BOOKS IN PRINT®

2000–2001

This edition of
BOOKS IN PRINT 2000-2001
was prepared by R.R. Bowker's Database Publishing Group in
collaboration with the Information Technology Department.

Drew Meyer, President & Chief Executive Officer
Michael Cairns, Vice President, Business Development
Dean Hollister, Vice President, Database Production
Randy Mysel, Vice President, Sales & Marketing
Andrew Grabois, Senior Managing Director, Bibliographies
Roy Crego, Managing Director, Books in Print Editorial
Angela D'Agostino, Senior Director, Product Development
Marin Mixon, Director, Marketing

International Standard Book Number/Standard Address Number Agency Publishers Authority Database
Doreen Gravesande, Director
Don Riseborough, Senior Managing Editor
Margot Cronin and Paula Kurdi, Senior Editors
Beverly Palacio and Joy Zichichi, Associate Editors
Kareem Douglas and Janet Weiss, Assistant Editors
Diana Fumando, SAN Senior Editor

Data Acquisition, Bibliographies Group
Joseph Kalina, Managing Editor
Nina Liana, Senior Editor
Gladys Osofisan, Assistant Editor

Quality Assurance & Web Content
Constance Harbison, Director, Quality Assurance
George Krubski, Managing Editor, Web Content, booksinprint.com
Christian Nielsen, Content Specialist Fiction, booksinprint.com
Myriam Nunez, Manager/Data Analysis, QA & Test
Brian Pickton, Senior Editor, Authority Control
Lisa Heft, Senior Editor, Quality Assurance
Jocelyn Kwiatkowski, Thomas Lucas, Michaela Weiland, Lynda Williams and
Steve Zaffuto, Assistant Editors

Subject Guide
Paula Entin, Senior Editor
Angela Barrett, Senior Associate Editor
Joseph V. Tondi, Associate Editor
Adrene Broomes, Assistant Editor

Electronic Data Interchange Group
Frank Accurso, Director
Mary Craig Daley, Managing Editor
Kathleen Keiderling, Managing Editor, Data Integration
Christopher Voser, Senior Editor
Brock Brunson, Associate Editor
Ila Joseph-Corley, Assistant Editor

Data Collection & Processing Group
Valerie Harris, Director of Operations, Tampa
Mervaine Ricks, Production Manager
Cheryl Patrick, Lead Project Coordinator
Rhonda McKendrick, Project Coordinator
Lori Burnett, Senior Data Entry Leader

Production
Carlton Dyce, Senior Director
Mitch Letterman, Senior Managing Editor
Melanie Koserowski, Xyvision Administrator/Senior Associate Desktop Publisher
Megan Roxberry, Senior Associate Desktop Publisher
Jeanne Audino, Monalisa Massiah and Maria Pirovano, Associate Desktop Publishers
Clarice D. Isaacs, Assistant Desktop Publisher

Editorial Systems Group
Gary Aiello, Vice President, Information Technology
Mark Heinzelman, Director
Frank Morris, Project Manager
Nana Rizinashvili and Youliang Zhou, Programmers

Computer Operations Group
Keith Moore, Manager, UNIX/Internet Systems
Nick Wikowski, Director, Network/Computer Operations
Jack Murphy, Supervisor

BOOKS IN PRINT®

2000–2001

VOLUME 1

AUTHORS ◆ A–D

New Providence, New Jersey

Published by
R.R. Bowker
A division of Reed Elsevier
121 Chanlon Rd., New Providence
New Jersey 07974

Drew Meyer, President and Chief Executive Officer

Telephone: 908-464-6800; Toll-free: 1-888-BOWKER2 (1-888-269-5372); Fax: 908-665-6688
E-mail address: info@bowker.com
URL: http://www.bowker.com

Readers may send any corrections and/or updates to the information in this work to R. R. Bowker through the corrections option on the Bowker Web site at http://www.bowker.com or may send e-mail directly to the address: Corrections@bowker.com. Publishers may update or add to their listings by accessing the Bowker Link Publisher Access System at http://www.bowkerlink.com. Books In Print is also available via subscription on the web at www.booksinprint.com.

International Standard Book Numbers
Set: 0-8352-4291-9
Volume 1: 0-8352-4292-7
Volume 2: 0-8352-4293-5
Volume 3: 0-8352-4294-3
Volume 4: 0-8352-4295-1
Volume 5: 0-8352-4296-X
Volume 6: 0-8352-4297-8
Volume 7: 0-8352-4298-6
Volume 8: 0-8352-4299-4
Volume 9: 0-8352-4300-1

International Standard Serial Number
0068-0214

Library of Congress Control Number
74-643574

Printed in the United States of America

ISBN 0-8352-4291-9

9 780835 242912

Contents of Volume 1

Contents of Volume 2

Contents of Volume 3

Contents of Volume 4

Contents of Volume 5

Contents of Volume 6

Contents of Volume 7

Contents of Volume 8

Contents of Volume 9

PREFACE

For more than fifty years, Books In Print has served the library and book trade communities as the definitive bibliographic resource. This 53rd edition—fully updated, and featuring more than 201,800 new titles and more than 265,000 new ISBNs—provides unparalleled coverage of the full range of books currently published or distributed in the United States.

STATISTICS

The 53rd edition of Books In Print contains over 1,680,100 active titles and over 1,779,820 active ISBNs published by 66,000 United States publishers. Bound in nine volumes, the set includes four volumes arranged by title and four by author. The ninth volume is devoted to publisher information and includes names, addresses (including E-mail and Web site addresses, when available) and ordering information for all publishers mentioned in the Author and Title volumes. Several useful publisher indexes are also provided.

RELATED PRODUCTS

In addition to the printed version, the Books In Print database (more than 3.4 million records, including OP titles, audiobooks and videos) can be searched by customers on Bowker's Web site, www.booksinprint.com. For further information about subscribing to this online service, please contact Bowker at 1-888-269-5372.

The Books In Print database is also available in many electronic formats. These include Books In Print on CD (available for Windows, DOS, and Macintosh systems); online access through CARL Corporation, The Dialog Corporation, DRA, EBSCO Publishing, The Gale Group, Information Access Company (IAC), Innovative Interfaces Inc., LEXIS®-NEXIS®, Micromedia (in Canada), OCLC, Inc., OVID Technologies, and SilverPlatter Information; as well as site-licensed raw data on magnetic media. Books Out-of-Print titles are also searchable on the Internet. Please visit our Web Site at http://www.bowker.com/bop for over 900,000 OP and OSI titles going back to 1979. Out-of-print titles are also available on the Books Out-of-Print PLUS CD-ROM (available quarterly) and through many online services.

COMPILATION

In order to be useful to subscribers, the information contained in Books In Print must be complete and accurate. Publishers are asked to review and correct their entries prior to each publication from the database, providing current price, publication date, availability status and ordering information, as well as recently published and forthcoming titles. Tens of thousands of entries are added or updated for each edition.

DATA ACQUISITION AND EDI

Bowker receives bibliographic information from publishers in many different formats: catalogs, Advance Book Information forms, checklists, phoned or faxed information, and most notably from Electronic Data Interchange. Publishers can also send corrections via www.bowkerlink.com.

Electronic Data Interchange (EDI) is a process by which participating publishers can submit their bibliographic information to Books In Print from their own databases.

Bowker's EDI system accepts publisher data 24 hours a day, 7 days a week. Methods of data transmission include the Internet (FTP), modem transfer, diskette, and magnetic tape. The benefits to this method are: no paper intervention, reduced costs, increased timeliness, and less chance of human error that can occur when re-keying information.

Bowker's EDI system is an outstanding tool for updating titles presently included in the Books In Print database, most notably price and status information. However, to communicate new title information to Books In Print via EDI, the quality of the publisher's textual data must be up to—or extremely close to—reference book standards.

Publishers wishing to obtain more information concerning Bowker's EDI system are encouraged to contact the EDI group at 908-771-7760 or 908-771-7728.

To ensure the accuracy, timeliness and comprehensiveness of data in Books In Print, Bowker has initiated discussions with the major publishers. This outreach entails analyzing the quality of all of a publisher's submissions to Books In Print, including EDI and paper-based sources, and working closely with the publisher to improve the content and timeliness of the information. This project also lays the groundwork for incorporating new valuable information into Books In Print. We are now collecting cover art, descriptive jacket and catalog copy, tables of content, contributor biographies, as well as awards won, bestseller listings, and review citations. Bowker makes this important, additional information available to customers who receive Books In Print in specific electronic formats and on our booksinprint.com web site.

CONTENT

The Books In Print database includes all types of books covering all topics. All editions and bindings are listed, including hardcover, paperbound, library binding, perfect binding, board books, spiral binding, text editions, teachers' and student editions, workbooks, lab manuals, and supplements. Books are excluded from entry for the following reasons:

» Books not distributed in the United States
» Books not available to the trade or general public for single or multiple copy purchase
» Free books not included with a title for sale
» Unbound material, pamphlets and booklets
» Periodicals and serials
» Books available only to members of an organization
» Subscription-only material
» Books sold only to schools
» Music manuscripts, sheet music, and librettos
» Certain sacred works, such as the Bhagavad Gita, Koran and Torah

Please note that Bibles are not included in the standard Books In Print products. Foreign publications are listed only when bibliographic information is submitted by a United States distributor who has rights to distribute such titles in the United States.

ISBN AGENCY

Each title included in Books In Print has been assigned an International Standard Book Number (ISBN) by the publisher. All ISBNs listed in this volume have been validated by using the check digit control, ensuring accuracy. ISBNs allow order transmission and bibliographic information updating using the Book Industry System Advisory Committee's (BISAC) standard format for data transmission. Publishers not currently participating in the ISBN system may request the assignment of an ISBN Publisher Prefix from the ISBN Agency by calling 908-665-6770, fax 908-665-2895, or through the ISBN/SAN Web site at www.bowker.com.

SAN AGENCY

Another listing feature in Books In Print is the Standard Address Number (SAN). The SAN is a unique identification number assigned to each address of an organization in or served by the publishing industry; it facilitates communications and repetitive transactions with other members of the industry.

The SAN functions in its application to activities such as purchasing, billing, shipping, receiving, paying, crediting and refunding, and can be used for any other communication or transaction between participating organizations. To obtain an application or further information on the SAN system, please contact Diana Fumando, SAN Senior Editor, by calling 908-771-7755, fax 908-665-2895, or visit the ISBN/SAN Web site at www.bowker.com.

HISTORY

The Books In Print bibliographic database was first introduced in 1948 as a listing of titles included in Bowker's Publishers Trade List Annual (PTLA). Since then it has grown from a one-volume work that covered 85,000 titles from 357 publishers, to today's multivolume authoritative resource encompassing some 1,680,100 active titles produced by more than 66,000 publishing houses. This growth reflects both the dramatic expansion of the publishing industry and Bowker's commitment to making Books In Print the most authoritative and comprehensive reference of its kind.

Our objective at R.R. Bowker is to find new ways to enable library and book trade professionals to do their job with greater ease and efficiency. We feel the accuracy and convenience Books In Print 2000-2001 offers in its many available formats demonstrates our commitment to this ideal. We are dedicated to maintaining Books In Print as the definitive bibliographic reference. We sincerely hope this edition meets your needs, and we welcome your comments and suggestions.

Updated information or corrections to the listings in Books In Print can now be submitted at any time via the Internet. Users may access the Bowker Web site at www.bowker.com and then follow the directions under the option "Have Corrections to one of our products?" This will enable them to contact our editors directly via e-mail. Publishers can submit updates and new titles to Books In Print by accessing the Bowker Link Publisher Access System at http://www.bowkerlink.com.

HOW TO USE BOOKS IN PRINT 2000-2001

Books In Print is designed to be easily searchable by both author and title. The set consists of nine volumes: four arranged alphabetically by author, four arranged alphabetically by title, and one containing publisher information and several useful indexes.

Entries in both the author and title indexes can include the following bibliographic information, when available: author, co-author, editor, co-editor, translator, co-translator, title, number of volumes, edition, Library of Congress Control Number, series information, page numbers, language if other than English, whether or not illustrated, grade range, year of publication, type of binding if other than cloth over boards, price, International Standard Book Number, publisher's order number, imprint and publisher. Entries marked with an asterisk are new to this edition of **Books In Print.**

How to Find an Author Entry

If a book has two authors or editors, a full bibliographic listing is included under the author or editor named first and the other is cross-referenced. Books with more than two authors or editors list only the name of the first followed by et al. Author names in Books In Print have been alphabetized using the following rules: Proper names beginning with

- "Mc" and "Mac" are filed in strict alphabetical order. For example, entries for contributor's names such as Mac Adam, MacAvory, and MacCarthy are located prior to the pages with entries for names such as McAdam, McCoy and McDermott.
- Compound names are listed under their first component and cross-referenced under their last. For example, Van Holland is listed under Van and cross-referenced under Holland.
- When author names are represented with initials, they are alphabetized before author first names. For example, Smith, H.C. appears before Smith, Harold A.

As a general rule, Dr., Mr., Mrs., and St., are filed in strict alphabetical order unless the author/publisher

SAMPLE ENTRY AUTHOR INDEX

1 ***De Vries, John.** 2 So Many Books, So Little Time: 3 A Reader's Dilemma. 4 3rd 5 rev. ed. 6 Kelly, Jane et al, eds. 7 LC 96-21340. 8 (About Readers Ser.: No. 33). 9 (Illus.) 10 155 p. 11 (YA). 12 (gr. 6 up). 13 2000. 14 pap. 15 25.95 16 x 17 (0-8352-5513-X, 18 B234, 19 Books Pr) 20 lib. bdg. 21 write for info. (0-8352-6612-4, B235, Books Pr) 22 Summertime Pubs.

***De Vries, John.** So Many Books, So Little Time: A Reader's Dilemma. 3rd rev. Kelly, Jane et al, eds. LC 96-21340. (About Readers Ser.: No. 33). (Illus.) 155 p. (YA). (gr. 6 up). 1998. text ed. 25.95x (0-8352-5513-X, B234, Books Pr); pap. text ed. write for info. (0-8352-6612-4, B235, Books Pr) Summertime Pubs.

KEY

1 Author
2 Title
3 Sub-Title
4 Edition Number
5 Edition Information
6 Editor(s)
7 Library of Congress Control Number
8 Series Title and Number
9 Illustrated
10 Number of Pages
11 Audience Code
12 Grade Range
13 Publication Year
14 Type of Binding
15 Price
16 "x" Indicating Short Discount
17 International Standard Book Number
18 Publisher's Order Number
19 Imprint or Foreign Publisher Symbol
20 Additional Binding Type
21 Price Information
22 Publisher's Symbol

requests that the title be filed as if it were spelled out. However, Dr. Seuss is filed under "Seuss" rather than as "Doctor Seuss".

The editors of **Books In Print** rely on publishers to provide standard spelling and format for each author. However, if a publisher is inconsistent in use of an author's name, there may be duplicate listings for that author in this volume. While most of these duplicate listings will appear in close proximity to each other, some may be quite far removed. An example of this is the use of Goethe for some titles and von Goethe for others. The editors have made every attempt to reduce variant forms of author's names in **Books In Print** and have cross-referenced many entries subject to this situation. It is still suggested that searches include all possible variant forms of author names.

How to Find a Title Entry

Titles in Books In Print have been alphabetized using the following rules:

- Initial articles of titles in English, French, German, Italian and Spanish have been deleted.
- Titles beginning with acronyms appear before those beginning with words. For example, B E A M A Directory precedes Baal, Babylon.
- As a general rule U.S. and UN are filed in strict alphabetical order unless the author/publisher requests that the title be filed as if it were spelled out.
- Titles beginning with numerals, including year dates, are filed alphabetically as if written out (17 found under Seventeen, etc.).

Prices Listed in Books In Print

The prices listed in Books In Print represent an effort on the part of publishers to be as accurate as possible. However, some price changes will occur before the next edition of the book is published. Users of this volume are encouraged to consult the **Books In Print Supplement**, published in March to access those changes. Prices printed are generally list prices, and trade discounts have not been indicated. The following symbol can be

SAMPLE ENTRY TITLE INDEX

(1) ***So Many Books, So Little Time:** (2) **A Reader's Dilemma.**
(3) 3rd (4) rev. ed. (5) John De Vries. (6) Ed. by Jane Kelly et al.
(7) LC 96-21340. (8) (About Readers Ser.: No. 33). (9) (Illus.)
(10) 155 p. (11) (YA). (12) (gr. 6 up). (13) 2000. (14) pap.
(15) 25.95 (16) x (17) (0-8352-5513-X, (18) B234,
(19) Books Pr); (20) lib. bdg. (21) write for info. (0-8352-66120-4,
B235, Books Pr) (22) Summertime Pubs.

***So Many Books, So Little Time: A Reader's Dilemma.**
3rd rev. ed. John De Vries. Ed. by Jane Kelly et al.
LC 96-21340. (About Readers Ser.: No. 33). (Illus.)
155 p. (YA). (gr. 6 up). 1998. text ed. 25.95x
(0-8352-5513-X, B234, Books Pr); pap. text ed.
write for info. (0-8352-6612-4, B235, Books Pr)
Summertime Pubs.

KEY

1. Title
2. Sub-Title
3. Edition Number
4. Edition Information
5. Author
6. Editor(s)
7. Library of Congress Control Number
8. Series Title and Number
9. Illustrated
10. Number of Pages
11. Audience Code
12. Grade Range
13. Publication Year
14. Type of Binding
15. Price
16. "x" Indicating Short Discount
17. International Standard Book Number
18. Publisher's Order Number
19. Imprint or Foreign Publisher Symbol
20. Additional Binding Type
21. Price Information
22. Publisher's Symbol

found after certain prices:
x...... *short discount; 20% or less (not uniformly provided by publishers)*

How to Find a Publisher/Distributor

Publisher and distributor names in Books In Print are generally abbreviated. Volume 9 contains the following indexes:

- Publisher Symbol Index—publishers listed alphabetically by symbol as used in bibliographic entries.
- Name Index—publishers listed alphabetically by abbreviated company name, with complete address and phone information.
- Publisher & Distributor Toll-Free and Fax Number Index–alphabetical listing of companies with address and toll-free telephone number and/or fax number(s).
- Wholesaler & Distributor Symbol Index—alphabetical listing with company name and address.
- Geographic Index to Wholesalers & Distributors—company names arranged by state.
- New Publishers–alphabetical listing of publishers new to the database for this edition.
- Inactive & Out-of-Business Publisher Index—alphabetical listing of companies that have gone out of business or cannot be located. (Information regarding the location of these companies is welcome and should be sent to: R.R. Bowker, 121 Chanlon Road, New Providence, NJ 07974, Attention: Publishers' Authority Database.)

Bibliographic entries containing "Pub. by" after the ISBN should be ordered from the company whose abbreviation appears at the end of the entry—not from the publisher.

Publisher entries preceded by a dagger and followed by the note "CIP" indicate publishers who participate in the "Cataloguing in Publication" program. For more information about this program, write the CIP offices of the Library of Congress, Washington, DC 20540.

Publisher entries printed in bold type indicate that the publisher is also listed in Publishers Trade List Annual 2000.

The Books In Print Family

In order to search books by subject, it is necessary to use the companion publication **Subject Guide to Books In Print**. Likewise, information on recently published works may not have been received in time for inclusion in Books In Print and should be searched in Books In Print Supplement. Books yet to be published will be found in the bimonthly publication Forthcoming Books.

Some books are better searched in other R.R. Bowker titles. For example, a more comprehensive listing of elementary and secondary school textbooks can be found in El-Hi Textbooks and Serials in Print, while Bowker's Law Books and Serials In Print -- A Multimedia Sourcebook contains several non-print media and serials indexes in addition to the law titles found in Books In Print.

LIST OF ABBREVIATIONS

abr.	abridged
adapt.	adapted
aft.	afterword
Amer.	American
anno.	annotated by
annot.	annotation(s)
ans.	answer(s)
app.	appendix
Apple II	Apple II disk
approx.	approximately
ARA	Arabic
assn.	association
audio	analog audio cassette
auth.	author
bd.	bound
bdg.	binding
bds.	boards
bibl(s).	bibliography(ies)
bk(s).	book(s)
bklet(s)	booklet(s)
boxed	boxed set, slipcase, or caseboard
Bro.	Brother
C	college audience level
CAN	Canada
CAT	Catalan
CHI	Chinese
co.	company
comm.	commission, committee
comment.	commentaries
comp.	compiled
cond.	condensed
contrib.	contributed
corp.	corporation
CRO	Croatian
CZE	Czech
DAN	Danish
dept.	department
des	designed
DEU	Germany
diag(s).	diagram(s)
digital audio	digital audio cassette
dir.	director
disk	software disk or diskette
dist.	distributed
Div.	Division
doz.	dozen
DUT	Dutch
ea.	each
ed.	edited, edition, editor
eds.	editions, editors
educ.	education
elem.	elementary
ency.	encyclopedia
ENG	English
enl.	enlarged
epil.	epilogue
exp.	expurgated
expr.	experiments
fac.	facsimile
fasc.	fascicule
fict.	fiction
fig(s).	figure(s)
FIN	Finnish
flmstrp.	filmstrip
footn.	footnotes
for.	Foreign
FRA	France
FRE	French
frwd.	foreword
gen.	general
GER	German
GBR	United Kingdom
GRE	Greek
gr.	grade(s)
hdbk.	handbook
HEB	Hebrew
HUN	Hungarian
Illus.	illustrated, illustration(s), illustrator(s)
in prep.	in preparation
incl.	includes, including
info.	information
inst.	institute
intro.	Introduction
IRL	Ireland
ISBN	International Standard Book Number
ISO	International Standards Organization
ITA	Italian
i.t.a.	initial teaching alphabet
J	juvenile audience level
JPN	Japanese
Jr.	Junior
jt. auth.	joint author
jt. ed.	joint editor
k	kindergarten audience level
KOR	Korean
lab	laboratory
lang(s).	languages(s)
LAT	Latin
LC	Library of Congress
lea.	leather
lib.	library
lib. bdg.	library binding
lit.	literature, literary
lp	record, album, long playing
ltd. ed.	limited edition
mac hd	144M, Mac high density disk
mac ld	800K, Mac high density disk
mass mkt.	mass market paperbound
math.	mathematics
mic. film	microfilm
mic form	microform
mod.	modern
mor.	morocco
MS(S)	manuscript(s)
natl.	national
net	net price (see publisher for specific pricing policies)
NLD	Netherlands
NOR	Norwegian
no(s).	number(s)
o.p.	out of print
orig.	original text, not a reprint (paperback)
o.s.i.	out of stock indefinitely
p.	pages
pap.	paper
per.	perfect binding
PER	Persian (Modern)
photos	photographer, photographs
POL	Polish
pop. ed.	popular edition
POR	Portuguese
prep.	preparation
probs.	problems
prog. bk.	programmed books
ps	preschool audience level
pseud.	pseudonym
pt(s).	part(s)
pub.	published, publisher, publishing
pubn.	publication
ref(s).	reference(s)
reprod(s).	reproduction(s)
ret.	retold by
rev.	revised
rpm.	revolution per minute (phono records)
RUS	Russian
SAN	Standard Address Number
S&L	Signed and Limited
SER	Serbian
sec.	section
sel.	selected
ser.	series
Soc.	society
sols.	solutions
s.p.	school price
SPA	Spanish
Sr.(after given name)	Senior
Sr.(before given name)	Sister
St.	Saint
subs.	subsidiary
subsc.	subscription
suppl.	supplement
SWE	Swedish
tech.	technical
text ed.	text edition
tr.	translated, translation, translator
trans.	transparencies
univ.	university
vdisk	videodisc
VHS	video, VHS format
vol(s).	volume(s)
wkbk.	workbook
x (after price)	short discount (20% or less)
YA	young adult audience level
yrbk.	yearbook
3.5 hd	1.44M, 3.5″ high density disk, DOS
3.5 ld	720, 3.5″ low density disk, DOS
5.25 hd	1.2M, 5.25″ high density disk, DOS
5.25 ld	360K, 5.25″ low density disk, DOS

PUBLISHERS WEEKLY BESTSELLERS LISTS

HARDCOVER NONFICTION

TITLE	AUTHOR	PUBLISHER	PRICE	HIGHEST RANK*	WEEKS ON LIST	ISBN
And the Crowd Goes Wild	Garner, Joe	Sourcebks	49.95	9	3	1-57071-460-6
Art of Happiness, The	Lama, The Dalai	Putnam Pub Group	22.95	8	52	1-57322-111-2
Body for Life	Phillips, Bill	HarpC	25.00	1	49	0-06-019339-5
Bodyguard's Story, The	Rees-Jones, Trevor	Warner Bks	25.95	10	4	0-446-52775-0
Camino	MacLaine, Shirley	PB	24.95	15	1	0-743-50072-0
Case Against Hillary Clinton, The	Noonan, Peggy	HarperTrade	24.00	11	7	0-06-039340-8
Century, The	Jennings, Peter	HarpC	60.00	1	30	0-385-48327-9
Cybill Disobedience	Shepherd, Cybill	HarpC	26.00	14	2	0-06-019350-6
Death of Innocence	Ramsey, John & Patsy	Nelson	24.99	13	4	0-7852-6816-2
Don't Sweat the Small Stuff in Love	Carlson, Richard	Hyperion	15.95	5	8	0-7868-6509-1
Don't Make Me Stop This Car!	Roker, Al	Scribner	24.00	7	1	0-684-86893-8
Dr. Atkins' Age-Defying Diet Revolution	Atkins, Robert C.	St Martin	24.95	11	2	0-312-25189-0
Dr. Shapiro's Picture Perfect Weight Loss	Shapiro, Howard	Rodale Pr Inc	29.95	6	2	1-57954-241-7
Duty	Greene, Bob	Morrow Avon	25.00	10	2	0-380-97849-0
Eating Well for Optimum Health	Weil, Andrew	Knopf	25.00	1(1)	13	0-375-40754-5
Every Day's a Party	Lagasse, Emeril	Morrow Avon	26.00	13	3	0-688-16430-7
Fair Ball	Costas, Bob	Broadway BDD	21.95	12	4	0-7679-0465-6
Faith of My Fathers	McCain, John	Random	25.00	2	15	0-375-50191-6
Fight Fat After Forty	Peeke, Pamela	Viking Penguin	24.95	15	1	0-670-88919-9
Flags of Our Fathers	Bradley, James	Bantam	24.95	5	7	0-553-11133-7
From Dawn to Decadence	Barzun, Jacques	HarpC	36.00	15	4	0-06-017586-9
From This Day Forward	Roberts, Cokie	Morrow Avon	24.00	10	5	0-688-16891-4
Galileo's Daughter	Sobel, Dava	Walker & Co	27.00	12	6	0-8027-1343-2
Greatest Generation Speaks, The	Brokaw, Tom	Random	19.95	2	12	0-375-50394-3
Greatest Generation, The	Brokaw, Tom	Random	24.95	1	57	0-375-50202-5
Guinness World Records 2000: Millennium Edition	Guinness Media Staff	Mint Pubs Inc	25.95	1	18	1-892051-00-1
Have a Nice Day!	Foley, Mick	HarperTrade	25.00	5	20	0-06-039299-1
Healing Grief	Van Praagh, James	Dutton Plume	23.95	11	2	0-525-94540-7
Heartbreaking Work of Staggerimg Genius, A	Eggers, Dave	S&S Trade	23.00	8	9	0-684-86347-2
Hell to Pay: The Unfolding Story of Hillary Rodham Clinton	Olson, Barbara	Regnery Pub	27.95			0-8952-6274-6
How to Know God	Chopra, Deepak	Harmony Bks	24.00	6	15	0-609-60078-8
In a Sunburned Country	Bryson, Bill	Broadway BDD	25.00	9	2	0-7679-0385-4
In the Heart of the Sea	Philbrick, Nathaniel	Viking Penguin	24.95	9	4	0-670-89157-6
It's Not About the Bike	Armstrong, Lance	Putnam Pub Group	24.95	12	4	0-399-14611-3
JonBenet	Thomas, Steve	St Martin	24.95	7	2	0-312-25326-5
Life: Our Century in Pictures	Stolley, Richard B.	Bulfinch Pr	60.00	14	6	0-8212-2633-9
Me Talk Pretty One Day	Sedaris, David	Little	22.95	8	2	0-316-77772-2
Measure of a Man	Poitier, Sidney	HarperSF	26.00	13	2	0-06-251607-8
Millionaire Mind, The	Stanley, Thomas J.	Andrews & McMeel	26.95	4	15	0-7407-0357-9
Necessary Journeys: Letting Ourselves Learn from Life	Snyderman, Nancy	Hyperion	19.95	10	3	0-7868-6513-X
No Such Thing as a Bad Day	Jordan, Hamilton	Longstreet	22.00	9	5	1-56352-578-X
Operator, The	King, Tom	Random	25.95	15	1	0-679-45754-2
Parenthood by Proxy	Schlessinger, Laura	HarperTrade	24.00	14	1	0-06-019125-2
Payne Stewart	Stewart, Tracey	Broadman	24.99	10	3	0-8054-2396-6
Peanuts: Golden Celebration, A	Schulz, Charles	HarpInfo	45.00	11	1	0-06-270244-0
Relationship Rescue	McGraw, Phillip	Hyperion	22.95	1(1)	17	0-7868-6631-4
Rock Says..., The	Layden, Joe	HarpC	26.00	1(7)	17	0-06-039298-3
Shrub: The Short but Happy Political Life of George W. Bush	Ivins, Molly	Random	19.95	12	4	0-375-50399-4
Simple Abundance	Breathnach, Sarah B.	Warner Bks	50.00	1	137	0-446-51913-8
Soul Stories	Zukav, Gary	S&S Trade	24.00	2	8	0-7432-0407-7
Standing for Something	Hinckley, Gordon	Crown Pub Grp	24.00	11	4	0-812-93317-6
Stickin'	Carville, James	S&S Trade	16.95	15	1	0-684-85773-1
Sugar Busters!	Steward, Leighton H.	Ballantine Pub Grp	22.00	1	194	0-345-42558-8

Ten Things I Wish I'd Known-Before I Went Out into the Real World	Shriver, Maria	Warner Bks	19.95	2	10	0-446-52612-6
'Tis	McCourt, Frank	Scribner	26.00	1	29	0-684-84878-3
Tuesdays with Morrie	Albom, Mitch	Doubleday	19.95	1(2)	136	0-385-48451-8
Vast Conspiracy, A	Toobin, Jeffrey	Random	25.00	6	5	0-375-50295-5
When Pride Still Mattered	Maraniss, David	S&S Trade	26.00	10	11	0-684-84418-4
Who Moved My Cheese?	Johnson, Spencer	Penguin Putnam	19.95	1(15)	26	0-399-14446-3

Data compiled from **Publishers Weekly** bestsellers listings, January - July 2000. *In the "Highest Rank" column, numbers in parentheses after a #1 bestseller indicate the number of weeks that this title reached the #1 ranking on the **Publishers Weekly** list during the six-month period noted above.

HARDCOVER FICTION

TITLE	AUTHOR	PUBLISHER	PRICE	HIGHEST RANK*	WEEKS ON LIST	ISBN
Anil's Ghost	Ondaatjie, Michael	Knopf	25.00	10	8	0-375-41053-8
Ashes of Victory	Weber, David	Baen Books	25.00	8	3	0-671-57854-5
Assassins	LaHaye, Tim	Tyndale Hse	22.99	3	11	0-8423-2920-X
Atlantis Found	Cussler, Clive	Putnam Pub Group	26.95	1	12	0-399-14588-5
Attorney, The	Martini, Steve	Putnam Pub Group	25.95	9	7	0-399-14536-2
Back Roads	O'Dell, Tawni	Viking Penguin	24.95	1(1)	9	0-670-89418-4
Before I Say Goodbye	Clark, Mary Higgins	S&S Trade	26.00	1(4)	9	0-684-83598-3
Beowulf	Heaney, Seamus	FS&G	25.00	9	9	0-374-11119-7
Blackout	Nance, John J.	Putnam Pub Group	23.95	15	1	0-399-14594-X
Bluest Eye, The	Morrison, Toni	Knopf	15.00	2	8	0-375-41155-0
Brethren, The	Grisham, John	Doubleday	27.95	1(8)	20	0-385-49746-6
Bridget Jones: Edge of Reason, The	Fielding, Helen	Viking Penguin	24.95	4	9	0-670-89296-3
Carolina Moon	Roberts, Nora	Putnam Pub Group	24.95	2	8	0-399-14592-3
Cat Who Robbed a Bank, The	Braun, Lillian J.	Putnam Pub Group	23.95	10	6	0-399-14570-2
City of God	Doctorow, E.L.	Random	25.00	11	4	0-679-44783-0
Cradle and All	Patterson, James	Little	25.95	2	1	0-316-69061-9
Daughter of Fortune	Allende, Isabelle	HarpC	26.00	3	16	0-06-019491-X
Day of Reckoning	Higgins, Jack	Putnam Pub Group	25.95	7	5	0-399-14585-0
Deep South	Barr, Nevada	Putnam Pub Group	23.95	10	1	0-399-14586-9
Demolition Angel	Crais, Robert	Doubleday	24.95	15	1	0-385-49584-6
Dragons of a Fallen Sun	Weis, Margaret	TSR Inc	27.95	11	2	0-7869-1564-1
Easy Prey	Sandford, John	Putnam Pub Group	25.95	1(1)	6	0-399-14613-X
Empty Chair, The	Deaver, Jeffrey	S&S Trade	25.00	6	6	0-684-85563-1
False Memory	Koontz, Dean	Bantam	26.95	1(1)	9	0-553-10666-X
Fierce Invalids Home from Hot Climates	Robbins, Tim	Bantam	27.50	11	6	0-553-10775-5
Fortune's Rocks	Shreve, Anita	Little	24.95	15	3	0-316-78101-0
Gap Creek	Morgan, Robert	Algonquin Bks	22.95	1(1)	14	1-56512-296-8
Gates of the Alamo, The	Harrigan, Stephen	Knopf	25.00	14	3	0-679-44717-2
Ghost Moon	Robards, Karen	Delacorte	24.95	15	2	0-385-31972-X
Girl with a Pearl Earring	Chevalier, Tracy	Dutton Plume	21.95	12	7	0-525-94527-X
He Shall Thunder in the Sky	Peters, Elizabeth	Morrow Avon	25.00	10	4	0-380-97659-5
Hearts in Atlantis	King, Stephen	Scribner	28.00	1	15	0-684-85351-5
Heir, The	Lindsey, Johanna	Morrow Avon	24.00	11	4	0-380-97536-X
Horse Heaven	Smiley, Jane	Knopf	26.00	13	5	0-375-40600-X
Hugger Mugger	Parker, Robert B.	Putnam Pub Group	23.95	6	5	0-399-14587-7
Human Stain, The	Roth, Philip	HM	26.00	13	3	0-618-05945-8
Hunting Badger	Hillerman, Tony	HarpC	26.00	6	15	0-06-019289-5
In the Fall	Lent, Jeffrey	Grove-Atltic	25.00	13	2	0-87113-765-8
Indwelling, The	LaHaye, Tim	Tyndale Hse	22.99	1(4)	4	0-8423-2928-5
Irresistible Forces	Steel, Danielle	Delacorte	26.95	4	8	0-385-31960-6
Lion's Game, The	DeMille, Nelson	Warner Bks	26.95	1(3)	16	0-446-52065-9
Looking Glass, The	Evans, Richard P.	S&S Trade	17.95	7	12	0-684-86781-8
Moment of Truth	Scottoline, Lisa	HarpC	25.00	9	7	0-06-019609-2
Monster	Kellerman, Jonathon	Random	25.95	8	9	0-679-45960-X
"O" is for Outlaw	Grafton, Sue	H Holt & Co	26.00	1	10	0-8050-5955-5
Off the Mangrove Coast	L'Amour, Louis	Bantam	16.95	14	1	0-553-80160-0
On Secret Service	Jakes, John	Dutton Plume	25.95	9	2	0-525-94544-X
Patient, The	Palmer, Michael	Bantam	24.95	12	4	0-553-10983-9
Personal Injuries	Turow, Scott	FS&G	27.00	1	13	0-374-28194-7
Plainsong	Haruf, Kent	Knopf	24.00	12	14	0-375-40618-2
Pop Goes the Weasel	Patterson, James	Little	26.00	1	13	0-316-69328-6
Ravelstein	Bellow, Saul	Viking Penguin	24.95	8	1	0-670-84134-X
Rogue Planet	Bear, Greg	Ballantine Pub Grp	26.00	8	4	0-345-43538-9
Run, The	Woods, Stuart	HarpC	26.00	9	6	0-06-019187-2
Saving Faith	Baldacci, David	Warner Bks	26.95	1	12	0-446-52577-4
Scandalmonger	Safire, William	S&S Trade	27.00	13	2	0-684-86719-2

HARDCOVER FICTION

continued

TITLE	AUTHOR	PUBLISHER	PRICE	HIGHEST RANK*	WEEKS ON LIST	ISBN
Search, The	Johansen, Iris	Bantam	24.95	5	2	0-553-80091-4
Secret Honor	Griffin, W.E.B.	Peng Put Young Read	25.95	11	6	0-399-14568-0
Secret of Shambhala, The	Redfield, James	Warner Bks	23.95	12	2	0-446-52308-9
Sick Puppy	Hiaasen, Carl	Knopf	25.00	2	11	0-679-45445-4
Soft Focus	Krentz, Jayne Ann	Putnam Pub Group	23.95	10	3	0-399-14578-8
Special Prisoner, The	Lehrer, Jim	Random	23.95	12	1	0-375-50371-4
Standoff	Brown, Sandra	Warner Bks	19.95	5	5	0-446-52701-7
Tara Road	Binchy, Maeve	Delacorte	24.95	2	28	0-385-33395-1
Timeline	Crichton, Michael	Knopf	26.95	1(1)	21	0-679-44481-5
Tough Cookie	Davidson, Diane M.	Bantam	23.95	7	5	0-553-10723-2
Vineyard, The	Delinsky, Barbara	S&S Trade	25.00	10	2	0-684-86484-3
Void Moon	Connelly, Michael	Little	24.95	11	2	0-316-15406-7
Waiting	Jin, Ha	Pantheon	24.00	15	1	0-375-40653-0
Walk to Remember, A	Sparks, Nicholas	Warner Bks	19.95	2	21	0-446-52553-7
Wedding, The	Steel, Danielle	Delacorte	26.95	1(2)	7	0-385-31437-X
Where You Belong	Bradford, Barbara Taylor	Doubleday	24.95	11	3	0-385-49275-8
White Teeth	Smith, Zadie	Random	24.95	9	2	0-375-50185-1
Wicked Widow	Quick, Amanda	Bantam	23.95	9	3	0-553-10087-4

Data compiled from **Publishers Weekly** bestsellers listings, January - July 2000. *In the "Highest Rank" column, numbers in parentheses after a #1 bestseller indicate the number of weeks that this title reached the #1 ranking on the **Publishers Weekly** list during the six-month period noted above.

MASS MARKET

TITLE	AUTHOR	PUBLISHER	PRICE	HIGHEST RANK*	WEEKS ON LIST	ISBN
All the Queen's Men	Howard, Linda	PB	7.50	14	2	0-671-56884-1
Angela's Ashes	McCourt, Frank	S&S Trade	7.99	1(1)	19	0-684-87215-3
Angels Flight	Connelly, Michael	Warner Bks	7.99	11	2	0-446-60727-4
Battlefield Earth	Hubbard, Ron	Bridge Pubns Inc	7.99	14	1	0-88404-681-8
Be Cool	Leonard, Elmore	Dell	7.50	8	3	0-440-23505-7
Bittersweet	Steel, Danielle	Dell	7.99	2	7	0-440-22484-5
Bittersweet Rain	Brown, Sandra	Warner Bks	6.99	9	5	0-446-60309-0
Black Friday	Patterson, James	Warner Bks	6.99	2	8	0-446-60932-3
Blind Man's Bluff	Sontag, Sherry	HarpC	7.99	8	9	0-06-103004-X
Carbohydrate Addict's Diet, The	Heller, Richard	NAL	6.99	1	25	0-451-17339-2
Carnal Innocence	Roberts, Nora	Bantam	7.50	6	4	0-553-29597-7
Cat Who Saw Stars, The	Braun, Lillian J.	Berkley Pub	6.99	8	5	0-515-12739-6
Celebration	Michaels, Fern	Kensgtn Pub Grp	6.99	13	1	0-8217-6452-7
Certain Prey	Sandford, John	Berkley Pub	7.99	1(1)	9	0-425-17427-1
Cider House Rules, The	Irving, John	Ballantine Pub Grp	7.99	1(1)	19	0-345-38765-1
Courtship, The	Coulter, Catherine	Berkley Pub	7.50	7	3	0-515-12721-3
Cowboy, The	Johnston, Joan	Dell	6.99	15	2	0-440-22380-6
Critical Mass	Martini, Steve	Berkley Pub	7.99	9	1	0-515-12648-9
Cuba	Coonts, Stephen	St Martin	7.99	12	4	0-312-97139-7
Dakota Born	Macomber, Debbie	Harlequin Bks	6.99	12	2	1-55166-576-X
Dark Tide I: Onslaught	Stackpole, Michael A.	Ballantine Pub Grp	6.99	8	4	0-345-42854-4
Dark Tide II: Ruin	Stackpole, Michael A.	Ballantine Pub Grp	6.99	6	2	0-345-42856-0
Devil's Teardrop, The	PB	PB	7.99	12	4	0-671-03844-3
Divide and Conquer	Clancy, Tom	Berkley Pub	7.99	7	1	0-425-17480-8
Dr. Atkins' New Diet Revolution	Atkins, Robert C.	Morrow Avon	6.99	1	176	0-380-72729-3
Eclipse Bay	Krentz, Jayne Ann	Berkley Pub	7.50	5	2	0-515-12801-5
Falcon at the Portal, The	Peters, Elizabeth	Morrow Avon	6.99	14	2	0-380-79857-3
False Pretenses	Coulter, Catherine	NAL	7.50	5	6	0-451-19968-5
First Lady	Phillips, Susan E.	Morrow Avon	6.99	6	4	0-380-80807-2
Fortune's Hand	Plain, Belva	Dell	7.99	6	3	0-440-22641-4
Girl Who Loved Tom Gordon, The	King, Stephen	PB	6.99	2	7	0-671-04285-8
Green Mile, The	King, Stephen	PB	7.99	1	18	0-671-03265-8
Hammer of Eden, The	Follet, Ken	Fawcett	7.99	4	7	0-449-22754-5
Hannibal	Harris, Thomas	Dell	7.99	1(4)	4	0-440-22467-5
High Five	Evanovich, Janet	St Martin	6.99	12	2	0-312-97134-6
Hush Money	Parker, Robert	Berkley Pub	7.50	7	4	0-425-17401-8
I Thee Wed	Quick, Amanda	Bantam	7.50	11	3	0-553-57410-8
Into the Garden	Andrews, V. C.	PB	7.99	7	2	0-671-00771-8
Irish Hearts	Roberts, Nora	Harlequin Bks	7.50	2	3	0-373-48400-3
Irish Rebel	Roberts, Nora	Harlequin Bks	4.50	4	3	0-373-24328-6
Jewel	Lott, Bret	PB	14.00	13	1	0-671-03818-4
Jewels of the Sun	Roberts, Nora	Berkley Pub	7.50	1	4	0-515-12677-2
Joining	Lindsey, Johanna	Morrow Avon	7.50	7	3	0-380-79333-4
Killing Game, The	Johansen, Iris	Bantam	6.99	2	4	0-553-58155-4
L.A. Requiem	Crais, Robert	Ballantine Pub Grp	6.99	12	3	0-345-43447-1
Lake News	Delinsky, Barbara	PB	7.99	8	2	0-671-03619-X
Liberty Falling	Barr, Nevada	Morrow Avon	6.99	13	3	0-380-72827-3
Mirror Image	Steel, Danielle	Dell	7.99	5	7	0-440-22477-2
Mistaken Identity	Scottoline, Lisa	HarpC	7.50	10	3	0-06-109611-3
On Mystic Lake	Hannah, Kristin	Ballantine Pub Grp	6.99	15	1	0-449-14967-6
One Wish	Miller, Linda L.	PB	6.99	15	1	0-671-53786-5
Outlaw Mountain	Jance, J.A.	Morrow Avon	6.99	13	2	0-380-79248-6
Path of Daggers, The	Jordan, Robert	Tor Bks	7.99	11	2	0-812-55029-3
Pearl Cove	Lowell, Elizabeth	Morrow Avon	7.50	9	2	0-380-78988-4
Perfect Storm, The	Junger, Sebastian	HarpC	6.99	2	41	0-06-101351-X
Prime Cut	Davidson, Diane M.	Bantam	6.50	12	5	0-553-57467-1

MASS MARKET
continued

TITLE	AUTHOR	PUBLISHER	PRICE	HIGHEST RANK*	WEEKS ON LIST	ISBN
Rain	Andrews, V.C.	PB	7.99	7	5	0-671-00767-X
Right Hand of Evil, The	Saul, John	Ballantine Pub Grp	7.99	10	2	0-449-00583-6
River's End	Roberts, Nora	Berkley Pub	7.99	1(3)	7	0-515-12783-3
Rules of Surrender	Dodd, Christina	Morrow Avon	6.99	15	1	0-380-81197-9
Saving Graces, The	Gaffney, Patricia	HarpC	6.99	9	7	0-06-109710-1
Seize the Night	Koontz, Dean	Bantam	7.99	5	7	0-553-58019-1
Send No Flowers	Brown, Sandra	Bantam	6.99	14	2	0-553-57601-1
Serpent: The Numan Files	Cussler, Clive	PB	7.99	7	5	0-671-02668-2
Shadow Watch	Clancy, Tom	Berkley Pub	7.99	6	7	0-425-17188-4
Simple Truth, The	Baldacci, David	Warner Bks	7.99	2	10	0-446-60771-1
Single & Single	Le Carre, John	PB	7.99	14	2	0-671-02797-2
Soldier Spies, The	Griffin, W.E.B.	Berkley Pub	7.50	15	2	0-515-12802-3
Soul of the Fire	Goodkind, Terry	Tor Bks	7.99	12	4	0-812-55149-4
Southern Cross	Cornwell, Patricia	Berkley Pub	7.99	3	1	0-425-17254-6
SSNN	Clancy, Tom	Berkley Pub	7.99	3	8	0-425-17353-4
Storming Heaven	Kyle, Mills	HarpC	6.99	15	2	0-06-101251-3
Sudden Change of Heart, A	Taylor Bradford, Barbara	Dell	7.99	14	1	0-440-23514-6
Sullivan's Island	Frank, Dorothea B.	Berkley Pub	6.99	10	3	0-515-12722-1
Testament, The	Grisham, John	Dell	7.99	1(12)	25	0-440-23474-3
Tom Clancy's Net Force	Clancy, Tom	Berkley Pub	7.99	4	6	0-425-17400-X
Tomorrow's Promise	Brown, Sandra	Harlequin Bks	6.99	15	1	1-55166-601-4
Transfer of Power	Flynn, Vince	PB	6.99	13	4	0-671-02320-9
Vector	Cook, Robin	Berkley Pub	7.99	6	4	0-425-17299-6
Week in the Zone, A	Sears, Barry	HarperCollins	6.99	14	1	0-06-103083-X
Welcome to the World, Baby Girl!	Flagg, Fannie	Ivy Books	7.50	14	9	0-804-11868-X
We'll Meet Again	Clark, Mary Higgins	PB	7.99	1(4)	8	0-671-00456-5
Witnesses in Death	Robb, J.D.	Berkley Pub	6.99	6	5	0-425-17363-1
Worst Fears Realized	Woods, Stuart	HarpC	7.50	8	3	0-06-101342-0

Data compiled from **Publishers Weekly** bestsellers listings, January 2000 - July 2000.
*In the "Highest Rank" column, numbers in parentheses after a #1 bestseller indicate the number of weeks that this title reached the #1 ranking on the **Publishers Weekly** list during the six-month period noted above.

TRADE PAPERBACK

TITLE	AUTHOR	PUBLISHER	PRICE	HIGHEST RANK*	WEEKS ON LIST	ISBN
American Psycho	Ellis, Bret Easton	Vin Bks	14.00	11	4	0-679-73577-1
Angela's Ashes	McCourt, Frank	S&S Trade	14.00	1	41	0-684-84267-X
Apollyon	LaHaye, Tim	Tyndale Hse	13.99	14	5	0-8423-2926-9
Black Hawk Down	Bowden, Mark	Viking Penguin	13.95	7	6	0-14-028850-3
Bluest Eye, The	Morrison, Toni	Dutton Plume	12.95	1(1)	5	0-452-28219-5
Bridget Jones's Diary	Fielding, Helen	Viking Penguin	12.95	7	16	0-14-028009-X
Carbohydrate Addict's Lifespan Program, The	Heller, Richard	Dutton Plume	15.95	1	18	0-452-27838-4
Chicken Soup for the Christian Family Soul	Canfield, Jack	Health Comm	12.95	8	1	1-55874-714-1
Chicken Soup for the Golden Soul	Canfield, Jack	Health Comm	12.95	12	2	1-55-874-725-7
Chicken Soup for the Mother's Soul	Canfield, Jack	Health Comm	12.95	1(1)	29	1-55874-460-6
Chicken Soup for the Teenage Soul	Canfield, Jack	Health Comm	12.95	2	88	1-55874-463-0
Chicken Soup for the Teenage Soul II	Canfield, Jack	Health Comm	12.95	1	33	1-55874-616-1
Chicken Soup for the Teenage Soul III	Canfield, Jack	Health Comm	12.95	1(1)	9	1-55874-761-3
Child Called "It", A	Pelzer, Dave	Health Comm	9.95	7	46	1-55874-366-9
Dr. Atkins' New Diet Cookbook	Atkins, Robert C.	M Evans	14.95	10	13	0-87131-794-X
Dr. Atkins' New Diet Revolution	Atkins, Robert C.	Morrow Avon	14.00	1	14	0-380-80368-2
East of the Mountains	Guterson, David	Harcourt	14.00	14	2	0-15-601104-2
Elegant Universe, The	Greene, Brian	Vin Bks	15.00	15	2	0-375-70811-1
ESPN	Patrick, Dan	Hyperion	12.95	15	1	0-7868-8539-4
Four Agreements, The	Ruiz, Don Miguel	Amber-Allen Pub	12.95	11	8	1-878424-31-9
Girl, Interrupted	Kaysen, Susanna	Vintage Pubng	12.00	7	20	0-679-74604-8
Girl's Guide to Hunting and Fishing	Bank, Melissa	Viking Penguin	12.95	2	7	0-14-029324-8
High Fidelity	Hornby, Nick	Berkley Pub	12.95	9	4	1-57322-821-4
Hours, The	Cunningham, Michael	St Martin	13.00	4	24	0-312-24302-2
Interpreter of Maladies: Stories	Lahiri, Jhumpa	HM	12.00	13	5	0-395-92720-X
Kiss of God	Ball, Marshall S.	Health Comm	9.95	15	2	1-55874-743-5
Left Behind	LaHaye, Tim	Tyndale Hse	12.99	12	30	0-8423-2912-9
Life Strategies	McGraw, Phillip	Hyperion	21.95	2	37	0-7868-6548-2
Map of the World, A	Hamilton, Jane	Doubleday	12.95	1(4)	15	0-385-72010-6
Memoirs of a Geisha	Golden, Arthur	Vin Bks	14.00	1	65	0-679-78158-7
Millionaire Next Door, The	Stanley, Thomas J.	PB	14.00	7	24	0-671-01520-6
New Song, A	Karon, Jan	Viking Penguin	12.95	8	8	0-14-027059-0
Old Farmers Almanac 2000, The	Hale, Judson	Yankee NH	5.95	5	14	1-57198-146-2
Organizing from the Inside Out	Morgenstern, Julie	H Holt & Co	14.00	10	4	0-8050-5649-1
Pilot's Wife, The	Shreve, Anita	Little	13.95	1	50	0-316-60195-0
Poisonwood Bible, The	Kingsolver, Barbara	HarpC	14.00	3	36	0-06-093053-5
Rich Dad Poor Dad	Kiyosaki, Robert	Warner Bks	15.95	1(1)	8	0-446-67745-0
Season Beyond a Kiss, A	Woodiwiss, Kathleen	Morrow Avon	14.00	1(3)	6	0-380-80793-9
Seat of the Soul, The	Zukav, Gary	S&S Trade	12.00	1(9)	67	0-671-69507-X
Snow Falling on Cedars	Guterson, David	Vin Bks	12.00	1(2)	11	0-679-76402-X
Take Time for Your Life	Richardson, Cheryl	Bantam	13.00	10	3	0-7679-0207-6
Talented Mr. Ripley, The	Highsmith, Patricia	Vin Bks	13.00	15	1	0-679-74229-8
Vinegar Hill	Ansay, Manette	Morrow Avon	13.00	1	13	0-380-73013-8
Walk in the Woods, A	Bill Bryson	Broadway BDD	13.00	12	22	0-7679-0252-1
Where the Heart Is	Letts, Billie	Warner Bks	12.00	1(1)	63	0-446-67221-1
While I was Gone	Miller, Sue	Ballantine Pub Grp	12.95	1(3)	14	0-345-43500-1
White Oleander	Fitch, Janet	Little	13.95	7	6	0-316-28495-5
World Almanac and Book of Facts 2000, The	Famighetti, Robert	Wrld Almnc	10.95	2	9	0-88687-847-0
Worst-Case Scenario Survival Handbook	Piven, Joshua	Chronicle Bks	14.95	13	6	0-8118-2555-8
Yesterday, I Cried	Vanzant, Iyanla	S&S Trade	13.00	14	1	0-684-86748-6

Data compiled from **Publishers Weekly** bestsellers listings from January 2000 - July 2000.
*In the "Highest Rank" column, numbers in parentheses after a #1 bestseller indicate the number of weeks that this title reached the #1 ranking on the **Publishers Weekly** list during the six-month period noted above.

BOOKS IN PRINT®
2000 - 2001
Volume 1
AUTHORS
A - D

A

A & C Black Staff. Writers' & Artists' Yearbook 1998. 704p. 1998. pap. 21.95 (0-7136-4721-3, Pub. by A & C Blk) Midpt Trade.
— Writers' & Artists' Yearbook, 2000. 1999. pap. text 19.95 (0-7136-5147-4) A & C Blk.
A & O Kika Staff, jt. auth. see Kira, Gene S.
A & T Staff. Get Started with Computer Concepts! (C). 1997. pap. 26.95 incl. cd-rom (0-7600-5589-0) Course Tech.
A & T Staff & Mendelsohn, Mac. Get Started with Microsoft Powerpoint 97! - Illustrated Interactive. (Illus.). 80p. 26.95 (0-7600-5341-3, Pub. by Course Tech) Thomson Learn.
A. A. I. C. C. Staff. Essays on International Law, 13 vols. (C). 1990. 100.00 (0-89771-314-1) St Mut.
***A. B. L. Coombes Anthology Staff.** With Dust Still in His Throat. Jones, Bill & Williams, Chris, eds. 224p. 2000. pap. 19.95 (0-7083-1578-X, Pub. by U Wales Pr) Paul & Co Pubs.
A. B. Publishing Staff. Adopting an Orphan. 1998. pap. text 6.95 (1-881545-87-3) Angelas Bkshelf.
— Come Home Mother. 1998. pap. text 6.95 (1-881545-92-X) Angelas Bkshelf.
— In the Twilight. 1998. pap. text 6.95 (1-881545-90-3) Angelas Bkshelf.
— Nobody Loves Me. 1998. pap. text 6.95 (1-881545-83-0) Angelas Bkshelf.
— Tom's Revenge. 1998. pap. text 6.95 (1-881545-91-1) Angelas Bkshelf.
A Blue Mountain Arts Collection. It's Great to Have a Sister Like You: A Collection. LC 98-42677. (Language of...Ser.). (Illus.). 48p. 1999. 14.95 (0-88396-481-3, L4813) Blue Mtn Art.
— The Language of Marriage: A Gift Two Hearts Will Always Share. LC 99-19311. (Language of...Ser.). (Illus.). 48p. 1999. 14.95 (0-88396-505-4, L5054) Blue Mtn Art.
— The Language of Success: A Gift for Those Who Follow Their Dreams. LC 99-18691. (Language of...Ser.). (Illus.). 48p. 1999. 14.95 (0-88396-504-6, L5046) Blue Mtn Art.
— The Language of Teaching: A Memorable Gift for Those Who Place a High Value on Education. LC 99-19315. (Language of...Ser.). (Illus.). 48p. 1999. 14.95 (0-88396-509-7, L5097) Blue Mtn Art.
— Thoughts to Share with a Wonderful Daughter: A Collection. LC 98-50181. (Language of...Ser.). 48p. 1999. 14.95 (0-88396-491-0) Blue Mtn Art.
— Thoughts to Share with a Wonderful Father: A Collection. LC 98-46834. (Language of...Ser.). (Illus.). 48p. 1999. 14.95 (0-88396-482-1, L4821) Blue Mtn Art.
— Thoughts to Share with a Wonderful Mother: A Collection. LC 98-46832. (Language of...Ser.). (Illus.). 48p. 1999. 14.95 (0-88396-487-2, L4872) Blue Mtn Art.
A Blue Mountain Arts Collection, ed. All I Want for Christmas Is You. LC 93-21906. (Illus.). 64p. 1993. 16.95 (0-88396-372-8) Blue Mtn Art.
— Be Proud of All You've Achieved: Poems on the Meaning of Success. LC 94-1656. 64p. 1999. pap. 7.95 (0-88396-374-4) Blue Mtn Art.
— Creeds of Life, Love & Inspiration: A Guidebook of Everyday Wisdom & Thought. LC 99-32260. (Illus.). 64p. 1999. pap. 8.95 (0-88396-520-8, B5208) Blue Mtn Art.
— En tu Alma Hay Nobleza, Hijo Mio.Tr. of There Is Greatness Within You, My Son. (ENG & SPA., Illus.). 64p. 1998. pap. 7.95 (0-88396-473-2) Blue Mtn Art.
— For a Special Teenager, Special Updated Edition: A Collection of Poems. LC 99-34278. 64p. 1999. 16.95 (0-88396-527-5, H5275) Blue Mtn Art.
A Blue Mountain Arts Collection, ed. For You, My Daughter: A Collection of Poems. LC 99-54096. 64p. 1984. pap. 8.95 (0-88396-552-6) Blue Mtn Art.
A Blue Mountain Arts Collection, ed. I Want Our Love to Last Forever: And I Know It Can If We Both Want It To. LC 94-6250. 64p. 1994. pap. 8.95 (0-88396-375-2) Blue Mtn Art.
***A Blue Mountain Arts Collection, ed.** The Language of Positive Thinking. LC 99-47783. 48p. 1999. 14.95 (0-88396-541-0) Blue Mtn Art.
A Blue Mountain Arts Collection, ed. Take Each Day One Step at a Time: Poems to Inspire & Encourage the Journey to Recovery: a Collection from Blue Mountain Arts. LC 94-34185. 64p. 1994. pap. 8.95 (0-88396-395-7) Blue Mtn Art.
— Teaching & Learning Are Lifelong Journeys: Thoughts on the Art of Teaching & the Meaning of Education. LC 99-15442. (Illus.). 48p. 1999. pap. 8.95 (0-88396-519-4, B5194) Blue Mtn Art.
— There Is Greatness Within You, My Son: A Collection of Poems. LC 94-31218. 64p. 1994. pap. 8.95 (0-88396-396-5) Blue Mtn Art.
A. Bogeng, Gustav, see Bogeng, Gustav A.
a Brandis, G. Brender, see Brender a Brandis, G.
A Brother of the Fraternity. Secret Symbols of the Rosicrucians of the 16th & 17th Centuries. 60p. 1998. reprint ed. pap. 16.95 (0-7661-0728-0) Kessinger Pub.
A. C. Bhaktivedanta Swami Prabhupada & Goswami, Satsvarupa D. Mukun-da-Mala-Stotra: The Prayers of King Kulasekhara. LC 92-31102. 157p. 1998. pap. 9.95 (0-89213-275-2) Bhaktivedanta.
A. C. E. Program of the Bedford Hills Correctional. Breaking the Walls of Silence: AIDS & Women in a New York State Maximum Security Prison. LC 92-35997. (Illus.). 336p. 1998. 29.95 (0-87951-500-7, Pub. by Overlook Pr) Penguin Putnam.
A. C. Gilbert Co. Staff. Gilbert American Flyer Instruction Book: For Operating & Assembling 3/16" Scale Trains & Accessories. (Illus.). 50p. 1997. reprint ed. pap. 9.25 (0-930429-06-0) Bibliographic Pr.
A. C. S. Staff. Clearing Our Environment: The Chemical Basis for Action. (C). 1991. text 400.00 (0-89771-541-1, Pub. by Intl Bk Distr) St Mut.
A., Clanchy. Essay Writing Student Text. 2nd ed. 1993. pap. write for info. (0-582-87188-3) Addison-Wesley.
A. D. G. La Nuit des Grands Chiens Malades. (FRE.). 217p. 1990. pap. 10.95 (0-7859-2155-9, 2070383253) Fr & Eur.
A. E. The Candle of Vision. 175p. 1996. pap. 15.00 (0-89540-298-X, SB-298) Sun Pub.
A. G. Library Staff, ed. A-Maze-Ing Day Amusement Park Fun. (American Girl Library Ser.). 1999. pap. text 1.95 (1-56247-735-8) Pleasant Co.
A. G. Publishing Editorial Staff. Christmas Graphics & Display. (Illus.). 208p. 1996. 69.95 (4-900781-06-1, Pub. by AG Pubs) Bks Nippan.
— The Form 2. LC 96-157227. (Illus.). 212p. 1996. 75.00 (4-900781-07-X, Pub. by AG Pubs) Bks Nippan.
A. H. A. Staff. A. H. A. Low-Salt Cookbook. 1992. pap. 15.00 (0-8129-2045-7, Times Bks) Crown Pub Group.
A. I. A. Staff. Environmental Resource Guide. 1996. pap. text 225.00 (0-471-15323-0) Wiley.
A. I. M. C. Staff. Company Insurance Handbook. (C). 1984. 325.00 (0-7855-4252-3, Pub. by Witherby & Co) St Mut.
A, James, jt. auth. see W, John.
A. Jay & Mike. Movie Star Confidential - The Super Adventures of Harry Chess Comics. (Illus.). 96p. (Orig.). 1989. pap. 10.95 (0-943595-16-9) Leyland Pubns.
A. Li Wan Po & G. Li Wan Po. OTC Medications: Symptoms & Treatment of Common Illnesses. (Illus.). 256p. 1991. pap. 31.95 (0-632-02954-4) Blackwell Sci.
A. M. Best Staff. Best's Loss Control Engineering Manual. annuals 500.00 (0-685-62527-3) A M Best.
— Best's Underwriting Guide. annuals 500.00 (0-685-62526-5) A M Best.
A. M. Homes Editors. The Safety of Objects. LC 99-14331. 176p. 1999. reprint ed. pap. 14.00 (0-688-17083-8, Wm Morrow) Morrow Avon.
A. M. Klein Symposium, University of Ottawa, 1974. The A. M. Klein Symposium. Mayne, Seymour, ed. & intro. by. LC 77-350191. (Re-Appraisals, Canadian Writers Ser.). 135p. 1975. reprint ed. pap. 41.90 (0-608-02207-1, 206287700004) Bks Demand.
"A Member of the Aristocracy" Staff. Manners & Rules of Good Society or Solecisms to be Avoided (1924) 280p. 1999. reprint ed. pap. 18.95 (0-7661-0824-4) Kessinger Pub.
A., Miller. Economics Today MacRo: The MacRo View. 9th ed. 1997. text 63.00 (0-673-98541-5) Addison-Wesley.
A. N. Parshin, ed. Algebraic Geometry V: Fano Manifolds. 250p. 1998. 99.00 (3-540-61468-0) Spr-Verlag.
A. N. T. Publications Staff & Smith, Jim B. The Last Mission - An Eye Witness Account by Jim B. Smith: The B-29 Raid That Ended WWII. (Illus.). 359p. 1995. text 40.00 (0-9647476-0-X) J B Smith.
A. P. W. A. Research Foundation Staff. Computer Assisted Mapping & Records Activity Manual. (CAMRAS Ser.: Pt. 1). 1979. 45.00 (0-917084-31-4) Am Public Works.
A. R. Bowman Memorial Museum Staff, jt. auth. see Crook County Historical Society Staff.
A. R. E. Editors, ed. see Thurston, Mark A.
A. R. E. Press Editors. The Christmas Story: As Told by Edgar Cayce. LC 96-11071. (Illus.). 56p. 1996. 14.95 (0-87604-356-2, 475) ARE Pr.
***A. R. E. Press Editors, ed.** Edgar Cayce's Healthy Diet & Recipe Guide. LC 98-21748. 192p. 1999. pap. 12.95 (0-87604-414-3, 539) ARE Pr.
A. S. A. Directors. American Spiritualist Assembly Minister's Handbook & Service Manual 1987. 78p. 1987. pap. 21.00 (0-939795-28-0) Amer Spirit.
A. S. A. Educations & Research Staff, ed. see Rizer, Arden C., Jr.
A. S. A. Staff, ed. see Rizer, Arden C., Jr.
***A T & T Staff.** A Practical Handbook of Speech Codes. (Discrete Mathematical & Applications Ser.). 256p. 2000. boxed set 79.95 (0-8493-8525-3) CRC Pr.
A&L New Media Staff. A & Lert: USMLE Step 1 Deluxe CD Sampler. 1997. write for info. incl. cd-rom (0-8385-0366-7, Apple Lange Med) McGraw.
***AA Grapevine, Inc. Staff.** AA Around the World: Adventures in Recovery. (Illus.). 164p. 2000. 5.00 (0-933685-31-9) A A Grapevine.
***Aa Publishing Staff.** Illustrated Guide to France. (Illus.). 256p. 2000. pap. 27.95 (0-393-31941-5, Norton Paperbks) Norton.
***Aaa.** AAA 1999 Britain Road Atlas. 144p. 1998. pap. 19.95 (1-56251-274-9) AAA.
***AAA Editorial Staff.** AAA Guide to National Park Vacations. 2000. pap. 18.95 (1-56251-322-2) AAA.
AAA Editorial Staff. AAA Guide to the National Parks. (Illus.). 320p. 1998. per. 18.00 (1-56251-245-5, Pub. by AAA) S&S Trade.
***AAA Editorial Staff.** AAA Travel Fun Book. (Illus.). (J). 1999. pap. 4.95 (1-56251-291-9, Pub. by AAA) S&S Trade.
— AAA World Passport to Safer Travel. 2000. pap. 8.95 (1-56251-321-4, Pub. by AAA) S&S Trade.
AAA Foundation Staff. On the Scene: Guide Roadside (Fifty Pack) (Emergency Care Ser.). 16p. 1995. pap. 25.00 (0-86720-525-3) Jones & Bartlett.
***AAA Road Atlas Staff.** AAA Mapscene Las Vegas: Map & Travel Guide. (Illus.). 1999. pap. 5.75 (1-56251-313-3) AAA.
— AAA North America Road Atlas: United States, Canada, Mexico 2000. (Road Atlas Ser.). (Illus.). 148p. 1999. pap. 10.95 (1-56251-292-7) AAA.
AAA Road Atlas Staff. AAA World Atlas 1999. 524p. 1998. 49.95 (1-56251-282-X) AAA.
***AAA Road Atlas Staff.** U. S. Interstate Road Atlas - French Edition - 2000 Edition. 81p. 1999. pap. 6.95 (0-7625-1141-9) Universal Map Enterprises Inc.
— U. S. Interstate Road Atlas - 2000 Edition. 81p. 1999. pap. 6.95 (0-7625-1140-0) Universal Map Enterprises Inc.
***AAA Staff.** AAA All-in-One Guide: London. (AAA All-in-One Guides Ser.). 1999. pap. 14.95 (1-56251-296-X, Pub. by AAA) S&S Trade.
— AAA Atlas. 151p. 1999. pap. 10.95 (0-7625-1138-9) Universal Map Enterprises Inc.
AAA Staff. AAA Autograph, 1998. (Illus.). 208p. 1997. pap. 12.95 (1-56251-252-8) AAA.
— AAA AutoGraph 1999: The New Car Shopper's Best Reference & Source for AAA Top Car Awards. 208p. 1999. pap. 13.95 (1-56251-281-1) AAA.
— AAA 1999 North American Road Atlas: The "Ultimate" Road Atlas of the United States, Canada, & Mexico. gif. ed. (Illus.). 148p. 1998. vinyl bd. 12.95 (1-56251-266-8) AAA.
— North America Road Atlas: United States, Canada, Mexico. (AAA North American Road Atlas Ser.). (Illus.). 152p. 1998. pap. 9.95 (1-56251-262-5, Pub. by AAA) S&S Trade.
— AAA North American Road Atlas 1997. 144p. 1996. pap. 9.95 (1-56251-229-3) AAA.
— AAA 1995 North America Road Atlas. 1994. 11.95 (1-56251-135-1) S&S Trade.
— ADR: A Practical Guide to Resolve Construction Disputes. 400p. 1994. boxed set 79.00 (0-8403-8970-1) Kendall-Hunt.
***AAA Staff.** Boston & New England. (Spiral Guides Ser.). (Illus.). 2000. pap. text 16.95 (1-56251-336-2) AAA.
— California. (Spiral Guides Ser.). 2000. pap. text 16.95 (1-56251-337-0) AAA.
AAA Staff. Ireland. (AAA All-in-One Guides Ser.). 1999. pap. 14.95 (1-56251-298-6, Pub. by AAA) S&S Trade.
— On & off the Record: Colosi on Negotiations. 144p. 1996. pap. text, per. 19.95 (0-8403-8585-4) Kendall-Hunt.
***AAA Staff.** Scotland. (AAA All-in-One Guides Ser.). 1999. pap. 14.95 (1-56251-297-8, Pub. by AAA) S&S Trade.
— Vancouver & the Canadian Rockies. (Spiral Guides Ser.). 2000. pap. text 16.95 (1-56251-338-9) AAA.
AAA Staff, jt. auth. see Universal Map Staff.
AAAB Staff. 4th International Wastepaper Conference, '97. 1997. 150.00 (1-85802-132-4, Pub. by Pira Pub) Bks Intl VA.
AAAI Press. AAAI-86: Proceedings of the 5th National Conference on Artificial Intelligence. 1990. pap. text 55.00 (0-262-51054-5) MIT Pr.
AAAI Press, compiled by. AAAI-88: Proceedings of the 7th National Conference on Artificial Intelligence. 1990. pap. text 55.00 (0-262-51056-1) MIT Pr.
AAAI Press Staff. AAAI 97: Proceedings of the Fourteenth National Conference on Artificial Intelligence. (Illus.). 1500p. 1997. pap. text 85.00 (0-262-51095-2) MIT Pr.
AAAI Press Staff. Proceedings from AAAI Eighth National Conference on Artificial Intelligence, 1990, 2 vols., Set. 1174p. 1990. pap. text 65.00 (0-262-51057-X) MIT Pr.
AAAI Press Staff, ed. AAAI, 98: Proceedings of the 15th National Conference on Artificial Intelligence. (Illus.). 1500p. 1998. pap. text 85.00 (0-262-51098-7) MIT Pr.
AAAI Press Staff, ed. AAAI 93: Proceedings of the Eleventh National Conference on Artificial Intelligence. (Illus.). 1000p. 1993. pap. text 75.00 (0-262-51071-5) MIT Pr.
— AAAI 92 Proceedings of the Tenth National Conference on AI. (Illus.). 1000p. 1992. pap. text 85.00 (0-262-51063-4) MIT Pr.
AAAI Staff. AAAI 1996: Proceedings of the Thirteenth National Conference on Artificial Intelligence, August 4-8, Portland, Oregon. LC 97-109153. (Illus.). 1500p. 1996. pap. text 80.00 (0-262-51091-X) MIT Pr.
— AAAI 00: Proceedings of the Seventeenth National Conference on Artificial Intelligence. 1200p. 2000. 85.00 (0-262-51112-6) MIT Pr.

A

AAALF (Seaman) Staff. Exercise & the Older Adult. 288p. 1998. per. 35.00 (0-87241-004-8) Kendall-Hunt.

***AAALF (Seaman) Staff.** Instructor's Manual to Accompany: Facilities Planning For Physical Activity & Sport. 9th ed. 34p. 1999. write for info. (0-7872-5994-2) Kendall-Hunt.

AAALF Staff. Facility Development. 9th ed. LC 99-71467. 480p. 1999. per. 50.00 (0-7872-5687-0, 41568701) Kendall-Hunt.

AAAS Office of Communications Staff, ed. Directory of AAAS Fellows, 1995. 237p. 1995. pap. 14.95 (0-87168-560-4) AAAS.

AABB Administrative Section Coordinating Committee, ed. Administrative Manual, Vol. 1. 3rd ed. LC 85-11061. (Illus.). 253p. 1985. pap. text 20.00 (0-915355-08-6) Am Assn Blood.

AABB Parentage Testing Committee, ed. Standards for Parentage Testing Laboratories. 2nd rev. ed. 24p. 1994. pap. text 20.00 (1-56395-037-5) Am Assn Blood.

Aaberg, Everett. Muscle Mechanics. LC 98-13154. (Illus.). 224p. 1998. pap. 19.95 (0-88011-796-6, PAAB0796) Human Kinetics.

— Resistance Training Instruction: Advanced Principles & Techniques for Fitness Professionals. LC 98-52411. (Illus.). 232p. 1999. pap. 27.00 (0-88011-801-6, PAAB0801) Human Kinetics.

Aaberg, J. C. Hymns & Hymnwriter of Denmark. 170p. reprint ed. 59.00 (0-932051-28-6) Rprt Serv.

Aaberson, Max, ed. see Carter, Lark P., et al.

AABGA Staff & AZH Staff. 1998 AABGA/AZH Salary Survey. rev. ed. Orig. Title: AABGA Salary Survey. 41p. 1998. 50.00 (0-934843-09-0) Am Assn Botanical Gdns.

Aaboe, Asger. Episodes from the Early History of Mathematics. LC 63-21916. (New Mathematical Library: No. 13). (Illus.). 133p. 1964. pap. text 17.50 (0-88385-613-1, NML-13) Math Assn.

Aaboe, Asger, et al. Saros Cycle Dates & Related Babylonian Astronomical Texts. LC 91-55342. (Transactions Ser.: Vol. 81, Pt. 6). (Illus.). 80p. (C). 1991. pap. 12.50 (0-87169-816-1, T816-AAA) Am Philos.

Aaby, Peter. The State of Guinea-Bissau: African Socialism or Socialism in Africa? (Research Report Ser.: No. 45). 35p. 1978. write for info. (91-7106-133-9, Pub. by Nordic Africa) Transaction Pubs.

Aaby, Peter, jt. ed. see Basu, Alaka.

AACC Commission on the Future of Community College. Building Communities: A Vision for a New Century. 49p. 1988. pap. 24.00 (0-87117-182-1, 1111) Comm Coll Pr Am Assn Comm Coll.

AACC Commission to Improve Minority Education Staff. Making Good on Our Promises: Moving Beyond Rhetoric to Action. 41p. 1993. pap. 15.00 (0-87117-258-5, 1356) Comm Coll Pr Am Assn Comm Coll.

AACC TDM-TOX Staff, ed. Drug Monitoring Data Pocket Guide II. 143p. 1994. 15.00 (0-915274-70-1, 625) Am Assn Clinical Chem.

Aach, Beverly W. A Moment with Bev. LC 97-67140. 92p. (Orig.). 1997. pap. 10.95 (1-57197-071-1) Pentland Pr.

AACN (American Association of Critical-Care Nurses) Staff. Core Curriculum for Critical Care Nursing. 5th ed. Eoyang, Thomas, ed. LC 97-36175. (Illus.). 752p. (C). 1998. pap. text 49.00 (0-7216-5147-X, W B Saunders Co) Harcrt Hlth Sci Grp.

AACN (American Association of Critical-Care Nurses) Staff. Core Curriculum for Critical Care Nursing: Instructor's Manual. 5th ed. (Illus.). 955p. Date not set. teacher ed. write for info. (0-7216-8343-6, W B Saunders Co) Harcrt Hlth Sci Grp.

AACN (American Association of Critical-Care Nurses) Staff. Neonatal Critical Care Nursing: Outline Core Content. 1997. pap. write for info. (0-7216-5898-9, W B Saunders Co) Harcrt Hlth Sci Grp.

AACP Staff. Shall I Study Pharmacy? 7th ed. 32p. 1980. pap. 0.75 (0-937526-08-8) AACP Alexandria.

AACTE Staff, ed. Alternative Paths to Teaching: A Directory of Post-Baccalaureate Programs. 2nd ed. 1996. 15.00 (0-89333-135-X) AACTE.

AAD Staff. Dermatology Self-Evaluation Program (DSEP) 276p. 1996. 350.00 (0-7872-2018-3) Kendall-Hunt.

Aadland, Dan. Horseback Adventures. (Illus.). 256p. 1995. 14.95 (0-87605-925-6) Howell Bks.

— Sketches from the Ranch. 256p. 1998. 29.95 (0-87605-291-X) Howell Bks.

— Sketches from the Ranch: A Montana Memoir. (Illus.). 256p. 1998. 29.95 (0-87605-078-X) Howell Bks.

— Vision Quests: A Guide to Adventures with Horses. LC 94-48909. (Illus.). 256p. 1995. pap. 30.00 (0-87605-990-6) Howell Bks.

***Aadland, Dan.** Women & Warriors of the Plains: The Pioneer Photography of Julia E. Tuell. 202p. 2000. reprint ed. pap. 18.00 (0-87842-417-2) Mountain Pr.

Aadland, Florence. The Big Love. 192p. 1986. 3.95 (0-446-30159-0) Warner Bks.

Aadnoy, Bernt S. Modern Well Design. (Illus.). 250p. (C). 1996. text 82.00 (90-5410-633-6, Pub. by A A Balkema) Ashgate Pub Co.

— Modern Well Design. LC 96-80206. 1997. 75.00 (0-88415-483-1, 5483) Gulf Pub.

Aaen, Bernhard. No Appointment Needed. 128p. 1981. pap. 5.99 (0-8280-0025-5) Review & Herald.

AAFCO Staff. Official Publication of Associaton of American Feed Control Officials, Inc. rev. ed. Haas, Earl M., ed. 336p. 1993. 20.00 (1-878341-04-9) AAFCO.

AAFP Staff. The American Academy of Family Physicians: Family Health & Medical Guide. (Illus.). 608p. 1996. 39.99 (0-8499-0839-6) Word Pub.

Aaftink, Herman J. Brand New Me: The Art of Authentic Living. Fisk, George W., ed. LC 95-10468. 252p. (Orig.). 1995. pap. 14.95 (0-9620507-4-1) Cosmic Concepts Pr.

AAG Staff, ed. Perception of Environment. (C). 1987. text 50.00 (81-85046-55-7, Pub. by Scientific Pubs) St Mut.

Aagaard, jt. auth. see Stenchever, Morton A.

***Aagaard, Jacob.** Easy Guide to the Sveshnikov Sicilian. 2000. pap. text 18.95 (1-85744-280-6) Cadgn Bks.

Aagaard, Johannes, jt. ed. see Meldgaard, Helle.

Aagaard-Mogensen, Lars, ed. The Idea of the Museum: Philosophical, Artistic & Political Questions. LC 87-5777. (Problems in Contemporary Philosophy Ser.: Vol. 6). (Illus.). 248p. 1989. lib. bdg. 89.95 (0-88946-334-4) E Mellen.

Aagaard-Mogensen, Lars, tr. see Hartnack, Justus.

Aage, Hans. Environmental Transition in Nordic & Baltic Countries. LC 98-28490. 256p. 1998. 85.00 (1-85898-629-X) E Elgar.

***Aagesen, Colleen & Blumberg, Margie.** Shakespeare for Kids: His Life & Times: 21 Activities. LC 98-49686. (Illus.). 149p. (J). (gr. 4-8). 1999. pap. 16.95 (1-55652-347-5) Chicago Review.

***Aageson, James W.** In the Beginning: Critical Concepts for the Study of the Bible. LC 99-87540. 160p. 2000. 45.00 (0-8133-6619-4); pap. 15.00 (0-8133-6620-8) Westview.

Aagot, Raaen. Grass of the Earth. Scott, Franklyn D., ed. LC 78-15850. (Scandinavians in America Ser.). 1979. reprint ed. lib. bdg. 23.95 (0-405-11658-6) Ayer.

Aagrawal, A. N. & Lal, K. Economics of Development & Planning. 2nd ed. 45.00 (0-7069-7138-8, Pub. by Vikas) S Asia.

Aagre, Scott, jt. auth. see Martin, Lance.

AAHE Staff, ed. Violence Intervention & Prevention Institute Proceedings. 92p. 1997. pap. 15.95 (0-88314-608-8) AAHPERD.

AAHE Staff, et al. The National Adolescent Student Health Survey - Survey Replication. 71p. (Orig.). Date not set. pap. 7.00 (0-88314-481-6, A4816) AAHPERD.

— National Health Education Standards: Achieving Health Literacy. 79p. (Orig.). 1995. pap. 3.00 (0-88314-611-8, 301-10035) AAHPERD.

AAHPERD Staff. Eating Disorders & Athletes: A Handbook for Coaches. Holliman, Susan C., ed. 90p. (Orig.). 1991. pap. 5.00 (0-8403-6689-2, 301-10023) AAHPERD.

— Physical Best Activity Guide for Elementary Level. (Physical Best Ser.). (Illus.). 248p. 1998. pap. text 24.00 (0-88011-962-4, BAAH0962) Human Kinetics.

— Physical Education for Lifelong Fitness: The Physical Best Teacher's Guide. LC 99-22701. (Physical Best Ser.). (Illus.). 408p. 1999. pap. 39.00 (0-88011-983-7) Human Kinetics.

AAHPM Staff. Hospice Core Curriculum. 196p. 1999. per. 75.00 (0-7872-5542-4, 41554201) Kendall-Hunt.

— Unipac Five: Communication & the Physician's Role on the Interdisc. LC 99-191374. 160p. 1998. spiral bd. 20.00 (0-7872-5144-5) Kendall-Hunt.

— Unipac Four: Management of Selected Nonpain Symtoms in the Ter. 1998. 20.00 (0-7872-1939-8) Kendall-Hunt.

— Unipac One: The Hospice/Palliative Medicine Medicine Approach to. LC 99-191374. 160p. 1998. spiral bd. 20.00 (0-7872-5081-3) Kendall-Hunt.

— Unipac Six: Ethics & Legal Decision Making When Caring for Termin. 1998. 20.00 (0-7872-1940-1) Kendall-Hunt.

— Unipac Three: Assessment & Treatment of Pain in Terminally Ill. 1998. 20.00 (0-7872-1938-X) Kendall-Hunt.

— Unipac Two: Alleviating Psychological & Spiritual Pain in the Terminally Ill. 1998. 20.00 (0-7872-1937-1) Kendall-Hunt.

AAIB Home Economics Workshop Cookbook Committee Staff. Food at Your Fingertips. large type ed. 116p. (J). (gr. 3 up). 1958. ring bd. 29.50 (0-317-01887-6, J-06850-00) Am Printing Hse.

Aaken, Ernst Van, see Van Aaken, Ernst.

***Aaker.** Strategic Market Management. 5th ed. 1999. pap. text 79.00 (0-471-37693-0) Wiley.

***Aaker, D., et al.** Marketing Research. 7th ed. 816p. 2000. write for info. (0-471-36340-5) Wiley.

Aaker, David A. Building Strong Brands. LC 95-9238. (Illus.). 256p. 1995. 27.50 (0-02-900151-X) Free Pr.

— Managing Brand Equity: Capitalizing on the Value of a Brand Name. 224p. 1991. 32.95 (0-02-900101-3) Free Pr.

***Aaker, David A.** Managing Brand Equity: Capitalizing on the Value of a Brand Name. (Illus.). 299p. 2000. reprint ed. 35.00 (0-7881-9336-8) DIANE Pub.

Aaker, David A. Search for the Consumer Interest. 1994. 25.00 (0-02-900053-X) S&S Trade.

— Strategic Market Management. 5th ed. LC 98-16155. (Illus.). 352p. 1998. pap. 58.95 (0-471-17743-1) Wiley.

Aaker, David A. & Biel, Alexander, eds. Brand Equity & Advertising: Advertising's Role in Building Strong Brands. (Advertising & Consumer Psychology Ser.). 384p. 1993. pap. 39.95 (0-8058-1284-9) L Erlbaum Assocs.

Aaker, David A. & Day, George S. Marketing Research: Private & Public Sector Decisions. LC 79-18532. (Wiley Series in Marketing). (Illus.). 648p. reprint ed. pap. 200.00 (0-7837-3502-2, 205783500008) Bks Demand.

Aaker, David A. & Joachimsthaler, Erich. Brand Leadership: Building Assets in an Information Economy. LC 99-89668. (Illus.). 368p. 2000. 29.50 (0-684-83924-5) Free Pr.

Aaker, David A., et al. Marketing Research. 6th ed. LC 97-21710. 792p. 1997. text 99.95 (0-471-17069-0) Wiley.

Aaker, David A., jt. auth. see Nelson, Jan C.

Aaker, Everett. Television Western Players of the '50s: A Biographical Encyclopedia of All Regular Cast Members in Western Series, 1949 Through 1959. LC 97-13647. (Illus.). 588p. 1997. lib. bdg. 95.00 (0-7864-0284-9) McFarland & Co.

Aaker, Jerry. Partners with the Poor: An Emerging Approach to Relief & Development. LC 92-35591. 1993. pap. 12.95 (0-377-00252-6) Friendship Pr.

Aaker, Jerry, ed. Livestock for a Small Earth: The Role of Animals in a Just & Sustainable World. LC 94-10382. (Illus.). 128p. 1994. pap. 18.95 (0-929765-28-1) Seven Locks Pr.

Aaker, Linda. A Woman's Odyssey: Journals, 1976-1992. LC 94-16038. 293p. 1994. 22.50 (0-929398-74-2) UNTX Pr.

Aakhus, Patricia. The Voyage of Mael Duin's Curragh. 2nd ed. (Irish Literature Ser.). 236p. 1989. pap. 12.95 (0-934257-31-0) Story Line.

Aakre, Nancy, ed. Miniatures. Cooper-Hewitt Museum. LC 82-72762. (Smithsonian Illustrated Library of Antiques). (Illus.). 128p. (Orig.). 1983. 9.95 (0-910503-45-1) Cooper-Hewitt Museum.

Aakre, Nancy, ed. see Buddensieg, Tilmann, et al.

Aakre, Nancy, ed. see Dee, Elain E. & Walton, Guy.

Aakre, Nancy, ed. see Lupton, Ellen.

Aakre, Nancy, ed. see Shinn, Deborah S.

Aakre, Nancy, ed. see Trapp, Kenneth R., et al.

Aal, Katharyn M. The Raccoon Book. LC 82-7831. (Illus.). 88p. 1982. pap. 5.95 (0-935526-05-6) McBooks Pr.

Aal, Katharyn M., et al. The Wings, the Vines. LC 82-24978. 96p. 1983. pap. 6.50 (0-935526-07-2) McBooks Pr.

***Aalam, Bryan O. & Bommer, Allan.** Design Fundamentals of Post-Tensioned Concrete Floors. (Illus.). 184p. 1999. pap. 54.00 (0-9674567-0-3) Adapt.

Aaland, Mikkel. Photoshop for the Web. 2nd ed. Koman, Richard, ed. (Illus.). 250p. (Orig.). 1999. pap. 29.95 (1-56592-641-2) OReilly & Assocs.

— The Sword of Heaven: A Five Continent Odyssey to Save the World. LC 99-38755. 262p. 1999. 24.00 (1-885211-44-9, 44-9, Pub. by Trvlers Tale) OReilly & Assocs.

***Aalderink, H., et al, eds.** Options for Closed Water Systems. (Water Science & Technology Ser.). 272p. 1999. pap. 163.00 (0-08-043642-1, Pergamon Pr) Elsevier.

Aalderink, R. H., et al, eds. Urban Storm Water Quality & Ecological Effects upon Receiving Waters: Proceedings of the Second IAWPRC Conference, Held in Wageningen, The Netherlands, 20-22 September 1989. (Water Science & Technology Ser.: No. 22). (Illus.). 318p. 1990. pap. 148.50 (0-08-040161-9, Pergamon Pr); pap. 60.00 (0-08-040162-7, Pergamon Pr) Elsevier.

Aalders, Carel A., jt. auth. see Van Gerven, Dirk.

Aalders, G. Charles. Bible Student's Commentary: Genesis, 2 vols. 1981. 29.95 (0-310-43968-X, 11755) Zondervan.

Aalders, G. J. D. Plutarch's Political Thought. (Verhandelingen der Koninklijke Nederlandse Akademie van Wetenschappen, Afd. Letterkunde, Nieuwe Reeks Ser.: No. 116). 68p. 1982. pap. text 25.00 (0-444-85554-8) Elsevier.

Aalders, Gerard & Wiebes, Cees. The Art of Cloaking Ownership: The Secret Collaboration & Protection of the German War Industry by the Neutrals: The Case of Sweden. (C). 1996. 29.95 (90-5356-179-X, Pub. by Amsterdam U Pr) U of Mich Pr.

Aalen, F. H. & Whelan, Kevin, eds. Dublin: City & County from Prehistory to Present. (County History & Society Ser.: No. 5). (Illus.). 900p. 1992. pap. 79.95 (0-906602-19-X, Pub. by Geography Pubns) Irish Bks Media.

Aalen, Sverre. Heilsverlangen und Heilsverwirklichung. (Arbeiten zur Literatur und Geschichte des Hellenistischen Judentums Ser.: Vol. XXI). (GER.). xxi, 70p. 1990. 41.50 (90-04-09257-9) Brill Academic Pubs.

***Aalfs, Janet E.** Reach. LC 99-64963. 86p. 1999. pap. 11.95 (0-9660459-2-0, Pub. by Perugia Pr) SPD-Small Pr Dist.

***Aalseth, Patricia T.** Code Trainer DX. 2000. 59.00 (0-8342-1757-0) Aspen Pub.

Aalseth, Patricia T. CodeBusters: A Quick Guide to Coding & Billing Compliance for Medical Practices. LC 98-43607. 32p. 1998. pap. 24.00 (0-8342-1317-6, 13176) Aspen Pub.

— CodeBusters' Coding Connection: A Documentation Guide for Compliant Coding. LC 98-52866. 320p. 1999. spiral bd. 29.00 (0-8342-1361-3) Aspen Pub.

Aalst, W. Van, see Van Aalst, W., ed.

Aalst, Wil Van Der, see Van Der Aalst, Wil.

Aalsvoort, jt. auth. see Cowie.

Aaltio, Maija-Hellikki. Finnish for Foreigners, Vol.3. (ENG & FIN.). pap. 39.95 (0-7859-7447-4, 9511019198); pap. 39.95 (0-7859-7448-2, 9511093282) Fr & Eur.

— Finnish for Foreigners Vol. 3: Reader. (ENG & FIN.). pap. 39.95 (0-7859-7449-0, 9511019198) Fr & Eur.

— Finnish for Foreigners Vol. 4: Oral Exercises. (ENG & FIN.). pap. 19.95 (0-7859-7450-4, 9511012312) Fr & Eur.

Aaltio, Maija-Hellikki. Finnish for Foreigners I, 8 cass., Vol. 1. unabridged ed. 236p. (C). pap. 225.00 incl. audio (0-88432-093-6, AFFN01) Audio-Forum.

— Finnish for Foreigners II, 3 cass., Vol. 2. unabridged ed. 215p. (C). pap. 85.00 incl. audio (0-88432-094-4, AFFN25) Audio-Forum.

Aaltio, Maija-Hellikki. Finnish Language Book for English Speaking People. (ENG & FIN.). 27.50 (0-87559-107-8) Shalom.

Aalto, Alvar, Foundation Staff. The Architectural Drawings of Alvar Aalto 1917-1939, Vol. 10: Villa Mairea 1938, Villa Mairea, 1938-1939. LC 93-27504. (Illus.). 384p. 1994. text 220.00 (0-8153-0599-0) Garland.

— The Architectural Drawings of Alvar Aalto 1917-1939, Vol. 11: Tallinn Art Museum, Kauttua Terrace House, Finnish Pavilion at the 1939 World's Fair in New York, & Other Buildings & Projects, 1937-1939. LC 93-27504. (Illus.). 368p. 1994. text 220.00 (0-8153-0600-8) Garland.

— The Architectural Drawings of Alvar Aalto 1917-1939, Vol. 7: Buildings & Plans for the A. Ahlstrom Company in Varkaus, & Tupe Houses, 1937-1939. LC 93-27504. (Illus.). 450p. 1994. text 220.00 (0-8153-0596-6) Garland.

— The Architectural Drawings of Alvar Aalto 1917-1939, Vol. 9: Buildings for the Tampella Company, Inkeroinen Elementary School, & Other Buildings & Projects, 1936-1939. LC 93-27504. (Illus.). 424p. 1994. text 220.00 (0-8153-0598-2) Garland.

Aalto, Madeleine & Knight, Trevor. International Network of Public Libraries Vol. 5: Fundraising: Alternative Financial Support for Public Library Services. LC 99-12675. (Illus.). 112p. 1999. pap. 16.50 (0-8108-3580-0) Scarecrow.

Aaltonen, Kalervo. Kalevala Tarot. LC 95-61762. 1997. pap. text 12.00 (0-88079-186-1, BK65) US Games Syst.

AAM Registrars Committee. Standard Facility Report. 2nd ed. 32p. 1998. pap. text 18.00 (0-931201-55-1) Am Assn Mus.

AAMI Staff. AAMI: Biological Evaluation of Medical Devices, 1996. (Standards & Recommended Practices Ser.). (Illus.). 286p. (Orig.). 1996. pap. 210.00 (1-57020-032-7, BIOT3-209) Assn Adv Med Instrn.

— AAMI: Breakthrough Management: A New Model for Hospital Technical Services. (Illus.). 75p. (Orig.). 1995. pap. 118.00 (1-57020-037-8, BRE-209) Assn Adv Med Instrn.

— AAMI: Designing, Testing & Labeling Reusable Medical Devices for Reprocessing in Health Care Facilities: A Guide for Manufacturer. (Illus.). 53p. (Orig.). 1994. pap. 90.00 (1-57020-029-7, TIR12-209) Assn Adv Med Instrn.

— AAMI: Dry Heat (Heated Air) Sterilizers. (Illus.). 20p. (Orig.). 1995. pap. 82.00 (1-57020-031-9, ST50-209) Assn Adv Med Instrn.

— AAMI: Hemodializer Blood Tubing. 2nd ed. (Illus.). 10p. (Orig.). 1994. pap. 70.00 (1-57020-027-0, RD17-209) Assn Adv Med Instrn.

— AAMI: Hemodialyzers. 2nd ed. (Illus.). 18p. 1996. pap. 70.00 (1-57020-059-9, RD16-209) Assn Adv Med Instrn.

— AAMI: Sterilization of Health Care Products - Requirements for Validation & Routine Control-Radiation Sterilization. (Illus.). 48p. (Orig.). 1994. pap. 95.00 (1-57020-033-5, ST1137-209) Assn Adv Med Instrn.

— AAMI: Sterilization Pt. 1: Good Hospital Practices 1995 Edition. (Standards & Recommended Practices Ser.). (Illus.). 450p. (Orig.). 1995. pap. 235.00 (1-57020-034-3, STBK5-1-209) Assn Adv Med Instrn.

— AAMI: 31st Annual Meeting Proceedings. (Illus.). (Orig.). 1996. pap. 25.00 (1-57020-036-X, AMP95-209) Assn Adv Med Instrn.

— AAMI Sterilization: Hospital Equipment & Industrial Process Control, 1995. (Standards & Recommended Practices Ser.). (Illus.). 450p. (Orig.). 1995. pap. 235.00 (1-57020-035-1, STBK5-2-209) Assn Adv Med Instrn.

— Ambulatory Electrocardiographs. (ANSI-AAMI American National Standard Ser.). (Illus.). 39p. (Orig.). 1994. pap. 90.00 (1-57020-022-X, EC38-209) Assn Adv Med Instrn.

— Automatic External Defibrillators & Remote-Control Defibrillators. (Illus.). 29p. (Orig.). 1993. pap. 82.00 (1-57020-000-9, DF39-209) Assn Adv Med Instrn.

— Biological Evaluation of Medical Devices. (Illus.). 286p. (Orig.). 1996. pap. 210.00 (1-57020-055-6, BIOT3-209) Assn Adv Med Instrn.

— Blood Pressure Transducers. 2nd rev. ed. (ANSI-AAMI American National Standard Ser.). (Illus.). 14p. (Orig.). 1994. pap. 70.00 (1-57020-023-8, BP22-209) Assn Adv Med Instrn.

— Cardiovascular Implants-Vascular Prostheses. rev. ed. (ANSI-AAMI American National Standard Ser.). (Illus.). 29p. (Orig.). 1994. pap. 82.00 (1-57020-025-4, VP20-209) Assn Adv Med Instrn.

— Computerized Maintenance Management Systems for Clinical Engineering. LC 97-223981. (AAMI Management Information Reports). (Illus.). 90p. (Orig.). 1994. pap. 75.00 (1-57020-013-0, MIR3-209) Assn Adv Med Instrn.

— Electrosurgical Devices. 2nd ed. (Illus.). 34p. 1993. pap. text 90.00 (1-57020-019-X, HF18-209) Assn Adv Med Instrn.

— Good Hospital Practice: Table-Top Dry Heat (Heated Air) Sterilization & Sterility Assurance in Dental & Medical Facilities. (Illus.). 27p. (Orig.). 1992. pap. 82.00 (0-910275-16-5, ST40-209) Assn Adv Med Instrn.

— Hospital Steam Sterilizers. (Illus.). 16p. 1994. pap. 70.00 (1-57020-016-5, ST8-209) Assn Adv Med Instrn.

— International Standards & Regulatory Harmonization: AAMI 1994 International Standards Conference on Medical Devices. (Conference Reports). (Illus.). 305p. (Orig.). 1994. pap. 150.00 (1-57020-021-1, ISP94-209) Assn Adv Med Instrn.

— Pacemaker Emergency Intervention System. (Illus.). 8p. (Orig.). 1993. pap. 62.00 (1-57020-009-2, PAC49-209) Assn Adv Med Instrn.

— Selection of Surgical Gowns & Drapes in Health Care Facilities. (AAMI Technical Information Report Ser.). (Illus.). 43p. (Orig.). 1994. pap. 90.00 (1-57020-024-6, TIR11-209) Assn Adv Med Instrn.

— Water Quality for Dialysis: Current Concepts in Hemodialyzer Reprocessing. 2nd ed. (Illus.). 59p. (Orig.). 1993. pap. 90.00 (1-57020-003-3, WQD-209) Assn Adv Med Instrn.

Aamidor, Abraham. Real Feature Writing. LC 98-45245. (LEA's Communication Ser.). 176p. 1999. 39.95 (0-8058-3179-7); pap. 19.95 (0-8058-3180-0) L Erlbaum Assocs.

An Asterisk (*) at the beginning of an entry indicates that the title is appearing for the first time.

Aamiry, M. A. Jerusalem: Arab Origin & Heritage. LC 77-30751. (Illus.). 62p. reprint ed. pap. 30.00 (*0-608-18742-9*, 203034500068) Bks Demand.

Aamodt. Human Relations & Interpersonal Effective. (Psychology). (C). 2000. pap. 40.95 (*0-534-35508-0*) Brooks-Cole.

Aamodt, Agnar, jt. ed. see Voloso, Manuela.

Aamodt, Alice, jt. auth. see Johnson, Sylvia A.

Aamodt, Donald. A Name to Conjure With. 272p. 1989. pap. 3.50 (*0-380-75137-2*, Avon Bks) Morrow Avon.

— A Troubling along the Border. 288p. (Orig.). 1991. mass mkt. 4.50 (*0-380-75827-X*, Avon Bks) Morrow Avon.

Aamodt, Michael G. Applied Industrial - Organizational Psychology. 529p. (C). 1990. pap. 54.75 (*0-534-13770-9*) Brooks-Cole.

— Applied Industrial - Organizational Psychology. 2nd ed. LC 95-17007. 1995. pap. 52.50 (*0-534-33880-1*) Brooks-Cole.

— Applied Industrial - Organizational Psychology. 2nd ed. (Psychology Ser.). 1995. mass mkt., suppl. ed. 15.75 (*0-534-33881-X*) Brooks-Cole.

— Applied Industrial - Organizational Psychology. 2nd ed. 1995. mass mkt., teacher ed. write for info. (*0-534-33882-8*) Brooks-Cole.

— Applied Industrial - Organizational Psychology. 3rd ed. LC 98-36520. (Psychology Ser.). 1999. pap. 80.95 (*0-534-35881-0*) Brooks-Cole.

Aamodt, Michael G. & Komorowski. SCAI '95. LC 95-75771. (Frontiers in Artificial Intelligence & Applications Ser.). (gr. 12). 1995. 98.00 (*90-5199-221-1*) IOS Press.

Aamodt, Terrie D. Bold Venture: A History of Walla Walla College. 320p. 1992. text 39.95 (*0-9631859-0-X*) Walla Walla Coll.

Aamot, Paul. Writing Insights: What Professional Writers Know about Structure & Content. 89p. 1993. pap. text 4.95 (*0-9637070-0-0*) Arden Pubs.

AAMVA Staff. COM 115: Fundamentals of Public Speaking. 2nd ed. 86p. (C). 1998. pap. text 11.95 (*0-7872-5305-7*, 41530501) Kendall-Hunt.

***AAMVA Staff.** The Fast Track to Vehicle Services Facts: A Motor Vehicle Regulations & Procedures Information Guide. 3rd ed. LC 99-202062. 242p. 1998. per. 50.00 (*0-7872-5398-7*) Kendall-Hunt.

Aanavi, Don. The Art of Mauna Kea: Asian & Oceanic Art at Mauna Kea Beach Hotel. Foster, Dorothy, ed. (Illus.). 180p. 1990. 65.00 (*0-86638-122-8*) EW Ctr HI.

Aandahl, Andrew R. Soils of the Great Plains: Land Use, Crops, & Grasses. LC 81-7435. (Illus.). 334p. reprint ed. pap. 103.60 (*0-8357-3787-X*, 203651700003) Bks Demand.

Aandahl, Frederick, ed. see Link, Arthur S., et al.

Aangeenbrug, Robert T., et al. A Bibliographic Analysis of Statewide Geographic Information Systems, 1970-1990. LC 92-20413. (CPL Bibliographies Ser.: No. 282). 1992. 10.00 (*0-86602-282-1*, Sage Prdcls Pr) Sage.

AANN Staff. Human Responses to Neurologic Dysfunction. 2nd ed. 700p. 1999. text. write for info. (*0-7216-2288-7*, W B Saunders Co) Harcrt Hlth Sci Grp.

Aans, ed. Bibliography of the Writings of Harvey Cushing. 3rd ed. 142p. 1993. 28.00 (*1-879284-26-X*) Am Assn Neuro.

AAOP (Striker) Staff. Strength of Materials in Orthotic & Prosthetic Design. 112p. 1996. 49.95 (*0-7872-1913-4*) Kendall-Hunt.

AAOS Committee on Professional Liability Staff. Medical Malpractice: A Primer for Orthopaedic Residents & Fellows. 73p. 1994. 25.00 (*0-89203-093-3*) Amer Acad Ortho Surg.

AAOS Staff. CPT/ICD 9 Cross-Reference for Orthopaedic Surgery. 640p. 1998. pap. 100.00 (*0-89203-207-3*) Amer Acad Ortho Surg.

— Emergency Care & Transport Section 1: Instructor's Resource Kit. 6th ed. (Emergency Care Ser.). 1995. spiral bd. 11.25 (*0-89203-135-2*, 02182) Jones & Bartlett.

— Emergency Care & Transport Section 2: Instructor's Resource Kit. 6th ed. (Emergency Care Ser.). 1995. spiral bd. 11.25 (*0-89203-136-0*, 02183) Jones & Bartlett.

— Emergency Care & Transport Section 3: Instructor's Resource Kit. 6th ed. (Emergency Care Ser.). 1995. spiral bd. 11.25 (*0-89203-137-9*, 02184) Jones & Bartlett.

— Emergency Care & Transport Section 4: Instructor's Resource Kit. 6th ed. (Emergency Care Ser.). 1995. spiral bd. 11.25 (*0-89203-138-7*, 02185) Jones & Bartlett.

— Emergency Care & Transport Section 5: Instructor's Resource Kit. 6th ed. (Emergency Care Ser.). 1995. spiral bd. 11.25 (*0-89203-139-5*, 02186) Jones & Bartlett.

— Emergency Care & Transport Section 6: Instructor's Resource Kit. 6th ed. (Emergency Care Ser.). 1997. spiral bd. 11.25 (*0-89203-140-9*, 02188) Jones & Bartlett.

— Emergency Care & Transport Section 7: Instructor's Resource Kit. 6th ed. (Emergency Care Ser.). 1995. spiral bd. 11.25 (*0-89203-141-7*, 02189) Jones & Bartlett.

— Emergency Care & Transport Section 8: Instructor's Resource Kit. 6th ed. (Emergency Care Ser.). 1995. spiral bd. 11.25 (*0-89203-142-5*, 02190) Jones & Bartlett.

— Emergency Care & Transport Basic: Instructor's Resource Kit. 6th ed. (Emergency Ser.). 1995. spiral bd. 11.25 (*0-89203-134-4*, 02181) Jones & Bartlett.

— Emergency Care & Transportation of the Sick & Injured. 6th rev. ed. (Emergency Care Ser.). (C). 1997. pap. text 52.00 (*0-89203-164-6*, 02328) Jones & Bartlett.

AAOS Staff. Emergency Care & Transportation of the Sick & Injured. 6th rev. ed. (Emergency Care Ser.). 784p. (C). 1997. text 52.00 (*0-89203-165-4*, 02332) Jones & Bartlett.

AAOS Staff. Emergency Care & Transportation of the Sick & Injured: Instructor Question Bank. 6th rev. ed. (Emergency Care Ser.). 1997. pap. 28.75 (*0-89203-180-8*, 02330) Jones & Bartlett.

— Emergency Care & Transportation of the Sick & Injured Instructor Workbook. 5th ed. (Emergency Care Ser.). 290p. 1994. pap., teacher ed. 25.00 (*0-89203-054-2*, 02069) Jones & Bartlett.

— EMTB: Student Workbook. 6th ed. (Emergency Care Ser.). 1997. pap., student ed. 25.50 (*0-89203-166-2*) Jones & Bartlett.

— Postgraduate Orthopaedic Fellowships, 1998. 400p. 1998. pap. 30.00 (*0-89203-206-5*) Amer Acad Ortho Surg.

— Winning at Risk. LC 99-192075. (Managed Care Ser.). 95p. 1997. pap. 45.00 (*0-89203-163-8*) Amer Acad Ortho Surg.

AAOS Staff, ed. Capitation & Other Managed Care Payment Systems for Orthopaedic Surgeons. 100p. 1996. pap. 45.00 (*0-89203-154-9*) Amer Acad Ortho Surg.

AAOS Staff & National Safety Council Staff. First Responder. 2nd ed. LC 96-48546. (Emergency Care Ser.). 544p. (C). 1997. pap. 40.00 (*0-86720-541-5*) Jones & Bartlett.

— First Responder: Instructor's Manual. 2nd ed. (Emergency Care Ser.). 192p. 1997. pap. 25.00 (*0-7637-0464-4*) Jones & Bartlett.

— First Responder: Student Workbook. (Emergency Care Ser.). 144p. 1995. pap., student ed. 10.95 (*0-86720-547-4*) Jones & Bartlett.

— First Responder: Student Workbook. 2nd ed. (Emergency Care Ser.). 168p. 1997. pap., student ed., wbk. ed. 24.00 (*0-7637-0477-6*) Jones & Bartlett.

— First Responder: Teaching Package. 2nd ed. (Emergency Care Ser.). 1997. boxed set 495.00 (*0-7637-0478-4*) Jones & Bartlett.

— First Responder: Test Bank. 2nd ed. (Emergency Care Ser.). 168p. 1997. pap. 50.00 (*0-7637-0465-2*) Jones & Bartlett.

AAOS/NSC Staff. First Responder. 1995. pap. 38.00 (*0-86720-530-X*) Jones & Bartlett.

***AAP Rights & Permissions Advisory Committee.** The New & Updated Copyright Primer: A Survival Guide to Copyright & the Permissions Process. rev. ed. Risher, Carol & Tyree, Nisha, eds. 101p. 2000. pap. 15.00 (*0-933636-37-7*) AAP.

Aapro, M. S. Innovative Antimetabolites in Solid Tumours. LC 94-30057. (ESO Monographs). 1994. write for info. (*0-387-58341-6*) Spr-Verlag.

— Innovative Antimetabolites in Solid Tumours. LC 94-30057. (ESO Monographs). 1994. 54.95 (*3-540-58341-6*) Spr-Verlag.

***Aapro, M. S.** Pediatric Emergencies for Prehospital Personnel. (Illus.). 256p. (C). 2000. pap. text 36.25 (*0-7637-1219-1*) JB Pubns.

Aapro, M. S. & Maraninchi, D., eds. The Role of Multiple Intensification in Medical Oncology. LC 97-40470. (ESO Monographs). (Illus.). vii, 54p. 1998. 39.00 (*3-540-63543-2*) Spr-Verlag.

Aapro, M. S., jt. ed. see Redmond, K.

AAPT Apparatus Committee Staff, ed. AAPT Apparatus Competition. (Occasional Publications). (Illus.). 224p. (Orig.). 1984. pap. text 15.00 (*0-917853-10-5*, OP-21) Am Assn Physics.

Aarabi, Bizhan, et al, eds. Missile Wounds of the Head & Neck, Vol. I. 270p. 95.00 (*1-879284-64-2*) Am Assn Neuro.

— Missile Wounds of the Head & Neck, Vol. II. 196p. 95.00 (*1-879284-66-9*) Am Assn Neuro.

A'aragon d'Ar Satumi & Blue Feather, Milina. Into the Realms of Joy: Testament to a Simple God & a Simple Way of Living. 224p. 1995. pap. 13.95 (*1-887135-00-6*) Jewell Pub NC.

Aarbakke, Jarle, et al, eds. Tumor Cell Differentiation: Biology & Pharmacology. LC 87-17012. (Experimental Biology & Medicine Ser.: Vol. 17). (Illus.). 360p. (C). 1987. 130.00 (*0-89603-134-9*) Humana.

***Aardahl, Jean.** Mormonism... Eternal Life or Eternal Death. Thurston, Pamela Sue, ed. 40p. 2000. mass mkt. 5.99 (*0-9675264-1-8*) A A Pubs.

— There Will Be No Divorce. Thomas, Sue, ed. 144p. 2000. mass mkt. 10.99 (*0-9675264-0-X*) A A Pubs.

Aardema, John, jt. illus. see Simic, Tim.

Aardema, Verna. Anansi Does the Impossible. LC 96-20033. (Illus.). 32p. (J). (ps-3). 1997. 16.00 (*0-689-81092-X*) S&S Childrens.

— Bimwili & The Zimwi. (Illus.). 1992. pap. 5.99 (*0-14-054608-1*) NAL.

— Bimwili & the Zimwi: A Tale from Zanzibar. (J). 1985. 10.19 (*0-606-03966-X*, Pub. by Turtleback) Demco.

— A Bookworm Who Hatched. LC 93-12002. (Meet the Author Ser.). (Illus.). 32p. (J). (gr. 2-5). 1995. 14.95 (*1-878450-39-5*, 705) R Owen Pubs.

— Borreguita & the Coyote. (J). 1998. pap. 6.99 (*0-679-88936-1*, Pub. by Random Bks Yng Read) Random.

— Borreguita & the Coyote. 1998. 13.19 (*0-606-12895-6*, Pub. by Turtleback) Demco.

— Bringing the Rain to Kapiti Plain. 1993. pap. 6.99 (*0-14-055252-9*) NAL.

— Bringing the Rain to Kapiti Plain. LC 80-25886. (Pied Piper Bks.). (Illus.). 32p. (J). (ps). 1981. 16.99 (*0-8037-0809-2*, Dial Yng Read) Peng Put Young Read.

— Bringing the Rain to Kapiti Plain. (J). (ps-3). 1992. pap. 5.99 (*0-14-054616-2*, PuffinBks) Peng Put Young Read.

Aardema, Verna. Bringing the Rain to Kapiti Plain: A Nandi Tale. (Reading Rainbow Bks.). 1981. 11.19 (*0-606-01606-6*, Pub. by Turtleback) Demco.

Aardema, Verna. Koi & the Kola Nuts: A Tale from Liberia. LC 97-46713. (Illus.). 32p. (J). (gr. k-5). 1999. 16.95 (*0-689-81760-6*) Atheneum Yung Read.

— Oh, Kojo! How Could You! 1993. pap. 5.99 (*0-14-054669-3*) NAL.

— Oh, Kojo! How Could You! An Ashanti Tale. 1984. 10.19 (*0-606-03880-9*, Pub. by Turtleback) Demco.

— Por Que Zumban los Mosquitos en los Oidos de la Gente.Tr. of Why Mosquitoes Buzz in People's Ears. (SPA., Illus.). 32p. (J). 1998. 16.99 (*0-8037-2298-2*, Dial Yng Read) Peng Put Young Read.

Aardema, Verna. Rabbit Makes a Monkey of Lion: A Swahili Tale. (Picture Puffin Ser.). (Illus.). (J). 1989. 11.19 (*0-606-02854-4*, Pub. by Turtleback) Demco.

— Traveling to Tondo: A Tale of the Nkundo of Zaire. 1991. 11.19 (*0-606-06065-0*, Pub. by Turtleback) Demco.

Aardema, Verna. Who's In Rabbit's House? 1992. pap. 6.99 (*0-14-054724-X*) NAL.

— Who's in Rabbit's House? A Masai Tale. (J). 1977. 11.19 (*0-606-02309-7*, Pub. by Turtleback) Demco.

— Why Mosquitoes Buzz in People's Ears: A West African Tale. LC 74-2886. (Illus.). 32p. (J). (ps-3). 1975. 16.99 (*0-8037-6089-2*, Dial Yng Read) Peng Put Young Read.

— Why Mosquitoes Buzz in People's Ears: A West African Tale. (J). 1975. 11.19 (*0-606-01884-0*, Pub. by Turtleback) Demco.

Aardema, Verna. Why Mosquitoes Buzz in People's Ears: A West African Tale. (J). (ps-4). pap. 12.95 incl. audio Weston Woods.

Aardema, Verna. Why Mosquitos Buzz in People's Ears. (J). 1980. pap. 2.95 (*0-590-10294-X*) Scholastic Inc.

Aardema, Verna & Clouse, Nancy. Sebugugu the Glutton: A Bantu Tale from Ruanda, Africa. (Illus.). 32p. (J). (gr. 2-4). 1993. 14.95 (*0-86543-377-1*) Africa World.

Aarebrot, Frank H., jt. auth. see Berglund, Sten.

Aarhus, Jeanne, ed. see Cumpton, Lonnie, et al.

Aarhus, Jeanne, ed. see Euling, Derrol, et al.

Aarli, J. A. & Toender, O. Immunological Aspects of Neurological Diseases. (Monographs in Neural Sciences: Vol. 6). (Illus.). xiv, 190p. 1980. pap. 42.75 (*3-8055-0814-X*) S Karger.

Aarnio, Aulis. Legal Reasoning, Vol. I. (C). 1992. lib. bdg. 125.00 (*0-8147-0606-1*) NYU Pr.

— The Rational As Reasonable: A Treatise on Legal Justification. (Law & Philosophy Library: No. 4). 288p. 1986. text 130.50 (*90-277-2276-5*) Kluwer Academic.

— Reason & Authority: A Treatise on the Dynamic Paradigm of Legal Dogmatics. LC 97-7848. 320p. 1997. text 82.95 (*1-85521-933-6*, Pub. by Ashgate Pub) Ashgate Pub Co.

Aarnio, Aulis & MacCormick, D. Neil, eds. Legal Reasoning, Set, Vols. I & II. (International Library of Essays in Law & Legal Theory). 1200p. (C). 1992. lib. bdg. 250.00 (*0-8147-0608-8*) NYU Pr.

— Legal Reasoning, Vol. II. (C). 1992. lib. bdg. 125.00 (*0-8147-0607-X*) NYU Pr.

Aaron. Answer Key to Accompany Little, Brown Compact Handbook. 3rd ed. (C). 1998. ring bd. write for info. (*0-321-01942-3*) Addson-Wesley Educ.

— Circlings. 2001. write for info. (*0-15-100373-4*) Harcourt.

— The Compact Reader. 4th ed. 1993. pap. text, teacher ed. 0.26 (*0-312-06645-7*) St Martin.

— The Compact Reader. 5th ed. 1996. pap. text, teacher ed. 10.00 (*0-312-13273-5*) St Martin.

— The Compact Reader. 6th ed. LC 98-87516. xxii, 376p. 1999. pap. text 30.95 (*0-312-17165-X*) St Martin.

— Frommer's Budget Travel Guide India on $40 a Day. 5th ed. 1996. per. 17.95 (*0-671-52016-4*) S&S Trade.

— International Labour Law Reports, Vol. 15, ILLR. 1997. 270.00 (*90-411-0280-9*) Kluwer Law Intl.

— Little Brown Essential Handbook for Business Writers. (C). 2000. spiral bd. Price not set. (*0-321-02697-7*) Addison-Wesley.

— Little Brown Essential Handbook for Technical Writers. (C). 2000. spiral bd. Price not set. (*0-321-02695-0*) Addison-Wesley.

Aaron, jt. auth. see Fowler.

Aaron, jt. auth. see Kennedy, Dorothy M.

Aaron, Benjamin. The First Annual Lecture. (Benjamin Aaron Annual Lecture Ser.). 30p. 1993. reprint ed. 7.00 (*0-89215-153-6*) U Cal LA Indus Rel.

Aaron, Benjamin, et al, eds. International Labour Law Reports, Vol. 4. 1986. lib. bdg. 179.00 (*90-247-3307-3*) Kluwer Academic.

Aaron, Benjamin, ed. see International Society for Labor Law & Social Secur.

Aaron Blake Publishers Staff. Working Actor's Guide to Los Angeles, 2000. 13th ed. 1999. pap. 39.00 (*0-937609-17-X*) Aaron Blake Pubs.

Aaron Blake Publishing Staff. The Working Actor's Guide to Los Angeles, 1999. 12th rev. ed. 1998. pap. 37.50 (*0-937609-15-3*) Aaron Blake Pubs.

Aaron, Brenda B. Soul Call. 70p. (Orig.). 1996. pap. write for info. (*1-57502-130-7*) Morris Pubng.

Aaron, Bud. ActiveX. LC 96-69519. 528p. 1996. per. 40.00 (*0-7615-0801-5*) Prima Pub.

— OS/2 Presentation Manager User's Guide. (Illus.). 380p. 1989. 28.95 (*0-8306-0736-6*, 3036); pap. 19.95 (*0-8306-9336-X*, 3036P) McGraw-Hill Prof.

— OS/2 Presentation Manager Developer's Guide. (Illus.). 480p. 1989. 34.95 (*0-8306-0346-8*, 3046); pap. 24.95 (*0-8306-9346-7*, 3046P) McGraw-Hill Prof.

Aaron, Carl. The Political Economy of Japanese Foreign Direct Investment in the U. K. & the U. S. Multinationals, Subnational Regions & the Investment Location Decision. LC 97-44367. (St. Antony's Ser.). 256p. 1998. text 69.95 (*0-312-21314-X*) St Martin.

Aaron, Chester. Duchess. LC 81-47755. 192p. (J). (gr. 7 up). 1982. lib. bdg. 11.89 (*0-397-31948-7*) HarpC Child Bks.

— Garlic Is Life. LC 95-40815. (Illus.). 224p. 1996. pap. 14.95 (*0-89815-806-0*) Ten Speed Pr.

***Aaron, Chester.** Garlic Kisses: Human Struggles - Garlic Connections. Urig, Douglas & Boatman, Dennis, eds. (Illus.). 176p. 2000. pap. 19.95 (*0-9701094-9-0*, 1-0027) Mostly Garlic.

Aaron, Chester. Gideon. LC 81-48066. 192p. (YA). (gr. 7 up). 1982. 11.95 (*0-397-31992-4*); lib. bdg. 11.89 (*0-397-31993-2*) HarpC Child Bks.

— The Great Garlic Book. LC 97-19655. (Illus.). 160p. 1997. pap. 14.95 (*0-89815-919-9*) Ten Speed Pr.

— Lackawanna. LC 83-47667. 224p. (YA). (gr. 7 up). 1986. lib. bdg. 11.89 (*0-397-32058-2*) HarpC Child Bks.

— Out of Sight, Out of Mind. LC 84-48356. 192p. (J). (gr. 6-9). 1985. lib. bdg. 11.89 (*0-397-32101-5*) HarpC Child Bks.

Aaron, Daniel. American Notes: Selected Essays. 288p. 1994. text 40.00 (*1-55553-195-4*) NE U Pr.

— Cincinnati, Queen City of the West, 1819-1838. LC 91-48133. (Urban Life & Urban Landscape Ser.). 364p. 1992. text 24.95 (*0-8142-0570-4*) Ohio St U Pr.

— Palabra por Palabra: Spanish Vocabulary Organizer. (Efficient Language Ser.). (SPA., Illus.). 68p. (Orig.). 1994. pap. 39.95 incl. disk (*1-884677-01-0*) Salix.

— The Unwritten War: American Writers & the Civil War. LC 86-40486. 402p. 1987. reprint ed. text 39.95 (*0-299-11390-6*) U of Wis Pr.

— Writers on the Left. LC 92-16360. 496p. 1992. pap. 20.50 (*0-231-08039-5*, Mrngside) Col U Pr.

***Aaron, Daniel, ed.** American Men & Women of Letters. 300-600p. 1999. 214.75 (*0-7910-4547-1*) Chelsea Hse.

Aaron, Daniel, ed. From a Darkened Room: The Inman Diary. (Inman Fund Ser.). (Illus.). 624p. 1996. pap. 17.95 (*0-674-45443-X*) HUP.

— Studies in Biography. (English Studies: No. 8). 200p. (C). 1978. 16.00 (*0-674-84651-6*); pap. 5.95 (*0-674-84652-4*) HUP.

Aaron, Daniel, ed. see Dos Passos, John.

Aaron, Daniel, ed. see Herrick, Robert.

Aaron, Daniel, ed. see Inman, Arthur C.

Aaron, Daniel, ed. see Longfellow, Henry Wadsworth.

Aaron, Daniel, ed. see Paine, Albert B.

Aaron, Daniel, ed. see Woodberry, George E. & Lewis, R. W. B.

Aaron, David. Agent of Influence. 480p. 1990. mass mkt. 4.95 (*0-380-71005-6*, Avon Bks) Morrow Avon.

— Crossing by Night. 416p. 1994. mass mkt. 5.99 (*0-380-72191-0*, Avon Bks) Morrow Avon.

— Crossing by Night. large type ed. LC 93-11442. 711p. 1993. reprint ed. lib. bdg. 22.95 (*0-7862-0008-1*) Thorndike Pr.

— Endless Light: The Ancient Path of the Kabbalah to Love, Spiritual Growth & Personal Power. LC 97-2453. 176p. 1997. 21.50 (*0-684-81873-6*) S&S Trade.

— Endless Light: The Ancient Path of the Kabbalah to Love, Spiritual Growth & Personal Power. 176p. 1998. reprint ed. pap. 12.00 (*0-425-16629-5*) Berkley Pub.

***Aaron, David.** Seeing God. 2001. 24.95 (*1-58542-080-8*, Tarcher Putnam) Putnam Pub Group.

Aaron, Dipley. Dipley's Don't You Believe It! Spurious & Ersatz New England Factoids. (Illus.). 128p. (Orig.). 1989. pap. 6.95 (*0-924771-10-0*, Covered Brdge Pr) Douglas Charles Ltd.

Aaron, Frani, intro. Phoenix Cuisine, Vol. 5. rev. ed. 160p. 1995. pap. 5.95 (*0-9632234-6-1*) R Hart Mktg.

Aaron, Frank. Phoenix Cuisine, 1992. 100p. 1992. 9.95 (*0-9632234-0-2*) R Hart Mktg.

— Phoenix Cuisine '99, Vol. 9. 1999. mass mkt. 7.95 (*1-893350-51-7*) R Hart Mktg.

Aaron, Frank, ed. Phoenix Cuisine, 1993, Vol. II. (Illus.). 120p. (Orig.). 1992. pap. 4.95 (*0-9632234-2-9*) R Hart Mktg.

***Aaron, Frank, ed.** Phoenix Cuisine 2000. (Illus.). 195p. 1999. pap. 8.95 (*1-893350-01-0*) R Hart Mktg.

Aaron, Frank, intro. Phoenix Cuisine. (Phoenix Cuisine Ser.: Vol. 4). 164p. 1994. pap. text 4.95 (*0-9632234-5-3*) R Hart Mktg.

— Phoenix Cuisine, Vol. 3. rev. ed. 150p. 1994. pap. text 4.95 (*0-9632234-4-5*) R Hart Mktg.

— Phoenix Cuisine, 1997, Vol. 6. rev. ed. (Illus.). 208p. 1996. pap. 7.95 (*0-9632234-9-6*) R Hart Mktg.

— Phoenix Cuisine 1998, Vol. 7. rev. ed. (Illus.). 194p. 1997. pap. 7.95 (*0-9632234-7-X*) R Hart Mktg.

Aaron, Frieda W. Bearing the Unbearable: Yiddish & Polish Poetry in the Ghettos & Concentration Camps. LC 89-11593. (SUNY Series in Modern Jewish Literature & Culture). 242p. (C). 1990. text 29.50 (*0-7914-0247-9*) State U NY Pr.

Aaron, Gregory. Weather Tracker's Kit. (Discovery Kit Ser.). (Illus.). 80p. (Orig.). (J). (gr. 4-7). 1991. 18.95 (*0-89471-998-X*) Running Pr.

***Aaron, Hank.** Chipper Jones: A Brace Legend in the Making. 2000. 24.95 (*1-887432-89-2*) Beckett Pubns.

Aaron, Hank. I Had a Hammer: The Hank Aaron Story. 1991. 11.09 (*0-606-01165-X*, Pub. by Turtleback) Demco.

Aaron, Hank & Wheeler, Lonnie. I Had a Hammer: The Hank Aaron Story. (Illus.). 480p. 1992. mass mkt. 6.99 (*0-06-109956-2*, Harp PBks) HarpC.

Aaron, Henry. On Social Welfare. LC 80-80680. (Illus.). 143p. 1980. 25.00 (*0-89011-549-4*) Abt Bks.

— On Social Welfare. (Illus.). 144p. 1984. lib. bdg. 58.50 (*0-8191-4102-X*) U Pr of Amer.

— Street Furniture. 1989. pap. 40.00 (*0-85263-864-7*, Pub. by Shire Pubns) St Mut.

***Aaron, Henry J.** Behavioral Dimensions Of Retirement Economics LC 99-6604. 1999. 18.95 (*0-8157-0063-6*) Brookings.

Aaron, Henry J. Economic Effects of Social Security. LC 82-73654. (Studies of Government Finance). 84p. 1982. pap. 10.95 (*0-8157-0029-6*) Brookings.

An Asterisk (*) at the beginning of an entry indicates that the title is appearing for the first time.

— The Peculiar Problem of Taxing Life Insurance Companies. LC 83-70788. (Studies of Government Finance). 46p. 1983. pap. 7.95 (*0-8157-0031-8*) Brookings.

— Retirement & Economic Behavior. 1984. pap. 16.95 (*0-8157-0035-0*) Brookings.

— Serious & Unstable Condition: Financing America's Health Care. 158p. 1991. 32.95 (*0-8157-0051-2*) Brookings.

— Shelter & Subsidies: Who Benefits from Federal Housing Policies? LC 72-306. (Brookings Institution Studies in Social Experimentation). 254p. reprint ed. pap. 78.80 (*0-608-14524-6*, 202535900043) Bks Demand.

— Who Pays the Property Tax? A New View. LC 75-19270. (Studies of Government Finance). 122p. reprint ed. pap. 37.90 (*0-8357-7074-5*, 203358700086) Bks Demand.

— Why Is Welfare So Hard to Reform? LC 72-13543. (Studies in Social Economics). 71p. 1973. pap. 10.95 (*0-8157-0019-9*) Brookings.

Aaron, Henry J., ed. Inflation & the Income Tax. LC 76-28669. (Studies of Government Finance). 1976. pap. 14.95 (*0-8157-0023-7*) Brookings.

— The Problem That Won't Go Away: Reforming U. S. Health Care Financing. 298p. (C). 1995. 42.95 (*0-8157-0010-5*) Brookings.

— Setting National Priorities: Policy for the '90s. 317p. (C). 1990. 34.95 (*0-8157-0048-2*); pap. 14.95 (*0-8157-0047-4*) Brookings.

— Social Security & the Budget: Proceedings of the First Conference of the National Academy of Social Insurance December 15th & 16th, 1988, Washington, D.C. LC 89-22570. (Illus.). 160p. (Orig.). (C). 1990. pap. text 22.50 (*0-8191-7602-8*); lib. bdg. 44.50 (*0-8191-7601-X*) U Pr of Amer.

Aaron, Henry J., et al, eds. Uneasy Compromise: Problems of a Hybrid Income-Consumption Tax. LC 88-464. 441p. 1988. pap. 19.95 (*0-8157-0045-8*); text 44.95 (*0-8157-0046-6*) Brookings.

— Values & Public Policy. 216p. (C). 1993. pap. 14.95 (*0-8157-0055-5*) Brookings.

— Values & Public Policy. 216p. (C). 1994. 34.95 (*0-8157-0056-3*) Brookings.

Aaron, Henry J. & Boskin, Michael J., eds. The Economics of Taxation. LC 79-3774. (Studies of Government Finance). 418p. 1980. 32.95 (*0-8157-0014-8*) Brookings.

Aaron, Henry J. & Gale, William G. A Citizen's Guide to Fundamental Tax Reform. 120p. 1997. pap. 10.95 (*0-8157-0049-0*) Brookings.

Aaron, Henry J. & Galper, Harvey. Assessing Tax Reform. LC 84-45979. (Studies of Government Finance). 145p. 1985. 32.95 (*0-8157-0038-5*) Brookings.

— Assessing Tax Reform. LC 84-45979. (Studies of Government Finance). 145p. 1986. pap. 12.95 (*0-8157-0037-7*) Brookings.

Aaron, Henry J. & Lougy, Cameran. The Comparable Worth Controversy. LC 85-48206. 57p. 1986. pap. 8.95 (*0-8157-0041-5*) Brookings.

Aaron, Henry J. & Pechman, Joseph A., eds. How Taxes Affect Economic Behavior. LC 81-1040. (Studies of Government Finance). 456p. 1981. 38.95 (*0-8157-0012-1*); pap. 16.95 (*0-8157-0011-3*) Brookings.

Aaron, Henry J. & Reischauer, Robert D. Countdown To Reform: The Great Social Security Debate / LC 98-37325. xii, 195 p. 1998. write for info. (*0-87078-430-7*) Century Foundation.

— There When You Need It: Saving Social Security for Future Generations of Americans. 240p. 1998. 24.95 (*0-87078-423-4*) Century Foundation.

— There When You Need It: Saving Social Security for Future Generations of Americans. LC 98-37325. 1998. 11.95 (*0-87078-429-3*) Century Foundation.

Aaron, Henry J. & Schultze, Charles L., eds. Setting Domestic Priorities: What Can Government Do? 318p. (C). 1992. 42.95 (*0-8157-0054-7*); pap. 18.95 (*0-8157-0053-9*) Brookings.

Aaron, Henry J. & Schwartz, William B. The Painful Prescription: Rationing Hospital Care. LC 83-45962. (Studies in Social Economics). 161p. 1984. 29.95 (*0-8157-0034-2*); pap. 11.95 (*0-8157-0033-4*) Brookings.

Aaron, Henry J. & Shoven, John B. Should Social Security Be Abolished? LC 99-12010. (Albert Hanson Lectures). (Illus.). 160p. 1999. 24.95 (*0-262-01174-3*) MIT Pr.

Aaron, Henry J., et al. Can America Afford to Grow Old? Paying for Social Security. 144p. 1989. pap. 10.95 (*0-8157-0043-1*) Brookings.

— Economic Choices, 1987. LC 85-48278. 126p. 1986. 32.95 (*0-8157-1040-2*); pap. 12.95 (*0-8157-1039-9*) Brookings.

Aaron, Henry J., ed. see Brookings Institution Staff.

Aaron, Henry J., jt. ed. see Reischauer, Robert D.

Aaron, Hilary. The Three Little Kittens in the Enchanted Forest: A Pop-Up Adventure. LC 94-79230. (Illus.). 16p. (J). (ps-2). 1995. 18.95 (*0-7868-0137-9*, Pub. by Hyprn Child) Little.

Aaron, Hugh. Business Not As Usual: How to Win Managing a Business Through Hard & Easy Times. Johnson, John A., ed. LC 92-62348. 240p. 1993. pap. 19.95 (*1-882521-00-5*) Stones Pt Pr.

— It's All Chaos: Tales of the Young, the Old & the Middle Aged. Feller-Roth, Barbara, ed. LC 95-72363. 272p. (Orig.). 1996. pap. text 15.00 (*1-882521-10-2*) Stones Pt Pr.

— Letters from the Good War: A Young Man's Discovery of the World. De Rosas, Ramon, ed. LC 96-68798. 750p. (Orig.). 1997. pap. 20.00 (*1-882521-04-8*) Stones Pt Pr.

— Suzy, Fair Suzy. large type ed. (Illus.). 32p. (J). (gr. k-4). 1998. pap. 8.95 (*1-882521-07-2*) Stones Pt Pr.

— When Wars Were Won. Feller-Roth, Barbara, ed. LC 95-69538. 280p. (Orig.). 1995. pap. text 16.00 (*1-882521-02-1*) Stones Pt Pr.

Aaron, James. Little Brown Essential Handbook for Writers. 3rd ed. LC 99-28869. 247p. (C). 1999. spiral bd. 16.00 (*0-321-04970-5*) Addson-Wesley Educ.

Aaron, Jan. Frommer's India from $40 a Day. 5th ed. 480p. 1996. 18.95 (*0-02-861123-3*) Macmillan.

— 101 Great Choices: New York City. LC 97-17560. (Illus.). 128p. 1996. pap. 7.95 (*0-8442-8987-6*, 89876, Passprt Bks) NTC Contemp Pub Co.

— 101 Great Choices: Washington, D.C. (Illus.). 128p. (Orig.). 1995. pap. 7.95 (*0-8442-8992-2*, 89922, Passprt Bks) NTC Contemp Pub Co.

Aaron, Jane. A Double Singleness: Gender & the Writings of Charles & Mary Lamb. 230p. (C). 1991. text 70.00 (*0-19-812890-8*) OUP.

Aaron, Jane, et al, eds. Our Sisters' Land: The Changing Identity of Women in Wales. (Illus.). 312p. 1994. pap. 24.95 (*0-7083-1247-0*, Pub. by Univ Wales Pr) Paul & Co Pubs.

Aaron, Jane & Gardiner, Barbara. When I'm Afraid. LC 98-12720. (Illus.). 36p. (J). (ps-2). 1998. text 15.00 (*0-307-44057-5*, Whitman Coin) St Martin.

— When I'm Angry. unabridged ed. LC 98-12721. (On My Own Biographies Ser.). (Illus.). 36p. (J). 1998. text 15.00 (*0-307-44019-2*, Whitman Coin) St Martin.

— When I'm Jealous, with a Parent's Guide to Jealousy. unabridged ed. LC 98-38562. (Illus.). 36p. 1998. text 15.00 (*0-307-44056-7*, Whitman Coin) St Martin.

— When I'm Sad, with a Parent's Guide to Sadness. unabridged ed. LC 98-36330. (Illus.). 36p. 1998. text 15.00 (*0-307-44058-3*, Whitman Coin) St Martin.

Aaron, Jane E. The Little, Brown Compact Handbook. 2nd ed. (Illus.). 320p. (C). 1997. text 22.66 (*0-673-99408-2*) Addson-Wesley Educ.

— The Little, Brown Compact Handbook. 2nd ed. 320p. 1995. spiral bd. 22.95 (*0-8230-5001-7*) Watsn-Guptill.

***Aaron, Jane E.** The Little, Brown Compact Handbook. 3rd ed. 416p. (C). 1998. spiral bd. 29.06 (*0-321-03796-0*) Addson-Wesley Educ.

— The Little, Brown Compact Handbook. 4th ed. LC 00-31024. 2000. write for info. (*0-321-07509-9*) Addson-Wesley Educ.

Aaron, Jane E., ed. The Compact Reader. 384p. 1984. teacher ed. write for info. (*0-318-57913-8*) St Martin.

Aaron, Jane E., jt. auth. see Fowler, H. Ramsey.

Aaron, Joe, jt. auth. see Jenkins, Jim.

Aaron, Joe, ed. see Chicago Jewish News Staff.

Aaron, Jonathan. Corridor: Poems. LC 91-50807. (Wesleyan Poetry Ser.). 59p. (C). 1992. pap. 12.95 (*0-8195-1203-6*, Wesleyan Univ Pr); text 25.00 (*0-8195-2200-7*, Wesleyan Univ Pr) U Pr of New Eng.

Aaron, Ken, ed. see Hester, William.

Aaron, Kevin J. Journey from Eden. LC 88-63512. (Illus.). 216p. (Orig.). 1989. pap. 8.95 (*0-9621490-0-4*) Cathedral Pubns.

Aaron, Marjorie. A Family Conspiracy. LC 88-92565. (Illus.). 64p. (Orig.). 1988. pap. 6.95 (*0-9621414-0-2*) MAQ Pubns.

Aaron, Martin H. & Wright, John H. The Appraisal of Religious Facilities. LC 97-19783. 1997. write for info. (*0-922154-39-2*) Appraisal Inst.

Aaron, Michael. Michael Aaron Piano Course: Lessons. Flatau, Carole, ed. 64p. (Orig.). 1994. pap. 5.95 (*0-89898-867-5*, 11004A) Wrner Bros.

Aaron, Michael. Michael Aaron Piano Course Vol. 24: Lessons. Flatau, Carole, ed. (Illus.). 64p. (Orig.). (J). (gr. k-1). 1994. pap. 5.95 (*0-89898-855-1*, 11001A) Wrner Bros.

Aaron, Michael. Michael Aaron Piano Course Vol. 24: Lessons. Flatau, Carole, ed. (Illus.). 64p. (Orig.). (J). (gr. 2). 1994. pap. 5.95 (*0-89898-859-4*, 11002A) Wrner Bros.

***Aaron, Michele.** Body's Perilous Pleasures: Dangerous Desires & Contemporary Culture. 2000. pap. 28.00 (*0-7486-0961-X*, Pub. by Edinburgh U Pr) Col U Pr.

Aaron, P. G. Dyslexia & Hyperlexia. (C). 1989. lib. bdg. 128.00 (*1-55608-079-4*) Kluwer Academic.

— Dyslexia & Hyperlexia: Diagnosis & Management of Developmental Reading Disabilities. (Neuropsychology & Cognition Ser.). 319p. (C). 1994. pap. text 73.00 (*0-7923-3155-9*) Kluwer Academic.

Aaron, P. G. & Baker, Catherine. Reading Disabilities in College & High School: Diagnosis & Management. LC 90-72124. (Illus.). 207p. 1991. pap. text 22.00 (*0-912752-23-8*) York Pr.

Aaron, P. G. & Joshi, R. Malatesha. Reading Problems: Consultation & Remediation. LC 92-3124. (School Practitioner Ser.). 285p. 1992. lib. bdg. 33.00 (*0-89862-365-0*) Guilford Pubns.

Aaron, Patricia J., ed. see Norwak, Mary.

Aaron, Phillip. Power to Create. 1991. pap. 12.95 (*0-9630418-0-0*) Pennington TX.

Aaron, Pietro. Compendiolo di Molti Dubbi, Segreti & Sentenze Intorno al Canto Fermo & Figurato. fac. ed. (Monuments of Music & Music Literature in Facsimile Ser., Series II: Vol. 66). (ITA.). 1974. lib. bdg. 35.00 (*0-8450-2266-0*) Broude.

— Libri Tres de Institutione Harmonica. fac. ed. (Monuments of Music & Music Literature in Facsimile, I Ser.: Vol. 67). (LAT.). 134p. 1976. lib. bdg. 35.00 (*0-8450-2267-9*) Broude.

— Lucidario in Musica di Alcune oppenioni Antiche et Moderne. fac. ed. (Monuments of Music & Music Literature in Facsimile Ser., Series II: Vol. 68). (Illus.). 1978. lib. bdg. 35.00 (*0-8450-2268-7*) Broude.

— Thoscanello de la Musica. fac. ed. (Monuments of Music & Music Literature in Facsimile Ser., Series II: Vol. 69). 1969. lib. bdg. 42.50 (*0-8450-2269-5*) Broude.

— Trattato . . . di Canto Figurato. fac. ed. (Monuments of Music & Music Literature in Facsimile Ser., Series II: Vol. 129). 1979. lib. bdg. 40.00 (*0-8450-2329-2*) Broude.

Aaron, Randi, jt. auth. see Zimmer, Judith.

Aaron, Richard I. Bankruptcy Law Fundamentals. LC 83-27535. 1984. ring bd. 145.00 (*0-87632-432-4*) West Group.

— Knowing & the Function of Reason. 1971. 25.00 (*0-19-824351-0*) OUP.

— Our Knowledge of Universals. (Studies in Philosophy: No. 40). 1975. lib. bdg. 29.95 (*0-8383-0108-8*) M S G Haskell Hse.

Aaron, Richard I., jt. auth. see Conard, Alfred F.

Aaron, Richard I., jt. auth. see Dix, George E.

Aaron, Richard I., jt. auth. see McCormick, Charles T.

Aaron, Robert, et al. The Gospel on Campus: A Handbook of Campus Ministry Programs & Resources. 2nd ed. Galligan-Stierle, Michael, ed. & pref. by. LC 96-185887. 240p. 1996. pap. text 16.95 (*1-57455-031-4*) US Catholic.

Aaron, Robin H., jt. auth. see Aaron, Ronald.

Aaron, Ronald & Aaron, Robin H. Improve Your Physics Grade. 256p. (Orig.). (C). 1984. pap. 43.95 (*0-471-89006-5*) Wiley.

Aaron, Stephen. Stage Fright: Its Role in Acting. LC 85-24649. 176p. 1986. 13.95 (*0-226-00018-4*) U Ch Pr.

— Stage Fright: Its Role in Acting. LC 85-24649. xx, 156p. 1993. pap. 9.95 (*0-226-00019-2*) U Ch Pr.

— Stage Fright: Its Role in Acting. LC 85-24649. 175p. reprint ed. pap. 54.30 (*0-608-09253-3*, 205405500002) Bks Demand.

Aaron, Stewart. Civil Discovery. Vol. L2. text 82.00 (*0-8205-2421-2*) Bender.

Aaron, Titus. Sexual Harassment. 70p. (YA). (gr. 7-12). 1992. pap. 6.95 (*1-57515-009-3*) PPI Pubng.

Aaron, Titus & Isaksen, Judith A. Sexual Harassment in the Workplace: A Guide to the Law & a Research Overview for Employers & Employees. LC 92-56628. 231p. 1993. pap. 32.50 (*0-89950-763-8*) McFarland & Co.

Aaron, Tossi, jt. auth. see Bisgaard, Erling.

Aaron, Tossi, ed. see Bisgaard, Erling & Stehouwer, Gulle.

***Aaron, Uche.** Tense & Aspect of Obolo Grammar & Discourse. LC 98-61265. (Publications in Linguistics: Vol. 128). 204p. 1999. pap. 29.00 (*1-55671-063-1*) S I L Intl.

Aaron, William. Mot pour Mot: French Vocabulary Organizer. (Efficient Language Ser.). (FRE., Illus.). 68p. (Orig.). 1994. pap. 39.95 incl. disk (*1-884677-00-2*) Salix.

Aaroni, Wallenrod. Fundamentals of Hebrew Grammar. 272p. 1978. pap. 11.95 (*0-88328-004-3*) Shilo Pub Hse.

Aaronian, Peg, ed. see Thiel, Michael F.

Aaronovitch, A. & Samson, S. Insurance Industry in the Countries of the E. E. C. (C). 1985. 108.00 (*0-7855-4132-2*, Pub. by Witherby & Co) St Mut.

Aaronovitch, Sam. The Road from Thatcherism: The Alternative Economic Strategy. LC 81-165154. 138 p. 1981. write for info. (*0-85315-534-8*) Lawrence & Wishart.

— The Ruling Class: A Study of British Finance Capital. LC 78-23485. 192p. 1979. reprint ed. lib. bdg. 55.00 (*0-313-20764-X*, AARC, Greenwood Pr) Greenwood.

Aaronovitch, Sam & Sawyer, Malcolm C. Big Business: Theoretical & Empirical Aspects of Concentration & Mergers in the United Kingdom LC 75-318049. xiv, 337p. 1975. write for info. (*0-333-14609-3*) Macmillan.

***Aaronovitch, Sam & Toporowski, Jan.** Political Economy & New Capitalism: Essays in Honour of Sam Aaronovitch. LC 99-22500. (Frontiers of Political Economy Ser.). 1999. text. write for info. (*0-415-20221-3*) Routledge.

Aarons, Edward S. Assignment--the Girl in the Gondola. (Assignment Ser.). 1979. mass mkt. 1.75 (*0-449-14165-9*, GM) Fawcett.

— Assignment Maltese Maiden. large type ed. (Adventure Travel Guide Ser.). 368p. 1992. 11.50 (*0-7089-2618-5*) Ulverscroft.

— Assignment Palermo. large type ed. 1989. pap. 16.99 (*0-7089-6741-8*, Linford) Ulverscroft.

— Assignment to Disaster. large type ed. (Linford Mystery Library). 368p. 1993. pap. 16.99 (*0-7089-7429-5*, Linford) Ulverscroft.

— Dark Destiny. large type ed. (Linford Mystery Library). 384p. 1995. pap. 16.99 (*0-7089-7796-0*, Linford) Ulverscroft.

— Escape to Love. large type ed. 368p. 1995. 27.99 (*0-7089-3251-7*) Ulverscroft.

— I Can't Stop Running. large type ed. (Linford Mystery Library). 1995. pap. 16.99 (*0-7089-7708-1*, Linford) Ulverscroft.

— The Net. large type ed. 1994. 27.99 (*0-7089-3179-0*) Ulverscroft.

— No Place to Live. large type ed. (Mystery Ser.). 1994. pap. 16.99 (*0-7089-7628-X*, Linford) Ulverscroft.

— Say It with Myrder. large type ed. (Linford Mystery Library). 368p. 1994. pap. 16.99 (*0-7089-7477-5*, Linford) Ulverscroft.

— Terror in the Town. large type ed. (Linford Mystery Library). 400p. 1995. pap. 16.99 (*0-7089-7712-X*, Linford) Ulverscroft.

— They All Ran Away. large type ed. (Linford Mystery Library). 352p. 1993. pap. 16.99 (*0-7089-7425-2*) Ulverscroft.

Aarons, Leroy. Prayers for Bobby: A Mother's Coming to Terms with the Suicide of Her Gay Son. LC 94-45141. 288p. 1996. pap. 14.00 (*0-06-251123-8*, Pub. by Harper SF) HarpC.

Aarons, Louis. Japanese Say Hello. rev. ed. (WordMate Ser.). (JPN.). 192p. (J). (gr. 9 up). 1996. spiral bd. 49.95 incl. audio (*1-887447-03-2*) WordMate.

Aarons, Louis. Spanish Say Hello. 2nd rev. ed. (WordMate Ser.). (SPA.). 181p. (gr. 9 up). 1996. pap., student ed., spiral bd. 39.95 incl. audio (*1-887447-00-8*) WordMate.

— Speed English. 2nd rev. ed. (JPN.). 200p. (YA). student ed. 59.95 incl. audio (*1-887447-02-4*) WordMate.

Aarons, Mark. Unholy Trinity: The Vatican, the Nazis, & Soviet Intelligence. LC 99-205288. 432p. 1998. pap. 16.95 (*0-312-18199-X*) St Martin.

***Aarons, Maureen.** Handbook of Autism: A Guide for Parents & Professionals. 2nd ed. 1999. pap. 24.99 (*0-415-16035-9*) Routledge.

— Handbook of Autism: A Guide for Parents & Professionals. 2nd ed. LC 98-49953. 1999. 75.00 (*0-415-16034-0*) Routledge.

Aarons, Maureen & Gittens, Tessa. Handbook of Autism: A Guide for Parents & Professionals. 144p. (C). 1991. pap. 24.99 (*0-415-05566-0*, A5984) Routledge.

Aarons, Victoria. Author As Character in the Works of Sholom Aleichem. LC 84-22703. (Studies in Art & Religious Interpretation: Vol. 3). 192p. 1989. lib. bdg. 79.95 (*0-88946-553-3*) E Mellen.

— A Measure of Memory: Storytelling & Identity in American Jewish Fiction. LC 95-13362. 1996. 35.00 (*0-8203-1773-X*) U of Ga Pr.

Aarons, Victoria & Salomon, Willis A., eds. Rhetoric & Ethics: Historical & Theoretical Perspectives. LC 90-21255. 220p. 1991. lib. bdg. 89.95 (*0-88946-212-7*) E Mellen.

Aaronsohn, Elizabeth. Going Against the Grain: Supporting the Student-Centered Teacher. LC 95-32535. 200p. 1996. 55.95 (*0-8039-6297-5*); pap. 24.95 (*0-8039-6298-3*) Corwin Pr.

Aaronson, Akiva. The Foundation of Judaism. 134p. 1997. 13.95 (*1-56871-108-5*) Targum Pr.

Aaronson, David E., jt. auth. see Simon, Rita J.

Aaronson, David F. Maryland Criminal Jury Instructions & Commentary. 2nd ed. 1,013p. 1988. 75.00 (*0-87473-335-9*, 60003-10, MICHIE) LEXIS Pub.

Aaronson, H. I., jt. ed. see Russell, K. C.

Aaronson, H. I., jt. ed. see Zackay, V. F.

Aaronson, Hubert I., ed. High-Temperature, High-Resolution Metallography. LC 67-26569. (Metallurgical Society Conference Ser.: Vol. 38). 391p. reprint ed. pap. 121.30 (*0-608-11335-2*, 200152700079) Bks Demand.

Aaronson, Hubert I., ed. see International Conference on Solid to Solid Phase T.

Aaronson, Jon. An Introduction to Infinite Ergodic Theory. LC 96-54848. (Mathematical Surveys & Monographs Ser.: Vol. 50). 284p. 1997. text 79.00 (*0-8218-0494-4*, SURV/50) Am Math.

Aaronson, P. I., et al, eds. International Symposium on Resistance Arteries - 5th International Symposium, Cambridge, September 1996: Abstracts. (Journal Ser.: Vol. 33, Supplement 2, 1996). (Illus.). 56p. 1996. pap. 24.50 (*3-8055-6376-0*) S Karger.

***Aaronson, P. I., et al.** Cardiovascular System at a Glance. LC 98-54927. (At a Glance Ser.). (Illus.). 1999. pap. 26.95 (*0-632-04971-5*) Blackwell Sci.

***Aaronson, Sharon.** Between Two Lands: For the Right Hand Alone. 1999. pap. 2.50 (*0-7390-0320-8*, 18997) Alfred Pub.

— Christmas Lites - Modern & Bright. 24p. 1994. pap. 4.95 (*0-7390-0779-3*) Alfred Pub.

— Christmas Stylings, Vol. 2. 24p. 1991. pap. 5.95 (*0-7390-0570-7*, 6045) Alfred Pub.

— Silent Night, Piano Duet. 8p. 1999. pap. 2.95 (*0-7390-0373-9*, 18978) Alfred Pub.

Aaronson, Sharon, ed. Rachmaninoff/Rhapsody on a Theme of Paganini. 4p. 1996. pap. 2.50 (*0-7390-0877-3*, 14322) Alfred Pub.

Aaronson, Sheldon, ed. Chemical Communication at the Microbial Level, Vol. I. 200p. 1982. 114.00 (*0-8493-5319-X*, QR96, CRC Reprint) Franklin.

— Chemical Communication at the Microbial Level, Vol. II. 200p. 1982. 114.00 (*0-8493-5320-3*, QR96, CRC Reprint) Franklin.

Aaronson, Stephanie & Cameron, Stephen V. Poverty in New York City, 1996: An Update & Perspectives. 92p. 1997. 12.00 (*0-88156-204-1*) Comm Serv Soc NY.

Aaronson, Stuart A., et al, eds. Oncogenes & Cancer: Proceedings of the Seventeenth International Symposium of the Princess Takamatsu Cancer Research Fund, June 1986. 320p. 1987. lib. bdg. 140.00 (*90-6764-101-4*, Pub. by VSP) Coronet Bks.

Aaronson, Susan A. Trade & the American Dream: A Social History of Postwar Trade Policy. LC 95-51058. (Illus.). 264p. 1996. pap. 18.95 (*0-8131-0874-8*); text 45.00 (*0-8131-1955-3*) U Pr of Ky.

Aaronson, William N., jt. auth. see Neuhaus, Ruby H.

AARP Staff. AARP Pharmacy Service Prescription Drug Handbook. rev. ed. (Illus.). 960p. 1992. pap. 18.00 (*0-685-52541-4*, Harper Ref) HarpC.

AARP Staff. Think of Your Future. 176p. 1995. pap. 24.95 (*0-06-263555-7*, HarpRes) HarpInfo.

AARP Staff. Think of Yr Future W. LC 96-132821. 272p. 1995. pap., wbk. ed. 24.95 (*0-06-263554-9*) HarpC.

Aarre, Bent. Spinnaker Handling. 2nd ed. Croft, Christopher & Firth, Anne, trs. from DAN.Tr. of Spilersejlads. (ENG., Illus.). 112p. 1993. pap. 14.95 (*0-924486-51-1*) Sheridan.

Aarrestad, Thomas. The Potter Giselle. LC 98-48021. (Illus.). 32p. (J). (ps-3). 2000. 14.95 (*1-57102-146-9*, Ideals Child) Hambleton-Hill.

***Aarsen, Carlyne.** A Mother at Heart. 2000. per. 4.50 (*0-373-87100-7*) Harlequin Bks.

Aarsen, Carolyn. The Cowboy's Bride. (Love Inspired Ser.: Bk. 67). 1999. per. 4.50 (*0-373-87067-1*, 1-87067-4) Harlequin Bks.

Aarsen, Carolyne. A Bride at Last. 1999. per. 4.50 (*0-373-87051-5*, 1-87051-8, Mira Bks) Harlequin Bks.

— Ever Faithful. (Love & Laughter Ser.). 1998. per. 4.50 (*0-373-87033-7*, Steeple Hill) Harlequin Bks.

***Aarsen, Carolyne.** A Family at Last. (Love Inspired Ser.). 2000. mass mkt. 4.50 (*0-373-87127-9*, 1871276) Harlequin Bks.

Aarsen, Carolyne. A Family-Style Christmas. (Love Inspired Ser.: Bk. 86). 2000. per. 4.50 (*0-373-87086-8*, 1-87086-4) Harlequin Bks.

— Homecoming. (Love Inspired Ser.). 1998. per. 4.50 (*0-373-87024-8*, Steeple Hill) Harlequin Bks.

Aarseth, Espen J. Cybertext: Perspectives on Ergodic Literature. LC 97-3554. (Illus.). 216p. 1997. text 45.00 (*0-8018-5578-0*); pap. text 14.95 (*0-8018-5579-9*) Johns Hopkins.

Aarsleff, Hans. The Study of Language in England, 1780-1860. LC 78-13573. 279p. 1979. reprint ed. lib. bdg. 55.00 (*0-313-21046-2*, AASL, Greenwood Pr) Greenwood.

Aarsleff, Hans, et al, eds. Papers in the History of Linguistics: Proceedings of the Third International Conference on the History of the Language Sciences (ICHoLS III), Princeton, 19-23 August 1984. LC 86-3528. (Studies in the History of Linguistics: Vol. 38). xxi, 680p. 1987. 177.00 (*90-272-4521-5*) J Benjamins Pubng Co.

Aarsleff, Hans, jt. auth. see Burchfield, Robert W.

Aarssen, Jeroen, jt. auth. see Backus, Ad.

Aarts, Bas. English Syntax & Argumentation. LC 97-11313. 320p. 1997. text 59.95 (*0-312-17574-4*) St Martin.

— Small Clauses in English: The Non-Verbal Types. LC 92-13313. (Topics in English Linguistics Ser.: No. 8). xi, 228p. (C). 1992. lib. bdg. 86.15 (*3-11-013487-X*) Mouton.

Aarts, Bas & Meyer, Charles F., eds. The Verb in Contemporary English: Theory & Description. 325p. (C). 1995. text 69.95 (*0-521-46039-5*) Cambridge U Pr.

Aarts, Emile H. & Korst, Jan. Simulated Annealing & Boltzmann Machines: A Stochastic Approach to Combinatorial Optimization & Neural Computing. LC 88-20871. 284p. 1989. 220.00 (*0-471-92146-7*) Wiley.

Aarts, Emile H., jt. auth. see Van Laarhoven, P. J.

Aarts, Emile L. & Lenstra, Jan K., eds. Local Search in Combinatorial Optimization. LC 96-36111. (Wiley-Interscience Series in Discrete Mathematics & Optimization). 522p. 1997. 159.95 (*0-471-94822-5*) Wiley.

Aarts, Flor & Van Els, Theo, eds. Contemporary Dutch Linguistics. fac. ed. LC 89-28805. 169p. (Orig.). 1990. reprint ed. pap. 52.40 (*0-7837-7798-1*, 204755400007) Bks Demand.

Aarts, J. M. & Nishiura, T. Dimension & Extensions. LC 92-44402. (North-Holland Mathematical Library: Vol. 48). 332p. 1993. 113.00 (*0-444-89740-2*, North Holland) Elsevier.

Aarts, Leo, et al, eds. Curing the Dutch Disease: An International Perspective on Disability. LC 96-84116. (International Studies on Social Security: Vol. 1). 192p. 1996. 63.95 (*1-85972-439-6*, Pub. by Avebry) Ashgate Pub Co.

Aarts, Leo J. & De Jong, Philip R. Economic Aspects of Disability Behavior. LC 92-25774. (Contributions to Economic Analysis Ser.: Vol. 207). 376p. 1992. 125.50 (*0-444-89462-4*, North Holland) Elsevier.

Aarts, N. J., ed. see European Congress on Thermography Staff.

Aartun, Kjell. Die Partikeln des Ugaritischen, Vol. 2. (Alter Orient und Altes Testament Ser.: Vol. 21). (GER.). x, 177p. 1978. text 29.50 (*3-7887-0567-1*, Pub. by NeukirchenerV) Eisenbrauns.

— Die Partilkeln des Ugaritischen Vol. 1: Adverbien, Verneinungspartikeln, Bekraftigungspartikeln, Hervorhebungspartikeln. (Alter Orient und Altes Testament Ser.: Vol. 21/1). (GER.). 124p. 1974. text 22.50 (*3-7887-0426-8*) NeukirchenerV.

Aas, G. & Riedmiller, A. Collins Nature Guide: Trees. 254p. 1996. 14.95 (*0-00-219993-9*, Pub. by HarpC) Trafalgar.

Aas-Rouxparis, Nicole. L' Espace Fictionnel dans la Mise en Scene de Claude Ollier. LC 90-5913. (American University Studies: Romance Languages & Literature: Ser. II, Vol. 142). (FRE.). 241p. (C). 1990. text 49.95 (*0-8204-1298-8*) P Lang Pubng.

AASCU Staff. Directory of Economic Development Programs at State Colleges & Universities. LC 88-16975. 188p. (C). 1989. pap. text 30.00 (*0-88044-094-5*); lib. bdg. 50.00 (*0-88044-095-3*) AASCU Press.

***Aase, Dawn.** Contextual Test of Articulation. LC 00-27316. 2000. pap. write for info. (*1-888222-49-2*) Thinking Pubns.

Aase, J. M. Diagnostic Dysmorphology: An Approach to the Patient with Multiple Congenital Anomalies. (Illus.). 308p. (C). 1990. text 59.50 (*0-306-43444-X*, Kluwer Plenum) Kluwer Academic.

Aasen, A., ed. Surgical Pathophysiology. xiii, 452p. 1990. text 176.00 (*3-7186-5038-X*, Harwood Acad Pubs) Gordon & Breach.

Aasen, A. O., et al, eds. Papers Dedicated to Egil Amundsen: On the Occasion of his 60th Birthday March 18, 1984. (Journal: European Surgical Research: Vol. 16, Supp. 2). (Illus.). iv, 172p. 1984. pap. 45.25 (*3-8055-3889-8*) S Karger.

Aasen, Clarence. Architecture of Siam: A Cultural History Interpretation. (Illus.). 344p. 1998. text 85.00 (*983-56-0027-9*) OUP.

Aasen, J. O., ed. North Sea Oil & Gas Reservoirs III: Proceedings of the Third North Sea Oil & Gas Reservoirs Conference Organized by the Norwegian Institute of Technology (NTH) Trondheim, Norway, November 30 - December 2, 1992. LC 93-8013. 430p. (C). 1994. lib. bdg. 310.00 (*0-7923-2304-1*) Kluwer Academic.

***Aasen, Larry.** North Dakota Images. (Images of America Ser.). (Illus.). 128p. 2000. pap. 18.99 (*0-7385-0763-6*) Arcadia Publng.

Aaseng, Jay, jt. auth. see Aaseng, Nathan.

Aaseng, Nathan. Aliens! (Grubstake Adventure Ser.). 80p. (J). 1995. pap. 5.99 (*0-8066-2838-3*, 9-2838) Augsburg Fortress.

— All-Star Line-up. 400p. (J). (gr. 4-7). 1995. pap. 9.99 (*0-7814-0203-4*) Chariot Victor.

— American Dinosaur Hunters. LC 96-6056. (Collective Biographies Ser.). (Illus.). 112p. (YA). (gr. 6 up). 1996. lib. bdg. 20.95 (*0-89490-710-7*) Enslow Pubs.

— America's Third-Party Presidential Candidates. LC 94-22102. (Profiles Ser.). (Illus.). 160p. (gr. 5-12). 1995. lib. bdg. 18.95 (*1-881508-19-6*) Oliver Pr MN.

— At Left Linebacker, Chip Demory. LC 87-30905. 128p. (J). (gr. 3-7). 1988. pap. 4.49 (*1-55513-921-3*, Chariot Bks) Chariot Victor.

— Athletes. LC 94-12469. (American Indian Lives Ser.). 144p. (J). 1995. 19.95 (*0-8160-3019-7*) Facts on File.

— Autoimmune Diseases. LC 94-49443. (Venture-Health & the Human Body Ser.). (Illus.). 112p. (YA). (gr. 7-12). 1995. lib. bdg. 22.00 (*0-531-12553-X*) Watts.

— Barry Sanders: Star Running Back. LC 93-6173. (Sports Reports Ser.). (Illus.). 104p. (J). (gr. 4-10). 1994. lib. bdg. 20.95 (*0-89490-484-1*) Enslow Pubs.

— Black Inventors. LC 96-40486. (American Profiles Ser.). (Illus.). 128p. (J). (gr. 5-12). 1997. 19.95 (*0-8160-3407-9*) Facts on File.

— Breaking the Sound Barrier. (YA). 1992. lib. bdg. 7.95 (*0-671-74213-2*, Julian Messner) Silver Burdett Pr.

— Business Builders in Computers. LC 98-54433. (Business Builders Ser.). (Illus.). 160p. (J). (gr. 5-12). 2000. lib. bdg. 19.95 (*1-881508-57-9*) Oliver Pr MN.

***Aaseng, Nathan.** Business Builders in Fast Food. Sterling, Denise, ed. (Business Builders Ser.: Vol. 3). (Illus.). 160p. (YA). (gr. 5-12). 2000. lib. bdg. 19.95 (*1-881508-58-7*) Oliver Pr MN.

Aaseng, Nathan. Business Builders in Oil. LC 98-50470. (Business Builders Ser.). (Illus.). 160p. (J). (gr. 5-12). 2000. lib. bdg. 19.95 (*1-881508-56-0*) Oliver Pr MN.

— Carl Lewis: Legend Chaser. LC 84-23348. (Sports Achievers Ser.). (Illus.). 56p. (J). (gr. 4-9). 1985. lib. bdg. 18.60 (*0-8225-0496-0*, Lerner Publctns) Lerner Pub.

— Charles Darwin: Revolutionary Biologist. LC 92-45281. (YA). (gr. 5 up). 1993. lib. bdg. 23.93 (*0-8225-4914-X*, Lerner Publctns) Lerner Pub.

***Aaseng, Nathan.** The Cherokee Nation vs. Georgia. LC 99-45621. (Famous Trials Ser.). (Illus.). 128p. (YA). (gr. 6-9). 2000. lib. bdg. 23.70 (*1-56006-628-8*) Lucent Bks.

Aaseng, Nathan. Construction: Building the Impossible. LC 98-51815. (Innovators Ser.). (Illus.). 144p. (J). (gr. 5-12). 1999. lib. bdg. 19.95 (*1-881508-59-5*) Oliver Pr MN.

— The Disease Fighters: The Nobel Prize in Medicine. (Nobel Prize Winners Ser.). (Illus.). 80p. (YA). (gr. 5 up). 1987. pap. 6.95 (*0-8225-9715-2*, First Ave Edns) Lerner Pub.

— Dwight Gooden: Strikeout King. (Sports Achievers Ser.). (Illus.). 56p. (J). (gr. 4-9). 1988. lib. bdg. 18.60 (*0-8225-0478-2*, Lerner Publctns) Lerner Pub.

— Ending World Hunger. LC 90-46207. (Science, Technology & Society Ser.). (Illus.). 144p. (YA). (gr. 9-12). 1991. lib. bdg. 24.00 (*0-531-11007-9*) Watts.

— Explorers for God. LC 98-18815. (Family Read-Aloud Collection). (Illus.). 128p. (J). (gr. k-7). 1998. 15.99 (*0-8066-3608-4*, 9-3608) Augsburg Fortress.

— Florence Griffith-Joyner: Dazzling Olympian. (Sports Achievers Ser.). (Illus.). 56p. (J). (gr. 4-9). 1989. lib. bdg. 18.60 (*0-8225-0495-2*, Lerner Publctns) Lerner Pub.

— Florence Griffith-Joyner: Dazzling Olympian. (Illus.). 56p. (J). (gr. 4-9). 1991. pap. 4.95 (*0-8225-9587-7*, First Ave Edns) Lerner Pub.

— Florence Griffith-Joyner: Dazzling Olympian. 1991. 10.15 (*0-606-12291-5*, Pub. by Turtleback) Demco.

— Genetics: Unlocking the Secrets of Life. LC 95-38804. (Innovators Ser.). (Illus.). 144p. (YA). (gr. 5-12). 1996. lib. bdg. 19.95 (*1-881508-27-7*) Oliver Pr MN.

— Great Justices of the Supreme Court. LC 92-18443. (Profiles Ser.). (Illus.). 160p. (YA). (gr. 5-12). 1992. lib. bdg. 18.95 (*1-881508-01-3*) Oliver Pr MN.

***Aaseng, Nathan.** The Impeachment of Bill Clinton. LC 99-39568. (Famous Trials Ser.). (Illus.). 128p. (YA). (gr. 6-9). 2000. lib. bdg. 23.70 (*1-56006-651-2*) Lucent Bks.

Aaseng, Nathan. Invertebrates. (Venture Bks.). (Illus.). 112p. (YA). (gr. 7-12). 1993. lib. bdg. 24.00 (*0-531-12550-5*) Watts.

— Jose Canseco: Baseball's Forty-Forty Man. (Sports Achievers Ser.). (Illus.). 56p. (J). (gr. 4-9). 1989. lib. bdg. 18.60 (*0-8225-0493-6*, Lerner Publctns) Lerner Pub.

— Jose Canseco: Baseball's Forty-Forty Man. (YA). 1989. pap. 4.95 (*0-8225-9586-9*, Lerner Publctns) Lerner Pub.

— The Locker Room Mirror: How Sports Reflect Society. LC 92-34582. (Illus.). 144p. (J). (gr. 5 up). 1993. 14.95 (*0-8027-8217-5*); lib. bdg. 15.85 (*0-8027-8218-3*) Walker & Co.

— Lost in the Forest. LC 96-18946. (Grubstake Adventure Ser.). 80p. (J). (gr. 5-9). 1996. pap. 5.99 (*0-8066-2790-5*, 9-2790, Augsburg) Augsburg Fortress.

— Meat-Eating Plants. LC 95-3827. (Weird & Wacky Science Ser.). (Illus.). 48p. (J). (gr. 4-10). 1996. lib. bdg. 18.95 (*0-89490-617-8*) Enslow Pubs.

***Aaseng, Nathan.** Multiple Sclerosis LC 99-34864. 2000. 25.00 (*0-531-11531-3*) Watts.

Aaseng, Nathan. Nature's Poisonous Creatures. (J). 1996. pap. 8.95 (*0-8050-4689-5*) H Holt & Co.

— Nature's Poisonous Creatures. LC 97-8728. (Scientific American Sourcebooks Ser.). 96p. (J). (gr. 5-9). 1997. 22.40 (*0-8050-4690-9*) TFC Bks NY.

— Navajo Code Talkers. LC 92-11408. 114p. (J). 1992. 15.95 (*0-8027-8182-9*); lib. bdg. 16.85 (*0-8027-8183-7*) Walker & Co.

***Aaseng, Nathan.** Navajo Code Talkers. (Illus.). 96p. (J). (gr. 3-6). 2000. reprint ed. pap. 7.95 (*0-8027-7589-6*) Walker & Co.

Aaseng, Nathan. The O. J. Simpson Trial: What It Shows Us about Our Legal System. (Illus.). 128p. (YA). (gr. 7 up). 1996. 15.95 (*0-8027-8404-6*); lib. bdg. 16.85 (*0-8027-8405-4*) Walker & Co.

— Overpopulation: Crisis or Challenge? LC 90-13121. (Science, Technology & Society Ser.). (Illus.). 160p. (YA). (gr. 9-12). 1991. lib. bdg. 24.00 (*0-531-11006-0*) Watts.

— Paris. LC 92-709. (Cities at War Ser.). (Illus.). 96p. (YA). (gr. 6 up). 1992. lib. bdg. 18.00 (*0-02-700010-9*, Mac Bks Young Read) S&S Childrens.

— The Peace Seekers: The Nobel Peace Prize. (Nobel Prize Winners Ser.). (Illus.). 80p. (J). (gr. 5 up). 1987. lib. bdg. 18.60 (*0-8225-0654-8*, Lerner Publctns) Lerner Pub.

— The Peace Seekers: The Nobel Peace Prize. (Illus.). 80p. (J). (gr. 5 up). 1991. pap. 5.95 (*0-8225-9604-0*, Lerner Publctns) Lerner Pub.

— Science vs. Pseudoscience. LC 93-30014. (Illus.). 112p. (YA). (gr. 9-12). 1994. lib. bdg. 24.00 (*0-531-11182-2*) Watts.

— Sneak Attack! LC 94-44807. (Grubstake Adventures Ser.). 80p. (J). (gr. 5-9). 1995. pap. 5.99 (*0-8066-2787-5*, 9-2787, Augsburg) Augsburg Fortress.

— Sports Great David Robinson. LC 91-41532. (Sports Great Bks.). (Illus.). 64p. (J). (gr. 4-10). 1992. lib. bdg. 17.95 (*0-89490-373-X*) Enslow Pubs.

— Sports Great David Robinson. rev. ed. LC 97-14982. (Sports Great Bks.). (Illus.). 64p. (J). (gr. 4-10). 1998. lib. bdg. 17.95 (*0-7660-1077-5*) Enslow Pubs.

— Sports Great John Stockton. LC 94-34940. (Sports Great Bks.). (Illus.). 64p. (J). (gr. 4-10). 1995. lib. bdg. 17.95 (*0-89490-598-8*) Enslow Pubs.

— Sports Great Kirby Puckett. LC 92-38433. (Sports Great Bks.). (Illus.). 64p. (J). (gr. 4-10). 1993. lib. bdg. 17.95 (*0-89490-392-6*) Enslow Pubs.

— Sports Great Michael Jordan. LC 92-11607. (Sports Great Bks.). (Illus.). 64p. (J). (gr. 4-10). 1992. lib. bdg. 17.95 (*0-89490-370-5*) Enslow Pubs.

— Sports Great Michael Jordan. rev. ed. LC 97-5539. (Sports Great Bks.). (Illus.). 64p. (J). (gr. 4-10). 1997. lib. bdg. 17.95 (*0-89490-978-9*) Enslow Pubs.

— Swamped! LC 95-10388. (Grubstake Adventures Ser.). 80p. (J). (gr. 5-9). 1995. pap. 5.99 (*0-8066-2788-3*, 9-2788, Augsburg) Augsburg Fortress.

***Aaseng, Nathan.** Teens & Drunk Driving. LC 99-16888. (Overview Ser.). (Illus.). 128p. (YA). (gr. 6-9). 2000. lib. bdg. 23.70 (*1-56006-518-4*) Lucent Bks.

— The Titanic. (Building History Ser.). (Illus.). 128p. (YA). (gr. 4-12). 1999. lib. bdg. 23.70 (*1-56006-569-9*) Lucent Bks.

Aaseng, Nathan. Top 10 Basketball Scoring Small Forwards. LC 98-44953. (Sports Top 10 Ser.). (Illus.). 48p. (YA). (gr. 4-10). 1999. lib. bdg. 18.95 (*0-7660-1152-6*) Enslow Pubs.

— Treacherous Traitors. LC 96-29861. (Profiles Ser.). (Illus.). 160p. (J). (gr. 5-12). 1997. lib. bdg. 18.95 (*1-881508-38-2*) Oliver Pr MN.

— True Champions: Great Athletes & Their Off-the-Field Heroics. LC 92-36942. (Illus.). 128p. (J). (gr. 5 up). 1993. 14.95 (*0-8027-8246-9*); lib. bdg. 15.85 (*0-8027-8247-7*) Walker & Co.

— Twentieth Century Inventors. (American Profiles Ser.). (Illus.). 144p. (YA). (gr. 5-12). 1991. 19.95 (*0-8160-2485-5*) Facts on File.

— Which Way Are You Leading Me, Lord? Bible Devotions & Activities for Boys. LC 84-21562. (Augsburg Young Readers Ser.). 112p. (Orig.). (J). (gr. 3-7). 1996. pap. 6.99 (*0-8066-2113-3*, 9-2113, Augsburg) Augsburg Fortress.

***Aaseng, Nathan.** The White House. LC 00-8238. (Building History Ser.). (Illus.). 2000. write for info. (*1-56006-708-X*) Lucent Bks.

Aaseng, Nathan. A Winning Season for the Braves. LC 82-72711. 128p. (J). (gr. 3-7). 1988. pap. 4.99 (*1-55513-950-7*, Chariot Bks) Chariot Victor.

***Aaseng, Nathan.** Women Olympic Champions. LC 00-8751. (History Makers Ser.). (Illus.). (J). 2000. lib. bdg. write for info. (*1-56006-709-8*) Lucent Bks.

Aaseng, Nathan. Yearbooks in Science: 1930-1939. (Yearbooks in Science Ser.). (Illus.). 80p. (J). (gr. 5-8). 1995. lib. bdg. 20.40 (*0-8050-3433-1*) TFC Bks NY.

— Yearbooks in Science: 1940-1949, 2. (Yearbooks in Science Ser.). (Illus.). 80p. (J). (gr. 5-8). 1995. lib. bdg. 20.40 (*0-8050-3434-X*) TFC Bks NY.

— You Are the Corporate Executive. LC 96-4570. (Great Decisions Ser.). (Illus.). 160p. (YA). (gr. 5-12). 1997. lib. bdg. 18.95 (*1-881508-35-8*) Oliver Pr MN.

— You Are the Explorer. LC 98-50136. (Great Decisions Ser.). (Illus.). 160p. (J). (gr. 5-12). 1999. lib. bdg. 18.95 (*1-881508-55-2*) Oliver Pr MN.

— You Are the General. LC 93-11661. (Great Decisions Ser.). (Illus.). 160p. (YA). (gr. 5-12). 1994. lib. bdg. 18.95 (*1-881508-11-0*) Oliver Pr MN.

— You Are the General II, 1800-1899. LC 94-46910. (Great Decisions Ser.). (Illus.). 160p. (YA). (gr. 5-12). 1995. lib. bdg. 18.95 (*1-881508-25-0*) Oliver Pr MN.

— You Are the Juror. LC 96-53046. (Great Decisions Ser.). (Illus.). 160p. (J). (gr. 5-12). 1997. lib. bdg. 18.95 (*1-881508-40-4*) Oliver Pr MN.

— You Are the President. LC 93-5776. (Great Decisions Ser.). (Illus.). 160p. (YA). (gr. 5-12). 1994. lib. bdg. 18.95 (*1-881508-10-2*) Oliver Pr MN.

— You Are the President II, 1800-1899. LC 93-46308. (Great Decisions Ser.). (Illus.). 160p. (YA). (gr. 5-12). 1994. lib. bdg. 18.95 (*1-881508-15-3*) Oliver Pr MN.

— You Are the Senator. LC 96-4569. (Great Decisions Ser.). (Illus.). 160p. (YA). (gr. 5-12). 1997. lib. bdg. 18.95 (*1-881508-36-6*) Oliver Pr MN.

— You Are the Supreme Court Justice. LC 93-46307. (Great Decisions Ser.). (Illus.). 160p. (YA). (gr. 5-12). 1994. lib. bdg. 18.95 (*1-881508-14-5*) Oliver Pr MN.

Aaseng, Nathan & Aaseng, Jay. Head Injuries. LC 95-44988. (Venture Bks.). (Illus.). 112p. (YA). (gr. 7-12). 1996. lib. bdg. 24.00 (*0-531-11267-5*) Watts.

Aaseng, Nathan & Sherer, Michael L. Night of Wonder: Service-Story for Christmas Eve. 1985. 3.50 (*0-89536-762-9*, 5869) CSS OH.

Aaseng, Rolf E. A Beginners' Guide to Studying the Bible. LC 91-28517. 112p. 1991. pap. 10.99 (*0-8066-2571-6*, 9-2571) Augsburg Fortress.

— Lift up Your Heads: He Is Coming Again. 1995. pap. 6.50 (*0-7880-0583-9*) CSS OH.

— Reflections in a Mission Mirror: Ancient Wisdom from Younger Churches. LC 98-35910. 72p. 1998. pap. 7.95 (*1-886513-07-4*) Kirk Hse Pubs.

***Aasent, Nathan.** The Cheetah. LC 99-50626. (Endangered Animals & Habitats Ser.). 128p. (YA). (gr. 4-12). 2000. lib. bdg. 18.96 (*1-56006-680-6*) Lucent Bks.

Aaserud, Finn. Redirecting Science: Niels Bohr, Philanthropy, & the Rise of Nuclear Physics. (Illus.). 369p. (C). 1990. text 69.95 (*0-521-35366-1*) Cambridge U Pr.

AASHTO Administrative Subcommittee on Computer Technology Staff. Computer Systems Index. 1987. 37.75 (*0-686-20962-1*, CSI) AASHTO.

AASHTO Staff. AASHTO 1914-1989: Moving America into the Future. (Reference Bks.). (Illus.). 288p. (Orig.). (C). 1990. pap. text 35.50 (*1-56051-007-2*, ANNV) AASHTO.

— Construction Manual for Highway Construction. rev. ed. (Construction & Right-of-Way Ser.). (Illus.). 236p. (C). 1990. text 36.50 (*1-56051-002-1*, CM-4) AASHTO.

— Guide for the Design of High Occupancy Vehicle Facilities. rev. ed. (Design & Traffic Ser.). (Illus.). 104p. (C). 1992. pap. text 26.00 (*1-56051-013-7*, GHOV-2) AASHTO.

— Guide for the Design of Park-&-Ride Facilities. (Design & Traffic Ser.). (Illus.). 96p. (Orig.). (C). 1992. pap. text 23.50 (*1-56051-012-9*, GPRF-1) AASHTO.

— Guide Specifications for Bridges Railings. (Illus.). 58p. (Orig.). (C). 1989. pap. 16.00 (*1-56051-037-4*, GSBR) AASHTO.

— Guide Specifications for Design & Construction of Segmental Concrete Bridges. (Illus.). (Orig.). (C). 1989. pap. 40.50 (*0-318-65196-3*, GSCB) AASHTO.

— Hot-Mix Asphalt Paving Handbook. (AASHTO Reports). (Illus.). 192p. (Orig.). (C). 1991. pap. text 36.25 (*1-56051-072-2*, MAPH) AASHTO.

— Model Drainage Manual. (Design & Traffic Ser.). (Illus.). 1368p. (Orig.). (C). 1991. pap. text 235.00 (*1-56051-010-2*, MDM-1) AASHTO.

— A Policy on Geometric Design of Highways & Streets. (Design & Traffic Ser.). (Illus.). i, 136p. (C). 1990. pap. text 37.00 (*1-56051-001-3*, GDHS-2) AASHTO.

— The States & the Interstates. (Reference Books & Proceedings). (Illus.). 236p. (Orig.). (C). 1991. pap. text 48.00 (*1-56051-011-0*, TSI) AASHTO.

— Transportation Landscape & Environmental Design. rev. ed. (Planning & Environment Ser.). (Illus.). 184p. (C). 1991. pap. text 48.50 (*1-56051-009-9*, HLED-2) AASHTO.

Aasland, Tertit. On the Move-to-the-Left in Uganda, 1969-1971. (Research Report Ser.: No. 26). 71p. 1974. write for info. (*91-7106-083-9*, Pub. by Nordic Africa) Transaction Pubs.

***Aaslid, Elisabeth & Schultz, Kate A.** Bring Your Muscles Back to Health. 256p. 2001. pap. 16.95 (*0-471-37891-7*) Wiley.

Aaslid, Rune, ed. Transcranial Doppler Sonography. (Illus.). 190p. 1992. 55.92 (*0-387-81935-5*) Spr-Verlag.

Aaslid, Rune, jt. auth. see Newell, David W.

Aasved, Mikal J. & Schaefer, James M. Who Needs Las Vegas? Gambling & Its Impacts in a Southwestern Minnesota Agricultural Community. (Illus.). 63p. (Orig.). (C). 1994. pap. text 35.00 (*0-7881-0862-X*) DIANE Pub.

AATG Staff, jt. contrib. by see Goethe Institut Staff.

Aatre, Vasu K., et al, eds. 1996 Symposium on Smart Materials, Structures & MEMS Vol. 3321. LC 98-213336. 878p. 1998. 141.00 (*0-8194-2762-4*) SPIE.

AAUP Staff. AAUP Directory, 1991-1992. 1991. pap. 14.95 (*0-945103-05-0*) U Ch Pr.

— The Association of American University Presses Directory, 1992-93. 226p. 1994. pap. 14.95 (*0-945103-06-9*) U Ch Pr.

— Association of American University Presses 1995-1996. LC 54-43046. 234p. 1997. pap. 14.95 (*0-945103-09-3*, Pub. by Assn Am Univ) U Ch Pr.

Aausc. 1990: Challenge in the 90's/Foreign Language Program. (Teaching Methods Ser.). (C). 1991. mass mkt. 11.95 (*0-8384-2548-8*) Heinle & Heinle.

— 1994: Faces in a Crowd. (Teaching Methods Ser.). (C). 1995. mass mkt. 25.95 (*0-8384-6367-3*) Heinle & Heinle.

— 1991: Assessing Foreign Language Proficiency. (Teaching Methods Ser.). (C). 1991. mass mkt. 11.95 (*0-8384-3915-2*) Heinle & Heinle.

— 1993: Dynamics of Language Learning. (Teaching Methods Ser.). 1994. pap. 19.95 (*0-8384-5456-9*) Heinle & Heinle.

— Research Issues: Language Program Direction. (C). 1999. 25.95 (*0-8384-1023-5*) Heinle & Heinle.

Aausc & Muyskens. Focus on Technology: New Ways of Learning & Teaching. (C). 1997. pap. 25.95 (*0-8384-7809-3*) Thomson Learn.

AAUW. The AAUW Report Action Guide. 8p. 1992. pap. 8.95 (*1-879922-04-5*) Am Assoc U Women.

— The AAUW Report Executive Summary. 8p. 1992. pap. 8.95 (*1-879922-03-7*) Am Assoc U Women.

A

An Asterisk (*) at the beginning of an entry indicates that the title is appearing for the first time.

A

— Achieving Gender Equity in the Classroom & on the Campus: The Next Steps. 308p. 1995. 21.95 (*1-879922-18-5*) Am Assoc U Women.

— How Schools Shortchange Girls: The AAUW Report. LC 98-162532. 169p. 1995. pap. 12.95 (*1-56924-821-4*) Marlowe & Co.

AAUW Staff. Gender & Race on Campus. 428p. 1997. 21.95 (*1-879922-19-3*) Am Assoc U Women.

— Separated by Sex: A Critical Look at Single-Sex Education for Girls. LC 98-5276. 95p. 1998. pap. 12.95 (*1-879922-16-9*) Am Assoc U Women.

AAUW, Thousand Oaks, CA Branch Members. Profiles of Women Past & Present: Women's History Monologues for Group Presentations, Vol. 1. rev. ed. LC 96-86656. (Illus.). 96p. (Orig.). 1996. pap. 14.95 (*0-9637756-2-6*) AAUW.

— Profiles of Women Past & Present: Women's History Monologues for Group Presentations, Vol. 2. LC 93-72554. (Illus.). 96p. (Orig.). 1996. pap. 14.95 (*0-9637756-1-8*) AAUW.

***Aav, Marianne & Stritzler-Levine, Nina, eds.** Finnish Modern Design: Utopian Ideals & Everyday Realities, 1930-97. (Illus.). 412p. 2000. pap. 35.00 (*0-300-08280-0*) Yale U Pr.

Aav, Marianne, et al. Finnish Modern Design: Utopian Ideals & Everyday Realities, 1930-1997. LC 97-44402. 1998. pap. write for info. (*0-300-07523-5*) Yale U Pr.

Aav, Marianne, ed. see Bard Graduate Center for Studies in the Decorative Arts Staff, et al.

Aaviksaar, A. Proceedings of the 11th International Conference on Phosphorus Chemistry. xiv, 470p. 1990. text 2001.00 (*2-88124-438-6*) Gordon & Breach.

Aay, Henk & Griffioen, Sander, eds. Geography & Worldview: A Christian Reconnaissance. LC 98-10839. 192p. (C). 1998. 40.00 (*0-7618-1042-0*); pap. 19.50 (*0-7618-1043-9*) U Pr of Amer.

Ab Amowicz, Rafa, et al. Clifford Algebras with Numeric & Symbolic Computations. LC 96-19921. 1996. write for info. (*3-7643-3907-1*, Pub. by Birkhauser) Princeton Arch.

AB Publishing Staff. Best Stories from the Best Book. 1991. pap. 6.95 (*1-878726-03-X*) Fam Hlth Pubns.

— Christ Our Savior: Gift Edition. 1991. pap. 5.99 (*1-878726-07-2*) Fam Hlth Pubns.

Aba, Adam. The Secret of the Doo Dah House. LC 91-89270. (Illus.). 192p. (J). (gr. 4-7). 1997. pap. 16.95 (*1-878756-51-6*) YCP Pubns.

ABA, Business Law Staff. Model Business Corporation Act Annotated, 4 vols. 3rd ed. 1985. write for info. (*0-318-65480-6*, H43899) P-H.

— Revised Model Nonprofit Corporation Act. 454p. 1988. write for info. (*0-318-65479-2*, H77939) P-H.

ABA Center for Pro Bono Staff & American Bar Association Staff. Pro Bono Delivery & Support: A Directory of Statewide Models. LC 98-157500. vi, 102p. 1998. write for info. (*1-57073-516-6*) Amer Bar Assn.

ABA, Center for Professional Responsibility Staff. Standards for Imposing Lawyer Sanctions. 63p. 1991. pap. 12.95 (*0-318-36471-9*, 561-0104) Amer Bar Assn.

— A Survey on the Teaching of Professional Responsibility. 27p. 1987. pap. 8.95 (*0-318-36473-5*, 561-0074) Amer Bar Assn.

ABA, Center on Children & the Law Staff, jt. auth. see Baker, Debra Ratterman.

ABA, Commission on Law & the Economy. Legal Advertising: The Illinois Experiment. 37p. 1985. pap. 12.50 (*0-685-14368-6*, 406-0008) Amer Bar Assn.

ABA, Commission on the Mentally Disabled. Ten Year Index: Mental & Physical Disability Law Reporter. 232p. 1987. pap. 65.00 (*0-685-21546-6*, 344-0007) Amer Bar Assn.

ABA, Committee on Comparative Procedure & Practice, jt. auth. see Cone, Sydney M.

ABA, Employee Benefits Committee, ed. Employee Benefits Law: 1996 Cumulative Supplement. 757p. 1996. pap., suppl. ed. 115.00 (*1-57018-016-4*, 1016) BNA Books.

ABA, Forum Committee on the Construction Industry & Fidelity & Surety Law Committee. Bankruptcy-Crisis in the Construction Industry, Thursday, January 27, 1983, the New York Hilton, New York, New York. LC 83-128770. 270p. 1983. 35.00 (*0-685-07625-3*, 557-0008) ABA Prof Educ Pubns.

ABA, General Practice Section Staff. Federal Procurement Regulations: Policy, Practice & Procedures. LC 87-71563. 547p. 1987. pap. 79.95 (*0-89707-312-6*, 515-0068) Amer Bar Assn.

ABA, House of Delegates. The Legislative History of the Model Rules of Professional Conduct: Their Development in the ABA House of Delegates. 216p. 1987. 39.95 (*0-318-36467-0*, 561-0078); pap. 29.95 (*0-318-36468-9*) Amer Bar Assn.

ABA, International Law & Practice Section Staff. Act of State & Extraterritorial Reach: Problems of Law & Policy. LC 83-72432. 136p. 1983. pap. 30.00 (*0-89707-119-0*, 521-0033) Amer Bar Assn.

— What Law Now for the Seas? LC 84-70164. 73p. 1984. pap. 8.00 (*0-89707-132-8*, 521-0034) Amer Bar Assn.

ABA-JAD National Conference of State Trial Judges, jt. auth. see National Judicial College Staff.

ABA, Labor & Employment Law Staff, et al, eds. Labor Arbitration: A Practical Guide for Advocates. 416p. 1990. trans. 55.00 (*0-87179-635-X*, 0635) BNA Books.

ABA, Law Student Division. Career Placement after Law School Graduation. 13p. 1986. pap. 15.00 (*0-318-36447-6*, 527-0023) Amer Bar Assn.

ABA, Legal Education & Admissions to the Bar Section Staff. The Challenges & Responsibilities of a Law School Board of Visitors. 19p. 1985. pap. 2.00 (*0-685-21545-8*, 529-0034) Amer Bar Assn.

— A Study of Contemporary Law School Curricula. 174p. 1987. pap. 4.00 (*0-318-36446-8*, 529-0033) Amer Bar Assn.

ABA, Public Contract Law Section Staff. The Architect-Engineer's Role under Superfund & Selecting a Professional Liability Insurance Policy. 88p. 1985. pap. 25.00 (*0-89707-169-7*, 539-0044) Amer Bar Assn.

ABA Staff. ABA Guide to Home Ownership: The Complete & Easy Guide to All the Law Every Home Owner Should Know. LC 94-40827. 193p. 1995. pap. 13.00 (*0-8129-2535-1*, Times Bks) Crown Pub Group.

— The ABA Guide to Wills & Estates: Everything You Need to Know about Wills, Trusts, Estates, & Taxes. 1995. pap. 13.00 (*0-8129-2536-X*, Times Bks) Crown Pub Group.

ABA, Tort & Insurance Practice Section Staff. Business Interruption Coverage. LC 87-71809. 165p. 1987. pap. 29.95 (*0-89707-318-5*, 519-0070) Amer Bar Assn.

Ababio-Clottey, Aeeshah & Clottey, Kokomon. Beyond Fear: Twelve Spiritual Keys to Racial Healing. LC 98-20399. 228p. 1999. pap. 12.95 (*0-915811-82-0*) H J Kramer Inc.

Abaco. Sound Guide for Physiology. 1995. 19.00 (*0-205-18373-5*) Allyn.

Abacus Development Group Staff. Netscape Plug-Ins. 1996. pap. text 29.95 incl. cd-rom (*1-55755-321-1*) Abacus MI.

— Zipping for Beginners. LC 97-129844. 1996. 14.95 incl. disk (*1-55755-306-8*) Abacus MI.

Abacus Publishing Staff. PC Bios Internals: Maximize Your PC's Bios. 1999. pap. text 29.95 (*1-55755-342-4*) Abacus MI.

Abacus Publishing Staff & Slaughter, Scott. Easy Digital Photography. 2nd ed. (Beginner's Ser.). 327p. 1999. pap. 29.95 (*1-55755-364-5*) Abacus MI.

Abacus Publishing Staff, PUBLISHING. Airport & Scenery Designer for Microsoft Flight Simulator 5.1 & Win95 6.0. 1997. 49.95 (*1-55755-331-9*) Abacus MI.

Abacus Staff. Flight Deck. pap. 39.95 incl. cd-rom (*1-55755-338-6*) Abacus MI.

Abacus Technology Corporation Staff. An Assessment of Flywheel Energy Storage Technology for Hybrid & Electric Vehicles (1996) rev. ed. (Flywheel Energy Information Ser.: Vol. I). (Illus.). 106p. 1996. lib. bdg. 125.00 (*0-89934-276-0*, BT945) Bus Tech Bks.

— Technology Assessments of Advanced Energy Storage Systems for Electric & Hybrid Electric Vehicles. (Electric Vehicle Information Ser.: Vol. VIII). (Illus.). 115p. 1996. pap. 85.00 (*0-89934-255-8*, BT035) Bus Tech Bks.

— Technology Assessments of Advanced Energy Storage Systems for Electric & Hybrid Electric Vehicles, Vol. 8. (Electric Vehicle Information Ser.). (Illus.). 115p. 1996. lib. bdg. 135.00 (*0-89934-256-6*, BT935) Bus Tech Bks.

Abad, Amading S. Professor Swami: Dream Interpretations Plus Mole Significance. Bliss, Angelie, ed. & tr. by. LC 96-84086. (Illus.). 112p. (Orig.). 1996. pap. 12.95 (*0-9651438-4-8*, Forever Yng Club) Air & Water King.

Abad de Santillan, Diego. Ricardo Flores Magon: Apostle of the Mexican Social Revolution. (Mexico Ser.). 1979. lib. bdg. 59.95 (*0-8490-2998-8*) Gordon Pr.

Abad, F. Diccionario de Linguistica de la Escuela Espanola. (SPA.). 284p. 1993. pap. 59.50 (*84-249-1042-7*) Elliots Bks.

Abad, Gemino H. Orion's Belt & Other Writings. LC 96-946490. 168p. 1997. pap. text 18.00 (*971-542-109-1*, Pub. by U of Philippines Pr) UH Pr.

Abad, Gemino H. & Hidalgo, Cristina P., eds. The Likhaan Book of Poetry & Fiction, 1995. LC 96-946561. 376p. 1997. pap. text 27.00 (*971-542-136-9*, Pub. by U of Philippines Pr) UH Pr.

Abad, Hector. The Joy of Being Awake. Budoff, Nathan, tr. 160p. 1996. pap. text 15.95 (*1-57129-020-6*) Brookline Bks.

Abad, J., et al, eds. New Perspectives in Quantum Field Theories: Proceedings of the XVI Gift International Seminar on Theoretical Physics, Jaca, Huesca, June 3-8, 1985. 490p. 1986. pap. 60.00 (*9971-5-0057-4*); text 131.00 (*9971-5-0048-5*) World Scientific Pub.

Abad, Javier & Fenoy, E. Marriage: A Path to Sanctity. 200p. 1997. pap. 9.95 (*971-11-7107-4*) Scepter Pubs.

Abad, Teresa. Inspirational Knowledge: Metaphysical Common Sense. LC 96-85537. 1996. mass mkt., per. 19.95 (*1-889131-01-6*) CasAnanda.

Abadan-Unat, Nermin. Women in Developing World: Evidence from Turkey. (World Affairs Ser.: Vol. 22, Bk. 1). (Orig.). 1986. pap. 9.95 (*0-87940-080-3*) Monograph Series.

Abadi, Jacob. Israel's Leadership, from Utopia to Crisis, 40. LC 93-9314. (Contributions to the Study of World History Ser.: No. 40). 216p. 1993. 62.95 (*0-313-27515-7*, ABF/, Greenwood Pr) Greenwood.

Abadi, Martin & Cardelli, Luca. A Theory of Objects. LC 96-17038. (Monographs in Computer Science). 396p. 1996. 39.95 (*0-387-94775-2*) Spr-Verlag.

Abadi, Martin & Ito, T., eds. Theoretical Aspects of Computer Software: Proceedings, 3rd International Symposium, TACS '97, Sendai, Japan, September 23-26, 1997. LC 97-33253. (Lecture Notes in Computer Science Ser.: Vol. 1281). xi, 639p. 1997. pap. 89.00 (*3-540-63388-X*) Spr-Verlag.

Abadi, Mauricio & Rogers, Susan. Reality &/or Realities. LC 95-5895. 1995. 35.00 (*1-56821-536-3*) Aronson.

Abadia, J., ed. see International Symposium on Iron Nutrition & Intera.

Abadie, Ann J., ed. see Faulkner, William.

Abadie, Ann J., jt. ed. see Fowler, Doreen.

Abadie, Ann J., jt. ed. see Harrington, Evans.

Abadie, Ann J., jt. ed. see Kartiganer, Donald M.

Abadie, M. J. Awaken Your Spiritual Self. LC 98-16311. 288p. 1998. pap. 10.95 (*1-58062-000-0*) Adams Media.

— Child Astrology: A Guide to Nurturing Your Child's Natural Gifts. LC 99-21309. (Illus.). 288p. 1999. 14.95 (*0-89281-722-4*, Destiny Bks) Inner Tradit.

***Abadie, M. J.** The Everything Angels Book: Discover the Guardians, Messengers & Heavenly Companions in Your Life. (Everything Ser.). (Illus.). 304p. 2000. pap. 12.95 (*1-58062-398-0*) Adams Media.

— Everything Herbal Remedies Book. LC 00-29292. 304p. 2000. pap. 12.95 (*1-58062-331-X*) Adams Media.

Abadie, M. J. The Everything Tarot Book. LC 99-40913. (Illus.). 304p. 1999. pap. 12.95 (*1-58062-191-0*) Adams Media.

***Abadie, M. J.** Teen Astrology. 2001. pap. 14.95 (*0-89281-823-9*, Bindu Bks) Inner Tradit.

Abadie, M. J. Your Psychic Potential. 320p. (Orig.). 1995. pap. 10.95 (*1-55850-475-3*) Adams Media.

Abadie, M. J., jt. auth. see Campbell, Joseph.

***Abadinsky.** Law & Justice. 5th ed. (Criminal Justice Ser.). 2001. 35.00 (*0-534-53398-1*) Wadsworth Pub.

Abadinsky. Organized Crime. 6th ed. LC 99-42094. (Criminal Justice Ser.). 1999. pap. text 60.95 (*0-534-54380-4*) Thomson Learn.

— Probation & Parole. 6th ed. 1996. pap. text, teacher ed. write for info. (*0-13-253709-5*) Allyn.

Abadinsky, Howard. The Criminal Elite: Professional & Organized Crime, 1. LC 83-1445. (Contributions to Criminology & Penology Ser.: No. 1). (Illus.). 190p. 1983. 37.50 (*0-313-23833-2*, ACE/, Greenwood Pr) Greenwood.

— Drug Abuse: An Introduction. 3rd ed. LC 96-28084. (Illus.). 400p. 1997. text 60.95 (*0-8304-1476-2*) Thomson Learn.

— Law & Justice: An Introduction to the American Legal System. 4th rev. ed. LC 97-12688. (Criminal Justice Ser.). (Illus.). 500p. (C). 1998. pap. text 42.95 (*0-8304-1482-7*) Thomson Learn.

— Probation & Parole: Theory & Practice. 4th ed. 448p. (C). 1990. boxed set. write for info. (*0-318-68288-5*) P-H.

Abadinsky, Howard, jt. auth. see Winfree, L. Thomas, Jr.

Abadir, Akef, tr. see Mahfouz, Naguib.

Abadir, Karim. Mathematics of Unit Root Econometrics. 1998. text 90.00 (*0-471-96650-9*) Wiley.

Abadir, Magdy, ed. Economics of Electronic Design, Manufacture & Test. (Frontiers in Electronic Testing Ser.). 192p. (C). 1994. text 125.00 (*0-7923-9471-2*) Kluwer Academic.

Abadzi, Helen. What We Know about Acquisition of Adult Literacy: Is There No Hope? LC 94-20038. 106p. 1994. pap. 22.00 (*0-8213-2862-X*, 12862) World Bank.

Abaelardus, Petrus. Opera, 2 vols., Set. vi, 1563p. 1970. reprint ed. 385.00 (*0-318-71447-7*) G Olms Pubs.

***Abagnale, Frank W., Jr. & Redding, Stan.** Catch Me If You Can: The Amazing True Story of the Most Extraordinary Liar in the History of Fun & Profit. 288p. 2000. pap. 14.00 (*0-7679-0538-5*) Broadway BDD.

Abajian, Diane. Praying & Doing the Stations of the Cross with Children. (Illus.). 24p. (J). (gr. 1-3). 1980. pap. 1.95 (*0-89622-118-0*) Twenty-Third.

Abajian, James T. De, see De Abajian, James T.

Abakumov, V. N., et al. Nonradiative Recombination in Semiconductors. (Modern Problems in Condensed Matter Sciences Ser.: Vol. 33). xviii, 320p. 1991. 232.75 (*0-444-88854-3*, North Holland) Elsevier.

Abakwue, S. A. Abundant Wealth. LC 97-93025. 138p. (Orig.). 1997. pap. 12.00 (*1-57502-403-9*, PO1290) Morris Pubng.

Abalakin, Victor K., jt. ed. see Lieske, Jay H.

Abalama, Katherine, jt. auth. see Small, Pauline.

Aballea, Martine & Sans, Jerome. Martine Aballea. (Illus.). 68p. 1992. pap. 20.00 (*2-908257-02-5*, Pub. by F R A C) Dist Art Pubs.

Aballi, Carlos F. Breve Apologia de la Cultura Cristiana Occidental. LC 90-82590. (Coleccion Cuba y sus Jueces). (SPA.). 64p. (Orig.). 1990. pap. 7.95 (*0-89729-567-6*) Ediciones.

Abalos, David T. La Comunidad Latina in the United States: Strategies of Transformation. LC 97-43953. 216p. 1998. 65.00 (*0-275-95892-2*, Praeger Pubs); pap. 19.95 (*0-275-95893-0*, Praeger Pubs) Greenwood.

— The Latino Family & the Politics of Transformation. LC 93-19612. (Praeger Series in Transformational Politics & Political Science). 192p. 1993. 55.00 (*0-275-94527-8*, Praeger Pubs) Greenwood.

— Latinos in the United States: The Sacred & the Political. LC 85-41010. 224p. 1988. pap. text 14.00 (*0-268-01278-4*) U of Notre Dame Pr.

— Strategies of Transformation Toward a Multicultural Society: Fulfilling the Story of Democracy. LC 95-37649. (Praeger Series in Transformational Politics & Political Science). 224p. 1996. 59.95 (*0-275-95270-3*, Praeger Pubs); pap. 19.95 (*0-275-95271-1*, Praeger Pubs) Greenwood.

Abalos, Inaki & Herreros, Juan. Areas of Impunity. 200p. (C). 1997. pap. 26.00 (*84-89698-17-1*) Dist Art Pubs.

Abalovich, M. B., et al. Ten Papers Translated from the Russian. LC 89-371. (Translations Ser.: Series 2, Vol. 142). 121p. 1989. 62.00 (*0-8218-3122-4*, TRANS2/142) Am Math.

Abanes, Richard. American Militias: Rebellion, Racism & Religion. 336p. (Orig.). 1996. pap. 14.99 (*0-8308-1368-3*, 1368) InterVarsity.

— Cults, New Religious Movements & Your Family: A Guide to Ten Non-Christian Groups Out to Convert Your Loved Ones. LC 97-35599. 1998. pap. 14.99 (*0-89107-981-5*) Crossway Bks.

— End-Time Visions: The Road to Armageddon? 432p. 1999. pap. 9.99 (*0-8054-1965-9*) Broadman.

— End-Time Visions: The Road to Armageddon? LC 97-44524. (Illus.). 416p. 1998. 25.95 (*1-56858-104-1*) FWEW.

Abanes, Richard, jt. auth. see House, H. Wayne.

Abangma, Julius. Soccer for Beginners: How to Understand & Play the Game of Soccer. LC 94-71946. (Illus.). 128p. (YA). (gr. 7-12). 1994. pap. 10.95 (*1-885392-07-9*) Allied Publishers.

Abangma, Samson N. Modes in Denya Discourse. LC 87-62710. (Publications in Linguistics: No. 79). (Illus.). 140p. (Orig.). 1987. pap. 22.00 (*0-88312-007-0*) S I L Intl.

Abanshin, Michael E. Eagles of the Luftwaffe Vol. 1: The Heinkel He-219 & He-111 in Detail. (Illus.). 96p. 1997. 44.95 (*1-884909-05-1*, 2001) Aviation Intl.

Abansmin, Michael E. Fighting Polikanpov. 64p. 1994. pap. 14.95 (*1-884909-01-9*) Aviation Intl.

Abao, Ritva, tr. see Gumbel, Dietrich.

***Abarbanel, Andrew.** Love Sick: Lessons on Relationships from Biological Psychiatry. 2000. pap. 18.95 (*0-923521-54-2*) Bull Pub.

Abarbanel, Andrew. Loving Madly/Loving Sanely. 240p. 1998. pap. 13.00 (*1-57566-251-5*, Knsington) Kensgtn Pub Corp.

Abarbanel, H. D. & Rabinovic, M. I. Introduction to Nonlinear Dynamics for Physicists. (Lecture Notes in Physics Ser.). 168p. 1993. text 45.00 (*981-02-1409-X*); pap. text 23.00 (*981-02-1410-3*) World Scientific Pub.

Abarbanel, H. D., et al. Analysis of Observed Chaotic Data: Springer Study Edition. (Institute for Nonlinear Science Ser.). (Illus.). 284p. 1997. pap. 29.95 (*0-387-98372-4*) Spr-Verlag.

Abarbanel, H. D., ed. see Garcia-Ojalvo, J. & Sancho, J.

Abarbanel, Henry D., jt. auth. see Simon, J. D.

Abarbanel, Judah. The Philosophy of Love. Friedeberg-Seeley, F. & Barnes, J. H., trs. 1977. lib. bdg. 250.00 (*0-8490-2433-1*) Gordon Pr.

Abarbanel, Karin. How to Succeed on Your Own: Overcoming Emotional Roadblocks on the Way from Cooperation to Cottage, from Employer to Entrepreneur. LC 93-24590. 320298p. 1995. 22.50 (*0-8050-1381-4*) H Holt & Co.

— How to Succeed on Your Own: Overcoming the Emotional Roadblocks on the Way from Corporate. 1995. pap. 12.95 (*0-8050-3555-9*) H Holt & Co.

Abarbanel, Karin, jt. auth. see Rue, Wendy.

Abarbanel, Stacey R. Smart Business Travel: How to Stay Safe When You're on the Road. LC 96-105946. 128p. (Orig.). 1994. pap. 12.95 (*0-912301-23-6*) First Bks.

Abarbenel, Don I. Abarbenel Al Hatorah, 3 Vols, Set. (HEB.). 45.00 (*0-87559-078-0*) Shalom.

Abarinov, Vladimir. The Murderers of Katyn. 250p. 1992. 19.95 (*0-7818-0032-3*) Hippocrene Bks.

Abarno, Robert. Agreement to Seek Reconciliation Through Christian Mediation (Agreeing to Agree in Obedience to God, Jo. 14: 21, 23; ICor. 6: 1-10; Jo. 15: 12) 3rd ed. 1996. write for info. (*0-9631575-9-0*) R Abarno.

Abarry, Abu S. & Garba, Mohammed. Introduction to Hausa: A Learner-Centered Approach. LC 99-20733. 1999. 21.95 (*0-86543-741-6*) Africa World.

Abarry, Abu S., jt. ed. see Asante, Molefi K.

Abart, Ellen M. Instant English--Ingles Instante: The Way to Enlarge Your Spanish Vocabulary with Cognates, Spanish Words which Look or Sound Like English Words--La Manera de Ampliar Su Vocabulario Ingles pidamente con Cognados, Palabras Espanolas que Parecen o Sonan a Palabras Inglesas. LC 90-86152. (ENG & SPA.). 200p. (Orig.). 1991. pap. 5.98 (*0-9628415-9-5*) Intrepid CO.

Abas, J. Rapid Turbo Pascal Graphics Tutor. (Illus.). 156p. 1992. pap. 38.00 (*0-7503-0206-2*); disk 175.00 (*0-7503-0280-1*) IOP Pub.

Abas, J. & Mondragon, J. R. Pascal an Interactive Text. (Illus.). 268p. 1990. pap. 42.00 (*0-7503-0020-5*); disk 175.00 (*0-7503-0023-X*) IOP Pub.

Abascal, Juan & Brucato, Laurel. Stress Mastery. (C). 2000. 24.00 (*0-13-634727-4*, Macmillan Coll) P-H.

Abasika, Etiese T. Mkpa. The Black Jesus: The Conspiracy & the Worlds Best Kept Secret. 4th rev. ed. Newswatch Book Ltd Staff, ed. (Illus.). 350p. (Orig.). 1999. reprint ed. pap. 25.00 (*1-893523-00-4*) Essene Research.

***Abata, Russell M.** A Christian's Guide to Self-Esteem. LC 99-71462. 64p. 1999. pap. 4.95 (*0-7648-0472-3*) Liguori Pubns.

Abatangelo, G. & Davidson, J. M., eds. Cutaneous Development, Aging & Repair. (FIDIA Research Ser.: Vol. 18). 360p. 1989. 150.00 (*0-387-96995-0*, 2801) Spr-Verlag.

Abate, Frank, ed. The Oxford American Desk Dictionary. (Illus.). 816p. 1998. 12.95 (*0-19-512673-4*) OUP.

— The Oxford American Dictionary & Language Guide. (Illus.). 1306p. 1999. 35.00 (*0-19-513449-4*) OUP.

— Oxford American Dictionary of Current English. LC 99-39972. (Illus.). 1008p. 1999. 17.95 (*0-19-513374-9*) OUP.

— The Oxford Desk Dictionary & Thesaurus: American Edition. 992p. 1997. 16.95 (*0-19-511214-8*) OUP.

— The Oxford Dictionary & Thesaurus: American Edition. LC 96-14847. 1856p. 1996. 35.00 (*0-19-509949-4*) OUP.

Abate, Frank & Byrd, Erick, eds. Easy German Bilingual Dictionary. LC 96-24343. (ENG & GER., Illus.). 464p. 1996. pap. 6.95 (*0-8442-0553-2*, 05532, Passprt Bks) NTC Contemp Pub Co.

Abate, Frank & Dioguardi, Ralph, eds. Easy Italian Bilingual Dictionary. (ENG & ITA., Illus.). 464p. 1996. pap. 6.95 (*0-8442-0097-2*) NTC Contemp Pub Co.

Abate, Frank, ed. see DK Publishing Staff.

***Abate, Frank A., ed.** Oxford Dictionary of People & Places. (Illus.). 896p. 2000. 27.50 (*0-19-513872-4*) OUP.

Abate, Frank R., ed. American Places Dictionary: A Guide to Populated Places, Natural Features, & Other United States Places, 4 vols. LC 93-12306. (Illus.). 1994. lib. bdg. 350.00 (*1-55888-747-4*) Omnigraphics Inc.

An Asterisk (*) at the beginning of an entry indicates that the title is appearing for the first time.

— American Places Dictionary Vol. 1: Northeast, 4 vols., Vol. 1. LC 93-12306. (Illus.). 1994. lib. bdg. 100.00 (*1-55888-146-8*) Omnigraphics Inc.

— American Places Dictionary Vol. 2: South, 4 vols., Vol. 2. LC 93-12306. (Illus.). 1994. lib. bdg. 100.00 (*1-55888-147-6*) Omnigraphics Inc.

— American Places Dictionary Vol. 3: Midwest, 4 vols., Vol. 3. LC 93-12306. (Illus.). 1994. lib. bdg. 100.00 (*1-55888-148-4*) Omnigraphics Inc.

— American Places Dictionary Vol. 4: West Appendices & Index, 4 vols., Vol. 4. LC 93-12306. (Illus.). 1994. lib. bdg. 100.00 (*1-55888-149-2*) Omnigraphics Inc.

— Omni Gazetteer of the United States of America: National Edition, 11 vols., Set. (Illus.). 9400p. 1991. lib. bdg. 1400.00 (*1-55888-336-3*) Omnigraphics Inc.

— Omni Gazetteer of the United States of America Vol. 1: New England. (Illus.). 396p. 1991. lib. bdg. 150.00 (*1-55888-325-8*) Omnigraphics Inc.

— Omni Gazetteer of the United States of America Vol. 2: Northeastern States. (Illus.). 720p. 1991. lib. bdg. 150.00 (*1-55888-326-6*) Omnigraphics Inc.

— Omni Gazetteer of the United States of America Vol. 3: Southeast. (Illus.). 786p. 1991. lib. bdg. 150.00 (*1-55888-327-4*) Omnigraphics Inc.

— Omni Gazetteer of the United States of America Vol. 4: South Central States. (Illus.). 1156p. 1991. lib. bdg. 150.00 (*1-55888-328-2*) Omnigraphics Inc.

— Omni Gazetteer of the United States of America Vol. 5: Southwestern States. (Illus.). 651p. 1991. lib. bdg. 150.00 (*1-55888-329-0*) Omnigraphics Inc.

— Omni Gazetteer of the United States of America Vol. 6: Great Lakes States. (Illus.). 757p. 1991. lib. bdg. 150.00 (*1-55888-330-4*) Omnigraphics Inc.

— Omni Gazetteer of the United States of America Vol. 7: Plains States. (Illus.). 495p. 1991. lib. bdg. 150.00 (*1-55888-331-2*) Omnigraphics Inc.

— Omni Gazetteer of the United States of America Vol. 8: Mountain States. (Illus.). 744p. 1991. lib. bdg. 150.00 (*1-55888-332-0*) Omnigraphics Inc.

— Omni Gazetteer of the United States of America Vol. 9: Pacific. (Illus.). 902p. 1991. lib. bdg. 150.00 (*1-55888-333-9*) Omnigraphics Inc.

— Omni Gazetteer of the United States of America Vol. 10: National Index. 1582p. 1991. lib. bdg. 150.00 (*1-55888-334-7*) Omnigraphics Inc.

— Omni Gazetteer of the United States of America Vol. 11: Appendices: U. S. Data Sourcebook. 570p. 1991. lib. bdg. 150.00 (*1-55888-335-5*) Omnigraphics Inc.

— The Pocket Oxford Dictionary & Thesaurus. 992p. 1999. pap. 12.95 (*0-19-513097-9*) OUP.

— Proper Names Master Index: A Comprehensive Index of More Than 200,000 Proper Names That Appear As Entries in Standard Reference Works, 2 vols., Set. LC 94-22479. 1600p. 1994. lib. bdg. 125.00 (*1-55888-837-3*) Omnigraphics Inc.

Abate, Frank R., jt. auth. see Dioguardi, Raffaele A.

Abate, Frank R., ed. see Byrd, Erick P.

Abate, Frank R., ed. see Dioguardi, Raffaele A.

Abate, Marco & Patrizio, Giorgio. Finsler Metrics--a Global Approach: With Applications to Geometric Theory. LC 94-35003. (Lecture Notes in Mathematics Ser.: Vol. 1591). x, 180p. 1994. 35.95 (*3-540-58465-X*) Spr-Verlag.

Abate, Randall, ed. Waste Management Solutions for Health Care Facilities. 500p. 1997. ring bd. 245.00 (*0-929321-37-5*) WEKA Pub.

Abate, Randall S. Directory of Environmental Law Education Opportunities at American Law Schools. 1997. 30.00 (*0-938609-09-2*) Graduate Group.

***Abate-Romano, Kathleen.** 222 Tips to Eliminate Your Fear of the Dentist. 259p. 1999. 26.95 (*0-9673658-0-5*) KAR Pubg.

Abatecola, John A. Fourth Avenue Sting. unabridged ed. Bartholomae, Barbara, ed. 206p. 1999. pap. 12.95 (*0-9665638-0-8*) Tadone Publ.

— Pico: The White Paper Act. LC 99-185553. 350p. 1998. text 24.50 (*0-9659628-0-6*) Tadone Publ.

Abatso, George & Abatso, Yvonne. How to Equip the African American Family: Issues & Guidelines for Building Strong Families. Birchett, Collen, ed. 183p. (Orig.). pap., teacher ed. 6.95 (*0-940955-18-0*, 9-2410) Urban Ministries.

— How to Equip the African American Family: Issues & Guidelines for Building Strong Families. Birchett, Colleen, ed. 239p. (Orig.). pap. text 7.95 (*0-940955-17-2*, 9-2734) Urban Ministries.

Abatso, Yvonne, jt. auth. see Abatso, George.

***Abatt, Corinne, et al, eds.** Century of Voices: Detroit Women Writers Anthology 1900-2000. 250p. 1999. pap. 16.00 (*0-9670318-0-X*) Detroit Women Wrts.

Abay, Estef. Die Keramik der Fruhbronzezeit in Anatolien: Mit Syrischen Affinitaten. (Altertumskunde des Vorderen Orients Ser.: Vol. 8). (GER., Illus.). xiv, 739p. 1997. text 133.00 (*3-927120-58-8*, Pub. by Ugarit-Verlag) Eisenbrauns.

Abaya, Hernando J. Looking Back in Anger. xv, 346p. (Orig.). (C). 1992. pap. 15.75 (*971-10-0477-1*, Pub. by New Day Pub) Cellar.

Abaygo, Kenn. Advanced Fugitive: Running, Hiding, Surviving, & Thriving Forever. LC 97-226708. (Illus.). 144p. 1997. pap. 15.00 (*0-87364-933-8*) Paladin Pr.

— Fugitive: How to Run, Hide, & Survive. 96p. 1993. pap. 12.00 (*0-87364-754-8*) Paladin Pr.

***Abaygo, Kenn.** The International Fugitive: Secrets of Clandestine Travel Overseas. 152p. 1999. pap. 17.00 (*1-58160-035-6*) Paladin Pr.

Abazah, Nizar & Muti Al-Hafiz, M. Tarikh 'Ulama' Dimashq fi Qarn al-Rabi' 'Ashar al-Hijri, 3 vols., Set. 1986. 47.95 (*1-57547-164-7*) Dar Al-Fikr.

— Tarikh 'Ulama' Dimashq fi Qarn al-Rabi' 'Ashar al-Hijri, Vol. 1. 1986. write for info. (*1-57547-165-5*) Dar Al-Fikr.

— Tarikh 'Ulama' Dimashq Fi Qarn Al-Rabi' 'Ashar al-Hijri, Vol. 2. 1986. write for info. (*1-57547-166-3*) Dar Al-Fikr.

— Tarikh 'Ulama' Dimashq fi Qarn al-Rabi' 'Ashar al-Hijri, Vol. 3. 1986. write for info. (*1-57547-167-1*) Dar Al-Fikr.

Abba, Dov Ben. Hebrew-English, English-Hebrew Dictionary: 35,000 Entries, Transliterated Hebrew Words in English Characters, English Words in Hebrew Characters. (ENG & HEB.). 700p. 1977. pap. 12.50 (*0-87559-215-5*) Shalom.

Abba, Giuseppe C. The Diary of One of Garibaldi's Thousand. Vincent, E. R., tr. from ITA. LC 80-24181. (Oxford Library of Italian Classics). (Illus.). 166p. 1981. reprint ed. lib. bdg. 59.50 (*0-313-22446-3*, ABDO, Greenwood Pr) Greenwood.

Abbad, Ibn. Letters on the Sufi Path. Renard, John, tr. 238p. 1996. 14.50 (*0-614-21303-7*, 715) Kazi Pubns.

Abbad y Lasierra, Inigo. Historia Geografica, Civil y Natural De la Isla De San Juan Bautista De Puerto Rico. 3rd ed. 320p. (C). 1979. pap. 7.20 (*0-8477-0800-4*) U of PR Pr.

Abbadi, Sabri. Die Personennamen der Inschriften aus Hatra. (Texte und Studien Zur Orientalistik Ser.: Vol. 1). xxviii, 217p. 1983. 30.00 (*3-487-07427-3*) G Olms Pubs.

Abbadie, L., et al, eds. Lamato: A Savannah Ecosystem. (Ecological Studies: Vol. TBA). (Illus.). 350p. 1997. 89.00 (*0-387-94844-9*) Spr-Verlag.

Abbagnano, N. Historia de la Pedadogia. (SPA.). 35.99 (*968-16-0637-X*, Pub. by Fondo) Continental Bk.

Abbagnano, Nicola. Dicc. de Filosofia. (SPA.). 39.99 (*968-16-1189-6*, Pub. by Fondo) Continental Bk.

Abbagnano, Nicolas. Introduccion a la Existencialismo. (Breviarios Ser.). (SPA.). pap. 7.99 (*968-16-0604-3*, Pub. by Fondo) Continental Bk.

Abbamont, Gary W. & Brescher, Antoinette. Test Smart! Ready-to-Use Test-Taking Strategies & Activities. LC 96-39568. 324p. 1997. pap. text, teacher ed. 29.95 (*0-87628-916-2*) Ctr Appl Res.

Abbamont, Gary W., jt. auth. see Brescher, Antoinette.

Abbarno, G. John, ed. Inherent & Instrumental Values: Excursion in Value Inquiry. 286p. 1998. 74.95 (*1-57309-269-X*); pap. 54.95 (*1-57309-268-1*) Intl Scholars.

***Abbas.** Faces of Christianity: A Photographic Journey. LC 00-38111. (Illus.). 328p. 2000. 60.00 (*0-8109-5728-0*, Pub. by Abrams) Time Warner.

Abbas, Abdul K., et al. Cellular & Molecular Immunology. 4th ed. LC 99-33582. (Illus.). 475p. 2000. pap. text. write for info. (*0-7216-8233-2*, W B Saunders Co) Harcrt Hlth Sci Grp.

Abbas, Abul K. & Flavell, R., eds. Genetic Models of Immune & Inflammatory Diseases. LC 95-46669. (Serono Symposia, U. S. A. Ser.). (Illus.). 176p. 1996. 110.00 (*0-387-94649-7*) Spr-Verlag.

Abbas, Abul K. & Lichtman, Andrew H. Cellular & Molecular Immunology. 3rd ed. Schmitt, William, ed. LC 96-49579. (Text & Review Ser.). (Illus.). 512p. 1997. pap. text 31.95 (*0-7216-4024-9*, W B Saunders Co) Harcrt Hlth Sci Grp.

Abbas, Ackbar. Contemporary Practices: Art & Experience. 128p. 1999. pap. text 24.95 (*2-906571-92-X*, Pub. by Editions Dis Voir) Dist Art Pubs.

— Hong Kong: Culture & the Politics of Disappearance. LC 96-41269. (Public Worlds Ser.: Vol. 2). 168p. (C). 1997. pap. 16.95 (*0-8166-2925-0*); text 39.95 (*0-8166-2924-2*) U of Minn Pr.

Abbas, Ackbar, ed. see International Conference on Literary Theory Staff.

Abbas, Adel M. His Throne Was on Water. LC 96 41514. (Illus.). 1996. pap. 14.95 (*0-915957-62-0*) amana pubns.

***Abbas, Adel M. A. & Fretwell, Anne P.** Science Miracles: No Sticks or Snakes. LC 99-88707. 2000. write for info. (*0-915957-97-3*) amana pubns.

Abbas, George E. Rhyme & Reason: Animal Lessons. (Illus.). 172p. 1998. pap. 12.95 (*0-9667117-0-X*, 001) Bib Concepts Comm.

Abbas, Jailan. Festivals of Egypt. (Illus.). 48p. (Orig.). (J). (gr. 3-8). 1995. pap. 7.50 (*977-5325-47-1*, Pub. by Hoopoe Bks) AMIDEAST.

Abbas, K. A. Indira Gandhi: The Last Post. 116p. 1985. 15.95 (*0-86132-116-2*) Asia Bk Corp.

— Janata in a Jam? 123p. 1978. 9.95 (*0-318-36592-8*) Asia Bk Corp.

— Twentieth March, a Day Like Any Other. 134p. (C). 1978. 11.95 (*0-7069-0610-1*, Pub. by Vikas) Asia Bk Corp.

Abbas, M. A. & Wong, Tak-Wai, eds. Literary Theory Today. LC 83-127859. 265p. 1981. reprint ed. pap. 82.20 (*0-608-01393-5*, 206215400002) Bks Demand.

Abbas, M. A., ed. see International Conference on Literary Theory Staff.

Abbas, Mahar A., jt. auth. see Holmin, Dalal A.

Abbas, Maher A. Beyond Phen-fen: Healthier, Safer, Medically Proven Weight-Loss. (Illus.). 150p. (Orig.). 1998. pap. 12.95 (*0-9656065-2-X*) SYTAC Pub.

— Beyond Phen-Fen: The Secrets to Modern, Healthier, Safer Weight-Loss. (Illus.). 224p. (YA). (gr. 10 up). 1998. pap. 12.95 (*0-9656065-3-8*) SYTAC Pub.

— Beyond the Magic Scalpel. LC 96-92946. 192p. (Orig.). 1997. pap. 11.95 (*0-9656065-0-3*) SYTAC Pub.

— Children of Ambiguity. LC 96-92947. (Illus.). 350p. (Orig.). 1998. pap. 13.95 (*0-9656065-1-1*) SYTAC Pub.

Abbas, Maher A. & Adame, Daniel D. College Students on the Go: Introduction to Health. 164p. (C). 1996. text 20.40 (*0-536-59261-6*) Pearson Custom.

Abbas, Maher A. & Spiegl, Marilyn J. Olive Oil Cookery: The Mediterranean Diet. 164p. (Orig.). 1995. pap. 12.95 (*0-913990-11-6*) Book Pub Co.

Abbas, Susan. Good-Bye, Glasses: A Comprehensive Guide to Radial Keratotomy, A Microsurgical Procedure to Permanently Correct Nearsightedness. (Illus.). 133p. (Orig.). 1990. pap. 14.95 (*0-9628886-0-5*) Patton Pub.

Abbaschian, G. J. & David, S. A., eds. Grain Refinement in Castings & Welds: Proceedings of a Symposium. LC 83-61027. (Conference Proceedings Ser.). (Illus.). 301p. reprint ed. pap. 93.40 (*0-608-17837-3*, 203259800080) Bks Demand.

Abbaschian, G. J., ed. see International Conference on Modeling of Casting &.

Abbaschian, R., et al, eds. A National Agenda in Materials Science & Engineering - Implementing the MS & E Report, Vol. NMSE. 52p. 1991. pap. 15.00 (*0-614-95846-6*) Materials Res.

Abbaschian, Reza, jt. auth. see Reed-Hill, Robert E.

Abbasi, I. A. Notes on Practice in Civil Courts. 15p. 1977. pap. 45.00 (*0-7855-1428-7*) St Mut.

Abbasi, S. A. Alternative Energy: Development & Management. 175p. 1995. pap. 275.00 (*81-7089-236-8*, Pub. by Intl Bk Distr) St Mut.

***Abbasi, S. A.** Environment Everyone: Bitter-Sweet Writings on Environment. (Illus.). 148p. 1998. 18.00 (*81-7141-439-7*, Pub. by Discovery Pub Hse) Nataraj Bks.

Abbasi, S. A. Environmental Impact of Water Resources Projects. (C). 1991. 28.00 (*81-7141-150-9*) S Asia.

— World's Worst Weed, Its Impact & Utilisation. 224p. 1993. pap. 225.00 (*0-7855-2717-6*, Pub. by Intl Bk Distr) St Mut.

Abbasi, S. A., et al. Hot Topics: Everyday Environmental Concerns. (Illus.). 228p. 2000. text 19.95 (*0-19-564534-0*) OUP.

Abbasi, Taher, jt. auth. see Kurup, Pran.

Abbass, D. K. & Zarzynski, Joseph W. The Radeau Land Tortoise: North America's Oldest Intact Warship. (Illus.). 32p. (YA). (gr. 7-12). 1994. pap. 4.95 (*0-937559-02-4*) M-Z Info.

Abbass, Jobe. Apostolic See in the New Eastern Code of Canon Law. LC 95-23875. 216p. 1995. text 89.95 (*0-7734-8976-2*) E Mellen.

Abbaszadegan, Morteza & AWWA Research Foundation Staff. Application of PCR Technologies for Virus Detection in Groundwater. LC 97-34412. 60p. 1998. 125.00 (*0-89867-934-6*, 90740) Am Water Wks Assn.

Abbat, William. Colloquial Who's Who. LC 65-27204. 256p. 1969. reprint ed. 18.95 (*0-405-03660-4*, Pub. by Blom Pubns) Ayer.

Abbate, Carolyn. Unsung Voices: Opera & Musical Narrative in the Nineteenth Century. 304p. 1991. text 49.50 (*0-691-09140-4*, Pub. by Princeton U Pr); pap. text 16.95 (*0-691-02608-4*, Pub. by Princeton U Pr) Cal Prin Full Svc.

Abbate, Carolyn & Parker, Roger, eds. Analyzing Opera: Verdi & Wagner. (California Studies in 19th Century Music: No. 6). 250p. 1988. 65.00 (*0-520-06157-8*, Pub. by U CA Pr) Cal Prin Full Svc.

Abbate, Janet. Inventing the Internet. LC 98-47647. (Illus.). 268p. 1999. 27.50 (*0-262-01172-7*) MIT Pr.

***Abbate, Janet.** Inventing the Internet. (Inside Technology Ser.). (Illus.). 282p. (C). 2000. pap. 16.95 (*0-262-51115-0*) MIT Pr.

Abbate, Janet, jt. ed. see Kahin, Brian.

Abbate, Marcia S. & LaChappelle, Nancy B. Pictures, Please! An Articulation Supplement. 290p. 1984. ring bd. 55.00 (*0-7616-2091-5*) Commun Skill.

Abbate, Matthew & Wagner, Allison, eds. El Dia de los Muertos. Grossi, Veronica & Anthor, Cecilia L., trs. from SPA. LC 87-8251.Tr. of Life of the Dead in Mexican Folk Art. (SPA., Illus.). 1995. reprint ed. pap. write for info. (*0-929865-14-6*) Mod Art Mus Ft Worth.

Abbate, Matthew, ed. see Canfield, Patrick M.

Abbatecola, Oronzo. Values in Art. (Illus.). 80p. 1994. pap. 20.95 (*0-8059-3533-9*) Dorrance.

Abbatt, F. & Mejia, A. Continuing the Education of Health Workers: A Workshop Manual. 185p. 1988. 35.00 (*92-4-154220-9*) World Health.

Abbatt, F., jt. auth. see Rotem, A.

Abbatt, F. R. Teaching for Better Learning: A Guide for Teachers of Primary Health Care Staff. 2nd ed. (ENG, FRE & SPA.). vii, 190p. 1992. pap. text 41.00 (*92-4-154442-2*, 1150377) World Health.

Abbatt, John Dilworth. A Victorian Quaker Courtship, 1853-1855. 1999. pap. 21.00 (*1-85072-043-6*, Pub. by W Sessions) St Mut.

Abbay, Alemseged. Re-Imagining Identity: The Divergent Paths of the Eritrean & Tigrayan Nationalist Struggles. LC 98-23736. 250p. 1998. 79.95 (*1-56902-071-X*); pap. 21.95 (*1-56902-072-8*) Red Sea Pr.

Abbe, Christopher J. Pilot's Pocket Decoder. LC 98-4210. 224p. 1998. pap. 14.95 (*0-07-007549-2*) McGraw.

Abbe de Saint-Denis, see Suger, pseud.

Abbe, Derek Van, see Van Abbe, Derek.

Abbe, Donald, et al. Lubbock & the South Plains. 2nd rev. ed. (Illus.). 128p. 1995. 29.95 (*0-89781-481-9*) Am Historical Pr.

Abbe, Dorothy. The Dwiggins Marionettes. LC 70-86956. (Puppet Library). 1970. 49.50 (*0-8238-0146-2*) Kalmbach.

— William Addison Dwiggins. 1974. 1.00 (*0-89073-018-0*, 141) Boston Public Lib.

Abbe, Dorothy, compiled by. Stencilled Ornament & Illustration. 1980. pap. 15.00 (*0-89073-064-4*, 223) Boston Public Lib.

Abbe, Elfriede. The Fern Herbal: Including the Ferns, the Horsetails & the Club Mosses. LC 84-45439. (Illus.). 120p. 1985. text 48.50 (*0-8014-1718-X*) Cornell U Pr.

Abbe, Ernst. Gesammelte Abhandlungen. (GER.). 1997. reprint ed. write for info. (*3-487-09120-8*) G Olms Pubs.

Abbe, George. Collected Poems. 1961. 5.95 (*0-87233-800-2*) Bauhan.

— Dreams & Dissent, Poems 1961-1970. 1970. 8.95 (*0-87233-016-8*) Bauhan.

— The Larks. (YA). (gr. 7 up). 1974. pap. 8.95 (*0-87233-033-8*) Bauhan.

— You & Contemporary Poetry. 1968. pap. 8.95 (*0-87233-010-9*) Bauhan.

Abbe, Kate. Joy Riding. Warren, Shirley, ed. 40p. (Orig.). 1992. pap. 6.00 (*1-877801-18-6*) Still Waters.

ABBE Research Department Staff. Alcohol (Ethanol)--Its Adverse, Harmful & Delayed Health Damage Including Cancer: Index of New Information with References. 150p. 1999. 47.50 (*0-7883-2216-8*); pap. 44.50 (*0-7883-2217-6*) ABBE Pubs Assn.

— Computer Dangers & Risks to Health for Consumers, Employees & Professionals: List of Affectations Including Mental Conditions. (Illus.). 120p. 1999. 47.50 (*0-7883-2156-0*); pap. 44.50 (*0-7883-2157-9*) ABBE Pubs Assn.

— Immigration & Migration of Ethnic Groups, Legal & Illegal Problems of Movements, Health Abuse & Politics: Index of New Information with References. (Illus.). 150p. 1999. 47.50 (*0-7883-2284-2*); pap. 44.50 (*0-7883-2285-0*) ABBE Pubs Assn.

— Jogging--Physical Health & Mental Effects & Improvements: Index of New Information with References. (Illus.). 150p. 1999. 47.50 (*0-7883-2204-4*); pap. 44.50 (*0-7883-2205-2*) ABBE Pubs Assn.

— Research--Its Care, Criticism, Variations, Opinions, Problems, Threats, Philosophy & Standards: Index of New Information with Bibliography. 150p. Date not set. 47.50 (*0-7883-2241-9*); pap. 44.50 (*0-7883-2242-7*) ABBE Pubs Assn.

— Research--Its Economics & Politics: Index of New Information with Bibliography. 150p. Date not set. 47.50 (*0-7883-2245-1*); pap. 44.50 (*0-7883-2246-X*) ABBE Pubs Assn.

— Research--Its Methods, Variations, Philosophy & Practicality: Index of New Information with Bibliography. 150p. Date not set. 47.50 (*0-7883-2237-0*); pap. 44.50 (*0-7883-2238-9*) ABBE Pubs Assn.

— Research--Its Phases & Some Historical Accounts: Index of New Information with Bibliography. 150p. Date not set. 47.50 (*0-7883-2243-5*); pap. 44.50 (*0-7883-2244-3*) ABBE Pubs Assn.

— Research--Its Statistics & Numerical Data: Index of New Information with Bibliography. 150p. Date not set. 47.50 (*0-7883-2235-4*); pap. 44.50 (*0-7883-2236-2*) ABBE Pubs Assn.

— Research--Legislation & Jurisprudence: Modern Phases & Trends: Index of New Information with Bibliography. 150p. Date not set. 47.50 (*0-7883-2239-7*); pap. 44.50 (*0-7883-2240-0*) ABBE Pubs Assn.

— Research Trends, Directions, Diversity, Specialities, Limitations & Regulations: Index of New Information with Bibliography. 150p. Date not set. 47.50 (*0-7883-2247-8*); pap. 44.50 (*0-7883-2248-6*) ABBE Pubs Assn.

— Walking As Exercise--Health Improvement, Disease Abatement & Stroke Prevention: Index of New Information with References. (Illus.). 150p. 1999. 47.50 (*0-7883-2186-2*); pap. 44.50 (*0-7883-2187-0*) ABBE Pubs Assn.

Abbe, T. & Howson, H. A. Colgate: Robert Colgate, the Immigrant: A Genealogy of the New York Colgates & Some Associated Lines. (Illus.). 464p. 1992. reprint ed. pap. 72.00 (*0-8328-2294-9*); reprint ed. lib. bdg. 82.00 (*0-8328-2293-0*) Higginson Bk Co.

Abbedut, jt. auth. see Elliott.

***Abbeduto.** Taking Sides: Education Psychology. 400p. 1999. pap. 18.44 (*0-07-235076-8*) McGraw.

Abbeduto, Leonard, jt. auth. see Rosenberg, Sheldon.

Abbeele, George Van Den, see Lyotard, Jean-Francois & Van Den Abbeele, George.

Abbeele, Georges Van Den, see Van Den Abbeele, Georges.

Abbell, Michael. International Extradition, 2 vols., Set. 1995. ring bd., suppl. ed. 295.00 (*0-935328-79-3*) Intl Law Inst.

Abbell, Michael, jt. auth. see Ristau, Bruno A.

Abbenes, J. G., et al. Greek Literary Theory after Aristotle. 352p. 1995. pap. 40.00 (*90-5383-365-X*) Paul & Co Pubs.

Abbett, R. W. American Civil Engineering Practice, Vol. 3. LC 56-11255. 1296p. reprint ed. 200.00 (*0-8357-9835-6*, 205509100003) Bks Demand.

Abbeville Press Staff. American Wildflowers: Address Book. 1997. pap. text 16.95 (*1-55859-768-9*) Abbeville Pr.

Abbeville Press Staff. Ansel Adams: The National Park Service Photographs. (Tiny Folios Ser.). (Illus.). 352p. 1996. pap. 11.95 (*1-55859-817-0*) Abbeville Pr.

— Art Journal: Abbeville Unbook. 1998. pap. text 9.95 (*0-7892-5387-9*) Abbeville Pr.

— Assorted Little Pebbles. 1998. 6.95 (*0-7892-0580-7*) Abbeville Pr.

— Assorted My First Color. 1998. 8.95 (*0-7892-0581-5*) Abbeville Pr.

— Barbie: In Fashion. (Tiny Folios Ser.). (Illus.). 328p. 1997. 11.95 (*0-7892-0404-5*) Abbeville Pr.

— Classic Cocktails: 1999 Wall Calendar. 1998. 12.95 (*0-7892-5373-9*) Abbeville Pr.

— Classic Journal: Abbeville Unbook. (Abbeville Anthologies Ser.). 1998. pap. text 9.95 (*0-7892-5388-7*) Abbeville Pr.

— Classic Unbook. 1998. pap. text 9.95 (*0-7892-5389-5*) Abbeville Pr.

— How Artists See Families, Work, Play, & Cities, Teacher's & Parents' ed. 1999. 10.95 (*0-7892-0369-3*) Abbeville Pr.

— Norman Rockwell: Address Book. 1992. 16.95 (*1-55859-202-4*) Abbeville Pr.

An Asterisk (*) at the beginning of an entry indicates that the title is appearing for the first time.

— Red Book. 1994. 10.95 (*1-55859-915-0*) Abbeville Pr.

— Treasures of the Uffizi: Mini ed. 1998. pap. text 11.95 (*0-7892-0575-0*) Abbeville Pr.

— White Book. 1994. 10.95 (*1-55859-916-9*) Abbeville Pr.

Abbeville Press Staff, ed. Assorted Modern Masters. 1998. pap. 14.95 (*0-7892-0593-9*) Abbeville Pr.

Abbeville Press Staff & Versace, Gianni. Vanitas: Designs. (Illus.). 272p. 1996. 75.00 (*1-55859-804-9*) Abbeville Pr.

Abbey, Aaron, ed. see Abbey, Rita D.

Abbey, Augustus. Technological Innovation: The R & D Work Environment. Dufey, Gunter, ed. LC 82-4883. (Research for Business Decisions Ser.: No. 49). 140p. 1982. reprint ed. pap. 43.40 (*0-8357-1335-0*, 207012300064) Bks Demand.

Abbey, Barbara. Barbara Abbey's Knitting Lace. Orig. Title: Knitting Lace. (Illus.). 144p. 1993. reprint ed. pap. 24.95 (*0-942018-05-2*) Schoolhouse WI.

*__Abbey, Beverly, ed.__ Instructional & Cognitive Impacts of Web-Based Education. LC 00-25657. 300p. (C). 2000. pap. 64.95 (*1-878289-59-4*) Idea Group Pub.

*__Abbey, Buck.__ U. S. Landscape Ordinances: An Annotated Reference Handbook. LC 98-24358. 456p. 1998. 80.00 (*0-471-29276-1*) Wiley.

Abbey, Charles J. The English Church & Its Bishops, 1700-1800, 2 vols. LC 77-130230. reprint ed. 145.00 (*0-404-00290-0*) AMS Pr.

Abbey, Cherie D., ed. Nineteenth-Century Literature Criticism, Vol. 14. 600p. 1987. 150.00 (*0-8103-5814-X*) Gale.

Abbey, Cherie D., ed. Nineteenth-Century Literature Criticism, Vol. 15. 600p. 1987. text 150.00 (*0-8103-5815-8*) Gale.

— Nineteenth-Century Literature Criticism, Vol. 16. 600p. 1987. text 150.00 (*0-8103-5816-6*) Gale.

Abbey, Cherie D. & Mullane, Janet, eds. Nineteenth-Century Literature Criticism, Vol. 17. LC 81-6943. 600p. 1988. 150.00 (*0-8103-5817-4*) Gale.

Abbey, Cherie D., jt. ed. see Harris, Laurie L.

Abbey, Duane C. The Ambulatory Patient Group Operations Manual. 360p. (C). 1996. text 195.00 (*0-7863-0842-7*, Irwn Prfssnl) McGraw-Hill Prof.

— Charge Master: Review Strategies for Improved Billing & Reimbursement. LC 97-16895. 1997. 175.00 (*0-7863-0997-0*, Irwn Prfssnl) McGraw-Hill Prof.

— Outpatient Services: Designing, Organizing & Managing Outpatient Resources. LC 97-41392. 250p. 1996. pap. text 60.00 (*0-7863-1085-5*, Irwn Prfssnl) McGraw-Hill Prof.

Abbey, Edward. Abbey's Road. 224p. 1991. pap. 12.95 (*0-452-26564-9*, Plume) Dutton Plume.

— The Best of Edward Abbey. LC 87-23568. Orig. Title: Slumgullion Stew. (Illus.). 400p. 1988. pap. 15.00 (*0-87156-786-5*, Pub. by Sierra) Random.

— Beyond the Wall: Essays from the Outside. LC 83-18346. 224p. 1995. pap. 11.95 (*0-8050-0820-9*, Owl) H Holt & Co.

— Black Sun: A Novel. lib. bdg. 19.95 (*0-8488-0900-9*) Amereon Ltd.

— Black Sun: A Novel. 160p. 1982. mass mkt. 5.99 (*0-380-58503-0*, Avon Bks) Morrow Avon.

— Black Sun: A Novel. 1991. reprint ed. lib. bdg. 21.95 (*1-56849-082-8*) Buccaneer Bks.

— Black Sun: A Novel. rev. ed. LC 90-36308. 176p. 1990. reprint ed. pap. 11.95 (*0-88496-319-5*) Capra Pr.

— Brave Cowboy. 320p. 1992. pap. 13.50 (*0-380-71459-0*, Avon Bks) Morrow Avon.

— Desert Solitaire: A Season in the Wilderness. LC 67-26166. (Ecological Main Event Ser.). 337p. 1991. mass mkt. 6.99 (*0-345-32649-0*) Ballantine Pub Grp.

— Desert Solitaire: A Season in the Wilderness. (Illus.). 288p. 1990. pap. 12.00 (*0-671-69588-6*, Touchstone) S&S Trade Pap.

— Desert Solitaire: A Season in the Wilderness. LC 87-36546. (Illus.). 255p. 1988. reprint ed. 37.50 (*0-8165-1057-1*) U of Ariz Pr.

— Down the River. (Illus.). 256p. 1991. pap. 12.95 (*0-452-26563-0*, Plume) Dutton Plume.

— Earth Apples: The Poetry of Edward Abbey. (Illus.). 128p. 1995. pap. 10.00 (*0-312-13479-7*, St Martin Griffin) St Martin.

— Fire on the Mountain. lib. bdg. 19.95 (*0-8488-0901-7*) Amereon Ltd.

— Fire on the Mountain. 1994. lib. bdg. 37.95 (*1-56849-457-2*) Buccaneer Bks.

— Fire on the Mountain. 192p. 1992. pap. 12.50 (*0-380-71460-4*, Avon Bks) Morrow Avon.

— The Fool's Progress: An Honest Novel. 528p. 1998. pap. 14.00 (*0-8050-5791-9*, Owl) H Holt & Co.

— The Fool's Progress: An Honest Novel. 528p. 1990. pap. 13.00 (*0-380-70856-6*, Avon Bks) Morrow Avon.

— Good News. 256p. 1991. pap. 12.95 (*0-452-26565-7*, Plume) Dutton Plume.

— Hayduke Lives! 308p. 1991. pap. 12.95 (*0-316-00413-8*) Little.

— Hayduke Lives! A Novel. 1998. pap. 12.95 (*0-316-19138-8*, Back Bay) Little.

— The Journey Home: Some Words in Defense of the American West. (Illus.). 256p. 1991. pap. 12.95 (*0-452-26562-2*, Plume) Dutton Plume.

— The Journey Home: Some Words in Defense of the American West. 1993. 23.75 (*0-8446-6706-4*) Peter Smith.

— The Monkey Wrench Gang. 22.95 (*0-8488-0902-5*) Amereon Ltd.

— Monkey Wrench Gang. LC 75-831. 387p. 1976. mass mkt. 6.99 (*0-380-00741-X*, Avon Bks) Morrow Avon.

— The Monkey Wrench Gang. 1991. reprint ed. lib. bdg. 37.95 (*1-56849-083-6*) Buccaneer Bks.

— The Monkey Wrench Gang. rev. ed. LC 75-831. (Illus.). 368p. 1999. reprint ed. 24.95 (*0-942688-18-X*) Dream Garden.

— Monkey Wrench Gang T. 368p. 1992. pap. 12.50 (*0-380-71339-X*, Avon Bks) Morrow Avon.

— One Life at a Time, Please. LC 87-8812. 240p. 1995. pap. 9.95 (*0-8050-0603-6*, Owl) H Holt & Co.

— The Serpents of Paradise: A Reader. Macrae, John, ed. 1995. 25.00 (*0-8050-3132-4*); pap. 12.95 (*0-8050-3133-2*, Owl) H Holt & Co.

— A Voice Crying in the Wilderness (Vox Clamantis in Deserto) Notes from a Secret Journal. 3rd ed. (Illus.). 112p. 1991. pap. 8.95 (*0-312-06488-8*) St Martin.

*__Abbey, Edward & Brinkley, Douglas.__ The Monkey Wrench Gang. 368p. 2000. pap. 13.00 (*0-06-095644-5*, Perennial) HarperTrade.

Abbey, Edward & Curtis, Jack. Confessions of a Barbarian; Red Knife Valley. LC 85-26939. (Back-to-Back Bks.: Vol. VII). 162p. (Orig.). 1986. pap. 7.50 (*0-88496-244-X*) Capra Pr.

Abbey, Edward, jt. auth. see Porter, Eliot.

Abbey, J. L. & Caygill, David. Estimulo de un Ajuste Propicio: El Caso de Ghana; Restructuracion de la Economia de Nueva Zelandia Desde 1984. LC HC0517.G6A33. (Conferencia Per Jacobsson de 1989 Ser.). (SPA.). 51p. reprint ed. pap. 30.00 (*0-608-08775-0*, 206941400004) Bks Demand.

— On Promoting Successful Adjustment: Some Lessons from Ghana; Economic Restructuring in New Zealand since 1984. LC HC0517.G6A33. (Per Jacobsson Lecture Ser.: Vol. 1989). 47p. reprint ed. pap. 30.00 (*0-608-08774-2*, 206941300004) Bks Demand.

— Pour un Ajustement Reussi: Quelques Enseignements a Tirer de l'Experience du Ghana; La Restructuration Economique en Nouvelle Zelande Depuis 1984. LC HC0517.G6A33. (Fondation Per Jacobsson Conference de 1989 Ser.). (FRE.). 53p. reprint ed. pap. 30.00 (*0-608-08776-9*, 206941500004) Bks Demand.

Abbey, J. R. Life in England in Aquatint & Lithography, 1770-1860: A Bibliographical Catalogue. (Illus.). 512p. 1991. reprint ed. 175.00 (*1-55660-129-8*) A Wofsy Fine Arts.

— Scenery of Great Britain & Ireland in Aquatint & Lithography, 1770-1860: A Bibliographical Catalogue. (Illus.). 488p. 1991. reprint ed. 175.00 (*1-55660-130-1*) A Wofsy Fine Arts.

— Travel in Aquatint & Lithography, 1770-1860 Vol. 1: World, Europe, Africa, Vol. 1. (Abbey Collection of Colour-Plate Books in Aquatint & Lithography, 1770-1860). (Illus.). 352p. 1991. reprint ed. 175.00 (*1-55660-131-X*) A Wofsy Fine Arts.

— Travel in Aquatint & Lithography, 1770-1860: A Bibliographical Catalogue, 2 vols. (Illus.). 1991. reprint ed. 325.00 (*1-55660-133-6*) A Wofsy Fine Arts.

— Travel in Aquatint & Lithography, 1770-1860: A Bibliographical Catalogue, 1 vol. 2nd ed. (Illus.). 740p. 1996. reprint ed. 175.00 (*1-55660-287-1*) A Wofsy Fine Arts.

— Travel in Aquatint & Lithography, 1770-1860 Vol. II: Asia, Oceania, Antarctica, America: A Bibliographical Catalogue. (Illus.). 464p. 1991. reprint ed. 175.00 (*1-55660-132-8*) A Wofsy Fine Arts.

Abbey, James R. Hospitality Sales & Advertising. 3rd rev. ed. LC 98-16675. (Illus.). 600p. (C). 1998. pap. 99.93 (*0-86612-174-9*) Educ Inst Am Hotel.

— Hospitality Sales & Marketing. LC 99-180367. (Illus.). 450p. (C). 1998. pap. write for info. (*0-86612-175-7*) Educ Inst Am Hotel.

Abbey, James R., jt. auth. see Astroff, Milton T.

Abbey, Karin, jt. auth. see Evans, G. Edward.

Abbey, L. M. & Zimmerman, J., eds. Dental Informatics: Integrating Technology into the Dental Environment. (Computers in Health Care Ser.). (Illus.). xiii, 348p. 1991. 75.00 (*0-387-97643-4*) Spr-Verlag.

Abbey, Lester. Highways: An Architectural Approach. (Illus.). 370p. 1992. text 63.95 (*0-442-00603-9*, VNR) Wiley.

Abbey, Lloyd R. Destroyer & Preserver: Shelley's Poetic Skepticism. LC 79-9166. 183p. reprint ed. pap. 56.80 (*0-7837-1815-2*, 204201500001) Bks Demand.

Abbey, Lynn. Beneath the Web. 320p. (Orig.). 1994. mass mkt. 4.99 (*0-441-00084-3*) Ace Bks.

— Jerlayne. 1999. mass mkt. 6.99 (*0-88677-809-3*, Pub. by DAW Bks) Penguin Putnam.

*__Abbey, Lynn.__ Nether Scroll. (Forgotten Realms Ser.). (Illus.). 320p. 2000. mass mkt. 6.99 (*0-7869-1566-8*) Wizards Coast.

— Out of Time. 2000. mass mkt. 5.99 (*0-441-00751-1*) Ace Bks.

Abbey, Lynn. Planeswalker. 1998. pap. 5.99 (*0-7869-1182-4*, Pub. by TSR Inc) Random.

— Siege of Shadows. 1996. mass mkt. 6.50 (*0-441-00306-0*) Ace Bks.

— The Temper of Wisdom. 1992. mass mkt. 4.99 (*0-446-36226-3*, Pub. by Warner Bks) Little.

— Unicorn & Dragon, Vol. 1. 240p. 1987. mass mkt. 3.50 (*0-380-75567-X*, Avon Bks) Morrow Avon.

— Unicorn & Dragon Vol. II: Conquest. 272p. 1988. pap. 6.95 (*0-380-75354-5*, Avon Bks) Morrow Avon.

— Wooden Sword. 1991. mass mkt. 4.99 (*0-441-90866-7*) Ace Bks.

Abbey, Lynn & Asprin, Robert L. Catwoman. 208p. 1992. mass mkt. 4.99 (*0-446-36043-0*) Warner Bks.

Abbey, Margaret. Amber Promise. large type ed. 265p. 1992. reprint ed. lib. bdg. 18.95 (*1-56054-425-2*) Thorndike Pr.

— Blood of the Boar. large type ed. LC 93-13142. 265p. 1993. lib. bdg. 18.95 (*1-56054-617-4*) Thorndike Pr.

— Brothers-in-Arms. large type ed. LC 92-43164. (Romance Ser.). 310p. 1993. lib. bdg. 19.95 (*1-56054-426-0*) Thorndike Pr.

— The Flight of the Kestrel. large type ed. LC 92-781. 291p. 1992. reprint ed. lib. bdg. 13.95 (*1-56054-374-4*) Thorndike Pr.

— Francesca. large type ed. (Candlelight Romance Ser.). 279p. 1992. reprint ed. lib. bdg. 16.95 (*1-56054-427-9*) Thorndike Pr.

— The Heart Is a Traitor. large type ed. LC 93-3643. 280p. 1993. lib. bdg. 19.95 (*1-56054-618-2*) Thorndike Pr.

— The Warwick Heiress. large type ed. LC 94-33760. (Nightingale Ser.). 269p. 1995. pap. 16.95 (*0-8161-7497-0*, G K Hall Lrg Type) Mac Lib Ref.

Abbey, Marguerite, et al. Glimpses of Childhood in the Old West, 1840-1940. (Yesteryears Ser.). (Illus.). 96p. (Orig.). 1995. pap. 12.95 (*0-9623233-3-0*) CA HPA.

Abbey, Merrill R. Day Dawns in Fire: America's Quest for Meaning. LC 75-36439. 128p. reprint ed. pap. 39.70 (*0-608-16957-9*, 202696600053) Bks Demand.

— The Epic of United Methodist Preaching: A Profile in American Social History. 216p. (Orig.). 1983. pap. text 22.00 (*0-8191-3692-1*); lib. bdg. 50.50 (*0-8191-3691-3*) U Pr of Amer.

— The Shape of the Gospel: Interpreting the Bible Through the Christian Year. LC 78-124751. 352p. 1970. write for info. (*0-687-38342-0*) Abingdon.

Abbey, Michael & Corey, Michael J. Oracle: A Beginner's Guide. (Oracle Press Ser.). 522p. 1995. pap. 29.95 (*0-07-882122-3*) McGraw.

— Oracle 8: A Beginner's Guide. (Illus.). 767p. 1997. pap. text 39.99 (*0-07-882393-5*, Oracle Press) Osborne-McGraw.

*__Abbey, Michael, et al.__ Oracle: A Beginner's Guide. 765p. 1999. pap. 44.99 (*0-07-212204-8*) Osborne Bks.

Abbey, Michael, jt. auth. see Corey, Michael J.

Abbey Press Printing Staff, tr. see Diede, Pauline N.

Abbey, Rita D. Rita Deanin Abbey. Abbey, Aaron, ed. LC 96-23835. (Rio Grande Ser.). (Illus.). 96p. 1997. 29.95 (*0-9652870-0-9*) Gan Or.

Abbey, Robert & Richards, Mark. A Practical Approach to Conveyancing. 466p. 1998. pap. 54.00 (*1-85431-732-6*, Pub. by Blackstone Pr) Gaunt.

*__Abbey, Robert & Richards, Mark.__ Practical Approach to Conveyancing. 2nd ed. 504p. 2000. pap. 50.00 (*1-85431-915-9*, Pub. by Blackstone Pr) Gaunt.

Abbey, Robert M. Q & A: Wills Probate & Administration. 226p. 1997. pap. 16.00 (*1-85431-607-9*, Pub. by Blackstone Pr) Gaunt.

Abbey, Robert M. & Richards, Mark B. Blackstone's Law Questions & Answers: Q&A Conveyancing. 2nd ed. 281p. 1999. pap. 24.00 (*1-85431-920-5*, Pub. by Blackstone Pr) Gaunt.

— Q & A Conveyancing. (Q & A Ser.). 272p. 1995. pap. 20.00 (*1-85431-407-6*, Pub. by Blackstone Pr) Gaunt.

Abbey, Ruth. Dream of Terror. large type ed. (Dales Large Print Ser.). 224p. 1996. pap. 18.99 (*1-85389-651-9*, Dales) Ulverscroft.

— From Montana's Mountains to Its Prairies. (Illus.). 96p. (Orig.). 1997. pap. 9.00 (*1-887804-09-9*) Cent Mont Pubng.

*__Abbey, Ruth.__ Nietzsche's Middle Period. LC 99-49373. 224p. 2000. text 45.00 (*0-19-513408-7*) OUP.

Abbey, Ruth. The Shadow Between. large type ed. (Dales Large Print Ser.). 284p. 1995. pap. 18.99 (*1-85389-535-0*, Dales) Ulverscroft.

Abbey, Sharon, jt. ed. see O'Reilly, Andrea.

Abbey, Sharon M. & O'Reilly, Andrea, eds. Redefining Motherhood: Changing Identities & Patterns. LC 98-187384. 300p. 1998. pap. 22.95 (*1-896764-06-1*, Pub. by Sec Story Pr) LPC InBook.

Abbey, Stella K. Mother Goose Sweeps History. LC 13-275. (Illus.). 1967. 2.99 (*0-686-00888-X*) S K Abbey.

Abbey, Susan E., jt. auth. see Demitrack, Mark A.

Abbey, Susan E., jt. ed. see Demitrack, Mark A.

Abbi, Anvita. Reduplication in South Asian Languages: An Areal, Typological & Historical Study. (C). 1992. 19.00 (*81-7023-310-0*, Pub. by Allied Pubs) S Asia.

Abbie, Lynn. The Dragons Within Me: Staying Alive! 218p. 1995. pap. 12.00 (*0-9647808-0-1*) Prosit Pr.

Abbin, Byrle M. Income Tax FID. 1995. 125.00 (*0-316-00417-0*, Aspen Law & Bus) Aspen Pub.

Abbin, Byrle M., et al. Income Taxation of Fiduciaries & Beneficiaries. annuals 1104p. 1997. pap. 125.00 (*1-56706-476-0*, 64760) Panel Pubs.

Abbin, Joseph. Blown Flathead. (Illus.). 120p. 1998. pap. 14.95 (*1-880047-64-0*) Creative Des.

Abbink, Emily. Colors of the Navajo. LC 97-26013. (Colors of the World Ser.). (Illus.). (J). 1998. 19.93 (*1-57505-207-5*, Carolrhoda); pap. 5.95 (*1-57505-269-5*, Carolrhoda) Lerner Pub.

— Missions of monterey Bay. (J). (gr. 4-7). 1999. pap. 5.95 (*0-8225-9835-3*) Lerner Pub.

Abbink, Emily. Missions of the Monterey Bay Area. LC 95-2843. (California Missions Ser.). (J). 1996. lib. bdg. 23.93 (*0-8225-1928-3*, Lerner Publctns) Lerner Pub.

*__Abbink, J. & Hesseling, Gerti.__ Election Observation & Democratization in Africa LC 99-15593. 2000. text 69.95 (*0-312-22394-3*) St Martin.

Abbink, Jon, jt. ed. see Aijmer, Goran.

Abbinnett, Ross. Truth & Social Science: From Hegel to Deconstruction. LC 97-62127. 200 p. 1998. write for info. (*0-8039-7593-7*) Sage.

Abbiss, J. B., jt. ed. see Pike, E. R.

Abbitt, Patricia L. Imaging in Obstetrics & Gynecology: A Teaching File. LC 96-37120. (Illus.). 384p. 1997. 89.00 (*0-683-18212-9*) Lppncott W & W.

— Ultrasound: A Pattern Approach. (Illus.). 472p. 1994. text 135.00 (*0-07-000031-X*) McGraw-Hill HPD.

Abblett, David E. & Abblett, Terry A. Cash Practice New Practice Survival Guide. (Illus.). 126p. (C). 1998. pap. text 29.95 (*0-9670283-0-2*) Abblett Chiro Prods.

Abblett, Terry A., jt. auth. see Abblett, David E.

Abbo, Fred E. Steps to a Longer Life. LC 78-31661. 220p. 1979. pap. 4.95 (*0-89037-211-X*) Anderson World.

Abbonen, M. Petit Vocabulaire du Var. (FRE.). 90p. 1993. 34.95 (*0-320-00903-3*) Fr & Eur.

*__Abborno, G. John M.__ The Ethics of Homelessness: Philosophical Perspectives. (Value Inquiry Book Ser.: Vol. 86). (Illus.). ix, 258p. 1999. 69.00 (*90-420-0787-7*); pap. 22.00 (*90-420-0777-X*) Editions Rodopi.

*__Abbot.__ Indian Ritual & Belief: The Keys of Power. 2000. 44.00 (*81-7304-339-6*, Pub. by Manohar) S Asia.

Abbot, Abiel. Letters Written in the Interior of Cuba. LC 75-37299. (Black Heritage Library Collection). 1977. reprint ed. 22.95 (*0-8369-8936-8*) Ayer.

Abbot, Abiel & Abbot, Ephraim. Abbot: A Genealogical Register of the Descendants of George Abbot, of Andover; George Abbot, of Rowley; Thomas Abbot, of Andover; Arthur Abbot of Ipswich; Robt. Abbot of Branford, Ct., & George Abbot of Norwalk, Ct. 217p. 1988. reprint ed. pap. 32.50 (*0-8328-0083-X*); reprint ed. lib. bdg. 40.50 (*0-8328-0082-1*) Higginson Bk Co.

Abbot, Abiel, et al. The American Republic & Ancient Israel. 1977. 23.95 (*0-405-10231-3*, 14482) Ayer.

Abbot, David. An Introduction to Reaction Kinetics. LC 67-7380. (Longman Concepts in Chemistry Ser.). 160p. reprint ed. pap. 49.60 (*0-608-10182-6*, 201633600003) Bks Demand.

Abbot, Ephraim, jt. auth. see Abbot, Abiel.

Abbot, Everett V. Justice & the Modern Law. xiv, 299p. 1997. reprint ed. 95.00 (*1-56169-248-4*) Gaunt.

— Justice & the Modern Law. xiv, 299p. 1987. reprint ed. 32.50 (*0-8377-1902-X*, Rothman) W S Hein.

Abbot, Francis E. Scientific Theism. LC 75-3012. (Philosophy in America Ser.). reprint ed. 39.50 (*0-404-59004-7*) AMS Pr.

— The Syllogistic Philosophy or Prolegomena to Science, 2 vols. LC 75-3013. (Philosophy in America Ser.). reprint ed. 115.00 (*0-404-59005-5*) AMS Pr.

— The Way Out of Agnosticism: or The Philosophy of Free Religion. LC 75-3014. (Philosophy in America Ser.). reprint ed. 34.50 (*0-404-59008-X*) AMS Pr.

Abbot, G. F. The Holy War in Tripoli. 1990. 150.00 (*1-85077-131-6*, Pub. by Darf Pubs Ltd) St Mut.

Abbot, George. A Briefe Description of the Whole Worlde. LC 78-25701. (English Experience Ser.: No. 213). 68p. 1970. reprint ed. 25.00 (*90-221-0213-0*) Walter J Johnson.

Abbot, Henry L. Siege Artillery in the Campaigns Against Richmond with Notes on the 15-Inch Gun. (Illus.). 192p. (C). 1986. reprint ed. 24.95 (*0-939631-04-0*) Thomas Publications.

Abbot-Hess, Mary. The Art of Cooking for the Diabetic. 496p. 1998. mass mkt. 7.50 (*0-451-19533-7*, Sig) NAL.

Abbot, James. Jane's World Railways: The International Authority on the Railway Technology of Today & Tomorrow, 1997-98. 39th ed. 1997. 390.00 (*0-7106-1563-9*) Janes Info Group.

Abbot, John. Birds of Georgia: Selected Drawings from the Houghton Library, Harvard University. LC 98-127263. (Illus.). 100p. 1997. boxed set 125.00 (*0-88322-040-7*) Beehive GA.

Abbot, John, et al. The Abbey Psalter: The Book of Psalms Used by the Trappist Monks of Genesee Abbey. LC 81-80871. 352p. 1981. 39.95 (*0-8091-0316-8*) Paulist Pr.

Abbot, John S., jt. auth. see Cody, William.

Abbot, Justin E. Bhanudas: The Poet Saint of Maharashtra. 1996. reprint ed. 16.00 (*81-7030-498-9*, Pub. by Sri Satguru Pubns) S Asia.

— Tukaram: The Poet Saint of Maharashtra. (C). 1996. 28.00 (*81-7030-497-0*, Pub. by Sri Satguru Pubns) S Asia.

Abbot, Kingsley. Back to the Beach: A Brian Wilson & the Beach Boys Reader. 256p. 1998. pap. 18.95 (*1-900924-02-1*, Pub. by Helter Skelter) Interlink Pub.

Abbot, Laura. Class Act. 1998. per. 4.25 (*0-373-70803-3*) Harlequin Bks.

— Une Femme Temperaire. (Amours d'Aujourd'Hui Ser.: No. 300). (FRE.). 1998. pap. 4.99 (*0-373-38300-2*, 1-38300-9) Harlequin Bks.

*__Abbot, Laura.__ Homecoming. (Superromance Ser.: Vol. 937). 2000. mass mkt. 4.50 (*0-373-70937-4*, 1-70937-7) Harlequin Bks.

Abbot, Laura. Mating for Life. LC 95-6888. (Superromance Ser.). 296p. 1995. per. 3.75 (*0-373-70639-1*, 1-70639-9) Harlequin Bks.

— This Christmas. 1996. per. 3.99 (*0-373-70721-5*, 1-70721-5) Harlequin Bks.

— Trial Courtship. (Superromance Ser.: Bk. 843). 1999. per. 4.25 (*0-373-70843-2*, 1-70843-7) Harlequin Bks.

— The Wedding Vow: Marriage by the Year 2000. (By the Year 2000 Ser.: No. 818). 1999. per. 4.25 (*0-373-70818-1*, 1-70818-9) Harlequin Bks.

— Where There's Smoke . . . (Women Who Dare Ser.). 1997. per. 3.99 (*0-373-70747-9*, 1-70747-0) Harlequin Bks.

*__Abbot, Marylyn.__ Gardening with Light & Color. (Illus.). 2000. 35.00 (*1-85626-324-X*, Pub. by Cathie Kyle) Trafalgar.

Abbot of Rumtek Monastery, jt. auth. see Rabjam, G.

Abbot, Philip & Levy, Michael B., eds. The Liberal Future in America: Essays in Renewal, 123. LC 84-12834. (Contributions in Political Science Ser.: No. 123). (Illus.). 210p. 1985. 57.95 (*0-313-23761-1*, ALF/, Greenwood Pr) Greenwood.

*__Abbot, Presley.__ Oxford Girl. 176p. 2000. mass mkt. 7.95 (*1-56201-173-1*, Pub. by Blue Moon Bks) Publishers Group.

Abbot, R. Tucker. Seashells, 2 vols. Rowland-Entwistle, Theodore, ed. LC 93-46147. (Science Nature Guides Ser.). (Illus.). 80p. (J). (gr. 3-6). 1994. 12.95 (*1-85028-264-1*, Silver Dolph) Advantage Pubs.

Abbot, Thomas K., tr. Kant's Introduction to Logic & His Essay on the Mistaken Subtilty of the Figures: 1885 Edition. (Key Texts Ser.). 108p. 1996. reprint ed. pap. 18.95 (*1-85506-163-5*) Bks Intl VA.

Abbot, Vicki. A New Owner's Guide to Maltese: AKC Rank #23. (New Owner's Guide to Ser.). (Illus.). 160p. 1997. 12.95 (*0-7938-2783-3*, JG-134) TFH Pubns.

An Asterisk (*) at the beginning of an entry indicates that the title is appearing for the first time.

Abbot, W. Panama & the Canal. 1976. lib. bdg. 250.00 (*0-8490-2404-8*) Gordon Pr.

Abbot, W. W., ed. The Papers of George Washington. (Revolutionary War Series, April-June 1776: Vol. 4). 1991. text 47.50 (*0-8139-1307-1*) U Pr of Va.

— The Papers of George Washington: February-December 1787. (Confederation Ser.: Vol. 5). 592p. 1997. lib. bdg. 47.50 (*0-8139-1672-0*) U Pr of Va.

— The Papers of George Washington: January-September 1788. (Confederation Ser.: Vol. 6). 608p. 1997. lib. bdg. 47.50 (*0-8139-1684-4*) U Pr of Va.

— The Papers of George Washington Vol. 3: Confederation Series: May 1785-March 1786. 654p. (C). 1994. text 47.50 (*0-8139-1506-6*) U Pr of Va.

— The Papers of George Washington, Colonial Series Vol. 8: June 1767-December 1771. 654p. (C). 1993. text 47.50 (*0-8139-1362-4*) U Pr of Va.

Abbot, W. W. & Twohig, Dorothy, eds. The Papers of George Washington: January - July 1784. (Confederation Ser.: Vol. 1). 600p. 1992. text 47.50 (*0-8139-1348-9*) U Pr of Va.

— The Papers of George Washington: January 1761-June 1767. LC 81-16307. (Colonial Ser.: Vol. 7). 586p. 1990. text 45.00 (*0-8139-1236-9*) U Pr of Va.

— The Papers of George Washington: January 1772-March 1774. (Colonial Ser.: Vol. 9). 704p. 1994. text 55.00 (*0-8139-1465-5*) U Pr of Va.

— The Papers of George Washington: July 1784 - May 1785. (Confederation Ser.: Vol. 2). 600p. 1992. text 47.50 (*0-8139-1349-7*) U Pr of Va.

— The Papers of George Washington: June-August 1776. (Revolutionary War Ser.: Vol. 5). 784p. 1993. text 67.50 (*0-8139-1447-7*) U Pr of Va.

— The Papers of George Washington: September 1789 - January 1790. (Presidential Ser.: Vol. 4). 627p. (C). 1993. text 65.00 (*0-8139-1407-8*) U Pr of Va.

Abbot, W. W., ed. see Twohig, Dorothy.

Abbot, W. W., ed. see Washington, George.

Abbot, William W. The Royal Governors of Georgia, 1754-1775. LC 59-9568. (Illus.). 208p. reprint ed. pap. 64.50 (*0-8357-3910-4*, 203664400004) Bks Demand.

— A Virginia Chronology, 1585-1783: "To Pass Away the Time" (Illus.). 78p. 1994. pap. 10.00 (*0-8063-4515-2*, 9015) Clearfield Co.

Abbotecola, Oronzo. Macrocosm: The Meaning of Numbers - The Key to the Cosmos. (Illus.). 29p. 1996. pap. 17.00 (*0-8059-3843-5*) Dorrance.

Abbotson, Susan, jt. auth. see Murphy, Brenda C. W.

***Abbotson, Susan C. W.** Student Companion to Arthur Miller. LC 99-89069. (Student Companions to Classic Writers Ser.). 184p. 2000. 29.95 (*0-313-30949-3*, GR0949, Greenwood Pr) Greenwood.

Abbott. Department & Discipline. LC 98-55981. 1999. pap. text 17.00 (*0-226-00099-0*) U Ch Pr.

— Free Response Tests for Mathematics Today Level 1. 1987. pap., suppl. ed. 16.00 (*0-15-350131-6*) Harcourt Schl Pubs.

— Free Response Tests for Mathematics Today Level 2. 1987. pap., suppl. ed. 16.00 (*0-15-350132-4*) Harcourt Schl Pubs.

— Free Response Tests for Mathematics Today Level 3. 1987. pap., suppl. ed. 12.75 (*0-15-350133-2*) Harcourt Schl Pubs.

— Free Response Tests for Mathematics Today Level 4. 1987. pap., suppl. ed. 12.75 (*0-15-350134-0*) Harcourt Schl Pubs.

— Free Response Tests for Mathematics Today Level 5. 1987. pap., suppl. ed. 13.25 (*0-15-350135-9*) Harcourt Schl Pubs.

— Free Response Tests for Mathematics Today Level 6. 1987. pap., suppl. ed. 13.25 (*0-15-350136-7*) Harcourt Schl Pubs.

— Free Response Tests for Mathematics Today Level 7. 1987. pap., suppl. ed. 13.75 (*0-15-350137-5*) Harcourt Schl Pubs.

— Free Response Tests for Mathematics Today Level 8. 1987. pap., suppl. ed. 13.75 (*0-15-350138-3*) Harcourt Schl Pubs.

— Mathematics Today, Level 1. 1987. pap., student ed. 21.75 (*0-15-350031-X*) Harcourt Schl Pubs.

— Mathematics Today, Level 2. 1987. pap., student ed. 21.75 (*0-15-350032-8*) Harcourt Schl Pubs.

— Mathematics Today, Level 3. 1987. pap., student ed. 40.00 (*0-15-350033-6*); pap., student ed. 28.75 (*0-15-350034-4*) Harcourt Schl Pubs.

— Mathematics Today, Level 8. 1987. text, teacher ed. 134.60 (*0-15-350048-4*) Harcourt.

— Mathematics Today, Level K. 1987. pap., student ed. 16.75 (*0-15-350030-1*) Harcourt Schl Pubs.

— Mathematics Today: Level 5. 1987. teacher ed. 91.00 (*0-15-350045-X*) Harcourt Schl Pubs.

— Mathematics Today: Level 6. 1987. teacher ed. 91.00 (*0-15-350046-8*) Harcourt Schl Pubs.

— Mathematics Today, 1985. (SPA.). 1985. 50.00 (*0-15-351094-3*); 30.50 (*0-15-351091-9*); 30.50 (*0-15-351092-7*); 50.00 (*0-15-351093-5*); pap. 21.75 (*0-15-350702-0*); pap. 21.75 (*0-15-350703-9*); pap. 16.75 (*0-15-350701-2*); pap. 20.25 (*0-15-351090-0*); pap., wbk. ed. 12.25 (*0-15-350738-1*); pap., wbk. ed. 9.75 (*0-15-350764-0*); pap., wbk. ed. 9.75 (*0-15-350765-9*); pap., wbk. ed. 11.25 (*0-15-350766-7*); pap., wbk. ed. 11.25 (*0-15-350768-3*); pap., wbk. ed. 11.25 (*0-15-350769-1*); pap., wbk. ed. 11.25 (*0-15-350767-5*) Harcourt Schl Pubs.

— Mathematics Today, 1987. (SPA.). 1987. pap., student ed. 31.50 (*0-15-350412-9*) Harcourt Schl Pubs.

— Mathematics Today, 1987, Level 1. (SPA.). 1987. pap., student ed. 31.50 (*0-15-350411-0*) Harcourt Schl Pubs.

— Mathematics Today, 1987, Level 2. 1987. teacher ed. 76.00 (*0-15-350042-5*); teacher ed. 84.00 (*0-15-350043-3*) Harcourt Schl Pubs.

— Mathematics Today, 1987, Level 5. 1987. student ed. 40.00 (*0-15-350036-0*) Harcourt Schl Pubs.

— Mathematics Today, 1987, Level 6. 1987. student ed. 40.50 (*0-15-350037-9*) Harcourt Schl Pubs.

— Mathematics Today, 1987, Level K. 1987. 68.00 (*0-15-350040-9*) Harcourt Schl Pubs.

— Mathematics Today, 1987: Level 4. 1987. 84.00 (*0-15-350044-1*) Harcourt Schl Pubs.

— Mathematics Today, 1995. (SPA.). 1985. 50.00 (*0-15-351095-1*) Harcourt Schl Pubs.

— Practice Workbook for Mathematics Today. 1987. pap., teacher ed. 20.50 (*0-15-350077-8*); pap., teacher ed. 15.50 (*0-15-350070-0*); pap., teacher ed. 18.75 (*0-15-350071-9*); pap., teacher ed. 18.75 (*0-15-350072-7*); pap., teacher ed. 20.50 (*0-15-350073-5*); pap., teacher ed. 20.50 (*0-15-350074-3*); pap., teacher ed. 20.50 (*0-15-350075-1*); pap., teacher ed. 20.50 (*0-15-350076-X*); pap., teacher ed. 20.50 (*0-15-350078-6*); pap., student ed. 9.00 (*0-15-350060-3*); pap., student ed. 9.75 (*0-15-350062-X*); pap., student ed. 11.25 (*0-15-350063-8*); pap., student ed. 11.25 (*0-15-350065-4*); pap., student ed. 11.25 (*0-15-350066-2*); pap., student ed. 12.25 (*0-15-350067-0*); pap., student ed. 12.25 (*0-15-350068-9*); pap., student ed. 9.75 (*0-15-350061-1*) Harcourt Schl Pubs.

— Pratice Workbook for Mathematics Today Level 4. 1987. pap., student ed. 11.25 (*0-15-350064-6*) Harcourt Schl Pubs.

— Problem Solving for Math Today, 1987, set. (J). (gr. 8). 1987. pap., wbk. ed. 127.95 (*0-15-350098-0*) Harcourt Schl Pubs.

— Problem Solving Workbook for Mathematics Today Level 1. 1987. pap., teacher ed. 79.75 (*0-15-350091-3*); pap., student ed. 9.00 (*0-15-350081-6*) Harcourt Schl Pubs.

— Problem Solving Workbook for Mathematics Today Level 2. 1987. pap., teacher ed. 79.75 (*0-15-350092-1*); pap., student ed. 9.00 (*0-15-350082-4*) Harcourt Schl Pubs.

— Problem Solving Workbook for Mathematics Today Level 3. 1987. pap., teacher ed. 93.75 (*0-15-350093-X*); pap., student ed. 10.50 (*0-15-350083-2*) Harcourt Schl Pubs.

— Problem Solving Workbook for Mathematics Today Level 4. 1987. pap., teacher ed. 93.75 (*0-15-350094-8*); pap., student ed. 10.50 (*0-15-350084-0*) Harcourt Schl Pubs.

— Problem Solving Workbook for Mathematics Today Level 5. 1987. pap., teacher ed. 93.75 (*0-15-350095-6*); pap., student ed. 10.50 (*0-15-350085-9*) Harcourt Schl Pubs.

— Problem Solving Workbook for Mathematics Today Level 6. 1987. pap., teacher ed. 93.75 (*0-15-350096-4*); pap., student ed. 10.50 (*0-15-350086-7*) Harcourt Schl Pubs.

— Problem Solving Workbook for Mathematics Today Level 7. 1987. pap., teacher ed. 127.75 (*0-15-350097-2*); pap., student ed. 13.00 (*0-15-350087-5*) Harcourt Schl Pubs.

— Problem Solving Workbook for Mathematics Today Level 8. 1987. pap., student ed. 13.00 (*0-15-350088-3*) Harcourt Schl Pubs.

— Standard Format Test Bank for Mathematics Today Level 1. 1987. pap., teacher ed., suppl. ed. 14.50 (*0-15-350121-9*) Harcourt Schl Pubs.

— Standard Format Test Bank for Mathematics Today Level 2. 1987. pap., teacher ed., suppl. ed. 14.50 (*0-15-350122-7*) Harcourt Schl Pubs.

— Standard Format Test Bank for Mathematics Today Level 3. 1987. pap., teacher ed., suppl. ed. 11.50 (*0-15-350123-5*) Harcourt Schl Pubs.

— Standard Format Test Bank for Mathematics Today Level 4. 1987. pap., teacher ed., suppl. ed. 11.50 (*0-15-350124-3*) Harcourt Schl Pubs.

— Standard Format Test Bank for Mathematics Today Level 5. 1987. pap., teacher ed., suppl. ed. 12.00 (*0-15-350125-1*) Harcourt Schl Pubs.

— Standard Format Test Bank for Mathematics Today Level 6. 1987. pap., teacher ed., suppl. ed. 12.00 (*0-15-350126-X*) Harcourt Schl Pubs.

— Standard Format Test Bank for Mathematics Today Level 7. 1987. pap., teacher ed., suppl. ed. 12.75 (*0-15-350127-8*) Harcourt Schl Pubs.

— Standard Format Test Bank for Mathematics Today Level 8. 1987. pap., teacher ed., suppl. ed. 12.75 (*0-15-350128-6*) Harcourt Schl Pubs.

— Twelve Shot. 1990. pap. 5.00 (*0-915990-04-0*) Z Pr.

— WordPerfect Works: Tutorial & Applications. (DF - Computer Applications Ser.). 1994. mass mkt. 17.95 (*0-538-63509-6*) S-W Pub.

Abbott, ed. Sedimentation & Tectonics in Coastal Southern California, No. T110. (IGC Field Trip Guidebooks Ser.). 64p. 1989. 21.00 (*0-87590-609-5*) Am Geophysical.

Abbott & Anon. Railroads One Hundred Years Ago. (Historical Ser.). (Illus.). 1980. pap. 3.50 (*0-89540-048-0*, SB-048) Sun Pub.

Abbott & Makeham. Agricultural Economics & Marketing in the Tropics. 1990. pap. text. write for info. (*0-582-02903-1*, Pub. by Addison-Wesley) Longman.

Abbott & Smith. Research Paper Development on Micro Soft Word 97. LC 98-22102. 179p. 1998. spiral bd. 36.80 (*0-13-674656-X*) P-H.

Abbott, jt. auth. see Janda.

***Abbott, Nancy C.** Journal of a Not-So-Perfect Daughter: Life Is Hardly Ever What You Expect. Thomas, Jerry, ed. LC 98-214950. 210p. 1998. pap. 5.97 (*0-8163-1650-3*) Pacific Pr Pub Assn.

Abbott, A. & Pendlebury, P. Business Law. 591p. (C). 1988. 135.00 (*0-7855-5681-8*, Pub. by Inst Pur & Supply) St Mut.

Abbott, Allan V. & Wilson, David G., eds. Human-Powered Vehicles. LC 95-10636. (Illus.). 288p. 1995. text 48.00 (*0-87322-827-8*, BABB0827) Human Kinetics.

Abbott, Andrea, jt. auth. see Leder, Sharon.

***Abbott, Andrew.** Chaos of Disciplines. 2000. pap. text 17.00 (*0-226-00101-6*); lib. bdg. 54.00 (*0-226-00100-8*) U Ch Pr.

Abbott, Andrew. Department & Discipline. LC 98-55981. 272p. 1999. lib. bdg. 45.00 (*0-226-00098-2*) U Ch Pr.

— The System of Professions: An Essay on the Division of Expert Labor. xvi, 452p. 1988. pap. text 22.50 (*0-226-00069-9*) U Ch Pr.

— The System of Professions: An Essay on the Division of Expert Labor. xvi, 450p. 1993. lib. bdg. 49.95 (*0-226-00068-0*) U Ch Pr.

Abbott, Ann A. Professional Choices: Values at Work. LC 87-34901. 163p. 1988. 18.95 (*0-87101-159-X*) Natl Assn Soc Wkrs.

Abbott, Anthony, ed. Publisher's Trade List Annual Index, 1903-1963. 150p. 1980. lib. bdg. 60.00 (*0-930466-25-X*) Mecklermedia.

— Publishers' Trade List Annual Index, 1964-1980. 175p. 1984. lib. bdg. 75.00 (*0-88736-015-7*) Mecklermedia.

Abbott, Anthony S. The Girl in the Yellow Raincoat. 65p. Date not set. pap. 8.95 (*0-932662-81-1*) St Andrews NC.

— The Great Gatsby. (Barron's Book Notes Ser.). (C). 1984. pap. 3.95 (*0-8120-3415-5*) Barron.

— A Small Thing Like-a-Breath. 93p. Date not set. pap. 8.95 (*1-879934-16-7*) St Andrews NC.

***Abbott, Austin.** Brief for the Trial of Civil Issues Before a Jury. viii, 201p. 1999. 65.00 (*1-56169-455-X*) Gaunt.

Abbott, Austin. Brief for the Trial of Criminal Cases. 2nd enl. ed. xx, 814p. 1994. reprint ed. 75.00 (*0-8377-1911-9*, Rothman) W S Hein.

***Abbott, Austin.** Trial Evidence: The Rules of Evidence Applicable on the Trial of Civil Actions Including Both Causes of Action & Defenses at Common Law, in Equity, & under the... LC 99-58132. xxx, 884p. 2000. reprint ed. 95.00 (*1-57588-612-X*) W S Hein.

Abbott, Barbara, ed. see Abbott, Marcia.

Abbott, Barbara, jt. ed. see Cowden, Frances B.

Abbott, Barry A., jt. auth. see Brandel, Roland E.

Abbott, Ben A., jt. ed. see Gerhart, Grant R.

Abbott, Berenice. Berenice Abbott, Photographer: A Modern Vision. (Illus.). 96p. (Orig.). 1989. pap. 14.95 (*0-87104-420-X*) NY Pub Lib.

— New York in the Thirties. LC 73-77375. Orig. Title: Changing New York. (Illus.). 97p. 1973. reprint ed. 11.95 (*0-486-22967-X*) Dover.

Abbott, Berenice, jt. auth. see Yochelson, Bonnie.

Abbott, Berenise. Shared Perspectives: The Printmaker & Photographer in New York, 1900-1950. (Illus.). 1994. pap. 15.00 (*0-910961-04-2*) Mus City NY.

Abbott, Bob. Supermazes: Thirty Mind Twisters for Puzzle Buffs, Game Nuts, & Other Smart People. 80p. 1997. pap., per. 14.00 (*0-7615-0701-9*) Prima Pub.

Abbott, Bonnie. Roam the Poet's Road. 1998. write for info. (*0-9660692-0-X*) Poetry Rd Pub.

Abbott, Brenda, ed. see Shattuck, Louise F.

Abbott, Bruce B., jt. auth. see Bordens, Kenneth S.

Abbott, C. B., jt. auth. see Lerner, Elaine.

Abbott, C. M. & Abbott, N. B. Journal of a Voyage from Liverpool to Australia in the Ship Othello 1833-1834. (C). 1988. 87.00 (*1-85072-029-0*, Pub. by W Sessions) St Mut.

Abbott, Candace F. Fruit-Bearer: What Can I Do for You, Lord? (Illus.). 280p. (Orig.). 1994. pap. 15.00 (*1-886068-00-3*) Fruit-Bearer.

Abbott, Candace F., ed. see Waters, Chris Ann.

Abbott, Carl. Boosters & Businessmen: Popular Economic Thought & Urban Growth in the Antebellum Middle West, 53. LC 80-1795. (Contributions in American Studies: No. 53). (Illus.). 266p. 1981. 65.00 (*0-313-22562-1*, ABB/, Greenwood Pr) Greenwood.

— The Metropolitan Frontier: Cities in the Modern American West. LC 93-11035. (Modern American West Ser.). (Illus.). 244p. 1993. 42.00 (*0-8165-1129-2*) U of Ariz Pr.

— The Metropolitan Frontier: Cities in the Modern American West. LC 93-11035. 244p. 1995. pap. 19.95 (*0-8165-1570-0*) U of Ariz Pr.

— The New Urban America: Growth & Politics in Sunbelt Cities. rev. ed. LC 86-40490. (Illus.). 350p. 1987. reprint ed. pap. 108.50 (*0-7837-9018-X*, 204977000003) Bks Demand.

— Political Terrain: Washington, D.C., from Tidewater Town to Global Metropolis. LC 98-41013. (Illus.). 272p. 1999. pap. 19.95 (*0-8078-4805-0*); lib. bdg. 39.95 (*0-8078-2478-X*) U of NC Pr.

— Portland: Planning, Politics & Growth in a Twentieth Century City. LC 82-21978. 360p. 1983. reprint ed. pap. 111.60 (*0-608-01404-4*, 206216700002) Bks Demand.

— Portland, Gateway to the Northwest. LC 97-74096. (Illus.). 264p. 1997. 39.95 (*0-9654754-3-3*) Am Historical Pr.

— Urban America in the Modern Age, 1920 to the Present. Eisenstadt, A. S. & Franklin, John H., eds. LC 86-6363. (American History Ser.). (Illus.). 192p. (C). 1987. pap. text 11.95 (*0-88295-840-2*) Harlan Davidson.

Abbott, Carl, et al, eds. Planning the Oregon Way: A 20-Year Evaluation. LC 93-36408. (Illus.). 352p. (C). 1994. text 27.95 (*0-87071-381-7*) Oreg St U Pr.

Abbott, Carl, et al. Colorado: A History of the Centennial State. 3rd rev. ed. LC 94-9340. (Illus.). 454p. (C). 1994. pap. text 29.95 (*0-87081-344-7*) Univ Pr Colo.

— Planning a New West: The Columbia River Gorge National Scenic Area. LC 96-39753. (Culture & Environment in the Pacific West Ser.). (Illus.). 224p. 1997. 26.95 (*0-87071-392-2*) Oreg St U Pr.

Abbott, Carl, jt. auth. see Goldfield, David.

Abbott, Cathy, jt. ed. see Jackson, Ian J.

Abbott, Charles C. The New York Bond Market, 1920-1930. LC 75-2618. (Wall Street & the Security Market Ser.). 1975. reprint ed. 26.95 (*0-405-06945-6*) Ayer.

***Abbott, Christopher.** Julian of Norwich: Autobiography & Theology. LC 98-56168. (Studies in Medieval Mysticism). 224p. 1999. 60.00 (*0-85991-548-4*) Boydell & Brewer.

Abbott, Claude C. The Life & Letters of George Darley. (BCL1-PR English Literature Ser.). 285p. 1992. reprint ed. lib. bdg. 79.00 (*0-7812-7507-5*) Rprt Serv.

Abbott, Craig S. Marianne Moore: A Descriptive Bibliography. LC 76-5922. (Series in Bibliography). 280p. 1977. 100.00 (*0-8229-3319-5*) U of Pittsburgh Pr.

Abbott, Craig S., ed. John Crowe Ransom: A Descriptive Bibliography. LC 97-62328. viii, 440p. 1999. 48.50 (*0-87875-503-9*) Whitston Pub.

Abbott, Dallas, jt. auth. see Menke, William.

Abbott, Damien. Encyclopaedia of Real Estate Terms. 200p. 1987. text 180.00 (*0-291-39702-6*, Pub. by Gower) Ashgate Pub Co.

***Abbott, Damien.** Encyclopedia of Real Estate Terms: Based on American & English Practice. 2nd ed. LC 00-190141. (Illus.). xl, 1432p. 2000. 145.00 (*0-9668946-8-5*) Delta Alpha.

Abbott, Dan. Colorado Midland Railway: Daylight Through the Divide. Anderson, Gary D., ed. (Illus.). 376p. 1996. reprint ed. 52.00 (*0-913582-45-X*) Sundance.

Abbott, Dana. Japanese Visitor's Guide to Silicon Valley. Tsumura, Ed, tr. (JPN., Illus.). (Orig.). 1994. pap. 15.99 (*0-9638781-0-7*) Silicon CA.

— Japanese Visitors' Guide to Silicon Valley. 2nd rev. ed. (JPN., Illus.). 136p. 1998. pap. 15.99 (*0-9638781-1-5*) Silicon CA.

— Silicon Valley Business Traveler's Guide: Easy Access to Sites Virtual & Tangible. (Illus.). 112p. (Orig.). 1997. pap. 12.95 (*0-9638781-8-2*) Silicon CA.

Abbott, Daniel J., jt. auth. see Clinard, Marshall B.

***Abbott, Dave.** Catch the Irish Laughter. 127p. 2000. pap. 17.95 (*0-9686024-0-1*) Inisfree.

***Abbott, David & Sayed, Yousry.** U.n.c.w. the Freshman Year 1999-00. 2nd ed. 220p. (C). 1999. per. 31.95 (*0-7872-6224-2*, 41622401) Kendall-Hunt.

Abbott, David P. Behind the Scenes with the Mediums. 5th rev. ed. 340p. 1996. reprint ed. pap. 25.00 (*0-7873-0014-4*) Hlth Research.

***Abbott, David R.** Ceramics & Community Organization among the Hohokam. LC 99-6768. 2000. 40.00 (*0-8165-1936-6*) U of Ariz Pr.

Abbott, David R., et al. Archaeology of the Pueblo Grande Platform Mound & Surrounding Features Vol. 1: Introduction to the Archival Project & History of Archaeological Research. LC 93-85695. (Pueblo Grande Museum Anthropological Papers: No. 1). (Illus.). 319p. (Orig.). 1993. 43.00 (*1-882572-02-5*); pap. 25.00 (*1-882572-03-3*) Pueblo Grande Mus.

Abbott, David W. & Levine, James P. Wrong Winner: The Coming Debacle in the Electoral College. LC 90-49220. 184p. 1991. 55.00 (*0-275-93780-1*, C3780, Praeger Pubs); pap. 18.95 (*0-275-93871-9*, B3871, Praeger Pubs) Greenwood.

Abbott, Deborah & Farmer, Ellen, eds. From Wedded Wife to Lesbian Life: Stories of Transformation. (Illus.). 290p. 1995. pap. 14.95 (*0-89594-766-8*) Crossing Pr.

Abbott, Deborah & Kisor, Henry. One TV Blasting & a Pig Outdoors. Tucker, Kathy, ed. LC 94-6649. (Illus.). 40p. (J). (gr. 2-6). 1994. lib. bdg. 14.95 (*0-8075-6075-8*) A Whitman.

***Abbott, Derek & Kish, Laszlo B., eds.** Unsolved Problems of Noise & Fluctuations: UPoN'99: Second International Conference. LC 00-100708. (AIP Conference Proceedings Ser.: Vol. 511). (Illus.). 578p. 2000. 150.00 (*1-56396-826-6*, Pub. by Spr-Verlag) Spr-Verlag.

Abbott, Diane L., et al. The Neighborhood's Catalogue: Lower East Side Planning & Design File. (Publications in Architecture & Urban Planning: No. R81-5). (Illus.). vi, 117p. 1987. reprint ed. 15.00 (*0-938744-18-6*) U of Wis Ctr Arch-Urban.

Abbott, Don P. Rhetoric in the New World: Rhetorical Theory & Practice in Colonial Spanish America. LC 95-41775. (Studies in Rhetoric/Communication). (Illus.). 140p. 1996. text 24.95 (*1-57003-085-5*) U of SC Pr.

***Abbott, Donald.** The Amber Flute of Oz. (Illus.). 128p. (J). (gr. 4 up). 1998. pap. 9.95 (*0-929605-88-8*) Books of Wonder.

Abbott, Donald. Father Goose in Oz. (Illus.). 121p. (J). (gr. 2 up). 1994. 34.95 (*0-929605-32-2*); pap. 9.95 (*0-929605-31-4*) Books of Wonder.

— How the Wizard Came to Oz. (Illus.). 120p. (J). (gr. 3 up). 1991. reprint ed. pap. 9.95 (*0-929605-15-2*) Books of Wonder.

Abbott, Donald. How the Wizard Came to Oz. (Illus.). 120p. (J). (gr. 3 up). 1991. reprint ed. 19.95 (*0-929605-24-1*) Books of Wonder.

Abbott, Donald. How the Wizard Saved Oz. (Illus.). 112p. (J). (gr. 3 up). 1996. pap. 12.95 (*0-929605-58-6*) Books of Wonder.

— The Magic Chest of Oz. (Illus.). 119p. (J). (gr. 3 up). 1993. pap. 9.95 (*0-929605-20-9*) Books of Wonder.

— The Speckled Rose of Oz. (Illus.). 104p. (J). (gr. 2 up). 1995. 34.95 (*0-929605-42-X*, Emerald Cty Pr); pap. 9.95 (*0-929605-43-8*) Books of Wonder.

Abbott, Donald P. Observing Marine Invertebrates: Drawings from the Laboratory. Hilgard, Galen H., ed. LC 87-9931. (Illus.). 408p. 1987. kivar 35.00 (*0-8047-1426-6*) Stanford U Pr.

— Observing Marine Invertebrates: Drawings from the Laboratory. fac. ed. Hilgard, Galen H., ed. LC 87-9931. (Illus.). 408p. 1987. pap. 30.00 (*0-7837-7266-1*, 204703900005) Bks Demand.

Abbott, Donald P., et al. Reef & Shore Fauna of Hawaii Section 6B: Ascidians. (Illus.). 62p. (C). 1997. pap. 19.95 (*0-930897-94-3*) Bishop Mus.

A

Abbott, Dori A. Great Crafts for Kids That Really Work & Don't Cost a Lot of Money! An Arts & Crafts Curriculum with 36 Lessons. (Illus.). 84p. (J). (gr. k-8). 1998. student ed., spiral bd. 19.95 (*0-9663784-1-5*) Smarr Pubs.

Abbott, Dorothy, ed. Mississippi Writers: An Anthology. LC 90-28947. (Center for the Study of Southern Culture Ser.). 1991. pap. 19.95 (*0-87805-503-7*); text 37.50 (*0-87805-479-0*) U Pr of Miss.

— Mississippi Writers Vol. 2: Reflections of Childhood & Youth: Nonfiction. LC 84-5131. (Center for the Study of Southern Culture Ser.). 736p. 1986. text 37.50 (*0-87805-233-X*) U Pr of Miss.

— Mississippi Writers Vol. 4: Reflections of Childhood & Youth, Drama. LC 84-5131. 1991. pap. 19.95 (*0-87805-238-0*); text 37.50 (*0-87805-237-2*) U Pr of Miss.

Abbott, Dorothy & Brown, Rosellen, eds. Mississippi Writers Vol. 3: Reflections of Childhood & Youth - Poetry. LC 84-5131. (Center for the Study of Southern Culture Ser.). 1987. text 37.50 (*0-87805-235-6*) U Pr of Miss.

***Abbott, Doug.** PCI Bus Demystified. (Demystified Ser.). 312p. 2000. pap. 49.95 (*1-878707-54-X*, Pub. by LLH Tech Pub) IPG Chicago.

Abbott, E. A. A Shakespearian Grammar. LC 72-3661. (Studies in Shakespeare: No. 24). 1972. reprint ed. lib. bdg. 75.00 (*0-8383-1571-2*) M S G Haskell Hse.

Abbott, E. C. & Smith, Helena H. We Pointed Them North: Recollections of a Cowpuncher. LC 55-9632. 1955. pap. 13.95 (*0-8061-1366-9*) U of Okla Pr.

Abbott, Edith. Historical Aspects of the Immigration Problem: Select Documents. LC 69-18753. (American Immigration Collection. Series 1). 1969. reprint ed. 40.95 (*0-405-00502-4*) Ayer.

— Immigration: Select Documents & Case Records. LC 69-18754. (American Immigration Collection. Series 1). 1969. reprint ed. 35.95 (*0-405-00501-6*) Ayer.

— Some American Pioneers in American Social Welfare. (Midway Reprint Ser.). 216p. (C). 1975. reprint ed. pap. text 8.75 (*0-226-00072-9*) U Ch Pr.

— Tenements of Chicago, 1908-1935. LC 78-112535. (Rise of Urban America Ser.). (Illus.). 1976. reprint ed. lib. bdg. 41.95 (*0-405-02431-2*) Ayer.

— Women in Industry. 408p. 1993. reprint ed. lib. bdg. 99.00 (*0-7812-5241-5*) Rprt Serv.

— Women in Industry: A Study in American Economic History. LC 70-89714. (American Labor, from Conspiracy to Collective Bargaining Ser., No. 1). 408p. 1979. reprint ed. lib. bdg. 30.95 (*0-405-02101-1*) Ayer.

Abbott, Edith & Breckinridge, Sophonisba P. Truancy & Non-Attendance in the Chicago Schools: A Study of the Social Aspects of the Compulsory Education & Child Labor Legislation of Illinois. LC 74-12526. (Rise of Urban America Ser.). 1978. reprint ed. 29.95 (*0-405-02432-0*) Ayer.

Abbott, Edith, et al. The Family & Social Service in the 1920s. LC 74-169361. (Family in America Ser.). 386p. 1979. 34.95 (*0-405-03885-2*) Ayer.

Abbott, Edith, jt. auth. see Breckinridge, Sophonisba P.

Abbott, Edwin A. Flatland. 158p. Date not set. 19.95 (*0-8488-2525-X*) Amereon Ltd.

— Flatland. (Illus.). 144p. 1983. pap. 12.00 (*0-06-463573-2*, EH 573) HarpC.

— Flatland. LC 98-11663. 1999. pap. 6.00 (*1-57062-438-0*, Pub. by Shambhala Pubns) Random.

***Abbott, Edwin A.** Flatland. large type ed. LC 99-14747. 1999. pap. 24.95 (*0-7838-8619-5*) Mac Lib Ref.

Abbott, Edwin A. Flatland. 160p. 1988. reprint ed. lib. bdg. 25.95 (*0-89966-576-4*) Buccaneer Bks.

— Flatland: A Parable of Spiritual Dimensions. LC 94-66629. 148p. 1995. pap. 8.99 (*1-85168-086-1*, Pub. by Onewrld Pubns) Penguin Putnam.

— Flatland: A Romance of Many Dimensions. (Illus.). 104p. (YA). 1998. pap. 10.95 (*1-892896-18-4*) Buy Books.

— Flatland: A Romance of Many Dimensions. 1984. mass mkt. 4.95 (*0-451-52290-7*, Sig) NAL.

— Flatland: A Romance of Many Dimensions. (Illus.). 130p. 1991. pap. 8.95 (*0-691-02525-8*, Pub. by Princeton U Pr) Cal Prin Full Svc.

— Flatland: A Romance of Many Dimensions. (Signet Classics). 1984. 10.05 (*0-606-03425-0*, Pub. by Turtleback) Demco.

— Flatland: A Romance of Many Dimensions. LC 98-5393. (Illus.). xv, 118p. 1998. pap. 8.95 (*0-14-043531-X*) Viking Penguin.

— Flatland: A Romance of Many Dimensions. rev. unabridged ed. (Illus.). 96p. 1992. pap. 1.00 (*0-486-27263-X*) Dover.

— Flatland: A Romance of Many Dimensions. 2nd ed. 1952. pap. 2.50 (*0-486-20001-9*) Dover.

***Abbott, Edwin A.** Paradosis. 240p. 1999. pap. 22.00 (*1-57910-294-8*) Wipf & Stock.

Abbott, Edwin A. St. Thomas of Canterbury: His Death & Miracles, 2 vols. in 1. LC 80-18216. (Crusades & Military Orders Ser.: Second Series). reprint ed. 74.50 (*0-404-16366-1*) AMS Pr.

***Abbott, Edwin A.** Silanus the Christian. 252p. 2000. pap. 9.95 (*0-594-04310-7*) Eightn Hundrd.

Abbott, Edwin A. & Burger, Dionys. Flatland/Sphereland. LC 82-48824. (Illus.). 352p. 1994. pap. 14.00 (*0-06-273276-5*, Harper Ref) HarpC.

Abbott, Edwin A. & Davies, David W. Flatland. (Illus.). 1978. reprint ed. 35.00 (*0-910330-21-2*) Grant Dahlstrom.

Abbott, Edwin A., see Square, A., pseud.

Abbott, Elisabeth, ed. see Pareto, Vilfredo.

Abbott, Elisabeth, tr. see Da Ponte, Lorenzo.

***Abbott, Elizabeth.** A History of Celibacy: From Athena to Elizabeth I, Leonardo da Vinci, Florence Nightingale, Ghandi & Cher. LC 99-87803. (Illus.). 496p. 2000. 29.50 (*0-684-84943-7*) Scribner.

Abbott, Elizabeth, tr. see Da Ponte, Lorenzo.

Abbott, Evelyn & Mansfield, E. D. A Primer of Greek Grammar. 1990. reprint ed. pap. text 14.95 (*0-89341-626-6*, Longwood Academic) Hollowbrook.

Abbott, Evelyn & Mansfield, Edwin D. A Primer of Greek Grammar: Accidence & Syntax. 230p. (C). 1977. reprint ed. pap. text 20.95 (*0-7156-1258-1*, Pub. by G Duckworth) Focus Pub-R Pullins.

Abbott, Fran W. & Mackenfuss, Pam. Working Right: Expressing Your True Colors in Life & Work. (Illus.). 50p. (C). 1990. pap. text. write for info. (*0-923400-01-X*) Phantom Pr.

Abbott, Frank F. The Common People of Ancient Rome: Studies of Roman Life & Literature. LC 65-23487. (J). (gr. 7 up). 1965. reprint ed. 30.00 (*0-8196-0157-8*) Biblo.

— A History & Description of Roman Political Institutions. 3rd ed. LC 63-10766. 451p. (J). (gr. 7 up). 1910. 30.00 (*0-8196-0117-9*) Biblo.

— Society & Politics in Ancient Rome: Essays & Sketches. LC 63-10767. 267p. (J). (gr. 7 up). 1909. 30.00 (*0-8196-0118-7*) Biblo.

Abbott, Frank F., tr. see Gentili, Albercio.

Abbott, Franklin. Mortal Love: Selected Poems, 1971-1998. 162p. 1999. pap. 14.00 (*0-9627616-3-X*, Pub. by RFD Pr) Bookazine Co Inc.

Abbott, Franklin, ed. Boyhood, Growing Up Male: A Multicultural Anthology. 2nd ed. LC 97-47771. 294p. 1998. pap. 15.95 (*0-299-15754-7*) U of Wis Pr.

***Abbott, Frederick M.** China in the World Trading System: Defining the Principles of Engagement. LC 98-205038. xiii, 222 p. 1998. 27.50 (*90-411-0631-6*) Kluwer Law Intl.

Abbott, Frederick M. Law & Policy of Regional Integration: The NAFTA & Western Hemispheric Integration in the World Trade Organization System. LC 94-42026. 1995. lib. bdg. 106.00 (*0-7923-3295-4*) Kluwer Academic.

Abbott, Frederick M. & Gerber, David J., eds. Public Policy & Global Technological Integration. LC 98-116502. 1997. 225.00 (*90-411-0655-3*) Kluwer Law Intl.

***Abbott, Frederick M., et al.** The International Intellectual Property System: Commentary & Materials. LC 99-37923. 1999. 85.00 (*90-411-9322-7*) Kluwer Law Intl.

Abbott, Gail, jt. auth. see Abbott, Gary.

Abbott, Gary & Abbott, Gail. St. Louis Gardeners' Directory, Vol. 1. (Illus.). 1994. 2.25 (*0-9643007-0-2*) Flora Fauna MO.

Abbott, Geoffrey. The Book of Execution: An Encyclopedia of Methods of Judicial Execution. (Illus.). 352p. 1995. mass mkt. 15.95 (*0-7472-4581-9*, Pub. by Headline Bk Pub) Trafalgar.

— Rack, Rope & Red-Hot Pincers: A History of Torture & Its Instruments. (Illus.). 243p. 1995. mass mkt. 13.95 (*0-7472-3984-3*, Pub. by Headline Bk Pub) Trafalgar.

Abbott, George. Three Men on a Horse. 1935. pap. 5.25 (*0-8222-1139-4*) Dramatists Play.

Abbott, George C. Debt Relief & Sustainable Development in Sub-Saharan Africa. 208p. 1993. 85.00 (*1-85278-513-6*) E Elgar.

***Abbott, George W. & Sporn, Lee S.** Trademark Counterfeiting LC 99-30477. 1999. ring bd. 165.00 (*0-7355-0551-9*) Panel Pubs.

***Abbott, Gerald.** In Touch With Industry: Industry Studies 1997. 428p. 1998. per. 20.00 (*0-16-061211-X*) USGPO.

— In Touch with Industry: Industry Studies 1998. 432p. 1999. per. 21.00 (*0-16-061230-6*) USGPO.

— In Touch with Industry: Industry Studies, 1999. 444p. 2000. per. 24.00 (*0-16-059196-1*) USGPO.

***Abbott, Gerald, ed.** In Touch with Industry: ICAF Industry Studies (1998) 250p. (C). 2000. reprint ed. pap. text 50.00 (*0-7881-8569-1*) DIANE Pub.

Abbott, Gerry, compiled by. Inroads into Burma: A Traveller's Anthology. (Oxford in Asia Paperbacks Ser.). (Illus.). 340p. 1998. pap. text 21.00 (*983-56-0034-1*) OUP.

***Abbott, Gerry & Khin Thant Han Staff.** The Folk-Tales of Burma: An Introduction By Gerry Abbott And Khin Thant Han. LC 00-22316. (Handbuch der Orientalistik, Dritte Abteilung, Sudostasien). 320p. 2000. 102.00 (*90-04-11812-8*) Brill Academic Pubs.

Abbott, Gordon, Jr. Saving Special Places: A Centennial History of the Trustees of Reservations: Pioneer of the Land Trust Movement. (Illus.). 352p. 1994. pap. 20.00 (*0-938864-19-X*) Ipswich Pr.

Abbott, Grace. The Immigrant & the Community. LC 70-145468. (American Immigration Library). xii, 303p. 1971. reprint ed. lib. bdg. 36.95 (*0-89198-000-8*) Ozer.

Abbott, H. Mark. Spirituality in a Mixed-Up Age. LC 98-118826. 208p. (Orig.). 1997. pap. 10.99 (*0-89367-208-4*) Light & Life Comm.

Abbott, H. Porter. Beckett Writing Beckett: The Author in the Autograph. LC 95-39559. 192p. 1996. text 35.00 (*0-8014-3246-4*) Cornell U Pr.

Abbott, Helen, ed. Selected Works: Seattle Art Museum. LC 91-9704. (Illus.). 208p. (Orig.). 1991. pap. 9.95 (*0-932216-35-8*) Seattle Art.

Abbott, Helen, ed. see Brown, Steven, et al.

Abbott, Helen, ed. see Godeau, Abigail S., et al.

Abbott, Helen, ed. see Lynch, Richard.

Abbott, Henry G. The American Watchmaker & Jeweler. (Illus.). 354p. 1989. pap. 19.95 (*0-930163-42-7*) Arlington Bk.

Abbott, Herman. History of Belfast (ME) to 1825. 18p. 1986. reprint ed. pap. 3.00 (*0-935207-37-6*) Danbury Hse Bks.

Abbott Hess, Mary, ed. Portion Photos of Popular Foods. 128p. 1997. spiral bd. 129.95 (*0-88091-162-X*) Am Dietetic Assn.

Abbott, Howard & Tyler, Mark. Safer by Design: A Guide to the Management & Law of Designing for Product Safety. 2nd ed. LC 96-34694. (Design Council Ser.). 352p. 1997. text 83.95 (*0-566-07707-8*, Pub. by Gower) Ashgate Pub Co.

Abbott, Ian, jt. auth. see Evans, Linda.

***Abbott, Ida O.** The Lawyers Guide to Mentoring. 2000. pap. 38.00 (*1-55733-020-4*) NALP.

Abbott, Ira H. & Von Doenhoff, Albert E. Theory of Wing Sections: Including a Summary of Airfoil Data. (Illus.). 693p. 1999. pap. 14.95 (*0-486-60586-8*) Dover.

Abbott, Isabella, ed. Taxonomy of Economic Seaweeds: With Reference to Some Pacific Species, Vol. VI. (Illus.). 230p. (Orig.). 1997. pap. text 10.00 (*1-888691-04-2*, T-040) U CA Calif Sea.

Abbott, Isabella A. La'au Hawaii: Traditional Hawaiian Uses of Plants. 162p. 1992. pap. 22.95 (*0-930897-62-5*) Bishop Mus.

— Marine Algae of California. xvi, 828p. (C). 1992. pap. 34.50 (*0-8047-2152-1*) Stanford U Pr.

— Marine Red Algae of the Hawaiian Islands. LC 99-22307. 465p. 1999. 60.00 (*1-58178-003-6*) Bishop Mus.

Abbott, Isabella A. & Hollenberg, George J. Marine Algae of California. LC 74-82774. (Illus.). xvi, 828p. 1976. 39.50 (*0-8047-0867-3*) Stanford U Pr.

Abbott, Isabella A., et al. Seaweeds. 2nd ed. (Pictured Key Nature Ser.). 152p. (C). 1978. text. write for info. (*0-697-04892-6*, WCB McGr Hill) McGrw-H Hghr Educ.

Abbott, J. Sind a Re-Interpretation of the Unhappy Valley. (C). 1992. 14.00 (*81-206-0759-7*, Pub. by Asian Educ Servs) S Asia.

Abbott, Jack H. In the Belly of the Beast: Letters from Prison. LC 90-50214. 192p. 1991. pap. 11.00 (*0-679-73237-3*) Vin Bks.

Abbott, Jack H. & Zack, Naomi. My Return. LC 86-43236. 213p. 1987. 29.95 (*0-87975-355-2*) Prometheus Bks.

Abbott, Jacob. Training Children in Godliness. McHugh, Michael J., ed. (Illus.). 144p. 1992. pap. text 4.95 (*1-930092-02-4*, CLP99505) Christian Liberty.

— Training Children in Godliness. McHugh, Michael J., ed. (Illus.). 144p. (YA). (gr. 6-9). 1992. text 8.00 (*1-930092-01-6*, CLP99505) Christian Liberty.

Abbott, Jacob. Wars of the Colonies. 291p. 1997. reprint ed. pap. 23.00 (*0-7884-0722-8*, A005) Heritage Bk.

— The Works of Jacob Abbott, 1803-1879, Set. reprint ed. lib. bdg. 500.00 (*0-685-18572-9*) Rprt Serv.

Abbott, Jacqui & Lonsdale, Alan. Academics Staff Appraisal. 141p. 1992. pap. 48.00 (*0-7300-1516-5*, Pub. by Deakin Univ) St Mut.

Abbott, James & Rice, Elaine. Designing Camelot: The Kennedy White House Restoration. LC 97-20251. (Illus.). 256p. 1997. 50.00 (*0-442-02532-7*, VNR) Wiley.

Abbott, James A. A Frenchman in Camelot: The Decoration of the Kennedy White House by Stephane Boudin. (Illus.). 40p. (Orig.). 1995. pap. write for info. (*0-9646659-0-5*) Boscobel Restoration.

Abbott, James A. & Rice, Elaine M. Designing Camelot. 260p. 1997. 50.00 (*0-471-29242-7*, VNR) Wiley.

— Designing Camelot: The Kennedy White House Restoration. 272p. 1999. pap. 29.95 (*0-471-37514-4*) Wiley.

Abbott, James C. Become the Manager of the Future. LC 95-69101. 284p. 1995. boxed set 39.95 (*1-887355-01-4*) R H Smith Pubs.

***Abbott, James C.** Optimize Your Operation: Stories, Tools & Lessons for Using the Principles of Process Management to Improve Your Quality. LC 99-62121. (Walkabout Ser.). (Illus.). 306p. 2000. 39.95 (*1-887355-04-9*) R H Smith Pubs.

Abbott, James C. Practical Understanding of Capability by Implementing Statistical Process Control. 2nd rev. ed. LC 95-69102. (Illus.). 338p. 1996. boxed set 39.95 (*1-887355-02-2*) R H Smith Pubs.

— Practical Understanding of Capability by Implementing Statistical Process Control. 3rd ed. LC 98-89305. (Illus.). 406p. 1999. 49.95 (*1-887355-03-0*) R H Smith Pubs.

Abbott, James E. Learn: When Dinosaurs Learned How to Dance. 128p. (C). 1994. pap. 19.95 (*1-885300-00-X*) Quality Mgmt.

— Quality Team Learning for Schools: A Principal's Perspective. LC 97-49869. 170p. 1998. 25.00 (*0-87389-384-0*, H0973) ASQ Qual Pr.

Abbott, Janet S. Mathematics Today: Level 7. 1987. 45.25 (*0-15-350038-7*) Harcourt Schl Pubs.

— Mathematics Today: Level 8. 1987. 45.25 (*0-15-350039-5*) Harcourt Schl Pubs.

Abbott, Jason, jt. auth. see Hampton, Mark.

Abbott, Jason, jt. auth. see Palan, Ronan.

Abbott, Jean T. & Gifford, Marilyn J. Prehospital Emergency Care: A Guide for Paramedics. 3rd ed. LC 95-49532. (Clinical Handbook Ser.). (Illus.). 382p. 1996. pap. text 23.95 (*1-85070-636-0*) Prthnon Pub.

Abbott, Jeffrey D., jt. auth. see Moran, Robert T.

Abbott, Jere. Lautrec-Redon. LC 74-86435. (Museum of Modern Art Publications in Reprint). (Illus.). 1969. reprint ed. 11.95 (*0-405-01527-5*) Ayer.

Abbott, John. David Crockett: His Life & Adventures. 1993. reprint ed. lib. bdg. 75.00 (*0-7812-5860-X*) Rprt Serv.

— The Mother at Home. 1998. pap. 7.49 (*0-87377-128-1*) GAM Pubns.

— Ride the Airwaves with Alfa & Zulu: Preparation for the Novice & No-Code Technician Amateur Radio Licenses. (Illus.). xii, 244p. (Orig.). 1998. pap. 14.95 (*0-9651088-0-5*) Abtronix.

***Abbott, John.** Ride the Airwaves with ALFA & ZULU: Technician Amateur Radio Ham License Manual. rev. ed. (Illus.). xii, 180p. 2000. pap. 14.95 (*0-9651088-1-3*) Abtronix.

Abbott, John. Sharing the City: Community Participation in Urban Management. LC 96-203882. (Illus.). 256p. 1996. 70.00 (*1-85383-323-1*, Pub. by Escan Pubns); pap. 32.00 (*1-85383-328-2*, Pub. by Escan Pubns) Island Pr.

Abbott, John, ed. Prevention of Fires & Explosions in Dryers: A User Guide. 2nd ed. 138p. 1990. 40.00 (*0-85295-257-0*, 9CH24) Gulf Pub.

Abbott, John, et al. Riding the Airwaves with Alpha & Zulu. (Illus.). 208p. 1995. pap. 14.95 (*0-917963-14-8*) Artsci Inc.

Abbott, John Cushman, ed. see Lienhard, Heinrich, et al.

***Abbott, John G., et al.** Acoustic Output Labeling Standard for Diagnostic Ultrasound Equipment: A Standard for How Manufacturers Should Specify Acoustic Output Data. (Illus.). 24p. 1998. pap. 30.00 (*1-930047-29-0*) Am Inst Ultrasound.

Abbott, John H. Courtright-Kortright Family, Descendants of Bastian Van L. Kortryk, a Native of Belgium Who Emigrated to Holland about 1615. 147p. 1997. reprint ed. pap. 22.50 (*0-8328-8086-8*); reprint ed. lib. bdg. 33.50 (*0-8328-8085-X*) Higginson Bk Co.

Abbott, John L. John Hawkesworth: Eighteenth-Century Man of Letters. LC 81-69811. 261p. 1982. reprint ed. pap. 81.00 (*0-608-01913-5*, 206256500003) Bks Demand.

Abbott, John S. Life of John Paul Jones. xi, 359p. 1985. reprint ed. 49.00 (*0-932051-77-4*) Rprt Serv.

— The Mother at Home: or The Principles of Maternal Duty. LC 72-169366. (Family in America Ser.). (Illus.). 198p. 1976. reprint ed. 17.95 (*0-405-03841-0*) Ayer.

— The Works of John Stevens Cabot Abbott, 1805-1877, Set. reprint ed. 500.00 (*0-685-18534-6*) Rprt Serv.

Abbott, John W. Nuances: The Soul of Hospice. 122p. 1997. pap. 14.95 (*0-936479-01-9*) Connecticut Hospice Inc.

***Abbott, Jonathan A.** Q Logic. LC 99-97026. 2000. pap. 10.95 (*0-533-13370-X*) Vantage.

Abbott, Jonathan A., ed. Small Animal Cardiology Secrets. (Secrets Ser.). (Illus.). 350p. 2000. pap. text 39.00 (*1-56053-352-8*) Hanley & Belfus.

Abbott, Justin E. Life of Eknath. reprint ed. 11.00 (*0-8364-0746-6*, Pub. by Motilal Bnarsidass) S Asia.

Abbott, Justin E. & Godbole, Narhar. Stories of Indian Saints. 1988. reprint ed. 36.00 (*81-208-0469-4*, Pub. by Motilal Bnarsidass) S Asia.

Abbott, Justin E., tr. see Eknath, Saint.

Abbott, Justin E., tr. see Mahipati.

Abbott, K. One Point Four Law. 288p. (C). 1987. 50.00 (*1-870941-06-3*) St Mut.

Abbott, Kate. Mystery at Echo Cliffs. LC 93-33849. (Illus.). 184p. (J). (gr. 5-9). 1994. pap. 11.95 (*1-878610-37-6*) Red Crane Bks.

Abbott, Katharine S. Nantucket Summers Vol. 1: The Story of a Family & a Very Special Cottage Called Sunycliffe. LC 96-67895. (Illus.). 176p. (Orig.). 1996. pap. 20.00 (*0-9651777-0-X*, 96001) Pinniped Pr.

Abbott, Keith. Erase Words. LC 76-58861. (Illus.). 1977. pap. 9.95 (*0-912652-35-7*) Blue Wind.

— Erase Words. deluxe limited ed. LC 76-58861. (Illus.). 1977. pap. 19.95 (*0-912652-36-5*) Blue Wind.

— The First Thing Coming. LC 87-18190. 226p. (Orig.). 1987. pap. 9.95 (*0-918273-31-5*) Coffee Hse.

— The French Girl. 42p. (Orig.). 1996. pap. 5.00 (*1-887289-14-3*) Rodent Pr.

— Gush: A Comic Novel about Unemployment. LC 75-9878. 140p. 1975. 29.95 (*0-912652-16-0*); pap. 12.95 (*0-912652-17-9*) Blue Wind.

— Gush: A Comic Novel about Unemployment. deluxe ed. LC 75-9878. 140p. 1975. 49.95 (*0-912652-18-7*) Blue Wind.

— Mordecai of Monterey. LC 84-72513. (Illus.). 224p. 1985. 13.95 (*0-933944-10-1*); pap. 8.95 (*0-933944-11-X*) City Miner Bks.

— Mordecai of Monterey. deluxe ed. LC 84-72513. (Illus.). 224p. 1985. 25.00 (*0-933944-21-7*) City Miner Bks.

— Putty. (Illus.). 1971. 29.95 (*0-912652-31-4*) Blue Wind.

— Rhino Ritz: An American Mystery. LC 78-23542. 1979. pap. 12.95 (*0-912652-43-8*) Blue Wind.

— Rhino Ritz: An American Mystery. deluxe limited ed. LC 78-23542. 1979. 49.95 (*0-912652-44-6*) Blue Wind.

Abbott-King, Janet P. Human Twinning As a Compensatory Mechanism: A Unifying Hypothesis. (Illus.). (Orig.). (C). 1989. pap. text 15.95 (*0-9621917-2-8*) Polar Pr.

Abbott-King, Janet P., jt. auth. see King, David T., Jr.

***Abbott, Kingsley, ed.** Calling Out Around the World: A Motown Reader. (Illus.). 2000. pap. 18.95 (*1-900924-14-5*, Pub. by Helter Skelter) Interlink Pub.

Abbott, L. & Pi, S. Y. Inflationary Cosmology. 712p. 1986. text 117.00 (*9971-978-64-4*); pap. text 49.00 (*9971-978-65-2*) World Scientific Pub.

Abbott, L. B. Special Effects: Wire, Tape & Rubber Band Style. Turner, George E., tr. LC 83-73058. 275p. 1984. 29.95 (*0-935578-06-4*) ASC Holding.

Abbott, L. K., jt. ed. see Robson, A. D.

Abbott, Laurence & Sejnowski, Terrence J., eds. Neural Codes & Distributed Representations: Foundations of Neural Computation. LC 98-14783. (Computational Neuroscience Ser.). (Illus.). 358p. 1998. pap. 30.00 (*0-262-51100-2*, Bradford Bks) MIT Pr.

Abbott, Lawrence. I Stand in the Center of the Good: Interviews with Contemporary Native American Artists. LC 93-36892. (American Indian Lives Ser.). (Illus.). xxii, 330p. (J). 1994. text 50.00 (*0-8032-1037-X*) U of Nebr Pr.

— The Listener's Book on Harmony. LC 74-27325. reprint ed. 34.50 (*0-404-12850-5*) AMS Pr.

Abbott, Lawrence F. Twelve Great Modernists. LC 76-84292. (Essay Index Reprint Ser.). 1977. 22.95 (*0-8369-1118-0*) Ayer.

Abbott, Lee K. Dreams of Distant Lives. 206p. 1990. pap. 10.00 (*1-877727-14-8*) White Pine.

— Living after Midnight: A Novella & Stories. LC 97-51224. 239p. 1998. pap. 16.95 (*0-8142-0792-8*, ABBLIX) Ohio St U Pr.

— Love Is the Crooked Thing. LC 96-15039. 182p. 1996. pap. 16.00 (*0-8142-0713-8*) Ohio St U Pr.

— Strangers in Paradise: Stories. LC 96-15038. 255p. 1996. pap. 17.00 (*0-8142-0712-X*) Ohio St U Pr.

— Wet Places at Noon. LC 97-20595. 204p. 1997. 22.95 (*0-87745-605-4*) U of Iowa Pr.

***Abbott, Lee K., et al.** The Putt at the End of the World. Standiford, Les, ed. LC 99-89030. 256p. 2000. 23.95 (*0-446-52600-2*, Pub. by Warner Bks) Little.

Abbott, Lemuel A. Descendants of George Abbott of Rowley, Mass. & of George Abbott, Sr., of Andover, Mass, 2 vols., Set. (Illus.). 1232p. 1988. reprint ed. pap. 156.00 (*0-8328-0085-6*); reprint ed. lib. bdg. 166.00 (*0-8328-0084-8*) Higginson Bk Co.

Abbott, Lesley & Moylett, Helen, eds. Early Interactions: Working with under Threes Responding to Children's Needs. LC 98-139486. 157p. 1998. 85.00 (*0-335-19840-6*); pap. 25.95 (*0-335-19839-2*) OpUniv Pr.

Abbott, Lesley & Pugh, Gillian. Training to Work in the Early Years. LC 98-3316. 189p. 1998. 85.00 (*0-335-20031-1*); pap. 26.99 (*0-335-20030-3*) OpUniv Pr.

Abbott, Lesley & Rodger, Rosemary. Quality Education in the Early Years. LC 94-16355. 224p. 1994. 98.95 (*0-335-19231-9*); pap. 22.95 (*0-335-19230-0*) OpUniv Pr.

Abbott, Leslie. Acting for Film & TV. (Illus.). 200p. 1993. pap. text 17.95 (*0-89863-165-3*) Star Pub CA.

— Active Acting: Exercises & Improvisations Leading to Performances. 192p. (C). 1987. pap. text 16.95 (*0-89863-114-9*) Star Pub CA.

Abbott, Linda & Smith, John R. Rainforest. (Illus.). 52p. 1994. pap. 12.95 (*0-936459-24-7*) Stained Glass.

— Some Thing's Fishy. (Illus.). 52p. 1993. pap. 12.95 (*0-936459-20-4*) Stained Glass.

Abbott, Linda, jt. auth. see Smith, John R.

Abbott, Linda M. Fresno: Valley of Abundance. Stochler, Sharon, ed. (Illus.). 248p. 1988. write for info. (*0-945347-00-6*) FCCCC.

Abbott, Louise. The Coast Way. (Illus.). 156p. (C). 1988. 125.00 (*0-7735-0671-3*, Pub. by McG-Queens Univ Pr) CUP Services.

— The Coast Way: A Portrait of the English on the Lower North Shore of the St Lawrence. (Illus.). 160p. (C). 1988. 65.00 (*0-7735-0654-3*, Pub. by McG-Queens Univ Pr) CUP Services.

Abbott, Louise C., jt. auth. see Jacobowitz, David M.

Abbott, Lyman. The Evolution of Christianity. vi, 258p. 1985. reprint ed. 59.00 (*0-7812-0801-7*) Rprt Serv.

— Henry Ward Beecher. LC 78-89428. (Black Heritage Library Collection). 1977. 32.95 (*0-8369-8500-1*) Ayer.

Abbott, Lyman, et al. The New Puritanism: During the Semi-Centennial Celebration of Plymouth Church, N.Y., 1847-1897. LC 70-39672. (Essay Index Reprint Ser.). 1977. 21.95 (*0-8369-2732-X*) Ayer.

Abbott, M. B. Computational Hydraulics: Elements of the Theory of Free Surface Flows. 344p. 1992. 84.95 (*1-85742-064-0*, Pub. by Avebury Technical) Ashgate Pub Co.

Abbott, M. B. & Minns, A. W. Computational Hydraulics. 2nd ed. 580p. 1998. text 144.95 (*0-291-39835-9*, Pub. by Ashgate Pub) Ashgate Pub Co.

Abbott, M. B. & Price, W. A., eds. Coastal, Estuarial, & Harbour Engineer's Reference Book. LC 93-6688. (Illus.). 768p. (C). 1994. 220.00 (*0-419-15430-2*, E & FN Spon) Routledge.

Abbott, Makeham. Agricultural Economics & Marketing in Tropics. 1990. pap. text. write for info. (*0-582-05623-3*, Pub. by Addison-Wesley) Longman.

***Abbott, Malvina E. J., et al.** California Criminal Law Procedure & Practice. 4th ed. LC 94-70697. 2000p. 1998. ring bd. 195.00 (*0-7626-0247-3*, CR-32112) Cont Ed Bar-CA.

Abbott, Marcia. My Face. Abbott, Barbara, ed. (Illus.). 44p. (J). (gr. 1-5). 1998. 12.50 (*0-9666097-0-0*) Forward Face.

Abbott, Margery P. An Experiment in Faith: Quaker Women Transcending Differences. 1995. pap. 4.00 (*0-87574-323-4*) Pendle Hill.

Abbott, Margery Post, ed. A Certain Kind of Perfection: An Anthology of Liberal & Evangelical Quaker Writings. LC 97-19674. 357p. 1997. pap. 20.00 (*0-87574-928-3*) Pendle Hill.

Abbott, Margot. The Last Innocent Hour. 1993. mass mkt. 5.99 (*0-312-92942-0*) St Martin.

Abbott, Marguerite, et al. Occupational Therapy. (Opportunities in...Ser.). (Illus.). 160p. 1990. 13.95 (*0-8442-6561-6*, VGM Career) NTC Contemp Pub Co.

— Occupational Therapy. (Opportunities in...Ser.). (Illus.). 160p. 1993. pap. 10.95 (*0-8442-6562-4*, VGM Career) NTC Contemp Pub Co.

***Abbott, Marguerite, et al.** Opportunities in Occupational Therapy Careers. rev. ed. LC 00-31995. (Opportunities Ser.). 2000. write for info. (*0-658-00473-5*, VGM Career) NTC Contemp Pub Co.

Abbott, Marti & Polk, Betty J. About Me. 1991. 9.99 (*0-8224-0491-5*) Fearon Teacher Aids.

— Books & Beyond Set, 3 bks., Set. (J). (gr. k-4). 27.99 (*1-56417-691-6*, FE7691) Fearon Teacher Aids.

— Celebrating Our Diversity. 1992. pap. 23.99 (*0-86653-989-1*) Fearon Teacher Aids.

— Celebrating Our Diversity: Using Multicultural Literature to Promote Cultural Awareness. (Illus.). 208p. (J). (gr. k-2). 1998. pap. text 25.00 (*0-7881-5265-3*) DIANE Pub.

— Clouds, Rain, Wind & Snow. 1991. 9.99 (*0-8224-1351-5*) Fearon Teacher Aids.

— Families. 1991. 9.99 (*0-8224-3168-8*) Fearon Teacher Aids.

Abbott, Mary. Family Ties: English Families, 1540-1920. LC 92-24886. (Illus.). 248p. (C). (gr. 13). 1993. pap. 22.99 (*0-415-09110-1*, B0015) Routledge.

— Life Cycles in England, 1560-1720: Cradle to Grave. LC 95-37392. 320p. (C). 1996. 85.00 (*0-415-10842-X*); pap. 24.99 (*0-415-10843-8*) Routledge.

Abbott, Mary L. Romantic Weekends in Texas. (Romantic Weekends Ser.). (Illus.). 276p. 1998. pap. 15.95 (*1-55650-834-4*) Hunter NJ.

Abbott, Mary L., ed. & intro. see De Dijin, Herman.

Abbott, Mary Lu. Travel Smart: Texas. 2nd ed. (Illus.). 256p. 1999. pap. 16.95 (*1-56261-449-5*, Travel Smart) Avalon Travel.

Abbott, Mary Lu, jt. ed. see Gayot, Alain.

Abbott, Michael, jt. auth. see Weeks, Sarah.

Abbott, Michael B. Hydroinformatics: Information Technology & the Aquatic Environment. 158p. 1991. 72.95 (*1-85628-832-3*, Pub. by Avebury Technical) Ashgate Pub Co.

Abbott, Michael B. & Refsgaard, Jens C., eds. Distributed Hydrological Modelling. (Water Science & Technology Library: Vol. 22). 1996. lib. bdg. 158.00 (*0-7923-4042-6*) Kluwer Academic.

Abbott, Michael M. & Van Ness, Hendrick. Schaum's Outline of Thermodynamics. 2nd rev. ed. LC 89-2576. 384p. (C). 1994. pap. 15.95 (*0-07-000042-5*) McGraw.

Abbott, Mike. Green Woodwork: Working with Wood the Natural Way. (Illus.). 208p. 1992. pap. 16.95 (*0-946819-18-1*, Pub. by Guild Master) Sterling.

Abbott, Mitchell E., et al. California Civil Appellate Practice, 2 vols. 3rd ed. Waxman, Robert N., ed. LC 96-85107. 2380p. 1996. ring bd. 159.00 (*0-7626-0008-X*, CP-32430) Cont Ed Bar-CA.

— California Civil Appellate Practice - 5-99 Update. 3rd ed. Waxman, Robert N., ed. LC 96-85107. 374p. 1999. ring bd. 59.00 (*0-7626-0331-3*, CP-32433) Cont Ed Bar-CA.

Abbott, Mitchell E., et al. California Civil Discovery Practice, 2 vols. 3rd ed. Compton, Linda A., ed. LC 98-71652. 1336p. 1998. ring bd. 179.00 (*0-7626-0188-4*, CP-32870) Cont Ed Bar-CA.

Abbott, N. B., jt. auth. see Abbott, C. M.

Abbott, Nabia. Aisha: The Beloved Mohammed. 230p. 1998. pap. 29.95 (*0-86356-007-5*, Pub. by Saqi) Intl Spec Bk.

— Aishah: The Beloved of Mohammed. LC 73-6264. (Middle East Ser.). 1973. reprint ed. 20.95 (*0-405-05318-5*) Ayer.

— Quaranic Commentary & Tradition: Studies in Arabic Literary Papyri, Vol. 2. LC 56-5027. (Oriental Institute Publications: No. 76). 1996. lib. bdg. 42.00 (*0-226-62177-4*, OIP76) U Ch Pr.

— Studies in Arabic Literary Papyri: Language & Literature, Vol. 3. LC 56-5027. (Oriental Institute Publications: No. 77). (Illus.). xvi, 216p. 1974. lib. bdg. 48.00 (*0-226-62178-2*) U Ch Pr.

— Two Queens of Baghdad, Mother & Wife of Harun Al-Rashid. LC 46-3799. 295p. reprint ed. pap. 91.50 (*0-608-11824-9*, 201122500074) Bks Demand.

Abbott, Nathan, ed. Brief Making & the Use of Law Books. LC 88-81235. (Legal Bibliographic & Research Reprint Ser.: Vol. 10). viii, 472p. 1988. reprint ed. lib. bdg. 47.50 (*0-89941-650-0*, 305630) W S Hein.

Abbott, P. Research into Practice: A Reader for Nurses & the Caring Professions. 2nd ed. LC 96-49631. (Social Science for Nurses & the Caring Professions Ser.). 1997. 94.00 (*0-335-19696-9*); pap. 30.99 (*0-335-19695-0*) OpUniv Pr.

— Research Meth Nurses. 2nd ed. (Social Science for Nurses & the Caring Professions Ser.). 1998. pap. 27.95 (*0-335-19697-7*) OpUniv Pr.

— Research Meth Nurses. 2nd ed. LC 97-42886. 200p. 1998. pap. 89.00 (*0-335-19698-5*) OpUniv Pr.

— Teach Yourself Algebra. 342p. 1995. pap. 10.95 (*0-8442-3904-6*, Teach Yrslf) NTC Contemp Pub Co.

— Teach Yourself Trigonometry. (Illus.). 208p. 1995. pap. 10.95 (*0-8442-3943-7*, Teach Yrslf) NTC Contemp Pub Co.

Abbott, P. & Lewry, S. Front Office: Procedures, Social Skills & Management. 2nd ed. 272p. 1999. pap. text 29.95 (*0-7506-4230-0*) Buttrwrth-Heinemann.

Abbott, P. & Neill, Hugh. Calculus. rev. ed. LC 98-65233. (Teach Yourself Ser.). (Illus.). 352p. 1998. pap. 14.95 (*0-8442-0041-7*, 00417, Teach Yrslf) NTC Contemp Pub Co.

— Teach Yourself Algebra. 2nd rev. ed. (Illus.). 352p. 1996. pap. 11.95 (*0-8442-3117-7*, Teach Yrslf) NTC Contemp Pub Co.

— Trigonometry. 2nd rev. ed. (Teach Yourself Ser.). 208p. 1998. pap. 11.95 (*0-8442-0042-5*, 00425) NTC Contemp Pub Co.

Abbott, P., jt. auth. see Thomas, N.

Abbott, P. E. & Tamplin, J. M. British Gallantry Awards. 334p. 1982. 100.00 (*0-902633-74-0*, Pub. by Picton) St Mut.

Abbott, P. L. Geology Pertaining to Archaeology, Drinkwater Lake Area, Fort Irwin, California. fac. ed. (Fort Irwin, Miscellaneous Reports). (Illus.). 31p. (C). 1996. reprint ed. pap. text 3.44 (*1-55567-522-0*) Coyote Press.

Abbott, Pamela & Lewry, S. Front Office: Procedures, Social Skills & Management. 264p. 1991. pap. 36.95 (*0-7506-0024-1*) Buttrwrth-Heinemann.

Abbott, Pamela & Payne, Geoff, eds. New Directions in the Sociology of Health. (Explorations in Sociology Ser.: No. 36). 240p. 1990. pap. 34.95 (*1-85000-787-X*, Falmer Pr) Taylor & Francis.

Abbott, Pamela & Sapsford, Roger. Women & Social Class. 240p. 1988. text 49.95 (*0-422-60990-0*, Pub. by Tavistock) Routldge.

Abbott, Pamela & Wallace, Claire. The Family & the New Right. 176p. 1992. 49.95 (*0-7453-0532-6*, Pub. by Pluto GBR) Stylus Pub VA.

— The Family & the New Right. 176p. (C). 1992. pap. 18.95 (*0-7453-0533-4*, Pub. by Pluto GBR) Stylus Pub VA.

— An Introduction to Sociology: Feminist Perspectives. 224p. (C). 1990. pap. text 18.95 (*0-415-01037-3*, A4052) Routledge.

— An Introduction to Sociology: Feminist Perspectives. 2nd ed. LC 95-49777. 352p. (C). 1996. pap. 22.99 (*0-415-12292-9*) Routledge.

— The Sociology of the Caring Professions. 200p. 1990. 65.00 (*1-85000-819-1*, Falmer Pr); pap. 34.95 (*1-85000-824-8*, Falmer Pr) Taylor & Francis.

Abbott, Pamela, jt. auth. see Ackers, Louise.

Abbott, Pamela, jt. auth. see Payne, Geoff.

Abbott, Pamela, jt. auth. see Sapsford, Roger.

Abbott, Pamela, jt. auth. see Sapsford, Roger.

Abbott, Patrick. Airships. (Album Ser.: No. 259). (Illus.). 32p. (C). 1989. pap. 6.25 (*0-7478-0084-7*, Pub. by Shire Pubns) Parkwest Pubns.

— The British Airship at War, 1914-1918. 152p. 1990. 50.00 (*0-86138-073-8*, Pub. by T Dalton) St Mut.

Abbott, Patrick L. Natural Disasters. 400p. (C). 1995. text. write for info. (*0-697-25493-3*, WCB McGr Hill) McGrw-H Hghr Educ.

— Natural Disasters. 448p. (C). 1997. per. write for info. (*0-07-114020-4*, WCB McGr Hill) McGrw-H Hghr Educ.

— Natural Disasters. 2nd ed. LC 98-23748. 416p. 1998. pap. 55.94 (*0-697-37439-4*) McGraw.

— Rise & Fall of San Diego: 150 Million Years of History Recorded in Seditientary Rocks. LC 99-35670. (Illus.). 208p. 1999. pap. 16.95 (*0-932653-31-6*) Sunbelt Pubns.

Abbott, Patrick L., ed. Cretaceous Stratigraphy Western North America. (Illus.). 233p. (Orig.). 1986. pap. 14.00 (*1-878861-26-3*) Pac Section SEPM.

— Geologic Studies in Baja California. (Illus.). 140p. (Orig.). 1989. pap. 12.00 (*1-878861-06-9*) Pac Section SEPM.

— Upper Cretaceous Depositional Systems, Southern California - Northern Baja California. (Illus.). 140p. (Orig.). 1984. pap. 5.00 (*1-878861-36-0*) Pac Section SEPM.

Abbott, Patrick L. & May, Jeffrey A., eds. Eocene Geologic History San Diego Region. (Illus.). 229p. 1991. pap. text 22.00 (*1-878861-61-1*) Pac Section SEPM.

Abbott, Paul. Ins & Outs of Mathematica. 920p. 1997. pap. text 34.95 (*0-387-94645-4*) Spr-Verlag.

Abbott, Paul, jt. auth. see Miyaji, Chikara.

Abbott, Paul B. The Gyroplane Flight Manual, Vol. 1. 6th rev. ed. (Illus.). 132p. (Orig.). 1996. pap. text 16.95 (*1-888723-00-9*) Abbott Co.

— How to License a Homebuilt Aircraft. 76p. 1994. pap. text 16.95 (*1-888723-03-3*) Abbott Co.

— Understanding the Gyroplane. 120p. 1994. pap. text 16.95 (*1-888723-01-7*) Abbott Co.

Abbott, Paul C. The Gyroplane Flight Manual. 5th ed. (Illus.). 61p. 1992. pap. 16.95 (*0-916413-19-5*) Aviation.

— How to License a Homebuilt Aircraft. 2nd ed. (Illus.). 61p. 1994. pap. 16.95 (*0-916413-20-9*) Aviation.

— Understanding the Gyroplane. 2nd ed. (Illus.). 85p. 1994. pap. 16.95 (*0-916413-21-7*) Aviation.

Abbott, Peter & Rodrigues, M. R. Modern African Wars Vol. 2: Angola & Mocambique, 1961-74. (Men-at-Arms Ser.: No. 202). (Illus.). 48p. pap. 11.95 (*0-85045-843-9*, 9135, Pub. by Ospry) Stackpole.

Abbott, Peter & Thomas, Nigel. Germany's Eastern Front Allies, 1941-45. (Men-at-Arms Ser.: No. 131). (Illus.). 48p. pap. 11.95 (*0-85045-475-1*, 9063, Pub. by Ospry) Stackpole.

— The Korean War, 1950-53. (Men-at-Arms Ser.: No. 174). (Illus.). 48p. 1986. pap. 12.95 (*0-85045-685-1*, 9106, Pub. by Ospry) Stackpole.

***Abbott, Philip.** Exceptional America: Newness & National Identity. LC 98-49947. (Major Concepts in Politics & Political Theory Ser.: Vol. 14). X, 251p. 1999. pap. text 26.95 (*0-8204-3912-6*) P Lang Pubng.

Abbott, Philip. The Exemplary Presidency: Franklin D. Roosevelt & the American Political Tradition. LC 89-20247. 248p. (C). 1990. pap. 17.95 (*0-87023-709-8*); lib. bdg. 35.00 (*0-87023-706-3*) U of Mass Pr.

— The Family on Trial: Special Relationships in Modern Political Thought. LC 80-26964. 256p. (C). 1981. 28.50 (*0-271-00282-4*) Pa St U Pr.

— Furious Fancies: American Political Thought in the Post-Liberal Era. 35. LC 79-7469. (Contributions in Political Science Ser.: No. 35). 265p. 1980. 59.95 (*0-313-20945-6*, AFF/, Greenwood Pr) Greenwood.

— Leftward Ho! V. F. Calverton & American Radicalism, 315. LC 92-21363. (Contributions in Political Science Ser.: No. 315). 248p. 1993. 62.95 (*0-313-28568-3*, ALH, Greenwood Pr) Greenwood.

— Political Thought in America: Conversations & Debates. 2nd rev. ed. LC 99-197252. 350p. (C). 1998. pap. text 22.95 (*1-57766-027-7*) Waveland Pr.

— States of Perfect Freedom: Autobiography & American Political Thought. LC 86-16248. 226p. 1987. 30.00 (*0-87023-542-7*) U of Mass Pr.

— Strong Presidents: A Theory of Leadership. LC 95-41758. 296p. 1996. pap. text 20.00 (*0-87049-932-7*); lib. bdg. 40.00 (*0-87049-931-9*) U of Tenn Pr.

Abbott, R. Tucker. Collectible Florida Shells. (Illus.). 64p. 1997. reprint ed. pap. 6.95 (*0-8200-0210-0*) Great Outdoors.

***Abbott, R. Tucker.** Seashells of North America, a Guide to Field Identification. (Golden Guide Ser.). 1998. 19.05 (*0-606-11822-5*, Pub. by Turtleback) Demco.

— Seashells of the World, a Guide to the Better-Known Species. (Golden Guide Ser.). 11.05 (*0-606-11823-3*, Pub. by Turtleback) Demco.

Abbott, R. Tucker & Morris, Percy A. A Field Guide to Shells of the Atlantic & Gulf Coasts & the West Indies. 4th ed. LC 94-14421. (Peterson Field Guide Ser.: Vol. 3). 512p. 1995. pap. 16.95 (*0-395-69779-4*) HM.

Abbott, Richard. Belo Horizonte: Around the World in 80 Years. LC 94-79311. (Illus.). 256p. (Orig.). 1995. pap. 14.95 (*1-882897-01-3*) Lost Coast.

Abbott, Richard H. Cotton & Capital: Boston Businessmen & Antislavery Reform, 1854-1868. LC 91-14137. 304p. (C). 1991. text 35.00 (*0-87023-749-7*) U of Mass Pr.

— The Republican Party & the South, 1855-1877: The First Southern Strategy. LC 85-16557. (Fred W. Morrison Series in Southern Studies). 317p. reprint ed. pap. 98.30 (*0-608-06015-1*, 206634300008) Bks Demand.

***Abbott, Robert.** The World as Information. 160p. 1999. pap. 24.95 (*1-871516-75-7*, Pub. by Intellect) Cromland.

Abbott, Robert, jt. auth. see Flanagan, William.

***Abbott, Robert F.** A Manager's Guide to Newsletters: Communicating for Results. LC 98-910997. (Illus.). 200p. 1999. 49.95 (*0-9683287-1-7*) Wrd Eng Pr.

Abbott, Robert J. Art & Reality: The Standard Reference Guide & Business Plan for Actively Developing Your Career As an Artist. 2nd ed. LC 97-10640. 288p. (Orig.). 1997. pap. text 29.95 (*0-929765-56-7*) Seven Locks Pr.

Abbott, Robert M. The Assemblies of God Evangelist: Life & Work. 48p. 1988. pap. 2.95 (*0-88243-695-3*) Gospel Pub.

Abbott, Roland W. The Million Dollar Rock. 82p. 1994. pap. 7.95 (*1-895387-47-7*) Creative Bk Pub.

— The Three Seas. LC 95-5022. 82p. 1987. reprint ed. pap. 7.95 (*0-920884-16-4*) Creative Bk Pub.

Abbott, Ronald R., et al. Going Digital: Electronic Images in the Library Catalog & Beyond. King, Mimi, ed. LC 95-41435. 88p. 1995. 9.00 (*0-8389-7814-2*) ALA.

Abbott, S. Ardis & Luddy, Jean A. Vernon & Historic Rockville. (Images of America Ser.). (Illus.). 128p. 1998. pap. 16.99 (*0-7524-0973-5*) Arcadia Publng.

Abbott, Scott H. Fictions of Freemasonry: Freemasonry & the German Novel. LC 90-12739. (Illus.). 240p. reprint ed. pap. 74.40 (*0-608-10554-6*, 20711740009) Bks Demand.

Abbott, Sheldon L. Automotive Brakes: A Text-Lab Manual. 2nd ed. (Illus.). 1987. pap. write for info. (*0-318-66994-3*) Macmillan.

— Automotive Power Trains. 2nd ed. 256p. 1987. pap. text 34.95 (*0-02-810010-7*); 7.28 (*0-02-810020-4*) Glencoe.

— Automotive Suspension Steering. 1982. 12.95 (*0-02-810110-3*) Macmillan.

— Automotive Transmissions. 2nd ed. 320p. 1987. teacher ed. 7.28 (*0-02-810290-8*) Glencoe.

— Automotive Transmissions. 2nd ed. 320p. 1988. pap. text 21.60 (*0-02-810280-0*) Glencoe.

Abbott, Sheldon L. & Hinerman, Ivan D. Automotive Brakes. 2nd ed. 477p. 1987. teacher ed. 7.28 (*0-02-810510-9*) Glencoe.

— Automotive Brakes. 2nd ed. 477p. 1987. pap. 35.83 (*0-02-810500-1*) Glencoe.

Abbott-Shim, Martha S. & Sibley, Annette M. Child Care Inventory: Administration Manual. LC 85-81658. 32p. (Orig.). 1986. pap. 12.95 (*0-89334-088-X*) Humanics Ltd.

— Child Care Inventory: Administration Manual & Test Booklet. LC 85-81658. 48p. (Orig.). 1986. pap., student ed. 22.95 (*0-89334-090-1*) Humanics Ltd.

Abbott, Shirley. Love's Apprentice: Confessions from the School of Romance. LC 97-44865. 288p. 1998. 23.00 (*0-395-67369-0*) HM.

— Love's Apprentice: The Romantic Education of a Modern Woman. 288p. 1999. pap. 13.00 (*0-395-95785-0*) HM.

Abbott, Shirley. Womenfolks: Growing up down South. LC 82-16880. 224p. 1983. 13.45 (*0-89919-156-8*, Pub. by Ticknor & Fields) HM.

Abbott, Shirley. Womenfolks: Growing up down South. 224p. 1998. reprint ed. 29.95 (*0-7351-0050-0*) Replica Bks.

— Womenfolks: Growing up down South. rev. ed. LC 98-5454. 224p. 1998. pap. 12.00 (*0-395-90144-8*) HM.

Abbott, Sidney & Love, Barbara, eds. Sappho Was a Right-On Woman. LC 77-160348. 1978. 8.95 (*0-8128-2406-7*, Scrbrough Hse) Madison Bks UPA.

***Abbott-Smith, G.** A Manual Greek Lexicon of the New Testament. 528p. 1999. pap. 24.95 (*0-567-08684-4*) T&T Clark Pubs.

Abbott-Smith, G. A Manual Greek Lexicon of the New Testament. 3rd ed. 528p. 1937. 34.95 (*0-567-01001-5*, Pub. by T & T Clark) Bks Intl VA.

Abbott-Smith, George & Bancroft, James. Bancroft. Charles Bancroft of Montreal: His Ancestors Thomas of England & Reading, Mass.; John of Lynnfield, Mass.; His Father James of Boston & His Descendants, 1640-1943. 126p. 1997. reprint ed. pap. 21.00 (*0-8328-7367-5*); reprint ed. lib. bdg. 31.00 (*0-8328-7366-7*) Higginson Bk Co.

Abbott, Stan R. Holy Spirit: The Anointing of God. (Illus.). 86p. (Orig.). 1984. pap. 2.95 (*0-915545-00-4*) S R Abbott Mini.

— Temple of Glory. 236p. (Orig.). 1986. pap. 5.95 (*0-915545-01-2*) S R Abbott Mini.

Abbott, Stephanie. Codependency: A Second-Hand Life. 11p. (Orig.). 1985. pap. 1.55 (*0-89486-317-7*, 5450B) Hazelden.

Abbott, Stephanie, ed. see Brown, Stephanie, et al.

Abbott, Stephen. And All My War Is Done. 154p. (C). 1989. text 59.00 (*0-946270-99-6*, Pub. by Pentland Pr) St Mut.

Abbott, Steve. Lives of the Poets. 1987. pap. 5.00 (*0-9607630-2-3*) Black Star.

— The Lizard Club. 159p. Date not set. 7.00 (*0-936756-71-3*) Autonomedia.

— A Short History of the Word. 32p. 1996. pap. 7.95 (*0-944754-34-1*) Pudding Hse Pubns.

— View Askew: Postmodern Investigations. (Illus.). 195p. (Orig.). 1989. pap. text 9.95 (*1-879594-13-7*) Androgyne Bks.

Abbott, Steve, et al. Hey, Good Lookin' Poems from the Poets Performance Troupe, Redkitchen. 46p. 1995. pap. 7.95 (*0-944754-31-7*) Pudding Hse Pubns.

Abbott, Sue. Building Gateway Partnerships: Process for Shaping the Future of Your Community. 172p. 1997. ring bd. 27.00 (*0-16-061683-2*) USGPO.

Abbott, Susan. Corporate Art Consulting. 350p. (Orig.). 1992. 89.95 (*1-879466-02-3*); pap. 69.95 (*1-879466-01-5*) Art Busn News.

— Corporate Art Consulting. LC 94-72316. (Illus.). 248p. (Orig.). 1994. pap. 89.95 (*1-879467-01-1*, 5825) Art Wrld Pr.

— Corproate Art Consulting. 256p. 1999. pap. 34.95 (*1-58115-034-2*) Allworth Pr.

— Standardized Testing. LC 98-181112. (Professional's Guide Ser.). 80p. 1997. pap., teacher ed. 9.95 (*1-57690-124-6*, TCM2124) Tchr Create Mat.

***Abbott, Susan.** Teaching Reading in the Middle Grades. 92p. 1999. pap., teacher ed. 9.95 (*1-57690-474-1*, TCM2474) Tchr Create Mat.

Abbott, Susan & Webb, Barbara. Fine Art Publicity: The Complete Guide for Galleries & Artists. LC 90-86153. 189p. 1991. pap. write for info. (*1-879466-00-7*) Art Busn News.

— Fine Art Publicity: The Complete Guide for Galleries & Artists. (Illus.). 190p. 1991. reprint ed. pap. 22.95 (*1-880559-48-X*) Allworth Pr.

Abbott, Susan S. Lessons: For Where There Is Love, There Is Hope - from a Mother Who Lost Her Child to Cancer. LC 96-14424. (Illus.). 1996. 4.95 (*1-56123-092-8*, LESC) Centering Corp.

Abbott, Susan W. Families of Early Milford, Connecticut. LC 78-66024. 875p. 1997. pap. 55.00 (*0-8063-0838-9*) Clearfield Co.

Abbott, T. K. Ephesians & Colossians: Critical & Exegetical Commentary. Driver, Samuel R. et al, eds. LC 40-15742. (International Critical Commentary Ser.). 392p. 1897. 39.95 (*0-567-05030-0*, Pub. by T & T Clark) Bks Intl VA.

Abbott, Thomas A., 3rd, ed. Health Care Policy & Regulation. (Topics in Regulatory Economics & Policy: 20). 272p. (C). 1995. lib. bdg. 107.50 (*0-7923-9540-9*) Kluwer Academic.

Abbott, Thomas K. Catalogue of Fifteenth-Century Books in the Library of Trinity-College, Dublin, & in Marsh's Library, Dublin. (Illus.). vi, 225p. 1977. reprint ed. 80.00 incl. 3.5 hd (*3-487-06319-0*) G Olms Pubs.

— Catalogue of the Manuscripts in the Library of Trinity-College, Dublin. (GER.). xxvi, 606p. 1980. reprint ed. write for info. (*3-487-06985-7*) G Olms Pubs.

Abbott, Thomas K., tr. see Kant, Immanuel.

Abbott, Tony. Attack of the Alien Mole Invaders. (Weird Zone Ser.). 1996. 8.09 (*0-606-10357-0*, Pub. by Turtleback) Demco.

— The Beast from Beneath the Cafeteria! (Weird Zone Ser.). 1996. 8.09 (*0-606-10032-6*, Pub. by Turtleback) Demco.

— The Brain That Wouldn't Obey! (Weird Zone Ser.). (Illus.). (J). (gr. 2-5). 1997. pap. 3.50 (*0-614-29038-4*, Little Apple) Scholastic Inc.

— The Brain That Wouldn't Obey! LC 49-244560. (Weird Zone Ser.). 1997. 8.09 (*0-606-10965-X*, Pub. by Turtleback) Demco.

***Abbott, Tony.** City in the Clouds. (Secrets of Droon Ser.). (Illus.). 88p. (J). (gr. 2-5). 1999. mass mkt. 2.99 (*0-590-10842-5*) Scholastic Inc.

Abbott, Tony. Cosmic Boy Versus Mezmo Head. (Weird Zone Ser.: No. 7). (J). 1997. mass mkt. 3.50 (*0-590-67439-0*, Little Apple) Scholastic Inc.

— Danger Guys. LC 93-29799. (Trophy Chapter Bk.: Vol. 1). (Illus.). 80p. (J). (gr. 2-5). 1994. pap. 4.25 (*0-06-440519-2*, HarpTrophy) HarpC Child Bks.

Abbott, Tony. Danger Guys. LC 93-29799. 1994. 9.15 (*0-606-06306-4*, Pub. by Turtleback) Demco.

Abbott, Tony. Danger Guys: Hollywood Halloween. LC 94-8593. (Trophy Chapter Bk.: Vol. 3). (Illus.). 96p. (J). (gr. 2-5). 1994. pap. 4.50 (*0-06-440522-2*, HarpTrophy) HarpC Child Bks.

Abbott, Tony. Danger Guys: Hollywood Halloween. LC 94-8593. (Trophy Chapter Bks.). 1994. 9.15 (*0-606-06308-0*, Pub. by Turtleback) Demco.

Abbott, Tony. Danger Guys & the Golden Lizard. LC 95-35944. (Trophy Chapter Bk.). (Illus.). 96p. (J). (gr. 2-5). 1996. pap. 3.95 (*0-06-442011-6*, HarpTrophy) HarpC Child Bks.

Abbott, Tony. Danger Guys & the Golden Lizard. LC 95-35944. (Danger Guys Ser.). 1996. 9.15 (*0-606-09178-5*, Pub. by Turtleback) Demco.

Abbott, Tony. Danger Guys Blast Off. LC 93-31806. (Trophy Chapter Bk.). (Illus.). 96p. (J). (gr. 2-5). 1994. pap. 4.50 (*0-06-440520-6*, HarpTrophy) HarpC Child Bks.

Abbott, Tony. Danger Guys Blast Off. LC 93-31806. (Trophy Chapter Bks.). 1994. 9.70 (*0-606-06307-2*, Pub. by Turtleback) Demco.

Abbott, Tony. Danger Guys Hit the Beach. LC 94-27519. (Trophy Chapter Bk.). (Illus.). 80p. (J). (gr. 2-5). 1995. pap. 4.50 (*0-06-440521-4*, HarpTrophy) HarpC Child Bks.

— Danger Guys Hit the Beach. 1995. 9.15 (*0-606-07410-4*, Pub. by Turtleback) Demco.

— Danger Guys on Ice. (J). 1995. 9.15 (*0-606-08442-8*, Pub. by Turtleback) Demco.

— Danger Guys On Ice. LC 95-671. (Trophy Chapter Bk.). (Illus.). 96p. (J). (gr. 4-7). 1995. pap. 3.95 (*0-06-442010-8*, HarpTrophy) HarpC Child Bks.

***Abbott, Tony.** The Fake Teacher. (Don't Touch That Remote Ser.: No. 2). (J). (gr. 3-6). 1999. pap. 3.99 (*0-671-02782-4*, Minstrel Bks) PB.

— Freak Week. (Don't Touch That Remote Ser.: No. 4). 176p. (J). (gr. 3-6). 2000. pap. 3.99 (*0-671-02784-0*, Minstrel Bks) PB.

Abbott, Tony. Gigantopus from Planet X! (Weird Zone Ser.). (Illus.). (J). (gr. 2-5). 1997. pap. 3.50 (*0-614-29039-2*, Little Apple) Scholastic Inc.

— Gigantopus from Planet X! (Weird Zone Ser.). (J). 1997. 8.60 (*0-606-12060-2*, Pub. by Turtleback) Demco.

***Abbott, Tony.** Golden Wasp. (Secrets of Droon Ser.: Vol. 8). (Illus.). 96p. (J). (gr. 2-5). 2000. pap. 2.99 (*0-439-18298-0*) Scholastic Inc.

Abbott, Tony. The Great Ice Battle, Vol. 5. Vol. 5. (Illus.). 87p. (gr. 2-5). 1999. mass mkt. 2.99 (*0-590-10843-3*, Little Apple) Scholastic Inc.

***Abbott, Tony.** The Hidden Stairs & the Magic Carpet. (Secrets of Droon Ser.: No. 1). (J). (gr. 2-5). 1999. pap. 2.99 (*0-590-10839-5*, Pub. by Scholastic Inc) Penguin Putnam.

Abbott, Tony. Incredible Shrinking Kids! (Weird Zone Ser.: No. 2). (J). (gr. 2-5). 1996. pap. 2.99 (*0-590-67434-X*) Scholastic Inc.

— Incredible Shrinking Kids! (Weird Zone Ser.). (J). 1996. 8.09 (*0-606-10031-8*, Pub. by Turtleback) Demco.

***Abbott, Tony.** Into the Land of the Lost. (Secrets of Droon Ser.: Vol. 7). (Illus.). (J). (gr. 2-5). 2000. pap. 2.99 (*0-439-18297-2*) Scholastic Inc.

— Journey to the Volcano Palace. (Secrets of Droon Ser.: No. 2). (Illus.). 85p. (J). (gr. 2-5). 1999. pap. 2.99 (*0-590-10841-7*, Pub. by Scholastic Inc) Penguin Putnam.

Abbott, Tony. The Mysterious Island. (Secrets of Droon Ser.: No. 3). (Illus.). (J). (gr. 2-5). 1999. pap. 2.99 (*0-590-10840-9*, Pub. by Scholastic Inc) Penguin Putnam.

— Orbit Wipeout! (J). 1995. mass mkt. 4.75 (*0-553-54235-4*) BDD Bks Young Read.

***Abbott, Tony.** Quest for the Queen. (Secrets of Droon Ser.: Vol. 10). (Illus.). (J). 2000. pap. 2.99 (*0-439-20784-3*) Scholastic Inc.

Abbott, Tony. Revenge of the Tiki Men! (Weird Zone Ser.). (J). 1997. 8.60 (*0-606-12062-9*, Pub. by Turtleback) Demco.

— Sitcom School. (Don't Touch That Remote Ser.: No. 1). (J). (gr. 3-6). 1999. pap. 3.99 (*0-671-02781-6*) PB.

***Abbott, Tony.** Sleeping Giant/Goll. (The Secrets of Droon Ser.: No. 6). (Illus.). 96p. (J). (gr. 2-5). 2000. pap. 3.99 (*0-590-10844-1*, Little Apple) Scholastic Inc.

Abbott, Tony. Space Bingo. (J). 1996. mass mkt. 4.75 (*0-553-54230-3*) BDD Bks Young Read.

— Stinky Business. (Don't Touch That Remote Ser.: No. 3). (Orig.). (J). (gr. 3-6). 2000. pap. 3.99 (*0-671-02783-2*) PB.

— Weird Zone. LC 49-122950. (Weird Zone Ser.: No. 4). (J). (gr. 5-7). 1996. pap. 2.99 (*0-590-67436-6*) Scholastic Inc.

— Weird Zone. (Weird Zone Ser.: No. 5). (J). 1997. mass mkt. 2.99 (*0-590-67437-4*) Scholastic Inc.

— Weird Zone, No. 6. (J). 1997. mass mkt. 3.50 (*0-590-67438-2*) Scholastic Inc.

— Weird Zone: Revenge of the Tiki Men!, Vol. 8. (Weird Zone Ser.: Vol. 8). 112p. (J). (gr. 2-5). 1997. pap. text 3.50 (*0-590-67440-4*) Scholastic Inc.

— Zombie Surf Commandos from Mars. (Weird Zone Ser.). 1996. 8.09 (*0-606-10030-X*, Pub. by Turtleback) Demco.

Abbott, Tony & Coville, Bruce. Snatched from Earth, Vol. 8. Vol. 8. (Illus.). 176p. (J). (gr. 3-6). 1909. mass mkt. 3.99 (*0-671-02657-7*) PB.

— There's an Alien in My Backpack. (Sixth Grade Alien Ser.: Vol. 9). 144p. 2000. 3.99 (*0-671-02658-5*, Minstrel Bks) PB.

Abbott, V. J., jt. auth. see Ingham, Allan E.

Abbott, Velma. From the Heart of Ohio. 1998. pap. write for info. (*1-58235-027-2*) Watermrk Pr.

Abbott, Verlin M., jt. auth. see Hall, Betty L.

***Abbott, Vicki.** Maltese. (Best of the Breed Library). (Illus.). 2000. write for info. (*1-58245-160-5*) Howell Bks.

Abbott, W. C. New York in the American Revolution. LC 72-7428. (American History & Americana Ser.: No. 47). 1973. reprint ed. lib. bdg. 75.00 (*0-8383-1668-9*) M S G Haskell Hse.

Abbott, W. H. Atmospheric Corrosion of Control Equipment. LC 93-84093. (MTI Publication Ser.: No. 38). (Illus.). 91p. 1993. reprint ed. pap. 30.00 (*0-608-06730-X*, 206692700009) Bks Demand.

Abbott, W. H., jt. auth. see Andrews, G. W.

Abbott, W. W., ed. see Washington, George.

Abbott, Walter F. Analytic Juror Rater. 142p. 1987. 15.50 (*0-8318-0588-9*, B588) Am Law Inst.

Abbott, Walter F. Surrogate Juries. LC 90-80485. 265p. 1990. 16.00 (*0-8318-0607-9*, B607) Am Law Inst.

***Abbott, Walter F. & Batt, John.** A Handbook of Jury Research. LC 99-62570. 798p. 1999. text 157.50 (*0-8318-0644-3*, B644) Am Law Inst.

Abbott, Walter F., et al. Jury Research: A Review & Bibliography. LC 92-75867. 346p. 1993. 27.00 (*0-8318-0638-9*, B638) Am Law Inst.

Abbott, Wilbur C. The New Barbarians. LC 75-179499. (Select Bibliographies Reprint Ser.). 1977. reprint ed. 19.95 (*0-8369-6628-7*) Ayer.

Abbott, Wilbur C., ed. The Writings & Speeches of Oliver Cromwell with an Introduction, Notes & a Sketch of His Life, Vol. I: 1599-1649. (Illus.). 786p. 1989. 125.00 (*0-19-821771-4*) OUP.

— The Writings & Speeches of Oliver Cromwell with an Introduction, Notes & a Sketch of His Life, Vol. II: The Commonwealth. (Illus.). 828p. 1989. 135.00 (*0-19-821772-2*) OUP.

— The Writings & Speeches of Oliver Cromwell with an Introduction, Notes, & a Sketch of His Life, Vol. III: The Protectorate. (Illus.). 992p. 1989. text 160.00 (*0-19-821773-0*) OUP.

— The Writings & Speeches of Oliver Cromwell with an Introduction, Notes & a Sketch of His Life, Vol. IV: The Protectorate. (Illus.). 1,100p. 1989. text 180.00 (*0-19-821774-9*) OUP.

***Abbott, William, et al.** Exactions & Impact Fees in California: A Comprehensive Guide to Policy, Practice & the Law. 2000. pap. text 45.00 (*0-923956-65-4*) Solano Pr.

Abbott, Willis J. The Story of Our Army: From Colonial Days to the Present. 1977. lib. bdg. 59.95 (*0-8490-2684-9*) Gordon Pr.

Abbott, Winston O. Come Climb My Hill. 1973. 9.95 (*0-918114-03-9*) Inspiration Conn.

— Come Walk among the Stars. deluxe ed. LC 66-29141. 1966. 9.95 (*0-918114-00-4*) Inspiration Conn.

— Have You Heard the Cricket Song. 1971. 9.95 (*0-918114-02-0*) Inspiration Conn.

— Letters from Chickadee Hill. (Illus.). 1978. 9.95 (*0-918114-04-7*) Inspiration Conn.

— Sing with the Wind. deluxe ed. LC 68-56014. 1968. 9.95 (*0-918114-01-2*) Inspiration Conn.

Abbotto. Seminars in Organic Synthesis. 1992. 109.00 (*88-85104-44-4*) CRC Pr.

Abbotts. Mathematics Today, 1987, Level 1. 1987. 76.00 (*0-15-350041-7*) Harcourt Schl Pubs.

***Abbotts, Adrian.** Naked Spirits: A Journey into Occupied Tibet. LC 97-216755. 288p. 1999. pap. 15.00 (*0-86241-617-5*, Pub. by Canongate Books) Interlink Pub.

Abbotts, I. L., ed. United Kingdom Oil & Gas Fields: Twenty-Five Years Commemorative Volume. (Geological Society Memoirs Ser.: No. 14). (Illus.). 582p. 1991. 134.00 (*0-903317-62-1*, 265, Pub. by Geol Soc Pub Hse) AAPG.

Abbou, A. Lexique Usuel des Nouvelles Technologies de Communicacion: French-English-Arabic. (ARA, ENG & FRE.). 173p. 1986. pap. 79.95 (*0-7859-7135-1*) Fr & Eur.

Abboud, et al. Advances in Internal Medicine, 43. (Illus.). 608p. (C). (gr. 13). 1997. text 79.00 (*0-8151-8317-8*, 21992) Mosby Inc.

Abboud, A. Robert. Money in the Bank: How Safe Is It? 200p. 1988. 24.00 (*1-55623-070-2*, Irwn Prfssnl) McGraw-Hill Prof.

***Abboud, Edward.** Israel's War Against the United States. 288p. (C). 2000. 29.95 (*0-9677915-3-7*) Vox VA.

Abboud, F. F. Elementary Modern Standard Arabic, No. I. 700p. 1996. pap. 29.95 (*0-614-21639-7*, 243) Kazi Pubns.

— Elementary Modern Standard Arabic, No. II. 500p. 1996. pap. 32.95 (*0-614-21640-0*, 244) Kazi Pubns.

Abboud, Francois M., jt. ed. see Shepherd, John T.

***Abboud, Frank E. & Grenon, Brian J., eds.** Photomask Technology & Management. 1999. pap. text 145.00 (*0-8194-3468-X*) SPIE.

Abboud, Frank E., jt. ed. see Grenon, Brian J.

Abboud, Hisham & Chase, Christopher. SuperLab LT: Experimental Software for Psychology Students. (Illus.). 50p. (Orig.). (C). 1997. pap. text 30.00 (*0-9661842-0-3*) Cedrus Corp.

Abboud, P. F., et al. Elementary Modern Standard Arabic, 2 vols., Pt. 1, Lessons 1-30. rev. ed. 656p. 1983. pap. text 31.95 (*0-521-27295-5*) Cambridge U Pr.

— Elementary Modern Standard Arabic, 2 vols., Pt. 2, Lessons 31-45. rev. ed. 496p. 1983. pap. text 28.95 (*0-521-27296-3*) Cambridge U Pr.

Abboushi, W. F. The Unmaking of Palestine. 1992. pap. 12.50 (*0-915597-74-8*) Amana Bks.

Abbri, Ferdinando, jt. ed. see Bensaude-Vincent, Bernadette.

Abbruzzese, G. & Brozzo, P., eds. Grain Growth in Polycrystalline Materials. 936p. 1992. text 283.00 (*0-87849-640-8*, Pub. by Trans T Pub) Enfield Pubs NH.

***Abbruzzetti, Massimo.** Darshan: A Collection of Short Stories. LC 99-94959. 2000. pap. 12.95 (*0-533-13235-5*) Vantage.

Abbruzzetti, Massimo. Encomium. 176p. 1998. pap. 9.95 (*1-56167-461-3*) Am Literary Pr.

Abbs. American Blueprint, Vol. 1. 1997. pap. write for info. (*0-582-22982-0*) Addison-Wesley.

— Blueprint. 1997. pap., student ed. write for info. (*0-582-09912-9*) Addison-Wesley.

— Building Strategies. 1997. pap. write for info. (*0-582-57945-7*) Addison-Wesley.

Abbs & Freebairn. Building Strategies. Date not set. pap. text, wbk. ed. write for info. (*0-582-57994-5*, Pub. by Addison-Wesley) Longman.

— Discoveries Tests Bk. 2. Date not set. pap. text. write for info. (*0-582-03178-8*, Pub. by Addison-Wesley) Longman.

— The Winning Team. 1993. pap. text, wbk. ed. write for info. (*0-582-21834-9*, Pub. by Addison-Wesley) Longman.

Abbs & Freebarin. Discoveries Tests Bk. 3. 1996. pap. text. write for info. (*0-582-03179-6*, Pub. by Addison-Wesley) Longman.

Abbs, jt. auth. see Malpas.

***Abbs, Barbara.** Conservatory: Month-by-Month. (Month-by-Month Gardening Ser.). (Illus.). 1999. pap. 14.95 (*0-7153-0830-0*) D & C Pub.

Abbs, Barbara. French Gardens: A Guide. LC 95-67047. (Gardeners Travel Ser.). 180p. 1994. per. 15.00 (*0-89831-041-5*) Sagapr.

— The Garden Lover's Guide to the Netherlands & Belgium. (Garden Lover's Guides Ser.). (Illus.). 100p. 1999. pap. 19.95 (*1-56898-162-7*) Princeton Arch.

Abbs, Emily. Discoveries Grammar Practice Book 1. 1997. pap. write for info. (*0-582-01823-4*) Addison-Wesley.

Abbs, Peter. A Is for Aesthetic: Essays on Creative & Aesthetic Education. 225p. 1989. pap. 37.95 (*1-85000-425-0*, Falmer Pr) Taylor & Francis.

— The Educational Imperative: A Defence of Socratic & Aesthetic Learning. LC 94-26375. 224p. 1994. 95.00 (*0-7507-0332-6*, Falmer Pr); pap. 34.95 (*0-7507-0333-4*, Falmer Pr) Taylor & Francis.

Abbs, Peter, ed. Living Powers: The Arts in Education. 250p. 1987. pap. 32.95 (*1-85000-168-5*, Falmer Pr) Taylor & Francis.

— The Symbolic Order: A Contemporary Reader on the Arts in Education. 370p. 1989. 85.00 (*1-85000-593-1*, Falmer Pr); pap. 39.95 (*1-85000-594-X*, Falmer Pr) Taylor & Francis.

Abbs, Peter, ed. & intro. see Gosse, Edmund.

Abbs, Susana. Popcorn, Vol. 3. 1996. pap. write for info. (*0-582-25558-9*) Addison-Wesley.

Abby Aldrich Rockefeller Folk Art Center Staff & Watson, Amy Z. The Folk Art Counting Book. (Illus.). 40p. 1992. 12.95 (*0-8109-3306-3*) Abrams.

Abby Communications Staff, ed. 1999-2000 Guide to Manufacturers' Reps. 176p. 1999. pap. 36.00 (*1-893677-04-4*) Abby Communs.

ABC-Clio Companion Staff, jt. auth. see Grossman, Mark.

ABC Educational Partnership Co. Staff. Microeconomics: Principles of Micro Economics Workbook. (C). 1994. 15.08 (*1-884775-01-2*) It Works.

— Microeconomics: Principles of Micro Economics Workbook. 210p. (C). 1995. 15.08 (*1-884775-00-4*) It Works.

ABC News Team Staff & Frady, Marshall. To Save Our Schools, to Save Our Children. LC 85-18798. (Illus.). 220p. 1986. 16.95 (*0-88282-013-3*) New Horizon NJ.

ABC Staff. Culturewatch. (Illus.). 160p. 1994. pap. text 27.93 (*0-13-137621-7*) P-H.

ABC Staff. Entwicklungsgeschichte der Erde Mit Einem ABC der Geologie, 2 vols., Set. (GER.). 800p. 1970. 35.00 (*0-8288-6532-9*, M-7363) Fr & Eur.

— Fach Lexikon ABC Automatisierung. (GER.). 739p. 1976. 45.00 (*0-8288-5692-3*, M7377) Fr & Eur.

— Fachlexikon ABC Biologie. 2nd ed. (GER.). 1972. 95.00 (*0-8288-6391-1*, M-7378) Fr & Eur.

— Fachlexikon ABC Chemie, 2 vols., Set. deluxe ed. (GER.). 1590p. 1976. 135.00 (*0-8288-5694-X*, M7379) Fr & Eur.

— Fachlexikon ABC Mathematik. (GER.). 624p. 1978. 75.00 (*0-8288-5242-1*, M7381) Fr & Eur.

— Fachlexikon ABC Physik, 2 vols., Set. (GER.). 1784p. 1974. 175.00 (*0-8288-6045-9*, M7383) Fr & Eur.

— Fachlexikon ABC Technik und Naturwissenschaft, Vols. 1 & 2. (GER.). 1970. 95.00 (*0-8288-6536-1*, M-7384) Fr & Eur.

ABC Staff & Duffy, Patricia. Focus on Innovators & Innovations: ABC News ESL Video Library. 160p. 1993. pap. text 27.93 incl. VHS (*0-13-007105-6*) P-H.

ABC Staff & Henly. Focus on American Culture. 160p. (C). 1993. pap. text 27.93 (*0-13-007113-7*) P-H.

ABC Staff & McPartland. Focus on Health. 160p. (C). 1993. pap. text 27.93 (*0-13-007121-8*) P-H.

ABC Staff & Stempleski, Susan. Focus on Environment. 160p. (C). 1993. pap. text 27.93 (*0-13-007097-1*) P-H.

ABC Staff, jt. auth. see Arcario, Paul J.

ABC Task Force Staff & Derman-Sparks, Louise. Anti-Bias Curriculum: Tools for Empowering Young Children. LC 88-63731. 149p. 1989. pap. 7.00 (*0-935989-20-X*, NAEYC #242) Natl Assn Child Ed.

Abcarian. Literature: The Human Experience. 7th ed. 1998. pap. text, teacher ed. 10.00 (*0-312-16656-7*) St Martin.

— Literature of Human Experience. 6th ed. 1993. pap. text 5.00 (*0-312-08409-9*) St Martin.

***Abcarian & Klotz.** Literature: Human Experience Shorter. 7th ed. 1999. pap. text 28.95 (*0-312-20691-7*) St Martin.

Abcarian, Richard & Klotz, Marvin. Literature: The Human Experience, Shorter with Essays. 5th ed. LC 90-71627. 960p. (C). 1991. pap. text, teacher ed. 2.66 (*0-312-06740-2*) St Martin.

Abcarian, Richard & Klotz, Marvin, eds. Literature: Reading & Writing, the Human Experience. 7th ed. LC 97-65206. 1460p. 1997. pap. text 50.95 (*0-312-15311-2*) St Martin.

— Literature: The Human Experience. 2nd rev. ed. 934p. (C). 1984. teacher ed. write for info. (*0-318-57731-3*) St Martin.

Abd al Ghani Abd al Khaliq. Hujjiyat al Sunnah: "The Legal Authoritativeness of the Sunnah" 2nd ed. (Silsilat Qadaya al Fikr al Islami Ser.: No. 1). (ARA.). 600p. (C). 1994. pap. 10.00 (*0-912463-24-4*); text 19.00 (*0-912463-23-6*) IIIT VA.

Abd al Hamid, Muhsin. Al Islam wa al Tanmiyah al Ijtima'iyah: (Islam & Social Development) 2nd ed. (Silsilat Qadaya al Fikr al Islami Ser.: No. 3). (ARA.). 153p. 1992. pap. 5.00 (*1-56564-049-7*) IIIT VA.

Abd al-Jabbar Danner. The Islamic Tradition: An Introduction. (C). 1992. text 29.95 (*0-933511-19-1*) Kazi Pubns.

Abd-Al-Kahir Ibn-Tahir ibn-Mahammad. Moslem Schisms & Sects: Being the History of the Various Philosophic Systems Developed in Islam. Seelye, Kate C., tr. LC 75-158216. (Columbia University. Oriental Studies: No. 15). 1920. 20.00 (*0-404-50505-8*) AMS Pr.

Abd Al-Monem, Mufid Al-Guindi. Spanish - Arabic Dictionary of Verbs, Grammar, & Conversation Terms (Diccionario Espanol-Arabe de Verbos, Gramatica y Temas de Conversacion. 2nd ed. (ARA & SPA.). 368p. 1974. 24.95 (*0-8288-4016-4*, S50423) Fr & Eur.

An Asterisk (*) at the beginning of an entry indicates that the title is appearing for the first time.

A

Abd Al-Qadir Al-Jilani. The Removal of Cares: Jala'Al-Khawatir. unabridged ed. Holland, Muhtar, tr. from ARA. LC 97-70846. 308p. 1997. pap. 24.95 (*1-882216-13-X*) Al-Baz Pub.
— Sufficient Provision for Seekers of the Path of Truth: (Al-Ghunya Li-Talibi Tariq Al-Haqq) unabridged ed. Holland, Muhtar, tr. from ARA. LC 95-75589. 169p. 1997. pap. 18.00 (*1-882216-11-3*) Al-Baz Pub.
— Sufficient Provision for Seekers of the Path of Truth Vol. 1: (Al-Ghunya Li-Talibi Tariq Al-Haqq) unabridged ed. Holland, Muhtar, tr. from ARA. LC 95-75589. 454p. 1997. pap. 28.00 (*1-882216-07-5*) Al-Baz Pub.
— Sufficient Provision for Seekers of the Path of Truth Vol. 2: (Al-Ghunya Li-Talibi Tariq Al-Haqq) unabridged ed. Holland, Muhtar, tr. from ARA. LC 95-75589. 318p. 1997. pap. 24.00 (*1-882216-08-3*) Al-Baz Pub.
— Sufficient Provision for Seekers of the Path of Truth Vol. 3: (Al-Ghunya Li-Talibi Tariq Al-Haqq) unabridged ed. Holland, Muhtar, tr. from ARA. LC 95-75589. 368p. 1997. pap. 26.00 (*1-882216-09-1*) Al-Baz Pub.
— Sufficient Provision for Seekers of the Path of Truth Vol. 4: (Al-Ghunya Li-Talibi Tariq Al-Haqq) unabridged ed. Holland, Muhtar, tr. from ARA. LC 95-75589. 410p. 1997. pap. 27.00 (*1-882216-10-5*) Al-Baz Pub.

Abd al-Rahman al-Jami. The Precious Pearl. Heer, Nicholas L., tr. from ARA. LC 78-12607. 237p. (C). 1992. pap. text 18.95 (*0-7914-1490-6*) State U NY Pr.

Abd al-Rahman Isma'il. Folk Medicine in Modern Egypt: Being the Relevant Parts of the Tibb al-Rukka, or Old Wives' Medicine, of 'Abd al-Rahman Isma'il. LC 77-87651. (Anthropology Ser.). (Illus.). reprint ed. 32.50 (*0-404-16407-2*) AMS Pr.

Abd-al-Salam, Al-Izz B. Al-Fitan wa-al-Balaya wa-al-Mihan wa-al-Razaya. (Writings of al-'Izz bin Abd-al-Salam Ser.). (ARA.). 32p. (Orig.). 1995. pap. 1.95 (*1-57547-223-6*) Dar Al-Fikr.
— Maqasid al-Salah. (Writings of Al-'Izz bin 'Abd-al-Salam Ser.). (ARA.). 48p. (Orig.). 1995. pap. 2.95 (*1-57547-226-0*) Dar Al-Fikr.
— Maqasid al-Sawm. (Writings of al-'Izz bin Abd-al-Salam Ser.). (ARA.). 64p. (Orig.). 1995. pap. 2.95 (*1-57547-224-4*) Dar Al-Fikr.

Abd-al-Salam, Al-Izz I. Ma'na Al-Iman Wa-al-Islam. (Writings of Al-'Izz ibn 'Abd-al-Salam Ser.). (ARA.). 32p. (Orig.). 1995. pap. 1.95 (*1-57547-225-2*) Dar Al-Fikr.

Abd al-Salam Nadvi. Umar Bin Abd Al-Aziz. 200p. (YA). (gr. 7-12). 1985. pap. 9.95 (*1-56744-406-7*) Kazi Pubns.

Abd al-Wahhab ibn Ali, Taj. Kitab Mu'id An-ni'am Wa-Mubid An-Niqam: The Restorer of Favours & the Restrainer of Chastisements. LC 78-53829. (Luzac's Semitic Text & Translation Ser.: Vol. 18). 1978. reprint ed. 45.00 (*0-404-11291-9*) AMS Pr.

Abd-al-Wahid Ulwani. Hadiqat al-Iman, 12 vols., Set. (J). 1993. pap. 14.95 (*1-57547-168-X*) Dar Al-Fikr.
— Hadiqat al-Iman, Vol. 1. (J). 1993. pap. write for info. (*1-57547-169-8*) Dar Al-Fikr.
— Hadiqat al-Iman, Vol. 2. (J). 1993. pap. write for info. (*1-57547-170-1*) Dar Al-Fikr.
— Hadiqat al-Iman, Vol. 3. (J). 1993. pap. write for info. (*1-57547-171-X*) Dar Al-Fikr.
— Hadiqat al-Iman, Vol. 4. (J). 1993. pap. write for info. (*1-57547-172-8*) Dar Al-Fikr.
— Hadiqat al-Iman, Vol. 5. (J). 1993. pap. write for info. (*1-57547-173-6*) Dar Al-Fikr.
— Hadiqat al-Iman, Vol. 6. (J). 1993. pap. write for info. (*1-57547-174-4*) Dar Al-Fikr.
— Hadiqat al-Iman, Vol. 7. (J). 1993. pap. write for info. (*1-57547-175-2*) Dar Al-Fikr.
— Hadiqat al-Iman, Vol. 8. (J). 1993. pap. write for info. (*1-57547-176-0*) Dar Al-Fikr.
— Hadiqat al-Iman, Vol. 9. (J). 1993. pap. write for info. (*1-57547-177-9*) Dar Al-Fikr.
— Hadiqat al-Iman, Vol. 10. (J). 1993. pap. write for info. (*1-57547-178-7*) Dar Al-Fikr.
— Hadiqat al-Iman, Vol. 11. (J). 1993. pap. write for info. (*1-57547-179-5*) Dar Al-Fikr.
— Hadiqat al-Iman, Vol. 12. (J). 1993. pap. write for info. (*1-57547-180-9*) Dar Al-Fikr.
— Mudhakkarat al-'Amm Sabur, 12 vols., Set. (J). 1993. pap. 16.95 (*1-57547-184-1*) Dar Al-Fikr.
— Mudhakkarat al-'Amm Sabur, Vol. 1. (J). 1993. pap. write for info. (*1-57547-185-X*) Dar Al-Fikr.
— Mudhakkarat al-'Amm Sabur, Vol. 2. (J). 1993. pap. write for info. (*1-57547-186-8*) Dar Al-Fikr.
— Mudhakkarat al-'Amm Sabur, Vol. 3. (J). 1993. pap. write for info. (*1-57547-187-6*) Dar Al-Fikr.
— Mudhakkarat al-'Amm Sabur, Vol. 4. (J). 1993. pap. write for info. (*1-57547-188-4*) Dar Al-Fikr.
— Mudhakkarat al-'Amm Sabur, Vol. 5. (J). 1993. pap. write for info. (*1-57547-189-2*) Dar Al-Fikr.
— Mudhakkarat al-'Amm Sabur, Vol. 6. (J). 1993. pap. write for info. (*1-57547-190-6*) Dar Al-Fikr.
— Mudhakkarat al-'Amm Sabur, Vol. 7. (J). 1993. pap. write for info. (*1-57547-191-4*) Dar Al-Fikr.
— Mudhakkarat al-'Amm Sabur, Vol. 8. (J). 1993. pap. write for info. (*1-57547-192-2*) Dar Al-Fikr.
— Mudhakkarat al-'Amm Sabur, Vol. 9. (J). 1993. pap. write for info. (*1-57547-193-0*) Dar Al-Fikr.
— Mudhakkarat al-'Amm Sabur, Vol. 10. (J). 1993. pap. write for info. (*1-57547-194-9*) Dar Al-Fikr.
— Mudhakkarat al-'Amm Sabur, Vol. 11. (J). 1993. pap. write for info. (*1-57547-195-7*) Dar Al-Fikr.
— Mudhakkarat al-'Amm Sabur, Vol. 12. (J). 1993. pap. write for info. (*1-57547-196-5*) Dar Al-Fikr.
— Uhibbu al-Madrasah, Vol. 2. (J). 1992. pap. write for info. (*1-57547-150-7*) Dar Al-Fikr.
— Uhibbu al-Madrasah, Vol. 3. (J). 1992. pap. write for info. (*1-57547-151-5*) Dar Al-Fikr.
— Uhibbu al-Madrasah, Vol. 4. (J). 1992. pap. write for info. (*1-57547-152-3*) Dar Al-Fikr.
— Uhibbu al-Madrasah, Vol. 5. (J). 1992. pap. write for info. (*1-57547-153-1*) Dar Al-Fikr.
— Uhibbu al-Madrasah, Vol. 6. (J). 1992. pap. write for info. (*1-57547-154-X*) Dar Al-Fikr.
— Uhibbu al-Madrasah, Vol. 7. (J). 1992. pap. write for info. (*1-57547-155-8*) Dar Al-Fikr.
— Uhibbu al-Madrasah, Vol. 8. (J). 1992. pap. write for info. (*1-57547-156-6*) Dar Al-Fikr.
— Uhibbu al-Madrasah, Vol. 9. (J). 1992. pap. write for info. (*1-57547-157-4*) Dar Al-Fikr.
— Uhibbu al-Madrasah, Vol. 10. (J). 1992. pap. write for info. (*1-57547-158-2*) Dar Al-Fikr.
— Uhibbu al-Madrasah, Vol. 11. (J). 1992. pap. write for info. (*1-57547-159-0*) Dar Al-Fikr.
— Uhibbu al-Madrasah, Vol. 12. (J). 1992. pap. 13.95 (*1-57547-160-4*) Dar Al-Fikr.

Abd-El-Hafiz, Salwa K. & Basili, Victor R. A Knowledge-Based Approach to Program Understanding. LC 95-4876. (Kluwer International Series in Engineering & Computer Science: No. 325). 119p. (C). 1995. text 91.00 (*0-7923-9605-7*) Kluwer Academic.

Abd El-Shahid, Marguerite N. Regional Economic Development: Theories & Strategies for Developing Countries. LC 96-129684. 49p. 1994. pap. 10.00 (*0-86602-304-6*, Sage Prdcls Pr) Sage.

Abd-El-Wahab, M. F., ed. Schistosomiasis in Egypt. 256p. 1982. 142.00 (*0-8493-6220-2*, RC182, CRC Reprint) Franklin.

Abd-El-Wahed, A. M. Automotive Engineering Dictionary: English-French-German-Arabic. (ARA, ENG, FRE & GER.). 436p. 1978. 75.00 (*0-8288-4864-5*, M9765) Fr & Eur.
— Chemical Technology Dictionary: English, French-German-Arabic. (ARA, ENG, FRE & GER.). 383p. 1974. 75.00 (*0-8288-5975-2*, M9759) Fr & Eur.
— Dictionary of Plastics Technology. El-Desouki, Handi Y., ed. (ARA, ENG, FRE & GER.). 1980. 75.00 (*0-8288-0731-0*, M9754) Fr & Eur.
— Iron & Steel Industry Dictionary. (ARA, ENG, FRE & GER.). 441p. 1974. 75.00 (*0-8288-6055-6*, M9760) Fr & Eur.
— Machine Tools Dictionary: English-French-German-Arabic. (ARA, ENG, FRE & GER.). 334p. 1977. 75.00 (*0-8288-5498-X*, M9757) Fr & Eur.
— Metal Forming Dictionary. (ARA, ENG, FRE & GER.). 386p. 1978. 75.00 (*0-8288-5251-0*, M9755) Fr & Eur.
— Radio & Television Dictionary. (ARA, ENG, FRE & GER.). 320p. 1980. 75.00 (*0-8288-0185-1*, M9762) Fr & Eur.
— Refrigeration & Air Conditioning Dictionary. (ARA, ENG, FRE & GER.). 395p. 1979. 75.00 (*0-8288-4833-5*, M9756) Fr & Eur.
— Technical Dictionary: English-French-German-Arabic. 297p. 1981. 29.95 (*0-7859-6880-6*, 3361000297) Fr & Eur.

Abd-El-Wahed, A. M., ed. see Zimaity, Muhammad A.

Abd-Elfattah, Anwar-Saad A. & Wechsler, Andrew S., eds. Purines & Myocardial Protection. (Developments in Cardiovascular Medicine Ser.: Vol. 161). 592p. (C). 1995. text 272.50 (*0-7923-3831-6*) Kluwer Academic.

Abd-ru-shin. En la Luz de la Verdad Tomo I: Mensaje del Grail. (SPA.). 226p. 1968. 12.00 (*0-317-05738-3*, Pub. by Stiftung Gralsbotschaft) Cambridge U Pr.
— En la Luz de la Verdad, Tomo II: Mensaje del Grail. (SPA.). 455p. 1975. 17.00 (*3-87860-057-7*, Pub. by Stiftung Gralsbotschaft) Cambridge U Pr.
— En la Luz de la Verdad, Tomo III: Mensaje del Grail. (SPA.). 501p. 1984. 17.00 (*3-87860-089-5*, Pub. by Stiftung Gralsbotschaft) Cambridge U Pr.
— Im Lichte der Wahrheit, Band I: Gralsbotschaft. (GER.). 220p. 1990. reprint ed. 12.00 (*3-87860-103-4*, Pub. by Stiftung Gralsbotschaft) Cambridge U Pr.
— Im Lichte der Wahrheit, Band II: Gralsbotschaft. (GER.). 432p. 1990. reprint ed. 17.00 (*3-87860-104-2*, Pub. by Stiftung Gralsbotschaft) Cambridge U Pr.
— Im Lichte der Wahrheit, Band III: Gralsbotschaft. (GER.). 459p. 1990. reprint ed. 17.00 (*3-87860-105-0*, Pub. by Stiftung Gralsbotschaft) Cambridge U Pr.
— Im Lichte der Wahrheit, Einbandige Ausgabe: Gralsbotschaft. (GER.). 1246p. 1992. reprint ed. 40.00 (*3-87860-203-0*, Pub. by Stiftung Gralsbotschaft) Cambridge U Pr.
— Im Lichte der Wahrheit Taschenbuch, Band I: Gralsbotschaft. (GER.). 219p. 1989. reprint ed. pap. 7.50 (*3-87860-172-7*, Pub. by Stiftung Gralsbotschaft) Cambridge U Pr.
— In the Light of Truth: Grail Message, 3 vols. 1079p. 1990. pap. 22.00 (*3-87860-189-1*, Pub. by Stiftung Gralsbotschaft) Cambridge U Pr.
— In the Light of Truth: The Grail Message, 3 vols., Set. 10th ed. 1062p. 1995. reprint ed. 39.00 (*1-57461-006-6*) Grail Found Pr.
— In the Light of Truth: The Grail Message, 3 Vol, Set. 17th ed. LC BP605.B43232. 1079p. 1995. reprint ed. pap. 29.00 (*1-57461-003-1*) Grail Found Pr.
— In the Light of Truth: The Grail Message, Vol. 1. 17th ed. LC BP605.B43232. 216p. 1995. reprint ed. pap. 12.00 (*1-57461-000-7*) Grail Found Pr.
— In the Light of Truth, Vol. I: The Grail Message. 1971. pap. 7.50 (*3-87860-173-5*) Grail Fndtn-Amer.
— Prayers, Given to Mankind Abd-Ru-Shin. 1966. pap. 5.00 (*3-87860-138-7*) Grail Fndtn-Amer.
— The Ten Commandments of God & the Lord's Prayer. 7th ed. LC BV4655.A2313 1995. 72p. 1995. reprint ed. 14.00 (*1-57461-007-4*) Grail Found Pr.
— The Ten Commandments of God & the Lord's Prayer. 8th ed. LC BV4655.A2313. 72p. 1995. reprint ed. pap. 9.00 (*1-57461-004-X*) Grail Found Pr.

Abdal-aziz, Aliyah F., ed. see Khalid, Anas.

Abdal-Haqq, Ismat. Professional Development Schools: A Directory of Projects in the United States. 2nd ed. 1995. 18.00 (*0-89333-130-9*) AACTE.
— Professional Development Schools: Weighing the Evidence. LC 97-21137. (Critical Issues in Teacher Education Ser.). 96p. 1997. 39.95 (*0-8039-6349-1*); pap. 16.95 (*0-8039-6350-5*) Corwin Pr.
— Resources on Professional Development Schools: An Annotated Bibliography & Resource Guide. 2nd ed. LC 97-76790. 1997. 18.00 (*0-89333-158-9*) AACTE.

Abdalati, Hammudah. The Family Structure in Islam. LC 77-79635. 1976. pap. 8.50 (*0-685-00342-6*) Am Trust Pubns.
— Islam in Focus. 211p. pap. write for info. (*1-882837-17-7*) W A M Y Intl.
— Islam in Focus. 2nd ed. LC 75-4382. (Illus.). 211p. 1975. pap. 5.00 (*0-89259-135-8*) Am Trust Pubns.

Abdalla, E. Two D-Gravity in Non-Critical Strings: Discrete & Contiuum Approaches. LC 94-7928. (Lecture Notes in Physics Ser.: Vol. 20). 1994. write for info. (*3-540-57805-6*) Spr-Verlag.
— Two D-Gravity in Non-Critical Strings: Discrete & Contiuum Approaches. LC 94-7928. (Lecture Notes in Physics Ser.: Vol. 20). 1994. 59.95 (*0-387-57805-6*) Spr-Verlag.

Abdalla, Elcio, et al. Non Perturbative Methods in Two Dimensional Quantum Field Theory. 700p. 1991. text 109.00 (*981-02-0462-0*); pap. text 61.00 (*981-02-0463-9*) World Scientific Pub.

Abdalla, Elcio, jt. ed. see Abdalla, Maria C.

Abdalla, Ismail & Sconyers, David, eds. Perspectives & Challenges in the Development of Sudanese Studies. LC 93-27049. 308p. 1993. text 99.95 (*0-7734-9333-6*) E Mellen.

Abdalla, Ismail H. Islam, Medicine, & Practitioners in Northern Nigeria. LC 97-1343. (Studies in African Health & Medicine: Vol. 6). 192p. 1997. text 79.95 (*0-7734-8655-0*) E Mellen.

Abdalla, Maria C. & Abdalla, Elcio, eds. Two Dimensional Models & String Theories. 228p. (C). 1988. text 77.00 (*9971-5-0580-0*) World Scientific Pub.

Abdallah, Anouar, et al. For Rushdie: A Collection of Essays by 100 Arabic & Muslim Writers. LC 93-46999. 1994. 27.50 (*0-8076-1354-1*); pap. 14.95 (*0-8076-1355-X*) Braziller.

Abdallah, Areski N. The Logic of Partial Information. LC 93-49421. (EATCS Monographs on Theoretical Computer Science). xxv, 715p. 1995. 98.00 (*0-387-56583-3*) Spr-Verlag.

Abdallah, Chaouki T., ed. Robot Control: Dynamics, Motion Planning, Analysis. LC 92-5764. (Illus.). 552p. (C). 1992. text 89.95 (*0-7803-0404-7*, PC0299-8) Inst Electrical.

Abdallah, Fadel. Iqra' Arabic Reader, Vol. 3. unabridged ed. Busool, Assad et al, eds. (Illus.). 170p. (J). (gr. 6-8). 1995. text 12.00 (*1-56316-010-2*) Iqra Intl Ed Fdtn.
— Iqra' Arabic Reader Workbook, Vol. I. unabridged ed. Busool, Assad & Tahrawi, Khalil, eds. (Illus.). 80p. (J). (gr. 1-3). 1993. 8.00 (*1-56316-004-8*) Iqra Intl Ed Fdtn.
— Iqra' Arabic Reader Workbook, Vol. 3. unabridged ed. Busool, Assad et al, eds. (Illus.). 100p. (J). (gr. 6-9). 1995. 8.00 (*1-56316-011-0*) Iqra Intl Ed Fdtn.
— Let's Read & Write Arabic, Vol. 1. 2nd ed. Busool, Assad & Tahrawi, Khalil, eds. 4p. (J). (gr. 1-5). 1996. reprint ed. pap. 4.00 (*1-56316-005-6*) Iqra Intl Ed Fdtn.
— Let's Read & Write Arabic, Vol. 2. 2nd ed. Busool, Assad & Tahrawi, Khalil, eds. (J). (gr. 1-5). 1996. reprint ed. pap. 4.00 (*1-56316-006-4*) Iqra Intl Ed Fdtn.

Abdallah, Fadel, ed. see Fannoun, Kathy.

Abdallah, Fadel, ed. see Ghazi, Abidullah & Ghazi, Tasneema K.

Abdallah, Fadel, ed. see Ghazi, Tasneema.

Abdallah, Fadel, ed. see Taimiyah, Sheikh A.

Abdallah, Fadel I. Iqra' Arabic Reader. Busool, Assad N. & Tahrawi, Khalil, eds. (Arabic Readers Ser.). (Illus.). 124p. 1995. pap. text 12.00 (*1-56316-008-0*) Iqra Intl Ed Fdtn.
— Iqra Arabic Reader 4. unabridged ed. Baugh, Carolyn, ed. LC 94-73184. (ARA.). 224p. (J). (gr. 4-6). 1997. pap. text 12.00 (*1-56316-013-7*) Iqra Intl Ed Fdtn.

***Abdallah, Fadel I.** Iqra Arabic Reader 4 Workbook, Vol. 4. Ghazi, Abidullah, ed. (Illus.). 72p. (YA). (gr. 6-8). 1998. pap. 8.00 (*1-56316-024-2*) Iqra Intl Ed Fdtn.

Abdallah, Fadel I. Iqra' Arabic Reader 2 Workbook. Busool, Assad N. & Ghazi, Abidullah, eds. LC 94-73184. (ARA & ENG., Illus.). 91p. (J). (gr. 4-5). 1998. wbk. ed. 12.00 (*1-56316-007-2*) Iqra Intl Ed Fdtn.

Abdallah, Fadel I., ed. from ARA. Our Book of Du'a' for Children. (Illus.). 25p. (Orig.). (J). (ps-1). 1994. pap. 5.00 (*1-56316-317-9*) Iqra Intl Ed Fdtn.

Abdallah, Hasan, jt. auth. see QURASHI, AL.

Abdallah, Hassan. A Dictionary of International Relations & Conference Terminology. (ARA & ENG.). 654p. 1982. 85.00 (*0-8288-2248-4*, F53990) Fr & Eur.
— A Dictionary of International Relations & Conference Terminology. (ARA & ENG.). 654p. 1982. 49.95 (*0-86685-298-0*, LDL2980, Pub. by Librairie du Liban) Intl Bk Ctr.

Abdallah, Umar F. The Islamic Struggle in Syria. LC 82-14210. 1983. 24.95 (*0-933782-10-1*) Mizan Pr.

Abdallah, Wagdy M. Internal Accountability: An International Emphasis. LC 84-2662. (Research for Business Decisions Ser.: No. 68). (Illus.). 130p. reprint ed. pap. 40.30 (*0-8357-1555-8*, 207035500088) Bks Demand.
— International Transfer Pricing Policies: Decision-Making Guidelines for Multinational Companies. LC 88-25258. 176p. 1989. 59.95 (*0-89930-294-7*, ATR, Quorum Bks) Greenwood.

***Abdallah, Wagdy M.** Managing Multinationals in the Middle East: Accounting & Tax Issues. LC 00-23932. 250p. 2000. 67.00 (*1-56720-267-5*, Q267, Quorum Bks) Greenwood.

Abdallah, Yohanna B. Yao: The Chiikala Cha Wayao. Sanderson, M., tr. 132p. 1973. 45.00 (*0-7146-2462-4*, BHA-02462, Pub. by F Cass Pubs) Intl Spec Bk.

Abdallatif. Abdallatif's Eines Arabischen Arztes, Denkwurdigkeiten Egyptens. xii, 348p. reprint ed. write for info. (*0-318-71477-9*) Lubrecht & Cramer.

Abdeen, Adnan. Dictionary of Accounting & Finance. (ARA & ENG.). 1980. 39.95 (*0-86685-275-1*, LDL2751, Pub. by Librairie du Liban) Intl Bk Ctr.

Abdeen, Adnan M. English-Arabic Dictionary for Accounting & Finance. 1980. 69.95 (*0-8288-0073-1*, M15620) Fr & Eur.

Abdel-Aal, H. K., et al, eds. Petroleum Economics & Engineering. 2nd ed. (Illus.). 456p. 1992. text 210.00 (*0-8247-8428-6*) Dekker.

Abdel-Aal, Hussein K. & Schmelzlee, Robert. Petroleum Economics & Engineering: An Introduction. LC 75-213. (Chemical Processing & Engineering Ser.: No. 6). (Illus.). 431p. reprint ed. pap. 133.70 (*0-7837-0917-X*, 204122200019) Bks Demand.

Abdel-Al, Mohamed. Weavers of Death. LC 96-207918. 158p. 1996. pap. 12.95 (*1-85756-285-2*, Pub. by Janus Pubng) Paul & Co Pubs.

Abdel-Aleem, Salah & Lowe, James E., eds. Cardiac Metabolism in Health & Disease. LC 97-42768. (Developments in Molecular & Cellular Biochemistry Ser.). 202p. 1998. 225.00 (*0-7923-8104-1*) Kluwer Academic.

Abdel-Aziz, M. Nuclear Proliferation & National Security. 238p. 1980. 21.95 (*0-318-37212-6*) Asia Bk Corp.

Abdel-Barr, Hussein A. The Market Structure of International Oil with Special Reference to the Organization of Petroleum Exporting Countries. Bruchey, Stuart, ed. LC 78-22653. (Energy in the American Economy Ser.). (Illus.). 1979. lib. bdg. 33.95 (*0-405-11958-5*) Ayer.

***Abdel-Fattah, Nabil, et al.** Road Freight & Privisation. 144p. 1999. 61.95 (*0-7546-1103-5*) Ashgate Pub Co.

Abdel-Fattah, Reda A. A Physician's Guide for Expert Witnessing. 175p. 1993. 105.00 (*1-883865-01-8*) Biomed Pr.
— Preventing TMJ & OS6's Injuries in Dental Practice. 352p. 1993. 207.00 (*0-8493-4725-4*) CRC Pr.

Abdel-Hamid, Tarek. Software Project Dynamics: An Integrated Approach. 288p. 1991. 52.60 (*0-13-822040-9*) P-H.

Abdel-Haq, Mohammed, jt. auth. see Al-Omar, Fuad.

Abdel, Jabbour & Nour, Jabbour A. Dictionnaire Francais-Arabe: Al Manhal. (ARA & FRE.). 1100p. 1985. 45.00 (*0-86685-415-0*, LD4153) Intl Bk Ctr.

***Abdel-Jaouad, Hedi.** Fugues de Barbarie: Les Ecrivains Maghrebins et le Surrealisme. (Illus.). 251p. 1998. pap. text 39.95 (*0-9665360-0-2*) Les Mains Secret.

Abdel-Kader. Life Personality & Writings of Al-Junayd. (Gibb Collection). 1962. pap. 20.00 (*0-7189-0223-8*, Pub. by Aris & Phillips) David Brown.

Abdel-Kader, Magdy. Investment Decisions in Advanced Manufacturing Technology: A Fuzzy Set Theory Approach. 16p. 1998. text 76.95 (*1-84014-561-7*) Ashgate Pub Co.

Abdel-Khalek, Goudal, jt. ed. see Tignor, Robert L.

Abdel-khalik, A. Rashad. Financial Reporting by Private Companies: Analysis & Diagnosis. LC 83-81884. (Financial Accounting Standards Board Research Report Ser.). (Illus.). 155p. (Orig.). 1983. pap. 15.00 (*0-910065-17-9*) Finan Acct Found.

Abdel-Khalik, Rashad. Blackwell Encyclopedic Dictionary of Accounting. LC 96-33131. 270p. 1997. 110.00 (*1-55786-941-3*) Blackwell Pubs.
— Blackwell Encyclopedic Dictionary of Accounting. LC 98-26080. (Blackwell Encyclopedia of Management Ser.). 320p. 1999. reprint ed. pap. 29.95 (*0-631-21187-X*) Blackwell Pubs.

Abdel-khalik, Rashad. Empirical Research in Accounting: A Methodological Viewpoint, Vol. 4. Ajinkya, Bipin B., ed. (Studies in Accounting Education). 125p. 1979. 12.00 (*0-86539-032-0*) Am Accounting.

Abdel-Khalik, Rashad, ed. Internal Control & the Impact of the Foreign Corrupt Practices Act. LC 82-17480. (University of Florida Accounting Ser.: No. 12). (Illus.). 239p. reprint ed. pap. 74.10 (*0-7837-4971-6*, 204463700004) Bks Demand.

Abdel-khalik, Rashad & Keller, Thomas F. Earnings or Cash Flows: An Experiment on Functional Fixation & the Valuation of the Firm. (Studies in Accounting Research: Vol. 16). 101p. 1979. 12.00 (*0-86539-028-2*) Am Accounting.

Abdel-Khalik, Rashad & Solomon, Ira, eds. Research Opportunities in Auditing: The Second Decade. 216p. 1989. 15.00 (*0-86539-070-3*) Am Accounting.

Abdel-Khalik, Rashad, ed. see Round Table Conference on Government Regulation of.

Abdel-Magid, Ahmed F., ed. Reductions in Organic Synthesis: Recent Advances & Practical Applications, Vol. 641. LC 96-26217. (Symposium Ser.: No. 641). (Illus.). 240p. 1996. text 89.95 (*0-8412-3381-0*, Pub. by Am Chemical) OUP.

Abdel-Magid, Isam M., et al. Modeling Methods for Environmental Engineers. LC 96-4980. 496p. 1996. disk 85.00 (*1-56670-172-4*, L1172) Lewis Pubs.

Abdel Magid, Isam Mohamed, see Rowe, Donald R. & Mohamed Abdel Magid, Isam.

Abdel-Malek, Kamal. America in an Arab Mirror: Images of America in Arabic Travel. text 45.00 (*0-312-22963-1*) St Martin.

An Asterisk (*) at the beginning of an entry indicates that the title is appearing for the first time.

A

Abdel-Malek, Kamal. Muhammad in the Modern Egyptian Popular Ballad. LC 95-18832. (Studies in Arabic Literature: Vol. 19). 1995. 93.00 (*90-04-10217-5*) Brill Academic Pubs.

— A Study of the Vernacular Poetry of Ahmad Fu'ad Nigm. LC 90-15065. (Studies in Arabic Literature: Vol. 12). 177p. 1990. 68.00 (*90-04-08933-0*) Brill Academic Pubs.

***Abdel-Malek, Kamal & Hallaq, Wael B., eds.** Tradition, Modernity, & Post modernity in Arabis Literature: Essay in Honor of Professor Issa F. Boullata. 580p. 2000. 119.00 (*90-04-11763-6*) Brill Academic Pubs.

***Abdel-Malek, Kamal & Jacobson, David C., eds.** Israeli & Palestinian Identities in History & Literature. LC 99-10907. 352p. 1999. text 49.95 (*0-312-21978-4*) St Martin.

Abdel-Malek, Kamal, jt. auth. see Asani, Ali S.

Abdel-Malek, Zaki N. The Closed List Classes of Colloquial Egyptian Arabic. (Janua Linguarum, Ser. Practica: No. 128). 240p. (Orig.). 1972. pap. text 76.15 (*90-279-2322-1*) Mouton.

Abdel-Massih, Ernest T. Advanced Moroccan Arabic. LC 74-161877. 244p. (C). 1974. pap. text 25.00 (*0-932098-08-8*) UM Ctr MENAS.

— A Computerized Lexicon of Tamazight: Berber Dialect of AYT Seghrouchen. LC 77-32220. (BER.). (C). 1971. pap. text 20.00 (*0-932098-06-1*) UM Ctr MENAS.

— A Course in Spoken Tamazight: Berber Dialects of the Middle Atlas. LC 79-32218. (C). 1970. pap. text 25.00 (*0-932098-04-5*) UM Ctr MENAS.

— An Introduction to Egyptian Arabic. rev. ed. LC 75-24784. (C). 1981. pap. text 25.00 (*0-932098-09-6*) UM Ctr MENAS.

— An Introduction to Moroccan Arabic. rev. ed. LC 74-154239. 1982. pap. text 25.00 (*0-932098-07-X*) UM Ctr MENAS.

— The Life & Miracles of Pope Kirillos VI. 139p. (Orig.). 1982. pap. text 3.00 (*0-932098-20-7*) St Mark Coptic Orthodox.

— A Reference Grammar of Tamazight. LC 72-32219. (C). 1970. pap. text 20.00 (*0-932098-05-3*) UM Ctr MENAS.

— A Sample Lexicon of Pan-Arabic. LC 75-18985. (ARA.). 1975. pap. text 10.00 (*0-932098-10-X*) UM Ctr MENAS.

— Tamazight Verb Stucture: A Generative Approach. LC 72-633892. (African Ser.: Vol. 2). (Orig.). 1968. pap. text 19.00 (*0-87750-160-2*) Res Inst Inner Asian Studies.

Abdel-Massih, Ernest T., et al, trs. from COP. The Divine Liturgy of St. Basil the Great. 257p. 1982. pap. 7.00 (*0-932098-19-3*) St Mark Coptic Orthodox.

Abdel-Massih, Ernest T., et al. A Comprehensive Study of Egyptian Arabic: A Reference Grammar of Egyptian Arabic: Grammatical & Linguistic Terms in Dictionary Form, Vol. III. LC 76-24957. (C). 1979. pap. text 25.00 (*0-932098-13-4*) UM Ctr MENAS.

— A Comprehensive Study of Egyptian Arabic: Conversation, Texts, Folk Literature, Cultural, Ethnological & Socio-Linguistic Notes, Vol. I. LC 76-24957. (C). 1978. pap. text 25.00 (*0-932098-11-8*) UM Ctr MENAS.

— A Comprehensive Study of Egyptian Arabic: Lexicon, Vol. IV. Incl. Pt. I. Egyptian Arabic - English: 34 Cultural Categories. LC 76-24957. 1979. Pt. II. English - Arabic: 34 Cultural Categories. LC 76-24957. 1979. LC 76-24957. (C). 1979. Set pap. text 25.00 (*0-932098-14-2*) UM Ctr MENAS.

— A Comprehensive Study of Egyptian Arabic: Proverbs & Metaphoric Phrases, Vol. II. LC 76-24957. (C). 1978. pap. text 25.00 (*0-932098-12-6*) UM Ctr MENAS.

***Abdel, Nabi H.** Nuclear Medicine Self-Study Program Oncology, Vol. IV. LC 98-49229. (Nuclear Medicine Self-Study Program IV Ser.: Unit 3). 49p. 1999. pap. 20.00 (*0-932004-61-X*) Soc Nuclear Med.

Abdel-Qadir, Ghazi. Sjamsi & Ali Baba in Town (Sjamsi en Ali Baba in de Stad) (Illus.). 26p. (J). (gr. k-3). 1998. 10.95 (*1-57379-070-2*, K1001) High-Scope.

Abdel-Rahim, Muddathir. Changing Patterns of Civilian-Military Relations in the Sudan. (Research Report Ser.: No. 46). 32p. 1978. write for info. (*91-7106-137-1*, Pub. by Nordic Africa) Transaction Pubs.

Abdel-Rohman, M., jt. auth. see Leipholz, Horst.

Abdel-Sayed, George, et al. Soil-Steel Bridges: Design & Construction. 357p. 1994. 60.00 (*0-07-003021-9*) McGraw.

Abdel Wahab, Farouk, ed. Modern Egyptian Drama: An Anthology. LC 72-94939. (Studies in Middle Eastern Literatures: No. 3). 1974. 30.00 (*0-88297-005-4*) Bibliotheca.

Abdelguerfi, Mahdi & Lavington, Simon, eds. Emerging Trends in Database & Knowledge Base Machines. LC 94-34327. 312p. 1995. 56.00 (*0-8186-6552-1*) IEEE Comp Soc.

Abdelguerfi, Mahdi & Wong, Kam-Fai. Parallel Database Techniques. LC 97-51310. 1998. 40.00 (*0-8186-8398-8*) IEEE Comp Soc.

Abdelhak, Mervat. Exercises in Health Information: Management of Strategic Resources. 1996. pap. text, wbk. ed. 23.00 (*0-7216-5133-X*, W B Saunders Co) Harcrt Hlth Sci Grp.

— Health Information Management Exams. 1996. 250.00 (*0-7216-5149-6*, W B Saunders Co) Harcrt Hlth Sci Grp.

— Review Manual of Health Information: Management of Strategic Resources. 1996. pap. text 31.50 (*0-7216-5148-8*, W B Saunders Co) Harcrt Hlth Sci Grp.

Abdelhak, Mervat, et al, eds. Health Information: Management of a Strategic Resource. (Illus.). 1996. teacher ed. write for info. (*0-7216-5151-8*, W B Saunders Co) Harcrt Hlth Sci Grp.

— Health Information: Management of a Strategic Resource, Textbook & Workbook Package. (Illus.). 784p. 1996. text, wbk. ed. 69.00 (*0-7216-5114-3*, W B Saunders Co) Harcrt Hlth Sci Grp.

Abdelhak, Mervat, et al. Health Information: Management of a Strategic Resource. (Illus.). 752p. 1996. text 52.50 (*0-7216-5132-1*, W B Saunders Co) Harcrt Hlth Sci Grp.

Abdelilah, Amalou. Digital Circuits: Engineers Tutor Series, 3 vols. (Illus.). (Orig.). pap. write for info. (*0-318-64993-4*); pap. 12.95 (*0-938862-67-7*); pap. 12.95 (*0-929704-04-5*) Weber Systems.

***Abdelkader, Dina.** Social Justice in Islam. LC 00-31936. 2000. write for info. (*1-56564-268-6*) IIIT VA.

Abdelkafi. Weddings in Tripolitania. 126p. 1987. 100.00 (*0-7855-1998-X*, Pub. by Darf Pubs Ltd) St Mut.

Abdelkafi, A. Weddings in Tripolitania. 126p. (C). 1989. 35.00 (*1-85077-945-7*, Pub. by Darf Pubs Ltd) St Mut.

***Abdelkarim, Abbas.** Change & Development in the Gulf. LC 98-34976. ix, 270p. 1999. write for info. (*0-333-73891-8*, Church St) LifeWay Christian.

Abdelkarim, Abbas. Change & Development in the Gulf. LC 98-34976. 304p. 1999. text 65.00 (*0-312-21658-0*) St Martin.

— Primitive Capital Accumulation in Sudan. 1992. text 42.50 (*0-7146-3324-0*, Pub. by F Cass Pubs) Intl Spec Bk.

Abdelkarim, Abbas, jt. auth. see Barnett, Tony.

Abdelkhalik, Rashad. Readings in Cost & Management Accounting. (AB - Accounting Principles Ser.). 1995. text 24.95 (*0-538-84477-9*) S-W Pub.

Abdellah, Faye G. & Levine, Eugene. Preparing Nursing Research for the 21st Century: Evolution, Methodologies, Challenges. LC 94-6045. 288p. 1994. 39.95 (*0-8261-8440-5*) Springer Pub.

Abdelnasser, Walid M. The Islamic Movement in Egypt: Perceptions of International Relations, 1967-1981. LC 93-24940. (Publication of the Graduate Institute of International Studies, Geneva). 320p. 1994. 76.50 (*0-7103-0469-2*) Routledge.

Abdelnoor, R. E. The Silver Burdett Mathematical Dictionary. LC 86-45568. (Illus.). 126p. (J). (gr. 5-12). 1986. 8.95 (*0-382-09485-9*); pap. 5.95 (*0-382-09309-7*) Silver Burdett Pr.

Abdelrahman, K. & Luque, E., eds. Parallel & Distributed Computing & Systems. LC 97-18498. (Illus.). 546p. 1996. pap. 152.00 (*0-88986-213-3*) Acta Pr.

Abdennour Samia. Egyptian Cooking. LC 98-18259. 199p. 1998. reprint ed. pap. 11.95 (*0-7818-0643-7*) Hippocrene Bks.

— Egyptian Cooking: A Practical Guide. 1985. pap. 20.00 (*977-424-026-X*, Pub. by Am Univ Cairo Pr) Col U Pr.

— Egyptian Cooking: A Practical Guide. LC 97-188881. 1997. pap. text 17.95 (*977-424-403-6*, Pub. by Am Univ Cairo Pr) Col U Pr.

— Middle Eastern Cooking: A Practical Guide. LC 97-144551. 1997. pap. text 17.95 (*977-424-401-X*, Pub. by Am Univ Cairo Pr) Col U Pr.

Abdenour, Thomas E. Sports Injury Care. (Fitness & Health Ser.). 264p. 1993. spiral bd. 21.25 (*0-86720-282-3*) Jones & Bartlett.

Abder-Raziq, M., jt. auth. see Kanawati, N.

Abderrahim, Hamid A., et al, eds. Reactor Dosimetry: Proceedings of the 9th International Symposium Prague, Czech Republic 26 September, 1996. 1000p. 1998. 148.00 (*981-02-3346-9*) World Scientific Pub.

Abdesslem, Habib. Foreign Language Lesson Discourse Analysis: The Teaching & Learning of English in Tunisian Schools. LC 92-19490. 408p. 1992. text 109.95 (*0-7734-9653-X*) E Mellen.

Abdi Abdulkadir Sheik-Abdi. Tales of Punt: Somali Folktales As Retold by Abdi Abdulkadir Sheik-Abdi. LC 93-91886. (Illus.). vii, 135p. (Orig.). 1993. pap. 11.95 (*0-9638802-2-5*) Dr Leisure.

— When a Hyena Laughs: A Somalian Novel. LC 94-77445. (Illus.). 275p. (Orig.). 1994. 29.95 (*0-9638802-5-X*); pap. 14.95 (*0-9638802-6-8*) Dr Leisure.

***Abdi, Herve.** Neural Networks. LC 98-46918. (University Papers Series.). 1999. 13.95 (*0-7619-1440-4*) Sage.

Abdi, Yakoub A., et al. Handbook of Drugs for Tropical Parasitic Infections. 2nd ed. 208p. 1995. 69.95 (*0-7484-0167-9*, Pub. by Tay Francis Ltd); pap. 34.95 (*0-7484-0168-7*, Pub. by Tay Francis Ltd) Taylor & Francis.

***Abdian, Geoffrey & Arvidson, P. Sven.** The Behavioral Elements & VQ: Understanding & Applying Character Values to Define & Achieve Your Values Quotient. Ourcharacter.com Technical Advisory Committee, ed. (Illus.). 165p. 1999. spiral bd. 19.95 (*1-930567-02-2*, Ourcharacter.com) Axios Pubng Corp.

— The Character Encyclopedia: A Comprehensive Character Reference Guide. 272p. 2000. 29.95 (*1-930567-13-8*, Ourcharacter.com) Axios Pubng Corp.

— CQ & the Behavioral Elements: How to Develop Your Personal & Professional Character Quotient. Ourcharacter.com Technical Advisory Committee, ed. (Illus.). 250p. 2000. spiral bd. 29.95 (*1-930567-03-0*, Ourcharacter.com) Axios Pubng Corp.

Abdian, Geoffrey, jt. auth. see Arvidson, P. Sven.

Abdill, George B. Civil War Railroads: A Pictorial Story of the War Between the States, 1861-1865. LC 98-46924. (Illus.). 192p. 1999. text 37.50 (*0-253-33536-1*) Ind U Pr.

Abdill, Margaret & Juppe, Denise, eds. Pets in Therapy. LC 97-16973. (Illus.). 214p. 1997. pap. 15.00 (*1-882883-29-2*, 312) Idyll Arbor.

Abdo & Daughters Staff. Kevin Costner: Reaching for the Stars. (Illus.). 32p. (YA). 1991. 18.49 (*1-56239-087-2*) ABDO Pub Co.

— Whitney Houston: Singer/Actress/Superstar. (Reaching for the Stars Ser.). (Illus.). 32p. (YA). 1994. lib. bdg. 19.93 (*1-56239-337-5*, ABDO & Dghtrs) ABDO Pub Co.

***Abdo, Geneive.** No God but God: Egypt & the Triumph of Islam. LC 99-58415. 240p. 2000. 25.00 (*0-19-512540-1*) OUP.

Abdo, John & Dachman, Kenneth A. Body Engineering: How to Reinvent the Way You Look & Feel. 1997. pap. 14.00 (*0-614-27363-3*, Perigee Bks) Berkley Pub.

Abdo, Sara C. Feininger in the Norton Simon Museum. (Illus.). 32p. (Orig.). 1994. pap. 8.95 (*0-915776-09-X*) NS Mus.

— Jawlensky in the Norton Simon Museum. (Illus.). 32p. (Orig.). 1990. pap. 8.95 (*0-915776-06-5*) NS Mus.

— Kandinsky in the Norton Simon Museum. (Illus.). 32p. (Orig.). 1994. pap. 8.95 (*0-915776-10-3*) NS Mus.

— Klee in the Norton Simon Museum. (Illus.). 32p. (Orig.). 1994. pap. 8.95 (*0-915776-11-1*) NS Mus.

Abdo, Sara C. & Williams, Gloria. Norton Simon Museum: A Brief Guide. (Illus.). 64p. (Orig.). 1996. pap. 6.00 (*0-915776-12-X*) NS Mus.

Abdoellah, Oekan S. Indonesian Transmigrants & Adaptation: An Ecological Anthropological Perspective. LC 93-9692. (Monographs: Vol. 33). 150p. (C). 1993. pap. 14.95 (*0-944613-19-5*) UC Berkeley Ctrs SE Asia.

Abdoh, et al. California Performance, Vol. 2. Leabhart, Thomas, ed. (Mime Journal Ser.). (Illus.). 229p. (Orig.). 1991. pap. 12.00 (*0-9611066-1-1*) Mime Jour.

***Abdoh, Salar.** The Poet Game: A Novel. LC 99-55845. 240p. 2000. text 23.00 (*0-312-20954-1*, Picador USA) St Martin.

Abdoh, Samir. The Syriac Christian Community: Historical & Contemporary Conditions. 120p. 1997. pap. 15.00 (*0-88206-209-3*) Caravan Bks.

Abdolah. Short Shorties. 1998. write for info. (*0-15-100335-1*) Harcourt.

***Abdolmohammadi, Mohammad J. & Usoff, Catherine.** The Assessment of Task Structure, Knowledge Base & Decision Aids for a Comprehensive Inventory of Audit Tasks. LC 99-89370. 2000. write for info. (*1-56720-294-2*, Quorum Bks) Greenwood.

Abdou, Hamed M. Dissolution, Bioavailability & Bioequivalence. LC 89-90760. 1989. 69.95 (*0-912734-20-5*) Mack Pub.

Abdou, J. & Keiding, H. Effectivity Functions in Social Choice. 208p. (C). 1991. lib. bdg. 131.50 (*0-7923-1147-7*) Kluwer Academic.

Abdou, Kamar M. & Hassanein, Ahmed T. The Concise Arabic-English Lexicon of Verbs in Context. (ARA & ENG.). 350p. 1992. pap. text 20.00 (*977-424-256-4*, Pub. by Am Univ Cairo Pr) Col U Pr.

Abdrabboh, Bob. Saudi Arabia: Forces of Modernization. 125p. (Orig.). 1985. pap. 9.95 (*0-915597-19-5*) Amana Bks.

Abduh, Muhammad. The Theology of Unity. LC 79-52560. (Islam Ser.). 1980. reprint ed. lib. bdg. 28.95 (*0-8369-9267-9*) Ayer.

***Abdul, Amani.** Home Born - Street Bred. 1999. 21.95 (*1-929985-03-7*); pap. 12.95 (*1-929985-02-9*) Angel Hrt Pub.

— Lyrics of an Angel: Poetry in Reality. 110p. 1999. pap. 12.95 (*1-929985-00-2*) Angel Hrt Pub.

Abdul Aziz Abdul Rahman, et al. The Maritime Economy of Malaysia. LC 98-944384. 119p. 1997. write for info. (*967-978-572-6*) Pelanduk.

Abdul-Aziz, Moudi M. King Abdul-Aziz & the Kuwait Conference, 1923-1924. Hatim, Basil & Buckley, Ron, trs. from ARA. 169p. 1998. pap. text 35.00 (*0-7881-5474-5*) DIANE Pub.

Abdu'l-Baha. Abdu'l-Baha in London. 127p. 1984. 8.75 (*0-900125-50-0*) Bahai.

— Abdu'l-Baha in London. 127p. 1988. pap. 7.95 (*0-900125-89-6*) Bahai.

— Contentment: Jewels from the Words of Abdu'l-Baha. 48p. 1995. pap. 5.95 (*1-870989-64-3*) Bahai.

— Forgiveness: Jewels from the Words of Abdu'l-Baha. (Illus.). 48p. 1997. pap. 5.95 (*1-870989-70-8*) Bahai.

— Friendship: Jewels from the Words of Abdu'l-Baha. 48p. 1994. pap. 5.95 (*1-870989-35-X*) Bahai.

— Hope: Jewels from the Words of 'Abou'l-Baha. (Illus.). 40p. 1996. pap. 5.95 (*1-870989-55-4*) Bahai.

— Love: Jewels from the Words of Abdu'l-Baha. 48p. 1994. pap. 5.95 (*1-870989-34-1*) Bahai.

— Memorials of the Faithful. 5th ed. Gail, Marzieh, tr. from PER. LC 97-219604. 204p. 1997. pap. 10.95 (*0-87743-242-2*) Bahai.

— Paris Talks: Addresses Given by Abdu'l-Baha in 1911. 224p. 1969. pap. 6.95 (*1-870989-61-9*) Bahai.

— Paris Talks: Addresses Given by Abdu'l-Baha in 1911. 224p. 1995. 13.95 (*1-870989-57-0*) Bahai.

— The Promulgation of Universal Peace: Talks Delivered by Abdu'l-Baha During His Visit to the United States & Canada in 1912. 2nd ed. LC 81-21689. 513p. 1982. 16.95 (*0-87743-172-8*, 103-039) Bahai.

— The Secret of Divine Civilization, pocket-sized. Gail, Marzieh & Khan, Ali-Kuli, trs. from PER. 126p. 1990. pap. 3.95 (*0-87743-219-8*) Bahai.

— Some Answered Questions. Barney, Laura C., tr. from PER. xviii, 324p. 1981. 15.95 (*0-87743-162-0*) Bahai.

— Some Answered Questions. Barney, Laura C., tr. from PER. LC 83-21353. xviii, 324p. 1984. pap. 3.95 (*0-87743-190-6*) Bahai.

— Tablet of the Heart: God & Me. Fisher, Betty J., ed. (Illus.). 56p. (J). (ps-2). 1987. lib. bdg. 10.95 (*0-87743-207-4*) Bahai.

— Tablets of the Divine Plan: Revealed by 'Abdu'l-Baha to the North American Baha'is. 144p. 1993. pap. 3.95 (*0-87743-233-3*) Bahai.

— A Traveler's Narrative: Written to Illustrate the Episode of the Bab. rev. ed. Browne, Edward G., tr. from PER. LC 79-19025. 110p. 1980. 11.95 (*0-87743-143-4*, 106-027) Bahai.

— Wisdom of the Master: The Spiritual Teachings of 'Abdu'l-Baha. Scholl, Steven, ed. LC 97-29993. (Illus.). 130p. 1997. pap. 10.95 (*1-883991-20-X*) Whte Cloud Pr.

Abdul-Baha & Universal House of Justice Staff. Selections from the Writings of Abdul-Baha. Gail, Marzieh, tr. from PER. LC 96-29279. 1996. pap. 3.95 (*0-87743-251-1*) Bahai.

Abdu'l-Baha, jt. auth. see Bahaullah.

Abdu'l-Baha, jt. auth. see Baha'u'llah.

Abdu'l-Baha, jt. auth. see Baha'u'llah, Bab.

Abdul-Baki, Kathryn K. Fields of Fig & Olive: Ameera & Other Stories of the Middle East. 217p. (Orig.). (YA). (gr. 10 up). 1991. 30.00 (*0-89410-725-9*, Three Contnts); pap. 14.00 (*0-89410-726-7*, Three Contnts) L Rienner.

***Abdul-Baki, Kathryn K.** Ghost Songs. LC 00-29812. 2000. pap. write for info. (*1-57889-098-5*) Passeggiata.

Abdul-Baki, Kathryn K. Tower of Dreams. 216p. 1995. 30.00 (*0-89410-816-6*, Three Contnts); pap. 14.00 (*0-89410-817-4*, Three Contnts) L Rienner.

Abdul Fattah Rashid Hamid. Self Knowledge & Spiritual Yearning. Quinlan, Hamid, ed. LC 82-70348. (Illus.). 116p. 1993. pap. 5.00 (*0-89259-127-7*) Am Trust Pubns.

Abdul-Hadi, Ayman S. Stock Markets of the Arab World. 208p. (C). 1988. lib. bdg. 52.50 (*0-415-00335-0*) Routledge.

Abdul Hameed Siddiqui. Islamic Concept of History. 12p. (Orig.). 1988. pap. 3.00 (*1-56744-303-6*) Kazi Pubns.

Abdul Hameed Siddiqui, tr. see Abu Muhammad Baghawi.

Abdul-Haqq, Adiyah Akbar. Sharing Your Faith with a Muslim. LC 80-16020. 192p. (Orig.). 1980. pap. 8.99 (*0-87123-553-6*) Bethany Hse.

Abdul-Jabaar, Kareem. Black Profiles in Courage: A Legacy of African-American Achievement. 288p. 1997. mass mkt. 6.99 (*0-380-73060-X*, Avon Bks) Morrow Avon.

***Abdul-Jabbar, Kareem.** Black Profiles in Courage: A Legacy of African-American Achievement. 288p. 2000. pap. 13.00 (*0-380-81341-6*, Perennial) HarperTrade.

Abdul-Jabbar, Kareem. Black Profiles in Courage: A Legacy of African-American Achievement. (Illus.). 256p. 1996. 22.00 (*0-688-13097-6*, Wm Morrow) Morrow Avon.

— Selected from Giant Steps. (Writers' Voices Ser.). 1990. 9.05 (*0-606-02138-8*, Pub. by Turtleback) Demco.

***Abdul-Jabbar, Kareem & Singular, Stephen.** A Season on the Reservation: My Sojourn with the White Mountain Apaches. LC 99-27743. 224p. 2000. 24.00 (*0-688-17077-3*, Wm Morrow) Morrow Avon.

Abdul-Jabbar, Kareem, jt. auth. see Knobler, Peter.

Abdul-Karim, Fadi W., jt. auth. see Lawrence, W. Dwayne.

Abdul-Karim, Fadi W., jt. ed. see Lawrence, W. Dwayne.

Abdul-Khaliq, Salim. The Untold Story of Blacks in Islam. 110p. (Orig.). 1994. pap. 7.00 (*1-56411-073-7*) Untd Bros & Sis.

Abdul, M. A. The Quran, Sh. Tabarsi's Commentary. 1991. 15.95 (*0-933511-27-2*) Kazi Pubns.

Abdul-Massih, George M. Lughat Al-Arab (The Arabic Language) Arabic Dictionary, Vol. I. (ARA.). 487p. 1993. 25.00 (*0-86685-580-7*, LDL5807, Pub. by Librairie du Liban) Intl Bk Ctr.

Abdul-Qadir Gilani, Muhyiddeen. The Endowment of Divine Grace & the Spread of Divine Mercy Vol. 1: Al-Fathu Rabbani. Al-Akili, Muhammad M., tr. from ARA. LC 90-63799. 240p. (Orig.). 1991. pap. 19.50 (*1-879405-01-6*) Pearl Pub Hse.

Abdul Qayyum Hazarvi, tr. see Al-Ghazali, Muhammad.

Abdul-Raheem, Tajudeen, ed. Pan-Africanism: Politics, Economy, & Social Change in the Twenty-First Century. LC 96-19795. 255p. (C). 1996. text 50.00 (*0-8147-0660-6*); pap. text 18.50 (*0-8147-0661-4*) NYU Pr.

Abdul Rahim AlFahim, ed. Two Hundred Hadith. 250p. 1993. pap. text 14.95 (*1-56744-483-0*) Kazi Pubns.

Abdul Rauf Feisal. Islam: A Sacred Law: What Every Muslim Should Know about the Shari Ah. LC 98-39399. 1999. write for info. (*0-939660-70-9*); pap. write for info. (*0-939660-71-7*) Threshold CA.

Abdul-Rauf, Muhammad. The Islamic View of Women & the Family. 160p. 1996. pap. 9.95 (*0-614-21388-6*, 1499) Kazi Pubns.

— The Islamic View of Women & the Family. 2nd ed. 175p. 1977. text 17.50 (*0-8315-0156-1*) Speller.

— Umar Al Faruq. LC 98-27998. 1998. write for info. (*1-881963-65-9*) Al-Saadawi Pubns.

Abdul-Rauf, Muhammad, tr. Arabic for English Speaking Students. 8th ed. LC 96-35050. 434p. (C). 1996. reprint ed. pap. 20.00 (*1-881963-00-4*) Al-Saadawi Pubns.

Abdul-Sabur, Najwak T. Not All Rhythm & Rhyme. 48p. 1999. pap. 6.95 (*0-9657247-1-9*) J & J Consultants.

Abdul, Uncle. Juice: Electricity for Pleasure & Pain. (Illus.). 150p. 1998. pap. 11.95 (*1-890159-06-9*) Greenery Pr.

Abdul Waheed Khan. Beacon Lights Bks. I-IV: True Tales for Children, 2 vol. set. 32p. (J). (gr. 1-6). 1985. pap. 6.50 (*1-56744-222-6*) Kazi Pubns.

***Abdul-Wahhab, Muhammad Morra.** Latin Kings Netas Bloods: Apartheid Prisons, Crime & Gangbangas. (Illus.). 82p. 1999. pap. 10.00 (*0-9676612-1-8*) Dar Us Salafyh.

Abdul Zahra Abdullah Ali. Insurance Development in the Arab World. (C). 1985. 730.00 (*0-7855-4149-7*, Pub. by Witherby & Co) St Mut.

Abdulagatov, I. M., et al. Thermodynamic Properties of Fluids & Fluid Mixtures. LC 99-17215. 350p. 1999. 97.50 (*1-56700-130-0*) Begell Hse.

Abdulai, Awudu & Delgado, Christopher L., eds. Re-Establishing Agriculture As a Priority for Development Policy in Sub-Saharan Africa. 1995. write for info. (*0-89629-333-5*) Intl Food Policy.

An Asterisk (*) at the beginning of an entry indicates that the title is appearing for the first time.

A

Abdulai, David. African Proverbs. Million, Charlotte, ed. (Illus.). 100p. (Orig.). 1996. 11.95 (0-9647012-3-5); pap. 5.95 (0-9647012-2-7) Konkori Intl.

— Poetical Eurythmics of an African Griot. limited unabridged ed. Kyambalesa, Henry, ed. 1997. pap. 9.95 (0-9647012-7-8, Dawn of a New Day) Konkori Intl.

— Sankofa: Stories, Proverbs & Poems of An African Childhood. Portis, Hattie et al, eds. (Illus.). 128p. (Orig.). 1995. pap. 14.95 (0-9647012-0-0) Konkori Intl.

Abdulai, David, ed. see Fann, Linsey.

Abdularahameana & Mayhofer, C. M. The Sarmdebsareasaka of Abdul Rahman: With Text. LC 98-909899. xvi, 259p. 1998. pap. 200.00 (81-208-1428-2, Pub. by Motilal Bnarsidass) St Mut.

Abdulaziz & Stover. Academic Reading Challenge. 240p. (C). 1988. pap. text 33.87 (0-13-000811-7) P-H.

Abdulaziz, Helen T. & Shenkarow, Ellen. Write It Right: Beginning Handwriting & Composition for Students of ESL. (Illus.). 208p. (C). 1986. pap. text 28.20 (0-13-969437-4) P-H.

*Abdulezer, Susan. Creating Multimedia Stories: HyperStudio 3.3. (Recipes4Success Ser.). (Illus.). 2000. 69.95 (0-9673308-9-0) Tech Learning Inc.

Abdulghafour, Gazi I., jt. auth. see Gogoi, Aparjita.

Abdulghani, Jasim M. Iraq & Iran: The Years of Crisis. LC 84-47945. 282p. 1984. reprint ed. pap. 87.50 (0-608-05918-8, 206625400008) Bks Demand.

AbdulHamid A. AbuSulayman. Towards an Islamic Theory of International Relations: New Directions for Methodology & Thought. 2nd rev. ed. (Islamization of Knowledge Ser.: No. 1). 240p. 1993. pap. 12.75 (0-912463-71-6); text 22.75 (0-685-39266-X) IIIT VA.

Abdulhamid Jodah Al Sahhar. The Prophet's Biography Series for Children, Nos. 1-10. Shahnaz, Mary & Quinlan, Hamid, eds. Outaiba Elhuwaib, tr. from ARA. LC 82-70350. Orig. Title: Kasas Alsyrah. (Illus.). 16p. 1982. pap. 2.00 (0-89259-025-4) Am Trust Pubns.

Abdulin, R. Z., et al. Vector Lyapunov Functions in Stability Theory. LC 95-54154. (Advanced Series in Mathematical Science & Engineering). 1996. write for info. (1-885978-20-0) Wrld Fed Pubs.

Abdulla. New Temple for Hathor at Memphis Vol. 1: Egyptology Today. 1978. pap. 32.50 (0-85668-089-3, Pub. by Aris & Phillips) David Brown.

Abdulla, Adnan K. Catharsis in Literature. LC 84-42839. 160p. 1985. 35.00 (0-253-31323-6) Ind U Pr.

Abdulla-Al-Joaid, et al. Water Sensitivity: Binder Validation. 104p. (C). 1994. pap. text 10.00 (0-309-05810-4, SHRP-A-402) SHRP.

Abdulla, Aman. Data Communications. (C). 2001. 50.25 (0-13-230475-9) P-H.

Abdulla, Jamal & McCarus, Ernest N., eds. Kurdish Essays. (Kurdish Readers Ser.: Vol. 2). ix, 147p. 1967. 14.00 (0-916798-62-3) UM Dept NES.

— Kurdish Short Stories. (Kurdish Readers Ser.: Vol. 3). ix, 115p. 1967. 14.00 (0-916798-63-1) UM Dept NES.

— Newspaper Kurdish. (Kurdish Readers Ser.: Vol. 1). vii, 115p. 1967. 14.00 (0-916798-61-5) UM Dept NES.

Abdulla, Jamal, jt. auth. see McCarus, Ernest N.

*Abdulla, Raficq. Words of Paradise: Selected Poems of Rumi. (Illus.). 112p. 2000. 19.95 (0-670-88935-0, Viking Studio) Studio Bks.

Abdulla, Ramjoo. Ramjoo's Diaries, 1922-1929: A Personal Account of Meher Baba's Early Work. LC 78-32145. 585p. 1979. reprint ed. 13.95 (0-915828-14-6) Sufism Reoriented.

Abdullabekov, K. N. Electromagnetic Phenomena in the Earth's Crust. Zeidler, Ryszard B., tr. from RUS. (Illus.). 160p. (C). 1991. text 110.00 (90-6191-171-0, Pub. by A A Balkema) Ashgate Pub Co.

Abdullaev, F. K. Random Waves in Nonlinear Dispersive Media. 250p. 1998. text 48.00 (981-02-2347-1) World Scientific Pub.

Abdullaev, Fatkhulla K. Theory of Solitons in Inhomogeneous Media. LC 93-29288. (Series in Nonlinear Science). 192p. 1994. 250.00 (0-471-94299-5) Wiley.

Abdullaev, Fatkhulla K., ed. Optical Solitons: Proceedings of the Workshop on Optical Solitons, Chipman-Tashkent, U. S. S. R., May 1989. 216p. (C). 1991. text 101.00 (981-02-0303-9) World Scientific Pub.

Abdullaev, Fatkhulla K., et al. Nonlinearity with Disorder 2: Proceedings of the Tashkent Conference, Tashkent, U. S. S. R. October 1-7, 1990. Bishop, A. R. & Pnevmatikos, S. N., eds. LC 92-19322. (Proceedings in Physics Ser.: Vol. 67). (Illus.). 350p. 1992. 108.95 (0-387-55474-2) Spr-Verlag.

— Optical Solitons. LC 93-13774. (Nonlinear Dynamics Ser.).Tr. of Optcheskie Solitony. 1993. 86.95 (0-387-51985-8) Spr-Verlag.

Abdullaev, Gasan M. & Dzhafarov, Taiar D. Atomic Diffusion in Semiconductor Structures. 1987. write for info. (2-88124-152-2) Gordon & Breach.

Abdullaev, Sandrilla S. Chaos & Dynamics of Rays in Waveguide Media. 311p. 1992. text 184.00 (2-88124-848-9) Gordon & Breach.

Abdullah. The Prophet's Speech at Tabuk. abr. ed. 16p. (Orig.). 1984. pap. 1.00 (0-916157-02-4) African Islam Miss Pubns.

Abdullah & Obaba, Al I. The Why & How of Burial & Death of a Muslim. (Illus.). 24p. (Orig.). (YA). 1985. pap. 1.50 (0-916157-03-2) African Islam Miss Pubns.

Abdullah, Achmed. Alien Souls. LC 75-121518. (Short Story Index Reprint Ser.). 1977. 20.95 (0-8369-3474-1) Ayer.

— Honourable Gentleman, & Others. LC 74-140324. (Short Story Index Reprint Ser.). 1977. 19.95 (0-8369-3716-3) Ayer.

— Swinging Caravan. LC 75-103485. (Short Story Index Reprint Ser.). 1977. 20.95 (0-8369-3077-0) Ayer.

— The Thief of Bagdad. 248p. 1987. 55.00 (1-85077-900-7, Pub. by Darf Pubs Ltd) St Mut.

Abdullah, Achmed & Pakenham, Thomas C. Dreamers of Empire. LC 68-57300. (Essay Index Reprint Ser.). 1977. 20.95 (0-8369-0099-5) Ayer.

Abdullah, Achmed, et al. Ten-Foot Chain. LC 73-116924. (Short Story Index Reprint Ser.). 1977. 16.95 (0-8369-3426-1) Ayer.

Abdullah Ali, Abdul Z. Insurance Development in the Arab World: An Analysis of the Relationship Between Available Domestic Retention Capacity & the Demand for International Reinsurance. (Illus.). 350p. 1985. lib. bdg. 213.50 (0-86010-707-8) G & T Inc.

Abdullah, Aslam. The Babari Masjid. 60p. 1991. pap. text 3.00 (1-881504-09-3) Minaret Pubns.

Abdullah, Bilal R. As-Suffah: A Radical Concept in Modern Islamic Social Services. 64p. 1996. pap. 7.50 (0-614-21542-0, 75) Kazi Pubns.

Abdullah, Fadel, ed. see Mohamed, Yasien & Haron, Muhammad.

Abdullah, Maisom. Capital Labor Substitutability in Malaysian Manufacturing. LC 91-25120. (Developing Economies of the Third World Ser.). 176p. 1991. text 10.00 (0-8153-0627-X) Garland.

Abdullah, Maisom Bt, see Bt Abdullah, Maisom.

Abdullah, Maryam Muhammad. Savannah a la Carte: A Savannah Symphony Women's Guild Cookbook. LC 98-61164. (Illus.). 1998. 24.95 (0-9665025-0-7) Savannah Symph.

Abdullah, Moha A. Small & Medium Enterprise in Malaysia: Policy Issues & Challenges. LC 98-73758. 234p. 1998. text 65.95 (1-84014-884-5, Pub. by Ashgate Pub) Ashgate Pub Co.

Abdullah, Moha A., jt. auth. see Chan, Raymond K.

*Abdullah, Moha Asri & Bakar, Isa Bin, eds. Small & Medium Enterprises in Asian Pacific Countries. 2000. lib. bdg. 59.00 (1-56072-796-9) Nova Sci Pubs.

Abdullah, Mohammed, jt. auth. see Morgan, J. Derald.

Abdullah, Morag M. Valley of the Giant Buddhas: Memoirs & Travel. 309p. 1993. 29.00 (0-86304-065-9, Pub. by Octagon Pr) ISHK.

Abdullah, Morag Murray. My Khyber Marriage. 272p. 1990. 24.00 (0-86304-055-1, Pub. by Octagon Pr) ISHK.

Abdullah, Omanii. I Wanna Be the Kinda Father My Mother Was: Reading Level 4 & Above. LC 92-35328. 64p. 1993. pap. 4.50 (0-88336-033-0); audio 9.95 (0-88336-623-1) New Readers.

*Abdullah, Sharif M. Creating a World That Works for All. LC 99-29159. 180p. 1999. pap. 15.00 (1-57675-062-0) Berrett-Koehler.

Abdullah, Sharif M. The Power of One: Authentic Leadership in Turbulent Times. 96p. 1991. pap. 10.00 (0-9632184-0-9) Forum Comm Trans.

— The Power of One: Authentic Leadership in Turbulent Times. 96p. 1995. pap. 10.00 (0-86571-325-1) New Soc Pubs.

Abdullah, T., ed. Arab & Islamic Studies in Honor of Marsden Jones. 1997. 29.95 (977-424-402-8) Col U Pr.

Abdullah, Taufik. Schools & Politics No. 50: The Kaum Muda Movement in West Sumatra 1927-1933. (Modern Indonesia Project Ser.). 257p. 1971. pap. 6.00 (0-87763-010-0) Cornell Mod Indo.

*Abdullah, Thabit A. J. Merchants, Mamluks & Murder: The Political Economy of Trade in Eighteenth-Century Basra. LC 00-26524. (C). 2000. pap. text 20.95 (0-7914-4808-8) State U NY Pr.

— Merchants, Mamluks & Murder: The Political Economy of Trade in Eighteenth-Century Basra. LC 00-26524. (C). 2001. text 62.50 (0-7914-4807-X) State U NY Pr.

Abdullah, Yahya Taher. The Mountain of Green Tea & Other Stories. Johnson-Davies, Denys, tr. 125p. 1992. pap. 10.00 (977-424-267-X, Pub. by Am Univ Cairo Pr) Col U Pr.

Abdullah Yusuf Ali. Roman Transliteration of the Holy Quran. 800p. (C). 1991. text 19.95 (1-56744-371-0) Kazi Pubns.

Abdullahi Ahmed-An-Na'im. Toward an Islamic Reformation: Civil Liberties, Human Rights & International Law. LC 89-21828. (Contemporary Issues in the Middle East Ser.). 240p. (C). 1990. text 39.95 (0-8156-2484-0) Syracuse U Pr.

Abdullahi, Ismail, ed. E. J. Josey: An Activist Librarian. LC 92-24085. (Illus.). 293p. 1992. 34.50 (0-8108-2584-8) Scarecrow.

Abdullayev, G. B. & Dzhafarov, T. D., eds. Atomic Diffusion in Semiconductor Structures, Vol. 1. x, 340p. 1987. text 779.00 (3-7186-0413-2) Gordon & Breach.

Abdulllah, Fadel, ed. see Ghazi, Abidullah & Ghazi, Tasneema K.

Abdulov, M. V. Phase Transformations & Rock Genesis. Chatterjee, A. K., ed. Ghose, Sankar, tr. from RUS. (Russian Translation Ser.: No. 107). 152p. (C). 1994. text 71.00 (90-5410-218-7, Pub. by A A Balkema) Ashgate Pub Co.

Abdulrab, Habib & Pecuchet, Jean-Pierre R., eds. Word Equations & Related Topics: Second International Workshop, IWWERT '91, Rouen, France, October 7-9, 1991 Proceedings. LC 93-29000. (Lecture Notes in Computer Science Ser.: Vol. 677). vii, 213p. 1993. 39.95 (0-387-56730-5) Spr-Verlag.

Abdulrahman, A. J., ed. Iraq. (World Bibliographical Ser.: No. 42). 163p. 1983. lib. bdg. 72.00 (0-903450-73-9) ABC-CLIO.

*Abdulrahman Bin, Ali Alhinai. Ceremonies & Celebrations of Oman. (Illus.). 240p. 2000. 64.00 (1-85964-130-X) Garnet Publishing Ltd.

AbdulRasheed, Shadeed A. Equality in America. LC 92-93906. 126p. (Orig.). 1993. 19.50 (0-9634231-1-8); pap. 8.50 (0-9634231-3-4); lib. bdg. 19.50 (0-9634231-2-6) SAAR Pubns.

Abdur Rehman Shad. Uthman ibn Affan: The Third Caliph of Islam. 96p. (YA). (gr. 10-12). 1985. pap. 3.50 (1-56744-409-1) Kazi Pubns.

Abdurahman, Bilal. Africa Revisited, 1972-1990. (Illus.). 55p. (YA). 1993. pap. text 10.00 (0-9619070-3-7) Ethno Modes Folkloric Workshop Inc.

— In the Key of Me: From Bedford-Stuy to Africa. (Illus.). 110p. pap. text 12.00 (0-9619070-2-9) Ethno Modes Folkloric Workshop Inc.

Abdus Samad Sharfuddin. The Black Stone. 24p. (Orig.). 1985. pap. 2.00 (1-56744-235-8) Kazi Pubns.

Abdushelishvili, M. G., et al. Contributions to the Physical Anthropology of Central Asia & the Caucasus. Field, Henry, ed. Heath, Barbara H., tr. LC 79-158217. (Harvard University, Peabody Museum of Archaeology & Ethnology, Russian Translation Ser.: Vol. 3, No. 2). 1968. lib. bdg. 115.00 (0-404-52645-4) AMS Pr.

*Abe, A., et al, eds. Biomedical Applications/Polymer Blends. (Advances in Polymer Science Ser.: Vol. 149). (Illus.). 210p. 1999. 166.00 (3-540-65933-1) Spr-Verlag.

Abe, A., ed. see Capek, I., et al.

Abe, A. B. Secret Revelations Manuscript. 55p. (Orig.). 1993. pap. 12.00 (0-9637922-1-0) Cherry Stne Bks.

*Abe, Atsuko. Japan & the European Union: Domestic Politics & Transnational Relations. LC 99-46722. 1999. write for info. (0-485-11556-5, Pub. by Athlone Pr) Humanities.

*Abe, Casio. Beat Takeshi vs. Takeshi Kitano. (Wicked Radiance Ser.: No. 1). 2000. pap. 22.95 (1-885030-29-0) Kaya Prod.

Abe, E. & Fitzgerald, R., eds. The Origins of Japanese Industrial Power: Strategies, Institutions & the Development of Organizational Capability. 186p. 1995. pap. 19.50 (0-7146-4157-X, Pub. by F Cass Pubs) Intl Spec Bk.

Abe, Etsuo & Fitzgerald, Robert, eds. The Origins of Japanese Industrial Power: Strategies, Institutions & the Development of Organizational Capability. LC 94-38512. 140p. 1995. 42.50 (0-7146-4623-7, Pub. by F Cass Pubs) Intl Spec Bk.

Abe, Etsuo & Gourvish, Terry, eds. Japanese Success? British Failure? Comparisons in Business Performance since 1945. LC 97-5483. (Illus.). 300p. (C). 1998. text 85.00 (0-19-829058-6) OUP.

Abe, Etsuo & Suzuki, Yoshitaka, eds. Changing Patterns of International Rivalry. 1991. text 57.50 (0-86008-475-2, Pub. by U of Tokyo) Col U Pr.

Abe, George. Residential Broadband. LC 97-81199. 1997. 50.00 (1-57870-020-5) Cisco Press.

— Residential Broadband. 1997. 50.00 (1-56205-813-4) New Riders Pub.

*Abe, George. Residential Broadband. 2nd ed. 500p. 1999. 50.00 (1-57870-177-5) Cisco Press.

Abe, H., et al, eds. Data Book on Mechanical Properties of Living Cells, Tissues, & Organs. (Illus.). 448p. 1996. 149.00 (4-431-70175-3) Spr-Verlag.

Abe, H. & Hoshi, M., eds. Diabetic Microangiopathy. (Frontiers in Diabetes Ser.: Vol. 3). (Illus.). xii, 500p. 1983. 240.00 (3-8055-3787-5) S Karger.

Abe, H. & Latchman, David. Stress Proteins. LC 98-42186. (Handbook of Experimental Pharmacology Ser.). 480p. 1999. 280.00 (3-540-65017-2) Spr-Verlag.

Abe, Hitoshi, et al. The Government & Politics of Japan. White, James W., tr. 230p. 1994. 29.50 (0-86008-501-5, Pub. by U of Tokyo) Col U Pr.

Abe, Joseph M., et al. Business Ecology: Giving Your Business the Natural Edge. LC 97-46458. (Illus.). 256p. 1998. pap. text 18.95 (0-7506-9955-8) Buttrwrth-Heinemann.

Abe, K., et al, eds. Kinins VA. (Advances in Experimental Medicine & Biology Ser.: Vol. 247A). (Illus.). 688p. 1989. 130.00 (0-306-43207-2, Plenum Trade) Perseus Pubng.

— Kinins VA, Pts. A & B. (Advances in Experimental Medicine & Biology Ser.: Vol. 247A). (Illus.). 688p. 1989. 240.00 (0-318-41974-2, Plenum Trade) Perseus Pubng.

— Kinins VB. (Advances in Experimental Medicine & Biology Ser.: Vol. 247B). (Illus.). 718p. 1989. 130.00 (0-306-43208-0, Plenum Trade) Perseus Pubng.

— Kinins VB, Pts. A & B. (Advances in Experimental Medicine & Biology Ser.: Vol. 247B). (Illus.). 718p. 1989. 240.00 (0-318-41975-0, Plenum Trade) Perseus Pubng.

Abe, K., jt. auth. see Ogino, Keizo.

Abe, K., jt. ed. see Nagasawa, Hiroshi.

Abe, Keith. Hawaii Aloha. 1986. write for info. (0-914916-76-9) Ku Paa.

Abe, Kobo. The Box Man: A Novel. Saunders, E. Dale, tr. from JPN. Orig. Title: Hakootoko. 178p. 1991. reprint ed. pap. 12.00 (0-86547-461-3) N Point Pr.

— The Face of Another. Saunders, E. Dale, tr. from JPN. Orig. Title: Tanin no kao. 256p. 1992. pap. 13.00 (4-7700-1634-4) Kodansha.

— Kangaroo Notebook: A Novel. Mori, Maryellen Toman, tr. LC 97-9204. 1997. pap. 12.00 (0-679-74663-3) Vin Bks.

— Secret Rendezvous: A Novel. De Angelis, Paul & Franklin, Helena, eds. Carpenter, Juliet Winters, tr. from JPN. Orig. Title: Mikkai. 192p. 1993. pap. 12.00 (1-56836-003-7) Kodansha.

— Three Plays. Keene, Donald, tr. & intro. by. LC 93-36358. 1993. 38.50 (0-231-08280-0) Col U Pr.

— Three Plays. Keene, Donald, tr. & intro. by. 1997. pap. text 17.00 (0-231-08281-9) Col U Pr.

— The Woman in the Dunes. Saunders, E. Dale, tr. from JPN. LC 90-50625. Orig. Title: Suna no onna. 256p. 1991. pap. 12.00 (0-679-73378-7) Vin Bks.

Abe, Kumiko, tr. see Urquidez, Benny.

Abe, M., et al. New Developments in Ion Exchange. 636p. 1991. 320.50 (0-444-98688-X) Elsevier.

Abe, Masao. Buddhism & Interfaith Dialogue. Heine, Steven, ed. LC 95-6926. 248p. (C). 1995. text 29.00 (0-8248-1751-6); pap. text 16.95 (0-8248-1752-4) UH Pr.

— A Study of Dogen: His Philosophy & Religion. Heine, Steven, ed. LC 90-93566. 224p. (C). 1991. text 59.50 (0-7914-0837-X); pap. text 19.95 (0-7914-0838-8) State U NY Pr.

— Zen & Comparative Studies. Heine, Steven, ed. LC 96-7546. 224p. 1996. text 28.00 (0-8248-1831-8); pap. text 15.95 (0-8248-1832-6) UH Pr.

— Zen & Western Thought. LaFleur, William R., ed. & intro. by. LC 83-24153. 332p. 1984. reprint ed. pap. text 16.00 (0-8248-1214-X) UH Pr.

Abe, Masao, ed. A Zen Life: D. T. Suzuki Remembered. (Illus.). 288p. (Orig.). 1986. pap. 19.95 (0-8348-0213-9) Weatherhill.

Abe, Masao, tr. see Nishida Kitaro.

Abe, Masayuki & Yokoyama, Naoki. Semiconductor Heterostructure Devices, Vol. 2. Ikoma, Toshiaki, ed. (Japanese Technology Reviews Ser.: Vol. 8). xii, 98p. 1989. pap. text 146.00 (2-88124-338-X) Gordon & Breach.

Abe, Mitsuyuki & Takahashi, Masaji, eds. Intraoperative Radiation Therapy: Proceedings of the Third International Symposium on Intraoperative Radiation Therapy, November 12-15, 1990, Kyoto, Japan. (Illus.). 300p. 1991. 91.00 (0-08-040702-1) McGraw.

Abe, Mitsuyuki, jt. ed. see Dobelbower, Ralph R., Jr.

Abe, Ryulchi. The Weaving of Mantra: Kukai & the Construction of Esoteric Buddhist Discourse. LC 98-36381. (Illus.). 593p. 1999. 40.00 (0-231-11286-6) Col U Pr.

*Abe, Ryuichi. The Weaving of Mantra: Kukai & the Construction of Esoteric Buddhist Discourse. 2000. reprint ed. pap. 19.50 (0-231-11287-4) Col U Pr.

Abe, Ryuichi & Haskel, Peter, trs. Great Fool: Zen Master Ryokan - Poems, Letters, & Other Writings. LC 95-42750. 376p. 1996. pap. text 28.00 (0-8248-1777-X) UH Pr.

Abe, Ryuzo. Statistical Mechanics. Yasushi Takahashi, tr. LC 74-84826. 188p. 1975. reprint ed. pap. 58.30 (0-608-01193-2, 206188200001) Bks Demand.

*Abe, Shana. Intimate Enemies. 400p. 2000. mass mkt. 5.99 (0-553-58199-6) Bantam.

— A Kiss at Midnight. (Meet Me at Midnight Ser.). 288p. 2000. mass mkt. 5.99 (0-553-58057-4) Bantam.

Abe, Shana. The Promise of Rain. 384p. 1998. mass mkt. 5.99 (0-553-57788-3) Bantam.

— A Rose in Winter. 400p. 1998. mass mkt. 5.50 (0-553-57787-5) Bantam.

— The Truelove Bride. 368p. 1999. mass mkt. 5.99 (0-553-58054-X) Bantam.

Abe, Shorzoe, jt. auth. see Mikesh, Robert C.

Abe, T. & Tsuta, T., eds. Advances in Engineering Plasticity & Its Applications (AEPA'96) Proceedings of the Asia-Pacific Symposium on Advances in Engineering Plasticity & its Applicatins - AEPA'96, Hiroshima, 21-24 August 1996. LC 96-217661. 952p. 1996. text 223.00 (0-08-042824-X, Pergamon Pr) Elsevier.

Abe, T. & Yamamaka, M., eds. Disseminated Intravascular Coagulation. (Bibliotheca Haemotologica Ser.: No. 49). (Illus.). xiv, 356p. 1983. 171.50 (3-8055-3726-3) S Karger.

Abe, T., ed. see International Symposium on Defects in Silicon, et al.

Abe, Takuya, et al, eds. Biodiversity: An Ecological Perspective. LC 96-13589. 294p. 1996. 79.95 (0-387-94702-7) Spr-Verlag.

*Abe, Takuya, et al. Termites: Evolution, Sociality, Symbioses, Ecology. LC 00-30653. 2000. write for info. (0-7923-6361-2) Kluwer Academic.

Abe, Y., et al, eds. New Trends in Nuclear Collective Dynamics: Proceedings of the Nuclear Physics Part of the Fifth Nishinomiya-Yukawa Memorial Symposium Nishinomiya, Japan, October 25-26, 1990. (Proceedings in Physics Ser.: Vol. 58). (Illus.). viii, 297p. 1992. 86.95 (0-387-53606-X) Spr-Verlag.

— Similarities & Differences Between Atomic Nuclei & Clusters: Toward a Unified Development of Cluster Science. LC 97-77601. (AIP Conference Proceedings Ser.: Vol. 416). (Illus.). xiv, 515p. 1999. write for info. (1-56396-714-6) Am Inst Physics.

— Towards a Unified Picture of Nuclear Dynamics. (Conference Proceeding Ser.: No. 250). 584p. 1992. 110.00 (0-88318-930-5) Am Inst Physics.

Abe, Yoshi. Japanese Phrasebook. 3rd ed. LC 99-220569. (Lonely Planet Phrasebooks). (Illus.). 256p. 1998. pap. text 6.95 (0-86442-616-X) Lonely Planet.

Abe, Yoshihiro, ed. Superconducting Glass-Ceramics in BSCCO: Fabrication Via Melting & Its Applications. LC 98-121488. 300p. 1997. text 48.00 (981-02-3204-7) World Scientific Pub.

Abe, Yukiko. Waves & Ripples Across the Pacific. (Illus.). 200p. 1993. 17.95 (1-57074-239-1) Greyden Pr.

*Abear, Donna. Mom... You're Not Naked, Are You? A Collection of Humor by Donna Abear. LC 00-190203. (Illus.). 256p. 2000. pap. 11.95 (0-9677101-0-3) Moonshadow Bks.

Abear, Donna. Sprucey, the Blue Christmas Tree: A One-Act Play. (Illus.). 36p. (J). (gr. k-8). 1997. pap. 3.50 (0-88680-439-6) I E Clark.

Abear, Gerald J., ed. see Richardson, Robert M.

Abebrase, Owusu E., et al. Criminal Litigation. 2nd ed. (London Guildhall-Cavendish Legal Practice Course Companion Ser.). 434p. 1996. pap. 34.00 (1-85941-006-5, Pub. by Cavendish Pubng) Gaunt.

Abecasis-Phillips, John A. Doing Business with the Japanese. LC 93-421. (Illus.). 176p. 1994. pap. 9.95 (0-8442-8392-4, 83924, NTC Business Bks) NTC Contemp Pub Co.

Abecassis De Laredo, E., ed. see Latin School of Physics Staff.

Abecassis, Michael M., jt. auth. see Stuart, Frank P.

An Asterisk (*) at the beginning of an entry indicates that the title is appearing for the first time.

A'Beckett, Gilbert A. Comic History of England, 2 vols. LC 72-158218. (Illus.). reprint ed. 76.50 (*0-404-00300-1*) AMS Pr.

Abed Al-Jabri, Mohammed. Arab-Islamic Philosophy. 150p. 1999. pap. 12.95 (*0-292-70480-1*) U of Tex Pr.

Abed, George T. & International Monetary Fund Staff. Fiscal Reforms in Low-Income Countries: Experience under IMF-Supported Programs, Vol. 160. LC 97-52372. (Occasional Paper Ser.). 1998. 18.00 (*1-55775-717-8*) Intl Monetary.

Abed-Kotob, Sana, jt. auth. see Sullivan, Denis J.

Abed, Laura W., jt. auth. see Wilkoff, William L.

Abed-Rabbo, Samir & Safie, Doris, eds. The Palestinian Uprising. 435p. (Orig.). 1990. pap. 19.95 (*0-937694-87-8*) Assn Arab-Amer U Grads.

Abed, Shukri B. Aristotelian Logic & the Arabic Language in Alfarabi. LC 89-77651. 226p. (C). 1990. pap. text 24.95 (*0-7914-0398-X*) State U NY Pr.

Abedi, Mehdi, jt. auth. see Fischer, Michael M.

Abedi, Mehdi, ed. & tr. see Taleqani, Mahmud & Mutahhari, Murtada.

Abedi, Mehdi, ed. & tr. see Talequani, Mahmud & Mutahhari, Murtada.

***Abedian, Iraj & Biggs, Michael.** Economic Globalisation & Fiscal Policy in South Africa. LC 99-165255. (Illus.). 576p. 1999. pap. text 37.00 (*0-19-571685-X*) OUP.

Abedian, Julia C. Exposing Federal Sponsorship of Job Loss: The Whitehall Plant Closing Campaign & "Runaway Plant" Reform. LC 95-37868. (Garland Studies on Industrial Productivity). (Illus.). 951026p. 1995. text 47.00 (*0-8153-1778-6*) Garland.

***Abedin, Zainul & Conner, Robert P.** Interpretation of Cardiac Arrhythmias: Self Assessment Approach. LC 99-16596. (Developments in Cardiovascular Medicine Ser.). 1999. write for info. (*0-7923-8576-4*) Kluwer Academic.

Abedin, Zainul & Conner, Robert P. Twelve Lead Egg Interpretation: The Self-Assessment Approach. 336p. 1989. pap. text 35.00 (*0-7216-2846-X*, W B Saunders Co) Harcrt Hlth Sci Grp.

Abee, Blanche H. Humphrey-Thomas - Thomas. Colonists of Carolina in the Lineage of Hon. W. D. Humphrey (Humphrey Family of Onslow County North Carolina & Thomas Family of Duplin County, North Carolina) (Illus.). 254p. 1997. reprint ed. pap. 39.50 (*0-8328-9261-0*); reprint ed. lib. bdg. 49.50 (*0-8328-9260-2*) Higginson Bk Co.

Abee, Cleveland. A First Report on the Relations Between Climates & Crops: U. S. Department of Agriculture, Weather Bureau Bulletin, No. 36. Egerton, Frank N., 3rd, ed. LC 77-74200. (History of Ecology Ser.). 1978. reprint ed. lib. bdg. 33.95 (*0-405-10370-0*) Ayer.

Abee, Steve. Bus. 120p. 1999. pap. text 9.00 (*1-888277-14-9*, Pub. by Incommcdo San Diego) Consort Bk Sales.

— King Planet. (Illus.). 150p. (Orig.). 1996. pap. 12.00 (*1-884615-14-7*) Incommcdo San Diego.

Abeel, David. Memoir of the Rev. David Abeel, D. D. Late Missionary to China. (American Biography Ser.). 315p. 1991. reprint ed. lib. bdg. 79.00 (*0-7812-8000-1*) Rprt Serv.

Abeel, Erica. Women Like Us. 401p. 1993. 22.95 (*0-685-71261-3*) Ticknor & Fields.

— Women Like Us, Vol. 1. 1995. mass mkt. 5.99 (*0-312-95506-5*, Pub. by Tor Bks) St Martin.

Abeel, Samantha. Reach for the Moon. LC 93-46417. (Illus.). 48p. (YA). 1994. 17.95 (*1-57025-013-8*) Pfeifer-Hamilton.

— What Once Was White? Williams, Roberta, ed. LC 93-77359. (Illus.). 48p. 1993. text 19.95 (*0-941653-13-7*) Village Pr Pubns.

Abeer Abu Saud. Qatari Women: Past & Present. (Illus.). 184p. (C). 1984. text 32.95 (*0-582-78372-0*) Longman.

Abegaz, Berhanu. Essays on Ethiopian Economic Development. (Making of Modern Africa Ser.). 368p. 1994. 91.95 (*1-85628-633-9*, Pub. by Avebry) Ashgate Pub Co.

— Manpower Development Planning: Theory & an African Case Study. (Making of Modern Africa Ser.). 240p. 1994. 72.95 (*1-85628-521-9*, Pub. by Avebry) Ashgate Pub Co.

Abegg, Jil, jt. auth. see Abegg, Myrlon.

***Abegg, Jimmy.** Ragamuffin Prayers. LC 99-98000. (Illus.). 160p. 2000. 16.99 (*0-7369-0303-8*) Harvest Hse.

Abegg, Lynda R. & Grillot, Peggy J. Savvy Secs: Street Wise & Book Smart. Treloar, Millicent, ed. LC 84-91839. 140p. (Orig.). 1985. pap. 9.95 (*0-9614131-0-7*) Abegg Grillot Ent.

Abegg, Lynda R., jt. auth. see Grillot, Peggy J.

Abegg, Martin, ed. Dead Sea Scroll Bible. 1999. 18.00 (*0-06-060064-0*) HarpC.

***Abegg, Martin, Jr., et al.** The Dead Sea Scrolls Bible: The Oldest Known Bible Translated for the First Time into English. LC 99-26866. 672p. 1999. 39.95 (*0-06-060063-2*) HarpC.

Abegg, Martin G., jt. auth. see Wacholder, Ben Z.

Abegg, Martin G., jt. ed. see Wacholder, Ben Z.

Abegg, Myrlon & Abegg, Jil. Eat Well...Stay Well...Spend Less! Build Your Immune Power . . . Double Your Buying Power. LC 97-61862. 212p. 1985. reprint ed. pap. text 14.95 (*1-57636-045-8*) SunRise Pbl.

Abegg, Von B. 100 Briefe Deutsch fur Export & Import: Langenscheidts Musterbriefe. (GER.). 160p. 1997. pap. 15.95 (*3-468-41112-X*) Langenscheidt.

Abegglen, James. Sea Change: Pacific Asia As the New World Industrial Center. 320p. 1994. 27.95 (*0-02-900155-2*) Free Pr.

Abegglen, James C. The Japanese Factory: Aspects of Its Social Organization. Coser, Lewis A. & Powell, Walter W., eds. LC 79-6982. (Perennial Works in Sociology). (Illus.). 1980. reprint ed. lib. bdg. 23.95 (*0-405-12082-6*) Ayer.

Abegglen, James C., et al. U. S. - Japan Economic Relations: A Symposium on Critical Issues. LC 80-620017. (Research Papers & Policy: No. 1). 57p. 1980. pap. 5.00 (*0-912966-25-4*) IEAS.

Abegglen, James C., jt. auth. see Warner, W. Lloyd.

Abegglen, Jean-Jacques. On Socialization in Hamadryas Baboons: A Field Study. LC 80-70316. (Illus.). 208p. 1984. 45.00 (*0-8387-5017-6*) Bucknell U Pr.

***Abegglen, Sue R.** Minute Minders. (Illus.). 96p. (YA). (gr. 5). 1998. pap. text 10.95 (*1-58037-071-3*, Pub. by M Twain Media) Carson-Dellos.

— Science Skills Made Easy. (Illus.). 96p. (YA). (gr. 5). 1999. pap. text 10.95 (*1-58037-095-0*, Pub. by M Twain Media) Carson-Dellos.

Abegunrin, Olayiwola. Nigeria & the Struggle for the Liberation of Zimbabwe: A Study of Foreign Policy of an Emerging Nation. LC 92-29433. 268p. 1992. text 89.95 (*0-7734-9178-3*) E Mellen.

Abehsera, Michael, tr. see Kervran, C. Louis.

Abehsera, Michel. Healing Power of Clay: The Natural Remedy for Dozens of Common Ailments. 128p. 1997. pap. text 9.95 (*0-8065-1942-8*, Citadel Pr) Carol Pub Group.

— Zen Macrobiotic Cooking. 1976. mass mkt. 4.95 (*0-380-01483-1*, Avon Bks) Morrow Avon.

— Zen Macrobiotic Cooking. 1971. reprint ed. pap. 9.95 (*0-8065-0893-0*, Citadel Pr) Carol Pub Group.

Abehsera, Michel, ed. & tr. see Dextreit, Raymond.

***Abeille, Anne & Rambow, Owen, eds.** Tree Adjoining Grammars: Mathematical, Computational & Linguistic Properties. (Lecture Notes Ser.: Vol. 107). 400p. (C). 2000. pap. text. write for info. (*1-57586-252-2*, Pub. by CSLI) Cambridge U Pr.

— Tree Adjoining Grammars: Mathematical, Computational & Linguistic Properties. (Lecture Notes Ser.: Vol. 107). 400p. (C). 2000. text. write for info. (*1-57586-251-4*, Pub. by CSLI) Cambridge U Pr.

Abel. Bio-Tech Architecture. 160p. 1998. pap. text 69.99 (*0-7506-3792-7*) Buttrwrth-Heinemann.

— Macroeconomics. 3rd ed. 672p. (C). 1997. text. write for info. (*0-201-33906-4*) Addison-Wesley.

— Organometallic Chemistry, Vol. 15. 1988. 296.00 (*0-85186-631-X*) CRC Pr.

— Speaking Respect. 1999. pap. text 21.00 (*0-226-00057-5*) U Ch Pr.

Abel & Clarke. Narrative of a Journey in the Interior of China. (Illus.). 420p. Date not set. 55.95 (*0-405-01711-1*) Arno Press.

Abel & Stone. Organometallic Chemistry, Vol. 9. 1991. 274.00 (*0-85186-571-2*) CRC Pr.

— Organometallic Chemistry, Vol. 10. 1989. 274.00 (*0-85186-581-X*) CRC Pr.

— Organometallic Chemistry, Vol. 11. 1989. 274.00 (*0-85186-591-7*) CRC Pr.

— Organometallic Chemistry, Vol. 12. 1989. 263.00 (*0-85186-601-8*) CRC Pr.

— Organometallic Chemistry, Vol. 13. 1988. 263.00 (*0-85186-611-5*) CRC Pr.

— Organometallic Chemistry, Vol. 19. 1990. 362.00 (*0-85186-671-9*) CRC Pr.

Abel, et al. Sprachbruecke Level 1: Einspr. Arbeitsheft 1 (Lektionen 1-7) (GER.). 129p. (C). 1988. pap. text 15.25 (*3-12-557150-2*, Pub. by Klett Edition) Intl Bk Import.

— Sprachbruecke Level 1: Einspr. Arbeitsheft 2 (Lektionen 8-15) (GER.). 144p. (C). 1989. pap. text 15.25 (*3-12-557160-X*, Pub. by Klett Edition) Intl Bk Import.

Abel, jt. auth. see Kane.

Abel, Andy & Bernanke, Ben. Conference Board Booklet T/a Web-enabled Version of Macroeconomics By Andy Abel & Ben Bernanke. 3rd ed. (C). 1998. ring bd. 32.81 (*0-321-04679-X*) Addison-Wesley.

Abel, Albert S. Towards a Constitutional Charter for Canada. LC 81-116198. 111p. reprint ed. pap. 34.50 (*0-8357-4133-8*, 203690500006) Bks Demand.

Abel, Allen. Flatbush Odyssey. LC 95-184431. (Illus.). 352p. 1995. 22.95 (*0-7710-0703-5*) McCland & Stewart.

— Flatbush Odyssey: A Journey Through the Heart of Brooklyn. (Illus.). 376p. 1996. pap. 14.95 (*0-7710-0704-3*) McCland & Stewart.

Abel, Andrew. Accompany Macroeconomics. 3rd ed. 304p. (C). 1997. pap. text, student ed. 24.00 (*0-201-49899-5*) Addison-Wesley.

— Macroeconomics. 3rd ed. (C). 1997. text. write for info. (*0-201-49897-9*) Addison-Wesley.

Abel, Andrew & Bernanke, Ben S. Macroeconomics. 2nd rev. ed. Toland, Beth, ed. (C). 1996. text 45.00 (*0-201-84788-4*) Addison-Wesley.

Abel, Andrew, ed. see Modigliani, Franco.

***Abel, Andrew B.** Macroeconomics. 4th ed. (C). 2001. text 86.00 (*0-201-44133-0*) Addison-Wesley.

Abel, Annie H. The American Indian & the End of the Confederacy, 1863-1866. LC 93-17686. viii, 419p. 1993. pap. 12.95 (*0-8032-5921-2*, Bison Books) U of Nebr Pr.

— The American Indian As Participant in the Civil War. 1988. reprint ed. lib. bdg. 79.00 (*0-7812-0727-4*) Rprt Serv.

— The American Indian As Slaveholder & Secessionist. 1988. reprint ed. lib. bdg. 79.00 (*0-7812-0728-2*) Rprt Serv.

— The American Indian in the Civil War, 1862-1865. LC 92-11003. (Illus.). ix, 403p. 1992. reprint ed. pap. 12.95 (*0-8032-5919-0*, Bison Books) U of Nebr Pr.

— The American Indian under Reconstruction. 1988. reprint ed. lib. bdg. 79.00 (*0-7812-0726-6*) Rprt Serv.

— History of Events Resulting in Indian Consolidation West of the Mississippi. LC 76-158219. reprint ed. 34.50 (*0-404-07116-3*) AMS Pr.

— Slaveholding Indians, 3 vols., Set. 1988. reprint ed. lib. bdg. 145.00 (*0-317-90022-6*) Rprt Serv.

— Slaveholding Indians, 3 vols., Set. LC 70-116268. 1925. reprint ed. 200.00 (*0-403-00471-3*) Scholarly.

— Slaveholding Indians: The American Indian As Participant in the Civil War, Vol. 2. LC 70-116268. 1919. reprint ed. 69.00 (*0-685-26253-7*) Scholarly.

— Slaveholding Indians: The American Indian As Slaveholder, Vol. 1. LC 70-116268. 1919. reprint ed. 69.00 (*0-685-26252-9*) Scholarly.

— Slaveholding Indians: The American Indian under Reconstruction, Vol. 3. LC 70-116268. 1919. reprint ed. 69.00 (*0-685-26254-5*) Scholarly.

Abel, Annie H., ed. Chardon's Journal at Fort Clark, 1834-1939. LC 77-140349. (Select Bibliographies Reprint Ser.). 1977. 24.95 (*0-8369-5592-7*) Ayer.

Abel, Annie H., ed. see Sibley, John.

Abel, Annie H., ed. see Tappan, Lewis.

Abel, Annie H., ed. & intro. see Chardon, F. A.

Abel, Armand, et al. Unity & Variety in Muslim Civilization. Von Grunebaum, Gustave E, ed. LC 55-11191. (Comparative Studies of Cultures & Civilizations: No. 7). 397p. reprint ed. pap. 123.10 (*0-608-18609-0*, 201361400087) Bks Demand.

Abel, Bernanke. Macroeconomics: The Brief Edition. (C). 1999. text. write for info. (*0-201-36010-1*) Addison-Wesley.

Abel, Brig H. & Grunner, Margit. Alles Gute: Resource Package. (GER.). 224p. 1989. teacher ed. 38.95 (*3-468-96890-6*) Langenscheidt.

Abel, Carl F. Carl Friedrich Abel: Six Selected Symphonies. Helm, Sanford, ed. (Recent Researches in Music of the Classic Era Ser.: Vol. RRC3). (Illus.). xi, 85p. 1977. pap. 35.00 (*0-89579-094-7*) A-R Eds.

Abel, Charles F. & Marsh, Frank H. In Defense of Political Trials, 336. LC 93-14129. 168p. 1993. 62.95 (*0-313-25111-8*, ADP/, Greenwood Pr) Greenwood.

— Punishment & Restitution: A Restitutionary Approach to Crime & the Criminal, 5. LC 83-22837. (Contributions in Criminology & Penology Ser.: No. 5). (Illus.). 214p. 1984. 62.95 (*0-313-23717-4*, ABP/) Greenwood.

Abel, Charles F., jt. ed. see Tetreault, Mary A.

***Abel, Chris.** Architecture & Identity: Responses to Cultural & Technological Change. 2nd ed. LC 99-51340. 288p. 2000. pap. 54.95 (*0-7506-4246-7*, Architectural Pr) Buttrwrth-Heinemann.

Abel, Chris. Architecture & Identity: Towards a Global Eco-Culture. LC 96-35728. 160p. 1997. pap. text 44.95 (*0-7506-0790-4*) Buttrwrth-Heinemann.

— Renault Centre: Architecture in Detail 04. (Architecture in Detail Ser.). 144p. 1991. pap. 44.95 (*0-471-28964-7*, VNR) Wiley.

— Renault Centre: Architecture in Detail 04. (Architecture in Detail Ser.). (Illus.). 144p. 1991. pap. 44.95 (*0-442-30826-4*, VNR) Wiley.

— Renault Centre: Swindon 1982 Foster Associates. (Architecture in Detail Ser.). (Illus.). 60p. (Orig.). 1997. pap. 29.95 (*1-85454-776-3*) Phaidon Pr.

Abel, D. & Ooi, B. C., eds. Advances in Spatial Databases: Proceedings of the Third International Symposium, SSD '93, Singapore, June 23-25, 1993. (Lecture Notes in Computer Science Ser.: Vol. 692). xiii, 529p. 1993. 73.95 (*0-387-56869-7*) Spr-Verlag.

Abel, Darrel. The Moral Picturesque: Studies in Hawthorne's Fiction. LC 87-26843. 336p. 1988. 28.95 (*0-911198-91-1*) Purdue U Pr.

Abel, David L. Patterns of Presumption: Reflections on How We View Reality. xi, 300p. 1998. 17.99 (*0-9657988-1-X*) LongView Press.

Abel, David W. What's That You Say? A Viewpoint Challenge. 167p. (Orig.). 1990. pap. 6.95 (*0-9627711-0-4*) D W Abel.

Abel, Don. Cooking with the Bad Guys: Recipes from the World's Most Notorious Kitchens. 1994. 13.95 (*0-87951-550-3*, Pub. by Overlook Pr) Penguin Putnam.

Abel, Donald C. Fifty Readings in Philosophy. LC 93-23607. 512p. (C). 1993. pap. 24.38 (*0-07-051518-2*) McGraw.

— Theories of Human Nature. 432p. (C). 1991. pap. 26.25 (*0-07-000050-6*) McGraw.

Abel, E. L. Fetal Alcohol Abuse Syndrome. LC 98-26505. (Illus.). 242p. (C). 1998. text 42.50 (*0-306-45666-4*, Kluwer Plenum) Kluwer Academic.

— Fetal Alcohol Syndrome & Fetal Alcohol Effects. LC 83-26898. (Illus.). 256p. (C). 1984. 49.00 (*0-306-41427-9*, Plenum Trade) Perseus Pubng.

— Marihuana: The First Twelve Thousand Years. LC 80-15606. (Illus.). 302p. (C). 1980. 44.50 (*0-306-40496-6*, Plenum Trade) Perseus Pubng.

***Abel, E. Lawrence.** Singing the New Nation: How Music Shaped the Confederacy, 1861-1865. LC 99-40645. (Illus.). 352p. 1999. 29.95 (*0-8117-0228-6*) Stackpole.

Abel, E. W. Organometallic Chemistry, Vol. 22. 506p. 1993. 341.00 (*0-85186-701-4*, R6701) CRC Pr.

Abel, E. W. & Stone, F. G. Organometallic Chemistry, Vol. 17. 502p. 1989. 330.00 (*0-85186-651-4*) CRC Pr.

Abel, Edward W. Organometallic Chemistry, Vol. 23. 456p. 1994. 341.00 (*0-85186-711-1*, R6711) CRC Pr.

Abel, Edward W. & Stone. Organometallic Chemistry, Vol. 8. 1991. 164.00 (*0-85186-690-5*) CRC Pr.

Abel, Eli, ed. What's News: The Media in American Society. 300p. 1981. 39.95 (*0-87855-448-3*) Transaction Pubs.

Abel, Elie. Leaking: Who Does It? Who Benefits? At What Cost? - A Twentieth Century Fund Paper. 75p. (C). 1987. text 18.95 (*0-87078-219-3*); pap. text 7.95 (*0-87078-218-5*) Century Foundation.

Abel, Elie, ed. What's News: The Media in American Society. LC 81-81414. 296p. 1981. text 19.95 (*0-917616-41-3*) ICS Pr.

Abel, Elizabeth. Virginia Woolf & the Fictions of Psychoanalysis. LC 89-4810. (Women in Culture & Society Ser.). 200p. 1989. 29.95 (*0-226-00079-6*) U Ch Pr.

— Virginia Woolf & the Fictions of Psychoanalysis. LC 89-4810. (Women in Culture & Society Ser.). xviii, 200p. (C). 1992. pap. text 13.95 (*0-226-00081-8*) U Ch Pr.

— Writing & Sexual Difference. LC 82-11131. (Phoenix Ser.). 322p. (C). 1982. pap. text 17.00 (*0-226-00076-1*) U Ch Pr.

Abel, Elizabeth, ed. Writing & Sexual Difference. LC 82-11131. 321p. reprint ed. pap. 99.60 (*0-608-09254-1*, 205405600002) Bks Demand.

Abel, Elizabeth, et al, eds. Female Subjects in Black & White: Race, Psychoanalysis, Feminism. LC 96-23683. (Illus.). 425p. 1997. 55.00 (*0-520-20629-0*, Pub. by U CA Pr); pap. 18.95 (*0-520-20630-4*, Pub. by U CA Pr) Cal Prin Full Svc.

— The Voyage In: Fictions of Female Development. LC 82-40473. 374p. 1983. reprint ed. pap. 116.00 (*0-608-02315-9*, 206295600004) Bks Demand.

Abel, Elizabeth & Abel, Emily K., eds. The Signs Reader: Women, Gender & Scholarship. LC 83-5781. 304p. 1983. pap. 14.95 (*0-226-00075-3*); lib. bdg. 25.00 (*0-226-00074-5*) U Ch Pr.

Abel, Elizabeth A. Photochemotherapy in Dermatology. LC 91-7109. (Illus.). 352p. 1992. text 90.00 (*0-89640-186-3*) Igaku-Shoin.

***Abel, Emily K.** Hearts of Wisdom: American Women Caring for Kin, 1850-1940. 352p. 2000. 49.95 (*0-674-00314-4*) HUP.

Abel, Emily K. Terminal Degrees: The Job Crisis in Higher Education. LC 83-26876. 253p. 1984. 45.00 (*0-275-91108-X*, C1108, Praeger Pubs) Greenwood.

— Who Cares for the Elderly? Public Policy & the Experiences of Adult Daughters. (Women in the Political Economy Ser.). 220p. 1991. 44.95 (*0-87722-814-0*) Temple U Pr.

— Who Cares for the Elderly? Public Policy & the Experiences of Adult Daughters. (Women in the Political Economy Ser.). 220p. 1992. pap. 22.95 (*0-87722-950-3*) Temple U Pr.

Abel, Emily K. & Nelson, Margaret K., eds. Circles of Care: Work & Identity in Women's Lives. LC 89-78197. (SUNY Series on Women & Work). 326p. (C). 1990. text 24.50 (*0-7914-0263-0*) State U NY Pr.

Abel, Emily K. & Pearson, M. L., eds. Across Cultures: The Spectrum of Women's Lives. (Studies in Gender & Culture: Vol. 4). iv, 156p. 1989. pap. text 29.00 (*0-677-22050-2*) Gordon & Breach.

Abel, Emily K., jt. ed. see Abel, Elizabeth.

Abel, Ernest L. Ancient Views on the Origins of Life. LC 72-656. 93p. 1973. 19.50 (*0-8386-1198-2*) Fairleigh Dickinson.

— Behavioral Teratogenesis & Behavioral Mutagenesis: A Primer in Abnormal Development. (Illus.). 254p. (C). 1989. text 49.50 (*0-306-43053-3*, Kluwer Plenum) Kluwer Academic.

— Behavioral Teratology: A Bibliography to the Study of Birth Defects of the Mind. LC 85-21946. 206p. 1985. lib. bdg. 55.00 (*0-313-25066-9*, ABT/, Greenwood Pr) Greenwood.

— A Dictionary of Drug Abuse Terms & Terminology. LC 83-22867. 137p. 1984. lib. bdg. 49.95 (*0-313-24095-7*, ADD/, Greenwood Pr) Greenwood.

— Fetal Alcohol Syndrome: An Annotated & Comprehensive Bibliography, 3 vols., I. 144p. 1981. 83.00 (*0-8493-6192-3*, RG629, CRC Reprint) Franklin.

— Fetal Alcohol Syndrome: An Annotated & Comprehensive Bibliography, 3 vols., II. 144p. 1982. 117.00 (*0-8493-6193-1*, CRC Reprint) Franklin.

— Fetal Alcohol Syndrome: An Annotated & Comprehensive Bibliography, 3 vols., III. 144p. 1982. 117.00 (*0-8493-6194-X*, CRC Reprint) Franklin.

— Fetal Alcohol Syndrome: An Annotated Bibliography. LC 85-25594. 170p. 1985. 65.00 (*0-275-92028-3*, C2028, Praeger Pubs) Greenwood.

— A Marihuana Dictionary: Words, Terms, Events & Persons Relating to Cannabis. LC 81-13427. 136p. 1982. lib. bdg. 55.00 (*0-313-23252-0*, ABM/, Greenwood Pr) Greenwood.

— Marihuana, Tobacco, Alcohol, & Reproduction. 256p. 1983. 146.00 (*0-8493-6480-9*, RG580, CRC Reprint) Franklin.

— Psychoactive Drugs & Sex. (Illus.). 242p. (C). 1985. 65.00 (*0-306-41869-X*, Plenum Trade) Perseus Pubng.

— The Roots of Anti-Semitism. LC 73-8286. 264p. 1975. 35.00 (*0-8386-1406-X*) Fairleigh Dickinson.

— Smoking & Reproduction: A Comprehensive Bibliography. LC 82-15660. 163p. 1982. lib. bdg. 55.00 (*0-313-23663-1*, ASR/, Greenwood Pr) Greenwood.

— Smoking & Reproduction: An Annotated Bibliography. 160p. 1984. 98.00 (*0-8493-6481-7*, Z6671, CRC Reprint) Franklin.

Abel, Ernest L., compiled by. Alcohol & Reproduction: A Bibliography. LC 82-6202. 219p. 1982. lib. bdg. 55.00 (*0-313-23474-4*, AAR/, Greenwood Pr) Greenwood.

— A Comprehensive Guide to the Cannabis Literature. LC 78-20014. 699p. 1979. lib. bdg. 115.00 (*0-313-20721-6*, ACG/, Greenwood Pr) Greenwood.

— Dictionary of Alcohol Use & Abuse: Slang, Terms & Terminology. LC 84-22521. 189p. 1985. lib. bdg. 75.00 (*0-313-24631-9*, ABA/, Greenwood Pr) Greenwood.

— Drugs & Sex: A Bibliography. LC 83-5656. 129p. 1983. lib. bdg. 42.95 (*0-313-23941-X*, ADS/, Greenwood Pr) Greenwood.

— Fetal Alcohol Exposure & Effects: A Comprehensive Bibliography. LC 85-9864. 309p. 1985. lib. bdg. 79.50 (*0-313-24632-7*, AFC/, Greenwood Pr) Greenwood.

— Homicide: A Bibliography, 11. LC 87-7553. (Bibliographies & Indexes in Sociology Ser.: No. 11). 182p. 1987. lib. bdg. 62.95 (*0-313-25901-1*, AHD/, Greenwood Pr) Greenwood.

An Asterisk (*) at the beginning of an entry indicates that the title is appearing for the first time.

— Lead & Reproduction: A Comprehensive Bibliography. LC 84-12846. 118p. 1985. lib. bdg. 59.95 (*0-313-24604-1*, ALR/, Greenwood Pr) Greenwood.

— Narcotics & Reproduction: A Bibliography. LC 83-13252. 215p. 1983. lib. bdg. 75.00 (*0-313-24052-3*, ABN/, Greenwood Pr) Greenwood.

— New Literature on Fetal Alcohol Exposure & Effects: A Bibliography, 1983-1988, 4. LC 89-28641. (Bibliographies & Indexes in Medical Studies: No. 4). 245p. 1990. lib. bdg. 65.00 (*0-313-27329-4*, ANL/, Greenwood Pr) Greenwood.

— Viruses & Reproduction: A Bibliography, 2. LC 88-16575. 329p. 1988. lib. bdg. 69.50 (*0-313-26439-2*, AVR/, Greenwood Pr) Greenwood.

Abel, Ernest L., ed. Fetal Alcohol Syndrome: From Mechanism to Prevention. LC 96-19080. 352p. 1996. boxed set 139.95 (*0-8493-7685-8*) CRC Pr.

Abel, Ernest L. & Buckley, Barbara E. The Handwriting on the Wall: Toward a Sociology & Psychology of Graffiti, 27. LC 76-50408. (Contributions in Sociology Ser.: No. 27). 156p. 1977. 39.95 (*0-8371-9475-X*, AVJ/, Greenwood Pr) Greenwood.

Abel, Francis L. & Newman, Walter H., eds. Functional Aspects of the Normal, Hypertrophied, & Failing Heart. (Developments in Cardiovascular Medicine Ser.). 1984. text 146.50 (*0-89838-665-9*) Kluwer Academic.

Abel, Friedhelm. The Kettenkrad. LC 91-60855. (Illus.). 48p. 1991. pap. 9.95 (*0-88740-315-8*) Schiffer.

Abel, Gunter. Nietzsche. Die Dynamik der Willen Zur Macht und die Ewige Wiederkehr Vol. 2: Um ein Vorwort Erweiterte Auflage. 504p. 1998. 36.00 (*3-11-015191-X*) De Gruyter.

Abel, Gunter & Salaquarda, Jorg, eds. Krisis der Metaphysik. xiv, 534p. (C). 1989. lib. bdg. 184.65 (*3-11-011269-8*) De Gruyter.

Abel, H., ed. Electrocardiology No. VI. (Advances in Cardiology Ser.: Vol. 28). (Illus.). xii, 248p. 1981. 136.75 (*3-8055-1185-X*) S Karger.

Abel, H., ed. see Congress on Electrocardiology, 1st, Wiesbaden, Oct.

Abel, H., ed. see International Congress on Electrocardiology Staff.

Abel Halvorsen, Sharon. Murder in Their Midst. LC 98-89649. 112p. 1999. pap. 13.50 (*0-88739-223-7*) Creat Arts Bk.

Abel, Istvan, et al. Money & Finance in the Transition to a Market Economy. LC 97-43508. 224p. 1998. 80.00 (*1-85898-228-6*) E Elgar.

Abel, Jackie, jt. auth. see Abel, Ken.

Abel, Jacob F. Einleitung in die Seelenlehre. (GER.). xxxiii, 465p. 1985. reprint ed. write for info. (*3-487-07605-5*) G Olms Pubs.

Abel, Janice. Community Shapers: Conversations with Retired Women. LC 97-151745. vii, 98p. 1997. pap. 13.95 (*0-9655739-0-7*) Abel Pub.

Abel, Janice, jt. auth. see Abel, Ruth A.

***Abel, Jessica.** Mirror, Window: An Artbabe Collection. (Illus.). 2000. pap. 12.95 (*1-56097-384-6*) Fantagraph Bks.

***Abel, Jessica & Glass, Ira.** Radio: An Illustrated Guide. (Illus.). 30p. 1999. 3.95 (*0-9679671-0-4*) WBEZ.

Abel, John F., ed. see International Association for Shell & Spatial Stru & Committee on Special Structures Staff, Structural.

***Abel, Kathleen.** Smile So Big. LC 97-2313. (J). 1998. 14.95 (*0-15-200671-0*) Harcourt.

Abel, Kathryn, et al, eds. Planning Community Mental Health Services for Women: A Multiprofessional Handbook. LC 95-38887. 280p. (C). 1996. 80.00 (*0-415-11455-1*); pap. 25.99 (*0-415-11456-X*) Routledge.

Abel, Ken. The Yiddishe Kup Dictionary. 64p. (Orig.). 1997. pap. 4.95 (*0-944214-13-4*) ABELexpress.

Abel, Ken & Abel, Jackie. The Tongue-in-Cheek Guide to Pittsburgh. (Illus.). 128p. (Orig.). 1997. reprint ed. pap. 4.95 (*0-944214-14-2*) ABELexpress.

Abel, Ken, jt. auth. see Chou, B. Ralph.

Abel, Kenneth. Bait. large type ed. LC 94-9344. 411p. 1994. lib. bdg. 23.95 (*0-8161-7436-9*, G K Hall Lrg Type) Mac Lib Ref.

— The Blue Wall. large type ed. 1996. 24.95 (*0-7862-0823-6*) Thorndike Pr.

***Abel, Kenneth.** Cold Steel Rain. 432p. 2000. 24.95 (*0-399-14662-8*) Putnam Pub Group.

Abel, Kenneth B. & Warfield, Guy W. The Maryland Corporation: Legal Aspects of Organization & Operation. (Corporate Practice Ser.: No. 71). 1997. 95.00 (*1-55871-362-X*) BNAC.

Abel, Kenneth F. Pennsylvania Gun Law Guide: What Every Handgun, Rifle or Shotgun Owner Must Know about Pennsylvania & Federal Gun Laws. 160p. (Orig.). 1996. pap. 7.95 (*0-944214-07-X*) ABELexpress.

Abel, Kerry. Drum Songs: Glimpses of Dene History. (McGill-Queen's Studies in Ethnic History). (Illus.). 368p. 1993. 60.00 (*0-7735-0992-5*, Pub. by McG-Queens Univ Pr); pap. 22.95 (*0-7735-1150-4*, Pub. by McG-Queens Univ Pr) CUP Services.

Abel, L. William, et al. Firefighting & Blowout Control. (Illus.). 450p. 1996. 95.00 (*0-9640030-9-0*, 03090) Gulf Pub.

***Abel, LaVerne.** Just Got to Thinkin' 1999. pap. write for info. (*1-58235-302-6*) Watermrk Pr.

Abel, LaVerne. The Moods of LaVerne. 1998. pap. write for info. (*1-57553-834-2*) Watermrk Pr.

Abel, Lionel, tr. see Pissarro, Camille.

Abel, Marianne, ed. Farm Wives & Other Iowa Stories. (Illus.). 138p. (Orig.). 1995. pap. 11.95 (*0-931209-57-9*) Mid-Prairie Bks.

Abel, Martin S. Occult Traumatic Lesions of the Cervical & Thoraco-Lumbar Vertebrae. 2nd ed. 392p. 1983. 42.50 (*0-87527-312-2*) Green.

Abel, Michael. Backpacking Made Easy, Vol. 1. rev. ed. LC 75-8529. (Illus.). 128p. 1975. pap. 7.95 (*0-87961-040-9*) Naturegraph.

Abel, Michele. The Art of Rubber Stamping: Easy As 1, 2, 3. 208p. 1991. pap. 14.95 (*0-9630756-0-8*) Creative MN.

— The Art of Rubber Stamping: Easy As 1-2-3. 2nd ed. 187p. 1995. pap. 16.95 (*0-9630756-2-4*) Creative MN.

— Rubber Stamping: Beyond the Basics. 184p. 1994. pap. 16.95 (*0-9630756-1-6*) Creative MN.

— Thanks for the Memories. 200p. 1998. pap. 19.95 (*0-9630756-3-2*) Creative MN.

Abel, Oliver. The Minimalist Griller Handbook. (Illus.). 208p. 1998. pap. 16.00 (*0-8059-4523-7*) Dorrance.

Abel, Othenio. Palaobiologie und Stammeschichte: Paleobiology & Phylogeny. Gould, Stephen Jay, ed. LC 79-8320. (History of Paleontology Ser.). (GER., Illus.). 1980. reprint ed. lib. bdg. 44.95 (*0-405-12701-4*) Ayer.

Abel, P. D. Water Pollution Biology. 1989. text 76.95 (*0-470-21394-9*) P-H.

— Water Pollution Biology. 2nd ed. 256p. 1997. 84.95 (*0-7484-0661-1*, Pub. by Tay Francis Ltd); pap. 34.95 (*0-7484-0619-0*, Pub. by Tay Francis Ltd) Taylor & Francis.

Abel, Peter. COBOL Programming: A Structured Approach. 3rd ed. 384p. (C). 1988. pap. text 48.20 (*0-13-139247-6*) P-H.

— IBM PC Assembly Language & Programming. 4th ed. LC 97-8688. 606p. (C). 1997. 73.00 (*0-13-756610-7*) P-H.

— Programming Assembler Language: IBM 370 Architecture & Assembly Language. 3rd ed. 528p. (C). 1989. text 44.20 (*0-13-728924-3*) P-H.

Abel, R. C., ed. see Chodkiewicz, K. & Abel, R. Christopher.

Abel, R. Christopher. The Pythagorean Brotherhood. Holmes, J. D., ed. (Orig.). 1997. pap. 4.95 (*1-55818-375-2*, Alexandrian) Holmes Pub.

Abel, R. Christopher & Hare, William L. Hermes Trismegistus: An Investigation of the Origin of the Hermetic Writings. 1996. reprint ed. pap. 4.95 (*1-55818-352-3*, Alexandrian) Holmes Pub.

Abel, R. Christopher & St. Luke, Hector. Master Craft of the Medieval Free Masons & Sacred Builders. 1997. reprint ed. pap. 6.95 (*1-55818-378-7*) Holmes Pub.

Abel, R. Christopher, jt. auth. see Chodkiewicz, K.

Abel, R. Christopher, jt. auth. see Maurer, Eduard.

Abel, R. Christopher, jt. auth. see Taylor, Allan N.

Abel, R. Christopher, ed. see Boulnois, Helen M.

Abel, R. Christopher, ed. see Potter, Edwin.

Abel, Reuben. Man Is the Measure. 320p. 1997. pap. 16.95 (*0-684-83636-X*) Free Pr.

— Man Is the Measure: A Cordial Invitation to the Central Problems of Philosophy. LC 75-16646. (Illus.). 1976. pap. 16.95 (*0-02-900110-2*) Free Pr.

— Pragmatic Humanism of F. C. S. Schiller. LC 70-158220. reprint ed. 24.50 (*0-404-00275-7*) AMS Pr.

Abel, Richard. The Book in the United States Today. LC 97-6314. 280p. 1997. pap. text 21.95 (*1-56000-972-1*) Transaction Pubs.

— Cine Goes to Town: French Cinema, 1896-1914. 574p. 1998. pap. text 29.95 (*0-520-07936-1*, Pub. by U CA Pr) Cal Prin Full Svc.

— French Cinema: The First Wave, 1915-1929. LC 83-43057. (Illus.). 695p. 1984. reprint ed. pap. 200.00 (*0-7837-8576-3*, 204939100011) Bks Demand.

— Lawyers. LC 98-150214. 1997. pap. 24.95 (*1-56584-392-4*, Pub. by New Press NY) Norton.

— Politics by Other Means: Law & the Struggle Against Apartheid. (After the Law Ser.). 600p. (C). 1995. pap. 23.99 (*0-415-90817-5*, B0758) Routledge.

— Politics by Other Means: Law in the Struggle Against Apartheid, 1980-1994. (After the Law Ser.). 664p. (C). 1995. 90.00 (*0-415-90816-7*, B0754) Routledge.

— The Red Rooster Scare: Making Cinema American, 1900-1910. LC 97-52074. 328p. 1999. 50.00 (*0-520-21203-7*, Pub. by U CA Pr) Cal Prin Full Svc.

— The Red Rooster Scare: or the Americanization of Early American Cinema. LC 97-52074. (Illus.). 328p. 1998. pap. 24.95 (*0-520-21478-1*, Pub. by U CA Pr) Cal Prin Full Svc.

Abel, Richard, ed. Silent Film. LC 95-12437. (Depth of Field Ser.). (Illus.). 300p. (C). 1995. text 52.00 (*0-8135-2225-0*); pap. text 20.00 (*0-8135-2226-9*) Rutgers U Pr.

Abel, Richard L. The Cine Goes to Town: French Cinema 1896-1914. LC 93-20640. 574p. 1994. 65.00 (*0-520-07935-3*, Pub. by U CA Pr) Cal Prin Full Svc.

— Speaking Respect. LC 97-30778. 380p. 1998. 30.00 (*0-226-00056-7*) U Ch Pr.

Abel, Richard L., ed. The Law & Society Reader. 450p. (C). 1995. text 55.00 (*0-8147-0617-7*); pap. text 20.00 (*0-8147-0618-5*) NYU Pr.

— Lawyers: A Critical Reader. 311p. 1997. 45.00 (*1-56584-324-X*, Pub. by New Press NY) Norton.

— The Politics of Informal Justice Vol. 2: Comparative Studies. LC 81-14920. (Studies on Law & Social Control). 1981. text 74.95 (*0-12-041502-X*) Acad Pr.

Abel, Richard L. & Lewis, Philip S., eds. Lawyers in Society: An Overview. LC 95-36935. 375p. 1995. pap. 19.95 (*0-520-20332-1*, Pub. by U CA Pr) Cal Prin Full Svc.

Abel, Robert. The Eye Care Revolution. 256p. 1999. pap. 14.00 (*1-57566-372-4*) Kensgtn Pub Corp.

— Full Tilt Boogie. LC 89-2418. 263p. 1989. 18.95 (*0-89924-065-8*); pap. 11.95 (*0-89924-064-X*) Lynx Hse.

— Ghost Traps. LC 90-34243. (Flannery O'Connor Award for Short Fiction Ser.). 168p. 1991. 19.95 (*0-8203-1252-5*) U of Ga Pr.

— The Relationship Toolbox: Tools for Love, Healing & Personal Empowerment. LC 97-71726. (Illus.). 500p. (Orig.). 1998. pap. 14.95 (*0-9657666-2-4*) Valntne Pub.

— Riding a Tiger: The Self-Criticism of Arnold Fisher. 168p. 1999. pap. 14.00 (*962-7160-50-4*, Pub. by Asia) Weatherhill.

Abel, Robert B. The Influence of Technical Cooperation on Reducing Tensions in the Middle East. LC 96-54912. 144p. 1997. 47.50 (*0-7618-0698-9*); pap. 29.50 (*0-7618-0699-7*) U Pr of Amer.

Abel, Ruth A. & Abel, Janice. From the Wishmore to You: Sisters Growing up in the '40s. LC 98-92729. (Illus.). vii, 125p. 1998. 27.95 (*0-9655739-2-3*); pap. 19.95 (*0-9655739-1-5*) Abel Pub.

Abel, Simone. Alphabet Sheep. (Illus.). 12p. (J). (ps-k). 1998. 7.95 (*0-7613-0395-2*) Millbrook Pr.

— Counting Sheep. (Illus.). 12p. (J). (ps). 1998. 7.95 (*0-7613-0396-0*) Millbrook Pr.

— Happy Birthday 1-Year-Old. (Illus.). 12p. (J). (ps). 1996. 8.99 (*0-8037-1921-3*, Dial Yng Read) Peng Put Young Read.

***Abel, Simone.** Baby's Bible Friends. (Baby Blessings Ser.). 8p. (J). 2000. 12.99 (*0-7847-1133-X*, 04313) Standard Pub.

Abel-Smith, B. & Leiserson, A. Poverty, Development & Health Policy. (Public Health Papers: No. 69). 109p. 1978. pap. text 10.00 (*92-4-130069-8*, 1110069) World Health.

Abel-Smith, Brian. Cost Containment & New Priorities in Health Care: A Study of the European Community. 160p. 1992. 66.95 (*1-85628-319-4*, Pub. by Avebry) Ashgate Pub Co.

— An Introduction to Health: Policy, Planning, & Financing. LC 94-7222. 1994. pap. text. write for info. (*0-582-23865-X*) Longman.

— An Introduction to Health: Policy, Planning & Financing. LC 94-7222. 1994. text. write for info. (*0-582-23866-8*) Longman.

— Legal Problems & the Citizen. 1973. text 26.00 (*0-435-82865-7*) Ashgate Pub Co.

Abel-Smith, Brian & Titmuss, Kay, eds. Philosophy of Welfare: Selected Writing of Richard M. Titmuss. 240p. (C). 1987. text 49.95 (*0-04-361063-3*); pap. text 18.95 (*0-04-361064-1*) Routledge.

Abel-Smith, Brian, jt. auth. see Titmuss, Richard M.

Abel, Sue. Reporting Waitangi: The Shaping of Television News. LC 97-221713. (Illus.). 176p. 1997. pap. 29.95 (*1-86940-176-X*, Pub. by Auckland Univ) Paul & Co Pubs.

Abel, Theodora M. Psychological Testing in Cultural Contexts. 1973. pap. 15.95 (*0-8084-0364-8*) NCUP.

Abel, Theodora M. & Metreaux, Rhoda. Culture & Psychotherapy. 1974. 24.95 (*0-8084-0368-0*); pap. 17.95 (*0-8084-0369-9*) NCUP.

Abel, Theodora Mead, tr. see Zarnuji, Burhan al-Din.

Abel, Theodore. Why Hitler Came into Power. 352p. 1986. pap. 18.50 (*0-674-95200-6*) HUP.

Abel, Ulf. National Museum, Stockholm. LC 96-110230. (Museum Ser.). (Illus.). 145p. 1995. 30.00 (*1-85759-048-1*) Scala Books.

Abel-Vidor, Suzanne, et al. Remember Your Relations: The Elsie Allen Baskets, Family & Friends. (Illus.). 128p. 1996. pap. 20.00 (*0-930588-80-0*) Heyday Bks.

Abela, George S., ed. Diagnostic & Therapeutic Cardiovascular Interventions II. 1992. 20.00 (*0-8194-0788-7*, 1642) SPIE.

— Lasers in Cardiovascular Medicine & Surgery: Fundamentals & Techniques. (Developments in Cardiovascular Medicine Ser.). (C). 1990. text 259.50 (*0-7923-0440-3*) Kluwer Academic.

Abelar, Taisha. The Sorcerers' Crossing: A Woman's Journey. 266p. 1993. reprint ed. pap. 13.95 (*0-14-019366-9*, Arkana) Viking Penguin.

Abelard, P., et al, eds. Euro Ceramics: ECERS V, Proceedings 5th Conference & Exhibition of the European Ceramic Society, Versailles, France, June 22-26, 1997, 3 vols. (Key Engineering Materials Ser.: Vols. 132-136). (Illus.). 2572p. (C). 1997. text 440.00 (*0-87849-761-7*, Pub. by Trans T Pub) Enfield Pubs NH.

Abelard, Peter. A Dialogue of a Philosopher with a Jew, & a Christian. viii, 187p. pap. 8.00 (*0-88844-269-6*) Brill Academic Pubs.

— Ethical Writings: The Complete Texts of Ethics & Dialogue Between a Philosopher, a Jew, & a Christian. Spade, Paul V., tr. LC 95-24270. (Hackett Classics Ser.). 256p. (C). 1995. pap. text 10.95 (*0-87220-322-0*); lib. bdg. 32.50 (*0-87220-323-9*) Hackett Pub.

— Ethics. Luscombe, D. E., ed. (Oxford Medieval Texts Ser.). (Illus.). 206p. 1971. text 95.00 (*0-19-822217-3*) OUP.

Abelard, Peter & Heloise. Love Letters of Abelard & Heloise. 1991. lib. bdg. 250.00 (*0-8490-4152-X*) Gordon Pr.

Abelda, Randy, et al, eds. Real World Micro. 7th ed. (Real World Readers Ser.). (Illus.). 128p. (C). 1998. pap. text 14.50 (*1-878585-37-1*) Dollars & Sense.

Abele, Jon R. About Starting Your Own Business: 95 Questions & Answers. (Illus.). 32p. 1993. pap. 1.80 (*0-88450-612-6*, 6116-N) Lawyers & Judges.

— Auto Accident Checklist. LC 94-43879. 128p. 1995. pap. text 21.00 (*0-913875-12-0*, 5120-N) Lawyers & Judges.

— Que Debe de Hacer Si Tiene un Accidente Automovilistico: 50 Preguntas y Respuestes.Tr. of 50 Questions & Answers about Automobile Accidents. (SPA.). 32p. 1993. pap. 1.80 (*0-913875-49-X*, 6122-N) Lawyers & Judges.

— What to Do If You Have an Auto Accident: 50 Questions & Answers (with Accident Scene Forms) (Illus.). 32p. 1993. pap. 1.80 (*0-88450-613-4*, 6114-N) Lawyers & Judges.

— You & Small Claims Court: 95 Questions & Answers. (Illus.). 32p. 1994. pap. 1.80 (*0-88450-611-8*, 6118-N) Lawyers & Judges.

Abele, Jon R. & Corey, Barry. Checklist: Damages in Personal Injury Cases. LC 97-52171. 72p. 1998. pap. 21.00 (*0-913875-37-6*, 5376-N) Lawyers & Judges.

Abele, Jon R., jt. auth. see Bakken, Gary.

Abele, Jon R., jt. auth. see Sindell, Joseph.

Abele, Lawrence, jt. ed. see Bliss, Dorothy E.

Abele, Manlio G. Structures of Permanent Magnets: Generation of Uniform Fields. LC 92-35449. 416p. 1993. 125.00 (*0-471-59112-2*) Wiley.

Abele, Rudolph R. Von, see Von Abele, Rudolph R.

Abeles, B., et al, eds. Energy & the Environment: Symposium Held on the Occasion of the 60th Birthday of George D. Cody, Annandale, U. S. A., May 18, 1990. 300p. 1992. text 93.00 (*981-02-0390-X*) World Scientific Pub.

Abeles, B., jt. ed. see Chang, R. P. H.

Abeles, Charles C. & Preston, Nathaniel S. Inside Information: Prevention of Abuse. 2nd ed. (Corporate Practice Series Portfolio: No. 15-2nd). 1987. 92.00 (*1-55871-232-1*) BNA.

Abeles, Francine F. The Mathematical Pamphlets of Charles Lutwidge Dodgson & Related Pieces Vol. 2: The Pamphlets. 1995. 65.00 (*0-930326-09-1*) L Carroll Soc.

Abeles, Francine F., ed. The Mathematical Pamphlets of Charles Lutwidge Dodgson & Related Pieces. (Pamphlets of Lewis Carroll Ser.: Vol. 2). (Illus.). 440p. (C). 1994. text 65.00 (*0-930326-08-3*) L Carroll Soc.

Abeles, Harold F., et al. Foundations of Music Education. 2nd ed. (Illus.). 408p. (C). 1994. 42.00 (*0-02-870011-2*, Schirmer Books) Mac Lib Ref.

Abeles, M. Corticonics: Neural Circuits of the Cerebral Cortex. (Illus.). 294p. (C). 1991. text 74.95 (*0-521-37476-6*) Cambridge U Pr.

— Local Cortical Circuits: An Electrophysiological Study. (Studies of Brain Function: Vol. 6). (Illus.). 110p. 1982. 38.95 (*0-387-11034-8*) Spr-Verlag.

Abeles, Marc. Quiet Days in Burgundy: A Study of Local Politics. McDermott, Annella, tr. (Cambridge Studies in Social & Cultural Anthropology: No. 79). (Illus.). 307p. (C). 1991. text 95.00 (*0-521-38302-1*) Cambridge U Pr.

Abeles, Norman, jt. auth. see Qualls, Sarah Honn.

Abeles, P. W. & Bardhan-Roy, B. K. Prestressed Concrete Designer's Handbook. 3rd ed. LC 98-206515. xxii, 556 p. 1981. write for info. (*0-7210-1232-9*) C & CA.

Abeles, Peter & Schwartz, Harry W. Planning for the Lower East Side. LC 72-88988. (Special Studies in U. S. Economic, Social & Political Issues). 1973. 32.00 (*0-275-28805-6*) Irvington.

Abeles, Robert H., et al. Biochemistry. 912p. (C). 1992. text 75.00 (*0-86720-212-2*) Jones & Bartlett.

Abeles, Ronald P., ed. Life-Span Perspectives & Social Psychology. 200p. 1987. text 39.95 (*0-89859-953-9*) L Erlbaum Assocs.

Abeles, Ronald P., et al, eds. Aging & Quality of Life. LC 94-6081. (Life Styles & Issues in Aging Ser.). 392p. 1994. 49.95 (*0-8261-8430-8*) Springer Pub.

Abeles, Ronald P., jt. ed. see Withey, Stephen B.

Abeles, Tom, jt. auth. see Morris, David.

Abelin, T. & Brzezinski, Z. Measurement in Health Promotion & Protection. (WHO Regional Publications, European Ser.: No. 22). 682p. 1987. text 80.00 (*92-890-1113-0*) World Health.

Abelkis, P. R. & Hudson, eds. Design of Fatigue & Fracture Resistant Structures - STP 761. 486p. 1982. 51.00 (*0-8031-0714-5*, STP761) ASTM.

Abelkis, P. R. & Potter, J. M., eds. Service Fatigue Loads Monitoring, Simulation, Analysis - STP 671. 298p. 1979. 29.50 (*0-8031-0721-8*, STP671) ASTM.

Abell. Exploration of Univ. 6th ed. 1991. 491.50 (*0-03-052609-4*, Pub. by Harcourt Coll Pubs) Harcourt.

— Exploration of Universe. 6th ed. (C). 1991. pap. text, teacher ed. 34.00 (*0-03-052608-6*) Harcourt Coll Pubs.

— Medical Office Projects Simulation. (Legal Office Procedures Ser.). 1999. pap. 15.75 (*0-538-72126-X*) S-W Pub.

— Modern Differential Equations. LC 95-70697. (C). 1996. text 94.50 (*0-03-098337-1*) Harcourt Coll Pubs.

— Modern Differential Equations: A Theory. (C). 1995. pap. text, student ed. 26.50 (*0-03-016202-5*) Harcourt Coll Pubs.

— Realm of the Universe. 5th ed. (C). 1992. pap. text, teacher ed. 28.00 (*0-03-074924-7*) Harcourt Coll Pubs.

— Realm of the Universe. 5th ed. (C). 1992. pap. text, teacher ed., suppl. ed. 40.50 (*0-03-074926-3*, Pub. by Harcourt Coll Pubs) Harcourt.

— Telecourse Project. 3rd ed. (C). 1992. pap. text, student ed. 28.50 (*0-03-096556-X*) Harcourt Coll Pubs.

Abell, et al. Statistics with Maple V. 608p. 1998. pap. write for info. (*0-12-041556-9*) Acad Pr.

Abell, Aaron I. American Catholicism & Social Action: A Search for Social Justice, 1865-1950. LC 80-16876. 306p. 1980. reprint ed. lib. bdg. 59.75 (*0-313-22513-3*, ABAC, Greenwood Pr) Greenwood.

Abell, Aaron I., ed. American Catholic Thought on Social Questions. LC 66-30548. (C). 1968. pap. write for info. (*0-672-60090-0*, AHS58, Bobbs) Macmillan.

***Abell, Alicia.** Tools for the Direct Access Trader: Hardware, Software, Resources & Everything Else You Need. (Direct Access Trader Ser.). (Illus.). 2001. 24.95 (*0-07-136248-7*) McGraw.

Abell, Alphonse R. Libraries: Index of Activities & Research. 150p. 1990. 47.50 (*1-55914-112-3*); pap. 44.50 (*1-55914-113-1*) ABBE Pubs Assn.

— Medical Periodicals: Index of Functions, History & Standards. LC 88-48002. 150p. 1989. 47.50 (*1-55914-086-0*); pap. 44.50 (*1-55914-087-9*) ABBE Pubs Assn.

Abell, Andrew, ed. Advances in Amino Acid Mimetics & Peptidomimetics, Vol. 1. 301p. 1998. 109.50 (*0-7623-0200-3*) Jai Pr.

A

Abell, Arthur M. Talks with Great Composers: Candid Conversations with Brahms, Puccini, Strauss, & Others. (Illus.). 192p. 1999. reprint ed. 29.95 (0-7351-0084-5) Replica Bks.

Abell, Barbara. Supermarket Development: CDC's & Inner City Economic Development. (Illus.). 80p. 1998. pap. 15.00 (1-889482-04-8) Nat Congress CED.

Abell, Derek F. Managing with Dual Strategies: Mastering the Present, Preempting the Future. 294p. 1993. 32.95 (0-02-900145-5) Free Pr.

Abell, Forrest A. Nine Tales. LC 96-71909. 112p. (Orig.). 1997. pap. 11.95 (1-56167-344-7) Am Literary Pr.

Abell, G. O. Early Evolution in the Universe. (International Astronomical Union Symposia Ser.). 1983. lib. bdg. 187.00 (90-277-1653-6) Kluwer Academic.

Abell, George O. Early Evolution Universe. (International Astronomical Union Symposia Ser.). 1983. pap. text 100.50 (90-277-1662-5) Kluwer Academic.

— Realm of the Universe: 1994 Version with Discover Special Issue & Astronomy Now! 94th ed. (C). 1994. pap. text 71.00 (0-03-006732-4) Holt R&W.

Abell, George O. & Peebles, P. J., eds. Objects of High Redshift: I. A. U. Symposium Los Angeles, Aug. 28 to 31, 1979. (International Astronomical Union Symposia Ser.: No. 92). 328p. 1980. lib. bdg. 104.50 (90-277-1118-6) Kluwer Academic.

Abell, George O., et al. Abell's Exploration of the Universe. 7th ed. (C). 1995. text 76.00 (0-03-001034-9, Pub. by SCP) Harcourt.

Abell, H. A. & Abell, L. P. Abell Family in America: Robert Abell of Rehobeth, MA: His English Ancestry & Immigrants; Abell Families in England. (Illus.). 339p. 1992. reprint ed. pap. 51.00 (0-8328-2607-3); reprint ed. lib. bdg. 61.00 (0-8328-2606-5) Higginson Bk Co.

Abell, Howard. The Day Trader's Advantage: How to Move from One Winning Position to the Next. 256p. 1996. 34.95 (0-7931-1778-X, 56803001) Dearborn.

***Abell, Howard.** The Day Trader's Advantage: How to Move from One Winning Position to the Next. 2nd ed. (Illus.). 240p. 2000. 35.00 (0-7931-3686-5, 56803002) Dearborn.

— Digital Day Trading: Moving from One Winning Stock Position to the Next. LC 99-17724. (Illus.). 288p. 1999. 40.00 (0-7931-3113-8) Dearborn.

— The Electronic Trading of Options. LC 99-49648. 256p. 2000. 40.00 (0-7931-3521-4, 56810801) Dearborn.

***Abell, Howard & Koppel, Robert.** The Market Savvy Investor: Profit from the Techniques of the Top Traders. LC 99-36071. 256p. 1999. 28.00 (0-7931-2792-0, 56807001) Dearborn.

***Abell, Howard, et al.** The Sixth Market: The Electronic Investor Revolution. 2000. 26.00 (0-7931-3913-9) Dearborn.

Abell, Howard, jt. auth. see Koppel, Robert.

Abell, John B. & Finnegan, Frederick W., Jr. Data & Data Processing Issues in the Estimation of Requirements for Aircraft Recoverable Spares & Depot Repair. LC 93-28343. 1993. pap. text 15.00 (0-8330-1434-X, MR-264-AF) Rand Corp.

Abell, John B., et al. Estimating Requirements for Aircraft Recoverable Spares & Depot Repair. LC 93-16450. 1993. pap. text 7.50 (0-8330-1332-7, R-4210-AF) Rand Corp.

Abell, John B., jt. auth. see Chenoweth, Mary E.

Abell, John B., jt. auth. see Miller, Louis W.

Abell, L. P., jt. auth. see Abell, H. A.

Abell, Mark. European Franchising. (Waterlow Publications: Vol. 1). 480p. 1991. write for info. (0-08-040868-0) Macmillan.

— European Franchising. (Waterlow Publications: Vol. 2). 480p. 1991. write for info. (0-08-040869-9) Macmillan.

— The Franchise Option: A Legal Guide. (Waterlow Publications). 176p. 1989. pap. 25.00 (0-08-040118-X, Pergamon Pr) Elsevier.

— The International Franchise Option, 7 pts., Set. (Waterlow Publications). 448p. 1990. 110.00 (0-08-040137-6) Macmillan.

Abell, Mark, ed. European Franchising, 2 vols. (Waterlow Publications). 960p. 1991. 390.00 (0-08-040871-0) Macmillan.

Abell, Martha & Braselton, James. Differential Equations with Mathematica. 2nd ed. LC 96-43813. (Illus.). 807p. (C). 1997. pap. text 44.95 (0-12-041550-X) Morgan Kaufmann.

— Mathematica by Example. 2nd ed. LC 96-43815. (Illus.). 603p. 1997. pap. text 44.00 (0-12-041552-6) Morgan Kaufmann.

***Abell, Martha L.** Differential Equations with Maple V. (Illus.). (C). 1999. pap. 59.95 (0-12-041560-7) Acad Pr.

Abell, Martha L. Modern Differential Equations: A Theory. (C). 1995. pap. text, teacher ed. 30.00 (0-03-016199-1) Harcourt Coll Pubs.

— Modified Differential Equations: Mathematical Laboratory Manual. (C). 1995. pap. text, lab manual ed. write for info. (0-03-016232-7) Harcourt Coll Pubs.

Abell, Martha L. & Braselton, James P. Maple V by Example. 2nd ed. LC 98-38819. (Illus.). 644p. (C). 1998. boxed set 44.95 incl. cd-rom (0-12-041558-5) Acad Pr.

Abell, Martha L., et al. Statistics with Mathematica. LC 98-27879. 1998. write for info. (0-12-041555-0) Acad Pr.

— Statistics with Mathematica. LC 98-27879. (Illus.). 632p. (C). 1998. pap. 49.95 (0-12-041554-2) Acad Pr.

Abell, Nancy L., et al. 1997 Employment Law Briefing Manual. 300p. 1997. ring bd., wbk. ed. 150.00 (1-890487-02-3) Ntl Employ Law.

Abell, Peter. Organizations As Bargaining & Influence Systems. LC 74-15208. (Illus.). 189p. 1975. write for info. (0-470-00160-7) Halsted Pr.

Abell, Peter, ed. Narrative Methods. 160p. 1993. pap. text 455.00 (2-88124-626-5) Gordon & Breach.

Abell, Richard B., ed. see Adamson, A. P.

***Abell, Roger.** MCSE Exam 70-216: Implementing & Adminstering a Microsoft Windows 2000 Network Infrastructure. 600p. 2000. pap. 39.99 (0-7897-2383-2) Que.

***Abell, Sam.** Seeing Gardens. 2000. 40.00 (0-7922-7956-5) Natl Geog.

Abell, Sam, photos by. University of Georgia. (Illus.). 112p. 1987. 37.50 (0-916509-22-2) Harmony Hse Pub.

Abell, Sam, jt. auth. see Ambrose, Stephen E.

Abell, Sam, jt. auth. see Smith, Roff M.

***Abell, Sandra K.** Science Teacher Education: An International Perspective. LC 00-41090. (Science & Technology Education Library). 2000. write for info. (0-7923-6455-4) Kluwer Academic.

Abell-Seddon, Brian. Museum Catalogues: A Foundation for Computer Processing. LC 88-114584. 238p. 1987. reprint ed. pap. 73.80 (0-7837-9270-0, 206000700004) Bks Demand.

Abell, Susan, jt. ed. see Barron, Mitch.

Abell, Troy D. Better Felt Than Said: The Holiness-Pentecostal Experience in Southern Appalachia. LC 81-86285. 216p. 1982. 19.95 (0-918954-35-5) Baylor Univ Pr.

Abell, Usher. Jazz Violin Solos. 52p. 1993. pap. 8.95 (1-56222-570-7, 94821) Mel Bay.

— Jazz Violin Studies. 152p. 1983. spiral bd. 10.95 (1-56222-336-4, 93954) Mel Bay.

— Jazz Violin Studies. 1986. audio 9.98 (1-56222-612-6, 93954C) Mel Bay.

— Jazz Violin Studies. 1993. pap., spiral bd. 19.95 incl. audio (0-7866-0954-0, 93954P) Mel Bay.

***Abell, Usher.** Jazz Violin Studies. 152p. 2000. spiral bd. 22.95 incl. audio compact disk (0-7866-5702-2, 93954BCD) Mel Bay.

Abell, Vivian, jt. auth. see Farlie, Barbara L.

Abell, Walter. Representation & Form: A Study of Aesthetic Values in Representational Art. 1988. reprint ed. pap. 3.95 (0-685-21478-8); reprint ed. lib. bdg. 49.00 (0-7812-0220-5) Rprt Serv.

— Representation & Form: A Study of Aesthetic Values in Representational Art. LC 36-17784. 172p. 1936. reprint ed. 16.00 (0-403-08900-X) Somerset Pub.

Abella, Alex. Dead of Night: A Novel. LC 98-21316. 320p. 1998. 23.00 (0-684-81426-9) S&S Trade.

Abella, Irving. On Strike: Six Key Labour Struggles in Canada, 1919-1949. 196p. 1975. 24.95 (0-88862-058-6, Pub. by J Lorimer) Formac Dist Ltd.

Abella, Irving, ed. On Strike: Six Key Labour Struggles in Canada. 196p. 1975. pap. 16.95 (0-88862-057-8, Pub. by J Lorimer) Formac Dist Ltd.

Abella, Irving M. Nationalism, Communism & Canadian Labour: The CIO, the Communist Party, & the Canadian Congress of Labour, 1935-1956. LC 72-80712. 268p. reprint ed. pap. 83.10 (0-608-13727-8, 202044800018) Bks Demand.

Abella, Irving M., et al. The Influence of the United States on Canadian Development: Eleven Case Studies. Preston, Richard A., ed. LC 72-81337. (Duke University, Commonwealth-Studies Center, Publication Ser.: No. 40). 281p. reprint ed. pap. 87.20 (0-608-11974-1, 202343700033) Bks Demand.

Abella, Kay T. Building Successful Training Programs: A Step-by-Step Guide. 176p. (C). 1986. 21.95 (0-201-00100-4) Addison-Wesley.

Abella, Manolo. Sending Workers Abroad. LC 97-181074. 120p. 1997. pap. 18.00 (92-2-108525-2) Intl Labour Office.

Abella, Olga. Grasping to What Is. 26p. (Orig.). (C). 1993. pap. text 6.00 (1-878173-06-5) Birnham Wood.

Abellan, Joaquin, ed. see Locke, John.

Abellera, Tom. The Teachings of Don Von: A Turnkey Way of Knowledge. LC 92-96956. (Illus.). 211p. (Orig.). 1992. pap. write for info. (0-9633942-0-7) Stochos Bks.

— The Teachings of Don Von: A Turnkey Way of Knowledge. (Illus.). 244p. (Orig.). 1994. write for info. (0-9633942-1-5) Stochos Bks.

Abello, Elizabeth, tr. see Moses, Marion.

Abello, Mireia B., tr. see Przeworski, Adam.

Abells, Chana B. The Children We Remember. LC 85-24876. (Illus.). 48p. (J). (gr. 2 up). 1986. 16.00 (0-688-06371-3, Grenwillow Bks) HarpC Child Bks.

Abells, Chana B. The Children We Remember. LC 85-24876. (Illus.). 48p. (J). (ps up). 1986. 15.93 (0-688-06372-1, Grenwillow Bks) HarpC Child Bks.

Abelman, Bob. Reclaiming the Wasteland: TV & Gifted Children. Runco, Mark A., ed. (Perspectives on Creativity Ser.). 256p. (C). 1995. text 55.00 (1-57273-014-5); pap. text 21.95 (1-57273-015-3) Hampton Pr NJ.

Abelman, Robert. Mass Communication: Issues & Perspectives. 230p. (C). 1990. text 28.40 (0-536-57747-1) Pearson Custom.

— Mass Communication: Issues & Perspectives. 2nd ed. 354p. (C). 1992. 48.00 (0-536-58182-7) Pearson Custom.

Abelman, Robert. Reaching a Critical Mass: A Critical Analysis of Television Entertainment. LC 97-22936. (Communication Ser.). 250p. 1997. 99.95 (0-8058-2199-6); pap. 55.00 (0-8058-2200-3) L Erlbaum Assocs.

— Some Children under Some Conditions: TV & the High Potential Kid. (Illus.). 95p. (Orig.). (C). 1994. pap. text 30.00 (0-7881-1339-9) DIANE Pub.

Abelman, Robert, et al, eds. Religious Television: Controversies & Conclusions. LC 89-78101. (Communication & Information Science Ser.). 376p. (C). 1989. text 78.50 (0-89391-643-9) Ablx Pub.

Abelman, Robert & Hoover, Stewart M. Religious Television: Controversies & Conclusions. Dervin, Brenda, ed. LC 89-78101. (Communication & Information Science Ser.). 376p. (C). 1989. pap. 39.50 (0-89391-644-7) Ablx Pub.

Abelman, Robert, et al. Television & the Exceptional Child: A Forgotten Audience. (Communication Ser.). 248p. 1992. pap. 27.50 (0-8058-0788-8); text 59.95 (0-8058-0787-X) L Erlbaum Assocs.

Abelmann, Jeryl, jt. auth. see Kronish, Miriam.

Abelmann, Nancy. Echoes of the Past, Epics of Dissent: A South Korean Social Movement. LC 95-35055. (Illus.). 467p. 1996. pap. 19.95 (0-520-20418-2, Pub. by U CA Pr) Cal Prin Full Svc.

— Echoes of the Past, Epics of Dissent: A South Korean Social Movement. LC 95-35055. (Illus.). 467p. (C). 1996. 60.00 (0-520-08590-6, Pub. by U CA Pr) Cal Prin Full Svc.

Abelmann, Nancy & Lie, John. Blue Dreams: Korean Americans & the Los Angeles Riots. (Illus.). 288p. 1995. text 33.95 (0-674-07704-0, ABEBLU) HUP.

Abelmann, Walter H., ed. Atlas of Heart Disease Vol. 2: Cardiomyopathies, Myocarditis & Pericardial Disease. LC 94-31947. 1994. text 134.00 (1-878132-24-5) Current Med.

Abelmann, Walter H., jt. ed. see Kawai, Chuichi.

Abeln, Susan H., et al. Essentials of Risk Control, 2 vols. 3rd ed. Head, George L., ed. LC 95-75959. 667p. (C). 1995. pap. 41.00 (0-89462-085-1, 5502/5503) IIA.

Abeln, Susan H., jt. auth. see Stewart, Darlene L.

Abeloff. Clinical Oncology. 2nd ed. LC 99-26164. (C). 1999. text 225.00 (0-443-07545-X) Church.

Abeloff, Martin D., ed. Complications of Cancer: Diagnosis & Management. LC 79-7563. 1980. text 70.00 (0-8018-2254-8) Johns Hopkins.

***Abeloff, Martin D., ed.** Oncology & Hematology, 2000: An Internet Resource Guide. (Physician Ser.). xvi, 500p. 2000. pap. 24.95 (0-9676811-0-3) eMedguides.

Abeloff, Martin D., et al, eds. Clinical Oncology. LC 95-744. 2,350p. 1995. text 221.00 (0-443-08941-8) Church.

Abelove, Henry. The Evangelist of Desire: John Wesley & the Methodists. LC 90-35420. 160p. 1990. 35.00 (0-8047-1826-1) Stanford U Pr.

— The Evangelist of Desire: John Wesley & the Methodists. xiv, 136p. (C). 1992. pap. 14.95 (0-8047-2157-2) Stanford U Pr.

Abelove, Henry, et al, eds. Lesbian & Gay Studies Reader. 800p. (gr. 13). 1993. pap. 28.99 (0-415-90519-2, A6621) Routledge.

Abelove, Joan. Go & Come Back. LC 97-36070. 177p. (YA). (gr. 6-12). 1998. 16.95 (0-7894-2476-2) DK Pub Inc.

***Abelove, Joan.** Go & Come Back. (Illus.). 192p. (YA). (gr. 7-12). 2000. pap. 5.99 (0-14-130694-7, PuffinBks) Peng Put Young Read.

— Go & Come Back. (Illus.). (J). 2000. 11.34 (0-606-18406-6) Turtleback.

Abelove, Joan. Saying It Out Loud. LC 98-33265. 144p. 1999. 15.95 (0-7894-2609-9) DK Pub Inc.

Abelow, Benjamin. Understanding Acid-Base. LC 97-3514. (Illus.). 250p. 1997. pap. 24.95 (0-683-18272-2) Lppncott W & W.

Abelow, Dan. Total Sex. 1988. mass mkt. 6.50 (0-425-11205-5) Berkley Pub.

***Abelquist, E. W.** Minimum Detectable Concentrations with Typical Radiation Survey Instruments for Various Contaminants & Field Conditions. 168p. 1998. per. 15.00 (0-16-062744-3) USGPO.

Abels, David. Do It with Your Shoes on & One Hundred Other Fun Ways to Spice up Your Sex Life. LC 93-95051. 128p. 1994. pap. 8.95 (1-884477-25-9) Three Cat Pr.

Abels, H. Finite Presentability of S-Arithmetic Groups. (Lecture Notes in Mathematics Ser.: Vol. 1261). vi, 178p. 1987. 34.95 (0-387-17975-5) Spr-Verlag.

Abels, Harriette S. Bermuda Triangle. LC 87-14029. (Mystery of...Ser.). (Illus.). 48p. (J). (gr. 5-6). 1987. lib. bdg. 12.95 (0-89686-340-9, Crstwood Hse) Silver Burdett Pr.

— Loch Ness Monster. LC 87-9027. (Mystery of...Ser.). (Illus.). 48p. (J). (gr. 5-6). 1987. text 12.95 (0-89686-343-3, Crstwood Hse) Silver Burdett Pr.

— The Pyramids. LC 87-15455. (Mystery of...Ser.). (Illus.). 48p. (J). (gr. 5-6). 1987. lib. bdg. 12.95 (0-89686-345-X, Crstwood Hse) Silver Burdett Pr.

Abels, Jules. Man on Fire: John Brown & the Cause of Liberty. LC 72-117961. 464p. reprint ed. pap. 143.90 (0-608-13758-8, 205168000001) Bks Demand.

Abels, Richard P. Alfred the Great: War, Kingship, & Culture in Anglo-Saxon England. LC 98-20930. (Medieval World Ser.). (C). 1998. text 72.95 (0-582-04048-5) Longman.

— Alfred the Great: War, Kingship & Culture in Anglo-Saxon England. LC 98-20930. (Medieval World Ser.). 373p. (C). 1998. pap. 32.46 (0-582-04047-7) Addison-Wesley.

Abelson, Amanda, jt. auth. see Abelson, Harold.

Abelson, Elaine S. When Ladies Go A-Thieving: Middle-Class Shoplifters in the Victorian Department Store. (Illus.). 320p. 1992. pap. text 19.95 (0-19-507142-5) OUP.

Abelson, Harold & Abelson, Amanda. LOGO for the Macintosh: An Introduction Through Object Logo. (Illus.). 400p. 1993. pap. 55.00 incl. disk (0-262-51070-7) MIT Pr.

Abelson, Harold & DiSessa, Andrea. Turtle Geometry: The Computer As a Medium for Exploring Mathematics. (Artificial Intelligence Ser.). (Illus.). 477p. 1981. 46.00 (0-262-01063-1) MIT Pr.

— Turtle Geometry: The Computer As a Medium for Exploring Mathematics. (Artificial Intelligence Ser.). (Illus.). 477p. 1986. pap. text 23.00 (0-262-51037-5) MIT Pr.

Abelson, Harold, et al. Structure & Interpretation of Computer Programs. (Electrical Engineering & Computer Science Ser.). 1989. disk 24.95 (0-262-51044-8) MIT Pr.

— Structure & Interpretation of Computer Programs. 2nd ed. LC 96-17756. (Illus.). 683p. 1996. 62.50 (0-262-01153-0) MIT Pr.

— Structure & Interpretation of Computer Programs. 2nd ed. LC 96-17756. 1996. pap. text 29.50 (0-262-51087-1) MIT Pr.

— Structure & Interpretation of Computer Programs. 2nd ed. (Illus.). 556p. (C). 1996. 76.56 (0-07-000484-6) McGraw.

Abelson, Harold, jt. auth. see Garfinkel, Simson.

Abelson, John N., et al, eds. Adenylyl Cyclase, G Proteins, & Guanylyl Cyclase. (Methods in Enzymology Ser.: Vol. 195). (Illus.). 512p. 1991. text 115.00 (0-12-182096-3) Acad Pr.

— Arachidonate Related Lipid Mediators. (Methods in Enzymology Ser.: Vol. 187). 683p. 1990. text 125.00 (0-12-182088-2) Acad Pr.

— Avidin-Biotin Technology. (Methods in Enzymology Ser.: Vol. 184). 746p. 1990. text 136.00 (0-12-182085-8) Acad Pr.

— Bacterial Pathogenesis. LC 97-202919. (Selected Methods in Enzymology Ser.: Vols. 235 & 236). (Illus.). 827p. 1997. 79.95 (0-12-175465-0) Morgan Kaufmann.

— Biochemical Spectroscopy. (Methods in Enzymology Ser.: Vol. 246). (Illus.). 816p. 1995. text 116.00 (0-12-182147-1) Acad Pr.

— Biomembranes Pt. R: Transport Theory: Cells & Model Membranes. (Methods in Enzymology Ser.: Vol. 171). 900p. 1989. text 157.00 (0-12-182072-6) Acad Pr.

— Biomembranes Pt. S: Transport Membrane Isolation & Characterization. (Methods in Enzymology Ser.: Vol. 172). 776p. 1989. text 167.00 (0-12-182073-4) Acad Pr.

— Biomembranes Pt. W: Cellular & Subcellular Transport: Epithelial Cells. (Methods in Enzymology Ser.: Vol. 192). 829p. 1990. text 146.00 (0-12-182093-9) Acad Pr.

— Carotenoids Pt. A: Chemistry, Separation, Quantitation, & Antioxidation. (Methods in Enzymology Ser.: Vol. 213). (Illus.). 538p. 1992. text 125.00 (0-12-182114-5) Acad Pr.

— Carotenoids Pt. B: Metabolism, Genetics, & Biosynthesis. (Methods in Enzymology Ser.: Vol. 214). (Illus.). 468p. 1993. text 104.00 (0-12-182115-3) Acad Pr.

— Cell Cycle Control. (Methods in Enzymology Ser.: Vol. 283). (Illus.). 678p. 1997. text 105.00 (0-12-182184-6) Morgan Kaufmann.

— Chemokine Receptors. (Methods in Enzymology Ser.: Vol. 288). (Illus.). 480p. 1997. text 99.95 (0-12-182189-7) Morgan Kaufmann.

— Combinatorial Chemistry. (Methods in Enzymology Ser.: Vol. 267). (Illus.). 493p. 1996. text 85.00 (0-12-182168-4) Acad Pr.

— Computer Methods for Macromolecular Sequence Analysis. (Methods in Enzymology Ser.: Vol. 266). (Illus.). 711p. 1996. text 110.00 (0-12-182167-6) Acad Pr.

— Cumulative Subject Index: Volumes 228, 230-262. (Methods in Enzymology Ser.: Vol. 265). (Illus.). 678p. 1996. text 95.00 (0-12-182166-8) Acad Pr.

— Cytochrome P450. (Methods in Enzymology Ser.: Vol. 206). (Illus.). 716p. 1991. text 125.00 (0-12-182107-2) Acad Pr.

Abelson, John N., et al, eds. Cytochrome P450, Pt. B. LC 96-209721. (Methods in Enzymology Ser.: Vol. 272). (Illus.). 468p. 1996. text 79.00 (0-12-182173-0) Acad Pr.

Abelson, John N., et al, eds. DNA Replication. (Methods in Enzymology Ser.: Vol. 262). (Illus.). 716p. 1995. text 104.00 (0-12-182163-3) Acad Pr.

— DNA Structure Pt. A: Synthesis & Physical Analysis of DNA. (Methods in Enzymology Ser.: Vol. 211). (Illus.). 619p. 1992. text 125.00 (0-12-182112-9) Acad Pr.

— DNA Structure Pt. B: Chemical & Electrophoretic Analysis of DNA. (Methods in Enzymology Ser.: Vol. 212). (Illus.). 501p. 1992. text 125.00 (0-12-182113-7) Acad Pr.

— Gene Expression Technology. (Methods in Enzymology Ser.: Vol. 185). 681p. 1990. text 121.00 (0-12-182086-6) Acad Pr.

— Guide to Techniques in Glycobiology. (Methods in Enzymology Ser.: Vol. 230). (Illus.). 567p. 1994. 53.00 (0-12-443665-X); text 104.00 (0-12-182131-5) Acad Pr.

— Guide to Techniques in Mouse Development. (Methods in Enzymology Ser.: Vol. 225). (Illus.). 1021p. 1993. text 125.00 (0-12-182126-9) Acad Pr.

— Guide to Techniques in Mouse Development. (Methods in Enzymology Ser.: Vol. 225). (Illus.). 1021p. 1993. 79.00 (0-12-736450-1) Acad Pr.

— Guide to Yeast Genetics & Molecular Biology. (Methods in Enzymology Ser.: Vol. 194). 933p. 1990. text 157.00 (0-12-182095-5) Acad Pr.

— Guide to Yeast Genetics & Molecular Biology. (Methods in Enzymology Ser.: Vol. 194). 933p. 1991. spiral bd. 66.00 (0-12-310670-2) Acad Pr.

— Hemoglobins Pt. C: Biophysical Methods. (Methods in Enzymology Ser.: Vol. 232). (Illus.). 725p. 1994. text 115.00 (0-12-182133-1) Acad Pr.

— Hemoglobins Pt. B: Biochemical & Analytical Methods. (Methods in Enzymology Ser.: Vol. 231). (Illus.). 743p. 1994. text 125.00 (0-12-182132-3) Acad Pr.

— Hormone Action Pt. K: Neuroendocrine Peptides. (Methods in Enzymology Ser.: Vol. 168). 906p. 1989. text 167.00 (0-12-182069-6) Acad Pr.

An Asterisk (*) at the beginning of an entry indicates that the title is appearing for the first time.

— Ion Channels. (Methods in Enzymology Ser.: Vol. 207). (Illus.). 917p. 1992. text 125.00 (*0-12-182108-0*) Acad Pr.

— Lipases Pt. B: Enzyme Characterization & Utilization, Pt. B. (Methods in Enzymology Ser.: Vol. 286). (Illus.). 563p. 1997. text 99.95 (*0-12-182187-0*) Morgan Kaufmann.

— Macromolecular Crystallography, Pt. A. (Methods in Enzymology Ser.: Vol. 276). (Illus.). 700p. 1997. text 99.00 (*0-12-182177-3*) Morgan Kaufmann.

— Mass Spectrometry. (Methods in Enzymology Ser.: Vol. 193). 890p. 1990. text 146.00 (*0-12-182094-7*) Acad Pr.

— Metallobiochemistry Pt. C: Spectroscopic & Physical Methods for Probing Metal Ion Environments in Metalloenzymes & Metalloproteins. (Methods in Enzymology Ser.: Vol. 226). (Illus.). 674p. 1993. text 115.00 (*0-12-182127-7*) Acad Pr.

— Metallobiochemistry Pt. D: Physical & Spectroscopic Methods for Probing Metal Ion Environments in Metalloproteins. (Methods in Enzymology Ser.: Vol. 227). (Illus.). 634p. 1993. text 115.00 (*0-12-182128-5*) Acad Pr.

— Metallobiochemistry Pt. B: Metallothionein & Related Molecules. (Methods in Enzymology Ser.: Vol. 205). (Illus.). 681p. 1991. text 125.00 (*0-12-182106-4*) Acad Pr.

— Methods in Enzymology Vol. 289: Solid-Phase Peptide Synthesis. (Illus.). 780p. 1997. text 110.00 (*0-12-182190-0*) Morgan Kaufmann.

— Methods in Enzymology Vol. 295: Energetics of Biological Macromolecules. (Illus.). 548p. (C). 1998. boxed set 99.95 (*0-12-182196-X*) Acad Pr.

— Molecular Design & Modeling - Concepts & Applications Pt. A: Proteins, Peptides, & Enzymes. (Methods in Enzymology Ser.: Vol. 202). (Illus.). 824p. 1991. text 125.00 (*0-12-182103-X*) Acad Pr.

— Molecular Design & Modeling - Concepts & Applications Pt. B: Antibodies & Antigens, Nucleic Acids, Polysaccharides, & Drugs. (Methods in Enzymology Ser.: Vol. 203). (Illus.). 764p. 1991. text 136.00 (*0-12-182104-8*) Acad Pr.

— Molecular Evolution: Computer Analysis of Protein & Nucleic Acid Sequences. (Methods in Enzymology Ser.: Vol. 183). 736p. 1990. text 146.00 (*0-12-182084-X*) Acad Pr.

— Molecular Evolution: Producing the Biochemical Data. (Methods in Enzymology Ser.: Vol. 224). (Illus.). 725p. 1993. text 104.00 (*0-12-182125-0*) Acad Pr.

— Molecular Motors & the Cytoskeleton. (Methods in Enzymology Ser.: Vol. 196). (Illus.). 559p. 1991. text 115.00 (*0-12-182097-1*) Acad Pr.

— Nuclear Magnetic Resonance, Pt. C. (Methods in Enzymology Ser.: Vol. 239). (Illus.). 813p. 1994. text. write for info. (*0-12-182140-4*) Acad Pr.

— Nuclear Magnetic Resonance Pt. A: Spectral Techniques & Dynamics. (Methods in Enzymology Ser.: Vol. 176). 530p. 1989. text 125.00 (*0-12-182077-7*) Acad Pr.

— Numerical Computer Methods. (Methods in Enzymology Ser.: Vol. 210). (Illus.). 718p. 1992. text 125.00 (*0-12-182111-0*) Acad Pr.

— Peptide Growth Factors, Pt. C. (Methods in Enzymology Ser.: Vol. 198). (Illus.). 578p. 1991. text 115.00 (*0-12-182099-8*) Acad Pr.

— Phospholipases. (Methods in Enzymology Ser.: Vol. 197). (Illus.). 640p. 1991. text 115.00 (*0-12-182098-X*) Acad Pr.

— Phospholipid Biosynthesis. (Methods in Enzymology Ser.: Vol. 209). (Illus.). 584p. 1992. text 125.00 (*0-12-182110-2*) Acad Pr.

— Platelets Pt. B: Receptors, Adhesion, Secretion. (Methods in Enzymology Ser.: Vol. 215). (Illus.). 526p. 1992. text 104.00 (*0-12-182116-1*) Acad Pr.

— Protein - DNA Interactions. (Methods in Enzymology Ser.: Vol. 208). (Illus.). 700p. 1991. text 125.00 (*0-12-182109-9*) Acad Pr.

— Protein Phosphorylation Pt. B: Analysis of Protein Phosphorylation, Protein Kinase Inhibitors, & Protein Phosphatases. (Methods in Enzymology Ser.: Vol. 201). (Illus.). 547p. (C). 1991. text 104.00 (*0-12-182102-1*) Acad Pr.

— Proteolytic Enzymes: Aspartic & Metallo Peptidases. (Methods in Enzymology Ser.: Vol. 248). (Illus.). 873p. 1995. text 121.00 (*0-12-182149-8*) Acad Pr.

— Ribosomes. (Methods in Enzymology Ser.: Vol. 164). 875p. 1988. text 146.00 (*0-12-182065-3*) Acad Pr.

— RNA Processing Pt. B: Specific Methods. (Methods in Enzymology Ser.: Vol. 181). 650p. 1990. text 136.00 (*0-12-182082-3*) Acad Pr.

— Vitamins & Coenzymes, Pt. I. (Methods in Enzymology Ser.: Vol. 279). (Illus.). 502p. 1997. text 99.00 (*0-12-182180-3*) Morgan Kaufmann.

— Vitamins & Coenzymes, Pt. J. (Methods in Enzymology Ser.: Vol. 280). (Illus.). 496p. 1997. text 99.00 (*0-12-182181-1*) Morgan Kaufmann.

— Vitamins & Coenzymes, Pt. K. (Methods in Enzymology Ser.: Vol. 281). (Illus.). 469p. 1997. text 99.00 (*0-12-182182-X*) Morgan Kaufmann.

Abelson, John N. & Simon, Melvin I., eds. Cumulative Subject Index: Volumes 135-139, 141-167. (Methods in Enzymology Ser.: Vol. 175). 272p. 1990. text 136.00 (*0-12-182076-9*) Acad Pr.

— Cumulative Subject Index: Volumes 168-174, 176-194. (Methods in Enzymology Ser.: Vol. 199). 312p. 1993. text 115.00 (*0-12-182100-5*) Acad Pr.

— Cumulative Subject Index: Volumes 195-198, 200-227. (Methods in Enzymology Ser.: Vol. 229). (Illus.). 389p. 1995. text 95.00 (*0-12-182130-7*) Acad Pr.

— Guide to Protein Purification. (Methods in Enzymology Ser.: Vol. 182). 894p. 1990. text 146.00 (*0-12-182083-1*); spiral bd. 71.00 (*0-12-213585-7*) Acad Pr.

— Methods in Enzymology Vol. 285: Cumulative Subject Index Vols. 263, 264, 266-289. (Methods in Enzymology Ser.: Vol. 285). (Illus.). 345p. 1998. boxed set 99.95 (*0-12-182186-2*) Morgan Kaufmann.

Abelson, John N., ed. see Colowick.

Abelson, John N., ed. see Simon, Melvin I.

Abelson, Mark B. Allergic Diseases of the Eye. LC 99-23446. (Illus.). 235p. 2000. text. write for info. (*0-7216-8679-6*, W B Saunders Co) Harcrt Hlth Sci Grp.

Abelson, Neva M. Topics in Blood Banking. LC 74-8253. 171p. reprint ed. pap. 53.10 (*0-608-12666-7*, 205599400043) Bks Demand.

Abelson, Norman. Trade Show Basics. 140p. 1987. 22.95 (*0-913247-07-3*); pap. 15.95 (*0-685-18704-7*) CCH INC.

Abelson, Paul. The Seven Liberal Arts: A Study in Medieval Culture. LC 76-176501. (Columbia University. Teachers College. Contributions to Education Ser.: No. 11). reprint ed. 39.50 (*0-404-55011-8*) AMS Pr.

***Abelson, Peter & Joyeux, Roselyne, eds.** Economic Forecasting. 336p. 2000. 39.95 (*1-86508-171-X*, Pub. by Allen & Unwin Pty) Paul & Co Pubs.

Abelson, Philip H. Enough of Pessimism: One Hundred Essays. LC 85-3924. 222p. 1985. 16.95 (*0-87168-310-5*, 85-05H) AAAS.

— Enough of Pessimism: One Hundred Essays. LC 85-3924. 223p. reprint ed. pap. 69.20 (*0-7837-6733-1*, 204636100011) Bks Demand.

Abelson, Philip H., ed. Biotechnology & Biological Frontiers. LC 84-21655. 516p. 1986. 51.00 (*0-87168-308-3*) AAAS.

— Biotechnology & Biological Frontiers. LC 84-21655. (AAAS Publication Ser.: No. 84-8). 526p. reprint ed. pap. 163.10 (*0-8357-7260-8*, 203145100074) Bks Demand.

— Energy: Use, Conservation, & Supply: A Special Science Compendium. LC 74-29004. (AAAS Miscellaneous Publications: No. 74-15). 160p. reprint ed. pap. 49.60 (*0-7837-0061-X*, 204030800016) Bks Demand.

— Food: Politics, Economics, Nutrition, & Research. LC 75-18785. (AAAS Miscellaneous Publications: No. 75-7). 208p. reprint ed. pap. 64.50 (*0-7837-0063-6*, 204031000016) Bks Demand.

— Health Care: Regulation, Economics, Ethics, Practice. LC 78-67824. (AAAS Publication: No. 78-12). 262p. reprint ed. pap. 81.30 (*0-7837-0067-9*, 204031400016) Bks Demand.

Abelson, Philip H., et al, eds. Neuroscience. LC 84-24524. (Illus.). 516p. (C). 1986. 54.50 (*0-87168-309-1*, 84-13S) AAAS.

— Neuroscience. LC 84-24524. (AAAS Publication: No. 84-13). (Illus.). 467p. reprint ed. pap. 144.80 (*0-8357-6436-2*, 203580700097) Bks Demand.

Abelson, Philip H. & Dorfman, Mary, eds. Advanced Technology. LC 80-67368. (AAAS Publication Ser.: No. 80-8). 167p. 1980. pap. 51.80 (*0-7837-0068-7*, 204031500016) Bks Demand.

Abelson, Philip H. & Hammond, Allen L., eds. Electronics, the Continuing Revolution: A Special Science Compendium. LC 77-77257. (AAAS Publication Ser.: No. 77-4). 223p. reprint ed. pap. 69.20 (*0-7837-0065-2*, 204031200016) Bks Demand.

— Energy II: Use Conservation & Supply. LC 78-59190. (AAAS Publication Ser.: No. 78-9). 207p. reprint ed. pap. 64.20 (*0-7837-0066-0*, 204031300016) Bks Demand.

— Materials: Renewable & Nonrenewable Resources. LC 76-7295. (AAAS Publication Ser.: No. 76-4). 208p. reprint ed. pap. 64.50 (*0-7837-0064-4*, 204031100016) Bks Demand.

Abelson, Philip H. & Kulstad, Ruth, eds. The Science Centennial Review. LC 80-69480. (AAAS Publication: No. 80-10). 192p. reprint ed. pap. 59.60 (*0-7837-0069-5*, 204031600016) Bks Demand.

Abelson, Phillip H., ed. see AEC Technical Information Center Staff, et al.

Abelson, Raziel. Ethics & Modern Life. 6th ed. 1995. pap. text 42.95 (*0-312-15761-4*) St Martin.

— Lawless Mind. LC 88-12358. 224p. (C). 1988. 32.95 (*0-87722-579-6*) Temple U Pr.

Abelson, Raziel & Friquegnon, Marie-Louise. Clarity & Vision: An Introduction to Phylosophy. 2nd ed. 320p. (C). per. write for info. (*0-7872-6725-2*) Kendall-Hunt.

Abelson, Raziel & Friquegnon, Marie-Louise. Ethics for Modern Life. 5th ed. (Professional Ethics in Education Ser.). 528p. (C). 1994. pap. 43.95 (*0-312-09967-3*) St Martin.

Abelson, Raziel & Friquegnon, Marie-Louise, eds. Ethics for Modern Life. 2nd ed. LC 81-48150. 428p. (C). 1982. pap. text 13.56 (*0-312-26601-4*) St Martin.

Abelson, Robert, jt. auth. see Schank, Roger C.

Abelson, Robert P. Statistics As Principled Argument. 232p. 1995. 59.95 (*0-8058-0527-3*); pap. 27.50 (*0-8058-0528-1*) L Erlbaum Assocs.

Aben, H. & Guillemet, C. Photoelasticity of Glass. LC 93-10032. 1993. 131.95 (*0-387-54841-6*) Spr-Verlag.

Aben Ragel, Aly. Libro Conplido en los Judizios de las Estrellas. Hilty, Gerald, ed. (SPA.). 273p. 1968. pap. 200.00 (*0-614-00232-X*) Elliots Bks.

Abend, Hallett. Pacific Charter: Our Destiny in Asia. LC 72-4478. (Essay Index Reprint Ser.). 1977. reprint ed. 20.95 (*0-8369-2932-2*) Ayer.

Abend, Nicole. Texas Provider Utilization & Financial Data. (Working Paper Ser.: Vol. 63). 61p. 1992. pap. 5.50 (*0-89940-545-2*) LBJ Sch Pub Aff.

Abend, Sander M., et al. Borderline Patients: Psychoanalytic Perspectives. Fine, Bernard D. et al, eds. LC 83-12750. (Kris Study Group Monographs: No. 7). viii, 255p. 1983. 37.50 (*0-8236-0576-0*) Intl Univs Pr.

Abendroth, jt. auth. see Adams.

Abendroth, Frank. Professional SQL Server 7.0. 500p. 1998. pap. 49.99 (*1-86100-177-0*, Pub. by Wrox Press) Wrox Pr Inc.

***Abendroth, John & Juricich, Mitch.** Hooked on Golf: Golf Courses of Northern California & Northern Nevada. Caskie, Jason, ed. (Illus.). 164p. 2000. pap. 9.95 (*0-9678969-0-8*) Bay Sprts Pub.

Abendroth, Thomas W., jt. auth. see Adams, Roy M.

Abendroth, Thomas W., jt. auth. see Stetter, Debra L.

Abendroth, Wolfgang. A Short History of the European Working Class. Jacobs, Nicholas & Trench, Brian, trs. LC 72-81766. 204p. 1972. reprint ed. pap. 63.30 (*0-7837-9614-5*, 206037100005) Bks Demand.

Abenheim, Donald. Reforging the Iron Cross: The Search for Tradition in the West German Armed Forces. LC 88-9969. 338p. reprint ed. pap. 104.80 (*0-608-06398-3*, 206675900008) Bks Demand.

Abenheimer, Karl M. Narcissism, Nihilism - Simplicity & Self: Studies in Literature As Psychology. Calder, Robert R., ed. (Aberdeen University Press Bks.). 160p. 1991. pap. text 16.91 (*0-08-041405-2*, Pub. by Aberdeen U Pr) Macmillan.

Abenoza, Pascual & Ackerman, A. Bernard. Neoplasms with Eccrine Differentiation. LC 89-7980. (Illus.). 536p. 1990. text 150.00 (*0-8121-1236-9*) Lppncott W & W.

Abensur, Nadine. Secrets from a Vegetarian Kitchen. (Illus.). 112p. 1997. 19.95 (*1-55670-549-2*) Stewart Tabori & Chang.

Abent, John A. Signs in the Heavens. LC 95-221011. 408p. (Orig.). 1995. pap. 15.99 (*1-56043-828-2*, Treasure Hse) Destiny Image.

Abentrod, Susan. 10 Minute Guide to Beating Debt. LC 96-68550. 144p. 1996. 10.95 (*0-02-861115-2*, Pub. by Macmillan) S&S Trade.

Aber, Adolf. Handbuch der Musikliteratur in Systematisch-Chronologischer Anordnung. 1967. reprint ed. 68.00 (*0-318-71726-3*) G Olms Pubs.

Aber, J. Lawrence, jt. auth. see Collins, Ann.

Aber, James S., et al. Glaciotectonic Landforms & Structures. (C). 1989. text 166.50 (*0-7923-0100-5*) Kluwer Academic.

Aber, Joanne. Getting a College Degree Fast: Testing Out & Other Accredited Short Cuts. LC 95-35979. 247p. 1996. pap. 17.95 (*1-57392-001-0*) Prometheus Bks.

Aber, John D. Terrestrial Ecosystems. 368p. (C). 1991. pap. text 57.50 (*0-03-047443-4*) Harcourt Coll Pubs.

***Aber, Linda.** In the Jungle. (Animals All Around Ser.). (Illus.). 18p. (J). (ps). 2000. bds. 5.99 (*1-57584-700-0*, Pub. by Rdrs Digest) S&S Trade.

***Aber, Linda & Brooks, Nan.** Dinosaur Days. (Illus.). 18p. (J). (ps-1). 2000. bds. 5.99 (*1-57584-388-9*) Rdrs Digest.

Aber, Linda Williams. My Super Sleepover Book. (Full House Michelle Ser.). 112p. (J). (ps-3). 1999. pap. 3.99 (*0-671-02701-8*) PB.

— My Totally Awesome Holiday Friendship Book. (Full House Michelle Ser.). (Illus.). 96p. (J). (gr. 2-4). 1997. per. 3.99 (*0-671-00840-4*) PB.

***Aber, Linda Williams.** Who's Got Spots? LC 99-88841. (Math Matters Ser.). (Illus.). (J). (gr. 1-3). 2000. pap. 4.95 (*1-57565-099-1*) Kane Pr.

Aber, Lynn B., jt. ed. see Miller, Harold L.

Aberbach, Alan D. The Ideas of Richard Wagner: An Examination & Analysis of His Major Aesthetic, Political, Economic, Social, & Religious Thoughts. rev. ed. 450p. (Orig.). (C). 1988. lib. bdg. 53.00 (*0-8191-6855-6*) U Pr of Amer.

— Richard Wagner: Mystic in the Making. LC 90-26688. 223p. (C). 1991. text 35.00 (*0-89341-662-2*, Longwood Academic) Hollowbrook.

— Richard Wagner's Religious Ideas: A Spiritual Journey. LC 96-49363. 312p. 1996. text 99.95 (*0-7734-8783-2*) E Mellen.

— Richard Wagner's Spiritual Pilgrimage. LC 98-12233. 298p. 1998. pap. 99.95 (*0-7734-8348-9*) E Mellen.

Aberbach, David. Charisma in Politics, Religion & the Media: Private Trauma, Public Ideals. LC 95-44389. 136p. (C). 1996. text 40.00 (*0-8147-0647-9*) NYU Pr.

— Imperialism & Biblical Prophecy, 750-500 BCE. LC 92-47228. (Illus.). 144p. (C). (gr. 13). 1993. 65.00 (*0-415-09500-X*) Routledge.

— Realism, Character, & Bias: The Fiction of Mendele Mocher Sefarim. (Littman Library of Jewish Civilization). 144p. 1993. 29.95 (*1-874774-07-2*); pap. 14.95 (*1-874774-08-0*) Intl Spec Bk.

— Revolutionary Hebrew, Empire & Crisis: Four Peaks in Hebrew Literature & Jewish Survival. LC 97-13467. 1997. text 42.50 (*0-8147-0673-8*) NYU Pr.

— Surviving Trauma: Loss, Literature, & Psychoanalysis. LC 89-50650. 204p. 1989. reprint ed. pap. 63.30 (*0-608-07877-8*, 205998400010) Bks Demand.

Aberbach, David, jt. auth. see Aberbach, Moses.

Aberbach, Jason, ed. see Owl, Michael W.

Aberbach, Joel & Walker, Jack. Detroit Longitudinal Study, 1967. 1974. write for info. (*0-89138-103-1*) ICPSR.

Aberbach, Joel D. Keeping a Watchful Eye: The Politics of Congressional Oversight. 288p. 1990. 36.95 (*0-8157-0060-1*); pap. 16.95 (*0-8157-0059-8*) Brookings.

Aberbach, Joel D., et al, eds. The Role of the State in Taiwan's Development. LC 93-33071. (Taiwan in the Modern World Ser.). 400p. (C). (gr. 13). 1994. text 88.95 (*1-56324-325-3*, East Gate Bk); pap. text 42.95 (*1-56324-326-1*, East Gate Bk) M E Sharpe.

***Aberbach, Joel D. & Rockman, Bert A.** In the Web of Politics: Three Decades of the U. S. Federal Executive. LC 99-50508. 248p. 2000. 42.95 (*0-8157-0062-8*); pap. 17.95 (*0-8157-0061-X*) Brookings.

Aberbach, Joel D. & Walker, Jack L. The Meanings of Black Power: A Comparison of White & Black Interpretations of a Political Slog. (Reprint Series in Political Science). (C). 1993. reprint ed. pap. text 5.00 (*0-8290-2764-5*, PS-421) Irvington.

Aberbach, Joel D., et al. Bureaucrats & Politicians in Western Democracies. 322p. 1982. pap. 18.00 (*0-674-08627-9*) HUP.

***Aberbach, Moses & Aberbach, David.** The Roman-Jewish Wars & Hebrew Cultural Nationalism. LC 99-54791. 2000. 65.00 (*0-312-23191-1*) St Martin.

Aberbach, Moshe. Labor, Crafts & Commerce in Ancient Israel. LC 94-213374. xii, 294p. 1994. text 30.00 (*965-223-860-0*, Pub. by Magnes Pr) Eisenbrauns.

Abercrombie, Barbara. Cat-Man's Daughter. LC 79-2676. 160p. (J). (gr. 6-9). 1981. 11.95 (*0-06-020030-8*) HarpC Child Bks.

— Charlie Anderson. (J). 1995. mass mkt. 4.95 (*0-689-80114-9*) Aladdin.

— Charlie Anderson. LC 89-2449. (Illus.). 32p. (J). (ps-3). 1990. lib. bdg. 16.00 (*0-689-50486-1*) McElderry Bks.

— Charlie Anderson. 1995. 10.15 (*0-606-07359-0*, Pub. by Turtleback) Demco.

— Michael & the Cats. LC 92-23950. (Illus.). 32p. (J). (ps-2). 1993. lib. bdg. 13.95 (*0-689-50543-4*) McElderry Bks.

Abercrombie, David. Elements of General Phonetics. 1979. 20.00 (*0-85224-028-7*, Pub. by Edinburgh U Pr) Col U Pr.

— Fifty Years in Phonetics: Selected Essays. (Illus.). 160p. 1991. 69.50 (*0-7486-0196-1*, Pub. by Edinburgh U Pr) Col U Pr.

Abercrombie, Esther, ed. see Williamston, Angela.

Abercrombie, Jay. Walks & Rambles in Ohio's Western Reserve: Discovering Nature & History in the Northeastern Corner. LC 95-43394. (Walks & Rambles Ser.). (Illus.). 208p. (Orig.). 1996. pap. 15.00 (*0-88150-285-5*, Pub. by Countryman) Norton.

— Walks & Rambles on the Delmarva Peninsula: A Guide for Hikers & Naturalists. LC 85-15813. (Walks & Rambles Ser.). (Illus.). 208p. (Orig.). 1985. pap. 13.00 (*0-942440-27-7*, Pub. by Countryman) Norton.

Abercrombie, John R. Computer Programs for Literary Analysis. LC 84-7214. 204p. 1984. spiral bd. 17.50 (*0-8122-1177-4*); disk 41.95 (*0-8122-3002-7*); disk 41.95 (*0-8122-3003-5*); disk 41.95 (*0-8122-3004-3*) U of Pa Pr.

Abercrombie, Lascelles. Epic. LC 73-102222. (Select Bibliographies Reprint Ser.). 1977. 21.95 (*0-8369-5107-7*) Ayer.

— Idea of Great Poetry. LC 73-99654. (Select Bibliographies Reprint Ser.). 1977. 21.95 (*0-8369-5083-6*) Ayer.

— The Idea of Great Poetry. 1988. reprint ed. lib. bdg. 59.00 (*0-7812-0111-X*) Rprt Serv.

— The Idea of Great Poetry. LC 72-131601. 231p. 1925. reprint ed. 17.00 (*0-403-00488-8*) Scholarly.

— Interludes & Poems. LC 79-50016. (One-Act Plays in Reprint Ser.). 1980. reprint ed. 30.00 (*0-8486-2040-2*) Roth Pub Inc.

— Principles of English Prosody, Pt. 1. LC 75-41000. (BCL Ser.: No. II). reprint ed. 24.50 (*0-404-14735-6*) AMS Pr.

— Principles of Literary Criticism. LC 78-21288. 160p. 1979. reprint ed. lib. bdg. 49.75 (*0-313-20025-4*, ABPL, Greenwood Pr) Greenwood.

— Revaluations: Studies in Biography. 1977. 19.95 (*0-8369-0821-X*) Ayer.

— Speculative Dialogues. 1988. reprint ed. lib. bdg. 49.00 (*0-7812-0108-X*) Rprt Serv.

— Speculative Dialogues. 1971. reprint ed. 39.00 (*0-403-00799-2*) Scholarly.

— The Theory of Poetry. LC 69-17712. 1969. reprint ed. 30.00 (*0-8196-0223-X*) Biblo.

— The Theory of Poetry. 1988. reprint ed. lib. bdg. 49.00 (*0-7812-0110-1*) Rprt Serv.

— The Theory of Poetry. LC 76-131602. 222p. 1924. reprint ed. 11.00 (*0-403-00489-6*) Scholarly.

— Thomas Hardy, a Critical Study. (BCL1-PR English Literature Ser.). 224p. 1992. reprint ed. lib. bdg. 79.00 (*0-7812-7549-0*) Rprt Serv.

Abercrombie, Lascelles, et al. Revaluations: Studies in Biography. LC 75-30773. (English Biography Ser.: No. 31). 1975. lib. bdg. 75.00 (*0-8383-2106-2*) M S G Haskell Hse.

Abercrombie, M. & Brachet, J., eds. Advances in Morphogenesis, 10 vols. Incl. Vol. 1. 1961. (*0-12-028601-7*); Vol. 2. 1963. (*0-12-028602-5*); Vol. 3. 1964. (*0-12-028603-3*); Vol. 4. 1965. (*0-12-028604-1*); Vol. 5. 1966. (*0-12-028605-X*); Vol. 6. 1967. (*0-12-028606-8*); Vol. 7. King, T. J., ed. 1968. (*0-12-028607-6*); Vol. 8. King, T. J., ed. 1970. (*0-12-028608-4*); Vol. 9. King, T. J., ed. 1971. (*0-12-028609-2*); Vol. 10. 1973. (*0-12-028610-6*); write for info. (*0-318-50204-6*) Acad Pr.

Abercrombie, M., et al. Diccionario de Biologia. (SPA.). 242p. 1978. pap. 24.95 (*0-8288-4881-5*, S50068) Fr & Eur.

Abercrombie, Neil. Blood of Patriots. 1997. mass mkt. 6.99 (*0-8125-6795-1*, Pub. by Forge NYC) St Martin.

Abercrombie, Neil, jt. auth. see Hoyt, Richard.

Abercrombie, Nicholas. Television & Society. (Illus.). 240p. (C). 1996. text 57.95 (*0-7456-1435-3*, Pub. by Polity Pr); pap. text 27.95 (*0-7456-1436-1*, Pub. by Polity Pr) Blackwell Pubs.

Abercrombie, Nicholas & Longhurst, Brian. Audiences: A Sociological Theory of Performance & Imagination. LC 97-62467. 197p. 1998. write for info. (*0-8039-8962-8*) Sage.

***Abercrombie, Nicholas & Warde, Alan, eds.** The Contemporary British Society Reader. 270p. 2000. 69.95 (*0-7456-2262-3*, Pub. by Polity Pr); pap. 34.95 (*0-7456-2263-1*, Pub. by Polity Pr) Blackwell Pubs.

***Abercrombie, Nicholas, et al.** Contemporary British Society. 3rd ed. (Illus.). 640p. 2000. text 74.95 (*0-7456-2296-8*, Pub. by Polity Pr); pap. text 39.95 (*0-7456-2297-6*, Pub. by Polity Pr) Blackwell Pubs.

Abercrombie, Nicholas, et al. The Dominant Ideologies. 272p. (C). 1990. pap. text 19.95 (*0-04-301299-X*) Routledge.

An Asterisk (*) at the beginning of an entry indicates that the title is appearing for the first time.

A

— The Dominant Ideology Thesis. 240p. 1980. text 60.00 (*0-04-301117-9*) Routledge.

— The Penguin Dictionary of Sociology. 3rd ed. 528p. 1995. pap. 14.95 (*0-14-051292-6*, Penguin Bks) Viking Penguin.

— Sovereign Individuals of Capitalism. 224p. (C). 1986. 55.00 (*0-04-301230-2*); pap. text 17.95 (*0-04-301231-0*) Routledge.

Abercrombie, Nicolas. Diccionario de Sociologia. (SPA.). 288p. 1986. pap. 26.95 (*0-7859-6000-7*, 8473606357) Fr & Eur.

Abercrombie, R. T. Abercrombie, the Abercrombies of Baltimore: Genealogical & Biographical Sketch of the Family of David Abercrombie Who Settled in Baltimore, MD in 1848. 35p. 1993. reprint ed. pap. 7.00 (*0-8328-3636-2*) Higginson Bk Co.

Abercrombie, Stanley. Corporate Interior Designs. (Illus.). 240p. 1997. 59.95 (*0-07-018243-4*) McGraw.

***Abercrombie, Stanley.** Corporate Interiors, No. 3. (Illus.). 360p. 1999. 59.95 (*1-58471-000-4*) Visual Refer.

Abercrombie, Stanley. Corporate Interiors No. 1: 33 Design Forms - 100 Projects. (Illus.). 312p. 1997. 59.95 (*0-934590-91-5*) Visual Refer.

— George Nelson: The Design of Modern Design. (Illus.). 384p. 1994. 65.00 (*0-262-01142-5*) MIT Pr.

***Abercrombie, Stanley.** George Nelson: The Design of Modern Design. (Illus.). 400p. (C). 2000. reprint ed. pap. 39.95 (*0-262-51116-9*) MIT Pr.

Abercrombie, Stanley. Hospitality & Restaurant Design. (Illus.). 200p. 1999. 49.95 (*0-934590-46-X*) Visual Refer.

Abercrombie, Stanley. Philosophy of Interior Design. LC 89-45506. (Illus.). 192p. 1991. pap. 25.00 (*0-06-430194-X*, Icon Edns) HarpC.

Abercrombie, Stanley, ed. Corporate Interiors, Vol. 2. 2nd ed. (Illus.). 428p. 1998. 59.95 (*0-934590-99-0*, 886978) Visual Refer.

Abercrombie, Stanley A., contrib. by. Dictionary of Terms Used in the Safety Profession. 3rd ed. 72p. 1988. pap. 25.00 (*0-939874-79-2*) ASSE.

Abercrombie, Thomas A. Pathways of Memory & Power: Ethnography & History among an Andean People. LC 96-38814. (Illus.). 552p. 1997. 60.00 (*0-299-15310-X*); pap. 27.00 (*0-299-15314-2*) U of Wis Pr.

Abercromby, John. The Pre- & Proto- Historic Finns, Both Eastern & Western, with the Magic Songs of the West Finns, 2 vols. LC 70-144523. (Grimm Library: Nos. 9-10). reprint ed. 74.50 (*0-404-53590-9*) AMS Pr.

Aberdeeb & North-East Scotland Family History Society Staff. The People of Skene & Kinellar, 1696: Taken from List of Pollable Persons in the Shires of Aberdeen, 1696 / LC 98-171185. 1998. write for info. (*1-900173-03-4*) Aberdeen & NE Scot.

Aberdeen and North-East Scotland Family History Society Staff, jt. auth. see Morgan, Dorothy H.

Aberdeen and North-East Scotland Family History Society Staff, jt. auth. see Spiers, Sheila M.

***Aberdeen, J. A.** Hollywood Renegades: The Society of Independent Motion Picture Producers. LC 00-9588. 336p. 2001. pap. 19.95 (*1-890110-24-8*) Cobblestone Ent.

Aberdeen Rare Books Staff. Nisbet's System of Heraldry, 2 vols. (C). 1988. 500.00 (*0-7855-3792-9*, Pub. by Aberdeen Rare Bks) St Mut.

— Register of the Great Seal of Scotland, 11 vols. (C). 1988. 2150.00 (*0-7855-3793-7*, Pub. by Aberdeen Rare Bks) St Mut.

Aberdeen, Scotland (Diocese Staff). Registrum Episcopatus Aberdonensis: Ecclesie Cathedralis Aberdonensis Regesta Que Extant in Unum Collecta, 2 vols. Innes, Cosmo N., ed. LC 77-38504. (Maitland Club, Glasgow. Publications: No. 63). 1845. 165.00 (*0-404-53065-6*) AMS Pr.

Aberdeen's Magazine of Masonry Construction Staff, ed. The Fireplace Book Vol. 2: An Idea Book of Fireplace Designs. (Illus.). 85p. (Orig.). 1995. pap. 24.95 (*0-924659-58-0*, 4515) Hanley.

Aberg, F. A. Medieval Moated Sites, Vol. 17. LC 79-306838. (CBA Research Report Ser.). 93p. 1978. 6.00 (*0-900312-58-0*) Council for British Archeology.

Aberg, J. A., jt. auth. see Volberding, P. A.

Aberg, Martin, et al, eds. Baltic Cities: Perspectives on Urban & Regional Change in the Baltic Sea Area. LC 99-182703. (Illus.). 253p. 1998. pap. 46.50 (*91-89116-03-8*, Pub. by Almqvist Wiksell) Coronet Bks.

Aberg, Nils F. The Anglo-Saxons in England During the Early Centuries after the Invasion. x, 219p. 1975. reprint ed. write for info. (*3-487-05723-9*) G Olms Pubs.

Aberg, Nina, tr. see Leo, Veronica & Daknewa, Tashi.

Aberg, Sally J., jt. auth. see Becom, Jeffrey.

Aberg, T., et al. Corpuscles & Radiation in Matter I. (Encyclopedia of Physics Ser.: Vol. 31). (Illus.). 670p. 1982. 282.95 (*0-387-11313-4*) Spr-Verlag.

Aberg, Ulf & Hancock, Walton M. Design Criteria of Predetermined Time Systems: With Special Reference to the MTM System. LC T 0060.M65A2. (Illus.). 35p. reprint ed. pap. 30.00 (*0-7837-5495-7*, 204526000005) Bks Demand.

Aberg, William. The Listening Chamber: Poems by William Aberg. LC 97-942. (Poetry Award Ser.). 1997. pap. 12.00 (*1-55728-463-6*) U of Ark Pr.

— The Listening Chamber: Poems by William Aberg. LC 97-942. (Poetry Award Ser.). 1997. 20.00 (*1-55728-464-4*) U of Ark Pr.

Aberg, Williams, ed. A Promise of Morning: Writings from Arizona Prisons. 1982. pap. 4.95 (*0-933188-21-8*) Blue Moon Pr.

***Abergel, Dianne.** Free Indeed! Psychology Treats but God Heals. 176p. 2000. pap. 9.99 (*1-890900-21-4*) Insight Intl.

***Abergel, Matthew.** Gay Stars: The Ultimate Gay Guys Guide to Astrology. 256p. 2000. per. 12.00 (*0-684-86607-2*) S&S Trade.

Abergel, Matthew. Work Your Stars! Using Astrology to Navigate Your Career Path, Shine on the Job & Guide Your Business Decisions. LC 99-22000. 384p. 1999. pap. 12.00 (*0-684-84995-X*, Fireside) S&S Trade Pap.

Aberger, Joseph P. Selling Your Business: Making the Right Moves/Avoiding Costly Mistakes. 48p. 1999. pap. 12.95 (*0-9670551-0-5*) Bus Val Servs.

Abergunrin, Olayiwola. Economic Dependence & Regional Cooperation in Southern Africa: SADCC & South Africa in Confrontation. LC 89-12585. (Studies in African Economic & Social Development: Vol. 2). 368p. 1990. lib. bdg. 99.95 (*0-88946-515-0*) E Mellen.

Aberjhani. I Made My Boy Out of Poetry: Poems, Stories, Dreams & Sho 'Nuff Truths. unabridged ed. 116p. 1998. pap. 9.95 (*0-9662356-5-7*) Aberjhani.

Aberlaitz & De Oreyegui, P. Buenaventura. Diccionario Vasco-Castellano, Castellano-Vasco de Voces Comunes a Dos o Mas Dialectos del Euskera. (SPA.). 14.95 (*0-7859-0865-X*, S3099) Fr & Eur.

Aberle, Bob. Clean & Quiet: The Guide to Electric Powered Flight. Fanelli, Frank, ed. (Illus.). (Orig.). 1995. pap. 12.95 (*0-924771-58-5*, Covered Brdge Pr) Douglas Charles Ltd.

Aberle, Craig L., jt. auth. see Xiradis-Aberle, Lori.

Aberle, D. F., et al. The Functional Prerequisites of a Society. (Reprint Series in Sociology). (C). 1993. reprint ed. pap. text 1.30 (*0-8290-2618-5*, S-1) Irvington.

Aberle, David F. The Peyote Religion among the Navaho. 2nd ed. LC 91-50310. (Illus.). 468p. 1991. reprint ed. pap. 24.95 (*0-8061-2382-6*) U of Okla Pr.

Aberle, Kathleen G. Ten Times More Beautiful: The Rebuilding of Vietnam. LC 78-14890. 275p. reprint ed. pap. 85.30 (*0-7837-3923-0*, 204377100010) Bks Demand.

Aberle, S. B. De, see De Aberle, S. B.

Aberley, Doug, ed. Boundaries of Home: Mapping for Local Empowerment. (Illus.). 144p. 1993. pap. 9.95 (*0-86571-272-7*) New Soc Pubs.

Aberlin, Jane S. Seniority Rules: A Light Look at Longevity. LC 97-91077. 1998. pap. 8.95 (*0-533-12559-6*) Vantage.

Aberly, Rachel, jt. auth. see Fritz, Suzanne.

Aberman, Rick, jt. auth. see Anderson, John.

Abern, Wendell. Bridge Is a Contact Sport: The First Humor Book on the Game of Bridge. (Illus.). 70p. (Orig.). 1995. pap. 8.95 (*0-9645895-0-8*) Carolivia.

Abernathy. Introduction to Computing with Multimedia. LC 97-17648. (Computer Science Ser.). (C). 1997. mass mkt. 46.95 (*0-534-23148-9*) PWS Pubs.

Abernathy, et al. A Stitch in Time: Lean Retailing & the Transformation of Manufacturing. LC 98-38224. (Illus.). 384p. 1999. 35.00 (*0-19-512615-7*) OUP.

Abernathy, Alta & Harris, Barbara. Bud & Me: The True Cross-Country Adventures of the Abernathy Boys. 2nd rev. ed. Rogers, William B., ed. (Illus.). 164p. 1998. 18.95 (*0-9662166-0-1*) Dove Creek Pr.

Abernathy, Ann & Thorpe, John G. The Oak Park Home & Studio of Frank Lloyd Wright. LC 88-10649. (Illus.). 48p. (Orig.). (gr. 6 up). 1988. pap. 8.95 (*0-945635-00-1*) F Lloyd Wright.

Abernathy, Beatrice. Once & for All. LC 93-74790. 1994. pap. 12.95 (*1-55673-891-9*, Express Pr) CSS OH.

Abernathy, C. David. An Exegetical Summary of I Peter. LC 98-61699. 190 p. 1998. pap. 17.00 (*1-55671-078-X*) S I L Intl.

Abernathy, C. R., et al, eds. Chemical Perspectives of Microelectronic Materials III. (Symposium Proceedings Ser.: Vol. 282). 725p. 1993. text 30.00 (*1-55899-177-8*) Materials Res.

Abernathy, C. R., et al, eds. Gallium Nitride & Related Materials II: Materials Research Society Symposium Proceedings, Vol. 468. LC 97-13305. 506p. 1997. text 71.00 (*1-55899-372-X*) Materials Res.

***Abernathy, C. R., et al, eds.** State-of-the-Art Program on Compound Semiconductors XXX. 264p. 1999. 62.00 (*1-56677-226-5*, PV 99-4) Electrochem Soc.

Abernathy, C. R., et al, eds. III-V Nitride Materials & Processes II. LC 98-158682. (Proceedings Ser.: Vol. 97-34). (Illus.). 294p. 1998. 48.00 (*1-56677-187-0*) Electrochem Soc.

Abernathy, Charles D. Detours: Biographies of Physically Disabled Achievers. 36p. (Orig.). 1988. pap. 5.95 (*0-9620745-0-0*); pap. text 3.95 (*0-9620745-1-9*) TEAM Savers.

Abernathy, Charles F. Civil Rights & Constitutional Litigation, Cases & Materials. 2nd ed. (American Casebook Ser.). 753p. (C). 1992. 57.50 (*0-314-92683-6*) West Pub.

— Law in the United States. 1995. 45.00 (*0-935328-76-9*) Intl Law Inst.

Abernathy, Charles M. Surgical Secrets. 1986. 22.95 (*0-8016-0070-7*) Mosby Inc.

Abernathy, Charles M. & Hamm, Robert M. Surgical Scripts: Master Surgeons Think Aloud about 43 Common Surgical Problems. LC 93-39297. 200p. 1994. 24.00 (*1-56053-119-3*) Hanley & Belfus.

Abernathy, Charles M., jt. ed. see Hamm, Robert M.

Abernathy, Charles O., et al, eds. Risk Assessment of Essential Elements. LC 94-75706. (Illus.). 320p. 1994. 45.00 (*0-944398-21-9*) ILSI.

Abernathy, Christina. Miss Abernathy's Concise Slave Training Manual. 96p. (Orig.). 1996. pap. text 11.95 (*0-9639763-9-7*) Greenery Pr.

— Training with Miss Abernathy: A Workbook for Erotic Slaves & Their Owners. 160p. 1998. pap. 11.95 (*1-890159-07-7*) Greenery Pr.

Abernathy, Estelle K. Pumpkin Corner. (Illus.). 160p. 1979. reprint ed. pap. 12.95 (*0-9608428-2-9*) Straw Patchwork.

Abernathy, Francis E. How the Critters Created Texas. 2nd rev. ed. LC 82-80440. (Illus.). 46p. (J). (gr. 1-6). 1998. lib. bdg. 14.95 (*0-936650-14-1*, Pub. by E C Temple) Sunbelt Media.

Abernathy, Jack. Living Monument: The Story of Grace Covenant Presbyterian Church. LC 89-81284. (Illus.). 168p. (Orig.). 1989. 100.00 (*0-9624718-0-1*); pap. 10.00 (*0-9624718-1-X*) Grace Covenant Presbyterian Church.

Abernathy, John H., jt. auth. see Shulman, Stephen N.

Abernathy, John R., ed. Weeds of Cotton: Characterization & Control. LC 92-6771. (Cotton Foundation Reference Bks.: No. 2). 1992. lib. bdg. 45.00 (*0-939809-02-8*) Cotton Found.

Abernathy, Kenneth & Allen, J. Thomas, Jr. Experiments in Computing: Laboratories for Introductory Computer Science in Think Pascal. 400p. (C). 1992. pap. 27.95 (*0-534-15421-2*) PWS Pubs.

— Experiments in Computing: Laboratories for Introductory Computer Science in Think Pascal. 400p. 1993. pap. 22.95 (*0-534-19417-6*) PWS Pubs.

Abernathy, M. Glenn & Perry Barbara, A. Civil Liberties under the Constitution. 6th ed. LC 92-23581. 485p. (C). 1993. pap. text 34.95 (*0-87249-854-9*) U of SC Pr.

Abernathy, Sydne, jt. ed. see Yascavage, Pam.

Abernathy, Thomas P. Historical Sketch of the University of Virginia. 1948. pap. 3.25 (*0-87517-033-1*) Dietz.

— South in the New Nation, 1789-1819. LC 61-15488. (History of the South Ser.: Vol. 4). (Illus.). xvi, 530p. 1961. text 55.00 (*0-8071-0004-8*) La State U Pr.

— South in the New Nation, 1789-1819. LC 61-15488. (History of the South Ser.: Vol. 4). (Illus.). xvi, 530p. 1961. pap. text 16.95 (*0-8071-0014-5*) La State U Pr.

Abernathy, William B. The Sin of Wages: Where the Conventional Pay System Has Led Us & How to Find a Way Out. LC 96-92835. 181p. (Orig.). 1996. pap. 12.00 (*0-9655276-0-3*) Abernathy & Assocs.

Abernathy, William J. The Productivity Dilemma: Roadblock to Innovation in the Automobile Industry. LC 78-1034. (Illus.). 279p. reprint ed. pap. 86.50 (*0-8357-6751-5*, 203540700095) Bks Demand.

Abernethy, B., et al. Biophysical Foundations of Human Movement. 450p. 1996. 79.95 (*0-7329-3047-2*, Pub. by Macmill Educ); pap. 39.95 (*0-7329-3048-0*, Pub. by Macmill Educ) Paul & Co Pubs.

Abernethy, Bruce, et al, eds. The Biophysical Foundations of Human Movement. LC 96-50009. (Illus.). 440p. (Orig.). (C). 1997. pap. text 32.00 (*0-88011-732-X*, BABE0732) Human Kinetics.

Abernethy, Bruce, jt. ed. see Snyder, Conrad W.

Abernethy, Burrjis, et al. 365 Meditations for Women. LC 89-194. 352p. 1989. pap. 12.00 (*0-687-41886-0*) Dimen for Liv.

Abernethy, Byron R., ed. see Stockwell, Elisha, Jr.

Abernethy, C. E. Abernethy's Ultimate Tenant Handbook. Baird, Cathryn, ed. 151p. 1997. pap. 18.95 (*0-9656465-1-3*) Abernethy Law Ofc.

***Abernethy, David B.** The Dynamics of Global Dominance: European Overseas Empires, 1415-1980. (Illus.). 492p. 2000. 35.00 (*0-300-07304-6*) Yale U Pr.

Abernethy, F. E., ed. Paisanos: A Folklore Miscellany. (Texas Folklore Society Publications: No. 41). (Illus.). 180p. 1978. reprint ed. 16.95 (*1-57441-059-8*) UNTX Pr.

— What's Going On? In Modern Texas Folklore. (Texas Folklore Society Publications: No. 40). (Illus.). 309p. 1976. 16.95 (*1-57441-058-X*) UNTX Pr.

Abernethy, F. E., et al, eds. Juneteenth Texas: Essays in African-American Folklore. LC 96-21854. (Texas Folklore Society Publications: Vol. 54). (Illus.). 364p. 1996. 29.95 (*1-57441-018-0*) UNTX Pr.

Abernethy, Francis, ed. Paisanos: A Folklore Miscellany. 1978. 15.00 (*0-88426-054-2*) Encino Pr.

Abernethy, Francis E. Legends of Texas' Heroic Age. (Texas History Ser.). (Illus.). 108p. (C). 1984. pap. text 9.95 (*0-89641-143-5*) American Pr.

— Singin' Texas. LC 93-39616. (Texas Folklore Society Publications). (Illus.). 183p. (Orig.). 1994. reprint ed. pap. 19.95 (*0-929398-71-8*) UNTX Pr.

— Texas Folklore Society, 1943-1971, Vol. 2. LC 92-12273. (Texas Folklore Society Publications: No. 53). (Illus.). 320p. 1994. 29.95 (*0-929398-78-5*) UNTX Pr.

— Texas Folklore Society, 1909-1943, Vol. I. LC 92-12273. (Texas Folklore Society Publications: No. 51). (Illus.). 326p. 1992. 29.95 (*0-929398-42-4*) UNTX Pr.

Abernethy, Francis E., ed. Between the Cracks of History: Essays on Teaching & Illustrating Folklore. LC 97-17598. (Texas Folklore Society Publications: Vol. 55). (Illus.). 284p. 1997. 27.00 (*1-57441-036-9*) UNTX Pr.

— The Bounty of Texas. LC 90-12417. (Texas Folklore Society Publications: No. 49). (Illus.). 232p. 1990. 19.95 (*0-929398-14-9*) UNTX Pr.

— Corners of Texas. LC 93-7447. (Texas Folklore Society Publication: No. 52). (Illus.). 319p. 1993. 19.95 (*0-929398-57-2*) UNTX Pr.

— Folk Art in Texas. LC 85-2001. (Texas Folklore Society Publications: No. 45). (Illus.). 209p. 1985. 35.00 (*0-87074-210-8*) UNTX Pr.

— Hoein' the Short Rows. LC 87-9756. (Texas Folklore Society Publications: No. 47). 238p. 1987. 19.95 (*0-87074-256-6*) UNTX Pr.

— Legendary Ladies of Texas. LC 94-16318. (Texas Folklore Society Publications: Vol. 43). (Illus.). 249p. (Orig.). 1994. reprint ed. pap. 17.95 (*0-929398-75-0*) UNTX Pr.

— Sonovagun Stew: A Folklore Miscellany. LC 85-14290. (Texas Folklore Society Publications: No. 46). (Illus.). 184p. 1985. 21.95 (*0-87074-211-6*) UNTX Pr.

— Texas Toys & Games. LC 87-10584. (Texas Folklore Society Publications: Vol. 48). (Illus.). 256p. 1997. reprint ed. pap. 16.95 (*1-57441-037-7*) UNTX Pr.

— What's Going On? (Texas Folklore Society Publications: Vol. 40). (Illus.). 1976. 20.00 (*0-88426-049-6*) Encino Pr.

***Abernethy, Francis Edward.** Built in Texas. 2nd ed. LC 00-29877. (Texas Folklore Society Publications: No. XLII). (Illus.). 292p. 2000. pap. write for info. (*1-57441-092-X*, Pub. by UNTX Pr) Tex A&M Univ Pr.

Abernethy, Jane F. & Tune, Suelyn C. Made in Hawaii. LC 83-4895. (Illus.). 140p. (J). (gr. 3-12). 1983. pap. 8.95 (*0-8248-0870-3*, Kolowalu Bk) UH Pr.

Abernethy, Kathy. Menopause & Hurt. 1997. pap. text 25.00 (*0-7020-2023-0*, Pub. by W B Saunders) Saunders.

Abernethy, Kenneth. Experiments in Computing: Think Pascal Without Disk. (Computer Science Ser.). 1992. mass mkt. 24.95 (*0-534-15422-0*) PWS Pubs.

Abernethy, Kenneth & Allen, Tom. Exploring Digital Domain - Window Version, Vol. 1. LC 98-49444. (Computer Science Ser.). (C). 1999. pap. 58.95 (*0-534-95516-9*) PWS Pubs.

Abernethy, Lloyd M. Benton Spruance: The Artist & the Man. LC 86-47620. (Illus.). 184p. 1988. 45.00 (*0-87982-517-0*) Art Alliance.

Abernethy, Peter, et al. English Novel Explication: Supplement One to January, 1975. LC 73-410. (Novel Explication Ser.). vii, 305p. (C). 1976. lib. bdg. 45.00 (*0-208-01464-0*) Shoe String.

Abernethy, Thomas P. From Frontier to Plantation in Tennessee: A Study in Frontier Democracy, No. 12--12. LC 78-12038. (Illus.). 392p. 1979. reprint ed. lib. bdg. 35.00 (*0-313-21124-8*, ABFF, Greenwood Pr) Greenwood.

— Three Virginia Frontiers. 1962. 16.50 (*0-8446-1001-1*) Peter Smith.

Abernethy, V. D. Population Politics: The Choices That Shape Our Future. LC 92-41791. (Illus.). 370p. (C). 1993. 26.50 (*0-306-44461-5*, Plen Insight) Perseus Pubng.

Abernethy, Virginia. Population Pressure & Cultural Adjustment. LC 78-11676. 189p. 1979. 35.95 (*0-87705-329-4*, Kluwer Acad Hman Sci) Kluwer Academic.

Abernethy, Virginia D. Population Politics: The Choices That Shape Our Future. LC 99-23301. 365p. 1999. pap. 26.95 (*0-7658-0603-7*) Transaction Pubs.

***Abers, Rebecca N.** Inventing Local Democracy: Grassroots Politics in Brazil. 280p. 2000. lib. bdg. 59.95 (*1-55587-893-8*) L Rienner.

Abersold, John & Howard, Wayne. Cases in Labor Relations: An Arbitration Experience. (Orig.). 1967. pap. text 15.95 (*0-685-03778-9*) P-H.

Abert, James G. Economic Policy & Planning in the Netherlands, 1950-1965. LC 69-15439. 298p. reprint ed. pap. 92.40 (*0-608-14192-5*, 202197200024) Bks Demand.

Abert, James G., ed. Program Evaluation at HEW: Research Versus Reality, 3 pts., Pt. 1. LC 79-17495. (Public Administration & Public Policy Ser.: No. 8). (Illus.). 423p. reprint ed. pap. 131.20 (*0-8357-3507-9*, 203451500001) Bks Demand.

— Program Evaluation at HEW: Research Versus Reality, 3 pts., Pt. 2. LC 79-17495. (Public Administration & Public Policy Ser.: No. 8). (Illus.). 407p. reprint ed. pap. 126.20 (*0-8357-3508-7*, 203451500002) Bks Demand.

— Program Evaluation at HEW: Research Versus Reality, 3 pts., Pt. 3. LC 79-17495. (Public Administration & Public Policy Ser.: No. 8). (Illus.). 328p. reprint ed. pap. 101.70 (*0-8357-3509-5*, 203451500003) Bks Demand.

Abert, James W. Expedition to the Southwest: An 1845 Reconnaissance of Colorado, New Mexico, Texas & Oklahoma. LC 99-30386. (Illus.). 144p. 1999. pap. 10.00 (*0-8032-5935-2*, Bison Books) U of Nebr Pr.

Aberth, John. Criminal Churchmen in the Age of Edward III: The Case of Bishop Thomas de Lisle. LC 95-49302. (Illus.). 296p. 1996. 50.00 (*0-271-01543-8*) Pa St U Pr.

***Aberth, John.** From the Brink of the Apocalypse: Confronting Famine, War, Plague & death in the Later Middle Ages. LC 00-38263. (Illus.). 288p. 2000. 26.00 (*0-415-92715-3*) Routledge.

Aberth, Oliver. Precise Numerical Methods Using C++ - KSO. LC 98-117803. (Illus.). 238p. 1998. text, boxed set 59.95 incl. cd-rom (*0-12-041750-2*) Acad Pr.

Abertini, Ippolio F. Clinical Consultations of Ippolito Francesco Albertini. Jarcho, Saul, tr. from ITA. & intro. by. (Illus.). 356p. 1990. lib. bdg. 24.95 (*0-317-03952-0*) F A Countway.

Abet. Rosicrucian Manual. 131p. 1996. reprint ed. spiral bd. 18.00 (*0-7873-0015-2*) Hlth Research.

Abet, Lothar, et al. Prenatal Diagnosis of Foetal Malformations & Diseases: Teaching Atlas of Amniofoetography. 88p. 1991. 65.00 (*3-05-500611-9*, Pub. by Akademie Verlag) Wiley.

Abetti, Pier A., jt. auth. see Maldifassi, Jose O.

Abeyaratne, Rohan, jt. ed. see Casey, James.

Abeyasingha, N. The Universal Catechism: A Homily Sourcebook. 65p. 1993. pap. 7.95 (*1-56929-010-5*, Pastoral Press) OR Catholic.

Abeykoon, P., et al. Reorientation of Medical Education Pt. 5: Introducing Problem-Based Learning in the South-East Asia Region. (WHO Regional Publications, South-East Asia Ser.: No. 18). viii, 42p. 1992. pap. 4.00 (*92-9022-164-X*, 1565018) World Health.

Abeykoon, P., jt. auth. see Mattock, N. M.

***Abeyratne, R. I.** Emergent Commercial Trends & Aviation Safety LC 99-20600. 1999. 109.95 (*1-84014-907-8*) Ashgate Pub Co.

Abeyratne, R. I. Legal & Regulatory Issues in International Aviation. LC 95-37807. 1996. 125.00 (*1-57105-010-8*) Transnatl Pubs.

***Abeyratne, R. I. R.** Aviation Trends in the New Millenium. LC 00-42044. 2000. write for info. (*0-7546-1299-6*, Pub. by Ashgate Pub) Ashgate Pub Co.

An Asterisk (*) at the beginning of an entry indicates that the title is appearing for the first time.

Abeyratne, Ruwantissa I. Aviation Security: Legal & Regulatory Aspects. LC 98-20262. 367p. 1998. text 101.95 (*1-84014-544-7*, Pub. by Ashgate Pub) Ashgate Pub Co.

Abeyratne, Sirimal. Anti-Export Bias in the Export-Oriented Economy of Sri Lanka. (Sri Lanka Studies: Vol. 1). 320p. 1994. pap. 28.50 (*90-5383-254-8*, Pub. by VU Univ Pr) Paul & Co Pubs.

***Abeyratne, Sirimal.** Economic Change & Political Conflict in Developing Countries: With Special Reference to Sri Lanka. LC 99-183827. 243p. 1999. pap. 35.00 (*90-5383-606-3*, Pub. by VU Univ Pr) Paul & Co Pubs.

Abeyta, Dorthy, ed. see ASCA Staff.

***Abeyta, Jennifer.** Coins. LC 99-58254. (Cool Collectibles Ser.). (Illus.). 48p. (J). (gr. 4-7). 2000. pap. 6.95 (*0-516-23529-X*) Childrens.

— Stamps. (High Interest Bks.). (Illus.). (J). 2000. 19.00 (*0-516-23334-3*) Childrens.

— Stamps. (High Interest Bks.). (Illus.). 48p. (J). (gr. 4-7). 2000. pap. write for info. (*0-516-23534-6*) Childrens.

***Abgrall, Jean-Marie.** Healing or Stealing: Medical Charlatans in the New Age. 244p. 2000. pap. 21.95 (*1-892941-51-1*, Pub. by Algora Pubng) Midpt Trade.

Abgrall, R., et al, eds. Hypersonic Flows for Reentry Problems, Vol. III: Proceedings of the INRIA-GAMNI - SMAI Workshop, Pt. II, Antibes, France, 15-19 April 1991. (Illus.). 1216p. 1993. 298.00 (*0-387-56189-7*) Spr-Verlag.

Abhau, Marcy, et al, eds. Architecture in Education: A Resource of Imaginative Ideas & Tested Activities. (Illus.). 191p. 1986. pap. text 25.00 (*0-9622908-0-7*) Fndtn Architecture.

Abhayadatta. Buddha's Lions. Robinson, James, tr. from TIB. LC 79-12397. (Tibetan Translation Ser.). (Illus.). 1979. 32.00 (*0-913546-60-7*); pap. 19.95 (*0-913546-61-5*) Dharma Pub.

Abhayananda, jt. auth. see Plotinus.

Abhayananda, S. Jnaneshvar: The Life & Works of the Celebrated Thirteenth Century Indian Mystic-Poet. (Illus.). 260p. (Orig.). 1989. pap. 11.95 (*0-914557-02-5*) Atma Bks.

***Abhayananda, S.** The Origin of Western Mysticism: Selected Writings of Plotinus. LC 99-38569. (Classics of Mystical Literature). 198p. 2000. pap. 19.95 (*0-914557-13-0*, Pub. by Atma Bks) ACCESS Pubs Network.

Abhayananda, S. The Supreme Self. 2nd rev. ed. LC 97-21590. 200p. 1998. pap. 14.95 (*0-914557-10-6*) Atma Bks.

— The Wisdom of Vedanta. 2nd rev. ed. 335p. (Orig.). 1998. pap. 14.95 (*0-914557-06-8*) Atma Bks.

Abhayananda, S., ed. see Thomas, a Kempis.

Abhayananda, Swami, tr. see Dattatreya.

Abhedananda, Swami. Doctrine of Karma. 1944. 6.95 (*0-87481-608-4*) Vedanta Pr.

— How to Be a Yogi. 6.95 (*0-87481-609-2*) Vedanta Pr.

— Human Affection & Divine Love. 64p. 1935. 4.95 (*0-87481-610-6*, Pub. by Ramakrishna Math) Vedanta Pr.

— India & Her People (1906) 286p. 1998. reprint ed. pap. 19.95 (*0-7661-0186-X*) Kessinger Pub.

— Journey into Kashmir & Tibet. 201p. 1988. 8.95 (*0-87481-643-2*, Pub. by Advaita Ashrama) Vedanta Pr.

— Life Beyond Death: A Critical Study of Spiritualism. 1946. pap. 7.95 (*0-87481-616-5*, Pub. by Rama Ved Math) Vedanta Pr.

— Ramakrishna Kathamrita: Memoirs of Ramakrishna. Orig. Title: Gospel of Ramakrishna. 266p. 1988. 7.95 (*0-87481-654-8*, Pub. by Rama Ved Math) Vedanta Pr.

— Reincarnation. 1947. 4.95 (*0-87481-604-1*, Pub. by Advaita Ashrama) Vedanta Pr.

— Songs Divine. Aiyer, P. S., tr. from SAN. 69p. 1985. pap. 5.95 (*0-87481-653-X*, Pub. by Ramakrishna Math) Vedanta Pr.

— A Study of Heliocentric Science. 1968. 5.95 (*0-87481-619-X*) Vedanta Pr.

— Vedanta Philosophy: Five Lectures on Reincarnation. 4th ed. 99p. 1976. reprint ed. spiral bd. 10.00 (*0-7873-0016-0*) Hlth Research.

— Vedanta Philosophy: Self-Knowledge (Atma-Jnana) 153p. 1998. reprint ed. pap. 16.95 (*0-7661-0126-6*) Kessinger Pub.

— Vedanta Philosophy Five Lectures on Reincarnation (1908) 100p. 1996. reprint ed. pap. 7.95 (*1-56459-886-1*) Kessinger Pub.

— Yoga Psychology. pap. 8.95 (*0-87481-614-9*, Pub. by Rama Ved Math) Vedanta Pr.

Abhijit, Dutta. Muslim Society in Transition: Titu Meer's Revolt. 241p. (C). 1987. 21.00 (*0-8364-2175-2*, Pub. by Minerva) S Asia.

Abhinavagupta. Paratrisika-Vivarana: The Secret of Tantric Mysticism. Baumer, Bettina, ed. Singh, Jaideva, tr. (C). 1988. 31.00 (*81-208-0462-7*, Pub. by Motilal Bnarsidass); pap. 21.00 (*81-208-0472-4*, Pub. by Motilal Bnarsidass) S Asia.

Abhyankar, K. D., ed. Treasures of Ancient Indian Astronomy. (C). 1993. 17.00 (*81-202-0354-2*, Pub. by Ajanta) S Asia.

Abhyankar, S. Ramification Theoretic Methods in Algebric Geometry. (Annals of Mathematics Studies: No. 43). 112p. 1959. pap. text 17.50 (*0-691-08023-2*, Pub. by Princeton U Pr) Cal Prin Full Svc.

Abhyankar, S. S. Resolution of Singularities of Embedded Algebraic Surfaces. 2nd ed. LC 98-9728. (Springer Monographs in Mathematics). x, 307p. 1998. 84.00 (*3-540-63719-2*) Spr-Verlag.

Abhyankar, S. S., et al. Algebraic Geometry: Papers Presented at the Bombay Colloquium. (Tata Institute of Fundamental Research Studies in Mathematics Ser.). 1970. 15.50 (*0-19-617607-7*) OUP.

Abhyankar, Shreeram S., ed. see Joint Summer Research Conference on Recent Develop.

Abhyanker, Shreeram S. Algebraic Geometry for Scientists & Engineers. LC 90-815. (SURV Ser.: Vol. 35). 295p. 1990. pap. 34.00 (*0-8218-1535-0*, SURV/35) Am Math.

Abi-Aad, Naji & Grenon, Michel. Instability & Conflict in the Middle East: People, Petroleum & Security Threats. (Illus.). 256p. 1997. text 65.00 (*0-312-17254-0*) St Martin.

Abichandani, P. Encyclopedia of Indian Literature Vol. 6: Supplementary Entries & Index. (C). 1995. 48.00 (*0-8364-2903-6*, Pub. by Indian Pubs) S Asia.

Abid, M., jt. ed. see Cheremisinoff, Nicholas P.

Abidi, A. H. The Gulf Crisis. (C). 1991. 29.00 (*81-7095-023-6*, Pub. by Lancer India) S Asia.

Abidi, A. H., ed. Indo-Gulf Economic Relations: Pattern, Prospects & Policies. (C). 1990. text 17.50 (*81-7076-025-9*, Pub. by Intellectual) S Asia.

Abidi, Asad A., et al. Integrated Circuits for Wireless Communications. LC 98-6333. 688p. 1998. 109.95 (*0-7803-3459-0*, PC5716-QOE) Inst Electrical.

Abidi, Mongi A. & Gonzalez, Ralph C., eds. Data Fusion in Robotics & Machine Intelligence. (Illus.). 546p. 1992. text 59.00 (*0-12-042120-8*) Acad Pr.

Abidi, Nigar F. Women Physicians: A Study in Roles & Role-Conflict. (Illus.). xvi, 244p. 1993. 24.00 (*81-85445-20-6*, Pub. by Manak Pubns Pvt Ltd) Nataraj Bks.

Abidi, S. A. Sufism in India. (C). 1992. 19.00 (*81-224-0418-9*) S Asia.

Abidin, Richard R. Early Childhood Parenting Skills Program Manual for the Mental Health Professional. (Illus.). 1996. pap. 32.00 (*0-911907-24-6*) Psych Assess.

— Early Childhood Parenting Skills Workbook for Parents. (Illus.). 1996. pap., wbk. ed. 14.00 (*0-911907-25-4*) Psych Assess.

Abidin, Richard R. Parenting Skills: Workbook & Trainer's Manual. 2nd ed. LC 81-13314. 85p. 1982. student ed. 20.95 (*0-89885-118-1*, Kluwer Acad Hman Sci) Kluwer Academic.

Abidine. Knopf Guide to Istanbul. (Illus.). 408p. 1993. pap. 26.00 (*0-679-74916-0*) Knopf.

Abif, Khafre K. & Neely, Teresa Y., eds. In Our Own Voices: The Changing Face of Librarianship. LC 95-36007. 460p. 1996. 47.50 (*0-8108-3074-4*) Scarecrow.

Abihider, Aftimios, ed. & illus. see Ofiesh, Mariam Namey.

Abiko, Bonnie F., tr. see Narazaki, Muneshige.

Abiko, Yasushi & Karmazyn, M. Protection Against Ischemia Reperfusion Damage of the Heart. LC 98-6390. 1998. write for info. (*4-431-70226-1*) Spr-Verlag.

Abiko, Yasushi, jt. ed. see Winbury, Martin M.

Abikoff, W. The Real Analytic Theory of Teichmueller Space. (Lecture Notes in Mathematics Ser.: Vol. 820). (Illus.). 144p. 1989. 34.95 (*0-387-10237-X*) Spr-Verlag.

Abikoff, William, et al, eds. The Mathematical Legacy of Wilhelm Mangus: Groups, Geometry, & Special Functions. LC 94-11625. (Contemporary Mathematics Ser.: Vol. 169). 499p. 1994. pap. 80.00 (*0-8218-5156-X*, CONM/169) Am Math.

Abildgaard, Noel, jt. auth. see Calvert, Robert.

Abildsoe, Deborah V., jt. auth. see Schloss, Irving S.

Abildtrup, Jens. Modern Time Series Analysis in Forest Products Markets. LC 98-49745. (Forestry Sciences Ser.). 5p. 1999. write for info. (*0-7923-5524-5*) Kluwer Academic.

Abilene Baptist History Committee. Strength for Today, Bright Hope for Tomorrow: Abilene Baptist Church Martinez, GA, 1774-1999. LC 98-68652. (Illus.). 416p. 1999. 29.95 (*1-57736-141-5*) Providence Hse.

Abimbola, Wande. Ifa: An Exposition of Ifa Literary Corpus. 2nd unabridged ed. (Illus.). 260p. 1997. reprint ed. pap. 24.95 (*1-890157-00-7*) Athelia-Henrietta.

— Ifa Divination Poetry. LC 73-86025. 179p. 1977. text 14.95 (*0-88357-023-8*) NOK Pubs.

— 3 West African Plays. (Illus.). 1977. 27.50 (*0-19-575325-9*) OUP.

Abinader, Elmaz. Children of the Roojme: A Family's Journey from Lebanon. LC 97-33200. (Illus.). 303p. (Orig.). 1997. pap. 14.95 (*0-299-15734-2*) U of Wis Pr.

— In the Country of My Dreams: Poetry by Elmaz Abinader. 68p. 1999. pap. 14.95 (*0-9653764-2-7*) Sufi Warrior.

Abinader, Elmaz, ed. see Jones, Diem.

Abinales, Patricio, ed. The Revolution Falters: The Left in Philippine Politics after 1986. (Southeast Asia Program Ser.: SEAP 15). 182p. (Orig.). 1996. pap. 15.00 (*0-87727-132-1*, SEAP 15) Cornell SE Asia.

Abingdon Press Staff. Abingdon Poster Book of Young Children: 16 Full Color Christian Posters. 32p. 1998. pap. 12.95 (*0-687-05601-2*) Abingdon.

— Celebrating Special Days: Worship Services for All Occasions. 64p. 1997. pap. 6.95 (*0-687-05278-5*) Abingdon.

— Destination Christmas: Advent Programs & Practices for Youth. LC 99-186995. 112p. 1998. pap. 15.95 (*0-687-06063-X*) Abingdon.

***Abingdon Press Staff.** Forgiveness, Faith & Character, People Who Are Different, Baptism & Communion, Telling the Story, Vol. 13. (Connect Ser.). 1999. pap. 20.00 (*0-687-72485-6*) Abingdon.

Abingdon Press Staff. More Welcome Speeches: Responses for All Occasions. LC 97-190845. 64p. 1997. 6.95 (*0-687-05298-X*) Abingdon.

***Abingdon Press Staff.** Would the Real Me Stand Up? Vol. 12: God & the Family, Loving God, the Journey to Peace. (Connect Ser.). 1999. pap. 20.00 (*0-687-72651-4*) Abingdon.

Abingdon Press Staff, compiled by. Celtic Prayers. (Illus.). 64p. 1997. 9.95 (*0-687-07847-4*) Abingdon.

Abington Publishing Staff, ed. Computer Technology in Welding: Third International Conference, June 1991. (Illus.). 400p. 1990. pap. 255.00 (*1-85573-010-3*, Pub. by Woodhead Pubng) Am Educ Systs.

Abiola, Kola. Dilogun: The Sixteen Cowries Divination System: The Soruce. unabridged ed. Akiwowo, Akinsola, ed. (African Traditional Religion Ser.). 273p. 1996. pap. write for info. (*0-9661740-0-3*) Zungo Pubns.

Abir-Am. Commemorations Osiris, Vol. 13. 2000. pap. text 25.00 (*0-226-00091-5*) U Ch Pr.

***Abir-Am.** Commemorations Osiris, Vol. 13. 2000. lib. bdg. 39.00 (*0-226-00090-7*) U Ch Pr.

***Abir-Am, P.** La Mise en Memoire de la Science. (FRE.). 336p. 1998. pap. text 44.00 (*90-5709-007-4*, edit archives) Gordon & Breach.

Abir-Am, Pnina G. Commemorations of Scientific Grandeur: The Politics of Collective Memory. 270p. 1999. pap. text 25.00 (*0-226-00093-1*); lib. bdg. 39.00 (*0-226-00092-3*) U Ch Pr.

Abir-Am, Pnina G & Outram, Dorinda, eds. Uneasy Careers & Intimate Lives: Women in Science, 1787-1979. (Douglass Series on Women's Lives & the Meaning of Gender). (Illus.). 400p. 1987. text 45.00 (*0-8135-1255-7*); pap. text 18.95 (*0-8135-1256-5*) Rutgers U Pr.

Abir, Mordechai. Oil, Power & Politics: Conflict in Arabia, the Red Sea & the Gulf. 210p. 1974. 47.50 (*0-7146-2990-1*, BHA-02990, Pub. by F Cass Pubs) Intl Spec Bk.

Abir, Mordechai & Yodfat, Aryeh Y. In the Direction of the Gulf: The Soviet Union & the Persian Gulf. 167p. 1977. 45.00 (*0-7146-3071-3*, BHA-03071, Pub. by F Cass Pubs) Intl Spec Bk.

Abir, Peter A. The Cosmic Conflict of the Church: An Exegetico-Theological Study. (European University Studies: Series 23, Vol. 547). (GER.). xxx, 365p. 1995. pap. 63.95 (*3-631-49352-5*) P Lang Pubng.

— The Cosmic Conflict of the Church: An Exegetico-Theological Study. LC 95-39864. (European University Studies: Series 23, Vol. 547). XXX, 365p. 1995. pap. 63.95 (*0-8204-2945-7*) P Lang Pubng.

Abiri, Michael M. Ultrasound Board Review: Questions & Answers for Self-Assessment. LC 98-41914. (Illus.). 192p. 1998. pap. 24.95 (*0-86577-815-9*) Thieme Med Pubs.

Abish, Walter. Alphabetical Africa. LC 73-89478. 160p. 1974. pap. 9.95 (*0-8112-0533-9*, NDP375, Pub. by New Directions) Norton.

— Eclipse Fever. (Nonpareil Bks.: Vol. 76). 352p. 1995. pap. 15.95 (*1-56792-036-5*) Godine.

— How German Is It=Wie Deutsch Ist Es. LC 80-20838. 256p. 1980. pap. 10.95 (*0-8112-0776-5*, NDP508, Pub. by New Directions) Norton.

— 99: The New Meaning. (Fiction Ser.). (Illus.). 112p. 1990. 20.00 (*0-930901-67-3*); pap. 8.00 (*0-930901-66-5*) Burning Deck.

— 99: The New Meaning. deluxe limited aut. ed. (Fiction Ser.). (Illus.). 112p. 1990. 30.00 (*0-930901-68-1*) Burning Deck.

Abitbol, Jean. Atlas of Laser Voice Surgery. LC 94-6939. (Illus.). 480p. 1995. pap. 250.00 (*1-56593-190-4*, 0569) Thomson Learn.

Abitbol, M. Maurice. Birth & Human Evolution: Anatomical & Obstetrical Mechanics in Primates. LC 95-42269. 256p. 1996. 95.00 (*0-89789-470-7*, Bergin & Garvey) Greenwood.

Abitbol, Michel. The Jews of North Africa During the Second World War. Zentelis, Catherine T., tr. LC 88-23247. 215p. reprint ed. pap. 66.70 (*0-608-10576-7*, 207119600009) Bks Demand.

Abitbol, Michel, jt. ed. see Gerber, Jane S.

Abiteboul, S., et al, eds. Nested Relations & Complex Objects in Databases. (Lecture Notes in Computer Science Ser.: Vol. 361). vi, 323p. 1989. 40.00 (*0-387-51171-7*) Spr-Verlag.

Abiteboul, S. & Kanellakis, Paris C., eds. ICDT Ninety: Proceedings of the Third International Conference on Database Theory, Paris, France, December 12-14, 1990. (Lecture Notes in Computer Science Ser.: Vol. 470). vii, 528p. 1990. 57.00 (*0-387-53507-1*) Spr-Verlag.

Abiteboul, S. & Shamir, E., eds. Automata, Languages, & Programming. (Lecture Notes in Computer Science Ser.: Vol. 820). 644p. 1994. 93.95 (*0-387-58201-0*) Spr-Verlag.

***Abiteboul, S. & Vercoustre, Anne-Marie, eds.** Research & Advanced Technology for Digital Libraries: Proceedings of the 3rd European Conference, ECDL'99, Paris, France, September 22-24, 1999. rev. ed. LC 99-51455. (Lecture Notes in Computer Science Ser.: Vol. 1696). xi, 494p. 1999. pap. 79.00 (*3-540-66558-7*) Spr-Verlag.

Abiteboul, Serge, et al, eds. Foundations of Databases. 685p. (C). 1994. text 53.44 (*0-201-53771-0*) Addison-Wesley.

Abiteboul, Serge & Hull, Richard. Foundations of Databases. 1995. pap. 71.25 (*0-201-71622-4*) Addison-Wesley.

Abiteboul, Serge, et al. Data on the Web: From Relations to Semistructured Data & XML. LC 99-46708. (Data Management Systems Ser.). 300p. 1999. 44.95 (*1-55860-622-X*, Pub. by Morgan Kaufmann) Harcourt.

Abitia, Fred P. The TEACCS Codex. 300p. 1990. 112.00 (*1-880944-00-6*); pap. 49.50 (*1-880944-01-4*) Atabichron.

Abitz, Diana, jt. auth. see McGuire, Charles.

Abitz, Friedrich. Baugeschichte und Dekoration des Grabes Ramses' VI. (Orbis Biblicus et Orientalis Ser.: Vol. 89). (GER.). 202p. 1989. text 38.00 (*3-7278-0637-0*, Pub. by Presses Univ Fribourg) Eisenbrauns.

— Pharao Als Gott: In Den Unterweltsbuchern des Neuen Reiches. (Orbis Biblicus et Orientalis Ser.: Vol. 146). (GER.). 219p. 1995. text 47.75 (*3-7278-1040-8*, Pub. by Presses Univ Fribourg) Eisenbrauns.

Abiuso, G. & Giglio, M., adapted by. Le Avventure di Pinocchio: Beginning Through Intermediate. (ITA., Illus.). 88p. (C). Date not set. pap. 9.95 (*0-8442-8023-2*, X8023-2) NTC Contemp Pub Co.

***Abiva, Huseyin, et al.** History of Muslim Civilization, Vol. 1. 2000. text. write for info. (*1-56316-455-8*) Iqra Intl Ed Fdtn.

Abiva, Huseyin, ed. see Abiva, Nilofer & Akhtar, Hina N.

Abiva, Huseyin, ed. see Al-Ahsan, Abdullah.

Abiva, Huseyin, ed. see Kolocotronis, Jamilah.

Abiva, Husryin. From the Lives of the Khulafa' Ar-Rashidun. Quraishi-Ahmed, Hudu & Liddle-Bhutt, Heidi, eds. LC 97-74714. (Illus.). 119p. (J). (gr. 4-7). 1998. pap. text 8.00 (*1-56316-379-9*) Iqra Intl Ed Fdtn.

Abiva, Nilofer & Akhtar, Hina N. History of Al-Khilafah Ar-Rashida Workbook. Abiva, Huseyin, ed. (Illus.). 109p. (YA). (gr. 5-7). 1997. wbk. ed. 6.00 (*1-56316-367-5*) Iqra Intl Ed Fdtn.

***Abiven, Jean.** 15 Days of Prayer with Saint Teresa of Avila. Hebert, Victoria & Sabourin, Denis, trs. from FRE. LC 99-55492. 128p. 2000. pap. 7.95 (*0-7648-0573-8*) Liguori Pubns.

***Abizadeh, Sorab & Mills, Allen.** The Return of Mitteleuropa: Socio-Economic Transition in Post-Communist Central Europe. LC 98-51004. 5p. 1998. 59.00 (*1-56072-643-1*) Nova Sci Pubs.

Abizadeh, Sorab & Yousefi, Mahmood, eds. Fiscal Systems & Economic Development: Case Studies of Selected Countries. LC 95-48997. (Illus.). 267p. (C). 1996. lib. bdg. 115.00 (*1-56072-294-0*) Nova Sci Pubs.

ABK Publishing Staff, ed. Handbook of Birds, Cages & Aviaries. (Illus.). 80p. 1998. pap. 19.95 (*0-9587102-9-5*) Avian Pubns.

Abker, Barbara J. Barb's Little Book. (Illus.). 52p. 1996. pap. write for info. (*1-57579-047-5*) Pine Hill Pr.

Abkowitz, Mark D. & Stammer, Robert E., Jr., eds. Microcomputer Applications Within the Urban Transportation Environment: Proceedings of a Conference Sponsored by the Urban Transportation Division. 824p. 1985. 9.00 (*0-87262-508-7*) Am Soc Civil Eng.

Abkowitz, Mark D. & Zografos, Kostas D., eds. State & Local Issues in Transportation of Hazardous Waste Materials: Toward a National Strategy. LC 91-18477. 292p. 1991. pap. text 6.00 (*0-87262-796-9*) Am Soc Civil Eng.

Abkowitz, Mark D., jt. ed. see Stammer, Robert E., Jr.

***Abkowitz, Stanley, ed.** The Emergence of the Titanium Industry & the Development of the Ti-6Al-4V Alloy Collection & Recollections. (Illus.). 42p. 1999. 30.00 (*0-87339-433-X*, 433X) Minerals Metals.

Ablameyko, Sergey V. Introduction to Interpretation of Graphic Images. LC 97-8930. (Tutorial Texts in Optical Engineering Ser.). 1997. pap. write for info. (*0-8194-2380-7*) SPIE.

Ablameyko, Sergey V. & Pridmore, Tony. Machine Interpretation of Line Drawing Images: Technical Drawings, Maps & Diagrams. LC 99-17199. 1999. write for info. (*3-540-76207-8*) Spr-Verlag.

Ablamowicz, R., et al, eds. Clifford Algebras with Numeric & Symbolic Computations. 1996. 64.50 (*0-8176-3907-1*) Spr-Verlag.

Ablamowicz, Rafal & Lounesto, Pertti, eds. Clifford Algebras & Spinor Structures: A Special Volume Dedicated to the Memory of Albert Crumeyrolle (1919-1992) LC 94-44743. (Mathematics & Its Applications Ser.: No. 321). 444p. (C). 1995. text 191.50 (*0-7923-3366-7*) Kluwer Academic.

***Ablan, Dan.** Inside Lightwave 6. 1999. pap. 55.00 incl. cd-rom (*0-7357-0919-X*) Macmillan Tech.

Ablan, Dan. LightWave Power Guide. LC 96-228499. 608p. 1996. 44.99 (*1-56205-633-6*) New Riders Pub.

Ablan, Dan & Hopkins, David. Inside Light Wave 5.5. 1997. 59.99 (*1-56205-799-5*) New Riders Pub.

Ablan, Jerry. Developing Intranet Applications with Java. LC 96-69063. 528p. 1996. 45.00 (*1-57521-166-1*) Sams.

***Ablard, John H., et al.** Innovative Contracting: Practical Approaches. (National Education Seminar Ser.). 208p. 1999. pap. 79.95 (*0-940343-96-7*, NES14) Natl Contract Mgmt.

Ablashi, D. V., et al, eds. Epstein-Barr Virus & Human Disease. LC 87-16869. (Experimental Biology & Medicine Ser.: Vol. 15). 530p. 1987. 125.00 (*0-89603-130-6*) Humana.

Ablashi, D. V., et al, eds. Epstein-Barr Virus & Human Disease, 1988. LC 89-15445. (Experimental Biology & Medicine Ser.: Vol. 20). 549p. 1989. 135.00 (*0-89603-165-9*) Humana.

— Epstein-Barr Virus & Human Disease, 1990. LC 91-20857. (Experimental Biology & Medicine Ser.: Vol. 24). (Illus.). 496p. 1991. 135.00 (*0-89603-221-3*) Humana.

Able, jt. auth. see Stone.

Able, Carl. Coptic Language. 1998. reprint ed. pap. 5.00 (*0-89979-098-4*) British Am Bks.

***Able, Deborah.** Hate Groups. rev. ed. LC 99-41174. (Issues in Focus Ser.). (Illus.). 112p. (YA). (gr. 6 up). 2000. lib. bdg. 20.95 (*0-7660-1245-X*) Enslow Pubs.

Able, Gene & Horan, Jack. Paddling South Carolina: A Guide to Palmetto State River Trails. 135p. 1990. reprint ed. 12.50 (*0-87844-101-8*) Sandlapper Pub Co.

Able, Kenneth P. Gatherings of Angels: Migrating Birds & Their Ecology. LC 98-47920. 1999. pap. 27.50 (*0-8014-8401-4*) Cornell U Pr.

Able, Kenneth P., ed. Gathering of Angels: Migrating Birds & Their Ecology. LC 98-47920. (Illus.). 192p. 1999. 27.50 (*0-8014-3362-2*) Cornell U Pr.

Able, Kenneth P., ed. see Hayes, Floyd E.

Able, Kenneth P., ed. see Pyle, Peter.

A

Able, Kenneth W. & Fahay, Michael P. The First Year in the Life of Estuarine Fishes in the Middle Atlantic Bight. LC 97-30312. (Illus.). xii, 342p. (C). 1998. text 67.00 (*0-8135-2500-4*) Rutgers U Pr.

Able, Linda. The Complete Guide to Publishing: An 'Its Easy!' Manual. (Complete Publishing Manuals Ser.: Vol. 2). 468p. (Orig.). (C). 1999. pap. 29.95 (*1-890357-06-5*) Fla Acad Pr.

— The Complete Guide to Seminars: An 'Its Easy!' Manual. (Complete Publishing Manuals Ser.: Vol. 3). 180p. (Orig.). 1999. pap. 24.95 (*1-890357-08-1*) Fla Acad Pr.

— The Complete Publisher's Resource Manual. (Complete Publishing Manuals Ser.: No. 1). 284p. 1999. pap. 22.95 (*1-890357-05-7*) Fla Acad Pr.

Able, Simone. Simone Abel's Colorful Sheep. 12p. (J). 1999. 7.95 (*0-7613-0993-4*, Copper Beech Bks) Millbrook Pr.

— Simone Abel's Shapely Sheep. 12p. (J). (gr. k-1). 1999. 7.95 (*0-7613-0992-6*, Copper Beech Bks) Millbrook Pr.

Able-Smith, Brian, et al. Choices in Health Policy: An Agenda for the European Union. (Illus.). 200p. 1995. text 82.95 (*1-85521-755-4*, Pub. by Dartmth Pub); pap. text 32.95 (*1-85521-762-7*, Pub. by Dartmth Pub) Ashgate Pub Co.

Ableman, Brian E. Swampland. LC 97-26986. (Habitats Ser.). (J). (gr. 2-3). 1997. 24.00 (*0-516-20743-1*) Childrens.

— Swampland. LC 97-26986. (Habitats Ser.). (J). 1998. pap. text 6.95 (*0-516-20374-6*) Childrens.

Ableman, Michael. On Good Land: The Autobiography of an Urban Farm. LC 97-30801. 144p. 1998. 18.95 (*0-8118-1921-3*) Chronicle Bks.

Ableman, Paul. Beyond Nakedness. (Illus.). 112p. (C). 1986. reprint ed. pap. 16.95 (*0-910550-56-5*) Events Unltd.

— I Hear Voices. LC 89-13879. 168p. 1990. 18.00 (*0-929701-05-4*); pap. 10.00 (*0-929701-04-6*) McPherson & Co.

— The Secret of Consciousness: How the Brain Tells 'the Story of Me' LC 98-54697. 1999. 14.95 (*0-7145-3053-0*) M Boyars Pubs.

— Tornado Pratt. LC 92-14922. 223p. 1992. 20.00 (*0-929701-25-9*); pap. 11.00 (*0-929701-26-7*) McPherson & Co.

— Waiting for God. LC 95-139787. (Illus.). 1995. 18.95 (*0-563-37086-6*, BBC-Parkwest) Parkwest Pubns.

Ableman, Paul & Dunn, John. Answers Please. (Illus.). 1996. pap. 7.95 (*0-563-37063-7*, BBC-Parkwest) Parkwest Pubns.

Ablemann, Nancy & Lie, John. Blue Dreams: Korean Americans & the Los Angeles Riots. (Illus.). 288p. 1997. reprint ed. pap. 17.50 (*0-674-07705-9*) HUP.

Abler, Elizabeth & American Rose Society. Guidelines for Judging Rose Arrangements: The Official American Rose Society Arrangement Judges Handbook. LC 98-178198. v, 95 p. 1998. write for info. (*0-9636340-4-6*) Am Rose Soc.

Abler, Ronald F., et al, eds. Geography's Inner Worlds: Pervasive Themes in Contemporary American Geography. LC 91-43478. (Illus.). 440p. (C). 1992. text 50.00 (*0-8135-1829-6*); pap. text 18.95 (*0-8135-1830-X*) Rutgers U Pr.

***Abler, Thomas S.** Hinterland Warriors & Military Dress: Exotic Costume & the Military Establishment. (Illus.). 256p. 1998. 65.00 (*1-85973-201-1*, Pub. by Berg Pubs) NYU Pr.

Abler, Thomas S., et al. A Canadian Indian Bibliography, 1960-1970. LC 75-300070. 748p. reprint ed. pap. 200.00 (*0-8357-7999-8*, 202648100049) Bks Demand.

Abler, Thomas S., ed. & intro. see Blacksnake, Governor.

Ables, C. The ASTD Trainer's Sourcebook Series, Customer Service. Roe, Richard L., ed. 250p. 1996. pap. text 39.95 (*0-07-053441-1*) McGraw.

***Ables, Hildred Hughes.** Ables: Charles David Ables Remembered. (Illus.). 250p. 1999. 30.00 (*1-892744-51-1*, A-151) Maloy.

— The Ables Family: Joe & Hildred. (Illus.). 1998. 30.00 (*1-892744-47-3*, A-147) Maloy.

— Hildred's Homespun Family Tree. (Illus.). 19p. 1997. pap. 8.00 (*1-892744-48-1*, A-148) Maloy.

— Miami Daily Record Herald: November 1917-Sept. 1922 Vital Records Index. 1990. 26.00 (*1-892744-53-8*, A-153) Maloy.

— Miami District Daily News: August 1917-March 1922 Vital Records Index. 1990. 26.00 (*1-892744-52-X*, A-152) Maloy.

Ables, Hildred Hughes, ed. Afton American Death Notices: 1900-1941 Newspaper Index. 62p. 1988. pap. 10.00 (*1-892744-04-X*, A-104) Maloy.

— Afton American Death Notices: 1942-1986 Newspaper Index. 92p. 1986. pap. 10.00 (*1-892744-05-8*, A-105) Maloy.

— The First United Methodist Church, Miami, Oklahoma, 1891-1984. 94p. 1985. pap. 10.00 (*1-892744-02-3*, A-102) Maloy.

— Funeral Home Records of Ottawa County, 1916-1936: Mitchelson Funeral Home. 65p. 1990. pap. 10.00 (*1-892744-54-6*, A-154) Maloy.

— Funeral Home Records of Ottawa County, 1934-1967: The Long, Fisk, Hutchens, Jim Thomas Records. 211p. 1998. pap. 25.00 (*1-892744-49-X*, A-149) Maloy.

— The Jones Book: Descendants of Jasper & Lou Jones. (Illus.). 166p. 1997. 50.00 (*1-892744-00-7*, A-100) Maloy.

— Miami Oklahoma News-Record No. 20: 1959-1960 Vital Records Index. 75p. 1990. 26.00 (*1-892744-26-0*, A-126) Maloy.

— Miami Oklahoma News-Record No. 21: 1961-1962 Vital Records Index. 75p. 1990. 26.00 (*1-892744-27-9*, A-127) Maloy.

— Miami Oklahoma News-Record No. 22: 1963-1964 Vital Records Index. 72p. 1990. 26.00 (*1-892744-28-7*, A-128) Maloy.

— Miami Oklahoma News-Record No. 23: 1965-1966 Vital Records Index. 108p. 1991. 26.00 (*1-892744-29-5*, A-129) Maloy.

— Miami Oklahoma News-Record No. 24: 1967-1968 Vital Records Index. 84p. 1991. 26.00 (*1-892744-30-9*, A-130) Maloy.

— Miami Oklahoma News-Record No. 25: 1969-1970 Vital Records Index. 96p. 1991. 26.00 (*1-892744-31-7*, A-131) Maloy.

— Miami Oklahoma News-Record No. 26: 1971-1972 Vital Records Index. 81p. 1992. 26.00 (*1-892744-32-5*, A-132) Maloy.

— Miami Oklahoma News-Record No. 27: 1973-1974 Vital Records Index. 80p. 1992. 26.00 (*1-892744-33-3*, A-133) Maloy.

— Miami Oklahoma News-Record No. 28: 1975-1976 Vital Records Index. 86p. 1992. 26.00 (*1-892744-34-1*, A-134) Maloy.

— Miami Oklahoma News-Record No. 29: 1977-1978 Vital Records Index. 87p. 1993. 26.00 (*1-892744-35-X*, A-135) Maloy.

— Miami Oklahoma News-Record No. 30: 1979-1980 Vital Records Index. 84p. 1993. 26.00 (*1-892744-36-8*, A-136) Maloy.

— Miami Oklahoma News-Record No. 31: 1981-1982 Vital Records Index. 81p. 1993. 26.00 (*1-892744-37-6*, A-137) Maloy.

— Miami Oklahoma News-Record No. 32: 1983-1984 Vital Records Index. 87p. 1994. 26.00 (*1-892744-38-4*, A-138) Maloy.

— Miami Oklahoma News-Record No. 33: 1985-1986 Vital Records Index. 85p. 1994. 26.00 (*1-892744-39-2*, A-139) Maloy.

— Miami Oklahoma News-Record No. 34: 1987-1988 Vital Records Index. 75p. 1994. 26.00 (*1-892744-40-6*, A-140) Maloy.

— Miami Oklahoma News-Record No. 35: 1989 Vital Records Index. 45p. 1995. 26.00 (*1-892744-41-4*, A-141) Maloy.

— Miami Oklahoma News-Record No. 36: 1990-1991 Vital Records Index. 104p. 1995. 26.00 (*1-892744-42-2*, A-142) Maloy.

— Miami Oklahoma News-Record No. 37: 1992-1993 Vital Records Index. 89p. 1995. 26.00 (*1-892744-43-0*, A-143) Maloy.

— Miami Oklahoma News-Record No. 38: 1994-1995 Vital Records Index. 88p. 1996. write for info. (*1-892744-44-9*, A-144) Maloy.

— Miami Oklahoma News-Record No. 39: 1996-1997 Vital Records Index. 100p. 1997. 26.00 (*1-892744-45-7*, A-145) Maloy.

— Miami Oklahoma News-Record No. 40: 1998-1999 Vital Records Index. 110p. 2000. 26.00 (*1-892744-46-5*, A-146) Maloy.

— Mt. Hope Cemetery: Afton, OK. 81p. 1988. pap. 10.00 (*1-892744-01-5*, A-101) Maloy.

— 1907 Census of Citizens of Miami, Oklahoma. 51p. 1986. pap. 10.00 (*1-892744-06-6*, A-106) Maloy.

— Unrecorded Burials & Corrected Data: A Supplement to the Gar Cemetery Index, Miami, OK. 66p. 1988. pap. 10.00 (*1-892744-03-1*, A-103) Maloy.

***Ables, Hildred Hughes & Bates, Daryl, eds.** Funeral Home Records of Ottawa County, 1918-September 1990: Cooper Funeral Home. 1999. 35.00 (*1-892744-50-3*, A-150) Maloy.

Ables, Hildred Hughes & Topliff, Audrey, eds. Miami Oklahoma News-Record No. 2: 1923-1924 Vital Records Index. 59p. 1981. 26.00 (*1-892744-08-2*, A-108) Maloy.

— Miami Oklahoma News-Record No. 3: 1925-1926 Vital Records Index. 67p. 1981. 26.00 (*1-892744-09-0*, A-109) Maloy.

— Miami Oklahoma News-Record No. 4: 1927-1928 Vital Records Index. 78p. 1982. 26.00 (*1-892744-10-4*, A-110) Maloy.

— Miami Oklahoma News-Record No. 5: 1929-1930 Vital Records Index. 95p. 1982. 26.00 (*1-892744-11-2*, A-111) Maloy.

— Miami Oklahoma News-Record No. 6: 1931-1932 Vital Records Index. 83p. 1983. 26.00 (*1-892744-12-0*, A-112) Maloy.

— Miami Oklahoma News-Record No. 7: 1933-1934 Vital Records Index. 94p. 1983. 26.00 (*1-892744-13-9*, A-113) Maloy.

— Miami Oklahoma News-Record No. 8: 1935-1936 Vital Records Index. 97p. 1984. 26.00 (*1-892744-14-7*, A-114) Maloy.

— Miami Oklahoma News-Record No. 9: 1937-1938 Vital Records Index. 108p. 1984. 26.00 (*1-892744-15-5*, A-115) Maloy.

— Miami Oklahoma News-Record No. 10: 1939-1940 Vital Records Index. 86p. 1985. 26.00 (*1-892744-16-3*, A-116) Maloy.

— Miami Oklahoma News-Record No. 11: 1941-1942 Vital Records Index. 86p. 1985. 26.00 (*1-892744-17-1*, A-117) Maloy.

— Miami Oklahoma News-Record No. 12: 1943-1944 Vital Records Index. 80p. 1986. 26.00 (*1-892744-18-X*, A-118) Maloy.

— Miami Oklahoma News-Record No. 13: 1945-1946 Vital Records Index. 60p. 1986. 26.00 (*1-892744-19-8*, A-119) Maloy.

— Miami Oklahoma News-Record No. 14: 1947-1948 Vital Records Index. 82p. 1987. 26.00 (*1-892744-20-1*, A-120) Maloy.

— Miami Oklahoma News-Record No. 15: 1949-1950 Vital Records Index. 71p. 1987. 26.00 (*1-892744-21-X*, A-121) Maloy.

— Miami Oklahoma News-Record No. 16: 1951-1952 Vital Records Index. 61p. 1988. 26.00 (*1-892744-22-8*, A-122) Maloy.

— Miami Oklahoma News-Record No. 17: 1953-1954 Vital Records Index. 90p. 1988. 26.00 (*1-892744-23-6*, A-123) Maloy.

— Miami Oklahoma News-Record No. 18: 1955-1956 Vital Records Index. 88p. 1989. 26.00 (*1-892744-24-4*, A-124) Maloy.

— Miami Oklahoma News-Record No. 19: 1957-1958 Vital Records Index. 81p. 1989. 26.00 (*1-892744-25-2*, A-125) Maloy.

— Ottawa County, OK, News-Papers: 1895-1922 Vital Statistics Index. 429p. 1980. 35.00 (*1-892744-07-4*, A-107) Maloy.

Ables, Timothy D. & Marascalco, Bobbie P. The Memorial Windows of Church of the Holy Trinity. (Illus.). 58p. (Orig.). 1992. pap. 20.00 (*0-9632630-8-0*) Church HT.

Ableson, John N., et al, eds. Reconstitution of Intracellular Transport. (Methods in Enzymology Ser.: Vol. 219). (Illus.). 438p. 1992. text 104.00 (*0-12-182120-X*) Acad Pr.

Ablett, W. H. English Trees & Tree Planting. (C). 1988. 170.00 (*0-7855-3239-0*, Pub. by Scientific) St Mut.

Abley, Mark. Glasburyon. LC 96-138740. 96p. 1994. pap. 14.95 (*1-55082-119-9*, Pub. by Quarry Pr) LPC InBook.

— The Ice Storm: January, 1998, Remembered in Pictures & in a Text. (Illus.). 1999. 29.95 (*0-7710-6100-5*) McCland & Stewart.

***Abley, Mark, ed.** Stories from the Ice Storm. (Illus.). 360p. 2000. text 22.95 (*0-7710-0653-5*) McCland & Stewart.

Abley, Sean & Booker, Mary. Attack of the Killer B-Movie Monologue Book. 100p. 1994. pap. 9.95 (*1-56850-036-X*) Chicago Plays.

Ablin, Arthur R. Supportive Care of Children with Cancer: Current Therapy & Guidelines from the Children's Cancer Group. 2nd ed. LC 97-26952. (Series in Hematology/Oncology). 192p. 1998. pap. text 29.95 (*0-8018-5727-9*) Johns Hopkins.

— Supportive Care of Children with Cancer: Current Therapy & Guidelines from the Children's Cancer Group. 2nd ed. LC 97-26952. (Series in Hematology/Oncology). 192p. 1999. text 65.00 (*0-8018-5726-0*) Johns Hopkins.

Ablin, Arthur R., ed. Supportive Care of Children with Cancer: Current Therapy & Guidelines from the Children's Cancer Group. LC 92-48869. (Johns Hopkins Series in Hematology - Oncology). 120p. 1993. pap. text 28.95 (*0-8018-4630-7*) Johns Hopkins.

Ablin, David A. & Hood, Marlowe, eds. The Cambodian Agony. 2nd ed. LC 90-21763. 496p. (C). (gr. 13). 1991. pap. text 38.95 (*0-87332-754-3*) M E Sharpe.

Ablin, Fred, ed. Contemporary Soviet Education: A Collection of Readings from Soviet Journals. LC 68-14428. 309p. reprint ed. pap. 95.80 (*0-608-14889-X*, 202614100048) Bks Demand.

Ablin, Richard J., ed. Handbook of Cryosurgery. LC 80-23431. (Science & Practice of Surgery Ser.: No. 1). 448p. reprint ed. pap. 138.90 (*0-7837-3341-0*, 204329900008) Bks Demand.

— Prostate As an Endocrine Gland. 232p. 1989. lib. bdg. 129.00 (*0-8493-5364-5*, QP257) CRC Pr.

— Prostatic Cancer. LC 81-12500. (Science & Practice of Surgery Ser.: No. 2). (Illus.). 341p. reprint ed. pap. 105.80 (*0-7837-0909-9*, 204121400019) Bks Demand.

Abling, Bina. Advanced Fashion Sketchbook. (Illus.). 133p. (C). 1995. text 47.00 (*0-87005-679-4*) Fairchild.

***Abling, Bina.** Fashion Rendering with Color. LC 00-39192. (Illus.). 2000. write for info. (*0-13-014460-6*) P-H.

***Abling, Bing.** Fashion Sketchbook. 3rd ed. (Illus.). 1998. pap. 42.00 (*1-56367-172-7*) Fairchild.

Ablon, Joan. Little People in America: The Social Dimensions of Dwarfism. LC 84-15910. 194p. 1984. 55.00 (*0-275-91109-8*, C1109, Praeger Pubs) Greenwood.

— Living with Difference: Families with Dwarf Children. LC 87-32790. 204p. 1988. 55.00 (*0-275-92901-9*, C2901, Praeger Pubs) Greenwood.

— Living with Genetic Disorder: The Impact of Neurofibromatosis 1. LC 99-11894. 216p. 1999. 59.95 (*0-86569-287-4*, T287, Auburn Hse) Greenwood.

Ablon, L. J., et al. Series in Mathematics Modules, Pts. 7, 8, 9, 10, 11. Incl. Module 7. Trigonometry with Applications. 1976. 7.95 (*0-8465-0261-5*); Module 8. Exponents & Logarithms. 1976. pap. text 6.36 (*0-8465-0262-3*); Module 9. Advanced Algebraic Techniques. 1976. 6.25 (*0-8465-0263-1*); Module 10. Functions & Word Problems. 1976. 6.25 (*0-8465-0264-X*); Module 11. Graphing Functions. 1976. pap. 1976. Set pap. 7.95 (*0-686-67410-3*) Benjamin-Cummings.

Ablon, Leon J., et al. Module I Numbers, 5 Modules, Module 1. 2nd ed. 1981. pap. text 8.95 (*0-8053-0131-3*) Addison-Wesley.

— Module II Polynomials, 5 Modules, Module 2. 2nd ed. 1981. pap. text 8.95 (*0-8053-0132-1*) Addison-Wesley.

— Module IV Algebric Fract, 5 Modules, Module 4. 2nd ed. 1981. pap. text 8.95 (*0-8053-0134-8*) Addison-Wesley.

— Module V Quadratic Equation, 5 Modules, Module 5. 2nd ed. 1981. pap. text 8.95 (*0-8053-0135-6*) Addison-Wesley.

— Series in Mathematics Modules, 5 Modules. 1981. pap. 9.75 (*0-685-42003-5*) Addison-Wesley.

Ablon, Leon J., ed. see Fitts, Gary.

Ablon, Steven L. Flying over Tasmania: Poems. LC 97-12753. 64p. (Orig.). 1997. pap. 10.00 (*1-56474-227-X*) Fithian Pr.

Ablon, Steven L., et al, eds. Human Feelings: Explorations in Affect Development & Meaning. LC 93-14309. 456p. 1993. text 59.95 (*0-88163-144-2*) Analytic Pr.

Ablon, Steven L., jt. ed. see Mack, John E.

Ablos, David T. The Latino Family & the Politics of Transformation. LC 93-19612. (Series in Transformational Politics & Political Science). 152p. 1993. pap. 19.95 (*0-275-94809-9*, Praeger Pubs) Greenwood.

Ablow, Keith Russell. Denial. LC 96-45408. 272p. 1997. 22.95 (*0-679-44211-1*) Pantheon.

— Denial. 1997. 24.00 (*0-614-27927-5*) Pantheon.

— Denial, Vol. 1. 358p. 2000. mass mkt. 6.99 (*0-312-96596-6*, Pub. by Tor Bks) St Martin.

— Medical School: Getting in, Staying in, Staying Human. 7th rev. ed. 1990. pap. 14.95 (*0-312-04349-X*) St Martin.

— Projection: A Novel. LC 99-21637. 320p. 1999. 24.00 (*0-679-44212-X*) Pantheon.

***Ablow, Keith Russell.** Projection: A Novel. 2000. mass mkt. 6.99 (*0-312-97574-0*) St Martin.

Ablow, Keith Russell. The Strange Case of Dr. Kappler: The Doctor Who Became a Killer. 1994. 19.95 (*0-02-900161-7*) Free Pr.

— To Wrestle with Demons. LC 94-3658. 158p. 1994. pap. text 9.95 (*0-7867-0166-8*) Carroll & Graf.

— Without Mercy. 1996. mass mkt. 5.99 (*0-312-95923-0*) St Martin.

Ablow, Keith Russell, jt. auth. see DePaulo, J. Raymond.

Ablowitz, M. A. & Clarkson, P. A. Solitons, Nonlinear Evolution Equations & Inverse Scattering. (London Mathematical Society Lecture Note Ser.: No. 149). 528p. (C). 1992. pap. text 59.95 (*0-521-38730-2*) Cambridge U Pr.

Ablowitz, M. J. & Segur, H. Solitons & the Inverse Scattering Transform. LC 81-50600. (Studies in Applied Mathematics: No. 4). x, 425p. 1982. text 87.00 (*0-89871-174-6*) Soc Indus-Appl Math.

Ablowitz, Mark J. & Fokas, Athanssios S. Complex Variables: Introduction & Applications. LC 96-48902. (Texts in Applied Mathematics Ser.: No. 16). (Illus.). 450p. (C). 1997. text 85.00 (*0-521-48058-2*); pap. text 36.95 (*0-521-48523-1*) Cambridge U Pr.

ABM Service Corp. Staff. National Directory of CB Radio Channels. LC 78-12796. 1979. 19.95 (*0-88280-064-7*); pap. 19.95 (*0-88280-065-5*) ETC Pubns.

Abma, J., et al. Fertility, Family Planning, & Women's Health: New Data from the 1995 National Survey of Family Growth. (Illus.). 114p. (C). 1998. pap. text 30.00 (*0-7881-7193-3*) DIANE Pub.

Abma, Joyce C. Fertility, Family Planning & Women's Health: New Data from the 1995 National Survey of Family Growth. 124p. 1997. pap. text 16.00 (*0-16-049093-6*) USGPO.

***Abma, R.** Bonds of Love: Methodic Studies of Prophectic Texts with Marriage Imagery: Isaiah 50:1-3 & 54:1-10, Hosea 1-3, Jeremiah 2-3. 250p. 1999. text 70.00 (*90-232-3509-6*, Pub. by Van Gorcum) Eisenbrauns.

Abma, Tineke A. & Stake, Robert E., eds. Advances in Program Evaluation Vol. 6: Telling Tales: On Narrative & Evaluation. Date not set. 78.50 (*0-7623-0433-2*) Jai Pr.

ABMP (Anchor) Staff. Disability Analysis Handbook: Tools for Independent Practice. LC 96-230350. 416p. 1996. pap. text, per. 60.00 (*0-7872-2670-X*) Kendall-Hunt.

— Medical Psychotherapy, Vol. 8. 240p. 1995. pap. text, per. 6.95 (*0-7872-0963-5*) Kendall-Hunt.

ABMP Staff. Advances in Medical Psychotherapy, Vol. 7. 272p. 1993. per. 8.95 (*0-8403-8524-2*) Kendall-Hunt.

— Disability Analysis in Practice. LC 99-188217. 412p. 1998. per. 60.00 (*0-7872-2135-X*, 41213501) Kendall-Hunt.

— Medical Psychotherapy, Vol. 10. 232p. 1999. per. 7.95 (*0-7872-5756-7*, 41575601) Kendall-Hunt.

Abnderson, S. H. & Hopmans, J. W., eds. Tomography of Soil - Water - Root Processes. LC 94-20002. (Publications: No. 36). 148p. 1994. pap. 21.00 (*0-89118-808-8*) Soil Sci Soc Am.

Abner, Alan K. Dead Reckoning: Experiences of a World War II Fighter Pilot. LC 96-48748. (Illus.). 134p. 1997. 24.95 (*1-57249-025-X*, Burd St Pr) White Mane Pub.

Abner, Allison & Villarosa, Linda. The Black Parenting Book: Caring for Our Children in the First Five Years. LC 98-28120. (Illus.). 432p. 1998. pap. 20.00 (*0-7679-0196-7*) Broadway BDD.

— Finding Our Way: The Teen Girls' Survival Guide. LC 95-35964. (Illus.). 336p. 1996. pap. 14.00 (*0-06-095114-1*, Perennial) HarperTrade.

Abner, Eddie, Jr. Three Social Plays of the Black Experience. LC 79-50129. 316p. (Orig.). (C). 1996. reprint ed. pap. text 35.00 (*0-9602508-0-8*) June Bugs Pub.

Abner, Monica Van den Branden, see Faragasso, Laura B.

Abner, Monica Vanden Branden, see Faragasso, Laura B. & Vanden Branden Abner, Monica.

Abner, Vernon. Getting the Spirit. LC 85-81966. (Illus.). 96p. (Orig.). 1985. pap. 5.95 (*0-935680-19-5*) Kentucke Imprints.

***Abnett, Dan.** First & Only. 288p. 2000. per. 6.95 (*0-671-78375-0*) PB.

— Gaunt's Ghosts III. 2000. per. 6.95 (*0-7434-1159-5*) PB.

— Ghostmaker. 288p. 2000. mass mkt. 6.95 (*0-671-78410-2*) PB.

— Hammers of Ulric. 288p. 2000. 6.95 (*0-671-78421-8*) PB.

Abnett, Dan & Lanning, Andy. Batman: Two Faces. O'Neil, Dennis, ed. (Illus.). 64p. 1998. pap. 4.95 (*1-56389-395-9*) DC Comics.

Abnett, Dan, jt. ed. see Hampton, Bo.

Abnett, William B., et al, eds. AccessAsia: A Guide to Specialists & Current Research 1994. 3rd ed. 462p. 1994. pap. 75.00 (*0-9631625-3-5*) Nat Bur Asian.

***Abney, A. H. & Darrell.** Interact for Macintosh to Accompany Elementary Algebra: A Prerequisite for Functions. (C). 1998. 25.00 (*0-201-43453-9*) Addison-Wesley.

An Asterisk (*) at the beginning of an entry indicates that the title is appearing for the first time.

Abney, Darrell H. Elementary Algebra: International Edition. 480p. (C). 1998. pap. text 49.00 (*0-201-43451-2*) Addison-Wesley.

***Abney, Darrell H.** Interact for Windows to Accompany Elementary Algebra: A Prerequisite for Functions. (C). 1998. pap. text 26.00 (*0-201-43455-5*) Addison-Wesley.

Abney, Darrell H. Intermediate Algebra: An Introduction to Applications Through Functions. annot. ed. (C). 1999. pap. text, teacher ed. write for info. (*0-201-87344-3*) Addison-Wesley.

— Intermediate Algebra: An Introduction to Functions Through Applications. 336p. (C). 1998. pap. text 57.00 (*0-201-85362-0*) Addison-Wesley.

***Abney, Darrell H.** Intermediate Algebra: An Introduction to Functions Through Applications. 320p. (C). 2000. text Price not set. (*0-201-85366-3*) Addison-Wesley.

— Intermediate Algebra: An Introduction to Functions Through Applications. annot. ed. 496p. (C). 1998. pap. text, teacher ed. 49.00 (*0-201-43450-4*) Addison-Wesley.

Abney, Don. The Louisiana Catahoula Leopard Dog. Luther, Luana, ed. LC 95-83697. (Illus.). 113p. (Orig.). 1996. pap. text 19.95 (*0-944875-44-0*) Doral Pub.

Abney, Glenn & Lauth, Thomas P. The Politics of State & City Administration. LC 85-14873. (SUNY Series in Public Administration). 260p. 1986. text 21.50 (*0-88706-255-5*) State U NY Pr.

Abney, Lisa, jt. ed. see Green, Suzanne Disheroon.

Abney, Russell, jt. auth. see Cornell, James.

Abney, Russell T., jt. auth. see Cornell, James L.

Abney, Tom O. & Keel, Brooks A., eds. The Cryptorchid Testis. 192p. 1989. lib. bdg. 139.00 (*0-8493-4751-3*, RJ477) CRC Pr.

Abney, W. D., jt. auth. see Robinson, Henry P.

Abnorman. Subway Stops: Collected Poems. LC 98-96354. 83p. 1998. pap. 11.95 (*1-879194-24-4*) GLB Pubs.

Abnous, Razmik, jt. auth. see Khoshafian, Setrag.

Abo-Khatwa, Ahmed N. Abo-Khatwa's English-Arabic Encyclopedia of Biology & Biochemistry. (ARA & ENG., Illus.). 1900p. (C). 1991. 36.00 (*0-9629071-0-3*) A N Abou-Khatwa.

Abo, Takaji, et al. Marshallese-English Dictionary. LC 76-26156. (PALI Language Texts, Micronesia Ser.). 626p. 1976. pap. text 25.00 (*0-8248-0457-0*) UH Pr.

Abo, Tetsuo. Hybrid Factory: The Japanese Production System in the United States. (Illus.). 352p. (C). 1994. text 65.00 (*0-19-507974-4*) OUP.

Aboba, Bernard. The Online User's Encyclopedia: Bulletin Boards & Beyond. LC 93-13304. 832p. (C). 1993. pap. text 34.95 (*0-201-62214-9*) Addison-Wesley.

Aboba, Bernard & Bassett, Britt. PC-Internet Connection: TCP Networking for DOS & Windows. 272p. pap. 34.95 (*1-883979-00-5*) MailCom.

Abodaher, D. Iacocca. 1989. pap. 4.50 (*0-8217-3018-5*) NAL.

Abodaher, David. Iacocca. 1985. mass mkt. 3.95 (*0-8217-1700-6*, Zebra Kensgtn) Kensgtn Pub Corp.

Abodeely, John E., et al. The NLRB & the Appropriate Bargaining Unit. rev. ed. LC 80-85252. (Labor Relations & Public Policy Ser.: No. 3). 359p. 1981. pap. 20.00 (*0-89546-028-9*) U PA Ctr Hum Res.

Abodunrin, Femi, et al, eds. Character Is Beauty: Redefining Yoruba Culture & Identity - Iwalewa-Haus, 1981-1886. LC 98-24254. 432p. 1997. 79.95 (*0-86543-623-1*); pap. 24.95 (*0-86543-624-X*) Africa World.

***Aboff, Marcie.** Open Your Eyes, Sidney Miffet! (Illus.). 12p. (J). (gr. k-2). 1999. pap. 3.75 (*1-880612-92-5*) Seedling Pubns.

Aboff, Marcie. Uncle Willy's Tickles. (Illus.). 32p. (J). 1996. pap. 8.95 (*0-945354-67-3*) Am Psychol.

Aboites, Luis. Breve Historia de Chihuahua (Concise History of Chihuahua) (Breves Historias de los Estados de Mexico Ser.). (SPA.). 1995. pap. 13.99 (*968-16-4539-1*, Pub. by Fondo) Continental Bk.

Aboites, Vicente. Fusion Nuclear por Medio del Laser. (Ciencia para Todos Ser.). (SPA.). pap. 6.99 (*968-16-4615-0*, Pub. by Fondo) Continental Bk.

— El Laser. (Ciencia para Todos Ser.). (SPA.). pap. 6.99 (*968-16-3578-7*, Pub. by Fondo) Continental Bk.

***Aboitiz, Christa, ed.** AutoWerke. 90p. 2000. write for info. (*3-7757-0901-0*, Pub. by Gerd Hatje) Dist Art Pubs.

Abokor, Axmed. The Camel in Somali Oral Tradition. 95p. 1987. pap. text 16.95 (*91-7106-269-6*) Transaction Pubs.

Abokor, Axmed C. Suugaania Geela: Jointly with the Somali Academy of Sciences & Arts. 103p. 1986. write for info. (*91-7106-259-9*, Pub. by Nordic Africa) Transaction Pubs.

Abolafia, Mitchel Y. Making Markets: Opportunism & Restraint on Wall Street. LC 96-20665. (Illus.). 240p. 1996. 32.50 (*0-674-54324-6*) HUP.

Abolofia, David. Dead. 1993. pap. 3.50 (*0-87129-294-7*, D57) Dramatic Pub.

Abolrous, Sam A. Learn C in Three Days. LC 92-11346. (Popular Applications Ser.). (Illus.). 288p. 1992. pap. 19.95 incl. disk (*1-55622-298-X*) Wordware Pub.

***Abolrous, Sam A.** Learn Pascal. LC 99-88051. (Illus.). 400p. 2000. pap. 39.95 (*1-55622-706-X*) Wordware Pub.

Abolrous, Sam A. Learn Pascal in Three Days. LC 93-12287. (Popular Applications Ser.). 288p. 1993. pap. 19.95 incl. disk (*1-55622-337-4*) Wordware Pub.

— Learn Pascal in Three Days. 2nd ed. LC 97-14638. 300p. 1997. pap. text 24.95 (*1-55622-567-9*) Wordware Pub.

Abondolo, Daniel M. Colloquial Finnish: The Complete Language Course. LC 96-32137. (Colloquials Ser.). (ENG & FIN., Illus.). 320p. 1998. pap. 22.99 (*0-415-11389-X*) Routledge.

— Colloquial Finnish: The Complete Language Course. LC 96-32137. (The Colloquial Ser.). (ENG & FIN., Illus.). 1998. pap. 49.99 incl. audio (*0-415-11391-1*) Routledge.

— Hungarian Inflectional Morphology. (Biblioteca Uralica Ser.: Vol. 9). 291p. (C). 1988. 90.00 (*963-05-4630-2*, Pub. by Akade Kiado) St Mut.

— The Uralic Languages. LC 96-29898. (Routledge Language Family Descriptions Ser.). 648p. (C). 1998. 215.00 (*0-415-08198-X*) Routledge.

Abonja, Simi, jt. ed. see Pearce, Tola O.

Aboobaker, M. The ABCs of Personal Financial Planning. LC 93-73900. (Illus.). 192p. 1994. pap. 14.95 (*0-9639296-0-7*) Creative Srvs.

Abood, Doris M. Lebanon: Bridge Between East & West. LC 73-84565. (Illus.). 40p. (J). (gr. 5-10). 1973. 3.50 (*0-913228-07-9*) Dillon-Liederbach.

Abood, Edward F. Underground Man. LC 72-97331. 189p. 1973. reprint ed. pap. 12.95 (*0-88316-048-X*) Chandler & Sharp.

Abood, Leo G., jt. ed. see Biel, John H.

Abood, Richard R. & Brushwood, David B. Pharmacy Practice & the Law. 370p. 1994. 53.00 (*0-8342-0321-9*, 20321) Aspen Pub.

— Pharmacy Practice & the Law. 2nd ed. LC 97-18903. 448p. 1997. 49.00 (*0-8342-0915-2*, 20915) Aspen Pub.

***Abood, Richard R. & Brushwood, David B.** Pharmacy Practice & the Law / 3rd ed. LC 00-33162. 2000. write for info. (*0-8342-1880-1*) Aspen Pub.

Abood, Salah M. Letters from the Streets of Exile. LC 97-93567. (Illus.). vi, 52p. 1997. pap. text. write for info. (*0-9658362-0-7*) Salah M Abood.

***Abood, Sheila & Keepnews, David.** Understanding Payment for Advanced Practice Nursing Services Vol. 1: Medicare Reimbursement. 144p. 2000. pap. write for info. (*1-55810-148-9*) Am Nurses Pub.

***Abootalebi, Ali Reza.** Islam & Democracy: State-Society Relations in Developing Countries, 1980-1994. LC 00-23016. (Comparative Studies of Democratization). 2000. write for info. (*0-8153-3735-3*) Garland.

Aborio, Portia. King Big Wig. (All Aboard Reading Picture Readers Ser.). (Illus.). 32p. (Orig.). (J). (ps-1). 1996. pap. 3.95 (*0-448-41498-8*, G & D) Peng Put Young Read.

— Pig Out! LC 95-79285. (All Aboard Reading Picture Readers Ser.). (Illus.). 32p. (Orig.). (J). (ps-1). 1997. pap. 3.99 (*0-448-41294-2*, G & D) Peng Put Young Read.

Aborisade, ed. Politics in Nigeria. (C). 1999. text. write for info. (*0-673-99284-5*) Addison-Wesley.

Aborisade, Oladimeji. Politics in Nigeria. (Longman Series in Comparative Politics). 250p. 1998. pap. 38.00 (*0-321-02539-3*) Addson-Wesley Educ.

Aborn, Allyson. Everything I Do You Blame on Me: A Book to Help Children Control Their Anger. Shore, Hennie M., ed. (Self-Esteem Ser.). (Illus.). 112p. (J). (gr. k-7). 1994. pap. 17.95 (*1-882732-10-3*) Childswork.

Aborn, Murray, ed. Telescience: Scientific Communication in the Information Age. (Annals Ser.: Vol. 495). 1988. 26.00 (*0-8039-2937-4*); pap. 17.00 (*0-8039-2938-2*) Sage.

***Aborn, Shana.** 30 Days to a More Spiritual Life. 208p. 2000. 17.95 (*0-385-49785-7*) Doubleday.

Abosch, Kenan S. & Gilbert, Dan. Improving Organizational Effectiveness Through Broadbanding. (Innovations Ser.: Vol. 2). (Illus.). 40p. (Orig.). 1996. pap. 39.95 (*1-57963-002-2*, A0102) Am Compensation.

Abosch, Kenan S. & Hand, Janice S. Life with Broadbands. (Illus.). 1998. pap. 125.00 (*1-57963-059-6*) Am Compensation.

Abosch, Kenan S., jt. auth. see Hand, Janice.

Abosh, Beverley & Collins, April, eds. Mental Illness in the Family: Issues & Trends. 224p. 1996. text 45.00 (*0-8020-2905-1*) U of Toronto Pr.

— Mental Illness in the Family: Issues & Trends. 224p. 1996. pap. text 15.95 (*0-8020-7412-X*) U of Toronto Pr.

Abou Bakr Ahmed Ba Kader, et al. Environmental Protection in Islam. 2nd ed. 120p. 1995. 16.00 (*2-8317-0115-5*, Pub. by IUCN) Island Pr.

Abou-Donia, M. B. Neurotoxicology. 444p. 1989. text 107.00 (*2-88124-406-8*) Gordon & Breach.

Abou-Donia, Mohammed B. Neurotoxicology. 640p. 1992. lib. bdg. 149.00 (*0-8493-8895-3*, RC347) CRC Pr.

Abou-El-Haj, Barbara. The Medieval Cult of Saints: Formations & Transformations. (Illus.). 476p. 1997. pap. text 25.95 (*0-521-58716-6*) Cambridge U Pr.

Abou El-Padl, Khaled. The Authoritative & Authoritarian in Islamic Discourses: A Contemporary Case Study. 2nd rev. ed. LC 98-195185. 118p. 1997. pap. text 9.95 (*1-891226-00-2*) Quill Pubs.

Abou, Selim. The Jesuit "Republic" of the Guaranis (1609-1768) & Its Heritage. Johnson, Lawrence J., tr. from FRE. LC 97-17439. (Illus.). 160p. 1997. 50.00 (*0-8245-1706-7*, Herdr & Herdr) Crossroad NY.

***Aboubaker Alwan, Daoud & Mibrathu, Yohanis.** Historical Dictionary of Djibouti. LC 00-40001. (African Historical Dictionaries Ser.). 2000. write for info. (*0-8108-3873-7*) Scarecrow.

Abouchar, Alan. Soviet Planning & Spatial Efficiency: The Prewar Cement Industry. LC 70-126203. (Indiana University Russian & East European Ser.: Vol. 39). 144p. reprint ed. pap. 44.70 (*0-608-30926-5*, 201581200097) Bks Demand.

Aboud, Frances E. Health Psychology in Global Perspective. LC 97-33937. (Cross-Cultural Psychology Ser.). 342p. 1998. 37.00 (*0-7619-0940-0*); pap. 17.99 (*0-7619-0941-9*) Sage.

Aboud, Jehad. Die Rolle des Konigs und Seiner Familie nach den Texten von Ugarit. (Forschungen zur Anthropologie und Religionsgeschichte Ser.: No. 27). xi, 217p. 1994. text 27.50 (*3-927120-20-0*, Pub. by UGARIT) Eisenbrauns.

Aboudi, J. Mechanics of Composite Materials: A Unified Micromechanical Approach. (Studies in Applied Mechanics: Vol. 29). 328p. 1991. 161.50 (*0-444-88452-1*, SAM 29) Elsevier.

Aboudi, Jacob, et al. Random Vibration & Reliability of Composite Structures. LC 91-67572. 200p. 1992. pap. text 49.95 (*0-87762-865-3*) Technomic.

Aboufadel, Edward & Schickler, Steven. Discovering Wavelets. LC 99-31029. 144p. 1999. 59.95 (*0-471-33193-7*) Wiley.

Aboujaoude, Frank, et al, eds. Natural Gas & Alternative Fuels for Engines: 1995: Proceedings: The ASME Internal Combustion Engine Division Spring Meeting (1995: Marietta, Ohio) LC 93-74680. (ICE Ser.: Vol. 24). 111p. 1995. pap. 70.00 (*0-7918-1304-5*, H00936) ASME.

***Aboul-Enein, Hassan Y.** Analytical & Preparative Separation Methods of Biomacromolecules LC 99-26367. (Illus.). 480p. 1999. text 195.00 (*0-8247-1996-4*) Dekker.

— Quality & Reliability in Analytical Chemistry. 2000. 79.95 (*0-8493-2376-2*) CRC Pr.

Aboul-Enein, Hassan Y. & Wainer, Irving W. The Impact of Stereochemistry on Drug Development & Use. LC 96-33491. (Chemical Analysis: A Series of Monographs on Analy). 728p. 1997. 110.00 (*0-471-59644-2*) Wiley.

Aboul-Fetouh, Hilmi M. Morphological Study of Egyptian Colloquial Arabic. (Janua Linguarum, Ser. Practica: No. 33). 1969. pap. text 75.40 (*90-279-0691-2*) Mouton.

Aboulafia, Mitchell. The Mediating Self: Mead, Sartre, & Self-Determination. LC 85-20378. 156p. 1986. 22.50 (*0-300-03523-3*) Yale U Pr.

— The Self-Winding Circle: A Study of Hegel's System. LC 82-210652. 124p. (C). 1982. 14.75 (*0-87527-307-6*) Green.

Aboulafia, Mitchell, ed. Philosophy, Social Theory & the Thought of George Herbert Mead. LC 90-30134. (SUNY Series in the Philosophy of the Social Sciences). 337p. 1991. text 21.50 (*0-7914-0359-9*) State U NY Pr.

***Aboulafia, Richard.** Jane's Gem Modern Civil Aircraft. 1999. pap. 10.00 (*0-00-472264-7*, HarpRes) HarpInfo.

Aboulker-Muscat, Colette. Alone with the One. (Illus.). 112p. 2000. pap. 35.00 (*1-883148-01-4*, Pub. by ACMI Pr) Midpt Trade.

— Mea Culpa: Tales of Resurrection. 177p. 1997. 35.00 (*1-883148-05-7*); pap. 20.00 (*1-883148-06-5*) ACMI Pr.

Aboulnaga, Taher, ed. see Ghanayem, Mohamed F.

Abouna, George M., ed. Current Status of Clinical Organ Transplantation. LC 84-1553. (Developments in Surgery Ser.). 1984. text 206.50 (*0-89838-635-7*) Kluwer Academic.

Abouna, George M., et al, eds. Organ Transplantation, 1990. (Developments in Surgery Ser.). (C). 1991. text 341.00 (*0-7923-1191-4*) Kluwer Academic.

Abourezk, Sanaa. Secrets of Healthy Middle Eastern Cuisine. LC 99-20256. 1999. 25.00 (*1-56656-310-0*) Interlink Pub.

***Abourezk, Sanaa.** Secrets of Healthy Middle Eastern Cuisine. (Illus.). 2000. pap. 17.95 (*1-56656-327-5*) Interlink Pub.

Abouriche, Nouredine, jt. auth. see Conseil International de la Language Francaise Sta.

***Abourjilie, Charlie.** Develooping Character for Classroom Success: Strategies to Increase Responsibility, Achievement & Motivation in Secondary Students. 98p. 2000. 12.00 (*1-892056-07-0*) Character Dev.

Abouseif, D. B. Minarets of Cairo. 1985. pap. 20.00 (*977-424-035-9*, Pub. by Am Univ Cairo Pr) Col U Pr.

Abousenna, Mona, jt. ed. see Wahba, Mourad.

Abousleiman, Y., et al, eds. Computer Methods & Water Resources IV. (Water Studies : No. 6). 311p. 1999. 198.00 (*1-85312-519-9*, 5199, Pub. by WIT Pr) Computational Mech MA.

About, Edmond. The Man with the Broken Ear. Holt, Henry, tr. LC 74-15941. (Science Fiction Ser.). 258p. 1975. reprint ed. 23.95 (*0-405-06271-0*) Ayer.

About Women Inc. Staff. Marketing Food to Women: How to Reach the Growing New Women's Food Product & Service Market. LC 98-145117. 35 p. 1997. write for info. (*1-890211-05-2*) About Women.

Abouv, Zhoumagaly & Oxtopcu, Kurtulus. Kazakh, Colloquial, Set. unabridged ed. 64p. 1994. 55.00 incl. audio (*0-88432-784-1*, AFKA10) Audio-Forum.

AbouZahr, C. & Royston, E., compiled by. Maternal Mortality: A Global Factbook. 608p. 1991. pap. text 50.00 (*92-4-159001-7*, 1930024) World Health.

Abouzeid, Leila. Return to Childhood: The Memoir of a Modern Moroccan Woman. LC 98-75404. 100p. 1998. pap. 10.95 (*0-292-70490-9*) U of Tex Pr.

Abouzeid, Lelia. The Year of the Elephant: A Moroccan Woman's Journey Toward Independence. Parmenter, Barbara M., tr. from ARA. (Modern Middle Eastern Literature in Translation Ser.). 129p. (Orig.). 1989. pap. 9.95 (*0-292-79603-X*) U of Tex Pr.

Abowd, John M. & Freeman, Richard B., eds. Immigration, Trade, & the Labor Market. (National Bureau of Economic Research Project Report Ser.). (Illus.). 448p. 1991. 57.50 (*0-226-00095-8*) U Ch Pr.

Abowitz, Kathleen K. Making Meaning of Community in an American High School. LC 99-34834. (Understanding Education & Policy Ser.). 224p. (C). 1999. 42.50 (*1-57273-206-7*) Hampton Pr NJ.

***Abowitz, Kathleen K.** Making Meaning of Community in an American High School. LC 99-34834. (Understanding Education & Policy Ser.). 224p. (C). 1999. pap. 19.95 (*1-57273-207-5*) Hampton Pr NJ.

Abp. Averky of Syracuse. Stand Fast in the Truth. 2nd rev. ed. Serfes, Demetrios, ed. Johnson, Seraphim, tr. (Illus.). 24p. 1995. pap. 4.00 (*0-912927-63-1*, D030) St John Kronstadt.

Abra, Jock. Assaulting Parnassus: Theoretical Views of Creativity. (Illus.). 616p. (Orig.). (C). 1988. lib. bdg. 65.50 (*0-8191-7054-2*) U Pr of Amer.

— The Motives for Creative Work. LC 96-51718. (Perspectives on Creativity Ser.). 288p. 1997. pap. 24.95 (*1-881303-93-4*) Hampton Pr NJ.

— Should Psychology Be a Science? Pros & Cons. LC 97-21853. 272p. 1998. 65.00 (*0-275-95476-5*, Praeger Pubs) Greenwood.

Abrabanel, Isaac. Abrabanel on Pirke Avot: A Digest of Rabbi Isaac Abravanel's "Nahalat Avot" Chill, Abraham, tr. from HEB. & intro. by. 503p. 1991. 32.95 (*0-87203-135-7*) Hermon.

Abraben, Emanuel E. Point of View: The Art of Architectural Photography. 202p. 1993. 62.95 (*0-442-00984-4*, VNR) Wiley.

Abraben, Emanuel M. Point of View: The Art of Architectural Photography. (Illus.). 202p. 1993. 62.95 (*0-471-28463-7*, VNR) Wiley.

Abrados, F. R. Nueva Sintaxis del Griego Antiguo. (SPA.). 840p. 1993. 200.00 (*84-249-1480-5*) Elliots Bks.

Abragam, A. L' Effet Mossbauer. (Documents on Modern Physics Ser.). vi, 70p. 1964. text 123.00 (*0-677-00015-4*) Gordon & Breach.

Abragam, Anatole. Principles of Nuclear Magnetism. (The International Series of Monographs on Physics: No. 32). (Illus.). 614p. 1983. pap. text 59.00 (*0-19-852014-X*) OUP.

— Reflections of a Physicist. 160p. 1986. pap. 36.00 (*0-19-851964-8*) OUP.

— Time Reversal: An Autobiography. (Illus.). 382p. 1989. 55.00 (*0-19-853926-6*) OUP.

Abraham. Advanced Ceramic Powders & Nano-Sized Ceramic Powders. 402p. 1994. 2850.00 (*1-56965-219-8*, GB102R) BCC.

— Burger's , Vol. 1. 6th ed. pap. text. write for info. (*0-471-37218-8*) Wiley.

— Color Atlas of the Human Anatomy. 4th ed. 1998. text 63.00 (*0-7234-2641-4*) Wolfe Pubng AZ.

— Electronic Ceramics: An Industry & Market Analysis. 341p. 1995. 2850.00 (*1-56965-223-6*, GB121R) BCC.

— Handbook of Nursing & Health Research: Design. 700p. 1996. 46.95 (*0-8016-7778-5*) Mosby Inc.

— Insurance Law & Regulations. 2nd ed. Date not set. pap. text, teacher ed. write for info. (*1-56662-261-1*) Foundation Pr.

***Abraham.** Making of the Indian Atomic Bomb. LC 98-27616. 180p. 1998. text 55.00 (*1-85649-629-5*, Pub. by Zed Books) St Martin.

Abraham. Social Psychology for Nurses. 286p. 1993. pap. 37.50 (*1-56593-552-7*, 0534) Singular Publishing.

Abraham & Flippo, Edwin B. Human Resources - Personnel Managing a Changing Workforce. 848p. 1991. 49.00 (*0-685-67137-2*, 49833) CCH INC.

Abraham & Kochummen, Sara. High Tech Ceramics Industry Review. 302p. 1995. 1500.00 (*1-56965-324-0*, DHC94) BCC.

Abraham, A. Iconography of Sensory Nerve Endings. 396p. (C). 1981. 204.00 (*963-05-2316-7*, Pub. by Akade Kiado) St Mut.

— Introduction to Orchids. (C). 1988. 160.00 (*0-7855-3295-1*, Pub. by Scientific) St Mut.

Abraham, A. J. The Awakening of Persia: The Reign of Nasr Al-Din Shah, 1848-1896. 72p. (Orig.). (C). 1993. pap. text 14.95 (*0-9628916-9-X*) Vande Vere.

***Abraham, A. J.** Khomeini, Islamic Fundamentalism & the Warriors of God: An Islamic Reader. 147p. 1999. pap. text 20.00 (*1-55605-293-6*) Wyndham Hall.

Abraham, A. J. The Lebanon War. LC 95-30698. 216p. 1996. 57.95 (*0-275-95389-0*, Praeger Pubs) Greenwood.

Abraham, A. Johnston. String Figures. Irvine, Keith, ed. LC 86-15518. (Folk Games Ser.). (Illus.). 1987. 27.00 (*0-917256-37-9*); pap. 16.00 (*0-917256-23-9*) Ref Pubns.

Abraham, Abie. Oh, God, Where Are You? LC 96-90313. (Illus.). 600p. 1996. 26.95 (*0-533-11987-1*) Vantage.

Abraham, Abraham. The Handbook on All Extraterrestrial Life. 52p. Date not set. pap. 14.00 (*1-889696-00-5*, 1) Abraham Assoc IL.

Abraham, Abraham K., et al, eds. Protein Synthesis: Translational & Post-Translational Events. LC 83-26463. (Experimental Biology & Medicine Ser.). 477p. 1984. 125.00 (*0-89603-060-1*) Humana.

Abraham, Abraham S. Comprehensive Guide to Medical Halachah. Orig. Title: Medical Halacha for Everyone. 1990. 25.95 (*0-87306-529-8*) Feldheim.

Abraham, Adam E. A Freed Man: An Emancipation Proclamation. 336p. Date not set. pap. 24.95 (*0-9700209-0-2*, Phaelos Bks) Phaelos Pubng.

— I am My Body, Not! (Illus.). 54p. (J). (gr. 1-10). 2000. 19.95 (*0-9700209-1-0*, Phaelos Bks) Phaelos Pubng.

— I am My Body, Not! deluxe ed. (Illus.). 56p. 2000. pap. 12.95 (*0-9700209-4-5*) Phaelos Pubng.

— I Am Spirit! deluxe ed. (Illus.). 36p. (YA). (gr. 8 up). 2000. 19.95 (*0-9700209-3-7*) Phaelos Pubng.

Abraham, Amy, jt. auth. see Brown, William C., Jr.

Abraham, Angela & Abraham, Ken. Jesus Loves Me Bible. LC 99-28445. Orig. Title: Hosanna Bible. 448p. (J). (ps-3). 1999. 16.99 (*0-8499-7501-8*) Tommy Nelson.

— Jesus Loves Me Devotional. LC 99-24993. (Illus.). 224p. 1999. 10.99 (*0-8499-5907-1*) Tommy Nelson.

— Praise & Worship: A Devotional for Little Ones. LC 95-13343. (Illus.). 224p. (J). (ps-3). 1996. 14.99 (*0-8499-1191-5*) Tommy Nelson.

Abraham, Angela, jt. auth. see Abraham, Ken.

Abraham, Angela, jt. compiled by see Abrahanm, Ken.

Abraham, Anthony L. & Crook, Richard. Brainstorm Vol. I: Monsters from the Id. LC 96-85001. (Illus.). 224p. 1996. pap. 9.95 (*1-889295-00-0*) Acolyte Media.

Abraham, Antoine J. Lebanon: A State of Siege, 1975-1984. 2nd ed. LC 85-51483. 69p. (C). 1989. pap. text 16.00 (*0-932269-21-4*) Wyndham Hall.

Abraham, Arthur. Mende Government & Politics under Colonial Rule: A Historical Study of Political Change in Sierra Leone 1890-1937. (Illus.). 1979. 29.50 (*0-19-711638-8*) OUP.

A

An Asterisk (*) at the beginning of an entry indicates that the title is appearing for the first time.

A

Abraham, Arthur, et al. The Encyclopaedia Africana Dictionary of African Biography Vol. 2: Sierra Leone-Zaire. Ofosu-Appiah, L. H., ed. LC 76-17954. (Illus.). 1979. 84.00 (*0-917256-06-9*) Ref Pubns.

Abraham, B., ed. Quality Improvement Through Statistical Methods. LC 97-51995. (Statistics for Industry & Technology Ser.). 450p. 1998. text 79.95 (*0-8176-4052-5*) Birkhauser.

***Abraham, Beatrice.** Thai Massage. (Illus.). 272p. 2000. pap. 18.95 (*965-494-117-1*) Astrolog Pub.

Abraham Ben Moses Ben Maimon. High Ways to Perfection of Abraham Maimonides. Rosenblatt, Samuel, tr. LC 74-158221. (Columbia University. Oriental Studies: No. 27). 1927. 24.50 (*0-404-50517-1*) AMS Pr.

Abraham, Bovas & Ledolter, Johannes. Statistical Methods for Forecasting. LC 83-7006. (Probability & Mathematical Ser.). 464p. 1983. 109.95 (*0-471-86764-0*, 1-346) Wiley.

Abraham, Bovas & Unnikrishnan, Nair N. Quality Improvement Through Statistical Methods. LC 97-51995. (Statistics for Industry & Technology Ser.). 1998. write for info. (*3-7643-4052-5*) Birkhauser.

Abraham, C. & Thomas, A. Microeconomics: Optimal Decision Making by Private Firms & Public Authorities. Jones, D. V., tr. from FRE. LC 79-188001. Orig. Title: Microeconomic, Decisions Optimal dans L'enterprise et dans la Nation. (Illus.). 507p. 1972. lib. bdg. 211.50 (*90-277-0237-3*) Kluwer Academic.

Abraham, C. M. Environmental Justice in India. LC 99-13933. (London-Leiden Series on Administration & Development : Vol. 2). 188p. 1999. 75.00 (*90-411-1169-7*) Kluwer Law Intl.

Abraham, Christian C. Manifesto of Destruction. 3rd ed. 104p. 1996. reprint ed. pap. 5.00 (*0-9654986-2-X*) IMXMI Pub.

Abraham, Claude. Pierre Corneille. LC 76-186715. (Twayne's World Authors Ser.). 169p. (C). 1972. lib. bdg. 17.95 (*0-8290-1745-3*) Irvington.

Abraham, Claude K. The Strangers: The Tragic World of Tristan l'Hermite. LC 66-64916. (University of Florida Humanities Monographs: No. 23). 83p. reprint ed. pap. 30.00 (*0-7837-5029-3*, 204469800004) Bks Demand.

Abraham, David. The Collapse of the Weimar Republic: Political Economy & Crisis. rev. ed. LC 86-27033. 366p. (C). 1986. 45.00 (*0-8419-1083-9*); pap. 20.00 (*0-8419-1084-7*) Holmes & Meier.

Abraham, Doc & Abraham, Katy. The Green Thumb Garden Handbook. (Illus.). 528p. 1992. pap. 18.95 (*1-55821-147-0*) Lyons Pr.

— The Green Thumb Garden Handbook. 536p. 1999. pap. 16.95 (*1-55821-905-6*) Lyons Pr.

— Green Thumb Wisdom: Garden Myths Revealed! McHale, Elizabeth, ed. LC 95-46682. (Illus.). 144p. (Orig.). 1996. pap. 12.95 (*0-88266-928-1*, 928-1, Storey Pub) Storey Bks.

— Growing Plants from Seed. (Illus.). 224p. 1991. pap. 13.95 (*1-55821-124-1*) Lyons Pr.

Abraham, E. C. Glycosylated Hemoglobins: Methods of Analysis & Clinical Applications. LC 85-15913. (Clinical & Biochemical Analysis Ser.: No. 19). 254p. reprint ed. pap. 78.80 (*0-7837-3367-4*, 204332500008) Bks Demand.

Abraham, Edward, jt. ed. see Shoemaker, William C.

Abraham, Edward P., et al. Launching the Antibiotic Era: Personal Accounts of the Discovery & Use of the First Antibiotics. Cohn, Zanvil A. & Moberg, Carol L., eds. 112p. 1990. 25.00 (*0-87470-047-7*) Rockefeller.

Abraham, Farid F. & Tiller, William A., eds. An Introduction to Computer Simulation in Applied Science. LC 72-83047. 233p. reprint ed. pap. 72.30 (*0-608-14547-5*, 202471400038) Bks Demand.

Abraham, Fern-Rae. Tin Craft: A Workbook. 2nd rev. ed. LC 93-46615. (Illus.). 32p. 1994. pap. 5.95 (*0-86534-098-6*) Sunstone Pr.

Abraham, Filip, et al, eds. Privatisations & Public Procurement in the European Union: Generale Bank Lectures, 1996-1997. LC 99-198884. (Leuven Law Ser.: No. 11). (Illus.). 141p. 1998. pap. 45.00 (*90-6186-872-6*, Pub. by Leuven Univ) Coronet Bks.

— Recent Economic & Legal Developments in European Environmental Policy: Generale Bank Lectures 1993-1994. (Law Ser.: Vol. 5). 272p. (Orig.). 1995. pap. 87.50 (*90-6186-703-7*, Pub. by Leuven Univ) Coronet Bks.

***Abraham, Filip, et al, eds.** Tax Policy & the Impending Economic & Monetary Union: Generale Bank Lectures 1997-1998. 148p. 1999. 39.50 (*90-6186-997-8*, Pub. by Leuven Univ) Coronet Bks.

Abraham, Francis & Morgan, John H. Sociological Thought: From Comte to Sorokin. LC 89-40442. 263p. (C). 1989. pap. text 20.00 (*1-55605-104-2*) Wyndham Hall.

Abraham, Fred. Macroeconomic Principles. 136p. (C). 1995. pap. text, per. 17.95 (*0-7872-1395-0*) Kendall-Hunt.

Abraham, Fred D. & Gilgen, Albert R. Chaos Theory in Psychology, 27. LC 94-29848. (Contributions in Psychology Ser.). 400p. 1995. 75.00 (*0-313-28961-1*, Greenwood Pr) Greenwood.

Abraham, Frederick D. & Gilgen, Albert R. Chaos Theory in Psychology. LC 94-29848. 400p. 1995. pap. 31.95 (*0-275-95140-5*, Praeger Pubs) Greenwood.

Abraham, Frederick D. & Shaw, Robert. Dynamical Systems: A Visual Introduction. (Illus.). 275p. 1992. spiral bd. 25.00 (*0-942344-12-X*, Pub. by Aerial Pr) Dakota Bks.

Abraham, Frederick D., et al. A Visual Introduction to Dynamical Systems Theory for Psychology. (Science Frontier Express Ser.). (Illus.). 290p. 1990. spiral bd. 25.00 (*0-942344-09-X*, Pub. by Aerial Pr) Dakota Bks.

Abraham-Frois, G., ed. Non-Linear Dynamics & Endogenous Cycles. LC 98-15193. (Lecture Notes in Economics & Mathematical Systems Ser.: Vol. 463). (Illus.). vi, 204p. 1998. pap. 61.00 (*3-540-64321-4*) Spr-Verlag.

Abraham-Frois, Gilbert, et al. Prices, Profits & Rhythms of Accumulation. Ben Ouagrham, Sonia, tr. LC 94-42383. 299p. (C). 1997. text 59.95 (*0-521-39532-1*) Cambridge U Pr.

Abraham Fund Staff. The Abraham Fund Directory of Institutions & Organizations Fostering Coexistence Between Jews & Arabs in Israel. Weiner, Anita et al, eds. 720p. (Orig.). (C). 1991. pap. 75.00 (*0-9629529-0-7*) Abraham Fund.

***Abraham, Garth, et al.** Martin Brassey's Commentary on the Labour Relations Act. 1999. ring bd. 96.50 (*0-7021-5118-1*, Pub. by Juta & Co) Gaunt.

***Abraham, Gary & Smith, Michael.** Kids' Hockey: The Parents' Guide. (Illus.). 176p. 2000. pap. 19.95 (*1-55209-545-2*) Firefly Bks Ltd.

Abraham, Gary A. Max Weber & the Jewish Question: A Study of the Social Outlook of His Sociology. 336p. 1992. text 34.95 (*0-252-01841-9*) U of Ill Pr.

***Abraham, George.** The Belles of Shangri-La. 2000. pap. 11.95 (*0-533-13472-2*) Vantage.

Abraham, Gerald. The Age of Beethoven, 1790-1830 LC 94-3835. (New Oxford History of Music Ser.). 1994. write for info. (*0-19-816455-6*) OUP.

— Dostoevski. LC 74-6398. (Studies in Dostoyevsky: No. 86). 1974. lib. bdg. 75.00 (*0-8383-1869-X*) M S G Haskell Hse.

— Nietzsche. LC 73-20387. (Nietzsche Ser.: No. 89). 1974. lib. bdg. 75.00 (*0-8383-1764-2*) M S G Haskell Hse.

— On Russian Music: Critical & Historical Studies of Glinka's Operas. LC 73-134046. (Essay Index Reprint Ser.). 280p. 1982. reprint ed. lib. bdg. 14.00 (*0-8290-0786-5*) Irvington.

— Tolstoy. LC 74-7018. (Studies in Tolstoy: No. 62). 1974. lib. bdg. 75.00 (*0-8383-1965-3*) M S G Haskell Hse.

Abraham, Gerald, ed. The Music of Sibelius. LC 74-23413. (Music Reprint Ser.). 218p. 1975. reprint ed. lib. bdg. 29.50 (*0-306-70716-0*) Da Capo.

— The New Oxford History of Music Vol. 6: Concert Music, Sixteen Thirty to Seventeen Fifty, Vol. 6. LC 85-2950. (Illus.). 806p. 1986. text 95.00 (*0-19-316306-3*) OUP.

Abraham, Gerald, tr. see Menke, Werner.

Abraham, Gerald E. Beethoven's Second-Period Quartets. 1988. reprint ed. lib. bdg. 49.00 (*0-7812-0265-5*) Rprt Serv.

— Beethoven's Second-Period Quartets. LC 70-181101. 79p. 1942. reprint ed. 49.00 (*0-403-01500-6*) Scholarly.

— Borodin: The Composer & His Music. LC 74-27324. (BCL Ser.: No. II). (Illus.). reprint ed. 32.50 (*0-404-12851-3*) AMS Pr.

— Borodin: The Composer & His Music: A Descriptive & Critical Analysis of His Works & a Study of His Value As an Art-Force. 205p. 1990. reprint ed. lib. bdg. 69.00 (*0-7812-9051-1*) Rprt Serv.

— Chopin's Musical Style. LC 79-25521. 116p. 1980. reprint ed. lib. bdg. 42.50 (*0-313-22251-7*, ABCM, Greenwood Pr) Greenwood.

— The Concise Oxford History of Music. (Illus.). 968p. 1985. pap. 27.50 (*0-19-284010-X*) OUP.

— Eight Soviet Composers. LC 71-106679. 102p. 1970. reprint ed. lib. bdg. 35.00 (*0-8371-3350-5*, ABSC, Greenwood Pr) Greenwood.

— Eight Soviet Composers. (Music Book Index Ser.). 102p. 1992. reprint ed. lib. bdg. 69.00 (*0-7812-9460-6*) Rprt Serv.

— A Hundred Years of Music: Music Book Index. 320p. 1993. reprint ed. lib. bdg. 89.00 (*0-7812-9562-9*) Rprt Serv.

— The Music of Sibelius: Music Book Index. 218p. 1993. reprint ed. lib. bdg. 79.00 (*0-7812-9621-8*) Rprt Serv.

— On Russian Music. LC 73-134046. (Essay Index Reprint Ser.). 1977. 18.95 (*0-8369-1900-9*) Ayer.

— On Russian Music. 1976. lib. bdg. 59.00 (*0-403-03757-3*) Scholarly.

— On Russian Music. 1988. reprint ed. lib. bdg. 49.00 (*0-7812-0272-8*) Rprt Serv.

— Rimsky-Korsakov. LC 75-41002. (BCL Ser.: No. II). reprint ed. 24.95 (*0-404-14500-0*) AMS Pr.

— Rimsky-Korsakov: Music Book Index. 142p. 1993. reprint ed. lib. bdg. 69.00 (*0-7812-9623-4*) Rprt Serv.

— Studies in Russian Music. LC 68-20285. (Essay Index Reprint Ser.). 1980. 20.95 (*0-8369-0133-9*) Ayer.

— Studies in Russian Music. 1988. reprint ed. lib. bdg. 49.00 (*0-7812-0107-1*) Rprt Serv.

— Studies in Russian Music. 1976. reprint ed. lib. bdg. 59.00 (*0-403-03700-X*) Scholarly.

— Tchaikovsky: Music Book Index. 144p. 1993. reprint ed. lib. bdg. 69.00 (*0-7812-9626-9*) Rprt Serv.

Abraham, Gerald E., ed. Grieg: A Symposium. LC 71-138196. 144p. 1971. reprint ed. lib. bdg. 35.00 (*0-8371-5549-5*, ABGR, Greenwood Pr) Greenwood.

— The New Oxford History of Music Vol. 8: The Age of Beethoven, 1790-1830. (Illus.). 768p. 1983. text 95.00 (*0-19-316308-X*) OUP.

— The New Oxford History of Music Vol. 9: Romanticism (1830-1890), Vol. 9. (Illus.). 956p. 1990. text 130.00 (*0-19-316309-8*) OUP.

— Schumann: A Symposium. LC 77-8051. 319p. 1977. reprint ed. lib. bdg. 69.50 (*0-8371-9050-9*, SCSY, Greenwood Pr) Greenwood.

Abraham, Gerald E., et al. The New Grove Russian Masters II: Rimsky-Korsakov, Skryabin, Rakhmaninov, Prokofiev, Shostakovich. (Orig.). 1986. 25.00 (*0-393-02283-8*) Norton.

Abraham, Guy E., ed. Radioassay Systems in Clinical Endocrinology. LC 81-862. (Basic & Clinical Endocrinology Ser.: No. 1). (Illus.). 687p. reprint ed. pap. 200.00 (*0-7837-0852-1*, 204116100019) Bks Demand.

Abraham, Henry. Nuclear Weapons & Nuclear War: A Source Book for Health Professionals. Cassel, Christine et al, eds. LC 83-24511. 553p. 1984. 65.00 (*0-275-91423-2*, C1423, Praeger Pubs) Greenwood.

— Where Art Thou Black Man: A Guide to Empower Black Men to Reach Their Potential. Shaffer, Tamara, ed. (Illus.). 112p. (Orig.). 1996. pap. 12.00 (*0-9651167-0-0*) Proj Restoration.

Abraham, Henry & Pfeffer, Irwin. Enjoying Global History. (YA). (gr. 10-12). 1996. pap. text 17.67 (*0-87720-890-5*) AMSCO Sch.

Abraham, Henry J. The Judicial Process: An Introductory Analysis of the Courts of the United States, England & France. 7th ed. LC 97-27311. (Illus.). 480p. (C). 1998. pap. text 31.95 (*0-19-509987-7*) OUP.

— The Judiciary: The Supreme Court in the Governmental Process. 9th ed. 288p. (C). 1993. text. write for info. (*0-697-12695-1*) Brown & Benchmark.

— The Judiciary: The Supreme Court in the Governmental Process. 10th ed. LC 96-25267. 325p. (C). 1996. text 50.00 (*0-8147-0652-5*); pap. text 18.50 (*0-8147-0653-3*) NYU Pr.

***Abraham, Henry J.** Justices, Presidents & Senators: A History of the U. S. Supreme Court Appointments from Washington to Clinton. rev. ed. LC 99-23000. 444p. 1999. pap. 29.95 (*0-8476-9605-7*, Pub. by Rowman) Natl Bk Netwk.

— Justices, Presidents & Senators: A History of the U. S. Supreme Court Appointments from Washington to Clinton. 4th ed. LC 99-23000. 444p. 1999. 75.00 (*0-8476-9604-9*) Rowman.

Abraham, Henry J. & Perry, Barbara. Freedom & the Court: Civil Rights & Liberties in the United States. 7th ed. 512p. (C). 1998. pap. text 32.95 (*0-19-509997-4*) OUP.

Abraham, Ivo, ed. see Bottrell, Melissa M., et al.

Abraham, James. The Bethesda Cancer Manual. 400p. pap. text 29.95 (*0-7817-2300-0*) Lppncott W & W.

Abraham, James M. A Time of Ignorance & Terror. 316p. 1999. pap. 22.50 (*0-9671462-0-8*) I & J Pubg.

***Abraham, Jay.** Getting Everything You Can Out of All You've Got: 21 Ways You Can Out-Think, Out-Perform & Out-Earn the Competition. LC 99-55044. 416p. 2000. text 24.95 (*0-312-20465-5*, Truman Talley) St Martin.

***Abraham, Jed H.** From Courtship to Courtroom: How Divorce Law Has Undermined Marriage for Men. LC 99-42588. 1999. pap. 14.95 (*0-8197-0692-2*); lib. bdg. 27.50 (*0-8197-0694-9*) Bloch.

Abraham, Jo Ann, ed. see Dowling, D. McDonald.

Abraham, John. Divide & School: Gender & Class Dynamics in Comprehensive Education. 210p. 1995. 89.95 (*0-7507-0390-3*, Falmer Pr) Taylor & Francis.

Abraham, John, ed. Divide & School: Gender & Class Dynamics in Comprehensive Education. LC 95-3992. 162p. 1995. pap. 27.95 (*0-7507-0391-1*, Falmer Pr) Taylor & Francis.

***Abraham, John & Lewis, Graham.** Regulating Medicines in Europe: Competition, Expertise & Public Health. LC 00-28615. 2000. pap. write for info. (*0-415-20878-5*) Routledge.

Abraham, Joseph, jt. auth. see Hirway, Indira.

Abraham, Julie. Are Girls Necessary? Lesbian Writing & Modern Histories. 272p. (C). 1995. pap. 24.99 (*0-415-91457-4*) Routledge.

— Are Girls Necessary? Lesbian Writing & Modern Histories. 272p. (C). (gr. 13 up). 1996. 70.00 (*0-415-91456-6*) Routledge.

Abraham, K. C. & Mbuy-Beya, Bernadette, eds. Spirituality of the Third World: A Cry for Life. LC 94-23357. 212p. (Orig.). 1994. pap. 20.00 (*0-88344-977-3*) Orbis Bks.

***Abraham, Katharine G., ed.** Geographic Profile of Employment & Unemployment, 1998. (Illus.). 157p. 2000. pap. text 30.00 (*0-7881-8903-4*) DIANE Pub.

Abraham, Katharine G. & Houseman, Susan N. Job Security in America: Lessons from Germany. 175p. (C). 1993. 34.95 (*0-8157-0076-8*); pap. 14.95 (*0-8157-0075-X*) Brookings.

Abraham, Katherine & McKersie, Robert B., eds. New Developments in the Labor Market: Toward a New Institutional Paradigm. 300p. 1990. 39.95 (*0-262-01118-2*) MIT Pr.

Abraham, Katy, jt. auth. see Abraham, Doc.

Abraham, Ken. Armed & Dangerous: Straight Answers from the Bible. (Inspirational Library Ser.). 272p. 1991. im. lthr. 4.97 (*1-55748-241-1*) Barbour Pub.

***Abraham, Ken.** Armed & Dengerous: Facing Today's Battles with the Word of God, Graduates Edition. 192p. 2000. pap. 0.99 (*1-57748-690-0*) Barbour Pub.

Abraham, Ken. Don't Bite the Apple 'Til You Check for Worms. LC 85-1729. 160p. (Orig.). (YA). (gr. 9). 1994. mass mkt. 5.99 (*0-8007-8620-3*, Spire) Revell.

— Fairways: Inspiration for the Golf Enthusiast. 1999. 12.99 (*1-57748-494-0*) Barbour Pub.

— Levantate y Pelea.Tr. of Stand up & Fight Back. (SPA.). 256p. (YA). 1995. 9.99 (*0-88113-298-5*, B067-2985) Caribe Betania.

Abraham, Ken & Abraham, Angela. Hosanna Bible. LC 93-593. (Illus.). 448p. (J). (ps-3). 1993. 16.99 (*0-8499-1036-6*) Tommy Nelson.

Abraham, Ken, jt. auth. see Abraham, Angela.

Abraham, Ken, jt. auth. see Boyce, Kim.

Abraham, Ken, jt. auth. see Croyle, John.

Abraham, Ken, jt. auth. see Stewart, Tracey.

Abraham, Ken, jt. auth. see Valdes, Jorge.

Abraham, Ken, ed. see Croyle, John.

Abraham, Kenneth S. Environmental Liability Insurance Law. 418p. 1992. 116.00 (*0-13-282765-4*) Aspen Law.

— The Forms & Functions of Tort Law: An Analytical Primer on Cases & Concepts. LC 97-182556. (Student Textbook Ser.). 287p. 1997. pap. text 15.75 (*1-56662-460-6*) Foundation Pr.

— Insurance Law & Regulation: Cases & Materials. (University Casebook Ser.). 752p. 1990. text 41.50 (*0-88277-791-2*) Foundation Pr.

— Insurance Law & Regulation: Cases & Materials. 2nd ed. (University Casebook Ser.). 735p. (C). 1995. text 44.50 (*1-56662-255-7*) Foundation Pr.

— Insurance Law & Regulation: Cases & Materials, Teachers Manual for Use With. (University Casebook Ser.). 139p. 1989. pap. text. write for info. (*0-88277-804-8*) Foundation Pr.

— Teacher's Manual for Use with Insurance Law & Regulation. 2nd ed. (University Casebook Ser.). Date not set. pap. text, teacher ed. write for info. (*0-614-07457-6*) Foundation Pr.

Abraham, Kinfe. Ethiopia: From Bullets to the Ballot Box: The Bumpy Road to Democracy & the Political Economy of Transition. LC 93-10805. xxvi, 300p. 1994. 45.95 (*0-932415-79-2*); pap. 16.95 (*0-932415-80-6*) Red Sea Pr.

— Missing Millions: Why & How Africa Is Underdeveloped. 1995. 49.95 (*0-86543-352-6*); pap. 16.95 (*0-86543-353-4*) Africa World.

— Politics of Black Nationalism: From Harlem to Soweto. LC 89-81532. 1991. 34.95 (*0-86543-155-8*); pap. 12.95 (*0-86543-156-6*) Africa World.

Abraham, Kurt. Balancing the Pairs of Opposites; The Seven Rays & Education; & Other Essays in Esoteric Psychology. LC 92-74332. (Illus.). 148p. (Orig.). 1993. pap. 9.95 (*0-9609002-5-X*) Lampus Pr.

— Introduction to the Seven Rays. LC 86-80170. 108p. (Orig.). 1986. pap. 8.50 (*0-9609002-2-5*) Lampus Pr.

— The Moon Veils Vulcan & the Sun Veils Neptune. LC 89-84728. 114p. (Orig.). 1989. pap. 10.50 (*0-9609002-4-1*) Lampus Pr.

— The Seven Rays & Nations - France & the United States Compared. LC 87-81909. 96p. (Orig.). 1987. pap. 9.80 (*0-9609002-3-3*) Lampus Pr.

— Techniques of Soul Alignment: The Rays, the Subtle Bodies, & the Use of Keywords. LC 97-93651. 125p. (Orig.). 1997. pap. 14.00 (*0-9609002-6-8*) Lampus Pr.

— Threefold Method for Understanding the Seven Rays & Other Essays in Esoteric Psychology. LC 84-81567. 120p. (Orig.). 1984. pap. 8.50 (*0-9609002-1-7*) Lampus Pr.

Abraham, Kurt B. Psychological Types & the Seven Rays, Vol. 1. LC 82-81863. 163p. (Orig.). 1983. pap. 15.00 (*0-9609002-0-9*) Lampus Pr.

Abraham, Laurie K. Mama Might Be Better off Dead: The Failure of Health Care in Urban America. LC 93-15514. 304p. 1993. 22.50 (*0-226-00138-5*) U Ch Pr.

— Mama Might Be Better off Dead: The Failure of Health Care in Urban America. xii, 302p. 1994. pap. 13.00 (*0-226-00139-3*) U Ch Pr.

Abraham, Lindy. Marvell & Alchemy. (Illus.). 384p. 1990. text 86.95 (*0-85967-774-5*, Pub. by Scolar Pr) Ashgate Pub Co.

Abraham, Lyndy. A Dictionary of Alchemical Imagery. LC 98-4544. (Illus.). 400p. (C). 1999. 80.00 (*0-521-63185-8*) Cambridge U Pr.

Abraham, Lyndy & Dee, Arthur. Arthur Dee: Fasciculus Chemicus. Linden, Stanton J., ed. Ashmole, Elias, tr. LC 96-31930. 216p. 1996. text 65.00 (*0-8153-0926-0*) Garland.

Abraham, M. Francis. Modern Sociological Theory: An Introduction. (Illus.). 320p. 1983. pap. text 15.95 (*0-19-561384-8*) OUP.

***Abraham, Margaret.** Speaking the Unspeakable: Marital Violence among South Asian Immigrants in the United States. LC 99-45632. (Illus.). 256p. 2000. text 52.00 (*0-8135-2792-9*) Rutgers U Pr.

— Speaking the Unspeakable: Marital Violence among South Asian Immigrants in the United States. LC 99-45632. (Illus.). 256p. (C). 2000. pap. 22.00 (*0-8135-2793-7*) Rutgers U Pr.

Abraham, Marilyn. First We Quit Our Jobs: How One Work Driven Couple Got on the Road to a New Life. LC 96-33579. 256p. 1997. pap. 11.95 (*0-440-50757-X*) Dell.

Abraham, Marilyn & MacGregor, Sandy. Happy Camper Cook Book. LC 98-49288. (Illus.). 144p. (Orig.). 1999. pap. 14.95 (*1-57416-024-9*) Clear Light.

Abraham, Martin. Betriebliche Sozialleistungen und die Regulierung Individueller Arbeitsverhaltnisse Vol. XII: Endogene Kooperation durch Private Institutionen. (Beitrage zur Gesellschaftsforschung Ser.: Bd. 17). (GER., Illus.). 232p. 1996. pap. 44.95 (*3-631-50016-5*) P Lang Pubng.

Abraham, Martin A., et al. Supercritical Fluids: Extraction & Pollution Prevention. LC 97-29085. (ACS Symposium Ser.: Vol. 670). 326p. 1997. text 115.00 (*0-8412-3517-1*) OUP.

Abraham, Mary. Restaurants of Detroit. 7th ed. 1996. pap. 11.95 (*0-937247-65-0*) Detroit Pr.

Abraham, Meera. Two Medieval Merchant Guilds of South India. (C). 1988. 34.00 (*81-85054-48-7*, Pub. by Manohar) S Asia.

***Abraham, Mel H.** Valuation Issues & Case Law Update: A Reference Guide. 329p. 2000. pap. 195.00 (*0-9701666-0-5*) NACAA.

Abraham, Michael C. Mommy . . . This Is Hard for Me: A Perspective on the Student with Special Needs Who Is Included Within the Regular Public School Classroom. (Illus.). 71p. 1998. pap. text 12.00 (*1-878276-60-3*) Educ Systs Assocs Inc.

***Abraham, Michael R. & Pavelich, Michael J.** Inquiries into Chemistry. 3rd ed. 340p. (C). 1999. pap. 22.95 (*1-57766-061-7*) Waveland Pr.

An Asterisk (*) at the beginning of an entry indicates that the title is appearing for the first time.

***Abraham, Moriah.** God's Mystic Grandson. 2000. pap. 14.95 (*0-533-13240-1*) Vantage.

Abraham, N. B., et al, eds. Instabilities & Chaos in Quantum Optics II. LC 88-12479. (NATO ASI Series B, Physics: Vol. 177). (Illus.). 404p. 1988. 120.00 (*0-306-42914-4*, Plenum Trade) Perseus Pubng.

— Measures of Complexity & Chaos. LC 89-37104. (NATO ASI Series B, Physics: Vol. 208). (Illus.). 486p. (C). 1989. 174.00 (*0-306-43387-7*, Plenum Trade) Perseus Pubng.

Abraham, N. B., et al. Measures of Complexity & Chaos (Ii) - Proceedings of the 2nd Workshop. 400p. 1994. text 109.00 (*981-02-1446-4*) World Scientific Pub.

Abraham, N. B., jt. auth. see Narducci, L. M.

Abraham, N. G., et al, eds. Molecular Biology of Hematopoiesis & Treatment of Leukemias & Lymphomas: 10th Symposium, Hamburg, Juli 1997: Abstracts. (Acta Haematologica Ser.: Vol. 98, Suppl. 1, 1997). vi, 128p. 1997. pap. 48.75 (*3-8055-6550-X*) S Karger.

— Molecular Biology of Hematopoiesis & Treatment of Leukemias & Lymphomas: 10th Symposium, Hamburg, July 1997 - Proceedings. (Acta Haematologica Ser.: Vol. 90, No. 3, 1998). (Illus.). 76p. 1998. pap. 43.50 (*3-8055-6681-6*) S Karger.

***Abraham, N. G., et al, eds.** Molecular Biology of Hematopoiesis & Treatment of Myeloproliferative Diseases: 11th Symposium, Bormio, June 1998: Proceedings. (Acta Haematologica Ser.: Vol. 101, No. 2). 50p. 1999. pap. 25.25 (*3-8055-6823-1*) S Karger.

Abraham, N. G., et al, eds. Molecular Biology of Hematopoiesis & Treatment of Myeloproliferative Diseases: 11th Symposium, Bornio, June 1998 - Abstracts. (Acta Haematologica Ser.: Vol. 100, Suppl. 1). iv, 72p. 1998. pap. 33.25 (*3-8055-6729-4*) S Karger.

***Abraham, Nabeel & Shryock, Andrew, eds.** Arab Detroit: From Margin to Mainstream. LC 99-54827. 2000. 49.95 (*0-8143-2811-3*); pap. 24.95 (*0-8143-2812-1*) Wayne St U Pr.

***Abraham, Nader G.** Molecular Biology of Hematopoiesis 6. LC 99-31967. 1999. write for info. (*0-306-46136-6*, Kluwer Plenum) Kluwer Academic.

Abraham, Nader G., et al, eds. Molecular Biology of Hematopoiesis 5. (Illus.). 737p. (C). 1996. text 179.00 (*0-306-45318-5*, Kluwer Plenum) Kluwer Academic.

— Molecular Biology of Hematopoiesis Proceedings: Proceedings. (Journal: Acta Haematologica: Vol. 95, No. 3-4, 1996). (Illus.). iv, 128p. 1996. pap. 44.00 (*3-8055-6319-1*) S Karger.

Abraham, Nicholas. Rhythms: On the Work, Translation, & Psychoanalysis. Thigpen, Benjamin, tr. from GER. LC 94-42455. (Meridian: Crossing Aesthetics Ser.). 184p. 1995. 35.00 (*0-8047-2502-0*) Stanford U Pr.

Abraham, Nicolas. Rhythms: On the Work, Translation, & Psychoanalysis. Thigpen, Benjamin, tr. from GER. LC 94-42455. (Meridian: Crossing Aesthetics Ser.). 184p. 1995. pap. 12.95 (*0-8047-2503-9*) Stanford U Pr.

Abraham, Nicolas & Torok, Maria. The Shell & the Kernel: Renewals of Psychoanalysis. Rand, Nicholas T., tr. LC 93-47621. (Illus.). 240p. 1994. pap. text 15.95 (*0-226-00088-5*); lib. bdg. 40.00 (*0-226-00087-7*) U Ch Pr.

Abraham, Norma J. Erik of the Dragon Ships. LC 83-50987. (Illus.). 163p. (Orig.). (J). (gr. 8-11). 1983. pap. 3.95 (*0-912661-00-3*) Woodsong Graph.

Abraham, P. A. Sherwood Anderson & the American Short Story. (C). 1995. write for info. (*81-85231-24-9*) Sterling Pubs.

Abraham, Paul & Mackey, Daphne. Get Ready: Interactive Listening & Speaking. (Illus.). 176p. (C). 1985. pap. text 20.00 (*0-13-353913-X*) P-H.

Abraham, Paul F. & Mackey, Daphne. Contact U. S. A. 3rd ed. 272p. 1996. pap. text 26.27 (*0-13-518754-0*) P-H.

***Abraham, Pearl.** Giving America. LC 98-22695. 309p. 1998. 22.95 (*1-57322-121-X*, Riverhead Books) Putnam Pub Group.

Abraham, Pearl. Giving up America. 320p. 1999. pap. text 12.95 (*1-57322-752-8*, Riverhead Books) Putnam Pub Group.

Abraham, Philip, jt. auth. see Antia, F. P.

Abraham-Podietz, Eva, jt. auth. see Fox, Anne L.

Abraham, R., et al. Manifolds, Tensor Analysis, & Applications. (Applied Mathematical Sciences Ser.: Vol. 75). (Illus.). 650p. 1996. 69.95 (*0-387-96790-7*) Spr-Verlag.

Abraham, R., ed. see Jas, F.

Abraham, R. J., et al. Introduction to NMR Spectroscopy. 286p. 1992. pap. 59.95 (*0-471-91894-6*) Wiley.

Abraham, Raimund. UnBuilt. LC 96-136043. (Illus.). 315p. 1996. 104.00 (*3-211-82671-8*) Spr-Verlag.

Abraham, Ralph. Dynamical Systems in 2-Dimensions. (Illus.). 225p. 1995. 39.95 (*0-387-94436-2*) Spr-Verlag.

— Foundations of Mechanics. 2nd ed. (C). 1994. pap. 71.00 (*0-201-40840-6*) Addison-Wesley.

— Foundations of Mechanics, Vol. 1. 3rd ed. (C). 1991. write for info. (*0-201-13186-2*) Addison-Wesley.

Abraham, Ralph & Shaw, Christopher D. Dynamics: The Geometry of Behavior. 3rd ed. (Illus.). 642p. 1997. spiral bd. 45.00 (*0-942344-16-2*, Pub. by Aerial Pr) Dakota Bks.

Abraham, Ralph, et al. Dynamical Systems in 2-Dimensions. LC 96-37581. (TELOS - the Electronic Library of Science). (Illus.). 288p. 1997. 59.95 incl. cd-rom (*0-387-94300-5*) Spr-Verlag.

Abraham, Ralph H. Chaos, Gaia, Eros: A Chaos Pioneer Uncovers the Three Great Streams of History. LC 94-2820. (Illus.). 288p. 1994. 18.00 (*0-06-250013-9*, Pub. by Harper SF) HarpC.

Abraham, Rebecca, jt. auth. see Seyoum, Belayneh.

Abraham, Richard. Alexander Kerensky: The First Love of the Revolution. 1990. pap. text 23.00 (*0-231-06109-9*) Col U Pr.

— Rosa Luxemburg: A Life for the International. LC 89-31671. (Women's Ser.). 185p. 1989. pap. 19.50 (*0-85496-182-8*) Berg Pubs.

Abraham, Roberta. Bibliography on Technology & Social Change in China & Japan. (Reports on Technology & Social Change). 262p. 1974. 12.00 (*0-945271-21-2*) ISU-CIKARD.

Abraham, Ronald J. & Lindquist, Timothy M. Whitepeak Corporation: Supplement. 1997. pap. 30.95 (*0-471-17131-X*) Wiley.

Abraham, S., ed. Carcinogenesis & Dietary Fat. (Prostaglandins, Leukotrienes, & Cancer Ser.). (C). 1989. text 258.00 (*0-7923-0117-X*) Kluwer Academic.

Abraham, Santosh G., jt. auth. see Hudak, David E.

***Abraham, Spencer, ed.** Visa Waiver Pilot Program: Congressional Hearing. (Illus.). 92p. (C). 2000. pap. text 20.00 (*0-7881-8764-3*) DIANE Pub.

***Abraham, Stephanie.** Boxer: Family Favorite. 224p. 1999. 24.95 (*1-58245-127-3*) Howell Bks.

Abraham, Stephanie. The Boxer: Owner's Guide to a Happy, Healthy Pet. (Owner's Guide to a Happy Healthy Pet Ser.). (Illus.). 160p. 1996. 12.95 (*0-87605-394-0*) Howell Bks.

Abraham, Suzanne & Llewellyn-Jones, Derek. Eating Disorders: The Facts. 4th ed. (Facts Ser.). (Illus.). 254p. 1996. pap. 19.95 (*0-19-262759-7*) OUP.

Abraham, Sylvia. How to Read the Tarot. LC 93-48787. (How to Ser.). (Illus.). 272p. 1994. pap. 4.99 (*1-56718-001-9*) Llewellyn Pubns.

— How to Use Tarot Spreads: Answers to Every Question. LC 97-24733. (How to Ser.). (Illus.). 288p. 1997. mass mkt. 4.99 (*1-56718-002-7*) Llewellyn Pubns.

Abraham, Theodore A. Do You Understand, Huh? A POW's Lament, 1941-1945. (Illus.). 237p. (Orig.). 1992. pap. 19.95 (*0-89745-143-0*) Sunflower U Pr.

Abraham, Thomas. Advanced Ceramics Opportunities: A Technical Economic & Market. LC 98-120864. 345p. 1997. 3650.00 (*1-56965-455-7*, GB-208) BCC.

— Carbon-Graphite Fibers, No. YGB-165A: Highlighting New Applications, U. S. & Global Markets, Players & New Developments. 1994. 2650.00 (*0-89336-203-4*, GB-165A) BCC.

— Diamond, Diamond-Like Carbon & CBN Films & Coated Products: A Technical Analysis Including Emerging Technologies, New Developments & Patents. LC 98-120914. 292p. 1997. 1500.00 (*1-56965-246-5*, GB-173T) BCC.

— High Tech Ceramics Industry Review. 295p. 1998. 1500.00 (*1-56965-507-3*, DHC96) BCC.

Abraham, Thomas, contrib. by. Advanced Glasses & Glass Ceramics-Materials, Processing, New Developments, Applications & Markets. (Report Ser.: No. GB-094R). 175p. 1996. 2750.00 (*1-56965-232-5*, GB-094R) BCC.

Abraham, Thomas, jt. auth. see Giese, Edward.

Abraham, Thomas, jt. auth. see Rittner, Mindy N.

***Abraham, Uri.** Losbuch for Concurrency. 250p. 1999. text 60.00 (*90-5699-199-X*, Harwood Acad Pubs) Gordon & Breach.

Abraham-Van de Mark, Eva, ed. Successful Home Birth & Midwifery: The Dutch Obstetric Model. LC 92-42901. 248p. 1993. 65.00 (*0-89789-295-X*, H295, Bergin & Garvey) Greenwood.

Abraham, W., et al, eds. Memory Mechanisms: A Tribute to G. V. Goddard. 400p. (C). 1990. pap. 59.95 (*0-8058-0277-0*); text 120.00 (*0-8058-0276-2*) L Erlbaum Assocs.

Abraham, W., intro. Losbuch In Deutschen Reimpaaren. fac. ed. (Codices Selecti A Ser.: Vol. XXXVIII). (GER., Illus.). 46p. 1972. lthr. 372.00 (*3-201-00790-0*, Pub. by Akademische Druck-und) Balogh.

Abraham, W. E. Mind of Africa. LC 63-9733. (Nature of Human Society Ser.). 1966. pap. text 3.00 (*0-226-00086-9*, P233) U Ch Pr.

Abraham, Werner. Diccionario de Terminologia Linguistica Actual. (SPA.). 512p. 1993. 79.50 (*84-249-0080-4*) Elliots Bks.

— Diccionario de Terminologia Linguistica Actual: Dictionary of Modern Linguistic Terminology. (SPA.). 511p. 1981. 85.00 (*0-8288-2027-9*, S60080) Fr & Eur.

— On the Formal Syntax of the Westgermania: Papers from the "Third Groningen Grammar Talks," Groningen, January 1981. (Linguistik Aktuell/Linguistics Today Ser.: No. 3). vi, 242p. 1983. 59.00 (*90-272-2723-3*) J Benjamins Pubng Co.

Abraham, Werner, ed. Discourse Particles: Descriptive & Theoretical Investigations on the Logical, Syntactic & Pragmatic Properties of Discourse Particles in German. LC 90-28425. (Pragmatics & Beyond Ser.: Vol. 12). viii, 338p. 1991. 89.00 (*1-55619-278-9*) J Benjamins Pubng Co.

— Ut Videam: Contributions to an Understanding of Linguistics for Pieter Verburg on the Occasion of His 70th Birthday. 300p. 1975. pap. 44.00 (*0-685-53313-1*) J Benjamins Pubng Co.

Abraham, Werner, et al, eds. Discourse Grammar & Typology: Papers in Honor of John W. M. Verhaar. LC 94-44089. (Studies in Language Companion Ser.: No. 27). xx, 352p. 1995. lib. bdg. 98.00 (*1-55619-379-3*) J Benjamins Pubng Co.

— Issues in Germanic Syntax. (Trends in Linguistics, Studies & Monographs: No. 44). x, 398p. (C). 1990. lib. bdg. 129.25 (*3-11-012205-7*) Mouton.

— Minimal Ideas: Syntactic Studies in the Minimalist Framework. LC 96-26359. (Linguistik Aktuell/Linguistics Today Ser.: Vol. 12). xii, 364p. 1996. pap. 29.95 (*1-55619-231-2*); lib. bdg. 89.00 (*1-55619-230-4*) J Benjamins Pubng Co.

Abraham, Werner & DeMeij, Sjaak. Topic Focus & Configurationality: Papers from the 6th Groningen Grammar Talks. Groningen, 1984. LC 85-17515. (Linguistik Aktuell/Linguistics Today Ser.: No. 4). v, 349p. 1986. 97.00 (*90-272-2724-1*) J Benjamins Pubng Co.

Abraham, Werner, ed. see Nedkilalkov, V. P.

Abraham, Willard. Parent Talk. LC 96-41025. (Illus.). 176p. (Orig.). 1996. pap. 14.95 (*1-57022-053-0*, ECS0530) ECS Lrn Systs.

Abraham, William J. Canon & Criterion in Christian Theology: From the Fathers to Feminism. 520p. 1998. text 110.00 (*0-19-826939-0*) OUP.

— An Introduction to the Philosophy of Religion. 250p. (C). 1984. pap. text 39.00 (*0-13-491887-8*) P-H.

— The Logic of Evangelism. 208p. (Orig.). (C). 1989. pap. 16.00 (*0-8028-0433-0*) Eerdmans.

— Unity, Liberty, & Charity: Building Bridges under Icy Waters. Messer, Donald E., ed. LC 96-11266. 1996. pap. 12.95 (*0-687-03306-3*) Abingdon.

— Waking from Doctrinal Amnesia: The Healing of Doctrine in the United Methodist Church. 128p. (Orig.). 1995. pap. 9.95 (*0-687-01718-1*) Abingdon.

Abraham, William J., ed. Evangelism: Essays by Albert Outler Cook. 1998. 19.95 (*1-885224-17-6*) Bristol Hse.

Abraham, William J. & Holtzer, Steven W., eds. The Rationality of Religious Belief: Essays in Honour of Basil Mitchell. 278p. 1987. 72.00 (*0-19-826675-8*) OUP.

Abraham, William J. & Prevost, Robert W., eds. How to Play Theological Ping-Pong: And Other Essays on Faith. LC 91-4481. 218p. reprint ed. pap. 67.60 (*0-7837-6564-9*, 204612900011) Bks Demand.

Abrahamian, Ervand. The Iranian Mojahedin. LC 88-51382. 315p. (C). 1992. reprint ed. pap. 20.00 (*0-300-05267-7*) Yale U Pr.

— The Iranian Mujahedin. LC 88-51382. 320p. (C). 1989. text 32.00 (*0-300-04423-2*) Yale U Pr.

— Khomeinism: Essays on the Islamic Republic. LC 92-39849. 1993. 60.00 (*0-520-08173-0*, Pub. by U CA Pr); pap. 18.95 (*0-520-08503-5*, Pub. by U CA Pr) Cal Prin Full Svc.

— Radical Islam: The Iranian Mojahedin. LC 88-177094. (Society & Culture in the Modern Middle East Ser.). viii, 307 p. 1989. write for info. (*1-85043-083-7*) I B T.

Abrahamian, Ervand. Tortured Confessions: Prisons & Public Recantations in Modern Iran. LC 98-42989. 284p. 1999. pap. 16.95 (*0-520-21866-3*, Pub. by U CA Pr) Cal Prin Full Svc.

***Abrahamian, Ervand.** Tortured Confessions: Prisons & Public Recantations in Modern Iran. LC 98-42989. 284p. 1999. 45.00 (*0-520-21623-7*, Pub. by U CA Pr) Cal Prin Full Svc.

***Abrahamov, Binyamin.** Islamic Theology: Traditionalism & Rationalism. 160p. 1999. 25.00 (*0-7486-1102-9*) Polygon.

Abrahamov, Binyamin, ed. Al-Kasim B. Ibrahim on the Proof of God's Existence: Kitab al-Dalil al-Kabir. (Islamic Philosophy, Theology & Science, Studies & Texts Ser.: Vol. V). xiii, 201p. 1990. 88.00 (*90-04-08985-3*) Brill Academic Pubs.

Abrahamov, Binyamin & Al-Mustarshid, Kitab. Anthropomorphism & Interpretation of the Qur'an in the Theology of al-Qasim Ibn Ibrahim. (Islamic Philosophy, Theology & Science, Studies & Texts Ser.: No. 26). (ARA & ENG.). 164p. 1996. 60.50 (*90-04-10408-9*) Brill Academic Pubs.

Abrahams, Allen, jt. auth. see Morganstern, Steven.

Abrahams, Athol D., ed. Hillslope Processes. (Binghamton Symposia in Geomorphology: International Ser.: No. 16). 400p. 1986. pap. text 90.00 (*0-04-551102-0*) Routledge.

Abrahams, Cecil. The Romantic Vision of Alex la Guma & Other Critical Essays. 1997. pap. 18.95 (*0-86543-579-0*) Africa World.

Abrahams, Cecil, ed. Memories of Home: The Writings of Alex La Guma. LC 91-70746. 106p. 1992. 29.95 (*0-86543-234-1*); pap. 9.95 (*0-86543-235-X*) Africa World.

— The Romantic Vision of Alex la Guma & Other Critical Essays. 261p. 59.95 (*0-86543-578-2*) Africa World.

— The Tragic Life: Bessie Head & Literature in Southern Africa. LC 90-81309. (C). 1990. 29.95 (*0-86543-176-0*); pap. 9.95 (*0-86543-177-9*) Africa World.

Abrahams-Curiel, Diana, tr. see Linssen, Robert.

Abrahams, D. Mark & Rizzardi, Fran. BLISS: The Berkeley Interactive Statistical System. (Orig.). (C). 1988. pap. text 37.50 (*0-393-95586-9*) Norton.

Abrahams, E. M. A Comparative Survey of Hindu, Christian, & Jewish Mysticism. LC 95-900086. (C). 1995. 28.00 (*81-7030-406-7*, Pub. by Sri Satguru Pubns) S Asia.

Abrahams, Edith, jt. auth. see Tauben, Carol.

Abrahams, Frank & Head, Paul. Case Studies in Music Education. 180p. (C). 1998. pap. 17.95 (*1-57999-026-6*) GIA Pubns.

Abrahams, Gerald. Technique in Chess. 2nd ed. 216p. 1973. reprint ed. pap. 5.95 (*0-486-22953-X*) Dover.

Abrahams, Harold J. Heroic Efforts at Meteor Crater, Arizona: Selected Correspondence Between Daniel Moreau Barringer & Elihu Thomson. LC 78-75170. 480p. 1983. 45.00 (*0-8386-2399-9*) Fairleigh Dickinson.

Abrahams, I. Campaigns in Palestine from Alexander the Great. (British Academy, London, Schweich Lectures on Biblical Archaeology Series, 1930). 1972. reprint ed. pap. 25.00 (*0-8115-1264-9*) Periodicals Srv.

Abrahams, I., tr. see Cassuto, U.

Abrahams, I., tr. see Urbach, E. E.

Abrahams, Israel. The Book of Delight & Other Papers. Katz, Steven, ed. LC 79-7124. (Jewish Philosophy, Mysticism & History of Ideas Ser.). 1980. reprint ed. lib. bdg. 29.95 (*0-405-12238-1*) Ayer.

— By-Paths in Hebraic Bookland. LC 77-174368. (Illus.). 1977. reprint ed. 19.95 (*0-405-08177-4*, Pub. by Blom Pubns) Ayer.

— Jewish Life in the Middle Ages. 452p. 1993. reprint ed. pap. 24.95 (*0-8276-0542-0*) JPS Phila.

Abrahams, Israel & Buchler, Adolf. The Foundations of Jewish Life: Three Studies. LC 73-2197. (Jewish People; History, Religion, Literature Ser.). 1979. 42.95 (*0-405-05263-4*) Ayer.

Abrahams, J. & Stollard, Paul. Fire from First Principles: A Design Guide to Building Fire Safety. (Illus.). 164p. 1991. pap. 27.95 (*0-419-15280-6*, E & FN Spon) Routledge.

Abrahams, Jeffrey. Mission Statement Book: 301 Corporate Mission Statements from America's Top Companies. rev. ed. LC 99-23607. 640p. 1999. pap. text 21.95 (*1-58008-132-0*) Ten Speed Pr.

Abrahams, John, jt. auth. see Stollard, P.

Abrahams, John R. The Manager's Guide to Centrex. LC 88-24218. 116p. reprint ed. pap. 36.00 (*0-7837-0412-7*, 204073400018) Bks Demand.

Abrahams, Jonathan. Clubsmarts: Buying Golf Clubs That Work. LC 93-43262. (Illus.). 96p. 1994. pap. 12.95 (*1-55821-272-8*) Burford Bks.

— First Tee: A Beginner's Guide to Golf. LC 95-50285. (Illus.). 168p. (Orig.). 1996. pap. 15.95 (*1-55821-445-3*, 14453) Burford Bks.

Abrahams, Lewis. New York Election Laws. lxi, 588p. 1950. suppl. ed. 40.00 (*0-89941-598-9*, 501850) W S Hein.

Abrahams, Lionel. Celibacy of Felix Greenspan. 181p. 1993. reprint ed. 21.95 (*0-89733-396-9*) Academy Chi Pubs.

Abrahams, Marc. The Best of Annals of Improbable Research. LC 97-14025. 256p. 1997. pap. text 14.95 (*0-7167-3094-4*) W H Freeman.

Abrahams, Marc, ed. Sex As a Heap of Malfunctioning Rubble: More of the Best of the Journal of Irreproducible Results. LC 92-50286. (Illus.). 208p. 1993. pap. 9.95 (*1-56305-312-8*, 3312) Workman Pub.

Abrahams, Mike & Sparham, Laurie. Still War: Photographs from the North of Ireland. Ziff, Trisha, ed. (Illus.). 128p. (Orig.). (C). 1990. pap. 20.00 (*0-941533-86-7*, NAB) I R Dee.

Abrahams, Olga. Flashcard, No. 3: Seiko & Spider's Thread. 1985. pap. 8.95 (*9971-972-25-5*) OMF Bks.

Abrahams, Paul P. The Foreign Expansion of American Finance & Its Relationship to the Foreign Economic Policies of the United States, 1907-1921. Bruchey, Stuart & Bruchey, Eleanor, eds. LC 76-4762. (American Business Abroad Ser.). 1976. 23.95 (*0-405-09262-8*) Ayer.

Abrahams, Paul W. OS/2 for the Impatient. (C). 1997. pap. text. write for info. (*0-201-59146-4*) Addison-Wesley.

Abrahams, Paul W. UNIX for the Hyperimpatient. 2nd ed. 1997. pap. text 29.95 (*0-201-41991-2*) Addison-Wesley.

Abrahams, Paul W. UNIX for the Impatient. 2nd ed. 1995. pap. text 29.25 (*0-201-60965-7*) Addison-Wesley.

— UNIX para Impacientes. (SPA.). 624p. (C). 1994. pap. text 28.33 (*0-201-62578-4*) Addison-Wesley.

Abrahams, Paul W. & Larson, Bruce R. Unix for Impatient Bk/Cd. 2nd ed. 896p. 1997. pap. text 54.95 (*0-201-41979-3*) Addison-Wesley.

— UNIX for the Impatient. 2nd ed. LC 95-14174. 864p. (C). 1996. pap. 29.95 (*0-201-82376-4*) Addison-Wesley.

***Abrahams, Paul W., et al.** XML for the Impatient. 352p. 2000. pap. 29.95 (*0-201-48554-0*) Addison-Wesley.

***Abrahams, Peter.** The Black Experience in the 20th Century: An Autobiography & Meditation. LC 00-31932. (Illus.). (C). 2001. write for info. (*0-253-33833-6*) Ind U Pr.

— Crying Wolf. LC 99-41500. (Illus.). 336p. 2000. 25.00 (*0-345-42385-2*) Ballantine Pub Grp.

Abrahams, Peter. The Fan. 1996. pap. 5.99 (*0-614-98107-7*) Warner Bks.

— The Fan. large type ed. LC 96-7733. 352p. 1996. lib. bdg. 24.95 (*1-57490-062-5*, Beeler LP Bks) T T Beeler.

— McMinn's Color Atlas of Human Anatomy. 4th ed. (Illus.). 1998. pap. text 40.00 (*0-7234-2772-0*, Pub. by Wolfe Pub) Mosby Inc.

— Mine Boy. (African Writers Ser.). 192p. (C). 1989. pap. 9.95 (*0-435-90562-7*, 90562) Heinemann.

— A Perfect Crime. 1999. mass mkt. 6.99 (*0-345-42680-0*) Ballantine Pub Grp.

***Abrahams, Peter.** A Perfect Crime. LC 98-48258. 1999. 28.95 (*0-7838-8476-1*) Macmillan Gen Ref.

Abrahams, Peter. Revolution, No. 9. 320p. 1993. mass mkt. 5.50 (*0-446-40156-0*, Pub. by Warner Bks) Little.

— A Wreath for Udomo. LC 83-45608. reprint ed. 45.00 (*0-404-20001-X*) AMS Pr.

Abrahams, Peter, jt. auth. see Ger, Ralph.

Abrahams, Peter H., et al. Problem Solving for Tutorials in Anatomy. LC 95-11349. Orig. Title: Pocket Examiner in Regional & Clinical Anatomy. 1995. reprint ed. pap. text 29.95 (*0-443-05285-9*) Church.

Abrahams, Peter H., jt. auth. see Weir, Jamie.

Abrahams, R. G. The Nyamwezi Today: A Tanzanian People in the 1970s. LC 80-41012. (Changing Cultures Ser.). 159p. reprint ed. pap. 45.40 (*0-608-15687-6*, 2031613) Bks Demand.

— The Peoples of Greater Unyamwezi, Tanzania (Nyamwezi, Sukuma, Sumbwa, Kimbu, Konongo) LC 67-111104. (Ethnographic Survey of Africa: East Central Africa Ser.: Pt. 17). 97p. reprint ed. pap. 30.10 (*0-8357-3207-X*, 205707700010) Bks Demand.

— The Political Organization of Unyamwezi. LC 67-12842. (Cambridge Studies in Social Anthropology: No. 1). 228p. reprint ed. pap. 65.00 (*0-608-17017-8*, 2027274) Bks Demand.

A

Abrahams, Ray. A Place of Their Own: Family Farming in Eastern Finland. (Cambridge Studies in Social & Cultural Anthropology: No. 81). (Illus.). 222p. (C). 1991. text 80.00 (0-521-38100-2) Cambridge U Pr.

— Vigilant Citizens: Vigilantism & the State. LC 98-25560. 224p. 1999. 57.95 (0-7456-1637-2); pap. 26.95 (0-7456-1638-0) Blackwell Pubs.

Abrahams, Ray, ed. After Socialism: Land Reform & Rural Social Change in Eastern Europe. LC 96-38. 256p. 1996. 59.95 (1-57181-910-X) Berghahn Bks.

Abrahams, Roger, et al, eds. By Land & by Sea: Folklore of Work & Leisure in Honor of Horace C. Beck. LC 85-80879. (Orig.). (C). 1985. pap. 20.00 (0-913714-68-2) Legacy Books.

Abrahams, Roger D. Afro-American Folktales: Stories from Black Traditions in the New World. (Pantheon Fairy Tale & Folklore Library). (J). 1985. 21.10 (0-606-03706-3, Pub. by Turtleback) Demco.

Abrahams, Roger D. Deep down in the Jungle: Negro Narrative Folklore from the Streets of Philadelphia. rev. ed. LC 78-124404. 287p. 1970. pap. text 26.95 (0-202-01092-9) Aldine de Gruyter.

Abrahams, Roger D., ed. African-American Folktales: Stories from Black Traditions in the New World. LC 98-42200. 1999. pap. 16.00 (0-375-70539-2) Pantheon.

— African Folktales: Traditional Stories of the Black World. LC 83-2474. (Fairy Tale & Folklore Library). 384p. 1983. pap. 18.00 (0-394-72117-9) Pantheon.

Abrahams, Roger D. & Rankin, Lois, eds. Counting-Out Rhymes: A Dictionary. LC 79-22260. (Publications of the American Folklore Society, Bibliographical & Special Ser.: No. 33). 263p. reprint ed. pap. 81.60 (0-7837-0090-3, 204036500016) Bks Demand.

Abrahams, Roger D., jt. auth. see Szwad, John F.

Abrahams, Roger D., jt. auth. see Zumwalt, Rosemary L.

Abrahams, S. C., ed. Accuracy in X-Ray Intensity Measurements. (Transactions of the American Crystallographic Association Ser.: Vol. 1). 112p. 1965. pap. 25.00 (0-686-60372-9) Polycrystal Bk Serv.

Abrahams, William, jt. auth. see Stansky, Peter.

Abrahams, William. Lillian Hellman Biography. 1995. write for info. (0-316-00433-2) Little.

Abrahamse, A., jt. auth. see Carroll, S.

Abrahamse, Allan. The Coming Wave of Violence in California. LC 98-120887. (Illus.). 13p. (Orig.). 1997. pap. 6.00 (0-8330-2537-6, DB-228-IF) Rand Corp.

Abrahamse, Allan, et al. The Costs of Excess Medical Claims for Automobile Personal Injuries. LC 95-221873. (Illus.). 28p. 1995. pap. text 6.00 (0-8330-1649-0, DB-139) Rand Corp.

— Three Strikes & You're Out: Estimated Benefits & Costs of California's New Mandatory-Sentencing Law. LC 94-37970. 1994. pap. text 13.00 (0-8330-1597-4, MR-509-RC) Rand Corp.

Abrahamse, Allan, jt. auth. see Vernez, George.

Abrahamse, Allan F. & Carroll, Stephen J. The Effects of a Choice Auto Insurance Plan on Insurance Costs. LC 95-16231. 74p. 1995. pap. text 13.00 (0-8330-1641-5, MR-540-ICJ) Rand Corp.

Abrahamse, Allan F., jt. auth. see Carroll, Stephen J.

Abrahamsen, Adele, jt. ed. see Bechtel, William.

Abrahamsen, Aron. Holiday in Heaven. 240p. 1998. pap. 12.95 (0-9662045-0-6) A & D Abrahamsen.

Abrahamsen, David. Confessions of Son of Sam. LC 84-21487. 256p. 1985. text 19.95 (0-231-05760-1) Col U Pr.

— Murder & Madness: The Secret Life of Jack the Ripper. 240p. 1993. mass mkt. 4.99 (0-380-71993-2, Avon Bks) Morrow Avon.

— The Psychology of Crime. LC 59-13606. 372p. reprint ed. pap. 115.40 (0-608-12521-0, 202497600040) Bks Demand.

— Who Are the Guilty? A Study of Education & Crime. LC 70-143306. 340p. 1972. reprint ed. lib. bdg. 69.50 (0-8371-5807-9, ABWG, Greenwood Pr) Greenwood.

Abrahamsen, Gunnar, et al, eds. Long-Term Experiments with Acid Rain in Norwegian Forest Ecosystems. LC 93-28646. (Ecological Studies: Vol. 104). 1993. 118.00 (0-387-94119-3) Spr-Verlag.

Abrahamsen, Martin A. & Scroggs, Claud L., eds. Agricultural Cooperation: Selected Readings. LC 57-7008. 590p. reprint ed. pap. 182.90 (0-8357-5266-6, 205583300039) Bks Demand.

Abrahamsen, Samuel. Norway's Response to the Holocaust: An Historical Perspective. LC 90-82993. (Illus.). 200p. 1991. pap. 13.95 (0-89604-117-4, Holocaust Library) US Holocaust.

— Say It in Norwegian. (Orig.). 1957. pap. 3.95 (0-486-20814-1) Dover.

Abrahamsen, Valerie A. Women & Worship at Phillipi: Diana, Artemis & Other Cults. LC 95-5491. (Illus.). 256p. 1995. per. 16.95 (1-885349-00-9) Astarte Shell Pr.

Abrahamson, Adele, jt. auth. see Bechtel, William.

Abrahamson, Charles, ed. The Holy Mountains of the World: Charged in Operation Starlight. LC 94-70169. (Illus.). 129p. (Orig.). 1994. pap. 14.95 (0-937249-14-9) Aetherius Soc.

Abrahamson, David. Magazine-Made America: The Cultural Transformation of the Postwar Periodical. Becker, Lee, ed. (Communication Ser.). 128p. (Orig.). (C). 1996. text 42.50 (1-57273-008-0); pap. text 18.95 (1-57273-009-9) Hampton Pr NJ.

Abrahamson, David, ed. The American Magazine: Research Perspectives & Prospects. LC 94-29798. 262p. 1995. pap. text 39.95 (0-8138-2484-2) Iowa St U Pr.

Abrahamson, Dean E., ed. The Challenge of Global Warming. LC 89-1830. (Illus.). 356p. 1989. text 45.00 (0-933280-87-4); pap. text 25.00 (0-933280-86-6) Island Pr.

Abrahamson, Debbie, et al. Advocacy, 1998-99. 3rd ed. (Inns of Court School of Law Ser.). 399p. 1998. pap. 42.00 (1-85431-770-9) Gaunt.

— Advocacy, 1997/98. 2nd ed. (Inns of Court School of Law Ser.). 392p. 1997. pap. 40.00 (1-85431-672-9, Pub. by Blackstone Pr) Gaunt.

— Professional Conduct, 1998-99. 3rd ed. LC 98-181977. (Inns of Court School of Law Ser.). 366p. 1998. pap. 42.00 (1-85431-773-3) Gaunt.

— Professional Conduct, 1997-98. 2nd ed. (Inns of Court School of Law Ser.). 362p. 1997. pap. 40.00 (1-85431-680-X, Pub. by Blackstone Pr) Gaunt.

Abrahamson, Irving. Against Silence: The Voice & Vision of Elie Wiesel, 3 vols., 1. 1188p. 1985. write for info. (0-89604-075-5, Holocaust Library) US Holocaust.

— Against Silence: The Voice & Vision of Elie Wiesel, 3 vols., 2. 1188p. 1985. write for info. (0-89604-076-3, Holocaust Library) US Holocaust.

— Against Silence: The Voice & Vision of Elie Wiesel, 3 vols., 3. 1188p. 1985. write for info. (0-89604-077-1, Holocaust Library) US Holocaust.

— Against Silence: The Voice & Vision of Elie Wiesel, 3 vols., Set. 1188p. 1987. 39.95 (0-89604-157-3, Holocaust Library) US Holocaust.

***Abrahamson, James A.** Confessions of a Diplomatic Pouch Clerk. (Illus.). 539p. 1999. pap. write for info. (0-7541-0422-2, Pub. by Minerva Pr) Unity Dist.

***Abrahamson, James L.** The Men of Secession & Civil War, 1859-1861. LC 99-89807. (American Crisis Ser.: No. 1). (Illus.). 208p. 2000. 55.00 (0-8420-2818-8); pap. 17.95 (0-8420-2819-6) Scholarly Res Inc.

Abrahamson, Jeffery, jt. auth. see Abrahamson, Patt.

Abrahamson, Joseph R. M - E: The God Within. 130p. 1992. 22.00 (0-9633462-0-2); pap., per. 10.00 (0-9633462-1-0) Waverly Pubns.

Abrahamson, Julia. A Neighborhood Finds Itself. 370p. 1972. reprint ed. 30.00 (0-8196-0268-X) Biblo.

Abrahamson, M. W. Engin Law & The Ice Contracts. 4th ed. 486p. (C). (gr. 13). 1979. 200.00 (0-419-16080-9) Chapman & Bkman.

Abrahamson, M. W. Engineering Law & the I.C.E. Contracts. 4th ed. 485p. 1979. mass mkt. 197.95 (0-85334-826-X) Elsevier.

Abrahamson, Mark. Grand Central Oyster Bar & Restaurant Cookbook. (Illus.). 376p. 1996. 27.50 (1-55670-534-4) Stewart Tabori & Chang.

— Out-of-Wedlock Births: The United States in Comparative Perspective. LC 97-43954. 184p. 1998. 55.00 (0-275-95662-8, Praeger Pubs); pap. 18.95 (0-275-95665-2, Praeger Pubs) Greenwood.

Abrahamson, Patt & Abrahamson, Jeffery. Brain Injury: A Family Tragedy. LC 97-11774. (Illus.). xx, 240p. 1997. 19.50 (1-882855-56-6) HDI Pubs.

Abrahamson, Robert L. Good English Models: A Handbook. LC 87-37341. (University of Maryland Series on Good English Writing). 1988. 8.95 (0-06-317502-9) HarpC.

Abrahamson, Royce L., jt. auth. see Pickle, Hal B.

Abrahamson, Seymour, jt. ed. see McElheny, Victor K.

Abrahamson, Seymour, jt. ed. see Peterson, Leif E.

Abrahamson, Stephen. Essays on Medical Education: (S. A.'s on Medical Education) LC 96-17730. 162p. 1996. lib. bdg. 32.50 (0-7618-0366-1) U Pr of Amer.

— Evaluation of Continuing Education in the Health Professions. 1985. lib. bdg. 80.50 (0-89838-168-1) Kluwer Academic.

Abrahamson, Vickie, jt. auth. see Janz, Wes.

Abrahamson, Warren G. & Weis, Arthur E. Evolutionary Ecology Across Three Trophic Levels: Goldenrods, Gallmakers, & Natural Enemies. LC 96-42051. (Monographs in Population Biology). 456p. 1997. text 75.00 (0-691-03733-7, Pub. by Princeton U Pr); pap. text 29.95 (0-691-01208-3, Pub. by Princeton U Pr) Cal Prin Full Svc.

Abrahamsson, Bengt. The Logic of Organizations. LC 92-33509. (Illus.). 200p. (C). 1993. text 42.00 (0-8039-5038-1); pap. text 22.95 (0-8039-5039-X) Sage.

— Why Organizations? How - & Why - People Organize. (Illus.). 312p. (C). 1993. text 45.00 (0-8039-5040-3); pap. text 23.95 (0-8039-5041-1) Sage.

Abrahamsson, Bernhard J. International Ocean Shipping: Current Concepts & Principles. (Illus.). 250p. 1980. pap. text 74.50 (0-89158-875-2) Westview.

Abrahamsson, Hans. The Origin of Death: Studies in African Mythology. Kastenbaum, Robert J., ed. LC 76-19555. (Death & Dying Ser.). 1979. reprint ed. lib. bdg. 25.95 (0-405-09551-1) Ayer.

Abrahamsson, Hans & Nilsson, Anders. Mozambique: The Troubled Transition. LC 95-21717. (Illus.). 256p. (C). 1995. text 65.00 (1-85649-323-7, Pub. by Zed Books) St Martin.

Abrahamsson, Kenneth. Adult Participation in Swedish Higher Education: A Study of Organizational Structure, Educational Design, & Current Policies. 121p. (Orig.). 1986. pap. text 33.00 (91-22-00850-0) Coronet Bks.

Abrahanm, Ken & Abraham, Angela, compiled by. A Treasury of Wisdom: Daily Inspiration from Favorite Christian Authors. LC 99-161901. 384p. 1998. lthr. 4.97 (1-57748-204-2) Barbour Pub.

Abrahart, Robert J., jt. auth. see Openshaw, Stan.

Abrahas, Roger D., et al, eds. Fields of Folklore: Essays in Honor of Kenneth S. Goldstein. (Illus.). 339p. (Orig.). 1919. pap. 514.95 (0-915305-05-4) Trickster Pr.

***Abrahm, J.** A Physician's Guide to Pain & Symptom Management in Cancer Patients LC 99-37061. 2000. 26.00 (0-8018-6246-9) Johns Hopkins.

Abrahms, Sally, jt. auth. see Smith, Gayle Rosenwald.

Abraitys, Vincent. The Backyard Wilderness: From the Canadian Maritimes to the Florida Keys. LC 74-80236. (Illus.). 208p. 1975. 10.95 (0-914366-02-5) Columbia Pub.

— Wayside Simples & Grateful Herbs. LC 76-19236. (Illus.). 1980. pap. 8.95 (0-914366-08-4) Columbia Pub.

Abram. Tourists & Tourism. LC 97-202749. 1997. 55.00 (1-85973-900-8, Pub. by Berg Pubs); pap. 19.50 (1-85973-905-9, Pub. by Berg Pubs) NYU Pr.

Abram, jt. auth. see Murdoch.

***Abram, Alvin.** The Light after the Dark: Six True Stories of Triumph after All Hope Has Gone... (Illus.). 304p. 1998. pap. 16.95 (1-55013-998-3, Pub. by Key Porter) Firefly Bks Ltd.

Abram, Dave, et al. The Rough Guide to South India. (Illus.). 352p. 2000. 19.95 (1-85828-469-4, Pub. by Rough Guides) Penguin Putnam.

Abram, David. The Rough Guide to Goa. 3rd ed. (Illus.). 304p. 1999. 16.95 (1-85828-441-4, Pub. by Rough Guides) Penguin Putnam.

— The Spell of the Sensuous: Perception & Language in a More-Than-Human World. 1997. pap. 14.00 (0-679-77639-7) Random.

Abram, David, et al. The Rough Guide to India. 3rd ed. (Illus.). 1344p. 1999. 24.95 (1-85828-445-7, Pub. by Rough Guides) Penguin Putnam.

Abram, Gary & O'Byrne, Bob. Distance to the Green: A Caddy's Lessons in Life, Business & Golf. 176p. (Orig.). 1997. pap. 12.95 (1-886816-06-9) Plan II Publ.

Abram, I. B. Jewish Tradition As Permanent Education. (Selecta Reeks Ser.: Vol. 50). vi, 284p. 1986. 20.00 (90-6472-072-X) Taylor & Francis.

Abram, Jaffe, ed. Puerto Rican Population of New York City. LC 74-14328. (Puerto Rican Experience Ser.). 65p. 1975. reprint ed. 13.95 (0-405-06226-5) Ayer.

Abram, Jan & Karnac, Harry. The Language of Winnicott: A Dictionary & Guide to Understanding His Work. LC 96-50065. 400p. 1997. 50.00 (1-56821-700-5) Aronson.

Abram, Jan, ed. see Green, Andre.

Abram, Joseph. Devanthery & Lamuniere: Four Examples. LC 96-219489. (Illus.). 96p. 1996. pap. 35.00 (3-7643-5435-6, Pub. by Birkhauser) Princeton Arch.

Abram, Joseph, et al. Columbia Documents of Architecture & Theory, Vol. 5. Tschumi, Bernard et al, eds. (Illus.). 170p. (Orig.). (C). 1995. pap. text 15.00 (1-883584-04-3) CUGSA.

Abram, Martin & Skidmore, Steve. Delta, Data & You. LC 84-22102. 131p. reprint ed. pap. 40.70 (0-608-17865-9, 203269500080) Bks Demand.

Abram, Norm. Measure Twice, Cut Once: Lessons from a Master Carpenter. (Illus.). 208p. (gr. 8). 1996. 18.00 (0-316-00494-4) Little.

— Mostly Shaker from the New Yankee Workshop. 1992. 35.00 (0-316-00473-1); pap. 22.00 (0-316-00475-8) Little.

— The New Yankee Workshop. (Illus.). 196p. 1989. 29.95 (0-316-00453-7); pap. 21.95 (0-316-00454-5) Little.

— New Yankee Workshop Kids' Stuff. LC 97-17889. (Illus.). 208p. 1998. pap. 19.95 (0-316-00492-8) Little.

Abram, Norm & Walker, Roland. The New Yankee Workshop Outdoor Projects. LC 93-42574. 204p. 1994. pap. 22.00 (0-316-00486-3) Little.

Abram, R. A. & Jaros, M., eds. Band Structure Engineering in Semiconductor Microstructures. (NATO ASI Ser.: Vol. 189). (Illus.). 400p. (C). 1988. text 155.00 (0-306-43080-0, Kluwer Plenum) Kluwer Academic.

Abram, Robert E., et al. Preparing for High Technology: CAD-CAM Programs. 79p. 1983. 6.50 (0-318-22175-6, RD234) Ctr Educ Trng Employ.

— Preparing for High Technology: Thirty Steps to Implementation. 49p. 1983. 6.50 (0-318-22178-0, RD232) Ctr Educ Trng Employ.

— Preparing for High Technology Bk. I: Programs That Work. 55p. 1982. 4.95 (0-318-22172-1, RD229) Ctr Educ Trng Employ.

Abram, Ruth. Send Us a Lady Physician: Women Doctors in America, 1835-1920. LC 85-13856. (Illus.). 1986. pap. 12.95 (0-393-30278-4) Norton.

Abram, Simone & Waldren, Jacqueline, eds. Anthropological Perspectives on Local Development: Knowledges & Sentiments in Conflict. LC 99-163030. (European Association of Social Anthropologists Ser.). (Illus.). 176p. (C). (gr. 13). 1998. 75.00 (0-415-18277-8, D6011); pap. 24.99 (0-415-18278-6, D6015) Routledge.

Abram, Stephen E., et al. The Pain Clinic Manual. (Illus.). 458p. 1990. pap. text 52.00 (0-397-50936-7) Lppncott W & W.

Abram, Victor P. Restoration of All Things. LC 62-18059. 149p. 1962. 6.00 (0-910840-07-5) Kingdom.

Abramchik, Lois. Is Your Family Like Mine? Cavallo, Barbara L., ed. (Illus.). 32p. (Orig.). (J). (gr. k-6). 1996. pap. 11.95 (0-9647145-0-7) Open Hrt Open Mind.

Abrames, J. Kenney. Striper Moon. (Illus.). 48p. 1994. pap. 15.95 (1-878175-67-X) F Amato Pubns.

Abramiam, Jackie. Conversations with Contemporary Armenian Artists. (Illus.). 200p. (Orig.). (C). 1990. pap. 12.50 (0-915597-78-0) Amana Bks.

Abramms, Bob, et al, eds. Cultural Diversity Fieldbook: Fresh Visions & Breakthrough Strategies for Revitalizing the U. S. Workplace. (Pacesetter Bks.). (Illus.). 272p. (Orig.). 1996. pap. 26.95 (1-56079-602-2, Petersons Pacesetter) Petersons.

Abramo, Tehilla, jt. auth. see Abramov, Yirmiyohu.

Abramo, Thomas J. Pediatric Conscious Sedation: Agents & Procedures-Specific Procedures, 2 vols., Pt. II. 84p. (C). (gr. 13). 1995. pap. text 155.00 (0-8151-0804-4) Mosby Inc.

Abramo, Thomas J. Pediatric Conscious Sedation Pt. I: Agents & Procedures, Package. 36p. 1996. write for info. (0-8151-0805-2) Mosby Inc.

— Pediatric Conscious Sedation Pt. II: Specific Procedures: Case Studies, Package. 48p. 1996. write for info. (0-8151-0808-7) Mosby Inc.

Abramoff. Cell Structure. Date not set. 1.20 (0-7167-9017-3) W H Freeman.

— Cell Structure & Function. Date not set. 1.20 (0-7167-9083-1) W H Freeman.

— Cellular Reproduction. Date not set. 1.50 (0-7167-9032-7); 1.20 (0-7167-9085-8) W H Freeman.

— Cellular Respiration. Date not set. 1.20 (0-7167-9088-2) W H Freeman.

— Chemical Aspects of Life. Date not set. 1.20 (0-7167-9011-4) W H Freeman.

— Chromosomal Basis of Hereditary. 1998. 1.20 (0-7167-9091-2) St Martin.

— Early Development of the Chick. Date not set. 1.20 (0-7167-9113-7) W H Freeman.

— Energy Capture: Photosynthesis. Date not set. 1.20 (0-7167-9024-6) W H Freeman.

— Enzymes. Date not set. 1.20 (0-7167-9087-4) W H Freeman.

— Expression of Gene Activity. Date not set. 1.20 (0-7167-9093-9) W H Freeman.

— Extraction of Proteins. Date not set. 1.50 (0-7167-9021-1) W H Freeman.

— Flowers & Fruits. 1998. 1.20 (0-7167-9101-3) St Martin.

— Human Genetics. Date not set. 1.20 (0-7167-9092-0) W H Freeman.

— Kingdom Animalia: Phylum Annel. Date not set. 1.20 (0-7167-9104-8) W H Freeman.

— Kingdom Animalia: Phylum Moll. Date not set. 1.20 (0-7167-9103-X) W H Freeman.

— Kingdom Fungi. Date not set. 1.50 (0-7167-9097-1) W H Freeman.

— Kingdom Monera, Vol. 1. Date not set. 1.20 (0-7167-9094-7) W H Freeman.

— Kingdom Plantae: The Bryophyte. Date not set. 1.50 (0-7167-9098-X) W H Freeman.

— Kingdom Plantae: The Vascular. Date not set. 1.50 (0-7167-9099-8) W H Freeman.

— Lab Manual. pap. text, lab manual ed. 16.00 (0-7167-2634-3) W H Freeman.

— Light Microscopy. Date not set. 1.50 (0-7167-9082-3) W H Freeman.

— Menedelian Genetics. Date not set. 1.20 (0-7167-9090-4) W H Freeman.

— Mitosis. Date not set. 1.20 (0-7167-9015-7) W H Freeman.

— Movement of Materials Through. Date not set. 1.50 (0-7167-9086-6) W H Freeman.

— Permeability of Cell Membranes. Date not set. 1.20 (0-7167-9020-3) W H Freeman.

— Photosynthesis. Date not set. 1.50 (0-7167-9089-0) W H Freeman.

— Plant Growth & Development. Date not set. 1.50 (0-7167-9118-8) W H Freeman.

— Respiration. Date not set. 1.20 (0-7167-9013-0) W H Freeman.

— Science of Biology. 1994. 60.80 (0-7167-2594-0) W H Freeman.

— Vertebrate Anatomy: External, Vol. 1. 2000. 1.50 (0-7167-9048-3) St Martin.

Abramoff, Larry, jt. auth. see Corey, Jack.

Abramoff, Lawrence J. Favorite Places of Worcester County: A Guide to Shopping, Dining, Recreation, Sightseeing, History, Facts & Fun. Tatnuck Bookseller & Sons Staff & Worcester Telegram & Gazette Staff, eds. LC 94-93946. 380p. (Orig.). 1995. pap. 13.95 (0-9636277-7-5) Chandler Hse.

Abramoff, Peter. Lab Separates in Biology. 1971. write for info. (0-7167-0600-8) W H Freeman.

Abramoff, Peter & Thompson, Robert G. Laboratory Outlines in Biology VI. 6th ed. LC 94-32653. 528p. (C). 1994. pap. text 32.95 (0-7167-2633-5) W H Freeman.

Abramoff, Peter & Thomson, Robert G. Laboratory Outlines in Biology. LC 90-3777. (Illus.). (C). 1991. pap. text 21.60 (0-7167-2142-2) W H Freeman.

— Laboratory Outlines in Biology. LC 90-3777. (Illus.). (C). 1991. teacher ed. 12.80 (0-7167-2208-9) W H Freeman.

Abramov, et al. Izbrannaia Proza Semidesiatykh: An Anthology of Russian Prose 1970s. LC 90-24236. (RUS.). 258p. (Orig.). 1990. pap. 14.00 (1-55779-028-0) Hermitage Pubs.

Abramov, A. & Avdohin, V. M. Oxidation of Sulfide Minerals in Benefication Processes. 336p. 1997. text 81.00 (90-5699-570-7) Gordon & Breach.

Abramov, Alexander P. Connectedness & Necessary Conditions for an Extremum. LC 97-49830. 199p. 1998. lib. bdg. 99.00 (0-7923-4910-5) Kluwer Academic.

Abramov, L. M., et al. Fifteen Papers on Topology & Logic. LC 51-5559. (Translations Ser.: Series 2, Vol. 39). 298p. 1964. 36.00 (0-8218-1739-6, TRANS2/39) Am Math.

— Fourteen Papers on Logic, Algebra, Complex Variables & Topology. LC 51-5559. (Translations Ser.: 2: Vol. 48). 396p. 1965. 44.00 (0-8218-1748-5, TRANS2/48) Am Math.

— Ten Papers on Functional Analysis & Measure Theory. LC 51-5559. (Translations Ser.: Series 2, Vol. 49). 268p. 1966. 35.00 (0-8218-1749-3, TRANS2/49) Am Math.

Abramov, O. V. High-Intensity Ultrasonics: Theory & Industrial Applications. 700p. 1998. text 180.00 (90-5699-041-1, ECU138) Gordon & Breach.

— Ultrasound in Liquid & Solid Metals. LC 93-25193. 512p. 1994. lib. bdg. 225.00 (0-8493-9355-8, TA369) CRC Pr.

Abramov, S. Zalman. Perpetual Dilemma: Jewish Religion in the Jewish State. LC 74-5897. 459p. 1976. 48.50 (0-8386-1687-9) Fairleigh Dickinson.

Abramov, Tehilla. Straight from the Heart: A Torah Perspective on Mothering Through Nursing. 156p. 1990. 17.95 (0-944070-18-3, Pub. by Targum Pr) Feldheim.

Abramov, Tehilla & Abramov, Yirmyohu. Our Family, Our Strength. 153p. 1997. 17.95 (1-56871-126-3, Pub. by Targum Pr) Feldheim.

An Asterisk (*) at the beginning of an entry indicates that the title is appearing for the first time.

Abramov, Tehilla & Touger, Malka. The Secret of Jewish Femininity: Insights into the Practice of Taharat Hamishpachah. 176p. 1988. 18.95 (*0-944070-04-3*, Pub. by Targum Pr) Feldheim.

Abramov, Tehilla, jt. auth. see Abramov, Yirmyohu.

Abramov, Valentin. Atlas of Arctic Icebergs: The Greenland, Barents, Kara, Laptev, East-Siberian, & Chukchi Seas, & the Arctic Basin. (Illus.). 78p. 1996. pap. 195.00 (*0-9644311-4-9*) Backbone Pubng.

Abramov, Yirmiyohu & Abramo, Tehilla. Harmony in the Home: An Educational Program for the Jewish Family. (Illus.). (J). (ps-5). 1996. pap. 12.95 (*1-56871-114-X*) Targum Pr.

Abramov, Yirmyohu & Abramov, Tehilla. Harmony in the Home: 25 Principles of Childrearing for Jewish Parents. 32p. 1996. pap. 12.95 (*1-56871-113-1*) Targum Pr.

Abramov, Yirmyohu, jt. auth. see Abramov, Tehilla.

Abramovic, Marina. The Bridge: El Puente. (Illus.). 302p. 1999. 45.00 (*84-482-1857-4*, Pub. by Charta) Dist Art Pubs.

— Objects Performance Video Sound. 144p. 1996. pap. 35.00 (*0-905836-88-X*, Pub. by Museum Modern Art) St Mut.

Abramovice, Ben. Long-Term Care Administration: The Management of Institutional & Non-Institutional Components of the Continuum of Care. LC 87-11949. (Series on Marketing & Health Services Administration: No. 1). 256p. (C). 1987. text 39.95 (*0-86656-399-7*) Haworth Pr.

Abramovich-Gomon, Alla. The Nenets' Song: A Microcosm of a Vanishing Culture. (Studies in Ethnomusicology: Vol. 4). (Illus.). 168p. 1999. text 74.95 (*1-84014-603-6*, Pub. by Ashgate Pub) Ashgate Pub Co.

Abramovich, I. I. & Klushin, I. G. Geodynamics & Metallogeny of Folded Belts. (Russian Translation Ser.: No. 78). (Illus.). 255p. (C). 1990. text 110.00 (*90-6191-932-0*, Pub. by A A Balkema) Ashgate Pub Co.

Abramovich, Ilya. Ne Zabyt' (Don't Forget) The Tragedy of Jews of Zin'kov. LC 90-85933. (RUS.). 112p. 1991. pap. text 10.00 (*0-911971-62-9*) Effect Pub.

Abramovich, Y. A., et al, eds. Functional Analysis & Economic Theory. LC 98-7945. (Illus.). viii, 296p. 1998. 109.00 (*3-540-64495-4*) Spr-Verlag.

***Abramovich, Y. A. & Kitover, A. K.** Inverses of Disjointness Preserving Operators. LC 99-54530. (Memoirs of the American Mathematical Society Ser.). 1999. write for info. (*0-8218-1397-8*) Am Math.

Abramovici, Miron, et al. Digital Systems Testing & Testable Design. rev. ed. 680p. 1994. 84.95 (*0-7803-1062-4*) Inst Electrical.

Abramovitc. Extra-Oral Radiography. (C). 1994. text. write for info. (*0-7216-2941-5*, W B Saunders Co) Harcrt Hlth Sci Grp.

Abramovitch, Henry Hanoch. The First Father: Abraham: the Psychology & Culture of a Spiritual Revolutionary. LC 92-42259. 1993. 42.50 (*0-8191-9027-6*) U Pr of Amer.

Abramovitch, R. A., ed. Reactive Intermediates, Vol. 2. LC 79-344. 614p. (C). 1982. 125.00 (*0-306-40594-6*, Plenum Trade) Perseus Pubng.

— Reactive Intermediates, Vol. 3. LC 82-15139. 644p. 1983. 125.00 (*0-306-40970-4*, Plenum Trade) Perseus Pubng.

Abramovits, Les, jt. auth. see Abromovitz, Hedy.

Abramovitsh, S. Y. Tales of Mendele the Book Peddler. 400p. 1996. pap. 15.00 (*0-8052-1013-X*) Schocken.

Abramovitz, Albert J., jt. ed. see Chatterjee, Pranab.

Abramovitz, Janet. Taking a Stand No. 140: Cultivating a New Relationship with the World's Forests. Peterson, Jane, ed. LC 98-60372. 70p. 1998. pap. 5.00 (*1-878071-42-4*) Worldwatch Inst.

Abramovitz, Janet N. Imperiled Waters, Impoverished Future: The Decline of Freshwater Ecosystems. 70p. (Orig.). 1996. pap. 5.00 (*1-878071-30-0*) Worldwatch Inst.

***Abramovitz, Janet N. & Mattoon, Ashley T.** Paper Cuts Vol. 149: Recovering the Paper Landscape. Peterson, Jane, ed. 80p. 1999. pap. 5.00 (*1-878071-51-3*) Worldwatch Inst.

Abramovitz, Janet N., jt. auth. see Borkenhagen, Lea M.

***Abramovitz, Les.** Long-Term Care Insurance Made Simple. LC 99-12994. 220p. 1999. pap. 14.95 (*1-885987-14-5*, ME094, Health Info Pr) Practice Mgmt Info.

Abramovitz, Melissa. Dependent Variables. 110p. (Orig.). 1991. pap. 9.99 (*0-945298-05-6*) Curtis Pubns.

Abramovitz, Mimi. Regulating the Lives of Women: Social Welfare Policy from Colonial Times to the Present. rev. ed. LC 96-9172. 412p. 1996. 40.00 (*0-89608-552-X*); pap. 22.00 (*0-89608-551-1*) South End Pr.

***Abramovitz, Mimi.** Under Attack, Fighting Back. 2nd rev. ed. LC 99-87575. 160p. 1999. pap. 15.00 (*1-58367-008-4*) Monthly Rev.

Abramovitz, Mimi. Under Attack, Fighting Back: Women & Welfare in the United States. (Conerstone Bks.). 1996. 26.00 (*0-85345-962-2*, Pub. by Monthly Rev) NYU Pr.

— Under Attack, Fighting Back: Women & Welfare in the United States. (Cornerstone Bks.). (Illus.). 160p. 1996. pap. 13.00 (*0-85345-963-0*, Pub. by Monthly Rev) NYU Pr.

Abramovitz, Moses. Approach to Price Theory for a Changing Economy. LC 73-38503. (Columbia University. Studies in the Social Sciences: No. 453). 1939. 27.50 (*0-404-51453-7*) AMS Pr.

— Evidences of Long Swings in Aggregate Construction since the Civil War. (Occasional Papers: No. 90). 252p. 1964. reprint ed. 65.60 (*0-87014-404-9*) Natl Bur Econ Res.

— Inventories & Business Cycles, with Special Reference to Manufacturer's Inventories. (Studies in Business Cycles: No. 4). 672p. 1950. reprint ed. 160.00 (*0-87014-087-6*) Natl Bur Econ Res.

— Resource & Output Trends in the United States since 1870. (Occasional Papers: No. 52). 23p. 1956. reprint ed. 20.00 (*0-87014-366-2*) Natl Bur Econ Res.

— The Role of Inventories in Business Cycles. (Occasional Papers: No. 26). 32p. 1948. reprint ed. 20.00 (*0-87014-341-7*) Natl Bur Econ Res.

— Thinking about Growth: And Other Essays on Economic Growth & Welfare. (Studies in Economic History & Policy: The United States in the Twentieth Century). (Illus.). 400p. (C). 1989. text 89.95 (*0-521-33396-2*) Cambridge U Pr.

— Thinking about Growth: And Other Essays on Economic Growth & Welfare. (Studies in Economic History & Policy: The United States in the Twentieth Century). (Illus.). 395p. (C). 1991. pap. text 21.95 (*0-521-40774-5*) Cambridge U Pr.

Abramovitz, Moses & Eliasberg, Vera F. The Growth of Public Employment in Great Britain. (General Ser.: No. 60). 168p. 1957. reprint ed. 43.70 (*0-87014-059-0*) Natl Bur Econ Res.

Abramowicz, D. Biocatalysis. 400p. (gr. 13). 1990. mass mkt. 146.95 (*0-442-23848-7*) Chapman & Hall.

Abramowicz, Hirsz. Profiles of a Lost World: Memoirs of East European. LC 98-27168. (Raphael Patai Series of Jewish Folklore & Anthropology). 1999. text 39.95 (*0-8143-2784-2*) Wayne St U Pr.

Abramowicz, Jacques S., jt. auth. see Jaffe, Richard.

Abramowicz, Marek A., et al, eds. Theory of Black Hole Accretion Disks. LC 99-187308. (Cambridge Contemporary Astrophysics Ser.). (Illus.). 293p. (C). 1998. text 69.95 (*0-521-62362-6*) Cambridge U Pr.

***Abramowicz, Marek A. & Sonego, Sebastiano.** Black Hole Physics in the Optical Space. 400p. 2000. 68.00 (*981-02-4116-X*) World Scientific Pub.

Abramowicz, Mark, ed. Drugs of Choice from the Medical Letter. rev. ed. 145p. 1999. 14.00 (*0-9660510-3-3*) Med Letter.

— Handbook of Antimicrobial Therapy: Revised Edition, 1998. rev. ed. 209p. 1998. 14.00 (*0-9660510-2-5*) Med Letter.

***Abramowicz, Mark, ed.** The Medical Letter Handbook of Antimicrobial Therapy: 2000 Edition. 214p. 2000. 12.00 (*0-9660510-6-8*) Med Letter.

***Abramowicz, R.** Clifford Algebras & Their Applications in Mathematical Physics, 2 vols. LC 00-34310. (Progress in Physics Ser.). (Illus.). 2000. write for info. (*3-7643-4183-1*) Birkhauser.

***Abramowicz, W. & Orlowska, M. E., eds.** BIS '99: Proceedings of the 3rd International Conference on Business Informaiton Systems, Poznan, Poland, April 14-16, 1999. LC 99-20261. xvi, 296p. 1999. pap. 109.00 (*1-85233-167-4*, Pub. by Spr-Verlag) Spr-Verlag.

***Abramowicz, Witold & Orlowska, M. E., eds.** BIS 2000: Fourth International Conference on Business Information Systems, Poznan, Poland, 12-13 April 2000. LC 00-28471. xiv, 306p. 2000. 96.00 (*1-85233-282-4*) Spr-Verlag.

Abramowitz, Adam, ed. see Polishuk, Peter.

Abramowitz, Alan I. & Segal, Jeffrey A. Senate Elections. LC 92-20733. (Illus.). 280p. (C). 1992. pap. text 20.95 (*0-472-08192-6*, 08192) U of Mich Pr.

— Senate Elections. LC 92-20733. (Illus.). 280p. (C). 1992. text 54.50 (*0-472-10345-8*, 10345) U of Mich Pr.

Abramowitz, Alan I. & Stone, Walter J. Nomination Politics: Party Activists & Presidential Choice. LC 84-17891. 158p. 1984. 52.95 (*0-275-91110-1*, C1110, Praeger Pubs) Greenwood.

***Abramowitz, Alton L.** Understanding Child Custody & Support. LC 98-183433. (Estate Planning & Administration Course Handbook Ser.). 384 p. 1998. 99.00 (*0-87224-478-4*) PLI.

Abramowitz, Amy D., et al. Telecommunications: Competition Issues in International Satellite Communications. (Illus.). 76p. (C). 1998. reprint ed. pap. text 30.00 (*0-7881-4308-5*) DIANE Pub.

Abramowitz, Bernard. Marriage & Family Life Code of the Jewish Faith. (HEB.). 16.00 (*0-87559-098-5*) Shalom.

Abramowitz, Bernard, ed. The Law of Israel. 29.95 (*0-910218-92-7*) Bennet Pub.

Abramowitz, Elkan & Williamson, Allan P. Corporate Sentencing: A Current Perspective. Merritt, Raymond W. & Ennico, Clifford M., eds. (Corporate Counseling Monograph). 147p. (Orig.). 1991. pap. 27.00 (*0-942954-43-2*) NYS Bar.

Abramowitz, Irving. Production Management: Concepts & Analysis for Operation & Control. LC 66-16835. (Illus.). 372p. reprint ed. pap. 115.40 (*0-608-11523-1*, 201244400081) Bks Demand.

Abramowitz, Isidore, ed. Great Prisoners: The First Anthology of Literature Written in Prison. LC 74-38782. (Essay Index Reprint Ser.). 1977. reprint ed. 44.95 (*0-8369-2563-7*) Ayer.

Abramowitz, Jack. Readings in American History, Bk. 2. (J). (gr. 4-5). 1987. pap. text 5.25 (*0-89525-862-5*) Ed Activities.

Abramowitz, Jack & Uva, Kenneth. Consumers & the Law. (YA). (gr. 7-12). 1987. pap. text 3.50 (*0-89525-871-4*) Ed Activities.

***Abramowitz, Leah.** Tales of Nehama. 2000. write for info. (*0-7657-6143-2*) Aronson.

Abramowitz, Mayer. Sacred Sword: A Novel about the Inquisition. 384p. 1992. 15.95 (*965-229-079-3*) Gefen Bks.

Abramowitz, Milton & Stegun, Irene A., eds. Handbook of Mathematical Functions with Formulas, Graphs & Mathematical Tables. (Illus.). 1046p. (C). 1965. pap. 26.95 (*0-486-61272-4*) Dover.

— Handbook of Mathematical Functions, with Formulas, Graphs, & Mathematical Tables. 10th ed. LC 64-60036. (National Bureau of Standards Applied Mathematics Ser.: No. 55). (Illus.). 1060p. 1972. 56.00 (*0-16-000202-8*, S/N 003-003-00279-8) USGPO.

Abramowitz, Morton, jt. auth. see Moorsteen, Richard.

Abramowitz, Morton I. China: Can We Have a Policy? LC 97-28082. 40p. 1997. pap. 5.95 (*0-87003-152-X*) Carnegie Endow.

***Abramowitz, Morton I.** U. S. Foreign Policy Toward North Korea: Next Steps. 2000. pap. text 7.00 (*0-87609-263-6*) Coun Foreign.

Abramowitz, Norman, jt. auth. see Nesbitt, William A.

***Abramowitz, Rachel.** Is That a Gun in Your Pocket? Women's Experience of Power in Hollywood. 400p. 2000. 26.95 (*0-679-43754-1*); 26.95 (*0-375-43754-1*) Random.

Abramowitz, Yosef I. Beyond Scandal: The Parent Guide to Sex, Lies & Leadership. xii, 129p. 1998. pap. 9.95 (*0-9664306-0-3*) JFL Bks.

Abramowitz, Yosef I. & Silverman, Susan. Jewish Family & Life. unabridged ed. 326p. 1998. pap. 15.00 (*0-307-44086-9*, Whitman Coin) St Martin.

Abramowski, Christina. Something Special. (Illus.). 32p. (J). (gr. 2-4). text 9.95 (*0-9634927-0-5*) Jr Leag Grnd Rapids.

Abramowski, Dwain & Davison, Sandra. Mountain Biking Michigan: Best Trails in Southern Michigan. (Illus.). 272p. 1997. pap. 13.95 (*1-882376-20-X*) Thunder Bay Pr.

Abramowski, Luise. Formula & Context: Studies in Early Christian. (Collected Studies: Vol. CS265). 300p. 1992. 109.95 (*0-86078-288-3*, Pub. by Variorum) Ashgate Pub Co.

***Abrams.** Art Listening. 1999. 10.00 (*0-7863-0374-3*) McGraw-Hill Prof.

Abrams. Biology of Lung Cancer: Diagnosis & Treatment. Rosen, Steven T. et al, eds. (Lung Biology in Health & Disease Ser.: Vol. 37). (Illus.). 384p. 1988. text 175.00 (*0-8247-7642-9*) Dekker.

— Birthday Book: The Metropolitan Museum of Art. rev. ed. (Illus.). 160p. 1996. 16.95 (*0-8109-1243-0*, Pub. by Abrams) Time Warner.

— Fourier Transform Spectroscopy. 1999. write for info. (*0-12-042510-6*) Acad Pr.

— A Glossary of Literary Terms. 7th ed. (C). 1998. pap. text 30.50 (*0-15-505452-X*) Harcourt Coll Pubs.

Abrams. Living Psalms 2001. 1997. pap. 9.99 (*0-8423-8869-9*) Tyndale Hse.

Abrams. The Nobel Peace Prize & the Laureatis. 2nd ed. 1998. 60.00 (*0-02-896900-6*) Mac Lib Ref.

— World Wide Web: Beyond the Basics. LC 98-6363. 483p. (C). 1998. pap. 37.40 (*0-13-954785-1*, Prentice Hall) P-H.

Abrams, ed. Proceedings of the 25th Annual Simulation Symposium. 248p. 1988. pap. 48.00 (*0-8186-0845-5*, ANS21-1) Soc Computer Sim.

***Abrams & Greenblatt.** The Anthology of English Literature: Middle Ages, Vol. 1. 7th ed. 1999. pap. text 20.25 (*0-393-97565-7*) Norton.

— The Anthology of English Literature: Romantic Period, Vol. 2. 7th ed. 1999. pap. text 20.25 (*0-393-97568-1*) Norton.

— The Anthology of English Literature: Victorian Age, Vol. 2. 7th ed. 1999. pap. text 20.25 (*0-393-97569-X*) Norton.

— The Anthology of English Literature: 16th/17th Century, Vol. 1. 7th ed. 1999. pap. text 20.25 (*0-393-97566-5*) Norton.

— The Anthology of English Literature: 18th Century, Vol. 1. 7th ed. 1999. pap. text 20.25 (*0-393-97567-3*) Norton.

— The Anthology of English Literature: 20th Century, Vol. 2. 7th ed. 1999. pap. text 20.25 (*0-393-97570-3*) Norton.

Abrams, et al. Use of Longer-Acting Agents in Cardiac Therapy: Recent Advances. Garbus, Stanley B., ed. 1989. 25.00 (*0-945986-11-4*) Health Care NJ.

Abrams, Alan. Special Treatment: The Untold Story of the Survival of Thousands of Jews in Hitler's Third Reich. (Illus.). 261p. 1985. 14.95 (*0-8184-0364-0*) Carol Pub Group.

Abrams, Albert. The Electronic Reactions of Abrams. 102p. 1993. reprint ed. spiral bd. 10.00 (*0-7873-0018-7*) Hlth Research.

— Human Energy. 52p. 1994. reprint ed. spiral bd. 14.00 (*0-7873-1161-8*) Hlth Research.

— New Concepts in Diagnosis & Treatment: Physico Clinical Medicine. 414p. 1996. reprint ed. spiral bd. 27.50 (*0-7873-0017-9*) Hlth Research.

Abrams, Ann, tr. see Porter, Jack N. & Merin, Yehuda, eds.

***Abrams, Ann U.** The Pilgrims & Pocahontas: Rival Myths of American Origin. LC F68.A16 1999. (Illus.). 432p. 1999. 28.00 (*0-8133-3497-7*, Pub. by Westview) HarpC.

Abrams, Anne. Clinical Drug Therapy: Rationals for Nursing Practice. 5th ed. LC 97-23562. 864p. 1997. pap. text 38.95 (*0-397-55372-2*) Lppncott W & W.

Abrams, Anne Collins. Clinical Drug Therapy: Rationales for Nursing Practice. 6th ed. 1056p. pap. text 44.95 (*0-7817-2121-0*) Lppncott W & W.

— Study Guide to Accompany Clinical Drug Therapy. 6th ed. pap. text. write for info. (*0-7817-1813-9*) Lppncott W & W.

Abrams, Arnie H. Educator's Guide to Macintosh Applications. LC 95-175734. 400p. (C). 1994. pap. text 44.00 (*0-205-16284-3*) Allyn.

— Educator's Guide to Macintosh Applications. (C). 1995. pap., teacher ed. write for info. (*0-205-16700-4*, H6700-2) Allyn.

Abrams, Arnie H. Multimedia Magic. LC 96-126498. 304p. (C). 1995. pap. text 43.00 (*0-205-17867-7*) Allyn.

Abrams, Aron. The Stock Market Crash of 1929. unabridged ed. 1987. pap. 7.95 incl. audio (*1-882071-22-0*, 024) B&B Audio.

Abrams, Barbara C. Estates of Grace: The Architectural Heritage of Religious Structures in Rye, N. Y. (Illus.). 20p. (Orig.). 1986. pap. text 4.00 (*0-9615327-1-8*) Rye Hist Soc.

***Abrams, Bernard & Stecker, Michael.** Structures in Space: Hidden Secrets of the Deep Sky. LC 99-35687. (Illus.). xi, 116p. 2000. pap. 39.95 incl. cd-rom (*1-85233-165-8*, Pub. by Spr-Verlag) Spr-Verlag.

Abrams, Bernard S., jt. auth. see Burnham, Archie C., Jr.

Abrams, Bill & American Marketing Association Staff. The Observational Research Handbook: Understanding How Consumers Live with Your Product. LC 99-44308. 304p. Date not set. 49.95 (*0-658-00073-X*, 00073X) NTC Contemp Pub Co.

Abrams, Brenda M., ed. Florida Family Law Reporter. text 280.00 (*0-8205-2103-5*) Bender.

Abrams, Brenda M., jt. auth. see Bender's Editors.

Abrams-Brill, Marietta, jt. auth. see Horowitz, Mark.

Abrams, Catherine M. Art Education: Theory & Practice. 303p. (C). 29.95 (*0-89641-243-1*) American Pr.

Abrams, Charles. Revolution in Land. Bruchey, Stuart, ed. LC 78-56679. (Management of Public Lands in the U. S. Ser.). (Illus.). 1979. reprint ed. lib. bdg. 28.95 (*0-405-11316-1*) Ayer.

Abrams, Charlotte. The Silents. LC 96-19638. (Illus.). 272p. 1996. 24.95 (*1-56368-055-6*, 2899) Gallaudet Univ Pr.

Abrams, Daniel. Sexual Symbolism & Merkavah Speculation in Medieval Germany: A Study of the Sod Ha-Egoz Texts. Schafer, Peter et al, eds. LC 98-114179. (Texts & Studies in Medieval & Early Modern Judaism). (ENG & HEB., Illus.). 228p. 1997. 115.00 (*3-16-146750-7*, Pub. by JCB Mohr) Coronet Bks.

Abrams, Daniel, ed. Assessment of Earthquake Engineering Research & Testing Capabilities in the United States: Proceedings. (Illus.). 304p. 1995. pap. 20.00 (*0-943198-48-8*, WP-01A) Earthquake Eng.

Abrams, Daniel, jt. auth. see Epstein, George.

Abrams, David, contrib. by. Duke-Elder's Practice of Refraction. 10th ed. LC 92-49141. 301p. 1993. text 74.95 (*0-443-03856-2*) Church.

Abrams, David M., jt. auth. see Bellak, Leopold.

Abrams, Dominic & Hogg, Michael, eds. Social Identity Theory: Constructive & Critical Advances. 1990. 72.95 (*0-387-91389-0*) Spr-Verlag.

Abrams, Dominic & Hogg, Michael A. Social Identity & Social Cognition. LC 98-29202. 320p. 1999. 59.95 (*0-631-20642-6*); pap. 27.95 (*0-631-20643-4*) Blackwell Pubs.

Abrams, Dominic, jt. auth. see Hogg, Michael.

Abrams, Douglas E. Civil Rico. 1995. suppl. ed. 100.00 (*0-316-00447-2*, Aspen Law & Bus) Aspen Pub.

— The Law of Civil RICO, Set. 624p. 1991. boxed set 150.00 (*0-316-00449-9*, 04499, Aspen Law & Bus) Aspen Pub.

Abrams, Douglas M. Conflict, Competition, or Cooperation? Dilemmas of State Education Policymaking. LC 92-43401. (SUNY Series, Education & Culture). 227p. (C). 1993. text 64.50 (*0-7914-1677-1*); pap. text 21.95 (*0-7914-1678-X*) State U NY Pr.

Abrams, Edwin D & Blackman, Edward B. Managing Low & Moderate Income Housing. LC 72-14209. (Special Studies in U. S. Economic, Social & Political Issues). 1973. 42.50 (*0-275-28816-1*) Irvington.

Abrams, Elliot M. How the Maya Built Their World: Energetics & Ancient Architecture. (Illus.). 192p. (C). 1994. pap. 15.95 (*0-292-70462-3*) U of Tex Pr.

Abrams, Elliott. Faith or Fear: How Jews Can Survive in a Christian America. LC 97-4966. 237p. 1997. 24.50 (*0-684-82511-2*) Free Pr.

— Security & Sacrifice: Isolation, Intervention, & American Foreign Policy. (Illus.). 150p. (Orig.). 1995. pap. 19.95 (*1-55813-049-7*) Hudson Instit IN.

— Shield & Sword: Neutrality & Engagement in American Foreign Policy. 1994. text 22.95 (*0-02-900165-X*) Free Pr.

— Undue Process: A Story of How Political Differences Are Turned into Crimes. 250p. 1992. text 27.95 (*0-02-900167-6*) Free Pr.

***Abrams, Elliott & Dalin, David G.** Secularism, Spirituality, & the Future of American Jewry. LC 99-17702. 1999. write for info. (*0-89633-190-3*) Ethics & Public Policy.

Abrams, Elliott & Johnson, James T. Close Calls: Intervention, Terrorism, Missile Defense & 'Just War' Today. LC 97-47718. 1998. write for info. (*0-89633-187-3*) Ethics & Public Policy.

Abrams, Elliott & Kagan, Donald. Honor among Nations: Intangible Interests & Foreign Policy. LC 98-18569. 1998. pap. write for info. (*0-89633-188-1*) Ethics & Public Policy.

Abrams, Gene, et al, eds. Methods in Module Theory. LC 92-23502. (Lecture Notes in Pure & Applied Mathematics Ser.: Vol. 140). (Illus.). 352p. 1992. pap. text 155.00 (*0-8247-8802-8*) Dekker.

Abrams, George H. J., jt. ed. see Malinowski, Sharon.

Abrams, H., et al, eds. MiCon 78: Optimization of Processing, Properties & Service Performance Through Microstructural Control - STP 672. 677p. 1979. 59.50 (*0-8031-0517-7*, STP672) ASTM.

Abrams, Halle, et al, eds. Optimization of Processing, Properties, & Service Performance Through Microstructural Control - STP 792. LC 82-71748. 341p. 1983. text 37.95 (*0-8031-0240-2*, STP792) ASTM.

Abrams, Harry N., Staff. The Cycladic Islands: An Adventure for Travelers & Archaeologists. 1997. 45.00 (*0-8109-5153-3*, Pub. by Abrams) Time Warner.

— Islamic Art: Art, Architecture & the Literary World. LC 96-46755. (Perspectives Ser.). (Illus.). 272p. 1997. pap. 24.95 (*0-8109-2710-1*, Pub. by Abrams) Time Warner.

— The Mystery of Magritte. 1997. 45.00 (*0-8109-5152-5*, Pub. by Abrams) Time Warner.

Abrams, Herbert L. Coronary Arteriography. 1982. 102.00 (*0-316-00469-3*, Little Brwn Med Div) Lppncott W & W.

An Asterisk (*) at the beginning of an entry indicates that the title is appearing for the first time.

A

— The President Has Been Shot: Confusion, Disability & the 25th Amendment. 424p. 1994. pap. 17.95 (0-8047-2325-7) Stanford U Pr.

Abrams, Herbert L. & Baum, Stanley. Abrams' Angiography: Vascular & Interventional Radiology. 4th ed. LC 96-24525. 1996. write for info. (0-316-08467-0, Little Brwn Med Div) Lppncott W & W.

Abrams, Herbert L., jt. auth. see McNeil, Barbara J.

Abrams, Howard B. Law of Copyright, 2 vols. LC 91-4402. (IP Ser.). 1991. ring bd. 240.00 (0-87632-741-2) West Group.

Abrams, Howard E. Federal Income Taxation of Parternships & Other Pass-Thru Entities. LC 93-19308. 281p. 1993. pap. 36.95 (0-87084-281-1) Anderson Pub Co.

***Abrams, Howard E. & Doernberg, Richard L.** Essentials of United States Taxation. LC 99-29262. 1024p. 1999. 190.00 (90-411-0964-1) Kluwer Law Intl.

Abrams, Howard E. & Doernberg, Richard L. Federal Corporate Taxation. 2nd ed. (University Textbook Ser.). 306p. 1990. pap. text 18.95 (0-88277-800-5) Foundation Pr.

— Federal Corporate Taxation. 3rd ed. (University Textbook Ser.). 345p. 1994. pap. text 18.95 (1-56662-228-X) Foundation Pr.

— Federal Corporate Taxation. 4th ed. LC 98-28101. (Paralegal). 343p. (C). 1998. pap. text 15.75 (1-56662-686-2) Foundation Pr.

Abrams, Irving. Haymarket Heritage: Memoirs of Irving Abrams. Boanes, Phyllis & Roediger, Dave, eds. 100p. 1986. pap. 10.95 (0-88286-176-X) C H Kerr.

Abrams, Irwin. Nobel Lectures in Peace 1971-1980. LC 97-159577. 184p. 1997. text 52.00 (981-02-1178-3); pap. text 21.00 (981-02-1179-1) World Scientific Pub.

— Nobel Lectures in Peace 1981-1990. 196p. 1997. text 52.00 (981-02-1180-5); pap. text 21.00 (981-02-1181-3) World Scientific Pub.

— The Nobel Peace Prize & the Laureates: An Illustrated Biographical History, 1901-1987. 1988. 45.00 (0-8161-8609-X, Hall Reference) Macmillan.

***Abrams, Irwin.** Words of Peace: Selections from the Speeches of the Nobel Peace Prize Laureates of the Twentieth Century. 3rd ed. 2000. 14.95 (1-55704-416-3) Newmarket.

Abrams, Irwin, ed. The Words of Peace: Selections from the Speeches of the Winners of the Nobel Peace Prize. LC 90-5851. (Illus.). 144p. 1990. 14.95 (1-55704-060-5, Pub. by Newmarket) Norton.

Abrams, Irwin, ed. The Words of Peace: Selections from the Speeches of the Winners of the Nobel Peace Prize. rev. ed. LC 95-38763. (Pocket Editions "Words of" Ser.). 160p. 1995. pap. 6.95 (1-55704-250-0, Pub. by Newmarket) Norton.

Abrams, Isabel. The Nature of Chicago: A Comprehensive Guide to Natural Sites in & Around the City. LC 96-51835. (Illus.). 272p. 1997. pap. 14.95 (1-55652-312-2) Chicago Review.

Abrams, Janet. If/Then: Play: Emerging Forms, Emerging Behaviors. 1999. pap. text 29.95 (90-72007-52-2) Bis NLD.

— Michael Graves: Buildings & Projects 1990-1994. (Illus.). 304p. 1995. 65.00 (0-8478-1901-9, Pub. by Rizzoli Intl); pap. 40.00 (0-8478-1902-7, Pub. by Rizzoli Intl) St Martin.

Abrams, Jason S., jt. auth. see Ratner, Steven R.

***Abrams, Jay B.** Quantitative Business Valuation: A Mathematical Approach for Today's Professionals. (Illus.). 2000. 95.00 (0-07-000215-0) McGraw.

Abrams, Jeremiah, jt. ed. see Zweig, Connie.

Abrams, Jerome H. & Cerra, Frank B., eds. Essentials of Surgical Critical Care: Clinical Cases & Practical Solutions (Case Book) LC 92-48762. (Illus.). 184p. 1992. pap. 25.00 (0-942219-32-5) Quality Med Pub.

Abrams, Jerome S. Abdominal Stomas: Indications, Operative Techniques, & Patient Care. LC 84-3670. 207p. reprint ed. pap. 64.20 (0-8357-7868-1, 203628500002) Bks Demand.

Abrams, Joanne, jt. ed. see Caratozzolo, Marie.

Abrams, Jodell. Enchanted Forest. (Troubador Ser.). (Illus.). 32p. (Orig.). (J). (ps up). 1995. pap. 5.95 (0-8431-3877-7, Price Stern) Peng Put Young Read.

Abrams, Jodell & Price, Stern, Sloan Publishing Staff. Enchanted Kingdom. rev. ed. (Troubador Ser.). (Illus.). 32p. (Orig.). (J). (gr. 1-7). 1998. pap. 5.99 (0-8431-7417-X, Price Stern) Peng Put Young Read.

Abrams, Jonathan. Ischemic Heart. 1991. 95.95 (0-316-00471-5, Little Brwn Med Div) Lppncott W & W.

Abrams, Jonathan, ed. A Contemporary Overview of Nitrate Therapy. (Illus.). 32p. (Orig.). 1987. pap. write for info. (0-943035-00-7) CoMed Comm.

Abrams, Judith. Simchat Torah: A Family Celebration. (Illus.). 24p. (Orig.). (J). (ps up). 1995. pap. 3.95 (0-929371-87-9) Kar-Ben.

— Sukkot: A Family Seder. LC 93-7551. (Illus.). 24p. (YA). (ps up). 1993. pap. 3.95 (0-929371-75-5) Kar-Ben.

Abrams, Judith Z. A Beginner's Guide to the Steinsaltz Talmud. LC 98-41125. 176p. 1999. 25.00 (0-7657-6047-9) Aronson.

— Judaism & Disabilities: Portrayals in Ancient Texts from the Tanach Through the Bavli. LC 98-17641. 304p. 1998. text 49.95 (1-56368-068-8) Gallaudet Univ Pr.

— Learn Talmud: How to Use The Talmud - The Steinsaltz Edition. LC 94-45558. 168p. 1995. pap. 20.00 (1-56821-463-4) Aronson.

— Rosh Hashanah - A Family Service. LC 90-4855. (Illus.). 32p. (Orig.). (J). (ps-4). 1990. pap. 3.95 (0-929371-16-X) Kar-Ben.

— Selichot - A Family Service. LC 90-4863. (Illus.). 24p. (J). (ps-4). 1990. pap. 3.95 (0-929371-15-1) Kar-Ben.

— Shabbat: A Family Service. LC 91-31640. (Illus.). 24p. (J). (ps-3). 1992. pap. text 3.95 (0-929371-29-1) Kar-Ben.

— The Talmud for Beginners Vol. 1: Prayer. LC 90-1211. 232p. 1991. 25.00 (0-87668-719-2) Aronson.

— The Talmud for Beginners Vol. 2: Text. LC 90-1211. 192p. 1993. pap. 25.00 (0-87668-597-1) Aronson.

— The Talmud for Beginners Vol. 3: Living in a Non-Jewish World. 192p. 1997. pap. 25.00 (0-7657-9967-7) Aronson.

— The Women of the Talmud. LC 94-22410. 224p. 1996. pap. 25.00 (1-56821-283-6) Aronson.

— Yom Kippur - A Family Service. LC 90-4862. (Illus.). 22p. (Orig.). (J). (ps-4). 1990. pap. 3.95 (0-929371-17-8) Kar-Ben.

Abrams, Judith Z. & Abrams, Steven A. Jewish Parenting: Rabbinic Insights. LC 94-6114. 312p. 1994. pap. 30.00 (1-56821-175-9) Aronson.

Abrams, Judith Z., ed. see Freeman, David.

Abrams, Karl, jt. auth. see Monroe, Manus.

Abrams, Karl J. Algae to the Rescue! Everything You Need to Know about Nutritional Blue-Green Algae. (Illus.). x, 200p. (Orig.). 1996. pap., mass mkt. 14.95 (1-889152-00-5) Logan Hse Publns.

— All A's with Algae Vol. 1: Energize Your Mind with Nutritional Blue-Green Algae. Baker, Cherie, ed. & illus. by. (Algae Nutrition Ser.). 70p. (Orig.). (YA). (gr. 9 up). 1997. pap., mass mkt. 12.95 (1-889152-01-3) Logan Hse Publns.

Abrams, Kenneth J. A Perfect Fish: Illusions in Fly Tying. LC 99-229058. 112p. 1999. 39.95 (1-57188-179-4) F Amato Pubns.

***Abrams, Kenneth J.** A Perfect Fish: Illusions in Fly Tying. LC 99-229058. (Illus.). 112p. 1999. pap. 29.95 (1-57188-138-7) F Amato Pubns.

Abrams, Kevin, jt. auth. see Lively, Scott.

Abrams, LeRoy. Illustrated Flora of the Pacific States, 4 vols., Set. Incl. Vol. 1. Ferns to Birthworts. (Illus.). xi, 557p. 1923. 85.00 (0-8047-0003-6); Vol. 2. Buckwheats to Kramerias. (Illus.). viii, 635p. 1944. 85.00 (0-8047-0004-4); Vol. 3. Geraniums to Figworts. (Illus.). viii, 866p. 1951. 85.00 (0-8047-0005-2); Vol. 4. Bignonias to Sunflowers. Ferris, Roxana S. (Illus.). v, 732p. 1960. 85.00 (0-8047-0006-0); (Illus.). 299.50 (0-8047-1100-3) Stanford U Pr.

Abrams, Lesley. Anglo-Saxon Glastonbury: Church & Endowment. (Studies in Anglo-Saxon History: Vol. 8). (Illus.). 394p. (C). 1996. 110.00 (0-85115-369-0) Boydell & Brewer.

Abrams, Lesley & Carley, James P., eds. The Archaeology & History of Glastonbury Abbey: Essays in Honour of the Nineteenth Birthday of C. A. Ralegh Radford. (Illus.). 361p. (C). 1991. 90.00 (0-85115-284-8) Boydell & Brewer.

Abrams, Leslie E. The History & Practice of Japanese Printmaking: A Selectively Annotated Bibliography of English Language Materials, 5. LC 83-16641. (Art Reference Collection Ser.: No. 5). 197p. 1984. lib. bdg. 59.95 (0-313-23188-5, AJP/) Greenwood.

Abrams, Liesa. His Other Girlfriend. (Love Stories Ser.). 192p. (YA). (gr. 7-12). 1999. mass mkt. 4.50 (0-553-49295-0) Bantam.

— Stolen Kisses. (Love Stories Ser.). (YA). (gr. 7-12). 1999. mass mkt. 3.99 (0-553-49288-8) BDD Bks Young Read.

Abrams, Lindsey. Global City Review Vol. 7: Totem & Taboo. 124p. 1996. pap. text 6.00 (1-887369-02-3) Global Cty Pr.

Abrams, Linsey, ed. Global City Review Vol. 5: Crime & Punishment. LC 95-79769. (Global City Review Ser.: No. 5). 120p. 1995. pap. 6.00 (0-9641292-7-2) Global Cty Pr.

Abrams, Lois M., jt. auth. see Penderghast, Thomas F.

Abrams, Lynn. Bismarck & the German Empire, 1871-1918. LC 94-22013. (Lancaster Pamphlets Ser.). 96p. (C). 1995. pap. 11.99 (0-415-07781-8, B2249) Routledge.

— The Orphan Country: Children of Scotland's Broken Homes, 1845 to the Present. 250p. 1998. pap. 60.00 (0-85976-497-4, Pub. by J Donald) St Mut.

Abrams, Lynn & Harvey, Elizabeth D., eds. Gender Relations in German History: Power, Agency & Experience from the Sixteenth to the Twentieth Century. LC 96-24759. (Illus.). 272p. 1997. pap. text 16.95 (0-8223-1896-2); lib. bdg. 49.95 (0-8223-1904-7) Duke.

Abrams, M. The Norton Anthology of English Literature. 6th ed. (C). 1996. text 40.00 (0-393-96806-5); text 55.75 (0-393-96807-3); text 55.75 (0-393-96935-5); pap. text 39.00 (0-393-96809-X); pap. text 39.00 (0-393-96810-3); pap. text 54.25 (0-393-96812-X); pap. text 39.00 (0-393-96936-3) Norton.

Abrams, M. The Norton Anthology of English Literature. 6th ed. (C). 1996. text 38.00 (0-393-96805-7); text 40.00 (0-393-96804-9); pap. text 36.00 (0-393-96811-1) Norton.

— Norton Anthology of English Literature. 6th ed. 1997. pap. 52.80 (0-393-98405-2) Norton.

Abrams, M., et al. Information Security Principles & Practice - Course Notes. (Illus.). 465p. (Orig.). (C). 1995. pap. 51.15 (0-942891-61-9) Comp Educ.

— Practical Security in a Networked Environment - Course Notes. (Illus.). 427p. (Orig.). (C). 1995. pap. 46.97 (0-942891-62-7) Comp Educ.

Abrams, M. H. The Correspondent Brute: Essays on English Romanticism. 208p. 1999. reprint ed. lib. bdg. 27.95 (0-7351-0101-9) Replica Bks.

— A Glossary of Literary Terms. 6th ed. 434p. (C). 1993. pap. text 30.50 (0-03-054982-5) Harcourt Coll Pubs.

***Abrams, M. H.** The Norton Anthology of English Literature, Vol. 1. 7th ed. LC 99-43298. 1999. pap. 52.25 (0-393-97487-1, Norton Paperbks) Norton.

— Norton Anthology of English Literature, Vol. 1. 7th ed. LC 99-43298. Vol. 1. 2974p. 1999. 53.50 (0-393-97486-3, Norton Paperbks) Norton.

— The Norton Anthology of English Literature, Vol. 2. 7th ed. 1999. pap. 52.25 (0-393-97491-X, Norton Paperbks) Norton.

— The Norton Anthology of English Literature, Vol. 2. 7th ed. LC 99-43298. Vol. 2. 1999. 53.50 (0-393-97490-1, Norton Paperbks) Norton.

Abrams, M. H., ed. The Norton Anthology of English Literature. 6th ed. (C). 1996. text 53.50 (0-393-96803-0) Norton.

Abrams, M. H., ed. The Norton Anthology of English Literature. 6th ed. (C). 1996. pap. text 37.50 (0-393-96808-1) Norton.

Abrams, M. J. & Murrer, Barry A., eds. Advances in Metals in Medicine, Vol. 1. 196p. 1993. 128.50 (1-55938-352-6) Jai Pr.

Abrams, Marc & Reynolds, Paul, Jr., eds. 6th Workshop on Parallel & Distributed Simulation (PADS '92) Newport Beach, California. 212p. 1992. 66.00 (1-56555-008-0, SS-24-3) Soc Computer Sim.

Abrams, Margaret. Awakened: A Novel. LC 54-7435. 350p. reprint ed. pap. 108.50 (0-8357-5933-4, 202921200059) Bks Demand.

Abrams, Marshall, et al. Enterprise Security: Integration with Open Systems - Course Notes. 430p. 1998. pap. 47.30 (0-942891-76-7) Comp Educ.

— Information Security Principles & Practice: Course Notes. 413p. (C). 1998. pap. 45.43 (0-942891-73-2) Comp Educ.

— Practical Security in Networks: Course Notes. 452p. 1998. pap. 49.72 (0-942891-75-9) Comp Educ.

— Recent Developments in Information Security: Course Notes. 447p. (C). 1998. pap. 49.17 (0-942891-74-0) Comp Educ.

***Abrams, Marshall D., et al, eds.** Information Security (1995) An Integrated Collection of Essays. (Illus.). 753p. 2000. reprint ed. text 40.00 (0-7881-9198-5) DIANE Pub.

Abrams, Mary, ed. Perspectives Whole Language Folio: A Folio of Articles from Perspectives in Education & Deafness. (Illus.). 62p. (J). 1991. pap. text, teacher ed. 6.95 (0-88095-205-9) Gallaudet U Pre Coll.

Abrams, Mary, ed. see Fleming, Linda F.

Abrams, Melvin S. Fire Safety of Concrete Structures. LC 83-71426. (American Concrete Institute Publication: No. SP-80). (Illus.). 314p. 1983. reprint ed. pap. 97.40 (0-608-07956-1, 206792900012) Bks Demand.

Abrams, Meyer H. Doing Things with Texts: Essays in Criticism & Critical Theory. 1991. pap. 14.95 (0-393-30747-6) Norton.

— Doing Things with Texts: Essays in Criticism & Literary Theory. 1989. 27.50 (0-393-02713-9) Norton.

— Mirror & the Lamp: Romantic Theory & the Critical Tradition. (Illus.). 406p. 1971. reprint ed. pap. text 16.95 (0-19-501471-5) OUP.

— Natural Supernaturalism: Tradition & Revolution in Romantic Literature. 550p. 1973. reprint ed. pap. 17.95 (0-393-00609-3) Norton.

Abrams, Meyer H., ed. English Romantic Poets: Modern Essays in Criticism. 2nd ed. 400p. 1975. pap. text 15.95 (0-19-501946-6) OUP.

— The Norton Anthology of English Literature, 001. 6th ed. LC 92-40016. (C). 1993. pap. write for info. (0-393-96288-1); text 50.00 (0-393-96287-3) Norton.

— The Norton Anthology of English Literature, Vol. 2. 6th ed. LC 92-40016. (C). 1993. text 50.00 (0-393-96289-X); pap. text 36.00 (0-393-96290-3) Norton.

— Wordsworth: A Collection of Critical Essays. 1972. 12.95 (0-685-03922-6, Spectrum IN) Macmillan Gen Ref.

***Abrams, Michael.** The Evolution Angel: An Emergency Physician's Lessons with Death & the Divine. LC 99-73439. 159p. 2000. pap. 12.95 (0-9671834-0-5, 6692, Pub. by Abundance Media) ACCESS Pubs Network.

Abrams, Michael, jt. auth. see Ellis, Albert.

Abrams, Michael, ed. see Krouse, John K.

Abrams, Michael A., jt. ed. see Schumacher, Dietmar.

Abrams, Michael C. CAD/CAM, CAE & PDM Computer Hardware Buyer's Guide. (Illus.). 55p. 1999. write for info. (0-934869-24-3) Cad-Cam Pub.

Abrams, Michael D. Eddie's Monster. LC 96-15962. (Illus.). 32p. (J). (gr. 1-5). 1996. 16.95 (0-7892-0230-1, Abbeville Kids); 9.98 (0-89660-102-1, Artabras) Abbeville Pr.

***Abrams, Nancy.** The Other Mother: A Lesbian's Fight for Her Daughter. LC 99-13125. (Living Out Ser.). 282p. 1999. text 50.00 (0-299-16490-X) U of Wis Pr.

Abrams, Nancy. The Other Mother: A Lesbian's Fight for Her Daughter. LC 99-13125. (Living Out Ser.). 269p. 1999. pap. 19.95 (0-299-16494-2) U of Wis Pr.

Abrams, Norman. Classics from the New Yankee Workshop. 216p. 1990. pap. 22.00 (0-316-00455-3) Little.

— Federal Criminal Law & Its Enforcement, 1996 Supplement To. 2nd ed. Beale, Sara S., ed. (American Casebook Ser.). 115p. 1996. pap. text. write for info. (0-314-20468-7) West Pub.

Abrams, Norman & Beale, Sara S. Federal Criminal Law & Its Enforcement. 2nd ed. (American Casebook Ser.). 1000p. (C). 1993. 65.00 (0-314-02217-1) West Pub.

Abrams, Ovid S. Metegee: The History & Culture of Guyana. LC 98-73091. 320p. 1998. pap. 24.95 (0-9660707-4-7, Ashanti Bks) Eldorado Pubns.

Abrams, P. H. Urodynamics. (Clinical Practice in Urology Ser.). (Illus.). 236p. 1986. 106.00 (0-387-11903-5) Spr-Verlag.

Abrams, P. H., jt. ed. see Gingell, J. C.

Abrams, Paul. Urodynamics. 2nd ed. LC 96-51999. 356p. 1997. 99.00 (3-540-19678-1) Spr-Verlag.

Abrams, Paul & Teillac, Pierre, eds. Identifying & Evaluation Urinary Incontinence in a Female Population/Patient Outcome Research: Success Criteria in BPH Management: Symposia Held During the Meeting of the European Association of Urology (EAU), Paris, September 1996. (European Urology Ser.: Vol. 32, Suppl. 2, 1997). (Illus.). iv, 54p. 1997. pap. 25.25 (3-8055-6539-9) S Karger.

***Abrams, Paul B.** The Sport of Cooking: A Gourmet Guide for Rookies. (Illus.). 144p. 2000. pap. 14.95 (1-892123-21-5) Capital VA.

***Abrams, Pete.** Sluggy Freelance: When Holidays Attack! (Illus.). 160p. 1999. pap. 12.95 (1-929462-00-X) Plan Nine Publ.

Abrams, Pete. Sluggy Freelance: Worship the Comic. (Illus.). 160p. 1999. pap. 12.95 (0-9660676-3-0) Plan Nine Publ.

Abrams, Peter. Sluggy Freelance: Is It Not Nifty? (Illus.). 160p. 1998. pap. 12.95 incl. mac ld (0-9660676-5-7) Plan Nine Publ.

Abrams, Peter D. The Law of Civil RICO. 1991. 145.00 (0-316-00479-0, Aspen Law & Bus) Aspen Pub.

Abrams, Peter D., et al. Spectrum I. (Spectrum Ser.). (Illus.). 92p. (YA). (gr. 7-12). 1987. pap. text, wbk. ed. 4.75 (0-13-826694-8, 20090) Prentice ESL.

Abrams, Philip. Historical Sociology. LC 82-61210. 372p. 1983. pap. text 18.95 (0-8014-9243-2) Cornell U Pr.

Abrams, R., ed. Environmental Education for the Next Generation, 1996: Professional Development & Teacher Training. 367p. 1997. pap. 15.00 (1-884008-54-2) NAAEE.

Abrams, Ray H., ed. The American Family in World War Two. LC 79-169365. (Family in America Ser.). 196p. 1977. reprint ed. 21.95 (0-405-03842-9) Ayer.

Abrams, Rebecca. When Parents Die: Learning to Live with the Loss of a Parent. 2nd ed. LC 98-45977. 1999. 75.00 (0-415-20065-2); pap. 20.99 (0-415-20066-0) Routledge.

***Abrams, Rhonda.** Wear Clean Underwear: Business Wisdom from Mom. 256p. 2000. pap. 12.95 (0-440-50907-6, Dell Trade Pbks) Dell.

Abrams, Rhonda M. The Successful Business Plan: Secrets & Strategies. 2nd ed. (Illus.). xxviii, 320p. 1999. reprint ed. pap. 27.95 (0-9669635-0-4, Running R Media) Rhonda.

— The Successful Business Plan: Secrets & Strategies. 3rd ed. 350p. 1999. pap. 27.95 (0-9669635-2-0) Rhonda.

— Wear Clean Underwear! Using Mom's Fundamental Lessons to Run an Extraordinary Business. LC 98-33310. 256p. 1999. 22.95 (0-375-50192-4) Villard Books.

Abrams, Richard. F 4-U Corsair at War. (Illus.). 160p. 1981. pap. 10.95 (0-685-04561-7, Scribners Ref) Mac Lib Ref.

Abrams, Richard K., et al. The Impact of the European Community's Internal Market on the EFTA, 1991. LC 90-24713. (Occasional Paper Ser.: No. 74). v, 66p. (Orig.). 1990. pap. 10.00 (1-55775-174-9) Intl Monetary.

Abrams, Richard K., jt. auth. see Johnson, G. G.

Abrams, Richard M. The Burdens of Progress, 1900-1929. Degler, Carl N., ed. LC 77-10900. (Scott, Foresman American History Ser.). 207p. reprint ed. pap. 64.20 (0-7837-3011-X, 204292900006) Bks Demand.

Abrams, Richard S. & Wexler, Paul. Medical Care of the Pregnant Patient. 404p. 1983. 49.95 (0-316-00470-7, Little Brwn Med Div) Lppncott W & W.

Abrams, Rita. Starting Up. 1990. bds. 9.95 (0-938971-46-8) JTG Nashville.

— Stepping Out. (J). 1991. audio 12.95 (0-938971-75-1) JTG Nashville.

Abrams, Robert, et al. Boomer Basics. 436p. 1999. 24.95 (0-07-135570-7) McGraw.

Abrams, Robert E., selected by. Treasures of Disney Animation Art. (Illus.). 320p. 1992. 49.98 (0-89660-031-9, Artabras); pap. 11.95 (1-55859-335-7) Abbeville Pr.

Abrams, Robert H., jt. auth. see Plater, Zygmunt J.

Abrams, Roger I. Legal Bases: Baseball & the Law. LC 97-28823. 240p. 1998. 27.95 (1-56639-599-2) Temple U Pr.

***Abrams, Roger I.** The Money Pitch: Baseball Free Agency & Salary Arbitration. LC 99-87922. (Illus.). 224p. 2000. 27.50 (1-56639-774-X) Temple U Pr.

Abrams, Ronald G., jt. auth. see Chambers, David W.

Abrams, Sam, ed. see Whitman, Walt.

Abrams, Sandy & Greer, William S. Infant-Toddler Health Record: Birth to 24 Months. Greer, Bill, ed. (Illus.). 120p. (Orig.). 1995. pap. 9.95 (0-9641332-4-5) Jormax Pubng.

Abrams, Sandy, et al. Child's Health Record: Two Years & Up. Caravella, Jack, ed. (Illus.). 120p. (Orig.). 1995. pap. 9.95 (0-9641332-5-3) Jormax Pubng.

— The Daily Baby's Log: Mother's Organizer & Record of Baby's Schedule. Caravella, Jack, ed. (Illus.). 120p. (Orig.). 1995. pap. 8.95 (0-9641332-3-7) Jormax Pubng.

***Abrams, Scott.** Using Journals with Reluctant Writers: Building Portfolios for Middle & High School Students. LC 99-50876. 112p. 2000. pap., wbk. ed. 24.95 (0-7619-7612-4); lib. bdg., wbk. ed. 55.95 (0-7619-7611-6) Corwin Pr.

***Abrams Staff.** Andy Warhol. (Illus.). 1999. 12.95 (0-8109-5806-6, Pub. by Abrams) Time Warner.

— Art History. rev. ed. (Illus.). 1999. pap. 10.00 (0-8109-2901-5, Pub. by Abrams) Time Warner.

— Art History, Vol. 1. rev. ed. (Illus.). 1999. 23.70 (0-8109-2905-8, Pub. by Abrams) Time Warner.

— Art History, Vol. 2. rev. ed. (Illus.). 1999. 23.70 (0-8109-2906-6, Pub. by Abrams) Time Warner.

— Art of Walt Disney. (Illus.). 1999. pap. 5.27 (0-8109-4212-7, Pub. by Abrams) Time Warner.

— At the End of the Century. (YA). 1998. pap. 18.00 (0-8109-2784-5, Pub. by Abrams) Time Warner.

— Aztec Art. (Illus.). 1998. pap. 7.70 (0-8109-2927-9, Pub. by Abrams) Time Warner.

— Cave of Altamira. (Illus.). (J). 1999. pap. 5.75 (0-8109-2727-6, Pub. by Abrams) Time Warner.

An Asterisk (*) at the beginning of an entry indicates that the title is appearing for the first time.

— Cindy Sherman. (Illus.). 1999. 12.95 (*0-8109-5808-2*, Pub. by Abrams) Time Warner.

— Claude Monet. 1999. 12.95 (*0-8109-5802-3*, Pub. by Abrams) Time Warner.

— Escape of Alexei. (YA). 1998. pap. 2.50 (*0-8109-2913-9*, Pub. by Abrams) Time Warner.

— Faeries. (YA). 1998. pap. 4.95 (*0-8109-2788-8*, Pub. by Abrams) Time Warner.

— Francis Bacon Retrospective. 1999. 20.00 (*0-8109-2925-2*, Pub. by Abrams) Time Warner.

— Henri Matisse. (Essential Ser.). (Illus.). 1999. 12.95 (*0-8109-5816-3*, Pub. by Abrams) Time Warner.

— Jan Vermeer. (Illus.). 1999. 12.95 (*0-8109-5801-5*, Pub. by Abrams) Time Warner.

— John James Audubon. (Illus.). 1999. 12.95 (*0-8109-5807-4*, Pub. by Abrams) Time Warner.

— Mary Cassat. (Illus.). (J). 1998. pap. 8.80 (*0-8109-2766-7*, Pub. by Abrams) Time Warner.

— Maxfield Parrish 1870-1966. 1999. pap. 12.50 (*0-8109-2931-7*, Pub. by Abrams) Time Warner.

— Nicholas & Alexandra. (YA). 1998. pap. 9.41 (*0-8109-2768-3*, Pub. by Abrams) Time Warner.

— Norman Rockwell. (Illus.). 1999. 12.95 (*0-8109-5824-4*, Pub. by Abrams) Time Warner.

— Pablo Picasso. (Illus.). 1999. 12.95 (*0-8109-5820-1*, Pub. by Abrams) Time Warner.

— Physics in the 20th Century. 1999. pap. 6.30 (*0-8109-2919-8*, Pub. by Abrams) Time Warner.

— Rene Magritte. (Illus.). 1999. 12.95 (*0-8109-5803-1*, Pub. by Abrams) Time Warner.

— Russell Laa. 1999. pap. 7.25 (*0-8109-2930-9*, Pub. by Abrams) Time Warner.

— Scythian Gold. 1999. 16.50 (*0-8109-2938-4*, Pub. by Abrams) Time Warner.

— Shamans of Prehistory. (Illus.). (YA). 1998. pap. 6.32 (*0-8109-2771-3*, Pub. by Abrams) Time Warner.

— Unknown Terrain: the Landscapes of Andrew Wyeth. (Illus.). (YA). 1998. pap. 6.50 (*0-8109-2769-1*, Pub. by Abrams) Time Warner.

— Van Gogh. (Illus.). 1999. pap. write for info. (*0-8109-2936-8*, Pub. by Abrams) Time Warner.

— Victorians. 1998. 35.00 (*0-8109-6350-7*, Pub. by Abrams) Time Warner.

— Willem De Kooning. (Essential Ser.). (Illus.). 1999. 12.95 (*0-8109-5811-2*, Pub. by Abrams) Time Warner.

Abrams, Stanley. Maryland Guide to Zoning Decisions: 1991 Supplement. 151p. 1998. pap. text 25.00 (*0-87473-854-7*, 60028-10, MICHIE) LEXIS Pub.

Abrams, Stanley, jt. auth. see Ansley, Norman.

Abrams, Stanley D. Guide to Maryland Zoning Decisions. 3rd ed. 537p. 1994. suppl. ed. 85.00 (*0-87473-999-3*, 60029-10, MICHIE) LEXIS Pub.

— Guide to Maryland Zoning Decisions: 1998 Cumulative Supplement. 3rd ed. 275p. 1998. suppl. ed. 85.00 (*0-327-00281-6*, 6003215) LEXIS Pub.

***Abrams, Stanley D.** Guide to Maryland Zoning Decisions, 1999 Cumulative Supplement: Pocketpart. 3rd ed. 300p. 1999. write for info. (*0-327-01669-8*, 6003216) LEXIS Pub.

Abrams, Steven A., jt. auth. see Abrams, Judith Z.

***Abrams, Stuart E.** More Than Conquerors. 2000. pap. 13.95 (*1-878647-58-X*) APU Pub Grp.

Abrams, Stuart E., jt. auth. see Fink, Robert S.

***Abrams, Susan L.** The New Success Rules for Women: 10 Surefire Strategies for Reaching Your Career Goals. LC 00-27647. 288p. 2000. 24.95 (*0-7615-2348-0*) Prima Pub.

Abrams, Susan L., jt. auth. see Harvey, Abner M.

Abrams, Susie, et al. Gray-Haired Grins & Giggles. 2nd abr. large type ed. Bigger, Margaret G., ed. LC 98-92498. (Illus.). 144p. 1998. pap. 13.95 (*0-9640606-7-1*) A Borough Bks.

— Gray-Haired Grins & Giggles: Guess What - Grammy & Grandy Have a Sense of Humor, Too! Bigger, Margaret G., ed. LC 95-77859. (Illus.). 128p. (Orig.). 1995. pap. 12.95 (*0-9640606-3-9*) A Borough Bks.

Abrams, Tom. A Bad Piece of Luck: A Novel. LC 94-78598. 128p. 1994. 19.95 (*0-942979-22-2*); pap. 9.95 (*0-942979-23-0*) Livingston U Pr.

***Abrams, Tom.** The Drinking of Spirits: Stories. 176p. 2000. 23.00 (*0-942979-69-9*) Livingston AL.

— The Drinking of Spirits: Stories. (Illus.). 176p. 2000. pap. 11.00 (*0-942979-70-2*) Livingston AL.

Abrams, Tony & Broder, Adam. Dead Man on Campus: Movie Tie-In. 1998. per. 6.50 (*0-671-02644-5*) PB.

Abramsky, L., ed. see Chapple, J.

Abramsky, S., et al, eds. Category Theory & Computer Science: Paris, France, September 3-6, 1991 Proceedings. (Lecture Notes in Computer Science Ser.: Vol. 530). vii, 301p. 1991. 43.00 (*0-387-54495-X*) Spr-Verlag.

***Abramsky, S., et al, eds.** Handbook of Logic in Computer Science: Algebraic & Logical Structures, Vol. 5. (Illus.). 544p. 2000. text 225.00 (*0-19-853781-6*) OUP.

Abramsky, S., et al, eds. Handbook of Logic in Computer Science: Semantic Structures, Vol. 1. (Illus.). 840p. 1993. text 198.00 (*0-19-853735-2*) OUP.

— Handbook of Logic in Computer Science: Semantic Structures, Vol. 2. (Illus.). 582p. 1993. text 225.00 (*0-19-853761-1*) OUP.

— Handbook of Logic in Computer Science Vol. 3: Semantic Structures, Vol. 3. (Illus.). 506p. 1995. text 198.00 (*0-19-853762-X*) OUP.

Abramsky, S. & Hankin, Chris, eds. Abstract Interpretation of Declarative Languages. LC 87-20899. (Computers & Their Applications Ser.). 284p. 1987. text 73.95 (*0-470-20971-2*) P-H.

Abramsky, S. & Maillbaum, T. S., eds. TAPSOFT '91 Vol. 1: Proceedings of the International Joint Conference on Theory & Practice of Software Development Brighton, U. K., April 8-12, 1991: Colloquium on Trees in Algebra & Programming (CAAP '91) (Lecture Notes in Computer Science Ser.: Vol. 493). viii, 455p. 1991. 57.00 (*0-387-53982-4*) Spr-Verlag.

— TAPSOFT '91 Vol. 2: Proceedings of the Internatioanl Joint Conference on Theory & Practice of Software Development Brighton, U. K., April 8-12, 1991: Advances in Distributed Computing (ADC) & Colloquium on Combining Paradigms for Software Development (CCPSD) (Lecture Notes in Computer Science Ser.: Vol. 494). viii, 482p. 1991. 57.00 (*0-387-53981-6*) Spr-Verlag.

Abramsky, S., et al. Handbook of Logic in Computer Science Vol. 4: Semantic Modelling. (Illus.). 666p. 1995. text 145.00 (*0-19-853780-8*) OUP.

Abramson. The Defense Is Ready. 320p. 1998. per. 14.00 (*0-671-02326-8*, Pocket Books) PB.

— Learning with LinkWay. (DF - Computer Applications Ser.). 1994. mass mkt., wbk. ed. 25.95 (*0-538-63668-8*) S-W Pub.

— Techpro: Information Processing/Keyboarding Simulation. (TA - Typing/Keyboarding Ser.). 1992. mass mkt. 17.25 (*0-538-61725-X*) S-W Pub.

Abramson, Alan J. & Salamon, Lester M. The Nonprofit Sector & the New Federal Budget. 138p. (Orig.). 1986. pap. text 19.50 (*0-87766-401-3*) Urban Inst.

Abramson, Albert. Electronic Motion Pictures: A History of the Television Camera. LC 74-4663. (Telecommunications Ser.). (Illus.). 228p. 1979. reprint ed. 26.95 (*0-405-06031-9*) Ayer.

— The History of Television, 1880-1941. LC 86-43091. (Illus.). 368p. 1987. lib. bdg. 49.95 (*0-89950-284-9*) McFarland & Co.

— Zworykin: Pioneer of Television. LC 94-7464. 384p. 1994. text 36.95 (*0-252-02104-5*) U of Ill Pr.

Abramson, Alexis. Home Safety for Seniors. LC 97-93125. (Illus.). 106p. (Orig.). 1997. pap. 10.95 (*0-9656918-0-2*) Mature Mart.

***Abramson, Allen.** Mythical Land, Legal Boundaries: Land Rites & Land Rights in Cultural & Historical Context. 2000. pap. text 22.50 (*0-7453-1570-4*) Pluto GBR.

***Abramson, Allen & Theodossopoulos, Dimitrios.** Land, Law & Environment: Mythical Land, Legal Boundaries. LC 00-9107. (Anthropology, Culture & Society Ser.). (Illus.). 2000. write for info. (*0-7453-1575-5*, Pub. by Pluto GBR) Stylus Pub VA.

Abramson, Betsy. Long Term Care Financing: A Consumer's Agenda for Action. 134p. 1989. 20.00 (*0-685-26153-0*) Ctr Public Rep.

Abramson, Betsy, et al. Advising Older Clients & Their Families, 2 vols. LC 96-50063. 1120p. 1997. ring bd. 250.00 (*0-945574-90-8*) State Bar WI.

Abramson, Betsy, jt. auth. see Meuer, Teresa.

Abramson, Bruce. The Expected-Outcome Model of Two-Player Games. (Research Notes in Artificial Intelligence Ser.). 200p. 1990. pap. text 34.95 (*1-55860-144-9*) Morgan Kaufmann.

Abramson, Carl, et al. Infectious Diseases of the Lower Extremity. (Illus.). 448p. 1991. 89.00 (*0-683-00040-3*) Lppncott W & W.

Abramson, Charles I. Invertebrate Learning: A Laboratory Manual & Source Book. LC 90-20660. (Illus.). 100p. 1990. pap. 14.95 (*1-55798-100-0*) Am Psychol.

— A Primer of Invertebrate Learning: The Behavioral Perspective. LC 94-4300. 273p. 1994. pap. 19.95 (*1-55798-228-7*) Am Psychol.

Abramson, Charles I., et al, eds. Russian Contributions to Inverterbrate Behavior. LC 95-40578. 248p. 1996. 75.00 (*0-275-94525-1*, Praeger Pubs) Greenwood.

Abramson, Chaya M. & Tscholkowsky, Esther. Who by Fire. 184p. 1995. 17.95 (*0-87306-742-8*); pap. 13.95 (*0-87306-746-0*) Feldheim.

*** Abramson, Daniel M.** Skyscraper Rivals: The AIG Building & the Architecture of Wall Street. (Illus.). 176p. 2000. 50.00 (*1-56898-244-5*) Princeton Arch.

Abramson, David H., jt. auth. see Sagerman, Robert H.

Abramson, Donald, jt. auth. see Koepfer, Helen R.

Abramson, Doris. It's Time. (Illus.). 104p. 1998. pap. 10.00 (*1-884540-40-6*) Haleys.

Abramson, Doris E. Negro Playwrights in the American Theatre, 1925-1959. LC 69-19457. 351p. reprint ed. pap. 108.90 (*0-608-14120-8*, 202428900036) Bks Demand.

Abramson, Edward. Emotional Eating: What You Need to Know Before Starting Your Next Diet. LC 97-45845. 1998. pap. text 17.95 (*0-7879-4047-X*) Jossey-Bass.

***Abramson, Edward.** Marriage Made Me Fat! (Illus.). 267p. 2000. mass mkt. 5.99 (*1-57566-556-5*) Kensgtn Pub Corp.

Abramson, Edward. To Have & to Hold. 256p. 1999. text 21.00 (*1-57566-421-6*) Kensgtn Pub Corp.

Abramson, Edward A. Bernard Malamud Revisited. (Twayne's United States Authors Ser.). 160p. 1993. 28.95 (*0-8057-7641-9*, Twyne) Mac Lib Ref.

— Chaim Potok. (United States Authors Ser.: No. 503). 176p. (C). 1986. 20.95 (*0-8057-7463-7*, Twyne) Mac Lib Ref.

Abramson, Glenda. Drama & Ideology in Modern Israel. LC 97-35221. (Illus.). 281p. (C). 1998. text 59.95 (*0-521-44159-5*) Cambridge U Pr.

— The Writing of Yehuda Amichai: A Thematic Approach. LC 89-4193. (SUNY Series in Modern Jewish Literature & Culture). 254p. (C). 1989. pap. text 24.95 (*0-88706-995-9*) State U NY Pr.

Abramson, Glenda, ed. The Experienced Soul: Studies in Amichai. LC 96-6694. 141p. (C). 1997. pap. 69.00 (*0-8133-2730-X*, Pub. by Westview) HarpC.

— Modern Jewish Mythologies. LC 99-26975. 200p. 1999. 39.95 (*0-87820-216-1*, Pub. by Hebrew Union Coll Pr) Wayne St U Pr.

Abramson, Glenda, ed. Modern Jewish Mythologies. 210p. Date not set. 39.95 (*0-8143-2893-8*) Wayne St U Pr.

Abramson, Glenda, ed. The Oxford Book of Hebrew Short Stories. 422p. 1996. 35.00 (*0-19-214206-2*) OUP.

— The Oxford Book of Hebrew Short Stories. 422p. 1997. reprint ed. pap. 15.95 (*0-19-288039-X*) OUP.

Abramson, Glenda & Parfitt, Tudor, eds. The Great Transition: The Recovery of the Lost Centres of Modern Hebrew Literature. (Oxford Centre for Postgraduate Hebrew Studies). 176p. (C). 1985. 56.50 (*0-8476-7437-1*) Rowman.

— Jewish Learning & the Academy: In Honour of Dr. David Patterson on the Occasion of His Seventieth Birthday. LC 93-5601. xvi, 321p. 1995. text 64.00 (*3-7186-5324-9*) Gordon & Breach.

Abramson, Glenda, tr. see Amichai, Yehuda.

Abramson, H. Norman, et al, eds. Technology Transfer Systems in the United States & Germany: Lessons & Perspectives. LC 97-76548. 150p. 1996. pap. text 43.00 (*0-309-05530-X*) Natl Acad Pr.

Abramson, Harold A. Psychological Problems in the Father-Son Relationship. LC 71-81849. 1969. 7.50 (*0-8079-0154-7*) October.

Abramson, Harvey & Dahl, V. Logic Grammars. (Symbolic Computation - Artificial Intelligence Ser.). (Illus.). 240p. 1989. 58.95 (*0-387-96961-6*) Spr-Verlag.

Abramson, Henry. A Prayer for the Government: Ukrainians & Jews in Revolutionary Times, 1917-1920. (Harvard Series in Ukrainian Studies; Harvard Center for Jewish Studies). (Illus.). 310p. (C). 1999. pap. 18.95 (*0-916458-87-3*) Harvard Ukrainian.

— A Prayer for the Government: Ukrainians & Jews in Revolutionary Times, 1917-1920. (Harvard Series in Ukrainian Studies; Harvard Center for Jewish Studies). (Illus.). 320p. (C). 1999. text 34.95 (*0-916458-88-1*) Harvard Ukrainian.

Abramson, Hilary. Student Athlete's Guide to College. 192p. 1999. pap. 12.00 (*0-375-75426-1*, Pub. by PRP NY) Random.

***Abramson, J. A.** Art in Nonliterate Societies: Structural Approaches & Implications for Sociocultural & System Theories. 1999. pap. write for info. (*0-932826-33-4*) New Issues MI.

Abramson, J. H. Making Sense of Data: A Self-Instruction Manual on the Interpretation of Epidemiological Data. 2nd ed. LC 93-36497. (Illus.). 416p. (C). 1994. pap. text 36.50 (*0-19-508969-3*) OUP.

— Survey Methods in Community Medicine: Epidemiological Studies, Programme Evaluation, Clinical Trials. 4th ed. (Illus.). 339p. 1990. pap. text 36.95 (*0-443-04196-2*) Church.

***Abramson, Jeffrey.** We, the Jury: The Jury System & the Ideal Democracy. 336p. 2000. pap. 17.95 (*0-674-00430-2*) HUP.

Abramson, Jerry, jt. auth. see Florio, James J.

Abramson, Joan. The Invisible Woman: Discrimination in the Academic Profession. LC 74-32627. 264p. reprint ed. pap. 81.90 (*0-608-14783-4*, 202564800045) Bks Demand.

Abramson, Joanne, et al. The Large Macaws: Their Care, Breeding & Conservation. Thomsen, Jorgen B., ed. (Illus.). 552p. 1996. lib. bdg. 170.00 (*0-9635964-0-3*) Raintree Pubns.

Abramson, Joanne, ed. see Naviaux, Barbara.

Abramson, Jon S., jt. ed. see Wheeler, J. Gary.

Abramson, Keith V. Top Ten Estate Planning Techniques for the 1990's. 160p. 1992. pap. 29.95 (*0-9635266-0-X*) Am Legal Pub.

Abramson, Lee W., et al. Slope Stability & Stablization methods. LC 95-16406. 656p. 1995. 120.00 (*0-471-10622-4*) Wiley.

Abramson, Leslie & Flaste, Richard. The Defense Is Ready: Life in the Trenches of Criminal Law. LC 96-37512. (Illus.). 304p. 1997. 24.50 (*0-684-81403-X*) S&S Trade.

Abramson, Leslie W. Judicial Disqualification under Canon 3 of the Code of Judicial Conduct. 2nd enl. ed. LC 91-73453. 96p. (Orig.). 1992. pap. 9.95 (*0-938870-53-X*) Am Judicature.

Abramson, Leslie W. & Edwards, Catherine D. Questions & Answers: Criminal Law. (Winning in Law School Ser.: Bk. 4). 155p. (Orig.). 1989. pap. text 12.95 (*0-915667-09-6*) Spectra Pub Co.

Abramson, Lillian. Not So Idle Notions. LC 94-46356. 128p. 1995. 15.95 (*0-944957-52-8*) Rivercross Pub.

Abramson, Lillian S., jt. auth. see Robinson, Jessie B.

Abramson, Lillian S., jt. ed. see Rudin, Jacob P.

Abramson, Lyn Y., ed. Social Cognition & Clinical Psychology: A Synthesis. LC 86-18453. 372p. 1988. lib. bdg. 47.95 (*0-89862-011-2*) Guilford Pubns.

Abramson, Marcia & Lovas, Paula M., eds. Aging & Sensory Change: An Annotated Bibliography. 80p. (Orig.). 1988. pap. 12.50 (*0-929596-00-5*) Gerontological Soc.

***Abramson, Marcie F.** Painless Word Problems. LC 00-31248. 2001. write for info. (*0-7641-1533-2*) Barron.

Abramson, Michael, et al, eds. Further & Higher Education Partnerships: The Future for Collaboration. LC 95-47027. 260p. (C). 1996. pap. 39.95 (*0-335-19597-0*) OpUniv Pr.

— Further & Higher Education Partnerships: The Future for Collaboration. LC 95-47027. 160p. 1996. 108.95 (*0-335-19598-9*) OpUniv Pr.

Abramson, Nils H. Light in Flight or the Holodiagram: The Columbi Egg of Optics, PM27. LC 96-33735. 1996. 80.00 (*0-8194-2107-3*) SPIE.

Abramson, P. B., ed. Guidebook to Light Water Reactor Safety Analysis. LC 84-22447. (Proceedings of the International Centre for Heat & Mass Transfer Ser.). (Illus.). 393p. 1985. 190.00 (*0-89116-262-3*) Hemisp Pub.

Abramson, Paul. A House Divided. (C). pap. text. write for info. (*0-393-97635-1*) Norton.

Abramson, Paul. The Journal of Sex Research, 1991, Vol. 28. 152p. 1991. pap. 74.00 (*0-317-03041-8*) Soc Sci Study Sex.

Abramson, Paul R. A Case for Case Studies: An Immigrant's Journal. 248p. (C). 1992. 49.95 (*0-8039-3695-8*); pap. 22.95 (*0-8039-3696-6*) Sage.

— Sarah: A Sexual Biography. LC 83-17983. 142p. (C). 1984. pap. text 19.95 (*0-87395-863-2*) State U NY Pr.

Abramson, Paul R. & Aldrich, John H. Change & Continuity in the 1996 Elections. LC 98-9251. 400p. (C). 1998. 28.95 (*1-56802-333-2*) Congr Quarterly.

Abramson, Paul R. & Inglehart, Ronald. Value Change in Global Perspective. LC 94-45178. 192p. 1995. pap. text 18.95 (*0-472-06591-2*, 06591) U of Mich Pr.

Abramson, Paul R. & Pinkerton, Steven D. With Pleasure: Thoughts on the Nature of Human Sexuality. (Illus.). 320p. 1995. text 30.00 (*0-19-509358-5*) OUP.

Abramson, Paul R. & Pinkerton, Steven D., eds. Sexual Nature, Sexual Culture. LC 94-36662. (Series on Sexuality, History, & Society). 434p. 1995. pap. text 19.95 (*0-226-00182-2*); lib. bdg. 65.00 (*0-226-00181-4*) U Ch Pr.

Abramson, Paul R., et al. Change & Continuity in the 1996 & 1998 Elections. LC 99-18220. 370p. 1999. pap. 30.95 (*1-56802-474-6*) Congr Quarterly.

Abramson, Paul R., jt. auth. see Murray, Joan.

Abramson, Phyllis L. Sob Sister Journalism, 23. LC 90-36637. (Contributions to the Study of Mass Media & Communications Ser.: No. 23). 144p. 1990. 49.95 (*0-313-26513-5*, AST, Greenwood Pr) Greenwood.

Abramson, Robert & Halset, Walter. Planning for Improved Enterprise Performance: A Guide for Managers & Consultants. (Management Development Ser.: No. 15). (Illus.). 170p. 1992. pap. 18.00 (*92-2-102082-7*) Intl Labour Office.

Abramson, Robert M. Rhythm Games: For Perception & Cognition. 36p. 1997. pap. 19.95 incl. audio compact disk (*0-913650-08-0*, M0599CD) Wrner Bros.

Abramson, Rudy, et al. Hallowed Ground: Preserving America's Heritage. LC 96-24513. 192p. 1996. 40.00 (*0-9650308-6-5*) Lickle Pubng.

Abramson, Shifa C., tr. see Ben-Hur, Raphaella B.

Abramson, Stacy, jt. auth. see Isay, David.

Abramson, Sue. Extended Frames. 32p. 1981. spiral bd. 10.00 (*0-930794-21-4*) Station Hill Pr.

Abramson, Susan & Stuchin, Marcie. Shops & Boutiques 2000: Designer Stores & Brand Imagery. LC 98-34462. 1998. pap. 45.00 (*0-86636-688-1*) PBC Intl Inc.

Abramson, Susan, jt. auth. see Stuchin, Marcie.

Abramson, Theodore, et al, eds. Handbook of Vocational Education Evaluation. LC 78-24256. 619p. 1979. reprint ed. pap. 191.90 (*0-608-00815-X*, 206160300010) Bks Demand.

Abramyan, E. A. Industrial Electron Accelerators & Applications. 300p. 1988. 115.00 (*0-89116-694-7*) Hemisp Pub.

Abranches, Carlos A., jt. auth. see Inter-American Commission on Human Rights.

Abranovic, Wynn A. Statistical Thinking & Data Analysis Methods for Managers. 950p. (C). 1997. 101.00 (*0-673-99296-9*) Addson-Wesley Educ.

Abranowitz, M., ed. see Treves, A., et al.

Abranson, Lillian. Hanukkah ABC. (Illus.). (J). (gr. 3-7). 1968. pap. 5.00 (*0-914080-60-1*) Shulsinger Sales.

***Abrantes, Fatima & Mix, Alan.** Reconstructing Ocean History: A Window into the Future. LC 99-52200. 1999. write for info. (*0-306-46293-1*, Kluwer Plenum) Kluwer Academic.

Abrantes, Roger. Dog Language: An Encyclopedia of Canine Behavior. Whitehead, Sarah, tr. from DAN.Tr. of Hundesprog. (Illus.). 295p. 1997. pap. 19.95 (*0-9660484-0-7*) Wakan Tanka.

— The Evolution of Canine Social Behavior. (Illus.). 80p. 1997. pap. 11.95 (*0-9660484-1-5*) Wakan Tanka.

Abrapalabra Staff, tr. see Sanchez-Ballate, Gerardo.

Abrash, Barbara & Egan, Catherine, eds. Mediating History: The MAP Guide to Independent Video by & about African Americans, Asian Americans, Latino, & Native American People. 200p. (C). 1992. pap. text 16.50 (*0-8147-0620-7*) NYU Pr.

Abrash, Henry I. & Hardcastle, Kenneth I. Chemistry. (Illus.). 708p. (C). 1993. reprint ed. text 95.00 (*1-878907-75-1*) TechBooks.

Abrate, Jayne, jt. ed. see Loughrin-Sacco, Steven J.

Abrate, Serge. Impact on Composite Structures. LC 97-16551. (Illus.). 300p. (C). 1998. text 64.95 (*0-521-47389-6*) Cambridge U Pr.

Abrauanel, Marty. Public Housing in a Competitive Market: An Example of How It Would Fare. (Illus.). 38p. (Orig.). (C). 1997. pap. text 30.00 (*0-7881-3764-6*) DIANE Pub.

Abravanel, Elliot D. & King Morrison, Elizabeth. Dr. Abravanel's Body Type Diet & Lifetime Nutrition Plan. rev. ed. LC 98-52981. 384p. (Orig.). 1999. pap. 13.95 (*0-553-38041-9*) Bantam.

Abravanel, Ernest, ed. see Stendhal, pseud.

Abravanel, Isaac. Principles of Faith (Rosh Amanah) Kellner, Menachem M., ed. & tr. by. from HEB. (Littman Library of Jewish Civilization). 272p. 1985. 26.00 (*0-19-710045-7*) OUP.

Abravanel, Isaac & Reines, Alvin J. Maimonides & Abrabanel on Prophecy. LC 73-119106. 321p. reprint ed. pap. 99.60 (*0-7837-0156-X*, 204045200017) Bks Demand.

Abreau, Kevin, ed. see Anderson, David M.

Abreau, Kevin, ed. see Anderson, David Martin.

Abreau, Kevin, ed. see Duffy, Chris.

Abrecht, Paul. Faith, Science & the Future. LC 79-7035. 240p. reprint ed. pap. 74.40 (*0-608-16836-X*, 202694200053) Bks Demand.

Abrell, Diana F. Pocket Guide to the Carriage Roads of Acadia National Park. 2nd expanded rev. ed. 40p. 1995. pap. 4.95 (*0-89272-349-1*) Down East.

A

An Asterisk (*) at the beginning of an entry indicates that the title is appearing for the first time.

Abrente. Diccionario Abrente de Terminos Economico-Financieros. (SPA.). 208p. 1989. pap. 21.95 (*0-7859-6420-7*, 8487402003) Fr & Eur.

Abrera, Bernard. Moths of Australia. 96p. 1984. 37.00 (*0-7855-0666-7*) St Mut.

Abrera, Josefa B. Doctoral Programs, Theses, & Graduates in Library & Information Science in the United States: An Analysis of the Published Literature, 1960-1980. (Occasional Papers: No. 183). 1988. pap. 2.50 (*0-685-34546-7*) U of Ill Grad Sch.

Abresch, Peter. Bloody Bonsai. (WWL Mystery Ser.: No. 321). 1999. per. 4.99 (*0-373-26321-X*, 1-26321-9, Wrldwide Lib) Harlequin Bks.

— Bloody Bonsai. 240p. 1998. 21.95 (*1-885173-34-2*) Write Way.

— Bloody Bonsai. large type ed. LC 98-53486. 1999. 26.95 (*0-7862-1787-1*) Thorndike Pr.

***Abresch, Peter.** Killing Thyme. 2000. mass mkt. 5.99 (*0-373-26356-2*, 1-26356-5) Harlequin Bks.

Abresch, Peter. Killing Thyme. (James P. Dandy Elderhostel Mystery Ser.: No. 2). 279p. 1999. 23.95 (*1-885173-68-7*) Write Way.

***Abresch, Peter.** Tip-a-Canoe. 272p. 2001. 23.95 (*1-885173-92-X*, Pub. by Write Way) Midpt Trade.

Abresch, Richard T. & Kern, Roger G. The Test Taking Advantage Strategy Manual. (Illus.). 181p. (YA). (gr. 10-12). 1990. pap. text 35.50 (*0-9627360-0-7*) Test Taking Advan.

***Abress, Monica Dwyer.** Quietly at Work: Township Government in America. LC 99-86138. (Illus.). 128p. 2000. pap. 18.95 (*1-58007-032-9*, Pub. by Specialty Pr) Voyageur Pr.

Abret, Helga & Grunewald, Michel, eds. Visions Allemandes de la France (1871-1914) Frankreich aus Deutscher Sicht (1871-1914) (Contacts Ser.: Series II, Vol. 15). (FRE.). 444p. 1995. 59.95 (*3-906754-04-9*, Pub. by P Lang) P Lang Pubng.

***Abreu, Ciao Fernando.** Whatever Happened to Dulce Veiga? A B-Novel. Frizzi, Adia, tr. from POR. & afterword by by. LC 00-37705. 192p. 2001. 35.00 (*0-292-70500-X*) U of Tex Pr.

***Abreu, Ciao Fernando & Frizzi, Adria.** Whatever Happened to Dulce Veiga? A B-Novel. LC 00-37705. (Texas Pan American Ser). 2001. pap. 15.95 (*0-292-70501-8*) U of Tex Pr.

Abreu, Daisy C., jt. auth. see Vargas, Nelida H.

Abreu, Domingo & Guerrero, Kelvin, eds. Parque Nacional del Este, D. R. Tomo 1: Recursos Terrestres. (SPA., Illus.). 134p. (Orig.). 1997. pap. 25.00 (*0-9643786-4-7*) Media Pubng.

Abreu-Felippe, Nicolas. El Lago. LC 91-75689. (Coleccion Caniqui). (SPA.). 124p. (Orig.). 1991. pap. 13.00 (*0-89729-619-2*) Ediciones.

Abreu, Ivan, jt. auth. see Matos, Libio.

Abreu, Jose, ed. see Covarrubias, Jorge.

Abreu, Marcelo & Verner, Dorte. Long-Term Brazilian Economic Growth, 1930-1994. LC 97-224735. (Long-Term Growth Ser.). 140p. 1997. pap. 25.00 (*92-64-15619-4*, 41-97-14-1, Pub. by Org for Econ) OECD.

Abreu, Maria I. & Rameh, Clea. Portugues Contemporaneo, 2 vols. Incl. Vol. 1. Portugues Contemporaneo I. LC 66-25520. 256p. 1972. pap. 12.95 (*0-87840-026-5*); Vol. 2. Portugues Contemporaneo 2. LC 66-25520. 346p. 1973. pap. 14.95 (*0-87840-025-7*); LC 66-25520. 1971. write for info. (*0-318-52679-4*) Georgetown U Pr.

Abreu, Maria I., jt. ed. see Sole, Carlos A., Jr.

Abreu, Rosendo. The Cambridge Program for the GED Social Studies Test. (GED Preparation Ser.). (Illus.). 272p. (Orig.). 1988. student ed. 3.30 (*0-8428-9394-6*) Cambridge Bk.

Abrev, Linda. Millions of Memories. 150p. 1999. 15.99 (*0-9670865-0-7*) Millions Memos.

Abrevaya, Elda. El Nino, Su Sufrimiento y la Pobreza. (SPA.). 160p. 1992. pap. write for info. (*0-929441-37-0*) Pubns Puertorriquenas.

Abrial, J. R. The B-Book: Assigning Programs to Meanings. LC 97-107195. 813p. (C). 1996. text 74.95 (*0-521-49619-5*) Cambridge U Pr.

Abrial, Jean-Raymond, et al. Formal Methods for Industrial Applications: Specifying & Programming the Steam Boiler Control. LC 96-39128. (Lecture Notes in Computer Science Ser.: Vol. 1165). 511p. 1996. 79.95 incl. cd-rom (*3-540-61929-1*) Spr-Verlag.

Abricka, Maria V., jt. auth. see Dessen, Cynthia S.

Abridged Ed. Treaties Establishing the European Communities. LC 88-163254. 649 p. 1987. write for info. (*92-825-7657-4*) Intl Pubns Serv.

***Abrie, Pieter L.** Design of RF & Microwave Amplifiers & Oscillators. LC 99-18043. (Microwave Library). 480p. 1999. 99.00 incl. cd-rom (*0-89006-797-X*) Artech Hse.

Abrignani, Catherine & Messenger, Bill. Alzheimer's Disease: Activities That Work. (Illus.). 123p. (C). 1991. 18.00 (*1-877735-34-5*, 2182PP) Prof Prnting & Pub.

Abrikosov, A. A. Fundamentals of the Theory of Metals. Beknazarov, A., tr. 630p. 1988. 190.00 (*0-444-87094-6*); pap. 83.50 (*0-444-87095-4*, North Holland) Elsevier.

Abrikosov, A. A., et al. Methods of Quantum Field Theory in Statistical Physics. Silverman, Richard A., tr. from RUS. 352p. (C). 1975. reprint ed. pap. 9.95 (*0-486-63228-8*) Dover.

— Quantum Field Theoretical Methods in Statistical Physics, Vol. 4. 1965. 166.00 (*0-08-013470-X*, Pub. by Pergamon Repr) Franklin.

Abril, Chi Qui, tr. see Diaz Agen, Manzani & Perez de Ayala, Juan, eds.

Abril de Esteve, Himilce. Ensenando Ortografia. (SPA.). 1975. pap. 6.00 (*0-89729-116-6*) Ediciones.

Abrill, jt. auth. see Brimhall.

Abrims, Ethel, ed. see Mincey, Melvin.

Abriola, L. M. Multiphase Migration of Organic Compounds in a Porous Medium: A Mathematical Model. (Lecture Notes in Engineering Ser.: Vol. 8). (Illus.). viii, 232p. 1984. 33.95 (*0-387-13694-0*) Spr-Verlag.

Abrioux, Yves. Ian Hamilton Finlay: A Visual Primer Introductory Notes & Commentaries. (Illus.). 312p. 1992. 55.00 (*0-262-01129-8*) MIT Pr.

Abrishaman, M. & Putnam, A. A. Effect of Furnace Design on Combustion Noise. 49p. 1977. pap. 3.75 (*0-318-12604-4*, M59077) Am Gas Assn.

***Abro, Ben.** Assassination! July 14. 2001. pap. 16.95 (*0-8032-5939-5*, Bison Books) U of Nebr Pr.

Abrohms, Alison. One Thousand & One Manipulatives for Math. 1993. pap. 16.95 (*0-590-49238-1*) Scholastic Inc.

Abrol, B. K., jt. auth. see Chopra, L. C.

Abrol, Prem N. Commercial Banking. (C). 1987. 28.00 (*0-8364-2176-0*, Pub. by Ashish Pub Hse) S Asia.

Abrol, Y. P., et al, eds. Impact of Global Climatic Changes on Photosynthesis & Plant Productivity. (C). 1991. text 80.00 (*81-204-0614-1*, Pub. by Oxford IBH) S Asia.

Abrol, Yash P., et al, eds. Photosynthesis: Photoreactions to Plant Productivity. LC 92-34817. 1993. text 308.00 (*0-7923-1943-5*) Kluwer Academic.

Abromeit, C., jt. ed. see Wollenberger, H.

Abromeit, Heidrun. Democracy in Europe: Legitimising Politics in a Non-State Polity. LC 98-24534. 192p. 1998. 39.95 (*1-57181-985-1*) Berghahn Bks.

Abromeit, Heidrun, et al. Adenauer to Kohl: The Development of the German Chancellorship. Padgett, Stephen, ed. LC 94-2059. 220p. 1994. 37.50 (*0-87840-556-9*) Georgetown U Pr.

Abromeit, Kathleen A., compiled by. An Index to African-American Spirituals for the Solo Voice, 76. LC 98-44409. (Music Reference Collection: Vol. 76). 216p. 1999. lib. bdg. 65.00 (*0-313-30577-3*) Greenwood.

Abromovitz, Hedy & Abramovits, Les. Insuring Quality: Bringing Quality to the Insurance Industry. (Illus.). 200p. 1997. lib. bdg. 39.95 (*1-57444-150-7*) St Lucie Pr.

Abromovitz, Hedy & Abromovitz, Les. Bring TQM on the QT to Your Organization: How to Implement Quality Management Without Shoving It Down Your Employees's Throats. 250p. (Orig.). 1993. pap. 10.00 (*0-945320-34-5*) Stat Process Contrl.

Abromovitz, Les. Family Insurance Handbook: The Complete Guide for the 1990s. 1990. 17.95 (*0-8306-8057-8*) McGraw-Hill Prof.

— Money for Nothing, Tips for Free. 168p. (Orig.). 1995. pap. 5.95 (*1-56245-185-5*) Great Quotations.

Abromovitz, Les, jt. auth. see Abromovitz, Hedy.

Abromowitz, Jack & Uva, Kenneth. The Constitution & the Government of the U. S. (YA). (gr. 7-12). 1987. pap. text 3.50 (*0-89525-747-5*) Ed Activities.

Abromowitz, Jennifer. Women Outdoors: The Best One Thousand Nine Hundred Books, Programs & Periodicals. LC 91-142632. (Illus.). 180p. (Orig.). 1990. pap. 28.00 (*0-9630956-0-9*) J Abromowitz.

Abroms, E. M. The Freedom of the Self: The Bio-Existential Treatment of Character Problems. (Critical Issues in Psychiatry Ser.). (Illus.). 262p. (C). 1993. 45.00 (*0-306-44370-8*, Plenum Trade) Perseus Pubng.

Abromson, Herman, ed. see Morley, Christopher.

Abrons, Richard. Every Day a Visitor. Page, Carolyn, ed. & illus. by. 196p. (Orig.). 1996. pap. 14.95 (*1-879205-68-8*) Nightshade Pr.

Abruna. Physical Chemistry. (C). pap. text, lab manual ed. write for info. (*0-7167-2668-8*) W H Freeman.

Abruna, H. D., ed. Electrochemical Interfaces: Modern Techniques for In-Situ Interface Characterization. 589p. 1991. lib. bdg. 95.00 (*0-89573-715-9*, Wiley-VCH) Wiley.

Abruna, H. D., ed. Electrochemical Interfaces: Modern Techniques for In-Situ Interface Characterization. 587p. 1991. 130.00 (*0-471-18725-9*) Wiley.

Abruscato. Elementary Science, 1986. 1986. text, teacher ed. 55.25 (*0-03-009307-4*) Harcourt Schl Pubs.

— Science, Grade 2, 1989. 1989. student ed. 36.00 (*0-03-011419-5*) Harcourt Schl Pubs.

— Science 1986. 1986. pap., teacher ed., wbk. ed. 13.50 (*0-03-003449-3*); pap., teacher ed., wbk. ed. 13.50 (*0-03-003453-1*); pap., teacher ed., wbk. ed. 14.25 (*0-03-003457-4*); pap., teacher ed., wbk. ed. 14.25 (*0-03-003459-0*); pap., wbk. ed. 8.25 (*0-03-003448-5*); pap., wbk. ed. 9.50 (*0-03-003454-X*); pap., wbk. ed. 9.50 (*0-03-003458-2*); text, teacher ed. 61.25 (*0-03-003164-8*); text, teacher ed. 67.25 (*0-03-003167-2*); text, teacher ed. 70.50 (*0-03-003168-0*); text, teacher ed. 73.25 (*0-03-003169-9*); text, teacher ed. 81.00 (*0-03-003172-9*); text, teacher ed. 58.50 (*0-03-003163-X*) Harcourt Schl Pubs.

— Science 1989. 1989. teacher ed. 61.75 (*0-03-011402-0*); teacher ed. 73.00 (*0-03-011404-7*); teacher ed. 80.00 (*0-03-011407-1*); teacher ed. 252.00 (*0-03-011974-X*); teacher ed. 263.25 (*0-03-011979-0*); teacher ed. 319.25 (*0-03-011984-7*); teacher ed. 325.00 (*0-03-011989-8*); teacher ed. 325.00 (*0-03-011994-4*); teacher ed. 325.00 (*0-03-011999-5*); pap., teacher ed., wbk. ed. 14.25 (*0-03-011423-3*); pap., teacher ed., wbk. ed. 14.25 (*0-03-011424-1*); pap., teacher ed., wbk. ed. 15.50 (*0-03-011427-6*); pap., teacher ed., wbk. ed. 15.50 (*0-03-011428-4*) Harcourt Schl Pubs.

Abruscato, Joe & Hassard, Jack. Whole Cosmos Catalog of Science Activities, Grades 4-8. 2nd ed. 1990. pap. 14.95 (*0-673-16753-4*, GoodYrBooks) Addson-Wesley Educ.

Abruscato, Joseph. Children, Computers, & Science Teaching. (Illus.). 224p. 1986. pap. text 26.00 (*0-13-131947-7*); pap. text 23.00 (*0-13-131939-6*) P-H.

***Abruscato, Joseph.** Elementary Science Content & Activities. 2000. pap. 40.00 (*0-205-33002-9*) Allyn.

— Methods for Teaching Children Science. 2000. pap. 40.00 (*0-205-33021-5*) Allyn.

— Teaching Children Science. 5th ed. LC 99-36512. 488p. (C). 1999. 72.00 (*0-205-28410-8*, Macmillan Coll) P-H.

Abruscato, Joseph. Whizbangers & Wonderments: Science Activities for Children. LC 99-28639. (Illus.). 312p. (C). 1999. pap. text 24.99 (*0-205-28409-4*, Macmillan Coll) P-H.

Abrutyn, Elias. Saunders Infection Control Reference Service. Biello, Lisa, ed. LC 96-38025. 1536p. 1997. text 295.00 (*0-7216-6443-1*, W B Saunders Co) Harcrt Hlth Sci Grp.

Abrutyn, Leslye, jt. auth. see Danielson, Charlotte.

Abruzzese, Roberta S., ed. Nursing Staff Development: Strategies for Success. 2nd ed. LC 95-49884. (Illus.). 368p. (C). (gr. 13). 1996. text 49.95 (*0-8151-0053-1*, 26131) Mosby Inc.

Abruzzi, William S. Dam That River! Ecology & Mormon Settlement in the Little Colorado River Basin. LC 93-17051. 236p. (C). 1993. lib. bdg. 46.50 (*0-8191-9126-4*) U Pr of Amer.

Abruzzini, Debbie & Boegler, Susan. Descripto Bingo. (Illus.). 128p. (J). (ps-5). 1996. spiral bd., wbk. ed. 29.95 (*1-58650-046-5*, BK-239) Super Duper.

Abruzzini, Debbie, jt. auth. see Boegler, Susan.

Abruzzo, Maria & Abruzzo, Thomas. Recovering Your Business. 188p. 1993. 19.95 (*0-9638710-0-5*) Tamp Computer.

Abruzzo, Thomas, jt. auth. see Abruzzo, Maria.

Abs, Hermann J., et al. Diccionario Abrente de Terminos Economico-Financieros. 9th ed. (SPA.). 880p. 1973. 275.00 (*0-7859-6900-4*, 3411012595) Fr & Eur.

Absalom, Roger. Italy Since 1800. LC 94-11465. (Present & Past Ser.). 352p. (C). 1995. text 71.95 (*0-582-02772-1*, 76982, Pub. by Addison-Wesley) Longman.

***Abse, Dannie.** Be Seated, Thou: Poems, 1989-1998. LC 99-45750. 138p. 2000. pap. 15.95 (*1-878818-83-X*, Pub. by Sheep Meadow) U Pr of New Eng.

Abse, Dannie. Dannie Abse. (Pocket Poet Ser.). 1963. pap. 3.95 (*0-8023-9036-6*) Dufour.

— Intermittent Journals. 256p. 1994. pap. 16.95 (*1-85411-109-4*, Pub. by Seren Bks) Dufour.

— Intermittent Journals. 256p. 1995. 35.00 (*1-85411-108-6*, Pub. by Seren Bks) Dufour.

— On the Evening Road. 64p. 1995. 15.95 (*0-09-178941-9*, Pub. by Hutchnson) Trafalgar.

— One-Legged on Ice. LC 82-20055. (Contemporary Poetry Ser.). 64p. (C). 1983. reprint ed. pap. 14.95 (*0-8203-0653-3*) U of Ga Pr.

— Remembrance of Crimes Past: Poems. LC 92-37208. 80p. (Orig.). 1993. pap. 9.95 (*0-89255-176-3*) Persea Bks.

— Sky in Narrow Streets. (QRL Poetry Bks.: Vol. XXVII). (WEL.). 1987. 35.00 (*0-614-06419-8*) Quarterly Rev.

— A Strong Dose of Myself LC 83-125379. 220p. 1983. write for info. (*0-09-151260-3*) Hutchnson.

— White Coat, Purple Coat: Collected Poems 1948-1988. 304p. 1991. 29.95 (*0-89255-153-4*) Persea Bks.

— White Coat, Purple Coat: Collected Poems 1948-1988. 288p. 1992. pap. 12.95 (*0-89255-177-1*) Persea Bks.

Abse, Dannie, ed. Twentieth Century Anglo-Welsh Poetry. LC 97-227971. 280p. 1997. 49.95 (*1-85411-182-5*, Pub. by Seren Bks); pap. 17.95 (*1-85411-183-3*, Pub. by Seren Bks) Dufour.

Abse, Dannie & Abse, Joan. The Music Lover's Literary Companion. 330p. 1995. pap. 14.95 (*0-86051-654-7*, Robson-Parkwest) Parkwest Pubns.

Abse, Dannie & Archard, Cary. Welsh Retrospective. LC 98-126189. 96p. 1998. pap. 17.95 (*1-85411-201-5*, Pub. by Seren Bks) Dufour.

Abse, Joan. The Art Galleries of Britain & Ireland: A Guide to Their Collections. LC 75-24944. (Illus.). 248p. (C). 1975. 28.50 (*0-8386-1850-2*) Fairleigh Dickinson.

***Abse, Joan, ed.** Letters from Wales. 324p. 2000. 42.95 (*1-85411-270-8*, Pub. by Seren Bks) Dufour.

Abse, Joan, jt. auth. see Abse, Dannie.

Abse, Leo. The Man Behind the Smile: Tony Blair & the Politics of Perversion. LC 97-122345. (Illus.). 1997. 28.95 (*1-86105-078-X*, Robson-Parkwest) Parkwest Pubns.

— Wotan, My Enemy: Can Britain Live with the Germans in the European Union? (Illus.). 274p. 1995. 29.95 (*0-86051-910-4*, Robson-Parkwest) Parkwest Pubns.

Abshagen, U. & Munnich, F. E., eds. Costs of Illness & Benefits of Drug Treatment. (Clinical Pharmacology Ser.: Vol. 4). (Illus.). 112p. 1990. text 42.00 (*3-88603-364-3*, Pub. by W Zuckschwerdt) Scholium Intl.

Abshear, J. R., et al. A Compendium of Trite Cliches, Hard Sayings & Sagacious Witticisms. LC 99-94888. 86p. 1999. pap. 19.95 (*0-9646750-2-1*) Abshear Pub.

Absher, Tom. Men & the Goddess: Feminine Archetypes in Western Literature. 192p. (Orig.). 1990. pap. 10.95 (*0-89281-268-0*) Inner Tradit.

Absher, W. O. Surry County, N. C., Court Minutes, 1768-1789, Vols. 1 & 2. 168p. 1985. pap. 18.50 (*0-89308-554-5*) Southern Hist Pr.

Abshire, David, ed. Egypt & Israel: Prospects for a New Era. 128p. (Orig.). (C). 1979. pap. text 24.95 (*0-87855-790-3*) Transaction Pubs.

Abshire, David M. & Brower, Brock. Putting America's House in Order: The Nation As a Family. LC 95-40577. 208p. 1996. 19.95 (*0-275-95431-5*, Praeger Pubs) Greenwood.

Abshire, David M. & Nurnberger, Ralph D., eds. The Growing Power of Congress. LC 80-28562. 328p. 1981. reprint ed. pap. 101.70 (*0-608-01495-8*, 205953900001) Bks Demand.

Abshire, Michael. Fund for the Improvement of Postsecondary Education: A School-to-career Winning Grant Proposal. 34p. write for info. (*0-8342-1737-6*) Aspen Pub.

— Rural Health Services Outreach: A Winning Grant Proposal. 80p. write for info. (*0-8342-1738-4*) Aspen Pub.

— School District Technology: A Winning Grant Proposal. 36p. write for info. (*0-8342-1739-2*) Aspen Pub.

Absi, E., jt. auth. see Kerisel, Jean.

Absi-Halabi, M., et al, eds. Catalysts in Petroleum Refining & Petrochemical Industries 1995: Proceedings of the 2nd International Conference on Catalysts in Petroleum Refining & Petrochemical Industries, Kuwait, 22-26 April 1995. LC 95-43385. (Studies in Surface Science & Catalysis: Vol. 100). 616p. 1996. text 250.00 (*0-444-82381-6*) Elsevier.

Absire, Alain. God's Equal. 272p. 1989. 21.95 (*0-15-136070-7*) Harcourt.

— Lazarus. 256p. 1988. 19.95 (*0-15-149250-6*) Harcourt.

Absolon, Karel B. The Antibacterial Effect of the Penicillium Mold: Billroth - 1874, Fleming - 1929. (Illus.). 110p. (C). 1994. pap. 24.50 (*0-614-04348-4*) Kabel Pubs.

— The Belle Epoque of Surgery: The Life & Times of Theodor Billroth, 2 vols., Set. enl. rev. ed. Orig. Title: The Surgeon's Surgeon. (Illus.). 312p. (Orig.). (C). 1995. text 59.50 (*0-930329-64-3*) Kabel Pubs.

— Bibliography of or about Theador Billroth: And His Pupils. (Illus.). 68p. (C). 1994. pap. text 19.50 (*0-930329-73-2*) Kabel Pubs.

***Absolon, Karel B.** Cell Theory - Histopathology: Its Origins - Foundation by Johannes Muller (1801-1858) (Illus.). (C). 1999. text 39.50 (*1-57529-079-0*) Kabel Pubs.

Absolon, Karel B. The Conquest of the Caves & Underground Rivers of Czechoslovakia's Macocha Abyss: A Historical & Technical Study of Their Exploration. (Illus.). 112p. (Orig.). 1987. pap. 39.50 (*0-930329-21-X*) Kabel Pubs.

***Absolon, Karel B.** The Development of an Academic Surgeon: The Young Theodor Billroth (1829-1894) 115p. 1999. 49.50 (*1-57529-080-4*) Kabel Pubs.

Absolon, Karel B. The Development of Emergency Medical Services in War & Peace. (Illus.). 102p. (Orig.). (C). 1994. pap. 24.50 (*0-614-04349-2*) Kabel Pubs.

— The Developmental Technology of Gastrectomy & Vagotomy. rev. ed. (Illus.). 178p. 1995. pap. 34.50 (*0-930329-97-X*) Kabel Pubs.

— Developmental Technology of Gastric Surgery. (Illus.). 152p. 1984. text 65.00 (*0-930329-01-5*); pap. text 42.50 (*0-930329-00-7*) Kabel Pubs.

— Developmental Technology of Gastric Surgery. 2nd rev. ed. Kabel Staff, ed. (Illus.). 200p. 1986. 42.50 (*0-930329-08-2*) Kabel Pubs.

— From G. Prochaska to J. E. Purkinje. (Illus.). 130p. (Orig.). 1987. pap. 39.50 (*0-930329-15-5*) Kabel Pubs.

Absolon, Karel B. From J. Prochaska to Jan E. Purkinje. (Illus.). 29.50 (*0-930329-39-2*) Kabel Pubs.

Absolon, Karel B. Grossmeister der Chirurgie (Theodor Billroth 1829-1894) Kern, Ernst et al, trs. Orig. Title: The Surgeon's Surgeon (Theodor Billroth 1829-1894). (GER., Illus.). 400p. (Orig.). 1989. pap. 39.50 (*0-930329-29-5*) Kabel Pubs.

— Happy Warrior: Theodor Billroth - Franco - Prussian War 1870. (Illus.). 104p. (C). 1994. pap. 24.50 (*0-614-04350-6*) Kabel Pubs.

***Absolon, Karel B.** Rober Remak (1815-1865) The First Jew Appointed to the Beslim Faculty. (Illus.). 60p. 1999. 39.50 (*1-57529-081-2*) Kabel Pubs.

Absolon, Karel B. The Study of Medical Sciences (Theodor Billroth & Abraham Flexner) An Analysis from Past to Present. (Illus.). 170p. 1986. pap. 49.50 (*0-930329-10-4*) Kabel Pubs.

— The Surgeon's Surgeon: Theodor Billroth (1829-1894), Vol. II. (Illus.). 232p. 1981. 28.50 (*0-87291-146-2*) Coronado Pr.

— The Surgeon's Surgeon Vol. 1: Theodor Billroth (1829-1894), Vol. 1. (Illus.). 1979. 25.00 (*0-87291-129-2*) Coronado Pr.

— The Surgeon's Surgeon Vol. 3: Theodor Billroth (1829-1894) (Illus.). 280p. 1987. 30.00 (*0-87291-163-2*) Coronado Pr.

***Absolon, Karel B.** The Surgeon's Surgeon - Theodor Billroth (1829-1894), Vol. IV. (Illus.). 1999. 29.50 (*0-930329-28-7*) Kabel Pubs.

— Theodor Billroth (1829-1894) 1999. 49.50 (*1-57529-012-X*) Kabel Pubs.

Absolon, Karel B. Theodor Billroth, 1829-1894. Brancato, Ubaldo, tr. (ITA., Illus.). 350p. (C). 1995. text 39.50 (*0-930329-76-7*) Kabel Pubs.

***Absolon, Karel B.** Wound Treatment (Past to Present) With Reference to Karl V. Reichenbach (Creosote) - Joseph Lister (Carbolic Acid) - Louis Pasteur (Asepsis) - Alexis Carrel (Dakin's Solution) - Theodor Billroth & Others. (Illus.). 1999. 39.50 (*1-57529-074-X*) Kabel Pubs.

Absolon, Karel B., ed. The Intimate Billroth: The Intimate Story of the Founder of Modern Surgery. (Illus.). 240p. 1985. pap. 39.50 (*0-930329-05-8*) Kabel Pubs.

— Three Unique Letters to Alexander Humboldt by Peter S. P. Pallas & Wilhelm H. Abich. fac. ed. (Illus.). 24p. (C). 1994. pap. 14.50 (*0-614-04352-2*) Kabel Pubs.

***Absolon, Karel B. & Billroth-Gottlieb, Hans.** The Intimate Billroth: Letters to His Confidante. (Billroth-Seegen Letters Ser.). 1999. 29.50 (*0-930329-32-5*) Kabel Pubs.

— Theodor Billroth Privat: Briefe Seiner Mitwisserin. (Billroth Seegen Briefe Ser.). (Illus.). 1999. 29.50 (*0-930329-16-3*) Kabel Pubs.

Absolon, Karel B. & Bufkova-Hankelova, Karla. The Tale of the Bad Macocha & the Fable of the Underground Punkva River. (Moravian Tales, Legends, Myths Ser.). (Illus.). 40p. (Orig.). (J). (gr. 4). 1984. pap. text 12.00 (*0-930329-02-3*) Kabel Pubs.

An Asterisk (*) at the beginning of an entry indicates that the title is appearing for the first time.

A

Absolon, Karel B. & Kern, Ernst, eds. Theodor Billroth Privat: Die Billroth Seegen Briefe. (Illus.). 291p. 1987. 39.50 (*0-930329-07-4*) Kabel Pubs.

Absolon, Karel B. & Sedwitz, J. Lee. The Antibacterial Effect of the Penicillium Mold: Billroth-1874 Fleming-1929. (Illus.). 110p. (Orig.). (C). 1994. text 24.50 (*0-930329-71-6*) Kabel Pubs.

— The Development of Emergency Medical Services in War & Peace. (Illus.). 102p. (Orig.). (C). 1994. pap. 34.50 (*0-685-71271-0*) Kabel Pubs.

— Happy Warrior - Theodor Billroth: Franco-Prussian War, 1870. (Illus.). 65p. (Orig.). 1994. pap. 29.50 (*0-685-71276-1*) Kabel Pubs.

— Happy Warrior - Theodor Billroth: Franco-Prussian War, 1870. (Illus.). 104p. (Orig.). (C). 1994. text 34.50 (*0-930329-68-6*) Kabel Pubs.

— Mechanism - Treatment - Prevention of Aspiration Pneumonia (Theodor Billroth) (Illus.). 102p. (C). 1999. text 29.50 (*0-930329-70-8*) Kabel Pubs.

Absolon, Karel B., ed. see Jonnard, Raymond.

Abster, W. D. Stokes County, N. C. Wills, 1790-1864, Vols. 1-4. 181p. 1985. pap. 21.50 (*0-89308-557-X*) Southern Hist Pr.

Abstreiter, Gerhard, et al, eds. Optical Spectroscopy of Low Dimensional Semiconductors: Proceedings of the NATO Advanced Study Intstitute, Ankara & Antalya, Turkey, 9-20 September 1996. LC 97-33653. (NATO Advanced Science Institutes Ser.: No. 344). 400p. 1997. text 217.50 (*0-7923-4728-5*) Kluwer Academic.

Abt, Clark C. Serious Games. LC 86-34021. 196p. (C). 1987. pap. text 21.50 (*0-8191-6148-9*); lib. bdg. 44.00 (*0-8191-6147-0*) U Pr of Amer.

— The Social Audit for Management: Problems & Possibilities. 1976. 30.00 (*0-89011-489-7*, REM-107) Abt Bks.

Abt, Clark C., ed. Problems in American Social Policy Research. LC 79-55772. (Illus.). 300p. 1980. text 30.00 (*0-89011-540-0*) Abt Bks.

Abt, Clark C., et al, eds. Perspectives on the Costs & Benefits of Applied Social Research. LC 78-67240. 1979. text 30.00 (*0-89011-520-6*) Abt Bks.

Abt, Clark C. & Hardy, Kathleen M., eds. AIDS & the Courts. (Illus.). 400p. 1990. 40.00 (*0-89011-615-6*); pap. 30.00 (*0-89011-616-4*); text 40.00 (*0-89011-640-7*) Abt Bks.

Abt, E., tr. see Stark, W.

***Abt, Helmut A.** Centennial Astrophysical Journal. 1999. pap. text 35.00 (*0-226-00186-5*) U Ch Pr.

— Centennial Astrophysical Journal. 2000. lib. bdg. 50.00 (*0-226-00185-7*) U Ch Pr.

Abt, Henry E. The Care, Cure, & Education of the Crippled Child: A Study of American Social & Professional Facilities to Care for, Cure, & Educate Crippled Children. LC 74-1659. (Children & Youth Ser.). (Illus.). 240p. 1974. reprint ed. 24.95 (*0-405-05941-8*) Ayer.

Abt, John & Myerson, Michael. Advocate & Activist: Memoirs of an American Communist Lawyer. LC 92-47040. 344p. 1993. text 29.95 (*0-252-02030-8*) U of Ill Pr.

Abt, Lawrence E. Acting Out. 1996. pap. 50.00 (*1-56821-778-1*) Aronson.

Abt, Lawrence E. & Weissman, Stuart L., eds. Acting Out. 2nd ed. LC 76-53942. 336p. 1976. reprint ed. 50.00 (*0-87668-287-5*) Aronson.

Abt, Lawrence E., jt. ed. see Rosner, Stanley.

***Abt, Regina, et al.** Dream Child: Creation & New Life in Dreams of Pregnant Women. 460p. 2000. pap. 33.00 (*3-85630-592-0*, Pub. by Daimon Pubs) Cassell & Continuum.

Abt, Samuel. In Pursuit of the Yellow Jersey: Bicycle Racing in the Year of the Tortured Tour. LC 98-75020. (Cycling Resources Ser.). (Illus.). 208p. 1999. pap. 16.95 (*1-892495-16-3*, 5163) Van der Plas.

***Abt, Samuel.** Lance Armstrong's Comeback from Cancer: A Scrapbook of the Tour de France Winner's Dramatic Career. LC 99-75679. (Illus.). 160p. 1999. pap. text 16.95 (*1-892495-25-2*, Pub. by Van der Plas) Seven Hills Bk.

Abt, Samuel. Pedaling to Glory: Victory & Drama in Professional Bicycle Racing. LC 97-3485. (Illus.). 160p. 1997. pap. 14.95 (*0-933201-83-4*) MBI Pubg.

— A Season in Turmoil: Lance Armstrong Replaces Greg LeMond As U. S. Cycling's Superstar. LC 96-11422. (Illus.). 176p. 1995. pap. 14.95 (*1-884737-09-9*) VeloPress.

Abt, Steven R. & Gessler, Johannes, eds. Hydraulic Engineering. (Conference Proceedings Ser.). 1280p. 1988. 109.00 (*0-87262-670-9*) Am Soc Civil Eng.

Abt, Steven R., et al. Water Resources Engineering 98, 2. LC 98-26983. 2000p. 1998. 199.00 (*0-7844-0359-7*) Am Soc Civil Eng.

Abt, Theodor. Progress Without Loss of Soul: A Wholistic Approach to Modernization Planning. Matthews, Boris L., tr. from GER. LC 89-890. (Illus.). 428p. 1989. 9.95 (*0-933029-36-5*); pap. 3.95 (*0-933029-19-5*) Chiron Pubns.

Abt, Vicki & Mustazza, Leonard. Coming after Oprah: Cultural Fallout in the Age of the TV Talk Show. LC 97-13986. 1997. 48.95 (*0-87972-751-9*); pap. 20.95 (*0-87972-752-7*) Bowling Green Univ Popular Press.

Abtertozzi. School of Meinong. 84.95 (*1-84014-374-6*) Ashgate Pub Co.

Abts, Henry W., III. How to Settle Your Living Trust. LC 98-39669. 384p. 1998. pap. 24.95 (*0-8092-2844-0*, 284400, Contemporary Bks) NTC Contemp Pub Co.

— The Living Trust. rev. ed. 368p. 1993. pap. 24.95 (*0-8092-3918-3*) NTC Contemp Pub Co.

— The Living Trust. rev. ed. LC 97-18356. (Illus.). 320p. 1997. pap. 24.95 (*0-8092-3031-3*, 303130, Contemporary Bks) NTC Contemp Pub Co.

Abu al-Fida. Geographie d'Aboulfeda, 2 vols. in 3, Set. Reinaud, M. & Guyard, S., trs. from ARA. (FRE.). 1128p. reprint ed. lib. bdg. 200.00 (*0-89241-181-3*) Caratzas.

Abu Al-Hasan & Ahmed-Ibn Ibrahim. The Arithmetic of Al-Uqlidisi. Saidan, A. S., tr. 1978. text 303.50 (*90-277-0752-9*) Kluwer Academic.

Abu al-Tayyib Ahmad ibn al-Husan, jt. auth. see Al-Mutanabbi.

Abu-Ala, Maududi. Birth Control. 1993. pap. 5.50 (*0-935782-52-4*) Kazi Pubns.

Abu-Amr, Ziad. Islamic Fundamentalism in the West Bank & Gaza: Muslim Brotherhood & Islamic Jihad. LC 93-28504. (Indiana Series in Arab & Islamic). 192p. (C). 1994. 32.50 (*0-253-30121-1*); pap. 12.95 (*0-253-20866-1*) Ind U Pr.

Abu Bakr al-Kalab Muhammad Muslehuddinadhi. Economics & Islam. 110p. (Orig.). 1980. pap. 3.95 (*1-56744-264-1*) Kazi Pubns.

Abu Bakr Ibn Tufail. The History of Hayy ibn Yaqzan. 180p. 1985. 200.00 (*1-85077-087-5*, Pub. by Darf Pubs Ltd) St Mut.

Abu-Bakr, Mohammed. Doctrines & Dogmas of the Mutazilites: The Rationalists of Islam. 84p. 1993. pap. 10.95 (*1-882250-06-0*) Purple Dawn.

— The Great Prophet Muhammad & His Famous Black Companions. 54p. 1993. pap. 6.50 (*1-882250-04-4*) Purple Dawn.

— Islamic Theocracy. 60p. 1993. pap. 5.95 (*1-882250-03-6*) Purple Dawn.

— Islam's Black Legacy: Some Leading Figures. 158p. 1993. 24.95 (*1-882250-08-7*) Purple Dawn.

***Abu-Bakr, Mohammed.** Living by Rational Faith: A Freethinker's Choice. LC 99-96361. 92p. 2000. pap. 12.00 (*0-9676815-0-2*) Intl Essay.

Abu-Bakr, Mohammed. Look Beyond Jesus to Muhammad. 57p. 1993. pap. 4.50 (*1-882250-07-9*) Purple Dawn.

Abu-Ghazaleh, Adnan. American Missions in Syria. 2nd ed. 94p. (Orig.). 1990. pap. 12.50 (*0-915597-25-X*) Amana Bks.

— History & Culture of the Ancient Middle East & North Africa. 145p. 1991. pap. 12.50 (*0-915597-84-5*) Amana Bks.

— Palestinian Arab Cultural Nationalism, 1919-1960. 135p. (Orig.). (C). 1990. pap. 12.50 (*0-915597-75-6*) Amana Bks.

***Abu-Ghazaleh, Talal.** Intellectual Property Laws of the Arab Countries. LC 00-32749. 2000. write for info. (*90-411-8842-8*) Kluwer Law Intl.

Abu-Habib, Lina. Gender & Disability: Women's Experiences in the Middle East. LC 98-133386. (Illus.). 64p. (C). 1997. pap. 9.95 (*0-85598-363-9*, Pub. by Oxfam Pub) Stylus Pub VA.

Abu-Haidar, J. A. Hispano-Arabic Literature & the Early Provencal Lyrics. 260p. 1998. 75.00 (*0-7007-1015-9*, Pub. by Curzon Pr Ltd) Paul & Co Pubs.

Abu Hakima. Eastern Arabia: Bahrain. 206p. 1986. 30.00 (*0-86685-528-9*, ABU6002) Intl Bk Ctr.

— Eastern Arabia: Kuwait. 1986. 30.00 (*0-86685-527-0*) Intl Bk Ctr.

Abu-Hakima, Ahmad M. Eastern Arabia: Historic Photographs, Vol. 1: Bahrain. (Illus.). 112p. (C). 1989. 35.00 (*0-903696-32-0*, Pub. by Hurtwood Pr Ltd) St Mut.

— Eastern Arabia: Kuwait, 1900-1936, Vol. 2. (Illus.). 208p. (C). 1989. 30.00 (*0-903696-00-2*, Pub. by Hurtwood Pr Ltd) St Mut.

— History of Eastern Arabia: Rise & Development of Bahrain, Kuwait & Wahhabi Saudi Arabia. 1988. 30.00 (*0-86685-473-8*) Intl Bk Ctr.

— The Modern History of Kuwait, 1750-1965. 1983. 35.00 (*0-7189-0259-9*) Intl Bk Ctr.

***Abu-Hakima, Sue & Willmott, Steven, eds.** Artificial Intelligence for Distributed Information Networking: Papers from the AAAI Workshop. (Technical Reports: Vol. WS-99-03). (Illus.). 92p. 1999. spiral bd. 25.00 (*1-57735-087-1*) AAAI Pr.

***Abu-Hamdiyyah, Mohammad.** The Qur'an: An Introduction to Its Message. LC 99-47371. (Illus.). 144p. 2000. pap. 17.99 (*0-415-22509-4*) Routledge.

— Qur'an - Introduction: An Introduction to Its Message. LC 99-47371. 152p. (C). 2000. text 60.00 (*0-415-22508-6*) Routledge.

Abu-Hassako, Taareid, ed. see Kamava, Connie H.

Abu-Husayn, Abdul-Rahim. Provincial Leaderships in Syria, Fifteen Seventy-Five to Sixteen Fifty. 230p. 1985. text 29.95 (*0-8156-6072-3*, Pub. by Am U Beirut) Syracuse U Pr.

Abu Husayn, Abdul-Rahim & Sa'Dawi, Saleh, eds. Christianity in the Ottoman Arab World: The State Records from the Muhimme Defteri, 1869-1922. (ARA.). 392p. 1998. pap. 40.00 (*0-88206-206-9*) Caravan Bks.

Abu-Izzeddin, Nejla M. The Druzes: A New Study of Their History, Faith, & Society. LC 92-31449. (Illus.). xii, 260p. 1993. 104.00 (*90-04-09705-8*) Brill Academic Pubs.

Abu-Jaber, Diana. Arabian Jazz. 388p. 1994. pap. 10.95 (*0-15-600048-2*) Harcourt.

***Abu-Jamal, Mumia.** All Things Censored. Hanrahan, Noelle, ed. (Illus.). 272p. 2000. 29.95 incl. cd-rom (*1-58322-022-4*) Seven Stories.

Abu-Jamal, Mumia. Death Blossoms: Reflections from a Prisoner of Conscience. LC 96-49924. (Illus.). 190p. 2000. reprint ed. pap. 12.00 (*0-87486-086-5*) Plough.

— Live from Death Row. 258p. 1995. 20.00 (*0-201-48319-X*) Addison-Wesley.

— Live from Death Row. 208p. 1996. pap. 12.50 (*0-380-72766-8*, Avon Bks) Morrow Avon.

Abu, Katharine, jt. auth. see Oppong, Christine.

Abu Khaldun Sati Al Husri. The Day of Maysalun: A Page from the Modern History of the Arabs. Glazer, Sidney, tr. from ARA. LC 66-29228. 1966. pap. 1.50 (*0-916808-06-8*) Mid East Inst.

Abu-Khalil, Shawqi. Al-Hadarah al-Arabiyah al-Islamiyah wa-Mujaz 'an Hadarat al-Sabiqah. 688p. 1994. 15.95 (*1-57547-013-6*) Dar Al-Fikr.

— Al-Hiwar Da'iman wa-Hiwar ma 'a Mustashriq. 192p. 1995. pap. 4.95 (*1-57547-014-4*) Dar Al-Fikr.

— Al-Insan bayna al-Ilm wa-al-Din. (Islamiyat Ser.) 288p. 1989. pap. 7.95 (*1-57547-011-X*) Dar Al-Fikr.

— Al-Islam wa-Harakat al-Taharrur al-Arabiyah. 248p. 1991. pap. 7.95 (*1-57547-006-3*) Dar Al-Fikr.

Abu Khalil, Shawqi. Al-Isqat fi Manahij al-Mustashriqin wa-al-Mubashshirin. 224p. 1995. pap. 6.95 (*1-57547-206-6*) Dar Al-Fikr.

Abu-Khalil, Shawqi. Al-Tasamuh fi al-Islam: Al-Mabda' wa-al-Tatbiq. (Hadha Huwa al-Islam Ser.). 144p. 1993. pap. 1.95 (*1-57547-017-9*) Dar Al-Fikr.

— Ara' Yahdimuha al-Islam. (Islamiyat Ser.). 128p. 1994. pap. 3.95 (*1-57547-003-9*) Dar Al-Fikr.

— Atlas al-Tarikh al-'Arabi wa-al-Islami. 128p. 1985. 12.95 (*1-57547-009-8*) Dar Al-Fikr.

— Fi al-Tarikh al-Islami. 352p. 1991. pap. 7.95 (*1-57547-020-9*) Dar Al-Fikr.

— Ghazwat al-Rasul al-A'zam, 10 vols., Set. 1993. pap. 23.95 (*1-57547-102-7*) Dar Al-Fikr.

— Ghazwat al-Rasul al-A'zam, Vol. 1. 1993. pap. write for info. (*1-57547-103-5*) Dar Al-Fikr.

— Ghazwat al-Rasul al-A'zam, Vol. 2. 1993. pap. write for info. (*1-57547-104-3*) Dar Al-Fikr.

— Ghazwat al-Rasul al-A'zam, Vol. 3. 1993. pap. write for info. (*1-57547-105-1*) Dar Al-Fikr.

— Ghazwat al-Rasul al-A'zam, Vol. 4. 1993. pap. write for info. (*1-57547-106-X*) Dar Al-Fikr.

— Ghazwat al-Rasul al-A'zam, Vol. 5. 1993. pap. write for info. (*1-57547-107-8*) Dar Al-Fikr.

— Ghazwat al-Rasul al-A'zam, Vol. 6. 1993. pap. write for info. (*1-57547-108-6*) Dar Al-Fikr.

— Ghazwat al-Rasul al-A'zam, Vol. 7. 1993. pap. write for info. (*1-57547-109-4*) Dar Al-Fikr.

— Ghazwat al-Rasul al-A'zam, Vol. 8. 1993. pap. write for info. (*1-57547-110-8*) Dar Al-Fikr.

— Ghazwat al-Rasul al-A'zam, Vol. 9. 1993. pap. write for info. (*1-57547-111-6*) Dar Al-Fikr.

— Ghazwat al-Rasul al-A'zam, Vol. 10. 1993. pap. write for info. (*1-57547-112-4*) Dar Al-Fikr.

— Uhibbu an Akun: Silsilat Qisas ll-Atfal, 20 vols., Set 640p. 1991. pap. 35.90 (*1-57547-120-5*) Dar Al-Fikr.

— Uhibbu an Akun: Silsilat Qisas ll-Atfal, Vol. 1. (J). 1991. pap. write for info. (*1-57547-121-3*) Dar Al-Fikr.

— Uhibbu an Akun: Silsilat Qisas ll-Atfal, Vol. 2. (J). 1991. pap. write for info. (*1-57547-122-1*) Dar Al-Fikr.

— Uhibbu an Akun: Silsilat Qisas ll-Atfal, Vol. 3. (J). 1991. pap. write for info. (*1-57547-123-X*) Dar Al-Fikr.

— Uhibbu an Akun: Silsilat Qisas ll-Atfal, Vol. 4. (J). 1991. pap. write for info. (*1-57547-124-8*) Dar Al-Fikr.

— Uhibbu an Akun: Silsilat Qisas ll-Atfal, Vol. 5. (J). 1991. pap. write for info. (*1-57547-125-6*) Dar Al-Fikr.

— Uhibbu an Akun: Silsilat Qisas ll-Atfal, Vol. 6. 1991. pap. write for info. (*1-57547-126-4*) Dar Al-Fikr.

— Uhibbu an Akun: Silsilat Qisas ll-Atfal, Vol. 7. 1991. pap. write for info. (*1-57547-127-2*) Dar Al-Fikr.

— Uhibbu an Akun: Silsilat Qisas ll-Atfal, Vol. 8. 1991. pap. write for info. (*1-57547-128-0*) Dar Al-Fikr.

— Uhibbu an Akun: Silsilat Qisas ll-Atfal, Vol. 9. 1991. pap. write for info. (*1-57547-129-9*) Dar Al-Fikr.

— Uhibbu an Akun: Silsilat Qisas ll-Atfal, Vol. 10. 1991. pap. write for info. (*1-57547-130-2*) Dar Al-Fikr.

— Uhibbu an Akun: Silsilat Qisas ll-Atfal, Vol. 11. 1991. pap. write for info. (*1-57547-131-0*) Dar Al-Fikr.

— Uhibbu an Akun: Silsilat Qisas ll-Atfal, Vol. 12. 1991. pap. write for info. (*1-57547-132-9*) Dar Al-Fikr.

— Uhibbu an Akun: Silsilat Qisas ll-Atfal, Vol. 13. 1991. pap. write for info. (*1-57547-133-7*) Dar Al-Fikr.

— Uhibbu an Akun: Silsilat Qisas ll-Atfal, Vol. 14. 1991. pap. write for info. (*1-57547-134-5*) Dar Al-Fikr.

— Uhibbu an Akun: Silsilat Qisas ll-Atfal, Vol. 15. 1991. pap. write for info. (*1-57547-135-3*) Dar Al-Fikr.

— Uhibbu an Akun: Silsilat Qisas ll-Atfal, Vol. 16. 1991. pap. write for info. (*1-57547-136-1*) Dar Al-Fikr.

— Uhibbu an Akun: Silsilat Qisas ll-Atfal, Vol. 17. 1991. pap. write for info. (*1-57547-137-X*) Dar Al-Fikr.

— Uhibbu an Akun: Silsilat Qisas ll-Atfal, Vol. 18. 1991. pap. write for info. (*1-57547-138-8*) Dar Al-Fikr.

— Uhibbu an Akun: Silsilat Qisas ll-Atfal, Vol. 19. 1991. pap. write for info. (*1-57547-139-6*) Dar Al-Fikr.

— Uhibbu an Akun: Silsilat Qisas ll-Atfal, Vol. 20. 1991. pap. write for info. (*1-57547-140-X*) Dar Al-Fikr.

— Uhibbu an A'rif Tarikh Ummati, 6 vols., Set. (Safhat min Tarikhina Ser.). 1993. pap. 7.95 (*1-57547-113-2*) Dar Al-Fikr.

— Uhibbu an A'rif Tarikh Ummati, Vol. 1. (Safhat min Tarikhina Ser.). 1993. pap. write for info. (*1-57547-114-0*) Dar Al-Fikr.

— Uhibbu an A'rif Tarikh Ummati, Vol. 2. (Safhat min Tarikhina Ser.). 1993. pap. write for info. (*1-57547-115-9*) Dar Al-Fikr.

— Uhibbu an A'rif Tarikh Ummati, Vol. 3. (Safhat min Tarikhina Ser.). 1993. pap. write for info. (*1-57547-116-7*) Dar Al-Fikr.

— Uhibbu an A'rif Tarikh Ummati, Vol. 4. (Safhat min Tarikhina Ser.). 1993. pap. write for info. (*1-57547-117-5*) Dar Al-Fikr.

— Uhibbu an A'rif Tarikh Ummati, Vol. 5. (Safhat min Tarikhina Ser.). 1993. pap. write for info. (*1-57547-118-3*) Dar Al-Fikr.

— Uhibbu an A'rif Tarikh Ummati, Vol. 6. (Safhat min Tarikhina Ser.). 1993. pap. write for info. (*1-57547-119-1*) Dar Al-Fikr.

Abu-Kishk, Bakir, jt. auth. see Prescott, James R.

Abu-Laban, Baha & Suleiman, Michael W., eds. Arab Americans: Continuity & Change. (Monographs: No. 24). 314p. (Orig.). 1989. pap. 19.75 (*0-937694-82-7*) Assn Arab-Amer U Grads.

Abu-Laban, Baha, jt. ed. see Abu-Lughod, Ibrahim.

Abu-Lebdeh, Hatem S. Conflict & Peace in the Middle East: National Perceptions & United States-Jordan Relations. LC 97-213721. 206p. (C). 1997. 52.00 (*0-7618-0811-6*); pap. 32.50 (*0-7618-0812-4*) U Pr of Amer.

Abu-Lughod, Ibrahim, ed. The Arab-Israeli Confrontation of June 1967: An Arab Perspective. LC 74-107607. 215p. reprint ed. pap. 66.70 (*0-8357-5700-5*, 201477200093) Bks Demand.

Abu-Lughod, Ibrahim & Abu-Laban, Baha, eds. Settler Regimes in Africa & the Arab World: The Illusion of Endurance. (Monographs: No. 4). 255p. 1974. 10.95 (*0-914456-06-7*); pap. text 6.95 (*0-914456-07-5*) Assn Arab-Amer U Grads.

Abu-Lughod, Ibrahim & Said, Edward W. Two Studies on the Palestinians Today & American Policy. (Information Papers: No. 17). 22p. (Orig.). (C). 1976. pap. 1.00 (*0-937694-33-9*) Assn Arab-Amer U Grads.

Abu-Lughod, Ibrahim A. Arab Rediscovery of Europe: A Study in Cultural Encounters. LC 62-21102. (Princeton Studies on the Near East). 199p. reprint ed. pap. 61.70 (*0-8357-5703-X*, 200059900033) Bks Demand.

Abu-Lughod, Janet L. Before European Hegemony: The World System A.D. 1250-1350. (Illus.). 464p. 1991. reprint ed. pap. text 19.95 (*0-19-506774-6*) OUP.

— New York, Chicago, Los Angeles: America's Global Cities. LC 99-20783. (Illus.). 580p. 1999. 39.95 (*0-8166-3335-5*, Pub. by U of Minn Pr) Chicago Distribution Ctr.

— New York, Chicago, Los Angeles: America's Global Cities LC 99-20783. 1999. write for info. (*0-8166-3336-3*) U of Minn Pr.

— Rabat: Urban Apartheid in Morocco. LC 80-7508. (Princeton Studies on the Near East). 405p. reprint ed. pap. 125.60 (*0-7837-1405-X*, 204175900023) Bks Demand.

— Sociology of the Twenty-First Century: Continuities & Cutting Edges. LC 99-22434. 216p. 2000. pap. text 17.00 (*0-226-00193-8*); lib. bdg. 45.00 (*0-226-00191-1*) U Ch Pr.

— The World System in the Thirteenth Century: Dead-End or Precursor? Adas, Michael, ed. (Essays on Global & Comparative History Ser.). 28p. 1994. pap. 6.00 (*0-87229-071-9*) Am Hist Assn.

Abu-Lughod, Janet L. & Hay, Richard, Jr., eds. Third World Urbanization. 1980. pap. 12.95 (*0-416-60141-3*, NO. 2866) Routledge.

Abu-Lughod, Janet L., et al. From Urban Village to "East Village" The Battle for New York's Lower East Side. LC 93-31977. (Illus.). 320p. (Orig.). (C). 1994. pap. text 27.95 (*1-55786-525-6*) Blackwell Pubs.

Abu-Lughod, Lila. Remaking Women: Feminism & Modernity in the Middle East. LC 97-46125. (Princeton Studies in Culture, Power & History). 314p. 1998. text 55.00 (*0-691-05791-5*, Pub. by Princeton U Pr); pap. text 16.95 (*0-691-05792-3*, Pub. by Princeton U Pr) Cal Prin Full Svc.

— Veiled Sentiments: Honor & Poetry in a Bedouin Society. (Illus.). 317p. 1987. pap. 18.95 (*0-520-06327-9*, Pub. by U CA Pr) Cal Prin Full Svc.

***Abu-Lughod, Lila.** Veiled Sentiments: Honor & Poetry in a Bedouin Society. 356p. 2000. pap. 18.95 (*0-520-22473-6*, Pub. by U CA Pr) Cal Prin Full Svc.

Abu-Lughod, Lila. Writing Women's Worlds: Bedouin Stories. (C). 1993. pap. 16.95 (*0-520-08304-0*, Pub. by U CA Pr) Cal Prin Full Svc.

Abu-Mostafa, Y. S., ed. Complexity in Information Theory. (Illus.). 150p. 1990. 45.95 (*0-387-96600-5*) Spr-Verlag.

Abu-Mostafa, Yaser, jt. ed. see Weigend, Andreas S.

Abu-Mostafa, Yaser S., et al, eds. Computational Finance. LC 99-30172. (Illus.). 650p. 1999. 95.00 (*0-262-01178-6*); pap. text 40.00 (*0-262-51107-X*) MIT Pr.

Abu Muhammad Baghawi. Mishkat al-Masabih, 3 vol. set. Abdul Hameed Siddiqui, tr. (ARA & ENG.). 950p. (C). 1988. text 59.00 (*1-56744-328-1*) Kazi Pubns.

Abu-Nimer, Mohammed. Dialogue, Conflict Resolution & Change: Arab-Jewish Encounters in Israel. LC 98-35837. (SUNY Series in Israeli Studies). 2p. (C). 1999. text 54.50 (*0-7914-4153-9*); pap. text 17.95 (*0-7914-4154-7*) State U NY Pr.

***Abu Odeh, Adnan.** Jordanians, Palestinians & the Hashemite Kingdom in the Middle East Peace Process. LC 99-35751. 1999. pap. 19.95 (*1-878379-88-7*) US Inst Peace.

Abu-Oden, Adrian, et al. U. N. Security Council Resolution 242: The Building Block of Peacemaking, Proceedings from the Washington Institute's Harris Symposium. LC 93-18860. 152p. 1993. pap. 14.95 (*0-944029-51-5*) Wash Inst NEP.

Abu-Rabi, A. Intellectual Origins of Islamic Resurgence in the Modern Arab World. 1996. write for info. (*0-614-21460-2*, 1436) Kazi Pubns.

Abu-Rabi', Ibrahim M. Intellectual Origins of Islamic Resurgence in the Modern Arab World. LC 94-44054. (SUNY Series in Near Eastern Studies). 370p. (C). 1995. pap. text 21.95 (*0-7914-2664-5*) State U NY Pr.

Abu-Rabia, Aref. Negev Bedouin & Livestock Rearing: Social, Economic & Political Aspects. LC 92-32092. 160p. 1994. 47.50 (*0-85496-319-7*, Pub. by Berg Pubs) NYU Pr.

Abu-Saud, Mahmoud. Concept of Islam. Quinlan, Hamid, ed. LC 83-70184. 147p. 1983. pap. 6.50 (*0-89259-043-2*) Am Trust Pubns.

Abu-Shumays, I. K., ed. see Society for Industrial & Applied Mathematics Staff, et al.

An Asterisk (*) at the beginning of an entry indicates that the title is appearing for the first time.

Abu-Taleb, Samy. Conversational Arabic in Seven Days. (BBC Phrase Bks.). (ARA., Illus.). 96p. 1995. pap. 8.95 (0-8442-4568-2, 45682, Passprt Bks) NTC Contemp Pub Co.

Abu-Taleb, Samy, ed. Conversational Arabic in Seven Days. (BBC Phrase Bks.). (ARA.). 96p. 1995. 14.95 incl. audio (0-8442-9145-5, Passprt Bks) NTC Contemp Pub Co.

Abu-Zahra, Nadia. Pure & Powerful: Studies in Contemporary Muslim Society. LC 97-146859. 1998. 45.00 (0-86372-179-6, Pub. by Garnet-Ithaca) LPC InBook.

*Abu-Zahra, Nadia. The Pure & the Powerful: Studies in Contemporary Muslim Society. 340p. 2000. pap. 21.00 (0-86372-269-5) Garnet-Ithaca.

Abu Zakariya An Nawawi. Riyad-us-Salihin, 2 pts., Pt. I. (ARA & ENG.). 1990. 20.00 (0-935782-69-9) Kazi Pubns.

— Riyad-us-Salihin, 2 pts., Pt. II. (ARA & ENG.). 1991. 20.00 (0-933511-38-8) Kazi Pubns.

— Riyad-us-Salihin, 2 pts., Set. (ARA & ENG.). 1989. 49.00 (1-56744-347-8) Kazi Pubns.

Abu-Zeid, Mahmoud A. & Biswas, Asit K. River Basin Planning & Management. LC 96-902104. (Water Resources Management Ser.: Vol. 4). (Illus.). 246p. 1996. text 24.95 (0-19-563755-0) OUP.

Abuaf, Niso & Schoess, Stephan. Foreign-Exchange Exposure Management. 1988. pap. 59.95 (0-88057-840-8) Exec Ent Pubns.

— Foreign-Exchange Exposure Management. 133p. 1994. pap. 99.95 (0-471-11293-3) Wiley.

*Abuan, Natalye, adapted by. The Emperor's New Groove. (Read-Aloud Storybook Ser.). (Illus.). 64p. (J). (ps-2). 2000. 6.99 (0-7364-0196-2) Mouse Works.

Abubakar, Ahmad. Africa & the Challenge of Development: Acquiescence & Dependency Versus Freedom & Development. LC 88-32290. 160p. 1989. 52.95 (0-275-93221-4, C3221, Praeger Pubs) Greenwood.

Abubakre, R. 'Deremi. Linguistic & Non-Linguistic Aspects of Qur'an Translating to Yoruba. (Studien Zur Sprachwissenschaft Ser.: Vol. 3). vi, 104p. 1986. 24.00 (3-487-07804-X) G Olms Pubs.

Abucar, Mohamed H. The Post-Colonial Society: The Algerian Struggle for Economic, Social, & Political Change, 1965-1990. (American University Studies Series XXI: Regional Studies: Vol. 14). 188p. (Orig.). (C). 1996. pap. text 29.95 (0-8204-2823-X) P Lang Pubng.

*Abucewicz, John A. Cast the First Stone. 200p. 2000. pap. 12.95 (1-891929-40-2) Four Seasons.

Abuchowski, A. Novel Therapeutics from Modern Biotechnology: From Laboratory to Human Testing. 1998. 299.00 (3-540-65025-3) Spr-Verlag.

Abuelo, J. Gary, ed. Renal Failure: Diagnosis & Treatment. LC 95-7920. (Developments in Nephrology Ser.: Vol. 37). 284p. (C). 1995. text 173.50 (0-7923-3438-8) Kluwer Academic.

*Abueva, Jose V. The Making of the Filipino Nation & Republic: From Barangays, Tribes, Sultanates & Colony (Ang Pagbubuo Ng Bansa at Republika Ng Pilipinas: Mula sa Mga Barangay, Tribu, Sultanato at Kolonya. LC 98-947826. (Pamana Ser.). (TAG & ENG.). 1078p. 1999. pap. text 120.00 (971-542-215-2, Pub. by U of Philippines Pr) UH Pr.

*Abueva, Jose V., et al, eds. The Philippines into the 21st Century: Future Scenarios for Governance, Democracy & Development, 1998-2025 (Ang Pilipinas Tungo Sa Ika-21 Dantaon: Pangkinabukasang Mga Senaryo para sa Pamamahala, Democracy, & Development, 1998-2025. LC 98-947827. (TAG & ENG.). 242p. 1999. pap. text 38.00 (971-542-210-1, Pub. by U of Philippines Pr) UH Pr.

Abuhaidar, Lamia, jt. auth. see Oussiemi, Maria.

Abuhamad, Alfred. Practical Guide to Fetal Echocardiography. LC 97-2780. (Illus.). 185p. 1997. text 63.00 (0-397-51674-6) Lppncott W & W.

Abujaber, Raouf S. Pioneers over Jordan: The Frontier of Settlement in Transjordan, 1850-1914. 352p. 1990. text 65.00 (1-85043-116-7, Pub. by I B T) St Martin.

Abukhalil, Asad. Historical Dictionary of Lebanon. LC 97-26849. (Asian Historical Dictionaries Ser.). 269p. 1998. 65.00 (0-8108-3395-6) Scarecrow.

AbuKhalil, As'ad, jt. auth. see Aruri, Naseer H.

Abul Ala Maududi, S. Moral Foundation of the Islamic Movement. Amin, Mohamed, tr. 56p. (Orig.). 1988. pap. 3.00 (1-56744-336-2) Kazi Pubns.

Abu'l-Fadl, Mirza. The Brilliant Proof. LC 98-12455. 1998. 14.95 (1-890688-00-2) Kalimat.

— Letters & Essays, 1886-1913. Cole, Juan R., tr. from PER. (Illus.). 210p. 1985. 19.95 (0-933770-36-7) Kalimat.

— Miracles & Metaphors. Cole, Juan R., tr. from ARA. (Illus.). 220p. 1982. pap. 19.95 (0-933770-22-7) Kalimat.

Abul-Fadl, Mona. Islam & the Middle East: The Aesthetics of a Political Inquiry. LC 90-5251. (Research Monographs: No. 2). 61p. (Orig.). 1990. pap. 5.00 (0-912463-74-0) IIIT VA.

— Where East Meets West: The West on the Agenda of the Islamic Revival. LC 90-45360. (Islamization of Knowledge Ser.: No. 10). 117p. (Orig.). 1992. pap. 6.00 (0-912463-73-2) IIIT VA.

Abul-Fadl, Mona, ed. Proceedings: Twenty-First Annual Conference of the Association of Muslim Social Scientists, Held in East Lansing, Michigan, October 30-November, 1992. LC 93-36577. (Issues in Contemporary Islamic Thought Ser.: No. 12). (Illus.). 589p. (Orig.). 1993. pap. 15.00 (1-56564-145-0) IIIT VA.

Abul-Fououh, Muhammad H. A Dictionary of Prophetic Tradition in Sahih Al-Bukhari Vol. 1, Vol. I. (ARA.). 556p. 1994. 45.00 (0-86685-609-9, LDL6099, Pub. by Librairie du Liban) Intl Bk Ctr.

Abul Futouh, Muhammad H. Emphasis Style in the Holy Qur'an. (ARA.). 292p. 1995. 35.00 (0-86685-646-3, LDL6463, Pub. by Librairie du Liban) Intl Bk Ctr.

Abul Hasan Ali Nadvi. Mercy for the Worlds. 32p. (Orig.). 1985. pap. 2.00 (1-56744-325-7) Kazi Pubns.

Abul-Huda, Samar N., tr. see Tifaschi, Al.

Abul-Husn, Latif. The Lebanese Conflict: Looking Inward. LC 97-36617. (Canberra Studies on Peace). 174p. 1997. 42.00 (1-55587-665-X) L Rienner.

Abulafia, Anna S., et al, eds. The Works of Gilbert Crispin. (Auctores Britannici Medii Aevi Ser.: Vol. VIII). (Illus.). 288p. 1987. 125.00 (0-19-726035-7) OUP.

Abulafia, David. Commerce & Conquest in the Mediterranean, 1100-1500. LC 93-18602. (Collected Studies: No. CS 410). 360p. 1993. 115.95 (0-86078-377-4, Pub. by Variorum) Ashgate Pub Co.

— Frederick the Second: A Medieval Emperor. (Illus.). 480p. 1992. pap. 17.95 (0-19-508040-8) OUP.

— Italy, Sicily & the Mediterranean, 1100-1400. (Collected Studies: No. CS250). 346p. (C). 1987. reprint ed. lib. bdg. 115.95 (0-86078-198-4, Pub. by Variorum) Ashgate Pub Co.

— A Mediterranean Emporium: The Catalan Kingdom of Majorca. 288p. (C). 1994. text 64.95 (0-521-32244-8) Cambridge U Pr.

— West Mediterrnean Kingdom. LC 97-20258. (Medieval World Ser.). (C). 1998. 68.44 (0-582-07821-0, Pub. by Addison-Wesley) Longman.

Abulafia, David, ed. The French Descent into Renaissance Italy, 1494-5: Antecedents & Effects. LC 95-34786. 512p. 1995. 99.95 (0-86078-550-5, Pub. by Variorum) Ashgate Pub Co.

— The New Cambridge Medieval History Vol. 5: C. 1198 - C. 1300. (Illus.). 900p. (C). 1999. text 120.00 (0-521-36289-X) Cambridge U Pr.

Abun-Nasr, Jamil M. A History of the Maghrib. 2nd ed. LC 74-25653. 432p. reprint ed. pap. 123.20 (0-608-12286-6, 2024410) Bks Demand.

— History of the Maqhrib in the Islamic Period. 512p. 1996. pap. 32.95 (0-614-21150-6, 449) Kazi Pubns.

AbuNabaa, Abdel A. Marketing in Saudi Arabia. LC 83-17819. 228p. 1984. 59.95 (0-275-91111-X, C1111, Praeger Pubs) Greenwood.

Abundant Life Staff. Abundant Life New Testament: Nuevo Testamento vida Abundante. 1987. pap. 3.75 (0-311-48771-8) Baptist Spanish.

— Abundant Life New Testament: Nuevo Testamento vida Abundante. 2000. pap. text 3.75 (0-311-48772-6) Baptist Spanish.

— La Biblia Vida Abundante. (SPA.). 1993. 16.99 (0-311-48820-X) Baptist Spanish.

— La Biblia Vida Abundante Abundant Life Bible. (SPA & ENG.). 2000. 32.99 (0-311-48823-4) Baptist Spanish.

— LaBiblia Vida Abundante Abundant Life Bible. 1993. 16.99 (0-311-48821-8) Baptist Spanish.

Abundis, Charlene. Don't Fence Me In. 375p. (Orig.). 1997. pap. 13.95 (0-9656058-0-9) Two Angels Pub.

Abunuwara, Ehab. Days of the Messiah: Pharaoh. 430p. 1996. mass mkt. 5.99 (1-55197-004-X) Picasso Publ.

AbuRahma, Ali F. & Bergan, John J., eds. Noninvasive Vascular Diagnosis. LC 98-50138. 1999. 265.00 (1-85233-128-3, Pub. by Spr-Verlag) Spr-Verlag.

Aburdene, Patricia & Naisbitt, John. Megatrends for Women: From Liberation to Leadership. 416p. 1993. pap. 12.50 (0-449-90825-9, Columbine) Fawcett.

Aburdene, Patricia, jt. auth. see Naisbitt, John.

Aburish, Said K. Arafat: From Defender to Dictator. (Illus.). 256p. 1998. 25.95 (1-58234-000-5) Bloomsbury Pubg.

— Arafat: From Defender to Dictator. 384p. 1999. pap. 15.95 (1-58234-049-8) Bloomsbury Pubg.

— A Brutal Friendship: The West & the Arab Elite. LC 98-3342. 416p. 1998. text 27.95 (0-312-18543-X) St Martin.

— Children of Bethany: The Story of a Palestinian Family. 256p. 1999. pap. 14.95 (1-58234-041-2) Bloomsbury Pubg.

— Children of Bethany: The Story of a Palestinian Family. LC 89-15414. 256p. 1989. 9.95 (0-253-30676-0) Ind U Pr.

— The Rise, Corruption & Coming Fall of the House of Saud. (Illus.). 326p. 1996. pap. 15.95 (0-614-19279-X) St Martin.

— Saddam Hussein: The Politics of Revenge. 2000. 27.95 (1-58234-050-1) Bloomsbury Pubg.

Aburrow-Newman, Alan. Christmas Storybook. (Illus.). 128p. (J). (ps-2). 1996. 7.98 (1-85854-553-6) Brimax Bks.

— Digby & the Big Flood. (Illus.). 24p. (J). (gr. k-3). 1996. 4.98 (1-85854-454-8) Brimax Bks.

— Digby Helps at the Zoo. (Illus.). 24p. (J). (gr. k-3). 1996. 4.98 (1-85854-452-1) Brimax Bks.

— Digby the Dinosaur. (Illus.). 24p. (J). (gr. k-3). 1996. 4.98 (1-85854-451-3) Brimax Bks.

— Digby the Firefighter. (Illus.). 24p. (J). (gr. k-3). 1996. 4.98 (1-85854-453-X) Brimax Bks.

— Digby to the Rescue. (Illus.). 88p. (J). (ps-3). 1997. 6.98 (1-85854-638-9) Brimax Bks.

Aburrow, Yvonne. Auguries & Omens: The Magical Lore of Birds. 1994. pap. 21.95 (1-898307-11-3, Pub. by Capall Bann Pubng) Holmes Pub.

— The Enchanted Forest: The Magical Lore of Trees. 1994. pap. 21.95 (1-898307-08-3, Pub. by Capall Bann Pubng) Holmes Pub.

— Magical Lore of Animals. (Orig.). 1997. pap. 23.95 (1-898307-80-6, Pub. by Capall Bann Pubng) Holmes Pub.

— The Sacred Grove: Mysteries of the Forest. 1994. pap. 22.95 (1-898307-12-1) Holmes Pub.

Abusabib, Mohamed A. African Art: An Aesthetic Inquiry. (Aesthetica Upsaliensia Ser.: No. 6). (Illus.). 171p. 1995. pap. 42.50 (91-554-3472-X) Coronet Bks.

Abushagur, Mustafa A. & Caulfield, H. John, eds. Selected Papers on Fourier Optics. LC 94-40115. (Milestone Ser.: Vol. 105). 1994. 50.00 (0-8194-1772-6) SPIE.

AbuSulayman, AbdulHamid. Azmat al 'Aql al Muslim: (Crisis in the Muslim Mind) LC 91-38922. (Silsilat al Manhajiyah al Islamiyah Ser.: No. 1). (ARA.). 243p. (Orig.). 1991. pap. 8.00 (1-56564-015-2) IIIT VA.

— Crisis in the Muslim Mind. DeLorenzo, Yusuf T., tr. from ARA. LC 93-24088. (Islamic Methodology Ser.: Vol. 1).Tr. of Azmat al-aql al Muslim. 160p. (Orig.). 1993. 20.00 (1-56564-137-X); pap. 10.00 (1-56564-138-8) IIIT VA.

— Qadiyat al Manhajiyah fi al Fikr al Islami: (The Issue of Methodology in Islamic Thought) (Rasa'il Islamiyat al Ma'rifah Ser.: No. 4). (ARA.). 42p. (Orig.). 1989. pap. 2.00 (1-56564-163-9) IIIT VA.

AbuSulayman, 'AbdulHamid, ed. Dalil Maktabat al Usrah al Muslimah: (Guide for the Muslim Family Book Collection) rev. ed. (Silsilat Islamiyat al Thaqafah Ser.: No. 1). (ARA.). 735p. 1991. pap. text 12.50 (0-912463-82-1) IIIT VA.

— Dalil Maktabat al Usrah al Muslimah: (Guide for the Muslim Family Book Collection) 2nd rev. ed. (Silsilat Islamiyat al Thaqafah Ser.: No. 1). (ARA.). 735p. 1991. text 20.00 (0-912463-81-3) IIIT VA.

Abut, H. Vector Quantization. LC 90-32686. (Illus.). 576p. 1990. text 77.95 (0-87942-265-3, PC02550) Inst Electrical.

Abuza'Kuk, Ali R. Roman Transliteration of the 28th Part of the Qur An: With Arabic Text. Ali, Abdullah Yusuf, tr. from ARA. LC 96-40482. 1997. write for info. (1-881963-61-6) Al-Saadawi Pubns.

Abuza'kuk, Ali R., ed. see Ali, Abdullah Y.

Abuza'kuk, Ali R., ed. & intro. see Ali, Abdullah Y.

ABW Staff. ABW (A Better World), 3 vols. Incl. Vol. 1. Back to the Future. 162p. 1996. per. 10.00 (0-9641885-1-1); Vol. 2. Is it Time to Break Away from the United Methodist Church? 18p. 1996. per. 5.00 (0-9641885-2-X); Vol. 3. Law of One. 114p. 1996. per. 7.00 (0-9641885-3-8); write for info. (0-9641885-0-3) ABW NE.

Abwunza, Judith. Women's Voices, Women's Power: Dialogues of Resistance from East Africa. LC 98-118625. 224p. (C). 1997. pap. 16.95 (1-55111-132-2) Broadview Pr.

Aby, Carroll D. A Guide to Money Market & Bond Investment Strategies. 130p. 1989. pap. text 32.95 (0-936176-17-2, Investors Intell) Chartcraft Inc.

Aby, Carroll D., Jr. Point & Figure Charting: The Complete Guide. rev. ed. LC 97-172657. 296p. 1996. 35.00 (0-934380-30-9, 538-A) Traders Pr.

Aby, Carroll D. & Vaughn, Donald E. Asset Allocation & Financial Market Timing: Techniques for Investment Professionals. LC 94-45275. 376p. 1995. 77.50 (0-89930-761-2, Quorum Bks) Greenwood.

Aby, Carroll D. & Vaugn, Donald E. A Charting Approach to Wall Street Profits. LC 89-80222. 312p. 1989. write for info. (0-936176-16-4) Chartcraft Inc.

Aby, Franklin S. Eby: Swiss Eby Family, Pioneer Millwrights & Millers of Lancaster Co. Pa. (Family Bulletin #2) (Illus.). 55p. 1997. reprint ed. pap. 11.00 (0-8328-8428-6); reprint ed. lib. bdg. 21.00 (0-8328-8427-8) Higginson Bk Co.

Aby, Franklin S., jt. auth. see Aby, Mavina S.

Aby, Mavina S. & Aby, Franklin S. Eby: The Aby Family of Peoria Co., Ill., the Eaby Family of Lancaster Co., Pa., Progeny of Theodorus Eby (1663-1732) of Lancaster Co., Pa. (Family Bulletin #4) (Illus.). 101p. 1997. reprint ed. pap. 17.00 (0-8328-8430-8); reprint ed. lib. bdg. 27.00 (0-8328-8429-4) Higginson Bk Co.

Aby, Stephen H. Sociology: A Guide to Reference & Information Sources. 2nd ed. LC 97-26613. (Reference Sources in the Social Sciences Ser.). 225p. 1997. lib. bdg. 42.00 (1-56308-422-8) Libs Unl.

Aby, Stephen H., compiled by. The IQ Debate: A Selective Guide to the Literature, 8. LC 90-13986. (Bibliographies & Indexes in Psychology Ser.: No. 8). 248p. 1990. lib. bdg. 65.00 (0-313-26440-6, AIQ/, Greenwood Pr) Greenwood.

*Aby, Stephen H. & Kuhn, James C., eds. Academic Freedom: A Guide to the Literature, 20. LC 99-59136. (Bibliographies & Indexes in Education Ser.: Vol. 20). 225p. 2000. lib. bdg. 75.00 (0-313-30386-X, Greenwood Pr) Greenwood.

Abzug. America & Holocaust, Vol. 1. LC 98-87517. 1999. pap. 10.95 (0-312-13393-6) St Martin.

— Essence of America. 2002. pap. write for info. (0-312-19205-3) St Martin.

— Rollo May. 1999. write for info. (0-201-40767-1) Addison-Wesley.

Abzug, Malcolm J. Computational Flight Dynamics. LC 98-12761. (AIAA Education Ser.). 470p. 1998. 94.95 incl. disk (1-56347-259-7) AIAA.

Abzug, Malcolm J. & Larrabee, E. Eugene. Airplane Stability & Control: A History of the Technologies That Made Aviation Possible. (Aerospace Ser.: No. 6). (Illus.). 390p. (C). 1997. text 59.95 (0-521-55236-2) Cambridge U Pr.

Abzug, Robert H. America & the Holocaust, 1933-1945: A Brief Documentary History. LC 98-87517. (Bedford Series in History & Culture). 230p. 1999. text 39.95 (0-312-21819-2) St Martin.

— Cosmos Crumbling: American Reform & Religious Imagination. 304p. (C). 1994. text 35.00 (0-19-503752-9) OUP.

— Cosmos Crumbling: American Reform & the Religious Imagination. 304p. (C). 1994. reprint ed. pap. text 21.95 (0-19-504568-8) OUP.

— Inside the Vicious Heart: Americans & the Liberation of Nazi Concentration Camps. LC 84-27252. (Illus.). 208p. 1987. pap. 15.95 (0-19-504236-0) OUP.

Ac, Saga I. Saga School: Moribana Style. 1996. pap. 10.95 (4-07-973234-1) Shufu No.

— Saga School: Seika Style. 1996. pap. 10.95 (4-07-973228-7) Shufu No.

— Saga School: Shogonka Style. 1996. pap. 10.95 (4-07-973211-2) Shufu No.

— Saga School Ikebana in Living. 1996. pap. 10.95 (4-07-973257-0) Shufu No.

— Saga School Principle Style. 1996. pap. 10.95 (4-07-973205-8) Shufu No.

Ac, Saka I. Saga School Heika. 1996. pap. 10.95 (4-07-973240-6) Shufu No.

AC/DC. AC/DC Bonfire: Guitar Tablature Edition. 1998. pap. 24.95 (0-8256-1652-2) Music Sales.

ACA Public Information Committee, 1990-1992 Staff. Improving Media Relations: A Handbook for Corrections. Phillips, Richard, ed. 44p. (Orig.). 1993. pap. 12.00 (0-929310-92-6) Am Correctional.

Academia Espanola Staff. Diccionario de la Lengua Castellana. (SPA.). 1989. 450.00 (0-7859-3369-7, 8478483985) Fr & Eur.

— Diccionario de la Lengua Castellana, Vol. 1. (SPA.). 1989. pap. 75.00 (0-7859-6321-9, 8478482059) Fr & Eur.

— Diccionario de la Lengua Castellana, Vol. 2. (SPA.). 1989. pap. 75.00 (0-7859-6322-7, 8478482067) Fr & Eur.

— Diccionario de la Lengua Castellana, Vol. 3. (SPA.). 1989. pap. 75.00 (0-7859-6323-5, 8478482075) Fr & Eur.

— Diccionario de la Lengua Castellana, Vol. 4. (SPA.). 1989. pap. 75.00 (0-7859-6324-3, 8478482083) Fr & Eur.

— Diccionario de la Lengua Castellana, Vol. 5. (SPA.). 1989. pap. 75.00 (0-7859-6325-1, 8478482091) Fr & Eur.

— Meyers Enzyklopaedisches Lexikon, Vol. 9. (SPA.). 1989. pap. 75.00 (0-7859-6350-2, 8478482040) Fr & Eur.

Academia Sinica, Kunming Inst. of Botany Staff, ed. Yunnan Camellias of China. (Illus.). 169p. 1986. text 75.00 (0-945345-10-0, Pub. by Sci Pr) Lubrecht & Cramer.

*Academic Committee on European Tax Law Staff. Family Taxation in Europe. Roch, Maria Teresa Soler, ed. LC 99-36255. 184p. 1999. pap. 90.00 (90-411-9755-9) Kluwer Law Intl.

Academic de Droit International de la Haye Staff. Recueil des Cours, 1983, Vol. 183. 1985. lib. bdg. 129.00 (90-247-3248-4) Kluwer Academic.

Academic Information Service, Inc. Staff. Tax Guide for College Teachers, 1994. rev. ed. 500p. 1992. pap. text 28.00 (0-916018-48-2) Acad Info Serv.

— Tax Guide for Engineers, 1994. 496p. (C). 1992. pap. text 30.00 (0-916018-47-4) Acad Info Serv.

Academic Media Staff. Waves, Tides & Currents. 1998. 43.00 (0-07-365959-2) McGraw.

— World Climates: Tropics. 1998. 39.00 (0-07-365961-4) McGraw.

Academic Press Staff. Academic Press Dictionary of Science & Technology: With CDROM. 1995. 84.00 (0-12-200401-9) Acad Pr.

*Academic Press Staff. Advances in Imaging & Electron Physics VIII. 250p. 1999. 130.00 (0-12-014753-X) Acad Pr.

— Encyclopedia of Separation Science, 10 vols. (Illus.). 7000p. 2000. 2900.00 (0-12-226770-2) Acad Pr.

— SciLogP. 136p. 1999. 895.00 (0-12-606309-5) Acad Pr.

Academic Press Staff. Table of Integrals, Series & Products. 5th ed. 1995. 84.00 incl. cd-rom (0-12-294756-8) Acad Pr.

*Academic Press Staff, et al. Methods in Microbiology Vol. 29: Genetic Methods for Diverse Prokaryotes. (Illus.). 560p. 1999. 59.95 (0-12-652340-1) Acad Pr.

Academic Solutions, Inc. Staff. The Arizona Constitution Study Guide. 6th rev. ed. LC 99-461813. 110p. (C). 1998. pap. text, student ed. 13.95 (0-9635364-5-1) Academic Solutions.

Academic Therapy Publications Staff. Directory of Facilities & Services for the Learning Disabled. 17th ed. 1998. pap. text 5.00 (1-57128-074-X) Acad Therapy.

Academie de Droit International de la Haye Staff. Receuil des Cours, 1980, No. IV. 380p. 1984. lib. bdg. 129.00 (90-247-2976-9) Kluwer Academic.

— Recueil des Cours. 1985. lib. bdg. 129.00 (90-247-3231-X) Kluwer Academic.

— Recueil des Cours. 1986. lib. bdg. 129.00 (90-247-3323-5) Kluwer Academic.

— Recueil des Cours. 1986. lib. bdg. 129.00 (90-247-3336-7) Kluwer Academic.

— Recueil des Cours. 1986. lib. bdg. 129.00 (90-247-3373-1) Kluwer Academic.

— Recueil des Cours - Collected Courses, Vol. 226. 432p. (C). 1992. lib. bdg. 129.00 (0-7923-1704-1) Kluwer Academic.

— Recueil des Cours - Collected Courses, Vol. 227 (1991-II) 432p. (C). 1992. lib. bdg. 129.00 (0-7923-1785-8) Kluwer Academic.

— Recueil des Cours, 1988, Vol. 212. 388p. (C). 1991. lib. bdg. 129.00 (0-7923-1411-5) Kluwer Academic.

— Recueil des Cours, 1984-85, Vol. 188. 1986. lib. bdg. 129.00 (90-247-3291-3) Kluwer Academic.

— Recueil des Cours, 1990-IV, Vol. 223. 416p. 1991. lib. bdg. 129.00 (0-7923-1524-3) Kluwer Academic.

Academie de Droit International de la Haye Staff, ed. General Index to the Collected Courses of the Hague Academy of International Law, Vols. 152-187. 404p. (C). 1994. lib. bdg. 129.00 (0-7923-2955-4, Pub. by M Nijhoff) Kluwer Academic.

— Receuil des Cours/Collected Courses, Vol. RADI 250. 1997. 215.00 (90-411-0419-4) Kluwer Law Intl.

— Receuil des Cours/Collected Courses, Vol. RADI 256. 1997. 215.00 (90-411-0420-8) Kluwer Law Intl.

— Recueil des Cours, Vol. 194. 1987. lib. bdg. 129.00 (90-247-3636-6) Kluwer Academic.

— Recueil des Cours, Vol. 200. 1987. lib. bdg. 129.00 (90-247-3644-7) Kluwer Academic.

An Asterisk (*) at the beginning of an entry indicates that the title is appearing for the first time.

— Recueil des Cours, Vol. 210, 1988-III. (C). 1989. lib. bdg. 129.00 (*0-7923-0398-9*) Kluwer Academic.
— Recueil des Cours, Vol. 214. (C). 1990. lib. bdg. 129.00 (*0-7923-0722-4*) Kluwer Academic.
— Recueil des Cours, Vol. 215 (1989-III) (C). 1990. lib. bdg. 129.00 (*0-7923-0815-8*) Kluwer Academic.
— Recueil des Cours, Vol. 216 (1989-IV) 416p. 1990. lib. bdg. 129.00 (*0-7923-1048-9*) Kluwer Academic.
— Recueil des Cours, Vol. 217 (1989-V) 456p. 1990. 117.00 (*0-07-923104-7*) Kluwer Academic.
— Recueil des Cours, Vol. 260.Tr. of Collected Courses. 416p. 1997. 129.00 (*90-411-0517-4*) Kluwer Academic.
— Recueil Des Cours 1993 IV: Collected Courses of the Hague Academy of International Law, Vol. 241. (C). 1994. 129.00 (*0-7923-2954-6*) Kluwer Academic.
— Recueil Des Cours III: Collected Courses of the Hague Academy of International Law 1993, Vol. 240. 500p. 1994. lib. bdg. 129.00 (*0-7923-2953-8*) Kluwer Academic.

***Academie de Droit International de la Haye Staff, ed.** Recueil des Cours Vol. 261: 1996.Tr. of Collected Courses. 432p. 1998. 129.00 (*90-411-1054-2*) Kluwer Law Intl.
— Recueil des Cours Vol. 263: 1997.Tr. of Collected Courses. 374p. 1997. 129.00 (*90-411-0539-5*) Kluwer Law Intl.
— Recueil des Cours Vol. 264: 1997.Tr. of Collected Courses. 416p. 1998. 129.00 (*90-411-1016-X*) Kluwer Law Intl.
— Recueil des Cours Vol. 265: 1997.Tr. of Collected Courses. 468p. 1999. 129.00 (*90-411-1178-6*) Kluwer Law Intl.
— Recueil des Cours Vol. 269: 1997.Tr. of Collected Courses. 464p. 1998. 129.00 (*90-411-1111-5*) Kluwer Law Intl.
— Recueil des Cours Vol. 271: 1998.Tr. of Collected Courses. 400p. 1999. 129.00 (*90-411-1210-3*) Kluwer Law Intl.

Academie de Droit International de la Haye Staff, ed. Recueil des Cours - Collected Courses, Vol. 219 (1989-VII) 416p. (C). 1993. lib. bdg. 129.00 (*0-7923-2140-5*) Kluwer Academic.
— Recueil des Cours - Collected Courses, Vol. 224 (1990-V) 416p. (C). 1993. lib. bdg. 129.00 (*0-7923-2317-3*) Kluwer Academic.
— Recueil des Cours - Collected Courses, Vol. 225 (1990-VI) 484p. (C). 1993. lib. bdg. 129.00 (*0-7923-2372-6*) Kluwer Academic.
— Recueil des Cours - Collected Courses, Vol. 229, 1991-IV. (C). 1992. lib. bdg. 129.00 (*0-7923-1984-2*) Kluwer Academic.
— Recueil des Cours - Collected Courses, Vol. 230 (1991-V) 423p. (C). 1993. lib. bdg. 129.00 (*0-7923-2472-2*) Kluwer Academic.
— Recueil des Cours - Collected Courses, Vol. 233 (1992-II) 416p. (C). 1993. lib. bdg. 129.00 (*0-7923-2409-9*) Kluwer Academic.
— Recueil des Cours - Collected Courses, Vol. 234, 1992, No. III. 436p. (C). 1993. lib. bdg. 129.00 (*0-7923-2260-6*) Kluwer Academic.
— Recueil des Cours - Collected Courses, Vol. 235, 1992-IV. 416p. (C). 1993. lib. bdg. 129.00 (*0-7923-2641-5*) Kluwer Academic.
— Recueil des Cours - Collected Courses, Vol. 236 (1992-V) 464p. (C). 1994. lib. bdg. 129.00 (*0-7923-2869-8*) Kluwer Academic.
— Recueil des Cours - Collected Courses, Vol. 239 (1993-II) 428p. (C). 1994. lib. bdg. 129.00 (*0-7923-2870-1*) Kluwer Academic.
— Recueil des Cours - Collected Courses, 1985-IV, Vol. 173. 444p. 1992. lib. bdg. 129.00 (*0-7923-2050-6*) Kluwer Academic.
— Recueil des Cours - Collected Courses, 1985-VI, Vol. 195. 1992. lib. bdg. 129.00 (*0-7923-2051-4*) Kluwer Academic.

***Academie de Droit International de la Haye Staff, ed.** Recueil des Cours (Collected Courses), Vol. 273. (ENG & FRE.). 416p. 1999. 129.00 (*90-411-1251-0*) Kluwer Law Intl.
— Recueil des Cours (Collected Courses), Vol. 274. (ENG & FRE.). 400p. 1999. text 129.00 (*90-411-1300-2*) Kluwer Law Intl.
— Recueil des Cours (Collected Courses) Vol. 250A: Index (Tomes) 1993-1994. 368p. 1999. text 129.00 (*90-411-1316-9*) Kluwer Law Intl.

Academie de Droit International de la Haye Staff, ed. Recueil des Cours (Collected Courses), 1997. (Recueil des Cours Ser.: No. 266). 430p. 1998. 129.00 (*90-411-0590-5*) Kluwer Law Intl.
— Recueil des Cours (Collected Courses), 1997. (Recueil des Cours Ser.: Vol. 267). 400p. 1998. 129.00 (*90-411-1006-2*) Kluwer Law Intl.

***Academie de Droit International de la Haye Staff, ed.** Recueil des Cours (Collected Courses) 1997, Vol. 268. (ENG & FRE.). 416p. 1999. text 129.00 (*90-411-1292-8*) Kluwer Law Intl.
— Recueil des Cours: Index Tomes Vol. 210A: 1987-1988.Tr. of Collected Courses: Index Volumes. 324p. 1997. 129.00 (*90-411-0533-6*) Kluwer Law Intl.
— Recueil des Cours: Index Tomes Vol. 220A: 1988-1990.Tr. of Collected Courses: Index Volumes. 368p. 1998. 129.00 (*90-411-1110-7*) Kluwer Law Intl.
— Recueil des Cours: Index Tomes Vol. 230A: 1990-1991.Tr. of Collected Courses: Index Volumes. 129p. 1998. 129.00 (*90-411-1137-9*) Kluwer Law Intl.

Academie de Droit International de la Haye Staff, ed. Recueil des Cours, 1988-I, Vol. 208. (C). 1988. lib. bdg. 129.00 (*0-7923-0058-0*) Kluwer Academic.
— Recueil des Cours, 1985-IV, Vol. 193. 1986. lib. bdg. 129.00 (*90-247-3424-X*) Kluwer Academic.
— Recueil des Cours, 1984, Vol. 189. (International Law Ser.). (C). 1989. lib. bdg. 129.00 (*0-7923-0057-2*) Kluwer Academic.
— Recueil des Cours, 1989-V, Vol. 217. (C). 1990. lib. bdg. 129.00 (*0-7923-1047-0*) Kluwer Academic.
— Recueil des Cours, 1989-VI, Vol. 218. 412p. (C). 1991. lib. bdg. 129.00 (*0-7923-1324-0*) Kluwer Academic.
— Recueil des Cours, 1989-I: 1989 - I, Vol. 213. (C). 1990. lib. bdg. 129.00 (*0-7923-0647-3*) Kluwer Academic.
— Recueil des Cours, 1987-II, Vol. 202. (C). 1988. lib. bdg. 129.00 (*90-247-3725-7*) Kluwer Academic.
— Recueil des Cours, 1987-III, Vol. 203. (C). 1988. lib. bdg. 129.00 (*90-247-3726-5*) Kluwer Academic.
— Recueil des Cours, 1987-IV, Vol. 204. (C). 1988. lib. bdg. 129.00 (*90-247-3742-7*) Kluwer Academic.
— Recueil des Cours, 1987-V: (1987 - V), Vol. 205. (C). 1989. lib. bdg. 129.00 (*0-7923-0322-9*) Kluwer Academic.
— Recueil des Cours, 1990-1, Vol. 220. 404p. (C). 1991. lib. bdg. 129.00 (*0-7923-1077-2*) Kluwer Academic.
— Recueil des Cours, 1990-II, Vol. 221. 406p. 1991. lib. bdg. 129.00 (*0-7923-1223-6*) Kluwer Academic.
— Recueil des Cours/Collected Courses, Vol. 257. 432p. 1997. 119.00 (*90-411-0440-2*) Kluwer Law Intl.
— Recueil des Cours/Collected Courses, Vol. 258. 460p. 1997. 119.00 (*90-411-0441-0*) Kluwer Law Intl.

Academie des Sciences Commerciales Staff. Dictionnaire Commercial. (FRE.). 1987. write for info. (*0-7859-7934-4*, 2-7101-0646-9) Fr & Eur.

Academie des Sciences Staff. Dictionary of Business: French-English-German. 3rd ed. (ENG, FRE & GER.). 1030p. 1994. 250.00 (*0-7859-8885-8*) Fr & Eur.

Academie Francaise Staff. Dictionnaire de l'Academia Francaise Vol. 1: A-Barattage. 9th ed. (FRE.). 116p. 1986. pap. 21.95 (*0-7859-7732-5*, 2110808926) Fr & Eur.
— Dictionnaire de l'Academie Francaise, Vol. 3. 9th ed. (FRE.). 1987. pap. 21.95 (*0-7859-7733-3*, 2110809205) Fr & Eur.
— Dictionnaire de l'Academie Francaise, Vol. 3. 9th ed. (FRE.). 1988. pap. 24.95 (*0-7859-7734-1*, 2110809531) Fr & Eur.
— Dictionnaire de l'Academie Francaise, Vol. 4. 9th ed. (FRE.). 1989. pap. 24.95 (*0-7859-7735-X*, 2110810521) Fr & Eur.
— Dictionnaire de l'Academie Francaise: A-Enz. (FRE.). 834p. 1992. 195.00 (*0-7859-7736-8*, 2110812494) Fr & Eur.
— Dictionnaire de l'Academie Francaise Vol. 5: Deux-Encyclique. 9th ed. (FRE.). 582p. 1990. pap. 28.95 (*0-7859-8620-0*, 211081117x) Fr & Eur.

***Academix Software Staff, ed.** TakeNote! (Illus.). 16p. 1999. pap. 33.00 (*0-205-30565-2*) Allyn.

Academy. Japanese Arch. 1988. pap. 21.95 (*0-312-02453-3*) St Martin.
— New Museology, Vol. 1. 1991. pap. 21.95 (*0-312-07141-8*) St Martin.
— Philosophy Arch Space, Vol. 1. 1992. pap. 25.00 (*0-312-07895-1*) St Martin.
— Post Modern Reader. 1992. 35.00 (*0-312-07896-X*) St Martin.

Academy Architecture Books Staff, et al. Mies Van Der Rohe: The European Works: An Architectural Monograph. (Academy Architecture Ser.). (Illus.). 112p. 1986. 45.00 (*0-312-53214-8*); pap. 30.00 (*0-312-53215-6*) St Martin.

Academy Editions Staff. Anglo American Suburbs. 1982. pap. 9.95 (*0-312-03717-1*) St Martin.
— Art & the Tectonic. (Orig.). 1991. pap. 21.95 (*0-312-05563-3*) St Martin.
— Contemporary Painting. (Art & Design Profiles Ser.: No. 26). (Illus.). 1992. pap. 26.95 (*0-312-08549-4*) Academy Ed UK.
— Marking the City Boundaries: Art & Design Profile 25. 1992. pap. 26.95 (*0-312-08107-3*) St Martin.
— Museums of the Last Generation. (Illus.). 144p. 1987. pap. 29.95 (*0-312-00451-6*) St Martin.
— New Architecture. 1991. pap. 21.95 (*0-312-04521-2*) St Martin.
— Peter Pran of Ellerbe Becket. (Architectural Monographs). 1993. 55.00 (*0-312-08689-X*) St Martin.
— Peter Pran of Ellerbe Becket: Recent Works. (Architectural Monographs: No. 24). 1993. pap. 38.00 (*0-312-08690-3*) St Martin.
— Pop Architecture: Architecture Design Profile 98. 1992. pap. 26.95 (*0-312-08108-1*) St Martin.
— Post-Modernism on Trial. 1991. pap. 19.95 (*0-312-06032-7*) St Martin.

Academy for Learning in Retirement Members. Ourselves - Then & Now: A Collection of Personal Essays. unabridged ed. Finnegan, Marianne G., ed. (Illus.). 288p. 1997. pap. 12.95 (*0-9659629-0-3*) Third Age Pr.

Academy Group Limited Staff. Aspects of Modern Art. 1990. pap. 21.95 (*0-312-04472-0*) St Martin.

Academy Group Ltd Staff. Alessi: The Design Factory. LC 95-142511. (Art & Design Monographs). (Illus.). 145p. 1994. pap. 54.95 (*1-85490-334-9*) Wiley.

Academy of American Poets Staff & Vedral, Joyce L. Fifty Years of American Poetry: Over 2000 Important Works by America's Modern Masters. 320p. 1995. mass mkt. 6.50 (*0-440-21877-2*) Dell.

Academy of Certified Hazardous Materials Staff. Hazardous Materials Mangement. LC 99-54563. (Engineering Handbook Ser.). 705p. 1999. 99.95 (*0-07-135173-6*) McGraw.

Academy of European Law Staff, ed. Collected Courses of the Academy of European Law: European Community Law, 1992, Vol. III, Bk. 1. (Collected Courses of European Law Ser.). 312p. (C). 1994. lib. bdg. 118.00 (*0-7923-3047-1*) Kluwer Academic.
— Collected Courses of the Academy of European Law: The Protection of Human Rights in Europe, 1992, Vol. III, Bk. 2. (Collected Courses of European Law Ser.). 420p. (C). 1994. lib. bdg. 118.00 (*0-7923-3154-0*) Kluwer Academic.
— Collected Courses of the Academy of European Law - Recueil des Cours de l'Academie de Droi Europeen Vol. I, Bk. 2: 1990 Community Law. 376p. (C). 1992. lib. bdg. 118.00 (*0-7923-1644-4*) Kluwer Academic.
— Collected Courses of the Academy of European Law - Recueil des Cours de l'Academie de Droit Europeen Vol. I, Bk. 1: 1990 Community Law. 384p. (C). 1992. lib. bdg. 118.00 (*0-7923-1603-7*) Kluwer Academic.

***Academy of European Law Staff, ed.** Collected Courses of the Academy of European Law (Recueil des Cours de l'Academie de Droit Europeen) Vol. VII, Bk. 2: 1996 European Community Law. (Collected Courses of the Academy of European Law Ser.: Vol. 14). (ENG & FRE.). 240p. 1999. text 117.00 (*90-411-1252-9*) Kluwer Law Intl.
— 1996 European Community Law, Vol. VII, Bk. 1. (Collected Courses of the Academy of European Law Ser.: Vol. 13).Tr. of Recueil des Cours de l'Academie de Droit Europeen. 416p. 1999. 129.00 (*90-411-1209-6*) Kluwer Law Intl.

Academy of Humanism Staff. Neo-Fundamentalism: The Humanist Response. LC 88-61449. 186p. 1988. 22.95 (*0-87975-452-4*) Prometheus Bks.

Academy of Humanism Staff, ed. Challenges to the Enlightenment: In Defense of Reason & Science. LC 93-41680. 319p. 1994. 27.95 (*0-87975-869-4*) Prometheus Bks.

Academy of Marine Sciences & Underwater Research Staff. Who's Who in Scuba Diving. Bachstein, Harry, ed. 436p. (C). 1992. 4.95 (*0-941332-28-4*, D500) Best Pub Co.

Academy of Marketing Science Staff. Developments in Marketing Science: Proceedings of the Annual Conference of the Academy of Marketing Science, Coral Gables, FL, May 28-31, 1997, Vol. 20, 1997. Wilson, Elizabeth J. & Hair, Joseph F., eds. LC 80-641158. (Illus.). 379p. reprint ed. pap. 117.50 (*0-608-10445-9*, 207108100020) Bks Demand.
— Developments in Marketing Science: Proceedings of the Annual Conference of the Academy of Marketing Science, Norfolk, VA, May 27-30, 1998, Vol. 21, 1998. Ford, John B. & Honeycutt, Earl D., eds. LC 80-641158. (Illus.). 559p. reprint ed. pap. 173.30 (*0-608-10447-7*, 207108200021) Bks Demand.
— Developments in Marketing Science: Proceedings of the Annual Conference of the Academy of Marketing Science, Phoenix, AZ, May 29-June 1, 1996, Vol. 19, 1996. Wilson, Elizabeth J. & Hair, Joseph F., eds. LC 80-641158. (Walter W. S. Cook Alumni Lectures: 1959). (Illus.). 333p. reprint ed. pap. 103.30 (*0-608-10445-0*, 207108000019) Bks Demand.
— Developments in Marketing Science Vol. 11-1989: Proceedings of the Eleventh Annual Conference of the Academy of Marketing Science, Montreal, Canada April 27-May 1, 1988. fac. ed. Bahn, Kenneth D., ed. LC 80-641158. 552p. 1988. reprint ed. pap. 171.20 (*0-7837-8120-2*, 204792700011) Bks Demand.
— Developments in Marketing Science Vol. 12-1989: Proceedings of the Thirteenth Annual Conference of the Academy of Marketing Science, Orlando, FL, May 17-20, 1989. fac. ed. Hawes, Jon M. & Thanopoulos, John, eds. LC 80-641158. 712p. 1989. reprint ed. pap. 200.00 (*0-7837-8119-9*, 204792600012) Bks Demand.
— Developments in Marketing Science Vol. 13-1990: Proceedings of the Thirteenth Annual Conference of the Academy of Marketing Science, New Orleans, LA, April 25-29, 1990. fac. ed. Dunlap, B. J., ed. LC 80-641158. 579p. 1990. reprint ed. pap. 179.50 (*0-7837-8117-2*, 204792400013) Bks Demand.
— Developments in Marketing Science Vol. 15-1992: Proceedings of the Annual Conference of the Academy of Marketing Science, San Diego, California, April 22-25, 1992. fac. ed. Crittenden, Victoria L., ed. LC 80-641158. 544p. 1992. reprint ed. pap. 168.70 (*0-7837-8116-4*, 204792300015) Bks Demand.
— Developments in Marketing Science Vol. 16-1993: Proceedings of the Annual Conference of the Academy of Marketing Science, Miami, FL, May 26-29, 1993. fac. ed. Levy, Michael & Grewal, Dhruv, eds. LC 80-641158. 717p. 1993. reprint ed. pap. 200.00 (*0-7837-8118-0*, 204792500016) Bks Demand.
— Developments in Marketing Science Vol. 17: Proceedings of the Annual Conference of the Academy of Marketing Science, Nashville, TN, June 1-4, 1994. Wilson, Elizabeth J. & Black, William C., eds. LC 80-641158. 491p. 1994. reprint ed. pap. 152.30 (*0-608-00730-7*, 206150600009) Bks Demand.
— Developments in Marketing Science Vol. 18: Proceedings of the Annual Conference of the Academy of Marketing Science, Orlando, FL, May 17-20, 1995. Gomes, Roger, ed. LC 80-641158. (Illus.). 260p. pap. 80.60 (*0-608-05157-8*, 206571800018) Bks Demand.
— Developments in Marketing Science Vol. 19: Proceedings of the Annual Conference of the Academy of Marketing Science, Phoenix, AZ, May 29-June 1, 1996. 25th anniversary ed. Wilson, Elizabeth J. & Hair, Joseph F., Jr., eds. LC 80-641158. (Illus.). 334p. pap. 103.60 (*0-608-05158-6*, 2065719) Bks Demand.
— Developments in Quality-of-Life Studies in Marketing Vol. 4: Proceedings of the Academy of Marketing Science's Fourth Quality-of-Life - Marketing Conference, Washington, DC, November 19-22, 1992. Sirgy, M. Joseph et al, eds. LC HF5411.A33. 219p. 1992. reprint ed. pap. 67.90 (*0-7837-8114-8*, 204792100008) Bks Demand.
— Developments in Quality-of-Life Studies in Marketing Vol. 5: Proceedings of the Fifth Quality-of-Life/ Marketing Conference, Williamsburg, VA, November 30-December 2, 1995. Meadow, H. Lee et al, eds. LC HF5411.A33. 224p. 1995. pap. 69.50 (*0-608-05107-1*, 206566800005) Bks Demand.
— International Conference on Services Marketing: Proceedings of the International Conference on Services Marketing Presented by the Academy of Marketing Science & the Marketing Department of Cleveland State Univ., Cleveland, OH, October 26-28, 1988. fac. ed. Thomas, Edward G., ed. LC HF5411.. (Special Conference Ser.: No. 5). 379p. 1988. reprint ed. pap. 117.50 (*0-7837-8125-3*, 204793200008) Bks Demand.
— Minority Marketing: Research Perspectives for the 1990's: Proceedings of the Minority Marketing Conference Presented by the Academy of Marketing Science & the University of Southern Mississippi, Long Beach, MS, October 14-16, 1993. fac. ed. King, Robert L., ed. LC HF5411.. (Special Conference Ser.: No. 6). 125p. 1993. reprint ed. pap. 38.80 (*0-7837-8115-6*, 204792200008) Bks Demand.
— Multicultural Marketing Conference, 1998: Proceedings, Montreal, Quebec, Canada, September 17-20, 1998. Chebat, Jean-Charles & Oumlil, A. Ben, eds. LC 99-1285. (Illus.). 567p. reprint ed. pap. 175.80 (*0-608-20286-X*, 207154400001) Bks Demand.
— World Marketing Congress: Proceedings of the Fifth Bi-Annual International Conference of the Academy of Marketing Science, Copenhagen, Denmark, August 11-14, 1991. fac. ed. Frankenberger, Kristina D. et al, eds. LC 89-110901. (International Conference Ser.: No. 5). 355p. 1991. reprint ed. pap. 110.10 (*0-7837-8122-9*, 204792900008) Bks Demand.
— World Marketing Congress: Proceedings of the Fourth Bi-Annual International Conference of the Academy of Marketing Science, Singapore, Republic of Singapore, July 16-19, 1989. Lazer, William et al, eds. LC 89-110901. (International Conference Ser.: No. 4). 435p. 1989. reprint ed. pap. 134.90 (*0-7837-8124-5*, 204793100008) Bks Demand.
— World Marketing Congress: Proceedings of the Seventh Bi-Annual World Marketing Congress, Melbourne, Australia, July 6-10, 1995, Vol. 7. Chandler, Peter et al, eds. LC 89-110901. 664p. 1995. pap. 200.00 (*0-608-05109-8*, 206566900007); pap. write for info. (*0-608-05110-1*, 2065669) Bks Demand.
— World Marketing Congress Vol. 3-1987: Proceedings of the Third Bi-Annual International Conference of the Academy of Marketing Science, Barcelona, Spain, August 23-26, 1987. fac. ed. Bahn, Kenneth D. & Sirgy, M. Joseph, eds. LC 89-110901. (International Conference Ser.: No. 3). 275p. 1987. reprint ed. pap. 85.30 (*0-7837-8123-7*, 204793000008) Bks Demand.
— World Marketing Congress Vol. 6-1993: Proceedings of the Sixth Bi-Annual International Conference of the Academy of Marketing Science, Istanbul, Turkey, July 15-19, 1993. fac. ed. Sirgy, M. Joseph et al, eds. LC 89-110901. 716p. 1993. reprint ed. pap. 200.00 (*0-7837-8121-0*, 204792800006) Bks Demand.

Academy of Motion Picture Arts & Sciences Staff. Annual Index to Motion Picture Credits, 1978. Ramsey, Verna, ed. LC 79-644761. 443p. 1979. lib. bdg. 195.00 (*0-313-20950-2*, AN78, Greenwood Pr) Greenwood.
— Annual Index to Motion Picture Credits, 1979. Ramsay, Verna, ed. LC 79-644761. 502p. 1980. lib. bdg. 195.00 (*0-313-20951-0*, AN79, Greenwood Pr) Greenwood.
— Annual Index to Motion Picture Credits, 1980. LC 79-644761. 521p. 1981. lib. bdg. 195.00 (*0-313-20952-9*, AN80, Greenwood Pr) Greenwood.
— Annual Index to Motion Picture Credits, 1981. LC 79-644761. 469p. 1982. lib. bdg. 195.00 (*0-313-20953-7*, AN81, Greenwood Pr) Greenwood.
— Annual Index to Motion Picture Credits, 1982. LC 79-644761. (Annual Index to Motion Picture Credits Ser.). 447p. 1983. lib. bdg. 195.00 (*0-313-24263-1*, AN82, Greenwood Pr) Greenwood.

Academy of Natural Sciences of Philadelphia Staff, ed. Catalog of the Library of the Academy of Natural Sciences of Philadelphia, 16 vols., Set. 1972. 1825.00 (*0-8161-0946-X*, G K Hall & Co) Mac Lib Ref.

Academy of Producer Insurance Studies, Inc. Staff. Understanding the Wholesale Insurance Market: An Educational Program. 82p. (Orig.). 1994. pap. text 20.00 (*1-878204-52-1*) APIS Inc.

Academy of Prosthodontics Staff. The Glossary of Prosthodontic Terms. LC 94-9176. 1994. write for info. (*0-318-72654-8*) Mosby Inc.

Academy of Religion & Mental Health Staff. Research in Religion & Health: Selected Projects & Methods. LC 59-15767. (Proceedings of the Fifth Academy Symposium Ser.: 1961). 175p. reprint ed. pap. 54.30 (*0-7837-0436-4*, 204075900018) Bks Demand.

Academy of Sciences & Technology in Berlin Staff, ed. Sonnenergie: Herausforderung Fur Forschung, Entwicklung und Internationale Zusammenarbeit. (Akademie der Wissenschaften zu Berlin, Forschungsbericht Ser.: Bd. 1). (GER., Illus.). xx, 281p. (C). 1991. pap. 52.35 (*3-11-012954-X*) De Gruyter.

Academy of Sciences & Technology in Berlin Staff, ed. see Albach, Horst.

Academy of Sciences & Technology in Berlin Staff, ed. see Fischer, Wolfram, et al.

Academy of Sciences & Technology in Berlin Staff, ed. see Mueller, Werner, et al.

Academy of Traditional Chinese Medicine, Shanghai. An Outline of Chinese Acupuncture. 305p. 17.50 (*0-317-31550-1*) Chans Corp.

Academy Staff. Free Space Architecture. 1992. pap. 26.95 (*0-312-07897-8*) St Martin.
— James Sterling Michael Wilford. 1991. pap. 21.95 (*0-312-05562-5*) St Martin.
— Modern Pluralism, Vol. 1. 1992. pap. 21.95 (*0-312-07539-1*) St Martin.

A

An Asterisk (*) at the beginning of an entry indicates that the title is appearing for the first time.

A

***Acadia National Park Staff.** Shoreline Discovery: A Guide to Acadia's Coastline. rev. ed. 26p. 1999. reprint ed. mass mkt., teacher ed. 2.95 (*1-888213-47-7*) Eastern National.

***Acadian House Publishing Staff.** Growing up in South Louisiana. 2000. 7.95 (*0-925417-35-1*) Acadian Hse Pub.

Acair Ltd. Staff. Summer Hunting a Prince: The Escape of Charles Edward Stuart. 96p. (C). 1992. text 35.00 (*0-86152-873-5*, Pub. by Acair Ltd) St Mut.

Acair Ltd. Staff, ed. A Chideachd Mo Ghaoil: Dain spioradail air an seinn le Cairistiona Sheadha. 1986. 40.00 (*0-86152-026-2*, Pub. by Acair Ltd); audio. write for info. (*0-7855-2558-0*, Pub. by Acair Ltd) St Mut.

— An Cogadh Mor Nineteen Fourteen to Nineteen Eighteen. 1985. 40.00 (*0-86152-016-5*, Pub. by Acair Ltd) St Mut.

— Eilean Fraoich. 1985. 65.00 (*0-7855-1348-5*, Pub. by Acair Ltd); pap. 50.00 (*0-7855-2997-7*, Pub. by Acair Ltd) St Mut.

— A Lewis Album from the Collection of Historical Photographs of Angus M. Macdonald, A. R. P. S. 1985. 65.00 (*0-86152-011-4*, Pub. by Acair Ltd) St Mut.

— RIS A Bhruthaich: Somhairle MacGill-eain, the Criticism & Prose Writing of Sorley Maclean. 1985. 90.00 (*0-86152-041-6*, Pub. by Acair Ltd) St Mut.

ACAM Press Staff. Object-Oriented Programming: Systems, Languages & Applications Oopsla '91 Conference. 1991. pap. text 35.50 (*0-201-55417-8*) Addison-Wesley.

Acamedica Press Staff. The Carewise Guide: Self-Care from Head to Toe. LC 94-72787. 448p. 1995. pap. 19.95 (*1-886444-00-5*) CareWise.

Acampora, A. S. An Introduction to Broadband Networks: LANs, MANs, ATM, B-ISDN, & Optical Networks for Integrated Multimedia Telecommunications. (Applications of Communications Theory Ser.). (Illus.). 350p. (C). 1994. 75.00 (*0-306-44558-1*, Plenum Trade) Perseus Pubng.

***Acampora, Ralph.** The Fourth Mega Market 1994-2006. (Illus.). 320p. 2000. 24.95 (*0-7868-6651-9*, Pub. by Hyperion) Time Warner.

— The Fourth Mega Market 1994-2006. 2001. pap. 15.95 (*0-7868-8562-9*, Pub. by Hyperion) Time Warner.

Acar, et al. New Macrolides, Azalides & Streptogramin in Clinical Practice. Neu, Harold C. et al, eds. (Infectious Disease & Therapy Ser.: Vol. 18). (Illus.). 568p. 1995. text 190.00 (*0-8247-9311-0*) Dekker.

Acar, Emmanual, jt. auth. see Satchell, Stephen.

Acar, Feride, jt. auth. see Ghuneps-Ayata, Aypse.

Acar, J., et al. Cardiopathies Valvulaires Acquises. (FRE., Illus.). 656p. 1985. 130.00 (*2-257-10441-2*) S M P F Inc.

Acar, M., et al, eds. Mechatronics: The Basis for New Industrial Development. 848p. 1994. 318.00 (*1-85312-367-6*) Computational Mech MA.

Acar, Memis, ed. Mechatronics Design in Textile Engineering: Proceedings of the NATO Advanced Study Institute on Advancements & Applications of Mechatronics Design in Textile Engineering, Side, Antalya, Turkey, April 5-16, 1992. (NATO Advanced Science Institutes Ser.: Series E). 328p. (C). 1994. text 213.00 (*0-7923-3204-0*) Kluwer Academic.

Acar, William, jt. auth. see Georgantzas, Nicholas C.

Acar, Yalcin B. & Seals, Roger K. Environmental Geotechnics. (C). 1998. 64.00 (*0-13-280496-4*, Macmillan Coll) P-H.

Acar, Yalcin B., ed. see ASCE Geotechnical Engineering Division Staff & ASCE Environmental Engineering Division Staff.

Acar, Yalcin B., jt. ed. see Usmen, Mumtaz A.

Acarnley, P. P. Stepping Motors: A Guide to Modern Theory & Practice. rev. ed. (Control Engineering Ser.: No. 19). 160p. 1992. pap. 39.00 (*0-86341-027-8*, CEO19Z) INSPEC Inc.

Acarya, Avadhutika A. Beyond the Superconscious Mind. (Illus.). 102p. (Orig.). 1989. pap. 6.00 (*0-88476-004-9*) Ananda Marga.

— Neo-Humanist Education: Education for a New World. (Illus.). 160p. (Orig.). 1989. pap. 4.95 (*0-88476-007-3*) Ananda Marga.

Acarya Mantreshwarananda Avadhuta, tr. see Prabhat Rainjan Sarkar.

Acarya Vijayananda Avadhuta, tr. see Prabhat Rainjan Sarkar.

Acaster, Linda. Hostage of the Heart. large type ed. (Large Print Ser.). 416p. 1996. 27.99 (*0-7089-3605-9*) Ulverscroft.

— A Wife for Winter Man. large type ed. (Large Print Ser.). 496p. 1996. 25.99 (*0-7089-3641-5*) Ulverscroft.

Acatos Publishing Staff. Mayer International Auction Records 1999. 6000p. 1999. 195.00 (*2-940033-49-8*, Pub. by Acatos Edit) Antique Collect.

Acatos, Sylvio & Bruggman, Maximilien. Pueblos: Prehistoric Indian Cultures of the Southwest. Fritzemeier, Barbara, tr. (Illus.). 240p. 1990. 45.00 (*0-8160-2437-5*) Facts on File.

ACC Research Project Editors, ed. The Pocket Price Guide to British Painting, 1830-1980. 160p. 1990. 25.00 (*1-85149-124-4*) Antique Collect.

ACCA Safety Task Team Staff. ACCA On-the Job Safety Handbook. (Illus.). 63p. 1997. pap. 50.00 (*1-892765-17-9*) Air Conditioning Cont.

Accad, Evelyn. The Excised. Bruner, David, tr. from FRE. LC 94-24659. 89p. 1994. pap. 8.50 (*0-89410-799-2*, Three Contnts) L Rienner.

Accad, Evelyne. Sexuality & War: Literary Masks of the Middle East. (Feminist Crosscurrents Ser.). 198p. (C). 1992. pap. text 18.50 (*0-8147-0615-0*) NYU Pr.

— Wounding Words: A Woman's Journal in Tunisia. Hahn, Cynthia T., tr. (African Writers Ser.). 1996. pap. 13.95 (*0-435-90523-6*, 90523) Heinemann.

Accad, Fouad E. Building Bridges: Christianity & Islam. LC 96-36968. 158p. (Orig.). 1997. pap. 10.00 (*0-89109-795-3*) NavPress.

Accademia Senese Degli Intronati Staff, ed. see Machiavelli, Niccolo, et al.

Accame, Silvio. Il Dominio Romano in Grecia Dalla Guerra Acaica Ad Augusto. LC 75-7302. (Roman History Ser.). (ITA.). 1975. reprint ed. 21.95 (*0-405-07179-5*) Ayer.

Accampo, Elinor A. Industrialization, Family Life, & Class Relations: Saint Chamond, 1815-1914. 320p. (C). 1988. 55.00 (*0-520-06095-4*, Pub. by U CA Pr) Cal Prin Full Svc.

Accardi, Art, ed. & photos by see DeFalco, Robert A.

Accardi, Bernard, et al, compiled by. Recent Studies in Myths & Literature, 1970-1990: An Annotated Bibliography. 29. LC 91-18070. (Bibliographies & Indexes in World Literature Ser.: No. 29). 264p. 1991. lib. bdg. 59.95 (*0-313-27545-9*, HSQ, Greenwood Pr) Greenwood.

Accardi, Carla. Carla Accardi. (Illus.). 560p. 1999. 125.00 (*88-86158-91-2*, Pub. by Charta) Dist Art Pubs.

Accardi, L. Quantum Probability & Related Topics, Vol. 8. 350p. 1993. text 100.00 (*981-02-1140-6*) World Scientific Pub.

— Quantum Probability & Related Topics, Vol. IX. 420p. 1994. text 106.00 (*981-02-2047-2*) World Scientific Pub.

— Quantum Probability & Related Topics: QP-PQ, Vol. 7. 350p. 1992. text 95.00 (*981-02-1011-6*) World Scientific Pub.

Accardi, L., ed. Quantum Probability & Related Topics. 500p. (C). 1991. pap. 48.00 (*981-02-0716-6*); text 113.00 (*981-02-0680-1*) World Scientific Pub.

— Quantum Probability & Related Topics, Vol. 7. LC 92-24406. 388p. 1992. pap. write for info. (*981-02-1979-2*) World Scientific Pub.

Accardi, L., et al, eds. Quantum Probability & Applications to the Quantum Theory of Irreversible Processes: Proceedings of the International Workshop Held at Villa Mondragone, Italy, Sept. 6-11, 1982. (Lecture Notes in Mathematics Ser.: Vol. 1055). vi, 411p. 1984. 49.95 (*0-387-12915-4*) Spr-Verlag.

— Quantum Probability & Applications, V: Proceedings of the Fourth Workshop, Held in Heidelberg, FRG, Sept. 26-30, 1988. (Lecture Notes in Mathematics Ser.: Vol. 1442). vi, 413p. 1990. 63.95 (*0-387-53026-6*) Spr-Verlag.

***Accardi, L., et al, eds.** Selected Papers of Takeyuki Hida. 500p. 2000. 94.00 (*981-02-4333-2*) World Scientific Pub.

Accardi, L. & Heyde, C. C., eds. Probability Towards 2000. LC 97-48856. (Lecture Notes in Statistics Ser.: Vol. 128). 366p. 1998. pap. 44.95 (*0-387-98458-5*) Spr-Verlag.

Accardi, L. & Von Waldenfels, W., eds. Quantum Probability & Applications, IV. (Lecture Notes in Mathematics Ser.: Vol. 1396). vi, 355p. 1989. 50.95 (*0-387-51613-1*) Spr-Verlag.

— Quantum Probability & Applications III. (Lecture Notes in Mathematics Ser.: Vol. 1303). vi, 373p. 1988. 54.95 (*0-387-18919-X*) Spr-Verlag.

Accardi, L. & Waldenfels, W. V., eds. Quantum Probability & Applications II. (Lecture Notes in Mathematics Ser.: Vol. 1136). vi, 534p. 1985. 64.95 (*0-387-15661-5*) Spr-Verlag.

Accardo. The Infernal Holmes: Dante in Baker Street. (Sherlockian Scholarship Ser.). write for info. (*1-55246-190-4*) Battered Silicon.

Accardo, Pasquale, ed. The Medical Almanac. LC 91-20882. (Illus.). 254p. 1992. 39.50 (*0-89603-181-0*) Humana.

Accardo, Pasquale J. Diagnosis & Detection: The Medical Iconography of Sherlock Holmes. LC 86-45057. 144p. 1987. 32.50 (*0-8386-3292-0*) Fairleigh Dickinson.

***Accardo, Pasquale J.** The Spencerian Holmes: Being the Annotated Manuscript of "The Hell of the Baskervilles" 1998. pap. 10.00 (*1-55246-056-8*) Battered Silicon.

***Accardo, Pasquale J., ed.** Attention Deficits & Hyperactivity in Children & Adults: Diagnosis, Treatment & Management. 2nd ed. (Pediatric Rehabilitation Ser.: Vol. 10). 710p. 2000. 85.00 (*0-8247-1962-X*) Dekker.

Accardo, Pasquale J., et al, eds. Attention Deficit Disorders & Hyperactivity in Children: Early Diagnosis & Intervention. (Pediatric Habilitation Ser.: Vol. 7). (Illus.). 424p. 1991. text 65.00 (*0-8247-8429-4*) Dekker.

***Accardo, Pasquale J., et al, eds.** Autism: Clinical & Research Issues. (Illus.). (C). 2000. Price not set. (*0-912752-48-3*) York Pr.

Accardo, Pasquale J., et al, eds. Behavior Belongs in the Brain: Neuro Behavioral Syndromes. LC 96-54476. (Illus.). (C). 1997. text 30.50 (*0-912752-41-6*) York Pr.

Accardo, Pasquale J. & Whitman, Barbara Y. Dictionary of Developmental Disabilities Terminology. (Illus.). 1996. 55.95 (*1-55766-245-2*); pap. 35.95 (*1-55766-112-X*) P H Brookes.

Accardo, Pasquale J., jt. auth. see Capute, Arnold J.

Accardy, Frank. Cover Me - Lord! (Christian Living Ser.). 1994. pap. 1.59 (*0-87509-568-2*) Chr Pubns.

Accattoli, Luigi. Life in the Vatican with John Paul II. 216p. 1999. pap. 29.95 (*0-7893-0252-7*, Pub. by Universe) St Martin.

— When a Pope Asks Forgiveness: The Mea Culpa's of John Paul II. Aumann, Jordan, tr. Orig. Title: Quando il Papa Chiede Perdono. 300p. 1998. pap. 16.95 (*0-8189-0808-4*) Alba.

— When a Pope Asks Forgiveness: The Mea Culpa's of Pope John Paul II. Aumann, Jordan, tr. LC 97-45147. 264p. 1998. pap. 16.95 (*0-8198-8295-X*) Pauline Bks.

Accawi, Anwar F. The Boy from the Tower of the Moon. LC 98-48921. 178p. (YA). 1999. 23.00 (*0-8070-7008-4*) Beacon Pr.

Accelerated Computer Training Staff, ed. How to Use WordPerfect 6.0 for Windows. 230p. 1995. teacher ed., spiral bd. 49.95 (*0-7402-0443-2*) Accelerated Comput Train.

Accents on Health, Inc., Staff, jt. auth. see Jones, Anita.

Access Communications Staff, ed. see Hieb, Constance.

Access Guides Staff. Boston. 4th ed. LC 97-215173. (Access Travel Guides Ser.). 224p. 1997. pap. 19.00 (*0-06-277197-3*, Harper Ref) HarpC.

— Caribbean Access. 3rd ed. LC 96-208499. 384p. 1996. pap. 20.00 (*0-06-277165-5*) HarpC.

— Mexico Access. 3rd ed. 272p. 1996. pap. 19.00 (*0-06-277166-3*) HarpC.

— Montreal & Quebec City Access. (Access Travel Guides Ser.). 160p. 1996. pap. 148.00 (*0-06-273136-X*, Access Trvl) HarpInfo.

— Wine Country France. 2nd ed. (Access Travel Guides Ser.). 256p. 1997. pap. 19.00 (*0-06-277193-0*, Access Trvl) HarpInfo.

Access Innovations, Inc. Staff. Filmstrip & Slide Set Finder, 1990: A Comprehensive Index to 35mm Educational Filmstrips & Slide Sets, Set, Vols. I-III. Morgan, Roy, ed. LC 90-60268. (NICEM Ser.). 2900p. 1990. 225.00 (*0-937548-15-4*) Plexus Pub.

***Access Press Staff.** Access Caribbean. 5th ed. (Illus.). 384p. 2000. pap. 20.00 (*0-06-277286-4*, Access Trvl) HarpInfo.

Access Press Staff. Access Florence & Venice. 4th ed. LC DG732.W865 1998. 304p. 1998. pap. 19.00 (*0-06-277222-8*, Access Trvl) HarpInfo.

***Access Press Staff.** Access Gay U.S.A. 2nd ed. (Access Travel Guides Ser.). (Illus.). 416p. 2000. pap. 20.00 (*0-06-277278-3*) HarpC.

Access Press Staff. Access London. 6th ed. (Illus.). 240p. 1998. pap. 20.00 (*0-06-277225-2*, Access Trvl) HarpInfo.

***Access Press Staff.** Access Nashville & Memphis. (Access Travel Guides Ser.). (Illus.). 240p. 2000. pap. 20.00 (*0-06-277250-3*) HarpC.

Access Press Staff. Access New York City. 8th ed. 336p. 1998. pap. 20.00 (*0-06-277235-X*, Access Trvl) HarpInfo.

— Access Orlando. 4th ed. 224p. 1997. pap. 19.00 (*0-06-277228-7*, Access Trvl) HarpInfo.

— Access Paris. 6th ed. 272p. 1998. pap. 19.00 (*0-06-277229-5*, Access Trvl) HarpInfo.

— Access San Francisco Restaurant 1997-1998. 256p. 1997. pap. 13.00 (*0-06-277219-8*, Access Trvl) HarpInfo.

— Cape Cod. 3rd ed. (Illus.). 208p. 1998. pap. 19.00 (*0-06-277220-1*, Access Trvl) HarpInfo.

— The Gay U. S. A. Guide. 416p. 1998. pap. 19.95 (*0-06-277212-0*, Access Trvl) HarpInfo.

— Hawaii. 7th ed. (Illus.). 192p. 1997. pap. 19.00 (*0-06-277223-6*, Access Trvl) HarpInfo.

— Las Vegas. 4th ed. (Illus.). 144p. 1997. pap. 19.00 (*0-06-277224-4*, Access Trvl) HarpInfo.

— Miami. 4th ed. (Illus.). 272p. 1997. pap. 19.00 (*0-06-277226-0*, Access Trvl) HarpInfo.

***Access Press Staff.** Miami & South Florida. 5th ed. 272p. 1999. pap. 19.00 (*0-06-277276-7*, HarpRes) HarpInfo.

Access Press Staff. Minneapolis & St. Paul. (Illus.). 256p. 1998. pap. 19.00 (*0-06-277234-1*, Access Trvl) HarpInfo.

— New Orleans. 3rd ed. LC 95-659042. (Illus.). 176p. 1997. pap. 19.00 (*0-06-277227-9*, Access Trvl) HarpInfo.

— Orlando & Central Florida. 5th ed. (Access Guides Ser.). 224p. 1999. pap. 19.00 (*0-06-277282-1*, HarpRes) HarpInfo.

— Philadelphia. 3rd ed. (Illus.). 192p. 1998. pap. 20.00 (*0-06-277230-9*, Access Trvl) HarpInfo.

— Washington, D. C. 6th ed. (Illus.). 240p. 1998. pap. 20.00 (*0-06-277232-5*, Access Trvl) HarpInfo.

Access Press Staff, ed. Access Cruise. 2nd ed. 2000. pap. 20.00 (*0-06-277283-X*) HarpC.

Access Publishing Staff. Beginner's Guide: Netscape Communicator 4.0.1. 1997. pap. text 19.99 (*1-57671-011-4*) INST Publishing.

— Microsoft Excel 97. (Beginner's Guide Ser.). 1997. pap. text 19.99 (*1-57671-039-4*) INST Publishing.

— Microsoft Word 97. (Beginner's Guide Ser.). 1997. pap. text 19.99 (*1-57671-013-0*) INST Publishing.

Access Staff. International Affairs Directory of Organizations. 2nd ed. LC 92-32969. 400p. 1992. lib. bdg. 75.00 (*0-87436-686-0*) ABC-CLIO.

— Study Guide Book. (Mathematics for Modern Living Ser.). 1980. pap. text 25.00 (*1-55740-000-8*) Magna Systems.

***Access Staff, ed.** Access Bible. 1999. 59.99 (*0-19-528255-8*) OUP.

Access Staff, ed. Bible: Access Ed. 1792p. 1999. 39.99 (*0-19-528218-3*); 42.99 (*0-19-528219-1*); pap. 27.99 (*0-19-528216-7*) OUP.

— Bible: Access Ed., A Companion for Life's Spiritual Journey. 2176p. 1999. pap. 29.99 (*0-19-528217-5*) OUP.

Access Staff, ed. see Wurman, Richard Saul.

Access U. S. A., Inc. Staff, ed. The Complete Guide to Immigration & Successful Living in the United States. (Illus.). 450p. 1994. pap. 59.95 (*0-9639667-2-3*) Access USA.

Accessible Space Team Staff. Accessible Design Review Guide: ADA Compliance for Architectural Plans & Specifications. (Illus.). 365p. 1996. 99.00 (*0-07-000189-8*) McGraw.

— Accessible Desk. 2000. write for info. (*0-07-135557-X*) McGraw.

Accetta, F. S., jt. ed. see Krauss, Lawrence M.

Accetta, Joseph S. & Shumaker, David L., eds. The Infrared & Electro-Optical Systems Handbook. LC 92-38055. 1993. 295.00 (*0-8194-1072-1*, PM10) SPIE.

***Accetta, Nicholas.** Duke Martin. LC 99-91260. 1999. 25.00 (*0-7388-0706-0*); pap. 18.00 (*0-7388-0707-9*) Xlibris Corp.

Accettura, P. Mark. The Michigan Estate Planning Guide: The Twenty Most Commonly Asked Estate Planning Questions. LC 99-90087. 200p. 1999. pap. 12.95 (*0-9669278-0-X*) Collinwood Pr.

ACCH Staff. Healthcare Environments for Children & Their Families. LC 97-69788. 320p. 1997. per. 39.95 (*0-7872-4336-1*) Kendall-Hunt.

Acchacoso, Theodore B. & Yamamoto, William S. AY's Neuroanatomy of C. Elegans for Computation. 304p. 1991. boxed set 131.95 (*0-8493-4234-1*, QM451) CRC Pr.

Acciardo, Marcia. Light Eating for Survival. (Illus.). 106p. (Orig.). 1978. pap. text 14.00 (*0-933278-05-5*) Twen Fir Cent.

***Accili, Domenico.** Genetic Manipulation of Receptor Expression & Function. LC 99-42182. (Receptor Biochemistry & Methodology Ser.). 275p. 2000. text 165.00 (*0-471-35057-5*) Wiley.

Accinelli, Robert. Crisis & Commitment: United States Policy Toward Taiwan, 1950-1955. LC 95-22269. 424p. (C). 1996. text 49.95 (*0-8078-2259-0*) U of NC Pr.

ACCIS Staff. Register of Development Activities of the United Nations System. 6th ed. 1105p. 45.00 (*92-1-100674-0*) UN.

Acclaim Books Staff. Hamlet, Odyssey, Huck Finn & Crime & Punishment. (Classics Illustrated Ser.). (Illus.). 1997. pap. text 179.64 (*1-57840-004-X*, Pub. by Acclaim Bks) Penguin Putnam.

— MacBeth, Oliver Twist, Connecticut Yankee in King Arthur's Court & Les Miserables. (Classics Illustrated Ser.). (Illus.). 1997. pap. text 179.64 (*1-57840-019-8*, Pub. by Acclaim Bks) Penguin Putnam.

— Midsummer's Night Dream, Great Expectations, Prince & the Pauper & Moby Dick. (Classics Illustrated Ser.). (Illus.). 1997. pap. text 179.64 (*1-57840-018-X*, Pub. by Acclaim Bks) Penguin Putnam.

— Tom Sawyer, Romeo & Juliet & Tale of Two Cities, Jane Eyre. (Classics Illustrated Ser.). 1997. pap. text 179.64 (*1-57840-000-7*, Pub. by Acclaim Bks) Penguin Putnam.

Acclaim Comics Staff. Hercules: The Making of a Hero. (Disney's Hercules Ser.). 1997. mass mkt. 5.95 (*1-57840-087-2*, Pub. by Acclaim Bks) Penguin Putnam.

— Power Rangers Turbo: Simple Simon Says & Other Stories. 1997. mass mkt. 4.50 (*1-57840-070-8*, Pub. by Acclaim Bks) Penguin Putnam.

— The Tick: Raw Justice. 1997. mass mkt. 4.50 (*1-57840-085-6*, Pub. by Acclaim Bks) Penguin Putnam.

— The Tick: Special 1. 1997. mass mkt. 4.50 (*1-57840-071-6*) Acclaim Bks.

Acclaim Comics Staff, ed. see Eliot, George, pseud.

***Acclaim Entertainment Staff.** Official Armorines Project Swarm Strategy Guide. (Illus.). 1999. pap. 12.99 (*1-57840-981-0*) Acclaim Bks.

— Official NBA Jam 2000 Play Book. (Illus.). 1999. pap. text. write for info. (*1-57840-984-5*) Acclaim Bks.

— Official Shadow Man Strategy Guide. (Illus.). 1999. pap. text 12.99 (*1-57840-987-X*) Acclaim Bks.

— Official WWF Attitude Strategy Guide. (Illus.). 1999. pap. text. write for info. (*1-57840-982-9*) Acclaim Bks.

Accola, Robert D. Topics in the Theory of Riemann Surfaces. LC 94-41550. (Lecture Notes in Mathematics Ser.: Vol. 1595). 1994. write for info. (*0-387-58721-7*) Spr-Verlag.

Accolas, Jean-Pierre, jt. ed. see Cogan, Timothy M.

Accolay, J. B. Concerto No. 1 in A Minor for the Violin. 16p. 1986. pap. 7.95 (*0-7935-5445-4*) H Leonard.

Accolti, Pietro. Perspective for Artists: Lo Inganno de Gl'occhi Prospettiva Practica, 1625. (Printed Sources of Western Art Ser.). (ITA., Illus.). 168p. 1981. reprint ed. boxed set 50.00 (*0-915346-60-5*) A Wofsy Fine Arts.

Accomazzo, Laura, jt. auth. see Moore, Robert J.

Acconci, Vito, jt. auth. see Finkelpearl, Tom.

Accone, Frank D., ed. see Scarlatti, Alessandro.

***Accordino, John J.** Captives of the Cold War Economy: The Struggle for Defense Conversion in American Communities. LC 99-88486. 224p. 2000. 65.00 (*0-275-96561-9*, Praeger Pubs) Greenwood.

Accordino, John J. The United States in the Global Economy: Challenges & Policy Choices. LC 92-11399. (Last Quarter Century: a Guide to the Issues & the Litereature Ser.: No. 2). 450p. (C). 1992. pap. text 38.00 (*0-8389-0591-9*) ALA.

***Accorsi, William.** 10 Button Book. LC 98-79765. (Illus.). 22p. (J). (ps). 1999. bds. 14.95 (*0-7611-1498-X*) Workman Pub.

Accounting & Auditing Publications Staff. AICPA Audit & Accounting Manual. 1584p. 1998. pap. 86.50 (*0-87051-230-7*, 007259) Am Inst CPA.

Accreditation Services Division Staff. 1998 Residency Directory, Vol. 2. rev. ed. 176p. 1997. pap. text 19.00 (*1-879907-74-7*, P509) Am Soc Hlth-Syst.

— 1998 Residency Directory, Vols. 1 & 2. rev. ed. 324p. 1997. pap. text 31.00 (*1-879907-73-9*, P508) Am Soc Hlth-Syst.

***Accreditation Services Division Staff.** 2000 Residency Directory, Vol. II. rev. ed. 272p. 1999. pap. text. write for info. (*1-58528-003-8*) Am Soc Hlth-Syst.

— 2000 Residency Directory, Vols. I & II. rev. ed. 506p. 1999. pap. text. write for info. (*1-58528-002-X*) Am Soc Hlth-Syst.

Accreditation Services Division Staff, contrib. by. 1999 Residency Directory, 2 vols. rev. ed. 448p. 1998. pap. text 31.00 (*1-879907-83-6*) Am Soc Hlth-Syst.

— 1999 Residency Directory, Vol. 2. rev. ed. 256p. 1998. pap. text 31.00 (*1-879907-84-4*) Am Soc Hlth-Syst.

Accredited Standards Committee C12 on Electricity. ANSI C12.1-1988, American National Standard Code for Electricity Metering. rev. ed. LC 88-46182. (Illus.). 200p. 1989. 51.50 (*1-55937-004-1*, SH12252) IEEE Standards.

An Asterisk (*) at the beginning of an entry indicates that the title is appearing for the first time.

Accredited Standards Committee on Electromagnetic. ANSI C63.4-1991, American National Standard for Methods of Measurement of Radio-Noise Emissions from Low-Voltage Electrical & Electronic Equipment in the Range of 9 kHz to 40 GHz. (Illus.). 64p. (Orig.). 1991. pap. 49.00 (*1-55937-086-6*, SH13896) IEEE Standards.

Accrocco, Joseph O. & Mayo, Jon. WHMIS Pocket Dictionary. 70p. 1991. 41.80 (*0-931690-28-5*) Genium Pub.

Accrocco, Joseph O. & Roy, Robert A. Right-to-Know Pocket Guide for School & University Employees. 88p. 1990. 41.80 (*0-931690-33-1*) Genium Pub.

Accrocco, Joseph O. & Wurth, Marilyn J. Diccionario de Bolsillo de las MSDS. 2nd ed. LC 87-26674.Tr. of MSDS Pocket Dictionary. (SPA.). 88p. 1994. reprint ed. pap. text. write for info. (*0-931690-27-7*) Genium Pub.

ACCT Federal Relations & Communications Staffs. Effective Advocacy: A Guide for Community College Trustees. 44p. 1994. pap., per. 15.00 (*1-886237-00-X*) Assn Commun Coll.

ACCU-Weather, Inc. Staff. ACCU-Data User's Guide 4.1. 304p. 1995. ring bd. 11.00 (*0-7872-1078-1*) Kendall-Hunt.

— Nexrad User's Guide 1.1. 64p. 1995. pap. text, ring bd. 5.00 (*0-7872-1098-6*) Kendall-Hunt.

Accu-Weather, Inc. Staff. On-Line with Accu-Weather: Instructional Modules in Meteorology. 80p. 1996. spiral bd. 9.75 (*0-8403-7132-2*) Kendall-Hunt.

Accurso, Frank. Machine Trades Projects & Procedures: Standard & Metric. LC 77-8691. 1978. pap. text 11.50 (*0-672-97101-1*, Bobbs) Macmillan.

***ACDM '00 Staff & Parmee, I. C.** Evolutionary Design & Manufacture: Selected Papers from ACDM '00. LC 00-37373. 2000. write for info. (*1-85233-300-6*) Spr-Verlag.

Ace. CIM Workbooks Promotional Practice. 208p. 1997. pap., wbk. ed. 39.95 (*0-7506-3580-0*) Buttrwrth-Heinemann.

***Ace.** Promotional Practice 1998-99. 208p. 2000. pap. text 34.95 (*0-7506-4031-6*) Buttrwrth-Heinemann.

Aced, Dan, ed. see Camara, Mary.

Acedo, Carmen & Illarnas, Felix. The Genus Bromus L. (Poaceae) in the Iberian Peninsula. (Phanerogamarum Monographiae Ser.: Tomus XXII). (Illus.). viii, 294p. 1998. 106.00 (*3-443-78004-0*, Pub. by Gebruder Borntraeger) Balogh.

***ACEEE Staff.** The Consumer's Guide to Home Energy Savings. 7th ed. Wilson, Alex, ed. (Illus.). 230p. 2000. pap. 8.95 (*0-918249-38-4*, Pub. by Am Coun Energy) Chelsea Green Pub.

— Green Guide to Cars & Trucks: Model Year 2000. DeCicco, John, ed. (Illus.). 128p. 2000. pap. 8.95 (*0-918249-39-2*, Pub. by Am Coun Energy) Chelsea Green Pub.

***Acello.** NCLEX-RN CMAT Review Cards. 3rd ed. (Illus.). 1999. boxed set 33.95 (*1-56930-092-5*) Skidmore Roth Pub.

Acello. Nursing Assisting: Essentials for Long Term Care. LC 98-17776. 384p. (C). 1998. pap. 30.95 (*0-8273-8450-5*) Delmar.

— Nursing Assisting: Essentials for Long-Term Care - IML. 224p. 1998. teacher ed. 13.95 (*0-8273-8451-3*) Delmar.

— Patient Care: Basic Skills for the Health Care Provider. 160p. 1998. pap. text, teacher ed. 20.95 (*0-7668-0182-9*) Delmar.

Acello, Barbara. Geriatric Survival Handbook. LC 98-117874. (Nurse's Survival Guide Ser.). 380p. (Orig.). (C). 1997. pap. 39.95 (*1-56930-061-5*) Skidmore Roth Pub.

— Infection Control Update, 1996. LC 96-32156. 1997. write for info. (*0-8273-8381-9*) Delmar.

— Nurse's Survival Handbook. 3rd ed. Sullivan, Molly, ed. 350p. (Orig.). (C). 1997. per. 39.95 (*1-56930-040-2*) Skidmore Roth Pub.

— Patient Care: Basic Skills for the Health Care Provider. LC 97-26953. 400p. (C). 1997. mass mkt. 30.95 (*0-8273-8423-8*) Delmar.

— Restorative Care for Certified Nursing Assistants. LC 99-17380. 304p. 1999. 25.95 (*0-8273-8141-7*) Delmar.

Acello, Barbara, jt. auth. see Kast, Barbara.

***Acena, Cristina M.** Una Aventura Con el Pollito Tito. 2000. 0.00 (*84-348-4975-5*) SM Ediciones.

Acena, Reis. Monetary Standards in Peripherals. LC 99-29989. 2000. text 75.00 (*0-312-22677-2*) St Martin.

ACER Staff. Card Games - Friendships Game. 1996. pap. 59.95 (*0-86431-192-3*, Pub. by Aust Council Educ Res) St Mut.

— Card Games - Qualities Game. 1996. pap. 59.95 (*0-86431-194-X*, Pub. by Aust Council Educ Res) St Mut.

— Cards Games - Feelings Game. 1996. pap. 59.95 (*0-86431-193-1*, Pub. by Aust Council Educ Res) St Mut.

Acerbo-Avalone, Nancy & Kremer, Katherine. Medical Malpractice Claims Investigation: A Step-by-Step Approach. LC 96-28261. 288p. 1997. pap. 59.00 (*0-8342-0860-1*, 20860) Aspen Pub.

Acerenza, Franca. Eyewear: Gli Occhiali. LC 96-50007. (Bella Cosa Ser.). 1997. pap. 12.95 (*0-8118-1870-5*) Chronicle Bks.

Acero, Alejandro. Acoustical & Environmental Robustness in Automatic Speech Recognition. LC 92-31211. (International Series in Engineering & Computer Science, VLSI, Computer Architecture, & Digital Screen Processing). (C). 1992. text 104.00 (*0-7923-9284-1*) Kluwer Academic.

***Acero, Raul.** Making Ceramic Sculptural: Techniques, Projects, Inspirations. Morgenthal, Deborah, ed. (Illus.). 160p. 2000. write for info. (*1-57990-175-1*, Pub. by Lark Books) Sterling.

Acers, Thomas E. Congenital Abnormalities of the Optic Nerve & Related Forebrain. LC 82-24962. (Illus.). 85p. reprint ed. pap. 30.00 (*0-8357-7638-7*, 205696100096) Bks Demand.

Acerson, Karen L. PC Magazine Guide to WordPerfect for Windows. (Guide to...Ser.). (Illus.). 1021p. (Orig.). 1991. pap. 27.95 (*1-56276-013-0*, Ziff-Davis Pr) Que.

***Acert, James.** Acret's California Construction Laws Annotated: 2000 Edition. annot. ed. 2000. pap. text 75.00 (*1-55701-327-6*) BNI Pubns.

Acervo. Diccionario de la Lengua Castellana, Vol. 6. (SPA.). 190p. 1982. 14.95 (*0-8288-2022-8*, S40787) Fr & Eur.

Aceto, Chris. Championship Bodybuilding: Chris Aceto's Instruction Book for Bodybuilding. 5th ed. (Illus.). 185p. 1999. reprint ed. 24.95 (*0-9669168-0-8*) Club Creavalle.

— Understanding Body Building Nutrition & Training. 204p. 1998. pap. 19.95 (*0-9669168-3-2*) Club Creavalle.

Aceto, Chris & Creavalle, Laura. The Health Handbook. 3rd ed. (Illus.). 141p. 1999. reprint ed. pap. text 19.95 (*0-9669168-5-9*) Club Creavalle.

Aceto, Luca. Action Refinement in Process Algebras. (Distinguished Dissertations in Computer Science Ser.: No. 3). 283p. (C). 1992. text 69.95 (*0-521-43111-5*) Cambridge U Pr.

Acevedo. Frontrunner High Flyer Workbook Intermediate. 1994. pap. text. write for info. (*0-582-07943-8*, Pub. by Addison-Wesley) Longman.

— Frontrunner 1. 1993. pap. text, student ed. write for info. (*0-582-07988-8*, Pub. by Addison-Wesley); pap. text, wbk. ed. write for info. (*0-582-08000-2*, Pub. by Addison-Wesley) Longman.

— Frontrunner 2. 1993. pap. text, student ed. write for info. (*0-582-07997-7*, Pub. by Addison-Wesley) Longman.

— Frontrunner 2. 1993. pap. text, wbk. ed. write for info. (*0-582-07941-1*, Drumbeat) Longman.

— Frontrunner 3. 1994. pap. text, student ed. write for info. (*0-582-07998-5*, Pub. by Addison-Wesley); pap. text, wbk. ed. write for info. (*0-582-07942-X*, Pub. by Addison-Wesley) Longman.

Acevedo Gonzales, Andino. Que Tiempos Aquellos! LC 84-25639. 1989. pap. 8.50 (*0-8477-0069-0*) U of PR Pr.

Acevedo, Jorge, jt. auth. see Goddard, Hule.

***Acevedo, Judith & Tokarski, Henry J.** Tokarski Meets Acevedo. Richburg, Shirley, ed. 2001. pap. 9.95 (*0-9658432-5-4*) Peoples MD.

Acevedo, Lucy, tr. see Zahner, Dee.

Acevedo, Mary E., tr. see Munoz, Silverio.

Acevedo, Pilar, tr. see Bishop, Gavin.

Acevedo, Pilar, tr. see Weninger, Brigitte.

Acevedo, Ramon L. Augusto D'Halmar: Novelista (Estudio De Pasion y Muerte Del Cura Deusto) LC 76-8011. (Coleccion Mente y Palabra). (SPA.). 204p. (Orig.). 1976. 5.00 (*0-8477-0530-7*); pap. 4.00 (*0-8477-0531-5*) U of PR Pr.

— No Mires Ahora . . . y Otros Cuentos. (Aqui y Ahora Ser.). 1997. pap. 6.95 (*0-8477-0317-7*) U of PR Pr.

— La Novela Centroamericana: Desde el Popol-vuh Hasta los Umbrales de la Novela Actual. LC 81-10316. (Coleccion Mente y Palabra). 503p. 1981. 15.00 (*0-8477-0584-6*); pap. 12.00 (*0-8477-0585-4*) U of PR Pr.

Acevedo, Rebeca, jt. auth. see Schaffer, Susan C.

Acevedo-Rodriguez, P. Flora of St. John, U. S. Virgin Islands. LC 96-34052. (Memoirs Ser.: Vol. 78). (Illus.). 1996. 49.95 (*0-89327-402-X*, MEM 78) NY Botanical.

Acevedo-Rodriguez, Pedro. Systematics of Serjania (Sapindaceae), Pt. I. LC 92-18033. (Memoirs Ser.: Vol. 67). 96p. 1993. pap. 15.50 (*0-89327-377-5*) NY Botanical.

Aceves, Joseph. Social Change in a Spanish Village. (Illus.). 144p. 1971. pap. 11.95 (*0-87073-755-4*) Schenkman Bks Inc.

***Aceves, Salvador M., ed.** Advanced Energy Systems Division: Proceedings ASME International Mechanical Engineering Congress & Exposition, Nashville, Tennesse, 1999. (AES Ser.: Vol. 39). 690p. 1999. 170.00 (*0-7918-1650-8*) ASME Pr.

Acey, Mark. Garfield's Christmas Tales. 1995. 10.15 (*0-606-07557-7*, Pub. by Turtleback) Demco.

ACF (Dreaver) Staff. Somatic Technique: A Simplified Method of Releasing Chronically Tight Muscles & Enhancing. LC 96-78756. 220p. 1997. pap. text, per. 49.95 (*0-7872-3015-4*) Kendall-Hunt.

ACF Staff. Behavioral Considerations in Patient Management. LC 96-78755. 240p. 1996. boxed set 69.00 (*0-7872-2729-3*) Kendall-Hunt.

— Clinical Laboratory Evaluation for the Chiropractic Profession. LC 97-72278. 272p. 1997. per. 49.95 (*0-7872-3400-1*) Kendall-Hunt.

Ach. Sociology Laboratory Activity Portfolio. 4th ed. 126p. 1998. pap. text 13.50 (*0-536-01335-7*) Pearson Custom.

Achabal, Dale, ed. see AMA Winter Educators' Conference Staff.

Achad, Frater. The Anatomy of the Body of God: Being the Supreme Revelation of Cosmic Consciousness. 120p. 1992. reprint ed. pap. 17.95 (*1-56459-140-9*) Kessinger Pub.

— Ancient Mystical White Brotherhood. 4th rev. ed. Rogge, Constance, ed. 186p. (Orig.). 1991. pap. text 10.95 (*0-926872-02-8*) Great Seal Pr.

— The Chalice of Ecstasy: Being the Inmost Secret of Parzival & the Holy Grail. 1994. pap. 6.95 (*1-55818-284-5*, Sure Fire) Holmes Pub.

— The Chalice of Ecstasy (1923) 85p. 1998. reprint ed. pap. 5.95 (*0-7661-0347-1*) Kessinger Pub.

— Crystal Vision Through Crystal Gazing. 116p. 1998. reprint ed. pap. 9.95 (*0-7661-0210-6*) Kessinger Pub.

— Crystal Vision Through Crystal Gazing. (Illus.). 116p. 1976. reprint ed. 11.00 (*0-911662-60-X*) Yoga.

— The Egyptian Revival: or the Evercoming Son in the Light of the Tarot. 126p. 1992. reprint ed. pap. 16.95 (*1-56459-202-2*) Kessinger Pub.

— Essence of the Practical Qabalah. (Illus.). 16p. 1994. pap. 4.95 (*1-55818-289-6*, Sure Fire) Holmes Pub.

— I. N. R. I. De Mysteriis Rosae Rubae et Aurae Crucis. 1990. reprint ed. pap. 4.95 (*1-55818-154-7*, Sure Fire) Holmes Pub.

— Liber Thirty-One. Greenfield, T. Allen, ed. (Illus.). 80p. 1998. pap. 9.95 (*1-891948-00-8*) Luxor Press.

— Melchizedek Truth Principles: From the Ancient Mystical White Brotherhood. 9th ed. 210p. (Orig.). 1963. pap. text 11.95 (*0-926872-01-X*) Great Seal Pr.

— Parzival: The Chalice of Ecstasy. 82p. 1976. reprint ed. 11.00 (*0-911662-59-6*) Yoga.

— Q. B. L.: or The Bride's Reception. 150p. 1992. reprint ed. pap. 17.95 (*1-56459-139-5*) Kessinger Pub.

— Thirty One Hymns to the Star Goddess. 1987. pap. 6.95 (*0-916411-63-X*, Sure Fire) Holmes Pub.

Achampong, Francis. Workplace Sexual Harassment Law: Principles, Landmark Developments, & Framework For Effective Risk Management. LC 99-18647. 264p. 1999. 69.50 (*1-56720-304-3*, Quorum Bks) Greenwood.

Achan, Vinod, jt. auth. see Borley, Neil R.

***Achankeng, Fuankem & Nkemnji, John Fonjia, eds.** Lebialem Issues & Challenges at Century End. 101p. 1999. pap. text 10.00 (*0-9663613-6-9*) Nkemnji Global.

Achar, A. & Venkanna, V. Law of Dowry Prohibition, with Rules, State Amendments & Allied Laws. (C). 1990. 93.00 (*0-89771-148-3*) St Mut.

Achar, K. Prabhakar, jt. auth. see Nair, P. K.

Acharay, V., ed. Catalogue of the Coins in the Prince of Wales Museum of Western India Bombay (The Sultans of Gujarat. (Illus.). 186p. 1988. reprint ed. 30.00 (*0-317-99946-X*, Pub. by M Manoharial) Coronet Bks.

Achard, Claude-Francois. Nuevo Diccionario de Sinonimos y Antonimos, Spa., 2 vols. 1425p. 1983. reprint ed. 350.00 (*0-8288-1719-7*, F8013) Fr & Eur.

Achard, Ken. The Fender Guitar. 2nd ed. (Illus.). 70p. 1990. reprint ed. pap. 17.95 (*0-933224-48-6*, T012) Bold Strummer Ltd.

— The History & Development of the American Guitar. (Illus.). 200p. 1990. reprint ed. pap. 24.95 (*0-933224-18-4*, T021) Bold Strummer Ltd.

Achard, Marcel. Jean de la Lune. (FRE.). 256p. pap. 10.95 (*0-7859-1769-1*, M2937) Fr & Eur.

Acharya, A. Christ Conspiracy: The Greatest Story Ever Told. 1999. pap. text 14.95 (*0-932813-74-7*) Advent Unltd.

Acharya, Amitav. An Arms Race in Post-Cold War Southeast Asia: Prospects for Control. 70p. (Orig.). (C). 1994. pap. text 35.00 (*0-7881-1281-3*) DIANE Pub.

— Arms Race in Post-Cold War Southeast Asia: Prospects for Control. 78p. 1994. pap. text 40.00 (*1-57979-202-2*) DIANE Pub.

Acharya, Amitav & Stubbs, Richard, eds. New Challenges for ASEAN: Emerging Policy Issues. LC 96-170023. (Canada & International Relations Ser.: Vol. 10). 218p. 1996. 62.00 (*0-7748-0521-8*, HC441) U of Wash Pr.

Acharya, Amitav, jt. ed. see Syrett, B. C.

Acharya, B S. Hadron Collider Physics. 550p. 1999. 140.00 (*981-02-3938-6*) World Scientific Pub.

Acharya, Jayaraj. The Nepala-Mahatmya of the Skandapurana: Legends on the Sacred Deities of Nepal. (Illus.). xvi, 320p. 1992. 33.00 (*81-85693-27-7*, Pub. by Nirala Pubns) Nataraj Bks.

Acharya, Jayaraj, ed. Women in Development: The Sericulture Experience in India. LC 93-911684. (C). 1995. 28.00 (*81-7341-009-7*, Pub. by Abhinav) S Asia.

Acharya, K. R., et al. Glycogen Phosphorylase B: Description of the Protein Structure. 132p. (C). 1991. text 44.00 (*981-02-0540-6*); pap. text 21.00 (*981-02-0541-4*) World Scientific Pub.

***Acharya, Kala, ed.** Dialogue: Hindu-Christian Cosmology & Religion. 1999. 58.00 (*81-7039-232-2*, Pub. by Somaiya Publns) S Asia.

Acharya, Madhu R. The Statistical Profile on Nepalese Women: An Update in the Policy Context. 1994. pap. 40.00 (*0-7855-0486-9*, Pub. by Ratna Pustak Bhandar) St Mut.

Acharya, Madhu R., ed. Nepal Encyclopedia. 1994. pap. 75.00 (*0-7855-0468-0*, Pub. by Ratna Pustak Bhandar) St Mut.

Acharya, Milly & Valmiki. The Ramayana for Young Readers. LC 98-908804. 62 p. 1998. 12.50 (*81-7223-285-3*) HarpC.

Acharya, Prasana K. Dictionary of Hindu Architecture. 1981. text 58.50 (*0-685-13704-X*) Coronet Bks.

— An Encyclopedia of Hindu Architecture. 1979. 64.50 (*0-8364-2601-0*, Pub. by M Manoharial) S Asia.

— Mansara on Architecture & Sculpture: Sanskrit Text with Critical Notes. 1979. reprint ed. 64.00 (*0-8364-2609-6*, Pub. by M Manoharial) S Asia.

Acharya, Prasanna K. Indian Architecture According to Manasara-Silpasastra. 1995. pap. 12.00 (*81-86142-70-3*, Pub. by Low Price) S Asia.

Acharya, R. S., et al, eds. Biomedical Image Processing & Three-Dimensional Microscopy. 1992. 20.00 (*0-8194-0814-X*, 1660) SPIE.

Acharya, Rohini. The Emergence & Growth of Biotechnology: Experiences in Industrialised & Developing Countries. LC 98-42884. (New Horizons in the Economics of Innovation Ser.). 160p. 1999. 65.00 (*1-85898-523-4*) E Elgar.

***Acharya, S., et al.** Economic Liberalisation in Nepal: Sequence & Process. 1998. pap. 23.00 (*0-7855-7539-1*) St Mut.

Acharya, Sabita. Pilgrimage in Indian Civilisation. LC 97-906047. xv, 270p. 1997. 30.00 (*81-86562-35-4*, Pub. by Manak Pubns Pvt Ltd) Nataraj Bks.

***Acharya, Sanjay.** Bhutan: Kingdom in the Himalaya. LC 99-932587. (Illus.). 96p. 1999. 19.95 (*81-7436-061-1*, Pub. by Reli Books) Nataraj Bks.

Acharya, Shuklendra. Law of Income Tax, 3 vols. (C). 1990. 195.00 (*0-89771-284-6*) St Mut.

Acharya, SriKumar. Changing Pattern of Education in Early Nineteenth-Century Bengal. (C). 1992. 34.00 (*81-85094-49-7*, Pub. by Punthi Pus) S Asia.

Achasova, S., et al. Parallel Substitution Algorithm. 232p. 1994. text 48.00 (*981-02-1777-3*) World Scientific Pub.

Achath, Sati. Fun with Hand Shadows. LC 96-19459. (Illus.). 160p. 1996. pap. 8.95 (*0-8092-3167-0*, 316700, Contemporary Bks) NTC Contemp Pub Co.

Achauer & Eriksson. The Art & Practice of Plastic Surgery Set. (Illus.). 3520p. 2000. text 595.00 (*0-8151-0984-9*, 29441) Mosby Inc.

Achauer, et al. The Art & Practice of Plastic Surgery, Vol.4. (C). (gr. 13). 2000. 195.00 (*0-8151-0999-7*, 29573) Mosby Inc.

Achaya, K. T. The Food Industries of British India. (Illus.). 324p. 1995. text 29.95 (*0-19-563418-7*) OUP.

— Ghani: The Traditional Oilmill of India. LC 92-17072. (Illus.). 128p. 1993. 30.00 (*0-917526-05-8*) Olearius Edns.

— A Historical Dictionary of Indian Food. LC 98-903528. 364p. 1998. 29.95 (*0-19-564254-6*) OUP.

Achbar, Mark, ed. Manufacturing Consent - Noam Chomsky & the Media: A Primer in Intellectual Self-Defence. LC 94-154599. (Illus.). 265p. 1998. 52.99 (*1-55164-003-1*, Pub. by Black Rose); pap. 23.99 (*1-55164-002-3*, Pub. by Black Rose) Consort Bk Sales.

Achberger, Karen R. Understanding Ingeborg Bachmann: Understanding Modern European & Latin American Literature. LC 94-18679. 230p. 1994. text 29.95 (*0-87249-994-4*) U of SC Pr.

***Achcar, Gilbert.** The Legacy of Ernest Mandel. 1999. 45.00 (*1-85984-703-X*, Pub. by Verso) Norton.

Ache, B. W., et al, eds. Perception of Complex Tastes & Smells. 450p. 1989. text 104.00 (*0-12-042990-X*) Acad Pr.

Ache, B. W., jt. ed. see Fidone, S. J.

Ache, Hans J., ed. Positronium & Muonium Chemistry: Based on a Symposium Sponsored by the Division of Physical Chemistry of the Chemical Institute of Canada at the Second Joint CIC/ACS Conference, Montreal, Canada, May 31-June 2, 1977. LC 79-11709. (Advances in Chemistry Ser.: No. 175). (Illus.). 384p. 1979. reprint ed. pap. 119.10 (*0-608-06753-9*, 206695000009) Bks Demand.

Acheampong, K., et al, eds. Fertilizer Use at the Village Level: Summary Proceedings of Workshop. LC 93-33830. (Special Publications: No. SP-20). 91p. 1993. pap. text 10.00 (*0-88090-105-5*) Intl Fertilizer.

Achebe, Chinua. Another Africa. LC 97-15412. (Illus.). 120p. 1998. 35.00 (*0-385-49038-0*) Doubleday.

— Anthills of the Savannah. 224p. 1997. pap. 10.95 (*0-385-26045-8*, Anchor NY) Doubleday.

— Arrow of God. LC 75-79409. (Anchor Literary Library). 240p. 1989. pap. 11.95 (*0-385-01480-5*, Anchor NY) Doubleday.

Achebe, Chinua. Beware Soul Brother. (African Writers Ser.). 68p. (C). 1972. pap. 8.95 (*0-435-90120-6*, 90120) Heinemann.

Achebe, Chinua. Chike & the River. 64p. 1966. pap. text 5.95 (*0-521-04003-5*) Cambridge U Pr.

— Conversations with Chinua Achebe. Lindfors, Bernth, ed. LC 97-6953. (Literary Conversations Ser.). xviii, 199p. 1997. pap. 17.00 (*0-87805-999-7*); text 45.00 (*0-87805-929-6*) U Pr of Miss.

— Girls at War: And Other Stories. 128p. 1991. pap. 12.00 (*0-385-41896-5*, Anchor NY) Doubleday.

***Achebe, Chinua.** Home & Exile. (The W.E.B. Du Bois Institute Ser.). 128p. 2000. 20.00 (*0-19-513506-7*) OUP.

Achebe, Chinua. Hopes & Impediments: Selected Essays. 208p. 1990. pap. 11.00 (*0-385-41479-X*, Anchor NY) Doubleday.

— A Man of the People. LC 66-22929. 160p. 1981. pap. 10.95 (*0-385-08616-4*, Anchor NY) Doubleday.

— No Longer at Ease. (C). 1961. 12.95 (*0-8392-1077-9*); pap. 7.95 (*0-8392-5008-8*) Astor-Honor.

— No Longer at Ease. LC 94-13428. 208p. 1994. pap. 7.95 (*0-385-47455-5*, Anchor NY) Doubleday.

— Things Fall Apart. LC 59-7114. (C). 1959. 15.95 (*0-8392-1113-9*); pap. 10.95 (*0-8392-5006-1*) Astor-Honor.

— Things Fall Apart. LC 94-13429. 209p. 1994. pap. 8.95 (*0-385-47454-7*, Anchor NY) Doubleday.

— Things Fall Apart. 208p. 1995. 15.00 (*0-679-44623-0*) Knopf.

— Things Fall Apart. 1994. 13.05 (*0-606-11979-5*, Pub. by Turtleback) Demco.

— Things Fall Apart. expanded ed. (African Writers Ser.). (Illus.). 208p. 1996. pap. 13.95 (*0-435-90525-2*) Heinemann.

— The Trouble with Nigeria. 68p. (C). 1984. pap. text 8.50 (*0-435-90698-4*, 90698) Heinemann.

Achebe, Chinua & Innes, C. L., eds. African Short Stories. (African Writers Ser.). 159p. (Orig.). (C). 1988. pap. 10.95 (*0-435-90536-8*, 90536) Heinemann.

Achebe, Chinua & Innes, Lynn, eds. The Heinemann Book of Contemporary African Short Stories. 256p. (C). 1992. pap. 9.95 (*0-435-90566-X*, 90566) Heinemann.

Achebe, Chinua & Iroaganachi, John. How the Leopard Got His Claws: With the Lament of the Deer. LC 72-93382. (Illus.). 32p. (J). (gr. 6 up). 1973. 11.95 (*0-89388-056-6*) Okpaku Communications.

Acheley, Thomas. A Most Lamentable & Tragicall Historie, Conteyning the Tyrannie Which Violenta Executed Upon Her Lover Didaco. LC 77-6840. (English Experience Ser.: No. 836). 1977. reprint ed. lib. bdg. 20.00 (*90-221-0836-8*) Walter J Johnson.

A

Achelis, Elisabeth. The Calendar for Everybody. LC 89-63208. xii, 141p. 1990. reprint ed. lib. bdg. 40.00 (1-55888-849-7) Omnigraphics Inc.

***Achelis, Steven B.** Technical Analysis from A to Z. 2nd ed. (Illus.). 430p. 2000. 39.95 (0-07-136348-3) McGraw.

Achelis, Steven B. Technical Analysis from A to Z: Covers Every Trading Tool from the Absolute Breadth Index to the Zig Zag. LC 95-223126. 350p. 1994. text 29.95 (1-55738-816-4, Irwn Prfssnl) McGraw-Hill Prof.

Achelis, Steven B., ed. see Raff, Gilbert L.

Achem, Sami R., et al, eds. Developments & Controversies in Gastrointestinal Motility: Journal. (Journal: Vol. 15, Suppl. 1, 1997). (Illus.). iv, 138p. 1997. pap. 41.75 (3-8055-6521-6) S Karger.

Achen, Christopher H. Interpreting & Using Regression. LC 82-42675. (Quantitative Applications in the Social Sciences Ser.: Vol. 29). 88p. 1982. pap. 10.95 (0-8039-1915-8) Sage.

Achen, Christopher H. & Phillips, Shively W. Cross-Level Inference. LC 94-22590. 258p. 1995. pap. text 18.95 (0-226-00220-9) U Ch Pr.

— Cross-Level Inference. LC 94-22590. 258p. 1995. lib. bdg. 55.00 (0-226-00219-5) U Ch Pr.

Achenbach, George. Goldmining in Foreclosure Properties. 3rd ed. 228p. (Orig.). 1994. 87.95 (0-471-03449-5); pap. 19.95 (0-471-03451-7) Wiley.

— Goldmining in Foreclosure Properties. 4th ed. LC 98-44991. (Illus.). 244p. (Orig.). 1999. pap. 19.95 (0-471-32934-7) Wiley.

Achenbach, J. D. Wave Propagation in Elastic Solids. (North-Holland Series in Applied Mathematics & Mechanics: Vol. 16). 426p. 1984. reprint ed. pap. 96.50 (0-7204-0325-1) Elsevier.

Achenbach, J. D., ed. Evaluation of Materials & Structures by Quantitative Ultrasonics. (CISM International Centre for Mechanical Sciences Ser.: Vol. 330). (Illus.). vi, 398p. 1993. 107.95 (0-387-82441-3) Spr-Verlag.

Achenbach, J. D. & Rajapakse, Y., eds. Solid Mechanics Research for Quantitative Non-Destructive Evaluation. (C). 1987. text 272.50 (90-247-3428-2) Kluwer Academic.

Achenbach, Joel. Captured by Aliens: The Search for Life & Truth in a Very Large Universe. LC 99-37592. 416p. 1999. 24.50 (0-684-84856-2) S&S Trade.

— Why Things Are: Answers to Every Essential Question in Life. 336p. 1991. pap. 10.00 (0-345-36224-1) Ballantine Pub Grp.

— Why Things Are Vol. 2, Vol. 2. 368p. (Orig.). 1993. pap. 10.00 (0-345-37798-2) Ballantine Pub Grp.

— Why Things Are & Why Things Aren't: The Answers to Life's Greatest Mysteries. (Illus.). 416p. 1996. pap. 11.00 (0-345-39288-4) Ballantine Pub Grp.

Achenbach, Thomas M. Assessment & Taxonomy of Child & Adolescent Psychopathology. LC 85-10798. (Developmental Clinical Psychology & Psychiatry Ser.: No. 3). 200p. (Orig.). 1985. reprint ed. pap. 62.00 (0-608-01091-X, 205940000001) Bks Demand.

— Developmental Psychopathology. 2nd ed. LC 82-2838. 770p. (C). 1982. text 89.95 (0-471-05536-0) Wiley.

— Empirically Based Taxonomy: How to Use Syndromes & Profiles Derived from the CBCL-4-18, TRF, & YSR. (Illus.). 212p. (Orig.). (C). 1993. pap. 25.00 (0-938565-25-7) U of VT Psych.

— Guide for the Caregiver - Teacher Report Form for Ages 2-5. (Illus.). 100p. (Orig.). 1997. pap. 10.00 (0-938565-47-8) U of VT Psych.

— Integrative Guide for the 1991 CBCL 4-18, YSR, & TRF Profiles. LC 90-72106. (Illus.). 211p. (Orig.). 1991. pap. 25.00 (0-938565-07-9) U of VT Psych.

— Manual for the Child Behavior Checklist - 2-3 & 1992 Profile. LC 92-60136. 210p. (Orig.). 1992. pap. 25.00 (0-938565-20-6) U of VT Psych.

— Manual for the Child Behavior Checklist 4-18 & 1991 Profile. LC 90-72107. (Illus.). 288p. (Orig.). 1991. pap. 25.00 (0-938565-08-7) U of VT Psych.

— Manual for the Teacher's Report Form & 1991 Profile. LC 90-72108. (Illus.). viii, 214p. (Orig.). 1991. pap. 25.00 (0-938565-10-9) U of VT Psych.

— Manual for the Young Adult Self-Report & Young Adult Behavior Checklist. LC 96-61686. (Illus.). 212p. (Orig.). 1997. pap. 25.00 (0-938565-45-1) U of VT Psych.

— Manual for the Youth Self-Report & 1991 Profile. LC 90-72109. (Illus.). 221p. (Orig.). 1991. pap. 25.00 (0-938565-09-5) U of VT Psych.

Achenbach, Thomas M. & McConaughy, Stephanie H. Empirically Based Assessment of Child & Adolescent Psychopathology: Practical Applications. (Developmental Clinical Psychology & Psychiatry Ser.: Vol. 13). 160p. (C). 1987. text 42.00 (0-8039-2924-2); pap. text 18.95 (0-8039-2925-0) Sage.

— Empirically Based Assessment of Child & Adolescent Psychopathology: Practical Applications. LC 96-10137. (Developmental Clinical Psychology & Psychiatry Ser.). 1996. 42.00 (0-8039-7247-4) Sage.

— Empirically Based Assessment of Child & Adolescent Psychopathology: Practical Applications. 2nd ed. LC 96-10137. (Developmental Clinical Psychology & Psychiatry Ser.: Vol. 13). 256p. 1996. pap. 18.95 (0-8039-7248-2) Sage.

Achenbach, Thomas M., et al. National Survey of Problems & Competencies among Four- to Sixteen-Year Olds. (Child Development Monographs: No. 225, Vol. 56, No. 3). (Illus.). 136p. 1992. pap. text 15.00 (0-226-00221-7) U Ch Pr.

Achenbach, Thomas M., jt. auth. see McConaughy, Stephanie H.

Achenbach, Thomas M., jt. auth. see Yignoe, Denise.

Achenbaum, W. Andrew. Crossing Frontiers: Gerontology Emerges As a Science. 294p. (C). 1995. text 69.95 (0-521-48194-5); pap. text 19.95 (0-521-55880-8) Cambridge U Pr.

— Old Age in the New Land: The American Experience since 1790. LC 77-28666. (Illus.). 251p. reprint ed. pap. 77.90 (0-8357-4333-0, 203713300007) Bks Demand.

— Social Security: Visions & Revisions. LC 86-4145. (Twentieth Century Fund Study Ser.). 294p. 1986. text 59.95 (0-521-32866-7) Cambridge U Pr.

— Social Security: Visions & Revisions. LC 86-4145. (Twentieth Century Fund Study Ser.). 320p. 1988. pap. text 20.95 (0-521-35766-7) Cambridge U Pr.

Achenbaum, W. Andrew & Albert, Daniel M. Profiles in Gerontology: A Biographical Dictionary. LC 95-8002. 416p. 1995. lib. bdg. 95.00 (0-313-29274-4, Greenwood Pr) Greenwood.

Achenbaum, W. Andrew, et al. Key Words in Sociocultural Gerontology. LC 96-5015. 192p. (Orig.). 1996. pap. 29.95 (0-8261-8590-8) Springer Pub.

— Orthodontics in an Aging Society. Carlson, David S., ed. LC 88-71195. (Craniofacial Growth Ser.: Vol. 22). (Illus.). 199p. 1989. 49.00 (0-929921-18-6) UM CHGD.

Achenbaum, W. Andrew, jt. ed. see Bengtson, Vern L.

Achenbaum, W. Andrew, jt. ed. see Schaie, K. Warner.

Achenbaum, W. Andrew, jt. ed. see Shenk, Dena.

Achenbaum, W. Andrew, jt. ed. see Trattner, Walter I.

***Acherkan, N.** Machine Tool Design, Vol. 1. 604p. 2000. pap. 56.25 (0-89875-046-6) U Pr Pacific.

— Machine Tool Design, Vol. 4. 496p. 2000. pap. 56.25 (0-89875-049-0) U Pr Pacific.

Acheson. Common Problems in Neuroophthalmology. 1996. text 115.00 (0-7020-1879-1) Bailliere Tindall.

— John Fowles. LC 97-46156. 160p. 1998. text 39.95 (0-312-21387-5) St Martin.

— Sam Becketts Artistic Theory. LC 96-27677. 264p. 1997. text 49.95 (0-312-16547-1) St Martin.

Acheson, A. W. Acheson. History of the Acheson Family on the Paternal Side. (Illus.). 60p. 1997. reprint ed. pap. 12.00 (0-8328-7199-0); reprint ed. lib. bdg. 22.00 (0-8328-7198-2) Higginson Bk Co.

Acheson, Alan. A History of the Church of Ireland. LC 97-224288. 304p. 1997. 69.95 (1-85607-210-X, Pub. by Columba Press) Intl Scholars.

Acheson, Alice B., ed. see Boscaljon, Karen.

Acheson, Alice B., ed. see Shanley, Mary K.

Acheson, Alice B., ed. see Sucher, Billie.

Acheson, Alison. The Half-Pipe Kidd. 164p. (YA). (gr. 7-12). 1997. pap. 6.95 (1-55050-120-8, Pub. by Coteau) Genl Dist Srvs.

Acheson, Arthur. Mistress Davenant. (Works of Arthur Acheson). v, 332p. 1985. reprint ed. 49.00 (0-7812-0818-1) Rprt Serv.

— Shakespeare & the Rival Poet. LC 79-113535. 1903. 29.50 (0-404-00277-3) AMS Pr.

— Shakespeare, Chapman & Sir Thomas More. LC 72-113536. reprint ed. 42.75 (0-404-00278-1) AMS Pr.

— Shakespeare's Lost Years in London. LC 79-152552. (Studies in Shakespeare: No. 24). 1971. reprint ed. lib. bdg. 75.00 (0-8383-1235-7) M S G Haskell Hse.

— Shakespeare's Sonnet Story, 1592-1598. LC 72-164658. (Studies in Shakespeare: No. 24). 1971. reprint ed. lib. bdg. 75.00 (0-8383-1322-1) M S G Haskell Hse.

Acheson, D. J. Elementary Fluid Dynamics. (Oxford Applied Mathematics & Computing Science Ser.). (Illus.). 406p. 1990. pap. text 39.95 (0-19-859679-0) OUP.

Acheson, David. From Calculus to Chaos: An Introduction to Dynamics. LC 98-121000. (Illus.). 278p. 1998. pap. text 27.95 (0-19-850077-7) OUP.

Acheson, David & Levinson, Robin. Safe Eating: Protecting Yourself Against E. Coli, Salmonella & Other Deadly Food Borne Pathogens. 352p. 1998. mass mkt. 6.50 (0-440-22659-7) Dell.

Acheson, Dean. A Democrat Looks at His Party. LC 76-48254. 199p. 1977. reprint ed. lib. bdg. 55.00 (0-8371-9332-X, ACDL, Greenwood Pr) Greenwood.

— The Pattern of Responsibility. Bundy, McGeorge, ed. LC 75-128070. xxi, 309p. 1972. reprint ed. 45.00 (0-678-03560-1) Kelley.

— Present at the Creation: My Years in the State Department. (Illus.). 848p. 1987. 29.95 (0-393-07448-X); pap. 19.95 (0-393-30412-4) Norton.

Acheson, Dean, et al. Official Conversations & Meetings of Dean Acheson, 1949-1953. LC 86-892618. (Presidential Documents Ser.). 5 p. 1980. write for info. (0-89093-354-5) U Pubns Amer.

Acheson, Donald. The Independent Inquiry into Inequalities in Health Report. xii, 164p. 1998. 45.00 (0-11-322173-8, HM21738, Pub. by Statnry Office) Balogh.

Acheson, Edna L. The Construction of Junior Church School Curricula. LC 73-176503. reprint ed. 37.50 (0-404-55331-1) AMS Pr.

Acheson, Edward G. A Pathfinder: Inventor, Scientist, Industrialist. (American Biography Ser.). 63p. 1991. reprint ed. lib. bdg. 59.00 (0-7812-8001-X) Rprt Serv.

Acheson, James M. Lobster Gangs of Maine. LC 87-40506. (Library of New England). (Illus.). 197p. 1988. pap. 14.95 (0-87451-451-7) U Pr of New Eng.

Acheson, James M., ed. Anthropology & Institutional Economics. LC 94-21983. (Monographs in Economic Anthropology: No. 12). (Illus.). 438p. (C). 1994. pap. text 39.00 (0-8191-9596-0); lib. bdg. 74.50 (0-8191-9595-2) U Pr of Amer.

Acheson, James M. & Arthur, Kateryna. Beckett's Later Fiction & Drama: Texts for Company LC 90-150311. xvii, 206 p. 1987. write for info. (0-333-39951-X) Macmillan.

Acheson, James M. & Huk, Romana, eds. Contemporary British Poetry: Essays in Theory & Criticism. LC 96-5029. 418p. (C). 1996. text 74.50 (0-7914-2767-6); pap. text 24.95 (0-7914-2768-4) State U NY Pr.

***Acheson, James M. & Riordan-Eva, Paul, eds.** Fundamentals of Clinical Opthalmology: Neuro-Opthalmology. (Illus.). 221p. 1999. text 71.95 (0-7279-1369-7) BMJ Pub.

Acheson, James M., jt. ed. see McCay, Bonnie J.

Acheson, Katherine O. The Diary of Anne Clifford, 1616-1619: A Critical Edition. LC 94-43066. (Renaissance Imagination Ser.). 240p. 1995. text 20.00 (0-8153-1932-0) Garland.

Acheson, Keith & Maule, Christopher. Much Ado about Culture: North American Trade Disputes. LC 99-48659. (Studies in International Economics). (Illus.). 388p. 1999. text 54.50 (0-472-11048-9, 11048) U of Mich Pr.

Acheson, Keith A. Techniques in the Clinical Supervision of Teachers: Preservice & Inservice Applications. 4th ed. 288p. 1997. pap., teacher ed. 53.95 (0-471-36436-3) Wiley.

Acheson, Nicholas & Williamson, Arthur, eds. Voluntary Action & Social Policy in Northern Ireland. 224p. 1995. 66.95 (1-85628-669-X, Pub. by Avebry) Ashgate Pub Co.

Acheson, Pamela. The Best of St. Thomas & St. John, U. S. Virgin Islands. 2nd ed. LC 98-48750. (Illus.). 144p. 1999. pap. 13.95 (0-9639905-1-9) Two Thous-Three Assocs.

— The Best of the British Virgin Islands. 2nd ed. LC 97-44960. (Illus.). 128p. (Orig.). 1998. pap. 13.95 (0-9639905-4-3) Two Thous-Three Assocs.

— The Best Romantic Escapes in Florida: A Lover's Guide to Exceptionally Romantic Inns, Resorts, Restaurants, Activities, & Experiences. LC 96-62029. 128p. 1997. pap. 13.95 (0-9639905-9-4) Two Thous-Three Assocs.

Acheson, Pamela & Myers, Richard B. More of the Best Romantic Escapes in Florida: A Lover's Guide to Exceptionally Romantic Inns, Resorts, Restaurants, Activities, & Experiences. LC 98-48766. 128p. 1999. pap. 13.95 (0-9639905-0-0) Two Thous-Three Assocs.

Acheson, Roy M., jt. auth. see Fee, Elizabeth.

Acheson, Roy M., jt. auth. see Matsumoto, Kiyoshi.

Acheson, Sam H. Joe Bailey, the Last Democrat. LC 79-124222. (Select Bibliographies Reprint Ser.). 1977. 24.95 (0-8369-5199-9) Ayer.

Acheson, T. W. St. John: The Making of a Colonial Urban Community. 310p. 1985. text 35.00 (0-8020-2586-2) U of Toronto Pr.

— Saint John: The Making of a Colonial Urban Community. 326p. 1992. pap. text 24.95 (0-8020-7380-8) U of Toronto Pr.

Achesone, James. The Military Garden: Instructions for All Young Souldiers. LC 74-80157. (English Experience Ser.: No. 637). 36p. 1974. reprint ed. 15.00 (90-221-0637-3) Walter J Johnson.

***Achey, Jeff.** Guide to Climbing Photography. LC 99-30219. (Illus.). 128p. 2000. 16.95 (0-8117-2728-9) Stackpole.

Achey, Jeff, ed. Climbing 1996 Wall Calendar. 1995. 14.95 (1-887216-02-2) Elk Mtn Pr.

Achgill, D. M., jt. ed. see Craft, W. J.

Achhammer, Angelika. Pleurotus Unter Stress: Oekophysiologische Untersuchungen Zu Wasserhaushalt und Sporulation. (Bibliotheca Mycologica: Vol. 141). (GER., Illus.). xii, 206p. 1992. 77.00 (3-443-59042-X, Pub. by Gebruder Borntraeger) Balogh.

Achiba, Y., et al, eds. Novel Forms of Carbon II Vol. 349: Materials Research Society Symposium Proceedings. LC 95-122054. 557p. 1994. text 30.00 (1-55899-249-9) Materials Res.

Achieser, N. I. Theory of Approximation. 317p. 1992. reprint ed. pap. 8.95 (0-486-67129-1) Dover.

Achiezer, N'Shei. The Easy & Delicious Cookbook. 1996. 15.95 (1-58330-016-3) Feldheim.

Achikeobi, Ezolabaagbo. Journey Through Breath. 1999. pap. text 10.95 (1-874509-76-X) XPr.

Achilladelis, Basil & Bowden, Mary E. Structures of Life: To Accompany an Exhibit by the Beckman Center for the History of Chemistry. (BCHOC Publication: No. 8). (Illus.). 36p. (Orig.). 1989. pap. 8.00 (0-941901-07-6) Chem Heritage Fnd.

Achille, Justin, jt. ed. see Hatch, Robert.

Achilles, Charles M. Let's Put Kids First, Finally: Getting Class Size Right. LC 99-6240. (One-Off Ser.). (Illus.). 216p. 1999. pap. 23.95 (0-8039-6807-8) Corwin Pr.

***Achilles, Charles M.** Let's Put Kids First, Finally: Getting Class Size Right. LC 99-6240. (One-Off Ser.). (Illus.). 216p. 1999. 53.95 (0-8039-6806-X) Corwin Pr.

Achilles, Charles M. & Ruskin, Karen B. Grantwriting, Fundraising & Partnerships: Strategies That Work! LC 95-33093. (Illus.). 200p. 1995. 55.95 (0-8039-6220-7); pap. 24.95 (0-8039-6221-5) Corwin Pr.

Achilles, Charles M., et al. Problem Analysis: Responding to School Complexity. LC 97-18980. 160p. 1997. 29.95 (1-883001-36-6) Eye On Educ.

Achilles, Charles M., jt. auth. see Hoover, Susan.

Achilles, Pat, tr. see Ellis, Susan J., et al.

Achilles, Paul S., ed. Psychology at Work. LC 74-156602. (Essay Index Reprint Ser.). 1977. reprint ed. 20.95 (0-8369-2262-X) Ayer.

Achilles, Rolf. Mies Van Der Rohe: Architect as Educator. (Illus.). 168p. 1986. pap. 25.00 (0-318-20183-6, 31718-8); lib. bdg. 39.95 (0-318-20182-8, 31716-1) IL Inst Tech.

Achilles, Tatius. The Most Delectable & Pleasant History of Clitiphon & Leucippe. Burton, W., tr. LC 77-6841. (English Experience Ser.: No. 837). 1977. reprint ed. lib. bdg. 30.00 (90-221-0837-6) Walter J Johnson.

***Achilli, Justin.** Brujah. (Clan Novel Ser.). 2000. pap. 14.95 (1-56504-267-0) White Wolf.

Achilli, Justin. Clanbook: Cappadocian. (Vampire Ser.). (Illus.). 72p. (Orig.). 1997. pap. 12.00 (1-56504-280-8, 2805) White Wolf.

— Clanbook: Giovanni. (Vampire Ser.). (Illus.). (Orig.). 1997. pap. 12.00 (1-56504-218-2, 2063) White Wolf.

***Achilli, Justin.** Fear & Loathing. (Aberrant Ser.). 2000. pap. 4.95 (1-56504-689-7) White Wolf.

— Giovanni. (Clan Novel Ser.). 288p. 2000. pap. text 5.99 (1-56504-826-1) White Wolf.

Achilli, Justin. Kindred of the East. (Vampire Ser.). 1998. 25.00 (1-56504-232-8) White Wolf.

***Achilli, Justin.** Mind's Eye Theatre: The Sabbat Guide. 2000. pap. 14.95 (1-56504-732-X) White Wolf.

— Subsidiaries: A Guide to Pentex. 2000. pap. text 17.95 (1-56504-358-8) White Wolf.

— Vampire Storytellers Handbook. rev. ed. 2000. 25.95 (1-56504-264-6) White Wolf.

Achilli, Justin & Dansky, Richard E. Guide to the Camarilla & Sabbat Limited Edition, 2 vols. (Vampire Ser.). (Illus.). 1999. boxed set 74.95 (1-56504-262-X, 2296) White Wolf.

Achilli, Justin & Heinig, Jess. Guide to the Sabbat. (Vampire Ser.). (Illus.). 224p. 1999. 25.95 (1-56504-263-8, 2303) White Wolf.

Achilli, Justin, et al. Kindred of the East Companion. (Vampire Ser.). (Illus.). 144p. 1999. pap. 19.95 (1-56504-223-9, 2901) White Wolf.

***Achilli, Justin, et al.** Vampire Storytellers Guide. limited ed. (Vampire Ser.). (Illus.). 224p. 1999. 49.95 (1-56504-273-5, 2294) White Wolf.

Achilli, Justin, ed. see Murphy, Kevin A.

Achim, Stephan. Sinn Als Bedeutung: Bedeutungstheoretische Untersuchungen zur Psychoanalyse Sigmund Freuds. (Quellen und Studien zur Philosophie: Vol. 24). (GER.). xvi, 174p. (C). 1989. lib. bdg. 78.25 (3-11-011949-8) De Gruyter.

Achim von Arnim, Ludwig. Ludwig Achim von Arnim's Novellas of 1812. Duncan, Bruce, tr. LC 97-41110. (Studies in German Language & Literature: Vol. 18). 228p. 1997. 89.95 (0-7734-8439-6) E Mellen.

Aching, Gerard. The Politics of Spanish American Modernismo: By Exquisite Design. LC 97-218373. (Studies in Latin American & Iberian Literature: Vol. 11). 192p. (C). 1997. text 54.95 (0-521-57249-5) Cambridge U Pr.

Achinstein, Asher. Buying Power of Labor & Post-War Cycles. LC 68-57563. (Columbia University. Studies in the Social Sciences: No. 292). reprint ed. 20.00 (0-404-51292-5) AMS Pr.

Achinstein, Peter. Concepts of Science: A Philosophical Analysis. LC 68-15451. 285p. 1968. reprint ed. pap. 88.40 (0-608-06721-0, 206691800009) Bks Demand.

— Particles & Waves: Historical Essays in the Philosophy of Science. (Illus.). 352p. 1991. pap. text 39.95 (0-19-506755-X, 6122) OUP.

Achinstein, Peter & Barker, Stephen F., eds. The Legacy of Logical Positivism in the Philosophy of Science. LC 69-15396. 10p. reprint ed. pap. 30.00 (0-608-10079-X, 200628500056) Bks Demand.

Achinstein, Peter & Hannaway, Owen, eds. Observation, Experiment, & Hypothesis in Modern Physical Science. 1985. 47.50 (0-262-01083-6, Bradford Bks) MIT Pr.

Achinstein, Peter & Snyder, Laura J., eds. Scientific Methods: Conceptual & Historical Problems. LC 93-47265. (Open Forum Ser.). 168p. (Orig.). (C). 1994. pap. 21.50 (0-89464-822-5) Krieger.

Achinstein, Peter, jt. ed. see Kargon, Robert.

Achinstein, Sharon. Milton & the Revolutionary Reader. LC 94-6647. (Literature in History Ser.). 344p. 1994. text 39.50 (0-691-03490-7, Pub. by Princeton U Pr) Cal Prin Full Svc.

Achinstein, Sharon, ed. Gender, Literature & the English Revolution. 190p. 1995. pap. text 176.00 (2-88449-152-X) Gordon & Breach.

Achkar, Edgar, et al. Clinical Gastroenterology. 2nd ed. (Illus.). 1992. text 115.00 (0-8121-1363-2) Lppncott W & W.

Achleitner, Friedrich. Adolf Krischanitz. 1994. pap. 34.95 (1-874056-42-0) Birkhauser.

***Achleitner, Friedrich.** Atelier 5. (Illus.). 192p. 2000. pap. write for info. (3-7643-6243-X) Birkhauser.

Achleitner, Friedrich, jt. text see Zumthor, Peter.

Achleitner, Herbert K., ed. Intellectual Foundations for Information Professionals. (Social Science Monographs). 213p. 1987. text 48.50 (0-88033-957-8, Pub. by East Eur Monographs) Col U Pr.

Achley, Alan A., jt. auth. see Duke, James A.

Achmad, Shaun, jt. auth. see Weinrank, Stanley.

Achmanova, O. S. Dictionary of Homonyms of the Russian Language. 3rd ed. (ENG & RUS.). 448p. 1986. 49.95 (0-8288-2000-7, M1254) Fr & Eur.

Achola, Paul P., et al, eds. Trends & the Future of University Education in Kenya. 134p. 1990. pap. text 10.95 (9966-835-84-9) Prof World Peace.

Achola, Paul P. W. & Msimuko, Arthur, eds. Development Through Self-Reliance in the SADDC Region. 170p. 1987. pap. text 14.95 (0-943852-26-9) Prof World Peace.

Achon, M. A., jt. auth. see Wittfoht, Annemarie.

Achour. Real Estate: Analysis & Appraisal. 400p. 1987. pap. 50.00 (0-409-80108-9, MICHIE) LEXIS Pub.

Achour, Christiane. Dictionnaire des Oeuvres Algeriennes en Langue Francais. (FRE.). 383p. 1990. pap. 95.00 (0-8288-7583-9, 2738409490) Fr & Eur.

Achrol, Ravi & Mitchell, Andrew, eds. AMA Educators' Proceedings, 1994 Vol. 5: Enhancing Knowledge Development in Marketing. 470p. 1994. pap. 50.00 (0-87757-252-6) Am Mktg.

Achte, K. A., et al. Alcoholic Psychoses in Finland. (Finnish Foundation for Alcohol Studies: Vol. 19). 1969. 4.00 (951-9192-08-5) Rutgers Ctr Alcohol.

Achtemeier, Elizabeth. The Committed Marriage. LC 76-7611. 224p. 1976. pap. 17.95 (0-664-24754-7) Westminster John Knox.

— Minor Prophets. LC 96-31321. (New International Biblical Commentary Ser.: Vol. 17). 390p. (C). 1996. pap. 11.95 (0-943575-05-2) Hendrickson MA.

— Nahum-Malachi. LC 85-45458. (Interpretation: A Bible Commentary for Teaching & Preaching Ser.). 216p. 1986. 25.00 (0-8042-3129-X) Westminster John Knox.

An Asterisk (*) at the beginning of an entry indicates that the title is appearing for the first time.

— Not Til I Have Done: A Personal Testimony. LC 98-39672. 136p. 1999. 18.00 (*0-664-22136-X*) Westminster John Knox.

— Preaching from the Minor Prophets: Texts & Sermon Suggestions. LC 97-38554. 155p. (Orig.). 1997. pap. 14.00 (*0-8028-4370-0*) Eerdmans.

— Preaching from the Old Testament. 200p. (Orig.). 1989. pap. 22.95 (*0-664-25042-4*) Westminster John Knox.

— Preaching Hard Texts of the Old Testament. LC 98-20141. 192p. 1998. pap. 14.95 (*1-56563-333-4*) Hendrickson MA.

Achtemeier, Elizabeth, jt. auth. see Achtemeier, Paul J.

Achtemeier, Elizabeth R. Not 'Til I Have Done: A Personal Testimony. LC 98-39672. 1999. 18.00 (*0-664-25809-3*) Westminster John Knox.

Achtemeier, Elizabeth R., et al. The Right Choice. Stallsworth, Paul T., ed. LC 96-51889. 144p. 1997. pap. 14.95 (*0-687-05079-0*) Abingdon.

***Achtemeier, Mark & Purves, Andrew.** Union in Christ: A Declaration for the Church. LC 99-25892. 1999. 8.95 (*1-57153-019-3*) Curriculm Presbytrn KY.

***Achtemeier, P. Mark & Purves, Andrew.** A Passion for the Gospel: Confessing Jesus Christ for the Twenty-First Century. 160p. 2000. pap. 14.95 (*0-664-50128-1*, Pub. by Geneva Press) Presbyterian Pub.

Achtemeier, Paul J. I Peter. Jay, Eldon, ed. LC 95-19564. (Hermeneia: A Critical & Historical Commentary on the Bible Ser.). 608p. 1996. 50.00 (*0-8006-6030-7*, 1-6030, Fortress Pr) Augsburg Fortress.

— The HarperCollins Bible Dictionary: Revised Edition. rev. ed. LC 96-25424. 1280p. 1996. 45.00 (*0-06-060037-3*, Pub. by Harper SF) HarpC.

— Harper's Bible Dictionary. write for info. (*0-06-060367-4*) HarpC.

— Inspiration & Authority: Nature & Function of Christian Scripture. rev. ed. LC 98-54748. Orig. Title: Inspiration of Scripture: Problems & Proposals. 160p. 1999. pap. 9.95 (*1-56563-363-6*) Hendrickson MA.

— The Inspiration of Scripture: Problems & Proposals. LC 80-10286. 188p. 1980. pap. 19.95 (*0-664-24313-4*) Westminster John Knox.

— Mark. 2nd enl. rev. ed. Krodel, Gerhard A., ed. LC 85-46020. (Proclamation Commentaries Ser.: the New Testament Witnesses for Preaching). 138p. 1986. pap. 14.00 (*0-8006-1916-1*, 1-1916, Fortress Pr) Augsburg Fortress.

— Romans. LC 84-47796. (Interpretation: A Bible Commentary for Teaching & Preaching Ser.). 240p. 1986. 25.00 (*0-8042-3137-0*) Westminster John Knox.

Achtemeier, Paul J., ed. The HarperCollins Bible Dictionary. 1996. 45.00 (*0-614-23034-9*) Harper SF.

Achtemeier, Paul J. & Achtemeier, Elizabeth. The Old Testament Roots of Our Faith. 8th rev. ed. 142p. 1994. pap. 9.95 (*1-56563-144-7*) Hendrickson MA.

Achtemeier, Paul J., jt. ed. see Mays, James L.

Achtemeier, Paul J., ed. see Society of Biblical Literature Staff.

Achten, Rik. First Principles & Our Way to Faith: A Fundamental-Theological Study of John Henry Newman's Notion of First Principles. LC 97-169339. (European University Studies: Series 23, Vol. 539). (GER.). 310p. 1995. pap. 57.95 (*3-631-49190-5*) P Lang Pubng.

Achtenberg, Anya. I Know What the Small Girl Knew: Poems. LC 82-81350. 65p. 1983. pap. 4.50 (*0-930100-11-5*) Holy Cow.

Achtenhagen, F., et al. Exchange Rate Management in Interdependent Economies: From Williamsburg to Louvre. (Handeln und Entscheiden in Konmplexen Okonomischen Situationen Ser.: Bd. 9). xviii, 172p. 1993. pap. 52.00 (*0-387-91472-2*) Spr-Verlag.

Achterberg, Dossey. Rituals of Healing. 384p. 1994. pap. 15.95 (*0-553-37347-1*) Bantam.

Achterberg, E. & Lanz, K. Enzyklopadisches Lexikon Fur des Geld, Bank und Borsen Wesen, 2 vols., Set. (GER.). 1967. 325.00 (*0-685-57717-1*, M7364) Fr & Eur.

Achterberg, Gerrit. But This Land Has No End. Boyce, Pieuke, tr. 1989. pap. text 9.95 (*0-88982-097-X*, Pub. by Oolichan Bks) Genl Dist Srvs.

— Hidden Weddings: Selected Poems. O'Loughlin, Michale, tr. from IRI. 72p. 1987. pap. 8.95 (*1-85186-022-3*) Dufour.

Achterberg, Jeanne. Imagery in Healing: Shamanism & Modern Medicine. LC 84-20748. (New Science Library). 256p. (Orig.). 1985. pap. 16.00 (*0-87773-307-4*, Pub. by Shambhala Pubns) Random.

— Imagery in Healing: Shamanism & Modern Medicine. (Orig.). 1985. pap. 18.00 (*0-394-73031-3*, Pub. by Shambhala Pubns) Random.

— Woman As Healer. LC 89-43314. 1991. pap. 17.00 (*0-87773-616-2*, Pub. by Shambhala Pubns) Random.

Achterberg, Jeanne & Lawlis, Frank. Bridges of the Bodymind. 2nd ed. (Illus.). xv, 375p. 1980. reprint ed. pap. text 30.00 (*0-918296-19-6*) Inst Personality & Ability.

Achterberg, Sandy. What Do You Think? Ideas & Opinions. (Illus.). 55p. (Orig.). (J). (gr. 3-10). 1995. pap. text 11.00 (*0-911943-40-4*) Leadership Pub.

Achterhof, Carole. He's a Keeper, I'm a Tosser. (Illus.). 200p. 1998. pap. 9.95 (*0-9625940-3-2*) Bare Bones Bks.

***Achterhof, Carole.** How to Pose with a Fish. (Illus.). 200p. 2000. pap. 9.95 (*0-9625940-4-0*) Bare Bones Bks.

Achterhof, Carole. Life with a Channel Surfer. LC 94-70345. (Illus.). 184p. (Orig.). 1994. pap. 9.95 (*0-9625940-2-4*) Bare Bones Bks.

Achtermeier, William O. Rhode Island Arms Makers & Gunsmiths, 1643-1883. LC 80-84583. (Illus.). 108p. 1980. 16.50 (*0-917218-15-9*) A Mowbray.

Achtman, Mark, et al, eds. Neisseriae, 1990: Proceedings of the 7th International Neisseria Conference Berlin, Federal Republic of Germany, Sept. 9-14, 1990. (Illus.). xx, 752p. (C). 1991. lib. bdg. 261.55 (*3-11-012712-1*) De Gruyter.

Achugar, Hugo. Mariposas Tropicales. (SPA.). 80p. 1986. pap. 8.50 (*0-910061-30-0*, 1404) Ediciones Norte.

— Poesia y Sociedad. (SPA.). 229p. 1988. pap. 12.00 (*0-318-39832-X*) Ediciones Norte.

Achugar, Hugo, et al, texts. Represion, Exilio y Democracia: La Cultura Uruguaya. (SPA.). 1987. 15.00 (*0-614-23155-8*) Edins Hispamerica.

Achuthan, N. S. Soviet Arms Transfer Policy in South Asia, 1955-1981. (C). 1988. 32.00 (*81-7062-037-6*, Pub. by Lancer India) S Asia.

Achziger, John, ed. see Lundahl, G. D. & Lundahl, Ruth C.

ACI Committee Staff. Building Code Requirements for Reinforced Concrete, 1989, with Commentary: ACI 318-89(92). ANSI 318R-89. rev. ed. 1992. 92.75 (*0-317-99889-7*, 318R-89BOW6) ACI.

— Cement & Concrete Terminology. 1990. pap. 54.50 (*0-685-85102-8*, 116R-90) ACI.

— TCI Manual of Concrete Inspection. 8th ed. 200p. 1992. 69.50 (*0-685-62675-X*, SP-2(92)BOW6) ACI.

ACI Committee 340. Design Handbook in Accordance with the Strength Design Method of ACI 318-89: Columns, Vol. 2. 1990. ring bd. 123.25 (*0-685-85093-5*, SP-17ABOW6) ACI.

ACI Committee 349. Code Requirements for Nuclear Safety Related Concrete Structures: ACI 349-85(90) 1985. 110.50 (*0-685-85087-0*, 349-85(90)BOW6) ACI.

ACI International Conference Staff. Evaluation & Rehabilitation of Concrete Structures & Innovations in Design: Proceedings ACI International Conference, Hong Kong, 1991, Vol. 1. Malhotra, V. M., ed. LC 91-76421. (American Concrete Institute Ser.: SP-128). 758p. 1992. reprint ed. pap. 200.00 (*0-608-04609-4*, 206537900001) Bks Demand.

— Evaluation & Rehabilitation of Concrete Structures & Innovations in Design Vol. 2: Proceedings ACI International Conference, Hong Kong, 1991. Malhotra, V. M., ed. LC 91-76421. (American Concrete Institute Ser.: SP-128). 743p. 1992. reprint ed. pap. 200.00 (*0-608-04610-8*, 206537900002) Bks Demand.

ACI Staff. Travel with or Without Pets: 25,000 Pets-R-Permitted Accomodations, Petsitters, Kennels & More! 6th ed. Nelson, M. E., ed. (Illus.). 512p. 1997. pap. 13.95 (*1-56471-797-6*) Annenberg.

Acidini-Luchinat, Cristina, ed. Treasures of Florence: The Medici Collection, 1400-1700. LC 98-186671. 224p. 1997. 85.00 (*3-7913-1867-5*, Pub. by Prestel) te Neues.

Acier, Marcel, ed. From Spanish Trenches. LC 78-63648. (Studies in Fascism: Ideology & Practice). 216p. reprint ed. 39.50 (*0-404-16898-1*) AMS Pr.

Acierno. Human Machine: How It Breaks Down. (C). 1989. pap. text 55.00 (*0-536-57360-3*) Pearson Custom.

***Acierno, L. J.** The History of Cardiology. (Illus.). 758p. 2001. pap. 55.00 (*1-85070-049-4*) Prthnon Pub.

Acierno, L. J. A History of Cardiology: Men, Ideas & Contributions. (History of Medicine Ser.). (Illus.). 758p. (C). 1994. 98.00 (*1-85070-339-6*) Prthnon Pub.

***Acierto, Maria G.** Building Community. 144p. 1999. 21.95 (*0-9642068-8-9*) Nyala Pubng.

Acikgenc, Alparslan. Being & Existence in Sadra & Heidegger. 211p. (C). 1997. pap. 18.00 (*0-934905-91-6*, Library of Islam) Kazi Pubns.

***Aciman, Andre.** False Papers. LC 00-27766. 288p. 2000. 23.00 (*0-374-29978-1*) FS&G.

Aciman, Andre. Out of Egypt: A Memoir. LC 95-34143. 1996. pap. 14.00 (*1-57322-534-7*, Riverhd Trade) Berkley Pub.

***Aciman, Andre, ed.** Letters of Transit: Reflections on Exile, Identity, Language & Loss. 2000. pap. 12.95 (*1-56584-607-9*, Pub. by New Press NY) Norton.

Aciman, Andre, ed. see Said, Edward W.

Acimovic, L. J. Problems of Security & Cooperation in Europe. 344p. 1981. lib. bdg. 129.50 (*90-286-0190-2*) Kluwer Academic.

Acinas, J. R., jt. ed. see Brebbia, Carlos A.

***Ackah, William B.** Pan-Africanism - Exploring the Contradiction: Politics, Identity & Development in Africa & the African Diaspora. (Interdisciplinary Research Series in Ethnic, Gender & Class Relations). 138p. 1999. text 61.95 (*1-84014-375-4*, Pub. by Ashgate Pub) Ashgate Pub Co.

Ackart, Robert. Breakfast Is Ready! 31 Complete Menus with Step-By-Step Recipes to Start Your Day. 94p. 1996. pap. 10.95 (*1-887678-01-8*) Finley-Greene Pubns.

— A Celebration of Vegetables: Menus for Festive Meat-Free Dining. LC 77-76469. (Illus.). 1979. pap. 6.95 (*0-689-70581-6*, 244) Atheneum Yung Read.

— Dinner Is Served! 50 Complete Menus with Step-By-Step Recipes for the Pleasure of Family & Friends. (Illus.). 200p. 1996. pap. 14.95 (*1-887678-05-0*) Finley-Greene Pubns.

— Lunch Is on the Table! 40 Complete Menus with Step-by-Step Recipes for Midday Enjoyment. (Illus.). 132p. 1960. pap. 12.95 (*1-887678-03-4*) Finley-Greene Pubns.

— Please Help Yourself! Self-Starting Ideas & Step-by-Step Recipes for Cocktail Parties & Elegant Buffet Meals. 132p. 1995. pap. 12.95 (*1-887678-07-7*) Finley-Greene Pubns.

Ackaway, Joseph C. Getting a Job in the 90s: A New Approach to Finding a Job in the 90's. LC 91-76453. 154p. (Orig.). 1991. pap. 9.95 (*0-9630157-1-0*) J C Ackaway.

Ackels, Ran. Immortal: Players Guide. 256p. 1996. 24.95 (*1-885681-03-8*) Precedence.

— Immortal: Pride Dracul. 96p. 1996. 14.95 (*1-885681-05-4*) Precedence.

— Immortal: The Invisible War. 288p. 1994. 24.95 (*1-885681-00-3*) Precedence.

Ackels, Ran & Von Griese, Brianna. Immortal: Lost Trinity. 128p. 1994. 19.95 (*1-885681-02-X*) Precedence.

— Immortal: Pilot Pack. 24p. 1994. 14.95 (*1-885681-01-1*) Precedence.

Ackelsberg, Martha A. Free Women of Spain: Anarchism & the Struggle for the Emancipation of Women. LC 90-42665. (Illus.). 250p. (Orig.). 1991. 42.00 (*0-253-30120-3*); pap. 15.95 (*0-253-20634-0*, MB-634) Ind U Pr.

Ackema, Peter. Issues in Morphosyntax. LC 99-21418. (Linguistik Aktuell/Linguistics Today Ser.: Vol. 26). viii, 310p. 1999. 75.00 (*1-55619-910-4*) J Benjamins Pubng Co.

Ackeman, Lowell, ed. The Biology, Husbandry & Health Care of Reptiles Vol. I: Biology. (Illus.). 382p. 1997. 79.95 (*0-7938-0501-5*, TS297) TFH Pubns.

Ackenheil, M., et al, eds. Implications of Psychopharmacology to Psychiatry: Biological, Nosological, & Therapeutical Concepts. 1995. 86.95 (*3-540-60533-9*) Spr-Verlag.

Ackenhusen. Real-Time Signal Processing: The Design & Implementation of Signal Processing. 500p. (C). 1999. 73.00 (*0-13-631771-5*, Macmillan Coll) P-H.

Ackenhusen, John G., ed. Signal Processing Technology & Applications. LC 94-46444. (Technology Update Ser.). 560p. 1995. write for info. (*0-7803-2469-2*) Inst Electrical.

Acker, Alan A., Sr. Broadcast Ministry Christianity on Idolatry. LC 98-142954. 109p. 1997. pap. 7.95 (*1-56794-134-6*, C2470) Star Bible.

Acker, Ally. Waiting for the Beloved. 8/8p. 10.95 (*1-888996-11-0*, Red Hen Press) Valentine CA.

Acker, Barbara & Hampton, Marion, eds. The Vocal Vision: Voice in Tomorrow's Theatre. LC 97-13927. 320p. 1997. pap. text 18.95 (*1-55783-282-X*) Applause Theatre Bk Pubs.

Acker, Bertie, tr. see De la Parra, Teresa.

Acker, Chris, ed. see Courtney, W. Keith.

Acker, David D. Skill in Communication - A Vital Element in Effective Management. (Illus.). 129p. (Orig.). (C). 1994. pap. text 25.00 (*1-56806-189-7*) DIANE Pub.

— Skill in Communication - A Vital Element in Effective Management. (Illus.). 140p. (Orig.). 1990. per. 6.00 (*0-16-024439-0*, 008-020-01218-1) USGPO.

Acker, Duane & Cunningham, Merle. Animal Science & Industry. 5th ed. LC 97-11218. 704p. 1997. 105.00 (*0-13-524901-5*) P-H.

Acker, Duane, jt. auth. see Cunningham, Merle.

Acker, E. D. Acker. Brief History of the Acker-Halbert Family, Composed of Biographical Sketches & Descent Diagrams. (Illus.). 177p. 1997. reprint ed. pap. 26.00 (*0-8328-7201-6*); reprint ed. lib. bdg. 36.00 (*0-8328-7200-8*) Higginson Bk Co.

Acker, Elizabeth Van, see Van Acker, Elizabeth.

Acker, G. Elaine. Life in a Rock Shelter: Prehistoric Indians of the Lower Pecos. LC 95-17291. (Illus.). (Orig.). 1996. pap. 19.95 (*0-937460-84-2*) Hendrick-Long.

Acker, G. H. Worm Gear Contact Temperatures. (Technical Papers: Vol. P251). (Illus.). 26p. 1944. pap. text 30.00 (*1-55589-423-2*) AGMA.

Acker, Georges van, see Nesbit, Roy Conyers & van Acker, Georges.

Acker, H., et al, eds. Chemoreceptors & Chemoreceptor Reflexes. LC 90-7230. (Illus.). 440p. 1990. 120.00 (*0-306-43593-4*, Plenum Trade) Perseus Pubng.

Acker, Helen. Four Sons of Norway. LC 72-117318. (Biography Index Reprint Ser.). 1977. 24.95 (*0-8369-8010-7*) Ayer.

Acker, Iris. The Secrets to Auditioning for Commercials. LC 90-20427. (Illus.). 128p. 1991. pap. 9.95 (*0-942963-04-0*) Distinctive Pub.

— What Got You Where You Are Today? LC 90-86069. (Illus.). 192p. 1991. pap. 12.95 (*0-942963-08-3*) Distinctive Pub.

Acker, J. W., ed. Lutheran Book of Prayer. rev. ed. LC 76-119916. 203p. 1970. 6.99 (*0-570-03005-6*, 06-1141) Concordia.

Acker, James. Basic Legal Research for Criminal Justice & the Social Sciences. rev. ed. LC 97-40978. 426p. 1998. pap. 28.00 (*0-8342-1013-4*, 10134) Aspen Pub.

Acker, James R., et al, eds. America's Experiment with Capital Punishment: Reflections on the Past, Present, & Future of the Ultimate Penal Sanction. LC 97-39985. 592p. 1998. pap. 35.00 (*0-89089-651-8*) Carolina Acad Pr.

Acker, James R. & Brody, David C. Criminal Procedure. LC 98-26479. xix, 788 p. 1998. 59.00 (*0-8342-1061-4*) Aspen Pub.

Acker, Jeannine K., jt. auth. see Schwandt, Rachel K.

Acker, Joan. Doing Comparable Worth: Gender, Class & Pay Equity. (Women in the Political Economy Ser.). 272p. (C). 1989. 39.95 (*0-87722-621-0*) Temple U Pr.

— Doing Comparable Worth: Gender, Class & Pay Equity. (Women in the Political Economy Ser.). 272p. 1991. pap. 22.95 (*0-87722-834-5*) Temple U Pr.

Acker, Joan R., et al. Working in the 21st Century: Gender & Beyond. unabridged ed. Glass, Judith, ed. (Dynamics of Gender in the Workplace Ser.: Vol. 1). 102p. 1994. pap. text 16.50 (*0-89215-186-2*) U Cal LA Indus Rel.

Acker, Jorge, ed. see Courtney, W. Keith.

Acker, Joseph, jt. auth. see Acker, William R.

Acker, Kathleen R. Love Takes Time. LC 96-90032. 1996. 11.95 (*0-533-11784-4*) Vantage.

Acker, Kathy. Blood & Guts in High School. LC 84-48118. 176p. 1989. pap. 12.00 (*0-8021-3193-X*, Grove) Grove-Atltic.

— Bodies of Work: Essays. 200p. (Orig.). 1996. pap. text 16.00 (*1-85242-425-7*) Serpents Tail.

— Don Quixote. LC 86-45260. 208p. 1989. pap. 11.00 (*0-8021-3192-1*, Grove) Grove-Atltic.

— Dust: A Creation Books Reader. Hunter, Jack D., ed. 160p. (Orig.). 1996. pap. 10.99 (*1-871592-44-5*) Creation Books.

— Empire of the Senseless. LC 88-19154. 240p. 1989. pap. 11.00 (*0-8021-3179-4*, Grove) Grove-Atltic.

— Great Expectations. LC 83-48312. 352p. 1989. pap. 8.95 (*0-8021-3155-7*, Grove) Grove-Atltic.

— Hannibal Lecter, My Father. 148p. 1991. pap. 6.00 (*0-936756-68-3*) Autonomedia.

— Hello, I'm Erica Jong. (Chapbook Ser.). (Illus.). 32p. (Orig.). 1982. pap. 3.00 (*0-936556-07-2*) Contact Two.

— In Memoriam to Identity. 272p. 1998. reprint ed. pap. 13.00 (*0-8021-3579-X*, Grove) Grove-Atltic.

Acker, Kathy. Literal Madness: Three Novels, My Death My Life by Pier Paulo Pasolini; Kathy Goes to Haiti; Florida. LC 87-14860. 352p. 1989. pap. 12.00 (*0-8021-3156-5*, Grove) Grove-Atltic.

Acker, Kathy. Low: Good & Evil in the Work of Nayland Blake. (Illus.). 39p. 1990. 20.00 (*0-902825-33-X*) Petersburg Pr.

— My Mother: Demonology: A Novel. LC 94-21534. 268p. 1994. pap. 11.00 (*0-8021-3403-3*, Grove) Grove-Atltic.

— N. Y. C. in 1979. (Illus.). 24p. (Orig.). 1981. pap. 3.00 (*0-917061-09-8*) Top Stories.

— Portrait of an Eye: Three Novels. LC 97-35003. 320p. 1998. pap. 14.00 (*0-8021-3543-9*, Grove) Grove-Atltic.

— Pussy, King of the Pirates. 288p. 1997. reprint ed. pap. 12.00 (*0-8021-3484-X*, Grove) Grove-Atltic.

— Pussycat Fever. (Illus.). 76p. (Orig.). 1995. pap. 7.00 (*1-873176-63-5*) AK Pr Dist.

Acker, Kathy, et al. The Artist in Society: Rights, Roles & Responsibilities. unabridged ed. Becker, Carl L. et al, eds. LC 95-70748. 112p. (Orig.). 1995. pap. 12.00 (*0-9647855-0-1*) New Art Exam.

— Spectacular Optical. Antlo-Suarez, Sandra & Madore, Michael, eds. (Illus.). 1998. pap., per. 12.00 (*1-888209-04-6*) PASSIM.

Acker, Loren E., et al. AIDS-Proofing Your Kids: A Step-by-Step Guide. Roehm, Michelle, ed. LC 91-43490. 176p. 1992. pap. 8.95 (*0-941831-72-8*) Beyond Words Pub.

Acker, Louis S., jt. auth. see Sakoian.

Acker, Louis S, jt. auth. see Sakoian, Frances.

Acker, Louis S., jt. auth. see Sokoian, Frances.

Acker, Paul. Revising Oral Theory: Formulaic Composition in Old English & Old Icelandic Verse. LC 98-11371. (Studies in Medieval Literature: Vol. 16). 150p. 1998. text 40.00 (*0-8153-3102-9*, H2104) Garland.

Acker, Randy & Fergus, Jim. A Field Guide - Dog First Aid: Emergency Care for Hunting, Working & Outdoor Dogs. (Illus.). 77p. 1994. spiral bd. 15.00 (*1-885106-04-1*) Wild Adven Pr.

Acker, Robert, tr. & afterword by see Wolfgruber, Gernot.

Acker, Sandra, ed. Teachers, Gender & Careers. 250p. 1989. pap. 34.95 (*1-85000-427-7*, Falmer Pr) Taylor & Francis.

Acker, Sandra & Piper, David W., eds. Is Higher Education Fair to Women? 256p. 1985. pap. 38.00 (*1-85059-002-8*) OpUniv Pr.

***Acker, Thomas S.** The Baroque Vortex: Velazquez, Calderon & Gracian under Philip IV. (Currents in Comparative Romance Languages & Literature Ser.: Vol. 23). 160p. (C). 2000. 42.95 (*0-8204-2367-X*) P Lang Pubng.

Acker, Toni. Tobey: A Tale of Transition. (Illus.). 40p. (YA). (gr. 7-12). 1987. pap. 5.95 (*0-942953-00-2*) Wonder Works Studio.

***Acker, Victor.** Celestin Freinet, 78. LC 00-20463. (Contributions to the Study of Education: Vol. 78). 2000. write for info. (*0-313-30994-9*) Greenwood.

Acker, William R. & Acker, Joseph. Kyudo: The Japanese Art of Archery. (Illus.). 88p. 1998. pap. 9.95 (*0-8048-2109-7*, Periplus Eds) Tuttle Pubng.

Ackerfors, Hans, et al. Introduction to the General Principles of Aquaculture. LC 93-29833. (Illus.). 178p. 1994. lib. bdg. 59.95 (*1-56022-012-0*) Haworth Jrnl Co-Edits.

Ackerknecht, Erwin H. Malaria in the Upper Mississippi Valley, 1760-1900. Rosenkrantz, Barbara G., ed. LC 76-25650. (Public Health in America Ser.). (Illus.). 1977. reprint ed. lib. bdg. 18.95 (*0-405-09805-7*) Ayer.

— Medicine & Ethnology: Selected Essays of Erwin H. Ackerknecht. Koelbing, H. & Walser, H., eds. LC 70-165334. 195p. reprint ed. 60.50 (*0-8357-9276-5*, 201402200088) Bks Demand.

— Medicine at the Paris Hospital, 1794-1848. LC 66-23003. 256p. reprint ed. pap. 79.40 (*0-7837-4487-0*, 204426400001) Bks Demand.

— Rudolph Virchow: Doctor, Statesman, Anthropologist & Virchow-Bibliographie 1843-1901, 2 vols. in 1. Schwalbe, J. & Cohen, I. Bernard, eds. LC 80-2112. (Development of Science Ser.). (Illus.). 1981. reprint ed. lib. bdg. 49.95 (*0-405-13832-6*) Ayer.

— A Short History of Medicine. rev. ed. LC 81-48194. 304p. (C). 1982. reprint ed. pap. 15.95 (*0-8018-2726-4*) Johns Hopkins.

Ackerley, C. J. & Gontarski, S.E. Demented Particulars: The Annotated Murphy. LC 98-87418. 255 p. 1998. write for info. (*1-892770-00-8*) Journal Beckett.

Ackerley, Chris & Clipper, Lawrence J. A Companion to under the Volcano. 492p. 1984. 49.95 (*0-7748-0199-9*) U of Wash Pr.

Ackerley, Gloria, ed. see Jackson, Eugene & Lopreato, Joseph.

Ackerley, J. R. Hindoo Holiday: An Indian Journal. LC 99-34710. 2000. pap. 12.95 (*0-940322-25-0*) NY Rev Bks.

An Asterisk (*) at the beginning of an entry indicates that the title is appearing for the first time.

A

— My Dog Tulip. LC 99-14568. 200p. 1999. reprint ed. pap. 12.95 (*0-940322-11-0*, Pub. by NY Rev Bks) Midpt Trade.

— My Father & Myself. LC 75-6884. (Illus.). 219p. 1975. reprint ed. pap. 3.95 (*0-15-662325-0*, Harvest Bks) Harcourt.

— My Father & Myself. LC 99-14566. 280p. 1999. reprint ed. pap. 12.95 (*0-940322-12-9*, Pub. by NY Rev Bks) Midpt Trade.

— We Think the World of You. 1961. 11.95 (*0-685-06622-3*) Astor-Honor.

— We Think the World of You. LC 99-34916. 211p. 2000. pap. text 12.95 (*0-940322-26-9*) NY Rev Bks.

Ackerley, Lisa, jt. auth. see Parkinson, Norman.

Ackerlind, Sheila R. King Dinis of Portugal & the Alfonsine Heritage. (American University Studies: History: Ser. IX, Vol. 69). XIV, 220p. (C). 1989. text 42.95 (*0-8204-0921-9*) P Lang Pubng.

— Patterns of Conflict: The Individual & Society in Spanish Literature to 1700. (American University Studies: Romance Languages & Literature: Ser. II, Vol. 105). 328p. (C). 1989. text 45.70 (*0-8204-0879-4*) P Lang Pubng.

Ackerlind, Sheila R., ed. Internationalism & the Three Portugals: The Memoirs of Francis Millet Rogers. LC 92-21766. (American University Studies: History: Ser. IX, Vols. 131). XII, 386p. (C). 1992. text 55.95 (*0-8204-1934-6*) P Lang Pubng.

***Ackerly, Brooke A.** A Feminist Theory of Social Criticism. LC 99-15848. (Contemporary Political Theory Ser.). 260p. (C). 2000. 54.95 (*0-521-65019-4*); pap. 19.95 (*0-521-65984-1*) Cambridge U Pr.

Ackerly, John. Nuclear Tibet. 64p. pap. 7.50 (*1-879245-06-X*) Intl Campaign Tibet.

Ackerly, John, ed. Essential Environmental Materials on Tibet. 2nd ed. 70p. (C). 1990. pap. 6.00 (*1-879245-02-7*) Intl Campaign Tibet.

— Tibetan Environment & Development News - Compilation. pap. 5.00 (*1-879245-07-8*) Intl Campaign Tibet.

Ackerly, Neal, et al. An Archaeological Survey of the Cholla-Saguaro Transmission Line Corridor. (Archaeological Ser.: Vol. 135, No. 1). (Illus.). 435p. 1979. 16.95 (*1-889747-55-6*) Ariz St Mus.

Ackerly, Sally M., jt. auth. see Riekes, Linda.

Ackerly, Sally M., ed. see Riekes, Linda.

Ackerman. The Earth's Atmosphere. (Earth Science Ser.). 2000. mass mkt. 40.00 (*0-534-51984-9*) Wadsworth Pub.

— Earth's Atmosphere. (Earth Science Ser.). 2000. pap., student ed. 14.00 (*0-534-37506-5*) Brooks-Cole.

Ackerman. Fluid & Electrolytes. 96p. 1994. pap., wbk. ed. 36.95 incl. VHS (*0-87434-708-4*) Springhouse Corp.

Ackerman. Microbiology. 1992. pap. text 49.00 (*0-7295-0352-6*, W B Saunders Co) Harcrt Hlth Sci Grp.

***Ackerman.** Professional Mobile Computing. (Illus.). 2000. pap. 49.99 (*1-86100-389-7*) Wrox Pr Inc.

Ackerman, A. Bernard. Clues to Diagnosis in Dermatopathology, Vol. III. (Illus.). 427p. 1993. 50.00 (*0-89189-354-7*) Am Soc Clinical.

— Neoplasms with Follicular Differentiation. LC 91-34968. (Illus.). 650p. 1992. text 150.00 (*0-8121-1542-2*) Lppncott W & W.

— Your Skin Is Showing. (Illus.). 32p. 1979. text 12.00 (*0-8121-1212-1*) Lppncott W & W.

Ackerman, A. Bernard, ed. Malignant Melanoma & Other Melanocytic Neoplasms. (Illus.). 352p. 1984. 53.50 (*0-685-24940-9*, MA1091) Mosby Inc.

Ackerman, A. Bernard & Delmut, Kerl. Pitfalls in Histopathologic Diagnosis of Malignant Melanoma. rev. ed. (Illus.). 900p. 1993. text 195.00 (*0-8121-1352-7*) Lppncott W & W.

Ackerman, A. Bernard & Raqaz. The Lives of Lesions: Chronology in Dermatopathology. (Illus.). 266p. 1984. text 94.50 (*0-8121-1215-6*) Lppncott W & W.

Ackerman, A. Bernard, et al. Clues to Diagnosis in Dermatopathology, Vol. I. LC 89-18029. (Illus.). 432p. 1991. text 160.00 (*0-89189-296-6*, 16-1-048-00) Am Soc Clinical.

— Differential Diagnosis in Dermatopathology, No. I. 2nd ed. LC 91-8881. (Illus.). 1992. text 125.00 (*0-8121-1383-7*) Lppncott W & W.

— Differential Diagnosis in Dermatopathology, Vol. 3. LC 92-23655. (Illus.). 202p. 1992. 125.00 (*0-8121-1580-5*) Lppncott W & W.

— Differential Diagnosis in Dermatopathology, Vol. 4. (Illus.). 228p. 1994. text 125.00 (*0-8121-1676-3*) Lppncott W & W.

— Histologic Diagnosis of Inflammatory Skin Diseases: An Algorithmic Method Based on Pattern Analysis. 2nd ed. LC 96-2903. 943p. 1997. 250.00 (*0-683-00010-1*) Lppncott W & W.

***Ackerman, A. Bernard, et al.** Neoplasms with Follicular Differentiation. LC 99-98185. (Histologic Diagnosis of Neoplastic Skin Diseases Ser.). 2000. write for info. (*1-893357-11-2*) Ardor Scrib.

Ackerman, A. Bernard, jt. auth. see Abenoza, Pascual.

Ackerman, A. Bernard, jt. auth. see Steffen, Charles.

Ackerman, A. Bernard, jt. ed. see Gottlieb, Geoffrey J.

Ackerman, A. Bernard, ed. see Weyers, Wolfgang.

Ackerman, Al. Ack's Hacks. 16p. (Orig.). 1984. pap. 4.00 (*0-935350-11-X*) Luna Bisonte.

— Meetings with Improbable Danglers: The Poets Meet John M. Bennett. (Illus.). 28p. 1998. pap. 5.00 (*0-935350-99-3*) Luna Bisonte.

Ackerman, Al & Salyer, Any. Son of Ark's Hacks; More Travesties, 2 bks. in 1. 1990. pap. 5.00 (*0-935350-26-8*); pap. write for info. (*0-935350-27-6*) Luna Bisonte.

***Ackerman, Alan L., Jr.** The Portable Theater: American Literature & the Nineteenth-Century Stage. LC 99-19382. (Illus.). 304p. 1999. 45.00 (*0-8018-6161-6*) Johns Hopkins.

Ackerman, Bernard. Clues to Diagnosis in Dermatopathology, Vol. II. 436p. 1992. text 50.00 (*0-89189-339-3*, D16-1-051-00) Am Soc Clinical.

Ackerman, Blaster A. Blaster: The Blaster Al Ackerman Omnibus. Stylites, Simeon et al, eds. (Illus.). 304p. (Orig.). 1994. pap. 12.95 (*0-945209-09-6*) Popular Reality.

Ackerman, Bruce. The Case Against Lameduck Impeachment. (Open Media Pamphlet Ser.). 80p. (Orig.). 1999. pap. 8.00 (*1-58322-004-6*, Pub. by Seven Stories) Publishers Group.

***Ackerman, Bruce.** We the People: Transformations. 528p. 2000. pap. 18.95 (*0-674-00397-7*) HUP.

Ackerman, Bruce. We the People Vol. 2: Transformations. 512p. 1998. 29.95 (*0-674-94847-5*) HUP.

Ackerman, Bruce & Golove, David. Is NAFTA Constitutional? LC 95-41094. 192p. (C). 1995. reprint ed. pap. text 14.50 (*0-674-46712-4*) HUP.

Ackerman, Bruce A. The Future of Liberal Revolution. LC 92-24558. 160p. (C). 1992. 27.50 (*0-300-05396-7*) Yale U Pr.

— The Future of Liberal Revolution. 160p. (C). 1992. pap. 15.00 (*0-300-05898-5*) Yale U Pr.

— Private Property & the Constitution. LC 76-47667. 1978. pap. 20.00 (*0-300-02237-9*) Yale U Pr.

— Private Property & the Constitution. LC 76-47667. 313p. reprint ed. pap. 97.10 (*0-8357-8752-4*, 203365800087) Bks Demand.

— Reconstructing American Law. 128p. 1984. 29.00 (*0-674-75015-2*) HUP.

— We the People: Foundations, Vol. 1. 369p. (C). 1991. text 24.95 (*0-674-94840-8*) Belknap Pr.

— We the People: Foundations, Vol. 1. Vol. 1. 384p. (C). 1993. pap. text 12.95 (*0-674-94841-6*) HUP.

Ackerman, Bruce A., ed. Economic Foundations of Property Law. 329p. 1925. 18.00 (*0-316-00644-0*) Aspen Pub.

Ackerman, Bruce A. & Alstott, Anne. The Stakeholder Society. LC 98-31559. 320p. 1999. 30.00 (*0-300-07826-9*) Yale U Pr.

***Ackerman, Bruce A. & Alstott, Anne.** The Stakeholder Society. LC 98-31559. 320p. 2000. pap. 13.95 (*0-300-08260-6*) Yale U Pr.

Ackerman, Bruce A. & Hassler, William T. Clean Coal: Dirty Air. LC 80-1089. (Illus.). 196p. 1981. pap. 16.00 (*0-300-02643-9*) Yale U Pr.

Ackerman, David & Bolme, Ed. Ecofront. (Cyberpunk Ser.). (Illus.). 80p. (Orig.). 1994. pap. 10.00 (*0-937279-50-1*, CP3341) Talsorian.

***Ackerman, David & Brown, Gregory, eds.** Selling to an ESOP: A Comprehensive Guide for Owners, Managers & Advisors. 6th ed. 280p. 2000. pap. 35.00 (*0-926902-63-6*) NCEO.

Ackerman, David, et al. When Gravity Fails. Quintanar, Derek & MacDonald, Michael, eds. (Cyberpunk Ser.). (Illus.). 88p. (C). 1991. pap. 12.00 (*0-937279-12-9*, CP3601) Talsorian.

Ackerman, Diane. Bats: Shadows in the Night. LC 96-6047. (J). (gr. 5-8). 1997. 18.00 (*0-517-70919-8*); lib. bdg. 19.99 (*0-517-70920-1*) Random.

— Curious Naturalist. 288p. 1998. pap. 24.00 (*0-7922-7356-7*) Natl Geog.

— Deep Play. LC 98-35067. 240p. 1999. 24.95 (*0-679-44879-9*) Random.

***Ackerman, Diane.** Deep Play. (Illus.). 256p. 2000. pap. 13.00 (*0-679-77135-2*) Vin Bks.

Ackerman, Diane. I Praise My Destroyer. LC 97-34464. 128p. 1998. 18.50 (*0-679-44878-0*) Random.

***Ackerman, Diane.** I Praise My Destroyer. 128p. 2000. pap. 12.00 (*0-679-77134-4*) Vin Bks.

— In Our Nature: Stories of Wildness. (Illus.). (J). 2000. 22.95 (*0-7894-2642-0*) DK Pub Inc.

Ackerman, Diane. Jaguar of Sweet Laughter: New & Selected Poems. LC 92-50642. 254p. 1993. pap. 12.00 (*0-679-74304-9*) Vin Bks.

— The Moon by Whalelight: And Other Adventures among Bats, Penguins, Crocodilians, & Whales. LC 92-50004. 1992. pap. 12.00 (*0-679-74226-3*) Vin Bks.

— A Natural History of Love. 1995. pap. 13.00 (*0-679-76183-7*) Vin Bks.

— A Natural History of the Senses. LC 91-50048. 352p. 1991. pap. 13.00 (*0-679-73566-6*) Vin Bks.

— A Natural History of the Senses. 1995. pap. 12.00 (*0-394-26953-5*) Vin Bks.

— The Rarest of the Rare: Vanishing Animals, Timeless Worlds. 1997. pap. 12.00 (*0-679-77623-0*) Vin Bks.

— Reverse Thunder. 97p. (Orig.). 1988. pap. 7.95 (*0-930829-09-3*) Lumen Inc.

***Ackerman, Diane.** The Senses of Animals. LC 99-20136. (J). 2000. 14.95 (*0-375-80400-5*); lib. bdg. 16.99 (*0-375-90400-X*) Knopf.

Ackerman, Diane. A Slender Thread: Rediscovering Hope at the Heart of Crisis. 294p. 1998. pap. 13.00 (*0-679-77133-6*) Vin Bks.

Ackerman, Diane & Mackin, Jeanne, eds. The Book of Love. LC 97-23049. 600p. 1998. 29.95 (*0-393-04589-7*) Norton.

Ackerman, Dorothy. A Quaker Looks at Yoga. LC 76-23909. (Orig.). 1976. pap. 4.00 (*0-87574-207-6*) Pendle Hill.

Ackerman, Edward A. Geography As a Fundamental Research Discipline. LC 58-14934. (University of Chicago, Department of Geography, Research Paper Ser.: No. 53). 39p. reprint ed. pap. 30.00 (*0-608-14700-1*, 205205300031) Bks Demand.

Ackerman, Edward A. & Lof, George O. Technology in American Water Development. LC 59-10066. 788p. reprint ed. pap. 200.00 (*0-7837-3147-7*, 204283900006) Bks Demand.

Ackerman, Edward A., jt. auth. see Whitaker, J. Russell.

Ackerman, Edward I., et al. Selected Papers on Analog Fiber-Optic Links. LC 98-7320. (Milestone Ser.). 1998. 118.00 (*0-8194-2945-7*) SPIE.

Ackerman, Evelyn. The Doll in Miniature. (Illus.). 256p. (Orig.). 1991. pap. 49.95 (*0-912823-09-7*, BT-112) Gold Horse.

Ackerman, Evelyn. The Genius of Moritz Gottschalk: Blue & Red Roof Dollhouses, Kitchens, Stables, & Other Miniature Structures. (Illus.). 224p. 1994. 49.00 (*0-912823-45-3*, BT-144, Pub. by Gold Horse) Dollmasters.

— My Favorite Patterns: For Dressing Antique Dolls, 1865-1925. (Illus.). 133p. 1993. pap. 29.95 (*0-912823-34-8*, BT-131, Pub. by Gold Horse) Dollmasters.

— My Favorite Patterns: For Dressing Antique Dolls 1865-1925. (Illus.). 119p. 1994. pap. 9.95 (*0-912823-47-X*, BT-143, Pub. by Gold Horse) Dollmasters.

— Under the Big Top with Schoenhut's Humpty Dumpty Circus. (Illus.). 169p. 1996. 49.00 (*0-912823-63-1*, BT-163, Pub. by Gold Horse) Dollmasters.

Ackerman, Evelyn B. Health Care in the Parisian Countryside, 1800-1914. LC 89-70063. (Illus.). 258p. (C). 1990. text 45.00 (*0-8135-1548-3*) Rutgers U Pr.

— Village of the Seine: Tradition & Change in Bonnieres. LC 78-58071. (Illus.). 187p. 1978. reprint ed. pap. 58.00 (*0-608-05314-7*, 206585200001) Bks Demand.

— Village on the Seine: Tradition & Change in Bonnieres, 1815-1914. LC 78-58071. (Illus.). 188p. 1978. 39.95 (*0-8014-1178-5*) Cornell U Pr.

Ackerman, Farrell & Webelhuth, Gert. A Theory of Predicates. LC 97-28186. (Lecture Notes Ser.). 500p. (C). 1998. 69.95 (*1-57586-087-2*); pap. text 27.95 (*1-57586-086-4*) CSLI.

Ackerman, Farrell, et al. Lexical Matters. Sag, Ivan A. & Szabolcsi, Anna, eds. LC 90-28772. (Center for the Study of Language & Information-Lecture Notes Ser.). 328p. (Orig.). (C). 1992. 64.95 (*0-937073-65-2*); pap. 21.95 (*0-937073-66-0*) CSLI.

Ackerman, Forrest J., ed. Science Fiction Classics: The Stories That Morphed into Movies. 448p. 1999. 15.95 (*1-57500-040-7*, Pub. by TV Bks) HarpC.

Ackerman, Frank. Hazardous to Our Wealth: Economic Policies in the 1980s. LC 83-51288. 195p. 1984. 30.00 (*0-89608-203-2*); pap. 8.00 (*0-89608-202-4*) South End Pr.

***Ackerman, Frank.** The Political Economy of Inequality. LC 99-48264. (Frontier Issues in Economic Thought Ser.). 2000. pap. write for info. (*1-55963-786-2*) Island Pr.

Ackerman, Frank. Reaganomics: Rhetoric vs. Reality. LC 82-80689. 166p. 1982. 35.00 (*0-89608-142-7*); pap. 7.50 (*0-89608-141-9*) South End Pr.

— Why Do We Recycle? Markets, Values, & Public Policy. 180p. (C). 1997. pap. 14.95 (*1-55963-505-3*) Island Pr.

***Ackerman, Frank, et al, eds.** The Changing Nature of Work. LC 98-35988. (Frontier Issues in Economic Thought Ser.: Vol. 4). 432p. 1998. text 60.00 (*1-55963-665-3*); pap. text 35.00 (*1-55963-666-1*) Island Pr.

Ackerman, Frank, et al, eds. Human Well-Being & Economic Goals. LC 97-36687. (Frontier Issues in Economic Thought Ser.: Vol. 3). 432p. 1997. text 50.00 (*1-55963-560-6*); pap. text 30.00 (*1-55963-561-4*) Island Pr.

Ackerman, G. P. Traffic School Home Study Booklet: California. (Illus.). 70p. 1999. pap. 19.95 (*0-9670958-0-8*) Zayco Inc.

Ackerman, Gerald M., jt. auth. see Zafran, Eric M.

Ackerman, Grant R., ed. U. N. Convention on Contracts for the International Sale of Goods Annotated. 1992. ring bd. 425.00 (*0-685-69647-2*, CISG) Warren Gorham & Lamont.

Ackerman, Hal. Wearable Parables: Proverbs for Program People. rev. ed. 1994. pap. 3.50 (*0-89230-247-X*) Do It Now.

Ackerman, Herbert S. Bogert, Five Bogert Families: Descendants of Evert, Jan Laurencz, Cornelis, Guysbert, & Harmense Myndertse Bogert. 528p. 1993. reprint ed. pap. 78.00 (*0-8328-3569-2*); reprint ed. lib. bdg. 88.00 (*0-8328-3568-4*) Higginson Bk Co.

— Bogert, More Bogert Families: Descendants of Cornelise Jansen, Gysbert Uyten, & Henry Bogert, with Other Bogert Families. 430p. 1993. reprint ed. pap. 66.00 (*0-8328-3567-6*); reprint ed. lib. bdg. 76.00 (*0-8328-3566-8*) Higginson Bk Co.

Ackerman, J. L. & Ellingson, W. A., eds. Advanced Tomographic Imaging Methods for the Analysis of Materials Vol. 217: Materials Research Society Symposium Proceedings. 219p. 1991. text 58.00 (*1-55899-109-3*) Materials Res.

Ackerman, James. Palladio. 1974. pap. 13.95 (*0-14-013500-6*, Viking) Viking Penguin.

Ackerman, James D. An Orchid Flora of Puerto Rico & the Virgin Islands. LC 95-3660. (Memoirs Ser.: Vol. 73). (ENG & SPA.). 1995. 35.00 (*0-89327-394-5*) NY Botanical.

Ackerman, James D. & Del Castillo De Mayada, Maruja. The Orchids of Puerto Rico & the Virgin Islands: Orquideas de Puerto Rico y las Islas Virgenes. (ENG & SPA., Illus.). 168p. 1993. 39.95 (*0-8477-2342-9*) U of PR Pr.

Ackerman, James S. The Architecture of Michelangelo. 2nd ed. LC 85-8671. (Illus.). 364p. 1986. pap. text 24.00 (*0-226-00240-3*) U Ch Pr.

— Distance Points: Studies in Theory & Renaissance Art & Architecture. (Illus.). 561p. 1994. pap. text 32.50 (*0-262-51077-4*) MIT Pr.

— Natural Sciences & the Arts: Aspects of Interaction from the Renaissance to the 20th Century. (Illus.). 178p. 1985. pap. text 47.50 (*91-554-1658-6*) Coronet Bks.

— The Villa: Form & Ideology of Country Houses. (A. W. Mellon Lectures in the Fine Arts, 1989: Vol. XXXV, No. 34). (Illus.). 304p. 1990. pap. text 35.00 (*0-691-00295-9*, Pub. by Princeton U Pr) Cal Prin Full Svc.

Ackerman, James S., et al. Teaching the Old Testament in English Classes. LC 72-93907. (Indiana University English Curriculum Studies). 511p. reprint ed. pap. 158.50 (*0-608-18244-3*, 205669100081) Bks Demand.

Ackerman, Jan. Fanners of the Flame. (Illus.). (Orig.). 1986. pap. 5.95 (*0-9616199-0-2*) J Ackerman.

Ackerman, Jane, tr. John of the Cross, the Living Flame of Love: Versions A & B. LC 94-31299. (Medieval & Renaissance Texts & Studies: Vol. 135).Tr. of LLama de Amor ViVa. 256p. 1997. reprint ed. 28.00 (*0-86698-143-8*, MR135) MRTS.

Ackerman, Janice S. Craft Cord Corral: Bead Stringing Projects for Everyone. Knight, Denise, ed. LC 94-72284. (Illus.). 52p. (Orig.). 1995. pap., per. 8.95 (*0-943604-45-1*, BOO/30) Eagles View.

Ackerman, Jay, jt. auth. see Heinick, Rick.

Ackerman, Jennifer. Longest Thread. 2001. 24.95 (*0-670-86063-8*) Viking Penguin.

— Notes from the Shore. 208p. 1996. pap. 11.95 (*0-14-017788-4*, Penguin Bks) Viking Penguin.

Ackerman, Jennifer G., ed. The Curious Naturalist. (Illus.). 1991. 41.95 (*0-87044-862-5*) Natl Geog.

Ackerman, Jerrold & Lipsitz, Lawrence, eds. Instructional Television: Status & Directions. LC 76-54241. (Illus.). 240p. 1977. 34.95 (*0-87778-096-X*) Educ Tech Pubns.

Ackerman, Jerry. Driver's Manual after You Get Your Driver's License. (Illus.). 22p. 1997. mass mkt. write for info. (*0-9659601-0-2*) Acks Seven.

Ackerman, John. Dylan Thomas: His Life & Work. 1996. pap. 17.95 (*0-333-63404-7*) St Martin.

— Finding Your Way: Personalized Practices for Spiritual Growth Through the Myers-Briggs Type Indicator. pap. 10.50 (*1-56699-113-7*, OD95) Alban Inst.

— Spiritual Awakening: A Guide to Spiritual Life in Congregations. LC 94-78335. 154p. 1994. pap. 14.75 (*1-56699-135-8*, AL156) Alban Inst.

— To Catch a Flying Star: A Scientific Theory of UFO's. (Illus.). 150p. 1989. pap. 15.00 (*0-912183-03-9*) Univelt Inc.

— Up the Lamb. 200p. 1998. 25.95 (*1-85411-187-6*, Pub. by Seren Bks) Dufour.

— Welsh Dylan. 160p. 1997. pap. 19.95 (*1-85411-179-5*, Pub. by Seren Bks) Dufour.

Ackerman, John, jt. auth. see Flower, Linda.

Ackerman, John, ed. see Thomas, Dylan.

Ackerman, Joseph, ed. see Symposium on Land Economics Research Staff.

Ackerman, K. Practical Handbook of Warehousing. 3rd ed. (Illus.). 612p. (C). (gr. 13). 1990. mass mkt. 84.95 (*0-412-09701-X*) Chapman & Hall.

Ackerman, Karen. Araminta's Paint Box. LC 88-35033. (Illus.). 32p. (J). (gr. 1-3). 1998. pap. text 5.99 (*0-689-82091-7*) Aladdin.

— Bingleman's Midway. LC 94-79154. (Illus.). 32p. (J). (gr. 2-5). 1995. 14.95 (*1-56397-366-9*) Boyds Mills Pr.

***Ackerman, Karen.** By the Dawn's Early Light. LC 92-35633. (Illus.). 32p. (J). (gr. k-3). 1999. pap. 5.99 (*0-689-82481-5*) Aladdin.

Ackerman, Karen. By the Dawn's Early Light: Al Amanecer. Ada, Alma F., tr. LC 93-34815. (ENG & SPA., Illus.). 32p. (J). (ps-3). 1994. 16.00 (*0-689-31788-3*); 14.95 (*0-689-31917-7*) Atheneum Yung Read.

— In the Park with Dad. (Illus.). 29p. (J). (ps-2). 1996. pap. 5.95 (*0-8198-3669-9*) Pauline Bks.

— The Leaves in October. LC 90-550. 128p. (J). (gr. 3-7). 1991. 13.95 (*0-689-31583-X*) Atheneum Yung Read.

— The Leaves in October. (J). 1991. 9.09 (*0-606-05420-0*, Pub. by Turtleback) Demco.

— The Night Crossing. (Illus.). 1995. pap. 4.50 (*0-679-87040-7*) Random.

— The Night Crossing. (J). 1995. 9.70 (*0-606-07944-0*, Pub. by Turtleback) Demco.

— Song & Dance Man. LC 87-3200. (Illus.). 32p. (J). (ps-2). 1988. lib. bdg. 16.99 (*0-394-99330-6*, Pub. by Knopf Bks Yng Read) Random.

— Song & Dance Man. 1992. 12.19 (*0-606-01543-4*, Pub. by Turtleback) Demco.

— This Old House. LC 91-20449. (Illus.). 40p. (J). (ps-1). 1992. lib. bdg. 14.95 (*0-689-31741-7*) Atheneum Yung Read.

— The Tin Heart. LC 89-6528. (Illus.). 32p. (J). (gr. 1-3). 1990. 13.95 (*0-689-31461-2*) Atheneum Yung Read.

***Ackerman, Karl.** Dear Will: A Novel. (Illus.). 320p. 2000. 23.50 (*0-684-83953-9*) S&S Trade.

Ackerman, Karl. The Patron Saint of Unmarried Women. large type ed. LC 94-28583. 399p. 1994. lib. bdg. 21.95 (*0-7862-0273-4*) Thorndike Pr.

Ackerman, Karl, ed. see Stephens, John L.

Ackerman, Kenneth B. Warehousing Profitably--An Update. 79.75 (*0-9631776-3-X*) K B Ackerman.

Ackerman, Kenneth B. Warehousing Profitably A Manager's Guide. (Illus.). 1994. text 69.75 (*0-9631776-1-3*) K B Ackerman.

— Words of Warehousing 2. 1995. pap. text 39.00 (*0-9631776-2-1*) K B Ackerman.

Ackerman, Kenneth B. & Searl, Hal. Warehousing Fundamentals. 398.00 (*0-9631776-4-8*) K B Ackerman.

Ackerman, Kenneth D. Gold Ring. 1990. pap. 12.95 (*0-88730-436-2*, HarpBusn) HarpInfo.

***Ackerman, Laurence D.** Identity Is Destiny: Leadership & the Roots of Value Creation. LC HD59.2.A28 1999. 250p. 2000. 27.95 (*1-57675-068-X*) Berrett-Koehler.

Ackerman, Lillian A., ed. A Song to the Creator: Traditional Arts of Native American Women of the Plateau. LC 96-32388. (Illus.). 132p. 1996. 29.95 (*0-8061-2876-3*); pap. 18.95 (*0-8061-2877-1*) U of Okla Pr.

An Asterisk (*) at the beginning of an entry indicates that the title is appearing for the first time.

Ackerman, Lillian A., jt. ed. see Klein, Laura F.

Ackerman, Lowell. The Biology, Husbandry & Health Care of Reptiles, 3 vols. (Illus.). 1997. text 195.00 (*0-7938-0504-X*, TS-300) TFH Pubns.

— Cat Behavior. LC 98-162141. (Illus.). 320p. 1996. 29.95 (*0-7938-0634-8*, TS-253) TFH Pubns.

— Dr. Ackerman's Book of the Boxer: AKC Rank #13. (Dr. Ackerman's Ser.). (Illus.). 96p. Date not set. 9.95 (*0-7938-2554-7*, BB-105) TFH Pubns.

— Dr. Ackerman's Book of the Chinese Shar Pei: AKC Rank #31. (Dr. Ackerman's Ser.). (Illus.). 96p. Date not set. 9.95 (*0-7938-2561-X*, BB-112) TFH Pubns.

— Dr. Ackerman's Book of the Collie: AKC Rank #29. (Dr. Ackerman's Ser.). (Illus.). 96p. Date not set. 9.95 (*0-7938-2558-X*, BB-109) TFH Pubns.

— Dr. Ackerman's Book of the Cocker Spaniel: AKC Rank #8. LC 98-163057. (Dr. Ackerman's Ser.). (Illus.). 96p. Date not set. 9.95 (*0-7938-2553-9*, BB-104) TFH Pubns.

— Dr. Ackerman's Book of the Dachshund. (Dr. Ackerman's Ser.). (Illus.). 96p. Date not set. 9.96 (*0-7938-2564-4*, BB-115) TFH Pubns.

— Dr. Ackerman's Book of the Dalmatian: AKC Rank #15. LC 98-163055. (Dr. Ackerman's Ser.). (Illus.). 96p. Date not set. 9.95 (*0-7938-2560-1*, BB-111) TFH Pubns.

— Dr. Ackerman's Book of the Doberman Pinscher: AKC Rank #20. LC 98-163054. (Dr. Ackerman's Ser.). (Illus.). 96p. Date not set. 9.95 (*0-7938-2556-3*, BB-107) TFH Pubns.

— Dr. Ackerman's Book of the German Shepherd: AKC Rank #3. LC 98-163056. (Dr. Ackerman's Ser.). (Illus.). 96p. Date not set. 9.95 (*0-7938-2551-2*, BB-102) TFH Pubns.

— Dr. Ackerman's Book of the Golden Retriever: AKC Rank #4. (Dr. Ackerman's Ser.). (Illus.). 96p. Date not set. 9.95 (*0-7938-2552-0*, BB-103) TFH Pubns.

— Dr. Ackerman's Book of the Great Dane: AKC Rank #32. (Dr. Ackerman's Ser.). (Illus.). 96p. Date not set. 9.95 (*0-7938-2565-2*, BB-116) TFH Pubns.

— Dr. Ackerman's Book of the Labrador Retriever: AKC Rank #1. (Dr. Ackerman's Ser.). (Illus.). 96p. Date not set. 9.95 (*0-7938-2562-8*, BB-113) TFH Pubns.

— Dr. Ackerman's Book of the Poodle: AKC Rank #6. (Dr. Ackerman's Ser.). (Illus.). 96p. Date not set. 9.95 (*0-7938-2557-1*, BB-108) TFH Pubns.

— Dr. Ackerman's Book of the Rottweiler: AKC Rank #2. LC 98-167124. (Dr. Ackerman's Ser.). (Illus.). 96p. Date not set. 9.95 (*0-7938-2550-4*, BB-101) TFH Pubns.

— Dr. Ackerman's Book of the Shih Tzu: AKC Rank #11. (Dr. Ackerman's Ser.). (Illus.). 96p. Date not set. 9.95 (*0-7938-2563-6*, BB-114) TFH Pubns.

— Dr. Ackerman's Book of the West Highland White Terrier: AKC Rank #36. (Dr. Ackerman's Ser.). (Illus.). 96p. Date not set. 9.95 (*0-7938-2559-8*, BB-110) TFH Pubns.

— Dr. Ackerman's Book of the Yorkshire Terrier: AKC Rank #9. (Dr. Ackerman's Ser.). (Illus.). 96p. Date not set. 9.95 (*0-7938-2555-5*, BB-106) TFH Pubns.

— Dog Owner's Healthcare Guide. (Illus.). 432p. 1996. 39.95 (*0-7938-0183-4*, TS214) TFH Pubns.

— Guide to Skin & Haircoat Problems in Dogs. LC 93-37070. (Illus.). 192p. 1994. pap. 21.95 (*0-931866-65-0*) Alpine Pubns.

— Owner's Guide to Cat Health. (Illus.). 208p. 1996. 34.95 (*0-7938-0595-3*, TS251) TFH Pubns.

— Skin & Coat Care for Cats. LC 98-163526. (Illus.). 160p. 1996. 29.95 (*0-7938-0633-X*, TS-250) TFH Pubns.

— Skin & Coat Care for Your Dog. (Illus.). 320p. 1996. 34.95 (*0-7938-2099-5*, TS249) TFH Pubns.

Ackerman, Lowell, ed. The Biology, Husbandry & Health Care of Reptiles Vol. II: Husbandry. (Illus.). 230p. 1997. text 49.95 (*0-7938-0502-3*, TS298) TFH Pubns.

— The Biology, Husbandry & Health Care of Reptiles Vol. III: Health Care. (Illus.). 446p. 1997. text 89.95 (*0-7938-0503-1*, TS299) TFH Pubns.

— Cat Health Encyclopedia. LC 99-207040. (Illus.). 320p. 1998. 59.95 (*0-7938-0506-6*, TS-302) TFH Pubns.

— Owner's Guide to Dog Behavior. (Illus.). 288p. 1996. 29.95 (*0-7938-2094-4*, TS252) TFH Pubns.

Ackerman, Lowell, jt. auth. see Nesbitt, Gene.

Ackerman, Lowell J. Canine Nutrition: What Every Owner, Breeder, & Trainer Should Know. LC 99-21068. (Illus.). 254p. 1999. pap. 17.95 (*1-57779-015-4*) Alpine Pubns.

Ackerman, M. & Hermann, Robert. Sophus Lie's, 1880 Transformation Group Paper. LC 75-17416. (Lie Groups: History, Frontiers & Applications: No. 1). 1975. 60.00 (*0-915692-10-4*) Math Sci Pr.

Ackerman, M., jt. auth. see Hermann, Robert.

Ackerman, Marc, jt. auth. see Sobel, Dean.

Ackerman, Marc J. Does Wednesday Mean Mom's House or Dad's? Parenting Together While Living Apart. LC 96-18380. 224p. 1996. pap. 17.95 (*0-471-13048-6*) Wiley.

***Ackerman, Marc J.** Essentials of Forensic Psychological Assessment. LC 99-18558. 294p. (C). 1999. pap. 29.95 (*0-471-33186-4*) Wiley.

Ackerman, Marc J. Psychological Experts in Personal Injury Actions, 1. 3rd ed. LC 98-193425. 1156p. 1998. boxed set. write for info. (*1-56706-921-5*) Panel Pubs.

***Ackerman, Marc J. & Kane, Andrew W.** Psychological Experts in Divorce Actions. 3rd ed. LC 98-194251. xxxiii, 1190 p. 1998. boxed set 148.00 (*1-56706-922-3*) Aspen Law.

Ackerman, Marjorie A. Pennsylvania. LC 93-73315. 1994. 39.95 (*1-55868-159-0*) Gr Arts Ctr Pub.

***Ackerman, Michele, et al.** "Someone Who Cares" A Guide to Hiring an In-Home Caregiver. rev. ed. (Illus.). 30p. 1998. pap. 10.00 (*0-9677434-0-0*) Ctr for Applied Gerontology.

Ackerman, Morris. Multiplex Man: And the One Penny Orange Mystery. LC 97-91725. 324p. (Orig.). 1997. pap. 9.95 (*0-9657743-0-9*) Chevy Chase.

Ackerman, N. R., et al, eds. Progress in Inflammation Research & Therapy. (Agents & Actions Supplements Ser.: Vol. 35). (Illus.). 208p. 1991. 128.50 (*0-8176-2529-1*) Birkhauser.

Ackerman, Nathan W. The Psychodynamics of Family Life: Diagnosis & Treatment of Family Relationships. LC 94-72519. 396p. 1995. pap. text 50.00 (*1-56821-341-7*) Aronson.

— Treating the Troubled Family. LC 94-71150. 320p. 1994. pap. 40.00 (*1-56821-268-2*) Aronson.

Ackerman, Ned. The Spirit Horse. LC 97-8547. 167p. (J). (gr. 5-9). 1998. 15.95 (*0-590-39650-1*) Scholastic Inc.

***Ackerman, Norman.** Fat No More: The Answer for the Dangerously Overweight. LC 99-17907. (Illus.). 250p. 1999. pap. 18.95 (*1-57392-692-2*) Prometheus Bks.

Ackerman, Norman. Radiology & Ultrasound of Urogenital Diseases in Dogs & Cats. LC 91-157208. (Illus.). 191p. reprint ed. pap. 59.30 (*0-608-08711-4*, 206927900003) Bks Demand.

Ackerman, Norman, jt. auth. see Burk, Ronald L.

***Ackerman, Peggy.** Bed & Breakfast U. S. A. 1999. 640p. 1999. pap. 19.95 (*0-452-28045-1*, Plume) Dutton Plume.

Ackerman, Peggy. Bed & Breakfast U. S. A. 1998. 784p. 1998. pap. 17.95 (*0-452-27874-0*, Plume) Dutton Plume.

***Ackerman, Peter.** My Favorite Bear. (Books for Young Learners). (Illus.). 12p. (J). (gr. k-2). 1999. pap. text 5.00 (*1-57274-336-0*, A2759) R Owen Pubs.

Ackerman, Peter & Kruegler, Christopher. Strategic Nonviolent Conflict. LC 93-2870. 392p. 1993. 65.00 (*0-275-93915-4*, C3915, Praeger Pubs); pap. 25.95 (*0-275-93916-2*, B3916, Praeger Pubs) Greenwood.

Ackerman, Phillip L. Learning & Individual Differences. LC 88-16317. (Psychology Ser.). 343p. (C). 1989. pap. text 27.95 (*0-7167-1985-1*) W H Freeman.

Ackerman, Phillip L., et al, eds. Learning & Individual Differences: Process, Trait, & Content Determinants. LC 98-31084. 1998. 49.95 (*1-55798-536-7*) Am Psychol.

Ackerman, Phyllis. Tapestry, the Mirror of Civilization. LC 74-108123. reprint ed. 45.00 (*0-404-00279-X*) AMS Pr.

Ackerman, Phyllis, ed. see Pope, Arthur U.

Ackerman, R. O. The Muzzleloader's Little Library. 1994. 6.00 (*1-877704-13-X*) Pioneer Pr.

Ackerman, Richard, et al. Making Sense As a School Principal: Persisting Questions, Creative Opportunities. (Education Ser.). 207p. 1995. 29.95 (*0-7879-0164-4*) Jossey-Bass.

Ackerman, Robert. Monarch Notes on Hardy's Tess of the D'Urbervilles. (Orig.). (C). 3.95 (*0-671-00619-3*, Arco) Macmillan Gen Ref.

— Silent Sons: A Book for & About Men. 240p. 1994. per. 11.00 (*0-671-89286-X*) S&S Trade Pap.

Ackerman, Robert, tr. see De Troyes, Chretien.

Ackerman, Robert J. A Husband's Little Black Book: Common Sense, Wit & Wisdom for a Better Marriage. 160p. 1994. 20.00 (*1-55874-349-9*); pap. 6.95 (*1-55874-317-0*, 3170) Health Comm.

— Perfect Daughters: Adult Daughters of Alcoholics. 200p. 1989. pap. 8.95 (*1-55874-040-6*) Health Comm.

— A Wife's Little Red Book: Common Sense, Wit & Wisdom for a Better Marriage. 180p. 1998. 20.00 (*1-55874-553-X*); pap. 6.95 (*1-55874-552-1*) Health Comm.

Ackerman, Robert J. & Joiner, Lee M. Too Old to Cry, Too Hurt to Laugh: Abused Teens in Today's America. 140p. 1989. pap. 9.95 (*0-8306-3407-X*) McGraw-Hill Prof.

Ackerman, Robert J. & Pickering, Susan E. Before It's Too Late: Helping Women in Controlling or Abusive Relationships. 175p. (Orig.). 1995. pap. 9.95 (*1-55874-345-6*, 3456) Health Comm.

Ackerman, Robert W. The Social Challenge to Business. LC 75-8921. 363p. reprint ed. pap. 112.60 (*0-7837-3833-1*, 204365400010) Bks Demand.

Ackerman, Robert W. & Dahood, Roger, eds. Ancrene Riwle: Introduction & Part One. LC 83-21987. (Medieval & Renaissance Texts & Studies: Vol. 31). 128p. 1989. reprint ed. 19.00 (*0-86698-055-5*, MR31) MRTS.

Ackerman, Robert W., jt. auth. see Toole, Virginia G.

Ackerman, Roger, et al. Process Quality Management & Improvement Guidelines. 2nd rev. ed. Annitto, Susan, ed. (AT&T Quality Library). (Illus.). 102p. (Orig.). 1988. reprint ed. pap. 29.95 (*0-932764-32-0*, 500-049) AT&T Customer Info.

— Process Quality Management & Improvement Guidelines. 2nd rev. ed. Annitto, Susan, ed. (AT&T Quality Library). (Illus.). 102p. (Orig.). 1988. pap. 24.95 (*0-614-07666-8*) AT&T Customer Info.

Ackerman, Ruth C. A Supplement to Twists & Turns, a Mother's Caring Journey: Two Children with Schizophrenia. (Illus.). 6p. 1997. pap. 3.00 (*0-9637493-1-5*) Paths of Life.

— Twists & Turns, a Mother's Caring Journey - Two Children with Schizophrenia. LC 93-94015. (Illus.). 149p. (Orig.). 1993. pap. 12.00 (*0-9637493-0-7*) Paths of Life.

Ackerman, Sandra. Discovering the Brain. 194p. 1991. 22.95 (*0-309-04529-0*) Natl Acad Pr.

Ackerman, Sheila. Just One Kiss. (Rainbow Romances Ser.: No. 905). 160p. 1994. 14.95 (*0-7090-4980-3*) Parkwest Pubns.

— Just One Kiss. large type ed. (Rainbow Romance Ser.). 256p. 1995. pap. 14.95 (*0-7089-7736-7*) Parkwest Pubns.

— Secrets from the Past. (Rainbow Romances Ser.). 160p. 1993. 14.95 (*0-7090-4916-1*) Parkwest Pubns.

— Secrets from the Past. large type ed. (Romance Ser.). 1994. pap. 16.99 (*0-7089-7612-3*, Linford) Ulverscroft.

Ackerman, Susan. Warrior, Dancer, Seductress, Queen: Women in Judges & Biblical Israel. LC 97-37992. (Anchor Bible Reference Library Ser.). 368p. 1998. 36.95 (*0-385-48424-0*) Doubleday.

Ackerman, Susan E., jt. auth. see Lee, Raymond L.

Ackerman, Susan Y. The Flying Pie & Other Stories. LC 96-39. 64p. (Orig.). (J). (gr. 1-5). 1996. pap. 10.99 (*0-8361-9032-7*) Herald Pr.

Ackerman, Terrence F. & Strong, Carson. A Casebook of Medical Ethics. 264p. 1989. pap. text 27.50 (*0-19-503917-3*) OUP.

Ackerman, Thomas. Guide to Careers in Federal Law Enforcement: Profiles of 225 High-Powered Positions & Surefire Tactics for Getting Hired. 280p. 1999. pap. 29.95 (*1-890394-33-5*, Sage Creek) Rhodes & Easton.

Ackerman, Walter. Out of Our People's Past: Sources for the Study of Jewish History. 1978. 7.50 (*0-8381-0221-2*) USCJE.

Ackerman, Wendayne, tr. see Kalff, Dora M.

Ackerman, William E. & Huneja, Mushtaque M. Obstetric Anesthesia Pearls. (Illus.). 280p. (C). 1992. pap. 37.95 (*0-8385-7173-5*, A7173-6, Apple Lange Med) McGraw.

Ackermann, A. & Diehl, V., eds. Malignancies of the Genitourinary Tract. LC 92-49944. 1993. write for info. (*3-540-54433-X*) Spr-Verlag.

Ackermann, Alfred M. Fishes (Tilapia) Index of New Information & Research Bible. rev. ed. 150p. 1997. 47.50 (*0-7883-1576-5*); pap. 44.50 (*0-7883-1577-3*) ABBE Pubs Assn.

***Ackermann, Alice.** Making Peace Prevail: Preventing Violent Conflict in Macedonia. 272p. 1999. 45.00 (*0-8156-2812-9*); pap. text 24.95 (*0-8156-0602-8*) Syracuse U Pr.

Ackermann, Barbara. You the Mayor? The Education of a City Politician. LC 88-14643. 281p. 1989. 57.95 (*0-86569-178-9*, T178, Auburn Hse) Greenwood.

Ackermann, D., jt. ed. see Tauber, Michael J.

Ackermann, Ernest. Learning to Use the WWW: Netscape 4. 1997. text 20.95 (*1-887902-28-7*) Franklin Beedle.

Ackermann, Ernest. Searching & Researching on the Internet & World Wide Web: The Information Specialist's Guide. 444p. 1998. pap. 29.95 (*1-887902-31-7*) Franklin Beedle.

***Ackermann, Ernest & Hartman, Karen.** The Information Searcher's Guide to Searching & Researching on the Internet & World Wide Web. 2nd ed. 436p. 2000. pap. 29.95 (*1-887902-58-9*, Pub. by Franklin Beedle) IPG Chicago.

— Internet & Web Essentials: What You Need to Know. (C). 2000. text. write for info. (*1-887902-40-6*) Franklin Beedle.

***Ackermann, Ernest & Hartman, Karen, eds.** Internet Today: Email, Searching & the World Wide Web. (Illus.). 286p. 1999. 55.00 (*1-57958-194-3*) Fitzroy Dearborn.

Ackermann, Ernest C. & Hartman, Karen. The Information Specialist's Guide to Searching & Researching on the Internet & the World Wide Web. 444p. 1998. 45.00 (*1-57958-117-X*) Fitzroy Dearborn.

***Ackermann, Ernest C. & Hartman, Karen.** The Information Specialist's Guide to Searching & Researching on the Internet & the World Wide Web. ed. LC 99-88539. 2000. write for info. (*1-887902-48-1*) Franklin Beedle.

— Internet Today: Email, Searching & the World Wide Web. LC 98-55746. 286p. 1999. text 35.99 (*1-887902-43-0*) Franklin Beedle.

— Searching & Researching on the Internet & the World Wide Web. LC 97-46514. 1997. pap. 29.95 (*1-887902-26-0*) Franklin Beedle.

***Ackermann, Ernest C. & Hartman, Karen.** Searching & Researching on the Internet & the World Wide Web. 486p. (C). 2000. pap. 29.95 (*1-887902-56-2*) Franklin Beedle.

***Ackermann, Ernest C., et al.** AP Computer Science A & AB. LC 98-66313. (Best Test Preparation for the Advanced Placement Examination Ser.). (Illus.). 451p. 1999. pap. 19.95 (*0-87891-278-9*) Res & Educ.

Ackermann, Fran, jt. auth. see Eden, Colin.

***Ackermann, Friedhelm.** Soziale Arbeit Zwischen Studium und Beruf: Eine Qualitativ-Empirische Studie Zur Berufseinmundung Von Absolventinnen Des Fachbereichs Sozialwesen. (GER., Illus.). 140p. 1999. 29.00 (*3-631-34648-4*) P Lang Pubng.

— Der Steininge Weg Zur Fachlichkeit Handlungskompetenz in der Sozialen Arbeit. 256p. 29.80 (*3-487-10960-3*, Pub. by G Olms Verlag) Lubrecht & Cramer.

Ackermann, H. & Dubow, M. Viruses of Prokaryotes: General Properties of Bacteriophages, Vol. 1. LC 87-9407. 216p. 1987. reprint ed. 123.00 (*0-8493-6056-0*, CRC Reprint) Franklin.

— Viruses of Prokaryotes: General Properties of Bacteriophages, Vol. 2. LC 87-9407. 256p. 1987. reprint ed. 145.00 (*0-8493-6057-9*, CRC Reprint) Franklin.

Ackermann, Hans-W. & Dubow, Michael S., eds. Viruses of Prokaryotes, 2 vols. 1987. 268.00 (*0-8493-6054-4*, QR342, CRC Reprint) Franklin.

— Viruses of Prokaryotes, 2 vols., Vol. I. 224p. 1987. write for info. (*0-318-62593-8*, CRC Reprint) Franklin.

— Viruses of Prokaryotes, 2 vols., Vol. II. 256p. 1987. write for info. (*0-318-62594-6*, CRC Reprint) Franklin.

Ackermann, Hans W., et al. Virus Life in Diagram. LC 98-149100. (Illus.). 232p. 1998. boxed set 74.95 (*0-8493-3126-9*) CRC Pr.

Ackermann, Hans-Wolfgang & Berthiaume, Laurent, eds. Atlas of Virus Diagrams. (Illus.). 160p. 1995. boxed set 84.95 (*0-8493-2457-2*, 2457) CRC Pr.

Ackermann, J. Sampled-Data Control Systems. LC 85-10012. (Communications & Control Engineering Ser.). (Illus.). 620p. 1985. 178.95 (*0-387-15610-0*) Spr-Verlag.

Ackermann, Jean. A Pride of Heroes: Candid Celebrations. v, 22p. (Orig.). (J). (gr. 8-12). 1984. pap. 6.00 (*0-9614506-0-6*) Box Four Twenty-Four.

Ackermann, Joan. The Batting Cage. 1999. pap. 5.25 (*0-8222-1654-X*) Dramatists Play.

— Marcus Is Walking: Scenes from the Road. 1999. pap. 5.25 (*0-8222-1655-8*) Dramatists Play.

— Off the Map. LC 99-222949. 1998. pap. 5.25 (*0-8222-1591-8*) Dramatists Play.

***Ackermann, Joan.** Summer Breeze. 2000. write for info. (*1-58235-568-1*) Watermrk Pr.

Ackermann, Jurgen, et al. Robust Control: Systems with Uncertain Physical Parameters. LC 93-27559. (Communications & Control Engineering Ser.). 1997. 109.00 (*0-387-19843-1*) Spr-Verlag.

Ackermann, Paul, et al, eds. Foods & Packaging Materials: Chemical Interactions. (Special Publication Ser.: No. 162). 250p. 1995. 79.95 (*0-85404-720-4*, R4720) CRC Pr.

Ackermann, Paul K., ed. see Brecht, Bertolt.

Ackermann, Paul K., ed. see Durrenmatt, Friedrich.

Ackermann, Paul K., ed. see Frisch, Max.

Ackermann, Peter. Kumiuta: Traditional Songs for Certificates - A Study of Their Texts & Implications. Schweiz, ed. (Swiss Asian Studies. Monographs: No. 10). 602p. 1990. pap. 122.80 (*3-261-04238-9*) P Lang Pubng.

Ackermann, Peter, ed. Hall 13: Expo 2000, Hanover. (Illus.). 64p. 1999. 29.95 (*3-7913-2018-1*) te Neues.

Ackermann, R. Therapie Urologischer Tumoren. (Illus.). 84p. 1991. pap. 35.00 (*3-8055-5294-7*) S Karger.

Ackermann, R. & Schroder, F. H., eds. Prostatic Hyperplasia: Etiology, Surgical & Conservative Management. (New Developments in Biosciences Ser.: No. 5). x, 154p. (C). 1989. pap. text 41.45 (*0-89925-528-0*) De Gruyter.

Ackermann, R., et al. Therapy of Urological Cancer.Tr. of Therapie Urologischer Tumoren. (Illus.). viii, 178p. 1991. pap. 35.00 (*3-8055-5369-2*) S Karger.

Ackermann, R. A. Cryogenic Regenerative Heat Exchangers. LC 97-13652. (International Cryogenics Monograph Ser.). (Illus.). 244p. (C). 1997. 89.50 (*0-306-45449-1*, Plenum Trade) Perseus Pubng.

Ackermann, Richard, et al. Environmental Action Programme for Central & Eastern Europe: Setting Priorities. LC 96-10238. (Report for the Environmental Action Programme for Central & Eastern Europe Ser.). 144p. 1998. pap. 22.00 (*0-8213-3179-5*, 13179) World Bank.

Ackermann, Rick & Buxton, Kathryn. The Coast of Maine Book: A Complete Guide. 4th ed. LC 98-53100. (Great Destinations Ser.). (Illus.). 320p. 1999. pap. 17.95 (*1-58157-006-6*) Berkshire Hse.

Ackermann, Robert J. A Data, Instruments & Theory: A Dialectical Approach to Understanding Science. LC 84-15938. 229p. 1985. reprint ed. pap. 71.00 (*0-608-02514-3*, 206315800004) Bks Demand.

— Heterogeneities: Race, Gender, Class, Nation, & State. LC 95-42343. 240p. 1996. 45.00 (*1-55849-013-2*); pap. 17.95 (*1-55849-014-0*) U of Mass Pr.

— Nietzsche: A Frenzied Look. LC 90-31323. 224p. 1990. 30.00 (*0-87023-722-5*) U of Mass Pr.

— Nietzsche: A Frenzied Look. LC 90-31323. 1993. pap. 16.95 (*0-87023-841-8*) U of Mass Pr.

— Religion As Critique. LC 84-16471. 184p. 1985. lib. bdg. 27.50 (*0-87023-462-5*) U of Mass Pr.

— Wittgenstein's City. LC 87-10895. 288p. (Orig.). (C). 1988. lib. bdg. 32.50 (*0-87023-589-3*) U of Mass Pr.

Ackermann, Roy L. Bildung & Verbildung in the Prose Fiction Works of Otto Julius Bierbaum. (European University Studies: German Language & Literature: Ser. 1, Vol. 101). 95p. 1974. pap. 24.80 (*3-261-01424-5*) P Lang Pubng.

Ackermann, Rudolph. Ackermann's Costume Plates: Women's Fashions in England, 1818-1828. Blum, Stella, ed. (Illus.). 120p. 1979. pap. 8.95 (*0-486-23690-0*) Dover.

Ackermann, Rudolph, ed. Neoclassical Ornamental Designs. LC 96-13357. (Pictorial Archive Ser.). (Illus.). 128p. 1996. 9.95 (*0-486-29224-X*) Dover.

Ackermann, William C., et al, eds. Man-Made Lakes: Their Problems & Environmental Effects. LC 73-86486. (Geophysical Monograph Ser.: Vol. 17). (Illus.). 847p. 1973. 35.00 (*0-87590-017-8*) Am Geophysical.

Ackermans, Gian & Ostermann, Ursula. Called by God's Goodness: A History of the Sisters of St. Francis of Penance & Christian Charity in the Twentieth Century. Serbacki, Mary, ed. LC 97-62073. (Illus.). 337p. 1997. pap. text 23.00 (*0-9661798-0-3*) Sisters St Francis.

Ackern, K. Van, see Van Ackern, K.

Ackers, Louise & Abbott, Pamela. Social Policy for Nurses & the Caring Professions. LC 95-49768. (Social Science for Nurses & the Caring Professions Ser.). 192p. (C). 1996. 88.00 (*0-335-19360-9*); pap. 23.95 (*0-335-19359-5*) OpUniv Pr.

Ackers, Peter, et al. Weirs & Flumes for Low Measurement. fac. ed. LC 78-317. (Illus.). 371p. 1978. pap. 115.10 (*0-7837-7669-1*, 204742200007) Bks Demand.

Ackerson, Anne W., ed. see Richards, Caroline C.

Ackerson, B. J. Phase Transitions in Colloidal Suspensions. 250p. 1990. text 530.00 (*0-677-26090-3*) Gordon & Breach.

Ackerson, Robert. Chrysler 300: America's Original Musclecar. (Illus.). 160p. 1996. 29.95 (*1-874105-65-0*, Pub. by Vloce Pub) Motorbooks Intl.

— Ford F100/F150 Pickup. (Illus.). 160p. 1997. 24.95 (*1-874105-83-9*, Pub. by Vloce Pub) Motorbooks Intl.

— Jeep. (Illus.). 160p. 1998. pap. 24.95 (*1-901295-41-9*, Pub. by Vloce Pub) Motorbooks Intl.

A

Ackerson, Robert C. Chevrolet High Performance. LC 94-77504. (Illus.). 608p. 1994. pap. 24.95 (*0-87341-326-1*, CH01) Krause Pubns.

*Ackerson, Robert C. Standard Catalog of 4 X 4's: A Comprehensive Guide to Four-Wheel Drive Vehicles Including Trucks. 2nd rev. ed. LC 92-71443. (Illus.). 736p. 2000. pap. 34.95 (*0-87341-899-9*, FX02) Krause Pubns.

Ackerson, Robert C. Standard Catalog of 4 x 4's: 1945-1993. LC 92-71443. (Illus.). 528p. 1993. pap. 24.95 (*0-87341-203-6*, FX01) Krause Pubns.

Ackerson, Robert C., jt. auth. see Kimes, Beverly R.

Ackerstein, Joan. The Americans with Disabilities Act: What Supervisors Need to Know. LC 93-10689. (Business Skills Express Ser.). 128p. 1993. pap. 10.95 (*1-55623-889-4*, Irwn Prfssnl) McGraw-Hill Prof.

Ackert. Facts & Figures. 3rd ed. (C). 1999. pap., teacher ed. 10.00 (*0-8384-0013-2*) Heinle & Heinle.

— Insights & Ideas. 2nd ed. 1995. teacher ed. 4.50 (*0-15-599904-4*) Harcourt Coll Pubs.

Ackert, Harriet R. Prodigal Souls: A Novel. LC 97-32023. 240p. 1998. pap. 14.95 (*1-56474-248-2*) Fithian Pr.

***Ackert, John J.** Pedro & the Irish Treasure. LC 99-64394. 1999. 25.00 (*0-7388-0500-9*); pap. 18.00 (*0-7388-0501-7*) Xlibris Corp.

Ackert, Patricia. Cause & Effect. 264p. (J). 1986. pap., teacher ed. 7.95 (*0-8384-2810-X*, Newbury) Heinle & Heinle.

— Cause & Effect. 2nd ed. (College ESL Ser.). (J). 1994. pap., teacher ed. 7.95 (*0-8384-3817-2*) Heinle & Heinle.

— Cause & Effect: Intermediate Reading Practice. 3rd ed. 1999. pap. text 26.95 (*0-8384-0874-5*) Heinle & Heinle.

— Concepts & Comments: A Reader for Students of English as a Second Language. 2nd ed. (C). 1986. pap. text, teacher ed. 3.00 (*0-03-071842-2*) Harcourt Coll Pubs.

— Facts & Figures. 261p. 1980. pap. 18.75 (*0-8384-2780-4*) Heinle & Heinle.

— Facts & Figures. (J). 1986. pap., teacher ed. 6.50 (*0-8384-2787-1*) Heinle & Heinle.

— Facts & Figures. 2nd ed. (College ESL Ser.). (J). 1994. mass mkt., teacher ed. 7.95 (*0-8384-3818-0*) Heinle & Heinle.

— Facts & Figures: Basic Reading Practice. 3rd ed. LC 98-43208. 1999. pap. text 26.95 (*0-8384-0865-6*) Heinle & Heinle.

— Insights & Ideas. 2nd ed. (C). 1995. pap. text 21.50 (*0-15-599719-X*, Pub. by Harcourt Coll Pubs) Harcourt.

— Please Write: A Beginning Composition Text for Students of ESL. (Illus.). 192p. (C). 1995. pap. text 28.60 (*0-13-683418-3*) P-H.

Ackert, Patricia & De Navarro, Nicki G. Facts & Figures: Basic Reading Practice. 2nd ed. LC 93-27954. 270p. (J). 1993. mass mkt. 25.95 (*0-8384-3813-X*) Heinle & Heinle.

Ackert, Patricia & Giroux De Navarro, Nikki S. Cause & Effect: Intermediate Reading Practice. 2nd ed. LC 93-42859. 225p. (J). 1994. pap. 25.95 (*0-8384-3814-8*) Heinle & Heinle.

Ackert, Patricia & Nebel, Anne. Concepts & Comments. 2nd ed. LC 96-80057. 256p. (C). 1997. pap. text 22.00 (*0-15-599718-1*, Pub. by Harcourt Coll Pubs) Harcourt.

Ackery, P. R., et al, eds. Carcasson's African Butterflies: An Annotated Catalogue of the Papilionidea & Hesperiaidea of the Afrotropical Region. (Illus.). 816p. 1995. 140.00 (*0-643-05561-4*, Pub. by CSIRO) Accents Pubns.

Ackery, P. R. & Vane-Wright, Richard I. Milkweed Butterflies: Their Cladistics & Biology. LC 83-7334. (Illus.). 450p. 1984. 79.50 (*0-8014-1688-4*) Cornell U Pr.

Ackery, Phillip R., jt. auth. see Vane-Wright, Richard I.

Ackes, Alfred E. The United States & the Global Struggle for Minerals. LC 78-11082. 365p. 1979. pap. 113.20 (*0-7837-8955-6*, 204966800002) Bks Demand.

Ackinclose, Timothy. Sabres & Pistols: The Civil War Career of Colonel Harry Gilmor, CSA. LC 97-120635. (Illus.). 288p. 1997. 25.00 (*1-879664-30-5*) Stan Clark Military.

"Harry Gilmor is one of the more interesting players in the sub-plot of partisan warfare along the upper Potomac. Tim Ackinclose's study of Gilmor is both scholarly & well written. It is a valuable contribution to Civil War literature."--Ted Alexander, Park Historian, Antietam National Battlefield. "Colonel Harry Gilmor has been overlooked too long as the subject of in-depth attention by serious historians. Mr. Ackinclose has now filled the gap with his well-researched biography of a fascinating wartime personality. His comprehensive work immediately sets the standard against which any future Gilmor biography must be measured."--P. James Kurapka, Sons of Confederate Veterans. "Mr. Ackinclose's biography challenges previous assumptions regarding Gilmor's role in the Civil War. Using the partisan's own memoirs as a guide, the author has scrupulously examined every event & detail to reveal the true nature of Harry Gilmor's exploits. This study provides fresh insight into partisan activities during the war & makes for dramatic reading."--David Dixon, Ph.D. "Mr. Ackinclose has vividly brought to life a true hell-for-leather Confederate horse soldier. As the author demonstrates in this thoroughly researched study, Harry Gilmor embodied the 'Cavalry Spirit'."--Michael Phipps. Stan Clark Military Books, 915 Fairview Avenue, Gettysburg, PA 17325; Phone: 717-337-1728; Fax: 717-337-0581.
Publisher Paid Annotation.

Acklam. First Certifcate Gold Coursebook. 1996. pap. text. write for info. (*0-582-25300-4*, Pub. by Addison-Wesley) Longman.

***Acklam & Burgess.** First Certificate Gold Greek Companion. 1998. pap. write for info. (*0-582-28755-3*) Addison-Wesley.

Acklam, Mohamed. Pre-Intermediate Choice Workbook Without Key. 1993. pap. write for info. (*0-582-07104-6*) Addison-Wesley.

Acklan, William H. Sterope: The Veiled Pleiad. LC 78-38637. (Black Heritage Library Collection). 1977. reprint ed. 22.95 (*0-8369-8963-5*) Ayer.

Ackland. At Home with Counting. (Illus.). 48p. 1994. pap. (*0-19-838130-1*) OUP.

— At Home with Letter Forms. (Illus.). 48p. 1994. pap. (*0-19-838129-8*) OUP.

— At Home with Pattern & Shape. (Illus.). 48p. 1994. pap. (*0-19-838131-X*) OUP.

Ackland, Diana, ed. see Insight Publishing Staff.

Ackland, Jenny. At Home with Numbers. (Illus.). 48p. 1993. pap. (*0-19-838117-4*) OUP.

— At Home with Reading. (Illus.). 48p. 1993. pap. (*0-19-838115-8*) OUP.

— At Home with Shape & Size. (Illus.). 48p. 1993. pap. (*0-19-838118-2*) OUP.

— At Home with Writing. (Illus.). 48p. 1993. pap. (*0-19-838116-6*) OUP.

***Ackland, Jon.** The Complete Guide to Endurance Training. 1999. pap. 16.95 (*0-7136-5017-6*) A & C Blk.

Ackland, Joss & Bayliss, Peter. 2ND SHEPHERDS PLAY CAS. abr. ed. LC 66-1757. 1972. audio 14.00 (*0-694-50026-7*, SWC 1032, Caedmon) HarperAudio.

Ackland, Len. Making a Real Killing: Rocky Flats & the Nuclear West. LC 99-6500. 296p. 1999. 34.95 (*0-8263-1877-0*) U of NM Pr.

Ackland, Len & McGuire, Steve, eds. Assessing the Nuclear Age. LC 85-82511. (Illus.). 384p. 1986. pap. 12.95 (*0-226-03873-4*) U Ch Pr.

Ackland, Len & McGuire, Steven, eds. Assessing the Nuclear Age. LC 85-82511. (Illus.). 400p. 1986. 24.95 (*0-941682-07-2*); pap. 12.95 (*0-941682-08-0*) Educ Found for Nucl Sci.

Ackland, Michael. Henry Handel Richardson. 124p. 1997. pap. text 26.00 (*0-19-553764-5*) OUP.

— Henry Kendall: Poetry, Prose & Selected Correspondence. (Orig.). 1993. pap. 16.95 (*0-7022-2308-5*, Pub. by Univ Queensland Pr) Intl Spec Bk.

— The Man & the Myths. (Miegunyah Press Ser.: 2:2). 368p. 1995. 49.95 (*0-522-84650-5*, Pub. by Melbourne Univ Pr) Paul & Co Pubs.

Ackland, Rodney. Absolute Hell. (Oberon Bks.). 142p. 1997. pap. 14.95 (*1-870259-19-X*) Theatre Comm.

— Ackland: Plays. (Oberon Bks.). 288p. 1997. pap. 18.95 (*1-870259-54-8*) Theatre Comm.

***Ackland, Rodney.** Ackland: Plays Two. (Oberon Bks.). 2000. pap. 20.95 (*1-84002-088-1*) Theatre Comm.

Ackland, Rodney & Vari, John. Farewell, Farewell, Eugene. 1961. pap. 5.25 (*0-8222-0385-5*) Dramatists Play.

Ackland, Rodney, tr. see Ostrovsky, Alexander.

Ackland-Snow, Nicola, et al. Fly: The Art of the Club Flyer. LC 96-34302. (Illus.). 96p. 1997. 24.95 (*0-8230-1854-7*) Watsn-Guptill.

Ackland, Timothy R., jt. ed. see Carter, J. E.

Ackland, Tom. The Disobedient Servant. (Illus.). 224p. 1998. pap. 10.95 (*0-575-40036-6*, Pub. by V Gollancz) Trafalgar.

Ackland, Valentine. The Nature of the Moment. LC 73-84871. 64p. 1974. 5.00 (*0-8112-0517-7*, Pub. by New Directions) Norton.

Acklen. Word 97 Essentials (Academic) LC 97-67231. 224p. 1997. 22.99 (*1-57576-825-9*) Sams.

Acklen, Jeannette T., et al. Tennessee Records: Bible Records & Marriage Bonds. 521p. 2000. reprint ed. pap. 39.95 (*0-8063-0000-0*, 20) Clearfield Co.

Acklen, L. Using Corel Wordperfect X. 700p. 1998. 29.99 (*0-7897-1620-8*) Que.

Acklen, Laura. Teach Yourself Microsoft Office 2000 in 10 Minutes. LC 98-86839. (Teach Yourself Ser.). (Illus.). 227p. 1999. pap. 12.99 (*0-672-31431-2*) Sams.

— Windows 95 on the Job Essentials. 1995. pap. text 22.99 (*1-57576-249-8*) Que Educ & Trng.

— Windows 95 Essentials. 1995. pap. text 22.99 (*1-57576-012-6*) Que Educ & Trng.

Acklen, Laura. Windows 95 Essentials. 2nd ed. 1996. 22.99 (*1-57576-632-9*, Pub. by Macmillan) S&S Trade.

Acklen, Laura. Word for Windows 95 Essentials. 1996. pap. text 22.99 (*1-57576-016-9*) Que Educ & Trng.

— Word 6 for Windows Essentials. LC 94-69260. 184p. 1995. 22.99 (*0-7897-0108-1*) Que.

— Word 97 Essentials Level I. 1997. teacher ed. 49.99 (*1-57576-807-0*) Que Educ & Trng.

— WordPerfect 7 for Windows 95 & Windows NT: Essentoials. LC 95-74873. 1996. pap. text 22.99 (*1-57576-018-5*) Que Educ & Trng.

Acklen, Laura, jt. auth. see Person, Ron.

Acklen, Laura, jt. auth. see Reisner, Trudi.

Ackleson, Steven G., ed. Ocean Optics XIII. Vol. 2963. 922p. 1997. 141.00 (*0-8194-2367-X*) SPIE.

Ackley. Essays from Contemporary Culture. 3rd ed. (C). 1995. pap. text, teacher ed. 32.00 (*0-15-502068-4*) Harcourt Coll Pubs.

— Essays from Contemporary Cultures. 3rd ed. LC 97-71821. (C). 1997. pap. text 31.50 (*0-15-505302-7*, Pub. by Harcourt Coll Pubs) Harcourt.

— Essays from Contemporary Curriculum. 2nd ed. (C). 1994. pap. text, teacher ed. 33.75 (*0-15-502084-6*) Harcourt Coll Pubs.

***Ackley, Betty J.** Nursing Diagnosis Handbook. 4th ed. (C). 1999. text 27.95 (*0-323-00786-4*) Mosby Inc.

Ackley, Betty J., ed. see Ladwig, Gail B.

Ackley, Clifford S. Photoimage--Printmaking, 60s to 90s: Museum of Fine Arts, Boston, July 7-September 27, 1998 & Des Moines Art Center, March 5-May 9, 1999. LC 98-66291. 92 p. 1998. 14.95 (*0-87846-463-8*) Mus Fine Arts Boston.

Ackley, Clifford S., ed. see Meyerowitz, Joel.

Ackley, Daisy B. Wagon Wheels A'Rollin. (Illus.). 331p. (Orig.). 1994. pap. 26.00 (*1-55613-899-7*) Heritage Bk.

Ackley, Dana C. Breaking Free of Managed Care: A Step-by-Step Guide to Regaining Control of Your Practice. LC 96-48406. 317p. 1997. lib. bdg. 37.95 (*1-57230-105-8*, 0105) Guilford Pubns.

***Ackley, Dana C.** Breaking Free of Managed Care: A Step-by-Step Guide to Regaining Control of Your Practice. 317p. 1999. pap. text 22.95 (*1-57230-524-X*, CO524) Guilford Pubns.

Ackley, David H. A Connectionist Machine for Genetic Hillclimbing. (C). 1987. text 84.00 (*0-89838-236-X*) Kluwer Academic.

Ackley, Edith F. Marionettes: Easy to Make Fun to Use. (Illus.). (J). (gr. 5-9). 1939. lib. bdg. 12.89 (*0-397-31409-4*) HarpC Child Bks.

Ackley, Harry. Criminal Defense: Jury Instructions. 318p. 1981. ring bd. 135.00 (*1-878337-15-7*) Knowles Pub Inc.

Ackley, John B. The Church of the Word: A Comparative Study of Word, Church & Office in the Thought of Karl Rahner & Gerhard Ebeling. LC 90-35342. (American University Studies: Theology & Religion: Ser. VII, Vol. 81). XVIII, 381p. (C). 1993. text 59.95 (*0-8204-1389-5*) P Lang Pubng.

Ackley, Katherine A. Essays from Contemporary Culture. 416p. (C). 1992. pap. text 33.00 (*0-15-522891-9*) Harcourt Coll Pubs.

— Perspectives on Contemporary Issues: Reading Across the Disciplines. LC 96-76367. 128p. (C). 1996. pap. text 33.00 (*0-15-502480-9*, Pub. by Harcourt Coll Pubs); pap. text, teacher ed. 28.00 (*0-15-502487-6*) Harcourt Coll Pubs.

— Women & Violence in Literature: An Essay Collection. LC 89-36391. 350p. 1990. text 15.00 (*0-8240-0693-3*, 1271) Garland.

Ackley, Katherine A., ed. Misogyny in Literature: An Essay Collection. LC 92-5103. (Illus.). 424p. 1992. text 20.00 (*0-8240-9774-2*, H1398) Garland.

***Ackley, Katherine Anne.** Essays from Contemporary Culture. 4th ed. LC 00-24345. 2000. write for info. (*0-15-507131-9*) Harcourt Coll Pubs.

Ackley, Kathleen C., ed. Affirming Faith: A Congregation's Guide to Confirmation. LC 96-41421. 328p. (Orig.). (YA). (gr. 7-11). 1996. pap. 24.95 (*0-8298-1065-X*) Pilgrim OH.

— Affirming the Faith: A Confirmand's Journal. LC 97-219227. (Illus.). 264p. (Orig.). (YA). (gr. 7-11). 1996. pap. 10.95 (*0-8298-1066-8*) Pilgrim OH.

Ackley, Kathleen C. & Deming, Lynne M., eds. In Good Company: A Woman's Journal for Spiritual Reflection, 2000. (Illus.). 344p. 1999. spiral bd. 16.95 (*0-8298-1308-X*) Pilgrim OH.

***Ackley, Kristina M.** 100 Top Internet Job Sites: Get Wired, Get Hired in Today's New Job Market. LC 99-89877. (Savvy CareerBuilder Ser.). 2000. pap. 12.95 (*1-57023-128-1*) Impact VA.

***Ackley, Laura & Miller, Phil.** Inside 3D Studio Max 3. 1300p. 1999. pap. 59.99 incl. cd-rom (*0-7357-0905-X*) New Riders Pub.

Ackley, Peggy J. It's a Boy. (Illus.). 1993. 6.95 (*0-8378-5298-6*) Gibson.

— It's a Girl. (Illus.). 1993. 6.95 (*0-8378-5299-4*) Gibson.

Ackley, Peggy J., jt. auth. see Jacobek, Kristi.

Ackley, R. J. & Greer. Spectrovision Incorporated. 1989. pap. text 23.00 (*0-13-004656-6*) P-H.

Ackley, Robert J., et al. Spectrovision Inc. A Business Communication Simulation. (Business Communications Ser.: No. 1-321). 21p. (C). 1984. pap. text 6.00 (*0-471-87996-7*) P-H.

Ackman, Geneva & Turnipseed, Susan. South Dakota: A Journey Through Time Activity Book. 48p. (YA). (gr. 3 up). 1998. pap. text, student ed. 9.00 (*1-57579-131-5*) Pine Hill Pr.

Ackman, Lars B., ed. Memory Functioning in Dementia. LC 92-11600. xii,300p. 1992. 157.00 (*0-444-88920-5*, North Holland) Elsevier.

Ackman, R. G. Marine Biogenic Lipids, Fats, & Oils, 2 vols., Vol. I. 368p. 1989. lib. bdg. 215.95 (*0-8493-4889-7*, QH91) CRC Pr.

— Marine Biogenic Lipids, Fats, & Oils, 2 vols., Vol. II. 416p. 1989. lib. bdg. 249.00 (*0-8493-4890-0*, QH91) CRC Pr.

***Ackoff, Russell L.** Ackoff's Best: His Classic Writings on Management. LC 98-24241. 356p. 1999. 29.95 (*0-471-31634-2*) Wiley.

Ackoff, Russell L. The Art of Problem Solving: Accompanied by Ackoff's Fables. 232p. 1987. pap. 24.95 (*0-471-85808-0*) Wiley.

— Creating the Corporate Future: Plan or Be Planned For. LC 80-28005. 312p. 1981. 49.95 (*0-471-09009-3*) Wiley.

— The Democratic Corporation: A Radical Prescription for Recreating Corporate America & Rediscovering Success. LC 93-35403. (Illus.). 272p. (C). 1994. 27.50 (*0-19-508727-5*) OUP.

— The Design of Social Research. LC 53-12546. 432p. reprint ed. pap. 134.00 (*0-608-16465-8*, 202675900052) Bks Demand.

— Progress in Operations Research, Vol. 1. LC 61-10415. (Operations Research Ser.: No. 5). 517p. reprint ed. 160.30 (*0-8357-9966-2*, 205157500089) Bks Demand.

— Re-Creating the Corporation: A Design of Organizations for the 21st Century. LC 99-13605. (Illus.). 352p. 1999. 30.00 (*0-19-512387-5*) OUP.

Ackoff, Russell L. & Emery, Fred. On Purposeful Systems. (Systems Inquiry Ser.). 296p. (C). 1982. reprint ed. pap. text 15.95 (*0-914105-00-0*) Intersystems Pubns.

Ackoff, Russell L., et al. A Guide to Controlling Your Corporation's Future. LC 84-14772. 165p. 1984. 27.95 (*0-471-88213-5*) Wiley.

— Revitalizing Western Economies: A New Agenda for Business & Government. LC 84-47977. (Joint Publication in the Jossey-Bass Management Series & the Jossey-Bass Social & Behavioral Science Ser.). 232p. reprint ed. pap. 72.00 (*0-7837-2509-4*, 204266800006) Bks Demand.

Ackoff, Russell L., jt. auth. see Rivett, Patrick.

Ackrill, J. L. Essays on Plato & Aristotle. LC 96-41722. 240p. 1997. text 60.00 (*0-19-823641-7*) OUP.

Ackrill, J. L., ed. Aristotle the Philosopher. (Oxford Paperbacks University Ser.). 168p. (Orig.). 1981. pap. text 21.95 (*0-19-289118-9*) OUP.

Ackrill, J. L., ed. see Aristotle.

Ackrill, Kate, jt. ed. see Bock, Gregory R.

Ackrill, Lindsay, tr. see Judson, J. L., ed.

Ackroyd. Social Psychology. 1998. pap. text 11.97 (*0-395-92152-X*) HM.

Ackroyd, Brian. World Satellite Communications. 1990. 99.95 (*0-8493-7703-X*, QA) CRC Pr.

Ackroyd, Carol. Technology of Political Control. 2nd ed. (C). pap. 19.95 (*0-86104-307-3*, Pub. by Pluto GBR) Stylus Pub VA.

Ackroyd, Dorothea. Bathtime Board Book. 1999. 3.95 (*1-58185-203-7*) Quadrillion Media.

— Bedtime Board Book. (Illus.). 12p. (ps-k). 1999. 3.95 (*1-58185-201-0*) Quadrillion Media.

***Ackroyd, Dorothea.** Eating & Drinking Bird Book. 1999. 3.95 (*1-58185-200-2*) Quadrillion Media.

Ackroyd, Dorothea. Playtime. 1999. 3.95 (*1-58185-202-9*) Quadrillion Media.

— What Can You Do? 1999. 3.95 (*1-58185-206-1*) Quadrillion Media.

— What Do You Hear? 1999. 3.95 (*1-58185-204-5*) Quadrillion Media.

— What Do You Know? 1999. 3.95 (*1-58185-207-X*) Quadrillion Media.

— What Do You See? 1999. 3.95 (*1-58185-205-3*) Quadrillion Media.

Ackroyd, Eric. A Dictionary of Dream Symbols: With an Introduction to Dream Psychology. 320p. 1993. pap. 9.95 (*0-7137-2363-7*, Pub. by Blandford Pr) Sterling.

Ackroyd, Joyce, tr. see Hakuseki, Arai.

Ackroyd, Neil & Lorimer, Robert. Global Navigation: A GPS User's Guide. 2nd ed. 223p. 1994. 80.00 (*1-85044-517-6*) LLP.

Ackroyd, Peter. Chatterton. 240p. 1996. pap. 12.00 (*0-8021-3480-7*, Grove) Grove-Atltic.

— English Music: A Novel. 416p. 1994. reprint ed. pap. 12.50 (*0-345-37613-7*) Ballantine Pub Grp.

— First Light. 336p. 1996. reprint ed. pap. 12.00 (*0-8021-3481-5*, Grove) Grove-Atltic.

— The Great Fire of London. LC 88-20838. 176p. 1995. pap. 11.95 (*0-226-00264-0*) U Ch Pr.

***Ackroyd, Peter.** The Life of Thomas Moore. 480p. 1999. pap. 17.50 (*0-385-49693-1*, Anchor NY) Doubleday.

— The Plato Papers: A Prophecy. LC 99-16573. 160p. 2000. 21.95 (*0-385-49768-7*, N A Talese) Doubleday.

— The Plato Papers: A Prophecy. 2001. reprint ed. pap. 12.00 (*0-385-49769-5*, Anchor NY) Doubleday.

Ackroyd, Peter, ed. see Wilde, Oscar.

Ackroyd, Peter, ed. & intro. see Wilde, Oscar.

Ackroyd, Peter R. Second Book of Samuel. LC 76-58074. (Cambridge Bible Commentary on the New English Bible, New Testament Ser.). (Illus.). 256p. 1977. pap. text 23.95 (*0-521-09754-1*) Cambridge U Pr.

Ackroyd, R. A. World According to Travis McGee. 21.95 (*0-8488-0510-0*) Amereon Ltd.

Ackroyd, Stephen. Data Collection Context. 2nd ed. LC 91-30756. (C). 1992. pap. text 24.95 (*0-582-05311-0*, Pub. by Addison-Wesley) Longman.

Ackroyd, Stephen, et al. New Technology & Practical Police Work: The Social Context of Technical Innovation. 100p. 1992. 113.00 (*0-335-09459-7*); pap. 41.95 (*0-335-09458-9*) OpUniv Pr.

ACL Staff. ACL Proceedings 1999 Annual Meeting. (C). 1999. pap. text 63.00 (*1-55860-609-2*) Morgan Kaufmann.

Acland, Charles R. & Buxton, William J., eds. Harold Innis in the New Century: Reflections & Refractions. 456p. 2000. 65.00 (*0-7735-1737-5*, Pub. by McG-Queens Univ Pr) CUP Services.

ACland, Charles R., jt. auth. see Buxton, William.

Acland, James H. Medieval Structure: The Gothic Vault. LC 72-76769. (Illus.). 264p. reprint ed. pap. 81.90 (*0-608-11390-5*, 201608500097) Bks Demand.

Acleto, Cesar O., et al, eds. Phycologia Latino-Americana, Vol. 1. (SPA., Illus.). 186p. 1981. text 45.00 (*3-7682-1297-1*) Lubrecht & Cramer.

ACLS Staff. Dictionary of Scientific Biography, Vols. 3 & 4. 1981. 190.00 (*0-684-16964-9*, Scribners Ref) Mac Lib Ref.

— Dictionary of Scientific Biography, Vols. 13 & 14. 1981. 190.00 (*0-684-16969-X*, Scribners Ref) Mac Lib Ref.

— Dictionary of Scientific Biography, Vols. 15 & 16. 1981. 190.00 (*0-684-16970-3*, Scribners Ref) Mac Lib Ref.

An Asterisk (*) at the beginning of an entry indicates that the title is appearing for the first time.

A

Acres, M. & Moldvay, Tom. Star Frontiers Mod, No. 1. 1982. 5.50 (0-394-52593-0) Random.

Acres, Mark. Death on the Docks. 1983. 5.50 (0-394-53162-0) Random.

— Dragon War. (Dark Divide Ser.: Bk. 2). 192p. (Orig.). 1994. mass mkt. 4.99 (0-380-77296-5, Avon Bks) Morrow Avon.

— Dragonspawn. 224p. (Orig.). 1994. mass mkt. 4.99 (0-380-77295-7, Avon Bks) Morrow Avon.

— Starspawn of Volturnus. 1983. 5.50 (0-394-53068-3) Random.

— Tomb of Lizard King. 1983. 5.50 (0-394-53152-3) Random.

Acres, Terry E. & Soderlund, David M., eds. Semiochemistry - Flavors & Pheromones: Proceedings of American Chemical Society Symposium, Washington, D.C. August 1983. (Illus.). x, 289p. 1985. 130.80 (3-11-010120-3) De Gruyter.

Acres, Wilfrid M. Bank of England from Within, 2 vols. 1991. reprint ed. lib. bdg. 99.00 (0-7812-0729-0) Rprt Serv.

***Acret, James.** The California Public Contract Code 2000 Edition. annot. ed. 2000. pap. 75.00 (1-55701-330-6) BNI Pubns.

Acret, James. National Construction Law Manual. 2nd ed. 1999. pap. 64.95 (1-55701-265-2) BNI Pubns.

***Acret, James & Ginn, David W.** California Construction Contracts & Disputes. 3rd ed. Griggs, Donald R., ed. LC 99-62003. 278p. 2000. 72.00 (0-7626-0400-X) Cont Ed Bar-CA.

***Acret, James, et al.** California Construction Contracts & Disputes, 2 vols. 3rd ed. Blanchette, Janis, ed. LC 99-62003. 1084p. 1999. ring bd. 179.00 (0-7626-0307-0, RE-33160) Cont Ed Bar-CA.

Acret, James, jt. auth. see Mead, Leon.

Acret, James. Architects & Engineers: Their Professional Responsibilities. LC 77-6379. 1977. text 95.00 (0-07-000187-1) McGraw.

— Attorney's Guide to California Construction Contracts & Disputes. LC 90-82521. 490p. 1990. 115.00 (0-88124-303-5, RE-31440) Cont Ed Bar-CA.

— California Construction Law Manual: Contractors Edition 1990. 1990. 45.00 (0-07-172279-3) Shepards.

— Construction Arbitration Handbook. 375p. 1985. text 110.00 (0-07-000228-2) Shepards.

— Construction Litigation Handbook. 477p. 1986. text 110.00 (0-07-000229-0) Shepards.

— National Mechanics Liens Handbook. 1998. pap. text 70.00 (1-55701-259-8) BNI Pubns.

— A Simplified Guide to Construction Law. 1996. pap. text 29.95 (1-55701-176-1) BNI Pubns.

Acrivos, Harold N. A Guide to Tropical & Sub-Tropical Vegetables. 54p. (Orig.). (C). 1988. 3.25 (0-9620198-0-1) Brevard Rare Fruit.

Acrivos, J. V., ed. Physics & Chemistry of Electrons & Ionsin Condensed Matter. 768p. 1984. text 315.50 (90-277-1799-0) Kluwer Academic.

"Across the River" East Bay Writers' Roundtable. Death & Doughnuts. LC 97-36293. (Griggs Anthology Ser.). 1997. write for info. (0-922530-06-8) Tantalus Bks.

Across the River East Bay Writers Roundtable Staff. Griggs Anthology: In the Beginning. LC 95-2796. 1995. write for info. (0-922530-03-3) Tantalus Bks.

ACS Committee on Chemistry & Public Affairs. Chemistry & the Food System. LC 80-11194. 138p. 1980. 14.95 (0-8412-0557-4); pap. 14.95 (0-8412-0563-9) Am Chemical.

ACS Committee on Professional Training Staff. ACS Directory of Graduate Research 1993. 1568p. 1993. 60.00 (0-8412-2723-3) Am Chemical.

ACS Software Staff. The Electronic Astrologer Reveals Your Horoscope. 1996. boxed set 59.95 incl. disk (0-935127-39-9) ACS Pubns.

ACS Staff. Louisiana Sampler Cookbook. 1980. pap. text 10.95 (0-87511-514-4) Claitors.

ACS Symposium on Highly Cross-Linked Polymer Networks. Polymer Networks: Structure & Mechanical Properties: Proceedings. Chompff, A. J. & Newman, S., eds. LC 73-163286. (Illus.). 507p. 1971. reprint ed. pap. 157.20 (0-608-05460-7, 206592900006) Bks Demand.

***Acs, Zoltan J.** Are Small Firms Important? Their Role & Impact. LC 98-51488. 1999. write for info. (0-7923-8415-6) Kluwer Law Intl.

Acs, Zoltan J. The Changing Structure of the American Economy: Lessons from the Steel Industry. LC 84-15930. 246p. 1984. 49.95 (0-275-91112-8, C1112, Praeger Pubs) Greenwood.

Acs, Zoltan J., ed. Small Firms & Economic Growth. LC 95-36670. (International Library of Critical Writings in Economics: Vol. 61). 1376p. 1996. 470.00 (1-85898-116-6) E Elgar.

Acs, Zoltan J., et al, eds. Entrepreneurship, Small & Medium Sized Enterprises & the Macroeconomy. LC 98-17417. (Illus.). 400p. (C). 1998. 69.95 (0-521-62105-4) Cambridge U Pr.

Acs, Zoltan J. & Audretsch, David B. Innovation & Small Firms. 296p. 1990. 38.50 (0-262-01113-1) MIT Pr.

Acs, Zoltan J. & Audretsch, David B., eds. The Economics of Small Firms: A Euoropean Challenge. (C). 1990. lib. bdg. 166.50 (0-7923-0484-5) Kluwer Academic.

— Innovation & Technological Change: An International Comparison. 216p. 1991. text 65.00 (0-472-10249-4, 10249) U of Mich Pr.

— Small Firms & Entrepreneurship: An East-West Perspective. 256p. (C). 1993. text 59.95 (0-521-43115-8) Cambridge U Pr.

Acs, Zoltan J. & Gerlowski, Daniel A. Managerial Economics & Organization. LC 95-31256. 464p. 1995. 98.00 (0-02-300292-1, Macmillan Coll) P-H.

Acs, Zoltan J. & Yin Yeung, Bernard, eds. Small & Medium-Sized Enterprises in the Global Economy. LC 98-40235. (Illus.). 192p. 1999. text 49.50 (0-472-11001-2, 11001) U of Mich Pr.

ACSA Elementary Education Committee. Principal's Handbook: Newsletter Extravaganza: Guidance, Resources & Samples for Use in Production of School Newsletters. 166p. 1998. ring bd. 45.00 (0-943397-46-4, 167) Assn Calif Sch Admin.

— Principal's Handbook: Proven Practical Strategies, Solutions & Samples for Use in the Day-to-Day Management of Your School. (Illus.). 450p. (J). (gr. k-8). 1996. ring bd. 95.00 (0-943397-39-1, 163) Assn Calif Sch Admin.

ACSA Middle Grades Education Committee. Middle School Matters: Tips from the Principal's Desk. 218p. 1998. ring bd. 70.00 (0-943397-45-6, 166) Assn Calif Sch Admin.

Acsay, Judit. Where to Eat in Budapest. 100p. 1989. 40.00 (963-13-3495-3, Pub. by Corvina Bks) St Mut.

***ACSI Staff.** Accreditation by School Progress: A School Improvement Process. 34p. 1999. 9.60 (1-58331-044-4) Assn Christ Sch.

— ACSI Elementary Mathematics: Fourth Grade - The Earth Below - Student Edition. (Enabling Educators Ser.). (Illus.). vii, 394p. (J). (gr. 3-4). 2000. student ed. 12.90 (1-58331-186-6) Assn Christ Sch.

— ACSI Elementary Mathematics: Fourth Grade - The Earth Below - Teacher Edition. (Enabling Educators Ser.). 2000. teacher ed. 85.00 (1-58331-187-4) Assn Christ Sch.

— ACSI Elementary Mathematics: Grade One - Life in the Sea - Student Work Text. (Enabling Educators Ser.). (Illus.). 366p. 1999. pap. text, student ed. 12.90 (1-58331-180-7) Assn Christ Sch.

— ACSI Elementary Mathematics: Grade Three - Life on the Land - Student Worktext. 362p. 1999. pap. text, student ed. 12.90 (1-58331-184-X) Assn Christ Sch.

— ACSI Elementary Mathematics: Grade Two - Life in the Air - Student Worktext. (Enabling Educators Ser.). (Illus.). 368p. 1999. pap. text, student ed. 12.90 (1-58331-182-3) Assn Christ Sch.

— ACSI Elementary Mathematics - Student: Grade One - Life in the Sea - Supplemental Exercises. (Enabling Educators Ser.). (Illus.). iv, 112p. (J). (gr. 1-2). 1999. student ed. 17.95 (1-58331-192-0) Assn Christ Sch.

— ACSI Elementary Mathematics - Student: Grade Three - Life on the Land - Supplemental Exercises. (Enabling Educators Ser.). iv, 112p. (J). (gr. 3-4). 1999. student ed. 17.95 (1-58331-194-7) Assn Christ Sch.

— ACSI Elementary Mathematics - Teacher Edition: Grade One - Life in the Sea. (Enabling Educators Ser.). (Illus.). xviii, 999p. 1999. teacher ed. 85.00 (1-58331-181-5) Assn Christ Sch.

— ACSI Elementary Mathematics - Teacher Edition: Grade Three - Life on the Land. (Enabling Educators Ser.). (Illus.). xviii, 1065p. 1999. 85.00 (1-58331-185-8) Assn Christ Sch.

— ACSI Elementary Mathematics - Teacher Edition: Grade Two - Life in the Air. (Enabling Educators Ser.). (Illus.). xviii, 1020p. 1999. teacher ed. 85.00 (1-58331-183-1) Assn Christ Sch.

— Christ & My Choices: Fifth Grade, Student Edition. (Elementary Bible Ser.). (Illus.). 176p. (J). (gr. 5-6). 2000. student ed. 11.25 (1-58331-112-2) Assn Christ Sch.

— Christian School Board Leadership: A Framework for Effective Governance. (Enabling Leadership Ser.). 95p. 2000. 58.00 (1-58331-042-8) Assn Christ Sch.

— Doing What's Right: First Grade Student Edition. (Character Foundation Curriculum Ser.). (Illus.). 96p. (J). (gr. 1-2). 2000. student ed. 8.50 (1-58331-142-4) Assn Christ Sch.

— Getting Started: Kindergarten, Student Edition. (Character Foundation Curriculum Ser.). (Illus.). 102p. (J). (gr. k-1). 2000. student ed. 8.50 (1-58331-140-8) Assn Christ Sch.

— God & Me: Kindergarten, Student Edition. (Elementary Bible Ser.). (Illus.). 161p. (J). (gr. k-1). 2000. student ed. 11.25 (1-58331-102-5) Assn Christ Sch.

— How Much Spring Is in Your Diving Board? A Career Planning Manual for Christian Young Adults. v, 199p. (YA). (gr. 11-13). 2000. student ed. 12.00 (1-58331-121-1) Assn Christ Sch.

— Let God Be God: A Study of the Attributes of God - Student Worktext. 116p. (YA). (gr. 9-11). 1999. student ed. 13.00 (1-58331-119-X) Assn Christ Sch.

— Mastering Bible Study Skills - Student Edition: Tools for Investigating God's Word. (Enabling Educators Ser.). (Illus.). 47p. (YA). (gr. 9-11). 1999. student ed. 13.00 (1-58331-128-9) Assn Christ Sch.

— Mastering Bible Study Skills - Teacher Edition: Tools for Investigating God's Word. (Enabling Educators Ser.). (Illus.). xi, 193p. 1999. teacher ed. 50.00 (1-58331-129-7) Assn Christ Sch.

— Native American Edition School Accreditation Manual: A Comprehensive Guide to the Accreditation Process. 106p. 2000. 9.60 (1-58331-045-2) Assn Christ Sch.

— Preschool Associate Credential Manual. 30p. 2000. 18.00 (1-58331-046-0) Assn Christ Sch.

— Reaching for Excellence Through ACSI Accreditation: An Introduction to the ACSI Process. 20p. 2000. 9.60 (1-58331-043-6) Assn Christ Sch.

ACSM Staff. ACSM's Fitness Book: A Proven Step-by-Step Program Prescribed by the Leading Experts in Health & Fitness. 2nd ed. LC 97-8611. (Illus.). 152p. 1997. 14.95 (0-88011-783-4, PACS0783) Human Kinetics.

— GIS-LIS '93, Vol. 1 & 2. 835p. 1993. 75.00 (0-614-06104-0, T725) Am Congrs Survey.

— GIS-LIS '94 (Phoenix, Arizona) 880p. 1994. pap. 65.00 (0-614-06100-8, T729) Am Congrs Survey.

— Metric Practice Guide for Surveying & Mapping. 11p. 1980. pap. 12.00 (0-614-06119-9, G400) Am Congrs Survey.

— Sample Contracts Manual. 38p. 1988. pap. 20.00 (0-614-06087-7, S286) Am Congrs Survey.

— The Surveyor in Court. 40p. 1975. pap. 12.00 (0-614-06114-8, S270) Am Congrs Survey.

ACSM Staff & ALTA Staff. Home Buyer Information Brochure. 6p. 1987. pap. 1.00 (0-614-06112-1, S284) Am Congrs Survey.

ACSM Staff & ASCE Staff. Definitions of Surveying & Associated Terms. 210p. 1978. pap. 18.00 (0-614-06117-2, S180) Am Congrs Survey.

ACSM Staff & ASPRS Staff. 1994 Annual Convention (Reno, Nevada) Vol. 1: ASPRS Proceedings. 762p. 1994. pap. 30.00 (0-614-06102-4, T727) Am Congrs Survey.

— 1994 Annual Convention (Reno, Nevada) Vol. 2: ACSM Proceedings. 353p. 1994. pap. 30.00 (0-614-06101-6, T728) Am Congrs Survey.

— 1993 Annual Convention (New Orleans) Vol. 3: ASPRS. 458p. 1993. 30.00 (0-614-06105-9, T724) Am Congrs Survey.

ACSM Staff, et al. The Glossary of the Mapping Sciences. 581p. 1994. 80.00 (0-614-06088-5, G500) Am Congrs Survey.

Act One Studios Staff. Act One Reports: Two Thousand Agencies, Theatres, Resources. 77p. 2000. pap. 6.00 (1-56850-007-6) Chicago Plays.

ACT Publishing Staff. College Planning/Search Book. 24th ed. 312p. (YA). (gr. 9-12). 1998. pap. 10.00 (1-56009-033-2) ACT.

ACT Staff & Vedral, Joyce L. Getting Into the ACT: Official Guide to the ACT Assessment. 2nd rev. ed. LC 97-73482. (Illus.). 556p. 1997. pap. 16.00 (0-15-600535-2) HUP.

ACT-UP - New York Women & AIDS Book Group Staff & New York Women's Handbook Group Staff. Women, AIDS, & Activism. 294p. 1990. 25.00 (0-89608-394-2); pap. 9.00 (0-89608-393-4) South End Pr.

Acta Instituti Atheniensis Staff, jt. ed. see Alroth, Brita.

***Actar Staff.** Fleeting Time. (Quaderns Ser.: Vol. 24). 2000. 29.95 (84-95273-17-9) Actar.

— Loops. (Quaderns Ser.: Vol. 23). 2000. 29.95 (84-95273-16-0) Actar.

Actar Staff. Operative Topographies, 20. (Quaderns Ser.). 1999. pap. text 25.00 (84-89698-84-8) Dist Art Pubs.

— State of the Question. (Quaderns Ser.). (Illus.). 180p. 2000. pap. 35.00 (84-89698-96-1) Dist Art Pubs.

Actenstucke. Zur Geschichte des Verhaltnisses von Staat und Kirche Im XIX.Jahrhundert. (GER.). 1587p. 1976. write for info. (3-487-05947-9) G Olms Pubs.

***Acting Through History Editorial Team Staff.** Acting Through History. LC 00-8631. 2000. pap. write for info. (0-88489-441-X) St Marys.

***Action Against Hunger Staff, ed.** The Geopolitics of Hunger, 2000-2001: Hunger & Power. 235p. 2000. pap. 22.00 (1-55587-901-2); lib. bdg. 49.95 (1-55587-925-X) L Rienner.

***Actium Publishing Staff.** 222 Ways to Promote Your Small Business on a Budget. (Illus.). 1999. pap. 13.95 (0-9657617-7-0) Actium Pub.

Activated Sludge Task Force Staff. Activated Sludge. LC 87-50920. (Manual of Practice, Operations & Maintenance Ser.: No. 9). 182p. 1987. pap. 38.00 (0-943244-97-8, MOM9PA) Water Environ.

***Active Education Film Staff, ed.** Microsoft Word 2000 Step-by-Step Courseware Expert Skills. LC 99-44097. (Illus.). 2000. pap., student ed. write for info. incl. cd-rom (0-7356-0984-5) Microsoft.

***Active Education Firm Staff, ed.** Microsoft Word 2000 Step-by-Step Courseware Core Skills. LC 99-44098. (Illus.). 2000. pap., student ed. write for info. incl. cd-rom (0-7356-0978-0) Microsoft.

***ActiveEducation Staff.** Microsoft Publisher 2000 Step by Step. LC 98-48192. 1999. pap. text 29.99 (1-57231-987-9) Microsoft.

Activity Bible Kids. Kid's Activity Bible, the Complete Text with Hundreds of Fascinating Puzzles & Fun Activities, 1. LC 99-187221. 1998. pap. text 12.99 (0-8423-3283-9) Focus Family.

Acton. A Critical Diction Russian. rev. ed. Date not set. text. write for info. (0-340-61453-6); text. write for info. (0-340-61454-4) St Martin.

Acton, Alfred, ed. The Letters & Memorials of Emanuel Swedenborg, Set, Vols. I & II. 1948. 16.00 (0-915221-04-7) Swedenborg Sci Assn.

— The Letters & Memorials of Emanuel Swedenborg, Vol. 1. 508p. 1948. 8.50 (0-915221-29-2) Swedenborg Sci Assn.

— The Letters & Memorials of Emanuel Swedenborg, Vol. 2. 803p. 1948. 8.50 (0-915221-30-6) Swedenborg Sci Assn.

Acton, Alfred, ed. & pref. see Swedenborg, Emanuel.

Acton, Alfred, ed. & tr. see Swedenborg, Emanuel.

Acton, Alfred, tr. & intro. see Swedenborg, Emanuel.

Acton, Avis. Behind the Chutes at Cheyenne Frontier Days: Your Pocket Guide to Rodeo. Garretson-Weibel, Cindy, ed. (Illus.). 112p. (Orig.). (YA). (gr. 6 up). 1991. pap. 7.95 (0-9627412-0-5) ABC Pub.

Acton, Avis, ed. see Arnold, Bess.

Acton, Bob. Walks on the Lizard. (C). 1989. pap. text 24.95 (0-85025-308-X, Pub. by Tor Mark Pr) St Mut.

Acton, Bryan & Duncan, Peter. Making Mead: A Complete Guide to the Making of Sweet & Dry Mead, Melomel, Metheglin, Hippocras, Pyment & Cyser. 68p. pap. 10.95 (0-9619072-8-2) G W Kent.

Acton, Connie. Learning Microsoft Works for Windows through Fun Projects: Version 4.0 for Windows 95. (Illus.). 165p. (YA). 1996. pap. text 16.95 (1-887281-08-8) Labyrinth CA.

Acton, Connie & Greene, Woody. Welcome to the World of Computers. (Illus.). 256p. (YA). 1995. pap. text 19.95 (1-887281-01-0) Labyrinth CA.

— Welcome to the World of Computers: Version 4.0 for Windows 95. (Illus.). 239p. (YA). 1996. pap. text 19.95 (1-887281-09-6) Labyrinth CA.

Acton, David. Hand of a Craftsman: The Woodcut Technique of Gustave Baumann. LC 96-75267. (Illus.). 144p. 1996. 39.95 (0-89013-297-6) Museum NM Pr.

— Master Drawings from the Worcester Art Museum. LC 97-48740. (Illus.). 288p. 1998. 75.00 (1-55595-146-5, Pub. by Hudson Hills) Natl Bk Netwk.

Acton, David & Goldman, Judith. Vincent Longo Prints, 1954-1955: A Selection. (Illus.). 40p. 1995. pap. 7.50 (1-885998-07-4) Hunter College.

Acton, David, et al. Gustave Baumann: Nearer to Art. (Illus.). 160p. 1993. 50.00 (0-89013-251-8) Museum NM Pr.

— Inspiring Reform: Boston's Arts & Crafts Movement. Davis Museum & Cultural Center Staff, ed. LC 96-86692. (Illus.). 200p. 1997. 75.00 (1-881894-08-8) WC Davis Mus & Cult.

Acton, Edward. Rethinking the Russian Revolution. (Reading History Ser.). 192p. 1990. text 49.50 (0-7131-6609-6, A4334, Pub. by E A) Routldge.

— Rethinking the Russian Revolution. (Reading History Ser.). 192p. 1995. pap. text 19.95 (0-7131-6530-8, A4338, Pub. by E A) St Martin.

— Russia. (C). 1989. pap. text 29.66 (0-582-49323-4) Addison-Wesley.

— Russia. (Present & the Past Ser.). 342p. (C). 1986. pap. text 24.75 (0-685-73796-9, 73577) Longman.

— Russia: The Tsarist & Soviet Legacy. 2nd ed. LC 94-11457. (Present & Past Ser.). 416p. (C). 1995. pap. 44.00 (0-582-08922-0, 76999) Longman.

Acton, Edward, et al, eds. Critical Companion to the Russian Revolution 1914-1921. LC 97-6945. 800p. 1997. 29.95 (0-253-33333-4) Ind U Pr.

Acton, Forman S. Numerical Methods That Work. rev. ed. (Spectrum Ser.). 560p. 1990. pap. text 41.95 (0-88385-450-3, NMTW) Math Assn.

— Thwart the Gremlins in Real Computing! Error Prevention in Scientific Calculations. LC 95-10606. 1995. 35.00 (0-691-03663-2) P-H.

Acton, H. B. The Morals of Markets & Related Essays. Gordon, David & Shearmur, Jeremy, eds. LC 92-42151. 284p. 1993. 20.00 (0-86597-106-4); pap. 7.50 (0-86597-107-2) Liberty Fund.

Acton, Harold. The Bourbons of Naples. (Lost Treasure Ser.). (Illus.). 750p. 1998. pap. 29.95 (1-85375-291-6) Prion.

— Modern Chinese Poetry. 1972. lib. bdg. 250.00 (0-87968-195-0) Krishna Pr.

— Three Extraordinary Ambassadors. LC 83-50109. (Walter Neurath Memorial Lectures). (Illus.). 64p. 1984. 12.95 (0-500-55015-8, Pub. by Thames Hudson) Norton.

Acton, Henry. Religious Opinions & Example of Milton, Locke, & Newton. LC 71-158223. reprint ed. 34.50 (0-404-00283-8) AMS Pr.

Acton, Jay & Bakalar, Nick. Green Diamonds: Investing in Minor League Baseball. 288p. 1993. 18.95 (0-8217-4150-0, Zebra Kensgtn) Kensgtn Pub Corp.

Acton, Jimmy C. Tales from the Sidewalk Benches. (Illus.). 103p. (Orig.). 1988. pap. 9.95 (0-943487-06-4) Sevgo Pr.

Acton, John E. The Correspondence of Lord Acton & Richard Simpson, Vol. 3. Altholz, Josef L. et al, eds. LC 75-112466. 377p. 1975. reprint ed. pap. 116.90 (0-608-12323-4, 2024407) Bks Demand.

— Essays in Religion, Politics & Morality Vol. 3: Selected Writings of Lord Acton. LC 85-4522. 776p. 1988. 20.00 (0-86597-050-5); pap. 7.50 (0-86597-051-3) Liberty Fund.

— Essays in the History of Liberty Vol. 1: Selected Writings of Lord Acton. Fears, J. Rufus, ed. LC 85-4522. 588p. 1985. 20.00 (0-86597-046-7); pap. 7.50 (0-86597-047-5) Liberty Fund.

— Essays in the Liberal Interpretation of History: Selected Papers. McNeill, William H., ed. LC 67-15313. (Classic European Historians Ser.). 449p. reprint ed. pap. 139.20 (0-608-13461-9, 202001600016) Bks Demand.

— Essays in the Study & Writing of History Vol. 2: Selected Writings of Lord Acton. Fears, J. Rufus, ed. LC 85-4522. 607p. (C). 1986. 20.00 (0-86597-048-3); pap. 7.50 (0-86597-049-1) Liberty Fund.

— Historical Essays & Studies. Figgis, J. N. & Laurence, R. V., eds. LC 67-23171. (Essay Index Reprint Ser.). 1977. 24.95 (0-8369-0134-7) Ayer.

— The History of Freedom. 98p. 1993. pap. 7.95 (1-880595-02-8) Acton Inst Stu Rel.

— History of Freedom, & Other Essays. Figgis, J. N. & Laurence, R. V., eds. LC 67-22048. (Essay Index Reprint Ser.). 1977. 29.95 (0-8369-0135-5) Ayer.

***Acton, John E.** Lectures on the French Revolution. LC 99-46818. 2000. 19.00 (0-86597-280-X); pap. 11.00 (0-86597-281-8) Liberty Fund.

Acton, John E. Lectures on the French Revolution. Figgis, John N. & Laurence, Reginald V., eds. LC 78-108814. (BCL Ser.: No. II). reprint ed. 62.50 (0-404-00284-6) AMS Pr.

Acton, Kenneth E. Starting in Video: The Costs & Resources Needed, Including a Directory of Christian Video Producers. (C). 1989. 29.00 (0-9510086-4-1, Pub. by Jay Bks) St Mut.

Acton, Lesley & McAulay, Paul. Repairing Pottery & Porcelain: A Complete Guide. LC 95-48175. (Illus.). 112p. 1996. pap. 18.95 (1-55821-486-0) Lyons Pr.

Acton, Lesley & McAuley, Paul J. Repairing Pottery & Porcelain: A Practical Guide. (Illus.). 128p. 1996. text. write for info. (90-5703-041-1, Harwood Acad Pubs) Gordon & Breach.

Acton, Mary. Learning to Look at Paintings. LC 97-160203. (Illus.). 272p. (C). 1997. 65.00 (*0-415-14889-8*); pap. 18.99 (*0-415-14890-1*) Routledge.

Acton, Patricia N. Invasion of Privacy: The Cross Creek Trial of Marjorie Kinnan Rawlings. LC 88-12036. (Illus.). 160p. 1988. 27.95 (*0-8130-0906-5*); pap. 14.95 (*0-8130-0908-1*) U Press Fla.

Acton, Patricia N., jt. auth. see Acton, Richard L.

Acton, Richard. A Brit among the Hawkeyes. LC 98-3666. 320p. 1998. 24.95 (*0-8138-2190-8*) Iowa St U Pr.

Acton, Richard L. & Acton, Patricia N. To Go Free: Iowa's Legal Heritage. LC 95-19307. (Illus.). 382p. 1995. text 39.95 (*0-8138-2178-9*) Iowa St U Pr.

Acton, Thomas, ed. Gypsy Politics & Traveller Identity. 203p. 1997. 59.95 (*0-900458-80-1*, Pub. by Univ of Herfordshire) Bold Strummer Ltd.

— Gypsy Politics & Traveller Identity. 174p. 1997. reprint ed. pap. 29.95 (*0-900458-75-5*, Pub. by Univ of Herfordshire) Bold Strummer Ltd.

— Scholarship & the Gypsy Struggle: Commitment in Romani Studies. 200p. 2000. pap. 35.95 (*1-902806-01-8*, Pub. by Univ of Herfordshire) Bold Strummer Ltd.

***Acton, Thomas & Mundy, Gary, eds.** Romani Culture & Gypsy Identity. 203p. 1999. reprint ed. pap. 33.95 (*0-900458-81-X*, Pub. by Univ of Herfordshire) Bold Strummer Ltd.

Acton, William. Prostitution, Considered in Its Moral, Social & Sanitary Aspects in London & Other Large Cities & Garrison Towns. 302p. 1972. reprint ed. 27.50 (*0-7146-2414-4*, BHA-02414, Pub. by F Cass Pubs) Intl Spec Bk.

Actor, Paul, et al, eds. Antibiotic Inhibition of Bacterial Cell Surface Assembly & Function. LC 87-30737. 679p. reprint ed. pap. 200.00 (*0-608-08629-0*, 206915200003) Bks Demand.

— Infections in the Immunocompromised Host: Laboratory Diagnosis & Treatment. LC 86-15091. (Advances in Experimental Medicine & Biology Ser.: Vol. 202). 220p. 1986. 65.00 (*0-306-42366-9*, Plenum Trade) Perseus Pubng.

***Actoveedication Staff.** Microsoft Web Publishing Step by Step. 368p. 2000. pap. 29.99 (*0-7356-1156-4*) Microsoft.

ACTR Staff. Business Russian. 216p. 1996. pap. text, per. 51.00 (*0-7872-0590-7*, 41059001) Kendall-Hunt.

ACTR Staff. Mir Rusky: The World of the Russians. 504p. 1997. text 54.95 (*0-7872-2471-5*, 41247101) Kendall-Hunt.

ACTR Staff. Political Russian: An Intermediate Course in Russian Language for International Relations. 3rd ed. 568p. 1996. pap., per. 46.00 (*0-7872-1904-5*, 41190401) Kendall-Hunt.

— Russian Faces & Voices. 444p. 1995. boxed set 44.95 (*0-7872-0504-4*, 41050401) Kendall-Hunt.

— Russian Faces & Voices. 160p. 1995. pap., per. 12.95 (*0-7872-1423-X*, 41142301) Kendall-Hunt.

— Russian Readings for Close Analysis. 288p. 1993. per. 34.00 (*0-8403-8587-0*) Kendall-Hunt.

— Russian Reference Grammar: Core Grammar in Functional Cont. LC 98-102155. 296p. 1997. per. 17.00 (*0-7872-4467-8*) Kendall-Hunt.

ACTR Staff. Russian Stage One Vol. 1: Live from Moscow, 1. 3rd ed. 625p. 1996. pap. text 48.00 (*0-8403-9964-2*, 40996401) Kendall-Hunt.

— Russian Stage One Vol. 1: Live from Moscow, 2. 1997. pap. text 48.00 (*0-7872-3296-3*) Kendall-Hunt.

ACTR Staff. Russian Stage Two: Grammar Supplement. 134p. 1996. pap. text, per. 12.00 (*0-7872-2926-1*) Kendall-Hunt.

— Russian Stage Two: Pak. 134p. 1996. 60.00 (*0-7872-2927-X*) Kendall-Hunt.

— Russian Stage Two: Video Edition. 158p. 1997. boxed set 80.00 (*0-7872-3962-3*, 41396201) Kendall-Hunt.

— Russian Themes: Video Resource. 192p. 1997. boxed set 99.95 (*0-7872-3757-4*) Kendall-Hunt.

— Stage One: Minirus. 256p. 1996. pap., per. 34.95 (*0-7872-1692-5*, 41169201) Kendall-Hunt.

ACTR Staff & Corlac. Russian Faces & Voices: Instructor's Manual. 94p. 1996. per. 12.95 (*0-7872-1425-6*) Kendall-Hunt.

ACTR Staff & Garza. Fundamentals of Russian Verbal Conjugation for Students & Teachers. 240p. 1993. per. 12.75 (*0-8403-8957-4*) Kendall-Hunt.

ACTR Staff & Simes. Years of Change: Reading the Russian Press. 2nd ed. LC 96-76183. 292p. 1996. pap. text, per. 42.00 (*0-7872-2202-X*, 41220201) Kendall-Hunt.

ACTR Staff & Simes-Timofejeva, Natasha. Scientific Russian: Readings in Russian Science & Technology. 176p. 1993. per. 32.00 (*0-8403-8586-2*, 40858601) Kendall-Hunt.

Acts, Hambler. How to Stop Smoking . . . in 50 Days! 60p. 1998. pap. 8.99 (*1-57532-181-5*) Press-Tige Pub.

***Acts, Random, ed.** Power of Kindness: Reconnecting to Friends, Family & the World. 336p. 2000. 6.98 (*1-56731-402-3*, MJF Bks) Fine Comms.

Actuaries Society Staff, ed. Health Care Symposium Proceedings: Risk Adjusters . . . Where Are We? LC 97-221974. 1996. pap. text 20.00 (*0-938959-40-9*) Soc Actuaries.

Acturi, Abbabus. The Other Land of Beautiful Things. (Illus.). 250p. (Orig.). 1992. pap. 12.95 (*1-880601-39-7*) Danon Pub.

Acuff, Daniel. What Kids Buy & Why: Psychological Secrets to Creating the Products That Kids Love. LC 97-33491. 224p. 1998. 27.50 (*0-684-83448-0*) Free Pr.

Acuff, Frank L. How to Negotiate Anything with Anyone, Anywhere Around the World. expanded ed. LC 97-20426. 336p. 1997. pap. 19.95 (*0-8144-7950-2*) AMACOM.

Acuna, Carlos H. & Gamarra, Eduardo A. Latin American Political Economy in the Age of Neoliberal Reform: Theoretical & Comparative Perspectives for the 1990's. Smith, William C. et al, eds. LC 93-44981. 232p. (C). 1994. pap. 21.95 (*1-56000-731-1*, Pub. by U Miami N-S Ctr) L Rienner.

Acuna, Rodolfo. Anything but Mexican: Chicanos in Contemporary Los Angeles. 225p. (C). 1996. 60.00 (*1-85984-936-9*, C0535, Pub. by Verso); pap. 20.00 (*1-85984-031-0*, C0536, Pub. by Verso) Norton.

***Acuna, Rodolfo.** Occupied America. 4th ed. LC 99-42046. 554p. (C). 1999. pap. text 46.00 (*0-321-04485-1*) Addison-Wesley.

Acuna, Rodolfo. Occupied America: A History of Chicanos. 3rd ed. 475p. (C). 1997. pap. 49.00 (*0-06-040163-X*) Addison-Wesley Educ.

— Sometimes There Is No Other Side: Chicanos & the Myth of Equality. LC 97-46840. 312p. 1998. 36.00 (*0-268-01762-X*); pap. 18.00 (*0-268-01763-8*) U of Notre Dame Pr.

— Sonoran Strongman: Ignacio Pesqueira & His Times. LC 73-76304. 191p. reprint ed. pap. 59.30 (*0-608-15552-7*, 205637900062) Bks Demand.

Acuna, Rodolfo F. A Community under Siege: A Chronicle of Chicanos East of the Los Angeles River, 1945-1975. (Monographs: No. 11). 540p. (Orig.). 1984. pap. 21.95 (*0-89551-066-9*, S301) UCLA Chicano Studies.

Acuna, Tathiana F. The United Nations Mission in El Salvador: A Humanitarian Law Perspective. LC 95-37528. (Nijhoff Law Specials Ser.: Vol. 14). 1995. pap. text 76.00 (*90-411-0123-3*) Kluwer Academic.

Acuna, Victor E., jt. auth. see Riley, Eugene W.

Acunto, Stephen B. Champions Boxing Guide. (Illus.). 58p. 1996. pap. write for info. (*0-9655051-0-3*) Am Assn Improv Boxing.

ACUPAE Group Staff, ed. see De LaFayette, Jean M.

ACUPAE Group Staff, ed. see De Lafayette, Jean M.

Acupuncture News Staff. How to Build-up a Successful Acupuncture Practice. 1976. 37.50 (*0-914322-04-4*) Chans Corp.

Acutt, Melinda & Mason, Pamela, eds. Environmental Valuation, Economic Policy & Sustainability: Recent Advances in Environmental Economics. LC 98-9836. 240p. 1998. 85.00 (*1-85898-753-9*) E Elgar.

***ACW Press Staff.** Rainbows in the Valley. 1999. pap. 8.95 (*0-9680260-1-X*) CVPL.

ACWC Staff. The Blackhorse Regiment in Vietnam, 1966-1972. 480p. 1997. 25.00 (*0-7872-3901-1*) Kendall-Hunt.

Acworth, Richard. The Philosophy of John Norris of Bemerton, 1657-1712. (Studien und Materialien Zur Geschichte der Philosophie Ser.: Vol. VI). 400p. 1979. 80.00 (*3-487-06884-2*) G Olms Pubs.

***Aczel.** The Compass of Philosophy. 2001. write for info. (*0-15-100506-0*) Harcourt.

Aczel. Complete Business Statistics. 3rd ed. 1996. student ed. 21.50 (*0-256-21856-0*) McGraw.

— Complete Business Stats Minitab Stud. 3rd ed. 1997. 89.00 (*0-07-561109-0*) McGraw.

Aczel & Meray, Tibor. The Revolt of the Mind. 449p. 1960. 8.75 (*0-685-55404-X*) Bookfinger.

Aczel, Amir D. Complete Business Statistics. 3rd ed. LC 95-36381. 768p. (C). 1996. text 71.25 (*0-256-13894-X*, Irwn McGrw-H) McGrw-H Hghr Educ.

— Complete Business Statistics. 4th ed. LC 98-36083. (Irwin/McGraw-Hill Series in Operations & Decision Sciences). 1998. 90.95 (*0-07-289302-8*) McGraw.

— Complete Business Statistics Mystat Software with QC Tools 3.50 IBM Disk. 2nd ed. 72p. (C). 1994. 5.95 (*0-256-19089-5*, Irwn McGrw-H) McGrw-H Hghr Educ.

— Fermat's Last Theorem: Unlocking the Secret of an Ancient Mathematical Problem. 160p. 1997. pap. 9.95 (*0-385-31946-0*) Doubleday.

— Fermat's Last Theorem: Unlocking the Secret of an Ancient Mathematical Problem. LC 96-9029. (Illus.). 147p. 1996. 18.00 (*1-56858-077-0*) FWEW.

***Aczel, Amir D.** God's Equation: Einstein, Relativity & the Expanding Universe. LC 99-36319. (Illus.). 272p. 1999. 22.00 (*1-56858-139-4*) FWEW.

Aczel, Amir D. How to Beat the I. R. S. at Its Own Game: Strategies to Avoid & Fight an Audit. LC 94-11051. 166p. 1994. pap. 8.95 (*1-56858-013-4*) FWEW.

***Aczel, Amir D.** The Mystery of the Aleph: Mathematics, the Kabbalah & the Search for Infinity. (Illus.). 304p. 2000. 24.95 (*1-56858-105-X*, Pub. by FWEW) Publishers Group.

Aczel, Amir D. Probability Vol. 1: The Book That Proves There Is Life in Outer Space. LC 98-16868. 230p. 2000. pap. 12.00 (*0-15-601080-1*, Harvest Bks) Harcourt.

***Aczel, Amir D.** Probability 1: Why There Must Be Intelligent Life in the Universe. LC 98-16868. 240p. 1998. 22.00 (*0-15-100376-9*) Harcourt.

Aczel, Amir D. Statistics: Concepts & Applications. LC 94-41399. 533p. (C). 1995. text 65.85 (*0-256-11935-X*, Irwn McGrw-H) McGrw-H Hghr Educ.

— Statistics, "Reading in Statistics" 128p. (C). 1995. text 13.75 (*0-256-18929-3*, Irwn McGrw-H) McGrw-H Hghr Educ.

— Statistics Students Companion. 136p. (C). 1995. text 23.75 (*0-256-18928-5*, Irwn McGrw-H) McGrw-H Hghr Educ.

Aczel, Amir D. & Doviak, Michael. Statistics Minitab Manual. 120p. (C). 1995. text 12.50 (*0-256-20064-5*, Irwn McGrw-H) McGrw-H Hghr Educ.

Aczel, Amir D., jt. auth. see Delurgio, Stephen.

Aczel, J. A Short Course on Functional Equations: Based upon Recent Applications to the Social & Behavioural Sciences. 1986. pap. text 55.50 (*90-277-2377-X*); lib. bdg. 100.00 (*90-277-2376-1*) Kluwer Academic.

Aczel, J., ed. Aggregating Clones, Colors, Equations, Iterates, Numbers, & Titles. (Aequationes Mathematicae Ser.: Vol. 50). 224p. 1995. pap. 39.50 (*3-7643-5243-4*) Spr-Verlag.

— Functional Equations: History, Applications & Theory. 1984. text 160.50 (*90-277-1706-0*) Kluwer Academic.

Aczel, J. & Dhombres, J. Functional Equations Containing Several Variables. (Encyclopedia of Mathematics & Its Applications Ser.: No. 31). (Illus.). 480p. 1989. text 135.00 (*0-521-35276-2*) Cambridge U Pr.

Aczel, Janos, ed. Aggregating Clones, Colors, Equations, Iterates, Numbers, & Tiles. LC 95-35258. 213p. 1995. 39.95 (*0-8176-5243-4*, QA431) Birkhauser.

Aczel, Peter. Non-Well-Founded Sets. LC 87-17857. (CSLI Lecture Notes Ser.: No. 14). 147p. 1988. 34.95 (*0-937073-21-0*); pap. 17.95 (*0-937073-22-9*) CSLI.

Aczel, Peter, et al, eds. Proof Theory. (Illus.). 316p. (C). 1993. text 59.95 (*0-521-41413-X*) Cambridge U Pr.

— Situation Theory & Its Applications, Vol. 3. (CSLI Lecture Notes Ser.: No. 37). 430p. 1993. 54.95 (*1-881526-09-7*); pap. 20.95 (*1-881526-08-9*) CSLI.

Aczel, Richard, tr. see Esterhazy, Peter.

Aczel, Richard, tr. see Kosztolanyi, Dezso.

Aczel, Tamas & Meray, Tibor. The Revolt of the Mind. LC 74-20275. 449p. 1975. reprint ed. lib. bdg. 75.00 (*0-8371-7851-7*, ACRM, Greenwood Pr) Greenwood.

Aczel, Thomas, ed. Mass Spectrometric Characterization of Shale Oils STP 902. LC 86-1203. (Special Technical Publication Ser.). (Illus.). 149p. 1986. text 29.00 (*0-8031-0467-7*, STP902) ASTM.

***Ad-Darqawi, Shaikh A.** Letters of a Sufi Master. 1998. pap. text 11.95 (*1-887752-16-1*) Fons Vitae.

Ad-Darqawi, Shaikh A. Letters of a Sufi Master: The Shaikh Al-'Arabi Ad-Darqawi. 2nd ed. Burckhardt, Titus, tr. from FRE. 38p. 1987. pap. 9.95 (*0-900588-00-4*) S Perennis.

Ad-Dimashqi, Shaikh W. Concerning the Affirmation of Divine Oneness Vol. 1: Risala Fit-Tawhid. Holland, Muhtar, tr. from ARA. LC 97-74907. 125p. 1998. pap. 15.00 (*1-882216-05-9*) Al-Baz Pub.

Ad-Din, Abu B. The Book of Certainty. 90p. 1996. pap. 9.95 (*0-614-21256-1*, 110) Kazi Pubns.

Ad Hoc Committee on Measurement Uncertainties. Determining & Reporting Measurement Uncertainties: Recommended Practice RP-12. (RP Ser.). (Illus.). 69p. 1995. reprint ed. 20.00 (*1-58464-020-0*) Natl Conf Stds Labs.

Ad Hoc Committee on Stewardship National Conf. of. Stewardship & Development in Catholic Dioceses & Parishes: Resource Manual. 26p. (C). 1996. pap. 2.95 (*1-57455-132-9*) US Catholic.

***Ad Me'ah Ve'esrim Plus.** Calendar for 154 Years, 1900-2053. 320p. 1999. 20.00 (*965-09-0099-3*, Pub. by R Mass Ltd) Lambda Pubs.

Ada. The American Dietetic Association's Complete Food & Nutrition Guide. 644p. 1996. 29.95 (*0-471-34658-6*) Wiley.

— The American Dietetic Association's Complete Food & Nutrition Guide. 656p. 1998. pap. 24.95 (*0-471-34659-4*) Wiley.

Ada. Calcium in Your Life. 168p. (Orig.). 1997. pap. 5.95 (*0-471-34667-5*) Wiley.

— Play Hard, Eat Right! A Parent's Guide to Sports Nutrition for Their Children. 160p. 1995. pap. 10.95 (*0-471-34695-0*) Wiley.

Ada. Snacking Habits for Healthy Living. 112p. 1997. pap. 8.95 (*0-471-34704-3*) Wiley.

Ada, A. F. Hagamos Caminos: Navegamos. 1986. text, student ed. 23.89 (*0-201-16584-8*) Addison-Wesley.

— Hagamos Caminos: Navegamos. 1987. pap. text, wbk. ed. 12.72 (*0-201-16785-9*) Addison-Wesley.

— Hagamos Caminos: Partimos. 1986. text 16.53 (*0-201-16580-5*); pap. text, student ed. 10.85 (*0-201-16781-6*) Addison-Wesley.

— Hagamos Caminos: Volamos. 1986. text 23.89 (*0-201-16583-X*) Addison-Wesley.

— Hagamos Caminos: Volamos. 1987. pap. text, student ed., wbk. ed. 11.77 (*0-201-16784-0*) Addison-Wesley.

Ada, Allma F. Mediopollito. (J). 1995. 21.95 (*0-385-44637-3*) BDD Bks Young Read.

Ada, Alma E., tr. see Clifton, Lucille.

Ada, Alma F. After the Storm. (Stories the Year 'Round Ser.). (J). (gr. k-12). 1998. pap. 7.95 (*1-56014-337-1*) Santillana.

— Amigos (Friends), Big Book. (Superbooks (Superlibros) Ser.). (ENG & SPA., Illus.). 26p. (J). (gr. k-1). 21.95 (*0-88272-501-7*) Santillana.

— El Arbol de Navidad. LC 96-38218.Tr. of Christmas Tree. (SPA., Illus.). 32p. (J). (ps-1). 1997. 14.45 (*0-7868-0151-4*, Pub. by Hyprn Child) Time Warner.

— El Arbol de Navidad: The Christmas Tree. LC 96-38218.Tr. of Christmas Tree. (SPA., Illus.). 32p. (J). (ps-1). 1997. lib. bdg. 14.89 (*0-7868-2123-X*, Pub. by Hyprn Child) Little.

— Barquitos de Papel. (Cuentos con Alma Ser.). (SPA., Illus.). 24p. (J). (gr. 3-9). 1993. 16.95 (*1-56492-118-2*) Laredo.

— Barriletes. (Cuentos con Alma Ser.). (SPA., Illus.). 24p. (J). (gr. 3-9). 1993. 16.95 (*1-56492-126-3*) Laredo.

— Bear's Walk Theme Link. (ESL Theme Links Ser.). (Illus.). (Orig.). 1993. ring bd. 99.50 (*1-56334-288-X*); 35.00 (*1-56334-287-1*); audio 10.50 (*1-56334-286-3*) Hampton-Brown.

— Caballito Blanco y Otras Poesias Favoritas: Green Small Book Set, 6 bks., Set. (Dias y Dias de Poesia Ser.). (SPA., Illus.). 40p. (Orig.). (J). (gr. 1-3). 1992. pap. 42.00 (*1-56334-118-2*) Hampton-Brown.

— El Canto del Mosquito (The Song of the Teeny-Tiny Mosquito) (Libros para Contar/Stories for the Telling Ser.). (SPA.). (J). (gr. k-1). pap. 5.95 (*0-88272-797-4*) Santillana.

***Ada, Alma F.** El Canto del Mosquito (The Song of the Teeny-Tiny Mosquito) (Libros para Contar/Stories for the Telling Ser.). (ENG & SPA.). (J). (gr. k-12). 1998. pap. 5.95 (*0-88272-806-7*) Santillana.

Ada, Alma F. El Canto del Mosquito (The Song of the Teeny-Tiny Mosquito), Big Book. (Libros para Contar/Stories for the Telling Ser.). (SPA.). (J). (gr. k-1). 1989. 18.95 (*0-88272-798-2*); 18.95 (*0-88272-807-5*) Santillana.

— Cinco Pollitos y Otras Poesias Favoritas: Tan Small Book Set, 6 bks., Set. (Dias y Dias de Poesia Ser.). (SPA., Illus.). 40p. (Orig.). (J). (ps-6). 1991. pap. 42.00 (*1-56334-117-4*) Hampton-Brown.

— Como Nacio el Arco Iris. (Cuentos para Todo el Ano). (SPA.). (J). (gr. k-12). 1995. pap. 7.95 (*1-56014-220-0*) Santillana.

— Dear Peter Rabbit. (SPA., Illus.). 32p. (J). (gr. k-3). 1997. pap. 6.99 (*0-689-80879-8*) S&S Bks Yung.

— Dear Peter Rabbit. LC 93-8459. (Illus.). 40p. (gr. k-3). 1997. per. 5.99 (*0-689-81289-2*) S&S Childrens.

Ada, Alma F. Dear Peter Rabbit. (J). 1997. 11.19 (*0-606-11246-4*, Pub. by Turtleback) Demco.

Ada, Alma F. Despues de la Tormenta. (Cuentos para Todo el Ano Ser.). (SPA.). (J). (gr. k-12). pap. 7.95 (*1-56014-226-X*) Santillana.

— Dias de Circo. (Cuentos con Alma Ser.). (SPA., Illus.). 24p. (J). (gr. 3-9). 1993. 16.95 (*1-56492-127-1*) Laredo.

— Dias y Dias Chart Set: Green Set. (Dias y Dias de Poesia Ser.). (SPA., Illus.). (Orig.). 1992. pap. 180.90 incl. audio (*1-56334-122-0*) Hampton-Brown.

— Dias y Dias de Poesia: Complete Program. (SPA.). (Orig.). (J). (ps-6). 1992. pap. 342.55 incl. audio (*1-56334-258-8*) Hampton-Brown.

— Dias y Dias de Poesia: Complete Program - Small Books, 36 bks. (SPA., Illus.). (Orig.). (J). (ps-6). 1992. pap. 556.75 incl. audio (*1-56334-259-6*) Hampton-Brown.

— Dias y Dias Green Chart Program with Small Books: Green Set. (Dias y Dias de Poesia Ser.). (SPA., Illus.). (Orig.). 1992. pap., teacher ed. 256.50 (*1-56334-120-4*) Hampton-Brown.

— Dias y Dias Tan Chart Program with Small Books: Tan Set. (Dias y Dias de Poesia Ser.). (SPA., Illus.). (Orig.). 1991. pap. 256.50 (*1-56334-119-0*) Hampton-Brown.

— The Empty Pinata. (Stories the Year 'Round Ser.). (J). (gr. k-12). 1998. pap. 7.95 (*1-56014-336-3*) Santillana.

— Una Extrana Visita (Strange Visitors), Big Book. (Libros para Contar/Stories for the Telling Ser.). (SPA., Illus.). (J). (gr. k-1). 1989. 18.95 (*0-88272-794-X*); 18.95 (*0-88272-803-2*) Santillana.

— Friends - Amigos. (ENG & SPA., Illus.). 26p. (J). (gr. k-2). 1989. 5.25 (*0-88272-500-9*) Santillana.

— El Gallo Que Fue a la Boda de Su Tio. (SPA.). 1998. 12.19 (*0-606-13364-X*, Pub. by Turtleback) Demco.

— Gathering the Sun: An Alphabet in Spanish & English. LC 96-3701. (ENG & SPA., Illus.). 40p. (J). (gr. k up). 1997. 16.00 (*0-688-13903-5*); lib. bdg. 15.93 (*0-688-13904-3*) Lothrop.

— Giraffe's Sad Tale. (ESL Theme Links Ser.). (Illus.). (Orig.). 1993. teacher ed., ring bd. 99.50 incl. audio (*1-56334-285-5*); 35.00 (*1-56334-284-7*); audio 10.50 (*1-56334-283-9*) Hampton-Brown.

— The Golden Cage. (Stories the Year 'Round Ser.). (J). (gr. k-12). 1998. pap. 7.95 (*1-56014-332-0*) Santillana.

— Hagamos Caminos Booklet. abr. ed. 1989. ring bd. 0.00 (*0-201-50879-6*) Addison-Wesley.

— La Hamaca de la Vaca. (Cuentos para Todo el Ano Ser.). (SPA., Illus.). 23p. (J). (gr. k-12). 1991. 7.95 (*1-56014-219-7*) Santillana.

— Hampton-Brown Pre-K Program, Set. (Dias y Dias de Poesia Ser.). (SPA., Illus.). 1993. 427.00 (*1-56334-424-6*) Hampton-Brown.

— How the Rainbow Came to Be. (Stories the Year 'Round Ser.). (J). (gr. k-12). 1997. pap. 7.95 (*1-56014-221-9*) Santillana.

— I Don't Want to Melt. (Stories the Year 'Round Ser.). (J). (gr. k-12). 1998. pap. 7.95 (*1-56014-333-9*) Santillana.

— I Love Saturdays y Domingos. LC 94-3362. (Illus.). (J). (gr. k-3). 2000. 16.00 (*0-689-31819-7*) Atheneum Yung Read.

— I Love Saturdays y Domingos. (J). 1999. 14.95 (*0-689-31979-7*) S&S Bks Yung.

— I Love Saturdays y Domingos. (SPA.). 2000. pap. 4.95 (*0-689-80591-8*) S&S Childrens.

— In the Cow's Backyard. (Stories the Year 'Round Ser.). (Illus.). 23p. (J). (gr. k-12). 1991. pap. 7.95 (*1-56014-275-8*) Santillana.

— In the Cow's Backyard: Big Book. (Stories the Year 'Round Ser.). (Illus.). (J). (gr. k-12). 1991. 22.95 (*1-56014-762-8*) Santillana.

— It Wasn't Me. (Stories the Year 'Round Ser.). (J). (gr. k-12). 1998. pap. 7.95 (*1-56014-334-7*) Santillana.

— La Jaula Dorada. (Cuentos para Todo el Ano Ser.). (SPA.). (J). (gr. k-12). pap. 7.95 (*1-56014-330-4*) Santillana.

— Jordi's Star. LC 95-11048. (Illus.). 32p. (J). (ps-3). 1996. 15.95 (*0-399-22832-2*, G P Putnam) Peng Put Young Read.

— The Kite. (Stories the Year 'Round Ser.). (Illus.). 23p. (J). (gr. k-12). 1992. pap. 7.95 (*1-56014-228-6*) Santillana.

***Ada, Alma F.** The Lizard & the Sun: La Lagartija y el Sol. 48p. (J). (gr. k-3). 1999. pap. 6.99 (*0-440-41531-4*) BDD Bks Young Read.

Ada, Alma F. The Lizard & the Sun/La Lagartija y el Sol: An Old Mexican Folk-Tale. Zubizarreta, Rosa, tr. LC 95-53283. (ENG & SPA., Illus.). 48p. (J). (gr. k-3). 1997. 16.95 (*0-385-32121-X*, DD Bks Yng Read) BDD Bks Young Read.

— Magical Encounter. 1994. pap. 15.50 (*0-88272-838-5*) Santillana.

— The Malachite Palace. Zubizarreta, Rosa, tr. from SPA. LC 95-44676. 32p. (J). (ps-3). 1998. 16.00 (*0-689-31972-X*) Atheneum Yung Read.

— Manzano, Manzano! (Big Book) (Cuento Mas Ser.). (SPA., Illus.). 24p. (Orig.). (J). (gr. k-3). 1989. pap. text 29.95 (*0-917837-09-6*) Hampton-Brown.

— Me Gustaria Tener (How Happy I Would Be) (Libros para Contar/Stories for the Telling Ser.). (SPA., Illus.). (J). (gr. k-1). 1989. pap. 5.95 (*0-88272-795-8*); pap. 5.95 (*0-88272-804-0*) Santillana.

— Me Gustaria Tener (How Happy I Would Be), Big Book. (Libros para Contar/Stories for the Telling Ser.). (SPA., Illus.). (J). (gr. k-1). 1989. 18.95 (*0-88272-796-6*); 18.95 (*0-88272-805-9*) Santillana.

— Me Llamo Maria Isabel. (SPA., Illus.). 64p. (J). (gr. 4-7). 1994. mass mkt. 15.00 (*0-689-31963-0*) Atheneum Yung Read.

— La Moneda de Oro (The Gold Coin) (SPA.). 1996. 11.95 (*84-241-3338-2*); pap. text 5.95 (*84-241-3364-1*) Lectorum Pubns.

— My Name Is Maria Isabel. Cerro, Ana M., tr. from SPA. LC 91-44910. (Illus.). 64p. (J). (gr. 2-5). 1993. 13.00 (*0-689-31517-1*) Atheneum Yung Read.

— My Name Is Maria Isabel: Spanish. (SPA.). 64p. (J). 1996. per. 4.99 (*0-689-81099-7*) S&S Childrens.

— No Fui Yo. (Cuentos para Todo el Ano Ser.). (SPA.). (J). (gr. k-12). pap. 7.95 (*1-56014-218-9*) Santillana.

— No Quiero Derretirme! (Cuentos para Todo el Ano Ser.). (SPA.). (J). (gr. k-12). pap. 7.95 (*1-56014-229-4*) Santillana.

— El Oso Mas Elegante (Big Book) (Cuento Mas Ser.). (SPA., Illus.). 24p. (Orig.). (J). (gr. k-3). 1989. pap. text 29.95 (*0-917837-10-X*) Hampton-Brown.

— El Panuelo de Seda. (Cuentos con Alma Ser.). (SPA., Illus.). 24p. (J). 1993. 16.95 (*1-56492-105-0*) Laredo.

— El Papalote. (Cuentos para Todo el Ano Ser.). (SPA., Illus.). 23p. (J). (gr. k-12). 1992. pap. 7.95 (*1-56014-227-8*) Santillana.

— El Patio de Mi Casa: Big Book. (Early Learning Packs Ser.). (SPA., Illus.). 16p. (Orig.). (J). (gr. 1-3). 1991. pap. text 29.95 (*1-56334-018-6*) Hampton-Brown.

— El Patio de Mi Casa: Small Book. (Early Learning Packs Ser.). (SPA., Illus.). 16p. (Orig.). (J). (gr. 1-3). 1991. pap. text 36.00 (*1-56334-088-7*) Hampton-Brown.

— Pavo para la Cena de Gracias? No, Gracias! (Cuentos para Todo el Ano Ser.). (SPA., Illus.). (J). (gr. k-12). pap. 7.95 (*1-56014-331-2*) Santillana.

— Pin, Pin, Sarabin. (Cuentos con Alma Ser.). (SPA., Illus.). 24p. (J). (gr. 3-9). 1993. 16.95 (*1-56492-130-1*) Laredo.

— La Pinata Vacia. (Cuentos para Todo el Ano Ser.). (SPA., Illus.). (J). (gr. k-12). pap. 7.95 (*1-56014-225-1*) Santillana.

— Pregones. (Cuentos con Alma Ser.).Tr. of Merchants. (SPA., Illus.). 24p. (J). (gr. 3-4). 1993. 16.95 (*1-56492-110-7*) Laredo.

— Querido Pedrin. (SPA., Illus.). (J). (gr. k-3). 1997. reprint ed. pap. 6.99 (*0-614-29084-8*) Aladdin.

— Quien Nacera Aqui? (Who's Hatching Here?), Big Book. (Libros para Contar/Stories for the Telling Ser.). (SPA., Illus.). (J). (gr. k-1). 18.95 (*0-88272-801-6*) Santillana.

— Quien Nacera Aqui? (Who's Hatching Here?), Big Book. (Libros para Contar/Stories for the Telling Ser.). (Illus.). (J). (gr. k-1). 1989. 18.95 (*0-88272-812-1*) Santillana.

— The Rooster Who Went to His Uncle's Wedding. (J). 1998. 11.19 (*0-606-13749-1*, Pub. by Turtleback) Demco.

— Rosa Alada. (Cuentos para Todo el Ano Ser.). (SPA.). (J). (gr. k-12). 1991. pap. 7.95 (*1-56014-224-3*) Santillana.

— A Rose with Wings. (Stories the Year 'Round Ser.). (J). (gr. k-12). 1998. pap. 7.95 (*1-56014-335-5*) Santillana.

— Sale el Oso (Big Book) (Rimas y Risas Green Ser.). (SPA., Illus.). 16p. (Orig.). (J). (gr. k-3). 1988. pap. text 29.95 (*0-917837-03-7*) Hampton-Brown.

— Sale el Oso (Small Book) (Rimas y Risas Green Ser.). (SPA., Illus.). 16p. (Orig.). (J). (gr. k-3). 1992. pap. text 6.00 (*1-56334-079-8*) Hampton-Brown.

— Los Seis Deseos de la Jirafa (Big Book) (Rimas y Risas Green Ser.). (SPA., Illus.). 16p. (Orig.). (J). (gr. k-3). 1988. pap. text 29.95 (*0-917837-02-9*) Hampton-Brown.

— Los Seis Deseos de la Jirafa (Small Book) (Rimas y Risas Green Ser.). (SPA., Illus.). 16p. (Orig.). (J). (gr. k-3). 1992. pap. text 6.00 (*1-56334-078-X*) Hampton-Brown.

— Una Semilla Nada Mas (Big Book) (Rimas y Risas Red Ser.). (SPA., Illus.). 16p. (Orig.). (J). (gr. k-3). 1990. pap. text 29.95 (*0-917837-56-8*) Hampton-Brown.

— Una Semilla Nada Mas (Small Book) (Rimas y Risas Red Ser.). (SPA., Illus.). 16p. (Orig.). (J). (gr. k-3). 1992. pap. text 6.00 (*1-56334-083-6*) Hampton-Brown.

— Sol Kit. (Spanish Elementary Ser.). (Illus.). 1989. pap. text 171.99 (*0-201-12755-5*) Addison-Wesley.

— La Sorpresa de Mama Coneja. (Cuentos para Todo el Ano Ser.). (SPA.). (J). (gr. k-12). 1991. pap. 7.95 (*1-56014-223-5*) Santillana.

— A Strange Visitor - Una Extrana Visita. (Libros para Contar Ser.). (Illus.). 26p. (Orig.). (J). (gr. k-2). 1989. 3.95 (*0-88272-802-4*); 3.95 (*0-88272-793-1*) Santillana.

— A Surprise for Mother Rabbit. (Stories the Year 'Round Ser.). (J). (gr. k-12). 1998. pap. 7.95 (*1-56014-280-4*) Santillana.

— El Susto del Fantasma. (Cuentos para Todo el Ano Ser.). (SPA.). (J). (gr. k-12). pap. 7.95 (*1-56014-222-7*) Santillana.

— Three Golden Oranges. LC 97-47570. (Illus.). 32p. (J). (gr. k-3). 1999. 17.00 (*0-689-80775-9*) S&S Childrens.

— Turkey for Thanksgiving Dinner? No Thanks! (Stories the Year 'Round Ser.). (J). (gr. k-12). 1998. pap. 7.95 (*1-56014-339-8*) Santillana.

***Ada, Alma F.** Under the Royal Palms: A Childhood in Cuba. LC 97-48887. (Illus.). 96p. (J). (gr. 3-7). 1998. 15.00 (*0-689-80631-0*) S&S Childrens.

Ada, Alma F. The Unicorn of the West: El Unicornio del Oeste. Zubizarreta, Rosa, tr. LC 92-7425. (SPA., Illus.). 32p. (J). (gr. 1-3). 1994. text 14.95 (*0-689-31916-9*) Atheneum Yung Read.

***Ada, Alma F.** What Are Ghosts Afraid Of? (Stories the Year 'Round Ser.). (J). (gr. k-12). 1998. pap. 7.95 (*1-56014-338-X*) Santillana.

Ada, Alma F. Where the Flame Trees Bloom. (Illus.). 80p. (J). 1994. 14.95 (*0-689-31900-2*) Atheneum Yung Read.

— Where the Flame Trees Bloom. (SPA.). (J). 2000. 14.00 (*0-689-80018-5*) Atheneum Yung Read.

— Who's Hatching Here? - Quien Nacera Aqui? (Libros para Contar Ser.). (ENG & SPA., Illus.). 24p. (J). (gr. k-2). 1989. 3.95 (*0-88272-811-3*); 3.95 (*0-88272-800-8*) Santillana.

— Yours Truly Goldilocks. LC 97-10696. (Illus.). 40p. (J). (ps-4). 1998. 16.00 (*0-689-81608-1*) Atheneum Yung Read.

Ada, Alma F., ed. Olmo y la Mariposa Azul. (Laredo Children's Bilingual Library). (Illus.). 24p. (J). (gr. k-3). 1992. lib. bdg. 7.50 (*1-56492-095-X*) Laredo.

Ada, Alma F., tr. La Natividad. rev. ed. LC 93-46976.Tr. of Nativity. (SPA., Illus.). 32p. (J). (ps up). 1994. pap. 4.95 (*0-15-200184-0*) Harcourt.

Ada, Alma F. & Zubizarreta, Rosalma, trs. Uncle Nacho's Hat (El Sombrero del Tio Nacho) LC 88-37090. (ENG & SPA., Illus.). 32p. (YA). (ps-3). 1993. pap. 6.95 (*0-89239-112-X*) Childrens Book Pr.

Ada, Alma F., et al. Choices & Other Stories from the Caribbean. LC 92-43134. (J). 1993. pap. 6.95 (*0-377-00257-7*) Friendship Pr.

— A Chorus of Cultures (Cultural Heritage Program with 12 Small Books) Developing Literacy Through Multicultural Poetry. (Illus.). 1993. 229.00 (*1-56334-338-X*) Hampton-Brown.

— A Chorus of Cultures (Cultural Heritage Program Without Small Books) Developing Literacy Through Multicultural Poetry. (Illus.). (Orig.). 1993. 185.00 (*1-56334-337-1*) Hampton-Brown.

— A Chorus of Cultures Poetry Anthology: Developing Literacy Through Multicultural Poetry. (Chorus of Cultures Ser.). (Illus.). 304p. (Orig.). (J). (gr. 1-6). 1993. pap., spiral bd. 49.95 (*1-56334-325-8*) Hampton-Brown.

Ada, Alma F., jt. auth. see Perl, Lila.

Ada, Alma F., tr. see Ackerman, Karen.

Ada, Alma F., tr. see Artell, Mike.

Ada, Alma F., tr. see Avery, Kristin.

Ada, Alma F., tr. see Baden, Robert.

Ada, Alma F., tr. see Blume, Judy.

Ada, Alma F., tr. see Butler, Andrea.

Ada, Alma F., tr. see Cabral, Len.

Ada, Alma F., tr. see Drescher, Henrik.

Ada, Alma F., tr. see Ehlert, Lois.

Ada, Alma F., tr. see Franklin, Kristine L.

Ada, Alma F., tr. see Greene, Inez.

Ada, Alma F., tr. see Guthrie, Woody.

Ada, Alma F., tr. see Hayes, Ann.

Ada, Alma F., tr. see Hutchins, Pat.

Ada, Alma F., tr. see Lester, Helen.

Ada, Alma F., tr. see Luenn, Nancy.

Ada, Alma F., tr. see Min, Laura.

Ada, Alma F., tr. see Mora, Pat.

Ada, Alma F., tr. see Piper, Watty.

Ada, Alma F., tr. see Pratt, Kristin J.

Ada, Alma F., tr. see Rylant, Cynthia.

Ada, Alma F., tr. see Snyder, Carol.

Ada, Alma F., tr. see Viorst, Judith.

Ada, Alma F., tr. see Williams, Sue.

Ada, Alma F., tr. see Wood, Audrey.

***Ada, Alma Flor.** Acuarela. (SPA., Illus.). 1999. pap. text 4.95 (*1-58105-422-X*) Santillana.

— Anton Pirulero. (SPA., Illus.). (ps-3). 1999. pap. text 7.95 (*1-58105-403-3*) Santillana.

— Asi Soy. (Puertas al Sol Ser.). (SPA., Illus.). 1999. pap. text 4.95 (*1-58105-412-2*) Santillana.

— Azul y Verde. (SPA., Illus.). 1999. pap. text 9.95 (*1-58105-417-3*) Santillana.

— Brocha y Pincel. (SPA., Illus.). 1999. pap. text 9.95 (*1-58105-419-X*) Santillana.

— Caballete. (SPA., Illus.). 1999. pap. text 9.95 (*1-58105-421-1*) Santillana.

— Caminos. (SPA., Illus.). 1999. pap. text 9.95 (*1-58105-415-7*) Santillana.

— Chuchurumbe. (SPA., Illus.). (ps-3). 1999. pap. text 8.95 (*1-58105-407-6*) Santillana.

— Colores. (SPA., Illus.). 1999. pap. text 4.95 (*1-58105-418-1*) Santillana.

— Crayones. (SPA., Illus.). 1999. pap. text 4.95 (*1-58105-420-3*) Santillana.

Ada, Alma Flor. Dear Peter Rabbit. LC 93-8459. (Illus.). 32p. (J). (gr. k-3). 1994. lib. bdg. 16.00 (*0-689-31850-2*) Atheneum Yung Read.

— Friend Frog. LC 97-45563. (Illus.). 32p. (J). 2000. 16.00 (*0-15-201522-1*, Gulliver Bks) Harcourt.

— The Gold Coin. Randall, Bernice, tr. from SPA. LC 93-14403. (Illus.). 32p. (J). (gr. k-3). 1994. mass mkt. 5.99 (*0-689-71793-8*) Aladdin.

— The Gold Coin. Randall, Bernice, tr. LC 90-32806. (Illus.). 32p. (J). (gr. k-3). 1991. lib. bdg. 16.00 (*0-689-31633-X*) Atheneum Yung Read.

— The Gold Coin. Randall, Bernice, tr. (J). 1994. 11.19 (*0-606-05846-X*, Pub. by Turtleback) Demco.

***Ada, Alma Flor.** Le Hamaca de la Vaca: O un Amigo Mas. (Cuentos para Todo el Ano (Little Books) Ser.). (SPA.). 2000. pap. text 7.95 (*1-58105-178-6*) Santillana.

— Lapices. (SPA., Illus.). 1999. pap. text 5.95 (*1-58105-424-6*) Santillana.

— Letras. (SPA., Illus.). 1999. pap. text 4.95 (*1-58105-402-5*) Santillana.

— Lienzo y Papel. (SPA., Illus.). 1999. pap. text 9.95 (*1-58105-423-8*) Santillana.

— Mambru. 1999. pap. text 7.95 (*1-58105-405-X*) Santillana.

— Me Gustaria Tener... (SPA.). (gr. k-3). 2000. pap. 5.95 (*1-58105-194-8*) Santillana.

Ada, Alma Flor. Me Llamo Maria Isabel. 1996. 10.19 (*0-606-10485-2*, Pub. by Turtleback) Demco.

— Mediopollito, a Folktale in Spanish & English. (Dell Picture Yearling Ser.). 1997. 11.19 (*0-606-11612-5*, Pub. by Turtleback) Demco.

***Ada, Alma Flor.** Mis Recuerdos. (Puertas al Sol Ser.). (SPA., Illus.). 1999. pap. text 4.95 (*1-58105-414-9*) Santillana.

— Mis Relatos. (Puertas al Sol Ser.). (SPA., Illus.). 1999. pap. text 4.95 (*1-58105-416-5*) Santillana.

— La Moneda de Oro.Tr. of Gold Coin. (SPA.). 1996. 11.15 (*0-606-13555-3*, Pub. by Turtleback) Demco.

Ada, Alma Flor. My Name is Maria Isabel. (J). 1995. 9.40 (*0-606-07908-4*) Turtleback.

— My Name Is Maria Isabel: Spanish. (J). 1996. pap. 4.95 (*0-689-31980-0*) S&S Bks Yung.

***Ada, Alma Flor.** Palabras. (SPA., Illus.). 1999. pap. text 4.95 (*1-58105-404-1*) Santillana.

— Pasos. (Puertas al Sol Ser.). (SPA., Illus.). 1999. pap. text 8.95 (*1-58105-411-4*) Santillana.

— Pimpon. (SPA., Illus.). (ps-3). 1999. pap. text 7.95 (*1-58105-401-7*) Santillana.

— La Pinata Vacia. (Cuentos para Todo el Ano (Little Books) Ser.). (SPA., Illus.). (J). 1999. pap. 7.95 (*1-58105-188-3*) Santillana.

— Poemas. (SPA., Illus.). 1999. pap. text 5.95 (*1-58105-408-4*) Santillana.

— Rimas. (SPA., Illus.). 1999. pap. text 4.95 (*1-58105-406-8*) Santillana.

— Sonrisas. (SPA., Illus.). 1999. pap. text 8.95 (*1-58105-409-2*) Santillana.

— El Susto de los Fantasmas. (Cuentos para Todo el Ano (Little Books) Ser.). (SPA.). (gr. k-3). 2000. pap. 7.95 (*1-58105-170-0*) Santillana.

— Voces. (SPA., Illus.). (gr. 4-7). 1999. pap. text 8.95 (*1-58105-413-0*) Santillana.

— Yo. (SPA., Illus.). 1999. pap. text 4.95 (*1-58105-410-6*) Santillana.

Ada, Alma Flor, see Flor Ada, Alma.

Ada, Alma Flor, tr. see Baker, Keith.

Ada, Alma Flor, tr. see Cherry, Lynne.

ADA Decision Systems Staff. DPL Decision Analysis Software for Microsft Windows: Advanced Version User Guide. 556p. 1995. pap. text, student ed. 108.95 incl. disk (*0-534-24816-0*) Wadsworth Pub.

— DPL Decision Analysis Software for Microsoft Windows: Standard Version User Guide. 441p. 1994. pap. text 45.25 incl. disk (*0-534-24810-1*) Wadsworth Pub.

***Ada-Europe International Conference on Reliable Software Technologies Staff, et al.** Reliable Software Technologies Ada Europe 2000: 5th Ada-europe International Conference on Reliable Software Technologies, Potsdam, Germany, June 26-30 2000 : Proceedings. LC 00-44020. 2000. pap. write for info. (*3-540-67669-4*) Spr-Verlag.

Ada, G. L. & Ramsay, Alistair J. Vaccines, Vaccination & the Immune Response. LC 96-31613. 272p. 1996. text 98.00 (*0-397-58761-9*) Lppncott W & W.

Ada, G. L., jt. ed. see Bankowski, Z.

Ada, Gordon L., ed. Strategies in Vaccine Design. LC 93-46422. (Medical Intelligence Unit Ser.). 232p. 1994. 99.00 (*1-57059-094-X*, LN9094) Landes Bioscience.

ADA/ADA Staff. The American Diabetes Association/The American Dietetic Association Family Cookbook, Vol. I. (Illus.). 448p. 1987. 23.00 (*0-671-76132-3*) S&S Trade.

— Being Vegetarian. (The Nutrition Now Series). 144p. 1996. pap. 6.95 (*0-471-34661-6*) Wiley.

Adab, Beverly J. Annotated Texts for Translation: English - French. LC 95-440508. (Topics in Translation Ser.: Vol. 5). (ENG & FRE.). 330p. 1996. 69.00 (*1-85359-320-6*, Pub. by Multilingual Matters); pap. 26.95 (*1-85359-319-2*, Pub. by Multilingual Matters) Taylor & Francis.

— Annotated Texts for Translation: French-English. LC 93-11423. (Topics in Translation Ser.: Vol. 3). 180p. 1993. 69.00 (*1-85359-206-4*, Pub. by Multilingual Matters); pap. 26.95 (*1-85359-205-6*, Pub. by Multilingual Matters) Taylor & Francis.

Adab, Beverly J., jt. auth. see Schaffner, Christina.

Adachi, Agnes. Child of the Winds: "My Mission with Raoul Wallenberg" LC 88-83367. (Illus.). 192p. 1989. lib. bdg. 19.95 (*0-9621930-0-3*) A Adachi.

— Four Seasons. 33p. (Orig.). 1995. pap. 7.50 (*0-9621930-3-8*) A Adachi.

— Gellert. LC 96-96954. 86p. (Orig.). 1994. pap. 12.00 (*0-9621930-5-4*) A Adachi.

— Homecoming. (Orig.). 1993. pap. 7.50 (*0-9621930-1-1*) A Adachi.

— Mabuto. 112p. 2000. pap. 11.00 (*0-8059-4676-4*) Dorrance.

— Short Stories. LC 95-94393. (Orig.). (YA). (gr. 9-12). 1995. pap. 10.00 (*0-9621930-2-X*) A Adachi.

— Wise Raoul. (Orig.). (J). (gr. 3-6). 1995. pap. 10.00 (*0-9621930-4-6*) A Adachi.

Adachi, Akeo, ed. Foundations of Computation Theory. 166p. (gr. 12). 1990. 63.00 (*90-5199-049-9*, Pub. by IOS Pr) IOS Press.

Adachi, Fumie, tr. & intro. see Matsuya Piece-Goods Store Staff, ed.

Adachi, Geraldine, ed. see Demura, Fumio.

Adachi, Geraldine, ed. see Demura, Fumio & Ivan, Dan.

Adachi, Geraldine, ed. see Toguchi, Seikichi.

Adachi, Hideo & Nagai, Jun. Three-Dimensional CT Angiography. LC 95-3482. 248p. 1995. text 162.00 (*0-316-00701-3*) Lppncott W & W.

Adachi, Jeff. Bar Breaker, vols 1 & 2. 1124p. (Orig.). (C). 1998. pap. 89.95 (*1-882278-04-6*) Survival Series.

— Bar Card Complete Set, 2 vols. (Illus.). (Orig.). (C). 1997. pap. 49.95 (*1-882278-07-0*) Survival Series.

— Bar Exam Survival Kit. 170p. (C). 1996. pap. text 29.95 (*1-882278-01-1*) Survival Series.

— Law School Survival Kit. 294p. (C). 1999. pap. text 29.95 (*1-882278-02-X*) Survival Series.

Adachi, Jeff & Wallack, Soloman. MBE Survival Kit: Guide to Success on the Multi-State Bar Exam. 443p. (Orig.). (C). 1998. pap. 29.95 (*1-882278-08-9*) Survival Series.

Adachi, Jonathan D. & Ioannidis, George. Primer on Corticosteroid-Induced Osteoporosis. 54p. pap. text 29.95 (*0-7817-2443-0*) Lppncott W & W.

Adachi, K. Minimum Japanese - Polish, Polish - Japanese Dictionary. (JPN & POL.). 1992. write for info. (*0-8288-7282-1*) Fr & Eur.

Adachi, Kelly. The Kids' Handbook. (Illus.). 112p. (J). (gr. 1 up). 1985. 7.95 (*0-8184-0365-9*); pap. 4.95 (*0-8184-0368-3*) Carol Pub Group.

Adachi, Masahisa. Imbeddings & Immersions. Hudson, Kiki, tr. from JPN. LC 93-7464. (Translations of Mathematical Monographs: Vol. 124). 183p. 1993. text 103.00 (*0-8218-4612-4*, MMONO/124) Am Math.

***Adachi, Mitsuru.** Short Program. (Illus.). 2000. pap. 16.95 (*1-56931-473-X*) Viz Commns Inc.

Adachi Office Staff, ed. see Batt, Deleece.

Adachi, S., ed. Properties of Aluminium Gallium Arsenide. (EMIS Datareviews Ser.: No. 7). 340p. 1993. boxed set 195.00 (*0-85296-558-3*, EM007) INSPEC Inc.

Adachi, Sadao. GaAs & Related Materials: Bulk Semiconducting & Superlattice Properties. LC 94-23457. 696p. 1994. text 106.00 (*981-02-1925-3*) World Scientific Pub.

***Adachi, Sadao.** Optical Properties of Crystaline & Amorphous Semiconductors: Materials & Fundamental Principles LC 99-23738. 1999. write for info. (*0-7923-8563-2*) Kluwer Academic.

Adachi, Sadao. Physical Properties of III-V Semiconductor Compounds: InP, InAs, GaAs, GaP, InGaAs, & InGaAsp. LC 92-7286. 336p. 1992. 140.00 (*0-471-57329-9*) Wiley.

Adachi, Sakyo, tr. see Webber, Bert.

Adachi, Toshihisa, et al, eds. Localisation & Bifurcation Theory for Soils & Rocks: Proceedings of the 4th International Workshop, Gifu, Japan, 28 September-2 October, 1997. (Illus.). 370p. (C). 1998. text 88.00 (*90-5809-004-3*) Ashgate Pub Co.

Adademiderinninbund, Deutschen, ed. Die Frauenfrage in Deutschland Bibliographie, 1931-1980, Vol. 10. (GER.). 957p. 1982. lib. bdg. 62.00 (*3-598-20187-7*) K G Saur Verlag.

Adagia-Hoven, R. Erasmi Opera Omnia. 350p. 1999. 190.50 (*0-444-82834-6*) Elsevier.

Adah, Samouhi Fawq el, see Fawq el Adah, Samouhi.

Adahan, Miriam. After the Chuppah: Making Marriage Work. (Miriam Adahan Handbook Ser.). 260p. 1994. 12.95 (*1-56871-070-4*) Targum Pr.

— Appreciating People: Including Yourself. 1989. 22.95 (*0-87306-485-2*) Feldheim.

— Awareness. LC 94-12976. (J). 1994. 24.95 (*0-87306-668-5*) Feldheim.

— Calm Down: Taking Control of Your Life. (The Miriam Adahan Handbook Ser.). 256p. 1995. 12.95 (*1-56871-082-8*) Targum Pr.

— E. M. E. T. T. A Step-by-Step Guide to Emotional Maturity Established Through Torah. 1987. 21.95 (*0-87306-410-0*) Feldheim.

— It's All a Gift. LC 92-13105. 1992. 24.95 (*0-87306-609-X*) Feldheim.

— The Miriam Adahan Handbook: Living with Kids Parents at Their Best. 250p. 1994. 12.95 (*1-56871-050-X*) Targum Pr.

— The Miriam Adahan Handbook: Nobody's Perfect - Maintaining Emotional Health, Vol. 1. 263p. 1994. 12.95 (*1-56871-047-X*) Targum Pr.

— Raising Children to Care: A Jewish Guide to Childrearing. 1988. 22.95 (*0-87306-456-9*) Feldheim.

— Sticks & Stones: Identifying & Avoiding All Forms of Abuse. LC 97-7351. 1997. 17.95 (*0-87306-793-2*) Feldheim.

Adahan, Miriam, contrib. by. Awareness. 1994. pap. 20.95 (*0-87306-671-5*) Feldheim.

Adahein, Miriam. 30 Seconds to Emotional Health. 1996. 17.95 (*0-87306-782-7*) Feldheim.

***Adahl, Karin, ed.** Islamic Art Collections: An International Survey. 288p. 1999. (*0-7007-1153-8*, Pub. by Curzon Pr Ltd) Paul & Co Pubs.

Adair. Frommer's Budget Travel Guide Mexico on $45 a Day, 1996. 1995. pap. 19.00 (*0-671-51885-2*) S&S Trade.

— Frommer's Comprehensive Travel Guide Puerto Vallarta, Manzanillo, Guadalajara 96-97. 1996. pap. 13.95 (*0-671-51934-4*) S&S Trade.

— Frommer's Mexico City. 1995. pap. 13.00 (*0-671-88493-X*) S&S Trade.

***Adair & Gillen.** Adair's Management Development Exercises. annuals 2000. boxed set 375.00 (*0-8464-4999-4*) Beekman Pubs.

Adair, Alistair S., jt. auth. see McCluskey, William J.

Adair, Alvis V. Desegregation: The Illusion of Black Progress. LC 83-25914. 208p. 1984. pap. text 22.50 (*0-8191-3767-7*) U Pr of Amer.

***Adair, Angela J.** Write Your Autobiography Using Memory Triggers: The Workbook for Awakening & Recording Memories. 98p. 1999. pap. 29.95 (*1-929072-02-3*) Deep South Pubng.

Adair, Audrey. Music Curriculum Activities Library. LC 87-8829. 112p. (C). 1987. pap. text 18.95 (*0-13-065707-7*) P-H.

An Asterisk (*) at the beginning of an entry indicates that the title is appearing for the first time.

Adair, Audrey J. Great Composers & Their Music History Unit 5: Fifty Ready to Use Activities. LC 87-8840. (Music Curriculum Activities Library: Vol. 5). 112p. (J). (gr. 3-9). 1987. pap. text 18.95 (*0-13-363797-2*, Parker Publishing Co) P-H.
— Musical Instruments & the Voices Grades 3-9: Fifty Ready-to-Use Activities. LC 87-8834. Vol. 4. 112p. (C). 1987. pap. text 18.95 (*0-13-606963-0*) P-H.
— Musicians in Action: Fifty Ready-to-Use Activities for Grades 3-9, Unit 7. LC 87-8833. (Classroom Music Activities Library: Vol. 7). 112p. (C). 1987. pap. text 18.95 (*0-13-607144-9*) P-H.
— Reading & Writing Music: Fifty Ready-to-Use Activities for Grades 3-9. LC 87-8830. (Music Curriculum Activities Library: Vol. 2). 112p. (C). 1987. pap. text 18.95 (*0-13-762196-5*) P-H.
— Ready-to-Use Music Activities Kit. LC 83-17480. 320p. (C). 1983. pap. text 32.95 (*0-13-762295-3*, Parker Publishing Co) P-H.
— Special Days Throughout the Year Unit 6: Fifty Ready-to-Use Activities. (Music Curriculum Activities Library). 112p. (J). (gr. 3-9). 1987. pap. text 18.95 (*0-13-826421-X*, Parker Publishing Co) P-H.
— Types of Musical Form & Composition: Fifty Ready-to-Use Activities. (Music Curriculum Activities Library). 112p. (C). 1987. pap. text 18.95 (*0-13-934985-5*) P-H.
***Adair, Cherry.** Kiss & Tell. 320p. 2000. mass mkt. 6.50 (*0-449-00683-2*) Ivy Books.
Adair, Cherry. The Mercenary. 1994. per. 2.99 (*0-373-25592-6*) Harlequin Bks.
— Le Serment du Solitaire. (Rouge Passion Ser.: Bk. 496). 1999. mass mkt. 3.50 (*0-373-37496-8*, 1-37496-6) Harlequin Bks.
Adair, Christy. Women & Dance: Sylphs & Sirens. LC 92-17279. (Illus.). 304p. (C). 1992. text 45.00 (*0-8147-0621-5*); pap. text 17.00 (*0-8147-0622-3*) NYU Pr.
Adair, D., jt. auth. see Hamilton, W. H.
Adair, Daryl & Vamplew, Wray. Sport in Australian History. LC 97-159539. (Australian Retrospectives Ser.). 184p. (Orig.). 1998. pap. 32.00 (*0-19-553590-1*) OUP.
Adair, David. A Davidian Testimony. 1997. 12.95 (*1-890503-08-8*) Mt Carmel Ctr.
Adair, Dick. Aloha Bear & the Meaning of Aloha. (Illus.). 24p. (J). (ps). 1987. 10.95 (*0-89610-077-4*) Island Heritage.
— The Story of Aloha Bear. (Illus.). 24p. (J). (ps). 1986. 10.95 (*0-89610-049-9*) Island Heritage.
— The Story of Aloha Bear. 1987. 13.95 incl. audio (*0-89610-074-X*) Island Heritage.
Adair, Douglas & Colbourn, Trevor. Fame & the Founding Fathers: Essays by Douglass Adair. LC 98-2875. 1998. 20.00 (*0-86597-192-7*); pap. 9.50 (*0-86597-193-5*) Liberty Fund.
Adair, Douglass, ed. see Adams, John & Rush, Benjamin.
Adair, Douglass, ed. see Oliver, Peter.
***Adair, Douglas G.** The Intellectual Origins of Jeffersonian Democracy: Republicanism, the Class Struggle & the Virtuous Farmer. Yellin, Mark E., ed. 272p. 2000. 65.00 (*0-7391-0124-2*); pap. 22.95 (*0-7391-0125-0*) Lxngtn Bks.
Adair, E. I Bought a Windmill. (Aberdeen University Press Bks.). (Illus.). 102p. 1978. pap. 8.00 (*0-08-023651-0*, Pergamon Pr) Elsevier.
Adair, Elizabeth. Flowers & Folk of the NE. 160p. 1998. pap. 24.00 (*1-84017-001-8*) St Mut.
Adair, Gene. George Washington Carver: Botanist. Huggins, Nathan I., ed. (Black Americans of Achievement Ser.). (Illus.). 124p. (YA). (gr. 5 up). 1989. pap. 8.95 (*0-7910-0234-9*) Chelsea Hse.
— George Washington Carver: Botanist. Huggins, Nathan I., ed. (Black Americans of Achievement Ser.). (Illus.). 124p. (YA). (gr. 5 up). 1989. lib. bdg. 19.95 (*1-55546-577-3*) Chelsea Hse.
— Thomas Alva Edison: Inventing the Electric Age. (Oxford Portraits in Science Ser.). (Illus.). 144p. (YA). (gr. 7 up). 1997. pap. 11.95 (*0-19-511981-9*) OUP.
— Thomas Edison: Inventing the Electric Age. (Oxford Scientists Ser.). (Illus.). 144p. (YA). (gr. 7 up). 1996. 22.00 (*0-19-508799-2*) OUP.
Adair, Gilbert. Love & Death on Long Island. LC 98-22274. 144p. 1998. pap. 12.00 (*0-8021-3592-7*, Grove) Grove-Atltic.
***Adair, Gilbert.** Movies. 2000. pap. 14.95 (*0-14-118084-6*) Viking Penguin.
Adair, Gilbert. Surfing the Zeitgeist. 256p. 1997. pap. 16.95 (*0-571-17991-6*) Faber & Faber.
Adair, Gilbert, tr. see Truffaut, Francois.
Adair-Heeley, Charlene. The Human Side of Just-in-Time: How to Make the Techniques Really Work. 325p. 1991. 29.95 (*0-8144-5031-8*) AMACOM.
Adair-Hoy, Angela, jt. auth. see Rose, M. J.
Adair, Ian. Magic Tricks: The Master's Secrets. 1995. 14.95 (*0-7858-0497-8*) Bk Sales Inc.
— One-Hundred Magic Tricks. 1991. 12.98 (*1-55521-729-X*) Bk Sales Inc.
Adair, James. The Works of James Adair, 1709-1783, Set. reprint ed. lib. bdg. 500.00 (*0-685-18555-9*) Rprt Serv.
Adair, James, jt. auth. see Verploegh, Harry.
Adair, James B. Adair History & Genealogy. (Illus.). 330p. 1991. reprint ed. pap. 51.50 (*0-8328-1802-X*); reprint ed. lib. bdg. 61.50 (*0-8328-1801-1*) Higginson Bk Co.
— Adair History & Genealogy. (Illus.). 408p. 1990. reprint ed. 37.50 (*0-89308-086-1*, FH 1) Southern Hist Pr.
Adair, James H. Applied Colloid & Surface Chemistry. 1999. 69.95 (*0-8493-8663-2*) CRC Pr.
Adair, James H., et al, eds. Handbook on Characterization Techniques for the Solid-Solution Interface. LC 93-33158. 1993. 74.00 (*0-944904-67-X*, G014) Am Ceramic.
— Science, Technology, & Applications of Colloidal Suspensions. LC 95-34341. (Ceramic Transactions Ser.: Vol. 54). 278p. 1995. 88.00 (*0-944904-96-3*, CT054) Am Ceramic.
Adair, James R. Saints Alive. LC 76-117319. (Biography Index Reprint Ser.). 1977. 20.95 (*0-8369-8011-5*) Ayer.
Adair, James R., ed. see Wiersbe, Warren W.
Adair, Janice, ed. see Adair, Michael.
Adair, Jean & Gregory, Helen. Menopause Country. (Illus.). 32p. (Orig.). 1996. pap. 5.50 (*0-941973-13-1*) Pinstripe Pub.
***Adair, John.** Decision Making & Problem Solving. 96p. 2000. pap. 17.95 (*0-8464-5026-7*) Beekman Pubs.
— Leadership Skills. 96p. 2000. pap. 17.95 (*0-8464-5102-6*) Beekman Pubs.
Adair, John. Navajo & Pueblo Silversmiths. LC 44-7567. (Civilization of the American Indian Ser.: No. 25). (Illus.). 264p. 1989. reprint ed. pap. 15.95 (*0-8061-2215-3*) U of Okla Pr.
Adair, John, jt. auth. see Leighton, Dorothea C.
Adair, John, jt. auth. see Worth, Sol.
Adair, John E. Puritans: Religion & Politics in Seventeenth-century England & America. LC 98-230233. x, 302 p. 1998. write for info. (*0-7509-2117-X*) Sutton Pub Ltd.
Adair, John Eric. By the Sword Divided: Eyewitness Accounts of the English Civil War. LC 98-195237. (History Paperbacks Ser.). (Illus.). 240p. 1998. pap. 21.95 (*0-7509-1858-6*, Pub. by Sutton Pub Ltd) Intl Pubs Mktg.
— Decision-Making & Problem Solving. 1997. pap. 24.00 (*0-85292-691-X*, Pub. by IPM Hse) St Mut.
— Developing Leaders. 1989. text 19.95 (*0-07-707076-3*) McGraw.
— Effective Leadership: A Self-Development Manual. 130p. 1983. text 59.95 (*0-566-02411-X*, Pub. by Gower) Ashgate Pub Co.
— Effective Teambuilding. 224p. 1986. text 59.95 (*0-566-02605-8*, Pub. by Gower) Ashgate Pub Co.
— Organization Communication Profile. (C). 1985. pap. 75.00 (*0-85171-083-2*, Pub. by IPM Hse) St Mut.
— Puritans: Religion & Politics in 17th Century England & America. LC 98-230233. 320p. 1998. pap. 24.95 (*0-7509-1950-7*, Pub. by Sutton Pub Ltd) Intl Pubs Mktg.
— Sir William Waller: The Campaigns of a Roundhead General. LC 97-164956. (Illus.). 1997. 45.00 (*0-7509-1312-6*, Pub. by Sutton Pub Ltd) Intl Pubs Mktg.
Adair, John Eric & Despres, David. Training for Communication: A Trainer's Manual. 89p. (C). 1985. ring bd. 225.00 (*0-85171-082-4*, Pub. by IPM Hse) St Mut.
Adair, John Eric & Despres, David, eds. A Handbook of Management Training Exercises Vol. 1. 157p. (C). 1987. ring bd. 285.00 (*0-85171-068-9*, Pub. by IPM Hse) St Mut.
— A Handbook of Management Training Exercises Vol. 2. 130p. (C). 1987. ring bd. 285.00 (*0-85171-078-6*, Pub. by IPM Hse) St Mut.
— A Handbook of Management Training Exercises Vol. 3. 130p. (C). 1987. ring bd. 285.00 (*0-85171-085-9*, Pub. by IPM Hse) St Mut.
Adair, John Eric & Gillen, Terry. Adair's Management Development Exercises. 1997. pap. 525.00 (*0-85292-684-7*, Pub. by IPM Hse) St Mut.
Adair, John Eric, et al. A Handbook of Management Training Exercises, Vol. 1. 160p. 1981. 350.00 (*0-7855-7319-4*) St Mut.
Adair, John Eric, jt. auth. see Young, Peter.
Adair, John Eric, ed. see Richards, John.
Adair, John G. Advances in Psychological Science: Social, Personal & Cultural Aspects. 580p. 1998. 94.95 (*0-86377-470-9*) L Erlbaum Assocs.
Adair, John R., jt. auth. see Harris, William J.
Adair, Kent T., jt. auth. see Li, Shiyou.
Adair, Lawrens. Glass Houses: Paper Men. 369p. (C). 1990. 80.00 (*1-875401-12-1*, Pub. by Boolarong Pubns) St Mut.
Adair, Margo. Essential Visualization Source: Combining Imagination, Intuition & Mindfulness for Healing Ourselves, Our Communities & Our Planet. 1999. pap. 14.00 (*0-609-80364-6*) Crown Pub Group.
— From Leadership to Empowerment. 23p. (Orig.). 1995. pap. 4.50 (*1-882098-25-0*) Tools Change.
Adair, Margo & Howell, Sharon. Breaking Old Patterns Weaving New Ties: Alliance Building. (Orig.). 1990. pap. 4.50 (*1-882098-24-2*) Tools Change.
— The Subjective Side of Politics. (Illus.). (Orig.). 1988. 3.50 (*1-882098-23-4*) Tools Change.
Adair, Marita. Frommer's Acapulco, Ixtapa & Taxco. 3rd ed. 1996. 13.95 (*0-02-861244-2*) Prntice Hall Bks.
— Frommer's Cancun, Cozumel & the Yucatan. 3rd ed. 1996. 14.95 (*0-02-861246-9*) Prntice Hall Bks.
— Frommer's Mexico. 560p. 1996. 18.95 (*0-02-861139-X*, P-H Travel) Prntice Hall Bks.
— Frommer's Mexico on 35$ a Day. 22nd ed. 1996. 19.95 (*0-02-861143-8*) Macmillan.
Adair, Marty. Frommer's Mexico 98. 704p. 1997. 19.95 (*0-02-861580-8*) Macmillan.
— Frommer's Portable Puerto Vallarta, Manzanillo, & Guadalajara. 4th ed. 176p. 1997. pap. 9.95 (*0-02-861581-6*) Macmillan.
Adair, Mary J., et al. Archeology & Paleoecology of the Central Great Plains: A Volume in the Central & Northern Plains Archeological Overview. LC 96-46225. (Arkansas Archeological Survey Research Ser.: No. 48). (Illus.). 292p. 1996. pap. 30.00 (*1-56349-079-X*, RS48) AR Archaeol.
Adair, Michael. Hey! You're Driving Me Crazy! The Definitive Guide for Handling the Stress & Anxiety of Driving. Adair, Janice, ed. LC 96-85166. (Illus.). 88p. (Orig.). (C). 1996. pap. 8.95 (*1-57502-220-6*, PO874) Morris Pubng.
Adair, Olivia & Havranek, Edward P., eds. Cardiology Secrets: Questions You Will Be Asked on Rounds, in the Clinic, on Oral Exams. (Secrets Ser.). (Illus.). 300p. (Orig.). 1994. pap. text 37.00 (*1-56053-104-5*) Hanley & Belfus.
Adair, Patricia M. The Waking Dream: A Study of Coleridge's Poetry. LC 68-71147. viii, 247p. 1967. write for info. (*0-7131-5000-9*) Arnld Pub.
Adair, Peggy. Chance. LC 90-82750. 200p. (Orig.). (YA). (gr. 6-12). 1990. pap. 4.95 (*0-9626803-9-7*) Deep Riv Pr.
Adair, R., et al. Brinca de Alegria Hacia la Primavera Con las Matematicas y Ciencias - Spring into Math & Science. (ENG & SPA.). 94p. (J). (gr. k-1). 1988. 16.95 (*1-881431-21-5*, 1403) AIMS Educ Fnd.
— Fall into Math & Science. (J). (gr. k-1). 1987. 16.95 (*1-881431-18-5*, 1101) AIMS Educ Fnd.
— Glide into Winter with Math & Science. (J). (gr. k-1). 1987. 16.95 (*1-881431-17-7*, 1102) AIMS Educ Fnd.
— Patine Al Invierno Con Matematicas y Ciencias - Glide into Winter with Math & Science. (ENG & SPA.) 105p. (J). (gr. k-1). 1987. 16.95 (*1-881431-20-7*, 1402) AIMS Educ Fnd.
Adair, Richard. Courtship, Illegitimacy & Marriage in Early Modern England. LC 95-37790. 272p. (C). 1996. text 79.95 (*0-7190-4252-6*, Pub. by Manchester Univ Pr) St Martin.
Adair, Robert K. The Great Design: Particles, Fields, & Creation. (Illus.). 384p. 1989. reprint ed. pap. 15.95 (*0-19-506069-5*) OUP.
— Physics of Baseball. LC 89-45623. (Illus.). 128p. (Orig.). 1990. pap. 7.95 (*0-00-001526-1*, Perennial) HarperTrade.
— The Physics of Baseball: 2nd Edition, Revised, Updated, & Enlarged. 2nd rev. ed. (Illus.). 160p. 1994. pap. 12.00 (*0-06-095047-1*, Perennial) HarperTrade.
Adair, Robin, et al. Spring into Math & Science. (J). (gr. k-1). 1987. 16.95 (*1-881431-16-9*, 1103) AIMS Educ Fnd.
***Adair, Sarah.** Information Sources for the Press & Broadcast Media. 2nd ed. LC 99-39789. (Guides to Information Sources Ser.). 256p. 1999. write for info. (*1-85739-261-2*) Bowker-Saur.
Adair, Sharilyn S. Where Is Jesus? LC 97-203007. 24p. (J). (ps-k). 1997. pap. 4.95 (*0-687-45869-2*) Abingdon.
— Zacchaeus Has a Good Day. LC 97-203008. 24p. (J). (gr. 1-4). 1997. pap. 4.95 (*0-687-05876-7*) Abingdon.
***Adair, Tama.** Austin's Best. Staton, Tracy, ed. (Illus.). 75p. 1999. pap. 19.95 (*0-9675270-0-7*, 0001) High Mountain.
Adair, Tammi. What the Angels Would Feed Their Babies. (Illus.). 50p. 1995. pap. 6.95 (*0-9649833-1-1*) T Adair.
Adair, Thomas H., jt. auth. see Hall, John E.
***Adair, Tom S.** Of Angels & Vipers: A Hawaiian Mystery. LC 99-91862. 2000. 25.00 (*0-7388-1342-7*); pap. 18.00 (*0-7388-1343-5*) Xlibris Corp.
— Poems for Love Letters: A Hawaiian Mystery. LC 99-91864. 2000. 25.00 (*0-7388-1344-3*); pap. 18.00 (*0-7388-1345-1*) Xlibris Corp.
Adair, Virginia. Living on Fire: A Collection of Poems. LC 99-52858. 176p. 2000. 22.00 (*0-375-50289-0*) Random.
Adair, Virginia H. Beliefs & Blasphemies. LC 97-47403 176p. 1998. 22.00 (*0-375-50017-0*) Random.
Adair, Virginia Hamilton. Ants on the Melon: A Collection of Poems. LC PS3551.D244A82 1999. 1998. pap. 12.95 (*0-375-75229-3*) Modern Lib NY.
***Adair, Vivyan C.** From Good Ma to Welfare Queen: A Genealogy of the Poor Woman in American Literature, Photography & Culture. (Literary Criticism & Cultural Theory Ser.). 200p. 2000. 55.00 (*0-8153-3651-9*) Garland.
Adair, William. The Frame in America, 1700-1900: A Survey of Fabrication Techniques & Styles. (Illus.). 50p. (Orig.). 1983. 15.00 (*0-317-03934-2*) Prof Picture Frame.
Adakai, Joline, tr. see Van Valkenburgh, A. Richard.
Adal. The Evidence of Things Not Seen. LC 74-31350. (Photography Ser.). (Illus.). 1975. 25.00 (*0-306-70722-5*) Da Capo.
Adalian, Paul T., jt. auth. see Duffy, Susan.
Adalian, Rouben P. & Masih, Joseph R., eds. Armenia & Karabagh Factbook. 2nd ed. (Illus.). 118p. 1996. pap. 10.00 (*0-925428-08-6*) Armenian Assembly.
Adalja, Varsha. Eni Sugandh (Gujerati) large type ed. (Charnwood Large Print Ser.). 1990. 27.99 (*0-7089-2270-8*, Charnwood) Ulverscroft.
Adam. Egyptian Activity Book. (Illus.). (J). 1998. 1.00 (*0-486-40079-4*) Dover.
— Longman Dictionary of Business English. 1994. pap. text write for info. (*0-582-25126-5*, Pub. by Addison-Wesley) Longman.
— Symbolistes et Decadents. Pakenham, ed. (Exeter French Texts Ser.: Vol. 70). (FRE.). 104p. Date not set. pap. text 19.95 (*0-85989-300-6*, Pub. by Univ Exeter Pr) Northwestern U Pr.
Adam, jt. auth. see Ghali, Wagdy R.
Adam, ed. see Balzac, Honore de.
Adam, ed. see Baudelaire, Charles.
Adam, A. Cantique de Noel: High E Flat Voice & Piano.Tr. of O Holy Night. (ENG & FRE.). 8p. 1986. pap. 3.95 (*0-7935-5338-5*, 50279730) H Leonard.
— Cantique de Noel: Low B Flat Voice & Piano.Tr. of O Holy Night. 8p. 1986. pap. 3.95 (*0-7935-5345-8*, 50279740) H Leonard.
— Cantique de Noel: Medium High D Flat Voice & Piano.Tr. of O Holy Night. (ENG & FRE.). 8p. 1986. pap. 3.95 (*0-7935-5341-5*, 50285970) H Leonard.
— Cantique de Noel: Medium Low in C Voice & Piano.Tr. of O Holy Night. 8p. 1986. pap. 3.95 (*0-7935-5342-3*, 50281510) H Leonard.
— Geoelectric & Geothermal Studies: East-Central Europe, Soviet Asia. 752p. (C). 1976. 150.00 (*963-05-0887-7*, Pub. by Akade Kiado) St Mut.
— Romanciers du XVII Siecle: Sorel Scarron, Furetiere, Mme. de La Fayette. deluxe ed. (Pleiade Ser.). (FRE.). 1512p. 72.95 (*2-07-010479-6*) Schoenhof.
— Truth Functions & the Problem of Their Realization by Two Terminal Graphs. 206p. (C). 1968. 50.00 (*963-05-3333-2*, Pub. by Akade Kiado) St Mut.
Adam, A. K. A Grammar for New Testament Greek. rev. ed. 224p. 1999. 34.95 (*0-687-01677-0*) Abingdon.
***Adam, A. K. M., ed.** Handbook of Postmodern Biblical Interpretation. 2000. pap. 29.99 (*0-8272-2971-2*) Chalice Pr.
— Postmodern Interpretations of the Bible - A Reader. 2000. pap. 29.99 (*0-8272-2970-4*) Chalice Pr.
Adam, Abdisalam A., tr. see Zino, Muhammad I.
Adam, Adolf. The Eucharistic Celebration: Source & Summit of Faith. 152p. (Orig.). 1994. pap. text 12.95 (*0-8146-6123-8*, Pueblo Bks) Liturgical Pr.
— The Key to Faith: Meditations on the Liturgical Year. Madigan, Patrick, tr. from GER. LC 97-51478. 176p. 1998. pap. 19.95 (*0-8146-2449-9*) Liturgical Pr.
— The Liturgical Year: Its History & Its Meaning after the Reform of the Liturgy. 308p. 1992. pap. 19.95 (*0-8146-6047-9*, Pueblo Bks) Liturgical Pr.
Adam, Agnes. Aunt Janet. Landes, William-Alan, ed. LC 97-7631. 72p. (Orig.). 1997. pap. 5.00 (*0-88734-718-5*) Players Pr.
Adam, Agnes. Between Two Thieves. 55p. (Orig.). 1996. pap. 5.00 (*0-88734-383-X*) Players Pr.
Adam, Agnes. Birds of Prey. LC 96-23874. 1996. pap. 5.00 (*0-88734-387-2*) Players Pr.
— A Bit of Land. LC 96-38348. 55p. (Orig.). 1996. pap. 5.00 (*0-88734-302-3*) Players Pr.
— Braidlands. LC 96-17886. 55p. (Orig.). 1996. pap. 6.00 (*0-88734-452-6*) Players Pr.
— Business Meeting. LC 96-25049. 55p. (Orig.). 1996. pap. 5.00 (*0-88734-363-5*) Players Pr.
— A Cameo from Cranford. 28p. (Orig.). 1996. pap. 5.00 (*0-88734-351-1*) Players Pr.
— Castles in the Air. LC 96-22100. 55p. (Orig.). 1996. pap. 5.00 (*0-88734-386-4*) Players Pr.
— Christmas. 28p. (Orig.). 1996. pap. 5.00 (*0-88734-352-X*) Players Pr.
— Coffee Morning. LC 96-23413. 55p. (Orig.). 1996. pap. 5.00 (*0-88734-365-1*) Players Pr.
— The Devil Goes Riding. LC 98-15149. 1998. pap. 5.00 (*0-88734-787-8*) Players Pr.
— A Great Occasion. LC 96-17479. 55p. (Orig.). 1996. pap. 5.00 (*0-88734-359-7*) Players Pr.
***Adam, Agnes.** Home Sweet Home. unabridged ed. LC 99-56580. 28p. (YA). (gr. 4-12). 1999. pap. 5.00 (*0-88734-764-9*) Players Pr.
Adam, Agnes. A Matter of Diplomacy. 32p. (Orig.). 1996. pap. 5.00 (*0-88734-356-2*) Players Pr.
— Miss Primrose's Husband. LC 98-55441. 28p. 1999. pap. 5.00 (*0-88734-828-9*) Players Pr.
— The Old Chest. Landes, William-Alan, ed. LC 98-52429. (Illus.). 28p. 1998. pap. 5.00 (*0-88734-822-X*) Players Pr.
— A Pearl of Great Price. LC 96-18029. 55p. (Orig.). 1996. pap. 5.00 (*0-88734-377-5*) Players Pr.
Adam, Ahmat. The Vernacular Press & the Emergence of Modern Indonesian Consciousness (1855 - 1913) (Studies on Southeast Asia: No. 17). (Orig.). (C). 1995. pap. text 16.00 (*0-87727-716-8*) Cornell SE Asia.
Adam, Alison. Artificial Knowing: Gender & the Thinking Machine. LC 97-16346. 216p. (C). 1998. 75.00 (*0-415-12962-1*); pap. 22.99 (*0-415-12963-X*) Routledge.
Adam, Alison & International Conference on Women, Work & Computer, eds. Women, Work & Computerization: Breaking Old Boundaries, Building New Forms: Proceedings of the IFIP TC9/WG 9.1 International Conference on Women, Work & Computerization Held in Manchester, U.K., 2-5 July, 1994. LC 94-37290. (IFIP Transactions A: Computer Science & Technology Ser.: Vol. A-57). 462p. 1994. pap. 149.00 (*0-444-81927-4*) Elsevier.
Adam, Andreas, jt. ed. see Watkinson, Anthony.
Adam, Andrew K. What Is Postmodern Biblical Criticism? LC 95-3485. (Guides to Biblical Scholarship Ser.). 96p. 1995. pap. 12.00 (*0-8006-2879-9*, 1-2879, Fortress Pr) Augsburg Fortress.
Adam, Andy & Gibson, Robert, eds. Practical Interventional Radiology of the Hepatobiliary System & Gastrointestinal Tract. 224p. 1994. text 98.50 (*0-340-55166-6*, Pub. by E A) OUP.
Adam, Andy & Rossi, Plinio. Biliary Tract Radiology. LC 96-29096. (Medical Radiology Ser.). (Illus.). 450p. 1996. 236.00 (*3-540-58776-4*) Spr-Verlag.
Adam, Antoine, jt. auth. see Diderot, Denis.
Adam, Antoine, ed. see Rimbaud, Arthur.
Adam, Antoine, ed. see Voltaire.
Adam, Arlie J., et al. Listening to Learn: A Handbook for Parents of a Hearing-Impaired Child. (Centennial Celebration Ser.). 110p. (Orig.). 1990. pap. text 19.95 (*0-88200-166-3*) Alexander Graham.
Adam, Auste, jt. auth. see Adam, Helen.
Adam, Barbara. Timescapes of Modernity: The Environment & Invisible Hazards. LC 97-23332. (Global Environmental Change Ser.). (Illus.). 256p. (C). 1998. 85.00 (*0-415-16274-2*) Routledge.
— Timescapes of Modernity: The Environment & Invisible Hazards. LC 97-23332. (Global Environmental Change Ser.). (Illus.). 256p. (C). 1998. pap. 24.99 (*0-415-16275-0*) Routledge.

— Timewatch: The Social Analysis of Time. 224p. (C). 1995. pap. text 26.95 (*0-7456-1461-2*) Blackwell Pubs.

Adam, Barbara & Allan, Stuart, eds. Theorizing Culture: An Interdisciplinary Critique after Postmodernism. (Illus.). 288p. (C). 1995. text 55.00 (*0-8147-0643-6*); pap. text 19.50 (*0-8147-0644-4*) NYU Pr.

Adam, Barry D. The Rise of a Gay & Lesbian Movement. (Social Movements Past & Present Ser.). 200p. 1987. 28.95 (*0-8057-9714-9*, Twyne) Mac Lib Ref.

— The Rise of a Gay & Lesbian Movement. rev. ed. LC 94-34364. (Social Movements Past & Present Ser.). 1995. 33.00 (*0-8057-3863-0*, Twyne); pap. 20.00 (*0-8057-3864-9*, Twyne) Mac Lib Ref.

Adam, Barry D., et al, eds. The Global Emergence of Gay & Lesbian Politics: National Imprints of a Worldwide Movement. LC 98-17218. 448p. 1998. text 59.95 (*1-56639-644-1*) Temple U Pr.

— The Global Emergence of Gay & Lesbian Politics: National Imprints of a Worldwide Movement. LC 98-17218. 448p. 1998. pap. text 22.95 (*1-56639-645-X*) Temple U Pr.

Adam, Barry D. & Sears, Alan. Experiencing HIV: Personal, Family & Work Relationships. LC 96-19248. 182p. 1996. 52.00 (*0-231-10120-1*); pap. 17.50 (*0-231-10121-X*) Col U Pr.

Adam, Bon. The Two Divinely Chosen Families & the New World Order. LC 97-178732. 1996. pap. write for info. (*1-86106-291-5*, Pub. by Minerva Pr) Unity Dist.

Adam, Bronwyn E., jt. ed. see Diamond, Robert M.

Adam-Casimiro, Niki, ed. & illus. see Mazel, David.

Adam, Charles, jt. auth. see Descartes, Rene.

***Adam, Christine.** The Adoption Option Complete Handbook, 2000-2001. LC 99-41662. 2000. pap. 24.95 (*0-7615-2007-4*) Prima Pub.

Adam, Christopher S., et al. Adjusting Privatization: Case Studies from Developing Countries. 400p. (C). 1993. pap. 29.95 (*0-435-08084-9*, 08084) Heinemann.

***Adam, David.** Border Lands: The Best of David Adam's Celtic Vision. LC 99-47011. 244p. 2000. 24.95 (*1-58051-070-1*) Sheed & Ward WI.

Adam, David. Celtic Book of Prayer. gif. ed. 156p. 1999. pap. 14.95 (*1-57098-310-0*) Roberts Rinehart.

— The Cry of the Deer: Meditations on the Hymn of St. Patrick. LC 88-39427. (Illus.). 176p. 1987. reprint ed. pap. 10.95 (*0-8192-1442-6*) Morehouse Pub.

***Adam, David.** A Desert in the Ocean: The Spiritual Journey According to St. Brendan the Navigator. 2000. pap. 11.95 (*0-8091-3994-4*) Grove-Atltic.

Adam, David. The Edge of Glory: Prayers in the Celtic Tradition. LC 87-31227. (Illus.). 120p. 1986. pap. 10.95 (*0-8192-1418-3*) Morehouse Pub.

— A Flame in My Heart: St. Aidan for Today. LC 98-30602. (Illus.). 176p. 1998. pap. 8.95 (*0-8192-1775-1*) Morehouse Pub.

***Adam, David.** Glimpses of Glory: Prayers for the Church Year C. 160p. 2000. pap. 11.95 (*0-8192-1865-0*) Morehouse Pub.

— Holy Island. 64p. 2000. pap. text 6.50 (*1-85311-165-1*) Canterbury Press Norwich.

Adam, David. The Open Gate: Prayers in the Celtic Tradition. LC 94-44757. (Illus.). 128p. 1995. pap. 9.95 (*0-8192-1640-2*) Morehouse Pub.

***Adam, David.** Power Lines: Celtic Prayers about Work. LC 99-87388. 128p. 2000. pap. 10.95 (*0-8192-1838-3*, 6279) Morehouse Pub.

Adam, David. The Rhythm of Life: Celtic Daily Prayer. LC 97-39554. 144p. 1997. pap. 10.95 (*0-8192-1715-8*) Morehouse Pub.

***Adam, David.** Traces of Glory: Prayers for the Church Year, Year B. LC 99-19746. 160p. 1999. pap. 11.95 (*0-8192-1824-3*) Morehouse Pub.

Adam, David, compiled by. The Wisdom of the Celts. LC 96-47030. (Wisdom Ser.). (Illus.). 48p. 1996. 8.00 (*0-8028-3833-2*) Eerdmans.

Adam, David R. Angie: The Littlest Elf. LC 97-94501. (Illus.). 32p. (J). (ps-6). 1997. pap. 7.95 (*0-9661318-0-0*, 3180) Hedge Corn.

Adam, E. Orgies Unlimited. 6.95 (*0-7472-4528-2*, Pub. by Headline Bk Pub) Trafalgar.

Adam, E., ed. Torrent of Portyngale. (EETS, ES Ser.: No. 51). 1974. reprint ed. 35.00 (*0-527-00257-7*) Periodicals Srv.

Adam, Eleanor. Ready-to-Use Illustrations of Children at Play: 95 Different Copyright-Free Designs Printed One Side. (Clip Art Ser.). (Illus.). 64p. 1993. text 5.95 (*0-486-27525-6*) Dover.

Adam, Eleanor J. Ready-to-Use Reading & Writing Silhouettes: 95 Different Copyright-Free Designs Printed One Side. (Clip Art Ser.). (Illus.). 64p. 1994. text 5.95 (*0-486-28183-3*) Dover.

Adam, Evelyn. To Be a Nurse. 2nd ed. (Illus.). 167p. 1990. pap. 32.00 (*0-920513-06-9*, Pub. by Saulnders) Saunders.

Adam, Frank. The Clans, Septs & Regiments of the Scottish Highlands. 8th ed. (Illus.). 624p. 1999. reprint ed. pap. 46.50 (*0-8063-0448-0*, 40, Pub. by Clearfield Co) ACCESS Pubs Network.

Adam, G. Visceral Perception: Understanding Internal Cognition. LC 98-19005. (Plenum Series in Behavioral Psychophysiology & Medicine). (Illus.). 200p. (C). 1998. text 49.50 (*0-306-45755-5*, Kluwer Plenum) Kluwer Academic.

Adam, Gerhard, jt. ed. see Debatin, J. F.

Adam, Gerold. Perception, Consciousness, Memory: Reflections of a Biologist. Takacsi-Nagy, K., tr. from HUN. LC 73-20153. (Illus.). 230p. 1980. reprint ed. pap. 71.30 (*0-608-05461-5*, 206593000006) Bks Demand.

Adam, Graeme M. Spain & Portugal. 1976. lib. bdg. 59.95 (*0-8490-2638-5*) Gordon Pr.

— Spain & Portugal, 2 vols., Set. 1980. lib. bdg. 199.00 (*0-8490-3183-4*) Gordon Pr.

Adam, H. Transactions of the International Vacuum Congress, 3rd, Stuttgart, June 1965, Vol. 2: Sessions 1-4. LC 59-6851. 1967. 368.00 (*0-08-011763-5*, Pub. by Pergamon Repr) Franklin.

— Transactions of the International Vacuum Congress, 3rd, 1965 Vol. 2: Sessions 5-8. 129.00 (*0-08-012126-8*, Pub. by Pergamon Repr) Franklin.

Adam, H., ed. Transactions: International Vacuum Congress, 3rd, Stuttgart, 1965, Vol. 1-2, Pts. 1-2. 1967. 108.00 (*0-08-012127-6*, Pub. by Pergamon Repr) Franklin.

***Adam, Hans C.** Edward S. Curtis. 1999. 39.99 (*3-8228-7183-4*) Benedikt Taschen.

Adam, Hans C. Karl Blassfeldt, 1865-1932. (Illus.). 359p. 1999. 39.99 (*3-8228-7438-8*) Taschen Amer.

***Adam, Hans-Christian.** Edward S. Curtis: Los Indios de Norteamerica. 1998. pap. 38.99 (*3-8228-8023-X*) Benedikt Taschen.

Adam, Hans Christian, ed. see Krase, Andreas.

Adam, Hargrave L., ed. Trial of George Chapman, No. 1. (Notable British Trials Ser.). x, 223p. 1995. reprint ed. 71.00 (*1-56169-155-0*) Gaunt.

— Trial of George Henry Lamson, No. 1. (Notable British Trials Ser.). 192p. 1995. reprint ed. 62.00 (*1-56169-146-1*) Gaunt.

Adam, Helen. The Bells of Dis. (Morning Coffee Chapbook Ser.). (Illus.). 18p. (Orig.). 1985. pap. 20.00 (*0-915124-92-0*) Coffee Hse.

— Ghosts & Grinning Shadows. 1979. pap. 8.00 (*0-914610-10-4*) Hanging Loose.

— Gone Sailing. limited ed. 1980. pap. 5.00 (*0-915124-29-7*) Toothpaste.

— San Francisco's Burning. 1985. 25.00 (*0-914610-43-0*); pap. 15.00 (*0-914610-33-3*) Hanging Loose.

— Selected Poems & Ballads. LC 74-77378. (Publication Ser.: No. 5b). (Illus.). 60p. 1975. 20.00 (*0-914496-04-2*) Helikon NY.

— Turn again to Me. 1977. 7.00 (*0-686-22908-8*); pap. 3.50 (*0-686-22909-6*) Kulchur Foun.

Adam, Helen & Adam, Auste. Stone Cold Gothic. 1984. 7.00 (*0-317-16221-7*); pap. 3.50 (*0-317-16222-5*) Kulchur Foun.

Adam, Hella. Plutarch's Schrift Non Posse Suaviter Vivi Secundum Epicurum. LC 72-96778. (Studien zur antiken Philosophie). (GER.). vi, 95p. (C). 1974. 38.00 (*90-6032-015-8*, Pub. by B R Gruner) Humanities.

Adam, Heribert & Giliomee, Hermann. Ethnic Power Mobilized: Can South Africa Change? LC 78-65492. 308p. 1979. 17.00 (*0-300-02377-4*) Yale U Pr.

Adam, Heribert & Moodley, Kogila A. The Opening of the Apartheid Mind: Options for the New South Africa. LC 92-36443. (Perspectives on Southern Africa Ser.: No. 50). (C). 1993. 35.00 (*0-520-08199-4*, Pub. by U CA Pr) Cal Prin Full Svc.

Adam, Heribert, et al. Comrades in Business: Post-Liberation Politics in South Africa. 256p. 1998. pap. 25.00 (*90-5727-022-6*, Pub. by Intl Bks) Paul & Co Pubs.

Adam, Hussein M. & Ford, Richard. Mending Rips in the Sky: Options for Somali Communities in the 21st Century. LC 97-10801. 1997. 89.95 (*1-56902-073-6*) Red Sea Pr.

Adam, Hussein M. & Ford, Richard, eds. Mending Rips in the Sky: Options for Somali Communities in the 21st Century. 630p. 1997. pap. 29.95 (*1-56902-074-4*) Red Sea Pr.

Adam, Ian, ed. This Particular Web: Essays on Middlemarch. LC 75-15844. 137p. reprint ed. pap. 42.50 (*0-8357-3628-8*, 203635600003) Bks Demand.

***Adam, J.** Mesons & Light Nuclei: Proceedings of the 7th Conference Prague-pruhonice, Czech Republic, 1998. 1999. 120.00 (*981-02-3885-1*) WSC Inst MA Studies.

Adam, J., ed. Plato: Crito. (Bristol Greek Texts Ser.). (GRE.). 128p. 1991. pap. 18.95 (*1-85399-032-9*, Pub. by Brist Class Pr) Focus Pub-R Pullins.

Adam, J., et al, eds. Mesons & Light Nuclei '95: Proceedings of the 6th International Conference, Straz pod Ralskem, Held July 3-7, 1995. LC 95-51699. (Few-Body Systems Ser.: Vol. 9). 527p. 1996. 159.00 (*3-211-82786-2*) Spr-Verlag.

Adam, J. A. & Bellomo, N., eds. A Survey of Models for Tumor-Immune System Dynamics. LC 96-38754. 332p. 1996. 75.00 (*0-8176-3901-2*) Birkhauser.

Adam, J. H. Longman Dictionary of Business English. Date not set. text. write for info. (*0-582-05029-4*, Pub. by Addison-Wesley) Longman.

Adam, Jacob. Zeit zur Abreise. Fehrs, J. & Heitmann, M., eds. (Haskala - Wissenschaftliche Abhandlungen Ser.: Vol. 5). (GER.). 161p. 1993. write for info. (*3-487-09772-9*) G Olms Pubs.

Adam, James. The Religious Teachers of Greece. LC 72-2565. (Select Bibliographies Reprint Ser.). 1977. reprint ed. 37.95 (*0-8369-6843-3*) Ayer.

— The Religious Teachers of Greece. LC 65-22806. (Library of Religious & Philosophical Thought). iv, 467p. 1966. reprint ed. lib. bdg. 37.50 (*0-678-09950-2*, Reference Bk Pubs) Kelley.

Adam, James M. Hypothermia - Ashore & Afloat: Proceedings of 3rd International " Action for Disaster " Conference, Aberdeen 1979. (Illus.). 216p. 1981. 48.00 (*0-08-025750-X*, Pergamon Pr) Elsevier.

Adam, James S. The Business Diaries of Sir Alexander Grant. 144p. (C). 1996. 38.00 (*0-85976-349-8*, Pub. by J Donald) St Mut.

***Adam, Jan.** Social Costs of Transformation to A Market Economy in Post-socialist Countries: The Case of Pola. LC 98-55364. 212p. 1999. text 69.95 (*0-312-22160-6*) St Martin.

Adam, Jan. Why Did Socialism Collapse in Central & East European Countries? The Case of Poland, Czechoslovakia & Hungary. 240p. 1996. text 75.00 (*0-312-12879-7*) St Martin.

Adam, Jean-Pierre. Roman Building: Materials & Technique. Mathews, Anthony S., tr. from FRE. LC 94-17349.Tr. of Construction Romaine. (Illus.). 364p. 1994. 57.50 (*0-253-30124-6*) Ind U Pr.

Adam, J.H. Longman Dictionary of Business English: English-Hungarian. 2nd ed. (ENG & HUN.). 809p. 1993. 150.00 (*0-7859-8882-3*) Fr & Eur.

Adam, Joseph. Christy: A Christmas Tree with Dreams. (Illus.). 18p. (J). (ps-3). 1996. 15.95 (*0-9653687-0-X*) Jamestwn Pr.

Adam, Judith. The New City Gardener: Natural Techniques & Necessary Skills for a Successful City Garden. (Illus.). 224p. 1999. pap. 24.95 (*1-55209-313-1*) Firefly Bks Ltd.

Adam, Karl. The Spirit of Catholicism. McCann, Justin, tr. LC 97-28325. 264p. 1997. pap. text 19.95 (*0-8245-1718-0*) Crossroad NY.

— The Spirit of Catholicism. 2nd ed. 252p. 1996. reprint ed. pap. 12.95 (*0-940535-85-8*, UP185) Franciscan U Pr.

Adam, Kelli. Internet Information Server Administration. 2000. pap. text 44.95 (*0-7357-0022-2*) New Riders Pub.

— MCSE Training Guide: TCP/IP. 2nd ed. LC 98-86323. (Training Guides). 1998. 49.99 (*1-56205-920-3*) New Riders Pub.

Adam Kring, Hilda, ed. From the Harmonist Kuche: Excerpts from & Commentary on the Housewife As Manager in the Kitchen, Pantry & the Kitchen Garden. (Illus.). 72p. 1998. 10.00 (*1-888578-06-8*) R E F Typesetting Pub.

Adam, M. The Little Entente & Europe (1920-1929) 330p. (C). 1993. 120.00 (*963-05-6320-7*, Pub. by Akade Kiado) St Mut.

— The Little Entente & Europe (1920-1929) 330p. (C). 1993. 120.00 (*963-05-6420-3*, Pub. by Akade Kiado) St Mut.

Adam, M., jt. auth. see Adam, S.

Adam, M., jt. auth. see Deyl, Z.

***Adam Media Corporation Staff, contrib. by.** The Everything Angels Mini Book: Discover the Heavenly Companions in Your Life. (Everything Mini Book Ser.). (Illus.). 192p. 2000. pap. 4.95 (*1-58062-387-5*) Adams Media.

— The Everything Astrology Mini Book. (Everything Mini Book Ser.). (Illus.). 192p. 2000. pap. 4.95 (*1-58062-385-9*) Adams Media.

— The Everything Baby Names Mini Book: Traditional to Original- Pick the Perfect Name! (Everything Mini Book Ser.). (Illus.). 192p. 2000. pap. 4.95 (*1-58062-391-3*) Adams Media.

— The Everything Bedtime Story Mini Book: 20 Favorite Family Classics to Make Bedtime Fun! (Everything Mini Book Ser.). (Illus.). 192p. 2000. pap. 4.95 (*1-58062-390-5*) Adams Media.

— The Everything Dreams Mini Book: Understand the Messages from Your Mind. (Everything Mini Book Ser.). (Illus.). 192p. 2000. pap. 4.95 (*1-58062-386-7*) Adams Media.

— The Everything Get Ready for Baby Mini Book: What You Need Before Baby Arrives! (Everything Mini Book Ser.). (Illus.). 192p. 2000. pap. 4.95 (*1-58062-389-1*) Adams Media.

— The Everything Love Spells Mini Book: Create Your Own Magic! (Everything Mini Book Ser.). (Illus.). 192p. 2000. pap. 4.95 (*1-58062-388-3*) Adams Media.

— Just What the Doctor Ordered: Health & Grooming in the Classic Age of Advertising. (Illus.). 32p. 2000. pap. 9.95 (*1-58062-376-X*) Adams Media.

— The Los Angeles JobBank. (JobBank Ser.). 520p. 2000. pap. 16.95 (*1-58062-381-6*) Adams Media.

— The Missouri JobBank. 3rd ed. (JobBank Ser.). 336p. 2000. pap. 16.95 (*1-58062-380-8*) Adams Media.

Adam, Michael. How to Tie Ties. LC 96-19462. (Illus.). 48p. 1996. 9.95 (*0-8069-9345-6*) Sterling.

Adam, Monika. Die Ubergangszone Von Buchen- und Fichtenwald in Den Noerdlichen Kalkalpen-Klimatische, Edaphische und Vegetationskundliche Aspekte Dargestellt Am Beispiel des Tamina- und Calfeisentales (SG-GR) (Dissertationes Botanicae Ser.: Band 255). (Illus.). xvi, 272p. 1995. pap. 83.00 (*3-443-64167-9*, Pub. by Gebruder Borntraeger) Balogh.

Adam, Nabil R. Electronic Commerce: Technical, Business & Legal Issues. LC 98-229064. 250p. 1998. 39.99 incl. cd-rom (*0-13-949082-5*) P-H.

Adam, Nabil R. & Bhargava, Bharat K., eds. Advanced Database Systems. LC 93-43688. (Lecture Notes in Computer Science Ser.). (Illus.). xv, 452p. 1993. 65.00 (*0-387-57507-3*) Spr-Verlag.

Adam, Nabil R. & Dogramaci, Ali, eds. Productivity Analysis at the Organizational Level. (Productivity Analysis Studies). 192p. 1981. lib. bdg. 71.50 (*0-89838-038-3*) Kluwer Academic.

Adam, Nabil R. & Gangopadhyay, Aryya. Database Issues in Geographic Information Systems. LC 97-8834. 136p. 1997. text 109.50 (*0-7923-9924-2*) Kluwer Academic.

Adam, Nabil R. & Yesha, Yelena, eds. Electronic Commerce: Current Research Issues & Applications. LC 95-52722. (Lecture Notes in Computer Science Ser.: No. 1028). 155p. 1996. pap. 36.00 (*3-540-60738-2*) Spr-Verlag.

Adam, Nabil R., jt. auth. see Dogramaci, Ali.

Adam, Nabil R., ed. see Bhargava, Bharat K.

Adam, Nabil R., jt. ed. see Dogramaci, Ali.

Adam, Nicky. Who's Who in British Opera. LC 93-12314. 600p. 1993. 69.95 (*0-85967-894-6*, Pub. by Scolar Pr); pap. text 34.95 (*1-85928-044-7*, Pub. by Scolar Pr) Ashgate Pub Co.

Adam of Usk. Chronicon Adae de Usk, A.D., 1377 to 1421. Thompson, Edward M., ed. LC 78-63447. (Pilgrimages Ser.). 392p. 1980. reprint ed. 57.50 (*0-404-16367-X*) AMS Pr.

Adam, Paul. Australian Rainforests. (Monographs on Biogeography: No. 6). (Illus.). 322p. 1994. reprint ed. pap. text 45.00 (*0-19-854872-9*) OUP.

***Adam, Paul.** Unholy Trinity. 376p. 2000. 25.95 (*1-55970-520-5*, Pub. by Arcade Pub Inc) Time Warner.

— Unholy Trinity. 488p. 2000. 31.99 (*0-7089-4225-3*) Ulverscroft.

Adam, Peter. Art of the Third Reich. (Illus.). 400p. 1992. 49.50 (*0-8109-1912-5*, Pub. by Abrams) Time Warner.

— Art of the Third Reich. (Illus.). 332p. 1995. pap. 19.95 (*0-8109-2615-6*, Pub. by Abrams) Time Warner.

— David Hockney & His Friends: Outlines. LC 98-148593. (Out Lines Ser.). (Illus.). 144p. 1997. pap. text 9.95 (*1-899791-55-8*) Stewart Tabori & Chang.

— Eileen Gray: Architect-Designer: A Biography. (Illus.). 335p. 1987. 39.95 (*0-8109-0996-0*) Abrams.

***Adam, Peter.** Eileen Gray - Architect/Designer: A Biography. rev. ed. LC 00-22522. (Illus.). 408p. 2000. 39.95 (*0-8109-4143-0*, Pub. by Abrams) Time Warner.

Adam, Peter. Speaking God's Words: A Practical Theology of Expository Preaching. LC 97-43516. 173p. 1998. pap. 15.99 (*0-8308-1522-8*, 1522) InterVarsity.

Adam, Rob. World's Most Powerful Rifles & Guns. 1991. 12.98 (*1-55521-712-5*) Bk Sales Inc.

Adam, Robert. Buildings: How They Work. LC 95-21850. (Illus.). 48p. (J). 1995. 14.95 (*0-8069-0958-7*) Sterling.

— Classical Architecture: A Comprehensive Handbook to the Tradition of Classical Style. (Illus.). 320p. 1991. 49.50 (*0-8109-3166-4*, Pub. by Abrams) Time Warner.

— The Works in Architecture of Robert & James Adam, 3 vols. in 1. LC 78-67644. (Scottish Enlightenment Ser.). reprint ed. 245.00 (*0-404-17233-4*) AMS Pr.

— World's Most Powerful Rifles & Handguns. 128p. 1996. write for info. (*1-57215-176-5*) World Pubns.

Adam, Robert E. Oceans of the World: Syllabus. 1978. pap. text 7.75 (*0-89420-041-0*, 233021); audio 70.85 (*0-89420-166-2*, 233000) Natl Book.

— U. S. Government: Executive Branch: Syllabus. (U. S. Government Ser.). (gr. 7-12). 1979. audio 150.05 (*0-89420-189-1*, 194000) Natl Book.

— U. S. Government: Executive Branch: Syllabus. (U. S. Government Ser.). (YA). (gr. 7-12). 1979. pap. text 8.95 (*0-89420-089-5*, 194030) Natl Book.

Adam, S. & Adam, M. Realization & Enlightenment. LC 96-96353. (Illus.). 157p. (Orig.). 1996. pap. 14.95 (*0-9649152-0-0*) M Smolko.

Adam, Sheila, et al. Critical Care Nursing. (Illus.). 460p. 1997. text 120.00 (*0-19-263023-7*); pap. text 69.50 (*0-19-263022-9*) OUP.

Adam-Smith, Derek, jt. auth. see Goss, David.

Adam Smith, Janet, see Smith, Janet Adam.

Adam, Stephen F. Microwave Theory & Applications. (Illus.). (C). 1992. reprint ed. text 60.00 (*0-9634284-0-3*) A Microwave Cnslt.

Adam, W. E., ed. Heart, Vol. 2. (Handbook of Nuclear Medicine Ser.). 466p. 1993. 315.00 (*1-56081-301-6*, Wiley-VCH) Wiley.

Adam, William. Vitruvius Scoticus: A Facsimile of a Rare & Important Book. reprint ed. 360.00 (*0-404-18136-8*) AMS Pr.

Adam, Winky. African Activity Book. 1999. pap. text 1.00 (*0-486-40492-7*) Dover.

***Adam, Winky.** Bugs Activity Book. (Little Activity Bks.). (Illus.). (J). 2000. pap. 1.00 (*0-486-40969-4*) Dover.

— Color by the Numbers. (Beginners Activity Bks.). (Illus.). (J). 1999. pap. 1.00 (*0-486-40793-4*) Dover.

— Cut-Paper Flower Stickers. (Illus.). (J). 1996. pap. 1.00 (*0-486-29212-6*) Dover.

— Flowers Follow-the-Dots. (Little Activity Bks.). 64p. (J). 1999. pap. text 1.00 (*0-486-40732-2*) Dover.

— Hooray for Halloween! (Glow-in-the-Dark Sticker Bks.). (Illus.). 16p. (J). (ps-k). 2000. pap. 4.99 (*0-448-42171-2*, Planet Dexter) Peng Put Young Read.

— Invisible Egyptian Magic Picture Book. (Little Activity Bks.). (Illus.). (J). 2000. pap. 1.00 (*0-486-41006-4*) Dover.

Adam, Winky. Knights Activity Book. (Illus.). 32p. (J). 1998. pap. 2.50 (*0-486-40356-4*) Dover.

— Let's Meet Allosaurus: And Other Jurassic Dinosaurs. (Illus.). 14p. (J). (ps-1). 1998. 4.99 (*0-689-81595-6*) Litle Simon.

— Let's Meet the Triceratops: And Other Cretaceious Dinosaurs. (Illus.). 14p. (J). (ps-1). 1998. 4.99 (*0-689-81596-4*) Litle Simon.

— Little Dinosaur ABC Coloring Book. (Illus.). 64p. (J). 1998. pap. 1.00 (*0-486-40301-7*) Dover.

***Adam, Winky.** Little Egyptian Mazes. (Little Activity Bks.). 64p. (J). 1999. pap. 1.00 (*0-486-40733-0*) Dover.

— My Ballet Activity Book. 1999. pap. text 1.00 (*0-486-40493-5*) Dover.

Adam, Winky. North American Indian Activity Book. (Illus.). 64p. (J). 1998. pap. 1.00 (*0-486-29824-8*) Dover.

***Adam, Winky.** Telling Time. (J). 2000. pap. 2.50 (*0-486-40794-2*) Dover.

Adama, Abimbola. Directory of African American Writers & Poets, 1992. 1992. pap. text 10.00 (*0-9629532-1-0*) Black Angels.

— Gifts from Spirit. 56p. 1992. pap. text 7.00 (*0-9629532-0-2*) Black Angels.

Adamac, Chris. The Complete Idiot's Guide to Adoption. LC 97-80971. 386p. 1997. 18.95 (*0-02-862108-5*) Macmillan Gen Ref.

Adamaitis, Joseph & Scott, Mary. Mortgage Lending - "From the Streets", Vol. 1. (Illus.). 150p. 1994. 149.00 (*1-885462-01-8*) New Eng Mortage.

— Mortgage Lending Inside the FHA & VA, Vol. 2. (Illus.). 150p. 149.00 (*1-885462-02-6*) New Eng Mortage.

Adamant, N. Hot Pursuit. mass mkt. 6.95 (*0-7472-4266-6*, Pub. by Headline Bk Pub) Trafalgar.

***Adamantopoulos, Konstantinos, et al.** EU Anti-Subsidy Law: Pursuing & Defending Complaints. 180p. 2000. pap. 92.00 (*1-902558-32-4*, Pub. by Palladian Law) Gaunt.

An Asterisk (*) at the beginning of an entry indicates that the title is appearing for the first time.

Adamany, David W. Financing Politics: Recent Wisconsin Elections. LC 79-84948. 318p. reprint ed. pap. 98.60 (*0-608-13892-4*, 202372700033) Bks Demand.

Adamany, David W. & Agree, George E. Political Money: A Strategy for Companion Financing in America. LC 75-11351. 254p. reprint ed. pap. 78.80 (*0-608-14599-8*, 202582000046) Bks Demand.

Adamatzky, Andrew I. Identification of Cellular Automata. 384p. 1994. 138.00 (*0-7484-0172-5*) Taylor & Francis.

Adamczyk, et al. Electricity & Magnetism. (Understanding Geography Ser.). (Illus.). 32p. (YA). (gr. 7-13). 1999. lib. bdg. 15.95 (*0-88110-590-2*, Usborne) EDC.

Adamczyk-Garbowska, Monika, jt. ed. see Polonsky, Antony.

Adamczyk, Peter, et al. Electricity & Magnetism. (Understanding Geography Ser.). (Illus.). 32p. (YA). (gr. 7-13). 1994. pap. 7.95 (*0-7460-0994-1*, Usborne) EDC.

Adamczyk, Richard. United States Army in World War II: Readers Guide. 183p. 1993. per. 13.00 (*0-16-037817-6*) USGPO.

Adamczyk, Werner. Feuer! An Artilleryman's Life on the Eastern Front. (Illus.). 405p. 1992. 25.00 (*0-916107-97-3*) Broadfoot.

Adame, Daniel D., jt. auth. see Abbas, Maher A.

Adame, Leonard, et al. Entrance. 1976. 5.00 (*0-912678-24-0*, Greenfld Rev Pr) Greenfld Rev Lit.

Adame, Samuel. Your Window Looking South. LC 96-90867. 1997. 21.95 (*0-533-12195-7*) Vantage.

Adamec, Christine. How to Live with a Mentally Ill Person: A Handbook of Day-to-Day Strategies. LC 95-42076. 256p. 1996. pap. 15.95 (*0-471-11419-7*) Wiley.

— Is Adoption for You? Essential Information for Making the Right Choice. LC 97-25121. 224p. 1998. pap. 14.95 (*0-471-18312-1*) Wiley.

***Adamec, Christine.** Moms with ADD: A Self-Help Manual. 2000. pap. 14.95 (*0-87833-175-1*) Taylor Pub.

Adamec, Christine. When Your Pet Dies: Dealing with Your Grief & Helping Your Children Cope. LC 97-122161. 192p. 1996. mass mkt. 4.99 (*0-425-15253-7*) Berkley Pub.

Adamec, Christine A. There Are Babies to Adopt. 272p. 1996. pap. 12.00 (*1-57566-013-X*) Kensgtn Pub Corp.

— There Are Babies to Adopt. 1996. pap. 12.00 (*0-8217-5225-1*) NAL.

— The Unofficial Guide to Eldercare. (Unofficial Guides Ser.). 354p. 1999. pap. 15.95 (*0-02-862456-4*, Pub. by Macmillan) S&S Trade.

***Adamec, Christine A.** Writing Freelance. (Illus.). 272p. 2000. pap. 19.95 (*1-55180-289-9*) Self-Counsel Pr.

Adamec, Christine A. & Pierce, William. The Encyclopedia of Adoption. (Illus.). 384p. 1991. 50.00 (*0-8160-2108-2*) Facts on File.

***Adamec, Christine A. & Pierce, William L.** The Encyclopedia of Adoption. 2nd ed. LC 99-40340. (Illus.). 416p. 2000. 60.00 (*0-8160-4041-9*) Facts on File.

Adamec, Ludwig W. Afghanistan's Foreign Affairs to the Mid-Twentieth Century: Relations with the U. S. S. R., Germany & Britain. fac. ed. LC 73-86450. (Illus.). 334p. pap. 103.60 (*0-7837-6964-4*, 204691400003) Bks Demand.

— Dictionary of Afghan Wars, Revolutions, & Insurgencies. LC 96-35600. (Wars, Revolution, & Civil Unrest Ser.: No. 1). 384p. 1996. 48.00 (*0-8108-3232-1*) Scarecrow.

— Historical Dictionary of Afghanistan. 2nd ed. LC 97-2878. (Asian/Oceanian Historical Dictionaries Ser.: No. 29). 499p. 1997. 58.00 (*0-8108-3312-3*) Scarecrow.

Adamek, Jiri. Foundations of Coding: Theory & Applications of Error-Correcting Codes with an Introduction to Cryptography & Information Theory. LC 90-20905. 352p. 1991. 129.95 (*0-471-62187-0*) Wiley.

— Theory of Mathematical Structures. 1983. text 220.00 (*90-277-1459-2*) Kluwer Academic.

Adamek, Jiri & McLane, S., eds. Categorial Topology & Its Relation to Analysis, in Algebra & Its Combinatorics. 488p. (C). 1989. text 123.00 (*9971-5-0966-0*) World Scientific Pub.

Adamek, Jiri & Rosicky, J. Locally Presentable & Accessible Categories. (London Mathematical Society Lecture Note Ser.: No. 184). (Illus.). 329p. (C). 1994. pap. text 49.95 (*0-521-42261-2*) Cambridge U Pr.

Adamek, Jiri & Trnkova, Vera. Automata & Algebras in Categories. (C). 1990. text 330.00 (*0-7923-0010-6*) Kluwer Academic.

Adamek, Maurine R. I'll Do Better Tomorrow, I Promise. 2nd ed. (Illus.). 32p. (J). (gr. 1-6). 1998. reprint ed. pap. 6.99 (*0-9669581-0-1*) Dreyer Pr.

***Adamek, Maurine Reynolds.** I'll Do Better Tomorrow, I Promise. (Illus.). 36p. 1999. 14.99 (*0-9669581-1-X*) Dreyer Pr.

Adamek, Raymond J., et al. The Triumph of Hope: The 1988 Pro-Life Year in Review & a Look to the Future. (Pro-Life Year in Review Ser.). 232p. (Orig.). (C). 1989. pap. 4.95 (*0-9620037-1-9*) NRLC Washington.

Adames, Jay. Christ & Your Problem - Chinese Edition. Lau, Deborah, tr. (CHI.). 33p. 1993. pap. 2.00 (*1-56582-034-7*) Christ Renew Min.

Adamha-Marc, jt. ed. see Stefano, George B.

Adami, Chris. Introduction to Artificial Life. LC 97-37605. (Illus.). 424p. 1997. 59.95 incl. cd-rom (*0-387-94646-2*) Spr-Verlag.

Adami, Christopher. Artificial Life: Proceedings of the Sixth International Conference on Artificial Life, 6. LC 98-22859. (Complex Adaptive Systems Ser.). 1998. pap. text 65.00 (*0-262-51099-5*) MIT Pr.

Adamiak, Richard. Justice & History in the Old Testament: The Evolution of Divine Retribution in the Historiographies of the Wilderness Generation. 2nd ed. 1985. 25.00 (*0-939738-08-2*) Adams Bk Co.

Adamian, Martin S., jt. auth. see Klem, Daniel.

Adamic, Kresimir J., jt. ed. see Herak, Janko N.

Adamic, Louis. Dynamite: A Century of Class Violence in America 1830-1930. rev. ed. 224p. (Orig.). 1984. reprint ed. pap. 12.00 (*0-946061-03-3*) Left Bank.

— Grandsons: A Story of American Lives. LC 74-26092. 384p. 1983. reprint ed. 52.50 (*0-404-58401-2*) AMS Pr.

— Grandsons: A Story of American Lives. LC 90-47472. (Proletarian Literature Ser.). xxviii, 406p. 2000. reprint ed. lib. bdg. 48.00 (*1-55888-300-2*) Omnigraphics Inc.

— Laughing in the Jungle: An Autobiography of an Immigrant in America. LC 69-18755. (American Immigration Collection. Series 1). 1969. reprint ed. 43.55 (*0-405-00503-2*) Ayer.

— My America: 1928-1938. LC 76-2050. (FDR & the Era of the New Deal Ser.). 1976. reprint ed. lib. bdg. 59.50 (*0-306-70801-9*) Da Capo.

— My America: 1928-1938. (American Biography Ser.). 669p. 1991. reprint ed. lib. bdg. 109.00 (*0-7812-8002-8*) Rprt Serv.

— The Native's Return. LC 74-34412. 358p. 1975. reprint ed. lib. bdg. 65.00 (*0-8371-7965-3*, ADNR, Greenwood Pr) Greenwood.

— The Native's Return: An American Immigrant Visits Yugoslavia & Discovers His Old Country. (American Biography Ser.). 370p. 1991. reprint ed. lib. bdg. 79.00 (*0-7812-8003-6*) Rprt Serv.

Adamic, Marc, jt. auth. see Walsh, Patricia.

Adamietz, I. A. Radiation Oncology of Gynecological Cancers. LC 96-29741. (Medical Radiology Ser.). 1997. write for info. (*3-540-56768-2*) Spr-Verlag.

Adamis, Eddie. Diccionario Basic del IBM-PC. (SPA.). 224p. 1985. pap. 55.00 (*0-8288-1364-7*, S60234) Fr & Eur.

Adamison, Cameron. Just Looking. (Illus.). 16p. (YA). (gr. 5-8). 1999. pap. 7.00 (*0-8059-4449-4*) Dorrance.

Adamjan, V. M., et al. Eleven Papers in Analysis. LC 51-5559. (Translations Ser.: Series 2, Vol. 95). 252p. 1970. 42.00 (*0-8218-1795-7*, TRANS2/95) Am Math.

— Nine Papers on Analysis. LC 78-5442. (Translations Ser.: Series 2, Vol. 111). 219p. 1978. 57.00 (*0-8218-3061-9*, TRANS2/111) Am Math.

Adamkewicz, Laura. Contemporary Biology Manual No. I, Vol. I. 3rd ed. 96p. (C). 1995. spiral bd. 8.95 (*0-8403-8774-1*) Kendall-Hunt.

— Contemporary Biology Manual No. II, Vol. II. 3rd ed. 80p. (C). 1995. spiral bd. 8.95 (*0-8403-8781-4*) Kendall-Hunt.

Adamnan, Saint. Vita Sancti Columbae. Reeves, William, ed. LC 79-174801. (Bannatyne Club, Edinburgh. Publications: No. 103). reprint ed. 94.50 (*0-404-52858-9*) AMS Pr.

Adamo, David Tuesday. Africa & the Africans in the Old Testament. LC 97-34254. 312p. 1997. pap. 55.00 (*1-57309-204-5*, U Pr W Africa) Intl Scholars.

Adamo, Jean-Marc. Multi-Threaded Object Oriented MPI-Based Message Passing Interface: The Arch Library. LC 98-18613. (Engineering & Computer Science Ser.). 200p. 1998. 120.00 (*0-7923-8165-3*) Kluwer Academic.

Adamo, John. Epigrams, Etc. A Dynamic Educational Resource. 112p. (Orig.). 1992. pap. 10.00 (*0-9633468-0-6*) J Adamo.

Adamo, Ralph. End of the World. LC 78-17913. (Lost Roads Poetry Ser.: No. 17). 1979. pap. 4.00 (*0-918786-18-5*) Lost Roads.

— Hanoi Rose: A Sequence of Poems. LC 89-63162. (Journal Press Bks.: Louisiana Legacy). (Illus.). 80p. (Orig.). 1989. pap. text 12.00 (*0-938498-08-8*) New Orleans Poetry.

— Sadness at the Private University. LC 77-79216. (Lost Roads Poetry Ser.: No. 3). 1978. pap. 3.00 (*0-918786-05-3*) Lost Roads.

Adamo-Tumminelli, Pat. A Guide to Pediatric Tracheotomy Care. 2nd ed. LC 93-24350. (Illus.). 90p. (C). 1993. pap. text, spiral bd. 29.95 (*0-398-05887-3*) C C Thomas.

Adamolekun, Ladipo, et al. Civil Service Reform in Francophone Africa: Proceedings of a Workshop, Abidjan, January 23-26, 1996. LC 97-9183. (Technical Papers). 176p. 1997. pap. 22.00 (*0-8213-3910-9*) World Bank.

Adamolekun, Lapido, et al. Civil Service Reform in Francophone Africa: Proceedings of a Workshop, Abidjan, January 23-26, 1996. (Technical Paper Ser.: No. 357F).Tr. of Reforme de la Fonction Publique en Afrique Francophone: Actes d'un Atelier, Abidjan, 23-26 Janvier 1996. 200p. 1997. pap. 22.00 (*0-8213-3863-3*, 13863) World Bank.

Adamolekun, Oladipupo, ed. Public Administration in Africa: Main Issues & Selected Country Studies. LC 99-10544. 440p. 1999. 70.00 (*0-8133-3653-8*, Pub. by Westview) HarpC.

Adamoli, Sabrina, et al. Organized Crime Around the World. 177p. 1998. pap. 30.00 (*951-53-1746-0*) Willow Tree NY.

Adamoli, Vida. Sons, Lovers, Etcetera. LC 97-182133. 250p. 1998. pap. 12.95 (*0-7472-5501-6*, Pub. by Headline Bk Pub) Trafalgar.

Adamov. Dayak: Ghetto 9. 1996. 14.95 (*1-882931-09-2*) Heavy Metal Magazine.

Adamov, Arthur. Adamov: Plays, Vol. I Contains Parody, Invasion, All Against All, Professor Taranne, Vol. 1. Meyer, Peter et al, trs. 200p. (Orig.). pap. 13.95 (*0-7145-4164-8*) Riverrun NY.

— L' Homme et l'Enfant. (FRE.). 256p. 1981. pap. 10.95 (*0-7859-1930-9*, 2070372618) Fr & Eur.

— Man & Child. Levy, Jo, tr. from FRE. LC 91-2145. 160p. 1991. 19.95 (*0-7145-4165-6*) Riverrun NY.

Adamov, Arthur & Fernando, Arrabal. Le Professeur Taranne & Pique-Nique en Campagne. Norrish, Peter, ed. 128p. (C). 1990. pap. 17.99 (*0-415-01713-0*) Routledge.

Adamovich, Brenda B., et al. Cognitive Rehabilitation of Closed Head Injured Patients: A Dynamic Approach. LC 90-50381. 160p. (Orig.). (C). 1985. pap. text 31.00 (*0-89079-389-1*, 1600) PRO-ED.

Adamovich, David R. The Heart: Fundamentals of Electrocardiography, Exercise Physiology, & Exercise Stress Testing. LC 83-50971. (Illus.). 414p. (Orig.). 1984. pap. 35.00 (*0-914363-00-X*) Sports Med Bks Inc.

***Adamovich, Inna.** The Christmas That Never Came. LC 99-65069. 1999. pap. 12.95 (*1-56167-559-8*) Am Literary Pr.

Adamovich, Shirley G., ed. The Road Taken: The New Hampshire Library Association, 1889-1989. LC 89-30525. (Illus.). 120p. 1989. 17.50 (*0-914659-40-5*, 30525) Phoenix Pub.

Adamovich, Shirley Gray. Reader in Library Technology. LC 75-8051. 236p. 1983. lib. bdg. 59.95 (*0-313-24042-6*, ZRJ/, Greenwood Pr) Greenwood.

Adamovics, John A. Analysis of Addictive & Misused Drugs. LC 94-22885. (Illus.). 800p. 1994. text 215.00 (*0-8247-9238-6*) Dekker.

Adamovics, John A., ed. Chromatographic Analysis of Pharmaceuticals. 2nd ed. LC 96-43177. (Chromatographic Science Ser.: Vol. 74). (Illus.). 544p. 1996. text 185.00 (*0-8247-9776-0*) Dekker.

Adamowicz, Elza. Surrealist Collage in Text & Image: Dissecting the Exquisite Corpse. LC 97-13546. (Studies in French: Vol. 56). (Illus.). 264p. (C). 1998. text 59.95 (*0-521-59204-6*) Cambridge U Pr.

Adamowicz, Joe. Hiking the Monadnock Region: 30 Day Hikes & Nature Walks in the Heart of New England. 2nd ed. Vaughan, Valerie, ed. LC 96-69273. (Illus.). 212p. 2000. pap. 12.95 (*1-889787-07-8*, Pub. by NE Cartographics) Midpt Trade.

Adamowicz, Wiktor L., et al, eds. Forestry, Economics & the Environment. (Illus.). 296p. 1996. text 75.00 (*0-85198-982-9*) OUP.

Adamowicz, Zofia & Zbierski, Pawel. Logic of Mathematics: A Modern Course of Classical Logic. LC 95-20818. (Pure & Applied Mathematics: A Wiley-Interscience Series of Texts, Monographs & Tracts). 272p. 1997. 74.95 (*0-471-06026-7*) Wiley.

Adamowski, Kaz, et al, eds. Water for World Development: Proceedings of the Sixth IWRA World Congress on Water Resources, 4 vols. 2814p. (Orig.). 1988. pap. 35.00 (*0-923227-02-4*) Intl Water Resc.

Adamowski, Kazimiera, jt. auth. see Hoff, Lee Ann.

Adamowski, Mary. The God That You Are. LC 93-93608. 119p. (Orig.). 1993. pap. 8.95 (*0-9638591-0-2*) Wind of Bliss.

Adams. Abuses of Punishment. LC 97-13512. 288p. 1998. pap. 18.95 (*0-312-17617-1*); text 55.00 (*0-312-17614-7*) St Martin.

— Adolescent Life. (Psychology). 1983. teacher ed. write for info. (*0-534-02048-8*) Wadsworth Pub.

— Album of American History, Vols. 1 & 2. 1981. 105.00 (*0-684-16845-6*) Mac Lib Ref.

— Album of American History, Vols. 3 & 4. 1981. 105.00 (*0-684-16846-4*) Mac Lib Ref.

— Album of American History, Vols. 5 & 6. 1981. 105.00 (*0-684-16847-2*) Mac Lib Ref.

— American Art. (Illus.). 2002. 50.00 (*0-07-232512-7*) McGraw.

— Art Across Time, 1. 1999. pap. 11.25 (*0-07-233886-5*) McGraw.

— Art Across Time, 2. 216p. 1999. pap. 11.25 (*0-07-233887-3*) McGraw.

— Astrology for Women. 1998. pap. 12.95 (*0-7322-5880-4*) HarpC.

— Atlas of Equine Surgery. LC 99-42010. 1999. text. write for info. (*0-7216-4643-3*, W B Saunders Co) Harcrt Hlth Sci Grp.

— Becoming Tania: A Novel of Love. 1990. 26.95 (*0-7710-0656-X*) McCland & Stewart.

— Body English with Answer Key. (C). 1997. text 11.75 (*0-673-19198-2*) Addson-Wesley Educ.

— Business Report Writing. 2nd ed. (C). 1988. pap. text, teacher ed. 27.75 (*0-03-013248-7*) Harcourt Coll Pubs.

— Caperoy. rev. ed. 1997. 30.00 (*0-8212-2409-3*, Pub. by Bulfinch Pr) Little.

— Communications Information Systems. (Graphic Comm Ser.). 1998. pap. 38.95 (*0-8273-6958-1*, VNR) Wiley.

— Communications Information Systems IRK. (Graphic Communications Ser.). 1997. teacher ed. 15.00 (*0-8273-6962-X*) Delmar.

— Connections. 2nd ed. (C). 1991. pap., teacher ed. write for info. (*0-321-40632-X*) Addison-Wesley.

— Conversations with Keith. 96p. (Orig.). 1997. pap. 9.95 (*1-882897-11-0*) Lost Coast.

***Adams.** Dementia Care. LC 98-36987. 1999. pap. text 39.95 (*0-7020-2278-0*) W B Saunders.

Adams. Developing Reading Versatility. 7th ed. LC 96-77628. (C). 1996. pap. text 53.00 (*0-03-018068-6*) Harcourt.

— Dictionary of American History, Vol. 1. 1977. 100.00 (*0-684-15071-9*) S&S Trade.

— Dictionary of American History, Vol. 2. 1977. 100.00 (*0-684-15072-7*) Mac Lib Ref.

— Dictionary of American History, Vol. 4. 1977. 100.00 (*0-684-15074-3*) Mac Lib Ref.

— Dictionary of American History, Vol. 5. 1977. 100.00 (*0-684-15075-1*) Mac Lib Ref.

— Dictionary of American History, Vol. 6. 1977. 100.00 (*0-684-15076-X*) Mac Lib Ref.

— Dictionary of American History 10 Vol Set: Includes Base Vols 1, 8 & 2 Vol Supplement, 8 Vols. 3848p. 1977. 900.00 (*0-684-80585-5*) S&S Trade.

— Disabled People. (Who Cares Ser.). (J). 1996. lib. bdg. 11.95 (*0-85953-864-8*) Childs Play.

***Adams.** Dollar Diplomacy. 216p. 2000. 70.95 (*1-84014-741-5*) Ashgate Pub Co.

Adams. Exercise Physiology. 3rd ed. LC 97-225294. 336p. 1997. spiral bd., lab manual ed. 33.13 (*0-697-29500-1*) McGraw.

— Exercise Physiology. 4th ed. 2001. 24.50 (*0-07-232903-3*) McGraw.

— First Steps: Front Page 2000. (C). 1999. pap. text 23.00 (*0-03-026377-8*) Harcourt.

— FIRST STEPS: OFFICE 2000 INTEG. (C). 1999. pap. text 23.00 (*0-03-026378-6*) Harcourt.

Adams. French Gardens 1500-1800. 1982. pap. 31.95 (*0-85967-664-1*) Ashgate Pub Co.

Adams. Harper Collins Concise Handbook Answer Key. (C). 1997. pap. text 13.00 (*0-06-502020-0*) Addison-Wesley.

— Harper Collins Concise Handbook for Writers. 576p. (C). 1997. pap., student ed. 13.00 (*0-06-502269-6*) Addson-Wesley Educ.

— Harper Collins Concise Handbook for Writers. (C). 1998. pap. 45.00 (*0-06-502536-9*) Addson-Wesley Educ.

— Harpercollins Concise Handbook & Exercises. LC 93-50599. 862p. (C). 1994. 45.00 (*0-06-040168-0*) Addison-Wesley Educ.

— Heartland of Cities. 1989. pap. text 24.95 (*0-226-00545-3*) U Ch Pr.

— A History of Art. LC 98-38707. 1998. 38.00 (*0-697-27479-9*, WCB McGr Hill) McGrw-H Hghr Educ.

— A History of Art, 2 vols. LC 98-38707. 1999. 38.00 (*0-697-27480-2*); text 58.00 incl. audio (*0-697-27478-0*, WCB McGr Hill) McGrw-H Hghr Educ.

— History of Western. 2nd ed. 1996. teacher ed. 9.06 (*0-697-28783-1*, WCB McGr Hill) McGrw-H Hghr Educ.

— History of Western Art. 2nd ed. 1996. 11.25 (*0-697-37593-5*, WCB McGr Hill) McGrw-H Hghr Educ.

— A History of Western Art. 3rd ed. 2000. 42.00 (*0-07-231717-5*) McGraw.

— Ideology & Politics in Britain Today. LC 98-28386. 2000. text 19.95 (*0-7190-5056-1*, Pub. by Manchester Univ Pr) St Martin.

— Ind Electronics Principles & Practices. 1985. wbk. ed. 28.83 (*0-07-000328-9*) McGraw.

***Adams.** Italian Renaissance Art. 2000. pap. 75.00 (*0-8133-3690-2*, Pub. by Westview); pap. 50.00 (*0-8133-3691-0*, Pub. by Westview) HarpC.

— Key Monuments of Baroque & Roco. 2000. pap. 23.00 (*0-8133-3430-6*, Pub. by Westview) HarpC.

— Key Monuments of the Italian. 2000. pap. 23.00 (*0-8133-3429-2*, Pub. by Westview) HarpC.

— Key Monuments of the 19th Century. 2000. 40.00 (*0-8133-3590-6*, Pub. by Westview); pap. 25.00 (*0-8133-3591-4*, Pub. by Westview) HarpC.

— Key Monuments of the 20th Century. 2000. 40.00 (*0-8133-3592-2*, Pub. by Westview); mass mkt. 25.00 (*0-8133-3593-0*, Pub. by Westview) HarpC.

Adams. Lecture Notes for Structures, Properties & Processing of Materials. (C). 1996. text. write for info. (*0-06-501217-8*) Addison-Wesley.

— Lives on Post. 1997. write for info. (*0-8212-2485-9*) Little.

— Macroeconomics. 6th ed. (C). 1998. pap. text, student ed. write for info. (*0-13-011236-4*) P-H.

— Mcrosoft PowerPoint 97. (C). 1998. pap. text 22.50 (*0-03-023726-2*) Harcourt Coll Pubs.

— Microsoft Access 97. (C). 1998. pap. text 22.50 (*0-03-023721-1*) Harcourt Coll Pubs.

— Microsoft Excel 97. (C). 1998. pap. text 22.50 (*0-03-023717-3*) Harcourt Coll Pubs.

— Microsoft Outlook 2000. (C). 1999. text 19.50 (*0-03-026381-6*) Harcourt.

— Modern Corporation Finance. (American Casebook Ser.). Date not set. text. write for info. (*0-314-06642-X*) West Pub.

— Monolith. rev. ed. 1997. 30.00 (*0-8212-2412-3*, Pub. by Bulfinch Pr) Little.

***Adams.** Moon of Reflection. 88p. 2000. pap. 12.95 (*1-882897-43-9*) Lost Coast.

Adams. Moondom, Vol. 1. rev. ed. 1997. 30.00 (*0-8212-2413-1*, Pub. by Bulfinch Pr) Little.

— Moonrise. rev. ed. 1997. 30.00 (*0-8212-2414-X*, Pub. by Bulfinch Pr) Little.

***Adams.** Multi-Level Marketing Made E-Z. 224p. 2000. pap. 17.95 (*1-56382-457-4*) E-Z Legal.

Adams. New Mexico Discovery Practice Manual. 1993. suppl. ed. 45.00 (*0-685-74338-1*, MICHIE) LEXIS Pub.

— The New World Media Textbook. (Mass Communication Ser.). 1919. pap. 35.00 (*0-534-57285-5*) Wadsworth Pub.

— Oaktree Security. 1997. 30.00 (*0-8212-2420-4*) Little.

— On Call: Surgery. (C). 1998. text. write for info. (*0-8089-2070-7*, Grune & Strat) Harcrt Hlth Sci Grp.

— Passion of Creation. LC 91-76299. 144p. (Orig.). 1992. pap. 9.95 (*1-879384-11-6*) Cypress Hse.

***Adams.** Philosophical Problems in the Law. 3rd ed. LC 99-19935. 608p. 1999. pap. 64.95 (*0-534-51903-2*) Thomson Learn.

Adams. Physiology 431 Study Guide. 4th ed. 332p. (C). 1997. spiral bd. 23.95 (*0-7872-2829-X*) Kendall-Hunt.

— Preparation: For Better Reading. 3rd ed. (C). 1988. pap. text, teacher ed. 27.50 (*0-03-013323-8*) Harcourt Coll Pubs.

— A Primer of Probability Logic. LC 97-20385. (Lecture Notes Ser.: No. 68). 450p. (C). 1998. 70.00 (*1-57586-067-8*); pap. 24.95 (*1-57586-066-X*) CSLI.

— Printing Technology. 4th ed. (Graphic Communications Ser.). 32p. 1996. text, teacher ed. 14.00 (*0-8273-6908-5*) Delmar.

— Psychophysiology of Low Back Pain. 1997. text 36.95 (*0-443-05259-X*, W B Saunders Co) Harcrt Hlth Sci Grp.

A

A

— Quick Summary & Documentation Guide: Harper Collins Concise Handbook. (C). 1997. pap. text 13.00 (*0-06-502268-8*) Addison-Wesley.
— Reading Beyond. 5th ed. (C). 1994. pap. text, teacher ed. 33.75 (*0-15-501786-1*) Harcourt Coll Pubs.
— The Reading Light. LC 95-60359. (C). 1995. pap. text 38.50 (*0-15-502398-5*, Pub. by Harcourt Coll Pubs) Harcourt.
— Readings Beyond Words. 6th ed. LC 99-64295. 384p. (C). 1999. text 50.00 (*0-15-508029-6*) Harcourt Coll Pubs.
— Readings Introduce Accounting 1. 280p. 1997. pap. text 36.20 (*0-536-00161-8*) Pearson Custom.
— Risk: The Policy Implications of Risk Compensation & Plural Rationalities. LC 95-88. 1995. 65.00 (*1-85728-067-9*, Pub. by UCL Pr Ltd); pap. write for info. (*1-85728-068-7*, Pub. by UCL Pr Ltd) Taylor & Francis.
— Rose Driftwood. 1993. 20.00 (*0-8212-2030-6*, Pub. by Bulfinch Pr) Little.
— Single Variable Calculus. 3rd ed. (C). 1995. text 43.96 (*0-201-82826-X*) Addison-Wesley.
— Solutions Manual for Structures, Properties & Processing of Materials. (C). 1998. pap. text. write for info. (*0-06-501216-X*) Addison-Wesley.
Adams. Stairway Forever. 1987. mass mkt. write for info. (*0-8125-3010-1*) Tor Bks.
Adams. Structures of Materials. (C). 1998. text. write for info. (*0-06-501215-1*) Addison-Wesley.
— Structures of Materials. (C). 1998. text. write for info. (*0-321-01058-2*) Addison-Wesley Educ.
Adams. Study Guide to Investment Math. pap. text 47.00 (*0-471-99882-6*) Wiley.
Adams. The Think, Read, React Plan for Writing. 6th ed. (C). 1993. pap. text 36.50 (*0-15-500798-X*, Pub. by Harcourt Coll Pubs) Harcourt.
— Think, Read, React, Plan, Write, & Rewrite. 6th ed. (C). 1993. pap. text, teacher ed. 4.50 (*0-15-500799-8*) Harcourt.
— The Tobacco Wars. LC 98-224165. (SWC-Economics Ser.). 1998. pap. 13.95 (*0-324-01296-9*) Thomson Learn.
— Twenty Years at Hull House. LC 98-87518. 1999. pap. 10.95 (*0-312-15706-1*) St Martin.
— The Two Headed God. LC 94-69726. 96p. (Orig.). 1995. pap. 9.95 (*1-879384-26-4*) Cypress Hse.
— Unicorn Peak. 1993. 20.00 (*0-8212-2029-2*, Pub. by Bulfinch Pr) Little.
— Urban Planning & Developing Process. LC 94-36313. 224p. 1994. 75.00 (*1-85728-021-0*, Pub. by UCL Pr Ltd); pap. 27.00 (*1-85728-022-9*, Pub. by UCL Pr Ltd) Taylor & Francis.
— Visions: Microsoft Office 97. (C). 1998. pap. text. write for info. (*0-03-023714-9*) Harcourt Coll Pubs.
— White House Ruin. 1993. 20.00 (*0-8212-2031-4*, Pub. by Bulfinch Pr) Little.
— Yosemite Winters. 1995. 30.00 (*0-8212-2183-3*, Pub. by Bulfinch Pr) Little.
Adams, ed. Dictionary of American History, No. 3. 1977. 100.00 (*0-684-15073-5*) Free Pr.
Adams & Abendroth. Illinois Estate Planning, Will Drafting & Estate Administration, No. 4. 300p. 1998. ring bd. 285.00 (*0-327-00319-7*, 81111-14) LEXIS Pub.
Adams & Slater. Mysteries of the Sky: Activities for Collaborative Groups. 232p. (C). 1998. per. 38.95 (*0-7872-5126-7*) Kendall-Hunt.
Adams, et al. Companion to Statistics. 2nd ed. 224p. (C). 1999. spiral bd. 34.95 (*0-7872-5791-5*, 41579101) Kendall-Hunt.
— Dictionary of American History, Vol. 7. 1977. 100.00 (*0-684-15077-8*) Mac Lib Ref.
— Dictionary of American History Index, Vol. 8. 1978. 100.00 (*0-684-15078-6*) Mac Lib Ref.
— How to Ace Calculus. LC 97-51944. 240p. 1998. pap. 14.95 (*0-7167-3160-6*) W H Freeman.
— Legacies: A History of Women & the Family in America, 1607-1870. 1987. 65.00 (*0-938545-04-3*) Jennings & Keefe.
— Statistics. 2nd ed. LC 99-474274. 608p. (C). 1999. per. 79.95 (*0-7872-5723-0*, 41572301) Kendall-Hunt.
— Student Handbook Formula: Physical Chemistry. 3rd ed. 64p. (C). 1997. pap. text 13.00 (*0-673-52342-X*) Addison-Wesley Educ.
Adams, jt. auth. see Daggett, Willard R.
Adams, jt. auth. see Daggett, Williard R.
Adams, jt. auth. see Griffin.
Adams, jt. auth. see Phillips.
Adams, ed. see Chesnaye Des Bois.
Adams, Paul E. Fail-Proof Your Business: Beat the Odds & Be Successful. LC 98-43249. 320p. 1999. pap. 15.95 (*0-944708-56-0*) Adams Hall.
Adams, Stacey, ed. see Mecham, Tisha.
Adams & Adams. Using Financial Accounting Information: A Decision Case Approach. LC 99-174342. (SWC-Accounting Ser.). 1998. pap. 67.95 (*0-324-00387-0*) Thomson Learn.
— Using Managerial Accounting Information: A Decision Case Approach. (SWC-Accounting Ser.). 1999. 67.95 (*0-324-00388-9*) Sth-Wstrn College.
Adams & Reese Staff. FIRREA Handbook. 830p. 1989. 35.00 (*0-9625110-0-5*) Adams & Reese.
Adams, A. Emblems in Glasgow. 167p. 1993. 60.00 (*0-85261-347-4*, Pub. by Univ of Glasgow) St Mut.
Adams, A. & Risley, S. A Genealogy of the Lake Family of Great Egg Harbor, New Jersey: Descendants of John Lake of Gravesend, Long Island, with Notes on the Gravesend & Staten Island Branches. (Illus.). 386p. 1993. reprint ed. pap. 60.00 (*0-8328-3046-1*); reprint ed. lib. bdg. 70.00 (*0-8328-3045-3*) Higginson Bk Co.
Adams, A., et al. English for Tomorrow. LC 96-54002. 1997. pap. 27.95 (*0-335-19780-9*) OpUniv Pr.
Adams, A. A., ed. see Technical Association of the Pulp & Paper Industry.
Adams, A. Dana. 4000 Preguntas y Respuestas sobre la Biblia. (SPA.). 1999. pap. 8.99 (*0-311-04037-3*) Casa Bautista.
Adams, A. E. & Mackenzie, W. S. A Color Atlas of Carbonate Sediments & Rocks under the Microscope. 1998. 90.00 (*0-470-29622-4*) Halsted Pr.
— A Color Atlas of Carbonate Sediments & Rocks under the Microscope. LC 98-171235. (Illus.). 192p. 1998. pap. 69.95 (*0-470-23749-X*) Wiley.
***Adams, A. E. & MacKenzie, W. S.** A Colour Atlas of Carbonate Sediments & Rocks under the Microscope. (Illus.). 180p. 1999. pap. 49.00 (*3-510-65193-6*, Pub. by E Schweizerbartsche) Balogh.
Adams, A. E. & MacKenzie, W. S. A Colour Atlas of Carbonate Sediments & Rocks under the Microscope. (Illus.). 192p. 1999. text 98.00 (*1-874545-83-9*); pap. text 45.00 (*1-874545-84-7*) OUP.
Adams, A. E., et al. Atlas of Sedimentary Rocks under the Microscope. LC 83-12379. 104p. 1984. pap. text 59.95 (*0-470-27476-X*) Halsted Pr.
Adams, A. E., jt. auth. see MacKenzie, W. S.
Adams, A. N. History of the Town of Fair Haven, VT. 516p. 1990. reprint ed. lib. bdg. 52.00 (*0-8328-1640-X*) Higginson Bk Co.
Adams, A. P. Recent Advances in Anaesthesia. 19th ed. 1996. pap. text 76.00 (*0-443-05306-5*, W B Saunders Co) Harcrt Hlth Sci Grp.
Adams, A. P. & Cashman, J. N., eds. Recent Advances in Anaesthesia & Analgesia, Vol. 20. (Illus.). 224p. 1998. pap. write for info. (*0-443-05988-8*) Church.
Adams, A. P., ed. see Hayes, Bernard.
***Adams, A. R.** Evil Memes: A Lexicon According to A. R. Adams. xx, 169p. 2000. pap. 10.00 (*0-9653746-1-0*) A R Adams.
Adams, A. R. The Fourth Constitution of the United States of America. LC 96-233097. xv, 150p. (Orig.). 1996. pap. 7.95 (*0-9653746-0-2*) A R Adams.
Adams, Abby. The Gardener's Gripe Book. LC 94-44834. (Illus.). 256p. 1996. pap. 10.95 (*1-56305-647-X*, 3647) Workman Pub.
— An Uncommon Scold. 272p. 1994. 8.00 (*0-671-88526-X*, Fireside) S&S Trade Pap.
Adams, Abigail. Golf Talk. (Charming Petites Ser.). 80p. 1996. 4.95 (*0-88088-796-6*) Peter Pauper.
Adams, Abigail & Adams, John. The Book of Abigail & John: Selected Letters of the Adams Family 1762-1784. Butterfield, L. H., ed. LC 97-49393. 424p. 1997. reprint ed. lib. bdg. 34.95 (*0-7351-0008-X*) Replica Bks.
Adams, Abigail L. Gone Fishin' LC 96-230642. (Charming Petites Ser.). 80p. 1996. 4.95 (*0-88088-799-0*) Peter Pauper.
Adams, Abigail S. Familiar Letters of John Adams & His Wife Abigail Adams ,During the Revolution. (Works of Abigail (Smith) Adams). 1989. reprint ed. lib. bdg. 79.00 (*0-7812-1402-5*) Rprt Serv.
— Familiar Letters of John Adams & His Wife Abigail Adams, During the Revolution. (American Biography Ser.). 424p. 1991. reprint ed. lib. bdg. 79.00 (*0-7812-8004-4*) Rprt Serv.
— Letters of Mrs. Adams: The Wife of John Adams. (Works of Abigail (Smith) Adams). 1989. reprint ed. lib. bdg. 79.00 (*0-685-27360-1*) Rprt Serv.
— New Letters of Abigail Adams, 1788-1801. (American Biography Ser.). 281p. 1991. reprint ed. lib. bdg. 69.00 (*0-7812-8005-2*) Rprt Serv.
— The Works of Abigail (Smith) Adams, 1744-1818. 1989. reprint ed. 600.00 (*0-685-18682-2*) Rprt Serv.
Adams, Abigail S. & Adams, John. The Book of Abigail & John: Selected Letters of the Adams Family, 1762-1784. Butterfield, L. H. et al, eds. LC 74-27938. (Illus.). 459p. 1976. 36.00 (*0-674-07855-1*) HUP.
— The Book of Abigail & John: Selected Letters of the Adams Family, 1762-1784. Butterfield, L. H. et al, eds. LC 74-27938. (Illus.). 459p. 1977. pap. text 9.95 (*0-674-07854-3*) HUP.
Adams, Abigail S., jt. auth. see Adams, John.
Adams, Adeline V. Amouretta Landscape & Other Stories. LC 79-103486. (Short Story Index Reprint Ser.). 1977. 19.95 (*0-8369-3192-0*) Ayer.
Adams, Adrian & So, Jaabe. A Claims to Land by the River: A Household in Senegal 1720-1994. (Illus.). 314p. 1996. text 90.00 (*0-19-820191-5*) OUP.
Adams, Adrian, tr. see Kourouma, Ahmadou.
Adams, Adrian, tr. see Ousmane, Sembene.
Adams, Adrienne. The Christmas Party. 2nd ed. LC 91-42159. (Illus.). 32p. (J). (ps-3). 1992. reprint ed. pap. 3.95 (*0-689-71630-3*) Aladdin.
— Easter Egg Artists. 1981. 11.19 (*0-606-00855-1*, Pub. by Turtleback) Demco.
— The Easter Egg Artists. LC 90-1097. (Illus.). 32p. (J). (ps-3). 1991. reprint ed. pap. 5.99 (*0-689-71481-5*) Aladdin.
— The Great Valentine's Day Balloon Race. LC 80-19527. (Illus.). 32p. (J). (ps-3). 1980. text 14.95 (*0-684-16640-2*) Scribner.
— The Great Valentine's Day Balloon Race. 2nd ed. LC 93-46114. (J). 1996. pap. 4.95 (*0-689-71847-0*) Aladdin.
— A Halloween Happening. LC 91-6907. (Illus.). 32p. (J). (ps-3). 1991. reprint ed. mass mkt. 3.95 (*0-689-71502-1*) Aladdin.
— A Woggle of Witches. LC 87-18703. (Illus.). 32p. (J). (ps-3). 1985. mass mkt. 4.95 (*0-689-71050-X*) Aladdin.
— Woggle of Witches. (J). 1971. 10.15 (*0-606-04426-4*, Pub. by Turtleback) Demco.
Adams, Aileen, ed. Victims of Crime Act of 1984 As Amended: A Report to the President & the Congress. (Illus.). 96p. (C). 1998. pap. text 20.00 (*0-7881-7430-4*) DIANE Pub.
Adams, Alan H., jt. auth. see Pressman, Alan H.
Adams, Alayne B., jt. auth. see Coiner.
Adams, Alayne B., jt. auth. see Coiner, Mayo L.
Adams, Alexander. Geronimo. (Quality Paperbacks Ser.). (Illus.). 381p. 1990. reprint ed. pap. 14.95 (*0-306-80394-1*) Da Capo.
Adams, Alexander B., ed. see Thoreau, Henry David.
Adams, Alfred Mac, tr. see Vargas Llosa, Mario.
***Adams, Alice.** After the War. LC 99-47104. 320p. 2000. 25.00 (*0-375-40683-2*) Knopf.
Adams, Alice. Almost Perfect. 256p. 1998. mass mkt. 14.00 (*0-671-02069-2*, Pocket Books) PB.
— Almost Perfect. large type ed. LC 93-49647. 441p. 1994. lib. bdg. 23.95 (*0-7862-0180-0*) Thorndike Pr.
— Caroline's Daughters. 366p. 1999. per. 14.00 (*0-671-02848-0*) S&S Trade.
— The Last Lovely City: Stories. LC 98-14585. 208p. 1999. 22.00 (*0-679-45441-1*) Knopf.
***Adams, Alice.** The Last Lovely City: Stories. 208p. 2000. reprint ed. per. 12.95 (*0-671-03618-1*, WSP) PB.
— Medicine Men. large type ed. LC 99-57691. 304p. 2000. lib. bdg. 28.95 (*1-58547-022-8*) Ctr Point Pubg.
Adams, Alice. Medicine Men: A Novel. LC 96-42001. 1997. 23.00 (*0-679-45440-3*) Knopf.
— Medicine Men: A Novel. 256p. 1998. mass mkt. 14.00 (*0-671-02067-6*, Pocket Books) PB.
— Second Chances. 366p. 1999. per. 14.00 (*0-671-02849-9*) S&S Trade.
— A Southern Exposure. 320p. 1996. pap. 12.00 (*0-449-91113-6*) Fawcett.
— A Southern Exposure. 1996. mass mkt. write for info. (*0-449-14949-8*) Fawcett.
— A Southern Exposure. large type ed. LC 96-10296. 1996. pap. 22.95 (*1-56895-324-0*) Wheeler Pub.
— A Southern Exposure: A Novel. LC 95-16109. 304p. 1995. 23.00 (*0-679-44452-1*) Knopf.
— Superior Women. 384p. 1985. mass mkt. 5.99 (*0-449-20746-3*, Crest) Fawcett.
— Superior Women. 384p. 1998. per. 14.00 (*0-671-02068-4*, Pocket Books) PB.
Adams, Alice D. The Neglected Period of Anti-Slavery in America, 1808-1831. 307p. 1973. reprint ed. 26.95 (*0-87928-034-4*) Corner Hse.
— The Neglected Period of Anti-Slavery in America, 1808-1831. (History - United States Ser.). 307p. 1992. reprint ed. lib. bdg. 89.00 (*0-7812-6157-0*) Rprt Serv.
Adams, Alice E. Reproducing the Womb: Images of Childbirth in Science, Feminist Theory, & Literature. (Illus.). 280p. 1994. text 45.00 (*0-8014-2945-5*); pap. text 16.95 (*0-8014-8161-9*) Cornell U Pr.
Adams, Alina. Annie's Wild Ride. 384p. 1998. mass mkt. 5.99 (*0-380-79472-1*, Avon Bks) Morrow Avon.
***Adams, Alina.** When a Man Loves a Woman. 384p. 2000. mass mkt. 6.50 (*0-440-23510-3*) Bantam Dell.
Adams, Alison, ed. Romance of Yder. (Arthurian Studies: No. VIII). 267p. 1983. 75.00 (*0-85991-133-0*) Boydell & Brewer.
Adams, Alison, et al, eds. Changing Face of Arthurian Romance: Essays on Arthurian Prose Romances in Memory of Cedric E. Pickford. (Arthurian Studies: Vol. XVI). 192p. 1986. 75.00 (*0-85991-227-2*) Boydell & Brewer.
Adams, Alison & Harper, Anthony J., eds. The Emblem in Renaissance & Baroque Europe: Tradition & Variety, Selected Papers of the Glasgow International Emblem Conference 13-17 August, 1990. (Symbola et Emblemata Ser.: Vol. 3). (Illus.). 286p. 1992. 107.50 (*90-04-09588-8*) Brill Academic Pubs.
Adams, Alison, et al. Methods in Yeast Genetics: A Laboratory Course Manual. LC 97-77211. (Illus.). 200p. (C). 1998. pap. text 61.00 (*0-87969-508-0*) Cold Spring Harbor.
Adams, Alison, ed. see Burton, Margie, et al.
Adams, Alison, ed. see Buxton, Paul K., et al.
Adams, Allaster. In Her Heart. LC 99-18661. 32p. 1999. pap. text 2.99 (*0-8341-1771-1*) Beacon Hill.
— In His Arms. LC 99-26330. 32p. 1999. pap. text 2.99 (*0-8341-1770-3*) Beacon Hill.
***Adams, Allen.** Making Merry with My Friends. (Illus.). (J). 1999. mass mkt. 10.95 (*0-7880-0998-2*) CSS OH.
Adams, Alph A. The Prince of Lost Kingdom. unabridged ed. LC 97-68759. 250p. 1997. pap. 11.95 (*0-9662823-0-2*) Gemini Pub Hse.
Adams, Alto, Jr. A Cattleman's Backcountry Florida. LC 84-20890. (Illus.). 54p. 1985. pap. 15.95 (*0-8130-0809-3*) U Press Fla.
Adams, Alto, Jr. & Gramling, Lee. A Florida Cattle Ranch. LC 98-25799. (Illus.). 102p. 1998. 24.95 (*1-56164-159-6*); pap. 18.95 (*1-56164-166-9*) Pineapple Pr.
Adams, Amy. Animals in the Library. (Illus.). 32p. (J). (gr. 1-6). 1996. pap. 12.00 (*1-888166-51-7*) Shining Lght.
— My Pet Iguana. large type ed. (Illus.). 32p. (J). (gr. 1-5). 1997. pap. 10.00 (*1-888166-54-1*) Shining Lght.
— A Pretzel of Peculiar Proportion. (J). (gr. 3-7). 1996. pap. 10.00 (*1-888166-50-9*) Shining Lght.
— The Tales of Poppit. 16p. (J). (gr. 1-3). 1995. pap. 10.00 (*1-888166-53-3*) Shining Lght.
***Adams, Andrea C.** Neurology for the Primary Care Physician. (Illus.). 300p. 2000. pap. text 35.00 (*0-8036-0538-2*) Davis Co.
Adams, Andrew. As Birds Flying: Jerusalem - Nineteen Seventeen. Raymond, E., ed. LC 91-76731. (Illus.). 160p. (Orig.). 1993. pap. 8.00 (*0-934666-45-8*) Artisan Pubs.
— Investment. (Banking & Finance Ser.). 420p. 1994. pap. text 12.50 (*1-85966-073-8*, Pub. by Graham & Trotman) Kluwer Academic.
— Ninja, the Invisible Assassins. Alston, Pat, ed. LC 75-130760. (Japanese Arts Ser.). (Illus.). 1970. 19.95 (*0-89750-030-X*, 302) Ohara Pubns.
Adams, Andrew N. The Descendants of James & William Adams of Londonderry, Now Derry, N. H. (Illus.). 87p. 1988. reprint ed. pap. 15.00 (*0-8328-0089-9*); reprint ed. lib. bdg. 23.00 (*0-8328-0088-0*) Higginson Bk Co.
— A Genealogical History of Henry Adams of Braintree, Mass., & His Descendants: Also John Adams, of Cambridge, Mass. (Illus.). 1246p. 1988. reprint ed. pap. 165.00 (*0-8328-0091-0*); reprint ed. lib. bdg. 173.00 (*0-8328-0090-2*) Higginson Bk Co.
— A Genealogical History of Robert Adams, of Newbury, Mass., & His Descendants, 1635-1900. (Illus.). 564p. 1988. reprint ed. pap. 86.50 (*0-8328-0093-7*); reprint ed. lib. bdg. 96.50 (*0-8328-0092-9*) Higginson Bk Co.
Adams, Andrew T., et al. Investment Mathematics & Statistics. LC 93-4922. 480p. (C). 1993. pap. text 57.50 (*1-85333-937-7*, Pub. by Graham & Trotman) Kluwer Academic.
Adams, Andy. Andy Adams' Campfire Tales. Hudson, Wilson M., ed. LC 75-29131. (Illus.). xxxi, 296p. 1976. reprint ed. pap. 15.95 (*0-8032-5835-6*, Bison Books) U of Nebr Pr.
— Cattle Brands: A Collection of Western Campfire Stories. LC 70-150534. (Short Story Index Reprint Ser.). 1977. reprint ed. 18.95 (*0-8369-3831-3*) Ayer.
— The Log of a Cowboy. 22.95 (*0-88411-929-7*) Amereon Ltd.
— The Log of a Cowboy. (Illus.). 416p. 1997. 7.98 (*1-56731-174-1*, MJF Bks) Fine Comms.
— The Log of a Cowboy. 387p. 1975. reprint ed. 26.95 (*0-87928-067-0*) Corner Hse.
— The Log of a Cowboy. 1993. reprint ed. lib. bdg. 75.00 (*0-7812-5861-8*) Rprt Serv.
— The Log of a Cowboy, Set. abr. ed. 1996. text 17.95 incl. audio (*1-57453-058-5*) Audio Lit.
***Adams, Andy.** The Log of a Cowboy: A Narrative of the Old Trail Days. (Illus.). 384p. 2000. pap. 10.00 (*0-618-08348-0*) HM.
Adams, Andy. The Log of a Cowboy: A Narrative of the Old Trail Days. LC 03-12817. (Illus.). x, 397p. 1964. pap. 10.95 (*0-8032-5000-2*, Bison Books) U of Nebr Pr.
***Adams, Andy.** The Log of a Cowboy: A Narrative of the Old Trail Days. 387p. 1999. reprint ed. text 20.00 (*0-7881-6379-5*) DIANE Pub.
Adams, Andy. The Ranch on the Beaver. LC 97-30607. (Illus.). xiv, 313p. 1997. pap. 12.95 (*0-8032-5930-1*, Bison Books) U of Nebr Pr.
— Wells Brothers: The Young Cattle Kings. LC 96-52808. (Illus.). xvii, 370p. 1997. pap. 12.95 (*0-8032-5929-8*, Bison Books) U of Nebr Pr.
***Adams, Ann.** At Home with Holistic Management: Creating a Life of Meaning. (Illus.). 169p. 1999. 20.00 (*0-9673941-0-4*) Ctr Holstc.
Adams, Ann. My Bible Word Book. LC 97-197416. (Illus.). 48p. (ps-2). 1997. 9.99 (*0-570-04882-6*, 56-1831) Concordia.
— The Silver Boat. (Illus.). 1990. pap. 11.50 (*0-938837-02-8*) Behav Sci Ctr Pubs.
***Adams, Ann.** The Silver Boat. (Illus.). iv, 34p. 2000. pap. 12.95 (*0-9678498-0-2*) Silver Boat Prods.
— The Silver Boat Coloring Book. (Illus.). 20p. 2000. pap. 9.00 (*0-9678498-1-0*) Silver Boat Prods.
Adams, Ann. The Silver Boat II: The Journey. (Illus.). 40p. (Orig.). 1994. pap. 11.50 (*0-938837-17-6*) Behav Sci Ctr Pubs.
Adams, Ann, ed. Beneath the Rain Shadow, Vol. III. (Illus.). 160p. 1999. pap. write for info. (*0-7392-0173-5*, PO3139) Morris Pubng.
Adams, Ann, ed. see Jones, Franklin, Sr.
***Adams, Ann-Charlotte Gavel & Leiren, Terje I., eds.** Stage & Screen: Studies in Scandinavian Drama & Film. (Illus.). 282p. (C). 2000. pap. 19.95 (*1-930721-00-5*) Dreamplay.
Adams, Ann J., ed. Rembrandt's "Bathsheba Reading King David's Letter" LC 97-18154. (Masterpieces in Western Painting Ser.). (Illus.). 224p. (C). 1998. text 54.95 (*0-521-45391-7*); pap. text 15.95 (*0-521-45986-9*) Cambridge U Pr.
Adams, Ann S. & Roberts, Arthur J., eds. Cardiac Colloquy: The First Comprehensive Video Textbook of Cardiac Surgery Technique. (Illus.). 205p. 1988. 595.00 (*0-944903-00-2*) Adams Pub Group.
Adams, Ann S., jt. auth. see Small, D. M.
Adams, Anna. Green Resistance: New & Selected Poems. LC 97-145642. 92p. 1997. pap. 17.95 (*1-870612-57-4*, Pub. by Enitha Pr) Dufour.
***Adams, Anna.** Her Daughter's Father. (Superromance Ser.: Vol. 896). 2000. mass mkt. 4.50 (*0-373-70896-3*) Harlequin Bks.
— The Marriage Contract. (Superromance Ser.). 2000. mass mkt. 4.50 (*0-373-70959-5*, 1709591) Harlequin Bks.
Adams, Anne. The Baker Book of Bible Travels for Kids. (Illus.). 192p. (gr. 3-7). 1999. 12.99 (*0-8010-4423-5*, New Kids Media) Baker Bks.
— Basic Administrative Law for Paralegals. LC 97-51671. 1998. pap. text 38.95 (*1-56706-631-3*) Aspen Law.
***Adams, Anne.** New Kids Book of Angel Visits. (New Kids Junior Reference Ser.). (Illus.). 96p. (J). (gr. k-4). 1999. 6.99 (*0-8010-4435-9*) Baker Bks.
— New Kids Book of Bible Animals. (Illus.). 96p. (J). (gr. k-4). 1999. 6.99 (*0-8010-4436-7*) Baker Bks.
— The New Kids Book of Bible Facts. 192p. (J). (gr. 1-10). 2000. 14.99 (*0-8010-4441-3*, New Kids Media) Baker Bks.
— New Kids Book of Bible Passages. 96p. (J). (gr. k-4). 1999. 6.99 (*0-8010-4434-0*) Baker Bks.
— New Kids Book of Bible People. (Illus.). 96p. (J). (gr. k-4). 1999. 6.99 (*0-8010-4437-5*) Baker Bks.
Adams, Anne, ed. see Fowler, Alex D.

An Asterisk (*) at the beginning of an entry indicates that the title is appearing for the first time.

A

***Adams, Anne B. & Nash-Cummings, Nancy.** Clean It, Fix It, Find It. Peat, Patricia B., ed. (Illus.). 206p. 1999. pap. 14.95 (*0-9670695-0-5*, Pub. by Four Footed Pr) Enfield Pubs NH.

Adams, Anne R. Tappan Zee Dress: Plain & Fancy, 1780-1930. (Illus.). 40p. 1984. pap. 4.00 (*0-911183-20-5*) Rockland County Hist.

Adams, Anne V. & Mayes, Janis A., eds. African Literature & Africa's Development. 176p. pap. 14.00 (*0-89410-735-6*) Cornell AS&RC.

— African Literature & Africa's Development, Vol. 13. 176p. 22.00 (*0-89410-734-8*) Cornell AS&RC.

Adams, Anne V., ed. see African Literature Association Staff.

Adams, Anne V., tr. see Opitz, May, et al, eds.

Adams, Annie. Booksellers Cookbook. 1989. pap. 14.95 (*0-9624839-0-7*) Cohn Thompson.

Adams, Annie E., tr. see Brandenburg, Erich.

Adams, Annmarie. Architecture in the Family Way: Doctors, Houses, & Men, 1870-1900. (Illus.). 352p. 1996. 49.95 (*0-7735-1386-8*, Pub. by McG-Queens Univ Pr) CUP Services.

Adams, Annmarie & McMurry, Sally, eds. Exploring Everyday Landscapes Vol. VII: Perspectives in Vernacular Architecture. LC 98-111049. (Illus.). 344p. (C). 1997. pap. text 30.00 (*0-87049-983-1*) U of Tenn Pr.

Adams, Annmarie, jt. ed. see McMurry, Sally.

Adams, Ansel. The American Wilderness. Stillman, Andrea G., ed. (Illus.). 146p. 1990. 150.00 (*0-8212-1799-2*, Pub. by Bulfinch Pr) Little.

— Ansel Adams: Centennial. 144p. 2001. write for info. (*0-8212-2515-4*) Little.

— Ansel Adams: Technical Writing. 1999. write for info. (*0-8212-2578-2*) Bulfinch Pr.

— Ansel Adams: The Centennial Postcard Book. 2001. pap. write for info. (*0-8212-2585-5*) Bulfinch Pr.

— Ansel Adams: Thirty Photographs, a Postcard Folio Book. (Illus.). 64p. 1994. 10.95 (*0-8212-2105-1*) Little.

— Ansel Adams Address Book. 214p. 1998. 25.00 (*0-8212-2510-3*) Little.

— Ansel Adams:Classic Images: Revised Edition. 2000. write for info. (*0-8212-2581-2*) Bulfinch Pr.

— Aspens: Northern New Mexico, 1958. 1997. 30.00 (*0-8212-2406-9*) Little.

***Adams, Ansel.** Born Free & Equal. Benti, Wynne & Michael, Bill, eds. (Illus.). 144p. 2000. pap. 29.95 (*1-893343-04-9*) Spotted Dog CA.

Adams, Ansel. Born Free & Equal. limited rev. ed. Medvec, Emily, ed. LC 84-21125. (Illus.). 44p. 1984. pap. 50.00 (*0-931547-00-8*, BFE, Photogram) Medvec.

— California: A Postcard Folio Book. (Illus.). 64p. 1998. 10.95 (*0-8212-2478-6*, Pub. by Bulfinch Pr) Little.

— The Camera. LC 80-11402. (Ansel Adams Photography Ser.: Bk. 1). (Illus.). 203p. 1980. 40.00 (*0-8212-1092-0*, Pub. by Bulfinch Pr) Little.

— Canyon de Chel. 1997. 30.00 (*0-8212-2391-7*) Little.

— Clearing Winter Storm - Yosemite. rev. ed. 1997. 30.00 (*0-8212-2410-7*, Pub. by Bulfinch Pr) Little.

— Color Photographs: A Postcard Folio Book. (Illus.). 30p. 1995. 10.95 (*0-8212-2240-6*, Pub. by Bulfinch Pr) Little.

— Examples: The Making of Forty Photographs. (Illus.). 180p. 1989. pap. 37.50 (*0-8212-1750-X*, Pub. by Bulfinch Pr) Little.

— Maroon Bells. 1995. 30.00 (*0-8212-2185-X*, Pub. by Bulfinch Pr) Little.

— Mount McKinley & Wonderlake Denali National Park,Alaska 1947. 1997. write for info. (*0-8212-2415-8*) Little.

— The National Parks: A Postcard Folio Book. (Illus.). 64p. 1995. 10.95 (*0-8212-2181-7*, Pub. by Bulfinch Pr) Little.

— Photographs of the Southwest. LC 76-10034. (Illus.). 1994. 50.00 (*0-8212-0699-0*, Pub. by Bulfinch Pr) Little.

— Pine Forest Snow. 1997. 30.00 (*0-8212-2421-2*) Little.

— The Portfolios of Ansel Adams. LC 77-71628. (Illus.). 1977. 45.00 (*0-8212-0723-7*, Pub. by Bulfinch Pr) Little.

— The Portfolios of Ansel Adams. 1981. 25.00 (*0-316-71395-3*) Little.

— The Print. LC 83-950. (Ansel Adams Photography Ser.: Bk. 3). (Illus.). 210p. 1983. 40.00 (*0-8212-1526-4*, Pub. by Bulfinch Pr) Little.

— Southwest: A Postcard Folio Book. 64p. 1996. 10.95 (*0-8212-2344-5*) Little.

— This is the American Earth. 96p. 1999. pap. write for info. (*0-8212-2274-0*) Little.

— Winter Photographs: A Postcard Folio Book. (Illus.). 64p. 1994. 10.95 (*0-8212-2135-3*, Pub. by Bulfinch Pr) Little.

— Yosemite. Stillman, Andrea G., ed. LC 95-12010. (Illus.). 112p. 1995. pap. 19.95 (*0-8212-2196-5*, Pub. by Bulfinch Pr) Little.

— Yosemite. 1995. 18.95 (*0-614-15013-2*) Little.

— Yosemite & the High Sierra. Stillman, Andrea G., ed. LC 94-8522. (Illus.). 136p. 1994. 50.00 (*0-8212-2134-5*, Pub. by Bulfinch Pr) Little.

— Yosemite National Park: A Postcard Folio Book. (Illus.). 64p. 1996. 9.95 (*0-8212-2283-X*, Pub. by Bulfinch Pr) Little.

Adams, Ansel, photos by. Ansel Adams: Classic Images. (Illus.). 111p. 1986. 40.00 (*0-8212-1629-5*, Pub. by Bulfinch Pr) Little.

— Ansel Adams: The National Park Service Photographs. LC 94-42782. (Illus.). 144p. 1995. 17.98 (*0-89660-056-4*, Artabras) Abbeville Pr.

Adams, Ansel & Alinder, Mary S. Ansel Adams: An Autobiography. (Illus.). 1985. 65.00 (*0-8212-1596-5*, Pub. by Bulfinch Pr) Little.

— Ansel Adams: An Autobiography. (Illus.). 312p. 1996. pap. 14.95 (*0-8212-2241-4*, Pub. by Bulfinch Pr) Little.

Adams, Ansel & Baker, Robert. The Camera. (Illus.). 224p. 1995. pap. 22.50 (*0-8212-2184-1*, Pub. by Bulfinch Pr) Little.

— The Negative. (Illus.). 288p. 1995. pap. 22.50 (*0-8212-2186-8*, Pub. by Bulfinch Pr) Little.

— The Print. (Illus.). 224p. 1995. pap. 22.50 (*0-8212-2187-6*, Pub. by Bulfinch Pr) Little.

***Adams, Ansel & Cunningham, Imogen.** Defining Modernism: Group F.64. (Illus.). 175p. 2000. pap. 25.00 (*0-933286-72-4*, Pub. by Frnds Photography) Dist Art Pubs.

Adams, Ansel & Newhall, Nancy. This Is the American Earth. (Illus.). 96p. 1995. 50.00 (*0-8212-2182-5*, Pub. by Bulfinch Pr) Little.

Adams, Ansel & Stillman, Andrea G. Ansel Adams' California. LC 97-9505. (Illus.). 112p. (gr. 8). 1997. 50.00 (*0-8212-2369-0*) Little.

***Adams, Ansel & Stillman, Andrea G.** The Grand Canyon. LC 99-89642. 112p. 2000. 21.95 (*0-8212-2650-9*, Pub. by Bulfinch Pr) Little.

Adams, Anthony. Hard at It. 310p. mass mkt. 6.95 (*0-7472-4952-0*, Pub. by Headline Bk Pub) Trafalgar.

Adams, Anthony & Jones, Esnor. Teaching Humanities in the Microelectronic Age. 128p. 1983. pap. 25.00 (*0-335-10196-8*) OpUniv Pr.

Adams, Anthony & Sterling, Leon S., eds. AI, 1992: Proceedings of the Fifth Australian Joint Conference on Artificial Intelligence: Hobart, Tasmania, 16-18 November 1992. LC 92-38726. 408p. 1992. text 109.00 (*981-02-1250-X*) World Scientific Pub.

Adams, Anthony & Tulasiewicz, Witold. The Crisis in Teacher Education: A European Concern? LC 94-46158. 160p. 1995. 85.00 (*0-7507-0284-2*, Falmer Pr); pap. 27.95 (*0-7507-0285-0*, Falmer Pr) Taylor & Francis.

Adams, Anthony P., et al, eds. Emergency Anaesthesia. 2nd ed. LC 97-21355. (Arnold Publication). (Illus.). 456p. 1998. pap. text 45.00 (*0-340-69219-7*, Pub. by E A) OUP.

Adams, Anthony P., et al. Emergency Anesthesia. (Illus.). 384p. 1987. text 48.00 (*0-03-013297-5*, W B Saunders Co) Harcrt Hlth Sci Grp.

Adams, April L., jt. auth. see Cernea, Michael M.

Adams, Arlene. Handbook for Literacy Tutors: A Practical Approach to Effective Informal Instruction in Reading & Writing. LC 98-53546. (Illus.). 204p. (Orig.). 1999. pap. text, spiral bd. 33.95 (*0-398-06940-9*) C C Thomas.

Adams, Arlin M. & Emmerich, Charles J. A Nation Dedicated to Religious Liberty: The Constitutional Heritage of the Religion Clauses. LC 90-36248. 188p. (C). 1990. pap. text 14.95 (*0-8122-1318-1*) U of Pa Pr.

Adams, Arlin M. & Thompson, Larry D. Final Report of the Independent Counsel in Re: Samuel R. Pierce, Jr., Vols. 1-3. LC 98-226950. 283p. 1998. pap. 28.00 (*0-16-049796-5*) USGPO.

Adams, Arretta. Angel on My Shoulder. unabridged ed. 250p. (Orig.). 1997. pap., per. 15.00 (*0-9653883-0-1*) A Adams.

Adams, Arthur. Past, Present & Future. (Godzilla Ser.). (Illus.). 1998. pap. text 17.95 (*1-56971-278-6*) Dark Horse Comics.

***Adams, Arthur E.** Moscow Nights. LC 99-96648. 2000. 23.95 (*0-533-13299-1*) Vantage.

Adams, Arthur E. Stalin & His Times. (Illus.). 243p. (C). 1986. reprint ed. pap. text 13.95 (*0-88133-250-X*) Waveland Pr.

Adams, Arthur E., ed. The Russian Revolution & Bolshevik Victory: Visions & Revisions. 3rd ed. LC 89-84256. (Problems in European Civilization Ser.). 495p. (C). 1990. pap. text 22.36 (*0-669-20877-9*) HM Trade Div.

Adams, Arthur G. The Catskills: An Illustrated Historical Guide with Gazetteer. 2nd rev. ed. LC 90-82351. (Illus.). xiv, 402p. 1990. reprint ed. pap. 22.00 (*0-8232-1301-3*) Fordham.

— The Hudson River Guidebook. (Illus.). xvii, 430p. 1996. 35.00 (*0-8232-1679-9*) Fordham.

— The Hudson River Guidebook. 2nd ed. (Illus.). xvii, 430p. 1996. pap. 25.00 (*0-8232-1680-2*) Fordham.

— The Hudson River Through the Years. (Illus.). xx, 340p. 1996. pap. 19.95 (*0-8232-1677-2*) Fordham.

— The Hudson River Through the Years. 2nd ed. LC 96-1737. (Illus.). xx, 340p. 1996. 35.00 (*0-8232-1676-4*) Fordham.

Adams, Arthur G., ed. The Hudson River in Literature: An Anthology. 2nd ed. LC 79-14862. (Illus.). x, 338p. 1988. reprint ed. pap. 19.95 (*0-8232-1202-5*) Fordham.

Adams, Arthur G. & Baxter, Raymond J. Railroad Ferries of the Hudson & the Stories of a Deck Hand. LC 99-14334. 272p. 1999. 35.00 (*0-8232-1953-4*, Pub. by Fordham); pap. 19.95 (*0-8232-1954-2*, Pub. by Fordham) BookMasters.

Adams, Arthur G., et al. Guide to the Catskills with Trail Guide & Maps. (Illus.). 440p. 1975. pap. 9.95 (*0-915850-01-X*) Walking News Inc.

Adams, Arthur G., ed. see Rajs, Jake.

Adams, Arthur J., jt. auth. see Shiffler, Ronald E.

Adams, Arvil V., jt. auth. see Wilson, Sandra.

***Adams, Ashley.** 'N Sync 'n Detail. 64p. 2000. pap. text 12.95 (*0-8256-1801-0*, Amsco Music) Music Sales.

Adams, Ashley. Omnibus Press Presents the Story of Britney Spears. (Illus.). 31p. (J). (gr. 4-7). 1999. pap. 9.95 (*0-8256-1744-8*, OP48149) Omnibus NY.

— The Story of N'Sync. (Illus.). 64p. 1999. pap. 9.95 (*0-8256-1760-X*) Music Sales.

Adams, Audra. The Bachelor's Bride. 1995. per. 3.25 (*0-373-05959-0*, 1-05959-1) Silhouette.

— Devil or Angel. (Desire Ser.). 1993. pap. 2.89 (*0-373-05783-0*, 5-05783-1) Silhouette.

— Encuentro Amoroso: The Bachelor's Bride. (SPA.). 1997. per. 3.50 (*0-373-35176-3*, 1-35176-6) Harlequin Bks.

— His Brother's Wife. (Desire Ser.). 1995. per. 3.25 (*0-373-05912-4*, 1-05912-0) Silhouette.

— His Brother's Wife. large type ed. (Silhouette Romance Ser.). 1996. lib. bdg. 19.95 (*0-373-59744-4*, G K Hall Lrg Type) Mac Lib Ref.

— Home Sweet Home. (Desire Ser.: No. 695). 1992. pap. 2.79 (*0-373-05695-8*, 5-05695-7) Harlequin Bks.

— Mommy's Hero. (Intimate Moments Ser.). 1996. per. 3.99 (*0-373-07743-2*, 1-07743-7) Silhouette.

— Rich Girl, Bad Boy. (Desire Ser.). 1994. per. 2.99 (*0-373-05839-X*, 5-05839-1) Silhouette.

Adams, Austin, jt. auth. see Edworthy, Judy.

***Adams, Ayin M.** The Color of Her Tears. (Illus.). 48p. 2000. pap. write for info. (*0-934172-52-8*, Pub. by WIM Pubns) NetRead Inc.

Adams, Azel. Creative Survival: A Narrative History of Azel Adams, The Forks, Maine. Butcher, Sally K., ed. LC 91-68485. (Illus.). 201p. (Orig.). 1992. pap. 12.95 (*0-9631912-1-7*) Old Bess Pub.

Adams, Barbara. Building a Bridge to Algebra. (C). pap. text 35.00 (*1-881592-30-8*) Hayden-McNeil.

— Egyptian Mummies. 2nd ed. (Egyptology Ser.: No.). (Illus.). 64p. 1992. pap. text 10.50 (*0-85263-944-5*, Pub. by Shire Pubns) Parkwest Pubns.

— Egyptian Objects in the Victoria & Albert Museum. (Egyptology Today Ser.: Vol. 3). 1979. pap. 32.95 (*0-85668-103-2*, Pub. by Aris & Phillips) David Brown.

— The Fort Cemetery at Hierakonolis. 260p. 1987. lib. bdg. 95.00 (*0-7103-0275-4*) Routledge.

— Hapax Legomena: Poems. Schultz, Patricia, ed. LC 90-37813. (Lewiston Poetry Ser.: Vol. 7). 64p. 1990. pap. 12.95 (*0-88946-849-4*) E Mellen.

— Predynastic Egypt. (Shire Egyptology Ser.). (Illus.). 76p. 1988. pap. text 12.00 (*0-85263-938-4*, Pub. by Shire Pubns) Lubrecht & Cramer.

— Sculptured Pottery from Koptos. (Petrie Collection) 1986. pap. 39.95 (*0-85668-389-2*, Pub. by Aris & Phillips) David Brown.

Adams, Barbara. A World of Tools. (Early Science Big Bks.). (Illus.). 16p. (J). (ps-2). Date not set. pap. 16.95 (*1-58273-115-2*) Newbridge Educ.

Adams, Barbara & Cialowicz, Krzysztof. Protodynastic Egypt. (Egyptology Ser.: No. 25). (Illus.). 64p. 1997. pap. 10.50 (*0-7478-0357-9*, Pub. by Shire Pubns) Parkwest Pubns.

Adams, Barbara, ed. see Bizjak, Gloria & IFSTA Instructor Staff.

Adams, Barbara, jt. ed. see Goodson, Carl.

Adams, Barbara, ed. see Griffith, Pam.

Adams, Barbara, jt. ed. see Hall, Richard.

Adams, Barbara, ed. see Hilley, Robert.

Adams, Barbara, ed. see Hilley, Robert & Pickering, Cindy.

Adams, Barbara, ed. see Pickering, Cindy.

Adams, Barbara, ed. see Walker, Susan S.

Adams, Barbara A. The Unprepossessing Mr. Ryan: Understanding Exemplary Legislative Leadership. LC 98-38621. 244p. 1998. 39.50 (*0-7618-1245-8*) U Pr of Amer.

Adams, Barbara E., jt. auth. see Clarke, John Henrik.

***Adams, Barbara Eleanor.** John Henrik Clarke: Master Teacher. LC 00-23104. 2000. pap. write for info. (*1-886433-20-8*) A&B Bks.

Adams, Barbara Johnston. The Go-Around Dollar. LC 90-26269. (Illus.). 32p. (J). (gr. 1-4). 1992. lib. bdg. 16.00 (*0-02-700031-1*, Mac Bks Young Read) S&S Childrens.

— New York City. LC 88-20245. (Downtown America Ser.). (Illus.). 60p. (J). (gr. 3 up). 1988. lib. bdg. 13.95 (*0-87518-384-0*) Silver Burdett Pr.

— New York City: Downtown America. (Illus.). 64p. (J). (gr. 4-7). 1996. pap. text 7.95 (*0-382-24794-9*) Silver Burdett Pr.

Adams, Barbara V. & Schuett, Stacey. Joey's Rowboat: Big Book. large type ed. (Little Books & Big Bks.). (Illus.). 8p. (J). (gr. k-2). 1997. pap. text 19.47 (*0-8215-0933-0*) Sadlier.

***Adams, Barry B.** Coming-to-Know: Recognition & the Complex Plot in Shakespeare. (Studies in Shakespeare: Vol. 10). 288p. (C). 2000. text 55.95 (*0-8204-4417-1*) P Lang Pubng.

Adams, Barry B. & Fitch, Lorne. Caring for the Green Zone: Riparian Areas & Grazing Management. LC 97-183033. 36 p. 1995. write for info. (*0-7732-1435-6*) APAB.

Adams, Barry B., ed. & intro. see Bale, John.

Adams, Barry G. Algebraic Approach to Simple Quantum Systems: With Applications to Perturbation Theory. LC 94-11900. (Illus.). 467p. 1994. 54.95 incl. 3.5 hd (*0-387-57801-3*) Spr-Verlag.

Adams, Barry J. Urban Stormwater Management Planning with Analytical Probabilistic Models. LC 99-42176. 376p. 2000. 80.00 (*0-471-33217-8*) Wiley.

Adams, Ben Q. & Newlin, Richard. R. C. Gorman: The Graphic Works. LC 87-51653. (JPN & SPA., Illus.). 256p. 1988. 125.00 (*0-9619950-0-9*) Tads Editions Ltd.

Adams, Benson D. Ballistic Missile Defense. LC 74-165800. (Policy Sciences Book Ser.). 288p. reprint ed. pap. 89.30 (*0-8357-5953-9*, 200776500064) Bks Demand.

Adams, Bernard. College Daze at Punxie: An Adult Look at College Teaching. 224p. 1999. pap. 15.00 (*0-910042-78-0*) Allegheny.

— The Religious Experiences of Tommy: An Adult Novel. LC 95-80596. 192p. (Orig.). 1996. pap. 9.95 (*0-910042-75-6*) Allegheny.

Adams, Bernard, tr. see Mikes, Keleman.

Adams, Bert N. The Family: The Sociological Interpretation. 5th ed. 450p. (C). 1995. pap. text 51.50 (*0-15-501925-2*, Pub. by Harcourt Coll Pubs) Harcourt.

Adams, Bert N., jt. auth. see Kadasham.

Adams, Bertram. Perry. An Incomplete History of the Descendants of John Perry of London, 1604-1955. (Illus.). 738p. 1991. reprint ed. pap. 105.00 (*0-8328-1992-1*); reprint ed. lib. bdg. 115.00 (*0-8328-1991-3*) Higginson Bk Co.

Adams, Beverly, ed. & intro. see Mellado, Justo P.

Adams, Bill. Yester Days I. (Illus.). 220p. 1992. reprint ed. pap. text 19.95 (*0-9634793-0-X*) Peoria Jrnl.

— Yester Days III. (Illus.). 209p. 1994. pap. text 19.95 (*0-9634793-2-6*) Peoria Jrnl.

— Yester Days II. (Illus.). 211p. 1993. pap. text 19.95 (*0-9634793-1-8*) Peoria Jrnl.

Adams, Bill & Brooks, Cecil. The Unwound Way. 352p. 1991. mass mkt. 4.99 (*0-345-37238-7*, Del Rey) Ballantine Pub Grp.

Adams, Billy. Ewan McGregor: The Story So Far. (Illus.). 272p. 1998. pap. 15.95 (*1-873631-80-4*, Pub. by B&W Pub) Firebird Dist.

— Ewan McGregor: The Unauthorized Biography. LC 99-32949. (Illus.). 280p. 1999. pap. 13.95 (*0-87951-704-2*, Pub. by Overlook Pr) Penguin Putnam.

Adams, Blair. Hallelu Yah: Knowing God Through His Name. LC 89-52009. 96p. (Orig.). 1988. pap. 8.95 (*0-916387-15-1*) Truth Forum.

Adams, Blair & Stein, Joel. Building Christian Character: A Guidebook Through the Elements of Christian Character. LC 89-51225. 203p. (Orig.). 1988. pap. 19.95 (*0-916387-13-5*) Truth Forum.

— Covenant Love: Its Nature, Commitment & Patterns. LC 89-51247. 225p. (Orig.). 1989. pap. 9.95 (*0-916387-18-6*) Truth Forum.

— The Right Words: The Grace of Writing. LC 89-51226. (Illus.). 160p. (Orig.). 1993. pap. 19.95 (*0-916387-28-3*) Truth Forum.

— Salvation Is of the Jews. 223p. (Orig.). 1988. pap. 9.95 (*0-916387-14-3*) Truth Forum.

— Who Owns the Children? Public Compulsion, Private Responsibility & the Dilemma of Ultimate Authority: Public Compulsion, Private Responsibility, & the Dilemma of Ultimate Authority. enl. rev. ed. LC 84-50087. 1991. pap. 16.95 (*0-916387-24-0*) Truth Forum.

— Who Owns the Children? Public Compulsion, Private Responsibility & the Dilemma of Ultimate Authority: Public Compulsion, Private Responsibility, & the Dilemma of Ultimate Authority. 5th enl. rev. ed. LC 84-50087. 1991. 26.95 (*0-916387-25-9*) Truth Forum.

— Wisdom's Children: Home Education & the Roots of Restored Biblical Culture. rev. ed. LC 88-51537. 602p. 1989. pap. 12.95 (*0-916387-11-9*) Truth Forum.

— The Writers Revision Handbook: Summary Points for Revising. 52p. 1993. pap. 4.95 (*0-916387-27-5*) Truth Forum.

Adams, Blair, et al. The Garden of God: Covenant As the Form That Holds God's Love, Including a New Testament View of Old Testament Law. LC 89-51247. 136p. (Orig.). 1989. pap. 8.95 (*0-916387-19-4*) Truth Forum.

— Guidelines for Teaching "Right Words" A Relational Approach to Writing. 4th ed. 208p. 1993. pap. 19.95 (*0-916387-29-1*) Truth Forum.

Adams, Blair, jt. auth. see Adams, Regina.

Adams, Blair, jt. ed. see Truth Forum Staff.

Adams, Bluford. E Pluribus Barnum: The Great Showman & the Making of U. S. Popular Culture. LC 96-31754. 1997. pap. 18.95 (*0-8166-2631-6*); text 47.95 (*0-8166-2630-8*) U of Minn Pr.

Adams, Bob. Adams Streetwise Business Forms - Complete with CD-ROM. LC 99-26116. 1999. pap. 24.95 incl. cd-rom (*1-58062-133-3*) Adams Media.

— Adams Streetwise Complete Business Plan: Create a Business Plan to Finance & Run a New or Existing Business. 352p. 1998. pap. 17.95 (*1-55850-845-7*) Adams Media.

— Adams Streetwise Small Business Start-Up. (Illus.). 450p. 1996. pap. 17.95 (*1-55850-581-4*) Adams Media.

— Streetwise Business Tips. LC 97-39654. xv, 240 p. 1997. pap. 8.95 (*1-55850-778-7*) Adams Media.

Adams, Bob & Veruki, Peter. Adams Streetwise Hiring Top Performers. LC 96-48008. 1997. pap. text 17.95 (*1-55850-684-5*) Adams Media.

Adams, Bob, et al. The Complete Resume & Job Search Book for College Students. 2nd ed. LC 98-33179. 240p. 1999. pap. 12.95 (*1-58062-136-8*) Adams Media.

Adams, Bob, et al. Streetwise Managing People: Lead Your Staff to Peak Performance. Adams Media Corporation Staff, ed. LC 97-34287. (Illus.). 369p. 1997. pap. 17.95 (*1-55850-726-4*) Adams Media.

Adams, Bob, jt. auth. see Stephens, Nancy J.

Adams, Brian. Deadly Karate Blows - The Medical Implications. rev. ed. LC 86-50088. 136p. (Orig.). 1986. reprint ed. pap. 10.95 (*0-86568-077-9*, 312) Unique Pubns.

— Grow Rich with Your Million Dollar Mind. 1991. pap. 10.00 (*0-87980-430-0*) Wilshire.

— How to Succeed: Unique Techniques for Achieving Personal Goals. 1985. pap. 10.00 (*0-87980-413-0*) Wilshire.

— Sales Cybernetics: New Scientific Techniques in Motivational Selling. 1985. pap. 10.00 (*0-87980-412-2*) Wilshire.

— Screen Acting: How to Succeed in Motion Pictures. LC 87-29682. (Illus.). 378p. 1987. pap. 17.95 (*0-943728-20-7*) Lone Eagle Pub.

Adams, Brian & Shirley, Graham, eds. Australian Cinema: The First Eighty Years. 326p. (C). 1990. pap. 24.95 (*0-86819-232-5*, Pub. by Currency Pr) Accents Pubns.

Adams, Bronte & Tate, Trudi, eds. That Kind of Woman. 304p. 1993. pap. 10.95 (*0-88184-963-4*) Carroll & Graf.

Adams, Brooke. Young Americans II: New American Art at the Saatchi Gallery. 1998. pap. text 24.95 (*0-9527453-7-2*, Pub. by Saatchi) Dist Art Pubs.

Adams, Bruce & Parr, John, eds. Boundary Crossers: Case Studies of How Ten of America's Metropolitan Regions Work. 179p. 1997. pap. 15.00 (*1-891464-07-8*) J M Burns Academy.

Adams, Bruce, ed. see Ciulla, Joanne B., et al.

A

Adams, Bruce, ed. see Couto, Richard, et al.

Adams, Bruce, ed. see Hollander, Edwin P., et al.

Adams, Bruce, ed. see Rapoport, Vitaly & Alexeev, Yuri.

Adams, Bruce A. The Politics of Punishment: Prision Reform in Russia, 1863-1917. LC 96-10422. (Illus.). 320p. 1996. lib. bdg. 35.00 (*0-87580-215-X*) N Ill U Pr.

Adams, Bruce F., ed. see Shulgin, V. V.

***Adams-Bullock, Ann & Hawk, Parmalee P.** Developing a Teaching Portfolio: A Guide for Preservice & Practicing Teachers. LC 00-31859. 2001. write for info. (*0-13-083040-2*) Prntice Hall Bks.

Adams-Bullock, Ann, jt. auth. see Foster-Harrison, Elizabeth S.

Adams, C. Help Your Child Recover from Sexual Abuse. 1995. pap. text 17.95 (*0-8020-7384-0*) U of Toronto Pr.

Adams, C. & Braden, R. Lock, Stock, & Barrel. deluxe limited ed. (Illus.). 198p. 1996. boxed set 60.00 (*1-57157-033-0*) Safari Pr.

Adams, C., ed. see Brizova, Joza, et al.

Adams, C. D., tr. Speeches. (Loeb Classical Library: No. 106). 552p. 1919. 18.95 (*0-674-99118-4*) HUP.

Adams, C. R., et al. Principles of Horticulture. 2nd ed. (Illus.). 204p. 1993. pap. 44.95 (*0-7506-1722-5*) Buttrwrth-Heinemann.

Adams, C. W. M. Color Atlas of Multiple Sclerosis. (Illus.). 1991. write for info. (*0-8151-0095-7*) Mosby Inc.

Adams, Candice. Perfectly Matched. 1994. per. 3.50 (*0-373-70616-2*, 1-70616-7) Harlequin Bks.

Adams, Candy L. Woman to Woman Golf Instructions. (Illus.). 168p. (Orig.). 1991. 24.95 (*0-937408-93-X*) GMI Pubns Inc.

Adams, Candy L., ed. see Adams, Walter E.

Adams, Canyon. Addiction in the White House: Disgrace of the U. S. Presidency. 192p. 1998. pap. 12.95 (*1-893172-14-7*) Epiphany Pr.

— The Beast Revealed: 666. LC 99-72546. 177p. 1999. pap. 12.95 (*1-893172-22-8*) Epiphany Pr.

***Adams, Canyon.** The Signs: Prophesy for 2000 A. D. & Beyond. LC 99-72260. 264p. 1999. pap. 12.95 (*1-893172-24-4*) Epiphany Pr.

Adams, Canyon. Spouse Hunt. 200p. (Orig.). 1998. pap. 12.95 (*1-893172-16-3*) Epiphany Pr.

Adams, Caren & Fay, Jennifer. Free of the Shadows: Recovering from Sexual Violence. 224p. 1990. pap. 12.95 (*0-934986-70-3*) New Harbinger.

— Helping Your Child Recover from Sexual Abuse. LC 88-37877. 176p. 1992. pap. 12.95 (*0-295-96806-0*) U of Wash Pr.

Adams, Carl R. Journeys Listening & Speaking, Bk. 1. 122p. 1998. pap. text 27.73 (*0-13-165036-X*) P-H.

Adams, Carl R. & Brown, Steven. Journeys, Bk. 2. 1997. pap. text 27.73 (*0-13-180332-8*, Prentice Hall) P-H.

***Adams, Carlisle.** Understanding the Public-Key Infrastructure: Concepts, Standards & Deployment Considerations. (Technology Ser.). 1999. 74.95 (*1-57870-166-X*) New Riders Pub.

Adams, Carlisle, jt. auth. see Heys, Howard.

Adams, Carmen. Claw. (J). 1995. pap. 3.50 (*0-590-60369-8*) Scholastic Inc.

— Song of the Vampire. 160p. (Orig.). 1996. mass mkt. 3.99 (*0-380-78031-3*, Avon Bks) Morrow Avon.

Adams, Carol. Guide to the Antique Shops of Britain: 1996. (Illus.). 800p. 1995. 29.50 (*1-85149-219-4*) Antique Collect.

— Guide to the Antique Shops of Britain 1996-1997. 25th ed. 1996. 29.50 (*1-85149-240-2*) Antique Collect.

— Guide to the Antique Shops of Great Britain, 1998-1999. 1998. 29.50 (*1-85149-281-X*) Antique Collect.

Adams, Carol, compiled by. Guide to the Antique Shops of Britain 1997-98. 26th ed. (Illus.). 800p. 1997. 29.50 (*1-85149-264-X*) Antique Collect.

Adams, Carol & Benoit, Monette. Double Take Drill-N-Test Q&A Dictation, 200 WPM. (Double-Take Ser.: Vol. II). (Orig.). 1996. pap. 22.95 (*1-881149-13-7*) CRRB.

— Double Take Drill-N-Test Q&A Dictation, 225 WPM. (Double-Take Ser.). (Orig.). 1996. pap. 22.95 (*1-881149-10-2*) CRRB.

— Just Jury Charge Dictation, 180 WPM. (Just Jury Charge Ser.: Vol. II). (Orig.). 1996. pap. 22.95 (*1-881149-14-5*) CRRB.

— Just Jury Charge Dictation, 200 WPM. (Just Jury Charge Ser.). (Orig.). 1996. pap. 22.95 (*1-881149-11-0*) CRRB.

Adams, Carol & Gill, Richard T. Economics: A Concise Micro/Macro Text Student Study Guide. 1993. pap. text, student ed. 21.95 (*1-55934-193-9*, 1193) Mayfield Pub.

Adams, Carol, et al. From Workshop to Warfare: The Lives of Medieval Women. 2nd ed. (Illus.). 46p. 1991. pap. 13.95 (*0-521-39983-1*) Cambridge U Pr.

— Under Control: Life in a Nineteenth Century Silk Factory. LC 83-7500. (Women in History Ser.). 48p. 1984. pap. 13.95 (*0-521-27481-8*) Cambridge U Pr.

Adams, Carol A. & Roberts, Clare B., eds. Financial Reporting by Multinationals. LC 96-2502. (Library of International Accounting: Vol. 5). 560p. 1996. 200.00 (*1-85898-193-X*) E Elgar.

Adams, Carol Hamblet, see Hamblet Adams, Carol.

***Adams, Carol J.** The Inner Art of Vegetarianism: Spiritual Practices for Body & Soul. 2000. pap. 14.95 (*1-930051-13-1*) Lantern Books.

— The Inner Art of Vegetarianism Workbook: Spiritual Practices for Body & Soul. 2000. pap. 15.00 (*1-930051-25-5*) Lantern Books.

Adams, Carol J. Neither Man nor Beast: Feminism & the Defense of Animals. LC 57-8649. 272p. 1995. pap. 15.95 (*0-8264-0803-6*) Continuum.

— The Sexual Politics of Meat: A Feminist-Vegetarian Critical Theory. (Illus.). 256p. 1991. pap. 16.95 (*0-8264-0513-4*) Continuum.

***Adams, Carol J.** The Sexual Politics of Meat: A Feminist-Vegetarian Critical Theory. 10th ed. LC 99-31195. 272p. 1999. pap. 18.95 (*0-8264-1184-3*) Continuum.

Adams, Carol J. Woman-Battering: Creative Pastoral Care & Counseling Ser. LC 94-9988. (Creative Pastoral Care & Counseling Ser.). 1994. pap. 15.00 (*0-8006-2785-7*, 1-2785, Fortress Pr) Augsburg Fortress.

Adams, Carol J., ed. Ecofeminism & the Sacred. LC 92-36883. 352p. 1994. pap. 19.95 (*0-8264-0667-X*) Continuum.

Adams, Carol J. & Donovan, Josephine, eds. Animals & Women: Feminist Theoretical Explorations. LC 95-17002. 392p. 1995. pap. 18.95 (*0-8223-1667-6*); lib. bdg. 59.95 (*0-8223-1655-2*) Duke.

Adams, Carol J. & Fortune, Marie M., eds. Violence Against Women & Children: A Christian Theological Sourcebook. 552p. 1995. pap. 29.95 (*0-8264-0830-3*) Continuum.

Adams, Carol J., jt. ed. see Donovan, Josephine.

***Adams, Carole & Adams, Phil.** Elephant Seals. 60p. 1999. pap. 6.95 (*0-9658776-9-8*) Cntrl Coast Pr.

Adams, Carole G. Basic Understandings for the Principle Approach of American Christian Education & the Christian Idea of the Child. Orig. Title: Beginnings in the Principle Approach: American Christian Education. (Illus.). 36p. 1998. pap. 3.00 (*0-912498-23-4*, BUPA) F A C E.

— The Noah Plan English Language Curriculum Guide: The Principle Approach Kindergarten Through Twelfth Grade. Youmans, Elizabeth L., ed. (Noah Plan Principle Approach Subject Curriculum Guides Ser.). (Illus.). 314p. 1998. pap. 40.00 (*0-912498-20-X*, EGC) F A C E.

Adams, Carole G., ed. see Slater, Rosalie J.

Adams, Caroline, et al. Laboratory Manual for Principles of Biology. 5th ed. 100p. 1995. pap. text, lab manual ed. 17.95 (*0-88725-225-7*) Hunter Textbks.

Adams, Caroline J. A Woman of Wisdom: Honoring, & Celebrating Who You Are. (Illus.). 176p. 1999. pap. 19.95 (*0-89087-874-9*) Celestial Arts.

***Adams, Caroline J.** Woman of Wisdom Companion Journal. (Illus.). 96p. 2000. 14.95 (*0-89087-998-2*) Celestial Arts.

***Adams, Carolyn.** Philadelphia: Neighborhoods, Division, & Conflict in a Postindustrial City. (Illus.). 210p. 1999. reprint ed. pap. text 17.00 (*0-7881-6747-2*) DIANE Pub.

Adams, Carolyn, et al. Philadelphia: Neighborhoods, Division & Conflict in a Postindustrial City. (Comparative American Cities Ser.). 272p. (C). 1991. 49.95 (*0-87722-842-6*) Temple U Pr.

— Philadelphia: Neighborhoods, Division, & Conflict in a Postindustrial City. (Comparative American Cities Ser.). 272p. 1993. pap. 16.95 (*1-56639-078-8*) Temple U Pr.

Adams, Carolyn, jt. auth. see Strandberg, Julie A.

Adams, Carolyn E. & Anthony, Ann, eds. Home Health Outcomes & Resource Utilization Integrating Today's Critical Priorities. (Council of Community Health Services Monograph Ser.: Vol. I). 150p. 1997. 23.95 (*0-88737-724-6*, 19-7246, NLN Pr) Natl League Nurse.

***Adams, Carolyn G.** Hunter Sutherlands Slave Manumissions & Sales in Hartford Co. Maryland 1775-1865. 121p. 1999. pap. 17.00 (*0-7884-1144-6*, A105) Heritage Bk.

Adams, Carolyn H. Stars over Texas. LC 96-33289. (Illus.). 1996. 9.95 (*1-57168-072-1*, Eakin Pr) Sunbelt Media.

Adams, Carolyn T. The Politics of Capital Investment: The Case of Philadelphia. LC 88-2274. (SUNY Series in Urban Public Policy). 202p. (C). 1988. text 24.50 (*0-88706-847-2*) State U NY Pr.

Adams, Cass, ed. The Soul Unearthed: Celebrating Wildness & Personal Renewal Through Nature. LC 96-17617. (New Consciousness Reader Ser.). 288p. (Orig.). 1996. pap. 14.95 (*0-87477-838-7*, Tarcher Putnam) Putnam Pub Group.

Adams, Cassandra, jt. auth. see Ching, Francis D. K.

Adams, Cassandra, jt. ed. see Elizabeth, Lynne.

Adams, Catherine, et al. Developmental Disorders of Language. 2nd ed. LC 97-2631. (Illus.). 256p. 1997. pap. 49.95 (*1-56593-863-1*, 1688) Singular Publishing.

Adams, Catherine E., ed. see Beyda, Vivian, et al.

Adams, Cathy & Violence Against Children Study Group Staff. Children, Child Abuse & Child Protection: Placing Children Centrally. LC 98-37307. 244p. 1999. pap. 32.00 (*0-471-98641-0*) Wiley.

Adams, Cecil. Return of the Straight Dope. 512p. (Orig.). 1994. pap. 10.95 (*0-345-38111-4*) Ballantine Pub Grp.

— Straight Dope. 1986. mass mkt. 5.95 (*0-345-33315-2*) Ballantine Pub Grp.

— The Straight Dope Tells All. 1998. pap. 10.95 (*0-345-42291-0*) Ballantine Pub Grp.

— The Straight Dope Tells All. 4th ed. LC 97-38612. 256p. 1998. pap. 10.95 (*0-345-42007-1*, Ballantine Epiphany) Ballantine Pub Grp.

Adams, Cecilia & Blank, Parthenia. Oregon Trail Diary of Twin Sisters Cecilia Adams & Parthenia Blank in 1852: The Unabridged Diary with Introduction & Contemporary Comments by Bert Webber. LC 90-12057. (Illus.). 86p. 1990. pap. 7.50 (*0-936738-48-0*) Webb Research.

Adams, Charl, ed. Affirmative Action in a Democratic South Africa. 164p. 1993. text 46.15 (*0-7021-2771-X*, Pub. by Juta & Co) Intl Spec Bk.

Adams, Charles. For Good & Evil: The Impact of Taxes on Civilization. 1994. pap. 16.95 (*1-56833-024-3*) Madison Bks UPA.

— For Good & Evil: The Impact of Taxes on the Course of Civilization. 2nd ed. LC 98-49954. (Illus.). 576p. 1999. 29.95 (*1-56833-123-1*, Pub. by Madison Bks UPA) Natl Bk Netwk.

— For Good & Evil: The Impact of Taxes upon the Course of Civilization. LC 92-33551. 552p. 1992. 29.95 (*0-8191-8631-7*) Madison Bks UPA.

— Oklahoma Discovery Practice Manual. 590p. 1987. ring bd. 120.00 (*0-327-01040-1*, 82233, MICHIE) LEXIS Pub.

***Adams, Charles.** Reading. LC 00-105239. (Postcard History Ser.). (Illus.). 128p. 2000. pap. 18.99 (*0-7385-0479-3*) Arcadia Publng.

Adams, Charles. Those Dirty Rotten Taxes. LC 97-51744. 256p. 1998. 24.50 (*0-684-84394-3*) Free Pr.

***Adams, Charles.** When in the Course of Human Events: Arguing the Case for Southern Secession. LC 99-41975. 1999. 24.95 (*0-8476-9722-3*) Rowman.

Adams, Charles C. Boontling: An American Lingo. rev. ed. (Illus.). 272p. (C). 1990. pap. 16.95 (*0-939665-05-0*) Mountain Hse Pr.

Adams, Charles C., 3rd. Guide to the Study of Animal Ecology. Edgerton, Frank N., ed. LC 77-74201. (History of Ecology Ser.). (Illus.). 1978. reprint ed. lib. bdg. 18.95 (*0-405-10371-9*) Ayer.

***Adams, Charles C.** Islam & Modernism in Egypt, Vol. 10. LC 99-53539. (Orientalism Ser.). 2000. write for info. (*0-415-20908-0*) Routledge.

Adams, Charles D., ed. Lysias: Selected Speeches. LC 79-123339. (Oklahoma Series in Classical Culture: Vol. 3). 408p. 1989. reprint ed. pap. 19.95 (*0-8061-1396-0*) U of Okla Pr.

Adams, Charles F. The Antinomian Controversy. LC 74-164507. 1976. reprint ed. lib. bdg. 25.00 (*0-306-70290-8*) Da Capo.

Adams, Charles F., Jr. Autobiography. (Works of Charles Francis Adams Jr. (1835-1915)). 1989. reprint ed. lib. bdg. 79.00 (*0-7812-1419-X*) Rprt Serv.

Adams, Charles F. California in the Year Two Thousand: A Look into the Future of the Golden State As It Approaches the Millennium. LC 92-29085. (Illus.). 256p. 1992. 21.95 (*0-87015-263-7*) Pacific Bks.

Adams, Charles F., Jr. Chapter of Erie. 152p. 1993. reprint ed. lib. bdg. 79.00 (*0-7812-5207-5*) Rprt Serv.

Adams, Charles F. Charles Francis Adams, 1807-1886, by His Son. Morse, John T., Jr., ed. LC 72-128955. (American Statesmen Ser.: No. 29). reprint ed. 45.00 (*0-404-50879-0*) AMS Pr.

— Charles Francis Adams, 1835-1915: An Autobiography. (History - United States Ser.). 224p. 1992. reprint ed. lib. bdg. 79.00 (*0-7812-6192-9*) Rprt Serv.

Adams, Charles F., Jr. Columbus & the Spanish Discovery of America. (Works of Charles Francis Adams Jr. (1835-1915)). 1989. reprint ed. lib. bdg. 79.00 (*0-7812-1411-4*) Rprt Serv.

Adams, Charles F. Dialect Ballads. LC 78-166640. (Illus.). 1971. reprint ed. 19.00 (*0-403-01415-8*) Scholarly.

— Heroes of the Golden Gate. LC 87-7013. (Illus.). 384p. 1987. 24.95 (*0-87015-256-4*) Pacific Bks.

— Heroes of the Golden Gate, Vol. PJ102C. LC 87-7013. (Illus.). 384p. 1999. reprint ed. pap. 15.95 (*0-87015-269-6*) Pacific Bks.

Adams, Charles F., Jr. History of Braintree. (Works of Charles Francis Adams Jr. (1835-1915)). 1989. reprint ed. lib. bdg. 79.00 (*0-7812-1409-2*) Rprt Serv.

— Lee at Appomattox. (Works of Charles Francis Adams Jr. (1835-1915)). 1989. reprint ed. lib. bdg. 79.00 (*0-7812-1414-9*) Rprt Serv.

— Lee at Appomattox, & Other Papers. 2nd ed. LC 77-134047. (Essay Index Reprint Ser.). 1977. 28.95 (*0-8369-1901-7*) Ayer.

Adams, Charles F. Life of John Adams, 2 vols., Set. LC 78-108455. 1971. reprint ed. 150.00 (*0-403-00470-5*) Scholarly.

— The Life of John Adams: Begun by John Quincy Adams, 2 vols., 1. rev. ed. (History - United States Ser.). 1992. reprint ed. write for info. (*0-7812-0161-6*) Rprt Serv.

— The Life of John Adams: Begun by John Quincy Adams, 2 vols., 2. rev. ed. (History - United States Ser.). 1992. reprint ed. write for info. (*0-7812-0162-4*) Rprt Serv.

— The Life of John Adams: Begun by John Quincy Adams, 2 vols., Set. rev. ed. (History - United States Ser.). 1992. reprint ed. lib. bdg. 150.00 (*0-7812-6138-4*) Rprt Serv.

— The Magnificent Rogues of San Francisco: A Galley of Fakers & Frauds, Rascals & Robber Barons, Scoundrels & Scalawags. LC 97-36488. (Illus.). 352p. 1998. 27.95 (*0-87015-262-9*) Pacific Bks.

— Massachusetts: Its Historians & Its History, an Object Lesson. (Works of Charles Frances Adams Jr. (1835-1915)). 110p. reprint ed. lib. bdg. 49.00 (*0-932051-10-3*) Rprt Serv.

Adams, Charles F., Jr. Massachusetts, Its Historians & Its History: An Object Lesson. LC 73-146849. (Select Bibliographies Reprint Ser.). 1977. reprint ed. 16.95 (*0-8369-5616-8*) Ayer.

— Memoir of Washington Irving. LC 70-148869. (Select Bibliographies Reprint Ser.). 1977. reprint ed. 19.95 (*0-8369-5641-9*) Ayer.

— Notes on Railroad Accidents. (Works of Charles Francis Adams Jr. (1835-1915)). 1989. reprint ed. lib. bdg. 79.00 (*0-7812-1407-6*) Rprt Serv.

— Railroads: Their Origin & Problems. Bruchey, Stuart, ed. LC 80-1294. (Railroads Ser.). 1981. reprint ed. lib. bdg. 23.95 (*0-405-13764-8*) Ayer.

— Railroads: Their Origin & Problems. (Works of Charles Francis Adams Jr. (1835-1915)). 1989. reprint ed. lib. bdg. 79.00 (*0-7812-1406-8*) Rprt Serv.

— Richard Henry Dana. (Works of Charles Francis Adams Jr. (1835-1915)). 1989. reprint ed. lib. bdg. 79.00 (*0-7812-1408-4*) Rprt Serv.

— Seward & the Declaration of Paris. (Works of Charles Francis Adams Jr. (1835-1915)). 1989. reprint ed. lib. bdg. 79.00 (*0-685-27453-5*) Rprt Serv.

— Studies: Military & Diplomatic. (Works of Charles Francis Adams Jr. (1835-1915)). 1989. reprint ed. lib. bdg. 79.00 (*0-7812-1416-5*) Rprt Serv.

— Studies, Military & Diplomatic, 1775-1865. LC 73-150168. (Select Bibliographies Reprint Ser.). 1977. 25.95 (*0-8369-5681-8*) Ayer.

Adams, Charles F. Studies, Military & Diplomatic, 1775-1865. LC 73-150168. (Select Bibliographies Reprint Ser.). 424p. 1982. reprint ed. 22.50 (*0-8290-0474-2*) Irvington.

Adams, Charles F., Jr. Three Episodes in Massachusetts History. (Works of Charles Francis Adams Jr. (1835-1915)). 1989. reprint ed. lib. bdg. 79.00 (*0-7812-1410-6*) Rprt Serv.

— Three Phi Beta Kappa Addresses. (Works of Charles Francis Adams Jr. (1835-1915)). 1989. reprint ed. lib. bdg. 79.00 (*0-7812-1415-7*) Rprt Serv.

— Trans-Atlantic Historical Solidarity. (Works of Charles Francis Adams Jr. (1835-1915)). 1989. reprint ed. lib. bdg. 79.00 (*0-7812-1418-1*) Rprt Serv.

Adams, Charles F. The Works of Charles Follen Adams, 1842-1918, Set. 1989. reprint ed. lib. bdg. 600.00 (*0-685-18559-1*) Rprt Serv.

Adams, Charles F., Jr. The Works of Charles Francis Adams Jr., 1835-1915, Set. 1987. reprint ed. lib. bdg. 800.00 (*0-685-18560-5*) Rprt Serv.

Adams, Charles F., Jr., ed. Correspondence Between John Adams & Mercy Warren Relating to Her History of the American Revolution, July-August, 1807. LC 72-2586. (American Women Ser.: Images & Realities). 202p. 1976. reprint ed. 21.95 (*0-405-04487-9*) Ayer.

— Russian Memoirs of John Quincy Adams: His Diary from 1809 to 1814. LC 74-115501. (Russia Observed, Series I). 1970. reprint ed. 29.95 (*0-405-03001-0*) Ayer.

Adams, Charles F., Jr. & Adams, Henry (Brooks). Chapters of Erie, & Other Essays. LC 66-22613. (Library of Early American Business & Industry: No. 8). 429p. 1967. reprint ed. 49.50 (*0-678-00220-7*) Kelley.

Adams, Charles F., Jr., jt. auth. see Nathan, Richard P.

Adams, Charles F., ed. see Adams, John Q.

Adams, Charles F., ed. see Adams, John Q., Jr.

Adams, Charles H. The Guardian of the Law: Authority & Identity in James Fenimore Cooper. LC 90-31994. 168p. 1991. lib. bdg. 35.00 (*0-271-00708-7*) Pa St U Pr.

Adams, Charles J., 3rd. Berks the Bizarre. 1995. pap. 9.95 (*1-880683-06-7*) Exeter Hse.

Adams, Charles J., III. Bucks County Ghost Stories. 186p. 1999. pap. 11.95 (*1-880683-13-X*) Exeter Hse.

— Cape May Ghost Stories, Bk. 2. 1997. pap. 8.95 (*1-880683-11-3*) Exeter Hse.

— Ghost Stories of Berks County (Pennsylvania) 215p. 1982. pap. 7.95 (*0-9610008-0-5*) Exeter Hse.

— Ghost Stories of Berks County (Pennsylvania), Bk. II. 150p. 1984. pap. 7.95 (*0-9610008-1-3*) Exeter Hse.

— New York City Ghost Stories. (Illus.). 185p. (Orig.). 1996. pap., per. 10.95 (*1-880683-09-1*) Exeter Hse.

— Pennsylvania Dutch Country Ghosts, Legends & Lore. (Illus.). 163p. 1994. pap. 10.95 (*1-880683-03-2*) Exeter Hse.

***Adams, Charles J.** Philadelphia Ghost Stories. 1998. pap. text 11.95 (*1-880683-12-1*) Exeter Hse.

— Philadelphia Ghost Stories. 1998. pap. 11.95 (*0-88068-312-0*) Profesores Universitarios Pro-Divulgacion Academica.

Adams, Charles J., III & Seibold, David J. Ghost Stories of the Lehigh Valley. (Illus.). 190p. 1993. pap. 9.95 (*1-880683-02-4*) Exeter Hse.

— Great Train Wrecks of Eastern Pennsylvania. (Illus.). 224p. (Orig.). 1992. pap. 12.95 (*1-880683-01-6*) Exeter Hse.

— Legends of Long Beach Island. (Illus.). 110p. 1985. pap. 7.95 (*0-9610008-2-1*) Exeter Hse.

— Pocono Ghosts Bk. 2: Legends & Lore. 1995. pap. 8.95 (*1-880683-08-3*) Exeter Hse.

— Shipwrecks & Legends: Round Cape May. (Illus.). 115p. 1987. pap. 8.95 (*0-9610008-5-6*) Exeter Hse.

Adams, Charles J., III, jt. auth. see Seibold, David J.

Adams, Charles J., III, jt. auth. see Trapani, Beth E.

Adams, Charles J., ed. see Conference on Iranian Civilization & Culture Staff.

Adams, Charles J., ed. see Crupi, Connie.

Adams, Charles J., III, ed. & intro. see Smith, Arthur C.

Adams, Charles K. Nature's Electricity. (Illus.). 176p. 1986. pap. 9.95 (*0-8306-2769-3*, NO. 2769) McGraw-Hill Prof.

— The Works of Charles Kendall Adams, 1835-1902, Set. 1987. reprint ed. lib. bdg. 800.00 (*0-685-18561-3*) Rprt Serv.

Adams, Charles L., intro. Frank Waters' People. (Studies in Frank Waters: Vol. XIV). 100p. (Orig.). 1992. pap. 10.00 (*1-878277-08-1*) Frank Waters Soc.

— Frank Waters' Readers. 100p. 1993. write for info. (*1-878277-10-3*) Frank Waters Soc.

— Studies in Frank Waters Vol. VI: The Papers from "Dialogues" 85p. (Orig.). (C). 1984. pap. 5.00 (*1-878277-00-6*) Frank Waters Soc.

— Studies in Frank Waters Vol. VII: An Appreciation. 113p. (Orig.). (C). 1985. pap. 5.00 (*1-878277-01-4*) Frank Waters Soc.

— Studies in Frank Waters Vol. VIII: Emergences. 98p. (Orig.). (C). 1986. pap. 5.00 (*1-878277-02-2*) Frank Waters Soc.

— Studies in Frank Waters Vol. IX: Flight from Fiesta. 79p. (Orig.). (C). 1987. pap. 5.00 (*1-878277-03-0*) Frank Waters Soc.

— Studies in Frank Waters Vol. X: Connections. (Illus.). 200p. (C). 1988. pap. 10.00 (*1-878277-04-9*) Frank Waters Soc.

— Studies in Frank Waters Vol. XII: The Form of the Novel. 100p. (Orig.). (C). 1990. pap. 10.00 (*1-878277-06-5*) Frank Waters Soc.

— Studies in Frank Waters Vol. XIII: "Frank Waters & the Land" 100p. (Orig.). 1991. pap. 10.00 (*1-878277-07-3*) Frank Waters Soc.

— Studies in Frank Waters Vol. XVI: Environmental Concerns. 100p. (Orig.). 1994. pap. 10.00 (*1-878277-11-1*) Frank Waters Soc.

An Asterisk (*) at the beginning of an entry indicates that the title is appearing for the first time.

Adams, Charles L., et al. Studies in Frank Waters Vol. 19: Insights. 99p. 1997. pap. 10.00 (*1-878277-14-6*) Frank Waters Soc.

Adams, Charles L., ed. see Evans-Wentz, W. Y.

Adams, Charles S. The Civil War in the Shenandoah Valley. 31p. 1995. pap. 5.95 (*1-888256-02-8*) CS Adams.

— The Civil War in Washington County, Maryland. (Illus.). 116p. (Orig.). 1996. pap. 16.00 (*1-888256-04-4*) CS Adams.

Adams, Charles S., ed. Alexander Robinson Boteler: Wheel Horse of Whiggery, Stonewall's Courier. (Illus.). 168p. 1998. pap. 24.00 (*1-888256-07-9*) CS Adams.

— Military Operations in Jefferson County, Virginia & West Virginia, 1861-1865. 52p. 1994. pap. 6.95 (*1-888256-00-1*) CS Adams.

— Roadside Markers in Maryland. 121p. 1997. pap. 16.00 (*1-888256-06-0*) CS Adams.

Adams, Charles S., ed. Roadside Markers in West Virginia. 90p. 1995. pap. 12.00 (*1-888256-03-6*) CS Adams.

Adams, Charles S. & Adams, Sean T. The Civil War in Frederick County, Maryland. 64p. 1995. pap. 13.95 (*1-888256-01-X*) CS Adams.

Adams, Charles S., ed. see Foster, B. G.

Adams, Charles W. New Mexico Discovery Practice Manual. 560p. 1994. ring bd. 115.00 (*0-409-25545-9*, MICHIE) LEXIS Pub.

— Oklahoma Discovery Practice Manual. 590p. 1993. ring bd. 120.00 (*0-614-05936-4*, MICHIE) LEXIS Pub.

— Oklahoma Discovery Practice Manual, 1987-1993. 590p. 1993. ring bd. 120.00 (*0-409-25104-6*, 82233-10, MICHIE) LEXIS Pub.

Adams, Charlie. Travels with Charlie: Days in the Broadcast Life of WSBT's Charlie Adams. 1998. pap. 18.95 (*1-888698-19-5*) Diamond Communications.

Adams-Chau, Lynda L. The Professional's Guide to Fund Raising, Corporate Giving, & Philanthropy: People Give to People. LC 87-32263. 192p. 1988. 52.95 (*0-89930-251-3*, ACP/, Quorum Bks) Greenwood.

***Adams, Cheryl O., et al.** Woman to Woman: Truths from Titus. 112p. 1999. teacher ed. 14.50 (*1-888220-06-6*); student ed. 14.50 (*1-888220-07-4*) Reality Living.

Adams, Cheryl O., jt. auth. see Fink, Joanne.

Adams, Chester H. A Guide for Judges in Child Support Enforcement. 173p. 1983. write for info. (*0-318-63278-0*) Natl Juv & Family Ct Judges.

***Adams, Chris.** A Neurosurgeon's Notebook. (Illus.). 19p. 1998. pap. 33.95 (*0-632-05154-X*) Blackwell Sci.

Adams, Chris, jt. auth. see Chester, Gary.

Adams, Christine. A Taste for Comfort & Status: A Bourgeois Family in Eighteenth-Century France. LC 98-54961. 2000. pap. 19.95 (*0-271-01956-5*) Pa St U Pr.

— Travel to Prague. 1992. 24.95 (*1-85043-312-7*, Pub. by I B T) St Martin.

Adams, Christine & Fruge, Ernest. Why Children Misbehave: And What to Do about It. LC 96-67939. (Illus.). 176p. (Orig.). 1996. pap. 14.95 (*1-57224-051-2*) New Harbinger.

Adams, Christine, et al. Visions & Revisions of Eighteenth-Century France. LC 96-31048. 1997. 45.00 (*0-271-01636-1*); pap. 16.95 (*0-271-01637-X*) Pa St U Pr.

***Adams, Christine A.** Gratitude Therapy. LC 99-73382. (Illus.). 88p. 1999. pap. 4.95 (*0-87029-332-X*, 20105) Abbey.

— Holy Relationships. LC 97-47708. 108p. 1998. 14.95 (*0-8192-1738-7*) Morehouse Pub.

Adams, Christine A. Living in Love: Connecting with the Power of Love Within. LC 93-24748. 200p. 1993. pap. 9.95 (*1-55874-278-6*) Health Comm.

— One-Day-at-a-Time Therapy. LC 90-80719. (Illus.). 72p. (Orig.). 1990. pap. 4.95 (*0-87029-228-5*, 20204-4) Abbey.

Adams, Christopher R. Building Better Warning Partnerships: National Weather Service Emergency Management Forum. (Illus.). 61p. (C). 1997. reprint ed. pap. text 30.00 (*0-7881-4153-8*) DIANE Pub.

Adams, Clairannette, ed. & illus. see Fitzgerald, Ernest E.

Adams, Clarks F. & Adams, John Q. Life of John Adams, 2 Vols. LC 68-24969. (American Biography Ser.: No. 32). 1969. reprint ed. lib. bdg. 150.00 (*0-8383-0151-7*) M S G Haskell Hse.

Adams, Clayton R., jt. ed. see Kelley, Judith H.

Adams, Clementina R. Common Threads: Themes in Afro-Hispanic Women's Literature. LC 96-61937. (SPA.). 335p. 1998. pap. 29.00 (*0-89729-827-6*) Ediciones.

***Adams, Clifford A.** Nutricines: Food Components in Health & Nutrition. 128p. 1999. pap. 80.00 (*1-897676-90-5*, Pub. by Nottingham Univ Pr) St Mut.

Adams, Clifford E. Plastics Gearing: Selection & Application. (Mechanical Engineering Ser.: Vol. 49). (Illus.). 400p. 1986. text 175.00 (*0-8247-7498-1*) Dekker.

Adams, Clifton. Doomsday Creek. large type ed. (Linford Western Library). 368p. 1992. pap. 16.99 (*0-7089-7177-6*) Ulverscroft.

— The Moonlight War. large type ed. (Linford Western Library). 320p. 1992. pap. 16.99 (*0-7089-7249-7*, Linford) Ulverscroft.

Adams, Clinton. Crayonstone: The Life & Work of Bolton Brown with a Catalogue of His Lithographs. LC 92-30157. (Illus.). 302p. 1993. reprint ed. pap. 93.70 (*0-608-07283-4*, 206751100009) Bks Demand.

— Picasso: Graphic Magician. 1998. 48.00 (*0-85667-494-X*) P Wilson Serv.

Adams, Clinton, ed. Second Impressions: Modern Prints & Printmakers Reconsidered. LC 97-157032. (Tamarind Papers). (Illus.). 112p. (C). 1996. pap. 29.95 (*0-8263-1672-7*) U of NM Pr.

Adams, Clinton, et al. Mexico Nine: Mexico Nueve. Downer, Kate, ed. Latin American Institute Staff, tr. (ENG & SPA., Illus.). 56p. (Orig.). 1988. pap. 16.00 (*0-9619735-0-1*) Tamarind Inst.

Adams, Colin C. The Knot Book: An Elementary Introduction to the Mathematical Theory of Knots. LC 93-49412. 306p. (C). 1994. text 32.95 (*0-7167-2393-X*) W H Freeman.

***Adams, Colin C.** The Knot Book: An Elementary Introduction to the Mathematical Theory of Knots. 2001. pap. 14.95 (*0-7167-4219-5*) W H Freeman.

***Adams, Colin C., et al.** How to Ace the Rest of Calculus: The Street Wise Guide, Including Multi-Variable Calculus. 2001. pap., student ed. 14.95 (*0-7167-4174-1*) W H Freeman.

Adams-Collier, Kathryn, ed. see Stokes, Lillian.

Adams, Corene, ed. see Boetticher, Budd.

Adams, Corene, ed. see Freeman, Don.

Adams, Corine. English Speech Rhythm & the Foreign Learner. (Janua Linguarum, Series Practica: No. 69). 1979. text 68.50 (*90-279-7716-X*) Mouton.

Adams, Courtney S., ed. French Chansons for Three Voices (ca. 1550), Pt. I. (Recent Researches in Music of the Renaissance Ser.: Vol. RRR36). (Illus.). xxix, 72p. 1982. pap. 35.00 (*0-89579-155-2*) A-R Eds.

— French Chansons for Three Voices (ca. 1550), Pt. II. (Recent Researches in Music of the Renaissance Ser.: Vol. RRR37). (Illus.). xxiii, 78p. 1982. pap. 35.00 (*0-89579-156-0*) A-R Eds.

Adams-Crymes, Phyllis. Mirror Images Vol. 1: Mirrors of Life. Hardbound, Inc., Staff, ed. Date not set. pap. 8.95 (*1-930659-00-8*) P Adams-Crymes.

— Mr. McGinnis's New Shoes. Hardbound, Inc., Staff, ed. (Children's Diary Ser.: Vol. 1). (Illus.). 27p. 2000. 17.00 (*1-930659-01-6*) P Adams-Crymes.

— My First Meal, Vol. 2. (Children's Diary Ser.). (Illus.). (J). (gr. k-3). 2000. pap. text. write for info. (*1-930659-02-4*) P Adams-Crymes.

Adams, Cynthia. The Mysterious Case of Sir Arthur Conan Doyle. LC 99-11668. (World Writers Ser.). (Illus.). 112p. (YA). (gr. 5 up). 1999. lib. bdg. 18.95 (*1-883846-34-X*) M Reynolds.

— World Famous Landmarks. 1998. pap. 14.95 (*1-56822-674-8*) Instruct Fair.

Adams, Cynthia & Jones, Peter. Interpersonal Skills & Health Professional Issues. 336p. pap. write for info. (*0-02-685483-X*); text 31.62 (*0-02-685482-1*) Glencoe.

Adams, Cynthia G. Exploring the United States on the Net. 1998. pap. 11.95 (*0-673-58638-3*) Addson-Wesley Educ.

— Exploring the World on the Net. (Illus.). 112p. 1998. pap. 11.95 (*0-673-57734-1*) Addson-Wesley Educ.

Adams, Cyril E. Lock, Stock & Barrel. 2nd ed. 1996. 24.95 (*1-57157-020-9*) Safari Pr.

Adams, Cyril E., ed. Mammalian Egg Transfer. 256p. 1982. 145.00 (*0-8493-6140-0*, QL739, CRC Reprint) Franklin.

Adams, D. Land for Industrial Development. (Illus.). 304p. (C). 1994. 80.00 (*0-419-19180-1*, E & FN Spon) Routledge.

***Adams, D. Briane, ed.** Potential Consequences of Climate Variability & Change to Water Resources in the United States. 424p. 1999. pap. 75.00 (*1-882132-45-9*, TPS-99-1) Am Water Resources.

Adams, D. J. Rachel Beats the Blizzard. 64p. (J). (gr. 1-6). 1998. pap. 5.95 (*0-9659630-1-2*) Tomorrows Girl.

Adams, D. K., jt. ed. see Bell, Ian F.

Adams, D. O., ed. see Stewart, H. Stephen.

Adams, D. Q., jt. ed. see Mallory, James.

Adams, D. R. & Hedberg, L. J. Function Spaces & Potential Theory. Berger, M. et al, eds. (Grundlehren der Mathematischen Wissenschaften Ser.: Bd. 314). 395p. 1995. 126.95 (*0-387-57060-8*) Spr-Verlag.

Adams, Dale, ed. see Jenny, Hans H.

Adams, Dan. The Child Influencers: Restoring the Lost Art of Parenting. (Illus.). 246p. (Orig.). 1990. pap. 9.95 (*0-9626349-0-5*) Home Team Pr.

Adams, Dana & Moore, Louis A. 4000 Questions & Answers on the Bible. 1996. pap. text 5.99 (*0-8054-1243-3*) Broadman.

Adams, Daniel. First Lady Down. 162p. (Orig.). 1996. pap. 4.99 (*0-9653326-5-9*) Alley Cat Pr.

Adams, Daniel J. From East to West: Essays in Honor of Donald G. Bloesch. LC 97-18953. 272p. 1997. 48.00 (*0-7618-0801-9*) U Pr of Amer.

***Adams, Daphne.** I Married Madam. (Sapphire Ser.). 2000. mass mkt. 9.95 (*0-352-33514-9*) Virgin Bks.

Adams, Darius M., et al. The Forest & Agricultural Sector Optimization Model (FASOM) Model Structure & Policy Applications. (Illus.). 60p. (C). 1997. reprint ed. pap. text 25.00 (*0-7881-4023-X*) DIANE Pub.

Adams, David. A Handbook of Diction for Singers: Italian, German, French. LC 98-12204. (Illus.). 192p. (C). 1998. pap. 19.95 (*0-19-512077-9*) OUP.

— Stage Welsh. Stephens, Meic, ed. (Changing Wales Ser.). 1996. pap. 11.95 (*0-8464-4740-1*) Beekman Pubs.

— The Three Little Pigs Go to Greasy Pete's. (Illus.). 40p. (J). (ps-3). 1994. pap. 5.95 (*0-9638421-8-8*); lib. bdg. 14.95 (*0-9638421-9-6*) Flatland Tales.

— Where We Came In: Poems. (Wild Dog Ser.). 64p. (Orig.). 1993. pap. 5.95 (*0-933087-26-8*) Bottom Dog Pr.

Adams, David, jt. auth. see Foreman, Tony.

Adams, David, ed. see Eckman, Frederick.

Adams, David, jt. ed. see Neuberger, James.

Adams, David A. Renewable Resource Policy: The Legal-Institutional Foundation. LC 93-6543. (Illus.). 580p. (C). 1993. text 58.00 (*1-55963-225-9*) Island Pr.

Adams, David D. Iowa Sportsman's Atlas. (Illus.). 1994. spiral bd. 19.95 (*1-56464-521-5*) Universal Map Enterprises Inc.

— Nebraska Sportsman's Atlas. (Illus.). 1994. spiral bd. 18.75 (*1-56464-686-6*) Universal Map Enterprises Inc.

Adams, David D., adapted by. Ohio Sportsman's Atlas. (Illus.). 1995. spiral bd. 21.95 (*0-7625-0054-9*) Universal Map Enterprises Inc.

Adams, David G. Bothy Nichts & Days. 100p. (C). 1996. pap. 30.00 (*0-85976-340-4*, Pub. by J Donald) St Mut.

Adams, David J. Cosmic X-Ray Astronomy. fac. ed. LC 80-491685. (Monographs on Astronomical Subjects: No. 6). (Illus.). 160p. 1980. reprint ed. pap. 49.60 (*0-7837-8001-X*, 204775700008) Bks Demand.

Adams, David J., et al. A Red Shadow of Steel Mills: Photos & Poems. Smith, Larry, ed. (Midwest Writers Ser.). (Illus.). 155p. (Orig.). 1991. pap. 8.95 (*0-933087-18-7*) Bottom Dog Pr.

***Adams, David K.** Religious & Secular Reform in America Ideas, Beliefs & Social Change. LC 98-47598. 1999. text 55.00 (*0-8147-0685-1*) NYU Pr.

Adams, David K., ed. Britain & Canada in the 1990s: Proceedings of a U. K. - Canada Colloquim. 158p. 1992. 67.95 (*1-85521-274-9*, Pub. by Dartmth Pub) Ashgate Pub Co.

Adams, David K. & Institute Research on Public Policy. Britain & Canada in the 1990s: Proceedings of a UK/Canada Colloquium, Leeds Castle, Kent, England. LC 92-146509. xi, 158p. 1991. write for info. (*0-88645-139-6*) IRPP.

***Adams, David Keith.** Religious & Secular Reform in America: Ideas, Beliefs & Social Change. LC 98-47598. 273p. 1999. pap. 20.00 (*0-8147-0686-X*) NYU Pr.

Adams, David L. & Morelan, Lyn. Forest Health in the Inland West: A Symposium. 64p. (Orig.). (C). 1995. pap. text 30.00 (*0-7881-1840-4*) DIANE Pub.

Adams, David L., jt. ed. see Sampson, R. Neil.

Adams, David M. Inorganic Solids: An Introduction to Concepts in Solid-State Structural Chemistry. LC 73-16863. 352p. reprint ed. pap. 109.20 (*0-608-14573-4*, 202492800040) Bks Demand.

Adams, David M. & Maine, Edward L. Business Ethics for the 21st Century. LC 97-21283. xvii, 590p. 1997. pap. text 45.95 (*1-55934-560-8*, 1560) Mayfield Pub.

Adams, David P. The Greatest Good to the Greatest Number: Penicillin Rationing on the American Home Front, 1940-1945. LC 90-6081. (American University Studies: History: Ser. IX, Vol. 93). (Illus.). VII, 228p. (C). 1991. text 38.95 (*0-8204-1284-8*) P Lang Pubng.

Adams, David R. & Hedberg, Lars I. Function Spaces & Potential Theory, Vol. 314. LC 95-23396. (Grundlehren der Mathematischen Wissenschaften Ser.). 1995. text. write for info. (*3-540-57060-8*) Spr-Verlag.

Adams, David T. Africa & the Africans in the Old Testament. LC 97-34254. 312p. 1998. 74.95 (*1-57309-205-3*, U Pr W Africa) Intl Scholars.

Adams, David W. Education for Extinction: American Indians & the Boarding School Experience, 1875-1928. LC 95-7638. (Illus.). 258p. 1997. reprint ed. pap. 17.95 (*0-7006-0838-9*) U Pr of KS.

— Education for Extinction: American Indians & the Boarding School Experience, 1875-1928. LC 95-7638. (Illus.). 408p. (C). 1997. reprint ed. 40.00 (*0-7006-0735-8*) U Pr of KS.

Adams, David W. & Deveau, Eleanor J., eds. Beyond the Innocence of Childhood: Factors Influencing Children & Adolescents' Perceptions & Attides Toward Death, Vol. 1. LC 95-20408. (Death, Value & Meaning Ser.). 203p. 1995. 34.95 (*0-89503-128-0*) Baywood Pub.

— Beyond the Innocence of Childhood: Helping Children & Adolescents Cope with Death & Bereavement, Vol. 3. LC 95-20407. (Death, Value & Meaning Ser.). 274p. 1995. 41.95 (*0-89503-130-2*) Baywood Pub.

— Beyond the Innocence of Childhood: Helping Children & Adolescents Cope with Life Threatening Illness & Dying, Vol. 2. LC 95-20406. (Death, Value & Meaning Ser.). 382p. 1995. 47.95 (*0-89503-129-9*) Baywood Pub.

Adams, Deborah. All the Crazy Winters. (Holiday Mysteries Ser.). 1992. mass mkt. 5.50 (*0-345-37076-7*) Ballantine Pub Grp.

— All the Dark Disguises. 1993. mass mkt. 4.99 (*0-345-37765-6*) Ballantine Pub Grp.

— All the Deadly Beloved. 1995. mass mkt. 5.99 (*0-345-39222-1*) Ballantine Pub Grp.

— All the Great Pretenders. (Orig.). 1992. mass mkt. 5.99 (*0-345-37075-9*) Ballantine Pub Grp.

***Adams, Deborah.** All the Hungry Mothers. 192p. 1999. pap. 14.95 (*1-57072-122-X*, Silver Dagger) Overmountain Pr.

— All the Hungry Mothers. (Jesus Creek Mysteries Ser.). 192p. 1999. reprint ed. 24.95 (*1-57072-106-8*, Silver Dagger) Overmountain Pr.

Adams, Deborah. Management Accounting for the Hospitality Industry. LC 98-119244. 1997. pap. text 33.95 (*0-304-32906-1*) Continuum.

Adams, Deborah, jt. auth. see Herman, Jeff.

Adams, Deborah B., ed. see Linhart, Letty.

Adams, Deborah B., ed. see Marsh, Laura.

Adams, Debra, ed. see McWhorter, Abner.

Adams, Dennis & Hamm, Mary E. Cooperative Learning: Critical Thinking & Collaboration Across the Curriculum. 2nd ed. (Illus.). 294p. 1996. 50.95 (*0-398-06587-X*); pap. 36.95 (*0-398-06588-8*) C C Thomas.

Adams, Dennis, et al. Veiled Histories: The Body, Place, & Public Art. Nouokov, Anna, ed. LC 97-66969. (Thinking Publically: Vol. 1). (Illus.). 192p. (Orig.). 1997. pap. 16.95 (*1-883831-07-5*) Critical Pr.

Adams, Dennis, jt. auth. see Hamm, Mary.

Adams, Dennis, jt. auth. see Hamm, Mary E.

Adams, Dennis, jt. auth. see Staniszewski, Mary A.

Adams, Dennis M. Diagnosis Documentation & Coding: The Key to Reimbursement & Capitation. LC 96-48064. 144p. (C). 1997. 40.00 (*0-7863-1000-6*, Irwn Prfssnl) McGraw-Hill Prof.

***Adams, Dennis M. & Hamm, Mary.** Literacy Today: Standards Across the Curriculum. LC 99-53868. (Reference Library of Social Science). 2000. pap. write for info. (*0-8153-3404-4*) Garland.

— Media & Literacy: Learning in an Electronic Age-Issues, Ideas & Teaching Strategies. 2nd ed. LC 99-48808. (Illus.). 244p. 2000. 31.95 (*0-398-07032-6*) C C Thomas.

— Media & Literacy: Learning in an Electronic Age-Issues, Ideas & Teaching Strategies. 2nd ed. LC 99-48808. 244p. 2000. 43.95 (*0-398-07031-8*) C C Thomas.

Adams, Dennis M. & Hamm, Mary E. New Designs for Teaching & Learning: Promoting Active Learning in Tomorrow's Schools. (Education Ser.). 366p. 1994. text 32.95 (*0-7879-0020-6*) Jossey-Bass.

Adams, Derek. The Adventures of Miles Diamond: The Case of the Missing Twin. (Orig.). 1993. mass mkt. 4.95 (*1-56333-118-7*, Badboy) Masquerade.

— Forbidden Love. 1998. mass mkt. 6.95 (*1-56333-645-6*, Badboy) Masquerade.

***Adams, Derek.** Forbidden Love. 2000. pap. 9.95 (*1-873741-37-5*) Millivres Bks.

Adams, Derek. Heat Wave. (Orig.). 1994. mass mkt. 4.95 (*1-56333-159-4*, Badboy) Masquerade.

— Mark of the Wolf. (Orig.). 1996. mass mkt. 5.95 (*1-56333-361-9*, Badboy) Masquerade.

— Miles Diamond & the Cretan Apollo. (Adventures of Miles Diamond Ser.). (Orig.). 1997. mass mkt. 5.95 (*1-56333-381-3*, Badboy) Masquerade.

— Miles Diamond & the Demon of Death. (Orig.). 1995. mass mkt. 4.95 (*1-56333-251-5*, Badboy) Masquerade.

— My Double Life. (Orig.). 1995. mass mkt. 5.95 (*1-56333-314-7*, Badboy) Masquerade.

Adams, Diane L. Lead Seals from Fort Michilimackinac, 1715-1781. (Archaeological Completion Reports: No. 14). (Illus.). 49p. (Orig.). 1989. pap. 8.00 (*0-911872-58-2*) Mackinac St Hist Pks.

Adams, Diane L., ed. Health Issues for Women of Color: A Cultural Diversity Health Perspective. 240p. 1995. 62.00 (*0-8039-7311-X*); pap. 27.50 (*0-8039-7312-8*) Sage.

***Adams, Doc.** Valley of Blood. large type ed. 240p. 2000. pap. 18.99 (*0-7089-5664-5*, Linford) Ulverscroft.

Adams, Dolph, jt. auth. see Carlisle, Dan.

Adams, Dolph, jt. auth. see Carlisle, Don.

Adams, Dolph O. & Hanna, Michael G., Jr., eds. Contemporary Topics in Immunobiology Vol. 13: Macrophage Action. LC 79-179761. 280p. 1984. 75.00 (*0-306-41536-4*, Plenum Trade) Perseus Pubng.

Adams, Don. Building Habitats for Reptiles: A Step by Step Guide. (Illus.). 40p. (Orig.). 1987. pap. 3.95 (*0-916005-07-0*) Silver Sea.

— James Merrill's Poetic Quest, 81. LC 96-35022. (Contributions to the Study of World Literature Ser.). 192p. 1997. 57.95 (*0-313-30250-2*) Greenwood.

Adams, Don & Goldbard, Arlene. Crossroads: Reflections on the Politics of Culture. LC 90-84237. 161p. (Orig.). 1990. pap. 13.95 (*0-9627234-0-1*) DNA Pr.

Adams, Don & Gottlieb, Esther E. Education & Social Change in Korea. LC 92-36748. (Reference Books in International Education, Vol. 27, Reference Library of Social Science: Vol. 23). 256p. 1993. text 46.00 (*0-8240-6635-9*, SS513) Garland.

Adams, Don C. & Salvaterra, Mary E. Block Scheduling: Pathways to Success. LC 97-143630. (Illus.). 1997. ring bd. write for info. (*1-56676-521-8*) Scarecrow.

Adams, Donald D., et al, eds. Cycling of Reduced Gases in the Hydrosphere Vol. 25: International Vereinig. F. Theoret. U. Angew. Limn.; Mitteil. (International Association of Theoretical & Applied Limnology, Communications Ser.: No. 25). (Illus.). x, 204p. 1996. pap. 46.00 (*3-510-52025-4*, Pub. by E Schweizerbartsche) Balogh.

Adams, Donald F., contrib. by. Test Methods for Composite Materials: December, 1996. 1997. ring bd. 179.95 (*1-56676-525-0*) Technomic.

Adams, Donald K., ed. see Polidori, John W.

Adams, Donald R. Canine Anatomy: A Systemic Study. LC 85-23114. (Illus.). 521p. 1986. reprint ed. pap. 161.60 (*0-608-07922-7*, 206789600011) Bks Demand.

Adams, Donald R., Jr. Wage Rates in Philadelphia, 1790-1830. LC 75-2572. (Dissertations in American Economic History Ser.). (Illus.). 1975. reprint ed. 31.95 (*0-405-07253-8*) Ayer.

Adams, Doris G. Iraq's People & Resources, Vol. XVIII. LC 80-19079. (University of California Publications in Social Welfare: Vol. XVIII). (Illus.). 160p. 1980. reprint ed. lib. bdg. 55.00 (*0-313-22759-4*, ADIP, Greenwood Pr) Greenwood.

Adams, Dorothy & Kurtz, Margaret A. The Legal Secretary: Terminology & Transcription. (Illus.). 1981. text 76.50 (*0-07-000330-0*) McGraw.

Adams, Dorothy A. & Esser, Peter D. Essential Elements of MRI & MRS. (Health Physics & Imaging Technology Ser.). 1999. 79.95 (*0-8493-9571-2*) CRC Pr.

Adams, Doug. Appropriating Australian Folk Dances into Sacred Dance. 1987. pap. 3.00 (*0-941500-45-4*) Sharing Co.

— Changing Biblical Imagery & Artistic Identity in 20th Century Liturgical Dance. 1984. pap. 3.00 (*0-941500-31-4*) Sharing Co.

— Children, Divorce & the Church. Schaller, Lyle E., ed. (Creative Leadership Ser.). 112p. (Orig.). 1992. pap. 12.95 (*0-687-06480-5*) Abingdon.

— Congregational Dancing in Christian Worship. rev. ed. 1984. pap. 9.95 (*0-941500-02-0*) Sharing Co.

— Eyes to See Wholeness: Visual Arts Informing Biblical & Theological Studies in Education & Worship. (Illus.). 220p. (Orig.). 1995. pap. 22.50 (*1-877871-86-9*, 3801) Ed Ministries.

A

— Humor in the American Pulpit from George Whitefield Through Henry Ward Beecher. rev. ed. 1992. pap. 12.95 (*0-941500-10-1*) Sharing Co.

— Involving the People in Dancing Worship: Historic & Contemporary Patterns. 1975. pap. 3.00 (*0-941500-11-X*) Sharing Co.

— Meeting House to Camp Meeting: Toward a History of American Free Church Worship from 1620-1835. 160p. (Orig.). 1981. pap. text 6.95 (*0-941500-26-8*) Sharing Co.

— Sacred Dance with Senior Citizens in Churches, Convalescent Homes, & Retirement Homes. 1982. pap. 3.00 (*0-941500-27-6*) Sharing Co.

— Transcendence with the Human Body in Art: George Segal, Stephen De Staebler, Jasper Johns, & Christo. (Illus.). 159p. 1995. reprint ed. 18.95 (*0-8245-1104-2*) Sharing Co.

Adams, Doug, ed. Dancing Christmas Carols. LC 78-63292. 136p. 1978. pap. 9.95 (*0-89390-006-0*) Resource Pubns.

Adams, Doug & Rock, Judith. Biblical Criteria in Modern Dance: Modern Dance As a Prophetic Form. 1979. pap. 3.00 (*0-941500-01-2*) Sharing Co.

Adams, Doug, jt. auth. see Fisher, Constance L.

Adams, Doug, jt. auth. see Taylor, Margaret F.

Adams, Doug, ed. see Blessin, Ann M.

Adams, Doug, ed. see Fisher, Constance L.

Adams, Doug, ed. see Hoeckmann, Olaf.

Adams, Doug, ed. see Huff, Joan.

Adams, Doug, ed. see Kirk, Martha A.

Adams, Doug, ed. see MacLeod, Marian B.

Adams, Doug, ed. see Packard, Dane.

Adams, Doug, ed. see Reed, Carlynn.

Adams, Doug, ed. see Sautter, Cynthia D.

Adams, Doug, ed. see Skidmore, Janet.

Adams, Doug, ed. see Smagatz-Rawlinson, Diane.

Adams, Doug, ed. see Taylor, Margaret F.

Adams, Doug, ed. see Winton-Henry, Cynthia.

Adams, Doug, ed. & intro. see De Sola, Carla.

Adams, Doug, ed. & intro. see Neilan, Ruth E.

Adams, Doug, ed. & intro. see Winton-Henry, Cynthia.

Adams, Douglas. Dirk Gently's Holistic Detective Agency. 1991. per. 6.99 (*0-671-74672-3*) PB.

— Dirk Gently's Holistic Detective Agency. 1987. 12.09 (*0-606-03771-3*, Pub. by Turtleback) Demco.

— Douglas Adams. 1986. pap. 15.80 (*0-671-91255-0*) PB.

— Douglas Adams, 4 vols. 1989. boxed set 18.00 (*0-671-92231-9*) PB.

— The Hitchhiker's Guide to the Galaxy. 216p. 1995. mass mkt. 6.99 (*0-345-39180-2*) Ballantine Pub Grp.

— The Hitchhiker's Guide to the Galaxy. LC 97-93348. 1997. pap. 11.00 (*0-345-41891-3*) Ballantine Pub Grp.

— The Hitchhiker's Guide to the Galaxy. 1991. mass mkt. 5.99 (*0-671-74606-5*) PB.

— The Hitchhiker's Guide to the Galaxy. 1997. 16.10 (*0-606-12336-9*, Pub. by Turtleback) Demco.

— The Hitchhiker's Guide to the Galaxy. 10th anniversary ed. 224p. 1989. reprint ed. 15.00 (*0-517-54209-9*) Crown Pub Group.

— Life, the Universe & Everything. Vol. 3. 232p. 1995. mass mkt. 6.99 (*0-345-39182-9*) Ballantine Pub Grp.

— Life, the Universe & Everything. 240p. 1991. per. 5.99 (*0-671-73967-0*) PB.

Adams, Douglas. Life, the Universe & Everything. (Hitchhiker's Trilogy Ser.). (J). 1982. 11.09 (*0-606-03137-5*, Pub. by Turtleback) Demco.

Adams, Douglas. The Long Dark Tea-Time of the Soul. 320p. 1991. per. 6.99 (*0-671-74251-5*) PB.

— The Long Dark Tea-Time of the Soul. 1988. 12.09 (*0-606-01764-X*, Pub. by Turtleback) Demco.

— Mostly Harmless. 288p. 1993. pap. 12.00 (*0-345-37933-0*) Ballantine Pub Grp.

— Mostly Harmless. 2000. mass mkt. 6.99 (*0-345-41877-8*) Ballantine Pub Grp.

— Mostly Harmless. large type ed. 272p. 1996. 24.95 (*1-85695-333-5*, Pub. by ISIS Lrg Prnt) Transaction Pubs.

— The Prostitute in the Family Tree: Discovering Humor & Irony in the Bible. LC 97-16943. 136p. 1997. pap. 12.00 (*0-664-25693-7*) Westminster John Knox.

— The Restaurant at the End of the Universe. Vol. 2. 245p. 1995. mass mkt. 6.99 (*0-345-39181-0*) Ballantine Pub Grp.

— The Restaurant at the End of the Universe. 1997. pap. 11.00 (*0-345-41892-1*) Ballantine Pub Grp.

— So Long & Thanks for All the Fish. 1999. mass mkt. 6.99 (*0-345-39183-7*) Ballantine Pub Grp.

— So Long & Thanks for All the Fish. 1985. 12.09 (*0-606-00985-X*, Pub. by Turtleback) Demco.

— The Ultimate Hitchhiker's Guide. LC 95-37384. (Illus.). 815p. 1996. 14.99 (*0-517-14925-7*) Random.

— The Ultimate Hitchhikers Guide. unabridged ed. 1999. 6.75 (*0-517-12485-8*) Random Hse Value.

Adams, Douglas & Carwardine, Mark. Last Chance to See. (Illus.). 240p. 1992. pap. 10.00 (*0-345-37198-4*) Ballantine Pub Grp.

Adams, Douglas, et al. The Hitchhiker's Guide to the Galaxy: The Authorized Collection. Kahan, Bob, ed. LC 98-156914. (Illus.). 144p. 1997. pap. 14.95 (*1-56389-271-5*, Pub. by DC Comics) Time Warner.

Adams, Douglas, jt. auth. see Jones, Terry.

Adams, Douglas Q. Essential Modern Greek Grammar. (Essential Grammar Ser.). 128p. (Orig.). 1987. pap. text 5.95 (*0-486-25133-0*) Dover.

— Tocharian Historical Phonology & Morphology. (Amer. Oriental Ser.: Vol. 71). xii, 199p. 1988. 35.00 (*0-940490-71-4*) Am Orient Soc.

Adams, Douglas Q., ed. Festschrift for Eric P. Hamp, Vol. 1, Pt. 1. LC 97-206511. (Journal of Indo-European Studies Monograph Ser.: No. 23). 184p. (C). 1997. pap. text 48.00 (*0-941694-57-7*) Inst Study Man.

Adams, Dunstan. What is Prayer? 9.95 (*0-85244-502-4*, 6213, Pub. by Gra1cewing) Morehouse Pub.

Adams, E. The Logic of Conditionals: An Application of Probability to Deductive Logic. LC 75-20306. (Synthese Library: No. 86). 169p. 1975. text 132.00 (*90-277-0631-X*, D Reidel) Kluwer Academic.

Adams, E., tr. see Sommer, Piotr.

Adams, E. Bryding. The Dwight & Lucille Beeson Wedgwood Collection. (Illus.). 401p. 1992. 70.00 (*0-931394-33-3*); pap. 45.00 (*0-931394-32-5*) Birmingham Mus.

Adams, E. Bryding, ed. Made in Alabama: A State Legacy. LC 95-37694. (Illus.). 232p. 1990. pap. 40.00 (*0-931394-40-6*) U of Ala Pr.

Adams, E. Charles. The Origin & Development of the Pueblo Katsina Cult. LC 90-48047. 235p. 1993. reprint ed. pap. 17.95 (*0-8165-1358-9*) U of Ariz Pr.

Adams, E. Charles, ed. River of Change: Prehistory of the Middle Little Colorado River Valley. (Archaeological Ser.: Vol. 185). (Illus.). 342p. 1996. pap. 24.95 (*1-889747-50-5*) Ariz St Mus.

Adams, E. Charles, jt. auth. see Spielmann, Katherine A.

Adams, E. D. & Ihas, Gary G., eds. Quantum Fluids & Solids, 1983: AIP Conference Proceedings No. 103, Sanibel Island, Florida. LC 83-72240. 512p. 1983. lib. bdg. 39.75 (*0-88318-202-5*) Am Inst Physics.

Adams, E. M. The Metaphysics of Self & World. 250p. 1991. 59.95 (*0-87722-784-5*) Temple U Pr.

— Religion & Cultural Freedom. LC 92-32677. (C). 1993. 59.95 (*1-56639-051-6*) Temple U Pr.

— A Society Fit for Human Beings. LC 96-52316. (SUNY Series in Constructive Postmodern Thought). 269p. (C). 1997. text 56.50 (*0-7914-3523-7*); pap. text 18.95 (*0-7914-3524-5*) State U NY Pr.

Adams, Earl. The Greyhound Handicapper. 70p. (Orig.). 1985. pap. 8.50 (*0-9612748-2-4*) E Adams.

— Handbook for Gamblers. 105p. 1983. pap. 9.50 (*0-9612748-1-6*) E Adams.

***Adams, Earl.** Splinters in My Mind. 55p. 1999. pap. 9.95 (*0-7414-0326-9*) Buy Books.

Adams, Eddie, jt. auth. see Cuomo, Kerry Kennedy.

Adams, Edgar. United States Store Cards. LC 80-70824. 1981. reprint ed. pap. 12.00 (*0-915262-60-6*) S J Durst.

Adams, Edgar H. Edgar H. Adams' Plates of Lyman H. Low's Hard Times Tokens. (Illus.). 38p. 1981. 35.00 (*0-88000-120-8*) Quarterman.

Adams, Edgar H., jt. ed. see Kozel, Nicholas J.

Adams Editors Staff, ed. Adams Resume Almanac. LC 94-8685. 1994. pap. 12.95 (*1-55850-358-7*) Adams Media.

***Adams, Edward.** Constructing The World: A Study in Paul's Cosmological Language. 320p. 2000. 49.95 (*0-567-08689-5*) T&T Clark Pubs.

Adams, Edward B. Art Treasures of Seoul: With Walking Tours. (Illus.). 272p. 1980. 25.00 (*0-89860-018-9*) Eastview.

— Herdboy & Weaver. (Korean Folk Story for Children Ser.). (Illus.). 32p. (J). (gr. 3). 1981. 10.95 (*0-8048-1470-8*, Pub. by Seoul Intl Tourist) Tuttle Pubng.

— Korea Guide. (Illus.). 1979. pap. 12.00 (*0-89860-026-X*) Eastview.

— Korea's Pottery Heritage, Vol. 1. (Illus.). 120p. 1986. 23.95 (*0-8048-1431-7*, Pub. by Seoul Intl Tourist) Tuttle Pubng.

— Palaces of Seoul. 1979. pap. 4.50 (*0-89860-027-8*) Eastview.

— Woodcutter & Nymph. (Korean Folk Story for Children Ser.). (Illus.). 32p. (J). (gr. 3). 1982. 10.95 (*0-8048-1471-6*, Pub. by Seoul Intl Tourist) Tuttle Pubng.

Adams, Edward B., ed. Blindman's Daughter. (Korean Folk Story for Children Ser.: Bk. 1). (Illus.). 32p. (J). (gr. 3). 1981. 10.95 (*0-8048-1472-4*, Pub. by Seoul Intl Tourist) Tuttle Pubng.

— Korean Cinderella. (Korean Folk Story for Children Ser.: Bk. 4). (Illus.). 32p. (J). (gr. 3). 1982. 10.95 (*0-8048-1473-2*, Pub. by Seoul Intl Tourist) Tuttle Pubng.

— Two Brothers & Their Magic Gourds. (Korean Folk Story for Children Ser.). (Illus.). 32p. (J). (gr. 3). 1981. 10.95 (*0-8048-1474-0*, Pub. by Seoul Intl Tourist) Tuttle Pubng.

Adams, Edward C. Tales of the Congaree. LC 86-30912. xx, 367p. (C). 1987. pap. 19.95 (*0-8078-4188-9*) U of NC Pr.

— Tales of the Congaree. O'Meally, Robert G., ed. LC 86-30912. (Illus.). 437p. reprint ed. pap. 135.50 (*0-608-06009-7*, 206633700008) Bks Demand.

Adams, Edward E. Total Quality Safety Management: An Introduction. LC 95-13971. (Illus.). 203p. (Orig.). 1995. pap. text 19.95 (*1-885581-03-3*, 4553) ASSE.

Adams, Edward S. Corporations & Other Business Associations, Statutes, Rules & Forms: 1997 Edition. annuals (Miscellaneous Ser.). 1146p. 1997. pap. text, suppl. ed. write for info. (*0-314-22738-5*) West Pub.

— MBA Concepts for Lawyers. 202p. 1997. pap. 35.00 (*0-943380-53-7*) PEG MN.

Adams, Edward S. & Matheson, John H. Corporations & Other Business Associations, Statutes, Rules & Forms, 1996 Edition. 1150p. (C). 1996. pap. text. write for info. (*0-314-20201-3*) West Pub.

Adams, Eileen. Making the Playground. 56p. 1993. pap. 10.00 (*0-948080-92-2*, Trentham Bks) Stylus Pub VA.

Adams, Elbridge. Joseph Conrad: The Man. LC 72-2130. (Studies in Conrad: No. 8). 1972. reprint ed. lib. bdg. 75.00 (*0-8383-1487-2*) M S G Haskell Hse.

Adams, Eleanor B. Bio-Bibliography of Franciscan Authors in Colonial Central America. (Bibliographical Ser.). 1953. 15.00 (*0-88382-101-X*) AAFH.

Adams, Elie M. Ethical Naturalism & the Modern World-View. LC 73-3019. 229p. 1973. reprint ed. lib. bdg. 69.50 (*0-8371-6820-1*, ADEN, Greenwood Pr) Greenwood.

***Adams, Elizabeth.** Color & Learn Medieval Times. Rogers, Kathy, ed. (Illus.). 32p. 1999. wbk. ed. write for info. (*1-56472-201-5*) Edupress Inc.

Adams, Elizabeth K. & Willetts, Keith J. The Lean Communications Provider: Managing Profitability in the Global Communications Market. (Illus.). 252p. 1996. 29.95 (*0-07-070306-X*) McGraw.

Adams, Ellen E. Tales of Early Fredonia. (Illus.). 155p. 1997. reprint ed. lib. bdg. 24.00 (*0-8328-6144-8*) Higginson Bk Co.

Adams, Eloi A. Madbury, Its People & Places. (Illus.). 152p. 1998. reprint ed. pap. 22.50 (*0-8328-9723-X*); reprint ed. lib. bdg. 29.50 (*0-8328-9722-1*) Higginson Bk Co.

Adams, Elsie B. Critical Essay on George Bernard Shaw. (Critical Essays on British Literature Ser.). 200p. (C). 1991. 49.00 (*0-8161-8858-0*, Hall Reference) Macmillan.

Adams, Elsie B., ed. G. B. Shaw: An Annotated Bibliography of Writings about Him, Volume II. (Annotated Secondary Bibliography Series on English Literature in Transition, 1880-1920). 1987. text 55.00 (*0-87580-121-8*) N Ill U Pr.

Adams, Emma H. To & Fro in Southern California: With Sketches in Arizona & New Mexico. Cortes, Carlos E., ed. LC 76-1220. (Chicano Heritage Ser.). 1977. reprint ed. 24.95 (*0-405-09481-7*) Ayer.

Adams, Ephraim D. British Interests & Activities in Texas, 1838-1846. 1963. 16.50 (*0-8446-1004-6*) Peter Smith.

— British Interests & Activities in Texas, 1838-1846. (BCL1 - United States Local History Ser.). 267p. 1991. reprint ed. lib. bdg. 79.00 (*0-7812-6306-9*) Rprt Serv.

— The Power of Ideals in American History. LC 75-98025. (BCL Ser.: No. II). reprint ed. 32.50 (*0-404-00285-4*) AMS Pr.

— The Power of Ideals in American History. (BCL1 - U. S. History Ser.). 159p. 1991. reprint ed. lib. bdg. 69.00 (*0-7812-6027-2*) Rprt Serv.

Adams, Eric. Francis Danby: Varieties of Poetic Landscape. LC 72-75185. (Illus.). 320p. reprint ed. pap. 99.20 (*0-608-11283-6*, 202197300024) Bks Demand.

Adams, Eric J. California Traveler: California Grassroots Tours - Selected Short Outings. (American Traveler Ser.: Vol. 27). 1993. pap. 4.95 (*1-55838-135-X*) R H Pub.

— California Traveler: Overnight in San Francisco - Enjoying a Short Visit. (American Traveler Ser.: Vol. 29). (Illus.). 48p. 1993. pap. 4.95 (*1-55838-147-3*) R H Pub.

— Loss of Innocence: A True Story of Juvenile Murder. 288p. (Orig.). 1991. mass mkt. 4.95 (*0-380-75987-X*, Avon Bks) Morrow Avon.

***Adams, Eric J. & Adams, Kathleen.** On the Day His Daddy Left. LC 00-8290. (Illus.). 24p. (J). (gr. k-4). 2000. lib. bdg. 14.95 (*0-8075-6072-3*) A Whitman.

Adams, Ernest C. & Hinde, G. W. Studies in the Law of Landlord & Tenant: The Adams Memorial Essays. 473p. 1976. boxed set 55.00 (*0-409-60640-5*, NZ, MICHIE) LEXIS Pub.

Adams, Eryn, pseud. King of the Shore. LC 93-78848. 300p. 1993. 16.99 (*0-9636634-0-2*) Hartway-Miller.

Adams, Eugene T., et al. American Idea. LC 73-117747. (Essay Index Reprint Ser.). 1977. 21.95 (*0-8369-1820-7*) Ayer.

Adams, Eugene W. The Legacy: A History of the Tuskegee University School of Veterinary Medicine. LC 94-74577. (Illus.). 312p. 1995. 32.50 (*0-9645067-1-8*) Media Ctr.

Adams, Evangeline. The Bowl of Heaven. 275p. 1995. pap. 22.00 (*0-89540-196-7*, SB-196, Sun Bks) Sun Pub.

Adams, Evangeline, jt. auth. see Crowley, Aleister.

Adams, Evangeline Smith, jt. auth. see Crowley, Aleister.

***Adams, Eve.** Christmas Eve. (Illus.). 10p. 2000. write for info. (*0-9538369-0-8*) E V Bks.

Adams, Evelyn. San Juan Islands Wildlife: A Handbook for Exploring Nature Year Around. (Illus.). 256p. 1995. pap. 14.95 (*0-89886-420-8*) Mountaineers.

Adams, Evelyn C. American Indian Education: Government Schools & Economic Progress. LC 70-165701. (American Education Ser, No. 2). 1979. reprint ed. 18.95 (*0-405-03690-6*) Ayer.

Adams, F., et al, eds. Inorganic Mass Spectrometry. LC 87-21561. (Series of Monographs on Analytical Chemistry & Its Applications). 404p. 1988. 195.00 (*0-471-82364-3*) Wiley.

Adams, F. & Dams, R. Applied Gamma-Ray Spectrometry. 2nd rev. ed. LC 79-114847. 1970. 341.00 (*0-08-006888-X*, Pub. by Pergamon Repr) Franklin.

Adams, F. C. Uncle Tom at Home: A Review of the Reviewers & Repudiators of Uncle Tom's Cabin by Mrs. Stowe. LC 78-107789. (Select Bibliographies Reprint Ser.). 1977. 20.95 (*0-8369-5210-3*) Ayer.

Adams, F. Gerard. The Business Forecasting Revolution. (Wharton Executive Library). (Illus.). 256p. 1986. text 27.50 (*0-19-503700-6*) OUP.

Adams, F. Gerard & Hickman, Bert G., eds. Global Econometrics: Essays in Honor of Lawrence R. Klein. (Illus.). 448p. 1983. 52.50 (*0-262-01071-2*) MIT Pr.

Adams, F. Gerard & Ichimura, Shinichi, eds. East Asian Development: Will the East Asian Growth Miracle Survive? LC 98-24556. 224p. 1998. 59.95 (*0-275-96411-6*, Praeger Pubs) Greenwood.

Adams, F. Gerard & James, William E., eds. Public Policies in East Asian Development: Facing New Challenges. LC 98-56628. 272p. 1999. 65.00 (*0-275-96444-2*, Praeger Pubs) Greenwood.

Adams, F. Gerard, et al. Economic Activity, Trade, & Industry in the U. S. - Japan - World Economy: A Macro Model Study of Economic Interactions. LC 92-28476. 240p. 1993. 65.00 (*0-275-94488-3*, C4488, Praeger Pubs) Greenwood.

Adams, F. L., compiled by. Pioneer History of Ingham County, Vol. I. (Illus.). 856p. 1997. reprint ed. lib. bdg. 87.50 (*0-8328-6760-8*) Higginson Bk Co.

Adams, Faith. El Salvador: Beauty among the Ashes. LC 85-6945. (Discovering Our Heritage Ser.). (Illus.). 136p. (YA). (gr. 5 up). 1986. text 14.95 (*0-87518-309-3*, Dillon Silver Burdett) Silver Burdett Pr.

— Nicaragua: Struggling with Change. LC 86-11608. (Discovering Our Heritage Ser.). (Illus.). 152p. (YA). (gr. 5 up). 1987. lib. bdg. 14.95 (*0-87518-340-9*, Dillon Silver Burdett) Silver Burdett Pr.

Adams Family. Adams Family Correspondence, 4 vols. Incl. Vols. 3-4. Volume 3, Apr. 1778-Sep. 1780; Volume 4. Oct. 1780-Sept. 1782. LC 63-14964. 979p. 1973. 114.50 (*0-674-00405-1*); LC 63-14964. (Adams Papers: No. 2). (Illus.). write for info. (*0-318-52993-9*) HUP.

Adams, Fanny. The World's Best Men Jokes. 96p. 1998. pap. 6.95 (*0-00-638816-7*, Pub. by HarpC) Trafalgar.

Adams, Fay G. The Initiation of an Activity Program into a Public School. LC 77-176504. (Columbia University, Teachers College, Contributions to Education Ser.: No. 598). reprint ed. 37.50 (*0-404-55598-5*) AMS Pr.

Adams, Faye. The Goodnight Loving Trail. Morrow, Linda, ed. 320p. (Orig.). 1995. mass mkt. 5.50 (*0-671-88299-6*) PB.

— Lady of the Gun. 1996. mass mkt. 5.99 (*0-671-52723-1*, Pocket Books) PB.

— Rosebud. Marrow, Linda, ed. 320p. (Orig.). 1994. mass mkt. 5.50 (*0-671-88298-8*) PB.

— Under a Texas Moon. 1996. mass mkt. 5.99 (*0-671-52727-4*) PB.

Adams, Faye A. Events at Allemangel. (Illus.). 192p. (Orig.). 1995. pap. text 40.00 (*0-9650598-8-X*) F A Adams.

***Adams, Fiona.** Argentina. (Culture Shock! Ser.). 2000. pap. 12.95 (*1-55868-529-4*) Gr Arts Ctr Pub.

Adams, Flora B. A Penny on the Stair & Other Poems. LC 98-16332. 96p. (J). (gr. 6-8). 1998. pap. 10.95 (*1-883911-27-3*) Brandylane.

Adams, Florence. Catch a Sunbeam: A Book of Solar Study & Experiments. LC 78-52820. (Illus.). (J). (gr. 3-7). 1978. 10.95 (*0-15-215197-4*, Harcourt Child Bks) Harcourt.

— Local Representation: Changing Realities, Emerging Theories. 200p. 1999. 50.00 (*0-8153-3370-6*) Garland.

Adams, Forrest, ed. Moss' Heart Disease in Infants, Children & Adolescents, 2 vols., Set. 4th ed. 1085p. 1989. text 172.00 (*0-683-00052-7*) Lppncott W & W.

Adams, Francine. Eurythmy for the Elementary Grades. Mitchell, David, ed. & illus. by. 96p. 1998. pap. 8.00 (*1-888365-07-2*) Assn Waldorf Schls.

Adams, Francis. Free School System of the United States. LC 73-89144. (American Education: Its Men, Institutions, & Ideas. Series 1). 1970. reprint ed. 17.95 (*0-405-01380-9*) Ayer.

— The Genuine Works of Hippocrates. 384p. 1972. reprint ed. 42.50 (*0-88275-002-X*) Krieger.

***Adams, Francis.** Globalization & the Dilemmas of the State in the South. LC 98-53721. (International Political Economy Ser.). 1999. text 69.95 (*0-312-22263-7*) St Martin.

Adams, Francis V. The Asthma Sourcebook. 2nd rev. ed. LC 98-231451. (Illus.). 256p. 1998. pap. 17.00 (*0-7373-0016-7*, 00167W) NTC Contemp Pub Co.

— The Asthma Sourcebook: Everything You Need to Know. (Illus.). 224p. 1996. pap. 16.00 (*1-56565-471-4*) Lowell Hse.

— The Breathing Disorders Sourcebook. LC 98-27806. 256p. 1998. pap. 17.00 (*0-7373-0006-X*, 0006XW) NTC Contemp Pub Co.

Adams, Frank. Jukeboxes, 1889-1993: Obscure, Mysterious & Innovative American Jukeboxes, Vol. 1. (Illus.). 182p. 1992. 29.95 (*1-56642-000-8*, R-550) A M C Corp.

Adams, Frank, ed. Bally Electronic Pinball Games: Repair Procedures & Module & Component Replacement. rev. ed. (Illus.). 60p. 1991. reprint ed. spiral bd. 27.00 (*1-56642-168-3*, R-13) A M C Corp.

— Bally Machines General Pinball Service Instructions. rev. ed. (Illus.). 58p. 1993. reprint ed. spiral bd. 27.00 (*1-56642-169-1*, R-112) A M C Corp.

— Bally Variety Bingo Type Pinball, 1954: Operating Instructions & Parts Catalog. rev. ed. (Illus.). 52p. 1993. reprint ed. spiral bd. 35.00 (*1-56642-159-4*, R-59) A M C Corp.

— Duo-Art Technical Manual: A Compilation of Service Manuals, Technical Charts, Photos. (Illus.). 72p. 1984. reprint ed. spiral bd. 27.00 (*0-913599-45-X*, R-36B) A M C Corp.

— Gottlieb & Co. Solid State Pinball Games, 1978: Service Manual. 2nd rev. ed. (Illus.). 94p. 1993. reprint ed. spiral bd. 35.00 (*1-56642-158-6*, R-34) A M C Corp.

— Jennings Chief-Type Slot Machines: Service & Parts Manual. rev. ed. (Illus.). 35p. 1993. reprint ed. spiral bd. 21.00 (*1-56642-157-8*, R-58) A M C Corp.

— RCA Victor Model CE-29, 1932: Service Notes & Schematic Jukebox. rev. ed. (Illus.). 8p. reprint ed. spiral bd. 12.50 (*1-56642-004-0*, R-5) A M C Corp.

— Seeburg Coon Hunt Ray-O-Lite Rifle Range Model G-5 & Coon Whiner Kit Type CWA-1: Installation & Operation Manual, Parts List & Schematics. rev. ed. (Illus.). 26p. 1992. reprint ed. spiral bd. 17.50 (*1-56642-003-2*, R-4) A M C Corp.

— Seeburg Multi Rayolite Rifle Range Model G-1 of 1939 Service Manual & Parts List. rev. ed. (Illus.). 64p. 1991. reprint ed. 29.50 (*0-939971-51-8*, R-527) A M C Corp.

— Seeburg Shoot the Bear, Ray-O-Lite Rifle Range Model G-4: Installation & Operation, Parts List & Schematic. rev. ed. (Illus.). 10p. 1992. reprint ed. spiral bd. 18.00 (*1-56642-010-5*, R-30) A M C Corp.

— Seeburg "1000" Series Background Music Systems &

Accessory Equipment for Models BSM2, BMCA1, BMC1, & BMU10: Service & Parts Manual. rev. ed. (Illus.). 142p. 1990. reprint ed. 35.00 (*1-56642-063-6*, R-390) A M C Corp.

Adams, Frank & Horton, Myles. Unearthing Seeds of Fire: The Idea of Highlander. LC 74-16653. 225p. 1975. pap. 9.95 (*0-89587-019-3*) Blair.

Adams, Frank, ed. see Seeburg Company Staff.

Adams, Frank D. Birth & Development of the Geological Sciences. 510p. 1990. pap. 10.95 (*0-486-26372-X*) Dover.

Adams, Frank J. Lectures on Lie Groups. LC 82-51014. (Midway Reprint Ser.). 192p. (C). 1983. pap. text 25.00 (*0-226-00530-5*) U Ch Pr.

Adams, Frank O. Sindon: A Layman's Guide to the Shroud of Turin. DeSalvo, John A., ed. LC 82-90138. (Illus.). 1982. 12.50 (*0-86700-008-2*, Synergy Bks) P Walsh Pr.

Adams, Frank T. James A. Dombrowski: An American Heretic, 1897-1983. LC 91-30565. (Illus.). 392p. (C). 1992. 49.50 (*0-87049-741-3*); pap. 22.50 (*0-87049-742-1*) U of Tenn Pr.

Adams, Frank T. & Hansen, Gary B. Putting Democracy to Work: A Practical Guide for Starting & Managing Worker-Owned Businesses. LC 92-28434. (Illus.). 352p. (Orig.). 1993. pap. 19.95 (*1-881052-09-5*) Berrett-Koehler.

— Putting Democracy to Work: A Practical Guide to Starting & Managing Worker-Owned Businesses. 2nd rev. ed. 324p. 1992. pap. 19.95 (*0-938493-19-1*) Hulogosi Inc.

Adams, Fred. Biology Laboratory Manual. 176p. (C). 1994. pap. text, spiral bd. 19.95 (*0-8403-9630-9*) Kendall-Hunt.

— Fred Adams' St. John's. (Illus.). 141p. 1994. reprint ed. pap. 9.55 (*0-920021-37-9*) Creative Bk Pub.

— The Great Fire of 1892. 80p. 1992. pap. 7.95 (*1-895387-16-7*) Creative Bk Pub.

— Potpourri of Old St. John's. (Illus.). 100p. 1991. pap. 9.55 (*0-920021-99-9*) Creative Bk Pub.

Adams, Fred, ed. Soil Acidity & Liming. 2nd ed. 380p. 1984. 25.00 (*0-89118-080-X*) Am Soc Agron.

***Adams, Fred & Laughlin, Greg.** Five Ages of the Universe: Inside the Physics of Eternity. LC 99-18139. (Illus.). 320p. 1999. 24.50 (*0-684-85422-8*) Free Pr.

— Five Ages of the Universe: Inside the Physics of Eternity. (Illus.). 288p. 2000. per. 14.00 (*0-684-86576-9*) S&S Trade.

Adams, Fred T. The Way to Modern Man: An Introduction to Human Evolution. LC 68-28011. (Anthropology & Education Ser.). 296p. reprint ed. pap. 91.80 (*0-608-14903-9*, 202598600048) Bks Demand.

Adams, Frederick U. Conquest of the Tropics: The Story of the Creative Enterprises Conducted by the United Fruit Company. Bruchey, Stuart & Bruchey, Eleanor, eds. LC 76-4766. (American Business Abroad Ser.). (Illus.). 1976. reprint ed. 40.95 (*0-405-09263-6*) Ayer.

— President John Smith: The Story of a Peaceful Revolution. LC 72-154428. (Utopian Literature Ser.). (Illus.). 1976. reprint ed. 25.95 (*0-405-03511-X*) Ayer.

Adams, Frida C., et al. Caring for Your Elderly at Home: How to Give Good Health Care. LC 89-51145. (Illus.). xxx, 179p. (Orig.). 1990. 21.95 (*0-685-27236-2*); pap. 14.95 (*0-685-27237-0*) Wasa-Trends Pub.

Adams, G. The Bilateral Bergman Shift. LC 86-17404. (Memoirs of the American Mathematical Society Ser.: Vol. 63/355). 75p. 1986. pap. 17.00 (*0-8218-2417-1*, MEMO 63/355) Am Math.

Adams, G. B. Civilization During the Middle Ages. 1972. 250.00 (*0-87968-873-4*) Gordon Pr.

Adams, G. Donald. Collecting & Restoring Antique Bicycles. 2nd ed. (Illus.). 370p. 1996. 32.50 (*0-9649537-0-6*); pap. 22.50 (*0-9649537-1-4*) Pedaling Hist.

— Museum Public Relations. LC 83-3708. (American Association for State & Local History Book Ser.). (Illus.). 248p. 1983. reprint ed. 34.95 (*0-910050-65-1*) AltaMira Pr.

Adams, G. E., et al, eds. Selective Activation of Drugs by Redox Processes. LC 90-14335. (NATO ASI Ser.: Vol. 198). (Illus.). 370p. (C). 1990. text 138.00 (*0-306-43735-X*, Kluwer Plenum) Kluwer Academic.

Adams, G. E., ed. see Gray, L. H., Conference Staff.

Adams, G. G., et al, eds. Advances in Information Storage & Processing Systems, 1995. (1995 International Mechanical Engineering Congress & Exposition Ser.: ISPS-Vol. 1). 168p. 1995. 72.00 (*0-7918-1734-2*, H01016) ASME.

Adams, G. G. W., et al. Kenerley Bankes's Clinical Ophthalmology: A Text & Colour Atlas. 4th ed. LC 99-12781. 188p. 1999. pap. text 45.00 (*0-7506-3908-3*) Buttrwrth-Heinemann.

Adams, Gail G. The Purchase of Order. LC 88-4724. (Flannery O'Connor Award for Short Fiction Ser.). 160p. 1995. pap. 12.95 (*0-8203-1734-9*) U of Ga Pr.

Adams, Gardner. Adams. John Adams & His Descendants, with Notes & Incidents. 139p. 1997. reprint ed. pap. 22.00 (*0-8328-7211-3*); reprint ed. lib. bdg. 32.00 (*0-8328-7210-5*) Higginson Bk Co.

***Adams, Garrett.** Advertising Your Business Made E-Z. 232p. 2000. pap. 17.95 (*1-56382-446-9*) E-Z Legal.

Adams, Gene M. Exercise Physiology. 2nd ed. 304p. (C). 1993. spiral bd., lab manual ed. write for info. (*0-697-12596-3*) Brown & Benchmark.

Adams, Geoffrey. The Call of Conscience: French Protestant Responses to the Algerian War, 1954-1962. LC 98-178116. (Editions SR Ser.: Vol. 21). (Illus.). 292p. 1998. pap. 29.95 (*0-88920-299-0*) W Laurier U Pr.

— The Huguenots & French Opinion, 1685-1787: The Enlightenment Debate on Toleration. 376p. (C). 1991. pap. 24.95 (*0-88920-209-5*); text 45.00 (*0-88920-217-6*) W Laurier U Pr.

Adams, George. Birdscaping Your Garden: A Practical Guide to Backyard Birds & the Plants That Attract Them. LC 93-43391. 1994. 29.95 (*0-87596-635-7*) Rodale Pr Inc.

— Birdscaping Your Garden: A Practical Guide to Backyard Birds & the Plants That Attract Them. 208p. 1998. pap. 18.95 (*0-87596-956-9*) Rodale Pr Inc.

— Insider's Price. Chelius, Jane, ed. 384p. (Orig.). 1993. mass mkt. 4.99 (*0-671-70171-1*) PB.

— Nature Ever New: Essays on the Renewal of Agriculture. 1979. pap. 7.50 (*0-916786-40-4*, Saint George Pubns) R Steiner Col.

Adams, George, tr. see Steiner, Rudolf.

Adams, George B. Constitutional History of England. 518p. 1997. reprint ed. 160.00 (*1-56169-256-5*) Gaunt.

— History of England from the Norman Conquest to the Death of John. LC 77-5634. (Political History of England Ser.: No. 2). reprint ed. 45.00 (*0-404-50772-7*) AMS Pr.

— Origin of the English Constitution. xii, 378p. 1986. reprint ed. 42.50 (*0-8377-1901-1*, Rothman) W S Hein.

Adams, George C., Jr. Structure & Meaning of Badarayana's Brahma Sutras: A Translation & Analysis of Adhyaya 1. (C). 1993. text 14.00 (*81-208-0931-9*, Pub. by Motilal Bnarsidass) S Asia.

Adams, George G., et al, eds. Information Storage & Processing Systems: Proceedings ASME International Symposium on Information Storage & Processing Systems, Anaheim, CA, 1998. LC 99-182518. (ISPS Ser.: Vol. 4). 107p. 1998. 90.00 (*0-7918-1583-8*) ASME.

— Information Storage & Processing Systems: Proceedings, 7th International Mechanical Engineering Congress & Exposition, Atlanta, GA, 1996. LC 96-78694. (ISPS Ser.: Vol. 2). 213p. 1996. pap. 84.00 (*0-7918-1529-3*, QA76) ASME.

— Information Storage & Processing Systems, 1997: Proceedings, ASME International Symposium on Information Storage & Processing Systems, Dallas, TX, 1997. LC 98-191007. (ISPS Ser.: Vol. 3). 91p. 1997. pap. 72.00 (*0-7918-1830-6*, QA76) ASME Pr.

Adams, George M. Better Than Gold. LC 79-167301. (Essay Index Reprint Ser.). 1977. reprint ed. 20.95 (*0-8369-2632-3*) Ayer.

Adams, George P. Idealism & the Modern Age. LC 75-3015. (Philosophy in America Ser.). reprint ed. 39.50 (*0-404-59009-8*) AMS Pr.

Adams, George R. Life on the Yukon, 1865-1867. Pierce, Richard A., ed. (Alaska History Ser.: No. 22). (Illus.). 219p. 1982. 24.00 (*0-919642-87-X*) Limestone Pr.

***Adams, George Rollie.** General William S. Harney: Prince of Dragoons. (Illus.). 352p. 2001. text 45.00 (*0-8032-1058-2*) U of Nebr Pr.

Adams, George W. Doctors in Blue: The Medical History of the Union Army in the Civil War. LC 96-22219. (Illus.). 253p. 1996. pap. 14.95 (*0-8071-2105-3*) La State U Pr.

Adams, George W. Educational Crossword Puzzles in History. (Illus.). 70p. (YA). (gr. 9-12). 1988. pap. text 4.90 (*0-921369-04-2*) J C George Ent.

Adams, Georgia. Moments with the Master. 156p. 1998. pap. 10.00 (*1-56469-042-3*) Harmony Hse Pub.

Adams, Georgie. The First Christmas. (Illus.). 19p. (J). (ps-3). 1997. bds. 12.99 (*0-8054-0175-X*) Broadman.

***Adams, Georgie.** The Good Shepherd Storybook. LC 98-50152. (Illus.). 96p. (J). (gr. k-5). 1999. 19.99 (*0-8054-1960-8*) Broadman.

Adams, Georgie. Highway Builders. (Illus.). 32p. (J). (ps-2). 1996. 14.95 (*1-55037-467-2*, Pub. by Annick) Firefly Bks Ltd.

— Highway Builders. (Illus.). 32p. (J). (ps-2). 1996. pap. 5.95 (*1-55037-466-4*, Pub. by Annick Pr) Firefly Bks Ltd.

***Adams, Georgie.** Noah's Ark. LC 99-19530. (Illus.). 24p. (J). (ps-1). 1999. 12.99 (*0-8054-2037-1*) Broadman.

Adams, Georgie. A Year Full of Stories: 366 Days of Story & Rhyme. LC 97-1407. (Illus.). 264p. (J). (ps-1). 1997. 29.95 (*0-385-32527-4*, DD Bks Yng Read) BDD Bks Young Read.

Adams, Gerald, ed. Adolescent Development: The Essential Readings. (Essential Readings in Developmental Psychology Ser.). 256p. 1999. 59.95 (*0-631-21742-8*); pap. 24.95 (*0-631-21743-6*) Blackwell Pubs.

Adams, Gerald & Crossman, Sharyn. Physical Attractiveness. LC 78-56850. 1979. 7.95 (*0-87212-122-4*) Libra.

Adams, Gerald, et al. Adolescent Life Experiences. 3rd ed. 1994. mass mkt., teacher ed. write for info. (*0-534-16237-1*) Brooks-Cole.

Adams, Gerald M. The Bells of Balangiga. (Illus.). 87p. 1998. 19.95 (*1-878117-20-3*); pap. 9.95 (*1-878117-19-X*) Lagumo Corp.

Adams, Gerald R., et al, eds. Adolescent Identity Formation. LC 92-353317. (Advances in Adolescent Development Ser.). (Illus.). 250p. 1992. reprint ed. pap. 77.50 (*0-608-07673-2*, 206776300010) Bks Demand.

— The Biology of Adolescent Behavior & Development. (Advances in Adolescent Development Ser.: Vol. 1). 384p. (C). 1989. text 58.00 (*0-8039-3403-3*); pap. text 26.00 (*0-8039-3404-1*) Sage.

— Biology of Adolescent Behavior & Development. LC 89-6144. (Advances in Adolescent Development Ser.). (Illus.). 320p. 1989. pap. 99.20 (*0-608-05064-4*, 206561900005) Bks Demand.

— Family Violence: Prevention & Treatment. (Issues in Children's & Families' Lives Ser.: Vol. 1). (Illus.). 304p. (C). 1993. text 52.00 (*0-8039-5246-5*); pap. text 25.50 (*0-8039-5247-3*) Sage.

Adams, Gerald R. & Gullotta, Thomas P. Adolescent Life Experiences. LC 82-20748. (Psychology Ser.). 600p. (C). 1983. mass mkt. 32.25 (*0-534-01242-6*) Brooks-Cole.

— Adolescent Life Experiences. 2nd ed. LC 88-23586. 503p. (C). 1989. mass mkt. 44.00 (*0-534-09876-2*) Brooks-Cole.

Adams, Gerald R., et al. Adolescent Identity Formation. (Advances in Adolescent Development Ser.: Vol. 4). (Illus.). 320p. 1992. pap. 26.00 (*0-8039-4616-3*) Sage.

— The Family-School Connection Vol. 2: Theory, Research & Practice. LC 95-11383. (Issues in Children's & Families' Lives Ser.: Vol. 2). (Illus.). 371p. 1995. 52.00 (*0-8039-7306-3*) Sage.

— Psychosocial Development During Adolescence: Progress in Developmental Contextualism. (Advances in Adolescent Development Ser.: Vol. 8). 346p. 1996. 37.00 (*0-7619-0532-4*) Sage.

Adams, Gerald R., et al. Psychosocial Development During Adolescence: Progress in Developmental Contextualism. (Advances in Adolescent Development Ser.: Vol. 8). 346p. 1996. pap. 16.99 (*0-7619-0533-2*) Sage.

Adams, Gerry. Before the Dawn: An Autobiography. LC 96-21191. (Illus.). 356p. 1997. 25.00 (*0-688-14312-1*, Wm Morrow) Morrow Avon.

***Adams, Gerry.** Before the Dawn: An Autobiography. 352p. 1998. reprint ed. pap. 15.00 (*0-688-16101-4*, Quil) HarperTrade.

Adams, Gerry. Cage Eleven. LC 93-12851. (Orig.). 1993. 11.45 (*1-879823-04-7*); pap. 7.45 (*1-879823-05-5*) Sheridan Sq Pr.

— Cage Eleven: Writings from Prison. 2nd ed. 160p. (Orig.). 1997. pap. 12.95 (*1-57098-131-0*) Roberts Rinehart.

— Falls Memories: A Belfast Life. (Illus.). 154p. 1994. pap. 10.95 (*1-879373-96-3*) Roberts Rinehart.

— Free Ireland: Towards a Lasting Peace. 240p. 1994. pap. 11.95 (*1-879373-95-5*) Roberts Rinehart.

— Irish Voice: The Quest for Peace. 256p. 1997. pap. text 14.95 (*1-57098-156-6*) Roberts Rinehart.

— The Street & Other Stories. LC 93-12328. 1993. 11.95 (*1-879823-02-0*); pap. 7.95 (*1-879823-03-9*) Sheridan Sq Pr.

— The Street & Other Stories. 2nd ed. 160p. 1997. pap. 12.95 (*1-57098-132-9*) Roberts Rinehart.

Adams, Gladys S. Buckland: The North West Section of Manchester. (Illus.). 123p. 1995. pap. 17.50 (*0-8328-4986-3*); lib. bdg. 27.50 (*0-685-02571-3*) Higginson Bk Co.

Adams, Gladys S. & Hoppe, L. H. Woodworth, from the Old Colony of New Plymouth to Nebraska, 1620-1920: History & Genealogy of the Family of Mildred Woodworth. (Illus.). 123p. 1995. reprint ed. lib. bdg 27.50 (*0-8328-4985-5*) Higginson Bk Co.

Adams, Glen, ed. see Mullan, John.

***Adams, Glen C., ed.** The Coeur d'Alene Indian Reservation. 92p. 1999. reprint ed. pap. 9.95 (*0-87770-692-1*) Ye Galleon.

Adams, Glenda. Games of the Strong. LC 88-63899. 186p. (C). 1989. pap. 8.95 (*0-943433-02-9*) Cane Hill Pr.

— The Hottest Night of the Century. LC 88-63894. 120p. (C). 1989. pap. 8.95 (*0-943433-03-7*) Cane Hill Pr.

— Longleg. LC 92-52964. 339p. 1992. pap. 9.95 (*0-943433-09-6*) Cane Hill Pr.

Adams, Gordon. The Iron Triangle: The Politics of Defense Contracting. 465p. 1981. pap. 24.95 (*0-87871-012-4*) Transaction Pubs.

***Adams-Gordon, Beverly L.** Home School High School & Beyond: A Time Management, Career Exploration, Organization & Study Skills Course. 4th rev. ed. (Illus.). (YA). (gr. 9-12). 1999. pap. text 19.95 (*1-888827-22-X*) Castlemoyle Bks.

Adams-Gordon, Beverly L. Home School, High School, & Beyond: A Time Management, Career Exploration, Organizational & Study Skills Course. 3rd rev. ed. LC 96-85082. (Illus.). 160p. (Orig.). (YA). (gr. 9-12). 1996. pap. text 17.95 (*1-888827-15-7*) Castlemoyle Bks.

— Spelling Power. 3rd rev. ed. LC 96-85073. (Illus.). 368p. 1997. pap., teacher ed. 49.95 (*1-888827-19-X*) Castlemoyle Bks.

— Unit Study Planning Workbook, Vol. 1. 164p. 1996. wbk. ed. 17.95 (*1-888827-17-3*) Castlemoyle Bks.

***Adams, Grace.** Freedom: The Story Behind Quiet Strength, Rosa Parks vs. OutKast Rappers & the Entertainment Industry. (Illus.). 220p. 2000. pap. text 35.00 (*1-877807-70-2*) Grace Pub MI.

Adams, Grace. Megabucking: DBA in America. LC 89-84485. (Illus.). 189p. (Orig.). 1989. pap. 24.95 (*1-877807-03-6*) Grace Pub MI.

— Workers on Relief. LC 74-137154. (Poverty U. S. A. Historical Record Ser.). 1977. reprint ed. 25.95 (*0-405-03091-6*) Ayer.

Adams, Grace, ed. Black Authors & Published Writers Directory, 1996-97. (Illus.). 320p. (Orig.). 1996. pap. 49.95 (*1-877807-50-8*) Grace Pub MI.

— Black Authors Books in Print, 1997-98. (Illus.). (Orig.). 1997. pap. 24.95 (*1-877807-60-5*) Grace Pub MI.

— National & International Black Journalist Directory, 1997-98: Print & Broadcast. (Illus.). (Orig.). 1997. pap. 24.95 (*1-877807-75-3*) Grace Pub MI.

Adams, Graham C. The Ottoneum Theater: An English Survivor from Seventeenth-Century Germany. LC 91-57961. (Studies in the Renaissance: No. 32). 1992. 39.50 (*0-404-62332-8*) AMS Pr.

Adams, Greg, jt. auth. see De Vries, Andre.

Adams, Gregg A. On Call: Surgery. (C). 1998. text. write for info. (*0-8089-2136-3*, Grune & Strat) Harcrt Hlth Sci Grp.

Adams, Gregg A. & Bresnick, Stephen D. On Call: Surgery. Schmitt, William, ed. LC 96-29954. (Illus.). 320p. 1997. pap. text 21.95 (*0-7216-6432-6*, W B Saunders Co) Harcrt Hlth Sci Grp.

Adams, Gregg A., jt. auth. see Bresnick, Stephen D.

Adams, Guy B. A Bibliography on a Human Theory of Organization. No. 1293. 1977. 5.50 (*0-686-19694-5*, Sage Prdcls Pr) Sage.

Adams, Guy B. & Balfour, Danny L. Unmasking Administrative Evil. LC 98-8931. (Advances in Public Administration Ser.). 207p. 1998. 54.00 (*0-7619-0668-1*); pap. 24.95 (*0-7619-0669-X*) Sage.

Adams, Guy B., jt. auth. see Ingersoll, Virginia H.

Adams, Guy B., ed. see Vickers, Geoffrey.

Adams, Guy B., jt. ed. see White, Jay D.

Adams, H. E., jt. ed. see Sutker, P. B.

Adams, H. J. The Eye of the Day & Tooth of the Lion. LC 92-71355. 48p. 1992. lib. bdg. 12.95 (*0-923687-18-1*) Celo Valley Bks.

***Adams, H. J.** Of Dragons, Kings, Sages & Little Folk. LC 99-63165. 120p. 1999. 22.50 (*0-923687-52-1*) Celo Valley Bks.

Adams, H. J. Once in the Wind of Morning. LC 95-74948. (Illus.). 208p. 1996. lib. bdg. 15.95 (*0-923687-37-8*) Celo Valley Bks.

***Adams, H. J.** The Song of the Blackbirds in the Reeds: In Which Great-Grandpa Nicholas Winslow Applewood Entertains Young Folk with Stories & Fables & Has Some Remarkable Betimes. LC 98-73039. 168p. 1998. 20.00 (*0-923687-48-3*) Celo Valley Bks.

Adams, H. J. To Hear Such Tunes. LC 93-71551. 64p. 1993. lib. bdg. 14.50 (*0-923687-27-0*) Celo Valley Bks.

Adams, H. J. With Dandelions to Tell the Hours: Tales of Some Gentle Little People. LC 92-71977. (Illus.). 160p. 1992. pap. 12.95 (*0-923687-55-6*) Celo Valley Bks.

Adams, H. M. Catalogue of Books Printed on the Continent of Europe, 1501-1600 in Cambridge Libraries, 2 vols. 1562p. 1999. 295.00 (*1-57898-124-7*) Martino Pubng.

Adams, H. P., jt. ed. see Bogousslavsky, J.

***Adams, H. Richard, ed.** Veterinary Pharmacology & Therapeutics. 1192p. 2000. 139.95 (*0-8138-1743-9*) Iowa St U Pr.

Adams, H. Richard, ed. Veterinary Pharmacology & Therapeutics. 7th ed. LC 95-15276. (Illus.). 1056p. (C). 1995. text 139.95 (*0-8138-1741-2*) Iowa St U Pr.

Adams, H. W., et al. The Faith Builder. 5.99 (*0-88019-060-4*) Schmul Pub Co.

Adams, Hannah. A Dictionary of All Religions & Religious Denominations: Jewish, Heathen, Mahometan, Christian, Ancient, & Modern. LC 92-15133. (American Academy of Religion, Classics in Religious Studies). 396p. 1992. 39.95 (*1-55540-727-7*, 01 05 08); pap. 24.95 (*1-55540-728-5*, 01 05 08) OUP.

Adams, Harold. The Barbed Wire Noose. 192p. 1987. 15.45 (*0-89296-250-X*, Pub. by Mysterious Pr) Little.

Adams, Harold. The Ditched Blonde: A Carl Wilcox Mystery. LC 95-11743. 168p. 1995. 19.95 (*0-8027-3263-1*) Walker & Co.

— The Ditched Blonde: A Carl Wilcox Mystery. (Carl Wilcox Mystery Ser.). 1998. pap. 7.95 (*0-8027-7555-1*) Walker & Co.

Adams, Harold. The Fourth Widow. 208p. 1986. 15.45 (*0-89296-231-3*, Pub. by Mysterious Pr) Little.

Adams, Harold. Hatchet Job: A Carl Wilcox Mystery. LC 96-24627. (Carl Wilcox Mystery Ser.). 176p. 1996. 19.95 (*0-8027-3286-0*) Walker & Co.

— The Ice Pick Artist: A Carl Wilcox Mystery. LC 97-23563. (Carl Wilcox Mystery Ser.). 240p. 1997. 21.95 (*0-8027-3310-7*) Walker & Co.

— Lead, So I Can Follow. LC 99-55556. (Carl Wilcox Mystery Ser.). 240p. 1999. 22.95 (*0-8027-3336-0*) Walker & Co.

***Adams, Harold.** Lead, So I Can Follow. (Carl Wilcox Mystery Ser.). 2000. pap. 8.95 (*0-8027-7596-9*) Walker & Co.

Adams, Harold. The Man Who Met the Train. LC 87-73206. (Carl Wilcox Mystery Ser.: No. 7). 240p. 1988. 15.95 (*0-89296-251-8*) Mysterious Pr.

— The Man Who Missed the Party: A Carol Wilcox Mystery. 192p. 1989. 16.95 (*0-89296-252-6*, Pub. by Mysterious Pr) Little.

— The Man Who Was Taller Than God. (Carl Wilcox Mystery Ser.). 1998. pap. 7.95 (*0-8027-7554-3*) Walker & Co.

— The Man Who Was Taller Than God: A Carl Wilcox Mystery. LC 92-13260. 156p. 1992. 18.95 (*0-8027-1239-8*) Walker & Co.

— No Badge, No Gun. LC 98-26095. (Carl Wilcox Mystery Ser.). 208p. 1998. 22.95 (*0-8027-3321-2*) Walker & Co.

— No Badge, No Gun. (Carl Wilcox Mystery Ser.). 212p. 1999. pap. 7.95 (*0-8027-7575-6*) Walker & Co.

— A Perfectly Proper Murder: A Carl Wilcox Mystery. LC 93-14721. 1993. 18.95 (*0-8027-3237-2*) Walker & Co.

— A Way with Widows. LC 94-1245. 142p. 1994. 18.95 (*0-8027-3190-2*) Walker & Co.

***Adams, Harold.** A Way with Widows. (Carl Wilcox Mystery Ser.). 156p. 1999. pap. 7.95 (*0-8027-7574-8*) Walker & Co.

Adams, Harold. A Way with Widows. large type ed. LC 94-31222. (Nightingale Ser.). 219p. 1995. pap. 17.95 (*0-7838-1144-6*, G K Hall Lrg Type) Mac Lib Ref.

— When Rich Men Die. 256p. 1988. pap. 3.50 (*0-380-70539-7*, Avon Bks) Morrow Avon.

Adams, Harold P. Handbook of Cerebrovascular Diseases. (Neurological Disease & Therapy Ser.: Vol. 17). (Illus.). 728p. 1993. text 255.00 (*0-8247-8820-6*) Dekker.

Adams, Harold P., Jr., et al. Management of Stroke: A Practical Guide for the Prevention, Evaluation & Treatment of Acute Stroke. 224p. 1998. pap. text 19.95 (*1-884735-35-5*) Prof Comms.

Adams, Harold W. & Stringham, Ray. Lawyer's Management Principles: A Course for Assistants, Student Syllabus. 1975. pap. text 9.95 (*0-89420-079-8*, 101028) Natl Book.

— Lawyer's Management Principles: A Course for Assistants, Student Syllabus. (gr. 11-12). 1975. audio 86.90 (*0-89420-200-6*, 101000) Natl Book.

An Asterisk (*) at the beginning of an entry indicates that the title is appearing for the first time.

A

Adams, Harry B. Preaching the Burden & the Joy. LC 96-1791. 168p. (Orig.). 1996. pap. 16.99 (*0-8272-2951-8*) Chalice Pr.
Adams, Hazard. The Academic Tribes. 2nd ed. LC 87-19051. 200p. 1987. text 24.95 (*0-252-01441-3*) U of Ill Pr.
— The Academic Tribes. 2nd ed. LC 87-19051. 200p. 1988. pap. text 10.95 (*0-252-06000-8*) U of Ill Pr.
— Antithetical Essays in Literary Criticism & Liberal Education. 292p. 1989. pap. 24.95 (*0-8130-0966-9*); lib. bdg. 44.95 (*0-8130-0955-3*) U Press Fla.
— The Book of Yeat's Vision: Romantic Modernism & Antithetical Tradition. LC 95-40619. 200p. (C). 1996. text 44.50 (*0-472-10623-6*, 10623) U of Mich Pr.
— The Book of Yeats's Poems. 304p. 1989. 49.95 (*0-8130-0944-8*) U Press Fla.
Adams, Hazard. The Book of Yeats's Vision: Romantic Modernism & Antithetical Tradition. (Illus.). 200p. (C). pap. text. write for info. (*0-472-08462-3*) U of Mich Pr.
Adams, Hazard. CRITICAL THEORY SINCE PLATO 2E. 2nd ed. 1350p. (C). 1992. text 77.50 (*0-15-516143-1*) Harcourt Coll Pubs.
— Joyce Cary's Trilogies: Pursuit of the Particular Real. 280p. 1986. reprint ed. pap. 24.95 (*0-8130-0851-4*) U Press Fla.
— Lady Gregory. (Irish Writers Ser.). 106p. 1973. 8.50 (*0-8387-1085-9*); pap. 1.95 (*0-8387-1207-X*) Bucknell U Pr.
— Many Pretty Toys. LC 98-21577. (SUNY Series in Postmodern Culture). 256p. (C). 1999. text 31.50 (*0-7914-4085-0*) State U NY Pr.
— Many Pretty Toys. LC 98-21577. (SUNY Series in Postmodern Culture). (C). 2000. pap. text 19.95 (*0-7914-4086-9*) State U NY Pr.
— Philosophy of the Literary Symbolic. LC 82-24785. (Illus.). xiv, 466p. 1983. pap. 34.95 (*0-8130-0771-2*) U Press Fla.
Adams, Hazard & Searle, Leroy, eds. Critical Theory since 1965. LC 86-13216. 904p. (C). 1986. pap. 39.95 (*0-8130-0844-1*) U Press Fla.
Adams, Hebron E. The Burodyssey of H. O. M. E. R. LC 93-90932. (Illus.). 96p. (Orig.). 1994. pap. 9.95 (*0-9632919-1-2*) Foxon Pr.
— The Foxons of Leicestershire & Wisconsin. LC 95-49145. 40p. (Orig.). 1996. pap. 9.95 (*0-9632919-2-0*) Foxon Pr.
— Historic Reston: The First Three Hundred Fifty Years. LC 92-72043. 48p. 1992. pap. text 6.95 (*0-9632919-0-4*) Foxon Pr.
Adams, Helen, jt. auth. see Melbourne, David.
Adams, Helen J. Understanding Retrogrades. LC 80-51517. 80p. 1980. 12.00 (*0-86690-056-X*, A1006-014) Am Fed Astrologers.
***Adams, Henry.** The Education of Henry Adams: An Autobiography. (American Heritage Library). 528p. 2000. pap. 12.00 (*0-618-05666-1*) HM.
Adams, Henry (Brooks). America's Economic Supremacy. LC 77-152155. (Essay Index Reprint Ser.). 1977. reprint ed. 18.95 (*0-8369-2477-0*) Ayer.
— America's Economic Supremacy. (Principle Works of Brooks Adams). 1989. reprint ed. lib. bdg. 79.00 (*0-7812-2570-1*) Rprt Serv.
— Chapters of Erie & Other Essays. (Works of Henry Adams). 1989. reprint ed. lib. bdg. 79.00 (*0-7812-1435-1*) Rprt Serv.
— The Degradation of the Democratic Dogma. 1990. 16.50 (*0-8446-1007-0*) Peter Smith.
— The Degradation of the Democratic Dogma. (Works of Henry Adams). 1989. reprint ed. lib. bdg. 79.00 (*0-7812-1445-9*) Rprt Serv.
— Democracy. Katopes, Peter, ed. 1991. 12.95 (*0-8084-0430-X*) NCUP.
— Democracy. Date not set. reprint ed. lib. bdg. 19.95 (*0-89190-525-1*, Queens House) Amereon Ltd.
— Democracy: An American Novel. 1983. pap. 12.95 (*0-452-00942-1*, Plume) Dutton Plume.
— Democracy: An American Novel. 1988. reprint ed. lib. bdg. 59.00 (*0-7812-1437-8*) Rprt Serv.
— Democracy: An American Novel. 1976. reprint ed. 59.00 (*0-403-05724-8*, Regency) Scholarly.
— The Emancipation of Massachusetts. (Principle Works of Brooks Adams). 1989. reprint ed. lib. bdg. 79.00 (*0-7812-0296-5*) Rprt Serv.
— Esther. LC 96-40052. 310p. 1997. pap. 9.95 (*1-57392-132-7*) Prometheus Bks.
***Adams, Henry (Brooks).** Esther. MacFarlane, Lisa, ed. & intro. by. LC 99-30000. 256p. 1999. pap. 9.95 (*0-14-044754-7*, Penguin Classics) Viking Penguin.
Adams, Henry (Brooks). Esther. Spiller, Robert E., ed. LC 83-5448. 1976. reprint ed. lib. bdg. 50.00 (*0-8201-1187-2*) Schol Facsimiles.
— Esther: A Novel. (Works of Henry Adams). 1989. reprint ed. lib. bdg. 79.00 (*0-7812-1439-4*) Rprt Serv.
— Handbook of American Paintings in the Nelson - Atkins Museum of Art, Kansas City, Missouri. LC 91-29780. (Illus.). 208p. (Orig.). (YA). 1991. pap. 4.95 (*0-942614-17-8*) Nelson-Atkins.
— Henry Adams: Selected Letters. Samuels, Ernest, ed. (Illus.). 587p. (C). 1992. 39.50 (*0-674-38757-0*) Belknap Pr.
— Historical Essays. reprint ed. 98.00 (*3-487-04645-8*) Adlers Foreign Bks.
— Historical Essays. (Works of Henry Adams). 1989. reprint ed. lib. bdg. 79.00 (*0-7812-1441-6*) Rprt Serv.
— Histories of the United States of America During the Administrations of Jefferson & Madison, 9 vols., Set. (Works of Henry Adams). 1989. reprint ed. lib. bdg. 810.00 (*0-7812-1440-8*) Rprt Serv.
— History of the U. S. During the Administrations of James Madison, Vol. 2. Harbert, Earl, ed. LC 85-23098. 1436p. 1986. 45.00 (*0-940450-35-6*, Pub. by Library of America) Penguin Putnam.
— History of the U. S. During the Administrations of Thomas Jefferson, Vol. 1. Harbert, Earl, ed. LC 85-23098. 1308p. 1986. 45.00 (*0-940450-34-8*, Pub. by Library of America) Penguin Putnam.
— History of the United States of America During the Administrations of Jefferson & Madison, 9 vols. 1980. lib. bdg. 995.00 (*0-8490-3148-6*) Gordon Pr.
— History of U. S. A. During the Administrations of Jefferson & Madison. abr. ed. Samuels, Ernest, ed. LC 78-66081. (Midway Reprint Ser.). xxii, 448p. 1979. pap. text 17.95 (*0-226-00512-7*, CAH) U Ch Pr.
— John Randolph. 20.95 (*0-89190-526-X*) Amereon Ltd.
— John Randolph. LC 95-33361. (American History Through Literature Ser.). 228p. (C). (gr. 13). 1995. 73.95 (*1-56324-652-X*); pap. 24.95 (*1-56324-653-8*) M E Sharpe.
— John Randolph. (Works of Henry Adams). 1989. reprint ed. lib. bdg. 79.00 (*0-7812-1438-6*) Rprt Serv.
— Law of Civilization & Decay. 1975. 250.00 (*0-87968-235-3*) Gordon Pr.
— Law of Civilization & Decay. (Principle Works of Brooks Adams). 1989. reprint ed. lib. bdg. 79.00 (*0-685-27364-4*) Rprt Serv.
— Law of Civilization & Decay: An Essay on History. LC 71-37125. (Essay Index Reprint Ser.). 1977. reprint ed. 23.95 (*0-8369-2478-9*) Ayer.
— Letters. (Works of Henry Adams). 1989. reprint ed. lib. bdg. 79.00 (*0-7812-1447-5*) Rprt Serv.
— The Letters of Henry Adams, 1858-1892, Vols. 1-3. Levenson, J. C. et al, eds. (Illus.). 2016p. 1983. 165.00 (*0-674-52685-6*) Belknap Pr.
— The Letters of Henry Adams, 1892-1918, Vols. 4-6. Levenson, J. C. et al, eds. LC 82-14673. (Illus.). 2400p. 1988. 225.00 (*0-674-52686-4*) HUP.
— Letters to a Niece & Prayer to the Virgin of Chartres. 1988. reprint ed. lib. bdg. 49.00 (*0-7812-1446-7*) Rprt Serv.
— Letters to a Niece & Prayer to the Virgin of Chartres. La Farge, Mabel, ed. 1970. reprint ed. 29.00 (*0-403-00490-X*) Scholarly.
— The Life of Albert Gallatin. (Works of Henry Adams). 1989. reprint ed. lib. bdg. 79.00 (*0-7812-1436-X*) Rprt Serv.
— The Life of George Cabot Lodge. (Works of Henry Adams). 1989. reprint ed. lib. bdg. 79.00 (*0-7812-1444-0*) Rprt Serv.
— The Life of George Cabot Lodge. LC 78-16619. 1978. reprint ed. 50.00 (*0-8201-1316-6*) Schol Facsimiles.
— Mont-Saint-Michel & Chartres. 1974. 250.00 (*0-87968-178-0*) Gordon Pr.
— Mont Saint Michel & Chartres. (Classics Ser.). 398p. 1986. pap. 14.95 (*0-14-039054-5*, Penguin Classics) Viking Penguin.
— Mont-Saint-Michel & Chartres. (Works of Henry Adams). 1989. reprint ed. lib. bdg. 79.00 (*0-7812-1442-4*) Rprt Serv.
— The New Empire. (Principle Works of Brooks Adams). 1989. reprint ed. lib. bdg. 79.00 (*0-685-27363-6*) Rprt Serv.
***Adams, Henry (Brooks).** New Empire. 2000. reprint ed. lib. bdg. 79.00 (*0-7812-2572-8*) Rprt Serv.
Adams, Henry (Brooks). Novels, Mont Saint Michel, the Education: Democracy; Esther; Mont Saint Michel & Chartres; Education of Henry Adams. Samuels, Ernest & Samuels, Jayne N., eds. LC 83-5448. 1246p. 1983. 40.00 (*0-940450-12-7*, Pub. by Library of America) Penguin Putnam.
Adams, Henry (Brooks). Tahiti. Spiller, Robert E., ed. LC 47-3845. (Illus.). 216p. 1976. reprint ed. 50.00 (*0-8201-1213-5*) Schol Facsimiles.
Adams, Henry (Brooks). Theory of Social Revolution. (Principle Works of Brooks Adams). 1989. reprint ed. lib. bdg. 79.00 (*0-7812-0285-X*) Rprt Serv.
— Thomas Hart Benton: Drawing from Life. LC 89-37316. (Illus.). 208p. 1990. pap. 24.95 (*1-55859-071-4*) Abbeville Pr.
— The United States in 1800. 142p. 1955. pap. text 9.95 (*0-8014-9014-6*) Cornell U Pr.
***Adams, Henry (Brooks).** The War of 1812. LC 99-38133. (Illus.). 394p. 1999. pap. 16.95 (*0-8154-1013-1*) Cooper Sq.
Adams, Henry (Brooks). The Works of Brooks Adams, 5 vols., Set. (Principle Works of Brooks Adams). 1989. reprint ed. lib. bdg. 79.00 (*0-685-27361-X*) Rprt Serv.
— The Works of Henry Adams, 1838-1918, Set. 1987. reprint ed. lib. bdg. 79.00 (*0-685-18563-X*) Rprt Serv.
Adams, Henry (Brooks), et al, eds. Albert Bloch: The American Blue Rider. LC 97-168755. (Illus.). 216p. 1997. 65.00 (*3-7913-1778-4*, Pub. by Prestel) te Neues.
Adams, Henry (Brooks), et al. American Drawings & Watercolors in the Collection of the Museum of Art, Carnegie Institute. LC 85-2984. (Illus.). 320p. (Orig.). 1985. pap. 19.95 (*0-88039-009-3*) Mus Art Carnegie.
Adams, Henry (Brooks), jt. auth. see Adams, Charles F., Jr.
Adams, Henry (Brooks), jt. auth. see James, Henry.
Adams, Henry (Brooks), jt. auth. see McFadden, David R.
Adams, Henry (Brooks), ed. see Joachimides, Christos.
Adams, Henry B. The Education of Henry Adams. Date not set. lib. bdg. 24.95 (*0-89190-844-7*) Amereon Ltd.
Adams, Henry B. The Education of Henry Adams. Samuels, Ernest, ed. (Riverside Edition Ser.). 600p. (C). 1973. pap. 13.96 (*0-395-16620-9*, RivEd) HM.
Adams, Henry B. The Education of Henry Adams. LC 96-15214. 1997. 18.50 (*0-679-60207-0*) Modern Lib NY.
— The Education of Henry Adams. Nadel, Ira, ed. LC 98-46268. (Oxford World's Classics Ser.). 552p. 1999. pap. 10.95 (*0-19-282369-8*) OUP.
— The Education of Henry Adams. 1999. pap. 12.95 (*0-679-64010-X*) Random.
— The Education of Henry Adams. Gooder, Jean, ed. & intro. by. 608p. 1995. pap. 12.95 (*0-14-044557-9*, Penguin Classics) Viking Penguin.
— The Education of Henry Adams. LC 90-45929. 530p. 1990. reprint ed. 34.95 (*0-87797-177-3*) Cherokee.
— The Education of Henry Adams. (Works of Henry Adams). 1989. reprint ed. lib. bdg. 79.00 (*0-7812-1443-2*) Rprt Serv.
***Adams, Henry Brooks.** Cardinal Pole. 252p. 2000. pap. 9.95 (*0-594-00174-9*) Eightn Hundrd.
— Democracy. 252p. 2000. pap. 9.95 (*0-594-04280-1*) Eightn Hundrd.
Adams, Henry C. Public Debts: An Essay in the Science of Finance. LC 75-2619. (Wall Street & the Security Market Ser.). 1975. reprint ed. 35.95 (*0-405-06946-4*) Ayer.
— Taxation in the United States, 1789-1816. LC 78-63745. (Johns Hopkins University. Studies in the Social Sciences. Thirtieth Ser. 1912: 5-6). reprint ed. 37.50 (*0-404-61015-3*) AMS Pr.
— Two Essays: Relation of the State to Industrial Action & Economics & Jurisprudence. Dorfman, Joseph, ed. LC 75-76510. (Reprints of Economic Classics Ser.). xi, 211p. 1969. reprint ed. 35.00 (*0-678-00494-3*) Kelley.
Adams, Henry E., ed. Handbook of Latin American Studies, Vol. 29: Social Sciences 1962-64. LC 36-32633. 1967. 49.95 (*0-8130-0001-7*) U Press Fla.
— Handbook of Latin American Studies, Vol. 30: Humanities 1965-1966. LC 36-32633. 1968. 49.95 (*0-8130-0266-4*) U Press Fla.
— Handbook of Latin American Studies, Vol. 31: Social Sciences 1963-1969. LC 36-32633. 1969. 49.95 (*0-8130-0294-X*) U Press Fla.
— Handbook of Latin American Studies, Vol. 32: Humanities 1966-1967. LC 36-32633. 1970. 49.95 (*0-8130-0316-4*) U Press Fla.
Adams, Henry E., jt. auth. see Tollison, C. David.
Adams, Henry E., jt. ed. see Pariseau, Earl J.
Adams, Henry G. & Arora, Sudhir. Total Quality in Radiology: A Guide to Implementation. LC 93-41954. 216p. 1994. boxed set 54.95 (*1-884015-07-7*) St Lucie Pr.
Adams, Henry H. English Domestic Or Homiletic Tragedy: 1575-1642. LC 65-16225. 1972. reprint ed. 22.95 (*0-405-08178-2*, Pub. by Blom Pubns) Ayer.
Adams, Henry H. & Hathaway, Baxter, eds. Dramatic Essays of the Neoclassic Age. LC 64-14692. 1972. 28.95 (*0-405-08179-0*, Pub. by Blom Pubns) Ayer.
Adams, Henry M. Prussian-American Relations, Seventeen Seventy-Five to Eighteen Seventy-One. LC 79-25884. 135p. 1980. reprint ed. lib. bdg. 49.50 (*0-313-22270-3*, ADPA, Greenwood Pr) Greenwood.
Adams, Herb. Chassis Engineering: Chassis Design, Building & Tuning for High Performance Handling. LC 92-37394. (Illus.). 160p. (Orig.). 1992. pap. 17.95 (*1-55788-055-7*, HP Books) Berkley Pub.
Adams, Herbert, ed. see Stephens, Christine & Jenness, Theodora R.
Adams, Herbert B. The Church & Popular Education. LC 78-63876. (Johns Hopkins University. Studies in the Social Sciences. Thirtieth Ser. 1912: 8-9). reprint ed. 37.50 (*0-404-61132-X*) AMS Pr.
— The Church & Popular Education. (Works of Herbert B. Adams). 84p. 1985. reprint ed. lib. bdg. 59.00 (*0-7812-0813-0*) Rprt Serv.
— The College of William & Mary. (Principle Works of Herbert Baxter Adams). 1989. reprint ed. lib. bdg. 79.00 (*0-7812-1468-8*) Rprt Serv.
— The Encouragement of Higher Education. (Principle Works of Herbert Baxter Adams). 1989. reprint ed. lib. bdg. 79.00 (*0-7812-1473-4*) Rprt Serv.
— German Origin of New England Towns. (Principle Works of Herbert Baxter Adams). 1989. reprint ed. lib. bdg. 79.00 (*0-7812-1462-9*) Rprt Serv.
— The Germanic Origin of New England Towns. LC 78-63731. (Johns Hopkins University. Studies in the Social Sciences. Thirtieth Ser. 1912: 2). reprint ed. 37.50 (*0-404-61002-1*) AMS Pr.
— Historical Scholarship in the U. S., 1876 to 1901. (Works of Herbert B. Adams). 314p. reprint ed. lib. bdg. 69.00 (*0-7812-0996-X*) Rprt Serv.
— Historical Scholarship in the United States, 1876-1901: As Revealed in the Correspondence of Herbert B. Adams. Holt, W. Stull, ed. LC 78-64173. (Johns Hopkins University. Studies in the Social Sciences. Thirtieth Ser. 1912: 4). reprint ed. 42.50 (*0-404-61282-2*) AMS Pr.
— Is History Past Politics? (Principle Works of Herbert Baxter Adams). 1989. reprint ed. lib. bdg. 79.00 (*0-7812-1478-5*) Rprt Serv.
— Jared Sparks & Alexis de Tocqueville. (Works of Herbert B. Adams). 49p. 1985. reprint ed. lib. bdg. 59.00 (*0-7812-0812-2*) Rprt Serv.
— Life & Writings of Jared Sparks. (Principle Works of Herbert Baxter Adams). 1989. reprint ed. lib. bdg. 79.00 (*0-7812-1477-7*) Rprt Serv.
— Life & Writings of Jared Sparks, 2 Vols, Set. LC 76-119924. (Select Bibliographies Reprint Ser.). 1977. 60.95 (*0-8369-5367-3*) Ayer.
— Maryland's Influence upon Land Cessions to the United States. LC 04-8520. 1885. 5.00 (*0-403-00136-6*) Scholarly.
— Maryland's Influence upon Land Cessions to the United States. LC 77-97563. (Johns Hopkins University. Studies in the Social Sciences. Tenth Ser. 1892:10-11). reprint ed. 32.50 (*0-404-00286-2*) AMS Pr.
— Methods of Historical study. (Principle Works of Herbert Baxter Adams). 1989. reprint ed. lib. bdg. 79.00 (*0-7812-1466-1*) Rprt Serv.
— Notes on the Literature of Charities. (Works of Herbert B. Adams). 48p. 1985. reprint ed. lib. bdg. 39.00 (*0-318-03786-6*) Rprt Serv.
— The Principle Works of Herbert Baxter Adams, Set. 1989. reprint ed. lib. bdg. 63.00 (*0-685-27424-1*) Rprt Serv.
— Public Educational Work in Baltimore. (Principle Works of Herbert Baxter Adams). 1989. reprint ed. lib. bdg. 79.00 (*0-7812-1481-5*) Rprt Serv.
— Public Libraries & Public Education. (Principle Works of Herbert Baxter Adams). 1989. reprint ed. lib. bdg. 79.00 (*0-7812-1482-3*) Rprt Serv.
— Saxon Tithing-Men in America. (Principle Works of Herbert Baxter Adams). 1989. reprint ed. lib. bdg. 79.00 (*0-7812-1464-5*) Rprt Serv.
— Seminary Libraries & University Extension. (Works of Herbert B. Adams). 33p. 1985. reprint ed. lib. bdg. 39.00 (*0-318-03785-8*) Rprt Serv.
— Seminary Notes on Recent Historical Literature. (Principle Works of Herbert Baxter Adams). 1989. reprint ed. lib. bdg. 79.00 (*0-7812-1475-0*) Rprt Serv.
— State Aide to Higher Education. (Principle Works of Herbert Baxter Adams). 1989. reprint ed. lib. bdg. 79.00 (*0-7812-1480-7*) Rprt Serv.
— The State & Higher Education. (Principle Works of Herbert Baxter Adams). 1989. reprint ed. lib. bdg. 79.00 (*0-7812-1474-2*) Rprt Serv.
— The Works of Herbert Baxter Adams, 1850-1901, Set. 1987. reprint ed. lib. bdg. 800.00 (*0-685-18564-8*) Rprt Serv.
Adams, Herbert B. & Wood, Henry. Columbus & His Discovery of America. LC 70-149681. (Johns Hopkins University. Studies in the Social Sciences. Tenth Ser. 1892:10-11: No. I). reprint ed. 32.50 (*0-404-00287-0*) AMS Pr.
Adams, Herbert D. The Knife That Saves: Memoirs of a Lahey Clinic Surgeon. (Illus.). xi, 369p. 1991. 28.95 (*0-88135-072-9*, Countway Lib Med) Watson Pub Intl.
Adams, Hetty. Peace in the Classroom: Practical Lessons in Living for Elementary-Age Children. (Illus.). 144p. 1994. pap., teacher ed. 16.00 (*1-895411-68-8*) Peguis Pubs Ltd.
Adams, Homer & Johnson, Sarah. The Teacher's Little Instruction Book: Little Bits of Wisdom from Teachers for Teachers. LC 98-170131. 160p. 1997. pap. 6.99 (*1-57757-005-7*) Honor Bks OK.
Adams, Homer J. Reminiscences of A. B. Mackey. Greathouse, Janice M., ed. (Centennial Ser.: Vol. 1). 140p. 1997. write for info. (*0-9657278-0-7*) Trevecca Nazarene.
***Adams, Homer J.** Trevecca: Tradition & Folklore. Greathouse, Janice M., ed. (Centennial Ser.: Vol. 3). 149p. 1999. 15.00 (*0-9657278-3-1*) Trevecca Nazarene.
Adams, Hope H., jt. auth. see Tortora, Gerard J.
Adams, Howard. The Education of Canadians, 1800-1867: The Roots of Separatism. LC 68-27289. 157p. reprint ed. pap. 48.70 (*0-7837-7004-9*, 204681800004) Bks Demand.
— A Tortured People: The Politics of Colonization. 208p. 1995. pap. 10.95 (*0-919441-77-7*, Pub. by Theytus Bks) Orca Bk Pubs.
— A Tortured People: The Politics of Colonization. rev. ed. 219p. 1999. pap. 14.95 (*0-919441-37-8*) Theytus Bks.
Adams, Howard G., contrib. by. Focusing on the Campus MILIEU. (C). 1993. 5.00 (*1-887284-01-X*) Natl Consortium.
— Making the Grade in Graduate School: Survival Strategy 101. (C). 1993. 5.00 (*1-887284-02-8*) Natl Consortium.
— Mentoring: An Essential Factor in the Doctoral Process for Minority Students. (C). 1992. 5.00 (*1-887284-05-2*) Natl Consortium.
— Recruiting Graduate Students. (C). 1997. 7.00 (*1-887284-39-7*) Natl Consortium.
— Successfully Negotiating the Graduate School Process. (C). 1990. 3.00 (*1-887284-06-0*) Natl Consortium.
— Thinking about Success: A Mentor's Guide. (C). 1996. 5.00 (*1-887284-26-5*) Natl Consortium.
— Thinking about Success: A Protege's Guide. (C). 1996. 5.00 (*1-887284-27-3*) Natl Consortium.
Adams, Howard G. & Scott, Sheila K., contrib. by. Fundamentals of Effective Mentoring. (C). 1997. 7.00 (*1-887284-36-2*) Natl Consortium.
— Report of the 1995 GEM Intern Mentorship Project. (C). 1995. 5.00 (*1-887284-21-4*) Natl Consortium.
— Transitioning New Hires into the Workplace. (C). 1995. 7.00 (*1-887284-22-2*) Natl Consortium.
Adams, Howard G., jt. contrib. by see Adams, Stephanie G.
Adams, Howard G., jt. contrib. by see Parris, Alyssia J.
Adams, Hume, et al. An Introduction to Neuropathology. 2nd ed. LC 93-4546. 1994. pap. text 59.95 (*0-443-04495-3*) Church.
Adams, I., tr. see Possekel, A. K.
Adams, Ian. Agent of Influence: A True Story. 233p. 1999. 24.95 (*0-7737-3126-1*) Genl Dist Srvs.
***Adams, Ian.** Agent of Influence: A True Story. 244p. 2000. pap. 22.95 (*0-7737-6115-2*) Stoddart Publ.
Adams, Ian. Ideology & Politics in Britain Today. LC 98-28386. (Politics Today Ser.). 1999. text 64.95 (*0-7190-5055-3*, Pub. by Manchester Univ Pr) St Martin.
— Political Ideology Today. (Politics Today Ser.). 208p. (C). 1993. text 19.95 (*0-7190-3347-0*) Manchester Univ Pr.
Adams, Ian, photos by. The Ohio Lands. (Illus.). 144p. 1995. 39.95 (*1-56313-739-9*) BrownTrout Pubs Inc.
— Ohio Lands. (Illus.). 1996. 39.95 (*0-7631-0739-5*) BrownTrout Pubs Inc.
***Adams, Ian, et al.** Stan Hywet Hall & Gardens. LC 99-55416. (Series on Ohio History & Culture). 2000. pap. 27.95 (*1-884836-60-7*) U Akron Pr.
Adams, Ian S. The Logic of Political Belief: A Philosophical Analysis of Ideology. 224p. (C). 1989. text 61.00 (*0-389-20886-8*) B&N Imports.
Adams, Inez B. & Adams, Tom. The Class of 1912. (Illus.). 120p. (Orig.). 1995. pap. 9.95 (*0-9648638-0-4*) T Berryhill.

An Asterisk (*) at the beginning of an entry indicates that the title is appearing for the first time.

***Adams, Irene.** Flight of Time. 1999. pap. write for info. (*1-58235-353-0*) Watermrk Pr.

Adams, J. Dictionary of Finance, English-Japanese. (ENG & JPN.). 1994. 25.00 (*0-7859-9735-0*) Fr & Eur.

— Grand Pianola Score. 144p. 1994. per. 60.00 (*0-7935-3628-6*, 50480554) H Leonard.

— Harmonielehre: Full Score Orchestra. 200p. 1992. per. 60.00 (*0-7935-1690-0*, 50488949) H Leonard.

— Harmonium - Choir/Orchestra: Full Score Poetry of Donne, Dickinson. 176p. 1988. per. 60.00 (*0-7935-4112-3*, 50480015) H Leonard.

Adams, J. So You Think You're Not Religious. pap. text 4.95 (*1-56101-049-9*) Cowley Pubns.

Adams, J. What Do You Do When Fear Overcomes You? 1992. pap. 25.00 (*0-87552-088-X*) P & R Pubng.

Adams, J., et al, eds. The Langlands Classification & Irreducible Characters for Real Reductive Groups. (Progress in Mathematics Ser.: Vol. 104). xii, 318p. 1992. 57.50 (*0-8176-3634-X*) Birkhauser.

Adams, J. & Rockmaker, Gordon. Industrial Electricity: Principles & Practices. 3rd ed. 1984. text 70.64 (*0-07-000327-0*) McGraw.

Adams, J., et al. Principles of Project Management: Collected Handbooks from the Project Management Institute. LC 96-51592. 307p. 1997. pap. 59.95 (*1-880410-30-3*) Proj Mgmt Inst.

Adams, J. Alan, jt. auth. see Rogers, David F.

Adams, J. C., et al, eds. Multicultural Education: Strategies for Implementation in Colleges & Universities. 152p. (C). Date not set. pap. text. write for info. (*1-885890-00-1*, 346811) IL Staff & Curriculum.

Adams, J. F. Lectures on Exceptional Lie Groups. Mahmud, Zafer & Mimura, Mamoru, eds. (Chicago Lectures in Mathematics). (Illus.). 128p. 1996. pap. text 19.95 (*0-226-00527-5*); lib. bdg. 45.00 (*0-226-00526-7*) U Ch Pr.

Adams, J. Frank. Selected Works, 2 vols. May, J. Peter & Thomas, Charles B., eds. (Illus.). 400p. (C). 1991. write for info. (*0-318-68319-9*) Cambridge U Pr.

— Stable Homotopy & Generalised Homology. (Chicago Lectures in Mathematics). 384p. 1974. pap. text 30.00 (*0-226-00524-0*) U Ch Pr.

Adams, J. G., III, jt. auth. see Honig, G. R.

Adams, J. M. Adams. History of the Adams & Evarts Families, Vol. I. 87p. 1997. reprint ed. pap. 16.50 (*0-8328-7213-X*); reprint ed. lib. bdg. 26.50 (*0-8328-7212-1*) Higginson Bk Co.

Adams, J. Mack & Haden, Douglas H. Computers: Appreciation, Applications, Implications: An Introduction. LC 73-1688. 600p. reprint ed. pap. 186.00 (*0-608-15110-6*, 201250400033) Bks Demand.

Adams, J. Mack, et al. An Introduction to Computer Science with Modula-2. LC 87-81175. (Computer Science Ser.). 480p. (C). 1988. pap. 53.75 (*0-669-12171-1*) Jones & Bartlett.

Adams, J. Maxwell. Electrical Safety: A Guide to the Causes & Prevention of Electrical Hazards. (Power Ser.: No. 19). 208p. 1994. boxed set 77.00 (*0-85296-806-X*, PO019) INSPEC Inc.

Adams, J. Michael & Faux, David D. Printing Technology: A Medium of Visual Communications. 3rd ed. 640p. 1987. pap. 48.95 (*0-8273-2775-7*) Delmar.

— Printing Technology: A Medium of Visual Communications. 3rd ed. 640p. 1987. pap., teacher ed. 14.00 (*0-8273-2776-5*) Delmar.

Adams, J. Michael, et al. Printing Technology. 4th ed. LC 95-34510. (Graphic Communications Ser.). 672p. (C). 1995. pap. 71.95 (*0-8273-6907-7*) Delmar.

Adams, J. N. Pelagonius, Veterinary Treatises & the Language of Veterinary Medicine in Latin. LC 95-3754. (Studies in Ancient Medicine: Vol. 11). ix, 695p. 1995. 257.00 (*90-04-10281-7*) Brill Academic Pubs.

Adams, J. N. & Davies, M. J., eds. A Bibliography of Nineteenth-Century Legal Literature, 3 vols. 3000p. (C). 1992. lib. bdg. (*0-907977-42-1*) Chadwyck-Healey.

Adams, J. N. & Mayer, R. G., eds. Aspects of the Language in Latin Poetry, Vol. 93. (Proceedings of the British Academy Ser.). 456p. 1999. text 70.00 (*0-19-726178-7*) OUP.

Adams, J. N., jt. auth. see Atiyah, P. S.

Adams, J. Q. & Welsch, Janice R., eds. Multicultural Education: Strategies for Implementation in Colleges & Universities, Vol. 2. 139p. (C). 1992. pap. text. write for info. (*1-885890-01-X*, 351921) IL Staff & Curriculum.

— A Multicultural Prism: Voices from the Field. (C). 1994. pap. text 10.00 (*1-885890-04-4*) IL Staff & Curriculum.

— Multicultural Prism: Voices from the Field, Vol. 2. 232p. (Orig.). 1996. pap. 10.00 (*1-885890-06-0*) IL Staff & Curriculum.

Adams, J. Q. & Welsch, Janide R., eds. Multicultural Education: Strategies for Implementation in Colleges & Universities, Vol. 3. 195p. (C). 1993. pap. text. write for info. (*1-885890-02-8*, 363211) IL Staff & Curriculum.

Adams, J. Q., jt. ed. see Welsch, Janice R.

Adams, J. S. Dictionary of Finance English-Chinese. (CHI & ENG.). 164p. 1996. pap. 25.00 (*0-9515066-2-5*, Pub. by AMCD) IBD Ltd.

— Dictionary of Finance English-Japanese. (ENG & JPN.). 150p. 1994. pap. 25.00 (*0-9515066-4-1*, Pub. by AMCD) IBD Ltd.

Adams, J. S. & Mathieson, T. I., eds. English-Chinese Dictionary of Finance: Ying Han Chin Jung Tzu Tien. LC HG0151.E56. (CHI & ENG.). 175p. 1992. reprint ed. pap. 54.30 (*0-608-04402-4*, 20651840000I) Bks Demand.

Adams, J. T. The Complete Concrete Masonry & Brick Handbook. 1983. mass mkt. 37.95 (*0-442-20830-8*) Chapman & Hall.

Adams, J. V. Last Trip to Vegas. LC 93-79463. 288p. (Orig.). 1993. pap. 5.00 (*0-9612454-1-7*) Jackrabbit.

***Adams, J. W. & Beaumont, R. P.** More Practice in Mathematics, Bk. 1. Goddard, T. R., ed. (J). (gr. 2-7). 1999. pap. 19.00 (*0-7217-2346-2*, Pub. by Schofield) St Mut.

— More Practice in Mathematics, Bk. 2. Goddard, T. R., ed. (J). (gr. 2-7). 1999. pap. 19.00 (*0-7217-2347-0*, Pub. by Schofield) St Mut.

— More Practice in Mathematics, Bk. 3. Goddard, T. R., ed. (J). (gr. 2-7). 1999. pap. 19.00 (*0-7217-2348-9*, Pub. by Schofield) St Mut.

— More Practice in Mathematics, Bk. 4. Goddard, T. R., ed. (J). (gr. 2-7). 1999. pap. 19.00 (*0-7217-2349-7*, Pub. by Schofield) St Mut.

— More Practice in Mathematics, Bk. 5. Goddard, T. R., ed. 1999. pap. 19.00 (*0-7217-2350-0*, Pub. by Schofield) St Mut.

— More Practice in Mathematics: Answer Book, Bk. 1. Goddard, T. R., ed. 1999. pap. 19.00 (*0-7217-2351-9*, Pub. by Schofield) St Mut.

— More Practice in Mathematics: Answer Book, Bk. 2. Goddard, T. R., ed. 1999. pap. 19.00 (*0-7217-2352-7*, Pub. by Schofield) St Mut.

— More Practice in Mathematics: Answer Book, Bk. 3. Goddard, T. R., ed. 1999. pap. 19.00 (*0-7217-2353-5*, Pub. by Schofield) St Mut.

— More Practice in Mathematics: Answer Book, Bk. 4. Goddard, T. R., ed. 1999. pap. 19.00 (*0-7217-2354-3*, Pub. by Schofield) St Mut.

— More Practice in Mathematics: Answer Book, Bk. 5. Goddard, T. R., ed. 1999. pap. 19.00 (*0-7217-2355-1*, Pub. by Schofield) St Mut.

Adams, Jack A. Human Factors Engineering. 432p. (C). 1988. text 59.20 (*0-02-300370-7*, Macmillan Coll) P-H.

Adams, Jack D. The Second Promise. LC 99-94271. (Illus.). 178p. 1999. pap. write for info. (*0-7392-0174-3*, PO3135) Morris Pubng.

***Adams, Jacob E.** Taking Charge of Curriculum: Teacher Networks & Curriculum Implementation. LC 00-21191. (Series on School Reform). (Illus.). 2000. pap. write for info. (*0-8077-3948-0*) Tchrs Coll.

Adams, Jad. Double Indemnity: Murder for Insurance. large type ed. (Illus.). 602p. 1997. 31.50 (*0-7089-3677-6*) Ulverscroft.

***Adams, Jad.** Madder Music Stronger Wine: The Life of Ernest Dowson Poet & Deca. 2000. text 29.50 (*1-86064-470-8*) I B T.

***Adams, Jad & Whitehead, Phillip.** The Dynasty: The Nehru - Gandhi Story. (Illus.). 352p. 2000. reprint ed. text 27.00 (*0-7881-9123-3*) DIANE Pub.

Adams, Jad & Whitehead, Phillip. The Dynasty: The Nehru-Gandhi Story. (Illus.). 368p. 1998. 27.00 (*1-57500-056-3*, Pub. by TV Bks) HarpC.

Adams, James. Landscaping with Herbs. LC 87-163339. (Illus.). 223p. 1987. 32.95 (*0-88192-073-8*) Timber.

Adams, James. New Spies. pap. 22.95 (*0-7126-7410-1*, Pub. by Random) Trafalgar.

Adams, James. The Next World War: Computers Are the Weapons & the Front Line Is Everywhere. LC 98-21135. 288p. 1998. 25.00 (*0-684-83452-9*) S&S Trade.

— The Prince Mammoth Pumpkin: A Parable. LC 97-36879. (Illus.). 48p. 1998. 14.95 (*0-8091-0492-X*) Paulist Pr.

***Adams, James.** Sellout: Aldrich Ames: The Spy Who Broke the CIA. (Illus.). 322p. 2000. reprint ed. 27.00 (*0-7881-9398-8*) DIANE Pub.

— So You Think You're Not Religious? 18.95 (*0-936384-99-9*) Cowley Pubns.

Adams, James. Spy Craft: The Great Game Guide. (Illus.). 300p. (Orig.). 1995. 19.99 (*1-56686-425-9*) Brady Pub.

Adams, James & Frischer, Patricia. Artist in the Market Place: Making your Living in the Fine Arts. LC 80-11273. 168p. 1980. 9.95 (*0-87131-315-4*) M Evans.

Adams, James, et al. Ambush: The War Between the SAS & the IRA. 200p. (Orig.). 1988. pap. 13.95 (*0-330-30893-9*, Pub. by Pan) Trans-Atl Phila.

Adams, James A. & Blinka, Daniel D. Pretrial Motions in Criminal Prosecutions. 764p. 1994. 95.00 (*1-55834-190-0*, MICHIE) LEXIS Pub.

— Prosecutor's Manual for Arrest, Search & Seizure. LC 98-85666. xvi, 648 p. 1998. 105.00 (*0-327-00210-7*, 60074-10) LEXIS Pub.

— Prosecutor's Manual for Arrest, Search & Seizure, 1999 Supplement. 70p. 1999. write for info. (*0-327-01499-7*, 6007310) LEXIS Pub.

Adams, James A., jt. auth. see Blinka, Daniel D.

Adams, James D. Shape of Books to Come. LC 72-167302. (Essay Index Reprint Ser.). 1977. reprint ed. 20.95 (*0-8369-2479-7*) Ayer.

— The Treasure Chest: An Anthology of Contemplative Prose. 402p. 1977. 23.95 (*0-8369-2883-0*) Ayer.

Adams, James E. Dandies & Desert Saints: Styles of Victorian Masculinity. 264p. 1995. pap. text 16.95 (*0-8014-8208-9*) Cornell U Pr.

— War Psalms of the Prince of Peace: Lessons from the Imprecatory Psalms. 1991. pap. 7.99 (*0-87552-093-6*) P & R Pubng.

Adams, James E., ed. A Treasury of Living Faith: Catholic Devotions for Every Day of the Year. (Illus.). 384p. 1991. 12.95 (*0-9629585-1-4*) Crtve Commns MO.

Adams, James E., jt. ed. see Miller, Andrew H.

Adams, James F., ed. see Buchanan, Joseph.

Adams, James F., jt. ed. see Thomson, William S.

Adams, James L. The Care & Feeding of Ideas: A Guide to Encouraging Creativity. LC 86-10895. 240p. 1986. pap. 13.00 (*0-201-10087-8*) Addison-Wesley.

— Conceptual Blockbusting. pap. write for info. (*0-318-60201-6*) Addison-Wesley.

— Conceptual Blockbusting. 3rd ed. 1988. 17.95 (*0-201-10149-1*) Addison-Wesley.

— Conceptual Blockbusting: A Guide to Better Ideas. 1986. pap. 9.95 (*0-201-10089-4*) Addison-Wesley.

— Conceptual Blockbusting: A Guide to Better Ideas. 3rd ed. 1990. pap. 13.00 (*0-201-55086-5*) Addison-Wesley.

— An Examined Faith: Social Context & Religious Committment. Beach, George K., ed. & intro. by. LC 90-21240. 356p. 1991. pap. 21.00 (*0-8070-1611-X*) Beacon Pr.

— Flying Buttresses, Entropy, & O-Rings: The World of an Engineer. (Illus.). 88p. (C). 1991. text 24.95 (*0-674-30688-0*) HUP.

— Flying Buttresses, Entropy, & O-Rings: The World of an Engineer. (Illus.). 272p. (C). 1993. pap. text 15.95 (*0-674-30689-9*) HUP.

— Not Without Dust & Heat: A Memoir. LC 94-62067. xiii, 465p. 1995. text 29.95 (*0-913552-55-0*) Exploration Pr.

— Voluntary Associations: Socio-cultural Analyses & Theological Interpretation. Engel, J. Ronald, ed. LC 86-80304. 410p. 1986. text 34.95 (*0-913552-34-8*); pap. text 20.95 (*0-913552-35-6*) Exploration Pr.

Adams, James L., ed. see Warren, Robert Penn.

Adams, James L., tr. see Tillich, Paul Johannes.

Adams, James L., tr. see Troeltsch, Ernst.

***Adams, James Mack.** Tybee Island, Georgia. (Images of America Ser.). (Illus.). 128p. 2000. pap. 18.99 (*0-7385-0576-5*) Arcadia Publng.

Adams, James N. The Latin Sexual Vocabulary. LC 90-4697. 284p. 1990. reprint ed. pap. text 19.95 (*0-8018-4106-2*) Johns Hopkins.

Adams, James N., compiled by. Cumulative Index, Journal of the Illinois State Historical Society, Vols. 26-50. 710p. 1968. 20.00 (*0-912154-17-9*) Ill St Hist Lib.

— General Index to Journal of the Illinois State Historical Society, Vols. 1-25. 714p. 1949. 20.00 (*0-912154-15-2*) Ill St Hist Lib.

— Illinois Place Names. LC 90-152740. 1989. 20.00 (*0-912226-24-2*) Ill St Hist Soc.

Adams, James O., ed. see Dearborn, John J.

Adams, James R. Chief: The Pride Is Back. Adams, Patricia, ed. (Illus.). (Orig.). 1988. pap. 12.95 (*0-9618060-3-6*) Sheer Joy Pr.

— Flickers from a Burning Candle. Adams, Patricia, ed. (Illus.). 200p. (Orig.). pap. 12.95 (*0-9618060-2-8*) Sheer Joy Pr.

— I, Bethlehem. Adams, Patricia, ed. LC 87-91348. (Illus.). 120p. (Orig.). 1987. pap. 9.95 (*0-9618060-1-X*) Sheer Joy Pr.

— I, Golgotha. Adams, Patricia, ed. (Illus.). 200p. 1987. pap. 9.95 (*0-9618060-0-1*) Sheer Joy Pr.

— Mr. North Carolina: Life & Times of a Great Legislator. (Illus.). 300p. 21.95 (*0-9618060-4-4*) Sheer Joy Pr.

— Mystery of the Eagle's Eye. Adams, Patricia, ed. (Illus.). 108p. (Orig.). (J). (gr. 3-6). 1995. pap. 7.95 (*0-9618060-7-9*) Sheer Joy Pr.

— The Seasons of Sin. (Illus.). 200p. 9.95 (*0-9618060-8-7*) Sheer Joy Pr.

— So You Can't Stand Evangelism? A Thinking Person's Guide to Church Growth. LC 94-21573. 192p. 1994. pap. 12.95 (*1-56101-096-0*) Cowley Pubns.

— So You Think You're Not Religious: A Thinking Person's Guide to the Church. LC 88-37625. 208p. (Orig.). 1989. pap. 9.95 (*0-936384-69-7*) Cowley Pubns.

— Torts: Suitable for Use with Epstein. (Cambridge Ser.). 289p. 1990. pap. text 16.00 (*0-685-54302-1*, Chicago Law Bk) Cambridge Law.

— Torts: Suitable for Use with Prosser. (Cambridge Ser.). 167p. 1988. pap. text 16.00 (*0-685-54300-5*, Chicago Law Bk) Cambridge Law.

— Voices Heard by the Master. Adams, Patricia, ed. (Illus.). 152p. (Orig.). 1991. pap. 9.95 (*0-9618060-5-2*) Sheer Joy Pr.

Adams, James R. & Frantz, Douglas. A Full Service Bank. Chelius, Jane, ed. 400p. 1993. per. 10.00 (*0-671-72912-8*) PB.

Adams, James R. & Mader, Robert D. Autopsy. LC 75-16017. (Illus.). 208p. 1976. reprint ed. pap. 64.50 (*0-8357-7586-0*, 205690700001) Bks Demand.

Adams, James T. The Adams Family. LC 73-21487. (Illus.). 364p. 1974. reprint ed. lib. bdg. 35.00 (*0-8371-6427-3*, ADAF, Greenwood Pr) Greenwood.

— Adams Family Records: Genealogical & Biographical History of All Branches of the Adams Family, Including Addams, Adam, Adamson, McAdams & Corresponding Names in Other Languages. (Illus.). 106p. 1997. reprint ed. pap. 19.00 (*0-8328-7209-1*); reprint ed. lib. bdg. 29.00 (*0-8328-7208-3*) Higginson Bk Co.

— The Epic of America. LC 80-19550. (Illus.). 446p. 1980. reprint ed. lib. bdg. 75.00 (*0-313-22377-7*, ADEA, Greenwood Pr) Greenwood.

— Henry Adams. (Illus.). 1970. reprint ed. 10.50 (*0-403-00491-8*) Scholarly.

— The History of New England, 3 vols., Set. (BCL1 - United States Local History Ser.). 1991. reprint ed. text 225.00 (*0-7812-6260-7*) Rprt Serv.

— History of the Town of Southampton (East of Canoe Place, New York) (Illus.). 424p. 1993. reprint ed. lib. bdg. 45.00 (*0-8328-3523-4*) Higginson Bk Co.

— Memorials of Old Bridgehampton. (Illus.). 399p. 1997. reprint ed. lib. bdg. 43.00 (*0-8328-6103-0*) Higginson Bk Co.

— New England in the Republic. 1989. reprint ed. lib. bdg. 79.00 (*0-7812-1507-2*) Rprt Serv.

— New England in the Republic, 1776-1850. (Works of James Truslow Adams). 438p. 1985. reprint ed. lib. bdg. 59.00 (*0-932051-16-2*) Rprt Serv.

— New England in the Republic, 1776-1850. (BCL1 - United States Local History Ser.). 438p. 1991. reprint ed. text 99.00 (*0-7812-6261-5*) Rprt Serv.

— New England in the Republic, 1776-1850. LC 70-144854. reprint ed. 39.00 (*0-403-00821-2*) Scholarly.

— Our Business Civilization: Some Aspects of Our American Culture. (BCL1 - U. S. History Ser.). 306p. 1991. lib. bdg. 89.00 (*0-7812-6018-3*) Rprt Serv.

— Our Business Civilization: Some Aspects of Our American Culture. LC 75-92608. reprint ed. 32.50 (*0-404-00288-9*) AMS Pr.

— Provincial Society, 1690-1763. (History - United States Ser.). 374p. 1991. reprint ed. lib. bdg. 99.00 (*0-7812-6093-0*) Rprt Serv.

— Revolutionary New England, 1691-1776. (BCL1 - United States Local History Ser.). 469p. 1991. reprint ed. text 99.00 (*0-7812-6262-3*) Rprt Serv.

— Tempo of Modern Life. LC 74-121444. (Essay Index Reprint Ser.). 1977. 23.95 (*0-8369-1691-3*) Ayer.

Adams, James T., ed. Atlas of American History. 2nd rev. ed. 320p. 1985. 85.00 (*0-684-18411-7*, Scribners Ref) Mac Lib Ref.

Adams, James T., ed. see American Geographical Society of New York Staff.

Adams, James W., jt. auth. see Creighton, James L.

Adams, Jan S. A Foreign Policy in Transition: Moscow's Retreat from Central America & the Caribbean, 1985-1992. LC 92-13683. 255p. 1992. pap. text 27.95 (*0-8223-1293-X*) Duke.

***Adams, Jane.** Fade to Grey. large type ed. 328p. 1999. 31.99 (*0-7089-4153-2*) Ulverscroft.

Adams, Jane. The Greenway. large type ed. 384p. 31.50 (*0-7089-3659-8*) Ulverscroft.

— The Transformation of Rural Life: Southern Illinois, 1890-1990. LC 94-4176. (Studies in Rural Culture). (Illus.). 352p. 1994. pap. text 19.95 (*0-8078-4479-9*); lib. bdg. 55.00 (*0-8078-2168-3*) U of NC Pr.

Adams, Jane, ed. All Anybody Ever Wanted of Me Was to Work: The Memoirs of Edith Bradley Rendleman. 213p. 1996. pap. 19.95 (*0-8093-2059-2*) S Ill U Pr.

Adams, Jane, ed. & intro. see Rendleman, Edith B.

Adams, Jane K. Occult Methods of Healing. 54p. 1997. reprint ed. pap. 9.95 (*0-7661-0066-9*) Kessinger Pub.

Adams, Jane M., jt. auth. see Scholinski, Daphne.

Adams, Janice E., jt. ed. see Adams, Robert P.

***Adams, Janine.** 25 Stupid Mistakes Dog Owners Make. 2000. pap. 16.95 (*0-7373-0490-1*, Pub. by Lowell Hse) NTC Contemp Pub Co.

— You Can Talk to Your Animals: Animal Communicators Tell You How. 224p. 2000. pap. 14.99 (*1-58245-177-X*) Howell Bks.

Adams, Janus. Freedom Days: 365 Inspired Moments in Civil Rights History. LC 97-21614. (Illus.). 432p. 1997. 22.95 (*0-471-19212-0*) Wiley.

— Freedom Days: 365 Inspired Moments in Civil Rights History. 420p. 1998. reprint ed. pap. 14.95 (*0-471-29104-8*) Wiley.

— Glory Days: 365 Inspired Moments in African-American History. 432p. 1996. pap. 13.50 (*0-06-092752-6*) HarpC.

— Sister Days: 365 Inspired Moments in African-American Women's History. LC 99-46894. 432p. 1999. 22.95 (*0-471-28361-4*) Wiley.

***Adams, Jay E.** Biblical Sonship: An Evaluation of the Sonship Discipleship Course. 1999. pap. 9.95 (*1-889032-15-8*) Timeless Texts.

— Life under the Son: Counsel from the Book of Ecclesiastes. 1999. pap. 9.95 (*1-889032-16-6*) Timeless Texts.

Adams, Jay Edward. Back to the Blackboard: Design for a Bibical Christian School. 2nd ed. 154p. 1998. reprint ed. pap. 9.95 (*1-889032-05-0*) Timeless Texts.

— The Biblical View of Self-Esteem, Self-Love, & Self-Image. LC 86-80705. 144p. 1986. pap. 7.99 (*0-89081-553-4*) Harvest Hse.

— A Call for Discernment. 2nd ed. 139p. 1987. reprint ed. pap. 9.95 (*1-889032-04-2*) Timeless Texts.

— Capacitado para Orientar. Orig. Title: Competent to Counsel. (SPA.). 328p. 1981. pap. 9.99 (*0-8254-1000-2*, Edit Portavoz) Kregel.

— Christ & Your Problems. 33p. 1973. pap. 1.99 (*0-87552-011-1*) P & R Pubng.

— The Christian Counselor's Casebook. (Jay Adams Library). 224p. 1986. pap. 15.99 (*0-310-51161-5*, 12128P) Zondervan.

— The Christian Counselor's Commentary: Galatians, Ephesians, Colossians, Philemon. 190p. 1995. 24.95 (*0-9643556-2-0*) Timeless Texts.

— The Christian Counselor's Commentary: I & II Corinthians. 190p. 1994. 24.95 (*0-9643556-1-2*) Timeless Texts.

— The Christian Counselor's Commentary: I & II Timothy & Titus. 144p. 1995. 24.95 (*0-9643556-5-5*) Timeless Texts.

— The Christian Counselor's Commentary: Proverbs, 2 vols., Vol. VI. 231p. 1997. 24.95 (*1-889032-03-4*) Timeless Texts.

— The Christian Counselor's Commentary: Romans, Philippians, First & Second Thessalonians. 240p. 1995. 24.95 (*0-9643556-6-3*) Timeless Texts.

— The Christian Counselor's Commentary: The Gospel of John & the Letters of John & Jesus, 11 vols., Vol. VIII. 211p. 1998. 24.95 (*1-889032-08-5*) Timeless Texts.

— The Christian Counselor's Commentary: The Gospel of Luke, No. 11, No. 8. 211p. Date not set. 24.95 (*1-889032-09-3*) Timeless Texts.

— The Christian Counselor's Commentary: The Gospels of Matthew & Mark, 11, No. 9. 1999. 24.95 (*1-889032-12-3*) Timeless Texts.

— The Christian Counselor's Commentary Vol. V: Hebrews, James, I & II Peter & Jude, 11 vols. 355p. 1996. 24.95 (*1-889032-01-8*) Timeless Texts.

— The Christian Counselor's Manual: The Practice of Nouthetic Counseling. (Jay Adams Library). 496p. 1986. teacher ed. 21.99 (*0-310-51150-X*, 12127) Zondervan.

— Christian Living in the Home. 1972. pap. 7.99 (*0-87552-016-2*) P & R Pubng.

— Christian Living in the World. 110p. 1998. pap. 9.95 (*1-889032-10-7*) Timeless Texts.

— The Christian's Guide to Guidance: How to Make Bibical Decisions in Everyday Life. 97p. 1998. pap. 8.95 (1-889032-06-9) Timeless Texts.

— Competent to Counsel: Introduction to Nouthetic Counseling. Smith, Michael, ed. (Jay Adams Library). 320p. 1986. 19.99 (0-310-51140-2, 12126) Zondervan.

— Counsel from Psalm 119. 140p. 1998. pap. 9.95 (1-889032-07-7) Timeless Texts.

— Essays on Biblical Preaching. (Jay Adams Library). 160p. 1986. pap. 7.95 (0-310-51041-4, 12116P) Zondervan.

— Essays on Counseling. (Jay Adams Library). 288p. 1986. pap. 8.95 (0-310-51171-2, 12129P) Zondervan.

— Four Weeks with God & Your Neighbor. 75p. 1978. pap. 5.99 (0-87552-020-0) P & R Pubng.

— From Forgiven to Forgiving: Learning to Forgive One Another God's Way. 175p. (Orig.). 1994. pap. 10.95 (1-879737-12-4) Calvary Press.

— Godliness Through Discipline. 1972. pap. 1.99 (0-87552-021-9) P & R Pubng.

— Godliness Through Discipline. 30p. (gr. 10). 1973. reprint ed. mass mkt. 2.99 (0-8010-0057-2) Baker Bks.

— Godliness Through Discipline - Chinese Edition. Wu, T. P., tr. (CHI.). 34p. 1989. pap. 1.50 (1-56582-075-4) Christ Renew Min.

— The Grand Demonstration: A Bibical Study of the So-Called Problem of Evil. 119p. 1991. pap. 7.95 (1-889032-02-6) Timeless Texts.

— Handbook of Church Discipline. (Jay Adams Library). 128p. 1986. pap. 14.99 (0-310-51191-7, 12131P) Zondervan.

— Helps for Counselors: A Mini-Manual for Christian Counseling. 64p. 1980. mass mkt. 5.99 (0-8010-0156-0) Baker Bks.

— How to Handle Trouble. 66p. 1982. pap. 3.99 (0-87552-076-6) P & R Pubng.

— How to Help People Change. (Jay Adams Library). 208p. 1986. pap. 12.99 (0-310-51181-X, 12130P) Zondervan.

— How to Overcome Evil. LC 83-3280. 116p. 1977. pap. 4.99 (0-87552-022-7) P & R Pubng.

— Insight & Creativity in Christian Counseling: An Antidote to Rigid & Mechanical Approaches. (Jay Adams Library). 144p. 1986. pap. 5.95 (0-310-51131-3, 12125P) Zondervan.

— The Language of Counseling & the Christian Counselor's Workbook. (Jay Adams Library). 160p. 1986. pap. 9.99 (0-310-51061-9, 12118P) Zondervan.

— Lectures on Counseling. (Jay Adams Library). 288p. 1986. pap. 8.95 (0-310-51121-6, 12124P) Zondervan.

— Liberacion: El Evangelo de Dios. 1980. pap. 3.50 (0-85151-417-0) Banner of Truth.

— Maintaining the Delicate Balance in Christian Living. 115p. 1998. pap. 9.95 (1-889032-11-5) Timeless Texts.

— Marriage, Divorce, & Remarriage in the Bible. (Jay Adams Library). 128p. 1986. pap. 10.99 (0-310-51111-9, 12123P) Zondervan.

— The Meaning & Mode of Baptism. 63p. 1975. pap. 4.99 (0-87552-043-X) P & R Pubng.

— Preaching with Purpose: The Urgent Task of Homiletics. (Jay Adams Library). 176p. 1986. pap. 14.99 (0-310-51091-0, 12121P) Zondervan.

— Ready to Restore. (Orig.). 1981. pap. 7.99 (0-87552-070-7) P & R Pubng.

— Shepherding God's Flock: A Handbook on Pastoral Ministry, Counseling, & Leadership. (Jay Adams Library). 544p. 1986. pap. 24.99 (0-310-51071-6, 12119P) Zondervan.

— Solving Marriage Problems: Biblical Solutions for Christian Counselors. (Jay Adams Library). 144p. 1986. pap. 10.99 (0-310-51081-3, 12120P) Zondervan.

— Teaching to Observe: The Counselor As Teacher. 140p. (Orig.). 1996. pap. 8.95 (0-9643556-8-X) Timeless Texts.

— A Theology of Christian Counseling: More Than Redemption. (Jay Adams Library). 352p. 1986. pap. 18.99 (0-310-51101-1, 12122P) Zondervan.

— A Thirst for Wholeness. 136p. 1997. pap. 8.95 (0-9643556-9-8) Timeless Texts.

— Truth Applied: Application in Preaching. 128p. 1990. mass mkt. 8.99 (0-310-51031-7) Zondervan.

— Tu Puedes Dejar de Preocuparte. (Serie Tu Puedes - You Can Ser.).Tr. of You Can Stop Worrying. (SPA.). 24p. 1992. pap. 1.79 (1-56063-147-3, 490481) Editorial Unilit.

— Tu Puedes Derrotar la Ira. (Serie Tu Puedes - You Can Ser.).Tr. of You Can Defeat Anger. (SPA.). 1982. (1-56063-148-1, 490482); pap. write for info. (0-614-27151-7) Editorial Unilit.

— Tu Puedes Endulzar Tu Amargo Matrimonio. (Serie Tu Puedes - You Can Ser.).Tr. of You Can Sweeten a Sour Marriage. (SPA.). 24p. 1982. pap. 1.79 (1-56063-149-X, 490483) Editorial Unilit.

— Tu Puedes Librarte del Habito de las Drogas. (Serie Tu Puedes - You Can Ser.).Tr. of You Can Kick the Drug Habit. (SPA.). 24p. 1982. pap. 1.79 (1-56063-150-3, 490484) Editorial Unilit.

— Tu Puedes Superar el Temor. (Serie Tu Puedes - You Can Ser.).Tr. of You Can Overcome Fear. (SPA.). 24p. 1982. pap. 1.79 (1-56063-151-1, 490485) Editorial Unilit.

— Tu Puedes Vencer la Depresion. (Serie Tu Puedes - You Can Ser.).Tr. of You Can Conquer Depression. (SPA.). 24p. 1982. pap. 1.79 (1-56063-152-X, 490486) Editorial Unilit.

— Update on Christian Counseling, 2 vols. (Jay Adams Library). 288p. 1986. pap. 9.45 (0-310-51051-1, 12117P) Zondervan.

Adams, Jay Edward. Vida Cristiana en el Hogar. (SPA.). 107p. pap. 5.95 (1-55883-027-8, 6701-0580C) Libros Desafio.

Adams, Jay Edward. What Do You Do-Depress. 1992. pap. text 25.00 (0-87552-087-1) P & R Pubng.

— What Do You Do-Hooked, 1. 1992. pap. text 25.00 (0-87552-089-8) P & R Pubng.

— What Do You Do-Marriage, 1. 1992. pap. text 25.00 (0-87552-090-1) P & R Pubng.

— What Do You Do When Anger Gets the Upper Hand? 1992. pap. text 25.00 (0-87552-086-3) P & R Pubng.

— What Do You Do-Worry, 1. 1992. pap. 25.00 (0-87552-091-X) P & R Pubng.

— What to Do about Worry - Chinese Edition. Choy, Cheuk, tr. (CHI.). 29p. 1983. pap. 2.00 (1-56582-078-9) Christ Renew Min.

— What to Do on Thursday: A Layman's Guide to the Practical Use of the Scriptures. rev. ed. 144p. 1995. reprint ed. pap. 8.95 (0-9643556-7-1) Timeless Texts.

— Winning The War Within: A Bibical Strategy for Spiritual Warfare. 152p. 1996. reprint ed. pap. 8.95 (1-889032-00-X) Timeless Texts.

***Adams, Jay Edward.** Wrinkled but Not Ruined: Counsel for the Elderly. 122p. 1999. pap. 9.95 (1-889032-13-1) Timeless Texts.

Adams, Jean, ed. Insect Potpourri: Adventures in Entomology. xiii, 336p. 1992. pap. 34.95 (1-877743-09-7) Sandhill Crane.

Adams, Jean, et al. Heroines of the Sky. LC 78-99615. (Essay Index Reprint Ser.). 1977. 30.95 (0-8369-1539-9) Ayer.

***Adams, Jean Ekman.** Clarence Goes Out West & Meets a Purple Horse. LC 99-48293. (Illus.). 32p. (J). (ps-1). 2000. 15.95 (0-87358-753-7, Rising Moon Bks) Northland AZ.

***Adams, Jean M., et al.** The Internet Guide for California Lawyers, 2000. Piatt, Norma, ed. LC 99-7520. 330p. 1999. pap. text 75.00 (0-7626-0368-2, MI-33210) Cont Ed Bar-CA.

Adams, Jean S. Virginia Indians: An Educational Coloring Book. (Illus.). 24p. (Orig.). (J). (gr. k-3). 1991. pap. 2.95 (1-884549-05-5) VA Mus Natl Hist.

Adams, Jeanette. Love Lyrics: Poetry by Jeanette Adams. (Illus.). 32p. (Orig.). 1982. pap. 5.00 (0-9627018-2-3) J Adams Pubns.

— Picture Me in a Poem: Poetry by Jeanette Adams. 2nd ed. (Illus.). 20p. (gr. k-8). 1980. pap. 5.00 (0-9627018-1-5) J Adams Pubns.

— Sukari: Poetry by Jeanette Adams. 2nd ed. (Illus.). 12p. (Orig.). 1979. pap. 5.00 (0-9627018-0-7) J Adams Pubns.

— Tales from Within the Rabbitry. (Illus.). 97p. (J). (gr. 2-7). 1999. text 20.00 (0-9672375-1-3); pap. text 11.95 (0-9672375-0-5) J Adams.

Adams, Jeanette N., jt. auth. see Maul, Susan K.

Adams, Jeanie. Going for Oysters. (J). (gr. 2-6). 1993. lib. bdg. 15.95 (0-8075-2978-8) A Whitman.

Adams, Jeanne. Getting People Involved in Life & Activities: Effective Motivating Techniques. LC 95-61706. 65p. (Orig.). 1995. pap. text 12.95 (0-910251-78-9, GPI82) Venture Pub PA.

Adams, Jeanne, et al. Fortran Top 90 - Ninety Key Features of Fortran 90. 252p. 1994. pap. 20.00 (0-9640135-0-9) Unicomp.

— The Key Features of F. 256p. (Orig.). 1996. pap. 30.00 (0-9640135-2-5) Unicomp.

Adams, Jeanne C., et al. Fortran 95 Handbook. LC 97-22057. (Scientific & Engineering Computation Ser.). (Illus.). 750p. 1997. pap. text 55.00 (0-262-51096-0) MIT Pr.

Adams, Jeff. The Conspiracy of the Text: The Place of the Narrative in the Development of Thought. 160p. 1987. 35.00 (0-7102-0799-9, 07999, Routledge Thoemms) Routledge.

— Job: Adventures in the Land of Uz. 655p. 1995. 19.95 (0-9643021-3-6) Reality Living.

— Philemon: Real Friendships in an Unreal World. Date not set. 14.95 (0-9643021-9-5) Reality Living.

— Psalm 119: A Journey into the Heart of God. 444p. 1993. 19.95 (0-9643021-2-8) Reality Living.

— Reality Living. 94p. 1990. 5.00 (0-9643021-0-1); pap. 3.50 (0-9643021-1-X) Reality Living.

— Salmo 119: Una Odisea Corazon de Dios.Tr. of Psalm 119. (SPA.). 320p. 1996. pap. 11.99 (0-8254-1004-5, Edit Portavoz) Kregel.

Adams, Jeff, ed. & pref. see Marquis, Don.

Adams, Jefferson, jt. auth. see Stiller, Werner.

Adams, Jeffrey, ed. Morike's Muses: Critical Essays on Eduard Morike. LC 89-48764. (GERM Ser.: Vol. 49). (Illus.). 250p. 1990. 45.00 (0-938100-75-0) Camden Hse.

***Adams, Jeffrey & Vogan, David A., eds.** Representation Theory of Lie Groups. LC 99-51732. (IAS/Park City Mathematics Ser.: Vol. 8). 340p. 2000. 49.00 (0-8218-1941-0) Am Math.

Adams, Jeffrey & Williams, Eric, eds. Mimetic Desire: Essays on Narcissism in German Literature from Romanticism to Post Modernism. LC 95-2819. (GERM Ser.). x, 226p. (C). 1995. 60.00 (1-879751-91-7) Camden Hse.

Adams, Jeffrey, et al. Representation Theory of Groups & Algebras. LC 92-43340. (Contemporary Mathematics Ser.: No. 145). 491p. 1993. pap. 50.00 (0-8218-5168-3, CONM/145) Am Math.

— Representation Theory of Groups & Algebras. LC 92-43340. (Contemporary Mathematics Ser.: No. 145). (Illus.). 503p. reprint ed. pap. 156.00 (0-608-09208-8, 205271200005) Bks Demand.

Adams, Jeffrey M., ed. see Jones, Warren H.

Adams, Jeffrey Q., jt. auth. see Clark, Robert M.

***Adams, Jenni.** Stress: A Friend for Life. 1998. pap. 25.95 (0-85207-318-6) C W Daniel.

Adams, Jenny L. Manual for a Technological Approach to Ground Stone Analysis. (Illus.). 81p. (Orig.). 1996. pap. 15.00 (1-886398-30-5) Desert Archaeol.

— Pinto Beans & Prehistoric Pots: The Legacy of Al & Alice Lancaster. (Archaeological Ser.: No. 183). (Illus.). 106p. 1994. pap. 14.95 (1-889747-48-3) Ariz St Mus.

Adams, Jeremy D., tr. see Pernoud, Regine & Clin, Marie-Veronique.

Adams, Jeremy Du Quesnay, tr. see Pernoud, Regine & Clin, Marie-Veronique.

Adams, Jerome. Latin American Heroes: Liberators & Patriots from 1500 to the Present. (Illus.). 368p. 1993. pap. 9.00 (0-345-38384-2) One Wrld.

Adams, Jerome & Yoder, Janice D. Effective Leadership for Woman & Men. LC 84-28440. 176p. 1985. text 73.25 (0-89391-168-2) Ablx Pub.

Adams, Jerome, jt. ed. see Morrison, Robert F.

Adams, Jerome R. Liberators & Patriots of Latin America: Biographies of 23 Leaders from Dona Marina (1505-1530) to Bishop Romero (1917-1980) LC 91-52511. (Illus.). 301p. (C). 1991. lib. bdg. 35.00 (0-89950-602-X) McFarland & Co.

— Notable Latin American Women: Twenty-Nine Leaders, Rebels, Poets, Battlers & Spies, 1500-1900. LC 94-40310. 197p. 1995. lib. bdg. 32.50 (0-7864-0022-6) McFarland & Co.

***Adams, Jessica.** Astrology for Women. 2nd ed. 1999. pap. 12.95 (0-7322-6433-2, Pub. by HarpC) Consort Bk Sales.

Adams, Jewel. Elise's Heart. 150p. (J). 1998. pap. 9.95 (1-890828-16-5, Pub. by Camden Ct) Origin Bk Sales.

Adams, Jim. Sprint Handicapping Explained. 208p. 1990. 46.00 (0-85131-407-4, Pub. by J A Allen) St Mut.

Adams, Jim, et al, contrib. by. Hostile Climate: Report on Anti-Gay Activity. 141p. 1998. pap. 12.95 (1-890780-02-2) People for the Am.

Adams, Jimmy. Baden Baden Nineteen Twenty-Five International Chess Tournament. (World's Greatest Chess Tournaments Ser.). (Illus.). 382p. 1991. 45.00 (0-939433-13-3) Caissa Edit.

Adams, Jimmy & Murst, Sarah, trs. Moscow 1935 International Chess Tournament. (Great Tournaments Ser.: Vol. 8). (Illus.). 356p. 1998. 45.00 (0-939433-52-4) Caissa Edit.

Adams, Jimmy, tr. see Kmoch, Hans.

Adams, Jimmy, tr. see Levenfish, Gregory.

Adams, Joanna Z. Intimate Connections. 1991. mass mkt. 4.50 (0-445-21064-8, Pub. by Warner Bks) Little.

Adams, Joel, et al. C++ An Introduction to Computing. 2nd ed. LC 97-29294. 868p. (C). 1997. pap. 68.00 (0-13-744392-7) P-H.

— Turbo C++ An Introduction to Computing. LC 95-41348. 1248p. (C). 1995. pap. 61.00 (0-13-439928-5) P-H.

Adams, Joey. From Gags to Riches. (American Autobiography Ser.). 336p. 1995. reprint ed. lib. bdg. 89.00 (0-7812-8439-2) Rprt Serv.

Adams, John. Archery. LC 96-12403. (Know the Sport Ser.). (Illus.). 48p. 1996. pap. 5.95 (0-8117-2830-7) Stackpole.

— Commercial Hiring & Leasing. 390p. 1989. boxed set 124.00 (0-406-10114-0, U.K., MICHIE) LEXIS Pub.

— Complete Guide to Video. (Illus.). 336p. 1997. pap. 29.95 (0-7906-1123-6) Prompt Publns.

— Correspondence Between John Adams & Mercy Warren. (American Biography Ser.). 436p. 1991. reprint ed. lib. bdg. 89.00 (0-7812-8007-9) Rprt Serv.

— A Defence of the Constitutions of Government of the United States of America, 3 vols, Set. reprint ed. 260.00 (3-511-05000-6) Adlers Foreign Bks.

— The Diary & Autobiography of John Adams, 4 vols., Set. Butterfield, L. H. et al, eds. LC 60-5387. (Adams Papers: No. 1). (Illus.). 1813p. 1961. 189.50 (0-674-20300-3) HUP.

— Earliest Diary of John Adams: June 1753-April 1754, September 1758-January 1759. Butterfield, L. H. et al, eds. LC 66-14442. (Adams Papers: No. 1). 142p. 1966. 21.50 (0-674-22000-5) HUP.

— Howard W. Sams Complete Guide to Audio. LC 97-68183. (Illus.). 336p. 1998. pap. 29.95 (0-7906-1128-7) Prompt Publns.

— Institutional Economics. 1980. lib. bdg. 126.00 (0-89838-022-7) Kluwer Academic.

— Letter of John Adams, Addressed to His Wife. (Works of John Adams). 286p. 1985. reprint ed. lib. bdg. 69.00 (0-932051-15-4) Rprt Serv.

— The Life of John Adams, Vol. 1. 1988. reprint ed. lib. bdg. 75.00 (0-317-90161-3) Rprt Serv.

***Adams, John.** Managing Water Supply & Sanitation in Emergencies. (Skills & Practice Ser.). 1999. pap. text 15.00 (0-85598-378-7) Oxfam Pubns.

— Mastering Electronics Workbench. (Illus.). 324p. 2000. pap. 39.95 (0-07-134483-7) McGraw-Hill Prof.

Adams, John. Merchandising Intellectual Property. 345p. 1987. boxed set 184.00 (0-406-10340-2, U.K., MICHIE) LEXIS Pub.

— Papers of John Adams Vols. 1 & 2: September 1755-April 1775. Taylor, Robert J. et al, eds. (Adams Papers: Series III). 876p. 1978. 107.00 (0-674-65441-2) Belknap Pr.

— Papers of John Adams Vols. 3 & 4: May 1775-August 1776, 2 vols., Set. Taylor, Robert J. et al, eds. (Adams Papers: Series III). 1110p. 1979. 107.00 (0-674-65442-0) Belknap Pr.

— Papers of John Adams Vols. 5 & 6: August 1776-July 1778, Set. Taylor, Robert J. et al, eds. (Adams Papers: Series III). (Illus.). 933p. (C). 1983. text 107.00 (0-674-65443-9) Belknap Pr.

***Adams, John.** The Political Writings of John Adams. 2000. 35.00 (0-89526-292-4) Regnery Pub.

Adams, John. Remarks on the Country Extending from Cape Palmas to the River Congo. 265p. 1966. reprint ed. 40.00 (0-7146-1783-0, BHA-01783, Pub. by F Cass Pubs) Intl Spec Bk.

— Topics in Algebraic & Analytic Geometry: Notes from a Course of Phillip Griffiths. rev. ed. LC 74-2968. (Mathematical Notes Ser.: No. 13). (Illus.). 227p. 1974. reprint ed. pap. 70.40 (0-608-06330-4, 206669100008) Bks Demand.

— Transforming Leadership: From Vision to Results. 2nd ed. LC 98-11219. 300p. 1998. pap. text 24.95 (0-917917-11-1) Miles River.

— Transforming Work. 2nd ed. LC 98-4765. 300p. 1998. pap. text 24.95 (0-917917-12-X) Miles River.

— Treatise on the Principles & Practice of the Action of Ejectment & the Resulting Action for Mense Profits. LC 97-25982. lxxi, 620p. 1997. reprint ed. 127.50 (0-8377-1913-5, Rothman) W S Hein.

— The Works of John Adams, 10 vols. LC 78-128978. reprint ed. 745.00 (0-404-00310-9) AMS Pr.

— Works of John Adams, Second President of the United States, 10 Vols, Set. LC 77-80620. (Select Bibliographies Reprint Ser.). reprint ed. 451.00 (0-8369-5020-8) Ayer.

— The Works of John Adams, 1704-1740, Set. 1987. reprint ed. lib. bdg. 63.00 (0-685-18565-6) Rprt Serv.

Adams, John & Adams, Abigail S. Familiar Letters of John Adams & His Wife Abigail Adams, During the Revolution. LC 79-117865. (Select Bibliographies Reprint Ser.). 1977. 24.95 (0-8369-5318-5) Ayer.

***Adams, John & Pigliaru, Francesco, eds.** Economic Growth & Change: National & Regional Patterns of Convergence & Divergence. LC 98-33209. 512p. 1999. 100.00 (1-85898-683-4) E Elgar.

Adams, John & Prichard, Jones K. Franchising: Practice & Precedents in Business Format Franchising. 3rd ed. 460p. 1990. boxed set 150.00 (0-406-13790-0, U.K., MICHIE) LEXIS Pub.

Adams, John & Rush, Benjamin. The Spur of Fame: Dialogues of John Adams & Benjamin Rush, 1805-1813. Schutz, John A. & Adair, Douglass, eds. LC 66-15694. (Huntington Library Publications). (Illus.). 321p. reprint ed. pap. 99.60 (0-7837-6684-X, 204630000011) Bks Demand.

Adams, John & Scaperlanda, Anthony, eds. The Institutional Economics of the International Economy. 256p. (C). 1996. lib. bdg. 109.00 (0-7923-9725-8) Kluwer Academic.

***Adams, John & Thompson, C. Bradley.** The Revolutionary Writings of John Adams. LC 99-46495. 2000. 19.00 (0-86597-284-2); pap. 11.00 (0-86597-285-0) Liberty Fund.

Adams, John, et al. The Crystal Sourcebook: From Science to Metaphysics. rev. ed. Milewski, John V. & Harford, Virginia L., eds. LC 87-13746. (Illus.). 370p. 1988. 34.95 (0-9618267-8-9); pap. 24.95 (0-9618267-9-7) Mystic Crystal Pubns.

***Adams, John, et al.** The Spur of Fame. LC 99-46817. 2000. 18.00 (0-86597-286-9) Liberty Fund.

— The Spur of Fame. LC 99-46817. 2000. pap. 9.00 (0-86597-287-7) Liberty Fund.

Adams, John, jt. auth. see Adams, Abigail.

Adams, John, jt. auth. see Adams, Abigail S.

Adams, John, jt. auth. see Martin, M. Dean.

Adams, John A., Jr. Damming the Colorado: The Rise of the Lower Colorado River Authority, 1933-1939. LC 90-32795. (Centennial Series of the Association of Former Students: No. 35). (Illus.). 184p. 1990. 33.95 (0-89096-426-2) Tex A&M Univ Pr.

Adams, John A. Mexican Banking & Investment in Transition. LC 96-38333. 272p. 1997. 72.95 (1-56720-054-0, Quorum Bks) Greenwood.

Adams, John A., Jr. Softly Call the Muster: The Evolution of a Texas Aggie Tradition. LC 93-36982. (Centennial Series of the Association of Former Students: Vol. 52). (Illus.). 116p. (C). 1994. pap. 9.95 (0-89096-586-2) Tex A&M Univ Pr.

Adams, John C. Outline of Orthopaedics. 10th ed. LC 85-14924. (Illus.). 514p. reprint ed. pap. 159.40 (0-8357-4655-0, 203758700008) Bks Demand.

— Sir Charles God Damn: The Life of Sir Charles G. D. Roberts. 264p. 1986. text 30.00 (0-8020-2595-1) U of Toronto Pr.

Adams, John C. & Hamblen, David L. Outline of Fractures. 10th ed. (Illus.). 302p. 1992. pap. text 49.95 (0-443-04371-X) Church.

— Outline of Fractures, Including Joint Injuries. 11th ed. LC 98-32447. 1999. write for info. (0-443-06027-4) Church.

— Outline of Orthopaedics. 12th ed. LC 95-6579. 1995. text 28.95 (0-443-05149-6) Church.

Adams, John C. & Stossel, Clifford A. Standard Orthopaedic Operations. 4th ed. (Illus.). 485p. 1992. text 169.95 (0-443-04351-5) Church.

Adams, John C., jt. auth. see Yarbrough, Stephen R.

Adams, John C., tr. see Calamandrei, Piero, Jr.

***Adams, John D.** Thinking Today As If Tomorrow Mattered: The Rise of a Sustainable Consciousness. LC 99-90449. (Illus.). 192p. 1999. pap. 14.95 (0-9672859-0-9) Eartheart Enter.

Adams, John F. Infinite Loop Spaces. LC 78-51152. (Annals of Mathematics Studies: No. 90). (Illus.). 225p. 1978. reprint ed. pap. 69.80 (0-608-06614-1, 206681100009) Bks Demand.

Adams, John H., et al. An Environmental Agenda for the Future. Cahn, Robert, ed. LC 85-19760. 155p. (Orig.). 1985. pap. 12.95 (0-933280-29-7) Island Pr.

Adams, John J. Internet Guide to the Electronics Industry. LC 96-72183. (Illus.). vi, 242 p. 1996. pap. 19.95 (0-7906-1092-2) Prompt Publns.

Adams, John J. & Wolenik, Robert. Build Your Own Home Theater. 2nd ed. Date not set. 24.95 (0-7506-7330-3) Buttrwrth-Heinemann.

Adams, John L. The Complete Guide to Florida Foundations, 1997. Passannante, Frances S., ed. (Orig.). 1997. pap. 90.00 (1-879543-17-6) FL Fund Pubns.

An Asterisk (*) at the beginning of an entry indicates that the title is appearing for the first time.

— Florida Scholarships. Passannante, Frances S., ed. Orig. Title: Your Guide to Florida Scholarships. 120p. (Orig.). 1997. pap. 24.00 (*1-879543-19-2*) FL Fund Pubns.

***Adams, John L., ed.** The Complete Guide to Florida Foundations, 2000. 12th rev. ed. 2000. pap. 90.00 (*1-879543-24-9*) FL Fund Pubns.

— Florida State Grant Programs, 2000-2001. 14th rev. ed. Orig. Title: Your Guide to State Programs. 2000. pap. 80.00 (*1-879543-25-7*) FL Fund Pubns.

Adams, John L., jt. ed. see Adams, Katherine H.

Adams, John N. Adams: Character Merchandising. 2nd ed. 445p. 1996. write for info. (*0-406-07767-3*, MICHIE) LEXIS Pub.

Adams, John N., ed. Essays for Clive Schmitthoff. 1983. 40.00 (*0-86205-059-6*, MICHIE) LEXIS Pub.

Adams, John N. & Pritchard Jones, K. V. Adams & Pritchard Jones: Franchising. 4th ed. 1997. write for info. (*0-406-08139-5*, APJF4, MICHIE) LEXIS Pub.

Adams, John P., et al. Elbow & Shoulder Pain. (Illus.). 369p. 1989. 65.00 (*0-87473-450-9*, 62025-10, MICHIE) LEXIS Pub.

— Hand & Wrist Pain. (Illus.). 523p. 1987. 65.00 (*0-87473-302-2*, 62010-10, MICHIE) LEXIS Pub.

— Pain: Cause, Effect, Evaluation, 6 vols., Set. (Illus.). 1987. 295.00 (*0-87473-463-0*, 62000-10, MICHIE) LEXIS Pub.

Adams, John Q. Argument of John Quincy Adams Before the Supreme Court of the United States in the Case of the United States vs. Cinque & Others: Africans Captured in the Schonner Amistad. LC 71-82164. (Anti-Slavery Crusade in America Ser.). 1978. reprint ed. 22.95 (*0-405-00601-2*) Ayer.

— Diary of John Quincy Adams: Nov. 1779-Dec. 1788, Set, Vols. 1 & 2. Allen, David G. et al, eds. LC 81-6197. (Adams Papers). (Illus.). 1017p. (C). 1982. 107.00 (*0-674-20420-4*) HUP.

— John Quincy Adams in Russia: Comprising Portions of the Diary of John Quincy Adams from 1809-1814. (American Biography Ser.). 662p. 1991. reprint ed. lib. bdg. 109.00 (*0-7812-8008-7*) Rprt Serv.

— Jubilee of the Constitution. LC 72-2657. (Select Bibliographies Reprint Ser.). 1977. reprint ed. 19.95 (*0-8369-6844-1*) Ayer.

— Lectures on Rhetoric & Oratory, 1810. LC 97-15685. (Scholars' Facsimiles & Reprints Ser.). 850p. 1997. 90.00 (*0-8201-1507-X*) Schol Facsimiles.

— Memoirs of John Quincy Adams, 12 vols. Adams, Charles F., ed. LC 71-134915. reprint ed. lib. bdg. 894.00 (*0-404-00330-3*) AMS Pr.

Adams, John Q., Jr. Memoirs of John Quincy Adams, Comprising Portions of His Diary from 1795 to 1848, 12 Vols, Set. Adams, Charles F., ed. LC 71-85454. (Select Bibliographies Reprint Ser.). 470.00 (*0-8369-5021-6*) Ayer.

Adams, John Q. Report of the Secretary of State upon Weights & Measures: Prepared in Obedience to a Resolution of the House of Representatives of the Fourteenth of December, 1819. Cohen, I. Bernard, ed. LC 79-7945. (Three Centuries of Science in America Ser.). 1980. reprint ed. lib. bdg. 25.95 (*0-405-12526-7*) Ayer.

— Speech of John Quincy Adams of Massachusetts, Upon the Right of the People, Men & Women, to Petition. LC 78-82163. (Anti-Slavery Crusade in America Ser.). 1978. reprint ed. 22.95 (*0-405-00602-0*) Ayer.

— Writings of John Quincy Adams, 7 vols., Set. Ford, Worthington C., ed. (History - United States Ser.). 1992. reprint ed. lib. bdg. 630.00 (*0-7812-6148-1*) Rprt Serv.

Adams, John Q., jt. auth. see Adams, Clarks F.

Adams, John Q., tr. see Gentz, Friedrich.

Adams, John Quincy. Wants of Man: A Poem Reprinted. 1999. 9.95 (*1-55709-453-5*, Pub. by Applewood) Consort Bk Sales.

Adams, John R. Books & Authors of San Diego. 252p. 1966. pap. 15.75 (*0-916304-01-9*) SDSU Press.

— Harriet Beecher Stowe. (United States Authors Ser.). 152p. 1989. 32.00 (*0-8057-7532-3*, TUSAS 42) Macmillan.

Adams, John R., ed. see Stowe, Harriet Beecher.

Adams, John S. Housing America in the 1980s. LC 86-42950. (Population of the United States in the 1980s: A Census Monograph Ser.). 1988. 65.00 (*0-87154-003-7*) Russell Sage.

Adams, John S. & Lukert, Barbara P. Osteoporosis: Genetics, Prevention & Treatment. LC 98-46837. (Endocrine Update Ser.). 308p. 1999. write for info. (*0-7923-8366-4*) Kluwer Academic.

Adams, John S. & VanDrasek, Barbara J. Minneapolis - St. Paul: People, Place, & Public Life. LC 93-2836. 248p. (C). 1993. 26.95 (*0-8166-2236-1*) U of Minn Pr.

Adams, John S., et al. Long Distance Commuting in Minnesota: Final Report. (Illus.). 93p. (Orig.). (C). 1995. pap. text 30.00 (*0-7881-2017-4*) DIANE Pub.

Adams, John S., ed. see Marshall, John.

Adams, John Stokes, jt. auth. see Barringer, Daniel Moreau.

Adams, John W. Be What You Are: Love. 96p. 1983. pap. 6.95 (*0-9602166-0-X*) Golden Key.

— Stars & Stripes Forever. (Illus.). 60p. 1992. 9.98 (*0-8317-6658-1*) Smithmark.

— Thirty Days to a Better Life. 1988. pap. 3.95 (*0-9602166-4-2*) Golden Key.

— The U. S. Expatriate's Handbook: A Guide to Living & Working Abroad. 1998. pap. write for info. (*0-9663171-0-6*) WVUC Busn & Econs.

— You & Your Deaf Child: A Self-Help Guide for Parents of Deaf & Hard of Hearing Children. LC 97-18820. Orig. Title: You & Your Hearing Impaired Child. 240p. 1997. 19.95 (*1-56368-060-2*, Clerc Bks) Gallaudet Univ Pr.

— You & Your Hearing-Impaired Child: A Self-Instructional Guide for Parents. LC 88-29948. (Illus.). 150p. 1988. pap. text 12.95 (*0-930323-40-8*, Clerc Bks) Gallaudet Univ Pr.

Adams, John W., jt. auth. see Riley, William B.

Adams, John W., tr. see Lungwitz, Anton.

Adams, Jon-K. Narrative Explanation: A Pragmatic Theory of Discourse. Martin, Richard & Schreyer, Rudiger, eds. LC 96-44830. (Aachen British & American Studies: Vol. 7). 170p. 1996. 38.95 (*3-631-30802-7*) P Lang Pubng.

Adams, Jon K. Pragmatics & Fiction. LC 86-26883. (Pragmatics & Beyond Ser.: VI-2). vi, 77p. 1986. pap. 29.00 (*0-915027-64-X*) J Benjamins Pubng Co.

***Adams, Jonathan.** Columns: Detail in Building. 96p. 1998. pap. 34.95 (*0-471-97807-8*) Wiley.

Adams, Jonathan S. & McShane, Thomas O. The Myth of Wild Africa: Conservation Without Illusion. (Illus.). 266p. 1997. pap. 16.95 (*0-520-20671-1*, Pub. by U CA Pr) Cal Prin Full Svc.

Adams, Joseph. Yeats & the Masks of Syntax: A Study in Connections. 190p. 1984. text 46.00 (*0-231-04818-1*) Col U Pr.

Adams, Joseph D. Between Us-Between the Lines. LC 88-92385. xii, 156p. (Orig.). 1989. pap. 9.95 (*1-880016-00-1*) Road Pubs.

Adams, Joseph D., compiled by. Criterion for Tune: Collections of Poems by Writers in Delaware, Maryland, Virginia, & the District of Columbia. (Poet's Domain Ser.: Vol. 11). 128p. (Orig.). 1995. pap. text 8.00 (*1-880016-19-2*) Road Pubs.

— Regional Voices: Collections of Poems by Writers in Maryland, Virginia & the District of Columbia. (Poet's Domain Ser.: Vol. 1). xiv, 50p. (Orig.). 1990. pap. 4.95 (*1-880016-02-8*) Road Pubs.

— Those Move Easiest Who Have Learned to Dance: Collections of Poems by Writers in Delaware, Maryland, Virginia, & the District of Columbia. (Poet's Domain Ser.: 10). 160p. (Orig.). 1994. pap. text 7.50 (*1-880016-15-X*) Road Pubs.

Adams, Joseph D., compiled by. And Not Alone the Aspiring Trees: Collections of Poems by Writers in Delaware, Maryland, Virginia, & the District of Columbia. (Poet's Domain Ser.: Vol. 8). xiv, 98p. (Orig.). 1993. pap. 6.95 (*1-880016-13-3*) Road Pubs.

— A Bundle of Grief...a Shovel of Stars: Collections of Poems by Writers in Maryland, Virginia, & the District of Columbia. (Poet's Domain Ser.: Vol. 4). xii, 84p. (Orig.). 1991. pap. 6.95 (*1-880016-07-9*) Road Pubs.

— Countless Silken Ties: Collections of Poems by Writers in Maryland, Virginia, & the District of Columbia. (Poet's Domain Ser.: Vol. 3). xii, 76p. 1991. pap. 5.95 (*1-880016-04-4*) Road Pubs.

— Footprints on the Sands of Time: Collections of Poems by Writers in Delaware, Maryland, Virginia, & the District of Columbia. (Poet's Domain Ser.: Vol. 7). xvi, 80p. (Orig.). 1993. pap. 6.95 (*1-880016-11-7*) Road Pubs.

— Nets to Catch the Wind: Collections of Poems by Writers in Maryland, Virginia, & the District of Columbia. (Poet's Domain Ser.: Vol. 6). xiv, 80p. (Orig.). 1992. pap. 6.95 (*1-880016-10-9*) Road Pubs.

— A Place for the Genuine: Collections of Poems by Writers in Maryland, Virginia, & the District of Columbia. (Poet's Domain Ser.: Vol. 2). xiv, 66p. (Orig.). 1990. pap. 5.95 (*1-880016-03-6*) Road Pubs.

— A Sense of Ocean & Old Trees: Collections of Poems by Writers in Maryland, Virginia, & the District of Columbia. (Poet's Domain Ser.: Vol. 5). xii, 68p. (Orig.). 1992. pap. 6.95 (*1-880016-08-7*) Road Pubs.

— Sewing at Once with a Double Thread: Collections of Poems by Writers in Delaware, Maryland, Virginia, & the District of Columbia. (Poet's Domain Ser.: Vol. 9). xiv, 98p. (Orig.). 1994. pap. 7.50 (*1-880016-14-1*) Road Pubs.

Adams, Joseph D., ed. A Little Nonsense: Collections of Works by Poets in Delaware, Maryland, Pennsylvania, Virginia, & the District of Columbia. (Poet's Domain Ser.: Vol. 14). 144p. (Orig.). 1997. pap. 10.00 (*1-880016-25-7*) Road Pubs.

— What One Beholds of a Woman Is the Least Part of Her: Collections of Poems by Writers in Delaware, Maryland, Virginia & the District of Columbia. (Poet's Domain Ser.: Vol. 12). 128p. 1995. pap. 8.00 (*1-880016-21-4*) Road Pubs.

Adams, Joseph D., ed. Straightway Dangerous: Collections of Poems by Writers in Delaware, Maryland, Pennsylvania, Virginia, & the District of Columbia. (Poet's Domain Ser.: Vol. 13). (Illus.). 144p. (Orig.). 1996. pap. 8.00 (*1-880016-23-0*) Road Pubs.

Adams, Joseph D., ed. see Allen, M. Ray.

Adams, Joseph D., ed. see Arthur, Robert P.

Adams, Joseph D., ed. see Awad, Joseph.

Adams, Joseph D., ed. see De Chazeau, Eunice.

Adams, Joseph D., ed. see Glasser, Jane E.

Adams, Joseph D., ed. see Hwahu, Jane.

Adams, Joseph D., ed. see Johnston, Agnes N.

Adams, Joseph D., ed. see Souders, Bruce.

Adams, Joseph D., ed. see Weinstein, Sharon.

Adams, Joseph D., ed. see Youkeles, Dollie C.

Adams, Joseph Q. Conventual Buildings of Blackfriars, London, & the Playhouses Constructed Therein. LC 76-113537. reprint ed. 32.50 (*0-404-00289-7*) AMS Pr.

Adams, Joseph Q., ed. Chief Pre-Shakespearean Dramas. LC 78-52734. (BCL Ser.: No. I & II). reprint ed. 67.50 (*0-404-18054-X*) AMS Pr.

Adams, Joseph Q., jt. ed. see Bradley, Jesse F.

Adams, Joseph Q., ed. see Herbert, Henry.

***Adams, Joseph S. & Solomon, Todd.** Domestic Partner Benefits: An Employer's Guide. 100p. 1999. 79.00 (*0-9670470-8-0*) Thompson Pub Grp.

Adams, Joyce. Apache Pride. 1. 320p. 1999. mass mkt. 4.99 (*0-8217-6282-6*) Kensgtn Pub Corp.

— Darling Cat. 320p. 1998. mass mkt. 4.99 (*0-8217-5900-0*, Zebra Kensgtn) Kensgtn Pub Corp.

***Adams, Joyce.** Jewish Community in Chattanooga, Tennessee. (Images of America Ser.). (Illus.). 128p. 1999. pap. 18.99 (*0-7385-0120-4*) Arcadia Publng.

Adams, Joyce. Moonlight Masquerade. 416p. 1994. mass mkt. 4.50 (*0-8217-4669-3*, Zebra Kensgtn) Kensgtn Pub Corp.

***Adams, Joyce.** Stryker's Bride. (Zebra Splendor Historical Romances Ser.). 2000. mass mkt. 4.99 (*0-8217-6601-5*, Zebra Kensgtn) Kensgtn Pub Corp.

Adams, Joyce. Tempting Tess. 352p. 1997. mass mkt. 4.99 (*0-8217-5539-0*, Zebra Kensgtn) Kensgtn Pub Corp.

Adams, Joyce, et al. Deck the Halls. 384p. 1999. reprint ed. mass mkt. 5.50 (*0-8217-5150-6*, Zebra Kensgtn) Kensgtn Pub Corp.

Adams, Juanita. Background Notes, Bulgaria: 1990, February. 7p. 1990. pap. 1.25 (*0-16-021121-2*) USGPO.

— Background Notes, Cape Verde: 1989, Nov. 6p. 1990. pap. 1.25 (*0-16-018572-6*) USGPO.

— Background Notes, Central African Republic: 1989, November. 6p. 1990. pap. 1.25 (*0-16-018573-4*) USGPO.

— Background Notes, Seychelles: 1989, November. 7p. 1990. pap. 1.25 (*0-16-018574-2*) USGPO.

Adams, Judith. Cheyenne: City of Blue Sky. 128p. 1988. 27.95 (*0-89781-229-8*, 5154) Am Historical Pr.

***Adams, Judith.** Queuing for Everest. (Illus.). 2000. pap. 14.95 (*1-84002-154-3*) Theatre Comm.

Adams, Judith A. & Perkins, Edwin J. The American Amusement Park Industry: A History of Technology & Thrills. (Twayne's Evolution of American Business Ser.: No. 7). 280p. 1991. 27.95 (*0-8057-9821-8*, Twyne); mass mkt. 16.95 (*0-8057-9822-6*, Twyne) Mac Lib Ref.

Adams, Judith P. Peacework: Life Stories of Women Peace Activists. (Oral History Ser.: No. 5). 320p. 1990. 15.95 (*0-685-29287-8*, Twyne); 25.95 (*0-8057-9106-X*, Twyne) Mac Lib Ref.

Adams, Judith Porter. Peacework: Oral Histories of Women Peace Activists. 1992. pap. 14.95 (*0-8057-9119-1*) Mac Lib Ref.

Adams, Julian & Merluzzi, Vincent J., eds. The Search for Antiviral Drugs: Case Histories from Concept to Clinic. LC 93-16405. (Illus.). xiii, 240p. 1993. 57.50 (*0-8176-3606-4*) Birkhauser.

Adams, Julian & Stratton, Kenneth. Press Time. 3rd ed. 1975. text 21.80 (*0-13-699041-X*) P-H.

Adams, Julian, jt. ed. see Merluzzi, Vincent J.

Adams, Julianne L. & DeBlack, Thomas A., eds. Civil Obedience: An Oral History of School Desegregation in Fayetteville, Arkansas, 1954-1965. LC 94-17831. (RJS., Illus.). 224p. 1994. pap. 14.00 (*1-55728-359-1*); text 24.00 (*1-55728-358-3*) U of Ark Pr.

Adams, K. Gary. William Schuman: A Bio-Bibliography 67. LC 98-13564. (Bio-Bibliographies in Music Ser.: Vol. 67). 288p. 1998. lib. bdg. 69.50 (*0-313-27359-6*, Greenwood Pr) Greenwood.

Adams, Karen. Numerology Up-to-Date: A Key to Your Fortune. 64p. 1996. reprint ed. spiral bd. 9.00 (*0-7873-1274-6*) Hlth Research.

Adams, Karen G. Moving: A Complete Checklist & Guice for Relocation 2nd ed. LC 99-17890. 1999. write for info. (*1-893067-00-9*) Silvercat Pubns.

Adams, Karen L. & Brink, Daniel T., eds. Perspectives on Official English: The Campaign for English As the Official Language of the U. S. A. (Contributions to the Sociology of Language Ser.: No. 57). x, 366p. (C). 1990. pap. 25.00 (*3-11-012792-X*); lib. bdg. 113.85 (*3-11-012325-8*) Mouton.

Adams, Karen L. & Hudak, Thomas J., eds. Papers from the Second Annual Meeting of the SE Asian Linguistics Society, 1992. (Illus.). xiii, 440p. 1994. pap. text 24.95 (*1-881044-08-4*) ASU Prog SE Asian.

Adams, Kat. Thursday's Child. (Desire Ser.). 1993. per. 2.39 (*0-373-05773-3*, 5-05773-2) Silhouette.

Adams, Katherine. Progressive Politics & the Training of America's Persuaders. LC 98-41195. 184p. 1999. 39.95 (*0-8058-3236-X*); pap. 19.95 (*0-8058-3237-8*) L Erlbaum Assocs.

***Adams, Katherine H.** A Group of Their Own: College Writing Courses & American Women Writers, 1880-1940. (C). 2001. pap. text 21.95 (*0-7914-4936-X*) State U NY Pr.

— A Group of Their Own: College Writing Courses & American Women Writers, 1880-1940. (C). 2001. text 65.50 (*0-7914-4935-1*) State U NY Pr.

Adams, Katherine H. A History of Professional Writing Instruction in American Colleges: Years of Acceptance Growth & Doubt. LC 92-35966. (SMU Studies in Composition & Rhetoric). 208p. 1993. text 22.50 (*0-87074-342-2*) SMU Press.

Adams, Katherine H. & Adams, John L., eds. Teaching Advanced Composition: Why & How. LC 90-35967. 298p. (Orig.). (C). (gr. 13). 1990. pap. text 23.00 (*0-86709-260-2*, 0260, Pub. by Boynton Cook Pubs) Heinemann.

Adams, Katherine H., jt. auth. see Keene, Michael L.

***Adams, Katherine J. & Gould, Lewis L., eds.** Inside the Natchez Trace Collection: New Sources for Southern History. LC 98-53364. (Illus.). 232p. 1999. text 35.00 (*0-8071-2363-3*) La State U Pr.

Adams, Katherine L., jt. auth. see Fisher, B. Aubrey.

Adams, Kathleen. Family Homework. (J). (ps-1). 1989. pap. 5.99 (*0-8224-3052-5*) Fearon Teacher Aids.

— Journal to the Self: 22 Paths to Personal Growth. 256p. (Orig.). 1990. mass mkt. 13.95 (*0-446-39038-0*, Pub. by Warner Bks) Little.

— Mightier Than the Sword: The Journal As a Path to Men's Self-Discovery. 256p. (Orig.). 1994. pap. 10.99 (*0-446-39464-5*) Warner Bks.

— The Way of the Journal: A Journal Therapy Workbook for Healing. 2nd rev. ed. LC 93-84727. 96p. (Orig.). 1998. pap. 18.95 (*0-9629164-2-0*, ADWJ) Sidran Pr.

Adams, Kathleen & Brosterman, Robert. The Complete Estate Planning Guide. rev. ed. LC 98-148228. 384p. 1998. mass mkt. 6.99 (*0-451-62876-4*) NAL.

Adams, Kathleen & Tiffany, Sharon. The Wild Woman: An Inquiry into the Anthropology of an Idea. 160p. 1985. 18.95 (*0-87073-213-7*); pap. 13.95 (*0-87073-243-9*) Schenkman Bks Inc.

A

Adams, Kathleen, jt. auth. see Adams, Eric J.

Adams, Kathleen J., jt. ed. see Hareven, Tamara K.

***Adams, Kathleen M. & Dickey, Sara, eds.** Home & Hegemony: Domestic Service & Identity Politics in South & Southeast Asia. LC 99-55617. (Illus.). 320p. (C). 2000. text 49.50 (*0-472-11106-X*, 11106) U of Mich Pr.

Adams, Kathy S. Vision Quest: A Young Man's Journey. (J). (gr. 6-9). 1995. pap. 10.95 (*0-9649555-0-4*) Eagles Path.

Adams, Keith, jt. auth. see Carney, Betty.

Adams, Ken. Bring Out the Genius in Your Child. LC 97-172418. (Illus.). 160p. 1997. pap. 14.95 (*0-7063-7466-5*, Pub. by WrLock) Sterling.

— Rodeos, Pig Races & Other Cowboy Stories. 128p. 1994. pap. 9.95 (*0-9638828-0-5*) Two Bit Pubns.

Adams, Kenneth. Foolishness of God. 1981. pap. 5.95 (*0-87508-036-7*) Chr Lit.

Adams, Kenneth & Rourke, Byron P., eds. The TCN Guide to Professional Practice in Clinical Neuropsychology. vi, 234p. 1992. 73.00 (*90-265-1242-2*); pap. 35.00 (*90-265-1243-0*) Swets.

Adams, Kenneth, jt. auth. see Toch, Hans.

Adams, Kenneth M. Silently Seduced: When Parents Make Their Children Partners. 118p. 1991. pap. 7.95 (*1-55874-131-3*) Health Comm.

Adams, Kenneth M., jt. ed. see Grant, Igor.

Adams, Kevin. North Carolina Waterfalls: Where to Find Them, How to Photograph Them. LC 93-35021. (Illus.). 210p. (Orig.). 1994. pap. 16.95 (*0-89587-110-6*) Blair.

Adams, Kevin & Casstevens, Martha. Wildflowers of the Southern Appalachians: How to Photograph & Identify Them. LC 95-51144. (Illus.). 1996. pap. 26.95 (*0-89587-143-2*) Blair.

***Adams, Kimberly VanEsveld.** Our Lady of Victorian Feminism: The Madonna in the Work of Anna Jameson, Margaret Fuller & George Eliot. (Illus.). 352p. (C). 2000. text 59.95 (*0-8214-1361-9*); pap. text 24.95 (*0-8214-1362-7*) Ohio U Pr.

Adams, L. High Speed Animation. 1991. 24.95 (*0-8306-6635-4*) McGraw-Hill Prof.

— Mink Raising. (Illus.). 222p. 1979. pap. 4.00 (*0-936622-15-6*) A R Harding Pub.

— Supercharged Graphics. 1991. 24.95 (*0-8306-6658-3*) McGraw-Hill Prof.

***Adams, L. Cecile.** Teacher's Guide to We Are the Church! (Illus.). 36p. 1999. pap. 5.95 (*1-890569-15-1*, 2811) Gnl Brd Glbl Minis.

— We Are the Church! (Illus.). 23p. (J). (gr. 4-6). 1999. pap. 3.50 (*1-890569-14-3*, 2810) Gnl Brd Glbl Minis.

Adams, L. Garry, ed. Advances in Brucellosis Research. LC 90-11118. (Illus.). 542p. 1990. 39.95 (*0-89096-447-5*) Tex A&M Univ Pr.

Adams, L. H. Penny Postcards: Growing up in a Small Southern Town During the Great Depression. LC 92-82731. 240p. (Orig.). 1992. pap. 15.00 (*0-9634655-0-3*) Abecedarian.

Adams, Larry E. Upon This Rock: An Inspirational Writing. (Illus.). 82p. 1999. pap. write for info. (*0-7392-0067-4*, PO2908) Morris Pubng.

Adams, Laura. Christabel. LC 98-13218. 256p. 1998. pap. 11.95 (*1-56280-214-3*) Naiad Pr.

***Adams, Laura.** The Dawning. LC 98-48241. 224p. 1999. pap. 11.95 (*1-56280-246-1*) Naiad Pr.

Adams, Laura. Night Vision. LC 97-10007. 256p. (Orig.). 1997. pap. 11.95 (*1-56280-182-1*) Naiad Pr.

Adams, Laurie. Connections. 2nd ed. 600p. (C). 1997. pap. text 58.00 (*0-673-46008-8*) Addson-Wesley Educ.

— High Performance Interactive Graphics: Modeling, Rendering & Animating for IBM PCs & Compatibles. 1991. 24.95 (*0-8306-6644-3*) McGraw-Hill Prof.

— Letting Go. 1980. 10.95 (*0-02-500270-8*) Macmillan.

— Saunders Ophthalmology Word Book. 4th ed. 368p. 1991. pap. text 35.00 (*0-7216-3672-1*, W B Saunders Co) Harcrt Hlth Sci Grp.

Adams, Laurie & Szaluta, Jacques, eds. Psychoanalysis & the Humanities. (Psychoanalytic Practice Monographs: No. 6). (Illus.). 176p. 1996. text 26.95 (*0-87630-743-8*) Brunner-Mazel.

Adams, Laurie S. Art & Psychoanalysis. LC 92-56205. 384p. 1994. pap. 30.00 (*0-06-430206-7*) HarpC.

Adams, Laurie S. A History of Western Art. (Illus.). 512p. (C). 1993. text. write for info. (*0-697-13182-3*) Brown & Benchmark.

— History of Western Art. (Illus.). 512p. 1994. 55.00 (*0-8109-3425-6*, Pub. by Abrams) Time Warner.

— A History of Western Art. 2nd ed. LC 95-80873. 560p. (C). 1996. text 58.00 (*0-697-28782-3*) Brown & Benchmark.

***Adams, Laurie S.** History of Western Art. 3rd ed. (Illus.). 576p. 2000. 79.95 (*0-07-243114-8*) McGraw.

Adams, Laurie S., ed. Methodologies of Art. LC 96-10778. 192p. 1996. pap. 25.00 (*0-06-430231-8*) HarpC.

Adams, Laurie S. & Baker, Susan J. A History of Western Art. 2nd ed. 176p. (C). 1996. text, student ed. 19.37 (*0-697-35384-2*) Brown & Benchmark.

— A History of Western Art: With Student Study Guide. 2nd ed. (C). 1996. student ed., ring bd. write for info. (*0-697-36741-X*) Brown & Benchmark.

Adams, Laurie S. & Pernis, Maria G. Federico da Montefeltro & Sigismondo Malatesta: The Eagle & the Elephant. LC 95-15469. (Studies in Italian Culture: Vol. 20). (Illus.). XV, 228p. (C). 1997. text 46.95 (0-8204-2816-7) P Lang Pubng.

Adams, Leah & Kostell, Patricia. Quotations for Early Childhood Educators. LC 98-35907. 1998. 9.00 (0-87173-146-0) ACEI.

Adams, Lee. High-Performance CAD Graphics. 1991. 24.95 (0-8306-6682-6); 24.95 (0-8306-6683-4); 24.95 (0-8306-6684-2); 24.95 (0-8306-6685-0) McGraw-Hill Prof.

— High Performance Graphics in C. 1991. 24.95 (0-8306-6671-0); 24.95 (0-8306-6672-9) McGraw-Hill Prof.

— High Performance Graphics in C: Animation & Simulation. (Illus.). 320p. 1988. 36.95 (0-8306-0249-6, 3049); pap. 29.95 (0-8306-9349-1, 3049) McGraw-Hill Prof.

— High Performance Interactive Graphics: Modeling, Rendering & Animating for IBM PCs & Compatibles. (Illus.). 320p. 1987. pap. 24.95 (0-8306-2879-7, 2879P) McGraw-Hill Prof.

— Lee Adams Visualization. 1991. 24.95 (0-8306-0721-8); 24.95 (0-8306-0741-2) McGraw-Hill Prof.

— Supercharged C Graphics, Quick. 1991. 24.95 (0-8306-6739-3) McGraw-Hill Prof.

— Supercharged C Graphics, Turbo. 1991. 29.95 (0-8306-6740-7) McGraw-Hill Prof.

— Supercharged Graphics: A Programmer's Source Code Toolbox. (Illus.). 400p. 1988. 29.95 (0-8306-0659-9, 2959); pap. 21.95 (0-8306-2959-9) McGraw-Hill Prof.

— Visual Basic for Windows Interactive Graphics Programming. 1994. pap. 39.95 (0-8306-4126-2, Windcrest) TAB Bks.

— Windows Interactive Graphics Programming. 1994. pap. 39.95 incl. disk (0-8306-3820-2, Windcrest) TAB Bks.

— Windows Visualization Programming with C-C Plus Plus: 3D Visualization, Simulation, & Virtual Reality. LC 93-32093. 1993. pap. text 39.95 (0-8306-3812-1, Windcrest) TAB Bks.

— Windows Visualization Programming with C/C++ 3D Visualization, Simulation & Virtual Reality. 1993. pap. 39.95 (0-07-000399-8) McGraw-Hill Prof.

Adams, Lee M. The Table Rock Basin in Barry County, Missouri. Chapman, Carl H., ed. (Memoir Ser.: No. 1). (Illus.). 63p. (Orig.). 1950. pap. 1.50 (0-943414-17-2) MO Arch Soc.

Adams, Leith & Burns, Keith. James Dean: Behind the Scenes. 1990. 29.95 (0-8065-1188-5, Citadel Pr) Carol Pub Group.

Adams, Leith & Burns, Keith, eds. James Dean: Behind the Scenes. (Illus.). 224p. 1992. pap. 19.95 (0-8065-1369-1, Citadel Pr) Carol Pub Group.

Adams, Lela C. Abstracts of Deed Books One & Two: Henry County, Virginia, Feb. 1776-July 1784. 188p. 1983. reprint ed. pap. 20.00 (0-89308-358-5, VA 43) Southern Hist Pr.

— Abstracts of Order Book No. "0," Patrick County, Virginia, 1791-August 1800. 130p. 1984. pap. 20.00 (0-89308-427-1) Southern Hist Pr.

— Abstracts of Pittsylvania County, Virginia, Wills 1767-1820. 408p. 1985. 37.50 (0-89308-581-2) Southern Hist Pr.

— Abstracts of Wills, Inventories & Accounts, Patrick County, Virginia, 1791-1823. 110p. 1972. pap. 17.50 (0-89308-356-9, VA 42) Southern Hist Pr.

— Henry County, Virginia, Will Abstracts, Vol. I & Vol. II: Seventeen Seventy-Seven to Eighteen Twenty. 120p. 1984. 17.50 (0-89308-544-8) Southern Hist Pr.

— Marriages of Patrick County, Virginia, 1791-1850. 165p. 1984. reprint ed. pap. 20.00 (0-89308-357-7, VA 46) Southern Hist Pr.

Adams, Len, jt. auth. see Holmes-Siedle, Andrew.

Adams, Leon D. The Commonsense Book of Wine. 5th rev. ed. 168p. pap. 8.95 (0-932664-76-8, 507) Wine Appreciation.

— Leon D. Adams' Commonsense Book of Wine. LC 75-6805. 240p. 1975. pap. 7.95 (0-685-42192-9) HM.

Adams, Leonard. William Wake's Gallican Correspondance & Related Documents, 1716-1731, 2 vols. (American University Studies: Series VII: Theology & Religion, Vol. 26). 810p. (C). 1988. text 114.00 (0-8204-0436-5) P Lang Pubng.

Adams, Leonard, ed. William Wake's Gallican Correspondence & Related Documents, 1716-1731, Vol. 3. (American University Studies: Theology & Religion: Ser. VII, Vol. 55). 402p. (C). 1989. text 51.50 (0-8204-1053-5) P Lang Pubng.

— William Wake's Gallican Correspondence & Related Documents, 1716-1731, Vol. 4. LC 87-21382. (American University Studies: Theology & Religion: Ser. VII, Vol. 56). 421p. 1990. text 60.50 (0-8204-1054-3) P Lang Pubng.

— William Wake's Gallican Correspondence & Related Documents, 1716-1731, Vol. 5. LC 87-21382. (American University Studies: Vol. 57). 390p. (C). 1991. text 54.95 (0-8204-1055-1) P Lang Pubng.

— William Wake's Gallican Correspondence & Related Documents, 1716-1731, Vol. 7. LC 87-21382. (American University Studies: Theology & Religion: Ser. VII, Vol. 134). 310p. (C). 1993. text 57.95 (0-8204-1882-X) P Lang Pubng.

— William Wake's Gallican Correspondence, 1716-1731, Vol. 6. LC 87-21382. (American University Studies: Theology & Religion: Ser. VII, Vol. 58). 439p. (C). 1992. text 62.95 (0-8204-1056-X) P Lang Pubng.

Adams, Leonie. High Falcon & Other Poems. (BCL1-PS American Literature Ser.). 48p. 1992. reprint ed. lib. bdg. 59.00 (0-7812-6912-1) Rprt Serv.

— Those Not Elect. (BCL1-PS American Literature Ser.). 50p. 1992. reprint ed. lib. bdg. 59.00 (0-7812-6913-X) Rprt Serv.

Adams, Lewis & Guz, Abraham, eds. Respiratory Sensation. (Lung Biology in Health & Disease Ser.: Vol. 90). (Illus.). 464p. 1996. text 180.00 (0-8247-8846-X) Dekker.

Adams, Lewis, jt. ed. see Semple, Stephen J.

Adams, Lewis M. Live at the Church. 7.00 (0-686-20820-X); pap. 3.50 (0-686-20821-8) Kulchur Foun.

***Adams, Lex W.** Finding Spiritual Peace. 133p. 1999. write for info. (0-9643206-2-2) Spirit of Truth.

Adams, Lex W. Treasures for the Heart. 100p. (Orig.). 1994. pap. write for info. (0-9643206-0-6) Spirit of Truth.

Adams, Lex W. & Adams, Lynn M. Strengthening the Spiritual Man. 125p. 1982. pap. write for info. (0-9643206-1-4) Spirit of Truth.

Adams, Linda & Lenz, Elinor. Be Your Best: Personal Effectiveness in Your Life & Your Relationships. rev. ed. 240p. 1989. pap. 9.95 (0-399-51563-1, Perigee Bks) Berkley Pub.

— Effectiveness Training for Women: E. T. W. 240p. 1987. pap. 8.95 (0-399-51371-X, Perigee Bks) Berkley Pub.

Adams, Linda, ed. see Penner, James.

Adams, Linda H., ed. see Bollard, Thomas S.

***Adams, Lisa.** FM. Hartman, Lauren, ed. Gleason, Mat, tr. (Illus.). 56p. 1999. pap. 15.00 (0-9669434-0-6, PI01) Peeps Island.

Adams, Lisa K. Dealing with Arguments. LC 97-4145. (Conflict Resolution Library). (J). 1997. lib. bdg. 15.93 (0-8239-5073-5, PowerKids) Rosen Group.

— Dealing with Hurt Feelings. 1999. pap. text 6.95 (1-56838-268-5) Hazelden.

— Dealing with Hurt Feelings. LC 97-4150. (Conlict Resolution Library). (J). 1997. lib. bdg. 15.93 (0-8239-5075-1, PowerKids) Rosen Group.

— Dealing with Lying. LC 97-4146. (Conlict Resolution Library). (J). 1997. lib. bdg. 15.93 (0-8239-5071-9, PowerKids) Rosen Group.

— Dealing with Someone Who Won't Listen. (Conflict Resolution Library). (Illus.). 24p. (J). (gr. k-4). 1998. pap. 6.95 (1-56838-267-7) Hazelden.

— Dealing with Someone Who Won't Listen. LC 97-1297. (Conflict Resolution Library). (J). 1997. lib. bdg. 15.93 (0-8239-5074-3, PowerKids) Rosen Group.

— Dealing with Stealing. LC 97-4147. (Conlict Resolution Library). (J). 1997. lib. bdg. 15.93 (0-8239-5072-7, PowerKids) Rosen Group.

— Dealing with Teasing. LC 97-4148. (Conflict Resolution Library). 24p. (J). (gr. k-4). 1997. lib. bdg. 15.93 (0-8239-5070-0, PowerKids) Rosen Group.

Adams, Lisa L. Gateway to New Life. (Illus.). 48p. 1995. write for info. (0-9641577-6-4) Spiral Triangle.

— Inner Flight: Poetry & Quilt Pictures. (Illus.). 42p. 1997. 60.00 (0-9641577-9-9) Spiral Triangle.

— Kalo: Taro. (Illus.). 24p. (Orig.). 1994. pap. 5.50 (0-9641577-1-3) Spiral Triangle.

— Petroglyphs. (Illus.). 32p. (Orig.). 1994. pap. 10.00 (0-9641577-5-6) Spiral Triangle.

— 'Uala: Sweet Potato. (ENG & HAW., Illus.). 24p. (Orig.). 1994. pap. 5.50 (0-9641577-2-1) Spiral Triangle.

— 'Ulu: Breadfruit. (Illus.). 24p. (Orig.). 1994. pap. 5.50 (0-9641577-3-X) Spiral Triangle.

Adams, Lizbeth, ed. see Dunn, Jeanette M. & Mutzebaugh, Carole A.

***Adams, Lloyd.** My Beloved Wife. 256p. 1999. pap. write for info. (0-9636577-7-1) Trego-Hill.

Adams, Lloyd L. Wetlands Overview: Problems with Acreage Data Persist. (Illus.). 93p. 1999. pap. text 20.00 (0-7881-7977-2) DIANE Pub.

Adams, Lloyd L., et al. Land Ownership: Similarities & Differences in the Management of Selected State & Federal Land Units. (Illus.). 57p. (C). 1998. pap. text 20.00 (0-7881-7552-1) DIANE Pub.

Adams, Louis W., jt. auth. see Rollo, Ned.

Adams, Lowell W. Urban Wildlife Habitats: A Landscape Perspective. LC 93-44211. (Wildlife Habitats Ser.: No. 3). 1994. pap. 16.95 (0-8166-2213-2) U of Minn Pr.

Adams, Lowell W. & Dove, Louise E. Wildlife Reserves & Corridors in the Urban Environment: A Guide to Ecological Landscape Planning & Resource Conservation. LC 88-61762. (Illus.). 91p. 1989. pap. 6.95 (0-942015-02-9) Urban Wildlife.

Adams, Lowell W. & Leedy, Daniel L., eds. Integrating Man & Nature in the Metropolitan Environment: Proceedings of a National Symposium on Urban Wildlife. LC 87-50323. (Illus.). 1987. pap. 14.95 (0-942015-00-2) Urban Wildlife.

— Wildlife Conservation in Metropolitan Environments: Proceedings of a National Symposium on Urban Wildlife. LC 91-60099. (Illus.). 264p. (Orig.). 1991. pap. 18.95 (0-942015-03-7) Urban Wildlife.

Adams, Loyce M. & Mazareth, J. L., eds. Linear & Nonlinear Conjugate Gradient-Related Methods. LC 96-68754. (Proceedings in Applied Mathematics Ser.: No. 85). xvi, 164p. 1996. pap. 34.00 (0-89871-376-5, PR85) Soc Indus-Appl Math.

Adams, Lucas G. Dome Story: Planning & Building a Geodesic Home. LC 99-162706. (Illus.). 73p. 1998. pap. 8.95 (1-891429-04-3) Armadillo Pubng.

***Adams, Lucas Grillis.** Domes to Decagons: Exploring Alternative Housing. (Illus.). 61p. 2000. pap. 8.95 (1-891429-06-X) Armadillo Pubng.

***Adams, Luke.** Hellfire. (Apache Law Ser.: Vol. 2). 176p. 2000. mass mkt. 3.99 (0-8439-4688-1, Leisure Bks) Dorchester Pub Co.

— The Lonely Gun. 176p. 1999. mass mkt. 3.99 (0-8439-4631-8, Leisure Bks) Dorchester Pub Co.

— Outlaw Town. (Apache Law Ser.: Vol. 3). 176p. 2000. mass mkt. 3.99 (0-8439-4732-2, Leisure Bks) Dorchester Pub Co.

***Adams, Lynn.** Irish Activity Book. (Little Activity Bks.). (Illus.). (J). 1998. pap. 1.00 (0-486-40000-X) Dover.

— Make Your Own Noah's Ark with Twenty-Three Stickers Book. (Little Activity Bks.). (Illus.). (J). 1995. pap. 1.00 (0-486-28928-1) Dover.

Adams, Lynn. A Moment of Time. 124p. 1999. pap. 8.95 (0-7392-0166-2, PO3125) Morris Pubng.

— My First Hidden Picture Coloring Book. (Illus.). (J). (gr. k-3). 1993. pap. 1.00 (0-486-27478-0) Dover.

Adams, Lynn. Bethlehem's Busy. (Picture Window Bks.). 10p. (J). (gr. 1-3). 1997. 11.99 (0-7847-0631-X, 03795) Standard Pub.

— The Real Mother Goose Merry Christmas Music Box. 12p. (J). (ps-k). 1997. 12.95 (0-590-93256-X, Cartwheel) Scholastic Inc.

Adams, Lynn & Goldbloom, Erwin. Racquetball Today. Perlee, Clyde, ed. 230p. (C). 1990. mass mkt. 19.25 (0-314-76958-7) West Pub.

Adams, Lynn & Magill, John, texts. St. Charles Avenue Streetcar Line: A Self-Guided Tour. (Illus.). 16p. 1994. pap. 4.95 (0-917860-38-1) Historic New Orleans.

Adams, Lynn & Schlemme, Roy. I Can Draw Bible Characters. (I Can Draw Ser.). 36p. (J). (gr. 1 up). 1997. pap. 4.95 (1-56010-237-3, ICD9) W Foster Pub.

Adams, Lynn, jt. auth. see Cristaldi, Kathryn.

Adams, Lynn M., jt. auth. see Adams, Lex W.

Adams, M. & McManus, F. Noise & Noise Law: A Practical Approach. 1994. pap. text 82.95 (0-471-93708-8) Wiley.

Adams, M. A., jt. ed. see Attiwill, P. M.

Adams, M. J. An Introduction to Optical Waveguides. LC 80-42059. (Illus.). 417p. reprint ed. pap. 129.30 (0-8357-6301-3, 203557400096) Bks Demand.

Adams, M. J., et al, eds. Dynamics of Complex Fluids: Proceedings of the 2nd Royal Society - Unilever Indo-U. K. Forum in Materials Science & Engineering. LC 98-23902. 450p. 1998. 86.00 (1-86094-086-2, Pub. by Imperial College) World Scientific Pub.

— Solid-Solid Interactions: Proceedings of the First Royal Society-Unilever Indo U. K. Forum in Materials Science. LC 97-102955. 448p. 1996. 86.00 (1-86094-010-2) World Scientific Pub.

Adams, M. J. & Henning, I. D. Optical Fibres & Sources for Communications. LC 90-47279. (Updates in Applied Physics & Electrical Technology Ser.). (Illus.). 192p. (C). 1990. text 75.00 (0-306-43711-2, Kluwer Plenum) Kluwer Academic.

Adams, M. J., jt. ed. see Briscoe, B. J.

***Adams, M. R. & Moss, M. O.** Food Microbiology. 2nd ed. (Illus.). 494p. 2000. pap. 44.95 (0-85404-611-9, Pub. by Royal Soc Chem) Spr-Verlag.

Adams, M. R. & Moss, M. O., eds. Food Microbiology. 398p. 1995. 49.95 (0-85404-509-0, R4509) CRC Pr.

Adams, Malcolm & Guillemin, Victor W. Measure Theory & Probability. LC 95-46511. 1995. write for info. (3-7643-3884-9) Birkhauser.

— Measure Theory & Probability. LC 95-46511. 205p. 1996. 29.50 (0-8176-3884-9) Birkhauser.

Adams, Marc. The Preacher's Son. 224p. 1996. 22.95 (1-889829-00-5) Window Books.

Adams, Marc, jt. auth. see Cliffe, Roger W.

Adams, Marcia. Christmas in the Heartland. 1997. pap. 17.00 (0-609-80261-5) C Potter.

— Cooking from Quilt Country: Hearty Recipes from Amish & Mennonite Kitchens. (Illus.). 1988. 30.00 (0-517-56813-6) C Potter.

— Heartland: The Best of the Old & the New from Midwest Kitchens. LC 90-27260. (Illus.). 272p. 1991. 30.00 (0-517-57533-7) C Potter.

— Marcia Adams' Christmas in the Heartland: Recipes, Decorations & Traditions for Joyous Celebrations. (Illus.). 176p. 1992. 25.00 (0-517-58572-3) C Potter.

— Marcia Adam's Heirloom Recipes: Hidden Treasures from America's Kitchens. LC 94-7662. (Illus.). 320p. 1994. 22.50 (0-517-59347-5) Crown Pub Group.

— New Recipes from Quilt Country: More Food & Folkways from the Amish & Mennonites. LC 97-22620. 304p. 1997. 30.00 (0-517-70562-1) C Potter.

***Adams, Marcia.** Recipes Remembered. LC 00-37596. (Illus.). 64p. 2000. 7.99 (0-517-20896-2) Random Hse Value.

Adams, Marcia. Shadow Patterns: A Novel of Dallas & Padre Island. 1997. pap. 18.95 (1-57860-022-7) Guild Pr IN.

Adams, Margaret, ed. Collectible Dolls & Accessories of the Twenties & Thirties from Sears, Roebuck & Co. Catalogs, 1921-1939. (Illus.). 144p. (Orig.). 1986. pap. 11.95 (0-486-25107-1) Dover.

Adams, Margaret L., et al. Office Leasing: Drafting & Negotiating the Lease, 2 vols. Stein, Carolyn J., ed. LC 96-83539. 1333p. 1996. ring bd. 179.00 (0-88124-961-0, RE-30890) Cont Ed Bar-CA.

Adams, Marian E., jt. auth. see Lifter, Marsha.

***Adams-Maricelli, Iona.** What If Your Face Froze that Way? (gr. k-2). 2000. pap. 5.95 (0-533-13255-X) Vantage.

Adams, Marilyn & Shanley, Mary F. Rhythm of the Seasons: A Journey Beyond Loss. LC 97-21495. (Illus.). 56p. 1997. 17.95 (1-882835-38-7) STA-Kris.

***Adams, Marilyn Fournet.** The Airplane Diaries. (Illus.). iv, 42p. 2000. 35.00 (0-615-11537-3) Nightbloom.

Adams, Marilyn J. Beginning to Read: Thinking & Learning about Print. (Illus.). 504p. 1994. pap. text 22.00 (0-262-51076-6, Bradford Bks) MIT Pr.

Adams, Marilyn J., et al. Phonemic Awareness in Young Children: A Classroom Curriculum. LC 97-21682. 208p. 1997. 24.95 (1-55766-321-1) P H Brookes.

***Adams, Marilyn Jager & Feehrer, Carl E.** Decision Making. (Odyssey Ser.). 2000. teacher ed., spiral bd. 5.00 (0-88106-145-X) Charlesbridge Pub.

Adams, Marilyn Jager, et al. Foundations of Reasoning. (Odyssey Ser.). (J). 1995. pap. text, student ed. 5.00 (0-88106-138-7, FR10) Charlesbridge Pub.

— Foundations of Reasoning: Teacher Manual. (Odyssey Ser.). (J). 1995. teacher ed., spiral bd. 15.00 (0-88106-137-9, FR15) Charlesbridge Pub.

— Foundations of Reasoning: Teacher Resource Book. (Odyssey Ser.). (J). 1995. ring bd. 90.00 (0-88106-400-9, FR20) Charlesbridge Pub.

Adams, Marilyn Jager, jt. auth. see Feehrer, Carl E.

***Adams, Marilyn M.** What Sort of Human Nature? Medieval Philosophy & the Systematics of Christology LC 99-6523. (Aquinas Lectures). 1999. write for info. (0-87462-166-6) Marquette.

Adams, Marilyn M. & Adams, Robert M., eds. The Problem of Evil. (Oxford Readings in Philosophy Ser.). 238p. 1991. pap. text 19.95 (0-19-824866-0) OUP.

Adams, Marilyn M., ed. see Wolter, Allan B.

Adams, Marilyn M., tr. see William of Ockham.

***Adams, Marilyn McCord.** Horrendous Evils & the Goodness of God. 2000. reprint ed. pap. 16.95 (0-8014-8686-6) Cornell U Pr.

***Adams, Marilynn F.** Porch People. Schilling, Leslie D., ed. LC 98-89233. (Illus.). 64p. (YA). 1999. 34.95 (1-893465-00-4) AuCajunal Pubg.

Adams, Marjorie P. Antiquarian Book Fair & Paper Show Directory 1987-1988. 120p. (Orig.). 1987. pap. 8.75 (0-317-62611-6) Parrott Pr.

Adams, Mark. Glimpses of an American Century: By a Mouse in the Halls of the Mighty. unabridged ed. LC 97-23605. (Illus.). 272p. 1997. 24.95 (0-915433-19-2) Packrat WA.

— How to Write So People Will Know What You're Trying to Say. (Shortcuts to Ignorance Ser.). 16p. 1980. pap. 1.95 (0-915433-05-2) Packrat WA.

— Particle Distributions in Hadronic & Nuclear Collisions. 300p. 1999. 78.00 (981-02-3786-3) World Scientific Pub.

Adams, Mark & Bradbury, Mark. Conflict & Development: Organizational Adaptation in Conflict Situations. (Research Discussion Papers). (C). 1995. pap. 15.95 (0-85598-320-5, Pub. by Oxfam Pub) Stylus Pub VA.

***Adams, Mark & Thomas, Nicholas.** Cook's Sites: Revisiting History. 196p. 1999. pap. 49.95 (1-877133-82-5, Pub. by Univ Otago Pr) Intl Spec Bk.

Adams, Mark, jt. auth. see Rapoport, Bernard.

Adams, Mark A. Seasons of Life. 48p. 1997. pap. write for info. (0-9652761-1-2) Kat & Mouse.

— Thoughts from Inside. 48p. (Orig.). 1996. pap. write for info. (0-9652761-0-4) Kat & Mouse.

Adams, Mark B., ed. The Evolution of Theodosius Dobzhansky: Essays on His Life & Thought in Russia & America. LC 93-42144. 264p. 1994. text 42.50 (0-691-03479-6, Pub. by Princeton U Pr) Cal Prin Full Svc.

— The Wellborn Science: Eugenics in Germany, France, Brazil & Russia. (Monographs in the History & Philosophy of Biology). 256p. 1990. text 70.00 (0-19-505361-3) OUP.

Adams, Mark D., et al, eds. Automated DNA Sequencing & Analysis. (Illus.). 368p. 1994. text 83.00 (0-12-717010-3) Acad Pr.

Adams, Mark E. Enthusi Adams: Developing a Successful Game Plan. 1999. 9.95 (0-9670245-0-1) E Adams Inc.

Adams, Martha O. Alzheimer's Disease: Courage for Those Who Care. LC 98-48409. 1999. pap. 16.95 (0-8298-1304-7) Pilgrim OH.

Adams, Martin, et al. Mechanics: Complete Advanced Level Mathematics. (Illus.). 616p. (YA). (gr. 11 up). 1999. pap. 43.50 (0-7487-3559-3, Pub. by S Thornes Pubs) Trans-Atl Phila.

Adams, Martin D. Sensor Modelling, Design & Data Processing for Autonomous Navigation in Confined Environments. LC 98-36913. (Illus.). 180p. 1998. 28.00 (981-02-3496-1) World Scientific Pub.

Adams, Martin R. Studies in the Literary Backgrounds of English Radicalism, with Special Reference to the French Revolution, No. 5--5. LC 68-28591. (Illus.). 330p. 1968. reprint ed. lib. bdg. 65.00 (0-8371-0000-3, ADSL, Greenwood Pr) Greenwood.

Adams, Mary. Epistles from the Planet Photosynthesis. LC 98-36816. (Contemporary Poetry Ser.). 72p. 1999. 19.95 (0-8130-1670-3); pap. 19.95 (0-8130-1672-X) U Press Fla.

Adams, Mary, ed. Science in the Changing World. LC 68-29188. (Essay Index Reprint Ser.). 1977. reprint ed. 20.95 (0-8369-0136-3) Ayer.

Adams, Mary, et al. Ecosystem Matters: Activity & Resource Guide for Environmental Educators. (Illus.). 225p. (Orig.). (C). 1995. pap. text 40.00 (0-7881-2453-6) DIANE Pub.

Adams, Mary, jt. auth. see Chamberlain, Martha.

Adams, Mary, tr. see Steiner, Rudolf.

Adams, Mary A. Whoopi Goldberg. 72p. 1996. pap. text 7.95 (0-382-39497-6) Silver Burdett Pr.

— Whoopi Goldberg: From Street to Stardom. LC 92-23766. (Taking Part Ser.). (Illus.). 64p. (J). (gr. 3 up). 1993. lib. bdg. 13.95 (0-87518-562-2) Silver Burdett Pr.

***Adams, Mary Anne.** Led by the Holy Spirit. (Illus.). 1999. 5.95 (1-929486-01-4) SonRises Bk Pubg.

***Adams, Mary Beth, et al.** The Contribution of Soil Science to the Development of & Implementation of Criteria & Indicators of Sustainable Forest Management: Proceedings of a Symposium Sponsored by the S-7 & S-11 Divisions of the Soil Science Society of America, the USDA Forest Service Northeastern Forest Experiment Station, & the Woods Hole Research Center. LC 98-61724. (Illus.). 1998. write for info. (0-89118-831-2) Soil Sci Soc Am.

Adams, Mary J., ed. see Adams, W. Howard.

Adams, Mary L. The Trouble with Normal: Postwar Youth & the Making of Heterosexuality. LC 98-116033. (Studies in Gender & History). (Illus.). 256p. 1997. text 50.00 (*0-8020-4202-3*); pap. text 19.95 (*0-8020-8057-X*) U of Toronto Pr.

Adams, Marylou. Brighten up at Breakfast: Helpful Tips for Heavenly Bodies. LC 81-51601. (Illus.). 120p. (J). (gr. 2-7). 1981. spiral bd. 7.95 (*0-9606248-0-5*) Starbright.

Adams, Matt. Business Tips from the World's Oldest Profession: How to Run Your Business Like the Best Whore in Town. 2000. pap. 14.95 (*0-9665796-3-1*) Insiders Guide.

— Hustlers, Escorts & Porn Stars: The Insider's Guide to Male Prostitution in America. LC 98-93365. 300p. 1998. pap. 24.95 (*0-9665796-0-7*) Insiders Guide.

— Hustlers, Escorts & Porn Stars: The Insider's Guide to Male Prostitution in America. 2nd ed. 1999. pap. 16.95 (*0-9665796-2-3*) Insiders Guide.

*__Adams, Matt.__ Newspapers in the E-Age: Re-Engineering for Electronic Commerce. (Gastric Stimulation for Wannabe Dinosaurs Ser.: Vol. 2). 180p. 1999. pap. 19.95 (*0-9665796-6-6*) Insiders Guide.

Adams, Matt. Newspapers in the E-Age Vol. 1: Re-Engineering for Electronic Commerce. LC 99-64868. (Gastric Stimulation for Wannabe Dinosaurs Ser.). 240p. 1999. pap. 16.95 (*0-9665796-5-8*) Insiders Guide.

Adams, Matthew D., jt. auth. see Stasz, Bird.

Adams, Maurianne. Gay Lesbianism. 56p. (C). 1994. 17.95 (*0-7872-0040-9*) Kendall-Hunt.

— Sexism. 106p. (C). 1994. 21.95 (*0-7872-0039-5*) Kendall-Hunt.

Adams, Maurianne, ed. Promoting Diversity in College Classrooms: Innovative Responses for the Curriculum. LC 85-644763. (New Directions for Teaching & Learning Ser.: No. TL 52). 100p. 1992. pap., student ed. 22.00 (*1-55542-745-6*) Jossey-Bass.

*__Adams, Maurianne, et al, eds.__ Readings for Diversity & Social Justice: An Anthology on Racism, Sexism, Classism, Anti-Semitism, Heterosexism & Ableism. 496p. 2000. 85.00 (*0-415-92633-5*); pap. 29.99 (*0-415-92634-3*) Routledge.

Adams, Maurianne, et al, eds. Teaching for Diversity & Social Justice: A Sourcebook for Teachers & Trainers. LC 96-37658. 392p. (C). 1997. pap. 23.99 (*0-415-91057-9*) Routledge.

— Teaching for Diversity & Social Justice: A Sourcebook for Teachers & Trainers. LC 96-37658. 392p. (C). 1997. 70.00 (*0-415-91056-0*) Routledge.

Adams, Maurianne & Bracey, John H., eds. Strangers & Neighbors: Relations Between Blacks & Jews in the United States. LC 99-30346. (Illus.). 800p. 1999. 70.00 (*1-55849-235-6*); pap. 29.95 (*1-55849-236-4*) U of Mass Pr.

Adams, Maurice L., ed. Rotor Dynamical Instability: Presented at the Applied Mechanics, Bioengineering, & Fluids Engineering Conference, Houston, Texas, June 20-22, 1983. LC 83-71215. (AMD Ser.: Vol. 55). 106p. pap. 32.90 (*0-7837-0203-5*, 204049900017) Bks Demand.

*__Adams, McCrea.__ Tipi. LC 00-25458. (Native American Homes Ser.). (Illus.). 2000. write for info. (*1-55916-275-9*) Rourke Bk Co.

Adams, McCrea, jt. ed. see Hochman, Steve.

Adams Media Corporation Staff. Adams Executive Recruiters Almanac. 1998. pap. 16.95 (*1-58062-029-9*) Adams Media.

— Atlanta JobBank, 2000. 13th ed. (JobBank Two Thousand Ser.). 464p. 1999. pap. text 16.95 (*1-58062-228-3*) Adams Media.

*__Adams Media Corporation Staff.__ Chicago JobBank, 2000. 528p. 1999. pap. 16.95 (*1-58062-232-1*) Adams Media.

— Dallas-Fort Worth JobBank, 2000. (JobBank Two Thousand Ser.). 448p. 1999. pap. 16.95 (*1-58062-233-X*) Adams Media.

Adams Media Corporation Staff. The Everything Christmas Book: Stories, Songs, Food, Traditions, Revelry & More. expanded ed. (Illus.). 480p. 2000. pap. 15.00 (*1-55850-697-7*) Adams Media.

— The JobBank Guide to Employment Services, 2000-2001 Edition. (JobBank Ser.). 432p. 1999. 230.00 (*1-58062-227-5*) Adams Media.

— Jobbank Guide to Health Care Companies. 608p. 1998. pap. 16.95 (*1-58062-030-2*) Adams Media.

— Los Angeles JobBank, 2000. 512p. 1999. pap. 16.95 (*1-58062-229-1*) Adams Media.

— The Minneapolis-St. Paul JobBank. 11th ed. Dipietro, Marcie, ed. (Illus.). 304p. 1999. pap. 16.95 (*1-58062-151-1*) Adams Media.

*__Adams Media Corporation Staff.__ The National JobBank, 2000 Edition. LC 90-640981. (JobBank Two Thousand Ser.). 1152p. 1999. 370.00 (*1-58062-226-7*) Adams Media.

Adams Media Corporation Staff. New Jersey JobBank. Graber, Steven et al, eds. (Illus.). 352p. 1999. pap. 16.95 (*1-58062-140-6*) Adams Media.

*__Adams Media Corporation Staff.__ New York JobBank, 2000 (Metro) 640p. 1999. pap. 16.95 (*1-58062-230-5*) Adams Media.

— Philadelphia JobBank, 2000 (Metro) 464p. 1999. pap. 16.95 (*1-58062-242-9*) Adams Media.

— San Francisco Bay Area JobBank, 2000. 512p. 1999. pap. 16.95 (*1-58062-234-8*) Adams Media.

Adams Media Corporation Staff. Seattle JobBank, 2000. 400p. 1999. pap. 16.95 (*1-58062-238-0*) Adams Media.

*__Adams Media Corporation Staff.__ Virginia JobBank. 3rd ed. 400p. 1999. pap. 16.95 (*1-58062-243-7*) Adams Media.

Adams Media Corporation Staff. Washington DC JobBank, 2000 (Metro) 480p. 1999. pap. 16.95 (*1-58062-231-3*) Adams Media.

*__Adams Media Corporation Staff, contrib. by.__ The Carolina JobBank. 6th ed. 368p. 1999. pap. 16.95 (*1-58062-240-2*) Adams Media.

— The Ohio JobBank. 10th ed. (Illus.). 400p. 1999. pap. 16.95 (*1-58062-241-0*) Adams Media.

Adams Media Corporation Staff, ed. Adams Cover Letter Almanac. (Almanacs Ser.). 768p. 1995. pap. 12.95 (*1-55850-497-4*) Adams Media.

— Adams Cover Letter Almanac & Disk. LC 96-7853. (Adams Almanacs). 762p. 1996. pap. 19.95 incl. 3.5 hd (*1-55850-619-5*) Adams Media.

— Adams Job Interview Almanac & CD-ROM. 1997. pap. text 19.95 incl. cd-rom (*1-55850-709-4*) Adams Media.

— Adams Resume Almanac & Disk. LC 96-15500. (Almanacs Sers). 762p. 1996. pap. 19.95 incl. 3.5 hd (*1-55850-618-7*) Adams Media.

— Connecticut JobBank: 1999 Edition. (JobBank Ser.). 320p. 1998. pap. 16.95 (*1-58062-082-5*) Adams Media.

— Detroit JobBank. 9th ed. 352p. 1999. pap. 16.95 (*1-58062-150-3*) Adams Media.

— The JobBank Guide to Computer & High-Tech Companies. 2nd ed. 704p. 1999. pap. 17.95 (*1-58062-139-2*) Adams Media.

— Las Vegas JobBank. 2nd ed. (JobBank Ser.). 304p. 1998. pap. 16.95 (*1-58062-031-0*) Adams Media.

— Missouri JobBank: 1999 Edition. 2nd ed. (JobBank Ser.). 336p. 1998. pap. 16.95 (*1-58062-083-3*) Adams Media.

— Pittsburgh JobBank: 1999 Edition. 2nd ed. (JobBank Ser.). 304p. 1998. pap. 16.95 (*1-58062-094-9*) Adams Media.

— The Portland, OR JobBank. 2nd ed. (JobBank Ser.). 320p. 1998. pap. 16.95 (*1-58062-032-9*) Adams Media.

— Tennessee JobBank. 4th ed. (JobBank Ser.). 320p. 1998. pap. 16.95 (*1-58062-039-6*) Adams Media.

— 365 Women Who Made a Difference. 1996. pap. text 6.95 (*1-55850-641-1*) Adams Media.

— 365 Women's Reflections on Men. 1996. pap. text 6.95 (*1-55850-642-X*) Adams Media.

Adams Media Corporation Staff, ed. see Adams, Bob, et al.

Adams Media Corporation Staff, ed. see DeVito, Carlo.

Adams Media Corporation Staff, jt. ed. see Ehrenstein, Emily.

Adams Media Corporation Staff, ed. see Segaloff, Nat.

Adams Media Corporation Staff, jt. ed. see Verucki, Peter.

*__Adams Media Editors.__ Adams Electronic Job Search Almanac 2001. 320p. 2000. pap. 10.95 (*1-58062-426-X*) Adams Media.

— Adams Jobs Almanac 2001. 952p. 2000. pap. 16.95 (*1-58062-443-X*) Adams Media.

— Mr. Cheap's Chicago: Shopping Bargains, Factory Outlets, Off-Price Stores, Discount Stores, Cheap Eats, Cheap Places to Stay & Affordable Fun Things to Do. 2nd ed. (Mr. Cheap's Ser.). 320p. 2000. pap. 9.95 (*1-58062-374-3*) Adams Media.

*__Adams Media Editors, ed.__ Adams Electronic Job Search Almanac 2000. 320p. 1999. pap. 10.95 (*1-58062-221-6*) Adams Media.

— Adams Jobs Almanac 2000. 952p. 1999. pap. 16.95 (*1-58062-220-8*) Adams Media.

Adams, Melinda, ed. see Marieb, Elaine N.

Adams, Melodie. What about Charlie? (Romance Ser.). 1993. pap. 2.69 (*0-373-08934-1*, 5-08934-7) Silhouette.

— What about Charlie? large type ed. LC 93-31003. 204p. 1994. lib. bdg. 14.95 (*0-7862-0124-X*) Thorndike Pr.

Adams, Mia. The Excyles. LC 96-111162. 353p. 1996. pap. 16.95 (*0-9649905-0-4*) Excelta Pubng.

The EXCYLES is an extraordinary true story about Mia Adams whose contacts with extraterrestrials & United States Government Intelligence Agents have changed her life forever! In 1988, conscious contact with alien intelligences catapulted her on a search for answers to questions about herself. As her personal spiritual journey unfolded, many incredible miracles & synchronicities manifested. Especially amazing is the romantic relationship that evolved with a government agent which yielded shocking answers & mysterious results. Included within these pages is a secret report written by the government agent outlining in detail the agendas of certain alien confederations on Earth & the special organized intelligence agencies' networks created to deal with them. Another main focus in the book is Mia's contacts & relationship to a group of interdimensional beings & their connection with a human group on Earth they call the Excyles. Cosmic revelations, expectations & insights are given to Mia in dialogue by Zarg & others from this interdimensional level. This is a unique, one of a kind true story that should be read by all those who care about the future of the United States of America & the transformation of planet Earth. To order: Excelta Publishing, Inc., P.O. Box 4530, Ft. Lauderdale, FL 33338. 954-561-8580. *Publisher Paid Annotation.*

Adams, Michael. Hardscrabbe: The Wet Mountain Poems. 30p. (Orig.). 1997. pap. 5.00 (*0-945884-15-X*) Longhand Pr.

— How to Tie Ties. 1999. 9.95 (*0-8069-6591-6*) Sterling.

*__Adams, Michael.__ Opencable Architecture. 400p. 1999. 50.00 (*1-57870-135-X*) Cisco Press.

Adams, Michael. Who's Afraid of Virginia Woolf? (Barron's Book Notes Ser.). 1985. pap. 2.50 (*0-8120-3549-5*) Barron.

— William Shakespeare's Othello. (Barron's Book Notes Ser.). (C). 1984. pap. 3.95 (*0-8120-3434-1*) Barron.

Adams, Michael, ed. The Middle East. rev. ed. LC 86-29274. (Handbooks to the Modern World Ser.). 883p. reprint ed. pap. 200.00 (*0-7837-1575-7*, 204186700024) Bks Demand.

Adams, Michael, et al. Jukeboxes. LC 95-45129. (Illus.). 144p. 1995. 35.00 (*0-88740-876-1*) Schiffer.

Adams, Michael, tr. see Galvez, Alfonso.

Adams, Michael, tr. see Galvez, Alfonso & Society of Jesus Christ the Priest Staff.

Adams, Michael, tr. see Members of the Faculty of Theology of the Universi & Casciaro, Jose M.

Adams, Michael A., et al. Shellfish & Public Health: Lead, Cadmium, Chromium, Arsenic, & Nickel in Shellfish. (Illus.). 212p. (Orig.). (C). 1994. pap. text 50.00 (*0-7881-0588-4*) DIANE Pub.

Adams, Michael C. The Best War Ever: America & World War II. LC 93-4364. (American Moment Ser.). (Illus.). 208p. (C). 1993. text 38.95 (*0-8018-4696-X*); pap. text 14.95 (*0-8018-4697-8*) Johns Hopkins.

— Fighting for Defeat: Union Military Failure in the East, 1861-1865. LC 91-42194. Orig. Title: Our Masters the Rebels. xiv, 256p. 1992. reprint ed. pap. 9.95 (*0-8032-1035-3*, Bison Books) U of Nebr Pr.

— The Great Adventure: Male Desire & the Coming of World War I. LC 89-46339. (Illus.). 196p. 1990. 9.25 (*0-253-30136-X*) Ind U Pr.

— The Great Adventure: Male Desire & the Coming of World War I. LC 89-46339. (Illus.). 183p. Date not set. reprint ed. pap. 56.80 (*0-608-20576-1*, 205449100002) Bks Demand.

— Our Masters the Rebels: A Speculation on Union Military Failure in the East, 1861-1865. LC 78-17107. 270p. reprint ed. pap. 83.70 (*0-7837-2213-3*, 205730300004) Bks Demand.

Adams, Michael H. Single-Camera Video: The Creative Challenge. 384p. (C). 1994. text. write for info. (*0-697-27934-0*) Brown & Benchmark.

Adams, Michael H. & Massey, Kimberley K. Introduction to Radio: Production & Programming. 288p. (C). 1994. text. write for info. (*0-697-15354-1*) Brown & Benchmark.

*__Adams, Michael Henry.__ Harlem: Lost & Found. (Illus.). 272p. 2000. 65.00 (*1-58093-070-0*, Pub. by Monacelli Pr) Penguin Putnam.

Adams, Michael V. The Multicultural Imagination: Race, Color, & the Unconscious. LC 96-7561. 296p. (C). 1996. pap. 27.99 (*0-415-13838-8*) Routledge.

— The Multicultural Imagination: Race, Color, & the Unconscious. LC 96-7561. (Illus.). 296p. (C). 1996 85.00 (*0-415-13837-X*) Routledge.

Adams, Michael W., et al, eds. Advances in Protein Chemistry Vol. 48: Enzymes & Proteins from Hyperthermophilic Microorganisms. (Illus.). 509p. 1996. text 90.00 (*0-12-034248-0*) Acad Pr.

Adams, Michael W. & Kelly, Robert M., eds. Biocatalysis at Extreme Temperatures: Enzyme Systems Near & Above 100 Degrees C. LC 92-16399. (ACS Symposium Ser.: Vol. 498). (Illus.). 215p. 1992. text 65.00 (*0-8412-2458-7*, Pub. by Am Chemical) OUP.

*__Adams, Michele & Russo, Gia.__ Baby Showers: Ideas & Recipes for the Perfect Party. LC 99-37291. (Illus.). 2000. pap. 14.95 (*0-8118-2678-3*) Chronicle Bks.

— Wedding Showers: Ideas & Recipes for the Perfect Party. LC 99-40620. (Illus.). 120p. 2000. pap. 14.95 (*0-8118-2677-5*) Chronicle Bks.

Adams, Mignon & Beck, Jeffrey, compiled by. User Surveys in College Libraries. (CLIP Note Ser.: No. 23). 118 p. (Orig.). (C). 1995. pap. 25.00 (*0-8389-7825-8*) Assn Coll & Res Libs.

Adams, Mike. Play Better Golf for Women. LC 97-72664. 1997. 27.95 (*0-8050-5694-7*) H Holt & Co.

Adams, Mike & Tomasi. The LAWs of the Golf Swing: Body-Type Your Swing & Master Your Game. LC 98-10674. (Illus.). 240p. 1998. 25.00 (*0-06-270815-3*) HarpC.

Adams, Mike & Tomasi, T. J. Play Better Golf: Lessons from the Academy of Golf at PGA National. 176p. 1996. 24.95 (*1-885203-35-7*) Jrny Editions.

*__Adams, Mike & Tomasi, T. J.__ Play Golf for Juniors: The Academy of Golf at PGA National. LC GV966.3.A33 2000. (Illus.). 144p. (YA). (gr. 5-12). 2000. pap. 19.95 (*1-55209-446-4*) Firefly Bks Ltd.

*__Adams, Mike, et al.__ Break 100 Now: From Hacker to Golfer in Just 90 Days. LC 97-26636. 176p. 1998. pap. 11.95 (*0-06-273480-6*, Perennial) HarperTrade.

Adams, Mike, et al. Play Better Golf for Seniors. LC 98-5945. (Illus.). 160p. 1999. 29.95 (*0-8050-5920-2*) H Holt & Co.

Adams, Mike J. & Barnett, Neil, eds. Chemometrics in Analytical Spectroscopy. (Royal Society of Chemistry Analytical Spectroscopy Monographs). 220p. 1995. 69.95 (*0-85404-555-4*, R4555) CRC Pr.

Adams, Milton, ed. see Briggs, Thomas.

Adams, Milton, ed. see Forrester, Margaret.

Adams, Milton, ed. see Konopka, Gisela.

Adams, Milton, ed. see Larson, Kathy.

Adams, Milton, ed. see Meadley, Walter.

Adams, Milton E., ed. see Azzam, Fouad.

Adams, Milton E., ed. see Brown, Kathy.

Adams, Milton E., ed. see Schaub, Janette.

Adams, Monni. Designs for Living: Symbolic Communication in African Art. 152p. (C). 1982. pap. 12.00 (*0-674-19969-3*) HUP.

Adams, Moody. How the Clinton Clergy Corrupted a President. 208p. 1999. pap. 11.99 (*0-937422-44-4*, 1039, Olive Pr SC) Midnight Call.

*__Adams, Moody.__ The Phantom's Dark Force. 230p. 1999. pap. 12.99 (*0-937422-47-9*, 1042, Olive Pr SC) Midnight Call.

Adams, Moody. The Titanic's Last Hero: John Harper: A Hero on the Titanic. 156p. 1997. pap. 9.99 (*0-937422-39-8*, 2171, Olive Pr SC) Midnight Call.

Adams, Mrs. John. Letters of Mrs. John Adams. 1988. reprint ed. lib. bdg. 75.00 (*0-7812-1401-7*) Rprt Serv.

*__Adams, N.__ Horrorscope (Special) 2000. mass mkt. 1.99 (*0-06-106263-4*) HarpC.

Adams, N. M., jt. auth. see Poole, A. L.

Adams, Nancy. Common Seaweeds of New Zealand. (Illus.). 96p. 1997. pap. 24.95 (*0-908812-70-1*, Pub. by Canterbury Univ) Accents Pubns.

— A Peacock Feather. LC 95-95219. (Illus.). 56p. 1995. 10.00 (*0-9655909-0-9*) N D Adams.

— Quick Bread Cook Book. 1996. ring bd. 6.95 (*1-885590-21-0*) Golden West Pub.

Adams, Nancy & Carter, Patricia. So Close. 80p. (Orig.). 1996. pap. 10.00 (*0-932616-55-0*, NPS100) Brick Hse Bks.

Adams, Nancy & Childs, Leigh. Word Sponges. 112p. 1997. pap. text 10.95 (*0-86651-195-4*) Seymour Pubns.

Adams, Nancy, jt. auth. see Childs, Leigh.

Adams, Nancy M. Seaweeds of New Zealand: An Illustrated Guide. (Illus.). 360p. (C). 1994. 79.95 (*0-908812-21-3*, Pub. by Canterbury Univ) Accents Pubns.

Adams, Nate. Energizers. 192p. (YA). 1994. pap. 9.99 (*0-310-37371-9*) Zondervan.

— Nine Character Traits Separating the Men from the Boys: Encouragement for Men Trying to Grow Up. LC 94-8449. 256p. 1994. pap. 9.99 (*1-55661-458-6*) Bethany Hse.

Adams, Nathaniel. Annals of Portsmouth. 400p. 1992. reprint ed. lib. bdg. 39.00 (*0-8328-2238-8*) Higginson Bk Co.

— Annals of Portsmouth, New Hampshire: Comprising a Period of Two Hundred Years from the First Settlement of the Town with Biographical Sketches... 412p. 1989. reprint ed. pap. 25.00 (*1-55613-225-5*) Heritage Bk.

Adams, Neal & Kuhlman, Larry. Kicks & Blowout Control. 2nd ed. LC 94-1884. 421p. 1994. 25.00 (*0-87814-419-6*) PennWell Bks.

Adams, Neal J. Drilling Engineering: A Complete Well Planning Approach. LC 84-1110. 976p. 1985. 125.95 (*0-87814-265-7*, P4366) PennWell Bks.

Adams, Nehemiah. Sable Cloud: A Southern Tale with Northern Comments. LC 78-138329. (Black Heritage Library Collection). 1977. 25.95 (*0-8369-8721-7*) Ayer.

— South-Side View of Slavery. LC 74-83939. (Black Heritage Library Collection). 1977. 17.95 (*0-8369-8501-X*) Ayer.

— The Works of Nehemiah Adams, 1806-1878, Set. 1987. reprint ed. lib. bdg. 500.00 (*0-685-18566-4*) Rprt Serv.

Adams, Neil. Greatest Batman Stories Ever Told. LC 89-212319. (DC Comics Collection). 352p. 1997. mass mkt. 15.95 (*0-930289-66-8*, Pub. by Warner Bks) Little.

Adams, Nellie F. & Walton, Bertha F. Fox Cousins by the Dozens: (Includes Allied Lines Aldridge, Ballard, Berryman, Brookshire, Conkwright, Fish Franklin, Haggard, Haley, Hughes, Parrish, Noe, Oliver, Todd, Tuttle, Vivion) 408p. 1992. reprint ed. pap. 59.50 (*0-8328-2423-2*); reprint ed. lib. bdg. 69.50 (*0-8328-2422-4*) Higginson Bk Co.

Adams, Nelson B., ed. see Northup, George T.

Adams, Nicholas, jt. auth. see Pepper, Simon.

Adams, Nicholas, ed. see Frommel, Christoph L.

Adams, Nicholas, jt. ed. see Frommel, Christoph L.

Adams, Nicholas D. Warehouse & Distribution Automation Handbook. 560p. 1996. 89.95 (*0-07-000400-5*) McGraw.

Adams, Nicholson, et al. Panorama de la Literatura Espanola. (SPA.). (C). 1994. pap. text 21.95 (*0-942566-17-3*) LinguaText.

Adams, Nicholson B. The Romantic Dramas of Garcia Gutierrez. 1976. lib. bdg. 59.95 (*0-8490-2542-7*) Gordon Pr.

— The Romantic Dramas of Garcia Gutierrez. 149p. 1922. 1.00 (*0-318-14303-8*) Hispanic Inst.

Adams, Nicholson B., et al, eds. Espana en Su Literatura. 3rd ed. (SPA.). (C). 1991. pap. 37.50 (*0-393-96060-9*) Norton.

Adams, Nicholson B., et al, eds. Hispanoamerica En Su Literatura. (C). 1965. pap. text 22.25 (*0-393-09660-2*) Norton.

Adams, Nicholson B., et al. Hispanoamerica En Su Literatura. 2nd ed. (C). 1993. pap. 37.50 (*0-393-96061-7*, Norton Paperbks) Norton.

Adams, Nigel. The Holden Mine: From Discovery to Production, 1896-1938. 87p. 1981. pap. 5.00 (*0-917048-53-9*) Wash St Hist Soc.

Adams, Nigel & Babcock, Lucia M., eds. Advances in Gas Phase Ion Chemistry, Vol. 3. 1998. 109.50 (*0-7623-0204-6*) Jai Pr.

Adams, Nigel, ed. see Babcock, Lucia M.

Adams, Nigel G. & Babcock, Lucia M., eds. Advances in Gas Phase Ion Chemistry, Vol. 4. 1999. 109.50 (*0-7623-0438-3*) Jai Pr.

Adams, Noah. Piano Lessons: Music, Love & True Adventures. 272p. 1997. pap. 12.95 (*0-385-31821-9*, Delta Trade) Dell.

*__Adams, Noland.__ Corvette: American Legend, 1958-1960. (Illus.). 256p. 1999. 24.95 (*1-880524-36-8*, 128443AP) Cars & Parts.

Adams, Noland. Corvette American Legend Vol. 1: The Beginning. (Illus.). 261p. 1996. boxed set 24.95 (*1-880524-20-1*) Cars & Parts.

— Corvette American Legend Vol. 2: 1954-55 Production. (Illus.). 206p. 1997. boxed set 24.95 (*1-880524-22-8*) Cars & Parts.

— Corvette American Legend, 1956. (Illus.). 208p. 1998. boxed set 24.95 (*1-880524-28-7*) Cars & Parts.

A

— Corvette Restoration & Technical Guide, 2 vols. 2nd ed. (Illus.). 1987. write for info. (*0-318-60843-X*) Auto Quarterly.
— Corvette Restoration & Technical Guide Vol. 1: 1953 - 1963. 2nd ed. (Illus.). 424p. 1987. 69.95 (*0-915038-57-9*, 3AQ0051) Auto Quarterly.
— Corvette Restoration & Technical Guide Vol. 2: 1963 - 1967, 2 vols. 2nd ed. LC 80-65894. (Illus.). 448p. 1987. 69.95 (*0-915038-42-0*, 3AQ0044) Auto Quarterly.
Adams, Norma & Cady, Foster, eds. Modeling Growth & Yield of Multipurpose Tree Species. 57p. 1988. pap. 10.00 (*0-933595-17-4*) Winrock Intl.
Adams, Norman. Haunted Scotland. (Illus.). 192p. 1998. pap. 13.95 (*1-85158-952-X*, Pub. by Mainstream Pubng) Trafalgar.
Adams, Norman & Singer, Joe. Drawing Animals. (Illus.). 160p. 1989. pap. 18.95 (*0-8230-1366-9*) Watsn-Guptill.
Adams, O. R. Adams' Lameness in Horses. 5th ed. LC 98-7679. 1998. write for info. (*0-683-07981-6*) Lppncott W & W.
Adams, Oscar S., jt. auth. see Deetz, Charles H.
Adams, Otto U. The Old Gardener. 13p. 1985. pap. 2.00 (*0-87770-372-8*) Ye Galleon.
Adams, P. Experiencing World History. text 45.00 (*0-8147-0690-8*); pap. text 20.00 (*0-8147-0691-6*) NYU Pr.
Adams, P. Wally Whale. (J). (ps-k). 1998. 9.99 (*0-85953-488-X*) Childs Play.
Adams, P. The Child's Play Museum. LC 90-46592. 24p. (J). (ps-2). 1976. 6.99 (*0-85953-094-9*, Pub. by Childs Play) Random House.
Adams, P. F., et al. Health Risk Behaviors among Our Nation's Youth: United States, 1992. LC 95-8593. (Vital & Health Statistics Ser.: Series 10, No. 192). 1995. write for info. (*0-08-406050-6*) Natl Ctr Health Stats.
Adams, P. F., jt. auth. see Griffiths, J. M.
Adams, P. H. & Entwistle, P. F. An Annotated Bibliography of Gilpinia Hercyniae (Hartig) European Spruce. 1981. 30.00 (*0-85074-051-7*) St Mut.
Adams, Pam. Alf 'n Bet's Handwriting Book. (Illus.). (J). (ps-3). 1993. pap. 4.99 (*0-85953-168-6*) Childs Play.
— All Kinds: Race & Colour. LC 90-45703. (Who Cares Ser.). 32p. (J). (gr. 4 up). 1990. 5.99 (*0-85953-363-8*); pap. 3.99 (*0-85953-353-0*) Childs Play.
— Away in a Manger. (J). 1996. 2.99 (*0-85953-923-7*) Childs Play.
— Baby Bubbles. 10p. (J). (gr. 3 up). 1981. 4.99 (*0-85953-265-8*) Childs Play.
— Croaky. 1999. pap. text 9.99 (*0-85953-614-9*) Childs Play.
— Disabled People. (Who Cares Ser.). 32p. (J). (gr. 4 up). 1990. 5.99 (*0-85953-361-1*); pap. 3.99 (*0-85953-351-4*) Childs Play.
— Dolly Dolphin's Play School. 10p. (J). 1981. 5.99 (*0-85953-266-6*) Childs Play.
— Elderly People. LC 90-45702. (Who Cares Ser.). 32p. (J). (gr. 4 up). 1990. 5.99 (*0-85953-362-X*); pap. 3.99 (*0-85953-352-2*) Childs Play.
— The Fairground. (Panorama Ser.). (Illus.). 32p. (J). (ps). 1984. 8.99 (*0-85953-194-5*, Pub. by Childs Play) Random House.
— First Day. (J). 1996. 2.99 (*0-85953-922-9*) Childs Play.
— First Nowell. (J). 1996. 2.99 (*0-85953-921-0*) Childs Play.
— The Frog. 44p. (J). 1985. 4.99 (*0-85953-259-3*) Childs Play.
— Froglet's Bathtime. (Illus.). 8p. (J). (gr. 3 up). 1981. 6.99 (*0-85953-329-8*) Childs Play.
— Gloria, Hosana. (J). 1996. 2.99 (*0-85953-924-5*) Childs Play.
— The Green-Eyed Monster. 32p. (J). (gr. 4 up). 1985. 6.99 (*0-85953-195-3*) Childs Play.
— Helpful Shoelace. LC 90-49236. 20p. (J). 1989. 7.99 (*0-85953-297-6*) Childs Play.
— The Helpful Shoelace. (FRE.). 20p. (Orig.). (J). 1989. 11.99 (*0-85953-452-9*); 11.99 (*0-85953-827-3*); 11.99 (*0-85953-563-0*) Childs Play.
— House That Jack Built. LC 99-57510. 1999. pap. text 19.99 (*0-85953-638-6*) Childs Play.
***Adams, Pam.** Kingfisher. 1999. pap. text 1.99 (*0-85953-863-X*) Childs Play.
Adams, Pam. Law & Order. LC 90-25106. (Who Cares Ser.). 32p. (J). 1990. pap. 3.99 (*0-85953-354-9*) Childs Play.
— Law & Order. (Who Cares Ser.). (ITA.). (J). 1990. pap. 3.99 (*0-85953-584-3*); pap. 3.99 (*0-85953-839-7*) Childs Play.
— Lift the Lid. (Toilet Training Ser.). (J). 1995. pap. 4.99 (*0-85953-722-6*) Childs Play.
— Lucky. (Illus.). 10p. (ps-1). 1999. pap. text 9.99 (*0-85953-613-0*) Childs Play.
— Magic Shoelaces. (FRE., Illus.). 32p. (J). 1989. pap. 3.99 (*0-85953-471-5*); pap. 3.99 (*0-85953-820-6*); pap. 3.99 (*0-85953-572-X*) Childs Play.
— Mrs. Honey's Dream. LC 92-40124. (Illus.). 32p. (J). 1993. pap. 3.99 (*0-85953-332-8*) Childs Play.
— Mrs. Honey's Glasses. LC 93-12368. (Illus.). 32p. (J). (ps-3). 1993. 7.99 (*0-85953-757-9*); pap. 3.99 (*0-85953-758-7*) Childs Play.
— Mrs. Honey's Hat. LC 90-46604. (Illus.). 24p. (J). (ps-2). 1980. 7.99 (*0-85953-099-X*, Pub. by Childs Play); pap. 3.99 (*0-85953-325-5*, Pub. by Childs Play) Random House.
— Mrs. Honey's Hat. (GRE.). (J). 1993. pap. 3.99 (*0-85953-821-4*) Childs Play.
— Mrs. Honey's Hat - Giant Lap Book. 32p. (J). (gr. k-3). 26.99 (*0-85953-829-X*) Childs Play.
***Adams, Pam.** Mrs. Honey's Hat Lap Book. LC 99-57507. 32p. (J). (ps-3). 1999. 26.99 (*0-85953-814-1*) Childs Play.
Adams, Pam. Mrs. Honey's Holiday. LC 92-41886. (Illus.). 32p. (J). 1993. 7.99 (*0-85953-755-2*); pap. 3.99 (*0-85953-756-0*) Childs Play.
— Myst Express. LC 90-45758. 24p. (J). 1989. 6.99 (*0-85953-180-5*) Childs Play.
— Noah's Ark. (Bath Bks.). 10p. (J). (gr. 3 up). 1981. 7.99 (*0-85953-267-4*) Childs Play.
***Adams, Pam.** Noah's Ark. 12p. 1999. 8.99 (*0-85953-586-X*) Childs Play.
— Noah's Ark, Giant Ed. 1999. 19.99 (*0-85953-579-7*) Childs Play.
Adams, Pam. The Ocean. (Panorama Ser.). 32p. (J). (ps). 1984. 9.99 (*0-85953-193-7*, Pub. by Childs Play) Random House.
— Oh, Soldier! Soldier! LC 90-48946. 16p. (J). (ps-3). 1990. pap. 6.99 (*0-85953-092-2*, Pub. by Childs Play) Random House.
— Old MacDonald. LC 99-57504. 1999. pap. text 19.99 (*0-85953-637-8*) Childs Play.
— On a Cold & Frosty Morning. (Soap Opera Ser.). 8p. (J). (gr. 4 up). 1990. 6.99 (*0-85953-442-1*) Childs Play.
***Adams, Pam.** Owl. 1999. pap. text 1.99 (*0-85953-862-1*) Childs Play.
Adams, Pam. Owls Number School. LC 90-48662. 24p. (J). 1989. 9.99 (*0-85953-166-X*) Childs Play.
***Adams, Pam.** Parrot. 1999. pap. text 1.99 (*0-85953-861-3*) Childs Play.
Adams, Pam. Playmates. (Baby Carriage Ser.). (Illus.). 8p. (J). (gr. 3 up). 1991. 6.99 (*0-85953-449-9*) Childs Play.
— Pocket Chameleon. (J). 1996. bds. 2.99 (*0-85953-918-0*) Childs Play.
— Pocket Earwig. (J). 1996. bds. 2.99 (*0-85953-916-4*) Childs Play.
— Pocket Fox. (J). 1996. bds. 2.99 (*0-85953-912-1*) Childs Play.
— Pocket Koala. (J). 1996. bds. 2.99 (*0-85953-917-2*) Childs Play.
— Pocket Mouse. (J). 1996. bds. 2.99 (*0-85953-911-3*) Childs Play.
— Pocket Panda. (J). 1996. bds. 2.99 (*0-85953-915-6*) Childs Play.
— Pocket Pony. (J). 1996. bds. 2.99 (*0-85953-913-X*) Childs Play.
— Pocket Python. (J). 1996. bds. 2.99 (*0-85953-910-5*) Childs Play.
— The Red-Eyed Monster. 32p. (J). (gr. 4 up). 1985. 6.99 (*0-85953-196-1*) Childs Play.
— Sing a Song of Sixpence. (J). 1998. 6.99 (*0-85953-627-0*) Childs Play.
— Sing a Song of Sixpence. LC 99-57505. 1999. pap. text 19.99 (*0-85953-639-4*) Childs Play.
— Six in a Bath. (Soap Opera Ser.). 8p. (J). (gr. 4 up). 1990. 4.99 (*0-85953-443-X*) Childs Play.
***Adams, Pam.** Snail. 1999. pap. text 1.99 (*0-85953-860-5*) Childs Play.
Adams, Pam. Ten Beads Tall. LC 90-1964. (Bead Frame Ser.). 16p. (J). 1989. 7.99 (*0-85953-242-9*); 11.99 (*0-85953-456-1*) Childs Play.
— This Is the House That Jack Built. LC 90-46922. (Illus.). 16p. (Orig.). (J). (ps-3). 1972. 13.99 (*0-85953-076-0*) Childs Play.
— This Old Man. LC 99-57503. (Illus.). (J). 2000. pap. text 19.99 (*0-85953-636-X*) Childs Play.
— Tingaling. (Illus.). 8p. (J). (gr. 4 up). 1981. 6.99 (*0-85953-328-X*) Childs Play.
— Ups & Downs. 44p. (J). (gr. 4 up). 1985. 4.99 (*0-85953-257-7*) Childs Play.
— Wally Whale & Friends. 10p. (J). (gr. 4 up). 1981. pap. 5.99 (*0-85953-268-2*) Childs Play.
— What on Earth? LC 90-45581. 24p. (J). 1989. 6.99 (*0-85953-165-1*) Childs Play.
— Who Cares about Law & Order? 32p. 1995. 7.99 (*0-85953-364-6*) Childs Play.
Adams, Pam. Alf 'N Bet. LC 92-14641. (J). 1992. 4.99 (*0-85953-167-8*) Childs Play.
— Day Dreams. LC 90-45583. (Imagination Ser.). 32p. (Orig.). (J). (ps-2). 1978. pap. 9.99 (*0-85953-105-8*, Pub. by Childs Play); pap. 3.99 (*0-85953-082-5*, Pub. by Childs Play) Random House.
— The Gingerbread Man. LC 90-45757. 24p. (J). (ps-2). 1981. 6.99 (*0-85953-107-4*, Pub. by Childs Play) Random House.
— The Gingerbread Man. (ITA.). (J). 1981. 9.99 (*0-85953-560-6*) Childs Play.
— How Many? (Motivation Ser.). 16p. (Orig.). (J). (ps-2). 1975. pap. 1.99 (*0-85953-045-0*, Pub. by Childs Play) Random House.
— If I Weren't Me. LC 90-46184. 24p. (J). (ps-2). 1981. 6.99 (*0-85953-108-2*, Pub. by Childs Play) Random House.
— Letters & Words. (Motivation Ser.). 16p. (Orig.). (J). (ps-2). 1975. pap. 1.99 (*0-85953-046-9*, Pub. by Childs Play) Random House.
— Magic. LC 90-46518. (Imagination Ser.). 32p. (Orig.). (J). (ps-2). 1978. 9.99 (*0-85953-104-X*, Pub. by Childs Play); pap. 3.99 (*0-85953-081-7*, Pub. by Childs Play) Random House.
— Magic. (Imagination Ser.). (SPA.). (Orig.). (J). 1978. pap. 6.99 (*0-85953-971-7*) Childs Play.
— Oh Soldier Soldier. (Books with Holes Ser.). (ITA.). (J). 1975. pap. 6.99 (*0-85953-594-0*) Childs Play.
— Oh, Soldier! Soldier! LC 90-48946. (Books with Holes Ser.). 16p. (J). (ps-2). 1978. 13.99 (*0-85953-093-0*, Pub. by Childs Play) Random House.
— Old MacDonald Had a Farm. (Books with Holes Ser.). (FRE.). 16p. (J). 1975. pap. 6.99 (*0-85953-461-8*); pap. 6.99 (*0-85953-592-4*) Childs Play.
— Old MacDonald Had a Farm. LC 90-46923. (Books with Holes Ser.). 16p. (J). (ps-2). 1975. pap. 6.99 (*0-85953-053-1*, Pub. by Childs Play) Random House.
— Pocket Bunny. (Pocket Pals Ser.). (J). 1995. bds. 2.99 (*0-85953-907-5*) Childs Play.
— Pocket Frog. (Pocket Pals Ser.). (J). 1995. bds. 2.99 (*0-85953-908-3*) Childs Play.
— Pocket Kitten. (Pocket Pals Ser.). (J). 1995. bds. 2.99 (*0-85953-905-9*) Childs Play.
— Pocket Puppy. (Pocket Pals Ser.). (J). 1995. bds. 2.99 (*0-85953-906-7*) Childs Play.
— Same & Different. (Motivation Ser.). 16p. (Orig.). (J). (ps-3). 1975. pap. 1.99 (*0-85953-043-4*, Pub. by Childs Play) Random House.
— There Were Ten in the Bed. LC 90-45580. 24p. (J). (ps-2). 1979. 6.99 (*0-85953-095-7*, Pub. by Childs Play) Random House.
— There Were Ten in the Bed. (GRE.). (J). 1979. 9.99 (*0-85953-826-5*); 9.99 (*0-85953-561-4*) Childs Play.
— This Is the House That Jack Built. (Books with Holes Ser.). (ITA.). (Orig.). (J). 1977. pap. 6.99 (*0-85953-593-2*) Childs Play.
— This Is the House That Jack Built. LC 90-46922. (Books with Holes Ser.). 16p. (Orig.). (J). (ps-2). 1977. pap. 6.99 (*0-85953-075-2*, Pub. by Childs Play) Random House.
— This Old Man. (Books with Holes Ser.). (FRE.). 16p. (J). 1974. pap. 6.99 (*0-85953-462-6*); pap. 6.99 (*0-85953-591-6*) Childs Play.
— This Old Man. LC 90-34327. (Books with Holes Ser.). 16p. (J). (ps-2). 1974. pap. 6.99 (*0-85953-026-4*, Pub. by Childs Play) Random House.
— What Is It? (Motivation Ser.). (Orig.). (J). (ps-2). 1975. pap. 1.99 (*0-85953-044-2*, Pub. by Childs Play) Random House.
Adams, Pam & Jones, Ceri. I Thought I Saw. LC 90-45582. (Imagination Ser.). (Illus.). (Orig.). (J). (ps-2). 1974. 6.99 (*0-85953-074-4*, Pub. by Childs Play); pap. 3.99 (*0-85953-029-9*, Pub. by Childs Play) Random House.
— I Thought I Saw. (Imagination Ser.). (SPA.). (Orig.). (J). 1974. pap. 6.99 (*0-85953-970-9*) Childs Play.
Adams, Pam & Jones, Ceri. A Book of Ghosts. LC 90-45584. (Imagination Ser.). 32p. (Orig.). (J). (ps-2). 1974. pap. 3.99 (*0-85953-028-0*, Pub. by Childs Play) Random House.
Adams, Pam & Twin, Michael. Rabbits Golden Rule Book. LC 90-2677. 24p. (J). 1989. 9.99 (*0-85953-298-4*) Childs Play.
Adams, Pam & Twinn, Michael. Rabbit's Golden Rule Book. (ITA.). (J). 1989. 9.99 (*0-85953-562-2*) Childs Play.
Adams, Pam, jt. auth. see Presland, John.
Adams, Pam, jt. auth. see Twinn, Michael.
Adams, Pam, jt. illus. see Taback, Simms.
Adams, Pamela J., et al. Flight Nursing Core Curriculum. unabridged ed. Krupa, Debra T., ed. 845p. 1997. pap. text 45.00 (*0-935890-12-2*) Emerg Nurses IL.
Adams, Pamela W. Advanced WordPerfect 6.1 for Windows. Baskett, Kathryn K. & Carnes, Susan D., eds. (Perfect Office Ser.). (Illus.). 70p. 1995. pap. text 26.03 (*1-58163-015-8*) CPI Train.
— Desktop Publishing with Microsoft Word 97. Davis, Jenell & Pressley, Sara, eds. (Microsoft Office 97 Ser.). (Illus.). 101p. 1998. pap. text 28.95 (*1-58163-066-2*) CPI Train.
***Adams, Pamela W.** Getting Started with Microsoft Office 2000. Davis, Jenell L. & Pressley, Sara R., eds. (Office 2000 Ser.). (Illus.). 140p. 1999. pap. 31.83 (*1-58163-090-5*) CPI Train.
Adams, Pamela W. Getting Started with Windows 98 & Office 97. Davis, Jenell L., ed. (Windows 98 Ser.). (Illus.). 116p. 1998. pap. text 31.83 (*1-58163-081-6*) CPI Train.
— Internet Basics with Netscape Communicator. Carnes, Susan D. & Baskett, Kathryn K., eds. (Internet Ser.). (Illus.). 109p. 1998. pap. text 31.83 (*1-58163-062-X*) CPI Train.
— Introduction to Computers for Teachers. Carnes, Susan D. & Pressley, Sara R., eds. (Educator's Ser.). (Illus.). 228p. 1998. pap. text 49.95 (*1-58163-065-4*) CPI Train.
***Adams, Pamela W.** Introduction to Microsoft Office 97. Davis, Jenell L., ed. (Office 97 Ser.). (Illus.). 170p. 1999. pap. 44.95 (*1-58163-094-8*) CPI Train.
Adams, Pamela W. Introduction to Paradox 5.0 for Windows. Baskett, Kathryn K. & Carnes, Susan D., eds. (Perfect Office Ser.). (Illus.). 71p. 1995. pap. text 26.03 (*1-58163-018-2*) CPI Train.
— Introduction to WordPerfect 6.1 for Windows. (Perfect Office Ser.). (Illus.). 76p. 1995. pap. text 26.03 (*1-58163-013-1*) CPI Train.
***Adams, Pamela W.** Learning to Use Computers with Windows 98. Davis, Jenell L. & Pressley, Sara R., eds. (Windows 98 Ser.). (Illus.). 152p. 1999. pap. text 31.83 (*1-58163-088-3*) CPI Train.
— Learning to Use Computers with Windows 95. Davis, Jenell L. & Pressley, Sara R., eds. (Windows 95 Ser.). (Illus.). 147p. 1999. pap. text 31.83 (*1-58163-087-5*) CPI Train.
Adams, Pamela W. Microsoft Excel 97 Advanced. Carpenter, Elizabeth & Pressley, Sara, eds. (Microsoft Office 97 Ser.). (Illus.). 100p. 1998. pap. text 28.95 (*1-58163-074-3*) CPI Train.
***Adams, Pamela W.** Microsoft Excel 2000: Introduction. Davis, Jenell L., ed. (Office 2000 Ser.). (Illus.). 122p. 1999. pap. 28.95 (*1-58163-092-1*) CPI Train.
Adams, Pamela W. Microsoft PowerPoint 97 Intermediate. Carpenter, Elizabeth & Pressley, Sara, eds. (Microsoft Office 97 Ser.). (Illus.). 53p. 1998. pap. text 28.95 (*1-58163-075-1*) CPI Train.
***Adams, Pamela W.** Microsoft PowerPoint 2000: Introduction. Davis, Jenell L., ed. (Office 2000 Ser.). (Illus.). 148p. 2000. pap. 28.95 (*1-58163-093-X*) CPI Train.
Adams, Pamela W. Microsoft Word 97 Advanced. Pressley, Sara R., ed. (Microsoft Office 97 Ser.). (Illus.). 116p. 1998. pap. text 28.95 (*1-58163-064-6*) CPI Train.
***Adams, Pamela W.** Microsoft Word 2000: Introduction. Davis, Jenell L. & Pressley, Sara R., eds. (Office 2000 Ser.). (Illus.). 131p. 1999. pap. 28.95 (*1-58163-091-3*) CPI Train.
Adams, Pamela W. Windows 98 Basics. Davis, Jenell L., ed. (Illus.). 154p. 1998. pap. text 31.83 (*1-58163-078-6*) CPI Train.
Adams, Pamela W. & Baskett, Kathryn. Excel 97 Introduction. Carnes, Susan, ed. (Microsoft Office 97). (Illus.). 86p. 1997. pap. text 28.95 (*1-58163-048-4*) CPI Train.
Adams, Pamela W. & Baskett, Kathryn K. Computer Survival Skills Using Office 97. 2nd rev. ed. Carnes, Susan D., ed. 187p. 1999. pap. text 44.95 (*1-58163-067-0*) CPI Train.
— Computer Survival Skills with Microsoft Office 95. Carnes, Susan D., ed. (Environments). (Illus.). 174p. (Orig.). 1997. pap. text 44.95 (*1-58163-049-2*) CPI Train.
— Corel WordPerfect 7.0. Carnes, Susan D., ed. (Corel Wordperfect Ser.). (Illus.). 165p. 1997. pap. text 53.58 (*1-58163-054-9*) CPI Train.
— Corel WordPerfect 7.0 Intermediate. Carnes, Susan D., ed. (Corel Office Ser.). (Illus.). 75p. 1997. pap. text 28.95 (*1-58163-052-2*) CPI Train.
— Corel WordPerfect 7.0 Introduction. Carnes, Susan D., ed. (Corel Office Ser.). (Illus.). 84p. 1997. pap. text 28.95 (*1-58163-051-4*) CPI Train.
— Excel 7.0 Advanced. Carnes, Susan D., ed. (Microsoft Office 95 Ser.). (Illus.). 86p. 1997. pap. text 28.95 (*1-58163-042-5*) CPI Train.
— Excel 7.0 Introduction. Carnes, Susan D., ed. (Microsoft Office 95 Ser.). (Illus.). 90p. 1997. pap. text 28.95 (*1-58163-040-9*) CPI Train.
— Excel 7.0 Intermediate. Carnes, Susan D., ed. (Microsoft Office 95 Ser.). (Illus.). 80p. 1997. pap. text 28.95 (*1-58163-041-7*) CPI Train.
— Getting Started with Microsoft Works 4.0. Carnes, Susan D., ed. (Operating Systems - Environment Ser.). (Illus.). 214p. 1997. pap. text 49.95 (*1-58163-050-6*) CPI Train.
— Getting Started with Personal Computers Using Office 97. Carnes, Susan D., ed. (Operating Systems/Environments Ser.). (Illus.). 123p. 1998. pap. text 28.95 (*1-58163-060-3*) CPI Train.
— Getting Started with Personal Computers with Microsoft Office 95. Carnes, Susan D., ed. (Operating Systems - Environment Ser.). (Illus.). 109p. 1997. pap. text 28.95 (*1-58163-000-X*) CPI Train.
— Intermediate WordPerfect 6.1 for Windows. Carnes, Susan D., ed. (Perfect Office Ser.). (Illus.). 82p. 1995. pap. text 26.03 (*1-58163-014-X*) CPI Train.
— Internet Basics with Internet Explorer 4.0. Carnes, Susan D., ed. (Internet Ser.). (Illus.). 112p. 1998. pap. text 31.83 (*1-58163-055-7*) CPI Train.
— Internet Basics with Netscape Navigator. Carnes, Susan D., ed. (Internet Ser.). (Illus.). 98p. (Orig.). 1997. pap. 31.83 (*1-58163-005-0*) CPI Train.
— Introduction to Microsoft Powerpoint 7.0. Carnes, Susan D., ed. (Microsoft Office 95 Ser.). (Illus.). 119p. 1997. pap. text 28.95 (*1-58163-043-3*) CPI Train.
— Microsoft Access 97 Introduction. Carnes, Susan D., ed. (Micrsoft Office 97 Ser.). (Illus.). 139p. 1998. pap. text 28.95 (*1-58163-059-X*) CPI Train.
— Microsoft Access 7.0 Introduction. Carnes, Susan D., ed. (Microsoft Office 95 Ser.). (Illus.). 122p. 1997. pap. text 28.95 (*1-58163-044-1*) CPI Train.
— Microsoft Excel 97. Carnes, Susan D., ed. (Microsoft Office 97 Ser.). 1997. pap. text 44.95 (*1-58163-073-5*) CPI Train.
— Microsoft Excel 97 Intermediate. Carnes, Susan D., ed. (Micrsoft Office 97 Ser.). (Illus.). 105p. 1997. pap. text 28.95 (*1-58163-058-1*) CPI Train.
— Microsoft Excel 7.0. Carnes, Susan D., ed. (Microsoft Office 95 Ser.). (Illus.). 166p. 1997. pap. text 44.95 (*1-58163-045-X*) CPI Train.
— Microsoft Powerpoint 97 Introduction. Carnes, Susan D., ed. (Micrsoft Office 97 Ser.). (Illus.). 129p. 1998. pap. text 28.95 (*1-58163-056-5*) CPI Train.
— Microsoft Word 97. Carnes, Susan D., ed. (Microsoft Office 97 Ser.). (Illus.). 183p. 1997. pap. text 44.95 (*1-58163-072-7*) CPI Train.
— Microsoft Word 97 Intermediate. Carnes, Susan D., ed. (Microsoft Office 97 Ser.). (Illus.). 103p. 1998. pap. text 28.95 (*1-58163-057-3*) CPI Train.
— Microsoft Word 7.0. Carnes, Susan D., ed. (Microsoft Office 95 Ser.). (Illus.). 161p. 1997. pap. text 44.95 (*1-58163-046-8*) CPI Train.
— Microsoft Word 7.0 Advanced. Carnes, Susan D., ed. (Microsoft Office 95 Ser.). (Illus.). 118p. 1997. pap. text 28.95 (*1-58163-039-5*) CPI Train.
— Microsoft Word 7.0 Intermediate. Carnes, Susan D., ed. (Microsoft Office 95 Ser.). (Illus.). 86p. 1997. pap. text 28.95 (*1-58163-038-7*) CPI Train.
— Microsoft Word 7.0 Introduction. Carnes, Susan D., ed. (Microsoft Office 95 Ser.). (Illus.). 82p. 1997. pap. text 28.95 (*1-58163-037-9*) CPI Train.
— Quattro Pro 6.0 Introduction. Carnes, Susan D., ed. (Perfect Office Ser.). (Illus.). 91p. 1995. pap. text 26.03 (*1-58163-017-4*) CPI Train.
— Windows 95 Basics. Carnes, Susan D., ed. (Operating Systems - Environment Ser.). (Illus.). 122p. 1995. pap. text 28.95 (*1-58163-003-4*) CPI Train.
— Word 97 Introduction. Carnes, Susan D., ed. (Microsoft Office 97 Ser.). (Illus.). 82p. 1997. pap. text 28.95 (*1-58163-047-6*) CPI Train.
Adams, Pamela W. & Carpenter, Elizabeth. Charting with Microsoft Excel 97. Davis, Jenell L., ed. (Microsoft Office 97 Ser.). (Illus.). 92p. 1998. pap. text 28.95 (*1-58163-070-0*) CPI Train.
***Adams, Pamela W. & Carpenter, Elizabeth.** Microsoft Access 2000: Introduction. Davis, Jenell L., ed. (Office 2000 Ser.). (Illus.). 150p. 2000. pap. 28.95 (*1-58163-095-6*) CPI Train.

An Asterisk (*) at the beginning of an entry indicates that the title is appearing for the first time.

***Adams, Pamela W. & Pressley, Sara R.** Computer Applications for Teachers. Davis, Jenell L., ed. (Educator's Ser.). (Illus.). 130p. 1999. pap. text 49.95 (*1-58163-079-4*) CPI Train.
— PowerPoint 97 for Teachers. Davis, Jennell L., ed. (Educator's Ser.). (Illus.). 200p. 1999. pap. text 49.95 (*1-58163-080-8*) CPI Train.
***Adams, Pamela W., et al.** Getting More Out of Windows 95. Davis, Jenell L., ed. & illus. by. (Educator's Ser.). 86p. 1999. pap. text 28.95 (*1-58163-089-1*) CPI Train.
Adams, Pamela W., ed. see Carpenter, Elizabeth & Martin, Rick.
Adams, Parveen. The Emptiness of the Image: Psychoanalysis & Sexual Differences. LC 95-12281. (Illus.). 192p. (C). 1995. pap. 21.99 (*0-415-04622-X*) Routledge.
Adams, Pat & Jacobs, Marc. Yo! Let's Eat!! A Cookbook for Teenagers . . . With Recipes from Teenagers. (Illus.). 96p. (YA). (gr. 8-12). 1994. ring bd. 7.95 (*1-878848-34-8*, 144F) Natl Res Ctr.
***Adams, Patch.** Docteur Tendresse. (French Audiobooks Ser.). (FRE.). 2000. audio 14.95 (*2-89517-080-0*, Pub. by Coffragants) Penton Overseas.
Adams, Patch. House Calls. Jacobs, Pamela D., ed. LC 98-34266. (Illus.). 170p. 1998. pap. 11.95 (*1-885003-18-8*) R D Reed Pubs.
Adams, Patch & Mylander, Maureen. Gesundheit! Bringing Good Health to You, the Medical System, & Society Through Physician Service, Complementary Therapies, Humor, & Joy. rev. ed. LC 99-187488. (Illus.). 224p. 1998. pap. 14.95 (*0-89281-781-X*, Inner Trad) Inner Tradit.
Adams, Patricia, jt. auth. see Savage, Karen.
Adams, Patricia, ed. see Adams, James R.
Adams, Patricia, ed. see Johnson, Judy & Johnson, Pushkin.
***Adams, Patricia F.** Current Estimates from the National Health Interview Survey, 1996. 209p. 1999. per. 22.00 (*0-16-050179-2*) USGPO.
— Health Risk Behaviors Among our Nation's Youth: United States, 1992. 55p. 1995. pap. 5.00 (*0-16-061436-8*) USGPO.
Adams, Paul. Health of the State. Gilbert, Neil & Specht, Harry, eds. LC 81-22647. (Studies in Social Welfare Policies & Programs). 198p. 1982. 52.95 (*0-275-90749-X*, C0749, Praeger Pubs) Greenwood.
— New Self-Hypnosis. 1978. pap. 10.00 (*0-87980-233-2*) Wilshire.
— 155 Legal Do's (And Dont's) for the Small Business. LC 96-17961. 256p. 1996. pap. 18.95 (*0-471-13161-X*) Wiley.
— The Sermon for Children. LC 94-73315. 1996. 12.95 (*1-55673-971-0*, Fairway Pr) CSS OH.
***Adams, Paul.** The Stranger from Melbourne, Frank Hardy: A Literary Biography, 1944-1975. 172p. 1999. 45.00 (*1-876268-40-9*, Pub. by Univ of West Aust Pr); pap. 34.95 (*1-876268-23-9*, Pub. by Univ of West Aust Pr) Intl Spec Bk.
Adams, Paul. Writing Right for Today's Mass Media. (Mass Communication Ser.). 400p. (C). 1998. pap. text 39.95 (*0-8304-1456-8*) Thomson Learn.
Adams, Paul & Nelson, Kristine E., eds. Reinventing Human Services: Community & Family Centered Practice. (Modern Applications of Social Work Ser.). 295p. 1995. pap. text 25.95 (*0-202-36098-9*); lib. bdg. 51.95 (*0-202-36097-0*) Aldine de Gruyter.
Adams, Paul, ed. see Archer, Helen M.
Adams, Paul, jt. ed. see Wegeng, Lana M.
Adams, Paul D., ed. see Trussell, Jennifer.
Adams, Paul L. A Primer of Child Psychology. 2nd ed. 1982. 19.00 (*0-316-03726-5*, Little Brwn Med Div) Lppncott W & W.
Adams, Paul L. & Fras, Ivan. Beginning Child Psychiatry. LC 87-32587. 624p. 1988. text 60.95 (*0-87630-493-5*) Brunner-Mazel.
Adams, Paul W., jt. auth. see Satterlund, Donald R.
Adams, Pauline. Somerville for Women: An Oxford College 1879-1993. (Illus.). 414p. (C). 1996. text 75.00 (*0-19-920179-X*); pap. text 30.00 (*0-19-920182-X*) OUP.
Adams, Pauline. Sounds Musical: A Music Course for Key Stage 2 (7-11 Years) : Teacher's Resource Book. LC 99-488189. 1997. write for info. (*0-19-320975-6*) OUP.
Adams, Pauline & Thornton, Emma S. A Populist Assault: Sarah E. Van De Vort Emery on American Democracy 1862-1895. LC 82-60665. (Illus.). 146p. 1982. 14.95 (*0-87972-203-7*) Bowling Green Univ Popular Press.
Adams, Pepper. The Bachelor Cure. (Silhouette Romance Ser.). 1994. per. 2.75 (*0-373-19003-4*, 5-19003-8) Harlequin Bks.
— The Bachelor Cure. (Romance Ser.). 1997. per. 143.64 (*0-373-91003-7*, 5-91003-9) Silhouette.
— Lady Willpower. (Romance Ser.). 1994. per. 2.75 (*0-373-08983-X*, 5-08983-4) Silhouette.
— Mad about Maggie: Fabulous Father. (Romance Ser.). 1993. per. 2.75 (*0-373-08964-3*, 5-08964-4) Silhouette.
— Rookie Dad. (Romance Ser.: No. 862). 1992. per. 2.69 (*0-373-08862-0*, 5-08862-0) Silhouette.
— That Old Black Magic. large type ed. 226p. 1992. reprint ed. lib. bdg. 13.95 (*1-56054-410-4*) Thorndike Pr.
Adams, Percy G. Travel Literature & the Evolution of the Novel. LC 83-19683. 380p. reprint ed. pap. 117.80 (*0-8357-4290-3*, 203708900007) Bks Demand.
Adams, Percy W. Adams: History of the Adams Family of North Staffordshire with Numerous Pedigree Charts & Notes on Allied Families. (Illus.). 480p. 1994. reprint ed. pap. 72.00 (*0-8328-4284-2*); reprint ed. lib. bdg. 82.00 (*0-8328-4283-4*) Higginson Bk Co.
Adams, Perrie M. & Pak, Charles Y., eds. Techniques of Patient-Oriented Research. LC 93-4602. 224p. 1993. text 54.00 (*0-7817-0107-4*) Lppncott W & W.
Adams, Peter. Art of Flowering Bonsai. LC 98-143570. (Illus.). 128p. 1998. 24.95 (*0-7063-7625-0*, Pub. by WrLock) Sterling.
***Adams, Peter.** At the Far Reach of Their Capacities: Case Studies of Dependent Authorship. 206p. 1999. pap. text 25.00 (*1-875659-07-2*, Pub. by Aust Assn Teach) Calendar Islands.
— Bonsai Landscapes. 128p. 1999. 27.95 (*0-7063-7767-2*) Ward & Ward.
— Homeopathy: Introductory Guide to Natural Medicine for the Whole Person. (New Perspectives Ser.). 2000. pap. 9.95 (*1-86204-663-8*, Pub. by Element MA) Penguin Putnam.
Adams, Peter. Homeopathy: Natural Medicine for the Whole Person. LC 96-34074. (Health Essentials Ser.). 128p. 1996. pap. 9.95 (*1-85230-879-6*, Pub. by Element MA) Penguin Putnam.
Adams, Peter, ed. Lexis - Nexis: The Legal Basics. 52p. 1995. 9.95 (*0-926578-12-X*) LEXIS-NEXIS.
— Lexis (R) Product Guide, 2 vols. 1992. ring bd. write for info. (*0-318-72160-0*); ring bd. write for info. (*0-318-72161-9*) LEXIS-NEXIS.
— Lexis (R) Product Guide, 2 vols., Set. 1992. ring bd. 85.00 (*0-926578-07-3*) LEXIS-NEXIS.
Adams, Peter B. & Lawson, Sheryl D. Dendrobium Kingianum: A Unique Australian Orchid. (Illus.). 197p. 1995. 45.00 (*1-875902-01-5*, Pub. by Central Queensland) Accents Pubns.
Adams, Peter D. Bonsai Design. (Illus.). 144p. 1996. pap. 19.95 (*0-7063-7447-9*, Pub. by WrLock) Sterling.
— Successful Bonsai Growing. rev. ed. (Illus.). 96p. (Orig.). 1996. pap. 10.95 (*0-7063-7439-8*, Pub. by WrLock) Sterling.
— Successful Bonsai Shaping. (Illus.). 128p. pap. 14.95 (*0-943955-70-X*, Trafalgar Sq Pub) Trafalgar.
— Workbook Basics. 471p. (C). 1997. spiral bd. 50.00 (*0-673-39924-9*) Addson-Wesley Educ.
Adams, Peter Dow. Harpercollins Concise Handbook & Exercises. (C). 1997. pap. 46.33 (*0-06-502537-7*) Addson-Wesley Educ.
— HarperCollins Concise Handbook for Writers. LC 93-50599. 565p. (C). 1994. pap. text 45.00 (*0-06-501994-6*) Addson-Wesley Educ.
Adams, Peter H. Antique Brass Wind Instruments: Identification & Value Guide. LC 97-80181. 160p. 1998. pap. 29.95 (*0-7643-0027-X*) Schiffer.
Adams, Peter J. Bermuda Countdown. 385p. mass mkt. 4.99 (*1-896329-83-7*) Picasso Publ.
Adams, Peter S. & Harrison, William, eds. Essentials of Cash Management. 6th ed. (C). 1998. pap. text 95.50 (*0-9614799-7-3*) Treasry Mgmt.
Adams, Phil, jt. auth. see Adams, Carole.
Adams, Phillip & Burton, Lee. Talkback: Emperors of Air LC 98-160494. x, 246 p. 1997. write for info. (*1-86448-325-3*) Allen & Unwin Pty.
***Adams, Phillip & Newell, Patrice.** Politically Incorrect Jokes from the Net. 2000. pap. 11.95 (*0-285-63445-3*, Pub. by Souvenir Pr Ltd) IPG Chicago.
Adams, Phylliss J. & Kronowitz, Ellen L. Pathways to Poetry: Poetry Fun for Grades 1-3. 288p. (J). (gr. 1-3). 16.99 (*0-86653-914-X*, FE0914) Fearon Teacher Aids.
— Pathways to Poetry: Poetry Fun for Grades 4-6. (J). (gr. 4-6). 16.99 (*0-86653-913-1*, FE0913) Fearon Teacher Aids.
— Pathways to Poetry: Poetry Fun for Preschool-Kindergarten. 256p. (J). (ps-6). 16.99 (*0-86653-915-8*, FE0915) Fearon Teacher Aids.
Adams-Price, Carolyn, ed. Creativity & Successful Aging: Theoretical & Empirical Approaches. LC 97-23168. (Illus.). 360p. 1997. 49.95 (*0-8261-9910-0*) Springer Pub.
Adams, Priscilla. Poetry - Windows & Mirrors: The Sketchbook Approach to Writing & Reading Poetry. LC 93-74573. (Illus.). 188p. (J). (gr. 6-10). 1995. pap. text 14.95 (*0-89089-571-6*) Carolina Acad Pr.
Adams, Q. M. Neither Male nor Female. 1977. per. 6.95 (*0-89985-104-5*) Christ for the Nations.
***Adams, R.** Eternal Prairie: Exploring Cemetery Traditions & Symbols. (Illus.). 128p. 1999. pap. 16.95 (*1-894004-33-7*) Fifth Hse Publ.
Adams, R., ed. see Adams, Shirley.
Adams, R. C. Social Survey Methods for Mass Media Research. 192p. 1989. 29.95 (*0-8058-0140-5*) L Erlbaum Assocs.
***Adams, R. F., et al.** Introduction to the American Legal System. 6th ed. 288p. (C). 2000. per. 29.95 (*0-929563-56-5*) Pearson Pubns.
Adams, R. G. Food from America's Bravest: A North American Experience in Firehouse Cooking. (Illus.). 232p. pap. 14.95 (*0-9638089-0-7*) Island Dog Pubns.
Adams, R. J. British Appeasement & the Origins of World War II. (Problems in European Civilization Ser.). 176p. (C). 1994. pap. text 18.36 (*0-669-33502-9*) HM Trade Div.
— British Politics & Foreign Policy in the Age of Appeasement, 1935-1939. 208p. (C). 1993. 39.50 (*0-8047-2100-9*) Stanford U Pr.
— Organic Reactions, Vol. 1. (Organic Reactions Ser.). 402p. 1942. 99.95 (*0-471-00462-6*) Wiley.
— Organic Reactions, Vol. 2. (Organic Reactions Ser.). 460p. 1944. 99.95 (*0-471-00495-2*) Wiley.
— Organic Reactions, Vol. 3. (Organic Reactions Ser.). 461p. 1946. 99.95 (*0-471-00528-2*) Wiley.
— Organic Reactions, Vol. 4. (Organic Reactions Ser.). 428p. 1948. 99.95 (*0-471-00561-4*) Wiley.
— Organic Reactions, Vol. 5. (Organic Reactions Ser.). 446p. 1949. 99.95 (*0-471-00594-0*) Wiley.
— Organic Reactions, Vol. 6. (Organic Reactions Ser.). 528p. 1951. 99.95 (*0-471-00627-0*) Wiley.
— Organic Reactions, Vol. 8. (Organic Reactions Ser.). 437p. 1954. 99.95 (*0-471-00693-9*) Wiley.
— Organic Reactions, Vol. 9. (Organic Reactions Ser.). 476p. 1957. 99.95 (*0-471-00726-9*) Wiley.
— Organic Reactions, Vol. 10. (Organic Reactions Ser.). 563p. 1959. 99.95 (*0-471-00759-5*) Wiley.
Adams, R. J., ed. The Great War, 1914-1918: Essays on the Military, Political, & Social History of the First World War. LC 89-20363. (Military History Ser.: No. 17). (Illus.). 208p. 1990. 39.50 (*0-89096-431-9*) Tex A&M Univ Pr.
Adams, R. J., jt. auth. see Meier, Nicholas.
***Adams, R J Q.** Bonar Law. LC 98-61602. 1p. 1999. 60.00 (*0-8047-3716-9*) Stanford U Pr.
***Adams, R. Jan.** Beauty Solutions for Women of Color. 2000. text 24.95 (*0-312-25310-9*) St Martin.
Adams, R. L. Cell Culture for Biochemists. 2nd rev. ed. (Laboratory Techniques in Biochemistry & Molecular Biology Ser.: Vol. 8). 364p. 1990. 215.50 (*0-444-81306-3*) Elsevier.
Adams, R. L. & Burdon, R. H. Molecular Biology of DNA Methylation. (Molecular Biology Ser.). (Illus.). xvi, 247p. 1985. 96.00 (*0-387-96161-5*) Spr-Verlag.
Adams, R. N. Electrochemistry at Solid Electrodes. (Monographs in Electroanalytical Chemistry & Electrochemistry Ser.: Vol. 1). (Illus.). 416p. 1969. text 165.00 (*0-8247-1005-3*) Dekker.
Adams, R. P., et al. Conservation of Plant Genes, II: Utilization of Ancient & Modern DNA. (Monographs in Systematic Botany from the Missouri Botanical Garden: No. 48). (Illus.). 276p. 1994. 31.95 (*0-915279-20-7*) Miss Botan.
— Texas Courts. 6th ed. 64p. (C). 1998. pap. text 15.50 (*0-929563-49-2*) Pearson Pubns.
Adams, Ramon. Western Words: A Dictionary of the Old West. (Illus.). 182p. 1997. pap. 11.95 (*0-7818-0590-2*) Hippocrene Bks.
Adams, Ramon F. Burs under the Saddle: A Second Look at Books & Histories of the West. LC 64-13593. 624p. 1989. pap. 21.95 (*0-8061-2170-X*) U of Okla Pr.
— Come An' Get It: The Story of the Old Cowboy Cook. LC 52-12299. (Illus.). 171p. (Orig.). 1952. pap. 9.95 (*0-8061-1013-9*) U of Okla Pr.
— The Cowboy Dictionary: The Chin Jaw Words & Whing-Ding Ways of the American West. LC 93-30210. 384p. 1994. pap. 10.95 (*0-399-51866-5*, Perigee Bks) Berkley Pub.
***Adams, Ramon F.** Cowboy Lingo. 272p. 2000. pap. 10.00 (*0-618-08349-9*) HM.
Adams, Ramon F. From the Pecos to the Powder: A Cowboy's Autobiography. LC 65-10113. (Illus.). 25 p. 1989. pap. 13.95 (*0-8061-2212-9*) U of Okla Pr.
— The Language of the Railroader. LC 77-22346. 192p. 1977. reprint ed. pap. 59.60 (*0-608-13296-9*, 205215200044) Bks Demand.
— More Burs under the Saddle: Books & Histories of the West. LC 77-18606. 200p. 1989. pap. 14.95 (*0-8061-2171-8*) U of Okla Pr.
— Six-Guns & Saddle Leather: A Bibliography of Books & Pamphlets on Western Outlaws & Gunmen. 2nd ed. LC 97-49974. 1998. 24.95 (*0-486-40035-2*) Dover.
Adams, Randy, jt. auth. see Sodaro, Craig.
Adams, Randy L., jt. auth. see Sodaro, Craig.
Adams, Ray. Serious Cycling for the Beginner. LC 77-73654. (Illus.). 88p. 1977. reprint ed. pap. 4.95 (*0-89037-115-6*) Anderson World.
Adams, Raymond. Science Learning in Victorian Schools, 1990. (C). 1992. 75.00 (*0-86431-108-7*, Pub. by Aust Council Educ Res) St Mut.
Adams, Raymond D. Principles of Neurology. 6th ed. 1998. 135.00 (*0-07-864230-2*) McGraw.
— Ulster Emigrants to Philadelphia, 1803-1850. 102p. 1998. pap. 15.00 (*0-8063-4615-9*) Clearfield Co.
Adams, Raymond D. & Victor, Maurice. Principles of Neurology. 5th ed. LC 92-48805. (Illus.). 1402p. 1993. text 79.00 (*0-07-000341-6*) McGraw-Hill HPD.
Adams, Raymond D., et al. Principles of Neurology. 6th rev. ed. (Illus.). 1440p. 1997. text 85.00 (*0-07-067439-6*) McGraw-Hill HPD.
— Principles of Neurology: Companion Handbook. 6th ed. LC 98-132505. (Illus.). 512p. 1997. text 32.00 (*0-07-000514-1*) McGraw-Hill HPD.
Adams, Raymond J., Jr. Avian Research at the Kalamazoo Nature Center 1970 to 1978. (Illus.). 86p. 1982. pap. 5.00 (*0-939294-11-7*, QL 677-5-A2) Beech Leaf.
Adams, Rebecca & Blieszner, Rosemary H., eds. Older Adult Friendship: Structure & Process. (Focus Editions Ser.: Vol. 103). 320p. 1989. text 59.95 (*0-8039-3143-3*) Sage.
— Older Adult Friendship: Structure & Process. (Focus Editions Ser.: Vol. 103). 320p. (C). 1989. pap. text 26.00 (*0-8039-3144-1*) Sage.
Adams, Rebecca, ed. see Adams, Shielly.
Adams, Rebecca, ed. see Adams, Shirley.
Adams, Rebecca G. & Allan, Graham, eds. Placing Friendship in Context. LC 98-15200. (Structural Analysis in the Social Sciences Ser.: No. 15). (Illus.). 222p. (C). 1998. text 54.95 (*0-521-58456-6*); pap. text 19.95 (*0-521-58589-9*) Cambridge U Pr.
Adams, Rebecca G. & Blieszner, Rosemary, eds. Older Adult Friendship: Structure & Process. LC 88-28287. (Sage Focus Editions Ser.: No. 103). 268p. 1989. reprint ed. pap. 83.10 (*0-608-04295-1*, 206507400012) Bks Demand.
***Adams, Rebecca G. & Sardiello, Robert.** DeadHead Social Science: "You Ain't Gonna Learn What You Don't Want to Know" 300p. 2000. 62.00 (*0-7425-0250-3*) Rowman.
— DeadHead Social Science: "You Ain't Gonna Learn What You Don't Want to Know" (Illus.). 288p. 2000. pap. 24.95 (*0-7425-0251-1*) Rowman.
***Adams, Rebecca G. & Sardiello, Robert, eds.** DeadHead Social Science: "You Ain't Goin' to Learn What You Don't Want to Know" (Illus.). 288p. 2000. pap. 24.95 (*0-7619-9073-9*) AltaMira Pr.
— DeadHead Social Science: "You Ain't Gonna Learn What You Don't Want to Know" LC 99-6841. (Illus.). 288p. 2000. 62.00 (*0-7619-9072-0*) AltaMira Pr.
Adams, Regina & Adams, Blair. Homestead Children: A Sampler of Children's Writings. LC 93-60490. 240p. (Orig.). 1993. pap. 19.95 (*0-916387-26-7*) Truth Forum.
— Journeys Home I: Coming to Home Birth. LC 89-50807. 299p. (Orig.). 1989. pap. 9.95 (*0-916387-17-8*) Truth Forum.
***Adams, Renee.** Cosmic Kate: The First Mission. LC 99-91408. (Illus.). 23p. (J). (ps-2). 1999. pap. write for info. (*0-9675994-0-7*) Make Believe.
Adams, Rex. Milagrosos Alimentos Curativos. 1998. 24.95 (*0-13-921081-4*) P-H.
— Milagrosos Alimentos Curativos. 320p. (C). 1998. pap. text 13.95 (*0-13-921073-3*) P-H.
***Adams, Rex.** Milagrosos Alimentos Curativos. (SPA.). 2000. pap. 14.00 (*0-7352-0195-1*) PH Pr.
Adams, Rex. Miracle Medicine Foods. 228p. (C). 1979. pap. text 9.95 (*0-13-585471-7*) P-H.
Adams, Rhenna L., jt. auth. see Torrado de Marcano, Ester.
Adams, Richard. Delaware Indians: A Brief History. 80p. 1995. reprint ed. pap. 8.95 (*0-910746-17-6*) Hope Farm.
— The Girl in a Swing. large type ed. 578p. 1982. 27.99 (*0-7089-8054-6*) Ulverscroft.
— Ideas for Science Projects. (Experimental Science Ser.). (YA). (gr. 9-12). 1998. pap. 9.95 (*0-531-15882-9*) Watts.
— Los Origenes de la Civilizacion Maya. (SPA.). 19.99 (*968-16-3254-0*, Pub. by Fondo) Continental Bk.
***Adams, Richard.** Outlandish Knight. 256p. 2000. 26.00 (*0-7278-5496-8*, Pub. by Severn Hse) Chivers N Amer.
— Physics Projects for Young Scientists. rev. ed. (Projects for Young Scientists Ser.). (Illus.). (J). 2000. pap. 6.95 (*0-531-16461-6*) Watts.
— The Plague Dogs. 480p. 1986. mass mkt. 5.95 (*0-449-21182-7*, Crest) Fawcett.
— The Plague Dogs. LC 98-48270. 1999. 26.95 (*0-7838-8489-3*) Macmillan Gen Ref.
Adams, Richard. Tales from Watership Dow. 352p. 1998. mass mkt. 6.99 (*0-380-72934-2*, Avon Bks) Morrow Avon.
— Tales from Watership Down. LC 96-17047. 1996. 23.00 (*0-679-45125-0*) Knopf.
***Adams, Richard.** Tales from Watership Down. 1998. 12.09 (*0-606-13835-8*, Pub. by Turtleback) Demco.
Adams, Richard. Tales from Watership Down. large type ed. LC 97-16196. 1997. 23.95 (*1-56895-449-2*) Wheeler Pub.
— Watership Down. 1996. 27.00 (*0-684-83605-X*, Scribners Ref) Mac Lib Ref.
— Watership Down. LC 73-6044. 429p. (YA). 1974. 40.00 (*0-02-700030-3*) Macmillan.
— Watership Down. LC 73-6044. 494p. 1976. mass mkt. 7.50 (*0-380-00293-0*, Avon Bks) Morrow Avon.
Adams, Richard. Watership Down. 1975. 12.09 (*0-606-05080-9*, Pub. by Turtleback) Demco.
Adams, Richard. Watership Down. large type ed. 642p. 1997. 24.95 (*0-7838-8081-2*, G K Hall Lrg Type) Mac Lib Ref.
— Watership Down. 1994. reprint ed. lib. bdg. 37.95 (*1-56849-250-2*) Buccaneer Bks.
— Watership Down. 20th anniversary ed. 480p. 1976. pap. 12.00 (*0-380-00428-3*, Avon Bks) Morrow Avon.
Adams, Richard & Goodwin, Peter. Physics Projects for Young Scientists. LC 98-40401. (Projects For Young Scientists Ser.). (YA). (gr. 9-12). 2000. 25.00 (*0-531-11667-0*) Watts.
Adams, Richard, et al. Robust Multivariable Flight Control. LC 94-3683. (Advances in Industrial Control Ser.). 1994. 65.95 (*0-387-19906-3*) Spr-Verlag.
Adams, Richard, ed. see Austen, Jane.
Adams, Richard, ed. see Dickens, Charles.
Adams, Richard, ed. see Hardy, Thomas.
Adams, Richard, ed. see Russell, Willy.
Adams, Richard, ed. see Shakespeare, William.
Adams, Richard, ed. see Sheridan, Richard Brinsley.
Adams, Richard C. Legends of the Delaware Indians & Picture Writing. Nichols, Deborah, ed. & intro. by. LC 97-23740. 128p. 1997. 25.95 (*0-8156-0487-4*) Syracuse U Pr.
***Adams, Richard C.** Legends of the Delaware Indians & Picture Writing. (The Iroquois & their Neighbors Ser.). (Illus.). 168p. 2000. pap. 15.95 (*0-8156-0639-7*) Syracuse U Pr.
Adams, Richard C. & Gardner, Robert. Ideas for Science Projects. rev. ed. LC 97-3457. (Experimental Science Ser.). (J). (gr. 5-9). 1997. 22.30 (*0-531-11347-7*) Watts.
— More Ideas for Science Projects. rev. ed. LC 97-5792. (Experimental Science Series Book). (Illus.). 160p. (J). (gr. 9 up). 1997. 24.00 (*0-531-11380-9*) Watts.
***Adams, Richard C. & Goodwin, Peter.** Engineering Projects for Young Scientists rev. ed. LC 99-30418. (Projects for Young Scientists Ser.). 2000. write for info. (*0-531-11668-9*) Watts.
Adams, Richard D. & Cotton, F. Albert, eds. Catalysis by Di- & Polynuclear Metal Cluster Complexes. LC 97-21333. (Chemistry of Metal Clusters Ser.). 533p. 1998. 135.00 (*0-471-23930-5*) Wiley.
Adams, Richard E. Ancient Civilizations of the New World. LC 97-15752. 176p. (C). 1997. pap. 20.00 (*0-8133-1383-X*, Pub. by Westview) HarpC.
— Prehistoric Mesoamerica. rev. ed. LC 90-50679. (Illus.). 480p. 1996. pap. 18.95 (*0-8061-2834-8*) U of Okla Pr.

A

A

***Adams, Richard E. & MacLeod, Murdo J., eds.** The Cambridge History of the Native Peoples of the Americas Vol. II: Mesoamerica, 2 vols. (Cambridge History of the Native Peoples of the Americas Ser.). 1664p. (C). 2000. 175.00 (*0-521-65205-7*) Cambridge U Pr.

Adams, Richard E. & MacLeod, Murdo J., eds. The Cambridge History of the Native Peoples of the Americas Vol. II, Pt. 2: Mesoamerica. (Cambridge History of the Native Peoples of the Americas Ser.). (Illus.). 768p. (C). 2000. 89.95 (*0-521-65204-9*) Cambridge U Pr.

Adams, Richard E. W. Rio Azul: An Ancient Maya City. LC 98-45078. 1999. 34.95 (*0-8061-3076-8*) U of Okla Pr.

***Adams, Richard E. W. & MacLeod, Murdo J., eds.** The Cambridge History of the Native Peoples of the Americas Vol 2, Pt. 1: Mesoamerica. LC 96-37349. (Cambridge History of the Native Peoples of the Americas Ser.). (Illus.). 896p. (C). 2000. 89.95 (*0-521-35165-0*) Cambridge U Pr.

Adams, Richard H., Jr. & He, Jane J. Sources of Income Inequality & Poverty in Rural Pakistan. LC 95-23924. (Research Reports: No. 102). 1995. write for info. (*0-89629-105-7*) Intl Food Policy.

Adams, Richard J., jt. auth. see Stuart, Simon N.

Adams, Richard M. School Nurse's Survival Guide: Ready-to-Use Tips, Techniques, & Materials for the School Health Professional. LC 95-18454. 368p. (C). 1995. spiral bd. 34.95 (*0-13-186727-X*, Pub. by P-H) S&S Trade.

***Adams, Richard M., II & Reinertson, Raymond N.** The GATF Guide to Digital Color Reproduction in Newspapers. LC 99-64454. (Illus.). 180p. (C). 1999. 75.00 (*0-88362-231-9*, 1560) GATFPress.

Adams, Richard M. & Romano, Frank. Computer-to-Plate: Automating the Printing Industry. 2nd rev. ed. LC 98-74334. 300p. (C). 1999. text 65.00 (*0-88362-217-3*, 14352) GATF.

***Adams, Richard M., II & Romano, Frank J.** Computer-to-Plate Primer. (Illus.). 120p. 1999. pap. 25.00 (*0-88362-236-X*, 1598) GATFPress.

***Adams, Richard M., II & Weisberg, Joshua B.** The GATF Practical Guide to Color Management. 2nd rev. ed. (Illus.). 260p. (C). 2000. 75.00 (*0-88362-248-3*, 15482) GATFPress.

Adams, Richard N. The Eighth Day: Social Evolution as the Self-Organization of Energy. LC 87-23295. (Illus.). 312p. 1988. pap. 16.95 (*0-292-72061-0*) U of Tex Pr.

***Adams, Rick A. & Pedersen, Scott C.** Ontogeny, Functional Ecology & Evolution of Bats. LC 99-57156. 2000. write for info. (*0-521-62632-3*) Cambridge U Pr.

***Adams, Rob & Adams, Terry.** The Bargain Hunter's Handbook: How to Buy Just about Anything for Next to Nothing. LC 99-23618. 192p. 1999. pap. 12.99 (*1-56414-410-0*) Career Pr Inc.

Adams, Rob & Adams, Terry. Success for Less: 100 Low-Cost Businesses You Can Start Today. LC 99-35029. (Illus.). 400p. 1999. pap. 14.95 (*1-891984-06-3*, Pub. by Entrepreneur) Natl Bk Netwk.

***Adams, Rob, et al.** How to Be a Teenage Millionaire: Start Your Own Business, Make Your Own Money & Run Your Own Life. 250p. 2000. pap. 16.95 (*1-891984-17-9*, Pub. by Entrepreneur) Natl Bk Netwk.

Adams, Robert. The Architecture & Art of Early Hispanic Colorado. LC 98-26177. 1998. pap. 27.50 (*0-87081-464-8*) Univ Pr Colo.

— Calculus Several Variables. 4th ed. 560p. (C). 1999. 79.95 (*0-201-64388-X*) Addison-Wesley.

— Eden. 1999. 75.00 (*1-56466-068-0*) Archer Fields.

— I Hear the Leaves & Love the Light. (Illus.). 48p. 40.00 (*3-923922-70-1*) Nazraeli Pr.

— Leibniz: Determinist, Theist, Idealist. 448p. 1998. reprint ed. pap. 19.95 (*0-19-512649-1*) OUP.

— Listening to the River: Seasons in the American West. (Illus.). 112p. 1994. 68.00 (*0-89381-565-9*) Aperture.

***Adams, Robert.** Notes for Friends. LC 99-29077. 80p. 1999. pap. 29.95 (*0-87081-545-8*) Univ Pr Colo.

Adams, Robert. Perfect Times, Perfect Places. (Illus.). 64p. 1988. 53.00 (*0-89381-299-4*) Aperture.

— The Personal Social Services: Clients, Consumers or Citizens? LC 95-49641. (Social Policy in Britain Ser.). 1996. pap. write for info. (*0-582-25875-8*, Pub. by Addison-Wesley) Longman.

— Proteus. (C). Date not set. pap. write for info. (*0-393-09974-1*, Norton Paperbks) Norton.

***Adams, Robert.** Single Variable Calculus. 4th ed. (C). 2000. text. write for info. (*0-201-66485-2*) Addison-Wesley.

Adams, Robert. To Make It Home: Photographs of the American West, 1965-1986. (Illus.). 176p. 1989. 114.00 (*0-89381-351-6*) Aperture.

— West from the Columbia: Views at the River Mouth. LC 94-74495. (Illus.). 84p. 1995. 76.00 (*0-89381-642-6*) Aperture.

— What We Bought: The New World. (Illus.). 202p. 1996. 40.00 (*3-89169-094-0*, 610591, Pub. by Sprengel Mus) Dist Art Pubs.

— Why People Photograph. LC 94-76843. (Illus.). 192p. 1994. 25.95 (*0-89381-597-7*) Aperture.

— Why People Photograph. LC 94-76843. (Illus.). 192p. 1996. pap. 19.95 (*0-89381-603-5*) Aperture.

Adams, Robert, photos by. Los Angeles Spring. (Illus.). 64p. 1986. 44.95 (*0-89381-220-X*) Aperture.

Adams, Robert & Norton, Andre, eds. Magic in Ithkar IV, No. 4. (Illus.). 288p. (Orig.). 1987. pap. 3.50 (*0-8125-4719-5*, Pub. by Tor Bks) St Martin.

Adams, Robert, et al. E. W., Centennial Essays in Honor of Edward Weston. Bunnell, Peter C. & Featherstone, David, eds. LC 86-80466. (Untitled Ser.: No. 41). (Illus.). 144p. (Orig.). 1986. pap. 4.98 (*0-933286-45-7*) Frnds Photography.

Adams, Robert, jt. auth. see Norton, Andre.

***Adams, Robert A.** Calculus: A Complete Course. 4th ed. (C). 1999. text. write for info. (*0-201-39607-6*) Addison-Wesley.

Adams, Robert A. Calculus of Several Variables. 3rd ed. 1996. text. write for info. (*0-201-87282-X*) Addison-Wesley.

— Calculus of Several Variables. 3rd ed. (C). 1996. text 51.95 (*0-201-88195-0*) Addison-Wesley.

Adams, Robert G. Firehouse Cooking. LC 97-49083. 224p. 1998. 7.99 (*0-517-18818-X*) Random Hse Value.

Adams, Robert M. Archaeological Investigations in Jefferson County, Missouri. Chapman, Carl H., ed. (Missouri Archaeologist Ser.: Vol. 11, Nos. 3 & 4). (Illus.). 71p. (Orig.). 1949. pap. 2.50 (*0-943414-28-8*) MO Arch Soc.

— Heartland of Cities: Surveys of Ancient Settlement & Land Use on the Central Floodplain of the Euphrates. LC 80-13995. (Illus.). 382p. reprint ed. pap. 118.50 (*0-608-09371-8*, 205411600004) Bks Demand.

— Irrigation's Impact on Society. Downing, Theodore E. & Gibson, McGuire, eds. LC 74-15602. (Anthropological Papers of the University of Arizona: No. 25). (Illus.). 191p. reprint ed. pap. 59.30 (*0-7837-5045-5*, 204472300004) Bks Demand.

— The Land & Literature of England: A Historical Account. (Illus.). 640p. 1986. reprint ed. pap. 19.95 (*0-393-30343-8*) Norton.

— Land Behind Baghdad: A History of Settlement on the Diyala Plains. LC 65-17279. 254p. reprint ed. pap. 78.80 (*0-608-16467-4*, 202676000052) Bks Demand.

— Leibniz: Determinist, Theist, Idealist. 448p. 1994. text 65.00 (*0-19-508460-8*) OUP.

— Occupational Skin Disease. 2nd ed. 624p. 1990. text 156.00 (*0-7216-2926-1*, 790026, W B Saunders Co) Harcrt Hlth Sci Grp.

— Occupational Skin Disease. 3rd ed. Fletcher, Judy, ed. LC 98-25698. (Illus.). 830p. 1999. text 125.00 (*0-7216-7037-7*, W B Saunders Co) Harcrt Hlth Sci Grp.

— Paths of Fire: An Anthropologist's Inquiry into Technology in the Making of the Modern West. 360p. 1996. text 29.95 (*0-691-02634-3*, Pub. by Princeton U Pr) Cal Prin Full Svc.

— Strains of Discord. LC 75-142601. (Essay Index Reprint Ser.). 1977. 18.95 (*0-8369-1917-3*) Ayer.

Adams, Robert M., ed. Erasmus. (Critical Editions Ser.). 1987. pap. write for info. (*0-393-95625-3*) Norton.

Adams, Robert M., et al, eds. Behavioral & Social Science Research: A National Resource, 2 pts., Pt. 1. LC 82-81776. (Illus.). 135p. reprint ed. pap. 41.90 (*0-8357-4263-6*, 203705900001) Bks Demand.

— Behavioral & Social Science Research: A National Resource, 2 pts., Pt. 2. LC 82-81776. (Illus.). 612p. reprint ed. pap. 189.80 (*0-8357-4264-4*, 203705900002) Bks Demand.

Adams, Robert M., jt. ed. see Adams, Marilyn M.

Adams, Robert M., ed. see Berkeley, George.

Adams, Robert M., ed. see Jonson, Ben.

Adams, Robert M., ed. see Kant, Immanuel.

Adams, Robert M., ed. see Meredith, George.

Adams, Robert M., ed. see More, Thomas.

Adams, Robert M., jt. ed. see Shapiro, Ian.

Adams, Robert M., ed. see Stendhal, pseud.

Adams, Robert M., ed. & tr. see Machiavelli, Niccolo.

Adams, Robert M., ed. & tr. see More, Thomas.

Adams, Robert M., tr. see Erasmus, Desiderius.

Adams, Robert Merrihew. Finite & Infinite Goods: A Framework for Ethics. LC 98-29122. 424p. 1999. text 45.00 (*0-19-512848-6*) OUP.

Adams, Robert P. Identification of Essential Oils by Ion Trap Mass Spectroscopy. 302p. 1989. text 84.00 (*0-12-044230-2*) Acad Pr.

Adams, Robert P. & Adams, Janice E., eds. Conservation of Plant Genes: DNA Banking & In Vitro Biotechnology. (Illus.). 345p. 1991. text 73.00 (*0-12-044140-3*) Acad Pr.

***Adams, Robert P. & Adams, Janice E., eds.** Conservation of Plant Genes III: Conservation & Utilization of African Plants. (Illus.). vii, 241p. 1999. 40.00 (*0-915279-56-8*) Miss Botan.

Adams, Robert T. Electronic Music Composition for Beginners. 2nd ed. 304p. (C). 1992. text. write for info. (*0-697-12492-4*) Brown & Benchmark.

Adams, Roger L. DNA Replication: In Focus. (Illus.). 96p. (C). 1991. pap. text 15.95 (*0-19-963216-2*, 12250) OUP.

Adams, Romanzo. Interracial Marriage in Hawaii: A Study of the Mutually Conditioned Processes of Acculturation & Amalgamation. LC 69-14907. (Criminology, Law Enforcement, & Social Problems Ser.: No. 65). (Illus.). 1969. reprint ed. 12.00 (*0-87585-065-0*) Patterson Smith.

***Adams, Ronald.** 100 Years of Big Trucks. (Crestline Ser.). (Illus.). 320p. 2000. 44.95 (*0-7603-0769-5*, 130098AP, Pub. by MBI Pubg) Motorbooks Intl.

Adams, Ronald G. What about Flying? LC 93-93883. 144p. (Orig.). 1993. pap. 8.95 (*0-9637307-0-3*) Wrds For You Pub.

Adams, Ronald J., et al. Street Survival: Tactics for Armed Encounters. LC 79-57196. (Illus.). 416p. 1980. text 31.95 (*0-935878-00-9*) Calibre Pr.

Adams, Rosemary K. What George Wore & Sally Didn't: Surprising Stories from America's Past. LC 98-40776. 1999. pap. 24.95 (*0-913820-21-0*) Chicago Hist.

***Adams, Rosemary K. & Platt, Harold, eds.** A Wild Kind of Boldness: The Chicago History Reader. LC 98-6687. (Illus.). 458p. 1998. 39.00 (*0-8028-3019-6*) Eerdmans.

***Adams Round Table Group Staff.** Murder among Friends. LC 99-51318. 2000. 21.95 (*0-425-16700-3*, Prime Crime) Berkley Pub.

Adams Round Table Staff. Justice in Manhattan. 1995. mass mkt. 5.50 (*0-425-15102-6*) Berkley Pub.

Adams Round Table Staff & Block, Lawrence. Murder on the Run. LC 97-23375. 336p. 1998. pap. 21.95 (*0-425-16146-3*, Prime Crime) Berkley Pub.

Adams, Roxana, ed. International Museum Day Resource Guide. (Professional Practice Ser.). (Illus.). 140p. 1997. ring bd. 14.00 (*0-931201-52-7*, PPD859) Am Assn Mus.

Adams, Roxana, ed. see Ritzenthaler, Tom.

Adams, Roxana, ed. see Serrell, Beverly.

Adams, Roxana J., ed. see Lister, Mary.

Adams, Roy. Communication & Delivery Systems for Librarians. 70p. 1990. text 63.95 (*0-566-05750-6*, Pub. by Gower) Ashgate Pub Co.

— The Sanctuary: Understanding the Heart of Adventist Theology. LC 92-14249. 1992. pap. 9.99 (*0-8280-0656-3*) Review & Herald.

Adams, Roy J. Comparative Industrial Relations. 176p. (C). 1991. mass mkt. 24.95 (*0-04-445967-X*, A8160) Thomson Learn.

— Information Technology & Libraries: A Future for Academic Libraries. (Information Technology Ser.). 192p. 1986. 34.00 (*0-7099-0577-7*, Pub. by C Helm) Routldge.

Adams, Roy J., ed. see Meltz, Noah M.

Adams, Roy M. Estate Planning Manual for Trust Officers. 3rd ed. LC 82-229355. (Illus.). 300p. 1992. 225.00 (*0-685-62689-X*) Am Bankers.

***Adams, Roy M. & Abendroth, Thomas W.** Illinois Estate Planning, Will Drafting & Estate Administration Forms. 3rd ed. 1000p. 1999. write for info. (*0-327-04909-X*, 8111211) LEXIS Pub.

Adams, Roy M., et al. Illinois Estate Planning, Will Drafting & Estate Administration Forms. 2nd ed. 1994. ring bd. 225.00 (*0-250-40735-3*, 81112-10, MICHIE) LEXIS Pub.

— Illinois Estate Planning, Will Drafting & Estate Administration Forms, 2 vols., Set. 2000p. 1993. spiral bd. 225.00 (*0-8342-0029-5*, MICHIE) LEXIS Pub.

Adams, Roy N. & Denman, Eugene D. Wave Propagation & Turbulent Media. LC 66-30179. (Modern Analytic & Computational Methods in Science & Mathematics Ser.). 134p. reprint ed. pap. 41.60 (*0-608-30461-1*, 200776600064) Bks Demand.

Adams, Royce. Risking Contact: Readings to Challenge Our Thinking. LC 96-76853. 640p. (C). 1997. pap. text 28.76 (*0-669-39327-4*); pap. text, teacher ed. 12.36 (*0-669-39329-0*) HM Trade Div.

Adams, Royce W., Jr., jt. auth. see Carman, Robert A.

Adams, Russ & Harmon, Craig. The Bar Code Book: Reading, Printing, & Specification of Bar Code Symbols. 3rd ed. 298p. 1989. pap. 19.95 (*0-911261-00-1*) Helmers Pub.

— Reading Between the Lines: An Introduction to Bar Code Technology. 4th ed. 298p. 1989. 34.00 (*0-911261-02-8*); pap. 23.95 (*0-685-34515-7*) Helmers Pub.

Adams, Russ & Lane, Joyce. The Black & White Solution: Bar Code & the IBM PC. 172p. (Orig.). 1987. pap. 19.95 (*0-911261-01-X*) Helmers Pub.

Adams, Russell B., Jr., ed. see Time-Life Books Editors.

Adams, Russell L. Great Negroes Past & Present. rev. ed. (Illus.). 205p. 1963. 29.95 (*0-910030-08-1*) African Am Imag.

Adams, Russell L., et al, eds. Neuropsychology for Clinical Practice: Etiology, Assessment, & Treatment of Common Neurological Disorders. LC 95-49944. 546p. 1996. 69.95 (*1-55798-298-8*, 431-7540) Am Psychol.

Adams, Ruth. One Little Candle. 4th ed. xii, 194p. 1994. 10.00 (*0-88053-314-5*, S-251) Macoy Pub.

Adams, Ruth & Cullen, Sue, eds. The Final Epidemic: Physicians & Scientists on Nuclear War. 266p. (Orig.). 1982. pap. 4.95 (*0-941682-00-5*) Educ Found for Nucl Sci.

Adams, Ruth, et al. Gathered Memories. viii, 142p. 1991. reprint ed. pap. 7.50 (*0-88053-308-0*, S-76) Macoy Pub.

Adams, Ruth S., jt. ed. see McNeill, William H.

Adams, S., jt. auth. see Holmes, M.

Adams, Sam. Persons, Places & Things. 139p. 1998. pap. 15.00 (*0-9665891-0-6*) P S Brown LA.

— Roland Mathias. 200p. 1995. pap. 10.95 (*0-7083-1285-3*, Pub. by Univ Wales Pr) Paul & Co Pubs.

***Adams, Sam.** T. J. Llewelyn Prichard. 130p. 2000. pap. 12.95 (*0-7083-1645-X*, Pub. by U Wales Pr) Paul & Co Pubs.

Adams, Sam. War of Numbers: An Intelligence Memoir. 251p. 1998. text 22.00 (*0-7881-5429-X*) DIANE Pub.

— War of Numbers: An Intelligence Memoir. LC 93-50207. 256p. 1994. 22.00 (*1-883642-23-X*) Steerforth Pr.

— War of Numbers: An Intelligence Memoir. LC 93-50207. 256p. 1995. pap. 13.00 (*1-883642-46-9*) Steerforth Pr.

Adams, Sam, ed. Seeing Wales Whole: Essays on the Literature of Wales. LC 98-213908. 176p. 1998. write for info. (*0-7083-1389-2*, Pub. by Univ Wales Pr) Paul & Co Pubs.

Adams, Sam & Mathias, Roland. The Shining Pyramid. 163p. (C). 1970. pap. 22.00 (*0-85044-484-5*, Pub. by Gomer Pr) St Mut.

Adams, Sam & Mathias, Roland, eds. The Shining Pyramid. 163p. 1970. pap. 30.00 (*0-85088-484-5*, Pub. by Gomer Pr) St Mut.

***Adams, Samuel.** Cattle Mutilations, an Elusive Prey. LC 00-130305. (Illus.). 128p. 2000. pap. write for info. (*1-57197-217-X*, Pub. by Pentland Pr) Assoc Pubs Grp.

Adams, Samuel, jt. auth. see Young, Ben.

Adams, Samuel H. Alexander Woollcott: His Life & His World. LC 77-130545. (Select Bibliographies Reprint Ser.). 1977. reprint ed. 25.95 (*0-8369-5518-8*) Ayer.

— Average Jones. LC 75-32731. (Literature of Mystery & Detection Ser.). (Illus.). 1976. reprint ed. 28.95 (*0-405-07861-7*) Ayer.

— Canal Town. Bergmann, Frank, ed. 476p. 1988. pap. 17.95 (*0-8156-0228-6*) Syracuse U Pr.

— From a Bench in Our Square. LC 72-103487. (Short Story Index Reprint Ser.). 1977. 21.95 (*0-8369-3213-7*) Ayer.

— Grandfather Stories. lib. bdg. 24.95 (*0-8488-1950-0*) Amereon Ltd.

— Grandfather Stories. LC 88-31918. (New York Classics Ser.). 336p. 1989. reprint ed. pap. text 17.95 (*0-8156-0232-4*) Syracuse U Pr.

— The Great American Fraud: A Series of Articles on the Patent Medicine Evil. 1976. reprint ed. 49.00 (*0-403-05771-X*, Regency) Scholarly.

— Our Square & the People in It. LC 78-106241. (Short Story Index Reprint Ser.). 1977. 25.95 (*0-8369-3277-3*) Ayer.

— Revelry. (BCL1-PS American Literature Ser.). 318p. 1992. reprint ed. lib. bdg. 89.00 (*0-7812-6914-8*) Rprt Serv.

— Tenderloin. 26.95 (*0-89190-894-3*) Amereon Ltd.

Adams, Samuel H., jt. auth. see White, Stewart E.

Adams, Sandi. What the Fly Heard: What Mediators Say Behind Closed Doors. (Illus.). iv, 65p. 1998. pap. 12.00 (*0-9666525-0-9*) Queen of Hrts.

Adams, Sandi, ed. see Beer, Jennifer E.

Adams, Sandra P., jt. auth. see Sieg, Kay W.

***Adams, Sandy.** Christmas Through the Eyes... 62p. 1999. pap. 0.99 (*0-9676661-3-9*) Calvary Dist.

***Adams, Sandy, et al.** Because He Lives: The Hope, Promise & Truth. 59p. 2000. pap. 0.99 (*0-9676661-8-X*) Calvary Dist.

Adams, Scott. Access Denied: Dilbert's Quest for Love in the Nineties. LC 96-84528. (Illus.). 80p. 1996. 4.95 (*0-8362-2191-5*) Andrews & McMeel.

— Always Postpone Meetings with Time-Wasting Morons. (Illus.). 112p. 1994. pap. 8.95 (*0-8362-1758-6*) Andrews & McMeel.

— The Boss: Nameless, Blameless & Shameless. LC 96-79237. (Illus.). 80p. 1997. 4.95 (*0-8362-3223-2*) Andrews & McMeel.

— Bring Me the Head of Willy the Mailboy. LC 94-79702. (Illus.). 128p. 1995. pap. 9.95 (*0-8362-1779-9*) Andrews & McMeel.

— Build a Better Life by Stealing Office Supplies: Dogbert's Big Book of Business. (Illus.). 112p. (Orig.). 1994. pap. 8.95 (*0-8362-1757-8*) Andrews & McMeel.

— Casual Day Has Gone Too Far. LC 96-97238. (Illus.). 128p. (Orig.). 1997. pap. 9.95 (*0-8362-2899-5*) Andrews & McMeel.

— Conversations with Dogbert. LC 96-224692. (Illus.). 48p. 1996. 6.95 (*0-8362-2197-4*) Andrews & McMeel.

— The Dilbert Bunch. LC 98-100878. (Illus.). 40p. 1997. 6.95 (*0-8362-2879-0*) Andrews & McMeel.

Adams, Scott. Dilbert Future: Adams,&Scott. abr. ed. 1997. audio 12.00 (*0-694-51842-5*, CPN 10109) HarperAudio.

Adams, Scott. The Dilbert Future: Thriving on Stupidity in the 21st Century. LC 97-7137. (Illus.). 258p. 1997. 25.00 (*0-88730-866-X*, HarpBusn) HarpInfo.

— The Dilbert Future: Thriving on Stupidity in the 21st Century. LC 97-7137. (Illus.). 274p. 1998. pap. 12.95 (*0-88730-910-0*, HarpBusn) HarpInfo.

— Dilbert Gives You the Business: A Dilbert Book. LC 99-61204. (Illus.). 224p. 1999. pap. 14.95 (*0-7407-0003-0*) Andrews & McMeel.

***Adams, Scott.** Dilbert Gives You the Business: A Dilbert Book. (Illus.). 224p. 1999. 19.95 (*0-7407-0338-2*) Andrews & McMeel.

Adams, Scott. Dilbert Postcard Book. (Illus.). 30p. 1996. pap. 8.95 (*0-8362-1331-9*) Andrews & McMeel.

— The Dilbert Principle: A Cubicle's-Eye View of Bosses, Meetings, Management Fads & Other Workplace Afflictions. LC 96-388. (Illus.). 352p. 1997. pap. 12.95 (*0-88730-858-9*, HarpBusn) HarpInfo.

— The Dilbert Principle: A Cubicle's Eye View of Bosses, Meetings, Management Fads & Other Workplace Afflictions. (Illus.). 336p. 1996. 22.00 (*0-88730-787-6*, HarpBusn) HarpInfo.

Adams, Scott. Dilbert Principle: Adams,&Scott. abr. ed. 1996. audio. write for info. (*0-694-51692-9*, CPN 10079, Pub. by HarperAudio) Lndmrk Audiobks.

Adams, Scott. Dogbert's Clues for the Clueless. LC 93-71864. (Illus.). 112p. (Orig.). 1993. pap. 8.95 (*0-8362-1737-3*) Andrews & McMeel.

— Dogbert's Top Secret Management Handbook. (Illus.). 112p. 1996. 16.00 (*0-88730-788-4*, HarpBusn) HarpInfo.

— Dogbert's Top Secret Management Handbook. (Illus.). 176p. 1997. pap. 11.95 (*0-88730-881-3*, HarpBusn) HarpInfo.

Adams, Scott. Dogbert's Top Secret Management Handbook: Adams,&Scott. abr. ed. 90p. 1996. audio. write for info. (*0-694-51772-0*, CPN 10097, Pub. by HarperAudio) Lndmrk Audiobks.

Adams, Scott. Don't Step in the Leadership: A Dilbert Book. LC 98-88670. (Dilbert Bks.). (Illus.). 127p. 1999. pap. 9.95 (*0-8362-7844-5*) Andrews & McMeel.

— Fugitive from the Cubicle Police. LC 96-84103. (Dilbert Bks.). (Illus.). 224p. (Orig.). 1996. pap. 12.95 (*0-8362-2119-2*) Andrews & McMeel.

— I'm Not Anti-Business, I'm Anti-Idiot. (Dilbert Bks.). (Illus.). 1998. pap. text 9.95 (*0-8362-5182-2*) Andrews & McMeel.

— It's Obvious You Won't Survive on Your Wits Alone. LC 95-79090. (Illus.). 224p. 1995. pap. 12.95 (*0-8362-0415-8*) Andrews & McMeel.

— Journey to Cubeville. LC 98-85334. (Dilbert Bks.). (Illus.). 224p. 1998. 19.95 (*0-8362-7175-0*); pap. 12.95 (*0-8362-6745-1*) Andrews & McMeel.

***Adams, Scott.** Joy of Work: Adams,&Scott. abr. ed. 1998. audio 12.00 (*0-694-51987-1*) HarperAudio.

Adams, Scott. The Joy of Work: How to Find Happiness at the Expense of Your Coworkers. LC 98-27083. (Illus.). 288p. 1998. 22.00 (*0-88730-871-6*, HarpBusn) HarpInfo.

— The Joy of Work: How to Find Happiness at the Expense of Your Coworkers. 272p. 2000. pap. 13.00 (*0-88730-895-3*, HarpBusn) HarpInfo.

An Asterisk (*) at the beginning of an entry indicates that the title is appearing for the first time.

— Medical Bibliography in an Age of Discontinuity. 244p. 1981. 14.00 (*0-8108-2433-7*) Scarecrow.
— No, You'd Better Watch Out. LC 97-225658. (Little Bks.). (Illus.). 80p. (J). 1997. 4.95 (*0-8362-3739-0*) Andrews & McMeel.
— Please Don't Feed the Egos: And Other Tips for Corporate Survival. LC 97-228609. (Illus.). 40p. 1997. 6.95 (*0-8362-3224-0*) Andrews & McMeel.
— Random Acts of Catness. LC 99-159374. (Little Bks.). (Illus.). 80p. 1998. pap. 4.95 (*0-8362-5277-2*) Andrews & McMeel.
***Adams, Scott.** Random Acts of Management. LC 99-68659. (Dilbert Bks.: No. 15). (Illus.). 128p. 2000. pap. 9.95 (*0-7407-0453-2*) Andrews & McMeel.
Adams, Scott. Seven Years of Highly Defective People: Scott Adams' Guided Tour of the Evolution of Dilbert. 256p. 1997. 19.95 (*0-8362-5129-6*) Andrews & McMeel.
— Seven Years of Highly Defective People: Scott Adams' Guided Tour of the Evolution of Dilbert. LC 97-72286. (Illus.). 256p. 1997. pap. 12.95 (*0-8362-3668-8*) Andrews & McMeel.
— Shave the Whales. LC 93-74266. (Illus.). 128p. 1994. pap. 9.95 (*0-8362-1740-3*) Andrews & McMeel.
— Still Pumped from Using the Mouse. LC 95-81471. (Dilbert Bks.). (Illus.). 128p. (Orig.). 1996. pap. 9.95 (*0-8362-1026-3*) Andrews & McMeel.
— Telling It Like It Isn't: A Tiptoe Approach to Communications - A Dilbert Little Book. LC 96-202412. (Illus.). 1996. 4.95 (*0-8362-1324-6*) Andrews & McMeel.
***Adams, Scott.** Treasury of Sunday Strips-Version 00. (Dilbert Bks.). (Illus.). 224p. (J). 2000. pap. 14.95 (*0-7407-0531-8*) Andrews & McMeel.
— Virginia: An Atlas of Virginia's Greatest Off-Road Bicycle Rides. 2nd ed. (Mountain Bike America Guidebks.). (Illus.). 336p. 2000. pap. 17.95 (*0-7627-0704-6*) Globe Pequot.
Adams, Scott. Work Is a Contact Sport. gif. ed. LC 96-86664. (Illus.). 80p. 1997. 4.95 (*0-8362-2878-2*) Andrews & McMeel.
— You Can't Schedule Stupidity. LC 99-159375. (Little Bks.). (Illus.). 80p. 1998. pap. 4.95 (*0-8362-5632-8*) Andrews & McMeel.
— You Don't Need Experience If You've Got Attitude. LC 96-224064. (Illus.). 48p. 1996. 6.95 (*0-8362-2196-6*) Andrews & McMeel.
***Adams, Scott & Fernandez, Martin.** Washington D. C./Baltimore: An Atlas of Northern Virginia & Maryland's Greatest Off-Road Bicycle Rides. 3rd ed. (Mountain Bike America Guidebks.). (Illus.). 304p. 2000. pap. 17.95 (*0-7627-0705-4*) Globe Pequot.
***Adams, Scott Charles.** . . . Never Dream. West, Carolyn, ed. 240p. 1999. pap. 15.00 (*0-9673045-0-4*) SC Adams.
Adams, Scott E. Bike Rides from Beaver Stadium: An Atlas of Central Pennsylvania's Greatest Bicycle Rides. (Illus.). 128p. (Orig.). 1992. pap. 9.95 (*1-882997-01-8*) Beachway Pr.
— Mountain Bike Madness in Central PA: An Atlas of Central Pennsylvania's Greatest Mountain Bike Rides. (Illus.). 142p. (Orig.). 1993. pap. 10.95 (*1-882997-02-6*) Beachway Pr.
— Mountain Bike Virginia: An Atlas of Virginia's Greatest Off-Road Bicycle Rides. 2nd ed. (Mountain Bike America Ser.). (Illus.). 224p. (YA). 1998. pap. 15.95 (*1-882997-11-5*) Beachway Pr.
— Mountain Bike Virginia: An Atlas of Virginia's Greatest Off-Road Bike Rides. (Mountain Bike America Ser.). (Illus.). 256p. (Orig.). 1995. pap. 12.95 (*1-882997-04-2*) Beachway Pr.
— The Washington-Baltimore Mountain Bike Book: Out of the Gridlock, into the Woods. LC 94-70940. (Illus.). 208p. (Orig.). 1994. pap. 12.95 (*1-882997-03-4*) Beachway Pr.
Adams, Scott E., ed. see Dunegan, Lizann.
Adams, Sean T., jt. auth. see Adams, Charles S.
Adams, Sexton & Griffin, Adelaide. Cases in Strategic Management. 3rd ed. 404p. (C). 1995. text 31.25 (*0-256-22294-0*, Irwn McGrw-H) McGrw-H Hghr Educ.
— Modern Personnel Management. LC 80-24173. (Illus.). 360p. (Orig.). reprint ed. pap. 111.60 (*0-608-18160-9*, 203285600081) Bks Demand.
Adams, Sheila K. Come Go Home with Me. LC 95-8516. 136p. 1997. 22.50 (*0-8078-2243-4*); pap. 12.95 (*0-8078-4536-1*) U of NC Pr.
Adams, Shelby L. Appalachian Legacy. LC 97-42794. (Illus.). 128p. 1998. 50.00 (*1-57806-048-6*); pap. 30.00 (*1-57806-049-4*) U Pr of Miss.
Adams, Shelby L., photos by. Appalachian Portraits. limited ed. LC 93-4688. (Illus.). 1993. 150.00 (*0-87805-706-4*) U Pr of Miss.
Adams, Sherman W. & Stiles, Henry R. The History of Ancient Wethersfield Vol. 1: The Narrative History, Vol. I. LC 74-83524. (Illus.). 1011p. 1995. reprint ed. 65.00 (*0-89725-073-7*, 1191) Picton Pr.
Adams, Sherman W. & Stiles, Henry R., eds. History of Ancient Wethersfield, Connecticut Vol. II: Genealogies & Biographies, Vol. II. LC 74-83524. (Illus.). 946p. 1984. reprint ed. 65.00 (*0-89725-068-0*, 1192) Picton Pr.
Adams, Shielly. The Sewing Connection Series: Series 17. Adams, Rebecca, ed. (Illus.). 64p. 1998. pap. 15.00 (*1-884389-37-6*, SCB017) Sewing Connection.
Adams, Shirley. Blouse Pattern Pizazz. (Illus.). 1982. VHS 24.95 (*1-884389-11-2*) Sewing Connection.
— Kitchen Angel, Vol. 1. (Illus.). 69p. 1997. ring bd. 30.00 (*0-9667340-0-9*) Clear Nutrition.
— The Sewing Connection: Series 1. rev. ed. (Illus.). 64p. 1994. 15.00 (*1-884389-23-6*) Sewing Connection.
— The Sewing Connection: Series 11. Adams, Rebecca, ed. (Series II). (Illus.). 64p. 1995. wbk. ed. 15.00 (*1-884389-24-4*) Sewing Connection.
— The Sewing Connection: Series 12. Adams, Rebecca, ed. (Illus.). 64p. 1995. pap., student ed. 15.00 (*1-884389-26-0*) Sewing Connection.
— The Sewing Connection: Series 13. Adams, Rebecca, ed. (Illus.). 64p. 1996. pap., wbk. ed. 15.00 (*1-884389-29-5*, SCB013) Sewing Connection.
— The Sewing Connection: Series 15. Adams, Rebecca, ed. (Illus.). 64p. 1997. pap. 15.00 (*1-884389-33-3*, SCB015) Sewing Connection.
— The Sewing Connection: Series 16. (Illus.). 64p. 1997. pap. 15.00 (*1-884389-35-X*, SCB016) Sewing Connection.
— The Sewing Connection Series: Series 1. (Illus.). 64p. 1990. VHS 59.95 (*1-884389-12-0*) Sewing Connection.
— The Sewing Connection Series: Series 10. Adams, Rebecca, ed. (Illus.). 64p. 1994. pap. text, student ed. 15.00 (*1-884389-21-X*, SCB010) Sewing Connection.
— The Sewing Connection Series: Series 2. (Illus.). 64p. 1991. student ed. 15.00 (*1-884389-01-5*); VHS 58.95 (*1-884389-13-9*) Sewing Connection.
— The Sewing Connection Series: Series 3. (Illus.). 64p. 1991. student ed. 15.00 (*1-884389-02-3*); VHS 58.95 (*1-884389-14-7*) Sewing Connection.
— The Sewing Connection Series: Series 4. (Illus.). 64p. 1991. student ed. 15.00 (*1-884389-03-1*); VHS 58.95 (*1-884389-15-5*) Sewing Connection.
— The Sewing Connection Series: Series 5. (Illus.). 64p. 1992. student ed. 15.00 (*1-884389-04-X*); VHS 58.95 (*1-884389-16-3*) Sewing Connection.
— The Sewing Connection Series: Series 6. (Illus.). 64p. 1992. student ed. 15.00 (*1-884389-05-8*); VHS 58.95 (*1-884389-17-1*) Sewing Connection.
— The Sewing Connection Series: Series 7. (Illus.). 64p. 1993. student ed. 15.00 (*1-884389-06-6*); VHS 58.95 (*1-884389-18-X*) Sewing Connection.
— The Sewing Connection Series: Series 8. (Illus.). 64p. 1993. student ed. 15.00 (*1-884389-07-4*); VHS 58.95 (*1-884389-19-8*) Sewing Connection.
— The Sewing Connection Series: Series 9. Adams, R., ed. (Illus.). 64p. 1994. pap. text, student ed. 15.00 (*1-884389-08-2*) Sewing Connection.
Adams, Shirley K. The Sewing Connection: Series 14. (Illus.). 64p. (Orig.). 1996. pap. text 15.00 (*1-884389-31-7*, SCB014) Sewing Connection.
Adams, Silas. The History of the Town of Bowdoinham (Maine), 1762-1912. LC 84-62118. (Illus.). 376p. 1985. reprint ed. 45.00 (*0-89725-055-9*, 1200) Picton Pr.
— History of the Town of Bowdoinham, 1762-1912. (Illus.). 295p. 1997. reprint ed. lib. bdg. 29.00 (*0-8328-5815-3*) Higginson Bk Co.
Adams, Silas W. The Federal Reserve System. 1979. lib. bdg. 59.95 (*0-8490-2915-5*) Gordon Pr.
— The Legalized Crime of Banking. 1979. lib. bdg. 250.00 (*0-8490-2957-0*) Gordon Pr.
— The United States Treasury System: Debt Bondage or a Debtless Economy. 1979. lib. bdg. 59.95 (*0-8490-3012-9*) Gordon Pr.
Adams, Simon. The DK Visual Timeline of the 20th Century. (Illus.). 48p. (J). 1996. 15.95 (*0-7894-0997-6*) DK Pub Inc.
***Adams, Simon.** Football. LC 99-32241. (Eyewitness Books). (J). (gr. 4-7). 1999. 15.95 (*0-7894-4725-8*) DK Pub Inc.
— The Handbook of Professional Selling & Sales Negotiation. 192p. 1996. pap. 33.50 (*0-273-62579-9*, Pub. by F T P-H) Trans-Atl Phila.
— Jazz: A Crash Course. (Crash Course Ser.). (Illus.). 144p. 1999. 14.95 (*0-8230-0979-3*) Watsn-Guptill.
— Titanic. LC 99-32241. (Eyewitness Books). (J). (gr. 4-7). 1999. 15.95 (*0-7894-4724-X*) DK Pub Inc.
Adams, Simon, ed. Household Accounts & Disbursement Books of Robert Dudley, Earl of Leicester, 1558-61, 1584-86. (Camden Fifth Ser.: No. 6). 534p. (C). 1996. text 59.95 (*0-521-55156-0*) Cambridge U Pr.
Adams, Simon & Rodriquez Salgado, Maria J. England, Spain & the Grand Armada, 1585-1589. 280p. (C). 1997. text 50.00 (*0-85976-300-5*, Pub. by J Donald) St Mut.
Adams, Simon, jt. auth. see Rodriquez, M. J.
Adams, Spencer L. The Long House of the Iroquois. LC 76-43640. (Illus.). reprint ed. 34.50 (*0-404-15475-1*) AMS Pr.
Adams, Stacy. Shoestring Memories: Through the Depression on a Hill Ranch. 208p. 1994. pap. 10.00 (*0-9640521-0-5*) Wild Rose Pr.
Adams, Stephanie G. & Adams, Howard G., contrib. by. Techniques for Effective Undergraduate Mentoring. (C). 1993. 5.00 (*1-887284-03-6*) Natl Consortium.
***Adams, Stephen.** California Family Law Practice. 14th rev. ed. 1800p. 1999. pap. text 275.00 (*1-890936-09-X*) CA Fam Law.
— Family Law Practice Nuts & Bolts: Nuts & Bolts, Set. 674p. 1998. pap. text, wbk. ed. 125.00 (*1-890936-00-6*) CA Fam Law.
Adams, Stephen. Poetic Designs: An Introduction to Meters, Verse Forms, & Figures of Speech. 240p. (C). 1997. pap. 16.95 (*1-55111-129-2*) Broadview Pr.
Adams, Stephen, et al, eds. Voices on the Glory. LC 99-165853. 1998. mass mkt. 5.99 (*0-87509-800-2*) Chr Pubns.
Adams, Stephen & Mandabach, Frederick A. Deductor XVII: Seventeenth California Edition. 17th rev. ed. (Illus.). 214p. 1999. spiral bd. 85.00 (*0-932663-74-5*) CA Fam Law.
Adams, Stephen & Ross, Donald. Revising Mythologies: The Composition of Thoreau's Major Works. LC 88-801. 285p. 1988. reprint ed. pap. 88.40 (*0-608-01439-7*, 206220100002) Bks Demand.
Adams, Stephen & Sevitch, Nancy. Court Companion 1996. rev. ed. 184p. 1996. spiral bd. 75.00 (*0-932663-92-3*) CA Fam Law.
Adams, Stephen, jt. auth. see Tocci, Christopher.
Adams, Stephen B. Mr. Kaiser Goes to Washington: The Rise of a Government Entrepreneur. LC 96-53391. (Luther Hartwell Hodges Series on Business, Society & the State). 251p. (gr. 13). 1997. 45.00 (*0-8078-2358-9*) U of NC Pr.
Adams, Stephen B. & Butler, Orville R. Manufacturing the Future: A History of Western Electric. LC 98-34294. 288p. (C). 1999. text 34.95 (*0-521-65118-2*) Cambridge U Pr.
Adams, Stephen P. Reinventing Your Career: Surviving a Layoff & Creating New Opportunities. pap. 9.99 (*0-8024-7361-X*) Northfield Pub.
— Reinventing Your Career: Surviving a Layoff & Creating New Opportunities. 160p. 1996. pap. 9.99 (*1-881273-61-X*) Northfield Pub.
***Adams, Steve.** Frontiers: Twentieth Century Physics LC 99-34590. 2000. 37.95 (*0-7484-0840-1*) Tay Francis Ltd.
— Oracle Ed1 Internal Services: For Waits, Latches, Locks & Memory. Russell, Deborah, ed. (Illus.). 150p. 1999. pap. 19.95 (*1-56592-598-X*) OReilly & Assocs.
Adams, Steve. Personal Finance with 1-2-3. (Orig.). 1990. pap. 24.95 (*0-13-660457-9*) P-H.
— Quick Guide to Financial Formulas for 1-2-3 Users. Hunt, ed. (Illus.). 350p. (Orig.). 1990. pap. 24.95 (*0-13-745134-2*) Brady Pub.
— Relativity: An Introduction to Space-Time Physics. LC 98-106738. 272p. 1997. pap. text 24.95 (*0-7484-0621-2*, Pub. by Tay Francis Ltd) Taylor & Francis.
— Using Quicken on the Mac: Tips & Techniques to Enhance Your Business Productivity. 1990. pap. 19.95 (*0-685-32930-5*) P-H.
Adams, Steve & Crago, Tracey. Marine Science Careers: A Sea Grant Guide to Ocean Opportunities. (Illus.). 40p. 1996. pap. text 5.00 (*0-9649529-0-4*) Maine-NHamp SGCP.
***Adams, Steve & Crago, Tracey, eds.** Marine Science Careers: A Sea Grant Guide to Ocean Opportunities. rev. ed. (Illus.). 32p. 2000. pap. text 5.00 (*0-9649529-2-0*) Maine-NHamp SGCP.
Adams, Steven. The Arts & Crafts Movement. 128p. 1996. write for info. (*1-57215-175-7*) World Pubns.
— The Barbizon School & the Origins of Impressionism. LC 95-128892. (Illus.). 240p. (C). 1994. text 55.00 (*0-7148-2919-6*, Pub. by Phaidon Press) Phaidon Pr.
— The Barbizon School & the Origins of Impressionism. (Illus.). 240p. 1997. pap. 35.00 (*0-7148-3623-0*, Pub. by Phaidon Press) Phaidon Pr.
Adams, Sue, et al. Graphics & Sound: Complete Lab. Shroeder, Bonnie, ed. (Illus.). 299.95 (*1-56177-028-0*, L183); Apple II 15.95 (*1-56177-027-2*, D183) CES Compu-Tech.
— Graphics & Sound Activity Book: Course Code 183-1. Schroeder, Bonnie, ed. (Illus.). 110p. (gr. 5). 1989. reprint ed. pap. 8.00 (*0-917531-49-3*) CES Compu-Tech.
— Graphics & Sound Activity Book, Teacher Edition: Course Code 183-1. rev. ed. Schroeder, Bonnie, ed. (Illus.). 130p. 1989. 19.95 (*0-917531-74-4*) CES Compu-Tech.
Adams, Susan. The Great Games Book: Over 30 Popular Games to Make & Play from Around the World. LC 97-16584. (J). (gr. 3-9). 1997. write for info. (*0-7894-2220-4*) DK Pub Inc.
— It's the Little Things: The Premarital Compatibility Test. 208p. 1995. pap. 8.95 (*0-8065-1634-8*, Citadel Pr) Carol Pub Group.
— The Marital Compatibility Test: Hundreds of Questions for Couples to Answer Together. LC 97-626. 160p. 1997. pap. 9.95 (*0-8065-1880-4*, Citadel Pr) Carol Pub Group.
***Adams, Susan.** The Marital Compatibility Test: 100's of Questions for Couples to Answer Together. LC 99-53973. 2000. 11.95 (*1-886039-46-1*) Addicus Bks.
Adams, Susan, ed. see Craighead, Joni.
Adams, Susan L. The Family Compatibility Test: Fun Questions for Moms, Dads & Kids to Ask Each Other. Colvin, Rod, ed. LC 96-47486. 175p. (Orig.). 1997. pap. 9.95 (*1-886039-27-5*) Addicus Bks.
Adams, T. Body English. 104p. 1997. pap. text 14.63 (*0-673-19189-3*) Addison-Wesley.
Adams, T. Dean, ed. see O'Halloran, Bethany J.
Adams, Ted, et al. Resident Evil: Magazine, No. 3. (Illus.). 56p. 1998. pap. write for info. (*1-58240-043-1*) Image Comics.
— Resident Evil: Magazine, No. 4. (Illus.). 56p. 1998. pap. 4.95 (*1-58240-045-8*) Image Comics.
Adams, Ted D., et al. Maintaining the Miracle Vol. 1: An Owner's Manual for the Human Body. (Illus.). 246p. reprint ed. pap. 17.95 (*0-9638937-7-7*) Capp Pubng.
Adams, Teresa & Smith, Stella. First Steps: Microsoft Word 97. 176p. (C). 1998. pap. text 13.00 (*0-03-023716-5*) Harcourt Coll Pubs.
***Adams, Teresa & Smith, Stella.** Microsoft Excel 2000. LC 99-61509. 2000. text. write for info. (*0-03-026133-3*) Harcourt Coll Pubs.
— Microsoft PowerPoint 2000. LC 99-61511. (Illus.). 2000. write for info. (*0-03-026142-2*) Harcourt Coll Pubs.
— Microsoft Word 2000. LC 99-61510. 2000. text. write for info. (*0-03-026137-6*) Harcourt Coll Pubs.
Adams, Teresa M., ed. Computing in Civil Engineering: Proceedings of the Fourth Congress Held in Conjunction with AEC Systems '97. LC 97-19516. 776p. 1997. 64.00 (*0-7844-0250-7*) Am Soc Civil Eng.
Adams, Terry, et al. Eye of the Beast. 1999. mass mkt. 6.50 (*0-312-96882-5*) St Martin.
— Eye of the Beast: The True Story of Serial Killer James Wood. LC 97-34332. (Illus.). 300p. (Orig.). 1997. pap. 16.95 (*1-886039-32-1*) Addicus Bks.
Adams, Terry, jt. auth. see Adams, Rob.
Adams, Thelma, ed. Censorship & First Amendment Rights: A Primer. 172p. 1991. pap. 10.00 (*1-879556-05-7*) ABA.
Adams, Thomas. Attitudes Through Idioms. 2nd ed. (College ESL Ser.). (J). 1993. text, suppl. ed. 7.95 (*0-8384-4251-X*) Heinle & Heinle.
***Adams, Thomas.** Concepts of Fitness. 170p. (C). 2000. spiral bd. 19.95 (*0-7872-7353-8*) Kendall-Hunt.
Adams, Thomas. The Design of Residential Areas: Basic Considerations, Principles & Methods. LC 73-2900. (Metropolitan America Ser.: Vol. 6). 334p. 1979. reprint ed. 31.95 (*0-405-05381-9*) Ayer.
— Guidelines for Surviving Heat & Cold: A Question-&-Answer Introduction to Protecting Yourself & Others from the Discomforts & Dangers of Summer & Winter. 143p. (C). 1992. pap. text 14.80 (*0-87563-403-6*) Stipes.
— Lore Power Is "Man" Power. 64p. 1981. pap. write for info. (*0-9609242-0-5*) T Adams.
— Physiology 432 Study Guide. 154p. (C). 1997. pap. text, spiral bd. 22.95 (*0-7872-3396-X*) Kendall-Hunt.
— Physiology 432 Study Guide. 5th ed. 298p. (C). 1998. spiral bd. 38.95 (*0-7872-4655-7*, 41465501) Kendall-Hunt.
— The Works of Thomas Adams, 3 vols. LC 72-158226. reprint ed. 65.00 (*0-404-00350-8*) AMS Pr.
— The Works of Thomas Adams, 3 vols. 502p. 1998. reprint ed. lib. bdg. 125.00 (*0-9651791-2-5*) Tanski Publns.
Adams, Thomas, et al. Physiology 431 Study Guide. 4th ed. 336p. (C). 1997. student ed., spiral bd. 29.95 (*0-7872-4403-1*) Kendall-Hunt.
Adams, Thomas B. Old Tom, Young Tom. 376p. 1988. 19.95 (*0-933905-11-4*); pap. 12.95 (*0-933905-12-2*) Claycomb Pr.
— Origins of Conflict: The United States in Central America, Selected Essays. Smith, Melden E., ed. 68p. (Orig.). 1989. pap. text 3.00 (*0-685-27234-6*) N Shore Cmnty Coll Pr.
Adams, Thomas F. Crime Scene Investigation. LC 99-27459. (Illus.). 180p. (C). 1999. pap. text 42.00 (*0-13-593427-3*) P-H.
— Police Patrol: Tactics & Techniques. LC 71-138484. (Essentials of Law Enforcement Ser.). 1971. 24.95 (*0-685-03898-X*) P-H.
Adams, Thomas K. U. S. Special Operations Forces in Action: The Challenge of Unconventional Warfare. LC 97-29160. 384p. (C). 1998. 59.50 (*0-7146-4795-0*, Pub. by F Cass Pubs); pap. 24.50 (*0-7146-4350-5*, Pub. by F Cass Pubs) Intl Spec Bk.
Adams, Thomas R. The American Controversy: A Bibliographical Study of the British Pamphlets about the American Disputes, 1764 to 1783, 2 vols. 1980. 60.00 (*0-914930-09-5*) Biblio Soc Am.
— The American Controversy: A Bibliographical Study of the British Pamphlets about the American Disputes, 1764 to 1783, Vol. 1. LC 77-76348. 566p. reprint ed. pap. 175.50 (*0-7837-6201-1*, 204592300001) Bks Demand.
— The American Controversy: A Bibliographical Study of the British Pamphlets about the American Disputes, 1764 to 1783, Vol. 2. LC 77-76348. 574p. reprint ed. pap. 178.00 (*0-7837-6202-X*, 204592300002) Bks Demand.
Adams, Thomas Randolph, et al. The Non-Cartographical Maritime Works Published by Mount & Page: A Preliminary Hand-List. LC 86-134845. (Occasional Papers of the Bibliographical Society). xiv, 54 p. 1985. write for info. (*0-948170-01-8*) CE38.
Adams, Thomas S., tr. see Levasseur, Emile.
Adams, Thomas W. & Cottrell, Alvin J. Cyprus Between East & West. LC 68-19429. (Washington Center of Foreign Policy Research. Studies in International Affairs: No. 7). 104p. reprint ed. pap. 32.30 (*0-608-11996-2*, 202299800031) Bks Demand.
Adams, Thomas W. & Kuder, Susan R. Attitudes Through Idioms. 2nd ed. LC 93-9042. (J). 1993. text 22.95 (*0-8384-3975-6*) Heinle & Heinle.
Adams, Tiffany. Employee Involvement Now! The NAM's Guide to Building Your Own Employee Involvement Program. LC 98-13872. (Public Affairs & Political Education Ser.: Vol. 1). 104p. 1998. 29.95 (*0-9630335-3-0*) Natl Assoc Mfrs.
Adams, Tim. Sun World. Hardy, Alice, ed. LC 78-74428. (A-1 Ser.). 4.00 (*0-686-24151-7*); pap. 8.00 (*0-686-24152-5*) Central FL Voters.
— Third World Out! Hardy, A. L., ed. LC 78-74429. 1978. pap. 14.00 (*0-686-23919-9*) Central FL Voters.
— Universal Salvation Agency. Hardy, Alice, ed. LC 78-74426. 9.00 (*0-686-24153-3*); pap. 1.50 (*0-686-24154-1*) Central FL Voters.
Adams, Timothy D. Telling Lies in Modern American Autobiography. LC 89-35380. xvi, 206p. (C). 1990. 34.95 (*0-8078-1888-7*) U of NC Pr.
Adams, Timothy Dow. Light Writing & Life Writing: Photography in Autobiography. LC 99-21544. (Illus.). 368p. 2000. 49.95 (*0-8078-4792-5*); lib. bdg. 49.95 (*0-8078-2513-1*) U of NC Pr.
Adams, Todd R. The Michael William Kaluta Treasury. (Illus.). 80p. (Orig.). 1988. pap. 9.95 (*0-9621421-0-7*) Glimmer Graph.
Adams, Tom. Grass Roots: How Ordinary People Are Changing America. 1991. 18.95 (*0-8065-1246-6*, Citadel Pr); pap. 9.95 (*0-8065-1232-6*) Carol Pub Group.
— Jump Start the HP-48G/GX Calculator. 2nd ed. 1998. pap. 19.95 (*1-881018-48-2*) Grt Lks Pr.
***Adams, Tom.** Jump Start the HP/48g/GX Calculator. 3rd ed. (Illus.). 1999. pap. 21.95 (*1-881018-30-X*) Grt Lks Pr.
Adams, Tom. An Ox in the Ditch: Nine Southern Stories of the Forties. 200p. 1995. pap. 12.95 (*0-9648638-1-2*) T Berryhill.
— Rape-! By Gov't Decree-1: (Winning Wars Without Heros) LC 92-71324. 216p. 1992. 14.95 (*0-8187-0159-5*) Harlo Press.

— Winning Wars Without Heroes, Vol. 1. LC 96-69098. (Illus.). 236p. (Orig.). 1996. pap. 11.95 (*1-882792-28-9*) Proctor Pubns.

*__Adams, Tom.__ Word Blitz! Learn over 700 of the Most Frequently Asked SAT Vocabulary Words Quickly & Easily with This Unique Book. LC 98-94903. viii, 152p. 2000. pap. 14.95 (*0-9669344-7-4*) Epsilon.

Adams, Tom & Armstrong, Kathryn. When Parents Age: What Children Can Do. 208p. (Orig.). 1996. reprint ed. mass mkt. 5.99 (*0-425-15262-6*) Berkley Pub.

Adams, Tom & Brandenburg, Betty, eds. Higman: A Collection. (Illus.). 286p. 1998. 24.95 (*0-9648638-4-7*); pap. 14.95 (*0-9648638-5-5*) T Berryhill.

Adams, Tom, jt. auth. see Adams, Inez B.

*__Adams, Tony.__ Addicted. 1999. mass mkt. 13.95 (*0-00-218795-7*, Pub. by HarpC) Trafalgar.

— Tony Adams Autobiography. 1998. 29.95 (*0-00-218794-9*, Pub. by HarpC) Trafalgar.

Adams, Tony, et al. Learning LOGO on the TRS-80 Color Computer. (Illus.). 174p. 1984. pap. 24.95 (*0-13-527961-5*) P-H.

Adams, Tony, jt. auth. see Tulasiewicz, Witold.

Adams, V. Dean. Water & Wastewater Examination Manual. (Illus.). 265p. 1990. lib. bdg. 75.00 (*0-87371-199-8*, L199) Lewis Pubs.

Adams, V. M., jt. ed. see McLeod, D. B.

Adams, Vincanne. Medical Science & Democratic Truth: Doctors & Revolution in Nepal. LC 97-18016. (Studies in Medical Anthropology: No. 6). (Illus.). 264p. (C). 1998. text 64.95 (*0-521-58486-8*); pap. text 24.95 (*0-521-58548-1*) Cambridge U Pr.

— Tigers of the Snow & Other Virtual Sherpas. LC 95-4618. 296p. 1996. text 52.50 (*0-691-03441-9*, Pub. by Princeton U Pr) Cal Prin Full Svc.

Adams, Vince & Askenazi, Abraham. Building Better Products with Finite Element Analysis. LC 98-28578. 624p. (C). 1998. pap. 63.95 (*1-56690-160-X*) Thomson Learn.

Adams, Virginia, et al, compiled by. On the Hill: A Photographic History of the University of Kansas. 2nd rev. ed. LC 93-1258. 1993. 25.00 (*0-7006-0611-4*) U Pr of KS.

Adams, Virginia M., ed. see Gooding, James H.

Adams, Vivian, jt. auth. see Boyd, Robert G.

Adams, Vyvyon, jt. auth. see Audax.

Adams, W. Concordance to the Plays of Shakespeare. 1973. 250.00 (*0-8490-1662-2*) Gordon Pr.

Adams, W. A., et al, eds. Exploratory Research & Development of Batteries for Electric & Hybrid Vehicles. LC 97-118965. (Proceedings Ser.: Vol. 96-14). (Illus.). 238p. 1996. 42.00 (*1-56677-158-7*) Electrochem Soc.

Adams, W. A. & Gibbs, R. J. Natural Turf for Sport & Amenity: Science & Management. 420p. 1994. pap. text 50.00 (*0-85198-720-6*) OUP.

Adams, W. A., et al. The Quest for Service Quality: Rx's for Achieving Excellence. 320p. 1992. 24.95 (*0-9632471-2-3*) Maxcomm.

— The Whole Systems Approach: Involving Everyone in the Company to Transform & Run Your Business. 240p. 1998. 24.95 (*1-890009-41-5*) Exec Excell.

Adams, W. A., ed. see Electrochemical Society Staff.

Adams, W. Davenport. Dictionary of English Literature: Being a Comprehensive Guide to English Authors & Their Works. 2nd ed. LC 89-26524. 708p. 1992. reprint ed. lib. bdg. 65.00 (*1-55888-898-5*) Omnigraphics Inc.

Adams, W. E. Our American Cousins: Being Personal Impressions of the People & Institutions of the United States, 1883. LC 92-12083. 388p. 1992. lib. bdg. 99.95 (*0-7734-9521-5*) E Mellen.

Adams, W. F. Barney: Barney (1634) - Hosmer (1635) Family Records. (Illus.). 133p. 1991. reprint ed. pap. 21.00 (*0-8328-2090-3*) Higginson Bk Co.

— The Life of Commodore Joshua Barney, U. S. Navy Hero, 1776-1812, Including Interesting Facts & General Material. (Illus.). 228p. 1993. reprint ed. pap. 36.00 (*0-8328-1681-7*); reprint ed. lib. bdg. 46.00 (*0-8328-1680-9*) Higginson Bk Co.

Adams, W. Howard. Cruise Control: So, You Want to Be Led by God's Spirit. 2nd ed. Adams, Mary J., ed. 200p. 1989. write for info. (*0-318-65921-2*) Sound Abundance.

Adams, W. M. Future Nature: A Vision for Conservation. (Illus.). 192p. 1996. pap. 25.00 (*1-85383-304-5*, Pub. by Escan Pubns) Island Pr.

— Wasting the Rain: Rivers, People, & Planning in Africa. LC 92-22825. 240p. (C). 1993. pap. 18.95 (*0-8166-2270-1*) U of Minn Pr.

Adams, W. M. & Pheng, Vatha. Flesh & Blood. LC 91-10068. 144p. 1991. write for info. (*1-878951-15-7*) Autumn Hse Pub.

Adams, W. M., jt. auth. see Mortimore, Michael.

Adams, W. Marsham. The House of the Hidden Places - A Clue to the Creed of Early Egypt from Egyptian Sources. (African Studies). 249p. reprint ed. 35.00 (*0-938818-74-0*) ECA Assoc.

Adams, W. Peter, ed. see International Geographical Congress (22nd: 1972: M.

Adams, W. Royce. Making the Grade. (C). 1997. pap. text, teacher ed. 37.96 (*0-669-35508-9*) HM Trade Div.

— Making the Grade. 2nd ed. 480p. (C). 1997. pap. text 38.76 (*0-669-35507-0*); pap. text, student ed. 19.16 (*0-669-35509-7*) HM Trade Div.

— Making the Grade: Strategies for Reading in the Social Sciences, Sciences, & Humanities. 462p. (C). 1992. pap. text 36.76 (*0-669-21379-9*); teacher ed. 37.96 (*0-669-28157-3*); 19.16 (*0-669-28158-1*) HM Trade Div.

*__Adams, W. Royce.__ Rairarubia. LC 99-21436. (Illus.). 144p. (J). (gr. 3-7). 1999. pap. 10.95 (*1-882897-36-6*) Lost Coast.

— Return to Rairarubia. LC 99-2146. 144p. (J). (gr. 3-7). 2000. pap. 10.95 (*1-882897-44-7*) Lost Coast.

Adams, W. Royce. Think, Read, React, Plan, Write, Rewrite. 5th ed. 368p. (C). 1986. teacher ed. write for info. (*0-318-69142-6*); pap. text. write for info. (*0-03-030819-4*) Harcourt Coll Pubs.

— Viewpoints: Reading Worth Thinking & Writing About. 2nd ed. 512p. (C). 1993. pap. text 31.96 (*0-669-27366-X*) HM Trade Div.

— Viewpoints: Readings Worth Thinking & Writing About. 2nd ed. (C). 1993. text, teacher ed. 2.66 (*0-669-27369-4*) HM Trade Div.

Adams, W. Royce & Patterson, Becky. Developing Reading Versatility. 7th ed. 76p. (C). 1996. pap. text, teacher ed. 33.50 (*0-03-018069-4*, Pub. by Harcourt Coll Pubs) Harcourt.

Adams, W. T., et al, eds. Population Genetics of Forest Trees: Proceedings of the International Symposium on Population Genetics of Forest Trees, Corvallis, Oregon, U. S. A. July 31-August 2, 1990. LC 92-18860. (Forestry Sciences Ser.: No. 42). 400p. (C). 1992. text 236.00 (*0-7923-1857-9*) Kluwer Academic.

Adams, W. W., et al, eds. Materials Science & Engineering of Rigid-Rod Polymers Vol. 134: Materials Research Society Symposium Proceedings. 699p. 1989. text 17.50 (*1-55899-007-0*) Materials Res.

Adams, Walter. Adam Smith Goes to Moscow: A Dialogue on Radical Reform. 184p. 1993. pap. text 14.95 (*0-691-00053-0*, Pub. by Princeton U Pr) Cal Prin Full Svc.

— Winning Blackjack. 80p. 1998. pap. 19.95 (*0-937408-73-5*) GMI Pubns Inc.

Adams, Walter, ed. The Structure of American Industry. 9th ed. LC 94-6773. 336p. (C). 1994. pap. text 52.00 (*0-02-300833-4*, Macmillan Coll) P-H.

Adams, Walter & Brick, James W. Adam Smith Goes to Moscow: A Dialogue on Radical Reform. LC 93-16275. 176p. 1993. text 39.50 (*0-691-03283-1*, Pub. by Princeton U Pr) Cal Prin Full Svc.

Adams, Walter, et al. Tariffs, Quotas, & Trade: The Politics of Protectionism. LC 78-66267. 330p. 1979. pap. text 24.95 (*0-917616-34-0*) Transaction Pubs.

Adams, Walter, jt. auth. see Mordock, John.

Adams, Walter E. Abortion: A Spiritual Holocaust. 60p. (Orig.). 1986. pap. 3.95 (*0-937408-38-7*) GMI Pubns Inc.

— The Black Hoods. 144p. 1993. pap. 6.95 (*0-937408-88-3*) GMI Pubns Inc.

— Blackjack Wizard. 70p. 1999. pap. 19.95 (*0-937408-72-7*) GMI Pubns Inc.

— Christian Psychology. Adams, Candy L., ed. 128p. (Orig.). 1990. pap. 5.95 (*0-937408-95-6*) GMI Pubns Inc.

— Death Mask. Adams, Candy L., ed. 1996. write for info. (*0-937408-79-4*) GMI Pubns Inc.

— Doc. 50p. 1996. write for info. (*0-937408-76-X*) GMI Pubns Inc.

— The Duffer, the Hacker, the Superb Club Thrower. Adams, Candy L., ed. (Illus.). 120p. (Orig.). 1989. pap. 5.95 (*0-937408-97-2*) GMI Pubns Inc.

— Future World. 128p. 1983. pap. 3.95 (*0-937408-25-5*) GMI Pubns Inc.

— The Heart Always Crys. Adams, Candy L., ed. 1996. write for info. (*0-937408-78-6*) GMI Pubns Inc.

— Heart Song. Adams, Candy L., ed. 1996. write for info. (*0-937408-80-8*) GMI Pubns Inc.

— Hellfire in the Earth. Adams, Candy L., ed. 232p. 1992. pap. 9.95 (*0-937408-91-3*) GMI Pubns Inc.

— Hidden Intervals of Time in Biblical Prophecy. 40p. (Orig.). 1988. pap. text 2.95 (*0-937408-98-0*) GMI Pubns Inc.

— An Honest Politician. 100p. 1996. 10.00 (*0-937408-81-6*) GMI Pubns Inc.

— In the Fury of Love. 250p. 1995. pap. 7.95 (*0-937408-83-2*) GMI Pubns Inc.

— Jesus Loves Me! Adams, Candy L., ed. 128p. (Orig.). 1990. pap. 5.95 (*0-937408-94-8*) GMI Pubns Inc.

— Kenneth Copeland Questioned! 50p. (Orig.). 1983. pap. 2.50 (*0-937408-26-3*) GMI Pubns Inc.

— A Life Worth Living. 100p. 1996. write for info. (*0-937408-77-8*) GMI Pubns Inc.

— Listen to the Prophets. Adams, Candy L., ed. 48p. (Orig.). 1990. pap. text 3.95 (*0-937408-96-4*) GMI Pubns Inc.

— Listen to the Prophets. 100p. (Orig.). write for info. (*0-944938-00-0*) Prophecy Pr.

— Parental Survival. 126p. (Orig.). 1984. pap. 6.95 (*0-937408-30-1*) GMI Pubns Inc.

— Pat Robertson in Error. 50p. (Orig.). 1983. pap. 2.95 (*0-937408-27-1*) GMI Pubns Inc.

— The Presidential Conspiracy. LC 93-78842. 400p. (Orig.). 1993. pap. text 11.95 (*0-937408-89-1*) GMI Pubns Inc.

— The Rapist. 180p. 1994. pap. 6.95 (*0-937408-87-5*) GMI Pubns Inc.

— The Rapist. 100p. 1996. 10.00 (*0-937408-82-4*) GMI Pubns Inc.

— The Rapist, Vol. III. 220p. 1995. pap. 6.95 (*0-937408-84-0*) GMI Pubns Inc.

— Souls in Jeopardy. 80p. (Orig.). 1987. pap. 3.95 (*0-937408-40-9*) GMI Pubns Inc.

— Sudden Destruction. Adams, Candy L., ed. 190p. 1992. pap. text 7.95 (*0-937408-90-5*) GMI Pubns Inc.

— Tithing: A Sixty Day Challenge to Financial Success. 56p. (Orig.). 1992. pap. 7.95 (*0-685-62270-3*) GMI Pubns Inc.

— The Tribulation Period Will Last Longer Than 7 Years. (Orig.). 1988. pap. 3.95 (*0-937408-99-9*) GMI Pubns Inc.

— Winning. 128p. (Orig.). 1985. pap. 4.95 (*0-937408-35-2*) GMI Pubns Inc.

— You Can Be Absolutely Irrefutably Supernaturally Healed by God Today. 100p. (Orig.). 1987. pap. 4.95 (*0-937408-39-5*) GMI Pubns Inc.

Adams, Walter E. & Brock, James W. Antitrust Economics on Trial: A Dialogue on the New Laissez-Faire. (Illus.). 160p. 1991. text 39.50 (*0-691-04291-8*, Pub. by Princeton U Pr); pap. text 14.95 (*0-691-00391-2*, Pub. by Princeton U Pr) Cal Prin Full Svc.

Adams, Walter H. Church Administration: A Handbook for Church Leaders. 1979. pap. 2.95 (*0-88027-001-2*) Firm Foun Pub.

*__Adams, Walter R., et al.__ Anthropology & Theology: God, Icons, & God-Talk. 2nd ed. LC 99-38233. 488p. 1999. pap. 37.50 (*0-7618-1477-9*) U Pr of Amer.

Adams, Walter R., ed. see American Anthropological Association Staff.

*__Adams, Wanda.__ Adams' Guide to Coding & Reimbursement: 1998 Update. (Illus.). 256p. 1998. text. write for info. (*0-323-00429-6*) Mosby Inc.

Adams, Wanda L. Guide to Coding & Reimbursement. LC 94-229708. 256p. (C). (gr. 13). 1994. pap. text 37.95 (*0-8151-0136-8*, 24217) Mosby Inc.

Adams, Ward R., et al. History of Arizona, 4 vols. Sloan, Richard E., ed. (Illus.). 2293p. 1997. reprint ed. lib. bdg. 199.00 (*0-8328-7044-7*) Higginson Bk Co.

Adams, Warren P., jt. auth. see Sherali, Hanif D.

Adams-Webber, J. R. Personal Construct Theory: Concepts & Applications. LC 78-8638. 251p. reprint ed. pap. 77.90 (*0-608-14906-3*, 202598500048) Bks Demand.

Adams-Webber, Jack R. The Construing Person. Mancuso, James C., ed. LC 81-12101. 309p. 1982. 40.95 (*0-275-90853-4*, C0853, Praeger Pubs) Greenwood.

Adams-Wells, Alethea, ed. Message in the Wind. LC 95-90233. 304p. 1995. 25.00 (*0-9645787-0-0*) Unole Pub.

Adams-Wells, Alethea A. Lady in the Moon. LC 96-90285. 247p. 1996. 20.00 (*0-9645787-1-9*) Unole Pub.

Adams, Willi P. The First American Constitutions: Republic Ideology & the Making of the State Constitutions in the Revolutionary Era. Kimber, Rita & Kimber, Robert, trs. LC 79-10887. 369p. 1980. reprint ed. pap. 114.40 (*0-608-08011-X*, 206797600001) Bks Demand.

— The German-Americans: An Ethnic Experience. Reichmann, Eberhard, ed. & tr. by. from GER. Rippley, LaVern J., tr. from GER. (Illus.). 45p. 1993. pap. 4.00 (*1-880788-01-2*) MKGAC & IGHS.

*__Adams, Willi Paul.__ The First American Constitutions: Republican Ideology & the Meaning of the State Constitutions in the Republican Era. expanded ed. LC 00-30457. 2000. pap. write for info. (*0-945612-78-8*) Madison Bks UPA.

Adams, William. Algebra with Applications. 384p. (C). 1995. pap. text, per. 52.95 (*0-7872-0996-1*) Kendall-Hunt.

— Calculus. 416p. (C). 1995. pap. text, per. 61.95 (*0-7872-1115-X*, 41111501) Kendall-Hunt.

— Companion to Algebra. 72p. (C). 1996. pap. text, spiral bd. 10.95 (*0-7872-2802-8*) Kendall-Hunt.

— Companion to Calculus. 64p. (C). 1996. pap. text, spiral bd. 10.95 (*0-7872-2803-6*) Kendall-Hunt.

— Companion to Finite Mathematics. 88p. (C). 1996. pap. text, spiral bd. 11.95 (*0-7872-2804-4*) Kendall-Hunt.

— Companion to Statistics: Basic Principles & Applications. 224p. (C). 1996. 20.95 (*0-7872-2303-4*) Kendall-Hunt.

*__Adams, William.__ Finite Mathematics, Models & Structures. rev. ed. 464p. (C). 1999. per. 61.95 (*0-7872-6444-X*, 41644403) Kendall-Hunt.

Adams, William. Get a Firmer Grip on Your Math. LC 96-75534. 298p. 1996. pap. text, per. 18.95 (*0-7872-1256-7*, 41156201) Kendall-Hunt.

— The Philosophical Roots of Anthropology. LC 98-26003. (Lecture Notes Ser.: No. 86). 350p. (C). 1998. pap. 19.95 (*1-57586-128-3*) CSLI.

— The Philosophical Roots of Anthropology. LC 98-26003. (CSLI Lecture Notes Ser.: Vol. 86). 450p. (C). 1998. text 59.95 (*1-57586-129-1*) CSLI.

— Winter Songs. 65p. 1998. 15.95 (*0-9667469-0-2*) Inst Readers.

Adams, William, ed. Historical Gazeteer & Biographical Memorial of Cattaraugus Co. (Illus.). 1164p. 1995. reprint ed. lib. bdg. 115.00 (*0-8328-4614-7*) Higginson Bk Co.

Adams, William, et al, eds. Afro-American Authors. LC 74-160035. (Multi-Ethnic Literature Ser.). (Illus.). 165p. (gr. 10-12). 1976. teacher ed. 8.24 (*0-685-02278-1*) HM.

— Asian-American Authors. (Multi-Ethnic Literature Ser.). 1976. teacher ed. 6.08 (*0-685-02280-3*) HM.

— Physical Geography of Africa. (Regional Environments Ser.). (Illus.). 452p. 1999. pap. text 35.00 (*0-19-823406-6*) OUP.

Adams, William & Knopp, Anthony. Brownsville: Portrait of a Border City. limited ed. (Illus.). 260p. 1997. 34.00 (*1-57168-207-4*) Sunbelt Media.

Adams, William & Schreibman, Fay, eds. Television Network News: Issues in Content Research. LC 78-64489. 1978. 6.50 (*0-932768-00-8*) CTS-GWU.

Adams, William, ed. see Paredes, Americo.

*__Adams, William A.__ A John Henry Moses Adventure Vol. 1: Capture. LC 99-91504. 2000. 25.00 (*0-7388-0844-X*); pap. 18.00 (*0-7388-0845-8*) Xlibris Corp.

Adams, William C. Foundations of Physical Education, Exercise & Sport Sciences. LC 90-37084. (Illus.). 296p. 1990. text 36.95 (*0-8121-1359-4*) Lppncott W & W.

— Media Influence on Presidential Candidates. (C). 1996. pap. text 13.95 (*0-8133-0172-6*) Westview.

Adams, William C., ed. Television Coverage of International Affairs. LC 81-15054. (Communication & Information Science Ser.). 272p. 1982. text 73.25 (*0-89391-103-8*) Ablx Pub.

— Television Coverage of the Middle East. LC 81-15049. (Communication & Information Science Ser.). 168p. 1981. text 73.25 (*0-89391-083-X*) Ablx Pub.

— Television Coverage of the 1980 Presidential Campaign. LC 83-3768. (Communication & Information Science Ser.). 196p. 1983. text 73.25 (*0-89391-104-6*) Ablx Pub.

Adams, William C., et al. Foundations of Physical Activity. 1968. pap. 7.60 (*0-87563-006-5*) Stipes.

Adams, William C., jt. auth. see Rodgers, Joann E.

Adams, William D. Shrubs & Vines for Southern Landscapes. fac. ed. LC 76-15455. (Illus.). 80p. pap. 30.00 (*0-7837-7408-7*, 204720200006) Bks Demand.

— Southern Flower Gardening. fac. ed. LC 79-29715. (Illus.). 94p. pap. 30.00 (*0-7837-7407-9*, 204720100006) Bks Demand.

*__Adams, William D. & Chaplin, Lois Trigg.__ The Texas Gardener's Book of Lists. 2000. pap. 17.95 (*0-87833-174-3*) Taylor Pub.

Adams, William D. & LeRoy, Thomas. Commonsense Vegetable Gardening for the South. LC 94-25304. (Illus.). 280p. 1995. 21.95 (*0-87833-876-4*) Taylor Pub.

Adams, William E. All the World is a Stage: And Every Actor Meets the Critic. (Illus.). 140p. 1997. mass mkt. 6.95 (*0-9639623-2-9*) Old Drum.

Adams, William E. Crats! 1993. pap. 6.95 (*0-9639623-0-2*) Old Drum.

— Memoirs of a Social Atom, 2 Vols. in 1. LC 67-29700. xix, 688p. 1968. reprint ed. 75.00 (*0-678-00349-1*) Kelley.

— My Yoke Is Easy & My Burden Is Light: A Current Technology Translation of the Bible. LC 97-91645. 100p. (Orig.). 1997. pap. text 6.95 (*0-9639623-1-0*) Old Drum.

Adams, William H. Denatured Visions: Landscape & Culture in the Twentieth Century. (Illus.). 144p. 1992. pap. 19.95 (*0-8109-6105-9*, Pub. by Abrams) Time Warner.

— Denatured Visions: Landscape & Culture in the 20th Century. (Illus.). 144p. 1991. pap. 19.95 (*0-87070-422-2*, 0-8109-6105-9, Pub. by Mus of Modern Art) Abrams.

— Famous Caves & Catacombs. LC 70-37773. (Essay Index Reprint Ser.). 1977. reprint ed. 25.95 (*0-8369-2577-7*) Ayer.

— Gardens Through History: Nature Perfected. (Illus.). 356p. 1991. 55.00 (*0-89659-919-1*) Abbeville Pr.

— Jefferson's Monticello. LC 83-6330. (Illus.). 288p. 1988. pap. 37.50 (*0-89659-950-7*) Abbeville Pr.

— Jefferson's Monticello. 2nd ed. (Illus.). 296p. 1998. 60.00 (*0-7892-0395-2*); pap. 39.95 (*0-7892-0184-4*) Abbeville Pr.

— Roberto Burle Marx: The Unnatural Art of the Garden. (Illus.). 80p. 1991. pap. 22.50 (*0-87070-197-5*, 0-8109-6096-6) Mus of Modern Art.

Adams, William H., ed. The Eye of Thomas Jefferson. LC 92-20309. (Illus.). 456p. (C). 1993. text 44.95 (*0-8262-0879-7*) U of Mo Pr.

— Jefferson & the Arts: An Extended View. LC 76-21951. 1976. text 45.00 (*0-8139-0931-7*) U Pr of Va.

Adams, William Howard. Nature Perfected: Gardens Through History. (Illus.). 356p. 1999. pap. text 39.95 (*0-7892-0458-4*) Abbeville Pr.

Adams, William Howard. The Paris Years of Thomas Jefferson. LC 97-12330. (Illus.). 368p. 1997. 35.00 (*0-300-06903-0*) Yale U Pr.

*__Adams, William Howard.__ The Paris Years of Thomas Jefferson. (Illus.). 368p. 2000. pap. 17.95 (*0-300-08261-4*) Yale U Pr.

Adams, William J. Restructuring the French Economy: Government & the Rise of Market Competition since World War II. 400p. 1989. 36.95 (*0-8157-0100-4*) Brookings.

— Statistics: Basic Principles & Applications. 808p. (C). 1994. pap. text, boxed set 63.95 (*0-8403-8964-7*) Kendall-Hunt.

Adams, William J., ed. Singular Europe: Economy & Polity of the European Community after 1992. LC 92-22674. (Illus.). 400p. (C). 1994. pap. text 32.50 (*0-472-06504-1*, 06504) U of Mich Pr.

Adams, William J., et al, eds. Aquatic Toxicology & Hazard Assessment, Vol. 10: STP 971. (Special Technical Publication Ser.). (Illus.). 960p. 1988. text 64.00 (*0-8031-0978-4*, STP971) ASTM.

Adams, William J. & Stoffaes, Christian, eds. French Industrial Policy. LC 85-48203. 228p. 1986. 34.95 (*0-8157-0098-9*); pap. 14.95 (*0-8157-0097-0*) Brookings.

Adams, William L. & Knopp, Anthony K. Brownsville: Portrait of a Border City. LC 97-15371. (Illus.). 256p. 1997. pap. 18.95 (*1-57168-174-4*, 714-4, Eakin Pr) Sunbelt Media.

Adams, William M. Green Development: Environment & Sustainability in the Third World. (Natural Environment Problems & Management Ser.). 272p. (C). 1992. pap. 24.99 (*0-415-08050-9*) Routledge.

Adams, William M. & Slikkerveer, L. Jan, eds. Indigenous Knowledge & Change in African Agriculture. (Studies in Technology & Social Change: Vol. 26). (Illus.). 166p. (Orig.). 1997. pap. text 18.00 (*0-945271-42-5*) ISU-CIKARD.

Adams, William M., ed. see Orme, Antony R.

Adams, William R. The Historic Buildings of Lake Wales. 120p. 1992. 34.75 (*1-881470-01-6*); lib. bdg. 17.85 (*1-881470-00-8*) So Herit FL.

— The Legend of Gomek. 32p. 1998. pap. text 6.95 (*1-881470-05-9*) So Herit FL.

— Roushi Kanren Yogo 222 Vol. 300: Union Terminology & Guide Book. Honda Hershey Institute Staff, tr. (JPN & ENG.). 210p. 1999. per. write for info. (*0-9669465-0-2*) H Hershey.

Adams, William R. & Fanning, Veronica, compiled by. Directory of International Resources for Indiana. LC 94-41027. (Project of the International Forum of the Indiana Humanities Council Ser.). (Illus.). 128p. 1995. pap. 14.95 (*0-253-20921-8*) Ind U Pr.

Adams, William S. Shaped by Images: One Who Presides. 120p. 1995. 18.95 (*0-89869-247-4*) Church Pub Inc.

Adams, William S. & Floyd, Michael H., eds. Our Heritage & Common Life: Essays Honoring Frank Eiji Sugeno, Frederic & Alma R. Duncalf Professor of Church History, the Episcopal Theological Seminary of Southwest, Austin, Texas. LC 94-9588. 194p. (C). 1994. lib. bdg. 42.00 (*0-8191-9520-0*) U Pr of Amer.

Adams, William Seth. Moving the Furniture: Liturgical Theory, Practice & Environment LC 99-22884. 1999. write for info. (*0-89869-316-0*) Church Pub Inc.

Adams, William W. & Loustaunau, Philippe. An Introduction to Grobner Bases. LC 94-19081. (Graduate Studies in Mathematics Ser.: Vol. 3). 289p. 1994. text 36.00 (*0-8218-3804-0*, GSM/3) Am Math.

Adams, William Y. The Ceramic Industries of Medieval Nubia, Pts. I & II. LC 85-15016. 688p. 1986. 95.00 (*0-8131-0500-5*) U Pr of Ky.

— Shonto: Study of the Role of the Trader in a Modern Navaho Community. (Bureau of American Ethnology Bulletins Ser.). 329p. 1995. lib. bdg. 99.00 (*0-7812-4188-X*) Rprt Serv.

Adams, William Y., ed. Shonto: A Study of the Role of the Trader in a Modern Navaho Community. 1988. reprint ed. lib. bdg. 75.00 (*0-7812-0219-1*) Rprt Serv.

Adams, Woody. Wait, Please Wait. xi, 80p. (Orig.). 1999. pap. 9.95 (*0-9672341-0-7*) Wood Frog Pubg.

Adamse, Michael. Anniversary: A Love Story. LC 97-32582. 250p. 1998. pap. 10.95 (*1-55874-542-4*) Health Comm.

***Adamse, Michael & Motta, Sheree.** Affairs of the Net: The Cybershrinks' Guide to Online Relationships. LC 99-55959. 250p. 2000. pap. 11.95 (*1-55874-787-7*, Simcha Press) Health Comm.

Adamse, Michael & Motta, Sheree. On-Line Friendship, Chat-Room Romance & Cybersex: Your Guide to Affairs of the Net. 250p. (Orig.). 1996. pap. 11.95 (*1-55874-418-5*, 4185) Health Comm.

***Adamsen, Paul B.** A Framework For Complex System Development. LC 99-86803. 240p. (C). 2000. boxed set 79.95 (*0-8493-2296-0*) CRC Pr.

Adamski. Introducing Microsoft Office 97 Professional New Perspective. 1997. pap. 42.00 (*0-7600-5422-3*) Course Tech.

Adamski & Hommel. New Perspectives on Access 97: Comprehensive Enhanced. 1998. 44.95 (*0-7600-7309-0*) Course Tech.

Adamski, et al. New Perspectives on Microsoft Office 97 Professional. (New Perspectives Ser.). 824p. (C). 1997. pap. 43.50 (*0-7600-5272-7*) Course Tech.

Adamski, jt. auth. see Pratt.

Adamski, G. Wisdom of the Masters of the Far East: Questions & Answers by Royal Order of Tibet, Vol. 1. 1996. reprint ed. spiral bd. 10.00 (*0-7873-0739-4*) Hlth Research.

Adamski, George. Inside the Spaceships: UFO Experiences of George Adamski 1952-1955. LC 80-80385. (Illus.). 296p. 1995. reprint ed. pap. 15.95 (*0-942176-01-4*) GAF Intl.

Adamski, Joe, ed. see Mennillo, Anthony.

Adamski, Joseph. Microsoft Access 2.0 for Windows: Comprehensive Edition. (New Perspectives Ser.). 600p. (C). 1996. pap. 42.95 (*0-7600-4582-8*) Course Tech.

Adamski, Joseph & Adamski, Judy. New Perspectives on Integrating Microsoft Office Professional for Windows 95. 10th ed. (New Perspectives Ser.). 264p. (C). 1996. pap. 30.95 (*0-7600-4576-3*) Course Tech.

Adamski, Joseph, et al. New Perspectives on Microsoft Access 97: Brief Edition. 10th ed. (New Perspectives Ser.). 160p. (C). 1997. pap. 21.95 (*0-7600-4552-6*) Course Tech.

— New Perspectives on Microsoft Access 97: Introductory Edition. 10th ed. (New Perspectives Ser.). 304p. (C). 1997. pap. 31.95 (*0-7600-5253-0*) Course Tech.

— Np On Ms Access97-comprehensiv. 10th ed. (NEW PERSPECTIVES). 552p. (C). 1997. pap. 31.50 (*0-7600-5259-X*) Course Tech.

Adamski, Joseph, jt. auth. see Pratt, Phil.

Adamski, Joseph, jt. auth. see Pratt, Philip J.

Adamski, Joseph J. Microsoft Access 7 for Windows 95: Comprehensive, Incl. instr. resource kit, labs, test mgr., files. (New Perspectives Ser.). (Illus.). 616p. 1996. pap. 42.95 (*0-7600-3543-1*) Course Tech.

— Microsoft Access 7 for Windows 95: Introductory, Incl. instr. resource kit, labs, test mgr., files. (New Perspectives Ser.). (Illus.). 304p. 1996. pap. 30.95 (*0-7600-3542-3*) Course Tech.

— Microsoft Access 2 for Windows - New Perspectives Introductory, Incl. instr. resource kit, test bank, transparency. (New Perspectives Ser.). (Illus.). 272p. (C). 1995. pap. 20.25 (*1-56527-148-3*) Course Tech.

— Microsoft Access 2 for Windows - New Perspectives Comprehensive, Incl. instr. resource kit, test bank, transparency. (New Perspectives Ser.). (Illus.). 600p. (C). 1995. mass mkt. 28.50 (*1-56527-987-5*) Course Tech.

— Word 2000 Expert. (C). 1999. pap. 20.00 (*0-619-00102-X*) Course Tech.

— Word 2000 Proficient. (C). 1999. pap. 15.00 (*0-619-00101-1*) Course Tech.

Adamski, Joseph J. & Adamski, Judy. Microsoft Office for Windows 95 Integrated - Advanced, Incl. instr. resource kit, test mgr., files. (New Perspectives Ser.). (Illus.). 504p. 1996. text. write for info. incl. 3.5 ld (*0-7600-4191-1*) Course Tech.

— Microsoft Office Professional for Windows 95 Integrated - Introductory, Incl. instr. resource kit, test mgr., files. (New Perspectives Ser.). (Illus.). 648p. 1996. pap. 56.95 (*0-7600-3579-2*) Course Tech.

Adamski, Joseph J. & Finnegan, Kathy. New Perspectives on Microsoft Access 2000 - Brief. 168p. per. 21.95 (*0-7600-7088-1*, Pub. by Course Tech) Thomson Learn.

Adamski, Joseph J., et al. New Perspectives on Microsoft Access 2000 - Introductory. 392p. per. 31.95 (*0-7600-7089-X*, Pub. by Course Tech) Thomson Learn.

Adamski, Joseph J., jt. auth. see Pratt, Philip J.

Adamski, Judy, jt. auth. see Adamski, Joseph.

Adamski, Judy, jt. auth. see Adamski, Joseph J.

Adamski, Judy, ed. see Mennillo, Anthony.

Adamski, M. Patricia, jt. auth. see Brodsky, Edward.

Adamski, Tony & Doyle, Tim. The Aviation Regulatory Process. (C). 1993. pap. text 25.00 (*1-881592-49-9*) Hayden-McNeil.

Adamson. Basic Law & the Legal Environment of Business. 1994. pap. text 57.50 (*0-256-12555-4*) McGraw.

— Digital Communications: A First Course. (Electronics Technology Ser.). 1997. teacher ed. 14.00 (*0-8273-6953-0*); text 66.95 (*0-8273-6952-2*) Delmar.

— Digital System Logic & Application. 2nd ed. (Electronics Technology Ser.). 1996. teacher ed. 14.00 (*0-8273-6028-2*) Delmar.

— Microcomputer Networks: Troubleshooting. (Electronics Technology Ser.). 1996. teacher ed. 18.76 (*0-8273-6955-7*); text 54.95 (*0-8273-6954-9*) Delmar.

— PC Maintenance & Repair. 1997. pap., wbk. ed. 7.00 (*0-8064-1318-2*, E40) Bergwall.

— Practise Your Conjunctions & Linkers. 1995. pap. text. write for info. (*0-582-09669-3*, Pub. by Addison-Wesley) Longman.

— Practise Your Tenses. 1990. pap. text. write for info. (*0-582-01446-8*, Pub. by Addison-Wesley) Longman.

— Systemic Physiology 5th ed. 1998. pap., lab manual ed. 8.25 (*0-07-230595-9*) McGraw.

Adamson & Gemes. The Language of Oysters. (Illus.). 168p. 1997. text 30.00 (*90-5703-101-9*) Gordon & Breach.

Adamson & Mietus, Norbert J. Applied Business Law. 13th ed. (LA - Business Law Ser.). 1987. mass mkt., wbk. ed. 15.95 (*0-538-12881-X*); mass mkt., wbk. ed. 16.95 (*0-538-12871-2*) S-W Pub.

— Applied Business Law. 13th abr. ed. (LA - Business Law Ser.). 1987. 2.95 (*0-538-12882-8*) S-W Pub.

— Db Applied Business Law: Microexam Applications. 13th ed. (LA - Business Law Ser.). 1988. 172.95 (*0-538-12876-3*) S-W Pub.

— Law for Business. 14th ed. (LA - Business Law Ser.). 1992. mass mkt., wbk. ed. 13.95 (*0-538-60957-5*) S-W Pub.

— Law for Business. 14th abr. ed. (LA - Business Law Ser.). 1992. pap., wbk. ed. 9.95 (*0-538-60959-1*); mass mkt. 44.95 (*0-538-60958-3*) S-W Pub.

— Microexam: Applied Business Law. 13th ed. (LA - Business Law Ser.). 1988. 172.95 (*0-538-12877-1*) S-W Pub.

Adamson, A. M. Marquesan Insects: Environment. (BMB Ser.: No. 139). 1969. reprint ed. 25.00 (*0-527-02245-4*) Periodicals Srv.

— Review of the Fauna of the Marquesas Islands & Discussion of Its Origin. (BMB Ser.: No. 159). 1974. reprint ed. 25.00 (*0-527-02267-5*) Periodicals Srv.

Adamson, A. P. Brief History of the Thirtieth Georgia Regiment. (Illus.). 161p. 1993. reprint ed. 20.00 (*1-881454-02-9*) Amer Hist Bks.

— Sojourns of a Patriot: The Field & Prison Papers of an Unreconstructed Confederate. Abell, Richard B. & Gecik, Faye, eds. LC 97-50520. (Journal of Confederate History Ser.: Vol. XIX). (Illus.). 200p. 1998. 26.95 (*1-889332-20-8*) So Herit Pr.

Adamson, Arthur. A Student's Guide for Projects, Field Studies & Research. enl. rev. ed. 96p. (C). 1986. 33.00 (*0-7855-4549-2*) St Mut.

Adamson, Arthur W. Physical Chemistry of Surfaces. 4th ed. LC 82-2711. (Illus.). 684p. reprint ed. pap. 200.00 (*0-7837-3525-1*, 205786000008) Bks Demand.

Adamson, Arthur W. & Fleischauer, Paul D., eds. Concepts of Inorganic Photochemistry. LC 84-5776. 456p. (C). 1984. reprint ed. lib. bdg. 47.50 (*0-89874-762-7*) Krieger.

Adamson, Arthur W. & Gast, Alice P. Physical Chemistry of Surfaces. 6th ed. LC 97-5929. 808p. 1997. 89.95 (*0-471-14873-3*) Wiley.

Adamson, Bob, jt. ed. see Agelasto, Michael.

Adamson, Bruce C. Oswald's Closest Friend: The George de Mohrenschildt Story, 9 vols., Set. 2nd rev. ed. McDonough, Dennis et al, eds. (Illus.). 1202p. 1996. 196.00 (*1-892501-03-1*) B C Adamson.

Adamson, Bruce Campbell. The Adamson Brothers Conspiracy & the Invention of "Lastex" the First Stretchable Clothing. large type ed. (Illus.). 50p. 1998. 10.00 (*1-892501-15-5*) B C Adamson.

— Allen Dulles' Paine Must be Let Luce. rev. ed. McDonough, Dennis et al, eds. (Oswald's Closest Friend Ser.: Vol. 6). (Illus.). 162p. 1996. 20.00 (*1-892501-09-0*) B C Adamson.

— America's First Conspiracy: The Story of Peggy Shippen & Benedict Arnold. large type ed. (Illus.). 80p. 1996. 15.00 (*1-892501-18-X*) B C Adamson.

— Diana the Queen of Hearts & the CIA/MI6 the Princedom of Darkness. large type rev ed. McDonough, Dennis & Schultz, Naomi, eds. (Oswald's Closest Friend Ser.: Vol. 9). (Illus.). 190p. 1998. 20.00 (*1-892501-12-0*) B C Adamson.

— H. L. Hunt Theory Ketchin up with JFK Assassination. McDonough, Dennis & Potter, Agnes H., eds. (Oswald's Closest Friend Ser.: Vol. 3). (Illus.). 90p. 1996. 15.00 (*1-892501-06-6*) B C Adamson.

— His Haitian Baby Was Not for Papa - Ties to LBJ. large type ed. Lomax, Dana et al, eds. (Oswald's Closest Friend Ser.: Vol. 5). (Illus.). 155p. 1996. 18.00 (*1-892501-08-2*) B C Adamson.

— The JFK Assassination Timeline Chart. 2nd rev. large type ed. Amerson, Andrew & Amerson, Susan, eds. 269p. 1996. 20.00 (*1-892501-02-3*) B C Adamson.

— Larry Flynt Kills JFK Assassination Article: After Flynt Offered $1,000,000 Reward for Proof of Conspiracy. large type ed. Knight, Donald, ed. (Illus.). 65p. 1998. 10.00 (*1-892501-14-7*) B C Adamson.

— The Life & Times of Captain George W. Ely, 1840-1922: Secretary of the New York Stock Exchange, 1874-1919. 3rd large type ed. Ely, George W., III et al, eds. (Illus.). 140p. 1996. 15.00 (*1-892501-01-5*) B C Adamson.

— Little Abner & His Ark: Abner Bartlett's Role in Constructing Largest Hotel in the World, The Waldorf-Astoria Hotel. large type ed. McDonough, Dennis, ed. (Illus.). 50p. 1998. 10.00 (*1-892501-13-9*) B C Adamson.

— Mr. McGhee You've Done It Again. rev. ed. Knight, Donald G. et al, eds. (Oswald's Closest Friend Ser.: Vol. 2). (Illus.). 83p. 1996. 15.00 (*1-892501-05-8*) B C Adamson.

— 1,000 Points of Light: The Public Remains in the Dark. large type rev. ed. Perez, Steve et al, eds. (Oswald's Closest Friend Ser.: Vol. 1). (Illus.). 168p. 1996. 18.00 (*1-892501-04-X*) B C Adamson.

— Spanish Fly Is Radioactive: The U. S. Dropped Four H-Bombs on Palomares, Spain. large type rev. ed. 40p. 1998. 10.00 (*1-892501-16-3*) B C Adamson.

— The Very First Cold Warrior - Dimitri Von Mohrenschildt. rev. ed. Potter, Agnes H. & McDonough, Dennis, eds. (Oswald's Closest Friend Ser.: Vol. 4). (Illus.). 130p. 1996. 15.00 (*1-892501-07-4*) B C Adamson.

— Wolfen Communism Without Trotsky. rev. ed. McDonough, Dennis & Potter, Agnes H., eds. (Oswald's Closest Friend Ser.: Vol. 8). (Illus.). 117p. 1996. 15.00 (*1-892501-11-2*) B C Adamson.

— Wrightmen Going in Wrong Directions. McDonough, Dennis et al, eds. (Oswald's Closest Friend Ser.: Vol. 7). (Illus.). 190p. 1996. 20.00 (*1-892501-10-4*) B C Adamson.

Adamson, Bruce Campbell & Foley, William. For Which We Stand: The Life & Papers of Rufus Easton. 3rd large type ed. Launer, Louis J., ed. (Illus.). 240p. 1996. 25.00 (*1-892501-00-7*) B C Adamson.

Adamson, Carlene A., ed. see Shelley, Percy Bysshe.

Adamson, Christopher. Data Warehouse Design Solutions. Venerable, Michael, ed. LC 98-17957. 544p. 1998. pap. 49.99 incl. cd-rom (*0-471-25195-X*) Wiley.

Adamson, D. A., jt. ed. see Williams, Martin A.

Adamson, Dave, jt. auth. see Hunt, Steve.

Adamson, David. Defending the World: The Politics & Diplomacy of the Environment. 250p. 1991. text 49.50 (*1-85043-302-X*, Pub. by I B T) St Martin.

— Living on the Edge. (Changing Wales Ser.). 46p. 1996. pap. 11.95 (*0-8464-4620-0*) Beekman Pubs.

***Adamson, David M., et al.** How Americans View World Population Issues: A Survey of Public Opinion. xxv, 123p. (C). 2000. pap. 15.00 (*0-8330-2823-5*, MR-1114) Rand Corp.

Adamson, David M., jt. auth. see Patterson, Sally.

***Adamson, Deborah.** Stormy the Baby Dolphin. (Illus.). (J). 2000. 15.95 (*1-57168-402-6*, Eakin Pr) Sunbelt Media.

— Stormy the Baby Dolphin. LC 99-58124. (Illus.). (J). 2000. 7.95 (*1-57168-386-0*, Eakin Pr) Sunbelt Media.

Adamson, Deborah, jt. auth. see Stav, Julie.

***Adamson, Diane G.** I Believe in Santa Claus. 2nd ed. (Illus.). 48p. (J). (ps-3). 1998. 15.95 (*0-9673571-0-1*) Di Adamson.

Adamson, Donald. International Hotel English. 176p. 1989. pap. text 26.80 (*0-13-473042-9*) P-H.

Adamson, Donald, tr. see Balzac, Honore de.

Adamson, Douglas. Beginning Karate. 96p. (C). 1996. pap. text, per. 32.95 (*0-7872-2085-X*, 41208501) Kendall-Hunt.

Adamson, Edward & Timlin, John. Art As Healing. 1991. pap. 18.95 (*0-904575-24-1*) Sigo Pr.

***Adamson, Eve.** Dachshunds. 1999. pap. 14.95 (*1-58245-148-6*) Howell Bks.

Adamson, Eve & Kays, Maureen. Breastfeeding: A Holistic Handbook. LC 98-235030. 288p. 1999. pap. 12.95 (*0-425-16316-4*) Berkley Pub.

Adamson, Eve, jt. auth. see Budilovsky, Joan.

Adamson, G. David & Martin, Daniel C., eds. Endoscopic Management of Gynecologic Disease. LC 94-48584 (Illus.). 464p. 1995. text 162.00 (*0-7817-0281-X*) Lppncott W & W.

Adamson, Gil. Help Me, Jacques Cousteau. LC 96-117576. 152p. 1995. pap. write for info. (*0-88984-161-6*) Porcup Quill.

Adamson, Gil & Connolly, Dawn. Mulder, It's Me: An X-Haustive X-Pose of the Woman Who Is Special Agent Dana Scully. (Illus.). 300p. 1997. pap. 16.95 (*1-55022-316-X*, Pub. by ECW) LPC InBook.

Adamson, Ginette & Myers, Eunice, eds. Continental, Latin-American & Francophone Women Writers, Vol. III. 260p. (C). 1997. 39.50 (*0-7618-0856-6*) U Pr of Amer.

— Continental, Latin-American & Francophone Women Writers, Vol. IV. 300p. 1997. 49.50 (*0-7618-0869-8*) U Pr of Amer.

— Continental, Latin-American & Francophone Women Writers Vol. 2: Selected Papers from the Wichita State University Conference on Foreign Literature, 1986-1987. LC 87-8105. 212p. (C). 1990. lib. bdg. 48.00 (*0-8191-7593-5*) U Pr of Amer.

Adamson, Hugh C. & Hainsworth, Philip. Historical Dictionary of the Bahai Faith. LC 97-2610. (Historical Dictionaries of Religions, Philosophies, & Movements Ser.: No. 17). 1997. 65.00 (*0-8108-3353-0*) Scarecrow.

Adamson, Hugh D. Variation Theory & Second Language Acquisition. fac. ed. LC 87-34198. (Illus.). 100p. 1988. reprint ed. pap. 31.00 (*0-7837-7799-X*, 204755500007) Bks Demand.

Adamson, I. A Set Theory Workbook. LC 97-36639. 150p. 1997. pap., wbk. ed. 29.50 (*0-8176-4028-2*) Birkhauser.

Adamson, Iain T. Data Structures & Algorithms: A First Course. LC 96-9537. 419p. 1996. pap. 27.50 (*3-540-76047-4*) Spr-Verlag.

— A General Topology. LC 95-34839. 1995. write for info. (*3-7643-3844-X*) Birkhauser.

— A General Topology. LC 95-34839. 152p. 1995. pap., wbk. ed. 29.50 (*0-8176-3844-X*) Birkhauser.

***Adamson, Isaac.** Tokyo Suckerpunch. 336p. 2000. pap. 13.00 (*0-380-81291-6*) Morrow Avon.

Adamson, J. C. & Mohan, Piare. Master Book of Wedding & Bridal Photography. 2nd ed. (Illus.). 165p. 1994. reprint ed. pap. 39.50 (*0-934420-17-3*, 1580) Studio Pr NE.

Adamson, James B. James. (New International Commentary on the New Testament Ser.). 227p. 1976. 30.00 (*0-8028-2515-X*) Eerdmans.

— James: The Man & His Message. fac. ed. LC 86-16240. 575p. (Orig.). 1989. reprint ed. pap. 178.30 (*0-7837-7942-9*, 204769800008) Bks Demand.

Adamson, Jane. Troilus & Cressida. 130p. 1988. pap. 13.95 (*0-8057-8704-6*) Macmillan.

Adamson, Jane, et al, eds. Renegotiating Ethics in Literature, Philosophy & Theory. LC 99-211222. (Literature, Culture, Theory Ser.: No. 29). 260p. (C). 1999. text 59.95 (*0-521-62079-1*); pap. text 19.95 (*0-521-62938-1*) Cambridge U Pr.

Adamson, Jay. MCSe TestPrep: Networking Essentials. 2nd ed. LC 98-87716. 400p. 1999. pap. 19.99 (*0-7357-0010-9*) New Riders Pub.

***Adamson, Jim, et al.** The Denny's Story: How a Company in Crisis Resurrected Its Good Name & Reputation. LC 99-47275. 224p. 2000. 24.95 (*0-471-36957-8*) Wiley.

Adamson, Joe. Bugs Bunny: Fifty Years & Only One Grey Hare. LC 90-4074. (Illus.). 192p. 1995. 35.00 (*0-8050-1190-0*); pap. 19.95 (*0-8050-1855-7*, Owl) H Holt & Co.

— Tex Avery: King of Cartoons. (Quality Paperbacks Ser.). (Illus.). 238p. 1985. reprint ed. pap. 15.95 (*0-306-80248-1*) Da Capo.

Adamson, Joe, ed. Byron Haskin. LC 84-14080. (Directors Guild of American Oral History Ser.: No. 1). (Illus.). 334p. 1997. 29.00 (*0-8108-1740-3*) Scarecrow.

Adamson, John. Basic Law the Legal Environment of Business. 260p. (C). 1994. text, student ed. 16.87 (*0-256-12554-6*, Irwn McGrw-H) McGrw-H Hghr Educ.

***Adamson, John.** The Princely Courts of Europe 1500-1750. 352p. 1999. 60.00 (*0-297-83653-6*) Weidenfeld & Nicolson.

Adamson, John, jt. auth. see Prior, Katherine.

Adamson, John E. Achievement Tests Law for Business. 15th ed. (LA - Business Law Ser.). (C). Date not set. pap. 7.95 (*0-538-68355-4*) S-W Pub.

— Basic Law & the Legal Environment of Business. LC 94-12327. (Irwin Legal Studies in Business Ser.). 640p. (C). 1994. text 50.95 (*0-256-11302-5*, Irwn McGrw-H) McGrw-H Hghr Educ.

— Externals & Essentials. LC 67-22049. (Essay Index Reprint Ser.). 1977. 19.95 (*0-8369-0137-1*) Ayer.

— Law for Business. 14th ed. (LA - Business Law Ser.). 1992. mass mkt. 49.95 (*0-538-60956-7*) S-W Pub.

— Law for Business & Personal Use. 15th ed. (LA - Business Law Ser.). (C). 1999. 62.95 (*0-538-68353-8*) S-W Pub.

— Law for Business & Personal Use. 15th ed. (Business Law). (C). 1999. student ed., wbk. ed. 11.75 (*0-538-68354-6*) S-W Pub.

Adamson, John E. & Mietus, Norbert J. Achievement Tests Law for Business. 14th ed. (LA - Business Law Ser.). 1992. 6.95 (*0-538-61285-1*) S-W Pub.

Adamson, Joseph. Melville, Shame, & the Evil Eye: A Psychoanalytic Reading. LC 96-8837. (SUNY Series in Psychoanalysis & Culture). 457p. (C). 1996. text 65.50 (*0-7914-3279-3*); pap. text 21.95 (*0-7914-3280-7*) State U NY Pr.

— Northrop Frye: A Visionary Life. LC 94-104728. (Illus.). 112p. (Orig.). 1993. pap. 9.95 (*1-55022-184-1*, Pub. by ECW) LPC InBook.

Adamson, Joseph & Clark, Hilary, eds. Scenes of Shame: Psychoanalysis, Shame, & Writing. LC 97-49913. (SUNY Series in Psychoanalysis & Culture). 288p. (C). 1998. text 65.50 (*0-7914-3975-5*); pap. text 21.95 (*0-7914-3976-3*) State U NY Pr.

Adamson, Joy. Born Free. LC 74-5073. (Illus.). 1994. reprint ed. lib. bdg. 44.95 (*1-56849-551-X*) Buccaneer Bks.

— Born Free: A Lioness of Two Worlds. LC 86-42972. 1987. 11.95 (*0-679-56141-2*) Pantheon.

***Adamson, Joy.** Born Free: A Lioness of Two Worlds. 224p. 2000. pap. text 14.95 (*0-375-71438-3*) Pantheon.

Adamson, Joy. Born Free, a Lioness of Two Worlds. LC 86-42972. (J). 1987. 20.10 (*0-606-03697-0*, Pub. by Turtleback) Demco.

Adamson, Judith. Graham Greene & Cinema. LC 84-12113. 191p. 1984. 29.95 (*0-937664-65-0*) Pilgrim Bks OK.

Adamson, Judith, jt. auth. see Korte, Leo J.

Adamson, Kay. Algeria: A Study in Competing Ideologies. LC 97-8712. 1997. pap. write for info. (*0-304-70013-4*, Pub. by Cassell) Sterling.

— Algeria: A Study in Competing Ideologies. LC 97-8712. 224p. 1998. 75.00 (*0-304-70012-6*, Pub. by Cassell) Cassell.

Adamson, L. Dangerous Games. 1995. mass mkt. 13.95 (*0-340-62872-3*, Pub. by Hodder & Stought Ltd) Trafalgar.

— Evil Acts. 1996. text 35.00 (*0-340-66019-8*, Pub. by Hodder & Stought Ltd) Trafalgar.

— Girl in Case. 1998. mass mkt. 15.95 (*0-340-66022-8*, Pub. by Hodder & Stought Ltd) Trafalgar.

— Lipstick & Lies. text 35.00 (*0-340-71317-8*, Pub. by Hodder & Stought Ltd) Trafalgar.

— Wish You Were Here. 1996. mass mkt. 13.95 (*0-340-63976-8*, Pub. by Hodder & Stought Ltd) Trafalgar.

A

Adamson, Lauren & Romski, Mary A. Communication & Language Acquisition: Discoveries from Atypical Development. LC 96-37329. 1997. 44.00 (*1-55766-279-7*) P H Brookes.

Adamson, Lauren B. Communication Development During Infancy. (Developmental Psychology Ser.). (C). 1996. pap. 24.00 (*0-8133-3011-4*, Pub. by Westview) HarpC.

Adamson, Lydia. Beware the Laughing Gull. (Lucy Wayles Mysteries Ser.). 1998. mass mkt. 5.99 (*0-451-19598-1*, Sig) NAL.

— A Cat in Wolf's Clothing: An Alice Nestleton Mystery. large type ed. LC 92-36501. (General Ser.). 223p. 1993. pap. 16.95 (*0-8161-5401-5*, G K Hall Lrg Type) Mac Lib Ref.

— A Cat of a Different Color. large type ed. (General Ser.). 200p. 1992. pap. 14.95 (*0-8161-5399-X*, G K Hall Lrg Type); lib. bdg. 18.95 (*0-8161-5398-1*, G K Hall Lrg Type) Mac Lib Ref.

***Adamson, Lydia.** A Cat of One's Own, 1. (Alice Nestleton Mystery Ser.). 208p. 2000. mass mkt. 5.99 (*0-451-19769-0*) NAL.

Adamson, Lydia. A Cat of One's Own. large type ed. LC 99-19149. 203p. 1999. 27.95 (*0-7862-1884-3*) Mac Lib Ref.

— A Cat on a Beach Blanket. (An Alice Nestleton Mystery Ser.). 1997. 22.95 (*0-614-27904-6*) NAL.

— A Cat on a Beach Blanket. 256p. 1998. mass mkt. 5.99 (*0-451-19259-1*, Sig) NAL.

— A Cat on Jingle Bell Rock. (Alice Nestleton Mystery Ser.). 1998. mass mkt. 5.99 (*0-451-19458-6*, Sig) NAL.

— A Cat on Stage Left: An Alice Nestleton Mystery. LC 97-44227. Vol. 16. (Illus.). 176p. 1998. 19.95 (*0-525-94419-2*) NAL.

— A Cat on Stage Left: An Alice Nestleton Mystery. large type ed. LC 98-24625. 222p. 1998. 30.00 (*0-7862-1559-3*) Thorndike Pr.

— A Cat on Stage Left: An Alice Nestleton Mystery, 1 vol., Vol. 16. Vol. 16. 175p. 1999. mass mkt. 5.99 (*0-451-19734-8*) NAL.

— A Cat under the Mistletoe. 240p. 1997. mass mkt. 5.99 (*0-451-19105-6*, Sig) NAL.

***Adamson, Lydia.** A Cat under the Mistletoe: An Alice Nestleton Mystery. LC 00-33758. 2000. write for info. (*0-7862-2651-X*) Thorndike Pr.

Adamson, Lydia. A Cat with No Regrets. 1999. pap. write for info. (*0-525-93811-7*) Viking Penguin.

— Dr. Nightingale Races the Outlaw Colt. (Deirdre Quinn Nightingale Mystery Ser.). 224p. 1998. mass mkt. 5.99 (*0-451-18815-2*, Sig) NAL.

***Adamson, Lydia.** Dr. Nightingale Races the Outlaw Colt: A Deirdre Quinn Nightingale Mystery. LC 00-21254. (Mystery Ser.). 2000. 27.95 (*0-7862-2486-X*) Thorndike Pr.

— Dr. Nightingale Seeks Greener Pastures. (Deirdre Quinn Nightingale Mystery Ser.). 2000. mass mkt. 5.99 (*0-451-20054-3*, Sig) NAL.

Adamson, Lydia. Dr. Nightingale Traps the Missing Lynx, 1 vol. 1999. mass mkt. 5.99 (*0-451-19773-9*) NAL.

***Adamson, Lydia, as told by.** Dr. Nightingale Traps the Missing Lynx. large type ed. LC 99-41962. (Thorndike Mystery Ser.). 1999. 26.95 (*0-7862-2204-2*) Thorndike Pr.

Adamson, Lynda G. American Historical Fiction: An Annotated Guide to Novels for Adults & Young Adults. annot. ed. LC 98-38044. 416p. 1998. 54.95 (*1-57356-067-7*) Oryx Pr.

— Historical Fiction for Children & Young Adults: An Annotated Bibliography of American & International Titles. LC 94-14435. 520p. 1994. 59.95 (*0-313-29008-3*, Greenwood Pr) Greenwood.

— Literature Connections to American History, K-6: Resources to Enhance & Entice. LC 97-14283. 542p. (gr. 5-6). 1997. lib. bdg. 33.50 (*1-56308-502-X*) Libs Unl.

— Literature Connections to American History, 7-12: Resources to Enhance & Entice. LC 97-19560. 624p. (YA). (gr. 7-12). 1997. lib. bdg. 34.50 (*1-56308-503-8*) Libs Unl.

— Literature Connections to World History, K-6: Resources to Enhance & Entice. LC 97-35952. 326p. 1998. lib. bdg. 30.00 (*1-56308-504-6*) Libs Unl.

— Literature Connections to World History, 7-12: Resources to Enhance & Entice. LC 97-35953. 511p. 1998. lib. bdg. 32.50 (*1-56308-505-4*) Libs Unl.

— Notable Women in American History: A Guide to Recommended Biographies & Autobiographies. LC 98-55350. 464p. 1999. 49.95 (*0-313-29584-0*, GR9584, Greenwood Pr) Greenwood.

— Notable Women in World History: A Guide to Recommended Biographies & Autobiographies. LC 97-33136. 416p. 1998. 49.50 (*0-313-29818-1*, Greenwood Pr) Greenwood.

— World Historical Fiction: An Annotated Guide to Novels for Adults & Young Adults. annot. ed. LC 98-39981. 719p. 1998. 54.95 (*1-57356-066-9*) Oryx Pr.

Adamson, M. R., tr. see Maritain, Jacques.

Adamson, Madeleine & Borgos, Seth. This Mighty Dream: Social Protest Movements in the United States. (Illus.). 128p. 1984. pap. 10.95 (*0-7102-0042-0*, Routledge Thoemms) Routledge.

Adamson, Margot, tr. see Maritain, Jacques.

Adamson, Mark. The New Jersey 2C Quizzer. 238p. 1999. ring bd. 39.95 (*1-885682-14-X*) Princeton Educ.

Adamson, Mark & Del Bagno, Daniel. New Jersey Attorney General Guidelines. 350p. (C). 1995. ring bd. 39.95 (*1-885682-03-4*) Princeton Educ.

— New Jersey Attorney General Guidelines. 3rd rev. ed. 418p. 1998. ring bd. 49.95 (*1-885682-13-1*) Princeton Educ.

Adamson, Mark & Del Bagno, Daniel R. The New Jersey 2C Quizzer. 218p. (C). 1996. ring bd. 39.95 (*1-885682-06-9*) Princeton Educ.

Adamson, Mark & DelBagno, Daniel. Attorney General Guidelines Quizzer. rev. ed. 240p. (C). 1997. ring bd. 39.95 (*1-885682-09-3*) Princeton Educ.

— The Law Enforcement Manual. 335p. (C). 1994. ring bd. 39.95 (*1-885682-01-8*) Princeton Educ.

Adamson, Mark, et al. The Law Enforcement Manual. rev. ed. 340p. 1997. ring bd. 39.95 (*1-885682-10-7*) Princeton Educ.

— New Jersey State Attorney General Guidelines Quizzer. 1994. 39.95 (*1-885682-00-X*) Princeton Educ.

Adamson, Mary J. A February Face. 1987. pap. 2.95 (*0-317-56973-2*) Bantam.

***Adamson, Mary Jo.** Blazing Tree. (Michael Merrick Mysteries Ser.). 272p. 2000. mass mkt. 5.99 (*0-451-20034-9*, Sig) NAL.

Adamson, Mathew, tr. see Bourdieu, Pierre.

Adamson, Matthew, tr. see Bourdieu, Pierre.

Adamson, Melitta W., ed. Food in the Middle Ages: A Book of Essays. LC 94-43057. (Medieval Casebooks Ser.: Vol. 12). 224p. 1995. text 47.00 (*0-8153-1345-4*, H1744) Garland.

Adamson, Nancy, et al. Feminist Organizing for Change: The Contemporary Women's Movement in Canada. 384p. 1989. pap. text 16.95 (*0-19-540658-3*) OUP.

Adamson, R. B., jt. auth. see Franklin, D.

Adamson, Richard. Bogota Bandit: The Outlaw Life of Charlie Mitten: Penalty King of Old Trafford. (Illus.). 192p. 1996. 34.95 (*1-85158-867-1*, Pub. by Mainstream Pubng) Trafalgar.

Adamson, Richard H., et al, eds. Heterocyclic Amines in Cooked Foods: Possible Human Carcinogens: 23rd International Symposium. (Proceedings of the Princess Takamatsu Cancer Research Fund Ser.). (Illus.). 306p. 1995. text 75.00 (*0-614-16034-0*) Specialist Journals.

Adamson, Robert. The Development of Modern Philosophy. Sorley, William R., ed. LC 76-165613. (Select Bibliographies Reprint Ser.). 1977. reprint ed. 25.95 (*0-8369-5920-5*) Ayer.

— Fichte. (Works of Robert Adamson). 222p. reprint ed. write for info. (*0-7812-0825-4*) Rprt Serv.

— Fichte: Philosophical Classics for English Readers. LC 76-94262. (Select Bibliographies Reprint Ser.). 1977. 21.95 (*0-8369-5036-4*) Ayer.

— Robert Adamson: Selected Poems, 1970-1989. 269p. 1990. pap. 19.95 (*0-7022-2323-9*, Pub. by Univ Queensland Pr) Intl Spec Bk.

— A Short History of Logic. Sorley, W. R., ed. (Reprints in Philosophy Ser.). reprint ed. lib. bdg. 39.50 (*0-697-00001-X*) Irvington.

Adamson, Robert, ed. The Clean Dark. 93p. (C). 1990. 105.00 (*0-9587801-2-9*, Pub. by Pascoe Pub) St Mut.

Adamson, Robin & Edelston, Brigitte. French Grammar. rev. ed. (Teach Yourself Ser.). (FRE.). 256p. 1999. pap. 11.95 (*0-8442-0225-8*, 02258) NTC Contemp Pub Co.

Adamson, Ronald B. & Van Swam, Leo F., eds. Zirconium in the Nuclear Industry: 7th International Symposium. LC 87-14537. (Special Technical Publication Ser.: No. 939). (Illus.). 815p. 1987. text 110.00 (*0-8031-0935-0*, STP938) ASTM.

Adamson, Sara. The Trainer. 2nd ed. (Orig.). 1998. reprint ed. mass mkt. 7.95 (*1-56333-686-3*, Rhinoceros) Masquerade.

Adamson, Seabron, et al. Energy Use, Air Pollution, & Environmental Policy in Krakow: Can Economic Incentives Really Help? (World Bank Technical Papers: Vol. 308). 84p. 1996. pap. 22.00 (*0-8213-3494-8*) World Bank.

Adamson, Stan, ed. Paul Nesbit's Longs Peak: Its Story & a Climbing Guide. rev. ed. LC 89-64298. (Illus.). 73p. 1990. pap. 6.95 (*0-9625445-0-7*) Mills Pub KS.

Adamson, Steven, et al. Advanced Satellite Communications: Potential Markets. LC 94-23429. (Advanced Computing & Telecommunications Ser.). (Illus.). 344p. 1995. 56.00 (*0-8155-1359-3*) Noyes.

Adamson, Suzanne & Harris, Eilish. The Reflexology Partnership: A Healing Bond. (Illus.). 160p. 1996. pap. 13.95 (*1-85626-149-2*, Pub. by Cathie Kyle) Trafalgar.

Adamson, Sylvia, et al, eds. Papers from the Fifth International Conference on English Historical Linguistics: Dedicated to the Memory of James Peter Thorne (1933-1988) LC 90-681. (Current Issues in Linguistic Theory Ser.: Vol. 65). xxi, 583p. 1990. 112.00 (*90-272-3562-7*) J Benjamins Pubng Co.

Adamson, Thomas A. Digital System Logic & Application. (Electronics Technology Ser.). 1989. pap., teacher ed. 16.00 (*0-8273-3113-4*) Delmar.

— Digital System Logic & Application. 2nd ed. (Electronics Technology Ser.). 1996. text 64.95 (*0-8273-6027-4*) Delmar.

— Electronic Communications. 2nd ed. 672p. 1992. mass mkt. 90.95 (*0-8273-5084-8*) Delmar.

— Electronic Communications: Systems & Circuits. 1988. pap., student ed. 24.95 (*0-8273-2641-6*); text 59.95 (*0-8273-2640-8*) Delmar.

— Electronic Communications: Systems & Circuits. 1988. pap., teacher ed. 15.00 (*0-8273-2642-4*) Delmar.

— Electronic Communications Lab Manual. 2nd ed. 1992. lab manual ed. 16.00 incl. disk (*0-8273-5912-8*) Delmar.

— Electronic Communications Lab Manual. 2nd ed. 1993. pap., lab manual ed. 30.25 (*0-8273-5237-9*) Delmar.

— Electronics Dictionary for Technicians. (C). 1992. pap. text 16.60 (*0-02-300820-2*, Macmillan Coll) P-H.

Adamson, Thomas A. & Antonakos, James L. Structured C for Engineering & Technology. 3rd ed. LC 97-20691. 861p. (C). 1997. pap. text 86.00 (*0-13-625229-X*) P-H.

Adamson, Tom. Advanced AC Circuits. Gorham, Kelly, ed. 29p. 1994. student ed. 7.00 (*0-8064-0326-8*, E23) Bergwall.

— Alternating Current Fundamentals. Gorham, Kelly, ed. 24p. 1993. student ed. 19.95 (*0-8064-0366-7*, E17) Bergwall.

— Electronic Circuit Troubleshooting. 20p. (YA). (gr. 10 up). 1995. pap., wbk. ed. 7.00 (*0-8064-0603-8*, E24) Bergwall.

— Electronic Communication Fundamentals. 32p. 1996. pap., wbk. ed. 7.00 (*0-8064-0451-5*, E70) Bergwall.

— Fiber Optics Explained. Gorham, Kelly, ed. 28p. 1994. student ed. 289.00 (*0-8064-0304-7*, E60) Bergwall.

***Adamson, Victor J.** That Kind Can Never Change... Can They? One Man's Struggle with His Homosexuality. LC 00-102924. 224p. 2000. pap. 11.99 (*1-56384-175-4*) Huntington Hse.

***Adamson, W. R.** The Book of Lights: Luminism's Ten Lights of Insight, Enlightenment, & Illumination. deluxe ed. LC 98-96525. 160p. 1999. pap. 14.95 (*0-9666474-0-8*) Ten Lights Pr.

Adamson, Walter L. Avant-Garde Florence: From Modernism to Fascism. LC 93-8062. (Studies in Cultural History). 368p. 1993. 46.95 (*0-674-05525-X*) HUP.

Adamthwaite, Anthony. Grandeur & Misery: France's Bid for Power in Europe, 1914-1940. LC 95-16078. 296p. 1995. pap. text 19.95 (*0-7131-6576-6*, A5508, Pub. by E A) OUP.

Adamthwaite, Anthony P. The Making of the Second World War. 2nd ed. (Historical Problems: Studies & Documents). (Illus.). 1977. pap. text 19.95 (*0-04-940057-6*) Routledge.

— The Making of the Second World War. 2nd ed. 240p. (C). 1989. pap. 23.99 (*0-415-90716-0*) Routledge.

Adamu, Abdalla U. Reform & Adaptation in Nigerian University Curricula, 1960-1992: Living on the Credit Line. LC 93-36834. (African Studies: Vol. 33). 304p. 1994. text 99.95 (*0-7734-9422-7*) E Mellen.

Adamy, Dave. Digital Communication: Overview Summary. (Overview Summaries Ser.). 32p. 1995. pap. 8.00 (*1-885897-08-1*) Lynx Pubng.

— Direction Finding Techniques: Overview Summary. (Overview Summaries Ser.). 32p. 1994. pap. 8.00 (*1-885897-05-7*) Lynx Pubng.

— Electronic Warfare Principles & Practice: Overview Summary. (Overview Summaries Ser.). 32p. 1995. pap. 8.00 (*1-885897-07-3*) Lynx Pubng.

— Electronic Warfare Simulation: Overview Summary. (Overview Summaries Ser.). 32p. 1995. pap. 8.00 (*1-885897-09-X*) Lynx Pubng.

— Practical Communication Theory. 160p. 1994. 49.95 (*1-885897-04-9*) Lynx Pubng.

— Proposal Preparation for Technical Staff Contributors. 110p. 1990. pap. 19.95 (*1-885897-01-4*) Lynx Pubng.

— Spread Spectrum Techniques: Overview Summary. (Overview Summaries Ser.). 32p. 1994. pap. 8.00 (*1-885897-06-5*) Lynx Pubng.

Adamy, Dave & Fisk, Terry. A Bird's Eye View of the EW Profession. (EW Cartoon Bks.). 96p. 1987. pap. 9.95 (*1-885897-00-6*) Lynx Pubng.

— EW Folks: Cartoons & Commentary on the Way They See the World. (EW Cartoon Bks.). 96p. 1992. pap. 9.95 (*1-885897-02-2*) Lynx Pubng.

***Adamy, David L.** Preparing & Delivering Effective Technical Presentations. 2nd ed. 297p. 2000. write for info. (*1-58053-017-6*) Artech Hse.

***Adamyan, V. M., et al, eds.** Differential Operators & Related Topics: Proceedings of the Mark Krein International Conference on Operator Theory & Applications, Odessa, Ukraine, August 18-22, 1997, 2 vols. Set. (Operator Theory Ser.). 880p. 2000. 250.00 (*3-7643-6289-8*) Birkhauser.

— Differential Operators & Related Topics Vol. I: Proceedings of the Mark Krein International Conference on Operator Theory & Applications, Odessa, Ukraine, August 18-22, 1997. (Operator Theory Ser.: Vol. 117). 432p. 2000. 140.00 (*3-7643-6287-1*, Pub. by Birkhauser) Spr-Verlag.

Adamyan, V. M., ed. see Mark Krein International Conference on Operator Theory & Applications Staff.

Adamz-Bogus, SDiane. Hatshepsut's Legacy: African & American Long Herstories. 250p. 2000. pap. 24.95 (*0-9650665-0-9*) Burning Bush CA.

Adamzewski & Brad, J. Hoofed Mammals of Alberta. 1993. pap. 19.95 (*1-55105-037-4*) Lone Pine.

Adamzik, Kirsten, et al, eds. Domanen- und Kulturspezifisches Schreiben. (Textproduktion und Medium Ser.: Bd. 3). (Illus.). VIII, 257p. 1997. pap. 40.95 (*3-631-31983-5*) P Lang Pubng.

Adamzik, Kirsten, jt. auth. see Niederhauser, Jurg.

Adan, Scott M. & Rollins, Kyle M. Damage Potential Index Mapping for Salt Lake Valley, Utah. (Miscellaneous Publication Ser.: Vol. 93-4). (Illus.). 64p. 1993. pap. 6.00 (*1-55791-323-4*, MP-93-4) Utah Geological Survey.

Adanson, M. Familles des Plantes, 2 vols. in 1. (Illus.). 1966. reprint ed. 225.00 (*3-7682-0345-X*) Lubrecht & Cramer.

Adanur, S., ed. Wellington Sears Handbook of Industrial Textiles. 848p. 1995. boxed set 189.95 (*1-85573-265-3*, Pub. by Woodhead Pubng) Am Educ Systs.

Adanur, Sabit. Paper Machine Clothing. LC 97-60981. 375p. 1997. text 79.95 (*1-56676-544-7*) Technomic.

Adanur, Sabit, ed. Wellington Sears Handbook of Industrial Textiles. LC 95-61229. 850p. 1995. text 199.95 (*1-56676-340-1*) Technomic.

Adany, Roza, ed. Tumor Matrix Biology. LC 94-44953. 272p. 1995. lib. bdg. 205.00 (*0-8493-4882-X*, 4882) CRC Pr.

Adaptive Environments Center, Inc. Staff. The ADA Action Guide for State & Local Governments. LC 93-6960. (Disability Law Practice Ser.). 170p. 1993. 32.90 (*0-934753-88-1*) LRP Pubns.

Adar, Evan. Spacion. LC 85-51325. 226p. 1986. 18.95 (*0-912159-03-0*) Center Pr CA.

Adar, Isaac, et al. The IBM Personal Computer: What You Should Know. rev. ed. LC 83-72637. (QED Personal Computing Ser.). 199p. reprint ed. pap. 61.70 (*0-608-15620-5*, 203174900076) Bks Demand.

Adar, Korwa G. Kenyan Foreign Policy Behavior Towards Somalia, 1963-1983. LC 92-46067. 242p. 1994. 45.00 (*0-8191-9041-1*) U Pr of Amer.

Adar, L., jt. ed. see Smilansky, M.

Adar Publications Staff, ed. see Doukhan, Jacques.

Adar, Z. The Book of Genesis: An Introduction to the Biblical Word. 165p. 1990. 12.00 (*965-223-727-2*, Pub. by Magnes Pr) Eisenbrauns.

Adare, Sierra. Backcountry Cooking: Feasts for Hikers, Hoofers, & Floaters. (Illus.). 246p. 1996. 16.95 (*1-886609-02-0*) Tamarack Bks.

***Adare, Sierra.** Greece: The Culture. (Illus.). (J). 1998. 13.40 (*0-606-18057-5*) Turtleback.

Adare, Sierra. What Editors Look For: How to Write Compelling Queries, Cover Letters, Synopses & Book Proposals. Republic of Texas Press Staff, ed. 160p. (Orig.). 1995. pap. 15.99 (*0-9646159-0-8*) Cougar Imprints.

— The Wyoming Guide. LC 99-19889. (Fulcrum State Travel Guide Ser.). (Illus.). 240p. 1999. pap. 17.95 (*1-55591-381-4*) Fulcrum Pub.

Adare, Sierra & Moulton, Candy V. Salt Lake City Uncovered. LC 96-40200. 320p. 1997. pap. 16.95 (*1-55622-534-2*, Seaside Pr) Wordware Pub.

Adare, Sierra S. Jackson Hole Uncovered. LC 96-446. 320p. 1997. pap. 16.95 (*1-55622-484-2*, Seaside Pr) Wordware Pub.

Adare, Viscount. Experiences in Spiritualism with Mr. D. D. Home. LC 75-36824. (Occult Ser.). 1976. reprint ed. 18.95 (*0-405-07937-0*) Ayer.

Adas, ed. Ideologies of Oppression. (C). 1998. text. write for info. (*0-321-01153-8*) Addson-Wesley Educ.

— World History, Vol. II. (C). 1996. text. write for info. (*0-673-99230-6*) Addison-Wesley.

Adas, Jane, ed. Corelli & His Contemporaries: Sonatas for Violin. LC 91-751665. (Eighteenth Century Continuo Sonata Ser.). 288p. 1991. text 50.00 (*0-8153-0174-X*) Garland.

— Early Eighteenth-Century French & German Masters: Sonatas for Violin. LC 91-751550. (Eighteenth Century Continuo Sonata Ser.: Vol. 3). 344p. 1991. text 50.00 (*0-8153-0176-6*) Garland.

— French & Italian Innovators: Continuo Sonatas for Violin. LC 91-751590. (Eighteenth Century Continuo Sonata Ser.: Vol. 4). 320p. 1991. text 50.00 (*0-8153-0177-4*) Garland.

— Late Eighteenth-Century Cello Sonatas: Continuo Sonatas for Cello. LC 91-751613. (Eighteenth Century Continuo Sonata Ser.: Vol. 8). 336p. 1991. text 50.00 (*0-8153-0181-2*) Garland.

— Late Eighteenth Century Masters: Continuo Sonatas for Violin. LC 91-755879. (Eighteenth Century Continuo Sonata Ser.: Vol. 6). 344p. 1992. text 50.00 (*0-8153-0179-0*) Garland.

— Late Eighteenth-Century Sonatas for Woodwinds Continuo Sonatas for Woodwinds: Continuo Sonatas for Woodwinds. LC 91-751612. (Eighteenth Century Continuo Sonata Ser.: Vol. 10). 360p. 1992. text 50.00 (*0-8153-0183-9*) Garland.

— Mid 18th Century Cello Sonatas: Continuo Sonatas for Cello. LC 91-755832. (18th Century Continuo Sonata Ser.: No. 7). 328p. 1992. text 100.00 (*0-8153-0180-4*) Garland.

— Mid Eighteenth-Century Masters: Continuo Sonatas for Violin. LC 91-752337. (Eighteenth Century Continuo Sonata Ser.: Vol. 5). 376p. 1991. text 50.00 (*0-8153-0178-2*) Garland.

— Veracini & His Contemporaries: Continuo Sonatas for Violin. LC 91-752425. (Eighteenth Century Continuo Sonata Ser.: Vol. 2). 296p. 1991. text 50.00 (*0-8153-0175-8*) Garland.

Adas, Michael. The Burma Delta: Economic Development & Social Change on an Asian Rice Frontier, 1852-1941. LC 73-15256. 272p. reprint ed. pap. 84.40 (*0-8357-9772-4*, 201535000093) Bks Demand.

— High Imperialism & the New History. (Essays on Global & Comparative History Ser.). 34p. 1994. pap. 6.00 (*0-87229-073-5*) Am Hist Assn.

— Machines As the Measure of Men: Science, Technology, & Ideologies of Western Dominance. LC 89-845. (Cornell Studies in Comparative History). (Illus.). 484p. 1990. reprint ed. pap. text 18.95 (*0-8014-9760-4*) Cornell U Pr.

— Prophets of Rebellion: Millenarian Protest Movements Against the European Colonial Order. LC 78-26775. 271p. reprint ed. pap. 84.10 (*0-7837-2453-5*, 204260600005) Bks Demand.

***Adas, Michael.** State, Market & Peasant in Colonial South & Southeast Asia. LC 98-19002. (Variorum Collected Studies Ser.: Vol. 616). 350p. 1998. text 99.95 (*0-86078-696-X*, Pub. by Variorum) Ashgate Pub Co.

***Adas, Michael, ed.** Agricultural & Pastoral Societies in Ancient & Classical History. (Critical Perspectives on the Past Ser.). 432p. 2001. 74.50 (*1-56639-831-2*); pap. 24.95 (*1-56639-832-0*) Temple U Pr.

Adas, Michael, ed. Islamic & European Expansion: The Forging of a Global Order. 380p. 1996. pap. 19.95 (*0-614-21153-0*) Kazi Pubns.

— Islamic & European Expansion: The Forging of a Global Order. LC 92-43872. (Critical Perspectives on the Past Ser.). 400p. 1993. 69.95 (*1-56639-067-2*); pap. 22.95 (*1-56639-068-0*) Temple U Pr.

— Technology & European Overseas Enterprise: Diffusion, Adaption & Adoption. LC 95-44267. (Expanding World Ser.: Vol. 7). 464p. 1996. 147.95 (*0-86078-525-4*, Pub. by Variorum) Ashgate Pub Co.

Adas, Michael, ed. see Abu-Lughod, Janet L.

Adas, Michael, ed. see Bentley, Jerry H.

An Asterisk (*) at the beginning of an entry indicates that the title is appearing for the first time.

Adas, Michael, ed. see Burstein, Stanley M.
Adas, Michael, ed. see Crosby, Alfred W.
Adas, Michael, ed. see Curtin, Philip De Armond.
Adas, Michael, ed. see Eaton, Richard M.
Adas, Michael, ed. see Kicza, John E.
Adas, Michael, ed. see McNeill, William H.
Adas, Michael, ed. see Stearns, Peter N.
Adas, Michael, ed. see Strobel, Margaret.
Adas, Michael, ed. see Tilly, Louise A.
Adas, Michael, ed. see Tucker, Judith E.
Adashi, Eli Y., et al, eds. Reproductive Endocrinology, Surgery, & Technology, 2 vols. (Illus.). 2560p. 1995. text 299.00 (*0-7817-0203-8*) Lppncott W & W.
Adashi, Eli Y. & Leung, Peter C., eds. The Ovary. LC 93-1668. (Comprehensive Endocrinology Ser.). 704p. 1993. text 165.00 (*0-7817-0079-5*) Lppncott W & W.
Adashi, Eli Y. & Thorner, Michael O., eds. The Somatotrophic Axis & the Reproductive Process in Health & Disease: Proceedings of the Symposium, Held October 28 to 31, 1993. LC 94-39174. 1995. 138.00 (*0-387-94419-2*) Spr-Verlag.
Adashko, J. George, tr. see Basov, N. G., ed.
Adashko, J. George, tr. see Bazarov, I. P.
Adashko, J. George, tr. see Borisova, Z. U.
Adashko, J. George, tr. see Kadomtsev, B. B., ed.
Adashko, J. George, tr. see Korobeinikov, V. P.
Adashko, J. George, tr. see Letov, Aleksandr M.
Adashko, J. George, tr. see Skobel'tsyn, D. V., ed.
Adasiak, Kathy T., jt. auth. see Dunne, Christine.
Adaskina, Natalia L. The Tretyakov Gallery, Moscow: A Panorama of Russian & Soviet Art, Painting, Graphic Art, Sculpture. (Illus.). 376p. 1983. 308.00 (*0-7855-1678-6*) St Mut.
Adatto, I. J., jt. auth. see Snider, Arthur J.
***Adatto, Kiku.** Picture Perfect: The Art & Artifice of Public Image Making. 200p. 1999. reprint ed. pap. text 12.00 (*0-7881-6243-8*) DIANE Pub.
Adawi, Nabil & Gulf Centre for Strategic Studies (London, England). The Two Holy Mosques in Saudi Arabia: Historical Context, Modern Developments & Cultural Significance. LC 95-137921. 86 p. 1994. write for info. (*1-871415-62-4*) Gulf Ctr.
Aday, Kathryn L., jt. auth. see Aday, Ron H.
Aday, Lu A. Designing & Conducting Health Surveys: A Comprehensive Guide. 2nd ed. LC 96-18108. 535p. 1996. 49.95 (*0-7879-0294-2*) Jossey-Bass.
Aday, Lu Ann. At Risk in America: The Health & Health Care Needs of Vulnerable Populations in the United States. LC 92-32437. (Health Ser.). 398p. 1993. text 47.95 (*1-55542-503-8*) Jossey-Bass.
Aday, Lu-Ann. Evaluating the Health Care System: Effectiveness, Efficiency, & Equity. 2nd ed. LC 98-12225. 334p. 1998. 45.00 (*1-56793-079-4*) Health Admin Pr.
Aday, Ron H., compiled by. Crime & the Elderly: An Annotated Bibliography, 8. LC 88-30051. (Bibliographies & Indexes in Gerontology Ser.). 131p. 1988. lib. bdg. 49.95 (*0-313-25470-2*, ACY, Greenwood Pr) Greenwood.
Aday, Ron H. & Aday, Kathryn L. Group Work with the Elderly: An Annotated Bibliography, 33. LC 96-42162. (Bibliographies & Indexes in Gerontology Ser.). 184p. 1997. lib. bdg. 69.50 (*0-313-29845-9*) Greenwood.
ADB Inc. Staff. Captain's Log, No. 18. (Illus.). 112p. 1999. pap. 14.95 (*1-58564-000-X*) Amarillo Design.
— Star Fleet Battles Module R2 (New Ships II) 2nd ed. 1999. pap. 17.95 (*1-58564-001-8*) Amarillo Design.
ADC Staff. ADC's Street Map of Cobb & N. Fulton Counties, Georgia. 6th ed. LC 93-675461. 95p. 1993. write for info. (*0-87530-129-0*) ADC Map People.
— ADC's Street Map of Raleigh, North Carolina & Vicinity Street Map. LC 90-675310. xxi, 40p. 1990. write for info. (*0-87530-135-5*) ADC Map People.
Adcock. Portfolio Optimisation. text. write for info. (*0-471-49101-2*) Wiley.
Adcock, Al. C-123 Provider in Action. (Aircraft in Action Ser.). (Illus.). 50p. 1992. pap. 8.95 (*0-89747-276-4*, 1124) Squad Sig Pubns.
Adcock, Al. Destroyer Escorts in Action. LC 98-138762. 1997. write for info. (*0-89747-378-7*) Squad Sig Pubns.
Adcock, Al. Escort Carriers CVE in Action. (Warships in Action Ser.). (Illus.). 50p. 1996. pap. 9.95 (*0-89747-356-6*, 4009) Squad Sig Pubns.
— F-14 Tomcat in Action. (Aircraft in Action Ser.). (Illus.). 50p. 1990. pap. 9.95 (*0-89747-247-0*, 1105) Squad Sig Pubns.
— H-3 Sea King in Action. (Aircraft in Action Ser.). (Illus.). 58p. 1995. pap. 9.95 (*0-89747-330-2*) Squad Sig Pubns.
***Adcock, Al.** U. S. Light Cruisers in Action. (Warships in Action Ser.: Vol. 12). (Illus.). 50p. 1999. pap. 9.95 (*0-89747-407-4*) Squad Sig Pubns.
— USS Alabama on Deck. (Illus.). 80p. 1999. pap. 14.95 (*0-89747-399-X*) Squad Sig Pubns.
Adcock, Arthur S. Glory That Was Grub Street. LC 72-99678. (Essay Index Reprint Ser.). 1977. 30.95 (*0-8369-1388-4*) Ayer.
Adcock, Betty. Difficult Wheel: Poems. (C). 1995. pap. 9.95 (*0-8071-2023-5*); text 17.95 (*0-8071-2022-7*) La State U Pr.
— Nettles: Poems. LC 83-726. 60p. 1983. pap. 7.95 (*0-8071-1103-1*) La State U Pr.
Adcock, Carol P. Geometric Maze Designs. (International Design Library). (Illus.). 48p. (Orig.). 1984. pap. 5.95 (*0-88045-048-7*) Stemmer Hse.
Adcock, Craig, et al. Terry Allen: Youth in Asia. Margolis, Nancy H., ed. (Illus.). 112p. (Orig.). (C). 1992. pap. 22.00 (*0-9611560-0-7*) SEC Contemp Art.
Adcock, Dennis. Strategic Marketing Management. Date not set. pap. text. write for info. (*0-471-86732-2*) Wiley.
— Strategic Marketing Management. LC 99-47600. 64p. 2000. pap. text 39.95 (*0-471-98169-9*) Wiley.
Adcock, Dennis & Bradfield, Ray. Marketing Principles & Practice. 3rd ed. 464p. (Orig.). 2000. pap. write for info. (*0-273-62798-8*) F T P H.
Adcock, Don, jt. auth. see Segal, Marilyn.
Adcock, Donald, ed. Literacy: Traditional, Cultural, Technology: Selected Papers from the 23rd Annual Conference of the IASL. 141p. 1994. pap. 25.00 (*1-890861-16-2*) IASL.
— Sustaining the Vision: Selected Papers from the 24th Annual Conference of the IASL. 180p. 1995. pap. 25.00 (*1-890861-18-9*) IASL.
— Sustaining the Vision - School Library Imperatives for the 21st Century: Selected Papers from the 25th Annual Conference of the IASL. 180p. 1996. pap. 25.00 (*1-890861-20-0*) IASL.
Adcock, Donald, et al, eds. Dreams & Dynamics: Selected Papers from the 22nd Annual Conference of the IASL. 78p. 1993. pap. 25.00 (*1-890861-15-4*) IASL.
Adcock, Edgar, et al, eds. Directory of Medical & Dental Schools Worldwide. 6th rev. ed. 280p. 1994. text 59.95 (*0-916524-48-5*) US Direct Serv.
Adcock, Fleur. Hotspur. 1986. pap. 6.95 (*1-85224-001-6*, Pub. by Bloodaxe Bks) Dufour.
— The Incident Book. Michie, Jonathan et al, eds. (Illus.). 490p. 1995. pap. text 24.95 (*0-19-828029-7*) OUP.
— Looking Back. 80p. 1998. pap. 13.95 (*0-19-288068-3*) OUP.
— Meeting the Comet. 24p. (Orig.). 1988. pap. 6.95 (*1-85224-054-7*, Pub. by Bloodaxe Bks) Dufour.
— Virgin & the Nightingale. 1983. 24.00 (*0-906427-55-X*, Pub. by Bloodaxe Bks); pap. 16.95 (*0-906427-56-8*, Pub. by Bloodaxe Bks) Dufour.
Adcock, Fleur, ed. Hugh Primas & the Archpoet. LC 93-46136. (Cambridge Medieval Classics Ser.: No. 2). 151p. (C). 1994. text 44.95 (*0-521-39546-1*) Cambridge U Pr.
Adcock, Fleur & Simms, Jacqueline, eds. The Oxford Book of Creatures. 400p. (C). 1996. 30.00 (*0-19-214226-7*) OUP.
Adcock, Fleur, et al. Fourpack No. 1, No. 1. 1986. pap. 12.95 (*1-85224-000-8*, Pub. by Bloodaxe Bks) Dufour.
***Adcock, Fleur, et al.** The Poetry Quartets, Vol. 2. 1999. 24.95 (*1-85224-469-0*, Pub. by Bloodaxe Bks) Dufour.
Adcock, Frank E. The Greek & Macedonian Art of War. LC 57-10495. (Sather Classical Lectures: No. 30). 1974. reprint ed. pap. 13.95 (*0-520-00005-6*, Pub. by U CA Pr) Cal Prin Full Svc.
— Roman Political Ideas & Practice. (Jerome Lectures). 128p. 1959. pap. text 13.95 (*0-472-06088-0*, 06088, Ann Arbor Bks) U of Mich Pr.
Adcock, Gene. Electro-Optical Surveillance. Edge, Ed, ed. LC 98-7459. (SecuritySource Library: Vol. III). (Illus.). 769p. 1999. text 300.00 (*1-884674-03-8*) CCS Security.
Adcock, Herschel C., Sr., et al. Construction Management Guide: Basic Business & Project Management for Contractors. (Illus.). 104p. 1995. spiral bd. 22.50 (*1-889834-01-7*) Nat Assn St Cntractrs.
— Construction Management Guide: Basic Business & Project Management for Contractors. 2nd rev. ed. (Illus.). 100p. 1999. spiral bd. 25.50 (*1-889834-08-4*) Nat Assn St Cntractrs.
— Construction Management Guide: Louisiana Edition. (Illus.). 158p. 1995. spiral bd. 27.50 (*1-889834-02-5*) Nat Assn St Cntractrs.
— Construction Management Guide: Louisiana Edition. 2nd rev. ed. 160p. 1998. spiral bd. 27.50 (*1-889834-05-X*) Nat Assn St Cntractrs.
***Adcock, Herschel C., Sr., et al.** Construction Management Guide: Louisiana Edition. 3rd rev. ed. 148p. 1999. 29.50 (*1-889834-10-6*) Nat Assn St Cntractrs.
Adcock, Herschel C., Sr., et al. Construction Management Guide: North Carolina Electrical Edition. 2nd rev. ed. (Illus.). 163p. 1999. spiral bd. 29.50 (*1-889834-09-2*) Nat Assn St Cntractrs.
***Adcock, Herschel C., Sr., et al.** Construction Management Guide: South Carolina Contractors' Licensing Board Edition. 180p. 2000. 25.00 (*1-889834-12-2*) Nat Assn St Cntractrs.
— Construction Management Guide: South Carolina Residential Builders' Edition. 160p. 2000. 25.00 (*1-889834-13-0*) Nat Assn St Cntractrs.
Adcock, Ian. Bentley Continental R. (Illus.). 192p. 1992. 300.00 (*1-85532-260-9*, Pub. by Ospry) Motorbooks Intl.
— Lotus Heritage. (Color Library). (Illus.). 128p. 1995. pap. 15.95 (*1-85532-508-X*, Pub. by Ospry) Motorbooks Intl.
Adcock, Ian, jt. ed. see Chung, K. Fan.
Adcock, John S. European Medical Device Directive: Self-Certification of Class I Devices. 120p. 1997. wbk. ed. 295.00 (*1-56993-001-5*) HISTECH.
— FDA Inspections: A Guide for Medical Device & Diagnostic Manufacturers. LC 97-50. 178p. 1997. 149.00 (*1-57491-046-9*) Interpharm.
Adcock, Kathleen. The Edge-Dwellers. LC 99-188341. 62p. 1998. pap. 8.00 (*1-57502-974-X*, PO2668) Morris Pubng.
Adcock, M. & White, R. Good-Enough Parenting: A Framework for Assessment. (C). 1989. 39.00 (*0-903534-57-6*, Pub. by Brit Ag for Adopt & Fost) St Mut.
Adcock, M. R. & Rowlands, O. The Administrative Parent: A Study of the Assumption of Parental Rights. (C). 1989. 60.00 (*0-903534-47-9*, Pub. by Brit Ag for Adopt & Fost) St Mut.
Adcock, Patrick. Muggsbottom & Me: A Study in Anglo-Arkansas Relations. LC 93-70993. 268p. 1993. 18.00 (*1-880909-10-3*) Baskerville.
Adcock, Thomas. Dark Maze. Chelius, Jane, ed. 320p. (Orig.). 1991. mass mkt. 5.50 (*0-671-72909-8*) PB.
— Devil's Heaven. 1996. mass mkt. 5.99 (*0-671-77043-8*) PB.
— Drown All the Dogs. Chelius, Jane, ed. 368p. 1995. mass mkt. 5.99 (*0-671-88329-1*) PB.
— Grief Street. 1998. per. 6.50 (*0-671-51987-5*, Pocket Books) PB.
— Sea of Green. 1989. 17.45 (*0-89296-384-0*, Pub. by Mysterious Pr) Little.
— Thrown Away Child. 266p. 1996. 21.00 (*0-671-51985-9*, PB Hardcover) PB.
— Thrown Away Child. 1997. per. 5.99 (*0-671-51984-0*) S&S Trade.
Adcock, Thomas L. Grief Street: A Neil Hockaday Mystery. LC 97-8279. 1997. 22.00 (*0-671-51986-7*) PB.
***Adcock, Virginia J.** The Second Day of June. 252p. 1999. pap. 14.00 (*0-9668884-2-1*) Wings Pubs.
***Adcock, William A.** Shaminism: A Guide For Life. 64p. 2000. pap. 6.95 (*1-84215-101-0*) Anness Pub.
Adcox, Diane. Intermediate Accounting Chapters 1-10: Working Papers. 5th ed. (C). 1994. pap. text, wbk. ed. 23.50 (*0-07-011194-4*) McGraw.
Adcox, Tom. Lessons from Life: Studies of Old Testament. 138p. 1993. pap. write for info. (*0-9636261-1-6*) Abund Life Bks.
— Symbols of the Holy Spirit. 51p. 1993. pap. write for info. (*0-9636261-0-8*) Abund Life Bks.
Adcroft, Patrice, jt. auth. see Teresi, Dick.
Adda, Lionel, ed. see Doherty, J. C.
Addabbo, Carole. Dina the Deaf Dinosaur. LC 97-70022. (Illus.). 32p. (J). (ps-5). 1998. 19.95 (*1-889262-04-8*) Hannacroix.
Addae, Akili & Oforiwaa, Yaa. The Wisdom of the Ages: Themes & Essences of Truth, Love, Struggle, & High-Culture in the Works of Ayi Kwei Armah & Kiarri T-H. Cheatwood. LC 91-68262. 80p. (Orig.). 1995. pap. 12.98 (*1-879289-01-6*) Native Sun Pubs.
Addae, Erriel K., ed. To Heal a People: Afrikan Scholars Defining a New Reality. LC 96-77308. 300p. (Orig.). 1996. pap. write for info. (*0-9644932-2-5*) Kujichagulia Pr.
Addams, Charles. My Crowd: The Original Addams Family & Other Ghoulish Creatures. 1991. pap. 10.95 (*0-671-77812-9*) S&S Trade.
— The World of Charles Addams. (Illus.). 1993. pap. 35.00 (*0-679-74813-X*) Knopf.
Addams, Jane. Democracy & Social Ethics: And Other Essays. reprint ed. 59.00 (*0-403-00824-7*) Scholarly.
— Democracy & Social Ethnics. 1988. reprint ed. lib. bdg. 75.00 (*0-7812-0225-6*) Rprt Serv.
— Excellent Becomes the Permanent. LC 77-107680. (Essay Index Reprint Ser.). 1977. 18.95 (*0-8369-1488-0*) Ayer.
— My Friend, Julia Lathrop. LC 74-1660. (Children & Youth Ser.). 246p. 1974. reprint ed. 24.95 (*0-405-05942-6*) Ayer.
— A New Conscience & an Ancient Evil. LC 76-169367. (Family in America Ser.). 236p. 1977. reprint ed. 24.95 (*0-405-03843-7*) Ayer.
— Newer Ideals of Peace. LC 71-137523. (Peace Movement in America Ser.). xviii, 243p. 1972. reprint ed. lib. bdg. 34.95 (*0-89198-050-4*) Ozer.
— On Education. LC 93-47022. 250p. (C). 1994. pap. 24.95 (*1-56000-734-6*) Transaction Pubs.
— Peace & Bread in Time of War. LC 83-80835. (NASW Classics Ser.). 264p. reprint ed. pap. 81.90 (*0-7837-6538-X*, 204567500007) Bks Demand.
— Social Thought of Jane Addams. Lasch, Christopher, ed. LC 65-22345. (Orig.). 1965. pap. 6.30 (*0-672-60110-9*, Bobbs) Macmillan.
— Social Thought of Jane Addams. Lasch, Christopher, ed. LC 82-7135. 300p. (Orig.). 1982. reprint ed. pap. text 16.95 (*0-8290-0338-X*) Irvington.
— The Spirit of Youth & the City Streets. LC 78-143047. 1982. 18.95 (*0-8434-0447-7*, Pub. by McGrath NH) Ayer.
— The Spirit of Youth & the City Streets. LC 72-76862. 192p. 1989. reprint ed. pap. text 10.95 (*0-252-00275-X*) U of Ill Pr.
— Twenty Years at Hull-House. (Prairie State Bks.). (Illus.). 328p. 1990. pap. text 15.95 (*0-252-06107-1*) U of Ill Pr.
— Twenty Years at Hull-House. 1992. reprint ed. lib. bdg. 31.95 (*0-89968-259-6*, Lghtyr Pr) Buccaneer Bks.
— Twenty Years at Hull-House: With Autobiographical Notes. LC 98-4875. (Twentieth-Century Classics Ser.). xxvi, 308p. 1998. pap. 12.95 (*0-14-118099-4*) Viking Penguin.
— Twenty Years at Hull-House: With Autobiographical Notes, 1 vol. LC 98-54661. 336p. 1999. mass mkt. 5.95 (*0-451-52739-9*) NAL.
Addams, Jane, et al. Philanthropy & Social Progress: Seven Essays. LC 75-108221. (Criminology, Law Enforcement, & Social Problems Ser.: No. 104). 1970. reprint ed. 15.00 (*0-87585-104-5*) Patterson Smith.
— Philanthropy & Social Progress: Seven Essays by Jane Addams, Robert A. Woods, Father J. O. S. Huntington, Prof. Franklin H. Giddings, & Bernard Bosanquet, Delivered Before the School of Applied Ethics at Plymouth, Mass. During the Session of 1892. LC 79-95059. (Select Bibliographies Reprint Ser.). 1977. 21.95 (*0-8369-5061-5*) Ayer.
Addams, Shay. Quest for Clues: The Manual of Swords. Ladyman, David, ed. (Quest for Clues Ser.: No. 6). (Illus.). 144p. (Orig.). 1993. pap. 16.95 (*0-929373-11-1*) Origin Syst.
Addams, Shay, ed. Quest for Clues, No. II. (Illus.). 200p. (Orig.). (C). 1989. pap. 29.95 (*0-929373-01-4*) Origin Syst.
— Quest for Clues, No. III. (Illus.). 198p. (Orig.). (YA). 1990. pap. 24.99 (*0-929373-02-2*) Origin Syst.
Addams, Shay & Ladyman, David, eds. Quest for Clues: The Book of Orbs. (Quest for Clues Ser.: No. 5). (Illus.). 144p. (Orig.). 1992. pap. 16.95 (*0-929373-10-3*) Origin Syst.
Addante, Joseph. Minute DOS. (Illus.). 192p. 1997. spiral bd. 24.95 incl. 3.5 hd (*0-9657970-0-7*) EDP Software.
Addante, Joseph A. Cash Register Trainer. (Illus.). 192p. 2000. 14.95 incl. 3.5 hd (*0-9657970-1-5*) EDP Software.
Addas, Calude. Quest for the Red Sulphur: The Life of Ibn' Arabi. Kingsley, Peter, tr. from FRE. (Golden Palm Ser.). 137p. 1995. 59.95 (*0-946621-44-6*, Pub. by Islamic Texts); pap. 19.95 (*0-946621-45-4*, Pub. by Islamic Texts) Intl Spec Bk.
***Addas, Claude.** Ibn Arabi & the Voyage of No Return. 1999. pap. 18.50 (*0-946621-74-8*) Islamic Texts.
Addas, Claude. Quest for the Red Sulphur: The Life of Ibn Arabi. 350p. 1996. pap. 19.95 (*0-614-21328-2*, 1029) Kazi Pubns.
Addelman, Ron, jt. auth. see Cajkler, Wasyl.
Addelson, Kathryn P. Impure Thoughts: Essays on Philosophy, Feminism, & Ethics. 1992. pap. 19.95 (*0-87722-960-0*) Temple U Pr.
— Moral Passages: Notes Toward a Collectivist Ethics. LC 94-20583. 272p. (C). 1994. pap. 19.99 (*0-415-91021-8*, B3836) Routledge.
— Moral Passages: Notes Toward a Collectivist Ethics. LC 94-20583. 256p. (C). (gr. 13). 1994. 70.00 (*0-415-91020-X*, B3832) Routledge.
Addelston. Prejudice. 2002. write for info. (*0-07-000505-2*) McGraw.
Addelstone, Carole. Many Paths, One Truth. LC 96-33087. (Illus.). 142p. (Orig.). 1997. lib. bdg. 25.95 (*0-89334-264-5*) Humanics Ltd.
Addeo, Carol, ed. see Addeo, Peter.
Addeo, Carolyn, jt. auth. see Addeo, Peter S.
Addeo, Edmond G., jt. auth. see Livingston-Wheeler, Virginia.
***Addeo, Peter.** Billings Diner's Club, 1999-2000. 4th ed. Addeo, Carol, ed. (Illus.). 117p. 1998. pap. 24.95 (*1-890019-09-7*) Big Sky Pubns.
— Bozeman-Livingston Diner's Club, 1998-1999. 4th deluxe ed. Addeo, Carol, ed. 121p. 1998. pap. 24.95 (*1-890019-08-9*) Big Sky Pubns.
— Bozeman-Livingston Diner's Club, 1999-2000. 5th deluxe ed. (Diner's Club Menu Bks.). (Illus.). 122p. 1999. pap. 24.95 (*1-890019-14-3*) Big Sky Pubns.
— Flathead Valley Diner's Club, 1999-2000. Addeo, Carol, ed. (Illus.). 120p. 1999. pap. 24.95 (*1-890019-12-7*) Big Sky Pubns.
— Missoula-Bitterroot Valley Diner's Club, 1999-2000. 6th deluxe ed. Addeo, Carol, ed. (Illus.). 114p. 1999. pap. 24.95 (*1-890019-10-0*) Big Sky Pubns.
Addeo, Peter, ed. see Harding, Martha.
Addeo, Peter S. & Addeo, Carolyn. Billings Diner's Club Menu Book 1998-99. 3rd ed. (Illus.). 145p. 1997. pap. text 24.95 (*1-890019-05-4*) Big Sky Pubns.
— Bozeman-Livingston Diner's Club Menu Book, 1997-98. 3rd ed. (Illus.). 128p. 1997. pap. text 24.95 (*1-890019-04-6*) Big Sky Pubns.
— Flathead Valley Diner's Club Menu Book 1997-98. 4th ed. (Illus.). 128p. 1997. pap. text 24.95 (*1-890019-03-8*) Big Sky Pubns.
— Great Falls Diner's Club Menu Book 1998-99. 3rd ed. (Illus.). 105p. 1997. pap. text 24.95 (*1-890019-06-2*) Big Sky Pubns.
— Helena Diner's Club Menu Book 1998-99. 2nd ed. (Illus.). 75p. 1997. pap. text 19.95 (*1-890019-07-0*) Big Sky Pubns.
— Missoula-Bitterroot Valley Diner's Club Menu Book, 1997-1998. 4th ed. (Illus.). 125p. 1997. pap. text 24.95 (*1-890019-02-X*) Big Sky Pubns.
Addeo, Peter S. & Jensen, Carolyn W. Billings Diner's Club Menu Book 1997-98. 3rd ed. (Illus.). 140p. 1996. pap. text 24.95 (*0-9628510-9-4*) Big Sky Pubns.
— Great Falls Diner's Club Menu Book 1997-98. 3rd ed. (Illus.). 125p. 1996. pap. text 24.95 (*1-890019-00-3*) Big Sky Pubns.
— Helena Diner's Club Menu Book 1997-98. 3rd ed. (Illus.). 60p. 1996. pap. text 19.95 (*1-890019-01-1*) Big Sky Pubns.
Addeo, Samuel J. Caribbean Journal: Notes in the Sun. 35p. 1994. pap. text 7.95 (*0-9642774-0-9*) BSP.
— Caribbean Journal: This Land Bonaire. Ashby, James, tr. (Illus.). 100p. (Orig.). 1995. pap. 8.99 (*0-9642774-1-7*) BSP.
— Caribbean Journal: This Land Bonaire. 2nd unabridged ed. (Illus.). 100p. (Orig.). 1996. reprint ed. pap. 11.95 (*0-9642774-3-3*) BSP.
— The Collected Letters & Journal Notes of Ignatio la Paloma d'Seville: After the Time of the Misty Eyes. unabridged ed. (Illus.). 76p. (Orig.). 1996. pap. 10.95 (*0-9642774-2-5*) BSP.
Addeo, Samuel J., ed. & intro. see De Mey, Dennis L.
Adderholdt, Miriam & Goldberg, Jan. Perfectionism: What's Bad about Being Too Good? LC 99-23088. 136p. (YA). (gr. 8 up). 1999. pap. text 12.95 (*1-57542-062-7*) Free Spirit Pub.
***Adderly, Brenda.** The Arthritis Cure Cookbook. 2000. reprint ed. pap. 14.95 (*0-89526-219-3*, LifeLine Press) Regnery Pub.
Adderly, Brenda. The Arthritis Cure Fitness Solution. LC 98-55567. (Illus.). 208p. 1999. 19.95 (*0-89526-359-9*) Regnery Pub.
***Adderly, Brenda.** The Arthritis Cure Fitness Solution. 2000. reprint ed. pap. 12.95 (*0-89526-244-4*, LifeLine Press) Regnery Pub.
Adderly, Brenda, ed. The Complete Guide to Pills. LC 97-143362. 1997. mass mkt. 6.99 (*0-345-40215-4*) Ballantine Pub Grp.

A

A

Adderly, Brenda, ed. The Doctor's Guide to Over-the-Counter Drugs. LC 98-208738. (Illus.). 1072p. (Orig.). 1998. mass mkt. 7.99 (0-446-60525-5, Pub. by Warner Bks) Little.

Adderly, Brenda & Das, Amal. The New Arthritis Cures: All the Treatments That Work for Your Arthritis Pain. 208p. 1999. 24.95 (0-89526-332-7, Pub. by Regnery Pub) Natl Bk Netwk.

Adderly, Brenda & De Angelis, Lissa. The Arthritis Cure Cookbook. LC 98-4516. (Illus.). 240p. 1998. 24.95 (0-89526-375-0) Regnery Pub.

Adderly, Brenda & Fox, Arnold. The Fat Blocker Diet. 224p. 1998. pap. 12.95 (0-312-19452-8) St Martin.

***Adderly, Brenda & Gordon, Jay.** Brighter Baby: Boost Your Child's Intelligence, Health & Happiness Though Infant Therapeutic Massage, the Mozart Effect & More: The Medically Proven Benefits of Baby Massage. LC 98-50803. (Illus.). 185p. 1999. 19.95 (0-89526-393-9) Regnery Pub.

Adderly, Brenda, jt. auth. see Beale, Brian.

Adderly, Brenda, jt. auth. see Crook, Thomas H., III.

Adderly, Brenda, jt. auth. see Fox, Arnold.

Adderly, Brenda, jt. auth. see Whitaker, Julian.

Adderly, Brenda D. Complete Guide to Nutritional Supplements. 1998. pap. 108.00 (0-7871-1782-X, Dove Audio) NewStar Media.

Adderly, Brenda D. Complete Guide to Nutritional Supplements: Everything You Need to Make Informed Choices For Optimum Health. 464p. 1998. pap. 18.00 (0-7871-1769-2, Dove Audio) NewStar Media.

Adderly, Brenda D. The Complete Guide to Pills. 1999. mass mkt. 6.99 (0-345-43453-6) Ballantine Pub Grp.

Adderly, Brenda D. & Fulde, Catherine P. The Healthy Heart Cookbook: Indulge Your Palate - Improve Your Health. (Illus.). 192p. 2000. pap. 19.95 (1-55867-236-2) Bristol Pub Ent CA.

Adderly, Brenda D., jt. auth. see Preuss, Harry G.

Adderly, James G. Stephen Remarx: The Story of a Venture into Ethics, 1893. Wolff, Robert L., ed. LC 75-485. (Victorian Fiction Ser.). 1976. lib. bdg. 73.00 (0-8240-1562-2) Garland.

Adderly, Julian. The Julian "Cannonball" Adderly Collection. 72p. 1995. per. 16.95 (0-7935-3173-X) H Leonard.

Adderson, Caroline. Bad Imaginings. 160p. 1993. pap. write for info. (0-88984-172-1) Porcup Quill.

Addesso, Patricia J. Management Would Be Easy . . . If It Weren't for the People. LC 96-19541. 192p. 1996. pap. 17.95 (0-8144-7915-4) AMACOM.

Addey, David. A Voyage Round Great Britain Vol. 1: Sheerness to Land's End in the Footsteps of William Daniell, R. A. (1769-1837) 160p. 1997. 100.00 (1-873376-34-0, Pub. by Spellmnt Pubs) St Mut.

— A Voyage Round Great Britain Vol. 2: Land's End to the Clyde in the Footsteps of William Daniell R. A. (1769-1837) 112p. 1997. 80.00 (1-873376-97-9, Pub. by Spellmnt Pubs) St Mut.

Addey, John M. Discrimination of Birth Types. 26p. 1974. 10.00 (0-86690-039-X, A1008-014) Am Fed Astrologers.

— Selected Writings. LC 76-46204. 232p. 1976. 13.00 (0-86690-057-8, A1011-014) Am Fed Astrologers.

Addi-Shir, Al-Sayyid. Dictionary of Persian Loan Words in the Arabic Language. (ARA, ENG & PER.). 1980. 25.00 (0-86685-128-3) Intl Bk Ctr.

Addicott, Frederick T., ed. Abscisic Acid. LC 81-23406. 607p. 1983. 115.00 (0-275-90932-8, C0932, Praeger Pubs) Greenwood.

Addicott, James P. & Butler, Charles F. Can You Afford to Grow Old? Solving the Crisis of Money & Healthcare in Retirement & Old Age. 240p. 1992. text 24.95 (1-55738-420-7, 420, Irwn Prfssnl) McGraw-Hill Prof.

Addie, Pauline. Wings on My Tennis Shoes. (American Autobiography Ser.). 198p. 1995. reprint ed. lib. bdg. 69.00 (0-7812-8440-6) Rprt Serv.

Addinall, M. F. & Addinall, N. Wild Mushrooms. 1988. pap. 26.95 (0-8464-4900-5) Beekman Pubs.

Addinall, Marie F., jt. auth. see Addinall, Nigel.

Addinall, N., jt. auth. see Addinall, M. F.

Addinall, Nigel. French Political Parties. LC 96-162230. 228p. 1995. pap. 17.95 (0-7083-1263-2, Pub. by Univ Wales Pr) Paul & Co Pubs.

Addinall, Nigel & Addinall, Marie F. Wild Mushrooms: How to Find, Identify & Cook Them. (Illus.). 96p. (C). 1992. 49.00 (0-7154-0724-4, Pub. by C Davies Pubs) St Mut.

Addinall, Peter. Philosophy & Biblical Interpretation: A Study in Nineteenth Century Conflict. 342p. (C). 1991. text 75.00 (0-521-40423-1) Cambridge U Pr.

Addington, Cornelia. The Wonder-Working Power of God. LC 87-70231. 152p. 1987. pap. 6.95 (0-87516-589-3) DeVorss.

Addington, Cornelia & Addington, Jack E. All about Prosperity & How You Can Prosper. LC 83-73342. (Orig.). 1984. pap. 9.95 (0-87516-533-8) DeVorss.

Addington, Cornelia, jt. auth. see Addington, Jack E.

Addington, Deborah. Blood Bound: Guidance for The Responsible Vampire. 1999. pap. text 11.95 (1-890159-08-5) Greenery Pr.

— A Hand in the Bush: The Fine Art of Vaginal Fisting. (Illus.). 120p. 1997. pap. 11.95 (1-890159-02-6) Greenery Pr.

Addington, Hugh M. Addington Vol. II: Including a Multitude of Related Families. (Illus.). 59p. 1997. reprint ed. pap. 12.00 (0-8328-7217-2); reprint ed. lib. bdg. 22.00 (0-8328-7216-4) Higginson Bk Co.

— History of the Family of Addington in the United States & England. 102p. 1991. reprint ed. 9.95 (0-932807-51-8) Overmountain Pr.

Addington, Jack E. All about Goals & How to Achieve Them. LC 77-80016. 1977. pap. 9.95 (0-87516-237-1) DeVorss.

Addington, Jack E. The Hidden Mystery of the Bible. LC 70-93549. 288p. 1996. reprint ed. pap. 12.95 (0-87516-626-2) DeVorss.

— Life Never Dies. 20p. pap. 3.00 (0-87516-626-1) DeVorss.

— Psychogenesis: Everything Begins in Mind. LC 79-145391. 212p. 1994. reprint ed. pap. 12.95 (0-87516-672-5) DeVorss.

— The Secret of Healing. 204p. 1979. pap. 10.95 (0-911336-80-X) Sci of Mind.

— Your Miracle Book: A Magic-Like Technique for Thinking Your Way to Abundance & Happiness. 24p. 1992. pap. 4.50 (0-87516-649-0) DeVorss.

Addington, Jack E. & Addington, Cornelia. How to Love & Be Loved: Drawing the Larger Circle. 160p. 1985. pap. 6.95 (0-87516-558-3) DeVorss.

— I Am the Way. LC 82-71191. 118p. (Orig.). 1982. pap. 4.95 (0-87516-486-2) DeVorss.

— The Joy of Meditation. LC 78-75078. 1979. pap. 8.95 (0-87516-292-4) DeVorss.

— The Perfect Power Within You. LC 73-87712. 167p. 1973. pap. 8.95 (0-87516-179-0) DeVorss.

— Your Needs Met. 156p. 1982. reprint ed. pap. 8.95 (0-87516-490-0) DeVorss.

Addington, Jack E., jt. auth. see Addington, Cornelia.

***Addington, Larry H.** America's War in Vietnam: A Short Narrative History. LC 99-41326. 224p. 2000. pap. 12.95 (0-253-21360-6); lib. bdg. 29.95 (0-253-33691-0) Ind U Pr.

Addington, Larry H. The Blitzkrieg Era & the German General Staff, 1865-1941. LC 75-163955. (Illus.). 302p. reprint ed. 93.70 (0-8357-9528-4, 205045300083) Bks Demand.

— The Patterns of War since the 18th Century. 2nd ed. LC 93-21544. (Illus.). 384p. (Orig.). (C). 1994. 36.95 (0-253-30132-7); pap. 15.95 (0-253-20860-2) Ind U Pr.

— The Patterns of War since the Eighteenth Century. (Illus.). 318p. (C). 1999. reprint ed. pap. text 20.00 (0-7881-6088-5) DIANE Pub.

— The Patterns of War Through the 18th Century. LC 89-45190. (Illus.). 176p. 1990. 25.95 (0-253-30131-9, MB 551) Ind U Pr.

— Patterns of War Through the 18th Century. LC 89-45190. (Illus.). 176p. 1990. pap. 12.95 (0-253-20551-4) Ind U Pr.

Addington, Lucile R. Lithic Illustration: Drawing Flaked Stone Artifacts for Publication. LC 85-8121. (Prehistoric Archeology & Ecology Ser.). (Illus.). xviii, 140p. 1986. lib. bdg. 41.00 (0-226-00634-4) U Ch Pr.

— Lithic Illustration: Drawing Flaked Stone Artifacts for Publication. LC 85-8121. (Prehistoric Archeology & Ecology Ser.). (Illus.). 253p. reprint ed. pap. 78.50 (0-608-09372-6, 205411700004) Bks Demand.

Addington, Luther P. The Story of Wise County (Virginia) (Illus.). 306p. 1988. reprint ed. 24.95 (0-932807-30-5) Overmountain Pr.

Addington, Robert M. History of Scott County, Virginia. LC 77-77267. (Illus.). 378p. 1994. reprint ed. pap. 30.00 (0-8063-0771-4, Pub. by Clearfield Co) ACCESS Pubs Network.

— History of Scott County, Virginia. (Illus.). 398p. 1992. reprint ed. 24.95 (0-932807-67-4) Overmountain Pr.

Addington, Susan, tr. see Kuga, Michio.

Addington, Thomas. Life at Work -- A Case for Skill. (Life@work Ser.). 1997. pap. 5.99 (0-8054-0183-0) Broadman.

Addington, Thomas, jt. auth. see Graves, Stephen.

Addink, A. D. & Spronk, N., eds. Exogenous & Endogenous Influences on Metabolic & Neural Control Vol. 2: Abstracts: Proceedings of the Third Congress of the European Society for Comparative Physiology & Biochemistry, August 31-September 3, 1981, Noorwijkerhout, Netherlands. (Illus.). 260p. 1982. 110.00 (0-08-028845-6, Pub. by Pergamon Repr) Franklin.

***Addis.** The Art of the Structural Engineer. 2nd ed. 2001. 75.95 (0-7506-4210-6) Buttrwrth-Heinemann.

Addis, William, ed. Structural & Civil Engineering Design. LC 98-49124. (Studies in the History of Civil Engineering: Vol. 12). (Illus.). 384p. 1999. text 157.95 (0-86078-761-3, Pub. by Ashgate Pub) Ashgate Pub Co.

Addis, Bill, jt. auth. see Walker, Derek.

Addis, Caren. Taking the Wheel: Autoparts Firms & the Political Economy of Industrialization in Brazil. LC 98-16934. 1999. 47.50 (0-271-01814-3); pap. 18.95 (0-271-01815-1) Pa St U Pr.

Addis, Denise, jt. auth. see Breman, Paul.

Addis, Elisabetta. Women Soldiers Vol. 1: Images & Realities. 1994. pap. 21.95 (0-312-12074-5) St Martin.

Addis, Elisabetta, et al. Women Soldiers: Images & Realities. Russo, Valeria E & Sebesta, Lorenza, eds. LC 93-39270. 1994. text 49.95 (0-312-12073-7) St Martin.

Addis, Faith. Taking the Biscuit. large type ed. (Non-Fiction Ser.). 320p. 1992. 27.99 (0-7089-2743-2) Ulverscroft.

***Addis, Gailyn.** Be Marilyn! Matching Marilyn's Magical Look. LC 00-26371. (Illus.). 2000. write for info. (1-57071-557-2) Sourcebks.

Addis, Ian. What Can the Matter Be & Other Stories. 96p. 1992. pap. 21.00 (1-85346-211-X, Pub. by David Fulton) Taylor & Francis.

Addis, Jeremy & Kelly, Shirley. The Irish Writers' Guide, 1996-1997. 168p. 1995. pap. 14.95 (1-874675-70-8) Dufour.

Addis, Jeremy & Kelly, Shirley, eds. Irish Writers' Guide, 1998-99. 2nd rev. ed. 208p. 1998. pap. 15.95 (1-899047-40-9, Pub. by A A Farmar) Irish Bks Media.

Addis, Laird. Of Mind & Music LC 98-55442. 1999. 29.95 (0-8014-3589-7) Cornell U Pr.

***Addis, Mark.** Wittgenstein: Making Sense of Other Minds. LC 99-73312. (Avebury Series in Philosophy). 1999. text 61.95 (0-7546-1043-8, Pub. by Ashgate Pub) Ashgate Pub Co.

Addis, Patricia K. Through a Woman's Eye: An Annotated Bibliography of American Women's Autobiographical Writings, 1946-1976. LC 82-10813. 621p. 1983. 45.00 (0-8108-1588-5) Scarecrow.

Addis, T. R. & Muir, R. M., eds. Research & Development in Expert Systems VII: Proceedings of the 10th Annual Technical Conference of the BCS Specialist Group, September, 1990. (British Computer Society Workshop Ser.). (Illus.). 325p. (C). 1990. text 74.95 (0-521-40403-7) Cambridge U Pr.

Addis, Tom, jt. ed. see Stender, Joachim.

Addison, Agnes. Romanticism & the Gothic Revival. 204p. 1967. reprint ed. 50.00 (0-87752-000-3) Gordian.

Addison, Alexander. Rise & Progress of Revolution. 1979. lib. bdg. 59.95 (0-8490-3000-5) Gordon Pr.

Addison, Alice A., ed. see Cressey, William W., et al.

Addison, C. C. The Chemistry of the Liquid Alkali Metals. fac. ed. LC 84-7496. (Illus.). 340p. 1984. reprint ed. pap. 105.40 (0-608-00986-5, 206184200012) Bks Demand.

Addison, C. G. & Macoy, Robert. The Knights of Templars & the Complete History of Masonic Knighthood from the Origin of the Orders to the Present Time. 634p. 1997. reprint ed. pap. 45.00 (0-7661-0019-7) Kessinger Pub.

Addison, Carole. Planning Investigative Projects: A Workbook for Social Services Practitioners. (C). 1988. 40.00 (0-7855-3735-X, Pub. by Natl Inst Soc Work); 40.00 (0-685-40353-X, Pub. by Natl Inst Soc Work); pap. 21.00 (0-902789-54-6, Pub. by Natl Inst Soc Work) St Mut.

Addison, Carolyn F. Archery Techniques. 2nd ed. 120p. (C). 1998. pap. text 12.95 (0-89641-237-7) American Pr.

Addison, Charles G. Damascus & Palmyra, 2 vols. LC 73-6265. (Middle East Ser.). 1973. reprint ed. 39.95 (0-405-05319-3) Ayer.

— History of the Knights Templar. 1997. pap. 16.95 (0-932813-40-2) Adventures Unltd.

— The Knights Templar History. rev. ed. LC 76-29832. reprint ed. 90.00 (0-404-15407-7) AMS Pr.

Addison, Claire. Where Flaubert Lies: Mythology & History. (Studies in French: No. 48). 408p. (C). 1996. text 69.95 (0-521-42016-4) Cambridge U Pr.

Addison, Corran, jt. auth. see Power, Scott.

Addison, Daniel D. Lucy Larcom: Life, Letters & Diary. LC 74-154143. (Select Bibliographies Reprint Ser.). 1977. reprint ed. 23.95 (0-8369-5759-8) Ayer.

Addison, Donna. CLI Ring Endless LI 1. 1982. 14.60 (0-394-07728-8) Random.

— CLU Gathering of Days. 1980. pap. 14.60 (0-394-66073-0) Random.

— CRA Arthur's Valentine. 1983. 11.96 (0-394-63145-5) Random.

— CRA Dinosaur Time. 1982. 11.96 (0-394-69185-7) Random.

— CRA Go Dog Go. 1982. 11.96 (0-394-62719-9) Random.

Addison, Donna & Khadka, Rup B. Nepalese: Taxation: A Path for Reform. 1994. pap. 147.00 (0-7855-7466-2, Pub. by Ratna Pustak Bhandar) St Mut.

Addison, Donna & Prachan, Babulall. Ratna's Nepali English Nepali Dictionary. 1997. pap. 47.00 (0-7855-7487-5, Pub. by Ratna Pustak Bhandar) St Mut.

Addison, Donna, jt. auth. see Lobel, Arnold.

Addison, G. M., et al, eds. Organic Acidureas. 1984. text 124.00 (0-85200-875-9) Kluwer Academic.

— Practical Developments in Inherited Metabolic Diseases. 1986. text 206.50 (0-85200-690-X) Kluwer Academic.

— Studies in Inherited Metabolic Diseases: Prenatal & Perinatal Diagnosis. (C). 1989. text 226.50 (0-7923-8916-6) Kluwer Academic.

Addison Gallery of American Art Staff. Catalogue of Permanent Collections. (Illus.). 66p. 1931. write for info. (1-879886-00-6) Addison Gallery.

Addison, Howard A. The Enneagram & Kabbalah: Reading Your Soul. LC 98-10641. 176p. 1998. pap. 15.95 (1-58023-001-6) Jewish Lights.

***Addison, Howard A.** Show Me Your Way: The Complete Guide to Exploring Interfaith Spiritual Direction. 208p. 2000. 21.95 (1-893361-12-8) SkyLight Paths.

***Addison, J.** A Treasury of Bird Lore. 1998. text 24.95 (0-233-99435-1, Pub. by Andre Deutsch) Trafalgar.

Addison, J. T., ed. see Mourmouras, I. A. & Arghyrou, M. G.

Addison, Jayne. About That Kiss. 1997. per. 3.25 (0-373-19202-9, 1-19202-0) Silhouette.

— A Precious Gift: Under the Mistletoe. (Romance Ser.). 1993. per. 2.75 (0-373-08980-5, 5-08980-0) Silhouette.

— Something Blue. (Romance Ser.). 1993. per. 2.75 (0-373-08944-9, 5-08944-6) Silhouette.

— Wild West Wife. 1995. per. 2.99 (0-373-19117-0, 1-19117-0) Silhouette.

Addison, Joanne & McGee, Sharon J., eds. Feminist Empirical Research: Emerging Perspectives on Qualitative Research & Teacher Research. LC 99-10531. 1999. pap. text 25.00 (0-86709-482-6, Pub. by Boynton Cook Pubs) Heinemann.

Addison, John, et al. Suleyman & the Ottoman Empire. Yapp, Malcolm & Killingray, Margaret, eds. (World History Program Ser.). (Illus.). (YA). (gr. 6-11). 1980. reprint ed. pap. text 5.90 (0-89908-013-8) Greenhaven.

Addison, John T., ed. Job Displacement: Consequences & Implications for Policy. LC 90-22623. (Labor Economics & Policy Ser.). 306p. (C). 1991. text 39.95 (0-8143-2285-9) Wayne St U Pr.

Addison, John T. & Siebert, W. Stanley. Regulating European Labour Markets: More Costs Than Benefits? (Hobart Paper Ser.: Vol. 138). 86p. 1999. pap. 19.95 (0-255-36420-2, Pub. by Inst Economic Affairs) Coronet Bks.

Addison, John T. & Welfens, Paul J., eds. Labor Markets & Social Security: Wage Costs, Social Security Financing & Labor Market Reforms in Europe. LC 97-47707. (Illus.). x, 389p. 1998. 99.00 (3-540-63784-2) Spr-Verlag.

Addison, Joseph. Addison: The Freeholder. Leheny, James, ed. (Illus.). 296p. 1980. text 100.00 (0-19-812494-5) OUP.

— Cato. Landes, William-Alan, ed. & intro. by. LC 96-122. 55p. (Orig.). 1996. pap. 7.00 (0-88734-293-0) Players Pr.

— The Coverley Papers from the Spectator. 1988. reprint ed. lib. bdg. 59.00 (0-7812-0704-5) Rprt Serv.

— The Coverley Papers from the Spectator. 1980. reprint ed. lib. bdg. 39.00 (0-686-71913-1) Scholarly.

— Criticism of Milton's Paradise Lost, from the Spectator, 1711-12. large type ed. Arber, Edward, ed. 152p. 1983. pap. 15.00 (0-87556-550-6) Saifer.

— Criticisms on Paradise Lost. (Works of Joseph Addison). 200p. 1985. reprint ed. lib. bdg. 39.00 (0-932051-91-X); reprint ed. lib. bdg. 59.00 (0-7812-0833-5) Rprt Serv.

— The De Coverly Papers. Meek, Joseph, ed. (Works of J. Addison). 128p. 1985. reprint ed. lib. bdg. 59.00 (0-932051-22-7) Rprt Serv.

— Essays in Criticism & Literary Theory. Loftis, John, ed. LC 74-76968. (Crofts Classics). 200p. (C). 1975. pap. text 4.95 (0-88295-106-8) Harlan Davidson.

— The Free-Holder, or Political Essays. 1976. reprint ed. 39.00 (0-403-05788-4, Regency) Scholarly.

— The Freeholder: Or, Political Essays. (Works of Joseph Addison). 311p. 1985. reprint ed. 69.00 (0-932051-53-7) Rprt Serv.

— Tatler & the Spectator. 617p. 1998. text 45.00 (0-312-16371-1) St Martin.

Addison, Joseph & Steele, Richard. Selected Essays from the Tatler, the Spectator, & the Guardian. McDonald, Daniel L., ed. LC 73-179472. (Library of Literature: No. 15). 1973. pap. 5.95 (0-672-60990-8, Bobbs) Macmillan.

Addison, Joseph, jt. auth. see Steele, Richard.

Addison-Licameli, Amy, ed. see Loh, Lily.

Addison, Linda D. Animated Objects. LC 97-27138. (Illus.). 112p. (Orig.). 1997. 14.95 (0-917053-10-9); pap. 7.95 (0-917053-09-5) Space And.

Addison, Lois A. & Fischer, Paul M. The Office Laboratory. 2nd ed. (Illus.). 433p. 1990. pap. text 75.00 (0-8385-7244-8, A7244-5) Appleton & Lange.

Addison, Medora C. Dreams & a Sword. LC 71-144719. (Yale Series of Younger Poets: No. 12). reprint ed. 18.00 (0-404-53812-6) AMS Pr.

Addison, Nancy K., ed. see Healey, Edward F.

Addison, Neil, jt. auth. see Lawson-Cruttenden, Timothy.

***Addison, Nicholas & Burgess, Lesley.** Learning to Teach Art & Design in the Secondary School. LC 99-41054. (Learning to Teach Subjects in the Secondary School Ser.). 248p. 2000. pap. write for info. (0-415-16881-3) Routledge.

Addison, Paul, tr. see Gutjahr, Lothar.

Addison, Paul S. Fractals & Chaos: An Illustrated Course. LC 97-18158. 1997. 126.00 (0-7503-0399-9); pap. 40.00 (0-7503-0400-6) IOP Pub.

Addison, R. Elaine, et al. Galloping Gourmets: The Other Side of Foxhunting. (Illus.). 200p. (Orig.). 1987. pap. 11.95 (0-9619378-0-7) Yadkin Val Hounds.

Addison, Richard B., jt. ed. see Packer, Martin J.

Addison, Shellei & Joyce, Kristin. Pearls. 1992. pap. 45.00 (0-13-655374-5) P-H.

Addison, Shellei, jt. auth. see Joyce, Kristin.

Addison, Terry. Rebuilding the Temple Within You. 48p. (C). 1999. pap. 4.95 (1-58169-028-2, Gazelle Pr) Genesis Comm Inc.

Addison, Tony, jt. auth. see Demery, Lionel.

Addison, W. E. Structural Principles in Inorganic Compounds. LC QD0156.A3. 200p. reprint ed. pap. 62.00 (0-608-10095-1, 200638300058) Bks Demand.

Addison, Wendy, ed. see Bennett, J. G., et al.

Addison, Wesley. Earth Science. 48.75 (0-201-21451-2) Addison-Wesley.

— Explorations Bk. 2: Activity Book. 1993. pap. 9.80 (0-201-19225-X) Addison-Wesley.

— Mathpass Interactive Cd Paper Instructions. 1p. (C). 1998. pap. text Price not set. (0-201-43692-2) Addison-Wesley.

***Addison, Wesley.** Proceedings: Annual Volume. 11th ed. 1999. pap. text 35.33 (0-201-61130-9) Addison-Wesley.

Addison-Wesley Editors. A Book Lover's Journal. 1986. 16.00 (0-201-10354-0) Addison-Wesley.

Addison-Wesley Germany Staff. Addison-Wesley Puzzle. (C). 1990. text. write for info. (0-201-55935-8) Addison-Wesley.

Addison-Wesley Longman, Inc. Staff. Addison Wesley Longman Author Guide. 128p. (C). 1998. text. write for info. (0-201-36621-5) Addison-Wesley.

— Longman Dictionary of American English. 2nd ed. LC 96-51562. 1996. pap. text 19.04 (0-8013-1823-8) Longman.

— Longman Dictionary of American English: A Dictionary for Learners of English. 2nd ed. LC 96-51562. 1997. text 29.39 (0-8013-1409-7) Longman.

— User Guide for Interactive Math V. 2.0. (C). 1998. pap. text. write for info. (0-201-38495-7) Addison-Wesley.

— Winter 1998 Book Express. 32p. (C). 1998. ring bd. write for info. (0-201-37948-1) Addison-Wesley.

Addison-Wesley Publishing Staff. Addison-Wesley: The First Fifty years, 1942-1992. 5th ed. LC 93-24799. 1995. write for info. (0-201-56700-8) Addison-Wesley.

Addison-Wesley Publishing Staff. The Art of Teaching ESL Staff Development Program. 1995. 20.20 (0-201-55480-1, 55480) Longman.

Addison-Wesley Publishing Staff. Big Bk Spnshed Tchrs Gd, Set. (ESOL Elementary Supplement Ser.). (Illus.). 16p. 1989. pap. 212.59 (0-201-19766-9) Addison-Wesley.

An Asterisk (*) at the beginning of an entry indicates that the title is appearing for the first time.

— Biotechnology. 1996. pap. text 27.96 (*0-201-86443-6*) Addison-Wesley.

— El Conejo la Tortuga - Big Book. (Spanish Elementary Ser.). (SPA., Illus.). 16p. (J). (gr. k-3). 1989. pap. text 31.75 (*0-201-19937-8*) Addison-Wesley.

— El Conejo la Tortuga - Little Book. (Spanish Elementary Ser.). (SPA., Illus.). 16p. (J). (gr. k-3). 1989. pap. text 4.50 (*0-201-19709-X*) Addison-Wesley.

— The Farmer & the Beet Little Book. (ESOL Elementary Supplement Ser.). (Illus.). 16p. (J). (gr. k-3). 1989. ring bd. 4.78 (*0-201-19053-2*) Addison-Wesley.

— Farmer & the Big Beet Book. (ESL Ser.). (Illus.). 16p. (J). (gr. k-2). 1989. 23.30 (*0-201-19318-3*) Addison-Wesley.

— La Gallinita Roja Big Book. (Spanish Elementary Ser.). (SPA., Illus.). 16p. (J). (gr. k-3). 1989. pap. text 31.75 (*0-201-19936-X*) Addison-Wesley.

— La Gallinita Roja, Spanish Little Book. (Spanish Elementary Ser.). (SPA., Illus.). 16p. (J). (gr. k-3). 1989. pap. text 4.50 (*0-201-19708-1*) Addison-Wesley.

— The Gingerbread Man. (ESL Ser.). (Illus.). 16p. (J). (gr. k-2). 1989. 23.30 (*0-201-19320-5*); pap. text 17.64 (*0-201-19064-8*) Addison-Wesley.

— The Gingerbread Man Little Book. (ESOL Elementary Supplement Ser.). (Illus.). 16p. (J). (gr. k-3). 1989. ring bd. 4.78 (*0-201-19054-0*) Addison-Wesley.

— Goldilocks & the Three Bears Little Book. (ESOL Elementary Supplement Ser.). (Illus.). 16p. (J). (gr. k-3). 1989. ring bd. 4.78 (*0-201-19055-9*) Addison-Wesley.

— Goldilocks Big Book. (ESL Ser.). (Illus.). 16p. (J). (gr. k-2). 1989. 23.30 (*0-201-19319-1*) Addison-Wesley.

— How the Moon Got in the Sky Little Book. (ESOL Elementary Supplement Ser.). (Illus.). 16p. (J). (gr. k-3). 1989. ring bd. 4.78 (*0-201-19359-0*) Addison-Wesley.

— Hw Moon Got Sky Big Book. (ESL Ser.). (Illus.). 16p. (J). (gr. k-2). 1989. 23.30 (*0-201-19325-6*) Addison-Wesley.

— Little Red Hen Big Book. (ESL Ser.). (Illus.). 16p. (J). (gr. k-2). 1989. 23.30 (*0-201-19323-X*) Addison-Wesley.

— The Little Red Hen Little Book. (ESOL Elementary Supplement Ser.). (Illus.). 16p. (J). (gr. k-3). 1989. pap. 4.78 (*0-201-19364-7*) Addison-Wesley.

— Las Matematicas de Addison Wesley: Suplemento de Practica 1. (SPA.). 168p. (C). 1995. pap. text 8.00 (*0-201-51862-7*) Addison-Wesley.

— Las Matematicas de Addison Wesley: Suplemento de Practica 2. (SPA.). 168p. (C). 1995. pap. text 8.00 (*0-201-51863-5*) Addison-Wesley.

— Las Matematicas de Addison Wesley: Suplemento de Practica 3. (SPA.). 140p. (C). 1995. pap. text 8.00 (*0-201-51864-3*) Addison-Wesley.

— Las Matematicas de Addison Wesley: Suplemento de Practica 4. (SPA.). 168p. (C). 1995. pap. text 8.00 (*0-201-51865-1*) Addison-Wesley.

Addison-Wesley Publishing Staff. Las Matematicas de Addison Wesley: Suplemento de Practica 5. 1995. pap. text. write for info. (*0-201-51866-X*) Addison-Wesley.

Addison-Wesley Publishing Staff. Las Matematicas de Addison Wesley: Suplemento de Practica 6. (SPA.). 168p. (C). 1995. pap. text 8.00 (*0-201-51867-8*) Addison-Wesley.

— Math Cad Intro to Introductory Physics. 386p. (C). 1992. pap. 39.40 (*0-201-54736-8*) Addison-Wesley.

— Math Quest 1. 1985. pap. text, student ed. 15.00 (*0-201-19100-8*) Addison-Wesley.

— Math Quest 3. LC 85-98688. (Illus.). 360p. 1986. pap. text, student ed. 26.56 (*0-201-19300-0*) Addison-Wesley.

— Newcomer Phonics. 96p. 1999. pap. text 14.60 (*0-201-43703-1*, Prentice Hall) P-H.

— The Rabbit & the Turnip. (ESL Ser.). (Illus.). 16p. (J). (gr. k-2). 1989. ring bd. 4.78 (*0-201-19360-4*) Addison-Wesley.

— Rabbit & Turnip Big Book. (ESL Ser.). (Illus.). 16p. (J). (gr. k-2). 1989. 23.30 (*0-201-19326-4*) Addison-Wesley.

— Ricitos de Oro - Little Book. (Spanish Elementary Ser.). (SPA., Illus.). 16p. (J). (gr. k-3). 1989. pap. text 4.50 (*0-201-19707-3*) Addison-Wesley.

— Ricitos de Oro y los Tres Osos Big Book. (Spanish Elementary Ser.). (SPA., Illus.). 16p. (J). (gr. k-3). 1989. pap. text 31.75 (*0-201-19935-1*) Addison-Wesley.

— Science. 1997. 319.00 (*0-201-31600-5*) Addison-Wesley.

— Special Education Program Level A. (ESOL Elementary Supplement Ser.). (Illus.). 16p. 1989. 32.95 (*0-201-19767-7*) Addison-Wesley.

— Special Education Program Level B. (ESOL Elementary Supplement Ser.). (Illus.). 16p. 1989. pap. text 212.59 (*0-201-19356-6*); pap. text, teacher ed. 32.95 (*0-201-19357-4*) Addison-Wesley.

— Summit: An Interactive Algebra Journey. 1997. 39.00 (*0-321-01928-8*) Addison-Wesley Educ.

— Thorndike Barnhart Children's Dictionary. (Illus.). 770p. (J). 1998. 17.95 (*0-673-12450-9*, Scott Frsmn) Addson-Wesley Educ.

— The Three Little Pigs. (ESL Ser.). 16p. (J). (gr. k-2). 1989. pap. 17.64 (*0-201-19066-4*) Addison-Wesley.

— Three Little Pigs Big Book. (ESL Ser.). 16p. (J). (gr. k-2). 1989. text 23.30 (*0-201-19322-1*) Addison-Wesley.

— The Three Little Pigs Little Book. (ESOL Elementary Supplement Ser.). (Illus.). 16p. (J). (gr. k-3). 1989. ring bd. 4.79 (*0-201-19058-3*) Addison-Wesley.

— Los Tres Cerditos - Big Book. (Spanish Elementary Ser.). (SPA., Illus.). 16p. (J). (gr. k-3). 1989. pap. text 31.75 (*0-201-19938-6*) Addison-Wesley.

— Los Tres Cerditos - Little Book. (Spanish Elementary Ser.). (SPA., Illus.). 16p. (J). (gr. k-3). 1989. pap. text 4.50 (*0-201-19710-3*) Addison-Wesley.

— TURNG PONTS MGT SYS 2. (Turning Points Ser.). (Illus.). 40p. 1989. pap. text 12.95 (*0-201-19718-9*) Addison-Wesley.

— Turning Point: Management System One. (Illus.). 32p. 1989. pap. text 19.11 (*0-201-19717-0*) Addison-Wesley.

Addison-Wesley Publishing Staff, ed. Advanced Dictionary. 1992. 33.56 (*0-673-12377-4*) Addison-Wesley Educ.

— Mathpass System Administrator Booklet. 34p. (C). 1998. ring bd. write for info. (*0-201-44045-8*) Addison-Wesley.

Addison-Wesley Publishing Staff & Aesop. Hare & the Tortoise: Esl Series. (ESL Ser.). (Illus.). 16p. (J). (gr. k-2). 1989. 23.30 (*0-201-19324-8*) Addison-Wesley.

— The Hare & the Tortoise Little Book. (ESOL Elementary Supplement Ser.). (Illus.). 16p. (J). (gr. k-3). 1989. ring bd. 4.79 (*0-201-19365-5*) Addison-Wesley.

Addison, pseud. Commerce Everyday Life. LC 97-74950. 368p. 1998. pap. 16.95 (*0-312-11597-0*) St Martin.

— Labour Markets in Europe Issues Harmonisation & Regulation. 1998. pap. 20.99 (*1-86152-418-8*) Thomson Learn.

Addiss, Stephen. The Art of Zen: Paintings & Calligraphy by Japanese Monks, 1600-1925. (Illus.). 224p. 1998. pap. 24.95 (*0-8109-2774-8*, Pub. by Abrams) Time Warner.

— Haiga: Takebe Socho & the Haiku-Painting Tradition. LC 95-2329. (Illus.). 134p. 1995. text 32.00 (*0-8248-1749-4*); pap. text 19.95 (*0-8248-1750-8*) UH Pr.

— How to Look at Japanese Art. LC 95-21879. (Illus.). 144p. 1996. pap. 19.95 (*0-8109-2640-7*, Pub. by Abrams) Time Warner.

***Addiss, Stephen.** Old Taoist: The Life, Art & Poetry of Kodojin. Chaves, Jonathan, tr. & comment by. (Illus.). 2000. 27.50 (*0-231-11656-X*) Col U Pr.

Addiss, Stephen. The World of Kameda Bosai. LC 84-2004. (Illus.). 127p. 1984. pap. 16.95 (*0-89494-019-8*) New Orleans Mus Art.

— The World of Kameda Bosai: The Calligraphy, Poetry, Painting & Artistic Circle of a Japanese Literatus. LC 84-2004. (Illus.). 128p. 1984. 35.00 (*0-7006-0251-8*) U Pr of KS.

Addiss, Stephen, ed. Tokaidoi I: Adventures on the Road in Old Japan. LC 80-53851. (Illus.). 120p. 1980. pap. 8.50 (*0-913689-06-8*) Spencer Muse Art.

Addiss, Stephen & Chu-tsing Li, eds. Catalogue of the Oriental Collection. LC 80-82048. (Illus.). 145p. 1980. pap. 8.50 (*0-685-57442-3*) Spencer Muse Art.

Addiss, Stephen & Erickson, Mary. Art History & Education. LC 92-24034. (Disciplines in Art Education, Contexts of Understanding Ser.). 256p. (C). 1993. 39.95 (*0-252-01970-9*); pap. text 15.95 (*0-252-06273-6*) U of Ill Pr.

Addiss, Stephen & Lombardo, Stanley, eds. Phoenix Papers: Twenty-Three Lawrence Poets. LC 93-83842. 140p. 1993. pap. write for info. (*0-9632475-1-4*) Penthe Pub.

Addiss, Stephen, et al. A Haiku Garden: The Four Seasons in Poems & Prints. LC 96-5137. (Illus.). 116p. 1996. 16.95 (*0-8348-0357-7*) Weatherhill.

— Haiku People, Big & Small: In Poems & Prints. LC 97-51890. (Illus.). 116p. 1998. 16.95 (*0-8348-0417-4*) Weatherhill.

— Japanese Quest for a New Vision: The Impact of Visiting Chinese Painters, 1600-1900. LC 86-60919. (Illus.). 136p. (Orig.). 1986. pap. 17.95 (*0-913689-24-6*) Spencer Muse Art.

— A Myriad of Autumn Leaves: Japanese Art from the Kurt & Millie Gitter Collection. LC 83-43150. (Illus.). 295p. 1983. pap. 29.95 (*0-89494-017-1*) New Orleans Mus Art.

— The Resonance of the Qin in East Asian Art. Barrett, J. May, ed. (CHI & ENG., Illus.). 144p. 1999. pap. 49.95 (*0-9654270-2-1*) China Institute Gallery.

Addiss, Stephen, jt. auth. see Seo, Audrey Y.

Addiss, Stephen, tr. see Lao-Tzu.

Addiss, Steve, jt. auth. see Seo, Audrey Y.

Additon, Grace. The Flavor of New England: A Sampler of Favorite Recipes. LC 92-70614. 363p. 1999. 8.98 (*0-88365-789-9*) Galahad Bks.

Addkison, Andrew R. & Kramer, Jack. One Hundred Garden Designs. 2nd rev. ed. LC 93-23824.Tr. of One Hundred Garden Plans. (Illus.). 288p. 1993. 22.95 (*1-55821-255-8*) Lyons Pr.

Addleman, Frank G. The Winning Edge. 228p. 1984. per. 10.00 (*0-671-76579-5*) S&S Trade.

Addleson, Mark. Equilibrium vs. Understanding: Towards the Rehumanization of Economics Within Social Theory. LC 95-11822. 304p. (C). (gr. 13). 1995. 85.00 (*0-415-12814-5*) Routledge.

Addleton, Jonathan S. Undermining the Centre: The Gulf Migration & Pakistan. (Illus.). 246p. 1992. text 45.00 (*0-19-577418-3*) OUP.

Addley, Ken. Occupational Stress: A Practical Approach. LC 97-27644. 256p. 1997. text 68.00 (*0-7506-2948-7*) Buttrwrth-Heinemann.

Addo, Ebenezer O. Kwame Nkrumah: A Case Study of Religion & Politics in Ghana. LC 97-18949. 236p. 1997. 55.00 (*0-7618-0785-3*) U Pr of Amer.

— Kwame Nkrumah: A Case Study of Religion & Politics in Ghana. 256p. 1999. pap. 23.50 (*0-7618-1318-7*) U Pr of Amer.

***Addo, Koffi.** Letter to a Son. 112p. 2000. pap. 11.00 (*0-8059-4779-5*) Dorrance.

***Addo, Michael K.** Human Rights Standards & the Responsibility of Transnational Corporations. LC 99-38087. 1999. 135.00 (*90-411-1246-4*) Kluwer Law Intl.

Addo, Peter E. Talking Drums: An Anthology of Poetry. 49p. 1999. pap. 8.00 (*0-8059-4478-8*) Dorrance.

Addonizio, Kim. In the Box Called Pleasure. LC 99-45089. 160p. 1999. pap. 12.95 (*1-57366-081-7*) Northwestern U Pr.

— Jimmy & Rita. LC 96-83953. (American Poets Continuum Ser.: Vol. 40). 70p. 1997. pap. 12.50 (*1-880238-41-1*) BOA Edns.

— The Philosopher's Club. LC 93-74021. (New Poets of America Ser.). 70p. 1994. pap. 10.00 (*1-880238-03-9*) BOA Edns.

— The Philosopher's Club. LC 93-74021. (New Poets of America Ser.: Vol. 14). 70p. 1994. 20.00 (*1-880238-02-0*) BOA Edns.

— Poetry Handbook. LC 96-40451. 224p. 1997. 23.00 (*0-393-04081-X*) Norton.

***Addonizio, Kim.** Tell Me. (American Poets Continuum Ser.: Vol. 61). 90p. 2000. 20.00 (*1-880238-90-X*); pap. 12.50 (*1-880238-91-8*) BOA Edns.

Addonizio, Kim & Laux, Dorianne. The Poet's Companion: A Guide to the Pleasures of Writing Poetry. LC 96-40451. 224p. 1997. pap. 13.00 (*0-393-31654-8*, Norton Paperbks) Norton.

Addonizio, Kim, et al. Sextet One: 6 Powerful American Voices. Di Suvero, Victor, ed. & intro. by. 1996. 17.50 (*0-938631-27-6*) Pennywhistle Pr.

Addonizio, Steven J. How to Save Money on Your Healthcare Costs: An Insider's Perspective. 63p. (Orig.). 1995. pap. 15.00 (*1-882194-15-2*) TN Valley Pub.

Address, Richard F., ed. A Time to Prepare: A Practical Guide for Individuals & Families in Determining One's Wishes for Extraordinary Medical Treatment & Financial Arrangements. 54p. (Orig.). 1994. pap. 6.95 (*0-8074-0534-5*, 243871) UAHC.

Addy, Cathryn L. The President's Journey: Issues & Ideals in the Community College. 164p. (C). 1995. text 30.95 (*1-882982-04-5*) Anker Pub.

Addy, Douglas P. Investigations in Pediatrics. (C). 1994. pap. text 63.00 (*0-7020-1737-X*) Harcourt.

Addy, Paul L., jt. auth. see Geis, A. John.

Addy, S. D. A Glossary of Words Used in the Neighbourhood of Sheffield: Including... & Customs. (English Dialect Society Publications: No. 57). 1969. reprint ed. pap. 45.00 (*0-8115-0478-6*) Periodicals Srv.

Addy, S. O. A Supplement to the Sheffield Glossary. (English Dialect Society Publications: No. 62). 1974. reprint ed. pap. 25.00 (*0-8115-0482-4*) Periodicals Srv.

Addy, Sharon H. Kidding Around Milwaukee: What to Do, Where to Go & How to Have Fun in Milwaukee. (Kidding Around Ser.). (Illus.). 144p. (J). (gr. 1-6). 1997. pap. 7.95 (*1-56261-362-6*) Avalon Travel.

— A Visit with Great-Grandma. Fay, Ann, ed. LC 88-20867. (Illus.). 32p. (J). (gr. 1-3). 1989. lib. bdg. 14.95 (*0-8075-8497-5*) A Whitman.

Addy, Sharon Hart. Right Here on This Spot. LC 96-15382. (Illus.). 32p. (J). (gr. k-2). 1999. 15.00 (*0-395-73091-0*) HM.

Addy, Steve. The Detroit Pistons: Four Decades of Motor City Memories. 263p. 1997. 39.95 (*1-57167-144-7*) Sports Pub.

Addy-Trout, Elaine, jt. auth. see Marquis, M. Ann.

Addyman, A. M., jt. auth. see Wilson, I. R.

Addyman, Peter & Morris, Richard, eds. The Archaeological Study of Churches. LC 77-365546. (Council for British Archaeology Research Report Ser.: No. 13). (Illus.). 96p. reprint ed. pap. 30.00 (*0-8357-5713-7*, 201402100088) Bks Demand.

Ade Ajayi, Jacob F., et al. The African Experience with Higher Education. 288p. (C). 1996. text 39.95 (*0-8214-1160-8*); pap. text 19.95 (*0-8214-1161-6*) Ohio U Pr.

Ade, Claudia & Erkert, Thomas. A Demographic Atlas of Austin. (Special Project Reports). (Illus.). 109p. 1987. pap. 8.00 (*0-89940-858-3*) LBJ Sch Pub Aff.

Ade, George. Artie, & Pink Marsh: Eighteen Ninety-Six to Eighteen Ninety-Seven. LC 63-22584. (Chicago in Fiction Ser). (Illus.). 236p. reprint ed. 73.20 (*0-8357-9641-8*, 201574800097) Bks Demand.

— Bang! Bang! A Collection of Stories Intended to Recall Memories of the Nickel Library Days When Boys Were Superhuman & Murder a Fine Art. LC 75-160929. (Short Story Index Reprint Ser.). (Illus.). 1977. reprint ed. 13.95 (*0-8369-3908-5*) Ayer.

— Doc Horne: A Story of the Streets & Town. LC 77-104402. reprint ed. pap. text 7.25 (*0-89197-734-1*); reprint ed. lib. bdg. 22.75 (*0-8398-0052-5*) Irvington.

— Fables in Slang. LC 83-46009. (Classics of Modern American Humor Ser.). (Illus.). reprint ed. 49.50 (*0-404-19925-9*) AMS Pr.

— Fables in Slang. (BCL1-PS American Literature Ser.). 200p. 1992. reprint ed. lib. bdg. 69.00 (*0-7812-6663-3*) Rprt Serv.

— The Girl Proposition. LC 74-96872. (Illus.). reprint ed. lib. bdg. 32.50 (*0-8398-0053-3*) Irvington.

— In Pastures New. LC 74-91072. reprint ed. lib. bdg. 32.50 (*0-8398-0054-1*) Irvington.

— People You Know. (Works of George Ade Ser.). 224p. 1985. reprint ed. 39.00 (*0-932051-62-6*) Rprt Serv.

— The Permanent Ade: The Living Writings of George Ade. (BCL1-PS American Literature Ser.). 347p. 1993. reprint ed. lib. bdg. 89.00 (*0-7812-6943-1*) Rprt Serv.

Ade, John. Newton County: Collection of Historical Facts & Personal Recollections Concerning Newton Co., from 1853 to 1911. (Illus.). 314p. 1997. reprint ed. lib. bdg. 37.50 (*0-8328-6661-X*) Higginson Bk Co.

Ade-Ridder, L. & Hennon, C. B., eds. Lifestyles of the Elderly: Diversity in Relationships, Health, & Caregiving. (Illus.). 256p. 1989. 37.00 (*0-89885-447-4*, Kluwer Acad Hman Sci) Kluwer Academic.

Adeajayi, J. F. & Peel, J. D., eds. People & Empires in African History: Essays in Memory of Michael Crowder. 254p. (C). 1992. text 49.95 (*0-582-08997-2*) Longman.

Adebayo, A. G. Embattled Federalism: History of Revenue Allocation in Nigeria, 1946-1990. LC 92-39232. (American University Studies: Economics: Ser. XVI, Vol. 9). XVI, 266p. (C). 1993. text 54.95 (*0-8204-1862-5*) P Lang Pubng.

Adebayo, Akanmu, jt. auth. see Falola, Toyin.

Adebayo, Augustus. Principles & Practice of Public Administration in Nigeria. LC 80-41173. 207p. reprint ed. pap. 64.20 (*0-608-18416-0*, 203049200069) Bks Demand.

Adebayo, Yinka. Age Ain't Nothin' but a Number. (Drummond Hill Crew Ser.). (J). 1998. mass mkt. 5.99 (*1-874509-33-6*, Pub. by X Pr) LPC InBook.

— Big Diss. (Drummond Hill Crew Ser.). 1999. pap. 5.99 (*1-874509-68-9*) X Pr.

— Boyz II Men. (J). 1998. mass mkt. 5.99 (*1-874509-29-8*, Pub. by X Pr) LPC InBook.

— Glamma Kids. (Drummond Hill Crew Ser.). 1999. pap. 6.99 (*1-874509-67-0*) X Pr.

— Livin' Large. (J). 1998. mass mkt. 5.99 (*1-874509-34-4*, Pub. by X Pr) LPC InBook.

***Adebayo, Yinka.** Ragga to Riches. 1999. pap. text 6.99 (*1-874509-69-7*) XPress.

Adebesin, Denise, jt. auth. see Adebesin, Larry.

Adebesin, Larry & Adebesin, Denise. Success - It's Your Birthright: Discover Who You Really Are & Learn How to Co-Control Your Destiny. 2nd rev. ed. 135p. 1997. reprint ed. pap. 12.95 (*0-9651929-8-9*) Enrichment Pub.

— Success: It's Your Birthright: Discover Who You Really Are & Learn: How to Co-Control Your Destiny, Experience Increased Health & Vitality, & Live the Lifestyle of Your Dreams. 136p. (Orig.) 1997. pap. 12.95 (*0-9651929-0-3*) Enrichment Pub.

Adebiyi, George A., jt. auth. see Russell, Lynn D.

Adeboye, E. A. As Pure As Light. 48p. 1986. pap. text 1.00 (*0-88144-076-0*) Christian Pub.

Adeboye, E. A., ed. The Crucified Life. 48p. (Orig.). 1985. pap. 0.95 (*0-88144-053-1*, CPS022) Christian Pub.

ADEC International Staff. Art Price Indicator International 99. 1792p. 1998. pap. 19.95 (*2-907129-14-7*, Pub. by ADEC-Prodn) Dealers Choice.

ADEC International Staff. Art Price Indicator International 1998. 98th ed. 1120p. 1997. pap. text 19.95 (*2-907129-11-2*, Pub. by ADEC Diffusion) New Eng Gallery.

ADEC Staff. ADEC International Art Price Annual 1997. 2300p. 1995. vinyl bd. 170.00 (*1-55660-257-X*) A Wofsy Fine Arts.

— Art Price Annual. 3272p. 1991. vinyl bd. 135.00 (*1-55660-253-7*) A Wofsy Fine Arts.

— Art Price Annual. 2747p. 1992. vinyl bd. 135.00 (*1-55660-254-5*) A Wofsy Fine Arts.

— Art Price Annual. 25226p. 1993. vinyl bd. 150.00 (*1-55660-255-3*) A Wofsy Fine Arts.

— Art Price Annual. 2636p. 1994. vinyl bd. 150.00 (*1-55660-256-1*) A Wofsy Fine Arts.

***ADEC Staff, ed.** ADEC 99 International Art Price Annual & Falk's Price Index: Annuaire Cotes. 3000p. 1999. 119.00 (*2-907129-15-5*, Pub. by ADEC Diffusion) New Eng Gallery.

Adede, A. O. International Environmental Law Digest: Instruments for International Responses to Problems of Environment & Development 1972-1992. 584p. 1993. 253.00 (*0-444-81626-7*) Elsevier.

— The System for Settlement of Disputes under the United Nations Convention on the Law of the Sea. LC 86-5373. (Publications on Ocean Development: Vol. 10). 1987. lib. bdg. 130.50 (*90-247-3324-3*) Kluwer Academic.

Adede, Rose. Joel Litu: African Quaker. LC 82-81325. 32p. 1982. pap. 1.00 (*0-87574-243-2*) Pendle Hill.

Adedeji. Comprehend & Master African Co. LC 99-488650. 1999. pap. 27.50 (*1-85649-763-1*); text 75.00 (*1-85649-762-3*) St Martin.

Adedeji, Adebayo. Towards A Dynamic African Economy: Selected Speeches & Lectures, 1975-1986. Senghor, Jeggan C., ed. (Illus.). 729p. (C). 1989. text 55.00 (*0-7146-3349-6*, Pub. by F Cass Pubs); pap. text 37.50 (*0-7146-4062-X*, Pub. by F Cass Pubs) Intl Spec Bk.

Adedeji, Adebayo, ed. The Indigenization of African Economics. 410p. (C). 1981. 55.00 (*0-8419-0708-0*, Africana); pap. 24.50 (*0-8419-0709-9*, Africana) Holmes & Meier.

— Renewal from the Roots? The Struggle for Democratic Development in Nigeria. LC 97-7839. 256p. (C). 1997. pap. 25.00 (*1-85649-510-8*); text 65.00 (*1-85649-509-4*, Pub. by Zed Books) St Martin.

Adedeji, Adebayo, et al, eds. The Challenge of African Economic Recovery & Development. 796p. 1991. text 55.00 (*0-7146-3388-7*, Pub. by F Cass Pubs); pap. text 35.00 (*0-7146-4074-3*, Pub. by F Cass Pubs) Intl Spec Bk.

Adedeji, Adebayo, et al. African Social Situation: Crucial Factors of Development & Transformation. (African Social Challenges Ser.: No. 2). 221p. 1990. lib. bdg. 60.00 (*0-905450-78-7*, Pub. by H Zell Pubs) Seven Hills Bk.

— Hard Bargaining Ahead: U. S. Trade Policy & Developing Countries. Preeg, Ernest H., ed. 224p. 1985. 32.95 (*0-88738-043-3*) Transaction Pubs.

— Hard Bargaining Ahead: U. S. Trade Policy & Developing Countries. Weintraub, Sidney, ed. 224p. 1985. pap. 17.95 (*0-87855-987-6*) Transaction Pubs.

Adedeji, Adeyemi A. The Law of Liberty: Victory Through Grace. LC 95-77407. 68p. (Orig.). 1995. pap. 5.99 (*0-88270-724-8*) Bridge-Logos.

Adedji, Adebayo, et al, eds. The Human Dimension of Africa's Persistent Economic Crisis: Selected Papers from the UN International Conference. 412p. 1991. 85.00 (*0-905450-40-X*, Pub. by H Zell Pubs) Seven Hills Bk.

Adedjouma, Davida, ed. The Palm of My Heart: Poetry by African American Children. LC 96-13426. (Illus.). 32p. (J). (ps up). 1996. 15.95 (*1-880000-41-5*) Lee & Low Bks.

— The Palm of My Heart: Poetry by African American Children. LC 96-13426. (Illus.). 32p. (YA). (ps up). 1998. pap. 6.95 (*1-880000-76-8*) Lee & Low Bks.

A

Adeduro, Amankwa. United States Marines Force Recons: A Black Hero's Story. 300p. (Orig.). 1994. pap. 16.95 (*0-86626-009-9*) AAIMS Pubs.

Adee, Donna. Miriam's Dilemma. (Miriam Ser.: No. 1). (Illus.). 160p. (J). (gr. 6-10). 1997. pap. 8.95 (*0-9654272-1-8*) Harvest KS.

Adee, Donna, et al. The Courtship of Miriam. LC 98-93866. (Miriam Ser.: Vol. 2). (Illus.). 200p. (YA). (gr. 7-12). 1998. pap. 8.95 (*0-9654272-2-6*) Harvest KS.

Adee, Lawrence E. & Underhill, Lee, Jr., eds. The Diary of Jannet Glendinning Adee. (Illus.). 338p. 1996. 35.00 (*0-9654586-0-1*) L E Adee.

Adee, Ronald R. Regulation S: The Safe Harbor for Offshore Securities Transactions. (Corporate Practice Ser.: No. 58-2). 1999. 95.00 (*1-55871-402-2*) BNA.

Adeeko, Adeleke. Proverbs, Textuality, & Nativism in African Literature. LC 97-40247. 176p. 1998. 49.95 (*0-8130-1562-6*) U Press Fla.

Adefope, Jide. After the Fall. 800p. 1997. 35.00 (*1-85884-093-7*, Pub. by Wernd Wrld Pr) Baker & Taylor.

Adefris, Assefa. Betrayal of the Emperor: An Ethiopian Remembers. Griffith, Joice, ed. Hailu, Amsale, tr. LC 99-162339. (Orig.). 1997. pap. 15.00 (*0-9659079-0-2*, 4078) Ethiopian Amer.

Adegbija, Efurosibina. Language Attitudes in Sub-Saharan Africa: A Sociolinguistic Overview. LC 94-5114. (Multilingual Matters Ser.: Vol. 103). 1994. 49.00 (*1-85359-239-0*, Pub. by Multilingual Matters) Taylor & Francis.

Adejom, Myrna, ed. see Queen, Linda M.

Adejunmobi, Moradewun. J. J. Rabearivelo, Literature & Lingua Franca in Colonial Madagascar, Vol. 12. (Francophone Cultures & Literatures Ser.). (Illus.). XXIV, 346p. (C). 1996. text 58.95 (*0-8204-2791-8*) P Lang Pubng.

Adekola, AbelFemi. Gateway to Personal Investment. 224p. (C). 1995. pap. 29.95 (*0-7872-1758-1*) Kendall-Hunt.

***Adel-Meguid, M., et al, eds.** Proteases as Targets for Therapy. LC 99-45434. (Handbook of Experimental Pharmacology Ser.: Vol. 140). (Illus.). 500p. 1999. 325.00 (*3-540-66118-2*) Spr-Verlag.

Adel, S. Prince of Silence. 272p. 1999. pap. 7.50 (*1-892614-12-X*, BWP-PS) Briarwood VA.

Adelaar, Robert S., ed. Injuries to the Foot & Ankle. LC 98-7630. (Illus.). 352p. 1998. text 125.00 (*0-397-51374-7*) Lppncott W & W.

Adelaar, Robert S., et al. Disorders of the Great Toe. LC 97-16222. (Monograph Ser.). (Illus.). 80p. 1997. pap. 38.00 (*0-89203-168-9*) Amer Acad Ortho Surg.

Adelaide, Debra. Motherlove 2: More Stories about Births, Babies & Beyond. LC 97-156315. 1997. write for info. (*0-09-183512-7*) Trafalgar.

Adelaide, Debra, jt. auth. see Cusack, Dymphna.

Adelard. Adelard of Bath, Conversations with His Nephew: "On the Same & the Different", "Questions on Natural Science" & "On Birds" Burnett, Charles, ed. LC 97-44298. (Cambridge Medieval Classics: No. 9). (Illus.). 293p. (C). 1998. text 74.95 (*0-521-39471-6*) Cambridge U Pr.

Adelard of Bath, tr. see Euclid.

Adelberg, Ellen & Currie, Claudia, eds. In Conflict with the Law: Women & the Canadian Justice System. 302p. 1993. pap. 18.95 (*0-88974-054-2*, Pub. by Press Gang Pubs) LPC InBook.

Adelberg, Michael S. Roster of the People of Revolutionary Monmouth County, New Jersey. 348p. pap. 32.50 (*0-8063-4677-9*) Clearfield Co.

Adele. Camus's l'Etranger: Fifty Years On. 1993. 45.00 (*0-333-53294-5*, Pub. by Macmillan) St Martin.

Adele, Geras. Pictures of the Night. (Egerton Hall Trilogy). 1998. 11.10 (*0-606-13704-1*, Pub. by Turtleback) Demco.

Adele, Lynne. Spirited Journeys: Self-Taught Texas Artists of the Twentieth Century. LC 97-212346. (Illus.). 207p. 1997. pap. 35.00 (*0-935213-42-2*, Pub. by J S Blanton Mus) U of Tex Pr.

Adelekan, Patricia A. African American Educators' Hall of Fame: Educators' Hall of Fame. (African American Educators' Hall of Fame Ser.). 24p. (Orig.). 1993. pap. 4.99 (*0-9620036-4-6*) Adelekan Pub Co.

— African American Educators' Hall of Fame: 1994 Edition, a Multi-Cultural Selection. 24p. (Orig.). 1994. pap. 4.99 (*0-9620036-5-4*) Adelekan Pub Co.

— African American Educators' Hall of Fame: 1995 Edition, a Multi-Cultural Selection. 24p. (Orig.). 1995. pap. 4.99 (*0-9620036-6-2*) Adelekan Pub Co.

Adeleke, S. A. & Neumann, P. M. Relations Related to Betweenness: Their Structure & Automorphisms. LC 97-35546. (Memoirs of the American Mathematical Society Ser.). 125p. 1998. pap. 43.00 (*0-8218-0623-8*) Am Math.

Adeleke, Tunde. UnAfrican Americans: Nineteenth-Century Black Nationalists & the Civilizing Mission. LC 97-50430. (Illus.). 216p. (C). 1998. 24.95 (*0-8131-2056-X*) U Pr of Ky.

Adeleke, Tunde, ed. Booker T. Washington - Interpretative Essays. LC 98-40433. (Black Studies: Vol. 4). 184p. 1998. lib. bdg. 79.95 (*0-7734-8260-1*) E Mellen.

Adeleke, Tuude. Songhay, 14 vols. Bond, George, ed. LC 95-1272. (Heritage Library of African Peoples: Set 2). (Illus.). 64p. (YA). (gr. 7-12). 1996. lib. bdg. 16.95 (*0-8239-1986-2*) Rosen Group.

Adeleye, Gabriel, et al. World Dictionary of Foreign Expressions: A Resource for Readers & Writers. LC 98-40788. 1999. 70.00 (*0-86516-422-3*) Bolchazy-Carducci.

Adelhelm, Michelle. Woman's Value Quiche & Pizza: Plus All Kinds of Pies & Pastries. 1999. pap. text 12.95 (*0-7981-3881-5*) Human & Rousseau.

Adelhofer, O., intro. Codex Vindobenesis Mexicanus 1. fac. ed. (Codices Selecti C Ser.: Vol. V). 65p. 1974. reprint ed. lthr. 600.00 (*3-201-00757-9*, Pub. by Akademische Druck-und) Balogh.

***Adeli.** Control, Optimization, & Smart Structures: High-Performance Bridges & Buildings of the Future. LC 99-21925. 288p. 1999. 79.95 (*0-471-35094-X*) Wiley.

Adeli, Hojjat. Knowledge Engineering Vol. 1: Fundamentals. (C). 1990. text 52.74 (*0-07-000355-6*) McGraw.

— Knowledge Engineering Vol. 2: Applications. (C). 1990. text 52.74 (*0-07-000357-2*) McGraw.

Adeli, Hojjat, ed. Advances in Design Optimization. (Illus.). 592p. (C). (gr. 13). 1994. 180.00 (*0-412-53730-3*, Chap & Hall NY) Chapman & Hall.

— Advances in Design Optimization. LC 93-32183. 1994. write for info. (*0-419-16960-1*, E & FN Spon) Routledge.

— Expert Systems in Construction & Structural Engineering. 384p. (gr. 13). 1988. text 95.50 (*0-412-28910-5*) Chapman & Hall.

— Microcomputer Knowledge-Based Expert Systems in Civil Engineering. (Symposium Proceedings Ser.). 220p. 1988. 5.00 (*0-87262-653-9*) Am Soc Civil Eng.

— Parallel & Distributed Processing in Structural Engineering. (Sessions Proceedings Ser.). 104p. 1988. 5.00 (*0-87262-640-7*) Am Soc Civil Eng.

— Parallel Processing in Computational Mechanics. (New Generation Computing Ser.: Vol. 2). (Illus.). 376p. 1991. text 165.00 (*0-8247-8557-6*) Dekker.

— Supercomputing in Engineering Analysis. (New Generation Computing Ser.: Vol. 1). (Illus.). 368p. 1991. text 165.00 (*0-8247-8559-2*) Dekker.

Adeli, Hojjat & Hung, Shih-Lin. Machine Learning: Neural Networks, Genetic Algorithms, & Fuzzy Systems. 211p. 1994. pap. 64.99 (*0-471-01633-0*) Wiley.

Adeli, Hojjat & Kamal, Osama. Parallel Processing in Structural Engineering. LC 92-42747. 1993. mass mkt. 104.95 (*1-85861-003-6*) Elsevier.

Adeli, Hojjat & Kumar, Sanjay. Distributed Computer-Aided Engineering. LC 98-38057. (Computer-Aided Electronics Ser.). 1998. boxed set 89.95 (*0-8493-2093-3*) CRC Pr.

***Adeli, Hojjat & Park, Hyo S.** Neurocomputing for Design Automation. LC 98-12674. (Computer-Aided Electronics Ser.). 240p. 1998. boxed set 94.95 (*0-8493-2092-5*) CRC Pr.

Adeli, Hojjat & Sierakowski, Robert L., eds. Mechanics Computing in 1990's & Beyond. LC 91-12840. 1352p. 1991. pap. text 15.00 (*0-87262-804-3*) Am Soc Civil Eng.

***Adeli, Hojjat & Soegiarso, Roesdiman.** High Performance Computing in Structural Engineering. LC 98-41242. (Computer-Aided Electronics Ser.). 249p. 1998. 85.00 (*0-8493-2091-7*) CRC Pr.

Adeli, Hojjat & Yu, George. Object-Oriented Computer-Aided Engineering. (C). 2001. 44.00 (*0-13-630872-4*, Macmillan Coll) P-H.

Adeli, Hojjat, ed. see IIS '97 & International Association of Science and Technology for Development Staff.

Adelio. A Journey to Philadelphia: or Memoirs of Charles Coleman Saunders. LC 78-64060. reprint ed. 47.50 (*0-404-17055-2*) AMS Pr.

Adelizzi, Jane U. & Goss, Diane, eds. A Closer Look: Perspectives & Reflections on College Students with Learning Disabilities. 240p. (Orig.). (C). 1995. pap. 20.00 (*0-9649752-0-3*) Curry College.

***Adelkhah, Fariba.** Being Modern in Iran. LC 99-27717. 2000. write for info. (*0-231-11941-0*) Col U Pr.

— Being Modern in Iran. LC 99-27717. 190p. 2000. 25.00 (*0-231-11940-2*) Col U Pr.

Adell, tr. see Alianza Staff.

Adell, Judith, et al, eds. A Guide to Non-Sexist Children's Books, Vol. 1: To 1976. LC 75-34396. (Illus.). 149p. 1976. pap. 8.00 (*0-915864-02-9*) Academy Chi Pubs.

— A Guide to Non-Sexist Children's Books, Vol. 1: To 1976. LC 75-34396. Vol. 1. (Illus.). 240p. 1976. 20.00 (*0-915864-01-0*) Academy Chi Pubs.

Adell, Sandra. Double Consciousness - Double Bind: Theoretical Issues in Twentieth-Century Black Literature. LC 93-49578. (Illus.). 192p. 1994. text 25.95 (*0-252-02109-6*) U of Ill Pr.

Adelman. The Decline of the Liberal Party, 1910-1931. (C). 1995. pap. 15.93 (*0-582-35327-0*) Addison-Wesley.

— The Rise of the Labor Party. 2nd ed. 141p. (C). 1989. pap. 15.93 (*0-582-35488-9*) Addison-Wesley.

— Unstable Angina Order. 1981. lib. bdg. 162.50 (*90-247-2486-4*, Pub. by M Nijhoff) Kluwer Academic.

Adelman & Shultz. The Pilgrim Must Embark: Living in Community. 1994. 125.00 (*1-56321-143-2*) L Erlbaum Assocs.

Adelman, jt. auth. see Alan, M.

Adelman, Andrew & Bainum, Peter M., eds. International Space Technical Applications, 19th Goddard Memorial Symposium, Mar. 26-27, 1981, Washington, D.C. (Science & Technology Ser.: Vol. 52). (Illus.). 186p. 1981. 30.00 (*0-87703-152-5*, Am Astronaut Soc); pap. 20.00 (*0-87703-153-3*, Am Astronaut Soc) Univelt Inc.

Adelman, Bob. Tijuana Bibles: Art & Wit in America's Forbidden Funnies, 1930-1950. LC 97-30672. 1997. 23.50 (*0-684-83461-8*, S&S Edns) Simon & Schuster.

Adelman, Bob, photos by. The Art of Roy Lichtenstein: Mural with Blue Brushstroke. LC 93-74353. (Illus.). 128p. 1994. reprint ed. pap. 19.45 (*1-55970-251-6*, Pub. by Arcade Pub Inc) Time Warner.

Adelman, Bob, jt. auth. see Johnson, Charles.

Adelman, Carol C., ed. International Regulation: New Rules in a Changing World Order. LC 88-23797. 250p. (C). 1988. 29.95 (*1-55815-026-9*); pap. 19.95 (*1-55815-027-7*) ICS Pr.

Adelman, Charles M. Cypro-Geometric Pottery: Refinements in Classification. (Studies in Mediterranean Archaeology: Vol. XLVII). (Illus.). 213p. (Orig.). 1976. pap. 42.50 (*91-85058-69-6*) P Astroms.

Adelman, Clifford. Knowledge Content of Computer Science in Higher Education & the Labor Market. 68p. 1997. pap. 6.50 (*0-16-063633-7*) USGPO.

— New College Course Map & Transcript Files: Changes in Course-taking & Achievement, 1972- 1993, Based on the Postsecondary Records from Two National Longitudinal Studies. LC 99-489149. 224p. 1999. per. 21.00 (*0-16-050152-0*) USGPO.

— New College Course Map & Transcript Files: Changes in Course-Taking & Achievement, 1972- 1993, Based on the Postsecondary Records from Two National Longitudinal Studies. 294p. 1995. pap. 19.00 (*0-16-063576-4*) USGPO.

— Women & Men of the Engineering Path: A Model for Analyses of Undergraduate Careers. LC 98-154855. 117p. 1998. pap. 16.00 (*0-16-049551-2*) USGPO.

Adelman, Deborah. The 'Children of Perestroika' Moscow Teenagers Talk about Their Lives & the Future. LC 90-25104. (Illus.). 280p. (gr. 13). 1991. 53.95 (*1-56324-000-9*) M E Sharpe.

— The 'Children of Perestroika' Moscow Teenagers Talk about Their Lives & the Future. LC 92-25104. (Illus.). 280p. (gr. 13). 1992. pap. 31.95 (*1-56324-001-7*) M E Sharpe.

— The 'Children of Perestroika' Come of Age: Young People of Moscow Talk about Life in the New Russia. LC 90-10936. 200p. (C). (gr. 13). 1994. pap. 30.95 (*1-56324-287-7*) M E Sharpe.

— The 'Children of Perestroika' Come of Age: Young People of Moscow Talk about Life in the New Russia. LC 90-10936. 200p. (J). (gr. 13). 1994. 52.95 (*1-56324-286-9*) M E Sharpe.

Adelman, Elizabeth, ed. see Rand McNally Staff & Cunningham, David.

Adelman, Elizabeth F., ed. Children's World Atlas. LC 96-675123. (Illus.). 96p. (J). (gr. 5-9). 1991. 14.95 (*0-528-83455-X*) Rand McNally.

Adelman, Gary. Anna Karenina: The Bitterness of Ecstasy. (Twayne's Masterwork Studies: No. 56). 160p. (C). 1990. 29.00 (*0-8057-8083-1*, Twayne); pap. 13.95 (*0-8057-8139-0*, Twayne) Mac Lib Ref.

— Heart of Darkness: Search for the Unconscious. (Masterwork Studies). 136p. 1987. 25.95 (*0-8057-7953-1*) Macmillan.

— Jude the Obscure: A Paradise of Despair. LC 92-10829. (Twayne's Masterworks Ser.: No. 94). 150p. (Orig.). 1992. 29.00 (*0-8057-9435-2*); pap. 13.95 (*0-8057-8563-9*) Macmillan.

Adelman, George. Neuroscience Year: Supplement 1 to the Encyclopedia of Neuroscience. 200p. 1989. 87.50 (*0-8176-3383-9*) Birkhauser.

***Adelman, George & Smith, Barry H.** Encyclopedia of Neuroscience. 2nd ed. LC 99-22323. 1999. write for info. (*0-444-50176-2*) Elsevier.

Adelman, George, jt. ed. see Smith, Barry.

***Adelman, Harold M.** Rheumatology - Questions & Answers. (Questions & Answers Ser.). (Illus.). 2000. pap. text 17.95 (*1-873413-73-4*) Merit Pub Intl.

Adelman, Harvey M., jt. auth. see Hall, Owen P., Jr.

Adelman, Howard, ed. Refugee Policy: Canada & the United States. 375p. 1991. pap. 14.50 (*0-934733-64-3*) CMS.

Adelman, Howard, et al, eds. Immigration & Refugee Policy: Australia & Canada Compared, Vol. 1. 335p. 1994. pap. text 49.90 (*0-8020-7608-4*) U of Toronto Pr.

— Immigration & Refugee Policy: Australia & Canada Compared, Vol. 2. 380p. 1994. pap. text 24.95 (*0-8020-7609-2*) U of Toronto Pr.

Adelman, Howard & Suhrke, Astri, eds. The Path of a Genocide: The Rwanda Crisis from Uganda to Zaire. 414p. 1999. 44.95 (*1-56000-382-0*) Transaction Pubs.

Adelman, Howard & Taylor, Linda. Learning Problems & Learning Disabilities: Moving Forward. LC 92-9363. 480p. (C). 1992. 43.00 (*0-534-18756-0*) Brooks-Cole.

Adelman, Howard S. & Taylor, Linda. On Understanding Intervention in Psychology & Education. LC 94-2986. 296p. 1994. 55.00 (*0-275-94888-9*, Praeger Pubs) Greenwood.

Adelman, Irma. Dynamics & Income Distribution: Selected Essays of Irma Adelman, Vol. 2. LC 94-48924. (Economists of the Twentieth Century Ser.). 432p. 1995. 100.00 (*1-85898-052-6*) E Elgar.

— Institutions & Development Strategies Vol. 1: Selected Essays of Irma Adelman. LC 94-48924. (Economists of the Twentieth Century Ser.). 400p. 1995. 100.00 (*1-85898-051-8*) E Elgar.

— Theories of Economic Growth & Development. viii, 164p. 1961. pap. 11.95 (*0-8047-0084-2*) Stanford U Pr.

Adelman, Irma, ed. Practical Approaches to Development Planning: Korea's Second Five-Year Plan. LC 69-19467. (Illus.). 320p. 1969. reprint ed. pap. 99.20 (*0-608-04079-7*, 206481100011) Bks Demand.

Adelman, Irma & Morris, Cynthia T. Economic Growth & Social Equity in Developing Countries. LC 73-80616. 273p. 1973. reprint ed. pap. 30.00 (*0-7837-6814-1*, 204664600003) Bks Demand.

— Economic Growth & Social Equity in Developing Countries. LC 73-80616. xiv, 260p. 1973. reprint ed. pap. 13.95 (*0-8047-0888-6*) Stanford U Pr.

— Society, Politics, & Economic Development: A Quantitative Approach. LC 67-21582. 317p. reprint ed. pap. 98.30 (*0-608-06037-2*, 206636900008) Bks Demand.

Adelman, Irma, jt. auth. see Morris, Cynthia T.

Adelman, Irma, jt. auth. see Taylor, J. Edward.

Adelman, Irving & Dworkin, Rita. The Contemporary Novel: A Checklist of Critical Literature on the English Language Novel since 1945. LC 96-17577. 1997. 125.00 (*0-8108-3103-1*) Scarecrow.

Adelman, Janet. The Common Liar: An Essay on Antony & Cleopatra. LC 72-91285. (Yale Studies in English: No. 181). 245p. reprint ed. pap. 76.00 (*0-8357-8697-8*, 203365900087) Bks Demand.

— Suffocating Mothers: Fantasies of Maternal Origin in Shakespeare's Plays, Hamlet to The Tempest. 320p. (C). 1991. pap. 21.99 (*0-415-90039-5*, A1139) Routledge.

Adelman, Jeremy. Frontier Development: Land, Labour, & Capital on the Wheatlands of Argentina & Canada, 1890-1914. LC 93-46770. (Oxford Historical Monographs). (Illus.). 344p. 1994. 70.00 (*0-19-820441-8*) OUP.

Adelman, Jeremy. Republic of Capital: Buenos Aires & the Legal Transformation of the Atlantic World LC 98-48249. 1999. 55.00 (*0-8047-3379-1*) Stanford U Pr.

Adelman, Jeremy, ed. Colonial Legacies: The Problem of Persistence in Latin American History. LC 98-35714. 320p. (C). (gr. 13). 1999. 75.00 (*0-415-92152-X*, D5927); pap. 22.99 (*0-415-92153-8*, D5931) Routledge.

Adelman, Jonathan R. Endgame: The Soviet & American Destruction of the Third Reich, June 1944-May 1945. 240p. 1988. text 31.00 (*0-8133-0384-2*) Westview.

— Prelude to the Cold War: The Tsarist, Soviet, & U. S. Armies in the Two World Wars. LC 88-2048. 287p. 1988. lib. bdg. 50.00 (*1-55587-123-2*) L Rienner.

— Revolution & Evolution. 1996. text 40.00 (*0-8133-0187-4*) Westview.

— Revolution & Evolution. (C). 1996. pap. text 16.95 (*0-8133-0188-2*) Westview.

— The Revolutionary Armies: The Historical Development of the Soviet & the Chinese People's Liberation Armies, 38. LC 79-7728. (Contributions in Political Science Ser.: No. 38). (Illus.). 230p. 1980. 55.00 (*0-313-22026-3*, ADR/) Greenwood.

— Torrents of Spring: Soviet & Post-Soviet Politics. LC 94-16403. 448p. (C). 1994. 44.38 (*0-07-000359-9*) McGraw.

Adelman, Jonathan R., ed. Superpowers & Revolution. LC 86-21273. 316p. 1986. 55.00 (*0-275-92166-2*, C2166, Praeger Pubs) Greenwood.

Adelman, Jonathan R. & Gibson, Cristann L. Contemporary Soviet Military Affairs: The Legacy of World War II. 256p. (C). (gr. 13). 1989. text 62.95 (*0-04-445031-1*) Routledge.

Adelman, Jonathan R. & Palmieri, Deborah A. The Dynamics of Soviet Foreign Policy. fac. ed. LC 88-24690. (Illus.). 367p. 1989. reprint ed. pap. 113.80 (*0-7837-8110-5*, 204791300008) Bks Demand.

Adelman, Kenneth L. & Augustine, Norman R. The Defense Revolution: Intelligent Downsizing of America's Military. 239p. 1990. 24.95 (*1-55815-074-9*) ICS Pr.

— The Defense Revolution: Intelligent Downsizing of America's Military. 239p. 1992. pap. 19.95 (*1-55815-075-7*) ICS Pr.

Adelman, Kenneth L., jt. auth. see Augustine, Norman.

Adelman, Leonard. Evaluating Decision Support & Expert Systems. LC 91-19337. (Series in Systems Engineering). 248p. 1991. 115.00 (*0-471-54801-4*) Wiley.

Adelman, Leonard & Riedel, Sharon L. Handbook for Evaluating Knowledge-Based Systems: Conceptual Framework & Compendium of Methods. LC 97-6499. 1997. text 148.50 (*0-7923-9906-4*) Kluwer Academic.

Adelman, Leonard, jt. auth. see Andriole, Stephen J.

Adelman, Linda. Writing & Thinking for Young Authors: Orange Level. Wright, Elena D., ed. (J). (gr. 3). 1994. teacher ed., ring bd. 125.00 (*0-88106-203-0*, W320) Charlesbridge Pub.

Adelman, Linda, et al. Writing & Thinking for Young Authors: Blue Level. Wright, Elena D., ed. (J). (gr. 4). 1995. teacher ed., ring bd. 125.00 (*0-88106-204-9*, W420) Charlesbridge Pub.

— Writing & Thinking for Young Authors: Gold Level. Wright, Elena D., ed. (J). (gr. 6). 1996. teacher ed., ring bd. 125.00 (*0-88106-206-5*, W620) Charlesbridge Pub.

— Writing & Thinking for Young Authors: Green Level. (J). (gr. 2). 1994. teacher ed., ring bd. 125.00 (*0-88106-202-2*, W220) Charlesbridge Pub.

— Writing & Thinking for Young Authors: Red Level. Wright, Elena D., ed. (J). (gr. 1). 1994. teacher ed., ring bd. 99.50 (*0-88106-201-4*, W120) Charlesbridge Pub.

— Writing & Thinking for Young Authors: Tan Level. Wright, Elena D., ed. (J). (gr. 5). 1994. teacher ed., ring bd. 125.00 (*0-88106-205-7*, W520) Charlesbridge Pub.

***Adelman, M.** German Shepherd Handbook. (Pet Handbks.). (Illus.). 2000. pap. text 9.95 (*0-7641-1332-1*) Barron.

Adelman, M. Patent Law Perspectives, 6 vols. 2nd ed. 1970. ring bd. 1280.00 (*0-8205-1532-9*) Bender.

Adelman, Mara B. & Frey, Lawrence R. The Fragile Community: Living Together with AIDS. (Everyday Communication Ser.). 136p. (C). 1996. text 32.50 (*0-8058-1843-X*); pap. text 16.50 (*0-8058-1844-8*) L Erlbaum Assocs.

Adelman, Mara B., jt. auth. see Albrecht, Terrance L.

Adelman, Mara B., jt. auth. see Levine, Deena R.

Adelman, Marcy. Lesbian Passages: True Stories Told by Women over 40. rev. ed. Orig. Title: Long Time Passing: Lives of Older Lesbians. 256p. 1996. pap. text 11.95 (*1-55583-365-9*) Alyson Pubns.

***Adelman, Marcy.** Midlife Lesbian Relationships: Friends, Lovers, Children & Parents. LC 00-31966. 2000. write for info. (*1-56023-142-4*) Harrington Pk.

Adelman, Marilyn M. & Cahill, Eileen M. Atlas of Sperm Morphology. LC 88-7867. (Illus.). 126p. 1989. 75.00 (*0-89189-275-3*) Am Soc Clinical.

Adelman, Mark R. & Johnson, Kurt E. Cell Biology: Review for New National Boards. LC 95-75532. (Illus.). 203p. 1995. pap. 25.00 (*0-9632873-8-9*) J & S Pub VA.

An Asterisk (*) at the beginning of an entry indicates that the title is appearing for the first time.

Adelman, Martin J., et al. Patent Law. LC 98-12716. (Paralegal). 1200p. 1998. text 49.25 (*0-314-06529-6*) West Pub.

Adelman, Melvin L. A Sporting Time: New York City & the Rise of Modern Athletics, 1820-1870. LC 85-13967. (Sport & Society Ser.). (Illus.). 408p. 1986. pap. text 15.95 (*0-252-06121-7*) U of Ill Pr.

Adelman, Morris A. The Economics of Petroleum Supply: Papers by M. A. Adelman 1962-1993. (Illus.). 556p. 1993. 65.00 (*0-262-01138-7*) MIT Pr.

— The Genie Out of the Bottle: World Oil since 1970. LC 95-8271. 350p. 1995. 47.50 (*0-262-01151-4*) MIT Pr.

— The World Petroleum Market. LC 72-4029. (Resources for the Future Ser.). (Illus.). 456p. (C). 1973. 37.00 (*0-8018-1422-7*) Johns Hopkins.

— The World Petroleum Market. LC 72-4029. 458p. reprint ed. pap. 142.00 (*0-7837-2179-X*, 204251700004) Bks Demand.

Adelman, Morris A., ed. A & P: A Study in Price-Cost Behavior & Public Policy. LC 59-14733. (Economic Studies: No. 113). (Illus.). 551p. 1959. 35.00 (*0-674-00050-1*) HUP.

Adelman, Nancy E. Uses of Time for Teaching & Learning. 106p. 1996. pap. 7.50 (*0-16-048870-2*) USGPO.

Adelman, Nancy E., et al. Racing with the Clock: Making Time for Teaching & Learning in School. LC 97-15313. 185p. (Orig.). 1997. text 39.00 (*0-8077-3649-X*); pap. text 17.95 (*0-8077-3648-1*) Tchrs Coll.

Adelman, P., jt. auth. see Vogel, S. A.

Adelman, Paul. The Decline of the Liberal Party, 1910-1931. 2nd ed. LC 95-14646. (Seminar Studies in History). (C). 1995. pap. text 11.25 (*0-582-27733-7*) Addison-Wesley.

— Gladstone Disraeli & Later. 3rd ed. LC 96-29168. (Seminar Studies in History). 144p. (C). 1997. pap. text 14.06 (*0-582-29322-7*, Pub. by Addison-Wesley) Longman.

— Gladstone Disraeli Later. 2nd ed. (C). 1995. pap. text 15.00 (*0-582-35332-7*) Longman.

— PEEL& CONSERVATV 1830 50. (C). 1989. pap. text 13.50 (*0-582-35557-5*) Addison-Wesley.

— Rise of the Labor Party. 3rd ed. (Seminar Studies in History). (C). 1996. pap. text 15.00 (*0-582-29210-7*) Addison-Wesley.

***Adelman, Penina V.** The Bible from Alef to Tav. (Illus.). 185p. (gr. 1-4). 1998. pap. 14.95 (*0-933873-22-0*) Torah Aura.

***Adelman, Phillip J. & Marks, Alan M.** Entrepreneurial Finance: Finance for Small Business. 2nd ed. 384p. 2000. pap. 42.67 (*0-13-085968-0*) P-H.

Adelman, Phillip J. & Marks, Alan M. Small Business Finance. LC 97-8385. 306p. 1997. pap. text 46.00 (*0-13-812983-5*) P-H.

Adelman, Richard C. Handbook of Biochemistry in Aging. Florini, James R., ed. LC 80-23060. (Series in Aging). 320p. 1981. 175.00 (*0-8493-3141-2*, QP86, CRC Reprint) Franklin.

Adelman, Richard C. & Roth, George S. Endocrine & Neuroendocrine Mechanisms of Aging. 232p. 1982. 99.95 (*0-8493-5811-6*, QP187) CRC Pr.

Adelman, Richard C. & Roth, George S., eds. Altered Proteins & Aging. 192p. 1983. 104.00 (*0-8493-5812-4*, QP86) CRC Pr.

— Testing the Theories of Aging. 304p. 1982. 304.00 (*0-8493-5829-9*, QP86, CRC Reprint) Franklin.

Adelman, Richard C., et al. Enzyme Induction in Aging & Protein Synthesis. LC 74-6131. 172p. 1974. text 39.00 (*0-8422-7222-4*) Irvington.

Adelman, Richard C., jt. auth. see Cristofalo, V.

Adelman, Roger M. & Phillips, Richard M. The Securities Enforcement Manual. LC 97-11812. 1997. write for info. (*1-57073-423-2*) Amer Bar Assn.

Adelman, Ronald D., jt. auth. see Breckman, Risa S.

Adelman, S., et al, eds. Automated Telescopes for Photometry & Imaging. (ASP Conference Series Proceedings: Vol. 28). 200p. 1992. 34.00 (*0-937707-47-3*) Astron Soc Pacific.

Adelman, S. J. & Wiese, W. L., eds. Astrophysical Applications of Powerful New Databases. (ASP Conference Series Proceedings: Vol. 78). 546p. 1995. 34.00 (*0-937707-97-X*) Astron Soc Pacific.

Adelman, Sam. From Apartheid to Liberation. (C). 1996. pap. text 18.95 (*0-7453-0512-1*) Westview.

— From Apsrtheid to Liberation. (C). 1996. text 44.00 (*0-7453-0511-3*) Westview.

Adelman, Sammy & Paliwala, Abdul, eds. Law & Crisis in the Third World. (African Discourse Ser.: No. 4). 344p. 1993. 65.00 (*0-905450-88-4*, Pub. by H Zell Pubs) Seven Hills Bk.

Adelman, Saul J., et al, eds. Hot Stars in the Galactic Halo. (Illus.). 404p. (C). 1994. text 74.95 (*0-521-46087-5*) Cambridge U Pr.

— Mass, Model Atmospheres & Spectrum Synthesis, Vol. 108. (ASP Conference Series Proceedings). 336p. 1996. 34.00 (*1-886733-28-7*) Astron Soc Pacific.

Adelman, Seymour. Rosenwald & Rosenbach: Two Philadelphia Bookmen. (Illus.). 40p. 1983. pap. 10.00 (*0-939084-15-5*) R Mus & Lib.

***Adelman, Todd & Behrend, Jodi.** Special Foods for Special Kids: Practical Solutions & Great Recipes for Children with Food Allergies. LC 99-67838. (Illus.). 160p. (ps up). 2000. pap. 16.95 (*1-885003-38-2*, Pub. by R D Reed Pubs) Midpt Trade.

Adelman, Urban, tr. see Jone, Heribert.

Adelman, William. Haymarket Revisited. (Illus.). 136p. 1976. 15.00 (*0-916884-08-2*) Ill Labor Hist Soc.

— Haymarket Revisited. (Illus.). 136p. 1986. pap. 5.95 (*0-916884-03-1*) Ill Labor Hist Soc.

— Haymarket Revisited: A Tour Guide & History. 140p. 1986. pap. 10.00 (*0-88286-197-2*) C H Kerr.

— Pilsen & the West Side. (Illus.). 100p. 1983. pap. 7.95 (*0-685-02463-6*) Ill Labor Hist Soc.

— Touring Pullman. 3rd ed. LC 72-80226. 46p. 1993. pap. 4.95 (*0-916884-05-8*) Ill Labor Hist Soc.

Adelman, William J., Jr. & Goldman, David E., eds. The Biophysical Approach to Excitable Systems: A Volume in Honor of Kenneth S. Cole on His 80th Birthday. LC 81-15759. 270p. 1981. 65.00 (*0-306-40784-1*, Plenum Trade) Perseus Pubng.

Adelman, Y., ed. see Rosenberg, A. J.

Adelmann. Soviet Philosophy Revisited. (Boston College Studies in Philosophy: No. 5). 104p. 1977. pap. text 94.00 (*90-247-1977-1*, Pub. by M Nijhoff) Kluwer Academic.

Adelmann, Arllys, jt. ed. see Whealy, Kent.

Adelmann, Dale. The Contribution of Cambridge Ecclesiologists to the Revival of Anglican Choral Worship, 1839-62. LC 97-39983. (Music in Nineteenth-Century Britain Ser.). 264p. 1998. text 74.95 (*1-85928-389-6*, Pub. by Ashgate Pub) Ashgate Pub Co.

Adelmann, F. J. Contemporary Chinese Philosophy. 1982. text 106.00 (*90-247-3057-0*) Kluwer Academic.

— Philosophical Investigations in the U. S. S. R. (Boston College Studies in Philosophy: No. 4). 146p. 1975. pap. text 71.50 (*90-247-1724-8*) Kluwer Academic.

Adelmann, F. J., ed. Authority. (Boston College Studies in Philosophy: No. 3). 131p. 1974. pap. text 57.00 (*90-247-1594-6*, Pub. by M Nijhoff) Kluwer Academic.

***Adelmann, G., et al, eds.** Ionotropic Glutamate Receptors in the CNS. LC 99-46477. (Handbook of Experimental Pharmacology Ser.: Vol. 141). (Illus.). 460p. 2000. 299.00 (*3-540-66120-4*) Spr-Verlag.

Adelmann, Howard B. Marcello Malpighi & the Evolution of Embryology, 5 vols. (Publications in the History of Science). (Illus.). 2548p. 1966. boxed set 250.00 (*0-8014-0004-X*) Cornell U Pr.

Adelmeyer, Moritz, jt. auth. see Iooss, Gerard.

Adelo, Samuel, tr. see Ruiz, Joseph J.

Adelphi. Modern Condition. 8th ed. 278p. (C). 1998. pap. text 24.75 (*0-536-01403-5*) Pearson Custom.

Adelphi-AIESEP 85 World Sport Conference (1985: Ad. Myths, Models, & Methods in Sport Pedagogy. Barrette, Gary T. et al, eds. LC 86-20094. (Illus.). 284p. 1987. reprint ed. pap. 88.10 (*0-608-06449-1*, 206728700009) Bks Demand.

Adelphus, Johannes. Johannes Adelphus: Ausgewaehlte Schriften, 3 vols, Vol. 1. Gotzkowsky, Bodo, ed. (Ausgaben Deutscher Literatur des XV bis XVIII Jahrhunderts Ser.). (C). 1974. 253.85 (*3-11-003382-8*) De Gruyter.

— Johannes Adelphus: Ausgewaehlte Schriften, 3 vols, Vol. 2. Gotzkowsky, Bodo, ed. (Ausgaben Deutscher Literatur des XV bis XVIII Jahrhunderts Ser.). (C). 1980. 269.25 (*3-11-007896-1*) De Gruyter.

— Johannes Adelphus: Ausgewaehlte Schriften, 3 vols, Vol. 3. Gotzkowsky, Bodo, ed. (Ausgaben Deutscher Literatur des XV bis XVIII Jahrhunderts Ser.). (C). 1980. 280.75 (*3-11-007897-X*) De Gruyter.

Adels, Jill H. The Wisdom of the Saints: An Anthology. 256p. 1989. reprint ed. pap. 16.95 (*0-19-505915-8*) OUP.

Adelsayed, Cindy. Connections to the Heart. (Illus.). 32p. (J). 1999. 22.95 (*1-57532-179-3*); pap. 11.99 (*1-57532-178-5*) Press-Tige Pub.

Adelsberg, David Van, see Van Adelsberg, David.

Adelsberger, Heimo H., et al, eds. Information Management in Computer Integrated Manufacturing: A Comprehensive Guide to State-of-the-Art CIM Solutions, Vol. IX. LC 95-25002. (Lecture Notes in Computer Science Ser.: Vol. 973). 665p. 1995. 79.00 (*3-540-60286-0*) Spr-Verlag.

Adelsberger, Lucie. Auschwitz: A Doctor's Story. Ray, Susan, tr. from GER. LC 95-20764. (Women's Life Writings from Around the World Ser.). 1995. text 26.95 (*1-55553-233-0*) NE U Pr.

Adelson, Alan & Lapides, Robert, eds. Lodz Ghetto: Inside a Community under Siege - Educational Package. (Illus.). 526p. 1989. text 59.95 (*0-9660440-2-9*, Jewish Herit Bks) Jewish Heritage.

Adelson, Alan, ed. see Sierakowiak, Dawid.

Adelson, Bruce. Brushing Back Jim Crow: The Integration of the Minor Leagues in the American South. LC 98-45122. (Illus.). 288p. 1999. 27.95 (*0-8139-1884-7*) U Pr of Va.

***Adelson, Bruce.** The Composite Guide to Field Hockey. LC 99-86455. (Illus.). 2000. pap. 5.95 (*0-7910-5872-7*) Chelsea Hse.

— The Composite Guide to Softball. LC 99-85979. (J). 2000. 16.95 (*0-7910-5867-0*) Chelsea Hse.

— Field Hockey. (Composite Guides Ser.). (Illus.). 2000. 16.95 (*0-7910-5863-8*) Chelsea Hse.

Adelson, Bruce. Grand Slam Trivia. LC 97-42297. (Sports Trivia Ser.). (Illus.). 64p. (J). 1998. pap. write for info. (*0-8225-9803-5*); lib. bdg. 23.95 (*0-8225-3314-6*) Lerner Pub.

— Hat Trick Trivia. LC 97-48485. (Illus.). (J). 1998. 22.60 (*0-8225-3315-4*) Lerner Pub.

— Hat Trick Trivia. LC 97-48485. (Illus.). 64p. (J). (gr. 4-8). 1998. pap. 6.95 (*0-8225-9806-X*, Lerner Publctns) Lerner Pub.

— Slam Dunk Trivia. LC 97-50006. (Illus.). (J). 1998. 22.60 (*0-8225-3313-8*) Lerner Pub.

— Slam Dunk Trivia. LC 97-50006. (Illus.). 64p. (J). (gr. 4-8). 1998. pap. 6.95 (*0-8225-9804-3*, Lerner Publctns) Lerner Pub.

***Adelson, Bruce.** Softball. LC 99-85979. (Composite Guides Ser.). (Illus.). 2000. pap. 5.95 (*0-7910-5876-X*) Chelsea Hse.

Adelson, Bruce. Touchdown Trivia. LC 97-46447. (Illus.). (J). 1998. 16.95 (*0-8225-3312-X*) Lerner Pub.

— Touchdown Trivia. LC 97-46447. (Lerner Sports Trivia Ser.). (Illus.). 64p. (J). 1998. pap. text 6.95 (*0-8225-9805-1*) Lerner Pub.

Adelson, Daniel, ed. Man As the Measure: The Crossroads. LC 77-184153. (Community Psychology Ser.: Vol. I). 146p. 1972. 35.95 (*0-87705-058-9*, Kluwer Acac Hman Sci) Kluwer Academic.

Adelson, Glenn, jt. auth. see Perlman, Dan L.

Adelson-Goldstein, Jayme. Listen First. (Illus.). 96p. 1991. pap. text, student ed. 9.95 (*0-19-434422-3*) OUP

— Real-Life English Bk. 2: A Competency-Based ESL Program for Adults. 1994. pap. text, student ed. 1.96 (*0-8114-3213-0*) Raintree Steck-V.

Adelson-Goldstein, Jayme. Real-Life English Bk. 2: A Competency-Based ESL Program for Adults. 1994. pap. 11.96 (*0-8114-3214-9*) Raintree Steck-V.

Adelson-Goldstein, Jayme, et al. The Basic Oxford Picture Dictionary. (Illus.). 112p. 1994. pap. text, student ed., wbk. ed. 7.95 (*0-19-434567-X*) OUP.

— The Basic Oxford Picture Dictionary: Picture Cards. 1994. 29.95 (*0-19-434565-3*) OUP.

— The New Oxford Picture Dictionary: Listening & Speaking Activity Book. (Illus.). 206p. 1993. pap. text 19.95 (*0-19-434365-0*) OUP.

Adelson-Goldstein, Jayme, jt. auth. see Creighton, Ann.

Adelson-Goldstein, Jayme, jt. auth. see Shapiro, Norma.

Adelson, Howard L. American Numismatic Society 1858-1958. (Illus.). 390p. 1958. 35.00 (*0-89722-045-5*) Am Numismatic.

Adelson, Joseph. Inventing Adolescence: The Political Psychology of Everyday Schooling. 320p. (C). 1985. 39.95 (*0-88738-026-3*) Transaction Pubs.

Adelson, Leslie A. Making Bodies, Making History: Feminism & German Identity. LC 92-37873. (Modern German Culture & Literature Ser.). xvi, 197p. (C) 1993. text 40.00 (*0-8032-1036-1*) U of Nebr Pr.

Adelson, Leslie A., tr. see Senocak, Zafer.

Adelson, Lester. The Pathology of Homicide: A Vade Mecum for Pathologist, Prosecutor & Defense Counsel. fac. ed. (Illus.). 992p. 1974. 141.95 (*0-398-03000-5*) C C Thomas.

Adelson, Robert G. Loran Cruise Plans: For Long Island Sound, Block Island Sound & Newport, Rhode Island, Vol. 2. 1986. 59.95 (*0-9615134-1-1*) Am Marine Corp.

— Loran Cruise Plans: For Massachusetts, Rhode Island, Cape Cod & the Islands, Vol. 1. 1985. 59.95 (*0-9615134-0-3*) Am Marine Corp.

Adelson, Roger. London & the Middle East: Money, Power, & War, 1902-1922. LC 94-36262. (Illus.). 320p. 1995. 42.50 (*0-300-06094-7*) Yale U Pr.

Adelson, Roger, ed. Speaking of History: Conversations with Historians, 1990-1995. LC 96-53683. (Illus.). 230p. (Orig.). 1997. pap. 18.95 (*0-87013-464-7*) Mich St U Pr.

Adelson-Velsky, G. M., jt. auth. see Kuznetsov, O. P.

Adelson, Warren, et al. Childe Hassam, Impressionist. LC 99-19610. 256p. 1999. 75.00 (*0-7892-0587-4*) Abbeville Pr.

— Sargent Abroad: Figures & Landscapes. LC 97-10517. (Illus.). 256p. 1997. 75.00 (*0-7892-0384-7*) Abbeville Pr.

***Adelsperger, Charlotte.** Through the Generations: The Unique Call of Motherhood. 20 bks. 2000. pap. 69.30 (*0-8341-1795-9*) Beacon Hill.

***Adelsperger, Charlotte & Hayes, Karen.** Through the Generations: The Unique Call of Motherhood. LC 99-44974. 56p. 2000. pap. 3.49 (*0-8341-1868-8*) Beacon Hill.

Adelstein. Business Communication in the Information Age. 1988. text 58.25 (*0-15-308501-0*) Holt R&W.

Adelstein, Amy. The Arts. LC 95-10243. (African American Life Ser.). 48p. (J). (gr. 4-6). 1995. lib. bdg. 23.93 (*1-57103-028-X*) Rourke Pr.

— Money. LC 97-6365. (Money & Me Ser.). 48p. (J). (gr. 3-8). 1998. lib. bdg. 22.60 (*0-86625-611-3*) Rourke Pubns.

Adelstein, James, ed. see Brill, A. Bertrand.

Adelstein, Michael. The Business of Better Writing. Samuels, Betty, ed. 200p. 1984. 36.00 (*0-910475-04-0*) KET.

— Business of Better Writing. Incl. Exercises to Lesson 1. 19p. 1984. pap. 3.00 (*0-910475-09-1*); Exercises to Lesson 2. 14p. 1984. pap. 3.00 (*0-910475-10-5*); Exercises to Lesson 3. 12p. 1984. pap. 3.00 (*0-910475-11-3*); Exercises to Lesson 4. 16p. 1984. pap. 3.00 (*0-910475-12-1*); 1984. pap. write for info. (*0-318-59006-9*) KET.

Adelstein, Michael E. Fanny Burney. LC 68-24282. (English Authors Ser.). 1968. lib. bdg. 20.95 (*0-8057-1072-8*) Irvington.

Adelstein, Michael E. & Pival, Jean G. The Reading Commitment. 2nd ed. 390p. (C). 1982. teacher ed. write for info. (*0-318-52975-0*) Harcourt Coll Pubs.

— The Writing Commitment. 5th ed. LC 91-78064. (Illus.). 624p. (C). 1993. reprint ed. text 44.50 (*0-15-500167-1*, Pub. by Harcourt Coll Pubs); reprint ed. pap. text 4.50 (*0-15-500302-X*) Harcourt Coll Pubs.

Adelstein, Michael E. & Sparrow, W. Keats. Business Communications. 2nd ed. 480p. (C). 1990. pap. text, teacher ed. 5.00 (*0-15-505609-3*) Dryden Pr.

Adelstein, Miriam, ed. Studies on the Works of Jose Donoso: An Anthology of Critical Essays. LC 89-13564. (Hispanic Literature Ser.: Vol. 5). 208p. 1990. lib. bdg. 89.95 (*0-88946-390-5*) E Mellen.

Adelstein, Robert S., ed. see International Conference on Cyclic Nucleotide Staf.

Adelstein, Robert S., ed. see Sixth International Conference on Cyclic Nucleotid.

Adelstein, S. James, ed. see Institute of Medicine, Committee on Biomedical Iso.

Adem, Alejandro. Group Representations: Cohomology, Group Actions, & Topology: Summer Research Institute on Cohomology, Representations, & Actions of Finite Groups, July 7-27, 1996, University of Washington, Seattle. LC 97-39874. 532p. 1997. text 99.00 (*0-8218-0658-0*) Am Math.

Adem, Alejandro, et al, eds. Homotopy Theory & Its Applications: A Conference on Algebraic Topology, August 9-13, 1993, Cocoyoc, Mexico. LC 95-15011. (Contemporary Mathematics Ser.: Vol. 188). 229p. 1995. pap. 49.00 (*0-8218-0305-0*, CONM/188) Am Math.

Adem, Alejandro & Milgram, Richard J. Cohomology of Finite Groups. LC 94-13318. (Grundlehren der Mathematischen Wisseschaften Ser.: Vol. 309). 1994. 103.95 (*0-387-57025-X*) Spr-Verlag.

Adema. Guillaume Apollinaire. 24.95 (*0-685-37180-8*, F82380) Fr & Eur.

Adema, ed. see Apollinaire, Guillaume.

Adema, F. & Radlk, Cupaniopsis. Sapindaceae: A Monograph. (Leiden Botanical Ser.: Vol. 15). (Illus.). 190p. 1991. pap. 37.00 (*90-71236-10-2*, Pub. by Rijksherbarium) Balogh.

Adema, Thomas J. Our Hills & Valleys: A History of the Helix-Spring Valley Region. LC 93-36144. (Illus.). 196p. (Orig.). 1993. pap. 14.95 (*0-918740-15-0*) San Diego Hist.

Ademola, Iyi-Eweka. Ibota: A Collection of Folk Tales from Benin. LC 96-92487. 61p. (Orig.). 1996. pap. 10.00 (*0-9656365-0-X*) Ogiso Pubn-Commun.

Ademola, Toye. Your Destiny Is in Your Hands. LC 99-165832. 181p. 1998. write for info. (*1-56043-213-6*) Destiny Image.

Ademuni-Odeke. Bareboat & Charter (Ship) Registration. LC 97-35077. 684p. 1998. 197.00 (*90-411-0513-1*) Kluwer Law Intl.

***Ademuni-Odeke.** Law of International Trade. 413p. 1999. pap. 44.00 (*1-85431-937-X*, 18459, Pub. by Blackstone Pr) Gaunt.

Ademuni-Odeke. Protectionism & the Future of International Shipping: The Nature, Development & Role of Flag Discriminations & Preferences, Cargo Reservations & Sabotage Restrictions, State Intervention & Maritime Subsidies. LC 83-25055. 1984. lib. bdg. 215.50 (*90-247-2918-1*) Kluwer Academic.

Ademuni-Odeke, Dr. Shipping in International Trade Relations. 600p. 1988. text 142.95 (*0-566-05371-3*, Pub. by Dartmth Pub) Ashgate Pub Co.

Aden, et al. Electronic Countermeasures. Boyd et al, eds. LC 78-69599. 1100p. 1978. reprint ed. 54.00 (*0-932146-00-7*) Peninsula CA.

Aden, John M. Pope's Once & Future Kings: Satire & Politics in the Early Career. LC 78-16618. 232p. reprint ed. pap. 72.00 (*0-8357-6538-5*, 203590000097) Bks Demand.

Aden, Paul. The Hosta Book. 2nd ed. LC 92-17024. (Illus.). 133p. 1992. pap. 19.95 (*0-88192-260-9*) Timber.

Aden, Roger C. Popular Stories & Promised Lands: Fan Cultures & Symbolic Pilgrimages. LC 98-19755. (Studies in Rhetoric & Communication). 26p. 1999. pap. 34.95 (*0-8173-0938-1*) U of Ala Pr.

Adenaike, Carolyn Keyes & Vansina, Jan. In Pursuit of History: Fieldwork in Africa. LC 96-30779. (Social History of Africa Ser.). 1996. 60.00 (*0-435-08990-0*, 08990); pap. 26.95 (*0-435-08992-7*, 08992) Heinemann.

Adenau, Debra, ed. Abstracts from Extramural Grant Program Meeting: Abstracts. (Journal Ser.: Vol. 14, Suppl. 1, 1996). (Illus.). viii, 112p. 1996. pap., suppl. ed. 36.50 (*3-8055-6284-5*) S Karger.

— Extramural Grant Program Meeting, Chicago, Illinois, June 1994, Abstracts Vol. 13, No. 1-2: Abstracts. (Journal Ser.: Vol. 13, No. 1 - 2, 1994). (Illus.). 106p. 1995. pap. 48.00 (*3-8055-6117-2*) S Karger.

— Extramural Grant Program 1996 Chicago, June 1996: Abstracts. (Journal: Vol. 15, Suppl. 1, 1997). (Illus.). xii, 130p. 1997. pap. 42.75 (*3-8055-6510-0*) S Karger.

Adenau, Debra L., ed. Extramural Grant Program, 1997: Chicago, June 1997 - Abstracts. (Blood Purification Ser.: Vol. 16, Suppl. 1, 1998). (Illus.). vi, 122p. 1998. pap. 39.25 (*3-8055-6676-X*) S Karger.

Adeney, Bernard T. Just War, Political Realism, & Faith. LC 88-16605. (American Theological Library Association Monograph: No. 24). 237p. 1988. 35.00 (*0-8108-2152-4*) Scarecrow.

— Strange Virtues: Ethics in Multicultural Perspective. 281p. (Orig.). 1995. pap. 19.99 (*0-8308-1855-3*, 1855) InterVarsity.

Adeney, Douglas, jt. auth. see Weckert, John.

Adeney, Miriam. How to Write. 56p. 1994. reprint ed. pap. 5.95 (*1-57383-028-3*) Regent College.

Adeney, Walter F. The Greek & Eastern Churches. LC 65-22087. (Library of Religious & Philosophical Thought). xiv, 634p. 1966. reprint ed. lib. bdg. 57.50 (*0-678-09951-0*, Reference Bk Pubs) Kelley.

Adeniji, P. Bodunrin. Lessons of History for the Nigerian Republic & Other World Essays. LC 98-61098. (Illus.). 72p. 1998. pap. 9.95 (*1-890306-13-4*) Warwick Hse.

***Adenle, Tola.** Deeper by a Tear: A Collection of Short Stories. LC 00-190179. 2000. 25.00 (*0-7388-1494-6*); pap. 18.00 (*0-7388-1495-4*) Xlibris Corp.

Adeoye, Oladimeji. The Morning of a Coup: The Dictatorship of Nigeria's Ibrahim B. Babamgida. 192p. (Orig.). 1995. pap. 19.95 (*1-886094-14-4*) Chicago Spectrum.

Adepoju, Aderanti, ed. The Impact of Structural Adjustment on the Population of Africa: The Implications for Education, Health & Employment. LC 93-20329. 148p. (C). 1993. pap. 25.00 (*0-435-08970-6*, 08970) Heinemann.

— Population & the Family: The Development Process in Africa. 240p. (C). 1996. text 59.95 (*1-85649-465-9*, Pub. by Zed Books); text 22.50 (*1-85649-466-7*) Zed Books.

Adepoju, Aderanti & Oppong, Christine. Gender, Work & Population in Sub-Saharan Africa. LC 93-50628. 245p. 1994. 45.00 (*0-435-08953-6*, 08953) Heinemann.

Ader, Bas Jan, et al. Bas Jan Ader. LC 98-56383. 72p. 2000. pap. 25.00 (*1-884355-04-8*, Pub. by U CA Fine Arts) Dist Art Pubs.

A

A

Ader, Michael J. & Wasch, William K. Understanding Medicare HMOS. (Illus.). 32p. (Orig.). 1997. pap. 9.95 (*1-890074-04-7*) CapitalHlth Pub.

Ader, Paul. The Big Win. 180p. 1984. 40.00 (*0-946270-04-X*, Pub. by Pentland Pr) St Mut.

— The Commander. 1985. 20.00 (*0-946270-19-8*, Pub. by Pentland Pr); pap. 15.00 (*0-946270-21-X*, Pub. by Pentland Pr) St Mut.

Ader, Robert, et al, eds. Psychoneuroimmunology. 2nd ed. 1218p. 1990. text 210.00 (*0-12-043782-1*) Acad Pr.

Ader, Robert, et al. Experimental Foundations of Behavioral Medicine: Conditioning Approaches. (Perspectives in Behavioral Medicine Ser.). 240p. 1988. 59.95 (*0-8058-0139-1*) L Erlbaum Assocs.

Adera, Edith Ofwona, jt. auth. see Rathgeber, Eva M.

Adera, Taddesse & Ahmed, Ali J., eds. Silence Is Not Golden: A Critical Anthology of Ethiopian Literature. 222p. (C). 1994. 49.95 (*0-932415-46-6*); pap. 16.95 (*0-932415-47-4*) Red Sea Pr.

Adereth, Max. Elsa Triolet & Louis Aragon: An Introduction to Their Interwoven Lives & Works. LC 93-42850. (Studies in French Literature: Vol. 17). 504p. 1994. text 119.95 (*0-7734-9647-5*) E Mellen.

Aderholdt, Kristel. Boredom Rx. (Illus.). 144p. (J). (gr. 1-8). 1991. 29.95 (*0-937857-19-X*, 1583) Speech Bin.

Aderkas, P. von, see Bonga, J. M. & Von Aderkas, P.

Aderman, James. Challenging Christianity: Leader's Guide. Fischer, William E., ed. (Bible Class Course for Young Adults Ser.). 48p. 1986. pap., student ed. 7.50 (*0-938272-25-X*, 22-2182) WELS Board.

— I'm Listening, Lord: Leader's Guide. Fischer, William E., ed. (Bible Class Course for Young Adults Ser.). 64p. 1984. pap. text 7.50 (*0-938272-19-5*, 22-2165) WELS Board.

— Is He the One? Fischer, William E., ed. (Bible Class Course for Young Adults Ser.). (Illus.). 64p. (J). (gr. 9-12). 1985. pap., student ed. 5.00 (*0-938272-20-9*, 22-2170) WELS Board.

Aderman, James & Fischer, William E. Challenging Christianity: Student's Guide. (Bible Class Course for Young Adults Ser.). (Illus.). 40p. 1986. pap., student ed. 4.00 (*0-938272-24-1*, 22-2181) WELS Board.

Aderman, James A. Face the Facts. LC 92-80013. 96p. (Orig.). 1992. pap. 9.99 (*0-8100-0425-9*, 12N1757) Northwest Pub.

— A Survival Guide to the Last Times. Fischer, William E., ed. (Bible Class Course for Young Adults Ser.). (Illus.). 36p. 1987. pap. text, student ed. 4.00 (*0-938272-30-6*, 22-2194) WELS Board.

— You Can't Lose. Fischer, William E., ed. (Bible Class Course for Young Adults Ser.). (Illus.). 36p. (Orig.). 1987. pap., teacher ed. 7.50 (*0-938272-28-4*, 22-2193); student ed. 4.00 (*0-938272-29-2*, 22-2192) WELS Board.

Aderman, James A. & Kelm, Paul E. I-Questions God Answers, Course 2. (Bible Class Course for Young Adults Ser.). (Illus.). 56p. 1989. pap. text, teacher ed. 7.50 (*0-938272-39-X*, 22-2219) WELS Board.

Aderman, Ralph M. Critical Essays of Washington Irving. (Critical Essays on American Literature Ser.). 280p. (C). 1990. 48.00 (*0-8161-8896-3*, G K Hall & Co) Mac Lib Ref.

Aderman, Ralph M., et al, eds. Letters of Washington Irving, 1839-1846, Vol. III. (Critical Editions Program Ser.). (C). 1982. 60.00 (*0-8057-8524-8*, Twyne) Mac Lib Ref.

Aderman, Ralph M., ed. see Irving, Washington.

Aderman, Ralph M., ed. see Rebreanu, Liviu.

Adero, Malaika, ed. Up South: Stories, Studies, & Letters of This Century's African American Migrations. LC 92-53733. (Illus.). 238p. 1994. pap. 12.95 (*1-56584-168-9*, Pub. by New Press NY) Norton.

Aders, Gebhard & Held, Werner. Stuka Dive Bombers-Pursuit Bombers-Combat Pilots - A Pictorial Chronicle of German Close-Combat Aircraft to 1945. LC 89-63368. (Illus.). 248p. 1990. 29.95 (*0-88740-216-X*) Schiffer.

Ades, Dawn. Art in Latin America: The Modern Era, 1820-1980. (Art - Latin American Studies). (Illus.). 384p. (C). 1989. 70.00 (*0-300-04556-5*) Yale U Pr.

— Art in Latin America: The Modern Era, 1820-1980. (Art - Latin American Studies). (Illus.). 384p. (C). 1993. pap. 35.00 (*0-300-04561-1*) Yale U Pr.

— Art Unsolved: The Outsider Collection with Essays by Dawn Ades & John Thompson. (Illus.). 120p. 1998. 35.00 (*0-85331-772-0*) Lund Humphries.

— Dali. 2nd rev. ed. LC 94-61060. (World of Art Ser.). (Illus.). 216p. 1995. pap. 14.95 (*0-500-20280-X*, Pub. by Thames Hudson) Norton.

***Ades, Dawn.** Dali's Optical Illusions. LC 99-38348. (Illus.). 208p. 1999. 45.00 (*0-300-08177-4*) Yale U Pr.

Ades, Dawn. Photomontage. rev. ed. LC 86-50313. (World of Art Ser.). (Illus.). 180p. 1986. reprint ed. pap. 14.95 (*0-500-20208-7*, Pub. by Thames Hudson) Norton.

— A Surreal Life: Edward James. 55.00 (*0-85667-493-1*, Pub. by P Wilson) Scala Books.

— Surrealist Art: The Lindy & Edwin Bergman Collection at the Art Institute of Chicago. Andreotti, Margherita & Jolles, Adam, eds. LC 96-61200. (World of Art Ser.). (Illus.). 246p. 1997. pap. 34.95 (*0-500-23711-5*, Pub. by Thames Hudson) Norton.

Ades, Dawn & Bradley, Fiona, eds. Salvador Dali: A Mythology. (Illus.). 168p. 1998. pap. 29.95 (*0-9660353-1-3*) S Dali Mus.

— Salvador Dali: A Mythology. (Illus.). 268p. 1998. pap. 35.00 (*1-85437-259-9*, Pub. by Tate Gallery) U of Wash Pr.

Ades, Dawn, et al. Marcel Duchamp. LC 98-61434. (World of Art Ser.). (Illus.). 224p. 1999. pap. 14.95 (*0-500-20322-9*, Pub. by Thames Hudson) Norton.

— The 20th-Century Poster: Design of the Avant-Garde. rev. ed. Friedman, Mildred, ed. (Illus.). 220p. 1990. reprint ed. pap. 29.95 (*1-55859-130-3*) Abbeville Pr.

Ades, E. W., jt. auth. see Highsmith, A.

Ades, Edwin W., et al, eds. Microbial Pathogenesis & Immune Response II: Proceedings of a New York Academy of Sciences Conference, October 25-28, 1995, Vol. 797. 1996. 90.00 (*1-57331-016-6*) NY Acad Sci.

Ades, Edwin W. & Lopez, C., eds. Natural Killer Cells & Host Defense. (Illus.). xiv, 302p. 1989. 256.75 (*3-8055-4791-9*) S Karger.

Ades, Hawley. Choral Arranging, Expanded Edition. 1983. 22.95 (*0-686-46895-3*, M224) Shawnee Pr.

Ades, John I. The Pizza Plot: And a Few Other Slices from Life. LC 88-37409. 160p. (Orig.). 1989. pap. 8.95 (*0-931832-22-5*) Fithian Pr.

Ades, Lisa, ed. see Burns, Ric & Sanders, James.

Ades, Lola. Floral Bouquets. (How to Draw & Paint Ser.). (Illus.). 32p. (Orig.). 1989. pap. 6.95 (*1-56010-036-2*, HT-218) W Foster Pub.

— How to Draw & Paint Flowers & Designs to Copy. (How to Draw & Paint Ser.). (Illus.). 32p. (Orig.). pap. 6.95 (*0-929261-22-4*, HT 157) W Foster Pub.

— Roses & Floral Bouquets. (How to Draw & Paint Ser.). (Illus.). 32p. (Orig.). 1989. pap. 6.95 (*0-929261-88-7*, HT214) W Foster Pub.

— Roses & Other Flowers. (How to Draw & Paint Ser.). (Illus.). 32p. (Orig.). 1989. pap. 6.95 (*0-929261-19-4*, HT130) W Foster Pub.

— Small Paintings That Sell. (How to Draw & Paint Ser.). (Illus.). 32p. (Orig.). 1989. pap. 6.95 (*0-929261-46-1*, HT201) W Foster Pub.

***Ades, Maurice, ed.** Industrial & Business Simulation Symposium. 220p. 1999. pap. 80.00 (*1-56555-167-2*) Soc Computer Sim.

Ades, Maurice & Fray, Roy, eds. Simulators International XIV Held in Atlanta, Georgia - April 1997. (Simulation Ser.: Vol. 29, No. 3). 286p. 1998. 120.00 (*1-56555-121-4*, SS-29-4) Soc Computer Sim.

Ades, Maurice & Griebenow, Ron, eds. Simulators International, Vol. 12. 290p. 1996. 120.00 (*1-56555-092-7*, SS-28-2) Soc Computer Sim.

***Ades, Maurice & Griebenow, Ron, eds.** Simulators International XV. Vol. 30. 305p. 1998. 50.00 (*1-56555-144-3*) Soc Computer Sim.

Ades, Maurice & Sharon, Ariel, eds. Simulators International, Vol. 12. 382p. 1995. 120.00 (*1-56555-049-8*, SS-27-3) Soc Computer Sim.

***Ades, Michael L., et al.** Land Use, Zoning & Private Controls on Real Estate. 3rd ed. 278p. 1998. pap. 48.00 (*1-58757-020-3*, GM028) Univ of KY.

Adesegun, T. Nokwari, ed. see Afrika, Llaila O.

Adeshina, R. Fola. My Survival As an African in America: A Story of My Struggle. Ford, Noni, ed. LC 96-107110. (Illus.). 152p. (Orig.). 1995. pap. text 12.95 (*0-9645896-0-5*) R F Adeshina.

Adesman, Marshall, jt. auth. see Holaday, J. Chris.

Adess, Nancy, ed. see Stallings, Betty & McMillion, Donna.

Adess, Nancy F., ed. see Evens, Jules G.

Adessa, Marea. Ladybug Porches & Seagulls in the Sky: Poems of Childhood. LC 89-81087. (Illus.). 70p. (Orig.). 1989. pap. 9.95 (*0-9624708-0-5*) Chesterworks Babcock.

Adesso, Vincent J. Psychological Perspectives on Women's Health. 360p. 1994. 27.95 (*1-56032-335-3*) Hemisp Pub.

Adeva, B. Electroweak Interactions, Neutrinos & QCD. 350p. 1999. 112.00 (*981-02-3940-8*) World Scientific Pub.

Adewale, Fama A. 1,000+ (African) Orisa - Yoruba Names. LC 98-91283. (ENG & YOR.). 200p. 1998. pap. 16.95 (*0-9644247-5-4*) ILE Orunmila.

Adewale-Somadhi, Aina. Fama's Ede Awo (Orisa Yoruba Dictionary) (YOR.). 200p. (Orig.). (C). 1996. pap. 19.95 (*0-9644247-3-8*) ILE Orunmila.

Adewale-Somadhi, F. A. & Somadhi, Ifabowale. Fundamentals of the Yoruba Religion (Orisa Worship) LC 94-79855. (Illus.). 251p. (Orig.). 1995. pap. 19.95 (*0-9644247-0-3*) ILE Orunmila.

Adewunm, jt. auth. see Osuntogun.

Adewunmi, Wole, jt. ed. see Osuntogun, Adeniyi.

***Adewusi, Olukemi, et al.** General Biology Lab Manual. 242p. (C). 1999. spiral bd., wbk. ed. 25.95 (*0-7872-6427-X*, 41642701) Kendall-Hunt.

Adey, A. D. & Andrew, M. G. Getting It Right: The Manager's Guide to Business Communication. 413p. 1993. reprint ed. pap. 37.00 (*0-7021-2453-2*, Pub. by Juta & Co) Intl Spec Bk.

Adey, Christopher. Orchestral Performance: A Guide for Conductors &Players. 450p. 1998. pap. 42.95 (*0-571-17724-7*) Faber & Faber.

Adey, Lionel. C. S. Lewis: Writer, Dreamer & Mentor. LC 97-46080. 312p. 1998. pap. 22.00 (*0-8028-4203-8*) Eerdmans.

Adey, Margaret & Albini, Louis. Galeria de Arte y Vida, Vol. 4. (SPA.). 1997. teacher ed. write for info. (*0-02-676596-9*) Glencoe.

— Tesoro Literario, Vol. 5. (SPA.). 1997. teacher ed. write for info. (*0-02-646512-4*) Glencoe.

Adey, Margaret, et al. Galeria Hispanica. 3rd ed. (Illus.). 1979. text 36.60 (*0-07-000361-0*) McGraw.

Adey, Philip, jt. auth. see Shayer, Michael.

Adey, R. A., et al, eds. Applications of Artificial Intelligence in Engineering X. 608p. 1995. 287.00 (*1-85312-316-1*) Computational Mech MA.

Adey, R. A., et al, eds. Applications of Artificial Intelligence in Engineering XII. annuals LC 97-67015. (AIENG Ser.: Vol. 12). 184p. 1997. 295.00 incl. cd-rom (*1-85312-471-0*, 4710) Computational Mech MA.

Adey, R. A., et al, eds. Simulation & Design of Microsystems & Microstructures. 350p. 1995. 183.00 (*1-85312-390-0*) Computational Mech MA.

Adey, R. A. & Renaud, P., eds. MICROSIM II: Simulation & Design of Microsystems & Microstructures. LC 97-67021. (MICROSIM Ser.: Vol. 2). 296p. 1997. 145.00 (*1-85312-501-6*, 5016) Computational Mech MA.

Adey, Robert. Locked Room Murders. 411p. 1994. 45.00 (*0-9628870-0-5*) Crossover Pr.

Adey, Robert A., ed. Engineering Software IV. 1200p. 1985. 135.00 (*0-931215-49-8*) Computational Mech MA.

— Engineering Software IV. 1200p. 1985. 149.00 (*0-685-10803-1*) Spr-Verlag.

— Parallel Processing in Engineering Applications: Proceedings of the First International Conference on Parallel Processing for Computational Mechanics, Southampton, 4-6 September 1990. 256p. 1990. 77.00 (*0-387-52962-4*) Spr-Verlag.

— Software for Engineering. (Progress in Engineering Ser.). 113p. 1985. pap. 46.00 (*0-931215-04-8*) Computational Mech MA.

— Software for Engineering Problems III. LC 90-81260. (Progress in Engineering Ser.). 184p. 1993. pap. text 75.00 (*0-945824-31-9*, 0480) Computational Mech MA.

Adey, Robert A., et al, eds. Applications of Artificial Intelligence in Engineering IX. LC 94-70403. (AIENG Ser.). 632p. 1994. 299.00 (*1-56252-208-6*, 284X) Computational Mech MA.

— Applications of Artificial Intelligence in Engineering VII. LC 92-70440. (AIENG Ser.). 1254p. 1992. 422.00 (*1-56252-102-0*, 1738) Computational Mech MA.

— Applications of Artificial Intelligence in Engineering X. LC 95-68893. (AIENG Ser.: Vol. 10). 608p. 1995. 287.00 (*1-56252-240-X*) Computational Mech MA.

— Boundary Element Starter Pack for Fracture Mechanics & Crack Growth, Stress Analysis & Acoustics. 1994. boxed set 544.00 (*1-56252-263-9*, 3390) Computational Mech MA.

— Knowledge Based Expert Systems in Engineering: Planning & Design. LC 87-71287. (AIENG Ser.: Vol. 2). 416p. 1987. 94.00 (*0-931215-59-5*) Computational Mech MA.

— Simulation & Design of Microsystems & Microstructures. LC 95-68883. 352p. 1995. 183.00 (*1-56252-314-7*, 3900) Computational Mech MA.

Adey, Robert A. & Rzevski, George, eds. Artificial Intelligence in Engineering VI. LC 91-72244. (AIENG Ser.). 1064p. 1991. 304.00 (*1-56252-069-5*, 141X) Computational Mech MA.

Adey, Robert A. & Sriram, D., eds. Applications of Artificial Intelligence to Engineering Problems: 1st International Conference, 2 vols. (AIENG Ser.). 1986. 208.00 (*0-931215-12-9*) Computational Mech MA.

Adey, Robert A. & Sriram, Duvvuru, eds. Applications of Artificial Intelligence to Engineering Problems, 2 vols. 1226p. 1986. 266.00 (*0-387-16349-2*) Spr-Verlag.

— Artificial Intelligence in Engineering: Tools & Techniques. LC 87-71288. (AIENG Ser.: Vol. 2). 416p. 1987. 84.00 (*0-931215-80-3*) Computational Mech MA.

— Knowledge Based Expert Systems for Engineering: Classification, Education, & Control. LC 87-71289. (AIENG Ser.: Vol. 2). 416p. 1987. 94.00 (*0-931215-81-1*) Computational Mech MA.

***Adey, Robert C. S., ed.** As It Might Have Been: A Collection of Sherlockian Parodies from Unlikely Sources. 179p. 1998. 31.50 (*1-899562-57-5*, Calabash Pr); pap. 21.50 (*1-899562-58-3*, Calabash Pr) Ash-Tree.

Adey, Walter H. & Loveland, Karen. Dynamic Aquaria: Building Living Ecosystems. 2nd ed. LC 97-80824. (Illus.). 498p. (C). 1998. pap. 49.95 (*0-12-043792-9*) Acad Pr.

Adey, Walter H., et al. Field Guidebook to the Reefs & Reef Communities of St. Croix, Virgin Islands. (Third International Symposium on Coral Reefs Ser.). (Illus.). 52p. 1977. pap. 6.00 (*0-932981-40-2*) Univ Miami A R C.

Adeyeye, Christianah, et al. Pharmaceutical Excipients: Towards the Twenty-First Century. 264p. 1995. ring bd. 159.95 (*1-56676-349-5*) Technomic.

Adgar & Kunstmann, Pierre. Le Gracial. LC 82-174243. (Publications Medievales de l'Universite d'Ottawa - University of Ottawa Mediaeval Texts & Studies: Vol. 8). (FRE.). 398p. 1982. reprint ed. pap. 123.40 (*0-608-02190-3*, 206286000003) Bks Demand.

Adger, Carolyn T., et al. Engaging Students: Thinking, Talking, Cooperating. LC 95-3733. (Illus.). 192p. 1995. pap. 24.95 (*0-8039-6231-2*) Corwin Pr.

— Making the Connection: Language & Academic Achievement Among African American Students Proceedings Of A Conference Of The Coalition On Language Diversity In Education / LC 98-52017. (Language in Education Ser.). 1999. write for info. (*1-887744-42-8*) Delta Systems.

Adger, Carolyn T., jt. ed. see Hoyle, Susan M.

Adger, David, et al, eds. Specifiers: Minimalist Approaches. (Illus.). 356p. 1999. pap. text 45.00 (*0-19-823814-2*) OUP.

Adger, Hoover, Jr. & McDonald, Eileen M. The Johns Hopkins Pediatric Substance Abuse Curriculum Manual. LC 93-27233. 416p. 1994. 195.00 (*0-8018-4802-4*) Johns Hopkins.

Adger, Susan. Write a Story for Your Child. 82p. 1997. pap. 11.95 (*0-933025-60-2*) Blue Bird Pub.

Adger, W. N., et al, eds. Climate Change Mitigation & European Land Use Policy. (A CAB International Publication). 368p. 1998. pap. text 90.00 (*0-85199-185-8*) OUP.

Adger, W. Neil & Brown, Katrina. Land Use & the Causes of Global Warming. LC 94-15145. 282p. 1995. 200.00 (*0-471-94885-3*) Wiley.

Adgey, A. J. Acute Phase of Ischemic Heart Disease & Myocardial Infarction. 1982. text 162.50 (*90-247-2675-1*) Kluwer Academic.

Adharyya, A. & Gupta, G. Practical Plant Physiology. (C). 1989. 50.00 (*0-89771-416-4*, Pub. by Current Dist) St Mut.

Adhe, Ama, jt. auth. see Tapontsang, Adhe.

Adhemar, Jean. The Caprices of Goya. (Illus.). 1951. 7.95 (*0-8288-3975-1*) Fr & Eur.

Adhikari & Bhandari. Environmental Economics Nepal. 1998. pap. 27.00 (*0-7855-7388-7*, Pub. by Ratna Pustak Bhandar) St Mut.

Adhikari, A., jt. auth. see Dhungel, D.

Adhikari, Jagannath. The Beginnings of Agarian Change: A Case Study in Central Nepal. 1996. pap. 160.00 (*0-7855-7363-1*, Pub. by Ratna Pustak Bhandar) St Mut.

Adhikari, Mohamed, jt. ed. see Switzer, Les.

Adhikari, Prakash Raj. Queens of the Shah Dynasty in Nepal: Dynasty in Nepal. 1997. pap. 40.00 (*0-7855-7483-2*, Pub. by Ratna Pustak Bhandar) St Mut.

Adhikari, Richard. Client/Server Application Development: Tools & Techniques. LC 94-21113. (Illus.). 197p. 1996. pap. 285.00 (*1-56607-033-3*) Comput Tech Res.

— Implementing Client/Server Technology. LC 94-1845. (Illus.). 162p. 1995. pap. 260.00 (*1-56607-030-9*) Comput Tech Res.

***Adhikari, S. & Bohle, S.** Food Crisis in Nepal. 1999. pap. 95.00 (*0-7855-7548-0*) St Mut.

***Adhikari, S. & Khadka, S.** Strategic Environmental Assessment. 1998. pap. 23.00 (*0-7855-7639-8*) St Mut.

***Adhikari, S. & Pyakuryal, S.** Environmental Economics in IUCN Nepal. 1999. pap. 34.00 (*0-7855-7541-3*) St Mut.

Adhikari, Sadhan K., adapted by. Variational Principles & the Numerical Solution of Scattering Problems. LC 97-24719. 323p. 1998. 94.95 (*0-471-18193-5*, Wiley-Interscience) Wiley.

Adhikary, A., jt. auth. see Ganguly, G.

Adhikary, A., jt. auth. see Sinha, S.

***Adhikary, D. P.** The History of Nepalese Nationalism. 1998. pap. 43.00 (*0-7855-7598-7*) St Mut.

Adhikarya, Ronny & Middleton, John. Communication Planning at the Institutional Level: A Selected Annotated Bibliography. ix, 99p. (Orig.). 1979. pap. text 6.00 (*0-86638-022-1*) EW Ctr HI.

ADHOC Corporate Investment Policy Committee. Investment Policy Guidebook for Corporate Pension Plan Trustees. LC 84-81691. 185p. 1984. pap. 10.00 (*0-89154-223-X*) Intl Found Employ.

Adhoute, B. G. Autologous Transfusion: Using Your Own Blood. (Illus.). x, 138p. 1992. 103.00 (*0-387-59554-6*) Spr-Verlag.

Adhvarindra, Dharmaraja. Vedanta Paribhasa. Madhavananda, Swami, tr. 263p. 1945. pap. 4.95 (*0-87481-072-8*, Pub. by Advaita Ashrama) Vedanta Pr.

Adhya, Sankar, et al, eds. RNA Polymerase & Associated Factors, Pt. A. (Methods in Enzymology Ser.: Vol. 273). (Illus.). 377p. 1996. text 79.00 (*0-12-182174-9*) Acad Pr.

Adhya, Sankar, et al, eds. RNA Polymerase & Associated Factors, Pt. B. (Methods in Enzymology Ser.: Vol. 274). (Illus.). 566p. 1996. text 89.00 (*0-12-182175-7*) Acad Pr.

***Adi Da Samra, Ruchira Avatar.** Real God Is the Indivisible Oneness of Unbroken Light: Reality, Truth & the "Non-Creator" God in the True World-Religion of Adidam. LC 99-64683. (Seventeen Companions of the True Dawn Horse Ser.). 346p. 1999. pap. 9.95 (*1-57097-055-6*) Dawn Horse Pr.

— The Truly Human New World-Culture of Unbroken Real-God-Man: The Eastern Versus the Western Traditional Cultures of Mankind. LC 99-64789. (Seventeen Companions of the True Dawn Horse Ser.: Vol. 2). 338p. 1999. pap. 9.95 (*1-57097-056-4*) Dawn Horse Pr.

Adi, Hakim. African Migrations. (Migrations Ser.). (Illus.). 48p. (J). (gr. 4-6). 1994. 5.00 (*1-56847-238-2*) Raintree Steck-V.

— West Africans in Britain, 1900-1960: Nationalism, Pan Africanism & Communism. LC 98-185891. 256p. 1998. pap. 22.50 (*0-85315-848-7*, Pub. by Lawrence & Wishart) NYU Pr.

Adi-Rubin, Margalit. Israeli Yemenite Embroidery. (Illus.). 84p. (Orig.). 1983. pap. 10.95 (*0-9611996-0-1*) M A R.

Adian, S. I. The Burnside Problem & Identities in Groups. Lennox, John C. & Wiegold, J., trs. from RUS. (Ergebnisse der Mathematik und Ihrer Grenzgebiete Ser.: Vol. 95). 1979. 65.00 (*0-387-08728-1*) Spr-Verlag.

Adian, S. I., et al, eds. Logical Foundations of Computer Science: 4th International Symposium, LFCS '97, Yaroslavl, Russia, July, 6-12, 1997, Proceedings. LC 97-20865. (Lecture Notes in Computer Science Ser.: No. 1234). ix, 431p. 1997. pap. 67.00 (*3-540-63045-7*) Spr-Verlag.

Adib-un-Rasul, Juba A. A Fearless Butterfly. 1995. pap. 10.00 (*0-936874-03-1*, QP-0001) Qiblah Pr.

Adibi. Dipeptides As New Substrates in Nutrition therapy Peptide als neue Substrate in der Ernaehrungstherapie. Adibi, S. A. et al, eds. (Beitraege zur Infusionstherapie und Klinische Ernaehrung Ser.: Vol. 17). (Illus.). viii, 196p. 1987. 55.00 (*3-8055-4613-0*) S Karger.

Adibi, S. A. Branched Chain Amino & Keto Acids in Health & Disease. Fekl, W. et al, eds. (Illus.). xiv, 572p. 1985. 129.75 (*3-8055-3996-7*) S Karger.

Adibi, S. A., ed. see Adibi.

***Adiccabandhu & Padmasri.** The Lion & the Jackal. (Illus.). 32p. (J). 1999. pap. 10.95 (*1-899579-13-3*, Pub. by Windhorse) Weatherhill.

— The Monkey King. (Illus.). 32p. (J). (ps-3). 1999. pap. 10.95 (*1-899579-09-5*, Pub. by Windhorse) Weatherhill.

— Siddhartha & the Swan. (Illus.). 32p. (J). 1999. pap. 10.95 (*1-899579-10-9*, Pub. by Windhorse) Weatherhill.

Adichie, Amanda N. Decisions. 64p. 1998. write for info. (*1-86106-422-5*, Pub. by Minerva Pr) Unity Dist.

Adickes. Human Diseases. 2000. pap. 39.95 (*0-8385-3930-0*, Medical Exam) Appleton & Lange.

An Asterisk (*) at the beginning of an entry indicates that the title is appearing for the first time.

— To Be Young Was Very Heaven: Women in New York Before the First World War. 224p. 2000. pap. 16.95 (*0-312-22335-8*) St Martin.

Adickes, Sandra. The Social Quest: The Expanded Vision of Four Women Travellers in the Era of the French Revolution. LC 91-17514. (American University Studies: History: Ser. IX, Vol. 92). 164p. 1991. 35.95 (*0-8204-0657-0*) P Lang Pubng.

***Adickes, Sandra.** To Be Young Was Very Heaven: Women in New York Before the First World War. large type ed. LC 98-17696. 1998. 26.95 (*0-7838-0184-X*, G K Hall & Co) Mac Lib Ref.

Adidevananda, Swami, tr. see Srinivasadasa.

Adie, Chris. Network Access to Multimedia Information. 67p. (Orig.). (C). 1995. pap. text 25.00 (*0-7881-1940-0*) DIANE Pub.

Adie, Chris, ed. A Survey of Distributed Multimedia: Research, Standards & Products. 150p. (Orig.). (C). 1993. pap. text 50.00 (*0-7881-0039-4*) DIANE Pub.

Adie, Douglas K. Monopoly Mail: Privatizing the United States Postal Service. 280p. (Orig.). 1988. 39.95 (*0-88738-203-7*); pap. 24.95 (*0-88738-747-0*) Transaction Pubs.

Adie, Michael, et al. Teaching Right & Wrong: Have the Churches Failed? (IEA Health & Welfare Unit Ser.: No. 3). 44p. 1994. pap. 14.95 (*0-255-36357-5*, Pub. by Inst Economic Affairs) Coronet Bks.

Adiele, Faith, et al. The Student Body: A Novel. 352p. 2000. pap. 13.95 (*0-615-11344-3*) MayaLuna Bks. In 1986, Brown University was rocked by news that some of its privileged students were entangled in a college prostitution ring. A decade later, The Student Body, a rollicking page-turner inspired by the Brown episode, was published to national acclaim. Authored by four Harvard classmates who collaborated under the pen-name of Jane Harvard, The Student Body is a work of singular vision & unexpected wit. The heroine of The Student Body is Toni Isaacs, an ambitious African-American undergard. A reporter for the Harvard Crimson, she pursues a tip that some of her classmates are turning tricks for cash. But as she uncovers the secret lives of some of her closest friends, she stumbles upon a deadly conspiracy involving a multinational drug company, a discredited scientist & a college prostitution ring that offers the very special attentions of the Ivy League - a conspiracy that threatens her own arrival. The novel is "a seamless, fast-paced work, filled with the topography & culture of Harvard" (Booklist, starred review); & "intricate & in-your-face smart" (L. A. Times). As The Baltimore Sun notes, the novel's "great strength is its ability simultaneously to celebrate & ridicule the earnest multicultural atmosphere of contemporary university life." More info at: http://www.thestudentbody.com. *Publisher Paid Annotation.

Adiga, C., et al. Chapter Sixteen of Rananujan's Second Notebook: Theta Functions & Q-Series. LC 84-24283. (Memoirs of the AMS Ser.: No. 53/315). 85p. 1985. pap. 19.00 (*0-8218-2316-7*, MEMO/53/315) Am Math.

Adiga, S. Object-Oriented Software Systems in Manufacturing. 1992. 69.50 (*0-442-31562-7*) Chapman & Hall.

Adigal, Ilango. Shilappadikaram: The Ankle Bracelet. Danielou, Alain, tr. LC 64-16823. (Orig.). 1965. pap. 12.95 (*0-8112-0001-9*, NDP162, Pub. by New Directions) Norton.

Adigard, Erik, jt. auth. see Betsky, Aaron.

***Adikari, Ambika P.** Urban & Environmental Planning in Nepal Analysis, Policies & Proposals. 1998. pap. 34.00 (*0-7855-7656-8*) St Mut.

Adil, Janeen R. Accessible Gardening for People with Physical Disabilities: A Guide to Methods, Tools, & Plants. LC 94-3548. (Illus.). 324p. (C). 1994. pap. 16.95 (*0-933149-56-5*) Woodbine House.

ADILKNO, Foundation for Advancement of Illegal Knowledge Staff. Cracking the Movement: Squatting Beyond the Media. 240p. Date not set. 7.00 (*0-936756-75-6*) Autonomedia.

— Media Archive. (New Autonomy Ser.). Orig. Title: Bilwet Media-Archief. 224p. 1998. pap. 14.00 (*1-57027-079-1*) Autonomedia.

Adilman, Mona, ed. Spirits of the Age. 192p. 1989. pap. 14.95 (*0-919627-07-2*, Pub. by Quarry Pr) LPC InBook.

Adimora-Ezeigbo, Akachi. The Buried Treasure. (Junior African Writers Ser.). (Illus.). 80p. (J). (gr. 3 up). 1992. pap. 3.88 (*0-7910-2908-5*) Chelsea Hse.

Adin, A., et al, eds. Environmental Quality & Ecosystem Stability. (Water Science & Technology Ser.: Vol. 27). 584p. 1993. pap. 272.50 (*0-08-042329-9*, Pergamon Pr) Elsevier.

Adin, A., jt. ed. see Ives, K. J.

Adinolfi, G., ed. Annuaire Europeen 1991 - European Yearbook 1991, Vol. XXXIX. 1256p. (C). 1993. lib. bdg. 381.00 (*0-7923-1959-1*) Kluwer Academic.

Adinolfi, G., ed. Annuaire Europeen 1990 - European Handbook 1990, Vol. XXXVIII. 1016p. (C). 1992. lib. bdg. 353.50 (*0-7923-1395-X*) Kluwer Academic.

Adinolfi, Joan. Tina's Diner. LC 96-7405. (Illus.). 32p. (J). (ps-3). 1997. per. 16.00 (*0-689-80634-5*) S&S Childrens.

Adinolfi, JoAnn. The Egyptian Polar Bear. (Illus.). 32p. (J). 1994. 14.95 (*0-395-68074-3*) HM.

Adinolfi, M., ed. Immunology & Genetics of Mammalian Reproduction: Some Controversial. (Journal: Experimental & Clinical Immunogenetics Ser.: Vol. 10, No. 2, 1993). (Illus.). 62p. 1993. pap. 47.00 (*3-8055-5867-8*) S Karger.

— Polymorphisms & Fertility. (Journal: Experimental & Clinical Immunogenetics Ser.: Vol. 2, No. 2). (Illus.). 88p. 1985. pap. 35.00 (*3-8055-4066-3*) S Karger.

Adinolfi, Matteo, ed. Genetics of Complement. (Journal: Experimental & Clinical Immunogenetics Ser.: Vol. 5, No. 2-3, 1988). (Illus.). 100p. 1988. pap. 31.50 (*3-8055-4860-5*) S Karger.

Adinolfi, Matteo & Davies, Angela F. Non-Isotopic In Situ Hybridization: Applications to Clinical Diagnosis & Molecular Gene. (Medical Intelligence Unit Ser.). 114p. 1994. 99.00 (*1-879702-85-1*, LN0285) Landes Bioscience.

Adinolfi, Ruggero, jt. auth. see Enck, John.

Adinoyi-ojo, Onukaba. Mbuti. 14 vols. Bond, George & Wyck, Gary V., eds. LC 94-22789. (Heritage Library of African Peoples). (Illus.). 64p. (YA). (gr. 7-12). 1995. lib. bdg. 16.95 (*0-8239-1998-6*) Rosen Group.

Adint, Victor. Drugs & Crime. rev. ed. LC 93-41862. (Drug Abuse Prevention Library). (Illus.). 64p. (YA). (gr. 7-12). 1997. lib. bdg. 15.95 (*0-8239-2604-4*) Rosen Group.

— Working Together Against Crime. (Library of Social Activism). (Illus.). 64p. (YA). (gr. 7-12). 1996. lib. bdg. 16.95 (*0-8239-2264-2*) Rosen Group.

Adiramled. The Art of Alchemy: The Generation of Gold, 4 vols., Set. 1994. pap. 16.95 (*1-55818-310-8*) Holmes Pub.

— The Art of Alchemy or the Generation of Gold: A Course of Practical Lessons in Metallic Transmutation for the Use of Occult Students Being a New Illumination Regarding the Secret Science of the Sages. 73p. 1993. reprint ed. pap. 12.95 (*1-56459-319-3*) Kessinger Pub.

Adirex, Paul. Mekong. 246p. 1995. pap. 17.95 (*974-89245-0-5*, Pub. by Aries Bks) Weatherhill.

— The Pirates of Tarutao. 246p. 1995. 24.95 (*974-89020-2-1*, Pub. by Aries Bks); pap. 17.95 (*974-88992-9-2*, Pub. by Aries Bks) Weatherhill.

— Until the Karma Ends. 246p. 1995. 24.95 (*974-89245-2-1*, Pub. by Aries Bks) Weatherhill.

Adirim, Isaak. Stagflation in the U. S. S. R. Young, Maureen, ed. (Illus.). 122p. (Orig.). 1983. pap. text 75.00 (*1-55831-003-7*) Delphic Associates.

Adirondack Mountain Club Staff, jt. auth. see Adirondack North Country Assoc., Staff.

Adirondack North Country Assoc., Staff & Adirondack Mountain Club Staff. Adirondack Park Mountain Bike Preliminary Trail & Route Listing. LC 95-12981. (Illus.). 280p. 1994. pap. 14.95 (*0-935272-77-1*) ADK Mtn Club.

Adisa, Opal P. It Begins with Tears. 1997. pap. 13.95 (*0-435-98946-4*) Heinemann.

— It Begins with Tears. (Caribbean Writers Ser.). 1997. 10.95 (*0-614-27263-7*) Heinemann.

— Tamarind & Mango Woman. 104p. 1993. pap. 11.95 (*0-920813-71-2*) Sister Vis Pr.

Adisa, Opal P. & Major, Devorah. Traveling Women. LC 89-83489. (Illus.). 103p. (Orig.). 1989. pap. 6.95 (*0-932693-01-6*) Jukebox Press.

Adiseshiah, Malcolm S. The Economics of Environment. 1987. 16.00 (*81-7062-034-1*) S Asia.

— Seventh Plan Perspectives, India. 1985. 26.00 (*0-8364-1449-7*, Pub. by Lancer India) S Asia.

Adiseshiah, Malcolm S., ed. The Economies of the States of the Indian Union. (C). 1989. 52.00 (*81-7062-057-0*, Pub. by Lancer India) S Asia.

— Forty Years of Economic Development: UN Agencies & India. 287p. (C). 1987. 31.00 (*81-7062-033-3*, Pub. by Lancer India) S Asia.

— Planning Perspectives of the Central Zone. 167p. (C). 1992. text 25.00 (*81-220-0261-7*, Pub. by Konark Pubs Pvt Ltd) Advent Bks Div.

— Price Policy. (C). 1987. 26.00 (*81-7062-027-9*, Pub. by Ashish Pub Hse) S Asia.

— Tax Policy: Proposals for Direct Tax Reform. (C). 1987. 14.00 (*81-7062-028-7*, Pub. by Lancer India) S Asia.

Adithan, M. & Pabla, B. S. Production Engineering, Estimating & Costing. 216p. 1990. text 25.00 (*81-220-0143-2*, Pub. by Konark Pubs Pvt Ltd) Advent Bks Div.

Adithan, M., jt. auth. see Pabla, B. S.

Aditjondro, George J. Is Oil Thicker Than Blood? A Study of Oil Companies Interests & Western Complicity in Indonesia's Annexation of East Timor. LC 98-28664. 3p. 1998. 69.00 (*1-56072-578-8*) Nova Sci Pubs.

Aditya, Anand. The Political Economy of Small States. 1997. pap. 30.00 (*0-7855-7482-4*, Pub. by Ratna Pustak Bhandar) St Mut.

Adiutori, Eugene T. The New Heat Transfer. 2nd ed. 434p. 1989. 39.95 (*0-9626220-0-1*) Ventuno Pr.

Adivar, Halide Edib. Turkey Faces West. LC 73-6266. (Middle East Ser.). 1973. reprint ed. 23.95 (*0-405-05320-7*) Ayer.

Adive, John R. The Verbal Piece in Ebira. (Publications in Linguistics: No. 85). 180p. 1989. pap. 13.00 (*0-88312-037-2*) S I L Intl.

Adix, Vern. Creative Dramatics: A Workbook of Games, Poems, Improvisations & Acting Stories. (Theatre Book Ser.). 44p. (YA). (gr. 8-12). 1986. pap. 9.95 (*1-57514-008-X*, 5000) Encore Perform Pub.

— Playmaking in the Classroom . . . And Elsewhere. (Theatre Book Ser.). 87p. 1991. pap. text 7.95 (*1-57514-013-6*, 5002) Encore Perform Pub.

— Puppetry: A Packet of Designs, Drawings & Ideas for & about Hand Puppets. (Encore Theatre Book Ser.). 93p. 1985. pap. 9.95 (*1-57514-010-1*, 5001) Encore Perform Pub.

— Theatre Scenecraft. rev. ed. 310p. 1981. pap. 22.50 (*0-87602-013-9*) Anchorage.

Adiyodi. Progress in Sexual Biology & Strategy Stucies, Vol. 9A, Progress in Male Gamete Ultrastructure an. 286p. 1999. 225.00 (*0-471-97163-4*) Wiley.

Adiyodi. Reproductive Biology Invertebrate. text. write for info. (*0-471-48968-9*); text. write for info. (*0-471-48969-7*) Wiley.

Adiyodi, K. G. Reproductive Biology of Invertebrates: Sexual Differentiation & Behaviour, Vol. 5, Sexual Differentiation and Behaviour. Adiyodi, Rita G., ed. LC 88-645030. (Reproductive Biology of Invertebrates Ser.). 536p. 1993. 460.00 (*0-471-93410-0*, Wiley-Liss) Wiley.

Adiyodi, K. G. & Adiyodi, Rita G., eds. Reproductive Biology of Invertebrates: Asexual Propagation & Reproductive Strategies, Vol. 6, Pt. A, Asexual Propagation and Reproductiv. (Reproductive Biology of Invertebrates Ser.: Vol. 6, Pt. A). 434p. 1993. 465.00 (*0-471-94118-2*) Wiley.

— Reproductive Biology of Invertebrates: Asexual Propagation & Reproductive Strategies, Vol. 6, Pt. B, Asexual Propagation and Reproductiv. LC 88-645030. 456p. 1995. 465.00 (*0-471-94119-0*) Wiley.

— Reproductive Biology of Invertebrates: Progress in Developmental Biology, Vol. 8. (progress). 382p. 1998. 250.00 (*0-471-96808-0*) Wiley.

— Reproductive Biology of Invertebrates: Progress in Gamete & Accessory Sex Gland Biology, Vol. 7. (Reproductive Biology of Invertebrates Ser.). 358p. 1998. 250.00 (*0-471-96648-7*) Wiley.

— Reproductive Biology of Invertebrates Vol. 1: Oogenesis, Oviposition & Oosorption. LC 81-16355. 796p. reprint ed. pap. 200.00 (*0-8357-6637-3*, 203529000001) Bks Demand.

— Reproductive Biology of Invertebrates Vol. 2: Spermatogenesis & Sperm Function. LC 81-16355. (Illus.). 718p. reprint ed. pap. 200.00 (*0-7837-4728-4*, 204451200002) Bks Demand.

— Reproductive Biology of Invertebrates, Vol. 4, Pt. A, Fertilization, Development & Parental Care, Vol. 4, Pt. A, Fertilization, Development and Pare. (Reproductive Biology of Invertebrates Ser.). 462p. 1989. 465.00 (*0-471-92269-2*) Wiley.

— Reproductive Biology of Invertebrates, Vol. 4, Pt. B, Fertilization, Development, & Parental Care, Vol. 4, Pt. B, Fertilization, Development, and Par. 552p. 199 . 465.00 (*0-471-92271-4*, Wiley-Liss) Wiley.

Adiyodi, K. G. & Adyodi, Rita G., eds. Reproductive Biology of Invertebrates Vol. 3: Accessory Sex Glands, Vol. 3, Accessory Sex Glands. 542p. 1993. 460.00 (*0-471-91466-5*) Wiley.

Adiyodi, K. G., jt. auth. see Bell, W. J.

Adiyodi, Rita G., ed. see Adiyodi, K. G.

Adiyodi, Rita G., jt. ed. see Adiyodi, K. G.

Adizes, I. Ciclos de Vida de la Organizacion. (SPA.). 335p. 1988. pap. 32.00 (*84-7978-127-0*, Pub. by Ediciones Diaz) IBD Ltd.

— How to Solve the Mismanagement Crisis: Diagnosis & Treatment of Management Problems. 1979. 24.95 (*0-8290-1326-1*) Irvington.

Adizes, Ichak. Corporate Lifecycles. (C). 1990. pap. text 16.95 (*0-13-174426-7*) P-H.

— How to Solve the Mismanagement Crisis: Diagnosis & Treatment of Management Problems. 300p. 1979. 24.95 (*0-937120-00-6*) Adizes Inst Inc.

— Managing Corporate Lifestyles. 2nd ed. LC 98-52210. 384p. (C). 1998. text 26.00 (*0-7352-0057-2*) PH Pr

— Managing the Performing Arts Organization: Founding Principles in the Management of the Arts. Griffin, Patrick H., ed. xii, 135p. (Orig.). 1997. pap. 19.95 (*0-937120-06-5*) Adizes Inst Inc.

— Mastering Change: The Power of Mutual Trust & Respect in Personal Life, Family Life, Business & Society. 240p. 1992. 19.95 (*0-937120-04-9*) Adizes Inst Inc.

— Mastering Change: The Power of Mutual Trust & Respect in Personal Life, Family Life, Business & Society. (Illus.). 243p. 1992. reprint ed. pap. write for info. (*0-937120-07-3*) Adizes Inst Inc.

— Pursuit of Prime: Maximize Your Company's Success with "The Adizes" Method. 304p. 1997. 22.95 (*1-888232-22-6*) Knowldge Exchange.

Adjali, Mia & Storms, Deborah. Study Guide to the United Nations. 48p. (Orig.). 1995. pap. text, teacher ed. 5.95 (*0-377-00293-3*) Friendship Pr.

Adjali, Mia & Storms, Deborah, eds. The Community of Nations. 128p. (Orig.). 1995. pap. 7.95 (*0-377-00292-5*) Friendship Pr.

Adjan, S., et al. Eleven Papers on Number Theory, Algebra & Functions of a Complex Variable. LC 51-5559. (Translations Ser.: Series 2, Vol. 46). 284p. 1965. 30.00 (*0-8218-1746-9*, TRANS2/46) Am Math.

Adjan, S. I., ed. Mathematical Logic, the Theory of Algorithms & the Theory of Sets: Dedicated to Academician Petr Sergeevic Novikov. LC 77-3359. (Proceedings of the Steklov Institute of Mathematics Ser.: No. 133). 274p. 1977. pap. 90.00 (*0-8218-3033-3*, STEKLO/133) Am Math.

Adjan, S I., ed. see Steklov Institute of Mathematics, Academy of Scien.

Adjangba, Anaumou J., ed. Food Production & Agriculture in Africa. 394p. 1988. pap. text 14.95 (*0-943852-81-1*) Prof World Peace.

Adjare, Stephen. The Golden Insect: A Handbook on Beekeeping for Beginners. 112p. 1984. pap. 14.50 (*0-946688-60-5*, Pub. by Intermed Tech) Stylus Pub VA.

Adjaye, Joseph K. Diplomacy & Diplomats in Nineteenth Century Asante. LC 96-18448. 310p. 1996. 59.95 (*0-86543-504-9*); pap. 18.95 (*0-86543-505-7*) Africa World.

Adjaye, Joseph K., ed. Time in the Black Experience. 167. LC 93-35843. (Contributions in Afro-American & African Studies: No. 167). 248p. 1994. 65.00 (*0-313-29118-7*, Greenwood Pr) Greenwood.

Adjaye, Joseph K., ed. see Andrews, Adrianne R.

Adjei, Akete L. & Gupta, Pramod K. Inhalation Delivery of Therapeutic Peptides & Proteins. LC 97-15722. (Lung Biology in Health & Disease Ser.). (Illus.). 952p. 1997. text 255.00 (*0-8247-9780-9*) Dekker.

Adjekum, Robert. From Africa to America: Life on Rocks. 200p. (C). 1989. text. write for info. (*0-318-65957-3*) R Adjekum.

Adjibolosoo, S. K., ed. International Perspectives on the Human Factor in Economic Development. LC 97-27933. 248p. 1998. 75.00 (*0-275-95967-8*, Praeger Pubs) Greenwood.

Adjibolosoo, Senyo. Rethinking Development Theory & Policy: A Human Factor Critique. LC 98-15650. 248p. 1999. 65.00 (*0-275-96348-9*, Praeger Pubs) Greenwood.

Adjibolosoo, Senyo, ed. The Significance of the Human Factor in African Economic Development. LC 94-8545. 280p. 1995. 65.00 (*0-275-94895-1*, Praeger Pubs) Greenwood.

Adjibolosoo, Senyo B., ed. Human Factor Engineering & the Political Economy of African Development. LC 95-51429. 208p. 1996. 62.95 (*0-275-95491-9*, Praeger Pubs) Greenwood.

Adjibolosoo, Senyo B., jt. ed. see Ezeala-Harrison, Fidelis.

***Adjibolosoo, Senyo B-S. K., ed.** The Human Factor in Shaping the Course of History & Development. LC 99-88691. 336p. 2000. 47.50 (*0-7618-1613-5*) U Pr of Amer.

Adjibolosoo, Senyo K. Global Development the Human Factor Way. LC 97-18062. 256p. 1998. 65.00 (*0-275-95966-X*, Praeger Pubs) Greenwood.

Adjmi, Morris, ed. Aldo Rossi: Architecture. LC 91-27398. (Illus.). 304p. 1991. 60.00 (*1-878271-15-6*); pap. 40.00 (*1-878271-16-4*) Princeton Arch.

Adjmi, Morris & Bertolotto, Giovanni, eds. Aldo Rossi: Drawings & Paintings 1981-1991. LC 93-21052. (Illus.). 224p. 1993. 60.00 (*1-878271-49-0*); pap. 40.00 (*1-878271-50-4*) Princeton Arch.

Adjoua. Alternative Dispute Resolution Essentials. (Paralegal Ser.). (C). 2001. pap. 29.75 (*0-7668-1139-5*) Thomson Learn.

Adjustment Administration, U. S. Department of Agriculture. Agricultural Adjustment. LC 75-27634. (World Food Supply Ser.). (Illus.). 1976. reprint ed. 35.95 (*0-405-07776-9*) Ayer.

***Adjutant General Staff, compiled by.** Records of Officers & Men of New Jersey in Wars 1791-1815. 305p. 1999. pap. 32.50 (*0-8328-9840-6*) Higginson Bk Co.

Adkerson, Donya L., jt. auth. see Carich, Mark S.

***Adkerson, Michelle.** How to Manage Problem Employees. Athey, Julie, ed. 96p. 2000. 47.00 (*0-925773-53-0*) M Lee Smith.

Adkin, Laurie E. The Politics of Sustainable Development: Citizens, Unions & the Corporations. LC 96-79518. (Illus.). 250p. 1996. 52.99 (*1-55164-081-3*, Pub. by Black Rose); pap. 28.99 (*1-55164-080-5*, Pub. by Black Rose) Consort Bk Sales.

Adkin, Mark, jt. auth. see Simpson, John.

Adkins. N. Scott Momaday. 1998. 22.95 (*0-8057-4005-8*, Twyne) Mac Lib Ref.

Adkins & Shackleton. Recollections: 10 Stories on 5 Themes. 1990. pap. text. write for info. (*0-17-556199-0*) Addison-Wesley.

Adkins, A. W., et al, eds. Human Virtue & Human Excellence. LC 91-2191. 309p. 1991. text 51.95 (*0-8204-1489-1*) P Lang Pubng.

Adkins, Amee, et al. Working Together: Grounded Perspectives on Interagency Collaboration. (Understanding Education & Policy Ser.). 272p. (C). 1998. text 55.00 (*1-57273-104-4*); pap. text 22.95 (*1-57273-105-2*) Hampton Pr NJ.

Adkins, Anne S. The Gift of Grief. Kelly, Jane, ed. 78p. (Orig.). 1991. pap. write for info. (*0-9621194-2-3*) Stratford NC.

Adkins, Arthur W. Merit & Responsibility: A Study in Greek Values. (Midway Reprint Ser.). 396p. 1975. reprint ed. pap. text 20.00 (*0-226-00728-6*) U Ch Pr.

— Poetic Craft in the Early Greek Elegists. LC 84-16203. 262p. 1985. lib. bdg. 42.00 (*0-226-00725-1*) U Ch Pr.

— Poetic Craft in the Early Greek Elegists. LC 84-16203. 262p. Date not set. reprint ed. 81.30 (*0-608-20976-7*, 205450400003) Bks Demand.

Adkins, Bernadine. Air Transport & EC Competition Law. LC 95-195161. 1994. 80.00 (*0-421-48610-4*, Pub. by Sweet & Maxwll) Gaunt.

Adkins, C. J. Equilibrium Thermodynamics. 3rd ed. LC 82-23634. 304p. 1984. pap. text 39.95 (*0-521-27456-7*) Cambridge U Pr.

Adkins, C. J., et al. Hopping & Related Phenomena Five: Proceedings of the 5th International Conference. 350p. 1994. text 109.00 (*981-02-1583-5*) World Scientific Pub.

Adkins, Cecil & Dickinson, Alis, eds. Doctoral Dissertations in Musicology. 7th ed. 545p. 1984. pap. 20.00 (*1-878528-04-1*) Am Musicological.

— Doctoral Dissertations in Musicology, February 1984-April 1995. 2nd ed. 406p. 1996. pap. 23.00 (*1-878528-03-3*) Am Musicological.

Adkins, Cecil, ed. see Vecchi, Orazio.

Adkins, Dinah. A Decade of Sucess: 10th Anniversary Survey of Business Incubators 1985-1995. 15p. 1996. pap. 18.00 (*1-887183-39-6*) NBIA.

Adkins, Dorcas. Simple Fountains for Indoors & Outdoors: 20 Step-by-Step Projects. LC 99-18137. (Illus.). 160p. 1999. 26.95 (*1-58017-190-7*) Storey Bks.

Adkins, E. Revenge in Laredo. 1987. pap. 2.50 (*0-8217-2173-9*) NAL.

A

A

Adkins, Erle. Big Bend Ambush. 224p. 1991. mass mkt. 3.50 (*0-8217-3421-0*, Zebra Kensgtn) Kensgtn Pub Corp.
— Pecos Blood. (Illus.). 224p. 1987. mass mkt. 2.50 (*0-8217-2101-1*, Zebra Kensgtn) Kensgtn Pub Corp.
— Two Guns from Texas. 1990. mass mkt. 2.95 (*0-8217-2925-X*, Zebra Kensgtn) Kensgtn Pub Corp.
Adkins, Frank. Chrysler Performance Upgrades. (Illus.). 112p. 1999. pap. 18.95 (*1-884089-40-2*, S-A Design) CarTech.
Adkins, Gary, ed. Communication Tips Collection, No. II: How to Do It Even Better. 2nd ed. 92p. 1992. pap. text 9.50 (*1-880331-03-9*) IL Assn Sch Bds.
Adkins, Gregory. Fast & Simple Techniques for Microsoft. Overacker, Roger, ed. & illus. by. ix, 113p. 1998. spiral bd. 29.95 (*0-9667949-0-7*) Gotcha Covered Enter.
Adkins, H. E. Treatise on the Military Band. 1977. lib. bdg. 59.95 (*0-8490-2763-2*) Gordon Pr.
Adkins, Hal. The Directory of Homebuilt Ultra Light Aircraft. (Illus.). 106p. (Orig.). 1982. pap. 10.00 (*0-910907-00-5*) Haljan Pubns.
Adkins, Hazel V., ed. Spinal Cord Injury. LC 85-4143. (Clinics in Physical Therapy Ser.: No. 6). (Illus.). 302p. reprint ed. pap. 93.70 (*0-8357-4653-4*, 203758400008) Bks Demand.
Adkins III, Andrew Z. Computerized Case Management Systems: Choosing & Implementing the Right Software for You. LC 98-73653. 1999. pap. 49.95 (*1-57073-609-X*) Amer Bar Assn.
Adkins, Jan. Art & Industry of Sandcastles. (Illus.). 64p. (J). (gr. k up). 1982. reprint ed. pap. 9.95 (*0-8027-7205-6*) Walker & Co.
— The Craft of Sail: A Primer of Sailing. LC 72-87347. 64p. 1984. pap. 10.95 (*0-8027-7214-5*) Walker & Co.
— Deadline for Final Art. 192p. 1990. 18.95 (*0-8027-5759-6*) Walker & Co.
***Adkins, Jan.** Dream Spinner: The Art of Roy Andersen. (Illus.). 166p. 1999. 60.00 (*0-9635642-4-2*) Settlers W Gall.
Adkins, Jan. From Here to There. 1999. 17.00 (*0-517-70925-2*) Random.
— How a House Happens. (Illus.). 32p. (J). (gr. 5 up). 1983. pap. 3.95 (*0-8027-7206-4*) Walker & Co.
— Inside: Seeing Beneath the Surface. 32p. 1984. pap. 4.95 (*0-8027-7215-3*) Walker & Co.
— Solstice: A Mystery of the Season. (Illus.). 128p. (YA). 1990. 12.95 (*0-8027-6970-5*); lib. bdg. 13.85 (*0-8027-6971-3*) Walker & Co.
— A Storm Without Rain. 1995. 18.00 (*0-8446-6809-5*) Peter Smith.
— Storm Without Rain. (J). 1993. 9.05 (*0-606-05626-2*, Pub. by Turtleback) Demco.
— String: Tying It up, Tying It Down. LC 91-25786. (Illus.). 48p. (YA). (gr. 5 up). 1992. lib. bdg. 13.95 (*0-684-18875-9*) Scribner.
— Toolchest: A Primer of Woodcraft. Cuyler, Margery, ed. LC 72-81374. (Illus.). 48p. 1973. pap. 4.95 (*0-8027-7218-8*) Walker & Co.
— The Wonder of Light: Big Book. Schaffer, Donna, ed. (Ranger Rick Science Spectacular Ser.). 16p. (J). (gr. 2-5). 1997. pap. text 16.95 (*1-56784-450-2*) Newbridge Educ.
— The Wonder of Light: Student Book. Schaffer, Donna, ed. (Ranger Rick Science Spectacular Ser.). 16p. (J). (gr. 2-5). 1997. pap. text 19.95 (*1-56784-475-8*) Newbridge Educ.
Adkins, Jan, ed. The Ragged Mountain Portable Wilderness Anthology. LC 93-8397. (Illus.). 144p. 1993. pap. 12.95 (*0-87742-370-9*, Ragged Mntain) McGraw-Hill Prof.
Adkins, Jan E., ed. The Ragged Mountain Portable Wilderness Anthology. 1993. pap. 12.95 (*0-07-000311-4*) McGraw-Hill Prof.
Adkins, Jeanette. Punctuation Made Easy. 112p. (C). 1997. pap. text 25.95 (*1-56226-353-6*) CAT Pub.
Adkins, Jeanette, jt. auth. see Branch, Elizabeth.
Adkins, Jo A., ed. The Reach of Song, 1989-1990. 224p. 1991. per. 9.00 (*0-918279-16-X*) GA State Poetry.
***Adkins, Kathleen.** Build Business Spreadsheets Using Excel. Matchett, Alastair, ed. (Illus.). 200p. 1998. pap. 39.95 (*1-891112-52-X*, AM0002) Adkins & Match.
— Build Business Spreadsheets Using Excel: New Updated for Excel 2000. 2nd ed. Matchett, Alastair, ed. (Illus.). 200p. 2000. pap. 39.95 (*1-891112-55-4*, AM0004) Adkins & Match.
***Adkins, Kathleen, et al.** Financial Business Box: Your Financial Skills Tool Kit, 3 vols. Matchett, Alastair, ed. 1999. boxed set 119.95 (*1-891112-53-8*, AM0005) Adkins & Match.
Adkins, Kathleen, ed. see Matchett, Alastair.
Adkins, Kathleen, ed. see Toy, Norman E.
Adkins, Leonard. The Caribbean - A Walking & Hiking Guide. 2nd ed. (Illus.). 368p. 1998. pap. 14.95 (*1-55650-848-4*) Hunter NJ.
***Adkins, Leonard.** 50 Hikes in Maryland: Walks, Hikes & Backpacks from the Allegheny Plateau to the Atlantic Ocean. 2000. pap. 16.95 (*0-88150-446-7*, Pub. by Countryman) Norton.
— 50 Hikes in Northern Virginia: Walks, Hikes & Backpacks from the Allegheny Mountains to the Chesapeake Bay. 2nd ed. LC 99-58150. (Illus.). 272p. 2000. pap. 16.95 (*0-88150-444-0*, Pub. by Countryman) Norton.
Adkins, Leonard M. The Appalachian Trail: A Visitor's Companion. LC 97-8059. (Illus.). 256p. 1997. pap. 14.95 (*0-89732-241-X*) Menasha Ridge.
— 50 Hikes in Northern Virginia: Walks, Hikes, & Backpacks from the Allegheny Mountains to the Chesapeake Bay. LC 93-17614. (Fifty Hikes Ser.). (Illus.). 272p. (Orig.). 1994. pap. 14.00 (*0-88150-278-2*, Pub. by Countryman) Norton.
— Seashore State Park: A Walking Guide. LC 89-49140. (Illus.). 64p. 1990. pap. 3.75 (*0-87033-406-9*, Tidewtr Pubs) Cornell Maritime.
— Virginia. (Adventure Guide). 1998. pap. text 15.95 (*1-55650-816-6*) Hunter NJ.
— Walking the Blue Ridge: A Guide to the Trails of the Blue Ridge Parkway. rev. ed. LC 92-17117. xiv, 521p. 1992. pap. 15.95 (*0-8078-4401-2*) U of NC Pr.
— Widlflowers of the Appalachain Trail. LC 98-53670. 128p. 1999. pap. 15.95 (*0-89732-295-9*) Menasha Ridge.
Adkins, Lesley. Introduction to the Romans. 1991. 12.98 (*1-55521-709-5*) Bk Sales Inc.
***Adkins, Lesley.** The Keys of Egypt: The Obsession to Decipher Egyptian Hieroglyphs. 320p. 2000. 25.00 (*0-06-019439-1*) HarpC.
— Keys to Egypt. 14.00 (*0-06-095349-7*) HarpC.
***Adkins, Lesley & Adkins, Roy.** Dictionary of Roman Religion. (Illus.). 304p. 2000. pap. 17.95 (*0-19-514233-0*) OUP.
Adkins, Lesley & Adkins, Roy A. Dictionary of Roman Religion. LC 95-8355. 304p. 1995. 40.00 (*0-8160-3005-7*) Facts on File.
***Adkins, Lesley & Adkins, Roy A.** Dictionary of Roman Religion. (Illus.). 288p. 2000. reprint ed. 25.00 (*0-7881-9456-9*) DIANE Pub.
Adkins, Lesley & Adkins, Roy A. Handbook to Life in Ancient Greece. LC 96-42111. 472p. 1997. 45.00 (*0-8160-3111-8*) Facts on File.
— Handbook to Life in Ancient Greece. LC 98-11568. (Illus.). 480p. 1998. pap. 18.95 (*0-19-512491-X*) OUP.
— Handbook to Life in Ancient Rome. (Illus.). 416p. 1994. 40.00 (*0-8160-2755-2*) Facts on File.
— Handbook to Life in Ancient Rome. LC 97-49394. (Illus.). 416p. 1998. pap. 19.95 (*0-19-512332-8*) OUP.
Adkins, Leslie & Adkins, Roy. The Handbook of British Archaeology. (Illus.). 319p. 1998. pap. 24.95 (*0-09-478330-6*, Pub. by Constable & Co) Trafalgar.
Adkins, Lisa. Gendered Work: Sexuality, Family & the Labour Market. LC 94-22206. 192p. 1994. write for info. (*0-335-19297-1*, Pub. by OpUniv Pr) Taylor & Francis.
— Gendered Work: Sexuality, Family & the Labour Market. LC 94-22206. 183p. 1995. pap. 27.50 (*0-335-19296-3*) Open Univ TX.
Adkins, Lisa & Leonard, Diana, eds. Sex in Question: French Feminism. 208p. 1995. 85.00 (*0-7484-0293-4*); pap. 27.95 (*0-7484-0294-2*) Taylor & Francis.
Adkins, Lisa & Merchant, Vicki, eds. Sexualizing the Social: Power & Organisation of Sexuality. 248p. 1996. pap. 19.95 (*0-312-16025-9*); text 59.95 (*0-312-16024-0*) St Martin.
Adkins, Lisa, jt. ed. see Holland, Janet.
Adkins, Mike. A Man Called Norman. 178p. 1989. pap. 9.99 (*0-929608-25-9*) Focus Family.
Adkins, Myrna A. & Ray, Charles. Intensive Training of Bilingual Workers in Mental Health & Cross-Cultural Communication. 93p. 1987. student ed. 25.00 (*0-940723-02-6*) SIIS.
Adkins, N. F. Fitz-Greene Halleck: An Early Knickerbocker Wit & Poet. 461p. 1993. reprint ed. lib. bdg. 99.00 (*0-7812-5265-2*) Rprt Serv.
Adkins, Paul. Codeword Dictionary a Compilation of Military Law Enforcement Codewords from 1904 to Present. LC 97-12140. 224p. 1997. pap. 12.95 (*0-7603-0368-1*) MBI Pubg.
Adkins, R. Benton, Jr. & Scott, H. William, Jr. Surgical Care for the Elderly. 2nd ed. LC 97-23283. 656p. 1997. text 129.00 (*0-7817-1450-8*) Lppncott W & W.
Adkins, R. T., ed. Information Sources in Polymers & Plastics. (Guides to Information Sources Ser.). (Illus.). 313p. 1989. text 75.00 (*0-408-02027-X*) Bowker-Saur.
Adkins, Roy, jt. auth. see Adkins, Lesley.
Adkins, Roy, jt. auth. see Adkins, Leslie.
Adkins, Roy A., jt. auth. see Adkins, Lesley.
Adkins, Stephanie H. The Wheat Field. LC 92-75006. (Orig.). 1992. pap. 9.95 (*0-9635140-0-8*) Atrax Pub.
***Adkins, Sue.** Cause Related Marketing: Who Cares Wins. 307p. 2000. pap. text 32.95 (*0-7506-4481-8*) Buttrwrth-Heinemann.
Adkins, Tom. Army Line Art, Vol. III. 48p. 1998. pap. 16.95 incl. cd-rom (*1-884778-52-6*) Old Mountain.
— Military Clip Art: Color Unit Patches. (Illus.). 32p. 1997. pap. text 12.95 incl. disk (*1-884778-26-7*) Old Mountain.
— Military Clip Art Vol. I: Color Military Clip Art. (Illus.). 36p. 1997. pap. text 12.95 incl. disk (*1-884778-25-9*) Old Mountain.
— Military Clipart: Air Assault. (Illus.). 48p. 1997. pap. text 16.95 incl. cd-rom (*1-884778-21-6*) Old Mountain.
— Military Clipart: Army Line Art, Vol. 2. (Illus.). 44p. 1997. pap. text 12.95 (*1-884778-20-8*) Old Mountain.
— Military Clipart: Rank Insignia. 36p. 1997. pap. text 16.95 incl. cd-rom (*1-884778-19-4*) Old Mountain.
— Military Clipart: Soviet. (Illus.). 40p. 1997. pap. text 12.95 incl. disk (*1-884778-32-1*) Old Mountain.
— Military Clipart: USAF Line Art, Vol. I. 40p. 1997. pap. text 16.95 incl. cd-rom (*1-884778-30-5*) Old Mountain.
— Military Clipart: USMC Line Art, Vol. I. (Illus.). 48p. 1997. pap. text 12.95 incl. disk (*1-884778-31-3*) Old Mountain.
— Military Clipart Vol. I: Army Line Art. (Illus.). 44p. 1997. pap. text 12.95 (*1-884778-18-6*) Old Mountain.
— Screen Savers: Rector Collection. (Illus.). 28p. 1997. pap. text 19.95 incl. disk (*1-884778-28-3*) Old Mountain.
— Screen Savers: Wolves. (Illus.). 28p. 1997. pap. text 12.95 incl. disk (*1-884778-36-4*) Old Mountain.
Adkins, Val. Creating Brochures & Booklets. (Graphic Design Basics Ser.). (Illus.). 128p. 1994. 26.99 (*0-89134-517-5*, North Lght Bks) F & W Pubns Inc.
Adkins, William A. & Weintraub, Steven H. Algebra: An Approach Via Module Theory. Ewing, J. H. et al, eds. LC 92-11951. (Graduate Texts in Mathematics Ser.: Vol. 136). (Illus.). 536p. 1992. 54.95 (*0-387-97839-9*); write for info. (*3-540-97839-9*) Spr-Verlag.
Adkins, Winthrop R. Adkins Life Skills Program: Career Development Series Unit 1; Exploring Who I Am & Where I Want to Go. 2nd ed. Davis, Donald D., ed. (Ten Unit Multi-Media Counseling - Learning Curriculum Ser.). 1985. pap. write for info. (*1-56223-001-8*) Inst Life Coping Skills.
— Adkins Life Skills Program: Career Development Series Unit 2: Exploring the World of Work. 2nd ed. Davis, Donald D., ed. (Ten Unit Multi-Media Counseling - Learning Curriculum Ser.). 1985. pap. write for info. (*1-56223-002-6*) Inst Life Coping Skills.
— Adkins Life Skills Program: Career Development Series Unit 3: Making Good Career Decisions. 2nd ed. Davis, Donald D., ed. (Ten Unit Multi-Media Counseling - Learning Curriculum Ser.). 1985. pap. write for info. (*1-56223-003-4*) Inst Life Coping Skills.
— Adkins Life Skills Program: Career Development Series Unit 4: Finding Job Information & Contacting Employers. 2nd ed. Davis, Donald D., ed. (Ten Unit Multi-Media Counseling - Learning Curriculum Ser.). 1985. pap. write for info. (*1-56223-004-2*) Inst Life Coping Skills.
— Adkins Life Skills Program: Career Development Series Unit 5: Using Employment Agencies & Personal Contacts. 2nd ed. Davis, Donald D., ed. (Ten Unit Multi-Media Counseling - Learning Curriculum Ser.). 1985. pap. write for info. (*1-56223-005-0*) Inst Life Coping Skills.
— Adkins Life Skills Program: Career Development Series Unit 6: Planning & Handling Time Effectively. 2nd ed. Davis, Donald D., ed. (Ten Unit Multi-Media Counseling - Learning Curriculum Ser.). 1985. pap. write for info. (*1-56223-006-9*) Inst Life Coping Skills.
— Adkins Life Skills Program: Career Development Series Unit 7: Developing a Career Plan. 2nd ed. Davis, Donald D., ed. (Ten Unit Multi-Media Counseling - Learning Curriculum Ser.). 1985. pap. write for info. (*1-56223-007-7*) Inst Life Coping Skills.
— Adkins Life Skills Program: Career Development Series Unit 8: Presenting Myself on Paper: Application Forms & Resumes. 2nd ed. Davis, Donald D., ed. (Ten Unit Multi-Media Counseling - Learning Curriculum Ser.). 1985. pap. write for info. (*1-56223-008-5*) Inst Life Coping Skills.
— Adkins Life Skills Program: Career Development Series Unit 9: Developing Effective Interviewing Skills. 2nd ed. Davis, Donald D., ed. (Ten Unit Multi-Media Counseling - Learning Curriculum Ser.). 1985. pap. write for info. (*1-56223-009-3*) Inst Life Coping Skills.
— Adkins Life Skills Program: Career Development Series Unit 10: Keeping a Job: Strategies That Help. 2nd ed. Davis, Donald D., ed. (Ten Unit Multi-Media Counseling - Learning Curriculum Ser.). 1985. pap. write for info. (*1-56223-010-7*) Inst Life Coping Skills.
***Adkins, Winthrop R., et al.** Adkins Life Skills Program: Career Development Series: "Como Decidirse por una Profesion Adecuada", 4, 3. (SPA.). 2000. pap. text. write for info. (*1-56223-023-9*) Inst Life Coping Skills.
— Adkins Life Skills Program: Career Development Series: "Como Desarrollar un Plan Para Alcanzar Metas Profesionales", 4 vols., Vol. 4. (Sistema Adkins). (SPA.). 2000. pap. text. write for info. (*1-56223-024-7*) Inst Life Coping Skills.
— Adkins Life Skills Program: Career Development Series: "Explorando Quien Soy Y A Donde Quiero Ir", 4 vols., Vol. 1. (SPA.). 53p. 2000. pap. text. write for info. (*1-56223-021-2*) Inst Life Coping Skills.
— Adkins Life Skilss Program: Career Development Series: "Explorando el Mundo del Trabajo", 4, 2. (SPA.). 51p. 2000. pap. text. write for info. (*1-56223-022-0*) Inst Life Coping Skills.
Adkinson, A. Wyle & Fry, N., eds. The House of Horror: The Story of Hammer Films. LC 74-146693. 1974. 19.95 (*0-89388-163-5*) Okpaku Communications.
Adkinson, Clarissa W. Bubba's Last Farewell. (J). (gr. 1-8). pap. write for info. (*1-885005-07-5*) LynHawk Pubng.
Adkinson, Robert. The Tarot. abr. ed. (Sacred Symbols Ser.). (Illus.). 80p. 1995. 10.00 (*0-500-06019-3*, Pub. by Thames Hudson) Norton.
Adkinson, Robert, ed. Ancient Egypt. LC 95-60474. (Sacred Symbols Ser.). (Illus.). 80p. 1995. 10.00 (*0-500-06013-4*, Pub. by Thames Hudson) Norton.
— The Buddha. LC 95-61826. (Sacred Symbols Ser.). (Illus.). 80p. 1996. 10.00 (*0-500-06023-1*, Pub. by Thames Hudson) Norton.
— The Celts. LC 95-60475. (Sacred Symbols Ser.). (Illus.). 80p. 1995. 10.00 (*0-500-06014-2*, Pub. by Thames Hudson) Norton.
— Christian Mysteries. LC 96-61233. (Sacred Symbols Ser.). (Illus.). 80p. 1997. 10.00 (*0-500-06026-6*, Pub. by Thames Hudson) Norton.
— The Mandala. LC 95-60472. (Sacred Symbols Ser.). (Illus.). 80p. 1995. 10.00 (*0-500-06020-7*, Pub. by Thames Hudson) Norton.
— The Maya. LC 95-61825. (Sacred Symbols Ser.). (Illus.). 80p. 1996. 10.00 (*0-500-06022-3*, Pub. by Thames Hudson) Norton.
— Native Americans, Vol. 7. LC 96-60181. (Sacred Symbols Ser.). (Illus.). 80p. 1996. 10.00 (*0-500-06025-8*, Pub. by Thames Hudson) Norton.
— Sacred Sex. LC 96-61177. (Sacred Symbols Ser.). (Illus.). 80p. 1997. 10.00 (*0-500-06027-4*, Pub. by Thames Hudson) Norton.
— Tao. LC 96-60180. (Sacred Symbols Ser.). (Illus.). 80p. 1996. 10.00 (*0-500-06024-X*, Pub. by Thames Hudson) Norton.
— The Tarot. LC 95-60473. (Sacred Symbols Ser.). (Illus.). 80p. 1995. 160.00 (*0-500-06021-5*, Pub. by Thames Hudson) Norton.
Adkison. Approaching Democracy. 1996. pap. text, student ed. 20.00 (*0-13-507385-5*) P-H.
***Adkison, Danny M. & Palmer, Lisa McNair.** The Oklahoma State Constitution: A Reference Guide. (Reference Guides to the State Constitutions of the United States Ser.: Vol. 32). 494p. 2000. lib. bdg. 138.00 (*0-313-27507-6*, AOS) Greenwood.
Adkison, Peter & McDonald, Michael. Sarista. (Talislanta Ser.). 72p. 1993. pap. 10.95 (*1-880992-15-9*) Wizards Coast.
Adkison, Peter, et al. The Primal Order. 236p. 1992. pap. 20.00 (*1-880992-00-0*) Wizards Coast.
Adkison, Ron. Best Easy Day Hikes: Grand Canyon. LC 98-11409. (Falcon Guides Ser.). (Illus.). 80p. 1998. pap. 6.95 (*1-56044-603-X*) Falcon Pub Inc.
— Best Easy Day Hikes: Grand Staircase Escalante & Glen Canyon Region. LC 98-220778. (Guide Ser.). (Illus.). 80p. 1998. pap. 6.95 (*1-56044-650-1*) Falcon Pub Inc.
— Best Easy Day Hikes: Northern Sierra. (Illus.). 96p. 1999. pap. 6.95 (*1-56044-693-5*) Falcon Pub Inc.
— Exploring Beyond Yelowstone: Hiking, Camping & Vacationing in the National Forests Surrounding Yellowstone & Grand Teton. LC 96-9265. 225p. 1996. pap. 15.95 (*0-89997-180-6*) Wilderness Pr.
— Hiking California. rev. ed. LC 96-39259. (Falcon Guides Ser.). (Illus.). 326p. 1996. pap. 15.95 (*1-56044-379-0*) Falcon Pub Inc.
— Hiking Grand Canyon National Park. LC 97-19745. (Illus.). 224p. (Orig.). 1997. pap. 14.95 (*1-56044-566-1*) Falcon Pub Inc.
— Hiking Grand Staircase - Escalante & the Glen Canyon Region. LC 98-22584. (Illus.). 346p. 1998. pap. 14.95 (*1-56044-645-5*) Falcon Pub Inc.
***Adkison, Ron.** Hiking Northern California. 3rd ed. LC 99-42149. (Falcon Guide Ser.). (Illus.). 326p. 2000. pap. 16.95 (*1-56044-701-X*) Falcon Pub Inc.
Adkison, Ron. Hiking Washington. LC 96-21416. (Illus.). 296p. 1996. pap. 15.95 (*1-56044-501-7*) Falcon Pub Inc.
— Hiking Wyoming's Wind River Range. LC 96-9104. (Illus.). 262p. (Orig.). 1996. pap. 16.95 (*1-56044-402-9*) Falcon Pub Inc.
— Utah's National Parks: Hiking & Vacationing in Utah's Canyon Country - Zion, Bryce, Arches, Canyonlands & Capitol Reef. LC 91-28496. (Illus.). 320p. (Orig.). 1991. pap. 14.95 (*0-89997-126-1*) Wilderness Pr.
Adkison, Sandra, tr. see Lucas, David J. & Veerman, David R.
Adkisson, Kathy. My Heart Flies. 128p. 1998. pap. write for info. (*0-9670067-0-8*) K Adkisson.
Adkoli, Anand, jt. auth. see Velpuri, Rama.
ADL. Skinhead International. LC 96-220748. 1995. pap. 7.50 (*0-88464-166-X*) ADL.
Adlam, J. C. Iran U. S. Claims Tribunal Reports, Vol. 23. (C). 1992. text 368.00 (*0-7855-0126-6*, Pub. by Grotius Pubns Ltd) St Mut.
Adland, P. G. Growing Stock Levels & Productivity Conclusions from Thinning & Spacing Trails in Young Pinus Patula Stands in Southern Tanzania. 1978. 40.00 (*0-85074-048-7*) St Mut.
Adlard, E. R., ed. Chromatography in the Petroleum Industry. LC 94-30628. (Journal of Chromotography Library: Vol. 56). 452p. 1995. 278.00 (*0-444-89776-3*) Elsevier.
Adlard, Edward R., jt. auth. see Handley, Alan J.
Adlard, John. A Biography of Arthur Diosy, Founder of the Japan Society: Home to Japan. LC 91-4247. (Japanese Studies: Vol. 2). 188p. 1991. lib. bdg. 79.95 (*0-7734-9758-7*) E Mellen.
Adlard, John, ed. The Fruit of That Forbidden Tree. 1980. pap. 7.50 (*0-85635-147-4*) Carcanet Pr.
Adlard, John, ed. see Wilmont, Earl of Rochester, John.
Adlard, P. G. & Richardson, K. F. Stand Density & Stem Taper in Pinus Patula: Schiede & Deppe. 1978. 40.00 (*0-85074-047-9*) St Mut.
Adlard, P. G. & Smith, J. P. Growth & Growing Space. 1981. 80.00 (*0-85074-054-1*) St Mut.
Adlard, P. G., et al. Wood Density Variation in Plantation-Grown Pinus Patula from the Viphya Plateau, Malawi. 1978. 45.00 (*0-85074-045-2*) St Mut.
Adleman, Debra. Waiting for the Lord: 19th Century Black Communities in Susquehanna County, Pennsylvania. LC 97-81057. (Illus.). 160p. 1997. pap. 19.95 (*0-89725-316-7*, 1838) Picton Pr.
Adleman, Jeanne. Racism in the Lives of Women: Testimony, Theory & Guides to Antiracist Practice. Enguidanos-Clark, Gloria M., ed. LC 94-20592. 1995. pap. 39.95 (*1-56023-863-1*, Harrington Park) Haworth Pr.
Adleman, Jeanne & Enguidanos-Clark, Gloria M., eds. Racism in the Lives of Women: Testimony, Theory & Guides to Antiracist Practice. LC 94-20592. 382p. (C). 1995. lib. bdg. 54.95 (*1-56024-918-8*, Harrington Park) Haworth Pr.
Adleman, L. M. & Huang, M. D. Primality Testing & Abelian Varieties over Finite Fields. (Lecture Notes in Mathematics Ser.: Vol. 1512). 142p. 1992. 29.95 (*0-387-55308-8*) Spr-Verlag.
Adleman, Leonard M., et al, eds. Algorithmic Number Theory: Proceedings of the First International Symposium, ANTS-I, Ithaca, NY, U. S. A., May 6-9, 1994. LC 94-238714. (Lecture Notes in Computer Science Ser.: Vol. 877). 1994. write for info. (*0-387-58691-1*) Spr-Verlag.
— Algorithmic Number Theory: Proceedings of the First International Symposium, ANTS-I, Ithaca, NY, U. S. A., May 6-9, 1994. LC 94-238714. (Lecture Notes in Computer Science Ser.: Vol. 877). 1994. 50.95 (*3-540-58691-1*) Spr-Verlag.
Adleman, Marvin, jt. auth. see Collins, John F.

An Asterisk (*) at the beginning of an entry indicates that the title is appearing for the first time.

Adler. American Drama, 1940-1960. 1997. pap. 18.00 (*0-8057-1621-1*, Twyne) Mac Lib Ref.
— Constructions of Deviance. (Adaptable Courseware-Softside Ser.). Date not set. pap. 33.00 (*0-534-56600-6*) Wadsworth Pub.
— Constructions of Deviance: Social Power, Context & Interaction. 3rd ed. LC 98-54759. (Sociology Ser.). 1999. 53.95 (*0-534-53912-2*) Wadsworth Pub.
— Contributions to the History of Herpetology. LC 89-50341. 1989. write for info. (*0-916984-19-2*) SSAR.
— Criminology. 4th ed. 2000. 51.74 (*0-07-232149-0*); 44.74 (*0-07-232150-4*) McGraw.
— Foundations of Education. (Education Ser.). 2001. pap. text 36.00 (*0-534-52247-5*) Brooks-Cole.
— Herpetology: Current Research. LC 92-61942. 1992. write for info. (*0-916984-27-3*) SSAR.
— How It's Done: An Invitation to Social Research. (Sociology-Upper Level Ser.). 400p. 1999. pap. 54.95 (*0-534-53325-6*) Wadsworth Pub.
— Interplay. 5th ed. (C). 1992. pap. text, teacher ed. 7.00 (*0-03-055494-2*) Harcourt Coll Pubs.
— Interplay. 6th ed. (C). 1995. pap. text, teacher ed. 49.75 (*0-15-502641-0*) Harcourt Coll Pubs.
***Adler.** Interplay. 8th ed. (C). 2000. pap. text. write for info. (*0-15-506956-X*) Harcourt Coll Pubs.
Adler. Introduction to Radiography. 1994. 325.00 (*0-7216-4612-3*) Harcourt.
— Looking Out, Looking In. 8th ed. (C). 1995. pap. text, teacher ed. 42.00 (*0-15-502739-5*) Harcourt Coll Pubs.
— Looking Out, Looking In. 9th ed. (C). 1998. text 47.50 (*0-15-505787-1*, Pub. by Harcourt Coll Pubs) Harcourt.
— Math for Life Sciences. 1998. pap., student ed. 30.95 (*0-534-35231-6*) Brooks-Cole.
— Math for Life Scientists. LC 97-38657. (Mathematics Ser.). 1998. mass mkt. 96.95 (*0-534-34816-5*) Wadsworth Pub.
— Math for Life Scientists: Preliminary Edition. LC 96-100817. (Mathematics Ser.). 1995. mass mkt. 58.95 (*0-534-34059-8*) Brooks-Cole.
— Padeia Proposal. 1998. pap. 8.00 (*0-684-84188-6*) S&S Trade.
***Adler.** Sociological Odyssey: An Introductory Sociology Reader. 2000. pap. 24.00 (*0-534-57053-4*) Wadsworth Pub.
Adler. Study Orchestration. 2nd ed. 400p. (C). 1989. 68.00 incl. audio (*0-393-99390-6*) Norton.
— Understanding Human Communication. 6th ed. (C). 1996. pap. text, teacher ed. 28.00 (*0-15-503287-9*) Harcourt Coll Pubs.
— Women's Colleges. 1994. pap. 17.00 (*0-685-71197-8*) Prntice Hall Bks.
— World Civilization, Vol. 2. Date not set. wbk. ed. write for info. (*0-314-09737-6*) West Pub.
— World Civilization Map Exercise Workbook. 1996. mass mkt., wbk. ed. 6.25 (*0-314-09412-1*) West Pub.
— World Civilizations. 1996. student ed. 15.25 (*0-314-09414-8*) West Pub.
— World Civilizations. 2nd ed. (History Ser.). 1999. text 88.95 (*0-534-56907-2*) Wadsworth Pub.
— World Civilizations, Vol. I. 2nd ed. LC 99-29867. (History Ser.). 1999. pap. 63.95 (*0-534-56908-0*) Wadsworth Pub.
— World Civilizations, Vol. II. 2nd ed. (History Ser.). 1999. pap. 63.95 (*0-534-56909-9*) Wadsworth Pub.
Adler, ed. About Education. (C). 1998. text. write for info. (*0-321-01120-1*) Addison-Wesley.
***Adler, A. & McGill.** International Dimensions of Organizational Behavior. 4th ed. (SWC-Management Ser.). (C). 2001. text 25.00 (*0-324-05786-5*) Sth-Wstrn College.
Adler, Alan, ed. Science-Fiction & Horror Movie Posters in Full Color. (Illus.). 48p. 1977. text 11.95 (*0-486-23452-5*) Dover.
Adler, Alan & Ramanan, S. Moduli of Abelian Varieties, Vol. VI. LC 96-39688. (Lecture Notes in Mathematics Ser.: Vol. 1644). 196p. 1996. pap. 43.00 (*3-540-62023-0*) Spr-Verlag.
Adler, Alan G., et al. Medical Evaluation of the Surgical Patient. (Blue Bk.). (Illus.). 304p. 1985. pap. text 36.95 (*0-7216-1146-X*, W B Saunders Co) Harcrt Hlth Sci Grp.
***Adler, Alan S. & Greenwald, David.** The Lawyer's Quick Guide to Word 97/2000. 1999. pap. 49.95 (*1-57073-733-9*) Amer Bar Assn.
Adler, Alfred. Cooperation Between the Sexes: Writings on Women & Men, Love & Marriage, & Sexuality. abr. ed. Ansbacher, Heinz L. & Ansbacher, Rowena R., eds. 192p. 1982. reprint ed. pap. 7.95 (*0-393-30019-6*) Norton.
— Cooperation Between the Sexes: Writings on Women, Love, Marriage & Its Disorders. LC 76-23804. 480p. 1980. reprint ed. 25.00 (*0-87668-443-6*) Aronson.
— Education of Children. LC 75-126155. 310p. 1978. pap. 3.95 (*0-89526-981-3*) Regnery Pub.
— Individual Psychology of Alfred Adler: A Systematic Presentation in Selections from His Writings. Ansbacher, Heinz L. & Ansbacher, Rowena R., eds. 544p. 1964. pap. 17.00 (*0-06-131154-5*, TB1154, Torch) HarpC.
— The Neurotic Constitution. LC 74-39684. (Select Bibliographies Reprint Ser.). 1980. reprint ed. 34.95 (*0-8369-9925-8*) Ayer.
— The Pattern of Life. 2nd ed. LC 81-71160. pap. 10.95 (*0-918560-28-4*) Adler Sch Prof Psy.
Adler, Alfred. Sight Singing: Pitch, Interval, Rhythm. 2nd ed. LC 96-28217. (C). 1997. pap. 24.00 (*0-393-97072-8*) Norton.
Adler, Alfred. Superiority & Social Interest: A Collection of Later Writings. Ansbacher, Heinz L. & Ansbacher, Rowena R., eds. 1979. reprint ed. pap. 14.95 (*0-393-00910-6*) Norton.
— Understanding Human Nature. Brett, Colin, tr. LC 97-49425. 250p. 1998. reprint ed. pap. 13.95 (*1-56838-195-6*) Hazelden.
— What Life Could Mean to You. LC 98-21894. 250p. 1998. reprint ed. pap. 12.95 (*1-56838-228-6*) Hazelden.
Adler, Alfred & Brett, Colin. Social Interest: Adler's Key to the Meaning of Life. 1998. pap. 14.95 (*1-85168-156-6*, Pub. by Element MA) Penguin Putnam.
— Understanding Life. LC 97-49424. 180p. 1998. reprint ed. pap. 13.95 (*1-56838-196-4*) Hazelden.
Adler, Allan R., ed. Litigation under the Federal Freedom of Information Act & Privacy Act, 1990. 15th ed. 494p. 1990. pap. text 45.00 (*0-86566-052-2*); pap. text, student ed. 15.00 (*0-685-11916-5*) ACLU DC.
— Litigation under the Federal Open Government Laws. 20th rev. ed. 500p. 1997. pap. 45.00 (*0-914031-27-9*) Amer Civil Lib.
— Litigation under the Federal Open Government Laws: The Freedom of Information Act, the Privacy Act, the Government in the Sunshine Act, the Federal Advisory Comm. Act. 18th ed. 512p. (Orig.). (C). 1993. pap. 45.00 (*0-86566-064-6*) Ctr Natl Security.
Adler, Allen H., ed. see Schwartz, Gary H.
Adler, Andrew & Coury, John E. The Theory of Numbers: A Text & Source Book of Problems. LC 94-41865. 416p. 1995. 57.50 (*0-86720-472-9*) Jones & Bartlett.
Adler, Andrew, ed. see Carey, MacDonald.
Adler, Andrew, ed. see Lanigan, Anne.
Adler, Andrew, ed. see Leibowitz, Alan.
Adler, Andrew, ed. see Sugar, Bert R.
Adler, Anne. Germany. 2nd ed. (Getting to Know Ser.). (Illus.). 48p. 1994. 8.95 (*0-8442-2178-3*, Natl Textbk Co) NTC Contemp Pub Co.
Adler, Anne G., et al, compiled by. Automation in Libraries, 1978-1982: A LITA Bibliography. LC 83-62104. (Library Hi Tech Monograph: No. 1). 1983. 40.00 (*0-87650-157-9*) Pierian.
Adler, Anne G. & Baber, Elizabeth A. Retrospective Conversion: From Cards to Computer. LC 84-81656. (Library Hi Tech Monograph: No. 2). 324p. 1984. 45.00 (*0-87650-177-3*) Pierian.
Adler, Arlene & Carlton, Rick, eds. Introduction to Radiography & Patient Care. LC 93-14806. (Illus.). 368p. 1993. pap. text 37.95 (*0-7216-3465-6*, W B Saunders Co) Harcrt Hlth Sci Grp.
Adler, Arlene M. & Carlton, Richard R. Introduction to Radiography & Patient Care. 2nd ed. Allan, Andrew, ed. LC 98-25697. (Illus.). 415p. (C). 1998. pap. text 35.00 (*0-7216-7662-6*, W B Saunders Co) Harcrt Hlth Sci Grp.
Adler, Arlene M., jt. auth. see Carlton, Richard R.
***Adler, Betsy B., et al.** Advising California Nonprofit Corporations, 2 vols. 2nd ed. Brown, Wendy L., ed. LC 98-71190. 1209p. 1998. ring bd. 179.00 (*0-7626-0177-9*, BU-32950) Cont Ed Bar-CA.
Adler, Betty. H.L.M. The Mencken Bibliography. LC 61-15699. 389p. reprint ed. pap. 120.60 (*0-608-11320-4*, 201147100078) Bks Demand.
Adler, Betty, compiled by. Man of Letters: Census of H. L. Mencken's Correspondence. (Orig.). 1969. 7.00 (*0-910556-03-2*) Enoch Pratt.
Adler, Bill, Jr. Cat's Letters to Santa. 96p. 1997. 5.99 (*1-57866-005-X*) Galahad Bks.
— Children's Letters to Santa Claus. LC 93-25377. (Illus.). (J). (ps-3). 1996. 9.95 (*1-55972-196-0*, Birch Ln Pr) Carol Pub Group.
— Diana: A Portrait in Her Own Words. LC 99-15270. 192p. 1999. 16.00 (*0-688-17003-X*, Wm Morrow) Morrow Avon.
— Do You Remember the Fifties? 128p. (Orig.). 1992. mass mkt. 3.99 (*0-380-76734-1*, Avon Bks) Morrow Avon.
— Do You Remember the Sixties? 128p. (Orig.). 1992. mass mkt. 3.99 (*0-380-76733-3*, Avon Bks) Morrow Avon.
— First, Kill All the Lawyers: Legal Proverbs, Epitaphs, Jokes & Anecdotes. LC 94-20353. 144p. 1994. 8.95 (*0-8065-1587-2*, Citadel Pr) Carol Pub Group.
— Five Hundred Great Facts about America. 240p. (Orig.). 1992. mass mkt. 4.50 (*0-380-76787-2*, Avon Bks) Morrow Avon.
Adler, Bill, Jr. Fred Astaire: A Wonderful Life: A Biography LC 87-25019. 191p. 1987. write for info. (*0-88184-376-8*) Carroll & Graf.
Adler, Bill, Jr. Generals: The New American Heroes. 215p. 1991. mass mkt. 4.50 (*0-380-76721-X*, Avon Bks) Morrow Avon.
— Great Lawyer Stories: From Courthouse to Jailhouse - Tall Tales, Jokes & Anecdotes. 144p. 1992. pap. 7.95 (*0-8065-1373-X*, Citadel Pr) Carol Pub Group.
Adler, Bill, Jr. Hip Kids' Letters from Camp. LC 75-142399. (J). 1971. write for info. (*0-688-31354-X*, Wm Morrow) Morrow Avon.
— If I Were President: Kids Talk about Running the Country. 128p. 2000. pap. 10.00 (*0-380-80562-6*) Morrow Avon.
— The Illustrated Book of World Records. LC 74-93. (Illus.). 123p. 1974. write for info. (*0-448-11760-6*, Tuffy) Putnam Pub Group.
— The Joe Dimaggio Reader. 1999. 18.00 (*0-688-17148-6*, Wm Morrow) Morrow Avon.
— Kids' E-Mail & Letters from Camp. 2000. 9.99 (*1-55853-827-5*) Rutledge Hill Pr.
Adler, Bill, Jr. The Letterman Wit: His Life & Humor. 144p. 1994. 14.95 (*0-7867-0075-0*) Carroll & Graf.
— The Letterman Wit: His Life & Humor. (Illus.). 160p. 1995. pap. 8.95 (*0-7867-0210-9*) Carroll & Graf.
— The Life & Humor of Robin Williams: A Biography. LC 99-15806. (Illus.). 224p. 1999. pap. 12.00 (*0-688-15245-7*, Wm Morrow) Morrow Avon.
— The Literary Agent's Guide to Getting Published & Making Money from Your Writing. LC 99-21349. 288p. 1999. pap. 14.95 (*1-892025-00-0*, Pub. by Claren Bks) IPG Chicago.
Adler, Bill, Jr. Motherhood, a Celebration. LC 87-739. ix, 116 p. 1987. write for info. (*0-88184-307-5*) Carroll & Graf.
Adler, Bill, Jr. One Hundred Ways to Love America. 1991. pap. 2.95 (*0-380-76746-5*, Avon Bks) Morrow Avon.
***Adler, Bill, Jr.** Outwitting Critters. 1998. pap. 12.95 (*0-676-57281-2*) Random.
Adler, Bill, Jr. Outwitting Critters: A Humane Guide for Confronting Devious Animals & Winning. LC 96-2750. 272p. 1997. pap. 12.95 (*1-55821-523-9*) Lyons Pr.
***Adler, Bill, Jr.** Outwitting Deer. LC 99-33059. (Illus.). 1999. pap. 14.95 (*1-55821-629-4*) Lyons Pr.
— Outwitting Mice. (Illus.). 224p. 2000. 14.95 (*1-58574-004-7*) Lyons Pr.
Adler, Bill, Jr. Outwitting Squirrels: 101 Cunning Stratagems to Reduce Dramatically the Egregious Misappropriation of Seed from Your Birdfeeder by Squirrels. 2nd ed. LC 88-20283. (Illus.). 188p. 1996. pap. 11.95 (*1-55652-302-5*) Chicago Review.
***Adler, Bill, Jr.** Outwitting the Neighbors: A Practical & Entertaining Guide to Achieving Peaceful Coexistence with Your Neighbors. 2000. pap. 14.95 (*1-58574-161-2*) Lyons Pr.
***Adler, Bill.** Quotable Birder. 2000. 20.00 (*1-58574-003-9*) Lyons Pr.
Adler, Bill, Jr. The Reagan Wit. LC 81-38509. 120p. 1992. 6.95 (*0-89803-090-0*) Jameson Bks.
— 365 Things to Do with Your Kids. LC 99-31190. 224p. 1999. pap. 12.95 (*0-8092-2611-1*, 261110, Contemporary Bks) NTC Contemp Pub Co.
— Uncommon Wisdom of Jacqueline Kennedy Onassis. xi, 156p. 1994. 12.95 (*0-8065-1592-9*, Citadel Pr) Carol Pub Group.
— Uncommon Wisdom of Jacqueline Kennedy Onassis: A Portrait in Her Own Words. 1999. pap. text 14.95 (*0-8065-2166-X*) Carol Pub Group.
***Adler, Bill, Jr.** Uncommon Wisdom of Oprah Winfrey: A Portrait in Her Own Words. 1999. pap. text 9.95 (*0-8065-2164-3*) Carol Pub Group.
Adler, Bill, Jr. The Uncommon Wisdom of Ronald Reagan: A Portrait in His Own Words. LC 96-575. 176p. (gr. 8). 1996. 14.95 (*0-316-05600-6*) Little.
Adler, Bill, Jr., compiled by. The Quotable Conservative: The Wit & Insight of Freedom's Most Passionate Advocates. (Illus.). 288p. 1995. 9.95 (*1-55972-291-6*, Birch Ln Pr) Carol Pub Group.
— Ross Perot: An American Maverick Speaks Out. LC 93-40570. v, 168p. 1994. 10.95 (*0-8065-1500-7*, Citadel Pr) Carol Pub Group.
— Wit & Wisdom of Abraham Lincoln. 1993. pap. 7.95 (*0-8065-1456-6*, Citadel Pr) Carol Pub Group.
Adler, Bill, Jr., ed. Cats' Letters to Santa. (Illus.). 96p. 1996. 10.95 (*0-7867-0123-4*) Carroll & Graf.
— Children's Letters to Socks: Kids Write to America's "First Cat" LC 93-46694. 64p. (YA). 1994. 9.95 (*1-55972-221-5*, Birch Ln Pr) Carol Pub Group.
— Kids' Letters from Camp. LC 93-46693. (Illus.). 64p. (YA). (gr. 7 up). 1994. 9.95 (*1-55972-226-6*, Birch Ln Pr) Carol Pub Group.
— The Reagan Wit: The Humor of the American President. LC 97-30824. 191p. 1998. 15.00 (*0-688-15514-6*, Wm Morrow) Morrow Avon.
— Time Machines. LC 97-29705. 382p. 1997. 24.00 (*0-7867-0493-4*) Carroll & Graf.
— The Uncommon Wisdom of Oprah Winfrey: A Portrait in Her Own Words. LC 96-37404. 334p. 1997. 14.95 (*1-55972-419-6*, Birch Ln Pr) Carol Pub Group.
— The Uncommon Wisdom of Oprah Winfrey: A Portrait in Her Own Words. 290p. 1999. text 15.00 (*0-7881-6097-4*) DIANE Pub.
Adler, Bill, Jr. & Cassiday, Bruce. The World of Jay Leno: His Humor & His Life. (Illus.). 192p. 1992. 15.95 (*1-55972-145-6*, Birch Ln Pr) Carol Pub Group.
Adler, Bill, Jr. & Chastin, Thomas. Who Killed the Robins Family? 192p. 1984. mass mkt. 3.50 (*0-446-32314-4*, Pub. by Warner Bks) Little.
Adler, Bill, Jr. & Fraser, Kristy. The Computer Support Directory: Voice, Fax, & Online Access Numbers. LC 94-47306. 1995. 12.95 (*0-07-000428-5*) McGraw.
Adler, Bill, Jr. & Houghton, P. Julie. America's Stupidest Business Decisions: 101 Blunders, Flops, & Screw Ups. LC 97-8566. (Illus.). 208p. (Orig.). 1997. pap. 9.95 (*0-688-15152-3*, Quil) HarperTrade.
Adler, Bill, Jr. & Malsberg, Edward. A Quiz Book: Interesting Facts That Inform & Entertain LC 77-78965. (Elephant Books Ser.). 94p. 1977. write for info. (*0-448-14294-5*, Tuffy) Putnam Pub Group.
— World's Worst Riddles & Jokes LC 76-6819. 110p. 1976. write for info. (*0-448-12586-2*, Tuffy) Putnam Pub Group.
Adler, Bill, Jr. & Pratt-Dewey, Beth. Ask Me Something I Don't Know. 224p. (Orig.). 1993. mass mkt. 4.99 (*0-380-76782-1*, Avon Bks) Morrow Avon.
Adler, Bill, Jr. & Presley, Elvis. Bill Adler's Love Letters to Elvis. LC 77-94852. 96p. 1978. write for info. (*0-448-14717-3*, Tuffy) Putnam Pub Group.
Adler, Bill, Jr. & Robin, Peggy. Billy Clinton's Letters from Camp. LC 97-291. (Illus.). 96p. 1997. pap. 8.95 (*0-7867-0417-9*) Carroll & Graf.
— The Star Fleet Academy Entrance Exam: Tantalizing Trivia from Classic Star Trek Voyager. LC 97-34763. 224p. 1995. pap. 9.95 (*0-8065-1695-X*, Citadel Pr) Carol Pub Group.
Adler, Bill, Jr. & Robin, Peggy, eds. Outwitting Toddlers. (Illus.). 192p. (Orig.). 1993. pap. 12.95 (*1-56565-032-8*) Lowell Hse.
Adler, Bill, see David, Jay, pseud.
Adler, Bill, ed. see David, Jay, pseud.
Adler, Bill, Jr., jt. auth. see Goodman, Gloria.
Adler, Bill, Jr., jt. auth. see Wagner, Ronald L.
Adler, Binyamin. The Vintage Haggadah: Veinah Shel Torah. Lavon, Yaakov, tr. 288p. 1998. 12.95 (*0-87306-642-1*) Feldheim.
Adler, Bruno, ed. Utopia: Dokumente der Wirklichkeit. (Bauhaus Ser.). 1990. reprint ed. pap. 110.00 (*3-601-00284-1*) Periodicals Srv.
***Adler, C. P.** Bone Diseases: The Diagnosis of Macroscopic, Histological & Radiological Structural Changes in the Skeleton. Steel, F., tr. LC 99-58725. (Illus.). xxix, 590p. 2000. 159.00 (*3-540-65061-X*) Spr-Verlag.
Adler, C. Q., ed. see Agnos, Peter.
***Adler, C. Ralph & Thurlow, Dave.** Soul of the Sky: Exploring the Human Side of Weather. LC 99-69401. (Illus.). 150p. 2000. pap. 12.95 (*0-931134-99-4*, Pub. by Mount Washington Observatory) ACCESS Pubs Network.
Adler, C. S. Always & Forever Friends. 176p. (J). 1990. pap. 3.99 (*0-380-70687-3*, Avon Bks) Morrow Avon.
— The Courtyard Cat. 176p. (J). (gr. 3-7). 1997. pap. 3.99 (*0-380-72829-X*, Avon Bks) Morrow Avon.
— Daddy's Climbing Tree. 144p. (J). (gr. 3-6). 1993. 15.00 (*0-395-63032-0*, Clarion Bks) HM.
— Eddie's Blue-Winged Dragon. 144p. (J). 1990. reprint ed. pap. 3.50 (*0-380-70768-3*, Avon Bks) Morrow Avon.
— Ghost Brother. 160p. (J). (gr. 4-8). 1990. 15.00 (*0-395-52592-6*, Clarion Bks) HM.
— Ghost Brother. 144p. (J). 1992. pap. 3.50 (*0-380-71386-1*, Avon Bks) Morrow Avon.
— Good-Bye Pink Pig. 176p. (J). (gr. 3-7). 1986. pap. 2.75 (*0-380-70175-8*, Avon Bks) Morrow Avon.
— Help, Pink Pig! 160p. 1991. pap. 2.95 (*0-380-71156-7*, Avon Bks) Morrow Avon.
— Her Blue Straw Hat. LC 96-50124. 112p. (J). (gr. 3-7). 1997. 16.00 (*0-15-201466-7*) Harcourt.
— Her Blue Straw Hat. LC 96-50124. 1997. pap. 5.00 (*0-15-201469-1*) Harcourt.
***Adler, C. S.** The Horse Her Father Gave Her. LC 00-25907. (Illus.). (J). 2000. write for info. (*0-618-04912-6*) HM.
Adler, C. S. The Lump in the Middle. 160p. (YA). 1991. pap. 3.50 (*0-380-71176-1*, Avon Bks) Morrow Avon.
— The Magic of the Glits. 96p. (J). 1987. pap. 2.50 (*0-380-70403-X*, Avon Bks) Morrow Avon.
— More Than a Horse. LC 96-42175. 192p. (J). (gr. 5-9). 1997. 15.00 (*0-395-79769-1*, Clarion Bks) HM.
— Not Just a Summer Crush. LC 98-11358. 128p. (J). (gr. 5-8). 1998. 15.00 (*0-395-88532-9*, Clarion Bks) HM.
— One Sister Too Many. LC 91-15530. 176p. (J). (gr. 3-7). 1991. reprint ed. pap. 3.95 (*0-689-71521-8*) Aladdin.
— The Silver Coach. 112p. (J). (gr. 3-7). 1988. pap. 2.50 (*0-380-75498-3*, Avon Bks) Morrow Avon.
— Some Other Summer. (J). (gr. 3-7). 1988. pap. 2.95 (*0-380-70515-X*, Avon Bks) Morrow Avon.
— That Horse Whiskey. 160p. (J). (gr. 3-7). 1996. pap. 3.99 (*0-380-72601-7*, Avon Bks) Morrow Avon.
— What's to Be Scared of, Suki? LC 95-50141. 176p. (J). (gr. 3-7). 1996. 13.95 (*0-395-77600-7*, Clarion Bks) HM.
Adler, C. S. Willie, the Frog Prince. LC 92-44113. 176p. (J). 1994. 15.00 (*0-395-65615-X*, Clarion Bks) HM.
Adler, C. S. Winning. LC 98-51935. 160p. (YA). (gr. 5-9). 1999. 14.00 (*0-395-65017-8*, Clarion Bks) HM.
— Youn Hee & Me. LC 94-31060. 192p. (J). (gr. 3-7). 1995. 12.00 (*0-15-200073-9*) Harcourt.
— Young He & Me. LC 94-31060. 192p. (J). (gr. 3-7). 1995. pap. 5.00 (*0-15-200376-2*) Harcourt.
Adler, Carol, ed. see Deiuliis, Guy.
Adler, Carol, ed. see Kelly, Dennis.
Adler, Carol, ed. see Simpson, Sheryl.
Adler, Carole S. Riding Whiskey. LC 93-30196. (Illus.). 160p. (J). 1994. 14.00 (*0-395-68185-5*) HM.
Adler, Chaim, jt. auth. see Inbar, Michael.
***Adler, Charles H. & Ahlskog, J. Eric, eds.** Parkinson's Disease & Movement Disorders: Diagnosis & Treatment Guidelines for the Practicing Physician. (Current Clinical Practice Ser.). 496p. 2000. 125.00 (*0-89603-607-3*) Humana.
Adler, Connie, ed. see Kingsbury, Lisa & Williams, Cam.
Adler, C.S. Youn Hee & Me. 1995. 10.10 (*0-606-10992-7*, Pub. by Turtleback) Demco.
Adler, Cy A. Ecological Fantasies: Death from Falling Watermelons. LC 73-80695. (Illus.). (Orig.). 1978. 24.00 (*0-914018-02-7*) Green Eagle Pr.
— Walking the Hudson, Batt to Bear: From the Battery to Bear Mountain. LC 96-95056. (Illus.). 164p. (Orig.). 1997. pap. 12.95 (*0-914018-04-3*, 7269) Green Eagle Pr.
Adler, Cy A., ed. see Tsuki, Tommi & Agnos, Peter.
Adler, Cyrus. I Have Considered the Days. (Illus.). 1969. 8.00 (*0-8381-3110-7*) USCJE.
— Jacob H. Schiff: His Life & Letters, 2 vols, Set. LC 72-1474. (Select Bibliographies Reprint Ser.). 1977. 46.95 (*0-8369-6818-2*) Ayer.
— Jacob H. Schiff: His Life & Letters, 2 vols., Set. 1968. reprint ed. 39.00 (*0-403-00134-X*) Scholarly.
— Walking Manhattan's Rim: The Great Saunter Around New York Island. Blanchard, Hal, ed. (Illus.). 1999. pap. 12.95 (*0-914018-12-4*) Green Eagle Pr.
Adler, Cyrus & Margalith, Aaron M. With Firmness in the Right: American Diplomatic Action Affecting Jews, 1840-1945. Davis, Moshe, ed. LC 77-70651. (America & the Holy Land Ser.). 1977. reprint ed. lib. bdg. 44.95 (*0-405-10222-4*) Ayer.
Adler, D., et al, eds. Materials Issues in Amorphous-Semiconductor Technology. (MRS Symposium Proceedings Ser.: Vol. 70). 1986. text 17.50 (*0-931837-36-7*) Materials Res.
Adler, David. Amazing Magnets. LC 82-17377. (Question & Answer Bks.). (Illus.). 32p. (J). (gr. 3-6). 1996. pap. 2.95 (*0-89375-895-7*) Troll Communs.
Adler, David. Cam Jansen & the Mystery of the Babe Ruth Baseball. (Cam Jansen Series). 57p. (J). (gr. 2-4). pap. 3.99 (*0-8072-1347-0*) Listening Lib.

A

A

— CAM Jansen & the Mystery of the Dinosaur Bones/CAM Jansen & the Mystery of the U.F.O. (Illus.). 128p. (J). (gr. 2-5). 2000. 5.99 (0-670-89365-X, Viking Child) Peng Put Young Read.

— Cam Jansen & the Stolen Diamonds/Cam Jansen & the Babe Ruth Baseball. (Illus.). 128p. (J). (gr. 2-5). 2000. 5.99 (0-670-89366-8, Viking Child) Peng Put Young Read.

Adler, David. George Washington's Wooden Teeth. 1998. 16.95 (0-8050-5114-7, Bks Young Read) H Holt & Co.

— A Houdini Club Magic Mystery: Magic Money. (First Stepping Stone Bks.). (Illus.). (J). (gr. 1-4). 1997. pap. 3.99 (0-614-28935-1) Random Bks Yng Read.

— Metric Handbook: Planning & Design Data. 2nd ed. LC 99-230878. 1999. pap. text 54.95 (0-7506-0899-4) Buttrwrth-Heinemann.

Adler, David. Metric Handbook CD Rom Version 1.1. Date not set. audio compact disk 330.00 (0-7506-4779-5, Architectural Pr) Buttrwrth-Heinemann.

Adler, David. A Picture Book of Martin Luther King, Jr. unabridged rev. ed. (Illus.). (J). (gr. 2-4). 1998. 24.95 incl. audio (0-87499-166-8) Live Oak Media.

***Adler, David.** A Picture Book of Martin Luther King, Jr.; Un Libro Illustrado Sobe Martin Luther King, Hijo, 2 bks., Set. unabridged ed. Mlawer, Teresa, tr. (J). 1999. pap. 29.95 incl. audio (0-87499-569-8) Live Oak Media.

Adler, David. We Remember the Holocaust. LC 87-21139. (Illus.). 160p. (YA). (gr. 6 up). 1995. 18.95 (0-8050-0434-3, Bks Young Read) H Holt & Co.

***Adler, David A.** America's Champion Swimmer: Gertrude Ederle. LC 98-54954. (Illus.). 32p. (J). (gr. k-4). 2000. 16.00 (0-15-201969-3, Gulliver Bks) Harcourt.

— America's Champion Swimmer: Gertrude Ederle. (Illus.). 32p. (gr. 1-4). 2000. 27.11 (0-7398-2197-0) Raintree Steck-V.

Adler, David A. Andy & Tamika. LC 98-39423. (Illus.). 144p. (J). 1999. 14.00 (0-15-201735-6) Harcourt.

— Andy & Tamika. LC 98-39423. 144p. (J). 1999. pap. 4.95 (0-15-201901-4, Gulliver Bks) Harcourt.

***Adler, David A.** Andy & Tamika. (Illus.). (J). 1999. 10.30 (0-606-18166-0) Turtleback.

Adler, David A. The Babe & I. LC 97-37580. (Illus.). 32p. (J). 1999. 16.00 (0-15-201378-4) Harcourt.

— Bible Fun Book: Puzzles, Riddles, Magic, & More. (Fun-to-Do Bks.). (Illus.). (Orig.). (J). (gr. 1-5). 1979. pap. 3.95 (0-88482-769-0) Hebrew Pub.

— Brothers in Egypt. (Prince of Egypt Ser.). 64p. 1998. pap. 3.99 (0-14-130218-6, PuffinBks) Peng Put Young Read.

— Calculator Riddles. LC 94-41874. (Illus.). 32p. (J). (gr. k-3). 1995. 14.95 (0-8234-1186-9); pap. 5.95 (0-8234-1269-5) Holiday.

***Adler, David A.** Cam Jansen & the Barking Treasure Mystery. LC 98-52517. (Illus.). 55p. (J). (ps-4). 1999. 13.99 (0-670-88516-9) Viking Penguin.

— Cam Jansen & the Birthday Mystery. LC 99-86039. (Cam Jansen Adventure Ser.: Vol. 20). (Illus.). 64p. (J). (gr. 2-5). 2000. 13.99 (0-670-88877-X, Viking Child) Peng Put Young Read.

— Cam Jansen & the Catnapping Mystery. (Cam Jansen Ser.: Vol. 18). (Illus.). 64p. (J). (gr. 2-5). 2000. pap. 3.99 (0-14-130897-4, PuffinBks) Peng Put Young Read.

Adler, David A. Cam Jansen & the Chocolate Fudge Mystery. (Cam Jansen Adventure Ser.). (J). 1995. 9.19 (0-606-07334-5, Pub. by Turtleback) Demco.

— Cam Jansen & the Ghostly Mystery. (Cam Jansen Ser.: Vol. 16). 64p. (J). (gr. 2-5). 1998. pap. 3.99 (0-14-038740-4, PuffinBks) Peng Put Young Read.

— Cam Jansen & the Ghostly Mystery. LC 96-15250. (Cam Jansen Adventure Ser.: Vol. 16). (Illus.). 64p. (J). (gr. 1-4). 1996. 13.99 (0-670-86872-8, Viking) Viking Penguin.

— Cam Jansen & the Mystery at the Haunted House. (Cam Jansen Ser.: No. 13). (Illus.). 64p. (J). (gr. 2-5). 1992. 13.99 (0-670-83419-X, Viking Child) Peng Put Young Read.

Adler, David A. Cam Jansen & the Mystery at the Haunted House. LC 91-28863. (Cam Jansen Adventure Ser.). 1994. 9.19 (0-606-06264-5, Pub. by Turtleback) Demco.

Adler, David A. Cam Jansen & the Mystery at the Monkey House. (Illus.). (J). (gr. 4). 1995. 9.00 (0-395-73242-5) HM.

— Cam Jansen & the Mystery at the Monkey House. LC 85-40443. (Cam Jansen Ser.). (Illus.). 56p. (J). (gr. 2-4). 1985. 13.99 (0-670-80782-6, Viking Child) Peng Put Young Read.

— Cam Jansen & the Mystery at the Monkey House. (Cam Jansen Ser.). 64p. (gr. 2-5). 1999. pap. 3.99 (0-14-130306-9, PuffinBks) Peng Put Young Read.

— Cam Jansen & the Mystery at the Monkey House. (Young Puffin Ser.). (J). 1993. 9.19 (0-606-05777-3, Pub. by Turtleback) Demco.

— Cam Jansen & the Mystery at the Monkey House. large type ed. (Illus.). 78p. (J). (gr. 4). 19.50 (0-614-20578-6, L-38180-00 APHB) Am Printing Hse.

Adler, David A. Cam Jansen & the Mystery of Flight 54. (Cam Jansen Ser.: No. 12). (Illus.). 64p. (J). (gr. 2-5). 1989. 13.99 (0-670-81841-0, Viking Child) Peng Put Young Read.

— Cam Jansen & the Mystery of Flight 54. (Cam Jansen Ser.). 64p. (J). 1999. pap. 3.99 (0-14-130459-6) Peng Put Young Read.

Adler, David A. Cam Jansen & the Mystery of Flight 54. (Cam Jansen Adventure Ser.). (J). 1992. 9.19 (0-606-01682-1, Pub. by Turtleback) Demco.

— Cam Jansen & the Mystery of the Babe Ruth Baseball. (Illus.). (J). (gr. 3). 1995. 8.60 (0-395-73229-8) HM.

— Cam Jansen & the Mystery of the Babe Ruth Baseball. LC 82-2621. (Cam Jansen Ser.: No. 6). (Illus.). 64p. (J). (gr. 2-5). 1982. 13.99 (0-670-20037-9, Viking Child) Peng Put Young Read.

— Cam Jansen & the Mystery of the Babe Ruth Baseball. (Cam Jansen Adventure Ser.). 1991. 9.19 (0-606-06146-0, Pub. by Turtleback) Demco.

— Cam Jansen & the Mystery of the Babe Ruth Baseball. large type ed. (Illus.). 86p. (J). (gr. 3). 21.50 (0-614-20579-4, L-38221-00 APHB) Am Printing Hse.

— Cam Jansen & the Mystery of the Babe Ruth Baseball, No. 6. Vol. 6. (Illus.). 64p. (J). (gr. 2-5). 1998. pap. 3.99 (0-14-130090-6, PuffinBks) Peng Put Young Read.

Adler, David A. Cam Jansen & the Mystery of the Carnival Prize. (Cam Jansen Adventure Ser.). (J). 1992. 9.19 (0-606-02446-8, Pub. by Turtleback) Demco.

Adler, David A. Cam Jansen & the Mystery of the Chocolate Fudge Sale. LC 93-18622. Vol. 14. (Illus.). 64p. (J). (gr. 2-5). 1993. 13.99 (0-670-84968-5, Viking Child) Peng Put Young Read.

— Cam Jansen & the Mystery of the Circus Clown. LC 82-50363. (Cam Jansen Ser.: No. 7). (Illus.). 64p. (J). (gr. 2-4). 1983. 13.99 (0-670-20036-0, Viking Child) Peng Put Young Read.

Adler, David A. Cam Jansen & the Mystery of the Circus Clown. LC 91-53035. (Cam Jansen Adventure Ser.). 1991. 9.19 (0-606-06262-9, Pub. by Turtleback) Demco.

Adler, David A. Cam Jansen & the Mystery of the Dinosaur Bones. LC 80-25132. (Cam Jansen Ser.: Vol. 3). (Illus.). 64p. (J). (gr. 4-7). 1981. 13.99 (0-670-20040-9, Viking Child) Peng Put Young Read.

— Cam Jansen & the Mystery of the Dinosaur Bones. (Puffin Chapters Ser.: Vol. 3). (Illus.). 64p. (J). (gr. 2-5). 1997. pap. 3.99 (0-14-038715-3, PuffinBks) Peng Put Young Read.

— Cam Jansen & the Mystery of the Dinosaur Bones. (Puffin Chapters Ser.). (J). 1997. 9.19 (0-606-04623-2, Pub. by Turtleback) Demco.

— Cam Jansen & the Mystery of the Gold Coins. LC 81-16158. (Cam Jansen Ser.: No. 5). (Illus.). 64p. (J). (gr. 2-5). 1982. 13.99 (0-670-20038-7, Viking Child) Peng Put Young Read.

— Cam Jansen & the Mystery of the Gold Coins. (Puffin Chapters Ser.: Vol. 5). (Illus.). 64p. (J). (gr. 2-5). 1998. pap. 3.99 (0-14-038954-7, PuffinBks) Peng Put Young Read.

Adler, David A. Cam Jansen & the Mystery of the Gold Coins. LC 91-53036. (Cam Jansen Adventure Ser.). 1991. 9.19 (0-606-06263-7, Pub. by Turtleback) Demco.

Adler, David A. Cam Jansen & the Mystery of the Monster Movie. LC 83-16693. (Cam Jansen Ser.: Vol. 8). (Illus.). 64p. (J). (gr. 4-7). 1984. 12.99 (0-670-20035-2, Viking Child) Peng Put Young Read.

— Cam Jansen & the Mystery of the Monster Movie. (Cam Jansen Ser.). (Illus.). 64p. (J). (gr. 2-5). 1992. pap. 3.99 (0-14-036021-2, PuffinBks) Peng Put Young Read.

Adler, David A. Cam Jansen & the Mystery of the Monster Movie. (Cam Jansen Adventure Ser.). (J). 1992. 9.19 (0-606-02443-3, Pub. by Turtleback) Demco.

Adler, David A. Cam Jansen & the Mystery of the Scary Snake. LC 97-2627. (Illus.). 64p. (J). (gr. 1-3). 1997. 13.99 (0-670-87517-1) Viking Penguin.

— Cam Jansen & the Mystery of the Stolen Corn Popper. (Cam Jansen Adventure Ser.). (J). 1992. 9.19 (0-606-01683-X, Pub. by Turtleback) Demco.

***Adler, David A.** Cam Jansen & the Mystery of the Stolen Corn Popper, 11. (Cam Jansen Ser.). 1999. pap. 3.99 (0-14-130461-8, PuffinBks) Peng Put Young Read.

Adler, David A. Cam Jansen & the Mystery of the Stolen Diamonds. (Illus.). 64p. (J). (gr. 2-5). 1997. pap. 3.99 (0-14-038580-0) Penguin Putnam.

Adler, David A. Cam Jansen & the Mystery of the Stolen Diamonds. (Cam Jansen Adventure Ser.). 1997. 9.19 (0-606-11182-4, Pub. by Turtleback) Demco.

Adler, David A. Cam Jansen & the Mystery of the Television Dog. (Cam Jansen Adventure Ser.). (J). 1991. 9.19 (0-606-04625-9, Pub. by Turtleback) Demco.

— Cam Jansen & the Mystery of the Television Dog. 64p. (J). (gr. 2-5). 1998. pap. 3.99 (0-14-038800-1) Viking Penguin.

— Cam Jansen & the Mystery of the U. F. O. LC 80-15580. (Cam Jansen Ser.: Vol. 2). (Illus.). 64p. (J). (gr. 4-7). 1980. 13.99 (0-670-20041-7, Viking Child) Peng Put Young Read.

Adler, David A. Cam Jansen & the Mystery of the U. F. O. LC 80-15580. (Cam Jansen Adventure Ser.). 1997. 9.19 (0-606-11183-2, Pub. by Turtleback) Demco.

Adler, David A. Cam Jansen & the Mystery of the U. F. O., No. 2. (Illus.). 64p. (J). (gr. 2-5). 1997. pap. 3.99 (0-14-038579-7, PuffinBks) Peng Put Young Read.

***Adler, David A.** Cam Jansen & the Scary Snake Mystery. 17th ed. (Cam Jansen Ser.: Vol. 17). (Illus.). 64p. (J). (gr. 2-5). 1999. pap. 3.99 (0-14-130363-8, PuffinBks) Peng Put Young Read.

Adler, David A. Cam Jansen & the Triceratops Pops Mystery. LC 95-4576. (Cam Jansen Ser.: No. 15). (Illus.). 56p. (J). (gr. 2-5). 1995. 13.99 (0-670-86027-1, Viking Child) Peng Put Young Read.

— Cam Jansen & the Triceratops Pops Mystery. (Puffin Chapters Ser.). (J). 1997. 9.19 (0-606-12641-4, Pub. by Turtleback) Demco.

***Adler, David A.** The Cam Jansen Fun Book. (Illus.). 32p. (J). (gr. 2-5). 2000. pap. 4.99 (0-14-056756-9, PuffinBks) Peng Put Young Read.

Adler, David A. Chanukah in Chelm. LC 96-53127. (Illus.). 32p. (J). (ps-3). 1997. 16.00 (0-688-09952-1); lib. bdg., lab manual ed. 15.93 (0-688-09953-X) Lothrop.

— Child of the Warsaw Ghetto. LC 94-27779. (Illus.). 32p. (J). (gr. 4-6). 1995. lib. bdg. 15.95 (0-8234-1160-5) Holiday.

— The Children's Book of Jewish Holidays. (ArtScroll Youth Ser.). (Illus.). 48p. (J). (gr. k-6). 1987. 13.99 (0-89906-810-3); pap. 8.99 (0-89906-811-1) Mesorah Pubns.

***Adler, David A.** Chocolate Fudge Mystery. (Cam Jansen Ser.). 64p. (J). 1999. pap. 3.99 (0-14-130648-3, PuffinBks) Peng Put Young Read.

Adler, David A. Christopher Columbus: Great Explorer. LC 90-28668. (Illus.). 48p. (J). (gr. k-3). 1991. lib. bdg. 15.95 (0-8234-0895-7) Holiday.

***Adler, David A.** Developing Business Strategies. LC 98-10049. 352p. 1998. 39.95 (0-471-18364-4) Wiley.

Adler, David A. The Dinosaur Princess & Other Prehistoric Riddles. LC 87-25121. (Illus.). 64p. (J). (gr. k-3). 1988. lib. bdg. 14.95 (0-8234-0686-5) Holiday.

***Adler, David A.** Dr. Martin Luther King, Jr. LC 00-24314. (Illus.). 2001. write for info. (0-8234-1572-4) Holiday.

Adler, David A. Easy Math Puzzles. LC 96-30921. (Illus.). 32p. (J). (gr. k-3). 1997. lib. bdg. 15.95 (0-8234-1283-0) Holiday.

Adler, David A. Eaton Stanley & the Mind Control Experiment. (Eaton Stanley Adventure Ser.). 1996. 8.70 (0-606-09226-9, Pub. by Turtleback) Demco.

Adler, David A. The Fourth Floor Twins & the Sand Castle Contest. (Fourth Floor Twins Ser.). (Illus.). (J). (gr. 2-5). 1988. 9.95 (0-318-37432-3, Viking Child) Peng Put Young Read.

— Fraction Fun. LC 96-10773. (Illus.). 32p. (J). (gr. k-3). 1996. lib. bdg. 16.95 (0-8234-1259-8) Holiday.

— Fraction Fun. (Illus.). 32p. (J). (ps up). 1996. reprint ed. pap. 6.95 (0-8234-1341-1) Holiday.

— Hanukkah Fun Book: Puzzles, Riddles, Magic & More. LC 76-47459. (Illus.). (J). (gr. 3-7). 1976. pap. 3.95 (0-88482-754-2) Hebrew Pub.

— Hanukkah Game Book: Games, Riddles, Puzzles & More. (Fun-to-Do Bks.). (Illus.). (J). (gr. 1-5). 1978. pap. 3.95 (0-88482-764-X) Hebrew Pub.

Adler, David A. Hiding from the Nazis. LC 96-38451. (Illus.). 32p. (J). (gr. 4-6). 1997. lib. bdg. 15.95 (0-8234-1288-1) Holiday.

Adler, David A. Hilde & Eli, Children of the Holocaust. LC 93-38229. (Illus.). 32p. (J). (gr. 4-6). 1994. 16.95 (0-8234-1091-9) Holiday.

— House on the Roof: A Sukkot Story. 1976. 10.15 (0-606-08774-5, Pub. by Turtleback) Demco.

— How Tall, How Short, How Far Away. LC 98-18802. (Illus.). (J). (ps-3). 1999. 16.95 (0-8234-1375-6) Holiday.

***Adler, David A.** How Tall, How Short, How Far Away. (Illus.). (gr. 4-7). 2000. 6.95 (0-8234-1632-1) Holiday.

Adler, David A. Jackie Robinson, He Was the First. LC 88-32394. (Illus.). 48p. (J). (gr. 2-5). 1989. lib. bdg. 15.95 (0-8234-0734-9) Holiday.

— Un Libro Ilustrado Sobre Martin Luther King, Hijo. Mlawer, Teresa, tr. from ENG. Orig. Title: A Picture Book of Martin Luther King, Jr.. (SPA., Illus.). 32p. (J). (ps-3). 1992. reprint ed. pap. 6.95 (0-8234-0991-0); reprint ed. lib. bdg. 15.95 (0-8234-0982-1) Holiday.

— Un Libro Ilustrado Sobre Martin Luther King, Hijo. unabridged ed. Orig. Title: A Picture Book of Martin Luther King, Jr.. (SPA., Illus.). (J). (gr. 1-6). 1993. 24.95 incl. audio (0-87499-297-4); pap. 15.95 incl. audio (0-87499-296-6) Live Oak Media.

— Un Libro Ilustrado Sobre Martin Luther King, Hijo, 4 bks., Set. unabridged ed. Orig. Title: A Picture Book of Martin Luther King, Jr.. (SPA., Illus.). (J). (gr. 1-6). 1993. pap., teacher ed. 37.95 incl. audio (0-87499-298-2) Live Oak Media.

— Lou Gehrig: The Luckiest Man Alive. LC 95-7997. (Illus.). 32p. (J). (gr. k-4). 1997. 16.00 (0-15-200523-4, Gulliver Bks) Harcourt.

***Adler, David A.** Lou Gehrig: The Luckiest Man Alive. 2001. pap. write for info. (0-15-202483-2) Harcourt.

Adler, David A. Lucky Stars. LC 94-33629. (Houdini Club Magic Mystery Ser.). (J). 1996. 9.19 (0-606-09579-9, Pub. by Turtleback) Demco.

— Magic Money. (First Stepping Stone Bks.). 1997. 9.19 (0-606-11590-0, Pub. by Turtleback) Demco.

— The Many Troubles of Andy Russell. LC 98-10788. (Illus.). 133p. (J). (gr. 3-5). 1998. 14.00 (0-15-201295-8) Harcourt.

— The Many Troubles of Andy Russell. LC 98-10788. (Illus.). 144p. (J). 1999. pap. 4.95 (0-15-201900-6, Voyager Bks) Harcourt.

— Martin Luther King, Jr. Free at Last. LC 86-4670. (Illus.). 48p. (J). (gr. k-3). 1986. lib. bdg. 15.95 (0-8234-0618-0) Holiday.

***Adler, David A.** My Writing Day. LC 99-11049. (Meet the Author Ser.). (Illus.). 32p. (J). (gr. 2-5). 1999. 14.95 (1-57274-326-3, 723) R Owen Pubs.

***Adler, David A.** Mystery at the Haunted House. (Cam Jansen Ser.). 64p. (J). 1999. pap. 3.99 (0-14-130649-1, PuffinBks) Peng Put Young Read.

Adler, David A. Mystery of the Monster Movie, 8 vols., Vol. 1 (Cam Jansen Ser.: Vol. 8). (Illus.). 64p. (gr. 2-5). 1999. pap. 3.99 (0-14-130460-X, PuffinBks) Peng Put Young Read.

— The Number on My Grandfather's Arm. (Illus.). 28p. (J). (gr. 1-3). 1987. 10.95 (0-8074-0328-8, 103641) UAHC.

— One Yellow Daffodil: A Hanukkah Story. LC 94-31374. (Illus.). 32p. (J). (gr. 1-5). 1999. pap. 6.00 (0-15-202094-2, Voyager Bks) Harcourt.

— Onion Sundaes: A Houdini Club Magic Mystery. (Houdini Club Magic Mystery Ser.). 1994. 9.19 (0-606-07063-X, Pub. by Turtleback) Demco.

— Our Golda: The Story of Golda Meir. (Women of Our Time Ser.). (Illus.). 64p. (J). (gr. 2-6). 1986. pap. 4.99 (0-14-032104-7, PuffinBks) Peng Put Young Read.

Adler, David A. Our Golda, the Story of Golda Meir. (Women of Our Time Ser.). (J). 1986. 9.70 (0-606-01704-6, Pub. by Turtleback) Demco.

— Parachuting Hamsters & Andy Russell. (Illus.). 144p. (YA). (gr. 4-7). 2000. 14.00 (0-15-202185-X, Harcourt Child Bks) Harcourt.

Adler, David A. Picture Book of Abraham Lincoln. LC 88-16393. (Illus.). 32p. (J). (gr. k-3). 1989. lib. bdg. 16.95 (0-8234-0731-4) Holiday.

— Picture Book of Abraham Lincoln. LC 88-16393. (Picture Book Biography Ser.). (Illus.). 26p. (J). (ps-3). 1990. pap. 6.95 (0-8234-0801-9) Holiday.

— A Picture Book of Abraham Lincoln. unabridged ed. (Illus.). (J). (gr. 2-4). 1990. 24.95 incl. audio (0-87499-159-5); pap. 15.95 incl. audio (0-87499-158-7) Live Oak Media.

— A Picture Book of Abraham Lincoln, 4 bks., Set. unabridged ed. (Illus.). (J). (gr. 2-4). 1990. pap. 37.95 incl. audio (0-87499-160-9) Live Oak Media.

— A Picture Book of Amelia Earhart. LC 96-54854. (Picture Book Biography Ser.). (Illus.). 32p. (J). (gr. 2-5). 1998. lib. bdg. 16.95 (0-8234-1315-2) Holiday.

***Adler, David A.** A Picture Book of Amelia Earhart. (Illus.). (J). 1998. pap. 6.95 (0-8234-1517-1) Holiday.

Adler, David A. A Picture Book of Anne Frank. LC 92-17283. (Illus.). 32p. (J). (gr. k-3). 1993. lib. bdg. 16.95 (0-8234-1003-X) Holiday.

— A Picture Book of Anne Frank. (Illus.). 32p. (J). (ps-3). 1994. pap. 6.95 (0-8234-1078-1) Holiday.

— A Picture Book of Anne Frank. unabridged ed. (Illus.). (J). (gr. 2-4). 1995. 24.95 incl. audio (0-87499-347-4); pap. 15.95 incl. audio (0-87499-346-6) Live Oak Media.

— A Picture Book of Anne Frank, 4 bks., Set. (Illus.). (J). (gr. 2-4). pap., teacher ed. 37.95 incl. audio (0-87499-348-2) Live Oak Media.

— A Picture Book of Benjamin Franklin. LC 89-20059. (Illus.). 32p. (J). (gr. k-3). 1990. lib. bdg. 16.95 (0-8234-0792-6) Holiday.

— A Picture Book of Benjamin Franklin. LC 89-20059. (Illus.). 32p. (J). (ps-3). 1991. pap. 6.95 (0-8234-0882-5) Holiday.

— A Picture Book of Christopher Columbus. LC 90-39211. (Illus.). 32p. (J). (gr. k-3). 1991. lib. bdg. 16.95 (0-8234-0857-4) Holiday.

— A Picture Book of Christopher Columbus. (Illus.). (J). (gr. k-3). 1992. reprint ed. pap. 6.95 (0-8234-0949-X) Holiday.

— A Picture Book of Christopher Columbus. unabridged ed. (Illus.). (J). (gr. 2-4). 1992. 24.95 incl. audio (0-87499-263-X); pap. 15.95 incl. audio (0-87499-262-1) Live Oak Media.

— A Picture Book of Christopher Columbus, 4 bks., Set. unabridged ed. (Illus.). (J). (gr. 2-4). 1992. pap., teacher ed. 37.95 incl. audio (0-87499-264-8) Live Oak Media.

— A Picture Book of Davy Crockett. (Illus.). 32p. (J). (ps-3). 1996. 16.95 (0-8234-1212-1); pap. 6.95 (0-8234-1343-8) Holiday.

— A Picture Book of Eleanor Roosevelt. LC 90-39212. (Illus.). 32p. (J). (gr. k-3). 1991. lib. bdg. 16.95 (0-8234-0856-6) Holiday.

— A Picture Book of Eleanor Roosevelt. (Illus.). 32p. (J). (ps-3). 1991. pap. 6.95 (0-8234-1157-5) Holiday.

— A Picture Book of Eleanor Roosevelt. unabridged ed. (J). (gr. 1-6). 1997. 24.95 incl. audio (0-87499-400-4) Live Oak Media.

— A Picture Book of Eleanor Roosevelt. unabridged ed. (J). (gr. 3-5). 1997. pap. 15.95 incl. audio (0-87499-399-7) Live Oak Media.

— A Picture Book of Eleanor Roosevelt, 4 bks., Set. (J). (gr. 3-5). 1997. pap., teacher ed. 37.95 incl. audio (0-87499-401-2) Live Oak Media.

— A Picture Book of Florence Nightingale. LC 91-43388. (Illus.). 32p. (J). (gr. k-2). 1992. lib. bdg. 16.95 (0-8234-0965-1) Holiday.

— A Picture Book of Florence Nightingale. (Illus.). (J). (gr. k-3). 1993. reprint ed. pap. text 6.95 (0-8234-1284-9) Holiday.

— A Picture Book of Frederick Douglass. LC 92-17378. (Illus.). 32p. (J). (gr. k-3). 1993. lib. bdg. 16.95 (0-8234-1002-1) Holiday.

— A Picture Book of Frederick Douglass. (Illus.). 32p. (J). (gr. k-3). 1993. pap. 6.95 (0-8234-1205-9) Holiday.

— A Picture Book of George Washington. LC 88-16384. (Illus.). 32p. (J). (gr. k-3). 1989. lib. bdg. 16.95 (0-8234-0732-2) Holiday.

— A Picture Book of George Washington. LC 88-16384. (Illus.). 30p. (J). (ps-3). 1990. pap. 6.95 (0-8234-0800-0) Holiday.

— A Picture Book of George Washington. unabridged ed. LC 88-16384. (Illus.). (J). (gr. 2-4). 1990. 24.95 incl. audio (0-87499-162-5); pap. 15.95 incl. audio (0-87499-161-7) Live Oak Media.

— A Picture Book of George Washington, 4 bks., Set. LC 88-16384. (Illus.). (J). (gr. 2-4). 1990. pap., teacher ed. 37.95 incl. audio (0-87499-163-3) Live Oak Media.

— A Picture Book of George Washington Carver. LC 98-20261. (Illus.). (J). (ps-3). 1999. lib. bdg. 15.95 (0-8234-1429-9) Holiday.

***Adler, David A.** A Picture Book of George Washington Carver. (Illus.). (gr. 4-7). 2000. 6.95 (0-8234-1633-X) Holiday.

Adler, David A. A Picture Book of Harriet Tubman. LC 91-19628. (Illus.). 32p. (J). (ps-3). 1992. lib. bdg. 16.95 (0-8234-0926-0) Holiday.

— A Picture Book of Harriet Tubman. 29p. (J). (ps-3). 1993. pap. 6.95 (0-8234-1065-X) Holiday.

— A Picture Book of Helen Keller. LC 89-77510. (Illus.). 32p. (J). (gr. k-3). 1990. lib. bdg. 16.95 (0-8234-0818-3) Holiday.

— A Picture Book of Helen Keller. LC 89-77510. (Illus.). (J). (gr. k-3). 1990. reprint ed. pap. 6.95 (0-8234-0950-3) Holiday.

— A Picture Book of Jackie Robinson. LC 93-27224. (Illus.). 32p. (J). (gr. k-3). 1994. lib. bdg. 16.95 (0-8234-1122-2) Holiday.

An Asterisk (*) at the beginning of an entry indicates that the title is appearing for the first time.

— A Picture Book of Jackie Robinson. LC 93-27224. (Illus.). 29p. (J). (gr. 1-4). 1994. reprint ed. pap. text 6.95 (*0-8234-1304-7*) Holiday.

— A Picture Book of Jesse Owens. (J). (gr. k-3). 1992. pap. text 6.95 (*0-8234-1066-8*) Holiday.

— A Picture Book of Jesse Owens. LC 91-44735. (Illus.). 32p. (J). (gr. k-3). 1992. lib. bdg. 16.95 (*0-8234-0966-X*) Holiday.

— A Picture Book of John F. Kennedy. LC 90-23589. (Illus.). 32p. (J). (gr. k-3). 1991. lib. bdg. 16.95 (*0-8234-0884-1*) Holiday.

— A Picture Book of John F. Kennedy. LC 90-23589. (Illus.). 32p. (J). (ps-3). 1992. pap. 6.95 (*0-8234-0976-7*) Holiday.

— A Picture Book of Louis Braille. LC 96-38453. (Illus.). 34p. (J). 1997. 16.95 (*0-8234-1291-1*) Holiday.

— A Picture Book of Louis Braille. (Illus.). (J). (ps-3). 1997. pap. text 6.95 (*0-8234-1413-2*) Holiday.

— A Picture Book of Martin Luther King, Jr. LC 89-1930. (Illus.). 32p. (J). (ps-3). 1989. lib. bdg. 16.95 (*0-8234-0770-5*) Holiday.

— A Picture Book of Martin Luther King, Jr. LC 89-1930. (Illus.). 32p. (J). (ps-3). 1990. pap. 6.95 (*0-8234-0847-7*) Holiday.

— A Picture Book of Martin Luther King, Jr. unabridged rev. ed. (Illus.). (J). (gr. 2-4). 1998. pap. 15.95 incl. audio (*0-87499-165-X*) Live Oak Media.

— A Picture Book of Martin Luther King, Jr., Set unabridged ed. (Illus.). (J). (gr. 2-4). 1998. pap., teacher ed. 37.95 incl. audio (*0-87499-167-6*) Live Oak Media.

— A Picture Book of Patrick Henry. LC 94-43849. (Illus.). 32p. (J). (gr. k-3). 1995. lib. bdg. 16.95 (*0-8234-1187-7*) Holiday.

— A Picture Book of Paul Revere. LC 94-9783. (Illus.). 32p. (J). (gr. k-3). 1995. lib. bdg. 16.95 (*0-8234-1144-3*) Holiday.

— A Picture Book of Paul Revere. (Illus.). (J). (gr. k-3). 1995. reprint ed. pap. text 6.95 (*0-8234-1294-6*) Holiday.

— A Picture Book of Robert E. Lee. (Illus.). (J). 1994. pap. 6.95 (*0-8234-1366-7*) Holiday.

— A Picture Book of Robert E. Lee. LC 93-22998. (Illus.). 32p. (J). (gr. k-3). 1994. lib. bdg. 16.95 (*0-8234-1111-7*) Holiday.

— A Picture Book of Rosa Parks. LC 92-41826. (Illus.). 32p. (J). (ps-3). 1993. pap. 6.95 (*0-8234-1177-X*) Holiday.

— A Picture Book of Rosa Parks. LC 92-41826. (Illus.). 32p. (J). (gr. k-3). 1993. lib. bdg. 16.95 (*0-8234-1041-2*) Holiday.

— A Picture Book of Rosa Parks. unabridged ed. (J). (ps-2). 1997. 24.95 incl. audio (*0-87499-397-0*); pap. 15.95 incl. audio (*0-87499-396-2*) Live Oak Media.

— A Picture Book of Rosa Parks, 4 bks., Set. unabridged ed. (J). (ps-2). 1997. pap., teacher ed. 37.95 incl. audio (*0-87499-398-9*) Live Oak Media.

— A Picture Book of Simon Bolivar. LC 91-19419. (Illus.). 32p. (J). (ps-3). 1992. lib. bdg. 16.95 (*0-8234-0927-9*) Holiday.

— A Picture Book of Sojourner Truth. LC 93-7478. (Illus.). 32p. (J). (gr. k-3). 1994. lib. bdg. 16.95 (*0-8234-1072-2*) Holiday.

— A Picture Book of Sojourner Truth. (Illus.). 32p. (J). (ps-3). 1994. pap. 6.95 (*0-8234-1262-8*) Holiday.

— A Picture Book of Thomas Alva Edison. LC 95-42533. (Illus.). (ps-3). 1996. pap. 6.95 (*0-8234-1414-0*) Holiday.

— A Picture Book of Thomas Jefferson. LC 89-20076. (Illus.). 32p. (J). (gr. k-3). 1990. lib. bdg. 16.95 (*0-8234-0791-8*) Holiday.

— A Picture Book of Thomas Jefferson. LC 89-20076. (Illus.). 32p. (J). (ps-3). 1991. pap. 6.95 (*0-8234-0881-7*) Holiday.

— A Picture Book of Thurgood Marshall. LC 96-37248. (Illus.). (ps-3). 1997. pap. 6.95 (*0-8234-1506-6*) Holiday.

— A Picture Book of Thurgood Marshall. LC 96-37248. (Picture Book Biographies Ser.). (Illus.). 32p. (J). (gr. k-3). 1997. lib. bdg. 16.95 (*0-8234-1308-X*) Holiday.

— Roman Numerals. LC 77-2270. (Crowell Young Math Bk.). (Illus.). 40p. (J). (ps-3). 1977. lib. bdg. 15.89 (*0-690-01302-7*) HarpC Child Bks.

— School Trouble for Andy Russell. LC 99-21184. (Illus.). 120p. (J). (gr. 2-4). 1999. 14.00 (*0-15-202190-6*, Gulliver Bks) Harcourt.

***Adler, David A.** School Trouble for Andy Russell. (Illus.). 128p. (J). (gr. 4-7). 2000. pap. 4.95 (*0-15-202496-4*, Harcourt Child Bks) Harcourt.

Adler, David A. Shape Up! Fun with Triangles & Other Polygons. LC 97-22236. (Illus.). 32p. (J). (gr. 2-5). 1998. lib. bdg. 15.95 (*0-8234-1346-2*) Holiday.

***Adler, David A.** Shape Up! Fun with Triangles & Other Polygons. (Illus.). (gr. 4-7). 2000. 6.95 (*0-8234-1638-0*) Holiday.

Adler, David A. Three-D, Two-D, One-D. LC 74-5156. (Young Math Ser.). (Illus.). 40p. (J). (gr. k-3). 1974. 10.95 (*0-690-00456-7*); lib. bdg. 12.89 (*0-690-00543-1*) HarpC Child Bks.

Adler, David A. Wacky Jacks. (Houdini Club Magic Mystery Ser.). 1994. 9.19 (*0-606-06855-4*, Pub. by Turtleback) Demco.

Adler, David A. We Remember the Holocaust. 160p. (J). (gr. 4-7). 1995. pap. 9.95 (*0-8050-3715-2*, Bks Young Read) H Holt & Co.

— Young Cam Jansen & the Dinosaur Game. LC 95-46463. (Viking Easy-to-Read Ser.). (Illus.). 32p. (J). (gr. k-3). 1996. 13.99 (*0-670-86399-8*, Viking Child) Peng Put Young Read.

— Young Cam Jansen & the Dinosaur Game: Level 2. (Young Cam Jansen Ser.). (Illus.). 32p. (J). (gr. k-3). 1998. pap. 3.99 (*0-14-037779-4*) Peng Put Young Read.

***Adler, David A.** Young Cam Jansen & the Dinosaur Game: Level 2. (Young Cam Jansen Ser.). (J). 1998. 9.19 (*0-606-13934-6*, Pub. by Turtleback) Demco.

— Young CAM Jansen & the Ice Skate Mystery. (Young Cam Jansen Ser.). (Illus.). 32p. (gr. k-3). 2000. pap. 3.99 (*0-14-130012-4*, PuffinBks) Peng Put Young Read.

Adler, David A. Young Cam Jansen & the Lost Tooth. (Illus.). 32p. (gr. k-3). 1999. pap. 3.99 (*0-14-130273-9*, PuffinBks) Peng Put Young Read.

— Young Cam Jansen & the Lost Tooth. LC 96-47357. (Viking Easy-To-Read Ser.). (Illus.). 32p. (J). (gr. k-3). 1997. 13.99 (*0-670-87354-3*) Viking Penguin.

— Young Cam Jansen & the Missing Cookie. LC 95-46462. (Viking Easy-to-Read Ser.). (Illus.). 32p. (J). (ps-3). 1996. 13.99 (*0-670-86772-1*, Viking Child) Peng Put Young Read.

— Young Cam Jansen & the Missing Cookie: Level 2. (Young Cam Jansen Ser.). (Illus.). 32p. (J). (gr. k-3). 1998. pap. 3.99 (*0-14-038050-7*, PuffinBks) Peng Put Young Read.

***Adler, David A.** Young Cam Jansen & the Missing Cookie: Level 2. (Young Cam Jansen Ser.). (J). 1998. 9.19 (*0-606-13935-4*, Pub. by Turtleback) Demco.

— Young Cam Jansen & the Pizza Shop Mystery. LC 99-41979. (Easy-to-Read Ser.). (Illus.). 32p. (J). (gr. k-3). 2000. 13.99 (*0-670-88861-3*, Viking Child) Peng Put Young Read.

Adler, David A., compiled by. The Kids' Catalog of Jewish Holidays. LC 96-17784. (Illus.). 244p. (Orig.). (J). 1996. pap. 15.95 (*0-8276-0581-1*) JPS Phila.

Adler, David A., ed. Treating Personality Disorders. LC 87-646993. (New Directions for Mental Health Services Ser.: No. 47). 1990. 25.00 (*1-55542-811-8*) Jossey-Bass.

Adler, David A, et al, eds. Physical Properties of Amorphous Materials. (Illus.). 456p. (C). 1985. text 132.00 (*0-306-41907-6*, Kluwer Plenum) Kluwer Academic.

— Physics of Disordered Materials. (Institute for Amorphous Studies). 868p. 1985. 165.00 (*0-306-42074-0*, Plenum Trade) Perseus Pubng.

***Adler, David A. & Adler, Peter S.** Heroes of the Revolution. LC 00-38843. (Illus.). 2001. write for info. (*0-8234-1471-X*) Holiday.

***Adler, David A. & Brown, Dan.** A Picture Book of Sacagawea. LC 99-37135. (Picture Book Biography Ser.). 32p. (J). (gr. k-3). 2000. 16.95 (*0-8234-1485-X*) Holiday.

Adler, David A & Fritzsche, Hellmut, eds. Tetrahedrally-Bonded Amorphous Semiconductors. (Institute for Amorphous Studies). 580p. 1985. 145.00 (*0-306-42076-7*, Plenum Trade) Perseus Pubng.

Adler, David A. & Natti, Susanna. Cam Jansen & the Mystery of the Carnival Prize. LC 84-3617. (Cam Jansen Ser.). (Illus.). 64p. (J). (gr. 2-5). 1984. 13.99 (*0-670-20034-4*, Viking Child) Peng Put Young Read.

Adler, David A., et al. Birthday Surprises: Ten Great Stories to Unwrap. Hurwitz, Johanna, ed. LC 94-26640. (Illus.). 128p. (YA). (gr. 5 up). 1995. 16.00 (*0-688-13194-8*, Wm Morrow) Morrow Avon.

Adler, David A., jt. auth. see Brookes, Diane.

Adler, David A., jt. ed. see Fritzche, Hellmut.

Adler, David E., jt. ed. see Bernstein, Michael A.

Adler, David G. & George, Larry N., eds. The Constitution & the Conduct of American Foreign Policy. LC 96-5057. 416p. 1996. pap. 19.95 (*0-7006-0756-0*) U Pr of KS.

— The Constitution & the Conduct of American Foreign Policy. LC 96-5057. 416p. 1996. 45.00 (*0-7006-0755-2*) U Pr of KS.

Adler, Dennis. The Art of the Automobile. Teberg, Pat, ed. LC 99-33362. (Illus.). 256p. 2000. 45.00 (*0-06-105128-4*, HarpRes) HarpInfo.

***Adler, Dennis. The Blue Book of Modern Black Powder Values. (Illus.). 125p. (C). 2000. write for info. (*1-886768-22-6*) Blue Bk Pubns.**
THE BLUE BOOK OF MODERN BLACK POWDER VALUES is a softcover reference & value guide for modern black powder firearms. With 96 pages of B&W value pricing & model information & over 24 pages of color, this book is designed as the sequel to Colt Blackpowder Reproductions & Replicas, in addition to being another stand alone Blue Book title. This book contains the most up-to-date information & pricing on almost all modern black powder firearms. Mfg. Sug. List Price: $12.95 + $2 S/H. Available from Baker & Taylor, or Ingram or directly from the publisher by calling toll free 1-800-877-4867, non-domestic 952-854-5229, fax 952-853-1486, or web site: www.bluebookinc.com *Publisher Paid Annotation.*

— Chrysler. LC 99-58170. (Illus.). 192p. 2000. 29.95 (*0-7603-0695-8*, 129826AP, Pub. by MBI Pubg) Motorbooks Intl.

Adler, Dennis. Colt Blackpowder Reproductions & Replicas. LC 98-87392. (Illus.). 288 p. (Orig.). 1998. pap. 29.95 (*1-886768-11-0*) Blue Bk Pubns.
COLT BLACKPOWDER REPRODUCTIONS & REPLICAS - A COLLECTOR'S & SHOOTER'S GUIDE is an illustrated volume on blackpowder firearms & recently manufactured reproductions/ replicas of such famous makes as Colt, Remington, etc. Included is a history of the Colt percussion revolver & similar makes, with photos. Reproductions are covered in detail, with many limited &/or special editions, & also guns manufactured by major Italian manufacturers, with an in-depth look at these factories & guns they have made for American companies & organizations. Chapters include practical percussion shooting & detailed loading information by gun & caliber, cowboy action shooting, & Civil War reenactment. Additionally, this publication has information on shooting & maintaining blackpowder pistol, as well as a complete blackpowder pricing guide with model descriptions providing the most up-to-date information on most recently manufactured makes & models. Dennis Adler is well-known in the automotive community for his photographic & literary achievements. This book is a visual masterpiece! Retail $29.95 plus $4.00 S/H. Available from Baker & Taylor, Ingram or directly from the publisher by calling 1-800-877-4867, non-domestic 612-854-5229, FAX 612-853-1486 or web site www.bluebookinc.com. *Publisher Paid Annotation.*

— Ferrari Road Cars. LC 97-2402. (Enthusiast Color Ser.). (Illus.). 96p. 1997. pap. 13.95 (*0-7603-0273-1*) MBI Pubg.

— Fifties Flashback: The American Car. (Illus.). 160p. 1996. 32.95 (*0-7603-0126-3*) MBI Pubg.

— Mercedes-Benz: 110 Years of Excellence. (Enthusiast Color Ser.). (Illus.). 96p. 1995. pap. 13.95 (*0-7603-0046-1*) MBI Pubg.

–The Nethercutt Collection: The Cars of San Sylmar. (Illus.). 208p. 2000. 35.00 (*1-886768-14-5*) Blue Bk Pubns.
The Nethercutt Collection - The Cars of San Sylmar is the official publication of the famous Nethercutt car collection, a museum located in San Sylmar, CA. Having collected major automotive marques since WW II, Mr. J. P. Nethercutt has amassed one of the world's most important automobile collections. Dennis Adler, an award winning automotive photographer & journalist with over 5,000 articles to his credit, was chosen by the museum to be the writer & photographer for this unique publication. A stunning visual masterpiece with many 2-page color spreads, no expense was spared to make this new 9x12 landscape book an extraordinary literary achievement. Not only are most of the more famous & well-known cars pictured & described, but all the cars are listed in a photo index. Additionally, there is a chapter on mechanical musical instruments, since the Nethercutt Museum also contains one of the world's best collections of these rare & unusual artifacts. Retail $35.00 + $4.00 S/H. Available from Baker & Taylor, Ingram or directly from the publisher by calling 1-800-877-4867, non-domestic 952-854-5229, fax 952-853-1486 or web site: www.bluebookinc.com. *Publisher Paid Annotation.*

— Packard. LC 98-8468. (Illus.). 156p. 1998. 39.95 (*0-7603-0482-3*) MBI Pubg.

— Porsche 911 Road Cars. LC 97-45035. (Sports Car Color History Ser.). (Illus.). 128p. 1998. pap. 21.95 (*0-7603-0365-7*) MBI Pubg.

— Speed & Luxury: The Great Cars. LC 97-20671. (Illus.). 160p. 1997. 29.95 (*0-7603-0486-6*) MBI Pubg.

Adler, Dennis, jt. auth. see Thaler, Mike.

Adler, Dennis A. Corvettes, 1953-1995. LC 95-77322. (Illus.). 176p. 1996. 49.95 (*0-87341-367-9*, COR01) Krause Pubns.

Adler, Doris R. The Log of the Sloop Advance. 1997. 15.00 (*1-886706-13-1*) Hickory Hse.

— Personal Property Tax Records for 1856 of Northampton Co., VA. 1996. 15.00 (*1-886706-14-X*) Hickory Hse.

Adler, Dorothy R. British Investment in American Railways, 1834-1898. Hidy, Muriel E., ed. LC 79-122437. 273p. reprint ed. pap. 84.70 (*0-7837-4342-4*, 204405200012) Bks Demand.

Adler, Dvorah. Mom's Come First: Enlightened Parenting. 180p. 1999. pap. 14.95 (*1-887472-58-4*, Pub. by Sunstar Pubng) Brodart.

Adler, E. Donny & Deeny K'Teemy Help the King. (Middos Ser.). (J). 1990. 7.99 (*0-89906-505-8*) Mesorah Pubns.

Adler, E. Fleeting Images. 1995. mass mkt. 15.95 (*0-340-41551-7*, Pub. by Hodder & Stought Ltd) Trafalgar.

***Adler, Edward.** Notes from a Dark Street. 2nd ed. iii, 219p. 2000. per. 18.95 (*0-931642-31-0*) Lintel.

***Adler, Elizabeth.** All or Nothing. 2000. mass mkt. 6.99 (*0-440-23496-4*) Dell.

Adler, Elizabeth A. All or Nothing. LC 99-31965. 336p. 1999. 23.95 (*0-385-33380-3*) Delacorte.

— Fortune Is a Woman. 592p. 1992. mass mkt. 6.99 (*0-440-21146-8*) Dell.

Adler, Elizabeth A. Indiscretions. 1995. mass mkt. 13.95 (*0-340-37370-9*, Pub. by Hodder & Stought Ltd) Trafalgar.

— Indiscretions. large type ed. LC 99-89394. 464p. 2000. lib. bdg. 27.95 (*1-58547-026-0*) Ctr Point Pubg.

Adler, Elizabeth A. Legacy of Secrets. LC 92-37239. 624p. 1994. mass mkt. 6.99 (*0-440-21657-5*) Dell.

— Legacy of Secrets. large type ed. LC 93-26431. 916p. 1993. lib. bdg. 23.95 (*1-56054-753-7*) Thorndike Pr.

— Legacy of Secrets. large type ed. LC 93-26431. 916p. 1994. pap. 16.95 (*1-56054-798-7*) Thorndike Pr.

— Leonie. 592p. 1987. mass mkt. 6.99 (*0-440-14662-3*) Dell.

— Now or Never. 448p. 1997. mass mkt. 6.99 (*0-440-22464-0*) Dell.

— Peach. 544p. 1989. mass mkt. 6.99 (*0-440-20111-X*) Dell.

— The Property of a Lady. 576p. 1991. mass mkt. 6.50 (*0-440-21014-3*) Dell.

— The Rich Shall Inherit. 560p. 1990. mass mkt. 6.99 (*0-440-20639-1*) Dell.

— The Secret of the Villa Mimosa. 416p. 1995. mass mkt. 6.99 (*0-440-21748-2*) Dell.

— The Secret of the Villa Mimosa. 1995. mass mkt. 6.50 (*0-614-15543-6*) Dell.

— The Secret of the Villa Mimosa. large type ed. LC 94-22937. 603p. 1995. lib. bdg. 24.95 (*0-7862-0324-2*) Thorndike Pr.

— Sooner or Later. 432p. 1998. mass mkt. 6.99 (*0-440-22465-9*) Dell.

— Sooner or Later. large type ed. LC 98-7712. (Romance Ser.). 1998. 26.95 (*1-56895-575-8*) Wheeler Pub.

Adler, Elizabeth W. Everyone's Guide to Successful Publications: How to Produce Powerful Brochures, Newsletters, Flyers & Business Communications, Start to Finish. (Illus.). 412p. (C). 1995. pap. 28.00 (*1-56609-027-X*) Peachpit Pr.

Adler, Elkan N., ed. Jewish Travellers in the Middle Ages: Nineteen Firsthand Accounts. 416p. 1987. reprint ed. pap. 10.95 (*0-486-25397-X*) Dover.

Adler, Ella & Knight, Kae. Ani Zachor; Ata Zachor: Moments in a Life. 56p. (C). 1998. pap. text 5.00 (*0-9648601-9-8*) Stella Matutina.

Adler, Elliot & Bachant, Janet Lee. Working in Depth: A Clinician's Guide to Framework & Flexibility in the Analytic Relationship. LC 98-4564. 1998. 60.00 (*0-7657-0160-X*) Aronson.

Adler, Emanuel. The International Practice of Arms Control. LC 92-10744. 301p. reprint ed. pap. 93.40 (*0-608-06290-1*, 206661900008) Bks Demand.

Adler, Emanuel & Barnett, Michael, eds. Security Communities. LC 98-10384. (Studies in International Relations: No. 62). (Illus.). 320p. (C). 1998. 69.95 (*0-521-63051-7*); pap. 24.95 (*0-521-63953-0*) Cambridge U Pr.

Adler, Emanuel & Crawford, Beverly. Progress in Post-War International Relations. 1991. text 61.50 (*0-231-07278-3*) Col U Pr.

— Progress in Post War International Relations. 497p. 1995. pap. 22.00 (*0-231-07279-1*) Col U Pr.

Adler, Emanuel, jt. ed. see Hanusch, Ferdinand.

Adler, Eve. Catullan Self-Revelation. Connor, W. R., ed. LC 80-2638. (Monographs in Classical Studies). (Illus.). 1981. lib. bdg. 34.95 (*0-405-14026-6*) Ayer.

— Dictionary of Russian Slang & Colloquial Expressions. (ENG & RUS.). 1995. pap. 11.95 (*0-8120-9085-3*) Barron.

Adler, Eve, tr. see Epstein, Mikhail.

Adler, Eve, tr. see Strauss, Leo.

Adler, Eve, tr. & intro. see Strauss, Leo.

Adler, F. W., jt. auth. see Hufbauer, G.

Adler, Felicia Rose. Master Dating: How to Meet & Attract Quality Men. unabridged ed. Iorio, Virginia, ed. LC 98-50194. (Illus.). 224p. 1999. pap. 12.95 (*0-911493-24-7*) Blue Sky.

Adler, Felix. The Reconstruction of the Spiritual Ideal. LC 77-27148. (Hibbert Lectures: 1923). reprint ed. 35.00 (*0-404-60422-6*) AMS Pr.

Adler, Frances P. Raising the Tents. 96p. 1993. 19.95 (*0-934971-34-X*); pap. 9.95 (*0-934971-33-1*) Calyx Bks.

Adler, Frances P., jt. auth. see Corser, Kira.

Adler, Frank, et al, eds. Automation & Industrial Workers: A Fifteen Nation Study & Cross-National Comparison, 4 pt. set, Vols. 1 & 2. (Vienna Centre Ser.). 1484p. 1986. text 295.00 (*0-08-033375-3*, Pub. by PPL) Elsevier.

Adler, Frank & Koval, Barbar. Automation & Industrial Workers Vol. 2, Pt. 1: A Cross National Comparison of 15 Countries, Vol. 2, Pts 1 & 2. LC 79-40811. (Vienna Centre Ser.). 911p. 1986. 181.00 (*0-08-028094-3*, K111, L120, Pub. by Pergamon Repr) Franklin.

Adler, Frank J. How to Buy Jewelery Wholesale. LC 98-96027. 1998. pap. 10.95 (*0-676-60126-X*) Hse Collectbls.

— How to Reduce Your Property Tax. LC 94-67414. (Illus.). 410p. 1995. pap. 19.95 (*1-57296-001-9*) FJA.

Adler, Franklin H. Italian Industrialists from Liberalism to Fascism: The Political Development of the Industrial Bourgeoisie, 1906-34. 478p. (C). 1995. text 74.95 (*0-521-43406-8*) Cambridge U Pr.

Adler, Freda. Nations Not Obsessed with Crime. (Wayne State University Law School Comparative Criminal Law Project Publications Ser.: Vol. 15). xx, 204p. 1983. 32.50 (*0-8377-0216-X*, Rothman) W S Hein.

Adler, Freda & Laufer, William S., eds. The Legacy of Anomie Theory. (Advances in Criminological Theory Ser.: Vol. 6). 370p. (C). 1994. text 49.95 (*1-56000-125-9*) Transaction Pubs.

— The Legacy of Anomie Theory Vol. 6: Advances in Criminological Theory. 449p. 1999. pap. 32.95 (*0-7658-0662-2*) Transaction Pubs.

— New Directions in Criminological Theory: Advances in Criminological Theory. (Advances in Criminological Theory Ser.: Vol. 4). 320p. (C). 1992. 44.95 (*1-56000-046-5*) Transaction Pubs.

Adler, Freda & Mueller, G. O., eds. Politics, Crime & the International Scene: An Inter-American Focus. x, 403p. 1972. reprint ed. pap. 12.00 (*0-8377-0203-8*, Rothman) W S Hein.

An Asterisk (*) at the beginning of an entry indicates that the title is appearing for the first time.

A

Adler, Freda & Mueller, Gerhard O. Criminal Justice: The Core Criminal Justice Careers Sourcebook. 2nd ed. 1996. pap. text. write for info. (*0-07-000503-6*) McGraw.

Adler, Freda, et al. Criminal Justice. LC 93-28243. 600p. (C). 1993. 76.56 (*0-07-000457-9*) McGraw.

— Criminal Justice. LC 93-28243. (C). 1994. pap., student ed. 17.19 (*0-07-000477-3*) McGraw.

— Criminal Justice: The Core. LC 95-33999. 405p. (C). 1995. pap. 54.69 (*0-07-000499-4*) McGraw.

— Criminal Justice: The Core. 2nd ed. LC 99-17716. 528p. 1999. pap. 51.25 (*0-07-228221-5*) McGraw.

— Criminology. 3rd ed. LC 97-12514. 576p. (C). 1997. 66.25 (*0-07-000509-5*) McGraw.

— Criminology: The Shorter Version. 3rd ed. LC 97-12515. 432p. (C). 1997. pap. 57.19 (*0-07-000512-5*) McGraw.

Adler, Freda, jt. ed. see Laufer, William S.

Adler, G. & Beglinger, C., eds. Cholecystokinin Antagonists in Gastroenterology: Basic & Clinical Status. (Illus.). xiii, 233p. 1991. 131.00 (*0-387-53582-9*) Spr-Verlag.

Adler, G., ed. see Jung, C. G.

Adler, G., ed. see Jung, C. G., et al.

Adler, Georg. Die Grundlagen der Karl Marxschen Kritik der Bestehenden Volkswirtschaft. 2nd ed. (GER.). x, 294p. 1977. reprint ed. write for info. (*3-487-02203-6*) G Olms Pubs.

Adler, Gerhard. Dynamics of the Self. 1991. pap. 14.95 (*0-904576-92-2*) Sigo Pr.

— The Living Symbol: A Case Study in the Process of Individuation. LC 61-9310. (Bollingen Ser.: No. 63). 491p. reprint ed. pap. 152.30 (*0-7837-0240-X*, 204054800017) Bks Demand.

— Studies in Analytical Psychology. LC 67-10652. (Illus.). 1967. 10.00 (*0-913430-14-5*) C G Jung Foun.

Adler, Gerhard, et al, eds. The Collected Works of C. G. Jung Vol. 9, Pt. 2: Aion - Researches into the Phenomenology of the Self. 2nd ed. Hull, R. F. C., tr. (Bollingen Ser.: No. 20). 353p. 1968. pap. 16.95 (*0-691-01826-X*, Pub. by Princeton U Pr); text 59.50 (*0-691-09759-3*, Pub. by Princeton U Pr) Cal Prin Full Svc.

— The Collected Works of C. G. Jung Vol. 16: The Practice of Psychotherapy. 2nd ed. Hull, R. F. C., tr. (Bollingen Ser.: No. 20). 416p. 1966. text 65.00 (*0-691-09767-4*, Pub. by Princeton U Pr) Cal Prin Full Svc.

— The Collected Works of C. G. Jung Vol. 17: The Development of Personality. Hull, R. F. C., tr. (Bollingen Ser.: No. 20). 1024p. 1954. pap. 15.95 (*0-691-01838-3*, Pub. by Princeton U Pr); text 49.50 (*0-691-09763-1*, Pub. by Princeton U Pr) Cal Prin Full Svc.

— Collected Works of C. G. Jung Vol. 19: General Bibliography of C. G. Jung's Writings. Hull, R. F. C., tr. LC 91-32917. (Bollingen Ser.: No. 20). 366p. 1991. text 49.50 (*0-691-09893-X*, Pub. by Princeton U Pr) Cal Prin Full Svc.

— The Collected Works of C. G. Jung Vol. 20: General Index. Hull, R. F. C., tr. LC 80-453172. (Bollingen Ser.: No. 20). 751p. 1979. text 89.50 (*0-691-09867-0*, Pub. by Princeton U Pr) Cal Prin Full Svc.

Adler, Gerhard, ed. see Jung, C. G.

Adler, Gerhard, ed. see Jung, C. G., et al.

***Adler, Glenn & Steinberg, Jonny.** From Comrades to Citizens: The South African Civics Movement & the Transition to Democracy. LC 99-53011. (International Political Economy Ser.). 264p. 2000. text 69.95 (*0-312-23102-4*) St Martin.

Adler, Glenn & Suarez, Doris, eds. Union Voices: Labor's Responses to Crisis. LC 91-38444. (SUNY Series in the Anthropology of Work). 321p. (C). 1992. text 64.50 (*0-7914-1247-4*); pap. text 21.95 (*0-7914-1248-2*) State U NY Pr.

***Adler, Glenn & Webster, Eddie.** Trade Unions & Democratization in South Africa. LC 99-23352. (International Political Economy Ser.). 238p. 2000. text 69.95 (*0-312-22253-X*) St Martin.

Adler, Gloria G. Mom to Mom: Commonsense Tips & Advice Every Mom Needs to Know. LC 97-32782. 144p. 1998. pap. 12.00 (*0-688-15793-9*, Wm Morrow) Morrow Avon.

Adler, Hanna. Lore's Life: At Eighty, a Time to Recall & Remember. LC 98-90458. 1998. pap. 10.95 (*0-533-12811-0*) Vantage.

***Adler, Hans & Hermand, Jost, eds.** Concepts of Culture. LC 98-46161. (German Life & Civilization Ser.: Vol. 28). IX, 211p. (C). 1999. text 47.95 (*0-8204-4141-4*) P Lang Pubng.

Adler, Hans, ed. see Grass, Gunter.

Adler, Hans, ed. see Herder, Johann G.

Adler, Hans-Peter. Das Akkadische des Konigs Tusratta von Mitanni. (GER.). xiii, 363p. 1976. text 17.50 (*3-7887-0503-5*, Pub. by NeukirchenerV) Eisenbrauns.

***Adler, Harry.** Train Your Brain: The Ultimate 21 Day Mental Skills Programme for Peak Performance. 1998. pap. text 16.95 (*0-7499-1809-8*, Pub. by Piatkus Bks) London Brdge.

Adler, Helmut E. & Rieber, Robert W., eds. Aspects of the History of Psychology in America 1892-1992. LC 94-42028. (Annals Ser.: Vol. 188). (Illus.). 147p. 1995. pap. 19.95 (*0-89766-867-7*) Am Psychol.

Adler, Henry, jt. auth. see Rich, Buddy.

Adler, Howard. One Hundred One Programming Tips & Tricks for the VIC-20 & Commodore 64. 128p. 1983. 8.95 (*0-86668-030-6*) ARCsoft.

— VIC-20 & Commodore 64 Computer Program Writing Workbook. 96p. 1983. 4.95 (*0-86668-811-0*) ARCsoft.

***Adler, Howard L., Jr., ed.** The Global Merger Notification Handbook. 1999. 310.00 (*1-874698-87-2*, Pub. by Cameron May) Gaunt.

Adler, Irit & Levy, Shem. Challenging Optical Picture Puzzles. (Illus.). 96p. 1996. pap. 5.95 (*0-8069-9440-1*) Sterling.

Adler, Irma, et al. Russian Express Track. (RUS.). 256p. 1995. 49.95 incl. audio (*0-8120-8242-7*) Barron.

Adler, Irving. The Environment. LC 75-35526. (Reason Why Ser.). (Illus.). (J). 1942. lib. bdg. 10.89 (*0-381-99617-4*) HarpC Child Bks.

— Food. LC 76-54783. (Reason Why Ser.). (Illus.). (J). (gr. 2-5). 1977. lib. bdg. 12.89 (*0-381-90051-7*) HarpC Child Bks.

— Hot & Cold. rev. ed. LC 74-9357. (Illus.). (J). (gr. 7-9). 1940. lib. bdg. 12.89 (*0-381-99990-4*, A34461) HarpC Child Bks.

— The Stars: Decoding Their Messages. rev. ed. LC 77-27665. (Illus.). 128p. (J). (gr. 5-12). 1980. lib. bdg. 11.89 (*0-690-03994-8*) HarpC Child Bks.

Adler, Irving & Adler, Ruth. Houses. LC 64-20708. (Reason Why Ser.). (Illus.). (J). (gr. 3-6). 1965. lib. bdg. 12.89 (*0-381-99967-X*, A35060) HarpC Child Bks.

Adler, J. Image Analysis. (Microscopy Handbook Ser.). (Illus.). 160p. 2000. pap. 34.95 (*0-387-91572-9*) Spr-Verlag.

Adler, Jacob. Claus Spreckels, the Sugar King in Hawaii. 320p. 1989. mass mkt. 5.95 (*0-935180-76-1*) Mutual Pub HI.

— Laugh, Jew, Laugh. London, Abraham, tr. LC 77-116925. (Short Story Index Reprint Ser.). 1977. 19.95 (*0-8369-3427-X*) Ayer.

— The Urgings of Conscience: A Theory of Punishment. (C). 1992. 59.95 (*0-87722-826-4*) Temple U Pr.

Adler, Jacob, ed. see Kamehameha, 4th.

Adler, Jacob H. The Reach of Art: A Study in the Prosody of Pope. LC 64-63900. (University of Florida Humanities Monographs: No. 16). 112p. reprint ed. pap. 34.80 (*0-7837-5030-7*, 204469900004) Bks Demand.

***Adler, Jacob P.** A Life on Stage. LC 99-31091. 416p. 1999. 30.00 (*0-679-41351-0*) Knopf.

Adler, Jane W., et al. Simple Justice: How Litigants Fare in the Pittsburgh Court Arbitration Program. LC 83-16016. 152p. 1983. pap. 15.00 (*0-8330-0518-9*, R-3071-1CJ) Rand Corp.

Adler, Janet. Arching Backward: The Mystical Initiation of a Contemporary Woman. (Illus.). 224p. 1995. 19.95 (*0-89281-577-9*, Destiny Bks) Inner Tradit.

— Arching Backward: The Mystical Initiation of a Contemporary Woman. LC 95-24266. 264p. 1996. pap. 14.95 (*0-89281-546-9*, Destiny Bks) Inner Tradit.

***Adler, Jasna & Jilek, Lubor.** Socialisme, Cultures, Histoire Itineraires et Representations: Melanges Offerts a Miklos Molnar. (Illus.). viii, 522p. 1999. 60.95 (*3-906762-46-7*) P Lang Pubng.

Adler, Jeanne W., jt. auth. see Stoddard, Seneca R.

Adler, Jeanne Winston, ed. In the Path of War: Children of the American Revolution Tell Their Stories. LC 98-37074. (Illus.). 160p. 1998. pap. 21.95 (*0-382-44367-5*) Cobblestone Pub Co.

Adler, Jeffrey S. Yankee Merchants & the Making of the Urban West: The Rise & Fall of Antebellum St. Louis. (Interdisciplinary Perspectives on Modern History Ser.). 284p. (C). 1991. text 57.95 (*0-521-41284-6*) Cambridge U Pr.

Adler, Jeremy & Fardon, Richard. Franz Steiner, Orientalism. LC 99-15631. 200p. 1999. pap. 19.50 (*1-57181-714-X*) Berghahn Bks.

***Adler, Jeremy & Fardon, Richard.** Franz Steiner, Orientalism. LC 99-15631. 200p. 1999. 69.95 (*1-57181-713-1*) Berghahn Bks.

Adler, Jeremy & Fardon, Richard. Franz Steiner, Taboo. LC 99-15631. 200p. 1999. 59.95 (*1-57181-711-5*); pap. 18.50 (*1-57181-712-3*) Berghahn Bks.

Adler, Joanne. 100 Colleges Where Average Students Can Excel. LC 96-78703. 1997. 14.95 (*0-02-861044-X*, Arc) IDG Bks.

Adler, Joe Anne. Stress: Just Chill Out! LC 96-32678. (Teen Issues Ser.). 104p. (YA). (gr. 6 up). 1997. lib. bdg. 20.95 (*0-89490-918-5*) Enslow Pubs.

Adler, John, ed. Responses to Shakespeare, 8 vols. 3200p. (C). 1998. 980.00 (*0-415-16321-8*) Routledge.

Adler, John, ed. see French, Charles F.

Adler, Jonathan H. Environmentalism at the Crossroads: Green Activism in America. 299p. (Orig.). 1995. pap. text 39.00 (*0-86587-570-7*) Gov Insts.

Adler, Jonathan N., jt. auth. see Plantz, Scott H.

Adler, Joseph. History of the U.S., Set, Vol. 1 & 2. 1088p. (C). 1995. pap. text, per. 88.95 (*0-7872-0967-8*) Kendall-Hunt.

— Restoring the Jews to Their Homeland: Nineteen Centuries in the Quest for Zion. LC 96-20616. xiv, 456p. 1997. 50.00 (*1-56821-978-4*) Aronson.

Adler, Joyce S. Dramatization of Three Melville Novels: With an Introduction on Interpretation by Dramatization. LC 92-5625. 200p. 1992. lib. bdg. 79.95 (*0-7734-9443-X*) E Mellen.

Adler, Judith. Artists in Office. LC 78-55941. 350p. 1979. 34.95 (*0-87855-281-2*) Transaction Pubs.

Adler, K. The Art of Accompanying & Coaching. LC 79-147128. (Music Reprint Ser.). 260p. 1971. reprint ed. lib. bdg. 35.00 (*0-306-70360-2*) Da Capo.

— The Art of Accompanying & Coaching. LC 79-147128. (Music Reprint Ser.). (Illus.). 260p. 1971. reprint ed. pap. 15.95 (*0-306-80027-6*) Da Capo.

***Adler, Karen.** Barbecued Ribs - Rubbed, Sauced & Glazed: A Collection of Recipes from the Best BBQ Cookbook Ever. (Illus.). 96p. 2000. pap. 9.95 (*0-925175-32-3*) Pig Out Pubns.

— The Best Little Barbecue Cookbook. 96p. 2000. pap. 4.95 (*0-89087-961-3*) Celestial Arts.

— The Best Little Grilling Cookbook. 96p. 2000. pap. 4.95 (*0-89087-962-1*) Celestial Arts.

— The Best Little Marinades Cookbook. 96p. 2000. pap. 4.95 (*0-89087-964-8*) Celestial Arts.

— The Best Little Sauces Cookbook. 96p. 2000. pap. 4.95 (*0-89087-965-6*) Celestial Arts.

Adler, Karen. Hooked on Fish on the Grill. rev. ed. 96p. (Orig.). 1994. pap. 9.95 (*0-925175-19-6*) Pig Out Pubns.

Adler, Karen & Fertig, Judith. QueQueens - Easy Grilling & Simple Smoking: Menus, Recipes & Tips Galore. 96p. (Orig.). 1997. pap. 9.95 (*0-925175-26-9*) Pig Out Pubns.

Adler, Karen & Stein, Shifra. Kansas City Cuisine: A Sampling of Restaurants & Their Recipes. rev. ed. 144p. 1995. pap. 14.95 (*1-878686-18-6*) Pig Out Pubns.

Adler, Karen & Wells, Carolyn. Pig Out on Kansas City Barbecue. (Illus.). 96p. (Orig.). Date not set. pap. 9.95 (*0-925175-21-8*) Pig Out Pubns.

Adler, Karen C. & Guthrie, Jane D. A Kansas City Christmas: Traditions & Recipes from the Heartland. LC 95-112764. (Illus.). 144p. (Orig.). 1994. pap. 14.95 (*1-878686-05-4*) Pig Out Pubns.

Adler-Kassner, Linda, et al, eds. Writing the Community: Concepts & Models for Service-Learning in Composition. (Service-Learning in the Disciplines Ser.). 224p. 1997. pap. 28.50 (*1-56377-006-7*) Am Assn Higher Ed.

Adler-Kassner, Linda & Harrington, Susanmarie, eds. Questioning Authority: Stories Told in School. (Illus.). 235p. (C). text 42.50 (*0-472-09759-8*, 09759); pap. text 22.95 (*0-472-06759-1*, 06759) U of Mich Pr.

Adler, Kathleen. Impressionism. (Illus.). 80p. 1999. pap. text 10.00 (*0-300-07690-8*) Yale U Pr.

— Unknown Inpressionists. 128p. 1990. text 40.00 (*0-7148-2452-6*) Phaidon Pr.

Adler, Kathleen & Garb, Tamar. Berthe Morisot. (Illus.). 128p. 1995. pap. 24.95 (*0-7148-3479-3*, Pub. by Phaidon Press) Phaidon Pr.

Adler, Keith. Advertising Resource Handbook. (Illus.). 248p. (Orig.). (C). 1988. pap. text 14.95 (*0-923044-01-9*) Ad Resources Inc.

***Adler, Kenneth B., et al, eds.** Oxygen/Nitrogen Radicals & Cellular Injury. (Illus.). 141p. (C). 2000. reprint ed. pap. text 30.00 (*0-7881-8538-1*) DIANE Pub.

Adler, Kief. Beyond the Staff of Life: The Wheatless, Dairyless Cookbook, Vol. 1. LC 76-43076. (Illus.). 80p. (Orig.). 1976. pap. 6.95 (*0-87961-075-1*) Naturegraph.

Adler, Kraig, jt. ed. see Halliday, Tim.

Adler, L. Ludwig Wittgenstein: Eine Existenzielle Deutung. 1976. 35.00 (*3-8055-2390-4*) S Karger.

Adler, Larry. Me & My Big Mouth! 1996. mass mkt. 5.99 (*1-85782-087-8*, Pub. by Blake Publng) Seven Hills Bk.

Adler, Laszlo, jt. auth. see Fitting, Dale.

Adler, Laura, jt. ed. see Morris, James M.

***Adler, Laure.** Marguerite Duras. 1999. 35.00 (*0-226-00758-8*) U Ch Pr.

Adler, Lee & Mayer, Charles S. Readings in Managing the Marketing Research Function. LC 80-11092. 199p. reprint ed. pap. 61.70 (*0-7837-2491-8*, 204265600005) Bks Demand.

Adler, Leonore L., ed. Cross-Cultural Research in Human Development: A Life-Span Perspective. LC 88-15536. (Illus.). 308p. 1989. 65.00 (*0-275-93048-3*, C3048, Praeger Pubs) Greenwood.

— International Handbook on Gender Roles. LC 92-45080. 552p. 1993. lib. bdg. 105.00 (*0-313-28336-2*, AIG, Greenwood Pr) Greenwood.

— Women in Cross-Cultural Perspective. LC 90-7376. 296p. 1991. 59.95 (*0-275-93658-9*, C3658, Praeger Pubs) Greenwood.

Adler, Leonore L. & Gielen, Uwe P., eds. Cross-Cultural Topics in Psychology. LC 93-40574. 272p. 1994. 75.00 (*0-275-94524-3*, Praeger Pubs); pap. 24.95 (*0-275-95062-X*, Praeger Pubs) Greenwood.

Adler, Leonore L. & Mukherji, Runi B. Spirit vs. Scalpel: Traditional Healing & Modern Psychotherapy. LC 94-29715. 248p. 1995. 62.95 (*0-89789-406-5*, Bergin & Garvey) Greenwood.

***Adler, Leonore Loeb & Gielen, Uwe P., eds.** Cross-Cultural Topics in Psychology. 2nd ed. LC 00-32379. 288p. 2001. 65.00 (*0-275-96972-X*, C6972, Praeger Pubs); pap. 65.00 (*0-275-96973-8*, C6972, Praeger Pubs) Greenwood.

Adler, Les K. The Red Image: American Attitudes Toward Communism in the Cold War Era. LC 91-31886. (Modern American History Ser.). 545p. 1992. text 35.00 (*0-8240-1905-9*) Garland.

Adler, Lillian W. & Castberg, C. Practice, Drill, & Review for Reading Hebrew. 1972. pap., wbk. ed. 4.95 (*0-87441-216-1*) Behrman.

— Reading Hebrew: Sefardic. 1972. pap. 8.95 (*0-87441-042-8*) Behrman.

Adler, Lillian W., jt. auth. see Yudell, Clifford.

***Adler, Lou.** Hire with Your Head: A Rational Way to Make a Gut Decision. LC 98-16189. 336p. 1998. 29.95 (*0-471-29294-X*, VNR) Wiley.

Adler, Louise, et al, eds. The Politics of Linking Schools & Social Services: The Yearbook of the Politics of Education Association, 1993. (Education Policy Perspectives Ser.). 224p. 1994. pap. 29.95 (*0-7507-0223-0*, Falmer Pr) Taylor & Francis.

Adler, Lucile. The Pink Madonna: Selected Poems. Merrill, Chris & Kleiner, Ellen, eds. (Illus.). 112p. 1997. pap. 12.00 (*0-9659508-0-8*) Juniper Pr NM.

Adler, Lucile, et al. Yefief 1: A Narrative of Culture at the End of the Century. limited ed. (Illus.). 176p. 1994. pap. 24.95 (*1-884434-00-2*) Images For Media.

Adler, Lynn. Centenarians: The Bonus Years. LC 89-26895. (Illus.). 348p. 1995. 25.00 (*0-929173-02-3*) Health Press.

Adler, M. N., tr. see Signer, Michael A.

Adler, Marcus N. Jazz Flute Etudes. 48p. 1997. pap. 12.95 (*0-7935-8517-1*) H Leonard.

Adler, Margie, ed. see Gregg, Cynthia R.

Adler, Margot. Drawing down the Moon. LC 97-145477. 1997. pap. 16.95 (*0-14-019536-X*) Viking Penguin.

— Heretic's Heart: A Journey Through Spirit & Revolution. LC 96-53538. 384p. 1997. 24.00 (*0-8070-7098-X*) Beacon Pr.

— Heretic's Heart: A Journey Through Spirit & Revolution. 1998. pap. 13.00 (*0-8070-7099-8*) Beacon Pr.

***Adler, Marion, et al.** Pets! 70p. 1999. pap. 5.95 (*0-87129-934-8*, P87) Dramatic Pub.

Adler, Martin W., et al, eds. Factors Affecting the Action of Narcotics. fac. ed. LC 78-2999. (Monographs of the Mario Negri Institute for Pharmacological Research). (Illus.). 796p. pap. 200.00 (*0-7837-7513-X*, 204699200005) Bks Demand.

Adler, Melvin J. A Pragmatic Logic for Commands. (Pragmatics & Beyond Ser.: No. I-3). viii, 131p. 1980. pap. 29.00 (*90-272-2501-X*) J Benjamins Pubng Co.

Adler, Michael, et al, eds. The Sociology of Social Security. 1991. text 70.00 (*0-7486-0258-5*, Pub. by Edinburgh U Pr) Col U Pr.

— The Sociology of Social Security. (Edinburgh Education & Society Ser.). 320p. 1992. pap. text 30.00 (*0-7486-0325-5*, Pub. by Edinburgh U Pr) Col U Pr.

Adler, Michael & Ziglio, Erio, eds. Gazing into the Oracle: The Delphi Method & Its Application to Social Policy & Public Health. 252p. 1994. 39.95 (*1-85302-104-0*) Taylor & Francis.

Adler, Michael, et al. Parental Choice & Educational Policy. (Edinburgh Education & Society Ser.). 228p. 1990. pap. 30.00 (*0-85224-656-0*, Pub. by Edinburgh U Pr) Col U Pr.

***Adler, Michael A.** Prehistoric Pueblo World, A. D. 1150-1350. (Illus.). 2000. pap. text 24.95 (*0-8165-2048-8*) U of Ariz Pr.

Adler, Michael A., ed. The Prehistoric Pueblo World, A. D., 1150-1350. LC 95-32452. (Illus.). 278p. 1996. 47.50 (*0-8165-1468-2*) U of Ariz Pr.

Adler, Michael H. Antique Typewriters, from Creed to Qwerty. LC 96-33429. 208p. (gr. 10). 1997. 39.95 (*0-7643-0132-2*) Schiffer.

Adler, Michael W., ed. ABC of AIDS, Vol. 4. 4th rev. ed. (Illus.). 102p. 1997. pap. 32.00 (*0-7279-1137-6*, Pub. by BMJ Pub) Login Brothers Bk Co.

— ABC of Sexually Transmitted Diseases. 3rd ed. (Illus.). 75p. 1995. pap. 24.00 (*0-7279-0889-8*) Login Brothers Bk Co.

Adler, Morris. Voice Still Speaks. Chinitz, Jacob, ed. LC 68-57433. 1969. text 25.00 (*0-8197-0052-5*) Bloch.

— The World of the Talmud. 1987. 5.95 (*0-394-20058-6*) Pantheon.

Adler, Mortimer J. Adler's Philosophical Dictionary. 224p. 1996. per. 11.00 (*0-684-82271-7*, Touchstone) S&S Trade Pap.

— Adler's Philosophical Dictionary: 125 Key Terms for the Philosopher's Lexicon. LC 95-7992. 223p. 1995. 20.50 (*0-684-80360-7*, B945, Touchstone) S&S Trade Pap.

— Aristotle for Everybody. 1997. per. 13.00 (*0-684-83823-0*) S&S Trade.

— Art & Prudence. Jowett, Garth S., ed. LC 77-11371. (Aspects of Film Ser.). 1978. reprint ed. lib. bdg. 54.95 (*0-405-11126-6*) Ayer.

— Art, the Arts, & the Great Ideas. 128p. 1994. 15.00 (*0-02-500243-0*) Macmillan.

— Art, the Arts, & the Great Ideas. 1995. pap. 11.00 (*0-684-80420-4*, Touchstone) S&S Trade Pap.

— The Common Sense of Politics. rev. ed. LC 95-32066. xxx, 265p. 1996. 29.95 (*0-8232-1666-7*); pap. 18.00 (*0-8232-1667-5*) Fordham.

— The Difference of Man & the Difference It Makes. LC 93-22673. xxxiv, 395p. (C). 1993. reprint ed. 35.00 (*0-8232-1534-2*); reprint ed. pap. 20.00 (*0-8232-1535-0*) Fordham.

— The Great Ideas: A Lexicon of Western Thought. LC 98-46395. 1008p. 1999. 55.00 (*0-684-85921-1*) S&S Trade.

— Great Ideas: One Hundred Two Essays. 958p. 1992. 45.00 (*0-02-500573-1*) Free Pr.

— How to Speak, How to Listen. 1997. per. 9.00 (*0-684-84647-0*) S&S Trade.

***Adler, Mortimer J.** How to Think about the Great Ideas: From the Great Books of Western Civilization. Weismann, Max, ed. LC 99-45251. (Illus.). 544p. 2000. pap. 24.95 (*0-8126-9412-0*) Open Court.

Adler, Mortimer J. How to Think about War & Peace. LC 95-49502. li, 307p. 1995. reprint ed. pap. text 18.00 (*0-8232-1643-8*) Fordham.

— How to Think about War & Peace. ii, 307p. (C). 1995. reprint ed. text 30.00 (*0-8232-1642-X*) Fordham.

— Platonism & Positivism in Psychology. LC 94-27446. 266p. 1994. pap. 24.95 (*1-56000-772-9*) Transaction Pubs.

— Reforming Education: The Opening of the American Mind. 320p. 1990. pap. 8.95 (*0-02-030175-8*) Macmillan.

— St. Thomas & the Gentiles. (Aquinas Lectures). 1938. 15.00 (*0-87462-102-X*) Marquette.

— A Second Look in the Rear-View Mirror: Further Autobiographical Reflections of a Philosopher at Large. LC 92-9169. 1994. pap. 10.00 (*0-02-016030-5*) Macmillan.

— Six Great Ideas. 1997. per. 10.00 (*0-684-82681-X*) S&S Trade.

— Six Great Ideas: Truth, Goodness, Beauty, Liberty, Equality, Justice. 243p. 1984. pap. 7.95 (*0-02-072020-3*, Collier S&S) S&S Trade.

— Ten Philosophical Mistakes. 1997. per. 10.00 (*0-684-81868-X*) S&S Trade.

— The Time of Our Lives: The Ethics of Common Sense. rev. ed. xv, 361p. 1996. 29.95 (*0-8232-1669-1*); pap. 18.00 (*0-8232-1670-5*) Fordham.

An Asterisk (*) at the beginning of an entry indicates that the title is appearing for the first time.

Adler, Mortimer J., ed. The Sciences Today. LC 75-4350. (Great Ideas Anthologies Ser.). (Illus.). 564p. 1977. 23.95 (*0-405-07173-6*) Ayer.

Adler, Mortimer J. & Van Doren, Charles. The Great Treasury of Western Thought: A Compendium of Important Statements & Comments on Man & His Institutions by the Great Thinkers in Western History. LC 77-154. 1171p. 1977. 49.50 (*0-8352-0833-8*) Bowker.

— How to Read a Book. 448p. 1992. 8.98 (*1-56731-010-9*, MJF Bks) Fine Comms.

— How to Read a Book. rev. ed. 426p. 1972. per. 13.00 (*0-671-21209-5*) S&S Trade.

Adler, Mortimer J., jt. auth. see Kelso, Louis O.

Adler, Mortimer J., jt. ed. see Hutchins, Robert M.

Adler, N., jt. ed. see Gerrits, A.

Adler, N. T., et al. Reproduction. (Handbook of Behavioral Neurobiology Ser.: Vol. 7). (Illus.). 820p. (C). 1985. text 175.00 (*0-306-41768-5*, Kluwer Plenum) Kluwer Academic.

Adler, Nanci D. Victims of Soviet Terror: The Story of the Memorial Movement. LC 92-46164. 200p. 1993. 55.00 (*0-275-94502-2*, C4502, Praeger Pubs) Greenwood.

***Adler, Nancy, et al.** Socioeconomic Status & Health in Industrial Nations: Social, Psychological & Biological Pathways. LC 99-52320. 1999. write for info. (*1-57331-211-8*) NY Acad Sci.

Adler, Nancy, tr. see Brunsson, Nils.

Adler, Nancy, tr. see Gardlund, Torsten.

Adler, Nancy, tr. see Gunnarsson, Torsten.

***Adler, Nancy E.** Socioeconomic Status & Health in Industrial Nations: Social, Psychological & Biological Pathways. annuals LC 99-52320. 1999. write for info. (*1-57331-212-6*) NY Acad Sci.

— Socioeconomic Status & Health in Industrial Nations: Social, Psychological & Biological Patterns. (Annals of the New York Academy of Science Ser.). 2000. pap. 34.95 (*0-8018-6545-X*) Johns Hopkins.

Adler, Nancy J. International Dimensions of Organizational Behavior. 2nd ed. 313p. (C). 1990. mass mkt. 21.50 (*0-534-92274-0*) S-W Pub.

— International Dimensions of Organizational Behavior. 3rd ed. LC 96-19520. (GI - Organizational Behavior Ser.). 1996. mass mkt. 41.95 (*0-538-86136-3*) S-W Pub.

— Intl Dimensions Organizational Behavior. (SWC-Management). 256p. 1986. mass mkt. 17.00 (*0-534-06258-X*) PWS Pubs.

Adler, Nancy J. & Izraeli, Dafna N., eds. Competitive Frontiers: Women Managers in a Global Economy. LC 93-19121. (Illus.). 460p. 1994. pap. 40.95 (*1-55786-510-8*) Blackwell Pubs.

— Women in Management Worldwide. LC 88-4520. 304p. (C). (gr. 13). 1989. pap. text 36.95 (*0-87332-570-2*) M E Sharpe.

Adler, Naomi. Play Me a Story: 9 Tales about Musical Instruments. LC 97-25708. (Barefoot Book of Musical Tales). (Illus.). 80p. (J). (gr. 3-5). 1997. 23.40 (*0-7613-0401-0*) Millbrook Pr.

Adler, Nicholas. Portraits from an Uninhabited Land. 1988. pap. write for info. (*0-318-63738-3*) Bantam.

Adler, Norman T., ed. Neuroendocrinology of Reproduction: Physiology & Behavior. LC 80-28245. 576p. 1981. 75.00 (*0-306-40600-4*, Plenum Trade); pap. 37.50 (*0-306-40611-X*, Plenum Trade) Perseus Pubng.

Adler, P., et al. Fluorides & Human Health. (Monographs: No. 59). 364p. 1970. pap. text 42.00 (*92-4-140059-5*, 1140059) World Health.

***Adler, P., et al.** Macromolecular Symposia 142. Guth, W. et al, eds. 225p. 1999. 105.00 (*3-527-29902-5*) Wiley.

Adler, P. M., ed. Multiphase Flow in Porous Media. 212p. (C). 1995. text 161.50 (*0-7923-3817-0*) Kluwer Academic.

Adler, Paramus. Data Mining. (C). 2000. pap. 26.00 (*0-13-083004-6*) P-H.

Adler, Patricia, ed. Fire in the Hills. 1992. pap. 19.95 (*0-9634167-0-7*) Phoenix Soc.

— In Good Company. 240p. (Orig.). 1999. pap. 12.95 (*0-9672885-1-7*) Live Wire Pr.

— The Poet's Domain: We Wear the Mask. 120p. (Orig.). 1999. pap. 10.95 (*0-9672885-0-9*) Live Wire Pr.

Adler, Patricia & Adler, Peter. Peer Power: Preadolescent Culture & Identity. LC 97-22516. xii, 255p. 1998. 48.00 (*0-8135-2459-8*); pap. 17.00 (*0-8135-2460-1*) Rutgers U Pr.

Adler, Patricia A. Wheeling & Dealing: An Ethnography of Upper-Level Drug Dealing & Smuggling Community. 224p. (C). 1993. pap. 18.50 (*0-231-08133-2*) Col U Pr.

Adler, Patricia A., et al, eds. The Social Dynamics of Financial Markets. LC 84-4340. (Contemporary Studies in Applied Behavioral Science: Vol. 2). 212p. 1984. 73.25 (*0-89232-435-X*) Jai Pr.

Adler, Patricia A. & Adler, Peter. Backboards & Blackboards. 288p. 1991. pap. text 21.00 (*0-231-07307-0*) Col U Pr.

— Constructions of Deviance: Social Power, Context, & Interaction. 588p. 1993. mass mkt. 36.95 (*0-534-21342-1*) Wadsworth Pub.

— Membership Roles in Field Research. (Qualitative Research Methods Ser.: Vol. 6). 96p. (C). 1987. text 24.00 (*0-8039-2760-6*); pap. text 10.50 (*0-8039-2578-6*) Sage.

Adler, Paul S., ed. Technology & the Future of Work. (Illus.). 352p. 1992. text 60.00 (*0-19-507171-9*) OUP.

Adler, Paul S. & Winograd, Terry, eds. Usability: Turning Technologies into Tools. (Illus.). 224p. 1992. text 65.00 (*0-19-507510-2*) OUP.

Adler, Peter. Momentum: A Theory of Social Action. LC 81-2718. (Sociological Observations Ser.: No. 11). 191p. reprint ed. pap. 59.30 (*0-8357-8465-7*, 203473300091) Bks Demand.

Adler, Peter & Barnard, Nicholas. African Majesty: The Textile Art of the Ashanti & Ewe. LC 92-70868. (Illus.). 192p. 1995. pap. 29.95 (*0-500-27844-X*, Pub. by Thames Hudson) Norton.

— Asafo! African Flags of the Fante. LC 92-70869. (Illus.). 96p. 1992. pap. 19.95 (*0-500-27684-6*, Pub. by Thames Hudson) Norton.

Adler, Peter, jt. auth. see Adler, Patricia.

Adler, Peter, jt. auth. see Adler, Patricia A.

Adler, Peter S. Beyond Paradise: Encounters in Hawaii Where the Tour Bus Never Runs. LC 93-13728. 1993. pap. 16.00 (*1-881987-01-9*) Ox Bow.

Adler, Peter S., jt. auth. see Adler, David A.

Adler, Phillip J. World Civilizations, 2 vols. Incl. Vol. 1. LC 95-34878. 350p. (C). 1996. 40.50 (*0-314-06800-7*); Vol. 2. LC 95-34878. 350p. (C). 1996. 40.50 (*0-314-06801-5*); 700p. (C). 1996. 56.75 (*0-314-06799-X*) West Pub.

Adler, Pierre M. Porous Media: Geometry & Transports. 560p. 1992. text 115.00 (*0-7506-9236-7*) Buttrwrth-Heinemann.

Adler, Pierre M. & Thovert, J. F. Fractures & Fracture Networks. LC 99-13863. (Theories & Applications of Transport in Porous Media Ser.). 1999. write for info. (*0-7923-5647-0*) Kluwer Academic.

***Adler, Pillip J.** World Civilizations since 1500, Vol. 2. 2nd ed. (History Ser.). (C). 2000. text 15.75 (*0-534-56911-0*) Wadsworth Pub.

Adler, R., et al, eds. A Practical Guide to Heavy Tails. LC 97-8731. 533p. 1997. 64.50 (*0-8176-3951-9*) Birkhauser.

Adler, R. L. & Marcus, B. Topological Entropy & Equivalence of Dynamical Systems. LC 79-15040. (Memoirs Ser.: No. 20/219). 84p. 1981. reprint ed. pap. 21.00 (*0-8218-2219-5*, MEMO/20/219) Am Math.

Adler, R. L. & Weiss, B. Similarity of Automorphisms of the Torus. LC 52-42839. (Memoirs Ser.: No. 1/98). 43p. 1970. pap. 16.00 (*0-8218-1298-X*, MEMO/1/98) Am Math.

Adler, Rachel. Engendering Judaism: A New Theology & Ethics. LC 97-18944. 260p. 1997. 24.95 (*0-8276-0584-6*) JPS Phila.

— Engendering Judaism: An Inclusive Theology & Ethics. LC 99-25989. 272p. 1999. pap. 15.00 (*0-8070-3619-6*) Beacon Pr.

Adler, Renata. Gone: The Last Days of the New Yorker. LC 99-49122. 256p. 2000. 24.50 (*0-684-80816-1*) S&S Trade.

***Adler, Renata.** In Private Capacity. 2001. 26.00 (*1-891620-90-8*) PublicAffairs NY.

Adler, Richard. The Future of Advertising: New Approaches to the Attention Economy. 60p. 1998. pap. 12.00 (*0-89843-223-5*) The Aspen Inst.

Adler, Richard. Information Literacy: Advancing Opportunities for Learning in the Digital Age. (Communications & Society Ser.). 45p. pap. 12.00 (*0-89843-262-6*) The Aspen Inst.

Adler, Richard, ed. Understanding Television: Essays on Television As a Social & Cultural Force. LC 81-47781. 456p. 1981. 65.00 (*0-275-90575-6*, C0575, Praeger Pubs) Greenwood.

Adler, Richard & Saffo, Paul. Consumer Market Strategies: Scenarios & Implications. 20p. 1985. 6.00 (*0-318-19208-X*, R-64) Inst Future.

Adler, Richard, et al. The Market for Teletext in the United States, 2 vols. 203p. 1983. 20.00 (*0-318-19202-0*, R-57) Inst Future.

Adler, Richard, jt. auth. see Lipinski, Hubert.

Adler, Richard P. Jobs, Technology & Employability: Redefining the Social Contract: A Report of the Aspen Institute Forum on Communications & Society. LC 99-174539. 62 p. 1998. 12.00 (*0-89843-241-3*) The Aspen Inst.

Adler, Robert & Landman, Jessica. The Clean Water Act 20 Years Later. LC 93-22632. 350p. 1993. text 60.00 (*1-55963-265-8*); pap. text 35.00 (*1-55963-266-6*) Island Pr.

Adler, Robert J. The Geometry of Random Fields. LC 80-40842. (Illus.). 292p. reprint ed. pap. 90.60 (*0-8357-6129-0*, 203420900089) Bks Demand.

— An Introduction to Continuity, Extrema, & Related Topics for General Gaussian Processes. LC 90-83130. (IMS Lecture Notes - Monographs: Vol. 12). vii, 160p. 1990. pap. 25.00 (*0-940600-17-X*) Inst Math.

Adler, Robert J., et al, eds. Stochastic Modelling in Physical Oceanography. LC 95-48417. (Progress in Probability Ser.: Vol. 39). xi, 467p. 1996. 84.50 (*0-8176-3798-2*) Birkhauser.

— Stochastic Modelling in Physical Oceanography. LC 95-48417. (Progress in Probability Ser.: Vol. 39). 1996. write for info. (*3-7643-3798-2*) Birkhauser.

Adler, Robert J., et al. A Practical Guide to Heavy Tails: Statistical Techniques for Analyzing Heavy Tailed Distributions. LC 97-8731. 1997. write for info. (*3-7643-3951-9*) Birkhauser.

Adler, Rodney R. Vertical Transportation for Buildings. LC 73-104976. (Elsevier Architectural Science Ser.). 238p. reprint ed. pap. 73.80 (*0-608-11653-X*, 200776000064) Bks Demand.

Adler, Roger, ed. see Carey, MacDonald.

Adler, Roger, ed. see Lanigan, Anne.

Adler, Roger, ed. see Leibowitz, Alan.

Adler, Roger, ed. see Sugar, Bert R.

Adler, Ronald B. Looking Out, Looking In. 8th ed. (C). 1995. text 47.50 (*0-15-501728-4*) Harcourt Coll Pubs.

Adler, Ronald B. & Elmhorst, Jeanne M. Communicating at Work: Principles & Practices for Business & the Professions. 5th ed. LC 95-41256. (C). 1995. pap. text 30.50 (*0-07-000478-1*) McGraw.

— Communicating at Work: Principles & Practices for Business & the Professions. 6th ed. LC 98-35487. 1998. 90.95 (*0-07-289303-6*) McGraw.

— Communicating at Work: Principles & Practices for Business & the Professions. 6th ed. LC 98-35487. 512p. 1998. pap. 45.00 (*0-07-303433-9*) McGraw.

Adler, Ronald B. & Rodman, George. Understanding Human Communication. 6th ed. LC 95-81785. 552p. (C). 1996. pap. text 47.50 (*0-15-503286-0*, Pub. by Harcourt Coll Pubs) Harcourt.

Adler, Ronald B. & Towne, Neil. Looking Out- Looking In. 7th ed. (Illus.). 450p. (C). 1993. text. write for info. (*0-318-69103-5*) Harcourt Coll Pubs.

Adler, Ronald B., et al. Interplay: The Process of Interpersonal Communication. 7th ed. LC 96-79891. 462p. (Orig.). (C). 1997. pap. text 47.00 (*0-15-503977-6*, Pub. by Harcourt Coll Pubs) Harcourt.

Adler, Ronald B., jt. auth. see Rodman, George.

Adler, Roy D., jt. ed. see Robinson, Larry M.

Adler, Roy L. & Weiss, Benjamin. Similarity of Automorphisms of the Torus. LC 52-42839. (American Mathematical Society Ser.: No. 98). (Illus.). 47p. 1970. pap. 30.00 (*0-608-05169-1*, 205259000001) Bks Demand.

Adler, Rudolph J. Biblical Beginnings: Archaeology & the Roots of Scripture. LC 85-16970. (Illus.). 320p. 1985. 17.95 (*0-13-076233-4*) P-H.

Adler, Ruth. A Day in the Life of the New York Times. 1981. 24.95 (*0-405-13782-6*) Ayer.

— Women of the Shtetl: Through the Eye of Y. L. Peretz. LC 78-69895. (Illus.). 152p. 1980. 26.50 (*0-8386-2356-0*) Fairleigh Dickinson.

— The Working Press. 1981. 24.95 (*0-405-13783-4*) Ayer.

Adler, Ruth, jt. auth. see Adler, Irving.

***Adler, Samuel.** Orchestration (C). 1999. text, wbk. ed. 45.25 (*0-393-98214-9*) Norton.

Adler, Samuel. The Study of Orchestration. 400p. (C). 1989. pap. text, teacher ed. write for info. (*0-393-95809-4*) Norton.

— The Study of Orchestration. 2nd ed. 400p. (C). 1989. 57.75 (*0-393-95807-8*) Norton.

— The Study of Orchestration. 2nd ed. (C). 1989. pap. text, wbk. ed. 23.75 (*0-393-95808-6*) Norton.

***Adler, Samuel.** The Study of Orchestration. 3rd ed. LC 99-55023. 2000. 40.50 (*0-393-97572-X*) Norton.

Adler, Samuel, jt. auth. see Barton, Andrew.

***Adler, Sara, et al.** Arbitration 1998: The Changing World of Dispute Resolution. 208p. 1998. 40.00 (*1-57018-174-8*, 1174-PR9) BNA Books.

Adler, Sebastian & McDonald, Robert. Christo: Collection on Loan Rothschild Bank. LC 81-84093. (Illus.). 144p. 1981. 19.95 (*0-934418-12-8*) Mus Contemp Art.

Adler, Selig. Isolationist Impulse: Its Twentieth Century Reaction. LC 74-15551. 538p. 1974. reprint ed. lib. bdg. 86.50 (*0-8371-7822-3*, ADII, Greenwood Pr) Greenwood.

Adler, Shelley. Alice's Hat: Poems. (Illus.). 75p. 1998. pap. 13.00 (*0-917232-32-1*) Gee Tee Bee.

Adler, Shelley, jt. auth. see Goodman, Florence J.

Adler, Shirley. Carving Spoons: Welsh Love Spoons, Celtic Knots, & Contemporary Favorites. (Illus.). 75p. 1997. pap. 14.95 (*1-56523-092-2*) Fox Chapel Pub.

Adler, Sinai. Your Rod & Your Staff. Barish, Tzvi, tr. & adapted by by. LC 95-41565. 1995. 17.95 (*0-87306-736-3*) Feldheim.

Adler, Sol. The Health & Education of the Economically Deprived Child. LC 67-26009. 194p. 1968. 10.50 (*0-87527-025-5*) Green.

Adler, Sol & King, Deborah A., eds. Oral Communication Problems in Children & Adolescents. 2nd ed. LC 93-10741. 240p. (C). 1993. 54.00 (*0-205-15089-6*) Allyn.

Adler, Stan. The Zen of Selling: The Way to Profit from Life's Everyday Lessons. LC 98-21612. 144p. 1998. 14.95 (*0-8144-0433-2*) AMACOM.

Adler, Stella. Book II of Script Interpretation. 1998. write for info. (*0-679-42443-1*) Knopf.

— Stella Adler on Ibsen, Strindberg, & Chekhov. Paris, Barry, ed. & pref. by. LC 98-38190. 352p. 1999. 27.50 (*0-679-42442-3*) Knopf.

***Adler, Stella.** Stella Adler on Ibsen, Strindberg & Chekhov. 352p. 2000. pap. 15.00 (*0-679-74698-6*) Knopf.

Adler, Stephen J., jt. ed. see Grunwald, Lisa.

Adler, Stephen L. Quaternionic Quantum Mechanics & Quantum Fields. (International Series of Monographs on Physics). 608p. 1995. text 95.00 (*0-19-506643-X*) OUP.

Adler, Stephen N., et al. A Pocket Manual of Differential Diagnosis. 3rd ed. LC 93-33819. 392p. 1994. pap. text 24.95 (*0-316-01109-6*) Lppncott W & W.

***Adler, Stephen N., et al.** A Pocket Manual of Differential Diagnosis. 4th ed. LC 99-42878. 352p. 1999. pap. text 24.95 (*0-7817-1943-7*) Lppncott W & W.

Adler, Sue. Mandela for Young Beginners. (Illus.). 64p. (J). (gr. 3). 1997. pap. 8.00 (*0-86316-174-X*) Writers & Readers.

Adler, Sue, et al. Managing Women: Feminism & Power in Educational Management. LC 92-34666. (Gender & Education Ser.). 144p. 1993. pap. 30.95 (*0-335-15780-7*) OpUniv Pr.

Adler, Susan A., jt. auth. see Pai, Young.

Adler, Susan M. Mothering, Education, & Ethnicity: The Transformation of Japanese American Culture. LC 98-8583. (Asian Americans). 203p. 1998. 53.00 (*0-8153-3159-2*) Garland.

Adler, Susan S. Meet Samantha: An American Girl. Thieme, Jeanne, ed. LC 98-16815. (American Girls Collection : Bk. 1). (Illus.). 61p. (YA). (gr. 2 up). 1986. pap. 5.95 (*0-937295-04-3*); lib. bdg. 12.95 (*0-937295-80-9*) Pleasant Co.

— Meet Samantha: An American Girl. (American Girls Collection: Bk. 1). (YA). (gr. 2 up). 1986. 11.15 (*0-606-02770-X*, Pub. by Turtleback) Demco.

— Samantha Learns a Lesson: A School Story. Thieme, Jeanne, ed. LC 98-16818. (American Girls Collection : Bk. 2). (Illus.). 72p. (YA). (gr. 2 up). 1986. text 12.95 (*0-937295-83-3*); pap. text 5.95 (*0-937295-13-2*) Pleasant Co.

— Samantha Learns a Lesson: A School Story. (American Girls Collection: Bk. 2). (Illus.). (YA). (gr. 2 up). 1986. 11.15 (*0-606-03451-X*, Pub. by Turtleback) Demco.

Adler, Susan S., et al. PNF in Practice: An Illustrated Guide. LC 93-5234. (Illus.). 240p. 1995. 49.95 (*0-387-52649-8*) Spr-Verlag.

***Adler, Susan S., et al.** PNF in Practice: An Illustrated Guide. 2nd rev. ed. (Illus.). xiii, 401p. 2000. pap. text 52.00 (*3-540-66395-9*) Spr-Verlag.

Adler, Susan S, et al. Samantha Boxed Set: Meet Samantha; Samantha Learns a Lesson; Samantha's Surprise; Happy Birthday, Samantha!; Samantha Saves the Day; Changes for Samantha. (American Girls Collection : Bks. 1-6). (Illus.). 432p. (YA). (gr. 2 up). 1991. boxed set 74.95 (*1-56247-050-7*); pap. text, boxed set 34.95 (*0-937295-77-9*) Pleasant Co.

Adler, T. C. van, see Van Adler, T. C.

Adler, Thomas P. American Drama, 1940-1960. LC 93-33791. (Critical History of American Drama Ser.). 272p. 1994. 33.00 (*0-8057-8957-X*, Twyne) Mac Lib Ref.

— Mirror on the Stage: The Pulitzer Plays As an Approach to American Drama. LC 86-21170. 192p. 1987. 39.95 (*0-911198-84-9*) Purdue U Pr.

Adler, Thomas P., jt. auth. see Woodman, Leonora.

***Adler, Tracy L. & Jacobson, Heidi Z.** Nature Is Not Romantic. (Illus.). 16p. 1999. pap. 5.00 (*1-885998-19-8*) Hunter College.

Adler, Tracy L., et al. News, Surprise, & Nostalgia. (Illus.). 24p. 1995. pap. text. write for info. (*1-885998-06-6*) Hunter College.

Adler, Tracy L., ed. see Brennan, Michael.

Adler, Ursula. A Critical Study of the American Nursing Home - the Final Solution. LC 91-8802. (Studies in Health & Human Services: Vol. 18). 242p. 1991. lib. bdg. 89.95 (*0-88946-383-2*) E Mellen.

Adler, W., et al. Exkursionsflora von Oesterreich (Field Guide to the Austrian Flora) (GER.). 1180p. 1994. 46.00 (*3-8001-3461-6*, Pub. by Eugen Ulmer) Balogh.

Adler, W. F., ed. Erosion: Prevention & Useful Application - STP 664. 637p. 1979. 55.00 (*0-685-00555-0*, STP664) ASTM.

Adler, Warren. Jackson Hole: Uneasy Eden. LC 97-8825. 224p. 1997. 24.95 (*0-943972-62-0*) Homestead WY.

— Never Too Late for Love. 288p. 1995. 22.95 (*0-943972-44-2*); pap. 14.95 (*0-943972-45-0*) Homestead WY.

— Private Lies. 352p. 1992. mass mkt. 4.99 (*0-380-71307-1*, Avon Bks) Morrow Avon.

— Random Hearts. 1999. mass mkt. 6.99 (*0-345-43612-1*) Ballantine Pub Grp.

— Senator Love. 256p. 1992. reprint ed. mass mkt. 3.99 (*0-8217-3998-0*, Zebra Kensgtn) Kensgtn Pub Corp.

— Twilight Child. 1989. pap. 3.95 (*0-317-02803-0*) NAL.

— We Are Holding the President Hostage. 304p. 1988. pap. 4.50 (*0-373-97072-2*) Harlequin Bks.

Adler, Wilfred. Piano Improvising. 128p. 1977. spiral bd. 11.95 (*0-87166-529-8*, 93410) Mel Bay.

Adler, William. Time Immemorial: Archaic History & Its Sources in Christian Chronography from Julius Africanus to George Syncellus. LC 88-13942. (Dumbarton Oaks Studies: Vol. 26). 200p. 1989. 19.50 (*0-88402-176-9*) Dumbarton Oaks.

Adler, William, jt. ed. see VanderKam, James C.

***Adler, William M.** Mollie's Job: A Story of Life & Work on the Global Assembly Line. LC 99-59825. 368p. 2000. 27.00 (*0-684-83779-X*, Scb1) S&S Trade.

Adler, Zsuzsanna. Rape on Trial. LC 86-15586. 224p. 1987. 49.95 (*0-7102-0804-9*, 08049, Routledge Thoemms) Routledge.

Adlerberg, Scott. Jungle Horses. (Orig.). 1998. pap. text 10.95 (*1-57532-069-X*) Press-Tige Pub.

— Spiders & Flies. (Orig.). 1998. pap. text 10.95 (*1-57532-068-1*) Press-Tige Pub.

Adlerblum, Nima H. Memoirs of Childhood: An Approach to Jewish Philosophy. Benheim, Els, ed. LC 98-5658. 327p. 1999. pap. 25.00 (*0-7657-6012-6*) Aronson.

— Study of Gersonides in His Proper Perspective. LC 73-158229. reprint ed. 27.50 (*0-404-00296-X*) AMS Pr.

Adlercreutz, Patrick, jt. ed. see Straathof, Adrie J. J.

Adlerman, Dan. Africa Calling: Nighttime Calling. LC 96-11961. (Illus.). 32p. (J). (ps-2). 1996. 15.95 (*1-879085-98-4*, Whispering Coyote) Charlesbridge Pub.

***Adlerman, Daniel, et al.** The Cool Black Pool. LC 00-36645. (Illus.). 2001. write for info. (*1-58089-058-X*, Whispering Coyote) Charlesbridge Pub.

Adlersflugel, Georg S. Winter Von, see Winter Von Adlersflugel, Georg S.

Adlerton, David. Parrots. (Illus.). 198p. 1992. 31.95 (*1-56465-100-2*, 16070) Tetra Pr.

Adley, Amanda R., jt. ed. see Anderson, Clinton W.

***Adlington, Robert.** The Music of Harrison Birtwistle. (Music in the Twentieth Century Ser.: No. 12). (Illus.). 244p. (C). 2000. 59.95 (*0-521-63082-7*) Cambridge U Pr.

Adlington, William, tr. see Apuleius, Madaurensis.

Adlkofer, F. & Thurau, K., eds. Effects of Nicotine on Biological Systems. (Advances in Pharmacological Sciences Ser.). 664p. 1991. 156.00 (*0-8176-2519-4*) Birkhauser.

Adlof, Linda, ed. see Sabolich, John.

Adlof, Linda, ed. see Sabolich, John A.

Adloff, Jean-Pierre & Guillaumont, Robert. Applied Radiochemistry. 448p. 1993. boxed set 157.95 (*0-8493-4244-9*, QD601) CRC Pr.

Adloff, Richard, tr. see Tholomier, Robert.

Adlor, Jack H. Rejected: The Chronicles of a Failed Writer. LC 97-73110. 166p. (Orig.). 1997. pap. 12.95 (*0-9655309-0-6*, 101) Ironweed Pr.

Admas, Roy M., et al. Illinois Estate Planning, Will Drafting & Estate Administration Forms, 2 vols. 2000p. 1993. suppl. ed. 82.00 (*0-685-74613-5*, MICHIE) LEXIS Pub.

Admassie, Yeraswork. Twenty Years to Nowhere: Property Rights, Land Management & Conservation in Ethiopia. LC 98-23169. 537p. 1997. 79.95 (*1-56902-060-4*); pap. 21.95 (*1-56902-061-2*) Red Sea Pr.

Administracao do Porto de Sines, Sines, Portugal, jt. auth. see Rubble Mound Structures Committee of the Waterway,.

Administracion de Fomento Economico Staff. Puerto Rico y el Mar: Un Programa de Accion Sobre Asuntos Marinos. 129p. 1974. pap. 5.00 (*0-8477-2300-3*) U of PR Pr.

Administrative Board, U.S. Catholic Conference Sta. Moral Principles & Policy Priorities for Welfare Reform. 12p. 1995. pap. text 1.25 (*1-57455-011-X*) US Catholic.

Administrative Review Council (Australia) Staff. Environmental Decisions & the Administrative Appeals Tribunal: Report to the Minister for Justice. LC 96-145401. (Parliamentary Paper/Parliament of the Commonwealth of Australia Ser.). xiii, 61 p. 1994. write for info. (*0-644-34932-8*, Pub. by Aust Gov Pub) Accents Pubns.

Admiraal, P. H., ed. Small Business in the Modern Economy. (Illus.). 200p. 1996. 58.95 (*0-631-20018-5*) Blackwell Pubs.

Admiraal, P. H., ed. see Lazonick, William, et al.

Admiralty Staff. His Majesty's Submarines. 3rd rev. ed. (World War II Monograph: Vol. 401). (Illus.). 43p. 1997. reprint ed. 17.95 (*1-57638-078-5*, M401H); reprint ed. pap. 7.95 (*1-57638-021-1*, M401S) Merriam Pr.

Admoni, W. G. Principles of Grammar Theory. Harden, Theo & Weydt, Harald, eds. LC 95-39815. X, 109p. 1995. pap. 29.95 (*0-8204-2911-2*, 68704) P Lang Pubng.

Admoni, Wladimir G. Principles of Grammar Theory. Harden, Theo & Weydt, Harald, eds. x, 109p. 1995. pap. 29.95 (*3-631-49183-2*) P Lang Pubng.

Adnan, Etel. The Arab Apocalypse. (Poetry Ser.). Orig. Title: L' Apocalypse Arabe. (Illus.). 80p. (Orig.). 1989. pap. 13.50 (*0-942996-09-7*) Post Apollo Pr.

— From A to Z Poetry. (Illus.). 30p. (Orig.). 1982. pap. 7.00 (*0-942996-00-3*) Post Apollo Pr.

— The Indian Never Had a Horse & Other Poems. 2nd ed. (Poetry Ser.). (Illus.). (Orig.). 1995. pap. 12.00 (*0-942996-04-6*) Post Apollo Pr.

— Journey to Mount Tamalpais. (Poetic Essay Ser.). (Illus.). 64p. (Orig.). 1986. pap. 10.95 (*0-942996-01-1*) Post Apollo Pr.

— Of Cities & Women: Letters to Fawwaz. LC 92-50342. 85p. 1993. pap. 11.00 (*0-942996-21-6*) Post Apollo Pr.

— Paris, When It's Naked. LC 92-50341. 115p. (Orig.). 1993. pap. 13.50 (*0-942996-20-8*) Post Apollo Pr.

— Sitt Marie-Rose. 5th ed. Kleege, Georgina, tr. from FRE. (Novel Ser.). 105p. (Orig.). 1998. pap. 11.00 (*0-942996-33-X*) Post Apollo Pr.

— The Spring Flowers Own & The Manifestations of the Voyage. (Illus.). 101p. (Orig.). 1990. pap. 12.00 (*0-942996-14-3*) Post Apollo Pr.

— There: In the Light & the Darkness of the Self & of the Other. LC 96-52155. 70p. (Orig.). 1997. pap. 13.00 (*0-942996-28-3*) Post Apollo Pr.

Adnan, Etel, et al. Russell Chatham. (Illus.). 61p. 1984. pap. 14.95 (*0-916947-00-9*) Winn Bks.

— Russell Chatham. deluxe limited ed. (Illus.). 61p. 1984. 175.00 (*0-916947-01-7*) Winn Bks.

Adnani, Muhammad. Dictionary of Common Mistakes in Modern Written Arabic: Arabic-Arabic. (ARA & ENG.). 1984. 35.00 (*0-86685-094-5*, Pub. by Librairie du Liban) Intl Bk Ctr.

Adnett, N. J. Labour Market Policy: A European Perspective. 2nd ed. LC 95-26702. 304p. (C). 1996. pap. text 30.94 (*0-582-24885-X*, Pub. by Addison-Wesley) Longman.

Adney, Edwin T. & Chappelle, Howard I. The Bark Canoes & Skin Boats of North America. LC 64-62636. (Illus.). 242p. 1983. reprint ed. pap. text 29.95 (*1-56098-296-9*) Smithsonian.

Adney, Tappan. The Klondike Stampede. LC 95-100641. (Illus.). 496p. 1994. pap. 19.95 (*0-7748-0490-4*) U of Wash Pr.

Ado, Gustave F. Macro-Sexology, Sex, Sweet Sour. LC 98-65642. 64p. 1998. pap. 9.95 (*1-57197-122-X*) Pentland Pr.

Ado, I. D., et al. Lie Groups. (Translations Ser. 1: Vol. 9). 534p. 1991. reprint ed. pap. 60.00 (*0-8218-1609-8*, TRANS1/9) Am Math.

***Adobe Creative Team Staff.** Adobe Acrobat 4.0 Classroom in a Book. 2nd ed. (Classroom in a Book Ser.). 384p. 2000. pap. 45.00 incl. cd-rom (*0-201-70284-3*) Adobe Pr.

Adobe Creative Team Staff. Adobe Acrobat 3.0 Classroom in a Book. (Classroom in a Book Ser.). 312p. 1997. 40.00 (*1-56830-365-3*) Adobe Pr.

***Adobe Creative Team Staff.** Adobe after Effects 4.0 Classroom in a Book. (Classroom in a Book Ser.). 384p. 1999. pap. text 45.00 incl. cd-rom (*0-201-65891-7*, Pub. by Adobe Pr) Peachpit Pr.

Adobe Creative Team Staff. Adobe after Effects 3.1 Classroom in a Book. (Classroom in a Book Ser.). 348p. 1997. 45.00 (*1-56830-369-6*) Adobe Pr.

— Adobe FAQ. 774p. 1997. pap. 50.00 (*1-56830-372-6*) Adobe Pr.

Adobe Creative Team Staff. Adobe Framemaker 5.5 Classroom in a Book. LC 96-80332. (Classroom in a Book Ser.). 351p. 1997. pap. text 45.00 incl. cd-rom (*1-56830-399-8*) Adobe Pr.

Adobe Creative Team Staff. Adobe GoLive 4.0 Classroom in a Book. (Classroom in a Book Ser.). 318p. 1999. pap. text 40.00 (*0-201-65889-5*, Pub. by Adobe Pr) Peachpit Pr.

***Adobe Creative Team Staff.** Adobe GoLive 4.0 Productivity Kit. 200p. 1999. pap. 35.00 (*0-201-65898-4*) Adobe Pr.

Adobe Creative Team Staff. Adobe Illustrator 8.0 Classroom in a Book. LC 98-84637. (Classroom in a Book Ser.). 300p. 1998. pap. 45.00 (*1-56830-470-6*) Adobe Pr.

— Adobe Illustrator for Macintosh: Classroom in a Book. 2nd ed. LC 96-216378. (Classroom in a Book Ser.). (Illus.). 320p. 1995. pap. 45.00 incl. cd-rom (*1-56830-234-7*) Adobe Pr.

— Adobe Illustrator 7.0 Classroom in a Book. (Classroom in a Book Ser.). 336p. 1997. pap. 45.00 (*1-56830-371-8*) Adobe Pr.

***Adobe Creative Team Staff.** Adobe InDesign Classroom in a Book. (Classroom in a Book Ser.). 456p. 1999. pap. 45.00 incl. cd-rom (*0-201-65893-3*, Pub. by Adobe Pr) Peachpit Pr.

— Adobe InDesign 1.5 Classroom in a Book. (Classroom in a Book Ser.). 2000. 45.00 (*0-201-71026-9*) Adobe Pr.

— Adobe LiveMotion Classroom in a Book. (Classroom in a Book Ser.). 2000. 35.00 (*0-201-70322-X*) Adobe Pr.

Adobe Creative Team Staff. Adobe PageMaker 6 for Macintosh: Classroom in a Book. LC 95-77726. (Classroom in a Book Ser.). (Illus.). 304p. 1995. pap. 45.00 (*1-56830-235-5*) Adobe Pr.

— Adobe PageMaker 6.5 Classroom in a Book. LC 97-70858. (Classroom in a Book Ser.). 324p. 1997. 45.00 (*1-56830-370-X*) Adobe Pr.

***Adobe Creative Team Staff.** Adobe PageMaker 6.5 Plus Productivity Kit. 192p. 1999. pap. text 25.00 (*0-201-65897-6*, Pub. by Adobe Pr) Peachpit Pr.

Adobe Creative Team Staff. Adobe Persuasion 4.0 Classroom in a Book. (Classroom in a Book Ser.). 195p. 1997. pap. 40.00 (*1-56830-316-5*) Adobe Pr.

***Adobe Creative Team Staff.** Adobe Photoshop 5.5 & Illustrator 8.0 Advanced. (Classroom in a Book Ser.). 408p. 2000. pap. 45.00 (*0-201-65900-X*) Adobe Pr.

— Adobe Photoshop 5.5 Classroom in a Book. (Classroom in a Book Ser.). 537p. 1999. pap. 45.00 incl. cd-rom (*0-201-65895-X*) Adobe Pr.

Adobe Creative Team Staff. Adobe Photoshop 5.0 Classroom in a Book. LC 98-84555. (Classroom in a Book Ser.). (Illus.). 300p. 1998. pap. 45.00 incl. cd-rom (*1-56830-466-8*) Adobe Pr.

— Adobe Premiere 5.0 Classroom in a Book. LC 98-84556. (Classroom in a Book Ser.). (Illus.). 378p. 1998. pap. 45.00 incl. cd-rom (*1-56830-467-6*) Adobe Pr.

— Adobe Premiere 4.0 for Windows: Classroom in a Book. (Classroom in a Book Ser.). (Illus.). 261p. 1995. pap. 50.00 (*1-56830-172-3*) Adobe Pr.

— Advanced Adobe PageMaker for Macintosh: Classroom in a Book. LC 95-81204. (Classroom in a Book Ser.). (Illus.). 312p. 1996. pap. 50.00 incl. cd-rom (*1-56830-261-4*) Adobe Pr.

— Photoshop 5.0 Productivity Kit. 192p. 1999. pap. text 39.99 (*1-56830-464-1*, Pub. by Adobe Pr) Peachpit Pr.

Adobe Creative Team Staff & Cohen, Luanne Seymour. Design Essentials. 3rd ed. 122p. 1999. 39.99 (*1-56830-472-2*) Adobe Pr.

Adobe Creative Team Staff, et al. Advanced Adobe Photoshop for Macintosh: Classroom in a Book. LC 94-76912. (Classroom in a Book Ser.). (Illus.). 202p. 1994. pap. text 50.00 (*1-56830-117-0*) Adobe Pr.

Adobe Creative Team Staff, jt. auth. see Faulkner, Andrew.

Adobe Creative Team Staff, jt. auth. see Fraser, Bruce.

Adobe Creative Team Staff, jt. auth. see Swanson, Becky.

Adobe Creative Team Staff, jt. auth. see Willmore, Ben.

***Adobe Systems, Inc.** PDF Reference. 2nd ed. 784p. 2000. pap. 49.95 incl. cd-rom (*0-201-61588-6*) Addison-Wesley.

Adobe Systems Inc. Staff. Adobe Premiere MacIntosh. Impress Group Staff & Prentice-Hall Staff, trs. LC 93-73013. (Classroom in a Book Ser.). (GER., Illus.). 320p. 1993. pap. text 44.95 (*3-930436-01-9*, Adobe) Hayden.

— Adobe Premiere MacIntosh. Impress Group Staff & Prentice-Hall Staff, trs. LC 93-78059. (Classroom in a Book Ser.). (JPN., Illus.). 320p. 1994. pap. text 44.95 (*4-8443-5413-2*, Adobe) Hayden.

— Adobe Type 1 Format. 2nd ed. (C). 1995. pap. text 16.95 (*0-201-60854-5*) Addison-Wesley.

— Postscript Language Reference. 3rd ed. LC 98-55489. 912p. (C). 1999. pap. text 49.95 (*0-201-37922-8*) Addison-Wesley.

— PostScript Language Reference Manual. 2nd ed. 784p. (C). 1990. pap. text 36.95 (*0-201-18127-4*) Addison-Wesley.

— PostScript Language Tutorial & Cookbook. 256p. (C). 1986. pap. text 26.95 (*0-201-10179-3*) Addison-Wesley.

— Programming the Display PostScript System with X. LC 93-7455. 624p. (C). 1993. pap. text 29.95 (*0-201-62203-3*) Addison-Wesley.

Adobe Systems Inc. Staff, et al. Adobe Photoshop for Macintosh. Impress Group Staff & Prentice-Hall Staff, trs. LC 93-78060. (Classroom in a Book Ser.). (JPN., Illus.). 320p. 1994. pap. text 44.95 (*4-8443-5412-4*, Adobe); pap. text 44.95 (*2-910565-00-9*, Adobe) Hayden.

— Design Essentials: Professional Studio Techniques. Wendling, Tanya, ed. Impress Group Staff & Prentice Hall Japan Staff, trs. LC 92-72409. (JPN., Illus.). 102p. (Orig.). 1992. pap. text 39.95 (*4-8443-5408-6*, Adobe) Hayden.

— Production Essentials. (Orig.). 1994. pap. text 39.95 (*0-685-75281-X*, Adobe) Hayden.

Adobe Systems Inc. Staff, ed. see Reid, Glenn C.

Adoboyde, Olagoke F. African. 305p. (Orig.). 1994. pap. 16.95 (*0-86626-003-X*) AAIMS Pubs.

Adoff. Jazzicals. (J). 2000. mass mkt. 17.00 (*0-689-80106-8*) S&S Bks Yung.

Adoff, Arnold. All the Colors of the Race. LC 81-11777. (Illus.). 64p. (J). (gr. 5 up). 1982. lib. bdg. 15.93 (*0-688-00880-1*) Lothrop.

— The Basket Counts. LC 98-47941. 46p. (YA). (gr. 5-8). 2000. 17.00 (*0-689-80108-4*) S&S Bks Yung.

— Birds. LC 81-47753. (Illus.). 64p. (J). (gr. k-5). 1982. lib. bdg. 11.89 (*0-397-31950-9*) HarpC Child Bks.

Adoff, Arnold. Black Is Brown Is Tan. (Illus.). 32p. (J). 15.95 (*0-06-028776-4*); 15.89 (*0-06-028777-2*) HarpC.

Adoff, Arnold. Black Is Brown Is Tan. LC 73-9855. (Illus.). 32p. (J). (ps-3). 1973. 15.95 (*0-06-020083-9*) HarpC Child Bks.

— Black Is Brown Is Tan. LC 73-9855. (Trophy Picture Bk.). (Illus.). 32p. (J). (ps-3). 1992. pap. 4.95 (*0-06-443269-6*, HarpTrophy) HarpC Child Bks.

Adoff, Arnold. Black Is Brown Is Tan: Re-Illustrated Edition. (Illus.). 32p. (J). 5.95 (*0-06-443644-6*) HarpC.

Adoff, Arnold. The Cabbages Are Chasing the Rabbits. LC 85-893. (Illus.). 32p. (J). (gr. k-3). 1985. 15.95 (*0-15-213875-7*, Harcourt Child Bks) Harcourt.

***Adoff, Arnold.** Daring Dog & Captain Cat. LC 98-52885. (J). 2001. 16.00 (*0-689-82599-4*) S&S Bks Yung.

Adoff, Arnold. Eats: Poems. (Reading Rainbow Bks.). (J). 1992. 9.15 (*0-606-01363-6*, Pub. by Turtleback) Demco.

— Friend Dog. LC 80-7773. (Illus.). 48p. (J). (gr. k-5). 1980. lib. bdg. 11.89 (*0-397-31912-6*) HarpC Child Bks.

— In for Winter, Out for Spring. Ingber, Bonnie V., ed. LC 90-33185. (Illus.). 43p. (J). (ps-3). 1991. 14.95 (*0-15-238637-8*) Harcourt.

— In for Winter, Out for Spring. LC 90-33185. (Illus.). 48p. 1997. pap. 7.00 (*0-15-201492-6*, Harcourt Child Bks) Harcourt.

— In for Winter, Out for Spring. (J). 1997. 12.20 (*0-606-11505-6*, Pub. by Turtleback) Demco.

— Love Letters. LC 96-19982. (Illus.). 40p. (J). (ps-3). 1997. 15.95 (*0-590-48478-8*) Scholastic Inc.

— Malcolm X. LC 99-21527. (Illus.). 64p. (J). (gr. 2-5). 2000. pap. 4.25 (*0-06-442118-X*) HarpC.

— My Black Me: A Beginning Book of Black Poetry. 84p. (J). (gr. 3-7). 1995. pap. 4.99 (*0-14-037443-4*, PuffinBks) Peng Put Young Read.

— My Black Me: A Beginning Book of Black Poetry. (J). 1995. 10.09 (*0-606-08573-4*, Pub. by Turtleback) Demco.

— Outside Inside Poems. LC 94-25179. (Illus.). 36p. (J). (gr. 1-5). 1995. pap. 5.00 (*0-15-200224-3*, Voyager Bks) Harcourt.

— Outside Inside Poems. (J). 1995. 10.20 (*0-606-07984-X*) Turtleback.

— The Return of Rex & Ethel. LC 91-23397. (Illus.). 40p. (J). (ps-3). 2000. 16.00 (*0-15-266367-3*, Harcourt Child Bks) Harcourt.

— Slow Dance Heartbreak Blues. LC 94-48242. (Illus.). 80p. (YA). (gr. 6 up). 1995. 15.00 (*0-688-10569-6*) Lothrop.

— Sports Pages. (Reading Rainbow Bks.). (J). 1990. 12.15 (*0-606-04543-0*, Pub. by Turtleback) Demco.

— Street Music: City Poems. LC 92-28539. (Illus.). 32p. (J). (gr. k-4). 1994. 15.95 (*0-06-021522-4*) HarpC Child Bks.

— Street Music: City Poems. LC 92-28539. (Illus.). 32p. (J). (gr. k-4). 1995. lib. bdg. 15.89 (*0-06-021523-2*) HarpC Child Bks.

— Touch the Poem. LC 95-34473. (Illus.). 32p. (J). (ps-3). 2000. 16.95 (*0-590-47970-9*, Blue Sky Press) Scholastic Inc.

Adoff, Arnold, ed. I Am the Darker Brother: An Anthology of Modern Poems by Black Americans. LC 96-31242. (J). 1997. pap. 4.99 (*0-689-80869-0*) S&S Bks Yung.

— I Am the Darker Brother: An Anthology of Modern Poems by Black Americans. LC 96-31242. (Illus.). 208p. (J). (gr. 5 up). 1997. per. 16.00 (*0-689-81241-8*) S&S Childrens.

— I Am the Darker Brother: An Anthology of Modern Poems by Black Americans. LC 96-31242. 1997. 10.09 (*0-606-11493-9*, Pub. by Turtleback) Demco.

— I Am the Darker Brother: An Anthology of Modern Poems by Negro Americans. (Illus.). (J). 1998. pap. 4.99 (*0-87628-443-8*) Ctr Appl Res.

— My Black Me: A Beginning Book of Black Poetry. (Illus.). 96p. (J). (gr. 4-7). 1994. 14.99 (*0-525-45216-8*, Dutton Child) Peng Put Young Read.

— The Poetry of Black America: Anthology of the Twentieth Century. LC 72-76518. 584p. (YA). (gr. 7 up). 1973. 25.95 (*0-06-020089-8*) HarpC Child Bks.

***Adogame, Afeosemime U.** Celestial Church of Christ. x, 251p. 1999. 45.95 (*3-631-34849-5*) P Lang Pubng.

Adogame, Afeosemime U. Celestial Church of Christ: The Politics of Cultural Identity in a West African Prophetic-Charismatic Movement. LC 99-23285. (Studies in the Intercultural History of Christianity: Vol. 115). X, 251p. 1999. pap. text 49.95 (*0-8204-4331-X*) P Lang Pubng.

Adolf, Barbara. The Employer's Guide to Child Care: Developing Programs for Working Parents. 2nd enl. rev. ed. LC 88-2343. (Illus.). 202p. 1988. 49.95 (*0-275-92891-8*, C2891, Praeger Pubs) Greenwood.

Adolf, Barbara & Rose, Karol. The Employer's Guide to Child Care: Developing Programs for Working Parents. LC 84-18003. 176p. 1985. 35.00 (*0-275-90051-7*, C0051, Praeger Pubs) Greenwood.

Adolf, Mary M., ed. see GMA Research Corporation Staff.

Adolfo Becquer, Gustavo, adapted by. La Corza Blanca, Level 2. (Leer en Espanol Ser.). (SPA.). (C). 1998. pap. 5.95 (*84-294-3593-X*) Santillana.

Adolph. Cognitive Motor Learning. LC 98-111048. 240p. 1997. pap. text 15.00 (*0-226-00766-9*) U Ch Pr.

— Methods in Molecular Genetics: Gene & Chromosome Analysis, 3 vols., Vols. 1, 2 & 5. 1994. 210.00 (*0-12-044355-4*) Acad Pr.

Adolph, A. L. & Lorenz, Rita. Enzyme Diagnosis in Diseases of the Heart, Liver & Pancreas. (Illus.). 124p. 1982. pap. 24.50 (*3-8055-3079-X*) S Karger.

Adolph, Andrea, et al, eds. Bite to Eat Place: An Anthology of Contemporary Food Poetry & Poetic Prose. LC 95-67899. 187p. (Orig.). 1995. pap. 14.95 (*0-9640933-1-6*) Redwood Coast.

Adolph, Harold P. & Bourne, Dave. Holyistic Attitudes: God's Prescription for Your Good Health. 1991. pap. 7.95 (*0-929292-16-2*) Hannibal Bks.

Adolph, Harold P. & Bourne, David. Como Evitar As Doencas.Tr. of Stop Making Yourself Sick. (POR.). 176p. 1991. pap. 4.95 (*0-8297-1638-6*) Vida Pubs.

Adolph, Kenneth W. Genome Research. LC 96-31105. 304p. 1996. spiral bd. 104.95 (*0-8493-4410-7*) CRC Pr.

— Human Genome Methods. LC 97-36261. 305p. 1997. lib. bdg. 89.95 (*0-8493-4411-5*) CRC Pr.

— Methods in Molecular Genetics Vol. 3: Molecular Microbiology Techniques, Pt. A. (Illus.). 398p. 1994. text 104.00 (*0-12-044305-8*) Acad Pr.

— Methods in Molecular Genetics, Vol. 2: Gene & Chromosome Analysis, Pt. B. (Illus.). 369p. 1993. text 104.00 (*0-12-044303-1*) Acad Pr.

Adolph, Kenneth W., ed. Advanced Techniques in Chromosome Research. (Illus.). 472p. 1991. text 215.00 (*0-8247-8430-8*) Dekker.

— Chromosomes: Eukaryotic, Prokaryotic & Viral, Vol. 1. 264p. 1989. boxed set 225.00 (*0-8493-4397-6*, QH600) CRC Pr.

— Chromosomes: Eukaryotic, Prokaryotic & Viral, Vol. 2. 240p. 1989. boxed set 225.00 (*0-8493-4398-4*, QH600) CRC Pr.

— Chromosomes: Eukaryotic, Prokaryotic & Viral, Vol. 3. 288p. 1989. boxed set 225.00 (*0-8493-4399-2*, QH600) CRC Pr.

— Chromosomes: Eukaryotic, Prokaryotic & Viral, Vols. I-III. 1989. 178.00 (*0-685-74181-8*) CRC Pr.

— Chromosomes & Chromatin, 3 vols. 608p. 1987. 127.00 (*0-8493-4355-0*, QH600, CRC Reprint); 109.00 (*0-8493-4356-9*, QH600, CRC Reprint); 101.00 (*0-8493-4357-7*, QH600, CRC Reprint) Franklin.

— Chromosomes & Chromatin, 3 vols., Set. 608p. 1987. 335.00 (*0-8493-4354-2*, QH600) CRC Pr.

— Methods in Molecular Genetics Vol. 4: Molecular Virology Techniques, Pt. A. (Illus.). 410p. 1994. text 104.00 (*0-12-044306-6*) Acad Pr.

— Methods in Molecular Genetics Vol. 5: Gene & Chromosome Analysis, Pt. C. (Illus.). 402p. 1994. text. write for info. (*0-12-044307-4*) Acad Pr.

— Methods in Molecular Genetics Vol. 6: Viral Gene Techniques, Vol. 6. (Illus.). 487p. 1995. text 90.00 (*0-12-044308-2*) Acad Pr.

— Methods in Molecular Genetics Vol. 8: Human Molecular Genetics, Vol. 8. (Illus.). 500p. 1996. text 85.00 (*0-12-044310-4*) Acad Pr.

— Microbial Genome Methods. 304p. 1996. 79.95 (*0-614-29958-6*, 4410H3Y) CRC Pr.

— Viral Genome Methods. 320p. 1996. spiral bd. 104.95 (*0-8493-4412-3*) CRC Pr.

Adolph, L. & Lorenz, Rita. Enzymdiagnostik bei Herz-Leber-und Pankreaserkrankungen. (GER.). 1978. 15.75 (*3-8055-2872-8*) S Karger.

Adolph, Steve. Dai Uy. 218p. 1991. 9.95 (*0-932572-17-0*) Phillips Pubns.

Adolphe, Bruce. The Mind's Ear. LC 91-35028. 72p. (Orig.). 1991. pap. 9.95 (*0-918812-71-2*, SE0183) MMB Music.

***Adolphe, Bruce.** The Musical Rexicon. (Illus.). 24p. (J). (ps-6). 2000. 3.95 (*0-9701249-0-2*) PollyRhythm.

Adolphe, Bruce. Of Mozart, Parrots & Cherry Blossoms in the Wind: A Composer Explores Mysteries of the Musical Mind. LC 99-40618. 240p. 1999. pap. 13.95 (*0-87910-286-1*) Limelight Edns.

— What to Listen for in the World. LC 96-27066. (Illus.). 112p. (Orig.). 1996. 17.95 (*0-87910-085-0*) Limelight Edns.

Adolphe, M., ed. Advances in Physiological Sciences, Vol. 10: Chemotherapy. limited ed. LC 78-41032. (Illus.). 220p. 1979. 40.00 (*0-08-023214-0*) Franklin.

Adolphe, Monique, ed. Biological Regulation of the Chondrocyte. 368p. 1992. lib. bdg. 219.00 (*0-8493-6733-6*, QP88) CRC Pr.

Adolphson, A., et al, eds. Analytic Number Theory & Diophantine Problems. (Progress in Mathematics Ser.: No. 70). 346p. 1987. 57.50 (*0-8176-3361-8*) Birkhauser.

Adolphson, Alan, et al, eds. P-Adic Methods in Number Theory & Algebraic Geometry. LC 92-20147. (Contemporary Mathematics Ser.: Vol. 133). 241p. 1992. pap. 39.00 (*0-8218-5145-4*, CONM/133) Am Math.

***Adolphson, Mikael S.** The Gates of Power: Monks, Courtiers & Warriors in Premodern Japan. LC 00-23448. 2000. pap. write for info. (*0-8248-2334-6*) UH Pr.

Adolphus, Stephen H., ed. Equality Postponed: Continuing Barriers to Higher Education in the 1980s. 156p. (Orig.). 1984. pap. 12.95 (*0-87447-188-5*) College Bd.

Adomat, Renee. Overseas Clinical Elective: A Survival Guide for Healthcare Workers. LC 96-25101. 176p. (Orig.). 1996. pap. text 29.95 (*0-632-04102-1*) Blackwell Sci.

Adomatis, Hans-Joachim, ed. see Murer, Jos.

Adomeit, Hannes. Imperial Overstretch: Germany in Soviet Policy from Stalin to Gorbachev : an Analysis Based on New Archival Evidence, Memoirs, & Interviews LC 98-208539. (Internationale Politik und Sicherheit Ser.). 609 p. 1998. write for info. (*3-7890-5133-0*) Nomos Verlags.

— Soviet Risk Taking & Crisis Behavior: A Theoretical & Empirical Analysis. 450p. (C). 1984. text 37.50 (*0-04-335043-7*); pap. text 15.95 (*0-04-335051-8*) Routledge.

Adomian, George. Applications of Nonlinear Stochastic Systems Theory to Physics. (C). 1988. text 169.00 (*90-277-2525-X*) Kluwer Academic.

— Solving Frontier Problems of Physics: The Decomposition Method. LC 93-39561. (Fundamental Theories of Physics Ser.: Vol. 60). 368p. (C). 1994. text 196.50 (*0-7923-2644-X*) Kluwer Academic.

Adomian, George, jt. auth. see Bellman, Richard Ernest.

***Adomites, Paul.** Cooperstown Baseball's Hall of Famers. LC 99-190406. 96 p. 1998. write for info. (*0-7853-3174-3*) Pubns Intl Ltd.

Adomites, Paul. The Cooperstown Review: The Forum of Baseball Literary Opinion, Vol. I. 196p. (Orig.). 1993. pap. 10.00 (*1-882974-00-X*) Sheraden Pub.

Adomites, Paul, ed. The Cooperstown Review: The Forum of Baseball Literary Opinion, Vol. 2. 204p. (Orig.). 1994. pap. text 10.00 (*1-882974-03-4*) Sheraden Pub.

— SABR Review of Books. (Illus.). 112p. 1987. pap. 6.00 (*0-910137-27-7*) Soc Am Baseball Res.

— SABR Review of Books. (Illus.). 112p. 1988. pap. 6.00 (*0-910137-33-1*) Soc Am Baseball Res.

— SABR Review of Books. (Illus.). 128p. 1989. pap. 7.00 (*0-910137-38-2*) Soc Am Baseball Res.

— SABR Review of Books. (Illus.). 147p. 1990. pap. 7.00 (*0-910137-42-0*) Soc Am Baseball Res.

Adomites, Paul, et al. Cooperstown Baseball's Hall of Famers. LC 97-176743. 96p. 1997. write for info. (*0-7853-2286-8*) Pubns Intl Ltd.

Adomites, Paul D., ed. SABR Review of Books. (Illus.). 112p. 1986. pap. 6.00 (*0-910137-23-4*) Soc Am Baseball Res.

Adomnan. Life of Columba. 2nd ed. Anderson, Alan D., ed. & tr. by. Anderson, Marjorie O., tr. (Oxford Medieval Texts Ser.). (Illus.). 344p. 1991. text 120.00 (*0-19-820215-6*) OUP.

***Adone, Claudio.** My Grandfather Jack the Ripper.Tr. of Mio Nonno Jack Lo Squartatore. 192p. (YA). (gr. 7-12). 2000. 19.00 (*1-928746-16-0*) Herodias.

Adone, Dany. The Acquisition of Mauritian Creole. LC 94-547. (Language Acquisition & Language Disorders (LALD) Ser.: No. 9). xii, 167p. 1994. lib. bdg. 40.00 (*1-55619-246-0*) J Benjamins Pubng Co.

Adoni, A., jt. ed. see Kahane, I.

***Adonis, A.** The Pages of Day & Night. 2001. pap. 15.95 (*0-8101-6081-1*) Northwestern U Pr.

Adonis, Ali Ahmed Sa'id. An Introduction to Arab Poetics. Cobham, Catherine, tr. 112p. 1991. text 22.50 (*0-292-73859-5*) U of Tex Pr.

— The Pages of Day & Night. Hazo, Samuel, tr. from ARA. LC 93-79810. 144p. 1994. 22.95 (*0-910395-96-9*) Marlboro Pr.

Adonis, Andrew. Making Aristocracy Work: The Peerage & the Political System in Britain, 1884-1914. LC 92-40926. (Oxford Historical Monographs). (Illus.). 324p. (C). 1993. text 57.00 (*0-19-820389-6*, Clarendon Pr) OUP.

Adonis, Andrew & Hames, Tim, eds. Conservative Revolution? The Thatcher-Reagan Decade in Perspective. 200p. 1994. text 79.95 (*0-7190-3668-2*, Pub. by Manchester Univ Pr) St Martin.

Adonisz, Belea. Interspecific & Intergeneric Crosses in Cultivated Plants. 262p. (C). 1992. pap. 195.00 (*963-05-6053-4*, Pub. by Akade Kiado) St Mut.

Adoplh, Kenneth W., ed. Methods in Molecular Genetics, Vol. 1: Gene & Chromosome Analysis, Pt. A. (Illus.). 404p. 1993. text 104.00 (*0-12-044301-5*) Acad Pr.

Adopt-A-Stream Foundation Staff. Field Guide to the Pacific Salmon: Including Salmon-Watching Sites in Alaska, British Columbia, Washington, Oregon, & Northern California. LC 92-22962. (Sasquatch Field Guide Ser.). (Illus.). 64p. (Orig.). 1992. pap. 5.95 (*0-912365-64-1*) Sasquatch Bks.

Adorini, L., ed. Selective Immunosuppression: Basic Concepts & Clinical Applications. (Chemical Immunology Ser.: Vol. 60). (Illus.). x, 166p. 1994. 151.50 (*3-8055-6034-6*) S Karger.

Adorini, L., jt. auth. see Martino, G.

Adorini, Luciano, ed. IL-12. (Chemical Immunology Ser.: Vol. 68, 1997). (Illus.). x, 204p. 1997. 194.00 (*3-8055-6526-7*) S Karger.

Adorjan, A. & Horvath, T. Sicilian: Sveshnikov Variation. (Chess Openings Ser.). 150p. 1987. 27.90 (*0-08-029735-8*, P115, Pergamon Pr) Elsevier.

Adorjan, Alexander S. Heat Transfer in LNG Engineering. 352p. 1990. 104.00 (*0-89116-899-0*) Hemisp Pub.

Adorjan, Carol. Cat Sitter Mystery. 80p. 1976. pap. 2.95 (*0-380-70094-8*, Avon Bks) Morrow Avon.

— The Copy Cat Mystery. 128p. (J). 1990. pap. 2.95 (*0-380-75743-5*, Avon Bks) Morrow Avon.

— I Can! Can You? rev. ed. Levine, Abby, ed. LC 90-37665. Orig. Title: Someone I Know. (Illus.). 24p. (J). (ps). 1990. lib. bdg. 13.95 (*0-8075-3491-9*) A Whitman.

Adorjan, Carol & Rasovsky, Yuri. WKID: Easy Radio Plays. LC 88-132. (Illus.). 80p. (J). (gr. 3-8). 1988. lib. bdg. 10.95 (*0-8075-9155-6*) A Whitman.

Adorjan, Carol M. Little Princess. (Troll Illustrated Classics). (Illus.). (J). 1988. 10.15 (*0-606-03607-5*, Pub. by Turtleback) Demco.

Adornato, Gary, ed. see Bake, Paul M.

Adorni, Giovanni & Zock, Michael, eds. Trends in Natural Language Generation: An Artificial Intelligence Perspective: Fourth European Workshop, EWNLG '93, Pisa, Italy, April 1993: Selected Papers. (Lecture Notes in Computer Science Ser.: Vol. 1036). 390p. 1996. pap. text 60.00 (*3-540-60800-1*) Spr-Verlag.

Adorni, Sergio, jt. auth. see Primorac, Karen.

Adorno, Calixta V. Juegos Infantiles de Puerto Rico. 266p. 1991. pap. 11.00 (*0-8477-2504-9*) U of PR Pr.

Adorno, Celeste F. Florida Ethics Guide for Legal Assistants. 2nd ed. LC 95-61034. 1995. per. 20.00 (*0-945979-77-0*, 288) FL Bar Legal Ed.

Adorno, Pedro L. Papiros de Babel. 526p. 1991. 23.85 (*0-8477-3237-1*) U of PR Pr.

Adorno, Rohena, et al. Iconografia Politica Del Nuevo Mundo. 118p. 1991. pap. 14.00 (*0-8477-3638-5*) U of PR Pr.

***Adorno, Rolena.** Guaman Poma: Writing & Resistance in Colonia Peru, Second Edition. 2nd ed. (Illus.). 247p. 2000. pap. 19.95 (*0-292-70503-4*) U of Tex Pr.

Adorno, Rolena & Pautz, Patrick C. Alvar Nunez Cabeza de Vaca: His Account, His Life, & the Expedition of Panfilo de Narvaez. LC 98-24032. 275p. 1999. text 275.00 (*0-8032-1454-5*) U of Nebr Pr.

Adorno, Rolena, et al. Guaman Poma de Ayala: The Colonial Art of an Andean Author. Ffolliott, Ann, ed. LC 91-78033. (Illus.). 114p. (Orig.). 1992. pap. 25.00 (*1-879128-04-7*) Americas Soc.

Adorno, Rolena, jt. ed. see Andrien, Kenneth J.

Adorno, Theodor W. Aesthetic Theory. Hullot-Kentor, Robert et al, eds. Tiedemann, Rolf, tr. LC 96-7729. (Theory & History of Literature Ser.: Vol. 88). 448p. (C). 1996. 39.95 (*0-8166-1799-6*) U of Minn Pr.

— Aesthetic Theory. Hullot-Kentor, Robert, ed. & tr. by. (Theory & History of Literature Ser.: Vo. 88). 448p. 1998. pap. 24.95 (*0-8166-1800-3*) U of Minn Pr.

— Beethoven: The Philosophy of Music. Tiedemann, Rolf, ed. Jephcott, Edmund, tr. LC 98-60570. 280p. 1998. 39.50 (*0-8047-3515-8*) Stanford U Pr.

— Critical Models: Interventions & Catchwords. Pickford, Henry W., tr. LC 97-39500. 400p. 1997. 39.50 (*0-231-07634-7*) Col U Pr.

***Adorno, Theodor W.** Critical Models: Interventions & Catchwords. 400p. 1999. pap. 18.50 (*0-231-07635-5*) Col U Pr.

Adorno, Theodor W. Culture Industry: Selected Essays on Mass Culture. Bernstein, J. M., ed. 192p. (C). 1991. pap. 24.99 (*0-415-05831-7*) Routledge.

— Hegel: Three Studies.Tr. of Drei Studien zu Hegel. (Illus.). 204p. 1994. pap. text 14.00 (*0-262-51080-4*) MIT Pr.

— In Search of Wagner. Livingstone, Rodney, tr. from GER. 159p. (Orig.). (C). 1985. pap. 19.00 (*0-86091-796-7*, Pub. by Verso) Norton.

***Adorno, Theodor W.** Introduction to Sociology. 2000. 39.50 (*0-8047-3933-1*) Stanford U Pr.

— The Jargon of Authenticity. Tarnowski, Knut & Will, Frederic, trs. from GER. LC 27-96701. 165p. (C). 1973. pap. 14.95 (*0-8101-0657-4*) Northwestern U Pr.

Adorno, Theodor W. Kierkegaard: Construction of the Aesthetic. Hullot-Kentor, Robert, tr. from GER. & frwd. by. LC 88-14389. (Theory & History of Literature Ser.: Vol. 61).Tr. of Kierkegaard: Konstruktion des Asthetischen. 166p. (Orig.). 1989. pap. 15.95 (*0-8166-1187-4*) U of Minn Pr.

— Mahler: A Musical Physiognomy. Jephcott, Edmund, tr. LC 88-14248. 192p. 1992. 30.00 (*0-226-00768-5*) U Ch Pr.

— Mahler: A Musical Physiognomy. 178p. (C). 1996. reprint ed. pap. text 14.00 (*0-226-00769-3*) U Ch Pr.

— Negative Dialectics. 2nd ed. 416p. (J). 1982. pap. 22.95 (*0-8264-0132-5*) Continuum.

— Notes to Literature, Vol. 1. Kritzman, Lawrence D. & Wolin, Richard, eds. Nicholsen, Shierry W., tr. from GER. (European Perspectives Ser.). 284p. (C). 1991. text 46.00 (*0-231-06332-6*) Col U Pr.

— Notes to Literature, Vol. 1. Kritzman, Lawrence D. & Wolin, Richard, eds. Nicholsen, Shierry W., tr. from GER. (European Perspectives Ser.). 284p. (C). 1993. pap. 19.50 (*0-231-06333-4*) Col U Pr.

— Notes to Literature, Vol. 2. Tiedemann, Rolf & Nicholsen, Shierry W., eds. (European Perspectives Ser.). 350p. (C). 1992. text 57.50 (*0-231-06912-X*) Col U Pr.

— Notes to Literature, Vol. 2. LC 90-27732. 350p. 1994. pap. 19.50 (*0-231-06913-8*) Col U Pr.

— Prisms. Weber, Samuel & Weber, Shierry, trs. from GER. 272p. (C). 1983. pap. text 14.95 (*0-262-51025-1*) MIT Pr.

***Adorno, Theodor W.** Problems of Moral Philosophy. 2000. 39.50 (*0-8047-3936-6*) Stanford U Pr.

— The Psychological Technique of Martin Luther Thomas' Radio Addresses. LC 00-24888. 2000. pap. write for info. (*0-8047-4003-8*) Stanford U Pr.

Adorno, Theodor W. Quasi una Fantasia: Essays on Modern Music. 2nd ed. 1998. pap. 20.00 (*1-85984-159-7*, Pub. by Verso) Norton.

— Sound Figures. LC 98-33460. (Meridian Ser.). 1999. pap. text 16.95 (*0-8047-3558-1*) Stanford U Pr.

***Adorno, Theodor W.** Sound Figures. LC 98-33460. (Meridian Ser.). 1999. 49.50 (*0-8047-3557-3*) Stanford U Pr.

Adorno, Theodor W. The Stars Come down to Earth & Other Essays on the Irrational in Culture. Crook, Stephen, ed. LC 94-12151. 240p. (C). (gr. 13). 1994. 70.00 (*0-415-10567-6*, B4753); pap. 22.99 (*0-415-10568-4*, B4757) Routledge.

***Adorno, Theodor W. & Benjamin, Walter.** The Complete Correspondence, 1928-1940: Theodor Adorno & Walter Benjamin. Lonitz, Henri, ed. Walker, Nicholas, tr. from GER. LC 99-10988. 384p. 1999. 39.95 (*0-674-15427-4*) HUP.

Adorno, Theodor W. & Eisler, Hanns. Composing for the Films. LC 94-17469. 195p. (C). 1994. pap. 29.95 (*0-485-12107-7*, Pub. by Athlone Pr); text 65.00 (*0-485-11454-2*, Pub. by Athlone Pr) Humanities.

Adorno, Theodor W., et al. German Essays on Music. Hermand, Jost & Gilbert, Michael, eds. LC 98-17039. (German Library). 324p. (C). 1993. 39.50 (*0-8264-0720-X*); pap. 19.95 (*0-8264-0721-8*) Continuum.

— German Sociology. Gerhardt, Uta, ed. LC 97-17939. (The German Library: No. 61). 324p. (C). 1998. 39.95 (*0-8264-0958-X*) Continuum.

— German Sociology. Gerhardt, Uta, ed. LC 97-17939. (German Library: Vol. 61). 324p. 1998. pap. 24.95 (*0-8264-0959-8*) Continuum.

— German 20th Century Philosophy: The Frankfurt School. Schirmacher, Wolfgang, ed. LC 96-45033. (The German Library). 257p. 1999. 39.50 (*0-8264-0966-0*); pap. 19.95 (*0-8264-0967-9*) Continuum.

Adorno, Theodor W., jt. auth. see Horkheimer, Max.

Adouze, Jean, et al, eds. Large Scale Structures of the Universe. (C). 1988. pap. text 99.50 (*90-277-2744-9*); lib. bdg. 220.50 (*90-277-2742-2*) Kluwer Academic.

Adovasio, James M. Basketry Technology: A Guide to Identification & Analysis. LC 77-70388. (Manuals on Archeology Ser.: No. 1). (Illus.). x, 182p. 1977. 18.00 (*0-202-33035-4*) Taraxacum.

ADP Context Software staff. Codelink - Anesthesiology. 1200p. (Orig.). 1997. pap. text 129.95 (*1-57066-106-5*, 9750) Practice Mgmt Info.

— Codelink - Obstetrics & Gynecology. 3rd rev. ed. 210p. 1998. pap. text 99.95 (*1-57066-107-3*, 9756) Practice Mgmt Info.

— Codelink - Ophthalmology. 3rd rev. ed. 260p. 1998 pap. text 99.95 (*1-57066-108-1*, 9751) Practice Mgmt Info.

— Codelink - Oral & Maxillary Surgery. 3rd ed. 315p. 1997. pap. text 99.95 (*1-57066-109-X*, 9752) Practice Mgmt Info.

— Codelink - Otolaryngology. 3rd rev. ed. 450p. 1998 pap. text 99.95 (*1-57066-111-1*, 9754) Practice Mgmt Info.

— Context Color-Coded ICD-9-CM, 1999, 2 vols. rev. ed. 900p. 1998. pap. text 44.95 (*1-57066-092-1*, 9927) Practice Mgmt Info.

***ADP Context Software staff & Davis, James B., eds.** Medical Fees in the United States 2000. 2000. pap. text 119.95 (*1-57066-167-7*, 20035) Practice Mgmt Info.

ADP Context Software staff & Davis, James B., eds. Medical Fees in the United States, 1999. 380p. 1999. pap. 119.95 (*1-57066-129-4*, 9935) Practice Mgmt Info.

***ADP Context Staff.** Codelink for Anesthesia, 2000. 4th rev. ed. 2000. pap. text. write for info. (*1-57066-169-3*) Practice Mgmt Info.

— Codelink for Maxillofacial Surgery, 2000. 3rd rev. ed. 340p. 2000. pap. text 99.95 (*1-57066-172-3*, 20052) Practice Mgmt Info.

— Codelink for OB/GYN, 2000. 3rd rev. ed. 250p. 2000. pap. text 99.95 (*1-57066-170-7*, 20056) Practice Mgmt Info.

— Codelink for Ophthalmology, 2000. 4th rev. ed. 300p. 2000. pap. text 99.95 (*1-57066-171-5*, 20051) Practice Mgmt Info.

— Codelink for Orthopaedics, 2000. 3rd rev. ed. 800p. 2000. pap. text 129.95 (*1-57066-173-1*, 20053) Practice Mgmt Info.

— Codelink for Otolaryngology, 2000. 4th rev. ed. 475p. 2000. pap. text 99.95 (*1-57066-174-X*, 20054) Practice Mgmt Info.

— Codelink for Plastic Surgery, 2000. 4th rev. ed. 2000. pap. text 99.95 (*1-57066-175-8*, 20055) Practice Mgmt Info.

ADP Hollander Interchange Staff. Classic Front End Manual, 1965-1979. LC 99-214681. (Hollander Classic Search Bks.). (Illus.). 210p. 1998. pap. 19.95 (*1-882437-82-9*) ADP-Hollander.

— The Hollander Interchange Manual: Body I. 64th rev. ed. (Illus.). 1032p. 1998. pap. 120.00 (*1-882437-91-8*) ADP-Hollander.

— The Hollander Interchange Manual: Body II. 64th rev. ed. (Illus.). 872p. 1998. pap. 120.00 (*1-882437-92-6*) ADP-Hollander.

— The Hollander Interchange Manual: Chassis I. 64th rev. ed. (Illus.). 768p. 1998. pap. 120.00 (*1-882437-96-9*) ADP-Hollander.

— The Hollander Interchange Manual: Chassis II. 64th rev. ed. (Illus.). 808p. 1998. pap. 120.00 (*1-882437-97-7*) ADP-Hollander.

— The Hollander Interchange Manual: Complete Set, 8 vols. 64th rev. ed. (Illus.). 6328p. 1998. pap. 399.00 (*1-882437-87-X*) ADP-Hollander.

— The Hollander Interchange Manual: Engine I. (Illus.). 568p. 1998. pap. 120.00 (*1-882437-94-2*) ADP-Hollander.

— The Hollander Interchange Manual: Engine II. 64th rev. ed. (Illus.). 976p. 1998. pap. 120.00 (*1-882437-95-0*) ADP-Hollander.

— The Hollander Interchange Manual: ID/Body, 4 vols. 64th rev. ed. (Illus.). 3208p. 1998. pap. 250.00 (*1-882437-88-8*) ADP-Hollander.

— The Hollander Interchange Manual: Identification I. 64th rev. ed. (Illus.). 640p. 1998. pap. 120.00 (*1-882437-89-6*) ADP-Hollander.

— The Hollander Interchange Manual: Identification II. 64th rev. ed. (Illus.). 664p. 1998. pap. 120.00 (*1-882437-90-X*) ADP-Hollander.

— The Hollander Interchange Manual: Mechanical Set. 4 vols. 64th rev. ed. (Illus.). 3120p. 1998. pap. 250.00 (*1-882437-93-4*) ADP-Hollander.

ADP Hollander Interchange Staff, ed. Camaro, 1967-1981. (Illus.). 368p. 1998. pap. 19.95 (*1-58132-001-9*) ADP-Hollander.

— Chevelle, 1964-1972. (Illus.). 312p. 1998. pap. 19.95 (*1-58132-002-7*) ADP-Hollander.

— Hollander Front End Manual, 1984 to 1998. 1998. pap. 49.95 (*1-58132-000-0*) ADP-Hollander.

— Mustang, 1965-1973. (Illus.). 252p. 1998. pap. 19.95 (*1-58132-004-3*) ADP-Hollander.

— Nova, 1965-1979. (Illus.). 312p. 1998. pap. 19.95 (*1-58132-005-1*) ADP-Hollander.

***Adrados, Francisco Rodriguez.** History of the Graeco Latin Fable: Fable during the Roman Empire & in the Middle Ages, II. Ray, Leslie A., tr. 650p. 2000. 232.00 (*90-04-11583-8*) Brill Academic Pubs.

Adrados, Francisco Rodriguez. A History of the Graeco-Latin Fable: Introduction & from the Origins to the Hellenistic Age, Vol. 1. Ray, Leslie A., tr. from SPA. LC 99-37200. (Mnemosyne, Supplements Ser.: 201). 760p. 1999. text 191.50 (*90-04-11454-8*) Brill Academic Pubs.

Adrados, Francisco Rodriguez, see Rodriguez Adrados, Francisco.

Adrain. Most Important Thing I Know. 192p. 1999. 6.98 (*1-56731-353-1*, MJF Bks) Fine Comms.

***Adrain, Lorne.** The Most Important Thing I Know About the Spirit of Sport: 101 Inspiring Messages From Athletes, Coaches, Sportswriters, And Commentators. LC 98-51011. 176p. 1999. 12.95 (*0-688-16400-5*, Wm Morrow) Morrow Avon.

Adrain, Lorne, ed. The Most Important Thing I Know: Life Lessons from Colin Powell, Stephen Covey, Maya Angelou & More Than 100 Other Individuals. gif. ed. LC 97-5890. 192p. 1997. 12.95 (*0-8362-2771-9*, Cader Bks) Andrews & McMeel.

***Adrain, Lorne A.** The Most Important Thing I Know About Love: Inspiring Messages From Eminent Writers, Poets, Musicians, Thinkers, And Others. LC 99-47934. (Most Important Thing I Know Ser.). 160p. 2000. 13.00 (*0-688-16401-3*, Wm Morrow) Morrow Avon.

Adreamine, Ltd. Staff, tr. see Ashton, Tia, et al.

Adreamine, Ltd. Staff, tr. see Ashton, Tita, et al.

Adreamine, Ltd. Staff, tr. see Hader, Steve, et al.

Adrett. Labour Market Policy. 1989. pap. text. write for info. (*0-582-00962-6*, Pub. by Addison-Wesley) Longman.

Adria, Marco. Peter Gzowski: An Electric Life. LC 96-151097. (Illus.). 170p. 1996. pap. 14.95 (*1-55022-166-3*, Pub. by ECW) Genl Dist Srvs.

— Peter Gzowski: An Electric Life. large type ed. (Illus.). 170p. 1996. pap. 15.95 (*1-55022-266-X*, Pub. by ECW) Genl Dist Srvs.

***Adria, Miguiel.** 1st Mies Van der Rohe Award for Latin American Architecture. (Illus.). 2000. pap. 25.00 (*84-95273-10-1*) Actar.

Adriaans, Pieter. Data Mining. LC 97-140818. 176p. (C). 1996. pap. text 24.99 (*0-201-40380-3*) Addison-Wesley.

Adriaansen, Willem L. & Waardenburg, J. G., eds. A Dual World Economy: Forty Years of Development Experience. (Illus.). 304p. 1992. text 35.00 (*0-19-562732-6*) OUP.

Adrian & Cooper. Biomechanics of Human. 2nd ed. 1995. teacher ed. 16.56 (*0-697-16243-5*) McGraw.

Adrian & Cooper, John M. Biomechanics of Human Movement. 3rd ed. 2000. text 42.00 (*0-697-29515-X*) McGraw.

Adrian & Storrs. Enjoy Trees: A Guide to Some Attractive Trees & Shrubs Found in Nepal. 1998. pap. 148.00 (*0-7855-7385-2*, Pub. by Ratna Pustak Bhandar) St Mut.

Adrian, Ann & Dennis, Judith. The Herbal Tea Book. 1981. pap. 2.95 (*0-87904-040-8*) Lust.

Adrian, Charles R. Some General Characteristics of Non-Partisan Elections. (Reprint Series in Social Sciences). (C). 1993. reprint ed. pap. text 5.00 (*0-8290-3424-2*, PS-3) Irvington.

Adrian, Charles R. & Fine, Michael R. State & Local Politics. (Political Science). 420p. (C). 1999. text 45.95 (*0-8304-1285-9*) Thomson Learn.

***Adrian, Christine.** Gob's Grief. 2001. 25.00 (*0-7679-0281-5*) Broadway BDD.

Adrian, Christine. A Step-by-Step Book about Tortoises. (Step-by-Step Ser.). (Illus.). 63p. (Orig.). 1987. pap. 5.95 (*0-86622-487-4*, SK-034) TFH Pubns.

Adrian, Dennis. Roger Brown & Friends in the Nineties. (Illus.). 8p. 1998. 5.00 (*1-890573-01-9*) V Every Smith.

— Seeing the Figure Now. unabridged ed. (Illus.). 64p. (Orig.). 1996. pap. 12.95 (*0-9637817-4-X*) Schl Art Inst.

— Sight Out of Mind: Essays & Criticism on Art. LC 85-8434. (Contemporary American Art Critics Ser.: No. 5). 243p. reprint ed. pap. 69.30 (*0-8357-1676-7*, 2070490) Bks Demand.

Adrian, Dennis, ed. Sylvia Sleigh: Invitation to a Voyage & Other Works. LC 89-61866. (Illus.). 38p. (Orig.). 1990. pap. 9.95 (*0-944110-42-8*) Milwauk Art Mus.

Adrian, Dennis & Born, Richard. The Chicago Imagist Print: Ten Artists' Works, 1958-1987 - a Catalogue Raisonne. Taylor, Sue, ed. LC 87-72605. (Illus.). 216p. (Orig.). 1987. pap. 25.00 (*0-935573-01-1*) D & A Smart Museum.

Adrian, Dennis, et al. Painting at Northwestern: Conger, Paschke, Valerio. (Illus.). 64p. (Orig.). (C). 1986. 30.00 (*0-941680-04-5*); pap. 15.00 (*0-941680-03-7*) M&L Block.

Adrian, Douglas J., jt. auth. see Adrian, James J.

Adrian, Jack. Pilgrimage to Hell. (Deathlands Ser.: No. 1). 384p. 1986. per. 4.99 (*0-373-63057-3*) Harlequin Bks.

***Adrian, Jack, ed.** The Ash-Tree Press Annual Macabre, 1999. xiv, 80p. 1999. 31.00 (*1-899562-88-5*) Ash-Tree.

— The Ash-Tree Press Annual Macabre, 1998. xvi, 88p. 1998. 31.00 (*1-899562-62-1*) Ash-Tree.

— The Ash-Tree Press Annual Macabre, 1997. 72p. 1997. 25.50 (*1-899562-37-0*) Ash-Tree.

Adrian, Jack, ed. Dashiell Hammett: A Retrospective Anthology. 352p. Date not set. 25.00 (*0-19-508500-0*) OUP.

Adrian, Jack, intro. Twelve Mystery Stories. (Oxford Twelves Ser.). 246p. 1998. pap. 9.95 (*0-19-288074-8*) OUP.

— Twelve Tales of Murder. (Oxford Twelves Ser.). 224p. 1998. pap. 9.95 (*0-19-288075-6*) OUP.

Adrian, Jack, ed. see Askew, Alice & Askew, Claude.

Adrian, Jack, ed. see Benson, E. F.

Adrian, Jack, ed. see Burrage, A. M.

A

An Asterisk (*) at the beginning of an entry indicates that the title is appearing for the first time.

A

Adrian, Jack, ed. see Burrage, Alfred McLelland.

Adrian, Jack, ed. see Capes, Bernard.

Adrian, Jack, jt. ed. see Cox, Michael.

Adrian, Jack, ed. see de Crespigny, Rose C.

Adrian, Jack, jt. ed. see Pronzini, Bill.

Adrian, Jack, ed. see Symons, Julian.

Adrian, Jack C. & Pronzini, Bill, eds. Hard-Boiled: An Anthology of American Crime Stories. 540p. 1995. 35.00 (*0-19-508499-3*) OUP.

Adrian, James J. Construction Claims: A Quantitative Approach. 306p. (C). 1993. reprint ed. pap. text 28.80 (*0-87563-442-7*) Stipes.

— Construction Estimating. 2nd ed. 536p. (C). 1993. text 54.80 (*0-87563-439-7*) Stipes.

— Construction Productivity Improvement. 470p. 1987. 42.25 (*0-444-01121-8*) P-H.

***Adrian, James J. & Adrian, Douglas J.** Construction Accounting: Financial, Managerial, Auditing & Tax. 3rd ed. 410p. 1998. pap. text 29.95 (*0-87563-845-7*) Stipes.

Adrian, James J. & Adrian, Douglas J. Total Productivity & Quality Management for Construction. 362p. (C). 1995. text 39.80 (*0-87563-552-0*) Stipes.

Adrian, Jean. Dictionnaire Agro-Alimentaire: Anglais-Francais, Francais-Anglais.Tr. of Dictionary Food Science. (ENG & FRE.). 346p. 1990. pap. 150.00 (*0-8288-2612-9*, F136010) Fr & Eur.

— Dictionnaire Agro-Alimentaire Anglais/Francais-Francais/Anglais. 2nd ed. (ENG & FRE.). 400p. 1996. 250.00 (*0-7859-9500-5*) Fr & Eur.

Adrian, Jean, et al. Dictionary of the Biochemistry of Food & Nutrition: Dictionnaire de Biochimie Alimentaire et de Nutrition. (ENG & FRE.). 320p. 1981. 125.00 (*0-8288-4440-2*, M9626) Fr & Eur.

Adrian, M. J., ed. Sports Women. (Medicine & Sport Science Ser.: Vol. 24). (Illus.). viii, 160p. 1987. 128.75 (*3-8055-4501-0*) S Karger.

Adrian, Marlene. Woman in Motion. LC 95-50086. (Illus.). 168p. 1995. 18.95 (*1-884724-04-3*); pap. 11.95 (*1-884724-03-5*) Women Diversity.

Adrian, Marlene J. & Cooper, John M. Biomechanics of Human Movement. 2nd ed. 592p. (C). 1994. text 53.00 (*0-697-16242-7*) Brown & Benchmark.

Adrian, P., ed. Environmental Pollution & Its Impact on Life in the Mediterranean Region, 1987: A Special Issue of the Journal Toxicological & Environmental Chemistry. x, 518p. 1989. text 1982.00 (*0-677-25840-2*) Gordon & Breach.

Adrian Pauw Symposium on Designing for Creep & Shr. Designing for Creep & Shrinkage in Concrete Structures: A Tribute to Adrian Pauw. LC 82-73066. (American Concrete Institute Publication: No. SP-76). 494p. 1982. reprint ed. pap. 153.20 (*0-608-01428-1*, 206219000002) Bks Demand.

Adrian, R. J., ed. Selected Papers on Laser Doppler Velocimetry. LC 93-10185. (Milestone Ser.: Vol. MS 78/HC). 1993. 55.00 (*0-8194-1298-8*) SPIE.

— Selected Papers on Laser Doppler Velocimetry. LC 93-10185. (Milestone Ser.: Vol. MS78). 1993. pap. 45.00 (*0-8194-1297-X*) SPIE.

Adrian, R. J., et al, eds. Developments in Laser Techniques & Fluid Mechanics: Selected Papers from the 8th International Symposium, Lisbon, Portugal, 8-11 July, 1996. LC 97-32248. 550p. 1997. text 179.00 (*3-540-63572-6*) Spr-Verlag.

***Adrian, R. J., et al, eds.** Laser Techniques Applied to Fluid Mechanics: Selected Papers from the Tenth International Symposium, Lisbon, Portugal, July 13-16, 2000. LC 00-26917. (Illus.). xi, 638p. 2000. 169.00 (*3-540-66738-5*) Spr-Verlag.

Adrian, Raeside. Dennis the Dragon. 32p. 1994. mass mkt. 5.95 (*0-385-25431-8*) Doubleday.

Adrian, Rhys, et al. Best Radio Plays of 1985: The BBC Giles Cooper Award Winners. 179p. (C). 1986. write for info. (*0-413-41640-2*, A0023, Methuen Drama) Methn.

Adrian, Richard H. Reviews of Physiology, Biochemistry, & Pharmacology, Vol. 88. (Illus.). 264p. 1981. 76.00 (*0-387-10408-9*) Spr-Verlag.

Adrian, Richard H., ed. Reviews of Physiology, Biochemistry & Pharmacology, Vol. 89. (Illus.). 260p. 1981. 70.00 (*0-387-10495-X*) Spr-Verlag.

— Reviews of Physiology, Biochemistry, & Pharmacology, Vol. 95. (Illus.). 235p. 1982. 76.00 (*0-387-11736-9*) Spr-Verlag.

Adrian, Richard H., et al, eds. Applications of Laser Anemometry to Fluid Mechanics. (Illus.). 575p. 1989. 155.95 (*0-387-51354-X*, 3184) Spr-Verlag.

— Reviews of Physiology, Biochemistry & Pharmacology, Vol. 90. (Illus.). 300p. 1981. 76.00 (*0-387-10657-X*) Spr-Verlag.

— Reviews of Physiology, Biochemistry & Pharmacology, Vol. 91. (Illus.). 240p. 1981. 67.00 (*0-387-10961-7*) Spr-Verlag.

— Reviews of Physiology, Biochemistry, & Pharmacology, Vol. 92. (Illus.). 220p. 1981. 67.00 (*0-387-11105-0*) Spr-Verlag.

— Reviews of Physiology, Biochemistry & Pharmacology, Vol. 94. (Illus.). 225p. 1982. 76.00 (*0-387-11701-6*) Spr-Verlag.

— Reviews of Physiology, Biochemistry & Pharmacology, Vol. 96. (Illus.). 194p. 1982. 72.00 (*0-387-11849-7*) Spr-Verlag.

— Reviews of Physiology, Biochemistry, & Pharmacology, Vol. 97. (Illus.). 176p. 1983. 67.00 (*0-387-12135-8*) Spr-Verlag.

Adrian, Richard H., et al. Applications of Laser Techniques to Fluid Mechanics: International Symposium Lisbon, Portugal, 5th, July 9-12, 1990. Dur O, D. F. et al, eds. (Illus.). 580p. 1991. 139.00 (*0-387-54318-X*) Spr-Verlag.

— Laser Techniques & Applications in Fluid Mechanics: Proceedings of the 6th International Symposium, Lisbon, Portugal, 20-23 July, 1992. Durao, D. F. et al, eds. (Illus.). 545p. 1993. 211.95 (*0-387-56879-4*) Spr-Verlag.

Adrian, Richard H., jt. ed. see Peachey, Lee D.

Adrian-Vallance. Practice Your Comparative. 1990. pap. write for info. (*0-582-01443-3*) Addison-Wesley.

Adrian, William B., jt. ed. see Hughes, Richard T.

Adriana, Leah, jt. auth. see Walker, Glenda.

Adriance, Guy W. & Brison, Fred R. Propagation of Horticultural Plants. 2nd ed. LC 79-9753. 308p. 1979. reprint ed. lib. bdg. 37.00 (*0-88275-965-5*) Krieger.

Adriance, Madeleine, ed. & tr. see Rezende, Ricardo.

Adriance, Madeleine C. Promised Land: Base Christian Communities & the Struggle for the Amazon. LC 94-42607. (SUNY Series in Religion, Culture, & Society). 202p. (C). 1995. text 59.50 (*0-7914-2649-1*); pap. text 19.95 (*0-7914-2650-5*) State U NY Pr.

Adriance, Thomas J. The Last Gaiter Button: A Study of the Mobilization & Concentration of the French Army in the War of 1870, 73. LC 87-25220. (Contributions in Military Studies Ser.: No. 73). 189p. 1987. 49.95 (*0-313-25469-9*, ALG/, Greenwood Pr) Greenwood.

Adriani, Gotz. Renoir: Oil Paintings, 1860-1917. LC 99-60273. (Illus.). 328p. 1999. pap. 60.00 (*0-300-07487-5*) Yale U Pr.

Adriani, John. Labat's Regional Anesthesia: Techniques & Clinical Applications. 4th ed. (Modern Concepts of Medicine Ser.). (Illus.). 748p. 1985. 75.00 (*0-87527-187-1*) Green.

Adriano, D. C. Trace Elements in the Terrestrial Environment. (Illus.). xix, 533p. 1985. 196.00 (*0-387-96158-5*) Spr-Verlag.

Adriano, D. C. & Havas, M., eds. Acidic Precipitation: Case Studies. (Advances in Environmental Science Ser.: Vol. 1). (Illus.). 312p. 1989. 219.00 (*0-387-96929-2*, 2468) Spr-Verlag.

Adriano, D. C. & Johnson, A. H., eds. Acidic Precipitation. (Advances in Environmental Science Ser.: Vol. 2). (Illus.). 435p. 1989. 337.00 (*0-387-97000-2*, 2837) Spr-Verlag.

Adriano, Domy C. Biochemistry of Trace Metal. 528p. 1992. lib. bdg. 110.00 (*0-87371-523-3*, L523) Lewis Pubs.

Adriano, Domy C., ed. Contamination of Groundwaters. 538p. 1994. boxed set 110.95 (*0-905927-44-3*) CRC Pr.

Adriano, Domy C. & Brisbin, I. Lehr, eds. Environmental Chemistry & Cycling Processes: Proceedings. LC 78-6603. (DOE Symposium Ser.). 946p. 1978. pap. 31.50 (*0-87079-302-0*, CONF-760429); fiche 9.00 (*0-87079-199-0*, CONF-760429) DOE.

Adriano, Mary. Among the Lilies. 617p. (Orig.). 1996. pap. 17.00 (*0-9651906-1-7*) Lily Pubns.

Adrianov, O. S. & Mering, T. A. Atlas of the Canine Brain. Domino, E. F., ed. Ignatieff, E., tr. LC 64-63010. (Illus.). 349p. 1964. 50.00 (*0-916182-01-0*) NPP Bks.

Adrianova, L. I. Introduction to Linear Systems of Differential Equations. Zhevandrov, Peter, tr. LC 95-35164. (Translations of Mathematical Monographs: Vol. 146). 204p. 1995. text 99.00 (*0-8218-0328-X*, MMONO/146) Am Math.

Adrichem, P. W. Van, see Wiepkema, P. R. & Van Adrichem, P. W., eds.

Adriel, Jean. Avatar. 285p. 1972. 9.95 (*0-940700-02-6*); pap. 6.95 (*0-940700-01-8*) Meher Baba Info.

Adrienne. Dictionary of Spoken American English (Dictionnaire de l'Americain Parle) Dictionnaire de l'Americain Parle. (ENG & FRE.). 735p. 1990. pap. 69.95 (*0-7859-4867-8*, M971) Fr & Eur.

— Fast French. 2nd ed. 200p. 1998. pap. 11.00 (*0-393-31669-6*) Norton.

— Francais Parle. LC 98-47251. (FRE.). 185p. 1999. pap. 12.00 (*0-393-31811-7*) Norton.

— French in 32 Lessons. 240p. 1997. reprint ed. pap. 11.00 (*0-393-31647-5*) Norton.

— German in 32 Lessons. rev. ed. 272p. 1997. pap. 12.00 (*0-393-31497-9*) Norton.

— Gesprochenes Deutsch. (GER.). 162p. 1999. pap. 12.00 (*0-393-31823-0*) Norton.

— Gimmick I: Italiano Parlato. 185p. 1984. pap. 8.95 (*0-393-30149-4*) Norton.

— Italian in 32 Lessons. (Gimmick Ser.). 240p. 1995. pap. 11.00 (*0-393-31346-8*, Norton Paperbks) Norton.

— Italiano Parlato. LC 98-47253. (ITA.). 185p. 1999. pap. 12.00 (*0-393-31812-5*) Norton.

— Spanish in 32 Minutes a Day. 224p. 1995. pap. 11.00 (*0-393-31305-0*, Norton Paperbks) Norton.

Adrienne, Carol. Encuentre Su Meta en la Vida. 1998. pap. 12.95 (*0-553-06093-7*) Bantam.

— The Numerology Kit. 192p. 1988. pap. 17.95 (*0-452-26081-7*, Plume) Dutton Plume.

— The Numerology Kit. 1989. pap. 12.95 (*0-317-02807-3*) NAL.

— The Purpose of Your Life: Finding Your Place in the World Using Synchronicity, Intuition, & Uncommon Sense. 320p. 1999. pap. 13.00 (*0-688-16625-3*, Wm Morrow) Morrow Avon.

— The Purpose of Your Life: Finding Your Place In The World Using Synchronicity, Intuition, And Uncommon Sense. LC 97-36912. 224p. 1998. 22.00 (*0-688-15512-X*, Wm Morrow) Morrow Avon.

— The Purpose of Your Life: Finding Your Place in the World Using Synchronicity, Intuition & Uncommon Sense, abr. ed. 1998. 16.95 incl. audio (*1-55927-512-X*) Audio Renaissance.

***Adrienne, Carol.** The Purpose of Your Life Experiential Guide. 2001. pap. 13.00 (*0-688-17802-2*) Morrow Avon.

Adrienne, Carol. The Purpose of Your Life Experiential Guide: Proven Exercises to Help You Find Your Way in the World. LC 99-12818. 320p. 1999. 22.00 (*0-688-16714-4*, Wm Morrow) Morrow Avon.

Adrienne, Carol, jt. auth. see Redfield, James.

Adrienne, Dawn. The Hawaiian Christmas Tree. (Illus.). 32p. (J). (gr. 2-5). 1999. 14.95 (*0-9667484-1-7*) Tamarind.

Adriex, Paul. Mekong. 246p. 1995. 24.95 (*974-89244-9-1*, Pub. by Aries Bks) Weatherhill.

Adrine-Robinson, Kenyette. Love Is a Child. Durant, Charlotte T. & Pye, Ethel, eds. (Illus.). 40p. (Orig.). 1992. pap. 4.00 (*0-913678-23-6*) New Day Pr.

Adrine-Robinson, Kenyette, ed. see Gaines, Edith M., et al.

Adrine, Ronald B. Ohio Domestic Violence Law. LC 98-208667. (Baldwin's Ohio Handbook Ser.). 693p. 1998. write for info. (*0-8322-0692-X*) Banks-Baldwin.

Adrogue, Horacio. Acid-Base & Electrolyte Disorders. (Contemporary Management in Critical Care Ser.: Vol. 1, No. 2). (Illus.). 240p. 1991. text 38.95 (*0-443-08829-2*) Church.

Adrogue, Horacio J. & Tobin, Martin J. Respiratory Failure. LC 96-9846. (Basics of Medicine Ser.). (Illus.). 248p. 1997. pap. text 42.95 (*0-86542-478-0*) Blackwell Sci.

Adrogue, Horacio J. & Wesson, Donald E. Acid-Base. LC 94-18243. (Basics of Medicine Ser.). 224p. 1994. pap. 10.95 (*0-86542-428-4*) Blackwell Sci.

— Acid-Base. LC 91-75540. (A & W Basics in Medicine Ser.). 204p. (C). 1991. text 29.95 (*0-9630670-0-1*) Libra & Gemini.

— Potassium. LC 94-17877. (Basics of Medicine Ser.). (Illus.). 248p. 1994. pap. 10.95 (*0-86542-427-6*) Blackwell Sci.

— Potassium. (A & W Basics in Medicine Ser.). 250p. 1992. text 29.95 (*0-9630670-1-X*) Libra & Gemini.

— Renal Failure. 224p. 1995. pap. 24.95 (*0-86542-430-6*) Blackwell Sci.

— Salt & Water. LC 94-18242. (Basics of Medicine Ser.). (Illus.). 320p. 1994. pap. 10.95 (*0-86542-426-8*) Blackwell Sci.

Adrosko, Rita J. Natural Dyes & Home Dyeing. (Illus.). 160p. 1971. reprint ed. pap. 5.95 (*0-486-22688-3*) Dover.

Adshead. China in World History. LC 99-27935. 2000. pap. 24.95 (*0-312-22565-2*) St Martin.

— China in World History. 2nd ed. 1997. pap. 24.95 (*0-333-62132-8*, Pub. by Macmillan) St Martin.

Adshead. Politics of the Archaic Peloponnese. 1986. 72.95 (*0-86127-024-X*) Ashgate Pub Co.

Adshead, Gwen & Brooke, Deborah, eds. Munchausen's Syndrome by Proxy: Current Issues in Assessment, Treatment & Research. 200p. 1999. 34.00 (*1-86094-134-6*) World Scientific Pub.

Adshead, Janet, ed. see Briginshaw, Valerie, et al.

Adshead-Lansdale, Janet, ed. Dance History: Introduction. 2nd ed. (Illus.). 320p. (Orig.). (C). 1994. pap. 24.99 (*0-415-09030-X*) Routledge.

Adshead-Lansdale, Janet, ed. Dancing Texts: Intertexuality in Interpretation. (Illus.). 272p. pap. 29.95 (*1-85273-064-1*) Princeton Bk Co.

Adshead, Paul. Around the World with Phineas Frog. LC 96-48630. (J). 1996. pap. text 7.99 (*0-85953-952-0*) Childs Play.

— Around the World with Phineas Frog. 1998. 13.99 (*0-85953-953-9*) Childs Play.

— The Chicken That Could Swim. (GRE.). (J). 1990. pap. 6.99 (*0-85953-803-6*); pap. 6.99 (*0-85953-552-5*) Childs Play.

— The Chicken That Could Swim. LC 90-34358. 32p. (J). (ps-3). 1990. 13.99 (*0-85953-294-1*); pap. 6.99 (*0-85953-346-8*) Childs Play.

— Chicken That Could Swim. (J). 1996. lib. bdg. 15.95 (*0-85953-890-7*) Childs Play.

— A Hug of Bears. LC 94-15266. (Illus.). 32p. (J). (gr. 2 up). 1994. 8.99 (*0-85953-934-2*) Childs Play.

— Incredible Reversing Peppermints. 128p. (J). (ps-3). 1993. 7.99 (*0-85953-514-2*) Childs Play.

— Incredible Reversing Peppermints. 1999. pap. text 5.99 (*0-85953-629-7*) Childs Play.

— One Odd Old Owl. 28p. (J). (ps-11). 1995. 13.99 (*0-85953-407-3*); pap. 7.99 (*0-85953-408-1*) Childs Play.

— One Odd Old Owl. (J). 1996. lib. bdg. 16.95 (*0-85953-886-9*) Childs Play.

— Peacock on the Roof. LC 90-49099. 32p. 1990. 13.99 (*0-85953-295-X*); pap. 6.99 (*0-85953-307-7*) Childs Play.

— Peacock on the Roof. (GRE.). (J). 1990. pap. 6.99 (*0-85953-804-4*) Childs Play.

— Peacock on the Roof. (J). 1996. lib. bdg. 15.95 (*0-85953-889-3*) Childs Play.

— Puzzle Island. (ITA.). (J). 1991. 13.99 (*0-85953-558-4*) Childs Play.

— Puzzle Island. LC 91-33416. (Illus.). 24p. (J). (gr. k-7). 1991. 13.99 (*0-85953-402-2*); pap. 7.99 (*0-85953-403-0*) Childs Play.

— Puzzle Island. (J). 1996. lib. bdg. 16.95 (*0-85953-885-0*) Childs Play.

— The Red Herring Mystery. (J). 1996. pap. 6.99 (*0-85953-955-5*) Childs Play.

— The Secret Hedgehog. LC 91-38897. 72p. (J). (gr. 4 up). 1991. 7.99 (*0-85953-510-X*) Childs Play.

— Trilby. 72p. (J). 1990. 7.99 (*0-85953-513-4*) Childs Play.

Adshead, Paul S. The Red Herring Mystery. LC 95-42317. (Illus.). (J). (gr. k-7). 1995. 13.99 (*0-85953-954-7*) Childs Play.

Adshead, S. A. Modernization of the Chinese Salt Administration, 1900-1920. LC 77-120315. (East Asian Monographs: No. 53). (Illus.). 294p. 1970. 40.50 (*0-674-58060-5*) HUP.

Adshead, Samuel A. China in World History. 2nd ed. LC 94-28743. 1995. text 55.00 (*0-312-12379-5*) St Martin.

— Material Culture in Europe & China, 1400-1800: The Rise of Consumerism. LC 96-45195. 256p. 1997. text 59.95 (*0-312-17285-0*) St Martin.

— The Philosophy of Religion in Nineteenth-Century England & Beyond LC 99-28275. 272p. 1999. text 65.00 (*0-312-22424-9*) St Martin.

Adsit, A., ed. Composites for Extreme Environments- STP 768. 188p. 1982. 24.00 (*0-8031-0698-X*, STP768) ASTM.

Adsit, Christopher B. Personal Disciplemaking Toolkit. 24p. Date not set. pap. 8.99 (*1-57902-021-6*) Integrtd Res.

Adsit, Kimberly S. & Gilstrap, Wendy R. Hooks, Books & Cooks. 1999. pap. 19.95 (*0-9671864-0-4*) HB&C Pr.

Adsit, N. R., jt. ed. see DiGiovanni, P. R.

Adsit, Norman W. Adsit. Descendants of John Adsit of Lyme, Ct. (Illus.). 226p. 1997. reprint ed. pap. 34.00 (*0-8328-7221-0*); reprint ed. lib. bdg. 44.00 (*0-8328-7220-2*) Higginson Bk Co.

Adsjibolosoo, Senoy. The Human Factor in Developing Africa. LC 94-42565. 240p. 1995. 59.95 (*0-275-95059-X*, Praeger Pubs) Greenwood.

Adson, John. Courtly Masquing Ayres, to 5 & 6 Parts, for Violins, Consorts, & Cornets. LC 77-6842. (English Experience Ser.: No. 838). 1977. reprint ed. lib. bdg. 25.00 (*90-221-0838-4*) Walter J Johnson.

***Adson, Patricia R.** Finding Your Own True North. LC 99-39605. 1999. pap. write for info. (*1-878287-38-9*) Type & Temperament.

— A Princess & Her Garden: A Fable of Awakening & Arrival. LC 99-60298. (Illus.). 64p. 2000. 16.95 (*1-883477-34-4*) Lone Oak MN.

Adu-Amankwah, Patrick A. The Moral Philosophy of R. M. Hare: A Vindication of Utilitarianism? LC 94-41395. (American University Studies V: Vol. 172). XXXV, 603p. (C). 1998. text 72.95 (*0-8204-2703-9*) P Lang Pubng.

Aducci, P., ed. Signal Transduction in Plants. LC 96-48484. (Molecular & Cell Biology Update Ser.). 1997. 88.00 (*0-8176-5307-4*); 88.00 (*3-7643-5307-4*) Birkhauser.

Aduddell, Robert, jt. auth. see Tatalovich, Raymond.

Adult Education Association of the U. S. A. Staff, jt. auth. see ERIC Staff.

Adult Education Association Staff. You Can Be a Successful Teacher of Adults. Langerman, Phillip D., ed. LC 74-81224. 186p. 1974. pap. 6.50 (*0-317-36197-X*) A A C E.

Adult Ya Reco Young. The Outsiders. 1979. 13.20 (*0-394-77997-5*) Random.

Advaita. Bridge to Eternity. 560p. 1987. pap. 8.95 (*0-87481-230-5*, Pub. by Advaita Ashrama) Vedanta Pr.

Advaita Ashrama Staff. Sarada Devi: A Biography in Pictures. (Illus.). 108p. 1989. 13.95 (*81-7505-078-0*, Pub. by Advaita Ashrama) Vedanta Pr.

Advaita Ashrama Staff, compiled by. Life of Sri Ramakrishna. 472p. 1940. pap. 8.95 (*81-7505-070-5*, Pub. by Advaita Ashrama) Vedanta Pr.

Advaita Ashrama Staff, ed. Ramakrishna: A Biography in Pictures. (Illus.). 1976. 14.95 (*0-87481-167-8*, Pub. by Advaita Ashrama) Vedanta Pr.

Advaita Ashrama Staff, ed. see Swami Vivekananda.

Advance Cal-Tech Inc. Staff. Let's Praise & Play: Children's Christian Mini-Piano Book. Kung, Edward, ed. (Illus.). 36p. (J). (ps-6). text. write for info. (*0-943759-00-5*) Advance Cal Tech.

Advance Thought Pub. Staff. The Science of Regeneration or Sex Enlightenment (1911) 162p. 1996. reprint ed. pap. 16.95 (*1-56459-932-9*) Kessinger Pub.

Advanced Computing Applications Group, JPL Section. Math, '77: Mathematical Subprograms for Fortran 77. 1994. pap. write for info. (*1-885644-00-0*) Fortner Sftware.

Advanced Estate Planning & Administration Seminar. Fourth Annual Advanced Estate Planning & Administration Seminar: April 24-26, 1983, the Tides Inn, Irvington, Virginia. 278p. 1984. write for info. (*0-318-57561-2*) Virginia Bar.

Advanced Information Systems, Inc. Staff, et al. Client/Server Unleashed. LC 95-74784. (Illus.). 744p. 1996. 45.00 incl. cd-rom (*0-672-30726-X*) Sams.

— Oracle Unleashed. LC 95-72326. (Illus.). 1404p. 1996. 59.99 incl. cd-rom (*0-672-30872-X*) Sams.

— Oracle Unleashed. 2nd ed. LC 97-67500. 1500p. 1997. 59.99 (*0-672-31148-8*) Mac USA.

Advanced Informations Staff, comment. Oracle Unleashed. 3rd ed. 1999. pap. text 49.99 (*0-672-31575-0*) Sams.

Advanced Life Support Group. Major Incident Medical Management & Support: The Practical Approach. 205p. 1995. pap. text 43.00 (*0-7279-0928-2*, Pub. by BMJ Pub) Login Brothers Bk Co.

Advanced Manufacturing Systems Exposition & Confer. Advanced Manufacturing Systems Exposition & Conference: Proceedings of the Conference Sessions, April 18-21, 1988, McCormick Place North, Chicago, IL. LC TS0176.. 923p. reprint ed. pap. 200.00 (*0-8357-5127-9*, 203291200081) Bks Demand.

— Advanced Manufacturing Systems Exposition & Conference: Proceedings of the Conference Sessions, December 15-17, 1987, Anaheim Convention Center, Anaheim, CA. LC TS0176.. 470p. reprint ed. pap. 145.70 (*0-8357-5126-0*, 203291000081) Bks Demand.

— Advanced Manufacturing Systems Exposition & Conference: Proceedings of the Conference Sessions, McCormick Place, Chicago, IL, June 24-26, 1986, Including 2nd International Conference on Simulation in Manufacturing: 4th International Conference on Automated Guided Vehicle Systems. LC TP0176.. 855p. reprint ed. pap. 200.00 (*0-8357-5125-2*, 202936800060) Bks Demand.

Advanced Mechanics & Engineering Ltd. Staff. Requirements for the Use of Mechanical Connections on the Pipeline Side of Risers above the Water. 1997. pap. 100.00 (*82-7257-518-3*, Pub. by Oljedirektoratet) St Mut.

An Asterisk (*) at the beginning of an entry indicates that the title is appearing for the first time.

Advanced Medicine Symposia Staff. Proceedings of the Advanced Medicine Symposia, 7th, 1971. Boucher, I. A., ed. 1971. pap. text 30.00 (*0-7855-7129-9*) St Mut.

Advanced Medicine Symposia Staff & Royal College of Physicians Staff. Proceedings of the Advanced Medicine Symposia, 10th, 1974. Ledingham, J. G., ed. (Illus.). 1974. pap. text 50.00 (*0-7855-7130-2*) St Mut.

— Proceedings of the Advanced Medicine Symposia, 11th, 1975. Lant, A. F., ed. (Illus.). 1975. pap. text 40.00 (*0-7855-7131-0*) St Mut.

***Advanced Paediatric Life Support Group Staff, ed.** Pre Hospital Pediatric Life Support. 203p. 1999. pap. 39.95 (*0-7279-1419-7*, Pub. by Brit Med Assn) Amer Coll Phys.

Advanced Research Projects Agency (ARPA) Staff. Defense Technology Conversion, Reinvestment, & Transition Assistance: Program Information Package & SBIR Program. 104p. (Orig.). (C). 1994. pap. text 30.00 (*0-7881-0360-1*) DIANE Pub.

Advanced Science Seminar (1964: Pinebrook Conferen. Cellular Ultrastructure of Woody Plants. Cote, Wilfred A., Jr., ed. LC 65-15857. 617p. reprint ed. pap. 191.30 (*0-608-15203-X*, 202739500055) Bks Demand.

Advanced Study Institute on ORD & CD (1971: Tierre. Fundamental Aspects & Recent Developments in Optical Rotatory Dispersion & Circular Dichroism: Proceedings of NATO Advanced Study Institute Held at Tirrenia (Pisa), Spetember 5-18, 1971. Ciardelli, F. & Salvadori, P., eds. LC 72-97936. 437p. reprint ed. pap. 135.50 (*0-608-15386-9*, 202925600059) Bks Demand.

Advanced Study Institute on Polar Cap Boundary Phe, et al. Polar Cap Boundary Phenomena: Proceedings of the NATO Advanced Study Institute on Polar Cap Boundary Phenomena, Longyearbyen, 4-13 June 1997. LC 98-9255. (NATO ASI Ser.). 1998. 184.00 (*0-7923-4976-8*) Kluwer Academic.

Advanced Study Institute Staff. Radiation Trapped in the Earth's Magnetic Field: Proceedings of the Advanced Study Institute, Bergen Norway, 1965. McCormac, Billy M., ed. (Astrophysics & Space Science Library: No. 5). 901p. 1966. text 338.00 (*90-277-0130-X*) Kluwer Academic.

Advanced Study Institute Symposium Staff & ESRO Symposium Staff. Earth's Magnetospheric Processes: Proceedings of the Advanced Study Institute ESRO Symposium, Cortina, Italy, 1971. McCormac, Billy M., ed. LC 70-188007. (Astrophysics & Space Science Library: No. 32). 417p. 1972. text 234.50 (*90-277-0231-4*) Kluwer Academic.

Advanced Summer Institute Staff. Magnetospheric Physics: Proceedings of the Advanced Summer Institute, Sheffield, England, 13-12 August, 1973. McCormac, Billy M., ed. LC 74-76472. (Astrophysics & Space Science Library: No. 44). 370p. 1974. lib. bdg. 165.00 (*90-277-0454-6*) Kluwer Academic.

Advancement Strategies Staff. Diversity Bingo: An Experiential Learning Event. 65p. 1992. student ed., ring bd. 99.95 (*0-88390-332-6*, Pfiffr & Co) Jossey-Bass.

Advances in Anesthesia Staff. Advances in Anesthesia, Vol. 4. LC 84-644411. 393p. reprint ed. pap. 121.90 (*0-8357-6296-3*, 203426100004) Bks Demand.

Advances in Cyclic Nucleotide & Protein Phosphoryl. Advances in Cyclic Nucleotide & Protein Phosphorylation Research, Vol. 1. fac. ed. LC 84-649078. (Illus.). 192p. pap. 59.60 (*0-7837-7147-9*, 204714800004) Bks Demand.

Advances in Endocrinology & Metabolism Staff. Advances in Endocrinology & Metabolism, Vol. 5, 1994. Mazzaferri, Ernest L., ed. LC 90-656463. 499p. 1994. reprint ed. pap. 154.70 (*0-608-02400-7*, 206304200005) Bks Demand.

Advances in Enzyme Regulation Staff. Advances in Enzyme Regulation, Vol. 36. Weber, G., ed. 466p. 1996. 613.00 (*0-08-044409-1*, Pergamon Pr) Elsevier.

Advances in Inflammation Research Staff. Advances in Inflammation Research Vol. 2. fac. ed. LC 78-55804. (Illus.). 227p. (C). pap. 70.40 (*0-7837-7381-1*, 204715600002) Bks Demand.

— Advances in Inflammation Research Vol. 4. fac. ed. LC 78-55804. (Illus.). 208p. pap. 64.50 (*0-7837-7382-X*, 204715600004) Bks Demand.

Advances in Internal Medicine Staff. Advances in Internal Medicine, Vol. 39, 1994. Schrier, Robert W., ed. LC 42-20729. 820p. 1994. reprint ed. pap. 200.00 (*0-608-02414-7*, 206305600039) Bks Demand.

Advances in Nephrology from the Necker Hospital St. Advances in Nephrology from the Necker Hospital, Vol. 12 - 1983. LC 73-154325. (Illus.). 374p. reprint ed. pap. 116.00 (*0-8357-7673-5*, 205700100012) Bks Demand.

— Advances in Nephrology from the Necker Hospital, Vol. 13 - 1984. LC 73-154325. (Illus.). 408p. reprint ed. pap. 126.50 (*0-8357-7674-3*, 205700200013) Bks Demand.

— Advances in Nephrology from the Necker Hospital, Vol. 14 - 1985. LC 73-154325. (Illus.). 544p. reprint ed. pap. 168.70 (*0-8357-7675-1*, 205700300014) Bks Demand.

Advances in Obstetrics & Gynecology Staff. Advances in Obstetrics & Gynecology, Vol. 1, 1994. Rock, John A., ed. LC 95-640986. 466p. 1994. reprint ed. pap. 144.50 (*0-608-02419-8*, 206306100001) Bks Demand.

Advances in Pathology & Laboratory Medicine Staff. Advances in Pathology & Laboratory Medicine, Vol. 5, 1992. Weinstein, Ronald S., ed. LC 91-337. 483p. 1992. reprint ed. pap. 149.80 (*0-608-02402-3*, 206304400005) Bks Demand.

Advances in Patient Care Conference Staff. Design & Use of Protocols: Proceedings of the Advances in Patient Care, Second Annual Conference, Feb. 15-22, 1975. Kallstrom, Marta & Yarnall, Stephen R., eds. (Illus.). 294p. 1975. 18.00 (*0-917054-02-4*) Med Communications.

— New Approaches to Counseling & Communication: How to Improve Your Skills in Patient Care: Proceedings of the Advances in Patient Care Conference, 4th, 1977. Zoog, Spring & Yarnall, Stephen R., eds. 1977. 20.00 (*0-917054-14-8*) Med Communications.

Advances in Pediatric Sport Sciences Staff. Advances in Pediatric Sport Sciences Vol. 1: Biological Issues. Boileau, Richard A., ed. LC 85-644893. (Illus.). 221p. 1989. reprint ed. pap. 68.60 (*0-608-06443-2*, 206728000001) Bks Demand.

— Advances in Pediatric Sport Sciences Vol. 2: Behavioral Issues. Gould, Daniel & Weiss, Maureen R., eds. LC 85-644893. (Illus.). 268p. 1989. reprint ed. pap. 83.10 (*0-608-06444-0*, 206728000002) Bks Demand.

Advances in Pediatrics Staff. Advances in Pediatrics, Vol. 31 - 1984. LC 42-22236. 516p. reprint ed. pap. 160.00 (*0-8357-7672-7*, 205700000031) Bks Demand.

— Advances in Pediatrics, Vol. 33. Barness, Lewis A., ed. LC 42-22236. (Illus.). 433p. 1986. reprint ed. pap. 134.30 (*0-8357-5560-6*, 203518900033) Bks Demand.

— Advances in Pediatrics, Vol. 40, 1993. Barness, Lewis A., ed. LC 42-22236. 478p. 1993. reprint ed. pap. 148.20 (*0-608-02398-1*, 206304000040) Bks Demand.

Advances in Photochemistry Staff. Advances in Photochemistry, Vol. 7. LC 63-13592. 424p. reprint ed. pap. 131.50 (*0-8357-5175-9*, 200649300059) Bks Demand.

Advances in Plastic & Reconstructive Surgery Staff. Advances in Plastic & Reconstructive Surgery, 2 vols., Vol. 2. Habal, Mutaz B. & Morain, William D., eds. LC 85-646246. 285p. reprint ed. pap. 88.40 (*0-8357-5557-6*, 203518700002) Bks Demand.

— Advances in Plastic & Reconstructive Surgery, 2 vols., Vol. 3. Habal, Mutaz B. & Morain, William D., eds. LC 85-646246. 333p. reprint ed. pap. 103.30 (*0-8357-5558-4*, 203518700003) Bks Demand.

Advances in Polyamine Research Staff. Advances in Polyamine Research, Vol. 2. fac. ed. Campbell, Robert A., ed. LC 77-83687. (Illus.). 395p. pap. 122.50 (*0-7837-7274-2*, 204703100002) Bks Demand.

Advances in Prostaglandin & Thromboxane Research S. Advances in Prostaglandin & Thromboxane Research, 1980, Vol. 7. LC 75-14588. 656p. 1980. reprint ed. pap. 200.00 (*0-608-00299-2*, 206025900007) Bks Demand.

Advances in Surgery Staff. Advances in Surgery, Vol. 21 - 1987. LC 65-29931. (Illus.). 320p. reprint ed. pap. 99.20 (*0-8357-7676-X*, 205700400021) Bks Demand.

Advances in Tracer Methodology. Advances in Tracer Methodology: A Collection of Papers Presented at the Eleventh Annual Symposium on Tracer Methodology, Vol. 4. Rothchild, Seymour, ed. LC 62-13475. 301p. reprint ed. pap. 93.40 (*0-8357-5191-0*, 202628400004) Bks Demand.

— Advances in Tracer Methodology: A Collection of Papers Presented at the Ninth & Tenth Symposium on Tracer Methodology, Vol. 3. Rothchild, Seymour, ed. LC 62-13475. 343p. reprint ed. pap. 106.40 (*0-8357-5190-2*, 202628300003) Bks Demand.

Advances in Trauma & Critical Care Staff. Advances in Trauma & Critical Care, Vol. 9, 1994. Maull, Kimball I., ed. LC 92-38051. 380p. 1994. reprint ed. pap. 117.80 (*0-608-02401-5*, 206304300009) Bks Demand.

Advani, Rukun. Beethoven among the Cows. (C). 1994. 12.50 (*0-02-516005-2*, Pub. by Ravi Dayal) S Asia.

Advani, Rukun, et al, eds. Civil Lines: New Writing from India. (C). 1994. pap. 9.50 (*0-86311-584-5*, Pub. by Ravi Dayal) S Asia.

Advani, S. G., et al, eds. Computer Aided Design in Composite Material Technology III. LC 91-77814. (CADCOMP Ser.: Vol. 3). 648p. 1992. 255.00 (*1-56252-094-6*, 1665) Computational Mech MA.

Advani, S. G., et al, eds. Computer Aided Design of Composite Material Technology III. 648p. 1992. 255.00 (*1-85312-166-5*) Computational Mech MA.

Advani, S. G., jt. ed. see Kumar, V.

Advani, S. G., jt. ed. see Siginer, Dennis A.

Advani, Sunjoo K. The Kinematic Design of Flight Simulator Motion-Bases. (Series 03 - Control & Simulation 04). (Illus.). 255p. 1998. pap. 47.50 (*90-407-1671-4*, Pub. by Delft U Pr) Coronet Bks.

Advani, Suresh G., ed. Flow & Rheology in Polymer Composites Manufacturing. LC 93-33455. (Composite Materials Ser.: No. 10). 626p. 1994. 205.50 (*0-444-89347-4*) Elsevier.

Advani, Suresh G. & Siginer, Dennis A., eds. Rheology & Fluid Mechanics of Nonlinear Materials, 1997: Proceedings, ASME International Mechanical Engineering Congress & Exposition, Dallas, TX, 1997. LC 97-76722. (FED - MD Ser.: Vols. 243 & 78). 261p. 1997. pap. 110.00 (*0-7918-1825-X*, TA357) ASME Pr.

Advantage International, Inc. Staff. Computers...Need to Know Basics. Exposure Unlimited Staff, ed. & illus. by. Date not set. 49.95 (*1-56756-093-8*) Advant Intl.

— Fraternal Software. 1992. 299.00 (*1-56756-024-5*); teacher ed. 25.00 (*1-56756-016-4*); disk 69.00 (*1-56756-010-5*, OD300I); disk 69.00 (*1-56756-011-3*, OD310M) Advant Intl.

— InfoQuest Services Software: Network Version 4.0. (C). 1992. 25.00 (*1-56756-015-6*); 1499.00 (*1-56756-021-0*, OD110I); 2250.00 (*1-56756-022-9*, OD120I); 5.25 hd 999.00 (*1-56756-006-7*, OD100I); mac hd 750.00 (*1-56756-007-5*, OD130M) Advant Intl.

— KeyMate - RideMate. 1992. 99.00 incl. disk (*1-56756-004-0*, OD400I); 99.00 incl. disk (*1-56756-005-9*, OD410M) Advant Intl.

— ListMan: List Management - Direct Mail & Telemarketing. 1992. 99.00 (*1-56756-003-2*, OD500I); 599.00 (*1-56756-023-7*, OD510I); student ed. 35.00 (*1-56756-018-0*) Advant Intl.

— Multiple Organizational Management Software (MOM) 1992. 1995.00 (*1-56756-008-3*, OD300I); 995.00 (*1-56756-009-1*, OD301I); student ed. 35.00 (*1-56756-019-9*) Advant Intl.

— My First Computer Book. (Illus.). 50p. 1992. student ed. 19.95 (*1-56756-002-4*, SAC200) Advant Intl.

— Pomp & Circumstance (P&C) Personnel Services Software. 1992. student ed. 35.00 (*0-685-66143-1*); disk 99.00 (*1-56756-014-8*, OD430I) Advant Intl.

— Software Boot Camp. Exposure Unlimited Staff, ed. & photos by by. (Illus.). 150p. 1996. spiral bd., wbk. ed. 29.99 (*1-56756-092-X*) Advant Intl.

— Student Organization Software. (C). 1992. 299.00 (*1-56756-025-3*, OD270I); teacher ed. 25.00 (*1-56756-017-2*); disk 69.00 (*1-56756-012-1*, OD250I); mac hd 69.00 (*1-56756-013-X*, OD260M) Advant Intl.

Advantage International, Inc. Staff, ed. see Tervo, Trace.

Advantage Media Staff. Successful Keyboarding: An Elementary Approach. (TE - Keyboarding Ser.). 1986. 53.95 (*0-538-28632-6*) S-W Pub.

Advantage Publishers Group Staff. Christmas at Home: Gifts, Recipes & Decorations for the Holidays. LC 98-28323. (Illus.). 160p. 1999. 14.98 (*1-57145-167-6*, Thunder Bay) Advantage Pubs.

— Cooking Italian Antipasti. LC 99-25760. (Cooking Italian Ser.). (Illus.). 128p. 1999. 9.98 (*1-57145-196-X*, Thunder Bay) Advantage Pubs.

— Cooking Italian Pasta. LC 99-27333. (Cooking Italian Ser.). (Illus.). 128p. 1999. 9.98 (*1-57145-195-1*, Thunder Bay) Advantage Pubs.

***Advantage Publishers Group Staff.** Seeing Sacramento, 1999-2000. 1999. pap. 5.00 (*0-9676177-1-5*) Advantage Pub CA.

***Advantage Publishing Staff & Botanica Editors.** Botanica's Roses: Over 1,000 Pages & over 2,000 Roses Listed. LC 00-39360. (Illus.). 2000. 19.95 (*1-57145-661-9*, Laurel Glen Pub) Advantage Pubs.

Advena, Jean C., compiled by. Drug Abuse Bibliography for 1972. LC 79-116588. 514p. 1974. 18.00 (*0-87875-046-0*) Whitston Pub.

— Drug Abuse Bibliography for 1973. LC 79-116588. xlii, 410p. 1975. 18.00 (*0-87875-057-6*) Whitston Pub.

— Drug Abuse Bibliography for 1970. LC 79-116588. 202p. 1971. 10.00 (*0-87875-016-9*) Whitston Pub.

— Drug Abuse Bibliography for 1971. LC 79-116588. 451p. 1972. 15.00 (*0-87875-025-8*) Whitston Pub.

Advena, Jean C., jt. ed. see Harding, Walter.

Advent. Do You Hear What I Hear. 1999. 8.00 (*1-56021-338-8*) W J Fantasy.

Adventura Books Editors. Gifts of the Wild: A Woman's Book of Adventure. LC 98-6000. (Illus.). 320p. 1998. pap. text 16.95 (*1-58005-006-9*) Seal Pr.

Adventure Architects Staff. Dzurlord. 256p. 1987. pap. 3.50 (*0-8125-6410-3*, Pub. by Tor Bks) St Martin.

Adventure Cycling Association Staff. Adventure Cycling in Michigan: Selected On- & Off-Road Rides. LC 97-3534. (Adventure Cycling In Ser.). (Illus.). 240p. 1997. pap. 14.95 (*0-89886-505-0*) Mountaineers.

— Adventure Cycling in Northern California: Selected On-& Off-Road Rides. LC 96-47852. (Illus.). 240p. (Orig.). 1997. pap. 14.95 (*0-89886-504-2*) Mountaineers.

Adventure House Staff. Mary Engelbreit Countdown to Christmas. 1998. 14.95 (*0-8362-7225-0*) Andrews & McMeel.

Adventure Publications. My Very Own Phone Book. (Jt. (ps-3). 1993. pap. 7.95 (*0-9635490-0-6*) Just Mom & Me.

Adventure Publications Staff. Best of Honey Giftpack. 1991. 9.95 (*0-934860-69-6*) Adventure Pubns.

— Best of Pancake & Waffle Giftpack. 108p. 1990. spiral bd. 17.95 (*0-934860-60-2*) Adventure Pubns.

— The Habits of Seven Highly Annoying People. LC 95-83147. (Illus.). 96p. (Orig.). 1995. pap. 7.00 (*1-887317-02-3*) Bad Dog Pr.

— Sisters Are Forever. (Small Wonders Ser.). 120p. 1995. spiral bd. 4.99 (*1-879127-53-9*) Lighten Up Enter.

— Thank You. (Small Wonders Ser.). 120p. 1995. spiral bd. 4.99 (*1-879127-52-0*) Lighten Up Enter.

Adventure Publications Staff, jt. auth. see Hinton, Pat C.

Adventure Publishing Staff, jt. auth. see Blacklock, Craig.

Adventure Staff. Birthday Wishes. (Small Wonders Ser.) 120p. 1995. spiral bd. 4.99 (*1-879127-54-7*) Lighten Up Enter.

— With Warmest Thanks. (Small Wonders Ser.). 120p. 1995. spiral bd. 4.99 (*1-879127-62-8*) Lighten Up Enter.

Adventure Staff, jt. auth. see Boysen, Claudia L.

Adventure Travel Society Staff, ed. see World Congress on Adventure Travel & Eco-Tourism S.

Adventurer Magazine Staff. Adventurer: 1753-1754, 2 vols. , Nos. 1-140. LC 68-58000. reprint ed. 245.00 (*0-404-19300-5*) AMS Pr.

***Adventures for Young Readers Staff.** Adventure Bible for Young Readers. (Illus.). (YA). 2000. 24.99 (*0-310-91142-7*); pap. 19.99 (*0-310-91143-5*) Zondervan.

***Adventures Imports Staff.** Assorted Guatemalan Fabrics Journals. (Illus.). 1999. pap. 3.00 (*1-892985-06-3*) Adventure Imports.

— Assorted Indonesian Batik Fabrics Journals. (Illus.). 1999. pap. 7.99 (*1-892985-07-1*) Adventure Imports.

— Journals in Hemp Fabric: Stamped. (Illus.). 1999. pap. 8.99 (*1-892985-08-X*) Adventure Imports.

Advertising Age Editors. How Procter & Gamble Became America's Leading Marketer. (Illus.). 128p. 1990. pap. 17.95 (*0-8442-3166-5*, NTC Business Bks) NTC Contemp Pub Co.

***Advertising Photography Assoc. Staff.** Advertising Photography in Japan, 2000. (Illus.). 240p. 1999. 89.95 (*4-89444-112-8*, Pub. by Pie Bks) Bks Nippan.

Advisory Committee on Development & Transfer of Bi. Technology Transfer, Working for Collaboration Commerce, & Competitiveness: Report of the Advisory Committee on Development & Transfer of Biotechnology. LC 95-620464. 68p. (Orig.). 1994. pap. write for info. (*0-945597-29-0*) NC Biotech Ctr.

Advisory Committee on Pollution of the Sea, London. Acops Yearbook 1986-1987. 120p. 1987. 35.00 (*0-317-66305-4*, Pergamon Pr) Elsevier.

Advisory Committee on Pollution of the Sea, London, ed. Marine Pollution: ACOPS Yearbook, 1990. (Advisory Committee on the Pollution of the Sea Ser.: Vol. 1). (Illus.). 188p. 1990. pap. 77.50 (*0-08-040809-5*, Pergamon Pr) Elsevier.

Advisory Group Aerospace Research Staff. Multilingual Aeronautical Dictionary. (DUT, ENG, FRE, GER & ITA.). 876p. 1980. 195.00 (*0-8288-0022-7*, M7770) Fr & Eur.

Advocacy Institute Staff. Change for the Better: Building New Dimensions in Public Interest Leadership. ix, 58p. 1991. pap. text 7.50 (*1-882215-02-8*) Advocacy Inst.

— The Elements of a Successful Public Interest Advocacy Campaign. 45p. (Orig.). (C). pap. text 7.50 (*1-882215-00-1*) Advocacy Inst.

— Taking Initiative: The 1990 Citizens' Movement. 115p. 1992. pap. text 15.00 (*1-882215-03-6*) Advocacy Inst.

Adwers, Robert E. Rudder, Stick & Throttle: Research & Reminiscences on Flying in Nebraska. LC 95-150059. (Illus.). x, 550p. (Orig.). 1993. pap. 25.00 (*0-9631699-4-7*) Making Hist.

Ady, C. M., ed. see Armstrong, Edward A.

Ady, Endre. Neighbours of the Night: Selected Short Stories. 176p. 1989. pap. 44.40 (*963-13-3901-7*, Pub. by Corvina Bks) St Mut.

Ady, Jean, jt. auth. see Sparks, John.

Ady, Julia M. Baldassare Castiglione: The Perfect Courtier, His Life & Letters, 1478-1529, 2 vols. LC 75-154138. (BCL Ser.: No. I). reprint ed. 87.50 (*0-404-09206-3*) AMS Pr.

— Beatrice D'Este, Duchess of Milan, 1475-1497. LC 71-154137. reprint ed. 43.50 (*0-404-09204-7*) AMS Pr.

— Christina of Denmark, Duchess of Milan & Lorraine, 1522-1590. LC 73-154140. reprint ed. 49.50 (*0-404-09205-5*) AMS Pr.

— Isabella D'Este, Marchioness of Mantua, 1474-1539, 2 vols. LC 79-154139. reprint ed. 145.00 (*0-404-09214-4*) AMS Pr.

— Jean-Francois Millet, His Life & Letters. LC 73-155629. reprint ed. 61.50 (*0-404-00297-8*) AMS Pr.

— The Pilgrim's Way from Winchester to Canterbury. LC 71-158231. reprint ed. 34.50 (*0-404-01399-6*) AMS Pr.

Ady, Ronald W. The Investment Evaluator: How to Size up Your Investments at a Glance. 274p. 1984. 22.50 (*0-13-503673-9*, Busn); pap. 9.95 (*0-317-07154-8*, Busn) P-H.

Adye, J. Payne. A Treatise on Court Marshall. 284p. reprint ed. 44.00 (*0-932051-70-7*) Rprt Serv.

Adyodi, Rita G., jt. ed. see Adiyodi, K. G.

Adzenyah, Abraham K., et al. Let Your Voice Be Heard! Songs from Ghana & Zimbabwe: Multipart & Game Songs Arranged & Annotated for Grades K-12. (Illus.). 167p. 1997. pap. 26.95 incl. audio compact disk (*0-937203-75-0*) World Music Pr.

Adzerikho, K. S., et al. Radiative Heat Transfer in Two-Phase Media. (ENG & RUS.). 208p. 1992. lib. bdg. 119.00 (*0-8493-9304-3*, TJ960) CRC Pr.

Adzhemyan, L. T., et al. The Field Theoretic Renormalization Group in Fully Developed Turbulence. Millard, P., tr. 208p. 1999. text 95.00 (*90-5699-145-0*) Gordon & Breach.

Adzic, R. R., et al, eds. Oxygen Electrochemistry. LC 95-61599. (Proceedings Ser.: Vol. 95-26). (Illus.). 246p. 1996. 42.00 (*1-56677-121-8*) Electrochem Soc.

Adzinyah, Abraham K., et al. Let Your Voice Be Heard! Songs from Ghana & Zimbabwe: (Call-&-Response, Multipart & Game Songs Arranged & Annotated for Grades K-12) 10th anniversary ed. (Illus.). 167p. (Orig.). 1997. pap. 26.95 incl. audio (*0-937203-76-9*) World Music Pr.

Adzomada, Kofi J. Dictionnaire Francais-Ewe. (FRE.). 245p. 1992. 75.00 (*0-7859-1019-0*, 2906718327) Fr & Eur.

Aeberhard, Kurt. Strategische Analyse: Empfehlungen zum Vorgehen & zu Sinnvollen Methodenkombinationen. (GER.). 351p. 1996. 55.95 (*3-906756-80-7*) P Lang Pubng.

Aebersold, Alicia, ed. Governors' Staff Directory, March 1994. 79p. (Orig.). 1994. pap. text 7.50 (*1-55877-182-4*) Natl Governor.

— Ideas That Work: Business & Environment. 151p. 1996. pap. 30.00 (*1-55877-262-6*) Natl Governor.

— Ideas That Work: Crime & Public Safety. 157p. 1996. pap. 30.00 (*1-55877-261-8*) Natl Governor.

— Ideas That Work: Education Reform. 173p. 1996. pap. 30.00 (*1-55877-263-4*) Natl Governor.

— Ideas That Work: Infrastructure. 133p. 1996. pap. 30.00 (*1-55877-264-2*) Natl Governor.

— Ideas That Work: Job Creation. 155p. 1996. pap. 30.00 (*1-55877-265-0*) Natl Governor.

— Ideas That Work: Self-Sufficiency. 135p. 1996. pap. 30.00 (*1-55877-266-9*) Natl Governor.

— Ideas That Work: Tax Policy. 95p. 1996. pap. 30.00 (*1-55877-267-7*) Natl Governor.

Aebersold, Alicia C., ed. Directory of Governors of the American States, Commonwealths, & Territories, January 1994. (Illus.). 68p. (Orig.). 1994. pap. text 8.95 (*1-55877-177-8*) Natl Governor.

— Directory of Governors of the American States, Commonwealths, & Territories, January 1995. (Illus.). 68p. (Orig.). 1995. pap. text 9.95 (*1-55877-229-4*) Natl Governor.

— Directory of Governors of the American States, Commonwealths, & Territories-1993. (Illus.). 68p. (Orig.). 1993. pap. text 8.95 (*1-55877-201-4*) Natl Governor.

— The Fiscal Survey of States, April 1993. 63p. (Orig.). 1993. pap. text 25.00 (*1-55877-208-1*) Natl Governor.

A

— The Fiscal Survey of States, April 1994. 46p. (Orig.). pap. text 25.00 (*1-55877-184-0*) Natl Governor.

— The Fiscal Survey of States, November 1994. 50p. (Orig.). 1994. pap. text 25.00 (*1-55877-227-8*) Natl Governor.

— The Fiscal Survey of States, October 1993. 45p. (Orig.). 1993. pap. text 25.00 (*1-55877-221-9*) Natl Governor.

— Governors' Staff Directory, April 1993. 80p. (Orig.). 1993. pap. text 7.50 (*1-55877-206-5*) Natl Governor.

— Governors' Staff Directory, September 1993. 80p. (Orig.). 1993. pap. text 7.50 (*1-55877-220-0*) Natl Governor.

— Governors' Staff Directory, September 1994. 80p. (Orig.). 1994. pap. text 9.95 (*1-55877-196-4*) Natl Governor.

Aebersold, Jo A. & Field, Mary L. From Reader to Reading Teacher. (Cambridge Language Education Ser.). (Illus.). 275p. (C). 1997. text 54.95 (*0-521-49705-1*); pap. text 20.95 (*0-521-49785-X*) Cambridge U Pr.

Aebersold, JoAnn, et al. Critical Thinking, Critical Choices: Listening & Speaking, Bk. 2. (Illus.). 256p. (C). 1985. pap. text 13.75 (*0-13-194127-5*) P-H.

Aebersold, Paul. Biotechnology Backstage. unabridged ed. 224p. 1998. 24.50 (*1-57529-064-2*) Kabel Pubs.

***Aebersold, William.** Seeds of Insanity. 273p. 1999. 17.00 (*0-9675384-0-8*) Alpha to Omega.

Aebi. Atlas of Microscopy Techniques. 260p. 1999. 115.00 (*0-12-044415-1*) Acad Pr.

Aebi, Andreas, tr. see Morgenthaler, Fritz.

Aebi, H., et al, eds. Einfuehrung in die Praktische Biochemie. 3rd ed. xii, 462p. 1982. pap. 65.25 (*3-8055-3448-5*) S Karger.

Aebi, M. & Regazzoni, P., eds. Bone Transplant. (Illus.). 380p. 1989. 144.00 (*0-387-50165-7*) Spr-Verlag.

Aebi, M., et al. AOASIF Principles in Spine Surgery: Techniques Recommended by the AOASIF Group, Spine Education Committee. LC 97-30417. 350p. 1998. write for info. (*3-540-62763-4*) Spr-Verlag.

Aebi, Magdalena. Kants Begruendung der "Duetschen Philosophie" (GER.). 525p. 1984. reprint ed. write for info. (*3-487-07382-X*) G Olms Pubs.

Aebi, Max, jt. ed. see Thalgott, John S.

Aebi, Philipp, jt. auth. see Osterwalder, Jurg.

Aebi, Robert. Schrodinger Diffusion Processes: Probability & Its Applications. 186p. 1996. 79.50 (*0-8176-5386-4*) Birkhauser.

Aebi, Tania. Maiden Voyage. LC 96-96662. 1996. pap. 10.00 (*0-345-41012-2*) Ballantine Pub Grp.

Aebi, Timothy P. & Kenney, Carolyn E. Smart Shopping: A Guide to Discount Stores in Utah. LC 94-69844. xxi, 327p. (Orig.). 1995. pap. 11.99 (*0-87579-834-9*, Shadow Mount) Deseret Bk.

Aebi, U. & Engel, J., eds. Cytoskeletal & Extracellular Proteins. (Biophysics Ser.: Vol. 3). (Illus.). 360p. 1989. 171.95 (*0-387-50067-7*) Spr-Verlag.

Aebischer, B. Symplectic Geometry: An Introduction Based on the Seminar in Bern in 1992. (Progress in Mathematics Ser.: No. 124). 256p. 1994. 49.50 (*3-7643-5064-4*); 49.50 (*0-8176-5064-4*) Birkhauser.

***Aebischer-Crettol, Eberhard.** Seelsorge und Suizid: Seelsorge Mit Hinterbliebenen, Die Von einem Suizid Betroffen Wurden. (Europaische Hochschulschriften Ser.: Reihe 23). 580p. 1999. 70.95 (*3-906764-27-3*) P Lang Pubng.

Aebischer, Paul. Mystere D'Adam. 119p. 1964. 9.95 (*0-8288-7496-4*) Fr & Eur.

Aeby, Jacquelyn. Counterfeit Love. large type ed. (Linford Romance Library). 256p. 1993. pap. 16.99 (*0-7089-7455-4*) Ulverscroft.

— Linnet's Folly. large type ed. (Linford Mystery Library). 256p. 1993. pap. 16.99 (*0-7089-7426-0*, Linford) Ulverscroft.

***Aeby, Jacquelyn.** Pipes of Margaree. large type ed. LC 99-42433. (Thorndike Candlelight Romance Ser.). 1999. 19.95 (*0-7862-2199-2*) Thorndike Pr.

AEC Technical Information Center Staff. Analysis of Essential Nuclear Reactor Materials. Rodden, Clement J., ed. LC 64-60035. 1291p. 1964. 40.00 (*0-87079-393-4*, TID-21384) DOE.

— Analysis of Essential Nuclear Reactor Materials. Rodden, Clement J., ed. LC 64-60035. 1291p. 1964. fiche 9.00 (*0-87079-136-2*, TID-21384) DOE.

— Biological Effects of External X & Gamma Radiation, Part 2. Zirkle, Raymond E., ed. (National Nuclear Energy Ser.: Vol. 22C). 487p. 1956. pap. 52.00 (*0-87079-146-X*, TID-5220); fiche 9.00 (*0-87079-147-8*, TID-5220) DOE.

— The Chemistry & Metallurgy of Miscellaneous Materials. Quill, Lawrence L., ed. (National Nuclear Energy Ser.: Div. IV, Vol. 19c). 172p. 1955. 9.00 incl. mic. film (*0-87079-162-1*, TID-5212); pap. 27.00 (*0-87079-161-3*, TID-5212) DOE.

— Determination of the Isotopic Composition of Uranium. Cameron, A. E., ed. (National Nuclear Energy Ser.: Div. I, Vol. 13). 173p. 1950. fiche 9.00 (*0-87079-452-3*, TID-5213) DOE.

— Environment of the Cape Thompson Region, Alaska, 2 vols. Wilimovsky, Norman & Wolfe, John N., eds. LC 66-60018. (AEC Technical Information Center Ser.). 1242p. 1966. pap. 39.25 (*0-87079-196-6*, PNE-481) DOE.

— The Environmental & Ecological Forum, 1970-1971. Kline, A. Burt, Jr., ed. LC 72-600120. 196p. 1972. pap. 27.00 (*0-87079-197-4*, TID-25857); fiche 9.00 (*0-87079-198-2*, TID-25857) DOE.

— Gas Bubble Disease: Proceedings. Fickeisen, D. H. & Schneider, M. J., eds. LC 75-619327. 131p. 1967. pap. 11.00 (*0-87079-023-4*, CONF-741033); fiche 9.00 (*0-87079-213-X*, CONF-741033) DOE.

— Metallurgy of Uranium & Its Alloys. Warner, J. C. et al, eds. (National Nuclear Energy Ser.: Div. IV, Vol. 12). 200p. 1953. 24.95 (*0-87079-273-3*, NNES-IV-12A); fiche 9.00 (*0-87079-453-1*, NNES-IV-12A) DOE.

— Meteorology & Atomic Energy: 1968. Slade, David H., ed. LC 68-60097. 450p. 1968. pap. 19.25 (*0-87079-274-1*, TID-24190); fiche 9.00 (*0-87079-275-X*, TID-24190) DOE.

— Nuclear Power Reactor Instrumentation Systems Handbook, 2 vols. Harrer, Joseph M. & Beckerley, James G., eds. LC 72-600355. fiche 9.00 (*0-87079-299-7*, TID-25952-P1); fiche 9.00 (*0-87079-300-4*, TID-25952-P2) DOE.

— Nuclear Power Reactor Instrumentation Systems Handbook, 2 vols., Vol. 1. Harrer, Joseph M. & Beckerley, James G., eds. LC 72-600355. 313p. 1973. pap. 16.00 (*0-87079-005-6*, TID-25952-P1) DOE.

— Nuclear Power Reactor Instrumentation Systems Handbook, 2 vols., Vol. 2. Harrer, Joseph M. & Beckerley, James G., eds. LC 72-600355. 285p. 1974. pap. 15.00 (*0-87079-144-3*, TID-25952-P2) DOE.

— Physical Mechanisms in Radiation Biology: Proceedings. Wood, Robert W. & Cooper, Raymond D., eds. LC 74-600124. 333p. 1974. pap. 16.25 (*0-685-01481-9*, CONF-721001); fiche 9.00 (*0-87079-303-9*, CONF-721001) DOE.

— Production & Separation of U-233: Collected Papers. Katzin, Leonard I., ed. (National Nuclear Energy Ser.: Div. IV, Vol. 17b). 323p. 1952. pap. 44.50 (*0-87079-383-7*, TID-5223); fiche 9.00 (*0-87079-341-1*, TID-5223) DOE.

— Production & Separation of U-233: Survey. Katzin, Leonard I. & Seaborg, Glenn Theodore, eds. (National Nuclear Energy Ser.: Div. IV, Vol. 17A). 236p. 1951. pap. 36.50 (*0-87079-384-5*, TID-5222); mic. film 9.00 (*0-87079-342-X*, TID-5222) DOE.

— Reactor Shielding Design Manual. Rockwell, Theodore, 3rd, ed. 467p. 1956. 52.00 (*0-87079-338-1*, TID-7004) DOE.

— Selected Measurement Methods for Plutonium & Uranium in the Nuclear Fuel Cycle. 2nd ed. Rodden, Clement J., ed. LC 72-600015. 416p. 1972. pap. 52.00 (*0-87079-354-3*, TID-7029); fiche 9.00 (*0-87079-355-1*, TID-7029) DOE.

— Separation of the Boron Isotopes. Murphy, George M., ed. (National Nuclear Energy Ser.: Div. III, Vol. 5). 459p. 1952. pap. 52.00 (*0-87079-349-7*, TID-5227); fiche 9.00 (*0-87079-350-0*, TID-5227) DOE.

— Symposium on Nuclear Energy & Latin American Development: Proceedings. 164p. 1968. pap. 18.95 (*0-87079-358-6*, PRNC-112); fiche 9.00 (*0-685-73232-0*) DOE.

— A Tropical Rain Forest: A Study of Irradiation & Ecology at El Verde, Puerto Rico, 3 Vols. Odum, Howard T. & Pigeon, Robert F., eds. LC 70-606844. 1684p. 1970. pap. 49.25 (*0-87079-230-X*, TID-24270); fiche 9.00 (*0-87079-340-3*, TID-24270) DOE.

— U. S. Research Reactors. Chastain, Joel W., ed. 76p. 1957. pap. 19.50 (*0-87079-380-2*, TID-7013); fiche 9.00 (*0-87079-483-3*, TID-7013) DOE.

AEC Technical Information Center Staff & Glasstone, Samuel. Public Safety & Underground Nuclear Detonations. 286p. 1971. 36.50 (*0-87079-315-2*, TID-25708) DOE.

AEC Technical Information Center Staff & Jaech, John L. Statistical Methods in Nuclear Material Control. LC 73-600241. 409p. 1973. 18.25 (*0-87079-343-8*, TID-26298); fiche 9.00 (*0-87079-344-6*, TID-26298) DOE.

AEC Technical Information Center Staff & Schaeffer, N. M. Reactor Shielding for Nuclear Engineers. LC 73-600001. 801p. 1973. pap. 28.00 (*0-87079-004-8*, TID-25951); fiche 9.00 (*0-87079-339-X*, TID-25951) DOE.

AEC Technical Information Center Staff & Sesonske, Alexander. Nuclear Power Plant Design Analysis. LC 73-600245. 497p. 1973. pap. 20.25 (*0-87079-009-9*, TID-26241); fiche 9.00 (*0-87079-287-3*, TID-26241) DOE.

AEC Technical Information Center Staff & Van Cleave, Charles. Late Somatic Effects of Ionizing Radiation. LC 68-62106. 315p. 1968. pap. 15.75 (*0-87079-253-9*, TID-24310); fiche 9.00 (*0-87079-254-7*, TID-24310) DOE.

AEC Technical Information Center Staff, et al. Developments in the Centrifuge Separation Project: AEC Technical Information Center. (National Nuclear Energy Ser.: Div. X, Vol. 1). 269p. 1951. 36.50 (*0-87079-179-6*, TID-5230); mic. film 10.00 (*0-87079-180-X*, TID-5230) DOE.

— Liquid Thermal Diffusion. Abelson, Phillip H., ed. (National Nuclear Energy Ser.: Div. IX, Vol. 1). 258p. 1958. 36.50 (*0-87079-259-8*, TID-5229); mic. film 9.00 (*0-87079-260-1*, TID-5229) DOE.

— Radiation Monitoring: A Programmed Instruction Book. 287p. 1967. pap. 36.50 (*0-87079-322-5*, EDM-123) DOE.

— Uranium Technology. (National Nuclear Energy Ser.: Div. VII, Vol. 2A). 238p. 1951. pap. 36.50 (*0-87079-227-X*, TID-5231); fiche 9.00 (*0-87079-463-9*, TID-5231) DOE.

— Vacuum Problems & Techniques. (National Nuclear Energy Ser.: Division I, Vol. 11). 289p. 1950. 36.50 (*0-87079-356-X*, TID-5210); fiche 9.00 (*0-87079-357-8*, TID-5210) DOE.

AEC Technical Information Center Staff, jt. auth. see Argonne National Laboratory Staff.

AEC Technical Information Center Staff, jt. auth. see Hutchison, Clyde A.

AEC Technical Information Center Staff, jt. auth. see Saenger, Eugene L.

AECT, Evaluation of Media Programs Committee. Evaluating Media Programs: District & School. (Illus.). 77p. 1980. student ed. 8.95 (*0-89240-039-0*) Assn Ed Comm Tech.

AECT Intellectual Freedom Commitee. Media, the Learner & Intellectual Freedom: A Handbook. (Orig.). 1979. pap. 8.95 (*0-89240-034-X*) Assn Ed Comm Tech.

AECT Program Standards Committee Task Force & Hitchens, Howard B. College Learning Resources Programs. 1977. pap. 7.95 (*0-89240-005-6*) Assn Ed Comm Tech.

AEDC Staff. Compensation & Benefits Survey, 1992. 48p. 1992. pap. text 75.00 (*0-9616567-3-5*) Amer Econ Dev Council.

Aedo, Carlos. Revision of Geranium Subgenus Erodioidea (Geraniaceae) (Systematic Botany Monographs: Vol. 49). 104p. 1996. pap. 14.00 (*0-912861-49-5*) Am Soc Plant.

Aedo, Cristian & Larranaga, Osvaldo, eds. Social Service Delivery Systems: An Agenda for Reform. 160p. (Orig.). 1994. pap. text 18.50 (*0-940602-76-8*) IADB.

AEE Staff. Women's Voices in Experiential Education. Warren, Karen J., ed. LC 96-76627. 320p. (Orig.). 1996. pap. text 23.95 (*0-7872-2059-0*) Kendall-Hunt.

AEE World Energy Engineering Congress Staff. Energy Engineering Technology: Proceedings of the AEE World Energy Engineering Congress, 1st. 45.00 (*0-915586-15-0*) Fairmont Pr.

***Aefksy, Fern.** Making Decisions about Diverse Learners: A Guide for Educators. LC 00-22350. 2000. write for info. (*1-883001-94-3*) Eye On Educ.

Aefsky, Fern. Inclusion Confusion: A Guide to Educating Students with Exceptional Needs. LC 95-16609. 80p. 1995. 39.95 (*0-8039-6283-5*); pap. 16.95 (*0-8039-6284-3*) Corwin Pr.

Aegean Institute of the Law of the Sea & Maritime, jt. auth. see Kariotis, Theodore C.

Aegerter, Roger. Golf Courses of Iowa. (Orig.). 1988. pap. 12.95 (*0-9622074-0-3*) R Aegerter.

— Golf Courses of Iowa. (Illus.). 232p. (Orig.). 1988. 12.95 (*0-317-93307-8*); pap. 11.95 (*0-317-93308-6*) R Aegerter.

— Golf Courses of Iowa. rev. ed. (Orig.). 1992. pap. 15.95 (*0-9622074-1-1*) R Aegerter.

Aegidius. On Ecclesiastical Power: De Ecclesiastica Potestate. Monahan, Arthur, tr. from LAT. LC 89-35825. (Texts & Studies in Religion: Vol. 41). 340p. 1990. lib. bdg. 99.95 (*0-88946-830-3*) E Mellen.

Aehlert, Barbara. ACLS: Quick Review Study Cards. 1994. pap. 18.00 (*0-8151-0343-3*) Mosby Inc.

— ACLS: Quick Review Study Guide. (Illus.). 320p. (C). (gr. 13). 1993. pap. text 13.95 (*0-8151-0007-8*) Mosby Inc.

— Aehlert's EMT-Basic Study Guide. LC 97-38043. (Illus.). 380p. 1997. 14.95 (*0-683-30217-5*) Lppncott W & W.

— ECG's Made Easy. (Illus.). teacher ed. write for info. (*0-8151-1380-3*); suppl. ed. write for info. (*0-8151-0092-2*) Mosby Inc.

— ECG's Made Easy. (Illus.). 272p. (C). (gr. 13). 1995. pap. text, teacher ed. 28.00 (*0-8151-0093-0*, 26655) Mosby Inc.

— ECGs Made Easy: With Pocket Reference. (Illus.). 400p. 1995. spiral bd. 31.00 (*0-8151-0094-9*, 26654) Mosby Inc.

— Pediatric Advanced Life Support. rev. ed. (Illus.). 240p. (C). (gr. 13). 1996. pap. text, student ed. 13.00 (*0-8151-1251-3*, 29598) Mosby Inc.

Aehlert, Barbara, et al. Aehlert's EMT-Basic Instructor's Kit. LC 98-6576. 1998. 39.95 (*0-683-30581-6*) Lppncott W & W.

Aein, Joseph M. An Optical Signal Processing Model for the Interferometric Fiber Optic Gyro Vol. 1: Deterministic Model. LC 95-13803. 62p. 1995. pap. text 7.50 (*0-8330-1642-3*, MR-482/1-ARPA) Rand Corp.

Aejmelaeus & Schmidt. The Traditional Prayer in the Psalms - & Literarische Studien zur Josephsgeschichte. (Beiheft zur Zeitschrift fuer die Alttestamentliche Wissenschaft Ser.: Vol. 167). vi, 310p. (C). 1986. lib. bdg. 126.95 (*3-11-010480-6*) De Gruyter.

Aelfric. Aelfric's Catholic Homilies: The Second Series. Godden, Malcolm, ed. (Series II SS 5: Series II). (Illus.). 486p. 1980. 58.00 (*0-19-722405-9*) OUP.

— Colloquy. Garmonsway, G. N., ed. (Old English Ser.). 1966. pap. text 5.95 (*0-89197-563-2*) Irvington.

— Lives of Three English Saints. Needham, G. I., ed. (Old English Ser.). 1966. pap. text 9.95 (*0-89197-564-0*) Irvington.

— A Testimonie of Antique. LC 73-36208. (English Experience Ser.: No. 214). 1970. reprint ed. 35.00 (*90-221-0214-9*) Walter J Johnson.

Aelian & Wilson, Nigel G. Historical Miscellany. Wilson, N. G., ed. & tr. by. LC 96-38637. (Loeb Classical Library). 1997. Price not set. incl. audio (*0-674-99535-X*) Belknap Pr.

Aelian, Claudius. On the Characteristics of Animals, 3 vols., 1. (Loeb Classical Library: No. 446, 448, 449). 390p. 1958. 19.95 (*0-674-99491-4*) HUP.

— On the Characteristics of Animals, 3 vols., 2. (Loeb Classical Library: No. 446, 448, 449). 1958. 19.95 (*0-674-99493-0*) HUP.

— On the Characteristics of Animals, 3 vols., Vol. 3. (Loeb Classical Library: No. 449). 452p. 1959. 19.95 (*0-674-99494-9*) HUP.

Aeling, John L., jt. ed. see Fitzpatrick, James E.

Aellen, Richard. Crux. 400p. 1991. mass mkt. 4.95 (*0-380-71200-8*, Avon Bks) Morrow Avon.

Aelly, ed. see Loti.

Aelred of Rievaulx. Aelred of Rievaulx, Historical Works. Freeland, Jane P. & Dutton, Marsha, eds. LC 93-46002. (Cistercian Fathers Ser.: No. 56). 1994. pap. write for info. (*0-87907-288-1*) Cistercian Pubns.

— Aelred of Rievaulx, Historical Works. Dutton, Marsha, ed. Freeland, Jane P., tr. LC 93-46002. (Cistercian Fathers Ser.: No. 56). 1997. write for info. (*0-87907-256-3*) Cistercian Pubns.

— The Mirror of Charity. Connor, Elizabeth, tr. from LAT. (Fathers Ser.: No. 17).Tr. of Speculum Caritatis. 352p. 1990. pap. 14.95 (*0-87907-717-4*) Cistercian Pubns.

— St. Ninian. MacDonald, Iain, ed. (Celtic Studies Ser.). 62p. 1994. pap. 4.95 (*0-86315-167-1*) Dufour.

— Spiritual Friendship. (Cistercian Fathers Ser.: No. 5). 144p. 1974. pap. 7.95 (*0-87907-705-0*) Cistercian Pubns.

— Treatises & the Pastoral Prayer. pap. 5.00 (*0-87907-902-9*) Cistercian Pubns.

Aemilianus, Palladius R. Obra de Agricultura, Traducida y Comentada en 1385 por Ferrer Sayol. Capuano, Thomas M., ed. (Dialect Ser.: No. 10). xxviii, 282p. 1990. 20.00 (*0-940639-45-9*) Hispanic Seminary.

Aemmer, Gail & Pyne, Lynette. Community Helpers. (Home Workbooks Ser.). (Illus.). 64p. (Orig.). (J). (ps-1). 1996. pap., wbk. ed. 2.49 (*0-88724-367-3*, CD-6864) Carson-Dellos.

— Manners. (Home Workbooks Ser.). (Illus.). 64p. (Orig.). (J). (ps-1). 1996. pap., wbk. ed. 2.49 (*0-88724-368-1*, CD-6865) Carson-Dellos.

Aendenroomer, Ton. Weld Pool Oscillation for Penetration Sensing & Control. (Illus.). 151p. (Orig.). 1996. pap. 82.50 (*90-407-1229-8*, Pub. by Delft U Pr) Coronet Bks.

Aeneas Tacticus. Military Essays. (Loeb Classical Library: No. 156). 19.95 (*0-674-99172-9*) HUP.

Aengus. Martyrology of St. Aengus. 1982. pap. 12.50 (*0-89981-057-8*) Eastern Orthodox.

Aeon Incorporated Staff, jt. auth. see Fine, Deborah.

Aepfelbacher, Franz C., jt. ed. see Messerli, Franz H.

Aepinus, Franz U. Aepinus's Essay on the Theory of Electricity & Magnetism: Introductory Monograph & Notes by R. W. Home. LC 78-10105. 528p. 1979. reprint ed. pap. 163.70 (*0-7837-9324-3*, 206006400004) Bks Demand.

Aepli, Martine. Korea. (Illus.). 139p. 1990. 49.50 (*0-7103-0367-X*, A4306) Routledge.

Aeppli, Dorothee, tr. see Polya, George & Szego, Gabor.

Aeppli, Ernest. Les Reves et Leur Interpretation. 308p. 1985. 19.95 (*2-920083-20-1*) Edns Roseau.

Aeppli, Felix. The Rolling Stones, 1962-1995: The Ultimate Guide. 610p. 1996. 145.00 (*0-907872-26-3*) Big Nickel.

Aeppli, Willi. Biography & Waldorf Education. Ritscher, Angelika V., tr. from GER.Tr. of Aus der Unterrichtspraxis an einer Rudolf Steiner Schule. 1987. pap. 3.50 (*0-88010-165-2*) Anthroposophic.

— Teacher, Child & Waldorf Education. Ritscher, Angelika V., tr. from GER.Tr. of Aus der Unterrichtspraxis an einer Rudolf Steiner Schule. 19p. 1987. pap. 3.50 (*0-88010-166-0*) Anthroposophic.

Aercke, Kristiaan, ed. Women Writing in Dutch. LC 93-37518. (Women Writers of the World Ser.: Vol. 1). 776p. 1994. text 35.00 (*0-8153-0231-2*) Garland.

Aercke, Kristiaan P. Gods of Play: Baroque Festive Performances As Rhetorical Discourse. LC 93-31052. (SUNY Series, The Margins of Literature). 284p. (C). 1994. text 64.50 (*0-7914-2049-3*); pap. text 21.95 (*0-7914-2050-7*) State U NY Pr.

Aerde, J. Van, see Van Aerde, J.

Aereboe, Friedrich. Der Einfluss des Krieges Auf die Landwirtschaftliche Produktion in Deutschland. (Wirtschafts-Und Sozialgeschichte des Weltkrieges (Osterreichische Und Ungarische Serie)). (GER.). 1927. 100.00 (*0-317-27455-4*) Elliots Bks.

Aerenson, Benjie. Lighting up the Two-Year Old. LC 99-215186. 1998. pap. 5.25 (*0-8222-1648-5*) Dramatists Play.

— The Possum Play: A Play in Two Acts LC 98-213913. 96 p. 1998. write for info. (*0-573-62436-4*) S French Trade.

Aerial Photography Services, Inc. Staff. Southern Sayin' 2.95 (*0-936672-30-7*) Aerial Photo.

***Aerni, April Laskey.** Valuing Us All: Feminist Pedagogy & Economics. LC 99-6459. 272p. (C). 1999. text 59.50 (*0-472-09704-0*, 09704); pap. text 23.95 (*0-472-06704-4*, 06704) U of Mich Pr.

Aero Medical Center Staff, tr. see Surgeon General, USAF Staff.

Aero Products Research, Inc., Department of Aviati. Flight Training Manual. LC 80-70568. 1981. pap. 9.95 (*0-912682-28-0*) Aero Products.

— Manual of Flight: Private & Commercial Pilot. 332p. 1973. pap. 14.95 (*0-685-62814-0*) Aero Products.

Aero Products Research, Inc., Industries Division. FCC Rules & Regulations 1977: Part 95, Citizens Radio Service. 1977. pap. 2.98 (*0-912682-16-7*) Aero Products.

— Official CB Crossword Puzzles for Big Dummy's. (Illus.). (J). (gr. 8 up). 1977. pap. 1.98 (*0-912682-18-3*) Aero Products.

Aero Products Research, Inc., Industries Division, ed. The Complete CB Dictionary. 1977. pap. 2.98 (*0-912682-17-5*) Aero Products.

Aero, Rita. Fodor's Walt Disney World for Adults: The Original Guide for Grown-Ups. 2nd rev. ed. (Illus.). 272p. 1995. pap. 14.00 (*0-679-03081-6*) Fodors Travel.

***Aero, Rita.** Rita Aeros Walt Disney World the Essential Guide to Amazing Vacat. (Illus.). 256p. 2000. pap. 19.95 (*0-312-25411-3*) St Martin.

Aero, Rita & Weiner, Elliot. The Brain Game: Twenty-Seven Fun-to Take Aptitude Tests. LC 83-61196. 175p. 1983. pap. 17.95 (*0-688-01923-4*, Quil) HarperTrade.

— The Mind Test. LC 81-2341. (Illus.). 192p. (Orig.). 1981. pap. 17.95 (*0-688-00401-6*, Quil) HarperTrade.

Aeronautical Institute of Sweden Staff, ed. see Humphreys, D. A.

Aerosmith Staff & Davis, Stephen. Walk This Way: The Autobiography of Aerosmith. (Illus.). 596p. 1999. mass mkt. 7.99 (*0-380-79531-0*, Avon Bks) Morrow Avon.

AeroSoft, Inc. Staff. GASPEx User Manual. 650p. (Orig.). 1997. pap. 110.00 (*0-9652780-1-8*) Aerosoft.

— GUST Version 1 User's Manual. 274p. 1998. pap. 50.00 (*0-9652780-2-6*) Aerosoft.

— GUST Version 1 User's Manual. 226p. 1998. pap. 50.00 (*0-9652780-3-4*) Aerosoft.

— Sense User's Manual. 176p. 1998. pap. 50.00 (*0-9652780-4-2*) Aerosoft.

Aerosol Measurement Workshop Staff. Aerosol Measurement. Lundgren, Dale A. et al, eds. LC 78-15424. (Illus.). 740p. reprint ed. pap. 200.00 (*0-8357-6719-1*, 203535400095) Bks Demand.

***Aerospace & Electronic Systems Society Staff.** 2000 IEEE/AIAA 19th Digital Avionics Systems Conference. Institute of Electrical & Electronics Engineers, Inc. Staff, ed. 2000p. 2000. pap. text. write for info. (*0-7803-6395-7*) IEEE Standards.

Aerospace Abstracts Database Staff. Physoelectric Transducers: Surface Acoustic Wave Devices. 1996. 85.00 (*0-614-18490-8*, 135P27) Info Gatekeepers.

Aerospace Corp. & IES Staffs, compiled by. 9th Aerospace Testing Seminar Proceedings, October, 1985. 300p. 1985. pap. 100.00 (*0-915414-87-2*) IEST.

Aerospace Daily Staff, et al. The Aviation & Aerospace Almanac, 1998. 1000p. 1997. pap. 75.00 (*0-07-006363-X*) McGraw.

Aerospace Industries Association Staff. Aerospace Facts & Figures, 1993-1994. 1993. pap. 15.00 (*0-685-70339-8*, AFF-94) AIAA.

Aerospace Publishing Ltd. Staff. World Air Power Journal, Vol. 9. Donald, David & Lake, Jon, eds. (Illus.). 160p. 1992. 24.95 (*1-880588-07-2*) AIRtime Pub.

Aerospace Testing Seminar Staff. Proceedings of Aerospace Testing Seminar, 2nd, Los Angeles, California, 17-18 March 1975. LC 62-38584. 340p. reprint ed. pap. 105.40 (*0-7837-1300-2*, 204144100020) Bks Demand.

— Proceedings of the Aerospace Testing Seminar, 6th, Los Angeles, California, 11-13 March, 1981. LC 62-38584. 261p. reprint ed. pap. 81.00 (*0-7837-1301-0*, 204144200020) Bks Demand.

— Proceedings of the Aerospace Testing Seminar, 7th, Los Angeles, California, 13-15 October 1982. LC 62-38584. 185p. reprint ed. pap. 57.40 (*0-7837-1302-9*, 204144300020) Bks Demand.

Aerospatiale Staff. International Dictionary of Aerospace Abbreviations. (ARN, ENG, FRE & GER.). 298p. 1987. pap. 65.00 (*2-85608-026-X*) IBD Ltd.

Aers, D., ed. see Milton, John.

Aers, David. Community, Gender & Individual Identity: English Writing, 1360-1430. 256p. 1989. 49.95 (*0-415-01378-X*) Routledge.

***Aers, David.** Faith, Ethics & Church: Writing in England, 1360-1409. LC 99-45714. 192p. 2000. 72.00 (*0-85991-561-1*, DS Brewer) Boydell & Brewer.

Aers, David, ed. Culture & History, 1350-1600: Essays on English Communities, Identities & Writing. 220p. (C). 1992. text 34.95 (*0-8143-2415-0*); pap. text 17.95 (*0-8143-2416-9*) Wayne St U Pr.

***Aers, David, ed.** Medieval Literature & Historical Inquiry: Essays in Honour of Derek Pearsall. LC 99-45485. 240p. 2000. 75.00 (*0-85991-555-7*, DS Brewer) Boydell & Brewer.

Aers, David & Staley, Lynn. The Powers of the Holy: Religion, Politics, & Gender in Late Medieval English Culture. LC 95-25309. 1996. 55.00 (*0-271-01541-1*); pap. 19.95 (*0-271-01542-X*) Pa St U Pr.

Aerssens, Jeroen. Molecular Analysis of a Chromosomal Translocation Breakpoint on the Short Arm of Chromosome 12. (Acta Biomedica Lovaniensia Ser.: No. 130). (Illus.). 111p. (Orig.). 1996. pap. 39.50 (*90-6186-743-6*, Pub. by Leuven Univ) Coronet Bks.

Aersten, Jan A. & Speer, Andreas, eds. Individuum und Individualitaet im Mittelalter. (Miscellanea Mediaevalia Ser.: Band 24). (GER.). xxiv, 877p. (C). 1995. lib. bdg. 415.40 (*3-11-014892-7*) De Gruyter.

Aerstin, F. & Street, G. Applied Chemical Process Design. LC 78-9104. (Illus.). 312p. (C). 1978. 59.50 (*0-306-31088-0*, Plenum Trade) Perseus Pubng.

***Aerts, Diederik.** Science, Technology & Social Change: The Orange Book of 'Einstein Meets Magritte' LC 99-29567. (Einstein Meets Magritte Ser.). 324p. 1999. 256.00 (*0-7923-5759-0*) Kluwer Academic.

***Aerts, Diederik & Pykacz, Jaroslaw.** Quantum Structures & the Nature of Reality: The Indigo Book of 'Einstein Meets Magritte' LC 99-27066. (Einstein Meets Magritte Ser.). 260p. 1999. 126.00 (*0-7923-5763-9*) Kluwer Academic.

***Aerts, Diederik, et al.** Einstein Meets Magritte: An Interdisciplinary Reflection: The White Book of Einstein Meets Magritte. LC 99-28097. 292p. 1999. 138.00 (*0-7923-5757-4*) Kluwer Academic.

— Science & Art: The Red Book of 'Einstein Meets Margritte' LC 99-27059. (Einstein Meets Magritte Ser.). 288p. 1999. 138.00 (*0-7923-5758-2*) Kluwer Academic.

— A World in Transition: Humankind & Nature. LC 99-29564. (Einstein Meets Magritte Ser.). 1999. 147.00 (*0-7923-5761-2*) Kluwer Academic.

— World Views & the Problem of Synthesis: The Yellow Book of 'Einstein Meets Magritte' LC 99-29566. (Einstein Meets Magritte Ser.). 392p. 1999. 189.00 (*0-7923-5760-4*) Kluwer Academic.

Aerts, Diederik, et al. Worldviews: From Fragmentation Towards Integration. LC 95-189267. 80p. 1994. pap. 12.00 (*90-5487-069-9*, Pub. by VUB Univ Pr) Paul & Co Pubs.

Aerts, E. Economic Planning in the Post-1945 Period: Proceedings of the Tenth International Economic History Congress, Leuven, Belgium, August 1990. Milward, Alan S., ed. (Studies in Social & Economic History: No. 7). 110p. (Orig.). 1990. pap. 32.50 (*90-6186-379-1*, Pub. by Leuven Univ) Coronet Bks.

Aerts, E., et al, eds. Liberalism & Paternalism in the 19th Century: Proceedings of the Tenth International Economic History Congress, Leuven, Belgium, August 1990. (Studies in Social & Economic History: No. 17). 137p. (Orig.). 1990. pap. 32.50 (*90-6186-389-9*, Pub. by Leuven Univ) Coronet Bks.

— Models of Regional Economies in Antiquity & the Middle Ages to the 11th Century: Proceedings of the 10th International Economic History Congress, Leuven, Belgium, August 1990. (Studies in Social & Economic History: No. 14). 95p. (Orig.). 1990. pap. 32.50 (*90-6186-386-4*, Pub. by Leuven Univ) Coronet Bks.

— Production, Marketing & Consumpton of Alcoholic Beverages since the Late Middle Ages: Proceedings of the Tenth International Economic History Congress, Leuven, Belgium, August 1990. (Studies in Social & Economic History: No. 18). 148p. (Orig.). 1990. pap. 32.50 (*90-6186-390-2*, Pub. by Leuven Univ) Coronet Bks.

— Structures & Dynamics of Agricultural Exploitations: Ownership, Occupation, Investment, Credit, & Markets: Proceedings of the Tenth International Economic History Congress, Leuven, Belgium, August 1990. (Studies in Social & Economic History: No. 5). 143p. (Orig.). 1990. pap. 32.50 (*90-6186-377-5*, Pub. by Leuven Univ) Coronet Bks.

— Women in the Labour Force - Comparative Studies on Labour Market & Organization of Work since the 18th Century: Proceedings of the Tenth International Economic History Congress, Leuven, Belgium, August 1990. (Studies in Social & Economic History: No. 11). 145p. (Orig.). 1990. pap. 32.50 (*90-6186-383-X*, Pub. by Leuven Univ) Coronet Bks.

Aerts, E. & Clark, P., eds. Metropolitan Cities & Their Hinterlands in Early Modern Europe: Proceedings of the 10th International Economic History Congress, Leuven, Belgium, August 1990. (Studies in Social & Economic History: No. 9). 100p. (Orig.). 1990. pap. 32.50 (*90-6186-381-3*, Pub. by Leuven Univ) Coronet Bks.

Aerts, E. & Crouzet, F., eds. Economic Effects of the French Revolutionary & Napoleonic Wars: Proceedings of the Tenth International Economic History Congress, Leuven, Belgium, August 1990. (Studies in Social & Economic History: No. 4). 135p. (Orig.). 1990. pap. 32.50 (*90-6186-376-7*, Pub. by Leuven Univ) Coronet Bks.

Aerts, E. & Thompson, F., eds. Ethnic Minority Groups in Towns & Countryside & Their Effects on Economic Development (1850-1940) Proceedings of the Tenth International Economic History Congress, Leuven, Belgium, August 1990. (Studies in Economic & Social History: No. 8). 137p. (Orig.). 1990. pap. 32.50 (*90-6186-380-5*, Pub. by Leuven Univ) Coronet Bks.

Aerts, E. & Tsubouchi, Y., eds. Economic & Demographic Development in Rice Producing Societies: Some Aspects of East-Asian Economic History, 1500-1900: Proceedings of the Tenth International Economic History Congress, Leuven, Belgium, August 1990. (Studies in Social & Economic History: No. 6). 161p. (Orig.). 1990. pap. 32.50 (*90-6186-378-3*, Pub. by Leuven Univ) Coronet Bks.

Aerts, E. & Valerio, N., eds. Growth & Stagnation in the Mediterranean World in the 19th & 20th Centuries: Proceedings of the Tenth International Economic History Congress, Leuven, Belgium, August 1990. (Studies in Social & Economic History: No. 13). 136p. (Orig.). 1990. pap. 32.50 (*90-6186-385-6*, Pub. by Leuven Univ) Coronet Bks.

Aerts, E. & Van der Wee, H., eds. Recent Doctoral Research in Economic History: Proceedings of the Tenth International Economic History Congress, Leuven, Belgium, August 1990. (Studies in Social & Economic History: No. 21). 204p. (Orig.). 1990. pap. 49.50 (*90-6186-393-7*, Pub. by Leuven Univ) Coronet Bks.

Aerts, E., jt. ed. see Van der Wee, H.

Aerts, R. & Heil, G. W., eds. Heathlands: Patterns & Processes in a Changing Environment. LC 92-41645. (Geobotany Ser.: Vol. 20). 238p. (C). 1993. text 200.50 (*0-7923-2094-8*) Kluwer Academic.

Aerts, W. J., et al, eds. Scholia: Studia ad Criticam. vi, 168p. 1985. pap. 35.00 (*90-6980-001-2*, Pub. by Egbert Forsten) Hod1der & Stoughton.

Aerts, W. J. & Gosman, M., eds. Exemplum et Similitudo: Alexander the Great & Other Heroes as Points of Reference in Medieval Literature. 191p. (Orig.). 1988. pap. 32.00 (*90-6980-018-7*, Pub. by Egbert Forsten) Hod1der & Stoughton.

Aerts, W. J., et al. Vincent of Beauvais & Alexander the Great. (Mediaevalia Groningana Ser.: Vol. VII). 187p. (Orig.). 1986. pap. 35.00 (*90-6980-009-8*, Pub. by Egbert Forsten) Hod1der & Stoughton.

Aerts, Willem J., ed. Michaelis Pselli: Historia Syntomos. (Corpus Fontium Historiae Byzantinae Ser.: Berolinensis Vol. XXX). xxx, 237p. (C). 1990. lib. bdg. 152.35 (*3-11-011219-1*) De Gruyter.

Aertsen, A. M., ed. Brain Theory: Spatio-Temporal Aspects of Brain Function. LC 93-15872. (Illus.). 318p. 1993. 169.50 (*0-444-89839-5*) Elsevier.

Aertsen, Ad & Braitenberg, Valentino. Brain Theory: Biological Basis & Computational Principles. LC 96-25113. 308p. 1996. 166.50 (*0-444-82046-9*) Elsevier.

Aertsen, Ad & Braitenberg, Valentino, eds. Information Processing in the Cortex: Experiments & Theory. LC 92-19742. (Illus.). 489p. 1992. 181.00 (*0-387-55391-6*) Spr-Verlag.

Aertsen, Ed H. & Bremmer, Rolf H., Jr., eds. Companion to Old English Poetry. LC 95-101228. 250p. (Orig.). 1993. pap. text 23.50 (*90-5383-116-9*, Pub. by VU Univ Pr) Paul & Co Pubs.

Aertsen, H. & Veldhoen, N. H., eds. Companion to Early Middle English Literature. 104p. 1993. pap. 15.00 (*90-6256-632-4*, Pub. by VU Univ Pr) Paul & Co Pubs.

Aertsen, H., jt. ed. see Veldhoen, N. H.

Aertsen, Henk & Jeffers, Robert J., eds. Historical Linguistics 1989: Papers from the 9th International Conference on Historical Linguistics, New Brunswick, 14-18 August 1989. LC 93-26004. (Current Issues in Linguistic Theory Ser.: No. 106). xviii, 538p. 1993. 115.00 (*1-55619-560-5*) J Benjamins Pubng Co.

Aertsen, Henk & MacDonald, Alasdair A., eds. Companion to Middle English Romance. 216p. 1991. pap. 34.95 (*90-6256-899-8*, Pub. by VU Univ Pr) Paul & Co Pubs.

Aertsen, Henk & Todd, Richard, eds. Chicago - Amsterdam: A Man of Two Cities, Essays in Memory of August J. Fry. 220p. 1997. pap. 22.50 (*90-5383-474-5*, Pub. by VUB Univ Pr) Paul & Co Pubs.

Aertsen, Jan A. Medieval Philosophy & the Transcendentals: The Case of Thomas Aquinas. LC 96-5485. (Studien und Texte zur Geistesgeschichte des Mittelalters Ser.: No. 52). x, 468p. 1996. 161.00 (*90-04-10585-9*) Brill Academic Pubs.

Aertssen, Kristen. Count on Me. (Count Me in Bks.: Bk. 4). (Illus.). 24p. (Orig.). (J). (ps-1). 1994. pap. 4.95 (*1-55037-362-5*, Pub. by Annick) Firefly Bks Ltd.

Aeschines. Aeschines Against Ctesiphon: On the Crown. Connor, W. R. & Richardson, Rufus B., eds. LC 78-18596. (Greek Texts & Commentaries Ser.). (ENG & GRE., Illus.). 1979. reprint ed. lib. bdg. 30.95 (*0-405-11437-0*) Ayer.

— Aeschinis Orationes. E Codicibus Partim Nunc Primum Excussis, Edidit Scholia ex Parteinedita, Adiecit Ferdinandus Schultz. LC 72-7905. (Greek History Ser.). (GRE & LAT.). 1973. reprint ed. 31.95 (*0-405-04776-2*) Ayer.

— Discours sur L'Ambasade. Connor, W. R., ed. LC 78-18585. (Greek Texts & Commentaries Ser.). (FRE & GRE.). 1979. reprint ed. lib. bdg. 19.95 (*0-405-11427-3*) Ayer.

Aeschliman, Gordon, ed. see Canales, Isaac.

Aeschliman, Gordon, ed. see Carney, Clandion.

Aeschliman, Gordon, ed. see Fisher, Mary.

Aeschliman, Gordon, ed. see Glasser, Arthur F.

Aeschliman, Gordon, ed. see Harrison, Dan.

Aeschliman, Gordon, ed. see Jayaprakash, Eva & Jayaprakash, Joshi.

Aeschliman, Gordon, ed. see Shelton, Chuck.

Aeschliman, Gordon, ed. see Truman, Bryan.

Aeschliman, Gordon, ed. see Webb, Jana.

Aeschliman, Michael D. The Restitution of Man: C. S. Lewis & the Case Against Scientism. rev. ed. LC 99-195728. 128p. 1998. pap. 12.00 (*0-8028-4491-X*) Eerdmans.

Aeschlimann, E. Dictionnaire des Miniaturistes du Moyen Age de la Renaissance. 2nd ed. D'Ancona, P., ed. (FRE.). 1972. 140.00 (*0-8115-0032-2*) Periodicals Srv.

Aeschylus. Aeschylus: Plays One. Raphael, Frederic & McLeish, Kenneth, trs. (Methuen World Dramatists Ser.). 153p. (Orig.). (C). 1991. pap. 14.95 (*0-413-65190-8*, A0584, Methuen Drama) Methn.

Aeschylus. Aeschylus: Plays Two. Raphael, Frederic & McLeish, Kenneth, trs. 129p. (C). 1991. pap. 9.95 (*0-413-65480-X*, A0595, Methuen Drama) Methn.

— Aeschylus: The Persians. Hall, Edith, ed. & tr. by. from GRE. (Classical Texts Ser.). 201p. 1996. 59.99 (*0-85668-596-8*, Pub. by Aris & Phillips); pap. 28.00 (*0-85668-597-6*, Pub. by Aris & Phillips) David Brown.

— Aeschylus - Index Analyticus Graecitatis Aeschyleae. Edinger, H. G., ed. (Alpha-Omega, Reihe A Ser.: Bd. II). (GER.). v, 474p. 1981. 120.00 (*3-487-06978-4*) G Olms Pubs.

— Aeschylus One: Oresteia, Agamemnon, the Libation Bearers, the Eumenides. Lattimore, Richmond, tr. & intro. by. LC 53-9655. 180p. 1969. pap. text 9.00 (*0-226-30778-6*, P306) U Ch Pr.

— Aeschylus Seven Against Thebes. Meagher, Robert E. tr. from GRE. xviii, 62p. (Orig.). 1996. pap. 8.00 (*0-86516-337-5*) Bolchazy-Carducci.

— Aeschylus Two; Four Tragedies: Prometheus Bound, Seven Against Thebes, the Persians, the Suppliant Maidens. Grene, David, ed. & tr. by. Lattimore, Richard, ed. Benardete, Seth G., tr. LC 56-11262. 1997. pap. text 6.95 (*0-226-30779-4*, P307) U Ch Pr.

— Agamemnon, 3 vols. Fraenkel, Eduard, ed. (Illus.). 1,070p. 1950. text 185.00 (*0-19-814101-7*) OUP.

— Agamemnon: A Play by Aeschylus - Translated from the Greek into English with Introduction, Notes, & Synopsis. unabridged ed. Rubenstein, Howard, tr. from GEC. LC 96-95453. 200p. (Orig.). 1998. pap. 19.95 (*0-9638886-4-1*) Granite Hills Pr.

— Agamemnon: Being of the House of Atreus. Landes, William-Alan, ed. & pref. by. 40p. 1995. pap. 7.00 (*0-88734-288-4*) Players Pr.

Aeschylus. Choephori. 456p. 1988. pap. text 30.00 (*0-19-872134-X*) OUP.

Aeschylus. The Choephoroe. unabridged ed. Landes, William-Alan, ed. LC 97-36883. 55p. 1997. pap. 7.00 (*0-88734-771-1*) Players Pr.

— The Eumenides. Landes, William-Alan, ed. LC 97-48796. 55p. 1998. pap. 7.00 (*0-88734-810-6*) Players Pr.

— Eumenides. Sommerstein, Alan H., ed. (Cambridge Greek & Latin Classics Ser.). 320p. (C). 1989. text 65.00 (*0-521-24084-0*); pap. text 24.95 (*0-521-28430-9*) Cambridge U Pr.

— The House of Atreus: Adapted from the Oresteia by John Lewin. LC 66-27418. (Minnesota Drama Editions Ser.: 2). 117p. reprint ed. pap. 36.30 (*0-608-14690-0*, 205583400039) Bks Demand.

— The Oresteia. Lloyd-Jones, Hugh, tr. LC 93-15929. 1994. 15.95 (*0-520-08328-8*, Pub. by U CA Pr) Cal Prin Full Svc.

— Oresteia. Meineck, Peter, tr. from GRE. & notes by. LC 98-37825. (HPC Classics Ser.). 288p. (C). 1998. pap. 8.95 (*0-87220-390-5*); lib. bdg. 32.95 (*0-87220-391-3*) Hackett Pub.

— The Oresteia, 2 vols., Set. 2nd ed. Thomson, G., ed. LC 74-489. 277p. 1966. lib. bdg. 98.50 (*0-317-54488-8*, Pub. by AM Hakkert) Coronet Bks.

— The Oresteia: Agamemnon, the Libation Bearers, the Eumenides. Fagles, Robert, tr. (Classics Ser.). 352p. 1984. pap. 9.95 (*0-14-044333-9*, Penguin Classics) Viking Penguin.

— The Oresteia Trilogy: Agamemnon, the Libation - Bearers & the Furies. unabridged ed. Morshead, E. D., tr. LC 96-13715. (Thrift Editions Ser.). 160p. 1996. reprint ed. pap. text 1.50 (*0-486-29242-8*) Dover.

— The Oresteian Trilogy. Vellacott, Philip, tr. Incl. Agamemnon. 1956. pap. Choephori. 1956. pap. Eumenides. (YA). (gr. 9 up). 1956. pap. (Classics Ser.). 208p. (Orig.). (YA). (gr. 9 up). 1956. Set pap. 9.95 (*0-14-044067-4*, Penguin Classics) Viking Penguin.

— The Persians. unabridged ed. Landes, William-Alan, ed. Potter, Robert, tr. from GRE. LC 98-2709. 55p. (Orig.). 1998. pap. 7.00 (*0-88734-779-7*) Players Pr.

— The Persians/Parsian: Persian Translation. Rouhani, Fu'ad, tr. LC 98-3406. (Illus.). 72p. 1999. pap. 10.00 (*0-936347-85-6*) IBEX.

— Prometheus Bound. Browning, Elizabeth Barrett, tr. from GRE. LC 92-53873. 70p. 1992. pap. 7.00 (*0-88734-252-3*) Players Pr.

— Prometheus Bound. Connor, W. R., ed. LC 78-18612. (Greek Texts & Commentaries Ser.). (Illus.). 1979. reprint ed. lib. bdg. 20.95 (*0-405-11451-6*) Ayer.

— Prometheus Bound. unabridged ed. (Thrift Editions Ser.). 64p. 1996. reprint ed. pap. text 1.00 (*0-486-28762-9*) Dover.

— Prometheus Bound & Other Plays. Vellacott, Philip, tr. Incl. Persians. (Orig.). 1961. pap. Seven Against Thebes. 1961. pap. Suppliants. 1961. pap. (Classics Ser.). 160p. (Orig.). 1961. Set pap. 8.95 (*0-14-044112-3*, Penguin Classics) Viking Penguin.

— Prometheus Bound & the Fragments of Prometheus Loosed. Wecklein, N., ed. (College Classical Ser.). (GRE.). iv, 178p. (Orig.). (C). 1981. reprint ed. pap. text 16.00 (*0-89241-126-0*); reprint ed. lib. bdg. 32.50 (*0-89241-358-1*) Caratzas.

— Scholia Graeca Ex Codicibus Aucta et Emendata. xviii, 548p. 1962. reprint ed. 120.00 (*0-318-70848-5*) G Olms Pubs.

— Septem Quae Supersunt Tragoediae. Page, Denys L., ed. (Oxford Classical Texts Ser.). 348p. 1973. text 32.00 (*0-19-814570-5*) OUP.

— The Seven Against Thebes. unabridged ed. Landes, William-Alan, ed. Morshead, E. D., tr. from GRE. LC 98-10977. 55p. 1998. pap. 7.00 (*0-88734-784-3*) Players Pr.

— The Seven Against Thebes - Septem Contra Thebas. 290p. 1994. reprint ed. pap. text 24.95 (*0-19-814999-9*) OUP.

Aeschylus. The Suppliants. Burian, Peter, tr. LC 90-9007. (Lockert Library of Poetry in Translation). 88p. reprint ed. pap. 30.00 (*0-608-20144-8*, 207141600011) Bks Demand.

Aeschylus. The Suppliants. unabridged ed. Landes, William-Alan, ed. Morshead, E. D., tr. from GRE. LC 98-50800. (Classic Plays Ser.). 55p. 1999. pap. 7.00 (*0-88734-785-1*) Players Pr.

— Suppliants & Other Dramas: Persians, Seven Against Thebes, Fragments, Prometheus Bound. rev. ed. Ewans, Michael, ed. & tr. by. LC 96-217957. (Everyman Paperback Classics Ser.). 312p. (C). 1996. pap. 7.50 (*0-460-87755-0*, Everyman's Classic Lib) Tuttle Pubng.

— Tragoediae. Von Wilamowitz-Moellendorff, Ulrich, ed. (GER.). xxxv, 382p. 1958. 120.00 (*3-296-10300-7*) G Olms Pubs.

Aeschylus, et al. The Oresteia/Apollo & Bacchus. Whallon, William, tr. & illus. by. LC 96-44037. (Oleander Language & Literature Ser.: Vol. 18). vi, 115p. 1997. 22.50 (*0-906672-58-9*); pap. 14.95 (*0-906672-59-7*) Oleander Pr.

Aesop. Aesop: Tales of Aethiop the African, Vol. 1. (Illus.). 64p. (J). (gr. 2-9). 1991. 6.95 (*1-877610-03-8*); audio 6.95 (*0-685-50185-X*) Sea Island.

— Aesop & Company: With Scenes from His Legendary Life. (Illus.). 64p. 1999. pap. 6.95 (*0-395-97496-8*) HM.

— Aesop for Children. (Illus.). 96p. (J). (ps-3). 1994. pap. 5.99 (*0-590-47977-6*) Scholastic Inc.

— Aesop for Children. LC 86-73175. (Illus.). 96p. (J). (gr. 2 up). 1984. reprint ed. 12.95 (*1-56288-039-X*) Checkerboard.

— Aesopica: A Series of Texts Relating to Aesop or Ascribed to Him Closely Connected with the Literary Tradition That Bears His Name, Vol. 1. Perry, Ben Edwin & Dorson, Richard M., eds. LC 80-797. (Folklore of the World Ser.). (ENG, GRE & LAT.). 1981. reprint ed. lib. bdg. 81.95 (*0-405-13337-5*) Ayer.

— Aesop's Fables. (Illus.). 32p. (J). (ps-3). 1991. 6.95 (*0-8362-4914-3*) Andrews & McMeel.

— Aesop's Fables. (Illus.). 48p. (J). (ps-3). 1997. 6.98 (*1-85854-573-0*) Brimax Bks.

— Aesop's Fables. (GRE., Illus.). 160p. (J). (gr. 2-3). 5.00 (*0-686-79630-6*) Divry.

— Aesop's Fables. (Illus.). 52p. (YA). 1990. pap. 4.95 (*1-57209-026-X*) First Classics.

— Aesop's Fables. 1991. lib. bdg. 250.00 (*0-8490-4157-0*) Gordon Pr.

— Aesop's Fables. LC 33-31662. (Illustrated Junior Library). (Illus.). 256p. (J). (gr. 4 up). 1947. 15.99 (*0-448-06003-5*, G & D) Peng Put Young Read.

— Aesop's Fables. (Illus.). 56p. (J). text 3.50 (*0-7214-1757-4*, Ladybrd) Penguin Putnam.

— Aesop's Fables. LC 97-8783. (Illus.). 56p. (J). 1997. 18.95 (*0-295-97641-1*) U of Wash Pr.

— Aesop's Fables. LC 84-19166. 32p. (Orig.). (J). (gr. 2-4). 1995. 14.95 (*0-8050-0210-3*, Bks Young Read) H Holt & Co.

— Aesop's Fables. 32p. (Orig.). (J). (gr. k-3). 1999. pap. 6.95 (*0-8050-6315-3*) H Holt & Co.

— Aesop's Fables. (Illus.). 48p. (J). (gr. k up). 1989. 12.95 (*0-8120-5958-1*) Barron.

A

— Aesop's Fables. (Pixies Ser.). (Illus.). 28p. (J). (ps up). 1991. 16.00 (*0-88708-108-8*, Picture Book Studio) S&S Childrens.
— Aesop's Fables. (Illus.). 288p. 1992. mass mkt. 4.95 (*0-451-52565-5*, Sig Classics) NAL.
— Aesop's Fables. (Illus.). 64p. (J). (gr. 2 up). 1992. 10.95 (*0-671-74116-0*, Silver Pr NJ); lib. bdg. 12.95 (*0-671-74117-9*, Silver Pr NJ) Silver Burdett Pr.
— Aesop's Fables. Kratoville, Betty Lou, ed. (Illus.). 80p. (J). (gr. 2-9). 1997. pap. text 14.00 (*1-57128-081-2*, 8081-2) High Noon Bks.
— Aesop's Fables. (Signet Classics). 1992. 10.05 (*0-606-01477-2*, Pub. by Turtleback) Demco.
— Aesop's Fables. large type ed. (Illus.). (J). (gr. 1-12). Date not set. lib. bdg. 22.95 (*0-88411-991-2*) Amereon Ltd.
— Aesop's Fables. Hull, Denison B., tr. LC 60-14237. 144p. reprint ed. pap. 44.70 (*0-8357-5215-1*, 205664900078) Bks Demand.
— Aesop's Fables, Vol. I. Hegeman, Kathryn T., ed. (J). (gr. 1-4). 1984. pap. 5.99 (*0-89824-051-4*) Trillium Pr.
— Aesop's Fables, Vol. II. Hegeman, Kathryn T., ed. (J). (gr. 1-4). 1984. pap. 5.99 (*0-89824-052-2*) Trillium Pr.
— Aesop's Fables, Vol. III. Hegeman, Kathryn T., ed. (J). (gr. 1-4). 1984. pap. 5.99 (*0-89824-053-0*) Trillium Pr.
— Aesop's Fables, Vol. IV. Hegeman, Kathryn T., ed. (J). (gr. 1-4). 1984. pap. 5.99 (*0-89824-054-9*) Trillium Pr.
— Aesop's Fables: A Classic Illustrated Edition. Higton, Bernard, ed. (Illus.). 96p. (J). 1990. 17.95 (*0-87701-780-8*) Chronicle Bks.
— Aesop's Fables: Illustrated Stories Collection. Random House Value Publishing Staff, ed. 1999. 6.99 (*0-517-20422-3*) Random Hse Value.
— Aesop's Fables: With a Life of Aesop. Keller, John E. & Keating, Louis Clark, trs. from SPA. (Studies in Romance Languages: No. 34). Orig. Title: La vida del Ysopet con sus fabulas hystoriadas. (Illus.). 256p. (C). 1993. text 45.00 (*0-8131-1812-3*) U Pr of Ky.
— Aesops Fables - Color Book. (J). 1972. pap. 2.95 (*0-486-21040-5*) Dover.
Aesop. Aesop's Funky Fables. (Illus.). 80p. (J). pap. 11.95 (*0-14-056246-X*, Pub. by Pnguin Bks Ltd) Trafalgar.
Aesop. Aesopus - Index Aesopi Fabularum. Garcia, Francisco M. & Lopez, Alfredo R., eds. (Alpha-Omega, Reihe A Ser.: Bd. CXVIII). (GER.). viii, 170p. 1991. write for info. (*3-487-09354-5*) G Olms Pubs.
— Androcles & the Lion. LC 89-1953. (Illus.). 32p. (J). (gr. k-3). 1989. pap. 5.95 (*0-8234-0906-6*) Holiday.
— Animal Fables from Aesop. (Illus.). 1991. 18.95 (*0-87923-913-1*) Godine.
— The Ant & the Grasshopper. Houghton Mifflin Company Staff, ed. (Literature Experience 1993 Ser.). (J). 1993. pap. 4.48 (*0-395-62579-3*) HM.
— The Ant & the Grasshopper. LC 99-18820. (Illus.). 32p. (J). (ps-3). 2000. 16.95 (*0-8234-1477-9*) Holiday.
— The City Mouse & the Country Mouse/The Lion & the Mouse, 2 bks., Set. (Stepping into English Ser.: Level 1). (YA). 1990. 39.50 incl. audio (*0-88432-985-2*, AFE441) Audio-Forum.
— The Complete Fables. Temple, Robert & Temple, Olivia, trs. LC 98-140244. xxv, 262p. 1998. pap. 8.95 (*0-14-044649-4*) Viking Penguin.
— The Exploding Frog: And Other Fables from Aesop. (Illus.). (J). (gr. 3 up). 1981. write for info. (*0-316-55577-0*) Little.
— Fables. L'Estrange, Roger, tr. LC 92-53179. (Illus.). 224p. (J). 1992. 13.95 (*0-679-41790-7*, Evrymans Lib Childs) Knopf.
— Fables. (Children's Library). 208p. 1998. pap. 3.95 (*1-85326-128-9*, 1289WW, Pub. by Wrdsworth Edits) NTC Contemp Pub Co.
— The Fables of Aesop. LC 93-48462. (Illus.). (J). 1994. 19.95 (*0-688-07051-5*) Lothrop.
— The Fables of Aesop Paraphrased in Verse, 1668. LC 92-24824. (Augustan Reprints Ser.: No. 1 (1965)). 1992. 50.00 (*0-404-70101-9*) AMS Pr.
— Fabulae Aesopicae: Renaissance Period. Berrigan, Joseph R., tr. from ENG. 1977. 15.00 (*0-87291-092-X*) Coronado Pr.
— The Fox & the Rooster: A Fable from Aesop. LC 97-20997. (J). 1998. 7.99 (*0-679-88821-7*) Random.
— The Fox & the Rooster: A Fable from Aesop. LC 97-20997. (J). 1998. lib. bdg. 9.99 (*0-679-98821-1*) Random.
— The Hare & the Tortoise. LC 80-28162. (Illus.). 32p. (J). (gr. k-3). 1996. pap. 3.95 (*0-89375-469-2*) Troll Communs.
— The Hare & the Tortoise. LC 96-6439. (Illus.). 32p. (J). (ps-3). 1996. 13.95 (*0-395-81368-9*) HM.
— Hare & the Tortoise. (Read Along With Me Ser.). (Illus.). 24p. (J). (ps-3). 1989. 2.25 (*1-56288-160-4*) Checkerboard.
— The Hare & the Tortoise; The Travelers & the Bear, 2 bks. in 1. (Aesop's Fables - Two in One Tales Ser.). (Illus.). 24p. (Orig.). (J). (gr. 1-4). 1993. pap. 2.50 (*1-56144-305-0*, Honey Bear Bks) Modern Pub NYC.
— The Hidden Picture Book of Aesop's Fables. LC 94-71032. (Illus.). 32p. (J). (ps-4). 1995. pap. 3.95 (*1-56397-259-X*) Boyds Mills Pr.
— El Leon y el Raton.Tr. of Lion & the Mouse. (J). 1997. pap. 3.95 (*0-8167-3065-2*) Troll Communs.
***Aesop.** The Lion & the Mouse. (Illus.). 32p. (J). (gr. k-3). 2000. 15.95 (*0-7358-1220-9*, Pub. by North-South Bks NYC) Chronicle Bks.
Aesop. The Lion & the Mouse. LC 80-28154. (Illus.). 32p. (J). (gr. k-3). 1981. lib. bdg. 15.85 (*0-89375-466-8*) Troll Communs.
— The Lion & the Mouse. (J). 1996. pap. 1.25 (*0-8167-0424-4*) Troll Communs.
— The Lion & the Mouse. LC 80-28154. (Illus.). 32p. (J). (gr. k-3). 1981. pap. 3.95 (*0-89375-467-6*) Troll Communs.
— The Lion & the Mouse. LC 97-220917. (Illus.). 16p. (J). 1998. write for info. (*0-8172-7266-6*) Raintree Steck-V.
— The Lion & the Mouse; The Wind & the Sun, 2 bks. in 1. (Aesop's Fables - Two in One Tales Ser.). (Illus.). 24p. (Orig.). (J). (gr. 1-4). 1993. pap. 2.50 (*1-56144-302-6*, Honey Bear Bks) Modern Pub NYC.
— The Morall Fabillis of Esope in Scottis Meter Be Maister Henrisone. LC 79-25964. (English Experience Ser.: No. 282). 104p. 1970. reprint ed. 25.00 (*90-221-0282-3*) Walter J Johnson.
— Once in a Wood: Ten Tales from Aesop. LC 92-24605. (Illus.). 64p. (J). (gr. 1 up). 1993. reprint ed. pap. 4.95 (*0-688-12268-X*, Wm Morrow) Morrow Avon.
— Select Fables of Esop & Other Fabulists. Dodsley, Robert, ed. LC 70-161796. (Augustan Translators Ser.). reprint ed. 49.50 (*0-404-54101-1*) AMS Pr.
— Subtyl Historyes & Fables of Esope. fac. ed. Caxton, William, ed. & tr. by. LC 76-177403. (English Experience Ser.: No. 439). 288p. 1970. reprint ed. 65.00 (*90-221-0439-7*) Walter J Johnson.
— The Sun & the Wind. (Illus.). 32p. (J). (gr. k-5). 1983. 3.95 (*0-87303-072-9*) Faith & Life.
— The Tortoise & the Hare. (J). (gr. 1 up). 1994. pap. 23.75 incl. cd-rom (*1-57135-057-8*) Living Bks.
— The Tortoise & the Hare. 1995. lib. bdg. 39.95 (*1-57135-061-6*) Living Bks.
— The Tortoise & the Hare: An Aesop Fable. LC 83-18668. (Illus.). 32p. (J). (gr. k-3). 1984. lib. bdg. 15.95 (*0-8234-0510-9*) Holiday.
— Town Mouse & Country Mouse. (Read Along With Me Ser.). (Illus.). 24p. (J). (ps-3). 1989. write for info. (*1-56288-161-2*) Checkerboard.
— Town Mouse & the Country Mouse. LC 78-18062. (Illus.). 32p. (J). (gr. k-3). 1979. lib. bdg. 15.95 (*0-89375-131-6*) Troll Communs.
— Town Mouse & the Country Mouse. LC 78-18062. (Illus.). 32p. (J). (gr. k-3). 1997. pap. 3.95 (*0-89375-109-X*) Troll Communs.
— The Town Mouse & the Country Mouse. LC 91-58761. (Illus.). 32p. (J). (ps up). 1992. 13.95 (*1-56402-102-5*) Candlewick Pr.
Aesop. The Town Mouse & the Country Mouse. LC 94-9789. (Bank Street Ready-to-Read Ser.). (Illus.). 48p. (J). 1997. pap. 4.50 (*0-553-37572-5*) Bantam.
Aesop. The Town Mouse & the Country Mouse. LC 98-6472. (Illus.). 32p. (J). (gr. k-3). 1998. lib. bdg. 15.88 (*1-55858-988-0*, Pub. by North-South Bks NYC) Chronicle Bks.
— The Town Mouse & the Country Mouse. LC 98-6472. (Illus.). 32p. (J). (gr. k-3). 1998. 15.95 (*1-55858-987-2*, Pub. by North-South Bks NYC) Chronicle Bks.
— The Town Mouse & the Country Mouse: The Boy Who Cried Wolf, 2 bks. in 1. (Aesop's Fables - Two in One Tales Ser.). (Illus.). 24p. (Orig.). (J). (gr. 1-4). 1993. pap. 2.50 (*1-56144-303-4*, Honey Bear Bks) Modern Pub NYC.
— The Wind & the Sun. LC 94-20301. (Illus.). 24p. (J). (gr. k-1). 1995. pap. 3.95 (*0-382-24657-8*) Silver Burdett Pr.
Aesop. Aesop's Fables. large type ed. 1993. 13.50 (*0-614-09814-9*, L-34099-00) Am Printing Hse.
Aesop & Caoursin, Guillaume. The Siege of Rhodes: The Book of Subtyl Histories & Fables of Esope. fac. ed. Kaye, John, tr. LC 75-14086. 344p. 1975. reprint ed. 60.00 (*0-8201-1154-6*) Schol Facsimiles.
***Aesop & Miles, Betty.** The Tortoise & the Hare. (Starting to Read Ser.). (J). 1998. 9.19 (*0-606-13858-7*, Pub. by Turtleback) Demco.
— The Tortoise & the Hare Ready to Read. LC 97-17355. (Ready-to-Read Ser.). (Illus.). 32p. (J). 1998. per. 15.00 (*0-689-81792-4*) S&S Bks Yung.
Aesop & Pearson, Maggie. The Fox & the Rooster & Other Tales. LC 97-16836. (Illus.). 80p. (J). (gr. 1-5). 1997. 14.95 (*1-888444-17-7*, 21017) Little Tiger.
Aesop, et al. Aesop's Fables. 80p. (J). (gr. 4-7). 1990. pap. 3.99 (*0-590-43880-8*) Scholastic Inc.
Aesop, jt. auth. see Addison-Wesley Publishing Staff.
Aesop, jt. auth. see Barnett, Carol.
Aesop, jt. auth. see Byrd, Don.
Aesop, jt. auth. see Craig, Helen.
Aesop, jt. auth. see Cullum, Albert.
Aesop, jt. auth. see De Paola, Tomie.
Aesop, jt. auth. see Dijs, Carla.
Aesop, jt. auth. see Dorizas, H.
Aesop, jt. auth. see Graczyk, Ed.
Aesop, jt. auth. see Handsford, S. A.
Aesop, jt. auth. see Heffelfinger, Ruth J.
Aesop, jt. auth. see Herman, Gail.
Aesop, jt. auth. see Ireland, Vicky.
Aesop, jt. auth. see Jones, Carol.
Aesop, jt. auth. see Lewis, Shari.
Aesop, jt. auth. see Mandeville, Bernard.
Aesop, jt. auth. see Martell, Ralph.
Aesop, jt. auth. see McCann, Dick.
Aesop, jt. auth. see McGovern, Ann.
Aesop, jt. auth. see Resnick, Jane P.
Aesop, jt. auth. see Rumble, Patricia B.
Aesop, jt. auth. see Sogabe, Aki.
Aesop, jt. auth. see Wallner, John.
Aesop, jt. auth. see Wylie, Kim E.
Aesop, jt. auth. see Yolen, Jane.
AESOP Enterprises, Inc. Staff & Crenshaw, Gwendolyn J. Akhenaton: Torchbearer of Light. (Heroes & Sheroes Ser.). 14p. (J). (gr. 3-12). 1991. pap. write for info. incl. audio (*1-880771-12-8*) AESOP Enter.
— Albert Einstein: Physicist & Peace Seeker. (Heroes & Sheroes Ser.). 12p. (J). (gr. 3-12). 1991. pap. write for info. incl. audio (*1-880771-10-1*) AESOP Enter.
— Aleksandr Sergeyevich Pushkin: Poetic Freedom Fighter for the People. (Heroes & Sheroes Ser.). 16p. (J). (gr. 3-12). 1991. pap. write for info. incl. audio (*1-880771-15-2*) AESOP Enter.
— Charles Richard Drew: A Navigator on the River of Life. (Heroes & Sheroes Ser.). 16p. (J). (gr. 3-12). 1991. pap. write for info. incl. audio (*1-880771-06-3*) AESOP Enter.
— George Washington Carver: A Scientist Glorifying the Glories of Nature. (Heroes & Sheroes Ser.). 16p. (J). (gr. 3-12). 1991. pap. write for info. incl. audio (*1-880771-04-7*) AESOP Enter.
— Harriet Tubman: Stand & Deliver. (Heroes & Sheroes Ser.). 20p. (J). (gr. 3-12). 1991. pap. write for info. (*1-880771-02-0*) AESOP Enter.
— Malcolm X: Developing Self-Esteem, Self-Love, & Self-Dignity. (Heroes & Sheroes Ser.). 27p. (J). (gr. 3-12). 1991. pap. write for info. incl. audio (*1-880771-00-4*) AESOP Enter.
— Martin Luther King, Jr. Personalism & the Sacredness of the Human Personality. (Heroes & Sheroes Ser.). 16p. (J). (gr. 3-12). 1991. pap. write for info. incl. audio (*1-880771-01-2*) AESOP Enter.
— Mary McLeod Bethune: We've Come This Far by Faith. (Heroes & Sheroes Ser.). 14p. (J). (gr. 3-12). 1991. pap. write for info. incl. audio (*1-880771-08-X*) AESOP Enter.
— Nzinga: Developing Determination & Persistence, Set. (Heroes & Sheroes Ser.). 16p. (J). (gr. 3-12). 1991. pap. write for info. incl. audio (*1-880771-14-4*) AESOP Enter.
— Queen Hatshepsut: Glorifying the Past for the Present & Future. (Heroes & Sheroes Ser.). 14p. (J). (gr. 3-12). 1991. pap. write for info. incl. audio (*1-880771-11-X*) AESOP Enter.
— Susan B. Anthony: A Crusader for Womanhood. (Heroes & Sheroes Ser.). 14p. (J). (gr. 3-12). 1991. pap. write for info. incl. audio (*1-880771-09-8*) AESOP Enter.
— Thomas Alva Edison: Persistent Dreamer & Doer. (Heroes & Sheroes Ser.). 14p. (J). (gr. 3-12). 1991. pap. write for info. incl. audio (*1-880771-13-6*) AESOP Enter.
Aesoph, Lauri M. Ailmentos Que Eliminan la Artritis. (SPA.). 320p. (C). 1998. pap. text 13.95 (*0-13-080424-X*) P-H.
***Aesoph, Lauri M.** Alimentos Que Eliminan la Artritis. (SPA.). 2000. pap. 14.00 (*0-7352-0193-5*) PH Pr.
Aesoph, Lauri M. How to Eat Away Arthritis. 2nd rev. expanded ed. LC 96-23887. 320p. (C). 1996. text 26.95 (*0-13-242900-4*) P-H.
— How to Eat Away Arthritis. 2nd rev. expanded ed. LC 96-23887. 320p. (C). 1996. pap. 13.95 (*0-13-242892-X*) P-H.
— Your Natural Health Makeover. 288p. (C). 1998. text 19.95 (*0-13-628660-7*); text 24.95 (*0-13-628652-6*) P-H.
Aesoph, Lauri M., ed. see Bonk, Melinda.
Aeur, Jim. Ernest Hemingway's The Old Man & the Sea. (Barron's Book Notes Ser.). (C). 1984. pap. 3.50 (*0-8120-3432-5*) Barron.
AEVAC, Inc. Staff, ed. see O'Keefe, Ruth A.
***Aeyels, D., et al, eds.** Stability & Stabilization of Nonlinear Systems. (Lecture Notes in Control & Information Sciences Ser.: Vol. 246). (Illus.). 400p. 1999. pap. 99.80 (*1-85233-638-2*, Pub. by Spr-Verlag) Spr-Verlag.
af Ornas, Anders Hjort, see Hjort af Ornas, Anders, ed.
Af Ornas, Anders, ed. see Mohamed Salih, M. A.
AFA Staff. Basic Principles of Astrology. 1962. 6.00 (*0-86690-052-7*, A1003-014) Am Fed Astrologers.
Afadrat Muhyiddin Ibn 'Arabi al-Hatimi at-Ta'i. Ibn 'Arabi: Divine Governance of the Human Kingdom. 300p. 1997. pap. 19.95 (*1-887752-05-6*) Fons Vitae.
Afagh, Fred, tr. see Merkin, David R.
Afanasev, Aleksandr. Russian Fairy Tales. LC 44-37884. (Fairy Tale & Folklore Library). 664p. (J). (gr. 6 up). 1976. pap. 18.00 (*0-394-73090-9*) Pantheon.
Afanas'Ev, Igor B. Superoxide Ion: Chemistry & Biological Implications, Vol. I. 208p. 1989. lib. bdg. 219.00 (*0-8493-5451-X*, QP535) CRC Pr.
Afanas'ev, Igor B. Superoxide Ion Vol. II: Chemistry & Biological Implications. 208p. 1991. lib. bdg. 219.00 (*0-8493-5452-8*, QP535) CRC Pr.
Afanasieff, Nicholas, et al. The Primacy of Peter: Essays in Ecclesiology & the Early Church. LC 92-6455. 182p. (Orig.). 1995. pap. text 11.95 (*0-88141-125-6*) St Vladimirs.
Afanasiev, A. N. Flying Ship: A Russian Folk-Tale. 1997. 15.95 (*0-86315-230-9*, Pub. by Floris Bks) Anthroposophic.
Afanasiev, Aleksandr, ed. Russian Adult Humor: Naughty Tales of Old Russia. Perkoff, G., tr. from RUS. (Illus.). 118p. (Orig.). 1996. pap. 7.95 (*1-57201-022-3*) Berkeley Slavic.
Afanasiev, Aleksandr A., ed. Erotic Tales of Old Russia. 2nd ed. Perkov, Yury, tr. & intro. by. (ENG & RUS., Illus.). 177p. (Orig.). 1988. pap. 7.95 (*0-933884-59-1*) Berkeley Slavic.
***Afanasiev, G. N.** Topological Effects in Quantum Mechanics LC 99-30411. (Fundamental Theories of Physics Ser.). 1999. write for info. (*0-7923-5800-7*) Kluwer Academic.
Afanasiev, V. A. & Zaikov, G. E., eds. Physical Methods in Chemistry. 182p. 1993. text 165.00 (*1-56072-063-8*) Nova Sci Pubs.
Afanasyev, Alexander. Russian Secret Tales: Bawdy Folktales of Old Russia. Legman, Gershon, tr. from RUS. & intro. by. (Illus.). lxxviii, 306p. 1998. reprint ed. pap. 29.95 (*0-8063-4778-3*, 7518) Clearfield Co.
Afanasyev, V. G. Dialectical Materialism. rev. ed. LC 87-3419. 156p. (Orig.). (C). 1987. pap. 4.25 (*0-7178-0656-1*) Intl Pubs Co.
— Historical Materialism: Part Two of Marxist Philosophy. rev. ed. LC 87-2647. 216p. (Orig.). (C). 1987. pap. 4.95 (*0-7178-0637-5*) Intl Pubs Co.
Afaque, Khan M. Gandhian Approach to Communalism: A Critical Study. 140p. 1986. 12.00 (*81-202-0163-9*, Pub. by Ajanta) S Asia.
Afarli, Tor A. The Syntax of Norwegian Passive Constructions. LC 92-17859. (Linguistik Aktuell - Linguistics Today Ser.: No. 7). xii, 177p. 1992. 50.00 (*1-55619-225-8*) J Benjamins Pubng Co.
Afary, Janet. The Iranian Constitutional Revolution, 1906-1911: Grassroots Democracy, Social Democracy, & the Origins of Feminism. LC 95-50433. (Illus.). 464p. (C). 1996. pap. 19.50 (*0-231-10351-4*) Col U Pr.
— The Iranian Constitutional Revolution, 1906-1911: Grassroots Democracy, Social Democracy, & the Origins of Feminism. LC 95-50433. (Illus.). 464p. (C). 1996. 47.50 (*0-231-10350-6*) Col U Pr.
AFBF Staff. Your Farm Bureau. 2nd ed. LC 96-78023. 272p. 1996. pap. text 15.00 (*0-7872-2880-X*) Kendall-Hunt.
Afcan, Paschal, tr. see Morack, Kathy.
***Afdem, John.** The Wizard of "IS" The Short, Ugly Story of the Impeachment of Billy Jeff Clinton & His Trailer-Park Presidency. 220p. 1999. pap. 14.00 (*0-7392-0272-3*, PO3353) Morris Pubng.
Afeltra, Louise R. Lovisa: Angel from Norway. LC 96-27675. (Illus.). 96p. (Orig.). 1997. pap. 9.95 (*1-56474-206-7*) Fithian Pr.
Afeman, Lydia. I Wanna Be a Sales Rep! The Insider's Guide to Landing Great-Paying Jobs in Sales. 192p. 1998. pap. 19.95 (*0-9662911-0-7*) L M Afeman.
Afendi, M. H. Curriculum & Teacher Education. 212p. 1996. pap. 14.50 (*0-614-21535-8*, 190) Kazi Pubns.
Affara, Gianni D, jt. auth. see Ulmer, Christopher.
Affentranger, Christoph. New Wood Architecture in Scandinavia. (Illus.). 240p. 1997. 75.00 (*3-7643-5458-5*, Pub. by Birkhauser) Princeton Arch.
Affiliated National Riding Commission, ed. National Riding Standards. rev. ed. 73p. 1981. pap. text 3.00 (*0-88314-154-X*, 303-10018) AAHPERD.
Affinito, Mona G. Helping with Forgiveness Decisions: A Brief Guide for Counselors. 80p. 1998. pap. 49.95 (*1-884937-50-0*) Manisses Communs.
***Affinito, Mona Gustafson.** When to Forgive: A Personal Guide. 168p. 1999. pap. 12.95 (*1-57224-175-6*) New Harbinger.
Affinity Communications. Sales & Marketing. (First Books for Business Ser.). (Illus.). 119p. 1996. pap. 12.00 (*0-07-001568-6*) McGraw.
Affinity Communications Staff. Apostles Little Instructions. 1999. pap. 8.95 (*0-452-27730-2*, Plume) Dutton Plume.
— Understanding Budgets. 1996. pap. 12.00 (*0-614-12589-8*) McGraw.
Affinity Communications Staff, ed. First Books for Business, 5 vols. (Illus.). 1996. pap. text 60.00 (*0-07-912985-4*) McGraw.
Affinity Publishing Editors. Millennium Journal. 384p. 1999. 6.95 (*1-928684-06-8*, Pub. by Affinity Pubg) BookWorld.
— Millennium Journal: Sports. 384p. 1999. 6.95 (*1-928684-00-9*, Pub. by Affinity Pubg) BookWorld.
— War. 384p. 1999. 6.95 (*1-928684-02-5*, Pub. by Affinity Pubg) BookWorld.
Affinity Publishing Group Staff. Flight. 384p. 1999. 6.95 (*1-928684-01-7*, Pub. by Affinity Pubg) BookWorld.
Affinnih, Yahya H. Occupational Commitment & the Mystique of Self-Employment among Lagos. LC 91-44506. 308p. 1992. lib. bdg. 99.95 (*0-7734-9951-2*) E Mellen.
Affleck, Ben & Damon, Matt. Good Will Hunting: A Screenplay. LC 97-44589. (Illus.). 168p. (J). 1997. pap. 10.45 (*0-7868-8344-8*, Pub. by Hyperion) Time Warner.
Affleck, Diane F. Just New from the Mills: Printed Cotton in America, Late 19th Early 20th Centuries. LC 87-61252. (Illus.). 108p. (Orig.). 1997. pap. text 15.00 (*0-937474-09-6*) Am Textile Hist.
Affleck, Diane L. & Hudon, Paul. Celebration & Remembrance: Commemorative Textiles in America, 1790-1990. LC 90-52859. 87p. (Orig.). 1990. pap. 15.00 (*0-937474-13-4*) Am Textile Hist.
Affleck, G., et al. Infants in Crisis: How Parents Cope with Newborn Intensive Care & Its Aftermath. Taylor, R. L. & Sternberg, L., eds. (Disorders of Human Learning, Behavior, & Communication Ser.). (Illus.). 168p. 1990. 89.95 (*0-387-97392-3*) Spr-Verlag.
Affleck, Mark E. Radarscan Issues Management. (Illus.). 98p. 1998. pap. 16.95 (*0-913869-06-6*) Issue Action Pubns.
Afflerbach, Lois & Franck, Marga, eds. The Emerging Field of Sociobibliography: The Collected Essays of Ilse Bry. 19. LC 76-28644. (Contributions in Librarianship & Information Science Ser.: No. 19). 251p. 1977. 67.95 (*0-8371-9289-7*, BRB/, Greenwood Pr) Greenwood.
Afflerbach, Peter, et al, eds. Authentic Reading Assessment: Practices & Possibilities. LC 93-11920. 328p. 1993. pap. 22.95 (*0-87207-765-9*) Intl Reading.
Afflerbach, Peter, jt. auth. see Pressley, Michael.
Afflerbach, Sabine. Zur Ontogenese der Kommasetzung Vom 7. Bis Zum 17. Lebensjahr: Eine Empirische Studie. (GER., Illus.). 274p. 1997. 54.95 (*3-631-31967-3*) P Lang Pubng.
Afflick, Martin. Caribbean Immigrants & Economic Adoption: A Caribbean Business Survey, 3 vols. (Illus.). 71p. 1990. pap. text. write for info. (*1-878433-05-9*) Caribbean Diaspora Pr.
Afflick, Martin, et al. Adjustment of Caribbean Immigrants in New York City: Social & Economic Dimensions, No. 1. 90p. (Orig.). Date not set. pap. write for info. (*1-878433-01-6*) Caribbean Diaspora Pr.
Afflolter. Perception, Interaction & Language: Interaction of Daily Living: The Roots of Development. 1991. 71.95 (*0-387-51150-4*) Spr-Verlag.

An Asterisk (*) at the beginning of an entry indicates that the title is appearing for the first time.

***Affolter, Felicie, et al.** Nonverbal Perceptual & Cognitive Processes in Children with Language Disorders: Toward a New Framework for Clinical Intervention. LC 00-34122. 2000. pap. 34.50 (*0-8058-3213-0*) L Erlbaum Assocs.

Affolter, James M. A Monograph of the Genus Lilaeopsis (Umbelliferae) Anderson, Christiane, ed. LC 85-1291. (Systematic Botany Monographs: Vol. 6). (Illus.). 140p. (Orig.). 1985. pap. 18.00 (*0-912861-06-1*) Am Soc Plant.

Afford, John & O'Neill, Deirdre. Contract State: Public Management & the Kennett Government. 192p. (C). 1996. pap. 54.00 (*0-7300-2111-4*, Pub. by Deakin Univ) St Mut.

Affron, Charles. Cinema & Sentiment. LC 82-2687. (Illus.). xii, 202p. 1982. 22.50 (*0-226-00820-7*) U Ch Pr.

— Cinema & Sentiment. LC 82-2687. (Illus.). 214p. Date not set. reprint ed. pap. 66.40 (*0-608-20977-5*, 205450500003) Bks Demand.

— A Stage for Poets: Studies in the Theatre of Hugo & Musset. LC 75-153847. (Princeton Essays in European & Comparative Literature Ser.). 274p. reprint ed. pap. 85.00 (*0-8357-7036-2*, 203340700085) Bks Demand.

Affron, Charles, ed. Eight & a Half. (Films in Print Ser.). 288p. 1987. text 35.00 (*0-8135-1210-7*); pap. text 17.00 (*0-8135-1211-5*) Rutgers U Pr.

Affron, Charles & Affron, Mirella. Sets in Motion: Art Direction & Film Narrative. LC 94-39443. (Illus.). 300p. (C). 1995. text 55.00 (*0-8135-2160-2*); pap. text 22.50 (*0-8135-2161-0*) Rutgers U Pr.

Affron, Matthew & Antliff, Mark. Fascist Visions: Art & Ideology in France & Italy. LC 97-8461. (ITA, FRE & ENG., Illus.). 336p. 1997. text 59.50 (*0-691-02738-2*, Pub. by Princeton U Pr); pap. text 19.95 (*0-691-02737-4*, Pub. by Princeton U Pr) Cal Prin Full Svc.

Affron, Mirella, jt. auth. see Affron, Charles.

Affron, Mirella J. & Rubinstein, E., eds. The Last Metro: Francois Truffaut, Director. (Films in Print Ser.). (Illus.). 160p. (C). 1985. 35.00 (*0-8135-1065-1*); pap. 17.00 (*0-8135-1066-X*) Rutgers U Pr.

Affrunti, Andy, Sr. A Personal Journal: Fifty Years at Motorola. rev. ed. 147p. 1994. 10.00 (*1-56946-004-3*) Motorola Univ.

Afgan, Naim, et al, eds. New Developments in Heat Exchangers. 696p. 1996. text 165.00 (*90-5699-512-X*, TJ263) Gordon & Breach.

Afgan, Naim H., ed. Archives of Heat Transfer, Vol. 1. LC 88-16245. (Archives of Heat Transfer Ser.). (Illus.). 466p. 1988. 185.00 (*0-89116-877-X*) Hemisp Pub.

— High Technology Park: A Guidebook for Design & Assessment. 146p. 1990. 132.00 (*1-56032-115-6*) Hemisp Pub.

Afgan, Naim H. & Spalding, D. Brian. Heat & Mass Transfer in Metallurgical Systems II. 1981. text 95.00 (*0-07-059805-3*) McGraw.

Afgan, Naim H., jt. ed. see Kline, Stephen J.

Afgan, Naim H., jt. ed. see Spalding, D. Brian.

Afgan, Naim H., jt. ed. see Van Swaaij, W. P.

Afghan, B. K. Analysis of Pesticides in Water: Significance, Principles, Techniques, & Chemistry of Pesticides, Vol. I. Chau, S. Y., ed. 216p. 1982. 144.00 (*0-8493-5210-X*, TP248) CRC Pr.

Afghan, B. K. & Chau, Alfred S., eds. Analysis of Trace Organics in the Aquatic Environment. 384p. 1989. lib. bdg. 259.00 (*0-8493-4626-6*, TD427) CRC Pr.

Afghan, B. K., jt. auth. see Chau, A. S.

Afghan, B. K., jt. ed. see Chau, Alfred S.

Afghani, Jamal A. An Islamic Response to Imperialism. Keddie, Nikki R., tr. 215p. 1996. pap. 15.95 (*0-614-21490-4*, 646) Kazi Pubns.

Afghari, Ali R., tr. see Beheshti, Ayatullah.

Afif, Kaissar A. And the Word Became Poem. De Graff Ajami, Barbara, ed. Ajami, Mansour, tr. & intro. by. LC 94-73623. (ARA & ENG., Illus.). 137p. (Orig.). (C). 1995. pap. 12.00 (*0-9626898-3-1*) Grindstone Pr.

Afifi, A. A. & Clark. Computer-Aided Multivariate Analysis. 2nd ed. (Illus.). 528p. 1996. lib. bdg. 105.00 (*0-412-99021-0*, Chap & Hall CRC) CRC Pr.

— Computer-Aided Multivariate Analysis. 3rd ed. 456p. 1996. boxed set 74.95 (*0-412-73060-X*, Chap & Hall CRC) CRC Pr.

Afifi, Abdelmonem & Lee, Martin. Electronic Companion to Biostatistics. Hefta, Gunder, ed. (Electronic Companion Ser.). (Illus.). 300p. (C). 1998. pap. text, wbk. ed. 29.95 (*1-888902-69-8*); pap. text, wbk. ed. 29.95 incl. cd-rom (*1-888902-70-1*) Cogito Lrning.

Afifi, Abdelmonem A. & Azen, Stanley P. Statistical Analysis: A Computer Oriented Approach. 2nd ed. 1979. text 114.00 (*0-12-044460-7*) Acad Pr.

Afifi, Adel K. & Bergman, Ronald A. Functional Neuroanatomy: Text & Atlas. LC 97-45690. (Illus.). 730p. 1997. pap. text 42.00 (*0-07-001589-9*) McGraw-Hill HPD.

***Afifi, Mohammed.** Little Songs in the Shade of Tamara: Translated from the Arabic by Lisa White with Afterword by Naguib Mafhouz, Nobel Prize Winning Author of Midaq Alley. White, Lisa, tr. from ARA. (Arabic Translation Award Ser.). Orig. Title: Taraniim Fii Dhil Tamaara. 112p. 2000. reprint ed. pap. 16.00 (*1-55728-614-0*) U of Ark Pr.

Afigbo, A. E. The Role of History As a Social Force. LC 79-88988. write for info. (*0-88357-013-0*); pap. write for info. (*0-88357-052-1*) NOK Pubs.

Afisher, W. Engineering for Nautical Students. 3rd rev. ed. (C). 1987. 75.00 (*0-85174-090-1*) St Mut.

Afkami, Bijan. One Percent Solution: Leadership Through Action. 1998. pap. 13.95 (*0-9664425-0-4*) SynEM Pr.

Afkhami, Gholam R. The Iranian Revolution: Thanatos on a National Scale. LC 85-61787. 276p. 1985. 12.00 (*0-916808-28-9*) Mid East Inst.

Afkhami, Mahnaz. Women in Exile. 208p. (C). 1994. pap. 14.95 (*0-8139-1543-0*) U Pr of Va.

Afkhami, Mahnaz, ed. Faith & Freedom: Women's Human Rights in the Middle East. 184p. 1995. 49.95 (*0-8156-2667-3*); pap. 19.95 (*0-8156-2668-1*) Syracuse U Pr.

Afkhami, Mahnaz & Friedl, Erika, eds. In the Eye of the Storm: Women in Postrevolutionary Iran. (Contemporary Issues in the Middle East Ser.). 300p. 1994. text 49.95 (*0-8156-2633-9*); pap. text 18.95 (*0-8156-2634-7*) Syracuse U Pr.

— Muslim Women & the Politics of Participation: Implementing the Beijing Platform. LC 97-25582. (Gender, Culture & Politics in the Middle East Ser.). 192p. 1997. 39.95 (*0-8156-2759-9*); pap. 19.95 (*0-8156-2760-2*) Syracuse U Pr.

***Afkhami, Mahnaz & Vazeri, Haleh.** Claiming Our Rights: Russian Edition. Filippova, Olga, ed. Toktakhodjaeva, Marfua, tr. (RUS.). 142p. 1999. 17.00 (*0-9669778-4-X*) Sistrhd Is Global.

Afkhami, Mahnaz & Vaziri, Haleh. Claiming Our Rights: A Manual for Women's Human Rights Education in Muslim Societies. 168p. 1996. 17.00 (*0-9669778-1-5*) Sistrhd Is Global.

***Afkhami, Mahnaz & Vaziri, Haleh.** Claiming Our Rights: Arabic Language Edition. (ARA.). 160p. 1999. 17.00 (*0-9669778-2-3*) Sistrhd Is Global.

— Claiming Our Rights: Azeri Edition. Horowitz, Dilshad, ed. Nassirova, Firangiz, tr. (AZE.). 135p. 1999. 22.00 (*0-9669778-3-1*) Sistrhd Is Global.

— Claiming Our Rights: Bangla/Bengali Edition. Kazi, Seema, tr. (BEN.). 66p. 1999. 17.00 (*0-9674159-1-8*) Sistrhd Is Global.

— Claiming Our Rights: Hindi Edition. Kazi, Seema, ed. (HIN.). 145p. 1999. 17.00 (*0-9669778-7-4*) Sistrhd Is Global.

— Claiming Our Rights: Malay Edition. Tahir, Sharifah, tr. (MAY.). 154p. 1999. 17.00 (*0-9669778-5-8*) Sistrhd Is Global.

— Claiming Our Rights: Persian Edition. Hekmat, Hormoz, tr. (PER.). 162p. 1999. 17.00 (*0-9669778-6-6*) Sistrhd Is Global.

— Claiming Our Rights: Urdu Language Edition. Kazi, Seema, tr. (URD.). 106p. 1999. 17.00 (*0-9674159-2-6*) Sistrhd Is Global.

— Claiming Our Rights: Uzbek Edition. Polatov, Abdummonob, ed. Toktakhodjaeva, Marfua, tr. (UZB.). 96p. 1999. 17.00 (*0-9669778-8-2*) Sistrhd Is Global.

***Afkhami, Mahnaz, et al.** Safe & Secure: Eliminating Violence Against Women & Girls in Muslim Societies. 164p. 1999. 22.00 (*0-9669778-0-7*) Sistrhd Is Global.

— Strategizing for Safety: Essays from the Expert Group Meeting on Eliminating Violence. 53p. 1999. 8.00 (*0-9674159-0-X*) Sistrhd Is Global.

***Aflalo, F. G.** Florida Enchantments. (Blue Water Classics Ser.). 512p. 2000. lthr. 65.00 (*1-56416-178-1*) Derrydale Pr.

***Aflalo, Frederick G.** Sunshine & Sport in Florida & the West Indies. LC 99-54104. 360p. 1999. lthr. 65.00 (*1-56416-179-X*) Derrydale Pr.

Afnan, Abul Qasim. Black Pearls: Servants in the Household of the Bab & Bahba.u.llbah. 2nd ed. LC 99-27903. 1999. 14.95 (*1-890688-03-7*) Kalimat.

Afnan, Soheil M. Avicenna, His Life & Works. LC 79-8705. 298p. 1980. reprint ed. lib. bdg. 38.50 (*0-313-22198-7*, AFAV, Greenwood Pr) Greenwood.

Afnor Staff. Dictionary of Computer Science. (ENG & FRE.). 611p. 1997. pap. 150.00 (*0-320-02173-4*) Fr & Eur.

Afnor Staff. Dictionary of Computer Science: French-English, English-French. (ENG & FRE.). 374p. 1989. pap. 95.00 (*0-7859-7740-6*, 2124869116) Fr & Eur.

— Dictionnaire de l'OSI: French-English. (ENG & FRE.). 176p. 1992. pap. 65.00 (*0-7859-8621-9*, 212481611x) Fr & Eur.

— Dictionnaire des Substances Chimiques Reglementees. (FRE.). 812p. 1987. pap. 395.00 (*0-7859-7738-4*, 2124201115) Fr & Eur.

— Textiles Vol. 1: Dictionnaire des Termes Normalises. 5th ed. (FRE.). 298p. 1988. pap. 145.00 (*0-7859-7737-6*, 2120707006) Fr & Eur.

Afnor Staff, ed. Dictionary of Computer Science. (ENG & FRE.). 626p. 1997. pap. 150.00 (*0-320-02393-1*) Fr & Eur.

Afolabi, Niyi. Golden Cage: Regeneration in Lusophone African Literature & Culture. LC 99-21332. 1999. write for info. (*0-86543-739-4*) Africa World.

Afolaian & Newsum. Use of English. 1983. pap. text. write for info. (*0-582-64236-1*, Pub. by Addison-Wesley) Longman.

Afolayan, Funso S., jt. auth. see Pemberton, John, III.

Afonja, Simi & Pearce, Tola O., eds. Social Change in Nigeria. LC 84-800. 269p. reprint ed. pap. 83.40 (*0-8357-2962-1*, 203922400011) Bks Demand.

Afon'kin, J. N. Russian-German Dictionary of Proverbs. (GER & RUS.). 287p. 1985. 19.95 (*0-8288-2285-9*, M15188) Fr & Eur.

Afonkin, Sergei & Hull, Tom. Russian Origami. LC 97-41444. 160p. 1998. pap. 15.95 (*0-312-16993-0*) St Martin.

Afonso, Anderson & Afonso, Corriea, eds. H. Heras Indological Studies. (C). 1990. 38.50 (*81-85002-11-8*, Pub. by Promilla) S Asia.

Afonso, Corriea, jt. ed. see Afonso, Anderson.

Afonso, Menco A. What Is the Nature of Authority in the Church? LC 96-10255. 108p. 1996. pap. text 19.50 (*0-7618-0286-X*) U Pr of Amer.

AFOSR-UTIAS Symposium on Aerodynamic Noise Staff. Aerodynamic Noise: Proceedings of AFOSR-UTIAS Symposium, Held at Toronto, 1968. LC 70-443578. 454p. reprint ed. pap. 140.80 (*0-8357-5212-7*, 201438200093) Bks Demand.

Afraid, Wanbli N., jt. auth. see Wood, Ted.

Afrajmovich, V. S. Bifurcation Theory & Catastrophe Theory. 1999. pap. text 49.95 (*3-540-65379-1*) Spr-Verlag.

Afrati, F. N. & Kolaitis, P. G., eds. Database Theory - ICDT '97 Vol. XIII: Proceedings, 6th International Conference, Delphi, Greece, January 8-10, 1997. LC 96-51632. (Lecture Notes in Computer Science Ser.: Vol. 1186). 477p. 1996. pap. 75.00 (*3-540-62222-5*) Spr-Verlag.

AFRC Technical Committee on Responses to Nutrients. The Nutrition of Goats No. 10. (A CAB International Publication). 136p. 1998. pap. text 40.00 (*0-85199-216-1*) OUP.

AFREPREN Staff. Rural Electrification in Africa. Ranganathan, V., ed. LC 92-28908. 240p. (C). 1992. text 55.00 (*1-85649-111-0*, Pub. by Zed Books) St Martin.

Afriat, A. & Selleri, F. Einstein, Podolsky & Rosen Paradox in Atomic, Nuclear, & Particle Physics. (Illus.). 264p. (C). 1998. text 79.50 (*0-306-45893-4*, Kluwer Plenum) Kluwer Academic.

Afriat, Cydney I. Electronic Fetal Monitoring. 256p. (C). 1989. 89.00 (*0-8342-0052-X*, 20052) Aspen Pub.

Afriat, S. N. Demand Functions & the Slutsky Matrix. LC 79-83973. (Princeton Studies in Mathematical Economics: Vol. 7). 282p. 1980. reprint ed. pap. 87.50 (*0-608-02876-2*, 206394000007) Bks Demand.

***Afriat, S. N.** Linear Dependence: Theory & Computation. LC 00-34933. 2000. write for info. (*0-306-46428-4*) Kluwer Academic.

Afriat, S. N. Logic of Choice & Economic Theory. 592p. 1987. 105.00 (*0-19-828461-6*) OUP.

— The Price Index. LC 77-2134. 203p. reprint ed. pap. 57.90 (*0-608-12285-8*, 2024409) Bks Demand.

Africa, Chris N. When Wolves Cry. 307p. Date not set. mass mkt. 4.99 (*1-55197-076-7*) Picasso Publ.

Africa Faith & Justice Network Staff, ed. The African Synod: Documents, Reflections, Perspectives. LC 95-26639. 240p. (Orig.). 1996. pap. 22.00 (*1-57075-038-6*) Orbis Bks.

Africa Information Service Staff, ed. see Cabral, Amilcar.

Africa, J. Simpson. History of Huntingdon & Blair Counties, Pennsylvania. (Illus.). 761p. 1992. reprint ed. lib. bdg. 77.50 (*0-8328-2443-7*) Higginson Bk Co.

Africa, Thomas W. The Immense Majesty: A History of Rome & the Roman Empire. LC 73-14536. 456p. (C). 1974. text 36.95 (*0-88295-700-7*) Harlan Davidson.

— The Immense Majesty: A History of Rome & the Roman Empire. (Illus.). 456p. (C). 1991. pap. text 26.95 (*0-88295-874-7*) Harlan Davidson.

Africa Watch Staff. Denying "The Honor of Living" Sudan, a Human Rights Disaster. 172p. 1990. pap. 15.00 (*0-929692-53-5*, Africa Watch) Hum Rts Watch.

— The Killings in South Africa: The Role of the Security Forces & the Response of the State. LC 90-85766. 36p. 1991. pap. 8.00 (*0-929692-76-4*, Africa Watch) Hum Rts Watch.

— Liberia - Flight from Terror: Testimony of Abuses in Nimba County. LC 90-82266. 30p. 1990. 5.00 (*0-929692-58-6*, Africa Watch) Hum Rts Watch.

— Where Silence Rules: The Suppression of Dissent in Malawi. LC 90-84931. 104p. 1990. pap. 10.00 (*0-929692-73-X*, Africa Watch) Hum Rts Watch.

— Zimbabwe, a Break with the Past: Human Rights & Political Unity. 114p. 1989. pap. 9.00 (*0-685-41312-8*, Africa Watch) Hum Rts Watch.

Africa Watch Staff & Human Rights Watch Prison Project Staff. South Africa: Prison Conditions in South Africa. LC 93-81326. 136p. (Orig.). 1994. pap. 10.00 (*1-56432-126-6*) Hum Rts Watch.

Africa Watch Staff, jt. auth. see Physicians for Human Rights Staff.

Africa World Press Staff. Africa: Africa World Press Guide to Educational Resources from & about Africa. LC 97-13312. 200p. 1997. pap. 21.95 (*0-86543-588-X*) Africa World.

— Art of African Fashion. 1999. 69.95 (*0-86543-725-4*); pap. text 29.95 (*0-86543-726-2*) Africa World.

— Emerging Perspectives on Ama Ata Aidoo. Azodo, Ada U. & Wilentz, Gay, eds. LC 98-7823. 500p. 1997. pap. 21.95 (*0-86543-581-2*) Africa World.

***African American Images Staff & Bush, Lawson.** Can Black Mothers Raise Our Sons? 1999. pap. 14.95 (*0-913543-64-0*, Pub. by African Am Imag) IPG Chicago.

African-American Institute Staff. Eritrea: Referendum on Independence, April 23-25, 1993. 175p. 1994. pap. text. write for info. (*1-885205-03-1*) African-Amer.

African-American Leaders in the Deep South. Five Grassroots Women Share Their Stories. (Common Ground Ser.: Vol. IV). (Illus.). 52p. (Orig.). 1989. pap. 5.00 (*1-884478-03-4*) Common Grnd.

African-American Poverty Rights Activists. Honoring a People's Prophet: Annie Armstead Smar. Jackson, Bennie et al, eds. (Common Ground Ser.: Vol. VIII). (Illus.). 110p. (Orig.). 1994. pap. 10.00 (*1-884478-07-7*) Common Grnd.

African Bibliographic Center Staff. Proceedings, 6 vols. LC 75-77167. (Special Bibliographic Ser.). 1969. reprint ed. lib. bdg. 150.00 (*0-8371-1066-1*, SBF&, Greenwood Pr) Greenwood.

African Bibliographic Center Staff, ed. Proceedings, Vol. 7, Nos. 1-2. (Special Bibliographic Ser.). reprint ed. lib. bdg. 25.00 (*0-8371-9916-6*, SBK&, Greenwood Pr) Greenwood.

African Center Staff. Debt-Conversion Schemes in Africa: How Theory Empowers Adult Literacy Learners. 143p. (C). 1992. text 35.00 (*0-435-08080-6*, 08080) Heinemann.

African Development Bank Staff. African Development Report, 1997: Fostering Private Development in Africa. (Illus.). 240p. 1997. pap. text 32.00 (*0-19-878215-2*) OUP.

African Development Bank Staff. African Development Report 1998: Africa in the World Economy, Human Capital Development in Africa, Economic & Social Statistics on Africa. (Illus.). 236p. 1998. pap. text 29.95 (*0-19-829421-2*) OUP.

***African Development Bank Staff.** African Development Report 2000. 224p. 2000. pap. text 29.95 (*0-19-829714-9*) OUP.

African Institution, London Staff. Review of the Colonial Slave Registration Acts. LC 78-149860. (Black Heritage Library Collection). 1977. 18.95 (*0-8369-8742-X*) Ayer.

African Islamic Mission Staff. One Hundred Amazing Facts about the Nubian Man & Woman. Obaba, Al I., ed. (Illus.). 124p. (Orig.). (YA). 1991. pap. text 8.95 (*0-916157-87-3*) African Islam Miss Pubns.

African Literature Association Staff. African Literature & Africa's Development: Mapping Intersections. Adams, Anne V. & Mayes, Janis A., eds. LC 97-32911. (Annual Selected Papers of the ALA). 328p. 1998. 69.95 (*0-86543-633-9*); pap. 19.95 (*0-86543-634-7*) Africa World.

— The Growth of African Literature: Twenty-Five Years after Dakar & Fourah Bay. Makward, Edris et al, eds. LC 98-10640. (Annual Selected Papers of the ALA Ser.). (FRE.). 328p. 1998. pap. 19.95 (*0-86543-659-2*) Africa World.

African Methodist Episcopal Church, First Episcopa. HIV-AIDS Prevention Education Curriculum & Guide for Ages 2 to 20 Plus. Wilson, Catherine W. & Cousin, Margaret J., eds. (Illus.). 62p. 1993. pap. text 35.00 (*0-9638634-0-1*) Home Mgmt.

Africanus, John L. A Geographical Histories of Africa. Jones, Luther, ed. Pory, John, tr. from ARA. LC 93-80611. (Illus.). 160p. (Orig.). 1994. pap. 17.95 (*0-9638686-0-8*) Jones Res & Pub.

Africanus Pontifex Staff. Not Born in Sin: The Return of Christ. (Illus.). 282p. 1998. per. 24.95 (*0-9662007-0-5*) Divine Minist.

Africanus, Sextus J. List of Olympian Victors. Rutgers, I., ed. 196p. 1980. pap. 20.00 (*0-89005-351-0*) Ares.

Africk, Henry. Elementary College Geometry: NYC Tech. (Adaptable Courseware Ser.). 1996. 17.50 (*0-534-49761-6*) Brooks-Cole.

Africville Genealogical Society Staff, ed. The Spirit of Africville. (Illus.). 124p. 1995. 34.95 (*0-88780-085-8*, Maritext); pap. 19.95 (*0-88780-084-X*, Pub. by Formac Publ Co) Formac Dist Ltd.

Afrika, Llaila O. African Holistic Health. rev. ed. Adesegun, T. Nokwari, ed. (Illus.). 300p. 1989. pap. 14.95 (*1-877610-00-3*) Sea Island.

Afrika, Llaila O., jt. auth. see Rose, Julio L.

Afrouz, Andy A. Practical Handbook Rock Mass Classification Systems: Modes of Ground Failure. 208p. 1992. boxed set 136.95 (*0-8493-3711-9*, QE431) CRC Pr.

Afsar, Mohammed N., ed. Millimeter & Submillimeter Waves & Applications III, Vol. 2842. 650p. 1996. 94.00 (*0-8194-2230-4*) SPIE.

— Millimeter & Submillimeter Waves & Applications IV, Vol. 3465. 1998. 124.00 (*0-8194-2920-1*) SPIE.

Afsarmanesh, Hamideh, jt. auth. see Camarinha-Matos, Luis M.

***Afsaruddin, Asma.** Hermeneutics & Honor: Negotiating Female "Public" Space in Islamic-ate Societies. (Middle Eastern Monographs: Vol. 32). 2000. pap. text 19.95 (*0-932885-21-7*) Harvard CMES.

Afsaruddin, Asma & Zahniser, A. H., eds. Humanism, Culture, & Language in the Near East: Studies in Honor of Georg Krotkoff. LC 96-51074. 464p. 1997. text 49.50 (*1-57506-020-5*) Eisenbrauns.

Afshar. Islam & Feminisms. 1999. pap. 19.95 (*0-312-22220-3*) St Martin.

Afshar, Ani. Beading Necklaces with Ani Afshar. LC 94-46707. (Illus.). 64p. (Orig.). 1995. pap. 12.95 (*0-88740-735-8*) Schiffer.

Afshar, Freydoun. Taxonomic Revision of the Superspecific Groups of the Cretaceous & Cenozoic Tellinidae. LC 72-98019. (Geological Society of America, Memoir Ser.: No. 119). 231p. reprint ed. pap. 71.70 (*0-608-13560-7*, 202546700044) Bks Demand.

Afshar, Haleh, ed. Women, State, & Ideology: Studies from Africa & Asia. LC 86-14432. 245p. (C). 1987. pap. text 24.95 (*0-88706-394-2*) State U NY Pr.

— Women, Work, & Ideology in the Third World. 280p. 1985. pap. 15.95 (*0-422-79710-3*, 9607, Pub. by Tavistock) Routldge.

Afshar, Haleh & Maynard, Mary, eds. The Dynamics of Race & Gender: Some Feminist Interventions. LC 93-45986. 224p. 1994. 75.00 (*0-7484-0211-X*, Pub. by Tay Francis Ltd); pap. 27.00 (*0-7484-0212-8*, Pub. by Tay Francis Ltd) Taylor & Francis.

Afshar, Iraj, ed. see Sayeed, Hassan T.

Afshar, Mahasti. The Immortal Hound: The Genesis & Transformation of a Symbol in Indo-Iranian Tradition. Lord, Albert B., ed. LC 90-32950. (Harvard Dissertations in Folklore & Oral Literature Ser.). 286p. 1990. reprint ed. text 20.00 (*0-8240-2789-2*) Garland.

***Afshear, Elraj & Eslami, Kambiz.** Iran & Iranian Studies. LC 98-84316. (ENG & PER.). x, 357, 35 p. 1998. write for info. (*0-9663442-0-0*) Zagros.

Aft, Laurence S. Fundamentals of Industrial Quality Control. LC 85-1378. (C). 1986. text. write for info. (*0-201-10901-8*); pap. text, student ed. 2.00 (*0-201-10902-6*) Addison-Wesley.

A

An Asterisk (*) at the beginning of an entry indicates that the title is appearing for the first time.

A

***Aft, Lawrence.** Work Measurement & Methods Improvement. 448p. 2000. 80.00 (0-471-37089-4) Wiley.

Aft, Lawrence S. Fundamentals of Industrial Quality Control. 3rd ed. LC 97-39332. (Illus.). 350p. 1997. lib. bdg. 42.50 (1-57444-151-5) St Lucie Pr.

— Productivity Measurement & Improvement. 2nd ed. 400p. (C). 1991. text 54.00 (0-13-728759-3) P-H.

***Aft, Richard N. & Ransohoff, Daniel J.** Painful Decisions, Positive Results: United Way & Community Chest, 1915-2000. (Illus.). 272p. (Orig.). 2000. pap. 20.00 (0-9676382-0-8) Comm Chest & Council.

***Aftab, Parry.** The Parent's Guide to Protecting Your Children in Cyberspace: How to Make Sure Your Child Navigates Safely Through the Perilous World of the Internet. (Illus.). 330p. 1999. pap. 12.95 (0-07-135752-1) McGraw.

Aftab, Parry. A Parents' Guide to the Internet: And How to Protect Your Children in Cyberspace. LC 97-61817. (Illus.). xxv, 328p. 1997. pap. 22.95 (0-9660491-0-1) SC Pr.

Aftabizadeh, A. R., ed. Differential Equations & Applications: Proceedings of the International Conference on Theory & Applications of Differential Equations. LC 89-9256. 1000p. 1990. pap. text 80.00 (0-8214-0942-5) Ohio U Pr.

Aftalion, Florin. The French Revolution: An Economic Interpretation. Thom, Martin, tr. (Illus.). 244p. (C). 1990. pap. text 17.95 (0-521-36810-3) Cambridge U Pr.

Aftalion, Fred. A History of the International Chemical Industry. Benfey, Otto Theodor, tr. LC 91-8179. (Chemical Sciences in Society Ser.). (Illus.). 440p. (C). 1991. text 49.95 (0-8122-8207-8) U of Pa Pr.

Aftandilian, Gregory L. Egypt's Bid for Arab Leadership: Implications for U. S. Policy. LC 93-7449. 96p. 1993. 10.95 (0-87609-146-X) Coun Foreign.

Aftel, Mandy. The Story of Your Life: Becoming the Author of Your Experience. 256p. 1996. 21.50 (0-684-81557-5) S&S Trade.

After School Inc. Staff. School Age Programs: Operations Manual for Site Supervisors. Middlebrooks, Anthony E., ed. (Illus.). 293p. 1998. ring bd. 70.00 (0-9665039-2-9) WI Youth.

— School-Age Programs: Personnel Policies & Procedures. 50p. 1998. ring bd. 35.00 (0-9665039-3-7) WI Youth.

Afterman. U. S. Securities Regulation of Foreign Issuers: Financial Reporting & Disclosure Practice. 1996. 250.00 (1-56706-200-8) Aspen Pub.

Afterman, Allan. GAAP Practice Manual, 2 vols. 1985. 260.00 (0-88712-198-5) Warren Gorham & Lamont.

Afterman, Allan & Jones, Rowan. Government Accounting & Auditing Disclosure Manual. 1991. 135.00 (0-7913-2025-1) Warren Gorham & Lamont.

Afterman, Allan B. Accounting & Auditing Update Service. 255.00 (0-685-69592-1, AAUS) Warren Gorham & Lamont.

— Handbook of SEC Accounting & Disclosure 1993 Annual. 172.00 (0-7913-0309-8) Warren Gorham & Lamont.

— International Accounting, Financial Reporting, & Analysis: A U. S. Perspective. 750p. 1995. 295.00 (0-7913-2472-9) Warren Gorham & Lamont.

— Public Accounting Practice Manual. 1993. pap. 130.00 (0-685-69599-9, CRP) Warren Gorham & Lamont.

— SEC Accounting & Reporting Update Service. 330.00 (0-685-69603-0, SARU) Warren Gorham & Lamont.

— SEC Regulation of Public Companies. LC 94-11319. (C). 1994. pap. text 33.80 (0-13-037185-8) Prntice Hall Bks.

— U. S. Securities Regulation of Foreign Issuers. 1996. ring bd. 185.00 (1-56706-297-0) Aspen Pub.

— U. S. Securities Regulation of Foreign Issuers: Financial Reporting & Disclosure Manual. LC 97-197574. 850p. 1997. 235.00 (90-411-0610-3) Kluwer Academic.

Afterman, Allan B. & Jones, Rowan. Governmental Accounting & Auditing Disclosure Manual. LC 91-67433. 1992. write for info. (0-7913-1145-7) Warren Gorham & Lamont.

— Governmental Accounting & Auditing Disclosure Manual. LC 93-244931. 1994. write for info. (0-7913-1735-8) Warren Gorham & Lamont.

Afterman, Allan B. & Jones, Rowan H. Accounting & Auditing Disclosure Manual. 1993. pap. 125.00 (0-685-69593-X, AADM) Warren Gorham & Lamont.

— Accounting & Auditing Disclosure Manual. 1994. pap. 125.00 (0-685-69594-8) Warren Gorham & Lamont.

— Governmental Accounting & Auditing Disclosure Manual. 1993. 135.00 (0-685-69611-1, GRAM) Warren Gorham & Lamont.

— Governmental Accounting & Auditing Disclosure Manual. 1994. 120.00 (0-685-69612-X) Warren Gorham & Lamont.

— Nonprofit Accounting & Auditing Disclosure Manual. 1992. ring bd. 135.00 (0-685-69608-1, NADM) Warren Gorham & Lamont.

Afterman, Allan B. & Roe, George. Accounting & Tax Highlights. 250.00 (0-685-69595-6, ATH) Warren Gorham & Lamont.

Afterman, Allen. Desire for White: New & Selected Poems. LC 91-22080. 109p. 1991. pap. 11.95 (1-878818-04-X, Pub. by Sheep Meadow) U Pr of New Eng.

— Kabbalah & Consciousness. 141p. (Orig.). 1997. pap. 12.95 (1-878818-59-7, Pub. by Sheep Meadow) U Pr of New Eng.

Afterman, Susan. Rain. 66p. (Orig.). 1988. pap. text 9.95 (0-7022-1617-8, Pub. by Univ Queensland Pr) Intl Spec Bk.

Afthonidou, Despoina. How to Eat Out in Greece: How to Understand the Menu & Make Yourself Understood. 1997. pap. text 6.95 (88-7301-096-2, Pub. by Gremese Intl) Natl Bk Netwk.

Afton, Jean, et al. Cheyenne Dog Soldiers: A Ledgerbook History of Coups & Combat. LC 96-44775. (Illus.). 434p. 1997. 59.95 (0-87081-435-4) Univ Pr Colo.

— Cheyenne Dog Soldiers: A Ledgerbook History of Coups & Combat. 1997. 49.95 (0-9658733-0-7) Univ Pr Colo.

***Afton, Jean, et al.** Cheyenne Dog Soldiers: A Ledgerbook History of Coups & Combat. (Illus.). 445p. 2000. reprint ed. pap. 24.95 (0-87081-574-1, Pub. by Univ Pr Colo) U of Okla Pr.

Afua. Heal Thyself for Health & Longevity. LC 98-14248. 1998. 19.95 (1-881316-50-5) A&B Bks.

Afua, Queen. Sacred Woman: A Guide to Healing the Feminine Body, Mind & Spirit. LC 99-41016. 464p. 2000. 28.00 (0-345-42348-8) One Wrld.

Afuah, Allan. Innovation Management: Strategies, Implementation & Profits. LC 97-9641. (Illus.). 416p. (C). 1997. 57.95 (0-19-511346-2) OUP.

***Afuah, Allan.** Internet Business Models & Strategies: Text & Cases. (Illus.). 2000. 50.95 (0-07-239724-1) McGraw.

***Afxentiou, Vasilis.** In Arms We Trust. 2000. pap. 18.00 (0-7388-2184-5) Xlibris Corp.

Afzal, Amir. Pure C Programming. LC 98-10224. 515p. 1998. pap. text 86.00 (0-13-840703-7) P-H.

***Afzal, Amir.** UNIX Unbounded: A Beginning Approach. 3rd ed. LC 99-12152. (Illus.). 429p. 1999. pap. text 85.00 (0-13-020030-1) P-H.

Afzal-Khan, Fawzia. Cultural Imperialism & the Indo-English Novel: Genre & Ideology in the Novels of R. K. Narayan, Anita Desai, Kamala Markandaya, & Salman Rushdie. LC 92-29782. 200p. 1993. pap. 18.95 (0-271-01013-4); lib. bdg. 40.00 (0-271-00912-8) Pa St U Pr.

***Afzal-Khan, Fawzia & Seshadri-Crooks, Kalpana.** The Pre-Occupation of Postcolonial Studies. LC 99-53103. 448p. 2000. 21.95 (0-8223-2521-7) Duke.

***Afzal-Khan, Fawzia & Seshadri-Crooks, Kalpana, eds.** The Pre-Occupation of Postcolonial Studies. (Illus.). 448p. 2000. text 64.95 (0-8223-2486-5) Duke.

Afzal-Ur-Rehman. Economic Doctrines of Islam, 4 Vols. 1981. pap. 39.50 (0-935782-81-8) Kazi Pubns.

Afzelius, A. Two Studies on Roman Expansion: An Original Anthology. LC 75-7301. (Roman History Ser.). (GER.). 1975. reprint ed. 31.95 (0-405-07178-7) Ayer.

Afzelius, B., jt. auth. see Bacetti, B.

Afzelius, Bjorn A., jt. auth. see Maunsbach, Arvid B.

Ag, Loher, jt. auth. see Barney, G. C.

AG Publishers Editors. Mac de Design, Vol. 2. (Illus.). 213p. 1997. 79.95 (4-900781-13-4, Pub. by AG Pubs Inc) Bks Nippan.

— P. O. P. Works. (Illus.). 216p. 1994. 69.95 (4-87246-303-X, Pub. by AG Pubs) Bks Nippan.

AG Publishers Editors, ed. Paperworks. (Illus.). 224p. 1996. 69.95 (4-900781-08-8, Pub. by AG Pubs) Bks Nippan.

Ag Sidiyene, Ehya & Bernus, Ed. Des Arbres et des Arbustes Spontanes de l'Adrar des Iforas (Mali) (Spontaneous Trees & Bushes of the Adrar des Iforas (Mali)) Etude Ethnolinguistique et Ethnobotanique (An Ethnolinguistic & Ethnobotanical Study)Tr. of Spontaneous Trees & Bushes of the Adrar des Iforas (Mali) - An Ethnolinguistic & Ethnobotanical Study. (FRE., Illus.). 138p. 1996. pap. 20.00 (2-7099-1325-9, Pub. by LInstitut Francais) Balogh.

Aga, Diana S., et al. Immunochemical Technology for Environmental Applications. LC 96-47943. (ACS Symposium Ser.: Vol. 657). 394p. 1997. text 125.00 (0-8412-3487-6, Pub. by Am Chemical) OUP.

Aga-Oglu, Kamer. The Williams Collection of Far Eastern Ceramics: Tonnancour Section. (Special Publications). (Illus.). 1975. pap. 4.00 (0-932206-75-1) U Mich Mus Anthro.

— The Williams Collection of Far Eastern Ceramics, Chinese, Siamese, & Annamese Ceramic Wares: Selected from the Collection of Justice & Mrs. G. M. Williams in the U. of Mich. Museum of Anthropology. (Special Publications). (Illus.). 1972. pap. 2.00 (0-932206-74-3) U Mich Mus Anthro.

***Agabian, Nancy.** Princess Freak. 161p. 2000. pap. 10.00 (1-892184-07-9) Beyond Baroque.

Agabin, Pacifico A. Unconstitutional Essays. 276p. 1996. pap. text 25.00 (971-542-077-X, Pub. by U of Philippines Pr) UH Pr.

Agace, Lucy. Lonely Planet Diving & Snorkeling Guide to Cocos Island. LC 96-37859. (Pisces Diving & Snorkeling Guides Ser.). 96p. 1997. pap. 14.95 (1-55992-092-0, 2092, Pisces Books) Lonely Planet.

Agache, Pierre G., jt. auth. see Leveque, Jean-Luc.

Agacinski, Sylviane. Aparte: Conceptions & Deaths of Soren Kierkegaard. LC 87-24072. 277p. 1988. pap. 29.95 (0-8130-0887-5) U Press Fla.

Agadjanian, Serge, jt. auth. see Eikelberner, George.

Agahd, Reinholdo, ed. see Varro, Marcus T.

Agaian, S., et al. Binary Polynomial & Nonlinear Digital Filters. LC 95-5438. (Monographs & Textbooks in Pure & Applied Mathematics: Vol. 191). (Illus.). 336p. 1995. text 167.50 (0-8247-9642-X) Dekker.

***Against the Clock.** Adobe Photoshop 5.0. LC 99-12147. 1999. pap. text 35.50 (0-13-021324-1); pap. text 25.00 (0-13-021323-3) S&S Trade.

Against the Clock. FreeHand 8.0: Advanced Digital Illustration. 1998. pap. text 33.33 (0-13-921487-9) P-H.

— Macintosh: Basic Operations. 1998. pap. text 33.33 (0-13-921461-5) P-H.

— Windows: Basic Operations. 1998. pap. text 33.33 (0-13-959149-4) P-H.

***Against the Clock.** Windows: Basic Operations & Student CD Package. 176p. (C). 1999. pap. text 33.33 (0-13-081240-4) P-H.

***Against the Clock, Inc. Staff.** Adobe Illustrator 8: An Introduction to Digital Illustration. LC 98-54898. 1999. write for info. (0-13-084009-2) P-H.

— Adobe Illustrator 8: An Introduction to Digital Illustration. 400p. 1999. pap. text 33.33 (0-13-084493-4, Prentice Hall) P-H.

— Adobe Illustrator 7: Advanced Digital Illustration & Student Cd. 304p. 1999. pap. text 33.33 (0-13-083980-9, Prentice Hall) P-H.

— Adobe Illustrator 7: An Introduction to Digital Illustration. 328p. 1999. pap. text 33.33 (0-13-084402-0, Prentice Hall) P-H.

— Adobe Indesign: Advanced Electronic Mechanicals. LC 00-27066. (Against the Clock Ser.). 368p. 2000. 33.33 (0-13-084008-4) P-H.

Against the Clock, Inc. Staff. Adobe Pagemaker 6.5: Advanced Electronic Mechanicals. LC 98-16288. (Against the Clock Ser.). 360p. (C). 1998. pap. text 33.33 (0-13-080505-X) P-H.

***Against the Clock, Inc. Staff.** Adobe Photoshop 5.5: Advanced Digital Images. LC 99-57428. 2000. write for info. (0-13-087994-0) P-H.

— Adobe Photoshop 4: An Introduction to Digital Images. 304p. 1999. pap. text 33.33 (0-13-083871-3, Prentice Hall) P-H.

— Adobe Photoshop 5: An Introduction to Digital Images. 375p. 1999. pap. text 33.33 (0-13-021745-X, Prentice Hall) P-H.

— Adobe Premiere 5: Digital Video Editing. 256p. 2000. spiral bd. 37.33 (0-13-086847-7, Prentice Hall) P-H.

— File Preparation: The Responsible Electronic Page & Student. 256p. 1998. pap. text 33.33 (0-13-083407-6, Prentice Hall) P-H.

— Macromedia (R) Director (R) 7: Creating Powerful Multimedia. LC 99-55647. 2000. write for info. (0-13-016658-8) P-H.

— MetaCreations Painter 5.5: A Digital Approach to Natural Art Media. LC 98-54897. 1999. 33.33 (0-13-013537-2) P-H.

— Microsoft Frontpage 2000: An Introduction to Web Design. LC 00-26995. (Illus.). 2001. write for info. (0-13-016697-9) P-H.

— Microsoft PowerPoint 2000: Presentation Graphics with Impact. LC 99-39275. 2000. write for info. (0-13-012639-X) P-H.

— Microsoft Publisher. LC 99-37113. (Against the Clock Ser.). 292p. 1999. spiral bd. 36.00 (0-13-012630-6) P-H.

— Quarkxpress 4: An Introduction to Electronic Mechanicals, R. 328p. 1999. pap. text 35.00 (0-13-022656-4, Prentice Hall) P-H.

Against the Clock, Inc. Staff. Preflight. LC 98-23213. 1998. pap. text. write for info. (0-13-095825-5) P-H.

***Against the Clock, Inc. Staff.** Preflight: An Introduction to File Analysis & Repair. 384p. 1998. pap. text 33.33 (0-13-020558-3, Prentice Hall) P-H.

— Quarkxpress 4: Advanced Electronic Mechanicals, Revised Edi. 346p. 1999. pap. text 33.33 (0-13-025609-9, Prentice Hall) P-H.

Agajanian, A. H., ed. Ion Implantation in Microelectronics: A Comprehensive Bibliography. LC 81-10753. (Computer Science Information Guides Ser.: Vol. 1). 266p. 1981. 95.00 (0-306-65198-X, Kluwer Plenum) Kluwer Academic.

Agalloco, J. P., jt. auth. see Carleton, F. J.

Agam, Giora. Industrial Chemicals: Chemicals in the Real World. LC 94-8946. (Industrial Chemistry Library: Vol. 6). 398p. 1994. 272.50 (0-444-88887-X) Elsevier.

— Phase Transfer Catalysts. LC 98-143423. 130p. 1998. 3450.00 (1-56965-388-7, C-207) BCC.

Agam, Ron. At the Wall. LC 97-31942. 1998. 24.95 (965-229-150-1, Pub. by Gefen Pub Hse) Gefen Bks.

Agam, Ya'acov, creator. The Agam Rainbow Torah: The Five Books of Moses. limited ed. 1993. 1800.00 (965-229-088-2) Gefen Bks.

Agama, P., ed. see Osho.

Agamben, Giorgio. The Coming Community. Hardt, Michael, tr. from ITA. LC 92-31387. (Theory out of Bounds Ser.: Vol. 1). 120p. (C). 1993. pap. 16.95 (0-8166-2235-3) U of Minn Pr.

— The End of the Poem: Studies in Poetics. Heller-Roazen, Daniel, tr. from ITA. LC 99-22592. (Meridian: Crossing Aesthetics Ser.). 148p. 1999. pap. 14.95 (0-8047-3022-9) Stanford U Pr.

— Homo Sacer: Sovereign Power & Bare Life. LC 97-36621. (Meridian Ser.). 1998. write for info. (0-8047-3217-5); pap. 17.95 (0-8047-3218-3) Stanford U Pr.

— Idea of Prose. Sullivan, Michael & Whitsitt, Sam, trs. from ITA. LC 94-11214. (SUNY Series, Intersections: Philosophy & Critical Theory). (Illus.). 138p. (C). 1995. text 39.50 (0-7914-2379-4); pap. text 14.95 (0-7914-2380-8) State U NY Pr.

— Infancy & History: Essays on the Destruction of Experience. Heron, Liz, tr. 256p. (C). 1993. pap. 19.00 (0-86091-645-6, B0523, Pub. by Verso) Norton.

— Infancy & History: The Destruction of Experience & the Origin of History. Heron, Liz, tr. 256p. (C). (gr. 13). 1993. 60.00 (0-86091-470-4, B0519, Pub. by Verso) Norton.

— Language & Death: The Place of Negativity. Pinkus, Karen E. & Hardt, Michael, trs. from ITA. (Theory & History of Literature Ser.: Vol. 78). xiii, 112p. (C). 1991. pap. 15.95 (0-8166-1937-9); text 39.95 (0-8166-1936-0) U of Minn Pr.

— The Man Without Content. Albert, Georgia, tr. from ITA. LC 99-21526. (Meridian: Crossing Aesthetics Ser.). 130p. 1999. pap. 14.95 (0-8047-3554-9) Stanford U Pr.

***Agamben, Giorgio.** Means Without End: Notes on Politics. LC 00-8712. (Theory Out of Bounds Ser.). 2000. write for info. (0-8166-3036-4) U of Minn Pr.

— Potentialities: Collected Essays. LC 99-39449. 1999. pap. text 18.95 (0-8047-3278-7) Stanford U Pr.

— Potentialities: Collected Essays in Philosophy. LC 99-39449. (Meridian Ser.). 307p. 1999. 55.00 (0-8047-3277-9) Stanford U Pr.

— Remnants of Auschwitz: The Witness & the Archive. LC 99-26013. 176p. 2000. 25.00 (1-890951-16-1) Zone Bks.

Agamben, Giorgio. Remnants of Auschwitz: The Witness & the Archive. LC 99-26013. 2000. write for info. (1-890951-17-X) Zone Bks.

— Stanzas: The Word & the Phantasm in Western Culture. Martinez, Ronald L., tr. from FRE. (Theory & History of Literature Ser.: Vol. 89). 224p. (C). 1992. pap. 16.95 (0-8166-2038-5); text 42.95 (0-8166-2037-7) U of Minn Pr.

Agami, A. & Kollaritsch. Annotated International Accounting Bibliography 1972-1981. 175p. 1983. 7.00 (0-86539-043-6) Am Accounting.

Agan, Donna D., ed. see Western Reserve Herb Society Staff.

***Agan, John.** Minden, Louisiana. (Images of America Ser.). (Illus.). 128p. 2000. pap. 18.99 (0-7385-0580-3) Arcadia Publng.

— Webster Parish, Louisiana. (Images of America Ser.). (Illus.). 128p. 2000. pap. 18.99 (0-7385-0604-4) Arcadia Publng.

Agan, Melissa, ed. see Cusick High School, Class of 'Ninety-Two Staff.

Aganbegyan, Abel. The Economic Challenge of Perestroika. Brown, Michael B., ed. Tiffen, Pauline M., tr. LC 88-3000. (Second World Ser.). (Illus.). 278p. 1988. 10.95 (0-253-32093-3) Ind U Pr.

Agannbegyan, Abel, et al, eds. Economics in a Changing World Vol. 1: System Transformation, Eastern & Western Assessments. 300p. 1994. text 79.95 (0-312-10641-6) St Martin.

Aganon, Virgilio, jt. auth. see Gregor, A. James.

Aganovic, Zoran & Gajic, Zijad. Linear Optimal Control of Bilinear Systems: With Applications to Singular Perturbations & Weak Coupling, Vol. X. Thoma, M., ed. (Lecture Notes in Control & Information Sciences: Vol. 206). 133p. 1995. 45.00 (3-540-19976-4) Spr-Verlag.

Agape Force. Bullfrogs & Butterflies. 16p. (J). Date not set. 1.19 (0-87123-761-X, 220761) Bethany Hse.

Agapiou, John S., jt. auth. see Stephenson, David A.

Agapito, J. F. Pillar Stability in Large Underground Openings: Applications from a Case Study in Competent, Jointed Rock. Raese, Jon W., ed. (Colorado School of Mines Quarterly Ser.: Vol. 81 No. 3 1986). (Illus.). 90p. 1986. pap. text 17.00 (0-918062-70-5) Colo Sch Mines.

Agapius, et al. The Rudder: Divine Canons of the Seven Decumenical & of Local Synods. Orthodox Christian Educational Society Staff & Makrakis, Apostolos, eds. Cummings, Denver, tr. Orig. Title: Pedalion. 1097p. (C). 1957. 79.95 (0-938366-00-9) Orthodox Chr.

***Agar.** Simply Explaining Small Animal Nutrition. 2000. pap. text 30.00 (0-7236-1077-0); pap. text 30.00 (0-7506-4575-X) Buttrwrth-Heinemann.

Agar, Emily, tr. see Mernissi, Fatima.

Agar, Heather & Lapham, Robert W. Drug Calculations for Nurses: A Step by Step Approach. 176p. 1995. pap. 14.99 (1-56593-600-0, 1228) Singular Publishing.

Agar, Herbert. Price of Power: America since Nineteen Forty-Five. LC 57-8575. (Chicago History of American Civilization Ser.). xii, 211p. 1957. pap. text 10.95 (0-226-00937-8, CHAC1) U Ch Pr.

— The Price of Power: America since Nineteen Forty Five. LC 57-8575. (Chicago History of American Civilization Ser.). 212p. reprint ed. pap. 65.80 (0-608-10910-X, 202001800016) Bks Demand.

Agar, Herbert & Tate, Allen, eds. Who Owns America? LC 71-99616. (Essay Index Reprint Ser.). 1977. 25.95 (0-8369-1540-2) Ayer.

Agar, Herbert, et al. The People's Choice, from Washington to Harding: A Study in Democracy. LC 90-46004. (Illus.). 356p. 1990. reprint ed. 34.95 (0-87797-178-1) Cherokee.

Agar, Jon. Science & Spectacle: The Work of Jodrell Bank in Postwar British Culture. (Studies in the History of Science, Technology & Medicine Ser.: Vol. 5). 284p. 1998. text 34.00 (90-5702-258-3, Harwood Acad Pubs) Gordon & Breach.

Agar, Michael. Language Shock: The Culture of Conversation. 288p. 1996. reprint ed. pap. 14.00 (0-688-14949-9, Wm Morrow) Morrow Avon.

— The Professional Stranger: An Informal Introduction to Ethnography. 2nd ed. (Illus.). 296p. 1996. pap. text 34.95 (0-12-044470-4) Acad Pr.

Agar, Michael H. Speaking of Ethnography. (Qualitative Research Methods Ser.: Vol. 2). 96p. (Orig.). 1985. 24.00 (0-8039-2561-1); pap. text 10.50 (0-8039-2492-5) Sage.

Agarawal, M. K., ed. Antihormones in Health & Disease. (Frontiers of Hormone Research Ser.: Vol. 19). (Illus.). viii, 200p. 1991. 178.50 (3-8055-5297-1) S Karger.

Agarawala, R. A. Bundi: The City of Painted Walls. (C). 1996. 82.00 (81-7320-019-X, Pub. by Agam Kala Prakashan) S Asia.

Agard. Poems in My Earphone. 1995. pap. text. write for info. (0-582-22587-6, Pub. by Addison-Wesley) Longman.

Agard, A. The Reportorie of Records at Westminster. LC 72-225. (English Experience Ser.: No. 291). 1971. reprint ed. 30.00 (90-221-0291-2) Walter J Johnson.

Agard, F. B. Spoken Romanian, Units 1-30. LC 74-1000. (Spoken Language Ser.). 342p. (gr. 9-12). 1976. pap. 20.00 (0-87950-315-7) Spoken Lang Serv.

Agard, F. B. & Agard, F. B. Spoken Romanian. LC 74-1000. (Spoken Language Ser.). 342p. (gr. 9-12). 1976. audio 75.00 (0-87950-317-3) Spoken Lang Serv.

Agard, F. B. & Agard, F. B. Spoken Romanian. LC 74-1000. (Spoken Language Ser.). 342p. (YA). (gr. 9-12). 1976. pap. 95.00 incl. audio (0-87950-314-9) Spoken Lang Serv.

Agard, F. B., et al. English for Speakers of Spanish. LC 75-26678. (Spoken English As a Foreign Language Ser.). xii, 403p. 1975. audio 70.00 (0-87950-311-4); audio 90.00 (0-87950-312-2) Spoken Lang Serv.

An Asterisk (*) at the beginning of an entry indicates that the title is appearing for the first time.

Agard, F. B., et al. English for Speakers of Spanish (El Ingles Hablado) LC 75-26678. (English for Foreigners Ser.). xii, 403p. 1975. pap. 20.00 (*0-87950-307-6*) Spoken Lang Serv.

Agard, F. B, jt. auth. see Agard, F. B.

Agard, Frederick B. A Course in Romance Linguistics Vol. 1: A Synchronic View. LC 83-20817. 254p. (C). 1984. pap. 24.95 (*0-87840-088-5*) Georgetown U Pr.

— A Course in Romance Linguistics Vol. 1: A Synchronic View. LC 83-20817. 254p. 1984. reprint ed. pap. 78.80 (*0-608-01816-3*, 206246500001) Bks Demand.

Agard, Frederick B. & DiPietro, Robert J. The Sounds of English & Italian. LC 65-25118. (Midway Reprint, Contrastive Structure Ser.). (Illus.). 84p. reprint ed. pap. 30.00 (*0-608-18217-6*, 205662100078) Bks Demand.

— The Sounds of English & Italian. LC 65-25118. (Midway Reprint Ser.). 76p. (C). 1974. reprint ed. pap. text 6.00 (*0-226-01020-1*) U Ch Pr.

***Agard, Johannes, et al.** Identity in Conflict. 2nd ed. LC 98-906079. xviii, 253 p. 1998. write for info. (*81-215-0844-4*) Coronet Bks.

Agard, John. From the Devil's Pulpit. LC 98-126203. 128p. 1998. pap. 17.95 (*1-85224-406-2*, Pub. by Bloodaxe Bks) Dufour.

— Life Doesn't Frighten Me at All. LC 89-26766. (Illus.). 88p. (YA). (gr. 6 up). 1995. 14.95 (*0-8050-1237-0*, Bks Young Read) H Holt & Co.

— Lovelines for a Goat-Born Lady. LC 90-60288. (Illus.). 80p. (Orig.). 1991. pap. 12.95 (*1-85242-201-7*) Serpents Tail.

— Mangoes & Bullets. 80p. (Orig.). 1991. pap. 12.95 (*1-85242-124-X*) Serpents Tail.

Agard, John. We Animals Would Like a Word with You. (J). 1997. 19.95 (*0-370-32333-5*, Pub. by Random) Trafalgar.

— We Animals Would Like a Word with You. (Illus.). 64p. (J). 1998. pap. 8.95 (*0-09-968851-4*, Pub. by Random) Trafalgar.

Agard, John & Paul, Korky. Brer Rabbit & the Great Tug-O-War. LC 97-44327. (Illus.). 32p. (J). (ps-2). 1998. 13.95 (*0-7641-5077-4*); pap. 6.95 (*0-7641-0513-2*) Barron.

Agard, John, ed. see Nichols, Grace.

Agard, Keoni K., jt. auth. see Dudley, Michael K.

Agard, Keoni Kealoha, jt. auth. see Dudley, Michael Kioni.

Agard, Lesley, jt. auth. see Chun-Lum, Sharlene.

AGARD-NATO Staff. Combustion & Propulsion: Colloquium on Energy Sources & Energy Conversion. (Agardographs Ser.: No. 81). x, 926p. 1967. text 789.00 (*0-677-10560-6*) Gordon & Breach.

— Low Temperature Oxidation. (Agardographs Ser.: No. 86). xiv, 412p. 1967. text 506.00 (*0-677-10540-1*) Gordon & Breach.

Agard, Walter R. The Greek Tradition in Sculpture. 1979. 12.95 (*0-405-10576-2*) Ayer.

Agard, William R. Humanities for Our Time. LC 68-29218. (Essay Index Reprint Ser.). 1977. reprint ed. 19.95 (*0-8369-0554-7*) Ayer.

Agardh, C. A. Species Algarum Rite Cognitae Cum Symonymus, Differentis Specificis et Descriptionibus Succinctis, 2 vols., Set. 1970. reprint ed. 69.30 (*90-6123-001-2*) Lubrecht & Cramer.

Agardh, Lennart, ed. Dynamic Materials Models in Computer Programs: Workshop Proceedings. (Illus.). 206p. (C). 1998. pap. text 40.00 (*0-7881-4817-6*) DIANE Pub.

Agardy, Frank P., jt. auth. see Nemerow, Nelson L.

Agardy, Franklin J., jt. auth. see Nemerow, Nelson L.

Agardy, Tundi. Marine Protected Areas & Ocean Conservation. 1997. text 69.95 (*0-12-044455-0*) Acad Pr.

Agari, Masahiko. Formula, Rhetoric, & the Word: Studies in Milton's Epic Style. LC 96-36864. 136p. 1997. pap. 29.95 (*3-906756-91-2*, Pub. by P Lang) P Lang Pubng.

Agarossi, Elena. A Nation Collapses: The Italian Surrender of September, 1943. LC 98-45622. 187p. (C). 2000. text 44.95 (*0-521-59199-6*) Cambridge U Pr.

Agarwal. Principles of Seed Pathology, Vol. II. 184p. 1987. 174.00 (*0-8493-4315-1*) CRC Pr.

***Agarwal, A., et al, eds.** Si Front-End Processing -- Physics & Technology of Dopant-Defect Interactions II: Materials Research Society Symposium Proceedings, Vol. 610. 2000. text 79.00 (*1-55899-518-8*) Materials Res.

Agarwal, A. K. North-Eastern Economy: Problems & Prospects. (C). 1988. 32.00 (*81-7099-056-4*, Pub. by Mittal Pubs Dist) S Asia.

Agarwal, Anant. Analysis of Cache Performance for Operating Systems & Multiprogramming. (C). 1989. text 91.50 (*0-7923-9005-9*) Kluwer Academic.

Agarwal, B. C., jt. ed. see Biswas, Asit K.

Agarwal, B. K. X-Ray Spectroscopy. (Optical Sciences Ser.: Vol. 15). (Illus.). 1979. 54.50 (*0-387-09268-4*) Spr-Verlag.

— X-Ray Spectroscopy: An Introduction. 2nd ed. Schawlow, Arthur L. et al, eds. (Optical Sciences Ser.: Vol. 15). (Illus.). xv, 419p. 1991. 64.95 (*0-387-50719-1*) Spr-Verlag.

Agarwal, Bhagwan D. & Broutman, L. J. Analysis & Performance of Fiber Composites. 2nd ed. LC 89-70653. (Society of Plastics Engineers Monographs). 472p. 1990. 125.00 (*0-471-51152-8*) Wiley.

— Analysis & Performance of Fiber Composites. 2nd ed. (Society of Plastics Engineers Monographs). 93p. 1990. pap., student ed. write for info. (*0-471-53994-5*) Wiley.

Agarwal, Bhoo, et al. A Humanistic Approach to Quality of Life: A Selected Bibliography, Nos. 1052-1054. 1976. 12.50 (*0-686-20398-4*, Sage Prdcls Pr) Sage.

Agarwal, Bina. A Field of One's Own: Gender & Land Rights in South Asia. (Cambridge South Asian Studies: No. 58). (Illus.). 594p. (C). 1995. pap. text 36.95 (*0-521-42926-9*) Cambridge U Pr.

— A Field of One's Own-Gender & Land Rights in South Asia. 1996. pap. 42.00 (*0-7855-7396-8*, Pub. by Ratna Pustak Bhandar) St Mut.

— Gender & Command over Property: An Economic Analysis of South Asia. 51p. 1994. pap. 8.00 (*81-85107-31-9*) Women Ink.

Agarwal, Bina, ed. The Structures of Patriarchy: The State, the Community & the Household. LC 88-706. (C). 1988. pap. 17.50 (*0-86232-773-3*, Pub. by Zed Books) St Martin.

Agarwal, Binod C., jt. auth. see Shah, Vimal P.

Agarwal, C. L. Law of Hundis & Negotiable Instruments. 9th ed. (C). 1989. 80.00 (*0-7855-5463-7*) St Mut.

Agarwal, D. P. The Copper Bronze Age in India. (Illus.). 286p. 1971. text 27.00 (*0-685-13646-9*) Coronet Bks.

Agarwal, D. P., et al, eds. Climate & Geology of Kashmir & Central Asia. (Current Trends in Geology Ser.: Vol. 6). xvi, 247p. 1985. 59.00 (*1-55528-064-1*, Pub. by Today Tomorrow) Scholarly Pubns.

Agarwal, D. P., et al. Alcohol Consumption & Alcoholism in Hungary: Ethnocultural, Epidemiological & Biomedical Aspects. LC 98-133662. 236p. 1997. 141.00 (*963-05-7377-6*, Pub. by Akade Kiado) St Mut.

Agarwal, Deepa. The Hilltop Mystery. LC 98-917363. 120 p. 1999. write for info. (*81-259-0683-5*) S Asia.

— There's Another Way! Stories of Peace, Love & Friendship. LC 98-917040. 103p. 1998. write for info. (*81-259-0596-0*) Vikas.

Agarwal, G. New Law on Inter-Corporate Loans & Inter-Corporate Investments. (C). 1989. 75.00 (*0-7855-6131-5*) St Mut.

Agarwal, G., ed. Company Minutes (Law, Practice & Procedure) with Draft Specimen Minutes. 2nd ed. (C). 1989. 75.00 (*0-7855-6130-7*) St Mut.

Agarwal, G. P., ed. see All India Symposium Staff.

Agarwal, G. S., ed. Practical Vedic Astrology: A Complete Self Learning Treatise. 1998. pap. 20.00 (*0-8364-5537-1*) S Asia.

Agarwal, G. S., et al. Fundamentals of Cavity Quantum Electrodynamics. 350p. 1995. text 58.00 (*981-02-1869-9*) World Scientific Pub.

Agarwal, Giriraj S. & Singh, Baljit, eds. Diamond Hindi-English Dictionary. 420p. (Orig.). 1993. pap. 6.95 (*1-881338-38-X*) Nataraj Bks.

Agarwal, Girish S., ed. Selected Papers on Fundamentals of Quantum Optics. LC 94-36850. (Milestone Ser.). 1994. 50.00 (*0-8194-1717-3*, MS103) SPIE.

— Selected Papers on Resonant & Collective Phenomena in Quantum Optics. LC 94-37447. (SPIE Milestone Ser.: Vol. MS 104). 1994. 50.00 (*0-8194-1718-1*) SPIE.

Agarwal, J. C., jt. auth. see Agarwal, S. P.

Agarwal, J. C., jt. ed. see Yannopoulos, John C.

Agarwal, J. S. Law Relating to Modvat. (C). 1988. 80.00 (*0-7855-6129-3*) St Mut.

Agarwal, Jamuna P. Pros & Cons of Third World Multinationals: A Case Study of India. 115p. 1985. lib. bdg. 42.50 (*3-16-344994-8*, Pub. by JCB Mohr) Coronet Bks.

Agarwal, Jamuna P., et al. EC Trade Policies Towards Associated Countries: Barriers to Success. x, 150p. 1985. lib. bdg. 56.50 (*3-16-344953-0*, Pub. by JCB Mohr) Coronet Bks.

— The International Competitiveness of Developing Countries for Risk Capital. (Kiel Institute Studies: No. 242). 155p. (Orig.). 1991. pap. 46.50 (*3-16-145879-6*) Coronet Bks.

Agarwal, Krishna, jt. auth. see Davis, W. Alan.

Agarwal, Krishna K. Programming with Structured Flowcharts. 142p. 1984. pap. text 13.50 (*0-89433-226-0*) Petrocelli.

Agarwal, M. K., ed. Hormone Antagonists. (Illus.). 734p. 1982. 138.50 (*3-11-008613-1*) De Gruyter.

— Principles of Recepterology. LC 83-15441. (Illus.). vii, 677p. 1983. 196.15 (*3-11-009558-0*) De Gruyter.

— Receptor Mediated Antisteroid Action. 523p. (C). 1987. lib. bdg. 229.25 (*3-11-011355-4*) De Gruyter.

Agarwal, M. K. & Yoshida, M., eds. Immunopharmacology of Endotoxicosis: Proceedings of the 5th International Congress of Immunology Satellite Workshop. Kyoto, Japan, August 27, 1983. LC 84-7650. (Illus.). xiv, 376p. 1984. 138.50 (*3-11-009887-3*) De Gruyter.

Agarwal, M. K., ed. see International Congress of Endocrinology Staff.

Agarwal, M. L. Handbook of Ophthalmology. 240p. (C). 1990. 70.00 (*81-85017-53-0*, Pub. by Interprint) St Mut.

— M. C. Q. in Ophthalmology. 185p. (C). 1991. 50.00 (*81-85017-54-9*, Pub. by Interprint) St Mut.

Agarwal, M. M. Essense of Vaisnavism. (C). 1992. text 19.50 (*81-202-0375-5*, Pub. by Ajanta) S Asia.

Agarwal, Manju. Tax Incentives & Investment Behavior. (C). 1988. 175.00 (*0-7855-4733-9*) St Mut.

Agarwal, N. K., jt. auth. see Gautam, Ashutosh.

Agarwal, P. N. Engineering Seismology. (C). 1991. 21.50 (*81-204-0571-4*, Pub. by Oxford IBH) S Asia.

Agarwal, Pankaj K. Intersection & Decomposition Algorithms for Arrangements of Curves in the Plane. 293p. (C). 1991. text 47.95 (*0-521-40446-0*) Cambridge U Pr.

Agarwal, Pankaj K., et al, eds. Robotics Vol. 3: The Algorithmic Perspective: 1998WAFR. LC 98-20972. (Workshop on the Algorithmic Foundations of Robotics Ser.: Vol. 3). (Illus.). 389p. (C). 1998. text 49.00 (*1-56881-081-4*) AK Peters.

Agarwal, Pankaj K., jt. auth. see Pach, Janos.

Agarwal, Pankaj K., jt. auth. see Sharir, Micha.

Agarwal, Priya. Passage from India: Post-Nineteen Sixty-Five Indian Immigrants & Their Children. (Illus.). 102p. 1991. 18.95 (*0-9630579-0-1*) Yuvati.

Agarwal, R. K. Disclosure in Company Accounts. (C). 1989. 140.00 (*0-7855-4815-7*) St Mut.

— Investment Allowance or Investment Deposit Scheme under New Income Tax Law, 1989. (C). 1989. 50.00 (*0-7855-3658-2*) St Mut.

— Practical Guide to Directors Report. (C). 1989. 140.00 (*0-7855-6128-5*) St Mut.

— Tax Planning for Different Categories of Assessees. (C). 1989. 120.00 (*0-7855-4732-0*) St Mut.

— Tax Planning for Different Tax Payers. (C). 1990. 90.00 (*0-89771-283-8*) St Mut.

Agarwal, R. K., jt. auth. see Jain, D. C.

Agarwal, R. S. Mind & Vision. 7th ed. 269p. 1996. pap. 9.95 (*81-7058-218-0*, Pub. by SAA) E-W Cultural Ctr.

— Secrets of Indian Medicine. 4th ed. 240p. 1996. pap. 6.95 (*81-7058-068-4*, Pub. by SAA) E-W Cultural Ctr.

— Yoga of Perfect Sight. (Illus.). 223p. 1995. pap. 5.95 (*81-7058-209-1*, Pub. by SAA) E-W Cultural Ctr.

— Yoga of Perfect Sight. 3rd ed. 1979. pap. 5.95 (*0-89744-948-7*) Auromere.

Agarwal, Ravi P. Boundary Value Problems from Higher Order Differential Equations. 310p. 1986. text 51.00 (*9971-5-0108-2*) World Scientific Pub.

— Focal Boundary Value Problems for Differential & Difference Equations. LC 98-9344. (Mathematics & Its Applications Ser.). 289p. 1998. 140.00 (*0-7923-4978-4*) Kluwer Academic.

Agarwal, Ravi P., ed. Contributions in Numerical Mathematics. Vol. 2. 1993. text 109.00 (*981-02-1437-5*) World Scientific Pub.

— Difference Equations & Inequalities: Theory, Methods & Applications. (Pure & Applied Mathematics Ser.: Vol. 155). (Illus.). 800p. 1991. text 215.00 (*0-8247-8675-9*) Dekker.

— Recent Trends in Differential Equations. (Series in Applicable Analysis: Vol. 1). 550p. 1992. text 81.00 (*981-02-0963-0*) World Scientific Pub.

Agarwal, Ravi P. & Chow, Y. M., eds. Numerical Mathematics, Singapore, 1988. (International Series of Numerical Mathematics: Vol. 86). 540p. 1988. 142.00 (*0-8176-2255-1*) Birkhauser.

Agarwal, Ravi P. & Lakshmikantham, V. Uniqueness & Nonuniqueness Criteria for Ordinary Differential Equations. (Series in Real Analysis). 324p. 1993. text 86.00 (*981-02-1357-3*) World Scientific Pub.

***Agarwal, Ravi P. & O'Regan, Donal, eds.** Integral & Integrodifferential Equations: Theory, Methods & Applications. (Series on Mathematical Analysis & Applications: Vol. 2). 331p. 2000. text 95.00 (*90-5699-221-X*, G & B Science) Gordon & Breach.

Agarwal, Ravi P. & Pang, Peter Y. Opial Inequalities with Applications in Differential & Difference Equations. LC 94-48292. (Mathematics & Its Applications Ser.: Vol. 320). 1995. text 180.50 (*0-7923-3365-9*) Kluwer Academic.

Agarwal, Ravi P. & Qu, Rubin. Computer Aided Geometric Design. LC 97-20485. (Lecture Notes in Mathematics & Computer Science Ser.). 1997. pap. write for info. (*0-9640398-7-7*) Dynamic Pubs.

Agarwal, Ravi P. & Wong, Patricia. Error Inequalities in Polynomial Interpolation & Their Applications. LC 93-15913. (Mathematics & Its Applications Ser.: Vol. 262). 376p. (C). 1993. text 214.50 (*0-7923-2337-8*) Kluwer Academic.

Agarwal, Ravi P. & Wong, Patricia J. Advanced Topics in Difference Equations. LC 97-8155. 507p. 1997. text 264.50 (*0-7923-4521-5*) Kluwer Academic.

***Agarwal, Ravi P., et al.** Oscillation Theory for Difference & Functional Differential. 352p. 2000. 152.00 (*0-7923-6289-6*, Kluwer Plenum) Kluwer Academic.

Agarwal, Ravi P., et al. Positive Solutions of Differential, Difference & Integral Equations. LC 98-49417. 12p. 1999. write for info. (*0-7923-5510-5*) Kluwer Academic.

Agarwal, Ritu & Ferratt, Thomas W. Coping with Labor Scarcity in Information Technology: Strategies & Practices for Effective Recruitment & Retention. (Practice-Driven Research in IT Management Ser.: No. 2). (Illus.). 138p. 1999. pap. 94.95 (*1-893673-02-2*) Pinnaflex Inc.

Agarwal, S. B., jt. ed. see Biswas, Asit K.

Agarwal, S. C. Diseases of Green Gram & Black Gram. 321p. (C). 1993. pap. 375.00 (*81-7089-161-2*, Pub. by Intl Bk Distr) St Mut.

— Fishery Management. 1990. 52.50 (*81-7024-282-7*, Pub. by Ashish Pub Hse) S Asia.

Agarwal, S. K. Environmental Issues & Themes. (Illus.). ix, 435p. 1997. 57.00 (*81-7024-853-1*, Pub. by APH Pubng) Nataraj Bks.

— Perspectives in Aridzone Ecology. (Recent Researches in Ecology, Environment & Pollution Ser.: Vol. 8). (Illus.). 225p. 1991. 59.00 (*1-55528-258-X*) Scholarly Pubns.

— Resource Ecology. 157p. 1993. pap. 125.00 (*81-85167-70-2*, Pub. by Print Hse) St Mut.

Agarwal, S. K., jt. ed. see Kumar, Vikram.

Agarwal, S. K., jt. ed. see Spivey, James J.

Agarwal, S. L. Apkritya Vidhi: (Law of Torts in Hindi) 2nd ed. (HIN.). (C). 1979. 25.00 (*0-7855-5408-4*) St Mut.

— Muslim Vidhi: Muslim Law in Hindi. 2nd ed. (HIN.). (C). 1980. 35.00 (*0-7855-5477-7*) St Mut.

Agarwal, S. P. & Agarwal, J. C. Educational & Social Uplift of Backward Classes, Pt. One: At What Cost & How? (C). 1991. text 44.00 (*81-7022-339-3*, Pub. by Concept) S Asia.

Agarwal, S. P. & Kanta, Naresh. Child Education in India. 1990. 16.00 (*81-7022-274-5*, Pub. by Concept) S Asia.

Agarwal, Sanjay K., jt. ed. see Spivey, James J.

***Agarwal, Sunita & Pallikaris, Ioannis.** Refractive Surgery. 500p. (C). 1999. text 125.00 (*81-7179-700-8*, Pub. by Jaypee Brothers) SLACK Inc.

Agarwal, Urmila. North Indian Temple Sculpture. (Illus.). (C). 1996. 52.50 (*81-215-0458-9*, Pub. by M Manoharlal) Coronet Bks.

Agarwal, V. Traditions & Trends in Indian Music. 82p. 1975. 7.95 (*0-318-36333-X*) Asia Bk Corp.

Agarwal, V. K. Analysis of Antibiotic & Drug Residues in Food Products of Animal Origin. (Illus.). 272p. (C). 1992. text 89.00 (*0-306-44199-3*, Kluwer Plenum) Kluwer Academic.

— Concentration of Economic Power & Monopolies in India. (C). 1989. 235.00 (*0-7855-4785-1*) St Mut.

— Consumer Protection in India. (C). 1989. 450.00 (*0-7855-3700-7*); 450.00 (*0-7855-4799-1*) St Mut.

Agarwal, V. K. & Sinclair, J. B. Principles of Seed Pathology, Vol. 1. LC 86-6147. 1987. 110.00 (*0-8493-4314-3*, SB732, CRC Reprint) Franklin.

Agarwal, V. K. & Sinclair, James B. Methods in Seed Pathology. 1999. 89.95 (*0-8493-2877-2*) CRC Pr.

Agarwal, V. S. Applied Botany for Mass Communications. (Illus.). 450p. 1988. 65.00 (*1-55528-094-3*, Pub. by Today Tomorrow) Scholarly Pubns.

— Drug Plants of India. (C). 1984. 65.00 (*0-7855-2276-X*, Pub. by Scientific) St Mut.

— Economic Plants of India. (C). 1988. 70.00 (*0-7855-2275-1*, Pub. by Scientific) St Mut.

— Perspective in Botanical Museum. (C). 1988. 110.00 (*0-7855-3238-2*, Pub. by Scientific) St Mut.

— Perspectives in Botanical Museum: With Preference to India. viii, 390p. 1983. 49.00 (*0-88065-233-0*) Scholarly Pubns.

Agarwal, Vijendra K. & Sinclair, James B. Principles of Seed Pathology, 2 vols. 352p. 1987. 279.90 (*0-8493-4313-5*, SB732) CRC Pr.

— Principles of Seed Pathology. 2nd ed. 560p. (C). 1996. boxed set 99.00 (*0-87371-670-1*, L670) Lewis Pubs.

Agarwala, Amar N. & Singh, S. P., eds. Economics of Underdevelopment: A Series of Articles & Papers. 512p. 1979. pap. text 12.95 (*0-19-560674-4*) OUP.

Agarwala, B. R. Supreme Court Practice & Procedure. (C). 1992. 250.00 (*0-89771-796-1*, Pub. by Eastern Book) St Mut.

— Supreme Court Practice & Procedure. 5th ed. (C). 1989. 200.00 (*0-7855-5412-2*) St Mut.

Agarwala, B. V. Facets of Coordination Chemistry. 268p. 1993. text 58.00 (*981-02-1438-3*) World Scientific Pub.

Agarwala, D. D. Guide to Revenue Law in U. P., 1901-1976. 986p. 1977. 210.00 (*0-7855-1425-2*) St Mut.

— Guide to Revenue Law in U. P., 1901-1982. 1406p. 1982. 345.00 (*0-7855-1423-6*) St Mut.

— Guide to Revenue Law in U. P. 1901-1989. 5th ed. (C). 1991. 100.00 (*0-7855-5434-3*) St Mut.

— Guide to Revenue Law in U. P. 1901-1990. 5th ed. (C). 1991. 110.00 (*0-7855-5592-7*) St Mut.

— Guide to Revenue Law in U. P., 1976-1982. 420p. 1982. 135.00 (*0-7855-1424-4*) St Mut.

Agarwala, Neena, jt. auth. see Snipes, Wallace.

Agarwala, P. N. A Case Study on Decision-Making in Selected Multinational Enterprises in India: Multinational Enterprises Programme, Working Paper, No. 38. ii, 44p. (Orig.). 1985. pap. 13.50 (*92-2-105121-8*) Intl Labour Office.

— Countertrade: A Global Perspective. 1990. text 27.50 (*0-7069-5284-7*, Pub. by Vikas) S Asia.

— The New International Economic Order. (Studies on the New International Economic Order). 350p. 1983. 88.00 (*0-08-028823-5*, Pergamon Pr) Elsevier.

Agarwala, R. A. Paintings from Central India. (C). 1987. 75.00 (*0-8364-2183-3*, Pub. by Agam) S Asia.

— Wall Paintings from Central India. (Illus.). (C). 1987. 74.95 (*0-317-66132-9*) Asia Bk Corp.

— Wall Paintings from Central India. (C). 1987. 78.50 (*0-8364-2203-1*, Pub. by Sundeep Prak) S Asia.

Agarwala, R. P., ed. Lasers in Materials Science. 307p. 1999. 99.00 (*0-87849-826-5*, Pub. by Trans T Pub) Enfield Pubs NH.

***Agarwala, R. P., ed.** Special Defects in Semiconducting Materials. (Solid State Phenomena Ser.: Vol. 71). (Illus.). 284p. 1999. text 90.00 (*3-908450-44-6*, Pub. by Scitec Pubns) Enfield Pubs NH.

Agarwala, R. P., ed. Surface Coatings for Advanced Materials. (Materials Science Forum Ser.: Vol. 246). (Illus.). 292p. (C). 1997. text 88.00 (*0-87849-749-8*, Pub. by Trans T Pub) Enfield Pubs NH.

Agarwala, Ramgopal. Econometric Model of India, 1848-1961. 188p. 1970. 45.00 (*0-7146-1200-6*, BHA-01200, Pub. by F Cass Pubs) Intl Spec Bk.

Agarwala, S. N., ed. see Seminar on Population Growth & India's Economic De.

Agarwala, V. P. Forests in India. 1990. reprint ed. 23.00 (*81-204-0041-0*, Pub. by Oxford IBH) S Asia.

Agarwala, V. S. & Brown, G. K., eds. Corrosion & Corrosivity Sensors. LC 94-214137. (Illus.). 295p. 1994. 54.00 (*1-877914-73-8*) NACE Intl.

Agarwala, Vinod S. & Ugiansky, Gilbert M., eds. New Methods for Corrosion Testing of Aluminum Alloys. LC 91-35946. (Special Technical Publication Ser.: No. 1134). (Illus.). 225p. 1992. text 65.00 (*0-8031-1435-4*, STP1134) ASTM.

Agashe, S. N. Paleobotany: Plants of the Past, Their Evolution, Paleoenvironment & Environment in Exploration of Fossil Fuels. rev. ed. 350p. 1996. pap. 39.00 (*1-886106-72-X*) Science Pubs.

Agashe, S. N., ed. 5th International Aerobiology Conference. (Illus.). 620p. (C). 1997. 120.00 (*1-886106-84-3*) Science Pubs.

— Recent Trends in Aerobiology, Allergy & Immunology. (Illus.). 332p. 1994. text 90.00 (*1-886106-02-9*) Science Pubs.

An Asterisk (*) at the beginning of an entry indicates that the title is appearing for the first time.

Agassant, J. F., et al. Polymer Processing: Principles & Modeling. 599p. 1991. 79.50 (*1-56990-000-0*) Hanser-Gardner.

Agassant, J. F., jt. auth. see Piau, J. M.

Agassi, Hamid H. Fallacies of Satanic Verses: Rushdiesm on Trial. 692p. 1994. pap. 24.75 (*0-9642343-0-0*) Tarmasal.

Agassi, J. & Jarvie, I. C., eds. Rationality: The Critical View. 490p. (C). 1987. pap. text 87.50 (*90-247-3455-X*, Pub. by M Nijhoff); lib. bdg. 180.50 (*90-247-3275-1*, Pub. by M Nijhoff) Kluwer Academic.

Agassi, Joseph. Faraday As a Natural Philosopher. LC 73-151130. (Illus.). 373p. reprint ed. pap. 115.70 (*0-608-18221-4*, 205662900078) Bks Demand.

— Liberal Nationalism for Israel: Towards an Israeli National Identity. LC 99-74061. Orig. Title: Ben Dat U-Le'om. (Illus.). 328p. 1999. 24.95 (*965-229-190-0*) Gefen Bks.

— Radiation Theory & the Quantum Revolution. LC 93-13904. 1993. 70.00 (*0-8176-2905-X*) Birkhauser.

— Science & Society: Selected Essays in the Sociology of Science. 550p. 1981. lib. bdg. 175.00 (*90-277-1244-1*, D Reidel) Kluwer Academic.

— Siblinghood of Humanity: An Introduction to Philosophy. 2nd ed. LC 91-16766. 296p. 1991. pap. 20.00 (*0-88206-511-4*) Caravan Bks.

— Technology: Philosophical & Social Aspects. 288p. 1985. pap. text 64.50 (*90-277-2045-2*, D Reidel); lib. bdg. 122.00 (*90-277-2044-4*, D Reidel) Kluwer Academic.

Agassi, Joseph & Cohen, Robert S., eds. Scientific Philosophy Today. 523p. 1981. pap. text 86.50 (*90-277-1263-8*, D Reidel); lib. bdg. 171.00 (*90-277-1262-X*, D Reidel) Kluwer Academic.

Agassi, Joseph, jt. auth. see Fried, Yehuda.

Agassi, Joseph, jt. auth. see Laor, Nathaniel.

Agassi, Judith B., jt. auth. see Buber, Martin.

***Agassi, Martine.** Hands Are Not for Hitting. (Illus.). 40p. (J). (ps-1). 2000. pap. 10.95 (*1-57542-077-5*) Free Spirit Pub.

Agassi, Menachem, ed. Soil Erosion, Conservation, & Rehabilitation. LC 95-40716. (Soils, Plants, & the Environment Bks.: Vol. 46). (Illus.). 424p. 1995. text 165.00 (*0-8247-8984-9*, S623) Dekker.

Agassiz, Alexander. Embryology of the Starfish. (Works of Alexander Agassiz). 1989. reprint ed. lib. bdg. 79.00 (*0-7812-1582-X*) Rprt Serv.

— North American Acalephae. (Works of Alexander Agassiz). 1989. reprint ed. lib. bdg. 79.00 (*0-7812-1581-1*) Rprt Serv.

— North American Starfishes. (Works of Alexander Agassiz). 1989. reprint ed. lib. bdg. 79.00 (*0-7812-1584-6*) Rprt Serv.

— Revision of the Echini. (Works of Alexander Agassiz). 1989. reprint ed. lib. bdg. 79.00 (*0-7812-1583-8*) Rprt Serv.

— The Works of Alexander Agassiz, 1837-1910. 1987. reprint ed. lib. bdg. 600.00 (*0-685-18567-2*) Rprt Serv.

Agassiz, Alexander, jt. auth. see Agassiz, Elizabeth.

Agassiz, Elizabeth & Agassiz, Alexander. Seaside Studies in Natural History: Marine Animals of Massachusetts Bay. LC 75-125726. (American Environmental Studies). (Illus.). 1975. reprint ed. 25.95 (*0-405-02651-X*) Ayer.

Agassiz, George R., ed. see Lyman, Theodore.

Agassiz, Louis. Contributions to the Natural History of the United States of America, 4 vols., Set. Sterling, Keir B., ed. LC 77-81094. (Biologists & Their World Ser.). (Illus.). 1978. reprint ed. lib. bdg. 132.95 (*0-405-10675-0*) Ayer.

— Contributions to the Natural History of the United States of America, 4 vols., Vol. 1. Sterling, Keir B., ed. LC 77-81094. (Biologists & Their World Ser.). (Illus.). 1978. reprint ed. 66.95 (*0-405-10676-9*) Ayer.

— Contributions to the Natural History of the United States of America, 4 vols., Vol. 2. Sterling, Keir B., ed. LC 77-81094. (Biologists & Their World Ser.). (Illus.). 1978. reprint ed. 66.95 (*0-405-10677-7*) Ayer.

— Etudes Critiques les Mollusques Fossiles: Memoire les Trigonies et Monographic Des Myes (Critical Studies on Fossil Mollusks. Gould, Stephen Jay, ed. LC 79-8323. (History of Paleontology Ser.). (FRE., Illus.). 1980. reprint ed. lib. bdg. 75.95 (*0-405-12702-2*) Ayer.

— Geological Sketches. 229p. 1985. reprint ed. 59.00 (*0-7812-0855-6*) Rprt Serv.

— The Intelligence of Louis Agassiz: A Specimen Book of Scientific Writings; Selected, with an Introduction & Notes. Davenport, Guy, ed. LC 83-18504. 237p. 1983. reprint ed. lib. bdg. 65.00 (*0-313-24249-6*, AGIN) Greenwood.

— Lake Superior: Its Physical Character: Vegetation, & Animals Compared with Those of Other & Similar Regions. LC 79-125727. (American Environmental Studies). 1972. reprint ed. 24.95 (*0-405-02652-8*) Ayer.

— Methods of Study in Natural History. LC 72-125728. (American Environmental Studies). 1974. reprint ed. 23.95 (*0-405-02653-6*) Ayer.

Agassiz, Louis & Gould, Augustus. Principles of Zoology, Touching the Structure, Development, Distribution, & Natural Arrangement of the Races of Animals Living & Extinct. LC 76-125729. (American Environmental Studies). (Illus.). 1974. reprint ed. 19.95 (*0-405-02654-4*) Ayer.

Agasso, Domenica. St. Mary Mazzarello.Tr. of Maria Mazzarello. 224p. (Orig.). 1996. pap. 9.95 (*0-8198-6989-9*) Pauline Bks.

— Thecla Merlo: Messenger of the Good News. Moore, John, tr. from ITA. (Illus.). 270p. (Orig.). 1994. pap. 8.50 (*0-8198-7376-4*) Pauline Bks.

Agasso, Renzo. The New Way of the Cross. (Illus.). 1996. pap. 45.00 (*0-85439-487-7*, Pub. by St Paul Pubns) St Mut.

Agate, James. Alarums & Excursions. LC 67-30169. (Essay Index Reprint Ser.). 1977. 20.95 (*0-8369-0138-X*) Ayer.

— Amazing Theatre. LC 76-91307. 1972. reprint ed. 24.95 (*0-405-08181-2*, Pub. by Blom Pubns) Ayer.

— Around Cinemas. LC 72-169323. (Literature of Cinema, Ser. 2). (Illus.). 286p. 1972. reprint ed. 20.95 (*0-405-03888-7*) Ayer.

— Around Cinemas: Second Series. LC 76-169324. (Literature of Cinema, Ser. 2). (Illus.). 300p. 1978. reprint ed. 24.95 (*0-405-03889-5*) Ayer.

— At Half-Past Eight: Essays on the Theatre 1921-1922. LC 70-91308. 1972. reprint ed. 24.95 (*0-405-08182-0*, Pub. by Blom Pubns) Ayer.

— Brief Chronicles. LC 79-92223. 1972. reprint ed. lib. bdg. 24.95 (*0-405-08183-9*, Pub. by Blom Pubns) Ayer.

— Buzz, Buzz! LC 73-91309. 1972. reprint ed. 20.95 (*0-405-08184-7*, Pub. by Blom Pubns) Ayer.

— Contemporary Theatre: 1923, 1924, 1925, 1926, 4 vols., Set. LC 74-91407. Date not set. 96.95 (*0-405-19057-3*) Ayer.

— Contemporary Theatre, 1925, Vol. 3. LC 74-91407. 312p. 1972. reprint ed. 23.95 (*0-405-08187-1*, Pub. by Blom Pubns) Ayer.

— Contemporary Theatre, 1924, Vol. 2. LC 74-91407. 325p. 1972. reprint ed. 24.95 (*0-405-08186-3*, Pub. by Blom Pubns) Ayer.

— Contemporary Theatre, 1926, Vol. 4. LC 74-91407. 389p. 1972. reprint ed. 24.95 (*0-405-08188-X*, Pub. by Blom Pubns) Ayer.

— Contemporary Theatre, 1923. LC 74-91407. 1972. reprint ed. 24.95 (*0-405-08185-5*, Pub. by Blom Pubns) Ayer.

— Immoment Toys. LC 77-86884. 264p. 1972. reprint ed. 20.95 (*0-405-08189-8*, Pub. by Blom Pubns) Ayer.

— More First Nights. LC 74-86886. 359p. 1972. reprint ed. 24.95 (*0-405-08190-1*, Pub. by Blom Pubns) Ayer.

— Playgoing: An Essay. LC 72-83870. 1972. reprint ed. 18.95 (*0-405-08191-X*, Pub. by Blom Pubns) Ayer.

— Rachel. LC 72-84504. 1972. 18.95 (*0-405-08192-8*, Pub. by Blom Pubns) Ayer.

— Red Letter Nights. LC 71-91886. 1972. reprint ed. 24.95 (*0-405-08193-6*, Pub. by Blom Pubns) Ayer.

— Short View of the English Stage, 1900-1926. LC 70-94263. (Select Bibliographies Reprint Ser.). 1977. 19.95 (*0-8369-5037-2*) Ayer.

— Short View of the English Stage, 1900-1926. LC 75-91887. 1972. reprint ed. 21.95 (*0-405-08194-4*, Pub. by Blom Pubns) Ayer.

— These Were Actors: Extracts from a Newspaper Cutting Book, 1811-1833. LC 72-91889. 1972. reprint ed. 17.95 (*0-405-08195-2*, Pub. by Blom Pubns) Ayer.

— Those Were the Nights. LC 77-91890. 1972. reprint ed. 20.95 (*0-405-08196-0*, Pub. by Blom Pubns) Ayer.

Agate, James E., ed. The English Dramatic Critics: An Anthology, 1660-1932. LC 83-45688. reprint ed. 49.50 (*0-404-20003-6*) AMS Pr.

Agate, May. Madame Sarah. LC 73-82817. 1972. reprint ed. 20.95 (*0-405-08197-9*, Pub. by Blom Pubns) Ayer.

Agathangelos. Patmowt'iwn Hayots: History of the Armenians. Thomson, Robert W., ed. LC 79-27282. (Classical Armenian Texts Ser.). 608p. 1980. reprint ed. 60.00 (*0-88206-027-9*) Caravan Bks.

Agathias. Agathiae Myrinaei Historiarum Libri Quinque. Keydell, Rudolfus, ed. (Corpus Fontium Historiae Byzantinae Ser.: Berolinensis Vol. 2). 232p. (C). 1967. 106.95 (*3-11-001348-7*) De Gruyter.

***Agathocleous, Tanya.** George Orwell: Battling Big Brother. (Oxford Portraits Ser.). (Illus.). 112p. (YA). 2000. lib. bdg. 22.00 (*0-19-512185-6*) OUP.

Agathocleus, Tanya. Museum New York. pap. 15.00 (*1-84166-034-5*, Pub. by Ellipsis) Norton.

Agawa, Hiroyuki. The Citadel in Spring. Rogers, Lawrence, tr. from JPN. 256p. 1991. 18.95 (*0-87011-960-5*) Kodansha.

— The Reluctant Admiral: Yamamoto & the Imperial Navy. Bester, John, tr. LC 79-84652. 397p. 1982. pap. 13.00 (*0-87011-512-X*) Kodansha.

***Agawa, Hiroyuki.** Reluctant Admiral: Yamamoto & the Imperial Navy. 2000. pap. 17.00 (*4-7700-2539-4*) Kodansha.

Agawu-Kakraba, Yaw B. Demythification in the Fiction of Miguel Delibes. LC 95-40413. (Currents in Comparative Romance Languages & Literatures Ser.: Vol. 40). 221p. (C). 1996. text 47.95 (*0-8204-3031-5*) P Lang Pubng.

Agawu, Kofi. African Rhythm: A Northern Ewe Perspective. (Illus.). 237p. (C). 1995. text 69.95 (*0-521-48084-1*) Cambridge U Pr.

Agawu, V. K. Playing with Signs. 168p. 1991. text 42.50 (*0-691-09138-2*, Pub. by Princeton U Pr) Cal Prin Full Svc.

Agay, Denes. The Baroque Period: Masters of the Seventeenth & Eighteenth Century. (Anthology of Piano Music Ser.: Vol. 1). 232p. 1981. pap. 19.95 (*0-8256-8041-7*, YK20212, Yorktown Mus) Music Sales.

— The Classical Period: Haydn, Mozart, Beethoven & Their Contemporaries. (Anthology of Piano Music Ser.: Vol. 2). 236p. 1981. pap. 19.95 (*0-8256-8042-5*, YK20220, Yorktown Mus) Music Sales.

— The First Classics for Piano, No. 2. (Recital Notebooks Ser.). (Illus.). 12p. 1965. pap. 3.95 (*0-8256-8051-4*, YK30070, Yorktown Mus) Music Sales.

— Intermediate Grades: Classics to Moderns. (Music for Millions Ser.: Vol. 37). 1962. pap. 11.95 (*0-8256-4037-7*, AM41617) Music Sales.

— An Introduction to Playing Folk Tunes: A Worldwide Collection of Melodic Gems from the Beginning Pianist. 32p. (Orig.). 1995. pap. 7.95 (*0-8256-8090-5*, YK21701, Amsco Music) Music Sales.

Agay, Denes. The Joy of Bach. 1968. pap. 11.95 (*0-8256-8011-5*, YK21004, Yorktown Mus) Music Sales.

Agay, Denes. The Joy of Baroque. 1974. pap. 11.95 (*0-8256-8015-8*, YK21012, Yorktown Mus) Music Sales.

— The Joy of Beethoven. LC 85-750996. 80p. 1983. pap. 11.95 (*0-8256-8026-3*, YK30039, Yorktown Mus) Music Sales.

— The Joy of Boogie & Blues, No. 1. 1968. pap. 11.95 (*0-8256-8010-7*, YK21020, Yorktown Mus) Music Sales.

— The Joy of Children's Favorites. (Illus.). 80p. 1989. pap. 11.95 (*0-8256-8074-3*, YK21392, Yorktown Mus) Music Sales.

— The Joy of Chopin. 1984. pap. 11.95 (*0-8256-8027-1*, YK20998, Yorktown Mus) Music Sales.

— The Joy of Claude Debussy. 1984. pap. 11.95 (*0-8256-8029-8*, YK21269, Yorktown Mus) Music Sales.

— Joy of Flute. (Illus.). 48p. 1993. pap. 11.95 (*0-7119-3259-X*, YK21616) Music Sales.

— The Joy of Mozart. 1983. pap. 11.95 (*0-8256-8025-5*, YK30021, Yorktown Mus) Music Sales.

— The Joy of Organ Music. (Illus.). 80p. 1967. pap. 11.95 (*0-8256-8007-7*, YK21095, Yorktown Mus) Music Sales.

— The Joy of Piano. (Orig.). 1964. pap. 11.95 (*0-8256-8002-6*, YK21103, Yorktown Mus) Music Sales.

— The Joy of Piano Duets. (Illus.). 80p. pap. 11.95 (*0-8256-8008-5*, YK21111, Yorktown Mus) Music Sales.

— Joy of Playing for Pleasure. 1994. pap. 11.95 (*0-8256-8075-1*, YK21491) Music Sales.

— The Joy of Ragtime. 1974. pap. 11.95 (*0-8256-8016-6*, YK21129, Yorktown Mus) Music Sales.

— The Joy of the Music of Denes Agay. 1980. pap. 11.95 (*0-8256-8024-7*, YK21228, Yorktown Mus) Music Sales.

— The Joy of the Music of Love. 80p. 1998. pap. 11.95 (*0-8256-8100-6*, YK21818) Music Sales.

— Learning to Play Piano, Bk. 2. rev. ed. (Illus.). 72p. 1992. pap. 8.95 (*0-8256-8070-0*, YK20493, Yorktown Mus) Music Sales.

— Learning to Play Piano, Bk. 3. rev. ed. (Illus.). 72p. 1992. pap. 8.95 (*0-8256-8071-9*, YK20501, Yorktown Mus) Music Sales.

— Learning to Play Piano, Bk. 4. rev. ed. (Illus.). 72p. 1993. pap. 8.95 (*0-8256-8072-7*, YK20519, Yorktown Mus) Music Sales.

— Learning to Play Piano Bk. 1: Primer. rev. ed. (Illus.). 72p. 1991. pap. 8.95 (*0-8256-8069-7*, YK20485, Yorktown Mus) Music Sales.

— Teaching Piano: A Comprehensive Guide & Reference Book for the Instructor, 2 vols. (Illus.). 702p. pap. 34.95 (*0-8256-8039-5*, YK30054) Omnibus NY.

— The Twentieth Century: Major Composers of Our Time. (Anthology of Piano Music Ser.: Vol. 4). 238p. 1971. pap. 19.95 (*0-8256-8044-1*, YK20246, Yorktown Mus) Music Sales.

Agay, Denes, ed. Anthology of Piano Music, Vol. 3: The Romantic Period. (Illus.). 244p. 1971. pap. 19.95 (*0-8256-8043-3*, YK20238, Yorktown Mus) Music Sales.

— Dearly Beloved-Wedding Songs. 1959. pap. 9.95 (*0-8256-4162-4*, AM42144) Music Sales.

— Easy Classics to Moderns. Vol. 17. 160p. 1985. pap. 11.95 (*0-8256-4017-2*, AM41484) Music Sales.

— An Introduction to Playing Duets. 31p. 1997. pap. text 7.95 (*0-8256-8096-4*, YK21777, Yorktown Mus) Music Sales.

— The Joy of Ballet Music. (Illus.). 80p. 1985. pap. 11.95 (*0-8256-8035-2*, YK21350, Yorktown Mus) Music Sales.

— The Joy of Bartok. (Illus.). 64p. 1984. pap. 11.95 (*0-8256-8034-4*, YK21319, Yorktown Mus) Music Sales.

— The Joy of Boogie & Blues, No. 2. (Illus.). 64p. 1985. pap. 11.95 (*0-8256-8036-0*, YK21368, Yorktown Mus) Music Sales.

— The Joy of Christmas. (Illus.). 80p. 1972. pap. 11.95 (*0-8256-8001-8*, YK21194, Yorktown Mus) Music Sales.

— The Joy of Classics. (Illus.). 80p. 1968. pap. 11.95 (*0-8256-8005-0*, YK21046, Yorktown Mus) Music Sales.

— The Joy of Classics to Pops. (Illus.). 80p. 1988. pap. 11.95 (*0-8256-8073-5*, YK21434, Yorktown Mus) Music Sales.

— The Joy of Disney. (Illus.). 64p. 1980. pap. 11.95 (*0-8256-8031-X*, WD10278, Yorktown Mus) Music Sales.

— The Joy of First Classics. (Illus.). 80p. 1987. pap. 11.95 (*0-8256-8066-2*, YK21376, Yorktown Mus) Music Sales.

— The Joy of First Classics, Bk. 2. (Illus.). 80p. 1989. pap. 11.95 (*0-8256-8077-8*, YK20568, Yorktown Mus) Music Sales.

— The Joy of First-Year Piano. (Illus.). 80p. 1972. pap. 11.95 (*0-8256-8013-1*, YK21053, Yorktown Mus) Music Sales.

— The Joy of Folk Songs. (Illus.). 80p. 1968. pap. 11.95 (*0-8256-8006-9*, YK21061, Yorktown Mus) Music Sales.

— The Joy of French Piano Music. (Illus.). 80p. pap. 11.95 (*0-8256-8033-6*, YK21293, Yorktown Mus) Music Sales.

— The Joy of Having Fun at the Piano. (Illus.). 80p. 1980. pap. 11.95 (*0-8256-8003-4*, YK30005, Yorktown Mus) Music Sales.

— The Joy of Jazz. (Illus.). 48p. 1968. pap. 11.95 (*0-8256-8004-2*, YK21087, Yorktown Mus) Music Sales.

— The Joy of Jazz, Bk. 2. (Illus.). 80p. 1987. pap. 11.95 (*0-8256-8067-0*, YK21384, Yorktown Mus) Music Sales.

— The Joy of Modern Piano Music. 80p. 1984. pap. 11.95 (*0-8256-8019-0*, YK21202, Yorktown Mus); pap. 11.95 (*0-86001-683-8*, YK21202, Yorktown Mus) Music Sales.

— The Joy of Modern Recital Repertory for Young Pianists. 80p. 1997. pap. 11.95 (*0-8256-8094-8*, YK21742) Music Sales.

— The Joy of Piano Entertainment. (Illus.). 80p. 1977. pap. 11.95 (*0-8256-8020-4*, YK21178, Yorktown Mus) Music Sales.

— The Joy of Recital Time. (Illus.). 80p. 1972. pap. 11.95 (*0-8256-8014-X*, YK21137, Yorktown Mus) Music Sales.

— The Joy of Romantic Piano Bk. 1: Early-to-Intermediate Grades. (Illus.). 80p. 1976. pap. 11.95 (*0-8256-8017-4*; YK21145, Yorktown Mus) Music Sales.

— The Joy of Romantic Piano Bk. 2: Intermediate-to-Early Advanced Grades. (Illus.). 80p. 1976. pap. 11.95 (*0-8256-8022-0*, YK21152, Yorktown Mus) Music Sales.

— The Joy of Russian Piano Music. (Illus.). 80p. pap. 11.95 (*0-8256-8032-8*, YK21285, Yorktown Mus) Music Sales.

— The Joy of Sacred Music. (Illus.). 80p. 1984. pap. 11.95 (*0-8256-8030-1*, YK41500, Yorktown Mus) Music Sales.

— The Joy of Sonatinas. (Illus.). 80p. 1972. pap. 11.95 (*0-8256-8012-3*, YK21160, Yorktown Mus) Music Sales.

— The Joy of Wedding Music. (Illus.). 80p. 1990. pap. 11.95 (*0-8256-8080-8*, YK21533, Yorktown Mus) Music Sales.

— Treasury of Popular Classics. (Illus.). 112p. 1987. pap. 12.95 (*0-8256-2096-1*, AM40361) Music Sales.

Agay, Denes, ed. An Introduction to Playing Sonatinas: A First Repetory for Early-Grade Pianists. 32p. 1997. 7.95 (*0-8256-8091-3*, YK 21693) Omnibus NY.

Agay, Denes, selected by. The Joy of Two Pianos, 2 bks., Set. (Illus.). 1989. pap. 14.95 (*0-8256-8076-X*, YK21459, Yorktown Mus) Music Sales.

— Sonatas & Sonatinas. (Classics to Moderns Ser.: No. MFM67). (Illus.). 208p. pap. 14.95 (*0-8256-4067-9*, AM48737) Music Sales.

Agay, Denes. The Joy of American Song Classics. 80p. 1997. pap. 11.95 (*0-8256-8089-1*, YK 20618) Music Sales.

— The Joy of Waltzes, Tangos & Polkas. 80p. 1998. pap. 11.95 (*0-8256-8103-0*, YK21842) Music Sales.

Agay, Denes & Goldstein, Jerome. The Joy of Clarinet. (Illus.). 80p. 1968. pap. 11.95 (*0-8256-8009-3*, YK21038, Yorktown Mus) Music Sales.

Agay, Denes & Metis, Frank. The Joy of Handel & the "Messiah" 80p. 1998. pap. 11.95 (*0-8256-8101-4*, YK21826) Music Sales.

— The Joy of Modern Blues. 80p. 1998. pap. 11.95 (*0-8256-8097-2*, YK21785) Music Sales.

Agay, Denes, jt. see Metis, Frank.

Agay, Denes, jt. auth. see Bachus, Nancy.

Agazarian, Yvonne & Peters, Richard. The Visible & Invisible Group. 302p. 1995. reprint ed. pap. text 36.00 (*1-85575-119-4*, Pub. by H Karnac Bks Ltd) Other Pr LLC.

— The Visible & Invisible Group: Two Perspectives on Group Psychotherapy & Group Process. 304p. 1989. pap. 17.95 (*0-415-03770-0*) Routledge.

Agazarian, Yvonne M. Systems-Centered Therapy for Groups. LC 97-3418. 328p. 1997. lib. bdg. 42.00 (*1-57230-195-3*, 0195) Guilford Pubns.

Agazzi, E., ed. Modern Logic - A Survey: Historical, Philosophical & Mathematical Aspects of Modern Logic & Its Applications. (Synthese Library: Vol. 149). 483p. 1980. text 206.50 (*90-277-1137-2*, D Reidel) Kluwer Academic.

Agazzi, E. & Cordero, Alberto, eds. Philosophy & the Origin & Evolution of the Universe. (Synthese Library: No. 217). 480p. 1991. text 185.50 (*0-7923-1322-4*) Kluwer Academic.

Agazzi, Evandro, ed. Philosophy of Mathematics Today. LC 96-49528. (Episteme EPIS Ser.: No. 22). 361p. (C). 1996. text 144.00 (*0-7923-4343-3*) Kluwer Academic.

— Probability in the Sciences. 280p. (C). 1988. lib. bdg. 137.50 (*90-277-2808-9*, Pub. by Kluwer Academic) Kluwer Academic.

— The Problem of Reductionism in Science. (Episteme Ser.). 236p. (C). 1991. lib. bdg. 122.00 (*0-7923-1406-9*, Pub. by Kluwer Academic) Kluwer Academic.

***Agazzi, Evandro & Pauri, Massimo.** The Reality of the Unobservable: Observability, Unobservability & Their Impact on the Issue of Scientific Realism. LC 00-38463. (Boston Studies in the Philosophy of Science). (Illus.). 2000. write for info. (*0-7923-6311-6*, Kluwer Plenum) Kluwer Academic.

Agbabian, Alidz. Fire & Water, Sister & Brother: An Armenian Myth. (Illus.). 32p. (Orig.). (J). (ps-2). 1998. pap. 12.00 (*0-9655507-2-9*) Dziludzar.

— Grag ou Tchur, Kuyr ou Yeghpayr: Haygagan Avantazuruyts. (ARM., Illus.). 32p. (Orig.). 1998. pap. 12.00 (*0-9655507-3-7*) Dziludzar.

— Tell Me Who Your Friend Is: An Armenian Folktale. (Illus.). 32p. (Orig.). (J). (ps-2). 1996. pap. 12.00 (*0-9655507-0-2*) Dziludzar.

— Useh Ov Eh Unkehrut: Haykahkan Johghohvurtakahn Badmoutiun.Tr. of Tell Me Who Your Friend Is. (ARM., Illus.). 32p. (Orig.). (J). (ps-2). 1996. pap. 12.00 (*0-9655507-1-0*) Dziludzar.

Agbaje, Adigun A. The Nigerian Press, Hegemony, & the Social Construction of Legitimacy, 1960-1983. LC 92-19202. 352p. 1992. lib. bdg. 99.95 (*0-7734-9555-X*) E Mellen.

Agbango, George, ed. Issues & Trends in Contemporary African Politics: Stability, Development, & Democratization. LC 96-18452. (Society & Politics in Africa Ser.: No. 1). 400p. (C). 1997. pap. text 32.95 (*0-8204-3130-3*) P Lang Pubng.

***Agbasiere, Joseph Therese & Ardener, Shirley.** Women in IGBO Life & Thought. LC 99-40300. 288p. 2000. pap. 25.99 (*0-415-22704-6*) Routledge.

***Agbasieri, Joseph-Theresa & Ardener, Shirley.** Women in Igbo Life & Thought. LC 99-40300. 288p. (C). 2000. text 85.00 (*0-415-22703-8*) Routledge.

Agbayani, Brian & Tang, Sze-Wing, eds. The Proceedings of the Fifteenth West Coast Conference on Formal Linguistics. (Proceedings of the West Coast Conference on Formal Linguistics Ser.). (Illus.). 544p. (C). 1997. 74.95 (*1-57586-079-1*); pap. 27.95 (*1-57586-078-3*) CSLI.

Agbenor, Pierre Richard & Montiel, Peter J. Development Macroeconomics. 2nd ed. LC 98-55310. 1999. 65.00 (*0-691-00677-6*, Pub. by Princeton U Pr) Cal Prin Full Svc.

Agbese, Pita O. & Ihonvbere, Julius O. Structural Adjustment & the Nigerian State. LC 97-2790. 1997. write for info. (*0-88258-196-1*) Howard U Pr.

Agbeti, John K. West African Church History No. 2: Christian Missions & Theological Training, 1842-1970. LC 86-149803. xv, 262p. 1991. pap. 64.00 (*90-04-09100-9*) Brill Academic Pubs.

An Asterisk (*) at the beginning of an entry indicates that the title is appearing for the first time.

Agbodeka, Francis. African Politics & British Policy in the Gold Coast 1868-1900: A Study in the Forms & Force of Protest. LC 73-175916. (Legon History Ser.). 218p. reprint ed. 67.60 (*0-8357-9446-6*, 201528500093) Bks Demand.

Agcaoili-Sombilla, Mercedita. Global Food Projections to 2020: Implications for Investment. Rosegrant, Mark A. & Perez, Nicostrato D., eds. (Illus.). 54p. (C). 1998. reprint ed. pap. text 20.00 (*0-7881-4337-9*) DIANE Pub.

Agcaoili, T. D. Collected Stories, Vol. 1. 128p. (Orig.). 1993. pap. 12.50 (*971-10-0479-8*, Pub. by New Day Pub) Cellar.

— Collected Stories Vol. 2: Stories of War. 149p. (Orig.). 1994. pap. 12.50 (*971-10-0539-5*, Pub. by New Day Pub) Cellar.

Agcaoili, T. D., ed. Philippine Writing: An Anthology. LC 76-98742. 351p. 1971. reprint ed. lib. bdg. 69.50 (*0-8371-3063-8*, AGPW, Greenwood Pr) Greenwood.

Age Concern England Staff. A Buyer's Guide to Sheltered Housing. (C). 1989. 35.00 (*0-86242-063-6*, Pub. by Age Concern Eng) St Mut.

— The Coming of Age in Europe: Older People in the European Community. (C). 1992. 65.00 (*0-86242-114-4*, Pub. by Age Concern Eng) St Mut.

— Your Home in Retirement: An Owner's Guide. (C). 1989. 25.00 (*0-86242-095-4*, Pub. by Age Concern Eng) St Mut.

Age, Mark. How to Do All Things: Your Use of Divine Power. 4th ed. LC 87-73244. (Illus.). 144p. 1988. reprint ed. pap. 7.00 (*0-912322-55-1*) Mark-Age.

Agee, Anne S., et al. The Basic Writer's Book. 3rd ed. LC 97-7220. 438p. 1997. pap. text 42.00 (*0-13-058637-4*) P-H.

Agee, Chris, ed. Scar on the Stone: Contemporary Poetry from Bosnia. 208p. 1998. pap. 19.95 (*1-85224-415-1*, Pub. by Bloodaxe Bks) Dufour.

Agee, Doris. Edgar Cayce on E. S. P. 224p. 1988. mass mkt. 3.95 (*0-446-35135-0*, Pub. by Warner Bks) Little.

Agee, E. M. & Assai, T., eds. Cloud Dynamics. 1982. text 162.50 (*90-277-1458-4*) Kluwer Academic.

Agee, Ida. Where's Curley Q? (Illus.). 32p. (Orig.). (J). (gr. k-4). 1995. pap. 3.50 (*0-9648344-0-5*) LCQ.

***Agee, James.** Agee on Film: Criticism & Comment on the Movies. Scorsese, Martin, ed. LC 99-42451. (Modern Library Movies Ser.). 406p. 2000. pap. 14.95 (*0-375-75529-2*) Modern Lib NY.

Agee, James. A Death in the Family. 320p. 1982. mass mkt. 6.50 (*0-553-27011-7*, Bantam Classics) Bantam.

— A Death in the Family. 1998. 17.10 (*0-606-13326-7*, Pub. by Turtleback) Demco.

***Agee, James.** A Death in the Family. LC 99-164384. 320p. 1998. pap. 12.00 (*0-375-70123-0*) Vin Bks.

— A Death in the Family. large type ed. LC 99-46448. 390p. 2000. lib. bdg. 28.95 (*1-58547-006-6*) Ctr Point Pubg.

Agee, James. James Agee: Selected Journalism. Ashdown, Paul, ed. LC 85-710. (Illus.). 228p. 1985. text 28.00 (*0-87049-466-X*) U of Tenn Pr.

— Let Us Now Praise Famous Men. (Illus.). 460p. 1989. pap. 16.95 (*0-395-48897-4*) HM.

— Let Us Now Praise Famous Men. LC 88-18110. (Illus.). 432p. 2000. 30.00 (*0-395-95771-0*) HM.

— Permit Me Voyage. LC 70-144740. (Yale Series of Younger Poets: No. 33). reprint ed. 18.00 (*0-404-53833-9*) AMS Pr.

Agee, James, et al. A Southern Appalachian Reader. Quillen, Rita et al, eds. LC 87-19589. (Illus.). 500p. (YA). (gr. 10-12). 1988. pap. text 14.95 (*0-913239-50-X*) Appalach Consortium.

Agee, James K. Ecosystem Management for Parks & Wilderness. LC 88-27673. (Illus.). 244p. 1989. 20.00 (*0-295-96817-6*) U of Wash Pr.

— Fire & Weather Disturbances in Terrestrial Ecosystems of the Eastern Cascades. (Illus.). 62p. 1998. reprint ed. 12.50 (*0-89904-940-0*, Ecosystems Resrch); reprint ed. pap. 6.50 (*0-89904-941-9*, Ecosystems Resrch) Crumb Elbow Pub.

— Fire Ecology of Pacific Northwest Forests. LC 93-2071. 505p. (C). 1993. text 60.00 (*1-55963-229-1*) Island Pr.

— Fire Ecology of Pacific Northwest Forests. 505p. (C). 1996. pap. text 38.00 (*1-55963-230-5*) Island Pr.

***Agee, Joel.** Twelve Years: An American Boyhood in East Germany. (Illus.). 1999. pap. 15.00 (*0-226-01050-3*) U Ch Pr.

Agee, Joel, tr. see Canetti, Elias.

Agee, Joel, tr. see Edvardson, Cordelia.

Agee, Joel, tr. see Loetscher, H., et al.

Agee, Joel, tr. see Meter, Leo.

Agee, Joel, tr. see Moser, Erwin.

Agee, Joel, tr. see Rilke, Rainer Maria.

Agee, Joel, tr. see Von Hentig, Hartmut.

Agee, Joel, tr. see Von Kleist, Heinrich.

Agee, Jon. The Bear in the Hat. (Michael di Capua Bks.). (Illus.). 32p. (J). 2000. 15.95 (*0-06-205187-3*) HarpC Child Bks.

***Agee, Jon.** The Bear in the Hat. (Michael di Capua Bks.). (Illus.). 32p. (J). 2000. lib. bdg. 15.89 (*0-06-205188-1*) HarpC Child Bks.

Agee, Jon. Dmitri the Astronaut. LC 94-75641. (Illus.). 32p. (J). (ps up). 1998. pap. 5.95 (*0-06-205925-4*) HarpC.

— Dmitri the Astronaut. LC 94-75641. (Michael di Capua Bks.). (Illus.). 32p. (J). (ps up). 1996. 14.95 (*0-06-205074-5*) HarpC Child Bks.

— Dmitri the Astronaut. (Trophy Picture Bks.). (J). 1998. 11.15 (*0-606-12916-2*, Pub. by Turtleback) Demco.

— Ellsworth. (Illus.). 32p. (J). (ps-3). 1989. pap. 3.95 (*0-374-42082-3*) FS&G.

***Agee, Jon.** Elvis Lives! And Other Anagrams. LC 99-38139. (Illus.). 80p. (YA). 2000. 15.00 (*0-374-32127-2*) FS&G.

— Go Hang a Salami! I'm a Lasagna Hog! And Other Palindromes. LC 91-31319. (Illus.). 80p. (YA). (gr. 2-6). 1992. 14.41 (*0-374-33473-0*) FS&G.

Agee, Jon. Go Hang a Salami! I'm a Lasagna Hog! And Other Palindromes. (Illus.). 80p. (J). 1994. pap. 6.95 (*0-374-44473-0*, Sunburst Bks) FS&G.

— If Snow Falls: A Story for December. LC 96-2299. 32p. (J). (ps-3). 1996. pap. 3.95 (*0-374-43565-0*) FS&G.

— If Snow Falls: A Story for December. LC 96-2299. 1996. 9.15 (*0-606-10221-3*, Pub. by Turtleback) Demco.

— The Incredible Painting of Felix Clousseau. LC 87-46072. (Illus.). 32p. (J). (ps-3). 1988. 15.00 (*0-374-33633-4*) FS&G.

— Incredible Painting of Felix Clousseau. 32p. (J). (gr. 4-8). 1990. pap. 4.95 (*0-374-43582-0*) FS&G.

— Ludlow Laughs. LC 85-45466. (Illus.). 32p. (J). (ps up). 1987. pap. 4.95 (*0-374-44663-6*) FS&G.

***Agee, Jon.** Palindromania. 2002. text. write for info. (*0-374-35730-7*) FS&G.

Agee, Jon. The Return of Freddy LeGrand. 32p. (J). (ps-3). 1992. 15.00 (*0-374-36249-1*) FS&G.

— The Return of Freddy LeGrand. (Illus.). 32p. (J). (ps-3). 1994. pap. 4.95 (*0-374-46230-5*) FS&G.

— Return of Freddy Legrand. (J). 1994. 10.15 (*0-606-08072-4*) Turtleback.

***Agee, Jon.** Sit On a Potato Pan, Otis! More Palindromes. LC 98-31783. (Illus.). 80p. (YA). (gr. 4 up). 1999. 14.41 (*0-374-31808-5*) FS&G.

Agee, Jon. So Many Dynamos! And Other Palindromes. LC 94-73749. (Illus.). 80p. (J). (gr. 2-6). 1994. 13.31 (*0-374-22473-0*) FS&G.

— So Many Dynamos! And Other Palindromes. (Illus.). 80p. (J). (ps-13). 1997. pap. 6.96 (*0-374-46905-9*, Sunburst Bks) FS&G.

— Who Ordered the Jumbo Shrimp. LC 97-78386. (Illus.). 80p. (J). (gr. 4 up). 1998. 12.95 (*0-06-205159-8*) HarpC.

Agee, Jon & Chase, Naomi F. Stacked. (Illus.). 20p. 1997. pap. 10.00 (*1-882329-11-2*) Garden St Pr.

Agee, Jon, jt. auth. see Steig, William.

Agee, Jonis. Bend This Heart. LC 89-7100. 160p. (Orig.). 1989. pap. 9.95 (*0-918273-51-X*) Coffee Hse.

— Mercury. LC 81-2998. (Illus.). 12p. (Orig.). 1981. pap. 15.00 (*0-915124-50-5*) Coffee Hse.

— South of Resurrection. 368p. 1998. pap. 12.95 (*0-14-024172-8*) Viking Penguin.

***Agee, Jonis.** Strange Angels. 2000. pap. 13.95 (*0-14-029186-5*) Viking Penguin.

Agee, Jonis. Taking the Wall. LC 99-35463. 180p. 1999. pap. 14.95 (*1-56689-088-8*, Pub. by Coffee Hse) SPD-Small Pr Dist.

— A .38 Special & a Broken Heart. LC 94-48076. (Coffee-to-Go-Short-Short Story Ser.). 128p. (Orig.). 1995. pap. 10.95 (*1-56689-032-2*) Coffee Hse.

— The Weight of Dreams. LC 98-54893. 387p. 1999. 24.95 (*0-670-88233-X*) Viking Penguin.

***Agee, Jonis.** Weight of Dreams. 2000. pap. 13.95 (*0-14-029188-1*) Viking Penguin.

Agee, Jonis, et al, eds. Border Crossings: A Minnesota Voices Project Reader. 288p. 1984. pap. 8.00 (*0-89823-054-3*) New Rivers Pr.

— Stiller's Pond: New Fiction from the Upper Midwest. 2nd enl. ed. 500p. 1991. pap. 15.95 (*0-89823-106-X*) New Rivers Pr.

Agee, M. J. End of the Age. 320p. 1994. mass mkt. 6.99 (*0-380-72181-3*, Avon Bks) Morrow Avon.

— Exit 2007: The Secret of Secrets Revealed. Bratt, Jean, ed. (Illus.). 322p. (Orig.). 1992. pap. 12.95 (*0-9629530-6-7*) Archer Pr.

— Heaven Found. 224p. 1997. mass mkt. 5.99 (*0-380-72699-8*, Avon Bks) Morrow Avon.

— Heaven Found: A Butter & Honey Star. (Illus.). 192p. (Orig.). 1996. pap. 12.00 (*0-9629530-7-5*) Archer Pr.

— Revelations 2000: Your Guide to Biblical Prophecy for the New Millennium. 448p. 1998. mass mkt. 6.99 (*0-380-73085-5*, Avon Bks) Morrow Avon.

Agee, P. M. Agee: A Record of the Agee Family. (Illus.). 330p. 1991. reprint ed. pap. 52.50 (*0-8328-1864-X*); reprint ed. lib. bdg. 62.50 (*0-8328-1863-1*) Higginson Bk Co.

Agee, Philip. On the Run. 480p. 1987. 19.95 (*0-8184-0419-1*) Carol Pub Group.

Agee, Phillip H. Introduction to Mass Communication. 13th ed. (C). 2000. pap. text. write for info. (*0-321-03428-7*) Addson-Wesley Educ.

Agee, Phillip H., et al. Introduction to Mass Communication. 11th ed. (C). 1993. text 30.75 (*0-673-46883-6*) Addson-Wesley Educ.

Agee, Phillip H., et al. Main Currents Mass Communications Edition. 2nd ed. 384p. (C). 1997. pap. text 44.00 (*0-06-040185-0*) Addson-Wesley Educ.

Agee, Phillip H., jt. auth. see Agee, Warren K.

Agee, Richard J. The Gardano Music Printing Firms, 1569-1611. (Eastman Studies in Music: No. 10). 544p. 1999. 95.00 (*1-58046-020-8*, 1071-9989, Pub. by Univ Rochester Pr) Boydell & Brewer.

Agee, Richard J., ed. see Festa, Costanzo.

Agee, Richard W. How to Play Bid Whist. (Orig.). 1981. pap. 5.95 (*0-9623578-0-4*) Agee Pub Co.

Agee, Warren K. & Agee, Phillip H. Introduction to Mass Communications. 11th ed. (C). 1994. text, teacher ed. 11.00 (*0-673-55259-4*) Addson-Wesley Educ.

Agee, Willaim C. Ralston Crawford: Painting & Visual Experience. (Illus.). 177p. 1983. 45.00 (*0-942642-08-2*) Twelvetrees Pr.

Agee, William. Donald Judd Colorist. 1999. 45.00 (*3-89322-878-0*, Ktchen Sink) Kitchen Sink.

Agee, William, intro. Michael Steiner: Bronze Sculpture 1979-89. (Illus.). 59p. 1990. pap. 25.00 (*1-58821-069-3*) Salander OReilly.

Agee, William, text. Arnold Friedman: The Last Years. (Illus.). 1989. pap. 25.00 (*1-58821-019-7*) Salander OReilly.

— Morton Livingston Schamberg. (Illus.). 42p. 25.00 (*1-58821-066-9*) Salander OReilly.

— Stuart Davis: The Breakthrough Years. (Illus.). 37p. 1987. pap. 40.00 (*1-58821-016-2*) Salander OReilly.

Agee, William, jt. text see Davis, Stuart.

Agee, William C. John Marin: Between Realism & Abstraction. (Illus.). 48p. 1997. mass mkt. write for info. (*0-87920-010-3*) Kennedy Gall.

Agee, William C. Kenneth Noland: The Circle Paintings, 1956-1963. De Lima Greene, Alison, ed. (Illus.). 96p. (Orig.). (C). 1993. pap. 25.00 (*0-89090-057-4*) Mus Fine TX.

— Sam Francis Paintings 1947-1992. LC 98-31923. (Illus.). 164p. 1999. 39.50 (*0-914357-65-4*, Pub. by Los Angeles Mus Contemp) RAM Publications.

Agee, William C., ed. Paths of Abstraction: Painting in New York, 1944-1981 Selections from the Ciba Art Collection. (Illus.). 70p. (Orig.). 1994. pap. 15.00 (*1-885998-00-7*) Hunter College.

Agee, William C., text. Donald Judd: Sculpture. (Illus.). 32p. (Orig.). 1994. pap. write for info. (*1-878283-46-4*) PaceWildenstein.

Agee, William C., et al. Fairfield Porter: An American Painter. LC 93-83244. (Illus.). 96p. 1993. pap. 18.00 (*0-943526-25-6*) Parrish Art.

Agee, William C., jt. auth. see Berman, Avis.

Ageel, M., jt. auth. see Sahai, H.

Ageel, Mohammad I., jt. auth. see Sahai, Hardeo.

Ageenko, F. L. Pronunciation Dictionary for Radio & Television Workers. 5th ed. (RUS.). 810p. 1984. 49.95 (*0-8288-1317-5*, M15226) Fr & Eur.

Ageev, A. L., jt. auth. see Vasin, V. V.

Ageikin, Iakov Semenovich. Off-the-Road Mobility of Automobiles. Kothekar, V. S., tr. from RUS. 245p. (C). 1987. text 116.00 (*90-6191-495-7*, Pub. by A A Balkema) Ashgate Pub Co.

— Off-the-Road Wheeled & Combined Traction Devices Theory & Calculation. Orig. Title: Vezdekhodnye kolesnye i kombinirovannye dvizhiteli. 219p. 1988. 168.00 (*90-6191-931-2*, Pub. by A A Balkema) Ashgate Pub Co.

— Off-the-Road Wheeled & Combined Traction Devices: Theory & Calculation. LC 87-904654. Orig. Title: Vezdekhodnye kolesnye i kombinirovannye dvizhiteli. xvii, 202 p. 1987. write for info. (*81-7087-013-5*) Oxonion Pr Pvt Ltd.

Agel, Charles. Monuments to the Industrial Revolution. (Illus.). 64p. 1998. pap. 20.00 (*0-89822-122-6*) Visual Studies.

Agel, Jerome. Words That Make America Great. LC 99-21543. 1999. pap. 16.95 (*0-375-70651-8*) Random.

***Agel, Jerome.** Words That Make America Great. 2000. 8.75 (*0-375-40904-1*) Random.

Agel, Jerome. The Words That Make America Great: An Interpretive Documentary History. 1996. 30.00 (*0-679-44959-0*) Random.

— Your Constitution. LC 87-3694. (J). 1987. 9.95 (*0-671-64458-0*) Litle Simon.

Agel, Jerome & Glanze, Walter. Pearls of Wisdom: A Harvest of Gems from All Ages. LC 87-45016. 160p. 1987. pap. 14.00 (*0-06-096200-3*, PL/6200, Perennial) HarperTrade.

Agel, Jerome, jt. auth. see Bernstein, Richard.

Agel, Jerome, jt. auth. see Bernstein, Richard B.

Agel, Jerry. Test Your Bible Power. 2nd ed. 1997. pap. 12.95 (*0-8038-9397-3*) Hastings.

Agelasto, Michael & Adamson, Bob, eds. Higher Education in Post-Mao China. LC 98-180622. 492p. 1998. pap. 47.50 (*962-209-450-3*, Pub. by HK Univ Pr) Coronet Bks.

Ageless Prophet. Electric Marijuana. limited ed. Young, Randy W., ed. & illus. by. (Dreambooks Ser.: Bk. 1). 112p. (Orig.). (J). 1994. pap. 9.50 (*0-9642042-0-7*) Diamond Sword.

Agell, Charlotte. I Slide into the White of Winter, Vol. 4. (Illus.). 40p. (J). (ps-4). 1994. 7.95 (*0-88448-115-8*) Tilbury Hse.

— I Swam with a Seal. LC 94-5652. (Illus.). 32p. (J). (ps-1). 1995. 12.00 (*0-15-200176-X*, Gulliver Bks) Harcourt.

— I Wear Long Green Hair in Summer. LC 93-33612. (Illus.). 32p. (J). (ps-4). 1994. 7.95 (*0-88448-113-1*) Tilbury Hse.

Agell, Charlotte. Mud Makes Me Dance in the Spring. LC 93-33610. (Illus.). 32p. (J). (ps-4). 1994. 7.95 (*0-88448-112-3*) Tilbury Hse.

Agell, Charlotte. The Sailor's Book. LC 94-43304. (Illus.). 32p. (J). 1995. pap. 5.00 (*0-15-200297-9*, Voyager Bks) Harcourt.

— To the Island. LC 97-48733. (Illus.). 32p. (J). (ps-k). 1998. 14.95 (*0-7894-2505-X*) DK Pub Inc.

— Up the Mountain. LC 98-44863. 32p. (J). 2000. 14.95 (*0-7894-2610-2*, D K Ink) DK Pub Inc.

— Wind Spins Me Around in the Fall, Vol. 3. (Illus.). 40p. (J). (ps-4). 1994. 7.95 (*0-88448-114-X*) Tilbury Hse.

Agell, Gun. Strengthen Your Immune System! 180p. 1994. pap. write for info. (*0-9640299-0-1*) G Agell.

Agell, Jonas. Effects of Capital Taxation: An Equilibrium Asset Market Approach. (Studia Oeconomiae Upsaliensia: No. 9). 123p. (Orig.). 1986. pap. text 33.75 (*91-554-1938-0*, Pub. by Uppsala Univ Acta Univ Uppsaliensis) Coronet Bks.

— Tax Reforms & Asset Markets. 182p. (Orig.). 1985. pap. text 48.00 (*91-7204-248-6*) Coronet Bks.

Agell, Jonas, et al. Incentives & Redistribution in the Welfare State: The Swedish Tax Reform. LC 97-18337. (ENG & SWE.). xiiim 247p. 1998. write for info. (*0-333-71201-3*) Macmillan Pr.

— Incentives & Redistribution of the Welfare State: The Swedish Tax Reform. LC 97-18337. 256p. 1998. text. write for info. (*0-312-21072-8*) St Martin.

Agell, Neus & Bachs, Oriol. Calcium & Calmodulin Function in the Cell Nucleus. LC 95-38991. (Molecular Biology Intelligence Unit Ser.). 149p. 1995. 69.00 (*1-57059-311-6*) Landes Bioscience.

Ageloff. An Introduction to Lotus 1-2-3 Release 2.3 & Release 2.4. (New Perspectives Ser.). 392p. pap. write for info. incl. disk (*1-56527-059-2*) Course Tech.

— Lotus 1-2-3/R2.4 for Business. 680p. (C). 1993. pap. write for info. (*1-56527-078-9*) Course Tech.

***Ageloff.** New Perspectives on Excel for Windows. (C). 1998. spiral bd. 44.95 (*0-7600-7000-8*) Course Tech.

Ageloff, Roy. An Introduction to dBase III Plus. 240p. 1997. write for info. (*1-56527-055-X*) Course Tech.

— Lotus 1-2-3 Release 2.3 for Business. (Illus.). 650p. (C). 1992. disk 49.95 (*1-878748-85-8*); disk 49.95 (*1-878748-86-6*); disk 30.95 (*1-878748-87-4*) Course Tech.

— Lotus 1-2-3 Release 2.2 for Business. 512p. (C). 1991. disk 53.50 (*1-878748-28-9*); disk 31.00 (*1-878748-39-4*); disk 53.50 (*1-878748-27-0*); disk 31.00 (*1-878748-38-6*) Course Tech.

— Paradox 5 for Windows - New Perspectives Introductory, Incl. instr. resource kit, test bank, transparency. (New Perspectives Ser.). (Illus.). 336p. (C). 1995. pap. 30.95 (*1-56527-538-1*) Course Tech.

— Paradox 5 for Windows - New Perspectives Comprehensive, Incl. instr. resource kit, test bank, transparency. (New Perspectives Ser.). (Illus.). 592p. 1995. pap. 42.95 (*1-56527-530-6*) Course Tech.

— Paradox Versions 1/4.5 for Windows - New Perspectives Introductory, Incl. instr. resource kit, test bank, transparency. LC 95-224497. (New Perspectives Ser.). (Illus.). 312p. 1994. text. write for info. (*1-56527-083-5*) Course Tech.

Ageloff, Roy & Hayen, Roger. Microsoft Excel 7 for Windows 95 - Advanced, Incl. instr. resource kit, Online comp., files. (New Perspectives Ser.). (Illus.). 696p. 1996. pap. 33.00 (*0-7600-3533-4*) Course Tech.

— New Perspectives on Microsoft Excel for Windows: Advanced. 696p. 1996. teacher ed. 18.50 (*0-7600-3971-2*) Course Tech.

— New Perspectives on Microsoft Excel 97: Advanced. (New Perspectives Ser.). 600p. 1997. pap. write for info. (*0-7600-5271-9*) Course Tech.

Ageloff, Roy, et al. Microcomputer Applications for Business: DOS, WordPerfect 5.1, Lotus 1-2-3 Release 2.2, dBASE III Plus. (Illus.). 864p. (C). 1992. pap. text 64.95 incl. 5.25 hd (*1-56527-018-5*); pap. text 44.95 incl. 5.25 hd (*1-878748-75-0*); pap. text 69.95 incl. 5.25 hd (*1-878748-77-7*) Course Tech.

— Microcomputer Applications for Business: DOS 6.0, dBase IV. (New Perspectives Ser.). pap. write for info. (*1-56527-174-2*) Course Tech.

— Microcomputer Applications for Business: DOS 6.0, WordPerfect 6.0, Lotus 1-2-3 Release 2.4, dBASE IV. (New Perspectives Ser.). 1072p. pap. write for info. (*1-56527-175-0*) Course Tech.

— Microcomputer Applications for Business: DOS/WP/123R2.4/dBIV. (New Perspectives Ser.). 952p. pap. write for info. (*1-56527-063-0*) Course Tech.

Ageloff, Roy, jt. auth. see Hommel, Charles.

Agen, Mel. Flamenco Music for Acoustic Guitar. 72p. 1997. pap. 17.95 incl. audio compact disk (*0-7866-3278-X*, 95326BCD) Mel Bay.

Agenblich, Anne, text. Anthony-Petr Gorny, Two Projects: Aye-I-Eye, Oui c'est la Morte. LC 95-81872. (Illus.). 42p. 1995. pap. 20.00 (*1-879173-25-5*) Locks Gallery.

Agenbroad, Larry. Before the Anasazi. (Illus.). 32p. 1990. pap. 5.95 (*0-89734-101-5*, PL61-2) Mus Northern Ariz.

Agenbroad, Larry D. The Huson-Meng Site: An Alberta Bison Kill in the Nebraska High Plains. (Illus.). 230p. (C). reprint ed. pap. write for info. (*0-318-65954-9*) L Agenbroad.

Agence de Cooperation Culturelle et Technique StafF, ed. Vocabulaire de L'Oceanologie. (FRE.). 431p. 1976. pap. 49.95 (*0-8288-5758-X*, M6560) Fr & Eur.

Agency for Instructional Technology Staff. Managing the Disruptive Classroom: Strategies for Educators Guide. (Orig.). 1993. pap. text 7.75 (*0-7842-0721-6*) Agency Instr Tech.

— Reinventing Our Schools Guide. (Orig.). 1993. pap. text 7.75 (*0-7842-0722-4*) Agency Instr Tech.

— There's Math in Deviled Eggs. 24p. (Orig.). 1993. pap. text 3.50 (*0-7842-0719-4*); VHS. write for info. (*0-7842-0720-8*) Agency Instr Tech.

— Workplace Readiness Business & Industry Edition: Problem Solving Instructor's Guide. 117p. (Orig.). 1995. pap. text. write for info. (*0-7842-0786-0*) Agency Instr Tech.

— Workplace Readiness Business & Industry Edition: Problem Solving Participant's Guide. 110p. (Orig.). 1995. pap. text. write for info. (*0-7842-0787-9*) Agency Instr Tech.

— Workplace Readiness Business & Industry Edition: Self-Management Instructor's Guide. 149p. (Orig.). 1995. pap. text. write for info. (*0-7842-0784-4*) Agency Instr Tech.

— Workplace Readiness Business & Industry Edition: Self-Management Participant's Guide. 145p. (Orig.). 1995. pap. text. write for info. (*0-7842-0785-2*) Agency Instr Tech.

— Workplace Readiness Business & Industry Edition: Teamwork Instructor's Guide. 136p. (Orig.). 1995. pap. text. write for info. (*0-7842-0782-8*) Agency Instr Tech.

— Workplace Readiness Business & Industry Edition: Teamwork Participant's Guide. 126p. (Orig.). 1995. pap. text. write for info. (*0-7842-0783-6*) Agency Instr Tech.

A

An Asterisk (*) at the beginning of an entry indicates that the title is appearing for the first time.

A

Agenda New York Staff. Agenda New York Special, 1992: Events Resources Directory. 1992. pap. 24.95 (*0-9628185-1-8*) Agenda NY.
— Agenda New York, 1991: Special Events Resource Directory. 1991. pap. 24.95 (*0-9628185-0-X*) Agenda NY.
— Agenda New York, 1993: Special Events Resource Directory. 1992. pap. 24.95 (*0-9628185-2-6*) Agenda NY.
Agenjo Cecilia, Cesar. Dansk Etymologisk Ordbog. 1330p. 1979. 225.00 (*0-8288-2388-X*, S37346) Fr & Eur.
Agenor, Pierre-Richard. Capital-Market Imperfections & the Macroeconomic Dynamics of Small Indebted Economies. LC 97-21900. (Princeton Studies in International Finance: Vol. 82). 64p. 1997. 13.50 (*0-88165-254-7*) Princeton U Int Finan Econ.
***Agenor, Pierre-Richard.** Economics of Adjustment & Growth. 2000. 69.95 (*0-12-044555-7*) Acad Pr.
Agenor, Pierre-Richard. Parallel Currency Markets in Developing Countries: Theory, Evidence, & Policy Implications. LC 92-32099. (Essays in International Finance Ser.: No. 188). 40p. 1992. pap. 10.00 (*0-88165-095-1*) Princeton U Int Finan Econ.
***Agenor, Pierre-Richard, et al, eds.** The Asian Financial Crisis: Causes, Contagion & Consequences. (Global Economic Institutions Ser.: No. 2). (Illus.). 448p. (C). 2000. 74.95 (*0-521-77080-7*) Cambridge U Pr.
Agenor, Pierre-Richard & Montiel, Peter J. Development Macroeconomics. LC 95-2853. 648p. 1996. text 55.00 (*0-691-03413-3*, Pub. by Princeton U Pr) Cal Prin Full Svc.
Agent, Maria Theresa Caen, jt. auth. see Warmack, William.
Ageoff, Roy, et al. Microcomputer Applications for Business: DOS, WordPerfect 5.1, Lotus 1-2-3 Release 2.2, dBASE III Plus. (Illus.). 864p. (C). 1992. pap. text 69.95 incl. 3.5 hd (*1-878748-78-5*) Course Tech.
***Ageorges, N. & Dainty, C.** Lasar Guide Star Adaptive Optics for Astronomy. (Illus.). 364p. 2000. 145.00 (*0-7923-6381-7*) Kluwer Academic.
Ager, Alastair. Refugees: Perspectives on the Experience of Forced Migration. LC 98-35943. 1999. pap. 35.00 (*0-304-33923-7*) Continuum.
***Ager, Alastair.** Refugees: Perspectives on the Experience of Forced Migration. LC 98-35943. 256p. 1999. 75.00 (*0-304-33922-9*) Continuum.
Ager, Alastair & Bendall, Sue, eds. Microcomputers & Clinical Psychology: Issues, Applications, & Future Developments. LC 91-12241. (Wiley Series in Clinical Psychology). 234p. 1991. reprint ed. pap. 72.60 (*0-608-04597-7*, 206536700003) Bks Demand.
Ager, Anne. Light Cuisine. 1987. 10.98 (*0-671-09186-7*) S&S Trade.
Ager, D. V., ed. see European Geological Societies Staff.
Ager, David. The Soccer Referee's Manual. LC 97-47664. (Illus.). 128p. 1998. pap. 16.95 (*1-57028-187-4*, 81874H, Mstrs Pr) NTC Contemp Pub Co.
***Ager, David.** The Soccer Referee's Manual. 3rd ed. LC 00-42908. 2001. write for info. (*0-8092-9735-3*, Contemporary Bks) NTC Contemp Pub Co.
***Ager, David J.** Handbook of Chiral Chemicals. LC 98-50969. (Illus.). 384p. 1999. text 165.00 (*0-8247-1058-4*) Dekker.
Ager, David J. & East, Michael B. Asymmetric Methodology in Organic Synthesis. LC 95-35877. (New Directions in Organic & Biological Chemistry Ser.). 512p. 1995. boxed set 139.95 (*0-8493-8942-9*, 8942) CRC Pr.
Ager, David J., jt. auth. see East, Michael B.
Ager, Dennis. Francophonie In The 1990's: Problems & Opportunities. LC 95-40872. 215p. 1995. 74.95 (*1-85359-324-9*, Pub. by Multilingual Matters); pap. 26.95 (*1-85359-323-0*, Pub. by Multilingual Matters) Taylor & Francis.
— Identity, Insecurity & Image: France & Language. LC 98-31849. 1999. 75.00 (*1-85359-443-1*); pap. text 24.95 (*1-85359-442-3*) Taylor & Francis.
Ager, Dennis, et al, eds. Language Education for Intercultural Communication. Vol. 96. LC 93-101. 1993. 74.95 (*1-85359-190-4*, Pub. by Multilingual Matters); pap. 29.95 (*1-85359-204-8*, Pub. by Multilingual Matters) Taylor & Francis.
Ager, Dennis E. Language Policy in Britain & France: The Processes of Policy. (Open L Ser.). 224p. 1997. text 99.50 (*0-304-33759-5*) Continuum.
Ager, J., tr. see Swedenborg, Emanuel.
Ager, John C. We Plow God's Fields: The Life of James G.K. McClure. (Illus.). 477p. 1991. 22.00 (*0-913239-63-1*); pap. 17.00 (*0-913239-68-2*) Appalach Consortium.
Ager, John C., jt. auth. see Swedenborg, Emanuel.
Ager, John C., ed. see Swedenborg, Emanual.
Ager, John C., ed. & tr. see Swedenborg, Emanuel.
Ager, John C., tr. see Swedenborg, Emanuel.
***Ager, Richard.** Art of Information of Communications Technology for Teachers. 144p. 2000. pap. 24.95 (*1-85346-622-0*) David Fulton.
Ager, Richard. Information & Communications Technology in Primary Schools: Children or Computers in Control? 1998. 28.95 (*1-85346-543-7*) Taylor & Francis.
Ager, Sheila L. Interstate Arbitrations in the Greek World, 337-90 B.C. LC 94-1292. (Hellenistic Culture & Society Ser.: Vol. 18). 544p. 1997. 75.00 (*0-520-08162-5*, Pub. by U CA Pr) Cal Prin Full Svc.
Ager, Susan. At Heart. Lorber, Helene, ed. 246p. 1996. pap. write for info. (*0-937247-67-7*) Detroit Pr.
Ager, Trygve M., tr. see Rolvaag, Ole Edvart.
Ager, Waldemar. On the Way to the Melting Pot: A Novel. Cleven, Harry T., tr. from NOR. LC 94-33998. (Prairie Classics Ser.: No. 4).Tr. of Paa Veien til Smeltepotten. 224p. 1995. pap. 14.95 (*1-879483-23-8*) Prairie Oak Pr.
Agera, Cassian R. Faith, Prayer & Grace: A Comparative Study in Ramanuja & Kierkegaard. (C). 1987. 25.00 (*0-8364-2347-X*, Pub. by Mittal Pubs Dist) S Asia.
***Agere, Sam.** Promoting Good Governance in the Public Sector, Vol. 11. (Managing the Public Service). 120p. 2000. pap. 16.95 (*0-85092-629-7*, Pub. by Comm Sec) Stylus Pub VA.
— Redefining Management Roles Vol. 10: Improving the Functional Relationship between Ministers & Permanent Secretaries. (Managing the Public Service). 120p. 2000. pap. 16.95 (*0-85092-614-9*, Pub. by Comm Sec) Stylus Pub VA.
***Agere, Sam, et al, eds.** Strengthening Management Development Institutions Vol. 9: Enhancing the Involvment of Management Development Institutions in the Public Service Reform Process. (Managing the Public Service). 96p. 2000. pap. 16.95 (*0-85092-585-1*, Pub. by Comm Sec) Stylus Pub VA.
***Agere, Sam & Jorm, Noella.** Designing Performance Appraisal, Vol. 12. 120p. 2000. pap. 16.95 (*0-85092-630-0*, Pub. by Comm Sec) Stylus Pub VA.
***Agere, Sam & Mandaza, Ibbo.** Improved Policy Analaysis & Management in Southern Africa Vol. 8: Rethinking Policy Analysis & Management Framework. (Managing the Public Service). 72p. 2000. pap. 16.95 (*0-85092-583-5*, Pub. by Comm Sec) Stylus Pub VA.
Agerer, R. Zur Oekologie der Mykorrhiza Pilze. (Bibliotheca Mycologica Ser.: vol. 97). (Illus.). 160p. 1985. pap. text 48.00 (*3-7682-1423-0*) Lubrecht & Cramer.
Ageron, Charles-Robert. Modern Algeria: A History from 1830 to the Present. LC 91-72492. 294p. 1992. 45.00 (*0-86543-266-X*); pap. 12.95 (*0-86543-267-8*) Africa World.
Agerschou, Hans, et al. Planning & Design of Ports & Marine Terminals. LC 83-7032. (Wiley-Interscience Publications). (Illus.). 330p. reprint ed. pap. 102.30 (*0-7837-3411-5*, 204337800008) Bks Demand.
***Agersnap, Soren.** Baptism & the New Life: A Study of Romans 6.1-14. 461p. 1999. 49.95 (*87-7288-654-4*, Pub. by Aarhus Univ Pr) David Brown.
***Agerston, Patricia.** And When He Came to Himself. 120p. 1999. pap. 10.00 (*0-7392-0217-0*) Morris Pubng.
Agerter, Sharlene R. & Glock, Waldo S. An Annotated Bibliography of Tree Growth & Growth Rings, 1950-1962. LC 64-17274. 188p. reprint ed. pap. 58.30 (*0-8357-5611-4*, 205533200017) Bks Demand.
Ageta, Hiroyuki, et al, eds. Towards Natural Medicine Research in the 21st Century: Proceedings of the International Symposium on Natural Medicines, Kyoto, Japan, 28-30 October 1997. LC 99-187096. (International Congress Ser.). 596p. 1998. 238.50 (*0-444-82898-2*, Excerpta Medica) Elsevier.
Agevi, Elijah, et al, eds. Lime & Alternative Binders in East Africa. 167p. 1995. pap. 29.50 (*1-85339-330-4*, Pub. by Intermed Tech) Stylus Pub VA.
Ageyev, M. Novel with Cocaine. unabridged ed. (World Classic Literature Ser.). (RUS.). pap. 6.95 (*2-87714-279-5*, Pub. by Bookking Intl) Distribks Inc.
***Aggarwal, A., et al, eds.** Algorithms & Computations: Proceedings of the 10th International Symposium, ISAAC'99, chennai, India, December 16-18, 1999. (Lecture Notes In Computer Science: 1741). xiii, 448p. 2000. pap. text (*3-540-66916-7*) Spr-Verlag.
Aggarwal, A., jt. auth. see Aggarwal, J.
Aggarwal, Alok, et al, eds. Proceedings of the Second Annual ACM-SIAM Symposium on Discrete Algorithms. (Proceedings in Applied Mathematics Ser.: No. 49). xiv, 482p. 1991. pap. 59.50 (*0-89871-271-8*) Soc Indus-Appl Math.
***Aggarwal, Anil, ed.** Web-Based Learning & Teaching Technologies: Opportunities & Challenges. LC 99-87117. (Illus.). 300p. (C). 2000. pap. 69.95 (*1-878289-60-8*) Idea Group Pub.
Aggarwal, Arjun P. Sexual Harassment: A Guide for Understanding & Prevention. 144p. 1992. pap. 21.95 (*0-409-90852-5*, MICHIE) LEXIS Pub.
Aggarwal, B. B. & Puri, R., eds. Human Cytokines: Their Role in Disease & Therapy, Vol. 2. 2nd ed. (Illus.). 608p. 1994. 149.95 (*0-86542-352-0*) Blackwell Sci.
Aggarwal, Bharat B. Human Cytokines Vol. 3: Handbook for Basic & Clinical Research. (Illus.). 1997. pap. text 90.00 (*0-86542-533-7*) Blackwell Sci.
Aggarwal, Bharat B., et al, eds. Human Cytokines: Handbook for Basic & Clinical Research, 2. LC 95-41187. 504p. 1996. pap. 69.95 (*0-86542-441-1*) Blackwell Sci.
Aggarwal, Bharwat & Puri, Raj. Human Cytokines, 3 vols. (Illus.). 1997. pap. 195.00 (*0-632-04333-4*) Blackwell Sci.
Aggarwal, C. I. Law of Hundis & Negotiable Instruments with Supplement, 1979. 9th ed. (C). 1979. 75.00 (*0-7855-4710-X*) St Mut.
***Aggarwal, Devi D.** Protocol in Srimad Bhagawat. LC 99-931371. 298p. 1999. write for info. (*81-7479-022-5*) S Asia.
Aggarwal, Ishwar D., jt. ed. see Sanghera, Jas S.
Aggarwal, J. & Aggarwal, A. A Text Book of SUPW, Vol. 1. 200p. 1997. pap. 60.00 (*81-209-0853-8*, Pub. by Pitambar Pub) St Mut.
— A Text Book of SUPW, Vol. 2. 160p. 1997. pap. 50.00 (*81-209-0976-3*, Pub. by Pitambar Pub) St Mut.
Aggarwal, J. C. Education Policy in India, 1992: Retrospect & Prospect. (Illus.). viii, 194p. 1992. 22.00 (*81-85402-20-5*, Pub. by Shipra Pubns) Nataraj Bks.
— Eight Five Year Plan: Planning & Development in India. (Illus.). vi, 232p. 1993. 22.00 (*81-85402-24-8*, Pub. by Shipra Pubns) Nataraj Bks.
— Modern History of Punjab: Relevant Select Documents. (C). 1992. 40.00 (*81-7022-431-4*, Pub. by Concept) S Asia.
Aggarwal, J. C. & Agrawal, S. P. Documentation Encyclopedia of UNESCO & Education, 2 pts., Set. (C). 1990. text 120.00 (*81-7022-329-6*, Pub. by Concept) S Asia.
Aggarwal, J. C. & Chowdry, N. K. Elections in India. (C). 1992. 27.50 (*81-85402-09-4*, Pub. by Concept) S Asia.
Aggarwal, J. C., jt. auth. see Agrasal, S. P.
Aggarwal, J. C., jt. auth. see Agrawal, S. P.
Aggarwal, J. C., jt. ed. see Agrawal, S. P.
Aggarwal, J. K., jt. ed. see Martin, Worthy N.
Aggarwal, Jagdishkumar K., ed. Multisensor for Computer Vision. LC 92-42968. 1993. write for info. (*3-540-55044-5*); 126.95 (*0-387-55044-5*) Spr-Verlag.
Aggarwal, K. K. Reliability Engineering. (Topics in Safety, Reliability & Quality Ser.). 396p. (C). 1993. text 227.50 (*0-7923-2524-9*) Kluwer Academic.
Aggarwal, M. L. Materia Medica of Human Mind. 783p. 1985. 29.95 (*0-318-36364-X*) Asia Bk Corp.
Aggarwal, M. L., jt. ed. see Saleem, M. A.
Aggarwal, M. R. Regional Economic Co-Operation in South Asia. 155p. 1979. 16.95 (*0-318-37268-1*) Asia Bk Corp.
Aggarwal, Partap C. Halfway to Equality: Harijans of India. 1983. 22.00 (*0-8364-1043-2*, Pub. by Manohar) S Asia.
Aggarwal, Praveen & Wali, Jyoti P. Diagnosis & Management of Common Poisoning. (Illus.). 524p. 1997. text 49.50 (*0-19-563957-X*) OUP.
Aggarwal, Purnima. My First ABC. (Illus.). (J). (ps). 1997. pap. 20.00 (*81-7289-131-8*, Pub. by Pitambar Pub) St Mut.
Aggarwal, R. L., et al, eds. Diluted Magnetic (Semimagnetic) Semiconductors. (MRS Symposium Proceedings Ser.: Vol. 89). 1987. text 17.50 (*0-931837-54-5*) Materials Res.
***Aggarwal, Raj.** Restructuring Japanese Business for Growth: Strategy, Finance, Management & Marketing Perspective LC 99-35796. 1999. write for info. (*0-7923-8583-7*) Kluwer Academic.
Aggarwal, Raj & Gibson, Charles. Discounting in Financial Accounting & Reporting: Issues in the Literature. LC 89-84511. 141p. (Orig.). 1989. pap. 25.00 (*0-910586-72-1*, 077-89) Finan Exec.
Aggarwal, Raj & Khera, Inder. Management Science: Cases & Applications. LC 79-65492. 1979. pap. text 21.00 (*0-8162-0096-3*); 8.00 (*0-685-02320-6*) Holden-Day.
Aggarwal, Raj & Schirm, David C., eds. Global Portfolio Diversification: Risk Management, Market Microstructure, & Implementaion Issues. (Illus.). 302p. 1994. text 69.95 (*0-12-044500-X*) Acad Pr.
Aggarwal, Raj K. International Business Finance: A Bibliography of Selected Business & Academic Sources. LC 84-2151. 297p. 1984. 65.00 (*0-275-91113-6*, C1113, Praeger Pubs) Greenwood.
— The Management of Foreign Exchange: Optimal Policies for a Multinational Company. rev. ed. Bruchey, Stuart, ed. LC 80-563. (Multinational Corporations Ser.). 1981. lib. bdg. 24.95 (*0-405-13359-6*) Ayer.
Aggarwal, S. K. Handbook of Journalism & Editorial Excellence. (C). 1992. text 22.00 (*81-7099-401-2*, Pub. by Mittal Pubs Dist) S Asia.
— Media Credibility LC 89-905747. xii, 246 p. 1989. write for info. (*81-7099-157-9*) S Asia.
Aggarwal, S. L. & Russo, S. Comprehensive Polymer Science: Second Supplement, No. 2. 700p. 1996. 376.75 (*0-08-042708-1*, Pergamon Pr) Elsevier.
Aggarwal, Santosh. Three Language Formula: An Educational Problem. (C). 1991. 28.00 (*81-212-0336-8*, Pub. by Gian Publng Hse) S Asia.
Aggarwal, V. B. A Complete Course in Certificate Computer Studies, Vol. 1. 128p. 1997. pap. 40.00 (*81-209-0738-8*, Pub. by Pitambar Pub) St Mut.
— Learning Computers, Bk. VI. 1997. pap. 38.00 (*81-209-0431-1*, Pub. by Pitambar Pub) St Mut.
— Learning Computers, Bk. VII. 1997. pap. 40.00 (*81-209-0432-X*, Pub. by Pitambar Pub); pap., wbk. ed. 20.00 (*81-209-0749-3*, Pub. by Pitambar Pub) St Mut.
— Learning Computers, Bk. VIII. 1997. pap. 36.00 (*81-209-0433-8*, Pub. by Pitambar Pub); pap., wbk. ed. 20.00 (*81-209-0662-4*, Pub. by Pitambar Pub) St Mut.
— Learning Computers, Bk. IX. 1997. pap. 40.00 (*81-209-0434-6*, Pub. by Pitambar Pub); pap., wbk. ed. 22.00 (*81-209-0655-1*, Pub. by Pitambar Pub) St Mut.
— Learning Computers, Bk. X. 1997. pap. 40.00 (*81-209-0653-5*, Pub. by Pitambar Pub); pap., wbk. ed. 20.00 (*81-209-0440-0*, Pub. by Pitambar Pub) St Mut.
— A Tutorial-CUM-Workbook OndBase III+ 112p. 1997. pap. 40.00 (*81-209-0800-7*, Pub. by Pitambar Pub) St Mut.
— A Tutorial of Lotus 1-2-3. 84p. 1996. pap. 30.00 (*81-209-0848-1*, Pub. by Pitambar Pub) St Mut.
Aggarwal, V. B. & Bagga, P. C. Practical Manual & Workbook on Computer Science. 124p. 1996. pap. 35.00 (*81-209-0443-5*, Pub. by Pitambar Pub) St Mut.
— Workbook in Cobol. 100p. 1996. pap. 20.00 (*81-209-0716-7*, Pub. by Pitambar Pub) St Mut.
Aggarwal, V. B. & Goel, M. P. Workbook in Basic. 184p. 1996. pap., wbk. ed. 50.00 (*81-209-0017-0*, Pub. by Pitambar Pub) St Mut.
Aggarwal, V. B., et al. Principles of Computer Science. 620p. 1990. pap. 120.00 (*81-209-0713-2*, Pub. by Pitambar Pub) St Mut.
Aggarwal, Vinod K. Debt Games: Strategic Interaction in International Debt Rescheduling. LC 95-30406. (Illus.). 626p. (C). 1996. pap. text 26.95 (*0-521-55552-3*) Cambridge U Pr.
— Debt Games: Strategic Interaction in International Debt Rescheduling. LC 95-30406. (Illus.). 626p. (C). 1996. text 69.95 (*0-521-35202-9*) Cambridge U Pr.
— Institutional Designs for a Complex World: Bargaining, Linkages & Nesting. LC 98-18839. 240p. 1998. pap. 17.95 (*0-8014-8464-2*) Cornell U Pr.
— Institutional Designs for a Complex World: Bargaining, Linkages & Nesting. LC 98-18839. (Illus.). 240p. 1998. text 45.00 (*0-8014-3460-2*) Cornell U Pr.
— International Debt Threat: Bargaining among Creditors & Debtors in the 1980s. LC 87-80549. (Policy Papers in International Affairs: No. 29). (Illus.). viii, 72p. (C). 1987. pap. text 5.95 (*0-87725-529-6*) U of Cal IAS.
Aggarwal, Vinod K. & Morrison, Charles E. Asia-Pacific Crossroads: Regime Creation & the Future of APEC. LC 97-50523. 448p. 1998. pap. 18.95 (*0-312-21148-1*) St Martin.
Aggarwal, Vinod K. & Morrison, Charles E., eds. Asia-Pacific Crossroads: Regime Creation & the Future of APEC, Vol. 1. LC 97-50523. 416p. 1998. text 55.00 (*0-312-21110-4*) St Martin.
Aggarwal, Y., jt. ed. see Sapra, C. L.
Aggarwala, R. & Balakrishman, N. Progressive Censoring: Theory, Methods & Applications. (Statistics for Industry & Technology Ser.). 256p. 2000. 69.95 (*0-8176-4001-0*) Birkhauser.
Aggeler, Geoffrey. Anthony Burgess: The Artist as Novelist. fac. ed. LC 78-12200. 253p. 1979. pap. 78.50 (*0-7837-8361-2*, 205917000009) Bks Demand.
— Nobler in the Mind: The Stoic-Skeptic Dialectic in English Renaissance Tragedy. LC 98-14035. 200p. 1998. 36.50 (*0-87413-661-X*) U Delaware Pr.
Agger, ed. How the Analyst's Work Shapes the Analyst. (Psychoanalytic Inquiry Ser.: Vol. 13, No. 3). 1993. 20.00 (*0-88163-942-7*) Analytic Pr.
— How the Analyst's Work Shapes the Analyst - II. (Psychoanalytic Inquiry Ser.: Vol. 16, No. 3). 1996. pap. 20.00 (*0-88163-938-9*) Analytic Pr.
— Sibling Relationships. (Psychoanalytic Inquiry Ser.: Vol. 8, No. 1). 1995. 20.00 (*0-88163-963-X*) Analytic Pr.
Agger, B. Decline of Discourse. 1990. pap. 34.95 (*1-85000-756-X*, Falmer Pr) Taylor & Francis.
Agger, Ben. Critical Social Theories: An Introduction. LC 97-34244. 224p. (C). 1997. pap. 24.00 (*0-8133-2174-3*, Pub. by Westview) HarpC.
— Critical Theory of Public Life: Knowledge, Discourse & Politics in an Age of Decline. (Critical Perspectives on Literacy & Education Ser.). 240p. 1991. 89.95 (*1-85000-966-X*, Falmer Pr) Taylor & Francis.
— Cultural Studies As Critical Theory. 224p. 1992. pap. 27.95 (*1-85000-965-1*, Falmer Pr) Taylor & Francis.
— The Discourse of Domination: From the Frankfurt School to Postmodernism. (Studies in Phenomenology & Existential Philosophy). 425p. 1992. pap. 19.95 (*0-8101-1029-6*) Northwestern U Pr.
— Fast Capitalism: A Critical Theory of Significance. fac. ed. LC 88-14432. 199p. 1989. pap. 61.70 (*0-7837-7605-5*, 204735800007) Bks Demand.
— Gender, Culture & Power: Toward a Feminist Postmodern Critical Theory. LC 93-14119. 192p. 1993. 55.00 (*0-275-94700-9*, C4700, Praeger Pubs) Greenwood.
***Agger, Ben.** Public Sociology: From Social Facts to Literary Acts. (New Social Formations Ser.). 272p. 2000. pap. text 19.95 (*0-8476-9841-6*) Rowman.
— Public Sociology: From Social Facts to Literary Acts. (New Social Formations Ser.). 272p. 2000. text 65.00 (*0-8476-9840-8*) Rowman.
Agger, Ben. Reading Science: A Literary, Political & Sociological Analysis. LC 89-80379. (Illus.). 272p. 1989. text 39.95 (*0-930390-93-8*) Gen Hall.
— Socio (onto) logy: A Disciplinary Reading. LC 88-10697. 440p. 1989. text 34.95 (*0-252-01558-4*) U of Ill Pr.
Agger, Ben, ed. A Brief Description of Recent Developments in the Theory of Social Structure, Suppl. 1. (Current Perspectives in Social Theory Ser.). 1995. 73.25 (*1-55938-875-7*) Jai Pr.
— Current Perspectives in Social Theory, Vol. 9. 238p. 1989. 73.25 (*0-89232-918-1*) Jai Pr.
— Current Perspectives in Social Theory, Vol. 10. 331p. 1990. 73.25 (*1-55938-063-2*) Jai Pr.
— Current Perspectives in Social Theory, Vol. 11. 329p. 1991. 73.25 (*1-55938-337-2*) Jai Pr.
— Current Perspectives in Social Theory, Vol. 12. 302p. 1992. 73.25 (*1-55938-442-5*) Jai Pr.
— Current Perspectives in Social Theory, Vol. 13. 246p. 1993. 73.25 (*1-55938-577-4*) Jai Pr.
— Current Perspectives in Social Theory, Vol. 14. 292p. 1994. 78.50 (*1-55938-694-0*) Jai Pr.
— Current Perspectives in Social Theory, Vol. 15. 275p. 1995. 73.25 (*1-55938-876-5*) Jai Pr.
— Current Perspectives in Social Theory, Vol. 16. 1996. 73.25 (*0-7623-0032-9*) Jai Pr.
Agger, Ben, et al, eds. Current Perspectives in Social Theory, Vol. 1. 394p. 1980. 78.50 (*0-89232-154-7*) Jai Pr.
— Current Perspectives in Social Theory, Vol. 3. 279p. 1983. 78.50 (*0-89232-297-7*) Jai Pr.
— Current Perspectives in Social Theory, Vol. 4. 358p. 1984. 73.25 (*0-89232-379-5*) Jai Pr.
— Current Perspectives in Social Theory, Vol. 7. 196p. 1986. 73.25 (*0-89232-713-8*) Jai Pr.
— Current Perspectives in Social Theory, Vol. 8. 345p. 1987. 73.25 (*0-89232-738-3*) Jai Pr.
Agger, Ben & McNall, Scott G., eds. Current Perspectives in Social Theory, Vol. 6. 328p. 1985. 73.25 (*0-89232-531-3*) Jai Pr.
Agger, Ben, ed. see McNall, Scott G.
Agger, Ben, ed. see McNall, Scott G. & Howe, Gary N.
Agger, Eugene E. The Budget in the American Commonwealths. LC 75-158232. (Columbia University. Studies in the Social Sciences: No. 66). reprint ed. 39.50 (*0-404-51066-3*) AMS Pr.
***Agger, Gunhild & Jensen, Jens F., eds.** The Aesthetics of Television. (Media & Cultural Studies: Vol. 2). 400p. 2000. 43.95 (*87-7307-623-6*, Pub. by Aalborg Univ) David Brown.

An Asterisk (*) at the beginning of an entry indicates that the title is appearing for the first time.

A

— Cylindrical Wormgearing Tolerance & Inspection Methods (Metric Edition) (ANSI/AGMA Standard Ser.: Vol. 2111-A98). 43p. 2000. pap. text 70.00 (*1-55589-717-7*) AGMA.

AGMA Technical Committee. Design & Selection of Components for Enclosed Gear Drives. (ANSI/AGMA Standard Ser.: No. 6001-C88). (Illus.). 23p. 1988. pap. text 60.00 (*1-55589-498-4*) AGMA.

— Design & Selection of Components for Enclosed Gear Drives. 4th rev. ed. (ANSI/AGMA Standard Ser.: Vol. 6001-D97). (Illus.). 41p. 1997. pap. text 80.00 (*1-55589-683-9*) AGMA.

— Design Guide for Vehicle Spur & Helical Gears. 2nd rev. ed. (ANSI/AGMA Standard Ser.: Vol. 6002-B93). (Illus.). 38p. 1993. pap. text 64.00 (*1-55589-009-1*) AGMA.

— Design Guidelines for Aerospace Gearing. rev. ed. (AGMA Standard Ser.: Vol. 911-A94). (Illus.). 97p. 2000. pap. text 91.00 (*1-55589-629-4*) AGMA.

— Design Manual for Bevel Gears. 3rd rev. ed. (ANSI/AGMA Standard Ser.: Vol. 2005-C96). (Illus.). 94p. 1988. pap. text 149.00 (*1-55589-667-7*) AGMA.

— Design Manual for Cylindrical Wormgearing. 3rd rev. ed. (ANSI/AGMA Standard Ser.: Vol. 6022-C93). 10p. 1993. pap. text 69.00 (*1-55589-041-5*) AGMA.

— Design Manual for Enclosed Epicyclic Gear Drives. rev. ed. (ANSI/AGMA Standard Ser.: Vol. 6023-A88). (Illus.). 50p. 2000. pap. text 80.00 (*1-55589-504-2*) AGMA.

— Design Manual for Parallel Shaft Fine-Pitch Gearing. (AGMA Standard Ser.: Vol. 917-B97). (Illus.). 84p. 1997. pap. 80.00 (*1-55589-694-4*) AGMA.

— Design of Industrial Double-Enveloping Wormgears. 3rd rev. ed. (ANSI/AGMA Standard Ser.: Vol. 6030-C87). (Illus.). 13p. 1994. pap. text 50.00 (*1-55589-493-3*) AGMA.

— Design Procedure for Aircraft Engine & Power Take-Off Bevel Gears. (Standard Ser.: Vol. 431.01). 31p. 1974. pap. text 30.00 (*1-55589-054-7*) AGMA.

— Explanatory Data as Basis for a Recommended Practice of AGMA for the Rating of Planetary & Spur Type Speed Reducers. (Technical Papers: Vol. P90A). (Illus.). 15p. 1938. pap. text 30.00 (*1-55589-126-8*) AGMA.

— Fine-Pitch on-Center Face Gears for 20-Degree Involute Spur Pinions. (AGMA Standard Ser.: Vol. 203.03). (Illus.). 23p. (Orig.). 1973. pap. text 35.00 (*1-55589-012-1*) AGMA.

— Flexible Coupling - Lubrication. 2nd rev. ed. (ANSI/AGMA Standard Ser.: Vol. 9001-B97). (Illus.). 6p. 1997. pap. text 38.00 (*1-55589-686-3*) AGMA.

— Flexible Couplings - Keyless Fits. rev. ed. (ANSI/AGMA Standard Ser.: Vol. 9003-A91). (Illus.). 21p. 1999. pap. text 48.00 (*1-55589-572-7*) AGMA.

***AGMA Technical Committee.** Flexible Couplings - Mass Elastic Properties & Other Characteristics. (ANSI/AGMA Standard Ser.: Vol. 9004-A99). 39p. 2000. pap. text 65.00 (*1-55589-715-0*) AGMA.

AGMA Technical Committee. Flexible Couplings - Potential Unbalance Classification. 3rd rev. ed. (ANSI/AGMA Standard Ser.: Vol. 9000-C90). (Illus.). 41p. 1996. pap. text 59.00 (*1-55589-549-2*) AGMA.

— Formats for Fine-Pitch Gear Specification Data. 3rd rev. ed. (AGMA Standard Ser.: Vol. 910-C90). (Illus.). 29p. 1995. pap. text 48.00 (*1-55589-571-9*) AGMA.

— Fundamental Rating Factors & Calculation Methods for Involute Spur & Helical Gear Teeth. 3rd rev. ed. (ANSI/AGMA Standard Ser.: Vol. 2001-C95). (Illus.). 70p. 1995. pap. text 159.00 (*1-55589-647-2*) AGMA.

— Fundamental Rating Factors & Calculation Methods for Involute Spur & Helical Gear Teeth (Metric Edition) 3rd rev. ed. (ANSI/AGMA Standard Ser.: Vol. 2101-C95). (Illus.). 70p. 1994. pap. text 133.00 (*1-55589-648-0*) AGMA.

— Gear-Cutting Tools Fine & Coarse-Pitch Hobs. (AGMA Standard Ser.: AGMA 120.01). 32p. 1975. pap. text 35.00 (*1-55589-007-5*) AGMA.

— Gear Materials & Heat Treatment Manual. 2nd rev. ed. (ANSI/AGMA Standard Ser.: Vol. 2004-B89). (Illus.). 78p. 1995. pap. text 96.00 (*1-55589-524-7*) AGMA.

— Gear Nomenclature, Definitions of Terms with Symbols. 6th ed. (ANSI/AGMA Standard Ser.: Vol. 1012-F90). (Illus.). 64p. 1990. pap. text 64.00 (*1-55589-551-4*) AGMA.

— Gear Power Rating for Cylindrical Grinding Mills, Kilns, Coolers & Dryers. 6th rev. ed. (ANSI/AGMA Standard Ser.: Vol. 6004-F88). (Illus.). 27p. 1996. pap. text 80.00 (*1-55589-499-2*) AGMA.

— Gear Sound Manual: Section I, Fundamentals of Sound As Related to Gears; Section II, Sources, Specifications, & Levels of Gear Sound; Section III, Gear-Noise Control. rev. ed. (AGMA Standard Ser.: Vol. 299.01). (Illus.). 56p. 1999. pap. text 69.00 (*1-55589-528-X*) AGMA.

— Gear Tooth Surface Texture with Functional Considerations. (AGMA Standard Ser.: Vol. 906-A94). (Illus.). 20p. 1994. pap. text 59.00 (*1-55589-634-0*) AGMA.

— Industrial Gear Lubrication. 4th rev. ed. (ANSI/AGMA Standard Ser.: Vol. 9005-D94). (Illus.). 15p. 1994. pap. text 80.00 (*1-55589-632-4*) AGMA.

— Information Sheet: Gear Scoring Design for Aerospace Spur & Helical Power Gears. rev. ed. (AGMA Standard Ser.: Vol. 217.01). 22p. 1999. pap. text 43.00 (*1-55589-020-2*) AGMA.

— Information Sheet: Systems Considerations for Critical Service Gear Drives. (AGMA Standard Ser.: AGMA 427.01). 13p. 1976. pap. text 30.00 (*1-55589-053-9*) AGMA.

— Information Sheet - Geometry Factors for Determining the Pitting Resistance & Bending Strength of Spur, Helical & Herringbone Gear Teeth. 2nd rev. ed. (AGMA Standard Ser.: Vol. 908-B89). (Illus.). 78p. 1999. pap. 80.00 (*1-55589-525-5*, 908B89) AGMA.

***AGMA Technical Committee.** Inspection Practices - Gear Blanks, Shaft Center Distance & Parallelism. (AGMA Standard Ser.: Vol. 915-3-A99). 9p. 2000. pap. text 30.00 (*1-55589-738-X*) AGMA.

AGMA Technical Committee. Load Classification & Service Factors for Flexible Couplings. (AGMA Standard Ser.: Vol. 922-A96). (Illus.). 6p. 1996. pap. text 38.00 (*1-55589-680-4*) AGMA.

***AGMA Technical Committee.** Materials for Marine Propulsion Gearing. (ANSI/AGMA Standard Ser.: Vol. 6033-B98). 48p. 2000. pap. text 80.00 (*1-55589-711-8*) AGMA.

— Materials for Marine Propulsion Gearing. (ANSI/AGMA Standard Ser.: Vol. 6133-B98). 48p. 2000. pap. text 70.00 (*1-55589-712-6*) AGMA.

AGMA Technical Committee. Measuring Instrument Calibration Pt. I: Involute Measurement (Metric Edition) (ANSI/AGMA Standard Ser.: Vol. 2110-A94). (Illus.). 39p. 2000. pap. text 55.00 (*1-55589-631-6*) AGMA.

***AGMA Technical Committee.** Measuring Instrument Calibration, Gear Pitch & Runout Measurements. (ANSI/AGMA Standard Ser.: Vol. 2114-A98). 33p. 2000. pap. text 64.00 (*1-55589-732-0*) AGMA.

AGMA Technical Committee. Measuring Instrument Calibration, Gear Tooth Alignment Measurement. (ANSI/AGMA Standard Ser.: Vol. 2113-A97). (Illus.). 33p. 1997. pap. text 55.00 (*1-55589-687-1*) AGMA.

***AGMA Technical Committee.** Method for Specifying the Geometry of Spur & Helical Gears. (AGMA Standard Ser.: Vol. 913-A98). 25p. 2000. pap. text 55.00 (*1-55589-714-2*) AGMA.

AGMA Technical Committee. Metric Usage. 3rd rev. ed. (AGMA Standard Ser.: Vol. 904-C96). (Illus.). 20p. 1989. pap. text 40.00 (*1-55589-681-2*) AGMA.

— Noise Control in Automobile Helical Gears. (Technical Papers: Vol. 299.02). 1963. pap. text 30.00 (*1-55589-145-4*) AGMA.

— Nomenclature for Flexible Couplings. (AGMA Standard Ser.: Vol. 510.03). 12p. 1984. pap. text 38.00 (*1-55589-062-8*) AGMA.

— Power Rating for Helical & Herringbone Gearing for Rolling Mill Service. 2nd rev. ed. (ANSI/AGMA Standard Ser.: Vol. 6005-B89). (Illus.). 33p. 1996. pap. text 75.00 (*1-55589-530-1*) AGMA.

— Practice for Enclosed Cylindrical Wormgear Speed Reducers & Gearmotors. 2nd rev. ed. (ANSI/AGMA Standard Ser.: Vol. 6034-B92). (Illus.). 37p. 1999. pap. text 53.00 (*1-55589-494-1*) AGMA.

— Practice for Helical & Herringbone Speed Reducers for Oilfield Pumping Units. rev. ed. (AGMA Standard Ser.: Vol. 422.03 (R1992)). 44p. 1998. pap. text 60.00 (*1-55589-050-4*) AGMA.

— Progress Report of Gear Rating Coordinating Committee. (Technical Papers: Vol. P101.04). (Illus.). 28p. 1952. pap. text 30.00 (*1-55589-131-4*) AGMA.

— Progress Report, Section 1, Bending Stress of Spur & Helical Gears. (AGMA Technical Papers: Vol. 101.02). (Illus.). 18p. 1951. pap. text 30.00 (*1-55589-129-2*) AGMA.

— Progress Report, Section 2, Scoring Factor (PVT) Values of Gear Teeth. (Technical Papers: Vol. P101.02A). (Illus.). 24p. 1951. pap. text 30.00 (*1-55589-130-6*) AGMA.

— Rating & Application of Single & Multiple Reduction Double-Enveloping Worm & Helical Worm Speed Reducers. 5th rev. ed. (ANSI/AGMA Standard Ser.: Vol. 6017-E86). (Illus.). 19p. 1994. pap. text 48.00 (*1-55589-013-X*) AGMA.

— Rating of Industrial Metal Spur Gears Research Report. (AGMA Technical Papers: Vol. P101.01). (Illus.). 29p. 1994. pap. text 30.00 (*1-55589-128-4*) AGMA.

AGMA Technical Committee. Rating the Pitting Resistance & Bending Strength of Generated Straight Bevel, Zerol Bevel, & Spiral Bevel Gear Teeth. rev. ed. (ANSI/AGMA Standard Ser.: Vol. 2003-B97). 75p. 1997. pap. 1388.00 (*1-55589-692-8*) AGMA.

AGMA Technical Committee. A Rational Method of Selecting Anti-Friction Bearings. (Technical Papers: Vol. P246). 5p. 1941. pap. text 30.00 (*1-55589-144-6*) AGMA.

— A Rational Procedure for the Preliminary Design of Minimum Volume Gears. rev. ed. (AGMA Standard Ser.: Vol. 901-A92). (Illus.). 37p. 1997. pap. text 32.00 (*1-55589-579-4*) AGMA.

***AGMA Technical Committee.** Recommended Practice for Carburized Aerospace Gearing. (AGMA Standard Ser.: Vol. 926-C99). 9p. 2000. pap. text 45.00 (*1-55589-758-4*) AGMA.

AGMA Technical Committee. Recommended Procedure for Carburized Aerospace Gearing. (Standard Ser.: Vol. 246.02A). 15p. 1983. pap. text 45.00 (*1-55589-027-X*) AGMA.

— Report of General Standardization Committee. (AGMA Technical Papers: Vol. P83B). 8p. 1930. pap. text 30.00 (*1-55589-125-X*) AGMA.

— Report of the Helical Gear Committee on Its Research Program Pts. 1-3: Durability Formula Analysis for Internal Helical Gearing; Theoretical Contact Length Determinations for Application to Durability Ratings of Helical Gears; Investi. (Technical Papers: Vol. P102). (Illus.). 30p. 1938. pap. text 30.00 (*1-55589-132-2*) AGMA.

***AGMA Technical Committee.** Sound for Enclosed Helical, Herringbone & Spiral Bevel Gear Drives. (ANSI/AGMA Standard Ser.: Vol. 6025-D98). 21p. 2000. pap. text 75.00 (*1-55589-718-5*) AGMA.

AGMA Technical Committee. Sound for Enclosed Helical, Herringbone & Spiral Bevel Gear Drives. 3rd rev. ed. (ANSI/AGMA Standard Ser.: Vol. 6025-C90). (Illus.). 19p. 1990. pap. text 60.00 (*1-55589-552-2*) AGMA.

***AGMA Technical Committee.** Specification for High Speed Helical Gear Units. (ANSI/AGMA Standard Ser.: Vol. 6011-H98). 46p. 2000. pap. text 85.00 (*1-55589-693-6*) AGMA.

AGMA Technical Committee. Specification for High Speed Helical Gear Units. 7th rev. ed. (ANSI/AGMA Standard Ser.: Vol. 6011-G92). (Illus.). 25p. 1992. pap. text 50.00 (*1-55589-575-1*) AGMA.

— Specification for Measurement of Linear Vibration on Gear Units. 2nd rev. ed. (ANSI/AGMA Standard Ser.: Vol. 6000-B96). (Illus.). 21p. 1994. pap. text 69.00 (*1-55589-666-9*) AGMA.

***AGMA Technical Committee.** Specifications for Powder Metallurgy Gears. (ANSI/AGMA Standard Ser.: Vol. 6008-A98). 17p. 2000. pap. text 53.00 (*1-55589-713-4*) AGMA.

AGMA Technical Committee. Spur Gear Durability Based on Critical Stress in Region of Single Tooth Contact. (Technical Papers: Vol. P102B). (Illus.). 14p. 1941. pap. text 30.00 (*1-55589-133-0*) AGMA.

— Standard for Gearmotors Using Spur, Helical, Herringbone, Straight Bevel, or Spiral Bevel Gears. rev. ed. (ANSI/AGMA Standard Ser.: Vol. 6019-E89). (Illus.). 103p. 1994. pap. 90.00 (*1-55589-531-X*) AGMA.

— Standard for Marine Gear Units: Rating. (ANSI/AGMA Standard Ser.: Vol. 6032-A94). (Illus.). 57p. 1994. pap. text 95.00 (*1-55589-633-2*) AGMA.

— Standard for Marine Propulsion Gear Units. (ANSI/AGMA Standard Ser.: Vol. 6033-A88). (Illus.). 43p. 1988. pap. text 65.00 (*1-55589-500-X*) AGMA.

— Standard for Shaft Mounted & Screw Conveyor Drives Using Spur, Helical, & Herringbone Gears. rev. ed. (ANSI/AGMA Standard Ser.: Vol. 6021-G89). (Illus.). 93p. 1994. pap. 90.00 (*1-55589-526-3*) AGMA.

— Standard for Spur, Helical, Herringbone, & Bevel Enclosed Drives. (ANSI/AGMA Standard Ser.: Vol. 6010-F97). (Illus.). 56p. 1997. pap. 149.00 (*1-55589-690-1*) AGMA.

— Standard for Spur, Helical, Herringbone, & Bevel Enclosed Drives. 5th ed. (ANSI/AGMA Standard Ser.: Vol. 6010-E88). (Illus.). 115p. 1988. pap. text 110.00 (*1-55589-523-9*, 6010E88) AGMA.

— Standard for Spur, Helical, Herringbone, & Bevel Enclosed Drives (Metric Edition) (ANSI/AGMA Standard Ser.: Vol. 6110-F97). 56p. 1997. pap. 128.00 (*1-55589-691-X*) AGMA.

— Standard 14.5 Inch Spur Gear Teeth. (Technical Papers: Vol. P90B). (Illus.). 49p. 1930. pap. text 30.00 (*1-55589-127-6*) AGMA.

— Style Manual for the Preparation of Standards, Information Sheets & Editorial Manuals. 6th rev. ed. (AGMA Standard Ser.: Vol. 900-F96). (Illus.). 38p. 1996. pap. text 30.00 (*1-55589-682-0*) AGMA.

— A Summary of Numerical Examples Demonstrating the Procedures for Calculating Geometry Factors for Spur & Helical Gears. rev. ed. (AGMA Standard Ser.: Vol. 918-A93). (Illus.). 42p. 1998. pap. text 64.00 (*1-55589-617-0*) AGMA.

— Surface Temper Etch Inspection after Grinding. 2nd rev. ed. (ANSI/AGMA Standard Ser.: Vol. 2007-B92). (Illus.). 8p. 1992. pap. text 38.00 (*1-55589-577-8*) AGMA.

— Symposium on Gear Tooth Finishing. (Technical Papers: Vol. P129.01). (Illus.). 56p. 1948. pap. text 30.00 (*1-55589-134-9*) AGMA.

— Tooth Proportions for Fine-Pitch, Spur & Helical Gears. 7th rev. ed. (ANSI/AGMA Standard Ser.: Vol. 1003-G93). 24p. 1999. pap. text 64.00 (*1-55589-015-6*) AGMA.

— Tooth Proportions for Plastic Gears. (ANSI/AGMA Standard Ser.: Vol. 1006-A97). (Illus.). 47p. 1997. pap. text 64.00 (*1-55589-684-7*) AGMA.

— Tooth Proportions for Plastic Gears (Metric Edition) (ANSI/AGMA Standard Ser.: Vol. 1106-A97). (Illus.). 47p. 1997. pap. text 59.00 (*1-55589-685-5*) AGMA.

AGMA Technical Committee & Wellauer, E. J. Coordinated Rating for the Strength of Gear Teeth Pts. I-III: Introduction - Discussion of Historical Background, Geometry Factors & Allowable Stress; Modifying Factors Used in AGMA Strength Ratings for Gear Teeth/ Method for Estimating. (Technical Papers: Vol. 229.03). 70p. 1956. pap. text 30.00 (*1-55589-142-X*) AGMA.

AGMA Technical Committee, et al. Fatigue Strength Characteristics of Gear Teeth. (Technical Papers: Vol. 229.02). (Illus.). 28p. 1954. pap. text 30.00 (*1-55589-141-1*) AGMA.

— Spur & Helical Gear Geometry Factors (J) Pts. I-III: Introduction & Use of the AGMA Geometry Factor; Manual Determinations for Helical Gear Tooth Geometry Factors; Determination of the AGMA Geometry Factor Using Computer Determination. (Technical Papers: Vol. P229.07). 87p. 1963. pap. text 30.00 (*1-55589-143-8*) AGMA.

AGMA/AWEA Technical Comm. Staff. Recommended Practices for Design & Specificiation of Gearboxes for Wind Turbine Generator Systems. (AGMA/AWEA Standard Ser.: Vol. 921-A97). (Illus.). 58p. 1997. pap. 75.00 (*1-55589-689-8*) AGMA.

Agmon, Marcy. Post Cold War U. S. Security Strategies for the Persian Gulf. LC 92-45222. 1993. pap. 7.50 (*0-8330-1312-2*, R-4268-AF/A) Rand Corp.

Agmon, Marcy, et al. Arms Proliferation Policy: Support to the Presidential Advisory Board. LC 96-177877. (Illus.). 158p. (Orig.). 1996. pap. text 20.00 (*0-8330-2403-5*, MR-771-OSD) Rand Corp.

Agmon, Marcy, jt. auth. see Tanham, George K.

Agmon, Tamir & Drobnick, Richard, eds. Small Firms in Global Competition. LC 92-40074. (Illus.). 160p. 1994. text 52.00 (*0-19-507825-X*) OUP.

Agmon, Tamir & Hekman, Christine R., eds. Trade Policy & Corporate Business Decisions. (Illus.). 256p. 1990. text 55.00 (*0-19-505538-1*) OUP.

Agmon, Tamir & Von Glinow, Mary A., eds. Technology Transfer in International Business. (Research Book from the International Business School & Research Program Ser.). (Illus.). 304p. 1991. text 52.00 (*0-19-506235-3*) OUP.

Agnaarsson, Ulfur, jt. auth. see Clayden, Graham.

Agnati, L. F., et al. Tropic Regulation of the Basal Ganglia: Focus on Dopamine Neurons. Fuxe, K. et al, eds. LC 93-34086. (Wenner-Gren International Ser.: 62). 628p. 1994. 209.00 (*0-08-042276-4*) Elsevier.

Agnati, Luigi F. & Fuxe, Kjell, eds. Quantitative Neuroanatomy in Transmitter Research. (Wenner-Gren International Symposia Ser.: Vol. 42). 432p. 1986. 95.00 (*0-306-42160-7*, Plenum Trade) Perseus Pubng.

Agnati, Luigi F., jt. ed. see Fuxe, Kjell.

Agnati, Luigi F., jt. ed. see Fuxe, K.

Agne, Russell M., jt. ed. see Clarke, John Henrik.

Agnelli, G. & Bueller, H. R., eds. The Diagnosis of Deep Vein Thrombosis & Pulmonary Embolism. (Journal Ser.: Vol. 25, No. 1-2, 1995). (Illus.). 88p. 1994. pap. 96.75 (*3-8055-6116-4*) S Karger.

Agnelli, Marella. The Agnelli Gardens at Villar Perosa: Two Centuries of a Family Retreat. LC 98-7763. (Illus.). 224p. 1998. 75.00 (*0-8109-1979-6*, Pub. by Abrams) Time Warner.

— Ninfa Gardens. 1999. 55.00 (*88-422-0797-7*, Pub. by U Allemandi) Antique Collect.

Agnello, Virginia & Garcia, Cindy. Vocal Rehabilitation: A Practice Book for Voice Improvement. 3rd ed. 1990. spiral bd. 24.00 (*0-89079-233-X*, 3652) PRO-ED.

Agnello, Virginia L. Vocal Rehabilitation: Let's Talk Voice. LC 93-5981. 1993. spiral bd. 14.00 (*0-89079-591-6*, 3659) PRO-ED.

Agnellus of Ravenna. Lectures on Galen's de Sectis. (Arethusa Monographs: No. 8). xviii, 181p. (C). 1981. pap. 10.00 (*0-930881-05-2*) Dept Classics.

Agner, Dwight. The Books of WAD, a Bibliography of the Books Designed by W. A. Dwiggins. limited rev. ed. LC 76-58639. (Illus.). 1977. 25.00 (*0-915346-26-5*) A Wofsy Fine Arts.

Agner, Dwight, jt. auth. see Lawson, Alexander S.

Agnes. Law & Gender Inequality: The Politics of Women's Rights in India. LC 99-938560. (Law in India Ser.). 268p. 1999. text 29.95 (*0-19-564587-1*) OUP.

Agnes Etherington Art Centre. Flaming Creatures: New Tendencies in Canadian Video : (exhibition) 1 October to 5 November 1997, Agnes Etherington Art Centre, Queen's University, Kingston, Canada. LC 98-171472. (Illus.). 1997. write for info. (*0-88911-748-9*) Queens U Inst Intergov.

Agnes Etherington Art Centre Staff. Edifice: May Chan, Dave Gordon, Jocelyn Purdie, Maureen Sheridan, Bill Roff, Scott Wallis: [Exhibition] 23 March-18 May, 1997, Agnes Etherington Art Centre. LC 98-171486. 24p. 1997. write for info. (*0-88911-744-6*) Queens U Inst Intergov.

Agnes, Kiss. New Techniques in Aqua Therapy. LC 98-46877. (Illus.). 330p. 1999. 19.95 (*1-58141-006-9*) Rivercross Pub.

Agnes, Michael. Webster's New World Pocket Misspeller's Dictionary. 2nd ed. LC 96-51674. 244p. 1997. 4.95 (*0-02-861720-7*) Macmillan.

Agnes, Michael, ed. see Laird, Charlton G. & Webster's New World Dictionaries Editors.

Agnes, Michael, ed. see Laird, Charlton G. & Webster's New World Dictionaries Editors.

Agnes, Michael, ed. see Laird, Charlton & Webster's New World Dictionaries Editors.

Agnes, Michael, ed. & frwd. see Websters New World Staff.

Agness, Marcia, jt. auth. see Baxter, Kathleen A.

Agnete, Kay. One Block Equals Many Quilts. LC 98-51824. (Illus.). 112p. 1998. per. 18.95 (*1-57432-719-4*, Am Quilters Soc) Collector Bks.

Agnew. Linear Algebra with Applications. (Math). 1978. mass mkt. 22.25 (*0-8185-0256-8*) Brooks-Cole.

— Standards-Based Language Arts Curriculum. LC 99-43271. 174p. (C). 2000. pap. text 26.00 (*0-205-28971-1*) Allyn.

— Triple-Controlled Timed Writings. 3rd ed. (TA - Typing/Keyboarding Ser.). 1992. mass mkt. 14.25 (*0-538-61174-X*) S-W Pub.

Agnew, Andrew. Agnew: The Hereditary Sheriffs of Galloway, Their Forebears & Friends, Their Courts & Customs of Their Times With Notes of the Early History, 2 vols., Set. (Illus.). 1992. reprint ed. pap. 143.00 (*0-8328-2475-5*); reprint ed. lib. bdg. 153.00 (*0-8328-2474-7*) Higginson Bk Co.

Agnew, Brad. Fort Gibson: Terminal on the Trail of Tears. LC 78-21391. (Illus.). 288p. 1989. pap. 13.95 (*0-8061-2207-2*) U of Okla Pr.

Agnew, Connie L., et al. Twins! Pregnancy, Birth & the First Year of Life with Twins. LC 97-14657. 320p. 1997. pap. 16.00 (*0-06-273460-1*, Perennial) HarperTrade.

Agnew, Daniel. History of the Region of Pennsylvania North of the Ohio & West of the Allegheny River. LC 75-146371. (First American Frontier Ser.). 1971. reprint ed. 18.95 (*0-405-02821-0*) Ayer.

Agnew, Eleanor & Robideaux, Sharon. My Mama's Waltz: A Book for Daughters of Alcoholic Mothers. LC 98-150433. 336p. 1998. 24.00 (*0-671-01385-8*, PB Hardcover) PB.

— My Mama's Waltz: A Book for Daughters of Alcoholic Mothers. 336p. 1999. pap. 14.00 (*0-671-01386-6*, PB Trade Paper) PB.

Agnew, George. Canadian Hospitals, Nineteen Twenty to Nineteen Seventy: A Dramatic Half Century. LC 73-78942. 320p. reprint ed. pap. 99.20 (*0-8357-7998-X*, 202348600033) Bks Demand.

An Asterisk (*) at the beginning of an entry indicates that the title is appearing for the first time.

Agnew, Hugh L. Origins of the Czech National Renascence. LC 92-36909. (Russian & East European Studies). 338p. (C). 1994. text 49.95 (*0-8229-3742-5*) U of Pittsburgh Pr.

Agnew, Irene, ed. Glossary of English & Russian Computer & Automated Control Systems Terminology. (ENG & RUS.). 1978. pap. 15.00 (*0-686-31723-8*) Agnew Tech-II.

Agnew, J. L., jt. auth. see Lee, F. D.

Agnew, Jean. Belfast Merchant Families in the Seventeenth Century. LC 96-219571. (Illus.). 256p. 1996. 49.50 (*1-85182-251-8*, Pub. by Four Cts Pr) Intl Spec Bk.

Agnew, Jean-Christophe. Worlds Apart: The Market & the Theater in Anglo-American Thought, 1550-1750. 280p. 1986. text 54.95 (*0-521-24322-X*) Cambridge U Pr.

— Worlds Apart: The Market & the Theater in Anglo-American Thought, 1550-1750. 280p. 1988. pap. text 19.95 (*0-521-37910-5*) Cambridge U Pr.

Agnew, Jeanne & Knapp, Robert C. Linear Algebra W/applications. 2nd ed. LC 82-20752. (Math). 400p. (C). 1983. mass mkt. 33.50 (*0-534-01364-3*) Brooks-Cole.

Agnew, Jeanne L. & Knapp, Robert C. Linear Algebra with Applications. 3rd ed. 392p. (C). 1989. text 72.95 (*0-534-09456-2*) Brooks-Cole.

Agnew, Jeremy. Exploring the Colorado High Country. LC 77-77959. (Illus.). 1977. pap. 4.95 (*0-918944-00-7*) Wildwood.

Agnew, John. Geopolitics: Revisioning World Politics. LC 97-35289. 150p. (C). 1998. pap. 18.99 (*0-415-14095-1*) Routledge.

— Geopolitics: Revisioning World Politics. LC 97-35289. (Illus.). 160p. (C). 1998. 60.00 (*0-415-14094-3*) Routledge.

— Rome. LC 94-44396. (World Cities Ser.). 204p. 1995. 100.00 (*0-471-94886-1*) Wiley.

Agnew, John, ed. Political Centralization & Decentralization in Europe & North America. (Orig.). 1990. pap. 15.00 (*0-944285-14-7*) Pol Studies.

— Political Geography. (Arnold Publications). (Illus.). 384p. 1996. text 75.00 (*0-340-67742-2*) OUP.

— Political Geography: A Reader. (Arnold Publications). (Illus.). 384p. 1996. pap. text 35.00 (*0-340-67743-0*) OUP.

Agnew, John, et al, eds. Human Geography in Theory: An Essential Anthology. (Illus.). 704p. (C). 1996. pap. 34.95 (*0-631-19461-4*) Blackwell Pubs.

Agnew, John & Askham, Gerry. Bulk in ISO Containers. (C). 1978. 60.00 (*0-906297-01-X*, Pub. by ICHCA) St Mut.

Agnew, John & Corbridge, Stuart. Mastering Space: Hegemony, Territory & International Political Economy. LC 94-22292. (Illus.). 336p. (C). 1995. pap. 25.99 (*0-415-09434-8*, B0132) Routledge.

Agnew, John & Duncan, James S., eds. The Power of Place: Bringing Together Geographical & Sociological Imaginations. 272p. 1989. 49.95 (*0-04-445281-0*) Routledge.

Agnew, John, et al. Thomas' Stowage. 3rd ed. (Illus.). 388p. (C). 1996. text 125.00 (*0-85174-625-X*) Sheridan.

Agnew, John, jt. auth. see Bish, Douglas.

Agnew, John, jt. auth. see Knox, Paul.

Agnew, John, jt. auth. see Knox, Paul L.

Agnew, John A. Place & Politics: The Geographical Mediation of State & Society. 228p. 1987. text 55.00 (*0-04-320177-6*) Routledge.

Agnew, John A., jt. auth. see Knox, Paul L.

Agnew, John A., jt. auth. see Szymanski, Richard.

Agnew, John B. & Young, Damian P., contrib. by. Chemeca '95: Winning in World Markets. LC 97-111305. (National Conference Proceedings 95 Ser.: Vol. 6). (Illus.). 694p. 1995. pap. 180.00 (*0-85825-641-X*, Pub. by Inst Engrs Aust-EA Bks) Accents Pubns.

Agnew, John H., jt. auth. see Wright, John S.

***Agnew, Jonathan.** Benson & Hedges Cricket Year 1998-99. 1999. 37.50 (*0-7475-4546-4*, Pub. by Blmsbury Pub) Trafalgar.

Agnew, Jonathan. Over to You, Aggers. (Illus.). 224p. 1998. 40.00 (*0-575-06454-4*, Pub. by V Gollancz) Trafalgar.

Agnew, Lea & Haden-Miller, Jo A. Atlanta & Its Lawyers: A Century of Vision: 1888-1988. (Illus.). 200p. 1988. 29.95 (*0-9621443-0-4*) Atlanta Bar.

Agnew, Lois P., jt. ed. see Enos, Richard L.

Agnew, Margaret C. Southern Living Microwave Cookbook. (Illus.). 266p. 1988. 19.95 (*0-8487-0725-7*) Oxmoor Hse.

Agnew, Michael, jt. auth. see Christians, Nick.

Agnew, Nancy L., ed. A Community Worthy of the Name: Selected Speeches by Nannerl O. Keohane. 240p. 1995. 15.00 (*0-9646418-0-1*) Wellesley MA.

Agnew, Neville, ed. Conservation of Ancient Sites on the Silk Road: Proceedings of an International Conference on the Conservation of Grotto Sites, Mogao Grottoes at Dunhuang. LC 96-30938. (Symposium Proceedings Ser.). (Illus.). 480p. (Orig.). 1997. pap. 75.00 (*0-89236-416-5*, Pub. by J P Getty Trust) OUP.

Agnew, Palmer W. & Kellerman, Anne S. Distributed Multi-Media: Technologies, Application & Opportunities in the Digital Information Industry. LC 95-16678. 448p. (C). 1996. pap. text 29.95 (*0-201-76536-5*) Addison-Wesley.

Agnew, Palmer W., et al. Multimedia in the Classroom. LC 95-18583. 308p. 1996. pap. text 50.00 (*0-205-16408-0*) Allyn.

***Agnew, Robert.** Juvenile Delinquency: Causes & Control. (Illus.). 350p. (C). 2000. pap. text. write for info. (*1-891487-47-7*) Roxbury Pub Co.

Agnew, Robert, jt. ed. see Passas, Nikos.

Agnew, Robert S., jt. ed. see Cullen, Francis T.

Agnew, Robin. Rebecca of Grand Hotel. (Illus.). 72p. (J). 1990. text 15.95 (*0-9627301-0-6*) Grand Hotel.

Agnew, Thomas, jt. auth. see Vollard, Ambroise.

Agnew, Una. A Button in Heaven: The Mystical Imagination of Parick Kavanagh. 272p. 1998. 64.95 (*1-85607-246-0*) Intl Scholars.

Agnew, V. Elite Women in Indian Politics. 163p. 1979. 14.95 (*0-7069-0745-0*) Asia Bk Corp.

Agnew, Vanessa, tr. see Kast, Verena.

Agnew, Vijay. In Search of a Safe Place: Abused Women & Culturally Sensitive Services. (Illus.). 304p. 1998. text 50.00 (*0-8020-4278-3*); pap. text 19.95 (*0-8020-8114-2*) U of Toronto Pr.

Agnihotri, A. Management of Crop Diseases. (C). 1992. 145.00 (*81-7136-039-4*, Pub. by Periodical Expert) St Mut.

Agnihotri, Pushpa. Poverty Amidst Prosperity: Survey of Slums. 261p. 1994. pap. 180.00 (*81-85880-47-6*, Pub. by Print Hse) St Mut.

Agnihotri, R. K. & Khanna, A. L., eds. English Language Teaching in India: Issues & Innovations. 256p. 1995. 42.00 (*0-8039-9248-3*) Sage.

— Second Language Acquisition: Socio-Cultural & Linguistic Aspects of English in India. (Research in Applied Linguistics Ser.: Vol. 1). 404p. 1994. 39.95 (*0-8039-9178-9*) Sage.

Agnihotri, Ram A. Artists & Their Films of Modern Hindi Cinema: Cultural & Socio-Political Impact on Society 1931-91, 3 vols., Set. (C). 1992. 88.00 (*81-7169-180-3*, Commonwealth) S Asia.

***Agnihotri, Ram A.** Film Stars in Indian Politics. LC 98-908750. 1998. 34.00 (*81-7169-506-X*, Pub. by Commonwealth) S Asia.

Agnihotri, Ram A. Social & Political Study of Modern Hindi Cinema. (C). 1990. 48.00 (*0-8364-2486-7*) S Asia.

Agnihotri, Rama K. & Khanna, Amrit L. Problematizing English in India. LC 97-7936. (Research in Applied Linguistics Ser.: Vol. 3). 168p. 1997. text 29.95 (*0-8039-9375-7*) Sage.

Agnihotri, Rama K., et al. Social Psychological Perspectives on Second Language Learning. LC 98-24122. (Research in Applied Linguistics Ser.). 1998. 34.00 (*0-7619-9260-X*); 34.00 (*81-7036-718-2*) Sage.

***Agnihotri, Satish B.** Sex Ratio Patterns in the Indian Population: A Fresh Exploration LC 99-37984. 1999. write for info. (*0-7619-9392-4*) Sage.

Agnihotri, V. K., jt. ed. see Mukherjee, Amitava.

***Agnihotri, V. P.** Disease Scenario in Crop Plants, Vols. 1 & 2. Misra, A. P. & Bhargava, K. S., eds. 1998. pap. 650.00 (*81-86249-06-0*, Pub. by Print Hse) St Mut.

Agnihotri, V. P., et al, eds. Perspectives in Phytopathology: Dr. R. S. Singh Festschrift Volume. (Illus.). xiii, 525p. (Orig.). 1989. 85.00 (*1-55528-167-2*) Scholarly Pubns.

Agnikhotri, R. C. Geomedical Environmental & Health Care: Study of Rundelkhand Region. (C). 1995. 27.00 (*0-614-13265-7*, Pub. by Rawat Pubns) S Asia.

***Agnoletti, M. & Anderson, S., eds.** Forest History: International Studies on Socioeconomic & Forest Ecosystem Change. LC 99-88765. (IUFRO Research Ser.). 400p. 2000. text 100.00 (*0-85199-419-9*) OUP.

— Methods & Approaches in Forest History. LC 99-86187. (IUFRO Research Ser.). 300p. 2000. text 85.00 (*0-85199-420-2*) OUP.

Agnoli, A., et al. Cerebral Metabolism in Aging & Neurological Disorders, Second Joint Meeting. Lechner, H. et al, eds. (Journal: Gerontology: Vol. 33, No. 3-4, 1987). (Illus.). 164p. 1987. pap. 95.75 (*3-8055-4640-8*) S Karger.

Agnon, Shmuel Yoseph. Agnon's Alef Bet: Poems. Friend, Robert, tr. from HEB. LC 97-38777. (Illus.). (J). 1998. 19.95 (*0-8276-0599-4*) JPS Phila.

— Eine Bibliographie Seiner Werke. Martin, Werner, ed. xi, 118p. 1980. 24.00 (*3-487-06972-5*) G Olms Pubs.

— A Book That Was Lost: And Other Stories. Mintz, Alan & Hoffman, Anne Golomb, eds. 448p. 1996. reprint ed. pap. 15.00 (*0-8052-1066-0*) Schocken.

***Agnon, Shmuel Yoseph.** The Bridal Canopy. 400p. 2000. pap. 24.95 (*0-8156-0640-0*) Syracuse U Pr.

— Only Yesterday. Harshav, Barbara, tr. 652p. 2000. 35.00 (*0-691-00972-4*, Pub. by Princeton U Pr) Cal Prin Full Svc.

Agnon, Shmuel Yoseph. Shira: A Novel. Shapiro, Zeva, tr. from HEB. LC 96-9552. (Library of Modern Jewish Literature). Orig. Title: Shirah. 585p. 1996. reprint ed. pap. 17.95 (*0-8156-0425-4*, AGSHP) Syracuse U Pr.

***Agnon, Shmuel Yoseph.** A Simple Story. Halkin, Hillel, tr. from HEB. LC 99-41900. 1999. pap. text 17.95 (*0-8156-0618-4*) Syracuse U Pr.

Agnon, Shmuel Yoseph & Glatzer, Nahum N., eds. Days of Awe: A Treasury of Jewish Wisdom for Reflection, Repentance & Renewal on the High Holy Days. Galpert, Maurice T., tr. LC 95-9026. 336p. 1995. pap. 15.00 (*0-8052-1048-2*) Schocken.

Agnos, D. Cadogan Chess: Easy Guide to Class Sicilia. 1999. pap. 18.95 (*1-85744-524-4*) Cadgn Bks.

Agnos, Peter. Cats of the West Side: Sex, Wisdom, Wild Habits Death. Picardo, Cheyenne, ed. (Illus.). 1999. 24.00 (*0-914018-11-6*) Green Eagle Pr.

— The Queer Dutchman Castaway: Castaway on Ascenscion. Adler, C. Q., ed. (Illus.). 144p. (Orig.). 1994. pap. 9.95 (*0-914018-03-5*) Green Eagle Pr.

— Wholly Mother Jones: Her Full-to-Bursting Life with Songs & Pictures. (Illus.). 110p. (Orig.). 1997. 24.95 (*0-914018-05-1*, 7270); pap. 16.95 (*0-914018-08-6*, 7271) Green Eagle Pr.

Agnos, Peter, jt. auth. see Tsuki, Tommi.

***Agnusdei, Donato & Compston, Juliet.** SERMS: A Novel Option to Maintain Health in the Postmenopause. (Illus.). 176p. 2000. pap. 65.00 (*1-85317-820-9*, Pub. by Martin Dunitz) Blackwell Sci.

Agocs, Sandor. The Troubled Origins of the Italian Catholic Labor Movement, 1878-1914. LC 87-31961. 253p. reprint ed. pap. 78.50 (*0-608-10621-6*, 207124300009) Bks Demand.

Agogino, A. M., ed. Design for Manufacture: Reducing Life Cycle Costs While Improving Time to Market & Product Quality. (DE Ser.: Vol. 51). 72p. 1992. 30.00 (*0-7918-1110-7*, G00754) ASME.

Agogino, George A., jt. auth. see Haynes, C. Vance.

Agombar, Fiona. Beat Fatigue with Yoga: A Step-by-Step Guide. LC 98-55286. (Illus.). 176p. 1999. pap. 10.95 (*1-86204-325-6*, Pub. by Element MA) Penguin Putnam.

Agonafer, A. & Fulton, R. E., eds. Computer Aided Design in Electronic Packaging. (DSC Ser.: Vol. 3). 92p. 1992. 30.00 (*0-7918-1127-1*, G00771) ASME.

Agonafer, D., ed. Solutions to CFD Benchmark Problems in Electronic Packaging. (HTD Ser.: Vol. 255). 64p. 1993. 30.00 (*0-7918-1168-9*, G00812) ASME.

***Agonafer, Dereje, et al, eds.** Advances in Electronic Packaging, 1999: Proceedings: The Pacific Rim-ASME International Intersociety Electronic & Photonic Packaging Conference (1999: Maui, HI) 2217p. 1999. 500.00 (*0-7918-1612-5*) ASME.

Agonafer, Dereje, et al, eds. Application of CAE/CAD to Electronic Packaging: Proceedings: International Mechanical Engineering Congress & Exposition (1996: Atlanta, Georgia) LC 96-79040. (EEP Ser.: Vol. 18). 123p. pap. 64.00 (*0-7918-1553-6*) ASME.

— CAE - CAD & Thermal Management Issues in Electronic Systems: Proceedings, ASME International Mechanical Engineering Congress & Exposition, Dallas, TX, 1997. LC 98-166447. (EEP - HTD Ser.: Vols. 23 & 356). 109p. 1997. pap. 72.00 (*0-7918-1852-7*, TK7816) ASME Pr.

Agonafer, Mulugeta. Africa in the Contemporary International Disorder: Crisis & Possibilities. 428p. (C). 1996. lib. bdg. 58.00 (*0-7618-0252-5*) U Pr of Amer.

— Contending Theories of Development in the Contemporary International Order - Disorder: Lessons from Kenya & Tanzania. 254p. (Orig.). (C). 1994. lib. bdg. 44.50 (*0-8191-9621-5*) U Pr of Amer.

Agoncillo, Teodoro A. Malolos: The Crisis of the Republic. LC 97-947310. xviii, 700 p. 1997. write for info. (*971-542-096-6*) U of Philippines Pr.

***Agonito, Rosemary.** Dirty Little Secrets: Sex in the Workplace. LC 99-91810. 224p. 2000. pap. 14.95 (*0-9673220-3-0*, Pub. by New Futures Pubns) ACCESS Pubs Network.

— Your Dream Made Easy: How to Start a Successful Business - A Step-by-Step Introduction with Worksheets. LC 99-90683. 184p. 2000. pap. 19.95 (*0-9673220-0-6*, Pub. by New Futures Pubns) ACCESS Pubs Network.

Agonito, Rosemary, ed. History of Ideas on Woman: A Source Book. LC 77-5061. 1978. pap. 15.95 (*0-399-50379-X*, Perigee Bks) Berkley Pub.

Agoos, Julie. Above the Land. LC 86-26675. 71p. 1987. 12.00 (*0-300-03861-5*) Yale U Pr.

— Calendar Year. LC 96-27457. 142p. 1999. pap. 15.95 (*1-878818-57-0*, Pub. by Sheep Meadow) U Pr of New Eng.

Agopian, L. & Miller, I. Rain Forest. (Thermatic Unit Ser.). (J). 1997. pap. 14.95 (*1-55734-674-7*) Tchr Create Mat.

Agopov & Koivu. Suomalais-Venalainen Maataloussanasto: Finnish-Russian Agricultural Dictionary. (FIN & RUS.). 282p. 1986. 195.00 (*0-8288-1182-2*, F22280) Fr & Eur.

Agopsowicz, William, jt. auth. see Swinton, Janet.

Agor, Weston H. The Chilean Senate: Internal Distribution of Influence. LC 79-165918. (Latin American Monographs: No. 23). 228p. reprint ed. pap. 70.70 (*0-8357-7720-0*, 203607700002) Bks Demand.

— The Logic of Intuitive Decision Making: A Research-Based Approach for Top Management. LC 86-8119. (Illus.). 200p. 1986. 57.95 (*0-89930-177-0*, ALI/, Quorum Bks) Greenwood.

Agori, Ken. Defenders of the Holy Grail. v, 147p. pap. 12.95 (*0-9676407-0-9*, Pub. by Elfstone Pubng) BookMasters.

Agoshkov, V. Boundary Value Problems for Transport Equations. LC 98-4737. (Modeling & Simulation in Science, Engineering & Technology Ser.). 278p. 1998. text 65.00 (*0-8176-3986-1*) Birkhauser.

Agoshkov, V. I. Boundary Value Problems for Transport Equations: Functional Spaces, Variational Statements, Regularity of Solutions. LC 98-4737. (Modeling & Simulation in Science, Engineering & Technology Ser.). 1998. write for info. (*3-7643-3986-1*) Birkhauser.

Agoshkov, V. I., jt. auth. see Marchuk, Gurii I.

Agosin, Manuel R., ed. Foreign Direct Investment in Latin America. LC 95-81780. (Inter-American Development Bank Ser.). 186p. (C). 1995. pap. text 18.50 (*1-886938-01-6*) IADB.

Agosin, Marjorie. An Absence of Shadows. Franzen, Cola & Kostopulos-Cooperman, Celeste, trs. from SPA. LC 98-37956. (Human Rights Ser.: Vol. 6). 128p. 1998. pap. 15.00 (*1-877727-92-X*) White Pine.

***Agosin, Marjorie.** The Alphabet in My Hands: A Writing Life. LC 99-23069. (Illus.). 200p. 2000. 24.00 (*0-8135-2704-X*) Rutgers U Pr.

Agosin, Marjorie. Always from Somewhere Else: A Memoir of My Chilean Jewish Father. Kostopulos-Cooperman, Celeste, tr. from SPA. (Helen Rose Scheuer Jewish Women's Ser.). (Illus.). 224p. 1998. 18.95 (*1-55861-195-9*) Feminist Pr.

***Agosin, Marjorie.** Always from Somewhere Else: A Memoir of My Chilean Jewish Father. 264p. 2000. pap. 11.95 (*1-55861-256-4*) Feminist Pr.

Agosin, Marjorie. Ashes of Revolt: Essays on Human Rights. LC 97-129800. 250p. (Orig.). 1996. pap. 15.00 (*1-877727-56-3*) White Pine.

— Council of the Fairies. 1997. pap. 11.95 (*1-885214-10-3*) Azul Edits.

— A Cross & a Star: Memoirs of a Jewish Girl in Chile. LC 94-3213. (Helen Rose Scheuer Jewish Women's Ser.). (Illus.). 224p. 1998. pap. 13.95 (*1-55861-176-2*) Feminist Pr.

— A Cross & a Star: Memoirs of a Jewish Girl in Chile. Kostopulos-Cooperman, Celeste, tr. 112p. 1997. pap. write for info. (*1-85964-112-1*) LPC InBook.

— A Cross & a Star: Memoirs of a Jewish Girl in Chile. LC 94-3213. (Illus.). 202p. (C). 1995. 19.95 (*0-8263-1573-9*) U of NM Pr.

— Dear Anne Frank: Poems. Schaaf, Richard, tr. from SPA. LC 93-73680. 128p. 1994. pap. 11.95 (*0-9632363-6-9*) Azul Edits.

— Dear Anne Frank: Poems. rev. ed. Schaaf, Richard et al, trs. LC 97-40296. (SPA & ENG.). 144p. 1998. reprint ed. pap. 11.95 (*0-87451-857-1*) U Pr of New Eng.

— A Dream of Light & Shadows: Portraits of Latin American Women Writers. LC 94-48679. 342p. 1995. 35.00 (*0-8263-1633-6*) U of NM Pr.

— Happiness. Horan, Elizabeth, tr. 238p. 1993. pap. 14.00 (*1-877727-34-2*) White Pine.

— Hogueras - Bonfires. Lindstrom, Naomi, tr. LC 90-84003. 152p. 1990. pap. 13.00 (*0-927534-07-X*) Biling Rev-Pr.

***Agosin, Marjorie.** Lluvia en el desierto (Rain in the Desert) Kostopolus-Cooperman, Celeste, tr. (SPA & ENG.). 112p. 1999. pap. 15.00 (*1-890932-09-4*) Sherman Asher Pub.

Agosin, Marjorie. Melodious Women: A Poetic Celebration of Extraordinary Women. Galmozzi, Monica Bruno, tr. from SPA. LC 97-42693. (Discoveries Ser.). 112p. 1997. pap. text 13.95 (*0-935480-91-9*) Lat Am Lit Rev Pr.

— The Mothers of Plaza de Mayo: The Story of Renee Epelbaum, 1976-1985. Molloy, Janice, tr. from SPA. LC 89-63626. (Illus.). 125p. (C). 1990. 29.95 (*0-932415-51-2*); pap. 9.95 (*0-932415-52-0*) Red Sea Pr.

— Sargasso. Franzen, Cola, tr. 224p. 1993. pap. 12.00 (*1-877727-27-X*) White Pine.

— Scraps of Life: The Chilean Arpilleras: Chilean Women & the Pinochet Dictatorship. Franzen, Cola, tr. from SPA. LC 87-61508. (Illus.). 190p. (C). 1987. 29.95 (*0-932415-28-8*); pap. 9.95 (*0-932415-29-6*) Red Sea Pr.

— Starry Night. Berg, Mary G., tr. LC 97-116486. 96p. (Orig.). 1996. pap. 12.00 (*1-877727-66-0*) White Pine.

— Tapestries of Hope, Threads: The Arpillera Movement in Chile, 1974-1994. LC 95-32448. (Illus.). 160p. (C). 1996. pap. 14.95 (*0-8263-1692-1*) U of NM Pr.

— Toward the Splendid City: Poems. Schaaf, Richard, tr. LC 94-6216. 1994. pap. 15.00 (*0-927534-46-0*) Biling Rev-Pr.

***Agosin, Marjorie.** Uncertain Travelers: Conversations with Jewish Women Immigrants to America. LC 99-30391. (Brandeis Series on Jewish Women). 221p. 1999. 24.95 (*0-87451-945-4*) U Pr of New Eng.

Agosin, Marjorie. Witches & Other Things. Miller, Yvette E., ed. Franzen, Cola, tr. LC 84-768. (Discoveries Ser.).Tr. of Brujas y Algo Mas. (ENG & SPA.). 150p. 1984. pap. 10.50 (*0-935480-16-1*) Lat Am Lit Rev Pr.

***Agosin, Marjorie.** A Woman's Gaze: Essays on Latin American Women Artists. LC 97-51385. 256p. 1998. pap. text 20.00 (*1-877727-85-7*) White Pine.

Agosin, Marjorie. Women in Disguise: Stories. Russell-Pineda, Diane, tr. from SPA. LC 95-75220. 168p. (C). 1996. pap. 14.95 (*1-885214-01-4*) Azul Edits.

— Women of Smoke: Latin American Women in Literature & Life. Lindstrom, Naomi, tr. LC 87-36203. (Discoveries Ser.). (ENG & SPA.). 150p. 1988. pap. 10.95 (*0-935480-34-X*) Lat Am Lit Rev Pr.

— Women of Smoke: Latin American Women in Literature & Life. Molloy, Janice, tr. LC 88-63387. 112p. 1989. 39.95 (*0-932415-42-3*); pap. 12.95 (*0-932415-43-1*) Red Sea Pr.

Agosin, Marjorie, ed. The House of Memory: Stories by Jewish Women Writers of Latin America. LC 99-10658. 250p. 1999. pap. 15.95 (*1-55861-209-2*, Pub. by Feminist Pr) Consort Bk Sales.

***Agosin, Marjorie, ed.** The House of Memory: Stories by Jewish Women Writers of Latin America. Horan, Elizabeth Rosa, tr. from SPA. LC 99-10658. (Helen Rose Scheuer Jewish Women's Ser.). 256p. 1999. 37.00 (*1-55861-208-4*, Pub. by Feminist Pr) Consort Bk Sales.

Agosin, Marjorie, ed. Landscapes of a New Land: Fiction by Latin American Women. 1989. 19.00 (*0-934834-88-1*); pap. 12.00 (*0-934834-96-2*) White Pine.

— Map of Hope: Women's Writing on Human Rights. LC 98-44985. 395p. (C). 1999. pap. 18.00 (*0-8135-2626-4*); text 49.00 (*0-8135-2625-6*) Rutgers U Pr.

***Agosin, Marjorie, ed.** Miriam's Daughters: Jewish Latin American Women Poets. Gordenstein, Roberta, tr. (SPA & ENG.). 224p. 2000. pap. 16.00 (*1-890932-13-2*, Pub. by Sherman Asher Pub) Partners-West.

Agosin, Marjorie, ed. Passion, Memory, & Identity: 20th Century Latin American Jewish Women Writers. LC 99-6197. 217p. 1999. 39.95 (*0-8263-2045-7*); pap. 18.95 (*0-8263-2049-X*) U of NM Pr.

— These Are Not Sweet Girls: Poetry by Latin American Women. LC 95-111754. Vol. 7. 368p. 2000. pap. 20.00 (*1-877727-38-5*, Pub. by White Pine) Consort Bk Sales.

— What Is Secret? No. 9: Short Stories by Chilean Women. LC 96-131637. (Secret Weaver Ser.: Vol. 9). 304p. (Orig.). 1996. pap. 17.00 (*1-877727-41-5*) White Pine.

— Women, Children & Human Rights. (Thematic Studies in Latin America Ser.). (C). 1996. pap. text 17.95 (*0-8133-1318-X*) Westview.

Agosin, Marjorie & Hall, Nancy, eds. A Necklace of Words: Short Fiction by Mexican Women. (Secret Weavers Ser.: Vol. 12). 148p. (Orig.). 1998. pap. 14.00 (*1-877727-73-3*) White Pine.

Agosin, Marjorie & Levison, Julie H., eds. Magical Sites: Women Travelers in 19th Century Latin America. LC 99-11291. 256p. 1998. pap. 17.00 (*1-877727-94-6*, Pub. by White Pine) Consort Bk Sales.

A

A

Agosin, Marjorie, et al. Chilean Folktales Retold. Kostopulos-Cooperman, Celeste, tr. 106p. (Orig.). 1992. pap. 9.95 (*0-88795-093-0*) Distributors.

— Maria Luisa Bombal: Apreciaciones Criticas. LC 87-70082. 280p. 1987. pap. 22.00 (*0-916950-73-5*) Biling Rev-Pr.

— Tapestries of Hope, Threads: The Arpillera Movement in Chile, 1974-1994. LC 95-32448. (Illus.). 160p. (C). 1996. 29.95 (*0-8263-1691-3*) U of NM Pr.

Agosta, John & Russell, Travis. Cellular Digital Packet Data Standards & Technology. LC 96-28768. (Illus.). 243p. 1996. pap. 50.00 (*0-07-000600-8*) McGraw.

***Agosta, Lou.** The Essential Guide to Data Warehousing. LC 99-40534. 526p. 1999. pap. text 34.99 (*0-13-085087-X*) P-H.

Agosta, Lucien L. E. B. White: The Children's Books. 1995. 32.00 (*0-8057-4631-5*, Twyne) Mac Lib Ref.

Agosta, William. Bombardier Beetles & Fever Trees: A Close-up Look at Chemical Warfare & Signals in Animals & Plants. LC 95-9533. (Illus.). 240p. 1995. 25.00 (*0-201-62658-6*, Health Sci) Addison-Wesley.

***Agosta, William C.** Thieves, Deceivers & Killers: Tales of Chemistry in Nature. LC 00-32627. 256p. 2000. 26.95 (*0-691-00488-9*) Princeton U Pr.

***Agosti, et al, eds.** Ants: Standard Methods for Measuring & Monitoring Biodiversity. 2000. 60.00 (*1-56098-858-4*) Smithsonian.

***Agosti, Donat, et al.** Ants: Standard Methods for Measuring & Monitoring Biodiversity. LC 00-21953. (Biological Diversity Handbook Ser.). (Illus.). 2000. pap. 26.95 (*1-56098-885-1*) Smithsonian.

Agosti, Maristella, ed. Information Retrieval & Hypertext. (Electronic Publishing Ser.). 304p. (C). 1996. text 115.00 (*0-7923-9710-X*) Kluwer Academic.

Agostinelli, Gianni. Migration-Development Interelationships: The Case of the Philippines. 33p. 1992. 5.00 (*0-934733-59-7*) CMS.

Agostini de del Rio, Amelia. Gramatica y Teoria Literaria: Guion Para el Estudiante. 2nd ed. 558p. (C). 1991. 7.50 (*0-8477-3104-9*) U of PR Pr.

Agostini, Pino. Encyclopedia of Italian Cooking. LC 98-25051. (Illus.). 416p. 1998. 34.95 (*1-57145-610-4*, Laurel Glen Pub) Advantage Pubs.

Agostini, Rosemary, ed. Medical & Orthopedic Issues of Active & Athletic Women. LC 94-75825. (Illus.). 300p. (Orig.). 1994. pap. text 50.95 (*1-56053-019-7*) Hanley & Belfus.

Agostinis, P. Protein Phosphatases: Substrate Specificity & Enzyme Regulation by Second-Site Phosphorylation. No. 1. 92p. (Orig.). 1988. pap. 22.00 (*90-6186-260-4*, Pub. by Leuven Univ) Coronet Bks.

Agostino De Del Rio, Amelia. Unamuno Multiple: Antologia. LC 81-10347. (Coleccion Mente y Palabra). 297p. 1982. 8.00 (*0-8477-0582-X*); pap. 7.00 (*0-8477-0583-8*) U of PR Pr.

Agostino, Paul. Created Writing: Poetry from New Angles. LC 95-4496. 140p. (C). 1995. pap. text 25.60 (*0-13-505280-7*) P-H.

— Engagements & Disengagements: New Poems. 128p. 1998. pap. 12.00 (*0-925062-14-6*) Writers Ink Pr.

AGOSTO, Inc. Staff. Photoshop Masters: The Artistic Creations of Twenty Adobe Photoshop Experts. (Illus.). 144p. 1998. pap. 29.99 (*1-56496-502-3*) Rockport Pubs.

AGOSTO, Inc. Staff, ed. Illustrator Masters: The Artistic Creations of Nineteen Adobe Illustrator Experts. (Illus.). 144p. 1999. pap. 29.99 (*1-56496-547-3*) Rockport Pubs.

— 3D & Web Masters: The Artistic Creations of Twenty-Three 3D & Web Experts. (Illus.). 144p. 1999. pap. 29.99 (*1-56496-548-1*) Rockport Pubs.

***Agosto, Noraida.** Michelle Cliff's Novels: Piecing the Tapestry of Memory & History. LC 98-42387. 208p. 1999. 49.95 (*0-8204-4255-0*) P Lang Pubng.

Agoston, G. A. Color Theory & Its Application in Art & Design. 2nd rev. ed. (Optical Sciences Ser.: Vol. 19). (Illus.). 300p. 1987. 72.95 (*0-387-17095-2*) Spr-Verlag.

Agoston, Max K. Algebraic Topology: A First Course. LC 75-18033. (Pure & Applied Mathematics Ser.: No. 32). (Illus.). 376p. reprint ed. pap. 116.60 (*0-8357-5307-7*, 203224100078) Bks Demand.

Agoston, Vilmos, ed. Autonomy: Challenge & - or Solution for the Central-European Minorities. Lengyel, Eva et al, trs. from HUN. 112p. (C). pap. 20.00 (*1-882785-07-X*) Matthias Corvinus.

***Agouris, P. & Stefanidis, A., eds.** Integrated Spatial Databases: Digital Images & GIS. LC 99-88771. (Lecture Notes in Computer Science Ser.: Vol. 1737). x, 317p. 2000. pap. 56.00 (*3-540-66931-0*) Spr-Verlag.

Agozino, Biko. Black Women & the Criminal Justice System: Towards the Decolonisation of Victimisation. LC 97-70346. 214p. 1997. 63.95 (*1-85972-643-7*, Pub. by Ashgate Pub) Ashgate Pub Co.

***Agozino, Biko, ed.** Theoretical & Methodological Issues in Migration Research: Interdisciplinary, Intergenerational & International Perspectives. 214p. 2000. text 61.95 (*1-84014-557-9*, Pub. by Ashgate Pub) Ashgate Pub Co.

AGPS Standards Section Staff, contrib. by. Australian Print Standards. 104p. 1995. (*0-644-42940-2*) AGPS Pr.

Agraham. Making of the Indian Atomic Bomb. LC 98-27616. 2000. pap. text 19.95 (*1-85649-630-9*, Pub. by Zed Books) St Martin.

Agrait, Gustavo. Beatus Ille en la Poesia Lirica del Siglo de Oro. (C). 3.75 (*0-8477-3100-6*); pap. 3.00 (*0-8477-3101-4*) U of PR Pr.

— De Hito en Hito: Siete Ensayos Sobre Literatura Espanola. LC 83-8864. (SPA.). 151p. 1983. pap. 5.00 (*0-8477-3508-7*) U of PR Pr.

— El Extrano Caso de...Quien? (SPA.). 170p. 1991. pap. 9.75 (*0-8477-3675-X*) U of PR Pr.

— Ocho Casos Extranos y Dos Casos Mas: Cuentos, 1930-1970. (UPREX, Ficcion Ser.: No. 4). 153p. (C). 1972. pap. 1.50 (*0-8477-0004-6*) U of PR Pr.

— Szomoru Vasarnap. LC 88-29642. 118p. (Orig.). 1989. pap. 6.95 (*0-8477-3632-6*) U of PR Pr.

Agrali, Salmon, jt. auth. see Swift, Lloyd.

Agrali, Selman, jt. auth. see Swift, Lloyd B.

Agramonte, Roberto. Marti y Su Concepcion de la Sociedad Tomo II, Parte 2: Patria y Humanidad 1. LC 81-10377. (Illus.). 394p. 1984. pap. 5.50 (*0-8477-3500-1*) U of PR Pr.

— Marti y Su Concepcion Del Mundo. 815p. (C). 1971. 7.50 (*0-8477-3102-2*) U of PR Pr.

— Sociologia: Curso Introductorio. LC 77-5905. (Illus.). 1978. pap. 8.00 (*0-8477-2443-3*) U of PR Pr.

Agramonte, Roberto D. Las Doctrinas Educativas y Politicas de Marti. (SPA.). 700p. 1991. pap. 35.00 (*0-8477-2497-2*) U of PR Pr.

— Teoria Sociologica: Exegesis de los Grandes Sistemas. LC 78-9810. (SPA.). 1024p. (C). 1981. pap. text 12.00 (*0-8477-2487-5*) U of PR Pr.

Agramonte, Roberto D. & De Rafael Rosa, Portada. Marti y Su Concepcion de la Sociedad, 2 pts., Tomo II. 1984. pap. 10.50 (*0-8477-3517-6*) U of PR Pr.

Agramonte, Roberto D. & Rosa, Portada de Rafael. Marti y Su Concepcion de la Sociedad Tomo II, Parte 1: Teoria General de la Sociedad. (Illus.). 232p. 1979. pap. 4.95 (*0-8477-2467-0*) U of PR Pr.

Agran, Edward G. Too Good a Town: William Allen White, Community, & the Emerging Rhetoric of Middle America. LC 98-19839. (Illus.). 256p. 1999. 30.00 (*1-55728-520-9*) U of Ark Pr.

***Agran, Edward G.** Too Good a Town: William Allen White, Community, & the Emerging Rhetoric of Middle America. LC 98-19839. (Illus.). 256p. 1999. pap. 16.00 (*1-55728-521-7*) U of Ark Pr.

Agran, Martin. Student-Directed Learning: Teaching Self-Determination Skills. LC 96-34861. (Special Education Ser.). (Illus.). 449p. 1996. 61.95 (*0-534-15942-7*) Brooks-Cole.

— Student-Directed Learning: Teaching Self-Determination Skills. (C). 1997. pap. text, teacher ed. write for info. (*0-534-34069-5*) Brooks-Cole.

Agran, Martin & Moore, Stephen C. How to Teach Self-Instruction of Job Skills. Browder, Diane M., ed. (Innovations Ser.). (Illus.). 48p. (C). 1994. pap. text 21.95 (*0-940898-34-9*) Am Assn Mental.

Agran, Martin & Wehmeyer, Michael L. Teaching Problem Solving to Students with Mental Retardation LC 99-26206. (Innovations Ser.). 1999. write for info. (*0-940898-62-4*) Am Assn Mental.

Agran, Rick. Crow Milk: Poems by Rick Agran. LC 97-208747. (Illus.). 80p. 1997. pap. 10.95 (*1-882291-55-7*) Oyster River Pr.

— Crowmilk. 56p. (Orig.). 1996. pap. 10.00 (*1-886963-02-9*) Kettle of Fish.

***Agran, Rick & Crill, Hildred.** Under the Legislature of Stars: Sixty-Two New Hampshire Poets. Kumin, Maxine & DeCarteret, Mark, eds. 112p. 1999. per. 15.00 (*1-882291-59-X*) Oyster River Pr.

Agranoff, Ann, jt. auth. see Anderes, Fred.

Agranoff, Bernard W., jt. auth. see Siegel, George J.

Agranoff, Raquel B. Risottos, Paellas & Other Rice Specialties. LC 97-195759. (Illus.). 176p. (Orig.). 1997. pap. 8.95 (*1-55867-166-8*, Nitty Gritty Ckbks) Bristol Pub Ent CA.

Agranoff, Raquel B. & Kane, Lois E. Ann Arbor Fresh: Recipes & Stories from the Ann Arbor Farmers' Market & the Kerrytown Historic District. LC 98-93340. (Illus.). 200p. 1998. pap. 15.50 (*0-9666191-0-2*) Agrakane Inc.

Agranoff, Robert, ed. Human Services on a Limited Budget. LC 83-4388. (Practical Management Ser.). (Illus.). 240p. (Orig.). (C). 1983. pap. 23.95 (*0-87326-038-4*) Intl City-Cnty Mgt.

Agranovic, Z. S., et al. Thirteen Papers on Functional Analysis. (Translations Ser.: Series 2, Vol. 90). 253p. 1970. 44.00 (*0-8218-1790-6*, TRANS2/90) Am Math.

Agranovich, M. Vladimir, jt. auth. see Kajzar, Francois.

Agranovich, Mikhal S. Generalized Methods of Eigenoscillations in the Diffraction Theory. 378p. 1999. 145.00 (*3-527-40092-3*) Wiley.

Agranovich, V. M. & Ginzburg, Vitaly L. Crystal Optics with Spatial Dispersion, & Excitons. 2nd ed. (Solid-State Sciences Ser.: Vol. 42). (Illus.). 455p. 1984. 97.95 (*0-387-11520-X*) Spr-Verlag.

Agranovich, V. M. & Mills, D. L., eds. Surface Polaritons: Electromagnetic Waves of Surfaces & Interfaces. (Modern Problems in Condensed Matter Sciences Ser.: Vol. 1). xvi, 718p. 1982. 342.50 (*0-444-86165-3*) Elsevier.

Agranovich, V. M., jt. auth. see Kajzar, F.

Agranovskii, M. L. Invariant Function Spaces on Homogeneous Manifolds of Lie Groups & Applications. LC 93-2029. (Translations of Mathematical Monographs: Vol. 126). 131p. 1993. text 71.00 (*0-8218-4604-3*, MMONO/126) Am Math.

Agras, W. Stewart. Eating Disorders. 144p. (C). 1987. pap. text 53.95 (*0-205-14263-X*, H4263, Longwood Div) Allyn.

— Overcoming Eating Disorders: A Cognitive-Behavioral Treatment for Bulimai Nervosa & Binge-Eati. 1999. pap. text 37.50 (*0-12-785054-6*) Acad Pr.

***Agras, W Stewart.** Overcoming Eating Disorders Client Workbook: A Cognitive-Behavioral Treatment for Bulimia Nervosa. 1999. pap. text, wbk. ed. 43.50 (*0-12-785055-4*) Acad Pr.

Agras, W. Stewart, ed. Behavior Modification: Principles & Clinical Applications. 2nd ed. 307p. 1978. 20.00 (*0-316-02031-1*, Little Brwn Med Div) Lppncott W & W.

Agrasal, S. P. & Aggarwal, J. C. Second Historical Survey of Women's Education in India, 1988-1994. (C). 1996. 52.00 (*81-7022-544-2*, Pub. by Concept) S Asia.

***Agrasbanchez, Rogelio.** Cine Mexicano: Poster Art from the Golden Age, 1936-1956. LC 00-34556. (Illus.). 2000. write for info. (*0-8118-3058-6*) Chronicle Bks.

Agrawal. Introduction to Financial Accounting. 3rd ed. 1995. 59.95 (*0-87393-474-1*) Dame Pubns.

— Introduction to Financial Accounting: Study Guide. 3rd ed. 1995. pap., student ed. 15.95 (*0-87393-500-4*) Dame Pubns.

— Introduction to Financial Accounting: Working Papers. 3rd ed. 1995. pap. 19.95 (*0-87393-501-2*) Dame Pubns.

— Mobile Computing. 1997. lib. bdg. 115.00 (*0-7923-9929-3*) Kluwer Academic.

— Proceedings of International Conference on Parallell Processing, 23rd, Vol. 1. 336p. 1994. 59.95 (*0-8493-2493-9*) CRC Pr.

— Receptor Characterization & Their Regulation. 232p. 1992. lib. bdg. write for info. (*0-8493-4230-9*, CRC Reprint) Franklin.

Agrawal, A. Studies on Nepali Language & Linguistics: A Bibliography. (C). 1991. text 60.00 (*0-7855-0157-6*, Pub. by Ratna Pustak Bhandar) St Mut.

Agrawal, A., ed. Bioprocess Parameter Control. (Advances in Biochemical Engineering-Biochemistry Ser.: Vol. 30). (Illus.). 210p. 1984. 81.00 (*0-387-13539-1*) Spr-Verlag.

Agrawal, A. N. India Economic Information Year Book 1992-93. 1993. reprint ed. 30.00 (*0-8364-2864-1*) S Asia.

— Indian Economy Problems of Development & Planning. 14th ed. (C). 1988. pap. 14.00 (*0-85226-015-6*) S Asia.

Agrawal, A. N., et al. India Economic Information Yearbook, 1990-91. (C). 1991. 35.00 (*81-214-0332-4*) S Asia.

***Agrawal, Anurag A., et al, eds.** Induced Plant Defenses Against Pathogens & Herbivores: Biochemistry, Ecology & Agriculture. 403p. 1999. 59.00 (*0-89054-242-2*) Am Phytopathol Soc.

Agrawal, Arun. Community in Conservation: Beyond Enchantment & Disenchantment. 93p. (C). 1998. spiral bd. write for info. (*0-9662380-0-1*) Conserv & Devel.

— Greener Pastures: Politics, Markets & Community Among a Migrant Pastoral People. LC 98-21274. 1999. pap. 17.95 (*0-8223-2122-X*); text. write for info. (*0-8223-2233-1*) Duke.

***Agrawal, Arun & Sivaramakrishnan, K., eds.** Agrarian Environments: Resources, Representations, & Rule in India. LC 00-27442. (Illus.). 336p. 2000. lib. bdg. 59.95 (*0-8223-2555-1*) Duke.

***Agrawal, Arun & Sivaramakrishnan, K. C.** Agrarian Environments: Resources, Representations & Rule in India. LC 00-27442. (Illus.). 336p. 2000. pap. 19.95 (*0-8223-2574-8*) Duke.

Agrawal, Arun, et al. Decentralization in Nepal: A Comparative Analysis: Participatory District Development Program. LC 98-43169. 96p. 1998. pap. 12.95 (*1-55815-507-4*) ICS Pr.

Agrawal, Ashvini. Rise & Fall of the Imperial Guptas. (C). 1989. 26.00 (*81-208-0592-5*, Pub. by Motilal Bnarsidass) S Asia.

Agrawal, B. D. Financial Accounting - Advanced. 1222p. 1990. 195.00 (*81-209-0019-7*, Pub. by Pitambar Pub) St Mut.

Agrawal, Brij N. Spacecraft Attitude, Dynamics & Control. (C). 2001. write for info. (*0-13-825092-8*, Macmillan Coll) P-H.

***Agrawal, C. Mauli, et al.** Synthetic Bioabsorbable Polymers for Implants. LC 00-40612. (STP Ser.). 2000. write for info. (*0-8031-2870-3*) ASTM.

Agrawal, D. P. & Kharakwal, J. S. Central Himalayas: An Archaeological, Linguistic & Cultural Synthesis. LC 98-907086. xx, 194 p. 1998. write for info. (*81-7305-132-1*) Aryan Bks Intl.

Agrawal, Devendra K. Receptor Characterization & Their Regulation. Date not set. write for info. (*0-8493-7819-2*) CRC Pr.

Agrawal, Devendra K., ed. Airway Smooth Muscle: Mod of Receptors & Response. 312p. 1990. lib. bdg. 202.00 (*0-8493-5904-X*, QP121) CRC Pr.

Agrawal, Devendra K. & Townley, Robert G. Inflammatory Cells & Mediators in Bronchial Asthma. (Illus.). 280p. 1990. lib. bdg. 175.00 (*0-8493-7294-1*, RC591) CRC Pr.

Agrawal, Devendra K., jt. ed. see Townley, Robert C.

Agrawal, G. P. Fiber-Optic Communication Systems. 2nd ed. LC 97-4040. (Microwave & Optical Engineering Ser.). 576p. 1997. 92.50 (*0-471-17540-4*) Wiley.

— Fiber Optics Communications Systems. 1996. 133.00 (*0-614-18448-7*, B25001) Info Gatekeepers.

Agrawal, Govind. Semiconductor Lasers: Past, Present, & Future. (Theoretical & Applied Optics Ser.). 360p. 1995. text 75.00 (*1-56396-211-X*) Am Inst Physics.

Agrawal, Govind P. Nonlinear Fiber Optics. 2nd ed. LC 94-44371. (Optics & Photonics Ser.). (Illus.). 592p. 1995. text 74.00 (*0-12-045142-5*) Acad Pr.

Agrawal, Govind P. & Boyd, Robert W., eds. Contemporary Nonlinear Optics. (Quantum Electronics Ser.). (Illus.). 496p. 1992. text 100.00 (*0-12-045135-2*) Acad Pr.

Agrawal, Govind R., et al. South-South Economic Cooperation: Problems & Prospects. (Research & Information System for Nonaligned & Other Developing Countries Ser.). xii, 263p. 1987. text 27.50 (*81-7027-102-9*, Pub. by Radiant Pubs) S Asia.

Agrawal, Hema. Society, Culture, & Mass Communication: Sociology of Journalism. LC 95-906161. (C). 1995. 27.50 (*81-7033-282-6*, Pub. by Har-Anand Pubns) S Asia.

Agrawal, J. C., jt. ed. see Zunde, Pranas.

Agrawal, Jagannath. Researches in Indian Epigraphy & Numismatics. (Illus.). xii, 133p. 1986. 18.00 (*0-685-67623-4*, Pub. by Sundeep Prak) Nataraj Bks.

Agrawal, Jai P. Power Electronic Systems: Theory & Design. 704p. (C). 2000. 98.00 (*0-13-442880-3*, Macmillan Coll) P-H.

— Power Electronics Applied. (C). 2001. 70.00 (*0-13-442872-2*, Macmillan Coll) P-H.

— Profiles of Power Electronics. (C). 2000. 68.00 (*0-13-442864-1*, Macmillan Coll) P-H.

Agrawal, K. C. Industrial Power Engineering Handbook. (Illus.). 1764p. Date not set. 149.95 (*0-7506-7351-6*) Buttrwrth-Heinemann.

Agrawal, Madhoolika, jt. auth. see Agrawal, Shashi B.

Agrawal, Madhu. Global Competitiveness in the Pharmaceutical Industry: The Effect of National Regulatory, Economic & Market Factors. LC 99-13600. 188p. 1999. lib. bdg. 69.95 (*0-7890-0715-0*, Pharmctl Prods) Haworth Pr.

Agrawal, Mamta. Education & Modernization: A Study of Hindu & Muslim Women. 1987. 17.50 (*0-8364-2088-8*, Pub. by Usha) S Asia.

Agrawal, O. P. Perspectives in Entomological Research. 1994. pap. 180.00 (*81-7233-075-8*, Pub. by Scientific Pubs) St Mut.

Agrawal, P. C. Oilseed in India. (C). 1990. 17.50 (*81-204-0553-6*, Pub. by Oxford IBH) S Asia.

Agrawal, P. K. India's Foreign Economic Relations. (C). 1991. 20.00 (*0-8364-2662-2*, Pub. by Chugh Pubns) S Asia.

— India's Move Towards Sustainable Development. 190p. 1996. pap. 150.00 (*81-7533-019-8*, Pub. by Print Hse) St Mut.

— Land Reforms in India: Constitutional & Legal Approach. 272p. (C). 1993. pap. 225.00 (*81-85880-09-3*, Pub. by Print Hse) St Mut.

— Motivation & Indian Bureaucracy. LC 94-906774. 119p. 1995. pap. 88.00 (*81-85880-66-2*, Pub. by Print Hse) St Mut.

Agrawal, P. K., ed. Carbon-13 NMR of Flavonoids. (Studies in Organic Chemistry: 39). 564p. 1989. 291.00 (*0-444-87449-6*) Elsevier.

— Environment Protection & Pollution Control in the Ganga. 173p. (C). 1994. pap. 120.00 (*81-85880-39-5*, Pub. by Print Hse) St Mut.

Agrawal, Pradeep, et al. Economic Restructuring in East Asia & India: Perspectives on Policy Reform. LC 94-43329. (International Political Economy Ser.). 270p. 1995. text 75.00 (*0-312-12537-2*) St Martin.

***Agrawal, Pradeep, et al.** Policy Regimes & Industrial Competitiveness: A Comparative Study of East Asia & India. LC 00-27831. (International Political Economy Ser.). 2000. write for info. (*0-312-23452-X*) St Martin.

Agrawal, R. C. Archaeological Remains in Western India. (C). 1989. 72.00 (*0-8364-2417-4*, Pub. by Agam) S Asia.

Agrawal, R. C., jt. ed. see Sharma, R. K.

Agrawal, R. L. Fundamentals of Plant Breeding & Hybrid Seed Production. (Illus.). 394p. 1998. 49.50 (*1-57808-029-0*) Science Pubs.

— Identifying Crop Varieties. (Illus.). 136p. 1997. 29.50 (*1-886106-90-8*, 6908) Science Pubs.

Agrawal, R. R. Medieval Revival & Its Influences on the Romantic Movement. 1990. 44.00 (*81-7017-262-4*, Pub. by Abhinav) S Asia.

Agrawal, Rakesh & Stolorz, Paul, eds. Proceedings of the Fourth International Conference on Knowledge Discovery & Data Mining. LC 98-210525. (Illus.). 392p. 1998. pap. text 60.00 (*1-57735-070-7*) AAAI Pr.

Agrawal, S. B., jt. ed. see Chaudhary, B. R.

Agrawal, S. P. Development of Library Services in India: Social Science Information. (C). 1989. 25.00 (*81-7022-233-8*, Pub. by Concept) S Asia.

— Festivals: National-International. 77p. 1984. 10.95 (*0-318-36316-X*) Asia Bk Corp.

Agrawal, S. P., ed. Development of Documentation in India: Social Science Information. (C). 1989. 44.00 (*81-7022-239-7*, Pub. by Concept) S Asia.

— Government & Politics in India: A Bibliographical Study of Contemporary Scenario Chronicling Rejiv Gandhi Era. (Concepts in Communication Informatics & Librarianship Ser.: No. 43). 1993. 34.00 (*81-7022-461-6*, Pub. by Concept) S Asia.

— Information India, 1991-92: Global View. (Concepts in Communication Informatics & Librarianship Ser.: No. 47). (C). 1993. 48.00 (*81-7022-308-3*, Pub. by Concept) S Asia.

— Media Utilization for the Development of Women & Children. (C). 1989. 23.00 (*81-7022-249-4*, Pub. by Concept) S Asia.

— Weaker Section in India: Undiscovered Past, Uncertain Present & Unpredictable Future Index to Writings in Indian Scholarly Journals & 10 National Newspapers Classified under 1500 Descriptors 1886-1900. (Concepts in Communication Informatics & Librarianship Ser.). (C). 1992. 50.00 (*81-7022-416-0*, Pub. by Concept) S Asia.

Agrawal, S. P. & Aggarwal, J. C. Development of Education in India. LC 98-909472. (Concepts in Communication Informatics & Librarianship Ser.). 447p. 1997. write for info. (*81-7022-661-9*) Concept.

— Third Historical Survey of Educational Development in India: Select Documents 1990-1992 LC 98-915889. (Concepts in Communication Informatics & Librarianship Ser.). 493p. 1994. write for info. (*81-7022-516-7*) Concept.

— Woman's Education in India. (C). 1992. 33.00 (*81-7022-318-0*, Pub. by Concept) S Asia.

Agrawal, S. P. & Aggarwal, J. C., eds. Nehru on Social Issues. (C). 1989. 30.00 (*81-7022-207-9*, Pub. by Concept) S Asia.

Agrawal, S. P., jt. auth. see Aggarwal, J. C.

Agrawal, Shashi B. & Agrawal, Madhoolika. Environmental Pollution & Plant Responses. LC 99-26504. 408p. 1999. boxed set 79.95 (*1-56670-341-7*) Lewis Pubs.

An Asterisk (*) at the beginning of an entry indicates that the title is appearing for the first time.

Agrawal, Sudhir, ed. Antisense Therapeutics. LC 96-3441. (Methods in Molecular Medicine Ser.: Vol. 1). (Illus.). 290p. 1996. 115.00 (*0-8109-305-8*) Humana.

— Protocols for Oligonucleotide Conjugates: Synthesis & Analytical Techniques. LC 93-23127. (Methods in Molecular Biology Ser.: Vol. 26). (Illus.). 390p. 1993. student ed., spiral bd. 99.50 (*0-89603-252-3*) Humana.

— Protocols for Oligonucleotides & Analogs: Synthesis & Properties. LC 93-7121. (Methods in Molecular Biology Ser.: Vol. 20). 516p. 1993. 119.50 (*0-89603-281-7*); pap. 99.50 (*0-89603-247-7*) Humana.

Agrawal, Sudhir, jt. ed. see Crooke, Stanley T.

Agrawal, Sunil K. & Fabien, Brian C. Optimization of Dynamic Systems. LC 99-21107. (Solid Mechanics & Its Applications Ser.). 221p. 1999. write for info. (*0-7923-5681-0*) Kluwer Academic.

Agrawal, Suphal P., ed. Superplastic Forming: Proceedings of a Symposium. LC 84-72936. (Conference Proceedings - American Society for Metals Ser.). (Illus.). 100p. reprint ed. pap. 31.00 (*0-8357-3559-1*, 203432300089) Bks Demand.

Agrawal, Surendra, ed. International Guide to Accounting Journals. 2nd ed. 360p. 1993. text 49.95 (*1-55876-067-9*) Wiener Pubs Inc.

***Agrawal, Usha.** Directory of Museums in India. 2000. 92.00 (*81-7574-087-6*, Pub. by Sundeep Prak) S Asia.

Agrawal, Vishwani D., jt. auth. see Cheng, Kwang-Ting.

Agrawala, A. K., et al, eds. Mission Critical Operating Systems. LC 91-33762. (Studies in Computer & Communications Systems: Vol. 1). 392p. (gr. 12). 1992. 75.00 (*90-5199-069-3*, Pub. by IOS Pr) IOS Press.

Agrawala, V. S., ed. see Bharati, Jahadhuru Swami Sri & Maharaja, Krsna Tirthaji.

Agrawala, V. S., ed. see Maharaja, Jagadguru S.

Agrawala, Vasudeva S. The Heritage of Indian Art: A Pictorical Presentation. (Illus.). 186p. 1984. 17.95 (*0-318-36275-9*) Asia Bk Corp.

Agre, Peter & Parker, John C. Red Blood Cell Membranes: Structure, Function, Clinical Implications. (Hematology Ser.: Vol. 11). (Illus.). 760p. 1989. text 250.00 (*0-8247-8022-1*) Dekker.

Agre, Peter C. & Cartron, Jean-Pierre, eds. Protein Blood Group Antigens of the Human Red Cell: Structure, Function, & Clinical Significance. LC 92-49755. (Johns Hopkins Series in Hematology/Oncology). (Illus.). 281p. 1992. reprint ed. pap. 87.20 (*0-608-05919-6*, 206625500008) Bks Demand.

Agre, Phil & Schuler, Douglas, eds. Reinventing Technology, Rediscovering Community. LC 96-36613. (Illus.). 272p. 1997. pap. 39.50 (*1-56750-259-8*); text 78.50 (*1-56750-258-X*) Ablx Pub.

Agre, Philip E. Computation & Human Experience. (Learning in Doing: Social, Cognitive & Computational Perspectives Ser.). (Illus.). 388p. (C). 1997. text 64.95 (*0-521-38432-X*); pap. text 21.95 (*0-521-38603-9*) Cambridge U Pr.

Agre, Philip E. & Rosenschein, Stanley J., eds. Computational Theories of Interaction & Agency. LC 96-6163. (Artificial Intelligence Ser.). (Illus.). 650p. 1996. pap. text 52.50 (*0-262-51090-1*) MIT Pr.

Agre, Philip E. & Rotenberg, Marc, eds. Technology & Privacy: The New Landscape. LC 97-7989. (Illus.). 336p. 1997. 30.00 (*0-262-01162-X*) MIT Pr.

Agre, Phillip E. & Rotenberg, Marc, eds. Technology & Privacy: The New Landscape. LC 97-7989. (Illus.). 324p. 1998. reprint ed. pap. text 15.00 (*0-262-51101-0*) MIT Pr.

Agreda, Mary. Mystical City of God: A Popular Abridgement, Vol. 1. abr. ed. Marison, Fiscar & Blatter, George J., trs. from SPA. LC 78-62255. 1993. reprint ed. pap. 18.50 (*0-89555-070-9*) TAN Bks Pubs.

Agreda, V. & Zoeller, J. Acetic Acid & Its Derivatives. (Chemical Industries Ser.: Vol. 49). (Illus.). 456p. 1992. text 215.00 (*0-8247-8792-7*) Dekker.

Agree, A. M., et al. Betz Handbook of Industrial Water Conditioning. 9th ed. LC 91-61770. 448p. 1991. 70.00 (*0-913641-00-6*) BetzDearborn.

***Agree, Emily M.** Aging Research in Europe: Demographic, Social & Behavioural Aspects. 90p. 1998. pap. 25.00 (*92-1-100762-3*) UN.

Agree, George E., jt. auth. see Adamany, David W.

Agrelius, M. Why Wait 'til I'm Dead? Buy This Book Now. 64p. (Orig.). 1986. pap. 4.95 (*0-936805-00-5*) Happy Val Whittier.

Agrelius, M., jt. auth. see Bough, G. Gordon.

Agren, Goran I. & Bosatta, Ernesto. Theoretical Ecosystem Ecology: Understanding Nutrient Cycles. (Illus.). 250p. (C). 1998. pap. text 29.95 (*0-521-64651-0*) Cambridge U Pr.

Agren, Gosta. Valley in the Midst of Violence: Selected Poems. McDuff, David, tr. from FIN. 110p. 1993. pap. 16.95 (*1-85224-236-1*, Pub. by Bloodaxe Bks) Dufour.

Agren, H., et al, eds. Studies of Brain Metabolism in Psychiatric Patients: Can Standards Be Drawn? (Journal of Neural Transmission: Suppl. 37). (Illus.). 100p. 1992. 63.95 (*0-387-82346-8*) Spr-Verlag.

Agren, J., et al. Computer Prediction of Phase Diagrams. 320p. Date not set. 150.00 (*0-901716-45-6*, Pub. by Inst Materials) Ashgate Pub Co.

Agren, Maria, ed. Iron-Making Societies: Early Industrial Development in Sweden & Russia, 1600-1900. LC 97-31843. (Illus.). 356p. 1998. 49.95 (*1-57181-955-X*) Berghahn Bks.

Agres, Stuart J., et al, eds. Emotion in Advertising: Theoretical & Practical Explorations. LC 90-30018. 408p. 1990. 75.00 (*0-89930-537-7*, Quorum Bks) Greenwood.

Agress, Lynne. The Feminine Irony: Women on Women in Early Nineteenth Century English Literature. (Illus.). 190p. 1984. reprint ed. pap. text 20.50 (*0-8191-4156-9*) U Pr of Amer.

Agrest, Diana, et al, eds. The Sex on Architecture. LC 96-5552. (Illus.). 320p. 1996. pap. 19.95 (*0-8109-2683-0*, Pub. by Abrams) Time Warner.

Agrest, Diana & Gandelsonas, Mario. Agrest & Gandelsonas, Works. LC 94-30361. (Illus.). 304p. 1994. 60.00 (*0-910413-28-2*); pap. 40.00 (*1-878271-90-3*) Princeton Arch.

Agrest, Diana, et al. The Imagined & Real Landscapes of Piranesi: Critical Writings in America. (Columbia Books of Architecture: Catalogue 4). (Illus.). 48p. (Orig.). (C). 1992. pap. 9.95 (*0-9623829-8-1*) CUGSA.

Agrest, Diana I. Architecture from Without. 137p. 1991. 37.50 (*0-262-01115-8*) MIT Pr.

Agresta, David, jt. auth. see Latham, Caroline.

Agresta, Lisa W. The Labrador Retriever: An Owner's Guide to a Happy, Healthy Pet. (Owner's Guide to a Happy, Healthy Pet Ser.). (Illus.). 160p. 1995. 12.95 (*0-87605-378-9*) Howell Bks.

Agresta, Ralph. The Best of Bass Jam Trax. 31p. 1997. pap. text 9.95 (*0-8256-1640-9*, AM945307) Music Sales.

— Blues Jam Trax for Guitar. 24p. 1997. pap. 10.95 incl. cd-rom (*0-8256-1605-0*, AM943107) Omnibus NY.

— Blues JamTrax. (JamTrax Ser.). (Illus.). 1991. pap. 9.95 (*0-8256-2583-1*, AM75888) Music Sales.

— Chicago Blues Jam Trax for Guitar. 32p. 1997. pap. 10.95 incl. audio compact disk (*0-8256-1603-4*, AN943085) Omnibus NY.

— Chords & Progressions for Rock Guitar. (Illus.). 88p. 1997. pap. 16.95 (*0-8256-1614-X*, AM943206) Music Sales.

— Classic Rock. (JamTrax Ser.). (Illus.). 1991. pap. 9.95 (*0-8256-1325-6*, AM87440) Music Sales.

— Harmonica Jam Trax. 31p. 1997. pap. text 9.95 (*0-8256-1641-7*, AM945318) Music Sales.

— Jazz Jam Trax for Guitar. 24p. 1997. pap. 10.95 incl. audio compact disk (*0-8256-1606-9*) Omnibus NY.

— Jazz JamTrax. (JamTrax Ser.). (Illus.). 1991. pap. 9.95 (*0-8256-2591-2*, AM75896) Music Sales.

— Modern Blues Jam Trax. (JamTrax Ser.). (Illus.). 1992. pap. 9.95 (*0-8256-1322-1*, AM87416) Music Sales.

— Modern Blues Jam Trax for Guitar. 28p. pap. 10.95 incl. audio compact disk (*0-8256-1604-2*, AM943096) Omnibus NY.

— Modern Rock Jam Trax. (JamTrax Ser.). (Illus.). 1992. pap. 9.95 (*0-8256-1323-X*, AM87424) Music Sales.

— More Blues Jam Trax for Guitar. (Illus.). 1993. pap. 9.95 (*0-8256-1364-7*, AM91303) Music Sales.

— More Blues Jam Trax for Guitar. 28p. pap. 10.95 incl. audio compact disk (*0-8256-1602-6*) Omnibus NY.

— Rock JamTrax. (JamTrax Ser.). (Illus.). 1991. pap. 9.95 (*0-8256-1269-1*, AM75870) Music Sales.

— Rock JamTrax for Guitar. 24p. 1997. pap. 10.95 incl. cd-rom (*0-8256-1607-7*) Omnibus NY.

— Rock JamTrax for Keyboard. (Illus.). 1993. pap. 9.95 (*0-8256-1268-3*, AM76647) Music Sales.

— Saxaphone JamTrax. rev. ed. 28p. 1998. pap. text 9.95 (*0-8256-1647-6*, AM945626) Music Sales.

— Twelve-Bar Blues Jams Trax for Guitar. 1994. pap. 9.95 (*0-8256-1415-5*, AM91476) Music Sales.

Agresti, Alan. Analysis of Ordinal Categorical Data. LC 83-23535. (Probability & Mathematical Statistics: Applied Probability & Statistics Section Ser.: No 1-287). 304p. 1984. 128.00 (*0-471-89055-3*) Wiley.

— Categorical Data Analysis. LC 89-22645. (Probability & Mathematical Statistics: Applied Probability & Statistics Section Ser.). 576p. 1990. 89.95 (*0-471-85301-1*) Wiley.

— An Introduction to Categorical Data Analysis. LC 95-21928. (Wiley Series in Probility & Mathematical Statistics). (Illus.). 312p. 1996. 79.95 (*0-471-11338-7*, Wiley-Interscience) Wiley.

Agresti, Alan & Finlay, Barbara. Statistical Methods for the Social Sciences. 3rd ed. LC 96-38408. 643p. 1997. 86.00 (*0-13-526526-6*) P-H.

Agresto, John. The Supreme Court & Constitutional Democracy. LC 83-45928. 192p. 1984. pap. text 14.95 (*0-8014-9277-7*) Cornell U Pr.

Agresto, John & Riesenberg, Peter, eds. The Humanist as Citizen. LC 81-4021. 276p. reprint ed. pap. 85.60 (*0-8357-3899-X*, 203663100004) Bks Demand.

Agria, Mary, jt. auth. see Jung, Shannon.

Agricola, Georgius. De Re Metallica. (Illus.). 638p. 1950. pap. 21.95 (*0-486-60006-8*) Dover.

Agricola, Johannes. Die Sprichwoertersammlungen, 2 vols. Gilman, Sander L., ed. (Ausgaben Deutscher Literatur des XV bis XVIII Jahrhunderts Ser.). 989p. (C). 1971. 707.70 (*3-11-003710-6*) De Gruyter.

Agricola, Martin. Musica Instrumentalis Deutsch 1528 und 1545, Erste und Vierte. Eitner, Robert, ed. (Publikation alterer praktischer und theoretischer Musikwerke Ser.: Vol. 20). (GER., Illus.). 1966. reprint ed. lib. bdg. 55.00 (*0-8450-1720-9*) Broude.

— Rudimenta Musices. fac. ed. (Monuments of Music & Music Literature in Facsimile Ser., Series II: Vol. 34). 1966. lib. bdg. 30.00 (*0-8450-2234-2*) Broude.

Agricola, Rudolph. De Inventione Dialectica Libri Tres. (GER.). 1976. reprint ed. write for info. (*3-487-05902-9*) G Olms Pubs.

Agricola, S. & Von Schmettow, B. Planung & Verwirklichung Von Freizeitangeboten. Moeglichkeiten & Formen der Partizipation. Schmitz-Scherzer, R., ed. (Psychologische Praxis Ser.: Band 50). 1976. 21.75 (*3-8055-2361-0*) S Karger.

Agricola, Sandra. Master Bedroom Poems. (Ohio Review Bks.). 72p. 1985. 9.95 (*0-942148-05-3*); pap. 5.95 (*0-942148-04-5*) Ohio Review.

— White Mercedes. (Ohio Review Bks.). 72p. 1988. 11.95 (*0-942148-09-6*); pap. 7.95 (*0-942148-08-8*) Ohio Review.

Agricultural & Food Research Council, Technical Co. Agricultural & Food Research Council Technical Committee on Responses to Nutrients: Nutritive Requirements of Ruminant Animals. (CAB International Publication). (Illus.). 50p. 1992. pap. text 35.00 (*0-85198-846-6*) OUP.

Agricultural Production Team Staff. Report on India's Food Crisis & Steps to Meet It. LC 75-26294. (World Food Supply Ser.). 1976. reprint ed. 23.95 (*0-405-07767-X*) Ayer.

Agricultural Research Council Staff. The Nutrient Requirements of Ruminant Livestock. 351p. (Orig.). 1980. pap. text 72.00 (*0-85198-459-2*) C A B Intl.

— The Nutrient Requirements of Ruminant Livestock Supplement, No. 1. 45p. (Orig.). 1984. pap. text 30.00 (*0-85198-528-9*) OUP.

Agricultural Tribunal of Investigation Staff. Final Report: Presented to Parliament by Command of His Majesty. LC 75-26316. (World Food Supply Ser.). (Illus.). 1976. reprint ed. 35.95 (*0-405-07793-9*) Ayer.

Agriculture Canada Staff. Hymenoptera of the World: An Identification Guide to Families. (Illus.). 680p. 1993. pap. 76.95 (*0-660-14933-8*, Pub. by Canadian Govt Pub) Accents Pubns.

Agriculture Canada Staff, jt. auth. see Mulligan, Gerald.

Agriculture Natural Resource Staff. Workforce Management for Farms & Horticultural Businesses: Finding, Training & Keeping Good Employees, Vol. 117. NRAES Staff, ed. LC 98-51670. 140p. 1999. pap. text 15.00 (*0-935817-37-9*) NRAES.

AgriData Staff. AgriData's Week-by-Week Marketing Journal. 64p. 1986. pap. 10.95 (*0-910939-16-0*) AgriData.

— Charting. 32p. 1982. pap. 9.95 (*0-685-16470-5*) AgriData.

Agriesti, David, tr. see Hopkins, John F.

Agrios, George N. Plant Pathology. 4th ed. LC 96-29221. (Illus.). xvi, 635p. 1997. text 59.95 (*0-12-044564-6*) Morgan Kaufmann.

Agrippa, Henry Cornelius. De Occulta Philosophia, Libri Tres. Compagni, Vittoria P., ed. LC 91-31186. (Studies in the History of Christian Thought: No. 48). (Illus.). vi, 660p. 1992. 233.00 (*90-04-09421-0*) Brill Academic Pubs.

— Declamation on the Nobility & Preeminence of the Female Sex. 128p. (C). 1996. pap. text 14.00 (*0-226-01059-7*) U Ch Pr.

— Declamation on the Nobility & Preeminence of the Female Sex. Rabil, Albert, Jr., ed. & tr. by. 128p. 1996. lib. bdg. 33.00 (*0-226-01058-9*) U Ch Pr.

— Occult Philosophy Bk. 4: Of Geomancy, Magical Elements, Astrological Geomancy, the Nature of Spirits, Magic of the Ancients. 217p. 1992. reprint ed. pap. 19.95 (*1-56459-170-0*) Kessinger Pub.

— The Philosophy of Natural Magic. 305p. 1996. reprint ed. spiral bd. 23.00 (*0-7873-0019-5*) Hlth Research.

— The Philosophy of Natural Magic. 307p. 1992. reprint ed. pap. 21.95 (*1-56459-160-3*) Kessinger Pub.

— The Three Books of Occult Philosophy. Tyson, Donald, ed. Freake, James, tr. LC 92-33147. (Llewellyn's Sourcebook Ser.). 1024p. 1994. pap. 39.95 (*0-87542-832-0*) Llewellyn Pubns.

— Three Books of Occult Philosophy or Magic. LC 79-8222. (Illus.). reprint ed. 39.50 (*0-404-18401-4*) AMS Pr.

— Three Books of Occult Philosophy or Magic. 288p. 1992. reprint ed. pap. 24.95 (*1-56459-199-9*) Kessinger Pub.

Agrofoglio, L. A., jt. auth. see Challand, S. R.

Agronin, Marc E., jt. auth. see Goodwin, Aurelie J.

Agronomov, A., et al. Problems & Exercises in Organic Chemistry. Mir Publishers Staff, tr. 400p. (C). 1975. 26.50 (*0-8464-0756-6*) Beekman Pubs.

Agruso, Susan, et al, eds. Physics Olympics Handbook. 26p. 1984. 14.00 (*0-917853-00-8*, OP-51) Am Assn Physics.

AGS Staff. Geriatrics at Your Fingertips. 160p. 1998. per. 9.95 (*0-7872-5474-6*, 41547401) Kendall-Hunt.

— Geriatrics Review Syllabus. 4th ed. 1999. boxed set 395.00 (*0-7872-5541-6*, 41554101) Kendall-Hunt.

— Pak: Wave 1 Anthem Connecticut. 1997. 8.47 (*0-7872-4577-1*) Kendall-Hunt.

— Pak: Wave 1 HMSA Hawaii. 1997. 8.47 (*0-7872-4589-5*) Kendall-Hunt.

AGSI Staff, jt. auth. see Leaver, Betty L.

Agterberg, F. P. Mineral Energy Resource Evaluation: Probabilistic Methods. write for info. (*0-318-56737-7*) Elsevier.

Agterberg, F. P., ed. Automated Stratigraphic Correlation. (Developments in Palaeontology & Stratigraphy Ser.: No. 13). 438p. 1990. 172.50 (*0-444-88253-7*) Elsevier.

Agthe, Dale. Windo Watchman Vol. II: Millions Prayed, God Responded, Witness the Impact. Pegues, Beverly & Strong, Deborah, eds. (Illus.). 375p. (Orig.). 1997. write for info. (*0-9644880-3-5*); pap. 14.99 (*0-9644880-1-9*) Christian Info.

Agtmael, Antoine W. Van, see Park, Keith K. & Van Agtmael, Antoine W., eds.

Agtuca, Jacqueline R. A Community Secret: For the Filipina in an Abusive Relationship. LC 93-23666. (Illus.). 80p. 1993. reprint ed. pap. 5.95 (*1-878067-44-3*) Seal Pr WA.

Agu, Ogonna. Search for Philosophic Truth by an African Inmate. 1998. pap. 14.95 (*0-907015-95-6*) Africa World.

Aguade, J., et al, eds. Algebraic Topology - Homotopy & Group Cohomology: Proceedings of a Conference Held in Barcelona, Spain, June 6-12, 1990. (Lecture Notes in Mathematics Ser.: Vol. 1509). x, 330p. 1992. pap. 49.00 (*0-387-55195-6*) Spr-Verlag.

Aguade, J. & Kane, R., eds. Algebraic Topology, Barcelona 1986. (Lecture Notes in Mathematics Ser.: Vol. 1298). x, 255p. 1988. 44.95 (*0-387-18729-4*) Spr-Verlag.

Aguado. Media Meteorology. 168p. 1999. pap., wbk. ed. 31.40 (*0-13-210858-5*) P-H.

***Aguado.** Meteorology. (gr. 12). 1999. pap. text, teacher ed. write for info. (*0-13-236662-2*) P-H.

— Meteorology. (gr. 12). 1999. pap. text, teacher ed. write for info. (*0-13-236621-5*, Prentice Hall) P-H.

Aguado & Burt. Understanding Weather & Climate. 474p. 1998. text 70.00 incl. disk (*0-13-210346-X*) P-H.

Aguado, Bill. Writerscorp Anthology. 192p. (gr. 7 up). 6.95 (*0-06-029288-1*); mass mkt. 14.89 (*0-06-447264-7*) HarpC.

***Aguado, Edward & Burt, James.** Understanding Weather & Climate. 2nd ed. 480p. 2000. 70.00 (*0-13-027394-5*, Prentice Hall) P-H.

Aguayo, Carlos A. & Biaggi, Virgilio. Diccionario de Biologia Animal. LC 76-41882. (SPA.). 581p. 1982. 15.00 (*0-8477-2318-6*) U of PR Pr.

Aguayo, Eduardo. Geodinamica de Mexico. (Ciencia para Todos Ser.). (SPA.). pap. 6.99 (*968-16-4535-9*, Pub. by Fondo) Continental Bk.

Aguayo, Juan M., tr. see Wade, Mary D.

Aguayo, Rafael. Dr. Deming: The American Who Taught the Japanese about Quality. 1990. 19.95 (*0-8184-0519-8*) Carol Pub Group.

— Dr. Deming: The American Who Taught the Japanese about Quality. (Illus.). 304p. 1991. per. 13.00 (*0-671-74621-9*) S&S Trade Pap.

Aguayo, Sergio. Myths & [Mis] Perceptions: Changing U. S. Elite Visions of Mexico. LC 97-51682. (U. S.-Mexico Contemporary Perspectives Ser.). 1998. pap. write for info. (*1-878367-36-6*) UCSD Ctr US-Mex.

Agudas Chassidsi Chabad Staff, jt. auth. see Ben-Ur, Aviva.

Aguecheek. My Unknown Chum. 1912. 25.00 (*0-8159-6208-8*) Devin.

Aguedas, jt. auth. see Conde.

Aguero, Felipe. Soldiers, Civilians, & Democracy: Post-Franco Spain in Comparative Perspective. LC 95-3399. 336p. 1995. text 49.95 (*0-8018-5085-1*) Johns Hopkins.

Aguero, Felipe & Stark, Jeffrey, eds. Fault Lines of Democracy in Post-Transition Latin America. 407p. 1998. pap. 25.95 (*1-57454-046-7*) U Miami N-S Ctr.

Aguero, Kathleen. The Real Weather. 1987. 15.00 (*0-914610-46-5*) Hanging Loose.

— The Real Weather. 1987. pap. 7.00 (*0-914610-42-2*) Hanging Loose.

Aguero, Kathleen, ed. Daily Fare: Essays from the Multicultural Experience. LC 92-15559. 248p. 1993. pap. 16.00 (*0-8203-1499-4*) U of Ga Pr.

Aguero, Kathleen & Goodman, Miriam. Thirsty Day & Permanent Wave. LC 76-55615. 88p. 1977. pap. 3.95 (*0-914086-17-0*) Alice James Bks.

Aguero, M., ed. Contribuciones Para el Estudio de la Pesca Artesanal en America Latina. (ICLARM Conference Proceedings Ser.: No. 35). (ENG & SPA.). 113p. 1992. per. write for info. (*0-614-23056-X*, Pub. by ICLARM) Intl Spec Bk.

Aguero, Max & Gonzalez, Exequiel. Managing Transboundary Stocks of Small Pelagic Fish: Problems & Options. LC 96-21473. (World Bank Discussion Papers: No. 329). 56p. 1996. pap. 22.00 (*0-8213-3659-2*) World Bank.

Agueros, Jack. Correspondence Between the Stonehaulers. 1991. 15.00 (*0-914610-94-5*); pap. 9.00 (*0-914610-93-7*) Hanging Loose.

— Dominoes & Other Stories from the Puerto Rican. LC 93-4849. 149p. 1993. 14.95 (*1-880684-11-X*) Curbstone.

— Sonnets from the Puerto Rican. 1996. 20.00 (*1-882413-23-7*); pap. 12.00 (*1-882413-22-9*) Hanging Loose.

Agueros, Jack, tr. see De Burgos, Julia.

Aguiar, Myriam Y. Sueno (Rimas al Recuerdo) LC 84-80617. (SPA.). 64p. (Orig.). 1984. pap. 6.00 (*0-89729-348-7*) Ediciones.

Aguiar, Neuma, ed. The Structure of Brazilian Development. LC 78-55936. 258p. 1979. 39.95 (*0-87855-138-7*) Transaction Pubs.

Aguiar, O. D., et al, eds. Omnidirectional Gravitational Radiation Observatory. 300p. 1997. text 54.00 (*981-02-3209-8*) World Scientific Pub.

Aguiar, Ricardo J. Veinte Cuentos Breves de la Revolucion Cubana. LC 87-80642. (Coleccion Caniqui). (SPA., Illus.). 84p. (Orig.). 1987. pap. 9.95 (*0-89729-440-8*) Ediciones.

***Aguiar, Sarah Appleton.** The Bitch Is Back: Wicked Women in Literature. LC 00-39506. 2001. pap. write for info. (*0-8093-2362-1*) S Ill U Pr.

Aguila, F. Del, see Del Aguila, F.

Aguilar. Martin Adan, el Hermoso Crepusculo. (SPA.). pap. 16.99 (*968-16-3791-7*, Pub. by Fondo) Continental Bk.

Aguilar, et al. The Community College: A New Beginning. 2nd ed. 340p. (C). 1997. per. 48.95 (*0-7872-4274-8*, 41427401) Kendall-Hunt.

Aguilar, Angelita, tr. see Morton, Arthur.

Aguilar, Angelita L., tr. Hay Mas Que Animales en Una Granja. (SPA.). (J). (gr. k-3). 1995. write for info. (*1-57842-003-2*) Delmas Creat.

Aguilar, Angelita L., tr. see Morton, Arthur.

Aguilar, Angelita L., tr. see Morton, Carl.

Aguilar, Angelita L., tr. see Morton, Delma.

Aguilar-Barajas, Ismael. An Evaluation of Industrial Estates in Mexico, 1970-1986. (Progress in Planning Ser.: No. 34). 96p. 1991. pap. 42.00 (*0-08-040772-2*, Pergamon Pr) Elsevier.

Aguilar-Benitez, M. Fundamental Physics: Selected Topics on High Energy & Astroparticle Physics. (High Energy Physics Ser.). 1998. 88.00 (*981-02-3587-9*) World Scientific Pub.

Aguilar-Benitez, M. & Cerrada, M. Physics at LEP: Seventeenth International Meeting on Fundamental Physics. 460p. (C). 1990. text 113.00 (*981-02-0227-X*) World Scientific Pub.

A

A

Aguilar-Carino, Maria L. Cordillera Tales. (Illus.). vii, 122p. 1990. pap. 12.50 (*971-10-0379-1*, Pub. by New Day Pub) Cellar.
Aguilar, Connie, ed. see Aguilar, Ricardo.
Aguilar, Dave & Robertson, Ken. Inside 3D Studio Max, Vol. II. 1997. pap. 54.99 (*0-614-28478-3*, New Riders Sftwre) MCP SW Interactive.
Aguilar, Eduardo. Re-Evaluation Counseling: A "Culturally Competent" Model for Social Liberation. 1995. pap. 2.00 (*1-885357-14-1*) Rational Isl.
Aguilar, Eduardo G. Boulevard of Heroes. Miller, Yvette E., ed. Miskowiec, Jay A., tr. LC 93-1491. (Discoveries Ser.). (SPA.). 192p. 1993. pap. 16.95 (*0-935480-62-5*) Lat Am Lit Rev Pr.
Aguilar, Enrique. El Crepusculo (The Twilight) 103p. 1971. pap. 3.50 (*1-57659-114-X*) Franciscan Inst.
— Pensamientos Sobre la Cultura Intelectural Y Moral (Thoughts on Intellectual & Moral Culture. 230p. 1967. pap. 7.00 (*1-57659-109-3*) Franciscan Inst.
— Sinfonias de Otono (Symphonies of Autumn) xii, 135p. 1962. pap. 3.50 (*1-57659-113-1*) Franciscan Inst.
Aguilar, Filomeno V., Jr. Clash of Spirits: The History of Power & Sugar Planter Hegemony on a Visayan Island. LC 98-16629. (Illus.). 336p. 1998. text 49.00 (*0-8248-1992-6*); pap. text 28.95 (*0-8248-2082-7*) UH Pr.
Aguilar, Francis J. General Managers in Action: Policies & Strategies. 2nd ed. 280p. (C). 1992. pap. text (*0-19-507730-X*) OUP.
— General Managers in Action: Policies & Strategies. 2nd ed. (Illus.). 736p. (C). 1992. text 69.95 (*0-19-507367-3*) OUP.
— Managing Corporate Ethics: Learning from America's Ethical Companies How to Supercharge Business. LC 93-5803. (Illus.). 192p. 1994. 30.00 (*0-19-508534-5*) OUP.
Aguilar, Francisco. History of the Foundation of the Town of Chamiquin. Feldman, Lawrence, ed. & tr. by. LC 87-81582. Orig. Title: Historia de la Fundacion de Chamiquin en la Provincia de Vera-paz. 152p. 1988. pap. 20.00 (*0-911437-30-4*) Labyrinthos.
Aguilar, Gaby O., ed. Mujeres del Mundo: Leyes y Politicas Que Afectan Sus Vidas Reproductivas: Latin America. unabridged ed. (Women of the World Ser.: Vol. 2). (SPA.). 225p. Date not set. pap. 25.00 (*1-890671-02-9*) Center Reprod.
— Women of the World Vol. 2: Laws & Policies Affecting Their Reproductive Lives - Latin America & the Caribbean. unabridged ed. 203p. 1997. pap. text 25.00 (*1-890671-03-7*) Center Reprod.
Aguilar-Henson, Marcela. Figura Cristalina. Cantu, Norma E., ed. (Illus.). 31p. (Orig.). 1983. pap. 5.00 (*0-913983-01-2*) M & A Edns.
Aguilar, Jorge. El Costo de las Ideas: Castro, Dictadura en Bancarrota. (SPA.). 220p. 1998. pap. 14.95 (*1-888683-17-1*) Wooster Bk.
Aguilar, Juan F. & Gonzalez, Armando E., eds. Basic Latin American Legal Materials, 1970-1975. (AALL Publications Ser.: No. 13). vi, 106p. 1977. pap. 17.50 (*0-8377-0111-2*, Rothman) W S Hein.
Aguilar, Julia. Poesia Popular Contempranea: Poesia General. (SPA.). 52p. 1992. pap. 4.99 (*1-882263-00-6*) J A Pubns.
Aguilar Leon, Luis. Cuba, Conciencia y Revolucion. (SPA.). 1972. pap. 15.00 (*0-89729-048-8*) Ediciones.
— Todo Tiene su Tiempo. (SPA.). 211p. 1997. pap. 18.00 (*0-89729-832-2*) Ediciones.
Aguilar, Leslie & Stokes, Linda. Multicultural Customer Service. (Business Skills Express Ser.). 160p. 1995. pap. 10.95 (*0-7863-0332-8*, Irwn Prfssnl) McGraw-Hill Prof.
Aguilar, Linda, et al. Orientation to the Community College. 356p. (C). 1996. pap. text, per. 37.95 (*0-7872-2475-8*) Kendall-Hunt.
Aguilar, Luis A. A Traves de una Rendija. SLUSA, Inc. Staff, ed. (SPA.). 80p. (Orig.). 1986. 6.00 (*0-917129-04-0*) SLUSA.
Aguilar, Luis E. De Como Se Me Murieron las Palabas y Otros Cuentos, Cantos y Cuestiones. (SPA., Illus.). 205p. 1984. 9.95 (*84-359-0385-0*) Ediciones.
Aguilar, Manuela. Cultural Diplomacy & Foreign Policy: German-American Relations, 1955-1968. (Studies in Modern European History: Vol. 19). X, 305p. (C). 1996. text 54.95 (*0-8204-2801-9*) P Lang Pubng.
Aguilar, Mario I. Being Oromo in Kenya. LC 97-51887. 325p. 1997. pap. text 19.95 (*0-86543-569-3*) Africa World.
— Being Oromo in Kenya. LC 97-51887. 325p. 1998. 69.95 (*0-86543-568-5*) Africa World.
— Recent Advances & Issues in Anthropology. (Frontiers of Science Ser.). (Illus.). 256p. 2000. text 44.95 (*1-57356-258-0*) Oryx Pr.
Aguilar, Mario I., ed. The Politics of Age & Gerontocracy in Africa. LC 98-27563. 250p. 1997. 79.95 (*0-86543-597-9*); pap. 21.95 (*0-86543-598-7*) Africa World.
Aguilar, Mila D. A Comrade Is As Precious As a Rice Seedling. 68p. (Orig.). 1987. reprint ed. pap. 6.95 (*0-913175-08-0*) Kitchen Table.
Aguilar, Mila D. Journey: An Autobiography in Verse, 1964-1995 LC 96-946498. (Likhaan / Sentro Ng Makathaing Pagsulat). xv, 220 p. 1996. write for info. (*971-542-116-4*) UH Pr.
Aguilar, Miriam E., jt. auth. see Lopez, Raymond.
Aguilar, Nelson. Giovanni Anselmo. Sands, Lucilla, ed. (Illus.). 48p. 1995. pap. 12.50 (*88-7757-054-7*) Dist Art Pubs.
Aguilar, Nona. The New No-Pill, No-Risk Birth Control: The Latest Findings on Natural Family Planning, the Method for Postponing Pregnancy Without Using Drugs, Chemicals, IUDs or Barrier Devices. LC 85-42927. (Illus.). 240p. 1985. pap. 12.95 (*0-89256-300-1*, Rawson Assocs) Macmillan.
Aguilar Peris, Jose, et al. Dictionary of Solar Energy: Diccionario de Energia Solar. (SPA.). 226p. 1982. pap. 39.95 (*0-8288-2294-8*, S21887) Fr & Eur.
***Aguilar, Rebeca.** Cristina's Secret, Vol. 1. 1999. mass mkt. 5.99 (*0-7860-1035-5*) Pinal County Schl Office.
Aguilar, Renato. Efficiency in Production: Theory & an Application on Kenyan Smallholders. (Gothenburg Economic Studies: No. 25). 182p. (Orig.). 1988. pap. 57.50 (*91-7900-561-6*) Coronet Bks.
***Aguilar, Ricardo.** Cuba Through the Eyes of an Exiled Generation. Aguilar, Connie & Aguilar, Roberto, eds. LC 99-90301.Tr. of Cuba a Traves de los Ojos de una Generacion de Exiliados. (ENG & SPA., Illus.). 68p. 1999. pap. 19.00 (*0-9672086-0-2*, BCV1) Envision Prodns.
Aguilar, Ricardo. Efrain Huerta. 118p. pap. 9.00 (*0-685-54696-9*, AGUEFR) Dos Pasos Ed.
Aguilar, Ricardo, et al, eds. Palabra Nueva: Poesia Chicana. (SPA.). (Orig.). pap. text 9.00 (*0-9615403-0-3*) Dos Pasos Ed.
Aguilar, Richard, et al. Sewage Sludge Application in Semiarid Grasslands: Effects on Vegetation & Water Quality. (Illus.). 108p. (Orig.). (C). 1995. pap. text 35.00 (*0-7881-1568-5*) DIANE Pub.
***Aguilar Rivera, Jose Antonio.** The Shadow of Ulysses: Public Intellectual Exchange across the U. S. Mexican Border. LC 00-41954. (Illus.). 2000. write for info. (*0-7391-0173-0*) Lxngtn Bks.
Aguilar, Roberto, ed. see Aguilar, Ricardo.
Aguilar, Rosario. The Lost Chronicles of Terra Firma. Hood, Edward W., tr. LC 97-189499. 186p. (Orig.). 1998. pap. 13.00 (*1-877727-62-8*) White Pine.
Aguilar-San Juan, Karin, ed. The State of Asian America: Activism & Resistance in the 1990s. (Race & Resistance Ser.). (Illus.). 395p. 1994. 40.00 (*0-89608-477-9*); pap. 22.00 (*0-89608-476-0*) South End Pr.
Aguilar, U. Juan, ed. see Bueno, Raul & Schmidt, Friedhlem.
Aguilera. Clin Dep Life Span. 2000. text. write for info. (*0-323-00944-1*) Harcourt.
***Aguilera, Carmen & Nicholson, H. B.** Coyolxauhqui-Chantico: Two Analyses of the Great Monument of Tenochtitlan. 140p. 2000. pap. 30.00 (*0-911437-73-8*) Labyrinthos.
Aguilera, Donna C. Crisis Intervention: Theory & Methodology. 8th ed. LC 97-20533. (Illus.). 360p. (C). (gr. 13). 1997. pap. text 33.00 (*0-8151-2604-2*, 31074) Mosby Inc.
Aguilera, Francisco & Shelby, Charmion, eds. Handbook of Latin American Studies, Vol. 12: 1946. LC 36-32633. 364p. 1946. 47.95 (*0-8130-0004-1*) U Press Fla.
— Handbook of Latin American Studies, Vol. 13: 1947. LC 36-32633. 239p. 1947. 49.95 (*0-8130-0005-X*) U Press Fla.
— Handbook of Latin American Studies, Vol. 14: 1948. LC 36-32633. 1948. 49.95 (*0-8130-0003-3*) U Press Fla.
Aguilera-Hellweg, Max. The Sacred Heart: An Atlas of the Body Seen Through Invasive Surgery. LC 97-5910. (Illus.). 128p. (gr. 8). 1997. 50.00 (*0-8212-2377-1*) Little.
***Aguilera, J. M. & Stanley, D. W.** Microstructural Principles of Food Processing & Engineering. 2nd ed. LC 99-31202. 350p. 1999. 125.00 (*0-8342-1256-0*, 12560) Aspen Pub.
Aguilera, Luis Gabriel. Gabriel's Fire: A Memoir. LC 99-16610. (Illus.). 304p. 2000. 22.00 (*0-226-01067-8*) U Ch Pr.
Aguilera-Malta, Demetrio. Babelandia. Earle, Peter, tr. from SPA. LC 84-9035. (Contemporary Literature Ser.). (Illus.). 375p. 1985. 29.95 (*0-89603-065-2*) Humana.
— Don Goyo. Brushwood, John S. & Brushwood, Carolyn, trs. from SPA. LC 80-81656. (Contemporary Literature Ser.). (Illus.). 200p. 1980. 24.95 (*0-89603-019-9*) Humana.
— Seven Serpents & Seven Moons. Rabassa, Gregory, tr. from SPA. LC 79-10516. (Texas Pan-American Ser.). (SPA.). 315p. reprint ed. pap. 97.70 (*0-8357-7735-9*, 203609200002) Bks Demand.
Aguilera, Robert. Naturally Fractured Reservoirs. 2nd ed. LC 95-18164. 720p. 1995. 145.95 (*0-87814-122-7*) PennWell Bks.
Aguilera, Roberto. Horizontal Drilling, Completion, & Production. (Contributions in Petroleum Geology & Engineering Ser.: Vol. 9). 352p. 1991. 85.00 (*0-87201-573-4*, 1573) Gulf Pub.
Aguinaldo, Emilio & Pacis, Vicente A. Second Look at America. 1957. 15.00 (*0-8315-0051-4*) Speller.
Aguino, Benigno S., Jr. Testament from a Prison Cell. Fernandez, Consuelo et al, eds. (Illus.). 190p. (Orig.). (C). 1989. 18.75 (*0-9621695-0-1*); pap. 7.95 (*0-9621695-1-X*) Philippine Jrnl.
Aguire, Kaye. Four in One Group Games: A Competency Based Guidance Curriculum for Grades 2-5. LC 98-65044. (Illus.). 128p. 1998. pap. 34.95 (*1-57543-060-6*) Mar Co Prods.
Aguirre. American Ethnicity. 3rd ed. 2000. pap. 29.74 (*0-07-231991-7*) McGraw.
— Closed Space. 2000. text 59.95 (*0-7190-2486-2*, Pub. by Manchester Univ Pr) St Martin.
Aguirre. Collective Behavior & Social Movement. 1996. 46.00 (*0-205-15978-8*) Allyn.
Aguirre, Adalberto, Jr. & Baker, David V. Notable Selections in Race & Ethnicity. 2nd ed. (Sources Ser.). (Illus.). 416p. 1998. pap. text 14.00 (*0-697-34332-4*, Dshkn McG-Hill) McGrw-H Hghr Educ.
Aguirre, Adalberto, Jr. & Baker, David V., eds. Sources: Notable Selections in Race & Ethnicity. LC 95-122. 416p. (C). 1995. text 14.95 (*1-56134-319-6*, Dshkn McG-Hill) McGrw-H Hghr Educ.
Aguirre, Adalberto, Jr. & Martinez, Ruben O. Chicanos in Higher Education: Issues & Dilemmas for the 21st Century. Fife, Jonathan D., ed. & frwd. by. (ASHE-ERIC Higher Education Reports: No. 93-3). 101p. (Orig.). 1993. pap. 24.00 (*1-878380-24-9*) GWU Grad Schl E&HD.
Aguirre, Adalberto, Jr. & Turner, Jonathan H. American Authenticity: The Dynamics & Consequences of Discrimination. LC 94-22093. (C). 1994. pap. text 35.00 (*0-07-000625-3*) McGraw.
Aguirre, Adalberto & Turner, Jonathan H. American Ethnicity: The Dynamics & Consequences of Discrimination. 2nd ed. LC 97-10257. 336p. (C). 1997. pap. 38.13 (*0-07-000627-X*) McGraw.
Aguirre, Alma, ed. see Molina, David.
Aguirre, Alonso A., jt. ed. see Chowdhury, N.
Aguirre, Angel. Diccionario Tematico de Antropologia. (SPA.). 694p. 1989. pap. 59.95 (*0-7859-6253-0*, S60822) Fr & Eur.
Aguirre, Blaise. The Fridges of Madison County. 82p. (Orig.). 1997. pap. 13.95 (*1-57502-414-4*, D01281) Morris Pubng.
Aguirre-Bravo, Celedonio & Villa-Salas, Avelino B., eds. Partnerships for Sustainable Forest Ecosystem Management: Fifth Mexico/U. S. Biennial Symposium. (Illus.). 419p. (Orig.). (C). 1996. pap. text 45.00 (*0-7881-2978-3*) DIANE Pub.
Aguirre, Carlos, jt. ed. see Salvatore, Ricardo D.
***Aguirre, Carlos A., et al, eds.** Reconstructing Criminality in Latin America. LC 99-41036. (Jaguar Books on Latin America: No. 19). 304p. 2000. 55.00 (*0-8420-2620-7*, SR Bks) Scholarly Res Inc.
— Reconstructing Criminality in Latin America. LC 99-41036. (Jaguar Books on Latin America: Vol. 19). 304p. 2000. pap. 18.95 (*0-8420-2621-5*, SR Bks) Scholarly Res Inc.
Aguirre, Carlos A., et al. Taxation in Sub-Saharan Africa: Pt. I: Tax Policy & Administration in Sub-Saharan Africa & Pt. II: A Statistical Evaluation of Taxation in Sub-Saharan Africa. (Occasional Paper Ser.: No. 8). 73p. 1981. pap. 5.00 (*1-55775-081-5*) Intl Monetary.
***Aguirre, David.** Waterman's Eye: The Life & Love of Emil Sigler. (Illus.). 230p. 2000. 39.95 (*0-9670339-6-9*) Rock Reef.
Aguirre, Edward. The United States in Prophecy: Prophetic Visions Warn America. LC 97-117145. (Illus.). 166p. (Orig.). 1996. mass mkt. 9.95 (*0-9650765-4-7*) Shiloh Pubng.
***Aguirre, Ernesto & Norton, Joseph J.** Reform of Latin American Banking Systems. 360p. 2000. 132.00 (*90-411-9736-2*) Kluwer Law Intl.
Aguirre, Felix. A Parent's Guide to Street Gangs. (Illus.). 145p. (Orig.). (C). 1993. pap. 15.00 (*0-927065-09-6*) Marin Chula Vista.
Aguirre, Fidel. Magnetismo de Jose Marti. LC 84-82243. (Coleccion Cuba y sus Jueces). (SPA., Illus.). 207p. (Orig.). 1985. pap. 9.95 (*0-89729-361-4*) Ediciones.
Aguirre-Happordt, Ingrid, jt. auth. see Blackburn, Jennifer.
Aguirre Hectrano, Fidel. Historia de los Hospitales Coloniales de Hispanoamerica Vol. XI: Peru. Camps, Janett, ed. (SPA., Illus.). Date not set. text 50.00 (*0-9641506-5-4*) Edit Interamerica.
Aguirre Jaime, A. Vigilancia Epidemiologica y Ordenadores. (SPA.). 231p. 1996. pap. 26.00 (*84-7978-266-8*, Pub. by Ediciones Diaz) IBD Ltd.
Aguirre, Jose A. De, see De Aguirre, Jose A.
Aguirre-Larson, Gina. Mi Nombre es Lupita y Tengo un Hijo Sordo: Folletos Informativos para Padres Precupados por la Audicion de Sus Hijos, 6 bks., Set. (SPA., Illus.). (Orig.). 1996. pap. 45.00 (*1-884362-16-8*) Butte Pubns.
Aguirre, Louis G., ed. see Boudreaux, Warren L.
Aguirre-Molina, Marilyn, jt. ed. see Molina, Carlos W.
Aguirre, Nataniel. Juan de la Rosa. Soldan, Alba M., ed. Waisman, Sergio G., tr. LC 97-27705. (Library of Latin America). (Illus.). 368p. 1998. 30.00 (*0-19-511327-6*) OUP.
— Juan de la Rosa. (Illus.). 368p. 1999. pap. 15.95 (*0-19-511328-4*) OUP.
Aguirre Rencurrell, Rafael A. Amanecer: Historias del Clandestinaje: (La Lucha de la Resistencia Contra Castro Dentro de Cuba) LC 96-84061. (Coleccion Cuba y sus Jueces). (SPA.). 119p. (Orig.). 1996. pap. 13.00 (*0-89729-803-9*) Ediciones.
Aguirre, Sylvia, tr. see CFKR Career Materials Staff.
Aguirre, Tania. Genetic & Functional Studies of the CU ZN Superoxide Dismutase Gene in Belgian Patients with Familial or Sporadic Amyotrophic Lateral Sclerosis. (Acta Biomedica Lovaniensia Ser.). (Illus.). 95p. 1998. pap. 39.50 (*90-6186-885-8*, Pub. by Leuven Univ) Coronet Bks.
Aguis, Dionisius A. & Hitchcock, Richard, eds. The Arab Influence in Medieval Europe: Folia Scholastica Mediterranea. 192p. 1997. pap. 19.95 (*0-86372-213-X*, Pub. by Garnet-Ithaca) LPC InBook.
Agulhon, Maurice. The French Republic, 1879-1992. Nevill, Antonia, tr. (History of France Ser.). (Illus.). (Orig.). 1995. pap. 25.95 (*0-631-19973-X*) Blackwell Pubs.
Agullo-Lopez, F. Electro-Optics: Phenomena, Materials & Applications. (Illus.). 345p. 1994. text 110.00 (*0-12-044512-3*) Acad Pr.
— Insulating Materials for Optoelectronics: New Developments. 400p. 1995. text 99.00 (*981-02-2230-0*) World Scientific Pub.
Agullo-Lopez, F. & Catlow, C. R. Point Defects in Materials. 445p. 1988. text 128.00 (*0-12-044510-7*) Acad Pr.
Agunga, Robert A. Developing the Third World: A Communication Approach. (Illus.). 365p. (C). 1997. lib. bdg. 85.00 (*1-56072-364-5*) Nova Sci Pubs.
Aguon, Katherine B. Chamorro, a Complete Course of Study. (Illus.). 300p. 1995. pap. text 35.00 (*0-9648411-0-X*) K B Aquon.
— Chamorro Grammar Guide. 250p. 1996. pap. text 35.00 (*0-9648411-1-8*) K B Aquon.
Agur, Anne, jt. auth. see Moore, Keith L.
Agur, Anne M., jt. auth. see Moore, Keith L.
***Agur, Anne M. R. & Lee, Ming J.** Grant's Atlas of Anatomy. 10th ed. LC 99-25481. 704p. 1999. pap. text 56.00 (*0-683-30264-7*) Lppncott W & W.
Agur, Anne M.R. & Lee, Ming J. Grant's Atlas of Anatomy. 10th ed. 784p. text 95.00 (*0-7817-2260-8*) Lppncott W & W.
Agur, Elie. Bobby Fischer: His Approach to Chess. 276p. 1993. text 24.95 (*1-85744-001-3*, Maxwell Macmillan) Macmillan.
Agus, Aharon R. Hermeneutic Biography in Rabbibic Midrash: The Gody of This Death & Life. LC 96-24493. (Studia Judaica: Vol. 16). ix, 262p. (C). 1996. lib. bdg. 124.45 (*3-11-015067-0*, 113/96) De Gruyter.
Agus, Carole. Killing Us Softly. 1998. write for info. (*0-609-60026-5*) Harmony Bks.
Agus, Jacob B. The Evolution of Jewish Thought. LC 73-2185. (Jewish People; History, Religion, Literature Ser.). 1978. reprint ed. 33.95 (*0-405-05251-0*) Ayer.
— High Priest of Rebirth: The Life, Times & Thought of Abraham Isaac Kuk. LC 79-189017. 242p. 1999. pap. 15.95 (*0-8197-0281-1*) Bloch.
— The Jewish Quest: Essays on Basic Concepts of Jewish Theology. LC 83-258. 264p. 1983. 25.00 (*0-88125-012-0*) Ktav.
Agus, Ronald E. The Binding of Isaac & Messiah: Law, Martyrdom, & Deliverance in Early Rabbinic Religiosity. LC 87-24496. (SUNY Series in Judaica: Hermeneutics, Mysticism, & Religion). 368p. (C). 1988. text 24.50 (*0-88706-735-2*) State U NY Pr.
Agus, Z., jt. ed. see Morad, M.
Agus, Z. S. & Kelepouris, E., eds. Cytosolic Calcium Measurements, Regulation & Biologic Significance in Epithelial Tissue. (Journal: Mineral & Electrolyte Metabolism Ser.: Vol. 14, No. 1, 1988). (Illus.). 96p. 1988. pap. 69.75 (*3-8055-4658-0*) S Karger.
Agusiobo, Obiora N., jt. auth. see Olaitan, Samson O.
Agusti, Anna. Tapies: The Complete Works, 1943-1960, Vol. 1. (Illus.). 546p. 1998. boxed set 99.95 (*3-89508-529-4*, 880030) Konemann.
— Tapies: The Complete Works, 1961-1968, Vol. 2. (Illus.). 546p. 1998. boxed set 99.95 (*3-89508-530-8*, 880031) Konemann.
— Tapies: The Complete Works, 1969-1975, Vol. 3. (Illus.). 546p. 1998. boxed set 99.95 (*3-89508-531-6*, 880032) Konemann.
— Tapies: The Complete Works, 1976-1981, Vol. 4. (Illus.). 546p. 1998. boxed set 99.95 (*3-89508-532-4*, 880033) Konemann.
Agusti, Anna, et al. Tapies: The Complete Works, 1969-1975, Vol. 3. LC 88-42714. (Illus.). 550p. 1992. 275.00 (*0-8478-1442-4*, Pub. by Rizzoli Intl) St Martin.
— Tapies Vol. 4: The Complete Works, 1976-1981. LC 88-42714. (Illus.). 500p. 1997. 275.00 (*0-8478-1829-2*, Pub. by Rizzoli Intl) St Martin.
Agusti, Jorge, et al, eds. Mammalian Evolution & Environmental Change in the Neogene of Europe Vol. 1: Hominoid Evolution & Climatic Change in Europe. LC 98-49430. (Illus.). 392p. 1999. 100.00 (*0-521-64097-0*) Cambridge U Pr.
Agustin, Jose. Ciudades Desiertas (Deserted Cities) 184p. 1995. pap. 12.50 (*0-679-76336-8*) Vin Bks.
Agustine, Sharon M., jt. ed. see Nolan, Marie T.
Agut, Shawn, jt. auth. see Pitucco, Anthony P.
Agutter. Understanding Biological Chemistry. (Biology Ser.). Date not set. text 32.50 (*0-412-49030-7*) Chapman & Hall.
Agutter, Paul S., jt. auth. see Taylor, Philip L.
Agwani, M. S., ed. The Gulf in Transition. 186p. 1987. 24.95 (*0-318-37271-1*) Asia Bk Corp.
Agyei, Alfred, tr. see Bystritskii, V. M. & Didenko, A. N., eds.
Agyei, William K. Fertility & Family Planning in the Third World: A Case Study of Papua New Guinea. 192p. 1985. lib. bdg. 49.50 (*0-685-19164-8*, Pub. by C Helm) Routldge.
Agyeman-Badu, Yaw, jt. auth. see Osei-Hwedie, Kwaku.
Agyeman-Duah, Baffour. The United States & Ethiopia: Military Assistance & the Quest for Security, 1953-1993. LC 94-8023. 274p. (C). 1994. lib. bdg. 48.50 (*0-8191-9523-5*) U Pr of Amer.
Agyeman, Janel W., ed. see Johnson, Alice W.
Agyeman, Janell W., ed. see Woods, Valerie L.
Agyeman, Opoku. Nkrumah's Ghana & East Africa: Pan-Africanism & African Interstate Relations. LC 91-55093. 240p. 1992. 38.50 (*0-8386-3456-7*) Fairleigh Dickinson.
— Pan-Africanism & Its Detractors: A Response to Harvard's Race-Effacing Universalists. LC 97-39566. 140p. 1997. text 69.95 (*0-7734-8432-9*) E Mellen.
***Agyemang, Attah-Poku.** African Stability & Integration: Regional, Continental & Diasporic Pan-African Realities. 192p. 2000. 37.50 (*0-7618-1596-1*) U Pr of Amer.
AH & MA Security Committee, jt. auth. see Ellis, Raymond C., Jr.
Ah Cheng. Unfilled Graves. 170p. 1995. pap. 7.95 (*0-8351-3145-9*) China Bks.
Ah Cheng, et al. The Time Is Not Yet Ripe. Bian, Ying, ed. Yang, Gladys et al, trs. from CHI. 382p. (Orig.). 1991. pap. 9.95 (*0-8351-2565-3*) China Bks.
Ah Nee-Benham, Maenette K. Case Studies for School Administrators: Managing Change in Education. LC 98-86274. 328p. 1998. text 39.95 (*1-56676-689-3*) Scarecrow.

An Asterisk (*) at the beginning of an entry indicates that the title is appearing for the first time.

***AHA, American Society for Healthcare Materials Man & NSC Staff.** Heartsaver Facts. (Illus.). 104p. (C). 1998. pap. text, teacher ed. 30.00 (*0-7637-0994-8*) JB Pubns.
Aha, David & Daniels, Jody J., eds. Case-Based Reasoning Integrations: Papers fom the AAAI Workshop. (Technical Reports: Vol. WS-98-15). (Illus.). 177p. 1998. spiral bd. 25.00 (*1-57735-068-5*) AAAI Pr.
Aha, David W., ed. Case-Based Reasoning: Papers from the 1994 AAAI Workshop. (AAAI Technical Reports). (Illus.). 188p. 1995. spiral bd. 25.00 (*0-929280-71-7*) AAAI Pr.
***Aha, David W., et al, eds.** Exploring Synergies of Knowledge Management & Case-Based Reasoning: Papers from the AAAI Workshop. (Technical Reports: Vol. WS-99-10). (Illus.). 99p. 1999. spiral bd. 25.00 (*1-57735-094-4*) AAAI Pr.
Aha, David W. & Ram, Ashwin, eds. Adaptation of Knowledge for Reuse: Papers from the 1995 Fall Symposium. (Technical Reports). (Illus.). 109p. 1995. spiral bd. 25.00 (*0-929280-94-6*) AAAI Pr.
Aha Punana Leo Curriculum Development Committee. He Hawai'i Au. (HAW., Illus.). 20p. (J). (gr. k). 1989. pap. 5.95 incl. audio (*1-890270-12-1*) Aha Punana Leo.
— He Mala'ai Ka'u. (HAW., Illus.). 28p. (J). (gr. k). 1989. pap. 5.95 incl. audio (*1-890270-15-6*) Aha Punana Leo.
— 'O Maile, Ka Pua'a. (HAW., Illus.). 28p. (J). (gr. k-1). 1989. pap. 5.95 incl. audio (*1-890270-06-7*) Aha Punana Leo.
Aha Punana Leo Curriculum Development Committee. Pai Ka Leo. (HAW., Illus.). 34p. (J). (ps-6). 1989. pap. 14.95 incl. audio (*1-880188-62-7*, Pub. by Bess Pr) Aha Punana Leo.
Aha Punana Leo Staff, tr. 'O Wau Kekahi I Ke Alualu Holoholona. (HAW., Illus.). 12p. (J). (gr. k). 1992. pap. 5.95 incl. audio (*1-890270-08-3*) Aha Punana Leo.
Ahad Ha-am, pseud. Ten Essays on Zionism & Judaism. LC 73-2202. (Jewish People; History, Religion, Literature Ser.). 1979. reprint ed. 29.95 (*0-405-05267-7*) Ayer.
Ahahui Olelo Hawaii Staff, tr. see Kajiyama, Kats.
Ahalt, J. Dawson, jt. auth. see Kosters, Marvin H.
Ahamd, Kh. J. Hundred Great Muslims. 572p. 1988. pap. 19.95 (*0-933511-16-7*) Kazi Pubns.
Ahamd, Syed B. Introduction to Qur'anic Script. (Illus.). 220p. 1998. pap. 29.95 (*0-7007-1069-8*, Pub. by Curzon Pr Ltd) Paul & Co Pubs.
Ahamed, Liaquat, jt. ed. see Edwards, Sebastian.
Ahamed, Syed V. & Lawrence, Victor B. Design & Engineering of Intelligent Communication Networks. LC 96-53503. 720p. (C). 1997. text 135.00 (*0-7923-9870-X*) Kluwer Academic.
— Intelligent Broadband Multimedia Networks: Generic Aspects & Architectures: Wireless, ISDN, Current & Future Intelligent Networks. LC 96-41385. 584p. (C). 1996. text 137.50 (*0-7923-9747-9*) Kluwer Academic.
— Intelligent Networks. (C). 2000. 50.00 (*0-13-474685-6*, Macmillan Coll) P-H.
Ahammad, Helal. Foreign Exchange & Trade Policy Issues in a Developing Country. LC 95-75574. 300p. 1995. text 79.95 (*1-85972-074-9*, Pub. by Avebry) Ashgate Pub Co.
Ahanotu, Austin M., ed. Religion, State & Society in Contemporary Africa: Nigeria, Sudan, South Africa, Zaire, & Mozambique. LC 91-28472. (American University Studies: Theology & Religion: Ser. VII, Vol. 111). 208p. (C). 1992. text 39.95 (*0-8204-1755-6*) P Lang Pubng.
Aharinejad, S. H. & Lametschwandtner, A. Microvascular Corrosion Casting in Scanning Electron Microscopy: Techniques & Applications. LC 92-48882. 400p. 1993. 159.00 (*0-387-82377-8*) Spr-Verlag.
Aharon, Shmuel Ben, see Ben Aharon, Shmuel.
Aharoni, Ada. Not in Vain: An Extraordinary Life. LC 97-76404. (Illus.). 240p. 1998. pap. 14.95 (*1-889409-18-9*) Ladybug Pr CA.
Aharoni, Ada, jt. ed. see Cronin, Gloria L.
Aharoni, Amikam. Introduction to the Theory of Ferromagnetism. (The International Series of Monographs on Physics: No. 93). (Illus.). 326p. 1996. text 85.00 (*0-19-851791-2*) OUP.
Aharoni, I. Kosher Italian Gourmet. 19.50 (*0-87559-227-9*) Shalom.
Aharoni, Israel. Eating Alfresco: The Best Street Food in the World. LC 98-30702. 144p. 1999. pap. 24.95 (*0-8109-2900-7*, Pub. by Abrams) Time Warner.
Aharoni, S. M. Synthesis, Characterization & Theory of Polymeric Networks & Gels. LC 92-26765. (Illus.). 370p. (C). 1992. text 120.00 (*0-306-44306-6*, Kluwer Plenum) Kluwer Academic.
Aharoni, S. M. & Edwards, S. F. Rigid Polymer Networks, Vol. 118. (Advances in Polymer Science Ser.). 256p. 1994. 150.00 (*0-387-58340-8*) Spr-Verlag.
Aharoni, Shaul M. N-Nylons: Their Synthesis, Structure & Properties. LC 97-183500. 622p. 1997. 295.00 (*0-471-96068-3*) Wiley.
Aharoni, Y. Investigations at Lachish: The Sanctuary & the Residency. (Monograph Series of the Sonia & Marco Nadler Institute of Archaeology: Vol. 4). (Illus.). xi, 116p. 1975. text 30.00 (*0-914594-02-8*, Pub. by Friends Archeol Inst) Eisenbrauns.
Aharoni, Yair. The Evolution & Management of State-Owned Enterprises. LC 77-8200. (In Business & Public Policy Ser.). 480p. 1986. text 34.95 (*0-88730-164-9*, HarpBusn) HarpInfo.
— The No-Risk Society. LC 81-6144. (Chatham House Series on Change in American Politics). 238p. (Orig.). reprint ed. pap. 73.80 (*0-8357-4825-1*, 203776200009) Bks Demand.
Aharoni, Yair, ed. Changing Roles of State Intervention in Services in an Era of Open International Markets. LC 96-12674. (SUNY Series in International Management). 333p. (C). 1997. text 73.50 (*0-7914-3227-0*); pap. text 24.95 (*0-7914-3228-9*) State U NY Pr.
— Coalitions & Competition: The Globalization of Professional Business Services. LC 93-6937. 256p. (C). (gr. 13). 1993. mass mkt. 77.95 (*0-415-08228-5*, B0181) Thomson Learn.
***Aharoni, Yair & Nachum, Lilach.** Globalization of Services: Some Implications for Theory & Practice. LC 99-88059. 280p. 2000. 100.00 (*0-415-22654-6*) Routledge.
Aharoni, Yohanan, et al. The Macmillan Bible Atlas. 3rd rev. ed. LC 77-4313. (Illus.). 192p. 1993. 35.00 (*0-02-500605-3*) Macmillan.
***Aharoni, Zvi.** Operation Eichmann: Pursuit & Capture. (Military Classics). 2000. pap. 9.95 (*0-304-35201-2*) Continuum.
Aharoni, Zvi. Operation Eichmann: The Truth Behind the Pursuit, Capture & Trial of Adolf Eichmann. Bogler, Helmut, tr. LC 97-21379. (Illus.). 192p. 1997. 22.95 (*0-471-19377-1*) Wiley.
Aharonian, Aharon G. Intermarriage & the Armenian-American Community. 118p. 1984. 21.00 (*0-9613300-0-7*) A G Aharonian.
Aharonian, Felix A. TeV Gamma-Ray Astrophysics: Theory & Observations Presented at the Heidelberg Workshop October 3-7, 1994. Volk, Heinrich J., ed. LC 95-47425. 448p. (C). 1996. text 191.50 (*0-7923-3854-5*) Kluwer Academic.
Aharonian, Kersam. A Historical Survey of the Armenian Case. LC 89-61388. 1989. write for info. (*0-936893-02-8*) Baikar.
Aharony, Amnon, jt. auth. see Stauffer, Dietrich.
Ahbe, Dottie & Pluta, Terry. Safety Always Matters. (Fire Safety Education Ser.). (Illus.). 32p. (J). (gr. 1-3). 1988. student ed. 2.00 (*0-9620584-4-0*) Safety Always Matters.
— Safety Always Matters. (Fire Safety Education Ser.). (Illus.). 32p. (J). (gr. 4-6). 1988. student ed. 2.00 (*0-9620584-5-9*) Safety Always Matters.
— Safety Always Matters. (Fire Safety Education Ser.). (Illus.). 32p. (J). (ps). 1991. student ed. 2.00 (*0-9620584-3-2*) Safety Always Matters.
— Safety Always Matters. (Fire Safety Education Ser.). (Illus.). 16p. (J). (ps). 1992. student ed. 0.59 (*0-9620584-0-8*) Safety Always Matters.
— Safety Always Matters. (Fire Safety Education Ser.). (Illus.). 16p. (J). (gr. 1-3). 1992. student ed. 0.59 (*0-9620584-1-6*) Safety Always Matters.
— Safety Always Matters. (Fire Safety Education Ser.). (Illus.). 16p. (J). (gr. 4-6). 1992. student ed. 0.59 (*0-9620584-2-4*) Safety Always Matters.
Ahd. My Big Dictionary. (C). 1994. pap. 18.95 (*0-395-70912-1*) HM.
Ahdar, Rex. Competition Law & Policy in New Zealand. lxi, 321p. 1991. pap. 70.00 (*0-455-21014-4*, Pub. by LawBk Co) Gaunt.
***Ahdar, Rex & Stenhouse, John, eds.** God & Government: The New Zealand Experiment. 200p. 1999. pap. 39.95 (*1-877133-80-9*, Pub. by Univ Otago Pr) Intl Spec Bk.
***Ahdar, Rex J.** Law & Religion. LC 00-40613. (Issues in Law & Society Ser.). 2000. pap. write for info. (*1-84014-757-1*, Pub. by Scolar Pr) Ashgate Pub Co.
Ahdieh, Robert B. Russia's Constitutional Revolution: Constitutional Structures, Legal Consciousness, & the Emergence of Constitutionalism from Below, 1985-1995. LC 96-6116. 208p. 1997. 30.00 (*0-271-01609-4*); pap. 14.95 (*0-271-01610-8*) Pa St U Pr.
Ahearn, Allen & Ahearn, Patricia. Author Price Guides, Vol. 2. 2nd rev. ed. 700p. 1997. 150.00 (*1-883060-09-5*) Quill & Brush Pr.
— Book Collecting, 2000: A Comprehensive Guide. rev. ed. LC 99-27244. 480p. 2000. 45.00 (*0-399-14574-5*, G P Putnam) Peng Put Young Read.
— Collected Books: The Guide to Values, 1997 Edition. LC 97-5397. 832p. 1997. 75.00 (*0-399-14279-7*, G P Putnam) Peng Put Young Read.
Ahearn, Allen, et al. Author Price Guides, Vol. 1. 2nd rev. ed. 725p. 1996. 150.00 (*1-883060-04-4*) Quill & Brush Pr.
— Author Price Guides, Vol. 2. 2nd rev. ed. 648p. 1993. ring bd. 150.00 (*1-883060-00-1*) Quill & Brush Pr.
— Author Price Guides, Vol. 3. 260p. 1996. ring bd. 186.00 (*1-883060-05-2*) Quill & Brush Pr.
Ahearn, Barry. William Carlos Williams & Alterity: The Early Poetry. (Cambridge Studies in American Literature & Culture: No. 75). 199p. (C). 1994. text 59.95 (*0-521-45200-7*) Cambridge U Pr.
Ahearn, Barry, ed. Pound/Cummings: The Correspondence of Ezra Pound & e. e. Cummings. LC 96-19031. 442p. (C). 1996. text 62.50 (*0-472-10298-2*, 10298) U of Mich Pr.
Ahearn, Cynthia. Philippine Brittlestars: Echinodermata: Ophiuroidea, Described by R. Koehler (1922): A Corrected & Annotated List of Type Specimens. LC 92-23874. (Smithsonian Contributions to Zoology Ser.: No. 537). 19p. reprint ed. pap. 30.00 (*0-7837-4381-5*, 204412100012) Bks Demand.
Ahearn, Daniel J., Jr. The Wages of Farm & Factory Laborers. LC 78-76649. (Columbia University. Studies in the Social Sciences: No. 518). 1969. reprint ed. 37.50 (*0-404-51518-5*) AMS Pr.
Ahearn, Edward J. Visionary Fictions: Apocalyptic Writing from Blake to the Modern Age. LC 95-46640. (Illus.). 224p. 1997. 32.50 (*0-300-06536-1*) Yale U Pr.
***Ahearn, Frederick L., Jr.** Psychosocial Wellness of Refugees: Issues in Qualitative & Quantitative Research. LC RC451.4.R43P77 1999. (Studies in Forced Migration). 2000. pap. 19.95 (*1-57181-205-9*); pap. 59.95 (*1-57181-204-0*) Berghahn Bks.
Ahearn, Frederick L., Jr. & Athey, Jean L., eds. Refugee Children: Theory, Research, & Services. LC 90-25554. (Series in Contemporary Medicine & Public Health). 240p. 1991. text 44.00 (*0-8018-4160-7*) Johns Hopkins.
Ahearn, Frederick L., Jr., jt. auth. see Cohen, Raquel E.
Ahearn, Joe & Clements, Brian, eds. Best Texas Writing 1996. 150p. (Orig.). 1997. pap. 15.00 (*0-9656345-1-4*) Rancho Loco Pr.
Ahearn, John, et al. The Sixth Day: Recent Developments in Figurative Sculpture. (Illus.). 24p. 1983. pap. 5.00 (*0-941548-04-X*) Ren Soc U Chi.
Ahearn, Joseph James. Philadelphia Naval Shipyard. (Images of America Ser.). 1999. pap. 14.99 (*0-7524-0873-9*) Arcadia Publng.
***Ahearn, Luke.** Designing 3D Games That Sell! (Illus.). 550p. 2000. pap. 49.95 (*1-58450-043-3*) Chrles River Media.
Ahearn, Marie L. The Rhetoric of War: Training Day, the Militia, & the Military Sermon, 95. LC 89-1919. (Contributions in American Studies: No. 95). 223p. 1989. 57.95 (*0-313-26619-0*, ARW, Greenwood Pr) Greenwood.
Ahearn, Patricia, jt. auth. see Ahearn, Allen.
Ahearne, Jeremy. Michel de Certeau. LC 95-70478. 240p. (Orig.). 1996. pap. 16.95 (*0-8047-2672-8*) Stanford U Pr.
Ahearne, John. Michel de Certeau. LC 95-70478. (Key Contemporary Thinkers Ser.). 240p. 1996. 45.00 (*0-8047-2670-1*) Stanford U Pr.
***Ahearne, John F.** The Responsible Researcher: Paths & Pitfalls. 1999. pap. text. write for info. (*0-914446-15-0*) Sigma Xi.
Ahearne, John F. & Blackburn, Charles F., eds. Vannevar Bush Science for the 21st Century No. II: Current & Future Challenges for Federal Support. 48p. (Orig.). 1996. pap. text. write for info. (*0-914446-10-X*) Sigma Xi.
Aheizer, N. I., et al. Nine Papers on Analysis. LC 51-5559. (Translations Ser.: Series 2, Vol. 22). 370p. 1962. 42.00 (*0-8218-1722-1*, TRANS2/22) Am Math.
Ahemd, Akbar S. & Hart, David M., eds. Islam in Tribal Societies: From the Atlas to the Indus. 320p. (Orig.). 1984. pap. 22.50 (*0-7100-9320-9*, Routledge Thoemms) Routledge.
Ahene, Rexford A. & Katz, Bernard S., eds. Privatization & Investment in Sub-Saharan Africa. LC 91-37511. 264p. 1992. 65.00 (*0-275-93374-1*, C3374, Praeger Pubs) Greenwood.
Aherin, Robert A., et al. Reducing Farm Injuries: Issues & Methods. LC 92-74621. 70p. 1992. pap. 23.50 (*0-929355-35-0*, C1692) Am Soc Ag Eng.
Ahern. Complete Problem Solving Introduction to Experimental Cell. 1996. 26.25 (*0-697-41857-X*, WCB McGr Hill) McGrw-H Hghr Educ.
— Cosmetology. 2nd ed. Date not set. pap. text, teacher ed. 41.00 (*0-314-99658-3*) West Pub.
— Cosmetology-Answers. 2nd ed. Date not set. pap. text, suppl. ed. 9.50 (*0-314-99656-7*) West Pub.
— The Golden Shield of LBF. 1999. mass mkt. 6.99 (*0-671-57825-1*) S&S Trade.
— Manicuring. Date not set. pap. text, teacher ed., wbk. ed. write for info. (*0-314-78617-1*); pap. text, wbk. ed. 15.00 (*0-314-78618-X*) West Pub.
Ahern, jt. auth. see Hubbard, T.
***Ahern, Annette.** Berger's Dual-citizenship Approach to Religion. LC 97-38843. (American University Studies: Vol. VII). 176p. 1999. 40.95 (*0-8204-3883-9*) P Lang Pubng.
Ahern, Barnabas. Mary, Queen of the Poor. (Queen of Apostles Ser.: Vol. VII). 19p. 1994. 0.65 (*0-911988-97-1*, 49736) AMI Pr.
Ahern, C., jt. auth. see Hettich, M.
Ahern, Colleen, ed. see Budy, Andrea H.
Ahern, Colleen, ed. see Dragone, Carol.
Ahern, Colleen, ed. see Sandy, Stephen.
Ahern, Daniel R. Nietzsche As Cultural Physician. LC 94-31510. 1995. 38.50 (*0-271-01425-3*) Pa St U Pr.
Ahern, David K., jt. auth. see Baer, Lee.
Ahern, Denise. The Bread & the Wine: John 13:1-38; 1 Corinthians 11:23-24. (Arch Bks.). (Illus.). 24p. (J). (gr. k-4). 1979. pap. 1.99 (*0-570-06127-X*, 59-1245) Concordia.
***Ahern, Dianne M.** Today I Was Baptized. (Illus.). 32p. 2000. 19.95 (*0-9679437-0-1*) Elan Systems.
Ahern, Emily M. Cult of the Dead in a Chinese Village. LC 72-97202. (Illus.). 296p. 1973. 35.00 (*0-8047-0835-5*) Stanford U Pr.
Ahern, Emily M. & Gates, Hill, eds. The Anthropology of Taiwanese Society. LC 79-64212. xvi, 491p. 1981. 59.50 (*0-8047-1043-0*) Stanford U Pr.
Ahern, Holly. Molecular & Cell Biology. 2nd ed. 112p. (C) 1999. spiral bd. 104.25 (*0-697-13640-X*, WCB McGr Hill) McGrw-H Hghr Educ.
Ahern, J., jt. ed. see Fabos, J. G.
Ahern, Jack. Plants in the Landscape: Environmental Design 335. 229p. (C). 1993. student ed. 22.46 (*1-56870-046-6*) RonJon Pub.
Ahern, James, jt. auth. see Peternel, Carolyn R.
Ahern, Jerry. Armageddon Conspiracy. 1984. pap. 2.50 (*0-373-62003-9*, Harlequin) Harlequin Bks.
— The Awakening. (Survivalist Ser.: No. 10). 1984. mass mkt. 2.50 (*0-8217-1478-3*, Zebra Kensgtn) Kensgtn Pub Corp.
— Carrying Concealed Weapons (CCW) How to Carry Concealed Weapons & Know When Others Are. Padua, Nancy, ed. (Illus.). 200p. (Orig.). 1996. pap. 14.95 (*0-941540-24-3*, 2030) Blacksmith Corp.
— The Doomsayer. (Survivalist Ser.: No. 4). (Orig.). 1981. mass mkt. 2.50 (*0-89083-893-3*, Zebra Kensgtn) Kensgtn Pub Corp.
— The End Is Coming. (Survivalist Ser.: No. 8). 1984. mass mkt. 2.50 (*0-8217-1374-4*, Zebra Kensgtn) Kensgtn Pub Corp.
— Master of D.E.A.T.H. 1985. pap. 2.50 (*0-373-62007-1*) Harlequin Bks.
— The Nightmare Begins. (Survivalist Ser.: No. 2). (Orig.). 1981. mass mkt. 2.50 (*0-89083-810-0*, Zebra Kensgtn) Kensgtn Pub Corp.
— Overlord. (Survivalist Ser.: No. 15). 224p. 1987. mass mkt. 2.50 (*0-8217-2070-8*, Zebra Kensgtn) Kensgtn Pub Corp.
— Pursuit. (Survivalist Ser.: No. 13). 240p. 1986. mass mkt. 2.50 (*0-8217-1877-0*, Zebra Kensgtn) Kensgtn Pub Corp.
— The Reprisal. (Survivalist Ser.: No. 11). 1986. mass mkt. 2.50 (*0-8217-1590-9*, Zebra Kensgtn) Kensgtn Pub Corp.
— Savage H. (Survivalist Ser.: No. 6). 1983. mass mkt. 2.50 (*0-8217-1243-8*, Zebra Kensgtn) Kensgtn Pub Corp.
— The Terror. (Survivalist Ser.: No. 14). 224p. 1987. mass mkt. 2.50 (*0-8217-1972-6*, Zebra Kensgtn) Kensgtn Pub Corp.
— War Mountain. (Survivalist Ser.: No. 25). 320p. 1993. mass mkt. 3.50 (*0-8217-4100-4*, Zebra Kensgtn) Kensgtn Pub Corp.
— The Web. (Survivalist Ser.: No. 5). 1983. mass mkt. 2.50 (*0-8217-1145-8*, Zebra Kensgtn) Kensgtn Pub Corp.
— Werewolves. 1990. mass mkt. 4.50 (*1-55817-335-8*, Pinncle Kensgtn) Kensgtn Pub Corp.
Ahern, Jerry & Ahern, S. A. The Takers River of Gold. 1985. mass mkt. 3.50 (*0-373-62402-6*) Harlequin Bks.
Ahern, Jerry & Ahern, Sharon. The Freeman. LC 91-31859. 372p. 1990. reprint ed. pap. 9.95 (*0-936783-07-9*) Merril Pr.
Ahern, Jerry J. West's Textbook of Cosmetology. 2nd ed. (Illus.). 509p. (C). 1986. pap. text 37.00 (*0-314-99125-5*) West Pub.
— West's Textbook of Manicuring. (Illus.). 107p. (Orig.). (C). 1986. 33.50 (*0-314-99126-3*) West Pub.
Ahern, John E. The Exergy Method of Energy Systems Analysis. LC 79-24500. (Illus.). 309p. reprint ed. pap. 95.80 (*0-8357-8675-7*, 205683200091) Bks Demand.
Ahern, Kathleen D. The Older Woman: The Able Self. rev. ed. LC 95-51444. (Studies on the Elderly in America). 118p. 1996. text 15.00 (*0-8153-2333-6*) Garland.
Ahern, Kevin B., tr. see Koch, Rudolf.
Ahern, Lawrence R. Bankruptcy Jury Manual. LC 98-141411. (West's Bankruptcy Ser.). 446 p. 1998. pap. 49.50 incl. disk (*0-314-23078-5*) West Pub.
— Bankruptcy Procedure Manual LC 98-145987. (West's Bankruptcy Ser.). 1468 p. 1998. write for info. (*0-314-23053-X*) West Pub.
Ahern, Lawrence R. & MacLean, Nancy F. Bankruptcy Jury Manual. LC 95-61778. xxvii, 387p. 1995. write for info. (*0-314-07703-0*) West Pub.
Ahern, Lawrence R., et al. Bankruptcy Rules Manual. LC 97-113498. (Bankruptcy Ser.). lxiii, 1433 p. 1996. write for info. (*0-314-20636-1*) West Pub.
Ahern, Mary & Malerstein, Abraham J. Psychotherapy & Character Structure: How to Recognize & Treat Particular Character Types. 260p. (C). 1993. text 22.50 (*0-9644089-2-9*) Cole Valley Pr.
Ahern, Mary, jt. auth. see Malerstein, Abraham J.
Ahern, Matt. Fishing with Matt Ahern...the Way It Was. Barrett, Linda, ed. (Illus.). 148p. (Orig.). 1993. pap. 12.95 (*0-923155-17-1*) Fisherman Lib.
Ahern, Maureen, tr. see Asturias, Miguel Angel.
Ahern, Maureen, tr. see Bernuy, J. Noriega, ed.
Ahern, Maureen, tr. see Bustamante, Cecilia.
Ahern, Maureen, tr. see Castellanos, Rosario.
Ahern, Maureen, tr. see Cisneros, Antonio.
Ahern, Mike & Duffy, Reid. Festerwood at Five: A "Novel" Approach to TV News. LC 98-72783. 250p. 1998. pap. 15.95 (*1-57860-061-8*) Guild Pr IN.
Ahern, Norman C., Jr. & Ahern, Yvonne. The Rented Christmas. 34p. (Orig.). 1993. pap. 4.00 (*1-57514-121-3*, 1079) Encore Perform Pub.
Ahern, Patrick. Maurice & Therese: The Story of a Love. LC 98-13268. (Illus.). 304p. 1998. 19.95 (*0-385-49261-8*) Doubleday.
***Ahern, Patrick.** Maurice & Therese: The Story of a Love. 2001. reprint ed. pap. 12.95 (*0-385-49740-7*) Doubleday.
Ahern, S. A., jt. auth. see Ahern, Jerry.
Ahern, Sharon, jt. auth. see Ahern, Jerry.
Ahern, Susan & Bailey, Kent G. Family-by-Choice: Creating Family in a World of Strangers. LC 96-11816. 240p. 1997. 19.95 (*0-925190-92-6*) Fairview Press.
Ahern, T. J. & Manning, M. C. Stability of Protein Pharmaceuticals Pt. A: Chemical & Physical Pathways of Protein Degradation. (Pharmaceutical Biotechnology Ser.: Vol. 2). (Illus.). 462p. (C). 1992. text 105.00 (*0-306-44152-7*, Kluwer Plenum) Kluwer Academic.
— Stability of Protein Pharmaceuticals Pt. B: In Vivo Pathways of Degradation & Strategies for Protein Stabilization. (Pharmaceutical Biotechnology Ser.: Vol. 3). (Illus.). 354p. (C). 1992. text 95.00 (*0-306-44153-5*, Kluwer Plenum) Kluwer Academic.
Ahern, Tom. The Capture of Trieste: Stories. (Burning Deck Fiction Ser.). 1978. 15.00 (*0-930900-45-6*); pap. 4.00 (*0-930900-46-4*) Burning Deck.
— Hecatombs of Lake. deluxe ed. 144p. 1984. 30.00 (*0-940650-30-4*) Sun & Moon CA.
— A Movie Starring the Late Cary Grant & an As-Yet Unsigned Actress. deluxe ed. (Treacle Story Ser.: No. 1). (Illus.). 32p. 1976. 12.50 (*0-914232-07-X*) McPherson & Co.
— Superbounce: Prose Poems. (Burning Deck Poetry Ser.). 28p. 1983. pap. 3.00 (*0-930901-12-6*) Burning Deck.
Ahern, Yvonne, jt. auth. see Ahern, Norman C., Jr.
Aherne, Pam & Thornber, Ann. Mathematics for All: An Interactive Approach Within Level 1. 2nd ed. 32p. 1993. pap. 16.00 (*1-85346-255-1*, Pub. by David Fulton) Taylor & Francis.
Aherne, William A. Morphometry. LC 82-185020. 1982. 49.50 (*0-7131-4403-3*) St Martin.

A

A

Aheron, Piper. From Avalon to Eden, North Carolina. (Images of America Ser.). (Illus.). 128p. 1997. pap. 16.99 (*0-7524-0824-0*) Arcadia Publng.

***Aheron, Piper Peters.** Greenville, South Carolina. (Images of America Ser.). (Illus.). 128p. 1999. pap. 18.99 (*0-7385-0144-1*) Arcadia Publng.

Aheron, Piper Peters. Oconee County, South Carolina. (Images of America Ser.). (Illus.). 128p. 1998. pap. 18.99 (*0-7524-0895-X*) Arcadia Publng.

Ahesaki, Masaharu. History of Japanese Religion: With Special Reference to the Social & Moral Life of the Nation. LC 95-14525. (Kegan Paul Japan Library: No. 3). (Illus.). 440p. 1996. 110.00 (*0-7103-0523-0*, Pub. by Kegan Paul Intl) Col U Pr.

AHF (Lehner) Staff. Know Your Body Activity Book: Grade 5. 72p. (J). (gr. 5). 1995. 6.50 (*0-7872-0800-0*) Kendall-Hunt.

— Know Your Body Curriculum: Grade 4 Activity Book. 80p. (J). (gr. 4). 1995. pap. text 6.50 (*0-7872-0798-5*, 41079801) Kendall-Hunt.

— KYB Grade 4 Activity Book. 80p. 1995. 5.00 (*0-7872-1034-X*, KYB) Kendall-Hunt.

AHF (Lehner) Staff, et al. Know Your Body: Grade 2, No. 2. 394p. 1996. teacher ed., ring bd. 65.00 (*0-7872-0795-0*) Kendall-Hunt.

— Know Your Body: Grade 3, No. 3. 374p. 1996. teacher ed., ring bd. 65.00 (*0-7872-0796-9*) Kendall-Hunt.

— Know Your Body Activity Book: Grade 6. 64p. (J). (gr. 6). 1995. 6.50 (*0-7872-0802-7*) Kendall-Hunt.

— Know Your Body Teacher's Guide: Grade K. rev. ed. (Illus.). 480p. 1996. teacher ed., ring bd. 65.00 (*0-7872-0793-4*) Kendall-Hunt.

— Know Your Body Teacher's Guide: Grade 4. 528p. 1996. teacher ed., ring bd. 65.00 (*0-7872-0797-7*) Kendall-Hunt.

Ahia, C. Emmanuel & Martin, Dan. The Danger to Self or Others Exception to Confidentiality. LC 93-7971. (Legal Ser.: Vol. 8). 764p. 1993. pap. text 18.95 (*1-55620-123-0*, 72308) Am Coun Assn.

Ahiagble, Gilbert & Meyer, Louise. Master Weaver from Ghana. LC 98-26514. (Illus.). 32p. (YA). (gr. 2-8). 1998. 18.00 (*0-940880-61-X*) Open Hand.

Ahiakpor, James C. W., ed. Keynes & the Classics Reconsidered. LC 98-3069. 1998. text 95.00 (*0-7923-8149-1*) Kluwer Academic.

Ahier. Jersey Sea Stories. (Jersey Heritage Editions Ser.). 40.00 (*0-86120-005-5*, Pub. by Aris & Phillips) David Brown.

Ahier, John. Education, Training & the Future of Work: Social, Political & Economic Contexts of Policy Development. 1999. 85.00 (*0-415-20208-6*) Routledge.

Ahiezer, N. I. & Krein, M. G. Some Questions in the Theory of Moments. Fleming, W. & Prill, D., trs. LC 63-22077. (Translations of Mathematical Monographs: Vol. 2). 265p. 1962. pap. 42.00 (*0-8218-1552-0*, MMONO/2) Am Math.

Ahiezer, N. I., et al. Fifteen Papers on Algebra. LC 51-5559. (Translations Ser.: Series 2, Vol. 50). 316p. 1966. 55.00 (*0-8218-1750-7*, TRANS2/50) Am Math.

— Fifteen Papers on Real & Complex Functions, Series, Differential & Integral Equations. LC 51-5559. (Translations Ser.: Series 2, Vol. 86). 282p. 1970. 47.00 (*0-8218-1786-8*, TRANS2/86) Am Math.

AHIMA, Ambulatory Care Section Staff. Ambulatory Care Documentation. (Illus.). 252p. 1997. pap. text 48.00 (*1-58426-009-2*, AB101597) Am Hlth Info.

Ahimaaz Ben Paltiel. The Chronicle of Ahimaaz. Salzman, Marcus, tr. LC 79-158233. (Columbia University. Oriental Studies: No. 18). reprint ed. 24.50 (*0-404-50508-2*) AMS Pr.

Ahimeir, Ora, jt. auth. see Eisenstadt, Samuel N.

Ahir, D. C. Asoka, the Great. LC 95-904667. (C). 1995. 22.50 (*81-7018-778-8*, Pub. by BR Pub) S Asia.

— Buddha Gaya Through the Ages. LC 94-905428. (C). 1995. 20.00 (*81-7030-409-1*, Pub. by Sri Satguru Pubns) S Asia.

— Buddhism in North India. (Illus.). (C). 1989. 50.00 (*81-85132-09-7*, Pub. by Classics India Pubns) S Asia.

***Ahir, D. C.** Buddhism in North India & Pakistan. LC 98-908066. 1998. 26.00 (*81-7030-586-1*, Pub. by Sri Satguru Pubns) S Asia.

Ahir, D. C. Buddhism in South India. (Bibliotheca Indo-Buddhica Ser.: No. 112). (C). 1992. 22.00 (*81-7030-332-X*) S Asia.

— Dr. Ambedkar & Punjab. (C). 1992. 14.00 (*81-7018-736-2*, Pub. by BR Pub) S Asia.

— Gautama Buddha. (C). 1994. text 6.50 (*81-7386-112-9*, Pub. by DK Pubs Ind) S Asia.

— Heritage of Buddhism. (C). 1989. 33.50 (*81-7018-552-1*) S Asia.

— Himalayan Buddhism Past & Present: Mahapandit Rahul Sankrityayan Centenary. (Bibliotheca Indo-Buddhica Ser.: No. 122). (C). 1993. 22.00 (*0-8364-2881-1*) S Asia.

— The Legacy of Dr. Ambedkar. (C). 1990. 140.00 (*0-89771-212-9*) St Mut.

— The Legacy of Dr. Ambedkar (Bharat Ratna) 1990. 42.00 (*81-7018-603-X*, Pub. by BR Pub) S Asia.

— Status of the Laity in Buddhism. (C). 1996. 16.00 (*81-7030-504-7*, Pub. by Sri Satguru Pubns) S Asia.

— Vipassanea: A Universal Buddhist Technique of Meditation. LC 98-915489. (Bibliotheca Indo-Buddhica Ser.). viii, 202p. 1999. write for info. (*81-7030-612-4*, Pub. by Sri Satguru Pubns) S Asia.

Ahir, D. C., ed. Panorama of Indian Buddhism: Selections from the Maha Bodhi Journal. LC 95-910357. (C). 1995. 42.00 (*81-7030-462-8*, Pub. by Sri Satguru Pubns) S Asia.

Ahir, D. C., ed. see Ambedkar, B. R.

Ahiram, Ephraim & Tovias, Alfred, eds. Whither EU-Israeli Relations? Common & Divergent Interests. LC 95-18748. (Ethnien, Regionen, Konflikte Ser.: Vol. 6). (Illus.). VI, 297p. 1995. pap. 57.95 (*3-631-47549-7*) P Lang Pubng.

Ahituv, N. & Berman, O. Operations Management of Distributed Service Networks: A Practical Quantitative Approach. (Applications of Modern Technology in Business Ser.). (Illus.). 310p. (C). 1988. 89.50 (*0-306-42864-4*, Plenum Trade) Perseus Pubng.

Ahituv, Shmuel, ed. Handbook of Ancient Hebrew Inscriptions: From the Period of the First Commonwealth & the Beginning of the Second Commonwealth (Hebrew, Philistine, Edomite) (Biblical Encyclopaedia Library: Vol. VII). (HEB.). 317p. 1992. pap. text 39.00 (*965-342-602-8*, Pub. by Bialik) Eisenbrauns.

Ahituv, Shmuel & Levine, Baruch, eds. The Early Biblical Period: Benjamin Mazar, Historical Studies. (Illus.). x, 266p. 1986. 64.50 (*965-221-005-6*) Brill Academic Pubs.

Ahituv, Shmuel, ed. see Mazar, Benjamin.

Ahjmed, Raisuddin & Hossain, Mahabub. Developmental Impact of Rural Infrastructure in Bangladesh. 150p. 1990. 10.00 (*0-89629-086-7*) Intl Food Policy.

Ahl, Diane C. Benozzo Gozzoli. LC 96-60714. (Illus.). 288p. 1996. 70.00 (*0-300-06699-6*) Yale U Pr.

— Leonardo da Vinci's Sforza Monument Horse - the Art & the Engineering: Proceedings of the Symposium Held Apr. 18-19, at Lafayette College & Lehigh University, & the Dent Projet Studio, Fogelsville, Pa. LC 94-36557. (Illus.). 152p. 1995. 55.00 (*0-934223-33-5*) Lehigh Univ Pr.

Ahl, Diane Cole, jt. ed. see Wisch, Barbara.

Ahl, Frederick. Metaformations: Soundplay & Wordplay in Ovid & Other Classical Poets. LC 84-23872. 336p. (C). 1985. 47.50 (*0-8014-1762-7*) Cornell U Pr.

— Sophocles' Oedipus: Evidence & Self-Conviction. LC 90-55733. 366p. 1991. text 49.95 (*0-8014-2558-1*); pap. text 18.95 (*0-8014-9929-1*) Cornell U Pr.

Ahl, Frederick & Roisman, Hannah M. The "Odyssey" Re-Formed. 352p. 1996. text 52.50 (*0-8014-3221-9*); pap. text 19.95 (*0-8014-8335-2*) Cornell U Pr.

Ahl, Frederick, tr. & intro. see Seneca, Lucius Annaeus.

Ahl, Valerie & Allen, Timothy F. Hierarchy Theory: A Vision, Vocabulary, & Epistemology. (Illus.). 192p. 1996. 52.00 (*0-231-08480-3*) Col U Pr.

Ahlander, Ann-Marie S. Environmental Problems in the Shortage Economy: The Legacy of Soviet Environmental Policy. (New Horizons in Environmental Economics Ser.). 192p. 1994. 80.00 (*1-85898-056-9*) E Elgar.

Ahlawat, Neerja. Women Organizations & Social Networks. LC 95-901640. (C). 1995. 20.00 (*81-7033-269-9*, Pub. by Rawat Pubns) S Asia.

Ahlback, Tore, ed. Dance, Music, Art & Religion: Based on Papers Read at the Symposium on Dance, Music & Art in Religion, Abo, Finland, 1994. (Illus.). 380p. (Orig.). 1996. pap. 67.50 (*951-650-834-0*) Coronet Bks.

— Old Norse & Finnish Religious & Cultic Place-Names. (Illus.). 507p. (Orig.). 1990. pap. 59.50 (*951-649-695-4*) Coronet Bks.

***Ahlberg.** Fast Fox Slow Dog: Slow Dogs Nose, Vol. 5. (Illus.). 32p. (J). 2000. pap. 9.95 (*0-14-056401-2*, Pub. by Pnguin Bks Ltd) Trafalgar.

Ahlberg, A. W. & Lundquist, N. Latin-Swedish Dictionary (Latinsk-Svensk Ordbok) 4th ed. (LAT & SWE.). 941p. 1982. 125.00 (*0-8288-1068-0*, M2818) Fr & Eur.

Ahlberg, Allan. Better Brown Stories. (Puffin Book Ser.). (J). 1998. 9.60 (*0-606-13198-1*, Pub. by Turtleback) Demco.

— Better Brown Stories. 112p. 1998. pap. 3.99 (*0-14-037369-1*) Viking Penguin.

— The Better Brown Stories. large type ed. (Illus.). (J). 1998. pap. 16.95 (*0-7540-6006-3*, Galaxy Child Lrg Print) Chivers N Amer.

— The Bravest Ever Bear. LC 98-51833. (Illus.). 32p. (J). (gr. 1-3). 2000. 15.99 (*0-7636-0783-5*) Candlewick Pr.

Ahlberg, Allan. Fast Fox & Slow Dog Bk. 1: Chicken, Chips & Peas. (Illus.). 32p. (J). pap. 9.95 (*0-14-056397-0*, Pub. by Pnguin Bks Ltd) Trafalgar.

— Fast Fox Slow Dog: Fast Fox Goes Crazy. 4th ed. (Illus.). 32p. (J). pap. 9.95 (*0-14-056400-4*, Pub. by Pnguin Bks Ltd) Trafalgar.

— Fast Fox Slow Dog: Hen House, Vol. 3. (Illus.). 32p. (J). pap. 9.95 (*0-14-056399-7*, Pub. by Pnguin Bks Ltd) Trafalgar.

— Fast Fox Slow Dog: Slow Dog Falling, Vol. 2. (Illus.). 32p. (J). pap. 9.95 (*0-14-056398-9*, Pub. by Pnguin Bks Ltd) Trafalgar.

Ahlberg, Allan. Ghost Train. ALC Staff, ed. LC 91-39838. (Illus.). 32p. (J). (gr. k up). 1992. mass mkt. 3.95 (*0-688-11659-0*, Wm Morrow) Morrow Avon.

— Ghost Train. (Funnybones Ser.). 1992. 9.15 (*0-606-01364-4*, Pub. by Turtleback) Demco.

— Giant Baby. 1997. pap. 3.99 (*0-14-036380-7*) Viking Penguin.

— Giant Baby. (J). 1999. pap. 3.99 (*0-14-038723-4*) Viking Penguin.

Ahlberg, Allan. Happy Families Master Tracks Train. (Illus.). 24p. (J). pap. 6.95 (*0-14-037881-2*, Pub. by Pnguin Bks Ltd) Trafalgar.

— Heard It in the Playground. (Illus.). (J). 1991. pap. 7.95 (*0-14-032824-6*, Pub. by Pnguin Bks Ltd) Trafalgar.

Ahlberg, Allan. It Was a Dark & Stormy Night. (Illus.). 32p. (J). (ps-3). 1999. text 13.99 (*0-670-85159-0*, Viking Child) Peng Put Young Read.

***Ahlberg, Allan.** It Was a Dark & Stormy Night. (Illus.). 32p. (J). (ps-3). 1999. pap. 5.99 (*0-14-055554-4*, PuffinBks) Peng Put Young Read.

— Master Bun: The Baker's Boy. (Illus.). (J). 1988. pap. 6.95 (*0-14-032344-9*, Pub. by Pnguin Bks Ltd) Trafalgar.

— Master Money the Millionaire: The Millionaire. 24p. (J). (gr. 3). 1981. pap. 6.95 (*0-14-031246-3*, Pub. by Pnguin Bks Ltd) Trafalgar.

— Mighty Slide. 96p. (YA). (gr. 7 up). 1990. pap. 7.95 (*0-14-032335-X*, Pub. by Pnguin Bks Ltd) Trafalgar.

— Miss Dirt: The Dustman's Daughter. (Illus.). 24p. (J). pap. 6.95 (*0-14-037882-0*, Pub. by Pnguin Bks Ltd) Trafalgar.

— Miss Dose: The Doctor's Daughter. (Illus.). (J). 1988. pap. 6.95 (*0-14-032346-5*, Pub. by Pnguin Bks Ltd) Trafalgar.

— Miss Jump the Jockey. (Illus.). 24p. (J). (gr. 3-6). 1980. pap. 6.95 (*0-14-031241-2*, Pub. by Pnguin Bks Ltd) Trafalgar.

— Mr. Creep the Crook. (Illus.). 24p. (J). 1988. pap. 6.95 (*0-14-032345-7*, Pub. by Pnguin Bks Ltd) Trafalgar.

Ahlberg, Allan. Mockingbird. LC 97-18207. (Illus.). 24p. (J). (ps-1). 1998. 14.99 (*0-7636-0439-9*) Candlewick Pr.

— Monkey Do. LC 97-36181. (Illus.). 32p. (J). (ps-k). 1998. 15.99 (*0-7636-0466-6*) Candlewick Pr.

Ahlberg, Allan. Mr. Cosmo the Conjuror. 24p. (J). 1980. pap. 6.95 (*0-14-031237-4*, Pub. by Pnguin Bks Ltd) Trafalgar.

— Mr. Tick the Teacher. 24p. (J). (gr. 3-6). 1981. pap. 6.95 (*0-14-031245-5*, Pub. by Pnguin Bks Ltd) Trafalgar.

— Mrs. Jolly's Joke Shop. (Illus.). 24p. (J). (gr. 3-6). 1988. pap. 6.95 (*0-14-032347-3*, Pub. by Pnguin Bks Ltd) Trafalgar.

— Mrs. Vole the Vet. (Illus.). 24p. (J). pap. 6.95 (*0-14-037880-4*, Pub. by Pnguin Bks Ltd) Trafalgar.

— Ms. Cliff the Climber. (Illus.). 24p. (J). 1997. pap. 6.95 (*0-14-037879-0*, Pub. by Pnguin Bks Ltd) Trafalgar.

Ahlberg, Allan. The Mysteries of Zigomar: Poems & Stories. LC 97-2035. (Illus.). 64p. (J). (gr. 1-7). 1997. 17.99 (*0-7636-0352-X*) Candlewick Pr.

— One, Two Flea: Level 4, Green. LC 98-88077. (Reading Together Ser.). (Illus.). 32p. (J). 1999. pap. write for info. (*0-7636-0859-9*) Candlewick Pr.

Ahlberg, Allan. Please Mrs. Butler. 1984. pap. 7.95 (*0-14-031494-6*, Pub. by Pnguin Bks Ltd) Trafalgar.

Ahlberg, Allan. The Snail House. LC 98-42389. (Illus.). 2000. write for info. (*0-7636-0711-8*) Candlewick Pr.

Ahlberg, Allan. Starting School. (Illus.). 32p. (J). pap. 9.95 (*0-14-050737-X*, Pub. by Pnguin Bks Ltd) Trafalgar.

— Woof. (Illus.). 160p. (J). pap. 9.95 (*0-14-038669-6*, Pub. by Pnguin Bks Ltd) Trafalgar.

Ahlberg, Allan, jt. auth. see Ahlberg, Janet.

Ahlberg, Allen, jt. auth. see Ahlberg, Janet.

Ahlberg, Ann. Children's Way of Handling & Experiencing Numbers. (Goteborg Studies in Educational Sciences: No. 113). 115p. 1997. pap. 37.50 (*91-7346-315-9*, Pub. by Almqvist Wiksell) Coronet Bks.

***Ahlberg, Ann.** Meeting Mathematics: Educational Studies with Young Children. (Goteborg Studies in Educational Sciences: No. 123). (Illus.). 236p. 1998. pap. 52.50 (*91-7346-332-9*, Pub. by Almqvist Wiksell) Coronet Bks.

Ahlberg, Beth M. Women, Sexuality & the Changing Social Order: The Impact of Government Policies on Reproductive Behavior in Kenya. (International Studies in Global Change). viii, 274p. 1991. pap. text 48.00 (*2-88124-499-8*) Gordon & Breach.

Ahlberg-Cornell, Gudrun. Myth & Epos in Early Greek Art: Representation & Interpretation. (Studies in Mediterranean Archaeology: Vol. C). (Illus.). 410p. (Orig.). 1992. pap. 97.50 (*91-7081-017-6*, Pub. by P Astroms) Coronet Bks.

Ahlberg-Cornell, Gudrun, ed. Herakles & the Sea-Monster in Attic Black-Figure Vase-Painting. (Acta Instituti Atheniensis Regni Sueciae Ser.: Vol. XXXIII). (Illus.). 172p. 1984. pap. 72.50 (*91-85086-79-7*, Pub. by P Astroms) Coronet Bks.

Ahlberg, Gudrun. Prothesis & Ekphora in Greek Geometric Art, Text & Figures, 2 vols. (Studies in Mediterranean Archaeology: Vol. XXXII). (Illus.). 385p. 1971. pap. 85.00 (*91-85058-50-5*, Pub. by P Astroms) Coronet Bks.

Ahlberg, Holly. Sedona 2001 & Beyond. (Illus.). 24p. 1998. pap. 8.95 (*1-891139-01-0*) Thorne Enterprises.

Ahlberg, Janet. Bear Nobody Wanted. 1993. 10.09 (*0-606-07268-3*, Pub. by Turtleback) Demco.

— Each Peach Pear Plum: An "I Spy" Story. (Picture Puffin Ser.). (J). 1986. 10.19 (*0-606-01453-5*, Pub. by Turtleback) Demco.

— Funnybones. (J). 1990. 10.15 (*0-606-04676-3*, Pub. by Turtleback) Demco.

Ahlberg, Janet. It Was a Dark & Stormy Night. (Illus.). 80p. pap. 7.95 (*0-14-130027-2*, Pub. by Pnguin Bks Ltd) Trafalgar.

Ahlberg, Janet. Jeremiah in the Dark Woods. (J). 1977. 10.19 (*0-606-04443-4*, Pub. by Turtleback) Demco.

— The Jolly Postman. (Illus.). (J). 1987. 9.95 (*0-434-92515-2*, Pub. by W Heinemann) Bentley Pubs.

— Starting School. (J). 1990. pap. 5.99 (*0-14-050843-0*, PuffinBks) Peng Put Young Read.

Ahlberg, Janet & Ahlberg, Allan. Adios Pequeno - Bye Bye, Baby. Puncel, Maria, tr. (SPA., Illus.). 28p. (J). (gr. k-1). 1990. write for info. (*84-372-6613-0*) Santillana.

— Baby Sleeps. (Illus.). 12p. (J). (ps). 1999. 5.95 (*0-316-03845-8*) Little.

— The Baby's Catalogue. (Illus.). 32p. (J). (ps). 1986. pap. 6.95 (*0-316-02038-9*) Little.

— Doll & Teddy. (Illus.). 12p. (J). (ps). 1999. 5.95 (*0-316-03846-6*) Little.

Ahlberg, Janet & Ahlberg, Allan. Each Peach, Pear, Plum. (Illus.). (J). pap. 9.95 (*0-14-050919-4*, Pub. by Pnguin Bks Ltd) Trafalgar.

Ahlberg, Janet & Ahlberg, Allan. Each Peach, Pear, Plum: An I-Spy Story. LC 79-16726. (Illus.). 32p. (J). (gr. k-3). 1979. 12.95 (*0-670-28705-9*, Viking Child) Peng Put Young Read.

— The Jolly Christmas Postman. (Illus.). 32p. (J). (gr. k-3). 1991. 17.95 (*0-316-02033-8*) Little.

— The Jolly Pocket Postman. LC 95-75601. (Illus.). 40p. (J). (gr. k-3). 1995. 19.95 (*0-316-60202-7*) Little.

— The Jolly Postman: Or Other People's Letters. LC 86-80044. (Illus.). 29p. (J). (ps-3). 1986. 17.95 (*0-316-02036-2*) Little.

— Peek-a-Boo Board Book. (Illus.). 32p. 1997. pap. 6.99 (*0-670-87192-3*) Viking Penguin.

— See the Rabbit. (Illus.). 12p. (J). (ps). 1999. 5.95 (*0-316-03847-4*) Little.

***Ahlberg, Janet & Ahlberg, Allan.** Starting School. 32p. (J). 1999. 19.95 (*0-670-81688-4*, Viking Child) Peng Put Young Read.

Ahlberg, Janet & Ahlberg, Allen. Peepo! (Illus.). (J). pap. 9.95 (*0-14-050384-6*, Pub. by Pnguin Bks Ltd) Trafalgar.

Ahlberg, Janet, et al. Blue Buggy. (Illus.). 12p. (J). (ps). 1999. 5.95 (*0-316-03848-2*) Little.

Ahlberg, Kersti, ed. AGA Gas Handbook: Properties & Uses of Industrial Gases. (Illus.). 582p. 1985. text 97.50 (*91-970061-1-4*) Coronet Bks.

Ahlberg, Mauri & Filho, Walter L., eds. Environmental Education for Sustainability: Good Environment, Good Life. (Environmental Education, Communication & Sustainability Ser.: Vol. 4). (Illus.). 300p. 1998. pap. text 48.95 (*0-8204-3612-7*) P Lang Pubng.

Ahlberg, Mauri & Filho, Walter Leal, eds. Environmental Education for Sustainability: Good Environment, Good Life. LC 98-229382. (Environmental Education, Communication & Sustainability Ser.: Vol. 4). 300p. 1998. pap. 48.95 (*3-631-33617-9*) P Lang Pubng.

Ahlberg, P. & Sundelof, L. Structure & Dynamics in Chemistry. (Illus.). 340p. (Orig.). 1978. pap. text 33.50 (*91-554-0793-5*) Coronet Bks.

Ahlberg, R. Sumerian & Japanese: A Comparative Language Study. vi, 142p. 1991. text 96.00 (*4-915809-50-1*) Gordon & Breach.

Ahlbom, Anders. Biostatistics for Epidemiologists. 224p. 1993. lib. bdg. 79.95 (*0-87371-912-3*, L912) Lewis Pubs.

Ahlbom, Anders, jt. auth. see Feychting, Maria.

Ahlbom, Jens, jt. auth. see Johansson, George.

Ahlborn, Richard. The Sculpted Saints of a Borderland Mission. LC 74-18171. (Illus.). 124p. 1974. pap. 7.50 (*0-915076-03-9*) SW Mission.

Ahlborn, Richard E., jt. auth. see Marshall, Howard W.

Ahlbrandt, Arlene. Larimer County, Colorado War Book. (Illus.). 126p. 1993. 35.00 (*0-88107-229-X*) Curtis Media.

Ahlbrandt, Calvin D. & Peterson, Allan C. Discrete Hamiltonian Systems: Difference Equations, Continued Fractions, & Riccati Equations. LC 96-45991. (Kluwer Texts in Mathematical Sciences Ser.). 374p. (C). 1996. lib. bdg. 175.00 (*0-7923-4277-1*) Kluwer Academic.

***Ahlbrandt, Patricia W.** Beaumaris. (Illus.). 168p. 1998. 13.50 (*1-55046-032-3*, Pub. by Boston Mills) Genl Dist Srvs.

Ahlbrandt, Roger S., Jr. Neighborhoods, People, & Community. (Environment, Development, & Public Policy: Public Policy & Social Services Ser.). 256p. 1984. 54.50 (*0-306-41542-9*, Plenum Trade) Perseus Pubng.

Ahlbrandt, Roger S., Jr., et al. A New Public Policy for Neighborhood Preservation. LC 79-12363. 276p. 1979. 65.00 (*0-275-90327-3*, C0327, Praeger Pubs) Greenwood.

Ahlbrandt, Roger S., et al. The Renaissance of American Steel: Lessons for Managers in Competitive Industries. (Illus.). 192p. 1996. 27.50 (*0-19-510828-0*) OUP.

Ahlbrecht, Martin. Entscheidungen unter Berucksichtigung des Zeitbezuges der Konsequenzen. (Europaische Hochschulschriften: Reihe 5: Bd. 1946). (GER., Illus.). 244p. 1996. pap. 44.95 (*3-631-30296-7*) P Lang Pubng.

Ahlburg, Dennis A., et al. The Impact of Population Growth on Well-Being in Developing Countries. LC 96-12883. (Population Economics Ser.). (Illus.). 360p. 1996. text 115.00 (*3-540-60709-9*) Spr-Verlag.

***Ahlefeld, Charlotte.** Liebe und Trennung: Charlotte Von Ahlefelds Briefe an Christian Friedrich Tieck Herausgegeben und Kommentiert Von James Trainer. 234p. 1999. pap. 42.95 (*3-906761-87-8*) P Lang Pubng.

Ahlem, Lloyd H. Living & Growing in Later Years. 112p. (Orig.). 1992. pap. write for info. (*0-9626063-1-6*) Covenant Benevolent Inst.

Ahlen, Ingemar, jt. ed. see Gustafsson, Lena.

Ahlen, J. Timothy, jt. auth. see Thomas, J. V.

Ahlenslager, Kathleen E. Glacier: The Story Behind the Scenery. LC 88-80118. (Illus.). 48p. (Orig.). 1988. pap. 7.95 (*0-88714-018-1*) KC Pubns.

Ahler, Stanley A. & Toom, Dennis L., eds. Archaeology of the Medicine Crow Site Complex (39BF2), Buffalo County, South Dakota. LC 96-620103. (Reports of Investigations: Vol. 51). 1995. pap. 20.00 (*0-89792-147-X*) Ill St Museum.

Ahler, Stephen R., et al. Late Archaic Components at Modoc Rock Shelter, Randolph County, Illinois. (Reports of Investigations: No. 48). (Illus.). 143p. 1992. pap. 12.00 (*0-89792-138-0*) Ill St Museum.

Ahler, Steven, et al. Archaeological Testing for the Smithland Pool, Illinois. (Center for Archaeological Investigations Research Paper Ser.: No. 13). (Illus.). xii, 290p. 1980. pap. 12.00 (*0-88104-027-4*) Center Archaeol.

Ahler, Steven R. & DePuydt, Peter J. A Report on the 1931 Powell Mound Excavations, Madison County, Illinois. (Reports of Investigations: No. 43). (Illus.). 40p. (C). 1987. pap. 5.00 (*0-89792-111-9*) Ill St Museum.

Ahlers & Allaire Staff, ed. see Zanzig, Thomas.

Ahlers, Claus, tr. see Hardy, George F.

An Asterisk (*) at the beginning of an entry indicates that the title is appearing for the first time.

Ahlers, David M. A New Look at Porfolio Management. Altman, Edward I. & Walter, Ingo I., eds. LC 76-10448. (Contemporary Studies in Economic & Financial Analysis: Vol. 5). 250p. 1977. 78.50 (*0-89232-012-5*) Jai Pr.

Ahlers, Glen-Peter, ed. Election Laws of the United States, 3 vols. LC 94-191407. 1995. ring bd. 275.00 (*0-379-01020-8*) Oceana.

Ahlers, Julia, et al, compiled by. Womenpsalms. 140p. 1992. pap. 6.95 (*0-88489-287-5*) St Marys.

Ahlers, Julia & Wilt, Michael. Christian Justice: Sharing God's Goodness. Allaire, Barbara, ed. (Illus.). 304p. (YA). (gr. 11-12). 1995. pap. text 14.00 (*0-88489-330-8*) St Marys.

Ahlers, Julia, et al. Growing in Christian Morality. 323p. (YA). (gr. 10-11). 1996. teacher ed., spiral bd. 24.95 (*0-88489-388-X*) St Marys.

— Growing in Christian Morality. rev. ed. (Illus.). 304p. 1996. pap. text 15.30 (*0-88489-387-1*) St Marys.

Ahlers, Julia, ed. see Koch, Carl, et al.

Ahlers, Nicole & Schonert, Jorg. Das Deutsche Versepos Zwischen 1848 Und 1914. 435p. 1998. 56.95 (*3-631-32591-6*) P Lang Pubng.

Ahlers, Rolf. The Barmen Theological Declaration of 1934: The Archeology of a Confessional Text. LC 86-5186. (Toronto Studies in Theology: Vol. 24). 264p. 1986. lib. bdg. 89.95 (*0-88946-768-4*) E Mellen.

— The Community of Freedom: Barth & Presuppositionless Theology. (American University Studies: Theology & Religion: Ser. VII, Vol. 40). XV, 655p. (C). 1989. text 84.95 (*0-8204-0564-7*) P Lang Pubng.

Ahlers, Rolf-Juergen & Reinhart, Gunther, eds. Rapid Prototyping & Flexible Manufacturing. LC 98-125242. (Europto Ser.: Vol. 3102). 160p. 1997. 59.00 (*0-8194-2522-2*) SPIE.

Ahlers, Rolf-Juergen, jt. ed. see Refregier, Philippe.

Ahlert, Gary, jt. auth. see Bloch, Sonny.

Ahlert, Gunter. Altern-Ergebnis Oekologischer Anpassung. (Illus.). x, 68p. 1996. pap. 49.75 (*3-8055-6361-2*) S Karger.

Ahles, Carol. Fine Machine Sewing: Easy Ways to Get the Look of Hand Finishing & Embellishing. LC 96-2876. (Illus.). 160p. 1996. pap. 24.95 (*1-56158-153-4*, 070257) Taunton.

Ahles, Harry E., jt. auth. see Magee, Dennis W.

Ahles, Harry E., ed. see MacKeever, Frank C.

***Ahlfeld, David & Mulligan, Ann.** Optimal Hydraulic Control of Groundwater Systems. 500p. 1999. 54.95 (*0-12-044830-0*) Acad Pr.

Ahlfors, L. V., et al. Some Problems of Mathematics & Mechanics. LC 76-4884. (Translations Ser.: Series 2, Vol. 104). 265p. 1976. 75.00 (*0-8218-3054-6*, TRANS2/104) Am Math.

Ahlfors, Lars V. Complex Analysis. 3rd ed. (Illus.). 336p. (C). 1979. 90.94 (*0-07-000657-1*) McGraw.

Ahlfors, Lars V., et al, eds. Advances in the Theory of Riemann Surfaces: Proceedings of the 1969 Stony Brook Conference. LC 72-121729. (Annals of Mathematics Studies: No. 66). 430p. 1971. reprint ed. pap. 133.30 (*0-608-06631-1*, 206682800009) Bks Demand.

Ahlfors, Lars V., intro. Lars Valerian Ahlfors: Collected Papers, 2 Vols., 1. 544p. 1983. 122.00 (*0-8176-3075-9*) Birkhauser.

— Lars Valerian Ahlfors: Collected Papers, 2 Vols., 2. 544p. 1983. 122.00 (*0-8176-3076-7*) Birkhauser.

— Lars Valerian Ahlfors: Collected Papers, 2 Vols., Set. 544p. 1980. 194.50 (*0-8176-3077-5*) Birkhauser.

Ahlfors, Lars V. & Sario, Leo. Riemann Surfaces. LC 59-11074. (Princeton Mathematical Ser.: No. 26). (Illus.). 396p. 1960. reprint ed. pap. 122.80 (*0-608-06610-9*, 206680700009) Bks Demand.

Ahlfors, U. G. Alcohol & Conflict. 1969. 4.00 (*951-9192-06-9*) Rutgers Ctr Alcohol.

Ahlgren, Andrew, jt. auth. see Rutherford, F. James.

Ahlgren, Gillian. The Human Person & the Church: Classic Texts in Perspective. LC 98-48315. 300p. 1998. pap. 25.00 (*1-57075-213-3*) Orbis Bks.

Ahlgren, Gillian T. Teresa of Avila & the Politics of Sanctity. 240p. 1996. text 39.95 (*0-8014-3232-4*) Cornell U Pr.

— Teresa of Avila & the Politics of Sanctity. 200p. 1998. pap. 15.95 (*0-8014-8572-X*) Cornell U Pr.

Ahlgren, Greg & Monier, Stephen R. Crime of the Century: The Lindbergh Kidnapping Hoax. (Illus.). 300p. 1993. 21.95 (*0-8283-1971-5*) Branden Bks.

Ahlgren, Inger & Hytenstam, Kenneth, eds. Bilingualism in Deaf Education Vol. 27. LC 96-150549. (International Studies on Sign Language & the Communication of the Deaf: Vol. 27). 312p. 1994. text 39.95 (*3-927731-54-4*, Pub. by Signum-Verlag) Gallaudet Univ Pr.

Ahlgren, James & MacDonald, John, eds. Gastrointestinal Oncology. LC 91-42124. (Illus.). 683p. 1992. reprint ed. pap. 200.00 (*0-608-07185-4*, 206741000009) Bks Demand.

Ahlgrim, Ryan. Morphed: New Life in Romans. (Generation Why Ser.). 35p. 1998. pap. 12.95 (*0-87303-277-2*) Faith & Life.

Ahlgrimm, M., jt. auth. see Harrison, M.

Ahlgrimm, Marla & Kells, John M. The HRT Solution: Optimizing Your Hormone Potential. LC 98-48480. 224p. 1999. pap. 9.95 (*0-89529-948-8*, Avery) Penguin Putnam.

***Ahlgrimm, Marla & Kells, John M.** Restoring Balance: An Individualized Approach to Hormone Replacement Therapy. 32p. 1998. pap. 3.95 (*1-890694-03-7*) IMPAKT Communs.

Ahlheim, Karl-Heinz. Diccionario Economia General y Empresa, Vol. 4. 5th ed. (SPA.). 768p. 1992. 65.00 (*0-8288-7721-1*, M7346) Fr & Eur.

— Duden Taschenbucher: Fremdworter Woerterbuch. (GER.). 368p. 1970. 29.95 (*0-7859-8347-3*, 3411011394) Fr & Eur.

— Schuelerduden - Die Psychologie: Scholar's Psychology Duden. (GER.). 408p. 1981. 35.00 (*0-8288-2205-0*, M15377) Fr & Eur.

Ahlin, John H. Maine Rubison: Downeast Settlers During the American Revolution. LC 66-29480. (Illus.). 224p. 1966. reprint ed. pap. 19.50 (*0-89725-320-5*, 1846) Picton Pr.

Ahlin, Lars. Cinnamoncandy. Weiss, Hanna K., tr. from SWE. LC 90-3043. (Library of World Literature in Translation: Vol. 1). 264p. 1990. reprint ed. text 20.00 (*0-8240-3183-0*) Garland.

Ahlquist, Cynthia. Llewellyn's Moon Sign Book & Gardening Almanac: 1999 Edition. annuals (Llewellyn's Moon Sign Book Ser.). (Illus.). 448p. 1998. pap. 6.95 (*1-56718-941-5*) Llewellyn Pubns.

Ahlquist, Cynthia, ed. Llewellyn's 1998 Daily Planetary Guide. 216p. (Orig.). 1997. spiral bd. 9.95 (*1-56718-934-2*) Llewellyn Pubns.

— Llewellyn's 1999 Magical Almanac. annuals (Illus.). 345p. 1999. pap. 6.95 (*1-56718-940-7*) Llewellyn Pubns.

— Llewellyn's 1999 Witches' Datebook. (Illus.). 144p. 1999. spiral bd. 9.95 (*1-56718-949-0*) Llewellyn Pubns.

— Llewellyn's Witches' Datebook 2000. 144p. 1999. pap. 9.95 (*1-56718-952-0*) Llewellyn Pubns.

Ahlquist, Cynthia, ed. see Llewellyn Staff.

Ahlquist, Cynthia, ed. see Star, Gloria.

Ahlquist, Jon E., jt. auth. see Sibley, Charles G.

Ahlquist, Karen E. Democracy at the Opera: Music, Theater, & Culture in New York City, 1815-60. LC 96-4494. (Music in American Life Ser.). 272p. 1997. text 29.95 (*0-252-02272-6*) U of Ill Pr.

Ahlqvist, Anders, ed. Diversions of Galway: Papers on the History of Linguistics from ICHoLS V. LC 92-24473. (Studies in the History of the Language Sciences: No. 68). xxvii, 384p. 1992. 100.00 (*1-55619-363-7*) J Benjamins Pubng Co.

***Ahlrichs, Nancy S.** Competing for Talent: Key Recruitment & Retention Strategies for Becoming an Employer of Choice. 274p. 2000. 32.95 (*0-89106-148-7*) Consulting Psychol.

Ahlskog, Gary & Sands, Harry, eds. Guide to Pastoral Counseling & Care. LC 98-49648. 415p. 1999. 60.00 (*1-887841-19-9*, 64117, Psychosocial) Intl Univs Pr.

Ahlskog, J. Eric, jt. ed. see Adler, Charles H.

Ahlstrand, Alan. Chevrolet Corvette: Automotive Repair Manual. LC 91-71157. (Haynes-U. S. Ser.). 373p. 1981. pap. 17.95 (*1-85010-723-8*) MBI Pubg.

— Honda Cr250/500r Owners Workshop Manual. LC 97-70909. (Motorcycle Repair Manual Ser.). (Illus.). 176p. 1998. pap. 23.95 (*1-56392-222-3*) Haynes Manuals.

Ahlstrand, Alan. Honda TRX300 ATV Owners Workshop Manual. (Owners Workshop Manuals Ser.). 1997. pap. 23.95 (*1-56392-125-1*) Haynes Manuals.

— Suzuki GSX-R & Katana GSX-F: Service & Repair Manual. (Service & Repair Manual Ser.). (Illus.). 1996. pap. 23.95 (*1-85960-284-3*) Haynes Manuals.

Ahlstrand, Alan & Haynes, John. Hyns Honda GL1200 Gold Wing, 1200 CC, 1984-1987. (Motorcycle Repair Manual Ser.). (Illus.). 208p. 1998. pap. 23.90 (*1-56392-199-5*) Haynes Manuals.

Ahlstrand, Alan, et al. Ford Escort & Mercury Lynx: Automotive Repair Manual, 1981-1990. 2nd ed. LC 91-75875. (Illus.). 368p. 1991. pap. 17.95 (*1-56392-004-2*) Haynes Manuals.

Ahlstrand, Alan, ed. see Beckstrom, Robert J. & Ortho Books-How to Staff.

Ahlstrand, Bruce, jt. auth. see Purcell, John.

Ahlstrom, Elbert H. A Quantitative Study of Rotatoria in Terwilliger's Pond, Put-In Bay, Ohio. (Bulletin Ser.: No. 30). 1934. pap. text 2.00 (*0-86727-029-2*) Ohio Bio Survey.

Ahlstrom, Gosta W. The History of Ancient Palestine. LC 93-16628. 990p. 1993. pap. 35.00 (*0-8006-2770-9*, 1-2770, Fortress Pr) Augsburg Fortress.

— The History of Ancient Palestine: From the Palaeolithic Period to Alexander's Conquest. Edelman, Diana, ed. (Journal for the Study of the Old Testament Supplement Ser.: No. 146). 1032p. 1992. 90.00 (*1-85075-367-9*, Pub. by Sheffield Acad) CUP Services.

Ahlstrom-Laakso, Salme. Drinking Habits Among Alcoholics. (Finnish Foundation for Alcohol Studies: Vol. 21). 1975. 8.00 (*951-9191-18-6*) Rutgers Ctr Alcohol.

Ahlstrom, Richard V., jt. auth. see Smiley, Francis E.

***Ahlstrom, Russell J.** It's All in Your Head. 80p. 1999. pap. 11.95 (*1-58244-033-6*) Rutledge Bks.

Ahlstrom, S. E. A Religious History of the American People. LC 72-151564. (Illus.). 1174p. 1974. pap. 27.00 (*0-300-01762-6*) Yale U Pr.

Ahlstrom, Sydney E. & Carey, Jonathan S. An American Reformation: A Documentary History of Unitarian Christianity. 512p. 1997. pap. 54.95 (*1-57309-208-8*) Intl Scholars.

Ahlstrom, Sydney E. & Mullin, Robert B. The Scientific Theist: A Life of Francis Ellingwood Abbot. LC 86-33128. 208p. 1987. 29.95 (*0-86554-236-8*, H208) Mercer Univ Pr.

Ahlstrom, Trudy & Devine, J. T. California Wine Winners, 1988. (Illus.). 128p. (Orig.). 1988. pap. 5.95 (*0-9614025-5-5*) Varietal Fair.

Ahlstrom, Trudy & Devine, J. T., eds. California Wine Winners, 1999: The Best of the 1998 Judgings. (Illus.). 216p. 1998. pap. 8.95 (*1-881796-05-1*) Varietal Fair.

— California Wine Winners, 1993: The Best of the 1992 Judgings. (Illus.). 160p. (Orig.). 1992. pap. 6.95 (*0-9614025-9-8*) Varietal Fair.

— California Wine Winners, 1995: The Best of the 1994 Judgings. (Illus.). 176p. (Orig.). 1994. pap. 6.95 (*1-881796-01-9*) Varietal Fair.

— California Wine Winners, 1996: The Best of the 1995 Judgings. annuals (Illus.). 176p. (Orig.). 1995. pap. 8.95 (*1-881796-02-7*) Varietal Fair.

Ahlstrom, Trudy, jt. ed. see Devine, J. T.

Ahlstrom, Trudy H. & Devine, J. T. California Wine Winners, 1983. 72p. (Orig.). 1984. pap. 4.95 (*0-9614025-0-4*) Varietal Fair.

— California Wine Winners, 1984. 96p. (Orig.). 1984. pap. 4.95 (*0-9614025-1-2*) Varietal Fair.

— California Wine Winners, 1985. 104p. (Orig.). 1985. pap. 5.95 (*0-9614025-2-0*) Varietal Fair.

— California Wine Winners, 1986. (Orig.). 1986. pap. 5.95 (*0-9614025-3-9*) Varietal Fair.

— California Wine Winners, 1987. (Illus.). (Orig.). 1987. pap. 5.95 (*0-9614025-4-7*) Varietal Fair.

— California Wine Winners, 1989. (Illus.). 128p. (Orig.). 1989. pap. 5.95 (*0-9614025-6-3*) Varietal Fair.

— California Wine Winners, 1991. (Illus.). 128p. (Orig.). 1990. pap. 5.95 (*0-9614025-7-1*) Varietal Fair.

— California Wine Winners, 1992: The Best from the 1991 Competitions. (Illus.). 128p. (Orig.). 1991. pap. 5.95 (*0-9614025-8-X*) Varietal Fair.

Ahlstrom, Winton M. & Havighurst, Robert J. Four Hundred Losers: Delinquent Boys in High School. LC 74-149914. (Jossey-Bass Behavioral Science Ser.). 262p. reprint ed. 81.30 (*0-8357-9321-4*, 201393500087) Bks Demand.

Ahlstroml, K. G. & Jonsson, M. Flexible Grouping of Pupils & Teamwork Between Teachers: 91-554-1098-8. 276p. (Orig.). 1980. pap. text 33.00 (*0-317-46415-9*) Coronet Bks.

Ahlswede, Rudolf & Wegener, Ingo. Search Problems. Wotschke, Jean E., tr. LC 87-8240. (Wiley-Interscience Series in Discrete Mathematics & Optimization). (Illus.). 296p. 1987. reprint ed. pap. 91.80 (*0-7837-9506-8*, 206025600005) Bks Demand.

Ahluwalea, Shashi. Profiles of Indian Prime Minister: Nehru to Narasimha Rao. (C). 1991. 34.00 (*81-7099-326-1*, Pub. by Mittal Pubs Dist) S Asia.

Ahluwalia, B. K. & Alhuwalia, S. Rajiv Gandhi: Breaking New Grounds. 202p. 1985. 34.95 (*0-318-36607-X*) Asia Bk Corp.

Ahluwalia, Bhagwat D., ed. Tomographic Methods in Nuclear Medicine: Physical Principles, Instruments, & Clinical Applications. 288p. 1989. lib. bdg. 195.00 (*0-8493-6198-2*, RC78) CRC Pr.

***Ahluwalia, D. P. S., et al.** White & Deadly: Sugar & Colonialism. LC 99-42760. (Horizons in Post-Colonial Studies). 194p. 1999. 59.00 (*1-56072-710-1*) Nova Sci Pubs.

Ahluwalia, D. P. S., jt. auth. see Ashcroft, Bill.

Ahluwalia, D. Pal. Post-Colonialism & the Politics of Kenya. (Illus.). 257p. (C). 1996. lib. bdg. 85.00 (*1-56072-387-4*) Nova Sci Pubs.

Ahluwalia, Gopal & Carliner, Michael. What Home Buyers Want. 124p. 1989. pap. 115.00 (*0-86718-466-3*) Home Builder.

Ahluwalia, H. P. Eternal Himalaya. 200p. (C). 1982. 180.00 (*81-85017-10-7*, Pub. by Interprint) St Mut.

— Ladakh: Nubra the Forbidden Valley. 176p. (C). 1988. 495.00 (*81-7002-023-9*, Pub. by Himalayan Bks) St Mut.

Ahluwalia, Isher Judge. Industrial Growth in India: Stagnation since the Mid-Sixties. (Illus.). 250p. 1985. 19.95 (*0-19-561787-8*) OUP.

— Productivity & Growth in Indian Manufacturing. (Illus.). 260p. 1992. 27.00 (*0-19-562763-6*) OUP.

Ahluwalia, Isher Judge & Little, I. M., eds. India's Economic Reforms & Development: Essays for Manmohan Singh. LC 98-902983. (Illus.). 412p. 1998. text 35.00 (*0-19-564403-4*) OUP.

Ahluwalia, Isher Judge, et al. Policy Reform in India. 168p. (Orig.). 1996. pap. 30.00 (*92-64-15308-X*, 41-96-10-1) OECD.

— Policy Reform in India. LC 97-914056. (Development Centre Seminars Ser.). 166p. (Orig.). 1997. pap. write for info. (*81-204-1188-9*) Oxford & IBH Pubng.

Ahluwalia, M. S. Social, Cultural & Economic History of Himachal Pradesh. LC 98-909493. 200p. 1998. write for info. (*81-7387-089-6*) Indus Pub.

Ahluwalia, Pal & Nursey-Bray, Paul. Post Colonial Condition: Contemporary Politics in Africa. 247p. 1997. text 75.00 (*1-56072-485-4*) Nova Sci Pubs.

Ahluwalia, Pal & Nursey-Bray, Paul. Post-Colonialism: Culture & Identity in Africa. LC 98-101330. (Horizons in Post Colonial Africa Ser.). 239p. 1997. lib. bdg. 85.00 (*1-56072-453-6*) Nova Sci Pubs.

Ahluwalia, S. K. Indian Forestry Scene. 234p. 1992. pap. 275.00 (*81-7089-165-5*, Pub. by Intl Bk Distr) St Mut.

Ahluwalia, Shashi. Raja Rammohun Roy & the Indian Renissance. (C). 1991. 28.00 (*81-7099-239-7*, Pub. by Mittal Pubs Dist) S Asia.

Ahlvin, Richard G. & Smoots, Vernon A. Construction Guide for Soils & Foundations. 2nd ed. LC 87-34639. (Practical Construction Guides Ser.). 304p. 1988. 120.00 (*0-471-80486-X*) Wiley.

Ahlwardt, Wilhelm. Linguistic & Non-Linguistic Aspects of Qur'an Translating to Yoruba, 10 vols., Set. (Handschriften-Verzeichnisse der Koniglichen Bibliothek Zu Berlin Ser.: Vols. VII-IX, XVI-XXII). (Illus.). lvi, 6042p. 1980. reprint ed. 1950.00 (*3-487-06932-6*) G Olms Pubs.

Ahmad. Canadian Financial Management: Problem Set. 2nd ed. (C). 1993. pap. 36.95 (*0-03-922959-9*) Harcourt Coll Pubs.

— The Optomechanical Engineer Handbook. 416p. 1998. 129.00 incl. cd-rom (*0-8493-9753-7*) CRC Pr.

Ahmad & Verghese. Converting Water into Wealth: Regional Co-Operation in Harnessing the Eastern Himalayan Rivers. 1994. pap. 30.00 (*0-7855-0433-8*, Pub. by Ratna Pustak Bhandar) St Mut.

Ahmad, ed. see Al-Biruni.

Ahmad, A., jt. auth. see Gupta, N. K.

Ahmad, Abdel G. & Mlay, Wilfred. Environment & Sustainable Development in Eastern & Southern Africa: Some Critical Issues. LC 97-28957. 243p. 1998. text 69.95 (*0-312-21047-7*) St Martin.

Ahmad, Abdussalam, ed. see Jiraki, Kalil.

Ahmad, Afzal. Indo-Portuguese Trade in Seventeenth Century (1600-1663) (C). 1991. 21.00 (*0-8364-2785-8*, Pub. by Gian Publng Hse) S Asia.

Ahmad, Aijaz. Lineages of the Present. (C). 65.00 (*1-85984-877-X*, Pub. by Verso) Norton.

***Ahmad, Aijaz.** Lineages of the Present: Ideological & Political Genealogies of Contemporary South Asia. 352p. (C). 2000. 35.00 (*1-85984-765-X*, Pub. by Verso) Norton.

Ahmad, Aijaz. Lineages of the Present: Political Essays. 1996. 48.00 (*81-85229-03-1*, Pub. by Manohar) S Asia.

— Lineages of the Present: Political Essays. 1997. pap. 20.00 (*1-85984-114-7*, Pub. by Verso) Norton.

***Ahmad, Aijaz, et al, eds.** A Singular Voice: Collected Writings of Michael Sprinker. 320p. 2001. 65.00 (*1-85984-796-X*, Pub. by Verso); pap. 22.00 (*1-85984-313-1*, Pub. by Verso) Norton.

Ahmad, Aijazuddin, ed. Social Structure & Regional Development: A Social Geography Perspective. 1993. 52.00 (*81-7033-182-X*, Pub. by Rawat Pubns) S Asia.

Ahmad, Akbar S. Towards Islamic Anthropology. 80p. (Orig.). 1986. pap. 7.50 (*0-317-52455-0*) New Era Publns MI.

Ahmad, Alia. Women & Fertility in Bangladesh. 176p. 1991. 27.50 (*0-8039-9682-9*) Sage.

Ahmad, Aliiaz, ed. see Ghalib, Miza A.

Ahmad, Ameerah H. Echoes & Visions: A Reflection on a Life of Poetry. (Illus.). 96p. 1997. pap. write for info. (*1-881316-77-7*) A&B Bks.

Ahmad, Anees. Handbook of Optomechanical Engineering. LC 96-41742. 416p. 1996. boxed set 169.95 (*0-8493-0133-5*) CRC Pr.

Ahmad, Anis. Muslim Women & Higher Education. 107p. 1992. pap. 4.95 (*1-56744-447-4*) Kazi Pubns.

Ahmad, Aqueil, ed. Science & Technology Policy for Economic Development in Africa. LC 92-40437. (International Studies in Sociology & Social Anthropology: Vol. 61). 1992. pap. 49.00 (*90-04-09659-0*) Brill Academic Pubs.

Ahmad, Ausaf. Indian Muslims: Issues in Social & Economic Development. (C). 1993. 18.00 (*81-85495-19-X*, Pub. by M Manoharial) S Asia.

Ahmad, Aziz. Studies in Islamic Culture in the Indian Environment. (Oxford India Paperbacks Ser.). 328p. 1999. pap. text 17.95 (*0-19-564464-6*) OUP.

Ahmad, Bihar A. Muslims in India Vol. 1: Their Educational, Demographic & Socio-Economic Status with Comparative Indicators for Hindus, Sikhs, Christians & Other Communities, Based on a Singular & Systematic Field Survey 1990-1993, No. 1. (C). 1993. 42.00 (*81-210-0317-2*, Pub. by Inter-India Pubns) S Asia.

Ahmad bin Abubakr Ibn Wahshiya. Ancient Alphabets: or The Long Desired Knowledge of Occult Alphabets Attained, & Hieroglypic Characters Explained: With an Account of the Egyptian Priests, Their Classes, Initiation, & Sacrifices. 2nd large type ed. Robb, Richard, ed. Hammer, Joseph, tr. (ARA & ENG., Illus.). 224p. Date not set. 35.00 (*0-913510-75-0*) Wizards.

Ahmad, Ehtisham, ed. Financing Decentralized Expenditures: An International Comparison of Grants. LC 96-20348. (Studies in Fiscal Federalism & State-Local Finance). 416p. 1997. 100.00 (*1-85898-448-3*) E Elgar.

Ahmad, Ehtisham, et al, eds. Reforming China's Public Finances. 1995. 24.00 (*1-55775-511-6*) Intl Monetary.

Ahmad, Ehtisham & Stern, Nicholas. The Theory & Practice of Tax Reform in Developing Countries. (Illus.). 362p. (C). 1991. text 80.00 (*0-521-26563-0*); pap. text 29.95 (*0-521-39742-1*) Cambridge U Pr.

***Ahmad, Eqbal.** Eqbal Ahmad: Confronting Empire: Interviews with David Barsamian. Barsamian, David, ed. 180p. 2000. 40.00 (*0-89608-616-X*, Pub. by South End Pr) Consort Bk Sales.

— Eqbal Ahmad: Confronting Empire: Interviews with David Barsamian. Barsamian, David, ed. LC 00-29159. (Illus.). 180p. 2000. pap. 16.00 (*0-89608-615-1*, Pub. by South End Pr) Consort Bk Sales.

***Ahmad, Farooq.** Consumer Protection in India: Problems & Prospects. LC 99-936399. 1999. 58.00 (*81-7648-068-1*, Pub. by Ashish Pub Hse) S Asia.

Ahmad, Fazl. Abu Bakr: First Caliph of Islam. (Heroes of Islam Ser.: Bk. 2). 100p. (Orig.). (YA). (gr. 7-12). 1984. pap. 3.50 (*1-56744-240-4*) Kazi Pubns.

— Aisha: The Truthful. (Heroes of Islam Ser.: Bk. 11). 140p. (Orig.). (YA). (gr. 7-12). 1984. pap. 3.50 (*1-56744-238-2*) Kazi Pubns.

— Ali, the Fourth Caliph of Islam. (Heroes of Islam Ser.: Bk. 5). 103p. (Orig.). (YA). (gr. 7-12). 1984. pap. 3.50 (*1-56744-243-9*) Kazi Pubns.

— Husain: The Great Martyr. (Heroes of Islam Ser.: Bk. 12). 150p. (Orig.). (YA). (gr. 7-12). 1984. pap. 3.50 (*1-56744-239-0*) Kazi Pubns.

— Khalid bin Walid: The Sword of Allah. (Heroes of Islam Ser.: Bk. 6). 115p. (Orig.). (YA). (gr. 7-12). 1984. pap. 3.50 (*1-56744-244-7*) Kazi Pubns.

— Mahmood of Ghazni. (Heroes of Islam Ser.: Bk. 8). 120p. (Orig.). (YA). (gr. 7-12). 1984. pap. 3.50 (*1-56744-246-3*) Kazi Pubns.

A

A

— Muhammad bin Qasim. (Heroes of Islam Ser.: Bk. 7). 95p. (Orig.). (YA). (gr. 7-12). 1984. pap. 3.50 (*1-56744-245-5*) Kazi Pubns.

— Muhammad the Prophet of Islam. (Heroes of Islam Ser.: Bk. I). 125p. (Orig.). (YA). (gr. 7-12). 1984. pap. 3.50 (*1-56744-236-6*) Kazi Pubns.

— Muhy-ud Din Alamgir Aurangzeb. (Heroes of Islam Ser.: Bk. 9). 103p. (Orig.). (YA). (gr. 7-12). 1984. pap. 3.50 (*1-56744-247-1*) Kazi Pubns.

— Omar: The Second Caliph of Islam. (Heroes of Islam Ser.: Bk. 3). 100p. (Orig.). (YA). (gr. 7-12). 1984. pap. 3.50 (*1-56744-241-2*) Kazi Pubns.

— Othman, the Third Caliph of Islam. (Heroes of Islam Ser.: Bk. 4). 95p. (Orig.). (YA). (gr. 7-12). 1984. pap. 3.50 (*1-56744-242-0*) Kazi Pubns.

— Some Companions of the Prophet, Pt. I. 115p. (YA). (gr. 4-10). 1985. pap. 3.50 (*1-56744-390-7*) Kazi Pubns.

— Some Companions of the Prophet, Pt. II. 115p. (YA). (gr. 4-10). 1985. pap. 3.50 (*1-56744-391-5*) Kazi Pubns.

— Some Companions of the Prophet, Pt. III. 115p. (YA). (gr. 4-10). 1985. pap. 3.50 (*1-56744-392-3*) Kazi Pubns.

— Sultan Tipu. (Heroes of Islam Ser.: Bk. 10). 120p. (Orig.). (YA). (gr. 7-12). 1984. pap. 3.50 (*1-56744-237-4*) Kazi Pubns.

Ahmad, Feroz. The Making of Modern Turkey. LC 93-20425. (Making of the Modern Middle East Ser.). 240p. (C). 1993. pap. 25.99 (*0-415-07836-9*, B0275) Routledge.

— The Making of Modern Turkey. LC 93-20425. (Making of the Modern Middle East Ser.). 240p. 1993. 55.00 (*0-415-07835-0*, B0271) Routledge.

Ahmad, Ghazi. Sayings of Muhammad. 76p. 1990. pap. 3.00 (*0-933511-47-7*) Kazi Pubns.

Ahmad, Gulzar. Battles of the Prophet of Allah, Vol. 1. 290p. (Orig.). 1986. pap. 12.95 (*1-56744-228-5*) Kazi Pubns.

— Battles of the Prophet of Allah, Vol. 2. 290p. (Orig.). 1986. pap. 12.95 (*1-56744-229-3*) Kazi Pubns.

Ahmad, Habeeb. Mysteries of Sound & Number. 1991. lib. bdg. 79.95 (*0-8490-4992-X*) Gordon Pr.

Ahmad, Hayat. Gas Pipeline Renewal: Insertion Technology. LC 89-48335. 224p. 1990. reprint ed. pap. 69.50 (*0-608-01576-8*, 206199600001) Bks Demand.

Ahmad, Husain. Technological Developments in Drugs & Pharmaceutical Industry in India. (C). 1988. 32.00 (*81-7013-004-2*, Pub. by Navarang) S Asia.

Ahmad, I. Letters from the Great Turke. LC 72-164. (English Experience Ser.: No. 292). 16p. 1971. reprint ed. 10.00 (*90-221-0292-0*) Walter J Johnson.

Ahmad, I., ed. see Metallurgical Society of AIME Staff.

Ahmad Ibn Abi Tahir Taifur. Kitab Bagdad, 2 pts. in 1. xxvi, 548p. reprint ed. write for info. (*0-318-71478-7*) G Olms Pubs.

Ahmad, Ilyas. The Social Contract & the Islamic State. 203p. 1981. 9.95 (*0-318-36777-7*) Asia Bk Corp.

Ahmad, Imad A. Signs in the Heavens. 174p. 1996. pap. 12.00 (*0-614-21610-9*, 1137) Kazi Pubns.

Ahmad, Imad-ad-Dean. Signs in the Heavens: A Muslin Astronomer's Perspective of Religion & Science. LC 92-90710. (Illus.). 174p. (Orig.). 1992. pap. 12.00 (*0-9627854-2-3*) Writers Inc.

Ahmad, Imadad D., jt. auth. see Lane, Rose W.

Ahmad, Imtiaz, ed. Caste & Social Stratification Among Muslims. 2nd ed. 1978. 16.00 (*0-8364-0050-X*) S Asia.

— Family, Kinship & Marriage among the Muslims. LC 77-74484. 1977. 18.50 (*0-88386-757-5*) S Asia.

— Ritual & Religion among Muslims in India. 1982. 20.00 (*0-8364-0852-7*, Pub. by Manohar) S Asia.

Ahmad, Iqbal, ed. see Minerals, Metals & Materials Society Staff.

Ahmad, Jalal A. The School Principal. Newton, John K., tr. (Studies in Middle Eastern Literatures: No. 4). 1983. pap. 12.00 (*0-88297-032-1*) Bibliotheca.

Ahmad, Jalal Al-e. Gharbzadegi: Weststruckness. Green, John & Alizadeh, Ahmad, trs. from PER. LC 82-61280. (Iran-e NO Literary Collection Ser.). (Illus.). 204p. (Orig.). 1982. pap. text 10.95 (*0-939214-07-5*) Mazda Pubs.

Ahmad, Jaleel. Import Substitution, Trade & Development. Altman, Edward I. & Walter, Ingo I., eds. LC 76-52015. (Contemporary Studies in Economic & Financial Analysis: Vol. 11). 236p. 1978. 78.50 (*0-89232-055-9*) Jai Pr.

Ahmad, K. Islam & the West. 1984. pap. 3.00 (*1-56744-074-6*) Kazi Pubns.

Ahmad, K., et al, eds. The Translator's Workbench: Tools & Terminology for Translation & Text Preprocessing in Europe. (Research Reports ESPRIT: Vol. 1). 185p. 1996. pap. 39.00 (*0-387-57645-2*) Spr-Verlag.

Ahmad, Khaliq. Business Practices in India. 1989. 30.00 (*0-8364-2571-5*, Pub. by Popular Prakashan) S Asia.

Ahmad, Khaliq, jt. ed. see Ahmad, Shamim.

Ahmad, Khurshid. Family Life in Islam. 38p. (Orig.). 1974. pap. 3.50 (*0-86037-016-X*) New Era Publns MI.

— Islam: Basic Principles & Characteristics. 24p. 1996. pap. 3.00 (*0-614-21426-2*, 572) Kazi Pubns.

— The Religion of Islam. 28p. (Orig.). 1985. pap. 3.00 (*1-56744-370-2*) Kazi Pubns.

Ahmad, Khurshid, ed. Islam: Its Meaning & Message. 279p. (Orig.). 1976. pap. 8.95 (*0-86037-000-3*, Pub. by Islamic Fnd) New Era Publns MI.

— Studies in Islamic Economics. 390p. (Orig.). 1980. 31.50 (*0-86037-066-6*, Pub. by Islamic Fnd); pap. 15.95 (*0-86037-067-4*, Pub. by Islamic Fnd) New Era Publns MI.

Ahmad, Khurshid, tr. see Maududi, Abul A.

Ahmad, Khurshid, tr. see Maududi, Sayyid A.

Ahmad, Khurshid, tr. & intro. see Al-Maudoodi, Abul A.

Ahmad, M. The Teaching of Islam. 208p. 1984. 150.00 (*1-85077-020-4*, Pub. by Darf Pubs Ltd) St Mut.

Ahmad, M. Munir & Sullivan, William G., eds. Flexible Automation & Integrated Manufacturing, 1994: Proceedings of the 4th International FAIM Conference. LC 94-18962. 875p. 1994. 195.00 (*1-56700-018-5*) Begell Hse.

Ahmad, M. Munir, jt. auth. see Eyada, Osama K.

Ahmad, Mabel L. Sound & Number: The Law of Destiny & Design. 128p. 1996. reprint ed. spiral bd. 12.00 (*0-7873-1275-4*) Hlth Research.

— Sound & Number: The Law of Destiny & Design. 130p. 1996. reprint ed. pap. 11.50 (*1-56459-928-0*) Kessinger Pub.

Ahmad, Marc & Ahmad, Omar. Building Massive Web Sites. (C). 1999. pap. 39.95 (*0-13-767534-8*) P-H.

Ahmad, Mohammad M. & Sullivan, William G. Factory Automation & Information Management: Proceedings of a Conference Held at the University of Limerick, Limerick, Ireland, March 13-15, 1991. 1016p. 1991. boxed set 189.00 (*0-8493-4210-4*, TK) CRC Pr.

— Flexible Automation & Intelligent Manufacturing, 1997: Proceedings of the Seventh International FAIM Conference, European Process Industries Competitiveness Centre, University of Teesside, Middlesbrough, England, June 25-27, 1997. LC 97-15432. 1997. write for info. (*1-56700-089-4*) Begell Hse.

Ahmad, Muhammad Ibn, see Ibn Ahmad, Muhammad.

Ahmad, Mumtaz. A Baluchi Glossary. LC 85-70270. 155p. 1985. text 35.00 (*0-931745-08-X*) Dunwoody Pr.

— Punjabi Reader in the Arabic Script. LC 90-80441. iv, 232p. 1992. 43.00 (*0-931745-65-9*) Dunwoody Pr.

— State Politics in Islam. 160p. (Orig.). 1986. pap. 8.00 (*0-89259-058-0*) Am Trust Pubns.

— Urdu Newspaper Reader. LC 85-70269. xiii, 322p. 1985. text 43.00 (*0-931745-06-3*) Dunwoody Pr.

Ahmad, Mumtaz, contrib. by. Punjabi Reader in the Arabic Script. 1992. audio 19.00 (*0-931745-89-6*) Dunwoody Pr.

Ahmad, N. Muslim Contribution to Geography. 1993. pap. 15.50 (*1-56744-155-6*) Kazi Pubns.

Ahmad, N., ed. Nitrogen Economy in Tropical Soils: Proceedings of the International Symposium on Nitrogen Economy in Tropical Soils Held January 9-14, 1994 in Trinidad, W. I. 444p. (C). 1996. text 294.00 (*0-7923-4094-9*) Kluwer Academic.

Ahmad, N. & Mermut, A., eds. Vertisols & Technologies for Their Management. LC 97-128936. (Developments in Soil Science Ser.: Vol. 24). (Illus.). 566p. 1996. 284.50 (*0-444-88789-X*) Elsevier.

Ahmad, Najma P. Hindustani Music. 1984. 18.50 (*0-8364-1218-4*, Pub. by Manohar) S Asia.

Ahmad, Naseeruddin & Rais, Sarwar. Himalayan Glaciers. LC 98-907617. 1998. 36.00 (*81-7024-946-5*, Pub. by Ashish Pub Hse) S Asia.

Ahmad, Nazeer, jt. auth. see Chang, Y. Austin.

Ahmad, Nazir. University Library Practices in Developing Countries. (Illus.). 220p. 1985. 55.00 (*0-7103-0058-1*) Routledge.

Ahmad, Nyla. Cybersurfer: The Owl Internet Guide for Kids. (Illus.). 72p. (J). 1996. pap. 19.95 incl. disk (*1-895688-50-7*, Pub. by Owl Bks) Firefly Bks Ltd.

Ahmad, Nyla, ed. see Thomas, Keltie.

Ahmad, Omair. A Tangle of Weeds. 1998. pap. write for info. (*1-57553-838-5*) Watermrk Pr.

Ahmad, Omar, jt. auth. see Ahmad, Marc.

Ahmad, P. Color & Learn Salat: Prayer. 32p. (J). 1979. pap. 3.95 (*0-935782-58-3*) Kazi Pubns.

Ahmad, Q. K., jt. ed. see Warrick, Richard A.

Ahmad, Qasim. Britain, Franco Spain & the Cold War, 1945-1950. LC 92-1114. (Modern European History Ser.: No. 2). 336p. 1992. text 30.00 (*0-8153-0737-3*) Garland.

Ahmad, Qazi S. Indian Cities: Characteristics & Correlates. LC 65-28148. (University of Chicago, Department of Geography, Research Paper Ser.: No. 102). 193p. reprint ed. pap. 59.90 (*0-7837-0388-0*, 204070900018) Bks Demand.

Ahmad, Qeyamuddin. Wahhabi Movement in India. (C). 1994. reprint ed. 32.50 (*81-7304-042-7*, Pub. by Manohar Bk Srv) S Asia.

***Ahmad, Rais.** Rural Banking & Economic Development. x, 277p. 1998. 25.00 (*81-7099-710-0*, Pub. by Mittal Pubns) Nataraj Bks.

Ahmad, Raja A., et al, trs. The Precious Gift. Orig. Title: Tuhft al-Nafis. (Illus.). 1982. 55.00 (*0-19-582507-1*) OUP.

Ahmad, Riaz. Quaid-I-Azam Jinnah: A Chronology. 169p. 1989. 12.50 (*1-56744-362-1*) Kazi Pubns.

Ahmad, S. F. Problems & Prospects of Cottage Industries in India. 1990. 33.50 (*81-7041-231-5*, Pub. by Anmol) S Asia.

Ahmad, S. H. The Hidden Mysteries of Number (1912) 62p. 1996. reprint ed. pap. 9.95 (*1-56459-856-X*) Kessinger Pub.

Ahmad, S. Mahmud. Towards Interest Free Banking. 1989. 22.00 (*0-933511-78-7*) Kazi Pubns.

Ahmad, Saghir. Class & Power in a Punjabi Village. LC 76-1663. 174p. reprint ed. pap. 54.00 (*0-7837-6986-5*, 204679800004) Bks Demand.

Ahmad, Saiyad F., ed. see Hassan, Syed K.

Ahmad, Sarfarazuddin. Rural Muslims in Transition. (C). 1991. 26.50 (*81-7169-170-6*, Pub. by Commonwealth) S Asia.

Ahmad, Shaikh, tr. see Iqbal, Muhammad.

Ahmad, Shakil, tr. see Saqr, Abdul B.

Ahmad, Shamim. Rural Marketing in India. (C). 1991. text 19.00 (*81-7024-407-2*, Pub. by Ashish Pub Hse) S Asia.

Ahmad, Shamim & Ahmad, Khaliq, eds. Business & Environment in India. (C). 1990. 22.00 (*81-7024-298-3*, Pub. by Ashish Pub Hse) S Asia.

Ahmad, Sheikh H. The Hidden Mysteries of Numbers. 59p. 1996. reprint ed. spiral bd. 12.00 (*0-7873-1064-6*) Hlth Research.

— The Mysteries of Sound & Number. abr. ed. 89p. 1983. reprint ed. pap. 10.00 (*0-7873-0020-9*) Hlth Research.

Ahmad, Sohrab, jt. auth. see Irons, Bruce.

Ahmad, Suleiman M., ed. see Hardy, Thomas.

Ahmad, Syed N. Capital in Economic Theory: Neo-Classical, Cambridge & Chaos. 512p. 1991. text 120.00 (*1-85278-201-3*) E Elgar.

— Origins of the Muslim Consciousness in India: A World-System Perspective, 29. LC 91-2529. (Contributions to the Study of World History Ser.: No. 29). 328p. 1991. 65.00 (*0-313-27331-6*, ASH, Greenwood Pr) Greenwood.

Ahmad, Taslim. The Quranic Way of Life. LC 97-90616. 121p. 1998. pap. 11.95 (*0-533-12446-8*) Vantage.

Ahmad, Tasneem, tr. see Mirat-Ul-Istalah.

Ahmad, V. U., jt. auth. see Ur-Rahman, A.

Ahmad, Viqar U. & Basha, Anwer. Handbook of Spectroscopic Data of Saponins. 1998. 395.00 (*0-8493-9491-0*) CRC Pr.

Ahmad, Viqar U. & Rahman, A. U. Handbook of Natural Products Data Vol. 2: Pentacyclic Triterpenoids. 1566p. 1994. 768.00 (*0-444-88200-6*) Elsevier.

***Ahmad, Viqar Uddin & Basha, Anwer.** Spectroscopic Data of Saponins: The Triterpenoid Glycosides. LC 00-29248. 2000. write for info. (*0-8493-0869-0*) CRC Pr.

***Ahmad, W. I.** Ethnicity, Disability & Chronic Illness. LC 99-41465. (Race, Health, & Social Care Ser.). 160p. 2000. pap. 32.95 (*0-335-19982-8*) OpUniv Pr.

Ahmad, Waqar I., ed. Race & Health in Contemporary Britain. LC 93-25331. 192p. 1993. pap. 35.95 (*0-335-15697-5*) OpUniv Pr.

Ahmad, Waqar I. & Atkin, Karl, eds. Race & Community Care. LC 95-50908. (Race, Health, & Social Care Ser.). 160p. 1996. 92.95 (*0-335-19463-X*); pap. 28.95 (*0-335-19462-1*) OpUniv Pr.

Ahmad, Wasim, jt. auth. see Jairajpuri, M. Shamim.

Ahmad, Yusuf J. & Muller, Frank G., eds. Integrated Physical, Socio-Economic & Environmental Planning, Vol. 10. (Natural Resources & the Environment Ser.). (Illus.). 216p. 1983. text 105.00 (*0-907567-18-5*, Tycooly Pub); pap. text 55.00 (*0-907567-19-3*, Tycooly Pub) Weidner & Sons.

Ahmad, Zahiruddin, tr. see Rgya-mTsho, Nag-dBan B.

Ahmad, Ziauddin, et al. Money & Banking in Islam. 299p. (Orig.). 1983. pap. 9.95 (*0-939830-27-2*, Pub. by Inst Pol Stud) New Era Publns MI.

Ahmadi. Iranian Islam. LC 98-9376. 281p. 1998. text 65.00 (*0-312-21433-2*) St Martin.

Ahmadian, M., ed. Advanced Automotive Technologies 1993. LC 89-46295. 419p. pap. 75.00 (*0-7918-1046-1*) ASME.

Ahmadjian, Vernon. Flowering Plants of Massachusetts. LC 78-19690. (Illus.). 608p. 1979. 45.00 (*0-87023-265-7*) U of Mass Pr.

— The Lichen Symbiosis. LC 92-42873. 264p. 1993. 79.95 (*0-471-57885-1*) Wiley.

Ahmadjian, Vernon, jt. auth. see Paracer, Surindar.

Ahman, Brita, jt. auth. see Faltskog, Agnetha.

Ahman, Sven, tr. see Menzinsky, George & Blomberg, Erik.

Ahman, Sven, tr. see Menzinsky, George, et al.

Ahman, Sven, tr. see Sjoman, Per, et al.

Ahmann, Elizabeth, ed. Home Care for the High-Risk Infant: A Family-Centered Approach. 2nd rev. ed. LC 96-7422. 256p. 1996. 57.00 (*0-8342-0750-8*) Aspen Pub.

Ahmann, Mathew H. The New Negro. LC 73-77031. 1969. reprint ed. 30.00 (*0-8196-0232-9*) Biblo.

Ahmann, R., et al, eds. The Quest for Stability: Problems of West European Security, 1918-1957. LC 92-28439. (Studies of the German Historical Institute, London). 558p. 1993. text 85.00 (*0-19-920503-5*) OUP.

Ahmansson, Gabriella. A Life & Its Mirrors: A Feminist Reading of L. M. Montgomery's Fiction. LC 91-164517. 1991. pap. 45.00 (*91-554-2673-5*, Pub. by Uppsala Univ Acta Univ Uppsaliensis) Coronet Bks.

Ahmed. Persistant Viral Infections. LC 98-24568. 738p. 1999. 320.00 (*0-471-98083-8*) Wiley.

***Ahmed, Nizam & Norton, Philip, eds.** Parliaments in Asia. LC 98-49311. (Library of Legislative Studies). 180p. 1999. 49.50 (*0-7146-4951-1*, Pub. by F Cass Pubs) Intl Spec Bk.

Ahmed, A. Diagnostic Breast Pathology: A Text & Colour Atlas. (Illus.). 151p. (C). 1992. write for info. (*0-443-03185-1*) Church.

— Geography of the Himalaya. (C). 1991. text 80.00 (*0-7855-0145-2*, Pub. by Ratna Pustak Bhandar) St Mut.

Ahmed, A. S. Thoughts of the Day. 24p. 1986. pap. 30.00 (*0-7223-2052-3*, Pub. by A H S Ltd) St Mut.

Ahmed, Aftab J. Aging Gracefully. (Good Health Guides Ser.). Date not set. pap. 3.95 (*0-87983-873-6*, 38736K, Keats Publng) NTC Contemp Pub Co.

— The Health Benefits of HGH. (Good Health Guides Ser.). 48p. 1998. pap. 3.95 (*0-87983-817-5*, 38175K, Keats Publng) NTC Contemp Pub Co.

***Ahmed, Aisha.** Islam for the Junior. large type ed. 58p. 2000. pap. text 5.00 (*1-879402-71-8*) Tahrike Tarsile Quran.

Ahmed, Akbar. Postmodernism & Islam: Predicament & Promise. LC 91-39584. 304p. (C). (gr. 13). 1992. pap. 24.99 (*0-415-06293-4*, A7179) Routledge.

Ahmed, Akbar, ed. Pakistan Society: Islam, Ethnicity & Leadership in South Asia. (Oxford Pakistan Paperbacks Ser.). (Illus.). 272p. 1997. reprint ed. pap. text 23.00 (*0-19-577837-5*) OUP.

Ahmed, Akbar & Shore, Chris, eds. The Future of Anthropology: Its Relevance to the Contemporary World. LC 95-34567. 280p. (C). 1995. pap. 25.00 (*0-485-12105-0*, Pub. by Athlone Pr); text 85.00 (*0-485-11445-3*, Pub. by Athlone Pr) Humanities.

Ahmed, Akbar S. Discovering Islam: Making Sense of Muslim History. 272p. 1989. 57.50 (*0-7102-1049-3*, 10493, Routledge Thoemms) Routledge.

— Discovering Islam: Making Sense of Muslim History. 272p. (C). 1989. pap. 22.99 (*0-415-03930-4*, A3525, Routledge Thoemms) Routledge.

— Discovering Islam: Making Sense of Muslim History & Society. 252p. 1996. pap. 16.95 (*0-614-21108-5*, 206) Kazi Pubns.

— Islam Today: A Short Introduction to the Muslim World. 272p. 1999. pap. 19.95 (*1-86064-257-8*, Pub. by I B T) St Martin.

— Jinnah, Pakistan & Islamic Identity: The Search for Saladin. LC 97-10613. (Illus.). 304p. 1997. pap. 20.99 (*0-415-14966-5*) Routledge.

— Jinnah, Pakistan & Islamic Identity: The Search for Saladin. LC 97-10613. (Illus.). 304p. (C). 1997. 75.00 (*0-415-14965-7*) Routledge.

— Living Islam: From Samarkand to Stornoway. LC 93-38378. (Illus.). 224p. 1994. 24.95 (*0-8160-3103-7*) Facts on File.

***Ahmed, Akbar S.** Living Islam: From Samarkand to Stornoway. (Illus.). 224p. 1999. 31.95 (*0-7351-0210-4*) Replica Bks.

Ahmed, Akbar S. Pakistan Society: Islam, Ethnicity & Leadership in South Asia. 300p. 1987. 25.00 (*0-19-577350-0*) OUP.

— Toward Islamic Anthropology. (Islamization of Knowledge Ser.: No. 2). 80p. (C). 1986. pap. text 5.00 (*0-912463-05-8*) IIIT VA.

Ahmed, Akbar S., ed. Pakistan: The Social Sciences' Perspective. (Illus.). 310p. 1990. text 21.00 (*0-19-577388-8*) OUP.

Ahmed, Akbar S. & Donan, Hastings, eds. Islam, Globalization, & Postmodernity. LC 94-15614. 240p. (C). 1994. pap. 24.99 (*0-415-09367-8*, B4734) Routledge.

Ahmed, Akber. Postmodernism in Islam. 294p. 1996. pap. 15.95 (*0-614-21168-9*, 970) Kazi Pubns.

Ahmed, Ali J. Daybreak Is Near... Literature, Clans & the Nation-State in Somalia. 232p. 1996. 59.95 (*1-56902-022-1*); pap. 18.95 (*1-56902-023-X*) Red Sea Pr.

Ahmed, Ali J., ed. Invention of Somalia. 282p. (C). 1994. 49.95 (*0-932415-98-9*); pap. 16.95 (*0-932415-99-7*) Red Sea Pr.

Ahmed, Ali J., jt. ed. see Adera, Taddesse.

Ahmed An-Na'im, Abdullahi. Toward an Islamic Reformation: Civil Liberties, Human Rights, & International Law. (Contemporary Issues in the Middle East Ser.). 270p. (Orig.). (C). 1996. pap. 19.95 (*0-8156-2706-8*, ANTIP) Syracuse U Pr.

Ahmed, Ashfaq. Power Electronics for Technology. LC 98-15732. 427p. 1998. 105.00 (*0-13-231069-4*) P-H.

Ahmed, Bashiruddin, jt. auth. see Eldersveld, Samuel J.

Ahmed, Borhanuddin. Generals of Pakistan & Bangladesh. 1993. 30.00 (*0-7069-6859-X*, Pub. by Vikas) S Asia.

Ahmed-Cawthorne, Francheska. Sista Girlfren' Breaks It down... When Mom's Not Around. 160p. 1996. pap. 9.00 (*0-684-81899-X*, Fireside) S&S Trade Pap.

Ahmed-Chamanga, Mohamed. Lexique Comorien (Shindzuani)-Francais. (FRE.). 240p. 1992. pap. 69.95 (*0-7859-1008-5*, 2738416632) Fr & Eur.

Ahmed, E., jt. auth. see Din, Shams U.

Ahmed, Ehsan. The Law & the Song: Hebraic, Christian, & Pagan Revivals in Sixteenth-Century France. LC 97-67748. 172p. (C). 1998. lib. bdg. 42.95 (*1-883479-19-3*) Summa Pubns.

Ahmed, Ehsan, ed. Economic Growth & Human Resource Development in an Islamic Perspective: Proceedings of the Fourth International Islamic Economics Seminar, 1992. LC 93-34903. (Islamization of Knowledge Ser.: No. 15). 107p. (Orig.). 1993. pap. 5.00 (*1-56564-146-9*) IIIT VA.

Ahmed, Ejaz. Commentaries on U. P. Cooperative Societies Act, 1965. 756p. 1984. 330.00 (*0-7855-1421-X*) St Mut.

— Law of Crimes. (C). 1988. 410.00 (*0-7855-3545-4*) St Mut.

— Law of Maintenance. (C). 1988. 85.00 (*0-7855-3560-8*) St Mut.

Ahmed, Ejaz, ed. Commentaries on U. P. Co-Operative Societies Act, 1965. 5th rev. ed. (C). 1989. 200.00 (*0-7855-5632-X*) St Mut.

Ahmed, F. & Almond, D. C. Field Mapping for Geology Students. (Illus.). 88p. 1983. pap. 18.95 (*0-04-550031-2*) Routledge.

Ahmed, F., jt. auth. see Ali, F.

Ahmed, Feroz. Infant Mortality among Black Americans. 110p. 1992. pap. text 10.00 (*1-56669-000-5*) Howard U Inst UAR.

Ahmed, H. & Spreadbury, P. J. Analogue & Digital Electronics for Engineers. (Illus.). 304p. 1984. pap. text 42.95 (*0-521-31910-2*) Cambridge U Pr.

Ahmed, Hasanuddin. An Easy Way to the Understanding of the Qur'an, Vol. 1. 168p. 1987. mass mkt. 5.00 (*0-911119-34-5*) Iqra Intl Ed Fdtn.

— An Easy Way to the Understanding of the Qur'an, Vol. 2. 135p. 1987. mass mkt. 5.00 (*0-911119-35-3*) Iqra Intl Ed Fdtn.

Ahmed, Huda Q., ed. see Halman, Hugh Talat.

Ahmed, Huda Q., ed. see Lemu, B. Aisha.

Ahmed, I., ed. Caste & Social Stratification among Muslim in India. 314p. 1978. 24.95 (*0-318-36798-X*) Asia Bk Corp.

Ahmed-Ibn Ibrahim, jt. auth. see Abu Al-Hasan.

An Asterisk (*) at the beginning of an entry indicates that the title is appearing for the first time.

Ahmed, Iftikhar. Technological Change & Agrarian Structure: A Study of Bangladesh (WEP Study) xiii, 136p. (Orig.). 1981. pap. 13.50 (*92-2-102543-8*) Intl Labour Office.

Ahmed, Iftikhar & Doeleman, Jacobus A., eds. Beyond Rio: The Environmental Issue & Sustainable Livelihoods in the Third World. LC 95-13883. (ILO Ser.). 336p. 1995. text 65.00 (*0-312-12712-X*) St Martin.

Ahmed, Imtiaz. Use of Waste Materials in Highway Construction. LC 92-541. (Illus.). 114p. 1993. 98.00 (*0-8155-1315-1*) Noyes.

Ahmed, Irshad & Morris, David. Replacing Petrochemicals with Biochemicals: A Pollution Prevention Strategy for the Great Lakes Region. LC 94-31806. 55p. (Orig.). 1994. 25.00 (*0-917582-96-9*) Inst Local Self Re.

Ahmed, Irshad, jt. auth. see Morris, David.

Ahmed, Ishtiaq. State, Nation & Ethnicity in Contemporary South Asia. 352p. 1998. pap. 24.95 (*1-85567-578-1*, Pub. by P P Pubs) Cassell & Continuum.

— State, Nation, Ethnicity & the Rise of Separatist Movements in Contemporary South Asia. LC 95-36993. 288p. 1996. 110.00 (*0-86187-747-0*) Bks Intl VA.

Ahmed, Jimmie. Poetic Potpourri. (Illus.). 53p. 1997. pap. 12.00 (*0-9656152-0-0*) Jimmie Ahmed.

Ahmed, K. Fanaticism, Intolerance & Islam. 1983. pap. 3.00 (*1-56744-005-3*) Kazi Pubns.

— Principles of Islamic Education. 1992. 3.00 (*1-56744-193-9*) Kazi Pubns.

Ahmed, Karima Y., jt. auth. see Clegg, Legrand, II.

Ahmed, Kassim. Hadith: A Re-Evaluation. 202p. (Orig.). 1997. pap. 7.50 (*1-881893-02-2*) Universal Unity.

Ahmed, Kazi M., jt. ed. see Tantaratana, Sawasd.

Ahmed, Khalil, et al. A Molecular & Cellular View of Protein Kinase CK2. LC 98-8321. (Developments in Molecular & Cellular Biochemistry Ser.). 16p. 1998. write for info. (*0-7923-8208-0*) Kluwer Academic.

Ahmed Khan, M. Basheer, ed. Perspectives on New Economic Policy. 1989. 14.00 (*81-202-0235-X*, Pub. by Ajanta) S Asia.

Ahmed, Kulsum. Renewable Energy Technologies: A Review of the Status & Costs of Selected Technologies. LC 93-46726. (Technical Papers: No. 240). 184p. 1994. pap. 22.00 (*0-8213-2744-5*, 12744) World Bank.

— Technological Development & Pollution Abatement: A Study of How Enterprises Are Finding Alternatives to Chlorofluorocarbons. LC 94-23780. (Technical Papers: No. 271). 66p. 1995. pap. 22.00 (*0-8213-3120-5*, 13120) World Bank.

Ahmed, Kulsum, jt. auth. see Anderson, Dennis.

Ahmed, Lalita. Vegetarian Cooking. 64p. 1995. 5.98 (*1-57215-022-X*) World Pubns.

Ahmed, Leila. A Border Passage. LC 98-39027. 303p. 1999. text 24.00 (*0-374-11518-4*) FS&G.

***Ahmed, Leila.** Border Passage: From Cairo to America--A Woman's Journey. 320p. 2000. pap. 13.95 (*0-14-029183-0*) Viking Penguin.

Ahmed, Leila. Women & Gender in Islam. 320p. 1996. 26.00 (*0-614-21400-9*, 1325); pap. 15.00 (*0-614-21399-1*, 1325) Kazi Pubns.

— Women & Gender in Islam: Historical Roots of a Modern Debate. 304p. (C). 1993. pap. 17.00 (*0-300-05583-8*) Yale U Pr.

Ahmed, Leila, jt. auth. see Al-Khalidi, Nancy.

Ahmed, M. Economics of Islam. 1982. 15.95 (*0-935782-87-7*) Kazi Pubns.

— A Model to Determine Benefits Obtainable from the Management of Riverine Fisheries of Bangladesh. (ICLARM Technical Reports: No. 28). 133p. 1991. per. write for info. (*971-8709-08-8*, Pub. by ICLARM) Intl Spec Bk.

— Status & Potential of Aquaculture in Small Waterbodies (Ponds & Ditches) in Bangladesh. (ICLARM Technical Reports: No. 37). 36p. 1992. write for info. (*971-8709-28-2*, Pub. by ICLARM) Intl Spec Bk.

Ahmed, M., et al. Aquaculture Technology Adoption in Kapasia Thana, Bangladesh: Some Preliminary Results from Farm Record-Keeping Data. (ICLARM Technical Reports: No. 44). 34p. 1995. write for info. (*971-8709-61-4*, Pub. by ICLARM) Intl Spec Bk.

— Household Socioeconomics, Resource Use & Fish Marketing in Two Thanas of Bangladesh. (ICLARM Technical Reports: No. 40). 82p. 1993. per. write for info. (*971-8709-41-X*, Pub. by ICLARM) Intl Spec Bk.

Ahmed, M. Aziz. Iqbal & Recent Exposition of Islamic Political Thoughts. 3rd ed. 64p. 1982. reprint ed. pap. 4.50 (*1-56744-030-4*) Kazi Pubns.

Ahmed, M. Farid. Capital Markets & Institutions in Bangladesh: Some Implications of Japanese Experience. LC 97-61066. (Illus.). 240p. 1997. text 69.95 (*1-84014-151-4*, Pub. by Ashgate Pub) Ashgate Pub Co.

Ahmed, Moudud. Democracy & the Challenge of Development: A Study of Politics & Military Interventions in Bangladesh. (C). 1995. 42.00 (*0-7069-9726-3*, Pub. by Vikas) S Asia.

Ahmed, N. U. Linear & Nonlinear Filtering for Engineers & Scientists. 250p. 1999. 42.00 (*981-02-3609-3*) World Scientific Pub.

Ahmed, N. U., et al. Engineer-in-Training (E. I. T.) Fundamentals of Engineering (F. E.) Exam - AM Portion. LC 97-67170. 800p. 1998. pap. 49.95 (*0-87891-077-8*) Res & Educ.

Ahmed, Nadir A. Ion Plating Technology: Developments & Applications. LC 86-32476. (Illus.). 183p. 1987. reprint ed. pap. 56.80 (*0-608-06821-7*, 206701800009) Bks Demand.

Ahmed, Naseem, creator. Rainbows: Stories & Customs from Around the World. 80p. 1996. teacher ed. 10.99 (*1-56417-855-2*, GA1561) Good Apple.

Ahmed, Nasir U. Semigroup Theory with Applications to Systems & Control. LC 90-49350. (Pitman Research Notes in Mathematics Ser.: Vol. 246). 298p. 1991. reprint ed. pap. 92.40 (*0-608-03600-5*, 206442300009) Bks Demand.

Ahmed, Nazeer & American Society of Civil Engineers Staff. Ground Water Protection Alternatives & Strategies in the U. S. A. LC 97-8835. 288p. 1997. 27.00 (*0-7844-0231-0*) Am Soc Civil Eng.

***Ahmed, Nizam & Norton, Philip, eds.** Parliaments in Asia. LC 98-49311. (Library of Legislative Studies). 180p. 1999. pap. 24.50 (*0-7146-8010-9*, Pub. by F Cass Pubs) Intl Spec Bk.

Ahmed Nomen Al-Madhaqi. Yemen & the U. S. A. A Super-Power & a Small-State Relationship, 1962-1992. 224p. 1996. text 65.00 (*1-85043-772-6*, Pub. by I B T) St Martin.

Ahmed, P. I. Living & Dying with AIDS. (Illus.). 296p. (C). 1991. 47.50 (*0-306-43851-8*, Plenum Trade) Perseus Pubng.

Ahmed, Paul I., ed. Living & Dying with Cancer. LC 80-27582. 343p. reprint ed. pap. 106.40 (*0-608-16261-2*, 205610000049) Bks Demand.

***Ahmed, Pervaiz.** Learning Through Knowledge Management. 288p. 2000. pap. 37.95 (*0-7506-4710-8*) Buttrwrth-Heinemann.

Ahmed, Rafeeuddin, et al. United Nations No. 21: Better Service, Better Value, Better Management Progress Report to the Secretary-General. (Illus.). 50p. 1998. pap. text 20.00 (*0-7881-7387-1*) DIANE Pub.

Ahmed, Rafiuddin. The Bengal Muslims 1871-1906: A Quest for Identity. 2nd ed. (Oxford University South Asian Studies Ser.). (Illus.). 302p. 1996. reprint ed. pap. text 14.95 (*0-19-563919-7*) OUP.

***Ahmed, Raisuddin.** Out of the Shadow of Famine: Evolving Food Markets & Food Policy in Bangladesh. 2000. pap. 35.00 (*0-8018-6476-3*) Johns Hopkins.

Ahmed, Raisuddin & Donovan, Cynthia. Issues of Infrastructural Development: A Synthesis of the Literature. LC 92-41875. 1992. write for info. (*0-89629-325-4*) Intl Food Policy.

***Ahmed, Raisuddin, et al.** Out of the Shadow of Famine: Evolving Food Markets & Food Policy in Bangladesh. LC 99-41406. 344p. 2000. write for info. (*0-8018-6333-3*) Johns Hopkins.

Ahmed, Raisuddin, jt. ed. see Mellor, John W.

Ahmed, S., jt. auth. see Brattsten, L. B.

***Ahmed, S. E., et al.** Applied Statistical Science III. 327p. 1998. 95.00 (*1-56072-581-8*) Nova Sci Pubs.

Ahmed, S. Z. East of Tien Shan: Unforgettable Journies into China's Ancient Past & Present. LC 98-93066. (Illus.). 262p. 1998. pap. 25.00 (*1-57502-842-5*, PO2312) Morris Pubng.

— The Tales of Imperial China & Asia. LC 97-94625. 182p. 1997. pap. 22.00 (*1-57502-641-4*, P01819) Morris Pubng.

— Travels in Shangri-La. LC 97-95349. 140p. (YA). 1998. pap. 20.00 (*1-57502-709-7*, PO1998) Morris Pubng.

— Twilight on the Silk Road. 1997. pap. text 22.00 (*1-57087-281-3*) Prof Pr NC.

Ahmed Sabri. When I Was a Boy in Turkey. LC 77-87624. (Illus.). reprint ed. 24.50 (*0-404-16450-1*) AMS Pr.

Ahmed, Sadiq. Appropriate Macroeconomic Management in Indonesia's Open Economy. LC 92-47503. (Discussion Papers: No. 191). 33p. 1993. pap. 22.00 (*0-8213-2338-5*, 12338) World Bank.

Ahmed, Safia N. Iqra Book of Verse: Bismillah (in the Name of Allah) (Illus.). 24p. (Orig.). (J). (ps-4). 1991. mass mkt. 5.00 (*1-56316-401-9*) Iqra Intl Ed Fdtn.

— Iqra' Book of Verse Vol. 2: Alhamdu Lillah. (Illus.). 24p. (Orig.). (J). (ps-4). 1991. mass mkt. 5.00 (*1-56316-402-7*) Iqra Intl Ed Fdtn.

Ahmed, Said B. The Swahili Chronicle of Ngazija. Harries, Lyndon, ed. (African Humanities Ser.). (Illus.). 136p. (Orig.). 1977. pap. text 10.00 (*0-941934-20-9*) Indiana Africa.

Ahmed, Saiyid S. Science & God. 11p. 1996. pap. 2.00 (*0-614-21607-9*, 1110) Kazi Pubns.

Ahmed, Salahuddin. The Dictionary of Muslin Names. LC 97-37518. 304p. 1998. pap. 13.95 (*0-8147-0675-4*); text 45.00 (*0-8147-0674-6*) NYU Pr.

Ahmed, Saleem. The Scrabble Word-Building Book. McCarthy, Paul, ed. 608p. (Orig.). 1991. per. 6.99 (*0-671-73456-3*) PB.

Ahmed, Samina, jt. ed. see Cortright, David.

Ahmed, Sara. Differences That Matter: Feminist Theory & Postmodernism. LC 98-20051. 230p. (C). 1999. text 54.95 (*0-521-59225-9*); pap. text 19.95 (*0-521-59761-7*) Cambridge U Pr.

***Ahmed, Sara.** Strange Encounters: Embodied Others in Post-Coloniality. LC 00-28076. 2000. write for info. (*0-415-20185-3*) Routledge.

— Thinking Through Feminism. LC 00-32845. (Transformations Ser.). 2000. write for info. (*0-415-22067-X*) Routledge.

***Ahmed, Shabbir.** When Is the Messiah Coming?? 35p. (YA). 2000. pap. 5.00 (*1-879402-73-4*) Tahrike Tarsile Quran.

— Why I Am Not a Christian! Islam As I Understand. 54p. 1999. text 10.00 (*1-879402-69-6*) Tahrike Tarsile Quran.

***Ahmed, Sirajuddin.** Sheikh Hasina: Prime Minister of Bangladesh. LC 98-909715. x, 375p. 1998. 36.00 (*81-7476-220-5*, Pub. by UBS Pubs) S Asia.

Ahmed, Syed. Incredible Journeys: Around the World. 144p. 1997. pap. 22.00 (*1-57087-316-X*) Prof Pr NC.

— Twilight on the Caucasus: Triumph & Tragedy of Imam Shayml Lion of Daghestan. 232p. 1997. pap. 22.00 (*1-57087-317-8*) Prof Pr NC.

Ahmed, Syed B. Introduction to Quranic Script: Calligraphic Introduction to the Quran. (Illus.). 184p. (C). 1985. text 32.50 (*0-7007-0182-6*, Pub. by Curzon Pr Ltd) Paul & Co Pubs.

Ahmed, Syed Noman. Rapid Rural Transformation Through Voluntary Action. 132p. 1997. pap. 100.00 (*81-7533-052-X*, Pub. by Print Hse) St Mut.

Ahmed, Syed Z. Ruwenzori: Mountains of the Moon. 168p. 1993. pap. 22.00 (*1-880365-72-3*) Prof Pr NC.

— Twilight of an Empire. 128p. 1995. pap. 22.00 (*1-57087-108-6*) Prof Pr NC.

Ahmed, Tarek H. Hydrocarbon Phase Behavior. LC 89-12003. (Contributions in Petroleum Geology & Engineering Ser.: No. 7). (Illus.). 432p. 1989. pap. 134.00 (*0-608-05077-6*, 206563200005) Bks Demand.

***Ahmed, Tarek H.** Reservoir Engineering Handbook. LC 99-53377. 880p. 2000. 155.00 (*0-88415-776-8*) Gulf Pub.

Ahmed, Viqar & Amjad, Rashid. The Management of Pakistan's Economy, 1947-1982. (UGC Series in Economics). (Illus.). 328p. 1985. pap. text 24.00 (*0-19-577316-0*) OUP.

Ahmed, Zafar U., ed. International Business Education Development. LC 96-12261. 93p. (C). 1996. 24.95 (*1-56024-816-5*, Intl Busn Pr) Haworth Pr.

Ahmet, Kemel, jt. auth. see Fallows, Stephen.

Ahmida, Ali A. The Making of Modern Libya: State Formation, Colonization, & Resistance, 1830-1932. LC 93-18526. (SUNY Series in the Social & Economic History of the Middle East). 222p. (C). 1994. text 22.50 (*0-7914-1761-1*) State U NY Pr.

***Ahmida, Ali Abdullatif.** Beyond Colonialism & Nationalism in North Africa. 1999. text 49.95 (*0-312-22287-4*) St Martin.

Ahmos, Zu-Bolton, II. A Niggered Amen. 1975. 6.85 (*0-941490-11-4*) Solo Pr.

Ahn. Tropical Soils & Fertilizer Use. 1992. pap. text. write for info. (*0-582-77507-8*, Pub. by Addison-Wesley) Longman.

Ahn, C. En Medio del Fuego.Tr. of Into the Fire. 9.99 (*0-7899-0615-5*, 497763) Editorial Unilit.

Ahn Carse, Adam Von, see Von Ahn Carse, Adam.

Ahn, Che. Into the Fire: How You Can Enter Renewal & Catch God's Holy Fire, 1. 168p. 1998. 16.99 (*0-8307-2343-9*) Gospel Lght.

— Moving from Renewal to Revival. 168p. 1998. pap. 10.99 (*0-8307-2149-5*) Gospel Lght.

***Ahn, Che, ed.** Hosting the Holy Spirit. 2000. pap. 11.99 (*0-8307-2584-9*, Renew) Gospel Lght.

***Ahn, Chong H. & Frazier, A. Bruno, eds.** Microfluidic Devices & Systems II. 322p. 1999. pap. text 84.00 (*0-8194-3474-4*) SPIE.

Ahn, Chong H., jt. ed. see Frazier, A. B.

Ahn, Gregor & Dietrich, Manfried, eds. Engel und Damonen: Theologische, Anthropologische, und Religionsgeschichtliche Aspekte des Guten und Bosen. (Forschungen zur Anthropologie und Religionsgeschichte Ser.: no. 29). (GER.). 1998. text 24.00 (*3-927120-31-6*, 29) Ugarit-Verlag.

Ahn, Junghyo. Silver Stallion: A Novel of Korea. LC 89-39219. 269p. 1993. pap. 13.00 (*1-56947-003-0*) Soho Press.

Ahn, Mark J., jt. auth. see Falloon, William D.

Ahn, S. H., et al. Asia Pacific Physics Conference: Proceedings of the Fourth, 2 vols. 1568p. 1991. pap. 83.00 (*981-02-0542-2*) World Scientific Pub.

— Asia Pacific Physics Conference: Proceedings of the Fourth, 2 vols., Set. 1568p. 1991. text 263.00 (*981-02-0538-4*) World Scientific Pub.

Ahn, S. S. Handbook of Endovascular Surgery: Vademecum. Obrand, D. I., ed. LC 97-31215. (Karger Landes Systems Publication Ser.). (Illus.). viii, 194p. 1997. 98.00 (*3-8055-6598-4*) S Karger.

Ahn, Samuel S. & Moore, Wesley S. Endovascular Surgery. 2nd ed. (Illus.). 612p. 1992. text 175.00 (*0-7216-4370-1*, W B Saunders Co) Harcrt Hlth Sci Grp.

Ahn, Samuel S., et al. Current Concepts in Endovascular Surgery. (Medical Intelligence Unit Ser.). 103p. 1994. 99.00 (*1-57059-000-1*, LN9000) Landes Bioscience.

Ahn Sang-soo. Bird Patterns: Asian Art Motifs from Korea. (Illus.). 200p. 1996. 42.50 (*89-7059-042-0*, Pub. by Ahn Graphics) Weatherhill.

Ahn, Seung-Joon. From State to Community: Rethinking South Korean Modernization. Chang, Hasok & Jacobson, Eric, eds. LC 94-18041. 128p. (Orig.). 1994. pap. 9.50 (*1-883930-02-2*) AIGIS Pubns.

Ahn, Stephan. Soren Kierkegaard's Ontologie der Bewusstseinsspharen: Versuch Einer Multidisziplinaren Gegenstandsuntersuchung. (GER.). xxi, 289p. 1997. text 27.00 (*3-927120-51-0*, Pub. by Ugarit-Verlag) Eisenbrauns.

Ahn, Steve J. Modern Global Cash Management Vol. 1: A Qualitative Approach. 2nd rev. ed. (Illus.). 402p. 1996. lib. bdg. 28.00 (*0-9650809-1-9*) GDI.

Ahnan, Katherine Van, see Van Ahnan, Katherine.

Ahne, James J., et al. Design & Implementation of a C-Band Single Antenna Polarimetric Active Radar Calibrator. LC TK6585.. (University of Michigan Reports: No. 027587-1-T). 120p. reprint ed. pap. 37.20 (*0-7837-6291-7*, 204600600010) Bks Demand.

Ahne, W. & Kurstak, Eduard, eds. Viruses of Lower Vertebrates. (Illus.). xiii, 518p. 1989. 139.00 (*0-387-50859-7*) Spr-Verlag.

Ahnebrink, L. The Influence of Zola on Frank Norris. (Essays & Studies on American Language & Literature: Vol. 5). 1969. reprint ed. pap. 25.00 (*0-8115-0186-8*) Periodicals Srv.

Ahnen, Katherine Von, see Von Ahnen, Katherine.

Ahnen, Pearl K. Legends & Legacies: (Memories) LC 95-95288. (Illus.). 200p. (Orig.). 1995. pap. 16.95 (*0-9649930-0-7*) Legna Pr.

Ahnert. Sound Reinforcement Engineering. LC 98-29583. 400p. 1998. pap. 144.95 (*0-415-23870-6*) Thomson Learn.

Ahnert, Frank. Introduction to Geomorphology. (Arnold Publications). (Illus.). 360p. 1998. pap. text 35.00 (*0-340-69259-6*) OUP.

Ahnish, Faraj A. The International Law of Maritime Boundaries & the Practice of States in the Mediterranean Sea. LC 92-25901. (Oxford Monographs in International Law). (Illus.). 448p. 1993. text 98.00 (*0-19-825739-2*, Clarendon Pr) OUP.

Ahnlund, Nils G. Gustav Adolf, the Great. Roberts, Michael, tr. from SWE. LC 83-10868. (Illus.). 314p. 1983. reprint ed. lib. bdg. 65.00 (*0-313-24115-5*, AHGU, Greenwood Pr) Greenwood.

Aho & Ullman. Foundations of Computer Science. (C). 1993. teacher ed. 49.60 (*0-7167-8256-1*) W H Freeman.

— Foundations of Computer Science. (C). 1994. text 50.40 (*0-7167-8281-2*) W H Freeman.

Aho, Alfred V. & Hopcroft, John E. The Design & Analysis of Computer Algorithms. 432p. (C). 1974. 54.38 (*0-201-00029-6*) Addison-Wesley.

Aho, Alfred V. & Ullman, Jeffrey D. Foundation of Computer Science. 786p. (C). 1994. text 70.95 (*0-7167-8284-7*) W H Freeman.

Aho, Alfred V., et al. The AWK Programming Language. LC 87-17566. (Computer Science Ser.). (Illus.). 210p. (C). 1988. pap. 44.00 (*0-201-07981-X*) Addison-Wesley.

— Compilers: Principles, Techniques, & Tools. LC 85-15647. 500p. (C). 1986. 69.00 (*0-201-10088-6*) Addison-Wesley.

— Data Structures & Algorithms. 400p. (C). 1983. 57.19 (*0-201-00023-7*) Addison-Wesley.

Aho, James. Politics Righteousness: Idaho Christian Patriotism. LC 90-30168. (Illus.). 320p. 1990. 24.95 (*0-295-96997-0*) U of Wash Pr.

— This Thing of Darkness: A Sociology of the Enemy. LC 94-12015. (Illus.). 224p. 1994. 22.50 (*0-295-97355-2*) U of Wash Pr.

Aho, James A. German Realpolitik & American Sociology: An Inquiry into the Sources & the Political Significance of the Sociology of Conflict. LC 73-21229. 346p. 1975. 40.00 (*0-8387-1453-6*) Bucknell U Pr.

— The Politics of Righteousness: Idaho Christian Patriotism. LC 90-30168. (Samuel & Althea Stroum Bks.). (Illus.). 334p. (C). 1995. pap. 14.95 (*0-295-97494-X*) U of Wash Pr.

— Religious Mythology & the Art of War: Comparative Religious Symbolisms of Military Violence, 3. LC 80-23465. (Contributions to the Study of Religion Ser.: No. 3). 258p. 1981. 59.95 (*0-313-22564-8*, ARM/, Greenwood Pr) Greenwood.

— The Things of the World: A Social Phenomenology. LC 98-23566. 184p. 1998. 55.00 (*0-275-96247-4*, Praeger Pubs); pap. 18.95 (*0-275-96248-2*, Praeger Pubs) Greenwood.

Aho, Jody. The Steamer William Irvin. LC 95-78442. 88p. 1995. pap. 9.95 (*0-932212-85-9*) Avery Color.

Aho, John V. A Butterfly in the Greenhouse. (Orig.). 1984. pap. 4.95 (*0-9613629-0-1*) Townsend Harbor.

— A Clearing of Daisies. (Orig.). 1985. pap. 5.00 (*0-9613629-1-X*) Townsend Harbor.

— East of Education. (Orig.). 1990. pap. text 5.00 (*0-9613629-4-4*) Townsend Harbor.

— Formal Strangers. (Orig.). 1987. pap. text 5.00 (*0-9613629-3-6*) Townsend Harbor.

— Juniper Hill. (Orig.). 1991. pap. text 5.00 (*0-9613629-5-2*) Townsend Harbor.

— Naked. (Orig.). 1986. pap. text 5.00 (*0-9613629-2-8*) Townsend Harbor.

Aho, Juhani. Forbidden Fruit & Other Stores. 93p. 1994. pap. 12.95 (*1-57216-009-8*) Penfield.

Aho, Margaret. The Only Light We Read By. 36p. 1997. pap. 15.00 (*0-931659-37-X*) Limberlost Pr.

— The Only Light We Read By. limited ed. 36p. 1997. 45.00 (*0-931659-38-8*) Limberlost Pr.

Aho, Marja-Leena. The Gift of Healing. (Orig.). 1996. pap. 14.95 (*0-9627954-2-9*) LifeTime OR.

Ahola, Tapani, jt. auth. see Furman, Ben.

Ahonen, Lauri. Missions Growth: A Case Study on Finnish Free Foreign Missions. LC 84-12636. 73p. (Orig.). 1984. pap. 5.95 (*0-87808-335-9*) William Carey Lib.

***Ahonen, Perti & Palonen, Kari, eds.** Disembalming Max Weber. 200p. 1999. pap. 22.95 (*951-39-0426-1*, Pub. by SoPhi Academic) Intl Spec Bk.

Ahonen, Pertti, ed. Tracing the Semiotic Boundaries of Politics. LC 93-25329. (Approaches to Semiotics Ser.: No. 111). (Illus.). ix, 399p. (C). 1993. lib. bdg. 160.00 (*3-11-013533-7*) Mouton.

Ahonen, Pertti & Salminen, Ari. Metamorphosis of the Administrative Welfare State: From Depoliticisation to Political Rationality. LC 98-137309. (Nordeuropaische Beitrage aus den Human- und Gesellschaftswissenschaften Ser.: Bd. 14). 214p. 1997. pap. 42.95 (*3-631-48494-1*) P Lang Pubng.

— Metamorphosis of the Administrative Welfare State: From Depoliticisation to Political Rationality. LC 98-137309. (Nordeuropaische Beitrage aus den Human- und Gesellschaftswissenschaften Ser.: Bd. 14). 214p. 1997. pap. 42.95 (*0-8204-3272-5*) P Lang Pubng.

Ahonen, Risto. Evangelisation Als Aufgabe der Kirche: Theologische Grundlegung Kirchlicher Evangelisation. Nembach, Ulrich, ed. (Forschungen zur Praktischen Theologie Ser.: Bd. 15). (GER.). 174p. 1996. 32.95 (*3-631-30034-4*) P Lang Pubng.

Ahooja-Patel, K., ed. World Economy in Transition: Essays Presented to Surendra Patel on his Sixtieth Birthday. 314p. 1986. text 94.50 (*0-08-031285-3*, Pergamon Pr) Elsevier.

Ahooja-Patel, Krisha. Development Distance Between Nations. (Illus.). xxiv, 291p. 1995. 35.00 (*81-7024-651-2*, Pub. by Ashish Pub Hse) Nataraj Bks.

***Ahooja-Patel, Krishna.** Women & Development. LC 99-935468. 1999. 32.00 (*81-241-0251-1*, Pub. by Har-Anand Pubns) S Asia.

A

A

Ahooja-Patel, Krishna. Women & Sustainable Development: An International Dimension. xvii, 206p. 1995. 20.00 (81-7024-650-4, Pub. by Ashish Pub Hse) Nataraj Bks.

***Ahouse, Jeremy J. & Barber, Jacqueline.** Fingerprinting. rev. ed. Bergman, Lincoln et al, eds. (Great Explorations in Math & Science (GEMS) Ser.). (Illus.). 72p. (J). (gr. 4-8). 2000. reprint ed. pap. 9.00 (0-924886-41-2, GEMS) Lawrence Science.

Ahouse, John. Upton Sinclair: A Descriptive Annotated Bibliography. 180p. (C). 1994. 55.00 (0-923980-35-0) Arundel Pr.

Ahouse, John B., jt. auth. see DeBoer, Kee.

Ahoy, Christopher K. & King, Frederick W. Manual for Selection of Consultants. rev. ed. Meraw, Ken et al, eds. LC 88-70743. (Illus.). 248p. (C). 1991. student ed. 85.00 (0-317-90976-2) Compr Facilities Mgmt.

Ahrari, M. E., ed. Change & Continuity in the Middle East: Conflict Resolution & Prospects for Peace. 256p. 1996. text 65.00 (0-312-12866-5) St Martin.

Ahrari, M. E. & Beal, James. The New Great Game in Muslim Central Asia. (Illus.). 91p. (C). 2000. reprint ed. pap. text 30.00 (0-7881-3492-2) DIANE Pub.

Ahrari, Mohammed E. The Dynamics of Oil Diplomacy: Conflict & Concensus. Bruchey, Stuart, ed. LC 80-608. (Multinational Corporations Ser.). 1981. lib. bdg. 49.95 (0-405-13360-X) Ayer.

— OPEC: The Failing Giant. LC 85-15040. 272p. 1986. 32.00 (0-8131-1552-3) U Pr of Ky.

Ahrari, Mohammed E., ed. Ethnic Groups & U. S. Foreign Policy, 186. LC 87-7512. (Contributions in Political Science Ser.: No. 186). 199p. 1987. 49.95 (0-313-25412-5, AEG/, Greenwood Pr) Greenwood.

Ahrari, Mohammed E. & Noyes, James H., eds. The Persian Gulf after the Cold War. LC 93-13535. 264p. 1993. 65.00 (0-275-94457-3, Praeger Pubs) Greenwood.

Ahrends, Frances. Good Cooking - from Grandma Ahrends & Her Family. Jones, Margaret H., ed. LC 96-230383. (Illus.). 326p. 1996. pap., spiral bd. 17.95 (0-934561-10-9) Propagation Pub.

Ahrendt, Delilah, jt. auth. see Curry, Sharon.

Ahrendt, Mary, et al. Private, No. 5. (Illus.). 93p. 1990. pap. 7.00 (1-881377-00-8) Private Lives.

Ahrens. Critical Care: Certification Practice Exams. 4th rev. ed. LC 97-15239. 690p. (C). 1997. spiral bd. 52.95 (0-8385-1474-X, A-1474-4, Apple Lange Med) McGraw.

— Essential Meteorology. Date not set. pap. text, teacher ed. write for info. (0-314-02046-2) West Pub.

— Essential Meteorology. 1993. pap., student ed. 15.25 (0-314-02047-0) West Pub.

— Essentials of Meteorology. 3rd ed. (Earth Science Ser.). 2000. 42.75 (0-534-57204-9) Wadsworth Pub.

— Essentials of Meteorology with InfoTrac. 2nd ed. (Earth Science Ser.). 1997. 42.75 incl. cd-rom (0-534-53774-X) Wadsworth Pub.

— Meteorology. (Adaptable Courseware-Hardside Ser.). Date not set. mass mkt. 39.96 (0-534-16072-7) Wadsworth Pub.

— Meteorology. 5th ed. Date not set. pap. text, teacher ed. write for info. (0-314-03305-X) West Pub.

— Meteorology. 5th ed. 1994. student ed. 17.75 (0-314-03970-8) West Pub.

— Meteorology Today. 6th ed. 1999. pap. text, student ed. 19.75 (0-534-37209-0) Brooks-Cole.

— Meteorology Today. 6th ed. (Earth Science Ser.). 1999. pap. 51.75 (0-534-55773-2) Wadsworth Pub.

— Meteorology Today: International Version. 6th ed. 1999. pap. text 51.75 (0-534-37379-8) Brooks-Cole.

— Meteorology Today w/Infotrac & Blue Skies Cd. 6th ed. LC 99-32123. 1999. pap. text 60.75 incl. cd-rom (0-534-37201-5) Brooks-Cole.

— Pharmacology. (National Veterinary Medical Ser.). 360p. 1996. pap. text 27.95 (0-683-00085-3) Lppncott W & W.

Ahrens, Art, jt. auth. see Gold, Eddie.

Ahrens, C. Donald. Essentials of Meteorology. 2nd ed. 1998. student ed. 17.25 (0-534-53769-3) Brooks-Cole.

— Essentials of Meteorology: An Invitation to the Atmosphere. Perlee, Clyde & Simon, eds. LC 92-41121. 450p. (C). 1993. pap. 40.25 (0-314-01245-1) West Pub.

— Essentials of Meterology: An Invitation to the Atmosphere. 2nd ed. LC 97-42051. (C). 1997. pap. 42.75 (0-534-53766-9) Wadsworth Pub.

— Meteorology Today: An Introduction to Weather, Climate & the Environment. 4th ed. Perlee, Clyde & Simon, eds. 576p. (C). 1991. text 54.75 (0-314-80905-8) West Pub.

— Meteorology Today: An Introduction to Weather, Climate & the Environment. 5th ed. Perlee, Simon, ed. LC 93-42121. 600p. (C). 1994. pap. 51.75 (0-314-02779-3) West Pub.

Ahrens, C. Lill, et al. Seasoned with Words: Stories, Memoirs & Poems about Food. (Colony House Collection Ser.: Vol. I). (Illus.). 192p. 1998. 22.50 (1-891535-01-3) Oregon Writers.

***Ahrens, Chip & Boxer, Daniel.** Maine Environmental & Land Use Statutes Deskbook. 700p. 1999. pap. text 95.00 (1-881758-58-3) Tower Pub ME.

Ahrens, Chris. Chris Ahrens' Greenhouse. (Illus.). 8p. 1990. 5.25 (0-86619-136-4) Vols Tech Asst.

— Joy Rides. 200p. 1998. pap. 14.95 (0-9640858-2-8) Chubasco Pubng.

— The Surfers Travel Guide: A Handbook to Surf Paradise. LC 96-166032. (Illus.). 225p. (Orig.). (YA). 1995. pap. 14.95 (0-9640858-1-X) Chubasco Pubng.

Ahrens, Chris M. Good Things Love Water: A Collection of Surf Stories. (Illus.). 160p. 1994. pap. 14.95 (0-9640858-0-1) Chubasco Pubng.

Ahrens, Christa, tr. see Flauhaus, Gunter.

Ahrens, Donald L., et al. Concrete & Concrete Masonry. rev. ed. (Illus.). 128p. 1996. pap. text 11.50 (0-913163-28-7, 176) Hobar Pubns.

Ahrens, Edward H. Patient-Oriented Research. (Illus.). 248p. 1992. text 39.95 (0-19-505156-4) OUP.

Ahrens, Edward P., Jr. The Perils of Imprudent Writing: How to Watch What You Write & Stay Out of Court. LC 97-90626. (Illus.). 96p. 1997. pap. 15.95 (0-9658381-3-7) Van Buren.

***Ahrens, Edward P., Jr.** The Perils of Imprudent Writing: How to Watch What You Write & Stay Out of Court. 2nd rev. ed. LC 99-71362. (Illus.). 144p. 1999. pap. 16.95 (0-9658381-6-1) Van Buren.

Ahrens, Heinrich L. De Graecae Linguae Dialectis, 2 vols., Set. xxx, 871p. 1971. reprint ed. 240.00 incl. 3.5 hd (3-487-04180-4) G Olms Pubs.

— Kleine Schriften. xv, 584p. 1977. reprint ed. 145.00 (3-487-06306-9) G Olms Pubs.

Ahrens, Herman C., Jr. Feeling Good about Yourself: Helping Youth Build Self-Esteem. (Looking up Ser.). 24p. (Orig.). 1983. pap. 1.95 (0-8298-0644-X) Pilgrim OH.

— Life with Your Parents: Encouraging Words for the Adolescent. LC 84-27371. (Looking up Ser.). 24p. 1983. pap. 1.95 (0-8298-0667-9) Pilgrim OH.

Ahrens, Jack. Father & Child. 36p. (Orig.). 1995. pap. write for info. (1-885206-18-6, Iliad Pr) Cader Pubng.

Ahrens, John. Preparing for the Future: An Essay on the Rights of Future Generations. (Studies in Social Philosophy & Policy: No. 2). 44p. (Orig.). 1983. pap. 18.95 (0-912051-00-0) Transaction Pubs.

Ahrens, Judy. The North Fork: Photographs from Fifteen Years at the Suffolk Times. (Illus.). 120p. 1993. write for info. (0-9637323-0-7) Lynn Loring Pub.

Ahrens, Kathleen M. Opportunities in Eye Care Careers. (Opportunities In . . . Ser.). (Illus.). 160p. pap. 12.95 (0-8442-8594-3, 297OIEC, VGM Career) NTC Contemp Pub Co.

Ahrens, L. H. Physics & Chemistry of Earth, Vol. 8. 1971. 115.00 (0-08-012630-8, Pergamon Pr) Elsevier.

— Physics & Chemistry of the Earth, Vol. 3. 1959. 200.00 (0-08-009157-1, Pergamon Pr) Elsevier.

— Physics & Chemistry of the Earth, Vol. 4. 1961. 200.00 (0-08-009455-4, Pergamon Pr) Elsevier.

— Physics & Chemistry of the Earth, Vol. 5. 1964. 200.00 (0-08-010191-7, Pergamon Pr) Elsevier.

— Physics & Chemistry of the Earth, Vol. 6. 1965. 175.00 (0-08-010426-6, Pergamon Pr) Elsevier.

— Physics & Chemistry of the Earth, Vol. 7. 1966. 200.00 (0-08-011765-1, Pergamon Pr) Elsevier.

— Physics & Chemistry of the Earth, Vol. 9. 1975. 165.00 (0-08-018017-5) Elsevier.

— Physics & Chemistry of the Earth, Vol. 10. (Illus.). 270p. 1980. 115.00 (0-08-020287-X, Pergamon Pr) Elsevier.

Ahrens, Matt, jt. ed. see Mirsky, Yehudah.

Ahrens, Matthias. Die Moosvegetation des Noerdlichen Bodenseegebietes. (Dissertationes Botanicae Ser.: Band 190). (GER., Illus.). vi, 681p. 1992. pap. 106.00 (3-443-64102-4, Pub. by Gebruder Borntraeger) Balogh.

Ahrens, Philip F., ed. see Pierce Atwood Environmental Department Staff, et al.

Ahrens, Prudence H. Salt-Free Baking at Home. 1985. pap. 10.95 (0-911506-19-5) Thueson.

Ahrens, Rhudiger, jt. auth. see Cope, Kevin Lee.

Ahrens, Robert H., Jr. Monarch Notes on Aeschylus' Plays. (Orig.). (C). 3.95 (0-671-00801-3, Arco) Macmillan Gen Ref.

***Ahrens, Robin I.** My Building. LC 97-62300. (Illus.). 32p. (J). (ps-1). 1998. 15.95 (1-890817-06-6, Pub. by Winslow Pr) Publishers Group.

***Ahrens, Robin Isabel.** Dee & Bee. LC 99-37945. (Illus.). 32p. (J). (ps-1). 2000. 14.95 (1-890817-26-0, Pub. by Winslow Pr) Publishers Group.

Ahrens, Rudiger, ed. see Panagopoulos, Nic.

Ahrens, T. J., ed. Global Earth Physics: A Handbook of Physical Constants. LC 94-44745. (AGU Reference Shelf Ser.: Vol. 1). 380p. 1995. 60.00 (0-87590-851-9) Am Geophysical.

— A Handbook of Physical Constants, 3 vols., Set. (AGU Reference Shelf Ser.: Vols. 1-3). 1000p. 1995. 160.00 (0-87590-854-3) Am Geophysical.

— Mineral Physics & Crystallography: A Handbook of Physical Constants. LC 95-3663. (AGU Reference Shelf Ser.: Vol. 2). 400p. 1995. 65.00 (0-87590-852-7) Am Geophysical.

— Rock Physics & Phase Relations: A Handbook of Physical Constants. LC 95-3664. (AGU Reference Shelf Ser.: Vol. 3). 270p. 1995. 50.00 (0-87590-853-5) Am Geophysical.

Ahrens, Thomas. Contrasting Involvements: A Study of Management Accounting Practices. (Management Organizations & Society Ser.: Vol. 1). 148p. 1999. text 38.00 (90-5702-351-2, Harwood Acad Pubs) Gordon & Breach.

— High Growth Companies: Driving the Tiger. 2nd ed. LC 98-25004. 220p. 1998. 74.95 (0-566-08030-3, Pub. by Gower) Ashgate Pub Co.

Ahrens, Thomas & Rutherford, Kim. Essentials of Oxygenation. (Nursing-Health Science Ser.). 194p. 1992. 56.25 (0-86720-332-3) Jones & Bartlett.

Ahrens, Thomas S. Hemodynamic Waveform Analysis. 1992. pap. text 39.95 (0-7216-4099-5, W B Saunders Co) Harcrt Hlth Sci Grp.

— Hemodynamic Waveform Recognition. (Illus.). 224p. 1993. pap. text 23.00 (0-7216-4313-2, W B Saunders Co) Harcrt Hlth Sci Grp.

***Ahrens, Tino.** From Dirac to Neutrino Oscillations. LC 00-41595. 2000. write for info. (0-7923-7886-5) Kluwer Academic.

***Ahrens, Toni.** Design Makes a Difference: Shipbuilding in Baltimore, 1795-1835. LC 99-183110. xviii, 205p. 1998. 20.00 (0-7884-1001-6) Heritage Bk.

Ahrensdorf, Peter J. The Death of Socrates & the Life of Philosophy: An Interpretation of Plato's Phaedo. LC 94-40812. 238p. (C). 1995. text 65.50 (0-7914-2633-5); pap. text 21.95 (0-7914-2634-3) State U NY Pr.

Ahrensdorf, Peter J., jt. auth. see Pangle, Thomas L.

Ahrensfeld, Janet L., et al. Special Libraries: A Guide for Management. 2nd ed. LC Z 0675.A2A43. (Illus.). 85p. reprint ed. pap. 30.00 (0-7837-1184-0, 204171300023) Bks Demand.

Ahrentzen, Sherry. Blurring Boundaries: Socio-Spatial Consequences of Working at Home. (Publications in Architecture & Urban Planning: No. R87-4). (Illus.). vii, 221p. (C). 1987. 20.00 (0-938744-53-4) U of Wis Ctr Arch-Urban.

— Hybrid Housing: A Contemporary Building Type for Multiple Residential & Business Use. (Publications in Architecture & Urban Planning: No. R92-1). (Illus.). 145p. (C). 1992. per. 18.00 (0-938744-77-1) U of Wis Ctr Arch-Urban.

Ahrikencheikh, Cherif & Seireg, Ali A. Optimized-Motion Planning: Theory & Implementation. 366p. 1994. 110.00 incl. disk (0-471-01903-8) Wiley.

Ahrne, Goran. Agency & Organization: Towards an Organizational Theory of Society. 160p. 1991. 45.00 (0-8039-8292-5); pap. 19.95 (0-8039-8293-3) Sage.

— Social Organizations: Interaction Inside, Outside & Between Organizations. 160p. 1994. 69.95 (0-8039-8920-2); pap. 24.95 (0-8039-8921-0) Sage.

Ahrne, Goran, et al, eds. Class & Social Organisation in Finland, Sweden & Norway. (Acta Universitatis Upsaliensis Studia Sociologica: No. 28). 154p. (Orig.). 1988. pap. 37.50 (91-554-2196-2, Pub. by Uppsala Univ Acta Univ Uppsaliensis) Coronet Bks.

Ahronheim. Handbook of Prescribing Medications for Geriatric Patients. 1992. pap. 34.95 (0-316-02042-7, A2305) Lppncott W & W.

Ahronheim, Judith & Weber, Doron. Final Passages: Positive Choices for the Dying & Their Loved Ones. 160p. 1992. 18.00 (0-671-78025-5) S&S Trade.

Ahronheim, Judith C., et al. Ethics in Clinical Practice. LC 99-42872. 508p. 1998. 59.00 (0-8342-1075-4, 10754) Aspen Pub.

Ahronheim, Judith C., jt. ed. see Rowe, John W.

***Ahroni, Jessie.** 101 Foot Care Tips for People with Diabetes. LC 99-55685. 128p. 2000. pap. 12.95 (1-58040-040-X, 0040XQ, Pub. by Am Diabetes) NTC Contemp Pub Co.

Ahroni, Reuben. The Jews of the British Crown Colony of Aden: History, Culture & Ethnic Relations. LC 94-18187. (Series in Jewish Studies: Vol. 12). xiv, 314p. 1994. 110.50 (90-04-10110-1) Brill Academic Pubs.

— Yemenite Jewry: Origins, Culture, & Literature. LC 84-48649. (Jewish Literature & Culture Ser.). (Illus.). 239p. 1986. reprint ed. pap. 74.10 (0-7837-3689-4, 205786700009) Bks Demand.

Ahronovitz, Ehoud & Fiorio, Christophe, eds. Discrete Geometry for Computer Imagery: Proceedings of the 7th International Workshop, DGCI 097, Montpellier, France, December 3-5, 1997, Vol. 134. LC 97-45949. (Lecture Notes in Computer Science Ser.: Vol. 1347). x, 255p. 1997. pap. 49.00 (3-540-63884-9) Spr-Verlag.

Ahrons, Constance. The Good Divorce. 320p. 1998. pap. 14.00 (0-06-092634-1, Perennial) HarperTrade.

Ahrons, Constance R. Divorced Families. 1989. pap. 10.95 (0-393-30622-4) Norton.

Ahronson, Meir & Or, Galia B. A Delicate Balance: Six Israeli Photographers. (Illus.). 64p. (Orig.). 1996. pap. 14.95 (0-9642772-1-2) Light Factory.

Ahrweiler, F. & Gilbert, N., eds. Computer Simulations in Science & Technology Studies. LC 98-39440. (Illus.). x, 244p. 1998. 78.00 (3-540-64871-2) Spr-Verlag.

Ahrweiler, Helene G. & Laiou, Angeliki E., eds. Studies on the Internal Diaspora of the Byzantine Empire. LC 96-53525. 1998. 30.00 (0-88402-247-1, ALBD) Dumbarton Oaks.

Ahrweiler, Petra. Analyzing Tabular Data: Loglinear & Logistic Models for Social Researchers. (Social Research Today Ser.: No. 1). 224p. 1993. pap. 25.00 (1-85728-091-1, Pub. by UCL Pr Ltd) Taylor & Francis.

— Researching Social Life. 352p. (C). 1993. text 65.00 (0-8039-8681-5); pap. text 22.95 (0-8039-8682-3) Sage.

Ahrweiler, Petra, et al, eds. Fordism & Flexibility: Divisions & Change. LC 91-23419. 160p. 1992. text 49.95 (0-312-06871-9) St Martin.

Ahrweiler, Petra & Conte, Rosaria, eds. Artificial Societies: The Computer Simulation of Social Life. LC 94-47440. 1995. 75.00 (1-85728-305-8, Pub. by UCL Pr Ltd) Taylor & Francis.

Ahrweiler, Petra & Monk, Andrew F., eds. Perspectives on HCI: Diverse Approaches. (Computers & People Ser.). (Illus.). 312p. 1995. text 63.00 (0-12-504575-1) Acad Pr.

Ahsan, Aitzaz. Indus Rediscovered: The Story of Pakistan. (Illus.). 430p. 1997. text 39.95 (0-19-577693-3) OUP.

Ahsan, I. Textbook of Surgery. 2nd ed. 410p. 1997. text 49.00 (90-5702-139-0, Harwood Acad Pubs); pap. text 25.00 (90-5702-140-4, Harwood Acad Pubs) Gordon & Breach.

Ahsan, M. M. Children's Book of Islam, Pts. One & Two. 56p. (J). 1996. pap. 3.95 (0-614-20996-X, 131) Kazi Pubns.

— Social Life under the Abbasids. 315p. 1979. 45.00 (0-86685-592-0) Intl Bk Ctr.

Ahsan, Manazir. Islam: Faith & Practice. (Illus.). 48p. (Orig.). 1980. pap. 3.00 (0-86037-001-1, Pub. by Islamic Fnd) New Era Publns MI.

Ahsan, Nilofer & Cramer, Lina. How Are We Doing? A Program Self-Assessment Toolkit for the Family Support Field. LC 98-51508. 135p. 1998. 32.50 (1-885429-22-3) Family Resource.

Ahsan, Tanveer. Process Analysis & Optimization of Direct Horizontal-Flow Roughing Filtration. (Illus.). 194p. (C). 1995. pap. text 52.00 (90-5410-635-2, Pub. by A A Balkema) Ashgate Pub Co.

Ahsanullah, M. History of the Islamic World. 311p. 1987. text 37.50 (0-89891-016-1, Pub. by Deep & Deep Pubns) Advent Bks Div.

Ahsanullah, M., ed. Applied Statistical Science Vol. 2: Papers in Honor of Professor Munir Ahmad. LC 98-117629. 267p. 1997. lib. bdg. 115.00 (1-56072-469-2) Nova Sci Pubs.

Ahsanullah, M. & Bhoj, D. S., eds. Applied Statistical Science. 285p. (C). 1996. lib. bdg. 95.00 (1-56072-405-6) Nova Sci Pubs.

***Ahsanullah, M. & Yildirim, F., eds.** Applied Statistical Science IV. 285p. 1999. 97.00 (1-56072-682-2) Nova Sci Pubs.

Ahsanullah, Mohammad. Record Statistics. (Illus.). 227p. (C). 1994. lib. bdg. 115.00 (1-56072-203-7) Nova Sci Pubs.

Ahsen, Akhter. Age Projection Test: Short-Term Imagery Treatment of Hysterias Phobias & Other Themes. LC 88-62767. 71p. 1988. pap. text. write for info. (0-913412-17-1) Brandon Hse.

— Aphrodite: The Psychology of Consciousness. LC 88-61344. 185p. 1988. pap. 14.95 (0-913412-25-2) Brandon Hse.

— Basic Concepts in Eidetic Psychotherapy. 434p. 1973. text 35.00 (0-913412-12-0) Brandon Hse.

— Eidetic Parents Test: Desk Volume. LC 89-62539. 96p. 1989. student ed. 19.95 (0-913412-01-5) Brandon Hse.

— Eidetic Parents Test & Analysis. 256p. 1972. 35.00 (0-913412-02-3) Brandon Hse.

— Ganesh: The Broken & the Misshapen. Invocation & Commentary on Consciousness. (Orig.). 1995. pap. 20.00 (0-913412-78-3) Brandon Hse.

— Hyponoia: The Underneath Sense of Being. 100p. (Orig.). (C). 1990. pap. text 9.95 (0-913412-36-8) Brandon Hse.

— Illuminations on the Path of Solomon. LC 94-239536. 627p. (Orig.). (C). 1994. pap. text 30.00 (0-913412-66-X) Brandon Hse.

— Imagery Paradigm: Imaginative Consciousness in the Experimental & Clinical Setting. LC 93-71037. 465p. (Orig.). 1993. pap. text 25.00 (0-913412-49-X) Brandon Hse.

— Manhunt in the Desert. 1979. pap. 9.95 (0-913412-26-0) Brandon Hse.

— New Surrealism. 542p. 1992. pap. 25.00 (0-913412-52-X) Brandon Hse.

— Oedipus at Thebes. LC 83-70541. 80p. (Orig.). 1984. pap. 9.95 (0-913412-35-X) Brandon Hse.

— Prolucid Dreaming. 312p. (C). 1992. pap. text 25.00 (0-913412-43-0) Brandon Hse.

— Psycheye. 288p. 1977. 30.00 (0-913412-47-3) Brandon Hse.

— Rhea Complex: A Detour Around the Oedipus Complex. LC 84-72149. 279p. 1984. 35.00 (0-913412-24-4) Brandon Hse.

— Trojan Horse: Imagery in Psychology, Literature, Art & Politics. LC 84-72150. 287p. 1984. 35.00 (0-913412-20-1) Brandon Hse.

— Unvividness Paradox: Dynamics of Imagery Formation. LC 89-62540. 250p. 1990. pap. text 24.95 (0-913412-46-5) Brandon Hse.

Ahsen, Akhter, ed. Behaviorists' Misconduct in Science. 200p. (C). 1990. pap. text 25.00 (0-913412-21-X) Brandon Hse.

— Imagery & Sociology. 368p. (Orig.). (C). 1991. pap. text 25.00 (0-913412-51-1) Brandon Hse.

— Mental Imagery Abstracts: The Journal of Mental Imagery, 1977-1989. LC 89-62538. 302p. 1989. pap. text 29.95 (0-913412-42-2) Brandon Hse.

Ahsen, Anette Von, see Von Ahsen, Anette.

AHSGR Staff, compiled by. Kuche Kochen. (Illus.). 238p. (J). (gr. 9-12). 1973. pap. text 18.00 (0-914222-10-4) Am Hist Soc Ger.

Ahterberg, E. & Lanz, K. Enzyklopadisches Lexikon Fur des Geld, Bank und Borsen Wesen, 2 vols., Set. (GER.). 1967. 325.00 (0-7859-0566-9, M7364) Fr & Eur.

Ahti, Teuvi, ed. see Nylander, William.

Ahti, Teuvo, ed. & pref. see Nylander, Wiliam.

Ahti, Teuvo, ed. & pref. see Nylander, William.

Ahto, Kimberly, ed. The Best of Art Culinaire, Issues 1-14. (Illus.). 328p. 1999. 38.00 (0-9623729-3-5) Culinaire.

Ahtone, Heather, et al, eds. Voices of Thunder: New Work from the Institute of American Indian Arts. (IAIA Anthology Ser.: No. 4). 184p. 1992. pap. text 8.00 (1-881396-03-7) IOA Indian Arts.

Ahtone, Heather & Coke, Allison H., eds. It's Not Quiet Anymore: New Work from the Institute of American Indian Arts. 1993. pap. 10.00 (1-881396-08-8) IOA Indian Arts.

Ahuadero, Francisco. Dictionary of Audiovisual Communication: Spanish-English, English-Spanish. (ENG & SPA.). 199p. 1991. pap. 49.95 (0-7859-7453-9, 8428318794) Fr & Eur.

Ahues, Mario, jt. auth. see Chatelin, Francois.

***Ahuja.** Handbook of Bio-Separations. (Separation Science & Technology Ser.). 684p. 2000. 159.95 (0-12-045540-4) Morgan Kaufmann.

Ahuja. Impurities Evaluation of Pharmaceuticals. LC 98-5185. (Illus.). 304p. 1998. text 135.00 (0-8247-9884-8) Dekker.

— Selectivity & Detectability Optimizations in HPLC. LC 88-38315. (Chemical Analysis Ser.). 624p. 1989. 195.00 (0-471-62645-7) Wiley.

Ahuja, Anil, jt. ed. see Evans, Rhodri.

Ahuja, B. N. Encyclopedia of General Knowledge. 540p. 1997. pap. 500.00 (81-209-1021-4, Pub. by Pitambar Pub) St Mut.

An Asterisk (*) at the beginning of an entry indicates that the title is appearing for the first time.

— Encyclopedia of India. 120p. 1998. pap. 195.00 (*81-209-1022-2*, Pub. by Pitambar Pub) St Mut.
— Encyclopedia of World. 418p. 1998. pap. 395.00 (*81-209-1010-9*, Pub. by Pitambar Pub) St Mut.
— Everyday Quiz. 264p. 1995. pap. 45.00 (*81-209-0824-4*, Pub. by Pitambar Pub) St Mut.
Ahuja, B. N. & Burn, Ashley. Pitambar's Encyclopaedia of General Knowledge & Current Affairs. 1992. 60.00 (*81-209-0000-6*, Pub. by Pitambar Pub) St Mut.
Ahuja, B. N. & Saxena, Paresh. Pitambar's Handbook of General Knowledge. 344p. (C). 1997. pap. 60.00 (*81-209-0516-4*, Pub. by Pitambar Pub) St Mut.
Ahuja, B. N., jt. auth. see Job, Alexander S.
Ahuja, D. R. Folklore of Rajasthan. 176p. 1980. 7.95 (*0-318-36320-8*) Asia Bk Corp.
Ahuja, Dilip. The Incremental Cost of Climate Change Mitigation Projects: First Steps Toward a Framework for Assessment. (Global Environment Facility (GEF) Working Paper Ser.: No. 9). 34p. 1994. pap. 22.00 (*1-884122-09-4*, 72209) World Bank.
Ahuja, H. N. Construction Performance Control by Networks. LC 76-4774. (Construction Management & Engineering Ser.). (Illus.). 660p. 1976. reprint ed. pap. 200.00 (*0-7837-3422-0*, 205774300008) Bks Demand.
Ahuja, Hira N. & Walsh, Michael A. Successful Methods in Cost Engineering. LC 82-17316. 398p. (Orig.). 1986. reprint ed. 51.95 (*0-471-86435-8*, JW) Krieger.
Ahuja, Hira N., et al. Project Management: Techniques in Planning & Controlling Construction Projects. 2nd ed. 520p. 1994. 99.00 (*0-471-59168-8*) Wiley.
Ahuja, Ila & Ahuja, M. Raj. Bhagavad Gita: A New Perspective - A Universal Message for the Modern Society. 1995. pap. 12.50 (*0-7069-9467-1*, Pub. by Vikas) S Asia.
Ahuja, Jay. Field of Dreams: A Guide to Visiting & Enjoying All 30 Major League Ballparks. LC 97-45700. (Illus.). 224p. 1998. pap. 17.95 (*0-8065-1965-7*) Carol Pub Group.
Ahuja, Kanta, et al, eds. Regime Transformations & Global Realignments: Indo-European Dialogues on the Post-Cold War World. (Indo-Dutch Studies on Development Alternatives: Vol. 11). (Illus.). 390p. (C). 1993. text 39.95 (*0-8039-9131-2*) Sage.
***Ahuja, Lajpat, et al.** Root Zone Quality Model: Modelling Management Effects on Water Quality & Crop Production. LC 97-61378. 372p. 2000. 98.00 (*1-887201-08-4*) WRP.
***Ahuja, M. L.** Electoral Politics & General Elections in India, 1952-1998. LC 98-908227. (Illus.). ix, 412p. 1998. 38.00 (*81-7099-711-9*, Pub. by Mittal Pubns) Nataraj Bks.
Ahuja, M. L. & Paul, Sharda. General Elections in India, 1989-1991. 250p. 1992. 27.95 (*81-7045-085-3*, Pub. by Manohar) S Asia.
Ahuja, M. R. Cancer Causes & Prevention. 1997. pap. 12.50 (*81-7476-159-4*, Pub. by UBS Pubs) S Asia.
Ahuja, M. R., ed. Micropropagation of Woody Plants. LC 92-14824. (Forestry Sciences Ser.: Vol. 41). 528p. 1992. text 307.50 (*0-7923-1807-2*) Kluwer Academic.
— Somatic Cell Genetics of Woody Plants. (Forestry Sciences Ser.). (C). 1988. text 120.00 (*90-247-3728-1*) Kluwer Academic.
— Woody Plant Biotechnology. (NATO ASI Ser.: Vol. 210). (Illus.). 392p. (C). 1991. text 150.00 (*0-306-44019-9*, Kluwer Plenum) Kluwer Academic.
Ahuja, M. R. & Libby, W. J., eds. Clonal Forestry. LC 92-25603. 1993. 158.95 (*0-387-52501-7*) Spr-Verlag.
— Clonal Forestry II: Conservation & Application. (Illus.). ix, 292p. 1993. 158.95 (*0-387-55174-8*) Spr-Verlag.
Ahuja, M. R., et al. Somatic Cell Genetics & Molecular Genetics of Trees. LC 96-30329. (Forestry Sciences Ser.). 1996. lib. bdg. 130.00 (*0-7923-4179-1*) Kluwer Academic.
Ahuja, M. Raj, jt. auth. see Ahuja, Ila.
Ahuja, Narendra, jt. ed. see Bowyer, Kevin.
Ahuja, O. P., jt. auth. see Jain, P. K.
Ahuja, Paul. On the DMZ. 26p. 1994. pap. 2.50 (*0-89567-124-7*) World View Forum.
Ahuja, Ram. Crime Against Women. 216p. 1987. 24.95 (*81-7033-022-X*) Asia Bk Corp.
— Indian Social System. (C). 1993. 38.00 (*81-7033-196-X*, Pub. by Rawat Pubns); pap. 14.00 (*81-7033-197-8*, Pub. by Rawat Pubns) S Asia.
— Rights of Women: A Feminist Perspective. (C). 1992. 20.00 (*81-7033-172-2*, Pub. by Rawat Pubns) S Asia.
— Social Problems in India. (C). 1992. 35.00 (*81-7033-138-2*, Pub. by Rawat Pubns) S Asia.
— Youth & Crime LC 96-904826. 176p. 1996. write for info. (*81-7033-334-2*) Rawat Pubns.
Ahuja, Ravindra K., et al. Network Flows: Theory, Algorithms, & Applications. 864p. 1993. 105.00 (*0-13-617549-X*) P-H.
Ahuja, Sarayu. Where the Streets Lead. LC 97-902620. (Illus.). 1997. write for info. (*0-14-025952-X*) Penguin Books.
Ahuja, Satinder. Chiral Separations by Chromatography. LC 98-55565. (An American Chemical Society Publication). (Illus.). 256p. 2000. text 85.00 (*0-8412-3631-3*) OUP.
— Trace & Ultratrace Analysis by HPLC. LC 91-7276. (Chemical Analysis: A Series of Monographs on Analytical Chemistry & Its Applications). 432p. 1991. 129.00 (*0-471-51419-5*) Wiley.
Ahuja, Satinder, ed. Chiral Separations: Applications & Technology. LC 96-3458. (ACS Professional Reference Bk.). (Illus.). 368p. 1996. text 105.00 (*0-8412-3407-8*, Pub. by Am Chemical) OUP.
— Chiral Separations by Liquid Chromatography. LC 91-4970. (ACS Symposium Ser.: No. 471). (Illus.). 239p. 1991. text 65.00 (*0-8412-2116-2*, Pub. by Am Chemical) OUP.
— Chromatography & Separation Chemistry: Advances & Developments. LC 85-28694. (Symposium Ser.: No. 297). (Illus.). viii, 312p. 1986. 57.95 (*0-8412-0953-7*, Pub. by Am Chemical) OUP.
— Chromatography & Separation Chemistry: Advances & Developments. LC 85-28694. 312p. reprint ed. pap. 96.80 (*0-608-03924-1*, 206437100009) Bks Demand.
— Chromatography of Pharmaceuticals: Natural, Synthetic, & Recombinant Products. LC 92-49380. (ACS Symposium Ser.: No. 512). (Illus.). 211p. 1992. text 65.00 (*0-8412-2498-6*, Pub. by Am Chemical) OUP.
— Ultrahigh Resolution Chromatography. LC 84-2792. (ACS Symposium Ser.: No. 250). 237p. 1984. lib. bdg. 49.95 (*0-8412-0835-2*) Am Chemical.
— Ultrahigh Resolution Chromatography. LC 84-2792. (ACS Symposium Ser.: No. 250). (Illus.). 240p. 1984. reprint ed. pap. 74.40 (*0-608-03134-8*, 206358700007) Bks Demand.
— Ultratrace Analysis of Pharmaceuticals & Other Compounds of Interests. LC 85-29407. (Chemical Analysus Ser.). 384p. 1986. 210.00 (*0-471-82673-1*) Wiley.
***Ahuja, Shyam, et al.** Dhurrie: Flatwoven Rugs of India. (Illus.). 272p. 2000. 125.00 (*1-85149-338-7*, Pub. by V&A Ent) Antique Collect.
Ahuja, Sunil & Dewhirst, Robert E. Goverment at Work: Issue Evolution, Passage, Implementation & Feedback. 242p. (C). per. 31.95 (*0-7872-6736-8*) Kendall-Hunt.
— Government at Work: Issue Evolution, Passage, Implementation & Feedback LC 98-67149. xii, 235 p. 1998. write for info. (*0-7872-5153-4*) Kendall-Hunt.
Ahuja, V. Design & Analysis of Computer Communication Networks. (C). 1982. text 81.00 (*0-07-000697-0*) McGraw.
Ahuja, Vijay. Network & Internet Security. (Illus.). 324p. 1999. reprint ed. pap. text 20.00 (*0-7881-6507-0*) DIANE Pub.
— Secure Commerce on the Internet. LC 96-30881. (Illus.). 298p. 1996. pap. text 29.95 (*0-12-045597-8*) Morgan Kaufmann.
Ahuja, Vinod, et al. Everyone's Miracle: Revisiting Poverty & Inequality in East Asia. LC 97-26454. (Directions in Development Ser.). 116p. 1997. pap. 22.00 (*0-8213-3979-6*, 13979) World Bank.
Ahulwalia, Shashi. Assassination of Rajiv Gandhi. (C). 1991. text 22.00 (*81-7099-315-6*, Pub. by Mittal Pubs Dist) S Asia.
Ahuwalia, H. P. Himalaya: A Practical Guide. Gerner, Manfred, ed. 469p. (C). 1992. 175.00 (*81-7002-004-2*, Pub. by Himalayan Bks) St Mut.
Ahvakana, F., as told by. Tikigagmigguuq (In Point Hope) (ESK.). 42p. 1973. pap. 3.50 (*0-933769-53-9*) Alaska Native.
Ai. Greed: Poems. 96p. 1994. pap. 10.00 (*0-393-31201-1*) Norton.
***Ai.** Vice: New & Selected Poems. LC 98-37334. 256p. 1999. 25.00 (*0-393-04705-9*) Norton.
Ai Camp, Roderic, ed. Democracy in Latin America: Patterns & Cycles. LC 95-30776. (Jaguar Books on Latin America: Vol. 10). 292p. 1995. 55.00 (*0-8420-2512-X*); pap. 18.95 (*0-8420-2513-8*) Scholarly Res Inc.
Ai, Fang. The Scholar & the Serving Maid. 209p. 1994. pap. 6.95 (*0-8351-3141-6*) China Bks.
— The Scholar & the Serving Maid: A Qing Dynasty Mystery. Fanquin, Yu & Samson, Esther, trs. 210p. 1994. pap. 10.95 (*7-5071-0224-6*) Cheng & Tsui.
***Ai, G.** Vice: New & Selected Poems. 272p. 2000. pap. 13.00 (*0-393-32018-9*) Norton.
Ai, G., et al, eds. The Magnetic & Velocity Fields of Solar Active Regions. (ASP Conference Series Proceedings: Vol. 46). xxxviii, 562 p. 1993. 34.00 (*0-937707-65-1*) Astron Soc Pacific.
Ai Gvhdi Waya. Path of the Mystic. 114p. 1997. pap. 11.95 (*0-929385-47-0*) Light Tech Pubng.
Ai, Minoru. Temporomandibular Dysfunction: Diagnosis & Treatment. (Dental Technique Ser.: No. 3). (Illus.). 46p. 1993. pap. 30.00 (*1-56386-013-9*, Ishiyaku EuroAmerica) Med Dent Media.
***AIA (Meister) Staff.** Cargoes from Three Continents: Ancient Mediterranean Trade in Modern Archaeology. 228p. 1999. per. 19.95 (*0-7872-6552-7*, 41655201) Kendall-Hunt.
AIA (Meister) Staff. Democracy 2500? LC 97-76100. 240p. 1997. per. 25.30 (*0-7872-4466-X*) Kendall-Hunt.
— 1997 Archaeological Fieldwork Opportunities Bulletin. 144p. 1997. pap. text 11.00 (*0-7872-3022-7*) Kendall-Hunt.
AIA Academy of Architecture for Health Staff, compiled by. Educational Facilities: 1995-1996 Review. 184p. 1996. 34.99 (*1-56496-224-5*) Rockport Pubs.
AIA Commitee on Designs for Historic Preservation. Historic Resource Facilities: 1997 Review. (Illus.). 192p. 1998. pap. 39.99 (*1-56496-507-4*) Rockport Pubs.
AIA Committee on Architecture for Health Staff. Health Facilities Review, Vol. 3. (Illus.). 168p. (Orig.). 1991. pap. 20.00 (*1-55835-036-5*) AIA Press.
AIA Committee on Architecture for Health Staff, ed. Health Facilities Review, Vol. 2. 128p. (Orig.). 1988. pap. 10.00 (*1-55835-017-9*) AIA Press.
AIA Committee on Architecture for Justice Staff. Justice Facilities Review, 1992-93. (Illus.). 84p. 1993. pap. 20.00 (*1-55835-089-6*, J247) AIA Press.
***AIA Committee on Architecture for Justice Staff.** Justice Facilities Review 1999-2000. (Illus.). 134p. 1999. pap. 40.00 (*1-879304-98-8*) AIA DC.
AIA, Southern Oregon Chapter Staff. Style & Vernacular: A Guide to the Architecture of Lane County, Oregon. (Illus.). 160p. (Orig.). 1983. pap. 9.95 (*0-87595-085-X*) Oregon Hist.
***AIA Staff.** The Architectural Firm Survey: 2000 AIA Report. (Illus.). 64p. 2000. pap. 95.00 (*1-57165-000-8*) AIA DC.
— Compensation at U. S. Architecture Firms 1999: The 1999 AIA Survey Report. (Illus.). 64p. 1999. pap. 32.00 (*1-879304-93-7*) AIA DC.
AIA Staff. Design for Aging: 1996-1997 Review. (Illus.). 160p. 1996. 39.99 (*1-56496-097-8*) Rockport Pubs.
— Directory of Professionals. 144p. 1994. pap. text, per. 12.00 (*0-7872-0332-7*) Kendall-Hunt.
***AIA Staff.** External Realtions of Early Age Crete 1100-600 BC. 406p. 2000. per. 118.95 (*0-7872-7183-7*) Kendall-Hunt.
AIA Staff. 1999 Archaeological Bulletin. 8th ed. 160p. 1998. per. 12.00 (*0-7872-5693-5*, 41569301) Kendall-Hunt.
***AIA Staff.** Sacred & Secular: Ancient Egyptian Ships & Boats. 176p. 2000. per. 77.75 (*0-7872-7182-9*) Kendall-Hunt.
AIA Staff, compiled by. Historic Facilities Review. (Illus.). 192p. 1997. 39.99 (*1-56496-225-3*) Rockport Pubs.
AIA Staff, jt. auth. see Meister.
AIAA-ASME Joint Fluids, Plasma Thermophysics, & Heat Transfer Staff. Three Dimensional Turbulent Shear Flows: Presented at 1982 AIAA-ASME Joint Fluids, Plasma, Thermophysics, & Heat Transfer Conference, St. Louis, Missouri, June 7-11, 1982. Carmi, S. et al, eds. LC 82-71168. (Illus.). 166p. reprint ed. pap. 51.50 (*0-8357-2875-7*, 203911100011) Bks Demand.
— Tube Bundle Thermalhydraulics: Presented at 1982 AIAA-ASME Joint Fluids, Plasma, Thermophysics & Heat Transfer Conference, St. Louis, Missouri, June 7-11, 1982. Pfund, P. A. et al, eds. LC 82-71169. 79p. reprint ed. pap. 30.00 (*0-8357-8771-0*, 203363400087) Bks Demand.
AIAA-ASME Joint Thermophysics & Heat Transfer Conf. Thermophysics & Heat Transfer Conference: Proceedings. Armaly, B. F. et al, eds. 1168p. 344.00 (*0-7918-1855-1*) ASME Pr.
AIAA-ASME Structures, Structural Dynamics & Materials Conference Staff. Structures & Materials: Collection of Technical Papers, 10th Conference, New Orleans, Louisiana, April 14-16, 1969. LC TA645.A3. (Illus.). 481p. reprint ed. pap. 149.20 (*0-608-30351-8*, 201645200004) Bks Demand.
AIAA-ASME Thermophysics & Heat Transfer Conference. Environmental Effects of Atmospheric Heat-Moisture Releases: Cooling Towers, Cooling Ponds, & Area Sources: Presented at the Second AIAA-ASME Thermophysics & Heat Transfer Conference, Palo Alto, California, May 24-26, 1978. Torrance, Kenneth E. & Watts, Robert G., eds. LC 78-52527. (Illus.). 123p. reprint ed. pap. 38.20 (*0-8357-2874-9*, 203911000011) Bks Demand.
— Heat Transfer in Electronic Equipment, 1986: Presented at the AIAA - ASME 4th Thermophysics & Heat Transfer Conference, Boston, Massachusetts, June 2-4, 1986. Bar-Cohen, A., ed. LC 86-185823. (HTD Ser.: Vol. 57). 253p. pap. 78.50 (*0-7837-0206-X*, 204050200017) Bks Demand.
***AIAA Design Engineering Committee on Standards & Society of Allied Weight Engineers Staff.** Recommended Practice: Mass Properties Control for Satellites, Missiles & Launch Vehicles. LC 99-89674 2000. pap. write for info. (*1-56347-387-9*) AIAA.
Aiach, Gilbert. Atlas of Rhinoplasty: Open & Endonasal Approaches. Madjiji, Azita et al, trs. (Illus.). 206p. 1995. text 175.00 (*0-942219-64-3*) Quality Med Pub.
Aiba, Shuichi, ed. Horizons of Biochemical Engineering. (Illus.). 384p. 1988. 105.00 (*0-19-856196-2*) OUP.
AIC Staff. Art Institute of Chicago Museum Studies. 1990. pap. 8.50 (*0-226-02817-8*) U Ch Pr.
— Art Institute of Chicago Studies. 1986. pap. 8.50 (*0-226-02809-7*) U Ch Pr.
Aicardi, Jean. Diseases of the Nervous System in Childhood. 2nd rev. ed. LC 98-172809. (Clinics in Developmental Medicine Ser.). (Illus.). 1100p. (C). 1998. text 260.00 (*1-898683-16-6*, Pub. by Mc Keith Pr) Cambridge U Pr.
— Epilepsy in Children. 2nd ed. (International Review of Child Neurology Ser.). 576p. 1993. text 110.00 (*0-7817-0111-2*) Lppncott W & W.
AICE, Center for Chemical Process Safety Staff. Guidelines on Technical Planning for On-Site Emergencies. LC 94-46234. 1995. 130.00 (*0-8169-0653-X*, G-31) Am Inst Chem Eng.
Aich, Dipak K. Emergence of Modern Bengali Elite: A Study of Progress in Education, 1854-1917. 1995. 20.00 (*81-85195-67-6*, Pub. by Minerva) S Asia.
AIChE Ammonia Plant Safety Committee Staff. Ammonia Plant Safety, Vol. 32. 260p. 1992. 50.00 (*0-8169-0574-5*, T-88) Am Inst Chem Eng.
— Ammonia Plant Safety, Vol. 34. 312p. 1994. 50.00 (*0-8169-0655-6*, T-94) Am Inst Chem Eng.
AIChE Ammonia Plant Safety Committee Staff & Delbov, W. J. Ammonia Plant Safety, Vol. 36. 330p. 1996. 165.00 (*0-8169-0708-0*, T-100) Am Inst Chem Eng.
AIChE Ammonia Plant Safety Committee Staff & Huurdeman, T. L. Ammonia Plant Safety, Vol. 35. 370p. 1995. 65.00 (*0-8169-0677-7*, T-96) Am Inst Chem Eng.
AIChE Design Institute for Emergency Relief System, et al, eds. Proceedings of the International Symposium on Runaway Reactions & Pressure Relief Design. (DIERS Proceedings Ser.). 764p. 1995. 115.00 (*0-8169-0676-9*, P-78) Am Inst Chem Eng.
AIChE Staff, ed. Conference & Workshop on Process Safety Management & Inherently Safer Processes. 504p. 1996. 29.00 (*0-8169-0700-5*, P-82) Am Inst Chem Eng.
— Release: A Model with Data to Predict Aerosol Rainout in Accidental Releases. LC 98-38811. 184p. 1998. 199.00 incl. cd-rom (*0-8169-0745-5*, G-50) Am Inst Chem Eng.
Aichele, D. & Schwegler, A. Blumen der Alpen (Flowers of the Alps) (Kosmos Naturfuehrer (Nature Guides) Ser.). (GER., Illus.). 192p. 1987. pap. 30.00 (*3-440-05730-5*, Pub. by Franckh-Kosmos) Balogh.
— Die Orchideen Europas (The Orchids of Europe) (Kosmos Naturfuehrer (Nature Guides) Ser.). (GER., Illus.). 192p. 1988. pap. 40.00 (*3-440-05829-8*, Pub. by Franckh-Kosmos) Balogh.
— Unsere Graeser (Our Grasses) (Kosmos Naturfuehrer (Nature Guides) Ser.). (GER., Illus.). 224p. 1991. 46.00 (*3-440-06201-5*, Pub. by Franckh-Kosmos) Balogh.
Aichele, Douglas B., ed. Professional Development for Teachers of Mathematics: 1994 Yearbook. (Illus.). 248p. 1994. 22.95 (*0-87353-366-6*) NCTM.
Aichele, George. Jesus Framed. LC 95-39726. (Biblical Limits Ser.). 216p. (C). 1996. 80.00 (*0-415-13862-0*); pap. 22.99 (*0-415-13863-9*) Routledge.
— Sign, Text, Scripture: Semiotics & the Bible. (SAP Title Ser.: Vol. 1). 163p. 1997. pap. 14.95 (*1-85075-691-0*, Pub. by Sheffield Acad) CUP Services.
Aichele, George & Pippin, Tina. Violence, Utopia, & the Kingdom of God: Fantasy & Ideology in the Bible. LC 97-49377. (Illus.). 176p. (C). 1998. 75.00 (*0-415-15667-X*); pap. 24.99 (*0-415-15668-8*) Routledge.
Aichele, George & Pippin, Tina, eds. The Monstrous & the Unspeakable: The Bible As Fantastic Literature. (Playing the Texts Ser.: Vol. 1). 246p. 1997. 74.00 (*1-85075-692-9*, Pub. by Sheffield Acad); pap. 24.50 (*1-85075-821-2*, Pub. by Sheffield Acad) CUP Services.
— Morgan Sportscar: The Early Years. 1997. write for info. (*1-85075-680-5*, Pub. by Sheffield Acad) CUP Services.
Aichele, Jean H. Galileo, the Tour Guide (a Summary of the Mission to Date) 102p. 1996. pap. 15.00 (*0-16-061850-9*) USGPO.
Aichele, Jean H., ed. Galileo, the Tour Guide: A Summary of the Mission to Date. (Illus.). 98p. (Orig.). (C). 1997. pap. text 30.00 (*0-7881-3987-8*) DIANE Pub.
Aichele, Ronald G. The Rights of Reason. Davies Group Staff, ed. & illus. by. 150p. (C). 1995. pap. 16.75 (*0-9630076-8-8*) Davies Grp.
Aichele, Tobias. Porsche 911 Forever Young. Albrecht, Peter, tr. from GER. (Illus.). 400p. (C). 1995. 69.95 (*0-929758-11-0*) Beeman Jorgensen.
— Porsche 911: Engine History & Development. LC 99-34042. (Illus.). 708p. 1999. text 39.95 (*0-7603-0702-4*, Pub. by MBI Pubg) Motorbooks Intl.
Aichelin, J. & Ardouin, D. Multiparticle Correlations & Nuclear Reactions, Corinne II. 500p. 1995. text 124.00 (*981-02-2118-5*) World Scientific Pub.
Aicher. Analogous Digital. 189p. 1994. 44.95 (*3-433-02403-0*) Wiley.
Aicher. World As Design. LC 95-184899. 193p. 1994. 44.95 (*3-433-02404-9*) Wiley.
Aicher, Joseph L. Designing Healthy Cities: Prescriptions, Principles, & Practice. LC 97-33431. 158p. (C). 1998. 29.50 (*0-89464-927-2*) Krieger.
Aicher, Peter J. Guide to the Aqueducts of Ancient Rome. LC 95-15513. (Illus.). xiv, 184p. 1995. 40.00 (*0-86516-271-9*); pap. 25.00 (*0-86516-282-4*) Bolchazy-Carducci.
Aiches, Alan Z., jt. auth. see Janson, Anthony F.
***Aichholzer, Doris.** Wildu Machen Ayn Guet Essen... Drei Mittelhochdeutsche Kochbucher; Erstedition, Ubersetzung, Kommentar. (GER.). 455p. 1999. 60.95 (*3-906762-44-0*, Pub. by P Lang) P Lang Pubng.
Aichholzer, Georg & Schienstock, Gerd, eds. Technology Policy: Towards an Integration of Social & Ecological Concerns. LC 93-37994. (Studies in Organization: No. 52). xiv, 418p. (C). 1994. lib. bdg. 89.95 (*3-11-013677-5*) De Gruyter.
Aichhorn, August. Delinquency & Child Guidance: Selected Papers of August Aichhorn. Fleischmann, Otto et al, eds. LC 64-8751. (Menninger Foundation Monograph Ser.: No. 1). 244p. 1967. 37.50 (*0-8236-1160-4*) Intl Univs Pr.
Aichinger, Gregor. Five Sacred Canzonettas. Hettrick, William E., ed. (Renaissance Recorder Ser.: No. 4). 1974. 2.75 (*0-913334-18-9*, CM1022) Consort Music.
— Gregor Aichinger: Cantiones Ecclesiasticae. Hettolick, William E., ed. (Recent Researches in Music of the Baroque Era Ser.: Vol. RRB13). xvi, 110p. 1972. pap. 45.00 (*0-89579-043-2*) A-R Eds.
— Gregor Aichinger: The Vocal Concertos. Hettrich, William E., ed. (Recent Researches in Music of the Baroque Era Ser.: Vol. RRB54-55). (Illus.). xxii, 192p. 1986. pap. 65.00 (*0-89579-213-3*, RRB54-55) A-R Eds.
— Three Marion Motets (a Three) Hettrick, William E., ed. (Renaissance Recorder Ser.: No. 6). 1975. 2.75 (*0-913334-25-1*, CM1026) Consort Music.
Aichinger, Ilse. Bound Man, & Other Stories. Mosbacher, Eric, tr. LC 72-144151. (Short Story Index Reprint Ser., Suppl. 1955-58). 1977. reprint ed. 12.95 (*0-8369-3766-X*) Ayer.
— Kleist, Moss, Fame. (GER.). 128p. 1991. pap. 9.00 (*3-596-11045-9*, Pub. by Fischer Tasch) Intl Bk Import.
Aichner, F., et al, eds. Three-Dimensional Magnetic Resonance Imaging: An Integrated Clinical Update of 3D-Imaging & 3D-Postprocessing: Proceedings of a Joint Meeting in Obergurgl, Austria, 23-27 March 1992. LC 94-20996. 300p. 1994. 125.00 (*0-86542-800-X*) Blackwell Sci.
Aichroth, Paul. Knee Surgery: Current Practice. 824p. 1992. text 262.50 (*0-88167-934-8*) Lppncott W & W.
Aicken, Frederick. The Nature of Science. 2nd ed. LC 90-46236. 162p. (C). 1991. pap. text 17.50 (*0-435-08310-4*, 08310) Heinemann.
Aicken, Mikel, jt. auth. see Kaye, D. H.
Aickman, Robert. Cold Hand in Mine. 1993. reprint ed. lib. bdg. 18.95 (*0-89968-416-5*, Lghtyr Pr) Buccaneer Bks.
— Sub Rosa: Strange Tales. 1993. reprint ed. lib. bdg. 18.95 (*0-89968-417-3*, Lghtyr Pr) Buccaneer Bks.

AICPA Accounting & Auditing Publications Staff. AICPA Audit & Accounting Manual: As of June 1, 1997. 1584p. 1997. pap. 84.00 (*0-87051-191-2*, 007258) Am Inst CPA.

AICPA Staff. AICPA Professional Standards, 2 vols. 2496p. 1998. pap. 119.00 (*0-87051-231-5*, 005018) Am Inst CPA.

— AICPA Technical Practice Aids. 1586p. 1998. pap. 86.50 (*0-87051-232-3*, 005058) Am Inst CPA.

— Checklists & Illustrative Financial Statements for Common Interest Realty Associations. 70p. 1998. pap. 33.75 (*0-87051-233-1*, 008714) Am Inst CPA.

— Checklists & Illustrative Financial Statements for Defined Benefit Pension Plans. 50p. 1998. pap. 33.75 (*0-87051-239-0*, 008720) Am Inst CPA.

— Checklists & Illustrative Financial Statements for Defined Contribution Pension Plans. 84p. 1998. pap. 33.75 (*0-87051-238-2*, 008713) Am Inst CPA.

— Checklists & Illustrative Financial Statements for Employee Health & Welfare Benefit Plans. 60p. 1998. pap. 33.75 (*0-87051-237-4*, 008721) Am Inst CPA.

— Checklists & Illustrative Financial Statements for Health Care Organizations. 120p. 1998. pap. 33.75 (*0-87051-236-6*, 008722) Am Inst CPA.

— Checklists & Illustrative Financial Statements for Not-for-Profit Organizations. 76p. 1998. pap. 33.75 (*0-87051-235-8*, 008723) Am Inst CPA.

— Checklists & Illustrative Financial Statements for State & Local Governmental Units. 120p. 1998. pap. 33.75 (*0-87051-234-X*, 008707) Am Inst CPA.

— Service Organizations: Applying SAS No. 70. rev. ed. LC 98-55959. (Auditing Practice Release Ser.). 160p. 1999. pap. 31.50 (*0-87051-246-3*, 021056) Am Inst CPA.

AICPA Staff, ed. Audit & Accounting Guide: Audits of Agricultural Producers & Agricultural Corporations. 156p. 1998. pap. 40.50 (*0-87051-218-8*, 012353) Am Inst CPA.

— Audit & Accounting Guide: Audits of Casinos. 94p. 1998. pap. 40.50 (*0-87051-212-9*, 013149) Am Inst CPA.

— Audit & Accounting Guide: Audits of Credit Unions. 196p. 1998. pap. 40.50 (*0-87051-220-X*, 012058) Am Inst CPA.

— Audit & Accounting Guide: Audits of Employee Benefit Plans. 350p. 1998. pap. 40.50 (*0-87051-207-2*, 012338) Am Inst CPA.

— Audit & Accounting Guide: Audits of Entities with Oil & Gas Producing Activities. 132p. 1998. pap. 40.50 (*0-87051-217-X*, 012105) Am Inst CPA.

— Audit & Accounting Guide: Audits of Federal Government Contractors. 192p. 1998. pap. 40.50 (*0-87051-213-7*, 012437) Am Inst CPA.

— Audit & Accounting Guide: Audits of Finance Companies. 128p. 1998. pap. 40.50 (*0-87051-223-4*, 012465) Am Inst CPA.

— Audit & Accounting Guide: Audits of Investment Companies. 304p. 1998. pap. 40.50 (*0-87051-215-3*, 012362) Am Inst CPA.

— Audit & Accounting Guide: Audits of Property & Liability Insurance Companies. 274p. 1998. pap. 40.50 (*0-87051-219-6*, 011921) Am Inst CPA.

— Audit & Accounting Guide: Audits of State & Local Governmental Units. 450p. 1998. pap. 40.50 (*0-87051-209-9*, 012057) Am Inst CPA.

— Audit & Accounting Guide: Banks & Savings Institutions. 390p. 1998. pap. 40.50 (*0-87051-222-6*, 011177) Am Inst CPA.

— Audit & Accounting Guide: Brokers & Dealers in Securities. 250p. 1998. pap. 40.50 (*0-87051-221-8*, 012180) Am Inst CPA.

— Audit & Accounting Guide: Construction Contractors. 200p. 1998. pap. 40.50 (*0-87051-210-2*, 012095) Am Inst CPA.

— Audit & Accounting Guide: Health Care Organizations. 250p. 1998. pap. 40.50 (*0-87051-214-5*, 012438) Am Inst CPA.

— Audit & Accounting Guides: Not-for-Profit Organizations. 384p. 1998. pap. 40.50 (*0-87051-216-1*, 013391) Am Inst CPA.

— Industry Audit Guide: Audits of Airlines. 106p. 1998. pap. 40.50 (*0-87051-208-0*, 013182) Am Inst CPA.

AICPA Staff, et al. Flexible Work Arrangements: A Guide for Public Accounting Firms. LC 97-25962. 146p. 1997. pap. 24.95 (*0-87051-190-4*, 090425) Am Inst CPA.

AICPA Staff, jt. auth. see Canadian Institute of Chartered Accountants Staff.

Aid, Frances M. Semantic Structures in Spanish: A Proposal for Instructional Materials. LC 72-96297. 152p. reprint ed. pap. 47.20 (*0-7837-6454-5*, 204645400012) Bks Demand.

Aid, Frances M., ed. see Colloquium on Hispanic Linguistics Staff.

Aida Negron De Montilla. La Americanizacion de Puerto Rico y el Sistema de Instruccion Publica. 2nd ed. LC 76-14880. (SPA.). 290p. 1990. reprint ed. pap. 9.95 (*0-8477-0101-8*) U of PR Pr.

Aidarous, Salah & Plevyak, Thomas. Telecommunications Network Management: Technology & Implementation. LC 97-38066. 352p. 1997. 69.95 (*0-7803-3454-X*, PC5711) Inst Electrical.

Aidarous, Salah & Plevyak, Thomas, eds. Telecommunications Network Management into the 21st Century: Techniques, Standards, Technologies, & Applications. LC 93-41040. 448p. 1995. 79.95 (*0-7803-1013-6*, PC03624) Inst Electrical.

AIDC Staff. Young German Architects: Junge Deutsche Architekten und Architektinnen. LC 98-13983. 159p. 1998. write for info. (*0-8176-5782-7*) Birkhauser.

Aidells, Bruce & Clark, Ron. Barbecuing, Grilling & Smoking. 128p. 1995. pap. 11.95 (*1-56426-074-7*) Cole Group.

***Aidells, Bruce & Kelly, Denis.** Bruce Aidells's Complete Sausage Book: Recipes from America's Premier Sausage Maker. LC 99-58199. (Illus.). 256p. 2000. pap. 19.95 (*1-58008-159-2*) Ten Speed Pr.

Aidells, Bruce & Kelly, Denis. The Complete Meat Cookbook: A Juicy & Authoritative Guide to Selecting, Seasoning & Cooking Today's Beef, Pork, Lamb, & Veal. LC 98-28216. 688p. 1998. 35.00 (*0-395-90492-7*) HM.

Aidells, Bruce & Kelly, Dennis. Good Meat. 1997. 30.00 (*0-684-81371-8*) S&S Trade.

Aidley, David J. The Physiology of Excitable Cells. 4th rev. ed. LC 97-46773. (Illus.). 550p. (C). 1998. text 90.00 (*0-521-57415-3*); pap. text 47.95 (*0-521-57421-8*) Cambridge U Pr.

Aidley, David J. & Stanfield, Peter R. Ion Channels: Molecules in Action. LC 96-230439. (Illus.). 319p. (C). 1996. text 74.95 (*0-521-49531-8*) Cambridge U Pr.

— Ion Channels: Molecules in Action. LC 96-230439. (Illus.). 319p. (C). 1996. pap. text 29.95 (*0-521-49882-1*) Cambridge U Pr.

Aidley, David J., jt. auth. see Keynes, R. D.

Aidman, Evan K. Winning Your Personal Injury Claim. LC 97-16712. (Legal Survival Guides Ser.). 224p. 1997. pap. 19.95 (*1-57071-165-8*, Sphinx Pubng) Sourcebks.

Aidoo, Ama Ata. Changes: A Love Story. LC 93-29102. (Women Writing Africa Ser.). 208p. 1993. 35.00 (*1-55861-064-2*); pap. 12.95 (*1-55861-065-0*) Feminist Pr.

— Dilemma of a Ghost: Anowa. (African Writers Ser.). (C). 1995. pap. text 12.19 (*0-582-27602-0*, Pub. by Addison-Wesley) Longman.

— No Sweetness Here & Other Stories. LC 95-18346. 170p. 1998. reprint ed. pap. 10.95 (*1-55861-119-3*) Feminist Pr.

— Our Sister Killjoy. LC 78-64625. 1979. 9.95 (*0-88357-064-5*); pap. 4.95 (*0-88357-065-3*) NOK Pubs.

— Our Sister Killjoy: Longman African Writers. 134p. (C). 1997. pap. 14.86 (*0-582-30845-3*) Longman.

Aidoo, Kofi. Men Ghost Africn Wri Ser. (Longman African Writers Ser.). (C). 1995. pap. 14.86 (*0-582-22871-9*) Addison-Wesley.

AIDS Committee. Going Home: A Family Facing AIDS. 1993. 87.25 (*0-697-24332-X*, WCB McGr Hill) McGraw-H Hghr Educ.

AIDS Foundation Dayton Staff & Volunteers. Positively Forward: A Handbook for HIV-Infected Persons. Ruggieri, L. & Loper, L., eds. (Illus.). 118p. (Orig.). 1989. pap. 5.00 (*0-685-30446-9*) AIDS Fndtn Dayton.

Aiello. Human Evolution. 320p. pap. write for info. (*0-471-35058-3*) Wiley.

Aiello. This World & the Next One. 113p. (Orig.). 1993. pap. 9.95 (*0-929385-44-6*) Light Tech Pubng.

Aiello, Alfonso. Tempo Di Colombo: The Times of Columbus. 28p. 1992. pap. text 10.95 (*0-9634106-9-5*) A Aiello.

— Tempo di Colombo, 1492-1992. 2nd rev. ed. (ITA., Illus.). 28p. 1992. pap. text 10.95 (*0-9634106-0-1*) A Aiello.

Aiello, Annette, jt. ed. see Quintero, Diomedes.

Aiello, Barbara & Shulman, Jeffrey. Business Is Looking Up: Featuring Renaldo Rodriguez. (Kids on the Block Bks.). (Illus.). 48p. (J). (gr. 5-8). 1991. lib. bdg. 13.95 (*0-8050-3136-7*) TFC Bks NY.

— Hometown Hero: Featuring Scott Whittaker. (Kids on the Block Bks.). (Illus.). 48p. (J). (gr. 5-8). 1995. lib. bdg. 13.95 (*0-941477-04-5*) TFC Bks NY.

— On with the Show! Featuring Brenda Dubrowski. (Kids on the Block Bks.). 56p. (J). (gr. 5-8). 1995. 13.95 (*0-941477-06-1*) TFC Bks NY.

— A Portrait of Me: Featuring Christine Kontos. (Kids on the Block Bks.). (Illus.). 48p. (J). (gr. 5-8). 1995. lib. bdg. 13.95 (*0-941477-05-3*) TFC Bks NY.

— Trick or Trouble: Featuring Brian McDaniel. (Kids on the Block Bks.). (Illus.). 56p. (J). (gr. 3-6). 1995. lib. bdg. 13.95 (*0-941477-07-X*) TFC Bks NY.

Aiello, J. C. Amelia. LC 98-96797. 222p. 1998. pap. 12.99 (*1-893191-00-1*, 9809AMEL08, Carmen Pr) J C Aiello Inc.

Aiello, J. R. & Baum, Abe, eds. Residential Crowding & Design. LC 79-357. (Illus.). 270p. 1979. 49.50 (*0-306-40205-X*, Plenum Trade) Perseus Pubng.

Aiello, Janet. Cats & Kittens Iron-on Transfer Patterns. 81st ed. (Illus.). 48p. (Orig.). 1983. pap. 3.95 (*0-486-24461-X*) Dover.

Aiello, Jerry L. Heiho: Martial Arts Concepts & Strategy. (Illus.). 100p. (Orig.). 1997. pap. text 29.95 (*1-883702-12-7*) Aiello Grp.

— The Warrior Legacy. 350p. 1995. pap. text 29.95 (*1-883702-10-0*) Aiello Grp.

— Zensho: American Philosophy & Intermediate Warrior Training Manual. 325p. (Orig.). 1994. pap. text 29.95 (*1-883702-06-2*) Aiello Grp.

Aiello, John. World Paper Money: Collectors Guide & Catalogue. 3rd ed. 312p. pap. 19.95 (*0-917515-00-5*) Sunrise NJ.

Aiello, Leslie & Dean, Christopher, eds. An Introduction to Human Evolutionary Anatomy. 596p. 1990. text 155.00 (*0-12-045590-0*) Acad Pr.

— An Introduction to Human Evolutionary Anatomy. 596p. (C). 1990. pap. text 59.95 (*0-12-045591-9*) Acad Pr.

Aiello, Leslie C., jt. ed. see Jablonski, Nina G.

Aiello, Luigia C., ed. Proceedings of the Ninth European Conference on Artificial Intelligence. 785p. 1998. pap. text 45.00 (*0-273-08822-X*) Morgan Kaufmann.

Aiello, Rit & Sloboda, John A., eds. Musical Perceptions. (Illus.). 304p. (C). 1994. pap. text 28.95 (*0-19-506476-3*) OUP.

Aiello, Robert J. The Deceivers. LC 98-72712. 300p. 1999. pap. 14.95 (*0-88739-187-7*) Creat Arts Bk.

***Aiello, Theresa G.** Child & Adolescent Treatment for Social Work Practice: A Rational PErspective For Beginning Clinicians. LC 99-17092. 288p. 1999. 32.95 (*0-684-84393-5*) S&S Trade.

Aiello, Theresa G., jt. auth. see Tosone, Carol.

Aieloski, Liz, ed. see Wolfrom, Joen.

Aiers, Andrew. When Things Go Wrong: Young People's Experience of Getting Access to the Complaints Procedure in Residential Care. 1998. pap. 43.00 (*1-899942-25-4*, Pub. by Natl Inst Soc Work) St Mut.

Aifantis, E. C. & Davison, L. W., eds. Media with Microstructures & Wave Propagation: Proceedings of the Conference, Houghton, MI, January 1983. 260p. 1985. pap. 130.00 (*0-08-031661-1*, Pergamon Pr) Elsevier.

Aifcr, ed. Dietary Phytochemicals in Cancer Prevention & Treatment: Proceedings of the American Institute for Cancer Research's Sixth Annual Research Conference Held in Washington, D. C., August 31-September 1, 1995. LC 96-24704. (Advances in Experimental Medicine & Biology Ser.: Vol. 401). (Illus.). 324p. (C). 1996. text 114.00 (*0-306-45365-7*, Kluwer Plenum) Kluwer Academic.

***AIGA Staff.** 18 Graphic Design Usa, Vol. 18. 18th ed. 1998. 59.95 (*0-688-15982-6*, Wm Morrow) Morrow Avon.

AIGA Staff. Graphic Design in the U. S. A. 19th ed. (Illus.). 1999. 45.00 (*0-688-16486-2*, Wm Morrow) Morrow Avon.

— Graphic Design U. S. A. No. 19: The Annual of the American Institute of Graphic Arts. 320p. 1999. pap. text 45.00 (*0-8230-7233-9*) Watsn-Guptill.

Aigaki, Dianne M. Trouble in Paradise: A Survivial Manual for Couples Who Are Parents. LC 86-72923. (Illus.). 304p. (Orig.). 1987. pap., student ed. 16.95 (*0-941941-01-9*) Dry Creek Pubns.

Aigbe, Sunday A. Theory of Social Involvement: A Case Study in the Anthropology of Religion, State, & Society. LC 92-28390. 280p. (C). 1993. lib. bdg. 52.50 (*0-8191-8873-5*) U Pr of Amer.

Aigen, Kenneth. Paths of Development in Nordoff-Robbins Music Therapy. LC 99-163018. 362p. (C). 1998. pap. text 57.50 incl. audio compact disk (*1-891278-03-7*) Barcelona Pubs.

Aiginger, Karl, ed. Applied Industrial Organization: Towards a Theory Based Empirical Industrial Organization. 250p. (C). 1995. lib. bdg. 87.50 (*0-7923-3051-X*) Kluwer Academic.

Aiginger, Karl & Finsinger, Jorg, eds. Applied Industrial Organization: Towards a Theory Based Empirical Industrial Organization. LC 94-29539. 1994. lib. bdg. 157.50 (*0-7923-3050-1*) Kluwer Academic.

Aigla, Jorge. The Aztec Shell. LC 94-34245. 84p. (Orig.). 1995. pap. 9.00 (*0-927534-49-5*) Biling Rev-Pr.

Aigla, Jorge H. Karate-Do & Zen, an Inquiry. LC 94-92304. 165p. 1994. pap. 17.95 (*0-9643148-4-3*) Do Pr.

— Sublunary. (Blue Ser.). (Illus.). 32p. (Orig.). 1989. pap. 4.00 (*0-938631-07-1*) Pennywhistle Pr.

Aigner, Hal. Adoption in America: Coming of Age. LC 86-60829. 216p. 1986. pap. 8.95 (*0-937572-02-0*) Paradigm Pr.

— Adoption in America Coming of Age. rev. ed. LC 92-14585. 240p. 1992. pap. 9.95 (*0-937572-04-7*) Paradigm Pr.

— Faint Trails: A Guide to Adult Adoptee-Birth Parent Reunification Searches. 102p. (Orig.). 1987. pap. 6.95 (*0-937572-03-9*) Paradigm Pr.

Aigner, K., ed. Regionale Chemotherapie der Leber. (Beitraege Zur Onkologie, Contributions to Oncology Ser.: Vol. 21). (Illus.). viii, 140p. 1985. 68.75 (*3-8055-4014-0*) S Karger.

Aigner, K., jt. ed. see Schwemmle, K.

Aigner, K. R., et al, eds. Regional Cancer Treatment. (Beitraege Zur Onkologie, Contributions to Oncology Ser.: Vol. 29). (Illus.). viii, 312p. 1988. 65.25 (*3-8055-4762-5*) S Karger.

Aigner, M., et al. Graph Theory: A Development from the 4-Color Problem. Boron, Leo F., tr. from GER. LC 86-77705. (Illus.). 233p. (Orig.). 1987. pap. 36.00 (*0-914351-03-6*) BCS Assocs.

Aigner, Martin. Combinatorial Search. (Teubner Series in Computer Science). 372p. 1988. 250.00 (*0-471-92142-4*) Wiley.

— Combinatorial Theory. LC 96-51833. (Classics in Mathematics Ser.). 483p. 1997. pap. 35.00 (*3-540-61787-6*) Spr-Verlag.

Aigner, Martin, ed. Higher Combinatorics. (Advanced Study Institutes Math & Physical Sciences Ser.: No. 31). 1977. text 106.00 (*90-277-0795-2*) Kluwer Academic.

Aigner, Martin & Ziegler, G. M. Proofs from "The Book" LC 98-34262. (Illus.). 210p. 1998. 29.00 (*3-540-63698-6*) Spr-Verlag.

Aigner, R. & Gillquist, J. Arthroscopy of the Knee. (Flexibook Ser.). (Illus.). 228p. 1991. text 32.50 (*0-86577-342-4*) Thieme Med Pubs.

Aigner, T. Storm Depositional Systems. (Lecture Notes in Earth Sciences Ser.: Vol. 3). vii, 174p. 1985. 27.95 (*0-387-15231-8*) Spr-Verlag.

Aigotti, Ronald E. The People's Cancer Guide Book: Practical Information to Help You Understand Cancer: Its Causes, Early Detection, Prevention, Symptoms, Treatments, & Cure. LC 95-76465. 427p. (Orig.). 1995. pap. 29.95 (*0-9648656-0-2*) Belletrist.

Aigrain, Philippe & Petkovic, Dragutin. Representation & Retrieval of Visual Media in Multimedia Systems. Zhang, Hong J., ed. LC 96-38482. 104p. (C). 1996. text 91.00 (*0-7923-9771-1*) Kluwer Academic.

AIHA Emergency Response Planning Committee. Emergency Response Planning Guidelines Series, 8 sets, Set. (Guide Ser.). 12.50 (*0-685-48780-6*) Am Indus Hygiene.

AIHA Engineering Committee. Engineering Field Reference Manual. 132p. 1984. 42.50 (*0-932627-08-0*) Am Indus Hygiene.

AIHA Ergonomics Committee, ed. Manual Material Handling: Understanding & Preventing Back Trauma. (Illus.). (C). 1993. reprint ed. pap. 40.00 (*0-932627-54-4*, 149-ER-89) Am Indus Hygiene.

AIHA Gas & Vapor Detection Systems Committee. Manual of Recommended Practice for Portable Direct-Reading Carbon Monoxide Indicators. Frazee, Patrick R., ed. 46p. 1985. 25.00 (*0-932627-22-6*) Am Indus Hygiene.

AIHA Noise Committee. Noise & Hearing Conservation Manual. 4th ed. 606p. 1986. 51.00 (*0-932627-21-8*) Am Indus Hygiene.

AIHA Nonionizing Radiation Committee. Non-Ionizing Radiation Guide Series. (Guide Ser.). 12.00 (*0-685-43790-6*) Am Indus Hygiene.

AIHA Nonionizing Radiation Committee, ed. Industrial Hygiene Auditing: A Manual for Practice. 135p. (C). 1994. pap. 46.00 (*0-932627-57-9*, 183-MA-94) Am Indus Hygiene.

— Radio-Frequency & Microwave Radiation. 2nd ed. (Nonionizing Radiation Guide Ser.). (Illus.). 33p. (C). 1994. pap. text 20.00 (*0-932627-59-5*, 187-EA-94) Am Indus Hygiene.

AIHA Respiratory Protection Committee. Respiratory Protection Monograph. 448p. 1985. 40.00 (*0-932627-20-X*) Am Indus Hygiene.

AIHA WEEL Committee. Workplace Environmental Exposure Level Guide Series, 17 sets, Set. (Guide Ser.). 15.00 (*0-685-43791-4*) Am Indus Hygiene.

Aihara, Chris. Nikkei Donburi: A Japanese American Cultural Survival Guide. LC 98-7207. (Illus.). (J). 1999. pap. 18.95 (*1-879965-18-6*) Polychrome Pub.

Aihara, Cornellia & Aihara, Herman. Natural Healing from Head to Toe: Traditional Macrobiotic Remedies. LC 93-4659. 464p. pap. 14.95 (*0-89529-496-6*, Avery) Penguin Putnam.

Aihara, Herman. Acid & Alkaline. 5th rev. ed. Hodson, Stan, ed. 121p. 1986. pap. 8.95 (*0-918860-44-X*) G Ohsawa.

— Kaleidoscope: Macrobiotic Articles, Essays & Lectures 1979-1985. Rothman, Sandy, ed. LC 86-80031. 338p. 1986. pap. 12.95 (*0-918860-43-1*) G Ohsawa.

Aihara, Herman, jt. auth. see Aihara, Cornellia.

Aihara, Herman, ed. see Ohsawa, George.

***Aihara, Kazunori.** Let's Find Pokemon. (Illus.). 22p. (J). (ps-3). 1999. pap. 11.95 (*1-56931-390-3*, Pub. by Viz Commns Inc) Publishers Group.

— Let's Find Pokemon!, No. 2. (Illus.). 32p. (ps-3). 2000. 11.95 (*1-56931-414-4*, Pub. by Viz Commns Inc) Publishers Group.

— Let's Find Pokemon! 3. (Let's Find Pokemon Ser.). (Illus.). (J). 2000. 11.95 (*1-56931-503-5*) Viz Commns Inc.

***Aihara, Kyoko.** Geisha. (Illus.). 128p. 2000. 27.95 (*1-85868-970-8*, Pub. by Carlton Bks Ltd) Natl Bk Netwk.

Aihara, Y., jt. ed. see Kawamura, R.

Aijaz, R. Matto. Management of Price Fluctuations. 285p. 1990. 120.00 (*81-7041-297-8*, Pub. by Scientific Pubs) St Mut.

Aijmer, Goran. Atomistic Society in Shatin--Hong Kong Valley. 1986. pap. 73.50 (*91-7346-158-X*, Pub. by Acta U Gothenburg) Coronet Bks.

***Aijmer, Goran & Abbink, Jon, eds.** The Meanings of Violence: A Cross-Cultural Perspective. 256p. 2000. 65.00 (*1-85973-435-9*, Pub. by Berg Pubs); pap. 24.50 (*1-85973-440-5*, Pub. by Berg Pubs) NYU Pr.

Aijmer, Goran & Ho, Virgil K. Cantonese Society at a Time of Change. 304p. 1998. pap. 32.50 (*962-201-832-7*, Pub. by Chinese Univ) U of Mich Pr.

Aijmer, Karin & Altenberg, Bengt, eds. English Corpus Linguistics. (Studies in Honour of Jan Svartvik). 400p. (C). 1991. text 34.95 (*0-582-05931-3*) Longman.

Aika, K. Ammonia: Catalysis & Manufacture. Nielsen, Anders, ed. LC 94-36677. 1995. 235.95 (*0-387-58335-1*) Spr-Verlag.

Aikawa, Hiroaki & Essen, Matts R. Potential Theory: Selected Topics. LC 96-27493. (Lecture Notes in Mathematics Ser.: Vol. 163). 200p. 1996. pap. 43.00 (*3-540-61583-0*) Spr-Verlag.

Aikawa, Jerry K. Magnesium: Its Biologic Significance. 144p. 1981. 99.00 (*0-8493-5871-X*, QP535) CRC Pr.

Aikema, Bernard. Jacopo Bassano & His Public: Moralizing Pictures in an Age of Reform, ca. 1535-1600. LC 95-30582. (Illus.). 280p. 1996. text 95.00 (*0-691-04395-7*, Pub. by Princeton U Pr) Cal Prin Full Svc.

— Tiepolo & His Circle: Drawings in American Collections. McCormick, Andrew, tr. (Illus.). 347p. 1996. 39.95 (*0-916724-90-5*) Harvard Art Mus.

Aikema, Bernard & Brown, Beverly L., eds. Renaissance Venice & the North: Crosscurrents in the Time of Durer, Bellini & Titian. (Illus.). 704p. 1999. 75.00 (*0-8478-2195-1*, Pub. by Rizzoli Intl) St Martin.

Aikema, Bernard & Tuijn, Marguerite. Tiepolo in Holland: Works by Giambattista Tiepolo & His Circle in Dutch Collections. LC 97-168289. (Illus.). 232p. 1997. pap. 40.00 (*90-6918-171-1*, Pub. by Boymans Mus) U of Wash Pr.

Aiken. Lady Catherines Necklace. 176p. 2000. text 21.95 (*0-312-24406-1*) St Martin.

— Legal & Ethical Issues in Health. 1999. pap. text. write for info. (*0-7216-6525-X*, W B Saunders Co) Harcrt Hlth Sci Grp.

Aiken, Al & Williams, Stuart. Optics for Sportsmen. 1993. 49.50 (*1-879356-26-0*) Wolfe Pub Co.

Aiken, B. The Waiter-Waitress Manual. 1976. text 10.12 (*0-07-000742-X*) McGraw.

An Asterisk (*) at the beginning of an entry indicates that the title is appearing for the first time.

Aiken, Bob & Freedman, Lew. Mutuk & Mukluks. 14.95 (*0-9671504-0-X*) Todd Commns.

Aiken, Carol. Spelling Skillbuilder. 2nd ed. (PS - Communication/English Ser.). (C). 1991. mass mkt. 17.75 (*0-538-70382-2*) S-W Pub.

Aiken, Charles S. The Cotton Plantation South since the Civil War. LC 97-30162. (Creating the North American Landscape Ser.). (Illus.). 448p. 1998. text 45.00 (*0-8018-5679-5*) Johns Hopkins.

Aiken, Conrad. The Charnel Rose, Senlin: A Biography & Other Poems. LC 79-156910. (Studies in Poetry: No. 38). 1972. reprint ed. lib. bdg. 75.00 (*0-8383-1247-0*) M S G Haskell Hse.

— The Clerk's Journal. LC 70-152799. 1971. 40.00 (*0-87130-022-2*) Eakins.

— The Clerk's Journal. deluxe limited ed. LC 70-152799. 1971. boxed set 75.00 (*0-87130-023-0*) Eakins.

Aiken, Conrad. Collected Poems, 1916-1970. 2nd ed. LC 79-120179. 1064p. 1970. text 45.00 (*0-19-501258-5*) OUP.

Aiken, Conrad. Jig of Forslin. 1964. pap. 5.95 (*0-8283-1443-8*, 32) Branden Bks.

— Scepticisms: Notes on Contemporary Poetry. LC 67-30170. (Essay Index Reprint Ser.). 1977. 18.95 (*0-8369-0140-1*) Ayer.

— Selected Letters of Conrad Aiken. Killorin, Joseph R., ed. LC 77-20620. (Illus.). 396p. reprint ed. pap. 122.80 (*0-8357-3749-7*, 203647500003) Bks Demand.

— Short Stories. LC 72-178434. (Short Story Index Reprint Ser.). 1977. reprint ed. 29.95 (*0-8369-4034-2*) Ayer.

Aiken, Conrad & Carle, S. Silent Snow, Secret Snow. 18p. 1974. pap. 3.50 (*0-87129-981-X*, S28) Dramatic Pub.

Aiken, Conrad & Lowry, Malcolm. The Letters of Conrad Aiken & Malcolm Lowry, 1929-1954. Sugars, Cynthia Conchita, ed. (Illus.). 350p. (C). 1992. pap. text 25.00 (*1-55022-168-X*, Pub. by ECW) Genl Dist Srvs.

Aiken, Coumba, tr. & illus. see Hammer, Roger A.

***Aiken, David.** Fire in the Cradle: Charleston's Literary Heritage. unabridged limited ed. xvi, 230p. 1999. 28.98 (*0-9675251-0-1*) Charleston Pr SC.

***Aiken, David & Newberry, Barbara.** Weatherford, Texas. (Images of America Ser.). (Illus.). 128p. 1999. pap. 18.99 (*0-7385-0110-7*) Arcadia Publng.

Aiken, David, jt. auth. see Aiken, Zora.

Aiken, David, ed. see Simms, William Gilmore.

Aiken, Eileen. Golden Remembrances: Of Monaca, Pennsylvania. LC 98-90704. (Illus.). 45p. (J). (gr. 5-8). 1999. per. 8.95 (*0-9667007-3-2*); boxed set 22.95 (*0-9667007-2-4*) Skeeter Hill.

— A Tract of Land Called Appetite. LC 98-90703. (Illus.). 44p. (J). (gr. 5-8). 1998. boxed set 22.95 (*0-9667007-0-8*) Skeeter Hill.

— A Tract of Land Called Appetite: The Story of Monaca, Pennsylvania. LC 98-90703. (Illus.). 44p. (J). (gr. 5-8). 1998. per. 8.95 (*0-9667007-1-6*) Skeeter Hill.

Aiken, Gayleen & Klein, Rachel. Moonlight & Music: The Enchanted World of Gayleen Aiken. LC 97-3656. (Illus.). 32p. 1997. 14.95 (*0-8109-4299-2*, Pub. by Abrams) Time Warner.

Aiken, George D. Pioneering with Wildflowers. 1994. pap. 12.95 (*0-911469-11-7*) A C Hood.

Aiken, George L. The Doom of Deville. (Works of George Aiken (1830-1876)). 1989. reprint ed. lib. bdg. 90.00 (*0-7812-1593-5*) Rprt Serv.

— The Emerald Ring. (Works of George Aiken (1830-1876)). 1989. reprint ed. lib. bdg. 90.00 (*0-7812-1592-7*) Rprt Serv.

— Josie. (Works of George Aiken (1830-1876)). 1989. reprint ed. lib. bdg. 90.00 (*0-7812-1594-3*) Rprt Serv.

— The Old Homestead. (Works of George Aiken (1830-1876)). 1989. reprint ed. lib. bdg. 79.00 (*0-7812-1591-9*) Rprt Serv.

— Orion: The Gold Beater. (Works of George Aiken (1830-1876)). 1989. reprint ed. lib. bdg. 90.00 (*0-7812-1589-7*) Rprt Serv.

— Uncle Tom's Cabin. (Works of George Aiken (1830-1876)). 1989. reprint ed. lib. bdg. 79.00 (*0-7812-1590-0*) Rprt Serv.

Aiken, George L. & Howard, George C. Uncle Tom's Cabin. Riis, Thomas L., ed. LC 94-1962. (Nineteenth-Century American Musical Theater Ser.: No. 5). (Illus.). 128p. 1994. text 79.00 (*0-8153-1366-7*) Garland.

Aiken, Ginny. Candy Kiss. 1996. mass mkt. 5.99 (*0-515-11941-5*, Jove) Berkley Pub.

— County Fair. 336p. 1997. mass mkt. 5.99 (*0-515-12021-9*, Jove) Berkley Pub.

— Crystal Memories. 304p. 1997. mass mkt. 5.99 (*0-515-12159-2*, Jove) Berkley Pub.

***Aiken, Ginny.** Lark, Vol. 2. (Bellamy's Blossoms Ser.). 2000. pap. 9.99 (*0-8423-3560-9*) Tyndale Hse.

— Magnolia. LC 99-57970. 280p. 2000. pap. 8.99 (*0-8423-3559-5*) Tyndale Hse.

Aiken, Ginny, et al. A Bouquet of Love. LC 98-47655. (Heart Quest Ser.). 377p. 1999. pap. 9.99 (*0-8423-3848-9*) Tyndale Hse.

— Dream Vacation. LC 99-51362. (HeartQuest Ser.). 300p. 2000. pap. text 9.99 (*0-8423-1899-2*) Tyndale Hse.

Aiken, Henry D., ed. Age of Ideology. LC 77-117748. (Essay Index Reprint Ser.). 1977. 21.95 (*0-8369-1821-5*) Ayer.

Aiken, Henry D., ed. see Hume, David.

Aiken Hodge, Jane. Bride of Dreams. large type ed. 464p. 1980. 29.99 (*0-7505-1251-2*) Ulverscroft.

***Aiken, Joan.** Black Hearts in Battersea. 240p. (YA). (gr. 5 up). 1999. pap. 5.95 (*0-395-97128-4*) HM.

Aiken, Joan. Blackground. large type ed. 339p. 1990. 22.95 (*1-85089-354-3*, Pub. by ISIS Lrg Prnt) Transaction Pubs.

— Cockatrice Boys. 224p. 1997. pap. 12.95 (*0-312-86390-X*) St Martin.

— Cold Shoulder Road. 288p. (J). 1997. pap. 4.50 (*0-440-41341-9*, YB BDD) BDD Bks Young Read.

— Cold Shoulder Road. LC 95-22176. (J). (gr. 5). 1996. 15.95 (*0-03-853218-2*) Delacorte.

— Cold Shoulder Road. LC 95-22176. 1997. 9.60 (*0-606-11218-9*, Pub. by Turtleback) Demco.

— Creepy Company: Ten Tales of Terror. (J). 1995. 9.09 (*0-606-07401-5*, Pub. by Turtleback) Demco.

***Aiken, Joan.** Cuckoo Tree. (Illus.). (J). 2000. 15.00 (*0-618-07024-9*); pap. 5.95 (*0-618-07023-0*) HM.

— Dangerous Games. (Illus.). 256p. (J). (gr. 3-7). 2000. pap. 4.99 (*0-440-41593-4*, Yearling) BDD Bks Young Read.

Aiken, Joan. Dangerous Games. LC 98-7610. 256p. (YA). (gr. 5 up). 1999. 15.95 (*0-385-32661-0*) Delacorte.

***Aiken, Joan.** Died on a Rainy Sunday. 128p. 1999. 21.95 (*0-7540-8550-3*, Black Dagger) Chivers N Amer.

— Died on a Rainy Sunday. large type ed. LC 99-14887. 175p. 1999. pap. 23.95 (*0-7862-1962-9*, G K Hall Lrg Type) Mac Lib Ref.

Aiken, Joan. A Fit of Shivers: Tales for Late at Night. 160p. (J). (gr. 4-7). 1995. pap. 4.50 (*0-440-41120-3*, YB BDD) BDD Bks Young Read.

— Foot in the Grave. LC 92-156011. 1992. 9.09 (*0-606-06383-8*, Pub. by Turtleback) Demco.

— El Gato Mog. 10th ed. (Barco de Vapor Ser.). (SPA.). (J). 1991. 11.05 (*0-606-05256-9*, Pub. by Turtleback) Demco.

— Give Yourself a Fright: Thirteen Tales of the Supernatural. 1995. 9.09 (*0-606-07580-1*, Pub. by Turtleback) Demco.

— The Haunting of Lamb House. large type ed. LC 92-44774. (General Ser.). 276p. 1993. reprint ed. lib. bdg. 18.95 (*1-56054-668-9*) Thorndike Pr.

— Is Underground. 1995. 9.09 9.09 (*0-606-07716-2*, Pub. by Turtleback) Demco.

— Jane Fairfax: Jane Austen's Emma, Through Another's Eyes. 256p. 1997. reprint ed. pap. 12.95 (*0-312-15707-X*) St Martin.

— The Last Slice of Rainbow: And Other Stories. LC 87-45271. (Charlotte Zolotow Bk.). (Illus.). 160p. (J). (gr. 3-7). 1988. 12.95 (*0-06-020042-1*) HarpC Child Bks.

— Midnight Is a Place. 288p. (J). (gr. 4-7). 1993. pap. 2.95 (*0-590-45496-X*) Scholastic Inc.

— Midnight Is a Place. (J). 1974. 8.05 (*0-606-05466-9*, Pub. by Turtleback) Demco.

— Morningquest. large type ed. 544p. 1994. 27.99 (*0-7089-3125-1*) Ulverscroft.

— Mortimer's Cross. LC 83-49475. (Charlotte Zolotow Bk.). (Illus.). 160p. (J). (gr. 3-6). 1984. 12.95 (*0-06-020032-4*) HarpC Child Bks.

— Nightbirds on Nantucket. 248p. (YA). (gr. 5). 1999. pap. 5.95 (*0-395-97185-3*) HM.

***Aiken, Joan.** Stolen Lake. (Illus.). (J). 2000. 15.00 (*0-618-07020-6*); pap. 5.95 (*0-618-07021-4*) HM.

Aiken, Joan. The Teeth of the Gale. LC 87-35050. (Charlotte Zolotow Bk.). 320p. (YA). (gr. 7 up). 1988. 14.95 (*0-06-020044-8*) HarpC Child Bks.

— Trouble with Product X. 190p. 1998. 19.50 (*0-7540-8524-4*, Black Dagger) Chivers N Amer.

— Up the Chimney Down. LC 85-42642. (Charlotte Zolotow Bk.). 256p. (J). (gr. 5 up). 1985. 12.95 (*0-06-020036-7*) HarpC Child Bks.

***Aiken, Joan.** The Way to Write for Children. 112p. 1998. pap. 16.95 (*0-14-027269-0*, Pub. by Pnguin Bks Ltd) Trafalgar.

Aiken, Joan. The Way to Write for Children. 128p. 1998. pap. 8.95 (*0-312-20048-X*) St Martin.

— The Wolves of Willoughby Chase. 176p. (J). (gr. k-6). 1987. pap. 4.99 (*0-440-49603-9*, YB BDD) BDD Bks Young Read.

— The Wolves of Willoughby Chase. LC 75-374349. (J). 1962. 9.60 (*0-606-03691-1*, Pub. by Turtleback) Demco.

***Aiken, Joan.** Wolves of Willoughby Chase. 2000. mass mkt. (*0-385-32790-0*) BDD Bks Young Read.

Aiken, Joan & Austen, Jane. Eliza's Daughter. large type ed. 433p. 1995. lib. bdg. 19.95 (*0-7862-0365-X*) Thorndike Pr.

— Emma Watson. LC 96-21595. 224p. 1996. 20.95 (*0-312-14593-4*) St Martin.

— Emma Watson: The Watsons Completed. large type ed. LC 97-9481. 1997. 24.95 (*1-56895-441-7*, Compass) Wheeler Pub.

— The Youngest Miss Ward. 320p. 1998. text 23.95 (*0-312-19375-0*) St Martin.

— The Youngest Miss Ward. large type ed. LC 98-55243. 1999. 30.00 (*0-7862-1826-6*) Mac Lib Ref.

Aiken, Joan L., ed. Haddonfield Historic Homes: Success Through Historic Preservation. LC 91-108808. (Illus.). 1991. 55.00 (*0-915180-33-2*) Harrowood Bks.

Aiken, John R. Utopianism & the Emergence of the Colonial Legal Profession: New York, 1664-1710. (Outstanding Studies in Early American History). 305p. 1989. reprint ed. 20.00 (*0-8240-6170-5*) Garland.

Aiken, Katherine G. Harnessing the Power of Motherhood: The National Florence Crittenton Mission, 1883-1925. LC 98-8979. (Illus.). 296p. 1998. text 38.00 (*1-57233-017-1*) U of Tenn Pr.

Aiken, Kenneth. Cruising Vermont's Scenic Roads: A Comprehensive Guide. LC 98-29364. (Illus.). 288p. 1998. pap. 15.95 (*0-89272-444-7*) Down East.

***Aiken, L. R.** Human Development in Adulthood. LC 97-51716. (Series in Adult Development & Aging). (Illus.). 416p. (C). 1998. 52.50 (*0-306-45734-2*, Plenum Trade) Perseus Pubng.

Aiken, Leona S. & West, Stephen G. Multiple Regression. (Illus.). 150p. 1991. 48.00 (*0-8039-3605-2*) Sage.

***Aiken, Lewis A.** Dying, Death & Bereavement. 4th ed. 416p. 2000. write for info. (*0-8058-3503-2*) L Erlbaum Assocs.

Aiken, Lewis A. Rating Scales & Checklists: Evaluating Behavior, Personality, & Attitudes. LC 95-39106. 320p. 1996. 69.50 incl. disk (*0-471-12787-6*) Wiley.

Aiken, Lewis R. Aging: An Introduction to Gerontology. 450p. 1994. 62.00 (*0-8039-5445-X*) Sage.

— Assessment of Adult Personality. LC 97-12115. 296p. 1997. 41.95 (*0-8261-9710-8*) Springer Pub.

— Assessment of Intellectual Functioning. 2nd ed. (Perspectives on Individual Differences Ser.). (Illus.). 424p. (C). 1996. 42.50 (*0-306-45152-2*, Kluwer Plenum) Kluwer Academic.

***Aiken, Lewis R.** Dying, Death & Bereavement. 4th ed. 416p. 2000. write for info. (*0-8058-3741-8*); pap. write for info. (*0-8058-3504-0*) L Erlbaum Assocs.

Aiken, Lewis R. Haunting Christmas Tales. 272p. (J). (gr. 4-7). 1993. pap. 3.50 (*0-590-46025-0*) Scholastic Inc.

— Human Differences. LC 99-11092. 352p. 1999. 69.95 (*0-8058-3091-X*); pap. 34.50 (*0-8058-3092-8*) L Erlbaum Assocs.

— Personality: Theories, Research & Applications. LC 92-30073. 512p. (C). 1992. text 61.00 (*0-13-658733-X*) P-H.

***Aiken, Lewis R.** Personality Assessment: Methods & Practices. 3rd ed. 592p. 1999. 59.00 (*0-88937-209-8*) Hogrefe & Huber Pubs.

Aiken, Lewis R. Psychological Testing & Assessment. 10th ed. LC 99-13723. 501p. (C). 1999. 89.00 (*0-205-29567-3*) Allyn.

— Questionnaires & Inventories: Surveying Opinions & Assessing Personality. LC 96-53659. (Illus.). 319p. 1997. 69.50 incl. disk (*0-471-16871-8*) Wiley.

— Tests & Examinations: Measuring Abilities & Performance. LC 97-41072. 293p. 1998. 69.50 incl. disk (*0-471-19263-5*) Wiley.

Aiken, Linda H. & Mechanic, David, eds. Applications of Social Science to Clinical Medicine & Health Policy. 500p. (C). 1986. pap. text 16.95 (*0-8135-1149-6*) Rutgers U Pr.

Aiken, Lisa. The Hidden Beauty of the Shema. 224p. 1997. 18.95 (*1-56871-115-8*, Pub. by Targum Pr) Feldheim.

— To Be a Jewish Woman. LC 91-31680. 312p. 1992. 40.00 (*0-87668-609-9*) Aronson.

— Why Me, God? A Jewish Guide for Coping with Suffering. LC 95-19572. 304p. 1996. 40.00 (*1-56821-535-5*) Aronson.

— Why Me God? A Jewish Guide for Coping & Suffering. LC 95-19572. 304p. 1997. pap. 30.00 (*0-7657-9954-5*) Aronson.

Aiken, Lisa, jt. auth. see Kirzner, Yitzchok.

Aiken, M. Iqiasuaq Avinnaq (The Lazy Mouse) (ESK.). 20p. (J). 1973. pap. 2.00 (*0-933769-47-4*) Alaska Native.

Aiken, Mary J., jt. auth. see House, Peggy.

Aiken, Nancy E. The Biological Origins of Art. LC 97-42064. (Human Evolution, Behavior & Intelligence Ser.). 200p. 1998. 55.00 (*0-275-95901-5*, Praeger Pubs) Greenwood.

Aiken, Nick. Prayers for Teenagers. 104p. (YA). 1992. pap. 5.99 (*0-551-01931-X*) Zondervan.

— Working with Teenagers. pap. 11.99 (*0-551-01649-3*) Zondervan.

Aiken, Peter. Hands-On VB5 for Web Development. LC 97-66857. 480p. 1997. per. 40.00 (*0-7615-0955-0*) Prima Pub.

— Teach Yourself Microsoft Word 2000 in 10 Minutes. LC 98-86986. (Teach Yourself Ser.). (Illus.). 227p. 1999. pap. 12.99 (*0-672-31441-X*) Sams.

Aiken, R. M. Information Processing 92 Vol. II: Education & Society. (IFIP Transactions A: Vol. A-13). 690p. 1992. pap. 195.75 (*0-444-89748-8*, North Holland) Elsevier.

Aiken, Rebecca B. Montreal Chinese Property Ownership & Occupational Change, 1881-1981. LC 87-45785. (Immigrant Communities & Ethnic Minorities in the U. S. & Canada Ser.: No. 20). 1988. 55.00 (*0-404-19430-3*) AMS Pr.

Aiken, Robert J. Aviation Safety: FAA Oversight of Repair Stations Needs Improvement. (Illus.). 91p. 1998. pap. text 20.00 (*0-7881-7205-0*) DIANE Pub.

Aiken, Robert S. Vanish Rain Forests. (Illus.). 212p. 1996. pap. text 45.00 (*0-19-854959-8*) OUP.

Aiken, S. B., et al. Wild Rice In Canada. (Illus.). 176p. (Orig.). 1988. pap. 18.95 (*1-55021-027-0*, Pub. by NC Ltd) U of Toronto Pr.

Aiken, S. Robert. Imperial Belvederes: The Hill Stations of Malaya. (Images of Asia Ser.). (Illus.). 96p. 1994. text 16.95 (*967-65-3037-9*) OUP.

Aiken, S. Robert & Leigh, Colin H. Vanishing Rain Forests: The Ecological Transition in Malaysia. (Oxford Monographs on Biogeography: No. 5). (Illus.). 224p. 1995. pap. 32.00 (*0-614-05437-0*) OUP.

Aiken, Steve. Satanism Vol. 1: Sacrilege, Silly or Serious? (Illus.). 48p. (Orig.). 1989. pap. text 10.00 (*1-877858-02-1*) Amer Focus Pub.

Aiken, Steve, ed. see Prihoda, Deborah.

Aiken, Susan Hardy. Isak Dinesen & the Engendering of Narrative. LC 89-20482. (Women in Culture & Society Ser.). 360p. 1990. pap. text 24.00 (*0-226-01113-5*); lib. bdg. 57.00 (*0-226-01112-7*) U Ch Pr.

Aiken, Susan Hardy, et al, eds. Changing Our Minds: Feminist Transformations of Knowledge. LC 87-9975. 171p. (C). 1988. text 23.50 (*0-88706-618-6*) State U NY Pr.

Aiken, Susan Hardy & Pinano. Making Worlds: Gender Metaphor, Materiality. LC 97-21106. (C). 1994. 35.00 (*0-8165-1779-7*) U of Ariz Pr.

— Making Worlds: Gender, Metaphor, Materiality. LC 97-21106. (C). 1997. pap. 17.95 (*0-8165-1780-0*) U of Ariz Pr.

Aiken, Susan Hardy, et al. Dialogues - Dialogi: Literary & Cultural Exchanges Between (Ex) Soviet & American Women. LC 93-8650. (Illus.). 440p. 1993. pap. text 19.95 (*0-8223-1390-1*); lib. bdg. 69.95 (*0-8223-1375-8*) Duke.

Aiken, Tonia, et al. Staying Healthy - The Later Years, Vol. 1. 220p. Date not set. pap. 14.95 (*1-885221-87-8*) BookPartners.

Aiken, Tonia D. Legal, Ethical, & Political Issues in Nursing. LC 93-46312. 297p. 1994. pap. 31.95 (*0-8036-0081-X*) Davis Co.

— Legal, Ethical, & Political Issues in Nursing. 2nd ed. 320p. pap. text 29.95 (*0-8036-0571-4*) Davis Co.

Aiken, William & LaFollette, Hugh, eds. World Hunger & Morality. 2nd rev. ed. LC 95-23514. 267p. (C). 1995. pap. text 24.40 (*0-13-448284-0*) P-H.

Aiken, Zora. Good Cruising: The Illustrated Essentials. LC 96-43714. (Illus.). 212p. 1996. pap. 18.95 (*0-07-000749-7*) McGraw.

Aiken, Zora & Aiken, David. Good Boatkeeping. LC 94-44224. (Illus.). 1995. pap. text 19.95 (*0-07-000747-0*) Intl Marine.

— Simple Tent Camping: The Basics of Camping from Car or Canoe. (Illus.). 224p. 1996. pap. 15.95 (*0-07-073021-0*, Ragged Mntain) McGraw-Hill Prof.

Aikenhead, Glen, jt. ed. see Solomon, Joan.

Aikens, C. Melvin. Excavations at Snake Rock Village & the Bear River No. 2 Site. LC 68-84289. (Utah Anthropological Papers: No. 87). reprint ed. 25.00 (*0-404-60687-3*) AMS Pr.

— Excavations in Southwest Utah. LC 67-2918. (Glen Canyon Ser.: No. 27). reprint ed. 45.00 (*0-404-60676-8*) AMS Pr.

— Fremont-Promontory-Plains Relationships. (Utah Anthropological Papers: No. 82). reprint ed. 21.00 (*0-404-60682-2*) AMS Pr.

***Aikens, C. Melvin.** Hogup Cave. (Anthropological Papers: No. 93). (Illus.). 300p. 1999. pap. 24.50 (*0-87480-613-5*) U of Utah Pr.

Aikens, C. Melvin. Hogup Cave. (Utah Anthropological Papers: No. 93). reprint ed. 24.00 (*0-404-60693-8*) AMS Pr.

— Virgin Kayenta Cultural Relationships. (Glen Canyon Ser.: No. 29). reprint ed. 22.50 (*0-404-60679-2*) AMS Pr.

Aikens, C. Melvin, ed. Current Status of CRM Archaeology in the Great Basin. (Bureau of Land Management-Nevada: No. 9). 250p. (C). 1986. pap. 27.50 (*1-55567-588-3*) Coyote Press.

Aikens, C. Melvin & Rhee, Song N., eds. Pacific Northeast Asia in Prehistory: Hunter-Fisher-Gatherers, Farmers, & Sociopolitical Elites. LC 92-26733. 236p. 1993. pap. 40.00 (*0-87422-092-0*) Wash St U Pr.

Aikens, C. Melvin, jt. auth. see Fowler, Don D.

Aikens, C. Melvin, jt. frwd. see Jennings, Jesse D.

Aikens, Curtis G. Curtis Cooks with Heart & Soul: Quick Healthy Cooking from the Host of TV's "From My Garden" LC 95-15122. 224p. 1995. 23.00 (*0-688-14012-2*, Hearst) Hearst Commns.

Aikens, David A., et al. Principles & Techniques for an Integrated Chemistry Laboratory. rev. ed. (Illus.). 420p. (C). 1984. reprint ed. pap. text 28.95 (*0-88133-102-3*) Waveland Pr.

Aikens, Diana. From an Appleseed... 64p. (J). (gr. 1-6). 1994. pap. 4.95 (*1-886182-00-0*) Heritage Edits.

Aikens, Diana M. Through a Miner's Eye . . . 60p. (J). (gr. 3-6). 1992. pap. 2.00 (*1-886182-01-9*) Heritage Edits.

Aikens, Susan, ed. see Davis, Andrew.

Aikey, Phillip. Algebra for All. (C). 1997. pap. 45.00 (*0-07-289548-9*) McGrw-H Hghr Educ.

Aikhafaji. Contemporary Strategic Management. Date not set. pap. 58.00 (*0-324-00606-3*) Sth-Wstrn College.

Aikhenvald, Alexandra V., jt. ed. see Dixon, R. M.

***Aikhenvald, Alexandra Y.** Classifiers: A Typology of Noun Categorization Devices. (Illus.). 480p. 2000. text 99.00 (*0-19-823886-X*) OUP.

Aikhenvald, Alexandra Y., jt. ed. see Dixon, R. M. W.

Aikhiezer, A. I. & Yastrzhembsky, I. Theory of Fundamental Interactions. 500p. 1995. text 82.00 (*981-02-1666-1*) World Scientific Pub.

Aikin, Jesse B. The Christian Minstrel. (Earlier American Music Ser.). 1992. 39.50 (*0-306-77326-0*) Da Capo.

Aikin, John. A View of the Life, Travels & Philanthropic Labours of the Late John Howard. 180p. 1994. reprint ed. 42.50 (*0-8377-1912-7*, Rothman) W S Hein.

Aikin, Judith P. Scaramutza in Germany: The Dramatic Works of Caspar Stieler. LC 88-25238. 239p. 1989. lib. bdg. 40.00 (*0-271-00656-0*) Pa St U Pr.

***Aikin, Olga.** Contracts. 264p. 2000. pap. 53.95 (*0-8464-5016-X*) Beekman Pubs.

Aikin, Olga. Contracts. 128p. (C). 1992. write for info. (*0-7855-2627-7*, Pub. by IPM Hse) St Mut.

— Contracts. 176p. (C). 1992. pap. text 95.00 (*0-85292-486-0*, Pub. by IPM Hse) St Mut.

Aikin, Ross R. Kilauea Point Lighthouse. pap. 6.95 (*0-681-02827-0*) Booklines Hawaii.

Aikin, W. A. The Voice: An Introduction to Practical Phonology. Rumsey, H. St. John, ed. LC 51-13505. 175p. reprint ed. pap. 54.30 (*0-608-10908-8*, 205124800092) Bks Demand.

***Aikins, Pat & Aikins, Larry.** The World of Ceramics: A Price Guide. (Illus.). 192p. 1999. pap. 29.95 (*0-89538-108-7*) L-W Inc.

Aikins, Pat & Aikins, Larry. The World of Kreiss Ceramics Vol. 1: A Price Guide. LC 99-193781. (Illus.). 224p. 1999. pap. 24.95 (*0-89538-098-6*) L-W Inc.

Aikins, Carrol, tr. see Grimm, George.

Aikins, Jan & Shrobe, Howard, eds. Innovative Applications of Artificial Intelligence 7, No. 7. (Illus.). 200p. (Orig.). 1995. pap. text 30.00 (*0-929280-81-4*) AAAI Pr.

Aikins, Jan, jt. ed. see Byrnes, Elizabeth.

An Asterisk (*) at the beginning of an entry indicates that the title is appearing for the first time.

A

Aikins, Larry. Pictorial Price Guide to Metal Lunch Boxes & Thermoses. rev. ed. (Illus.). 218p. 1999. reprint ed. pap. 19.95 (*0-89538-007-2*) L-W Inc.

— Vinyl & Plastic Lunch Boxes. 2nd rev. ed. (Illus.). 159p. 1995. pap. 14.95 (*0-89538-015-3*) L-W Inc.

Aikins, Larry, jt. auth. see Aikins, Pat.

Aikk, Juha. Do We Need Minority Rights? Conceptual Issues. LC 96-41627. (International Studies in Human Rights). 1996. lib. bdg. 88.50 (*90-411-0309-0*, Pub. by M Nijhoff) Kluwer Academic.

Aikman, David. Great Souls: Six Who Changed the Century. LC 97-32773. 1997. 22.99 (*0-8499-0965-1*) Word Pub.

***Aikman, David.** Great Souls: Six Who Changed the Century. 388p. 2000. reprint ed. text 23.00 (*0-7881-6975-0*) DIANE Pub.

Aikman, David. When the Almond Tree Blossoms. 1995. mass mkt. 5.99 (*0-8499-3641-1*) Word Pub.

Aikman, Duncan, ed. Taming of the Frontier. LC 67-26711. (Essay Index Reprint Ser.). 1980. 31.95 (*0-8369-0141-X*) Ayer.

Aikman, Lonelle. The Living White House. 9th ed. 152p. 1996. 6.50 (*0-912308-55-9*) White House Hist.

***Aikman, Lonnelle.** The Living White House. (Illus.). 151p. (C). 1998. pap., pap. text 25.00 (*0-7881-7408-8*) DIANE Pub.

Aikman, Lonnelle. Nous le Peuple. 1982. pap. 2.50 (*0-916200-01-9*) US Capitol Hist.

— We the People: The Story of the United States Capitol. 14th ed. National Geographic Society Staff, ed. LC 91-65042. (Illus.). 144p. 1991. reprint ed. pap. 3.00 (*0-916200-10-8*) US Capitol Hist.

— Wir, das Volk. 2nd ed. Vidal, Paul, tr. (GER., Illus.). 144p. 1983. pap. 2.50 (*0-916200-02-7*) US Capitol Hist.

Aikman, Lonnelle & National Geographic Society Editorial Staff. The Living White House. 9th ed. 152p. 1996. pap. 5.00 (*0-912308-54-0*) White House Hist.

Aikman, Sheila. Intercultural Education & Literacy: An Ethnographic Study of Indigenous Knowledge & Learning in the Peruvian Amazons. LC 98-51682. (Studies in Written Language & Literacy: Vol. 7). x, 232p. 1999. 79.00 (*1-55619-385-8*) J Benjamins Pubng Co.

Aikman, Tom G. Boss Gardener: The Life & Times of John McLaren. (Illus.). 118p. (Orig.). 1988. pap. 9.95 (*0-917583-18-3*) Lexikos.

Aikman, Troy. Mind, Body & Soul. 1998. 50.00 (*1-892049-10-4*) Benchmark Press.

— Things Change. LC 95-5479. (Illus.). 40p. (J). 1995. 14.95 (*0-87833-888-8*) Taylor Pub.

Aikman, Z. Susanne. A Primer: The Art of Native American Beadwork. (Illus.). 64p. 1980. reprint ed. pap. 6.95 (*0-9629155-0-5*) Morning Flower.

Aikman, Z. Susanne. Bead Workbook Designer Pages to Color. 16p. (Orig.). 1991. pap. 2.95 (*0-9629155-1-3*) Morning Flower.

***Aikten, Ian.** The Contemporary Australian Poets: An Anthology. LC 98-226148. 256p. 1998. pap. 27.50 (*0-7486-0948-2*, Pub. by Edinburgh U Pr); lib. bdg. 70.00 (*0-7486-0970-9*, Pub. by Edinburgh U Pr) Col U Pr.

Ailbhe. The Rule of St. Ailbhe. 1990. reprint ed. pap. 2.95 (*0-89981-111-6*) Eastern Orthodox.

Aileen, Joyce. Michael Landon: The Triumph & the Tragedy. 1991. mass mkt. 4.50 (*0-8217-3651-5*, Zebra Kensgtn) Kensgtn Pub Corp.

Ailes, Adrian, jt. auth. see Chesshyre, Hubert.

Ailes, Roger. You Are the Message. 1996. pap. 12.95 (*0-614-12578-2*) Doubleday.

Ailes, Roger & Kraushar, Jon. You Are the Message: Getting What You Want by Being Who You Are. 240p. 1989. pap. 14.95 (*0-385-26542-5*) Doubleday.

Ailey, Alvin, Jr. & Bailey, A. Peter. Revelations: The Autobiography of Alvin Ailey. LC 94-16684. (Illus.). 256p. 1994. 18.95 (*1-55972-255-X*, Birch Ln Pr) Carol Pub Group.

***Ailey, Alvin, Jr. & Bailey, A. Peter.** Revelations: The Autobiography of Alvin Ailey. (Illus.). 210p. 1999. reprint ed. 29.95 (*0-7351-0080-2*) Replica Bks.

***Ailhaud, Gerard, ed.** Adipose Tissue Protocols. (Methods in Molecular Biology Ser.: Vol. 155). 334p. 2000. 89.50 (*0-89603-747-9*) Humana.

Ailor, W. H., ed. Engine Coolant Testing: State of the Art - STP 705. 374p. 1980. 32.50 (*0-8031-0331-X*, STP705) ASTM.

Ailsby. Waffen SS: The Illustrated History, 1923-1945. LC 98-48056. (Illus.). 224p. 1998. 29.95 (*0-7603-0564-1*) MBI Pubg.

***Ailsby, Christopher.** Hitler's Sky Warriors: German Paratroopers in Action, 1939-1945. (Illus.). 2000. 32.95 (*1-57488-282-1*) Brasseys.

Ailsby, Christopher. SS: Roll of Infamy. LC 97-28593. (Illus.). 1997. 24.95 (*0-7603-0409-2*) MBI Pubg.

Ailsby, Christopher. SS: Hell on the Eastern Front. 192p. 1997. 80.00 (*1-86227-031-7*, Pub. by Spellmnt Pubs) St Mut.

— Waffen SS: An Unpublished Record 1923-1945. (Illus.). 224p. 1999. 45.00 (*0-283-06345-9*, Pub. by S1 & J) Trans-Atl Phila.

Aim, K. Turkey: Perfect Food. 1993. pap. 3.99 (*0-425-14093-8*) Berkley Pub.

Aim, Meredith. Incentives in Marketing & Motivation. LC 98-67752. 512p. 1998. per. 27.96 (*0-7872-5407-X*) Kendall-Hunt.

Aim, Roger B., jt. ed. see Vigneswaran, Saravanamuthu.

Aiman, E. J., ed. Infertility: Diagnosis & Management. (Clinical Perspectives in Obstetrics & Gynecology Ser.). (Illus.). 260p. 1984. 129.00 (*0-387-90940-0*) Spr-Verlag.

Aimar, Lucien, et al. Frozen Desserts. (Illus.). 192p. 1997. 55.00 (*0-471-16066-0*) Wiley.

Aimard, Paule. El Lenguaje Del Nino. (SPA.). pap. 7.99 (*968-16-4074-8*, Pub. by Fondo) Continental Bk.

AIME, Iron & Steel Society Staff. Process Technology Conference, 9th, Proceedings, Detroit Meeting, March 25-28, 1990 Vol. 9: Use of Instrumentation to Optimize the Continuous Casting Process. LC 82-197229. 203p. pap. 63.00 (*0-7837-2203-6*, 204254100004) Bks Demand.

— Transactions of the Iron & Steel Society of AIME, Vol. 5. LC 83-122618. (Illus.). 116p. reprint ed. pap. 36.00 (*0-8357-8393-6*, 203300700005) Bks Demand.

AIME Meeting Staff. Gold & Silver: Leaching, Recovery, & Economics: Proceedings from the 110th AIME Meeting, Chicago, Illinois, February 22-26, 1981. fac. ed. Schlitt, W. Joseph, ed. LC 81-68558. (Illus.). 154p. 1981. reprint ed. pap. 47.80 (*0-7837-7855-4*, 204761400007) Bks Demand.

AIME, Metallurgical Society Staff. Electro & Thermo-Transport in Metals & Alloys: A Symposium. Hummel, R. E. & Huntington, H. B., eds. LC 77-76059. 165p. reprint ed. pap. 51.20 (*0-608-12292-0*, 202377100034) Bks Demand.

— High-Strength Powder Metallurgy Aluminum Alloys: Proceedings of a Symposium Sponsored by the Powder Metallurgy Committee of the Metallurgical Society of AIME, Held at the 111th AIME Annual Meeting, Dallas, Texas, February 17-18, 1982. Koczak, Michael J. & Hildeman, Gregory J., eds. LC 82-63094. (Metallurgical Society of AIME, Conference Proceedings Ser.). 419p. reprint ed. pap. 129.90 (*0-608-16269-8*, 202666400051) Bks Demand.

— Homogenization & Annealing of Aluminum & Copper Alloys: Proceedings of a Symposium Sponsored by the Non-Ferrous Metals Committee of the Metallurgical Society & the Annealing & Recovery Committee of MSD - ASM International, Cincinnati, Ohio, October 12-13, 1987. Merchant, Harish D. et al, eds. LC 88-60120. 271p. reprint ed. pap. 84.10 (*0-7837-2207-9*, 205245700004) Bks Demand.

— Light Metals, 1987: Proceedings of the Technical Sessions Sponsored by the TMS Light Metal Committee at the 116th Annual Meeting, Denver, Colorado, February 24-26, 1987. Zabreznik, R. D., ed. LC TN0773.A43. 900p. reprint ed. pap. 200.00 (*0-7837-2210-9*, 205246000004) Bks Demand.

— Noble Metal Alloys: Phase Diagrams, Alloy Phase Stability, Thermodynamic Aspects, Properties & Special Features: Proceedings of the TMS Alloy Phase Committee, the TMS Thermodynamics Committee, & American Society for Metals Alloy Phase Diagram Data Committee, Held at the Metallurgical Society of AIME Annual Meeting, February 24-28, 1985. Massalski, T. B. et al, eds. LC 85-29754. 370p. reprint ed. pap. 114.70 (*0-7837-2209-5*, 205245900004) Bks Demand.

— Novel NDE Methods for Materials: Proceedings of a Symposium. Rath, Bhakta B., ed. LC 83-62891. (Conference Proceedings - The Metallurgical Society of AIME Ser.). (Illus.). 205p. reprint ed. pap. 63.60 (*0-8357-5543-6*, 203515800093) Bks Demand.

— Processing of Metal & Ceramic Powders: Proceedings of a Symposium, Sponsored by the Powder Metallurgical Society of AIME & Basic Science Division of the American Ceramic Society ...Louisville, KY, October 12-14, 1981. German, Randall M. & Lay, K. W., eds. LC 82-61009. 345p. reprint ed. pap. 107.00 (*0-608-16944-7*, 205614700050) Bks Demand.

— Thermomechanical Processing of Aluminum Alloys: Processings of a Symposium Sponsored by the TMS-AIME Heat Treatment Committee at the TMS Fall Meeting in St. Louis, MO, October 18, 1978. Morris, James G., ed. LC 79-88848. 233p. reprint ed. pap. 72.30 (*0-608-16964-1*, 205614800050) Bks Demand.

AIME, Society of Mining Engineers Staff. Froth Flotation Fiftieth Anniversary Volume. Fuerstenau, D. W., ed. LC 63-46768. (Rocky Mountain Fund Ser.). 691p. reprint ed. pap. 200.00 (*0-608-14448-7*, 202501800040) Bks Demand.

Aimeric De Peguilhan. Poems. LC 70-128941. reprint ed. 34.50 (*0-404-50724-7*) AMS Pr.

Aimesbury, Richard. Doubles. LC 96-90025. (Orig.). 1996. pap. 17.95 (*0-533-11777-1*) Vantage.

Aimone, Alan C. & Aimone, Barbara A. A User's Guide to the Official Records of the American Civil War. LC 93-9261. (Illus.). 101p. 1993. pap. 12.00 (*0-942597-38-9*) White Mane Pub.

Aimone, Barbara A., jt. auth. see Aimone, Alan C.

AIMR Staff, et al. Selected Chapters - Business One Irwin. 2nd ed. 1991. per. write for info. (*1-55623-765-0*, Irwn Prfssnl) McGraw-Hill Prof.

Ain-Globe, Leah, jt. ed. see Eisenberg, Azriel.

Aina, Dunni. How to Achieve Wealth, Success, & Happiness: A New Success Book for the 1990s. LC 91-65360. 136p. (Orig.). 1992. 9.95 (*0-9629129-0-5*) Worldwide Pubs.

Ainar, R. Sathyanatha. History of the Nayaks of Madura. (C). 1991. reprint ed. 27.00 (*81-206-0532-2*, Pub. by Asian Educ Servs) S Asia.

***Aine, C. J., et al, eds.** Biomag96: Proceedings of the 10th International Conference on Biomagnetism. LC 99-42829. (Illus.). 1187p. 1999. 129.00 (*0-387-98915-3*) Spr-Verlag.

Ainger, Alfred. Charles Lamb. Morley, John, ed. LC 68-58369. (English Men of Letters Ser.). reprint ed. lib. bdg. 34.50 (*0-404-51701-3*) AMS Pr.

— Charles Lamb. (BCL1-PR English Literature Ser.). 191p. 1992. reprint ed. lib. bdg. 69.00 (*0-7812-7585-7*) Rprt Serv.

— Lectures & Essays, 2 vols., Set. LC 76-158235. reprint ed. 67.50 (*0-404-00360-5*) AMS Pr.

Ainger, Andrew, ed. see Ennals, Richard, et al.

Aini, A. A., ed. see Mughniyyah, Muhammad J.

Aini, A. A., ed. see Suhufi, S. M.

Aini, Amir A., ed. see Al-Khoei, Ayattullah A.

Aini, Amirali, ed. see Jordac, George.

Aini, Sadreddin. Death of the Usurer. (Middle Eastern Ser.: No. 26). 350p. (Orig.). 1995. pap. write for info. (*0-936665-23-8*) Jahan Bk Co.

Ainian, Alexander M. From Rulers' Dwellings to Temples: Architecture, Religion & Society in Early Iron Age Greece (1100-700 B. C.) (Studies in Mediterranean Archaeology: Vol. CXXI). (Illus.). 590p. (Orig.). 1997. pap. 126.00 (*91-7081-152-0*, Pub. by P Astroms) Coronet Bks.

***Ainina, M. Fall.** A Field Guide to Internationalizing Business Education. LC 00-22646. 2000. write for info. (*0-9678682-0-3*) U TCtr Intl Bus Ed & Research.

Ainlay, Stephen. Day Brought Back My Night: Ageing & New Vision Loss. 176p. 1989. 29.95 (*0-415-00764-X*) Routledge.

Ainlay, Stephen C., et al, eds. The Dilemma of Difference: A Multidisciplinary View of Stigma. LC 86-15086. (Perspectives in Social Psychology Ser.). (Illus.). 286p. (C). 1986. 59.00 (*0-306-42304-9*, Plenum Trade) Perseus Pubng.

Ainley. Learning Policy. LC 99-18546. 236p. 1999. text 69.95 (*0-312-22230-0*) St Martin.

***Ainley, Beulah.** Black Journalists, White Media. 180p. 1998. pap. 22.50 (*1-85856-058-6*, Trentham Bks) Stylus Pub VA.

Ainley, David G. & Boekelheide, Robert J., eds. Seabirds of the Farallon Islands: Ecology, Dynamics, & Structure of an Upwelling-System Community. (Illus.). 488p. 1990. 69.50 (*0-8047-1530-0*) Stanford U Pr.

Ainley, David G., et al. The Marine Ecology of Birds in the Ross Sea, Antarctica. 97p. 1984. 15.00 (*0-943610-39-7*) Am Ornithologists.

Ainley, John. Primary Schooling in Victoria. (C). 1990. pap. 55.00 (*0-86431-064-1*, Pub. by Aust Council Educ Res) St Mut.

Ainley, John & Sheret, Michael. Progress Through High School. (C). 1992. pap. 65.00 (*0-86431-138-9*, Pub. by Aust Council Educ Res) St Mut.

Ainley, Pat. Class & Skill: Changing Divisions of Knowledge & Labor. 160p. 1993. pap. 31.95 (*0-304-32679-8*); text 100.00 (*0-304-32681-X*) Continuum.

— Vocational Education & Training. Wragg, C. E., ed. (Education Matters Ser.). 144p. 1990. pap. text 29.95 (*0-304-31948-1*) Continuum.

Ainley, Pat & Corney, Mark. Training for the Future: The Rise & Fall of the Manpower Services Commission. 160p. 1990. pap. text 37.95 (*0-304-31861-2*) Continuum.

Ainley, Patrick. Degrees of Difference: Higher Education in the 1990s. LC 97-187089. 256p. (C). 1994. pap. 25.00 (*0-85315-804-5*, Pub. by Lawrence & Wishart) NYU Pr.

— Young People Leaving Home. 160p. 1991. 33.95 (*0-304-32446-9*); text 95.00 (*0-304-32443-4*) Continuum.

Ainley, Patrick & Bailey, Bill. The Business of Learning. LC 97-224029. (Illus.). 224p. 1997. 90.00 (*0-304-33981-4*); pap. 29.95 (*0-304-33982-2*) Continuum.

***Ainley, Patrick & Rainbird, Helen.** Apprenticeship. 224p. 1999. 59.95 (*0-7494-2728-0*, Kogan Pg Educ) Stylus Pub VA.

Ainley, Rosa. Death of a Mother: Daughters' Stories. 260p. 1995. pap. text 13.00 (*0-04-440928-1*) NYU Pr.

***Ainley, Rosa.** Dyke London. 1999. pap. 12.95 (*1-899858-74-1*, Pub. by Ellipsis) Norton.

Ainley, Rosa. The Space Files: Exploring Bodies, Space, & Gender. LC 97-33186. (Illus.). 264p. (C). 1998. 85.00 (*0-415-15489-8*); pap. 25.99 (*0-415-15490-1*) Routledge.

— What Is She Like? Lesbian Identities from 1950s to 1990s. Date not set. pap. 21.95 (*0-304-32900-2*, Pub. by Cassell) LPC InBook.

Ainley, Stephen C., jt. ed. see Hunter, James D.

***Ainsa, Patricia.** Teaching Children with Aids. LC 99-53192. (Symposium Ser.: Vol. 60). 120p. 2000. 59.95 (*0-7734-7823-X*) E Mellen.

Ainsbury, Robert D. DOS 6 Secrets. (Secrets Ser.). 400p. 1993. pap. 39.95 (*1-878058-70-3*) IDG Bks.

Ainscough, Carolyn & Toon, Kay. Breaking Free: A Self-Help Guide for Adults Who Were Sexually Abused As Children. LC 93-37229. 256p. 1993. pap. 12.95 (*1-55561-057-9*) Fisher Bks.

***Ainscough, Carolyn & Toon, Kay.** Surviving Childhood Sexual Abuse: Practical Self-Help for Adults Who Were Sexually Abused as Children. LC 00-35431. 256p. 2000. pap. 14.00 (*1-55561-225-3*) Fisher Bks.

— Surviving Childhood Sexual Abuse Workbook. 224p. 2000. pap., wbk. ed. 14.00 (*1-55561-290-3*) Fisher Bks.

Ainscow, Mel. Effective Schools for All. write for info. (*1-85346-164-4*) Taylor & Francis.

— Special Needs in the Classroom: A Teacher Education Guide. LC 94-195528. 240p. 1994. pap. write for info. (*1-85302-248-9*, Pub. by Jessica Kingsley) Taylor & Francis.

— Understanding the Development of Inclusive Schools. LC 99-218329. 192p. 1999. 85.00 (*0-7507-0735-6*, Falmer Pr); pap. text 26.95 (*0-7507-0734-8*, Falmer Pr) Taylor & Francis.

Ainscow, Mel & Florek, Anton. Special Educational Needs: Towards a Whole School Approach. (Illus.). 168p. (Orig.). 1990. pap. 24.95 (*0-8464-1475-9*) Beekman Pubs.

Ainscow, Mel & Tweddle, David. Early Learning Skills Analysis. 4th ed. 208p. 1984. pap. 34.95 (*0-8464-4331-7*) Beekman Pubs.

— Encouraging Classroom Success. 80p. (Orig.). 1989. pap. 24.95 (*0-8464-1477-5*) Beekman Pubs.

Ainscow, Mel, et al. Creating the Conditions for School Improvement: A Handbook of Staff Development Activities. LC 95-112522. 176p. 1994. pap. 29.95 (*1-85346-310-8*, Pub. by David Fulton) Taylor & Francis.

— School Improvement in an Era of Change. LC 94-12563. 240p. 1994. pap. 21.95 (*0-8077-3390-3*) Tchrs Coll.

Ainscow, Mel, jt. auth. see West, Mel.

Ainscow, Mel, jt. ed. see Booth, Tony.

Ainsley, Michael. I Knew You Were Waiting. 2nd rev. ed. 64p. 1999. reprint ed. pap. 9.95 (*1-58446-006-7*, Legacy OH) Temple Pubg.

***Ainsley, Robert.** The Bluffer's Guide to the Internet: Bluff Your Way in the Internet. (Bluffer's Guides Ser.). 64p. 1999. pap. 5.95 (*1-902825-51-9*) Oval Bks.

— The Bluffer's Guide to University: Bluff Your Way in University. (Bluffer's Guides Ser.). 64p. 1999. pap. 5.95 (*1-902825-66-7*) Oval Bks.

Ainsley, Robert. Encyclopedia of Classical Music. 1999. pap. text 22.95 (*1-85868-628-8*, Pub. by Carlton Bks Ltd) Natl Bk Netwk.

***Ainsley, Robert, ed.** Classical Music. (Illus.). 272p. 2000. 30.00 (*0-7881-9405-4*) DIANE Pub.

***Ainsley, Robert & Rae, Alexander C.** The Bluffer's Guide to Computers: Bluff Your Way in Computers. (Bluffer's Guides Ser.). 64p. 1999. pap. 5.95 (*1-902825-88-8*) Oval Bks.

Ainsley, Ron. Bluff Your Way on the Internet. Taute, Anne, ed. 64p. 1996. pap. 5.99 (*1-85304-580-2*, Pub. by Ravette Bks) Assoc Pubs Grp.

Ainslie, Dorothy. Strangled Waters. LC 96-61790. 192p. (Orig.). 1997. pap. 15.00 (*1-883893-90-9*) WinePress Pub.

Ainslie, Douglas, tr. see Barbey d'Aurevilly, Jules.

Ainslie, Douglas, tr. see Croce, Benedetto.

Ainslie, Hew. Scottish Songs, Ballads, & Poems. LC 75-144578. reprint ed. 37.50 (*0-404-08550-4*) AMS Pr.

— The Works of Hew Ainslie, 1792-1878, Set. 1987. reprint ed. lib. bdg. 600.00 (*0-685-18570-2*) Rprt Serv.

Ainslie, Patricia. Maine Probate Procedure. Duthie, Beth, ed. (Illus.). 72p. 1993. ring bd., suppl. ed. 27.00 (*0-614-03139-7*, MICHIE) LEXIS Pub.

Ainslie, Ricardo. No Dancin' in Anson: An American Story of Race & Social Change. LC 95-18805. 368p. 1995. 27.50 (*1-56821-585-1*) Aronson.

Ainslie, Ricardo C. The Psychology of Twinship. LC 96-46672. 288p. 1997. pap. 40.00 (*1-56821-664-5*) Aronson.

Ainslie, Ricardo C., ed. The Child & the Day Care Setting: Qualitative Variations & Development. LC 84-6836. 209p. 1984. 79.50 (*0-275-91114-4*, C1114, Praeger Pubs) Greenwood.

Ainslie, Susan, jt. auth. see Tenberg, Richard.

Ainslie, Susan, jt. auth. see Tenburg, Richard.

Ainslie, Susan, jt. auth. see Tender, Reinhard.

Ainslie, Tom. Ainslie's Complete Guide to Thoroughbred Racing. (Illus.). 352p. 1988. per. 14.00 (*0-671-65655-4*, Fireside) S&S Trade Pap.

— Ainslie's Complete Hoyle. LC 74-32023. 526p. 1979. per. 16.00 (*0-671-24779-4*) S&S Trade.

— How to Gamble in a Casino. 224p. 1987. pap. 10.00 (*0-671-63952-8*, Fireside) S&S Trade Pap.

Ainslie, Tom & Ledbetter, Bonnie. Body Language of Horses. LC 79-26995. (Illus.). 224p. 1980. 20.00 (*0-688-03620-1*, Wm Morrow) Morrow Avon.

Ainslie, W. Materia Indica, 2 vols., Set. (C). 1988. reprint ed. 100.00 (*0-7855-2257-3*, Pub. by Scientific) St Mut.

— Materia Indica, Vol. 1. xxxiv, 654p. 1979. reprint ed. 300.00 (*0-7855-6645-7*, Pub. by Intl Bk Distr) St Mut.

— Materia Inidica, Vol. 1. (C). 1979. text 325.00 (*0-89771-539-X*, Pub. by Intl Bk Distr) St Mut.

Ainslie, W. S. Naval Nostalgia. 1985. 40.00 (*0-946270-27-9*, Pub. by Pentland Pr) St Mut.

Ainsworth. Ainsworth & Bisby's Dictionary of the Fungi. 8th ed. 615p. 1995. 125.00 (*0-7859-9261-8*) Fr & Eur.

— Intro. Accounting. 1996. pap. 25.94 (*0-256-25691-8*) McGraw.

— Introduction Accounting, 2. 2nd ed. 240p. 1999. pap. 19.69 (*0-07-030690-7*) McGraw.

— Introduction Accountingtg, 1. 2nd ed. 224p. 1999. pap. 19.69 (*0-07-030689-3*) McGraw.

***Ainsworth.** Introduction to Accounting. 2nd ed. LC 99-34638. 968p. 1999. 89.69 (*0-07-030676-1*) McGraw.

Ainsworth. Introduction to Accounting, 1. 2nd ed. 280p. 1999. pap. 19.69 (*0-07-030684-2*) McGraw.

— Introduction to Accounting, 2. 2nd ed. 304p. 1999. pap. 19.69 (*0-07-030685-0*) McGraw.

— Introduction to Accounting, Vol. 1. abr. ed. 1996. 45.00 (*0-256-23372-1*, Irwn McGrw-H) McGrw-H Hghr Educ.

Ainsworth & Bisby, Frank A. Dictionary of the Fungi. 7th ed. 445p. 1983. 125.00 (*0-8288-5172-7*, M9711) Fr & Eur.

Ainsworth, A. W., ed. Advances in Speech, Hearing & Language Processing, Vol. 1. 340p. 1990. 78.50 (*1-55938-210-4*) Jai Pr.

— Advances in Speech, Hearing & Language Processing, Vol. 2. 296p. 1992. 78.50 (*1-55938-300-3*) Jai Pr.

Ainsworth, Catherine H. American Calendar Customs, Vol. II. LC 79-55784. 110p. (Orig.). 1980. 12.00 (*0-933190-07-7*) Clyde Pr.

— American Folk Foods. LC 84-72828. (Illus.). 224p. (Orig.). 1984. 12.00 (*0-933190-12-3*) Clyde Pr.

— Black & White & Said All Over-Riddles: Riddles. LC 72-5461. (Folklore Bks.). 36p. (J). (ps-12). 1976. 5.00 (*0-933190-02-6*) Clyde Pr.

— Family Life of Young Americans. LC 85-72144. 272p. (Orig.). (J). (ps-12). 1986. 12.00 (*0-933190-13-1*) Clyde Pr.

— Folktales of America, Vol. I. LC 80-66300. (Folktales & Legends Ser.). 124p. (Orig.). (J). (ps-12). 1980. 12.00 (*0-933190-08-5*) Clyde Pr.

— Folktales of America, Vol. II. LC 80-66300. (Folktales & Legends Ser.). 212p. (Orig.). (J). (ps-12). 1982. 12.00 (*0-933190-09-3*) Clyde Pr.

— Folktales of America, Vol. III. LC 80-66300. (Folktales & Legends Ser.). 224p. (Orig.). (J). (ps-12). 1987. 12.00 (*0-933190-15-8*) Clyde Pr.
— Games & Lore of Young Americans. LC 83-70191. 251p. (Orig.). (J). (ps-12). 1983. 12.00 (*0-933190-10-7*) Clyde Pr.
— Jump Rope Verses Around the United States. LC 75-4827. (Folklore Bks.). 24p. (J). (ps-12). 1976. 5.00 (*0-933190-01-8*) Clyde Pr.
— Legends of New York State. 2nd ed. LC 78-54873. (Folklore Bks.). 99p. (J). (ps-12). 1983. 12.00 (*0-933190-11-5*) Clyde Pr.
— Superstitions from Seven Towns of the United States. LC 43-7320. (Folklore Bks.). 64p. (J). (ps-12). 1973. 5.00 (*0-933190-00-X*) Clyde Pr.

Ainsworth-Davis, James R. Thomas H. Huxley. LC 70-158236. (English Men of Science Ser.: No. 2). reprint ed. 39.50 (*0-404-07892-3*) AMS Pr.

Ainsworth, Deborah, ed. see Evans-Baker, Kathleen.

Ainsworth, Ford. The Bridge: A Drama in One-Act. (Illus.). 28p. 1982. pap. 3.25 (*0-88680-013-7*) I E Clark.
— Farewell to Galatea: A Comedy in One Act. (Illus.). 35p. 1978. pap. 3.25 (*0-88680-050-1*) I E Clark.
— Persephone: A One-Act Comedy. (Illus.). 40p. 1977. pap. 3.25 (*0-88680-149-4*) I E Clark.
— Persephone: Director's Script. (Illus.). 40p. 1977. pap. 10.00 (*0-88680-150-8*) I E Clark.
— The River Between: A Drama in 3 Acts. (Illus.). 68p. 1991. pap. 4.00 (*0-88680-348-9*) I E Clark.
— The Sheep Thief: Adaptation of the Second Shepherds' Play. (Illus.). 24p. 1979. pap. 3.25 (*0-88680-175-3*) I E Clark.

Ainsworth, Frank. Family Centered Group Care: Model Building. LC 97-74444. (Illus.). 176p. 1997. text 59.95 (*1-84014-121-2*, Pub. by Ashgate Pub) Ashgate Pub Co.

Ainsworth, Frank & Fulcher, Leon C., eds. Group Care for Children. 308p. 1981. pap. 14.95 (*0-422-77850-8*, NO. 3541, Pub. by Tavistock) Routldge.

Ainsworth, Frank, jt. ed. see Fulcher, Leon C.

Ainsworth, G. C., jt. ed. see Mordue, J. E.

Ainsworth, Henry. Annotations on the Pentateuch & Psalms, 2 vols., Set. 1991. reprint ed. 70.00 (*1-877611-35-2*) Soli Deo Gloria.
— Annotations on the Pentateuch & Psalms, 2 vols., Vol. 1. 779p. 1991. reprint ed. 35.00 (*1-877611-33-6*) Soli Deo Gloria.
— Annotations on the Pentateuch & Psalms, 2 vols., Vol. 2. 745p. 1991. reprint ed. 35.00 (*1-877611-34-4*) Soli Deo Gloria.
— A True Confession of the Faith, Which Wee Falsley Called Brownists, Doo Hold. LC 78-26338. (English Experience Ser.: No. 158). 24p. 1969. reprint ed. 25.00 (*90-221-0158-4*) Walter J Johnson.

Ainsworth, Henry & Johnson, Francis. An Apologie or Defence of Such True Christians As Are Commonly Called Brownists. LC 70-25742. (English Experience Ser.: No. 217). 1970. reprint ed. 45.00 (*90-221-0217-3*) Walter J Johnson.

Ainsworth, J., ed. Index of Wills Proved in the Prerogative Court of Canterbury, Vol. 9: 1671-1675. 1969. reprint ed. 90.00 (*0-8115-1510-9*) Periodicals Srv.

Ainsworth, Jackie. An Account to Settle: The Story of the United Bank Workers (Sorwuc) 128p. 1979. pap. write for info. (*0-88974-012-7*, Pub. by Press Gang Pubs) LPC InBook.

***Ainsworth, Jim.** Good Food Guide 2000. 740p. 1999. pap. 24.95 (*0-85202-777-X*) Cimino Pub Grp.

Ainsworth, Jim. Good Food Guide 1999. (Which? Books Travel Guides). 1998. pap. 24.95 (*0-85202-717-6*, Pub. by Which) Cimino Pub Grp.
— The Mitchell Beazley Red Wine Guide: A Complete Introduction to Choosing Red Wines. (Illus.). 192p. 1999. 21.95 (*1-84000-196-8*, Pub. by Mitchell Beazley) Antique Collect.
— The Mitchell Beazley White Wine Guide: A Complete Introduction to Choosing White Wines. (Illus.). 192p. 1999. 21.95 (*1-84000-197-6*, Pub. by Mitchell Beazley) Antique Collect.

***Ainsworth, Jim H.** Biscuits Across the Brazos. (Illus.). vi, 82p. 2000. 15.00 (*0-9679483-0-4*) Season Harvest.

Ainsworth, Jim H. The CPA's Guide to a Successful Financial Planning Practice: Selling Financial Investments & Marketing Advisory Services. LC 94-17917. 264p. 1995. 85.00 (*0-471-07687-2*) Wiley.
— How to Become a Successful Financial Consultant: Making a Living Investing Other People's Money. LC 96-16259. 240p. 1997. 29.95 (*0-471-15561-6*) Wiley.

***Ainsworth, Jim T. & Rudloff, DeLoyd E.** Crossing over Cachino - History of Kennard, Texas. 448p. 1998. 50.00 (*1-878096-48-6*, Epigram Pr) Best E TX Pubs.

Ainsworth, John. The Art of Indoor Bonsai: Cultivation Tropical, Sub-Tropical & Tender Bonsai. 128p. 1992. pap. 19.95 (*0-943955-58-0*, Trafalgar Sq Pub) Trafalgar.

Ainsworth, Katherine. The McCallum Saga: The Story of the Founding of Palm Springs. LC 96-52785. 1996. 28.00 (*0-9618724-1-1*) Palm Springs CA.

***Ainsworth, Ken.** Building a Shelf & a Bike Rack. (Illus.). 32p. (J). (gr. 1-7). 1998. pap. 5.95 (*1-55037-513-X*, Pub. by Annick); lib. bdg. 16.95 (*1-55037-555-5*, Pub. by Annick) Firefly Bks Ltd.
— Building a Solitaire Game & a Pegboard, 2 vols. (Illus.). 32p. (J). (gr. 1-7). 1998. 16.95 (*1-55037-554-7*, Pub. by Annick) Firefly Bks Ltd.
— Building a Solitaire Game & a Pegboard, 2 vols. (Building Together Ser.: No. 1). (Illus.). 24p. (J). (gr. 1-7). 1998. pap. 5.95 (*1-55037-512-1*, Pub. by Annick) Firefly Bks Ltd.

Ainsworth, Ken. Carly's Stories. (Illus.). 24p. (J). (ps-1). 1995. pap. 5.95 (*1-55037-380-3*, Pub. by Annick); text 16.95 (*1-55037-381-1*, Pub. by Annick) Firefly Bks Ltd.

Ainsworth, L. K., jt. ed. see Kirwan, Barry I.

Ainsworth, Larry. Student-Generated Rubrics: An Assessment Model to Help All Students Succeed. LC 98-187161. 80p. 1997. pap. text 15.95 (*1-57232-921-1*) Seymour Pubns.

Ainsworth, Leonard H., jt. auth. see Ainsworth, Mary D.

***Ainsworth, M., et al, eds.** The Graduate Student's Guide to Numerical Analysis '98: Lecture Notes from the VIII EPSRC Summer School in Numerical Analysis. LC 99-32314. (Series in Computational Mathematics: Vol. 26). x, 252p. 1999. 95.00 (*3-540-65752-5*) Spr-Verlag.

Ainsworth, M., ed. see Light, W. A. & Marletta, M.

Ainsworth, M. D., et al. Patterns of Attachment: A Psychological Study of the Strange Situation. 416p. 1978. 99.95 (*0-89859-461-8*) L Erlbaum Assocs.

Ainsworth, Mark, et al, eds. Wavelets, Multilevel Methods & Elliptic PDE's. LC 97-221671. (Numerical Mathematics & Scientific Computation Ser.). (Illus.). 314p. (C). 1997. text 49.95 (*0-19-850190-0*) OUP.

***Ainsworth, Mark & Oden, J. Tinsley.** A Posteriori Error Estimation in Finite Element Analysis. (Pure & Applied Mathematics: A Wiley-Interscience Series of Texts, Monographs & Tracts). 256p. 2000. 84.95 (*0-471-29411-X*) Wiley.

Ainsworth, Martha, et al. The Impact of Female Schooling on Fertility & Contraceptive Use: A Study of Fourteen Sub-Saharan Countries. (LSMS Working Papers: No. 106). (FRE.). 90p. 1995. pap. 22.00 (*0-8213-3328-3*, 13328) World Bank.

Ainsworth, Martha, jt. auth. see Feyisetan, Bamikale J.

Ainsworth, Martha, jt. auth. see Shaw, R. Paul.

Ainsworth, Mary D. An Evaluation of Adjustment Based upon the Concept of Security. LC 41-14467. (University of Toronto, Studies , Child Development: No. 18). 72p. reprint ed. pap. 30.00 (*0-608-16347-3*, 202654500050) Bks Demand.
— Infancy in Uganda: Infant Care & the Growth of Love. LC 67-16039. (Illus.). 491p. 1967. reprint ed. pap. 152.30 (*0-608-04070-3*, 206480200011) Bks Demand.

Ainsworth, Mary D. & Ainsworth, Leonard H. Measuring Security in Personal Adjustment. LC 58-37947. 112p. reprint ed. pap. 34.80 (*0-608-30643-6*, 201411000094) Bks Demand.

Ainsworth, Maryan W. Gerard David: Purity of Vision in an Age of Transition. LC 98-30075. (Illus.). 360p. 1998. 75.00 (*0-8109-6523-2*, Pub. by Abrams) Time Warner.
— Petrus Christus: Renaissance Master of Bruges. LC 93-47600. (Illus.). 232p. 1994. pap. 35.00 (*0-87099-695-9*) Metro Mus Art.

Ainsworth, Maryan W., ed. see Metropolitan Museum of Art (New York, N. Y.) Staff.

Ainsworth, Oliver M., ed. see Milton, John.

Ainsworth, Oliver M., ed. & intro. see Milton, John.

Ainsworth, Patricia. The Devil's Hole. large type ed. 352p. 1987. 27.99 (*0-7089-1566-3*) Ulverscroft.
— Portrait in Gold. large type ed. 416p. 1986. 27.99 (*0-7089-1496-9*) Ulverscroft.
— Understanding Depression. LC 99-35416. (Understanding Health & Sickness Ser.). (Illus.). 120p. 2000. 28.00 (*1-57806-168-7*); pap. 12.00 (*1-57806-169-5*) U Pr of Miss.

Ainsworth, Penne. The Flint Hills Salon: A Case Analysis. 2nd ed. 80p. 1996. pap. 25.95 (*0-471-13829-0*) Wiley.
— Introduction to Accounting. 2nd ed. 1999. pap. 1450.00 (*0-07-030688-5*) McGraw.

Ainsworth, Penne & Deines, Dan. Introduction to Accounting: An Integrated Approach, Chapters 1-13. 576p. (C). 1996. text 35.95 (*0-256-12383-7*, Irwn McGrw-H) McGrw-H Hghr Educ.
— Introduction to Accounting: An Integrated Approach. 576p. (C). 1995. text 20.00 (*0-256-19696-6*, Irwn McGrw-H) McGrw-H Hghr Educ.

Ainsworth, Penne, et al. Introduction to Accounting. 152p. (C). 1996. text 17.50 (*0-256-24349-2*, Irwn McGrw-H) McGrw-H Hghr Educ.
— Introduction to Accounting, 1. 224p. (C). 1996. pap., text 17.50 incl. disk (*0-256-24348-4*, Irwn McGrw-H) McGrw-H Hghr Educ.
— Introduction to Accounting Vol. 1: An Integrated Approach. 1072p. (C). 1996. text 65.95 (*0-256-23308-X*, Irwn McGrw-H) McGrw-H Hghr Educ.
— Introduction to Accounting Vol. 2, Chapters 14-25: An Integrated Approach. 576p. (C). 1996. text 35.95 (*0-256-23374-8*, Irwn McGrw-H) McGrw-H Hghr Educ.
— Introduction to Accounting (Annual Report Package) (C). 1996. text 35.95 (*0-256-22116-2*, Irwn McGrw-H) McGrw-H Hghr Educ.
— Introduction to Accounting Ready Notes, 2. 144p. (C). 1996. text 17.50 (*0-256-24713-7*, Irwn McGrw-H) McGrw-H Hghr Educ.

***Ainsworth, Peter B.** Psychology & Crime: Myths & Reality / LC 99-36913. (Criminology Ser.). 2000. write for info. (*0-582-41424-5*) Addison-Wesley.

Ainsworth, Peter B. Psychology, Law, & Eyewitness Testimony. LC 98-19886. (Psychology of Crime, Policing, & Law Ser.). 208p. 1998. 110.00 (*0-471-96931-1*) Wiley.
— Psychology, Law, & Eyewitness Testimony. LC 98-19886. (Psychology of Crime, Policing, & Law Ser.). 208p. 1999. pap. 35.50 (*0-471-98238-5*) Wiley.

Ainsworth, Peter F. Jean Froissart & the Fabric of History: Truth, Myth, & Fiction in the Chroniques. 352p. 1991. 79.00 (*0-19-815864-5*) OUP.

Ainsworth, Ralph M. Profitable Grain Trading. LC 80-53316. (Illus.). 256p. 1980. reprint ed. text 25.00 (*0-934380-04-X*, 32) Traders Pr.

Ainsworth, Richard E. Roses Forever. (Illus.). 152p. (Orig.). 1996. pap. 7.99 (*0-9655298-0-0*) R E Ainsworth.

Ainsworth, Ruth. Little Yellow Taxi & His Friends. 1997. 12.95 (*0-7188-2554-3*, Lutterworth-Parkwest) Parkwest Pubns.
— Mermaid's Tales. 1997. 14.95 (*0-7188-2460-1*, Lutterworth-Parkwest) Parkwest Pubns.

Ainsworth, Stanley & Fraser, Jane. If Your Child Stutters: A Guide for Parents, No. 11. 3rd ed. 54p. 1988 pap. 1.00 (*0-933388-23-3*) Stuttering Fnd Am.

Ainsworth, T. L., et al. Recent Progress in Many-Body Theories, Vol. 3. (Illus.). 520p. (C). 1992. text 139.50 (*0-306-44246-9*, Kluwer Plenum) Kluwer Academic.

Ainsworth-Vaughn, Nancy. Claiming Power in Doctor-Patient Talk. (Oxford Studies in Sociolinguistics). (Illus.). 224p. 1998. pap. 19.95 (*0-19-509607-X*); text 49.95 (*0-19-509606-1*) OUP.

Ainsworth, W. A. Speech Recognition by Machine. (Computing Ser.: No. 12). 216p. 1988. 95.00 (*0-86341-115-0*, CM012) INSPEC Inc.

Ainsworth, W. A., ed. Advances in Speech Hearing & Language Processing: In Preparation, Winter 1997, Vol. 4. Date not set. 78.50 (*0-7623-0154-6*) Jai Pr.
— Cochlear Nucleus: Structure & Function in Relation to Modeling, Vol. 3. 616p. 1996. 157.00 (*1-55938-430-1*) Jai Pr.

***Ainsworth, W. H.** The Admirable Crichton. 252p. 2000. pap. 9.95 (*0-594-02931-7*) Eightn Hundrd.
— Boscobel: or The Royal Oak. 252p. 2000. pap. 9.95 (*0-594-04295-X*) Eightn Hundrd.
— The Constable de Bourbon. 252p. 2000. pap. 9.95 (*0-594-00177-3*) Eightn Hundrd.
— Guy Fawkes: or The Gunpowder Treason. 252p. 2000. pap. 9.95 (*0-594-00048-3*) Eightn Hundrd.
— The Lancashire Witches. 252p. 2000. pap. 9.95 (*0-594-01483-2*) Eightn Hundrd.
— The Miser's Daughter. 252p. 2000. pap. 9.95 (*0-594-02926-0*) Eightn Hundrd.
— Old St. Paul's. 252p. 2000. pap. 9.95 (*0-594-0017[illegible]-4*) Eightn Hundrd.
— Saint James's. 252p. 2000. pap. 9.95 (*0-594-00168-4*) Eightn Hundrd.

***Ainsworth, W. Harrison.** The Constable of the Tower. LC 99-80201. (Library of Classical Historical Fiction). 340p. 1999. pap. 16.95 (*0-594-00156-0*) Eightn Hundrd.

Ainsworth, William H. Auriol: Or, the Elixir of Life. Reginald, R. & Menville, Douglas A., eds. LC 75-46248. (Supernatural & Occult Fiction Ser.). (Illus.). 1976. reprint ed. lib. bdg. 23.95 (*0-405-08108-1*) Ayer.
— Rookwood: A Romance, 3 vols., bk.2. LC 79-8225 (Illus.). reprint ed. 84.50 (*0-404-61758-1*) AMS Pr.

Ainsworth, William H., jt. auth. see Bulwer Lytton, Edward.

Ainsztein, R., tr. see Baklanov, Grigory.

Aintry, Jack. Last Ride to Rocky Mesa. 224p. 1989. mass mkt. 2.95 (*0-8217-2689-7*, Zebra Kensgtn) Kensgtn Pub Corp.
— Nebraska Ambush. 224p. 1989. mass mkt. 2.95 (*0-8217-2586-6*, Zebra Kensgtn) Kensgtn Pub Corp.

Ainworth, Maryan W., et al. Art & Autoradiography: Insights Into the Genesis of Paintings of Rembrandt, Van Dyck, & Vermeer. Wasserman, Rosanne, ed. (Illus.). 112p. 1987. 50.00 (*0-87099-285-6*, 0-8109-6445-7) Metro Mus Art.

Ainyette, Ivan G. Neuropsychological Case Histories: A Comparative Analysis. unabridged ed. LC 96-93032. (Illus.). 304p. 1998. text 50.00 (*0-9655600-0-7*) NY Neurosci Pr.

Aiono, Uluaipou-o-Malo, jt. auth. see Merrill, Philip.

AIP Conference on Advanced Accelerator Concepts 1. Advanced Accelerator Concepts Vol. 335: AIP Conference Proceedings. Schoessow, Paul, ed. LC 95-78225. (Conference Proceedings Ser.: Vol. 335). (Illus.). 854p. 1995. 170.00 incl. cd-rom (*1-56396-476-7*) Am Inst Physics.

AIP Conference Staff. Laser Acceleration of Particles. Channell, Paul J., ed. LC 82-73361. (AIP Conference Proceedings Ser.: No. 91). 276p. 1982. lib. bdg. 32.00 (*0-88318-190-8*) Am Inst Physics.
— Tetrahedrally Bonded Amorphous Semiconductors: Proceedings of the Conference, No. 20, Yorktown Heights. Brodsky, M. et al, eds. LC 74-80145. 369p. 1974. 16.00 (*0-88318-119-3*) Am Inst Physics.
— Transport Phenomena, 1973: AIP Conference Proceedings, No. 11. Kestin, J., ed. LC 73-80682. 346p. 1973. 14.00 (*0-88318-110-X*) Am Inst Physics.

AIPCR-PIACR Staff. French-English - English-French Dictionary of Road Transportation Technology. 642p. 1992. 99.75 (*2-84060-000-5*, Pub. by La Maison Du Dict) IBD Ltd.
— French-English--English-French Dictionary of Road Transportation Technology. (ENG & FRE.). 642p. 1992. 95.00 (*0-7859-8861-0*) Fr & Eur.

Aiple, Richard. Sparks of Life: A Collection of Thoughts about Life & Love. LC 97-76827. (Illus.). 56p. 1998. pap. 14.95 (*1-885221-79-7*) BookPartners.

Aiqouni, K. H., ed. see Wohlfahrt, Franz.

Air & Gas Structural Design Committee, contrib. by. The Structural Design of Air & Gas Ducts for Power Stations & Industrial Boiler Applications: Air & Gas Duct Structural Design Committee of the Civil Engineers. LC 95-24709. 312p. 1995. 30.00 (*0-7844-0112-8*) Am Soc Civil Eng.

Air & Waste Management Association Staff. Air Pollution Engineering Manual. Buonicore, Anthony J. & Davis, Wayne T., eds. (Illus.). 928p. 1992. text 147.95 (*0-442-00843-0*, VNR) Wiley.
— Air Waste & Environmental Research Faculty Profile. Synergistic Technologices, Inc. Staff et al, eds. LC 92-2439. 384p. 1993. pap. 98.95 (*0-442-01265-9*, VNR) Wiley.

***Air & Waste Management Association Staff & Davis, Wayne T.** Air Pollution Engineering Manual. 2nd ed. LC 99-56637. 912p. 2000. 149.00 (*0-471-33333-6*) Wiley.

Air & Waste Management Association Staff & Synergistic Technologies, Inc. Staff. Air, Waste & Environmental Research Faculty Profile Directory. Hughes, Gary C. et al, eds. (Environmental Engineering Ser.). 378p. 1992. pap. 125.00 (*0-471-28516-1*, VNR) Wiley.

Air Chart Systems Staff. Aviation Topographic Atlas. (Illus.). spiral bd. 59.00 (*1-889776-00-9*) Air Chart.

Air-Conditioning & Refrigeration Institute Staff. Refrigeration & Air Conditioning. 2nd ed. (Illus.). 779p. 1987. pap. text, student ed., lab manual ed. 25.00 (*0-13-770223-X*) P-H.

Air Conditioning Contractors of America Staff. ACCA Guide to Safety & Loss Control. 325p. Date not set. pap. 100.00 (*1-892765-16-0*) Air Conditioning Cont.
— A Contractor's Guide: Strategies for Fighting Unfair Utility Competition. 1996. pap. 80.00 (*1-892765-21-7*) Air Conditioning Cont.
— Financial Analysis for Your HVACR Contracting Industry. (Illus.). 30p. 1995. pap. 40.00 (*1-892765-20-9*) Air Conditioning Cont.
— Understanding the Friction Chart - TT1O2. 12p. 1967. pap. 15.00 (*1-892765-10-1*) Air Conditioning Cont.

Air Conditioning Staff. Refrigeration & Air Conditioning. 3rd ed. LC 97-344. 1072p. 1997. 88.00 (*0-13-323775-3*) P-H.

Air Data, Inc. Staff, ed. Homebuilt Aircraft Directory: The Buyer's Guide to Almost 300 Homebuilt Aircraft Designs. 2nd ed. (Illus.). 157p. 1992. pap. 24.95 (*1-881460-00-2*) Homebuilt Bk.

Air, Dorothy H., jt. auth. see Hassan, Aftab.

Air Force Association. Air Force Fifty. LC 98-60442. 192 p. 1998. write for info. (*1-56311-409-7*) Turner Pub KY.

Air Force Cambridge Research Staff & Peiser, H. Crystal Growth: Proceedings of the International Conference on Crystal Growth, Boston, June 1966. LC 66-29611. 1967. 381.00 (*0-08-011690-6*, Pub. by Pergamon Repr) Franklin.

Air Force Staff. Air Force FAR Supplement. 1996. ring bd. 175.00 (*1-56726-076-4*) Mgmt Concepts.

Air, Gillian M., jt. ed. see Laver, W. Graeme.

AIR, Inc. Staff. Airlines Flying Through Time: A Financial & Historical Overview of the Major Airlines. 2nd ed. 160p. 1998. reprint ed. pap. 34.00 (*1-891726-05-6*) Aviation Info.

Air Pollution Control Conference Staff. Integrated Environmental Control for Coal-Fired Power Plants; Presented at the Air Pollution Control Conference, Denver, Colorado, February 22-25, 1981. Hesketh, Howard E., ed. LC 81-65775. (Illus.). 162p. reprint ed. pap. 50.30 (*0-8357-2896-X*, 203913200011) Bks Demand.

Air Rescue Association Staff. USAF Air Rescue. limited ed. LC 97-60390. 120p. 1997. write for info. (*1-56311-363-5*) Turner Pub KY.

Aira, Cesar. The Hare. Caistor, Nick, tr. from ACE. LC 97-679. 248p. 1998. pap. 16.99 (*1-85242-291-2*) Serpents Tail.

Airaghi. Multiskilling: Dietary Assisting for the Health Care Provider. 2nd rev. abr. ed. LC 98-51789. (Allied Health Ser.). 64p. (C). 1999. pap. 21.95 (*0-7668-0514-X*) Delmar.

Airaksinen, Timo. Ethics of Coercion & Authority: A Philosophical Study of Social Life. LC 87-35766. 232p. (C). 1988. text 49.95 (*0-8229-3583-X*) U of Pittsburgh Pr.
— Of Glamor, Sex, & De Sade. LC 90-35686. 1990. 37.50 (*0-89341-591-X*, Longwood Academic) Hollowbrook.

***Airaksinen, Timo.** The Philosophy of H. P. Lovecraft: The Route to Horror. LC 98-9852. (New Studies in Aesthetics: Vol. 29). VIII, 251p. (C). 1999. text 49.95 (*0-8204-4022-1*, 40221) P Lang Pubng.

Airaksinen, Timo. The Philosophy of the Marquis de Sade. 224p. (C). 1995. pap. 22.99 (*0-415-11229-X*, C0187) Routledge.
— The Philosophy of the Marquis de Sade. LC 94-29578. 208p. (C). (gr. 13). 1995. 80.00 (*0-415-11228-1*, C0186) Routledge.

Airaksinen, Timo & Bertman, Martin A. Hobbes: War among Nations. 208p. 1989. text 82.95 (*0-566-05769-7*, Pub. by Avebry) Ashgate Pub Co.

Airaksinen, Timo & Gasparski, Wojciech W., eds. Practical Philosophy & Action Theory. LC 92-34585. (Praxiology: the International Annual of Practical Philosophy & Methodology Ser.: Vol. 2). 319p. (C). 1993. text 49.95 (*1-56000-094-5*) Transaction Pubs.

Airasian. Assessment in the Classroom. 2nd ed. LC 99-31296. 320p. 1999. pap. 31.55 (*0-07-228953-8*) McGraw.
— Classroom Assessment. 2nd ed. 1993. teacher ed. 21.56 (*0-07-000771-3*) McGraw.

Airasian, Peter W. Assessment in the Classroom. LC 95-20310. (C). 1995. pap. text 24.50 (*0-07-000772-1*) McGraw.
— Assessment in the Classroom. LC 95-20310. 1995. write for info. (*0-07-000773-X*) McGraw.

Airasian, Peter W. & Gullickson, Arlen R. Teacher Self-Evaluation Tool Kit. LC 96-2538. (Illus.). 96p. 1996. pap. 22.95 (*0-8039-6517-6*) Corwin Pr.
— Teacher Self-Evaluation Tool Kit. (Illus.). 96p. 1996. 51.95 (*0-8039-6516-8*) Corwin Pr.
— Teacher Self-Evaluation Tool Kit. 96p. 1997. wbk. ed. 49.95 (*2-8106-6516-8*); pap., wbk. ed. 19.95 (*2-8106-6517-6*) NEA.

Airasian, Peter W., et al. Minimal Competency Testing. LC 79-3994. (Illus.). 248p. 1979. 39.95 (*0-87778-138-9*) Educ Tech Pubns.

Airasian, Peter W., jt. auth. see Gay, L. R.

Airbrush Action Magazine Staff, compiled by. Airbrush Action 4: The Best New Airbrush Illustration. (Illus.). 192p. 1997. 39.99 (*1-56496-200-8*) Rockport Pubs.

A

Airbrush Action Magazine Staff, ed. Airbrush Action 4. (Illus.). 192p. 1995. pap. 39.99 (*1-56496-208-3*) Rockport Pubs.

Aird, Alisdair, ed. The Good Guide to Britain, 1998: Fabulous Things to Do & See in Britain. (Illus.). 960p. 1997. 22.95 (*0-09-185244-7*, Pub. by Ebury Pr) Trafalgar.

***Aird, Alisdair, ed.** The Good Guide to Britain 2000: Fabulous Things to Do & See in Britain. (Illus.). 992p. 1999. pap. 24.95 (*0-09-187095-X*, Pub. by Ebury Pr) Trafalgar.

Aird, Alisdair, ed. Good Pub Guide, 1998. (Illus.). 1056p. 1997. pap. 22.95 (*0-09-181475-8*, Pub. by Ebury Pr) Trafalgar.

— The Good Pub Guide, 1999. (Illus.). 1056p. 1998. pap. 24.95 (*0-09-181476-6*, Pub. by Ebury Pr) Trafalgar.

***Aird, Alisdair, ed.** The Good Pub Guide 2000. (Illus.). 1056p. 1999. pap. 24.95 (*0-09-186792-4*, Pub. by Ebury Pr) Trafalgar.

Aird, Catherine. After Effects. large type ed. (Nightingale Ser.). 250p. 1997. pap. 18.95 (*0-614-25110-9*, G K Hall Lrg Type) Mac Lib Ref.

— A Going Concern. large type ed. LC 94-34004. (Nightingale Ser.). 235p. 1995. pap. 17.95 (*0-7838-1134-9*, G K Hall Lrg Type) Mac Lib Ref.

***Aird, Catherine.** Henrietta Who? large type ed. LC 00-21437. 268p. 2000. pap. 21.95 (*0-7838-9003-6*, G K Hall Lrg Type) Mac Lib Ref.

— The Religious Body: The First C.D. Sloan Mystery. 2000. 21.95 (*0-7540-8561-9*, Black Dagger) Chivers N Amer.

— Stiff News. LC 98-48257. 222 p. 1999. write for info. (*0-7540-3643-X*) Chivers N Amer.

Aird, Catherine. Stiff News. LC 98-47610. 240p. 1998. text 21.95 (*0-312-20023-4*) St Martin.

— Stiff News. LC 98-48257. 1999. pap. text 20.95 (*0-7838-8477-X*) Thorndike Pr.

Aird, Edwin. Basic Physics for Medical Imaging. 224p. 1988. pap. 70.00 (*0-7506-1796-9*) Buttrwrth-Heinemann.

***Aird, Forbes.** Automotive Math Handbook. LC 99-57010. (Illus.). 160p. 2000. pap. 14.95 (*0-7603-0696-6*, 129821AP, Pub. by MBI Pubg) Motorbooks Intl.

Aird, Forbes. High Performance Hardware: Fastener Technology for Auto Racers & Enthusiasts. LC 98-49146. 176p. 1999. pap. 16.95 (*1-55788-304-1*, HP Books) Berkley Pub.

— How to Restore Auto Electrics. (Illus.). 128p. 1996. pap. 19.95 (*0-7603-0120-4*) MBI Pubg.

— Mechanic's Guide to Precision Measurement Tools - Power Pro: Power Pro. LC 99-17761. (Illus.). 128p. 1999. pap. 19.95 (*0-7603-0545-5*) MBI Pubg.

— Race Car Chassis Design & Construction. LC 97-14012. (PowerPro Ser.). (Illus.). 128p. 1997. pap. 19.95 (*0-7603-0283-9*) MBI Pubg.

— Racer's Encyclopedia of Metals, Fibers & Materials. (Power Pro Ser.). (Illus.). 128p. 1994. pap. 19.95 (*0-87938-916-8*) MBI Pubg.

Aird, Forbes & Elston, Malco. How to Tune & Modify Carburetors for High Performance. LC 97-35972. (Power Tech Ser.). (Illus.). 160p. 1997. pap. 16.95 (*0-7603-0421-1*) MBI Pubg.

Aird, Forbes D. Fiberglass & Composite Materials: An Enthusiast's Guide to High Performance Non-Metallic Materials for Automotive Racing & Marine Use. LC 95-25236. 176p. 1996. pap. 17.95 (*1-55788-239-8*, HP Books) Berkley Pub.

Aird, Hazel B. Henry Ford: Young Man with Ideas. (J). 1986. 10.05 (*0-606-03225-8*, Pub. by Turtleback) Demco.

Aird, Hazel B. & Ruddiman, Catherine. Henry Ford: Young Man with Ideas. LC 86-10756. (Childhood of Famous Americans Ser.). (Illus.). 192p. (J). (gr. 2-6). 1986. reprint ed. mass mkt. 4.95 (*0-02-041910-4*) Macmillan.

Aird, John. Slaughter of the Innocents: Coercive Birth Control in China. 150p. 1990. 24.75 (*0-8447-3703-8*, AEI Pr) Am Enterprise.

Aird, John S. The Size, Composition & Growth of the Population of Mainland China. LC 76-38047. (China Classic & Contemporary Works in Reprint Ser.). reprint ed. 41.50 (*0-404-56901-3*) AMS Pr.

***Aird, Leet Paul.** Loon Laughter: Ecological Fables & Nature Tales. 1999. pap. 11.95 (*1-55041-390-2*) Fitzhenry & W Ltd.

Aird, Robert B. Foundations of Modern Neurology: A Century of Progress. LC 93-25683. 315p. 1994. reprint ed. pap. 97.70 (*0-608-05830-0*, 205979500007) Bks Demand.

Aird, Robert B., et al. The Epilepsies: A Critical Review. LC 84-6768. (Illus.). 320p. 1984. reprint ed. pap. 99.20 (*0-608-07213-3*, 206743800009) Bks Demand.

Aird, William M. St. Cuthbert & the Normans: The Church of Durham, 1071-1153. LC 98-23148. (Studies in the History of Medieval Religion: Vol. 14). (Illus.). 328p. 1998. 75.00 (*0-85115-615-0*, Boydell Pr) Boydell & Brewer.

Aires, Elizabeth. Men & Women in Interaction: Reconsidering the Differences. 304p. 1996. pap. 19.95 (*0-19-510358-0*) OUP.

Airey, N., jt. auth. see Thorn, R.

Airey, Theresa. Creative Photo Printing. LC 96-23298. (Illus.). 160p. 1996. 29.95 (*0-8174-3725-8*, Amphoto) Watsn-Guptill.

Airey, W. T., et al. New Zealand: Chapters by W. T. G. Airey (And Others) LC 81-23727. (United Nations Ser.). (Illus.). 329p. 1982. reprint ed. lib. bdg. 69.50 (*0-313-23410-8*, BENZ, Greenwood Pr) Greenwood.

Airguide Publications, Inc. Staff. The Baja Traveler. 2nd ed. Garcia, Brenda, ed. LC 86-72692. (Illus.). 363p. 1991. pap. text 24.00 (*0-934754-03-9*) Airguide Pubns.

Airhart, Arnold E. Acts. Greathouse, William M. & Taylor, Willard H., eds. (Bible Exposition Ser.: Vol. 5). 196p. 1977. 14.99 (*0-8341-0316-8*) Beacon Hill.

Airhart, John. Voyage to Olympus. 250p. (Orig.). 1997. pap. 9.95 (*0-9659308-9-0*) Erica Hse.

Airhart, Phyllis D. Serving the Present Age: Revivalism, Progressivism & the Methodist Tradition in Canada. 232p. 1992. 60.00 (*0-7735-0882-1*, Pub. by McG-Queens Univ Pr) CUP Services.

Airhart, Phyllis D. & Bendroth, Margaret L., eds. Faith Traditions & the Family. LC 96-16562. (Studies in the Family, Religion, & Culture). 184p. 1996. pap. 18.00 (*0-664-25581-7*) Westminster John Knox.

Airhihenbuwa, Collins O. Health & Culture: Beyond the Western Paradigm. LC 95-2551. (Illus.). 176p. 1995. 44.00 (*0-8039-7156-7*); pap. 19.95 (*0-8039-7157-5*) Sage.

Airiau, Roland, et al. Circuit Synthesis with VHDL. LC 93-42978. (International Series in Engineering & Computer Science, VLSI, Computer Architecture, & Digital Screen Processing: Vol. 261). 240p. (C). 1994. lib. bdg. 105.00 (*0-7923-9429-1*) Kluwer Academic.

Airlie, Shiona M. Thistle & Bamboo: The Life & Times of Sir James Stewart Lockhart. (Illus.). 276p. 1990. 29.95 (*0-19-584211-1*) OUP.

Airola, Paavo O. Are You Confused? The Authoritative Answers to Controversial Questions. 224p. 1984. pap. 7.95 (*0-932090-04-4*) Health Plus.

— Cancer: Causes, Prevention & Treatment-the Total Approach. 48p. 1984. pap. 3.95 (*0-932090-05-2*) Health Plus.

— Everywoman's Book. (Illus.). 640p. 1984. 17.95 (*0-932090-00-1*); pap. 14.95 (*0-932090-10-9*) Health Plus.

— Everywoman's Book: Dr. Airola's Practical Guide to Holistic Health. (Health Plus Bk.). 640p. 1984. pap. 12.95 (*0-685-53939-3*) NTC Contemp Pub Co.

— How to Get Well: Dr. Airola's Handbook of Natural Healing. 304p. 1984. 14.95 (*0-932090-03-6*) Health Plus.

— How to Keep Slim, Healthy & Young with Juice Fasting. 80p. 1971. pap. 6.95 (*0-685-42168-6*) Health Plus.

— Hypoglycemia: A Better Approach. 192p. 1977. pap. 7.95 (*0-932090-01-X*) Health Plus.

— The Miracle of Garlic. 48p. 1984. pap. 3.95 (*0-932090-08-7*) Health Plus.

— Stop Hair Loss. 32p. 1984. pap. 2.95 (*0-932090-06-0*) Health Plus.

— Swedish Beauty Secrets. 48p. 1984. pap. 3.95 (*0-932090-07-9*) Health Plus.

— There Is a Cure for Arthritis. 228p. (C). 1988. pap. text 10.95 (*0-13-914698-9*) P-H.

— Worldwide Secrets for Staying Young. 208p. 1984. pap. 6.95 (*0-932090-12-5*) Health Plus.

Airola, Paavo O. & Lines, Anni M. The Airola Diet & Cookbook. (Health Plus Bk.). 1984. 12.95 (*0-685-53936-9*) NTC Contemp Pub Co.

— The Airola Diet & Cookbook: World Famous Diet of Supernutrition for Superhealth. (Illus.). 288p. 1984. 12.95 (*0-932090-11-7*) Health Plus.

Airozo, Diana, jt. ed. see Warmbrodt, Robert D.

AIRP Workshop, et al. Interdisciplinary Computer Vision: Applications & Changing Needs : 22nd Aipr Workshop, 13-15 October 1993, Washington, D. C. LC 94-65652. vii, 237p. 1994. write for info. (*0-8194-1390-9*) SPIE.

Airport Committee. Airport Service Area Lighting. (Recommended Practices Ser.). (Illus.). 9p. 1987. pap. 10.00 (*0-87995-035-8*, RP-14-87) Illum Eng.

Airports Conference Staff. Airports, Key to Air Transportation System: Proceedings of the Airports Conference, Atlanta 1971. LC 73-171782. 297p. 1971. reprint ed. pap. 92.10 (*0-8357-5289-5*, 201011800073) Bks Demand.

Airs, John & Ball, Chris. Taking Time to Act: A Guide to Cross-Curricular Drama. LC 94-43586. 164p. 1995. pap. 16.95 (*0-435-08666-9*, 08666) Heinemann.

Airs, Malcolm. The Making of the English Country House, 1500-1640 LC 76-379881. viii, 208 p. 1975. write for info. (*0-85139-378-0*) Arch Pr Bks.

— Tudor & Jacobean Country House: A Building History. LC 97-159919. 1997. 33.95 (*0-7509-0737-1*, Pub. by Sutton Pub Ltd) Intl Pubs Mktg.

— The Tudor & Jacobean Country House: A Building History. (Illus.). 256p. 1998. pap. 24.95 (*0-7509-1788-1*, Pub. by Sutton Pub Ltd) Intl Pubs Mktg.

Airst, Randall. How to Avoid Environmental Liability: A Practical Guide for Real Estate Owners, Lenders & Professionals. 2nd ed. Stann, Susan, ed. (Illus.). 435p. 1996. text 125.00 (*1-886509-04-2*); pap. text 95.00 (*1-886509-05-0*) Marga Environ.

Airst, Randall L. How to Avoid Environmental Liability: A Practical Guide for Corporations, Financial Institutions & Professionals. 550p. (C). 1994. spiral bd., per. 125.00 (*0-614-03968-1*) Marga Environ.

— How to Avoid Environmental Liability: A Practical Guide for Real Estate Owners, Lenders & Professionals. rev. ed. Stann, Susan, ed. 1994. 125.00 (*1-886509-00-X*) Marga Environ.

***Airth, Rennie.** River of Darkness. LC 99-55209. 2000. 28.95 (*0-7862-2334-0*) Thorndike Pr.

— River of Darkness. 2000. pap. 6.99 (*0-14-029196-2*) Viking Penguin.

— River of Darkness. large type ed. 520p. 2000. write for info. (*0-7089-4165-6*) Ulverscroft.

Airy, Anne, ed. see Gerrard, Keith & Perkins Cole Liability Law Group Staff.

Airy, George B. & Cohen, I. Bernard, eds. Gravitation. LC 80-2113. (Development of Science Ser.). (Illus.). 1981. lib. bdg. 23.95 (*0-405-13833-4*) Ayer.

Airy, Helen L. Whatever Happened to Billy the Kid? Another Viewpoint. LC 92-9629. (Illus.). (Orig.). 1992. pap. 12.95 (*0-86534-185-0*) Sunstone Pr.

***AIS Editorial Staff.** Strategic Report on Employer Managed Care Purchasing in 40 Metro Areas. 389p. 1999. spiral bd. 527.00 (*0-929156-57-9*) Atlantic Info Services Inc.

— Strategic Report on Hospitals in 40 Metro Areas. 724p. 1999. spiral bd. 387.00 (*0-929156-72-2*) Atlantic Info Services Inc.

— Strategic Report on Managed Care Plans in 40 Metro Areas. 464p. 1999. spiral bd. 567.00 (*0-929156-58-7*) Atlantic Info Services Inc.

***AIS Editorial Staff, ed.** 43 Practical Medicare Compliance Strategies for Physician Group Practices. 43p. 1999. spiral bd. 47.00 (*0-929156-62-5*) Atlantic Info Services Inc.

— HMO & PBM Strategies for Pharmacy Benefits. 2nd rev. ed. 265p. 1999. pap. 389.00 (*0-929156-73-0*) Atlantic Info Services Inc.

— Managed Care Contracting & Capitation Strategies. 37p. 1998. spiral bd. 9.00 (*0-929156-40-4*) Atlantic Info Services Inc.

— 73 Practical Strategies for Medicare Compliance. 2nd rev. ed. 85p. 1998. spiral bd. 54.00 (*0-929156-74-9*) Atlantic Info Services Inc.

Aisa, Maria Del Carmen Herrero, see Del Carmen Herrero Aisa, Maria, notes.

Aisa, P. A. Brana, jt. auth. see Ramiro, J. M. Santamaria.

***Aisbett, Bev.** Living with It: A Survivor's Guide to Panic Attacks. 1999. pap. 8.95 (*0-207-18040-7*, Pub. by Colns) Consort Bk Sales.

Aisbett, Janet E., et al. On (K-Z-n) & K-Fq(t)-(t2) LC 85-15802. (Memoirs of the American Mathematical Society Ser.: No. 329). 200p. 1985. pap. 24.00 (*0-8218-2330-2*, MEMO/57/329C) Am Math.

***Aisbett, Mark.** So You Wanna Be a Stuntman: The Official Stuntman's Guidebook. 96p. 1999. per. 19.95 (*0-9684865-0-9*) Lif5drivers.

AISC Manual Committee. Manual of Steel Construction Allowable Stress Design. 9th rev. ed. (Illus.). 1144p. (C). 1991. text 72.00 (*1-56424-000-2*, M016) Am Inst Steel Construct.

AISE Staff. The Lubrication Engineers Manual. 2nd ed. LC 96-85885. (Illus.). 650p. 1996. text 245.00 (*0-930767-01-2*) Assn Iron & Steel.

— Specifications for Electric Overhead Traveling Cranes for Steel Mill Service. (Technical Papers: Vol. P257). (Illus.). 48p. 1949. pap. text 30.00 (*1-55589-457-7*) AGMA.

AISE Staff, et al. The Making, Shaping & Treating of Steel. 10th ed. LC 84-81539. (Illus.). 1572p. 1985. text 125.00 (*0-930767-00-4*, 6357Z) Assn Iron & Steel.

AISE Steel Foundation Staff, jt. auth. see Fruehan, R. J.

Aisen, Mindy L., ed. Orthotics in Neurologic Rehabilitation. 160p. 1992. pap. 34.95 (*0-939957-47-7*) Demos Medical.

***Aisen, Mindy L., ed.** Prosthetics - Amputations - Orthotics - Orthopedics & Spinal Cord Injury & Other Neurological Disorders. (Illus.). 59p. (C). 2000. pap. text 20.00 (*0-7881-8674-4*) DIANE Pub.

Aisen, Mindy L., ed. Sexual & Reproductive Neurorehabilitation. LC 97-12460. (Current Clinical Neurology Ser.). (Illus.). 256p. 1997. 125.00 (*0-89603-376-7*) Humana.

Aisen, Paul, et al. Alzheimer's Disease - Questions & Answers, 2nd Edition. 2nd ed. (Questions & Answers Ser.). (Illus.). 154p. 1999. pap. 17.95 (*1-873413-52-1*) Merit Pub Intl.

Aisenberg. Patent Law. 2nd ed. 1992. 95.00 (*0-316-02052-4*, Aspen Law & Bus) Aspen Pub.

— Patent Law Precedent. 1991. 95.00 (*0-316-02043-5*, Aspen Law & Bus) Aspen Pub.

Aisenberg, Alan C. Malignant Lymphoma: Biology, Natural History & Treatments. LC 90-13686. (Illus.). 395p. 1991. text 54.50 (*0-8121-1382-9*) Lppncott W & W.

Aisenberg, Andrew R. Contagion: Disease, Government & the 'Social Question' in Nineteenth-Century France. LC 98-36505. 294p. 1998. 45.00 (*0-8047-3395-3*) Stanford U Pr.

Aisenberg, Gino & Montes, Elizabeth. Bursting with Joy - Una Celebracion! (Illus.). (Orig.). (J). (gr. 1-8). 1992. teacher ed. 15.95 (*1-55944-025-2*) Franciscan Comns.

Aisenberg, Irwin M. Attorney's Dictionary of Patent Claims: Legal Materials & Practice Commentaries, 2 vols., Set. 1985. ring bd. 470.00 (*0-8205-1546-9*) Bender.

Aisenberg, Katy. Ravishing Images: Ekphrasis in the Poetry & Prose of William Wordsworth, W. H. Auden, & Philip Larkin. (American University Studies: Vol. 158). VIII, 206p. (C). 1995. text 41.95 (*0-8204-2031-X*) P Lang Pubng.

Aisenberg, Nadya. Before We Were Strangers. LC 89-82065. 96p. 1990. pap. 15.95 (*0-948259-81-7*, Pub. by Forest Bks) Dufour.

— A Common Spring: Crime Novel & Classic. LC 79-84638. 1980. 16.95 (*0-87972-141-3*); pap. 9.95 (*0-87972-142-1*) Bowling Green Univ Popular Press.

— Leaving Eden: Poems. LC 95-60233. 96p. 1996. pap. 14.95 (*1-85610-039-1*, Pub. by Forest Bks) Dufour.

— We Animals: Poems of Our World. LC 88-35043. 1989. pap. 10.95 (*0-87156-685-0*, Pub. by Sierra) Random.

Aisenberg, Nadya & Harrington, Mona. Women of Academe: Outsiders in the Sacred Grove. LC 87-30067. 224p. 1988. pap. 17.95 (*0-87023-607-5*) U of Mass Pr.

Aish, Caroline, jt. auth. see Rolley, Katrina.

Aish Hatorah Women's Organization Staff, compiled by. The Taste of Shabbos, The Complete Cookbook. 1987. 19.95 (*0-87306-426-7*) Feldheim.

Aisher, Robin. Racing Skipper. 96p. (C). 1990. text 59.00 (*0-906754-69-0*, Pub. by Fernhurst Bks) St Mut.

Aisner, Joseph, ed. Lung Cancer. LC 84-12095. (Contemporary Issues in Clinical Oncology Ser.: No. 3). (Illus.). 352p. reprint ed. pap. 109.20 (*0-7837-6257-7*, 204596900010) Bks Demand.

Aisner, Joseph, et al, eds. Comprehensive Textbook of Thoracic Oncology. LC 95-2030. (Illus.). 992p. 1996. 149.00 (*0-683-00062-4*) Lppncott W & W.

Aisner, Joseph, ed. see Chang, Paul.

Aissaoui, D. M., et al, eds. Applications of Paleomagnetism to Sedimentary Geology. (Special Publications: Vol. 49). (Illus.). 209p. 1993. text 86.00 (*1-56576-002-6*) SEPM.

Aissing, Alena. Russian Dictionaries: Selected Bibliography, 1960-1990. LC 90-23731. 81p. 1991. 12.95 (*0-912526-52-1*) Lib Res.

Aistrip, Joseph A. The Southern Strategy Revisited: Republican Top-Down Advancement in the South. LC 94-41601. (Illus.). 312p. 1996. 39.95 (*0-8131-1904-9*) U Pr of Ky.

Ait. Caring for Children. (Early Childhood Education Ser.). 1992. pap., teacher ed. 9.00 (*0-8273-5405-3*) Delmar.

***Ait.** Communication 2000 Certification & Testing Tools. 1998. 28.95 (*0-538-68876-9*) Thomson Learn.

— Diversity in the Workplace. 1997. pap. 120.00 (*0-538-68003-2*) Thomson Learn.

— Engineering & Industry. 1997. pap. 120.00 (*0-538-68007-5*) Thomson Learn.

— Ethics in Workplace. 1997. pap. 120.00 (*0-538-68004-0*) Thomson Learn.

— Health Service. 1997. pap. 120.00 (*0-538-68005-9*) Thomson Learn.

— Learn Good, Skills at Work: Using Resources, 15 Vols. (Tech Prep Ser.). 1999. pap. 110.00 (*0-538-68964-1*) Sth-Wstrn College.

— Learner's Guide, Skills at Work: Applying Technology, Vol. 3. (Tech Prep Ser.). 1999. pap., student ed. 8.50 (*0-538-68968-4*) Sth-Wstrn College.

— Learner's Guide, Skills at Work: Developing Interpersonal Skills, Vol. 2. (Tech Prep Ser.). 1999. pap. 8.50 (*0-538-68973-0*) Sth-Wstrn College.

— Learner's Guide, Skills at Work: Using Resources. (Tech Prep Ser.). 1999. pap. 8.50 (*0-538-68958-7*) Sth-Wstrn College.

— Learner's Guide, Skills at Work Module 4: Understanding Systems. (Tech Prep Ser.). 1999. pap. 8.50 (*0-538-69001-1*) Sth-Wstrn College.

— Learner's Guide, Skills at Work Module 5: Acquiring Information. (Tech Prep Ser.). 1999. pap. 8.50 (*0-538-69008-9*); pap. 110.00 (*0-538-69013-5*) Sth-Wstrn College.

— Learning Guide- Skills at Work Module 3: Applying Technology, 15 Vos. (Tech Prep Ser.). 1999. pap. 110.00 (*0-538-68999-4*) Sth-Wstrn College.

— Learning Guide, Skills at Work Module 2: Developing Interpersonal Skills, 15 Vols. (Tech Prep Ser.). 1999. pap. 110.00 (*0-538-68979-X*) Sth-Wstrn College.

— Learning Guide, Skills at Work Module 4: Understanding Systems. 1999. pap. 110.00 (*0-538-69006-2*) Sth-Wstrn College.

— Science Links. 1997. pap., student ed. 3.25 (*0-538-67100-9*) Thomson Learn.

Ait. The Teacher's Links: Science Links. (Applied Science Ser.). 1997. mass mkt. 100.95 (*0-538-67842-9*) S-W Pub.

AIT - University of Wisconsin Staff. Caring for Infants & Toddlers. 36p. (Orig.). 1993. pap. 6.95 (*0-7842-0666-X*) Agency Instr Tech.

Ait-Kaci, Hassan. Warren's Abstract Machine: A Tutorial Reconstruction. 1991. pap. write for info. (*0-262-69146-9*) MIT Pr.

AIT-Maryland State Dept of Education Staff. Everybody's School House Guide. 200p. (Orig.). 1996. pap. text. write for info. (*0-7842-0805-0*) Agency Instr Tech.

AIT-PDK Staff. John I. Goodlad: New Schools, New Teachers (Facilitator's Guide) (Orig.). 1993. pap. text 6.95 (*0-7842-0718-6*) Agency Instr Tech.

— Positive Insights on Education Guide. 40p. (Orig.). 1997. pap. text 7.95 (*0-7842-0817-4*) Agency Instr Tech.

AIT Staff. Comm 2000, Learner's Guide, Mod. 1. (EJ - Tech Prep Ser.). 1995. mass mkt. 8.95 (*0-538-63495-2*) S-W Pub.

— Comm 2000, Learner's Guide, Mod. 2. (EJ - Tech Prep Ser.). 1995. pap. 8.95 (*0-538-63569-X*) S-W Pub.

— Comm 2000, Learner's Guide, Mod. 3. (EJ - Tech Prep Ser.). 1995. mass mkt. 8.95 (*0-538-63574-6*) S-W Pub.

— Comm 2000, Learner's Guide, Mod. 4. (EJ - Tech Prep Ser.). 1995. mass mkt. 8.95 (*0-538-63579-7*) S-W Pub.

— Comm 2000, Learner's Guide, Mod. 5. (EJ - Tech Prep Ser.). 1995. pap. 8.95 (*0-538-63584-3*) S-W Pub.

— Comm 2000, Learner's Guide, Mod. 6. (EJ - Tech Prep Ser.). 1995. mass mkt. 8.95 (*0-538-63589-4*) S-W Pub.

— Comm 2000, Learner's Guide, Mod. 7. (EJ - Tech Prep Ser.). 1995. mass mkt. 8.95 (*0-538-63594-0*) S-W Pub.

— Comm 2000, Learner's Guide, Mod. 8. (EJ - Tech Prep Ser.). 1995. mass mkt. 8.95 (*0-538-63599-1*) S-W Pub.

— Comm 2000, Learner's Guide, Mod. 9. (EJ - Tech Prep Ser.). 1995. mass mkt. 8.95 (*0-538-63604-1*) S-W Pub.

— Comm 2000, Learner's Guide, Mod. 10. (EJ - Tech Prep Ser.). 1995. mass mkt. 8.95 (*0-538-63609-2*) S-W Pub.

— Earth, the Environment, & Beyond from Science Source. Grewar, Mindy, ed. 40p. (Orig.). (YA). (gr. 7-12). 1992. text 7.95 (*0-7842-0605-8*) Agency Instr Tech.

— Every Child Can Succeed: An Action Guide. Eakin, Sybil, ed. 36p. (Orig.). 1992. pap. text 5.95 (*0-7842-0600-7*) Agency Instr Tech.

— Every Child Can Succeed: Facilitator's Guide for the Essential Elements Component. Eakin, Sybil, ed. 56p. (Orig.). 1992. pap. text 6.50 (*0-7842-0602-3*) Agency Instr Tech.

— Every Child Can Succeed: Facilitator's Guide for the Successful School Component. Eakin, Sybil, ed. 40p. (Orig.). 1992. pap. text 6.25 (*0-7842-0601-5*) Agency Instr Tech.

— Every Child Can Succeed: Readings for School Improvement. Eakin, Sybil, ed. 416p. (Orig.). 1992. 24.95 (*0-7842-0603-1*) Agency Instr Tech.

An Asterisk (*) at the beginning of an entry indicates that the title is appearing for the first time.

— Families & Schools: Teaming for Success, Facilitator's Guide. 24p. (Orig.). 1995. pap. text 8.95 (*0-7842-0779-8*) Agency Instr Tech.

— Looking from the Inside/Out. 104p. (Orig.). (J). (gr. 2-4). 1996. pap. text 8.95 (*0-7842-0812-3*) Agency Instr Tech.

— Mathmedia. (YA). (gr. 7-12). 1995. teacher ed. 24.95 (*0-7842-0815-8*) Agency Instr Tech.

— Our Human Body from Science Source. Grewar, Mindy, ed. 32p. (Orig.). (YA). (gr. 7-12). 1992. text 7.95 (*0-7842-0604-X*) Agency Instr Tech.

— The Road to School-to-Work: Facilitator's Guide. 32p. (Orig.). 1995. pap. text 7.95 (*0-7842-0778-X*) Agency Instr Tech.

— The Road to School-to-Work: School Implementation Resource Guide. 136p. (Orig.). 1995. pap. text 14.95 (*0-7842-0777-1*) Agency Instr Tech.

AIT Staff, jt. auth. see Bracey, Gerald W.

AIT-WDCN Nashville, TN Staff. Front Row Center. 45p. (Orig.). (YA). (gr. 7-12). 1995. pap. text, teacher ed. 5.95 (*0-7842-0810-7*) Agency Instr Tech.

AIT-WI Education Communication Board Staff. Teaching Early Literacy Guide. 200p. (Orig.). 1996. pap. text 8.95 (*0-7842-0806-9*) Agency Instr Tech.

AIT/General Learning Corp./Wisconsin Educational C. Mathematics Is Elementary (Guide) 96p. (Orig.). (J). (gr. 2-4). 1996. pap. text 7.95 (*0-7842-0814-X*) Agency Instr Tech.

AIT/Kauffman Foundation Staff. The "E" & Me Student Guide: The Entrepreneur in You. 96p. (YA). (gr. 11-12). 1998. pap. text, student ed. 65.50 (*0-7842-0871-9*) Agency Instr Tech.

— The "E" & Me Teacher's Guide: The Entrepreneur in You. 108p. 1998. pap. text, teacher ed. write for info. (*0-7842-0870-0*) Agency Instr Tech.

Aita, Carolyn, ed. see Materials Research Society Staff.

Aita, Paul, ed. see Scherer, Bonnie.

Aitchinson, James. Brain Scans. LC 99-220143. 64p. 1994. pap. 21.00 (*1-898218-91-9*) St Mut.

***Aitchisen, S.** Toward Sustainable Tourism in the Everest Region of Nepal. 1998. pap. 50.00 (*0-7855-7653-3*) St Mut.

Aitchison, C. U., ed. Treaties & Engagements Relating to Arabia & the Persian Gulf. 350p. (C). 1987. reprint ed. lib. bdg. 95.00 (*1-85207-076-5*, Pub. by Archive Editions) N Ross.

***Aitchison, Cara, et al.** Leisure & Tourism Landscapes: Social & Cultural Geographies. LC 00-30820. (Illus.). 2000. write for info. (*0-415-17060-5*) Routledge.

Aitchison, Ian J. & Hey, A. J. Gauge Theories in Particle Physics. 2nd ed. (Graduate Student Series in Physics). (Illus.). 588p. 1989. pap. 57.00 (*0-85274-328-9*) IOP Pub.

Aitchison, Ian J. & Paton, J. E., eds. Progress in Nuclear Physics, Vol. 13: Rudolf Peierls & Theoretical Physics - Proceedings of the Peierls Symposium. 1977. 89.00 (*0-08-020606-9*, Pergamon Pr); pap. 18.25 (*0-08-021621-8*, Pergamon Pr) Elsevier.

Aitchison, Ian J., et al. Plots, Quarks & Strange Particles: Proc of the Dalitz Conference, 1990. 220p. 1991. pap. 28.00 (*981-02-0471-X*); text 84.00 (*981-02-0470-1*) World Scientific Pub.

Aitchison, J. Cassell Guide to Written English. 256p. 1998. pap. 12.95 (*0-304-34963-1*) Continuum.

— The Statistical Analysis of Compositional Data. (Monographs on Statistics & Applied Probability). 400p. 1986. text 49.95 (*0-412-28060-4*, 9864) Chapman & Hall.

Aitchison, J. & Lauder, I. J. Statistical Concepts & Applications in Medicine. (Monographs on Statistics & Applied Probability). (Illus.). 400p. 1993. 60.00 (*0-412-30430-9*) Chapman & Hall.

Aitchison, J. W. & Carter, Harold. A Geography of the Welsh Language, 1961-1991. LC 95-228007. xi, 130p. 1994. pap. 19.95 (*0-7083-1236-5*, Pub. by Univ Wales Pr) Paul & Co Pubs.

Aitchison, James. The Golden Harvester: The Vision of Edwin Muir. 224p. (C). 1988. text 31.90 (*0-08-036400-4*, Pub. by Aberdeen U Pr) Macmillan.

— Second Nature. 100p. 1990. pap. text 13.00 (*0-08-037986-9*, Pub. by Aberdeen U Pr) Macmillan.

Aitchison, Jean. The Articulate Mammal. 3rd ed. 292p. 1989. pap. text 16.95 (*0-04-445355-8*) Routledge.

— The Articulate Mammal: An Introduction to Psycholinguistics. 4th rev. ed. LC 97-50244. 320p. (C). 1998. 75.00 (*0-415-16866-X*); pap. 24.99 (*0-415-16791-4*) Routledge.

— Language Change: Progress or Decay? 2nd ed. (Approaches to Linguistics Ser.). 270p. (C). 1991. pap. text 18.95 (*0-521-42283-3*) Cambridge U Pr.

— The Language Web: The Power & Problem of Words, the 1996 BBC Reith Lectures. (The 1996 BBC Reith Lectures). (Illus.). 152p. (C). 1997. pap. text 16.95 (*0-521-57475-7*) Cambridge U Pr.

— The Language Web: The Power & Problem of Words, the 1996 BBC Reith Lectures. LC 96-43929. (1996 BBC Reith Lectures). (Illus.). 152p. (C). 1997. text 49.95 (*0-521-57385-8*) Cambridge U Pr.

— The Seeds of Speech: Language Origin & Evolution. (Approaches to Linguistics Ser.). 293p. (C). 1996. text 54.95 (*0-521-46246-0*); pap. text 18.95 (*0-521-46793-4*) Cambridge U Pr.

***Aitchison, Jean.** The Seeds of Speech: Language Origin & Evolution. (Canto Book Ser.). (Illus.). 304p. 2000. pap. 13.95 (*0-521-78571-5*) Cambridge U Pr.

— Teach Yourself Linguistics 5/e. 5th ed. (Teach Yourself Ser.). 240p. 2000. pap. 12.95 (*0-8442-2668-8*, Teach Yrslf) NTC Contemp Pub Co.

Aitchison, Jean. Words in the Mind. 2nd ed. (Illus.). 288p. 1994. pap. text 28.95 (*0-631-18921-1*) Blackwell Pubs.

Aitchison, Jean, contrib. by. International Thesaurus of Refugee Terminology. (C). 1989. lib. bdg. 189.00 (*0-7923-0504-3*) Kluwer Academic.

Aitchison, Jean & United Nations High Commissioner for Refugees Staff. UNHCR International Thesaurus of Refugee Terminology. 2nd ed. 592p. 80.00 (*92-1-000052-8*) UN.

***Aitchison, Jim.** Cutting Edge Advertising: How to Create the World's Best Print for Brands in the 21st Century. (Illus.). 352p. (C). 1999. pap. text 29.99 (*0-13-012897-X*) P-H.

Aitchison, John. An Ensign in the Peninsular War: The Letters of John Aitchison. Thompson, W. F., ed. (Illus.). 352p. 1995. pap. 12.95 (*0-7181-3840-6*, Penguin Bks) Viking Penguin.

Aitchison, John & Brown, J. A. The Lognormal Distribution: With Special References to Its Uses in Economics. LC 58-1106. (University of Cambridge, Dept. of Applied Economics, Occasional Papers: No. 5). (Illus.). 194p. reprint ed. pap. 55.30 (*0-608-18268-0*, 2032993) Bks Demand.

***Aitchison, John & Carter, Harold.** Language, Economy & Society: The Changing Fortunes of the Welsh Language in the Twentieth Century. 192p. 2000. pap. 32.00 (*0-7083-1552-6*, Pub. by U Wales Pr) Paul & Co Pubs.

Aitchison, Kathy J., et al. First Episode on Psychosis. 138p. 1999. pap. 39.95 (*1-85317-435-1*) Martin Dunitz.

Aitchison, M. Caught in the Crossfire. 1995. 6.99 (*1-85792-149-6*, Pub. by Christian Focus) Spring Arbor Dist.

Aitchison, N. B. Armagh & the Royal Centres in Early Medieval Ireland: Monuments, Cosmology & the Past. (Illus.). 368p. (C). 1994. 81.00 (*1-873448-02-3*, Pub. by Cruithne Pr) Boydell & Brewer.

***Aitchison, Nick.** Macbeth: Man & Myth. 1999. 34.95 (*0-7509-1891-8*, Pub. by Sutton Publng) Intl Pubs Mktg.

— Scotland's Stone of Destiny: Myth, History & Nationhood. (Illus.). 176p. 2000. 32.50 (*0-7524-1465-8*, Pub. by Tempus Pubng) Arcadia Publng.

Aitchison, Robert G., jt. compiled by see Shurtleff, William R.

Aitchison, Stewart. Grand Canyon National Park. (Pocket Portfolio Ser.: Vol. 2). (Illus.). 32p. (Orig.). 1997. pap. 5.95 (*0-939365-52-9*); pap. 6.95 (*0-939365-76-6*); pap. 6.95 (*0-939365-75-8*); pap. 6.95 (*0-939365-74-X*); pap. 6.95 (*0-939365-73-1*) Panorama Intl.

***Aitchison, Stewart.** Grand Canyon, Window of Time. (Illus.). 2000. pap. 8.95 (*1-58071-007-7*) Panorama Intl.

Aitchison, Stewart. Lake Powell - Glen Canyon National Recreation Area. Nicholas, Jeff, ed. (Pocket Portfolio Ser.: Vol. 13). (Illus.). 32p. 1999. pap. 5.95 (*1-58071-000-X*, Pub. by Panorama Intl) Falcon Pub Inc.

***Aitchison, Stewart.** Longstreet Highroad Guide to the Arizona Mountains & Grand Canyon. LC 00-104188. (Longstreet Highroad Coastal Ser.). (Illus.). 352p. 2000. pap. 18.95 (*1-56352-593-3*) Longstreet.

Aitchison, Stewart. A Naturalist's Guide to Hiking the Grand Canyon. LC 84-15035. 172p. 1985. pap. 8.95 (*0-13-610221-2*) P-H.

— Red Rock - Sacred Mountain: The Canyons & Peaks from Sedona to Flagstaff. LC 92-19896. (Illus.). 128p. (Orig.). 1992. pap. 5.95 (*0-89658-215-9*) Voyageur Pr.

— A Traveler's Guide to Monument Valley. LC 93-15911. (Illus.). 64p. (Orig.). 1993. pap. 3.95 (*0-89658-225-6*) Voyageur Pr.

— Wilderness Areas of the Colorado Plateau. (Illus.). 32p. 1989. pap. 4.95 (*0-89734-098-1*, PL60-4) Mus Northern Ariz.

— A Wilderness Called Grand Canyon. LC 90-25373. (Illus.). 128p. 1993. pap. 19.95 (*0-89658-227-2*) Voyageur Pr.

Aitchison, Stewart & Grubbs, Bruce. Hiking Arizona. rev. ed. LC 99-24183. (Falcon Guides Ser.). (Illus.). 237p. 1996. reprint ed. pap. 14.95 (*1-56044-463-0*) Falcon Pub Inc.

Aitchison, Stewart & Yazzie, Susie. Monument Valley Navajo Tribal Park. Leach, Nicky, ed. (Visual Interpretation Ser.). (Illus.). 48p. 1994. pap. 7.95 (*0-939365-38-3*) Panorama Intl.

Aitchison, Will. Factfinding & Arbitration. 278p. 1991. pap. 29.95 (*1-880607-05-0*) Labor Rel Info.

— The FLSA - a User's Manual. 2nd ed. LC 98-215264. 453p. 1997. pap. 29.95 (*1-880607-12-3*) Labor Rel Info.

— Model Firefighter's Contract: A Labor Perspective. LC 97-211698. 215p. 1994. pap. 29.95 (*1-880607-08-5*) Labor Rel Info.

— Model Law Enforcement Contract: A Labor Perspective. 3rd ed. LC 99-462511. 414p. 1999. pap. 29.95 (*1-880607-14-X*) Labor Rel Info.

— The Rights of Firefighters. 2nd ed. 378p. 1997. pap. 29.95 (*1-880607-11-5*) Labor Rel Info.

— The Rights of Law Enforcement Officers. 3rd ed. LC 97-210439. 539p. 1996. pap. 29.95 (*1-880607-10-7*) Labor Rel Info.

***Aitchison, Will.** The Rights of Law Enforcement Officers. 4th ed. 540p. 2000. pap. 29.95 (*1-880607-16-6*) Labor Rel Info.

Aitcin. High Strength Concrete. LC 98-230236. (Modern Concrete Technology Ser.). (Illus.). 624p. (C). 1998. 100.00 (*0-419-19270-0*, E & FN Spon) Routledge.

Aitelli, Peter & Dietrich, Debra M. Research Guide to Professional Law. LC 85-8695. (Legal Research Guides Ser.: Vol. 1). vii, 86p. 1985. 42.00 (*0-89941-453-2*, 303700) W S Hein.

Aithal, K. Parameswara. A Descriptive Catalogue of the Sanskrit & Other Indian Manuscripts of the Chandra Shum Shere Collection in the Bodleian Library, Pt. III. 260p. 1999. pap. 105.00 (*0-19-951388-0*) OUP.

— Veda-Laksana Vedic Ancillary Literature: A Descriptive Bibliography. (C). 1993. 54.00 (*81-208-1120-8*, Pub. by Motilal Bnarsidass) S Asia.

Aitkan, Bill. Using the Psion Series 3a. (Orig.). 1996. pap. 34.95 (*1-898307-26-1*, Pub. by Capall Bann Pubng) Holmes Pub.

Aitken. Behavioural Sciences for Health. (C). 1996. pap. text 55.00 (*0-7020-1964-X*) Harcourt.

— Teaching Tenses. 1992. pap. text. write for info. (*0-17-555920-1*) Addison-Wesley.

Aitken, jt. auth. see Handy, Charles.

Aitken, A. C. To Catch the Spirit: The Memoir of A. C. Aitken. LC 97-117776. 124p. 1996. pap. 29.95 (*0-908569-99-8*, Pub. by Univ Otago Pr) Intl Spec Bk.

Aitken, A. J., et al, eds. A Dictionary of the Older Scottish Tongue Pt. 42: Ru-Sanct: From the Twelfth Century to the End of the Seventeenth. (Dictionary of the Older Scottish Tongue Ser.). 120p. 1993. pap. text 52.00 (*0-08-030683-7*) OUP.

Aitken, A. J. & Stevenson, James A. A Dictionary of the Older Scottish Tongue: From the Twelfth Century to the End of the Seventeenth, No. 37. LC 38-21689. 120p. 1993. pap. text 52.00 (*0-08-030676-4*) OUP.

— A Dictionary of the Older Scottish Tongue Pt. 36: From the Twelfth Century to the End of the Seventeenth. LC 38-21689. 120p. 1993. pap. text 52.00 (*0-08-030673-X*) OUP.

— A Dictionary of the Older Scottish Tongue Pt. 39: From the Twelfth Century to the End of the Seventeenth. LC 38-21689. 120p. 1993. pap. text 52.00 (*0-08-030678-0*) OUP.

— A Dictionary of the Older Scottish Tongue Pt. 41: From the Twelfth Century to the End of the Seventeenth. 140p. 1994. pap. text 55.00 (*0-08-030680-2*) OUP.

Aitken, A. J. & Stevenson, James A., eds. A Dictionary of the Older Scottish Tongue: From the Twelfth Century, Pts. XXVII-XXXI. (Dictionary of the Older Scottish Tongue Ser.: Vol. 5). 620p. 1994. text 230.00 (*0-08-028490-6*) OUP.

— A Dictionary of the Older Scottish Tongue: From the Twelfth Century to the End of the Seventeenth, 6 vols. LC 38-21689. 1988. 1050.00 (*0-08-030675-6*, Pub. by Aberdeen U Pr) Macmillan.

— A Dictionary of the Older Scottish Tongue: From the Twelfth Century to the End of the Seventeenth. LC 38-21689. (Dictionary of the Older Scottish Tongue Ser.: No. 38). 120p. 1993. pap. text 52.00 (*0-08-030677-2*) OUP.

— A Dictionary of the Older Scottish Tongue: From the Twelfth Century to the End of the Seventeenth, Pt. 33. 120p. 1993. pap. text 52.00 (*0-08-030394-3*) OUP.

— A Dictionary of the Older Scottish Tongue: From the Twelfth Century to the End of the Seventeenth, Pt. 40. (Dictionary of the Older Scottish Tongue Ser.). 120p. 1993. pap. text 52.00 (*0-08-030679-9*) OUP.

— A Dictionary of the Older Scottish Tongue Pt. 32: From the Twelfth Century to the End of the Seventeenth. 120p. 1993. pap. text 52.00 (*0-08-030393-5*) OUP.

— A Dictionary of the Older Scottish Tongue Pt. 34: From the Twelfth Century to the End of the Seventeenth. (DOST Ser.). 120p. 1993. pap. text 52.00 (*0-08-030395-1*) OUP.

— A Dictionary of the Older Scottish Tongue Pt. 35: From the Twelfth Century to the End of the Seventeenth. (Dictionary of the Older Scottish Tongue Ser.). 120p. 1993. pap. text 52.00 (*0-08-030396-X*) OUP.

— A Dictionary of the Older Scottish Tongue Vol. 7 (37-41) From the Twelfth Century to the End of the Seventeenth. LC 38-21689. 600p. 1994. text 230.00 (*0-08-030681-0*) OUP.

Aitken, A. J., et al. A Dictionary of the Older Scottish Tongue Vols. 1-7: From the Twelfth Century to the End of the Seventeenth. (Dictionary of the Older Scottish Tongue Ser.: No. 7). 4200p. 1990. 1900.00 (*0-08-030682-9*, Pub. by Aberdeen U Pr) Macmillan.

Aitken, Alexander C. Determinants & Matrices. LC 82-24168. (University Mathematical Texts Ser.). 144p. 1983. reprint ed. lib. bdg. 49.75 (*0-313-23294-6*, AIDE, Greenwood Pr) Greenwood.

Aitken, Bill. Exploring Indian Railways. (Illus.). 308p. 1994. 26.00 (*0-19-563109-9*) OUP.

Aitken, C., ed. Psychosomatics & Pleasure: Proceedings of the Twenty-Third Annual Conference of the Society for Psychosomatic Research Held at the Royal College of Physicians, London, 19-20 November 1979. 88p. 1981. pap. 24.00 (*0-08-026797-1*, Pergamon Pr) Elsevier.

Aitken, C. G. Statistics & the Evaluation of Evidence for Forensic Scientists. (Statistics in Practice Ser.). 276p. 1995. 110.00 (*0-471-95532-9*) Wiley.

Aitken-Christie, Jenny, et al, eds. Automation & Environmental Control in Plant Tissue Culture. LC 94-14890. 592p. (C). 1994. text 340.00 (*0-7923-2841-8*) Kluwer Academic.

***Aitken, Doug.** Parkett, No. 57. 2000. pap. 32.00 (*3-907582-07-1*) Parkett Verlag AG.

Aitken, Doug, jt. auth. see Kuipers, Dean.

Aitken, E., ed. Russian Poetry for Intermediates. rev. ed. (Russian Texts Ser.). (RUS.). 1996. pap. 16.95 (*1-85399-415-4*, Pub. by Brist Class Pr) Focus Pub-R Pullins.

Aitken, Elaine. A Web of Gold. (Rainbow Romances Ser.: No. 899). 160p. 1994. 14.95 (*0-7090-4971-4*) Parkwest Pubns.

Aitken, G. A. The Life of Richard Steele, 2 vols. LC 68-24893. (English Biography Ser.: No. 31). (Illus.). 1968. reprint ed. lib. bdg. 150.00 (*0-8383-0152-5*) M S G Haskell Hse.

Aitken, G. A., ed. see Steele, Richard.

Aitken, George, ed. see Defoe, Daniel.

Aitken, George A. Later Stuart Tracts. LC 64-16748. (Arber's an English Garner Ser.). 1964. reprint ed. 65.00 (*0-8154-0003-9*) Cooper Sq.

— The Life & Works of John Arbuthnot, M. D., Fellow of the Royal College of Physicians. (BCL1-PR English Literature Ser.). 516p. 1992. reprint ed. lib. bdg. 99.00 (*0-7812-7318-8*) Rprt Serv.

— The Life of Richard Steele, 2 vols., Set. (BCL1-PR English Literature Ser.). 1992. reprint ed. lib. bdg. 150.00 (*0-7812-7407-9*) Rprt Serv.

Aitken, George A., ed. see Steele, Richard.

Aitken, George A., ed. see Steele, Richard & Addison, Joseph.

Aitken, Gill, et al. Psychology, Discourse & Social Practice: From Regulation to Resistance. LC 97-121064. 208p. 1996. 69.95 (*0-7484-0503-8*, Pub. by Tay Francis Ltd); pap. 24.95 (*0-7484-0504-6*, Pub. by Tay Francis Ltd) Taylor & Francis.

Aitken, Gillon, ed. see Naipaul, V. S.

Aitken, Gillon, tr. see Pushkin, Aleksandr.

Aitken, H. Peter. Access & Affordability: Strategic Planning Perspectives for Independent Schools. 1994. pap. 32.00 (*0-934338-80-9*) NAIS.

Aitken, Hugh. The Piece As a Whole: Studies in Holistic Musical Analysis. 136p. 1997. pap. 17.95 (*0-275-96038-2*, Praeger Pubs) Greenwood.

— The Piece As a Whole: Studies in Holistic Musical Analysis, 45. LC 97-2714. (Contributions to the Study of Music & Dance: Vol. 45). 136p. 1997. 49.95 (*0-313-30061-5*, Greenwood Pr) Greenwood.

Aitken, Hugh G. The Continuous Wave: Technology & American Radio, 1900-1932. LC 84-22265. (Illus.). 607p. reprint ed. pap. 188.20 (*0-7837-4330-0*, 204403400012) Bks Demand.

— Scientific Management in Action: Taylorism at Watertown Arsenal, 1908-1915. LC 84-26462. 288p. 1985. reprint ed. pap. 89.30 (*0-608-02940-8*, 206400600008) Bks Demand.

Aitken, Hugh G., jt. auth. see Easterbrook, W. T.

Aitken, I. D., jt. auth. see Martin, W. B.

Aitken, J. Compilation of Litanies & Vesper Hymns. 136p. 25.00 (*0-87556-551-4*) Saifer.

Aitken, J. F., ed. see Howell, J. A.

Aitken, J. K. The Elements of Drafting. 9th ed. 133p. 1995. pap. 32.00 (*0-455-21320-8*, Pub. by LawBk Co) Gaunt.

— Piesse: The Elements of Drafting. 8th ed. xvi, 137p. 1991. pap. 25.00 (*0-455-21023-3*, Pub. by LawBk Co) Gaunt.

Aitken, Johan L. Masques of Morality: Female in Fiction. 190p. pap. 12.95 (*0-88961-113-0*, Pub. by Womens Pr) LPC InBook.

Aitken, John. Compilations of Litanies & Vesper Hymns. 1954. 25.00 (*0-87556-004-0*) Saifer.

Aitken, John & Mills, George. Scientific Problem Solving: An Introduction to Technology. (J). (gr. 4-6). 1989. pap. 12.99 (*0-8224-6324-5*) Fearon Teacher Aids.

Aitken, Jonathan. Nixon: A Life. (Illus.). 640p. 1996. pap. 17.95 (*0-89526-720-9*) Regnery Pub.

***Aitken, Judie.** Love Beyond Time. (Time Passages Romance Ser.). 2000. mass mkt. 5.99 (*0-515-12744-2*, Jove) Berkley Pub.

***Aitken, Julia.** Easy Entertaining Cookbook. (Illus.). 192p. 1999. pap. 17.95 (*0-7788-0013-X*) Firefly Bks Ltd.

Aitken, K. T. Proverbs. 1993. pap. 22.00 (*0-7152-0533-1*, Pub. by St Andrew) St Mut.

Aitken, Keith. The Bairns O'Adam: The Story of the STUC. 326p. 1997. 23.95 (*0-7486-6200-6*, Pub. by Polygon) Subterranean Co.

***Aitken, Kenneth.** Mastering ADHD: Handbook for Parents & Clinicians. 160p. 2000. pap. 18.95 (*1-85302-800-2*) Jessica Kingsley.

Aitken, Larry P., jt. auth. see Haller, Edwin W.

Aitken, Leila. Dressmaking: A Step-by-Step Course. LC 93-43378. (Illus.). 160p. 1994. 27.95 (*0-8069-0627-8*) Sterling.

— The Flower Arranger's Garden Month-by-Month. LC 95-232135. (Illus.). 144p. 1995. 24.95 (*0-7153-0296-5*, Pub. by D & C Pub) Sterling.

— Flower Arranger's Garden Month by Month. (Illus.). 144p. 1998. pap. 14.95 (*0-7153-0709-6*, Pub. by D & C Pub) Sterling.

Aitken, Lynda & Griffin, Gabriele. Gender Issues in Elder Abuse. 224p. 1996. 69.95 (*0-8039-7522-8*); pap. 24.95 (*0-8039-7523-6*) Sage.

Aitken, M. J., et al, eds. The Origin of Modern Humans & the Impact of Chronometric Dating. (Illus.). 288p. 1993. text 49.50 (*0-691-03242-4*, Pub. by Princeton U Pr) Cal Prin Full Svc.

Aitken, M. J., jt. auth. see Taylor, R. E.

Aitken, Margaret, ed. In My Small Corner: Memories of an Orcadian Childhood. 160p. 1998. pap. 24.00 (*1-84017-002-6*) St Mut.

Aitken, Maria. Style: Acting in High Comedy. (Applause Acting Ser.). (Illus.). 160p. 1996. pap. 12.95 (*1-55783-214-5*) Applause Theatre Bk Pubs.

Aitken, Maria, ed. see Caine, Michael.

Aitken, Maria, ed. see Callow, Simon.

Aitken, Martin J. An Introduction to Optical Dating: The Dating of Quaternary Sediments by the Use of Photon-Stimulated Luminescence. (Illus.). 280p. 1998. text 130.00 (*0-19-854092-2*) OUP.

— Science-Based Dating in Archaeology: Longman Archaeology Series. (Archaeology Ser.). (Illus.). 288p. (C). 1989. text 49.95 (*0-582-05498-2*) Longman.

Aitken, Murray, et al. Statistical Modelling in GLIM. (Oxford Statistical Science Ser.). (Illus.). 392p. 1989. pap. text 45.00 (*0-19-852203-7*) OUP.

Aitken, Peter. The Complete Idiot's Guide to 1-2-3 for Windows. 2nd ed. 328p. 1994. 16.95 (*1-56761-485-X*, Alpha Ref) Macmillan Gen Ref.

***Aitken, Peter.** Developing Solutions with Office 2000 Components & Vba. LC 00-27557. 528p. 2000. pap. 49.99 (*0-13-026305-2*, Prentice Hall) P-H.

A

An Asterisk (*) at the beginning of an entry indicates that the title is appearing for the first time.

A

Aitken, Peter. Digital Camera Design Guide. 10th ed. (CTI Ser.). 250p. (C). 1997. pap. 45.00 incl. cd-rom (*1-57610-184-3*) Coriolis Grp.
— Show Me Word for Windows 6.0. 1993. 12.95 (*1-56761-347-0*, Alpha Ref) Macmillan Gen Ref.
— Teach Yourself Internet Programming with Visual Basic 6 in 21 Days. LC 98-87212. 500p. 1998. pap. 29.99 (*0-672-31459-2*) Sams.
— Teach Yourself Word 97 in 10 Minutes. LC 98-84892. 1998. 12.99 (*0-672-31336-7*) Sams.
— Ten Minute Guide to Word for Windows 95. (Illus.). 175p. 1995. 12.99 (*0-7897-0379-3*, Alpha Ref) Macmillan Gen Ref.
— 10 Minute Guide to Word 97. LC 96-70780. 208p. 1996. 14.99 (*0-7897-1019-6*) Que.
***Aitken, Peter & Jones, Bradley L.** Sams Teach Yourself C in 21 Days. 5th ed. 1999. pap. 29.99 (*0-672-31766-4*) Sams.
Aitken, Peter, jt. auth. see Jones, Brad.
Aitken, Peter G. Quicken: Self Teaching Guide. LC 92-782. 384p. 1992. pap. 19.95 (*0-471-54889-8*) Wiley.
— Sams Teach Yourself C in 21 Days: Complete Complier Edition. 710p. (Orig.). 1998. pap. text 49.99 (*0-672-31260-3*) Sams.
— Visual Basic 6 Programming Explorer. LC 98-34270. 704p. 1998. pap. 49.99 (*1-57610-281-5*) Coriolis Grp.
Aitken, R. Alan, ed. Asymmetric Synthesis. LC 91-46601. 224p. (Orig.). 1992. 155.00 (*0-7514-0059-9*, A4212, Pub. by B Acad & Prof) Routldge.
— Asymmetric Synthesis. 256p. (Orig.). 1991. 125.00 (*0-412-02451-9*, A4212, Chap & Hall NY) Chapman & Hall.
Aitken, Robert. The Dragon Who Never Sleeps: Verses for Zen Buddhist Practice. LC 92-33717. 82p. 1992. pap. 9.50 (*0-938077-60-0*) Parallax Pr.
— Encouraging Words: Zen Buddhist Teachings for Western Students. 256p. 1994. pap. 13.00 (*0-679-75652-3*) Pantheon.
— The Gateless Barrier. 332p. 1991. pap. 15.00 (*0-86547-442-7*) N Point Pr.
— The Mind of Clover: Essays in Zen Buddhist Ethics. LC 84-60680. 202p. (Orig.). 1982. pap. 12.00 (*0-86547-158-4*) N Point Pr.
— Original Dwelling Place: Zen Buddhist Essays. 256p. 1997. pap. text 13.50 (*1-887178-41-4*, Pub. by Counterpt DC) HarpC.
— The Practice of Perfection: The Paramitas from a Zen Buddhist Perspective. LC 97-5488. 240p. 1997. pap. text 13.50 (*1-887178-40-6*, Pub. by Counterpt DC) HarpC.
Aitken, Robert. Taking the Path of Zen. LC 82-81475. Vol. 1. (Illus.). 150p. (Orig.). 1982. pap. 11.00 (*0-86547-080-4*) N Point Pr.
Aitken, Robert. A Zen Wave: Basho's Haiku & Zen. LC 78-13243. (Illus.). 192p. 1979. reprint ed. pap. 16.95 (*0-8348-0137-X*) Weatherhill.
Aitken, Robert, jt. auth. see Leithwood, Kenneth.
Aitken, Robert, ed. see Hanh, Thich Nhat.
Aitken, Robert T. Ethnology of Tubuai. (BMB Ser.: No. 70). 1972. reprint ed. 30.00 (*0-527-02176-8*) Periodicals Srv.
Aitken, Rosemary. The Tinner's Daughter. 375p. 1997. 27.00 (*1-85797-637-1*, Pub. by Orion Pubng Grp) Trafalgar.
***Aitken, Rosemary.** The Tinner's Daughter. 1999. pap. 13.95 (*0-7528-2760-X*, Pub. by Orion Pubng Grp) Trafalgar.
Aitken, Stuart A., ed. see International Symposium on Visually Handicapped In, et al.
Aitken, Stuart C. Family Fantasies & Community Space. LC 97-17634. (Illus.). 272p. 1998. 50.00 (*0-8135-2461-X*); pap. 20.00 (*0-8135-2462-8*) Rutgers U Pr.
— Putting Children in Their Place. Cromley, Robert & Cromley, Ellen, eds. LC 94-7839. (Resource Publications in Geography). (C). 1994. pap. text 15.00 (*0-89291-216-2*) Assn Am Geographers.
Aitken, Stuart C. & Zonn, Leo E., eds. Place, Power, Situation & Spectacle: A Geography of Film. 278p. (C). 1994. pap. text 26.95 (*0-8476-7826-1*); lib. bdg. 71.50 (*0-8476-7825-3*) Rowman.
Aitken, W. B. Beekman: Distinguished Families in America Descended from Wilhelmus Beekman & Jan Tomasse Van Dyke. (Illus.). 264p. 1992. reprint ed. pap. 42.00 (*0-8328-2632-4*); reprint ed. lib. bdg. 52.00 (*0-8328-2631-6*) Higginson Bk Co.
Aitken, Wayne. An Arithmetic Riemann-Roch Theorem for Singular Arithmetic Surfaces. LC 95-52304. (Memoirs of the American Mathematical Society Ser.: Vol. 573). 174p. 1996. pap. 43.00 (*0-8218-0407-3*, MEMO/120/573) Am Math.
Aitken, Wayne, jt. auth. see Foster, David.
***Aitken, Will.** Realia. 2000. 0.00 (*0-679-31040-1*) Random.
Aitken, William H. A Problem-Solving Approach to Pension Funding & Valuation. 2nd ed. 405p. (C). 1996. pap. text 52.50 (*1-56698-200-6*) Actex Pubns.
Aitkenhead, A. R., jt. auth. see Smith, G.
Aitkenhead, Alan R. Textbook of Anesthesia. 3rd ed. 1996. pap. text 69.95 (*0-443-05056-2*) Church.
Aitkenhead, Donna. Bicycling the Atlantic Coast: A Complete Route Guide, Florida to Maine. LC 92-41896. (Illus.). 256p. (Orig.). 1993. pap. 14.95 (*0-89886-303-1*) Mountaineers.
— Central Oregon Wilderness Areas: (Cascades to the Coast) (Illus.). 112p. 1994. pap. 8.95 (*0-911518-83-5*) F Amato Pubns.
— Northern Oregon Wilderness Areas. (Illus.). 112p. 1995. pap. 8.95 (*0-911518-87-8*) F Amato Pubns.
Aitkens, Maggie. Kerry: A Teenage Mother. LC 94-897. (Illus.). 48p. (J). (gr. 4-8). 1994. lib. bdg. 19.93 (*0-8225-2556-9*, Lerner Publctns) Lerner Pub.
Aitkin. Stability & Change in Australian Politics. (Australian National University Press Ser.). 1982. pap. text 37.00 (*0-08-032822-9*, Pergamon Pr) Elsevier.
Aitkin, Donald, et al. Australian National Political Attitudes, 1967. 1975. write for info. (*0-89138-117-1*) ICPSR.
Aitkin, Lindsay. Hearing - The Brain & Auditory Communication in Marsupials. LC 97-36128. (Zoophysiology Ser.: Vol. 36). (Illus.). 150p. 1998. 109.00 (*3-540-62946-7*) Spr-Verlag.
Aitkin, Lindsay, ed. The Auditory Midbrain: Structure & Function in the Central Auditory Pathway. LC 85-14358. (Contemporary Neuroscience Ser.). 246p. 1986. 89.50 (*0-89603-085-7*) Humana.
Aitkin, Rosemary. The Girl from Penvarris. 358p. 1996. pap. 17.95 (*0-7528-0065-5*, Pub. by Weidenfeld & Nicolson) Trafalgar.
Aitmatov, Chingiz. The Day Lasts More Than a Hundred Years. French, John, tr. from RUS. LC 83-48135. 368p. 1983. pap. 14.95 (*0-253-20482-8*, MB 482) Ind U Pr.
***Aitmatov, Chingiz.** Jamila. Lukner, R. F., tr. from RUS. 47p. 2000. pap. 9.00 (*0-911005-39-0*) Dallas Inst Pubns.
Aito, Antero & Jarvisalo, J. Trace Elements in Health & Disease. 1991. 132.00 (*0-85186-976-9*) CRC Pr.
Aiton, E. J., et al. The Harmony of the World by Johannes Kepler. LC 93-72555. (Memoirs Ser.: Vol. 209). (Illus.). 600p. (C). 1997. 45.00 (*0-87169-209-0*, M209-AIE) Am Philos.
Aiton, E. J., tr. see Kepler, Johannes.
Aityan, S. K., et al, eds. Proceedings of Neural, Parallel & Scientific Computations, Vol. 1. (Illus.). 520p. (Orig.). (C). 1995. 100.00 (*0-9640398-9-3*); pap. 75.00 (*0-9640398-8-5*) Dynamic Pubs.
Aivanhov, Omraam M. Angels & Other Mysteries of the Tree of Life. 2nd ed. (Izvor Collection: Vol. 236). (Illus.). 207p. 1996. reprint ed. pap. 8.95 (*1-895978-07-6*, Pub. by Prosveta) Prosveta USA.
— The Book of Divine Magic. 2nd ed. (Izvor Collection: No. 226). 208p. 1993. reprint ed. pap. 7.95 (*2-85566-442-X*, Pub. by Prosveta) Prosveta USA.
— The Book of Revelations: A Commentary. (Izvor Collection: Vol. 230).Tr. of Approche de la Cite Celeste; Commentaires Sur l'Apocalypse. (Illus.). 190p. 1991. pap. 7.95 (*2-85566-491-8*, Pub. by Prosveta) Prosveta USA.
— Christmas & Easter in the Initiatic Tradition. 2nd rev. ed. (Izvor Collection: Vol. 209). (Illus.). 154p. 1987. pap. 7.95 (*2-85566-397-0*, Pub. by Prosveta) Prosveta USA.
— Cosmic Balance: The Secret of Polarity. 2nd ed. (Izvor Collection Ser.: Vol. 237). (Illus.). 262p. 1998. pap. 7.95 (*2-85566-710-0*, Pub. by Prosveta) Prosveta USA.
— Cosmic Moral Law. 4th ed. (Complete Works: Vol. 12). (Illus.). 284p. 1999. pap. 14.95 (*2-85566-445-4*, Pub. by Prosveta) Prosveta USA.
— Creation: Artistic & Spiritual. 2nd ed. (Izvor Collection: Vol. 223). 203p. 1987. pap. 7.95 (*2-85566-402-0*, Pub. by Prosveta) Prosveta USA.
— Daily Meditations, Vol. 8. 370p. 1997. pap. 12.95 (*1-895978-11-4*) Prosveta USA.
***Aivanhov, Omraam M.** Daily Meditations 2000. (Illus.). 366p. 1999. pap. 8.95 (*2-85566-779-8*, Pub. by Prosveta) Prosveta USA.
— Education Begins Before Birth. 168p. 1982. mass mkt. 7.95 (*2-85566-374-1*, Pub. by Prosveta) Prosveta USA.
Aivanhov, Omraam M. Education Begins Before Birth. (Izvor Collection: Vol. 203). (Illus.). 168p. 1982. pap. 6.95 (*0-911857-02-8*) Prosveta USA.
— The Egregor of the Dove or the Reign of Peace. 2nd rev. ed. (Izvor Collection: Vol. 208). Orig. Title: Under the Dove, the Reign of Peace. 172p. 1987. pap. 7.95 (*2-85566-403-9*, Pub. by Prosveta) Prosveta USA.
— Freedom, the Spirit Triumphant. 2nd rev. ed. (Izvor Collection: Vol. 211). 160p. 1986. pap. 7.95 (*2-85566-385-7*, Pub. by Prosveta) Prosveta USA.
— The Fruits of the Tree of Life: The Cabbalistic Tradition. LC 91-70255. (Complete Works: Vol. 32). (Illus.). 314p. 1991. reprint ed. pap. 14.95 (*0-911857-09-5*) Prosveta USA.
— Golden Rules for Everyday Life. (IAAE Occasional Papers: Vol. 227). 158p. 1994. pap. 7.95 (*2-85566-472-1*, Pub. by Prosveta) Prosveta USA.
***Aivanhov, Omraam M.** Golden Rules for Everyday Life. 4th ed. 158p. 2000. pap. 7.95 (*1-895978-17-3*, Pub. by Prosveta) Prosveta USA.
— Hacia una Civilizacion Solar. 4th ed. (SPA.). 147p. 1995. pap. 7.95 (*2-85566-195-1*, Pub. by Prosveta) Prosveta USA.
Aivanhov, Omraam M. Harmony. 2nd rev. ed. (Complete Works: Vol. 6). 265p. 1988. pap. 14.95 (*2-85566-439-X*, Pub. by Prosveta) Prosveta USA.
— Harmony & Health. (Izvor Collection: Vol. 225). 178p. 1988. pap. 7.95 (*2-85566-443-8*) Prosveta USA.
— Hope for the World: Spiritual Galvanoplasty. 3rd ed. (Izvor Collection: Vol. 214). (Illus.). 197p. 1984. pap. 7.95 (*2-85566-306-7*, Pub. by Prosveta) Prosveta USA.
— In Spirit & in Truth. 2nd ed. (Izvor Collection: Vol. 235). 215p. 1998. pap. 7.95 (*1-895978-06-8*, Pub. by Prosveta) Prosveta USA.
— The Key to the Problems of Existence. 3rd rev. ed. (Complete Works: Vol. 11). (Illus.). 243p. 1988. pap. 14.95 (*2-85566-313-X*, Pub. by Prosveta) Prosveta USA.
— Know Thyself: Jnana Yoga, Pt. 1. 3rd ed. (Complete Works: Vol. 17). (Illus.). 246p. 1995. pap. 14.95 (*2-85566-446-2*, Pub. by Prosveta) Prosveta USA.
— Know Thyself: Jnana Yoga, Pt. 2. 2nd ed. LC 94-900036. (Complete Works: Vol. 18). (Illus.). 259p. 1994. pap. 14.95 (*1-895978-02-5*, Pub. by Prosveta) Prosveta USA.
— Life & Work in an Initiatic School Pt. 1: Training for the Divine. (Complete Works: Vol. 30). (Illus.). 264p. 1996. pap. 14.95 (*1-895978-09-2*, Pub. by Prosveta) Prosveta USA.
— Life Force. 3rd ed. (Complete Works: Vol. 5). (Illus.). 262p. 1993. pap. 14.95 (*2-85566-419-5*, Pub. by Prosveta) Prosveta USA.
— Light Is a Living Spirit. 2nd rev. ed. (Izvor Collection: Vol. 212). (Illus.). 146p. 1987. pap. 7.95 (*2-85566-391-1*, Pub. by Prosveta) Prosveta USA.
— The Living Book of Nature. 2nd rev. ed. (Izvor Collection: Vol. 216). (Illus.). 224p. 1987. pap. 7.95 (*2-85566-396-2*, Pub. by Prosveta) Prosveta USA.
— Looking into the Invisible: Intuition, Clairvoyance, Dreams. 3rd ed. (Izvor Collection: Vol. 228). 217p. 1995. pap. 7.95 (*2-85566-469-1*, Pub. by Prosveta) Prosveta USA.
Aivanhov, Omraam M. Love & Sexuality. 4th ed. 283p. 1997. pap. 14.95 (*2-85566-740-2*, Pub. by Prosveta) Prosveta USA.
Aivanhov, Omraam M. Love & Sexuality, Pt. I. 3rd ed. (Complete Works: Pt. I, Vol. 14). (Illus.). 250p. 1989. pap. 14.95 (*2-85566-423-3*, Pub. by Prosveta) Prosveta USA.
— Love & Sexuality, Pt. II. 4th ed. (Complete Works: Vol. 15). 301p. 1992. pap. 14.95 (*2-85566-440-3*, Pub. by Prosveta) Prosveta USA.
— Man Master of His Destiny. (Izvor Collection: Vol. 202). 194p. 1989. pap. 7.95 (*0-911857-01-X*) Prosveta USA.
Aivanhov, Omraam M. Man, Master of His Destiny. 194p. 1982. mass mkt. 7.95 (*2-85566-377-6*, Pub. by Prosveta) Prosveta USA.
Aivanhov, Omraam M. Man's Psychic Life: Elements & Structures. (Izvor Collection: Vol. 222). (Illus.). 205p. 1987. pap. 7.95 (*2-85566-389-X*, Pub. by Prosveta) Prosveta USA.
— Man's Subtle Bodies & Centers: The Aura, the Solar Plexus, the Chakras. 4th ed. (Izvor Collection: Vol. 219). (Illus.). 154p. 1986. pap. 7.95 (*2-85566-383-0*, Pub. by Prosveta) Prosveta USA.
— Man's Two Natures, Human & Divine. 3rd rev. ed. (Izvor Collection: Vol. 213). (Illus.). 152p. 1984. pap. 7.95 (*2-85566-326-1*, Pub. by Prosveta) Prosveta USA.
— The Mysteries of Fire & Water. (Izvor Collection: No. 232). 173p. 1993. pap. 7.95 (*2-85566-545-0*, Pub. by Prosveta) Prosveta USA.
— The Mysteries of Yesod. 3rd ed. (Complete Works: Vol. 7). (Illus.). 217p. 1988. pap. 14.95 (*2-85566-109-9*, Pub. by Prosveta) Prosveta USA.
— A New Dawn: Society & Politics in the Light of Initiatic Science, Pt. 1. 2nd ed. (Complete Works: Vol. 25). (Illus.). 267p. 1990. pap. 14.95 (*2-85566-486-1*, Pub. by Prosveta) Prosveta USA.
— A New Earth: Methods, Exercises, Formulas, Prayers. 5th ed. (Complete Works: Vol. 13). (Illus.). 248p. 1995. pap. 13.95 (*2-85566-622-8*, Pub. by Prosveta) Prosveta USA.
— New Light on the Gospels. 2nd ed. (Izvor Collection: Vol. 217). 181p. 1985. pap. 7.95 (*2-85566-339-3*, Pub. by Prosveta) Prosveta USA.
— On the Art of Teaching from the Initiatic Point of View. 3rd ed. (Complete Works: Vol. 29). (Illus.). 242p. 1989. pap. 14.95 (*2-85566-274-5*, Pub. by Prosveta) Prosveta USA.
— The Path of Silence. (Izvor Collection: Vol. 229). 167p. 1990. pap. 7.95 (*2-85566-473-X*) Prosveta USA.
Aivanhov, Omraam M. The Path of Silence. 2nd ed. 167p. 1995. pap. 7.95 (*1-895978-19-X*, Pub. by Prosveta) Prosveta USA.
Aivanhov, Omraam M. Philosophy of Universality. 2nd rev. ed. (Izvor Collection: Vol. 206). 178p. 1988. pap. 7.95 (*2-85566-420-9*, Pub. by Prosveta) Prosveta USA.
— The Powers of Thought. 2nd ed. LC 91-70253. (Izvor Collection: No. 224). 230p. 1991. reprint ed. pap. 7.95 (*0-911857-08-7*) Prosveta USA.
— The Second Birth. (Complete Works of O. M. Aivanhov: Vol. 1). 210p. 1981. reprint ed. pap. 14.95 (*0-87516-418-8*) DeVorss.
— Seeds of Happiness. (Izvor Collection: Vol. 231). 203p. 1992. pap. 7.95 (*2-85566-522-1*, Pub. by Prosveta) Prosveta USA.
— Sexual Force or the Winged Dragon. 5th rev. ed. (Izvor Collection: Vol. 205). 138p. 1987. pap. 7.95 (*2-85566-299-0*, Pub. by Prosveta) Prosveta USA.
— Spiritual Alchemy. 2nd rev. ed. (Complete Works: Vol. 2). (Illus.). 234p. 1989. pap. 14.95 (*2-85566-371-7*, Pub. by Prosveta) Prosveta USA.
— The Splendour of Tipharet. 3rd rev. ed. (Complete Works: Vol. 10). (Illus.). 319p. 1994. pap. 14.95 (*1-895978-05-X*, Pub. by Prosveta) Prosveta USA.
— The Symbolic Language of Geometrical Figures. 3rd ed. (Izvor Collection: Vol. 218). 152p. 1985. pap. 7.95 (*2-85566-366-0*, Pub. by Prosveta) Prosveta USA.
— Toward a Solar Civilization. (Izvor Collection: Vol. 201). (Illus.). 148p. 1982. pap. 7.95 (*0-911857-00-1*) Prosveta USA.
— The Tree of Knowledge of Good & Evil. 3rd ed. (Izvor Collection: Vol. 210). (Illus.). 160p. 1988. pap. 7.95 (*2-85566-283-4*, Pub. by Prosveta) Prosveta USA.
— True Alchemy or the Quest for Perfection. 2nd ed. (Izvor Collection). (Illus.). 191p. 1986. pap. 7.95 (*2-85566-384-9*, Pub. by Prosveta) Prosveta USA.
— The True Meaning of Christ's Teaching. (Izvor Collection: Vol. 215). (Illus.). 203p. 1989. pap. 7.95 (*2-85566-322-9*) Prosveta USA.
— Truth: Fruit of Wisdom & Love. (Izvor Collection: Vol. 234). 227p. 1994. pap. 8.95 (*1-895978-03-3*, Pub. by Prosveta) Prosveta USA.
— What Is a Spiritual Master? 3rd ed. (Izvor Collection: Vol. 207). 185p. 1989. pap. 7.95 (*2-85566-300-8*, Pub. by Prosveta) Prosveta USA.
— The Yoga of Nutrition. 2nd ed. LC 91-70254. (Izvor Collection: No. 204). 139p. 1991. pap. 7.95 (*0-911857-10-9*) Prosveta USA.
— Youth, Creators of the Future. 2nd ed. 194p. 1993. pap. 7.95 (*1-895978-01-7*, Pub. by Prosveta) Prosveta USA.
— The Zodiac, Key to Man & to the Universe. 2nd ed. (Izvor Collection: Vol. 220). (Illus.). 176p. 1989. pap. 7.95 (*2-85566-369-5*, Pub. by Prosveta) Prosveta USA.
Aivazis, M. Group Theory in Physics: Problems & Solutions. 124p. (C). 1991. pap. text 15.00 (*981-02-0486-8*) World Scientific Pub.
Aivazjan, S. A., et al. Twenty-Two Papers on Statistics & Probability. LC 61-9803. (Selected Translations in Mathematical Statistics & Probability Ser.: Vol. 6). 274p. 1966. 49.00 (*0-8218-1456-7*, STAPRO/6) Am Math.
Aiver, Moriel N. All You Really Need to Know about MRI Physics. unabridged ed. (Illus.). 140p. 1996. pap. text 45.00 (*0-9660982-2-6*, AAMRIP); spiral bd. 45.00 (*0-9660982-0-X*, AAMRIP) Simply Physics.
Aixala, Jerome, ed. see Arrupe, Pedro.
Aixala, Jerome, tr. see Dalmases, Candido de.
Aixela, Javier F., tr. see Puncel, Maria, ed.
Aixela, Javier F., tr. see Vasquez, Juan J., ed.
Aiya-oba, Anthony A. Elements of Nuclear Philosophy. (Illus.). 250p. 1997. 25.00 (*0-87291-174-8*) Coronado Pr.
Aiyangar, M. B., jt. tr. see Rangacharya, M.
Aiyangar, M. Srinivasa. Tamil Studies: Essays on the History of the Tamil People, Language, Religion & Literature. LC 98-904955. xix, 427 p. 1998. write for info. (*81-206-0029-0*) Asian Educ Servs.
Aiyangar, Narayan. Essays on Indo-Aryan Mythology. 656p. 1986. reprint ed. 34.00 (*0-8364-1712-7*, Pub. by Manohar) S Asia.
Aiyangar, S. Krishnaswami. Evolution of Hindu Administrative Institutions in South India. (C). 1994. text 28.00 (*81-206-0966-2*, Pub. by Asian Educ Servs) S Asia.
— Some Contributions of South India to Indian Culture. (C). 1995. 34.00 (*81-206-0999-9*, Pub. by Asian Educ Servs) S Asia.
***Aiyangar, S. Krishnaswami, ed.** Vijayanagara: History & Legacy. 2000. 148.50 (*81-7305-168-2*, Pub. by Aryan Bks Intl) S Asia.
Aiyangar, Srinivasa. Tamil Studies. (Illus.). 428p. 1986. reprint ed. 22.00 (*0-8364-1714-3*, Pub. by Abhinav) S Asia.
Aiyappan, A., jt. auth. see Mahadevan, Kuttan.
Aiyar, A. Arms & Explosives. (C). 1988. 275.00 (*0-7855-3702-3*) St Mut.
— The Law Lexicon. (C). 1990. 165.00 (*0-89771-131-9*) St Mut.
Aiyar, A., ed. The Art of Cross Examination, Civil & Criminal. (C). 1990. 225.00 (*0-89771-248-X*) St Mut.
Aiyar, A. N. Indian Tax Laws, 1988. (C). 1989. 210.00 (*0-7855-3659-0*) St Mut.
Aiyar, B. R. The Fatal Rumour: A Nineteenth-Century Indian Novel. Blackburn, Stuart, tr. from TAM. LC 99-932092. (School of Oriental & African Studies). (Illus.). 196p. 1999. 17.95 (*0-19-564261-9*) OUP.
Aiyar, Indira S. Durga As Mahisasuramardini: A Dynamic Myth of Goddess. LC 97-906378. 388p. 1997. 59.00 (*81-212-0510-7*, Pub. by Gyan Publishing Hse) Nataraj Bks.
Aiyar, K. N. Thirty Minor Upanishads: Including the Yoga Upanishads. 300p. 1980. reprint ed. 16.95 (*0-935548-00-9*) Codex Pr.
Aiyar, M. S. Thiagaraja: A Great Musician Saint. 238p. 1986. reprint ed. 20.00 (*0-8364-1766-6*, Pub. by Usha) S Asia.
Aiyar, Mani S. In Rajiv's Footprints: One Year in Parliament. 1993. 30.00 (*81-220-0306-0*, Pub. by Konark Pubs Pvt Ltd) Advent Bks Div.
— Pakistan Papers. (C). 1995. pap. 11.00 (*81-7476-007-5*, Pub. by UBS Pubs) S Asia.
***Aiyar, Mani S.** Rajiv Gandhi's India: Politics: Nationhood, Ethnicity, Pluralism, & Conflict Resolution, Vol. 1. 1998. 52.00 (*81-7476-196-9*, Pub. by UBS Pubs) S Asia.
***Aiyar, Mani S., ed.** Rajiv Gandhi's India Vol. 2: Economics: People in Democracy & Development & Conflict Resolution. 1998. 28.00 (*81-7476-197-7*, Pub. by UBS Pubs) S Asia.
***Aiyar, Mani S. & Rasgotra, M., eds.** Rajiv Gandhi's India Vol. 3: Foreign Policy: Ending the Quest for Dominance & Conflict Resolution. 1998. 27.00 (*81-7476-198-5*, Pub. by UBS Pubs) S Asia.
Aiyar, Mani S., jt. ed. see Kumar, Ravinder.
Aiyar, R. Swaminatha. Dravidian Theories. (C). 1987. 26.00 (*81-208-0331-0*, Pub. by Motilal Bnarsidass) S Asia.
***Aiyejiana, Funso.** The Legend of the Rockhills & Other Stories. 212p. 1999. pap. 15.95 (*0-920661-78-5*, Pub. by TSAR Pubns) SPD-Small Pr Dist.
Aiyengar, Devi S. I Am Hindu, 8 vols. (Religions of the World Ser.). (Illus.). 24p. (J). (gr. k-4). 1996. lib. bdg. 15.93 (*0-8239-2381-9*, PowerKids) Rosen Group.
Aiyer, K. Narayanaswami, tr. Laghu-Yoga-Vasistha. 1987. 26.95 (*0-8356-7497-5*) Theos Pub Hse.
Aiyer, P. S., tr. see Abhedananda, Swami.
Aiyer, T. Law of Provincial Insolvency. (C). 1988. 60.00 (*0-7855-3559-4*) St Mut.
Aizaki, Naoaki, ed. Photomask & X-Ray Mask Technology IV, Vol. 3096. LC 98-122044. 518p. 1997. 99.00 (*0-8194-2516-8*) SPIE.
— Photomask & X-Ray Mask Technology V. LC 98-227293. (Proceedings of SPIE Ser.: Vol. 3412). 630p. 1998. 116.00 (*0-8194-2864-7*) SPIE.
Aizan, Yamaji. Essays on the Modern Japanese Church: Christianity in Meiji Japan. Squires, Graham, tr. from JPN. LC 99-47907. (Michigan Monograph Series in Japanese Studies: Vol. 27). viii, 196p. 2000. 28.95 (*0-939512-93-9*) U MI Japan.
Aizawa, Kiyoharu, et al, eds. Visual Communications & Image Processing '99. 1570p. pap. text 179.00 (*0-8194-3124-9*) SPIE.
Aizawa, M., jt. auth. see Kajiyama, Tisato.
Aizawa, M., jt. ed. see Kajiyama, Tisato.
Aizeki, Y., jt. auth. see Suzuki, O.

An Asterisk (*) at the beginning of an entry indicates that the title is appearing for the first time.

A

An Asterisk (*) at the beginning of an entry indicates that the title is appearing for the first time.

A

Akaha, Tsuneo & Langdon, Frank, eds. Japan in the Posthegemonic World. LC 92-32013. 296p. 1993. pap. text 19.95 (*1-55587-385-5*) L Rienner.

Akahira, M. & Takeuchi, K. Asymptotic Efficiency of Statistical Estimators: Concepts & Higher Order Asymptotic Efficiency. (Lecture Notes in Statistics Ser.: Vol. 7). 256p. 1981. 58.95 (*0-387-90576-6*) Spr-Verlag.

Akahira, Masafumi, jt. auth. see Takeuchi, Kei.

Akahito, et al. Springs of Japanese Wisdom. (Illus.). 22p. 1997. 4.95 (*3-85788-317-0*, Pub. by Quellen Verlag) Assoc Pubs Grp.

Akahori, Satoru & Omishi, Ray. Sorcerer Hunters. (Illus.). 192p. (YA). (gr. 7 up). 1999. pap. 11.95 (*1-892213-22-2*, Mixx Manga) Mixx Enter Inc.

Akahori, T. A New Approach to the Local Embedding Theorem of CR-Structure for N Greater Than or Equal to 4 (the Local Solvability for the Operator b in the Abstract Sense) LC 87-1433. (Memoirs of the American Mathematical Society Ser.: No. 67/366). 257p. 1987. pap. 34.00 (*0-8218-2428-7*, MEMO/67/366) Am Math.

Akai. Instructors Manual to Accompany Applied Numerical Methods. 280p. 1994. pap. text 17.95 (*0-471-30918-4*) Wiley.

Akai, H., jt. ed. see Terakura, K.

Akai, Hiromu, jt. ed. see King, Robert C.

Akai, K., et al, eds. Weak Rock: Soft, Fractured & Weathered Rock: Proceedings of the International Symposium, Tokyo, 21-24 September 1981, 3 vols. 1549p. 1981. text 634.00 (*90-6191-209-1*, Pub. by A A Balkema) Ashgate Pub Co.

Akai, K., et al, eds. Weak Rock, Soft Fractured & Weathered Rock, Vol. 2. 1981. 216.00 (*90-6191-207-5*) Ashgate Pub Co.

Akai, Koichi, et al. Geotechnical Reconnaissance of the Effects of the January 17, 1995, Hyogoken-Nanbu Earthquake, Japan. (Illus.). 151p. (C). 1997. reprint ed. pap. text 35.00 (*0-7881-2538-9*) DIANE Pub.

Akai, Shin-ichi, et al. Bulk Crystal Growth Technology, Vol.1. (Japanese Technology Reviews Ser.: Vol. 4). viii, 192p. 1989. pap. text 156.00 (*2-88124-289-8*) Gordon & Breach.

Akai, Terence J. Applied Numerical Methods for Engineers. LC 93-6374. 410p. 1993. text 89.95 (*0-471-57523-2*) Wiley.

Akaike, H. & Kitagawa, G., eds. The Practice of Time Series Analysis. LC 98-31331. (Statistics in Engineering & Physical Science Ser.). 400p. 1999. 49.95 (*0-387-98658-8*) Spr-Verlag.

Akaike, H. & Nakagawa, T. Statistical Analysis & Control of Dynamic Systems. (C). 1989. text 202.50 (*90-277-2786-4*) Kluwer Academic.

Akaike, Hirotsugu, jt. auth. see Kitagawa, G.

Akaishi, Y., et al, eds. Developments of Nuclear Cluster Dynamics. 368p. (C). 1989. text 99.00 (*9971-5-0746-3*) World Scientific Pub.

Akaishi, Y., et al. Cluster Model & Other Topics. (International Review of Nuclear Physics Ser.: Vol. 4). 520p. 1987. pap. 46.00 (*9971-5-0078-7*); text 131.00 (*9971-5-0077-9*) World Scientific Pub.

Akaiwa, Yoshihiko. Introduction to Digital Mobile Communication. LC 97-4310. 456p. 1997. 89.95 (*0-471-17545-5*) Wiley.

***Akakwe, Michael.** Company Policy: The Rage Behind the Mask. 2000. pap. 9.99 (*0-9678579-0-2*) Pipedream Pr.

Akal Staff. Diccionario de Geografia. (SPA.). 624p. 1991. 125.00 (*0-7859-6237-9*, 8476006810) Fr & Eur.

— Diccionario de Teminos Literarios. (SPA.). 600p. 1990. 125.00 (*0-7859-6235-2*, M2815) Fr & Eur.

Akal, Tuncay & Berkson, Jonathon M., eds. Ocean Seismo-Acoustics: Low-Frequency Underwater Acoustics. (NATO Conference Series IV, Marine Sciences: Vol. 16). 896p. 1986. 165.00 (*0-306-42266-2*, Plenum Trade) Perseus Pubng.

Akalaitis, JoAnne. Green Card. 1991. pap. 6.95 (*0-88145-082-0*) Broadway Play.

Akalank Pub. Staff. Reservations for Backward Classes: Mandal Commission Report of the Backward Classes Commission. (C). 1990. 53.00 (*0-89771-132-7*) St Mut.

Akalu, Aster. The Nuer View of Biological Life: Nature & Sexuality in the Experience of the Ethiopian Nuer. (Regiae Societatis Humaniorum: Scripta Minora, Ser. 1988-1989: Pt. 1). (Illus.). 60p. (Orig.). 1989. pap. 32.50 (*91-22-01283-4*) Coronet Bks.

Akama, Seiki. Logic, Language & Computation. LC 96-52738. (Applied Logic Ser.: APLS Vol. 5). 260p. (C). 1997. text 97.50 (*0-7923-4376-X*) Kluwer Academic.

Akamatis, Iannis, jt. auth. see Ginouves, Rene.

Akamatsu, T. John, et al, eds. Family Health Psychology. (Series in Applied Psychology: Social Issues & Questions). 240p. 1992. 69.95 (*1-56032-247-0*) Taylor & Francis.

Akamatsu, Tsutomu. The Theory of Neutralization & the Archiphoneme in Functional Phonology. LC 87-28723. (Current Issues in Linguistic Theory Ser.: No. 43). xxi, 533p. (C). 1988. 130.00 (*90-272-3537-6*) J Benjamins Pubng Co.

Akan, A. Osman. Urban Stormwater Hydrology: A Guide to Engineering Calculations. LC 92-62441. 275p. 1992. text 99.95 (*0-87762-967-6*) Technomic.

Akan, Obasi H. & Harvey-Akan, Lynn. FamilyTies: Fun Activities for Collecting Family Historical & Heritage Information. (Illus.). 46p. 1998. pap., wbk. ed. 14.95 (*0-9663782-0-2*) Twenty Fourth Cent.

Akanatsu, Anne. Give & Take: Exchanging Information in Business. (Longman American Business English Skills Ser.). 1p. 1995. pap. text 13.00 (*0-582-08419-9*) Addison-Wesley.

Akansu. Multiresolution Signal Decomposition. 2nd ed. 450p. 1998. write for info. (*0-12-047141-8*) Acad Pr.

Akansu, Ali N. & Haddad, Richard A. Multiresolution Signal Decomposition: Transforms, Subbands, & Wavelets. LC 92-18629. (Telecommunications Ser.). (Illus.). 376p. 1992. text 59.00 (*0-12-047140-X*) Acad Pr.

***Akansu, Ali N. & Medley, Michael J.** Wavelet, Subband, & Block Transforms in Communications & Multimedia. LC 99-21060. (International Series in Engineering & Computer Science). xxi, 408 p. 1999. write for info. (*0-7923-8507-1*) Kluwer Academic.

Akansu, Ali N. & Smith, Mark J., eds. Subband & Wavelet Transforms: Design & Applications. LC 95-40664. (International Series in Engineering & Computer Science, Natural Language Processing & Machine Translation: No. 340). 472p. (C). 1995. text 115.00 (*0-7923-9645-6*) Kluwer Academic.

Akao, Yoji. Despliegue de Funciones de Calidad: Integracion de Necesidades Del Cliente En el Diseno Del Producto. (Illus.). 389p. (Orig.). 1993. pap. 65.00 (*84-87022-88-X*) Productivity Inc.

Akao, Yoji, ed. Hoshin Kanri: Policy Deployment for Successful TQM. LC 91-16513. 207p. 1991. 65.00 (*0-915299-57-7*) Productivity Inc.

— Quality Function Deployment: Integrating Customer Requirements into Product Design. LC 89-43209. (Illus.). 387p. 1990. 85.00 (*0-915299-41-0*) Productivity Inc.

Akao, Yoji, et al. Hoshin Planning (Policy Deployment) Tutorial: From the Eighth Symposium on QFD. (Illus.). 67p. 1996. pap. 75.00 (*1-889477-80-X*) QFD Inst.

Akao, Yoji, jt. ed. see Mizuno, Shigeru.

***Akapelwa, M.** Recital. 75p. 2000. pap. write for info. (*0-7541-0595-4*, Pub. by Minerva Pr) Unity Dist.

Akar, Azade. Authentic Turkish Designs. LC 92-4843. (Design Library). (Illus.). 48p. 1992. pap. 4.95 (*0-486-27211-7*) Dover.

— Treasury of Turkish Designs: Six Hundred Seventy Motifs from Iznik Pottery. (Pictorial Archive Ser.). (Illus.). 128p. 1988. pap. 8.95 (*0-486-25594-8*) Dover.

Akard, Freddie C., et al. United States Taekwon-Do Federation Handbook of Tournament Rules & Regulations. 4th ed. Sereff, Charles E., ed. (Illus.). 94p. (Orig.). 1993. per. 6.00 (*0-9622129-6-2*) Lilley Gulch.

Akard, Freddie C., ed. see Mitchell, Richard L.

Akard, Patrick. Return of the Market: The Politics of the U. S. Economic Policy from Carter to Clinton. 1998. pap. 21.95 (*0-8133-2927-2*) Westview.

— Return of the Market: The Politics of the U. S. Economic Policy from Carter to Clinton. 1999. pap. 59.00 (*0-8133-2926-4*) Westview.

Akare, Thomas. The Slums. (African Writers Ser.). 192p. (Orig.). (C). 1981. pap. 7.95 (*0-435-90241-5*, 90241) Heinemann.

Akarli, Engin D. The Long Peace: Ottoman Lebanon, 1861-1920. LC 92-18987. 1993. 55.00 (*0-520-08014-9*, Pub. by U CA Pr) Cal Prin Full Svc.

Akas, Kardy, jt. auth. see Hari, Mani.

***Akash, Munir & Mattawa, Khaled, eds.** Post Gibran: Anthology of New Arab American Writing. (Illus.). 460p. 2000. pap. 19.95 (*0-9652031-3-1*) Syracuse U Pr.

Akashi, H. Control Science & Technology for the Progress of Society: Proceedings, 7 vols. LC 81-23491. (IFAC Proceedings Ser.). 3800p. 1982. 1832.00 (*0-08-027580-X*, Pub. by Pergamon Repr) Franklin.

Akashi, K., et al, eds. Powder Preparation/Rapid Quenching: Materials Research Society International Symposium Proceedings-IMAM-3. 645p. 1989. text 17.50 (*1-55899-032-1*, IMAM-3) Materials Res.

Akashi, Kinji. Cornelius Van Bynkershoek: His Contribution to the Development of International Law. LC 98-21378. (International Law in Japanese Perspective Ser.). 1998. 84.00 (*90-411-0599-9*) Kluwer Law Intl.

Akasofu, S. I. Aurora Borealis: The Amazing Northern Lights. Henning, Robert A. et al, eds. LC 72-92087. (Alaska Geographic Ser.: Vol. 6, No. 2). (Illus.). 95p. 1979. reprint ed. pap. 19.95 (*0-88240-124-6*) Alaska Geog Soc.

Akasofu, S. I. & Kan, J. R., eds. Physics of Auroral Arc Formation. (Geophysical Monograph Ser.: Vol. 25). 465p. 1981. 32.00 (*0-87590-050-X*) Am Geophysical.

Akasofu, Syun-Ichi. Physics of Magnetospheric Substorms. (Astrophysics & Space Science Library: No. 47). 1977. lib. bdg. 245.50 (*90-277-0748-0*) Kluwer Academic.

Akasofu, Syun-Ichi, ed. Dynamics of the Magnetosphere. (Astrophysics & Space Science Library: No. 78). 1979. text 211.50 (*90-277-1052-X*) Kluwer Academic.

Akasofu, Syun-Ichi & Kamide, Y., eds. The Solar Wind & the Earth. (C). 1987. lib. bdg. 204.50 (*90-277-2471-7*) Kluwer Academic.

Akass, Ron. Essential Health & Safety for Managers: A Guide to Good Practice in the European Union. 284p. 1994. 78.95 (*0-566-07332-3*, Pub. by Gower) Ashgate Pub Co.

Akass, Ron. What Every Manager Needs to Know about Health. 288p. 1996. pap. 34.95 (*0-566-07734-5*) Ashgate Pub Co.

Akatsuka, I., ed. Biology of Economic Algae. (Illus.). 545p. 1995. 150.00 (*90-5103-093-2*, Pub. by SPB Acad Pub) Balogh.

Akatsuka, Isamu, ed. Introduction to Applied Phycology. (Illus.). iv, 683p. 1990. 160.00 (*90-5103-052-5*, Pub. by SPB Acad Pub) Balogh.

Akatsuka, Noriko, ed. Japanese - Korean Linguistics, Vol. 4. 1995. pap. text 24.95 (*1-881526-64-X*) CSLI.

Akatsuka, Noriko, et al, eds. Japanese - Korean Linguistics, Vol. 7. 720p. (C). 1998. pap. 29.95 (*1-57586-116-X*); text 74.95 (*1-57586-117-8*) CSLI.

— Japanese/Korean Linguistics, Vol. 5. 400p. (Orig.). (C). 1996. 69.95 (*1-57586-045-7*) CSLI.

— Japanese/Korean Linguistics, Vol. 5. 400p. (Orig.). (C). 1996. pap. 25.95 (*1-57586-044-9*) CSLI.

Akavia, Gideon. Decisive Victory & Correct Doctrine: Cults in French Military Thought. 94p. (Orig.). 1993. pap. 12.00 (*0-935371-26-5*) CFISAC.

Akavia, Miriam. An End to Childhood. McLeary, Michael P. & Goldman, Jeanette, trs. 112p. 1994. pap. 22.50 (*0-85303-294-7*, Pub. by M Vallentine & Co) Intl Spec Bk.

Akawie, Alice L., et al. California Title Insurance Practice. 2nd rev. ed. Blanchette, Janis LaRoche & Sherlin, Johanna, eds. LC 97-65421. 688p. 1997. ring bd. 129.00 (*0-7626-0063-2*, RE-32620) Cont Ed Bar-CA.

— California Title Insurance Practice: 1/98 Update. 2nd ed. Blanchette, Janis L., ed. LC 97-65421. 478p. 1998. ring bd. 44.00 (*0-7626-0176-0*, RE-32621) Cont Ed Bar-CA.

Akay, Metin. Biomedical Signal Processing. LC 93-25710. 377p. 1994. text 58.00 (*0-12-047145-0*) Acad Pr.

— Detection & Estimation Methods for Biomedical Sygnals. LC 95-44630. (Illus.). 268p. 1996. text, boxed set 84.95 incl. 3.5 hd (*0-12-047145-4*) Acad Pr.

***Akay, Metin.** Nonlinear Biomedical Signal Processing. LC 00-27777. 2000. write for info. (*0-7803-6011-7*) IEEE Standards.

Akay, Metin, ed. Time-Frequency & Wavelets in Biomedical Signal Processing. LC 97-19866. 768p. 1997. 129.95 (*0-7803-1147-7*, PC5619) Inst Electrical.

***Akay, Metin & Marsh, Andy.** Virtual Reality Technologies in Medicine. 360p. 2001. 110.00 (*0-471-38863-7*) Wiley.

Akazawa, T., et al, eds. Neandertals & Modern Humans in Western Asia. LC 98-35581. (Illus.). 552p. (C). 1998. 79.50 (*0-306-45924-8*, Plenum Trade) Perseus Pubng.

Akazawa, Takeru, et al, eds. The Other Visualized: Depictions of the Mongoloid Peoples. (Illus.). 274p. 1993. pap. 33.50 (*0-86008-509-0*, Pub. by U of Tokyo) Col U Pr.

Akazawa, Takeru & Sakaguchi, Yutaka, eds. Paleolithic Site of the Douara Cave & Paleogeography of Palmyra Basin in Syria: 1984 Excavations, Part IV. (Illus.). 276p. 1987. text 69.50 (*0-86008-415-9*, Pub. by U of Tokyo) Col U Pr.

Akazawa, Takeru, jt. ed. see Hanihara, Kazuro.

Akbar, Fatollah. The Eye of an Ant: Persian Proverbs & Poems Rendered into English Verse. LC 94-48744. 102p. (Orig.). 1995. pap. 10.00 (*0-936347-56-2*) IBEX.

Akbar, Fatollah, tr. Eye of an Ant: Persian Proverbs & Poems. 283p. 1996. pap. 10.00 (*0-614-21642-7*, 1385) Kazi Pubns.

Akbar Khan, Ali, jt. auth. see Ruckert, George.

Akbar, Khatija. Madhubala: Her Life Her Films. LC 97-901433. (C). 1997. pap. 14.00 (*81-7476-153-5*, Pub. by UBS Pubs Dist) S Asia.

Akbar, M. Entrepreneurship & Indian Muslims. (C). 1990. 31.00 (*81-85445-01-X*, Pub. by Manak Pubns Pvt Ltd) Nataraj Bks.

Akbar, M. J. India: The Siege Within Challenges to a Nation's Unity. LC 96-903073. (C). 1996. 14.00 (*81-7476-076-8*, Pub. by UBS Pubs Dist) S Asia.

Akbar, M. K. Pakistan from Jinnah to Sharif. LC 97-904082. vi, 360p. 1997. 45.00 (*81-7099-656-2*, Pub. by Mittal Pubs Dist) Nataraj Bks.

— Pakistan Today. 237p. 1998. 26.00 (*81-7099-700-3*, Pub. by Mittal Pubs Dist) Nataraj Bks.

Akbar, M. M. The Orations of Muhhamad, the Prophet of Islam. 106p. 1991. 8.50 (*81-7151-047-7*) Asia Bk Corp.

Akbar, Na'im. Breaking the Chains of Psychological Slavery. rev. ed. 95p. 1996. pap. 10.00 (*0-935257-05-5*) Mind Prods Assocs.

— Chains & Images of Psychological Slavery. 76p. (Orig.). (C). reprint ed. pap. 3.50 (*0-933821-00-X*) New Mind Prod.

— The Community of Self. rev. ed. 80p. 1985. pap. 8.00 (*0-935257-00-4*) Mind Prods Assocs.

— Light from Ancient Africa. LC 94-96248. 85p. (Orig.). 1994. pap. 9.95 (*0-935257-02-0*) Mind Prods Assocs.

— Light from Ancient Africa. 1994. 15.00 (*0-935257-03-9*) Mind Prods Assocs.

— Natural Psychology & Human Transformation. rev. ed. 65p. 1995. pap. 8.00 (*0-935257-04-7*) Mind Prods Assocs.

— Visions for Black Men. LC 91-65248. 95p. 1992. reprint ed. pap. 10.00 (*0-935257-01-2*) Mind Prods Assocs.

Akbar, Na'im & Nu'Man, Muhammad A. From Miseducation to Education. rev. ed. 26p. (Orig.). 1985. reprint ed. pap. 2.75 (*0-933821-01-8*) New Mind Prod.

Akbulut, S. & King, H. Topology of Real Algebraic Sets. (Mathematical Sciences Research Institute Publications: Vol. 25). x, 249p. 1991. 63.95 (*0-387-97744-9*) Spr-Verlag.

Akbulut, Selman, et al, eds. Proceedings of Govoka Geometry - Topology Conference, 1993. (Illus.). 110p. (C). Date not set. pap. 20.00 (*975-403-010-3*) Intl Pr Boston.

— Proceedings of Govoka Geometry - Topology Conference, 1994. (Illus.). 88p. (C). Date not set. pap. 20.00 (*975-403-023-5*) Intl Pr Boston.

— Proceedings of Govoka Geometry - Topology Conference, 1995. 139p. (C). Date not set. 25.00 (*975-403-040-5*) Intl Pr Boston.

— Proceedings of Govoka Geometry - Topology Conference, 1996. (Illus.). 131p. (C). Date not set. 25.00 (*975-403-071-5*) Intl Pr Boston.

Akbulut, Selman, ed. see Conference on Real Algebraic Geometry & Toplogy St.

Akca, Nancy, ed. see Porter, David B.

Akcakaya, H. Resit & Ferson, Scott. RAMAS - Space: Spatially Structured Population Models for Conservation Biology. 114p. 1990. teacher ed. 495.00 (*1-884977-05-7*); disk 295.00 (*1-884977-04-9*) Applied Biomath.

Akcakaya, H. Resit, et al. Applied Population Ecology: Principles & Computer Exercises Using RAMAS EcoLab 1.0. (Illus.). xii, 255p. (Orig.). 1997. pap. text. write for info. incl. disk (*1-884977-23-5*); pap. text. write for info. (*1-884977-22-7*) Applied Biomath.

— Applied Population Ecology: Principles & Computer Exercises Using RAMAS EcoLab 2.0. 2nd rev. ed. (Illus.). xii, 285p. 1998. pap. text 95.00 incl. disk (*1-884977-26-X*); pap. text 95.00 (*1-884977-25-1*) Applied Biomath.

***Akcakaya, H. Resit, et al.** Applied Population Ecology Using RAMAS Ecolab: Principles & Computer Exercises Using RAMAS EcoLab 2.0. 2nd rev. ed. 272p. (C). 1999. pap. text 39.95 incl. cd-rom (*0-87893-028-0*) Sinauer Assocs.

Akcakaya, H. Resit, jt. auth. see Ferson, Scott.

Akcora, Rustem. Use of Contilever Jack-up Drilling Rigs for Cost Effective Satellite & Marginal Field Development. 1989. 125.00 (*90-6314-552-7*, Pub. by Lorne & MacLean Marine) St Mut.

Akcora, Rustem, ed. Use of Cantilever Jack-up Drilling Rigs for Cost Effective Satellite & Marginal Field Developments. (C). 1989. 95.00 (*0-89771-727-9*, Pub. by Lorne & MacLean Marine) St Mut.

Akdogan, Haluk. The Integration of International Capital Markets: Theory & Empirical Evidence. 208p. 1995. 95.00 (*1-85898-131-X*) E Elgar.

***Ake, Anne.** The Apache. LC 00-8758. (Indigenous Peoples of North America Ser.). (Illus.). 2001. write for info. (*1-56006-616-4*) Lucent Bks.

Ake, Anne. The Gorilla. LC 98-53231. (Overview Ser.). (Illus.). 128p. (YA). (gr. 4-12). 1999. lib. bdg. 23.70 (*1-56006-492-7*) Lucent Bks.

Ake, Claude. Democracy & Development in Africa. 173p. (C). 1995. 38.95 (*0-8157-0220-5*) Brookings.

Ake, Claude & World Institute for Development Economics Research. Why Humanitarian Emergencies Occur: Insights from the Interface of State, Democracy, & Civil Society. LC 98-178546. (Research for Action Ser.). 13p. 1997. write for info. (*952-9520-47-6*) UN.

Ake, Jeffrey J. Agressive Exporting: How to Make Your Small Company into an International Tiger. 216p. 1995. pap. 10.95 (*1-888249-02-1*) Intl Vision.

— Channing: Paradigm Transition Fuge. LC 96-134475. 136p. 1995. text 19.95 (*1-888249-01-3*) Intl Vision.

— Youthful Musings: A Book of Poetry. 68p. 1995. pap. 6.95 (*1-888249-00-5*) Intl Vision.

Akehurst, F. R., tr. The Etablissements de Saint Louis: Thirteenth-Century Law Texts from Tours, Orleans, & Paris. LC 96-20334. (Middle Ages Ser.). 160p. 1996. text 32.50 (*0-8122-3350-6*) U of Pa Pr.

Akehurst, F. R., tr. from FRE. The Coutumes de Beauvaisis of Philippe de Beaumanoir. LC 91-31497. (Middle Ages Ser.). 792p. (C). 1992. text 79.95 (*0-8122-3105-8*) U of Pa Pr.

Akehurst, F. R. & Davis, Judith M., eds. A Handbook of the Troubadours. 508p. 1995. pap. 24.95 (*0-520-07976-0*, Pub. by U CA Pr) Cal Prin Full Svc.

Akehurst, F. R. & Van D'Elden, Stephanie C. The Stranger in Medieval Society. LC 97-21249. (Medieval Cultures Ser.). 1998. 44.95 (*0-8166-3031-3*); pap. 17.95 (*0-8166-3032-1*) U of Minn Pr.

Akehurst, G. & Gadrey, J., eds. Economics of Services. (Illus.). 200p. 1988. text 32.50 (*0-7146-3337-2*, Pub. by F Cass Pubs) Intl Spec Bk.

Akehurst, Gary & Alexander, Nicholas, eds. The Internationalisation of Retailing. 208p. (C). 1996. 35.00 (*0-7146-4648-2*, Pub. by F Cass Pubs); pap. 19.50 (*0-7146-4174-X*, Pub. by F Cass Pubs) Intl Spec Bk.

— Retail Employment. LC 96-14521. (Retailing Ser.). 200p. (Orig.). (C). 1996. pap. 21.00 (*0-7146-4177-4*, Pub. by F Cass Pubs) Intl Spec Bk.

— Retail Marketing. LC 96-14526. (Retailing Ser.). 200p. (Orig.). (C). 1996. pap. 21.00 (*0-7146-4175-8*, Pub. by F Cass Pubs) Intl Spec Bk.

— Retail Structure. LC 96-14523. (Retailing Ser.). 200p. (Orig.). (C). 1996. pap. 21.00 (*0-7146-4176-6*, Pub. by F Cass Pubs) Intl Spec Bk.

Akehurst, Gary, jt. ed. see Alexander, Nicholas.

Akehurst, Ken. Everyones Gone to the Hereafter. 184p. 1985. pap. 11.95 (*0-85435-414-X*, Pub. by C W Daniel) Natl Bk Netwk.

— Everyone's Guide to the Hereafter. 128p. (Orig.). pap. 17.95 (*0-8464-4188-8*) Beekman Pubs.

Akehurst, Michael B. A Modern Introduction to International Law. rev. ed. LC 86-28828. 1987. pap. text 24.95 (*0-04-341037-5*) Routledge.

Akehurst, Michael B., jt. auth. see Malanczuk, Peter.

Akehurst, Richard. Games Guns & Rifles: Percussion to Hammerless. (Illus.). 192p. 1993. 39.95 (*0-948253-61-4*, Pub. by Sportmans Pr) Trafalgar.

Akel, Abdullatif A. Agony in Limbo. Ciulla, A. J., ed. (Illus.). 388p. (C). 17.95 (*0-913791-01-6*) Rubicon Bks.

Akel, D'Ann, jt. auth. see Dinaburg, Kathy.

Akelman. Hand & Wrist Injuries. 1999. text. write for info. (*0-7216-6966-2*) Harcourt.

Akeman, Thom. The Best Ever Guide to the Monterey Peninsula & Carmel Area. 4th rev. ed. (Illus.). 192p. 1999. pap. 15.95 (*0-9623209-4-3*) Kaskaskia Pr.

Akemann, C. & Anderson, J. Lyapunov Theorems for Operator Algebras. LC 91-28168. (Memoirs Ser.). 88p. 1991. pap. 19.00 (*0-8218-2516-X*, MEMO/94/458) Am Math.

Akemann, C. & Shultz, F. Perfect C: Algebras. LC 85-4018. (Memoirs of the AMS Ser.: No. 55/326). 117p. 1986. pap. 22.00 (*0-8218-2327-2*, MEMO/55/326) Am Math.

Aken, David C. Van, see Van Aken, David C.

Aken, K. M., jt. ed. see Carron, L. T.

Aken, Mark J. Van, see Van Aken, Mark J.

Aken, Norman van, see Van Aken, Norman.

Aken, W. G. Van, see Van Aken, W. G.

An Asterisk (*) at the beginning of an entry indicates that the title is appearing for the first time.

Akenhead, Robert, jt. auth. see Cottington, Jack.

Akens, David S. How to Write Everything Better & Get It Published. 224p. (Orig.). 1996. pap. 8.95 (*0-87397-316-X*, Strode Pubs) Circle Bk Service.

— John Glenn: First American in Space. 17.95 (*0-88411-900-9*) Amereon Ltd.

Akens, David S. & Klein, Eugene L. Computers in Plain English. Duran, Paul & Duran, Jennie, eds. (Illus.). 120p. 1997. pap. 18.95 (*0-87397-997-4*) Circle Bk Service.

Akens, Jean. High Desert Treasures: The State Parks of Southeastern Utah. LC 89-82357. (Illus.). 64p. (Orig.). 1990. pap. 4.50 (*0-944123-03-1*) Four Crnrs UT.

— Ute Mountain Tribal Park: The Other Mesa Verde. (Illus.). 96p. (Orig.). 1995. pap. 8.50 (*0-944123-00-7*) Four Crnrs UT.

Akens, Jean, ed. see Stanton, Bette L.

Akenside, Mark. The Poetical Manuscripts of Mark Akenside. (Illus.). 32p. (Orig.). 1988. pap. 15.00 (*0-943184-02-9*) Amherst Coll Pr.

— Poetical Works. (BCL1-PR English Literature Ser.). 353p. 1992. reprint ed. lib. bdg. 89.00 (*0-7812-7317-X*) Rprt Serv.

— Poetical Works of Mark Akenside. Dyce, Alexander, ed. LC 71-94924. reprint ed. 54.00 (*0-404-00299-4*) AMS Pr.

Akenson, Don. At Face Value: The Life & Times of Eliza McCormack & John White. 264p. (C). 1990. 55.00 (*0-7735-0765-5*, Pub. by McG-Queens Univ Pr) CUP Services.

— At Face Value: The Life & Times of Eliza McCormack & John White. 262p. (C). 1992. pap. 22.95 (*0-7735-0948-8*, Pub. by McG-Queens Univ Pr) CUP Services.

Akenson, Donald. Surpassing Wonder: The Invention of the Bible & the Talmuds. LC 98-230652. 672p. 1998. 39.95 (*0-15-100418-8*) Harcourt.

Akenson, Donald H. Being Had: Historians, Evidence & the Irish in North America. 243p. 1985. text 38.00 (*0-88835-014-7*) P D Meany.

— The Church of Ireland: Ecclesiastical Reform & Revolution, 1880-1885. LC 76-151565. 428p. reprint ed. pap. 132.70 (*0-608-30399-2*, 201319700085) Bks Demand.

— Conor: A Biography of Conor Cruise O'Brien. (Illus.). 576p. 1994. text 39.95 (*0-8014-3086-0*) Cornell U Pr.

— Conor: A Biography of Conor Cruise O'Brien: Anthology, Vol. 2. (Illus.). 376p. 1994. 34.95 (*0-7735-1256-X*, Pub. by McG-Queens Univ Pr) CUP Services.

— Conor: A Biography of Conor Cruise O'Brien: Narrative. (Illus.). 608p. 1994. 34.95 (*0-7735-1255-1*, Pub. by McG-Queens Univ Pr) CUP Services.

— God's Peoples: Covenant & Land in South Africa, Israel, & Ulster. LC 92-8758. (Illus.). 416p. 1992. text 39.95 (*0-8014-2755-X*) Cornell U Pr.

— If the Irish Ran the World: Montserrat, 1630-1730. LC 96-901080. (Illus.). 288p. 1997. text 60.00 (*0-7735-1630-1*, Pub. by McG-Queens Univ Pr); pap. text 22.95 (*0-7735-1686-7*, Pub. by McG-Queens Univ Pr) CUP Services.

— The Irish Diaspora: A Primer. 330p. Date not set. pap. 15.95 (*0-85389-663-1*) Dufour.

— The Irish Diaspora: A Primer. (Illus.). 265p. 1993. text 38.00 (*0-88835-038-4*) P D Meany.

— The Irish Diaspora: A Primer. (Illus.). 319p. 1997. reprint ed. pap. 15.95 (*0-88835-001-5*) P D Meany.

— A Mirror to Kathleen's Face: Education in Independent Ireland, 1922-1960. 240p. (C). 1975. 39.95 (*0-7735-0203-3*, Pub. by McG-Queens Univ Pr) CUP Services.

— Small Differences: Irish Catholics & Irish Protestants, 1815-1922: An International Perspective. (Studies in the History of Religion). 256p. (C). 1988. 60.00 (*0-7735-0636-5*, Pub. by McG-Queens Univ Pr) CUP Services.

— Small Differences: Irish Catholics & Irish Protestants, 1815-1922: An International Perspective. (Illus.). 236p. 1999. reprint ed. pap. 18.00 (*0-7881-6129-6*) DIANE Pub.

— Small Differences: Irish Catholics & Irish Protestants, 1815-1922: An International Perspective. (McGill-Queen's Studies in the History of Religion Ser.). 256p. (C). 1991. reprint ed. pap. text 22.95 (*0-7735-0858-9*, Pub. by McG-Queens Univ Pr) CUP Services.

— The United States & Ireland. LC 73-82348. (American Foreign Policy Library). 322p. reprint ed. pap. 99.90 (*0-7837-4444-7*, 205797400012) Bks Demand.

Akenson, Donald H., ed. Canadian Papers in Rural History, Vol. 1. LC 79-304789. 113p. 1978. reprint ed. pap. 35.10 (*0-608-03793-1*, 206465300001) Bks Demand.

— Canadian Papers in Rural History, Vol. 2. LC 79-304789. 172p. reprint ed. pap. 53.40 (*0-608-03794-X*, 206465300002) Bks Demand.

— Canadian Papers in Rural History, Vol. 3. LC 79-304789. 256p. 1996. reprint ed. pap. 79.40 (*0-608-03795-8*, 206465300003) Bks Demand.

— Canadian Papers in Rural History, Vol. 4. LC 79-304789. 338p. pap. 104.80 (*0-608-03796-6*, 206465300004) Bks Demand.

— Canadian Papers in Rural History, Vol. 5. LC 79-304789. 375p. reprint ed. pap. 116.30 (*0-608-03797-4*, 206465300005) Bks Demand.

— Canadian Papers in Rural History, Vol. 6. LC 79-304789. 353p. reprint ed. pap. 109.50 (*0-608-03798-2*, 206465300006) Bks Demand.

— Canadian Papers in Rural History, Vol. 7. LC 79-304789. 406p. reprint ed. pap. 125.90 (*0-608-03799-0*, 206465300007) Bks Demand.

— Canadian Papers in Rural History, Vol. 8. LC 79-304789. 327p. reprint ed. pap. 101.40 (*0-608-03800-8*, 206465300008) Bks Demand.

— Canadian Papers in Rural History, Vol. 9. LC 79-304789. 418p. reprint ed. pap. 129.60 (*0-608-03801-6*, 206465300009) Bks Demand.

— Canadian Papers in Rural History, Vol. 10. LC 79-304789. 313p. reprint ed. pap. 97.10 (*0-608-03802-4*, 206465300010) Bks Demand.

Akenson, Donald Harman. The Irish in Ontario: A Study in Rural History. (Illus.). 416p. 1984. 60.00 (*0-7735-0430-3*, Pub. by McG-Queens Univ Pr) CUP Services.

— The Irish in Ontario: A Study in Rural History. (Illus.). 448p. 1985. pap. 24.95 (*0-7735-0591-1*, Pub. by McG-Queens Univ Pr) CUP Services.

***Akenson, Donald Harman.** Saint Saul: A Skeleton Key to the Historical Jesus. 336p. 2000. 27.50 (*0-19-514157-1*) OUP.

— Surpassing Wonder: The Invention of the Bible & the Talmuds. 672p. write for info. (*0-7735-1781-2*, Pub. by McG-Queens Univ Pr) CUP Services.

Akenson, James E., jt. ed. see Wolfe, Charles K.

Aker. What Comes in 2 3 & 4. (C). 1998. pap. 5.95 (*0-87628-368-7*) S&S Trade.

Aker, Benny C. & McGee, Gary B., eds. Signs & Wonders in Ministry Today. 128p. (Orig.). 1996. pap. 7.99 (*0-88243-346-6*) Gospel Pub.

Aker, Don. Of Things Not Seen. unabridged ed. 176p. (YA). (gr. 7 up). 1997. mass mkt. 5.99 (*0-7736-7435-7*) STDK.

— Stranger at Bay. unabridged ed. 256p. (J). (gr. 7 up). 1998. pap. 4.95 (*0-7736-7468-3*) Stoddart Publ.

Aker, Frank. October, 1973: The Arab-Israeli War. LC 85-751. (Illus.). ix, 185p. (C). 1985. lib. bdg. 27.50 (*0-208-02066-7*, Archon Bks) Shoe String.

Aker, Frank & Norval, Morsan. Breaking the Strangle Hold: The Liberation of Grenada. 130p. (Orig.). 1984. pap. 4.95 (*0-9613968-0-6*) Gun Ownrs Fund.

Aker, George. Adult Education Procedures, Methods, & Techniques: A Classified & Annotated Bibliography 1953-1963. 1965. 5.00 (*0-87060-089-3*, PRE 2) Syracuse U Cont Ed.

Aker, J. Brooke. Law of Wills in Pennsylvania: Drafting, Interpreting, Contesting with Forms. LC 83-72488. (Illus.). 567p. 1999. ring bd. 109.50 (*1-887024-35-2*) Bisel Co.

— Pennsylvania Probate, Estates & Fiduciaries Code Annotated. 1999. ring bd. 109.50 (*1-887024-62-X*) Bisel Co.

Aker, J. Brooke, et al. Mental Capacity: Medical & Legal Aspects of the Aging. (Trial Practice Ser.). 372p. 1977. text 95.00 (*0-07-000756-X*) Shepards.

Aker, J. Brooke, jt. auth. see Smith, M. Paul.

Aker, James C., ed. see Eskesen, Sherri L.

***Aker, Joe C. & Zvonkovic, Gary, photos by.** Rafael Moneo: Audrey Jones Beck Building, Museum of Fine Arts, Houston. (Opus Ser.: Vol. 36). (Illus.). 60p. 2000. 42.00 (*3-930698-36-6*) Edition A Menges.

Aker, John & Biddle, Chuck. CRNA Guide to Ambulatory Anesthesia. (Illus.). 608p. 1997. 65.00 (*0-07-057127-9*) McGraw.

Aker, John, jt. auth. see Zaglaniczny, Karen L.

Aker, Saundra N. & Lenssen, Polly. A Guide to Good Nutrition During & after Chemotherapy & Radiation. 3rd rev. ed. LC 87-83467. (Illus.). 147p. 1988. pap. 5.00 (*0-945278-00-4*) Hutchinson Cancer Res Ctr.

Aker, Sharon. The Mac Almanac. (Illus.). 960p. (Orig.). 1994. pap. 29.95 (*1-56276-143-9*, Ziff-Davis Pr) Que.

— Word Tips & Techniques. 1992. pap. text. write for info. (*0-201-60888-X*) AddVantage Lrn.

Aker, Sharon Z. Macintosh Companion: The Basics & Beyond. 608p. 1991. pap. text 22.95 (*0-201-57754-2*) Addison-Wesley.

— Xtras for System 7. 128p. 1992. pap. text 24.95 (*0-201-60853-7*) Addison-Wesley.

Aker, Sharon Z., jt. auth. see Wolfson, Richard.

***Aker, Sharon Zardetto.** The Macintosh Bible. 7th ed. LC 99-167870. (Illus.). 1024p. (C). 1998. pap. 34.99 (*0-201-87483-0*, Pub. by Peachpit Pr) Addison-Wesley.

Aker, Suzanne. What Comes in Twos, Threes & Fours? LC 89-3548. (J). (ps-k). 1992. pap. 5.95 (*0-671-79247-4*) S&S Bks Yung.

— What Comes in Twos, Threes & Fours? 1992. 11.15 (*0-606-13095-0*, Pub. by Turtleback) Demco.

— What Comes in 2's, 3's & 4's? LC 89-35482. (Illus.). 32p. (J). (ps-k). 1992. lib. bdg. 15.00 (*0-671-67173-1*) S&S Childrens.

***Akeret, Robert.** Photolanguage: How Photos Reveal the Fascinating Stories of Our Lives & Relationships. (Illus.). 240p. 2000. 29.95 (*0-393-04968-X*) Norton.

Akeret, Robert. Tales from Travelling Couch: A Psychotherapist Revisits His Most Memorable Patients. 240p. 1996. pap. 13.00 (*0-393-31498-7*) Norton.

Akeret, Robert U. Tales from a Traveling Couch: A Psychotherapist Revisits His Most Memorable Patients. 235p. 1998. text 22.00 (*0-7881-5941-0*) DIANE Pub.

Akerholm, Johnny & Giovannini, Alberto, eds. Exchange Rate Policies in the Nordic Countries. 320p. (C). 1994. 37.50 (*1-898128-11-1*) Brookings.

Akerley, Ben E. The X-Rated Bible: An Irreverent Survey of Sex in the Scriptures. (Illus.). 428p. 1985. pap. 14.00 (*0-910309-19-1*, 5000) Am Atheist.

— The X-Rated Bible: An Irreverent Survey of Sex in the Scriptures. rev. ed. (Illus.). 430p. 1999. pap. 14.95 (*0-922915-55-5*) Feral Hse.

Akerley, John. Programming with VisualAge for Java Version 2, 2nd Edtion. 2nd ed. 500p. 1999. pap. text 49.99 (*0-13-021298-9*) P-H.

Akerlof, George A. An Economic Theorist's Book of Tales: Essays That Entertain the Consequences of New Assumptions in Economic Theory. (Illus.). 206p. 1984. pap. text 20.95 (*0-521-26933-4*) Cambridge U Pr.

Akerlof, George A. & Yellen, Janet, eds. Efficiency Wage Models of the Labor Market. (Illus.). 192p. 1986. text 64.95 (*0-521-32156-5*) Cambridge U Pr.

Akerlund, A. Swedish-Spanish Dictionary: Svensk-Spansk Ordbok (Esselte) (SPA & SWE.). 389p. 1984. 49.95 (*0-8288-1069-9*, M2815) Fr & Eur.

Akerman, Joe. American Brahman: A History of the American Brahman Breed & the American Brahman Breeders Association. (Illus.). 384p. 1982. 17.50 (*0-318-12445-9*) Am Brahman Breeders.

— American Brahman: A History of the American Brahman Breed & the American Brahman Breeders Association. deluxe ed. (Illus.). 384p. 1982. ring bd. 52.50 (*0-318-12446-7*) Am Brahman Breeders.

Akerman, Johan. Economic Progress & Economic Crises. LC 79-13175. (Illus.). x, 190p. 1979. reprint ed. lib. bdg. 35.00 (*0-87991-952-3*) Porcupine Pr.

— Theory of Industrialism: Causal Analysis & Economic Plans. LC 80-21155. (Illus.). 332p. 1980. reprint ed. lib. bdg. 45.00 (*0-87991-859-4*) Porcupine Pr.

Akerman, John Y., ed. Letters from Roundhead Officers. LC 73-158237. (Bannatyne Club, Edinburgh. Publications: No. 101). reprint ed. 57.50 (*0-404-52849-X*) AMS Pr.

Akerman, John Y., ed. see Guy, Henry.

Akerman, N., ed. The Necessity of Friction: 19 Essays on a Vital Force. 336p. 1993. 71.95 (*0-387-91470-6*, Spr-Verlag.

Akerman, Nordal, ed. The Necessity of Friction. LC 97-22525. 336p. (C). 1998. pap. 28.00 (*0-8133-3434-9*, Pub. by Westview) HarpC.

Akerman, Sue. Two Cushions & a Quilt. 2nd ed. Turpin-Delport, Lesley, ed. & illus. by. 78p. 1994. reprint ed. pap. 19.95 (*0-9583873-1-1*, Pub. by Triple T Pubng) Quilters Res.

Akerman, Susanna. Queen Christina of Sweden & Her Circle: The Transformation of a Seventeenth-Century Philosophical Libertine. LC 90-42995. (BSIH Ser.: No. 21). xv, 339p. 1991. 108.00 (*90-04-09310-9*) Brill Academic Pubs.

— Rose Cross over the Baltic: The Spread of Rosicrucianism in Northern Europe. LC 98-6871. viii, 264p. 1998. 90.50 (*90-04-11030-5*) Brill Academic Pubs.

Akermark, Spiliopoulou. Justifications of Minority Protection in International Law, Vol. ISHR 50. LC 97-17064. (International Studies in Human Rights). 1997. 102.00 (*90-411-0424-0*, Pub. by M Nijhoff) Kluwer Academic.

Akeroyd, J. Collins Wild Guide: Wild Flowers. 255p. 1996. pap. 12.95 (*0-00-220004-X*, Pub. by HarpC) Trafalgar.

Akeroyd, John. 3-D Plant. LC 99-180635. (Eyewitness Books). (Illus.). 56p. (J). (gr. 4-7). 1998. spiral bd. 16.95 (*0-7894-3453-9*) DK Pub Inc.

Akeroyd, Richard H. Reason & Revelation: From Paul to Pascal. LC 91-18226. 130p. (C). 1991. pap. 12.95 (*0-86554-405-0*, P097) Mercer Univ Pr.

Akeroyd, Richard H., tr. see Schlumberger, Jean.

Akers, A. E. Akers Family of Franklin County, Va., Combined with the Boone, Cannaday, Hickman & Pridgen Families. (Illus.). 159p. 1998. reprint ed. pap. 23.00 (*0-8328-7223-7*); reprint ed. lib. bdg. 33.00 (*0-8328-7222-9*) Higginson Bk Co.

Akers, Angela, jt. auth. see Duncan, King.

Akers, Angela D. The O+ Factor: Stories of People Who Have Overcome Obstacles on the Road to Success. 150p. 1998. pap. 7.95 (*0-936497-49-1*) Seven Worlds.

Akers, Ashley, jt. auth. see Akers, Gary.

Akers, Charlene. First & Foremost: A Guide to Northern California's Independent Bookstores. (Illus.). 216p. (Orig.). 1996. pap. 12.95 (*0-930588-90-8*) Heyday Bks.

***Akers, Charlene.** Obesity. LC 99-46398. (Overview Ser.). 128p. (YA). (gr. 4-12). 2000. 18.96 (*1-56006-662-8*) Lucent Bks.

Akers, Charlene. Open to the Public: A Guide to the Museums of Northern California. (Illus.). 352p. (Orig.). 1994. pap. 14.95 (*0-930588-72-X*) Heyday Bks.

Akers, Charles W. Abigail Adams. 2nd ed. LC 99-462646. 240p. (C). 1999. pap. text 20.20 (*0-321-04370-7*) Addison-Wesley Educ.

— Abigail Adams: An American Woman. LC 79-2241. (Library of American Biography). (C). 1980. text 19.00 (*0-673-39318-6*) Addson-Wesley Educ.

— Abigail Adams: An American Woman. LC 79-2241 (Library of American Biography). (Illus.). x, 207p. 1980. 15.95 (*0-316-02041-9*) Little.

Akers, David J., ed. Creative Application of Materials Engineering. LC 89-39536. 64p. 1989. pap. text 5.00 (*0-87262-733-0*, 733) Am Soc Civil Eng.

Akers, David W. A Handbook of Twentieth-Century United States Gold Coins. (Illus.). 184p. 1988. text 29.95 (*0-943161-19-3*); pap. text 19.95 (*0-943161-14-2*) Bowers & Merena.

Akers-Douglas, Adrian. Flying? No Fear! A Handbook for Apprehensive Flyers. 1998. pap. 9.95 (*1-84024-056-7*, Pub. by Summers) Howell Pr VA.

Akers-Douglas, Frank & Snelgrove, John. Butterworths Personal Tax: Self Assessment & Simplification. (Orig.). 1994. pap. 27.95 (*0-406-04528-3*, MICHIE) LEXIS Pub.

Akers-Douglas, Frank & Snelgrove, John H. Butterworths Personal Tax: Self-Assessment & Simplification. 2nd ed. 1996. ring bd. write for info. (*0-406-99652-0*, BPTS1ASET, MICHIE) LEXIS Pub.

Akers, Gary & Akers, Ashley. Kentucky - Land of Beauty: Paintings by Gary Akers. Akers, Lynn R., ed. (Illus.). 1998. 79.95 (*0-9664145-0-0*) G L Galleries.

Akers, James D. The Life & Goal Planner: How to Win the Achievement Game. 117p. (Orig.). 1988. pap. 19.95 (*0-9621678-0-0*) J D Akers & Assocs.

Akers, James E., jt. ed. see Wagner, Carmen.

Akers, Joan, et al. Name That Portion: Fractions, Percents, & Decimals. Anderson, Catherine et al, eds. (Investigations in Number, Data, & Space Ser.). (Illus.). 178p. (Orig.). (J). (gr. 5-6). 1996. pap., teacher ed. 22.95 (*0-86651-990-4*, DS21426) Seymour Pubns.

— Shapes, Halves, & Symmetry: Geometry & Fractions. Anderson, Catherine et al, eds. (Investigations in Number, Data, & Space Ser.). (Illus.). 209p. (Orig.). (J). (gr. 2). 1996. pap., teacher ed. 32.95 incl. mac ld (*1-57232-217-9*, 21648) Seymour Pubns.

— Shapes, Halves, & Symmetry: Geometry & Fractions. rev. ed. Anderson, Catherine et al, eds. LC 97-207392. (Investigations in Number, Data, & Space Ser.). (Illus.). 219p. (Orig.). (J). (gr. 2 up). 1997. pap. text 32.95 (*1-57232-656-5*, 43803) Seymour Pubns.

***Akers, John K.** This We Believe: The Good News of Jesus Christ for the World. 2000. 0.00 (*0-310-23428-X*) Zondervan.

***Akers, Keith.** The Lost Religion of Jesus: Simple Living & Nonviolence in Early Christianity. 2000. pap. 20.00 (*1-930051-26-3*) Lantern Books.

Akers, Keith. A Vegetarian Sourcebook: The Nutrition, Ecology, & Ethics of a Natural Foods Diet. 4th rev. ed. (Illus.). 256p. 1993. pap. 10.95 (*0-945528-00-0*) Vegetarian Pr.

Akers, Laura, jt. auth. see Severson, Herbert H.

Akers, Linda, jt. auth. see Walker, Jane R.

Akers, Lynn R., jt. auth. see Ewen, Dale R.

Akers, Lynn R., ed. see Akers, Gary & Akers, Ashley.

Akers, Michael J. Parenteral Quality Control: Sterility, Pyrogen, Particulate, & Package Integrity Testing. 2nd rev. ed. LC 93-25667. (Advances in Parenteral Sciences Ser.: Vol. 5). (Illus.). 400p. 1993. text 130.00 (*0-8247-9088-X*) Dekker.

***Akers, Michelle.** The Game & the Glory. 2000. pap. 7.99 (*0-310-70025-6*) Zondervan.

***Akers, Michelle & Lewis, Gregg.** The Game & the Glory: An Autobiography. LC 99-87980. (Illus.). 224p. 2000. 19.99 (*0-310-23529-4*) Zondervan.

Akers, Michelle & Nash, Tim. Standing Fast: Battles of a Champion. (Orig.). 1997. pap. 12.95 (*1-887791-04-3*) JTC Sports.

Akers, Michelle & Nelson, Judy. Face to Face with Michelle Akers. (Illus.). 87p. Date not set. pap. 4.99 (*1-57902-049-6*) Integrtd Res.

Akers, Monte. Flames after Midnight: Murder, Vengeance, & the Desolation of a Texas Community. LC 98-29775. 240p. 1999. pap. 14.95 (*0-292-70487-9*) U of Tex Pr.

Akers, Nancy R. The Lilac Garland. large type ed. LC 90-35647. 276p. 1990. reprint ed. lib. bdg. 18.95 (*1-56054-013-3*) Thorndike Pr.

Akers, Phyllis. Let the Brother Go If... LC 99-37848. 1999. pap. text 7.95 (*1-890194-38-7*) Pines One.

Akers, Regina & Weiner, Herb. Beyond Tacos: Mexican Cuisine. 68p. 1984. pap. 7.50 (*0-937383-00-7*) Kitchen Wisdom.

Akers, Ronald L. Criminological Theories: Introduction & Evaluation. 2nd ed. LC 96-19834. 271p. (C). 1996. pap. text. write for info. (*0-935732-51-9*) Roxbury Pub Co.

— Criminological Theories: Introduction & Evaluation. 3rd ed. LC 99-27748. 271p. (C). 2000. pap. text. write for info. (*1-891487-38-8*) Roxbury Pub Co.

— Deviant Behavior: A Social Learning Approach. 2nd ed. (Sociology - Introductory Level Ser.). Date not set. pap., teacher ed. write for info. (*0-534-02233-2*) Wadsworth Pub.

— Deviant Behavior: A Social Learning Approach. 3rd ed. 436p. (C). 1992. reprint ed. text 83.00 (*1-878907-66-2*) TechBooks.

— Social Learning & Social Structure: A General Theory of Crime & Deviance. LC 97-10291. 1997. text 55.00 (*1-55553-310-8*) NE U Pr.

***Akers, Ronald L., ed.** Criminological Theories: Introduction & Evaluation. 259p. 1999. 55.00 (*1-57958-168-4*) Fitzroy Dearborn.

***Akers, Tim, ed.** Short Stories for Students, Vol. 6. 350p. 1999. text 60.00 (*0-7876-3606-1*, GML00299-113235, Gale Res Intl) Gale.

Akerson, Akerson, Charles B. The Appraiser's Workbook. 2nd ed. LC 96-24808. 1996. write for info. (*0-922154-30-9*) Appraisal Inst.

***Akerson, Charles B.** Capitalization Theory & Techniques: Study Guide, with Financial Tables Computed by Financial Publishing Company, Boston. 2nd ed. Appraisal Institute Staff & Financial Publishing Company Staff, eds. LC 00-26606. 2000. write for info. (*0-922154-58-9*) Appraisal Inst.

Akerson, Charles B. Capitalization Theory & Techniques Study Guide. 258p. 1984. pap., student ed., spiral bd. 20.00 (*0-911780-73-4*) Appraisal Inst.

Akerson, Charles B., rev. The Internal Rate of Return in Real Estate Investments. rev. ed. 29p. 1988. pap. 8.00 (*0-685-21957-7*) Appraisal Inst.

Akerson, James, jt. auth. see Myllymaki, Theodora.

Akerson, James M., jt. ed. see Estrin, Norman F.

Akerstrom, Ake. Berbati Vol. 2: The Pictorial Pottery. (Acta Instituti Atheniensis Regni Sueciae Ser.: Vol. XXXVI:2). (Illus.). 190p. 1987. pap. 97.50 (*91-85086-96-7*, Pub. by P Astroms) Coronet Bks.

Akerstrom-Hougen, Gunilla. The Calendar & Hunting Mosaics of the Villa of the Falconer in Argos: A Study in Early Byzantine Iconography. (Acta Instituti Atheniensis Regni Sueciae Ser.: Series 4, XXIII). (Illus.). 54p. (Orig.). 1974. pap. 87.50 (*91-85086-10-X*, Pub. by P Astroms) Coronet Bks.

Akerstrom, Malin. Betrayal & Betrayers: The Sociology of Treachery. 196p. (C). 1990. 44.95 (*0-88738-358-0*) Transaction Pubs.

— Crooks & Squares: Lifestyles of Thieves & Addicts in Comparison to Conventional People. 254p. (C). 1993. pap. text 24.95 (*1-56000-653-6*) Transaction Pubs.

A

Akeson, Wayne H. Knee Ligaments: Structure, Function, Injury, & Repair. 2nd ed. 608p. text 130.00 (0-7817-1817-1) Lppncott W & W.

Akesson, et al. Thompson's Core Textbook of Anatomy. 2nd ed. (Illus.). 586p. 1989. spiral bd. 39.95 (0-397-50849-2) Lppncott W & W.

Akesson, Lynn, jt. ed. see Lundin, Susanne.

Akesson, N. B. & Yates, W. E. The Use of Aircraft for Mosquito Control, Oct. 1982. 96p. 1982. 10.00 (0-686-84357-6) Am Mosquito.

Akesson, N. B., jt. ed. see Kaneko, Thomas M.

Akesson, Samuel K., ed. see True, Adiaha.

Akey, Stephen. College. LC 95-31739. 128p. (Orig.). 1996. pap. 12.95 (0-914061-55-0) Orchises Pr.

Akgakaya, H. Resit. Ramas/GIS: Linking GIS with Metapopulation Dynamics. (Illus.). 230p. (C). 1993. text 995.00 (1-884977-16-2); text 1495.00 incl. disk (1-884977-17-0) Applied Biomath.

— Ramas/Metapop: Metapopulation Viability Analysis. (Illus.). 185p. (C). 1994. text 395.00 (1-884977-14-6); text 595.00 incl. disk (1-884977-15-4) Applied Biomath.

Akgul, Mustafa, et al, eds. Combinatorial Optimization: New Frontiers in Theory & Practice. LC 92-10793. (NATO ASI Series F: Computer & Systems Sciences, Special Programme AET: Vol. 82). xi, 334p. 1992. write for info. (3-540-55439-4); 94.00 (0-387-55439-4) Spr-Verlag.

Akhandananda. In the Lap of the Himalayas. 1988. pap. 2.00 (0-87481-540-1, Pub. by Ramakrishna Math) Vedanta Pr.

Akhandananda, Swami. The Call of the Spirit: Conversations with Swami Akhandananda, a Direct Disciple of Sri Ramakrishna. LC 99-931326. 170 p. 1984. write for info. (81-7120-466-X) Vedanta Pr.

— Service of God in Man. 186p. 1979. pap. 2.95 (0-87481-503-7) Vedanta Pr.

Akhavan, J. The Chemistry of Explosives. 186p. 1998. pap. 34.95 (0-85404-563-5) Spr-Verlag.

Akhavan, Payam & Howse, Robert, eds. Yugoslavia, the Former & Future: Reflections by Scholars from the Region. 180p. (C). 1995. pap. 16.95 (0-8157-0253-1) Brookings.

— Yugoslavia, the Former & Future: Reflections by Scholars from the Region. LC 95-7556. 181p. (C). 1995. 34.95 (0-8157-0254-X) Brookings.

Akhavi, Shahrough. Religion & Politics in Contemporary Iran. LC 79-22084. 255p. (C). 1980. text 64.50 (0-87395-408-4); pap. text 21.95 (0-87395-456-4) State U NY Pr.

Akhemtov, N. Inorganic Chemistry. 640p. 1975. 25.00 (0-8464-1262-4) Beekman Pubs.

Akhenaton, Sri. Crystal Communion: Lovelight Meditations. LC 90-61184. (Illus.). 354p. (Orig.). 1994. pap. 21.95 (0-9621839-4-6) Portal MD.

— The Dawning: Coming of Age. LC 94-73981. (Illus.). 166p. 1998. pap. 13.95 (0-9621839-7-0) Portal MD.

— Discussion of Spiritual Attunement & Soul Evolution, Vol. II. LC 92-80153. 273p. (Orig.). 1992. pap. 12.95 (0-9621839-5-4) Portal MD.

— Loving Touch: The Sacred Covenant of Divine Communion. LC 96-72257. (Illus.). 331p. 1998. pap. 24.95 (0-9621839-8-9) Portal MD.

— Reflections from the Golden Mind. LC 93-86392. 92p. 1994. 12.95 (0-9621839-6-2) Portal MD.

Akhenaton, Susu, jt. auth. see DeVone, James M., Sr.

Akhiezer, A. I. & Akhiezer, I. Plasma Electrodynamics Vol. 2: Non Linear Theory & Fluctuations. LC 74-332. (International Series of Monographs in Natural Philosophy: Vol. 80: 2). 1975. 147.00 (0-08-018016-7, Pub. by Pergamon Repr) Franklin.

***Akhiezer, A. I. & Peleminsky, S. V.** Fields & Fundamental Interactions. 512p. 1999. text 110.00 (90-5699-148-5, Harwood Acad Pubs) Gordon & Breach.

Akhiezer, A. I. & Shul'ga, N. F. High Energy Electrodynamics in Matter. 400p. 1996. text 66.00 (2-88449-014-0) Gordon & Breach.

Akhiezer, A. I., et al. Nuclear Electrodynamics. Gribkova, J., tr. (Series in Nuclear & Particle Physics). (Illus.). 420p. 1993. write for info. (3-540-54906-4) Spr-Verlag.

— Nuclear Electrodynamics. Gribkova, J., tr. from RUS. LC 92-43795. (Series in Nuclear & Particle Physics). (Illus.). 480p. 1994. 137.95 (0-387-54906-4) Spr-Verlag.

Akhiezer, I., jt. auth. see Akhiezer, A. I.

Akhiezer, N. I. Calculus of Variations. vi, 280p. 1988. text 376.00 (3-7186-4805-9) Gordon & Breach.

— Elements of the Theory of Elliptic Functions. McFaden, H. H., tr. LC 89-18452. (Translations of Mathematical Monographs: Vol. 79). 237p. 1990. 102.00 (0-8218-4532-2, MMONO/79) Am Math.

— Lectures on Integral Transforms. LC 88-19393. (Translations of Mathematical Monographs: No. 70). 108p. 1988. text 57.00 (0-8218-4524-1, MMONO/70) Am Math.

Akhiezer, N. I. & Glazman, I. M. Theory of Linear Operators in Hilbert Space. Nestell, Merlynd, tr. from RUS. LC 93-6143. (ENG.). 378p. 1993. reprint ed. pap. 10.95 (0-486-67748-6) Dover.

Akhiezer, N. I. & Mcfaden, H. H. Elements of the Theory of Elliptic Functions. LC 89-18452. (Translations of Mathematical Monographs: Vol. 79). 237p. 1990. pap. 49.00 (0-8218-0900-8) Am Math.

Akhiezev, A. I. & Peletminskii, S. V. Methods of Statistical Physics. Schukin, M., tr. (International Series in Natural Philosophy: Vol. 104). (Illus.). 462p. 1981. text 207.00 (0-08-025040-8, Pub. by Pergamon Repr) Franklin.

Akhlaq, A., jt. auth. see Fiqh, Tawhid.

Akhmadi, Heri. Breaking the Chains of Oppression of the Indonesian People Vol. 59: Defense Statement at His Trial on Charges of Insulting the Head of State, Bandung, June 7-10, 1979. (Modern Indonesia Project Ser.). 201p. 1981. pap. 8.75 (0-87763-001-1) Cornell Mod Indo.

Akhmanov, S. A., et al, eds. Optics of Femtosecond Laser Pulses. 384p. 1992. 75.00 (0-88318-851-1) Am Inst Physics.

Akhmanov, S. A. & Khokhlov, R. V. Problems of Nonlinear Optics. Sen, R., ed. Jacobi, N., tr. from RUS. LC 78-131021. xiii, 294p. 1972. text 312.00 (0-677-30400-5) Gordon & Breach.

Akhmanov, S. A. & Nikitin, S. Y. Physical Optics. LC 96-48892. (Illus.). 502p. 1997. text 115.00 (0-19-851795-5) OUP.

Akhmanova, O., ed. Dictionary of Homonyms of the Russian Language. (ENG & RUS.). 448p. (C). 1986. 59.00 (0-7855-6427-6, Pub. by Collets) St Mut.

Akhmanova, O. & Wilson, E. English-Russian & Russian-English Dictionary. 1055p. (C). 1988. 75.00 (0-569-09031-8, Pub. by Collets) St Mut.

— Russian-English Dictionary. 33rd ed. 534p. (C). 1988. 100.00 (0-569-08924-7, Pub. by Collets) St Mut.

Akhmanova, O. S. English - Russian Dictionary. 32nd ed. Wilson, E. A., ed. (ENG & RUS.). 656p. 1987. reprint ed. 7.95 (0-8285-0586-1) Firebird NY.

— English - Russian Russian - English Dictionary. 4th ed. Wilson, E. A., ed. (ENG & RUS.). 672p. (C). 1993. reprint ed. 21.95 (0-8285-5283-5) Firebird NY.

— Russian-English Dictionary. 34th rev. ed. Wilson, E. A., ed. (ENG & RUS.). 536p. 1987. 7.95 (0-8285-0607-8) Firebird NY.

Akhmanova, O. S. & Wilson, E. Diccionario de Geografia. (SPA.). 1055p. 1988. 22.95 (0-8288-7391-7, M2909) Fr & Eur.

— English-Russian Dictionary. (ENG & RUS.). 639p. 1979. 14.95 (0-8288-5454-8, M9115) Fr & Eur.

Akhmanova, O. S. & Wilson, Elizabeth A., eds. English-Russian Russian-English Dictionary. 1056p. 1988. 12.95 (0-8285-5186-3) Firebird NY.

Akhmanova, Olga. Phonology, Morphonology, Morphology. LC 72-159459. (Janua Linguarum, Ser. Minor: No. 101). 135p. 1971. pap. text 42.35 (90-279-1748-5) Mouton.

Akhmanova, Olga & Mikael'an, Galina. The Theory of Syntax in Modern Linguistics. LC 69-13300. (Janua Linguarum, Ser. Minor: No. 68). (Orig.). 1969. pap. text 52.35 (90-279-0683-1) Mouton.

Akhmatova, Anna Andreevena. The Complete Poems of Anna Akhmatova. 3rd rev. ed. Reeder, Roberta, ed. Hemschemeyer, Judith, tr. from RUS. (Illus.). 948p. 1997. pap. 29.00 (0-939010-27-5) Zephyr Pr.

— My Half-Century: Selected Prose. Meyer, Ronald, ed. LC 97-14774. 1997. pap. 18.95 (0-8101-1485-2) Northwestern U Pr.

— Poem Without a Hero & Selected Poems. Mayhew, Lenore & McNaughton, William, trs. from RUS. LC 89-60154. No. 14. 193p. 1989. 17.95 (0-932440-51-7); pap. 9.95 (0-932440-50-9) Oberlin Coll Pr.

— Poems. Coffin, Lyn, tr. from RUS. 1983. pap. 10.95 (0-393-30014-5) Norton.

— Poems of Akhmatova. Kunitz, Stanley & Hayward, Max, trs. LC 97-19949. (RUS & ENG.). 192p. 1997. pap. 13.00 (0-395-86003-2) HM.

— Selected Poems. McKane, Richard, tr. from RUS. LC 88-51306. 256p. 1988. reprint ed. pap. 21.00 (1-85224-063-6, Pub. by Bloodaxe Bks) Dufour.

***Akhmatova, Anna Andreevena.** Selected Poems of Anna Akhmatova. 2000. pap. 16.95 (0-939010-61-5) Zephyr Pr.

Akhmatova, Anna Andreevena. Twenty Poems of Anna Akhmatova. Kenyon, Jane & Dunham, Vera Sandomirsky, trs. from RUS. 54p. 1985. pap. 8.95 (0-915408-30-9) Ally Pr.

— U Samago Moria. (RUS.). 36p. (C). 1994. reprint ed. pap. text 4.00 (0-933884-62-1) Berkeley Slavic.

— You Will Hear Thunder: Akhmatova: Poems. Thomas, D. M., tr. LC 84-62245. 146p. 1985. reprint ed. pap. 14.95 (0-8214-0806-2) Ohio U Pr.

Akhmatova, Anna Andreevena, et al. Rossiia Glazami Zhenshchin: Literaturnaia Antologiia. LC 89-11681. (RUS., Illus.). 192p. (Orig.). 1989. pap. 10.00 (0-938920-94-4) Hermitage Pubs.

Akhmatova, Anna Andreevena, jt. auth. see Stallworthy, Jon.

Akhmatova, Anna Andreevena, jt. auth. see Wells, David.

Akhmedov, Akhmed-Djabir. Azerbaijan Cookery. 230p. 1986. 12.95 (0-8285-3799-2) Firebird NY.

Akhmedov, Ismail. In & Out of Stalin's GRU. LC 83-17018. 222p. 1984. lib. bdg. 49.95 (0-313-27008-2, U7008, Greenwood Pr) Greenwood.

Akhmedov, S., et al. Eleven Papers on Differential Equations. LC 85-1315. (AMS Translations Series-Two: Series 2, Vol. 126). 114p. 1985. text 62.00 (0-8218-3089-9, TRANS2/126) Am Math.

Akhmerov, R. R., et al. Measures of Noncompactness & Condensing Operators. (Operator Theory: Advances & Applications Ser.: Vol. 55). 260p. 1992. 129.00 (0-8176-2716-2) Birkhauser.

Akhmetzyanov, M. K., et al. Photomechanics '95: 11-14 September, 1995, Novosibirsk, Russia. LC 96-68789. vii, 176p. 1996. pap. write for info. (0-8194-2177-4) SPIE.

Akhoury, R., et al, eds. Gauge Theories: Past & Future. (Series in 20th Century Physics: Vol. 1). 368p. 1992. pap. write for info. (981-02-1029-9) World Scientific Pub.

Akhoury, R., et al. Gauge Theories - Past & Future: In Commemoration of the 60th Birthday of Professor M. Veltman. 368p. 1992. text 109.00 (981-02-1028-0) World Scientific Pub.

Akhrem, Afanasii A. & Titov, Yurii A. Total Steroid Synthesis. Hazzard, B. J., tr. from RUS. LC 69-12525. (Illus.). 374p. 1970. reprint ed. pap. 116.00 (0-608-05477-1, 20659460006) Bks Demand.

Akhrori, K. A., jt. auth. see Arzumanov, S. D.

Akhtar, Hina & Quraishi, Huda, eds. Seven Surahs: For the Classroom. unabridged ed. LC 96-79298. 126p. (YA). (gr. 6-12). 1996. pap. text 8.00 (1-56316-114-1) Iqra Intl Ed Fdtn.

Akhtar, Hina, ed. see Akhter, Syed H.

Akhtar, Hina, ed. see Lemu, B. A.

Akhtar, Hina N., jt. auth. see Abiva, Nilofer.

Akhtar, Hina N., ed. see Lemu, B. Aisha.

***Akhtar, Hina Naseem.** Islamic Morals & Manners for Children. Quraishi-Ahmed, Huda & Liddle-Bhutt, Heidi, eds. (Teachings of the Qur'an Ser.: Vol. II). (Illus.). 101p. (J). (gr. 3-7). 1998. wbk. ed. 6.00 (1-56316-119-2) Iqra Intl Ed Fdtn.

Akhtar, Masood, et al. Sudden Cardiac Death. (Illus.). 637p. 1994. text 99.00 (0-683-00063-2) Lppncott W & W.

Akhtar, Masood, jt. auth. see Young, Raymond A.

Akhtar, Rais, ed. Contemporary Approaches to Indian Geography: Essays in Honour of Professor Mohammad Shafi. LC 97-906036. (Illus.). xxxiii, 396p. 1997. 70.00 (81-7024-871-X, Pub. by APH Pubng) Nataraj Bks.

— Disease, Ecology & Health: Readings in Medical Geography. 1990. 48.00 (81-7033-095-5, Pub. by Rawat Pubns) S Asia.

— Health Care Patterns & Planning in Developing Countries, 29. LC 89-25941. (Contributions in Medical Studies: No. 29). 360p. 1991. 75.00 (0-313-26745-6, AHC/, Greenwood Pr) Greenwood.

— Health Disease in Tropical Africa: Geographical & Medical Viewpoints. xii, 520p. 1987. text 312.00 (3-7186-0300-4) Gordon & Breach.

— Themes in Medical Geography: Environment & Health. 1991. 78.50 (81-7024-332-7, Pub. by Ashish Pub Hse) S Asia.

Akhtar, Saghir, ed. Delivery Strategies for Antisense Oligonucleotide Therapeutics. 320p. 1995. boxed set 239.95 (0-8493-4778-5, 4778) CRC Pr.

***Akhtar, Salman.** Broken Structures: Severe Personality Disorder & Their Treatment. 2000. pap. text 50.00 (0-7657-0255-X) Aronson.

Akhtar, Salman. The Hidden Knot. 68p. 1985. pap. 4.00 (0-9615818-0-8) S Akhtar.

***Akhtar, Salman.** Immigration & Identity: Turmoil, Treatment & Transformation. LC 99-28892. 9248p. 1999. 40.00 (0-7657-0232-0) Aronson.

Akhtar, Salman. Inner Torment: Living Between Conflict & Fragmentation. LC 97-50487. 1998. 45.00 (0-7657-0159-6) Aronson.

— Quest for Answers: A Primer of Understanding & Treating Severe Personality Disorders. LC 94-22794. 1995. pap. 40.00 (1-56821-364-6) Aronson.

— Turned to Light LC 98-96921. 52p. 1998. write for info. (0-9661852-4-2) Adams Pr IL.

Akhtar, Salman, et al, eds. The Birth of Hatred: Developmental, Clinical & Technical Aspects of Intense Aggression. LC 94-23614. 1996. 35.00 (1-56821-428-6) Aronson.

— The Internal Mother: Conceptual & Technical Aspects of Object Constancy. LC 95-31219. 1996. 40.00 (1-56821-651-3) Aronson.

Akhtar, Salman & Kramer, Selma. Brothers & Sisters: Developmental, Dynamic & Technical Aspects of the Sibling Relationship. LC 98-54403. xii, 187p. 1999. pap. 22.00 (0-7657-0203-7) Aronson.

— The Colors of Childhood: Separation-Individuation Across Cultural, Racial, & Ethnic Diversity. LC 97-45188. (Illus.). 248p. 1998. 40.00 (0-7657-0155-3) Aronson.

— Intimacy & Infidelity: Separation-Individuation Perspectives. LC 96-4644. 200p. 1996. 40.00 (1-56821-775-7) Aronson.

***Akhtar, Salman & Kramer, Selma, eds.** Thicker Than Blood: Bonds of Fantasy & Reality in Adoption. LC 00-20263. 2000. pap. 30.00 (0-7657-0266-5) Aronson.

Akhtar, Salman & Parens, Henri, eds. Beyond the Symbiotic Orbit: Advances in Separation-Individuation Theory Essays in Honor of Selma Kramer, M. D. 472p. 1991. 55.00 (0-88163-109-4) Analytic Pr.

Akhtar, Salman, jt. auth. see Volkan, Vamik D.

Akhtar, Salman, jt. ed. see Kramer, Selma.

Akhtar, Shabbir. A Faith for All Seasons: Islam & the Challenge of the Modern World. 263p. (Orig.). 1991. text 28.50 (0-929587-54-5); pap. text 12.95 (0-929587-63-4) I R Dee.

— A Faith for All Seasons: Islam & the Challenge of the Modern World. 255p. (Orig.). 1996. 29.95 (0-614-21411-4, 283); pap. 14.50 (0-614-21410-6, 283) Kazi Pubns.

***Akhtar, Shakil.** Media, Religion & Politics in Pakistan. 300p. 2000. text 24.95 (0-19-579174-6) OUP.

Akhtar, Syed W. The Early Imamiyyah Shiite Thinkers. (C). 1988. 35.00 (81-7024-196-0, Pub. by Ashish Pub Hse) S Asia.

Akhtathusein, A. Tayebali, et al. Stiffness of Asphalt-Aggregate Mixes. 101p. (Orig.). (C). 1994. pap. text 15.00 (0-309-05768-X, SHRP-A-388) SHRP.

Akhter, Javeed, jt. auth. see Braibanti, Ralph.

Akhter, Syed H. Essence of Islam: According to the Qur'an & the Traditions. unabridged ed. Akhtar, Hina et al, eds. LC 97-68442. 333p. 1998. pap. text 15.00 (1-56316-412-4) Iqra Intl Ed Fdtn.

Akhund, Igbal. Memoirs of a Bystander: A Life in Diplomacy. LC 97-172304. (Illus.). 528p. 1997. pap. text 42.00 (0-19-577736-0) OUP.

***Akhund, Iqbal.** Trial & Error: The Advent & Eclipse of Benazir Bhutto. (Illus.). 350p. 2000. text 24.95 (0-19-579160-6) OUP.

Aki, K., jt. auth. see Wang, R.

Aki, Keiiti & Dmowska, Renata, eds. Relating Geophysical Structures & Processes: The Jeffreys Volume. LC 93-28483. (Geophysical Monograph, Vol. 76; IUGG Ser.: Vol. 16). 133p. 1993. 27.00 (0-87590-467-X) Am Geophysical.

Aki, Keiiti & Richards, Paul G. Quantitative Seismology: Theory & Methods, Vol. I. LC 79-17434. (Geology Ser.). (Illus.). 573p. (C). 1980. text 43.20 (0-7167-1058-7) W H Freeman.

Aki, Keiiti, jt. auth. see Wu, Ru-Shan.

Aki, Keiiti, jt. ed. see Stuart, W. D.

Aki, Keiiti, jt. ed. see Wang, Ren.

Aki, Keiiti, jt. ed. see Wu, Ru-Shan.

Akiba, Hiroya. Structural Changes in Foreign Exchange Markets. (Illus.). xi, 318p. 1994. 39.00 (81-7024-602-4, Pub. by Ashish Pub Hse) Nataraj Bks.

Akiba, Kin-ya, ed. Chemistry of Hypervalent Compounds. LC 98-6578. 432p. 1998. 145.00 (0-471-24019-2) Wiley.

Akiba, Okon. Nigerian Foreign Policy Towards Africa: Continuity & Change. LC 96-19565. (American University Studies X: Vol. 45). XIII, 230p. (C). 1998. pap. text 26.95 (0-8204-3371-3) P Lang Pubng.

Akifyev. Mechanisms in Productive Chromosones of Aberrat & Eukary, Vol. 10, No. 3. 54p. 1997. pap. text 27.00 (3-7186-5829-1, Harwood Acad Pubs) Gordon & Breach.

Akihisa, Toshihiro, jt. auth. see Goad, L. John.

Akiko, Yosano. Tangled Hair: Love Poems of Yosano Akiko. Maloney, Dennis & Oshiro, Hide, trs. (Illus.). 48p. 1986. pap. 7.50 (0-934834-05-9) White Pine.

Akil. From Niggas to Gods. LC 95-140584. (Illus.). 251p. (Orig.). 1993. pap. 12.95 (1-56411-064-8) Untd Bros & Sis.

— From Niggas to Gods: Escaping Negativity & Becoming God. 247p. 1996. pap. 14.95 (0-9648181-1-6) New Gen Pub.

— The Image, the Character & the Responsibility of the Goddess Blackwoman. 54p. (Orig.). 1994. pap. 6.00 (1-56411-129-6) Untd Bros & Sis.

— There Are Only Two Religions in the Whole World. 1996. pap. 7.95 (1-56411-116-4) Untd Bros & Sis.

Akil, H. & Lewis, J. W., eds. Neurotransmitters & Pain Control. (Pain & Headache Ser.: Vol. 9). (Illus.). x, 306p. 1987. 128.00 (3-8055-4579-7) S Karger.

***Akimaru, Haruo & Kawashima, Keonosuke.** Teletraffic: Theory & Applications. 2nd ed. LC 99-26228. (Telecommunication Networks & Computer Systems Ser.). xix, 226p. 1999. 119.00 (1-85233-162-3, Pub. by Spr-Verlag) Spr-Verlag.

Akimaru, Haruo & Kawashima, Konosuke. Teletraffic: Theory & Applications. LC 92-21122. (Telecommunications Networks & Computer Systems Ser.). 1993. 78.95 (0-387-19805-9) Spr-Verlag.

Akimoto, Haruo, ed. see Epilepsy International Symposium Staff.

Akimoto, Minoji, jt. ed. see Brinton, Laurel J.

Akimoto, S. & Manghnani, Murli H. High Pressure Research in Geophysics. 1982. text 358.50 (90-277-1439-8) Kluwer Academic.

Akimushkin & Ivanov. St. Petersburg Muraqqa' (Illus.). 352p. 1996. 475.00 (88-7813-607-7, Pub. by Art Bks Intl) Partners Pubs Grp.

Akin, David & Robbins, Joel, eds. Money & Modernity: State & Local Currencies in Melanesia. LC 98-40182. (Association of Social Anthropology in Oceania Monographs). (Illus.). 256p. 1999. pap. 19.95 (0-8229-5689-6); text 45.00 (0-8229-4087-6) U of Pittsburgh Pr.

Akin, Bernetia, ed. see Brathwaite, Christopher.

Akin, Camille, ed. see Bury, Don & Heischman, Larry.

Akin, Camille, ed. see Koehler, Dan M.

Akin, Camille, ed. see Salvaneschi, Luigi.

Akin, Cavit & Smith, Jared, eds. Gas, Oil & Coal Biotechnology Vol. I: Proceedings of a Conference Held in 1988. vi, 462p. 1988. 75.00 (0-910091-73-0) Inst Gas Tech.

— Gas, Oil, Coal & Environmental Biotechnology II. viii, 587p. 1990. 75.00 (0-910091-77-3) Inst Gas Tech.

— Gas, Oil, Coal & Environmental Biotechnology III. viii, 546p. 1991. 75.00 (0-910091-80-3) Inst Gas Tech.

***Akin, Charlotte A.** The Long Road Called Goodbye. (Illus.). 340p. 2000. 25.00 (1-881871-33-9, Pub. by Creighton U Pr); pap. write for info. (1-881871-34-7, Pub. by Creighton U Pr) BookMasters.

Akin, E. Recurrence in Topological Dynamics: Furstenberg Families & Ellis Actions. LC 97-24363. (University Series in Mathematics). (Illus.). 276p. (C). 1997. text 75.00 (0-306-45550-1, Kluwer Plenum) Kluwer Academic.

Akin, E., ed. see Lyubich, Y. I.

Akin, Edward N. Flagler: Rockefeller Partner & Florida Baron. LC 87-2070. (Illus.). 320p. reprint ed. pap. 99.20 (0-7837-0575-1, 204091900019) Bks Demand.

— Flagler: Rockefeller Partner & Florida Baron. (Florida Sand Dollar Bk.). (Illus.). 320p. 1992. reprint ed. pap. 19.95 (0-8130-1108-6) U Press Fla.

Akin, Ethan. The General Topology of Dynamical Systems. LC 92-41669. (Graduate Studies in the Mathematical Sciences: Vol. 1). 261p. 1993. text 36.00 (0-8218-3800-8, GSM/1) Am Math.

— Hopf Bifurcation in the Two Locus Genetic Model. LC 83-6438. (Memoirs of the American Mathematical Society Ser.: No. 44/284). 190p. 1983. pap. 24.00 (0-8218-2284-5, MEMO/44/284) Am Math.

— Simplicial Dynamical Systems. LC 99-14982. (Memoirs Ser.). 1999. write for info. (0-8218-1383-8) Am Math.

Akin, Herbert L. 1999. LC 81-80962. (Illus.). 260p. 1981. 4.95 (0-938736-03-5) Life Enrich.

Akin, J. Ed. Applications & Implementation of Finite Element Methods. 1984. pap. text 56.00 (0-12-047652-5) Acad Pr.

An Asterisk (*) at the beginning of an entry indicates that the title is appearing for the first time.

— Finite Elements for Analysis & Design. (Computational Mathematics & Applications Ser.). (Illus.). 560p. 1994. text 79.00 (*0-12-047653-3*); pap. text 53.00 (*0-12-047654-1*) Acad Pr.

*Akin, James. The Journal of James Akin Jr., Oregon Trail, 1852. (Illus.). 33p. 1999. reprint ed. pap. 6.95 (*0-87770-699-9*) Ye Galleon.

Akin, James. Mass Confusion: The Do's & Don'ts of Catholic Worship. 2nd expanded ed. 244p. 1998. pap. 15.95 (*1-888992-05-0*) Catholic Answers.

***Akin, James.** Papacy. 80p. 2000. pap. 7.95 (*1-888992-09-3*) Catholic Answers.

Akin, John E., ed. see American Society of Mechanical Engineers Staff.

Akin, John S., et al. The Demand for Primary Health Services in the Third World. LC 84-18153. (Illus.). 272p. 1985. 61.50 (*0-8476-7355-3*, R7355) Rowman.

Akin, Johnnye. Crayfish International Cookbook. Woolfolk, Doug, ed. (Illus.). 210p. (Orig.). 1981. spiral bd. 9.95 (*0-86518-023-7*) Moran Pub Corp.

Akin, Johnnye, et al, eds. Language Behavior: A Book of Readings in Communication. LC 77-110948. (Janua Linguarum, Ser. Major: No. 41). 1970. text 90.80 (*90-279-1244-0*) Mouton.

Akin, Johnnye, et al. Terms Used in Whitewater Kayaking in Colorado; Collegiate Slang - Aspects of Word Formation & Semantic Change; The Vocabulary of Race Relations in a Prison. (Publications of the American Dialect Society: No. 51). 46p. 1969. pap. 4.60 (*0-8173-0651-X*) U of Ala Pr.

Akin, Katy. Impassioned Cows by Moonlight. 72p. 1975. pap. 5.00 (*0-914610-02-3*) Hanging Loose.

Akin, Mary. Come Walk with Me. (Illus.). 260p. (Orig.). (C). 1993. 19.95 (*1-880047-13-6*); pap. text 12.95 (*1-880047-08-X*) Creative Des.

Akin, Richard H. The Private Investigator's Basic Manual. 208p. 1979. 37.95 (*0-398-03520-2*); pap. 24.95 (*0-398-06002-9*) C C Thomas.

Akin, Terri & Schilling, Dianne. Everybody Wins! 100 Games Children Should Play. (Illus.). 151p. 1993. teacher ed. 15.95 (*0-614-15847-8*) Innerchoice Pub.

Akin, Terri, et al. Character Education in America's Schools. 170p. (Orig.). (J). (gr. 1-6). 1995. pap. text 21.95 (*1-56499-026-5*, IP9029) Innerchoice Pub.

***Akin, Terri, et al.** Helping Kids Manage Grief, Fear & Anger. (Illus.). 120p. (J). (gr. 3-8). 1999. pap. text 16.95 (*1-56499-040-0*, Pub. by Innerchoice Pub) Jalmar Pr.

Akin, Terri, et al. Insights: A Self & Career Awareness Program for the Elementary Grades. 220p. (Orig.). (J). (gr. k-6). 1991. pap. text, teacher ed. 26.95 (*0-9625486-3-4*, IP4863) Innerchoice Pub.

Akin, Terry, et al. The Best: Self-Esteem Activities for the Elementary Grades. (Illus.). 224p. (Orig.). (J). (gr. k-6). 1990. pap., teacher ed. 26.95 (*0-9625486-2-6*, IP4862) Innerchoice Pub.

Akin, Wallace E. Global Patterns: Climate, Vegetation & Soils. LC 90-50227. (Illus.). 384p. 1991. 49.95 (*0-8061-2309-5*) U of Okla Pr.

Akinade, Akintunde E., jt. ed. see Irvin, Dale T.

Akinchan, S. Caste Class & Politics: Emerging Horizons of Political Sociology. x, 326p. 1995. 30.00 (*81-212-0486-0*, Pub. by Gyan Publishing Hse) Nataraj Bks.

Akindale, R. A. The Organization & Promotion of World Peace: A Study of Universal-Regional Relationships. LC 74-79987. 223p. reprint ed. pap. 69.20 (*0-608-09958-9*, 202642000049) Bks Demand.

Akindele, Akin O. The Military Franchise. 170p. 1993. pap. 14.95 (*1-880365-97-9*) Prof Pr NC.

— Utopia, Euphoria, Myopia. LC 98-89526. 375p. 1998. text 25.00 (*0-7388-0249-2*); pap. text 15.00 (*0-7388-0250-6*) Xlibris Corp.

Akiner. Caspian: Politics, Energy, Security. 200p. 1999. text 59.95 (*0-312-17381-4*) St Martin.

Akiner, Shirin. The Formation of Kazakh Identity. LC 96-147080. (Former Soviet South Papers). 83p. (C). 1995. pap. 12.95 (*1-899658-03-3*) Brookings.

— Islamic Peoples of the Soviet Union. (Illus.). 451p. 1983. 50.00 (*0-7103-0025-5*) Routledge.

— Islamic Peoples of the Soviet Union. rev. ed. 480p. 1987. lib. bdg. 79.50 (*0-7103-0188-X*) Routledge.

— Sustainable Development in Central Asia. LC 98-34842. 240p. 1998. text 55.00 (*0-312-21931-8*) St Martin.

— Tajikistan: Disintegration or Reconciliation? (Central Asian & Caucasian Prospects Ser.). 96p. 1998. pap. 12.95 (*1-86203-061-8*, Pub. by Royal Inst Intl Affairs) Brookings.

Akiner, Shirin, ed. Cultural Change & Continuity in Central Asia. 320p. 1992. 85.00 (*0-7103-0351-3*, A3942) Routledge.

— The Early History of Central Asia. 320p. 1991. 78.50 (*0-7103-0350-5*, A3930) Routledge.

— Economic & Political Trends in Central Asia. 320p. 1991. 78.50 (*0-7103-0352-1*, A3938) Routledge.

— Mongolia Today. 320p. 1991. 75.00 (*0-7103-0345-9*, A3934) Routledge.

— Political & Economic Trends in Central Asia. 350p. 1994. text 69.50 (*1-85043-516-2*, Pub. by I B T) St Martin.

Akiner, Shirin, et al, eds. Sustainable Development in Central Asia. LC 96-219909. 240p. 1996. 75.00 (*0-7007-0419-1*, Pub. by Curzon Pr Ltd) Paul & Co Pubs.

Akiner, Shirin, jt. ed. see Barnett, Robert.

Akingbade, Harrison O. From Slave to Bishop: Samuel Ajayi Crother. LC 96-69278. 128p. (Orig.). 1996. pap. 9.95 (*1-884570-52-6*) Research Triangle.

Akinjide, Richard, ed. see Elias, T. O.

Akinlabi, Akinbiyi, ed. Theoretical Approaches to African Linguistics. 1995. per. 19.95 (*0-86543-463-8*) Africa World.

— Theoretical Approaches to African Linguistics. (Trends in African Linguistics Ser.: Vol. 1). 430p. 1995. 69.95 (*0-86543-462-X*) Africa World.

Akinmola, Bankole O. Heirs of the Kingdom. 96p. 1998. pap. 8.00 (*0-9668148-0-0*) B O Akinmola.

Akinmusuru, J. O., et al, eds. Soil Mechanics & Foundations Engineering: Proceedings of the 9th Regional Conference for Africa, Lagos, 15-18 Sept 1987, 2 vols. 850p. 1987. text 407.00 (*90-6191-717-4*, Pub. by A A Balkema) Ashgate Pub Co.

Akinrinade, Olusola & Barling, J. Kurt, eds. Economic Development in Africa. 220p. 1992. 49.00 (*0-86187-909-0*, Pub. by P P Pubs) Cassell & Continuum.

***Akins, Ellen.** Hometown Brew. LC 97-49477. 224p. 1998. 4.99 (*0-679-44795-4*) Knopf.

Akins, Ellen. World Like a Knife. LC 91-15802. (Poetry & Fiction Ser.). 144p. 1991. text 32.50 (*0-8018-4288-3*) Johns Hopkins.

Akins, Faren R., et al. Parent-Child Separation: Psychosocial Effects on Development. LC 81-7304. 368p. 1981. 95.00 (*0-306-65196-3*, Kluwer Plenum) Kluwer Academic.

Akins, H. D. & Lew, Ellen F. Rice: A Food for All Seasons. (Illus.). 250p. 1989. pap. 10.00 (*0-9623005-0-0*) H D Akins.

Akins, Harold D., jt. auth. see Lew, Ellen F.

Akins, Kathleen, ed. Perception. (Vancouver Series in Cognitive Science). 352p. 1996. pap. text 40.00 (*0-19-508462-4*) OUP.

— Perception, Vol. 5. (Vancouver Series in Cognitive Science). 352p. 1996. text 70.00 (*0-19-508461-6*) OUP.

***Akins, Marcia, et al.** 1001 Things You Always Wanted to Know about Visual FoxPro. Hosier, John, ed. 588p. 2000. pap. 49.95 (*0-9655093-3-8*) Hentzenwerke.

Akins, Terri, et al. Feelings Are Facts: Helping Children Understand, Manage & Learn from Their Feelings. Schilling, Dianne, ed. (Illus.). 96p. 1993. pap., teacher ed. 14.95 (*1-56499-010-9*, IP9010) Innerchoice Pub.

— Getting It Together: Drug Prevention Activities for the Classroom. 40p. (J). (gr. 4-6). 1991. pap., teacher ed. 13.95 (*1-56499-004-4*, IP9004) Innerchoice Pub.

Akins, Terri, jt. auth. see Palomares, Susanna.

Akins, Tom, et al. The Internal Consultant's Guide. rev. ed. (Illus.). 200p. 1996. spiral bd., wbk. ed. 75.00 (*0-9629679-5-5*) Miller Howard Cnslt.

Akins, V. & Harada, H., eds. Automated IC Manufacturing. LC 92-70529. (Proceedings Ser.: Vol. 92-8). 283p. 1992. 36.00 (*1-56677-004-1*) Electrochem Soc.

Akinsanya, Adeoye. Multinationals in a Changing Environment: A Study of Business & Government Relations in the Third World. LC 83-24592. 208p. 1984. 69.50 (*0-275-91115-2*, C1115, Praeger Pubs) Greenwood.

Akinsheye, Dayo, jt. auth. see Akinsheye, Dexter.

Akinsheye, Dayo, ed. see Akinsheye, Dexter.

Akinsheye, Dayo, ed. see Gibbs, C. R.

Akinsheye, Dexter. African American Inventor Math Pack Workbook. Akinsheye, Dayo, ed. (Illus.). 20p. (Orig.). (J). (gr. 2-5). 1992. pap. text, wbk. ed. 4.50 (*1-877835-53-6*) TD Pub.

— African American Inventors Study Print Series: Two Teacher's Guides & a Set of 40 study prints. Akinsheye, Dayo, ed. 1992. 59.99 (*1-877835-84-6*) TD Pub.

— Discovering American History. Akinsheye, Dayo, ed. (African American Inventors & Scientists Workbook & Coloring Book Ser.). (Illus.). 20p. (Orig.). (J). (gr. 2-3). 1992. pap. 5.00 (*1-877835-70-6*) TD Pub.

Akinsheye, Dexter & Akinsheye, Dayo. I Want to Be... (Illus.). 56p. (J). (gr. k-4). 1992. reprint ed. pap. 12.00 (*1-877835-47-1*); reprint ed. pap. text 5.00 (*1-877835-48-X*) TD Pub.

Akintoba, Tayo O. African States & Contemporary International Law: A Case Study of the 1982 Law of the Sea Convention & the Exclusive Economic Zone. LC 95-43172. (Publications on Ocean Development: Vol. 26). 181p. 1995. lib. bdg. 99.50 (*90-411-0144-6*, Pub. by M Nijhoff) Kluwer Academic.

Akintoye, Stephen A. Emergent African States: Topics in Twentieth Century African History. LC 77-363585. (Illus.). 256p. reprint ed. pap. 79.40 (*0-8357-6104-5*, 203447700090) Bks Demand.

Akinyela, Makungu M. Culture & Power in Practice: Cultural Democracy & the Family Support Movement. 14p. pap. 7.00 (*1-885429-17-7*) Family Resource.

Akinyemi, Rowena. Rain Forests. (Illus.). 24p. 1996. pap. text 6.95 (*0-19-422803-7*) OUP.

— Remember Miranda. (Illus.). 44p. 1997. pap. text 5.95 (*0-19-421691-8*) OUP.

Akio, Terumasa. Me & Alves: A Japanese Journey. Matsui, Susan, tr. (Illus.). 24p. (J). 1993. pap. 4.95 (*1-55037-222-X*, Pub. by Annick); lib. bdg. 14.95 (*1-55037-223-8*, Pub. by Annick) Firefly Bks Ltd.

Akira Isihara. Condensed Matter Physics. (Illus.). 376p. 1991. text 75.00 (*0-19-506286-8*) OUP.

Akira Kudo & Hara, Terushi, eds. International Cartels in Business History: The International Conference on Business History, No. 18. 300p. 1992. 58.50 (*0-86008-487-6*, Pub. by U of Tokyo) Col U Pr.

Akira, Oki, jt. ed. see Reid, Anthony.

Akira, Suehiro. Capitol Accumulation in Thailand, 1855-1985. (Illus.). 446p. 1998. pap. text 22.50 (*974-390-005-5*) U of Wash Pr.

Akira, Yuyama, tr. see Numata Center for Buddhist Translation & Research.

Akisada, Masayoshi & Fujimoto, Yoshihide. Soft Tissue Roentgenography in Diagnosis of Thyroid Cancer: Detection of Psammoma Bodies by Spot-tangential Projection. LC 74-176722. 143p. reprint ed. pap. 44.40 (*0-608-12989-5*, 202471000038) Bks Demand.

Akishev, Alisher. Iskusstvo Mifologiia Sakov. (RUS.). 176p. 1984. 50.00 (*0-7855-0955-0*) St Mut.

Akishina, T., jt. auth. see Teskova, S.

Akiskal, H. S., jt. ed. see Burton, S. W.

Akiskal, Hagop S. Dysthymia & the Spectrum of Chronic Depressions. Cassano, Giovanni B., ed. LC 97-11003. 228p. 1997. lib. bdg. 32.00 (*1-57230-089-2*) Guilford Pubns.

Akita, George. Foundations of Constitutional Government in Modern Japan, 1868-1900. LC 65-13835. (Harvard East Asian Ser.: No. 23). 303p. reprint ed. pap. 94.00 (*0-7837-2214-1*, 205730400004) Bks Demand.

Akita, Y. Techniques Used in Nepalese Image Making. (C). 1991. text 60.00 (*0-7855-6973-1*, Pub. by Ratna Pustak Bhandar) St Mut.

Akitt, James W., jt. auth. see Mann, Brian E.

Akivis, M. A. & Goldberg, V. V. An Introduction to Linear Algebra & Tensors. rev. ed. Silverman, Richard A., ed. LC 77-78589. 167p. (C). 1977. reprint ed. pap. 6.95 (*0-486-63545-7*) Dover.

— Projective Differential Geometry of Submanifolds. LC 93-10725. (North-Holland Mathematical Library: No. 49). (Illus.). 374p. 1993. 149.50 (*0-444-89771-2*, North Holland) Elsevier.

Akivis, M. A. & Rosenfeld, B. A. Elie Cartan, 1869-1951. Ivanov, Simeon, ed. Goldberg, V. V., tr. from RUS. LC 93-6932. (Translations of Mathematical Monographs: Vol. 123). 317p. 1993. text 153.00 (*0-8218-4587-X*, MMONO/123) Am Math.

Akivis, Maks A. & Goldberg, Vladislav V. Conformal Differential Geometry & Its Generalizations. LC 96-31348. (Pure & Applied Mathematics: A Wiley-Interscience Series of Texts, Monographs & Tracts). 400p. 1996. 99.95 (*0-471-14958-6*, Wiley-Interscience) Wiley.

Akiwowo, Akinsola, ed. see Abiola, Kola.

Akiyama, Aisaburo. Buddhist Hand-Symbol. LC 78-72367. reprint ed. 39.50 (*0-404-17214-8*) AMS Pr.

Akiyama, C. & Akiyama, N. Learn Japanese the Fast & Fun Way. (Fast & Fun Way Language Bks.). (JPN & ENG.). 256p. 1990. pap. 16.95 (*0-8120-4365-0*) Barron.

Akiyama, Carol. Japanese Idioms. 1996. pap. 7.95 (*0-8120-9045-4*) Barron.

— 2001 Japanese/English Idioms. (JPN & ENG.). 1995. pap. text 13.95 (*0-8120-9433-6*) Barron.

Akiyama, Carol & Akiyama, Nobuo. Japanese Grammar. (JPN & ENG.). 256p. 1991. vinyl bd. 6.95 (*0-8120-4643-9*) Barron.

— Japanese Vocabulary. (JPN & ENG.). 256p. 1991. vinyl bd. 6.95 (*0-8120-4743-5*) Barron.

— Learn Japanese the Fast & Fun Way. 2nd rev. ed. LC 98-73386. (ENG & JPN., Illus.). 256p. 1999. pap. 16.95 (*0-7641-0623-6*); pap., boxed set 39.95 incl. audio (*0-7641-7271-9*) Barron.

Akiyama, Carol, et al. Japanese on the Road, Level 2. (Languages on the Road Ser.). (ENG & JPN.). 1992. pap. 11.95 incl. audio (*0-8120-7935-3*) Barron.

Akiyama, Carol, jt. auth. see Akiyama, Nobuo.

Akiyama, J., et al, eds. Graph Theory & Combinatorics. 300p. (C). 1992. text 70.00 (*981-02-0588-0*) World Scientific Pub.

***Akiyama, J., et al.** Discrete & Computational Geometry: Second Japanese Conference, JCDCG '98, Tokyo, Japan, December 9-12, 1998, Revised Papers. LC 00-23693. (Lecture Notes in Computer Science Ser.: Vol. 1763). viii, 333p. 2000. pap. 56.00 (*3-540-67181-1*) Spr-Verlag.

Akiyama, Kaneo. Function Analysis: Systematic Improvement of Quality & Performance. Dillon, Andrew P., tr. from JPN. LC 91-8681. 269p. 1991. 60.00 (*0-915299-81-X*) Productivity Inc.

Akiyama, M., ed. Design Technology of Fusion Reactors. 636p. (C). 1990. text 109.00 (*9971-5-0727-7*) World Scientific Pub.

Akiyama, Masayuki, ed. see Aldridge, Alfred O.

Akiyama, N., jt. auth. see Akiyama, C.

Akiyama, Nobuo & Akiyama, Carol. Japanese. 290p. 1995. pap. 10.95 (*0-8120-9046-2*) Barron.

— Japanese at a Glance. 3rd ed. LC 97-50301. (ENG & JPN.). 464p. 1998. pap. 8.95 (*0-7641-0320-2*) Barron.

— Japanese for the Business Traveler. (Business Dictionaries Ser.). (JPN & ENG.). 300p. (Orig.). 1994. pap. 11.95 (*0-8120-1770-6*) Barron.

Akiyama, Nobuo, et al. Now You're Talking: Japanese in No Time. 2nd ed. (ENG & JPN.). 1998. pap. 15.95 incl. audio (*0-7641-7165-8*) Barron.

Akiyama, Nobuo, jt. auth. see Akiyama, Carol.

Akiyama, Nubuo. SR Japanese. (SR Japanese Ser.). 1990. pap. 6.60 (*0-8325-9649-3*, Natl Textbk Co); pap. text 7.95 (*0-8325-9648-5*, Natl Textbk Co) NTC Contemp Pub Co.

Akiyama, Shinobu. A Revision of the Genus Lespedeza Section Macrolespedeza: (Leguminosae) (Illus.). 142p. 1988. 79.50 (*0-86008-429-9*, Pub. by U of Tokyo) Col U Pr.

Akiyama, Takamasa, jt. auth. see Ishiguro, Masayasu.

***Akizuki, Risu.** Survival in the Office: The Evolution of Japanese Working Women. 2000. pap. 12.00 (*4-7700-2695-1*) Kodansha.

— Survival in the Office: The Evolution of Japanese Working Women. 2001. pap. 12.00 (*4-7700-2696-X*) Kodansha.

— Survival in the Office: The Evolution of Japanese Working Women. 180p. 1999. pap. 12.00 (*4-7700-2390-1*, Pub. by Kodansha Intl) Kodansha.

— Survival in the Office: The Evolution of Japanese Working Women. 144p. 2000. pap. 12.00 (*4-7700-2502-5*); pap. 12.00 (*4-7700-2501-7*) Kodansha Intl.

Akizuki, Ryomin. New Mahayana: Buddhism for a Post-Modern World. Heisig, James W. & Swanson, Paul L., trs. from JPN. LC 90-83802. 208p. 1991. pap. 15.00 (*0-89581-900-7*) Asian Humanities.

Akizuki, Tatsuichiro. Nagasaki, 1945. Honeycombe, Gordon, ed. (Illus.). 168p. 1982. pap. 5.95 (*0-7043-3382-1*, Pub. by Quartet) Charles River Bks.

Akkad, Abbas M. Bilal: The First Muadhdhin of the Prophet of Islam. 90p. 1996. pap. 4.95 (*0-614-21702-4*, 104) Kazi Pubns.

***Akkan, Suzan H., compiled by.** Dictionary of Turkish Acronyms & Abbreviations: A Selected List, 1928-1998. LC 98-88341. xvi, 231p. 1999. pap. 24.95 (*1-892381-01-X*) Turko-Tatar.

— Dictionary of Turkish Acronyms & Abbreviations: A Selected List, 1928-1998. LC 98-88341. xvi, 231p. (C). 1999. 49.95 (*1-892381-00-1*) Turko-Tatar.

Akkas, Nuri. Progress on Biomechanics. (NATO Advanced Study Institutes Ser.). 395p. 1979. text 122.00 (*90-286-0479-0*) Kluwer Academic.

Akkas, Nuri, ed. Biomechanics of Active Movement & Division of Cells: Proceedings of the NATO ASI on Biomechanics of Active Movement & Division of Cells, Held in Istanbul, Turkey, Sept. 19-29, 1993. LC 94-15684. (NATO ASI Series H: Cell Biology: Voll 84). 1994. 307.95 (*0-387-57951-6*) Spr-Verlag.

— Biomechanics of Cell Division. LC 87-12349. (NATO ASI Series A, Life Sciences: Vol. 132). 382p. 1987. 105.00 (*0-306-42592-0*, Plenum Trade) Perseus Pubng.

Akker, H. P. Van Den, see Graamans, K. & Van Den Akker, H. P., eds.

Akkerboom, J. C. Testing Problems with Linear or Angular Inequality Constraints. (Lecture Notes in Statistics Ser.: Vol. 62). xii, 291p. 1990. 63.95 (*0-387-97232-3*) Spr-Verlag.

Akkerman, A. Thermal Physics Reviews Vol. 4, Pt. 4: Application of High-Current Charged Particle Beams in Dynamic High-Pressure Physics, Vol. 4. (Soviet Technology Reviews Ser.: Section B). 79p. 1992. pap. text 148.00 (*3-7186-5397-4*, Harwood Acad Pubs) Gordon & Breach.

Akkerman, F., ed. Vitae of Rudolph Agricola. annot. ed. (Medieval & Renaissance Texts & Studies: No. 190). 1998. 26.00 (*0-86698-232-9*, MR190) MRTS.

Akkerman, Fokke, et al. Northern Humanism Between 1469 & 1625. LC 99-17135. 250p. 1999. write for info. (*90-04-11314-2*) Brill Academic Pubs.

Akkerman, J. N., ed. Energetics of Secretion Responses, Vol. 1. LC 88-278. 176p. 1988. 185.00 (*0-8493-5906-6*, QH604, CRC Reprint) Franklin.

Akkerman, Jan N., ed. Energetics of Secretion Responses, Vol. 2. LC 88-278. 160p. 1988. 98.00 (*0-8493-5907-4*, QH604, CRC Reprint) Franklin.

***Akkerman, Mark.** Deep Six. 160p. 2000. reprint ed. pap. 5.95 (*1-930535-00-7*) Star Dists.

Akkerman, Tjitske & Stuurman, Siep. Perspectives on Feminist Thought in European History: From the Middle Ages to the Present. LC 97-25914. 256p. (C). 1998. 90.00 (*0-415-15220-8*) Routledge.

Akkermans, A. D., et al, eds. Frankia Symbioses: Proceedings of the Workshop on Frankia Symbioses, Wageningen, September 5-6, 1983. 258p. 1984. text 168.50 (*90-247-2967-X*) Kluwer Academic.

— Molecular Microbial Ecology Manual. LC 95-31285. 512p. (C). 1995. text 209.50 (*0-7923-3698-4*) Kluwer Academic.

— Molecular Microbial Ecology Manual, Set. LC 95-16332. 1995. write for info. (*0-7923-3411-6*) Kluwer Academic.

— Molecular Microbial Ecology Manual, Vol. 1. LC 95-16332. 1995. write for info. (*0-7923-3410-8*) Kluwer Academic.

Akkermans, E., et al, eds. Mesoscopic Quantum Physics: Proceedings of the Les Houches Summer School, Session LXI, 28 June-29 July, 1994. (Houches Summer School Proceedings Ser.: Vol. 61). (FRE.). 836p. 1995. 273.00 (*0-444-82293-3*) Elsevier.

Akkermans, Louis M., et al, eds. Gastric & Gastroduodenal Motility, 4. LC 84-16090. (Surgical Science Ser.: Vol. 4). 244p. 1984. 65.00 (*0-275-91420-8*, C1420, Praeger Pubs) Greenwood.

Akkermans, Louis M., jt. auth. see Smout, Andre J.

Akkermans, Peter M. Villages in the Steppe: Later Neolithic Settlement & Subsistence in the Balikh Valley, Northern Syria. LC 93-40086. (Archaeological Ser.: No. 5). (Illus.). xvi, 351p. 1993. pap. 37.50 (*1-879621-10-X*); lib. bdg. 50.00 (*1-879621-11-8*) Intl Mono Prehstry.

Akkermans, Peter M., ed. Tell Sabi Abyad - The Late Neolithic Settlement: Report on the Excavations of the University of Amsterdam (1988) & the National Museum of Antiquities Leiden (1991-1993) in Syria. LC 96-220500. 556p. 1996. text 139.50 (*90-6258-078-5*, Pub. by Netherlands Inst) Eisenbrauns.

Akl, Fred A., jt. ed. see Jong, Ing-Chang.

Akl, Selim G. Parallel Computation: Models & Methods. LC 96-42310. 608p. 1996. pap. 78.00 (*0-13-147034-5*) P-H.

Akl, Selim G., et al, eds. Advances in Computing & Information - ICCI '90: Proceedings of the International Conference on Computing & Information Niagara Falls, Canada, May 23-26, 1990. (Lecture Notes in Computer Science Ser.: Vol. 468). viii, 529p. 1991. 55.00 (*0-387-53504-7*) Spr-Verlag.

— Algorithms & Data Structures: 4th International Workshop, WADS '95, Kingston, Canada, August 16-18, 1995, Proceedings, Vol. IX. LC 95-23124. (Lecture Notes in Computer Science Ser.: Vol. 955). (Illus.). 519p. 1995. 81.00 (*3-540-60220-8*) Spr-Verlag.

Aklaev, Airat R. Democratization & Ethnic Peace: Patterns of Ethnopolitical Crisis Management in a Post-Soviet Setting. LC 99-72330. 8p. 1999. 74.95 (*1-84014-972-8*) Ashgate Pub Co.

Aklaev, Airat R., et al. Ethnopolitical Crises & Transitions to Violence: Legitimacy & Identity in the Republics of the Former Soviet Union. LC 95-211990. 1994. pap. write for info. (*0-919117-85-6*) PRI.

Akland, Eleanor. Ever Sure, Ever True. (Illus.). 108p. 1984. per. 5.00 (*0-614-24750-0*) Tesseract SD.

A

Aklcamo, I. Edward. Fundamentals of Microbiology. 2nd ed. LC 86-13972. (Biology Ser.). (Illus.). 900p. (C). 1986. text. write for info. (0-201-11780-0) Addison-Wesley.

***Aklecha, Vishwajit.** Object-Oriented Frameworks Using C++ & Corba Gold Book. LC 99-23782. 574p. 1999. pap. 39.99 (1-57610-403-6) Coriolis Grp.

Aklonis, John J. & MacKnight, William J. Introduction to Polymer Viscoelasticity. 2nd ed. LC 82-17528. 320p. 1983. 99.00 (0-471-86729-2) Wiley.

Aklu, Chaitram. Caribbean Trivia. 96p. 1993. pap. 7.95 (1-880365-39-1) Prof Pr NC.

Akmajian, Adrian & Heny, Frank W. An Introduction to the Principles of Transformational Syntax. LC 74-3054. 544p. 1980. pap. text 24.50 (0-262-51022-7) MIT Pr.

Akmajian, Adrian, et al. Linguistics: An Introduction to Language & Communication. 4th ed. LC 95-11668. 530p. 1995. pap. text 32.00 (0-262-51086-3) MIT Pr.

— Linguistics: An Introduction to Language & Communication. 4th ed. LC 95-11668. 530p. 1995. 55.00 (0-262-01150-6) MIT Pr.

Akmajian, Diran, ed. see Pignolet De Monteclair, Michel.

Akmakjian, Alan P. California Picnic. Stone, Ken, ed. LC 93-145122. (Illus.). (Orig.). 1992. pap. 3.50 (0-930715-12-8) M F Pr.

— California Picnic & Other Poems. LC 95-71196. 80p. 1996. 29.95 (0-89002-233-X); pap. 9.95 (0-89002-330-1) Northwoods Pr.

— Let the Sun Go. Stone, Ken, ed. LC 93-145132. (Illus.). (Orig.). 1992. pap. 3.50 (0-930715-11-X) M F Pr.

Akmal, Naim & Usmani, Arthur M., eds. Polymers in Sensors: Theory & Practice. LC 98-13989. (Symposium Ser.: No. 690). (Illus.). 320p. 1998. text 110.95 (0-8412-3550-3, Pub. by Am Chemical) OUP.

Akmal, Naim, jt. ed. see Usmani, Arthur M.

Akman, V. Unobstructed Shortest Paths in Polyhedral Environments. (Lecture Notes in Computer Science Ser.: Vol. 251). vii, 103p. 1987. 26.00 (0-387-17629-2) Spr-Verlag.

Akman, V., et al, eds. Intelligent CAD Systems II. (Eurographic Seminars Ser.). (Illus.). x, 324p. 1989. 71.95 (0-387-50914-3) Spr-Verlag.

***Akmon, Nancy.** Peter Rabbit Celebrates Christmas. Akmon, Roni, ed. (Illus.). 48p. 1999. 8.95 (1-884807-45-3, EC745) Blushing Rose.

— Treasured Memories: Victorian Photograph Album. (Illus.). 14p. 1999. 10.95 (1-884807-41-0, EC741) Blushing Rose.

Akmon, Nancy, ed. Alice in Wonderland Coloring Book. (Illus.). 54p. (J). 1996. pap. 6.95 (1-884807-20-8, EC721) Blushing Rose.

***Akmon, Nancy & Akmon, Roni.** Little Gardener. 84p. (J). 2000. 18.95 (1-884807-48-8, EC748) Blushing Rose.

Akmon, Nancy & Akmon, Roni. A Posy of Roses: Victorian Photograph Album. (Illus.). 26p. 1996. 19.95 (1-884807-15-1) Blushing Rose.

***Akmon, Nancy & Akmon, Roni.** Roosevelt Bears Coloring Book. (Illus.). 52p. 2000. 7.95 (1-884807-49-6, EC 749) Blushing Rose.

Akmon, Nancy & Akmon, Roni. Sweet Memories: Victorian Photograph Album. (Illus.). 12p. 1996. 10.95 (1-884807-16-X) Blushing Rose.

***Akmon, Nancy & Akmon, Roni.** Tea Time. 84p. 2000. 18.95 (1-884807-46-1) Blushing Rose.

***Akmon, Nancy & Akmon, Roni, eds.** Christmas ABC: Story/Stickerbook. (Illus.). 28p. 1999. 10.95 (1-884807-42-9, EC742) Blushing Rose.

— Hollyberries of Christmas. (Illus.). 36p. 1999. 8.95 (1-884807-44-5, EC744) Blushing Rose.

— Rhymes for Children: Story/Stickerbook. (Illus.). 28p. 1999. 10.95 (1-884807-43-7, EC743) Blushing Rose.

Akmon, Nancy, jt. auth. see Akmon, Roni.

Akmon, Nancy C. Baby Album. (Illus.). 84p. 1992. text 35.00 (1-884807-10-0, EC71) Blushing Rose.

— Best of Friends: A Giftbook with Envelope. (Illus.). 49p. 1998. 6.95 (1-884807-27-5, EC705) Blushing Rose.

— The Best Yet to Be: A Giftbook with Envelope. (Illus.). 49p. 1998. 6.95 (1-884807-28-3, EC704) Blushing Rose.

— Christmas Album. (Illus.). 84p. 1992. 29.95 (0-926684-05-1) Blushing Rose.

— Come to My Tea Party: A Cookbook for Children. rev. ed. LC 98-160284. (Illus.). 84p. (J). (gr. 3-6). 1997. 13.95 (1-884807-33-X, EC713) Blushing Rose.

— Happy Birthday! Photo Album & Journal. (Illus.). 1998. 13.95 (1-884807-32-1, EC727) Blushing Rose.

— Mothers & Daughters: A Giftbook with Envelope. (Illus.). 49p. 1998. 6.95 (1-884807-25-9, EC706) Blushing Rose.

— My Sister: A Giftbook with Envelope. (Illus.). 49p. 1998. 6.95 (1-884807-26-7, EC709) Blushing Rose.

— Nuestro Bebe.Tr. of Our Baby. (SPA., Illus.). 56p. 1997. 33.95 (1-884807-23-2) Blushing Rose.

— Our Baby. (Illus.). 56p. 1997. 35.00 (1-884807-17-8, EC7) Blushing Rose.

— School Life: Photo Album & Journal. (Illus.). 1998. 13.95 (1-884807-31-3, EC726) Blushing Rose.

— Travel Journal: Photo Album & Journal. (Illus.). 1998. 13.95 (1-884807-30-5, EC725) Blushing Rose.

— Wedding Album. (Wedding Album Ser.). (Illus.). 84p. 1994. 35.95 (1-884807-00-3, EC712) Blushing Rose.

— Wedding Album: Floral Cover Version. (Wedding Album Ser.). (Illus.). 84p. 1995. 35.95 (1-884807-12-7, EC710) Blushing Rose.

— Wedding Floral Guest Book. (Wedding Album Ser.). (Illus.). 84p. 1996. 13.95 (1-884807-18-6, EC719) Blushing Rose.

Akmon, Nancy C., ed. Angels: Messengers from Heaven. (Illus.). 32p. 1994. text 8.95 (1-884807-09-7) Blushing Rose.

— My Baby Photograph Album: Victorian Photograph Album. (Illus.). 14p. 1997. 10.95 (1-884807-11-9) Blushing Rose.

Akmon, Nancy C. & Akmon, Roni. The Language of Flowers: Flower Dictionary, Poetry & Flowers. LC 96-134275. (Illus.). 32p. 1995. 8.95 (1-884807-13-5) Blushing Rose.

— Wedding Guest Book. (Wedding Album Ser.). 84p. 1994. 13.95 (1-884807-04-6, EC714) Blushing Rose.

***Akmon, Roni & Akmon, Nancy.** Cottage Garden. (Illus.). 24p. 2000. 19.95 (1-884807-47-X, EC 747) Blushing Rose.

— Roosevelt Bears Traveling Adventures. (Illus.). 28p. 2000. 10.95 (1-884807-50-X, EC 750) Blushing Rose.

Akmon, Roni, jt. auth. see Akmon, Nancy.

Akmon, Roni, jt. auth. see Akmon, Nancy C.

Akmon, Roni, jt. auth. see Cogan, Nancy.

Akmon, Roni, ed. see Akmon, Nancy.

Akmon, Roni, jt. ed. see Akmon, Nancy.

Akmon, Roni, tr. & des. see Cogan Akmon, Nancy.

Akner, Lois F. Parent-H to Survive. 1994. pap. 12.00 (0-688-13791-1, Quil) HarperTrade.

Akobundu, I. Okezie. Weed Science in the Tropics. LC 87-8128. 538p. reprint ed. pap. 166.80 (0-8357-7540-2, 203626300001) Bks Demand.

Akoev, G. N. & Andrianov, Y. N. Sensory Hair Cells: Synaptic Transmission. LC 93-7183.Tr. of Sinapticheskaia Peredacha v Retsoptarakh Akustiko-Lateralnoi Sistemy. 1993. 211.95 (0-387-56186-2) Spr-Verlag.

Akoh & Min, eds. Food Lipids. LC 98-14950. (Illus.). 840p. 1998. text 225.00 (0-8247-9985-2) Dekker.

Akoh, Casimir C. & Swanson, Barry G., eds. Carbohydrate Polyesters As Fat Substitutes. LC 94-577. (Food Science & Technology Ser.: Vol. 62). (Illus.). 288p. 1994. text 150.00 (0-8247-9062-6) Dekker.

Akoh, J. A. Dialysis Acess: Current Practice. 300p. 1999. 56.00 (1-86094-169-9) Imperial College.

***Akoka, Jacky, et al, eds.** Conceptual Modeling ER'99: 18th International Conference on Conceptual Modeling, Paris, France, November 15-18, 1999, Proceedings. LC 99-51449. (Lecture Notes In Computer Science: Vol. 1728). xv, 539p. 1999. pap. 85.00 (3-540-66686-9) Spr-Verlag.

Akoneck, Oya, ed. see De LaFayette, Jean M.

Akong Tulku, Rinpoche, jt. auth. see Wittenhafer, Donald E.

Akopian, A., ed. Industrial Potential of Russia: Analytical Study Based on Fixed Asset Statistics to 1992. 117p. (C). 1992. lib. bdg. 395.00 (1-56072-080-8) Nova Sci Pubs.

Akopjan, S. A., et al. Fifteen Papers on Analysis. LC 51-5559. (Translations Ser.: Series 2, Vol. 72). 276p. 1968. 49.00 (0-8218-1772-8, TRANS2/72) Am Math.

Akos, Karoly, jt. auth. see Hari, Maria.

Akos, Gyorgy, et al, eds. 5th Congress on Modern Optics. LC 99-220852. (Proceedings of SPIE Ser.: Vol. 3573). 646p. 1998. 116.00 (0-8194-3038-2) SPIE.

Akosu, Tyohdauah. The Writing of Ezekiel (Es'kia) Mphahlele, South African Writer: Literature, Culture & Politics. LC 95-3003. 332p. 1996. 99.95 (0-7734-2285-4) E Mellen.

Akoun, J. A. Cote des Lithos, Gravures, Sculptures, Bronzes 1993. 4th ed. (FRE.). 480p. 1992. pap. 75.00 (0-8288-7317-8, 285171169) Fr & Eur.

— Cote des Peintres, 1993. 7th ed. (FRE.). 680p. 1993. 75.00 (0-8288-7228-7, 2859171169) Fr & Eur.

Akoval, Guneri. Frontiers in the Science & Technology of Polymer Recycling. LC 98-26192. (NATO ASI Series E). 1998. write for info. (0-7923-5190-8) Kluwer Academic.

***Akovali, G. & Mansurov, Z. A., eds.** The Role of Government & Research Institutes in the Planning of Research & Development in some Central Asian & Caucasian Republics. (NATO Science Series: Vol. 32). 288p. 2000. 83.00 (1-58603-022-1) IOS Press.

Akovali, Guneri, ed. The Interfacial Interactions in Polymeric Composites. LC 92-41725. (NATO Advanced Study Institutes Series E, Applied Sciences: No. 230). 1993. text 294.00 (0-7923-2108-1) Kluwer Academic.

Akovlevich, I., jt. auth. see Khinchin, Aleksandra.

Akpalu, Vinoko. When Sorrow-Song Descends on You. Barkan, Stanley H., ed. Awoonor, Kofi, tr. (Cross-Cultural Review Chapbook Ser.: No. 14). (ENG & EWE.). 16p. 1992. 15.00 (0-89304-876-3); pap. 5.00 (0-89304-877-1) Cross-Cultrl NY.

— When Sorrow-Song Descends on You. Barkan, Stanley H., ed. Awoonor, Kofi, tr. (Cross-Cultural Review Chapbook Ser.: No. 14: African Ghanaian Poetry 1). (ENG & EWE.). 16p. 1992. 15.00 (0-89304-813-5); pap. 5.00 (0-89304-838-0) Cross-Cultrl NY.

Akpan, Ememobong M., jt. auth. see Akpan, Michael E.

Akpan, Juliana, jt. auth. see Akpan, Michael.

Akpan, Juliana M., jt. auth. see Akpan, Michael E.

Akpan, Juliana M., jt. ed. see Akpan, Michael E.

Akpan, Michael & Akpan, Juliana. Updates on Human Immuno-Deficiency Virus Which Causes the A.I.D.S. Disease & the Third World. 88p. (Orig.). 1993. pap. 8.95 (1-56411-048-6) Untd Bros & Sis.

Akpan, Michael E. & Akpan, Ememobong M. The Power of Positive Thinking: From Poverty to Fame. LC 92-75966. 182p. 1992. pap. text 15.00 (0-9634998-0-7) Ebewos Afr-Am.

Akpan, Michael E. & Akpan, Juliana M. Basic Information You Need to Start & Succeed in Your Own Business. 53p. 1992. pap. write for info. (0-9634998-1-5) Ebewos Afr-Am.

— Overcoming Barriers in Family Life & Sex Education from African Perspective, 2 vols., 1. LC 93-71701. (Illus.). 114p. (Orig.). 1993. pap. 13.95 (0-9634998-2-3) Ebewos Afr-Am.

— Overcoming Barriers in Family Life & Sex Education from African Perspective, 2 vols., 2. LC 93-71701. (Illus.). 114p. (Orig.). 1993. pap. 15.00 (0-9634998-5-8) Ebewos Afr-Am.

Akpan, Michael E. & Akpan, Juliana M., eds. An Eclectic Collection of Poems for All Peoples All Generations & All Ages. LC 93-71571. 137p. 1993. pap. 10.00 (0-9634998-4-X) Ebewos Afr-Am.

Akpan, N. Public Administration in Nigeria. 1982. pap. text. write for info. (0-582-64398-8, Pub. by Addison-Wesley) Longman.

Akpan, Ntieyong U. Struggle for Succession, 1966-1970: Personal Account of the Nigerian Civil War. 220p. 1972. pap. 22.50 (0-7146-2949-9, BHA-02949, Pub. by F Cass Pubs) Intl Spec Bk.

Akpeki, Tesse. A Force for Change: Enhancing the Quality of Women's Involvement on Boards. LC 98-234846. 60 p. ;p. 1997. write for info. (0-7199-1529-5) NCVO Pubns.

Akpinar, Aylin. Male's Honour & Female's Shame: Gender & Ethnic Identity Constructions among Turkish Divorcees in the Migration Context. LC 98-139457. 172p. 1998. write for info. (91-506-1261-1) Uppsala Universitet.

Akram Diya' al Umari. The Madinan Society at the Time of the Prophet Vol. 1: Its Characteristics & Organization. An Attempt to Apply the Rules of the Muhaddithun in the Criticism of Historical Reports. Khattab, Huda, tr. from ARA. LC 89-2185. 250p. (C). 1991. text 19.95 (0-912463-36-8); pap. text 10.95 (0-912463-37-6) IIIT VA.

— The Madinan Society at the Time of the Prophet Vol. 2: The Jihad Against the Mushrikun. An Attempt to Apply the Rules of the Muhaddithun in the Criticism of Historical Reports. Khattab, Huda, tr. from ARA. LC 89-2185. 250p. (C). 1991. pap. 10.95 (0-912463-39-2); text 19.95 (0-912463-38-4) IIIT VA.

Akramkhodzhaev, A. M., et al. Geology & Exploration of Oil- & Gasbearing Ancient Deltas. Rao, P. M., tr. (Russian Translation Ser.: No. 69). (RUS.). 214p. (C). 1989. text 123.00 (90-6191-907-X, Pub. by A A Balkema) Ashgate Pub Co.

Akrasanee, Narongchai, ed. see Pacific Trade & Development Conference Staff.

Akre, J., ed. Infant Feeding: The Physiological Basis. (FRE & SPA.). 108p. 1990. pap. text 20.00 (92-4-068670-3, 0036701) World Health.

Akre, Roger D., et al. Insects Did It First. LC 92-38722. (Illus.). 1992. pap. 13.00 (0-87770-517-8) Ye Galleon.

Akresh, Murray S., et al. Retiree Health Benefits: How to Cope with the Accounting, Actuarial, & Management Issues. Barth, Claire & Strand, Jennifer, eds. (Bold Step Ser.). (Illus.). 134p. (Orig.). 1991. pap. 40.00 (0-86641-194-1, 91156) Inst Mgmt Account.

Akridge, J. R. & Balkanski, M., eds. Solid State Microbatteries. LC 90-6769. (NATO ASI Ser.: Vol. 217). (Illus.). 450p. (C). 1990. text 162.00 (0-306-43505-5, Kluwer Plenum) Kluwer Academic.

Akrigg, Helen B. British Columbia Place Names. 3rd ed. LC 98-115245. 320p. 1998. pap. text 19.95 (0-7748-0637-0) U BC Pr.

***Akright, Carol.** Funding Your Dreams Generation to Generation: Intergenerational Financial Planning to Ensure Your Family's Health, Wealth & Prosperity. 2001. pap. 19.95 (0-7931-3713-6) Dearborn.

Akrill, Caroline. Not Quite a Horsewoman. 187p. (C). 1990. pap. 21.00 (0-85140-727-7, Pub. by J A Allen) St Mut.

— Not Quite a Horsewoman. 230p. 1995. pap. 35.00 (0-85131-643-3, Pub. by J A Allen) Trafalgar.

— Showing the Ridden Pony. 174p. (C). 1990. 52.00 (0-85131-513-5, Pub. by J A Allen) St Mut.

— Showing the Ridden Pony. 3rd rev. ed. (Illus.). 1996. 46.00 (0-85131-649-2, Pub. by J A Allen) Trafalgar.

Akritas, Alkiviadis G. Elements of Computer Algebra with Applications. LC 88-14870. 448p. 1989. 160.00 (0-471-61163-8) Wiley.

Akron Art Museum Staff, jt. auth. see New Museum of Contemporary Art Staff (New York, N.

Akron-Summit County Public Library, Science & Technology Staff, ed. Science Fair Project Index, 1973-1982. LC 83-3353. 729p. 1983. 62.50 (0-8108-1605-9) Scarecrow.

Akron-Summit County Public Library Staff. Science Fair Project Index, 1985-1989: For Grades K-8. Bishop, Cynthia et al, eds. LC 92-22221. 563p. (J). (gr. k-8). 1992. 58.00 (0-8108-2555-4) Scarecrow.

Akron-Summit County Public Library Staff, et al, eds. Science Fair Project Index, 1981-1984. LC 86-6571. 692p. 1986. 50.00 (0-8108-1892-2) Scarecrow.

Akrotirianakis, Stavros N. Byzantium Comes to Southern California: The Los Angeles Greek Orthodox Community. 368p. 1994. pap. text 11.95 (1-880971-04-6) Light&Life Pub Co MN.

Akroyd, T. Concrete Properties & Manufacture. LC 61-11155. 1962. 154.00 (0-08-009595-X, Pub. by Pergamon Repr) Franklin.

Aksakov, Sergei. The Family Chronicle. Beverley, M. C., tr. from RUS. LC 85-7977.Tr. of Semeinaia Khronika. 227p. 1985. reprint ed. lib. bdg. 67.50 (0-313-24835-4, AKFCH, Greenwood Pr) Greenwood.

— Notes of a Provincial Wildfowler. Windle, Kevin, tr. from RUS. LC 98-16062. (Studies in Russian Literature & Theory). (Illus.). 216p. 1998. text 29.95 (0-8101-1391-0) Northwestern U Pr.

— Notes on Fishing. Hodge, Thomas P., tr. LC 97-14128. 280p. 1997. 30.00 (0-8101-1366-X) Northwestern U Pr.

Aksan, Virginia H. An Ottoman Statesman in War & Peace: Ahmed Resmi Efendi, 1700-1783. xviii, 253p. 1995. 107.00 (90-04-10116-0) Brill Academic Pubs.

Aksay, I., et al, eds. Processing Science of Advanced Ceramics Vol. 155: Materials Research Society Symposium Proceedings, Vol. 155. 387p. 1989. text 17.50 (1-55899-028-3) Materials Res.

Aksay, I. & Sarikaya, M. Biomimetics: Design & Processing of Materials. (Polymers & Complex Materials Ser.). 352p. (C). 1995. text 69.95 (1-56396-196-2, AIP Pr) Spr-Verlag.

Aksay, I. A., et al, eds. Atomic & Molecular Processing of Electronic & Ceramic Materials: Preparation, Characterization & Properties. (Materials Research Society Conference Proceedings Ser.: Vol. AMEC). 1988. text 17.50 (0-931837-85-5) Materials Res.

Akselsen, Bjorn, ed. & photos by see Hastings, Pattie B. & Armstrong, Linda.

Aksenov, V. L., et al. Neutron Scattering by Ferroelectric. 406p. (C). 1989. text 77.00 (9971-5-0193-7) World Scientific Pub.

Aksent'ev, L. A., et al. Fourteen Papers Translated from the Russian. LC 87-12578. (Translations Ser. 2: Vol. 136). 154p. 1987. 59.00 (0-8218-3112-7, TRANS2/136) Am Math.

***Aksionczyk, Nicholas M.** A Second Look at Fundamentalism, the Scopes Trial, & Inherit the Wind. LC 98-72685. 1999. write for info. (0-932766-51-X, Inst Creation) Master Bks.

Aksit, Mehmet, et al, eds. ECOOP'97 - Object-Oriented Programming: 11th European Conference, Jyvaskyla, Finland, June 9-13, 1997, Proceedings. LC 97-20574. (Lecture Notes in Computer Science Ser.: No. 1241). xi, 531p. 1997. pap. 79.00 (3-540-63089-9) Spr-Verlag.

Aksomaitis, A., et al. Twenty-Nine Papers on Statistics & Probability. (Selected Translations in Mathematical Statistics & Probability Ser.: Vol. 9). 315p. 1971. 51.00 (0-8218-1459-1, STAPRO/9) Am Math.

***Aksonov, A.I.** Moskovisea Saga. 6th ed. 1999. 19.95 (5-87113-066-6) Distribks Inc.

Aksoy, A. G. & Khamsi, M. A. Nonstandard Methods in Fixed Point Theory. Ewing, J. H. et al, eds. (Universitext Ser.). (Illus.). ix, 139p. 1990. 49.95 (0-387-97364-8) Spr-Verlag.

Aksoy, Ercument G. The Problem of the Multiple Interpretation of Ricardo. Breit, William & Elzinga, Kenneth G., eds. LC 91-13684. (Political Economy & Public Policy Ser.: Vol. 8). 314p. 1991. 78.50 (1-55938-289-9) Jai Pr.

Aksoy, M., ed. Benzene Carcinogenicity. (Cancer Specialists & Hematologists Ser.). 192p. 1988. 100.00 (0-8493-6670-4, RC643, CRC Reprint) Franklin.

***Aksoy, Majvor S.** The Journeys of a Fragile Heart. LC 00-190048. 144p. 2000. pap. 19.95 (1-56167-615-2, Five Star Spec Ed) Am Literary Pr.

Akst, Daniel. St. Burl's Obituary. LC 96-43962. 376p. 1997. pap. 12.00 (0-15-600514-X, Harvest Bks) Harcourt.

— St. Burl's Obituary. LC 95-52568. 370p. 1996. 22.95 (1-878448-68-4) MacMurray & Beck.

Aksu-Koc & Slobin, Dan I., eds. The Acquisition of Turkish: The Crosslinguistic Study of Language. (Crosslinguistic Study of Language Acquisition Ser.). 64p. 1986. pap. 16.00 (0-89859-848-6) L Erlbaum Assocs.

Aksu-Koc, Ayhan. The Acquisition of Aspect & Modality: The Case of Past Reference in Turkish. (Cambridge Studies in Linguistics). 264p. 1988. text 64.95 (0-521-33119-6) Cambridge U Pr.

Aksyonov, Vassily. The Destruction of Pompeii & Other Stories. (Contemporary Russian Prose Ser.). 183p. 1991. pap. 9.95 (0-679-73441-4) Vin Bks.

Aksyonov, Vassily. Generations of Winter. 1995. pap. 15.00 (0-679-76182-9) Vin Bks.

***Aksyonov, Vassily.** Moskovskie Slova I Slovechki: Proiskhozhdenie Moskovskikh Poslovits, Pogovorok, Rechenii & Pesen. 8th ed. 1999. pap. 9.95 (5-87113-022-4) Distribks Inc.

Aksyonov, Vassily. The New Sweet Style: A Novel. LC 99-13313. 496p. 1999. 29.95 (0-679-44401-7) Random.

— Quest for an Island. 250p. 1987. 17.95 (1-55554-020-1) PAJ Pubns.

***Aksyonov, Vassily.** Your Murderer. Gerould, Daniel, tr. (Russian Theatre Archive Ser.: Vol. 21). 70p. 1999. text 31.00 (90-5755-103-9, Harwood Acad Pubs) Gordon & Breach.

Aksyonov, Vassily. Zatovarennaya Bochkotara - Randevu. 2nd ed. Poliak, Gregory, ed. (RUS., Illus.). 100p. (Orig.). reprint ed. pap. 7.50 (0-940294-02-8) Silver Age Pub.

Aksyonov, Vassily, et al. Za Trideviat Zemel: Antologiia Emigrantskoi Prozy 1980s. LC 92-21114. (RUS.). 162p. (Orig.). 1992. pap. 12.00 (1-55779-022-1) Hermitage Pubs.

Aksyonov, Vassily, jt. intro. see Draitser, Emil.

Aktan, Okan H., jt. auth. see Krueger, Anne O.

Aktas, Gulen, et al, eds. Strings & Symmetries: Proceedings of the Gursey Memorial Conference I, Held at Istanbul, Turkey, 6-10 June 1994. LC 95-12986. (Lecture Notes in Physics Ser.: Vol. 447). xii, 398p. 1995. 101.95 (3-540-59163-X) Spr-Verlag.

Akter Banu, U. A. Razia, see Razia Akter Banu, U. A., ed.

Aktlsenko, U. P., jt. auth. see Hritonenko, Natali.

Aktolun, C. & Tauxe, W. Newlon. Nuclear Oncology. LC 99-10449. 500p. 1999. 189.00 (3-540-64760-0) Spr-Verlag.

Akton, Okan, jt. auth. see Krueger, Anne O.

***Aktories, K., et al, eds.** Bacterial Protein Toxins. (Handbook of Experimental Pharmacology Ser.: 145). xxiv, 732p. 2000. (3-540-66125-5) Spr-Verlag.

Aktories, K., et al. GTPases in Biology. Dickey, Burton F. & Birnbaumer, Lutz, eds. LC 93-21636. (Handbook of Experimental Pharmacology Ser.: Vol. 108). 1994. 424.00 (0-387-56773-9) Spr-Verlag.

An Asterisk (*) at the beginning of an entry indicates that the title is appearing for the first time.

Aktouf, Chouki, et al. Basic Concepts & Advances in Fault-Tolerant Computing Design. (Series on Stability, Vibration & Control of Systems). 400p. 1998. 68.00 (*981-02-3259-4*) World Scientific Pub.

AKTRIN Furniture Information Center Staff & Centro Studi Industria Leggera Staff. The Furniture Industry in Eastern Europe. LC 97-27944. (Illus.). 201p. 1997. pap. 1000.00 (*0-921577-72-9*) AKTRIN.

— The Furniture Industry in Latin America. LC 97-27892. (Illus.). 119p. 1997. pap. 1000.00 (*0-921577-70-2*) AKTRIN.

— The Furniture Industry in Mexico. LC 98-31343. 100p. 1998. spiral bd. 1000.00 (*0-921577-85-0*) AKTRIN.

Aktrin Research Institute Staff. The Furniture Industry in the Middle East & Africa. LC 98-23101. (Illus.). 100p. 1998. spiral bd. 1000.00 (*0-921577-84-2*) AKTRIN.

Aktrin Research Institute Staff & Centro Studi Industria Leggera Staff. The Furniture Industry in India. LC 98-14241. (Illus.). 100p. 1998. pap. 1000.00 (*0-921577-79-6*) AKTRIN.

— The Furniture Industry in Japan. LC 97-35564. (Illus.). 89p. 1997. spiral bd. 1000.00 (*0-921577-68-0*) AKTRIN.

— The Furniture Industry in the United States & Canada. LC 98-14159. (Illus.). 243p. 1998. spiral bd. 1000.00 (*0-921577-80-X*) AKTRIN.

Aktrin Research Institute Staff, jt. auth. see McCormack, Thomas W.

Aktrin Research Institute Staff, jt. auth. see Wille, Stefan.

***Aku, Edmund.** Re-Defining Community: A Discourse on Community & the Pluralism of Today's World with Personalist Underpinnings. (European University Studies: Vol. 692). 253p. 2000. pap. 42.95 (*0-8204-4733-1*) P Lang Pubng.

Akudinoba. Under the Sign of Darkness. 67.95 (*1-85521-992-1*) Ashgate Pub Co.

Akudinobi, Jude G., jt. auth. see Zegeye, Abebe.

Akulenko, Leonid D., ed. Problems & Methods of Optimal Control. LC 94-14889. (Mathematics & Its Applications Ser.: Vol. 286). 360p. (C). 1994. text 220.50 (*0-7923-2855-8*) Kluwer Academic.

Akulin, V. M. & Karlov, N. V. Intense Resonant Interactions in Quantum Electronics. Beiglbock, W. et al, eds. Tselikova, O. N. & Potapchouck, V. S., trs. from RUS. (Texts & Monographs in Physics). (Illus.). 312p. 1991. 75.95 (*0-387-53574-8*) Spr-Verlag.

Akulov, Vladimir P., jt. ed. see Wess, Julius.

Akural, Sabri, ed. Turkic Culture: Continuity & Change. 2nd ed. LC 87-80268. (Turkish Studies). (Illus.). 196p. (C). 1993. pap. text 15.95 (*1-878318-06-3*) IN Univ Turkish.

Akural, Sabri M. & Basgoz, Ilhan, eds. Turkic Culture: Continuity & Change. (Turkish Studies: Vol. 6). 186p. (C). 1987. 11.95 (*0-685-29324-6*) IN Univ Turkish.

Akurgal, Mango & Ettinghausen Staff. Les Tresors de Turque. (FRE.). 252p. 1966. 95.00 (*0-8288-4002-4*) Fr & Eur.

Akutagawa, Donald & Whitman, Terry. Mind Your Own Business: My Turf, Your Space, Our Place. Lewis, Lynne E., ed. LC 94-66620. 220p. (Orig.). 1994. pap. write for info. (*0-614-05037-5*) Brownell & Carroll.

Akutagawa, Ryunosuke. Cogwheels & Other Stories. Norman, Howard, tr. from JPN. 80p. 1994. pap. 9.95 (*0-88962-182-9*) Mosaic.

— Essential Akutagawa: Rashomonm Hell Screen, Cogwheels, a Fools Life & other Short Fiction. 240p. 1999. pap. text 10.95 (*1-56886-061-7*, Pub. by Marsilio Pubs) Consort Bk Sales.

— Hell Screen & Other Stories. Norman, W. H., tr. LC 78-98800. 177p. 1970. reprint ed. lib. bdg. 52.50 (*0-8371-3017-4*, AKHS, Greenwood Pr) Greenwood.

— Hell Screen; Cogwheels; A Fool's Life. Date not set. 12.00 (*0-941419-03-7*, Eridanos Library) Marsilio Pubs.

***Akutagawa, Ryunosuke.** Kappa. Bownas, Geoffrey, tr. 144p. 2000. pap. 10.95 (*0-8048-3251-X*) Tuttle Pubng.

Akutagawa, Ryunosuke. Kappa. Shiojiri, Seiichi, tr. LC 71-98801. 136p. 1970. reprint ed. lib. bdg. 35.00 (*0-8371-3064-6*, AKKA, Greenwood Pr) Greenwood.

— Kappa: A Satire. Bownas, Geoffrey, tr. from JPN. LC 79-157260. 142p. 1971. pap. 9.95 (*0-8048-0994-1*) Tuttle Pubng.

— Rashomon. LC 52-9665. (Illus.). 120p. 1999. reprint ed. pap. 11.00 (*0-87140-173-8*) Norton.

Akutagawa, Ryunosuke. Rashomon & Other Stories. Takashi, Kojima, tr. LC 52-9665. (Illus.). 1970. pap. 7.95 (*0-87140-214-9*, Pub. by Liveright) Norton.

Akutagawa, Ryunosuke. Rashomon & Other Stories. Kojima, Takashi, tr. from JPN. LC 83-50837. (Illus.). 102p. 1952. pap. 9.95 (*0-8048-1457-0*) Tuttle Pubng.

Akutsu, T. & Koyanagi, H. Heart Replacement: Artificial Heart 5-The 5th International Symposium on Artificial Heart & Assist Devices, January 26-27, 1995, Tokyo, Japan. 428p. 1996. 289.00 (*4-431-70169-9*) Spr-Verlag.

Akutsu, T. & Koyanagi, H., eds. Artificial Heart, No. 3: Proceedings of the 3rd International Symposium on Artificial Heart & Assist Devices February 16-17, 1990, Tokyo, Japan. (Illus.). 384p. 1992. 187.00 (*0-387-70065-X*) Spr-Verlag.

Akwa, Dika. Bible de la Sagesse Bantoue: Choix d'Aphorismes, Devinettes et Mots d'Espirts du Cameroun et du Gabon. (B. E. Ser.: No. 128). (FRE.). 1955. 25.00 (*0-8115-3055-8*) Periodicals Srv.

Akwanga, Amechi. Orimili: One Man's Struggle for Power in Pre-Colonial Nigeria. (African Writers Ser.). 186p. (C). 1991. pap. 8.95 (*0-435-90670-4*, 90670) Heinemann.

Akwe:kon Press Staff, jt. auth. see National Museum of the American Indian (NMAI) Staf.

Akweenda, S. International Law & the Protection of Namibia's Territorial Integrity: Boundaries & Territorial Claims. LC 97-16415. 388p. 1997. 195.00 (*90-411-0412-7*) Kluwer Law Intl.

Akwule, Raymond. Global Telecommunications: The Technology, Administration & Policies. 208p. 1992. text 46.95 (*0-240-80032-X*, Focal) Buttrwrth-Heinemann.

Akyea, E. Ofori. Ewe. LC 96-32826. (Heritage Library of African Peoples: Set 2). (Illus.). 64p. (YA). (gr. 7-12). 1996. lib. bdg. 17.95 (*0-8239-1980-3*, D1980-3) Rosen Group.

Akyeampong, Emmanuel Kwaku. Drink, Power & Cultural Change: A Social History of Alcohol in Ghana, "1800 to Recent Times" LC 96-32887. (Social History of Africa Ser.). 1996. 60.00 (*0-435-08994-3*, 08994); pap. 23.95 (*0-435-08996-X*, 08996) Heinemann.

Akyuz, O., jt. ed. see Odabasi, Halis.

Akyuz, Yilmaz. East Asian Development: New Perspectives. LC 98-30180. 160p. 1998. 37.50 (*0-7146-4934-1*, Pub. by F Cass Pubs); pap. 18.50 (*0-7146-4494-3*, Pub. by F Cass Pubs) Intl Spec Bk.

Akzhigitov, G. N. English-Russian Dictionary of Medical & Biological Abbreviations A-Z. 426p. (C). 1992. 32.95 (*0-8285-5162-6*) Firebird NY.

— English-Russian Medical Dictionary. 604p. (C). 1992. 29.95 (*0-8285-4998-2*) Firebird NY.

Akzin, Benjamin & Drov, Yehezkel. Israel: High-Pressure Planning. LC 66-17521. (National Planning Ser.: No. 5). 122p. pap. 37.90 (*0-608-13880-0*, 202039300017) Bks Demand.

***Al.** Macmillan Compendium of Twenty First Century. LC 98-50677. 999p. 1998. 125.00 (*0-02-864977-X*) Macmillan Gen Ref.

Al. Macmillan Profiles Scientists Entrepreneurs. LC 98-28744. 389p. (J). 1998. 75.00 (*0-02-864983-4*) Macmillan Gen Ref.

— Macmillan Profiles Tycoons Entrepreneurs. LC 98-39089. 349p. 1998. per. 75.00 (*0-02-864982-6*) Macmillan Gen Ref.

Al-Adawiyyah, Rabi'a. Doorkeeper of the Heart. Upton, Charles, tr. 56p. 1996. pap. 8.00 (*0-614-21265-0*, 214) Kazi Pubns.

Al-Ahsan, Abdullah. The History of Al-Khilafah Ar-Rashidah. unabridged ed. Durkee, Noura & Abiva, Huseyin, eds. LC 94-75416. (Illus.). 80p. (Orig.). (J). (gr. 6-8). 1994. pap. text 8.00 (*1-56316-366-7*) Iqra Intl Ed Fdtn.

Al-Akaidi, Marwan, jt. ed. see Verbraeck, Alexander.

Al-Akili, Imam M., ed. & tr. see Al-Asfahani, Al-Hafiz A.

Al-Akili, Muhammad. Defeating the Evil Eye. 128p. (Orig.). 1993. pap. 8.95 (*1-879405-08-3*) Pearl Pub Hse.

— Natural Healing with Tibb Medicine: Medicine of the Prophet. 320p. 1996. pap. 16.95 (*0-614-21556-0*, 888) Pearl Pub Hse.

— Qur'an Selected Commentaries. LC 93-92766. 240p. (Orig.). 1993. pap. 11.95 (*1-879405-09-1*) Pearl Pub Hse.

Al-Akili, Muhammad, tr. Beauty of the Righteous & the Ranks of the Elite. 448p. 1996. pap. 21.95 (*0-614-21253-7*, 1503) Pearl Pub Hse.

— Quran: Selected Commentaries. 238p. 1996. pap. 11.95 (*0-614-21065-8*, 1041) Pearl Pub Hse.

— Shaikh Muhyidden A. Qaid Gilani (al-Fathu Rabbani) 130p. 1996. pap. 16.50 (*0-614-21345-2*, 1126) Pearl Pub Hse.

Al-Akili, Muhammad, tr. see Seerin, Ibn.

Al-Akili, Muhammad M. Ibn Seerin's Dictionary of Dreams According to Islamic Inner Traditions: (Tafsir-ul Ahlam) LC 91-61405. 548p. (Orig.). (C). 1991. 24.50 (*1-879405-03-2*) Pearl Pub Hse.

Al-Akili, Muhammad M., tr. see Abdul-Qadir Gilani, Muhyiddeen.

Al-Akili, Muhammad M., tr. see Al-Jawziyya, Ibn A.

Al-Akili, Muhammad M., tr. see Shaikh Muhyiddeen Abdul-Qadir Gilani.

***Al-Ali, Nadje.** Secularism, Gender & the State in the Middle East: The Egyptian Women's Movement. (Cambridge Middle East Studies Ser.). 275p. 2000. write for info. (*0-521-78022-5*); pap. write for info. (*0-521-78504-9*) Cambridge U Pr.

Al-Amin bin Ali al Mazru'i, Shaykh. The History of the Mazru'i Dynasty of Mombasa. Ritchie, J. M., ed. & tr. by. from ARA. LC 96-171054. (Fontes Historiae Africanae, Series Arabica). (Illus.). 268p. 1996. text 75.00 (*0-19-726158-2*) OUP.

Al-Amin, Imam J. Revolution by the Book: The Rap Is Live. 174p. 1996. pap. 12.00 (*0-614-21699-0*, 1078) Kazi Pubns.

Al-Amin, Jamil. Revolution by the Book: The Rap Is Live. LC 93-2726. 174p. 1993. pap. 12.00 (*0-9627854-3-1*) Writers Inc.

Al-Amir, Daisy. The Waiting List. Parmenter, Barbara M., tr. from ARA. (Modern Middle Eastern Literature in Translation Ser.). 100p. (C). 1995. pap. text 8.95 (*0-292-79067-8*, Pub. by Ctr Mid East Stud) U of Tex Pr.

Al-Ammari, Ahmad. Al-Muwajahah Al-Hadariyah: Al-Maghrib Namudhahajan, Vol. 1. LC 96-33945. (Silsilat Al-Rasail Al-Jamiiyah Ser.: No. 20). 1996. write for info. (*1-56564-239-2*) IIIT VA.

— Al-Muwajahah Al-Hadariyah: Al-Maghrib Namudhahajan, Vol. 2. LC 96-33945. (Silsilat Al-Rasail Al-Jamiiyah Ser.: No. 20). 1996. write for info. (*1-56564-240-6*) IIIT VA.

Al-Amriki, Mawlana Y., tr. see Ullah, Qazi T.

Al-'Anani, Hasan. Freedom & Responsibility in Quranic Perspective. Kayani, M. S., tr. 218p. 1990. pap. 12.50 (*0-89259-105-6*) Am Trust Pubns.

Al-Andalusi, Sa'id. Science in the Medieval World: Book of the Categories of Nations. Salem, Sema'an I. & Kumar, Alok, trs. from ARA. (History of Science Ser.). 118p. (C). 1996. pap. 11.95 (*0-292-70469-0*) U of Tex Pr.

Al-Andalusi, Said. Science in the Medieval World: Book of the Categories of Nations. Kumar, Alok, ed. Salem, Sema'an I., tr. 144p. 1996. 29.00 (*0-614-21609-5*, 1112) Kazi Pubns.

Al-Ani, Salman H. Arabic Phonology: An Acoustical & Physiological Investigation. (Janua Linguarum, Ser. Practica: No. 61). 104p. 1970. pap. text 41.55 (*90-279-0727-7*) Mouton.

Al-Ani, Salmon H., compiled by. Fred Walter Householder Bibliography. (Arcadia Bibliographica Virorum Eruditorum Ser.: Fasc. 6). 1984. 18.00 (*0-931922-16-X*) Eurolingua.

Al-Anon Family Group Headquarters, Inc. Staff. Alateen: Hope for Children of Alcoholics. LC 73-82710. 115p. 1973. pap. 5.50 (*0-910034-20-6*) Al-Anon.

— Alateen's Fourth Step Inventory. 48p. 1989. pap. 2.50 (*0-910034-60-5*) Al-Anon.

— As We Understood. LC 85-71379. 269p. 1985. 8.50 (*0-910034-56-7*) Al-Anon.

— Blueprint for Progress. 60p. 1987. pap. 2.50 (*0-910034-59-1*) Al-Anon.

— Courage to Be Me: Living with Alcoholism. LC 96-79465. (Illus.). 326p. (Orig.). (J). 1996. pap. 9.00 (*0-910034-30-3*) Al-Anon.

— Courage to Change: One Day at a Time in Al-Anon II. LC 92-71379. 384p. 1992. 10.00 (*0-910034-79-6*) Al-Anon.

— The Dilemma of the Alcoholic Marriage. LC 70-132133. 100p. 1971. pap. 7.00 (*0-910034-18-4*) Al-Anon.

— Forum Favorites, 4 vols., Vol. 1. LC 82-73095. 423p. 1982. pap. 16.00 (*0-910034-51-6*) Al-Anon.

— Forum Favorites, Vol. IV. LC 91-72776. 144p. 1993. 5.00 (*0-910034-90-7*) Al-Anon.

— From Survival to Recovery: Growing Up in An Alcoholic Home. LC 94-72327. 304p. 1994. 13.00 (*0-910034-97-4*, B-21) Al-Anon.

— Having Had a Spiritual Awakening... LC 98-71773. (Illus.). 180p. 1998. 10.00 (*0-910034-33-8*, B-25 Al-Anon.

— Homeward Bound. 144p. 1993. pap. 2.50 (*0-910034-85-0*) Al-Anon.

— How Al-Anon Works for Families & Friends of Alcoholics. LC 95-75626. 400p. 1995. 11.00 (*0-910034-26-5*, B-22) Al-Anon.

— Living with Sobriety: Another Beginning. 144p. 1993. pap. 2.50 (*0-910034-58-3*) Al-Anon.

— One Day at a Time in Al-Anon. LC 72-85153. 1989. 8.00 (*0-910034-21-4*) Al-Anon.

— One Day at a Time in Al-Anon. large type ed. LC 72-85153. 1989. 10.00 (*0-910034-63-X*) Al-Anon.

— Paths to Recovery: Al-Anon's Steps, Traditions & Concepts. LC 97-70986. 383p. 1997. 15.00 (*0-910034-31-1*) Al-Anon.

— Sexual Intimacy & the Alcoholic Relationship. 144p. 1993. pap. 2.50 (*0-910034-87-7*) Al-Anon.

Al-Arabi. Tarjuman Al-Ashwaq. Nicholson, Reynold, tr. 155p. 1911. pap. 10.95 (*0-7229-5134-5*) Theos Pub Hse.

Al-Arabi, Ibn. The Bezels of Wisdom. Austin, R. W., tr. 302p. 1996. pap. 12.00 (*0-614-21254-5*, 101) Kazi Pubns.

Al-Arabi, Muhyiddin. The Seals of Wisdom. (Sacred Texts Ser.). (Illus.). (Orig.). (C). 1983. pap. 12.75 (*0-88695-010-4*) Concord Grove.

Al-Araby, Abdullah. El Islam al Descubierto.Tr. of Islam Unveiled. (ENG & SPA.). 56p. (Orig.). 1997. pap. 2.50 (*0-9656683-1-2*) Pen vs The Sword.

— Islam Unveiled. 6th rev. ed. 56p. (Orig.). 1987. pap. 2.50 (*0-9656683-0-4*) Pen vs The Sword.

Al-Asfahani, Al-Hafiz A. The Beauty of the Righteous & Ranks of the Elite: Hilyat-ul AwiliyaWa Tabaqat al-Asfiya. Al-Akili, Imam M., ed. & tr. by. LC 92-64267. (ARA.). 450p. (Orig.). 1995. pap. 21.95 (*1-879405-11-3*) Pearl Pub Hse.

Al-Ashqar, Umar S. The World of the Jinn & Devils. Zarabozo, Jamaal A., tr. from ARA.Tr. of A'Lam Jinn Wa Shayateen. 255p. 1998. pap. 11.00 (*1-891540-02-5*) Al-Basheer Co.

Al-Assaf, A. F. & Schmele, June. The Textbook of Total Quality in Healthcare. LC 93-31083. (Illus.). 312p. 1993. boxed set 57.95 (*0-9634030-4-4*) St Lucie Pr.

Al-Ati, Hammudah A. Family Structure in Islam. 209p. 1996. pap. 6.50 (*0-614-21506-4*, 288) Kazi Pubns.

Al-Attas, S. N. Aims & Objectives of Islamic Education. 168p. 1996. 13.50 (*0-614-21533-1*, 17) Kazi Pubns.

Al-Aug, Abdul K., jt. ed. see Taminian, Lucine.

Al-Awadhi, N., et al, eds. Restoration & Rehabilitation of the Desert Environment. LC 96-19949. 306p. 1996. 244.00 (*0-444-82471-5*) Elsevier.

Al-awajl, Ibrahim. Ten Tents of the Tribe: (bilingual) text 40.00 (*1-873395-60-4*) St Martin.

Al-Azami, Muhammad M. On "Schacht's Origins of Muhammadan Jurisprudence" 1996. pap. 24.95 (*0-946621-46-2*, Pub. by Islamic Texts) Intl Spec Bk.

— On "Schacht's Origins of Muhammadan Jurisprudence" LC 84-2270. 500p. 1986. text 26.00 (*0-471-89145-2*) Wiley.

— On "Schacht's Origins of Muhammadan Jurisprudence" 237p. 1995. reprint ed. pap. 14.95 (*0-946621-49-7*, Pub. by Islamic Texts) Intl Spec Bk.

Al-Azmeh, Aziz. Arabic Thought & Islamic Society. 320p. 1986. 59.95 (*0-7099-0584-X*, Pub. by C Helm) Routldge.

— Ibn Khaldun. 186p. 1996. pap. 21.95 (*0-614-21709-1*, 478) Kazi Pubns.

— Ibn Khaldun: An Essay in Reinterpretation. 192p. 1982. 49.50 (*0-7146-3130-2*, BHA-03130, Pub. by F Cass Pubs) Intl Spec Bk.

— Islams & Modernities. (Phronesis Ser.). 160p. (C). 1993. 60.00 (*0-86091-451-8*, B2495, Pub. by Verso) Norton.

Al Azmeh, Aziz. Islams & Modernities. 2nd rev. ed. LC 96-48963. (C). 1996. pap. 19.00 (*1-85984-106-6*) Routledge.

Al-Azmeh, Aziz. Reconstituting Islam. (Occasional Papers Ser.). iii, 28p. 1996. pap. 3.95 (*1-929218-12-5*) Georgetwn U Ctr Muslim.

Al-Azmeh, Aziz, ed. Islamic Law: Social & Historical Contexts. 1986. 52.50 (*0-7099-0588-2*, Pub. by C Helm) Routldge.

— Islamic Law: Social & Historical Contexts. 224p. (C). 1988. lib. bdg. 52.50 (*0-415-00477-2*) Routledge.

***Al-Azzawi, F.** Hormone Replacement Therapy & the Endometrium. (Illus.). 200p. 2001. 58.00 (*1-85070-092-3*) Prthnon Pub.

Al-Badani, Mostafa, tr. see Al-Haddad, Imam A.

Al-Badawi, Mostafa, tr. see Ibn Alawi, Imam Abdallah.

Al Baharna, H. M. British Extra-Territorial Jurisdiction in the Gulf, 1913-1971. 350p. 1998. lib. bdg. 90.00 (*1-85207-840-5*) N Ross.

Al-Banna, Shaheed H. What Is Our Message? 46p. (Orig.). 1985. pap. 3.00 (*1-56744-416-4*) Kazi Pubns.

***Al-Barazi, Tammam & Wines, Leslie.** Rumi: A Spiritual Biography. (Lives & Legacies Ser.). 2001. 19.95 (*0-8245-2352-0*) Crossroad NY.

Al-Barzinji, Suhaib J. Working Principles for an Islamic Model in Mass Media Communication. LC 97-46723. (Academic Dissertations Ser.). 1998. 8.00 (*1-56564-264-3*) IIIT VA.

Al-Basha, Abdur R. Portraits: Lives of the Companions of Prophet Muhammad (Peace Be Upon Him) Al-Osh, Alexandra S., tr. LC 93-18486.Tr. of Suwar Min Hayat Al-Sahabah. 1993. write for info. (*1-56923-003-X*) Inst Islamic.

— Portraits: Lives of the Companions of Prophet Muhammad (Peace Be Upon Him), 1. Al-Osh, Alexandra S., tr. LC 93-18486.Tr. of Suwar Min Hayat Al-Sahabah. 1993. write for info. (*1-56923-000-5*) Inst Islamic.

Al-Batal, Mahmoud, ed. Al Arabiyya No. 2: AATA Monographs in Arabic Studies. (C). pap. text 35.00 (*0-9621530-1-X*) AM Assn Teach.

Al-Batal, Mahmoud, et al. Al-Kitaab: A Textbook for Beginning Arabic. LC 95-6982. Orig. Title: Textbook for Beginning Arabic. 480p. 1995. pap. 35.00 (*0-87840-291-8*) Georgetown U Pr.

— Alif Baa: Introduction to Arabic Letters & Sounds. LC 95-6981. Orig. Title: Introduction to Arabic Letters & Sounds. 224p. 1995. pap. text 20.00 (*0-87840-292-6*) Georgetown U Pr.

— The Teaching of Arabic As a Foreign Language: Issues & Directions. LC 95-22101. (Al-Arabiyya Monograph Ser.: No. 2). 359p. 1995. 30.00 (*0-9621530-9-5*) AM Assn Teach.

Al-Bayati, Abdul W. Love, Death & Exile: Poems Translated from Arabic. Frangieh, Bassam K., tr. from ARA. LC 90-20394. 314p. (Orig.). (C). 1991. pap. 14.95 (*0-87840-218-7*) Georgetown U Pr.

Al-Bayati, Basil. The City & the Mosque. (Illus.). 70p. 1998. text 25.00 (*0-7881-5473-7*) DIANE Pub.

— Community & Unity. (Academy Architecture Ser.). (Illus.). 144p. 1983. 35.00 (*0-312-15298-1*) St Martin.

Al-Biruni. Alberuni's India: An Account of the Religion, Philosophy, Literature, Geography, Chronology, Astronomy , Customs, Laws & Astrology of India about AD 1030, 2 vols. in l. Sachau, Edward C., tr. reprint ed. text 54.00 (*81-215-0562-3*) Coronet Bks.

— The Chronology of Ancient Nations. Sachau, Edward C., ed. xvi, 464p. reprint ed. lib. bdg. 90.00 (*0-89241-178-3*) Caratzas.

Al-Biruni. India. 3rd ed. Ahmad, ed. 1995. reprint ed. 6.00 (*81-237-0289-2*, Pub. by Natl Bk Trust) S Asia.

Al-Bitar, Bashshar, jt. auth. see Al-Subayi, Adnan.

Al-Bukhari, Sahih. Sahih Al-Bukhari: The Early Years of Islam. Asad, Muhammad, tr. from ARA. 306p. 1938. reprint ed. 33.00 (*0-939660-05-9*, Pub. by Dar Al-Andalus) Threshold CA.

Al-Buraey, Muhammad, jt. auth. see Muhammad Abdullah.

Al-Bustani, Abdullah. Arabic Dictionary: Al Wafi. (ARA.). 728p. 1991. 45.00 (*0-86685-095-3*, LDL0953, Pub. by Librairie du Liban) Intl Bk Ctr.

Al-Chalabi, Fadhil J. OPEC at the Crossroads. (Illus.). 252p. 1989. 92.00 (*0-08-037526-X*, Pergamon Pr) Elsevier.

An Asterisk (*) at the beginning of an entry indicates that the title is appearing for the first time.

A

Rd., Boxford, MA 01921. Toll-free 877-887-2828. Fax 978-887-3960. E-mail: IElissaAmal;@aol.com, website: http://AngelwiththeGoldenGlow.com, add $5 for single copy shipping, credit cards accepted. ***Publisher Paid Annotation.***

Al, Curtis Et. Inventions to Biology. 5th ed. 1994. 59.60 (*0-87901-787-2*) St Martin.

Al-Dahir, H. Abdul. Muhammad: A Prophecy Fulfilled. 111p. 1996. pap. 8.00 (*0-614-21674-5*, 807) Kazi Pubns.

***Al-Daif, Rashid.** Dear Mr. Kawabata. 176p. 2000. pap. 12.95 (*0-7043-8113-3*, Pub. by Quartet) Interlink Pub.

— This Side of Innocence. Haydar, Paula, tr. 2000. pap. 12.95 (*1-56656-383-6*) Interlink Pub.

Al-Deen, Hana S. Noor, see Noor Al-Deen, Hana S.

***Al-Dekhayel, Abdulkarim.** Kuwait: Oil, State & Political Legitmation. 252p. 2000. 62.00 (*0-86372-250-4*, Pub. by Garnet-Ithaca) LPC InBook.

Al-Diftar, Sheikh I. Hajj. 72p. 1991. pap. text 3.00 (*1-881504-03-4*) Minaret Pubns.

Al-Dimashqi, Ibn 'Asakir. A Biography of Jesus by Ibn 'Asakir of Damascus (1105-1176) Ali Mourad, Suleiman, ed. 386p. 1996. pap. 40.00 (*0-88206-207-7*) Caravan Bks.

Al-Din, Minhaj. General History of Muhammadan Dynasties of Asia from 810 to 1260 AD, 2 vols., Set. Raverty, H. C., tr. from PER. reprint ed. text 77.50 (*0-685-13415-6*) Coronet Bks.

Al-Din Tusi, Nasir. Contemplation & Action. Badakhchani, Seyyed H., tr. & intro. by. 160p. 1998. text 59.50 (*1-85043-908-7*) St Martin.

Al-Doory, Y. & DiSalvo, A. F. Blastomycosis. (Current Topics in Infectious Disease Ser.). (Illus.). 288p. (C). 1991. text 75.00 (*0-306-43958-1*, Kluwer Plenum) Kluwer Academic.

Al-Doory, Yousef. Laboratory Medical Mycology. LC 79-22500. 420p. reprint ed. pap. 130.20 (*0-7837-1478-5*, 205717300023) Bks Demand.

Al-Doory, Yousef & Domson, Joanne F., eds. Mould Allergy. LC 83-14951. (Illus.). 299p. reprint ed. pap. 92.70 (*0-8357-7639-5*, 205696200096) Bks Demand.

Al-Ebraheem, Hassan A. Kuwait & the Gulf: Small States & the International System. 113p. (Orig.). 1984. pap. text 6.95 (*0-932568-08-4*) GU Ctr CAS.

Al-Ekabi, Hussain, jt. ed. see Ollis, David F.

Al-Eyd, Kadhim A. Oil Revenues, Absorptive Capacity & Prospects for Accelerated Growth. LC 79-18596. 188p. 1979. 62.95 (*0-275-90328-1*, C0328, Praeger Pubs) Greenwood.

Al-Fahim, Mohammed. From Rags to Riches: A Story of Abu Dhabi. 1998. text 39.50 (*1-86064-233-0*, Pub. by I B T) St Martin.

Al-Fallouji, M. A. R. Postgraduate Surgery: The Candidate's Guide. 2nd ed. LC 97-22534. 688p. 1998. pap. text 155.00 (*0-7506-1591-5*) Buttrwrth-Heinemann.

Al-Farabi. Short Commentary on Aristotle's Prior Analytics. Rescher, Nicholas, tr. LC 63-10581. 132p. reprint ed. pap. 41.00 (*0-608-10175-3*, 201048700068) Bks Demand.

Al-Farabi, Abu N. On the Perfect State. 500p. (C). 1997. 59.95 (*1-871031-71-0*) Kazi Pubns.

Al Fara'id, jt. auth. see Samarra'i, Ibrahim A.

Al-Faraj, Sami, et al. Common Ground on Iraq-Kuwait Reconciliation. Thompson, Brent, ed. LC 97-80818. 125p. 1998. 12.95 (*0-9647474-1-3*) Srch Common Grd.

Al-Faris, Abdul-Razak F. OPEC & the Market: A Study of Oil Price Rigidity, Determination, & Differentials. LC 93-81258. (Illus.). 156p. 1994. 26.00 (*0-918714-41-9*) Intl Res Ctr Energy.

Al-Farsy, Fouad. Modernity & Tradition: The Saudi Equation. (Illus.). 360p. 1990. 77.00 (*0-7103-0395-5*, A5214) Routledge.

— Saudi Arabia: A Case Study in Development. 300p. (Orig.). 1986. 59.50 (*0-7103-0128-6*, 01286) Routledge.

Al Farugi, I. R. Towards Islamic Arabic. 64p. (Orig.). 1986. pap. 5.00 (*0-317-52453-4*) New Era Publns MI.

— Trialogue of Abrahamic Faiths. 88p. (Orig.). 1986. pap. 7.50 (*0-317-52454-2*) New Era Publns MI.

Al-Faruqi, Ismail R. The Cultural Atlas of Islam. 512p. 1996. 89.00 (*0-614-21622-2*, 186) Kazi Pubns.

— Islam. LC 94-45213. (Illus.). 82p. 1994. pap. 6.95 (*0-915957-21-3*) amana pubns.

Al-Faruqi, Isma'il R. Islamic Da'wah: Its Nature & Demands. 19p. (Orig.). pap. 3.00 (*0-89259-064-5*) Am Trust Pubns.

Al-Faruqi, Ismail R., ed. Trialogue of the Abrahamic Faiths: Papers Presented to the Islamic Studies Group of American Academy of Religion. 4th ed. LC 95-5120. (Issues of Islamic Thought Ser.: No. 1). 1995. 7.50 (*0-915957-25-6*) amana pubns.

Al-Faruqi, Ismail R. & Al-Faruqi, Lois L. The Cultural Atlas of Islam. 115.00 (*0-685-66743-X*) Tahrike Tarsile Quran.

Al-Faruqi, Llamya. Woman, Muslim Society, & Islam. American Trust Publications, ed. LC 87-51271. 160p. 1987. pap. 1.50 (*0-89259-068-8*) Am Trust Pubns.

Al Faruqi, Lois L., ed. An Annotated Glossary of Arabic Musical Terms. LC 81-4129. (ARA & ENG.). 511p. 1981. lib. bdg. 125.00 (*0-313-20554-X*, AFM/, Greenwood Pr) Greenwood.

Al-Faruqi, Lois L., jt. auth. see Al-Faruqi, Ismail R.

Al-Fattah. Muslim Brothers & the Palestine Question, 1928-1947. (Modern Middle East Studies). 256p. 1998. text 59.50 (*1-86064-214-4*, Pub. by I B T) St Martin.

Al-Fayyumi, Nathanael Ibn, see Ibn Al-Fayyumi, Nathanael.A

al Funisi, khayr. Surest Path: The Political Treatise of a Nineteenth-Century Muslim Statesman. Brown, Leon C., tr. LC 67-25399. (Middle Eastern Monographs: No. 16). 190p. 1990. 5.00 (*0-674-85695-3*) HUP.

Al-Furqan Islamic Heritage Foundation (London, England). The Codicology of Islamic Manuscripts: Proceedings of the 2nd Conference of Al-Furqean Islamic Heritage Foundation, 4-5 December, 1993. Dutton, Yasin, ed. LC 96-153810. (ENG & ARA.). x, 145p. 1995. write for info. (*1-873992-15-7*) Al-Furqan Islamic.

Al-Furqan Islamic Heritage Foundation (London, England), et al. The Conservation & Preservation of Islamic Manuscripts: Proceedings of the Third Conference of Al-Furqean Islamic Heritage Foundation : 18th-19th November 1995) Ibish, Yusuf & Atiyeh, George Nicholas, eds. LC 96-969675. xiv, 212 p. 1996. write for info. (*1-873992-19-X*) Al-Furqan Islamic.

Al-Gailani, Lamia W. Studies in the Chronology & Regional Style of Old Babylonian Cylinder Seals. (Bibliotheca Mesopotamica Ser.: Vol. 23). x, 154p. 1988. pap. 21.00 (*0-89003-172-X*) Undena Pubns.

— Studies in the Chronology & Regional Style of Old Babylonian Cylinder Seals. (Bibliotheca Mesopotamica Ser.: Vol. 23). (Illus.). x, 154p. 1988. 29.00 (*0-89003-173-8*) Undena Pubns.

Al-Gallaf, Yousif. Compute Arabia. 2nd ed. 1990. pap. write for info. (*0-318-63376-0*) Meghan-Kiffer.

Al-Ghanem, Salwa. The Reign of Mubarak-Al-Sabah: Sheikh of Kuwait, 1896-1915. 272p. 1998. 59.50 (*1-86064-350-7*, Pub. by I B T) St Martin.

Al-Ghazali. Abstinence in Islam. Farah, Caesar E., tr. (Islamic Studies: No. 1). 1992. 25.00 (*0-88297-049-6*) Bibliotheca.

***Al-Ghazali.** Al-Ghazali's Deliverance from Error & Other Works: Al-Munqidh min al-Dalal. 2nd rev. ed. McCarthy, R. J., tr. LC 99-68059. Orig. Title: Freedom & Fulfillment. 333p. 2000. pap. 29.95 (*1-887752-27-7*, Pub. by Fons Vitae) Words Distrib.

Al-Ghazali. Disciplining the Soul, Vol. 1. Winter, T. J., ed. & tr. by. from ARA. (Al-Ghazali Ser.). 136p. 1995. 59.95 (*0-946621-42-X*, Pub. by Islamic Texts); pap. 24.95 (*0-946621-43-8*, Pub. by Islamic Texts) Intl Spec Bk.

— Inner Dimensions of Islamic Worship. Holland, Muhtar, tr. from ARA. 142p. (Orig.). 1983. pap. 6.95 (*0-86037-125-5*, Pub. by Islamic Fnd) New Era Publns MI.

— Invocation & Supplications. rev. ed. Winter, T. J., ed. Nakamura, Kojito, tr. from ARA. & pref. by. (Al-Ghazali Ser.). 138p. 1995. 44.95 (*0-946621-12-8*, Pub. by Islamic Texts); pap. 19.95 (*0-946621-14-4*, Pub. by Islamic Texts) Intl Spec Bk.

— Muslim Character. 220p. 1988. pap. 6.50 (*1-56744-154-8*) Kazi Pubns.

— The Ninety-Nine Beautiful Names of God. Burrell, David B. et al, trs. from ARA. (Al-Ghazali Ser.). 138p. 1995. reprint ed. 52.95 (*0-946621-30-6*, Pub. by Islamic Texts); reprint ed. pap. 21.95 (*0-946621-31-4*, Pub. by Islamic Texts) Intl Spec Bk.

— On the Duties of Brotherhood. 1991. 8.95 (*1-56744-173-4*) Kazi Pubns.

— On the Duties of Brotherhood in Islam. Holland, Muhtar, tr. from ARA. 95p. (Orig.). 1980. pap. 4.95 (*0-86037-068-2*, Pub. by Islamic Fnd) New Era Publns MI.

— The Remembrance of Death & the Afterlife. Winter, T. J., ed. & tr. by. from ARA. (Al-Ghazali Ser.). 138p. 1995. reprint ed. 59.95 (*0-946621-09-8*, Pub. by Islamic Texts); reprint ed. pap. 24.95 (*0-946621-13-6*, Pub. by Islamic Texts) Intl Spec Bk.

Al-Ghazali, Imam. The Proper Conduct of Marriage in Islam (Adab An-Nikah) Book 12 of Ihya Ulumud-Din, Vol. 1. Holland, Muhtar, tr. from ARA. LC 98-84302. 120p. 1998. pap. 16.00 (*1-882216-14-8*) Al-Baz Pub.

Al-Ghazali, M. Muslim's Character. 240p. pap. write for info. (*1-882837-23-1*) W A M Y Intl.

Al-Ghazali, Muhammad. Al-Ghazali on Disciplining the Soul & on Breaking the Two Desires. Winter, T. J., tr. 1996. pap. 24.95 (*0-614-21247-2*, 20); pap. 24.95 (*0-614-21540-4*, 20) Kazi Pubns.

— The Alchemy of Happiness. Field, Claud, tr. 136p. 1996. pap. 4.00 (*0-614-21248-0*, 27) Kazi Pubns.

— Confessions of al-Ghazali. Field, Claude, tr. 70p. (Orig.). 1987. pap. 4.95 (*1-56744-256-0*) Kazi Pubns.

— Duties of Brotherhood in Islam. 95p. 1996. pap. 7.50 (*0-614-21266-9*, 218) Kazi Pubns.

— Faith & Practice of Al-Ghazali. Watt, William M., tr. 155p. 1996. pap. 8.50 (*0-614-21275-8*, 281); pap. 7.50 (*0-614-21409-2*, 281) Kazi Pubns.

— Inner Dimensions of Islamic Worship. Holland, Muhtar, tr. 145p. 1996. pap. 10.50 (*0-614-21291-X*, 502) Kazi Pubns.

— Invocations & Supplications. Nakamura, Kajito, tr. 132p. 1996. pap. 18.95 (*0-614-21461-0*, 521) Kazi Pubns.

— Letters of al-Ghazali. Qayyum, Abdul, tr. 150p. (Orig.). 1986. pap. 4.50 (*1-56744-322-2*) Kazi Pubns.

— The Mysteries of Almsgiving. Faris, N. A., tr. 1994. pap. 4.95 (*1-56744-163-7*) Kazi Pubns.

— Mysteries of the Human Soul. Abdul Qayyum Hazarvi, tr. 64p. (Orig.). 1985. pap. 7.50 (*1-56744-343-5*) Kazi Pubns.

— The Ninety-Nine Beautiful Names of God. Burrell, David B., tr. 205p. 1996. pap. 30.75 (*0-614-21186-7*, 895) Kazi Pubns.

— Remembrance & Prayer: The Way of the Prophet Muhammad. De Lorenzo, Yusuf T., tr. 232p. 1996. pap. 14.95 (*0-614-21331-2*, 1072) Kazi Pubns.

— The Remembrance of Death & the Afterlife. Winter, T. J., tr. 350p. 1996. pap. 21.95 (*0-614-21189-1*, 1073) Kazi Pubns.

Al-Ghazzali. Just Balance. 1986. pap. 6.50 (*1-56744-113-0*) Kazi Pubns.

— The Mysteries of Almsgiving. Faris, Nabik A., tr. 1966. 19.95 (*0-8156-6002-2*, Pub. by Am U Beirut) Syracuse U Pr.

Al-Ghazzali, Abu Hamid Muhammad. The Alchemy of Happiness. annot. rev. ed. Daniel, Elton L., ed. Field, Claud, tr. from PER. LC 91-9523. (Sources & Studies in World History). 160p. (C). (gr. 13). 1991. text 58.95 (*1-56324-004-1*); pap. text 27.95 (*1-56324-005-X*) M E Sharpe.

Al-Ghunaymi al-Maydani, Abd-al-Ghani. Sharh al-'Aqidah al-Tahawiyah al-Mussamat "Bayan al-Sunnah wa-al-Jama'ah" (ARA.). 160p. (Orig.). 1995. pap. 3.95 (*1-57547-228-7*) Dar Al-Fikr.

Al-Gita, Kashif, ed. The Shia Origin & Faith. Haq, M. Fazal, tr. from ARA. 284p. 1984. pap. 3.00 (*0-941724-23-9*) Islamic Seminary.

Al-Gwaiz, M. A. Theory of Distributions. (Pure & Applied Mathematics Ser.: Vol. 159). (Illus.). 272p. 1992. text 160.00 (*0-8247-8672-6*) Dekker.

***Al-Haaza, Nasser.** The Creation: The Odyssey of the Pharaohs. 176p. 2000. pap. 15.00 (*0-8059-4792-2*) Dorrance.

Al-Haddad, Habib A. Key to the Garden. 154p. 1996. pap. 12.95 (*0-614-21299-5*, 1647); pap. 12.95 (*0-614-21438-6*, 1647) Kazi Pubns.

Al-Haddad, Imam A. The Book of Assistance. 142p. 1996. pap. 10.95 (*0-614-21255-3*, 109) Kazi Pubns.

— Gifts for the Seeker. 76p. 1996. 12.95 (*0-614-21279-0*, 335) Kazi Pubns.

— The Lives of Man. 98p. 1996. pap. 9.95 (*0-614-21182-4*, 728) Kazi Pubns.

— The Lives of Man: A Guide to the Human States: Before Life, in the World, & after Death. Murad, Abdal-Hakim, ed. Al-Badani, Mostafa, tr. 97p. 1998. pap. 11.95 (*1-887752-14-5*) Fons Vitae.

Al-Haj, Majid. Education, Empowerment, & Control: The Case of the Arabs in Israel. LC 93-48104. (SUNY Series in Israeli Studies). 249p. (C). 1995. text 57.50 (*0-7914-2201-1*); pap. text 18.95 (*0-7914-2202-X*) State U NY Pr.

Al-Haj, Muhammed U. The Muslim Law of Inheritance. 225p. 1986. 19.95 (*0-318-37194-4*) Asia Bk Corp.

Al-Haj Yahya, Tawfiq. Al-Tibb al-Badil (Al-Tibb al-Tabi'i) 256p. Date not set. pap. 5.95 (*1-57547-216-3*) Dar Al-Fikr.

Al-Hakim, Tawfiq. Fate of a Cockroach & Other Plays. Johnson-Davies, Denys, tr. from ARA. 184p. 1980. reprint ed. pap. 12.95 (*0-89410-197-8*, Three Contnts) L Rienner.

— In the Tavern of Life & Other Stories. Hutchins, William M., ed. & tr. by. LC 95-19994. 232p. 1998. pap. 18.95 (*0-89410-649-X*, Three Contnts); lib. bdg. 40.00 (*0-89410-648-1*, Three Contnts) L Rienner.

— Plays, Prefaces & Postscripts of Tawfiq al-Hakim Vol. 1: Theater of the Mind. Hutchins, William M., tr. & intro. by. LC 80-80887. 301p. 1981. 15.00 (*0-89410-148-X*, Three Contnts); pap. 8.95 (*0-89410-134-X*, Three Contnts) L Rienner.

— Plays, Prefaces & Postscripts of Tawfiq al-Hakim Vol. 2: Theater of Society. Hutchins, William M., tr. & intro. by. LC 80-80887. 350p. 1984. 15.00 (*0-89410-280-X*, Three Contnts) L Rienner.

— The Prison of Life: An Autobiography. Cachia, Pierre A., tr. from ARA. 160p. 1993. pap. 22.50 (*977-424-279-3*, Pub. by Am Univ Cairo Pr) Col U Pr.

— The Return of the Spirit. Hutchins, William M., tr. from ARA. 288p. (Orig.). 1990. reprint ed. 35.00 (*0-89410-425-X*, Three Contnts); reprint ed. pap. 15.00 (*0-89410-426-8*, Three Contnts) L Rienner.

Al-Hakim, Tawfiq & Eban, A. S. Maze of Justice: Diary of a Country Prosecutor. 160p. 1989. text 25.00 (*0-292-75112-5*) U of Tex Pr.

Al-Halveti, Shaykh T., tr. see Gilani, Shaykh A.

Al-Halveti, Shaykh T., tr. see Yahyaal-Suhrawardi, Hazrat S. & Bayrak, Tosun.

Al-Halveti, Sheikh T. The Most Beautiful Names. 100p. 1996. pap. 13.00 (*0-614-21184-0*, 805); pap. 13.00 (*0-614-21315-0*, 805) Kazi Pubns.

Al Hamid, Muhsin Abd, see Abd al Hamid, Muhsin.

Al Haqq, Jad A., jt. auth. see Mu'asir, Nadwat I.

Al-Hariri, Mokhless. Washington Sentinels. 224p. 1992. 43.00 (*0-9624483-3-8*) GDG Pubns.

— Washington Sentinels. limited ed. 224p. 1992. 75.50 (*0-9624483-2-X*) GDG Pubns.

Al-Hariri-Rifai, Mokhless, jt. auth. see Al-Hariri-Rifai, Wahbi.

Al-Hariri-Rifai, Wahbi & Al-Hariri-Rifai, Mokhless. The Heritage of the Kingdom of Saudi Arabia. (Illus.). 1989. write for info. (*0-9624483-0-3*) GDG Pubns.

Al-Harizi, Judah. The Book of Tahkemoni, 2 vols. Segal, David, tr. from HEB. & intro. by. (Littman Library of Jewish Civilization). 528p. 2001. 87.50 (*1-874774-03-X*) Intl Spec Bk.

Al-Harkan, Saud. To Where the Birds Migrate. 250p. (Orig.). 1994. pap. 5.99 (*0-9642938-3-8*) Ravenala Pubns.

— Water & Clay. 136p. 1994. 39.95 (*0-9642938-1-1*) Ravenala Pubns.

Al-Hasan, Saiyid Zafar, see Zafar al-Hasan, Saiyid.

Al-Hasan, Shaybani M. The Islamic Law of Nations: Shaybani's Siyar. Khadduri, Majid, tr. & intro. by. LC 66-14377. 331p. 1966. reprint ed. pap. 102.70 (*0-608-04053-3*, 206478900011) Bks Demand.

Al-Hashimi, Bashir. The Art of PSpice: Analogue & Digital Circuit Simulation. LC 94-26861. (Illus.). 272p. 1995. boxed set 79.95 (*0-8493-7895-8*) CRC Pr.

Al-Hassan, Ahmad Y. Islamic Technology: An Illustrated History. 304p. 1996. pap. 28.95 (*0-614-21603-6*, 657) Kazi Pubns.

Al-Hassan, Ahmad Y. & Hill, Donald. Islamic Technology: An Illustrated History. (Illus.). 320p. (C). 1992. pap. text 29.95 (*0-521-42239-6*) Cambridge U Pr.

Al-Hassan, Bello S. Reduplication in the Chadic Languages: A Study of Form & Function. LC 97-43633. (European University Studies, Series 21: Vol. 191). XX, 249p. (C). 1997. pap. text 48.95 (*0-8204-3518-X*) P Lang Pubng.

Al-Hassani, Bakir. Language of the Qur'an. 1990. 20.00 (*0-685-66738-3*, 43) Tahrike Tarsile Quran.

— Language of the Quran: A Concise Text of Arabic Grammar with Ample Applications from the Quran & the Hadith. 120p. 1996. pap. 12.95 (*0-614-21058-5*, 1377) Kazi Pubns.

Al-Hatimy, Said A. Woman in Islam: A Comparative Study. 160p. 1996. pap. 5.95 (*0-614-21397-5*, 1579) Kazi Pubns.

Al-Hibri, Azizah, ed. Hypatia, Issue No. 2. 100p. 1985. pap. 19.25 (*0-08-031851-7*, Pergamon Pr) Elsevier.

Al-Hibri, Azizah & Simons, Margaret A., eds. Hypatia Reborn: Essays in Feminist Philosophy. LC 89-46334. (Illus.). 360p. 1990. 42.00 (*0-253-32744-X*); pap. text 7.50 (*0-253-20585-9*, MB 585) Ind U Pr.

Al-Hibshi, Abdullah M., ed. City of Divine & Earthly Joys: The Description of San'a. Mackintosh-Smith, Tim, tr. from ARA.Tr. of Sayyid Jamal Al-Din Ali Ibn Abdullah Ibn Al-Qasim Ibn Al-Mu'ayyad Bi'llah Muhammad Ibn Al-Qasim Ibn Muhammad Al-Shahari. Date not set. write for info. (*1-882557-07-7*) Am Inst Yemeni.

Al-Himyari, Ibn. Al-Rawd al-Mi'tar FiKhabar al-Aqtar. (ARA.). 1975. 40.00 (*0-86685-358-8*) Intl Bk Ctr.

Al-Hiyari, Mustafa. Jerusalem under the Fatimids & the Crusaders. 208p. 1994. pap. 15.00 (*0-88206-208-5*) Caravan Bks.

Al, Huang C. L. Thinking Body, Dancing Mind: Taosports for Extraordinary Performance in Athletics. 336p. 1994. pap. 14.95 (*0-553-37378-1*) Bantam.

Al-Huda, Bint. Prosperous Ending. Talebian, Fatemeh, tr. 156p. (J). 1997. pap. 12.95 (*1-871031-72-9*) Kazi Pubns.

Al-Hujwiri. The Kashf Al-Mahjub "The Revelation of the Veiled" An Early Persian Treatise on Sufism. Nicholson, Reynold A., tr. from PER. (Gibb Memorial Ser.: Vol. 17). 464p. reprint ed. pap. 28.00 (*0-7189-0203-3*, Pub. by Aris & Phillips) David Brown.

Al-Husayn, Ibn & Al-Sulami. The Way of Sufi Chivalry. 122p. 1996. pap. 10.95 (*0-614-21379-7*, 1293); pap. 10.95 (*0-614-21563-3*, 1293) Kazi Pubns.

Al-Husry, Khaldun S. Origins of Modern Arab Political Thought. LC 80-11794. 184p. 1980. reprint ed. 25.00 (*0-88206-037-6*) Caravan Bks.

***Al-I'Keem-Onaiwu.** Connection Between Sexuality & Spirituality. 162p. 1999. pap. write for info. (*0-7541-0866-X*, Pub. by Minerva Pr) Unity Dist.

Al-Ilah al-Nabhan, Abd & Bin Mukhtar Tulaymat, Ghazi. Al Lubab fi 'Ilal al-bina' wa-al-I'rab li-Abi al-Baqa' Abdillah ibn al-Husayn al-'Ukburi, 2 vols., Set. 1200p. 1994. 35.95 (*1-57547-200-7*) Dar Al-Fikr.

— Al Lubab fi 'Ilal al-bina' wa-al-I'rab li-Abi al-Baqa' Abdillah ibn al-Husayn al-'Ukburi, Vol. 1. 1994. write for info. (*1-57547-201-5*) Dar Al-Fikr.

— Al Lubab fi 'Ilal al-bina' wa-al-I'rab li-Abi al-Baqa' Abdillah ibn al-Husayn al-'Ukburi, Vol. 2. 1994. write for info. (*1-57547-202-3*) Dar Al-Fikr.

Al-Iraqi, Ahmad. The Book of Knowledge Acquired Concerning the Cultivation of Gold, Kitab Al-'Ilm Al-Muktasab Fi Zira'at' Adh-Dhahab, the Arabic Text Edited with English Translation & Critical Notes. Holmyard, E. J., ed. 1986. text 95.00 (*0-935548-09-2*) Codex Pr.

Al-Ishsh, Yusuf. Al-Dawlah al-Umawiyah wa-al-Ahdath Allati Sabaqat/ha wa-Mahhadat Laha Ibtida'an min Fitnat 'Uthman. (ARA.). 376p. (Orig.). 1995. pap. 7.95 (*1-57547-230-9*) Dar Al-Fikr.

Al-Iskandari, Ibn A. The Key to Salvation. Danner, Mary A., tr. 1996. pap. 21.95 (*0-614-21298-7*, 688) Kazi Pubns.

— The Key to Salvation: A Sufi Manual of Invocation. Koury-Danner, Mary, tr. from ARA. & intro. by. LC 94-145373. (Golden Palm Ser.). (Orig.). 1995. 39.95 (*0-946621-26-8*, Pub. by Islamic Texts) Intl Spec Bk.

Al-Issa, Ihsan, ed. Handbook of Culture & Mental Illness: An International Perspective. 391p. 1995. 57.50 (*0-8236-2288-6*) Intl Univs Pr.

Al-Issa, Ihsan & Tousignant, Michel, eds. Ethnicity Immigration & Psychopathology. LC 97-14149. (Series on Stress & Coping). 316p. (C). 1997. 49.50 (*0-306-45479-3*, Plenum Trade) Perseus Pubng.

Al-Jaar, Robert Y. & Desrochers, Alan A. Applications of Petri Nets in Manufacturing Systems: Modeling, Control, & Performance Analysis. LC 94-4198. 348p. 1994. 89.95 (*0-87942-295-5*, PC02907) Inst Electrical.

Al-Jabarti, Abal R. Napoleon in Egypt: A Chronicle of the French Occupation, 1788. Moreh, S., tr. from ARA. (Illus.). 196p. (C). 1993. text 39.95 (*1-55876-069-5*); pap. text 16.95 (*1-55876-070-9*) Wiener Pubs Inc.

Al Jadir, Saad M. Kunuz. 352p. 275.00 (*9981-871-06-0*, Pub. by LAK Intl) Antique Collect.

Al-Jafari, Fatima S. Digest of Muslim Names: Beautiful Muslim Names & Their Meaning. LC 97-19308. (ARA.). 1997. write for info. (*0-915957-68-X*) Amana Corp.

***al-Jahiz.** The Book of Misers: Al-Bukhala. Serjeant, R. B., tr. 288p. 2000. pap. 25.00 (*1-85964-141-5*) Garnet Publishing Co.

al-Jahiz. Epistle on Singing Girls Vol. 2: Approaches to Arabic Literature. Beeston, ed. 1980. 59.95 (*0-85668-165-2*, Pub. by Aris & Phillips); pap. 22.00 (*0-85668-181-4*, Pub. by Aris & Phillips) David Brown.

***Al-Jahiz, Abu Uthman Amir Ibn Bahir.** Sobriety & Mirth: A Selection of the Shorter Writings of al-Jahiz. Colville, Jim, tr. 320p. 2001. text 110.00 (*0-7103-0697-0*) Col U Pr.

Al-Jamal, Mahmoud, tr. see Muhammad al-Jamal, Shaykh.

An Asterisk (*) at the beginning of an entry indicates that the title is appearing for the first time.

Al-Jamal, Samer, photos by. Lebanon: A Journey of Beauty. (Illus.). 188p. 1994. 49.95 (*0-9642784-0-5*) Cedar Creative.

al-Jamal, Shaykh Muhammad, see Muhammad al-Jamal, Shaykh.

Al-Jarrahi, Abdussamad, ed. see Badawi, Jamal A.

Al-Jarrahi, Abdussamad, tr. see Boisard, Marcel A.

Al-Jassar, A., jt. auth. see Alawi, H.

Al-Jassim, M. & Gee, J. M., eds. NCPV Photovoltaics Program Review: Proceedings of the 15th Conference. LC 99-60143. (Conference Proceedings Ser.: Vol. 462). 850p. 1999. (*1-56396-836-3*) Am Inst Physics.

Al-Jawziyya, Ibn A. Natural Healing with Tibb Medicine: Medicine of the Prophet. Al-Akili, Muhammad M., tr. LC 92-85137. 384p. (Orig.). (C). 1994. pap. 16.95 (*1-879405-07-5*) Pearl Pub Hse.

al-Jawziyya, Ibn Qayyim, see Qayyim al-Jawziyya, Ibn.

Al-Jazri, Allamah M. A Comprehensive Collection of Short Prayers: Al-Hisnul Hasin. 302p. (Orig.). 1995. text 14.95 (*1-56744-504-7*) Kazi Pubns.

Al-Jazzar, Ibn. Ibn Al-Jazzar on Sexual Diseases & Their Treatment Bk. 6: A Critical Edition of Zad Al-Musafir Wa-Gut Al-Hadir: Provisions for the Traveller & Nourishment for the Sedentary. LC 96-36415. (Sir Henry Wellcome Asian Ser.). 417p. 1997. 127.50 (*0-7103-0569-9*, Pub. by Kegan Paul Intl) Col U Pr.

Al-Jerrahi, Lex H. Atom from the Sun of Knowledge. 390p. 1996. pap. 19.95 (*0-614-21252-9*, 81) Kazi Pubns.

Al-Jerrahi, Muzaffer O. Adornment of Hearts. Rogers, Louis, ed. Holland, Muhtar & Freidrich, Sixtina, trs. from TUR. 145p. (Orig.). 1992. pap. 9.95 (*1-879708-01-9*) Pir Pubns.

— Ashki's Divan. Rogers, Louis, ed. Holland, Muhtar & Friedrich, Sixtina, trs. from TUR. 140p. (Orig.). 1992. pap. 9.95 (*1-879708-02-7*) Pir Pubns.

— Blessed Virgin Mary. Rogers, Louis, ed. Holland, Muhtar, tr. from TUR. 81p. (Orig.). 1992. pap. 9.95 (*1-879708-04-3*) Pir Pubns.

— The Garden of Dervishes. Roers, Louis, ed. Holland, Muhtar, tr. from TUR. 86p. (Orig.). 1992. pap. 9.95 (*1-879708-03-5*) Pir Pubns.

— Irshad: Wisdom of a Sufi Master. Holland, Muhtar, tr. from TUR. 725p. 1991. 29.95 (*1-879708-00-0*) Pir Pubns.

***Al-Jibaly, Muhummad.** The Beard - Between the Salaf & Khalaf. unabridged ed. (Enter into Islam Completely Ser.: Vol. 1). 47p. 1999. pap. 3.50 (*1-891229-31-1*) Al-Kitaab & As-Sunnah.

— The Final Request: The Islamic Will & Testament. unabridged ed. (Inevitable Journey Ser.: Vol. 214). 148p. 1999. pap. 8.00 (*1-891229-02-8*) Al-Kitaab & As-Sunnah.

— Funerals: Regulations & Exhortations. unabridged ed. (Inevitable Journey Ser.: Vol. 314). (Illus.). 348p. 1998. pap. 13.00 (*1-891229-03-6*) Al-Kitaab & As-Sunnah.

— Knowing Allah. large type ed. (Eemaan Made Easy Ser.). (Illus.). 63p. (J). (gr. 2). 1998. pap. 5.00 (*1-891229-05-2*) Al-Kitaab & As-Sunnah.

— Knowing the Angels. large type ed. (Eemaan Made Easy Ser.: Vol. 2). (Illus.). 102p. (J). (gr. 2). 1999. pap. 7.00 (*1-891229-06-0*) Al-Kitaab & As-Sunnah.

— Life in Al-Barzakh. unabridged ed. (Inevitable Journey Ser.: Vol. 414). 126p. 1998. pap. 7.00 (*1-891229-04-4*) Al-Kitaab & As-Sunnah.

— The Night Prayers: Qiyam & Tarawih. 2nd unabridged ed. 198p. 1999. pap. 9.00 (*1-891229-22-2*) Al-Kitaab & As-Sunnah.

— Sickness: Regulations & Exhortations. unabridged ed. (Inevitable Journey Ser.). 171p. 1998. pap. 8.00 (*1-891229-01-X*) Al-Kitaab & As-Sunnah.

— Smoking - A Social Poison. (Enter into Islam Completely Ser.: Vol. 2). 51p. 1999. pap. 3.50 (*1-891229-32-X*) Al-Kitaab & As-Sunnah.

Al-Jibouri, Yasin T. The Ninety-Nine Attributes of Allah: ASMAAA-UL-HUSNAA. 177p. 1997. 20.00 (*1-879402-56-4*); pap. text 12.00 (*1-879402-55-6*) Tahrike Tarsile Quran.

Al-Jilani, Hadrat'Abd A. The Secret of Secrets. Bayrak, Tosun, tr. from TUR. & intro. by. LC 93-110643. (Golden Palm Ser.). 138p. (Orig.). 1992. pap. 18.95 (*0-946621-29-2*, Pub. by Islamic Texts) Intl Spec Bk.

Al-Jilani, Shaikh A. Fifteen Letters (Khamsata Ashara Maktuban) Vol. 1: The Maktubat. AlMuttaqi, Ali H. & Holland, Muhtar, trs. from ARA. LC 97-80418. 72p. 1997. pap. 10.00 (*1-882216-16-4*) Al-Baz Pub.

Al-Jili, Abd A. Universal Man. Burckhardt, Titus & Culme-Seymour, Angela, trs. from ARA. (Illus.). 102p. 1983. reprint ed. pap. 15.00 (*0-904975-15-0*, Pub. by Beshara) Beshara Fndtn.

Al-Johani, M., intro. The Encyclopedia of Religions & Sects. 2nd ed. (ARA.). 575p. pap. write for info. (*1-882837-09-6*) W A M Y Intl.

Al-Johani, Maneh. The Truth about Jesus. 24p. pap. write for info. (*1-882837-12-6*) W A M Y Intl.

Al-Johani, Maneh, tr. see Yakan, Fathi.

Al J's Sports Connections Ltd. Staff. The Winning Strategy: For Provincial Sports Lotteries. LC 98-226786. 220p. 1996. pap. 15.95 (*0-7737-5841-0*) Stoddart Publ.

***Al-Jumaily, Ghanim A. & SPIE Staff.** Optical Metrology: Proceedings of a Conference, Held July 18-19,1999, Denver, Colorado LC 99-32250. (Critical Reviews of Optical Science & Technology Ser.). 1999. write for info. (*0-8194-3235-0*) SPIE.

Al-Jundi, Assef, et al. Our Own Clues: Poets of the Lake Z. 2nd ed. 96p. (C). 1993. pap. text 8.50 (*0-9639676-0-6*) Our Lady Lake.

Al-Kabbani, Shaykh H. The Naqshbandi Sufi Way: History & Guidebook of the Saints of the Golden Chair. LC 99-211185. (Illus.). 504p. 1995. 99.00 (*0-934905-34-7*) Kazi Pubns.

***Al-Kafrawl, Said.** Hill of Gypsies & Other Stories. 1999. 14.50 (*977-424-480-X*, Pub. by Am Univ Cairo Pr) Col U Pr.

Al-Kalali, Nayef, tr. see Kabbani, Nizar.

Al-Kausar, Tawfik, intro. Islamic Students Organizations: Role & Challenges, Proceedings of International Conference. 2nd ed. (ARA.). 425p. (YA). 1985. pap. write for info. (*1-882837-03-7*) W A M Y Intl.

— Muslim Minorities in the World Vol. 2: Research Papers & Proceedings of the 6th International Conference of Wamy. (ARA.). 479p. (Orig.). pap. write for info. (*1-882837-07-X*) W A M Y Intl.

Al-Khafaji, Amir W. & Andersland, Orlando B. Geotechnical Engineering & Soil Testing. (Illus.). 714p. 1995. text 85.95 (*0-19-510719-5*) OUP.

Al-Khafaji, Amir W. & Tooley, John R. Computerized Numerical Analysis. (Illus.). 250p. (C). 1995. spiral bd. 69.95 (*0-03-001752-1*) OUP.

— Numerical Methods in Engineering Practice. (Illus.). 656p. 1995. text 76.95 (*0-03-001757-2*) OUP.

— Numerical Methods in Engineering Practice. 642p. 1986. student ed. write for info. (*0-03-001753-X*) SCP.

Al-Khalidi, Nancy & Ahmed, Leila. Sandwich Maker Cookbook. viii, 217p. 1991. pap. 12.95 (*0-9632393-0-9*) NALA Pubs.

Al-Khalifa, Shaikh A. & Rice, Michael, eds. Bahrain Through the Ages: The History. 2nd ed. (Illus.). 450p. 1993. 99.95 (*0-7103-0272-X*, A5027) Routledge.

Al-Khalifah, Hamad ibn Isa. First Light: Modern Bahrain & Its Heritage. LC 94-10622. (Illus.). 220p. 1995. 59.50 (*0-7103-0494-3*) Routledge.

***Al-Khalil, Samir.** Republic of Fear: The Inside Story of Saddam's Iraq. 310p. 2000. reprint ed. pap. text 13.00 (*0-7881-9181-0*) DIANE Pub.

Al-Khalil, Samir. Republic of Fear: The Inside Story of Saddam's Iraq. rev. ed. 310p. 1998. pap. text 13.00 (*0-7881-5715-9*) DIANE Pub.

***Al-Khalili, J. S.** Black Holes, Wormholes & Time Machines. LC 99-46327. 256p. 1999. pap. 16.50 (*0-7503-0560-6*) IOP Pub.

Al-Kharrat, Edwar. City of Saffron. Liardet, Frances, tr. from ARA. 192p. 1990. 19.95 (*0-7043-2693-0*, Pub. by Quartet) Interlink Pub.

— Girls of Alexandria. 256p. 1993. 19.95 (*0-7043-7006-9*, Pub. by Quartet) Interlink Pub.

Al-Khatib, A. S. A New Dictionary of Scientific & Technical Terms: English-Arabic. 6th ed. (ARA & ENG.). 751p. Date not set. 125.00 (*0-7859-7136-X*) Fr & Eur.

Al-Khayyat, Ridha, jt. auth. see El-Sayed, Khalil.

Al-Khazendar, Sami. Jordan & the Palestinian Question: The Role of Islamic & Left Forces in Foreign Policy-Making. 224p. 1997. 40.00 (*0-86372-221-0*, Pub. by Garnet-Ithaca) LPC InBook.

Al-Khoei, Ayatullah A. Articles of Islamic Acts: Tawzih-ul-masail. rev. ed. Aini, Amir A., ed. Haq, Muhammad F., tr. from PER. 664p. (C). 1991. reprint ed. 18.00 (*0-941724-21-2*) Islamic Seminary.

Al-Khouri, Touma. The Contemplations of Judas Iscariot: A Trilogy for Christ. LC 96-135457. (Trilogy for Christ Ser.: Pt. 3). 260p. 1996. per. 10.95 (*1-879038-24-2*) Oakwood Pubns.

— Of Preaching in America. (Trilogy for Christ Ser.: Pt. 2). 300p. 1995. per. 10.95 (*1-879038-23-4*) Oakwood Pubns.

— Orthodox Fathers, Orthodox Faith. LC 96-135457. (Trilogy for Christ Ser.: Pt. 1). 392p. 1994. per. 10.95 (*1-879038-20-X*) Oakwood Pubns.

Al-Kilani. Dictionary of Computer Terminology. (ARA & ENG.). 1987. 49.95 (*0-86685-425-8*) Intl Bk Ctr.

— Dictionary of Computer Terminology. (ARA., Illus.). 378p. 1988. 49.95 (*0-86685-438-X*, LDL438X, Pub. by Librairie du Liban) Intl Bk Ctr.

Al-Kindi. The Medical Formulary: or Aqrabadhin of Al-Kindi. Levy, Martin, tr. LC 65-12105. (Publications in Medieval Science). 424p. reprint ed. pap. 131.50 (*0-608-20448-X*, 207170100002) Bks Demand.

Al-Kisai. Tales of the Prophets (Qisas al-Anbiya) In Islamic Jurisprudence. Thackston, Wheeler, tr. from PER. 380p. (Orig.). (C). 1997. 49.95 (*1-871031-01-X*) Kazi Pubns.

Al-Kusayer, Tawfik, intro. Islamic Da'wah: Proceedings of the Fifth International Conference of Wamy, 1982. 522p. (Orig.). 1986. pap. write for info. (*1-882837-24-X*) W A M Y Intl.

— Islamic Media & Human Relations: Proceedings of the Third International Conference of Wamy, 1976. 668p. pap. write for info. (*1-882837-02-9*) W A M Y Intl.

Al-Kush, Maajid. Toil & Struggle. 40p. 1996. write for info. (*0-9627663-3-X*) Designer Comns.

Al-Kuzbari, Salma H., ed. & tr. see Gibran, Kahlil.

Al-Kuzbari, Salma H., jt. tr. see Bushrui, Suheil.

Al-Issa, Ihsan, ed. Al-Junun: Mental Illness in the Islamic World. LC 99-41683. 300p. 1999. 48.00 (*0-8236-3337-3*, 03337) Intl Univs Pr.

Al-Ma'ani, Sultan. Nordjordanische Ortsnamen. (Texte und Studien Zur Orientalistik Ser.: Bd. 7). (GER.). xiv, 326p. 1992. write for info. (*3-487-09632-3*) G Olms Pubs.

Al-Mabuk, Radhi, jt. auth. see Vernon, Ann.

Al-Maghut, Muhammad. The Fan of Swords. Jayyusi, May & Nye, Naomi S., trs. 62p. 1991. 16.00 (*0-89410-685-6*, Three Contnts); pap. 10.00 (*0-89410-686-4*, Three Contnts) L Rienner.

— Joy Is Not My Profession. Harris, Michael, ed. Asfour, John & Burch, Alison, trs. from ARA. (Signal Editions Ser.). 64p. (Orig.). 1994. pap. 12.00 (*1-55065-050-5*, Pub. by Vehicule Pr) Genl Dist Srvs.

Al-Malaika, S., et al. Chemistry & Technology of Polymer Additives. LC 99-13887. (Illus.). 294p. 1999. 180.00 (*0-632-05338-0*) Blackwell Sci.

Al-Mamun, Allama. Sayings of Muhammad. 1990. pap. 6.95 (*0-8065-1169-9*, Citadel Pr) Carol Pub Group.

Al-Mansour, Khalid A. Betrayal by Any Other Name: An Honest Appraisal of Black & Hispanic American Leadership over the Last 100 Years. 800p. (Orig.). (C). 1993. pap. 29.95 (*1-883136-14-8*) First Afr Arabian.

— Lost Books of Africa Rediscovered - We Charge Genocide. (Illus.). 976p. (Orig.). (C). 1995. pap. 29.95 (*1-883136-15-6*) First Afr Arabian.

— Rise 'n Unite - The Black Man's Back. 985p. (Orig.). (C). 1995. pap. 29.95 (*1-883136-16-4*) First Afr Arabian.

Al-Marayati, Abid A. Diplomatic History of Modern Iraq. 1961. 9.95 (*0-8315-0108-1*) Speller.

Al-Marayati, Abid A., ed. International Relations of the Middle East & North Africa. 500p. 1984. pap. 19.95 (*0-87073-830-5*); text 24.95 (*0-87073-824-0*) Schenkman Bks Inc.

Al-Masiri, Tahrir A. Ishkaliyat al Tahayyuz: Al-Amal Al-Kamilah Li-Nadwat Ishkaliyat Al-Tahayyuz Fi Al-Ulum Al-Tabiiyah Wa-Al-Ijtimaiyah Wa-Al-Insaniyah, Vol. 1. LC 96-33880. (Silsilat Al-Manhajiyah Al-Islamiyah Ser.: No. 9). 1996. write for info. (*1-56564-236-8*) IIIT VA.

— Ishkaliyat al Tahayyuz: Al-Amal Al-Kamilah Li-Nadwat Ishkaliyat Al-Tahayyuz Fi Al-Ulum Al-Tabiiyah Wa-Al-Ijtimaiyah Wa-Al-Insaniyah, Vol. 2. LC 96-33880. (Silsilat Al-Manhajiyah Al-Islamiyah Ser.: No. 9). 1996. write for info. (*1-56564-237-6*) IIIT VA.

Al-Maudoodi, Abul A. Towards Understanding Islam. Ahmad, Khurshid, tr. & intro. by. 116p. (YA). 1985. reprint ed. pap. write for info. (*1-882837-25-8*) W A M Y Intl.

***Al-Mawardi, Al-Ahkam A.** The Ordinances of Government: Al-Ahkam al-Sultaniyya. Wahba, Wafaa, tr. (Great Books of Islamic Civilization Ser.). 312p. 2000. pap. 25.00 (*1-85964-140-7*) Garnet Publishing Co.

Al-Mazidi, Feisal. The Future of the Gulf: The Legacy of the War & the Challenges of the 1990s. 112p. 1994. text 125.00 (*1-85043-789-0*, Pub. by I B T) St Martin.

al Mazru'i, Shaykh Al-Amin bin Ali, see Al-Amin bin Ali al Mazru'i, Shaykh.

Al-Mefty, Ossama. Operative Atlas for Meningiomas. LC 97-2086. (Illus.). 660p. 1997. text 195.00 (*0-7817-0152-X*) Lppncott W & W.

Al-Mefty, Ossama, ed. Meningiomas. 656p. 1990. text 176.00 (*0-88167-713-2*, 2188) Lppncott W & W.

Al-Mefty, Ossama, jt. auth. see Eisenberg, Mark.

Al-Meraie, Abdulrahman M. Prisoners of Aristotle. LC 84-80999. 189p. (C). 1984. 16.95 (*0-930371-00-3*) Epistemics.

Al-Moajil, Abdullah H. & Benharbit, Abdelali. Basic Mathematics: A Precalculus Course for Science & Engineering. LC 80-41685. 320p. reprint ed. pap. 99.20 (*0-8357-5980-6*, 203040000069) Bks Demand.

Al-Mubarak, A. F. The Future World Order. 412p. 1998. pap. 20.00 (*1-883058-55-4*) Global Pubns.

Al-Mubarak, Hani. Uhibbu an A'rif A'lam Ummati: Sirat Rijal Sana'u al-Tarikh, 6 vols., Set. 96p. (J). 1993. pap. 7.95 (*1-57547-141-8*) Dar Al-Fikr.

— Uhibbu an A'rif A'lam Ummati: Sirat Rijal Sana'u al-Tarikh, Vol. 1. (J). 1993. pap. write for info. (*1-57547-142-6*) Dar Al-Fikr.

— Uhibbu an A'rif A'lam Ummati: Sirat Rijal Sana'u al-Tarikh, Vol. 2. (J). 1993. pap. write for info. (*1-57547-143-4*) Dar Al-Fikr.

— Uhibbu an A'rif A'lam Ummati: Sirat Rijal Sana'u al-Tarikh, Vol. 3. (J). 1993. pap. write for info. (*1-57547-144-2*) Dar Al-Fikr.

— Uhibbu an A'rif A'lam Ummati: Sirat Rijal Sana'u al-Tarikh, Vol. 4. (J). 1993. pap. write for info. (*1-57547-145-0*) Dar Al-Fikr.

— Uhibbu an A'rif A'lam Ummati: Sirat Rijal Sana'u al-Tarikh, Vol. 5. (J). 1993. pap. write for info. (*1-57547-146-9*) Dar Al-Fikr.

— Uhibbu an A'rif A'lam Ummati: Sirat Rijal Sana'u al-Tarikh, Vol. 6. (J). 1993. pap. write for info. (*1-57547-147-7*) Dar Al-Fikr.

Al-Mufid, Shaykh. Kitab Al-Irshad: The Book of Guidance. Howard, I. K., tr. 620p. 1996. pap. 15.95 (*0-614-21181-6*, 697) Kazi Pubns.

Al-Mujahid, Sharif. Quaid-I-Azam Jinnah: Studies in Interpretation. 810p. 1989. 39.95 (*1-56744-363-X*) Kazi Pubns.

Al-Mukaffah. Kalilat wa Dumma: Short Stories in Arabic. 1983. pap. 16.00 (*0-86685-543-2*) Intl Bk Ctr.

Al-Munif, Abd Al-Rahman. Endings. 152p. 1993. 15.95 (*0-7043-2651-5*, Pub. by Quartet) Interlink Pub.

Al-Mustalah, et al. Dictionary of Computer Science. (ARA & ENG., Illus.). 240p. 1989. 39.95 (*0-86685-504-1*, LDL5041, Pub. by Librairie du Liban) Intl Bk Ctr.

Al-Mustarshid, Kitab, jt. auth. see Abrahamov, Binyamin.

Al-Mutanabbi & Abu al-Tayyib Ahmad ibn al-Husan. Poems of Al-Mutanabbi: A Selection with Introduction, Translations & Notes. Arberry, Arthur J., tr. LC 66-17060. 161p. reprint ed. pap. 45.90 (*0-608-10870-7*, 2051447) Bks Demand.

Al-Mutawa, Naif. To Bounce or Not to Bounce. (Illus.). 32p. (J). 1996. 9.00 (*0-9651807-0-0*); pap. 15.00 (*0-9651807-1-9*) N AL-Mutawa.

Al-Mutawa, Subhi A. Kuwait City Parks: A Critical Review of Their Design, Facilities, Programs, & Management. (Illus.). 125p. 1986. text 55.00 (*0-7103-0068-9*) Routledge.

Al-Muzaffar, Muhammad. The Faith of Shi'a Islam. LC 83-50153. 89p. (C). pap. 4.95 (*0-940368-26-9*, 21) Tahrike Tarsile Quran.

Al-Naamani, Houda. I Was a Point, I Was a Circle: An Elegiac Ode. Sara, Solomon I., tr. from ARA. (Dual Arabic-English Texts Ser.). 66p. 1993. pap. 10.00 (*0-89410-723-2*, Three Contnts) L Rienner.

Al-Nabawiyya, Al-Sira. Life of the Prophet Muhammad, 4. (Life of the Prophet Muhammad Ser.). 1999. 95.00 (*1-85964-040-0*) Garnet Publishing Ltd.

— Life of the Prophet Muhammad, Vol. 3. 1999. 95.00 (*1-85964-009-5*) Garnet Pubg.

Al-Nadim, Ibn. The Catalog. 500p. (C). 1997. 79.95 (*1-871031-62-1*) Kazi Pubns.

Al-Nafie, Abdulatif H., jt. auth. see Watts, David.

Al-Nafussi, Awatif I. & Hughes, David E. Histological Diagnosis of Tumours by Pattern Analysis: An A-Z Guide. LC 97-160230. (Illus.). 832p. 1997. text 195.00 (*0-340-58606-0*, Pub. by E A) Routldge.

***Al-Nafzawi, Muhammad.** The Perfumed Garden of Sensual Desire. Colville, Jim, tr. 81p. 1999. 110.00 (*0-7103-0644-X*, Pub. by Kegan Paul Intl) Col U Pr.

Al-Naq Ib, Ahmadibn L. Reliance of the Traveller: A Classic Manual of Islamic Sacred Law. Keller, Noah H., tr. from ARA. LC 97-27651. 1264p. 1997. 29.95 (*0-915957-72-8*) Amana Corp.

***Al-Naqshbandi, Shaykh Nazim.** Defending Truth. 64p. (C). 2000. pap. 10.00 (*1-898863-18-0*, Pub. by Zero Prods) Kazi Pubns.

— Natural Medicine. 64p. (C). 2000. pap. 7.50 (*1-898863-10-5*, Pub. by Zero Prods) Kazi Pubns.

— Peace & Waste. 100p. (C). 2000. pap. 9.95 (*1-898863-13-X*, Pub. by Zero Prods) Kazi Pubns.

— Princess Diana's Death. 64p. (C). 2000. pap. 9.50 (*1-898863-14-8*, Pub. by Zero Prods) Kazi Pubns.

— Pure Hearts. 64p. (C). 2000. pap. 12.00 (*1-898863-19-9*, Pub. by Zero Prods) Kazi Pubns.

— Secret Desires. 64p. (C). 2000. pap. 14.95 (*1-898863-08-3*, Pub. by Zero Prods) Kazi Pubns.

— Star from Heaven. 64p. (C). 2000. pap. 12.00 (*1-898863-04-0*, Pub. by Zero Prods) Kazi Pubns.

Al-Nassir, A. A. Sibawaihi the Phonologist. (Library of Arabic Linguistics). 240p. 1992. 115.00 (*0-7103-0356-4*, A3926) Routledge.

Al-Nauimi, Najeeb & Meese, Richard, eds. International Legal Issues Arising under the United Nations Decade of International Law. LC 95-33946. 1995. lib. bdg. 272.00 (*90-411-0107-1*, Pub. by M Nijhoff) Kluwer Academic.

Al-Niffari. Mawaqif & Mukhatabat. (Gibb Memorial New Ser.: Vol. 9). 1935. 64.50 (*0-906094-22-4*, Pub. by Aris & Phillips) David Brown.

Al-Nihlawi, Abd-al-Rahman. Usul al-Tarbiyah al-Islamiyah wa-Asalibuha fi al-Bayt wa-al-Madrasah wa-al-Mujtama. 1983. pap. 4.95 (*1-57547-008-X*) Dar Al-Fikr.

Al-Nowaihi, Magda M. The Poetry of Ibn Khafajah: A Literary Analysis. LC 92-21985. (Studies in Arabic Literature: Vol. 16). 176p. 1993. 83.00 (*90-04-09660-4*) Brill Academic Pubs.

Al-Nuayyim, Abd M. Al-Istishraq Fi Al-Al-Sirah Al-Nabawiyah: Dirasah Tarikhayah Li-Ara (Watt, Brukilman, Wa-Wilhawzin) Mugaranah Bi-Al-Ruyah Al-Islamiyah. LC 96-33947. (Silsilat Al-Rasail Al-Jamiiyah Ser.: No. 21). 1996. write for info. (*1-56564-238-4*) IIIT VA.

Al-Omar, Fuad & Abdel-Haq, Mohammed. Islamic Banking: Theory, Practice & Challenges. 198p. (C). 1996. text 55.00 (*1-85649-343-1*, Pub. by Zed Books) St Martin.

Al-Osh, Alexandra S., tr. see Al-Basha, Abdur R.

Al-Othman, Nasser. With Their Bare Hands. 1984. pap. text. write for info. (*0-582-78375-5*, Pub. by Addison-Wesley) Longman.

Al-Qadi, Wadad, ed. Studia Arabica et Islamia: Festschrift for Ihsan Abbas. 1981. 175.00 (*0-8156-6058-8*, Pub. by Am U Beirut) Syracuse U Pr.

Al-Qadir Al-Jilani, Abd. Sufficient Provision for Seekers of the Path of Truth: Al-Ghunya Li-Talibi Tariq Al-Haqq, 5 vols. Holland, Muhtar, tr. LC 95-75589. 1738p. 1997. pap. 110.00 (*1-882216-12-1*) Al-Baz Pub.

Al-Qaradawi, Yusuf. The Lawful & the Prohibited in Islam. Siddiqui, Mohammed M. et al, trs. from ARA. LC 80-81562. Orig. Title: Al-Halal Wal-Haram Fil Islam. (ENG.). 355p. (Orig.). 1981. pap. 10.00 (*0-89259-016-5*) Am Trust Pubns.

Al-Qaradawl, Yusuf. Non Muslims in the Islamic Society. Hamad, Khalil M. & Shah, Sayed M., trs. LC 83-72763. 68p. (Orig.). 1985. reprint ed. pap. 3.75 (*0-89259-049-1*) Am Trust Pubns.

Al-Qardawi, Y. Islamic Education & Hassan Al-Banna. 1988. 10.50 (*1-56744-093-2*) Kazi Pubns.

Al-Qasimi, Sultan Muhammad. The Myth of Arab Piracy in the Gulf. LC 85-22411. 450p. 1986. 49.95 (*0-7099-2106-3*, Pub. by C Helm) Routldge.

Al-Qazzaz, Ayad. Women in the Arab World: An Annotated Bibliography. (Bibliography Ser.: No. 2). 39p. (Orig.). 1975. pap. text 2.00 (*0-937694-15-0*) Assn Arab-Amer U Grads.

— Women in the Middle East & North Africa: An Annotated Bibliography. 190p. 1977. pap. 7.50 (*0-292-79009-0*) U of Tex Pr.

Al-Qazzaz, Ayad & Oweiss, Ibrahim M. Two Studies on Israel. (Information Papers: No. 13). 29p. (Orig.). 1974. pap. text 1.00 (*0-937694-29-0*) Assn Arab-Amer U Grads.

Al-Qibrisi, Shaykh N. Mercy Oceans: Teachings of Maulana Abdullah al-Faiza ad-Daghestani. 190p. (Orig.). 1980. pap. 4.75 (*0-939830-11-6*) New Era Publns MI.

Al-Quaradauir, Yusuf. Islamic Awakening Between Rejection & Extremism. LC 82-74123. (Illus.). 95p. 1983. pap. 7.50 (*0-89259-040-8*) Am Trust Pubns.

Al-Qubrusi, Shaykh N. Islam the Freedom to Serve. 96p. (C). 1997. pap. 6.95 (*1-871031-56-7*) Kazi Pubns.

Al-Qushayri. Principles of Sufism. Von Schlegell, B. R., tr. from ARA. LC 92-82685. 366p. 1993. text 29.95 (*0-933782-21-7*); pap. text 19.95 (*0-933782-20-9*) Mizan Pr.

Al-Qushayri, Abdul K. Sufi Book of Virtue. Harris, Rabia T., tr. 1997. pap. text 24.95 (*1-56744-531-4*) Kazi Pubns.

Al-Qushayri, Abul Q. Sufi Book of Spiritual Ascent. Harris, Rabia T., tr. 380p. (C). 1997. pap. 19.95 (*1-56744-530-6*) Kazi Pubns.

A

Al-Radi, Nuha. Baghdad Diaries. LC 99-187025. 152p. 1998. pap. 16.95 (*0-86356-095-4*, Pub. by Saqi) Intl Spec Bk.

Al-Radi, Selma, et al. The Amiriya in Rada: The History & Restoration of a 16th-Century Madrasa in the Yemen. (Oxford Studies in Islamic Art: No. XIII). (Illus.). 216p. 1998. text 67.00 (*0-19-728023-4*) OUP.

Al-Radi, Selma M. Phlamoudhi Vounari: A Sanctuary Site in Cyprus. (Studies in Mediterranean Archaeology: Vol. LXV). (Illus.). 136p. (Orig.). 1983. pap. 52.50 (*91-86098-10-1*, Pub. by P Astroms) Coronet Bks.

Al-Ramlyn, Lenin. In Plain Arabic. Allouba, Esmat, tr. 144p. 1995. 25.00 (*977-424-342-0*, Pub. by Am Univ Cairo Pr) Col U Pr.

Al-Rasheed, Madawi. Iraqi Assyrian Christians in London: The Construction of Ethnicity. LC 98-44213. (Studies in Sociology: Vol. 21). 260p. 1998. lib. bdg. 89.95 (*0-7734-8251-2*) E Mellen.

— Politics in an Arabian Oasis: The Rashidi Tribal Dynasty. 224p. 1991. text 70.00 (*1-85043-320-8*) I B T.

Al-Rashid, Mohammad. The Veiled Sun. LC 90-44315. 1991. 22.95 (*0-87949-327-5*) Ashley Bks.

Al-Rawahy, Hamood H. A Guide to Your Marriage: What the West Could Learn from Eastern Cultures on Marriage. LC 98-90212. 86p. 2000. pap. 10.95 (*0-533-12733-5*) Vantage.

Al-Rawandi, Ibn. Islamic Mysticism: A Secular Perspective. LC 99-57689. 260p. 2000. 32.95 (*1-57392-767-8*) Prometheus Bks.

Al-Rawas, Ali Ahmed. Oman in Early Islamic History. 275p. 2000. 62.00 (*0-86372-238-5*, Pub. by Garnet-Ithaca) LPC InBook.

Al-Rawi, Rosina-Fawzia. Grandmother's Secrets: The Ancient Rituals & Healing Power of Belly Dancing. Arav, Monique, tr. LC 98-38638. 1998. 25.00 (*1-56656-302-X*) Interlink Pub.

***Al-Rawi, Rosina-Fawzia B.** Grandmother's Secrets: The Ancient Rituals & Healing Power of Belly Dancing. LC 98-38638. 2000. pap. 25.00 (*1-56656-326-7*) Interlink Pub.

Al-Rubaei, Mohamed & Emery. Flow Cytometry Applications in Cell Culture. (Illus.). 344p. 1995. text 150.00 (*0-8247-9614-4*) Dekker.

Al-Rubeai, M., ed. Apoptosis. (Advances in Biochemical Engineering/Biotechnology Ser.: Vol. 62). (Illus.). xi, 193p. 1998. 139.00 (*3-540-64153-X*) Spr-Verlag.

Al-Rubeai, Mohamed. Cell Engineering. LC 99-30730. 302p. 1999. write for info. (*0-7923-5790-6*) Kluwer Academic.

Al-Rumi, Yakut. Moujam al Buldan, 5 vols. 1967. 95.00 (*0-86685-497-5*) Intl Bk Ctr.

***Al-Sabah, Meshal.** Reflections of an Arab Prince: Taking Our Past into Our Future. 300p. 2001. text 40.00 (*0-7103-0699-7*) Col U Pr.

— Reflections of an Arab Prince: Taking Our Past into Our Future. 480p. 1997. 42.50 (*0-7103-0596-6*, Pub. by Kegan Paul Intl) Col U Pr.

Al-Sabbagh, Ibn. The Mystical Teachings of Al-Shadhili. Douglas, Elmer, tr. 274p. 1996. pap. 19.95 (*0-614-21322-3*, 880) Kazi Pubns.

Al-Sabi, Hilal. Rusum Dar Al-Khila Fah (Rules & Regulations of Abbasid Court) Salem, Elie A., ed. 1977. 19.95 (*0-8156-6046-4*, Pub. by Am U Beirut) Syracuse U Pr.

Al-Sa'Dawi, Nawal. Death of an Ex-Minister. 1991. pap. write for info. (*0-413-42100-7*, Methuen Drama) Methn.

— Innocence of the Devil. 1998. pap. 15.95 (*0-520-21652-0*, Pub. by U CA Pr) Cal Prin Full Svc.

— Memoirs of a Woman Doctor. Cobham, Catherine, tr. 1989. pap. 8.95 (*0-87286-223-2*) City Lights.

Al-Sadr, Ayatullah B. He His Messenger & His Message: Al-Mursil, Ar-Rasul, Ar-Risalah. rev. ed. Rizwani, RAza H., ed. Ansari, M. A., tr. from ARA. 114p. (C). reprint ed. pap. 5.00 (*0-941724-12-3*) Islamic Seminary.

Al-Salam, Debra D., jt. auth. see Koralek, Derry G.

Al-Salihi, Joan. Follow-Me: Caravans of Poems. Omar, Najwa, tr.Tr. of Alam & Amal (Suffering & Pain). (ARA & ENG., Illus.). 150p. 1997. 6.00 (*0-9656771-0-9*) F Al-Salihi.

Al-Saltana, Taj. Crowning Anguish: Memoirs of a Persian Princess from the Harem to Modernity, 1884-1914. Vanzan, Anna & Neshati, Amin, trs. from PER. LC 93-3329. (Illus.). 352p. 1993. 29.95 (*0-934211-35-3*); pap. 17.95 (*0-934211-36-1*) Mage Pubs Inc.

Al-Sam, S. & Lakhani, Sunil R., eds. An Atlas of Pseudomalignant Conditions. LC 98-3605. (Illus.). 384p. 1998. text 195.00 (*0-340-64616-0*) OUP.

Al-Samarqandi. Chahar Maqala: The Four Discourses of Nidhami-I-Arudi-I-Samarqandi. (Gibb Memorial Old Ser.: Vols. 11-12). 1921. pap. 14.50 (*0-906094-06-2*, Pub. by Aris & Phillips) David Brown.

Al-Sayari, S. S. & Zoetl, J. G., eds. Quaternary Period in Saudi Arabia One. (Illus.). 1978. 75.00 (*0-387-81448-5*) Spr-Verlag.

Al-Saydawi, Yusuf. Al-'Arabiyah bayna Kharakufski wa-Dakk al-Bab. (ARA.). 64p. (Orig.). 1995. pap. 1.95 (*1-57547-229-5*) Dar Al-Fikr.

Al-Sayh Abu Ishaq Ibrahim Al-Sirazi & Chaumont, Eric. Kitab Al-Luma Fi Usul Al-Figh: Traite de Theorie Legale Musulmane. (Studies in Comparative Legal History). (FRE.). Date not set. write for info. (*1-882239-09-1*) Robbins Collection.

Al-Shabab, Omar S. Interpretation & the Language of Translation. 128p. 1996. pap. 18.95 (*1-85756-231-3*, Pub. by Janus Pubng) Paul & Co Pubs.

Al-Shabab, Omar S., jt. auth. see Baka, Farida.

***Al-Shafei, Khalil, ed.** Engineering for Calcareous Sediments: Proceedings of the 2nd International Conference, Bahrain, 21-24 February 1999, 2 vols. (Illus.). 550p. (C). 1999. text 175.00 (*90-5809-037-X*, Pub. by A A Balkema) Ashgate Pub Co.

Al-Shafii. Risala: Treatise on the Foundations of Islamic Jurisprudence. 368p. 1996. 40.00 (*0-614-21208-1*, 1082) Kazi Pubns.

Al-Shafii, Al-Imam. Al-Shafiis Risala: Treatise on the Foundations of Islamic Jurisprudence. Khadduri, Majiid, tr. from ARA. 379p. 1997. pap. 34.95 (*0-946621-61-6*, Pub. by Islamic Texts) Intl Spec Bk.

— Al-Shafiis Risala: Treatise on the Foundations of Islamic Jurisprudence. 2nd ed. Khadduri, Majid, tr. from ARA. & intro. by. 380p. 1995. 19.95 (*0-946621-15-2*, Pub. by Islamic Texts) Intl Spec Bk.

Al-Shaikh, Al, ed. see American Society of Mechanical Engineers Staff.

Al Shaikh-Ali, A. S., ed. see Alwani, Taha J.

Al Shaikh-Ali, A. S., tr. see Alwani, Taha J.

Al-Shaikh, B. & Stacey, S. Essentials of Anaesthetic Equipment. (Illus.). 147p. 1995. write for info. (*0-443-05069-4*) Church.

Al-Sharif, Abdu, ed. Political Studies on Yemen. (Translations of Western-Language Articles into Arabic for Use in Yemeni Universities Ser.: Vol. 1). 1996. write for info. (*1-882557-03-4*) Am Inst Yemeni.

Al-Sharqawi, Abdel R. Egyptian Earth. Stewart, Desmond, tr. from ARA. 264p. (C). 1990. text 24.95 (*0-292-72071-8*) U of Tex Pr.

Al-Shaykh, Hanan. Beirut Blues. Cobhaim, Catherine, tr.Tr. of Barid Bayrut. 384p. 1996. pap. 12.95 (*0-385-47382-6*, Anchor NY) Doubleday.

— I Sweep the Sun off Rooftops: Stories. Cobham, Catherine, tr. from ARA. LC 98-15876. 288p. 1998. pap. 12.00 (*0-385-49127-1*, Anchor NY) Doubleday.

— The Story of Zahra. Ford, Peter, tr. from ARA. LC 93-3678. 224p. 1996. pap. 13.95 (*0-385-47206-4*, Anchor NY) Doubleday.

— The Story of Zahra. 192p. 1996. pap. 9.00 (*0-614-21395-9*, 1171) Kazi Pubns.

— Women of Sand & Myrrh. Cobham, Catherine, tr. 288p. 1992. reprint ed. pap. 11.95 (*0-385-42358-6*, Anchor NY) Doubleday.

Al-Sheikh, Aal, ed. Islam & Civilization & Role of the Muslim Youth Vol. 1: Research Papers & Proceedings of 4th International Conference of Wamy. 747p. (Orig.). 1985. pap. write for info. (*1-882837-05-3*) W A M Y Intl.

Al-Sheikh, Aal, ed. Muslim Minorities in the World: Research Papers & Proceedings of the 6th International Conference of Wamy. (ARA.). 507p. (Orig.). pap. write for info. (*1-882837-08-8*) W A M Y Intl.

Al-Sheikh, H. E., intro. Issues from the Contemporary Islamic Thoughts: Research Papers & Proceedings of the 2nd International Conference of Wamy. 3rd ed. (ARA.). 433p. (YA). 1984. reprint ed. pap. write for info. (*1-882837-01-0*) W A M Y Intl.

***Al Sheikly, Sami Sattar.** Das agyptische Dorf Karnak im Werk von Yahya at Tahir Abdallah. 210p. 2000. 35.95 (*3-906764-54-0*, Pub. by P Lang) P Lang Pubng.

Al-Sihah, Ghawamid. Dictionary of Roots of Difficult Words. (ARA.). 224p. 1997. 29.95 (*0-86685-690-0*) Intl Bk Ctr.

Al-Sihah, Ghawamid. Dictionary on the Roots of Difficult Words: Al-Safadi. (ARA.). 1996. 19.95 (*0-86685-685-4*) Intl Bk Ctr.

Al-Subayi, Adnan & Al-Bitar, Bashshar. Qira'ah fi "Kitab al-Hubb wa-al-Tibb wa-al-Mu'jizat" 168p. 1995. pap. 4.95 (*1-57547-207-4*) Dar Al-Fikr.

***Al-Sudairi, Abdulaziz.** A Vision of the Middle East: An Intellectual Biography of Albert. 2000. text 35.00 (*1-86064-581-X*, Pub. by I B T) St Martin.

Al-Sudairi, Amir A. The Desert Frontier of Arabia: Al-Jawf Through the Ages. LC 95-197475. (Illus.). 176p. 1995. 39.95 (*0-905743-75-X*, Pub. by Stacey Intl) Intl Bk Ctr.

Al Sudais, Muhammad. Selection of Current Najdi-Arabic Proverbs. (ARA.). 301p. 1993. 29.95 (*0-86685-643-9*, LDL6609, Pub. by Librairie du Liban) Intl Bk Ctr.

***Al-Suhrawardi, Shihab al-Din.** The Philosophy of Illumination. Walbridge, John & Ziai, Hossein, trs. from ARA. (Islamic Translation Ser.).Tr. of Hikmat al-Ishraq. xlvii, 323p. 2000. 29.95 (*0-8425-2457-6*, Pub. by Brigham) U Ch Pr.

Al-Sulami, jt. auth. see Al-Husayn, Ibn.

Al Sulami, Ibn A. The Way of Sufi Chivalry: Futuwwah. 192p. 1991. reprint ed. pap. 10.95 (*0-89281-317-2*) Inner Tradit.

Al-Sultan, Khaled S. & Rahim, M. A. Optimization in Quality Control. LC 97-150. 1997. lib. bdg. 143.00 (*0-7923-9889-0*) Kluwer Academic.

Al-Sunaidi, Julie, ed. see Smith, Audrey.

Al-Suwaidi, Ahmed. Finance of International Trade in the Gulf. LC 93-40699. (Arab & Islamic Laws Ser.). 480p. (C). 1994. lib. bdg. 186.50 (*1-85333-947-4*, Pub. by Graham & Trotman) Kluwer Academic.

Al-Suwaidi, Jamal S., ed. Iran & the Gulf: A Search for Stability. LC 96-61057. (Illus.). 425p. 1997. text 59.50 (*1-86064-143-1*) I B T.

Al-Swailmi, Saleh, jt. auth. see Terrel, Ronald L.

Al-Tabari. History of al-Tabari 425: The Reunification of the Abbasid Caliphate. Bosworth, C. E., tr. 250p. 1996. pap. 16.95 (*0-614-21141-7*, 425) Kazi Pubns.

— History of al-Tabari No. 01: General Introduction & from the Creation to the Flood. Rosenthal, Franz, tr. 450p. 1996. pap. 24.95 (*0-614-21112-3*, 402) Kazi Pubns.

— History of al-Tabari No. 02: Prophets & Patriarchs. Brinner, William M., tr. 200p. 1996. pap. 16.95 (*0-614-21113-1*, 403) Kazi Pubns.

— History of al-Tabari No. 03: Children of Israel. Perlmann, Moshe, tr. 200p. 1996. pap. 16.95 (*0-614-21114-X*, 405) Kazi Pubns.

— History of al-Tabari No. 04: Ancient Kingdoms. Perlmann, Moshe, tr. 200p. 1996. pap. 16.95 (*0-614-21115-8*, 405) Kazi Pubns.

— History of al-Tabari No. 06: Muhammad at Mecca. Watt, William M., tr. 178p. 1996. pap. 14.95 (*0-614-21116-6*, 433) Kazi Pubns.

— History of al-Tabari No. 07: The Foundation of the Community. McDonald, M. V., tr. 184p. 1996. pap. 18.95 (*0-614-21117-4*, 434) Kazi Pubns.

— History of al-Tabari No. 09: The Last Years of the Prophet. Poonawala, Ismail K., tr. 250p. 1996. pap. 19.95 (*0-614-21118-2*, 406) Kazi Pubns.

— History of al-Tabari No. 10: The Conquest of Arabia. Donner, Fred M., tr. 180p. 1996. pap. 18.95 (*0-614-21119-0*, 407) Kazi Pubns.

— History of al-Tabari No. 11: The Challenge to the Empire. Blankinship, Khalid Y., tr. 160p. 1996. pap. 16.95 (*0-614-21120-4*, 408) Kazi Pubns.

— History of al-Tabari No. 12: The Battle of al-Qadisiyyah & the Conquest of Syria & Palestine. Friedmann, Yohanan, tr. 250p. 1996. pap. 19.95 (*0-614-21121-2*, 435) Kazi Pubns.

— History of al-Tabari No. 13: The Conquest of Iraq, Southwestern Persia, & Egypt. Juynboll, Gautier H., tr. 250p. 1996. pap. 15.95 (*0-614-21122-0*, 409) Kazi Pubns.

— History of al-Tabari No. 14: The Conquest of Iran AD 641-643. Smith, Margaret, tr. 230p. 1996. pap. 17.95 (*0-614-21123-9*, 436) Kazi Pubns.

— History of al-Tabari No. 15: The Crisis of the Early Caliphate. Humphreys, R. Stephen, tr. 290p. 1996. pap. 18.95 (*0-614-21124-7*, 410) Kazi Pubns.

— History of al-Tabari No. 16: The Community Divided: the Caliphate of 'Ali, AD 656-657/AH 35-36. Brockett, Adrian, tr. 288p. 1996. pap. 20.95 (*0-614-21125-5*, 411) Kazi Pubns.

— History of al-Tabari No. 17: The First Civil War: from the Battle of Siffin to the Death of Ali, AD 656-661/AH 36-40. Hawting, G. R., tr. 224p. 1996. pap. 19.95 (*0-614-21126-3*, 412) Kazi Pubns.

— History of al-Tabari No. 18: Between Civil Wars: the Caliphate of Mu'awiyah. Morony, Michael G., tr. 200p. 1996. pap. 16.95 (*0-614-21127-1*, 413) Kazi Pubns.

— History of al-Tabari No. 19: The Caliphate of Yazid b. Mu'awiyah. Howard, I. K., tr. 248p. 1996. pap. 17.95 (*0-614-21128-X*, 414) Kazi Pubns.

— History of al-Tabari No. 20: The Collapse of Sufyanid Authority & the Coming of Marwanids. Hawting, G. R., tr. 246p. 1996. pap. 20.95 (*0-614-21129-8*, 415) Kazi Pubns.

— History of al-Tabari No. 21: Victory of the Marwanids. Fishbein, Michael, tr. 350p. 1996. pap. 17.95 (*0-614-21130-1*, 416) Kazi Pubns.

— History of al-Tabari No. 22: The Marwanid Restoration. Rowson, Everett, tr. 210p. 1996. pap. 16.95 (*0-614-21131-X*, 417) Kazi Pubns.

— History of al-Tabari No. 23: The Zenith of the Marwanid House. Hinds, Martin, tr. 250p. 1996. pap. 19.95 (*0-614-21132-8*, 418) Kazi Pubns.

— History of al-Tabari No. 24: The Empire in Transition. Powers, David S., tr. 250p. 1996. pap. 16.95 (*0-614-21133-6*, 419) Kazi Pubns.

— History of al-Tabari No. 25: The End of Expansion. Blankinship, Khalid Y., tr. 250p. 1996. pap. 19.95 (*0-614-21134-4*, 420) Kazi Pubns.

— History of al-Tabari No. 26: The Waning of the Umayyad Caliphate. 230p. 1996. pap. 18.95 (*0-614-21135-2*, No. 26) Kazi Pubns.

— History of al-Tabari No. 27: The Abbasid Revolution. Williams, John A., tr. 200p. 1996. pap. 17.95 (*0-614-21136-0*, 422) Kazi Pubns.

— History of al-Tabari No. 28: Abbasid Caliphate Affirmed: AD 753-763/136-145 AH. 326p. 1995. pap. 20.95 (*0-614-21137-9*, 437) Kazi Pubns.

— History of al-Tabari No. 29: Al-Mansur & Al-Mahdi. Kennedy, Hugh, tr. 280p. 1996. pap. 16.95 (*0-614-21138-7*, 423) Kazi Pubns.

— History of al-Tabari No. 30: The Abbasid Caliphate in Equilibrium. Bosworth, C. E., tr. 320p. 1996. pap. 25.95 (*0-614-21139-5*, 424) Kazi Pubns.

— History of al-Tabari No. 31: The War Between Brothers, AD 809-813. Fishbein, Michael, tr. 218p. 1996. pap. 17.95 (*0-614-21140-9*, 438) Kazi Pubns.

— History of al-Tabari No. 33: Storm & Stress along the Northern Frontier of the Abbasid Caliphate. Bosworth, C. E., tr. 238p. 1996. pap. 18.95 (*0-614-21142-5*, 426) Kazi Pubns.

— History of al-Tabari No. 34: Incipient Decline. 310p. 1996. pap. 17.95 (*0-614-21143-3*, 427) Kazi Pubns.

— History of al-Tabari No. 35: The Crisis of the Abbasid Caliphate. Saliba, George, tr. 200p. 1996. pap. 15.95 (*0-614-21144-1*, 428) Kazi Pubns.

— History of al-Tabari No. 36: The Revolt of the Zanu. Waines, David, tr. 230p. 1996. pap. 16.95 (*0-614-21145-X*, 439) Kazi Pubns.

— History of al-Tabari No. 37: The Abbasid Recovery. Fields, Phillip, tr. 200p. 1996. pap. 16.95 (*0-614-21146-8*, 429) Kazi Pubns.

— History of al-Tabari No. 38: The Return of the Caliphate to Baghdad. Rosenthal, Franz, tr. 240p. 1996. pap. 10.95 (*0-614-21147-6*, 430) Kazi Pubns.

Al-Tabataba'i, Muhammad H. Shi'ite Islam. Nasr, Seyyed Hossein, tr. LC 74-8289. 253p. (C). 1979. pap. text 19.95 (*0-87395-390-8*) State U NY Pr.

***Al-Tahawy, Miral.** The Tent. 160p. 1998. 19.50 (*977-424-473-7*, Pub. by Am Univ Cairo Pr) Col U Pr.

Al-Tajir, Mahdi A. Language & Linguistic Origins in Bahrain: The Baharnah Dialect of Arabic. (Library of Arabic Linguistics). 188p. 1983. 99.00 (*0-7103-0024-7*) Routledge.

Al Tamimi Essam, jt. auth. see Price, Richard.

Al-Theeb, Solaiman, tr. see Healey, John F., ed.

Al-Tikriti, Navil, et al. Identifying A Small Enterprise Project: The Handicrafts Industry in Belize. (Pew Case Studies in International Affairs). 50p. (C). 1993. pap. text 3.50 (*1-56927-156-9*) Geo U Inst Dplmcy.

Al-Timimi, Kais & MacKrell, John. Step: Towards Open Systems: STEP Fundamentals & Business Benefits. (Illus.). 130p. 1996. pap. 79.95 (*1-889760-00-5*) CIMdata Inc.

Al Tulab, Munjid & El Mashreq, Dar. Arabic Student Dictionary. (ARA.). 1979. 29.95 (*2-7214-2118-2*) Intl Bk Ctr.

Al-Ubaidi, Maan R., ed. see Ghanayem, Mohamed F.

***Al-Udhari, Abdullah.** Classical Poems by Arab Women: A Bilingual Anthology. (ARA & ENG.). 2000. 38.50 (*0-86356-096-2*); pap. 19.50 (*0-86356-047-4*) Saqi.

Al-Uqdah, Jannah. Teaching Our Babies to Read: A Guide for African American Parents. LC 93-90748. 64p. (Orig.). 1993. pap. 4.00 (*0-9638046-0-X*) Al-Uqdah Ent.

Al-Wahab, Ibrahim. Law Dictionary (English-Arabic) 320p. 1972. 29.95 (*0-86685-082-1*, LDL0811, Pub. by Librairie du Liban) Intl Bk Ctr.

Al-Wahhab Bakr, 'Abd, jt. auth. see Crecelius, Daniel.

Al-Warraki, Nariman N. & Hassanein, Ahmed T. The Connectors in Modern Standard Arabic. (World XEgypt Ser.). 210p. 1995. pap. 22.50 (*977-424-354-4*, Pub. by Am Univ Cairo Pr) Col U Pr.

Al-Weshah, Radwan A., jt. ed. see Stout, Glenn E.

Al Yahya, Mohammad A. Kuwait: Fall & Rebirth. LC 93-15346. 140p. 1993. 59.95 (*0-7103-0463-3*, B2525) Routledge.

Al-Yassin, Ibrahim M. Growth Potential of Dental Epithelium in Tissue Culture. 180p. 1984. 90.00 (*0-7103-0073-5*) Routledge.

Al-Yassini, Ayman. Religion & State in the Kingdom of Saudi Arabia. (Special Studies on the Middle East). 190p. 1985. text 54.50 (*0-8133-0058-4*) Westview.

Al-Zahrawi. On Surgery & Instruments. 288p. (C). 1997. text 40.00 (*0-934905-81-9*, Library of Islam) Kazi Pubns.

Al-Zaibag, Muayed & Duran, Carlos, eds. Valvular Heart Disease. LC 93-46486. (Fundamental & Clinical Cardiology Ser.: Vol. 20). (Illus.). 760p. 1994. text 235.00 (*0-8247-8861-3*) Dekker.

Al-Zuhayli, Muhammad. Tarikh Al-Qada' Fi Al-Islam. 592p. 1995. 16.95 (*1-57547-198-1*) Dar Al-Fikr.

Al-Zuhayli, Wahbah. Al-Fiqh al-Islami wa-Adillatuh, 8 vols., Set. 6752p. 1989. 119.95 (*1-57547-046-2*) Dar Al-Fikr.

— Al-Fiqh al-Islami wa-Adillatuh, Vol. 1. 1989. write for info. (*1-57547-047-0*) Dar Al-Fikr.

— Al-Fiqh al-Islami wa-Adillatuh, Vol. 2. 1989. write for info. (*1-57547-048-9*) Dar Al-Fikr.

— Al-Fiqh al-Islami wa-Adillatuh, Vol. 3. 1989. write for info. (*1-57547-049-7*) Dar Al-Fikr.

— Al-Fiqh al-Islami wa-Adillatuh, Vol. 4. 1989. write for info. (*1-57547-050-0*) Dar Al-Fikr.

— Al-Fiqh al-Islami wa-Adillatuh, Vol. 5. 1989. write for info. (*1-57547-051-9*) Dar Al-Fikr.

— Al-Fiqh al-Islami wa-Adillatuh, Vol. 6. 1989. write for info. (*1-57547-052-7*) Dar Al-Fikr.

— Al-Fiqh al-Islami wa-Adillatuh, Vol. 7. 1989. write for info. (*1-57547-053-5*) Dar Al-Fikr.

— Al-Fiqh al-Islami wa-Adillatuh, Vol. 8. 1989. write for info. (*1-57547-054-3*) Dar Al-Fikr.

— Al-Tafsir al-Munir fi al-Aqidah wa-al-Shari ah wa-al-Manhaj, 16 vols., Set. 10280p. 1991. 79.95 (*1-57547-055-1*) Dar Al-Fikr.

— Al-Tafsir al-Munir fi al-Aqidah wa-al-Shari ah wa-al-Manhaj, Vol. 1. 1991. write for info. (*1-57547-056-X*) Dar Al-Fikr.

— Al-Tafsir al-Munir fi al-Aqidah wa-al-Shari ah wa-al-Manhaj, Vol. 2. 1991. write for info. (*1-57547-057-8*) Dar Al-Fikr.

— Al-Tafsir al-Munir fi al-Aqidah wa-al-Shari ah wa-al-Manhaj, Vol. 3. 1991. write for info. (*1-57547-058-6*) Dar Al-Fikr.

— Al-Tafsir al-Munir fi al-Aqidah wa-al-Shari ah wa-al-Manhaj, Vol. 4. 1991. write for info. (*1-57547-059-4*) Dar Al-Fikr.

— Al-Tafsir al-Munir fi al-Aqidah wa-al-Shari ah wa-al-Manhaj, Vol. 5. 1991. write for info. (*1-57547-060-8*) Dar Al-Fikr.

— Al-Tafsir al-Munir fi al-Aqidah wa-al-Shari ah wa-al-Manhaj, Vol. 6. 1991. write for info. (*1-57547-061-6*) Dar Al-Fikr.

— Al-Tafsir al-Munir fi al-Aqidah wa-al-Shari ah wa-al-Manhaj, Vol. 7. 1991. write for info. (*1-57547-062-4*) Dar Al-Fikr.

— Al-Tafsir al-Munir fi al-Aqidah wa-al-Shari ah wa-al-Manhaj, Vol. 8. 1991. pap. write for info. (*1-57547-063-2*) Dar Al-Fikr.

— Al-Tafsir al-Munir fi al-Aqidah wa-al-Shari ah wa-al-Manhaj, Vol. 9. 1991. write for info. (*1-57547-064-0*) Dar Al-Fikr.

— Al-Tafsir al-Munir fi al-Aqidah wa-al-Shari ah wa-al-Manhaj, Vol. 10. 1991. write for info. (*1-57547-065-9*) Dar Al-Fikr.

— Al-Tafsir al-Munir fi al-Aqidah wa-al-Shari ah wa-al-Manhaj, Vol. 11. 1991. write for info. (*1-57547-066-7*) Dar Al-Fikr.

— Al-Tafsir al-Munir fi al-Aqidah wa-al-Shari ah wa-al-Manhaj, Vol. 12. 1991. write for info. (*1-57547-067-5*) Dar Al-Fikr.

— Al-Tafsir al-Munir fi al-Aqidah wa-al-Shari ah wa-al-Manhaj, Vol. 13. 1991. write for info. (*1-57547-068-3*) Dar Al-Fikr.

— Al-Tafsir al-Munir fi al-Aqidah wa-al-Shari ah wa-al-Manhaj, Vol. 14. 1991. write for info. (*1-57547-069-1*) Dar Al-Fikr.

An Asterisk (*) at the beginning of an entry indicates that the title is appearing for the first time.

— Al-Tafsir al-Munir fi al-Aqidah wa-al-Shari ah wa-al-Manhaj, Vol. 15. 1991. write for info. (*1-57547-070-5*) Dar Al-Fikr.
— Al-Tafsir al-Munir fi al-Aqidah wa-al-Shari ah wa-al-Manhaj, Vol. 16. 1991. write for info. (*1-57547-071-3*) Dar Al-Fikr.
— Al-Tafsir al-Wajiz wa-Mu'jam Ma'ani al-Qur'an al-'Aziz. (ARA.). 160p. 1995. 19.95 (*1-57547-227-9*) Dar Al-Fikr.
— Al-Tafsir al-Wajiz'ala Hamish al-Qur'an al-'Azim: Wa-ma'ahu Asbab al-Nuzul wa-Qawa'id al-Tartil. 646p. 1995. 23.95 (*1-57547-000-4*) Dar Al-Fikr.
— Al-Wajiz fi Usul al-Fiqh. 248p. 1994. pap. 6.95 (*1-57547-205-8*) Dar Al-Fikr.
Ala, M., et al, eds. Seventy-Five Years of Progress in Oil Field Science & Technology: A Symposium to Mark the 75th Anniversary of the Foundation of the Oil Technology Course at the Royal School of Mines, Imperial College of Science, Technology & Medicine, 12 July 1988. (Illus.). 215p. (C). 1991. text 136.00 (*90-6191-108-7*, Pub. by A A Balkema) Ashgate Pub Co.
Ala Maudoodi, Abul. Come Let Us Change This World. 4th ed. Siddique, Kaukab, tr. from URD. & intro. by. 151p. 1986. pap. 5.00 (*0-942978-05-6*) Am Soc Ed & Rel.
ALA Reference & Adult Services Division Ad Hoc Co. Reference Sources for Small & Medium-Sized Libraries. 5th ed. Lang, Jovian P., ed. LC 92-10007. 352p. (C). 1992. pap. text 40.00 (*0-8389-3406-4*) ALA.
ALA Resources & Technical Services Division Staff. Guide to Performance Evaluation of Library Materials Vendors. 1989. pap. text 15.00 (*0-8389-3369-6*) ALA.
Ala, Salvatore. Clay of the Maker. LC 99-178517. 1998. pap. 10.00 (*0-88962-663-4*) Mosaic.
***ALA Staff.** ALA's Guide to Best Reading in 1999. 1999. 29.95 (*0-8389-8013-9*) ALA.
ALA Staff. PC LAN Systems for the Small Law Firm. 96p. 1993. per. 49.95 (*0-8403-8578-1*) Kendall-Hunt.
— Software Selection . . . Law Firms. 96p. 1993. per. 49.95 (*0-8403-8960-4*) Kendall-Hunt.
— Telephone & Peripheral Systems for Law Firms. 112p. 1993. per. 75.00 (*0-8403-8582-X*) Kendall-Hunt.
Ala'Aldeen, Dlawer A. & Hormaeche, Carlos E., eds. Molecular & Clinical Aspects of Bacterial Vaccine Development. LC 94-43839. 376p. 1995. 285.00 (*0-471-95564-7*) Wiley.
Alaba, John O. Starting Your Own Business & Making It a Success. 68p. 1998. pap. 20.00 (*0-9664674-0-X*) TFS Publ.
Alabado, Ceres S., ed. see Vigilia, Corazon S.
Alabama ACEP Staff & Campbell, John E. Basic Trauma Life Support. (Illus.). 224p. (C). 1985. teacher ed. 17.95 (*0-89303-363-4*) P-H.
Alabama Historical Quarterly Staff. Alabama Census Returns, 1820: And an Abstract of Federal Census of Alabama, 1830. LC 67-28599. (Illus.). 192p. 1999. reprint ed. pap. 21.50 (*0-8063-0003-5*) Clearfield Co.
Alabama Pattern Jury Instructions Committee. Alabama Pattern Jury Instructions: Civil. 2nd ed. LC 93-79024. 644p. 1993. 190.00 (*0-317-04336-6*) West Group.
***Alabama Study Group of the Afro-American Genealogical & Historical Society of Chicago Staff.** An Index of Headstones in Lincoln Cemetery - Chicago, Illinois. (Illus.). 587p. 2000. pap. 34.50 (*0-7884-1375-9*, 1375) Heritage Bk.
Alabama Symposium on English & American Literature. Signs & Symbols in Chaucer's Poetry. Hermann, John P. & Burke, John J., Jr., eds. LC 80-11064. (Illus.). 267p. 1981. pap. 82.80 (*0-7837-8379-5*, 205918900009) Bks Demand.
Alabaster, Henry. Wheel of the Law. (Illus.). 386p. 1998. reprint ed. pap. 24.95 (*0-7661-0426-5*) Kessinger Pub.
Alabaster, Oliver. Dieta de la Fibra. 1997. pap. text 17.98 (*970-05-0660-6*) Grijalbo Edit.
***Alabiso, Vincent, et al, eds.** Flash! The Associated Press Covers the World. (Illus.). 208p. 2000. pap. 24.95 (*0-8109-2793-4*, Pub. by Abrams) Time Warner.
Alabiso, Vincent & Zoeller, Chuck, eds. Flash! The Associated Press Covers the World. LC 97-40307. (Illus.). 208p. (YA). 1998. 39.95 (*0-8109-1974-5*, Pub. by Abrams) Time Warner.
Alabuzhev, P., et al. Vibration Protecting & Measuring Systems with Quasi-Zero Stiffness. (Applications of Vibration Ser.). 100p. 1989. 85.00 (*0-89116-811-7*) Hemisp Pub.
Alaca Company Staff, ed. Cotton's Journey from Seed to You Presented by Clever Cotton, No. III. (Illus.). 8p. 1995. student ed. 1.50 (*0-9641484-5-5*) Alaca.
Alaca Company Staff, ed. see Yribarren, Rick & Yribarren, Janette.
Alacoque, Margaret M. & Sisters of the Visitation Staff. Autobiography of St. Margaret Mary. LC 86-50148. 141p. 1995. reprint ed. pap. 6.00 (*0-89555-295-7*) TAN Bks Pubs.
Alacoque, St. Margaret M. The Letters of St. Margaret Mary Alacoque. Herbst, Clarence A., tr. from FRE. LC 97-60910. 285p. 1997. reprint ed. pap. 13.50 (*0-89555-605-7*, 1526) TAN Bks Pubs.
Aladar, Sarbu. The Reality of Appearances, Vision & Representation in Emerson, Hawthorne & Melville: Vision & Representation in Emerson, Hawthorne & Melville. 276p. 1996. pap. 60.00 (*963-05-7314-8*, Pub. by Akade Kiado) St Mut.
Aladdin. Trucks. LC 90-49260. (Eye Openers Ser.). (Illus.). 24p. (J). (ps-k). 1991. 7.95 (*0-689-71405-X*) Aladdin.
Aladdin, ed. see Kindersley, Dorling.
Aladdin, ed. see Royston, Angela.
Aladdin Company Staff. Aladdin "Built in a Day" House Catalog, 1917. 17th ed. (Illus.). 128p. 1995. pap. text 10.95 (*0-486-28591-X*) Dover.
Aladdin Paperbacks Publishing Staff. Ben Affleck, Vol.8. (Scene Ser.). (Illus.). 32p. 1999. pap. 6.99 (*0-689-82547-1*) Aladdin.
***Aladdin Paperbacks Publishing Staff.** Brandy, Vol. 6. (Scene Ser.). (Illus.). 32p. 1999. pap. 6.99 (*0-689-82545-5*) Aladdin.
— Newberry Awards. 1998. pap. 143.10 (*0-689-00462-1*) Aladdin.
Aladjem, A., jt. ed. see Lewis, F. A.
Aladjem, Henrietta. The Challenges of Lupus: Insights & Hope. LC 98-47123. 254p. 1999. pap. 14.95 (*0-89529-881-3*, Avery) Penguin Putnam.
— A Decade of Lupus: Selections from Lupus News. 288p. (Orig.). 1991. pap. text 12.00 (*0-9608660-9-4*) Lupus Found Am.
Aladjem, Silvio & Vidyasagar, Dharmapuri. Atlas of Perinatology. (Illus.). 508p. 1982. text 180.00 (*0-7216-1080-3*, W B Saunders Co) Harcrt Hlth Sci Grp.
Aladro-Font, Jordi, ed. Homenaje a Don Luis Monguio. (Homenajes Ser.: No. 13). (SPA.). 1997. 22.00 (*0-936388-82-X*) Juan de la Cuesta.
***Alaerts, G. J.** Water Sector Capacity Building: Concepts & Instruments. 455p. 1999. 90.00 (*90-5410-421-X*, Pub. by A A Balkema) Ashgate Pub Co.
Alaez, J. A., jt. ed. see Murthy, T. K.
Alagappa, Muthia & Inoguchi, Takashi, eds. International Security Management & the United Nations. LC 99-6178. 320p. 1998. pap. 24.95 (*92-808-1001-4*, Pub. by UN Univ Pr) Brookings.
Alagappa, Muthiah. Asian Security Practice: Material & Ideational Influences. LC 98-16563. 860p. 1998. 75.00 (*0-8047-3347-3*); pap. 29.95 (*0-8047-3348-1*) Stanford U Pr.
— Democratic Transition in Asia: The Role of the International Community. (Illus.). 51p. (Orig.). (C). 1994. pap. text 25.00 (*0-7881-1364-X*) DIANE Pub.
— The National Security of Developing States: Lessons from Thailand. LC 86-17497. 288p. (C). 1986. 55.00 (*0-86569-152-5*, Auburn Hse) Greenwood.
Alagappa, Muthiah, ed. Building Confidence, Resolving Conflicts: Proceedings of the Second Asia-Pacific Roundtable. 155p. 1990. 75.00 (*0-7103-0372-6*, A4534) Routledge.
— In Search of Peace: Confidence Building & Conflict Reduction in the Pacific. 72p. 1990. 45.00 (*0-7103-0375-0*, A4119) Routledge.
— Political Legitimacy in Southeast Asia: The Quest for Moral Authority. LC 95-1075. (Contemporary Issues in Asia & the Pacific Ser.). 448p. 1995. 60.00 (*0-8047-2504-7*); pap. 19.95 (*0-8047-2560-8*) Stanford U Pr.
Alagar, V. S. & Missaoui, R. Object-Oriented Technology for Database & Software Systems. LC 95-33010. 300p. 1995. 74.00 (*981-02-2170-3*) World Scientific Pub.
Alagar, V. S. & Nivat, Maurice, eds. Algebraic Methodology & Software Technology: 4th International Conference, AMAST '95, Montreal, Canada, July 3-7, 1995: Proceedings. LC 95-20081. (Lecture Notes in Computer Science Ser.: No. 936). (Illus.). 591p. 1995. 94.00 (*3-540-60043-4*) Spr-Verlag.
Alagar, V. S. & Periyasamy, K. Specification of Software Systems. LC 98-16912. (Graduate Texts in Computer Science Ser.). 420p. 1998. 59.95 (*0-387-98430-5*) Spr-Verlag.
Alagar, Vangalur S., et al, eds. Formal Methods in Databases & Software Engineering: Proceedings of the Workshop on Formal Methods Databases & Software Engineering , Montreal, Canada, 15-16 May 1992. LC 93-3821. 1993. 69.00 (*0-387-19812-1*) Spr-Verlag.
Alagh, Y. K. Economic LD Imensions of the Sardar Sarovar Project. (C). 1995. 26.00 (*81-241-0333-X*, Pub. by Har-Anand Pubns) S Asia.
— Indian Development Planning & Policy: An Alternative View. 1991. text 30.00 (*0-7069-5560-9*, Pub. by Vikas) S Asia.
Alagh, Y. K., ed. Narmada & Environment: An Assessment. (C). 1995. 62.50 (*0-614-08521-7*, Pub. by Har-Anand Pubns) S Asia.
Alagh, Yoginder K. Indian Development Planning & Policy: A Re-Evaluation. rev. ed. 1997. reprint ed. 27.50 (*0-7069-8569-9*, Pub. by Vikas) S Asia.
Alagh, Yoginder K., ed. Process of Industrialization & Technological Alternatives. (C). 1988. 34.00 (*81-7062-044-9*, Pub. by Lancer International) S Asia.
Alagic, S. Object-Oriented Database Programming. (Texts & Monographs in Computer Science). (Illus.). 320p. 1988. 75.95 (*0-387-96754-0*) Spr-Verlag.
— Relational Database Technology. (Texts & Monographs in Computer Science). (Illus.). 275p. 1986. 79.95 (*0-387-96276-X*) Spr-Verlag.
Alagic, S. & Arbib, Michael A. The Design of Well-Structured & Correct Programs. 4th ed. (Texts & Monographs in Computer Science). (Illus.). x, 292p. 1991. reprint ed. 79.95 (*0-387-90299-6*) Spr-Verlag.
Alagich, Richard. Soccer: Winning Through Technique & Tactics. (Illus.). 488p. 1995. pap. 29.95 (*0-07-470228-9*) McGraw.
Alagille, Daniel & Odievre, Michel. Liver & Biliary Tract Disease in Children. LC 79-12254. 375p. reprint ed. pap. 116.30 (*0-608-13286-1*, 205575900037) Bks Demand.
Alahow-to-Parent. The ALAHOW-to-Parent Group Manual. 172p. (Orig.). 1989. pap. text. write for info. (*0-318-66436-4*) Alahow-To-Parent.
Alahydoian, Ruth. A Study of the Success Rates of State CDBG Economic Development Loans. (Illus.). 61p. (C). 1999. reprint ed. pap. text 20.00 (*0-7881-4382-4*) DIANE Pub.
Alailima, Fay. Aggie Grey: A Samoan Saga. 144p. 1989. pap. 15.95 (*0-935180-79-6*) Mutual Pub HI.
***Alaimo, Robert J.** Handbook of Chemical Health & Safety. LC 99-52958. 2000. write for info. (*0-8412-3670-4*) Am Chemical.
***Alaimo, Stacy.** Undomesticated Ground: Recasting Nature as Feminist Space. 2000. pap. write for info. (*0-8014-8643-2*) Cornell U Pr.
Alain. Les Arts et les Dieux. deluxe ed. (FRE.). 1488p. 1979. 110.00 (*0-8288-3412-1*, F80950) Fr & Eur.
— Diccionario de Terminos Literarios. (FRE & SPA.). 384p. 1990. pap. 11.95 (*0-7859-1673-3*, F80950) Fr & Eur.
— Les Passions et la Sagesse. (FRE.). 95.00 (*0-8288-3413-X*, F81190) Fr & Eur.
— Les Passions et la Sagesse. (FRE.). 1480p. 1960. text 115.00 (*0-7859-7572-1*, F81190) Fr & Eur.
— Propos. deluxe ed. (Pleiade Ser.: Vol. 2). (FRE.). 1408p. 1973. 95.00 (*0-7859-4642-X*, F33650) Fr & Eur.
— Propos, Vol. 1. deluxe ed. (Pleiade Ser.). (FRE.). 1424p. 1956. 95.00 (*0-7859-4636-5*, F21170) Fr & Eur.
Alain, Dumort & Paprotte, Wolf. Road to the Information Society: New Technologies for Education & Training, EUR 16675. 267p. 1996. pap. 45.00 (*92-827-7850-8*, CD-NA-16671-ENC, Pub. by Comm Europ Commun) Bernan Associates.
Alain-Fournier. Le Grand Meaulnes. (FRE., Illus.). 1989. write for info. (*0-7859-3562-2*, F81562) Fr & Eur.
Alain-Fournier. Le Grand Meaulnes: B Level. text 8.95 (*0-88436-110-1*) EMC-Paradigm.
Alain-Fournier. Le Grand Meaulnes & Miracles: Or the Lost Domain. Russell, R. B. & Eckersley, Adrian, trs. 283p. 1998. 49.95 (*1-872621-38-4*, Pub. by Tartarus Pr) Firebird Dist.
— Le Grande Meaulnes. Davison, Frank, tr. from FRE. (Classics Ser.). 736p. 1991. pap. 10.95 (*0-14-018282-9*, Penguin Classics) Viking Penguin.
— Miracles. (FRE.). 223p. 1988. pap. 11.95 (*0-7859-3144-9*, 2253047066) Fr & Eur.
Alain, Hermano. Flora de Cuba, Vol. 5. 362p. 1962. 3.50 (*0-8477-2319-4*); pap. 2.50 (*0-8477-2302-X*) U of PR Pr.
Alain, Hermano, jt. auth. see Leon, H.
Alain, S. J. How to Start & Run Your Own Business. (Book & Cassette Tape Ser.). (Illus.). (Orig.). 1986. pap. 49.00 (*0-934493-03-0*) AlphaVideo Grp.
Alajbegovic, Jusuf H. & Mockor, Jiri. Approximation Theorems in Commutative Algebra: Classical & Categorical Methods. LC 92-26603. (Mathematics & Its Applications East European Ser.: Vol. 59). 1992. text 208.00 (*0-7923-1948-6*) Kluwer Academic.
Alajoki, Elmer. God Is Love. (Illus.). 238p. 1995. write for info. (*1-887034-01-3*) Laestadian Lutheran.
Alali, A. Odasuo & Byrd, Gary W. Terrorism & the News Media: A Selected, Annotated Bibiliography. LC 94-2923. 214p. 1994. pap. 42.50 (*0-89950-904-5*) McFarland & Co.
Alali, A. Odasuo & Eke, Kenoye K. Media Coverage of Terrorism: Methods of Diffusion. (Focus Editions Ser.: Vol. 130). (Illus.). 272p. 1991. text 59.95 (*0-8039-4190-0*); pap. text 26.00 (*0-8039-4191-9*) Sage.
Alali, A. Odasuo & Eke, Kenoye K., eds. Media Coverage of Terrorism: Methods of Diffusion. LC 90-28310. (Sage Focus Editions Ser.: Vol. 130). 160p. reprint ed. pap. 49.60 (*0-608-09788-8*, 206996200007) Bks Demand.
Alam, A., jt. ed. see Sen, S.
***Alam, Ahmad.** Wandering Thoughts - A Collection of Poems. 1999. pap. write for info. (*1-58235-029-5*) Watermrk Pr.
Alam, Assadollah. The Diaries of Assadollah Alam Vol. I: 1347-1348. Alikhani, Alinaghi, ed. (PER.). 414p. 1992. 25.00 (*0-936347-57-0*) IBEX.
— The Diaries of Assadollah Alam Vol. II: 1349-1351. Alikhani, Alinaghi, ed. (PER.). 424p. 1993. 25.00 (*0-936347-58-9*) IBEX.
— The Diaries of Assadollah Alam Vol. III: 1952. Alikhani, Alinaghi, ed. LC 95-15505. (PER.). 378p. 1996. 25.00 (*0-936347-59-7*) IBEX.
***Alam, Edward Joseph.** Out of the Shadows Into Reality: Philosophical Exposition of John Newman's Grammar of Assent. 200p. 2000. pap. 7.00 (*0-9634349-6-9*, Pub. by Notre Dame Univ) Platform Intl.
Alam, Fakrul. Bharati Mukherjee. LC 95-10832. (Twayne's United States Authors Ser.: Vol. 653). 1995. 32.00 (*0-8057-3997-1*, Twyne) Mac Lib Ref.
Alam, Ghayur, jt. auth. see Jacobsson, Staffan.
***Alam, Glynn M.** Dive Deep & Deadly. LC 99-50923. 2000. pap. 12.95 (*0-9661072-9-2*) Avocet Pr.
Alam, Javeed. Domination & Dissent: Peasants & Politics. xi, 170p. 1985. 12.00 (*81-85010-00-5*) Nataraj Bks.
— India: Living with Modernity. LC 99-933484. 254p. 1999. text 27.00 (*0-19-564525-1*) OUP.
Alam, K., ed. Agricultural Development in North-East India: Constraints & Prospects. 1993. 30.00 (*81-7100-471-7*, Pub. by Deep & Deep Pubns) S Asia.
Alam, M. K., jt. ed. see Guceri, Selcuk I.
Alam, M. Shahid. Governments & Markets in Economic Development Strategies: Lessons from Korea, Taiwan, & Japan. LC 88-27442. 198p. 1989. 52.95 (*0-275-92935-3*, C2935, Praeger Pubs) Greenwood.
***Alam, M. Shahid.** Poverty from the Wealth of Nations: Integration & Polarization in the Global Economy since 1760. LC 99-46992. 224p. 2000. text 69.95 (*0-312-23018-4*) St Martin.
Alam, Maktoob & Thomson, Ronald H. Handbook of Natural Products from Marine Invertebrates Pt. 1 Phylum Mollusca. 288p. 1997. text 72.00 (*90-5702-253-2*, Harwood Acad Pubs) Gordon & Breach.
Alam, Manzoor & Alikhan, Fatima, eds. Perspectives on Urbanization & Migration, India & U. S. S. R. xxiv, 538p. 1987. 26.50 (*81-8364-2155-8*, Pub. by Allied Pubs) S Asia.
Alam, Manzoor & Kidwai, Atiya H. Regional Imperatives in Utilization & Management of Resources: India & the U. S. S. R. 1987. 58.50 (*0-8364-2256-2*, Pub. by Concept) S Asia.
***Alam, Mohammad S. & Thompson, Brian J.** Selected Papers on Optical Pattern Recognition Using Joint Transform Correlation LC 99-16224. (Milestone Ser.). 1999. write for info. (*0-8194-3470-1*) SPIE.
Alam, Mohammed B. Aspects of American Government. (Illus.). viii, 187p. 1994. 25.00 (*81-7024-653-9*, Pub. by Ashish Pub Hse) Nataraj Bks.
Alam, Mohammed B., ed. Essays on Nuclear Proliferation. (C). 1995. 28.00 (*0-7069-9065-X*, Pub. by Vikas) S Asia.
Alam, Muzaffar. The Crisis of Empire in Mughal North India: Awadh & the Punjab, 1707-1748. (Illus.). 384p. 1988. text 39.95 (*0-19-561892-0*) OUP.
— The Crisis of Empire in Mughal North India: Awadh & the Punjab 1707-1748. (Oxford India Paperbacks Ser.). 384p. 1993. pap. 5.95 (*0-19-563000-9*) OUP.
***Alam, Muzaffar, ed.** Making of Indo-Persian Culture: Indian & French Studies. 2000. 58.00 (*81-7304-210-1*, Pub. by Manohar) S Asia.
Alam, Muzaffar & Subrahmanyam, Sanjay, eds. The Mughal State, 1526-1750. LC 98-909289. (Oxford in India Readings Ser.). 548p. 1998. text 35.00 (*0-19-563905-7*) OUP.
Alam, S. M. The State, Class Formation, & Development in Bangladesh. 262p. 1995. lib. bdg. 48.00 (*0-7618-0079-4*) U Pr of Amer.
Alam, Sher. Lasers Without Inversion. LC 97-6632. (Tutorial Texts in Optical Engineering Ser.). 1997. pap. write for info. (*0-8194-2514-1*) SPIE.
***Alam, Sher.** Lasers Without Inversion & Electromagnetically Induced Transparency. 1998. 80.00 (*0-8194-3040-4*) SPIE.
Alam, V. Emergency Power in Indian Democracy. 1986. 120.00 (*0-7855-1809-6*, Pub. by Archives Pubs) St Mut.
Alamares, Jay. The Existential Wage-Slave Hymnal. ii, 45p. 1996. pap. 6.00 (*1-888662-04-2*) Vinegar Hill.
Alamares, Jay. Lost Rhythm Avenue. 48p. 1997. pap. 8.00 (*1-888662-13-1*) Vinegar Hill.
Alamdari, F. Displacement Ventilation Performance - Office Space Application. 1993. pap. 60.00 (*0-86022-388-4*, Pub. by Build Servs Info Assn) St Mut.
Alamdari, F. & Eagles, N. Displacement Ventilation & Chilled Ceilings. 1996. pap. 100.00 (*0-86022-433-3*, Pub. by Build Servs Info Assn) St Mut.
Alamdari, F., jt. auth. see BSRIA Staff.
Alamdari, F., jt. auth. see Fishwick, P. J.
Alamdari, F., jt. auth. see Rose, P. M.
Alameddine, Rabih. Koolaids: The Art of War. LC 98-4879. 256p. 1998. text 23.00 (*0-312-18693-2*) St Martin.
— Koolaids: The Art of War. 256p. 1999. pap. 13.00 (*0-312-20658-5*, Picador USA) St Martin.
***Alameddine, Rabih.** Koolaids: The Art of War, a Novel. 245p. 2000. reprint ed. 23.00 (*0-7881-9338-4*) DIANE Pub.
Alameddine, Rabih. The Perv: Stories. LC 99-25993. 208p. 1999. text 21.00 (*0-312-20041-2*, Picador USA) St Martin.
Alameida, Roy K. Na Mo'olelo Hawai'i O Ka Wa Kahiko: Stories of Old Hawaii. LC 99-205062. (Illus.). 128p. 1997. pap. 12.95 (*1-57306-026-7*); pap., teacher ed. 8.95 (*1-57306-065-8*) Bess Pr.
Alamgir, Mohivddin & Arora, Poonam. Providing Food Security for All. (Studies in Rural Poverty: An International Fund for Agricultural Development Ser.). 304p. (C). 1991. text 50.00 (*0-8147-0603-7*) NYU Pr.
Alami, Rachid, jt. ed. see Steel, Sam.
Alamichel, Marie-Francoise & Brewer, Derek S., eds. The Middle Ages after the Middle Ages in the English-Speaking World. LC 96-54703. 176p. 1997. 75.00 (*0-85991-508-5*) Boydell & Brewer.
Alamo, Katherine, ed. see Sharpe, Rick.
***Alampalli, Sreenivas, ed.** Structural Materials Technology. LC 00-100229. 455p. 2000. text 219.00 (*1-56676-949-3*) Technomic.
Alampi. Federal Data Base Finder. 4th ed. 1995. 130.00 (*0-7876-0361-9*) Gale.
Alampi, Frank, tr. see Bonaldo, Nadia.
Alampi, Janet. Pregnancy & Prayer. (Illus.). 80p. (Orig.). 1995. pap. 3.95 (*0-8198-5892-7*) Pauline Bks.
Alampi, Janet, tr. see Bonaldo, Nadia.
Alamuddin, Najib. The Flying Sheikh LC 87-182718. 290p. 1987. write for info. (*0-7043-2627-2*) Quartet.
Alamuddin, Nura S. & Starr, Paul D. Crucial Bonds: Marriage Among the Lebanese Druze. LC 78-10465. 128p. 1980. 25.00 (*0-88206-024-4*) Caravan Bks.
Alan Bell, Peter, et al. Accidental Justice: The Dilemmas of Tort Law. 288p. 1999. pap. text 17.00 (*0-300-07857-9*) Yale U Pr.
Alan, Carter. U2: The Road to POP. rev. ed. LC 97-228526. (Illus.). 256p. 1997. pap. 14.95 (*0-571-19930-5*) Faber & Faber.
Alan, Carter, jt. auth. see Dawson, Dinky.
Alan, Elizabeth. The Heir. LC 98-68271. 212p. 1999. pap. 9.95 (*1-57197-153-X*) Pentland Pr.
Alan, Jabbour, jt. auth. see Carl, Lindahl.
Alan, John, ed. Black Brown & Red: The Movement for Freedom among Black, Chicano, Latino, & Indian. (Illus.). 78p. (Orig.). 1975. pap. 0.75 (*0-914441-09-4*) News & Letters.
Alan, John, jt. auth. see Turner, Lou.
Alan, Lloyd. Night of the Gargoyle. (House of Horrors). (J). 1995. 9.05 (*0-606-08455-X*, Pub. by Turtleback) Demco.
***Alan, M. & Adelman.** 20 Common Problems in Geriatrics. (Illus.). 552p. 2000. pap. 45.00 (*0-07-000518-4*) McGraw.
Alan of Lille. Anticlaudianus, or the Good & Perfect Man. Sheridan, James J., tr. from LAT. 251p. pap. 14.86 (*0-88844-263-7*) Brill Academic Pubs.
— The Plaint of Nature. Sheridan, James J., tr. from LAT. viii, 256p. pap. 13.14 (*0-88844-275-0*) Brill Academic Pubs.
Alan, Richard. The Gemstone File: Sixty Years of Corrupt Manipulation in World Government Detailing the Events Surrounding the Assassination of JFK. LC 92-70202. (Illus.). 416p. (Orig.). 1992. pap. 29.95 (*0-9631704-5-7*) Gemstone Pub.

A

A

Alan, Rose. Don't Ever Forget Me. LC 86-46441. 1988. 15.00 (*0-87212-204-2*) Libra.

Alan Shawn Feinstein World Staff, ed. The Hunger Report, 1993. 102p. 1994. pap. text 13.00 (*2-88449-118-X*) Gordon & Breach.

Alan Sutton Publishing Inc. Staff. Ring of Words: Poems from the Daily Telegraphy/Arvon Foundation International Poetry Competition. 1999. pap. text 14.00 (*0-7509-1981-7*) A Sutton.

***Alan, Vaughan.** Doorways to Higher Consciousness, Vol. I. LC 97-78001. 1998. 19.95 (*0-9636489-3-4*) Celest Pr.

Alana-Leah, Stacia, jt. auth. see Mardyks, Raymond.

***Alanahally, Srikrishna & Giridhar, P. P.** Gendethimma = Parasangada Gendethimma. LC 99-933820. (Modern Indian Novels in Translation Ser.). xiii, 173 p. 1998. write for info. (*0-333-92330-8*, Pub. by S1 & J) Trafalgar.

Aland, B., intro. Das Neue Testament Auf Papyrus: II. Die Paulinischen Briefe, Part1: Roem, 1. Kor., 2 Kor. rev. ed. (Arbeiten zur Neutestamentlichen Testforschung Ser.: No. 12). lviii, 418p. (C). 1989. lib. bdg. 119.25 (*3-11-012248-0*) De Gruyter.

Aland, Barbara & Juckel, Andreas, eds. Das Neue Testament in Syrischer Uberlieferung II. Die Paulinsichen Briefe Teil 1: Romer- und 1. Korinthebrief. (Arbeiten zur Neutestamentlichen Textforschung Ser.: Vol. 14). ix, 644p. 1991. lib. bdg. 315.40 (*3-11-011139-X*) De Gruyter.

— Das Neue Testament in Syrischer Ueberlieferung II - Die Paulinischen Briefe Teil 2: Korintherbrief, Galaterbrief, Epheserbrief, Philipperbrief und Kolosserbrief. (Arbeiten zur Neutestamentlichen Textforschung Ser.: Band 23). (GER.). viii, 582p. (C). 1995. lib. bdg. 292.35 (*3-11-014613-4*) De Gruyter.

Aland, Barbara, jt. auth. see Aland, Kurt.

Aland, Kurt. Supplementa: Zu den Neutestamentlichen und den Kirchengeschichtlichen Entwurfen. viii, 516p. (C). 1990. lib. bdg. 152.35 (*3-11-012142-5*) De Gruyter.

Aland, Kurt, ed. Die Alten Uebersetzungen des Neuen Testaments, die Kirchenvaeterzitate und Lektionare: Der Gegenwaertige Stand Ihrer Erforschung und Ihre Bedeutung fuer die Griechische Textgeschichte. (Arbeiten zur Neutestamentlichen Textforschung Ser.: No. 5). xxiv, 590p. (C). 1972. 142.35 (*3-11-004121-9*) De Gruyter.

— Glanz & Niedergang der Deutschen Universitaet: 50 Jahre Deutscher Wissenschafts-Geschichte in Briefen an und Von Hans Lietzmann, 1892-1942. 1979. 142.35 (*3-11-004980-5*) De Gruyter.

— Die Korrespondenz Heinrich Melchior Muehlenbergs aus der Anfangszeit des Deutschen Luthertums in Nordamerika: Band III: 1763-1768. (Texte zur Geschichte des Pitismus, Abt. III August Hermann Franke, Handschriftlicher Nachlass, Band 4 Ser.). xiii, 715p. (C). 1990. lib. bdg. 306.15 (*3-11-011968-4*) De Gruyter.

— Die Korrespondenz Heinrich Melchior Muehlenbergs aus der Anfangszeit des Deutschen Luthertums in Nordamerika: Band IV, 1769-1776. (Texte zur Geschichte des Pietismus, Abt. III, August Hermann Francke, Handschriftlicher Nachlass Ser.: Bd. 5). (GER.). xvi, 773p. (C). 1993. lib. bdg. 360.00 (*3-11-012842-X*) De Gruyter.

— Repertorium der Griechischen Christlichen Papyri Pt. I: Biblische Papyri, Altes Testament, Neues Testament, Varia, Apokryphen. (Patristische Texte und Studien: Vol. 18). 473p. (C). 1976. 142.35 (*3-11-004674-1*) De Gruyter.

— Text und Textwert der Griechischen Handschriften des Neuen Testaments II: Die Paulinischen Briefe, 1. (Arbeiten zur Neutestamentlichen Testforschung Ser.). (GER.). xxii, 806p. (C). 1991. lib. bdg. 215.40 (*3-11-013442-X*) De Gruyter.

— Text und Textwert der Griechischen Handschriften des Neuen Testaments II: Die Paulinischen Briefe, 2. (Arbeiten zur Neutestamentlichen Testforschung Ser.). (GER.). vi, 819p. (C). 1991. lib. bdg. 215.40 (*3-11-013443-8*) De Gruyter.

— Text und Textwert der Griechischen Handschriften des Neuen Testaments II: Die Paulinischen Briefe, 3. (Arbeiten zur Neutestamentlichen Testforschung Ser.). (GER.). vi, 658p. (C). 1991. lib. bdg. 175.40 (*3-11-013444-6*) De Gruyter.

— Text und Textwert der Griechischen Handschriften des Neuen Testaments II: Die Paulinischen Briefe, 4. (Arbeiten zur Neutestamentlichen Testforschung Ser.). (GER.). vi, 941p. (C). 1991. lib. bdg. 244.65 (*3-11-013445-4*) De Gruyter.

— Text und Textwert der Grieschischen Handschriften des Neuen Testaments Drei, Die Apostelgeschichte, 2 vols., No. 1, Untersuchungen und Ergaenzungsliste. (Arbeiten zur Neutestamentlichen Textforschung Ser.: Nos. 20-21). (GER.). xii, 719p. (C). 1993. lib. bdg. 215.40 (*3-11-014055-1*) De Gruyter.

— Text und Textwert der Grieschischen Handschriften des Neuen Testaments Drei, Die Apostelgeschichte, 2 vols., No. 2, Hauptliste. (Arbeiten zur Neutestamentlichen Testforschung Ser.: Nos. 20-21). (GER.). ix, 806p. (C). 1993. lib. bdg. 221.55 (*3-11-014056-X*) De Gruyter.

Aland, Kurt, et al, eds. Kurzgefasste Liste der Griechischen Handschriften des Neuen Testaments. 2nd rev. ed. (Arbeiten zur Neutestamentlichen Textforschung Ser.: Bd. 1). (GER.). 541p. (C). 1994. lib. bdg., suppl. ed. 167.70 (*3-11-011986-2*) De Gruyter.

Aland, Kurt & Aland, Barbara. The Text of the New Testament. rev. ed. 1995. pap. 25.00 (*0-8028-4098-1*) Eerdmans.

Aland, Kurt & Rosenbaum, Hans-Udo, eds. Repertorium der Griechischen Christlichen Papyri Pt. II: Kirchenvaeter-Papyri, Teil 1: Beschreibungen. (Patristische Texte Und Studien: Bd. 42). (GER.). cxxix, 580p. (C). 1995. lib. bdg. 260.00 (*3-11-006798-6*) De Gruyter.

Aland, Kurt, jt. ed. see Institut fuer Neutestamentliche Textforschung, Mue.

Alanen, et al. Agricultural Reform in the Kokhoz. 72.95 (*1-84014-738-5*) Ashgate Pub Co.

***Alanen, Arnold R. & Melnick, Robert.** Preserving Cultural Landscapes in America LC 99-38598. (Center Books on Contemporary Landscape Design Ser.). 2000. 22.50 (*0-8018-6264-7*) Johns Hopkins.

Alanen, Lilli, et al. Commonality & Particularity in Ethics. LC 96-43910. 448p. 1997. text 55.00 (*0-312-17231-1*) St Martin.

Alanen, Yrjo O. Schizophrenia: Its Origins & Need-Adapted Treatment. LC 98-153236. (Illus.). 334p. 1997. pap. text 42.50 (*1-85575-156-9*, Pub. by H Karnac Bks Ltd) Other Pr LLC.

Alanen, Yrjo O., et al, eds. Early Treatment for Schizophrenic Patients: Scandinavian Psychotherapeutic Approaches. 162p. 1994. pap. 18.00 (*82-00-41197-4*) Scandnvan Univ Pr.

Alangari, Haifa. The Struggle for Power in Arabia: Ibn Saud, Hussein & Great Britain, 1914-1924. LC 99-233111. 234p. 1998. boxed set 45.00 (*0-86372-216-4*) Garnet-Ithaca.

Alaniz, Yolanda & Wong, Nellie, eds. Voices of Color. LC 98-21193. 1999. pap. 12.95 (*0-932323-05-7*) Red Letter Pr.

Alanko, Kristiina, jt. auth. see Kauppinen, Kirsti.

***Alano, Annemarie E., ed.** 1999 Hart Gulf States Petroleum Directory. 9th rev. ed. (Illus.). 746p. 1999. per. 129.00 (*1-58271-012-0*) Phillips Business.

Alano, Becky. Teaching the Novel. Morgan, Mary, ed. (Teaching Resources in the ERIC Database (TRIED) Ser.). 1989. pap. 14.95 (*0-927516-06-3*) ERIC-REC.

Alao, A., ed. see Toyin, Falola & Ajayi, A.

Alao, Abiodun. Brothers at War: Dissident & Rebel Activities in Southern Africa. 224p. 1994. text 65.00 (*1-85043-816-1*, Pub. by I B T) St Martin.

— The Burden of Collective Goodwill: The International Involvement in the Liberian Civil War. LC 97-77892. 246p. 1998. text 63.95 (*1-84014-318-5*, Pub. by Ashgate Pub) Ashgate Pub Co.

***Alao, Abiodun, et al.** Peacekeepers, Politicians & Warlords: The Liberian Peace Process. LC 99-6832. 192p. 1999. 19.95 (*92-808-1031-6*) UN Univ Pr.

***Alaofin, Victor.** Structural Adjustment Program & Agricultural Tradables: The Case of Cocoa Farming in Nigeria. Vol. 5. 188p. 1999. pap. 39.95 (*3-631-35057-0*) P Lang Pubng.

— Structural Adjustment Program & Agricultural Tradables: The Case of Cocoa Farming in Nigeria. LC 99-41559. (European University Studies, Series 5: Vol. 2474). 188p. (C). 1999. pap. text 39.95 (*0-8204-4350-6*) P Lang Pubng.

Alaolmolki, Nozar. The Persian Gulf Region in the Twenty-First Century: Stability & Change. 226p. (Orig.). 1996. pap. text 34.00 (*0-7618-0480-3*); lib. bdg. 54.00 (*0-7618-0479-X*) U Pr of Amer.

— Struggle for Dominance in the Persian Gulf: Past, Present & Future Prospects. LC 91-7327. (American University Studies: Political Science: Ser. X, Vol. 31). XIII, 322p. 1991. 49.95 (*0-8204-1590-1*) P Lang Pubng.

Alaoui, Brahim, ed. Delacroix in Morocco. LC 95-139857. (Illus.). 240p. 1994. 55.00 (*2-08-013572-4*, Pub. by Flammarion) Abbeville Pr.

Alaphilippe, Francois & Karaquillo, Jean-Pierre. Dictionnaire Juridique Sport. (FRE.). 1990. write for info. (*0-7859-7843-7*, 2-247-01093-8) Fr & Eur.

Alapi, Krisztina. Hungarian Handy Extra Dictionary. (Handy Extra Dictionaries Ser.). 209p. (Orig.). 1993. pap. 8.95 (*0-7818-0164-8*) Hippocrene Bks.

Alarcbon, Walter, jt. auth. see Salazar, Marbia C.

Alarcon. El Sombrero de Tres Picos. unabridged ed. (SPA.). pap. 5.95 (*84-410-0043-3*, Pub. by Bookking Intl) Distribks Inc.

Alarcon, Francisco J., ed. Lead: A Boot Camp & Intensive Parole Program: The Final Impact Evaluation. (Illus.). 155p. (C). 1998. pap. text 30.00 (*0-7881-7172-0*) DIANE Pub.

***Alarcon, Francisco X.** Angels Ride Bikes & Other Fall Poems. 32p. (J). 1999. 21.27 (*0-516-21696-1*) Childrens.

Alarcon, Francisco X. Angels Ride Bikes & Other Fall Poems (Los Angeles Andanen Bicicleta y Otros Poemas de Otono) LC 98-56507. (ENG & SPA., Illus.). 32p. (J). (gr. 1-3). 2000. 15.95 (*0-89239-160-X*, Pub. by Childrens Book Pr) Publishers Group.

— De Amor Oscuro - Of Dark Love: Poems. limited ed. Rich, Adrienne & Aragon, Francisco, trs. (ENG & SPA., Illus.). 44p. 1991. boxed set 560.00 (*0-939952-09-2*) Moving Parts.

— From the Bellybutton of the Moon & Other Summer Poems. (J). 1998. 21.27 (*0-516-21647-3*) Childrens.

— From the Bellybutton of the Moon & Other Summer Poems/Del Ombligo de la Luna y Otros Poemas de Verano. LC 97-37457. (ENG & SPA., Illus.). 32p. (YA). (gr. 1 up). 1998. 15.95 (*0-89239-153-7*) Childrens Book Pr.

***Alarcon, Francisco X.** It Doesn't Have to Be This Way. 32p. (J). 1999. 21.27 (*0-516-21698-8*) Childrens.

Alarcon, Francisco X. Laughing Tomatoes & Other Spring Poems (Jitomates Risuenos y Otros Poemas de Primavera) (ENG & SPA., Illus.). (J). 1997. 21.27 (*0-516-20545-5*) Childrens.

— Laughing Tomatoes & Other Spring Poems (Jitomates Risuenos y Otros Poemas de Primavera) LC 96-7459. (ENG & SPA., Illus.). (J). (ps-3). 1997. 15.95 (*0-89239-139-1*) Childrens Book Pr.

— Loma Prieta. Funkhouser, Christopher, ed. (ENG & SPA., Illus.). 32p. (Orig.). 1990. pap. 3.00 (*0-9627192-1-8*) We Pr.

— Snake Poems: An Aztec Invocation. McEvoy, ion, ed. LC 91-30469. 176p. 1992. pap. 11.95 (*0-8118-0161-6*) Chronicle Bks.

Alarcon, Francisco X., jt. ed. see Colombi, M. Cecelia.

Alarcon, Francisco X., tr. see Garza, Carmen L.

Alarcon, Francisco X., tr. see Moroney, Lynn & Ata, Te.

Alarcon, Hernando Ruiz De, see Ruiz de Alarcon, Hernando.

Alarcon, Jorge, et al. The Social Accounting Framework for Development: Concepts, Construction & Applications. 290p. 1991. text 75.95 (*1-85628-164-7*, Pub. by Avebry) Ashgate Pub Co.

***Alarcon, Jorge A. & Segura, Liliana A.** Rescate Arqueologico en el Municipio de Aguazul - Casanare. (SPA., Illus.). 152p. 1998. pap. 9.50 (*1-877812-55-2*) UPLAAP.

Alarcon, Juan Ruiz De, see Ruiz De Alarcon, Juan.

Alarcon, Justo S. & Cardenas, Lupe. El Espacio Literario de Juan Bruce Novoa y La Literatura Chicana: Un Analisis Metacritico del Texto.Tr. of Juan Bruce Novoa's Theory of Chicano Literary Space: A Metacritical Analysis of the Text. (SPA., Illus.). 111p. (Orig.). (C). 1993. pap. 22.00 (*0-927065-15-0*) Marin Chula Vista.

Alarcon, Karen B. Louella Mae, She's Run Away! LC 96-12319. (Illus.). 32p. (J). (gr. 1-4). 1997. 14.95 (*0-8050-3532-X*) H Holt & Co.

Alarcon, L. F., ed. Lean Construction. (Illus.). 512p. (C). 1997. text 116.00 (*90-5410-648-4*, Pub. by A A Balkema) Ashgate Pub Co.

Alarcon, Norma. Adaline Kent Award, 1994: Armando Rascon: Occupied Aztlan. Guiu, Inmaculada, tr. from ENG. LC 94-65445. (ENG & SPA., Illus.). 42p. (Orig.). 1994. pap. 5.00 (*0-930495-23-3*) San Fran Art Inst.

Alarcon, Norma, tr. see Castillo, Ana, ed.

Alarcon, Pedro. El Final de Norma. (Clasicos Ser.). (SPA.). 180p. 1997. pap. write for info. (*0-929441-90-7*) Pubns Puertorriquenas.

Alarcon, Pedro A. De, see De Alarcon, Pedro A.

Alarcon, Pedro Antonio de. El Capitan Veneno: El Sombrero de Tres Picos. (SPA.). pap. 13.95 (*84-239-0037-1*, Pub. by Espasa Calpe) Continental Bk.

— El Sombrero de Tres Picos. (SPA.). pap. 11.50 (*84-206-0107-1*, Pub. by Alianza Editorial) Continental Bk.

Alarcon, R. & Butler, M. Electronuclear Physics with Internal Targets: The Blast Detector. 268p. 1993. text 81.00 (*981-02-1126-0*) World Scientific Pub.

***Alarcon, Renato D., et al.** Personality Disorders & Culture: Clinical & Conceptual Interactions. LC 97-46371. 310p. 1998. 75.00 (*0-471-14964-0*) Wiley.

Alarcon, Ricardo, jt. auth. see Castro, Fidel.

Alarcon, Ruiz De, see De Alarcon, Ruiz.

Alarcos Llorach, Emilio. Gramatica de la Lengua Espanola. Real Academia Espano Staff, ed. LC 94-230223. (Coleccion Nebrija-Bello). (SPA.). 408p. 1994. pap. text 29.95 (*84-239-7840-0*) Elliots Bks.

Alarid, Brian D., ed. see Bailey, Brian J.

Alarid, Waldo. Santa Fe Shadows Whisper: A History of the Alarid & Moya Families. Garcia-Simms, Charlene, ed. LC 97-195729. (Illus.). 176p. (Orig.). 1997. pap. 14.95 (*0-9628974-5-0*) El Escrito.

Alarid, William M. Free Help from Uncle Sam to Start Your Own Business or Expand the One You Have. 4th rev. ed. Scott, Curt, ed. LC 96-37763. (Illus.). 304p. 1997. pap. 15.95 (*0-940673-66-5*) Puma Pub Co.

***Alarid, William M.** Free Help from Uncle Sam to Start Your Own Business (Or Expand the One You Have) 5th rev. ed. Lawrence, Sidney, ed. 304p. 2000. pap. 17.95 (*0-940673-75-4*) Puma Pub Co.

Alarid, William M. Money Sources for Small Business: How You Can Find Private, State, Federal & Corporate Financing. 2nd rev. ed. Scott, Curt, ed. LC 96-6814. 224p. (Orig.). 1998. pap. 19.95 (*0-940673-73-8*) Puma Pub Co.

Alarid, William M. & Berle, Gustav. Free Help from Uncle Sam to Start Your Own Business, Or Expand the One You Have. 3rd ed. (Illus.). 300p. 1992. pap. text 13.95 (*0-940673-54-1*) Puma Pub Co.

Alario, Anthony J. Practical Guide to the Care of the Pediatric Patient. (Illus.). 800p. (C). (gr. 13). 1997. spiral bd. 35.95 (*0-8151-0150-3*, 26341) Mosby Inc.

Alario, Margarita. Environmental Destruction, Risk Exposure & Social Asymmetry: Case Studies of the Environmental Movement's Action. 148p. (Orig.). (C). 1994. pap. text 27.50 (*0-8191-9728-9*); lib. bdg. 46.50 (*0-8191-9727-0*) U Pr of Amer.

***Alaroon, P. A.** El Sombrero De Tres Picos. (SPA.). 1999. 13.00 (*84-481-0987-2*, McGrw-H College) McGrw-H Hghr Educ.

Alas, Leopoldo (Clarin). A Hoax - Supercheria: Supercheria. Nimetz, Michael, tr. from SPA. LC 94-36510. (Hispanic Literature Ser.: Vol. 24). 64p. 1995. text 39.95 (*0-7734-8978-9*) E Mellen.

Alas, Leopoldo (Clarin), ed. The Moral Tales. Stackhouse, Kenneth A., tr. from SPA. 218p. (Orig.). (C). 1988. lib. bdg. 47.00 (*0-913969-12-5*) Univ Pub Assocs.

Alas, Rosy A., tr. see Cherry, Winky.

***Alaska.** Alaska Related Laws to the Insurance Laws. LC 97-76069. 1999. write for info. (*0-89246-490-9*) NILS Pub.

Alaska Airmen's Assoc. Staff. Alaska Airmen's Association Logbook: For Alaska, NW Canada & Russia. 2nd ed. Bowers, Don, ed. (Illus.). 198p. 1994. pap. 29.95 (*1-884646-04-2*) Maverick Dist.

Alaska Brotherhood, Herman, ed. see Kavelin, Archimandrite L.

Alaska Flyfishers Club Staff & Derksen, Dirk V. Fly Patterns of Alaska. rev. ed. (Illus.). 80p. 1993. 29.95 (*1-878175-32-7*); pap. 19.95 (*1-878175-31-9*) F Amato Pubns.

***Alaska Geographic Editors.** The Best of Alaska Geographic. Rennick, Penny, ed. (Illus.). 148p. 2000. pap. 24.95 (*1-56661-049-4*) Alaska Geog Soc.

Alaska Geographic Society Staff. Alaska National Interest Lands: D-2 Lands. LC 81-10979. (Alaska Geographic Ser.: Vol. 8, No. 4). (Illus.). 242p. (Orig.). 1981. pap. 19.95 (*0-88240-159-9*) Alaska Geog Soc.

— Alaska Peninsula. Rennick, Penny, ed. LC 72-92087. (Alaska Geographic Ser.: Vol. 21, No. 1). (Illus.). 112p. 1994. pap. 19.95 (*1-56661-018-4*) Alaska Geog Soc.

— Alaska Whales & Whaling. Henning, Robert, ed. (Alaska Geographic Ser.: Vol. 10, No. 1). (Illus.). 144p. 1978. reprint ed. pap. 19.95 (*0-88240-114-9*) Alaska Geog Soc.

— Alaska's Bears. Rennick, Penny, ed. LC 72-92087. (Alaska Geographic Ser.: Vol. 20, No. 4). (Illus.). 112p. 1993. pap. 19.95 (*1-56661-014-1*) Alaska Geog Soc.

— Alaska's Railroads. Rennick, Penny, ed. LC 72-92087. (Alaska Geographic Ser.: Vol. 19, No. 4). (Illus.). 96p. 1992. pap. 19.95 (*1-56661-006-0*) Alaska Geog Soc.

— Alaska's Volcanoes. Rennick, Penny, ed. LC 72-92087. (Alaska Geographic Ser.: Vol. 18, No. 2). (Illus.). 96p. pap. 19.95 (*0-88240-197-1*) Alaska Geog Soc.

— Anchorage. Rennick, Penny, ed. LC 72-92087. (Alaska Geographic Ser.: Vol. 23-1). (Illus.). 128p. (Orig.). 1996. pap. 21.95 (*1-56661-030-3*) Alaska Geog Soc.

— Arctic National Wildlife Refuge. Rennick, Penny, ed. LC 72-92087. (Alaska Geographic Ser.: Vol. 20, No. 3). (Illus.). 96p. (Orig.). 1993. pap. 19.95 (*1-56661-012-5*) Alaska Geog Soc.

— Brooks Range. Rennick, Penny, ed. LC 72-92087. (Alaska Geographic Ser.: Vol. 23-3). (Illus.). (Orig.). 1996. pap. 19.95 (*1-56661-032-X*) Alaska Geog Soc.

— The Chilkat River Valley. (Alaska Geographic Ser.: Vol. 11, No. 3). (Illus.). 112p. 1984. pap. 9.95 (*0-88240-203-X*) Alaska Geog Soc.

— Climbing Alaska. Rennick, Penny, ed. (Alaska Geographic Ser.: Vol. 25-3). (Illus.). 96p. 1998. pap. 21.95 (*1-56661-042-7*) Alaska Geog Soc.

— The Copper Trail. Rennick, Penny, ed. LC 72-92087. (Alaska Geographic Ser.: Vol. 16, No. 4). (Illus.). 96p. 1989. pap. 19.95 (*0-88240-191-2*) Alaska Geog Soc.

— Denali. Rennick, Penny, ed. LC 75-79112. (Alaska Geographic Ser.: Vol. 15, No. 4). (Illus.). 96p. (Orig.). 1995. reprint ed. 19.95 (*0-88240-186-6*) Alaska Geog Soc.

— Frontier Flight. Rennick, Penny, ed. (Alaska Geographic Ser.: Vol. No. 4). (Illus.). 112p. 1998. pap. 21.95 (*1-56661-043-5*) Alaska Geog Soc.

— Islands of the Seals: The Pribilofs. LC 82-8708. (Alaska Geographic Ser.: Vol. 9, No. 3). (Illus.). 128p. (Orig.). 1982. pap. 19.95 (*0-88240-169-6*) Alaska Geog Soc.

— Katmai Country. LC 75-79112. (Alaska Geographic Ser.: Vol. 16, No. 1). (Illus.). 96p. 1989. pap. 19.95 (*0-88240-188-2*) Alaska Geog Soc.

— The Lower Yukon River. Rennick, Penny, ed. LC 72-92087. (Alaska Geographic Ser.: Vol. 17, No. 4). (Illus.). 96p. pap. 19.95 (*0-88240-195-5*) Alaska Geog Soc.

— The Middle Yukon River. Rennick, Penny, ed. LC 72-92087. (Alaska Geographic Ser.: Vol. 17, No. 3). (Illus.). 96p. pap. 19.95 (*0-88240-194-7*) Alaska Geog Soc.

— Moose, Caribou, & Muskox. Rennick, Penny, ed. LC 72-92087. (Alaska Geographic Ser.: Vol. 23-4). (Illus.). (Orig.). 1997. pap. 19.95 (*1-56661-033-8*) Alaska Geog Soc.

— Nome, City of the Golden Beaches. LC 84-294. (Alaska Geographic Ser.: Vol. 11, no. 1). (Illus.). 184p. 1984. pap. 19.95 (*0-88240-201-3*) Alaska Geog Soc.

— Northwest Territories. Harrington, Richard, ed. LC 72-92087. (Alaska Geographic Ser.: Vol. 12, No. 3). (Illus.). 136p. 1985. pap. 9.95 (*0-88240-204-8*) Alaska Geog Soc.

— The Nushagak River. (Alaska Geographic Ser.: Vol. 17, No. 1). (Illus.). 96p. pap. 19.95 (*0-88240-192-0*) Alaska Geog Soc.

— Prince William Sound. Rennick, Penny, ed. LC 72-92087. (Alaska Geographic Ser.: Vol. 20-1). (Illus.). 112p. 1993. pap. 19.95 (*1-56661-008-7*) Alaska Geog Soc.

— Restoring Alaska Vol. 26, No.1: Legacy of an Oil Spill. Rennick, Penny, ed. LC 72-92087. (Illus.). 112p. 1999. pap. 21.95 (*1-56661-046-X*) Alaska Geog Soc.

— Rich Earth: Alaskas Mineral Industry. Campbell, L. J. & Rennick, Penny, eds. (Alaska Geographic Ser.: Vol. 22, No. 3). (Illus.). 96p. 1995. pap. 19.95 (*1-56661-027-3*) Alaska Geog Soc.

— Southeast Alaska. Rennick, Penny, ed. LC 72-92087. (Alaska Geographic Ser.: Vol. 20-2). (Illus.). 128p. 1993. pap. 19.95 (*1-56661-010-9*) Alaska Geog Soc.

— The Tanana Basin. Rennick, Penny, ed. LC 72-92087. (Alaska Geographic Ser.: Vol. 16, No. 3). (Illus.). 96p. 1989. pap. 19.95 (*0-88240-190-4*) Alaska Geog Soc.

— Up the Koyukuk. LC 83-15343. (Alaska Geographic Ser.: Vol. 10, no. 4). (Illus.). 152p. 1983. pap. 9.95 (*0-88240-200-5*) Alaska Geog Soc.

— Yukon Territory. Rennick, Penny, ed. (Alaska Geographic Ser.: Vol. 25-2). (Illus.). 128p. (Orig.). 1998. pap. 21.95 (*1-56661-041-9*) Alaska Geog Soc.

Alaska Geographic Society Staff, ed. Alaska's Farms & Gardens. LC 84-6455. (Alaska Geographic Ser.: Vol. 11 No. 2). (Illus.). 144p. (Orig.). 1984. pap. 19.95 (*0-88240-202-1*) Alaska Geog Soc.

— Alaska's Oil-Gas & Minerals Industry. LC 82-16312. (Alaska Geographic Ser.: Vol. 9, No. 4). (Illus.). 216p. 1982. pap. 9.95 (*0-88240-170-X*) Alaska Geog Soc.

An Asterisk (*) at the beginning of an entry indicates that the title is appearing for the first time.

— Alaska's Seward Peninsula. LC 72-92087. (Alaska Geographic Ser.: Vol. 14, No. 3). (Illus.). 109p. (Orig.). 1987. pap. 19.95 (*0-88240-182-3*) Alaska Geog Soc.

— Backcountry Alaska. LC 72-92087. (Alaska Geographic Ser.: Vol. 13, No. 2). (Illus.). 1987. pap. 19.95 (*0-88240-177-7*) Alaska Geog Soc.

— British Columbia's Coast: The Canadian Inside Passage. LC 72-92087. (Alaska Geographic Ser.: Vol. 13, No. 3). (Illus.). 200p. 1972. pap. 19.95 (*0-88240-178-5*) Alaska Geog Soc.

— Dogs of the North. (Alaska Geographic Ser.: Vol. 14, No. 1). (Illus.). 120p. 1987. pap. 21.95 (*0-88240-180-7*) Alaska Geog Soc.

— The Stikine River. LC 79-20674. (Alaska Geographic Ser.: Vol. 6, No. 4). (Illus.). 1979. pap. 9.95 (*0-88240-133-5*) Alaska Geog Soc.

— The Upper Yukon Basin. LC 72-92087. (Alaska Geographic Ser.: Vol. 14, No. 4). (Illus.). 120p. 1987. pap. 19.95 (*0-88240-183-1*) Alaska Geog Soc.

— Where Mountains Meet the Sea: Alaska's Gulf Coast. LC 72-92087. (Alaska Geographic Ser.: Vol. 13, No. 1). (Illus.). 192p. pap. 19.95 (*0-88240-175-0*) Alaska Geog Soc.

Alaska Geographic Society Staff & Doogan, Mike. Dawson City. Rennick, Penny, ed. LC 72-92087. (Alaska Geographic Ser.: Vol. 15, No. 2). (Illus.). 94p. (Orig.). 1989. pap. 19.95 (*0-88240-185-8*) Alaska Geog Soc.

Alaska Geographic Society Staff & Evangelista, Mark. Alaska's Weather. LC 72-92087. (Alaska Geographic Ser.: Vol. 18, No. 1). (Illus.). 96p. pap. 19.95 (*0-88240-196-3*) Alaska Geog Soc.

Alaska Geographic Society Staff & Freeburn, Laurence. The Silver Years of the Alaska Canned Salmon Industry: An Album of Historical Photos. (Alaska Geographic Ser.: Vol. 3, No. 4). (Illus.). 168p. 1991. reprint ed. pap. 19.95 (*0-88240-082-7*) Alaska Geog Soc.

Alaska Geographic Society Staff, jt. auth. see Campbell, L. J., & Staff.

Alaska Geographic Society Staff, jt. auth. see Campbell Staff, L. J.

Alaska Geographic Society Staff, jt. auth. see Simpson, Sherry.

Alaska Geographic Staff, ed. see Rennick, Penny.

Alaska Northwest Books Staff. Alaska Almanac: Facts about Alaska. 23rd ed. (Illus.). 1999. pap. text 11.95 (*0-88240-520-9*, Alaska NW Bks) Gr Arts Ctr Pub.

Alaska Rainforest Tours Staff. Alaska: The Alaska Catalog for Independent Travelers. rev. ed. 96p. (Orig.). 1996. pap. 4.95 (*0-9643593-3-2*) Alaska Rainforest.

***Alastair Sawday Staff.** French Bed & Breakfast. 5th ed. Cooke-Yarborough, Ann, ed. (Alastair Sawday's Special Places to Stay Ser.). (Illus.). 432p. 2000. pap. 19.95 (*0-7627-0719-4*) Globe Pequot.

— Ireland. 2nd ed. Greenwood, Simon, ed. (Alastair Sawday's Special Places to Stay Ser.). (Illus.). 256p. 2000. pap. 19.95 (*0-7627-0722-4*) Globe Pequot.

— Paris Hotels. 2nd ed. Cooke-Yarborough, Anne, ed. (Alastair Sawday's Special Places to Stay Ser.). (Illus.). 192p. 2000. pap. 14.95 (*0-7627-0724-0*) Globe Pequot.

— Spain & Portugal. 3rd ed. (Illus.). 2000. pap. 19.95 (*0-7627-0723-2*) Globe Pequot.

***Alastair Sawday Staff, ed.** British: Hotels, Inns & Other Places. (Alastair Sawday's Special Places to Stay Ser.). (Illus.). 2001. pap. 19.95 (*0-7627-0772-0*) Globe Pequot.

Alasuutari, Pertti. Desire & Craving: A Cultural Theory of Alcoholism. LC 91-22457. (SUNY Series in New Social Studies on Alcohol & Drugs). 226p. (C). 1992. pap. text 21.95 (*0-7914-1098-6*) State U NY Pr.

— Researching Culture: Qualitative Method & Cultural Studies. 240p. (C). 1995. 69.95 (*0-8039-7830-8*); pap. 24.95 (*0-8039-7831-6*) Sage.

Alaszewski, et al. Risk & Welfare: Policies, Strategies, & Practice. LC 98-14539. 166p. 1998. 85.00 (*0-335-19870-8*); pap. 27.95 (*0-335-19869-4*) OpUniv Pr.

Alatalo, Frances & Anderson, Lori, eds. North by Choice: Tahquamenon Area Poems. (Illus.). 112p. (Orig.). 1991. pap. 12.95 (*0-9629546-0-8*) Newberry News.

Alatalo, Rauno V., jt. auth. see Hoglund, Jacob.

Alatalo, Rauno V., jt. auth. see Lundberg, Arne.

Alatalo, Sally & Wilson, Anne. Imperfect Sutures. (Illus.). 16p. (Orig.). 1995. pap. 15.00 (*1-888636-02-5*) Sara Ranchouse.

Alatalo, Sally, ed. see Rhymer, Eve.

Alatas, Syed H. Corruption: Its Nature, Causes & Functions. 213p. 1990. 80.95 (*1-85628-045-4*, Pub. by Avebry) Ashgate Pub Co.

— Intellectuals in Developing Societies. 130p. 1977. 35.00 (*0-7146-3004-7*, BHA-03004, Pub. by F Cass Pubs) Intl Spec Bk.

— Myth of the Lazy Native. 267p. 1977. 49.50 (*0-7146-3050-0*, BHA-03050, Pub. by F Cass Pubs) Intl Spec Bk.

Alatenhofen. Word. (C). 1989. text. write for info. (*0-201-52275-6*) Addison-Wesley.

Alatis, James E., ed. Georgetown University Round Table '90/Linguistics, Language Teaching & Language Acquisition: The Interdependence of Theory, Practice & Research. LC 58-31607. (Illus.). 531p. 1990. pap. 21.00 (*0-87840-125-3*) Georgetown U Pr.

— Georgetown University Round Table '91/Linguistics & Language Pedagogy: The State of the Art. LC 58-31607. 620p. 1991. pap. 35.00 (*0-87840-126-1*) Georgetown U Pr.

— Georgetown University Round Table on Languages & Linguistics, 1989: Language Teaching, Testing & Technology: Lessons from the Past with a View Toward the Future. (Georgetown Univ. Round Table Ser.). 411p. (Orig.). 1989. pap. 16.95 (*0-87840-124-5*) Georgetown U Pr.

— Georgetown University Round Table on Languages & Linguistics 1994: Educational Linguistics, Cross-Cultural Communication, & Global Interdependence. LC 58-31607. (Georgetown Univ. Round Table Ser.). 412p. (Orig.). 1995. pap. 35.00 (*0-87840-129-6*) Georgetown U Pr.

Alatis, James E., et al, eds. Georgetown University Round Table on Languages & Linguistics 1995: Linguistics & the Education of Language Teachers: Ethnolinguistic, Psycholinguistic, & Sociolinguistic Aspects. 752p. 1995. pap. 40.00 (*0-87840-130-X*) Georgetown U Pr.

— Georgetown University Round Table on Languages & Linguistics 1996: Linguistics, Language Acquisition, & Language Variation: Current Trends & Future Prospects. 296p. (Orig.). (C). 1996. pap. 37.50 (*0-87840-131-8*) Georgetown U Pr.

Alatis, James E. & Staczek, John J., eds. Perspectives on Bilingualism & Bilingual Education. LC 85-5457. 462p. (Orig.). reprint ed. pap. 143.30 (*0-7837-7083-9*, 204689500004) Bks Demand.

Alatis, James E., ed. see Georgetown University Round Table Meeting on Lingu.

Alatis, James E., ed. see Georgetown University Round Table on Languages & L.

Alatis, James E., ed. see Georgetown University Roundtable on Languages & Li.

Alatorre, Antonio. El Apogeo del Castellano. (Fondo 2000 Ser.). (SPA.). pap. 2.99 (*968-16-5043-3*, Pub. by Fondo) Continental Bk.

— Los 1,001 Anos de la Lengua Espanola (1,001 Years of the Spanish Language) (SPA.). 343p. 1989. pap. 16.99 (*968-16-3116-1*, Pub. by Fondo) Continental Bk.

Alatriste, Lucero. Let's Buy & Sell in Spanish!Tr. of Compremos y Vendamos en Espanol!. (SPA.). 800p. 1995. pap. 35.00 (*0-9648353-0-4*) L Alatriste.

Alatriste, Sealtiel. Tan Pordiosero el Cuerpo (So Beggary the Body) (SPA.). 136p. 1987. pap. 7.99 (*968-16-2634-6*, Pub. by Fondo) Continental Bk.

Alauddin. Develop Governance & Environment. LC 98-30663. 1999. text 79.95 (*0-312-21997-0*) St Martin.

Alauddin, Mahammad & Tisdell, C. A. The Environment & Economic Development in South Asia: An Overview from Bangladesh. LC 97-36092. 242p. 1998. text 69.95 (*0-312-21106-6*) St Martin.

Alaupovic, P., jt. ed. see Malmendier, C. L.

Alauzen, Andre. Dictionnaire des Peintres et Sculpteurs de Provence-Alpes-Cote d'Azur. (FRE.). 522p. 1986. 165.00 (*0-7859-8128-4*, 2862761311) Fr & Eur.

Alavi, A. & Axford, J. S. Glycoimmunology: Proceedings of the Third Jenner International Glycoimmunology Meeting Held in Il Ciocco, Tuscany, Italy, October 11-14, 1994, Vol. 1. (Advances in Experimental Medicine & Biology Ser.: Vol. 376). (Illus.). 306p. 1995. 105.00 (*0-306-45102-6*, Kluwer Plenum) Kluwer Academic.

Alavi, Abass, jt. auth. see Bohrer, Stanley P.

Alavi, Bozorg, et al. Stories from Iran, 1921-1991: A Chicago Anthology. Moayyad, Heshmat, ed. Perry, John et al, trs. from PER. LC PK6449.E7 S86 1992. (Illus.). 576p. 1992. 35.00 (*0-934211-28-0*) Mage Pubs Inc.

— Stories from Iran, 1921-1991: A Chicago Anthology. Moayyad, Heshmat, ed. Perry, John et al, trs. from PER. LC PK6449.E7 S86 1992. (Illus.). 576p. 1992. pap. 19.95 (*0-934211-33-7*) Mage Pubs Inc.

Alavi, Bozorg, jt. auth. see Junker, Heinrich.

Alavi, Christine, ed. Problem-Based Learning in a Health Sciences Curriculum. LC 94-35357. 224p. (C). 1995. 80.00 (*0-415-11207-9*, C0059); pap. 27.99 (*0-415-11208-7*, C0060) Routledge.

Alavi, Hamza & Harriss, John, eds. South Asia. (Sociology of "Developing Societies" Ser.). 288p. (C). 1989. 28.00 (*0-85345-779-4*, Pub. by Monthly Rev); pap. 16.00 (*0-85345-778-6*, Pub. by Monthly Rev) NYU Pr.

Alavi, Hamza, jt. ed. see Halliday, Fred.

Alavi, Hamza, jt. ed. see Shanin, Teodor.

Alavi, Karima, jt. auth. see Douglass, Susan L.

Alavi, Rokiah. Industrialization in Malaysia: Import Substitution & Infant Industry Performance. LC 95-26780. (Studies in the Growth Economies of Asia Ser.: Vol. 7). (Illus.). 232p. (C). 1996. 85.00 (*0-415-14476-0*) Routledge.

Alavi, Seema. The Sepoys & the Company: Tradition & Transition in Northern India 1770-1830. (Illus.). 340p. (C). 1996. text 22.00 (*0-19-563484-5*) OUP.

— The Sepoys & the Company: Tradition & Transition in Northern India, 1770-1830. (Illus.). 340p. 1998. reprint ed. pap. 19.95 (*0-19-564595-2*) OUP.

Alavi, Y. & Schwenk, A., eds. Graph Theory, Combinatorics, & Algorithms: Proceedings of the Seventh Quadrennial International Conference on the Theory & Applications of Graphs, Vol. 1. LC 94-29109. 648p. 1995. 42.01 (*0-471-30439-5*) Wiley.

— Graph Theory, Combinatorics, & Algorithms: Proceedings of the Seventh Quadrennial International Conference on the Theory & Applications of Graphs, 2 vols., Vol. 2. LC 94-29109. 1268p. 1995. 395.00 (*0-471-30437-9*) Wiley.

— Graph Theory, Combinatorics, & Algorithms: Proceedings of the Seventh Quadrennial International Conference on the Theory & Applications of Graphs, Vol. 2. 656p. 1995. 42.01 (*0-471-30438-7*) Wiley.

Alavi, Y., jt. auth. see Hsieh, P. F.

Alawi, H., et al, eds. Solar Energy & the Arab World. (Illus.). 502p. 1983. 30.00 (*0-08-030571-7*, Pergamon Pr) Elsevier.

Alawi, H. & Al-Jassar, A. Solar Energy Arab World: 1st Arab International Solar Energy Conference Kuwait 12/83. LC 83-17410. 1983. reprint ed. 225.00 (*0-08-030570-9*, Pub. by Pergamon Repr) Franklin.

***Alaya, Flavia.** Under the Rose: A Confession. LC 99-35835. (Cross-Cultural Memoir Ser.). (Illus.). 400p. 1999. 25.95 (*1-55861-221-1*, Pub. by Feminist Pr) Consort Bk Sales.

Alaya, Flavia & Van Rensalier, Dolores. Bridge Street to Freedom: Landmarking a Station on the Underground Railroad. unabridged ed. LC 99-181170. (Illus.). 72p. 1999. pap. write for info. (*0-927351-04-8*) Ramapo College.

***Alaye, Sundiata.** Empty Promises Private Pain: A Light Out of Darkness. unabridged ed. Farrell, Kelley, ed. 384p. 1999. pap. 15.95 (*0-9673566-0-1*) Moyo Pr.

Alaye, Sundiata N., ed. see Rasul, Chuma W.

Alayeto, Ofelia. Sofia Casanova (1861-1958) Spanish Woman Poet, Journalist, & Author. LC 92-22741. (Scripta Humanistica Ser.: Vol. 89). 1992. 54.50 (*0-916379-95-7*) Scripta.

Alayna. Rag Doll: A Journey of Healing & Integration. LC 97-72778. 107p. 1997. pap. 11.00 (*0-9658490-0-7*) M M Pubns.

Alazami, M. M., ed. El Paco Hacia el Paraiso: Dichos de Muhammad el Enviado de Dios. 2nd rev. ed. Safi, Ahmad M., tr. from ARA. LC 94-5296. (SPA.). 304p. (Orig.). 1995. pap. 6.95 (*0-915957-18-3*) amana pubns.

***Alazka.** Brick Wall: That Is All. LC 99-91898. 177p. 1999. 25.00 (*0-7388-1358-3*); pap. 18.00 (*0-7388-1359-1*) Xlibris Corp.

***Alazraki, Jaime.** Critical Essays on Julio Cortbazar LC 99-34318. (Critical Essays on World Literature Ser.). 1999. write for info. (*0-7838-0384-2*, G K Hall & Co) Mac Lib Ref.

Alazraki, Jaime. Jorge Luis Borges. LC 77-136494. (Essays on Modern Writers Ser.: No. 57). 48p. 1971. pap. text 12.00 (*0-231-03283-8*) Col U Pr.

Alazraki, Jaime, et al, eds. Homenaje a Andres Iduarte. (ENG & SPA., Illus.). 1976. 15.00 (*0-89217-000-X*) American Hispanist.

Alazraki, Jaime & Ivask, Ivar, eds. The Final Island: The Fiction of Julio Cortazar. LC 77-21912. (Illus.). 1978. 27.95 (*0-8061-1436-3*) U of Okla Pr.

Alb, Martin C. And Scripture Cannot Be Broken: The Form & Function of the Early Christian Testimonia Collections. LC 99-11377. (Supplements to Novum Testamentum Ser.). 1999. write for info. (*90-04-11417-3*) Brill Academic Pubs.

***Alba, Alicia de, et al.** Curriculum in the Postmodern Condition. LC 99-58774. (Counterpoints Ser.: Vol. 103). 103p. (C). 2000. pap. text 29.95 (*0-8204-4176-7*) P Lang Pubng.

Alba, Alicia Gaspar De, see Gaspar De Alba, Alicia.

Alba, Alicia Gaspar De, see Gaspar de Alba, Alicia.

Alba, De-Anna. Cauldron of Change: Myths, Mysteries & Magick of the Goddess. 234p. (Orig.). 1994. pap. 14.95 (*1-878980-08-4*) Delphi IL.

Alba, Eleodoro M., jt. auth. see Gall, Norman.

Alba, Francisco. The Population of Mexico: Trends, Issues, & Policies. LC 81-1432. (Illus.). 150p. (C). 1981. 34.95 (*0-87855-359-2*) Transaction Pubs.

Alba, Gene. Mutley Goes Diving! (Mutley's True Life Adventures Ser.). 1998. 14.95 (*0-89346-878-9*) Heian Intl.

— Mutley Goes to Snow Mountain. (Mutley's True Life Adventures Ser.). 32p. (J). (ps-6). 1999. 14.95 (*0-89346-877-0*) Heian Intl.

Alba, Jose G. Moreno de, see Moreno de Alba, Jose G.

Alba, Jose G. Moreno De, see Moreno De Alba, Jose G.

Alba, Joseph & Hutchinson, Wes, eds. Advances in Consumer Research Vol. 25: Proceedings of the 1997 Conference. 1998. 59.00 (*0-915552-40-X*) Assn Consumer Res.

Alba, Juanita. Calor: A Story of Warmth for All Ages. (ENG & SPA.). 1994. 19.95 (*1-880507-26-9*) Lectorum Pubns.

Alba, Kathy. Morgan's Summit. 186p. mass mkt. 5.99 (*1-55197-415-0*) Picasso Publ.

Alba, Orlando. Vocabulario Basico del Espanol. (SPA.). 400p. 1996. pap. text 16.95 (*1-56328-118-X*) Edit Plaza Mayor.

Alba, Richard D. Ethnic Identity: The Transformation of White America. 390p. (C). 1990. 45.00 (*0-300-04737-1*) Yale U Pr.

— Ethnic Identity: The Transformation of White America. 390p. (C). 1992. reprint ed. pap. 20.00 (*0-300-05221-9*) Yale U Pr.

— Italian Americans: Into the Twilight of Ethnicity. (Illus.). 240p. (C). 1985. pap. text 17.00 (*0-317-11601-0*) P-H.

Alba, Richard D., ed. Ethnicity & Race in the U. S. A. Towards the Twenty-First Century. 192p. 1988. pap. text 13.95 (*0-415-00772-0*) Routledge.

Alba-Tercedor, J. & Sanchez-Ortega, A., eds. Overview & Strategies of Ephemeroptera & Plecoptera. xiv, 588p. 1991. 95.00 (*1-877743-08-9*) Sandhill Crane.

Alba, Victor. The Communist Party in Spain. Smith, Vincent G., tr. from SPA. LC 82-19339. 475p. 1983. 54.95 (*0-87855-464-5*) Transaction Pubs.

— Lincoln. LC 90-156584. (Memoria de La Historia Ser.). 1998. pap. 14.95 (*84-320-4520-9*) Planeta.

— Pancho Villa y Zapata. LC 95-133981. (Memoria de La Historia Ser.). 1998. pap. 19.95 (*84-08-01176-6*) Planeta.

— Transition in Spain: From Franco to Democracy. Lotito, Barbara, tr. LC 77-28117. 334p. 1978. 44.95 (*0-87855-225-1*) Transaction Pubs.

Alba, Victor & Schwartz, Stephen. Spanish Marxism vs. Soviet Communism: A History of the P. O. U. M. 448p. 1988. 49.95 (*0-88738-198-7*) Transaction Pubs.

Alba, Victor, jt. auth. see Harris, Louis K.

***Albach, H., et al, eds.** Theory of the Firm: Erich Gutenberg's Foundations & Further Developments. LC HB241.T496 1999. (Illus.). x, 351p. 2000. 82.95 (*3-540-66318-5*) Spr-Verlag.

Albach, Horst. Cultural & Technical Innovation: A Cross-Cultural Analysis & Policy Recommendations. Academy of Sciences & Technology in Berlin Staff, ed. LC 93-44230. (Academy of Sciences & Technology in Berlin, Research Report Ser.: No. 9). (Illus.). xxv, 1072p. (C). 1993. lib. bdg. 283.10 (*3-11-013947-2*, 4-94) De Gruyter.

— The Transformation of Firms & Markets: A Network Approach to Economic Transformation Processes in East Germany. LC 97-104421. (Studia Oeconomiae Negotiorum: No. 34). (Illus.). 114p. (Orig.). 1994. pap. 36.50 (*91-554-3236-0*) Coronet Bks.

Albahari, David. Tsing. (Writings from an Unbound Europe Ser.). 100p. 1997. pap. 14.95 (*0-8101-1568-9*) Northwestern U Pr.

— Words Are Something Else. Elias-Bursac, Ellen, tr. (Writings from an Unbound Europe). 200p. 1996. pap. 15.95 (*0-8101-1306-6*); text 49.95 (*0-8101-1305-8*) Northwestern U Pr.

Albaiges, J., ed. Analytical Chemistry of PCBs. LC 93-15433. (Current Topics In Environmental & Toxicological Chemistry Ser.: Vol. 16). ix, 409p. 1993. text 131.00 (*2-88124-938-8*) Gordon & Breach.

— Eighteenth International Symposium on Environmental Analytical Chemistry, & Fourth International Congress on Analytical Techniques in Environmental Chemistry: Barcelona, September 5-8, 1988. viii, 256p. 1990. pap. text 904.00 (*0-677-26010-5*) Gordon & Breach.

— Marine Pollution. (Proceedings of the Arab School of Science & Technology Ser.). (Illus.). 225p. 1989. 115.00 (*0-89116-862-1*) Hemisp Pub.

Albaiges, J. & Frei, R. W., eds. Fate of Hydrocarbons in the Environment: An Analytical Approach. (Current Topics In Environmental & Toxicological Chemistry Ser.: Vol. 10). x, 374p. 1986. text 176.00 (*2-88124-139-5*) Gordon & Breach.

Albaiges, J., jt. auth. see International Congress on Analytical Techniques in.

Albaiges, J., jt. ed. see Frei, R. W.

Albaiges, Juan, ed. Proceedings of the Italian National Program for Antarctica Research. 250p. 1994. pap. text 883.00 (*2-88449-008-6*) Gordon & Breach.

— Proceedings of the 5th Workshop on the Chemistry & Fate of Modern Pesticides. 342p. 1996. pap. text 60.00 (*90-5699-074-8*) Gordon & Breach.

Albainy, Tracey, et al. Woven Splendor: Five Centuries of European Tapestry in the Detroit Institute of Arts. (Illus.). 88p. (Orig.). 1996. pap. 14.95 (*0-89558-146-9*) Det Inst Arts.

Albajes, Ramon. Integrated Pest & Disease Management in Greenhouse Crops. LC 99-18112. (Developments in Plant Pathology Ser.). 1999. write for info. (*0-7923-5631-4*) Kluwer Academic.

Albala-Bertrand, J. M. The Political Economy of Large Natural Disasters: With Special Reference to Developing Countries. LC 92-28248. (Illus.). 272p. 1993. text 65.00 (*0-19-828765-8*, Clarendon Pr) OUP.

Albala-Bertrand, Luis, jt. ed. see UNESCO Staff.

Albala, David. Atlas of Normal Endourologic Appearances. LC 97-42492. 208p. 1998. text 135.00 (*0-397-51676-2*) Lppncott W & W.

Albala, Elie. Computer Acronyms & Abbreviations: Over 4000 Entries & What They Stand for, a Practical Dictionary for Computer Users. 96p. (Orig.). 1992. pap. 12.95 (*0-921993-06-4*) Alpel Publ.

Albalak, Ramon J. Polymer Devolatilization. (Plastics Engineering Ser.: Vol. 33). (Illus.). 736p. 1996. text 250.00 (*0-8247-9627-6*) Dekker.

Alban, Billie T., jt. auth. see Bunker, Barbara B.

Alban, Francis & Ferrara, Christopher A. Il Sacerdote Di Fatima. Orig. Title: Fatima Priest. (ITA.). mass mkt. write for info. (*0-9663046-3-2*) Good Counsel.

Alban, Francisco S., tr. see Fisk, Nicholas.

Alban Institute Action Research Team on Conflict Management. Pacific Asian American Ministry in a Time of Shifting Paradigms: The Example of Asian American Conflict Management. pap. 7.50 (*1-56699-163-3*, OD117) Alban Inst.

Alban, Lester E. Systematic Analysis of Gear Failures. LC 85-70125. (Illus.). 240p. 1985. reprint ed. pap. 74.40 (*0-608-07914-6*, 205267100012) Bks Demand.

Albanese. America: Religions & Religion. 3rd ed. LC 97-53209. (Religion Ser.). 1998. 55.95 (*0-534-50457-4*) Wadsworth Pub.

— Criminal Justice. 288p. 1999. pap. text, student ed. 22.00 (*0-205-29388-3*) Allyn.

Albanese, et al. Management. rev. ed. 1997. 74.95 (*0-87393-330-3*) Dame Pubns.

Albanese, Andrew. Graduation Day. LC 97-53253. 256p. 1998. 22.00 (*0-688-16033-6*, Wm Morrow) Morrow Avon.

***Albanese, Andrew & Trissler, Brandon, eds.** Graduation Day: The Best of America's Commencement Speeches. 264p. 2000. reprint ed. 22.00 (*0-7881-9272-8*) DIANE Pub.

Albanese, Catherine L. America: Religions & Religion. 389p. (C). 1981. pap. write for info. (*0-534-00928-X*) Wadsworth Pub.

— America: Religions & Religion. 2nd ed. 548p. (C). 1991. pap. 35.25 (*0-534-16488-9*) Wadsworth Pub.

— A Cobbler's Universe: Religion, Poetry, & Performance in the Life of a South Italian Immigrant. LC 97-39582. (Illus.). 226p. 1997. pap. 22.95 (*0-8264-0875-3*) Continuum.

— Nature Religion in America: From the Algonkian Indians to the New Age. LC 89-39561. (Chicago History of American Religion Ser.). (Illus.). 284p. 1991. pap. text 17.00 (*0-226-01146-1*) U Ch Pr.

— Nature Religion in America: From the Algonkian Indians to the New Age. LC 89-39561. (Chicago History of American Religion Ser.). (Illus.). 284p. 1993. 24.95 (*0-226-01145-3*) U Ch Pr.

A

An Asterisk (*) at the beginning of an entry indicates that the title is appearing for the first time.

Albanese, Denise. New Science, New World. LC 95-47757. (Illus.). 264p. 1996. pap. text 16.95 (*0-8223-1768-0*); lib. bdg. 49.95 (*0-8223-1759-1*) Duke.

Albanese, Gayle, jt. auth. see Justis, Eileen Garrison.

Albanese, James V. Kuukee Birds: The Complete Anthology. (Illus.). 130p. 1997. pap. 25.99 (*0-9653892-1-9*) J V Albanese.

Albanese, James V. & Albanese, Joseph O. Food Faith: I Wrote This Book for the Money. (Illus.). 130p. 1996. pap., wbk. ed. 25.95 (*0-9653892-2-7*) J V Albanese.

Albanese, Jay, ed. Contemporary Issues in Organized Crime. 220p. (C). 1995. pap. text 25.00 (*1-881798-04-6*, Criminal Justice) Willow Tree NY.

***Albanese, Jay S.** Criminal Justice. LC 98-50830. 584p. (C). 1999. text 60.00 (*0-205-19354-4*, Macmillan Coll) P-H.

— Criminal Justice, 2000 Update: Interactive Edition. 584p. 1999. 63.00 incl. cd-rom (*0-205-31884-3*) Allyn.

Albanese, Jay S. Dealing with Delinquency: An Investigation of Juvenile Justice. (Illus.). 138p. (Orig.). 1985. pap. text 15.00 (*0-8191-4449-5*); lib. bdg. 43.50 (*0-8191-4448-7*) U Pr of Amer.

— Justice, Privacy, & Crime Control. 68p. (Orig.). 1984. pap. text 13.50 (*0-8191-4173-9*) U Pr of Amer.

— Organized Crime in America. 3rd ed. LC 95-76762. (Illus.). 265p. (C). 1995. pap. 31.95 (*0-87084-028-2*) Anderson Pub Co.

— White Collar Crime in America. LC 94-2292. 320p. (C). 1994. pap. text 26.20 (*0-02-301261-7*, Macmillan Coll) P-H.

Albanese, Jay S. & Pursley, Robert D. Crime in America: Some Existing & Emerging Problems. LC 92-9904. 416p. (C). 1992. pap. text 33.80 (*0-13-191446-4*) P-H.

Albanese, Joseph A. & Nutz, Patricia A. Mosby's 1999 Nursing Drug Reference & Review Cards. 9th ed. 300p. (C). (gr. 13). 1998. text 29.95 (*0-8151-2056-7*, 27777) Mosby Inc.

***Albanese, Joseph A. & Nutz, Patricia A.** Mosby's 2000 Nursing Drug Reference & Review Cards. 10th ed. 448p. (C). 1999. text. write for info. (*0-323-00795-3*) Mosby Inc.

Albanese, Joseph O., jt. auth. see Albanese, James V.

Albanese, Laura L., ed. see Higdon, Rose M. & Higdon, Hal.

***Albanese, Laurie.** Lynelle by the Sea. LC 99-42638. 240p. 2000. 22.95 (*0-525-94536-9*, Dutt) Dutton Plume.

***Albanese, Laurie Lico.** Lynelle by the Sea. 2001. reprint ed. pap. 13.00 (*0-452-28218-7*, Plume) Dutton Plume.

Albanese, Paul J., ed. Psychological Foundations of Economic Behavior. LC 87-38476. 190p. 1988. 57.95 (*0-275-92742-3*, C2742, Praeger Pubs) Greenwood.

Albanese, R., ed. Electromagnetic Non-Destructive Evaluation. LC 97-75196. 450p. Date not set. 65.00 (*90-5199-375-7*) IOS Press.

Albanese, Ralph, Jr. Le Dynamisme de la Peur Chez Moliere: Une Analyse Socio - Culturelle de Dom Juan, Tartuffe, et L'Ecole Des Femmes. LC 76-9061. (Romance Monographs: No. 19). 1976. 26.00 (*84-399-5071-3*) Romance.

— Moliere a l'Ecole Republicaine: De la Critique Universitaire aux Manuels Scolaires (1870-1914) (Stanford French & Italian Studies: No. 72). 176p. 1991. pap. 56.50 (*0-915838-88-5*) Anma Libri.

***Albanese, Yvonne.** Answers: A Divine Connection. 2001. pap. 13.95 (*1-57174-192-5*) Hampton Roads Pub Co.

Albanesi, Franco. Montessori Class Management. LC 90-83194. 172p. (C). 1990. pap. 23.00 (*0-9628008-0-5*) Albanesi Educ Ctr.

Albani, Emma. Forty Years of Song. Farkas, Andrew, ed. LC 76-29924. (Opera Biographies Ser.). (Illus.). 1977. reprint ed. lib. bdg. 33.95 (*0-405-09667-4*) Ayer.

Albani, Matthias, et al. Studies in the Book of Jubilees. LC 98-198374. viii, 344p. 1997. write for info. (*3-16-146793-0*) JCB Mohr.

Albano, A., ed. see Green, M., et al.

Albano, Antonio & Morrison, Ron, eds. Persistent Object Systems: Proceedings of the 5th International Workshop, San Miniato (Pisa), Italy, 1-4 September 1992. LC 92-27164. (Workshops in Computing Ser.). 1993. 79.00 (*0-387-19800-8*) Spr-Verlag.

Albano, Charles. Transactional Analysis on the Job & Communicating with Subordinates. rev. ed. Rendero, Thomasine, ed. LC 75-20236. 183p. reprint ed. pap. 56.80 (*0-608-12971-2*, 202392800034) Bks Demand.

***Albano, David.** He's Been Faithful. 1999. pap. write for info. (*1-58235-175-9*) Watermrk Pr.

— He's Been Faithful: Inspirational Poetry for Healing, Encourgment & Worship. 64p. 1999. pap. 9.99 (*1-57921-193-3*, Pub. by WinePress Pub) BookWorld.

Albano, John R. Haircutting at Home. 1995. pap. 4.50 (*0-425-14814-9*); pap. text 4.50 (*0-425-14688-X*) Berkley Pub.

Albano, Lou. The Complete Idiot's Guide to Pro-Wrestling. 352p. 1998. pap. text 16.95 (*0-02-862395-9*) Macmillan Gen Ref.

Albano, Lou & Ricciuti, Edward R. The Wit & Wisdom of Lou Albano. (Illus.). 96p. (Orig.). 1986. pap. 5.95 (*0-9616263-0-5*) WWF Bks.

Albano, Michael J., et al. Surviving Divorce in Kansas City. LC 96-93102. 100p. (Orig.). 1997. pap. 15.95 (*0-9656174-0-8*) L Sanchez.

— Surviving Divorce in Kansas City. 2nd rev. ed. 84p. (Orig.). 1998. pap. 9.95 (*0-9656174-1-6*) L Sanchez.

Albano, P. The Seventh Carrier. 1987. pap. 4.50 (*0-8217-3612-4*) NAL.

Albano, Peter. Assault of the Supercarrier. 448p. 1996. mass mkt. 4.99 (*0-8217-5314-2*) Kensgtn Pub Corp.

— Challenge of the Seventh Carrier. 384p. 1993. mass mkt. 3.99 (*0-8217-4096-2*, Zebra Kensgtn) Kensgtn Pub Corp.

— Ordeal of the Seventh Carrier. 384p. 1992. mass mkt. 3.99 (*0-8217-3932-8*, Zebra Kensgtn) Kensgtn Pub Corp.

— Quest of the Seventh Carrier. 1989. mass mkt. 3.95 (*0-8217-2599-8*, Zebra Kensgtn) Kensgtn Pub Corp.

— Return of the Seventh Carrier. 400p. 1987. mass mkt. 3.95 (*0-8217-2093-7*, Zebra Kensgtn) Kensgtn Pub Corp.

— Revenge of Seventh Carrier. 1992. mass mkt. 3.99 (*0-8217-3631-0*, Zebra Kensgtn) Kensgtn Pub Corp.

— The Seventh Carrier. 1987. mass mkt. 3.95 (*0-8217-2056-2*, Zebra Kensgtn) Kensgtn Pub Corp.

— Super Carrier. 384p. 1994. mass mkt. 4.50 (*0-8217-4490-9*, Zebra Kensgtn) Kensgtn Pub Corp.

— Trial of the Seventh Carrier. 1990. mass mkt. 3.95 (*0-8217-3213-7*, Zebra Kensgtn) Kensgtn Pub Corp.

Albano, Peter. Waves of Glory. 336p. 1989. mass mkt. 3.95 (*0-445-20731-0*) Warner Bks.

Albano, Peter. The Young Dragons. 352p. 1992. mass mkt. 4.99 (*0-8217-3904-2*, Zebra Kensgtn) Kensgtn Pub Corp.

Albano, Robert A. Middle English Historiography. LC 92-38882. (American University Studies: English Language & Literature: Ser. IV, Vol. 168). 254p. (C). 1993. text 51.95 (*0-8204-2136-7*) P Lang Pubng.

Albano, Roberta & Giaquinto, Carol. Dental Assisting Test Preparation. LC 95-23664. 192p. 1995. pap. text 43.00 (*0-8359-4944-3*, Pub. by P-H) S&S Trade.

Albano, Roberta, et al. Dance in Italy: From the 18th Century to the Present Day. Pappacena, Flavia, ed. (Illus.). 192p. 2000. 32.50 (*88-7301-150-0*, Pub. by Gremese Intl) Natl Bk Netwk.

***Albanov, Valerian.** In the Land of White Death: An Epic Story of Survival in the Siberian Arctic. (Exploration Ser.). 272p. 2000. pap. 14.95 (*0-679-78361-X*) Modern Lib NY.

Albany Institute of History & Art Staff. The Natural Palette: Hudson River Artists & the Land. Fiore, Jenny & Mack, Stevie, eds. (J). (gr. 4-12). 1997. teacher ed. 94.95 incl. VHS (*0-945666-60-8*) Crizmac.

Albarede, Francis. Introduction to Geochemical Modeling. 564p. 1996. pap. text 40.95 (*0-521-57804-3*) Cambridge U Pr.

— Introduction to Geochemical Modelling. LC 93-49747. (Illus.). 450p. (C). 1995. text 110.00 (*0-521-45451-4*) Cambridge U Pr.

Albarede, J. L., et al, eds. Sleep Disorders & Insomnia in the Elderly. 232p. 1993. 39.95 (*0-8261-8171-6*) Springer Pub.

Albarede, J. L., jt. ed. see Vellas, Bruno J.

Albarella, Jacqueline. The Basic Make-up Workbook. (Illus.). 1980. pap. 12.95 (*0-914620-03-7*) Alpha Pr.

Albarella, Joan. Agenda for Murder. 1998. pap. 11.99 (*1-883061-20-2*) Rising AZ.

***Albarella, Joan.** Called to Kill. 205p. 2000. pap. 12.00 (*1-883061-28-8*) Rising AZ.

Albarella, Joan. Mirror Me. (Illus.). 50p. 1973. pap. 3.00 (*0-914620-01-0*) Alpha Pr.

— Poems for the Asking. (Illus.). 24p. 1975. pap. 2.00 (*0-914620-02-9*) Alpha Pr.

— Spirit & Joy. 12p. 1993. write for info. (*0-914620-04-5*) Alpha Pr.

Albarelli, Dean. Cheaters & Other Stories. 224p. 1997. pap. 12.95 (*0-312-18064-0*) St Martin.

***Albarez, Paul & Auchter, Norma.** Salon Violin Gems Violin Solo. 56p. 1999. pap. 9.95 (*0-7866-1645-8*, 95691) Mel Bay.

Albarracin-Sarmiento, Carlos. Estructura del 'Martin Fierro' (Purdue University Monographs in Romance Languages: No. 9). (SPA.). xx, 336p. 1982. 78.00 (*90-272-1719-X*) J Benjamins Pubng Co.

Albarran, Alan & Chan-Olmsted, Sylvia, eds. Global Media Economics: Commercialization, Concentration & Integration of World Media Markets. LC 98-14142. (Illus.). 362p. 1998. text 54.95 (*0-8138-2690-X*) Iowa St U Pr.

Albarran, Alan B. Management of Electronic Media. LC 96-19353. (Radio/TV/Film Ser.). (C). 1996. 87.95 (*0-534-26274-0*) Wadsworth Pub.

— Media Economics: Understanding Markets, Industries, & Concepts. LC 96-513. (Illus.). 238p. 1996. pap. text 36.95 (*0-8138-2128-2*) Iowa St U Pr.

***Albarran, Alan B., ed.** Understanding the Web: The Social, Political & Economic Dimensions of the Intern. (Illus.). 297p. 2000. 39.95 (*0-8138-2527-X*) Iowa St U Pr.

Albats, Yevgenia. A State Within the State: The KGB & Its Hold on Russia--Past, Present & Future. 320p. 1994. text 25.00 (*0-374-18104-7*) FS&G.

Albaugh, Gaylord P. History & Annotated Bibliography of American Religious Periodicals & Newspapers Established from 1730 Through 1830, 2 vols., Set. 1544p. 1994. 125.00 (*0-944026-53-2*, 42181) Oak Knoll.

Albaugh, Stephen L. Aesthetic Knowledge. 94p. (C). 1989. text. write for info. (*0-318-65315-X*) Iowa Inst Philos.

— The Present Opposition Between Art & Theory. 175p. (C). 1989. text. write for info. (*0-318-65314-1*) Iowa Inst Philos.

Albaugh, William. The William Albaugh Collection. 11 bks. Kusrow, Bruce, ed. (Illus.). 1994. reprint ed. 300.00 (*1-56837-253-1*) Broadfoot.

Albaugh, William, III & Steuart, Richard D. Handbook of Confederate Swords. (William Albaugh Collection). (Illus.). 127p. 1993. reprint ed. 30.00 (*1-56837-268-X*) Broadfoot.

Albaugh, William A., III. The Confederate Brass-Framed Colt & Whitney. (William Albaugh Collection). (Illus.). 105p. 1993. reprint ed. 25.00 (*1-56837-265-5*) Broadfoot.

— Confederate Edged Weapons. 198p. 1993. 30.00 (*1-884849-05-9*) R&R Bks.

— Confederate Faces: Photographs of Confederates. (William Albaugh Collection). (Illus.). 229p. 1993. reprint ed. 45.00 (*1-56837-260-4*) Broadfoot.

— More Confederate Faces: Photographs of Confederates. (William Albaugh Collection). (Illus.). 233p. 1993. reprint ed. 45.00 (*1-56837-259-0*) Broadfoot.

— Photographic Supplement of Confederate Swords. (William Albaugh Collection). (Illus.). 235p. 1993. reprint ed. 35.00 (*1-56837-266-3*) Broadfoot.

— Tyler Texas C. S. A. (William Albaugh Collection). (Illus.). 235p. 1993. reprint ed. 25.00 (*1-56837-263-9*) Broadfoot.

Albaugh, William A., III & Simmons, Edward N. Confederate Arms. (William Albaugh Collection). (Illus.). 278p. 1993. reprint ed. 35.00 (*1-56837-264-7*) Broadfoot.

Albaugh, William A., III, et al. Confederate Handguns. (William Albaugh Collection). (Illus.). 250p. 1993. reprint ed. 35.00 (*1-56837-261-2*) Broadfoot.

Albaugh, William S., III. Confederate Edged Weapons. (William Albaugh Collection). (Illus.). 224p. 1993. reprint ed. 35.00 (*1-56837-267-1*) Broadfoot.

Albaugh, William S., III & Steuart, Richard D. The Original Confederate Colt. rev. ed. (William Albaugh Collection). (Illus.). 62p. 1993. reprint ed. 25.00 (*1-56837-262-0*) Broadfoot.

Albaum-Feinstein, Andrea. DSM-IV Crosswalk: Guidelines for Coding Mental Health Information. 132p. 1999. pap. text 60.00 (*1-58426-000-9*, AC200298) Am Hlth Info.

Albaum, Gerald, et al. International Marketing & Export Management. 3rd ed. 446p. (C). 1998. pap. 70.00 (*0-201-41964-5*, Prentice Hall) P-H.

Albayrak, S., jt. ed. see Veldhuijsen, H.

***Albayrak, Sahin, ed.** Intelligent Agents for Telecommunication Applications: 3rd International Workshop, IATA'99, Stockholm, Sweden, August 9-10, 1999: Proceedings. LC 99-46865. (Lecture Notes in Computer Science Ser.: Vol. 1699). ix, 191p. 1999. pap. 45.00 (*3-540-66539-0*) Spr-Verlag.

Albayrak, Sahin & Garijo, Francisco J., eds. Intelligent Agents for Telecommunication Applications: Proceedings of the 2nd International Workshop, IATA'98, Paris, France, July 4-7, 1998. LC 98-29746. (Lecture Notes in Artificial Intelligence Ser.: Vol. 1437). xii, 251p. 1998. pap. 49.00 (*3-540-64720-1*) Spr-Verlag.

***Albban, Juan Pedro Viqueira.** Propriety & Permissiveness in Bourbon Mexico. Lipsett-Rivera, Sonya, tr. from SPA. LC 99-19888. 280p. 1999. 55.00 (*0-8420-2466-2*) Scholarly Res Inc.

Albban, Juan Pedro Viqueira, et al. Propriety & Permissiveness in Bourbon Mexico. LC 99-19888. (Latin American Silhouettes Ser.). 280p. 1999. pap. 19.95 (*0-8420-2467-0*) Scholarly Res Inc.

Albe, Frederick, jt. auth. see Wisner, Nancy C.

Albeck, Chanoch. Einfuehrung in die Mischna. (Studia Judaica: Vol. 6). 493p. (C). 1971. 89.25 (*3-11-006429-4*) De Gruyter.

Albee, Arden L. Annual Review of Earth & Planetary Sciences, Vol. 14. Wetherill, George W. et al, eds. LC 72-82137. (Illus.). 1986. text 55.00 (*0-8243-2014-X*) Annual Reviews.

Albee, Beverly J., et al. The Atlas of Vascular Plants. 26.00 (*0-940378-09-4*) Utah Mus Natural Hist.

Albee, Edward. The American Dream: And Zoo Story: Two Plays. LC 97-10444. 1997. pap. 9.95 (*0-452-27889-9*, Plume) Dutton Plume.

— The American Dream, The Death of Bessie Smith, Fam & Yam: Three Plays. 1962. pap. 5.25 (*0-8222-0030-9*) Dramatists Play.

— Box & Quotations from Chairman Mao Tse-Tung: Two Inter-Related Plays. 1968. pap. 5.25 (*0-8222-0139-9*) Dramatists Play.

— Counting the Ways, & Listening: Two Plays. 1977. pap. 5.25 (*0-8222-0242-5*) Dramatists Play.

— Delicate Balance. LC 96-30725. 1997. pap. 9.95 (*0-452-27809-0*, Plume) Dutton Plume.

Albee, Edward. Delicate Balance. unabridged ed. LC 73-750754. 1988. audio 30.00 (*0-694-50925-6*, SWC 360, Caedmon) HarperAudio.

Albee, Edward. Finding the Sun. 1994. pap. 5.25 (*0-8222-1327-3*) Dramatists Play.

— Fragments. LC 96-162847. 1995. pap. 5.25 (*0-8222-1421-0*) Dramatists Play.

— Icons & Idols: A Photographer's Chronicle of the Arts, 1960-1995. (Illus.). 160p. 1998. 40.00 (*0-8230-4025-9*) Watsn-Guptill.

— The Lady from Dubuque: A Play in Two Acts. 1980. pap. 5.25 (*0-8222-0628-5*) Dramatists Play.

— Lee Krasner - Collages & Paintings. Hynes, Mary B., ed. LC 98-60141. (Illus.). 34p. 1998. pap. 12.00 (*0-9655319-3-7*) Tasende Gallery.

— Marriage Play. LC 96-208087. 1995. pap. 5.25 (*0-8222-1422-9*) Dramatists Play.

— The Plays, Vol. 3. Incl. All Over. 1982. Counting the Ways & Listening. 1982. Seascape. 1982. 1982. Set pap. 9.95 (*0-689-70615-4*) Atheneum Yung Read.

— Sandbox. 1983. pap. 3.95 (*0-451-12819-2*, AE2819, Sig) NAL.

— The Sandbox & The Death of Bessie Smith. 1989. pap. 6.95 (*0-317-02810-3*) NAL.

— Seascape. 1975. pap. 5.25 (*0-8222-1004-5*) Dramatists Play.

***Albee, Edward.** Three Tall Women. 128p. 1999. pap. 5.33 (*0-452-27400-1*) Addson-Wesley Educ.

Albee, Edward. Three Tall Women. LC 95-118164. 1994. pap. 5.25 (*0-8222-1420-2*) Dramatists Play.

— Tiny Alice. 1965. pap. 5.25 (*0-8222-1154-8*) Dramatists Play.

— Who's Afraid of Virginia Woolf? 1962. pap. 5.25 (*0-8222-1249-8*) Dramatists Play.

— Who's Afraid of Virginia Woolf? 256p. 1983. mass mkt. 6.99 (*0-451-15871-7*, Sig) NAL.

— Zoo Story & The Sandbox: Two Short Plays. 1961. pap. 5.25 (*0-8222-1295-1*) Dramatists Play.

Albee, Edward, compiled by. John McLaughlin: Western Modernism/Eastern Thought. LC 96-6930. (Illus.). 96p. 1996. pap. 22.50 (*0-940872-22-6*, 620732) Laguna Beach.

Albee, Edward, pref. Stephanie Brody Lederman: October 7-November 13, 1992. LC 92-36452. 1992. write for info. (*0-933699-27-1*) Hillwood Art.

Albee, Edward & Rubin, David S. Selections from the Edward Albee Collection. LC 88-82766. (Illus.). 28p. (Orig.). 1988. pap. text 8.00 (*0-941972-07-0*) Freedman.

Albee, Edward, et al. Ethics of Change: Government's Role in the Arts & Humanities. Blagdan, Donna & Kesler, Russ, eds. (Proceedings of the February Forum Ser.: Vol. 3). (Illus.). 110p. (Orig.). 1989. pap. text. write for info. (*1-882070-04-6*) Atlantic Ctr Arts.

Albee, Edward, jt. auth. see Cooper, Giles.

Albee, Edward, jt. auth. see Hudson River Editions Staff.

Albee, Edward A. Who's Afraid of Virginia Wolf? & Other Works. 1972. 3.95 (*0-671-00907-9*, Arco) Macmillan Gen Ref.

Albee, Ernest. A History of English Utilitarianism: 1902 Edition. 448p. 1996. reprint ed. 48.00 (*1-85506-056-6*) Bks Intl VA.

Albee, Fred. Surgeon's Fight to Rebuild Men. (American Autobiography Ser.). 270p. 1995. reprint ed. lib. bdg. 79.00 (*0-7812-8441-4*) Rprt Serv.

Albee, George W. & Gullotta, Thomas P., eds. Primary Prevention Works. (Issues in Children's & Families' Lives Ser.: Vol. 6). 454p. 1996. 59.95 (*0-7619-0467-0*); pap. 27.95 (*0-7619-0468-9*) Sage.

Albee, George W., et al. Improving Children's Lives: Global Perspectives on Prevention. (Primary Prevention of Psychopathology Ser.: Vol. 14). (Illus.). 416p. (C). 1992. 56.00 (*0-8039-4610-4*) Sage.

Albee, John. New Castle, Historic & Picturesque: With the Bi-Centennial Souvenir, 1693-1893. (Illus.). 205p. 1998. reprint ed. lib. bdg. 29.00 (*0-8328-9725-6*) Higginson Bk Co.

Albee, Louise R., ed. The Bartlett Collection: A List of Books on Angling. 180p. 1996. reprint ed. 50.00 (*1-888262-22-2*) Martino Pubng.

Albee, Parker B., Jr. & Freeman, Keller C. Shadow of Suribachi: Raising the Flags on Iwo Jima. LC 94-34304. 232p. 1995. 49.95 (*0-275-95063-8*, Praeger Pubs) Greenwood.

Albee, Parker Bishop, Jr. Letters from Sea, 1882-1901: Joanna & Lincoln Colcord's Seafaring Childhood. LC 99-43369. (Illus.). 224p. 1999. 35.00 (*0-88448-214-6*) Tilbury Hse.

Albee, Robert L. Power Thinking: The Secret of Success. 139p. (Orig.). 1989. pap. text 8.95 (*0-9624441-0-3*) Writers Express.

— Shrimp Diet for Giants: 365 Shrimp Recipes to Bust Yer Gut! (Illus.). 160p. (Orig.). 1996. pap. text, otabind 11.95 (*0-9624441-2-X*) Writers Express.

Albee, Sarah. Allegra's Colors! 26p. (YA). (ps up). 1996. 3.50 (*0-689-80844-5*) S&S Childrens.

— Allegra's Shapes. 26p. (J). (ps up). 1996. 3.50 (*0-689-80843-7*) S&S Childrens.

***Albee, Sarah.** Best Friends. (Road to Writing Mile 5 Ser.). (Illus.). (J). 2000. pap. 3.99 (*0-307-45501-7*) Gldn Bks Pub Co.

Albee, Sarah. Big Bird at Bat. (Illus.). (J). 1995. 4.99 (*0-679-87090-3*) Random.

***Albee, Sarah.** Blue's Lunchbox. (Blue's Clues Shaped Paperback Ser.: No. 6). (Illus.). 16p. (J). (gr. k-3). 2000. pap. 3.99 (*0-689-83099-8*, Simon Spot) Litle Simon.

— Blue's Travel Game. (Blue's Clues Shaped Paperback Ser.: No. 5). (Illus.). 16p. (J). (ps-2). 2000. pap. 3.99 (*0-689-83098-X*, Simon Spot) Litle Simon.

Albee, Sarah. Curious Little Duckling. (Illus.). 24p. (Orig.). (J). (ps-2). 1997. pap. 3.95 (*0-8167-3738-X*, Whistlstop) Troll Communs.

***Albee, Sarah.** Double Trouble: A Story about Twins. (Illus.). 24p. (J). (ps). 2000. 2.99 (*0-375-80448-X*, Pub. by Random Bks Yng Read) Random.

Albee, Sarah. The Dragon's Scales. LC 97-40337. (Step into Reading & Math Ser.: A Step 2 Book). (Illus.). 48p. (J). (gr. k-3). 1998. pap. 3.99 (*0-679-88381-9*) Random.

— The Dragon's Scales. LC 97-40337. (Step into Reading & Math Ser.: A Step 2 Book). 48p. (J). (gr. k-3). 1998. lib. bdg. 11.99 (*0-679-98381-3*, Pub. by Random Bks Yng Read) Random.

— The Dragon's Scales. (Step into Reading & Math Ser.: A Step 2 Book). (J). (gr. 1-3). 1998. 9.19 (*0-606-13960-5*, Pub. by Turtleback) Demco.

***Albee, Sarah.** Elmo Loves You. (J). 2001. mass mkt. 4.99 (*0-375-81208-3*, Pub. by Random Bks Yng Read) Random.

— Elmo's Ducky Day. LC 99-31288. (Pictureback Ser.). (Illus.). 24p. (J). (ps-3). 2000. pap. 3.25 (*0-375-80483-8*, Pub. by Random Bks Yng Read) Random.

— Elmo's First Babysitter. 24p. (J). 2001. mass mkt. 1.99 (*0-375-81149-4*) Random Bks Yng Read.

— Ernie's Joke Book. 24p. (J). 2001. mass mkt. 3.25 (*0-375-81155-9*, Pub. by Random Bks Yng Read) Random.

— Great Outdoors. (Road to Reading Mile 3 Ser.). (Illus.). (J). 2000. pap. 3.99 (*0-307-45450-9*) Gldn Bks Pub Co.

— I Can Do It! Featuring Jim Henson's Sesame Street Muppets. (Step into Reading Ser.: A Step 1 Book). (J). (ps-1). 1997. 9.19 (*0-606-12730-5*, Pub. by Turtleback) Demco.

— If You're Happy & You Know It. 24p. (J). 2001. mass mkt. (*0-375-81154-0*) Random Bks Yng Read.

— Imagine That! (Road to Writing Mile 5 Ser.). (Illus.). (J). 2000. pap. 3.99 (*0-307-45500-9*) Gldn Bks Pub Co.

Albee, Sarah. James's Treasure Hunt. (Peek 'n' Seek Board Bks.). (Illus.). 14p. (J). (ps-k). 1997. 4.99 (*0-689-81302-3*) S&S Childrens.

An Asterisk (*) at the beginning of an entry indicates that the title is appearing for the first time.

— Lindi's Costume Parade. (Stickers & Shapes Ser.). (J). 2000. mass mkt. 3.99 (0-689-81307-4) S&S Childrens.

***Albee, Sarah.** Me, Myself & I. (Illus.). (J). 2000. pap. 3.99 (0-307-45451-7) Gldn Bks Pub Co.

Albee, Sarah. Mr. Ron's Favorite Animals. (Peek 'n' Seek Board Bks.). (Illus.). 14p. (J). (ps-k). 1997. 4.99 (0-689-81301-5) S&S Childrens.

***Albee, Sarah.** Monkeys. LC 98-47463. (Very First Things to Know about Ser.). (Illus.). 32p. (J). (ps-2). 1999. bds. 8.95 (0-7611-1134-4) Workman Pub.

— My Baby Bro is Little Monster. 24p. (J). 2001. mass mkt. 1.99 (0-375-81148-6) Random Bks Yng Read.

Albee, Sarah. My Best Friend Is Out of This World. LC 98-12754. (Road to Reading Ser.). (Illus.). 32p. (J). 1998. pap. 3.99 (0-307-26202-2, 26202) Gldn Bks Pub Co.

***Albee, Sarah.** My New Pet Is the Greatest. LC 98-8772. (Road to Reading Ser.). (Illus.). 32p. (J). 1999. pap. 3.99 (0-307-26208-1, Whitman Coin) St Martin.

Albee, Sarah. Sesame Street: Elmo's Noisy Day. Loredo, Betsy, ed. (Magic Touch Talking Bks.). (Illus.). (J). (ps-2). 1997. 19.99 (1-888208-37-6) Hasbro.

***Albee, Sarah.** Shall We Dance? (Jellybean Bks.). (Illus.). 24p. (J). (ps). 2000. 2.99 (0-375-80449-8) Random.

Albee, Sarah. Space Invaders! LC PZ7.A3174Sp 1998. (Ready to Read). (Illus.). 32p. (J). (ps-3). 1998. pap. 3.99 (0-689-82130-1, Simon Spot) Litle Simon.

— Spotty Can't Sleep ! Including Toy. (Fisher-Price Playbks.). (Illus.). 14p. (J). (gr. k-3). 1997. bds. 6.99 (1-57584-179-7, Pub. by Rdrs Digest) Random.

***Albee, Sarah.** Spring Fever. 24p. (J). 2001. mass mkt. 1.99 (0-375-81150-8) Random Bks Yng Read.

Albee, Sarah. There's a Ghost in My House. LC 96-221688. (Illus.). 24p. (Orig.). (J). (ps-3). 1996. pap. 3.95 (0-8167-4113-1, Whistlstop) Troll Communs.

— The Twelve Days of Christmas. LC 96-75580. (Little Golden Bks.). (J). 1996. 2.29 (0-307-98787-6, 98787, Goldn Books) Gldn Bks Pub Co.

***Albee, Sarah.** Watch Out for Banana Peels & Other Important Sesame Street Safety Tips. LC 99-15920. (Pictureback Ser.). (Illus.). 24p. (J). 2000. pap. 3.25 (0-375-80482-X, Pub. by Random Bks Yng Read) Random.

Albee, Sarah. What Do I Hear? What Do I Hear? 14p. (J). (ps up). 1996. pap. 4.99 (0-689-80842-9) S&S Childrens.

— What Do I See? What Do I See? 14p. (J). 1996. 4.99 (0-689-80841-0) S&S Childrens.

— What Do People Do? A Learn-About Book. (Fisher Price CarryAlong Playbks.). (Illus.). 20p. (J). (gr. k-3). 1997. bds. 10.99 (1-57584-185-1, Pub. by Rdrs Digest) Random.

Albee, Sarah & Sesame Street Staff. I Can Do It! Featuring Jim Henson's Sesame Street Muppets. LC 96-53135. (Step into Reading Ser.: A Step 1 Book). (Illus.). 32p. (J). (ps-1). 1997. pap. 3.99 (0-679-88687-7, Pub. by Random Bks Yng Read) Random.

Albee, Sarah, et al. 6 Wild Adventures. (Lunch Box Library). (Illus.). 208p. (J). (gr. 3-5). 1997. pap. text 6.95 (0-7611-0678-2, 10678) Workman Pub.

Albee, Sarah, jt. auth. see Yablonsky, Buster.

Albelda, Ra. On the Margin the Feminist Impact on Economics & Feminism. LC 97-12263. 1997. 33.00 (0-8057-9759-9, Twyne) Mac Lib Ref.

Albelda, Randy, et al, eds. Alternatives to Economic Orthodoxy: A Reader in Political Economy. LC 86-33899. (Illus.). 358p. 1987. reprint ed. pap. 111.00 (0-7837-9963-2, 206069000006) Bks Demand.

Albelda, Randy & Tilly, Chris. Glass Ceilings & Bottomless Pits: Women's Work, Women's Poverty. 224p. (Orig.). 1997. 40.00 (0-89608-566-X); pap. 18.00 (0-89608-565-1) South End Pr.

Albelda, Randy, et al. Mink Coats Don't Trickle Down: The Economic Attack on Women & People of Color. LC 87-63363. 64p. 1988. pap. 5.00 (0-89608-328-4) South End Pr.

— Unlevel Playing Fields: Understanding Wage Inequality & Discrimination. LC 96-36356. (Illus.). 256p. (C). 1996. pap. 23.44 (0-07-000968-6) McGraw.

Albelda, Randy P., et al, eds. Alternatives to Economic Orthodoxy. LC 86-33899. 424p. (C). (gr. 13). 1987. pap. text 40.95 (0-87332-413-7) M E Sharpe.

Albeniz, contrib. by. Guitar Music of Spain No. 2: Volume 2. 1994. 24.95 (0-7119-3304-9, AM90241) Omnibus NY.

— Spanish Classics for GT Tablature Albeni. 1994. 33.95 (0-7119-3411-8, AM91080) Omnibus NY.

Albeniz, I. Albentz Piano Album: Centennial Edition. 96p. 1994. 14.95 (0-7935-3041-5) H Leonard.

— Isaac Albeniz Masterpieces. (Piano Solo Ser.). 64p. 1984. pap. 8.95 (0-7935-2566-7, 00009325) H Leonard.

Albeniz, Isaac. Iberia & Espana. 192p. 1987. pap. 10.95 (0-486-25367-8) Dover.

— Suite Espanola, Opus 47. Stang, Aaron, ed. 36p. (C). 1985. pap. text 12.95 (0-7692-1284-0, EL02800) Wrner Bros.

Albensi, Bill. The Colony of New Sweden. 37p. 1987. pap. 3.00 (0-930950-27-5) Nopoly Pr.

— Lenape & the Colony of New Sweden. LC 87-15207. 183p. 1987. 14.75 (0-930950-17-8); pap. 8.75 (0-930950-18-6) Nopoly Pr.

Alber, A. F. Interactive Computer Systems: Videotex & Multimedia. LC 93-3393. (Illus.). 454p. (C). 1993. 79.50 (0-306-44395-3, Plenum Trade) Perseus Pubng.

Alber, Antone F. Multimedia: A Management Perspective. (C). 1995. pap. 72.95 (0-534-21312-X) Wadsworth Pub.

Alber, Charles J., ed. see Semanov, Vladimir I.

Alber, Glenn, ed. see Migliaro, Marco W.

Alber, Hans D. Materials with Memory: Initial-Boundary Value Problems for Constitutive Equations with Internal Variablees. Dold, A. & Takens, F., eds. LC 98-9337. (Lecture Notes in Mathematics Ser.: Vol. 1682). x, 166p. 1998. pap. 33.00 (3-540-64066-5) Spr-Verlag.

***Alber, J. & Scholkopf, M.** Seniorenpolitik: Die Soziale Lage Alterer Menschen in Deutschland Und Europa.Tr. of Senior Citizen's Policy:The Social Situation of Older People in Germany & Europe. (GER.). 424p. 1998. text 55.00 (90-5708-045-1); pap. text 40.00 (90-5708-046-X) Gordon & Breach.

Alber, M., et al, eds. Current & Future Directions in Applied Mathematics. LC 97-182. 272p. 1997. 38.50 (0-8176-3956-X) Birkhauser.

Alber, Mark, et al. Current & Future Directions in Applied Mathematics. LC 97-182. 1997. write for info. (3-7643-3956-X) Birkhauser.

Alber, Miller. Exceptional Children: Intro to Special Education. 6th ed. (C). 1999. pap. text 15.25 (0-13-025749-4) P-H.

Alber, S. I., et al. Eleven Papers on Analysis. LC 51-5559. (Translations Ser.: Series 2, Vol. 14). 332p. 1960. reprint ed. 38.00 (0-8218-1714-0, TRANS2/14) Am Math.

Albera, A. E. Making Roses Behave. (Illus.). 1960. spiral bd. 4.95 (0-87505-244-4) Borden.

Alberda, A. T. & Vemer, Hendricus M., eds. Pioneers in Invitro Fertilization: Proceedings of a Symposium Held in Oss, the Netherlands, November 5, 1993. LC 94-48589. (Studies in Profertility Ser.: Vol. 3). (Illus.). 122p. 1995. 65.00 (1-85070-566-6) Prthnon Pub.

Alberda, T., et al, eds. Food from Dry Lands: An Integrated Approach to Planning of Agricultural Development. LC 92-21701. (System Approaches for Sustainable Agricultural Development Ser.: Vol. 1). (C). 1992. text 171.00 (0-7923-1877-3) Kluwer Academic.

Alberes. Esthetique et Morale chez Giraudox. 1957. 24.95 (0-7859-0342-9, F104470) Fr & Eur.

Alberg, Kari. Gratitude: A Record of Your Blessings. (Illus.). 144p. 1998. spiral bd. 19.95 (1-55670-810-6) Stewart Tabori & Chang.

***Alberg, Robert.** Lighthouses. (Illus.). 48p. 1999. pap. 23.00 (1-929602-00-6) Lighthouse Gift.

Alberg, Tom A., jt. auth. see Archie, Peter B.

Alberger, Patricia L. & Smith, Virginia C., eds. Communicating University Research. 137p. 1985. pap. 10.00 (0-89964-238-1, 26601) Coun Adv & Supp Ed.

Alberghina, L., et al, eds. Lipases: Structure, Mechanisms & Genetic Engineering. (GBF Monographs: Vol.16). (Illus.). 441p. (Orig.). 1991. pap. 131.00 (3-527-28332-3, Wiley-VCH) Wiley.

***Alberghina, Lilia, ed.** Protein Engineering for Industrial Biotechnology. 388p. 2000. text 110.00 (90-5702-412-8, Harwood Acad Pubs) Gordon & Breach.

Albergotti, William Greer. Abigail's Story, Tides at the Doorstep: The Mackays, LaRoches, Jenkinses & Chisolms of Low Country, South Carolina, 1671-1897. LC 99-20684. 1999. 100.00 (0-87152-524-0) Reprint.

Alberi, G., et al, eds. Applications of Physics to Medicine & Biology: Proceedings of the International Confernece, Trieste, Italy, March 30-April 3, 1983. 688p. 1983. 108.00 (9971-950-42-1) World Scientific Pub.

Alberich, ed. see Kennett-Barrington.

***Albericio, Fernando & Kates, Steven A.** Solid-Phase Synthesis: A Practical Guide. LC 00-28154. (Illus.). 2000. write for info. (0-8247-0359-6) Dekker.

Alberico, W. M. & Sciuto, S. Symmetry & Simplicity in Physics: A Symposium on the Occasion of Sergio Fubini's 65 Birthday. 232p. 1995. text 81.00 (981-02-2048-0) World Scientific Pub.

Alberigo, Giuseppe, ed. The Reception of Vatican II. 362p. 1994. pap. 60.00 (0-86012-167-4, Pub. by Srch Pr) St Mut.

— Where Does the Church Stand?, Vol. 146. (Concilium Ser.). 128p. (Orig.). 1981. 6.95 (0-8164-2313-X) Harper SF.

Alberigo, Giuseppe, et al, eds. The Bible As Cultural Heritage. 150p. (Orig.). 1995. pap. 15.00 (0-88344-882-3) Orbis Bks.

— The Reception of Vatican II. O'Connell, Matthew J., tr. from FRE. LC 87-15175. 384p. 1988. pap. 19.95 (0-8132-0654-5) Cath U Pr.

Alberigo, Giuseppe & Komonchak, Joseph A., eds. The History of Vatican II 1959-1965 Vol. 1: Announcing & Preparing Vatican II Toward a New Era in Catholicism, Vol. I. LC 95-42334. 650p. 1996. 80.00 (1-57075-049-1) Orbis Bks.

— History of Vatican III. 654p. 1999. 80.00 (1-57075-153-6) Orbis Bks.

— The History of Vatican II Vol. II: Formation of the Council's Identity, Oct 62-Sept 63. 2nd abr. rev. ed. 654p. 1997. 80.00 (1-57075-147-1) Orbis Bks.

Alberink, Ivo B., jt. auth. see Pestman, Wiebe R.

Alberione, James. Queen of Apostles Prayerbook. rev. ed. 384p. (J). 1991. pap. 9.95 (0-8198-6200-2) Pauline Bks.

Alberione, James. Queen of Apostles Prayerbook. rev. ed. 384p. (J). 1991. vinyl bd. 12.95 (0-8198-6202-9) Pauline Bks.

Alberione, James. Thoughts. 170p. (C). 1996. pap. 39.95 (0-85439-233-5, Pub. by St Paul Pubns) St Mut.

Alberman, Eva, jt. ed. see Poswillo, David E.

Alberman, Eva, jt. ed. see Stanley, Fiona.

Albern, William F. & Morris, M. D. Factory Constructed Housing Developments: Planning, Design & Construction. LC 96-29774. 236p. 1997. lib. bdg. 49.95 (0-8493-7481-2) CRC Pr.

Alberoni, Francesco. Movement & Institution. LC 84-3181. (European Perspectives Ser.). 448p. 1984. text 81.00 (0-231-04884-X) Col U Pr.

Alberro, Alexander. Dan Graham Models to Projects 1978 to 1995. (Illus.). 52p. (Orig.). Date not set. pap. write for info. (0-944219-13-6) M Goodman Gallery.

Alberro, Alexander, et al, contrib. by. Lawrence Weiner. LC 98-230645. (Colour Library). (Illus.). 128p. 1998. pap. 14.95 (0-7148-3755-5, Pub. by Phaidon Press) Phaidon Pr.

Alberro, Alexander & Stimson, Blake, eds. Conceptual Art: A Critical Anthology. LC 98-52388. (Illus.). 569p. 1999. pap. 50.00 (0-262-01173-5) MIT Pr.

***Alberro, Alexander & Stimson, Blake, eds.** Conceptual Art: A Critical Anthology. (Illus.). 624p. (C). 2000. reprint ed. pap. 29.95 (0-262-51117-7) MIT Pr.

Alberro, Alexander, et al. Tracing Cultures: Art History, Criticism, Critical Fiction. 176p. 1995. pap. 17.95 (0-87427-092-8) Dist Art Pubs.

— Tracing Cultures: Art History Criticism Critical Fiction. (Illus.). 176p. 1994. pap. 15.95 (0-614-14990-8) Whitney Mus.

Alberro, Alexander, ed. see Graham, Dan.

Alberro, Elaine. Forever True. (Encanto Ser.). 1999. mass mkt. 5.99 (0-7860-0669-2) Kensgtn Pub Corp.

***Alberro, Elaine.** Heart of Gold/Corazon de Oro. (Encanto Ser.). 400p. 2000. mass mkt. 5.99 (0-7860-1060-6, Pinncle Kensgtn) Kensgtn Pub Corp.

Alberro, Solange. Inquisicion y Sociedad en Mexico, 1571-1700 (The Inquisition & Society in Mexico, 1571-1700) (SPA.). 624p. 1988. pap. 21.99 (968-16-2994-9, Pub. by Fondo) Continental Bk.

Albers. Urban Planning in Western Europe since 1945. 400p. 1997. text. write for info. (0-419-20220-X, E & FN Spon) Routledge.

Albers, Jan. John Burgoyne (1722-1792) (Illus.). 96p. pap. 14.95 (1-884592-13-9) Images from the Past.

Albers, Anne C., et al. Comprehensive Care of the Pediatric Patient: Prehospital Through Rehabilitation. Broome, Marion E., ed. 249p. Date not set. pap. text 16.00 (0-935890-25-4) Emerg Nurses IL.

Albers, Cheryl. The Sociology of Families: Readings. LC 99-6035. 1999. write for info. (0-7619-8610-3) Sage.

Albers, Christina E. Readers Guide to Short Stories of Henry James. LC 97-6444. 1997. 85.00 (0-8161-9099-2, G K Hall & Co) Mac Lib Ref.

Albers, Dave. Child of the Sun: A Cuban Legend. LC 95-13230. (Legends of the World Ser.). 32p. (J). (gr. 2-6). 1997. lib. bdg. 18.60 (0-8167-3747-9) Troll Communs.

— Child of the Sun: A Cuban Legend. LC 95-13230. (Legends of the World Ser.). 32p. (J). (gr. 2-6). 1997. pap. 4.95 (0-8167-3748-7) Troll Communs.

Albers, Donald J., et al, eds. More Mathematical People: Contemporary Conversations. LC 94-21956. 375p. 1994. pap. text 45.00 (0-12-048251-7) Acad Pr.

Albers, Donald J., et al, eds. New Directions in 2-Year College Mathematics. (Illus.). xxi, 491p. 1985. 65.95 (0-387-96145-3) Spr-Verlag.

Albers, Donald J., et al. International Mathematical Congresses: An Illustrated History 1893-1986 Including ICM 1986. 2nd rev. ed. (Illus.). v, 64p. 1987. 60.95 (0-387-96479-7) Spr-Verlag.

***Albers, Everett C.** Lewis & Clark Meet the American Indians: As Told by Seaman the Dog. (Illus.). 32p. (J). (ps-11). 1999. pap. 3.95 (0-9674002-0-1) United Printing.

Albers, Everett C., ed. Mostly Amusing, Always Amazingly True Memories: North Dakota Seniors Tell Their Stories. LC 96-70617. (Illus.). 178p. (Orig.). 1996. pap. 10.00 (0-9654579-0-7) N Dakota Hum.

Albers, Everett C., et al, eds. Behold Our New Century: 20th Century Visions of America. LC 98-86507. 264p. 1998. 17.95 (0-9664256-0-X); pap. 10.95 (0-9664256-1-8) Chautauqua Soc.

Albers, Everett C. & Tweton, D. Jerome. The Way It Was: The North Dakota Experience, 8 bks. Incl. No. 1. Sod-Busters. LC 95-95347. (Illus.). 112p. (Orig.). 1996. pap. 12.95 (0-9650778-0-2); No. 2. Norwegian Homesteaders. LC 98-89183. 112p. 1998. pap. 12.95 (0-9650778-2-9); No. 3. Cowboys & Ranchers. 112p. 1999. pap. 12.95 (0-9650778-3-7); pap. Price not set. (0-9650778-1-0) Grass Rts.

***Albers, Everett C. & Tweton, D. Jerome, eds.** The Way It Was - The North Dakota Frontier Experience Bk. 4: Germans from Russia Settlers. (Illus.). 112p. 1999. pap. 12.95 (0-9650778-4-5) Grass Rts.

***Albers, Everett C. & Weisgerber, Rebecca J.** One Hundred or So: North Dakota Centenarians at the End of the 20th Century. 128p. 2000. pap. 19.95 (0-9654579-3-1) N Dakota Hum.

Albers, Everett C., jt. ed. see Henke, Warren A.

Albers, Everett C., ed. see Patzman, Barbara J.

Albers, Gregg R. Counseling & AIDS. (Resources for Christian Counseling Ser.: Vol. 24). 224p. 18.99 (0-8499-0695-4) Word Pub.

— Counseling the Sick & Terminally Ill. (Resources for Christian Counseling Ser.: Vol. 20). 211p. 18.99 (0-8499-0693-8) Word Pub.

Albers, H. G. & Bolton, S. Testen und Prufen in der Grundstufe. Neuner, Gerd, ed. (Fernstudienangebot Ser.). (GER.). 200p. 1996. 11.25 (3-468-49673-7) Langenscheidt.

Albers, Henry H. Saudi Arabia: Technocrats in a Traditional Society. (American University Studies Anthropology & Sociology: Ser. XI, Vol. 33). XII, 230p. (C). 1989. text 35.95 (0-8204-1095-0) P Lang Pubng.

Albers, Henry H. & Davis, Ann K. The Wonderful World of Christmas Trees. LC 97-73829. 110p. (Orig.). 1997. pap. 21.95 (0-931209-69-2) Mid-Prairie Bks.

Albers, Jan. Hands on the Land: A History of the Vermont Landscape. LC 98-31767. (Illus.). 320p. 1999. 35.00 (0-262-01175-1) MIT Pr.

Albers, Josef. Interaction of Color. (Illus.). 1994. cd-rom 130.00 (0-300-05995-7) Yale U Pr.

— Interaction of Color. rev. ed. LC 74-15585. (Illus.). 74p. 1975. pap. 12.00 (0-300-01846-0) Yale U Pr.

***Albers, Josef.** Josef Albers: Werke auf Papier. (Illus.). 192p. 2000. 60.00 (3-87909-599-X, Pub. by Wienand) Nazraeli Press.

***Albers, Lawrence.** Handbook of Psychiatric Drugs: 2002 Edition. rev. ed. (Current Clinical Strategies Ser.). 109p. 2000. pap. 28.95 incl. cd-rom (1-881528-95-2) Current Clin Strat.

Albers, Lawrence. Handbook of Psychiatric Drugs, 1998-99 Edition: Current Clinical Strategies. 102p. 1998. pap. 8.75 (1-881528-54-5) Current Clin Strat.

***Albers, Lawrence J., et al.** Handbook of Psychiatric Drugs: 2001-2002 Edition. rev. ed. (Current Clinical Strategies Ser.). 109p. 2000. pap. 9.95 (1-881528-94-4) Current Clin Strat.

Albers, Maura & Cvikota, Tom, eds. Just Add Color: A Children's Coloring Book with Drawings by Contemporary Artists. (Illus.). 36p. (Orig.). (J). 1991. pap. text 19.95 (0-9627744-0-5) HBP NY.

Albers, Michelle, jt. ed. see Pawlak, Laura.

Albers Mohrman, Susan, et al, eds. Tomorrow's Organization: Crafting Winning Capabilities in a Dynamic World. LC 97-42831. 1998. pap. text 32.95 (0-7879-4004-6) Jossey-Bass.

Albers, Patricia. Shadows, Fire, Snow: The Life of Tina Modotti. LC 98-45727. (Illus.). 304p. 1999. 30.00 (0-609-60069-9) C Potter.

Albers, Patricia & Medicine, Beatrice. The Hidden Half: Studies of Plains Indian Women. LC 82-23906. 286p. (Orig.). 1983. pap. text 23.25 (0-8191-2957-7); lib. bdg. 53.00 (0-8191-2956-9) U Pr of Amer.

***Albers, Peter H., et al.** Environmental Contaminants & Terrestrial Vertebrates: Effects on Populations, Communities & Ecosystems. (Illus.). 2000. write for info. (1-880611-39-2, SETAC Pr) SETAC.

Albers, Randall, ed. Hair Trigger Vol. 19: A Story Workshop Anthology. 256p. (Orig.). 1997. pap. 7.95 (0-932026-47-8) Columbia College Chi.

— Hair Trigger 20: A Story Workshop Anthology. 300p. 1998. pap. write for info. (0-932026-50-8) Columbia College Chi.

— Hair Trigger 18: A Story Workshop Anthology. 179p. (Orig.). 1996. pap. 7.95 (0-932026-40-0) Columbia College Chi.

Albers, Robert H. Shame: A Faith Perspective. 148p. 1995. pap. text 12.95 (1-56024-957-9, Harrington Park) Haworth Pr.

— Shame: A Faith Perspective. LC 94-29610. 148p. 1995. lib. bdg. 39.95 (1-56024-935-8) Haworth Pr.

***Albers, Ron.** Defending Your Client in a Misdemeanor Case: Part 1, 2 - Fall 1999 Action Guide, 2 vols. Waxman, Robert, ed. 160p. 1999. 58.00i (0-7626-0386-0) Cont Ed Bar-CA.

Albers, S. Brave Bear & the Ghosts: A Sioux Legend. LC 96-5977. (Native American Lore & Legends Ser.). (Illus.). 48p. (J). (gr. 4-8). 1996. lib. bdg. 16.95 (0-86593-429-0) Rourke Corp.

— Coyote & the Grasshopper: A Pomo Legend. LC 96-5114. (Native American Lore & Legends Ser.). 48p. (J). (gr. 4-8). 1996. lib. bdg. 16.95 (0-86593-427-4) Rourke Corp.

— First Woman & the Strawberry: A Cherokee Legend. LC 96-9040. (Native American Lore & Legends Ser.). 48p. (J). (gr. 4-8). 1996. lib. bdg. 16.95 (0-86593-431-2) Rourke Corp.

— Red Hawk & the Sky Sisters: A Shawnee Legend. LC 96-9111. (Native American Lore & Legends Ser.). 48p. (J). (gr. 4-8). 1996. lib. bdg. 16.95 (0-86593-432-0) Rourke Corp.

— Song of the Hermit Thrush: An Iroquois Legend. LC 96-5113. (Native American Lore & Legends Ser.). 48p. (J). (gr. 4-8). 1996. lib. bdg. 16.95 (0-86593-428-2) Rourke Corp.

— Sunflower's Promise: A Zuni Legend. LC 96-9039. (Native American Lore & Legends Ser.). 48p. (J). (gr. 4-8). 1996. lib. bdg. 16.95 (0-86593-430-4) Rourke Corp.

Albers, Steven H. Front-Page Preaching. LC 98-13254. 112p. 1998. 10.99 (0-570-05327-7) Concordia.

Albers, Vernon M. Underwater Acoustics Instrumentation. LC 76-84217. 99p. reprint ed. pap. 30.70 (0-608-30413-1, 205112200078) Bks Demand.

Albers, Walter A., jt. ed. see Schwing, Richard C.

Albers, Wulf, et al. Understanding Strategic Interaction: Essays in Honor of Reinhard Selten. LC 96-38555. (Illus.). 517p. 1996. 149.50 (3-540-61490-7) Spr-Verlag.

Albersheim, Walter J. The Conscience of Science & Other Essays. LC 82-50162. 237p. 1982. 9.95 (0-912057-34-3, 501910) GLELJ AMORC.

***Alberstat, Philip.** Independent Producers' Guide to Film & TV Contracts. 256p. 1999. pap. text 47.95 (0-240-51583-8, Focal) Buttrwrth-Heinemann.

Alberstat, Philip. Media Production Agreements. LC 96-6431. 336p. (C). 1996. 85.00 (0-415-13668-7) Routledge.

Alberston, Bruce, jt. auth. see Wilson, Fred.

Alberswerth, Roy F. & Payden, Deborah A. Talking with Your Child about the Church Year. LC 92-27562. (Growing Together Ser.). 32p. 1992. pap. 2.25 (0-8298-0864-7) Pilgrim OH.

Albert. Great Traditions in Ethics. 4th ed. (Philosophy Ser.). 1980. pap. 13.00 (0-534-26255-4) Wadsworth Pub.

— History of Ophthalmology, Vol. 7. 1995. pap. text 125.00 (0-7923-3401-9) Kluwer Academic.

***Albert.** Principles in Practicing Ophthalmology, Vol. 6. 2nd ed. LC 99-29496. (C). 1999. text 950.00 (0-7216-7500-X, W B Saunders Co) Harcrt Hlth Sci Grp.

Albert. The Secrets of Hiding. (J). 1999. per. 4.95 (0-02-041130-8) S&S Childrens.

— Simon & Schuster Two Minute Crosswords, No. 3. 1995. pap. 5.95 (0-684-80263-5, Fireside) S&S Trade Pap.

A

Albert, et al, compiled by. The Story of Berwick. (Illus.). 166p. 1995. reprint ed. lib. bdg. 29.50 (*0-8328-4688-0*) Higginson Bk Co.

***Albert & Skolnik.** Hard Times: Narratives of Human Consequences of Social Welfare Programs. (Social Work Ser.). 2001. pap. 30.00 (*0-534-35918-3*) Wadsworth Pub.

Albert, A. A. & Kaplansky, I., eds. Finite Groups. LC 50-1183. (Proceedings of Symposia in Pure Mathematics Ser.: Vol. 1). 110p. 1959. reprint ed. pap. 32.00 (*0-8218-1401-X*, PSPUM/1) Am Math.

Albert, A. Adrian, ed. The Collected Mathematical Papers of Leonard Eugene Dickson, Vol. 6. LC 69-19943. (AMS/Chelsea Ser.). 714p. 1997. text 49.00 (*0-8284-0306-6*) Am Math.

Albert, A. Adrian, ed. see Dickson, Leonard E.

Albert, Abraham A. Modern Higher Algebra. LC 38-2937. (University of Chicago Science Ser.). 331p. reprint ed. pap. 102.70 (*0-608-30091-8*, 201699800005) Bks Demand.

— Solid Analytic Geometry. LC QA0553.A5819. 174p. reprint ed. pap. 54.00 (*0-608-30105-1*, 201698300006) Bks Demand.

— Structure of Algebras. LC 41-9. (Colloquium Publications: Vol. 24). 210p. 1939. reprint ed. pap. 45.00 (*0-8218-1024-3*, COLL/24) Am Math.

Albert, Adelin & Harris, Eugene K. Multivariate Interpretation of Clinical Laboratory Data. (Statistics: Textbooks & Monographs: Vol. 75). (Illus.). 328p. 1987. text 137.50 (*0-8247-7735-2*) Dekker.

Albert, Adelin, jt. auth. see Harris, Eugene K.

Albert, Adrien & Serjeant, E. P. The Determination of Ionization Constants: A Laboratory Manual. 3rd ed. (Illus.). 150p. 1984. 47.50 (*0-412-24290-7*, NO. 6848) Chapman & Hall.

Albert, Alphaeus H. Record of American Uniform & Historical Buttons: Bicentennial Edition. LC 76-58596. (Illus.). 511p. 1977. 40.00 (*0-9613581-7-3*) North South Trader.

Albert, Barbara. The Love of Friends: A Celebration of Women's Friendship. 288p. 1997. pap. 11.00 (*0-425-16058-0*) Berkley Pub.

Albert, Bill. Desert Blues. LC 93-36289. 188p. 1994. 22.00 (*1-877946-49-4*) Permanent Pr.

— Desert Blues. 188p. 1995. pap. text 16.00 (*1-877946-65-6*) Permanent Pr.

Albert, Bill & Graves, Adrian, eds. World Sugar Economy in War. 272p. 1988. lib. bdg. 55.00 (*0-415-00127-7*) Routledge.

Albert, Bill, jt. auth. see Reynolds, Simon.

Albert-Birot, Pierre. Grabinoulor. Wright, Barbara, tr. from FRE. & pref. by. LC 86-72567. 100p. 1987. 20.00 (*0-916583-18-X*) Dalkey Arch.

***Albert-Birot, Pierre.** Grabinoulor. LC 00-20972. 99p. 2000. pap. 10.95 (*1-56478-245-X*, Pub. by Dalkey Arch) Chicago Distribution Ctr.

Albert, Burt. Fat Free Meetings: How to Keep Them Fast, Focused & Fun! LC 96-41970. 224p. 1996. pap. 16.95 (*1-56079-597-2*, Petersons Pacesetter) Petersons.

Albert, Burton. Journey of the Nightly Jaguar. (J). 1999. mass mkt. 16.00 (*0-689-31981-9*) Atheneum Yung Read.

— Journey of the Nightly Jaguar: Spanish Paperback Edition. (J). 2000. pap. 4.95 (*0-689-80590-X*) S&S Bks Yung.

— Journey of the Nightly Jaguar: The Mayan Sun at Night Becomes a Jaguar Stalking the Jungle. LC 94-14456. (Illus.). 32p. (J). (gr. k-3). 1996. 16.00 (*0-689-31905-3*) Atheneum Yung Read.

— The Pirates of Bat Cave Island. (Illus.). 24p. (J). 1997. per. 12.95 (*0-689-81284-1*) S&S Childrens.

— What Makes My Daddy Best? (Illus.). 26p. (J). (ps-2). 1998. pap. 3.99 (*0-689-81230-2*) S&S Childrens.

— What Makes My Mommie Best? (Illus.). 24p. (J). (ps-2). 1998. pap. 3.99 (*0-689-81801-7*, 875355Q) Litle Simon.

— Where Does the Trail Lead? (Illus.). 40p. (J). (ps-3). 1991. pap. 16.00 (*0-671-73409-1*) S&S Bks Yung.

— Where Does the Trail Lead? LC 90-21450. (Illus.). 40p. (J). (ps-3). 1993. pap. 5.95 (*0-671-79617-8*) S&S Bks Yung.

— Windsongs & Rainbows. LC 92-12012. (Illus.). (J). (ps-2). 1993. pap. 14.00 (*0-671-76004-1*) S&S Bks Yung.

Albert, C., ed. Geometrie Symplectique et Mecanique. (Lecture Notes in Mathematics Ser.: Vol. 1416). v, 289p. 1990. 39.50 (*0-387-52191-7*) Spr-Verlag.

Albert, C. L., jt. ed. see Coggan, D. A.

***Albert, Carl.** Little Giant: The Life & Times of Speaker Carl Albert. 400p. 1999. pap. 14.95 (*0-8061-3200-0*) U of Okla Pr.

Albert, Charles S., jt. auth. see Gerhard, Johann.

Albert, Charles T. & Levin, Edward J. Maryland Real Estate Leasing Forms. 1994. ring bd., suppl. ed. 85.00 (*0-685-74616-X*, MICHIE) LEXIS Pub.

— Maryland Real Estate Leasing Forms, 2 vols., Set. 1020p. 1994. spiral bd. 269.00 incl. disk (*0-87189-065-8*, 81590-10, MICHIE) LEXIS Pub.

Albert, D., ed. Knowledge Structures. (Illus.). xxiii, 256p. 1995. 119.00 (*0-387-57664-9*) Spr-Verlag.

Albert, D. M. Source Book of Ophthalmology. (Illus.). 416p. 1995. 99.95 (*0-86542-240-0*) Blackwell Sci.

Albert, Dalia N. En el Diario Asombro de lo Humano. Carvajal, Pepe, ed. (Luna Poetica Ser.). 82p. 1989. pap. write for info. (*0-942347-00-5*) Ediciones Puerto.

— Los Petalos de la Rosa. Carvajal, Pepe, ed. (SPA.). 28p. 1993. pap. write for info. (*0-942347-01-3*) Ediciones Puerto.

— Vamos a Subir la Voz para Morir Mariposas. Carvajal, Pepe, ed. (Illus.). 23p. 1989. pap. write for info. (*0-942347-02-1*) Ediciones Puerto.

Albert, Daniel A., et al. Reasoning in Medicine: An Introduction to Clinical Inference. LC 87-3243. (Johns Hopkins Series in Contemporary Medicine & Public Health). 280p. reprint ed. pap. 86.80 (*0-7837-4261-4*, 204395300012) Bks Demand.

Albert, Daniel M. The History of Ophthalmology. LC 96-9847. (Illus.). 350p. 1996. text 125.00 (*0-86542-378-4*) Blackwell Sci.

***Albert, Daniel M., ed.** The Best of Archives of Ophthalmology. 250p. 1999. 50.00 (*1-57947-058-0*) AMA.

Albert, Daniel M. & Brightbill, Frederick S. Ophthalmic Surgery: Principles & Techniques. LC 98-34615. (Illus.). 1998. 399.00 (*0-632-04337-7*) Blackwell Sci.

Albert, Daniel M. & Jakobiec, Frederick A. Atlas of Clinical Ophthalmology, 2 vols.Set, Set. LC 95-1015. (Illus.). 480p. 1995. text 235.00 (*0-7216-3417-6*, W B Saunders Co) Harcrt Hlth Sci Grp.

Albert, Daniel M. & Jakobiec, Frederick A., eds. Principles & Practice of Ophthalmology, 6 vols., Set. (Illus.). 1993. text 825.00 (*0-7216-6592-6*, W B Saunders Co) Harcrt Hlth Sci Grp.

— Principles & Practice of Ophthalmology: Clinical Practice, 5 vols., Set. LC 93-7247. (Illus.). 1993. text 695.00 (*0-7216-3418-4*, W B Saunders Co) Harcrt Hlth Sci Grp.

Albert, Daniel M. & Jokobiec, Frederick A., eds. Principles & Practice of Ophthalmology: Basic Sciences, Vol. 1. LC 93-12658. (Illus.). 1435p. 1993. text 195.00 (*0-7216-3416-8*, W B Saunders Co) Harcrt Hlth Sci Grp.

Albert, Daniel M., et al. Herpesvirus: Recent Studies, 3 vols., Vol. 2. LC 73-13558. 1974. 25.50 (*0-8422-7169-4*) Irvington.

Albert, Daniel M., jt. auth. see Achenbaum, W. Andrew.

Albert, Dave & Melvin, George F. New England Diesels. LC 75-27730. (Illus.). 1977. 28.95 (*0-916160-01-7*) G R Cockle.

Albert, David. Difficult Scriptures: Coming to Grips with the Law of Moses in the Worldwide Church of God. LC 96-90252. 200p. (Orig.). 1996. pap. 14.95 (*1-889174-50-5*, 9096) Tyler Hse.

Albert, David, jt. auth. see MacKrell, John.

***Albert, David H.** And the Skylark Signs with Me: Adventures in Homeschooling & Community-Based Education. 240p. 1999. pap. 16.95 (*0-86571-401-0*, Pub. by New Soc Pubs) Consort Bk Sales.

Albert, David Z. Quantum Mechanics & Experience. (Illus.). 232p. 1993. 37.95 (*0-674-74112-9*) HUP.

— Quantum Mechanics & Experience. (Illus.). 224p. (C). 1994. pap. 17.00 (*0-674-74113-7*) HUP.

***Albert, David Z.** Time & Chance. (Illus.). 224p. 2000. 29.95 (*0-674-00317-9*) HUP.

Albert, Dietrich & Lukas, Josef, eds. Knowledge Spaces: Theories, Empirical Research, & Applications. LC 99-11094. 240p. 1998. 49.95 (*0-8058-2799-4*) L Erlbaum Assocs.

***Albert, Donald P., et al, eds.** Spatial Analysis, GIS & Remote Sensing: Applications in the Health Sciences. (Illus.). 250p. 2000. 69.95 (*1-57504-101-4*, Ann Arbor Press) Sleepng Bear.

Albert, Donna. Beautiful American Marine. LC 82-90348. (Illus.). 74p. (Orig.). 1982. pap. 5.95 (*0-9608924-0-0*) DJA Writ Circle.

— No-Sew Special Effects. (Illus.). 128p. 1996. pap. 19.95 (*0-8019-8718-0*) Krause Pubns.

Albert, Ethel M., et al. Great Traditions in Ethics. 5th ed. 394p. (C). 1984. pap. write for info. (*0-534-02815-2*) Wadsworth Pub.

— Great Traditions in Ethics. 6th ed. 409p. (C). 1987. pap. write for info. (*0-534-08130-4*) Wadsworth Pub.

Albert, Floyd. Even Commas: Poems. LC 95-21911. 64p. 1995. 14.95 (*0-7734-2743-0*, Mellen Poetry Pr) E Mellen.

Albert, Frank. One-Strike Stopping Power. (Illus.). 176p. 1993. pap. 15.00 (*0-87364-714-9*) Paladin Pr.

Albert, Fred. Barkitecture. LC 98-46089. (Illus.). 96p. 1999. 24.95 (*0-7892-0373-1*) Abbeville Pr.

Albert, G. Peter. Intellectual Property Law in Cyberspace. LC 99-29759. 944p. 1999. 175.00 (*1-57018-165-9*, 1165-PR9) BNA Books.

Albert, Gail, ed. Service-Learning Reader: Reflections & Perspectives on Service. 375p. (Orig.). (C). 1998. pap. text 38.00 (*0-536-01242-3*) Pearson Custom.

Albert, George, ed. The Cash Box Country Album Charts, 1964-1988. LC 89-27934. 300p. 1989. 35.00 (*0-8108-2273-3*) Scarecrow.

Albert, George & Hoffmann, Frank. The Cash Box Country Singles Charts, 1958-1982. LC 84-1266. 605p. 1984. 45.00 (*0-8108-1685-7*) Scarecrow.

Albert, George & Hoffmann, Frank, eds. The Cash Box Black Contemporary Singles Charts, 1960-1984. LC 85-22078. (Cash Box Ser.: Vol. 3). 716p. 1986. 50.00 (*0-8108-1853-1*) Scarecrow.

Albert, George, jt. auth. see Hoffmann, Frank.

***Albert, George D.** History of the County of Westmoreland, Pennsylvania, with Biographical Sketches of Many of the Pioneers & Prominent Men. LC 98-74101. Orig. Title: '. 727p. 1998. reprint ed. write for info. (*1-55856-286-9*, 293) Closson Pr.

Albert, George D., ed. History of the County of Westmoreland. (Illus.). 496p. 1995. reprint ed. lib. bdg. 53.00 (*0-8328-5111-6*) Higginson Bk Co.

Albert, Georgia, tr. see Agamben, Giorgio.

Albert, Georgia, tr. see Frey, Hans-Jost.

Albert, Greg, ed. Basic Figure Drawing Techniques. (Basic Technique Ser.). (Illus.). 128p. 1994. pap. 16.99 (*0-89134-551-5*, North Lght Bks) F & W Pubns Inc.

Albert, Greg & Wolf, Rachel R., eds. Basic Drawing Techniques. (Basic Technique Ser.). (Illus.). 128p. 1991. pap. 16.99 (*0-89134-388-1*, 30332, North Lght Bks) F & W Pubns Inc.

— Basic Oil Painting Techniques. (Basic Technique Ser.). (Illus.). 128p. 1993. pap. 16.99 (*0-89134-463-2*, 30477, North Lght Bks) F & W Pubns Inc.

— Basic Watercolor Techniques. (Basic Technique Ser.). (Illus.). 144p. 1991. pap. 16.99 (*0-89134-387-3*, 30331, North Lght Bks) F & W Pubns Inc.

Albert, Greg, jt. ed. see Long, Jennifer.

Albert, Gretchen D. Scribble Art: Kindergarten & Preschool. (Illus.). 85p. (J). (ps-3). 1980. pap. text 5.80 (*0-686-28105-5*) GDA Pubns.

Albert, Gwen & Sparling, Kent. Green, Green. Mycue, Edward, ed. (Took Modern Poetry in English Ser.: No. 32). (Illus.). 32p. (Orig.). 1992. pap. 8.00 (*1-879457-34-2*) Norton Coker Pr.

Albert, Gwendolyn. Dogs. Mycue, Edward, ed. (Took Modern Poetry in English Ser.: No. 13). (Illus.). 28p. (Orig.). 1991. pap. 5.00 (*1-879457-11-3*) Norton Coker Pr.

***Albert, Hans.** No Latitude for Fools. LC 99-91656. 2000. 25.00 (*0-7388-1156-4*); pap. 18.00 (*0-7388-1157-2*) Xlibris Corp.

Albert, J. D. The Touchstone of Sincerity. 256p. 1986. pap. 7.50 (*0-85398-223-6*) G Ronald Pub.

Albert, J. Leach, et al, eds. Automata, Languages & Programming: Proceedings of ICALP International Colloquium, 18th, Madrid, Spain, July 8-12, 1991. (Lecture Notes in Computer Science Ser.: Vol. 510). xii, 763p. 1991. 79.95 (*0-387-54233-7*) Spr-Verlag.

Albert, Jacques. Teach Yourself Microsoft Windows 2 & Windows 386. 197p. 1989. ring bd. 79.95 incl. disk (*0-929533-12-7*) Tutorland.

Albert, James. Jim Bakker: Miscarriage of Justice? LC 97-22581. 544p. 1997. 39.95 (*0-8126-9369-8*); pap. 18.95 (*0-8126-9370-1*) Open Court.

***Albert, James & Rossman, Allan J.** Workshop Statistics: Discovery with Data, a Bayesian Approach. (Workshop Mathematics Project Ser.). 350p. (C). 2000. pap. 44.95 (*1-930190-12-3*) Key Coll.

Albert, James, jt. auth. see Lane, Louise.

Albert, James A. The Broadcaster's Legal Guide for Conducting Contests & Promotions. LC 85-60744. 237p. 1985. 34.95 (*0-933893-08-6*) Precept Pr.

— Pay Dirt: Divorces of the Rich & Famous. (Illus.). 250p. 1989. 19.95 (*0-8283-1927-8*) Branden Bks.

— Pay Dirt: Divorces of the Rich & Famous. (Illus.). 268p. 1998. text 17.00 (*0-7881-5289-0*) DIANE Pub.

Albert, James H. Bayesian Computation Using Minitab. (C). 1996. pap. 39.95 (*0-534-51781-1*) Wadsworth Pub.

Albert, James H. & Johnson, Valen E. Ordinal Data Modeling. Fienberg, S. et al, eds. LC 98-51801. 312p. 1999. 65.00 (*0-387-98718-5*) Spr-Verlag.

Albert, Jamme. Sabaean Inscriptions from Mahram Bilgis (Marib) LC 62-10311. (American Foundation for the Study of Man Ser.: Vol. 3). 557p. reprint ed. pap. 172.70 (*0-608-10851-0*, 200519900050) Bks Demand.

Albert, Janice M., ed. see Higgins, Richard L.

Albert, Jeffrey, jt. auth. see McAuliffe, William E.

Albert, John G., jt. ed. see Showalter, Dennis.

Albert, Jon. The Best Caesar Salad You've Ever Had! or Your Money Back! 52p. 1992. text 10.95 (*0-9633619-0-2*) Albert Co CA.

Albert, Jonathan, ed. see Beck, John & Starr, Ronald.

Albert, Joseph. Osmo's Autobearography. (Who's There Bears? Ser.: Vol. 1). (Illus.). 24p. (J). (ps-2). 1997. write for info. (*1-891376-00-4*) Fluffyville USA.

— Osmo's Who's Playing Where? (Who's There Bears? Ser.: Vol. 2). (Illus.). 24p. (J). (ps-2). 1997. write for info. (*1-891376-01-2*) Fluffyville USA.

Albert, Judith C. & Albert, Stewart E., eds. The Sixties Papers: Documents of a Rebellious Decade. 372p. 1984. 59.95 (*0-275-91116-0*, C1116, Praeger Pubs); pap. 26.95 (*0-275-91781-9*, B1781, Praeger Pubs) Greenwood.

Albert, Karen. Albert & Company Degree Program Guide. (Illus.). 95p. (Orig.). 1995. pap. 295.00 (*0-614-10992-2*) Albert & Co.

— Albert & Company Executive Development Programs Guide 1995-96. 9th ed. (Executive Development Programs Ser.). (Illus.). 520p. reprint ed. pap. 425.00 (*0-614-10990-6*) Albert & Co.

— Albert & Company Executive Development Programs Guide 1996-97. 10th ed. (Executive Development Programs Ser.). 590p. Date not set. reprint ed. pap. 425.00 (*0-614-10991-4*) Albert & Co.

— Albert & Company Technology Management Program Guide. (Executive Development Programs Guide: Technology Management Program Ser.). 65p. 1995. reprint ed. pap. write for info. (*0-614-10989-2*) Albert & Co.

— Approach to Career Management. 1979. pap. write for info. (*1-879715-16-3*) Albert & Co.

— Executive Development Programs Compendium, 1991, Vol. 1: General Management Programs. 102p. 1990. write for info. (*1-879715-07-4*) Albert & Co.

— Executive Development Programs Compendium, 1991, Vol. 2: Functional Management Programs. 138p. 1990. write for info. (*1-879715-08-2*) Albert & Co.

— Guide to Executive Development Programs in Manufacturing. 1989. pap. write for info. (*1-879715-09-0*) Albert & Co.

— Stress Management. 1979. pap. write for info. (*1-879715-15-5*) Albert & Co.

Albert, Karin, tr. see Zhao, Qingquan.

Albert, Katherine A. Get a Good Nights Sleep. LC 96-21034. 1996. 21.50 (*0-684-80428-X*) S&S Trade.

— Get a Good Night's Sleep: How to Conquer Your Insomnia Without Drugs or Medication. 208p. 1997. per. 11.00 (*0-684-83527-4*, Fireside) S&S Trade Pap.

***Albert, Ken.** Fishing in Northern California, 2000-2001 Edition. 8th rev. ed. (Illus.). 240p. 2000. pap. 14.95 (*0-934061-38-6*) Marketscope Bks.

Albert, Ken. Fishing in Southern California - 1999-2000 Edition: The Complete Guide. 7th rev. ed. (Illus.). 240p. 1999. pap. 14.95 (*0-934061-36-X*) Marketscope Bks.

Albert, Leonard. Evangelism Breakthrough. 1990. teacher ed. 9.95 (*0-87148-319-X*) Pathway Pr.

Albert, Linda. Cooperative Discipline Handbook. (Cooperative Discipline Ser.). 1990. teacher ed. 14.95 (*0-88671-362-5*, 4002) Am Guidance.

Albert, Linda & DeSisto, Pete. Cooperative Discipline. LC 95-77062. ix, 182p. 1996. write for info. (*0-7854-0042-7*) Am Guidance.

Albert, Linda, jt. auth. see Einstein, Elizabeth A.

Albert, Lois, ed. see Holmes, Mary A. & Gilbert, Claudette M.

Albert, Lois E. An Archeological Survey along the Red River: The Kemp Bottoms Area, Bryan County, Oklahoma. (Archeological Resource Survey Report: Vol. 19). (Illus.). 166p. (C). 1984. pap. text 5.00 (*1-881346-12-9*) Univ OK Archeol.

— An Archeological Survey in the James Fork Watershed, LeFlore County, Oklahoma. (Archeological Resource Survey Report: No. 28). (Illus.). 204p. (C). 1987. pap. text 7.00 (*1-881346-19-6*) Univ OK Archeol.

Albert, Marilyn S. & Moss, Mark B., eds. Geriatric Neuropsychology. LC 88-10004. 316p. 1988. lib. bdg. 45.00 (*0-89862-722-2*) Guilford Pubns.

Albert, Marina F. Friedrich Schlegel's Theorie des Witzes Und Sein Roman Lucinde. (Studies in Modern German Literature: Vol. 59). (GER.). IX, 172p. (C). 1995. text 41.95 (*0-8204-2211-8*) P Lang Pubng.

Albert, Mark. Eccentric Muscle Training in Sports & Orthopaedics. LC 90-26175. (Illus.). 171p. 1991. reprint ed. pap. 53.10 (*0-7837-9749-4*, 206047700005) Bks Demand.

Albert, Mark R. & Yates, John T., Jr. The Surface Scientists's Guide to Organometallic Chemistry. LC 86-25937. (Illus.). xiii, 200p. 1987. text 59.00 (*0-8412-1003-9*, Pub. by Am Chemical) OUP.

Albert, Martin L. & Knoefel, Janice E., eds. Clinical Neurology of Aging. 2nd rev. ed. (Illus.). 728p. 1994. reprint ed. text 145.00 (*0-19-507167-0*) OUP.

Albert, Martin L., jt. auth. see Helm-Estabrooks, Nancy.

Albert, Marv & Fischler, Stan. Marv Albert's Sports Quiz Book LC 74-7549. 205p. 1976. write for info. (*0-448-11797-5*, G & D) Peng Put Young Read.

Albert, Marvin. A Dancer's Progress & Schrodinger's Cat. 93p. 1993. 20.00 (*0-9634859-0-3*); pap. 11.95 (*0-9634859-1-1*) Alex Pr & Print.

***Albert, Marvin H.** Three Rode North. large type ed. LC 99-38384. 1999. 21.95 (*1-56895-768-8*, Wheeler) Wheeler Pub.

Albert-Matesz, Rachel, jt. auth. see Matesz, Don.

***Albert, Mathias, et al, eds.** Civilizing World Politics: Society & Community Beyond the State. LC 99-44888. 352p. 1999. pap. 28.95 (*0-8476-9803-3*); text 69.00 (*0-8476-9802-5*) Rowman.

Albert, Matilde. El Reino de la Memoria. (Aqui y Ahora Ser.). 1997. 6.95 (*0-8477-0329-0*) U of PR Pr.

***Albert, Merrill K.** The Big Casino. LC 99-95017. 1999. pap. 9.95 (*0-533-13267-3*) Vantage.

Albert, Michael. Stop the Killing Train: Radical Visions for Radical Change. 243p. 1994. 35.00 (*0-89608-471-X*); pap. 15.00 (*0-89608-470-1*) South End Pr.

— Thinking Forward: Learning to Conceptualize Economic Vision. 224p. pap. 13.95 (*1-894037-00-6*) Arbeiter Ring.

Albert, Michael & Dellinger, David, eds. Beyond Survival: New Directions for the Disarmament Movement. 365p. 1983. 35.00 (*0-89608-176-1*); pap. 12.00 (*0-89608-175-3*) South End Pr.

Albert, Michael & Hahnel, Robin. Looking Forward: Participatory Economics for the Twenty-First Century. Orig. Title: Participatory Economics. (Illus.). 154p. 1991. 25.00 (*0-89608-406-X*); pap. 16.00 (*0-89608-405-1*) South End Pr.

— Marxism & Socialist Theory: Socialism in Theory & Practice. LC 80-85407. 303p. (C). 1981. 35.00 (*0-89608-076-5*); pap. 8.50 (*0-89608-075-7*) South End Pr.

— Political Economy of Participatory Socialism. 176p. 1990. text 55.00 (*0-691-04274-8*, Pub. by Princeton U Pr) Cal Prin Full Svc.

— Socialism Today & Tomorrow. LC 81-50138. 406p. (C). 1981. 35.00 (*0-89608-078-1*); pap. 9.50 (*0-89608-077-3*) South End Pr.

Albert, Michael, et al. Liberating Theory. LC 86-13032. 197p. 1986. 25.00 (*0-89608-307-1*) South End Pr.

Albert, Michael, jt. auth. see Hahnel, Robin.

***Albert, Michael B.** The New Innovators: Global Patenting Trends in Five Sectors. (Illus.). 54p. 2000. pap. text 20.00 (*0-7881-8787-2*) DIANE Pub.

Albert, Michel. Capitalism vs. Capitalism: How America's Obsession with Individual Achievement & Short-Term Profit Has Led It to the Brink of Collapse. Haviland, Paul, tr. from FRE. LC 93-4542. 260p. 1993. reprint ed. 25.95 (*1-56858-004-5*) FWEW.

Albert, Michelle & Rooney, A., eds. Jumbo Shrimp: A New Anthology of Short - Short Fiction by Emerging & Experienced Writers. 86p. 1997. pap. 8.95 (*1-891051-04-0*) Back Cover Pr.

Albert, Mimi. Skirts. 259p. 1994. 19.00 (*1-880909-13-8*) Baskerville.

Albert, Nachum. Destruction of Slonim Jewry: The Story of the Jews During the Holocaust. Rosenfeld, Max, ed. & tr. by. from YID. LC 90-81303. (Illus.). 400p. 1990. pap. 13.95 (*0-89604-137-9*, Holocaust Library) US Holocaust.

Albert, Neil. An Appointment in May: A Dave Garrett Mystery. LC 96-1198. (Dave Garrett Mystery Ser.). 288p. 1996. 20.95 (*0-8027-3279-8*) Walker & Co.

— Cruel April: A Dave Garrett Mystery. large type ed. (Niagara Large Print Ser.). 1996. 27.99 (*0-7089-5826-5*) Ulverscroft.

— The February Trouble: A Dave Garrett Mystery. 235p. 1992. 19.95 (*0-8027-1244-4*) Walker & Co.

— The January Corpse. 192p. 1991. 18.95 (*0-8027-3206-2*) Walker & Co.

An Asterisk (*) at the beginning of an entry indicates that the title is appearing for the first time.

— Tangled June: A Dave Garrett Mystery. LC 97-1350. 246p. 1997. 20.95 (*0-8027-3305-0*) Walker & Co.

Albert, Octavia V. The House of Bondage. LC 70-37580. (Black Heritage Library Collection). 1977. reprint ed. 23.95 (*0-8369-8956-2*) Ayer.

— The House of Bondage: Or Charlotte Brooks & Other Slaves. (Schomburg Library of Nineteenth-Century Black Women Writers). (Illus.). 224p. 1991. reprint ed. pap. 9.95 (*0-19-506784-3*) OUP.

— The House of Bondage or Charlotte Brooks & Other Slaves. (Schomburg Library of Nineteenth-Century Black Women Writers). 224p. 1988. text 35.00 (*0-19-505263-3*) OUP.

Albert, Paul, et al, eds. AIDS Practice Manual. 3rd ed. 1990. pap. write for info. (*0-9602188-7-4*) Natl Lawyers Guild.

Albert, Peter J. Religion in a Revolutionary Age: Perspectives on the American Revolution. Hoffman, Ronald, ed. LC 93-13544. 1994. text 39.50 (*0-8139-1448-5*) U Pr of Va.

Albert, Peter J. & Hoffman, Ronald, eds. We Shall Overcome: Martin Luther King, Jr. & the Black Freedom Struggle. LC 92-42144. (Illus.). 304p. 1993. reprint ed. pap. 14.95 (*0-306-80511-1*) Da Capo.

Albert, Peter J. & Miller, Harold L., eds. The American Federation of Labor Records: The Samuel Gompers Era, 1877-1937. 67p. 1981. pap. write for info. (*0-87020-190-5*) Chadwyck-Healey.

***Albert, Peter J. & Palladino, Grace, eds.** The Samuel Gompers Papers Vol. 8: Progress & Reaction in the Age of Reform, 1909-13. 608p. 2000. text 100.00 (*0-252-02564-4*) U of Ill Pr.

Albert, Peter J., jt. ed. see Hoffman, Ronald.

Albert, Peter J., jt. ed. see Kaufman, Stuart B.

Albert, Phyllis C. The Modernization of French Jewry: Consistory & Community in the Nineteenth Century. LC 76-50680. 472p. reprint ed. pap. 146.40 (*0-7837-2995-2*, 204294600006) Bks Demand.

Albert, Phyllis C., jt. ed. see Malino, Frances.

Albert, Rachel. Cooking with Rachel: Creative Vegetarian & Macrobiotic Cuisine. Ruggles, Laurel, ed. LC 89-85012. (Illus.). 328p. 1989. pap. 12.95 (*0-918860-49-0*) G Ohsawa.

***Albert, Raymond.** Law & Social Work Practice: A Legal System Approach. 2nd ed. (Social Work Ser.). (Illus.). 560p. 2000. 59.95 (*0-8261-4891-3*) Springer Pub.

Albert, Richard C. Damming the Delaware: The Rise & Fall of Tocks Island Dam. LC 86-43197. (Illus.). 224p. 1988. 40.00 (*0-271-00481-9*) Pa St U Pr.

Albert, Richard E. Alejandro's Gift. LC 93-30199. (Illus.). 32p. (J). 1994. 14.95 (*0-8118-0436-4*) Chronicle Bks.

— Alejandro's Gift. (Illus.). 32p. (J). (ps-1). 1996. pap. 6.95 (*0-8118-1342-8*) Chronicle Bks.

***Albert, Richard K., et al.** Comprehensive Respiratory Medicine. LC 99-14698. 1999. text. write for info. (*0-7234-3118-3*) Wolfe Pub.

Albert, Richard N. An Annotated Bibliography of Jazz Fiction & Jazz Fiction Criticism, 52. LC 96-8937. (Bibliographies & Indexes in World Literature Ser.: No. 52). 136p. 1996. lib. bdg. 59.95 (*0-313-28998-0*, Greenwood Pr) Greenwood.

Albert, Roald. Medical Engineering Dictionary in Four Languages. (ENG, FRE, GER & RUS.). 550p. 1994. 150.00 (*3-86117-051-5*) IBD Ltd.

Albert-Robatto, Matilde. Redaccion y Estilo. 6th ed. Marle, Inc. Staff, ed. 400p. pap. 20.00 (*0-9627933-0-2*) A L Matilde.

Albert, Robert. To Sow a Seed. (C). 1990. text 31.00 (*0-7223-2553-3*, Pub. by A H S Ltd) St Mut.

Albert, Robert S., ed. Genius & Eminence. LC 92-12055. (International Series in Experimental Social Psychology: Vol. 22). 428p. 1992. pap. text 34.95 (*0-08-037765-3*, Prgamon Press) Buttrwrth-Heinemann.

— Genius & Eminence. 2nd ed. LC 92-12055. (International Series in Experimental Social Psychology: Vol. 22). 1992. 95.00 (*0-08-037764-5*, Prgamon Press) Buttrwrth-Heinemann.

Albert, Robert S., jt. ed. see Runco, Mark A.

Albert, Ronald & Hahnewald, Harry, eds. Eight Language Dictionary of Medical Technology. LC 78-40828. 1979. 270.00 (*0-08-023763-0*, Pub. by Pergamon Repr) Franklin.

Albert, Roy & Shaul, David Leedom, compiled by. A Concise Hopi & English Lexicon. LC 84-9197. vi, 204p. 1985. 46.00 (*90-272-2015-8*) J Benjamins Pubng Co.

Albert, S. Concerto for Cello & Orchestra: Piano Reduction. 64p. 1993. pap. 35.00 (*0-7935-3138-1*) H Leonard.

— Tribute for Violin & Piano. 16p. 1995. pap. 20.00 (*0-7935-4383-5*, 50482201) H Leonard.

Albert, Sam. As Is. 140p. 1983. pap. 7.95 (*0-931694-20-5*) Wampeter Pr.

Albert Schweitzer Institute for the Humanities Sta, jt. auth. see Schweitzer, Albert.

Albert, Sheila. Contratando, O Director Executivo: Guia Pratico para o Processo de Buscae Selecao.Tr. of Hiring the Chief Executive. (POR.). 27p. (Orig.). 1996. pap. write for info. (*0-925299-60-X*) Natl Ctr Nonprofit.

— Hiring the Chief Executive: A Practical Guide to the Search & Selection Process. 28p. 1993. pap. text 16.00 (*0-925299-27-8*) Natl Ctr Nonprofit.

Albert, Shirley. Doll Party. LC 93-12685. (All Aboard Reading Ser.). (Illus.). 32p. (J). (ps-1). 1994. pap. 3.99 (*0-448-40182-7*, G & D) Peng Put Young Read.

— The Polly Pocket Cookbook. LC 96-13578. (Step into Reading Ser.: A Step 2 Book). (Illus.). (J). (ps-3). 1996. lib. bdg. 11.99 (*0-679-97484-9*) Random.

Albert, Shirley & Herman, Gail. The Polly Pocket Cookbook. (Step into Reading Ser.: A Step 2 Book). (Illus.). (J). (gr. 1-3). 1996. pap. 3.99 (*0-679-87484-4*) Random.

Albert, Stan & Cecil, David R. Ssri Probability. LC 92-41666. (Six Sigma Research Institute Ser.). 1993. pap. text 21.95 (*0-201-63409-0*) Addison-Wesley.

Albert, Stephen. Sun's Heat from Distant Hills: Tenor & Orchestra Piano Reduction. 32p. 1993. pap. 18.95 (*0-7935-2244-7*) H Leonard.

— Treestone: Piano Vocal Reduction. 136p. 1993. per. 50.00 (*0-7935-2916-6*) H Leonard.

Albert, Stephen L. & Seneca, Lucius Annaeus. Into Eclipse: For Tenor & Orchestra Score. 112p. 1993. per. 75.00 (*0-7935-2435-0*, 50481145) H Leonard.

Albert, Steven & Bradley, Keith. Managing Knowledge: Experts, Agencies & Organisations. 227p. (C). 1997. text 64.95 (*0-521-56150-7*); pap. text 20.95 (*0-521-59887-7*) Cambridge U Pr.

***Albert, Steven M. & Logsdon, Rebecca G.** Assessing Quality of Life in Alzheimer's Disease. LC 99-88404. 2000. pap. write for info. (*0-8261-1333-8*) Springer Pub.

Albert, Stewart E., jt. ed. see Albert, Judith C.

Albert, Susan W. Writing from Life: Telling Your Soul's Story. LC 96-20142. (Inner Work Bks.). 240p. (Orig.). 1997. pap. 16.95 (*0-87477-848-4*, Tarcher Putnam) Putnam Pub Group.

***Albert, Susan Wittig.** Chile Death. (China Bayles Mystery Ser.: No. 7). 306p. 1999. reprint ed. mass mkt. 6.50 (*0-425-17147-7*, Prime Crime) Berkley Pub.

Albert, Susan Wittig. Chile Death: A China Bayles Mystery. LC 98-13766. 288p. 1998. 21.95 (*0-425-16539-6*, Prime Crime) Berkley Pub.

— Hangman's Root: A China Bayles Mystery. 272p. 1995. mass mkt. 5.99 (*0-425-14898-X*) Berkley Pub.

— Hangman's Root: A China Bayles Mystery. 288p. 1994. 20.00 (*0-684-19677-8*, Scribners Ref) Mac Lib Ref.

— Hangman's Root: A China Bayles Mystery. large type ed. LC 94-49704. 319p. 1995. pap. 19.95 (*0-7838-1246-9*, G K Hall Lrg Type) Mac Lib Ref.

***Albert, Susan Wittig.** Lavender Lies. (China Bayles Mysteries Ser.). 2000. mass mkt. 6.50 (*0-425-17700-9*) Berkley Pub.

Albert, Susan Wittig. Lavender Lies: A China Bayles Mystery. LC 99-33252. (China Bayles Mystery Ser.: No. 8). 306p. 1999. 21.95 (*0-425-17032-2*, Prime Crime) Berkley Pub.

— Love Lies Bleeding: A China Bayles Mystery. LC 96-53666. 320p. 1997. pap. 21.95 (*0-425-15969-8*, Prime Crime) Berkley Pub.

— Love Lies Bleeding: A China Bayles Mystery. (China Bayles Mystery Ser.). 320p. 1998. reprint ed. pap. 5.99 (*0-425-16611-2*, Prime Crime) Berkley Pub.

***Albert, Susan Wittig.** Mistletoe Man: A China Bayles Mystery. LC 99-87021. 2000. 21.95 (*0-425-17673-8*) Berkley Pub.

Albert, Susan Wittig. Rosemary Remembered: A China Bayles Mystery. LC 95-15062. 304p. 1995. pap. 19.95 (*0-425-14937-4*, Prime Crime) Berkley Pub.

— Rosemary Remembered: A China Bayles Mystery. 1996. mass mkt. 5.99 (*0-425-15405-X*) Berkley Pub.

— Rueful Death: A China Bayles Mystery. LC 95-26165. 320p. 1996. 21.95 (*0-425-15469-6*) Berkley Pub.

— Rueful Death: A China Bayles Mystery. 1997. mass mkt. 5.99 (*0-614-27730-2*, Prime Crime) Berkley Pub.

— Rueful Death: A China Bayles Mystery. 288p. 1997. reprint ed. mass mkt. 5.99 (*0-425-15941-8*, Prime Crime) Berkley Pub.

— Thyme of Death: A Mystery Introducing China Bayles. 1994. mass mkt. 6.99 (*0-425-14098-9*) Berkley Pub.

— Witches' Bane: A China Bayles Mystery. 272p. 1994. reprint ed. mass mkt. 5.99 (*0-425-14406-2*, Prime Crime) Berkley Pub.

Albert, Thomas Milton, jt. auth. see Oppel, Andrew J.

Albert, Tim. Medical Journalism: A Writers Guide. 1995. write for info. (*1-85775-088-8*, Radcliffe Med Pr) Scovill Paterson.

— Medical Journalism: The Writer's Guide. 2nd ed. 1995. pap. 24.95 (*1-870905-28-8*, Radcliffe Med Pr) Scovill Paterson.

— Winning the Publications Game: How to Get Published Without Neglecting Your Patients. LC 96-36426. 1996. write for info. (*1-85775-183-3*, Radcliffe Med Pr) Scovill Paterson.

***Albert, Tim, ed.** A-Z of Medical Writing. 145p. 2000. pap. 27.50 (*0-7279-1487-1*, Pub. by BMJ Pub) Login Brothers Bk Co.

Albert, Todd A., et al. Surgical Approaches to the Spine. LC 96-29395. (Illus.). 272p. 1997. text 125.00 (*0-7216-4554-2*, W B Saunders Co) Harcrt Hlth Sci Grp.

***Albert, Todd J. & Vaccaro, Alexander R.** Physical Examination of the Spine. (Illus.). 232p. 2001. pap. 39.95 (*0-86577-916-3*) Thieme Med Pubs.

Albert, Toni. Ben & Me: A Study Guide. Friedland, Joyce & Kessler, Rikki, eds. (Novel-Ties Ser.). (J). (gr. 2-5). 1991. pap. text 15.95 (*0-88122-566-5*) Lrn Links.

— Charley Skedaddle: A Study Guide. Friedland, J. & Kessler, R., eds. (Novel-Ties Ser.). (J). (gr. 4-7). 1992. pap. text, student ed. 15.95 (*0-88122-725-0*) Lrn Links.

— Eco-Pack: The Remarkable Rainforest & The Incredible Coral Reef, 2 bks. (Illus.). 128p. (Orig.). (J). (gr. 3-8). 1996. pap. 19.95 (*0-9640742-2-2*) Trickle Creek.

***Albert, Toni.** I Heard the Willow Weep. LC 99-75629. (Illus.). 32p. (J). (gr. k-5). 2000. 15.95 (*1-929432-00-3*, Pub. by Trickle Creek); pap. 7.95 (*1-929432-01-1*, Pub. by Trickle Creek) Educational Bk Distributors.

Albert, Toni. The Incredible Coral Reef: Another Active-Learning Book for Kids. LC 96-60150. (Illus.). 64p. (Orig.). (J). (gr. 3-8). 1998. pap. 10.95 (*0-9640742-1-4*) Trickle Creek.

— A Kid's Fall EcoJournal: With Nature Activities for Exploring the Season. LC 96-61931. (Illus.). 56p. (Orig.). (J). (gr. 3 up). 1997. pap. text 9.95 (*0-9640742-5-7*) Trickle Creek.

— A Kid's Spring EcoJournal: With Nature Activities for Exploring the Season. LC 96-61929. (Illus.). 56p. (Orig.). (J). (gr. 3 up). 1997. pap. text 9.95 (*0-9640742-3-0*) Trickle Creek.

— A Kid's Summer EcoJournal: With Nature Activities for Exploring the Season. LC 96-61930. (Illus.). 56p. (J). (gr. 3 up). 1998. pap. 9.95 (*0-9640742-4-9*) Trickle Creek.

— A Kid's Winter EcoJournal: With Nature Activities for Exploring the Season. LC 96-61932. (Illus.). 56p. (J). (gr. 3 up). 1998. pap. 9.95 (*0-9640742-6-5*) Trickle Creek.

— Nothing but the Truth: A Study Guide. Friedland, J. & Kessler, R., eds. (Novel-Ties Ser.). (J). (gr. 5-7). 1994. pap. text 15.95 (*1-56982-071-6*) Lrn Links.

— Prairie Songs: A Study Guide. Friedland, J. & Kessler, R., eds. (Novel-Ties Ser.). (J). (gr. 4-6). 1993. pap. text, student ed. 15.95 (*0-88122-882-6*) Lrn Links.

— The Remarkable Rainforest: An Active-Learning Book for Kids. LC 94-60401. (Illus.). 64p. (Orig.). (J). (gr. 3-8). 1994. pap. 10.95 (*0-9640742-0-6*) Trickle Creek.

— The War with Grandpa: A Study Guide. Friedland, Joyce & Kessler, Rikki, eds. (Novel-Ties Ser.). (J). (gr. 4-6). 1991. pap. text 15.95 (*0-88122-578-9*) Lrn Links.

— Words by Heart: A Study Guide. Friedland, J. & Kessler, R., eds. (Novel-Ties Ser.). (J). (gr. 5-7). 1992. pap. text, student ed. 15.95 (*0-88122-724-2*) Lrn Links.

Albert, Vicky N. Welfare Dependence & Welfare Policy: A Statistical Study, 8. LC 88-15495. (Studies in Social Welfare Policies & Programs: No. 8). 211p. 1988. 59.95 (*0-313-26175-X*, AWD/, Greenwood Pr) Greenwood.

***Albert, W., et al, eds.** Quality of Life & Psychosomatics: In Mechanical Circulation in Heart Transplantation. x, 118p. 1998. 38.00 (*3-7985-0991-3*) Spr-Verlag.

Albert, Walter, ed. see Cendrars, Blaise.

Albert Whitman Publishing Staff. Let's Collect Coins! 3rd unabridged ed. LC 96-210610. (Illus.). 96p. 1996. pap. text 3.50 (*0-307-99381-7*, Whitman Coin) St Martin.

Albert, Wilda & King, Kelly. Great American Garage Sale. (Illus.). 35p. (Orig.). pap. 3.95 (*0-943983-05-3*) Natl Direct.

Alberta Alcohol and Drug Abuse Commission, jt. auth. see Clark, Stewart C.

Alberta, Eric. Programming for Students with Special Needs. LC 96-206208. 1995. write for info. (*0-7732-1834-3*) APAB.

Alberta, Eric & Maier, Art. The Official Price Guide to Antiques & Collectibles. 16th ed. 784p. 1998. pap. 15.95 (*0-87637-962-5*) Hse Collectbls.

Alberta Hospital Edmonton, Recreation Therapy Staf. Protocols for Recreation Therapy Programs. Kellard, Jill, ed. LC 95-60642. 132p. (C). 1995. pap. 24.95 (*0-910251-73-8*, PRT79) Venture Pub PA.

Alberta-Montana International Partnership Staff. Alberta-Montana Discovery Guide: Museums, Parks & Historic Sites. (Illus.). 358p. 1998. ring bd. 12.95 (*0-7732-1240-X*) APAB.

Alberta Staff. Review of Cumulative Impact of Program & Service Changes for Seniors. LC 97-218288. iii, 43 p. 1996. write for info. (*0-7732-5313-0*) APAB.

— Volunteering: How to Build Your Career by Helping Others. 48 P. ;p. 1998. (*0-7732-1729-0*) APAB.

— Volunteering & Career Building: A Guide for Career Practitioners, Educators, & Volunteer Managers. 44p. 1998. (*0-7732-1731-2*) APAB.

Alberta Staff, jt. auth. see Berry, D. K.

Alberta Staff, jt. auth. see Gunson, John.

***Albertalli & Nilsen.** Roles of the Teacher. (C). 2001. text 48.00 (*0-7668-1539-0*) Delmar.

Albertazzi, A., et al, eds. Nutritional & Pharmacological Strategies in Chronic Renal Failure. (Contributions to Nephrology Ser.: Vol. 81). (Illus.). x, 290p. 1991. 29.75 (*3-8055-5189-4*) S Karger.

Albertazzi, L. Shapes of Forms: From Gestalt Psychology & Phenomenology to Ontology & Mathematics. LC 98-36377. (Synthese Library). 1998. 140.00 (*0-7923-5246-7*) Kluwer Academic.

***Albertazzi, Liliana.** Meaning & Cognition: A Multidisciplinary Approach. LC 00-40314. (Converging Evidence in Language & Communication Research Ser.). 2000. write for info. (*1-55619-681-4*) J Benjamins Pubng Co.

Albertazzi, Liliana, et al, eds. The School of Franz Brentano. LC 95-39650. (Nijhoff International Philosophy Ser.: No. 52). 1995. text 220.50 (*0-7923-3766-2*) Kluwer Academic.

Albertazzi, Liliana, jt. auth. see Leclercq-k, Jacques.

Albertazzi, Ralph, jt. auth. see Fisher, David.

Alberte-Hallam, Teresa, et al. Microcomputer Use Lab Manual. 1985. write for info. incl. disk (*0-318-67043-7*) Harcourt.

Albertelli, Pilo. Gli Eleati: Testimonianze & Frammenti. LC 75-13249. (History of Ideas in Ancient Greece Ser.). (ITA.). 1976. reprint ed. 25.95 (*0-405-07286-4*) Ayer.

Albertet de Sestero. Les Poesies Du Troubadour Alberte... Boutiere, Jean, ed. LC 80-2173. reprint ed. 24.50 (*0-404-19001-4*) AMS Pr.

Alberti. Konkordanz Zu Leon Battista Albertis, 3 vols. Nunez, Javier F., ed. (GER.). 2156p. write for info. (*0-318-70583-4*) G Olms Pubs.

***Alberti, A.** Aspasius: The Earliest Existant Commentary on Aristotles's Ethics. LC 98-46649. (Peripatoi Ser.). 1998. 114.85 (*3-11-016081-1*) De Gruyter.

***Alberti, Anthony.** Wiretaps: A Complete Guide for the Law & Criminal Justice Professional. LC 98-55582. 275p 1999. 69.95 (*1-57292-142-0*) Austin & Winfield.

***Alberti, Bart.** -ine Poems: In the Manner of Animals. (Poetry Manga Ser.). (Illus.). 128p. 2000. pap. 9.95 (*1-886163-07-3*) SoloZone.

Alberti, Benjamin, jt. auth. see Politis, Gustavo.

Alberti, Benjamin, jt. ed. see Politis, Gustavo.

Alberti, Eduard. Lexikon der Schleswig-Holstein-Lauenburgischen und Eutinischen Schriftsteller Von 1829-1882, 4 vols., Set. 1983. write for info. incl. fiche (*0-318-71884-7*) G Olms Pubs.

Alberti, Gerd & Norton, Roy A., eds. Porose Integumental Organs of Oribatid Mites: Acari, Oribatida. (Zoologica Ser.: Vol. 146). (Illus.). 143p. 1997. pap. 122.00 (*3-510-55033-1*) Lubrecht & Cramer.

Alberti, Giorgio, jt. auth. see Whyte, William F.

Alberti, Johanna. Eleanor Rathbone. (Women of Ideas Ser.). 1996. pap. 19.95 (*0-8039-8876-1*) Sage.

— Eleanor Rathbone. LC 96-67388. (Women of Ideas Ser.). 176p. (C). 1996. 55.00 (*0-8039-8875-3*) Sage.

Alberti, John, ed. The Canon in the Classroom: The Pedagogical Implications of Canon Revision in American Literature. LC 94-19101. (Wellesley Studies in Critical Theory, Literary History & Culture: No. 3). 376p. 1994. text 25.00 (*0-8153-1416-7*, H1762) Garland.

— The Heath Anthology of American Literature. 2nd ed. 942p. (C). 1994. pap. text, teacher ed. 2.66 (*0-669-32974-6*) HM Trade Div.

Alberti, Leon Battista. The Family in Renaissance Florence Bk. 3: I Libri Della Famiglia. Watkins, Renee N., tr. & pref. by. 118p. (C). 1994. pap. text 9.95 (*0-88133-821-4*) Waveland Pr.

— Konkordanz Zu Leon Battista Albertis de Re Aedificatoria, 3 vols. (Alpha-Omega, Reihe B Ser.: Bd. 7). (GER.). 2212p. 1996. write for info. (*3-487-09945-4*) G Olms Pubs.

— On Painting. Kemp, Martin, ed. Grayson, Cecil, tr. (Illus.). 112p. 1991. pap. 12.95 (*0-14-043331-7*, Penguin Classics) Viking Penguin.

— On Painting. Spencer, John R., tr. from ITA. LC 76-22485. (Illus.). 141p. 1976. reprint ed. lib. bdg. 38.50 (*0-8371-8974-8*, ALOP, Greenwood Pr) Greenwood.

— On Painting: De Pictura Praestantissima, 1540. (Printed Sources of Western Art Ser.). (LAT.). 128p. 1981. reprint ed. pap. 35.00 (*0-915346-55-9*) A Wofsy Fine Arts.

— On the Art of Building in Ten Books. Rykwert, Joseph et al, trs. (Illus.). 470p. 1991. pap. text 29.50 (*0-262-51060-X*) MIT Pr.

— The Ten Books of Architecture: The 1755 Leoni Edition. 336p. 1987. pap. 16.95 (*0-486-25239-6*) Dover.

— The Use & Abuse of Books: De Commodis Litterarum Atque Incommodis. Neu Watkins, Renee, tr. 55p. (C). 1999. 5.95 (*1-57766-049-8*) Waveland Pr.

Alberti, Leon Battista, jt. auth. see Biermann, Veronica.

***Alberti, Miranda.** Cuisines of the World: Italy. LC 99-462006. (Illus.). 2000. 14.98 (*1-57145-257-5*, Thunder Bay) Advantage Pubs.

Alberti, Peter M. & Uhlmann, Armin. Stochasticity & Partial Order. 1982. text 94.00 (*90-277-1350-2*) Kluwer Academic.

Alberti, Peter W., ed. Personal Hearing Protection in Industry. LC 81-40748. (Illus.). 621p. 1982. reprint ed. pap. 192.60 (*0-7837-9574-2*, 206032300005) Bks Demand.

Alberti, Peter W. & Ruben, Robert J., eds. Otologic Medicine & Surgery, Vol. 1. LC 88-1022. (Illus.). 1037p. reprint ed. pap. 200.00 (*0-7837-6824-9*, 204665600001) Bks Demand.

— Otologic Medicine & Surgery, Vol. 2. LC 88-1022. (Illus.). 949p. reprint ed. pap. 200.00 (*0-7837-6825-7*, 204665600002) Bks Demand.

Alberti, Rafael. Andalusian Whore. Barken, Stanley H., ed. Scheer, Linda & Swann, Brian, trs. (Review Chapbook Ser.: No. 29: Spanish Poetry 1). (ENG & SPA.). 48p. 1992. 15.00 (*0-89304-967-0*); pap. 5.00 (*0-89304-968-9*) Cross-Cultrl NY.

— Andalusian Whore: Mini. Barken, Stanley H., ed. Scheer, Linda & Swann, Brian, trs. (Review Chapbook Ser.: No. 29: Spanish Poetry 1). (ENG & SPA.). 48p. 1992. 15.00 (*0-685-26547-1*); pap. 5.00 (*0-685-26548-X*) Cross-Cultrl NY.

— Antologia Poetica. (SPA.). pap. 14.25 (*84-206-1759-8*, Pub. by Alianza Editorial) Continental Bk.

— Antologia Poetica. 4th ed. (SPA.). 264p. 1989. pap. 11.95 (*0-7859-5138-5*, S19845) Fr & Eur.

— Antologia Poetica. 7th ed. 160p. 1991. pap. 8.95 (*0-7859-5147-4*) Fr & Eur.

— Cal y Canto. 2nd ed. (SPA.). 112p. 1988. pap. 9.95 (*0-7859-5146-6*, S19846) Fr & Eur.

— Concerning the Angels. Sawyer-Laucanno, Christopher, tr. from SPA. 200p. 1995. pap. 12.95 (*0-87286-297-6*) City Lights.

***Alberti, Rafael.** Imagen Primera De... 1999. pap. 18.95 (*84-322-0767-5*) Planeta.

Alberti, Rafael. The Lost Grove: Autobiography of a Spanish Poet in Exile. Berns, Gabriel, ed. & tr. by. LC 74-79760. 1977. pap. 13.95 (*0-520-04265-4*, Pub. by U CA Pr) Cal Prin Full Svc.

— Maravillas Con Variaciones Acrosticas en el Jardin de Miro. deluxe limited aut. ed. (Ediciones Especiales y de Bibliofilo Ser.). (CAT., Illus.). 118p. 1975. 17500.00 (*84-343-0226-8*) Elliots Bks.

— The Other Shore: 100 Poems by Rafael Alberti. Chantikian, Kosrof, ed. Elgorriaga, Jose A. & Paul, Martin, trs. from SPA. LC 80-84602. (Modern Poets in Translation Ser.: Vol. I). xiii, 234p. (C). 1981. 25.95 (*0-916426-05-X*); pap. 15.95 (*0-916426-06-8*) KOSMOS.

— Rome: Danger to Pedestrians. Swann & Scheer, trs. (QRL Poetry Bks.: Vol. XXV). (SPA.). 1984. 20.00 (*0-614-06409-0*) Quarterly Rev.

— To Painting. 1999. pap. text 17.95 (*0-8101-1725-8*, Hydra Bks) Northwestern U Pr.

— To Painting: A Bilingual Collection. (ENG & SPA., Illus.). 253p. 1997. 29.95 (*0-8101-1351-1*, Hydra Bks) Northwestern U Pr.

Alberti, Robert E. Stand up, Speak Out, Talk Back. 1990. mass mkt. 5.50 (*0-671-73588-8*) PB.

Alberti, Robert E. & Emmons, Michael L. Manual for Assertiveness Trainers: 1990 Edition with 1995 Supplement. 3rd ed. LC 90-5326. 160p. 1995. pap. 10.95 (*0-915166-14-3*) Impact Pubs CA.

–Your Perfect Right: A Guide to Assertive Living. 7th rev. ed. LC 95-18417. 256p. 1995. pap. 12.95 (*0-915166-12-7*) Impact Pubs CA.
Twenty-fifth Anniversary Edition of the assertiveness handbook MOST RECOMMENDED BY PSYCHOLOGISTS -- fifth most recommended among ALL self-help books according to a national survey! This over one-million copy bestseller is packed with examples & exercises, with new material on living in a multicultural society, making the decision to express yourself, new recommendations on anger expression & anxiety treatment. Topics include: Assertiveness Builds Equal Relationships...It's Not What You Say, It's How You Say It! Intimacy & Sexuality...Assertiveness Works at Work, Too...Handling Difficult People...Deciding When to Be Assertive...Helping Others Deal With the New Assertive You. Available nationally through all the major wholesalers or direct from the publisher.
Publisher Paid Annotation.

Alberti, Robert E., jt. auth. see Fisher, Bruce.

Alberti, W. E. & Sagerman, Robert H., eds. Radiotherapy of Intracular & Orbital Tumors. LC 92-48365. (Medical Radiology Ser.). 1993. write for info. (*3-540-17686-1*); 299.00 (*0-387-17686-1*) Spr-Verlag.

Albertiin, David M. It's a Matter of Life & Faith Vol. 2: The Apostle's Creed & the Lord's Prayer. LC 96-47408. 1997. pap. 27.50 (*0-7880-0357-7*) CSS OH.

Albertin, David M. It's a Matter of Life & Faith Vol. 1: Baptism, Confession, Absolution, the Office of the Keys & Holy Communion. LC 96-47408. 1997. pap. 21.95 (*0-7880-0356-9*) CSS OH.

— It's a Matter of Life & Faith Vol. 3: The Ten Commandments. LC 96-47408. 1997. pap. 20.25 (*0-7880-0358-5*) CSS OH.

Albertin, L., et al. Load Carrying Capacity of Nitrided Gears. (Nineteen Ninety-Four Fall Technical Meeting Ser.: Vol. 94FTM4). (Illus.). 10p. 1994. pap. text 30.00 (*1-55589-638-3*) AGMA.

***Albertin, Steven E.** Against the Grain - Words for a Politically Incorrect Church: Gospel Sermons for Sundays after Pentecost (Last Third), Cycle B. LC 99-32757. 120p. 1999. pap. 11.25 (*0-7880-1503-6*) CSS OH.

Albertina, Vienna, jt. auth. see Sammiung, Graphische.

Albertine, Susan, ed. A Living of Words: American Women in Print Culture. LC 94-19670. (Illus.). 272p. (C). 1995. text 38.00 (*0-87049-867-3*) U of Tenn Pr.

Albertini, Alberto, et al, eds. Biotechnology in Clinical Medicine. LC 87-42921. 384p. 1987. reprint ed. pap. 119.10 (*0-608-00353-0*, 206107000007) Bks Demand.

— Biotechnology of Plasma Proteins: Haemostasis, Thrombosis & Iron Proteins. (Current Studies in Hematology & Blood Transfusion: No. 58). (Illus.). x, 216p. 1991. 182.75 (*3-8055-5250-5*) S Karger.

— Molecular Probes: Technology & Medical Applications. LC 88-32473. (Illus.). 316p. 1989. reprint ed. pap. 98.00 (*0-608-00587-8*, 206117400007) Bks Demand.

Albertini, Bianca & Bagnoli, Alessandra. Carlo Scarpa: Architecture in Details. Mills, Donald, tr. from ITA. (Illus.). 240p. 1988. 80.00 (*0-262-01107-7*) MIT Pr.

Albertini, Francesco, et al. Clinical Consultation & Letters by Ippolito Francesco Albertini, Francesco Torti, & Other Physicians. (Illus.). lxix, 356p. 1989. 24.95 (*0-88135-089-3*, Sci Hist) Watson Pub Intl.

Albertini, J. A. Cuando la Sangre Mancha. De Fana, Angel, ed. (SPA., Illus.). 466p. 1997. pap. 19.95 (*1-890829-00-5*) DFana Editions.

Albertini, Jean. Dictionnaire Francais-Corse. (FRE.). 349p. 1974. pap. 49.95 (*0-8288-6028-9*, M6001) Fr & Eur.

Albertini, Jean, ed. see Rolland, Romain.

Albertini, Jose A. Tierra de Extranos. LC 82-8440. (Coleccion Caniqui). (SPA.). 160p. (Orig.). 1983. pap. 9.95 (*0-89729-327-4*) Ediciones.

Albertini, Rudolf Von, see Von Albertini, Rudolf.

Albertinus, Aegidius. Der Landstortzer: Gusmann von Al-Farche Oder Picaro Genannt. (Barockromane Ser.). 753p. 1975. reprint ed. 150.00 (*3-487-05442-6*) G Olms Pubs.

Alberto. Negrero. 1996. 9.95 (*84-01-46987-2*) Plaza.

***Alberto, Eliseo.** Caracol Beach. Grossman, Edith, tr. LC 99-58954. 320p. 2000. 25.00 (*0-375-40540-2*) Knopf.

Alberto, Eliseo. Infonne Contra Mi Mismo. 1998. pap. 19.95 (*968-19-0339-0*) Santillana.

***Alberto, Paul & Troutman, Anne C.** Applied Behavior Analysis for Teachers. 5th ed. LC 98-19203. (Illus.). 514p. 1999. 58.33 (*0-13-079760-X*) P-H.

Alberton, Kathleen. The ABCs of Family Court: A Children's Guide. LC 88-120423. (Illus.). 54p. (J). (gr. 1-12). 1987. pap. 1.50 (*0-9619599-0-8*) NYC Law Dept.

Albertos, Jose L. & Suarez, Luisa S. Manual de Estilo. Centro Tecnico de la Sociedad Staff & Interamericana de Prensa Staff, eds. (SPA.). 224p. (Orig.). (C). 1993. pap. text 21.00 (*0-89730-225-7*, Inter Am Pr) R J Berg.

Albertos, P., et al, eds. Control Engineering Solutions: A Practical Approach. LC 97-115145. (IEE Control Engineering Ser.: No. 54). 300p. 1996. 82.00 (*0-85296-829-9*, CE054) INSPEC Inc.

Albertos, P., jt. ed. see Kopacek, Peter.

Alberts, A. The Islands. Beekman, E. M., ed. Koning, Hans, tr. from DUT. LC 82-21882. (Library of the Indies). Orig. Title: De Eilanden. (Illus.). 160p. 1983. lib. bdg. 22.50 (*0-87023-385-8*) U of Mass Pr.

— Islands: A Novel of the East Indies. (Library of the Indies). 138p. 1999. pap. 11.95 (*962-593-261-5*) Tuttle Pubng.

Alberts, Betty, jt. auth. see National Research Council Staff.

***Alberts, Bray.** Molecular Biology of the Cell & the Hypercell. 3rd ed. (Illus.). 1999. 95.95 (*0-8153-3623-3*) Garland.

Alberts, Bruce. Essential Cell Biology: An Introduction to the Molecular of the Cell. LC 97-17039. 768p. 1997. pap. text 46.00 (*0-8153-2971-7*) Garland.

Alberts, Bruce & Bray, Dennis. The Art of Molecular Biology of the Cell: For Mac & Windows. 3rd ed. 1996. 44.00 (*0-8153-2158-9*) Garland.

Alberts, Bruce, et al. Essential Cell Biology: An Introduction to the Molecular Biology of the Cell. LC 97-17039. (Illus.). 764p. 1997. text 65.95 (*0-8153-2045-0*) Garland.

— Molecular Biology of the Cell. 2nd ed. LC 88-38275. (Illus.). 1308p. 1989. text 63.00 (*0-8240-3695-6*) Garland.

— Molecular Biology of the Cell. 3rd ed. LC 93-45907. 1408p. 1994. text 73.95 (*0-8153-1619-4*) Garland.

— Molecular Biology of the Cell. 3rd rev. ed. LC 93-45907. (Illus.). 1408p. 1994. pap. text 63.00 (*0-8153-1620-8*) Garland.

Alberts, David. The Expressive Body: Physical Characterization for the Actor. LC 97-16177. 1997. pap. 17.95 (*0-435-07030-4*) Heinemann.

— Rehearsal Management For Directors. LC 94-49122. 160p. 1995. pap. 15.95 (*0-435-08665-0*, 08665) Heinemann.

— Talking about Mime: An Illustrated Guide. LC 94-18094. 120p. 1994. pap. 14.95 (*0-435-08641-3*, 08641) Heinemann.

Alberts, David E. Fresh Start Credit After Bankruptcy. 28p. 1998. pap. 34.95 (*0-9670210-0-6*) Fresh Start.

Alberts, David S. Defensive Information Warfare. (Illus.). 80p. 1997. pap. text 25.00 (*0-7881-4695-5*) DIANE Pub.

— The Unintended Consequence of Information Age Technologies: Avoiding the Pitfalls, Seizing the Initiative. (Illus.). 62p. 1997. pap. text 25.00 (*0-7881-4705-6*) DIANE Pub.

Alberts, David S. & Czerwinski, Thomas J. Complexity, Global Politics, & National Security. LC 97-24301. 1997. write for info. (*1-57906-046-3*) Natl Defense.

Alberts, David S. & Surwit, Earl A., eds. Ovarian Cancer. (Cancer Treatment & Research Ser.). 1985. text 153.00 (*0-89838-676-4*) Kluwer Academic.

Alberts, David S., et al. The Information Age: An Anthology on Its Impacts & Consequences. LC 97-23702. 1997. write for info. (*1-57906-041-2*) Natl Defense.

— Network Centric Warfare: The Face of Battle in the 21st Century. LC 98-53271. (CCRP Publication Ser.). 1999. write for info. (*1-57906-019-6*) Natl Defense.

Alberts, David S., jt. ed. see Surwit, Earl A.

Alberts, Don E. The Battle of Glorieta: Union Victory in the West. LC 98-5216. (Illus.). 224p. 1998. 29.95 (*0-89096-825-X*) Tex A&M Univ Pr.

***Alberts, Don E.** The Battle of Glorieta: Union Victory in the West. (Illus.). 248p. 2000. pap. 16.95 (*1-58544-100-7*) Tex A&M Univ Pr.

Alberts, Don E., ed. Rebels on the Rio Grande: The Civil War Journal of A.B. Peticolas. (Illus.). 187p. 1993. pap. 12.95 (*0-9636915-0-3*) Merit Pr NM.

***Alberts, Emma Deix.** What the Hell Was I Thinking? 280p. 2000. pap. 14.95 (*0-9638215-3-9*, Kells Bks) Kells Media.

Alberts, Emma F. All That Is Familiar: A Collection of Poems. LC 97-77072. (Illus.). 60p. 1998. pap. 9.95 (*0-9638215-1-2*) Kells Media.

Alberts, Emma F., et al. Cobblestones: A Collection of Modern Writings. LC 97-77072. 68p. 1998. pap. 10.95 (*0-9638215-5-5*) Kells Media.

Alberts, Emma Feix, see DeRenzis, Roxanne & Feix Alberts, Emma, eds.

Alberts, Fred G. Geographic Names of the Antarctic. 1995. 858p. 1995. per. 47.00 (*0-16-061860-6*) USGPO.

Alberts, Gerard G., jt. auth. see White, Carolynne C.

Alberts, J. J., jt. ed. see Pomeroy, L. R.

Alberts, Joye, jt. auth. see Schwarz, Gretchen.

Alberts, Laurie. Goodnight Silky Sullivan. 192p. (Orig.). (C). 1995. pap. 17.95 (*0-8262-1009-0*) U of Mo Pr.

— Lost Daughters. LC 98-48770. (Hardscrabble Bks. Ser.). 217p. 1999. 22.95 (*0-87451-898-9*) U Pr of New Eng.

— The Price of Land in Shelby. LC 96-24556. (Hardscrabble Bks.). 330p. 1996. pap. 14.95 (*0-87451-844-X*); text 30.00 (*0-87451-782-6*) U Pr of New Eng.

Alberts, Louw & Chikane, Frank, eds. The Road to Rustenburg: The Church Looking Forward to a New South Africa. LC 92-119117. (Illus.). 294p. 1991. reprint ed. pap. 91.20 (*0-7837-6727-7*, 204635500011) Bks Demand.

Alberts, Mark J. Genetics of Cerebrovascular Disease. LC 98-18758. (Illus.). 500p. 1998. 120.00 (*0-87993-584-7*) Futura Pub.

Alberts, Michael J. The Handbook for the Cheated Investor: What to Do If You've Been Had. 105p. (Orig.). 1989. pap. 14.95 (*0-685-26493-9*) IIPL.

***Alberts, Nancy.** No Toys on Sunday. LC 98-11434. (Illus.). 32p. (J). (ps-4). 1998. 16.95 (*0-8192-1740-9*) Morehouse Pub.

Alberts, Nancy. Second-Grade Star. (Illus.). (J). (gr. 1-4). 1996. pap. 3.50 (*0-590-25234-8*) Scholastic Inc.

Alberts, Nancy Markham. Elizabeth's Beauty. LC 97-3562. (Illus.). 32p. (J). (ps-5). 1997. 16.95 (*0-8192-1677-1*) Morehouse Pub.

Alberts, Robert C. George Rogers Clark & the Winning of the Old Northwest. (Illus.). 63p. 1998. pap. text 20.00 (*0-7881-4796-X*) DIANE Pub.

— George Rogers Clark & the Winning of the Old Northwest. 72p. 1989. pap. 5.50 (*0-16-003424-8*) USGPO.

Alberts, Robert C., ed. see Berck, Eva.

Alberts, Robert C., ed. see Madous, H. Michael & Newman, Eric P.

Alberts, T. E., ed. Proceedings of the ASME Dynamic Systems & Control Division Vol. 57: International Mechanical Engineering Congress & Exposition - Proceedings of the ASME Dynamic Systems & Control Division, 2 vols., Set, Vols. 1 & 2. LC 95-81282. (1995 ASME International Mechanical Engineering Congress & Exposition Ser.: DSC-Vol. 57). 1120p. 1995. 350.00 (*0-7918-1746-6*, H01025) ASME.

***Alberts, Timothy J., et al.** The Art of Making Beautiful Fashion Doll Shoes. (Illus.). 112p. 1999. 24.95 (*0-87588-561-6*, H5704) Hobby Hse.

Alberts, William W. The Corporate Merger. Segall, Joel E., ed. LC 77-354354. (Studies in Business: Ser. 3 Vol. 10). 318p. Date not set. reprint ed. pap. 98.60 (*0-608-20978-3*, 205450600003) Bks Demand.

Alberts, William W. & Segall, Joel E., eds. Corporate Merger. LC 66-13888. (Studies in Business & Society). xxx, 288p. 1966. lib. bdg. 17.00 (*0-226-01233-6*) U Ch Pr.

Albertsen, June. Two Are Twins. LC 86-70195. (Illus.). 31p. (J). (ps-3). 1987. pap. 5.95 (*0-9615839-0-8*) Double Talk.

Albertsen, Ken. Key to the Airways: Directory Guide to Courier & Consolidated Flights. 6th ed. 32p. 1998. 15.00 (*1-879338-35-1*) Albertsens.

— Metaphysical & Paranormal Hocus Pocus: Why People Embellish Reality with Myths. (Illus.). 142p. 1998. pap. 14.00 (*1-879338-18-1*) Albertsens.

Albertson, Alice O. Nantucket Wild Flowers. LC 73-80640. (Illus.). 1973. reprint ed. 10.00 (*0-913728-02-0*) Theophrastus.

Albertson, Bruce, jt. auth. see Wilson, Fred.

Albertson, Charles C. Death & Afterwards (1906) 106p. 1998. reprint ed. pap. 12.95 (*0-7661-0550-4*) Kessinger Pub.

Albertson, Chris. Bessie. LC 79-163353. 253p. 1974. pap. 8.95 (*0-8128-1700-1*, Scrbrough Hse) Madison Bks UPA.

Albertson, Clinton, ed. Anglo-Saxon Saints & Heroes. LC 67-16652. 375p. reprint ed. pap. 116.30 (*0-7837-0437-2*, 204076000018) Bks Demand.

Albertson, Dean. Roosevelt's Farmer: Claude R. Wickard in the New Deal. LC 74-23430. (FDR & the Era of the New Deal Ser.). 1975. reprint ed. lib. bdg. 49.50 (*0-306-70702-0*) Da Capo.

Albertson, Dean & Ferrell, Robert H. Main Problems in American History Vol. 5: The New Deal & President Roosevelt an American Foreign Policy. abr. ed. (PaperBook Series in History). (Illus.). 128p. (C). 1996. pap. text 2.25 (*1-877891-36-3*) Paperbook Pr Inc.

Albertson, Dorothy L. RPM Unlimited: A Business Machines Practice Set. 2nd ed. (Illus.). (gr. 9-12). 1980. 14.56 (*0-07-000955-4*) McGraw.

Albertson, Dorothy L. & Fillmore-Hoyt, Cathy. A Business Machines Practice Set: RPM Unlimited. 3rd ed. 240p. 1989. pap. text 10.60 (*0-07-000962-7*) McGraw.

Albertson, Ellen. He's a Fork, She's a Spoon: Recipes for a Long, Loving Life Together, the Cooking Couple. 192p. 1998. pap. text 14.95 (*0-9646649-1-7*) Alexandria Camb.

Albertson, Ellen, jt. auth. see Albertson, Michael.

Albertson, Fred C. Catalogue of the Cypriote Sculptures & Terracottas in the Kelsey Museum of Archaeology, the University of Michigan. (Studies in Mediterranean Archaeology: Vol. XX: 14). (Illus.). 65p. (Orig.). 1991. pap. 52.50 (*91-7081-038-9*, Pub. by P Astroms) Coronet Bks.

Albertson, James H. Astride the Winged Horse. 152p. 1995. pap. 12.50 (*0-9645358-0-7*) Candlewood Pub.

Albertson, Joan. Letters Home to Minnesota: Second Minnesota Volunteers. 270p. 1992. pap. 27.95 (*0-9630286-1-8*) PD Enter.

Albertson, Jon. Falklands Fiasco. Hooper, Anne, ed. (Air Adventure Ser.). (Illus.). 284p. (YA). (gr. 12). 1989. 16.95 (*0-9621448-1-9*) Aeolus Bks.

— Naked in the Twisted Sky. Hooper, N. John & Hooper, Anne, eds. (Air Adventure Ser.: Vol. I). 300p. (YA). (gr. 12). 1989. 16.95 (*0-9621448-2-7*) Aeolus Bks.

— Valley of the Condor. Hooper, Anne, ed. (Air Adventure Ser.: Vol. III). 300p. (YA). (gr. 12). 1990. write for info. (*0-9621448-3-5*) Aeolus Bks.

Albertson, Lucie. Crystal Swan. 1998. pap. write for info. (*1-58235-008-6*) Watermrk Pr.

Albertson, M. L. & Kia, R. A., eds. Design of Hydraulic Structures 89: Proceedings of the Second International Symposium on Design of Hydraulic Structures, Fort Collins, Colorado, 26-29 June 1989. 502p. (C). 1989. text 123.00 (*90-6191-898-7*, Pub. by A A Balkema) Ashgate Pub Co.

***Albertson, M. Lee.** The Budget Planner: Get a Grip. 35p. 1999. 19.95 (*0-9677068-0-7*) Albertson Enter.

Albertson, Maurice L., et al, eds. Paranormal Research. 1016p. (Orig.). (C). 1988. pap. text 35.00 (*0-317-91341-7*) Rocky Mtn Rsch Inst.

Albertson, Michael & Albertson, Ellen. Food As Foreplay: Recipes for Romance, Love & Lust. LC 95-78452. (Illus.). 192p. (Orig.). 1996. pap. 14.95 (*0-9646649-0-9*) Alexandria Camb.

Albertson, Michael O. & Hutchinson, Joan P. Discrete Mathematics with Algorithms. LC 88-235. 560p. 1988. text 95.95 (*0-471-84902-2*) Wiley.

Albertson, Mila, ed. 1997-98 Greeting Care Industry Directory: A Comprehensive Guide to the Products & Services of the Greeting Card Industry. 9th ed. 332p. 1997. pap. 95.00 (*0-938369-30-X*) Grtng Card Creat Netwk.

— 1997-98 Directory of Greeting Card Sales Representatives. 4th ed. 286p. 1997. pap. 95.00 (*0-938369-31-8*) Greeting Card Assn.

Albertson, Mila & Riviere, Nancy, eds. Greeting Card Creative Network Annual Talent Directory, 1992. 3rd ed. (Illus.). 1993. pap. 25.00 (*0-938369-17-2*) Greeting Card Assn.

Albertson, Mila, ed. see McDermott, Marianne.

Albertson, Orris E., et al. Dewatering Municipal Wastewater Sludges. LC 90-23202. (Pollution Technology Review Ser.: No. 202). (Illus.). 189p. 1991. 79.00 (*0-8155-1266-X*) Noyes.

Albertson, Ralph. A Survey of Mutualistic Communities in America. LC 72-2934. (Communal Societies in America Ser.). reprint ed. 31.50 (*0-404-10700-1*) AMS Pr.

Albertson, Rebecca & Geideman, Cybele. How to Braid Quality Custom Tack: Easy to Follow Styles & Techniques 22 Illustrated Tack Projects. 8th rev. ed. Jones, John O., ed. Orig. Title: The Art of Braiding Quality Custom Tack. (Illus.). 72p. (J). (gr. 3-12). 1998. 23.00 (*0-9611536-0-1*) U-Braid-It.

Albertson, Timothy E., jt. auth. see Peterson, Steven L.

Albertsson, Ann-Christine & Huang, Samuel J., eds. Degradable Polymers, Recycling, & Plastics Waste Management: Proceedings. LC 95-21646. (Plastics Engineering Ser.: Vol. 29). (Illus.). 336p. 1995. text 165.00 (*0-8247-9668-3*) Dekker.

Albertsson-Wikland, K. & Ranke, M. B., eds. Turner Syndrome in a Life Span Perspective: Research & Clinical Aspects : Proceedings of the 4th International Symposium, Gothenburg, 12-21 May, 1995. (International Congress Ser.: Vol. 1089). 340p. 1995. 212.50 (*0-444-82188-0*) Elsevier.

Albertsson-Wikland, Kerstin, et al, eds. Clinical Pediatric Endocrinology: Serono Symposia Workshop, Arles, France, September 8-9, 1997. (Hormone Research Ser.: Vol. 49, Supplement 2, 1998). (Illus.). iv, 82p. 1998. 37.50 (*3-8055-6700-6*) S Karger.

Albertus, F. Tysk-Dansk: Dansk-Tysk Ordbog. (DAN & GER.). 532p. 1982. 39.95 (*0-8288-4424-0*, M1293) Fr & Eur.

Albertus, Frater. Alchemist's Handbook. LC 74-21127. (Illus.). 128p. (Orig.). 1987. reprint ed. pap. 12.50 (*0-87728-655-8*) Weiser.

— Praxis Spagyrica Philosophica & From One to Ten, 2 vols. in 1. LC 97-48438. (Illus.). 144p. 1998. reprint ed. 37.95 (*0-87728-892-5*) Weiser.

Albertus, Frater, ed. Golden Manuscripts. 160p. 1993. reprint ed. pap. 16.95 (*1-56459-303-7*) Kessinger Pub.

***Albertus, Karen.** Come & See: A Lectionary-Based Christian Initiation Process Using Catholic... Leader Edition. 4th ed. 2000. teacher ed. 24.95 (*0-86716-410-7*) St Anthony Mess Pr.

— Come & See: A Lectionary-Based Christian Initiation Process Using Catholic... Participant Edition. 4th ed. 2000. 19.95 (*0-86716-411-5*) St Anthony Mess Pr.

Albertus, Karen. Come & See: A Lectionary-Based Christian Initiation Process Using Catholic Updates. 3rd ed. 1995. teacher ed., ring bd. 24.95 (*0-86716-197-3*) St Anthony Mess Pr.

— Come & See: An RCIA Process Based on the Complete Lectionary Using Catholic Updates. 3rd ed. 1995. student ed., ring bd. 19.95 (*0-86716-198-1*) St Anthony Mess Pr.

Albertus, Karen, et al. Critical Thinking Activities to Improve Writing Skills A1: Descriptive Mysteries. (Illus.). 40p. (YA). (gr. 4 up). 1989. pap. 11.95 (*0-89455-387-9*) Crit Think Bks.

— Critical Thinking Activities to Improve Writing Skills A1: Where-Abouts. (Illus.). 52p. (YA). (gr. 4 up). 1989. pap. 11.95 (*0-89455-386-0*) Crit Think Bks.

Albertus Magnus. Albertus Magnus: Egyptian Secrets. 9.95 (*0-685-72555-3*) Wehman.

— Egyptian Secrets: or White & Black Art for Man & Beast. 210p. 1993. reprint ed. pap. 16.95 (*1-56459-356-8*) Kessinger Pub.

***Albertus Magnus.** On Union with God. 96p. 2000. 14.95 (*0-8264-4998-0*) Continuum.

Albertus Magnus, jt. auth. see Bonin, Theraese M.

Albertus, Saxonia D. Perutilis Logica. (Documenta Semiotica Ser.: Vol. 6). (GER.). 103p. 1974. reprint ed. write for info. (*3-487-05253-9*) G Olms Pubs.

— Sophismata. (GER.). 218p. 1975. reprint ed. write for info. (*3-487-05584-8*) G Olms Pubs.

Alberty. Physical Chemistry. 2nd ed. 384p. 1996. pap. 36.95 (*0-471-16028-8*) Wiley.

Alberty, Beth & Dropkin, Ruth, eds. The Open Education Advisor: Training, Role & Function of Advisors to the Open Corridor Program. Descriptions of Specific Help to Teachers. 92p. 1975. pap. 3.50 (*0-918374-10-3*) City Coll Wk.

Alberty, Beth & Weber, Lillian. Continuity & Connection in Curriculum. 1979. pap. 3.50 (*0-918374-03-0*) City Coll Wk.

Alberty, Beth, et al. Taking Root: The Workshop Center at City College. 45p. (Orig.). (C). 1983. pap. 3.00 (*0-317-45084-0*) City Coll Wk.

Alberty, Beth, jt. auth. see Weber, Lillian.

Alberty, Robert A. & Silbey, Robert J. Physical Chemistry. 2nd ed. LC 96-4841. 960p. 1996. text 106.95 (*0-471-10428-0*) Wiley.

***Alberty, Robert A. & Silbey, Robert J.** Physical Chemistry. 3rd ed. 980p. (C). 2000. text 111.95 (*0-471-38311-2*) Wiley.

Alberty, Steven. Advising Small Businesses, 3 vols., Set. 1990. 350.00 (*0-685-30632-1*) West Group.

Albertyn. Interpreting CT Head Scans. 1996. pap. text 39.00 (*0-443-05029-5*, W B Saunders Co) Harcrt Hlth Sci Grp.

Albertyn, Chris & McCann, Mike. Alcohol, Employment & Fair Labour Practice. xvi,252p. 1993. pap. write for info. (*0-7021-2820-1*, Pub. by Juta & Co) Gaunt.

Albertz, R. & Otto, S., eds. Religion und Gesellschaft: Studien zu Ihrer Wechselbeziehung in den Kulturen des Antiken Vorderen Orients. (Alter Orient und Altes Testament Ser.). (GER.). viii, 220p. 1997. text 51.00 (*3-927120-54-5*, 248, Pub. by Ugarit-Verlag) Eisenbrauns.

Albertz, Rainer. A History of Israelite Religion in the Old Testament Period Vol. I: From the Beginnings to the End of the Monarchy. Bowden, John, tr. (Old Testament Library: Vol. 1). 384p. 1994. 32.00 (*0-664-21846-6*) Westminster John Knox.

— A History of Israelite Religion in the Old Testament Period Vol. 2: From the Exile to the Maccabees. Bowden, John, tr. (Old Testament Library: Vol. 2). 1994. 32.00 (*0-664-21847-4*) Westminster John Knox.

Alberus, Erasmus. Novum Dictionarii Genus. (Documenta Linguistica, Reihe I: Worterbucher Des Vol. 15 & 16. Jahrhunderts Ser.). (GER.). 840p. 1975. reprint ed. 240.00 (*3-487-05602-X*) G Olms Pubs.

Albery, Faxon F. Michael Ryan, Capitalist. LC 74-22766. (Labor Movement in Fiction & Non-Fiction Ser.). 1976. reprint ed. 38.50 (*0-404-58402-0*) AMS Pr.

Albery, Kari. One Day at Time: A Journal of Inspiration. 160p. 1996. spiral bd. 15.95 (*1-55670-520-4*) Stewart Tabori & Chang.

Albery, Nicholas & McCosker, Karen, eds. A Poem a Day. LC 96-32784. 485p. 1996. pap. 18.00 (*1-883642-38-8*) Steerforth Pr.

Albery, Nick. Time Out Book of Country Walks. 384p. 1997. pap. 19.95 (*0-14-026544-9*, Pub. by Pnguin Bks Ltd) Trafalgar.

Albes, Zita M. The Child under Stress - Dyslexia? 106p. (C). 1986. 50.00 (*0-86236-007-2*, Pub. by Granary) St Mut.

Albet, Carlos Rubio. Saga. LC 97-60043. (SPA.). 188p. 1997. pap. 14.95 (*1-882573-08-0*, Zinnia Bks) Serena Bay.

Albet, Maguy, jt. auth. see St. Onge, Ronald.

Albet, Montserrat. Mozart Un Genio Musical. 1998. pap. 19.95 (*84-08-01042-5*) Planeta.

***Albeverio, S. & Kurasov, P.** Singular Perturbations of Differential Operators. (London Mathematical Society Lecture Note Ser.: No. 271). 448p. (C). 2000. pap. text 44.95 (*0-521-77912-X*) Cambridge U Pr.

Albeverio, S., et al. Advances in Dynamical Systems & Quantum Physics. 372p. 1995. text 128.00 (*981-02-1821-4*) World Scientific Pub.

— Noncommutative Distributions: Unitary Representation of Gauge Groups & Algebras. LC 93-9942. (Pure & Applied Mathematics Ser.: Vol. 175). (Illus.). 208p. 1993. text 125.00 (*0-8247-9131-2*) Dekker.

— Stochastic Processes, Physics & Geometry II. 756p. 1995. text 162.00 (*981-02-2141-X*) World Scientific Pub.

Albeverio, Sergio, et al, eds. Ideas & Methods in Quantum & Statistical Physics, Vol. 2: In Memory of Raphael Hoegh-Krohn. (Illus.). 556p. (C). 1992. text 90.00 (*0-521-41930-1*) Cambridge U Pr.

Albeverio, Sergio A. Stochastic Processes: Mathematics & Physics. Blanchard, P. & Streit, Ludwig, eds. (Lecture Notes in Mathematics Ser.: Vol. 1250). vi, 359p. 1987. 52.95 (*0-387-17797-3*) Spr-Verlag.

Albeverio, Sergio A., ed. Trends & Development in the Eighties: Proceedings of the International Workshop on Bielefeld Encounters in Physics & Mathematics IV. 436p. 1985. 70.00 (*9971-966-77-8*) World Scientific Pub.

Albeverio, Sergio A., et al, eds. Advances in Analysis, Probability, & Mathematical Physics: Contributions of Nonstandard Analysis. LC 94-35635. (Mathematics & Its Applications Ser.: Vol. 314). 1994. text 153.00 (*0-7923-3191-5*) Kluwer Academic.

— Ideas & Methods in Analysis, Stochastics, & Applications, Vol. 1: In Memory of Raphael Hoegh-Krohn. (Illus.). 523p. (C). 1992. text 90.00 (*0-521-41929-8*) Cambridge U Pr.

— Stochastic Aspects of Classical & Quantum Systems. (Lecture Notes in Mathematics Ser.: Vol. 1109). ix, 227p. 1985. 37.95 (*0-387-13914-1*) Spr-Verlag.

— Stochastic Processes: Physics & Geometry International Conference. 760p. (C). 1990. text 173.00 (*981-02-0019-6*) World Scientific Pub.

— Stochastic Processes & Their Applications in Mathematics & Physics. (C). 1990. text 226.50 (*0-7923-0894-8*) Kluwer Academic.

— Stochastic Processes in Classical & Quantum Systems. (Lecture Notes in Physics Ser.: Vol. 262). xi, 551p. 1986. 78.95 (*0-387-17166-5*) Spr-Verlag.

— Stochastic Processes in Physics & Engineering. (C). 1988. text 195.50 (*90-277-2659-0*) Kluwer Academic.

— Stochastics, Algebra & Analysis in Classical & Quantum Dynamics. (C). 1990. text 166.50 (*0-7923-0637-6*) Kluwer Academic.

Albeverio, Sergio A., et al. Resonances Models & Phenomena. Ferreira, L. S. & Streit, Ludwig, eds. (Lecture Notes in Physics Ser.: Vol. 211). vi, 359p. 1984. 42.95 (*0-387-13880-3*) Spr-Verlag.

— Solvable Models in Quantum Mechanics. (Texts & Monographs in Physics). 480p. 1988. 136.95 (*0-387-17841-4*) Spr-Verlag.

— Stochastic Processes: Mathematics & Physics. Blanchard, P. & Streit, Ludwig, eds. (Lecture Notes in Mathematics Ser.: Vol. 1158). vi, 257p. 1986. 48.95 (*0-387-15998-3*) Spr-Verlag.

Albi, Charles & Jones, William C. Otto Perry: Master Railroad Photographer. LC 82-4201. (Illus.). 336p. 1982. 30.00 (*0-918654-32-7*) CO RR Mus.

Albi, Johnna. Greens Glorious Greens. 288p. 1996. pap. 16.95 (*0-312-14108-4*) St Martin.

Albi, Linda, et al. Mothering Twins: From Hearing the News to Beyond the Terrible Twos. 416p. (Orig.). 1993. per. 14.00 (*0-671-72357-X*) S&S Trade Pap.

Albiach, Anne-Marie. Etat. 1989. pap. 10.00 (*0-942433-13-0*) Awede Pr.

— A Geometry: 3 Poems. Waldrop, Keith & Waldrop, Rosmarie, trs. from FRE. (Serie d'Ecriture Supplement: Vol. 3). 28p. 1998. pap. 5.00 (*1-886224-31-5*) Burning Deck.

— Mezza Voce. Simas, Joseph et al, trs. from FRE. (Poetry Ser.). 164p. (Orig.). 1988. pap. 12.95 (*0-942996-11-9*) Post Apollo Pr.

— Vocative Figure. 2nd rev. ed. Barnett, Anthony & Simas, Joseph, trs. from FRE. 48p. 1992. reprint ed. pap. 12.00 (*0-907954-18-9*, Pub. by Allardyce Barnett) SPD-Small Pr Dist.

Albiani, Joseph, et al. The Crucifixion: What Really Happened & Why. LC 99-229531. (Yeshuahen Yosef Ser.). 96p. 1999. pap. 12.95 (*0-9670535-0-1*) Joy Publs.

Albias, H., et al, eds. Attribute Grammars, Applications & Systems: International Summer School SAGA Prague, Czechoslovakia, June 4-13, 1991 Proceedings. (Lecture Notes in Computer Science Ser.: Vol. 545). ix, 513p. 1991. 53.95 (*0-387-54572-7*) Spr-Verlag.

Albietz, F. N., jt. auth. see Hartigan, T. R.

Albin. Lotus 1-2-3 for Windows Release 4 & 5, Easy Reference Guide. (DF - Computer Applications Ser.). 1995. mass mkt. 9.95 (*0-538-63690-4*) S-W Pub.

Albin, Barbara & Holek, Julia. Crafts for Religious Education. (Illus.). 174p. (Orig.). 1987. pap. 10.95 (*1-55588-144-0*) St Michael Guild.

Albin, Cecilia & Saunders, Harold H. Sinai II: The Politics of International Mediation. (Pew Case Studies in International Affairs). 114p. 1991. pap. text 3.50 (*1-56927-421-5*) Geo U Inst Dplmcy.

Albin, Edgar A., et al. Selections from the Permanent Collection of the Springfield Art Museum. Landwehr, William C., ed. LC 80-53333. 100p. 1980. pap. text 5.00 (*0-934306-03-6*) Springfield.

Albin, Francis M. Consumer Economics & Personal Money Management. 2nd ed. (Illus.). 496p. (C). 1988. 78.00 (*0-13-168048-X*) P-H.

Albin, Francis M., ed. Anh-Viet Viet-Anh Tu Dien Ke Toan. Thomson, Cecile P. et al, trs. LC 92-80731.Tr. of English-Vietnamese Vietnamese-English Accounting Dictionary. (ENG & VIE.). 342p. (Orig.). 1992. pap. 24.95 (*0-9626407-1-9*) Paper Tig Pr.

— Business Vietnamese. Thi Thanh Hieu, Dao et al, trs. (VIE.). 48p. (Orig.). 1995. pap. text 3.50 (*0-9626407-2-7*) Paper Tig Pr.

— Concise English-Vietnamese Accounting Dictionary. Dao Thi Thanh Hieu & Huynh Ngoc Phu'oc, trs.Tr. of Tu Dien Ke Toan Anh-Viet Suc Tich va Gian Luoc. 192p. 1997. pap. 21.95 (*0-9626407-4-3*) Paper Tig Pr.

— English-Vietnamese Business-Finance Pocket Dictionary. 2nd ed. Dao Thi Thanh Hieu & Huynh Ngoc Phu'oc, trs.Tr. of Anh-Viet Tu Dien Bo Tui Kinh Doanh-Tai Chinh Chuyen Khoa. 208p. 1997. pap. 14.95 (*0-9626407-6-X*) Paper Tig Pr.

Albin, James R. Bay Area Directory. 208p. 1994. pap. 85.95 (*0-916210-94-4*) J R Albin.

— Bay Area Employment Agency & Executive Recruiter Directory. 50p. 1994. 49.95 (*0-916210-79-0*) J R Albin.

— Employer Directory. 200p. 1997. 99.95 (*0-614-14821-9*) J R Albin.

— Los Angeles Employer Directory. 200p. 1994. 99.95 (*0-916210-81-2*) J R Albin.

Albin, Maurice S., ed. Textbook of Neuroanesthesia: With Neurosurgical & Neuroscience Perspectives. LC 96-24790. (Illus.). 1500p. 1996. text, teacher ed. 175.00 (*0-07-000966-X*) McGraw-Hill HPD.

Albin, Mel & Johnson, Noel. Financial Planning with Employee Benefits: A Guide for Employees. Crisp, Michael G., ed. LC 89-61793. (Fifty-Minute Ser.). (Illus.). 105p. (Orig.). 1989. pap. 10.95 (*0-931961-90-4*) Crisp Pubns.

Albin, Peter S. & Foley, Duncan K. Barriers & Bounds to Rationality: Essays on Economic Complexity & Dynamics in Interactive Systems. LC 97-33634. (Studies in Complexity). 296p. 1998. text 35.00 (*0-691-02676-9*, Pub. by Princeton U Pr) Cal Prin Full Svc.

Albin, R. C., jt. ed. see Thompson, G. B.

Albin, Robert C., et al. Cattle Feeding: A Guide to Management. 2nd rev. ed. (Illus.). 272p. 1996. pap. 25.95 (*0-9627761-2-2*) Trafton Printing.

Albin, Steven J. Basket Maker, Vol. 1. Press, Cody, ed. (Illus.). 32p. (J). (gr. 2). 1992. 10.95 (*0-9632943-0-X*) Sleepy Zebra.

Albing, Mary. Seasons to Celebrate: God's Children Celebrate the Church Year. 64p. 1994. pap. 10.99 (*0-8066-2722-0*, 10-27220, Augsburg) Augsburg Fortress.

Albini, A. & Fasani, E., eds. Drugs: Photochemistry & Photostability. (Special Publications: No. 225). 354p. 1998. 120.00 (*0-85404-743-3*) Spr-Verlag.

Albini, Angelo, ed. Heterocyclic N-Oxides. 328p. 1991. lib. bdg. 244.00 (*0-8493-4552-9*, QD401) CRC Pr.

Albini, B., ed. see International Convocation on Immunology Staff.

Albini, Joseph L. American Mafia: Genesis of a Legend. LC 70-147120. (Orig.). (C). 1971. pap. text 12.95 (*0-89197-014-2*) Irvington.

Albini, Louis, jt. auth. see Adey, Margaret.

Albinoni, Tomaso. Adagio in G Minor on a Theme of T. Albinoni: Full Score for Strings & Orchestra. 1986. pap. 6.95 (*0-7935-5548-5*) H Leonard.

— Tomasco Albinoni: Twelve Cantatas, Opus 4. Talbot, Michael, ed. (Recent Researches in Music of the Baroque Era Ser.: Vol. RRB31). (Illus.). xix, 100p. 1979. pap. 40.00 (*0-89579-111-0*, RRB31) A-R Eds.

— Tomaso Albinoni: Pimpinone - Intermezzi Comici Musicali. Talbot, Michael, ed. (Recent Researches in Music of the Baroque Era Ser.: Vol. RRB43). (Illus.). xxx, 77p. 1983. pap. 35.00 (*0-89579-169-2*) A-R Eds.

— Tomaso Albinoni: Sonatas & Suites, Opus 8 - For Two Violins, Violon Cello & Basso Continuo. Harris, C. David, ed. (Recent Researches in Music of the Baroque Era Ser.: Vol. RRB51). (Illus.). xi, 102p. 1986. pap. 40.00 (*0-89579-207-9*) A-R Eds.

— Tomaso Albinoni: Sonatas & Suites, Opus 8 - For Two Violins, Violon Cello & Basso Continuo. Harris, C. David, ed. (Recent Researches in Music of the Baroque Era Ser.: Vol. RRB52). (Illus.). 99p. 1986. pap. 35.00 (*0-89579-208-7*) A-R Eds.

Albinski, Henry S. ANZUS, the United States & Pacific Security. LC 87-10548. (Asian Agenda Reports: No. 17). 76p. (Orig.). (C). 1987. pap. text 8.50 (*0-8191-6374-0*); lib. bdg. 27.00 (*0-8191-6373-2*) U Pr of Amer.

— Australian Policies & Attitudes Toward China. LC 66-10548. 527p. reprint ed. pap. 163.40 (*0-8357-8809-1*, 205228100085) Bks Demand.

— Politics & Foreign Policy in Australia: The Impact of Vietnam & Conscription. LC 76-101128. 240p. reprint ed. 74.40 (*0-8357-9114-9*, 201787800010) Bks Demand.

Albinski, Henry S., ed. Strategic Imperatives & Western Responses in the South & Southwest Pacific. 462p. (C). 1986. vinyl bd. 18.00 (*0-317-91351-4*) Pac Forum.

Albinski, Nan B. The Directory of Resources for Australian Studies in North America. 211p. 1992. 15.00 (*0-7326-0435-4*, Pub. by Natl Ctr Austln) Austlia-NZ Studies.

— Women's Utopias in Nineteenth & Twentieth Century Fiction. 224p. 1988. lib. bdg. 59.50 (*0-415-00337-X*) Routledge.

***Albinson, Clare.** In Harmony with Your Horse. (Illus.). 128p. 2001. pap. 6.95 (*0-7160-2129-3*, Pub. by Elliot RW Bks) Midpt Trade.

— Riding & Schooling. 224p. 2000. pap. 9.95 (*0-7160-2118-8*, Pub. by Elliot RW Bks) Midpt Trade.

Albinson, Jack. A Hand for the Wheel: The Mel Kenyon Story. (Illus.). 102p. 1997. 20.00 (*0-9627653-8-4*) Witness Prods.

— The Oily Grail: A Story of the Indy 500. LC 73-87667. 101p. 1974. write for info. (*0-513-01322-9*) Denison.

Albinus, Fabricus. The Confession of Pontius Pilate. Shehadi, Beshara, tr. 1991. lib. bdg. 79.95 (*0-8490-5011-1*) Gordon Pr.

***Albinus, Lars.** The House of Hades: Studies in Ancient Greek Eschatology. (Studies in Religion: Vol. 2). (Illus.). 224p. (C). 2000. 24.95 (*87-7288-833-4*, Pub. by Aarhus Univ Pr) David Brown.

Albion, Mark. Making a Life, Making a Living: Reclaiming Your Purpose & Passion in Business & in Life. LC 99-30166. 256p. 2000. 23.95 (*0-446-52404-2*, Pub. by Warner Bks) Little.

***Albion, Mark.** Making a Life, Making a Living: Reclaiming Your Purpose & Passion in Business & in Life. 2000. pap. 13.95 (*0-446-67651-9*) Warner Bks.

Albion, Mark S. Advertising's Hidden Effects: Manufacturers' Advertising & Retailing Pricing. LC 82-6776. 332p. 1983. 24.95 (*0-86569-111-8*, Auburn Hse) Greenwood.

Albion, Mark S. & Farris, Paul W. Advertising Controversy: Evidence on the Economic Effects of Advertising. LC 80-24645. 245p. (C). 1981. 62.95 (*0-86569-057-X*, Auburn Hse) Greenwood.

Albion, Robert G. Introduction to Military History. LC 75-158240. (Illus.). 1971. reprint ed. 37.50 (*0-404-00303-6*) AMS Pr.

— Naval & Maritime History: An Annotated Bibliography. 4th rev. ed. LC 73-186863. ix, 370p. 1972. 14.95 (*0-913372-05-6*) Mystic Seaport.

Albion, Robert G., et al. New England & the Sea. LC 72-3694. (American Maritime Library: Vol. 5). (Illus.). xiv, 303p. 1972. pap. 18.00 (*0-913372-23-4*) Mystic Seaport.

Albion, Robert Greebhalgh. Forests & Sea Power: The Timber Problem of The Royal Navy, 1652-1862. LC 99-50337. 1999. 34.95 (*1-55750-021-5*) Naval Inst Pr.

Albis, Robert V. Poet & Audience in the Argonautica of Apollonius. 168p. 1996. 52.50 (*0-8476-8315-X*); pap. 21.95 (*0-8476-8316-8*) Rowman.

Albisetti, James C. Schooling German Girls & Women: Secondary & Higher Education in the Nineteenth Century. LC 88-9991. (Illus.). 365p. reprint ed. pap. 113.20 (*0-608-06419-X*, 206663200008) Bks Demand.

Albiston, Steven K., jt. auth. see Hammon, Darrel L.

Albitz, Paul, jt. auth. see Liu, Cricket.

Albizati, K. F., et al. Synthesis of Marine Natural Products No. 1: Terpenoids. Scheuer, Paul J., ed. (Bioorganic Marine Chemistry Ser.: Vol. 5). (Illus.). xi, 280p. 1992. 172.95 (*0-387-54375-9*) Spr-Verlag.

— Synthesis of Marine Natural Products No. 2: Nonterpenoids. Scheuer, Paul J., ed. (Bioorganic Marine Chemistry Ser.: Vol. 6). (Illus.). xi, 322p. 1992. 172.95 (*0-387-54376-7*) Spr-Verlag.

Albl, Martin, et al, eds. Directions in New Testament Methods. (Studies in Theology). 129p. 1993. pap. 15.00 (*0-87462-626-9*) Marquette.

Alblas, Henk. Complete Compiler Course. text. write for info. (*0-471-87739-5*) Wiley.

Albo, Gregory, et al, eds. A Different Kind of State: Popular Power & Democratic Administration. 248p. (C). 1993. pap. text 26.00 (*0-19-540907-8*) OUP.

Albo, Maria Elena, tr. "iHagalo o Haga Dieta" - Moderacion no Privacion: Un Sistema Conelque Realmente Puede Vivir: Controlando su Peso en Elmundo Actual.Tr. of Do It! or Diet - Moderation Not Deprivation. (SPA., Illus.). 124p. 1983. spiral bd. 15.00 (*0-9659120-2-7*) Michelle Present.

***Albo, Mike.** Hornito: My Lie Life. LC 00-38669. 224p. 2000. 23.00 (*0-688-17436-1*, Wm Morrow) Morrow Avon.

Albo, Shana. Infertility Solutions: Natural Approaches. LC 99-35378. (Illus.). 224p. 2000. pap. 12.95 (*0-89529-919-4*, Avery) Penguin Putnam.

***Albohm, Marjorie, et al.** Reimbursement for Athletic Trainers. 200p. (C). 2000. pap. text 24.00 (*1-55642-408-6*) SLACK Inc.

Albohm, Marjorie J., jt. auth. see Ritter, Merrill A.

Albom, Mitch. Live Albom, No. I. 1996. mass mkt. 6.95 (*0-937247-06-5*) Detroit Pr.

— Live Albom, No. II. 1996. pap. 9.95 (*0-937247-54-5*) Detroit Pr.

— Live Albom, No. III. 1996. pap. 9.95 (*0-937247-71-5*) Detroit Pr.

— Live Albom, No. IV. 1996. pap. 12.95 (*0-937247-66-9*) Detroit Pr.

— Tuesdays with Morrie: An Old Man, a Young Man & Life's Greatest Lesson. LC 96-52535. 208p. 1997. 21.00 (*0-385-48451-8*) Doubleday.

***Albom, Mitch.** Tuesdays with Morrie: An Old Man, a Young Man & Life's Greatest Lesson. large type ed. 2000. pap. 10.95 (*1-56895-967-2*) Wheeler Pub.

Albom, Mitch & Coulter, Catherine. Tuesdays with Morrie: An Old Man, a Young Man & Life's Greatest Lesson. large type ed. LC 98-6713. 1998. 25.95 (*1-56895-557-X*, Wheeler) Wheeler Pub.

Albon, George. Empire Life. (Littoral Bks.). 72p. 1998. pap. 10.95 (*1-55713-376-X*, Pub. by Sun & Moon CA) Consort Bk Sales.

— Possible Floor. 1990. pap. 3.50 (*0-938979-35-3*) EG Bksellers.

Albon, Robert & Stafford, David. Rent Control. 144p. 1987. lib. bdg. 55.00 (*0-7099-5411-5*, Pub. by C Helm) Routldge.

Albone, Eric S. Mammalian Semiochemistry: The Investigation of Chemical Signals Between Mammals. LC 83-10231. 372p. 1984. 411.00 (*0-471-10253-9*) Halsted Pr.

Albores-Saavedra, Jorge, et al. Histological Typing of Tumours of the Gallbladder & Extrahepatic Bile Ducts: In Collaboration with Pathologists in 5 Countries. 2nd ed. (Illus.). 96p. 1994. 48.00 (*0-387-52838-5*) Spr-Verlag.

Albores-Saavedra, Jorge, jt. ed. see Henson, Donald Earl.

Albores-Saavedra, Jorge, jt. ed. see Henson, Donald.

Alborg, J. L. Historia de la Literatura Espanola: Edad Media y Renacimiento, Vol. 1. 2nd ed. (SPA.). 1082p. 1993. 150.00 (*84-249-3126-2*) Elliots Bks.

— Historia de la Literatura Espanola: El Romanticismo, Vol. 4. (SPA.). 952p. 1993. 150.00 (*84-249-3146-7*) Elliots Bks.

— Historia de la Literatura Espanola: El Siglo XVIII, Vol. 3. (SPA.). 980p. 1993. 150.00 (*84-249-3130-0*) Elliots Bks.

— Historia de la Literatura Espanola: Epoca Barroca, Vol. 2. 2nd ed. (SPA.). 996p. 1993. 150.00 (*84-249-3128-9*) Elliots Bks.

— Sobre Critica y Criticos (Historia de la Literatura Espanola: Parentesis Teorico Que Apenas Tiene Que Ver Con la Presente Historia. (SPA.). 1006p. 1993. 200.00 (*84-249-1465-1*) Elliots Bks.

Alborg, J. L., jt. auth. see Ballesteros, M.

***Alborghetti, Marci.** Miracle of the Myrrh. LC 00-20551. (Illus.). 32p. (J). (gr. k-4). 2000. 16.95 (*1-890817-16-3*, Pub. by Winslow Pr) Publishers Group.

Alborghetti, Stephen P., ed. see Gove, Thomas P.

Alborn, Timothy L. Conceiving Companies: Joint-Stock Politics in Victorian England. LC 97-33482. 320p. (C). 1998. 85.00 (*0-415-18079-1*) Routledge.

Alborna-Salado, Juan. Antirreflexiones. LC 92-73337. (Coleccion Cuba y sus Jueces). (SPA.). 102p. (Orig.). 1992. pap. 12.00 (*0-89729-652-4*) Ediciones.

Albornoz, Fernando, ed. The Auxiliaries. Quiroga, Roberto, tr. (Rotary Drilling Ser.: Unit I, Lesson 9). (SPA., Illus.). 60p. (Orig.). 1983. pap. text 14.00 (*0-88698-037-2*, 2.10922) PETEX.

— Rotary, Kelly & Swivel. Quiroga, Roberto, tr. (Rotary Drilling Ser.: Unit I, Lesson 4). (SPA., Illus.). 69p. (Orig.). 1982. pap. text 14.00 (*0-88698-032-1*, 2.10422) PETEX.

— The Rotary Rig & Its Components. Carmona-Agosto, Vivian, tr. (Rotary Drilling Ser.: Unit I, Lesson 1). (SPA., Illus.). 47p. (Orig.). 1980. pap. 14.00 (*0-88698-029-1*, 2.10132) PETEX.

Albornoz, Fernando, tr. see Carmona-Agosto, Vivian, ed.

Albornoz, Fernando, tr. see Leecraft, Jodie, ed.

Alborough, Jez. Can You Jump Like a Kangaroo? LC 95-71698. (Animal Pop-Up Bks.). (Illus.). 12p. (J). (ps). 1996. 7.99 (*1-56402-880-1*) Candlewick Pr.

— Can You Peck Like a Hen? LC 95-71699. (Animal Pop-Up Bks.). (Illus.). 12p. (J). (ps). 1996. 7.99 (*1-56402-881-X*) Candlewick Pr.

— Cuddly Dudley. LC 92-52994. (Illus.). 32p. (J). (ps-3). 1995. reprint ed. pap. 4.99 (*1-56402-505-5*) Candlewick Pr.

Alborough, Jez. Donde Esta Mi Osito?Tr. of Where's My Teddy?. 1995. 17.15 (*0-606-10403-8*, Pub. by Turtleback) Demco.

Alborough, Jez. Donde Esta Mi Osito? Where's My Teddy? (SPA.). 18p. (J). (gr. k-1). 1995. pap. 11.95 (*1-56014-582-X*) Santillana.

***Alborough, Jez.** Duck in a Truck. (Illus.). 16p. (J). (ps-3). 1999. pap. 10.98 (*1-58048-064-0*) Sandvik Pub.

Alborough, Jez. Duck in the Truck. LC 99-60934. (Illus.). 40p. (J). (ps-1). 2000. 14.95 (*0-06-028685-7*) HarpC.

— Hide-&-Seek. LC 93-28542. (Illus.). 32p. (J). (ps up). 1994. pap. 5.99 (*1-56402-369-9*) Candlewick Pr.

***Alborough, Jez.** Hide-and-Seek: A Flip-the-Flap Book. LC 93-28542. (Illus.). 32p. (J). 1999. pap. 3.99 (*0-7636-0690-1*, Pub. by Candlewick Pr) Penguin Putnam.

— Hug. (Illus.). 32p. (YA). (ps up). 2000. 14.99 (*0-7636-1287-1*) Candlewick Pr.

A

An Asterisk (*) at the beginning of an entry indicates that the title is appearing for the first time.

A

Alborough, Jez. Ice Cream Bear. LC 97-10119. (Illus.). 32p. (Orig.). (J). (ps-k). 1997. pap. 5.99 *(0-7636-0293-0)* Candlewick Pr.

— It's the Bear! LC 94-10510. 1996. 11.19 *(0-606-09482-2,* Pub. by Turtleback) Demco.

— It's the Bear! LC 94-10510. (Illus.). 32p. (J). (ps-3). 1996. reprint ed. pap. 4.99 *(1-56402-840-2)* Candlewick Pr.

— It's the Bear!, Set. LC 94-10510. (J). (ps-3). 1994. 15.95 *(1-56402-486-5)* Candlewick Pr.

***Alborough, Jez.** Math Together: Green Books. (Illus.). (YA). (ps up). 2000. pap. 19.99 *(0-7636-0954-4)* Candlewick Pr.

— Math Together: Yellow Books. (Illus.). (YA). (ps up). 2000. 19.99 *(0-7636-0947-1)* Candlewick Pr.

Alborough, Jez. My Friend Bear. LC 97-32557. (Illus.). 32p. (J). (ps-2). 1998. 16.99 *(0-7636-0583-2)* Candlewick Pr.

— There's Something at the Mail Slot. LC 94-22619. (Illus.). (J). (ps up). 1995. pap. 4.99 *(1-56402-523-3)* Candlewick Pr.

— Watch Out! Big Bro's Coming! (Illus.). (J). (ps-3). 1997. 16.99 *(0-614-28640-9)* Candlewick Pr.

— Watch Out! Big Bro's Coming! LC 96-30318. (Illus.). 32p. (J). (ps-3). 1997. 16.99 *(0-7636-0130-6)* Candlewick Pr.

— Watch Out! Big Bro's Coming! LC 96-30318. (Illus.). 32p. (J). (ps-3). 1998. pap. 6.99 *(0-7636-0584-0)* Candlewick Pr.

— Where's My Teddy? LC 91-58765. (Illus.). 32p. (J). (ps up). 1992. 15.95 *(1-56402-048-7)* Candlewick Pr.

— Where's My Teddy? LC 91-58765. (Illus.). 32p. (J). (ps up). 1994. pap. 4.99 *(1-56402-280-3)* Candlewick Pr.

— Where's My Teddy? (Little Book Cards Ser.). (Illus.). (J). 1997. pap. 3.29 *(0-7636-0220-5)* Candlewick Pr.

— Where's My Teddy? 1994. 11.19 *(0-606-06093-6,* Pub. by Turtleback) Demco.

— Where's My Teddy? Big Book. LC 91-58765. (Illus.). (J). 1995. pap. 19.99 *(1-56402-468-7)* Candlewick Pr.

***Alborough, Jez.** Whose Socks Are Those? A Flip-the-Flap Book. LC 98-73215. (Illus.). 32p. (J). (ps). 1999. pap. 3.99 *(0-7636-0688-X,* Pub. by Candlewick Pr) Penguin Putnam.

Albors-Llorens, Albertina. Private Parties in European Community Law: Challenging Community Measures. 310p. 1996. text 80.00 *(0-19-826080-6)* OUP.

Albota, Mihail. Dictionary of Geodesics, Photogrametrics-Teledicton & Cartography: Dictionar de Geodezie, Fotogrammetrie-Teledetectie si Cartografie. 548p. 1980. write for info. *(0-8288-0361-7,* M15715) Fr & Eur.

Albouy, Pierre, ed. see Hugo, Victor.

Albouy, Yves. Marginal Cost Analysis & Pricing of Water & Electrical Power: Methodology Notes. 230p. 1983. 18.50 *(0-940602-10-5)* IADB.

Albovias, Benjamin C. Immigration to the United States. 160p. 1988. reprint ed. pap. text 14.95 *(0-9621331-0-8)* B C Albovias.

Albowitz, B., et al, eds. Structural & Functional Organization of the Neocortex: Proceedings of a Symposium in the Memory of Otto D. Creutzfeldt, May 1993. LC 94-16023. 1994. write for info. *(0-387-57205-8)* Spr-Verlag.

Albracht, F., ed. see Ebeling, H.

Albrand, Martha. After Midnight. 1976. pap. 0.95 *(0-380-01009-7,* Avon Bks) Morrow Avon.

***Albrant, Daniel H., ed.** The American Pharmaceutical Association Drug Treatment Protocols. LC 99-72581. (Illus.). 457p. (C). 1999. text 100.00 *(0-917330-98-6)* Am Pharm Assn.

***Albrant, Daniel H. & Harteker, Linda R.** The Pharmacy Student Companion: Your Road Map to Pharmacy Education & Careers. 3rd rev. ed. Meade, Vicki L., ed. 157p. (C). 1999. pap. 20.00 *(0-917330-94-3)* Am Pharm Assn.

Albrecht. Communicating in Organizations. (C). 1996. pap. text, teacher ed. 28.00 *(0-15-502744-1)* Harcourt Coll Pubs.

***Albrecht.** Principles of Dressage. 2000. 19.95 *(0-85131-569-0,* Pub. by J A Allen) Trafalgar.

Albrecht & Stice, James D. Survey of Accounting. (AB - Accounting Principles Ser.). (C). 1998. pap. 83.95 *(0-538-84617-8)* S-W Pub.

— Survey of Accounting. (AB - Accounting Principles Ser.). (C). 1999. pap., student ed. 19.00 *(0-538-87324-8)* S-W Pub.

Albrecht, jt. auth. see Hvass.

Albrecht, jt. auth. see Skousen.

Albrecht, Adalbert, tr. see Aschaffenburg, Gustav.

Albrecht, Adalbert, tr. see Kohler, Josef.

Albrecht, Bob & Inman, Don. Mastering QBasic & QuickBasic. LC 93-39036. 1993. write for info. *(0-02-802581-4)* Glencoe.

Albrecht, Bob, et al. Teach Yourself Visual Basic. (Illus.). 512p. 1995. pap. text 24.95 *(0-07-882078-2)* McGraw.

Albrecht, Bruce A., jt. auth. see Bohren, Craig F.

Albrecht, Carl W. & Watkins, Reed A. Cross-Reference to Names of Ohio Skippers & Butterflies: Insecta, Lepidoptera, Hesperoidea & Papilionoidea. (Informative Circular Ser.: No. 12). 1983. pap. text 4.00 *(0-86727-095-0)* Ohio Bio Survey.

Albrecht-Carrie, Rene. Italy from Napoleon to Mussolini. LC 49-50178. 316p. reprint ed. pap. 98.00 *(0-608-15780-5,* 203101100073) Bks Demand.

Albrecht, Catherine, ed. see Drouin, Marie J., et al.

Albrecht, Christian. Schleiermacher's Theorie der Froemmigkeit: Ihr Wissenschaftlicher Ort und Ihr Systematischer Gehalt In den Reden, In der Glausbenslehre und In der Dialektikk. (Schleiermacher-Archiv Ser.: No. 15). (GER.). xvii, 350p. 1993. lib. bdg. 152.35 *(3-11-014172-8)* De Gruyter.

***Albrecht, Daniel E.** Rites in the Spirit: A Ritual Approach to Pentecostal/Charismatic Spirituality. (Journal of Pentecostal Theology Supplement Ser.: No. 17). 280p. 1999. pap. 21.95 *(1-84127-017-2,* Pub. by Sheffield Acad) CUP Services.

Albrecht, Don E. & Murdock, Steve H. The Sociology of U. S. Agriculture: An Ecological Perspective. LC 89-77423. (Illus.). 257p. 1990. reprint ed. pap. 79.70 *(0-608-00040-X,* 206080600006) Bks Demand.

***Albrecht, Donald & Broikos, Chrysanthe B., eds.** On the Job: Design & the American Office. (Illus.). 128p. 2000. pap. 24.95 *(1-56898-241-0)* Princeton Arch.

***Albrecht, Donald, et al.** Design Culture Now: National Design Triennial. (Illus.). 208p. 2000. pap. 29.95 *(1-56898-218-6)* Princeton Arch.

Albrecht, Donald, et al. The Work of Charles & Ray Eames: A Legacy of Invention. LC 97-4086. (Illus.). 205p. 1997. 49.50 *(0-8109-1799-8,* Pub. by Abrams) Time Warner.

Albrecht, Donald, ed. & intro. see Reed, Peter S., et al.

***Albrecht, Donna.** I Love to Tell the Story: Favorite Bible Stories of Famous People. 1999. pap. 13.00 *(0-425-17230-9)* Berkley Pub.

Albrecht, Donna G. Buying a Home When You're Single. 208p. 1994. pap. 14.95 *(0-471-02499-6)* Wiley.

— Promoting Your Business with Free Publicity. 1996. pap. text 16.95 *(0-89384-305-9)* P-H.

— Raising a Child Who Has a Physical Disability. LC 94-41908. 228p. 1995. pap. 12.95 *(0-471-04240-4)* Wiley.

Albrecht, Douglas & Ziderman, Adrian. Deferred Cost Recovery for Higher Education: Student Loan Programs in Developing Countries. (Discussion Papers: No. 137). 68p. 1991. pap. 22.00 *(0-8213-1952-3,* 11952) World Bank.

— Financing Universities in Developing Countries. (Stanford Series on Education & Public Policy 16: No. 16). 176p. 1994. 85.00 *(0-7507-0352-0,* Falmer Pr); pap. 27.95 *(0-7507-0353-9,* Falmer Pr) Taylor & Francis.

Albrecht, E. Logic, Semiotics & Methodology: Logik, Semiotik, Methodologie. (GER & RUS.). 290p. 1983. 39.95 *(0-8288-2276-X,* M15207) Fr & Eur.

Albrecht, Earl. Altar Prayer Workbook B: (Common-Luth), Series B. 1984. wbk. ed. 10.50 *(0-89536-688-6,* 4865) CSS OH.

— Altar Prayer Workbook C (C-L-RC), Series C. 1985. wbk. ed. 10.50 *(0-89536-758-0,* 5864) CSS OH.

Albrecht, Ernest. The New American Circus. LC 95-2792. (Illus.). 280p. 1995. 29.95 *(0-8130-1364-X)* U Press Fla.

Albrecht, Ernest J. A Ringling by Any Other Name: The Story of John Ringling North & His Circus. LC 88-35639. (Illus.). 405p. 1989. 41.50 *(0-8108-2206-7)* Scarecrow.

Albrecht, Ernst & Mathieu, Martin. Banach Algebras '97: Proceedings of the 13th International Conference on Banach Algebras Held at the Heinrich Fabri Institute of the University of Tubingen in Blaubeuren, July 20-August 3, 1997. LC 98-29387. 566p. 1998. 148.95 *(3-11-015466-8)* De Gruyter.

Albrecht, Gary L. The Disability Business: Political Economy of Rehabilitation in America. (Library of Social Research: Vol. 190). 320p. (C). 1992. text 59.95 *(0-8039-3630-3);* pap. text 26.00 *(0-8039-3631-1)* Sage.

Albrecht, Gary L., ed. Advances in Medical Sociology, Vol. 1. 329p. 1990. 78.50 *(1-55938-092-6)* Jai Pr.

— Advances in Medical Sociology Vol. 6: Case & Care Management. 1996. 78.50 *(1-55938-986-9)* Jai Pr.

— A Reconsideration of Health Behavior Change Models, Vol. 4. (Advances in Medical Sociology Ser.). 280p. 1994. 78.50 *(1-55938-758-0)* Jai Pr.

— The Sociology of Physical Disability & Rehabilitation. LC 75-33544. (Contemporary Community Health Ser.). (Illus.). 319p. 1976. reprint ed. pap. 98.90 *(0-608-00895-8,* 206168900010) Bks Demand.

— The Sociology of Physical Disability & Rehabilitation. LC 75-33544. (Contemporary Community Health Ser.). 613p. (C). 1982. reprint ed. pap. 12.95 *(0-8229-5341-2)* U of Pittsburgh Pr.

Albrecht, Gary L. & Fitzpatrick, Ray, eds. Quality of Life in Health Care. (Advances in Medical Sociology Ser.: Vol. 5). 311p. 1994. 78.50 *(1-55938-838-2)* Jai Pr.

Albrecht, Gary L. & Levy, Judith A., eds. Advances in Medical Sociology, Vol. 2. 322p. 1991. 78.50 *(1-55938-252-X)* Jai Pr.

Albrecht, Gary L. & Zimmerman, Rick, eds. The Social & Behavioral Aspects of AIDS, Vol. 3. (Advances in Medical Sociology Ser.). 227p. 1993. 78.50 *(1-55938-439-5)* Jai Pr.

Albrecht, Gene H. The Craniofacial Morphology of the Sulawesi Macaques: Multivariate Analysis As a Tool in Systematics. (Contributions to Primatology Ser.: Vol. 13). (Illus.). 1977. 64.50 *(3-8055-2694-6)* S Karger.

Albrecht, Gloria. The Character of Our Communities: Toward an Ethic of Liberation for the Church. 192p. (Orig.). 1995. pap. 16.95 *(0-687-00283-4)* Abingdon.

Albrecht, Grace, ed. see Brandt, Betty.

Albrecht, Guenter & Ludwig-Mayerhofer, Wolfgang, eds. Diversion & Informal Social Control. LC 95-30679. (Prevention & Intervention in Childhood & Adolescence: No. 17). xii, 457p. (C). 1995. lib. bdg. 84.95 *(3-11-014948-6)* De Gruyter.

Albrecht, Guenther. Lexikon Deutschsprachiger Schriftsteller, Vol. 1. (GER.). 1974. 75.00 *(0-7859-0408-5,* M7204) Fr & Eur.

— Lexikon Deutschsprachiger Schriftsteller, Vol. 2. (GER.). 1974. 75.00 *(0-7859-0409-3,* M7205) Fr & Eur.

Albrecht, Gunter & Otto, Hans-Uwe, eds. Social Prevention & the Social Sciences: Theoretical Controversies, Research Problems, & Evaluation Strategies. (Prevention & Intervention in Childhood & Adolescence Ser.: No. 11). xii, 638p. (C). 1991. lib. bdg. 89.95 *(3-11-012387-8,* 148-91) De Gruyter.

Albrecht, H. & Leppa, S. Criminal Law/Environment. 259p. 1992. pap. 25.00 *(951-47-6439-0,* Criminal Justice) Willow Tree NY.

Albrecht, Hans-Christian, jt. ed. see Heward, Roger.

Albrecht, Hans J., et al, eds. Laser-Tissue Interaction & Tissue Optics II. (Europto Ser.: Vol. 2923). 212p. 1996. 66.00 *(0-8194-2325-4)* SPIE.

Albrecht, Harald. Untersuchungen Zur Veranderung der Segetalflora an Sieben Bayerischen Ackerstandorten Zeischen Den Erhebungszeitraumen 1951-68 und 1986-88. (Dissertationes Botanicae Ser.: Band 141). (GER., Illus.). xvi, 202p. 1989. pap. 48.00 *(3-443-64055-9,* Pub. by Gebruder Borntraeger) Balogh.

Albrecht, Helga, jt. auth. see Helbig, Gerhard.

Albrecht, Helmuth. Technische Bildung Zwischen Wissenschaft und Praxis. (GER.). 1997. write for info. *(3-487-07819-8)* G Olms Pubs.

Albrecht, James E. The Life & Times of a Country Doctor. (Illus.). 280p. 1993. pap. 18.00 *(0-9639102-0-5)* Jjea enter.

Albrecht, James W., et al. Moses Code: Modeling the Experimentally Organized Economy, Technical Documentation. (Industrial Institute for Economic & Social Research Report Ser.: No. 36). (Illus.). 354p. (Orig.). 1989. pap. 84.00 *(91-7204-322-9)* Coronet Bks.

Albrecht, James W., ed. see Industrial Institute for Economic & Social Researc.

Albrecht, Julius. Numerische Behandlung von Differentialgleichungen Mit Besonderer Berucksichtigung Freier Randwertaufgaben. Collatz, Lothar & Hammerlin, Gunther, eds. (International Series of Numerical Mathematics: No. 39). (GER., Illus.). 280p. 1980. 55.50 *(0-8176-0986-5)* Birkhauser.

Albrecht, Julius, et al, eds. Numerical Treatment of Eigenvalue Problems Vol. 5: Workshop in Oberwolfach, February 25 - March 3, 1990. (International Series of Numerical Mathematics: Vol. 96). (ENG & GER.). 256p. 1991. 96.00 *(0-8176-2575-5)* Birkhauser.

Albrecht, Julius & Collatz, Lothar, eds. Numerische Behandlung von Eigenwertaufgaben. (International Series of Numerical Mathematics: Vol. 2, No. 43). (GER., Illus.). 203p. pap. 38.95 *(3-7643-1067-7)* Birkhauser.

Albrecht, Julius, et al. Numerical Treatment of Eigenvalue Problems, Vol. 3. (International Series of Numerical Mathematics: Vol. 69). (ENG & GER.). 216p. 1984. 49.95 *(3-7643-1605-5)* Birkhauser.

Albrecht, Karl. At America's Service. 1992. mass mkt. 13.99 *(0-446-39316-9,* Pub. by Warner Bks) Little.

— At America's Service, American Management Association Edition: How Corporations Can Revolutionize the Way They Treat Their Customers. 252p. 1988. text 3.50 *(1-55623-168-7,* Irwn Prfssnl) McGraw-Hill Prof.

— Brain Power: Learn to Improve Your Thinking Skills. 320p. 1980. per. 14.00 *(0-671-76198-6)* S&S Trade.

***Albrecht, Karl.** Corporate Radar: Tracking the Forces That Are Shaping Your Business. LC 99-30448. (Illus.). 256p. 1999. 27.95 *(0-8144-0504-5)* AMACOM.

Albrecht, Karl. The Northbound Train: Finding the Purpose, Setting the Direction, Shaping the Destiny of Your Organization. LC 93-49388. 224p. 1994. 22.95 *(0-8144-0233-X)* AMACOM.

— The Only Thing That Matters: Bringing the Power of the Customer into the Center of Your Business. LC 17-171. 256p. 1992. 23.00 *(0-88730-541-5,* HarpBusn) HarpInfo.

— The Only Thing That Matters: Bringing the Power of the Customer into the Center of Your Business. LC 92-54853. (Illus.). 256p. 1993. pap. 13.50 *(0-88730-639-X,* HarpBusn) HarpInfo.

— Service Within: Solving the Middle Management Leadership Crisis. 200p. 1990. 35.00 *(1-55623-353-1,* Irwn Prfssnl) McGraw-Hill Prof.

— Stress & the Manager: Making It Work for You. (Illus.). 1979. pap. 8.95 *(0-13-852673-7)* P-H.

Albrecht, Karl & Albrecht, Steve. Added Value Negotiating: The Breakthrough Method for Building Balanced Deals. LC 92-43739. 205p. 1993. 25.00 *(1-55623-967-X,* Irwn Prfssnl) McGraw-Hill Prof.

Albrecht, Karl & Zemke, Ron. Service America! Doing Business in the New Economy. 1990. mass mkt. 13.99 *(0-446-39092-5,* Pub. by Warner Bks) Little.

***Albrecht, Kay M.** Innovations: The Comprehensive Infant Curriculum. (Illus.). 416p. 2000. pap. 39.95 *(0-87659-213-2)* Gryphon Hse.

— Innovations: The Comprehensive Toddler Curriculum. (Illus.). 416p. 2000. pap. 39.95 *(0-87659-214-0)* Gryphon Hse.

Albrecht, Klaus, et al, eds. Oskar Kokoschka. (Illus.). 230p. 1991. 65.00 *(3-7913-1132-8,* Pub. by Prestel) te Neues.

Albrecht, Kurt. Dogmen der Reitkunst. (Documenta Hippologica Ser.). (GER., Illus.). 128p. 1996. reprint ed. write for info. *(3-487-08368-X)* G Olms Pubs.

— Meilensteine Auf Dem Wege zur Hohen Schule. (Documenta Hippologica Ser.). (GER., Illus.). 147p. 1996. write for info. *(3-487-08253-5)* G Olms Pubs.

Albrecht, Maryann H. Cultural Diversity; Exercises, Cases, Resources. 207p. (C). 1997. pap. text 19.95 *(0-87563-743-4)* Stipes.

Albrecht, Maryann H., et al. Growing: A Woman's Guide to Career Satisfaction. 320p. 1984. spiral bd. 22.95 *(0-942560-12-4)* Brace-Park.

Albrecht, Michael. Kants Antinomie der Praktischen Vernunft. (Studien und Materialien Zur Geschichte Der Philosophie: Bd. 21). (GER.). 243p. 1978. write for info. *(3-487-06749-8)* G Olms Pubs.

— Matthew. (People's Bible Teachings Ser.). 275p. 1996. pap. 13.99 *(0-8100-0582-4,* 15N0576) Northwest Pub.

Albrecht, Michael V. Die Parenthese in Ovids Metamorphosen und Ihre Dichterische Funktion. (Spudasmata Ser.: Vol. 7). (GER.). 233p. 1994. write for info. *(3-487-00907-2)* G Olms Pubs.

Albrecht, Michael V. & Schmeling, Gareth L. A History of Roman Literature: From Livius Andronicus to Boethius, with Special Regard to Its Influence on World Literature, 2 vols. LC 96-38926. (Mnemosyne, Bibliotheca Classica Batava: Supplementum). 1996. write for info. *(90-04-10709-6);* write for info. *(90-04-10711-8)* Brill Academic Pubs.

Albrecht, Miguel A. & Egret, Daniel, eds. Databases & On-Line Data in Astronomy. (C). 1991. lib. bdg. 97.00 *(0-7923-1247-3)* Kluwer Academic.

Albrecht, Miguel A., jt. ed. see Egret, Daniel.

Albrecht, Peter, tr. see Aichele, Tobias.

Albrecht, Peter A. & Backes, Otto. Crime Prevention & Intervention: Legal & Ethical Problems. viii, 286p. (C). 1989. lib. bdg. 95.75 *(3-11-011741-X)* De Gruyter.

Albrecht, R. Geometric Modelling: Dagstuhl 1993. Hagen, H. et al, eds. LC 95-7042. (Computing Ser.: Suppl. 10). (Illus.). 372p. 1995. 129.00 *(3-211-82666-1)* Spr-Verlag.

— Gmelin-Organoiron Compounds, Pt. 4. 8th ed. Slawisch, A., ed. (Illus.). 296p. 1986. 1100.00 *(0-387-93530-4)* Spr-Verlag.

— MS Excel 3.0. (C). 1991. text. write for info. *(0-201-55931-5)* Addison-Wesley.

Albrecht, R., ed. Systems: Theory & Practice. (Advances in Computing Science Ser.). (Illus.). vii, 314p. 1998. pap. 79.95 *(3-211-83206-8)* Spr-Verlag.

Albrecht, R., et al, eds. Computer Aided Systems Theory - EUROCAST '95: A Selection of Papers from the Fifth International Workshop on Computer Aided Systems Theory, Innsbruck, Austria, May 22-25, 1995: Proceedings. (Lecture Notes in Computer Science Ser.: Vol. 1030). 539p. 1996. pap. 81.00 *(3-540-60748-X)* Spr-Verlag.

Albrecht, R. & Plura, M. Stepping up to OS-2 Warp. 1995. 19.95 *(1-55755-269-X)* Abacus MI.

Albrecht, R. & Somer, H. Reorganorhenium Compounds, Pt. 4. 8th ed. (Gmelin Handbook of Inorganic & Organometallic Chemistry Ser.). (Illus.). 296p. 1997. 1231.00 *(3-540-93734-X)* Spr-Verlag.

Albrecht, R., et al. Validation Numerics: Theory & Applications. (Computing Ser.: Suppl. 9). (Illus.). 300p. 1993. 126.95 *(0-387-82451-0)* Spr-Verlag.

Albrecht, R., jt. auth. see Rautenbach, R.

Albrecht, Renate & Schubler, Werner. Paul Tillich: Sein Leben. (GER., Illus.). 187p. 1994. 37.95 *(3-631-46487-8)* P Lang Pubng.

Albrecht, Renate & Schussler, Werner, eds. Schluessel zum Werk von Paul Tillich: Textgeschichte und Bibliographie sowie Register zu den Gesammelten Werken. (Gesammelte Werke Ser.: Band 14). 344p. (C). 1990. lib. bdg. 67.70 *(3-11-012039-9)* De Gruyter.

***Albrecht, Rick & Albrecht, Wendy.** Legacy. Boethcher, Pete et al, eds. 320p. 2000. pap. 19.95 *(0-9700389-0-9)* Visions of Help.

Albrecht, Rudolf, et al, eds. Astronomical Data Analysis Software & Systems VII. (Conference Series Proceedings: Vol. 145). 527p. 1998. 52.00 *(1-886733-65-1)* Astron Soc Pacific.

Albrecht, Ruth, jt. auth. see Havighurst, Robert J.

***Albrecht, Sally & Althouse, Jay.** Let the Earth Resound: SoundPax Instrumental Accompaniment Packet. 1999. pap. 20.00 *(0-7390-0748-3,* 18650) Alfred Pub.

— Shakin' It Up! Date not set. pap. write for info. incl. audio compact disk *(0-7390-0848-X,* 19808) Alfred Pub.

— Shakin' It Up! Teacher's Handbook. Date not set. pap., teacher ed. write for info. *(0-7390-0846-3,* 19806) Alfred Pub.

Albrecht, Sally K. Choral Music in Motion. 85p. (Orig.). 1984. pap. 14.95 *(0-939139-02-2)* Music In Action.

— Choral Music In Motion, Vol. 2: Movement for Larger Groups. (Illus.). 100p. (Orig.). 1989. pap. text 19.95 *(0-939139-06-5,* 107) Music In Action.

— Everyday Songs. 1995. pap. 39.95 incl. audio compact disk *(0-88284-837-2)* Alfred Pub.

— Rhythm to the Rescue. 1997. pap. 49.95 incl. audio compact disk *(0-88284-840-2)* Alfred Pub.

— Santa's Shopping Network, Director's Score. 36p. 1995. pap. 19.95 *(0-7390-0266-X,* 11636) Alfred Pub.

— Santa's Shopping Network Edition Performance Pack. 1995. pap. 54.95 *(0-7390-0267-8,* 11639) Alfred Pub.

— Santa's Shopping Network Edition Student 5 Pack. 1995. pap. 22.50 *(0-7390-0268-6,* 11637) Alfred Pub.

Albrecht, Sally K. & Althouse, Jay. Santa's Stuck in the '50s, Director's Score. 48p. 1999. pap. 19.95 *(0-7390-0086-1,* 18727) Alfred Pub.

— Santa's Stuck in the '50s: Performance Pack Edition. 1999. pap. 54.95 *(0-7390-0088-8,* 18730) Alfred Pub.

— Santa's Stuck in the '50s: Preview Pack Edition. 1999. pap. 12.95 incl. audio compact disk *(0-7390-0087-X,* 18729) Alfred Pub.

— Santa's Stuck in the '50s: Student 5-pk Edition. 1999. pap. 22.50 *(0-7390-0095-0,* 18728) Alfred Pub.

Albrecht, Sally K. & Smith, Melinda. School House Raps. 1999. pap. 34.95 incl. audio compact disk *(0-7390-0083-7,* 18740) Alfred Pub.

Albrecht, Sally K., jt. auth. see Althouse, Jay.

Albrecht, Stan L., et al. Divorce & Remarriage: Problems, Adaptations & Adjustments, 42. LC 82-24250. (Contributions in Women's Studies: No. 42). (Illus.). 211p. 1983. 55.00 *(0-313-23616-X,* ALD/, Greenwood Pr) Greenwood.

Albrecht, Steve. Crisis Managment for Corporate Self-Defense: How to Protect Your Organization in a Crisis...How to Stop a Crisis Before It Starts. 256p. 1996. 24.95 *(0-8144-0265-8)* AMACOM.

— Ethical Workplace. 1998. pap. 12.95 *(1-56052-486-3)* Crisp Pubns.

— Fear & Violence on the Job: Prevention Solutions for the Dangerous Workplace. LC 97-3617. 248p. 1997. pap. 25.00 *(0-89089-658-5)* Carolina Acad Pr.

— The Paralegal's Desk Reference: Up-to-the-Minute Information-Gathering Techniques for Today's Paralegal. 224p. 1993. per. 12.95 (*0-671-84715-5*, Arc) IDG Bks.
— Streetwork: The Way to Police Officer Safety & Survival. 256p. 1992. pap. 19.95 (*0-87364-650-9*) Paladin Pr.
Albrecht, Steve, jt. auth. see Albrecht, Karl.
Albrecht, Steve, jt. auth. see Clemens, John K.
Albrecht, Steven. General Chemistry Lab Manual. 2nd ed. 312p. (C). 1999. spiral bd. 29.95 (*0-7872-5705-2*, 41570501) Kendall-Hunt.
— Service, Service, Service. Date not set. pap. 9.95 (*1-55850-758-2*) Adams Media.
Albrecht, Steven & Morrison, John. Contact & Cover: Two-Officer Suspect Control. 164p. 1992. pap. 23.95 (*0-398-06003-7*) C C Thomas.
— Contact & Cover: Two-Officer Suspect Control. 164p. (C). 1992. text 36.95 (*0-398-05773-7*) C C Thomas.
Albrecht, T., ed. The Changing Complexion of DNA Viruses. (Journal: Intervirology: Vol. 31, Nos. 1-2, 1990). (Illus.). 184p. 1990. pap. 161.75 (*3-8055-5103-7*) S Karger.
***Albrecht, Terrance.** Rezeption und Zeitlichkeit des Werkes Christoph Heins. 2000. 35.95 (*3-631-35837-7*) P Lang Pubng.
Albrecht, Terrance L. & Adelman, Mara B. Communicating Social Support. LC 87-4962. 317p. 1987. reprint ed. pap. 98.30 (*0-608-01103-7*, 205941200001) Bks Demand.
Albrecht, Terrance L. & Back, Betsy W. Communications in Complex Organizations: A Relational Approach. LC 96-77467. 322p. (C). 1996. text 59.00 (*0-15-500317-8*) Harcourt Coll Pubs.
Albrecht, Terrance L., jt. ed. see Philipsen, Gerry.
Albrecht, Theodore. Ludwig Van Beethoven: A Guide to Research. (Composer Resource Manuals Ser.). 900p. lib. bdg. 121.00 (*0-8240-8807-7*) Garland.
Albrecht, Theodore, ed. Letters to Beethoven & Other Correspondence. LC 95-43793. (North American Beethoven Studies: Vol. 1). lii, 279p. 1996. text 65.00 (*0-8032-1033-7*) U of Nebr Pr.
Albrecht, Theodore, ed. Letters to Beethoven & Other Correspondence, Vol. 2. LC 95-43793. (North American Beethoven Studies). (Illus.). xxiv, 302p. 1996. text 65.00 (*0-8032-1039-6*) U of Nebr Pr.
Albrecht, Theodore, ed. Letters to Beethoven & Other Correspondence, Vol. 3. LC 95-43793. (North American Beethoven Studies). (Illus.). xxiv, 365p. 1996. text 65.00 (*0-8032-1040-X*) U of Nebr Pr.
Albrecht, Ulrich. The History of the Soviet Armaments Industry. 400p. 1993. text 85.00 (*3-7186-5313-3*) Gordon & Breach.
Albrecht, Ulrich, et al. Der Griff Nach Dem Atomaren Feuer Vol. 2: Uberarbeitete Auflage. 2nd ed. (GER.). 248p. 1997. 31.95 (*3-631-32244-5*) P Lang Pubng.
Albrecht, W., jt. ed. see Lunenschloss, J.
Albrecht, W. P. Hazlitt & the Creative Imagination. LC 65-26727. xii, 204p. 1965. 25.00 (*0-7006-0001-9*) U Pr of KS.
— The Sublime Pleasures of Tragedy. LC 75-11896. x, 206p. 1975. 29.95 (*0-7006-0135-X*) U Pr of KS.
Albrecht, W. Steve & Skousen, K. Fred. Accounting Concepts & Application. 7th ed. LC 98-8494. (AB - Accounting Principles Ser.). 1998. mass mkt. 94.95 (*0-538-87624-7*) S-W Pub.
— Accounting Concepts & Applications. 5th ed. (AB - Accounting Principles Ser.). 1995. pap., student ed. 25.95 (*0-538-84420-5*) S-W Pub.
— Accounting Concepts & Applications: Chapters 1-14. 5th ed. (AB - Accounting Principles Ser.). 1995. pap., student ed. 25.95 (*0-538-84419-1*) S-W Pub.
— Accounting Concepts & Applications: Working Papers Chapters 13-26, Vol. 2. 5th ed. (AB - Accounting Principles Ser.). 1995. pap., wbk. ed. 26.95 (*0-538-84418-3*) S-W Pub.
— Accounting Concepts & Applications: Working Papers Chapters 2-14, Vol. 1. 5th ed. (AB - Accounting Principles Ser.). 1995. pap. 26.95 (*0-538-84417-5*) S-W Pub.
— Financial Accounting. 6th ed. (AB - Accounting Principles Ser.). (C). 1996. mass mkt., suppl. ed. 22.95 (*0-538-84416-7*) S-W Pub.
— Management Accounting: Concepts & Applications. 7th ed. (SWC-Accounting). 1998. pap., student ed. 19.00 (*0-538-87627-1*) S-W Pub.
Albrecht, W. Steve, et al. A Common Body of Knowledge for the Practice of Internal Auditing. (Illus.). 157p. 1992. pap. text 35.00 (*0-89413-138-9*, A849) Inst Inter Aud.
— Financial Accounting. 6th ed. LC 95-10725. (C). 1995. pap. 75.95 (*0-538-84317-9*) S-W Pub.
— Fraud: Bringing Light to the Dark Side of Business. 250p. 1994. text 32.50 (*1-55623-760-X*, Irwn Prfssnl) McGraw-Hill Prof.
— Guide to Fraud Investigations, 2 vols. Incl. Vol. 1. 1996. ring bd. (*0-7646-0096-6*); Vol. 2. 1996. ring bd. (*0-7646-0097-4*); 225.00 (*0-7646-0095-8*) Prctnrs Pub Co.
— Guide To Fraud Investigations, 2 vols. Incl. Vol. 1. 1998. ring bd. 225.00 (*0-7646-0400-7*); Vol. 2. 1998. ring bd. 225.00 (*0-7646-0401-5*); 225.00 (*0-7646-0399-X*) Prctnrs Pub Co.
Albrecht, Wendy, jt. auth. see Albrecht, Rick.
Albrecht, Wilbur, ed. see Powys, John Cowper.
Albrecht, William A. The Albrecht Papers, Vol. II. Walters, Charles, Jr., ed. LC 83-81673. 192p. 1983. 20.00 (*0-911311-07-6*) Acres USA.
— The Albrecht Papers, Vol. III. Walters, Charles, Jr., ed. LC 88-82608. (Illus.). 397p. 1989. 20.00 (*0-911311-18-1*) Acres USA.
— The Albrecht Papers, Vol. IV. LC 92-71281. 250p. 1992. pap. 20.00 (*0-911311-23-8*) Acres USA.
— The Albrecht Papers Vol. 1: Foundation Concepts. rev. ed. Walters, Charles, Jr., ed. (Albrecht Papers). (Illus.). 515p. 1996. 30.00 (*0-911311-05-X*) Acres USA.
Albrechts, Louis, et al, eds. An Enlarged Europe: Regions in Competition? (Regional Policy & Development Ser.: No. 6). 286p. 1995. pap. 49.50 (*1-85302-188-1*) Taylor & Francis.
— Regional Policy at the Crossroads: European Perspectives. 220p. 1988. 30.00 (*1-85302-021-4*, Pub. by Jessica Kingsley) Taylor & Francis.
***Albrechtsen, D., et al, eds.** Perspectives on Foreign & Second Language Pedagogy. (Illus.). 304p. 1999. pap. 31.50 (*87-7838-385-4*, Pub. by Odense Univ) Intl Spec Bk.
Albrechtsen, Dagfinn. Extracorporeal Renal Surgery & Autotransplantation. Brekke, Inge B. & Flatmark, Audum, eds. LC 97-17144. (Illus.). 200p. 1997. 120.00 (*3-540-62761-8*) Spr-Verlag.
***Albree, Joe, et al.** A Station Favorable to the Pursuits of Science: Primary Materials in the History of Mathematics at the United States Military Academy. LC 99-51659. (History of Mathematics Ser.: Vol. 18). 272p. 2000. 59.00 (*0-8218-2059-1*) Am Math.
Albregts, Melisa & Cape, Elizabeth. Best Friends: Tons of Crazy, Cool Things to Do with Your Girlfriends. LC 98-25691. (Illus.). 152p. (J). (gr. 3-6). 1998. pap. 12.95 (*1-55652-326-2*) Chicago Review.
Albregtse, Dirk, et al. Taxpayer Protection in the European Union. LC 98-11726. (EFS Brochures Ser.). 1998. 86.00 (*90-411-9668-4*) Kluwer Law Intl.
Albregtse, Dirk, ed. see Simons, Fons & Foundation for European Fiscal Studies Staff.
***Albrektson, J. Raymond.** Living Large: How to Live Well--Even on a Little. LC 99-44168. 208p. 2000. pap. 10.95 (*1-57856-227-9*) Waterbrook Pr.
Albrektsson, Thomas & Zarb, George A., eds. The Branemark Osseointegrated Implant. (Illus.). 262p. 1989. text 69.50 (*0-86715-208-7*) Quint Pub Co.
***Albretti, A.** Slovene Phrase Finder. (Collins Gem Phrase Finder Ser.). (GER & SLV.). 256p. 2000. pap. 6.50 (*0-00-470883-0*, Pub. by HarpC) Trafalgar.
Albretti, Andrea. Colloquial Slovene: A Complete Language Course. LC 95-3675. (Colloquials Ser.). (ENG & SLO.). 338p. (gr. 13). 1995. pap. 22.99 (*0-415-08946-8*) Routledge.
— Colloquial Slovene: A Complete Language Course. (SLO.). 336p. 1995. pap., pap. text 45.00 incl. audio (*0-415-08948-4*) Routledge.
— Slovene. (Illus.). 256p. 1998. pap. 26.95 incl. audio (*0-8442-0031-X*, 0031X, Teach Yrslf) NTC Contemp Pub Co.
— Slovene: A Complete Course for Beginners. (ENG & SLV., Illus.). 256p. 1997. pap. 16.95 (*0-8442-0034-4*, 00344, Teach Yrslf) NTC Contemp Pub Co.
Albright. Acting: The Creative Process. 2nd ed. (Speech & Theater Ser.). 1974. pap. 10.50 (*0-8221-0046-0*) Wadsworth Pub.
— Acting: The Creative Process. 3rd ed. (Speech & Theater Ser.). 1982. pap. 37.50 (*0-534-01171-3*) Wadsworth Pub.
— Houses of the Pale Moon. 1995. mass mkt. 6.95 (*1-56201-080-8*, Pub. by Blue Moon Bks) Publishers Group.
— Managerial Statistics. LC 99-55993. (Business Statistics). 937p. 1999. pap. 86.95 (*0-534-34981-1*) Brooks-Cole.
***Albright.** Operative Techniques in Pediatric Neurosurgery. (Illus.). 352p. 2000. 179.00 (*0-86577-846-9*) Thieme Med Pubs.
Albright. Quantitative Methods for Managers. LC 98-48547. (Business Statistics Ser.). 996p. 1999. pap. 93.95 (*0-534-26124-8*) Wadsworth Pub.
***Albright.** Ukraine & European Security. LC D1065.U38A4 1999. 1999. text 65.00 (*0-312-22294-7*) St Martin.
Albright, et al. Student Primer Data Analysis & Decision Making W/micro Excel. (Business Statistics). 2000. pap. text 14.00 (*0-534-36190-0*) Brooks-Cole.
Albright, jt. auth. see Ingram.
Albright, jt. auth. see Winston.
Albright, A. L., jt. ed. see Neville, B.
Albright, A. Leland, et al. Principles & Practice of Pediatric Neurosurgery. LC 98-29770. (Illus.). 1472p. 1999. 239.00 (*0-86577-799-3*) Thieme Med Pubs.
Albright, Alex Wilson. Texas Courts: Pretrial : Cases & Materials, 1997-1998. 2nd ed. LC 97-216075. xii, 580 p. 1997. write for info. (*0-9648201-9-6*) Grail & Tucker.
Albright, Alison, jt. auth. see Neufeldt, Alfred.
Albright, Alto, et al. Alto's Cut-by-Cut How-to-Cut Mat Designs: Collection. Hurrey, Clair E., ed. (Illus.). 56p. (Orig.). 1997. pap. write for info. (*0-9658215-0-1*) Altos EZ Mat.
Albright, Ann C. Choreographing Difference: The Body & Identity in Contemporary Dance. LC 97-17034. (Illus.). 244p. 1997. pap. 19.95 (*0-8195-6321-8*, Wesleyan Univ Pr) U Pr of New Eng.
***Albright, Barbara.** Margaritas: Recipes for Margaritas & South-of-the-Border Snacks. (Illus.). 2000. 4.95 (*0-7407-1033-8*) Andrews & McMeel.
Albright, Barbara & Weiner, Jerry. Wild about Brownies. (Wild about Ser.). 1985. pap. 9.95 (*0-8120-2911-9*) Barron.
Albright, Barbara & Weiner, Leslie. More Muffins: 76 Recipes for Moist, Delicious, Fresh-Baked Muffins. LC 99-34013. (Illus.). 128p. 1999. pap. 8.95 (*0-312-24313-8*) St Martin.
— Mostly Muffins. (Illus.). 104p. 1984. pap. 6.95 (*0-312-54916-4*) St Martin.
— Totally Teabreads: Quick & Easy Recipes for More than 60 Delicious Quick Breads & Spreads. LC 93-43659. (Illus.). 144p. (Orig.). 1994. pap. 7.95 (*0-312-10561-4*) St Martin.
Albright, Barbara, jt. auth. see Guisewite, Cathy.
Albright, Barbara, jt. auth. see Weiner, Leslie.
Albright, Barbara, ed. see Maxwell House Staff.
Albright, Barbara, ed. see Philbin, Regis & Gifford, Kathie Lee.
Albright, Carol B. & Parrino, Maria, eds. Italian American Autobiographies. (Italian Americana Publications). 144p. (Orig.). (C). 1993. pap. text 10.00 (*1-883386-00-4*) U RI Col Cont Educ.
Albright, Carol R. & Haugen, Joel, eds. Beginning with the End: God, Science, & Wolfhart Pannenberg. LC 97-114. 476p. 1997. 42.95 (*0-8126-9325-6*); pap. 24.95 (*0-8126-9326-4*) Open Court.
Albright, Carol R., jt. auth. see Ashbrook, James B.
Albright, Claribel. Albright. Some Records of the Albright Family, with Additional Findings. (Illus.). 151p. 1997. reprint ed. pap. 23.00 (*0-8328-7225-3*); reprint ed. lib. bdg. 33.00 (*0-8328-7224-5*) Higginson Bk Co.
Albright College - Freedman Gallery Staff. Contemporary Hispanic Shrines. LC 89-85133. 1989. write for info. (*0-941972-09-7*) Freedman.
Albright, Daniel. Lyricality in English Literature. LC 84-10455. 286p. 1985. reprint ed. pap. 88.70 (*0-608-02665-4*, 206331800004) Bks Demand.
— Personality & Impersonality: Lawrence, Woolf & Mann. LC 77-23873. 328p. Date not set. reprint ed. pap. 101.70 (*0-608-20979-1*, 205450700003) Bks Demand.
— Quantum Poetics: Yeats, Pound, Eliot & the Science of Modernism. (Illus.). 317p. (C). 1997. text 64.95 (*0-521-57305-X*) Cambridge U Pr.
— Representation & the Imagination: Beckett, Kafka, Nabokov, & Schoenberg. LC 80-26976. (Chicago Original Paperback Ser.). viii, 230p. (C). 1981. pap. text 24.00 (*0-226-01252-2*) U Ch Pr.
— Representation & the Imagination: Beckett, Kafka, Nabokov & Schoenberg. LC 80-26976. (Illus.). 247p. reprint ed. pap. 76.60 (*0-608-09438-2*, 205423800005) Bks Demand.
— Stravinsky: The Music Box & the Nightingale. (Monographs on Musicology: Vol. 9). viii, 88p. 1989. pap. text 17.00 (*2-88124-295-2*) Gordon & Breach.
— Tennyson: The Muses' Tug-of-War. LC 86-1546. (Virginia Victorian Studies). 267p. reprint ed. pap. 82.80 (*0-7837-4360-2*, 204407000012) Bks Demand.
— Untwisting the Serpent: Modernism in Music, Literature & Other Arts. LC 98-47950. 1999. lib. bdg. 70.00 (*0-226-01253-0*) U Ch Pr.
— Untwisting the Serpent: Modernism in Music, Literature & Other Arts. LC 98-47950. (Illus.). 376p. 1999. pap. text 25.00 (*0-226-01254-9*) U Ch Pr.
Albright, Daniel, ed. see Ehrenpreis, Irvin.
Albright, Daniel, ed. see Morley, Michael.
Albright, Daniel, jt. tr. see Vienken, Heinz J.
Albright, David, et al. Challenges of Fissile Material Control. O'Neill, Kevin, ed. LC 98-75828. (Illus.). xviii, 118p. 1999. pap. 15.95 (*0-9669467-0-7*, FM1) Inst Sci.
— Plutonium & Highly Enriched Uranium, 1996: World Inventories, Capabilities, & Policies. (SIPRI Publication). (Illus.). 534p. 1997. text 79.00 (*0-19-828009-2*) OUP.
— World Inventory of Plutonium & Highly Enriched Uranium, 1992. LC 92-31562. (Illus.). 272p. 1993. text 42.00 (*0-19-829153-1*) OUP.
Albright, David E. The U. S. S. R. Sub-Saharan Africa in the 1980s, 101. (Washington Papers: No. 101). 144p. 1983. pap. 11.95 (*0-275-91558-1*, B1558, Praeger Pubs) Greenwood.
Albright, David E., ed. Communism in Africa. LC 78-13813. 288p. reprint ed. pap. 89.30 (*0-608-18245-1*, 205669200081) Bks Demand.
Albright, David E., jt. auth. see Lovell, John P.
Albright, Diane R., jt. auth. see Ericson, Jane H.
Albright, E. M. Spenser's Cosmic Philosophy of Religion. LC 72-100730. 1970. reprint ed. pap. 50.00 (*0-8383-0001-4*) M S G Haskell Hse.
***Albright, Elizabeth K.** Pediatric History & Physical Examination. 4th ed. (Current Clinical Strategies Ser.). 90p. 2000. pap. 9.95 (*1-881528-92-8*) Current Clin Strat.
— Pediatric History & Physical Examination: 2000 Edition. rev. ed. (Current Clinical Strategies Ser.). 90p. 2000. pap. 28.95 (*1-881528-93-6*) Current Clin Strat.
Albright, Evelyn M. Dramatic Publications in England, 1580-1640. LC 77-131246. 424p. (C). 1971. reprint ed. 75.00 (*0-87752-127-1*) Gordian.
Albright, Frank, jt. auth. see Bowen, Richard L.
Albright, Fred. Polyrhythmic Studies for Snare Drum. 72p. (YA). 1997. pap. text 14.95 (*0-7692-0946-7*, 0105B) Wrner Bros.
Albright, Fuller & Ellsworth, Read. Uncharted Seas. 124p. 1990. 24.95 (*0-318-50058-2*) JBK Pub.
— Uncharted Seas. deluxe ed. 124p. 1990. ring bd. 59.95 (*0-945892-02-0*) JBK Pub.
Albright, H. D., ed. see Antoine, Andre.
Albright, Horace. The Birth of the National Park Service. 1985. 15.95 (*0-614-10448-3*, L115) Natl Parks & Cons.
Albright, Horace M. Creating The National Park Service: The Missing Years. LC 98-43916. 1999. 34.95 (*0-8061-3116-0*) U of Okla Pr.
— Creating the National Park Service: The Missing Years. 384p. 1999. pap. text 17.95 (*0-8061-3155-1*) U of Okla Pr.
Albright, Horace M. & Taylor, Frank J. Oh, Ranger! 14th rev. ed. Jones, William R., ed. (Illus.). 176p. 1981. reprint ed. pap. 6.95 (*0-89646-068-1*) Vistabooks.
Albright, Horace M., et al. National Park Service: The Story Behind the Scenery. LC 86-81514. (Illus.). 96p. 1987. 17.50 (*0-88714-009-2*); pap. 7.95 (*0-88714-010-6*) KC Pubns.
Albright, Ivan. Hail to the Pure. limited ed. 1982. 2500.00 (*0-89659-015-1*) Abbeville Pr.
Albright, J. L. & Arave, C. W. The Behaviour of Cattle. LC 97-13554. (CAB International Publication). (Illus.). 320p. (C). 1997. text 95.00 (*0-85199-196-3*) OUP.
Albright, Jack E. Galliant's Journey: The Key to Successful Living. (Illus.). 64p. (Orig.). 1995. pap. 8.00 (*0-9655923-0-8*) Albright Pub.
Albright, Jason W. Greensboro, 1808-1904: Facts, Figures, Traditions & Reminiscences. (Illus.). 134p. 1997. reprint ed. pap. 18.00 (*0-8328-6898-1*); reprint ed. lib. bdg. 28.00 (*0-8328-6897-3*) Higginson Bk Co.
Albright, Jim. Creating the Advertising Message. LC 91-14088. 286p. (C). 1992. pap. text 46.95 (*0-87484-884-9*, 884) Mayfield Pub.
Albright, Jim & Albright, Kim Y. Fight Right! A Christian Approach to Conflict. (Generation Why Ser.: Vol. 3:7). 36p. (J). (gr. 9-12). 1998. pap. 12.95 (*0-87303-279-9*) Faith & Life.
***Albright, Joseph & Kunstel, Marcia.** Bombshell: The Secret Story of America's Unknown Atomic Spy Conspiracy. (Illus.). 399p. 1999. reprint ed. text 27.00 (*0-7881-6806-1*) DIANE Pub.
***Albright, Judith A.** Internet Travel Resources: A Comprehensive Guide to Travel Web Sites. (Illus.). 126p. 1999. spiral bd. write for info. (*0-9673287-0-5*) Notebook Pubns.
— Road Travelers Online: 202 Useful Web Sites for Everything You Would Ever Want to Know Before Planning a Road Trip in the U. S. or Canada. (Illus.). 65p. 1999. spiral bd. 11.95 (*0-9673287-1-3*) Notebook Pubns.
Albright, Judith M. Mary & the Children of Medjugorje & You. LC 89-62765. (Illus.). 32p. 1989. pap. 3.00 (*1-877678-05-8*) Queenship Pub.
— Our Lady at Garabandal. LC 92-75070. (Illus.). 100p. 1992. pap. 5.95 (*1-880033-04-6*) Queenship Pub.
Albright, Kim Y., jt. auth. see Albright, Jim.
Albright-Knox Art Gallery Staff. Thirty-Seventh Western New York Exhibition. LC 78-53046. (Illus.). 1978. 3.50 (*0-914782-18-5*) Buffalo Fine-Albrght-Knox.
Albright-Knox Art Gallery Staff, jt. auth. see Nash, Steven A.
***Albright, L. Barry.** Biostratigraphy & Vertebrate Paleontology of the San Timoteo Badlands, Southern California. LC 99-43047. (Publications in Geological Sciences: Vol. 144). 134p. 2000. pap. 23.00 (*0-520-09836-6*, Pub. by U CA Pr) Cal Prin Full Svc.
Albright, Leland A., et al. Principles & Practice of Pediatric Neurosurgery. LC 98-29770. 1999. 239.00 (*3-13-114691-5*) Thieme Med Pubs.
***Albright, Letha.** Tulsa Time. (Dark Oak Mysteries Ser.). 2000. pap. 7.50 (*1-892343-12-6*) Oak Tree Pub.
Albright, Lisa, ed. see Ratnavira, Natalie Ann.
Albright, Louis. Environment Control for Animals & Plants. LC 90-62260. 453p. 1990. 92.25 (*0-929355-08-3*, M0390) Am Soc Ag Eng.
Albright, Lyle, et al. Pyrolysis: Theory & Industrial Practice. 446p. 1983. text 152.00 (*0-12-048880-9*) Acad Pr.
Albright, Lyle F. Processes for Major Addition-Type Plastics & Their Monomers. 2nd ed. LC 80-12568. 304p. 1985. lib. bdg. 37.50 (*0-89874-074-6*) Krieger.
Albright, Lyle F., et al, eds. Nitration: Recent Laboratory & Industrial Developments. LC 96-11096. (ACS Symposium Ser.: No. 623). (Illus.). 296p. 1996. text 105.00 (*0-8412-3393-4*, Pub. by Am Chemical) OUP.
— Novel Production Methods for Ethylene, Light, Hydrocarbons & Aromatics. (Chemical Industries Ser.: Vol. 46). (Illus.). 576p. 1991. text 250.00 (*0-8247-8588-6*) Dekker.
Albright, Lyle F. & Baker, R. Terry, eds. Coke Formation on Metal Surfaces. LC 82-16335. (ACS Symposium Ser.: No. 202). 321p. 1982. lib. bdg. 42.95 (*0-8412-0745-3*) Am Chemical.
— Coke Formation on Metal Surfaces. LC 82-16335. (ACS Symposium Ser.: No. 202). (Illus.). 328p. 1982. reprint ed. pap. 101.70 (*0-608-03215-8*, 206373400007) Bks Demand.
Albright, Lyle F. & Crynes, Billy L., eds. Industrial & Laboratory Pyrolyses. LC 76-28733. (ACS Symposium Ser.: No. 32). 1976. 43.95 (*0-8412-0337-7*) Am Chemical.
— Industrial & Laboratory Pyrolyses. LC 76-28733. (ACS Symposium Ser.: Vol. 32). 520p. 1976. reprint ed. pap. 161.20 (*0-608-03556-4*, 206427500008) Bks Demand.
Albright, Lyle F. & Goldsby, Arthur R., eds. Industrial & Laboratory Alkylations. LC 77-23973. (ACS Symposium Ser.: No. 55). 1977. 43.95 (*0-8412-0385-7*) Am Chemical.
— Industrial & Laboratory Alkylations. fac. ed. LC 77-23973. (ACS Symposium Ser.: No. 55). 472p. 1994. pap. 146.40 (*0-7837-7719-1*, 205253000007) Bks Demand.
Albright, Lyle F. & Hanson, Carl, eds. Industrial & Laboratory Nitrations. LC 75-38712. (ACS Symposium Ser.: No. 22). 1976. 38.95 (*0-8412-0306-7*) Am Chemical.
Albright, Lyle F., jt. auth. see DeWitt, David P.
Albright, Madeleine K. Poland: The Role of the Press in Political Change, 102. LC 83-16144. (Washington Papers). 168p. 1983. pap. 13.95 (*0-275-91559-X*, B1559, Praeger Pubs) Greenwood.
Albright, Martina & Burke, Sally, eds. Wit, Wisdom & Humor: From the Apple Orchard School. LC 98-93653. (Illus.). 196p. 1998. pap. 19.95 (*1-57502-958-8*, PO2630) Morris Pubng.
Albright, Mary, jt. auth. see Carr, Clay.
Albright, Michael J. & Graf, David L., eds. Teaching in the Information Age: The Role of Educational Technology. LC 85-644763. (New Directions for Teaching & Learning Ser.: No. TL 51). 100p. 1992. 22.00 (*1-55542-744-8*) Jossey-Bass.
Albright, Naomi. Angel Blue. 99p. 1993. spiral bd. 10.00 (*1-882218-00-0*) Blue Star Pubs.
— The Great White Forest-King. 170p. (YA). 1992. per. 14.95 (*1-882218-01-9*) Blue Star Pubs.

A

— Path of the Star. 193p. 1992. spiral bd. 14.75 (*1-882218-04-3*) Blue Star Pubs.

— The Teachings on Living Things & Protection Dolls. 80p. 1992. spiral bd. 16.95 (*1-882218-05-1*) Blue Star Pubs.

Albright, P. Crow Indian Photographer: The Work of Richard Throssel. LC 96-4498. (Illus.). 247p. 1997. 75.00 (*0-8263-1754-5*); pap. 37.95 (*0-8263-1755-3*) U of NM Pr.

Albright, Patricia, et al. Giant Book of Bulletin Boards, No. 2395. Cicciarelli, Joellyn T., ed. (Illus.). 224p. (J). (gr. k-3). 1998. pap. 16.98 (*1-57471-371-X*) Creat Teach Pr.

Albright, Peter. The Complete Book of Complementary Therapies. LC 96-39297. (Illus.). 176p. 1997. 29.95 (*1-882606-72-8*) Peoples Med Soc.

Albright, Peter, ed. Acupressure. LC 95-25135. 64p. 1996. 12.95 (*0-02-860833-X*) Macmillan Info.

— Aromatherapy. LC 95-37893. (Naturally Better Ser.). 64p. 1996. 12.95 (*0-02-860832-1*) Macmillan.

— Herbal Remedies. LC 95-37892. (Naturally Better Ser.). 64p. 1996. 12.95 (*0-02-860834-8*) Macmillan.

Albright, Priscilla, jt. auth. see Albright, Rodney.

Albright, Raymond & Johnson, Robbin. Study Group Papers on American Commercial Diplomacy in Asia, Vol. 2. 1998. pap. 5.00 (*0-87609-216-4*) Coun Foreign.

***Albright, Rick & Trunzo, Deborah, eds.** National Directory of Drug Abuse & Alcoholism Treatment Programs (1998) 550p. (C). 2000. pap. text 60.00 (*0-7567-0165-1*) DIANE Pub.

Albright, Robert, et al, eds. Looking to the New Millenium: New Jersey's Plan for Higher Education. 42p. 1998. reprint ed. pap. text 20.00 (*0-7881-4152-X*) DIANE Pub.

Albright, Rodney & Albright, Priscilla. Hiking the Great Smoky Mountains. 4th ed. LC 98-37831. (Illus.). 160p. 1998. pap. 10.95 (*0-7627-0224-9*) Globe Pequot.

— Short Nature Walks on Long Island. 6th ed. Wendt, Robert, ed. LC 98-5453. (Short Nature Walks Ser.). (Illus.). 176p. 1998. pap. 10.95 (*0-7627-0216-8*) Globe Pequot.

Albright, Roger. Five Hundred Forty-Seven Tips for Saving Energy in Your Home. rev. ed. 128p. 1991. reprint ed. pap. 7.95 (*0-88266-677-0*) Storey Bks.

— Five Hundred Forty-Seven Tips for Saving Energy in Your Home. rev. ed. 128p. 1991. reprint ed. 17.95 (*0-88266-678-9*) Storey Bks.

Albright, Ronald C., Jr. Electronic Communication Systems for Home & Office. LC 89-42857. 256p. 1989. per. 16.95 (*0-8019-7993-5*) NP-Chilton.

Albright, Ronald T. & Compton, Bridget R. Internal Consulting Basics: Developing & Implementing Incentive Plans. (Building Blocks Ser.: Vol. 35). (Illus.). 27p. (Orig.). 1996. pap. 24.95 (*1-57963-036-7*, A0235) Am Compensation.

Albright, Ruth N. Vedic Declension of the Type Vrkis: A Contribution to the Study of the Feminine Noun Declension in Indo-European. (LD Ser.: No.1). 1927. pap. 25.00 (*0-527-00747-1*) Periodicals Srv.

Albright, S. Christian. Student Execustat 3.0: Miniguide. 152p. 1993. pap. 20.95 (*0-534-22014-2*) Wadsworth Pub.

Albright, S. Christian, jt. auth. see Winston, Wayne L.

Albright, Spencer D., III. Systematized Abbreviation-Related Dermatopathology Software (SARDS) Reference Manual. 1989. write for info. incl. disk (*0-318-65958-1*); write for info. incl. disk (*0-318-65959-X*) S Albright.

Albright, Thomas. Art in the San Francisco Bay Area, 1945-1980: An Illustrated History. LC 84-24112. 360p. 1985. pap. 45.00 (*0-520-05518-7*, Pub. by U CA Pr) Cal Prin Full Svc.

Albright, Thomas & Butterfield, Jan. Oliver Jackson. LC 82-61511. (Illus.). 32p. 1982. pap. 7.95 (*0-932216-10-2*) Seattle Art.

Albright, Thomas A. & Burdett, Jeremy K. Problems in Molecular Orbital Theory. LC 92-25944. (Illus.). 296p. 1992. pap. text 27.95 (*0-19-507175-1*) OUP.

Albright, Thomas A., et al. Orbital Interactions in Chemistry. LC 84-15310. 464p. 1985. 99.95 (*0-471-87393-4*) Wiley.

Albright, Thomas B. Twenty First Century Blueprint. LC 93-85850. 254p. 1994. pap. 12.95 (*0-933451-21-0*) Twty-Frst Ctry.

— 21st Century Turfs, Powers, Solutions. unabridged ed. LC 96-90450. 265p. (Orig.). 1996. 21.95 (*1-888264-00-4*); pap. 12.95 (*1-888264-04-7*) Twty-Frst Ctry.

***Albright, Thomas B.** The United States Government: Save Me Some Pie. LC 99-90803. 320p. 1999. 21.95 (*1-888264-14-4*) Twty-Frst Ctry.

Albright, Townsend. How to Hold It All Together When You've Lost Your Job. LC 95-30142. (Illus.). 192p. 1995. pap. 9.95 (*0-8442-4395-7*, VGM Career) NTC Contemp Pub Co.

***Albright, Verne R.** The Long Way to Los Gatos. (Illus.). 384p. 1999. 29.95 (*0-9658533-2-2*) Amigo Pubns.

Albright, Victor E. Shakespearian Stage. LC 79-158241. reprint ed. 29.50 (*0-404-00304-4*) AMS Pr.

Albright, William D. Out of Anger with Love: Poems Collection. 1993. pap. 9.95 (*0-9637935-0-0*) Davis Comm Grp.

Albright, William F. The Proto-Sinaitic Inscriptions & Their Decipherment. LC 73-248003. (Harvard Theological Studies: No. 22). 50p. reprint ed. pap. 30.00 (*0-608-18593-0*, 201750500007) Bks Demand.

— Yahweh & the Gods of Canaan: An Historical Analysis of Two Contrasting Faiths. xiv, 294p. 1990. reprint ed. text 29.50 (*0-931464-01-3*) Eisenbrauns.

Albright, William F. & Mann, C. S., eds. Matthew. LC 77-150875. (Anchor Bible Ser.: Vol. 26). 576p. 1971. 37.50 (*0-385-08658-X*, Anchor NY) Doubleday.

Albright, Winston. Managerial Statistics. (Business Statistics Ser.). 2000. pap. text, student ed. 15.00 (*0-534-37139-6*) Brooks-Cole.

Albrigo, L. G., jt. auth. see Davies, F. S.

Albring, Manfred, et al, eds. Innovationen in der Arzneimitteltherapie: Definition, Medizinische Umsetzung und Finanzierung Bad Orber Gesprache Uber Kontroverse Themen Im Gesundheitswesen 25.-27.10.1996. (Allokation Im Marktwirtschaftlichen System Ser.: Bd. 40). (GER., Illus.). 157p. 1997. 24.95 (*3-631-31942-8*) P Lang Pubng.

Albritton, Carla M. Supplyisms: A Navy Supply-Type's Handbook for Comic Relief Afloat & Ashore. (Illus.). ix, 132p. (Orig.). 1996. pap. 6.95 (*0-9653458-0-7*) C M Albritton.

Albritton, Clarice. Beyond the Lighthouse. LC 77-83447. (Illus.). 1978. pap. 4.95 (*0-87516-243-6*) DeVorss.

— The Untold Story: Jesus Son of God. LC 83-73188. 1983. pap. 5.95 (*0-318-00817-3*) W P Brownell.

Albritton, Clarice & Newby, Grace. A Lamp unto Our Faith. LC 76-24514. 1976. pap. 4.95 (*0-87516-218-5*) DeVorss.

Albritton, Claude C., ed. Charles Lyell on North American Geology: An Original Anthology. LC 77-6524. (History of Geology Ser.). (Illus.). 1978. lib. bdg. 56.95 (*0-405-10446-4*) Ayer.

— History of Geology Series, 37 vols. (Illus.). 1978. lib. bdg. 1286.50 (*0-405-10429-4*) Ayer.

Albritton, Claude C., ed. see Association of American Geologists & Naturalists a.

Albritton, Claude C., Jr., ed. see Bakewell, Robert.

Albritton, Claude C., Jr., ed. see Buckland, William.

Albritton, Claude C., ed. see Clarke, John M.

Albritton, Claude C., Jr., ed. see Cleaveland, Parker.

Albritton, Claude C., Jr., ed. see Conybeare, W. D. & Phillips, William R.

Albritton, Claude C., Jr., ed. see Cuvier, Georges.

Albritton, Claude C., Jr., ed. see Davison, Charles.

Albritton, Claude C., Jr., ed. see Gilbert, Grove Karl.

Albritton, Claude C., Jr., ed. see Greenough, George B.

Albritton, Claude C., Jr., ed. see Hooke, Robert.

Albritton, Claude C., ed. see Kirwan, Richard.

Albritton, Claude C., Jr., ed. see Lambrecht, K. & Quenstedt, W. A.

Albritton, Claude C., ed. see Literary & Philosophical Society of New York Staff, Jr. & Clinton, DeWitt.

Albritton, Claude C., Jr., ed. see Lyell, Charles.

Albritton, Claude C., ed. see Marcou, Jules, Jr.

Albritton, Claude C., ed. see Mariotte, Edme.

Albritton, Claude C., jt. ed. see Merrill, George P.

Albritton, Claude C., Jr., ed. see Miller, Hugh G.

Albritton, Claude C., Jr., ed. see Moore, Nathaniel F.

Albritton, Claude C., Jr., ed. see Murray, John.

Albritton, Claude C., Jr., ed. see Parkinson, James.

Albritton, Claude C., Jr., ed. see Phillips, John.

Albritton, Claude C., Jr., ed. see Phillips, William R.

Albritton, Claude C., Jr., ed. see Ray, John.

Albritton, Claude C., Jr., ed. see Scrope, George P.

Albritton, Claude C., Jr., ed. see Sherley, Thomas.

Albritton, Claude C., Jr., ed. see Whiston, William.

Albritton, Claude C., Jr., ed. see White, George W.

Albritton, Claude C., Jr., ed. see Whitehurst, John.

Albritton, Claude C., Jr., ed. see Woodward, Horace B.

Albritton, Claude C., Jr., ed. see Woodward, John.

Albritton, Daniel L. & Watson, Robert T. Scientific Assessment of Stratospheric Ozone: 1989, Vol. 1. (Illus.). 486p. 1996. reprint ed. pap. text 50.00 (*0-7881-3205-9*) DIANE Pub.

Albritton, Frankie P., Jr. Health Care Insurance Reform in the United States: A Market Approach with Application from the Federal Republic of Germany. LC 92-31546. 108p. (C). 1993. lib. bdg. 39.50 (*0-8191-8896-4*) U Pr of Amer.

Albritton, John. Cisco IOS Essentials. LC 99-12964. (Cisco Technical Expert Ser.). (SPA., Illus.). 466p. 1999. pap. 55.00 (*0-07-134743-7*) McGraw.

***Albritton, John.** Cisco LOS--IP Essentials. 1999. pap. 55.00 (*0-07-135633-9*) McGraw-Hill Prof.

***Albritton, Robert.** Dialectics & Deconstruction in Political Economy. LC 99-21774. 1999. text 69.95 (*0-312-22447-8*) St Martin.

Albritton, Robert, jt. ed. see Sekine, Thomas T.

Albritton, Sabra, et al. You Are Not Alone. Raval, Devyani S. et al, eds. (Illus.). 216p. 1998. pap. 19.95 (*0-9666425-0-3*, 98022) Childs Med Ventures.

Albritton, Sarah C., jt. auth. see Pearman, Roger R.

Albrizio, Ann, jt. auth. see Lustig, Osnat.

Albrizio, Eileen. Messy on the Inside. (Illus.). 82p. 1999. pap. 10.00 (*1-889289-32-9*) Ye Olde Font Shoppe.

***Albrizio, Eileen, et al.** Come Like Water: The 1998 Connecticut Scam Team. 40p. 1998. 5.00 (*1-889289-19-1*) Ye Olde Font Shoppe.

Albro, John A., ed. see Shepard, Thomas.

Albro, Ward S. Always a Rebel: Ricardo Flores Magon & the Mexican Revolution. LC 92-6074. (Illus.). 220p. 1992. 24.95 (*0-87565-108-9*) Tex Christian.

— To Die on Your Feet: The Life, Times & Writing of Praxedis Guerrero. LC 96-20198. (Illus.). 224p. 1996. 25.00 (*0-87565-163-1*) Tex Christian.

Albronda, Mildred. Douglas Tilden: Portrait of a Deaf Sculptor. 1980. pap. 4.95 (*0-932666-03-5*) T J Pubs.

Albrough, Jez & Ashforth, Camila. The Candlewick Book of Bear Stories. LC 95-17580. (Illus.). 90p. (J). (ps-3). 1995. 19.99 (*1-56402-653-1*) Candlewick Pr.

Albrow, Martin. Do Organizations Have Feelings? LC 97-7099. 200p. (C). 1997. 75.00 (*0-415-11546-9*) Routledge.

Albrow, Martin. Do Organizations Have Feelings? LC 97-7099. 200p. (C). 1997. pap. 22.99 (*0-415-11547-7*) Routledge.

Albrow, Martin. Global Age: State & Society Beyond Modernity. LC 96-69671. 1997. pap. text 16.95 (*0-8047-2870-4*) Stanford U Pr.

— Max Weber's Construction of Social Theory. LC 90-33088. 300p. 1991. pap. 16.95 (*0-312-04754-1*) St Martin.

— Sociology: The Basics. LC HM1.A625 1999. (Basics of Business Ser.). 1999. pap. 14.99 (*0-415-17264-0*) Routledge.

Albrow, Martin & King, Elizabeth, eds. Globalization, Knowledge & Society. (Illus.). 280p. (C). 1990. text 45.00 (*0-8039-8323-9*); pap. text 18.95 (*0-8039-8324-7*) Sage.

Albrow, Martin, tr. see Luhmann, Niklas.

Albu, Susan H. & Arndt, Elizabeth E. Here's Savannah. LC 95-134040. 112p. 1994. pap. 6.95 (*0-9640597-1-1*) Albu & Arndt.

— Savannah Trivia. 58p. 1993. pap. 6.95 (*0-9640597-0-3*) Albu & Arndt.

Albucasis. De Chirurgia, 2 vols. in 1. xxix, 642p. reprint ed. write for info. (*0-318-71479-5*) G Olms Pubs.

***Albues, Tereza.** Pedra Canga. 140p. 2000. pap. 12.95 (*1-892295-70-9*) Green Integer.

Albulafia, Anna S. Christians & Jews in Dispute: Disputational Literature & the Rise of Anti-Judaism in the West (c. 1000-1150) LC 98-71753. (Variorum Collected Studies Ser.: Vol. 621). 310p. 1998. text 89.95 (*0-86078-674-9*, Pub. by Variorum) Ashgate Pub Co.

Album, Stephen. A Checklist of Popular Islamic Coins. 1993. pap. 8.00 (*0-9636024-0-3*) S Album.

Albuquerque, Afonso De, see De Albuquerque, Afonso.

Albuquerque, Klaus De, see McElroy, Jerome L. & De Albuquerque, Klaus.

Albuquerque Museum Staff. Drawing the Borderline: Artist-Explorers of the U. S.-Mexico Boundary Survey. Hall, Dawn, ed. LC 96-83034. (Historians of the Frontier & American West Ser.). (Illus.). 167p. (Orig.). 1996. pap. 29.95 (*0-8263-1752-9*) U of NM Pr.

Albuquerque, Severino J. Violent Acts: A Study of Violence in Contemporary Latin American Theatre. LC 90-34750. (Latin American Literature & Culture Ser.). 298p. (C). 1990. text 39.95 (*0-8143-2243-3*); pap. text 19.95 (*0-8143-2244-1*) Wayne St U Pr.

Albuquerque, Teresa. Anjuna: Profile of a Village in Goa. (C). 1987. 27.00 (*81-85002-06-1*, Pub. by Promilla) S Asia.

— Urbs Prima in India: An Epoch in the History of Bombay, 1840-1865. 1985. 28.00 (*81-85002-00-2*, Pub. by Promilla) S Asia.

Albuquerque Tribune Staff, ed. see Galagher, Tim.

Albuquerque Tribune Staff, ed. see Hansel, Kathleen.

Alburger, James. The Art of Voice Acting: The Craft & Business of Performing for Voice-Over. LC 98-38070. 256p. 1998. pap. text 19.95 (*0-240-80340-X*, Focal) Buttrwrth-Heinemann.

Alburt, L. Test & Improve Your Chess: A Grandmaster Method of Chess Evaluation. (Chess Ser.). 100p. 1989. 27.90 (*0-08-032041-4*, Pergamon Pr); pap. 15.90 (*0-08-032042-2*, Pergamon Pr) Elsevier.

***Alburt, Lev.** Chess Training Pocket Book: 300 Most Important Positions & Ideas. 2nd ed. (Illus.). 2000. pap. text 17.95 (*1-889323-14-4*, Chess Info & Res) L Alburt.

— Chess Training Pocketbook. 1997. pap. 17.95 (*1-889323-04-7*) L Alburt.

Alburt, Lev. Test & Improve Your Chess. 127p. 1994. text 12.95 (*1-85744-061-7*) S&S Trade.

***Alburt, Lev & Krogeur, Nikolai.** Just the Facts! Winning Endgame Play. Lawrence, Al, ed. (Comprehensive Chess Course Ser.: Vol. 7). 2p. 1999. pap. 19.95 (*1-889323-06-3*, Pub. by L Alburt) Norton.

Alburt, Lev & Palatnik, Sam. Chess Strategy for the Tournament Player. Lawrence, Albert, ed. (Comprehensive Chess Course Ser.: Vol. 5). (Illus.). 352p. 1997. pap. 23.95 (*1-889323-05-5*) L Alburt.

Alburt, Lev & Parr, Larry. The Secrets of the Russian Chess Masters Vol. 1: Fundamentals of the Game, 2 vols., Vols. 1 & 2. LC 96-50896. (Illus.). 224p. (C). 1997. 25.00 (*0-393-04115-8*) Norton.

— The Secrets of the Russian Chess Masters Vol. 2: Beyond the Basics, 2 vols., Vol. 2. LC 96-50896. (Illus.). 224p. (C). 1997. 25.00 (*0-393-04116-6*) Norton.

Alburt, Lev, jt. auth. see Palatnik, Sam.

Alburt, Lev, jt. auth. see Pelts, Roman.

Albury, David, compiled by. The Quizmaster's Scottish Quiz Book. 128p. 1996. pap. 8.95 (*0-7486-6217-0*, Pub. by Polygon) Subterranean Co.

Albury, Gale. The Moonlight Unicorn. LC 94-90363. (Illus.). 14p. (Orig.). (J). (ps-8). 1994. pap. 4.00 (*0-9642344-0-8*) TEA Printers & Pubs.

— Tale of the Purple Ants. LC 95-61782. (Illus.). 20p. (Orig.). (J). (ps-8). 1995. pap. 4.50 (*0-9642344-1-6*) TEA Printers & Pubs.

Albury, Lois. Rags to Riches. (Illus.). 248p. 1997. write for info. (*1-57502-607-4*, PO1750) Morris Pubng.

***Albury Publishing Staff.** Free at Last: Breaking the Cycle of Generational Curses. 2000. 12.99 (*1-57778-124-4*) Albury Pub.

Albury Publishing Staff. God Will Make a Way: When There Seems to Be No Way. 1999. 17.99 (*1-57778-099-X*) Albury Pub.

— God's Answers to Your Every Question. (Q&A Promise Book Ser.: Vol. 1). 192p. 1998. pap. 5.99 (*1-57778-093-0*, Pub. by Albury Pub) Appalach Bk Dist.

— God's Answers to Your Every Question: For Fathers. (Q&A Promise Book Ser.: Vol. 2). 192p. 1998. pap. 5.99 (*1-57778-038-8*, Pub. by Albury Pub) Appalach Bk Dist.

— God's Answers to Your Every Question: For Mothers. (Q&A Promise Book Ser.: Vol. 3). 192p. 1998. pap. 5.99 (*1-57778-047-7*, Pub. by Albury Pub) Appalach Bk Dist.

— God's Answers to Your Every Question: For Students. (Q&A Promise Book Ser.: Vol. 4). 192p. (YA). 1998. pap., student ed. 5.99 (*1-57778-041-8*, Pub. by Albury Pub) Appalach Bk Dist.

***Albury Publishing Staff.** Israel: The Fifth Gospel, a Biblical Guide to the Holy Land. (Illus.). 384p. 2000. pap. 21.99 (*1-57778-153-8*) Albury Pub.

Albury Publishing Staff, ed. see Wommack, Andrew.

Albury, Randall. The Politics of Objectivity. 79p. (C). 1995. pap. 21.00 (*0-949823-10-4*, Pub. by Deakin Univ) St Mut.

Albury, W. R., jt. ed. see Slezak, Peter.

Albury, W. R., tr. see Bonnot de Condillac, Etienne.

***Albus, Anita.** The Art of Arts: Recollections of Painting. LC 00-20320. 2000. 35.00 (*0-375-40099-0*) Knopf.

Albus, James S. Brains, Behavior & Robotics. 352p. 1981. write for info. (*0-318-58966-4*) New World Bks.

— Peoples' Capitalism: The Economics of the Robot Revolution. LC 75-44585. 157p. 1976. 10.50 (*0-917480-01-5*); pap. 6.95 (*0-917480-00-7*) New World Bks.

Albus, James S. & Meystel, Alex M. Intelligent Systems: Architecture, Design, Control. LC 99-23427. (Series in Intelligent Systems). 640p. 1999. text 89.95 (*0-471-19374-7*) Wiley.

Albus, Volker. Dear Gast/Dear Guest: Zum Stand Der Heimat Auf Zeit/On the State of the Short-Stay Home. 1997. pap. text 29.90 (*3-930698-82-X*) Edition A Menges.

— Icons of Design: The 20th Century. 192p. 2000. 29.95 (*3-7913-2306-7*, Pub. by Prestel) te Neues.

Albyn, Carole L. & Webb, Lois S. The Multicultural Cookbook for Students. LC 92-41634. (Illus.). 312p. 1993. pap. 29.50 (*0-89774-735-6*) Oryx Pr.

ALC Staff, ed. see Ahlberg, Allan.

ALC Staff, ed. see Avi.

ALC Staff, ed. see Child, Lydia Maria.

ALC Staff, ed. see Clifford, Eth.

ALC Staff, ed. see Haskins, James.

ALC Staff, ed. see Hurwitz, Johanna.

ALC Staff, ed. see Isadora, Rachel.

ALC Staff, ed. see Kellogg, Steven.

ALC Staff, ed. see Monson, A. M.

ALC Staff, ed. see Prelutsky, Jack.

ALC Staff, ed. see Pryor, Bonnie.

ALC Staff, ed. see Simon, Seymour.

Alcabes, Abraham, jt. auth. see Jones, James A.

Alcabes, Sylvan. UPCO's Review of Biology. 2nd ed. (Upco's Science Ser.). (Illus.). 288p. (YA). (gr. 9-12). 1988. pap. text 3.00 (*0-937323-05-5*) United Pub Co.

Alcabes, Sylvan, jt. auth. see UPCO's Review of Biology Staff.

Alcacer, Luis, ed. Conducting Polymers: Special Applications. (C). 1987. text 161.50 (*90-277-2529-2*) Kluwer Academic.

— The Physics & Chemistry of Low Dimensional Solids. (NATO Advanced Study Institutes Series C, Mathematical & Physical Sciences: No. 56). 436p. 1980. text 148.50 (*90-277-1144-5*) Kluwer Academic.

Alcade, Javier G. Development, Decay, & Social Conflict: An International & Peruvian Perspective. (World in Change Ser.: Vol. II). 216p. (C). 1991. pap. text 26.50 (*0-8191-8461-6*); lib. bdg. 59.50 (*0-8191-8460-8*) U Pr of Amer.

Alcala, Angel, ed. The Spanish Inquisition & the Inquisitional Mind. 1987. text 84.00 (*0-88033-952-7*, SC49, Pub. by East Eur Monographs) Col U Pr.

Alcala, Gaspar. History of New Mexico, Sixteen-Ten. Espinos, Gilberto & Hodge, F. W., eds. LC 67-24716. (Quivira Society Publications, Vol. 4). 1967. reprint ed. 25.95 (*0-405-00074-X*) Ayer.

Alcala, Kathleen. The Flower in the Skull: A Novel. LC 97-32553. 182p. 1998. 22.95 (*0-8118-1916-7*) Chronicle Bks.

— The Flower in the Skull: A Novel. LC 98-56462. 192p. (C). 1999. pap. 12.00 (*0-15-600634-0*, Harvest Bks) Harcourt.

— Mrs. Vargas & the Dead Naturalist. LC 92-4469. 192p. 1992. 19.95 (*0-934971-26-9*); pap. 9.95 (*0-934971-25-0*) Calyx Bks.

— Spirits of the Ordinary. LC 98-12914. 256p. (C). 1998. pap. 12.00 (*0-15-600568-9*) Harcourt.

— Spirits of the Ordinary: A Tale of Casas Grandes. LC 96-15665. 204p. 1997. 22.95 (*0-8118-1447-5*) Chronicle Bks.

***Alcala, Kathleen.** Treasures in Heaven: A Novel. LC 99-87726. 2000. 22.95 (*0-8118-2953-7*) Chronicle Bks.

Alcala, Larry. The Best of Larry Alcala's Mang Ambo, Bk. 2. (Illus.). 66p. (Orig.). 1993. pap. 8.75 (*971-10-0523-9*, Pub. by New Day Pub) Cellar.

— The Best of Mang Ambo. (Illus.). 132p. (Orig.). 1989. pap. 6.50 (*971-10-0372-4*, Pub. by New Day Pub) Cellar.

Alcala, V. O., ed. A Bibliography of Education in the Caribbean. 1976. lib. bdg. 59.95 (*0-8490-1498-0*) Gordon Pr.

Alcala-Zamora, Pedro De, see De Alcala-Zamora, Pedro.

Alcalay, Ammiel. After Jews & Arabs: Remaking Levantine Culture. 288p. (C). 1992. pap. 19.95 (*0-8166-2155-1*); text 49.95 (*0-8166-2154-3*) U of Minn Pr.

— The Cairo Notebooks. 76p. (Orig.). 1994. pap. 9.50 (*0-935162-13-5*) Singing Horse.

***Alcalay, Ammiel.** Memories of Our Future. LC 99-34696. 330p. 1999. pap. 14.95 (*0-87286-360-3*, Pub. by City Lights) SPD-Small Pr Dist.

Alcalay, Ammiel, ed. Keys to the Garden: New Israeli Writing. 400p. (Orig.). 1996. pap. 18.95 (*0-87286-308-5*) City Lights.

Alcalay, Ammiel, ed. see Dizdareivc, Zlatko.

Alcalay, Ammiel, ed. see Hukanovic, Rezak.

Alcalay, Ammiel, tr. see Bruchac, Joseph, et al.

Alcalay, Ammiel, tr. see Kozer, Jose.

Alcalay, Ammiel, tr. see Mehmedinovic, Semezdin.

Alcalay, Reuben. Complete Set of Hebrew-English-Hebrew Dictionaries, 5 vols. (HEB & ENG.). 7201p. 129.00 (*0-87559-214-7*) Shalom.

Alcalay, Reuben. English-Hebrew Dictionary, 3 vols. (ENG & HEB.). 2135p. 1987. 75.00 (*0-87559-213-9*) Shalom.

— Hebrew-English Dictionary, Vol. 2. (ENG & HEB.). 1442p. 1987. 65.00 (*0-87559-212-0*) Shalom.

Alcalde, Fernando, tr. see Siegenthaler, Kathrin & Pfister, Marcus.

Alcalde, Gonzalo, jt. auth. see Sagasti, Francisco R.

Alcalde, Javier G. The Idea of Third World Development: Emerging Perspectives in the United States & Britain, 1900-1950. Thompson, Kenneth W., ed. LC 87-8154. (Exxon Education Foundation Series on Rhetoric & Political Discourse: Vol. 8). 258p. (Orig.). (C). 1987. pap. text 24.00 (*0-8191-6304-X*, Pub. by White Miller Center) U Pr of Amer.

Alcaly. The Complete Hebrew-English/English-Hebrew Dictionary. (ENG & HEB.). 2000p. 1996. 295.00 (*0-7859-9625-7*) Fr & Eur.

Alcamo. The Foundations of Human Genetics. 450p. text. write for info. (*0-471-31785-3*) Wiley.

Alcamo, Edward. Anatomy Coloring Book. 1997. pap. 18.00 (*0-679-77849-7*) Random.

— Fundamentals of Microbiology. 4th ed. (C). 1996. 54.00 (*0-8053-0337-5*) Benjamin-Cummings.

Alcamo, Edward, jt. auth. see Elson, Lawrence M.

***Alcamo, Edward I.** DNA Technology. 2nd ed. LC 99-68792. (Illus.). 416p. 1999. 59.95 (*0-12-048920-1*) Acad Pr.

Alcamo, I. Edward. AIDS: The Biological Basis. 304p. (C). 1992. text. write for info. (*0-697-12061-9*, WCB McGr Hill) McGrw-H Hghr Educ.

— AIDS: The Biological Basis. 2nd ed. LC 96-83692. 320p. (C). 1996. text 42.50 (*0-697-15882-9*, WCB McGr Hill) McGrw-H Hghr Educ.

— Anatomy & Physiology the Easy Way. LC 95-45605. (Barron's Easy Way Ser.). 496p. 1996. pap. 13.95 (*0-8120-9134-5*) Barron.

— DNA Technology: The Awesome Skill. 320p. (C). 1996. text. write for info. (*0-07-114021-2*, WCB McGr Hill) McGrw-H Hghr Educ.

— Fundamental Microbiology. 5th ed. LC 96-43386. 896p. (C). 1996. 100.00 (*0-8053-0532-7*) Addison-Wesley.

— Fundamentals of Microbiology. 3rd ed. (C). 1991. text 59.25 (*0-8053-0020-1*) Benjamin-Cummings.

— Fundamentals of Microbiology. 4th ed. LC 93-46618. (C). 1994. pap. text, student ed. 18.75 (*0-8053-0327-8*) Benjamin-Cummings.

***Alcamo, I. Edward.** Fundamentals of Microbiology. 6th ed. (Illus.). 864p. (C). 2000. text 75.00 (*0-7637-1067-9*) JB Pubns.

Alcamo, I. Edward. LAB MNL Fundmtl Microbio. 5th ed. 320p. (C). 1997. pap. text, lab manual ed. 32.00 (*0-8053-0534-3*) Addison-Wesley.

— Microbiology. (Blond's Medical Guides Ser.). (Illus.). 181p. (Orig.). (C). 1994. pap. text 19.99 (*0-945819-41-2*) Sulzburger & Graham Pub.

— Microbiology Quick Review. (Cliffs Quick Reviews Ser.). (Illus.). 101p. (Orig.). 1996. pap. text 9.95 (*0-8220-5333-0*, Cliff) IDG Bks.

— Microgames & Puzzles. (Illus.). 120p. 1996. pap. text 15.95 (*0-89863-184-X*) Star Pub CA.

— Schaum's Outline of Microbiology. LC 97-12020. (Illus.). 409p. (C). 1997. pap. 15.95 (*0-07-000967-8*) McGraw.

— S/G Fundamental Microbiology. 5th ed. 304p. (C). 1997. pap. text, student ed. 23.00 (*0-8053-0533-5*) Addison-Wesley.

Alcamo, I. Edward & Princeton Review Publishing Staff. Biology Coloring Workbook. (Princeton Review Ser.). 288p. 1998. pap., wbk. ed. 18.00 (*0-679-77884-5*) Random.

Alcamo, J., ed. Coping with Crisis in Eastern Europe's Environment: Coping with Challenge. (Illus.). 325p. (C). 1993. text 85.00 (*1-85070-433-3*) Prthnon Pub.

Alcamo, J., et al, eds. Global Change Scenarios of the 21st Century: Results from the IMAGE 2.1 Model. LC 98-31164. 312p. 1998. 115.00 (*0-08-043447-9*, Pergamon Pr) Elsevier.

Alcamo, John. Casino Gambling Behind the Tables. LC 97-75252. 256p. 1997. pap. 7.99 (*0-914839-44-6*) Gollehon Pr.

Alcamo, Joseph. The RAINS Model of Acidification: Science & Strategies in Europe. (C). 1990. lib. bdg. 171.00 (*0-7923-0781-X*) Kluwer Academic.

Alcamo, Joseph, ed. Image 2.0: Integrating Modeling of Global Climate Change. LC 94-15442. 328p. (C). 1994. text 186.50 (*0-7923-2860-4*) Kluwer Academic.

Alcamo, Joseph & Bartnicki, Jerzy, eds. Atmospheric Computations to Assess Acidification in Europe. (C). 1990. text 122.00 (*0-7923-0160-9*) Kluwer Academic.

Alcantara. Aspects of Public Health Nursing. Ashurkov, ed. (Public Health Papers: No. 4). 185p. 1961. 5.00 (*92-4-130004-3*) World Health.

Alcantara, Adriana C. Reminiscences & Other Stories. 132p. (Orig.). 1993. pap. 10.75 (*971-10-0493-3*, Pub. by New Day Pub) Cellar.

Alcantara, Alejandro, tr. see Emley, Douglas.

Alcantara, Cynthia Hewitt de, see Hewitt de Alcantara, Cynthia, ed.

***Alcantara, Isabel & Egnolff, Sandra.** Frida Kahlo & Diego Rivera. (Pegasus Library Ser.). (Illus.). 128p. 1999. 25.00 (*3-7913-2164-1*, Pub. by Prestel) te Neues.

Alcantara, Pelagio & Diaz, Manuel S., eds. Ilocano Harvest: A Collection of Short Stories in English by Contemporary Ilocano Writers. (Orig.). (C). 1989. pap. 10.75 (*971-10-0342-2*, Pub. by New Day Pub) Cellar.

Alcantara, Ricardo, jt. auth. see Doumerc, Beatriz.

Alcantara, S. Peter. A Golden Treatise of Mental Prayer. Hollings, G. S., ed. LC 77-18960. 185p. reprint ed. 57.40 (*0-8357-9135-1*, 201909600010) Bks Demand.

Alcantra, Ricardo. Dog & Cat. LC 98-29896. (Illus.). 32p. (J). (gr. k-3). 1999. lib. bdg. 16.90 (*0-7613-1420-2*, Copper Beech Bks) Millbrook Pr.

Alcaraz, Daniel. Diccionario Practico de la Lengua Espanola del Nuevo Mundo. (SPA., Illus.). 294p. 1995. pap. 7.95 (*0-8442-7969-2*, 79692) NTC Contemp Pub Co.

Alcaraz, Manuel, et al. Sexual Hormones: Influence on the Electrophysiology of the Brain. LC 74-4137. 223p. 1974. text 31.00 (*0-8422-7214-3*) Irvington.

Alcaraz Varo, Enrique. Dictionary of Legal Terms Spanish-English - English-Spanish. 4th ed. (ENG & SPA.). 694p. 1997. reprint ed. 69.95 (*84-344-0509-1*, Pub. by Ariel Editorial) IBD Ltd.

Alcaraz Varo, Enrique. Dictionary of Economic, Financial & Commercial Terms, Spanish-English/English-Spanish. (ENG & SPA.). 1252p. 1996. 195.00 (*0-7859-9468-8*) Fr & Eur.

Alcaro, Marion Walker. Walt Whitman's Mrs. G: A Biography of Anne Gilchrist. 1991. 42.50 (*0-8386-3381-1*) Fairleigh Dickinson.

— Walt Whitman's Mrs. G: A Biography of Anne Gilchrist. LC 89-46136. (Illus.). 288p. 1991. 42.50 (*0-685-48674-5*) Fairleigh Dickinson.

Alcatena, Enrique, jt. auth. see Wagner, John.

Alcatena, Quique, jt. auth. see Barriero, Enrique.

Alcayaga, Lucila Godoy y, see Mistral, Gabriela, pseud.

Alcazar, Miguel, ed. see Segovia, Andres.

Alcena, Valiere. African American Health Book: A Prescription for Improvement. LC 95-19784. (Illus.). 272p. 1996. pap. 12.95 (*0-8065-1719-0*, Citadel Pr) Carol Pub Group.

— AIDS the Expanding Epidemic - What the Public Needs to Know: A Multicultural Overview. 204p. (Orig.). 1994. 24.99 (*0-9633365-1-7*) Alcena Med Comms.

— The Status of Health of Blacks in the United States of America: A Prescription for Improvement. 256p. 1992. pap. text 30.95 (*0-8403-7394-5*) Kendall-Hunt.

Alcena, Veliere. The African-American Health Book: A Prescription for Improvement. LC 93-44652. 1994. 18.95 (*1-55972-214-2*, Birch Ln Pr) Carol Pub Group.

Alcerro, Angela, jt. auth. see Carney, John.

Alcerro, Angela, jt. auth. see Carney, John P.

Alces & Hansford. Sales, Leases & Bulk Transfers. 1989. teacher ed. write for info. (*0-8205-0387-8*) Bender.

Alces, jt. auth. see Benfield.

Alces, Peter & Howard, Margaret. Bankruptcy, Teacher's Manual. (American Casebook Ser.). 181p. (C). 1995. pap. text, teacher ed. write for info. (*0-314-06753-1*) West Pub.

Alces, Peter, et al. Uniform Commercial Code Transaction Guide: Analysis & Forms, 4 vols. 1992. 420.00 (*0-685-28166-3*) West Group.

Alces, Peter A. Intellectual Property Law. LC 93-79049. xxxii, 736 p. 1994. 145.00 (*0-316-77960-1*, Aspen Law & Bus) Aspen Pub.

— Law of Fraudulent Transactions, No. 2200. 1989. suppl. ed. 59.00 (*0-7913-1202-X*); boxed set, suppl. ed. 135.00 (*0-7913-0310-1*) Warren Gorham & Lamont.

— The Law of Suretyship & Guaranty. 320p. 1996. 135.00 (*0-7913-2615-2*) Warren Gorham & Lamont.

Alces, Peter A. Sales, Leases & Bulk Transfers 1989. annuals 1989. text 51.00 (*0-8205-2887-0*) Bender.

Alces, Peter A. & Beafield, Marion W., Jr. Payment Systems, Teacher's Manual to Accompany Cases & Materials On. (American Casebook Ser.). 200p. 1993. pap. text. write for info. (*0-314-02808-0*) West Pub.

Alces, Peter A. & Benfield, Marion W., Jr. Payment Systems: Cases, Materials, & Problems. LC 93-20285. (American Casebook Ser.). 576p. (C). 1993. 52.50 (*0-314-01973-1*) West Pub.

Alces, Peter A. & Howard, Margaret. Bankruptcy, Cases & Materials on. (American Casebook Ser.). 704p. (C). 1995. 57.50 (*0-314-04894-4*) West Pub.

Alces, Peter A. & See, Harold F. The Commercial Law of Intellectual Property. 768p. 1994. boxed set 155.00 (*0-316-77962-8*, 79601) Aspen Law.

***Alch, Mark.** How to Become a Millionaire: A Straight-Forward Approach to Accumulating Personal Wealth. LC 99-65086. 240p. 1999. 20.00 (*1-56352-606-9*) Longstreet.

Alcharizi, Yehuda, tr. see Maimonides.

Alchemy, Jack. For Sex & Free Roadmaps. (Illus.). 1976. pap. 1.50 (*0-917402-01-4*) Downtown Poets.

Alchian. Exchange & Production 1st. (SWC-Economics). 1968. pap. 10.50 (*0-534-04335-6*) S-W Pub.

— Exchange & Production 2nd. 2nd ed. (SWC-Economics). 1977. pap. 21.50 (*0-534-00493-8*) S-W Pub.

Alchian, Armen A. Economic Forces at Work. LC 77-1327. 1977. 15.00 (*0-913966-30-4*); pap. 7.00 (*0-913966-35-5*) Liberty Fund.

Alchian, Armen A., ed. see Koopmans, Tjalling C.

Alchin, Carrie A. Ear Training for Teacher & Pupil. LC 74-27326. 152p. 1982. reprint ed. 34.50 (*0-404-12852-1*) AMS Pr.

Alchon, Guy. The Invisible Hand of Planning: Capitalism, Social Science, & the State in the 1920s. LC 84-42873. 263p. reprint ed. pap. 81.60 (*0-608-06401-7*, 206676200008) Bks Demand.

Alchon, Suzanne A. Native Society & Disease in Colonial Ecuador. (Cambridge Latin American Studies: No. 71). (Illus.). 165p. (C). 1992. text 57.95 (*0-521-40186-0*) Cambridge U Pr.

Alchourron, C. E. & Bulygin, E. Normative Systems. LC 75-170895. (Library of Exact Philosophy: Vol. 5). (Illus.). 1972. 69.95 (*0-387-81019-6*) Spr-Verlag.

Alciat, Andreas. Emblematum Liber. (Emblematische Cabinet Ser.). 88p. 1977. reprint ed. 55.00 (*3-487-06144-9*) G Olms Pubs.

Alciato, Andrea. Emblemata: Lyons, 1550. Manning, John, ed. Knott, Betty I., tr. LC 95-26294. (Emblem Ser.). 450p. 1996. 99.95 (*1-85928-002-1*, Pub. by Scolar Pr) Ashgate Pub Co.

Alciatore, David G., jt. auth. see Histand, Michael B.

Alciere, Rose M. Creating Help for Windows Applications. (Popular Applications Ser.). 144p. 1995. pap. 15.95 (*1-55622-448-6*) Wordware Pub.

Alcina, Juan F., ed. see De la Vega, Garcilaso.

Alciun, Albinus. The Book of Jasher. 291p. 1997. reprint ed. pap. 23.00 (*0-7873-0000-4*) Hlth Research.

***Alcivar-Warren, Acacia, et al, eds.** Proceedings of the Aquaculture Species Genome Mapping Workshop: May 18-19, 1997, University of Massachusetts Dartmouth, North Dartmouth, Massachusetts. (NRAES Ser.: Vol. 124). 85p. 1999. pap. text 12.00 (*0-935817-46-8*) NRAES.

Alcman. The Parthenon. Connor, W. R., ed. LC 78-81590. (Greek Texts & Commentaries Ser.). 1979. reprint ed. lib. bdg. 22.95 (*0-405-11432-X*) Ayer.

Alcock. Short History of Europe: From the Greeks & Romans to the Present Day. LC 97-34338. 256p. 1998. pap. 18.95 (*0-312-21036-1*); text 59.95 (*0-312-21003-5*) St Martin.

— Understanding Poverty. 1997. text 19.95 (*0-333-56759-5*, Pub. by Macmillan) St Martin.

Alcock, ed. Social Economy & the Democratic State. (C). 1989. pap. 19.50 (*0-85315-718-9*, Pub. by Lawrence & Wishart) NYU Pr.

Alcock, A. Carcinological Fauna of India. 700p. 1968. pap. 175.00 (*0-7855-2720-6*, Pub. by Intl Bks & Periodicals) St Mut.

— A Descriptive Catalogue of the Indian Deep-Sea Fished in the Indian Museum. Talwar, P. K., ed. (Illus.). 228p. (C). 1994. text 195.00 (*1-881570-44-4*) Science Pubs.

— Materials for a Carcenological Fauna of India, 1895-1900, 6pts. in 1. 1968. 160.00 (*3-7682-0544-4*) Lubrecht & Cramer.

Alcock, Anne. Showing & Ringcraft Explained LC 78-319016. (Horseman's Handbook Ser.). 96p. 1978. write for info. (*0-7063-5574-1*, Pub. by WrLock) Sterling.

Alcock, Anne. They're Off. 144p. 1990. pap. 35.00 (*0-85131-299-3*, Pub. by J A Allen) St Mut.

Alcock, Anne, jt. auth. see Sherred, Alison.

Alcock, Anthony. The Life of Samuel of Kalamun. 1983. pap. 39.95 (*0-85668-219-5*, Pub. by Aris & Phillips) David Brown.

Alcock, Anthony, tr. see Assmann, Jan.

***Alcock, Antony Evelyn.** A History of the Protection of Regional Cultural Minorities in Europe: From the Edict of Nantes to the Present Day. LC 00-30889. 2000. write for info. (*0-312-23556-9*) St Martin.

Alcock, Dana. Memory Bank Handbook. 257p. 1997. pap. 9.95 (*0-9656170-0-9*) Danas Gifts.

Alcock, Deborah. The Romance of Protestantism: Tales of Trials & Victory. LC 99-35037. 1999. 9.90 (*0-921100-88-4*) Inhtce Pubns.

Alcock, Donald. Illustrating BASIC: A Simple Programming Language. (Illus.). 144p. 1977. pap. text 22.95 (*0-521-21704-0*) Cambridge U Pr.

— Illustrating BBC Basic. 194p. 1986. pap. text 21.95 (*0-521-31495-X*) Cambridge U Pr.

— Illustrating C. 2nd ed. (Illus.). 222p. (C). 1994. spiral bd. 24.95 (*0-521-46821-3*) Cambridge U Pr.

— Illustrating FORTRAN. (Illus.). 144p. 1983. spiral bd. 25.95 (*0-521-28810-X*) Cambridge U Pr.

— Illustrating Pascal. (Illus.). 192p. 1987. pap. text 26.95 (*0-521-33695-3*) Cambridge U Pr.

Alcock, James. Science & Supernature: A Critical Appraisal of Parapsychology. LC 89-70033. 192p. 1990. 31.95 (*0-87975-548-2*) Prometheus Bks.

***Alcock, Jim & Carment, Bill.** A Textbook of Social Psychology. 5th ed. 608p. 2000. 99.93 (*0-13-026354-0*) P-H.

Alcock, John. Animal Behavior: An Evolutionary Approach. 6th ed. LC 97-27347. (Illus.). 640p. (C). 1997. text 67.95 (*0-87893-009-4*) Sinauer Assocs.

— In a Desert Garden: Love & Death among the Insects. LC 97-589. (Illus.). 192p. 1997. 27.50 (*0-393-04118-2*) Norton.

— In a Desert Garden: Love & Death among the Insects. LC 98-51808. 192p. 1999. 17.95 (*0-8165-1970-6*) U of Ariz Pr.

***Alcock, John.** In a Desert Garden: Love & Death among the Insects. (Illus.). 186p. 2000. reprint ed. text 27.00 (*0-7881-9246-9*) DIANE Pub.

Alcock, John. The Kookaburras' Song: Exploring Animal Behavior in Australia. LC 88-4740. (Illus.). 218p. 1988. 24.95 (*0-8165-1050-4*) U of Ariz Pr.

— The Masked Bobwhite Rides Again. LC 93-15416. 186p. (Orig.). 1993. pap. 17.95 (*0-8165-1405-4*); lib. bdg. 36.00 (*0-8165-1387-2*) U of Ariz Pr.

— Mons Perfectionis. LC 74-28823. (English Experience Ser.: No. 706). 1974. reprint ed. 20.00 (*90-221-0706-X*) Walter J Johnson.

— Sonoran Desert Spring. LC 84-16468. (Illus.). 196p. 1985. 19.95 (*0-226-01258-1*) U Ch Pr.

— Sonoran Desert Spring. LC 84-16468. (Illus.). 196p. 1988. pap. 9.95 (*0-226-01260-3*) U Ch Pr.

— Sonoran Desert Spring. LC 84-16468. (Illus.). 206p. reprint ed. pap. 63.90 (*0-608-08826-9*, 206946500004) Bks Demand.

— Sonoran Desert Spring. LC 93-41190. (Illus.). 134p. 1994. reprint ed. pap. 17.95 (*0-8165-1399-6*) U of Ariz Pr.

— Sonoran Desert Summer. LC 89-20235. 187p. 1990. 33.95 (*0-8165-1150-0*) U of Ariz Pr.

— Sonoran Desert Summer. LC 89-20235. (Illus.). 187p. 1994. reprint ed. pap. 17.95 (*0-8165-1438-0*) U of Ariz Pr.

— Spousage of a Virgin to Christ. LC 74-80158. (English Experience Ser.: No. 638). (Illus.). 19p. 1974. reprint ed. 15.00 (*90-221-0638-1*) Walter J Johnson.

Alcock, John, jt. auth. see Sherman, Paul W.

Alcock, John, jt. auth. see Thornhill, Randy.

Alcock, John P. Five Generations of the Family of Burr Harrison of Virginia, 1650-1800. viii, 284p. (Orig.). 1991. pap. 25.00 (*1-55613-378-2*) Heritage Bk.

Alcock, John W. & Gillette, M. L. Monitoring Acid-Base Titrations with a pH Meter. Stanitski, C. L., ed. (Modular Laboratory Program in Chemistry Ser.). 16p. (C). 1997. pap. text 1.50 (*0-87540-494-4*) Chem Educ Res.

Alcock, John W., jt. auth. see Gillette, Marcia L.

Alcock, Leslie. Arthur's Britain. 1970. pap. 8.95 (*0-14-021396-1*, Penguin Bks) Viking Penguin.

Alcock, Leslie. Arthur's Britain: History & Archaeology, AD 367-634. LC 72-176453. xviii, 415p. 1971. write for info. (*0-7139-0245-0*, A Lane) Viking Penguin.

— "By South Cadbury Is That Camelot ..." the Excavation of Cadbury Castle 1966-1970. LC 73-151573. (New Aspects of Antiquity Ser.). 224 p. 1972. write for info. (*0-500-39011-8*) Thames Hudson.

Alcock, Leslie & Camelot Research Committee Staff. Was This Camelot? Excavations at Cadbury Castle, 1966-1970. LC 72-82214. (New Aspects of Archaeology Ser.). 224p. 1972. write for info. (*0-8128-1505-X*) Madison Bks UPA.

Alcock, Leslie, et al. Cadbury Castle, Somerset: The Early Medieval Archaeology. LC 95-227586. x, 188p. 1995. 65.00 (*0-7083-1275-6*, Pub. by Univ Wales Pr) Paul & Co Pubs.

Alcock, Leslie, jt. ed. see Austin, David.

Alcock, N. W., contrib. by. Coordination Chemistry. LC 94-47046. (Structure & Bonding Ser.: Vol. 82). 1995. write for info. (*0-387-58761-6*) Spr-Verlag.

Alcock, Pete, et al, eds. The Student's Companion to Social Policy. LC 97-10142. (Illus.). 320p. (C). 1997. text 73.95 (*0-631-20239-0*); pap. text 31.95 (*0-631-20240-4*) Blackwell Pubs.

Alcock, Peter. Social Policy in Britain: Themes & Issues. 272p. 1996. text 49.95 (*0-312-16201-4*) St Martin.

Alcock, Rutherford. Capital of the Tycoon, 2 vols., Set. 1863. 35.00 (*0-403-00241-9*) Scholarly.

Alcock, Susan E. Graecia Capta: The Landscapes of Roman Greece. (Illus.). 329p. 1996. pap. text 22.95 (*0-521-56819-6*) Cambridge U Pr.

— Sandy Pylos: An Archaeological History from Nestor to Navarino. Davis, Jack L., ed. LC 97-40652. (Illus.). 390p. 1998. 50.00 (*0-292-71594-3*, DAVSAN); pap. 24.95 (*0-292-71595-1*, DAVSAP) U of Tex Pr.

Alcock, Susan E. & Osborne, Robin, eds. Placing the Gods: Sanctuaries & Sacred Space in Ancient Greece. (Illus.). 282p. (C). 1996. pap. text 28.00 (*0-19-815060-1*) OUP.

Alcock, Susan E., jt. ed. see Osborne, Robin.

Alcock, Susan E., ed. see Pausanias.

Alcock, Vivien. The Cuckoo Sister. LC 96-52040. 240p. (J). 1997. pap. 4.95 (*0-395-81651-3*) HM.

— The Haunting of Cassie Palmer. LC 81-15230. 1982. 9.95 (*0-440-03538-4*) Dell.

— The Haunting of Cassie Palmer. LC 96-31657. 192p. (J). 1997. pap. 6.95 (*0-395-81653-X*) HM.

— The Monster Garden. LC 88-6900. 160p. (J). (gr. 5-9). 1988. 13.95 (*0-440-50053-2*) Delacorte.

— The Mysterious Mr. Ross. LC 87-5455. 160p. (YA). (gr. 5-9). 1987. 14.95 (*0-385-29581-2*) Delacorte.

— The Red-Eared Ghosts. (J). (gr. 5-9). 1997. 15.95 (*0-614-28825-8*) HM.

— The Red-Eared Ghosts. LC 96-1209. 272p. (J). (gr. 5-7). 1997. 15.95 (*0-395-81660-2*) HM.

— Red Eared Ghosts. 272p. (J). (gr. 5-9). 1998. pap. 4.95 (*0-395-88394-6*) HM.

— Singer to the Sea God. 208p. (J). (gr. 4-7). 1995. pap. 3.99 (*0-440-41003-7*) Dell.

— Singer to the Sea God. (YA). (gr. 9-12). 1996. 18.50 (*0-8446-6887-7*) Peter Smith.

— Singer to the Sea God. 1995. 9.09 (*0-606-08165-8*) Turtleback.

— The Stonewalkers. LC 97-28196. 176p. 1998. pap. 4.95 (*0-395-81652-1*) HM.

— The Stranger at the Window. LC 97-14195. 208p. (J). (gr. 5-9). 1999. 16.00 (*0-395-81661-0*) HM.

***Alcock, Vivien.** The Stranger at the Window. LC 97-14195. 208p. (YA). (gr. 5-9). 1999. pap. 4.95 (*0-395-94329-9*, Sandpiper) HM.

Alcock, Vivien. The Sylvia Game. LC 96-53109. 224p. (J). 1997. pap. 4.95 (*0-395-81650-5*) HM.

— Travelers by Night. LC 85-1663. (Illus.). 192p. (J). (gr. 4-6). 1985. 14.95 (*0-385-29406-9*) Delacorte.

— The Trial of Anna Cotman. LC 96-31658. 224p. (J). 1997. pap. 6.95 (*0-395-81649-1*) HM.

***Alcoff, Eduardo & Mendieta, Eduardo.** Thinking from the Underside of History. 352p. 2000. pap. 22.95 (*0-8476-9651-0*) Rowman.

— Thinking from Underside History. 352p. 2000. 70.00 (*0-8476-9650-2*) Rowman.

Alcoff, Linda & Potter, Elizabeth, eds. Feminist Epistemologies. LC 92-11309. (Thinking Gender Ser.). 272p. (C). (gr. 13). 1992. pap. 19.99 (*0-415-90451-X*, A5820) Routledge.

Alcoff, Linda M. Epistemology: The Big Questions. LC 97-51452. (Philosophy Ser.). 496p. 1998. 62.95 (*0-631-20579-9*); pap. 29.95 (*0-631-20580-2*) Blackwell Pubs.

— Real Knowing: New Versions of the Coherence Theory. 272p. 1996. text 37.50 (*0-8014-3047-X*) Cornell U Pr.

Alcohol Anonymous World Services Inc. Staff. Alcoholics Anonymous. (VIE.). 1991. 8.50 (*0-916856-44-5*) AAWS.

— Alcoholics Anonymous. (SPA.). 1993. 5.00 (*0-916856-57-7*); 7.95 (*0-916856-49-6*) AAWS.

A

— Alcoholics Anonymous. (SWA.). 1993. 14.00 (*0-916856-47-X*) AAWS.

Alcoholic Anonymous World Services Inc. Staff. Alcoholics Anonymous. (SPA.). 154p. 1983. pap. write for info. (*0-916856-09-7*) AAWS.

Alcoholics Anonymous, Archives of the General Serv. Alcoholics Anonymous Nineteen Thirty-Nine to Nineteen Forty-Two. 1985. 50.00 (*0-916856-17-8*) AAWS.

Alcoholics Anonymous World Services, Inc., Staff. AA en Prisiones: De Preso a Preso. Orig. Title: AA in Prison: Inmate to Inmate. (SPA.). 136p. 1991. pap. 2.95 (*0-916856-46-1*) AAWS.

— Alcoholics Anonymous. LC 76-4029. 400p. 1939. 3.60 (*0-916856-00-3*) AAWS.

— Alcoholics Anonymous. (RUS.). 181p. 1989. pap. 2.75 (*0-916856-25-9*) AAWS.

— Alcoholics Anonymous. (CHI.). 1990. write for info. (*0-916856-35-6*) AAWS.

Alcoholics Anonymous World Services, Inc. Staff. Alcoholics Anonymous. (ROM.). write for info. (*0-916856-40-2*) AAWS.

— Alcoholics Anonymous. (THA.). 1993. 8.55 (*0-916856-58-5*) AAWS.

— Alcoholics Anonymous. (PER.). 1993. 8.55 (*0-916856-50-X*) AAWS.

Alcoholics Anonymous World Services, Inc., Staff. Alcoholics Anonymous. (TAG.). write for info. (*0-916856-56-9*) AAWS.

— Alcoholics Anonymous. rev. ed. (SPA.). 1990. pap. 3.50 (*0-916856-19-4*) AAWS.

Alcoholics Anonymous World Services, Inc. Staff. Alcoholics Anonymous: The Story of How Many Thousands of Men & Women Have Recovered from Alcoholism. 576p. 1986. pap. 3.20 (*0-916856-18-6*) AAWS.

Alcoholics Anonymous World Services, Inc., Staff. Alcoholics Anonymous Comes of Age: A Brief History of Alcoholic Anonymous. LC 57-10949. 333p. 1957. 3.70 (*0-916856-02-X*) AAWS.

— Alcoholics Anonymous World Services, Inc. (HUN.). 1990. pap. 2.50 (*0-916856-38-0*) AAWS.

Alcoholics Anonymous World Services, Inc. Staff. As Bill Sees It - Como lo ve Bill. rev. ed. (SPA.). 1993. 2.50 (*0-916856-54-2*) AAWS.

— Daily Reflections: A Book of Reflections by AA Members for AA Members. 382p. 1990. pap. 5.25 (*0-916856-37-2*) AAWS.

— Los Doce Pasos y Las Doce Tradiciones.Tr. of Twelve Steps & Twelve Traditions. (ENG & SPA.). 196p. (Orig.). 1985. pap. 2.50 (*0-916856-16-X*) AAWS.

Alcoholics Anonymous World Services, Inc., Staff. Dr. Bob & Good Oldtimers & Pass It On. 1894. spiral bd. 7.70 (*0-916856-13-5*) AAWS.

— Latvian Twelve Steps & Twelve Traditions. 1993. 8.45 (*0-916856-61-5*) AAWS.

— Lithuanian "Living Sober" 1993. 8.40 (*0-916856-60-7*) AAWS.

Alcoholics Anonymous World Services, Inc. Staff. Little Big Book (Alcoholics Anonymous) 164p. 1993. 4.00 (*0-916856-59-3*) AAWS.

Alcoholics Anonymous World Services, Inc., Staff. Llegamos a Creer - Came to Believe. (SPA.). 1987. 2.50 (*0-916856-21-6*) AAWS.

— Pass It On: The Story of Bill Wilson & How the A. A. Message Reached the World. LC 84-72766. 432p. 1984. 6.50 (*0-916856-12-7*) AAWS.

— Twelve Steps & Twelve Traditions. (LIT.). 192p. 1953. pap. 5.25 (*0-916856-48-8*) AAWS.

Alcoholics Anonymous World Services, Inc. Staff. Twelve Steps, Twelve Traditions, 5 vols. (HUN.). 1993. 8.45 (*0-916856-52-6*) AAWS.

Alcoholics Anonymous World Services, Inc., Staff, ed. Alcoholics Anonymous. (ARA.). 1990. pap. 4.00 (*0-916856-34-8*) AAWS.

— Alcoholics Anonymous. (TUR.). 1991. 9.90 (*0-916856-36-4*) AAWS.

Alcoholics Anonymous World Services, Inc. Staff, ed. Alcoholics Anonymous. (CZE.). 1990. pap. 2.50 (*0-916856-28-3*) AAWS.

— Alcoholics Anonymous. (LIT.). 1991. pap. 6.50 (*0-916856-39-9*) AAWS.

Alcoholics Anonymous World Services, Inc., Staff, ed. Alcoholics Anonymous. large type ed. 573p. 1990. reprint ed. 12.00 (*0-916856-33-X*) AAWS.

Alcoholism Symposium Staff. Alcoholism, a Multidisciplinary Approach: Proceedings of the Symposium on Alcoholism, Amsterdam, May 1978. Mendlewicz, Julien & Van Praag, Herman M., eds. (Advances in Biological Psychiatry Ser.: Vol. 3). (Illus.). 1979. pap. 48.00 (*3-8055-2977-5*) S Karger.

Alcomo, Edward I. DNA Technology: The Awesome Skill. 256p. (C). 1995. text 42.50 (*0-697-21248-3*, WCB McGr Hill) McGrw-H Hghr Educ.

Alcon, Susan. Treasures from the Sea. 24p. 1995. pap. text 5.95 (*0-87487-743-1*) Summy-Birchard.

Alcorn. Handbook Introductory Economics. 168p. (C). 2000. pap. text 18.40 (*0-536-01582-1*) Pearson Custom.

***Alcorn.** Social Issues in Technology: A Format for Investigation. 3rd ed. LC 99-23787. 291p. 1999. 66.00 (*0-13-020681-4*) P-H.

Alcorn, jt. auth. see Ebborn.

Alcorn, Alfred. The Long Run of Myles Mayberry. LC 98-54296. (Illus.). 240p. 1999. pap. 13.00 (*1-58195-001-2*, Pub. by Zoland Bks) Consort Bk Sales.

— Murder in the Museum of Man. 273p. 1998. pap. 13.00 (*0-944072-78-X*) Zoland Bks.

Alcorn, Andrew, et al. Managed Care Pt. C: Integrating the Delivery & Financing of Health Care. Hopkins, Julie, ed. (HIAA Insurance Education Ser.). (Illus.). 233p. 1998. pap. text 30.00 (*1-879143-46-1*) Health Ins Assn Am.

Alcorn, Bob J., jt. auth. see Humphrey, Janice H.

Alcorn, Charles L., jt. auth. see Nicholson, Charles L.

Alcorn, Dennis. Wink at Success, Flirt with Serenity: An Affirmative Guide to Personal Peace. LC 92-73377. 112p. (Orig.). 1992. pap. 9.95 (*0-9633857-0-4*) Blue Canoe.

Alcorn, Edgar G. The Duties & Liabilities of Bank Directors. Bruchey, Stuart, ed. LC 80-1128. (Rise of Commercial Banking Ser.). 1981. reprint ed. lib. bdg. 18.95 (*0-405-13628-5*) Ayer.

***Alcorn, Ellenor M.** English Silver in the Museum of Fine Arts, Boston Vol. 2: Silver from 1697 Including Irish & Scottish Silver. (Illus.). 416p. 2000. 85.00 (*0-87846-480-8*) Mus Fine Arts Boston.

Alcorn, Gordon A. Silent Wings. (Illus.). 83p. 1982. pap. 5.95 (*0-87770-277-2*) Ye Galleon.

Alcorn, J. R. The Birds of Nevada. LC 88-80743. (Illus.). 450p. 1988. 55.00 (*0-9620221-0-1*) Fairview West Pub.

— Tinnemaha. (Illus.). 155p. 1991. 24.95 (*0-9620221-1-X*) Fairview West Pub.

***Alcorn, Jo Lynn.** Easy Holiday & Seasonal Art Projects with Paper. 80p. 1999. pap. 10.95 (*0-590-43371-7*) Scholastic Inc.

Alcorn, John. The Master Scratch Builders: Tips & Techniques from the Master Aircraft Modelers. LC 98-89832. (Illus.). 224p. 1999. 45.00 (*0-7643-0795-9*) Schiffer.

Alcorn, John, et al. Scratch Built! A Celebration of the Static Scale Airplane Modeler's Craft. LC 93-83060. (Illus.). 144p. (Orig.). 1993. pap. 24.95 (*0-88740-417-0*) Schiffer.

Alcorn, Marianne S., jt. ed. see Shimpock-Vieweg, Kathy.

Alcorn, Marshall W. Narcissism & the Literary Libido: Rhetoric, Text, & Subjectivity. (Literature & Psychoanalysis Ser.). 1997. pap. text 20.00 (*0-8147-0665-7*) NYU Pr.

Alcorn, Marshall W., Jr. & Alcorn, Marshall W., Jr. Narcissism & the Literary Libido: Rhetoric, Text, & Subjectivity. 300p. (C). 1993. text 50.00 (*0-8147-0614-2*) NYU Pr.

Alcorn, Marshall W., Jr., jt. auth. see Alcorn, Marshall W., Jr.

Alcorn, Pat B. Success & Survival in the Family Owned Business. 272p. 1986. mass mkt. 9.95 (*0-446-38326-0*, Pub. by Warner Bks) Little.

— Success & Survival in the Family Owned Business. LC 80-28976. 265p. 1982. reprint ed. pap. 82.20 (*0-608-08411-5*, AU0034600062) Bks Demand.

Alcorn, Paul A. Ethics in Technology. 256p. (C). 2000. 66.00 (*0-13-660192-8*, Macmillan Coll) P-H.

Alcorn, Peter, et al. Drug Law in the Code States. 235p. 1993. 64.00 (*1-86287-112-4*, Pub. by Federation Pr) Gaunt.

***Alcorn, Randy.** Deadline. 1999. audio 19.99 (*1-57673-318-1*) Multnomah Pubs.

— Dominion. 612p. 2000. pap. 14.99 (*1-57673-661-X*, Pub. by Multnomah Pubs) GL Services.

— Edge of Eternity. 336p. 1998. 119.60 (*1-57856-165-5*) Waterbrook Pr.

Alcorn, Randy. Edge of Eternity: A Novel. 336p. 1998. 14.95 (*1-57856-085-3*) Waterbrook Pr.

***Alcorn, Randy.** Edge of Eternity: A Novel. 336p. 1999. pap. 11.95 (*1-57856-295-3*) Waterbrook Pr.

— In Light of Eternity: Perspectives on Heaven. 176p. 1999. 1.11 (*1-57856-299-6*) Waterbrook Pr.

— Lord Foulgrin's Letters. LC 00-8460. 2000. 14.99 (*1-57673-679-2*) Multnomah Pubs.

— Prolife Answers to Pro-Choice Arguments. 2000. pap. 10.99 (*1-57673-751-9*) Multnomah Pubs.

Alcorn, Randy. Prolife Answers to Prochoice Arguments. Morris, Rod, ed. LC 92-15392. 294p. 1992. pap. 10.99 (*0-88070-472-1*, Multnomah Bks) Multnomah Pubs.

— Your Money & Possessions: Making Them Count for Eternity. 436p. 1989. pap. 10.99 (*0-8423-8731-5*) Tyndale Hse.

Alcorn, Rowena. Timothy - Nez Perce Chief, Life & Times, 1800-1891. 72p. 1996. pap. 9.95 (*0-87770-362-0*) Ye Galleon.

Alcorn, Stephen, jt. auth. see Pinkney, Andrea Davis.

Alcorn, Susan, ed. see Robbins, Curt.

***Alcorta, Joe H., Sr.** Essential Spanish for Bankers. (SPA & ENG.). 32p. 1999. pap. 3.95 (*0-9624264-3-1*) Hermenegildo Pr.

— La Historia de un Famoso Equipo: Los Dallas Cowboys. (Illus.). 412p. 1989. 9.95 (*0-9624264-1-5*) Hermenegildo Pr.

Alcorta, Joe H., Sr. Speak Spanish in 60 Days. (ENG & SPA.). 76p. 1991. reprint ed. pap. text 9.95 (*0-9624264-2-3*) Hermenegildo Pr.

Alcorta, Ludovico. Flexible Automation in Developing Countries. LC 98-11152. (UNU/Intech Studies in New Technology & Development). (Illus.). 416p. (C). 1998. 110.00 (*0-415-19153-X*) Routledge.

Alcosser, Murray, jt. auth. see Eldridge, Niles.

Alcosser, Sandra. Except by Nature. 82p. 1998. pap. 12.95 (*1-55597-273-X*) Graywolf.

— A Fish to Feed All Hunger. LC 85-29619. 80p. reprint ed. pap. 30.00 (*0-8357-2556-1*, 204024700015) Bks Demand.

— A Fish to Feed All Hunger. 2nd ed. Trusky, Tom, ed. LC 85-29619. 70p. 1993. reprint ed. pap. 6.95 (*0-916272-55-9*) Ahsahta Pr.

Alcott, A. Bronson. Concord Days. 1969. pap. 15.00 (*0-87556-005-9*) Saifer.

— How Like an Angel Came I Down: Conversations with Children on the Gospels. 384p. (Orig.). 1991. reprint ed. pap. 18.95 (*0-940262-38-X*, Lindisfarne) Anthroposophic.

— New Connecticut. 1970. reprint ed. 15.00 (*0-87556-007-5*) Saifer.

— Ralph Waldo Emerson. (Illus.). 81p. 1983. reprint ed. pap. 15.00 (*0-87556-553-0*) Saifer.

— Sonnets & Canzonets. (Illus.). 1969. reprint ed. 15.00 (*0-87556-008-3*) Saifer.

— Table Talk. 208p. 1969. 20.00 (*0-87556-010-5*) Saifer.

— Tablets. 208p. 1969. reprint ed. 20.00 (*0-87556-011-3*) Saifer.

Alcott, A. Bronson, ed. Conversations with Children on the Gospels (Record of Conversations on the Gospels, Held in Mr. Alcott's School, Unfolding the Doctrine & Discipline of Human Culture), 2 vols. LC 72-4948. (Romantic Tradition in American Literature Ser.). 616p. 1976. reprint ed. 44.95 (*0-405-04621-9*) Ayer.

Alcott, Amos. Doctrine & Discipline of Human Culture. 27p. 1998. reprint ed. lib. bdg. 69.00 (*0-7812-4797-7*) Rprt Serv.

Alcott, Amos B. Concord Days. (Works of Amos Bronson Alcott). 1989. reprint ed. lib. bdg. 79.00 (*0-685-27409-8*) Rprt Serv.

— Concord Days. 276p. 1998. reprint ed. lib. bdg. 79.00 (*0-7812-4783-7*) Rprt Serv.

— Conversations with Children on the Gospel. (Works of Amos Bronson Alcott). 1989. reprint ed. lib. bdg. 79.00 (*0-7812-0300-7*) Rprt Serv.

— Doctrine & Discipline of Human Culture. (Works of Amos Bronson Alcott). 1989. reprint ed. lib. bdg. 79.00 (*0-685-27397-0*) Rprt Serv.

— Emerson (Anonymous) (Works of Amos Bronson Alcott). 1989. reprint ed. lib. bdg. 79.00 (*0-685-27411-X*) Rprt Serv.

— New Connecticut. (Works of Amos Bronson Alcott). 1989. reprint ed. lib. bdg. 79.00 (*0-685-27407-1*) Rprt Serv.

— Ralph Waldo Emerson. 1978. lib. bdg. 200.00 (*0-8490-7766-4*) Gordon Pr.

— Ralph Waldo Emerson. LC 68-24930. (American Biography Ser.: No. 32). 1969. reprint ed. lib. bdg. 75.00 (*0-8383-0908-9*) M S G Haskell Hse.

— Ralph Waldo Emerson. (Works of Amos Bronson Alcott). 1989. reprint ed. lib. bdg. 79.00 (*0-685-27413-6*) Rprt Serv.

— Ralph Waldo Emerson: An Estimate of His Character & Genius, in Prose & Verse. (BCL1-PS American Literature Ser.). 81p. 1992. reprint ed. lib. bdg. 59.00 (*0-7812-6705-6*) Rprt Serv.

— Sonnets & Canzonets. LC 72-86166. reprint ed. 27.50 (*0-404-00305-2*) AMS Pr.

— Sonnets & Canzonets. (Works of Amos Bronson Alcott). 1989. reprint ed. lib. bdg. 79.00 (*0-685-27406-3*) Rprt Serv.

— Sonnets & Canzonets. (BCL1-PS American Literature Ser.). 149p. 1992. reprint ed. lib. bdg. 69.00 (*0-7812-6666-1*) Rprt Serv.

— Table Talk. (Works of Amos Bronson Alcott). 1989. reprint ed. lib. bdg. 79.00 (*0-685-27408-X*) Rprt Serv.

— Table-Talk. (BCL1-PS American Literature Ser.). 178p. 1992. reprint ed. lib. bdg. 69.00 (*0-7812-6667-X*) Rprt Serv.

— Tables. (Works of Amos Bronson Alcott). 1989. reprint ed. lib. bdg. 79.00 (*0-685-27410-1*) Rprt Serv.

Alcott, James A. A History of Cowles Media Company. LC 98-15417. 1998. 29.95 (*0-86573-862-9*); pap. 19.95 (*0-86573-863-7*) Creat Pub Intl.

Alcott, Louisa May. Alternative Alcott. Showalter, Elaine, ed. & intro. by. (American Women Writers Ser.). 400p. 1988. pap. 16.00 (*0-8135-1272-7*) Rutgers U Pr.

— Aunt Jo's Scrap-bag. (Works of Louisa May Alcott). 1989. reprint ed. lib. bdg. 79.00 (*0-7812-1630-3*) Rprt Serv.

— Behind a Mask: The Unknown Thrillers of Louisa May Alcott. Stern, Madeleine B., ed. & intro. by. Date not set. lib. bdg. 22.95 (*0-88411-096-6*, Aeonian Pr) Amereon Ltd.

— Behind a Mask: The Unknown Thrillers of Louisa May Alcott. Stern, Madeleine B., ed. & intro. by. LC 97-165375. 320p. 1997. reprint ed. pap. 12.00 (*0-688-15132-9*, Quil) HarperTrade.

— Behind a Mask: The Unknown Thrillers of Louisa May Alcott, Vol. 1. Stern, Madeleine B., ed. & intro. by. 1995. 23.00 (*0-688-00338-9*, Wm Morrow) Morrow Avon.

Alcott, Louisa May. Diana & Persis. Elbert, Sarah, ed. LC 77-11663. (Individual Publications). (Illus.). 1978. lib. bdg. 18.95 (*0-405-10521-5*) Ayer.

Alcott, Louisa May. Eight Cousins. (J). Date not set. pap. 2.95 (*0-8167-0462-7*) Little.

— Eight Cousins. (Works of Louisa May Alcott). 1989. reprint ed. lib. bdg. 79.00 (*0-7812-1633-8*) Rprt Serv.

— Eight Cousins: Or the Aunt Hill. LC 95-39506. (Illus.). 260p. (J). (gr. 4-7). 1996. pap. 9.95 (*0-316-03086-4*) Little.

— The Feminist Alcott: Stories of a Woman's Power. Stern, Madeleine B., ed. & intro. by. 279p. 1996. text 47.50 (*1-55553-265-9*); pap. text 17.95 (*1-55553-266-7*) NE U Pr.

— Flower Fables. Shealy, Daniel, ed. (Illus.). 112p. (J). 1998. 22.00 (*0-9660933-0-5*) OKey-Doke.

— Flower Fables. (Works of Louisa May Alcott). 1989. reprint ed. lib. bdg. 79.00 (*0-7812-1624-9*) Rprt Serv.

— Freaks of Genius: Unknown Thrillers of Louisa May Alcott, 28. Shealy, Daniel et al, eds. LC 90-22398. (Contributions to the Study of Popular Culture Ser.: No. 28). 256p. 1991. 59.95 (*0-313-27627-7*, SKE, Greenwood Pr) Greenwood.

— From Jo March's Attic: Stories of Intrigue & Suspense. Stern, Madeleine B. & Shealy, Daniel, eds. (Illus.). 160p. 1993. text 24.95 (*1-55553-177-6*) NE U Pr.

— Hospital Sketches. LC 92-47062. 96p. 1989. reprint ed. pap. 7.95 (*0-918222-78-8*) Applewood.

— Hospital Sketches. (Works of Louisa May Alcott). 1989. reprint ed. lib. bdg. 79.00 (*0-7812-1625-7*) Rprt Serv.

— The Inheritance. Myerson, Joel & Shealy, Daniel, eds. LC 97-26241. 149p. 1998. pap. 10.95 (*0-14-043666-9*, Penguin Classics) Viking Penguin.

— The Inheritance. 192p. 1998. mass mkt. 5.99 (*0-14-027729-3*) Viking Penguin.

***Alcott, Louisa May.** Inheritance. (Illus.). (J). 1998. 11.34 (*0-606-18412-0*) Turtleback.

Alcott, Louisa May. The Inheritance. large type ed. LC 97-32441. 1997. 26.95 (*1-56895-505-7*) Wheeler Pub.

— Jack & Jill. 352p. Date not set. 25.95 (*0-8488-2671-X*) Amereon Ltd.

— Jack & Jill. (J). 1997. write for info. (*0-316-03778-8*) Little.

— Jack & Jill. (Illus.). 304p. (J). (gr. 4-6). 1999. pap. 8.95 (*0-316-03084-8*) Little.

— Jack & Jill. (Works of Louisa May Alcott). 1989. reprint ed. lib. bdg. 79.00 (*0-7812-1638-9*) Rprt Serv.

— Jo's Boys. (J). 1988. 23.95 (*0-8488-0411-2*) Amereon Ltd.

— Jo's Boys. 336p. 1995. mass mkt. 4.95 (*0-553-21449-7*) Bantam.

***Alcott, Louisa May.** Jo's Boys. LC 99-32233. (Children's Thrift Classics Ser.). (Illus.). 80p. (J). 1999. pap. 1.00 (*0-486-40789-6*) Dover.

Alcott, Louisa May. Jo's Boys. (Illus.). (YA). (gr. 5 up). 1996. pap. 4.99 (*0-14-036714-4*, Viking) Viking Penguin.

— Jo's Boys. (Works of Louisa May Alcott). (J). 1989. reprint ed. lib. bdg. 79.00 (*0-7812-1642-7*) Rprt Serv.

— Jo's Boys & How They Turned Out. LC 94-17447. 336p. (J). (gr. 4-6). 1994. pap. 7.95 (*0-316-03103-8*) Little.

— The Journals of Louisa May Alcott. Myerson, Joel et al, eds. (Illus.). 352p. 1989. 24.95 (*0-316-59362-1*) Little.

— The Journals of Louisa May Alcott. Myerson, Joel et al, eds. LC 97-20998. 400p. 1997. pap. 21.95 (*0-8203-1950-3*) U of Ga Pr.

— Little Men: Life at Plumfield with Jo's Boys. Date not set. 20.95 (*0-8488-1476-2*) Amereon Ltd.

— Little Men: Life at Plumfield with Jo's Boys. LC 94-17448. 288p. (J). (gr. 4-6). 1994. pap. 8.95 (*0-316-03104-6*) Little.

— Little Men: Life at Plumfield with Jo's Boys. LC 94-17448. (J). (gr. 7-10). 1994. 16.95 (*0-316-03108-9*) Little.

— Little Men: Life at Plumfield with Jo's Boys. 1986. mass mkt. 4.95 (*0-451-52275-3*, Sig Classics) NAL.

— Little Men: Life at Plumfield with Jo's Boys. (Classics for Young Readers Ser.). (Illus.). 608p. (YA). (gr. 5 up). 1995. pap. 4.99 (*0-14-036713-6*, PuffinBks) Peng Put Young Read.

— Little Men: Life at Plumfield with Jo's Boys. 384p. (J). (gr. 4-7). 1987. pap. 3.99 (*0-590-41279-5*, Apple Paperbacks) Scholastic Inc.

— Little Men: Life at Plumfield with Jo's Boys. (J). 1997. pap. 2.95 (*0-8167-1471-1*) Troll Communs.

— Little Men: Life at Plumfield with Jo's Boys. (Puffin Classics). (J). 1994. 9.09 (*0-606-07797-9*, Pub. by Turtleback) Demco.

— Little Men: Life at Plumfield with Jo's Boys. large type ed. LC 95-33070. 460p. (J). 1995. 23.95 (*0-7838-1468-2*, G K Hall Lrg Type) Mac Lib Ref.

— Little Men: Life at Plumfield with Jo's Boys. (J). 1983. reprint ed. lib. bdg. 18.95 (*0-89966-409-1*) Buccaneer Bks.

— Little Men: Life at Plumfield with Jo's Boys. (Works of Louisa May Alcott). (J). 1989. reprint ed. lib. bdg. 79.00 (*0-7812-1629-X*) Rprt Serv.

— Little Women. (Keepsake Collection Bks.). (J). 1998. boxed set 3.99 (*1-57145-101-3*, Thunder Bay) Advantage Pubs.

***Alcott, Louisa May.** Little Women. (Classics Ser.). 704p. (J). (gr. 4-7). 2000. pap. 5.99 (*0-689-83531-0*) Aladdin.

Alcott, Louisa May. Little Women. Date not set. lib. bdg. 19.95 (*0-614-25286-5*) Amereon Ltd.

— Little Women. (Andre Deutsch Classics). 264p. (J). (gr. 5-8). 1996. 9.95 (*0-233-99040-2*, Pub. by Andre Deutsch) Trafalgar.

— Little Women. (Read-Along Ser.). (YA). 1994. pap., student ed. 34.95 incl. audio (*0-88432-965-8*, S23935) Audio-Forum.

— Little Women. 480p. (YA). 1983. mass mkt. 3.95 (*0-553-21275-3*, Bantam Classics) Bantam.

— Little Women. (Young Reader's Christian Library). (Illus.). 192p. (J). (gr. 3-7). 1998. pap. 1.39 (*1-57748-229-8*) Barbour Pub.

***Alcott, Louisa May.** Little Women. Gerver, Jane E., ed. LC 99-14752. (Eyewitness Classics Ser.). 64p. (gr. 2). 1999. 14.95 (*0-7894-4767-3*) DK Pub Inc.

— Little Women. LC 99-48534. (Juvenile Classics). (Illus.). 608p. (J). 2000. pap. 3.00 (*0-486-41023-4*) Dover.

Alcott, Louisa May. Little Women. 93p. 1941. pap. 5.50 (*0-87129-320-X*, L27) Dramatic Pub.

— Little Women. 1997. pap. 4.50 (*1-57514-326-7*, 1051) Encore Perform Pub.

— Little Women. (Classic Collection). 1997. 15.99 (*1-56179-552-6*) Focus Family.

— Little Women. (Illus.). 192p. (J). 2.98 (*1-56156-371-4*) Kidsbks.

— Little Women. (Illus.). 524p. (YA). (gr. 7 up). 1968. 19.95 (*0-316-03095-3*) Little.

— Little Women. (Illus.). (J). (gr. 3-7). 1968. 19.95 (*0-685-47121-7*) Little.

— Little Women. (English As a Second Language Bk.). 1981. pap. text 4.46 (*0-582-53489-5*) Longman.

— Little Women. (Modern Library College Editions). 603p. (C). 1983. pap. 8.44 (*0-07-554389-3*) McGraw.

— Little Women. (J). 1981. pap. 6.00 (*0-685-06605-3*) Modern Lib NY.

— Little Women. (Little Brown Notebooks). 1998. 9.99 (*1-897954-77-8*, Pub. by Mus Quilts Pub) Sterling.

— Little Women. write for info. (*0-614-22111-0*, Sig Classics) NAL.

— Little Women. 480p. (J). (gr. 3 up). 1983. mass mkt. 3.95 (*0-451-52341-5*, Sig Classics) NAL.

— Little Women, 4 vols. 40.00 (*0-614-30531-4*) NAVH.

— Little Women. Bassett, Jennifer, ed. (Illus.). 78p. 1995. pap. text 5.95 (*0-19-422756-1*) OUP.

— Little Women. Alderson, Valerie, ed. & intro. by. (Oxford World's Classics Ser.). 526p. 1998. pap. 6.95 (*0-19-283434-7*) OUP.

— Little Women. 1994. mass mkt. 5.99 (*0-671-51764-3*) PB.

***Alcott, Louisa May.** Little Women. 1998. pap. 7.00 (*0-582-40194-1*) Pearson Educ.

Alcott, Louisa May. Little Women. 32p. (J). (ps-3). 1994. pap. 2.95 (*0-590-22537-5*, PuffinBks) Peng Put Young Read.

— Little Women. (Puffin Classics Ser.). (Illus.). 669p. (J). (gr. 5-9). 1997. pap. 6.99 (*0-14-038022-1*, PuffinBks) Peng Put Young Read.

— Little Women. Vogel, Malvina, ed. (Great Illustrated Classics Ser.: Vol. 4). (Illus.). 240p. (J). (gr. 3-6). 1989. 9.95 (*0-86611-955-8*) Playmore Inc.

— Little Women. LC 93-38237. (Step into Classics Ser.). 108p. (J). (gr. 4-7). 1994. pap. 3.99 (*0-679-86175-0*, Pub. by Random Bks Yng Read) Random.

— Little Women. 510p. (J). (gr. 4-7). 1994. pap. 3.95 (*0-590-20350-9*) Random Hse Value.

— Little Women. (Classics Ser.). 368p. (YA). (gr. 5 up). 1995. pap. 3.99 (*0-14-036668-7*) Random Hse Value.

— Little Women. 400p. (J). 1998. 5.99 (*0-517-18954-2*) Random Hse Value.

***Alcott, Louisa May.** Little Women. (Giant Classics). 688p. (YA). 2000. 8.98 (*0-7624-0565-1*, Courage) Running Pr.

Alcott, Louisa May. Little Women. (Illustrated Classics Ser.). (J). 1988. 2.98 (*0-671-09222-7*) S&S Trade.

— Little Women. (YA). 1996. 37.50 (*0-87557-135-2*) Saphrograph.

***Alcott, Louisa May.** Little Women. 608p. (gr. 4-7). 2000. pap. 6.99 (*0-439-10136-0*) Scholastic Inc.

Alcott, Louisa May. Little Women. (Little Brown Notebook Ser.). (Illus.). 256p. 1995. 6.95 (*0-8069-3975-3*) Sterling.

— Little Women. 480p. 1994. pap. 2.50 (*0-8125-2333-4*, Pub. by Tor Bks) St Martin.

— Little Women. 1997. pap. 4.95 (*0-89375-707-1*) Troll Communs.

— Little Women. 1962. 10.10 (*0-606-00974-4*, Pub. by Turtleback) Demco.

— Little Women. LC 93-38237. (Bullseye Step into Classics Ser.). 1994. 9.09 (*0-606-09566-7*, Pub. by Turtleback) Demco.

— Little Women. Showalter, Elaine, ed. & intro. by. 608p. (J). 1989. pap. 7.95 (*0-14-039069-3*, Penguin Classics) Viking Penguin.

— Little Women. (Children's Library). 1998. pap. 3.95 (*1-85326-116-5*, 1165WW, Pub. by Wrdsworth Edits) NTC Contemp Pub Co.

— Little Women. (J). 1940. 6.00 (*0-87602-150-X*) Anchorage.

— Little Women. (YA). 1994. pap. 3.99 (*0-671-51902-6*, Minstrel Bks) PB.

— Little Women. abr. ed. 256p. (J). (gr. 4-7). 1986. pap. 4.50 (*0-590-43797-6*, Apple Classics) Scholastic Inc.

— Little Women. abr. large type ed. (Illus.). 32p. (J). (gr. k up). 1995. pap. 14.95 (*1-886201-05-6*) Nana Banana.

— Little Women. adapted ed. (Living Classics Ser.). (Illus.). 32p. (J). (gr. 3-7). 1997. 14.95 (*0-7641-7047-3*) Barron.

— Little Women. deluxe ed. (Illus.). 656p. (J). (gr. 4 up). 1947. 18.99 (*0-448-06019-1*, G & D) Peng Put Young Read.

— Little Women. deluxe ed. LC 97-60825. (Illus.). 288p. (J). 1997. pap. 16.99 (*0-670-87706-9*, Viking Child) Peng Put Young Read.

— Little Women. large type ed. 665p. 1998. lib. bdg. 25.00 (*0-939495-51-1*) North Bks.

— Little Women. large type ed. 336p. (J). 1987. 27.99 (*0-7089-8384-7*, Charnwood) Ulverscroft.

— Little Women. (YA). (gr. 6 up). 1983. reprint ed. lib. bdg. 18.95 (*0-89966-408-3*) Buccaneer Bks.

— Little Women. LC 96-39462. (Children's Thrift Classics Ser.). (Illus.). 96p. (J). 1997. reprint ed. pap. text 1.00 (*0-486-29634-2*) Dover.

— Little Women. (Illus.). 352p. (J). 1993. reprint ed. 25.00 (*0-88363-203-9*) H L Levin.

— Little Women. 559p. (J). 1998. reprint ed. lib. bdg. 24.00 (*1-58287-046-2*) North Bks.

— Little Women. (Works of Louisa May Alcott). (J). 1989. reprint ed. lib. bdg. 79.00 (*0-7812-1627-3*) Rprt Serv.

***Alcott, Louisa May.** Little Women. unabridged ed. (Wordsworth Classics). (YA). (gr. 6-12). 1998. 5.27 (*0-89061-116-5*, R1165WW, Jamestwn Pub) NTC Contemp Pub Co.

Alcott, Louisa May. Little Women. 2nd ed. (Illus.). 62p. 1993. pap. text 5.95 (*0-19-585271-0*) OUP.

— Little Women: Adapted for the Stage. (Illus.). 95p. 1995. pap. 4.00 (*0-88680-412-4*, 412-4) I E Clark.

— Little Women: Book & Charm Keepsake. 48p. (J). (gr. 4-7). 1994. 12.95 (*0-590-22538-3*) Scholastic Inc.

— Little Women: Meg, Joe, Beth, & Amy. (Great Stories Ser.). (Illus.). 526p. (J). 1999. pap. 9.99 (*1-56179-744-8*) Focus Family.

— Little Women: Or Meg, Jo, Beth & Amy. LC 93-18943. (Little Classics Ser.). (Illus.). 308p. (J). (gr. 4-8). 1995. 15.95 (*0-8050-2767-X*, Bks Young Read) H Holt & Co.

— Little Women: Or Meg, Jo, Beth & Amy. LC 94-5865. (Everyman's Library of Children's Classics). 384p. (J). 1994. 14.95 (*0-679-43642-1*, Evrymans Lib Childs) Knopf.

— Little Women: Or Meg, Jo, Beth & Amy. LC 94-17444. 502p. (J). (gr. 4-6). 1994. 18.95 (*0-316-03107-0*) Little.

— Little Women: Or Meg, Jo, Beth & Amy. LC 94-17444. 502p. (J). (gr. 7-10). 1994. pap. 9.95 (*0-316-03105-4*) Little.

— Little Women & Good Wives. 464p. 1994. reprint ed. pap. text 5.95 (*0-460-87141-2*, Everyman's Classic Lib) Tuttle Pubng.

— Little Women & Little Men. 1995. 29.95 (*0-679-44610-9*, Evrymans Lib Childs) Knopf.

***Alcott, Louisa May.** Little Women Book & Charm. (J). 2001. write for info. (*0-694-01527-X*, HarpFestival) HarpC Child Bks.

Alcott, Louisa May. Little Women; Little Men; Jo's Boys. (J). (gr. 4-6). 1994. pap. text, boxed set 25.85 (*0-316-03106-2*) Little.

— A Long Fatal Love Chase. 368p. 1996. mass mkt. 6.99 (*0-440-22301-6*) Dell.

— A Long Fatal Love Chase. large type ed. 1997. pap. 23.95 (*0-7862-0623-3*) Thorndike Pr.

— The Lost Stories of Louisa May Alcott. Shealy, Daniel, ed. LC 95-6897. 1995. 10.95 (*0-8065-1654-2*) Carol Pub Group.

— The Lost Stories of Louisa May Alcott, Set. unabridged ed. Stern, Madeleine B. et al, eds. 1995. 16.95 incl. audio (*1-882071-53-0*, 393003, Pub. by B&B Audio) Lndmrk Audiobks.

***Alcott, Louisa May.** Louisa May Alcott. LC 99-57115. (Portable Library). 704p. 2000. pap. 16.95 (*0-14-027574-6*, Penguin Bks) Viking Penguin.

Alcott, Louisa May. Louisa May Alcott: An Intimate Anthology. LC 97-16454. 432p. 1997. 18.00 (*0-385-48722-3*) Doubleday.

Alcott, Louisa May. Louisa May Alcott: Her Girlhood Diary. Ryan, Cary, ed. LC 93-22343. (Illus.). 56p. (YA). (gr. 5 up). 1997. 14.95 (*0-8167-3139-X*) BrdgeWater.

Alcott, Louisa May. Louisa May Alcott: Her Girlhood Diary. Ryan, Cary, ed. LC 93-22343. (Illus.). 56p. (YA). (gr. 5 up). 1995. pap. 4.95 (*0-8167-3150-0*, Troll Medallion) Troll Communs.

— Louisa May Alcott: Her Girlhood Diary. 1993. 10.15 (*0-606-07811-8*, Pub. by Turtleback) Demco.

Alcott, Louisa May. Louisa May Alcott: Her Life, Letters & Journals. (American Biography Ser.). 404p. 1991. reprint ed. lib. bdg. 89.00 (*0-7812-8009-5*) Rprt Serv.

Alcott, Louisa May. Louisa May Alcott on Race, Sex, & Slavery. Elbert, Sarah, ed. & intro. by. LC 96-48085. (Illus.). 1997. text 42.50 (*1-55553-308-6*); pap. text 15.95 (*1-55553-307-8*) NE U Pr.

— Louisa May Alcott Unmasked: Collected Thrillers. Stern, Madeleine B., ed. & intro. by. (Illus.). 780p. 1995. text 55.00 (*1-55553-225-X*); pap. text 24.95 (*1-55553-226-8*) NE U Pr.

— Louisa May Alcott Unmasked: Collected Thrillers, Set. unabridged ed. Stern, Madeleine B., ed. & intro. by. 1996. 16.95 incl. audio (*1-882071-63-8*, 393916, Pub. by B&B Audio) Lndmrk Audiobks.

Alcott, Louisa May. Louisa May Alcott's Fairy Tales & Fantasy Stories. Shealy, Daniel, ed. LC 91-43144. (Illus.). 432p. (J). 1992. pap. 24.95 (*0-87049-758-8*) U of Tenn Pr.

Alcott, Louisa May. Louisa May Alcott's Little Women at Christmas. LC 99-13474. (J). 1999. 14.95 (*0-8249-4161-6*) Ideals.

— Louisa's Wonder Book: An Unknown Alcott Juvenile. Stern, Madeline B., ed. LC 76-358119. (Clarke Historical Press Juvenile Ser.: No. 1). Orig. Title: Will's Wonder Book. (Illus.). (J). 1975. reprint ed. 7.50 (*0-916699-08-0*) CMU Clarke Hist Lib.

— Lulu's Library. (Works of Louisa May Alcott). 1989. reprint ed. lib. bdg. 79.00 (*0-7812-1641-9*) Rprt Serv.

— A Marble Woman: Unknown Thrillers of Louisa May Alcott. Stern, Madeleine B., ed. Orig. Title: Plots & Counterplots. 320p. 1995. reprint ed. pap. 11.00 (*0-380-72677-7*, Avon Bks) Morrow Avon.

— Marmee's Surprise: A Little Women Story. LC 95-30266. (Step into Reading Ser.: A Step 3 Book). (Illus.). (J). (gr. 2-3). 1997. pap. 3.99 (*0-679-87579-4*, Pub. by Random Bks Yng Read); lib. bdg. 11.99 (*0-679-97579-9*, Pub. by Random Bks Yng Read) Random.

Alcott, Louisa May. Marmee's Surprise: A Little Women Story. (Step into Reading Ser.: A Step 3 Book). (J). (gr. 2-3). 1997. 9.19 (*0-606-12765-8*, Pub. by Turtleback) Demco.

Alcott, Louisa May. Modern Magic. Stern, Madeleine B., ed. & intro. by. Date not set. lib. bdg. 23.95 (*0-8488-1881-4*) Amereon Ltd.

— Modern Magic. LC 95-2830. 294p. 1995. 14.50 (*0-679-60171-6*) Modern Lib NY.

— A Modern Mephistopheles. (J). Date not set. lib. bdg. 16.95 (*0-8488-0412-0*) Amereon Ltd.

— A Modern Mephistopheles. LC 87-8026. 437p. 1987. pap. 17.95 (*0-275-92780-6*, B2780, Praeger Pubs) Greenwood.

— A Modern Mephistopheles. (Works of Louisa May Alcott). 1989. reprint ed. lib. bdg. 79.00 (*0-7812-1636-2*) Rprt Serv.

— A Modern Mephistopheles: And, Taming a Tartar. Stern, Madeleine B., ed. & intro. by. LC 87-8026. 437p. 1987. 59.95 (*0-275-92754-7*, C2754, Praeger Pubs) Greenwood.

Alcott, Louisa May. Moods. Elbert, Sarah, ed. LC 90-48069. (American Women Writers Ser.). 284p. (C). 1991. pap. text 16.00 (*0-8135-1670-6*) Rutgers U Pr.

— Moods. (Works of Louisa May Alcott). 1989. reprint ed. lib. bdg. 79.00 (*0-7812-1626-5*) Rprt Serv.

— Mujercitas. (SPA., Illus.). (J). 1998. pap. 6.95 (*84-01-46257-6*) Plaza.

Alcott, Louisa May. An Old-Fashioned Girl. LC 96-29254. 352p. (J). (gr. 4-6). 1997. pap. 9.95 (*0-316-03775-3*) Little.

— An Old-Fashioned Girl. LC 96-29254. (J). 1999. 25.01 (*0-316-03809-1*) Little.

— An Old-Fashioned Girl. (J). 1997. pap. 2.95 (*0-8167-1462-2*) Troll Communs.

Alcott, Louisa May. An Old-Fashioned Girl. (Puffin Classics). (J). 1996. 10.09 (*0-606-11700-8*, Pub. by Turtleback) Demco.

Alcott, Louisa May. An Old-Fashioned Girl. (Illus.). 368p. (YA). (gr. 5-9). 1996. pap. 5.99 (*0-14-037449-3*) Viking Penguin.

— An Old-Fashioned Girl. (Works of Louisa May Alcott). 1989. reprint ed. lib. bdg. 79.00 (*0-7812-1628-1*) Rprt Serv.

***Alcott, Louisa May.** An Old-Fashioned Girl, Vol. 1. LC 98-36885. (Chapter Book Charmers Ser.). 80p. (J). (gr. 2-5). 1999. 2.99 (*0-694-01287-4*, HarpFestival) HarpC Child Bks.

Alcott, Louisa May. An Old-Fashioned Thanksgiving. LC 93-36951. 62p. 1990. pap. 5.95 (*1-55709-135-8*) Applewood.

— An Old-Fashioned Thanksgiving. LC 93-20352. (Illus.). 40p. (J). (gr. k-3). 1993. 13.95 (*0-8249-8620-2*, Ideals Child) Hambleton-Hill.

— An Old-Fashioned Thanksgiving. LC 73-15698. (Illus.). 72p. (J). (gr. 4-6). 1974. 12.95 (*0-397-31515-5*) HarpC Child Bks.

— An Old-Fashioned Thanksgiving. LC 89-1908. (Illus.). 32p. (J). (gr. 4-6). 1989. lib. bdg. 14.95 (*0-8234-0772-1*) Holiday.

— An Old-Fashioned Thanksgiving. LC 93-20352. (Illus.). 40p. (J). (gr. k-3). 1995. reprint ed. pap., per. 5.95 (*1-57102-053-5*, Ideals Child) Hambleton-Hill.

— On Picket Duty & Other Tales. 1988. reprint ed. lib. bdg. 49.00 (*0-7812-0078-4*) Rprt Serv.

***Alcott, Louisa May. The Poems of Louisa May Alcott. LC 99-51490. (American Classics Ser.). 147p. 2000. pap. 15.95 (*0-9655309-5-7*) Ironweed Pr.**
The Poems of Louisa May Alcott is the first comprehensive volume of her poems, many of which are collected here for the first time. This book will delight & surprise those who know Louisa May Alcott principally through her fiction. All Ironweed American Classics books are printed on acid-free paper. Available to trade via Baker & Taylor, Brodart, & Ingram. *Publisher Paid Annotation.*

Alcott, Louisa May. Proverb Stories. (Works of Louisa May Alcott). 1989. reprint ed. lib. bdg. 79.00 (*0-7812-1639-7*) Rprt Serv.

— Quatre Filles du Docteur March. (Folio - Junior Ser.: No. 413). (FRE., Illus.). (J). (gr. 5-10). 1993. 10.95 (*2-07-033413-9*) Schoenhof.

***Alcott, Louisa May.** Quiet Little Woman: Family & Children's Edition. 2000. 14.99 (*1-56292-771-X*) Honor Bks OK.

Alcott, Louisa May. The Quiet Little Women: A Christmas Story. (Illus.). 128p. 1999. 14.99 (*1-56292-616-0*) Honor Bks OK.

— Rose in Bloom. 354p. Date not set. 25.95 (*0-8488-2198-X*) Amereon Ltd.

— Rose in Bloom. (Illus.). (J). (gr. 7 up). 1976. 19.95 (*0-316-03098-8*) Little.

— Rose in Bloom. (Puffin Classics Ser.). (Illus.). 326p. (YA). (gr. 5 up). 1995. pap. 4.99 (*0-14-037451-5*, PuffinBks) Peng Put Young Read.

— Rose in Bloom. (Works of Louisa May Alcott). 1989. reprint ed. lib. bdg. 79.00 (*0-7812-1634-6*) Rprt Serv.

— Rose in Bloom: A Sequel to Eight Cousins. LC 95-19929. 336p. (J). (gr. 4-6). 1995. pap. 9.95 (*0-316-03089-9*) Little.

— The Selected Letters of Louisa May Alcott. Myerson, Joel et al, eds. LC 95-8400. 1995. pap. 19.95 (*0-8203-1740-3*) U of Ga Pr.

— Shawl Straps. (Works of Louisa May Alcott). 1989. reprint ed. lib. bdg. 79.00 (*0-7812-1631-1*) Rprt Serv.

— Short Stories. unabridged ed. (Thrift Editions Ser.). 64p. 1996. pap. text 1.00 (*0-486-29063-8*) Dover.

— Silver Pitchers & Other Stories. (Works of Louisa May Alcott). 1989. reprint ed. lib. bdg. 79.00 (*0-7812-1635-4*) Rprt Serv.

***Alcott, Louisa May.** The Sketches of Louisa May Alcott. (Ironweed American Classics Ser.). 273p. 2001. pap. 22.95 (*0-9655309-8-1*) Ironweed Pr.

Alcott, Louisa May. Spinning Wheel Stories. (Works of Louisa May Alcott). 1989. reprint ed. lib. bdg. 79.00 (*0-7812-1640-0*) Rprt Serv.

— Taming a Tartar. 88p. Date not set. 16.95 (*0-8488-2646-9*) Amereon Ltd.

— Transcendental Wild Oats: And Excerpts from the Fruitlands Diary. LC 76-355426. 1995. pap. text 6.95 (*1-55832-039-3*) Harvard Common Pr.

— Under the Lilacs. (Illus.). 272p. (J). (gr. 4-6). 1996. pap. 9.95 (*0-316-03087-2*) Little.

— Under the Lilacs. (J). 1997. pap. 2.95 (*0-8167-1472-X*) Troll Communs.

— Under the Lilacs. (Works of Louisa May Alcott). 1989. reprint ed. lib. bdg. 79.00 (*0-7812-1637-0*) Rprt Serv.

— Work. (Works of Louisa May Alcott). 1989. reprint ed. lib. bdg. 79.00 (*0-7812-1632-X*) Rprt Serv.

— Work: A Story of Experience. Kasson, Joy S., ed. & intro. by. LC 93-43988. 320p. 1994. pap. 11.95 (*0-14-039091-X*, Penguin Classics) Viking Penguin.

— Work: A Story of Experience. Hardwick, Elizabeth, ed. LC 76-51662. (Rediscovered Fiction by American Women Ser.). (Illus.). 1977. reprint ed. lib. bdg. 29.95 (*0-405-10042-6*) Ayer.

— Work: A Story of Experience. 1976. reprint ed. 39.00 (*0-403-05873-2*, Regency) Scholarly.

— The Works of Louisa May Alcott. (J). (gr. 5-6). 40.95 (*0-88411-173-3*) Amereon Ltd.

— The Works of Louisa May Alcott, 1832-1888, Set. 1987. reprint ed. lib. bdg. 63.00 (*0-685-18574-5*) Rprt Serv.

Alcott, Louisa May & Blaisdell, Robert. Little Men: Life at Plumfield with Jo's Boys. LC 97-11716. (Children's Thrift Classics Ser.). (Illus.). (J). 1997. pap. 1.00 (*0-486-29805-1*) Dover.

Alcott, Louisa May & Longest, David. Little Women of Orchard House. 116p. 1998. pap. 5.50 (*0-87129-857-0*, L95) Dramatic Pub.

Alcott, Louisa May & Thorne, Jenny. Little Women. LC 78-2919. (Illustrated Classics). (J). 1978. write for info. (*0-8393-6210-2*) Raintree Steck-V.

Alcott, Louisa May, jt. auth. see Emerson, Charlotte.

Alcott, Louisa May, jt. auth. see Keyser, Elizabeth Lennox.

Alcott, Louisa May, jt. auth. see Pfeffer, Susan Beth.

Alcott, Louisa May, jt. auth. see Tierney, Tom.

Alcott, Monique. Le Journal de Delphine. (Serie Rouge). 65p. (C). 1994. pap. 7.50 (*0-521-44979-0*) Cambridge U Pr.

Alcott, Ron. Building Classic Salmon Flies. Richardson, Arleigh D., 3rd, ed. LC 95-18384. (Illus.). 200p. 1995. 35.00 (*0-88150-314-2*, Pub. by Countryman) Norton.

Alcott, Sarah. Young Amelia Earhart: A Dream to Fly. LC 91-24974. (Illus.). 32p. (J). (gr. k-2). 1997. pap. 3.50 (*0-8167-2529-2*) Troll Communs.

— Young Clara Barton: Battlefield Nurse. LC 95-8110. (First-Start Biography Ser.). (Illus.). 32p. (J). (gr. k-2). 1995. pap. text 3.50 (*0-8167-3767-3*) Troll Communs.

— Young Clara Barton: Battlefield Nurse. LC 95-8110. (First-Start Biography Ser.). (Illus.). 32p. (J). (gr. k-2). 1997. lib. bdg. 17.25 (*0-8167-3766-5*) Troll Communs.

Alcott, William A. Confessions of a School Master. LC 77-89145. (American Education: Its Men, Institutions, & Ideas. Series 2). 1974. reprint ed. 19.95 (*0-405-01381-7*) Ayer.

— The Physiology of Marriage. LC 79-180551. (Medicine & Society in America Ser.). 266p. 1972. reprint ed. 20.95 (*0-405-03931-X*) Ayer.

— The Works of William Andrus Alcott, 1798-1859, Set. 1987. reprint ed. lib. bdg. 500.00 (*0-685-18575-3*) Rprt Serv.

— The Young Husband: or Duties of Man in the Marriage Relation. LC 70-169368. (Family in America Ser.). (Illus.). 392p. 1976. reprint ed. 25.95 (*0-405-03844-5*) Ayer.

— The Young Wife, or Duties of Woman in the Marriage Relation. LC 73-169369. (Family in America Ser.). (Illus.). 382p. 1974. reprint ed. 25.95 (*0-405-03845-3*) Ayer.

Alcouffe, Daniel & Durand, Jannic. Louvre, Objets d'Art. (Illus.). 128p. 1995. 30.00 (*0-302-00675-3*) Scala Books.

Alcouffe, R., et al. Monte-Carlo Methods & Applications in Neutronics, Photonics & Statistical Physics. (Lecture Notes in Physics Ser.: Vol. 240). viii, 483p. 1985. 53.95 (*0-387-16070-1*) Spr-Verlag.

Alcover, Aina, tr. see Thoele, Sue P.

Alcover, Amiris. Medicina y Sentido Comun. LC 87-83264. (Coleccion Textos). (SPA.). 205p. (Orig.). 1988. pap. 9.95 (*0-89729-470-X*) Ediciones.

Alcover, Anthony M., et al. Diccionari Catala Valencia Balear: Obra Completa, 10 vols. (CAT.). 1985. 1495.00 (*0-8288-2080-5*, S31549) Fr & Eur.

Alcover, Norbert. Eight Day Retreat with St. Ignatius of Loyola. 254p. (C). 1996. pap. 39.95 (*0-85439-388-9*, Pub. by St Paul Pubns) St Mut.

Alcoze, Thom. Multiculturalism in Mathematics, Science, & Technology: Reading & Activities. pap. 32.00 (*0-201-29595-4*) Addison-Wesley.

***Alcraft, Rob.** Cambodia. LC 98-44398. (Visit to Ser.). 32p. (J). 1999. lib. bdg. write for info. (*1-57572-845-1*) Heinemann Lib.

— Chemical Disasters. LC 99-34942. (World's Worst Ser.). 1999. lib. bdg. write for info. (*1-57572-987-3*) Heinemann Lib.

Alcraft, Rob. Germany. LC 99-18086. (A Visit to Ser.). 1999. write for info. (*1-57572-852-4*) Heinemann Lib.

— Mexico. LC 98-37737. (Visit to Ser.). (Illus.). 32p. (J). 1999. lib. bdg. 13.95 (*1-57572-848-6*) Heinemann Lib.

***Alcraft, Rob.** Nuclear Disasters. LC 99-27879. (World's Worst Ser.). 1999. lib. bdg. write for info. (*1-57572-989-X*) Heinemann Lib.

— Oil Disasters. LC 99-27878. (World's Worst Ser.). 1999. lib. bdg. write for info. (*1-57572-990-3*) Heinemann Lib.

— Shipping Disasters. LC 99-34941. (World's Worst Ser.). 1999. lib. bdg. write for info. (*1-57572-991-1*) Heinemann Lib.

A

A

— Space Disasters. LC 99-34943. 1999. write for info. (*1-57572-992-X*) Heinemann Lib.
— Zoom City (Intermediate) LC 98-11592. (Illus.). 32p. (J). (gr. 3-8). 1998. 17.95 (*1-57572-717-X*) Heinemann Lib.
***Alcraft, Rob & Spilsbury, Louise.** Fire Disasters. LC 99-37350. (World's Worst Ser.). 1999. lib. bdg. write for info. (*1-57572-988-1*) Heinemann Lib.
Alcraft, Rob & Sprague, Sean. Mexico. LC 95-52957. (Worldfocus Ser.). (J). 1998. 18.50 (*1-57572-078-7*) Heinemann Lib.
ALCTS, Acquisition of Library Materials Staff & Hamilton, Marsha J. Guide to Preservation in Acquisition Processing. LC 92-45636. (Acquisitions Guidelines Ser.: No. 8). 34p. (C). 1993. pap. text 10.00 (*0-8389-0611-7*) ALA.
Alcuaz, Marie De, see De Alcuaz, Marie.
Alcuin. The Bishops, Kings & Saints of York. Godman, Peter, ed. (Oxford Medieval Texts Ser.). 332p. 1983. text 89.00 (*0-19-822262-9*) OUP.
***Alcuins, Flaccus Albinus, tr.** The Book of Jasher: With Testimonies & Notes. 73p. 1998. pap. 5.00 (*0-944379-20-6*) CPA Bk Pub.
Alcuinus, Flaccus A., tr. The Book of Jasher: One of the Sacred Books of the Bible Long Lost or Undiscovered. 90p. 1993. reprint ed. pap. 14.95 (*1-56459-340-1*) Kessinger Pub.
Alcyon, Clara. Hearts & Gizzards: Motherhood in Motion. 120p. 1998. pap. 15.95 (*1-58244-003-4*) Rutledge Bks.
Alcyone, pseud. At the Feet of the Master. 1999. 2.75 (*81-7059-125-2*) Theos Pub Hse.
— At the Feet of the Master. reprint ed. pap. text 5.00 (*0-911662-17-0*) Yoga.
Alda, Arlene. Arlene Alda's ABC: What Do You See? LC 93-24999. (Illus.). 32p. (J). (ps-k). 1993. reprint ed. 12.95 (*1-883672-01-5*) Tricycle Pr.
— Arlene Alda's 1 2 3: What Do You See? LC 98-5966. (Illus.). 24p. (J). (ps-k). 1998. 12.95 (*1-883672-71-6*) Tricycle Pr.
— Hurry Granny Annie. LC 99-11180. (Illus.). 32p. (J). (ps-2). 1999. 14.95 (*1-883672-72-4*) Tricycle Pr.
Alda, Frances. Men, Women & Tenors. LC 72-107790. (Select Bibliographies Reprint Ser.). 1977. 29.95 (*0-8369-5174-3*) Ayer.
— Men, Women & Tenors. LC 75-149653. reprint ed. 32.50 (*0-404-00306-0*) AMS Pr.
— Men, Women & Tenors. (Music Book Index Ser.). 307p. 1992. reprint ed. lib. bdg. 89.00 (*0-7812-9473-8*) Rprt Serv.
***Aldag, Ramon J. & Antonioni, David.** Mission Values & Leadership Styles in Credit Unions. 90p. 1999. pap. 100.00 (*1-880572-42-7*, 1752-54) Filene Res.
Aldag, Ramon J. & Stearns, Timothy M. Management. (SWC-Management). (C). 1987. mass mkt. 47.00 (*0-538-07702-6*, G70) S-W Pub.
Aldag, Ramon J., jt. auth. see Grube, Jean A.
Aldag, Raymond & Joseph, Buck. NYT Leadership & Vision: 25 Keys to Motivation. LC 99-27688. 104p. 1999. pap. 12.95 (*0-86730-780-3*) Lebhar Friedman.
Aldama, A. A., et al, eds. Computational Methods in Water Resources XI Vol. 1: Computational Methods in Surface Flow & Transport Problems. LC 96-8526. 752p. 1996. 277.00 (*1-85312-477-X*, 477X) Computational Mech MA.
— Computational Methods in Water Resources XI Vol. 2: Computational Methods in Subsurface Flow & Transport Problems. LC 96-85276. 520p. 1996. 217.00 (*1-85312-487-7*, 4877) Computational Mech MA.
Aldama, A. A. & Aparicio, J., eds. Computational Methods in Water Resources XI, 2 vols., Set. LC 96-85276. (Computational Methods in Water Resources Ser.: Vol. 11). 1272p. 1996. 387.00 (*1-85312-488-5*, 488-5) Computational Mech MA.
Aldama, A. M. De, see De Aldama, A. M.
Aldama, Antonio M. De, see De Aldama, Antonio M.
Aldan, Daisy. The Annihilation of the Cathares: Thirteenth Century Holocaust. 1989. pap. 4.95 (*0-913152-50-1*) Folder Edns.
— Between High Tides: Poems. (C). 1978. pap. 9.95 (*0-913152-00-5*) Folder Edns.
— Breakthrough. 1971. lib. bdg. 12.95 (*0-913152-02-1*) Folder Edns.
— Foundation Stone Meditation by Rudolf Steiner. 1981. pap. 2.50 (*0-916786-53-6*, Saint George Pubns) R Steiner Col.
— A Golden Story: Novella. (C). 1979. pap. 9.95 (*0-913152-06-4*) Folder Edns.
— In Passage. LC 87-71465. 136p. 1987. pap. 9.95 (*0-913152-10-2*); lib. bdg. 19.95 (*0-913152-09-9*) Folder Edns.
— Or Learn to Walk on Water: Poems by Daisy Aldan. (Illus.). 1971. 4.50 (*0-913152-15-3*) Folder Edns.
— Poetry & Consciousness. 1985p. 1985. pap. 3.50 (*0-913152-16-1*) Folder Edns.
— Shakespeare & Spectator Consciousness. 1987. pap. 4.50 (*0-913152-18-8*) Folder Edns.
— Stones: Poems by Daisy Aldan. (Illus.). 1973. 5.95 (*0-913152-20-X*) Folder Edns.
— Verses for the Zodiac. (Illus.). 1975. 12.95 (*0-913152-23-4*); pap. 5.95 (*0-913152-22-6*) Folder Edns.
Aldan, Daisy, tr. see Steffen, Albert.
Aldan, Daisy, tr. see Steiner, Rudolf.
Aldan, Daisy, tr. see Witzenman, Herbert.
Aldan, Daisy, tr. & reader see Mallarme, Stephane.
Aldana, jt. auth. see Bishop.
Aldana, Jacquelyn. The 15-Minute Miracle. Masters, Laurie, ed. LC 97-94033. (Illus.). 160p. 1998. pap. 16.95 (*0-9656741-7-7*, 299-2450) Inner Wisdom CA.
— My Miracle Manifestation Manual. Sands, Gillian & Supreme Editing Team Staff, eds. 128p. 1999. pap. 15.95 (*0-9656741-4-2*) Inner Wisdom CA.
Aldana, Maria J., jt. ed. see Mellado, Joaquin.
Aldana, Patricia, ed. Jade & Iron: Latin American Tales from Two Cultures. Hazelton, Hugh, tr. (Illus.). 64p. (J). (gr. 2 up). 1996. 18.95 (*0-88899-256-4*) Publishers Group.
Aldana, Patricia, tr. see De Sahagun, Bernardino.
***Aldana, Steven G. & George, James.** Lifestyle Management for Patients with Coronary Heart Disease. 416p. (Orig.). (C). 1999. per. 32.95 (*0-7872-5801-6*) Kendall-Hunt.
Aldanov, Mark. Nightmare & Dawn. Carmichael, Joel, tr. LC 73-21489. 343p. 1974. reprint ed. lib. bdg. 65.00 (*0-8371-6406-0*, ALND, Greenwood Pr) Greenwood.
Aldanov, Mark A. Zagadka Tolstogo. LC 79-91652. (Brown University Slavic Reprint Ser.: No. 7). 138p. reprint ed. pap. 42.80 (*0-608-13566-6*, 202239400026) Bks Demand.
Aldape, Virginia. Enrichment Collection Resource Guide. Yarnaught, Paula, ed. (Guide for Enrichment Collection). (Illus.). 48p. (Orig.). 1995. pap., teacher ed. 8.99 (*1-885101-36-8*) Writers Pr ID.
Aldape, Virginia T. Nicole's Story: A Book about a Girl with Juvenile Rheumatoid Arthritis. LC 95-35622. (Illus.). (J). 1996. lib. bdg. 19.95 (*0-8225-2578-X*, Lerner Publctns) Lerner Pub.
Aldape, Virginia T. & Kossacoff, Lillian S. David, Donny & Darren: A Book About Identical Triplets. LC 96-33551. (J). 1997. lib. bdg. 21.27 (*0-8225-2584-4*, Lerner Publctns) Lerner Pub.
Aldapuerta, Jesus I. The Eyes: Emetic Fables from the Andalusian de Sade. 88p. (YA). (gr. 12). 1996. pap. 10.95 (*0-9523288-3-6*, Pub. by Headpress) AK Pr Dist.
Aldaraca, Bridget, et al, eds. Nicaragua in Revolution: The Poets Speak. LC 80-16304. (Studies in Marxism: Vol. 5). 301p. 1980. 18.95 (*0-930656-10-5*); pap. 8.95 (*0-930656-09-1*) MEP Pubns.
Aldaraca, Bridget & Baker, Edward. Spanish Grammar. LC 85-14162. (College Outline Ser.). 250p. (C). 1986. pap. text 10.25 (*0-15-601689-3*) Harcourt Coll Pubs.
Aldaraca, Bridget A. El Angel del Hogar: Galdos & the Ideology of Domesticity in Spain. LC 91-30892. (Studies in the Romance Languages & Literatures). 260p. 1992. pap. 37.50 (*0-8078-9243-2*) U of NC Pr.
Alday, Salvador C., tr. Reinflamando la Llama. (SPA.). 30p. 1991. pap. 1.95 (*0-8146-5023-6*) Liturgical Pr.
Alday, U. Colloquial Spanish. (SPA.). 15p. 1995. pap., pap. text 29.99 incl. cd-rom (*0-415-12682-7*) Routledge.
Aldaz, Ana-Marie, tr. see Scorza, Manuel.
Aldaz, Anna-Marie, tr. see Castro, Rosalia de.
Aldaz, Anna-Marie, tr. see Scorza, Manuel.
Aldaz, Arra-Marie. The Past of the Future: The Novelistic Cycle of Manuel Scorza. LC 90-6178. (American University Studies: Latin American Literature: Ser. XXII, Vol. 8). XI, 193p. (C). 1991. text 35.00 (*0-8204-1287-2*) P Lang Pubng.
Aldaz, C. Marcelo, et al, eds. Etiology of Breast & Gynecological Cancers. Vol. 396. LC 96-40180. 296p. 1997. 225.00 (*0-471-16901-3*) Wiley.
Aldaz, Jose D. Como Ahorrar & Cuando No Se Puede: Una Guia que te Ayudara a Mejorar tu Situacion Economica. (SPA., Illus.). 64p. 1999. pap. 7.99 (*0-9671051-0-2*) Cora Pubg.
Aldbrook, Mark & Hemming, Charles. The Folding Screen. (Illus.). 144p. 1999. 50.00 (*0-8478-2179-X*, Pub. by Rizzoli Intl) St Martin.
Aldcroft, Derek H. The European Economy, 1914-1990. 3rd rev. ed. LC 92-38193. 320p. (C). 1993. pap. 27.99 (*0-415-09160-8*) Routledge.
— The Inter-War Economy: Britain 1919-1939. LC 70-20963. 441p. 1971. text 81.00 (*0-231-03517-9*) Col U Pr.
— Studies in the Interwar European Economy. LC 96-40442. 240p. 1997. text 78.95 (*1-85928-360-8*, Pub. by Scolar Pr) Ashgate Pub Co.
Aldcroft, Derek H. & Catterall, Ross, eds. Rich Nations - Poor Nations: The Long-Run Perspective. LC 95-19498. (Illus.). 240p. 1996. 95.00 (*1-85898-059-3*) E Elgar.
Aldcroft, Derek H. & Morewood, Steven. Economic Change in Eastern Europe since 1918. 296p. (Orig.). 1995. 90.00 (*1-85278-819-4*) E Elgar.
— Economic Change in Eastern Europe since 1918. LC 94-16370. 296p. (Orig.). (C). 1996. pap. 25.00 (*1-85278-823-2*) E Elgar.
Aldcroft, Derek H. & Oliver, Michael J. Exchange Rate Regimes in the Twentieth Century. LC 98-21063. 224p. 1998. 85.00 (*1-85898-320-7*) E Elgar.
Aldcroft, Derek H. & Oliver, Michael J. Trade Unions in the Modern World. 68.95 (*1-85928-370-5*) Ashgate Pub Co.
Aldcroft, Derek H. & Slaven, Anthony, eds. Enterprise & Management: Essays in Honour of Peter L. Payne. 336p. 1995. 86.95 (*1-85928-111-7*, Pub. by Scolar Pr) Ashgate Pub Co.
***Aldcroft, Derek H. & Sutcliffe, Anthony, eds.** Europe in the International Economy, 1500 to 2000. LC 99-12897. 304p. 1999. 90.00 (*1-85898-670-2*) E Elgar.
Aldcroft, Derek H. & Ville, Simon P., eds. The European Economy, 1750-1914: A Thematic Approach. LC 93-27921. 1994. text 29.95 (*0-7190-3599-6*) Manchester Univ Pr.
Aldcroft, Derek H., jt. auth. see Catterall, Ross.
Aldcroft, Derek H., ed. see Freeman, Michael.
Aldea Vaquero, Quintin. Diccionario de Historia Ecclesiastica de Espana, 4 vols. (SPA.). 3200p. 1972. 195.00 (*0-7859-3335-2*, 8400038835) Fr & Eur.
— Diccionario de Historia Eclesiastica de Espana, 4 vols., Vol. 1 Suppl. (SPA.). 1987. pap. 195.00 (*0-318-72224-0*, 8400064313) Fr & Eur.
Aldebaran. Nixon & the Foxes of Watergate. 1968. pap. 2.95 (*0-918680-12-3*) Griffon House.
Aldebol, Tony. Army Air Force & United States Air Force Decorations, Medals, Ribbons, Badges & Insignia, 1941-1947 & 1947-1997. 2nd ed. (Illus.). 124p. 1999. 29.95 (*1-884452-05-1*, Pub. by MOA Press); pap. 24.95 (*1-884452-04-3*, Pub. by MOA Press) Stackpole.
Aldecoa. Cuentos: Level C Books. text 8.95 (*0-88436-283-3*) EMC-Paradigm.
Aldecoa, Francisco & Keating, Michael, eds. Paradiplomacy in Action: The Foreign Relations of Subnational Governments. LC 99-20579. 248p. 1999. pap. 26.50 (*0-7146-8018-4*, Pub. by F Cass Pubs) Intl Spec Bk.
***Aldecoa, Francisco & Keating, Michael, eds.** Paradiplomacy in Action: The Foreign Relations of Subnational Governments. LC 99-20579. 248p. 1999. 52.50 (*0-7146-4971-6*, Pub. by F Cass Pubs) Intl Spec Bk.
Aldemir, T., et al, eds. Reliability & Safety Assessment of Dynamic Process Systems. (NATO ASI Series F: Computer & Systems Sciences, Special Programme AET: Vol. 120). 236p. 1994. 71.95 (*0-387-57148-5*) Spr-Verlag.
Alden, Aimee N. Collector's Encyclopedia of Early Noritake. 216p. 1995. 24.95 (*0-89145-637-6*, 3961) Collector Bks.
***Alden, Andrew.** Annotated Bibliography for Adult Day Care. (Illus.). 106p. 1999. pap. 20.00 (*0-938744-98-4*) U of Wis Ctr Arch-Urban.
Alden, Carroll S. The United States Navy, a History. (History - United States Ser.). 508p. 1993. reprint ed. lib. bdg. 99.00 (*0-7812-4838-8*) Rprt Serv.
Alden, Carroll S. & Earle, Ralph. Makers of Naval Tradition. LC 76-167303. (Essay Index Reprint Ser.). 1977. reprint ed. 30.95 (*0-8369-2733-8*) Ayer.
Alden, Charles H., ed. Eliab Alden of Middleborough, MA, & Cairo, NY. 55p. 1995. pap. 11.00 (*0-8328-4442-X*) Higginson Bk Co.
— Eliab Alden of Middleborough, MA & Cairo, NY. 55p. 1995. lib. bdg. 21.00 (*0-8328-4443-8*) Higginson Bk Co.
Alden, Chevy. Black Falcon. LC 88-50158. 257p. 1988. 20.95 (*0-9619991-5-2*) Tri-Pacer Pr.
— How to Get Published - Guaranteed. Cook, Richard, ed. LC 93-60906. (Illus.). 376p. 1994. pap. 21.95 (*0-9619991-6-0*) Tri-Pacer Pr.
— How to Write, Publish & Sell Your Own Aviation Books. Cook, Richard, ed. LC 97-90914. (Illus.). 376p. (Orig.). 1998. pap. 21.95 (*0-9619991-3-6*) Tri-Pacer Pr.
***Alden, Chris.** Mozambique & the Construction of the New African State: From Negotiations to Nation Building. LC 00-33317. 2000. write for info. (*0-312-23594-1*) St Martin.
Alden, Chris & Daloz, Jean-Pascal, eds. Paris, Pretoria & the African Continent: The International Relations of States & Societies in Transition. 256p. 1996. text 69.95 (*0-312-15824-6*) St Martin.
Alden, Daisy, tr. see Steffen, Albert.
Alden, Dauril. The Making of an Enterprise: The Society of Jesus in Portugal, Its Empire, & Beyond--1540-1750. LC 94-4820. 1995. 75.00 (*0-8047-2271-4*) Stanford U Pr.
— Royal Government in Colonial Brazil: With Special Reference to the Administration of the Marquis of Lavradio, Viceroy, 1769-1779. LC 68-26064. (Illus.). 583p. reprint ed. pap. 180.80 (*0-608-17461-0*, 202994200066) Bks Demand.
Alden, Dauril & Dean, Warren, eds. Essays Concerning the Socioeconomic History of Brazil & Portuguese India. LC 76-53761. (Illus.). 261p. reprint ed. pap. 81.00 (*0-7837-5095-1*, 204479400004) Bks Demand.
***Alden, Douglas & Stoll, Charles S.** How to Invest in the Stock Market Without Going CRAZY! The Winning Points Program. Streit, Anita, ed. (Illus.). 160p. 2000. pap. 24.95 (*0-9654605-2-5*) Fortune Pr Pubs.
Alden, Douglas, jt. ed. see Thompson, William J.
Alden, Douglas W., ed. French XX Bibliography: Critical & Biographical Reference for the Study of French Literature Since 1885, No. 37. LC 77-648803. (Orig.). 1985. pap. 72.00 (*0-933444-45-1*) Assoc Univ Prs.
— Introduction to French Masterpieces. (FRE.). 1948. 32.95 (*0-89197-240-4*); pap. text 12.50 (*0-89197-241-2*) Irvington.
Alden, Douglas W., et al, eds. French Twentieth Bibliography: Critical & Bibliographical References for the Study of French Literature Since 1885, No. 44. LC 77-648803. 696p. 1993. 98.00 (*0-945636-55-5*) Susquehanna U Pr.
— French Twentieth Bibliography: Critical & Biographical References for the Study of French Literature since 1885, No. 43. LC 77-648803. 488p. (C). 1992. 86.00 (*0-945636-41-5*) Susquehanna U Pr.
— French XX Bibliography: Critical & Biographical Reference for French Literature since 1885. LC 77-648803. 600p. 1989. 86.00 (*0-941664-99-6*) Susquehanna U Pr.
— French XX Bibliography: Critical & Biographical Reference for French Literature since 1885, No. 38. LC 77-648803. (Illus.). 448p. 1987. 86.00 (*0-941664-28-7*) Susquehanna U Pr.
— French XX Bibliography: Critical & Biographical Reference for French Literature since 1885, No. 39. LC 77-648803. 440p. 1988. 86.00 (*0-941664-86-4*) Susquehanna U Pr.
Alden, Douglas W. & Brooks, Richard A., eds. A Critical Bibliography of French Literature Vol. 6: The 20th Century, 3 pts., Set. 1980. 235.00 (*0-8156-2204-X*) Syracuse U Pr.
Alden, Douglas W. & Hoy, Peter C., eds. French XX Bibliography. LC 77-648803. (Critical & Biographical References for the Study of French Literature since 1885 Ser.: No. 42). 472p. 1992. 86.00 (*0-945636-36-9*) Susquehanna U Pr.
Alden, Douglas W. & Thompson, William J., eds. French XX Bibliography, Vol. 47. LC 77-648803. 560p. 1996. pap. 105.00 (*0-945636-95-4*) Susquehanna U Pr.
— French XX Bibliography Issue 46. LC 77-648803. 560p. 1995. pap. 105.00 (*0-945636-86-5*) U Delaware Pr.
— French XX Bibliography Issue 48: Critical & Biographical References for the Study of French Literature since 1885, Vol. X, No. 3. LC 77-648803. 560p. 1997. 105.00 (*1-57591-005-5*) Susquehanna U Pr.
Alden, Douglas W., et al. French XX Bibliography, No. 45. 552p. 1994. 98.00 (*0-945636-68-7*) Susquehanna U Pr.
Alden, Douglas W., jt. ed. see Thompson, William J.
Alden, Douglas W., tr. see Faivre, Mario.
Alden, E. & Shaw, H. Alden: Descendents of Polly & Ebenezer Alden, Who were 6th in Descent from John Alden, the Pilgrim. 100p. 1994. reprint ed. pap. 19.50 (*0-8328-4288-5*); reprint ed. lib. bdg. 29.50 (*0-8328-4287-7*) Higginson Bk Co.
Alden, Frank W. Alden. John Alden of Ashfield, Massachusetts & Chautauqua County, New York: His Alden Ancestors & His Descendants. 84p. 1995. reprint ed. pap. 17.00 (*0-8328-4862-X*); reprint ed. lib. bdg. 27.00 (*0-8328-4849-2*) Higginson Bk Co.
Alden, George H. New Governments West of the Alleghenies Before 1780: Introductory to a Study of the Organization & Admission of New States. LC 70-106117. (First American Frontier Ser.). (Illus.). 1971. reprint ed. 12.95 (*0-405-02822-9*) Ayer.
Alden, Gracie T. Life's Inspirations. (Illus.). 40p. 1998. pap. 6.00 (*1-892609-01-0*) Gracie Pub.
— Whispers of the Heart. (Illus.). 48p. 1998. pap. 6.00 (*1-892609-00-2*) Gracie Pub.
Alden, Grant & Blackstock, Peter, eds. No Depression: An Introduction to Alternative Country Music. 256p. 1998. pap. 16.95 (*1-891847-00-7*, D010024, Pub. by Dowling Pr) Music Sales.
Alden, Grant, ed. see Gilbert, Jeff.
Alden, Henry M. Magazine Writing & the New Literature. LC 70-175686. (Select Bibliographies Reprint Ser.). (C). 1977. reprint ed. 23.95 (*0-8369-5030-5*) Ayer.
— A Study of Death: Works of Henry Mills Alden. (Works of Henry Mills Alden). vii, 335p. 1985. reprint ed. 49.00 (*0-685-10448-6*) Rprt Serv.
Alden, Henry M., jt. ed. see Howells, William Dean.
Alden, Isabel. Four Girls at Chautaugua. (Grace Livingston Hill Ser.: Vol. 9). 1996. mass mkt. 5.99 (*0-8423-3186-7*) Tyndale Hse.
Alden, Isabella. Chautauqua Girls at Home. (Grace Livingston Hill Ser.: Vol. 14). 1997. pap. 5.99 (*0-8423-3190-5*) Tyndale Hse.
— Cunning Workmen. (Grace Livingston Hill Ser.: Vol. 20). 1997. pap. 4.99 (*0-8423-3196-4*) Tyndale Hse.
— Ester Ried Yet Speaking. (Grace Livingston Hill Library: No. 12). 1996. mass mkt. 5.99 (*0-8423-3188-3*) Tyndale Hse.
— Ester Ried Yet Speaking. large type ed. LC 98-39415. 352p. 1998. 22.95 (*0-7838-0375-3*, G K Hall Lrg Type) Mac Lib Ref.
— Four Mothers at Chautauqua, No. 15. (Grace Livingston Hill Ser.). 1997. pap. 5.99 (*0-8423-3191-3*) Tyndale Hse.
— Grace Livingston Hill Library: Chrissy's Endeavor. 1997. pap. 5.99 (*0-8423-3189-1*) Tyndale Hse.
— Judge Burnham's Daughters. (Grace Livingston Hill Ser.: Vol. 10). 1996. pap. 5.99 (*0-8423-3185-9*) Tyndale Hse.
— A New Graft on the Family Tree. (Grace Livingston Hill Library: No. 17). 1997. pap. 5.99 (*0-8423-3193-X*) Tyndale Hse.
— Overruled. (Grace Livingston Hill Ser.: Vol. 19). 1997. pap. 5.99 (*0-8423-3195-6*) Tyndale Hse.
— Profiles. (Grace Livingston Hill Ser.: Vol. 16). 1997. pap. 5.99 (*0-8423-3192-1*) Tyndale Hse.
— Ruth Erskin's Crosses. (Grace Livingston Hill Library: No. 11). 1996. mass mkt. 5.99 (*0-8423-3187-5*) Tyndale Hse.
— What She Said/Meant. (Grace Livingston Hill Library: No. 18). 1997. pap. 4.99 (*0-8423-3194-8*) Tyndale Hse.
***Alden, Isabella & Hill, Grace Livingston.** Grace Livingston Hill Collection No. 4: Finding of Jasper Holt/Miranda/The Witness/Divers Women. (Grace Livingston Hill Collections). 450p. 1999. pap. 4.97 (*1-57748-508-4*) Barbour Pub.
Alden, Isabella, jt. auth. see Hill, Grace Livingston.
***Alden, Isabella M.** Three People. (Christian Fiction Ser.). 2000. 23.95 (*0-7862-2437-1*) Thorndike Pr.
Alden, J., et al. Forest Development in Cold Climates. LC 93-898. (NATO ASI Ser.: Vol. 244). (Illus.). 580p. (C). 1993. text 155.00 (*0-306-44480-1*, Kluwer Plenum) Kluwer Academic.
Alden, Jay. Backward Chaining: Teaching Task Performance. Langdon, Danny G., ed. LC 77-25132. (Instructional Design Library). (Illus.). 96p. 1978. 27.95 (*0-87778-110-9*) Educ Tech Pubns.
Alden, Jay & American Society for Training & Development Staff. A Trainer's Guide to Web-Based Instruction: Getting Started on Intranet- & Internet-Based Training LC 98-70594. (Learning Technologies Ser.). xi, 81 p. 1998. write for info. (*1-56286-084-4*) Am Soc Train & Devel.
Alden, Jean F., tr. see Twain, Mark, pseud.
Alden, Jeremy & Boland, Philip, eds. Regional Development Strategies: A European Perspective. LC 95-44356. (Regional Policy & Development Ser.: Vol. 15). 325p. 1996. 34.95 (*1-85302-356-6*, Pub. by Jessica Kingsley) Taylor & Francis.
Alden, Jill. Contemporary American Indian Beadwork: The Exquisite Art. LC 99-72192. (Illus.). 112p. 1999. pap. 29.95 (*0-9670040-0-4*) Dolph Pubg.
Alden, Joan. Before Our Eyes. LC 93-30089. 152p. (Orig.). 1993. pap. 8.95 (*1-56341-033-8*); lib. bdg. 18.95 (*1-56341-034-6*) Firebrand Bks.

— A Boy's Best Friend. LC 92-8061. (Illus.). 32p. (J). (ps-2). 1992. 12.95 (*1-55583-203-2*, Alyson Wonderland) Alyson Pubns.

Alden, John. Alden: The Story of a Pilgrim Family from the Mayflower to the Present Time (1899), with Autobiography, Recollections, Letters, Incidents & Genealogy. (Illus.). 441p. 1994. lib. bdg. 78.00 (*0-8328-4285-0*) Higginson Bk Co.

— Alden: The Story of a Pilgrim Family from the Mayflower to the Present Time (1899), with Autobiography, Recollections, Letters, Incidents & Genealogy. (Illus.). 441p. 1994. reprint ed. pap. 68.00 (*0-8328-4286-9*) Higginson Bk Co.

— The First South. 1990. 16.50 (*0-8446-1013-5*) Peter Smith.

— Printers & Printing in Philately. 76p. (C). 1987. 35.00 (*0-7855-2241-7*, Pub. by Picton) St Mut.

Alden, John D. Salvage Man: Edward Ellsberg & the U. S. Navy. LC 97-26226. (Illus.). 352p. 1997. 37.50 (*1-55750-027-4*) Naval Inst Pr.

— U. S. Submarine Attacks During World War II. LC 89-30878. (Illus.). 320p. 1989. 26.95 (*0-87021-767-4*) Naval Inst Pr.

Alden, John E. Eaton Family of Dedham & the Powder House Rock. (Illus.). 67p. 1997. reprint ed. pap. 13.50 (*0-8328-8420-0*); reprint ed. lib. bdg. 23.50 (*0-8328-8419-7*) Higginson Bk Co.

Alden, John L. & Kane, John M. Design of Industrial Ventilation Systems. 5th ed. LC 81-19194, (Illus.). 260p. 1982. 36.95 (*0-8311-1138-0*) Indus Pr.

Alden, John R. George Washington: A Biography. LC 83-25585. (Southern Biography Ser.). (Illus.). 326p. 1996. pap. 19.95 (*0-8071-2126-6*) La State U Pr.

— A History of the American Revolution. (Quality Paperbacks Ser.). (Illus.). 592p. 1989. pap. 17.95 (*0-306-80366-6*) Da Capo.

— John Stuart & the Southern Colonial Frontier: A Study of Indian Relations, War, Trade, Land Problems in the Southern Wilderness, 1754-1775. LC 66-29459. (Illus.). 384p. 1966. reprint ed. 75.00 (*0-87752-001-1*) Gordian.

— South in the Revolution, 1763-1789. LC 57-12096. (History of the South Ser.: Vol. 3). (Illus.). xvi, 442p. 1957. text 50.00 (*0-8071-0003-X*); pap. text 16.95 (*0-8071-0013-7*) La State U Pr.

— Stephen Sayre: American Revolutionary Adventurer. LC 83-771. 231p. 1983. pap. 71.70 (*0-7837-8526-7*, 204933500011) Bks Demand.

Alden, Joseph. The Works of Joseph Alden, 1807-1885, Set. 1987. reprint ed. lib. bdg. 500.00 (*0-685-18578-8*) Rprt Serv.

Alden, Karl R. The City of God: Conversations on the Doctrines of the New Church. 224p. 1990. reprint ed. pap. 12.00 (*0-945003-02-1*) General Church.

Alden, Laura. Megalosaurio (Megalosaurus) (Libros Sobre Dinosaurios! Ser.). (SPA., Illus.). 32p. (J). (gr. k-4). 1994. lib. bdg. 21.36 (*1-56766-142-4*) Childs World.

— Ornitomimo (Ornithomimus) (Libros Sobre Dinosaurios! Ser.). (SPA., Illus.). 32p. (J). (gr. k-4). 1994. lib. bdg. 21.36 (*1-56766-145-9*) Childs World.

— Thanksgiving. LC 93-13019. (Circle the Year with Holidays Ser.). (Illus.). 32p. (J). (gr. 1-2). 1993. pap. 3.95 (*0-516-40688-4*) Childrens.

Alden, Marueen J. Bronze Age Population Fluctuations in the Argolid from the Evidence of Mycenaean Tombs. (Studies in Mediterranean Archaeology & Literature: No. 15). 436p. (Orig.). 1981. pap. 57.50 (*91-86098-00-4*, Pub. by P Astroms) Coronet Bks.

Alden, Norbert G. Medical Schools - Activities, Trends & Progress: Index of New Information with Authors, Subjects & Bibliography. 180p. 1993. 47.50 (*1-55914-804-7*); pap. 44.50 (*1-55914-805-5*) ABBE Pubs Assn.

Alden, Patricia. Social Mobility in the English Bildungsroman: Gissing, Hardy, Bennett, & Lawrence. 158p. 1986. pap. 24.95 (*0-7734-1996-9*) E Mellen.

Alden, Patricia, et al, eds. African Studies & the Undergraduate Curriculum. LC 93-50942. 340p. 1994. pap. text 26.50 (*1-55587-445-2*) L Rienner.

Alden, Patricia & Tremaine, Louis. Nuruddin Farah. LC 98-33279. (World Authors Ser.). 15p. 1999. write for info. (*0-8057-1667-X*, Twyne) Mac Lib Ref.

Alden, Paulette B. Crossing the Moon: A Journey Through Infertility. LC 96-76411. 304p. 1998. pap. 11.95 (*0-14-027209-7*) Viking Penguin.

— Feeding the Eagles. (Short Fiction Ser.). 192p. 1989. pap. 8.00 (*1-55597-116-4*) Graywolf.

Alden, Peter. Field Guide to Mammals Coloring Book. (Illus.). 64p. 1987. pap. 6.95 (*0-395-44091-2*) HM.

— Peterson First Guide to Mammals of North America. 1987. 10.05 (*0-606-04508-2*, Pub. by Turtleback) Demco.

Alden, Peter & National Audubon Society Staff. National Audubon Society Field Guide to California. LC 97-31243. 447p. 1998. 19.95 (*0-679-44678-8*) Random.

— National Audubon Society Field Guide to Florida. LC 97-31242. 447p. 1998. 19.95 (*0-679-44677-X*) Random.

— National Audubon Society Field Guide to New England. LC 97-31241. 448p. 1998. 19.95 (*0-679-44676-1*) Random.

— National Audubon Society Field Guide to the Pacific Northwest. LC 97-31246. 448p. 1998. 19.95 (*0-679-44679-6*) Random.

Alden, Peter, et al. The National Audubon Society Field Guide to African Wildlife. LC 95-5543. (Illus.). 992p. 1995. 20.45 (*0-679-43234-5*) Knopf.

Alden, Peter, jt. auth. see Peterson, Roger T.

Alden, Ray. Advanced Speaker Design. rev. ed. LC 96-135555. (Illus.). 124p. (C). 1995. reprint ed. pap. 19.95 (*0-7906-1070-1*) Prompt Publns.

— Audio Systems Technology: Level III. 2000. pap. text 34.95 (*0-7906-1178-3*) Prompt Publns.

Alden, Raymond M. A Shakespeare Handbook. Campbell, Oscar J., ed. LC 75-109639. (Select Bibliographies Reprint Ser.). 1977. 26.95 (*0-8369-5248-0*) Ayer.

— Why the Chimes Rang. (Illus.). 44p. 1989. reprint ed. lib. bdg. 17.95 (*0-89966-595-0*) Buccaneer Bks.

— Why the Chimes Rang. LC 94-78669. (Illus.). 39p. 1994. reprint ed. 14.95 (*1-878208-46-2*) Guild Pr IN.

— Why the Chinese Rang. 46p. Date not set. 16.95 (*0-8488-2199-8*) Amereon Ltd.

Alden, Raymond M., ed. English Verse. LC 77-121032. reprint ed. 69.50 (*0-404-00308-7*) AMS Pr.

— Poems of the English Race. LC 77-149099. (Granger Index Reprint Ser.). 1977. 27.95 (*0-8369-6224-9*) Ayer.

— Shakespeare. LC 73-113539. reprint ed. 39.50 (*0-404-00307-9*) AMS Pr.

Alden, Richard. English Grammar Review. 262p. (C). 1992. pap. text 31.46 (*1-56226-103-7*) CAT Pub.

— Fundamentals of Grammar & Writing. 3rd ed. 386p. (C). 1994. pap. text 41.20 (*1-56226-199-1*) CAT Pub.

— Fundamentals of Grammar & Writing, Instructor's Guide. 3rd ed. 52p. 1994. pap. text, teacher ed. write for info. (*1-56226-200-9*) CAT Pub.

— Fundamentals of Grammar & Writing Test Bank. 80p. (C). 1990. pap. text. write for info. (*1-56226-033-2*) CAT Pub.

— Preparing for the GED Essay Test. 140p. (C). 1990. pap. text 17.07 (*1-56226-017-0*) CAT Pub.

Alden, Richard & Onuoha, Everest C. Fundamentals of Grammar & Writing. 356p. (C). 1996. pap. text 36.95 (*1-56226-296-3*) CAT Pub.

Alden, Richard, jt. auth. see Brand, Joan.

Alden, Richard, jt. auth. see Goodyear, John.

Alden, Richard, jt. auth. see Haney, Gloria.

Alden, Richard, jt. auth. see Jacobs, Greg.

Alden, Richard, jt. auth. see Mather, Jean.

Alden, Richard, jt. auth. see Mitchell, Carolyn.

Alden, Richard, jt. auth. see Strumpf, Michael.

Alden, Richard, jt. auth. see Weiser, David.

Alden, Richard, jt. auth. see Wilson, Paige.

Alden, Richard H., jt. auth. see Chester, Thomas.

Alden, Rio. Panda Bear's Journey: A Heroic Tale of Heart & Home. (Illus.). 32p. (Orig.). 1994. pap. 8.95 (*1-878321-09-9*, Compassion Pr) Compassion Bks.

Alden, Robert. Los Salmos I. (Comentario Biblico Portavoz Ser.). Orig. Title: Psalms. (SPA.). 336p. 1994. pap. 9.99 (*0-8254-1001-0*, Edit Portavoz) Kregel.

Alden, Robert L. Job. LC 93-39262. (New American Commentary Ser.: Vol. 11). 432p. 1994. 27.99 (*0-8054-0111-3*, 4201-11) Broadman.

— Psalms, Vol. 2. (Everyman's Bible Commentary Ser.). 1975. pap. 9.99 (*0-8024-2019-2*) Moody.

— Psalms: Songs of Discipleship. (Everyman's Bible Commentary Ser.: Vol. 3). 1975. pap. 9.99 (*0-8024-2020-6*) Moody.

Alden, Roland, jt. auth. see Blissmer, Robert H.

Alden, Sharyn. Up North Wisconsin: A Region for All Seasons. Stoga, Stan, ed. LC 99-70830. (Illus.). 172p. 1999. pap. 14.95 (*0-915024-69-1*) Trails Media.

Alden, Timothy. A Collection of American Epitaphs: Inscriptions with Occasional Notes, 5 vols. Kastenbaum, Robert J., ed. LC 76-19556. (Death & Dying Ser.). 1977. reprint ed. lib. bdg. 99.95 (*0-405-09594-5*) Ayer.

Alden, Todd. Rene Magritte, 1 (Essential Ser.). 1999. 12.95 (*0-8362-1936-8*) Andrews & McMeel.

Alden, Vernon R. Speaking for Myself: The Personal Reflections of Vernon R. Alden: University President, Corporate Director, International Entrepreneur. LC 97-36704. (Illus.). 233p. 1997. 24.95 (*0-9650743-2-3*); pap. 19.95 (*0-9650743-3-1*) Ohio Univ Lib.

Alden, William L. Told by the Colonel. (Illus.). 1971. reprint ed. 19.00 (*0-403-01435-2*) Scholarly.

Aldenderfer, Mark S. Montane Foragers: Asana & the South-Central Andean Archaic. LC 97-40225. (Illus.). 344p. 1998. text 39.95 (*0-87745-621-6*) U of Iowa Pr.

Aldenderfer, Mark S., ed. Domestic Architecture, Ethnicity, & Complementarity in the South-Central Andes. LC 92-35091. (Illus.). 188p. 1993. text 47.95 (*0-87745-400-0*) U of Iowa Pr.

— Quantitative Research in Archaeology: Progress & Prospects. LC 86-15564. (Illus.). 312p. reprint ed. pap. 96.80 (*0-7837-4576-1*, 204410500003) Bks Demand.

Aldenderfer, Mark S. & Blashfield, Roger K. Cluster Analysis. (Quantitative Applications in the Social Sciences Ser.: Vol. 44). 96p. (C). 1984. pap. text 10.95 (*0-8039-2376-7*) Sage.

Aldenham, Lord, ed. see Degeste, Beatrix Chanson.

Aldenkamp, A. P. & Stores, G. Education & Epilepsy: Proceedings of an International Workshop on Education & Epilepsy. x, 146p. 1988. 40.75 (*90-265-0885-9*) Swets.

Aldenkamp, Albert P., et al, eds. Epilepsy in Children & Adolescents. LC 95-90097. 336p. 1995. boxed set 189.95 (*0-8493-7659-9*, 7659) CRC Pr.

Alder. Canine Practice No. 2. 2nd ed. 1996. pap. text 49.00 (*0-7020-2082-6*, W B Saunders Co) Harcrt Hlth Sci Grp.

— Feline Practice No. 2. 2nd ed. 1996. pap. text 49.00 (*0-7020-2081-8*, W B Saunders Co) Harcrt Hlth Sci Grp.

— Hire with Your Head Not Your Gut. (Business Technology Ser.). 1998. pap. 24.95 (*0-442-02644-7*, VNR) Wiley.

Alder & Moore. ADA Compliance Manual for Employers, Issue 2. 2nd ed. 131p. 1998. pap. write for info. (*0-327-00594-7*, 8012913) LEXIS Pub.

Alder, jt. auth. see Moore.

Alder, B., ed. see Kirkwood, John G.

Alder, Beth. Psychology of Health: Application of Psychology for Health Professionals. 208p. 1995. text 48.00 (*3-7186-5761-9*, Harwood Acad Pubs); pap. text 20.00 (*3-7186-5762-7*, Harwood Acad Pubs) Gordon & Breach.

***Alder, Beth.** Psychology of Health: Applications of Psychology for Health Professionals. 2nd ed. 324p. 1999. text 42.00 (*90-5702-493-4*, Harwood Acad Pubs); pap. text 24.00 (*90-5702-494-2*, Harwood Acad Pubs) Gordon & Breach.

Alder, Bill. What Book Publishers Won't Tell You: A Literary Agent's Guide to the Secrets of Getting Published. 224p. 1997. pap. text 12.95 (*0-8065-1926-6*, Citadel Pr) Carol Pub Group.

Alder, C. & Wundersitz, J. Family Conferencing & Juvenile Justice. LC 95-169761. 220p. 1994. pap. 35.00 (*0-642-19881-0*, Pub. by Aust Inst Criminology) Acvent Bks Div.

***Alder, Christine, ed.** Juvenile Crime & Juvenile Justice: Toward 2000 & Beyond. (Research & Public Policy Ser.: Vol. 14). 68p. 1999. pap. 75.00 (*0-642-24053-*', Pub. by Aust Inst Criminology) St Mut.

Alder, Christine, jt. ed. see White, Rob.

Alder, Daryl, ed. Sport on Film & Video: The North American Society for Sport History Guide. LC 93-27967. 204p. 1993. pap. 34.50 (*0-8108-2739-5*) Scarecrow.

Alder, David A. The Children of Chelm. (Story Bks.). (Illus.). (J). (gr. 1-5). 1979. pap. 5.00 (*0-88482-773-9*) Hebrew Pub.

— Happy Thanksgiving. 1999. pap. 3.95 (*0-14-054275-2*) NAL.

Alder, Debora, ed. see McGonagle, Cindy.

Alder, Elizabeth. The King's Shadow. LC 93-34159. 272p. (YA). (gr. 7-12). 1997. mass mkt. 4.50 (*0-440-22011-4*) Dell.

— The King's Shadow. LC 93-34159. 192p. (J). (gr. 7 up). 1995. 17.00 (*0-374-34182-6*) FS&G.

— The King's Shadow. (J). 1997. 9.09 (*0-606-11000-3*, Pub. by Turtleback) Demco.

Alder, Elmer. Breaking into Print: Being a Compilation of Papers Wherein Each of a Select Group of Authors Tells of the Difficulties of Authorship & How Such Trials Are Met. LC 68-55840. (Essay Index Reprint Ser.). 1977. reprint ed. 18.95 (*0-8369-0247-5*) Ayer.

Alder, Felix. Creed & Deed: A Series of Discourses. LC 76-38430. (Religion in America, Ser.: 2). 254p. 1972. reprint ed. 19.95 (*0-405-04051-2*) Ayer.

***Alder, George, et al.** Redemption & Responsibility: A Few Hours with George Alder. Tiffin, Gary & Bollenbaugh, Mick, eds. 179p. 1999. pap. 17.00 (*1-57910-323-5*) Wipf & Stock.

***Alder, Harry.** How to Boost Your Intelligence. 2000. pap. 14.95 (*0-7494-3220-9*) Kogan Page Ltd.

— How to Live Longer: Discover How to Add More Enjoyable Years to Your Life Expectancy. 208p. 2000. pap. 15.95 (*1-85703-605-0*, Pub. by How To Bks) Midpt Trade.

Alder, Harry. NLP - Neuro Linguistic Programming: The Art & Science of Getting What You Want. 224p. 1997. pap. 14.95 (*0-7499-1489-0*, Pub. by Piatkus Bks) London Brdge.

— NLP for Managers: How to Achieve Excellence at Work. 240p. 1998. pap. text 14.95 (*0-7499-1643-5*, Pub. by Piatkus Bks) London Brdge.

— NLP for Trainers: Communicating for Excellence. LC 95-49799. (Training Ser.). 1996. pap. write for info. (*0-07-709134-5*) McGraw.

***Alder, Harry.** Quick Fix Your Emotional Intelligence. 192p. 2000. pap. 9.95 (*1-85703-653-0*, Pub. by How To Bks) Midpt Trade.

— Remembering Names & Faces. 64p. 2000. pap. 9.95 (*1-85703-592-5*, Pub. by How To Bks) Midpt Trade.

— The Ultimate How to Book. LC 99-40391. 1999. 43.95 (*0-566-08151-2*) Ashgate Pub Co.

Alder, Harry & Morris, Karl. Masterstroke: Use the Power of Your Mind to Improve Your Golf with NLP. (Illus.). 176p. (Orig.). 1997. pap. text 13.95 (*0-7499-1715-6*, Pub. by Piatkus Bks) London Brdge.

Alder, Harry, jt. auth. see Temporal, Paul.

***Alder, Holly.** Story Time Crafts for Kids, Vol. 1. LC 00-27003. (Illus.). 128p. 2000. pap. 16.99 (*1-58180-059-2*, North Lght Bks) F & W Pubns Inc.

— Storytime Crafts for Kids, Vol. 2. LC 00-27003. (Illus.). 128p. (J). 2000. pap. 16.99 (*1-58180-088-6*, North Lght Bks) F & W Pubns Inc.

Alder, Jacqueline, jt. auth. see Kay, Robert.

Alder, John, jt. auth. see Aldous, Grahame L.

Alder, Jonathan E. Jesus Never Was a Christian. Sherry, Patrick, ed. LC 87-81321. 224p. (Orig.). 1987. pap. 10.95 (*0-943847-02-8*) Jonathan Edward.

Alder, Jonathan L. Sexual Harassment: Discrimination & Other Claims. 380p. 1994. spiral bd. 80.00 incl. disk (*0-250-48600-8*, MICHIE) LEXIS Pub.

— When Business Gets Personal. 1993. 135.00 incl. disk (*0-250-48604-0*, MICHIE) LEXIS Pub.

Alder, Jonathan L. & Moore, Maureen F. ADA Compliance Manual for Employers. 1994. ring bd., suppl. ed. 40.00 (*0-685-74455-8*, MICHIE) LEXIS Pub.

— Labor & Employment in Louisiana. 1994. ring bd., suppl. ed. 45.00 (*0-614-03666-6*, MICHIE) LEXIS Pub.

Alder, Jonathan L., jt. auth. see Moore, Maureen F.

Alder, Ken. Engineering the Revolution. 496p. 1999. pap. 22.95 (*0-691-00969-4*, Pub. by Princeton U Pr) Cal Prin Full Svc.

— Engineering the Revolution: Arms & Enlightenment in France, 1763-1815. LC 96-25139. 472p. 1997. text 59.50 (*0-691-02671-8*, Pub. by Princeton U Pr) Cal Prin Full Svc.

Alder, Lory. Paris Is Fun: A Bilingual Guide. 1969. 12.00 (*0-7207-0225-9*) Transatl Arts.

Alder, Phillip. Get Smarter at Bridge. 240p. 1994. pap. text 12.95 (*0-9642034-0-5*) P Alder.

Alder, Phillip, ed. see Truscott, Alan.

Alder, Piet Van, see Van Alder, Piet.

Alder, Roger W., et al. Mechanism in Organic Chemistry. LC 72-147196. (Illus.). 388p. reprint ed. pap. 120.30 (*0-8357-6433-8*, 203580400097) Bks Demand.

Alder, Vera S. Finding of the Third Eye. 188p. 1973. reprint ed. pap. 8.95 (*0-87728-056-8*) Weiser.

— Initiation of the World. 252p. 1972. pap. 14.95 (*0-87728-057-6*) Weiser.

***Alder, Vera Stanley.** The Fifth Dimension. 240p. 2000. pap. 14.95 (*1-57863-165-3*) Weiser.

— The Initiation of the World. LC 99-49830. 252p. 2000. pap. 14.95 (*1-57863-166-1*) Weiser.

Alder, Vicki. Mysteries in the Scriptures: Enlightenment Through Ancient Beliefs. 326p. 1991. 13.95 (*0-9626559-1-0*) V Alder.

— The Signs of the Last Days: A Scriptural Guide to the Future. (Illus.). 248p. 1990. 12.95 (*0-9626559-0-2*) V Alder.

Alder, William H. & Nordin, Albert A. Immunological Techniques Applied to Aging Research. 256p. 1981. 141.00 (*0-8493-5809-4*, QP86, CRC Reprint) Franklin.

Alderborn, Goran, jt. ed. see Nystrom, Christer.

Alderete, Betty, tr. see Dickens, Charles.

Alderete, Betty, tr. see McDonough, Jerome.

Alderete, Jillian T. Footprints of Faith. 1998. pap. write for info. (*1-57553-870-9*) Watermrk Pr.

Alderette, Betty, tr. see McDonough, Jerome.

Alderfer, Clayton P. & Cooper, Cary L., eds. Advances in Experiential Social Processes, Vol. 2. LC 77-22060. (Illus.). 341p. reprint ed. pap. 105.80 (*0-8357-5163-5*, 203043300002) Bks Demand.

Alderfer, Clayton P., jt. ed. see Cooper, Cary L.

Alderfer, E. G. The Ephrata Commune: An Early American Counterculture. LC 85-1044. (Illus.). 288p. 1985. pap. 19.95 (*0-8229-5801-5*) U of Pittsburgh Pr.

Alderfer, Hannah, et al. Caught Looking: Feminism, Pornography & Censorship. (Illus.). 96p. (Orig.). 1987. pap. 10.00 (*0-9617884-0-2*) Caught Looking.

Alderfer, Owen. The Minister's Manual: King James Version. rev. ed. 1970. reprint ed. 8.95 (*0-916035-04-2*) Evangel Indiana.

— The Minister's Manual: New International Version. 192p. 1991. 10.95 (*0-916035-47-6*) Evangel Indiana.

Alderfer, Richard, jt. auth. see Ulloth, Dana R.

Alderfer, Rick A. Marketing Your Restaurant: So Easy, Effective, & Inexpensive Ideas That You Can Use Today! LC 98-90424. 84p. 1998. pap. 12.95 (*0-9664822-0-4*) Strategic Pr.

Alderink, Larry J. Creation & Salvation in Ancient Orphism. LC 81-5772. (American Philological Association, American Classical Studies: Vol. 8). 150p. reprint ed. pap. 46.50 (*0-608-08681-9*, 206920400003) Bks Demand.

Alderman. Railway Interest. 344p. 1993. 65.95 (*0-7512-0232-0*) Ashgate Pub Co.

Alderman & Hanley. Clinical Medicine for the Occupational Physician. (Occupational Safety & Health Ser.: Vol. 7). (Illus.). 552p. 1982. text 210.00 (*0-8247-7957-6*) Dekker.

Alderman, Annabel. Family Man. LC 99-230471. 128p. 1999. 18.95 (*0-86554-646-0*) Mercer Univ Pr.

Alderman, Betty. Modern Redwork Designs. LC 99-40081. 96p. 1999. per. 16.95 (*1-57432-733-X*) Collector Bks.

Alderman, Bill & Wilson, Eleanore. Recreational Vehicles: Finding the Best Buy. 2nd ed. LC 96-85975. (Illus.). 123p. 1996. pap. 9.95 (*1-56625-070-6*) Bonus Books.

Alderman, E. & Kennedy, C. The Right to Privacy. (YA). 1997. pap. 14.00 (*0-679-74434-7*) Vin Bks.

Alderman, Ellen & Kennedy, Caroline. In Our Defense: The Bill of Rights in Action. LC 90-48844. 432p. 1992. pap. 13.50 (*0-380-71720-4*, Avon Bks) Morrow Avon.

— The Right to Privacy. 405p. 1999. reprint ed. text 27.00 (*0-7881-6359-0*) DIANE Pub.

Alderman, Eric. Expert Advisor. LC 87-12658. (Expert Advisor Ser.). (Illus.). 352p. 1988. pap. 17.95 (*0-201-05755-7*) Addison-Wesley.

Alderman, Eric & Pfister, Michelle M. Expert Advisor: WordPerfect 5.0. 350p. 1989. pap. text 19.95 (*0-201-51734-5*) Addison-Wesley.

Alderman, G., compiled by. Energy & Protein Requirements of Ruminants. (Illus.). 176p. (Orig.). 1993. pap. text 40.00 (*0-85198-851-2*) OUP.

Alderman, Geoffrey. London Jewry & London Politics, 1889-1986. 192p. 1989. 49.95 (*0-415-02204-5*) Routledge.

— Modern Britain, 1700-1980: A Domestic History. 256p. (C). 1986. 52.50 (*0-7099-0537-8*, Pub. by C Helm) Routldge.

— Modern British Jewry. 416p. 1992. 95.00 (*0-19-820145-1*) OUP.

— Modern British Jewry. (Illus.). 444p. 1998. reprint ed. pap. text 35.00 (*0-19-820759-X*) OUP.

— Pressure Groups & Government in Great Britain. LC 83-733. 172p. reprint ed. pap. 53.40 (*0-7837-1592-7*, 204188400024) Bks Demand.

— Response in the Yield of Milk Constituents to the Intake of Nutrients by Dairy Cows. LC 99-177989. 112p. 1998. text 35.00 (*0-85199-284-6*) OUP.

***Alderman, Gillian.** Lilith's Castle. 1999. mass mkt. 12.95 (*0-00-648272-4*, Pub. by HarpC) Trafalgar.

Alderman, Harold. Downturn & Economic Recovery in Ghana: Impacts on the Poor. (Monographs). (Illus.). 121p. (C). 1991. pap. text 12.00 (*1-56401-010-4*) Cornell Food.

— Nutritional Status in Ghana & Its Determinants. (Working Papers). (C). 1990. pap. text 7.00 (*1-56401-101-1*) Cornell Food.

— Poverty, Household Food Security, & Nutrition in Rural Pakistan. LC 93-39211. (Research Report Ser.: Vol. 96). 1993. write for info. (*0-89629-099-9*) Intl Food Policy.

— Social Assistance in Albania: Decentralization & Targeted

A

A

Transfers. LC 98-23193. (Living Standards Measurement Study Working Papers: No. 134). 60p. 1998. pap. 22.00 (*0-8213-4245-2*, 14245) World Bank.

Alderman, Harold, et al, eds. Child Growth & Nutrition in Developing Countries: Priorities for Action. (C). Date not set. 49.95 (*0-614-10594-3*); pap. 19.95 (*0-614-10595-1*) Cornell Food.

— Child Growth & Nutrition in Developing Countries: Priorities for Action. (Food Systems & Agrarian Change Ser.). (Illus.). 496p. 1994. pap. text 29.95 (*0-8014-8189-9*) Cornell U Pr.

Alderman, Harold & CFNPP Staff. Food Security & Grain Trade in Ghana. (Working Papers). 84p. (Orig.). (C). 1992. pap. 7.00 (*1-56401-128-3*) Cornell Food.

Alderman, Harold & Shively, Gerald. Prices & Markets in Ghana. (Working Papers). (C). 1991. pap. text 7.00 (*1-56401-110-0*) Cornell Food.

Alderman, Harold, et al. A Comparison of Ghanaian Civil Servants' Earning Before & after Retrenchment. (Working Papers: No. 64). 24p. 1994. pap. 7.00 (*1-56401-164-X*) Cornell Food.

Alderman, Harold, jt. auth. see Sahn, David E.

Alderman, Harold, jt. ed. see Srivastava, Jitendra P.

Alderman, J. Anthony. Wildflowers of the Blue Ridge Parkway. LC 96-47698. (Illus.). 268p. (C). 1997. pap. 9.50 (*0-8078-4651-1*) U of NC Pr.

Alderman, John P. Twenty-Ninth Virginia Infantry. (Virginia Regimental Histories Ser.). (Illus.). 143p. 1989. 19.95 (*0-930919-66-1*) H E Howard.

Alderman, Karen C., jt. auth. see Levitan, Sar A.

Alderman, Kay. Motivation for Achievement: Possibilities for Teaching & Learning. 304p. 1999. pap. 29.95 (*0-8058-3077-4*) L Erlbaum Assocs.

Alderman, Lesley, jt. auth. see Cheney, Karen.

Alderman, Linda. Why Did Daddy Die? Helping a Child Cope with the Loss of a Parent. 1991. pap. 8.95 (*0-671-74670-7*) PB.

Alderman, Margaret. Each New Sunrise: Meditations in Maturity. 88p. 1999. pap. 7.95 (*0-88489-569-6*) St Marys.

Alderman, Margaret & Burns, Josephine. Praying with Elizabeth Seton. Koch, Carl, ed. LC 93-143874. (Companions for the Journey Ser.). (Illus.). 120p. 1992. pap. 8.95 (*0-88489-282-4*) St Marys.

Alderman, Pat. Greasy Cove in Unicoi County, TN. (Illus.). 48p. 1975. pap. 4.95 (*0-932807-03-8*) Overmountain Pr.

— Nancy Ward - Dragging Canoe. (Illus.). 90p. 1978. pap. 7.95 (*0-932807-05-4*) Overmountain Pr.

— One Heroic Hour at King's Mountain. (Illus.). 94p. 1968. pap. 7.95 (*0-932807-40-2*) Overmountain Pr.

— The Overmountain Men. (Illus.). 308p. 1970. reprint ed. 22.95 (*0-932807-15-1*); reprint ed. pap. 17.95 (*0-932807-16-X*) Overmountain Pr.

— Tilson Grist Mill. (Illus.). 49p. 1981. pap. 3.95 (*0-932807-07-0*) Overmountain Pr.

Alderman, Richard. Know Your Rights! 5th ed. LC 97-13340. 238p. 1997. pap. 13.95 (*0-88415-420-3*, 5420) Gulf Pub.

— Texas Deceptive Trade Practices. 3rd ed. LC 94-72967. 576p. 1994. pap. 48.75 (*0-916081-37-0*) J Marshall Pub Co.

Alderman, Richard & Dole, Richard F. A Transactional Guide to the Uniform Commercial Code, 2 vols. 2nd ed. 1349p. 1983. 21.50 (*0-8318-0400-9*, B400/B581) Am Law Inst.

— A Transactional Guide to the Uniform Commercial Code, 1987 Supplement, 2 vols. 2nd ed. 1349p. 1987. pap., suppl. ed. 2.70 (*0-8318-0581-1*, B581) Am Law Inst.

Alderman, Richard & Oldham, Tom. Your Texas Business. 2nd ed. 364p. 1992. pap. 27.95 (*0-88415-024-0*, 5024) Gulf Pub.

Alderman, Richard M. The Lawyer's Guide to the Texas Deceptive Trade Practices Act. 370p. Date not set. ring bd. 120.00 (*0-409-25430-4*, 82587, MICHIE) LEXIS Pub.

— The Lawyer's Guide to the Texas Deceptive Trade Practices Act, Issue 16. 201p. 1998. ring bd. write for info. (*0-327-00689-7*, 8258918) LEXIS Pub.

***Alderman, Richard M.** Texas Deceptive Trade Practices Act. 2nd ed. 550p. 1999. ring bd. 179.00 (*0-327-10204-7*, 8258711) LEXIS Pub.

Alderman, Robert. How to Make More Money at Interior Design. 192p. (C). 1982. 18.95 (*0-685-05995-2*) Inter Design.

Alderman, Robert L. How to Prosper As an Interior Designer: A Business & Legal Guide. LC 96-43760. 288p. 1997. 54.95 (*0-471-16223-X*) Wiley.

Alderman, Sharon. A Handweaver's Notebook: Swatch Collections from Handwoven Magazine. LC 90-38089. (Illus.). 144p. (Orig.). 1990. pap. 18.00 (*0-934026-57-2*) Interweave.

Alderman, Tracy. The Scarred Soul: Understanding & Ending Self-Inflicted Violence. LC 97-66073. (Illus.). 224p. (Orig.). 1997. pap. 14.95 (*1-57224-079-2*) New Harbinger.

Alderman, Tracy & Marshall, Karen. Amongst Ourselves: A Self-Help Guide to Living with Dissociative Identity Disorder. LC 98-66702. 176p. 1998. pap. 14.95 (*1-57224-122-5*) New Harbinger.

Alders, Carine, et al, eds. Linking with Farmers: Networking for Low-External-Input & Sustainable Agriculture. LC 99-939620. (Illus.). 200p. 1993. pap. 25.00 (*1-85339-210-3*, Pub. by Intermed Tech) Stylus Pub VA.

Alders, Koos, et al, eds. Monetary Policy in a Converging Europe: Papers & Proceedings of an International Workshop Organised by De Nederlandsche Bank & the Limburg Institute of Financial Economics. LC 95-35840. 1996. write for info. (*0-614-08575-6*) Kluwer Academic.

Aldersey-Williams, Hugh. The Most Beautiful Molecule: The Discovery of the Buckyball. LC 95-12422. 340p. 1995. 24.95 (*0-471-10938-X*) Wiley.

— The Most Beautiful Molecule: The Discovery of the Buckyball. (Illus.). 340p. 1997. pap. 16.95 (*0-471-19333-X*) Wiley.

Aldersmith, H., jt. auth. see Davidson, D.

Alderson. Mansex Fine: Religion, Manliness & Imperialism in Nineteenth-Century Britain. 25p. 1998. text 79.95 (*0-7190-5275-0*, Pub. by Manchester Univ Pr) St Martin.

***Alderson.** Surfing: A Beginner's Manual. (Illus.). 93p. 2000. pap. 16.95 (*1-898660-24-7*, Pub. by Fernhurst Bks) Motorbooks Intl.

Alderson, Anthony D. The Structure of the Ottoman Dynasty. LC 81-23751. 186p. 1982. reprint ed. lib. bdg. 75.00 (*0-313-22522-2*, ALSO, Greenwood Pr) Greenwood.

Alderson, Brian. Edward Ardizzone, a Preliminary Hand-List of His Illustrated Books, 1929-1970. LC 74-179329. 64p. 1972. write for info. (*0-900002-12-3*) Oak Knoll.

— Ezra Jack Keats: A Bibliography & Catalogue. LC 97-27860. (Illus.). 240p. 1998. 75.00 (*1-56554-007-7*) Pelican.

— Ezra Jack Keats: Artist & Picture-Book Maker. LC 93-43206. (Illus.). 224p. 1994. 50.00 (*1-56554-006-9*) Pelican.

— Tale of the Turnip. LC 98-35831. (Illus.). 32p. (J). 1999. text 12.99 (*0-7636-0494-1*) Candlewick Pr.

Alderson, Brian, tr. & selected by see Andersen, Hans Christian.

Alderson, Daniel. Talking Back to Poems: A Working Guide for the Aspiring Poet. LC 95-39441. 128p. 1996. pap. 9.95 (*0-89087-795-5*) Celestial Arts.

Alderson, Daniel & Simon, Jon. Sat: See You at the Top. 120p. 1995. pap. 9.95 (*0-89087-747-5*) Celestial Arts.

***Alderson, David.** Ireland in Proximity: History, Gender & Space. LC 99-30780. 1999. pap. 24.99 (*0-415-18958-6*) Routledge.

***Alderson, David, et al, eds.** Ireland in Proximity: History, Gender, Space. LC 99-30780. 208p. (C). 1999. text. write for info. (*0-415-18957-8*) Routledge.

Alderson, Evan, et al, eds. Reflections on Cultural Policy: Past, Present, Future. 160p. (C). 1993. text 35.00 (*0-88920-215-X*) W Laurier U Pr.

Alderson, Frederick. Outdoor Games. (Junior Reference Ser.). (Illus.). 64p. (J). (gr. 6 up). 1980. 14.95 (*0-7136-2031-5*) Dufour.

— View North: A Long Look at Northern England. LC 68-23825. (Illus.). 283p. 1968. 29.95 (*0-678-05577-7*) Kelley.

Alderson, J. Charles, et al, eds. Reviews of English Language Proficiency Tests. 88p. 1987. pap. 16.50 (*0-939791-31-5*) Tchrs Eng Spkrs.

Alderson, J. Charles & Beretta, Alan, eds. Evaluating Second Language Education. (Cambridge Applied Linguistics Ser.). 384p. (C). 1992. text 69.95 (*0-521-41067-3*); pap. text 27.95 (*0-521-42269-8*) Cambridge U Pr.

Alderson, J. Charles, et al. Language Test Construction & Evaluation. (Cambridge Language Teaching Library). 320p. (C). 1995. text 59.95 (*0-521-47255-5*); pap. text 22.95 (*0-521-47829-4*) Cambridge U Pr.

***Alderson, James.** Midnight at Noon. 1998. spiral bd. 6.00 (*1-929326-34-3*) Hal Bar Pubg.

Alderson, Jo B. & Rennert, Kate A. Wisconsin's Early French Habitants. 208p. 1998. pap. 19.00 (*0-7884-0895-X*, A411) Heritage Bk.

Alderson, John. Principled Policing: Protecting the Public with Integrity. 185p. 1998. pap. 39.00 (*1-872870-71-6*, Pub. by Waterside Pr) Gaunt.

Alderson, L. W. Gingko Leaves & Cello Grass. 1978. pap. 5.00 (*0-686-24038-3*) Bellevue Pr.

— Gingko Leaves & Cello Grass. deluxe ed. 1978. 7.50 (*0-686-85711-9*) Bellevue Pr.

Alderson, Lawrence. Rare Breeds. (Album Ser.: No. 118). (Illus.). 32p. pap. 4.75 (*0-7478-0279-3*, Pub. by Shire Pubns) Parkwest Pubns.

— Rare Breeds. 1989. pap. 25.00 (*0-7478-0002-2*, Pub. by Shire Pubns) St Mut.

Alderson, Lawrence, ed. Genetic Conservation of Domestic Livestock. 240p. 1990. text 57.00 (*0-85198-669-2*) C A B Intl.

Alderson, Lawrence & Bodo, Imre, eds. Genetic Conservation of Domestic Livestock, Vol. 2. (Illus.). 304p. 1992. text 90.00 (*0-85198-809-1*) OUP.

Alderson, Leona. Healthy Food Choices. LC 94-60900. 245p. 1994. otabind 14.95 (*0-945383-98-3*) Teach Servs.

Alderson, M. R., et al, eds. Hodgkin's Disease III: Occurrence & Diagnosis. LC 73-23030. (Hodgkin's Disease Ser.: Vol. 3). 155p. 1974. text 24.00 (*0-8422-7195-3*) Irvington.

Alderson, Michael, tr. see Novo, Salvador.

Alderson, Nannie T. & Smith, Helena H. A Bride Goes West. LC 42-12918. (Illus.). viii, 273p. 1969. reprint ed. pap. 10.95 (*0-8032-5001-0*, Bison Books) U of Nebr Pr.

Alderson, Priscilla. Children's Consent to Surgery. LC 93-1413. 224p. (C). 1993. 122.00 (*0-335-15733-5*); pap. 37.95 (*0-335-15732-7*) OpUniv Pr.

***Alderson, Priscilla.** Young Children's Rights: Exploring Beliefs, Principles & Practice. 2000. pap. 22.95 (*1-85302-880-0*) Jessica Kingsley.

Alderson, R. H., ed. Design of the Electron Microscope Labora. (Practical Methods in Electron Microscopy Ser.: Vol. 4). 130p. 1975. pap. 35.50 (*0-7204-4260-5*, North Holland) Elsevier.

— Design of the Electron Microscope Laboratory. (Practical Methods in Electron Microscopy Ser.: Vol. 4). 1975. pap. 21.00 (*0-444-10816-5*, North Holland) Elsevier.

Alderson, Richard. No Holiness, No Heaven! 105p. (Orig.). 1986. pap. 6.50 (*0-85151-495-2*) Banner of Truth.

Alderson, Sue A. Ida & the Wool Smugglers. (Illus.). 32p. (J). (ps-2). 1990. pap. 5.95 (*0-88899-119-3*, Pub. by Grndwd Bks) Publishers Group.

— The Not Impossible Summer. unabridged ed. 112p. (Orig.). (YA). (gr. 3 up). 1983. pap. 4.95 (*0-7736-7286-9*) STDK.

— Pond Seasons. LC 96-932115. (Illus.). 32p. (J). 1997. 15.95 (*0-88899-283-1*) Publishers Group.

Alderson, Sue Ann. Bonnie McSmithers Is at It Again! (Annikins Ser.: Vol. 9). (Illus.). 24p. (Orig.). (J). (ps-2). 1990. pap. 0.99 (*1-55037-110-X*, Pub. by Annick) Firefly Bks Ltd.

— Bonnie McSmithers You're Driving Me Dithers. (Annikins Ser.: Vol. 9). (Illus.). 24p. (J). (ps-2). 1990. pap. 0.99 (*1-55037-108-8*, Pub. by Annick) Firefly Bks Ltd.

— Hurry Up, Bonnie! (Annikins Ser.: Vol. 9). (Illus.). 32p. (Orig.). (J). (ps-2). 1990. pap. 0.99 (*1-55037-109-6*, Pub. by Annick) Firefly Bks Ltd.

— Wherever Bears Be. LC 98-34405. (Illus.). (J). 1999. 14.95 (*1-883672-77-5*) Tricycle Pr.

Alderson, Tom. Michelson in the Desert: Stories. LC 86-16159. 88p. (Orig.). 1987. pap. 12.95 (*0-8262-0621-2*, 83-36299) U of Mo Pr.

Alderson, Valerie, ed. & intro. see Alcott, Louisa May.

***Alderson, Wayne T.** Surf U. K. 2nd ed. (Illus.). 2000. pap. 21.95 (*1-898660-68-9*) Fernhurst Bks.

Alderson, Wayne T. Surf UK. (Illus.). 159p. 1998. pap. 19.95 (*1-898660-09-3*) Golden Turtle Pr.

Alderson, Wayne T. & McDonnell, Nancy A. Theory R Management: How to Utilize Value of the Person Leadership Principles of Love, Dignity & Respect. LC 94-12159. 239p. 1994. 20.00 (*0-8407-9148-8*) Value of the Person.

Alderson, William N. Pine Mountain Groups Network Analysis Reference Guide: The Definitive Resource for the Network Analyst. 8th rev. ed. (Illus.). 78p. 1998. pap. 65.00 (*1-58392-000-5*) Pine Mt.

Alderson, William T. & Low, Shirley P. Interpretation of Historic Sites. 2nd rev. ed. LC 96-1396. (American Association for State & Local History Book Ser.). 202p. 1985. reprint ed. pap. 22.95 (*0-7619-9162-X*) AltaMira Pr.

Alderson, Wroe. Marketing Behavior & Executive Action. Assael, Henry, ed. LC 78-222. (Century of Marketing Ser.). 1979. reprint ed. lib. bdg. 44.95 (*0-405-11162-2*) Ayer.

Alderton. Foxes, Wolves & Wild Dogs. LC 99-165658. (Of the World Ser.). (Illus.). 192p. 1998. pap. 17.95 (*0-7137-2753-5*, Pub. by Blandford Pr) Sterling.

— Turtles & Tortoises. LC 99-165642. (Of the World Ser.). (Illus.). 192p. 1998. pap. 17.95 (*0-7137-2391-2*, Pub. by Blandford Pr) Sterling.

— Wild Cats. (Of the World Ser.). (Illus.). 192p. 1998. pap. 17.95 (*0-7137-2752-7*, Pub. by Blandford Pr) Sterling.

Alderton, Catherine, et al. An International History of Mammalogy Vol. 2: (Covering Africa-in Part; Southwest Pacific-in Part; the Americas-in Part; Europe-in Part) Sterling, Keir B., ed. LC 82-18865. (Illus.). 400p. 2000. 50.00 (*0-910485-02-X*); pap. 40.00 (*0-910485-03-8*) One World Pr.

Alderton, D. Castles & Palaces. (Information Ser.). (Illus.). 32p. (J). 3.25 (*0-7214-1741-8*, Ladybrd) Penguin Putnam.

— Jungle Animals. (Information Ser.). 32p. (J). text 3.25 (*0-7214-1745-0*, Ladybrd) Penguin Putnam.

— Keeping African Grey Parrots. (Illus.). 128p. 1989. 17.95 (*0-86622-957-4*, TS-111) TFH Pubns.

Alderton, David. The Atlas of Quails. (Illus.). 144p. 1992. text 47.95 (*0-86622-145-X*, TS-179) TFH Pubns.

— A Birdkeeper's Guide to Pet Birds. (Illus.). 118p. 1995. 10.95 (*1-56465-174-6*, 16081) Tetra Pr.

— A Birdkeeper's Guide to Breeding Birds. (Illus.). 118p. 1996. 10.95 (*1-56465-159-2*, 16083) Tetra Pr.

— A Birdkeeper's Guide to Budgies. (Illus.). 118p. 1996. 10.95 (*1-56465-152-5*, 16087) Tetra Pr.

— A Birdkeeper's Guide to Cockatiels. (Illus.). 95p. 1996. 10.95 (*1-56465-143-6*, 16095) Tetra Pr.

— A Birdkeeper's Guide to Cockatoos. (Illus.). 95p. 10.95 (*3-89356-037-8*, 16090) Tetra Pr.

— Birdkeepers Guide to Cockatoos. (Illus.). 1990. 11.95 (*1-56465-192-4*, 16090) Tetra Pr.

— A Birdkeeper's Guide to Finches. (Illus.). 118p. 1994. 10.95 (*1-56465-125-8*, 16084) Tetra Pr.

— A Birdkeeper's Guide to Long-Tailed Parrots. (Illus.). 95p. 1996. 10.95 (*1-56465-157-6*, 16078) Tetra Pr.

— A Birdkeeper's Guide to Softbills. (Illus.). 118p. 10.95 (*3-923880-71-5*, 16082) Tetra Pr.

***Alderton, David.** The Cage Bird Question & Answer Manual. (Illus.). 208p. 2000. 16.95 (*0-7641-5237-8*) Barron.

Alderton, David. Caring for Your Pet Bird. (101 Essential Tips Ser.). (Illus.). 72p. 1997. pap. 4.95 (*0-7894-1077-X*) DK Pub Inc.

— Cat & Kitten Care. (Practical Guide Ser.). (Illus.). 118p. 1995. 11.95 (*1-56465-154-1*, 16041) Tetra Pr.

— Cats. LC 92-7611. (Eyewitness Handbooks Ser.). (Illus.). 256p. 1992. 29.95 (*1-56458-073-3*); pap. 18.95 (*1-56458-070-9*) DK Pub Inc.

— Cats. LC 94-24739. (DK Pockets Ser.). (Illus.). 128p. (YA). (gr. 7 up). 1995. pap. 6.95 (*1-56458-886-6*) DK Pub Inc.

***Alderton, David.** Complete Book of Finches & Softbills. (Illus.). 2000. 29.95 (*0-7938-0511-2*) TFH Pubns.

Alderton, David. Complete Guide to Bird Care. LC 98-27516. (Illus.). 112p. 1998. 19.95 (*0-87605-038-0*) Howell Bks.

— The Complete Guide to Tropical Aquarium Fish Care. LC 98-35560. 112p. 1998. 19.95 (*0-87605-040-2*) Howell Bks.

— Crocodiles & Alligators of the World. (Illus.). 192p. 1998. pap. 17.95 (*0-7137-2382-3*, Pub. by Blandford Pr) Sterling.

— Crocodiles & Alligators of the World. (Of the World Ser.). (Illus.). 190p. 1991. lib. bdg. 29.95 (*0-8160-2297-6*) Facts on File.

— The Dog Care Manual. (Illus.). 160p. 1994. pap. 18.95 (*0-8120-9163-9*) Barron.

— Dogs. LC 92-53450. (Eyewitness Handbooks Ser.). (Illus.). 320p. 1993. 29.95 (*1-56458-179-9*); pap. 17.95 (*1-56458-176-4*) DK Pub Inc.

— The Exotic Pet Survival Manual: A Comprehensive Guide to Keeping Snakes, Lizards, Other Reptiles, Amphibians, Insects, Arachnids, & other Invertebrates. LC 96-47001. (Illus.). 160p. 1997. pap. 16.95 (*0-8120-9797-1*) Barron.

— Foxes, Wolves & Wild Dogs of the World. LC 92-46595. 192p. 1994. 29.95 (*0-8160-2954-7*) Facts on File.

— The Handbook of Cage & Aviary Birds. (Illus.). 496p. 1997. pap. 16.95 (*0-7137-2654-7*, Pub. by Blandford Pr) Sterling.

— Horses. LC 94-31844. (DK Pockets Ser.). (Illus.). 128p. (YA). (gr. 7 up). 1995. pap. 6.95 (*1-56458-890-4*) DK Pub Inc.

— The International Encyclopedia of Petcare. LC 97-36138. 192p. 1997. 27.95 (*0-87605-547-1*) Macmillan.

— Looking after Cage Birds. (Illus.). 128p. 1996. pap. 14.95 (*0-7137-2578-8*, Pub. by Blandford Pr) Sterling.

— My Cat. (Pet Photo Album Ser.). (Illus.). 24p. (J). (gr. 2-6). 1997. 15.95 (*0-7613-0249-2*) Millbrook Pr.

— My Dog. (Pet Photo Album Ser.). (Illus.). 24p. (J). (gr. 2-6). 1997. 15.95 (*0-7613-0239-5*) Millbrook Pr.

— Parrots. (Illus.). 128p. text 24.95 (*0-905483-91-X*, Pub. by Whittet Bks) Diamond Farm Bk.

— Parrots & Macaws. (Birdkeeper's Guide Ser.). (Illus.). 96p. 11.95 (*3-923880-74-X*, 16086) Tetra Pr.

— A Petkeeper's Guide to Hamsters & Gerbils. (Illus.). 118p. 1995. 10.95 (*1-56465-128-2*, 16053) Tetra Pr.

— A Petkeeper's Guide to Rabbits & Guinea Pigs. (Illus.). 120p. 1995. 10.95 (*1-56465-137-1*, 16054) Tetra Pr.

— A Petkeeper's Guide to Reptiles & Amphibians. (Illus.). 118p. 1995. 10.95 (*1-56465-156-8*, 16055) Tetra Pr.

***Alderton, David.** Rodents of the World. 192p. 1999. pap. text 19.95 (*0-7137-2789-6*) Blandford Pr.

Alderton, David. Rodents of the World. LC 96-15285. 192p. 1996. 29.95 (*0-8160-3229-7*) Facts on File.

— A Step-by-Step Book about Stick Insects. (Illus.). 64p. 1992. pap. 5.95 (*0-86622-349-5*, SK043) TFH Pubns.

— The Tiger Inside. LC 97-46177. 144p. 1998. pap. 21.95 (*0-87605-611-7*) Howell Bks.

— Turtles & Tortoises of the World. (Of the World Ser.). (Illus.). 191p. 1988. 29.95 (*0-8160-1733-6*) Facts on File.

— Wild Cats of the World. LC 92-38774. (Illus.). 192p. 1993. 29.95 (*0-8160-2736-6*) Facts on File.

— The Wolf Within. 144p. 1998. pap. 21.95 (*0-87605-612-5*) Howell Bks.

— You & Your Pet Bird. 1992. pap. 17.00 (*0-679-74061-9*) McKay.

Alderton, Mary. Sweden. (Blue Guide Ser.). (Illus.). 448p. 1995. pap. 24.00 (*0-393-31271-2*, Norton Paperbks) Norton.

Alderton, Patricia, jt. auth. see Kerry, Iris.

Alderton, Therese. Crimson Deception. 320p. 1986. mass mkt. 2.95 (*0-8217-1913-0*, Zebra Kensgtn) Kensgtn Pub Corp.

— Second Season. 1992. mass mkt. 3.99 (*0-8217-3640-X*, Zebra Kensgtn) Kensgtn Pub Corp.

Alderweireldt, F. C., jt. ed. see Pandit, U. K.

Aldfrith, et al. Old Irish Wisdom Attributed to Aldfrith of Northumbria: An Edition of Briathra Flainn Fhina Maic Ossu. LC 99-34089. (Medieval & Renaissance Texts & Studies: Vol. 205). 1999. 28.00 (*0-86698-247-7*) MRTS.

Aldgate, jt. auth. see Richards.

Aldgate, Anthony. Britain Can Take It: The British Cinema in the Second World War. 256p. 1994. pap. 25.00 (*0-7486-0508-8*, Pub. by Edinburgh U Pr) Col U Pr.

— Censorship & the Permissive Society: British Cinema & Theatre, 1955-1965. (Illus.). 184p. 1995. text 49.95 (*0-19-811241-6*) OUP.

***Aldgate, Anthony.** Windows on the Sixties. 2000. pap. 22.50 (*1-86064-383-3*) I B T.

Aldgate, Jane, jt. ed. see Hill, Malcolm.

Aldhous, J. R. Chemicals & Forestry: A Review of Pesticides & Other Chemicals For Forestry & Amenity Tree. LC 99-24932. (Forestry Ser.). 1999. 95.00 (*0-86380-199-4*) Research Studies Pr Ltd.

Aldhous, J. R. & Mason, W. L., eds. Forest Nursery Practice. (Forestry Commission Bulletin Ser.: No. 111). 268p. 1994. pap. 50.00 (*0-11-710323-3*, HM03233, Pub. by Statnry Office) Bernan Associates.

***Aldhouse-Green, Miranda & Howell, Raymond.** Celtic Wales. (Illus.). 160p. 2000. pap. 14.95 (*0-7083-1532-1*, Pub. by U Wales Pr) Paul & Co Pubs.

Aldi, Kim. Preparing the Assembly to Celebrate. (Preparing for Liturgy Ser.). 48p. 1997. pap. 3.95 (*0-8146-2500-2*) Liturgical Pr.

Alding, Peter. The C. I. D. Room. large type ed. (Linford Mystery Library). 1991. pap. 16.99 (*0-7089-7153-9*) Ulverscroft.

— Circle of Danger. large type ed. 1991. 27.99 (*0-7089-2510-3*) Ulverscroft.

— Despite the Evidence. large type ed. (Linford Mystery Library). 416p. 1992. pap. 16.99 (*0-7089-7301-9*) Ulverscroft.

— Field of Fire. large type ed. (Linford Mystery Library). 338p. 1992. pap. 16.99 (*0-7089-7261-6*) Ulverscroft.

— Guilt Without Proof. large type ed. 1991. 27.99 (*0-7089-2456-5*) Ulverscroft.

— A Man Condemned. large type ed. (Dales Mystery Ser.). 192p. 1992. pap. 18.99 (*1-85389-302-1*, Dales) Ulverscroft.

— Murder among Thieves. large type ed. 320p. 1992. 27.99 (*0-7089-2564-2*) Ulverscroft.

An Asterisk (*) at the beginning of an entry indicates that the title is appearing for the first time.

***Aldinger, Fritz, et al.** Precursor-Derived Ceramics: Synthesis, Structure & High-Temperature Mechanical Properties. 314p. 1999. 180.00 (*3-527-29814-2*) Wiley.

Aldington, Richard. Artifex: Sketches & Ideas. (Essay Index Reprint Ser.). 1977. 23.95 (*0-8369-1438-4*) Ayer.

— Bubb Booklets: The Letters of Richard Aldington to Charles Clinch Bubb. (Illus.). 64p. 1988. 40.00 (*0-930126-25-4*) Typographeum.

— Collected Poems. LC 78-64002. (Des Imagistes: Literature of the Imagist Movement Ser.). 248p. reprint ed. 34.50 (*0-404-17075-7*) AMS Pr.

— French Studies & Reviews. LC 67-23172. (Essay Index Reprint Ser.). 1977. 19.95 (*0-8369-0142-8*) Ayer.

— French Studies & Reviews. LC 67-23172. (Essay Index Reprint Ser.). 247p. reprint ed. lib. bdg. 18.00 (*0-8290-0481-5*) Irvington.

— In Winter. (Illus.). 16p. 1987. 50.00 (*0-930126-21-1*) Typographeum.

— Lawrence of Arabia: A Biographical Inquiry. LC 75-36506. (Illus.). 448p. 1976. reprint ed. lib. bdg. 35.00 (*0-8371-8634-X*, ALLA, Greenwood Pr) Greenwood.

— Life for Life's Sake: A Book of Reminiscences. LC 78-64003. (Des Imagistes Ser.). 416p. reprint ed. 55.00 (*0-404-17076-5*) AMS Pr.

— Literary Studies & Reviews. LC 68-16901. (Essay Index Reprint Ser.). 1977. 19.95 (*0-8369-0143-6*) Ayer.

— Roads to Glory. (Short Story Index Reprint Ser.). 1977. 20.95 (*0-8369-3666-3*) Ayer.

Aldington, Richard & H. D. Richard Aldington & H. D. The Later Years in Letters. Zilboorg, Caroline C., ed. & comment by. LC 94-24440. 1995. text 79.95 (*0-7190-4570-3*, Pub. by Manchester Univ Pr) St Martin.

Aldington, Richard, ed. see Lawrence, D. H.

Aldington, Richard, ed. see Wilde, Oscar.

Aldington, Richard, ed. & tr. see De Gourmont, Remy.

Aldington, Richard, tr. see De Laclos, Pierre-Ambroise.

Aldington, Richard, tr. see Nerval, Gerard De.

Aldington, Richard, tr. see Voltaire.

Aldis, Allan. Barbary Slavedriver. 1998. pap. 9.95 (*1-897809-52-2*) Silver Moon.

Aldis, Dorothy. Hiding. (Illus.). 32p. (J). 1993. pap. 5.95 (*1-55074-342-2*) Kids Can Pr.

Aldis, Dorothy & Collins, Heather. Hiding. (FRE.). (J). pap. 7.99 (*0-590-24195-8*) Scholastic Inc.

Aldis, Julie. The Maple Syrup Book. 96p. 2000. 19.95 (*1-55046-207-5*, Pub. by Boston Mills) Genl Dist Srvs.

Aldis, Rodney. Polar Lands. LC 91-34170. (Ecology Watch Ser.). (Illus.). 48p. (J). (gr. 5 up). 1992. lib. bdg. 13.95 (*0-87518-494-4*, Dillon Silver Burdett) Silver Burdett Pr.

— Rainforests. LC 91-20595. (Ecology Watch Ser.). (Illus.). 48p. (J). (gr. 4-6). 1991. lib. bdg. 13.95 (*0-87518-495-2*, Dillon Silver Burdett) Silver Burdett Pr.

— Towns & Cities. LC 91-35801. (Ecology Watch Ser.). (Illus.). 48p. (J). (gr. 5 up). 1992. lib. bdg. 13.95 (*0-87518-496-0*, Dillon Silver Burdett) Silver Burdett Pr.

Aldisert, Ruggero J. The Judicial Process, Text, Materials & Cases. 2nd ed. (American Casebook Ser.). 128p. (C). 1996. pap. text, teacher ed. write for info. (*0-314-09617-5*) West Pub.

— JUDICIAL PROCESS-TEXT/MATERIALS & CASES 2E. 2nd ed. LC 95-47145. (Paralegal). 900p. (C). 1996. text 45.00 incl. disk (*0-314-06776-0*) West Pub.

— Logic for Lawyers. 3rd ed. LC 97-215508. 268p. 1997. pap. 37.95 (*1-55681-538-7*) Natl Inst Trial Ad.

— Logic for Lawyers: A Guide to Clear Legal Thinking. 1992. LC 89-31818. 1992. pap. 29.95 (*0-87632-743-9*) West Group.

— Opinion Writing. 338p. 1993. reprint ed. text. write for info. (*0-314-84548-8*) West Pub.

— Winning on Appeal: Better Briefs & Oral Argument. LC 92-25687. 1992. 49.95 (*0-87632-851-6*) West Group.

— Winning on Appeal: Better Briefs & Oral Argument. rev. ed. LC 97-126282. 382p. 1996. pap. 42.95 (*1-55681-506-9*) Natl Inst Trial Ad.

***Aldiss, Allan.** Hacienda. 1998. pap. 8.95 (*1-897809-47-6*) Silver Moon.

— Slaves for the Sheik. 1999. pap. 9.99 (*1-897809-59-X*) Silver Moon.

Aldiss, Brian W. Bury My Heart at W.H. Smith's: A Writing Life. LC 91-139793. 221p. 1990. write for info. (*0-340-53661-6*) St Martin.

Aldiss, Brian W. The Detached Retina: Aspects of SF & Fantasy. LC 95-133. 280p. 1995. 45.00 (*0-8156-2681-9*); pap. 19.95 (*0-8156-0370-3*) Syracuse U Pr.

Aldiss, Brian W. Forgotten Life. 1989. 24.95 (*0-385-25211-0*) Doubleday.

— Frankenstein Unbound. 1990. mass mkt. 4.95 (*0-446-36036-8*) Warner Bks.

— Last Orders. 223p. 1990. mass mkt. 3.95 (*0-88184-617-1*) Carroll & Graf.

— New Arrivals, Old Encounters: 12 Stories. LC 79-2642. 224p. 1979. 25.00 (*0-06-010055-9*) Ultramarine Pub.

— Non-Stop. 268p. 1989. pap. 3.95 (*0-88184-492-6*) Carroll & Graf.

— A Romance of the Equator: Best Fantasy Stories LC 90-129407. 345 p. 1989. 13.95 (*0-575-04211-7*) V Gollancz.

— The Saliva Tree. 1993. reprint ed. lib. bdg. 18.95 (*0-89968-326-6*, Lghtyr Pr) Buccaneer Bks.

— The Saliva Tree & Other Strange Growths. LC 79-28703. 232p. 1981. reprint ed. 25.00 (*0-89366-147-3*) Ultramarine Pub.

— This World & Nearer Ones. 262p. 1981. pap. 16.95 (*0-938075-41-1*) Ocean View Bks.

— Trillion Year Spree. 528p. 1988. pap. 9.95 (*0-380-70461-7*, Avon Bks) Morrow Avon.

— The Twinkling of an Eye: My Life As an Englishman. LC 98-51197. 496p. 1999. text 32.50 (*0-312-19346-7*) St Martin.

Aldiss, Brian W. & Harrison, Harry, eds. Science Fiction Horizons, 2 vols. LC 74-15942. (Science Fiction Ser.). (Illus.). 64p. 1977. reprint ed. 17.95 (*0-405-06320-2*) Ayer.

***Aldiss, Brian W. & Penrose, Roger.** White Mars: Or, The Mind Set Free: A 21st Century Utopia. 256p. 2000. text 22.95 (*0-312-25473-3*) St Martin.

Aldiss, Brian W., jt. auth. see Stone, Geo.

Aldissi, M., ed. Intrinsically Conducting Polymers - An Emerging Technology: Proceedings of the NATO Advanced Research Workshop on 'Applications of Intrinsically Conducting Polymers', Burlington, Vermont, U. S. A. October 12-15, 1992. 240p. (C). 1993. text 164.50 (*0-7923-2456-0*) Kluwer Academic.

Aldissi, M., jt. auth. see Hyer, D. K.

Aldophus, Bernard A., jt. auth. see Smith, David E., Jr.

Aldous. Sports Turf Management Handbook. 430p. 1999. text 125.00 (*0-7506-8954-4*) Buttrwrth-Heinemann.

Aldous, Christopher. Police in Occupation Japan: Control Corruption & Resistance to Reform. (Routledge Studies in the Modern History of Asia: 1). 328p. (C). 1997. 90.00 (*0-415-14526-0*) Routledge.

Aldous, Clarence M., jt. auth. see Mendall, Howard L.

Aldous, D. J. Probability Approximations Via the Poison Clumping Heuristic. (Applied Mathematical Sciences Ser.: Vol. 77). (Illus.). xv, 269p. 1988. 69.95 (*0-387-96899-7*) Spr-Verlag.

Aldous, D. J., et al. Ecole d'Ete de Probabilites de Saint-Flour XIII - 1983. Hennequin, P. L., ed. (Lecture Notes in Mathematics Ser.: Vol. 1117). (Illus.). ix, 490p. 1985. 54.95 (*0-387-15203-2*) Spr-Verlag.

***Aldous, David.** International Turf Management Handbook. LC 99-36136. 1999. write for info. (*0-8493-0681-7*) CRC Pr.

— International Turf Management Handbook. 1999. ring bd. 99.95 (*0-8493-0102-5*) CRC Pr.

Aldous, David, et al, eds. Discrete Probability & Algorithms. LC 95-151. (IMA Volumes in Mathematics & Its Applications Ser.: Vol. 72). (Illus.). 175p. 1995. 59.95 (*0-387-94532-6*) Spr-Verlag.

Aldous, David & Pemantle, Robin. Random Discrete Structures. LC 95-44886. (IMA Volumes in Mathematics & Its Applications Ser.: Vol. 76). 248p. 1995. 59.95 (*0-387-94623-3*) Spr-Verlag.

Aldous, David J. & Propp, James, eds. Microsurveys in Discrete Probability: DIMACS Workshop, June 2-6, 1997. LC 98-4520. (DIMACS Ser.: Vol. 41). (Illus.). 220p. 1998. 39.00 (*0-8218-0827-3*, DIMACS/41) Am Math.

Aldous, Grahame L. & Alder, John. Applications for Judicial Review: Law & Practice of the Crown. 2nd ed. 230p. 1993. pap. 70.00 (*0-406-00576-1*, U.K., MICHIE) LEXIS Pub.

Aldous, Joan. Family Careers: A Rethinking. 301p. 1996. 59.95 (*0-8039-5179-5*); pap. 27.95 (*0-8039-5180-9*) Sage.

Aldous, Joan, ed. Two Paychecks: Life in Dual Earner Families. LC 82-10538. (Sage Focus Editions Ser.: No. 56). 247p. reprint ed. pap. 76.60 (*0-8357-4739-5*, 203765900009) Bks Demand.

Aldous, Joan & Hill, Reuben. International Bibliography of Research in Marriage & the Family, Vol. 1, 1900-1964. LC 67-63014. 516p. reprint ed. pap. 160.00 (*0-608-14676-5*, 205583500001) Bks Demand.

Aldous, Joan, jt. ed. see D'Antonio, William V.

Aldous, Joan, jt. ed. see Klein, David M.

***Aldous, Joan M. & Wilson, Robin J.** Graphs & Applications: An Introductory Approach. LC 99-56960. (Illus.). xi, 444p. (C). 2000. pap. 49.95 incl. cd-rom (*1-85233-259-X*, Pub. by Spr-Verlag) Spr-Verlag.

Aldous, Joan M., jt. auth. see Dolan, Alan.

Aldous, Kate, jt. ed. see Pearson, Maggie.

Aldous, Kathy, jt. auth. see Plenk, Bruce.

Aldous, Richard & Lee, Sabine. Harold MacMillan: Aspects of a Political Life. LC 98-38450. 288p. 1999. text 69.95 (*0-312-21906-7*) St Martin.

Aldous, Richard & Lee, Sabine, eds. Harold Macmillan & Britain's World Role. LC 95-14917. 230p. 1995. text 65.00 (*0-312-12578-X*) St Martin.

Aldred, Cyril. Akhenaten: King of Egypt. LC 87-51153. (Illus.). 320p. 1991. reprint ed. pap. 24.95 (*0-500-27621-8*, Pub. by Thames Hudson) Norton.

— Egypt to the End of the Old Kingdom. LC 82-80981. (Illus.). 1982. reprint ed. pap. 12.95 (*0-500-29001-6*, Pub. by Thames Hudson) Norton.

— Egyptian Art. LC 84-51309. (World of Art Ser.). (Illus.). 252p. 1985. pap. 14.95 (*0-500-20180-3*, Pub. by Thames Hudson) Norton.

— The Egyptians. 2nd rev. ed. LC 98-60040. (Illus.). 224p. 1998. pap. 16.95 (*0-500-28036-3*, Pub. by Thames Hudson) Norton.

— Tut-Ankh-Amen & His Friends. (J). (gr. 6-8). 1977. pap. 4.95 (*0-88388-043-1*) Bellerophon Bks.

— Tutankhmun. (Illus.). (J). (gr. 5). 1978. pap. 3.50 (*0-88388-059-8*) Bellerophon Bks.

Aldred, David. Castles & Cathedrals: The Architecture of Power. (Cambridge History Programme Ser.). (Illus.). 64p. (C). 1993. pap. 13.95 (*0-521-42842-4*) Cambridge U Pr.

Aldred, Guy. Bakunin. LC 79-179272. (Studies in Philosophy: No. 40). 1971. lib. bdg. 75.00 (*0-8383-1259-4*) M S G Haskell Hse.

Aldred, Guy A. Bakunin's Writings. 1973. 250.00 (*0-87968-049-0*) Gordon Pr.

Aldred, Heather, ed. Pregnancy & Birth Sourcebook. LC 97-36154. (Health Reference Ser.: Vol. 31). 1997. lib. bdg. 78.00 (*0-7808-0216-0*) Omnigraphics Inc.

— Sports Injuries Sourcebook: Health Reference Series. LC 99-29624. (Health Reference Ser.). 600p. 1999. lib. bdg. 78.00 (*0-7808-0218-7*) Omnigraphics Inc.

Aldred, Heather E., ed. Women's Health Concerns Sourcebook: Basic Information about Health Issues That Affect Women, Featuring Facts about Menstruation & Other Gynecological Concerns. LC 97-17093. (Health Reference Ser.: Vol. 27). (Illus.). 580p. 1997. 78.00 (*0-7808-0219-5*) Omnigraphics Inc.

Aldred, Joe D., ed. Preaching with Power: Sermons by Black Preachers. 160p. 1998. pap. 16.50 (*0-304-70439-3*) Continuum.

***Aldred, Ken.** Superpowers in The Post-cold War Era. LC 99-12667. 1999. text 65.00 (*0-312-22262-9*) St Martin.

Aldred, Lisa. Thurgood Marshall: Supreme Court Justice. Huggins, Nathan I., ed. (Black Americans of Achievement Ser.). (Illus.). 124p. (YA). (gr. 5 up). 1990. pap. 8.95 (*0-7910-0245-4*); lib. bdg. 19.95 (*1-55546-601-X*) Chelsea Hse.

Aldred, Margaret. Awaken Heart. 1980. per. 1.50 (*0-373-58051-7*) Harlequin Bks.

Aldred, Sophie & Tucker, Mike. Ace! The Inside Story of the End of an Era. LC 97-105015. (Dr. Who Missing Adventures Ser.). (Illus.). 128p. 1996. text 24.95 (*1-85227-574-X*, Pub. by Virgin Bks) London Brdge.

Aldredge-Clanton, Jann. God, a Word for Girls & Boys. (Illus.). 160p. (Orig.). 1993. pap. 12.95 (*0-9629898-3-5*) Glad River.

— In Search of the Christ-Sophia: An Inclusive Christology for Liberating Christians. LC 94-61249. 192p. (Orig.). 1995. pap. 14.95 (*0-89622-629-8*) Twenty-Third.

***Aldredge-Clanton, Jann.** In Whose Image? rev. ed. LC 00-9489. 2001. pap. 14.95 (*0-8245-1881-0*) Crossroad NY.

Aldredge-Clanton, Jann. Praying with Christ-Sophia: Services for Healing & Renewal. LC 96-60419. 160p. (Orig.). 1996. pap. 19.95 (*0-89622-697-2*) Twenty-Third.

Aldrete, Bernardo. Del Origen y Principio de la Lengua Castellana O Romance Que Hoy Se Usa en Espana. 371p. 1970. reprint ed. 126.40 incl. 3.5 hd (*0-318-71611-9*) G Olms Pubs.

Aldrete, Gregory S. Gestures & Acclamations in Ancient Rome. LC 98-56501. (Illus.). 256p. 1999. 38.00 (*0-8018-6132-2*) Johns Hopkins.

Aldrich. Espionage, Security & Intelligence in Britain 1945-1970. LC 98-28364. 256p. 2000. text 69.95 (*0-7190-4955-5*, Pub. by Manchester Univ Pr) St Martin.

— Introduction to Hospitality. 2nd ed. (C). 1998. pap. text, student ed. 20.00 (*0-13-011851-6*) P-H.

Aldrich, et al. Evoked Potential Audiometry: Fundamentals & Applications. LC 98-23831. 260p. 1998. 68.00 (*0-13-299603-0*) P-H.

Aldrich, Anne Hazard. Notes from Myself: A Guide to Creative Journal Writing. LC 97-6786. 160p. 1998. pap. 11.95 (*0-7867-0433-0*) Carroll & Graf.

Aldrich, B. S. Home-Coming. 23.95 (*0-8488-0067-2*) Amereon Ltd.

Aldrich, Bess S. Across the Smiling Meadow & Other Stories. Date not set. lib. bdg. 19.95 (*0-8488-0068-0*) Amereon Ltd.

— Bess Streeter Aldrich Treasury. large type ed. Date not set. lib. bdg. 31.95 (*0-88411-232-2*, Aeonian Pr) Amereon Ltd.

— Bess Streeter Aldrich Treasury. 320p. reprint ed. lib. bdg. 33.95 (*0-88411-263-2*) Amereon Ltd.

— The Collected Short Works, 1907-1919. Petersen, Carol M., ed. & intro. by. LC 94-19005. xiv, 246p. 1995. text 50.00 (*0-8032-1038-8*) U of Nebr Pr.

— The Cutters. large type ed. 220p. 1992. reprint ed. lib. bdg. 19.95 (*1-56054-501-1*) Thorndike Pr.

— The Cutters. 275p. 1975. reprint ed. lib. bdg. 23.95 (*0-88411-254-3*) Amereon Ltd.

— The Drum Goes Dead. 339p. 1975. reprint ed. lib. bdg. 12.95 (*0-88411-256-X*) Amereon Ltd.

— Journey into Christmas. 265p. reprint ed. lib. bdg. 22.95 (*0-88411-262-4*) Amereon Ltd.

— Journey into Christmas & Other Stories. LC 85-8559. (Illus.). v, 265p. 1985. reprint ed. pap. 10.95 (*0-8032-5908-5*, Bison Books) U of Nebr Pr.

— A Lantern in Her Hand. LC 93-39763. ix, 307p. 1994. pap. 10.00 (*0-8032-5922-0*, Bison Books) U of Nebr Pr.

— A Lantern in Her Hand. LC 96-34910. 256p. (YA). (gr. 8 up). 1997. pap. 4.99 (*0-14-038428-6*) Viking Penguin.

— A Lantern in Her Hand. 278p. Date not set. reprint ed. lib. bdg. 21.95 (*0-88411-260-8*) Amereon Ltd.

— The Lieutenant's Lady. 275p. 1975. reprint ed. lib. bdg. 24.95 (*0-88411-252-7*) Amereon Ltd.

— The Lieutenant's Lady. LC 87-4994. iv, 277p. 1987. reprint ed. pap. 13.50 (*0-8032-5914-X*, Bison Books) U of Nebr Pr.

— Man Who Caught the Weather & Other Stories. 293p. 1975. reprint ed. lib. bdg. 23.95 (*0-88411-258-6*) Amereon Ltd.

— Miss Bishop. 336p. 1975. reprint ed. lib. bdg. 25.95 (*0-88411-255-1*) Amereon Ltd.

— Miss Bishop. LC 86-6969. iv, 337p. 1986. reprint ed. pap. 14.95 (*0-8032-5909-3*, Bison Books) U of Nebr Pr.

— Mother Mason. large type ed. LC 93-17772. 219p. 1993. lib. bdg. 20.95 (*1-56054-502-X*) Thorndike Pr.

— Mother Mason. 268p. 1975. reprint ed. lib. bdg. 22.95 (*0-88411-257-8*) Amereon Ltd.

— Mother Mason. LC 86-25111. v, 269p. 1987. reprint ed. pap. 11.95 (*0-8032-5913-1*, Bison Books) U of Nebr Pr.

— The Outsider & Other Stories. 20.95 (*0-8488-0161-X*) Amereon Ltd.

— The Rim of the Prairie. LC 25-19624. xii, 352p. 1966. pap. 12.95 (*0-8032-5002-9*, Bison Books) U of Nebr Pr.

— The Rim of the Prairie. 296p. reprint ed. lib. bdg. 26.95 (*0-88411-259-4*) Amereon Ltd.

— Romance in G Minor. 25.95 (*0-8488-0066-4*) Amereon Ltd.

— Song of Years. large type ed. LC 91-30615. 735p. 1992. lib. bdg. 20.95 (*1-56054-275-6*) Thorndike Pr.

— A Song of Years. 490p. 1975. reprint ed. lib. bdg. 30.95 (*0-88411-251-9*) Amereon Ltd.

— Song of Years. LC 91-17881. 405p. 1991. reprint ed. pap. 12.95 (*0-8032-5918-2*, Bison Books) U of Nebr Pr.

— Spring Came on Forever. large type ed. LC 92-41150. 418p. 1993. reprint ed. lib. bdg. 20.95 (*1-56054-503-8*) Thorndike Pr.

— Spring Came on Forever. 333p. reprint ed. lib. bdg. 25.95 (*0-88411-261-6*) Amereon Ltd.

— Spring Came on Forever. LC 84-19671. vii, 333p. 1985. reprint ed. pap. 13.95 (*0-8032-5907-7*, Bison Books) U of Nebr Pr.

— The Victory of Connie Lee. 25.95 (*0-8488-0160-1*) Amereon Ltd.

— A White Bird Flying. LC 87-30057. ii, 222p. 1988. pap. 9.95 (*0-8032-5915-8*, Bison Books) U of Nebr Pr.

— A White Bird Flying. 335p. 1975. reprint ed. lib. bdg. 25.95 (*0-88411-253-5*) Amereon Ltd.

A

***Aldrich, Bess S. & Petersen, Carol M.** The Collected Short Works, 1920-1954. LC 98-19283. xvi, 321p. 1999. text 50.00 (*0-8032-1052-3*) U of Nebr Pr.

Aldrich, Bess Streeter. A Lantern in Her Hand. (J). 1997. 10.09 (*0-606-11546-3*, Pub. by Turtleback) Demco.

Aldrich, Bob. ABC's of AFV's: A Guide to Alternative Fuel Vehicles. (Illus.). 112p. 1997. reprint ed. pap. text 25.00 (*0-7881-4593-2*) DIANE Pub.

Aldrich, Brian C., ed. Housing in Asia: Problems & Perspectives. 1990. 20.00 (*81-7033-101-3*, Pub. by Rawat Pubns) S Asia.

Aldrich, Brian C. & Sandhu, Ranvinder S. Housing the Urban Poor Policy & Practice in Developing Countries. 420p. 1995. pap. 212.50 (*81-7036-462-0*, Pub. by Print Hse) St Mut.

Aldrich, C. K. The Medical Interview: Gateway to the Doctor-Patient Relationship. 2nd enl. rev. ed. (Illus.). 164p. 1999. pap. 24.95 (*1-85070-014-1*) Prthnon Pub.

Aldrich, C. Knight. The Medical Interview: Gateway to the Doctor Patient Relationship. LC 93-18395. (Illus.). 126p. 1993. 17.95 (*1-85070-487-2*) Prthnon Pub.

Aldrich, C. Knight, ed. see Sherman, Francis T.

Aldrich, Caroline, ed. Bulgaria. (C). 1995. 50.00 (*0-929851-35-8*) Am Assn Coll Registrars.

Aldrich, Charles R. Primitive Mind & Modern Civilization. LC 79-98401. reprint ed. 27.50 (*0-404-00309-5*) AMS Pr.

Aldrich Chemical Company, jt. auth. see Pouchert, Charles J.

Aldrich, Daniel G., Jr. & Mayer, Lorenzo. Mexico & the United States: Neighbors in Crisis. LC 93-924. (Great Issues of the Day Ser.: No. 6). (Illus.). x, 390p. 1993. pap. 35.00 (*0-89370-445-8*) Millefleurs.

Aldrich, Dorothy. Historic Colorado City: Town with a Future. Feitz, Leland, ed. (Illus.). 80p. 1996. pap. 5.95 (*0-936564-41-5*) Little London.

Aldrich, Dorothy, jt. ed. see Schwartz, Dorothy.

***Aldrich, Douglas F.** Mastering the Digital Marketplace: Practical Strategies for Competitiveness in the New Economy. LC 99-26880. 336p. 1999. 29.95 (*0-471-34546-6*) Wiley.

Aldrich, Earl M. The Modern Short Story in Peru. LC 66-22860. 224p. 1966. reprint ed. pap. 69.50 (*0-608-01901-1*, 206255300003) Bks Demand.

Aldrich, Edward. Drawing & Painting Animals: How to Capture the Essence of Wildlife Art. LC 98-24730. (Illus.). 1998. 29.95 (*0-8230-3606-5*) Watsn-Guptill.

Aldrich, Elizabeth. Daily Use of the Ephemeris. LC 84-72294. 86p. 1971. 7.00 (*0-86690-286-4*, A2406-014) Am Fed Astrologers.

— From the Ballroom to Hell: Grace & Folly in Nineteenth-Century Dance. (Illus.). 250p. (Orig.). 1991. pap. 19.95 (*0-8101-0913-1*) Northwestern U Pr.

Aldrich, Frank T., jt. auth. see Lounsbury, John F.

Aldrich, Frederick. Absolute Zero. LC 98-68263. 448p. 1999. 28.95 (*1-57197-144-0*) Pentland Pr.

Aldrich, Gary W. Unlimited Access: An FBI Agent Inside the Clinton White House. LC 99-18400. (American History Ser.). 1999. 26.95 (*0-7838-8583-0*) Mac Lib Ref.

— Unlimited Access: An FBI Agent Inside the Clinton White House. LC 95-26817. 1996. 24.95 (*0-89526-454-4*) Regnery Pub.

— Unlimited Access: An FBI Agent Inside the Clinton White House. LC 98-161435. (Illus.). 288p. 1998. pap. 15.95 (*0-89526-406-4*) Regnery Pub.

Aldrich, Gary W. & Davis, Mark. Speak No Evil. LC 98-35210. 288p. 1998. 24.95 (*0-89526-358-0*) Regnery Pub.

Aldrich, George. Walpole As It Was & As It Is: Containing the Complete Civil History of the Town from 1749 to 1879, Also...a History of the 150 Families that Settled in the Town Previous to 1820... (Illus.). 404p. 1995. reprint ed. lib. bdg. 42.50 (*0-8328-4646-5*) Higginson Bk Co.

Aldrich, George H., ed. The Jurisprudence of the Iran-United States Claims Tribunal. 606p. 1996. text 150.00 (*0-19-825805-4*) OUP.

Aldrich, Harl P. Charles A. Bragg Memorial Lecture: The New Technology. 25.00 (*0-614-05238-6*, CBML10811.5M) ASFE.

Aldrich, Henry, et al. Henry Aldrich: Selected Anthems & Motet Recompositions. Shay, Robert, ed. (Recent Researches in Music of the Baroque Era Ser.: Vol. RRB85). (Illus.). xiv, 120p. 1998. pap. 45.00 (*0-89579-393-8*) A-R Eds.

Aldrich, Henry C. & Todd, William J., eds. Ultrastructure Techniques for Microorganisms. (Illus.). 548p. (C). 1986. text 150.00 (*0-306-42251-4*, Kluwer Plenum) Kluwer Academic.

Aldrich, Howard, et al. Population Perspectives on Organizations. 110p. (Orig.). 1986. pap. text 37.50 (*91-554-1909-7*, Pub. by Uppsala Univ Acta Univ Uppsaliensis) Coronet Bks.

An Asterisk (*) at the beginning of an entry indicates that the title is appearing for the first time.

Aldrich, James A. Centennial: A Century of Island Newspapers. LC 85-28488. (Illus.). 194p. 1985. pap. 24.95 (*0-941238-04-0*, Penobscot Bks) Penobscot Bay.

Aldrich, James M. Fair Winds, Stormy Seas: 50 Years of Maine Maritime Academy. LC 91-50653. (Illus.). 150p. 1991. pap. 18.85 (*0-941238-09-1*, Penobscot Bks) Penobscot Bay.

Aldrich, James R. Pollution Prevention Economics: Financial Impacts on Business & Industry. (Illus.). 192p. 1995. 45.00 (*0-07-000993-7*) McGraw.

***Aldrich, Joe.** Lifestyle Evangelism: Learning to Open Your Life to Those Around You. 252p. 1999. pap. 6.99 (*1-57673-651-2*) Multnomah Pubs.

Aldrich, Joe. Secrets of Wisdom from Mama's Heart. 1999. pap. 14.99 (*0-8499-5403-7*) Word Pub.

***Aldrich, Joe, et al.** Classic Critical Concern, Set. 1999. pap. 19.99 (*1-57673-282-7*) Multnomah Pubs.

Aldrich, John. Lakesport's Ancient Homes: Recollections of Major John Aldrich . . . And of the Homes of Lakeport in 1844 with Notes of Their Occupants Then & Later. (Illus.). 86p. 1997. reprint ed. pap. 15.00 (*0-8328-6003-4*) Higginson Bk Co.

Aldrich, John, et al. American Government: People, Institutions, & Policies, 2 vols. 2nd ed. (C). 1990. pap. text 3.96 (*0-395-52944-1*) HM.

— American Government: People, Institutions, & Policies, 2 vols. 2nd ed. (C). 1990. pap. text 5.96 (*0-395-52946-8*); pap. text, teacher ed. 2.76 (*0-395-52943-3*) HM.

— American Government: People, Institutions, & Policies, 2 vols. 2nd ed. (C). 1990. 53.56 (*0-395-52945-X*) HM.

— American Government: People, Institutions, & Politics. LC 85-80687. 608p. (C). 1985. audio 5.00 (*0-395-40816-4*) HM.

Aldrich, John F. Single Wing Offense with the Spinning Fullback. LC 83-7060. (Illus.). 183p. 1983. reprint ed. pap. 52.20 (*0-608-00104-X*, 2060869) Bks Demand.

Aldrich, John H. Before the Convention: Strategies & Choices in Presidential Nomination Campaigns. LC 79-27752. (Illus.). xiv, 258p. 1980. pap. text 7.95 (*0-226-01270-0*, P888); lib. bdg. 30.00 (*0-226-01269-7*) U Ch Pr.

— Why Parties? The Origin & Transformation of Political Parties in America. LC 94-36879. (American Politics & Political Economy Ser.). 360p. 1995. pap. text 16.95 (*0-226-01272-7*) U Ch Pr.

— Why Parties? The Origin & Transformation of Political Parties in America. LC 94-36879. (American Politics & Political Economy Ser.). 360p. 1997. lib. bdg. 48.00 (*0-226-01271-9*) U Ch Pr.

Aldrich, John H. & Nelson, Forrest D. Linear Probability, Logit, & Probit Models. LC 84-51766. (Quantitative Applications in the Social Sciences Ser.: Vol. 45). 95p. 1984. pap. 10.95 (*0-8039-2133-0*) Sage.

Aldrich, John H., jt. auth. see Abramson, Paul R.

Aldrich, John K. Ghosts of Boulder County: A Guide to the Ghost Towns & Mining Camps of Boulder County, Colorado. rev. ed. 53p. 1990. pap. text 6.95 (*1-883425-03-4*) Cent Graphics.

— Ghosts of Chaffee County: A Guide to the Ghost Towns & Mining Camps of Chaffee County, & Eastern Gunnison County, Colorado. rev. ed. 64p. 1992. pap. text 6.95 (*1-883425-08-5*) Cent Graphics.

— Ghosts of Clear Creek County: A Guide to the Ghost Towns & Mining Camps of Clear Creek County, Colorado. rev. ed. 60p. 1997. pap. text 6.95 (*1-883425-02-6*) Cent Graphics.

— Ghosts of Gilpin County: A Guide to the Ghost Towns & Mining Camps of Gilpin County, Colorado. rev. ed. 52p. 1996. pap. text 6.95 (*1-883425-01-8*) Cent Graphics.

— Ghosts of Lake County: A Guide to the Ghost Towns & Mining Camps of Lake County, & Eastern Pitkin County, Colorado. rev. ed. 57p. 1997. pap. text 6.95 (*1-883425-07-7*) Cent Graphics.

— Ghosts of Northern Colorado: A Guide to the Ghost Towns & Mining Camps of Eagle, Grand, Jackson, Routt, & Larimer Counties, Colorado. rev. ed. 52p. 1991. pap. text 6.95 (*1-883425-11-5*) Cent Graphics.

— Ghosts of Park County: A Guide to the Ghost Towns & Mining Camps of Park County, Colorado. rev. ed. 50p. 1994. pap. text 6.95 (*1-883425-04-2*) Cent Graphics.

— Ghosts of Pitkin County: A Guide to the Ghost Towns & Mining Camps of Pitkin & Northern Gunnison Counties, Colorado. rev. ed. 57p. 1992. pap. text 6.95 (*1-883425-10-7*) Cent Graphics.

— Ghosts of Summit County: A Guide to the Ghost Towns & Mining Camps of Summit County, Colorado. rev. ed. 60p. 1997. pap. text 6.95 (*1-883425-06-9*) Cent Graphics.

— Ghosts of Teller County: A Guide to the Ghost Towns & Mining Camps of Teller County, Colorado. 50p. 1994. pap. text 6.95 (*1-883425-05-0*) Cent Graphics.

— Ghosts of the Eastern San Juans: A Guide to the Ghost Towns & Mining Camps of the Eastern San Juan Mountains, Colorado. 50p. 1997. pap. text 6.95 (*1-883425-12-3*) Cent Graphics.

— Ghosts of the Sangre de Cristo Area: A Guide to the Ghost Towns & Mining Camps of the Greater Sangre de Cristo Mountains, Colorado. rev. ed. 54p. 1997. pap. text 6.95 (*1-883425-09-3*) Cent Graphics.

— Ghosts of the Western San Juans Vol. I: A Guide to the Ghost Towns & Mining Camps of Ouray, San Juan, & Hinsdale Counties, Colorado. rev. ed. 64p. 1998. pap. text 6.95 (*1-883425-13-1*) Cent Graphics.

— Ghosts of the Western San Juans Vol. II: A Guide to the Ghost Towns & Mining Camps of San Miguel, La Plata, & Delores Counties, Colorado. 50p. 1997. pap. text 6.95 (*1-883425-14-X*) Cent Graphics.

Aldrich, John W. Ecogeographical Variation in Size & Proportions of Song Sparrows (Melospizamelodia) (Ornithological Monographs: No. 35). (Illus.). x, 134p. 1984. pap. 15.00 (*0-943610-43-5*) Am Ornithologists.

Aldrich, Jonathan. Death of Michelangelo. Hunting, Constance, ed. 40p. (Orig.). 1985. pap. 7.95 (*0-913006-33-5*) Puckerbrush.

Aldrich, Joseph C. Gentle Persuasion: Creative Ways to Introduce Your Friends to Christ. Halliday, Steve, ed. LC 88-19828. (Illus.). 240p. 1988. pap. 10.99 (*0-88070-253-2*, Multnomah Bks) Multnomah Pubs.

Aldrich, Kathleen. Out of the Dark. LC 94-48662. 106p. (J). 1995. pap. 6.49 (*0-89084-799-1*, 086942) Bob Jones Univ.

Aldrich, Keith, tr. Apollodorus: The Library of Greek Mythology. 298p. 1975. 25.00 (*0-87291-072-5*) Coronado Pr.

Aldrich, Lance, jt. auth. see Wise, Gary.

Aldrich-Langen, Caroline. Australia. LC 83-19723. (World Education Ser.). (Illus.). 276p. (Orig.). 1983. pap. text 12.00 (*0-910054-78-9*) Am Assn Coll Registrars.

— The Educational System of Australia: An Update of the 1983 World Education Series Volume. 74p. 1990. pap. 12.00 (*0-929851-05-6*) Am Assn Coll Registrars.

— Understanding the Admissions Process in U. S. Higher Education: A Case Study Approach. LC 93-35556. (PIER World Education Series Special Report). 24p. 1993. pap. text 25.00 (*0-929851-18-8*) Am Assn Coll Registrars.

Aldrich-Langen, Caroline, ed. Methods & Skills for Research on Foreign Educational Systems: A Report on the 1994 NAFSA/EAIE Seminars, June 3-5, University of Miami, Coral Gables, Florida, November 22-23, Cambridge, England. LC 95-34230. 1995. 15.00 (*0-929851-68-4*) Am Assn Coll Registrars.

Aldrich-Langen, Caroline & Sellew, Kathleen T., eds. The Admission & Placement of Students from Central America. (Workshop Reports). 236p. 1988. 25.00 (*0-614-23471-9*, 5347) Am Assn Coll Registrars.

Aldrich, Lanning. Majorca: The Art of Living. 208p. 1998. 50.00 (*1-55670-847-5*) Stewart Tabori & Chang.

Aldrich, Leigh S. Covering the Community: A Diversity Handbook for Media. LC 98-58151. (A Diversity Stylebook for Media Ser.). 1999. write for info. (*0-7619-8513-1*) Pine Forge.

Aldrich, Lewis C. History of Franklin & Grand Isle Counties, Vermont. (Illus.). 821p. 1992. reprint ed. lib. bdg. 80.00 (*0-8328-2255-8*) Higginson Bk Co.

Aldrich, Lewis C., ed. History of Bennington County, Vermont. (Illus.). 584p. 1993. reprint ed. lib. bdg. 59.50 (*0-8328-3208-1*) Higginson Bk Co.

— History of Clearfield County, with Illustrations & Biographical Sketches of Some of Its Prominent Men & Pioneers. (Illus.). 731p. 1997. reprint ed. lib. bdg. 75.00 (*0-8328-6402-1*) Higginson Bk Co.

— History of Erie County, Ohio. 653p. 1993. reprint ed. lib. bdg. 66.00 (*0-8328-2782-7*) Higginson Bk Co.

— History of Henry & Fulton Counties, with Illustrations & Biographical Sketches of Some of Its Prominent Men & Pioneers. (Illus.). 712p. 1997. reprint ed. lib. bdg. 74.50 (*0-8328-6325-4*) Higginson Bk Co.

— History of Yates County, with Illustrations & Biographical Sketches of the Prominent Men & Pioneers. (Illus.). 671p. 1997. reprint ed. lib. bdg. 68.50 (*0-8328-6284-3*) Higginson Bk Co.

Aldrich, Lewis C. & Holmes, Frank R., eds. History of Windsor County, Vermont. (Illus.). 1005p. 1993. reprint ed. lib. bdg. 99.50 (*0-8328-3172-7*) Higginson Bk Co.

Aldrich, Linda K., ed. see Chambers, Marjorie B.

Aldrich, Maria. Girl Rearing: A Memoir of a Girlhood Gone Astray. LC 98-5400. 192p. 1998. 24.95 (*0-393-02748-1*) Norton.

Aldrich, Mark. Safety First: Technology, Labor, & Business in the Building of American Work Safety, 1870-1939. LC 96-28998. (Studies in Industry & Society). (Illus.). 440p. 1997. text 49.95 (*0-8018-5405-9*) Johns Hopkins.

Aldrich, Mark & Buchele, Robert. The Economics of Comparable Worth. LC 85-26821. 208p. 1986. text 34.95 (*0-88730-073-1*, HarpBusn) HarpInfo.

Aldrich, Megan. Gothic Revival. (Illus.). 240p. 1997. pap. 35.00 (*0-7148-3631-1*, Pub. by Phaidon Press) Phaidon Pr.

Aldrich, Michael S. Sleep Medicine: Normal Sleep & Its Disorders. LC 98-30554. (Contemporary Neurology Ser.: Vol. 53). (Illus.). 408p. 1999. text 110.00 (*0-19-512957-1*) OUP.

Aldrich, Michele L., jt. ed. see Leviton, Alan E.

Aldrich, Mildred. A Hilltop on the Marne Being Letters Written June 3-September 8, 1914. (American Biography Ser.). 187p. 1991. reprint ed. lib. bdg. 59.00 (*0-7812-8010-9*) Rprt Serv.

— On the Edge of the War Zone, From the Battle of the Marne to the Entrance of the Stars & Stripes. (American Biography Ser.). 311p. 1991. reprint ed. lib. bdg. 69.00 (*0-7812-8011-7*) Rprt Serv.

— Told in a French Garden, August, 1914. (Short Story Index Reprint Ser.). 1977. 20.95 (*0-8369-3327-3*) Ayer.

Aldrich-Moodie, Benjamin & Kwong, Jo. Environmental Education. (IEA Studies in Education, No. 3: No. 9). 126p. 1997. pap. 27.50 (*0-255-36442-3*, Pub. by Inst Economic Affairs) Coronet Bks.

Aldrich, Nancy. Keeping Childhood. rev. ed. (Illus.). 123p. 1989. pap. 15.00 (*0-9623583-0-4*) Childhood Pr.

Aldrich, Nancy C., et al. Complying with the Americans with Disabilities Act, ADA: A Guide for Health Care Facilities. (Illus.). 560p. (Orig.). 1992. pap. 60.00 (*0-87258-591-3*, 055980) Am Hospital.

Aldrich, Nelson W., Jr. Old Money: The Mythology of Wealth in America. 2nd expanded ed. LC 96-84663. 352p. 1996. pap. 16.95 (*1-880559-64-1*) Allworth Pr.

Aldrich, Nicole M. Feelings Between God & Me. 1997. pap. write for info. (*1-57553-525-4*) Watermrk Pr.

Aldrich, R. J. & Kremer, R. J. Principles in Weed Management. 2nd ed. LC 96-28049. (Illus.). 1997. 64.95 (*0-8138-2023-5*) Iowa St U Pr.

Aldrich, Richard. Concert Life in New York, Nineteen Hundred to Nineteen Twenty-Three. Johnson, Harold, ed. LC 78-156603. (Essay Index Reprint Ser.). 1977. reprint ed. 39.95 (*0-8369-2263-8*) Ayer.

— Concert Life in New York, 1902-1923. (Music Book Index Ser.). 795p. 1992. reprint ed. lib. bdg. 109.00 (*0-7812-9503-3*) Rprt Serv.

— History in the National Curriculum. 120p. (Orig.). 1990. pap. 21.95 (*0-8464-1416-3*) Beekman Pubs.

— The Key to the South: Britain, the United States, & Thailand During the Approach of the Pacific War, 1929-1942. (South-East Asian Historical Monographs). (Illus.). 440p. 1993. text 55.00 (*0-19-588612-7*) OUP.

— Musical Discourse, from the New York Times. LC 67-28740. (Essay Index Reprint Ser.). 1977. 20.95 (*0-8369-0144-4*) Ayer.

— School & Society in Victorian Britain: Joseph Payne & the New World of Education. LC 94-17106. (Studies in the History of Education: Vol. 935, Vol. 1). (Illus.). 317p. 1994. text 54.00 (*0-8153-1558-9*, SS935) Garland.

Aldrich, Richard, ed. In History & in Education: Essays Presented to Peter Gordon. 256p. (C). 1996. 45.00 (*0-7130-0201-8*, Pub. by Woburn Pr) Intl Spec Bk.

Aldrich, Richard & Gordon, Peter. Biographical Dictionary of North American & European Educationists. (Illus.). 528p. 1997. 49.50 (*0-7130-0193-3*, Pub. by Woburn Pr); 49.50 (*0-7130-0205-0*, Pub. by Woburn Pr); pap. 25.00 (*0-7130-4022-X*, Pub. by Woburn Pr); pap. 25.00 (*0-7130-4025-4*, Pub. by Woburn Pr) Intl Spec Bk.

— Dictionary of British Educationists. (Illus.). 276p. 1989. text 35.00 (*0-7130-0177-1*, Pub. by Woburn Pr); pap. text 19.50 (*0-7130-4011-4*, Pub. by Woburn Pr) Intl Spec Bk.

Aldrich, Richard, tr. see Lehmann, Lilli.

Aldrich, Richard J. Espionage, Security & Intelligence in Britain 1945-1970. LC 98-28364. (Documents in Contemporary History Ser.). 256p. 1998. pap. 29.95 (*0-7190-4956-3*) St Martin.

***Aldrich, Richard J.** Intelligence & the War Against Japan: Britain, America & the Politics of Secret Service. LC 99-29697. (Illus.). 483p. 2000. 34.95 (*0-521-64186-1*) Cambridge U Pr.

Aldrich, Richard J., ed. British Intelligence, Strategy & the Cold War, 1945-1951. (Illus.). 368p. (C). (gr. 13). 1992. 120.00 (*0-415-07851-2*, A7516) Routledge.

***Aldrich, Richard J., et al, eds.** The Clandestine Cold War in Asia, 1945-65: Western Intelligence, Propaganda, Security & Special Operations. (Illus.). 312p. 2000. 57.50 (*0-7146-5045-5*, Pub. by F Cass Pubs); pap. 24.50 (*0-7146-8096-6*, Pub. by F Cass Pubs) Intl Spec Bk.

Aldrich, Richard J. & Hopkins, Michael F. Intelligence, Defence & Diplomacy: British Policy in the Post War World. LC 93-6365. (Studies in Intelligence). 270p. 1994. 47.50 (*0-7146-3498-0*, Pub. by F Cass Pubs); pap. 24.50 (*0-7146-4140-5*, Pub. by F Cass Pubs) Intl Spec Bk.

Aldrich, Robert. France & the South Pacific since, 1940. LC 93-6783. 440p. (C). 1993. text 34.00 (*0-8248-1558-0*) UH Pr.

— The Seduction of the Mediterranean: Writing, Art & Homosexual Fantasy. LC 92-40812. 1993. write for info. (*0-415-03277-6*) Routledge.

— The Seduction of the Mediterranean: Writing, Art & Homosexual Fantasy. LC 92-40812. (Illus.). 288p. (C). (gr. 13). 1993. pap. 27.99 (*0-415-09312-0*) Routledge.

— Seduction of the Mediterranean: Writing, Art & Homosexual Fantasy. LC 91-40812. (Illus.). 288p. (C). (gr. 13). 1993. 80.00 (*0-415-03227-X*) Routledge.

Aldrich, Robert & Connell, John. France's Overseas Frontier: The Departements et Territoires d'Outre-mer. (Illus.). 367p. (C). 1992. text 74.95 (*0-521-39061-3*) Cambridge U Pr.

— The Last Colonies. LC 97-39275. (Illus.). 272p. (C). 1998. 59.95 (*0-521-41461-X*) Cambridge U Pr.

Aldrich, Robert & Connell, John, eds. France in World Politics. 256p. 1989. 56.95 (*0-415-03506-6*) Routledge.

Aldrich, Robert, jt. auth. see Tipton, Frank B.

Aldrich, Robert, jt. ed. see Carroll, John M.

Aldrich, Robert, jt. ed. see Tipton, Frank B.

Aldrich, Robert A. & Bartok, John W., Jr. Greenhouse Engineering. (NRAES Ser.: Vol. 33). (Illus.). 212p. 1984. pap. text 30.00 (*0-935817-57-3*, NRAES-33) NRAES.

Aldrich, Robert S. Robert Aldrich's los Gatos. (Illus.). 1997. write for info. (*0-9661471-0-3*) Metro Publng.

Aldrich, Ruth I., ed. see Holcroft, Thomas.

Aldrich, Sandra. Will I Ever Be Whole Again? Surviving the Death of Someone You Love. LC 99-19406. 171p. 1999. 16.99 (*1-58229-012-1*) Howard Pub LA.

Aldrich, Sandra, jt. auth. see Jones, Wanda.

Aldrich, Sandra P. Bless Your Socks Off: Unleashing the Power of Encouragement. LC 97-47627. 1998. pap. text 9.99 (*1-56179-579-8*) Focus Family.

— Men Read Newspapers, Not Minds: And Other Things I Wish I'd Known When I First Married. LC 96-9174. 180p. 1996. pap. 10.99 (*0-8423-8175-9*) Tyndale Hse.

***Aldrich, Sandra P.** 101 Upward Glances. 2000. pap. 10.99 (*0-8423-3604-4*) Tyndale Hse.

Aldrich, Sandra P. & Valentine, Bobbie. Heartprints: Celebrating the Power of a Simple Touch. 208p. 1999. 13.95 (*1-57856-039-X*) Waterbrook Pr.

***Aldrich, Sandra P. & Valentine, Bobbie.** Heartprints: Celebrating the Power of a Simple Touch. 208p. 1999. 111.60 (*1-57856-201-5*) Waterbrook Pr.

Aldrich, Sandra P., jt. auth. see Fuller, Cheri.

Aldrich, Sandra P., jt. auth. see Gabre-Tsadick, Marta.

Aldrich, Steve. Casino Blackjack: Your Best Bet. (Illus.). 1989. 6.00 (*0-9622229-1-7*) Zauberman Pr.

— A Powerful Memory: A Key to Success. 1989. 5.00 (*0-9622229-0-9*) Zauberman Pr.

Aldrich, Terry M. Rates of Return on Investment in Technical Education in the Ante-Bellum American Economy. LC 75-2573. (Dissertations in American Economic History Ser.). (Illus.). 1975. 37.95 (*0-405-07254-6*) Ayer.

Aldrich, Thomas Bailey. Cloth of Gold. (Works of Thomas Bailey Aldrich). 1989. reprint ed. lib. bdg. 79.00 (*0-685-27378-4*) Rprt Serv.

— Flower & Thorn. (Works of Thomas Bailey Aldrich). 1989. reprint ed. lib. bdg. 79.00 (*0-685-58458-5*) Rprt Serv.

Aldrich, Thomas Bailey. Friar Jerome's Beautiful Book. (Works of Thomas Bailey Aldrich). 1989. reprint ed. lib. bdg. 79.00 (*0-7812-1666-4*) Rprt Serv.

Aldrich, Thomas Bailey. From Ponkapog to Pesth. (Works of Thomas Bailey Aldrich). 1989. reprint ed. lib. bdg. 79.00 (*0-7812-1679-6*) Rprt Serv.

— Judith & Holofernes. (Works of Thomas Bailey Aldrich). 1989. reprint ed. lib. bdg. 79.00 (*0-685-56070-8*) Rprt Serv.

— Marjorie Daw & Other People. (Short Story Index Reprint Ser.). 1977. 20.95 (*0-8369-3230-7*) Ayer.

— Marjorie Daw & Other People. (Works of Thomas Bailey Aldrich). 243p. reprint ed. 44.00 (*0-7812-0819-X*) Rprt Serv.

— Marjorie Daw & Other People. (Works of Thomas Bailey Aldrich). 1989. reprint ed. lib. bdg. 79.00 (*0-7812-1665-6*) Rprt Serv.

— Marjorie Daw & Other Stories. (Short Story Index Reprint Ser.). 1977. 20.95 (*0-8369-3231-5*) Ayer.

— Marjorie Daw & Other Stories. 1972. reprint ed. lib. bdg. 18.00 (*0-8422-8001-4*) Irvington.

— Marjorie Daw & Other Stories. (C). 1986. reprint ed. pap. text 6.95 (*0-8290-1943-X*) Irvington.

— Mercedes & Later Lyrics. (Works of Thomas Bailey Aldrich). 1989. reprint ed. lib. bdg. 79.00 (*0-7812-1667-2*) Rprt Serv.

— An Old Town by the Sea. (Works of Thomas Bailey Aldrich). 1989. reprint ed. lib. bdg. 79.00 (*0-7812-1680-X*) Rprt Serv.

— Pompinea. (Works of Thomas Bailey Aldrich). 1989. reprint ed. lib. bdg. 79.00 (*0-685-27379-2*) Rprt Serv.

Aldrich, Thomas Bailey. Ponkapog Papers. LC 70-84293. (Essay Index Reprint Ser.). 1977. 15.95 (*0-8369-1073-7*) Ayer.

— Ponkapog Papers. (Works of Thomas Bailey Aldrich). 1989. reprint ed. lib. bdg. 79.00 (*0-7812-1681-8*) Rprt Serv.

Aldrich, Thomas Bailey. Prudence Palfrey. (Works of Thomas Bailey Aldrich). 1989. reprint ed. lib. bdg. 79.00 (*0-7812-1672-9*) Rprt Serv.

— The Queen of Sheba. (Works of Thomas Bailey Aldrich). 1989. reprint ed. lib. bdg. 79.00 (*0-7812-1673-7*) Rprt Serv.

— Quite So. (Works of Thomas Bailey Aldrich). 1989. reprint ed. lib. bdg. 79.00 (*0-7812-1678-8*) Rprt Serv.

— A Rivermouth Romance. (Works of Thomas Bailey Aldrich). 1989. reprint ed. lib. bdg. 79.00 (*0-7812-1674-5*) Rprt Serv.

— A Sea Turn & Other Matters. LC 76-81258. (Short Story Index Reprint Ser.). 1977. 20.95 (*0-8369-3010-X*) Ayer.

— A Sea Turn & Other Matters. (Works of Thomas Bailey Aldrich). 1989. reprint ed. lib. bdg. 79.00 (*0-7812-1677-X*) Rprt Serv.

— The Stillwater Tragedy. LC 68-20001. (Americans in Fiction Ser.). 333p. reprint ed. pap. text 5.95 (*0-89197-949-2*); reprint ed. lib. bdg. 32.00 (*0-8398-0055-X*) Irvington.

— The Stilwater Tragedy. (Works of Thomas Bailey Aldrich). 1989. reprint ed. lib. bdg. 79.00 (*0-7812-1675-3*) Rprt Serv.

— The Story of a Bad Boy. 20.00 (*0-614-30542-X*) NAVH.

— The Story of a Bad Boy. (Works of Thomas Bailey Aldrich). 1989. reprint ed. lib. bdg. 79.00 (*0-7812-1669-9*) Rprt Serv.

— The Story of a Bad Boy. rev. ed. LC 96-1905. (Hardscrabble Bks. Ser.). (Illus.). 312p. 1996. reprint ed. pap. 14.95 (*0-87451-794-X*) U Pr of New Eng.

— Two Bites at a Cherry, with Other Tales. 1972. reprint ed. lib. bdg. 30.00 (*0-8422-8002-2*) Irvington.

— Two Bites at a Cherry, with Other Tales. (C). 1986. reprint ed. pap. text 6.95 (*0-8290-2044-6*) Irvington.

— Two Bites at a Cherry, with Other Tales. (Works of Thomas Bailey Aldrich). 1989. reprint ed. lib. bdg. 79.00 (*0-7812-1676-1*) Rprt Serv.

— William Towers. (Works of Thomas Bailey Aldrich). 1989. reprint ed. lib. bdg. 79.00 (*0-685-27374-1*) Rprt Serv.

— The Works of Thomas Bailey Aldrich, 1836-1907, Set. 1987. reprint ed. lib. bdg. 500.00 (*0-685-18584-2*) Rprt Serv.

— Writings of Thomas Bailey Aldrich, 9 vols. reprint ed. 373.50 (*0-404-00370-2*) AMS Pr.

Aldrich, Tim E., et al. Environmental Epidemiology & Risk Assessment. (Industrial Health & Safety Ser.). 274p. 1992. 110.00 (*0-471-29066-1*, VNR) Wiley.

Aldrich, Vickie. The Collaborative Learning Manual. 221p. (C). 1994. pap. text 35.66 (*0-201-59930-9*) Addison-Wesley.

***Aldrich, Vickie.** Mom Has a New Boyfriend, What about Me? (Illus.). vi, 26p. (J). (ps-3). 2000. pap. 7.95 (*0-615-11547-0*) Aldrich Crow.

Aldrich, Virgil C. The Body of a Person. LC 88-19017. 114p. (Orig.). (C). 1988. pap. text 15.00 (*0-8191-7106-9*) U Pr of Amer.

Aldrich, Winifred. Fabric, Form & Flat Pattern Cutting. (Illus.). 208p. (Orig.). 1996. pap. 29.95 (*0-632-03917-5*) Blackwell Sci.

— Metric Pattern Cutting for Children's Wear & Babywear: From Birth to 14 Years 3rd ed. LC 99-19986. 1999. write for info. (*0-632-05265-1*) Blackwell Sci.

— Metric Pattern Cutting for Menswear: Including Unisex Clothes & Computer Aided Design. 3rd ed. (Illus.). 180p. 1996. pap. 32.95 (*0-632-04113-7*) Blackwell Sci.

Aldrich, Winifred, ed. CAD in Clothing & Textiles: A Collection of Expert Views. 2nd ed. LC 94-19280. 1994. pap. 32.95 (*0-632-03893-4*) Blackwell Sci.

Aldridge. A Possible Tree. LC 92-13704. (Illus.). 32p. (J). (gr. k-3). 1998. per. 5.99 (*0-689-82131-X*) S&S Childrens.

Aldridge, A. Owen. The Dragon & the Eagle: The Presence of China in the American Enlightenment. LC 93-1060. (Illus.). 288p. 1993. text 39.95 (*0-8143-2455-X*) Wayne St U Pr.

— The Reemergence of World Literature: A Study of Asia & the West. LC 84-40806. 232p. 1986. 35.00 (*0-87413-277-0*) U Delaware Pr.

— Thomas Paine's American Idealogy. LC 83-40239. 328p. 1984. 45.00 (*0-87413-260-6*) U Delaware Pr.

Aldridge, Alan. Power, Authority & Restrictive Practices: A Sociological Essay on Industrial Relations LC 77-358899. xviii, 135p. 1976. 5.00 (*0-631-17230-0*) Blackwell Pubs.

— Religion in the Contemporary World: A Sociological Introduction. LC 99-26047. 256p. (C). 2000. text 59.95 (*0-7456-2082-5*, Pub. by Polity Pr); pap. text 24.95 (*0-7456-2083-3*, Pub. by Polity Pr) Blackwell Pubs.

Aldridge, Alan, ed. The Beatles Illustrated Lyrics. (Illus.). 268p. 1991. pap. 27.95 (*0-395-59426-X*) HM.

Aldridge, Alan, et al. The Gnole. (Illus.). 115p. 1996. pap. 14.95 (*0-7493-2224-1*) Buttrwrth-Heinemann.

Aldridge, Alan, ed. see Beatles.

Aldridge, Alexandra. The Scientific World View in Dystopia. LC 84-2724. (Studies in Speculative Fiction: No. 3). 107p. reprint ed. pap. 33.20 (*0-8357-1572-8*, 207053100001) Bks Demand.

Aldridge, Alfred O. Benjamin Franklin & Nature's God. LC 67-13409. 287p. reprint ed. pap. 89.00 (*0-8357-7132-6*, 202336500032) Bks Demand.

— Crosscurrents in the Literatures of Asia & the West: Essays in Honor of A. Owen Aldridge. Akiyama, Masayuki & Leung, Yiu-Nam, eds. LC 97-10229. (Illus.). 240p. 1997. 27.50 (*0-87413-639-3*) U Delaware Pr.

— Early American Literature: A Comparatist Approach. LC 82-47580. 335p. 1982. reprint ed. pap. 103.90 (*0-608-04519-5*, 206526400001) Bks Demand.

— Voltaire & the Century of Light. LC 75-2978. 456p. 1975. reprint ed. pap. 141.40 (*0-608-02502-X*, 206314600004) Bks Demand.

Aldridge, Anna C. Roadmap to D. C. Probate. 170p. 1997. 34.95 (*0-9656135-0-X*) Washington Law Pub.

Aldridge, B. B. Lapham Family in America: 13,000 Descendants, Including Descendants of John, Devonshire, Eng. to Providence, RI, 1673, & Thomas, Kent, Eng. to Scituate, MA, 1634, Also Genealogical Notes of Other Lapham Families. 552p. 1991. reprint ed. pap. 85.00 (*0-8328-1794-5*); reprint ed. lib. bdg. 95.00 (*0-8328-1793-7*) Higginson Bk Co.

Aldridge, Bertha B. Beal. John Beal the Centenarian & Descendants: Fourteen Generations, 1588-1956; Also Other Beal Families from England. 263p. 1997. reprint ed. pap. 39.50 (*0-8328-7445-0*); reprint ed. lib. bdg. 49.50 (*0-8328-7444-2*) Higginson Bk Co.

Aldridge, Bill, et al. Energy Sources & Natural Fuels. (Illus.). 80p. 1993. pap. text 12.95 (*0-87355-115-X*) Natl Sci Tchrs.

Aldridge, Bill G., et al. Energy Sources & Natural Fuels, Vol. 2. Tobia, E. & Marshall, S., eds. LC 96-67614. (Illus.). 108p. 1996. pap. text 12.95 (*0-87355-140-0*, PB129X) Natl Sci Tchrs.

Aldridge, Bob & Aldridge, Janet. Children & Nonviolence. LC 87-4126. 136p. (Orig.). 1987. pap. 10.95 (*0-932727-17-4*); lib. bdg. 16.95 (*0-932727-18-2*) Hope Pub Hse.

Aldridge, Bryan, et al. McDowell County, NC Cemeteries. 252p. 1995. pap. 25.00 (*1-888549-00-9*) Appalachan Pr.

Aldridge, Carrie. Are You Weighted Down? Southern, Elva, ed. Chesley, Ed, tr. (Illus.). 181p. (Orig.). 1997. pap. write for info. (*0-9658312-0-5*) C Aldridge.

***Aldridge, Christian.** The Book of Gray. 2nd ed. (Illus.). 108p. 2000. pap. 12.00 (*0-9660736-6-5*, HG1103) Hubris Games.

— Dacartha Prime. (Illus.). 140p. 2000. pap. 20.00 (*0-9660736-4-9*, HG1004) Hubris Games.

Aldridge, Christian. Story Engine: Universal Rules. (Illus.). 102p. 1998. pap. 22.95 (*0-9660736-0-6*) Hubris Games.

***Aldridge, Christian & Schatz, Michael.** Tales from the Empire. (Illus.). 96p. 1998. pap. 15.00 (*0-9660736-1-4*, HG1002) Hubris Games.

Aldridge, Daniel W., Jr., ed. The Aldridge Historically Black College Guide. 249p. 1983. pap. text 12.95 (*0-317-03146-5*) Aldridge Group.

Aldridge, David. Music Therapy in Palliative Care: New Voices. LC 98-45893. 1999. pap. text 26.95 (*1-85302-739-1*) Taylor & Francis.

— Music Therapy Research & Practice in Medicine: From Out of the Silence. 352p. 1996. pap. text 32.95 (*1-85302-296-9*, Pub. by Jessica Kingsley) Taylor & Francis.

— Music Therapy with Children, Vol. 1. 1999. pap. 27.95 (*1-85302-757-X*) Jessica Kingsley.

— Suicide: The Tragedy of Hopelessness. LC 98-152420. 300p. 1998. pap. 28.95 (*1-85302-444-9*, Pub. by Jessica Kingsley) Taylor & Francis.

Aldridge, Delores. Black Male-Female Relationships: A Resource Book of Selected Materials. 256p. 1989. pap. text 34.95 (*0-8403-5553-X*) Kendall-Hunt.

— Focusing: Black Male - Female Relationships. 1991. 7.95 (*0-88378-140-9*) Third World.

Aldridge, Delores P. & Rodgers-Rose, LaFrancis, eds. River of Tears: The Politics of Black Women's Health. 174p. (Orig.). (C). 1993. pap. text 13.95 (*0-934185-01-8*) Traces Inst.

***Aldridge, Delores P. & Young, Carlene.** Out of the Revolution: The Development of Africana Studies. LC 99-87501. 2000. write for info. (*0-7391-0111-0*) Lxngtn Bks.

Aldridge, James, jt. auth. see Kyle, Thomas G.

Aldridge, Janet, jt. auth. see Aldridge, Bob.

Aldridge, Jean P. & Crouch, Phoebe F. For All the World to See. LC 93-72627. 338p. 1993. 20.00 (*0-9637753-0-8*) Aldridge-Crouch.

Aldridge, Jerry. Self-Esteem: Loving Yourself at Every Age. LC 93-11765. 152p. (Orig.). 1993. pap. 16.95 (*0-9637034-0-4*) Religious Educ.

Aldridge, Jerry, et al. Jumpstarters: Integrating Environmental Print Throughout the Curriculum. 94p. 1995. teacher ed. write for info. (*0-9648892-0-X*) Campus Press.

— No Easy Answers: Helping Children with Attention & Activity Level Differences. LC 97-51877. 80p. 1998. pap. text 15.00 (*0-87173-140-1*) ACEI.

Aldridge, Jerry, jt. auth. see Cowles, Milly.

Aldridge, Jerry, jt. auth. see Sibley, Joyce.

Aldridge, John. Vintage Guide to Drum Collecting. (Illus.). 180p. 1994. pap. 24.95 (*0-931759-79-X*, 00000167) Centerstream Pub.

Aldridge, John, jt. auth. see Cook, Rob.

Aldridge, John W. After the Lost Generation. LC 79-142602. (Essay Index Reprint Ser.). 1977. 34.49 (*0-8369-2141-0*) Ayer.

— Classics & Contemporaries. 256p. 1992. 29.95 (*0-8262-0822-3*) U of Mo Pr.

— In Search of Heresy: American Literature in an Age of Conformity. LC 74-3618. 208p. 1982. reprint ed. lib. bdg. 97.50 (*0-8371-7452-X*, AEALSH, Greenwood Pr) Greenwood.

— Talents & Technicians: Literary Chic & the New Assembly-Line Fiction. 160p. 1992. text 18.00 (*0-684-18789-2*) S&S Trade.

— Time to Murder & Create: The Contemporary Novel in Crisis. LC 79-39113. (Essay Index Reprint Ser.). 1980. reprint ed. 29.95 (*0-8369-2682-X*) Ayer.

Aldridge, Josephine H. A Possible Tree. LC 92-13704. (Illus.). 32p. (J). (gr. k-3). 1993. lib. bdg. 16.00 (*0-02-700407-4*, Mac Bks Young Read) S&S Childrens.

Aldridge, Lester, jt. auth. see Ryan, Michael W.

Aldridge, M. Dayne & Swamidass, Paul M. Cross - Functional Management of Technology: Cases & Readings. LC 95-46606. 320p. (C). 1996. text 41.50 (*0-256-19429-7*, Irwn McGrw-H) McGrw-H Hghr Educ.

Aldridge, M. Gene, et al. Game Plan for the Denver World Trade Center: Corporate Welfare of Market Reality? 26p. 1989. pap. text 8.00 (*1-57655-128-8*) Independ Inst.

Aldridge, Marion D. The Pastor's Guidebook: A Manual for Worship. LC 83-70213. 160p. 1984. 16.99 (*0-8054-2312-5*, 4223-12) Broadman.

Aldridge, Marion D. The Pastor's Guidebook: Pastor's Guidebook for Special Occasions. LC 88-24113. (Orig.). 1988. pap. 19.99 (*0-8054-2318-4*, 4223-18) Broadman.

Aldridge, Marion D. & Lewis, Kevin, eds. The Changing Shape of Protestantism in the South. 112p. (Orig.). 1996. pap. text 15.00 (*0-86554-518-9*, MUP/P146) Mercer Univ Pr.

Aldridge, Maurice V. The Elements of Mathematical Semantics. (Trends in Linguistics, Studies & Monographs: No. 66). x, 262p. 1992. lib. bdg. 113.85 (*3-11-012957-4*) Mouton.

Aldridge, Mavis. Critical Thinking: Proverbs. 110p. (C). 1999. per. 27.95 (*0-7872-5749-4*, 41574903) Kendall-Hunt.

— Diversity in Oneness. 192p. 1996. pap. text 25.95 (*0-7872-0583-4*) Kendall-Hunt.

Aldridge, Meryl & Hewitt, Nicholas, eds. Controlling Broadcast: Access Policy & Practice in North America & Europe. LC 93-37271. (Fulbright Papers: No. 13). 1994. text 89.95 (*0-7190-4277-1*) Manchester Univ Pr.

Aldridge, Michelle, ed. Child Language. LC 95-23852. 223p. 1995. 59.00 (*1-85359-316-8*, Pub. by Multilingual Matters) Taylor & Francis.

Aldridge, Michelle & Wood, Joanne. Interviewing Children: A Guide for Child Care & Forensic Practitioners. LC 98-28995. (Child Care & Protection Ser.). 248p. 1998. 100.00 (*0-471-97052-2*) Wiley.

— Interviewing Children: A Guide for Child Care & Forensic Practitioners. LC 98-28995. (Child Care & Protection Ser.). 248p. 1999. pap. 35.50 (*0-471-98207-5*) Wiley.

Aldridge, Richard. Driving North. LC 89-9252. (Illus.). 64p. (Orig.). 1989. pap. 9.95 (*0-945980-09-4*) Nrth Country Pr.

— Red Pine, Black Ash. LC 80-18598. (Illus.). 143p. 1980. 10.00 (*0-89621-062-6*) Nrth Country Pr.

Aldridge, Richard, ed. Speaking of New England: The Place & Her People: 72 Poems by 56 of Her Poets, Past & Present. LC 93-15597. 112p. 1993. pap. 12.95 (*0-945980-41-8*) Nrth Country Pr.

Aldridge, Richard J. Palaeobiology of Conodonts. LC 86-211414. (British Micropalaeontological Society Ser.). 264p. 1987. text 74.95 (*0-470-20788-4*) P-H.

Aldridge, Robert, jt. auth. see Myers, Ched.

Aldridge, Robert C. Counterforce Syndrome: A Guide to U. S. Nuclear Weapons & Strategic Doctrine. rev. ed. (Illus.). 86p. 1979. pap. 4.95 (*0-89758-008-7*) Inst Policy Stud.

— First Strike: The Pentagon's Strategy for Nuclear War. LC 82-61148. (Illus.). 325p. 1983. 35.00 (*0-89608-155-9*); pap. 9.00 (*0-89608-154-0*) South End Pr.

Aldridge, Ruth. I Remember When. LC 93-26926. (Voyages Ser.). (Illus.). (J). 1994. 4.25 (*0-383-03750-6*) SRA McGraw.

Aldridge, Sarah. Amantha. 240p. (Orig.). 1995. pap. 10.95 (*0-9646648-0-1*) A&M Bks.

— Magdalena. 336p. 1995. reprint ed. pap. 9.95 (*0-9646648-1-X*) A&M Bks.

— Misfortune's Friend. 2nd ed. LC 84-29610. 296p. (Orig.). 1996. reprint ed. pap. 8.95 (*0-9646648-2-8*) A&M Bks.

— Nina in the Wilderness. LC 97-93762. 288p. 1997. 18.00 (*0-9646648-4-4*); pap. 11.95 (*0-9646648-3-6*) A&M Bks.

Aldridge, Sue. Children's Party Cakes. (Illus.). 88p. 1999. 19.95 (*1-85368-986-6*, Pub. by New5 Holland) Sterling.

Aldridge, Susan. Magic Molecules: How Drugs Work. LC 98-21346. (Illus.). 282p. (C). 1998. 24.95 (*0-521-58414-0*) Cambridge U Pr.

— The Thread of Life: The Story of Genes & Genetic Engineering. (Illus.). 270p. (C). 1996. 29.95 (*0-521-46542-7*) Cambridge U Pr.

— The Thread of Life: The Story of Genes & Genetic Engineering. (Canto Book Ser.). (Illus.). 272p. (C). 1998. reprint ed. pap. 12.95 (*0-521-62509-2*) Cambridge U Pr.

Aldridge, Tim. Restoring Oil Painting: A Practical Guide. (Illus.). 80p. 1987. 15.95 (*0-900873-60-4*, Pub. by Bishopsgte Pr); pap. 11.95 (*0-900873-62-0*, Pub. by Bishopsgte Pr) Intl Spec Bk.

— Restoring Oil Paintings. 1985. 40.00 (*0-7855-2948-9*, Pub. by Bishopsgate Pr Ltd) St Mut.

— Restoring Oil Paintings. 1985. pap. 29.00 (*0-7855-2949-7*) St Mut.

***Aldridge, Victoria.** Ben Morgan's Mistake. large type ed. 1999. 25.99 (*0-263-15910-8*, Pub. by Mills & Boon) Ulverscroft.

Aldridge, W., jt. auth. see Marrant, John.

Aldrige, Norman. Mechanisms & Concepts in Toxicology. 288p. 1996. 99.95 (*0-7484-0413-9*); 44.95 (*0-7484-0414-7*) Taylor & Francis.

***Aldrin, Edwin Eugene, Jr. & Barnes, John.** The Return. LC 00-22710. 358p. 2000. 25.95 (*0-312-87424-3*) Forge NYC.

Aldrin, Edwin Eugene (Buzz), Jr & Barnes, John. Encounter with Tiber. 1996. 21.95 (*0-614-96779-1*) Warner Bks.

— Encounter with Tiber. 656p. 1997. reprint ed. mass mkt. 6.50 (*0-446-60404-6*, Pub. by Warner Bks) Little.

Aldroandi, Ulisses. Delle Statue Antiche, Che Per Tutta Roma, in Diversi Luoghi, e Case si Veggono. xxiv, 315p. 1975. reprint ed. 80.00 incl. 3.5 hd (*3-487-05674-7*) G Olms Pubs.

Aldroubi, Akram, et al, eds. Wavelet Applications in Signal & Image Processing V, Vol. 3169. LC 98-122618. 608p. 1997. 107.00 (*0-8194-2591-5*) SPIE.

Aldroubi, Akram & Lin, Enbing. Wavelets, Multiwavelets, & Their Applications Vol. 216: AMS Special Session on Wavelets, Multiwavelets, & Their Applications, April 5-6, 1995, San Diego, California, Vol. 216. LC 97-38981. (Contemporary Mathematics Ser.). 175p. 1998. pap. 49.00 (*0-8218-0793-5*) Am Math.

Aldroubi, Akram & Unser, Michael, eds. Wavelets in Medicine & Biology. LC 95-46327. 640p. 1996. boxed set 94.95 (*0-8493-9483-X*) CRC Pr.

Aldrovandi, R. & Pereira, J. G. An Introduction to Geometrical Physics. LC 95-16285. 300p. 1995. text 97.00 (*981-02-2232-7*) World Scientific Pub.

Alduenda, Eileen, et al. Sustainable Design: A Plan Book for Sonoran Desert Dwellings. (Illus.). 112p. 1999. pap. 12.95 (*0-9670011-0-2*) Tucson Inst.

Aldus, P. J. Mousetrap: Structure & Meaning in Hamlet. LC 76-42263. 250p. reprint ed. pap. 77.50 (*0-608-15376-1*, 202932300060) Bks Demand.

Aldwell, Edward & Schachter, Carl. Harmony & Voice Leading. 2nd ed. 624p. (C). 1988. text 75.00 (*0-15-531519-6*, Pub. by Harcourt Coll Pubs) Harcourt.

— WKBK A-HARMONY & VOICE LDG 2/E. 2nd ed. 624p. (C). 1989. student ed. 29.00 (*0-15-531520-X*) Harcourt Coll Pubs.

— WKBK B-HARMONY & VOICE LDG 2/E, Wkbk. B. 2nd ed. 624p. (C). 1989. 29.00 (*0-15-531521-8*) Harcourt Coll Pubs.

Aldwell, S. W. Wingfield: It's Church, Castle & College. (Illus.). 128p. 1995. 40.00 (*0-937543-06-3*) Wingfield Family Soc.

***Aldwin, Carolyn M.** Stress, Coping & Developing: An Integrative Perspective. LC 94-18295. 331p. 1999. pap. text 21.95 (*1-57230-543-6*, C0543) Guilford Pubns.

Aldwin, Carolyn M. Stress, Coping & Development: A Integrative Perspective. LC 94-18295. 331p. 1994. lib. bdg. 40.00 (*0-89862-261-1*, 2261) Guilford Pubns.

Aldwinckle, H. S., jt. ed. see Jones, A. L.

Aldwinckle, Russell. Jesus: A Savior or the Savior? Religious Pluralism in Christian Perspective. LC 81-19033. viii, 232p. 1982. text 15.95 (*0-86554-023-3*, MUP-H024) Mercer Univ Pr.

Aldwinckle, Russell F. The Logic of the Believing Mind. LC 94-40520. ii, 638p. 1995. write for info. (*0-7734-9068-X*) E Mellen.

Aldy, Catherine, ed. see Breeden, Terri & Ralph, Sharon.

Aldy, Catherine, ed. see Cook, Shirley.

Aldy, Catherine, ed. see Groeber, Joan.

Aldyne, Nathan. Canary: A Daniel Valentine & Clarisse Lovelace Mystery. LC 99-47254. (Orig.). 1999. reprint ed. pap. 10.00 (*1-55583-443-4*, Alyson Bks) Alyson Pubns.

— Cobalt. LC 99-165462. 200p. 1998. pap. 10.00 (*1-55583-441-8*) Alyson Pubns.

— Slate: A Daniel Valentine & Clarissa Lovelace Mystery. 234p. 1999. reprint ed. pap. 10.00 (*1-55583-442-6*) Alyson Pubns.

— Vermilion. 220p. 1997. pap. 10.95 (*1-55583-434-5*) Alyson Pubns.

Ale, John C. Partnership Law for Securities Practitioners. LC 92-12345. (Securities Law Ser.). 1992. ring bd. 145.00 (*0-87632-896-6*) West Group.

Alea, Pat & Mullins, Patricia A. The Best Work of Your Life. LC 98-2889. 256p. 1998. pap. write for info. (*0-399-52434-7*) Putnam Pub Group.

Aleamoni, Lawrence M., ed. Techniques for Evaluating & Improving Instruction. LC 85-644763. (New Directions for Teaching & Learning Ser.: No. 31). 1987. 22.00 (*1-55542-935-1*) Jossey-Bass.

***Aleandri, Emelise.** Italian-American Immigrant Theatre-NYC. (Images of America Ser.). 128p. 1999. pap. 18.99 (*0-7385-0097-6*) Arcadia Publng.

Aleaz, K. P. The Gospel of Indian Culture. LC 94-902477. (C). 1995. 32.00 (*81-85094-74-8*, Pub. by Punthi Pus) S Asia.

— Harmony of Religions: The Relevance of Swami Vivekananda. (C). 1993. text 30.00 (*81-85094-59-4*, Pub. by Punthi Pus) S Asia.

Alec Thomas Archives Staff. Gone for a Soldier: The Civil War Memoirs of Private Alfred Bellard. Donald, David H., ed. 1991. pap. 19.95 (*0-316-08838-2*) Little.

Alechinsky, Pierre, jt. auth. see Gibson, Michael.

Alecian, Serge & Girard, Pierre. Changing Functions of Lower & Middle Management in France. (Illus.). 108p. (Orig.). (C). 1993. pap. text 40.00 (*0-7881-0139-0*) DIANE Pub.

Aleck, Jonathan, jt. ed. see Sack, Peter.

Alecson, Deborah G. Lost Lullaby. LC 94-11712. 1995. 30.00 (*0-520-08870-0*, Pub. by U CA Pr) Cal Prin Full Svc.

Alecson, Deborah Golden. Altenative Treatments for Children Within the Autistic Spectrum. (Good Health Guides Ser.). 1999. pap. 3.95 (*0-87983-965-1*, 39651K, Keats Publng) NTC Contemp Pub Co.

Alecto Historical Editions Board Staff, ed. Domesday Book Studies. (Illus.). x, 179p. 1987. lib. bdg. 150.00 (*0-948459-51-4*) Omnigraphics Inc.

***Aleda, Shirley, ed.** The Beach Book: A Literary Companion. LC 98-34381. 264p. 1999. pap. 14.95 (*1-889330-27-2*, Pub. by Sarabande Bks) Consort Bk Sales.

***Aledort, Andy.** At the Millennium's Edge: Exploring the Great Rock Stylists of Our Times. (Guitar Presents Ser.). 1999. pap. 14.95 (*1-57560-221-0*) Cherry Lane.

Aledort, Andy, ed. Joe Satriani - Surfing with the Alien (Guitar - Vocal) (Illus.). 80p. (Orig.). 1990. pap. text 19.95 (*0-89524-414-4*, Pub. by Cherry Lane) H Leonard.

Aledort, Andy, jt. ed. see Phillips, Mark.

Aledort, Louis M., et al, eds. Inhibitors to Coagulation Factors. (Advances in Experimental Medicine & Biology Ser.: Vol. 386). (Illus.). 324p. (C). 1996. text 107.00 (*0-306-45196-4*, Kluwer Plenum) Kluwer Academic.

— Outpatient Medicine. fac. ed. LC 78-51280. (Illus.). 335p. pap. 103.90 (*0-7837-7182-7*, 204711700005) Bks Demand.

Aleechawa. Sister Leaves. (Illus.). 350p. 1998. pap. 16.00 (*0-9645787-4-3*) Unole Pub.

Aleem, Maruls A. The Code of Three. LC 96-96743. (Illus.). 1996. pap. 7.95 (*0-9653969-0-8*) MAA Publns.

Aleem, Marvis A. Challenges in the Techno-Society. LC 97-94049. (Illus.). 105p. 1997. pap. 9.95 (*0-9653969-2-4*) MAA Publns.

***Aleem, Marvis A.** Elements of the Enviro-World. LC 99-95321. (Illus.). iii, 107p. 1999. pap. 11.95 (*0-9653969-3-2*) MAA Publns.

Aleem, Shamim. The Suicide: Problems & Remedies. LC 94-905770. (Illus.). xii, 124p. (C). 1994. 16.00 (*81-7024-657-1*, Pub. by Ashish Pub Hse) Nataraj Bks.

— Women, Police & Social Change. (C). 1991. text 15.00 (*81-7024-408-0*, Pub. by Ashish Pub Hse) S Asia.

Aleem, Shamin, ed. Women's Development Problems & Prospects. (Illus.). xii, 237p. (C). 1996. 32.00 (*81-7024-741-1*, Pub. by APH Pubng) Nataraj Bks.

Aleene. Best of Aleene's Creative Living, Bk. 2. (Illus.). 144p. 1998. pap. 14.95 (*0-8487-1676-0*, 108710) Oxmoor Hse.

***Alef, Daniel.** Pale Truth: A Novel. LC 00-9450. 2000. write for info. (*0-9700174-1-3*) Maxit Pubng.

Alef, Edward R. & Berg, Daniel. The Learning Factory. LC 96-28703. 114p. 1996. pap. text 14.50 (*0-7618-0465-X*) U Pr of Amer.

Alef, Gustave. Rulers & Nobles in Fifteenth-Century Muscovy. (Collected Studies: No. CS172). 354p. (C). 1983. reprint ed. lib. bdg. 124.95 (*0-86078-120-8*, Pub. by Variorum) Ashgate Pub Co.

Alef, Kassem & Nannipieri, Paolo, eds. Methods in Applied Soil Microbiology & Biochemistry. (Illus.). 608p. 1995. boxed set 90.00 (*0-12-513840-7*) Acad Pr.

Alefeld, Georg & Radermacher, reinhard. Heat Conversion Systems. LC 93-829. 304p. 1993. boxed set 99.95 (*0-8493-8928-3*, TJ265) CRC Pr.

Alefeld, Gotz, et al, eds. Scientific Computing & Validated Numerics. 341p. 1996. pap. 149.95 (*3-527-40102-4*) Wiley.

— Scientific Computing & Validated Numerics: Proceedings of the International Symposium on Scientific Computing, Computer Arithmetic & Validated Numbers SCAN-95 Held in Wuppertal, Germany, September 26-29, 1995. (Mathematical Research Ser.: Vol. 90). (Illus.). 341p. 1996. pap. 120.75 (*3-05-501737-4*, Wiley-VCH) Wiley.

Alefeld, Gotz & Herzberger, Jurgen. Introduction to Interval Computations. Rockne, Jon, tr. from GER. (Computer Science & Applied Mathematics Ser.). 1983. text 100.00 (*0-12-049820-0*) Acad Pr.

Alefeld, Gotz, ed. see Herzberger, Jurgen.

Alefgeld, Gotz & Herzberger, Jurgen, eds. Numerical Methods & Error Bounds: Proceedings of the IMACS-GAMM International Symposium on Numerical Methods & Errors Bounds Held in Oldenburg, Germany, July 9-12, 1995. (Mathematical Research Ser.: Vol. 89). (Illus.). 305p. 1996. pap. 83.95 (*3-05-501696-3*, Wiley-VCH) Wiley.

A

An Asterisk (*) at the beginning of an entry indicates that the title is appearing for the first time.

Alegi. Italian Income Tax. 1994. lib. bdg. 197.50 (*90-6544-814-4*) Kluwer Academic.

Alegret, Nancy L., jt. auth. see Philabaum, Dabney M.

Alegret, S., ed. Developments in Solvent Extraction. 1988. text 54.95 (*0-470-21251-9*) P-H.

Alegria, A., jt. ed. see Colmenero, J.

Alegria, Ciro. Broad & Alien Is the World. LC 62-17709. 434p. 1973. 45.00 (*0-85036-171-0*) Dufour.

— Broad & Alien Is the World. LC 62-17709. 474p. 1984. pap. 24.95 (*0-85036-282-2*) Dufour.

— Broad & Alien Is the World. 434p. 1987. 40.00 (*0-317-61293-X*); pap. 18.95 (*0-317-61294-8*) Dufour.

Alegria, Claribel. Family Album. Hopkinson, Amanda, tr. from SPA. LC 91-55413. 191p. (Orig.). 1991. pap. 10.95 (*0-915306-94-8*) Curbstone.

— Flowers from the Volcano. unabridged ed. Forche, Carolyn, tr. LC 82-70893. (Pitt Poetry Ser.). (ENG & SPA.). 103p. 1982. pap. 32.00 (*0-608-07698-8*, 206778800010) Bks Demand.

— Fugues. Flakoll, Darwin J., tr. from SPA. LC 93-25965. 143p. (Orig.). 1993. pap. 10.95 (*1-880684-10-1*) Curbstone.

— Luisa in Realityland. Flakoll, Darwin J., tr. LC 87-71705. 152p. 1987. 17.95 (*0-915306-70-0*) Curbstone.

— Luisa in Realityland. Flakoll, Darwin J., tr. LC 87-71705. 152p. 1988. pap. 9.95 (*0-915306-69-7*) Curbstone.

— El Nino Que Buscaba a Ayer (The Boy Who Searched for Yesterday) (Encuento/Literary Encounters Ser.). 1997. pap. text 10.95 (*968-494-072-6*) Donars.

*__Alegria, Claribel.__ Sorrow. Forche, Carolyn, tr. from SPA. & intro. by. LC 99-27585. 104p. 1999. pap. 13.95 (*1-880684-63-2*, Pub. by Curbstone) SPD-Small Pr Dist.

Alegria, Claribel. Thresholds: Umbrales: Poems. Flakoll, Darwin J., tr. from SPA. LC 96-21329. 70p. 1996. pap. 10.95 (*1-880684-36-5*) Curbstone.

— Woman of the River. Flakoll, Darwin J., tr. from SPA. LC 88-4775. (Poetry Ser.). 112p. (Orig.). 1989. pap. 10.95 (*0-8229-5409-5*); text 19.95 (*0-8229-3594-5*) U of Pittsburgh Pr.

Alegria, Claribel & Flakoll, Darwin J. Ashes of Izalco. LC 89-62125. 174p. (Orig.). 1989. 17.95 (*0-915306-83-2*) Curbstone.

— Death of Somoza: The First Person Story of the Guerrillas Who Assassinated the Nicaraguan Dictator. LC 95-36159. 162p. 1996. pap. 12.95 (*1-880684-26-8*) Curbstone.

— Tunnel to Canto Grande. LC 95-37983. 148p. 1996. pap. 12.95 (*1-880684-34-9*) Curbstone.

Alegria, Claribel & Flakoll, Darwin J., eds. On the Front Line: Guerrilla Poems of El Salvador. LC 89-62126. 90p. (Orig.). 1989. pap. 7.95 (*0-915306-86-7*) Curbstone.

Alegria, Claribel, et al. Ashes of Izalco. LC 89-62125. 174p. (Orig.). 1998. pap. 12.95 (*0-915306-84-0*) Curbstone.

Alegria, Claribel, ed. see Benedetti, Mario.

Alegria, Claribel, tr. see Urias, Alfonso Q.

Alegria, Fernando. Allende: A Novel. Janney, Frank, tr. from SPA. LC 92-441. 320p. (C). 1993. 45.00 (*0-8047-1998-5*) Stanford U Pr.

— Allende: A Novel. xiv, 303p. 1994. pap. 13.95 (*0-8047-2326-5*) Stanford U Pr.

— Changing Centuries: Selected Poems. 2nd ed. Kessler, Stephen, tr. & pref. by. LC 88-6794. (Discoveries Ser.). (ENG & SPA.). 133p. 1988. pap. 11.95 (*0-935480-37-4*) Lat Am Lit Rev Pr.

— The Funhouse. LC 85-73355. 152p. (Orig.). 1986. pap. 9.00 (*0-934770-52-2*) Arte Publico.

— The Maypole Warriors. Miller, Yvette E., ed. Lozano, Carlos, tr. from SPA. LC 92-21222. (Discoveries Ser.). 192p. 1992. pap. 16.95 (*0-935480-58-7*) Lat Am Lit Rev Pr.

— Nueva Historia de la Novela Hispanoamericana. (Rama Ser.). (SPA.). 450p. 1986. pap. 22.50 (*0-910061-29-7*, 1505) Ediciones Norte.

— Paradise Lost or Gained. LC 91-11258. 240p. (Orig.). 1991. pap. 11.00 (*1-55885-037-6*) Arte Publico.

Alegria, Fernando L., Jr. A Guide to State-Level Policies, Practices, & Procedures: Enhancing Employment Opportunities for Older Workers. Feinstein, Gerry, ed. 50p. (Orig.). 1992. pap. text 15.00 (*1-55877-144-1*) Natl Governor.

Alegria, Idsa, jt. auth. see Pico, Isabel.

Alegria Ortega, Idsa E. La Comision del Status de Puerto Rico: Su Historia y Significacion. (SPA.). x, 216p. 1982. pap. 6.00 (*0-8477-0869-1*) U of PR Pr.

— La Comision del Status de Puerto Rico: Su Historia y Significacion. LC 80-25739. 214p. 1982. pap. text 6.00 (*0-8477-8869-5*) U of PR Pr.

Alegria, Ricardo. Taino: Pre-Colombian Art & Culture from the Caribbean. LC 97-42053. 1997. pap. text 35.00 (*1-885254-82-2*, Pub. by Monacelli Pr) Penguin Putnam.

Alegria, Ricardo E. Ball Courts & Ceremonial Plazas in the West Indies. (Publications in Anthropology: No. 79). 1983. pap. 12.50 (*0-913516-15-5*) Yale U Anthro.

Alegria, Ricardo E., et al. Taino: Pre-Columbian Art & Culture from the Caribbean. Bercht, Fatima & Brodsky, Estrellita, eds. (ENG & SPA., Illus.). 56p. 1997. pap. 15.00 (*1-882454-05-7*) El Museo Barrio.

Alegria, Ricardo E., jt. auth. see Rouse, Irving.

Aleichem, Sholem. The Bloody Hoax: Jewish Literature & Culture. LC 91-11717. (Jewish Literature & Culture Ser.). 400p. 1992. 29.95 (*0-253-30401-6*) Ind U Pr.

— Favorite Stories: Tales of Sholom Aleichem. 1988. 23.95 (*0-8488-0414-7*) Amereon Ltd.

— The Jackpot: A Folk-Play in 4 Acts. Zumoff, Barnett, tr. from YID. 107p. (Orig.). (C). 1989. pap. 7.50 (*1-877909-40-8*) Jwsh Bk Ctr Wrkmns Cir.

— More Favorite Tales. 1988. 25.95 (*0-8488-0413-9*) Amereon Ltd.

— Nineteen to the Dozen: Monologues & Bits & Bobs of Other Things. Frieden, Ken, ed. Gorelick, Ted, tr. LC 97-29985. (Judaic Traditions in Literature, Music, & Art Ser.). 177p. 1997. 24.95 (*0-8156-0477-7*) Syracuse U Pr.

*__Aleichem, Sholem.__ Nineteen to the Dozen: Monologues & Bits & Bobs of Other Things. Frieden, Ken, ed. Gorelick, Ted, tr. 192p. 2000. pap. 17.95 (*0-8156-0634-6*) Syracuse U Pr.

Aleichem, Sholem. Tevye the Dairyman & the Railroad Stories. 1996. pap. 15.00 (*0-8052-1069-5*) Random Hse Value.

— A Treasury of Sholom Aleichem Children's Stories. Shevrin, Aliza, tr. from YID. & selected by by. LC 96-14590. (Illus.). 368p. (J). 1996. 30.00 (*1-56821-926-1*) Aronson.

— Why Do the Jews Need a Land of Their Own? Leftwich, Joseph & Chertoff, Mordecai S., trs. LC 83-45297. 242p. 1984. 19.95 (*0-8453-4774-8*, Cornwall Bks) Assoc Univ Prs.

*__Aleichem, Sholem & Leviant, Curt.__ Happy New Year! & Other Stories. LC 00-31777. (Thrift Editions Ser.). 2000. pap. write for info. (*0-486-41419-1*) Dover.

Aleichem, Sholem, jt. auth. see Lifson, David S.

Aleinikoff, T. Alexander. Between Principles & Politics: The Direction of U. S. Citizenship Policy. LC 98-73643. (International Migration Policy Issues Ser.). 76 p. 1998. pap. 10.95 (*0-87003-153-8*) Carnegie Endow.

— From Migrants to Citizens: Membership in a Changing World. 1999. pap. text 24.95 (*0-87003-159-7*) Carnegie Endow.

Aleinikoff, T. Alexander, et al, eds. Immigration & Nationality Laws of the U. S. Selected Statutes, Regulations & Forms. 661p. (C). 1995. pap. 16.50 (*0-314-06817-1*) West Pub.

Aleinikoff, T. Alexander & Martin, David A. Immigration & Nationality Laws of the U. S. Selected Statutes, Regulations & Forms. 525p. (C). 1993. reprint ed. pap. text 16.00 (*0-314-01073-4*) West Pub.

Aleinikoff, T. Alexander, et al. Immigration Process & Policy. 3rd ed. LC 95-12826. (American Casebook Ser.). 1096p. (C). 1995. text 53.00 (*0-314-06104-5*) West Pub.

Aleinikoff, T. Alexander, jt. auth. see Garvey, John H.

Aleinikoff, Thomas, et al. Immigration: Process & Policy 1997 Supplement To. 3rd ed. (American Casebook Ser.). 119p. (C). 1996. pap. text. write for info. (*0-314-21945-5*) West Pub.

— Immigration, Process & Policy, Teacher's Manual to Accompany. 3rd ed. (American Casebook Ser.). 153p. 1995. pap. text. write for info. (*0-314-07345-0*) West Pub.

Aleinikoff, Thomas A., et al. Immigration: Process & Policy. 4th ed. LC 98-17101. (Paralegal). 1150p. (C). 1998. text 47.25 (*0-314-23149-8*) West Pub.

Aleixandre, Vicente. The Cave of Night. Bartman, Joeffrey, tr. 1980. 6.85 (*0-941490-19-X*) Solo Pr.

*__Aleixandre, Vicente.__ Destruction or Love: La Destruccibon O el Amor. LC 00-35780. (Illus.). 280p. 2000. 49.50 (*1-57591-051-9*) Susquehanna U Pr.

Aleixandre, Vicente. A Longing for the Light: Selected Poems of Vicente Aleixandre. Hyde, Lewis, ed. Kessler, Stephen et al, trs. from SPA. 284p. 1985. reprint ed. pap. 10.00 (*0-914742-89-2*) Copper Canyon.

— Poemas Amorosos. (SPA.). 120p. 1960. 6.95 (*0-8288-7024-1*, BC283) Fr & Eur.

Aleixandre, Vicente. Shadow of Paradise. Harter, Hugh A., tr. 232p. 1993. pap. 18.95 (*0-520-08257-5*, Pub. by U CA Pr) Cal Prin Full Svc.

Alejaldre, C. & Carreras, B. A., eds. Transport & Confinement in Toroidal Devices: Second Workshop on Magnetic Confinement Fusion. (Illus.). 176p. 1992. pap. 92.00 (*0-7503-0184-8*) IOP Pub.

Alejando, Alis, tr. see Bofill, Francesc.

Alejandro, Alis, tr. Goldilocks & the Three Bears (Ricitos de Oro y los Tres Osos) LC 97-28902. (ENG & SPA., Illus.). 32p. (J). (ps-2). 1998. pap. 6.95 (*0-8118-1835-7*) Chronicle Bks.

— Jack & the Beanstalk (Juan y los Frijoles Magicos) LC 97-28901. (ENG & SPA., Illus.). 32p. (J). (gr. k-2). 1998. pap. 6.95 (*0-8118-1843-8*) Chronicle Bks.

Alejandro, Alis, tr. see Grejniec, Michael.

Alejandro, Alis, tr. see Janovitz, Marilyn.

Alejandro, Alis, tr. see Mata, Marta.

Alejandro, Ann. Beauty Parlor Poems. Bixby, Robert, ed. 31p. (Orig.). 1995. pap. 6.00 (*1-882983-20-3*) March Street Pr.

Alejandro, Carlos F. Diaz, see Diaz Alejandro, Carlos F.

Alejandro, Carlos F. Diaz, see Bacha, Edmar L. & Diaz Alejandro, Carlos F.

Alejandro, Reynaldo. The Food of the Philippines. (Illus.). 120p. 1999. 16.95 (*962-593-245-3*) Tuttle Pubng.

— The Philippine Cookbook. (Illus.). 256p. 1985. reprint ed. pap. 14.95 (*0-399-51144-X*, Perigee Bks) Berkley Pub.

Alejandro, Reynaldo, jt. auth. see O'Boyle, Lily G.

Alejandro, Roberto. Hermeneutics, Citizenship, & the Public Sphere. LC 92-23077. (SUNY Series in Political Theory: Contemporary Issues). 291p. (C). 1993. text 64.50 (*0-7914-1487-6*); pap. text 21.95 (*0-7914-1488-4*) State U NY Pr.

— The Limits of Rawlsian Justice. LC 97-165585. 248p. 1997. text 39.95 (*0-8018-5678-7*) Johns Hopkins.

Alejo, Robert, jt. auth. see Schmid, Sigi.

Alekhine, A. On the Road to the World Championship, Nineteen Twenty-Three to Twenty-Seven. Neat, Kenneth P., ed. Feather, C. J., tr. LC 84-3051. (Chess Ser.). (Illus.). 250p. 1984. 29.95 (*0-08-029731-5*, Pergamon Pr) Elsevier.

Alekhine, Alexander. My Best Games of Chess, 1908-1937. 581p. 1985. reprint ed. pap. 13.95 (*0-486-24941-7*) Dover.

— One Hundred-Seven Great Chess Battles, 1938-1945, Vol. 945. 256p. 1992. reprint ed. pap. 7.95 (*0-486-27104-8*) Dover.

Aleksander. Designing Intelligent Systems. (C). 1987. mass mkt. 24.95 (*1-85091-252-1*) ITCP.

Aleksander, I. Introduction to Neural Computing. 2nd ed. 1995. pap. write for info. (*0-412-60390-X*) Chapman & Hall.

Aleksander, Igor. Designing Intelligent Systems: An Introduction. (Illus.). 166p. 1984. 22.95 (*0-89059-043-5*, 590435) Productivity Inc.

— Impossible Minds: My Neurons, My Consciousness. 380p. 1996. pap. 25.00 (*1-86094-030-7*); pap. text 8.50 (*1-86094-036-6*) World Scientific Pub.

— Intro to Neutral Computing. 1990. pap. 38.95 (*0-442-31218-0*) Chapman & Hall.

Aleksander, Igor & Morton, Helen. An Introduction to Neural Computing. 2nd ed. (Illus.). 288p. 1995. pap. 32.95 (*1-85032-167-1*) ITCP.

Aleksandrjan, R. A., et al. Partial Differential Equations. LC 76-8428. (Translations Ser.: Series 2, Vol. 105). 346p. 1976. 84.00 (*0-8218-3055-4*, TRANS2/105) Am Math.

Aleksandrov, A. A., jt. ed. see Sytchev, V. V.

Aleksandrov, A. D. Mathematics: Its Content, Methods & Meaning. LC 99-33023. 1120p. 1999. pap. text 29.95 (*0-486-40916-3*) Dover.

Aleksandrov, A. D., et al, eds. Mathematics Vol. 2: Its Content, Methods, & Meaning, 3 vols. 2nd ed. Gould, S. H., tr. 1969. reprint ed. pap. text 16.00 (*0-262-51004-9*) MIT Pr.

— Mathematics Vol. 3: Its Content, Methods, & Meaning, 3 vols. 2nd ed. Gould, S. H., tr. 1969. reprint ed. pap. text 16.00 (*0-262-51003-0*) MIT Pr.

Aleksandrov, A. D. & Zalgaller, V. A. Intrinsic Geometry of Surfaces. Danskin, J. M., tr. LC 66-30492. (Translations of Mathematical Monographs: Vol. 15). 327p. 1967. text 44.00 (*0-8218-1565-2*, MMONO/15) Am Math.

Aleksandrov, A. D. & Zalgaller, V. A., eds. Two-Dimensional Manifolds of Bounded Curvature: Proceedings. (Proceedings of the Steklov Institute of Mathematics Ser.: No. 76). 183p. 1967. pap. 58.00 (*0-8218-1876-7*, STEKLO/76) Am Math.

Aleksandrov, A. D., et al. Eleven Papers on Topology, Function Theory, & Differential Equations. LC 51-5559. (Translations Ser.: Series 2, Vol. 1). 304p. 1955. 37.00 (*0-8218-1701-9*, TRANS2/1) Am Math.

— Nine Papers on Topology, Lie Groups, & Differential Equations. LC 51-5559. (Translations Ser.: Series 2, Vol. 21). 416p. 1962. 45.00 (*0-8218-1721-3*, TRANS2/21) Am Math.

— Ten Papers on Differential Equations & Functional Analysis. LC 51-5559. (Translations Ser.: Series 2, Vol. 68). 264p. 1968. 49.00 (*0-8218-1768-X*, TRANS2/68) Am Math.

Aleksandrov, Huri. Moscow. 358p. 1984. 39.00 (*0-7855-0925-9*) St Mut.

Aleksandrov, Michail. On the Dynamics of Cables with Application to Marine Use. LC VM0791.A434. (University of Michigan, Dept. of Naval Architecture & Marine Engineering, Report Ser.: No. 76). 32p. reprint ed. pap. 30.00 (*0-608-13482-1*, 202263000028) Bks Demand.

Aleksandrov, Nikolai. Two Leaps Across Chasm: A Russian Mystery. 256p. 1992. text 20.00 (*0-684-19415-5*) S&S Trade.

Aleksandrov, P., ed. Topology: A Collection of Papers. LC 85-7326. (Proceedings of the Steklov Instittute of Mathematics Ser.: Vol. 154). 333p. 1985. pap. 111.00 (*0-8218-3086-4*, STEKLO/154) Am Math.

Aleksandrov, P. S., ed. English-Russian Dictionary of Mathematical Terms. 2nd rev. ed. 416p. (C). 1994. 21.95 (*0-8285-5170-7*) Firebird NY.

Aleksandrov, P. S., et al. Ten Papers on Topology. LC 51-5559. (Translations Ser.: Series 2, Vol. 30). 358p. 1963. 42.00 (*0-8218-1730-2*, TRANS2/30) Am Math.

Aleksandrov, V. N. & Megson, G. M. Parallel Algorithms for Knapsack Type Problems. 280p. 1997. text 61.00 (*981-02-2120-7*) World Scientific Pub.

Aleksandrov, Yu A. Bubble Chambers. Frisken, William R., tr. LC 66-14342. 382p. reprint ed. pap. 118.50 (*0-8357-7451-1*, 205519200011) Bks Demand.

Aleksandrova, Z. Dictionary of Russian Synonyms. 5th ed. (ENG & RUS.). 600p. (C). 1986. 95.00 (*0-7855-6466-7*, Pub. by Collets) St Mut.

Aleksandrova, Z. E. Dictionary of Synonyms of the Russian Language. 5th ed. (ENG & RUS.). 400p. 1986. 49.95 (*0-8288-2001-5*, M1973) Fr & Eur.

Aleksandrowicz, J., tr. see Geremek, Bronislaw.

Aleksandrowicz-Pedich, Lucyna, tr. see Wisniewski, Tomasz.

Aleksanova, Irene, tr. see Dezin, Aleksei A.

Alekseenko, N. N. Radiation Damage of Nuclear Power Plant Pressure Vessel Steels. LC 97-26106. (Russian Materials Monographs). 292p. 1997. 40.00 (*0-89448-564-4*) Am Nuclear Soc.

Alekseenko, S. V., et al. Wave Flow of Liquid Films. 313p. 1994. 135.00 (*1-56700-021-5*) Begell Hse.

Alekseev, A., et al, eds. Integrable Models & Strings: Proceedings of the Third Baltic Rim Student Seminar Held at Helsinki, Finland, 13-17 September 1993. LC 94-34259. (Lecture Notes in Physics Ser.: Vol. 436). 1994. write for info. (*0-387-58453-6*) Spr-Verlag.

— Integrable Models & Strings: Proceedings of the Third Baltic Rim Student Seminar Held at Helsinki, Finland, 13-17 September 1993. (Lecture Notes in Physics Ser.: Vol. 436). 1994. 69.95 (*3-540-58453-6*) Spr-Verlag.

Alekseev, A. I. Fedor Petrovich Litke. Arndt, Kathy, ed. LeComte, Serge, tr. from RUS. (Rasmuson Library Historical Translation: Volume X). (Illus.). xviii, 262p. (Orig.). (C). 1996. pap. 18.00 (*0-912006-86-2*) U of Alaska Pr.

Alekseev, Aleksandr I. The Destiny of Russian America, 1741-1767. Pierce, Richard A., ed. Ramsay, Marina, tr. from RUS. (Alaska History Ser.: No. 34). (Illus.). 1990. 35.00 (*0-919642-13-6*) Limestone Pr.

— Odyssey of a Russian Scientist: I. G. Voznesenskii in Alaska, California & Siberia, 1839-1849. Pierce, Richard A., ed. Follette, Wilma, tr. from RUS. (Alaska History Ser.: No. 30). (Illus.). 1987. 22.00 (*0-919642-05-5*) Limestone Pr.

*__Alekseev, Andrei.__ The Golden Deer of Eurasia: Scythian & Sarmatian Treasures from the Russian Steppes the Hermitage, Saint Petersburg & the Archaeological Museum, U. F. A. (Illus.). 460p. 2000. 65.00 (*0-300-08510-9*) Yale U Pr.

Alekseev, D. I. Dictionary of Abbreviations of the Russian Language. (ENG & RUS.). 486p. 1983. write for info. (*0-8288-0752-3*, M15485) Fr & Eur.

— Shorter Dictionary of Spoken Russian: Abkuerzungswoertereuch der Russischen Sprache. 3rd ed. (GER & RUS.). 1983. 29.95 (*0-8288-1162-8*, M15324) Fr & Eur.

Alekseev, P., ed. English-Russian Frequency Glossary on Physics. 288p. (C). 1980. 160.00 (*0-7855-5037-2*, Pub. by Collets) St Mut.

Alekseev, P. F., et al. Thermophysical Properties of Organosilicon Compounds. 300p. 1996. 75.00 (*1-56700-037-1*) Begell Hse.

Alekseev, P. M. English-Russian Glossary of Physics Terms. (ENG & RUS.). 288p. 1980. 60.00 (*0-7855-7157-4*) St Mut.

Alekseev, Peter A. Cerkovnyi Slovar'ili Istolkovanie Slavenskich Takze Malovrazumitel'nych Drevnich I Inojazycnych Recenij, 2 vols. (GER.). xix, 1280p. 1976. 378.00 (*3-487-06133-3*) G Olms Pubs.

Alekseev, V. M., et al. Optimal Control. Volosov, V. M., tr. from RUS. LC 87-6935. (Contemporary Soviet Mathematics Ser.). 322p. 1987. reprint ed. pap. 99.90 (*0-608-09370-X*, 205411500002) Bks Demand.

— Thirteen Papers on Differential Equations. (Translations Ser.: Series 2, Vol. 89). 300p. 1970. 49.00 (*0-8218-1789-2*, TRANS2/89) Am Math.

Alekseev, V. P., et al. Contributions to the Archaeology of Armenia. Field, Henry, ed. Krimgold, Arlene, tr. (Harvard University, Peabody Museum of Archaeology & Ethnology, Russian Translation Ser.: Vol. 3, No. 3). reprint ed. lib. bdg. 76.50 (*0-404-52646-2*) AMS Pr.

Alekseeva, E. A., jt. auth. see Posypaiko, V. I.

Alekseeva, T. A., jt. auth. see Gay, William.

Alekseeva, T. A., jt. ed. see Gay, William C.

Alekseeva, T. V. Artists of the Venetsianov School. 420p. 1982. 86.00 (*0-7855-1566-6*) St Mut.

— Artists of the Venetsianov School. (Illus.). 420p. 1982. 104.00 (*0-7855-0694-2*) St Mut.

Alekseeva, T. V., et al. Machines for Earthmoving Work: Theory & Calculations. Sivaramakrishnan, M. M., tr. from RUS. 529p. (C). 1985. text 220.00 (*90-6191-447-7*, Pub. by A A Balkema) Ashgate Pub Co.

Alekseyev, Mikhail. Russian Market in Government Securities. (Euromoney Country Guide Ser.). 1997. 170.00 (*1-85564-585-8*, Pub. by Euromoney) Am Educ Systs.

Alekseyev, Veniamin & Lundkvist, Sven, eds. State & Minorities: A Symposium on National Processes in Russia & Scandinavia. (Illus.). 128p. 1997. pap. 32.50 (*91-7402-267-9*) Coronet Bks.

Aleksiev, Archimandrite S. Forgotten Medicine: The Mystery of Repentance. Doynova, Ralitsa, tr. LC 94-66581. (Spiritual Writings of Archimandrite Seraphim Aleksiev Ser.). (Illus.). 72p. 1995. pap. 5.00 (*0-614-30953-0*) St Herman Pr.

Aleksiev, Archimandrite S. The Meaning of Suffering & Strife & Reconciliation, 2 vols. in 1. Doynova, Ralitsa, tr. LC 94-69053. (Spiritual Writings of Archimandrite Seraphim Aleksiev Ser.). (BUL., Illus.). 112p. 1996. pap. 8.95 (*0-938635-86-7*) St Herman Pr.

Aleksiuk, Michael. Power Therapy: Maximizing Health Through Self-Efficacy. LC 96-17394. 392p. 1996. 22.50 (*0-88937-138-5*) Hogrefe & Huber Pubs.

Alekzander, Terri, ed. Fresh Ideas in Brochure Design. LC 97-13998. (Fresh Ideas Ser.). (Illus.). 160p. 1997. 31.99 (*0-89134-755-0*, North Lght Bks) F & W Pubns Inc.

Alem, Raja. Hyattombs Hyattombs. 176p. 1997. 29.00 (*0-7103-0595-8*, Pub. by Kegan Paul Intl) Col U Pr.

Alema, W. D., ed. Politics & Economics of Japan: An Annotated Bibliography. 82p. (C). 1992. pap. text 95.00 (*1-56072-049-2*) Nova Sci Pubs.

*__Aleman, Manuel M.__ Lo Irracional En la Literatura: Prologo Luis A. Acosta. Membrives, Eva P., ed. (SPA.). 252p. 1999. 39.95 (*3-906762-29-7*) P Lang Pubng.

Aleman, Mateo. The Rogue: or The Life of Guzman De Alfarache, 4 vols. Mabbe, James, tr. (Tudor Translations, Second Ser.: No. 2-5). reprint ed. 230.00 (*0-404-51970-9*) AMS Pr.

Aleman, Miguel. Miguel Aleman Contesta: Ensayo. LC 75-620022. (Encuesta Politica, Mexico Ser.: No. 4). 68p. reprint ed. pap. 30.00 (*0-608-17159-X*, 202731800055) Bks Demand.

*__Aleman, Sara, et al, eds.__ Therapeutic Interventions with Ethnic Elders: Health & Social Issues. LC 99-45998. (Illus.). 220p. 2000. lib. bdg. 39.95 (*0-7890-0272-8*) Haworth Pr.

Aleman, Serafin. Aprender Ingles: Curso Comparado de la Gramatica y la Pronunciacion del Ingles al Castellano. LC 96-85449. (Coleccion Textos Ser.). (ENG & SPA.). 191p. (Orig.). 1997. pap. 16.00 (*0-89729-809-8*, 809-8) Ediciones.

— Juegos de Vida y Muerte: El Suicidio la Novela Galdosiana. LC 77-88535. 1978. pap. 7.95 (*0-89729-182-4*) Ediciones.

An Asterisk (*) at the beginning of an entry indicates that the title is appearing for the first time.

— Pronunciacion Simplificada del Ingles Con un Resumen de la Gramatica Inglesa. LC 94-71460. (Coleccion Textos). 176p. 1994. pap. 19.00 (*0-89729-734-2*) Ediciones.

Aleman, Steven R., jt. auth. see Jones, Nancy L.

Alemany, A., et al. Transfer Phenomena in Magnetohydrodynamic & Electroconducting Flows: Selected Papers of the Pamir Conference Held in Aussois, France, 22-26 September 1997. LC 98-43900. (Fluid Mechanics & Its Applications Ser.). 14p. 1999. write for info. (*0-7923-5532-6*) Kluwer Academic.

***Alemany, Agustbi.** Sources on the Alans: A Critical Compilation. LC 00-41423. (Handbook of Oriental Studies, Section Eight, Central Asia). 2000. write for info. (*90-04-11442-4*) Brill Academic Pubs.

Alemany-Dessaint, Veronique. Orfevrerie Francaise. deluxe ed. (FRE.). 216p. 1991. 195.00 (*0-8288-7301-1*, 2705900357) Fr & Eur.

Alemany, Norah, tr. see Maury, Inez.

Alemayehu, Dereje. The Crisis of Capitalist Development in Africa: The Case of Cote d'Lvoire. LC 97-203664. 1997. pap. text 24.95 (*3-8258-3014-4*) Transaction Pubs.

Alemayehu, Makonnen. Industrialization in Africa. LC 99-14464. 450p. 1998. 89.95 (*0-86543-652-5*); pap. 24.95 (*0-86543-653-3*) Africa World.

Alembert, Jean L., jt. auth. see Diderot, Denis.

Alemian-Goldberg, Sandy. Congratulations... It's an Angel: The Gift of Talia. Hewitt, Linda V., ed. (Illus.). 192p. 1999. pap. 14.95 (*0-9672065-0-2*) LifeCraft Pubg.

Alemna, A. Anaba. Oral Literature in African Libraries: Implications for Ghana. 45p. 1993. 6.00 (*0-941934-64-0*) Indiana Africa.

Alen, A. Belgian Constitutional Law. 1992. pap. text 76.50 (*90-6544-633-8*) Kluwer Academic.

Alen, Andre, ed. Constitutional Law. (International Encyclopedia of Laws Ser.). 1991. ring bd. 115.00 (*0-685-58993-5*) Kluwer Law Intl.

— Constitutional Law. (International Encyclopedia of Laws Ser.). 1992. ring bd. 117.00 (*90-6544-944-2*) Kluwer Law Intl.

Alen, R., jt. auth. see Sjostrom, Eero.

Alen, Rupert, jt. auth. see Dahlquist, Anna M.

Alencar, Jose de. Iracema. Villaca, Alcides & Lindstrom, Naomi, eds. Landers, Clifford E., tr. from SPA. LC 99-45927. (Library of Latin America). 176p. 2000. 30.00 (*0-19-511547-3*) OUP.

— Iracema: A Legend of Brazil. Villaca, Alcides & Lindstrom, Naomi, eds. Landers, Clifford E., tr. from SPA. LC 99-45927. 176p. 2000. pap. 14.95 (*0-19-511548-1*) OUP.

— Iracema, the Honey-Lips: A Legend of Brazil. Burton, Isabel, tr. 1976. lib. bdg. 59.95 (*0-8490-2076-X*) Gordon Pr.

Alencar, Jose de. Senhora: Profile of a Woman. Edinger, Catarina F., tr. from POR. LC 93-791. (Texas Pan American Ser.). 225p. (C). 1994. pap. 12.95 (*0-292-70450-X*); text 30.00 (*0-292-70449-6*) U of Tex Pr.

Alencar Xavier, Yanko Marcius de, see Marcius de Alencar Xavier, Yanko.

Alenick, Jerome B., ed. Real Estate Development Manual. LC 90-70402. (Illus.). 585p. 1990. text 150.00 (*0-7913-0550-3*) Warren Gorham & Lamont.

Alenicyn, J. E., ed. Extremal Problems of the Geometric Theory of Functions: Proceedings. (Proceedings of the Steklov Institute of Mathematics Ser.: Vol. 94). 167p. 1969. pap. 60.00 (*0-8218-1894-5*, STEKLO/94) Am Math.

Alenicyn, Ju. E., et al. Fifteen Papers on Series & Functions of Complex Variables. LC 51-5559. (Translations Ser.: Series 2, Vol. 43). 320p. 1964. 38.00 (*0-8218-1743-4*, TRANS2/43) Am Math.

Alenier, Karren L. Bumper Cars: Gertrude Said She Took Him for a Ride. (Premier Ser.: No. 2). 32p. (Orig.). 1996. pap. 6.00 (*0-9654421-1-X*) Mica Press.

— The Dancer's Muse. (Dialogues on Dance Ser.: No. 2). (Illus.). 25p. (Orig.). 1981. pap. 5.95 (*0-915380-12-9*) Ommation Pr.

— Wandering on the Outside. 2nd ed. LC 74-30470. (Illus.). 1979. per. 8.00 (*0-915380-00-5*) Word Works.

Alenier, Karren L., ed. Whose Woods These Are. LC 83-50101. 176p. 1983. pap. 8.00 (*0-915380-18-8*) Word Works.

Alenier, Karren L., et al, eds. Winners: A Retrospective of the Washington Prize. LC 98-61423. 300p. 1999. pap. text 20.00 (*0-915380-43-9*) Word Works.

Alenitsyn, Alexander G., et al. Concise Handbook in Physics & Mathematics. LC 97-21519. 528p. 1997. 49.95 (*0-8493-7745-5*, NP7745) CRC Pr.

Aleotti, Vittoria. Ghirlanda de Madrigali a Quatro Voci. Carruthers, C. Ann, ed. (Music at the Courts of Italy Ser.: Vol. 1). (Illus.). 1995. lib. bdg. 75.00 (*0-8450-7701-5*) Broude.

Aler, F. Vernon. Aler's History of Martinsburg & Berkeley County, West Virginia. 452p. 1993. reprint ed. lib. bdg. 47.00 (*0-8328-3497-1*) Higginson Bk Co.

Alera, Don B. Frederique: The True Story of a Youth Transformed into a Girl. Orpen, Valerie, tr. from FRE. (Illus.). 163p. 1998. 34.95 (*1-897767-08-0*, Pub. by Delectus Bks) Xclusiv Distrib.

Alera, Don Brennus. Frederique: The True Story of a Youth Transformed into a Girl. 1999. mass mkt. 7.95 (*1-58419-002-7*) Masq Bks.

Aleramo, Sibilla. A Woman. Delmar, Rosalind, tr. from ITA. (Illus.). 200p. 1980. pap. 15.95 (*0-520-04949-7*, Pub. by U CA Pr) Cal Prin Full Svc.

Alerich & Herman. Electric Motor Control. 6th ed. LC 97-34500. 352p. 1998. mass mkt. 58.95 (*0-8273-8456-4*) Delmar.

Alerich, jt. auth. see Keljik, Jeff.

Alerich, Walter & Keljik, Jeff. Electricity 4: Motors, Controls, Alternators. 6th ed. (Electrical Trades Ser.). (Illus.). 336p. 1996. mass mkt. 34.95 (*0-8273-6593-4*) Delmar.

Alerich, Walter, et al. Electricity: Motors, Generators, Controls, No. 3. 6th ed. LC 95-42330. (Electrical Trades Ser.). 240p. 1996. pap. 34.95 (*0-8273-6594-2*) Delmar.

Alerich, Walter N. Electric Motor Control. 4th ed. (Electrical Trades Ser.). (Illus.). (C). 1989. pap., teacher ed. 15.00 (*0-8273-3040-5*) Delmar.

— Electric Motor Control. 5th ed. LC 92-10097. 333p. 1993. mass mkt. 54.95 (*0-8273-5250-6*) Delmar.

— Electric Motor Control. 5th ed. LC 92-10097. 37p. 1993. teacher ed. 15.50 (*0-8273-5251-4*) Delmar.

— Electrical Construction Wiring. (Illus.). 476p. 1971. pap. 18.96 (*0-8269-1420-9*) Am Technical.

Alerich, Walter N., jt. auth. see Herman, Stephen L.

Alerich, Walter N., jt. auth. see Kubala, Thomas S.

Alerman, Sune, et al, eds. Chance & Change: Social & Economic Studies in the Historical Demography in the Baltic Area. (Odense Studies in History & Social Sciences: No. 52). 294p. (Orig.). 1978. pap. 28.50 (*87-7492-248-3*, Pub. by Odense Universitets Forlag) Coronet Bks.

Alers-Montalvo, Manual. The Puerto Rican Migrants of New York City. LC 83-45349. (Immigrant Communities & Ethnic Minorities in the U. S. & Canada Ser.: No. 8). 1985. 37.50 (*0-404-19400-1*) AMS Pr.

Alers, Rochelle. Careless Whispers. LC 94-77077. 189p. 1994. pap. 8.95 (*1-885478-00-3*, Pub. by Genesis Press) BookWorld.

— Gentle Yearning. 1998. pap. 10.95 (*1-885478-24-0*, Pub. by Genesis Press) BookWorld.

— Happily Ever After. (Arabesque Ser.). 224p. 1994. mass mkt. 4.99 (*0-7860-0064-3*, Pinncle Kensgtn) Kensgtn Pub Corp.

***Alers, Rochelle.** Harvest Moon, Vol. 1. 1999. mass mkt. 4.99 (*1-58314-056-5*) BET Bks.

Alers, Rochelle. Heaven Sent. 320p. 1998. pap. 4.99 (*0-7860-0530-0*) Kensgtn Pub Corp.

— Hidden Agenda. (Arabesque Ser.). 288p. 1997. mass mkt. 4.99 (*0-7860-0384-7*, Pinncle Kensgtn) Kensgtn Pub Corp.

— Hideaway. (Arabesque Ser.). 1995. mass mkt. 4.99 (*0-7860-0135-6*, Pinncle Kensgtn) Kensgtn Pub Corp.

— Home Sweet Home. (Arabesque Ser.). 1996. mass mkt. 4.99 (*0-7860-0276-X*, Pinncle Kensgtn) Kensgtn Pub Corp.

***Alers, Rochelle.** Just Before Dawn. 256p. 2000. mass mkt. 5.99 (*1-58314-103-0*, Arabesq) BET Bks.

Alers, Rochelle. Reckless Surrender. LC 97-199201. 206p. 1997. pap. 6.95 (*1-885478-17-8*, Pub. by Genesis Press) BookWorld.

— Summer Magic. 1999. mass mkt. 4.99 (*1-58314-012-3*) Kensgtn Pub Corp.

— Vows. (Arabesque Ser.). 288p. 1997. mass mkt. 4.99 (*0-7860-0463-0*, Pinncle Kensgtn) Kensgtn Pub Corp.

***Alers, Rochelle, et al.** Della's House of Style. 368p. 2000. pap. 6.50 (*0-312-97497-3*, St Martins Paperbacks) St Martin.

Alers, Rochelle, et al. Rosie's Curl & Weave. 311p. 1999. mass mkt. 5.99 (*0-312-96828-0*) St Martin.

***Alers, Rochelle, et al.** Welcome to Leo's. 2000. mass mkt. 6.50 (*0-312-97588-0*) St Martin.

***Alerson, Sue Ann.** Wherever Bears Be: A Story for Two Voices. (Illus.). (J). (ps-3). 1999. bds. 15.95 (*1-896580-18-1*, Pub. by T1rad Bks) Tricycle Pr.

Alerstam, Thomas. Bird Migration. Christie, David A., tr. & pref. by. (Illus.). 428p. (C). 1993. pap. text 44.95 (*0-521-44822-0*) Cambridge U Pr.

Alerts, E., ed. see Eichengreen, Barry J.

Alesandro, John, ed. Marriage Studies, Vol. IV. 188p. 1990. pap. 7.00 (*0-943616-48-4*) Canon Law Soc.

Alesch, Daniel J. & Petak, William J. The Politics & Economics of Earthquake Hazard Mitigation: Unreinforced Masonry Buildings in Southern California. (Program on Environment & Behavior Monograph Ser.: No. 43). 300p. (Orig.). (C). 1986. pap. 20.00 (*0-685-28117-5*) Natural Hazards.

***Alescovskii, V. B., ed.** Macromolecular Symposia 136. 150p. 1999. 65.00 (*3-527-29804-5*) Wiley.

Aleshinsky, Sergi, et al. Human Factors Engineering in the Soviet Union: Selected Papers with Analysis. (Illus.). 323p. (Orig.). 1989. pap. text 100.00 (*1-55831-107-6*) Delphic Associates.

Aleshire, Daniel O. Comprendamos Al Joven de Hoy: Understanding Today's Youth. Rivas De Jara, Orquidea, ed. & tr. by. from ENG. (SPA.). 160p. (Orig.). 1993. pap. 6.50 (*0-311-11903-4*) Casa Bautista.

— Faithcare: Ministering to All God's People Through the Ages of Life. LC 87-30880. 180p. 1988. pap. 17.95 (*0-664-24054-2*) Westminster John Knox.

Aleshire, Joan. Cloud Train. LC 82-80305. 58p. 1982. 8.95 (*0-89672-099-3*); pap. 4.95 (*0-89672-098-5*) Tex Tech Univ Pr.

— This Far. (QRL Poetry Bks.: Vol. XXVII). 1987. 35.00 (*0-614-06421-X*) Quarterly Rev.

— The Yellow Transparents. LC 96-86553. 100p. 1997. pap. 12.95 (*1-884800-13-0*) Four Way Bks.

Aleshire, Keith. Upgrading & Repairing PCs. 8th ed. 1998. wbk. ed. 32.00 (*1-58076-003-1*) Que Educ & Trng.

Aleshire, Peter. The Fox & the Whirlwind: General George Cook & Geronimo, a Paired Biography. LC 99-36279. 384p. 2000. text 30.00 (*0-471-32575-9*) Wiley.

Aleshire, Sara B. Asklepios at Athens: Epigraphic & Prosopographic Essays on Athenian Healing Cults. (Illus.). xii, 256p. 1992. pap. 74.00 (*90-5063-068-5*, Pub. by Gieben) J Benjamins Pubng Co.

— The Athenian Asklepieion: The People, Their Dedications, & the Inventories. (Illus.). 416p. 1989. pap. 80.00 (*90-5063-025-1*, Pub. by Gieben) J Benjamins Pubng Co.

Aleshkovsky, Peter. Skunk: A Life. (Glas Ser.: No. 15). 186p. 1998. pap. 14.95 (*5-7172-0033-1*) I R Dee.

Aleshkovsky, Yuz (Iosif). A Ring in a Case. LC 95-10115.Tr. of Eine Kleine Nachtmusik. 248p. 1995. 24.95 (*0-8101-1138-1*) Northwestern U Pr.

Aleshovesky, Yuz. Kangaroo. Glenny, Tamara, tr. from RUS. LC 98-54876. 290p. 1999. reprint ed. pap. 13.50 (*1-56478-216-6*) Dalkey Arch.

Alesi, Gladys E. How to Prepare for the U. S. Citizenship Test. 4th ed. 272p. 1996. pap. 12.95 (*0-8120-9328-3*) Barron.

***Alesi, Gladys E.** How to Prepare for the U. S. Citizenship Test. 5th ed. LC 99-32624. 272p. 2000. 14.95 (*0-7641-0767-4*) Barron.

Alesii, Brenda C. Boston Sports Quiz. 1991. pap. 9.95 (*0-8065-1212-1*, Citadel Pr) Carol Pub Group.

Alesii, Brenda C. & Locche, Daniel. Chicago Sports Quiz. LC 92-19305. (Illus.). 208p. 1992. pap. 9.95 (*0-8065-1372-1*, Citadel Pr) Carol Pub Group.

— Los Angeles Sports Quiz. LC 92-19306. (Illus.). 240p. 1992. pap. 10.95 (*0-8065-1381-0*, Citadel Pr) Carol Pub Group.

— Philadelphia Sports Quiz: Phillies, Athletics, Eagles 76ers, Warriors, Flyers. LC 92-38084. 1993. 9.95 (*0-8065-1416-7*, Citadel Pr) Carol Pub Group.

— Washington-Baltimore Sports Quiz: Senators, Orioles, Redskins, Colts, Bullets, Capitals. LC 92-38083. 1993. 9.95 (*0-8065-1424-8*) Carol Pub Group.

Alesii, Brenda C., jt. auth. see Locche, Daniel A.

Alesii, Brenda C., ed. see Stedler, Richard.

Alesina, Alberto & Carliner, Geoffrey, eds. Politics & Economics in the '80s. (Illus.). 306p. 1991. pap. text 21.00 (*0-226-01281-6*) U Ch Pr.

— Politics & Economics in the '80s. (Illus.). 320p. 1992. lib. bdg. 45.00 (*0-226-01280-8*) U Ch Pr.

Alesina, Alberto & Rosenthal, Howard. Partisan Politics, Divided Government, & the Economy. LC 93-48512. (Political Economy of Institutions & Decisions Ser.). 298p. (C). 1995. text 69.95 (*0-521-43029-1*) Cambridge U Pr.

Alesina, Alberto & Rosenthal, Howard. Partisan Politics, Divided Government, & the Economy. LC 93-48512. (Political Economy of Institutions & Decisions Ser.). 298p. (C). 1995. pap. text 19.95 (*0-521-43620-6*) Cambridge U Pr.

Alesina, Alberto & Roubini, Nouriel. Political Cycles & the Macroeconomy. LC 97-14051. (Illus.). 300p. 1997. 45.00 (*0-262-01161-1*) MIT Pr.

— Political Cycles & the Macroeconomy. 300p. 1997. pap. text 22.50 (*0-262-51094-4*) MIT Pr.

Alesina, Alberto, et al. BPEA 1, 1998. 1998. pap. 17.00 (*0-8157-1195-6*) Brookings.

Aleskerov, F. T. Arrovian Aggregation Models. LC 99-11147. (Theory & Decision Library). 1999. write for info. (*0-7923-8451-2*) Kluwer Academic.

Aleskerov, F. T., jt. auth. see Alzermant, M.

Aleskjavicene, A., et al. Twenty-Four Papers on Statistics & Probability. LC 61-9803. (Selected Translations in Mathematical Statistics & Probability Ser.: Vol. 7). 302p. 1968. 51.00 (*0-8218-1457-5*, STAPRO/7) Am Math.

— Twenty-Two Papers on Statistics & Probability. LC 61-9803. (Selected Translations in Mathematical Statistics & Probability Ser.: Vol. 11). 279p. 1973. 45.00 (*0-8218-1461-3*, STAPRO/11) Am Math.

Aleskovsky, Ruth & Simon, Robert M. The Repetitive Strain Injury Handbook: A Complete Guide to Prevention, Related Issues & an 8-Step Recovery Plan. LC 99-36203. (Illus.). 224p. 2000. 15.00 (*0-8050-5930-X*, Owlet BYR) H Holt & Co.

Alessandra, Anthony J. & Barrera, Rick. Collaborative Selling: How to Gain the Competitive Advantage in Sales. LC 93-13175. 256p. 1993. 75.00 (*0-471-59664-7*); pap. 19.95 (*0-471-59665-5*) Wiley.

Alessandra, Anthony J., jt. auth. see Hunsaker, Phillip L.

Alessandra, Joseph R. 13 Eyes. Alessandra, Lee, ed. 113p. (YA). (gr. 10 up). 1999. pap. 5.95 (*0-9671255-0-2*) Netherfield NJ.

Alessandra, Lee, ed. see Alessandra, Joseph R.

Alessandra, Tony. Charisma: Seven Keys to Developing the Magnetism That Leads to Success. LC 97-1145. 304p. 1998. 24.00 (*0-446-52049-7*, Pub. by Warner Bks) Little.

***Alessandra, Tony.** Charisma: Seven Keys to Developing the Magnetism That Leads to Success. 288p. 2000. mass mkt. 13.95 (*0-446-67598-9*, Pub. by Warner Bks) Little.

Alessandra, Tony & Hunsaker, Phillip L. Communicating At Work. (Illus.). 224p. (Orig.). 1993. pap. 11.00 (*0-671-78855-8*, Fireside) S&S Trade Pap.

Alessandra, Tony & O'Connor, Michael J. The Platinum Rule: Discover the Four Basic Business Personalities - & How They Can Lead You to Success. 304p. 1998. mass mkt. 12.99 (*0-446-67343-9*, Pub. by Warner Bks) Little.

Alessandra, Tony, et al. Non-Manipulative Selling. 256p. 1992. pap. 13.00 (*0-671-76448-9*, Fireside) S&S Trade Pap.

— People Smarts: Powerful Techniques for Turning Every Encounter into a Mutual Win. Ross, Marilyn, ed. 350p. 1989. 19.95 (*0-685-30408-6*) Keynote Pub.

— The Sales Manager's Idea-a-Day Guide. rev. ed. LC 96-71226. 343p. 1996. pap. 29.95 (*0-85013-261-4*) Dartnell Corp.

— The Sales Professional's Idea-a-Day Guide. rev. ed. LC 96-71223. 363p. 1996. pap. 29.95 (*0-85013-260-6*) Dartnell Corp.

Alessandrello, Anna. The Earth. LC 94-2874. (Beginnings Origins & Evolution Ser.).Tr. of Terra. (Illus.). 40p. (J). (gr. 3-10). 1994. lib. bdg. 24.26 (*0-8114-3331-5*) Raintree Steck-V.

Alessandri, C., jt. ed. see Aliabadi, M. H.

Alessandrini, Anthony. Frantz Fanon: Critical Perspectives. LC 98-34514. 1999. 75.00 (*0-415-18975-6*); pap. 24.99 (*0-415-18976-4*) Routledge.

***Alessandrini, Anthony.** Numerologia: Manual Practico. 1999. pap. text 6.95 (*84-270-2140-2*) E Martinez Roca.

Alessandrini, Charles A. & Wert, I. Gregg Van. Beyond the Bottom Line: A Painless Look at Finance & Accounting for the Nonfinancial Executive. Guder, Robert F., ed. (The Practical Executive's Bookshelf Ser.). 146p. 1995. 14.95 (*0-910187-09-6*) Economics Pr.

Alessandrini, Jodi & Kinser, Kathy. Puppy Stuff. (Illus.). 144p. 1997. 24.95 (*0-9647465-6-5*) Pallachip Pubng.

Alessandro, Nini. Ida della Torre. (Italian Opera Ser., 1810-1840). 255p. 1986. text 30.00 (*0-8240-6576-X*) Garland.

***Alesse, Craig.** Basic 35mm Photo Guide: For Beginning Photographers. 5th ed. (Illus.). 112p. 2000. pap. 12.95 (*1-58428-030-1*) Amherst Media.

Alesse, Craig. Don't Take My Picture! 2nd ed. LC 97-77816. (Illus.). 104p. 1997. pap. 9.95 (*0-936262-60-5*) Amherst Media.

Alessi & Trollip. Computer Based Instruction. 3rd ed. 432p. 2000. pap. 49.33 (*0-205-27691-1*) Allyn.

Alessi, Alberto. Alessi. (Illus.). 130p. 1998. pap. 4.95 (*3-8290-1377-9*, 520754) Konemann.

Alessi, Bob, jt. auth. see Moore, Casey.

Alessi, James G., ed. Production & Neutralization of Negative Ion & Beams. LC 85-71695. (Conference Proceeding Ser.: No. 158). 784p. 1987. lib. bdg. 85.00 (*0-88318-358-7*) Am Inst Physics.

***Alessi, John.** The Greatest Mystery of All. 2000. pap. 10.95 (*0-533-13409-9*) Vantage.

Alessi, Michael De, see De Alessi, Michael.

Alessi, Paul T., jt. ed. see Bernard, John D.

Alessi, Stephen M. & Trollip, Stanley R. Computer-Based Instruction: Methods & Development. 2nd ed. LC 90-22106. 432p. 1991. pap. 61.00 (*0-13-168592-9*) P-H.

Alessi, V., jt. auth. see Salerno, G.

Alessia, Joseph. The Poetry of Dino Frescobaldi: Romance Language & Literature. LC 83-5482. (American University Studies: Romance Languages & Literature: Ser. II, Vol. 2). 157p. (Orig.). (C). 1983. pap. text 15.80 (*0-8204-0008-4*) P Lang Pubng.

Alessia, Joseph, tr. see Turco, Lewis H.

Alessio, Antonio & Haines, Claudia P., eds. L' Enigma Pirandello. (Biblioteca di Quaderni d'Italianistica Ser.: Vol. 5). 338p. (Orig.). (C). 1988. pap. 25.00 (*0-9691979-3-4*, Pub. by Can Soc Ital Stu) Speedimpex.

Alessio, Luis & Munoz, Hector. Marriage & the Family: The Domestic Church. Owen, Aloysius, tr. from SPA. LC 82-6853. 121p. 1982. pap. 3.95 (*0-8189-0433-X*) Alba.

Alessio, Piemontese. A Booke Conteining...Experienced Medicines: The Fourth & Finall Booke of His Secretes. Androse, R., tr. LC 77-6846. (English Experience Ser.: No. 841). 1977. reprint ed. lib. bdg. 35.00 (*90-221-0841-4*) Walter J Johnson.

— The Second Part of the Secretes of Maister Alexis of Piemont. Ward, W., tr. LC 77-6843. (English Experience Ser.: No. 839). 1977. reprint ed. lib. bdg. 20.00 (*90-221-0839-2*) Walter J Johnson.

***Alesso, H. Peter.** E-Video: How to Produce Internet Video as Broadband Technologies Converge. 320p. 2000. pap. text 44.95 (*0-201-70314-9*) Addison-Wesley.

Alethia, I. M. The Coupling. 300p. (Orig.). 1995. pap. 18.95 (*0-9646354-0-2*) Callon Pr Inc.

Aletti, Ann & Brinkley, Jeanne. Altering Ready-to-Wear Fashions. (gr. 10-12). 1976. teacher ed. 1.28 (*0-317-00011-X*); text 20.48 (*0-317-00010-1*) Glencoe.

Aletti, Vince. Male/Female. 1999. 29.95 (*0-89381-881-X*) Aperture.

Aletto, P. Ross. Stretch Your Gas Dollars. LC 79-54982. (Illus.). 72p. (Orig.). 1979. pap. 2.95 (*0-935126-00-7*) E & C Bks.

Aleva, G. J., jt. auth. see Bardossy, Gy.

Alevizatos, Dorothy C., jt. auth. see Percival, Robert V.

Alevizon, William S. Beachcomber's Guide to Florida Marine Life. LC 94-17568. 184p. 1994. pap. 12.95 (*0-88415-128-X*, 5128) Gulf Pub.

— Pisces Guide to Caribbean Reef Ecology. LC 93-2430. 128p. 1994. pap. 15.95 (*1-55992-077-7*, Pisces Books) Lonely Planet.

Alex. Yo Te Amo (I Love You) (SPA.). 4.99 (*0-685-74988-6*, 490250) Editorial Unilit.

Alex, Alain J., ed. see European Conference on the Spectroscopy of Biologi.

Alex-Assensoh, Yvette M. Black & Multiracial Politics in America. text 55.00 (*0-8147-0662-2*); pap. text 21.00 (*0-8147-0663-0*) NYU Pr.

Alex-Assensoh, Yvette M. Neighborhoods, Family, & Political Behavior in Urban America: Political Behavior & Orientations. Bingham, Richard D., ed. LC 98-5122. (Contemporary Urban Affairs Ser.). (Illus.). 197p. 1998. 45.00 (*0-8153-2381-6*) Garland.

Alex, Ben. David Livingstone: The Missionary Who Discovered Africa. (Heroes of Faith & Courage Ser.). (Illus.). 42p. (J). (gr. 4-9). 1995. 11.99 (*1-56476-474-5*, 6-3474, Victor Bks) Chariot Victor.

— David Livingstone: The Missionary Who Discovered Africa. (Heroes of Faith & Courage Ser.). (Illus.). 43p. (J). (gr. 3-12). 1998. reprint ed. pap. 7.99 (*1-884543-21-9*) O M Lit.

— Dietrich Bonhoeffer: The Pastor Who Followed Christ to the Cross. (Heroes of Faith & Courage Ser.). (Illus.). 49p. (J). (gr. 3-12). 1998. reprint ed. pap. 7.99 (*1-884543-18-9*) O M Lit.

A

An Asterisk (*) at the beginning of an entry indicates that the title is appearing for the first time.

A

— Florence Nightingale: The Lady with the Lamp in Battle. (Heroes of Faith & Courage Ser.). (Illus.). 49p. (J). (gr. 3-12). 1998. pap. 7.99 (1-884543-16-2) O M Lit.

— Hudson Taylor. (Heroes of Faith & Courage Ser.). (Illus.). 42p. (J). (gr. 4-9). 1995. 11.99 (1-56476-476-1, 6-3476, Victor Bks) Chariot Victor.

— Hudson Taylor: The Missionary Who Won a Nation by Prayer. (Heroes of Faith & Courage Ser.). (Illus.). 51p. (J). (gr. 3-12). 1998. pap. 7.99 (1-884543-14-6) O M Lit.

— Martin Luther: German Monk Who Changed the Church. (Heroes of Faith & Courage Ser.). (Illus.). 51p. (J). (gr. 3-12). 1998. reprint ed. pap. 7.99 (1-884543-13-8) O M Lit.

— Martin Luther: The German Monk Who Changed the Church. (Heroes of Faith & Courage Ser.). (Illus.). 42p. (J). (gr. 4-9). 1995. 11.99 (1-56476-475-3, 6-3475, Victor Bks) Chariot Victor.

— Mother Teresa: The Woman Who Served God with Her Hands. (Heroes of Faith & Courage Ser.). (Illus.). 42p. (J). (gr. 4-9). 1995. 11.99 (1-56476-477-X, 6-3477, Victor Bks) Chariot Victor.

— St. Augustine: Bishop of Hippo/Father of the Church. (Heroes of Faith & Courage Ser.). (Illus.). 49p. (J). (gr. 3-12). 1998. reprint ed. pap. 7.99 (1-884543-19-7) O M Lit.

***Alex, Ben.** Soren Kierkegaard - An Authentic Life: The Life & Writings of an Extraordinary Christian Philosopher. 120p. 2000. 16.95 (1-896836-41-0, Pub. by NStone Publ) Logos Prods.

Alex, Ben. William Carey: Shoemaker Who Pioneered Modern Missions. (Heroes of Faith & Courage Ser.). (Illus.). 49p. (J). (gr. 3-12). 1998. reprint ed. pap. 7.99 (1-884543-15-4) O M Lit.

Alex, Gary E., jt. auth. see Byerlee, Derek.

Alex, Kirk. Blood, Sweat & Chump Change: Taxi Tales & Vignettes. 220p. 2000. pap. 11.95 (0-939122-26-X) Tucumcari.

— Working the Hard Side of the Street: Selected Stories - Poems - Screams. 360p. (Orig.). 1998. pap. 14.95 (0-939122-25-1) Tucumcari.

Alex, Kurt, tr. see Michaeli, Walter, et al.

Alex, Kyra. The First Five Years. write for info. (1-57074-318-5) Greyden Pr.

***Alex, Lynn M.** Iowa's Archaeological Past. LC 99-33566. (Bur Oak Book Ser.). (Illus.). 420p. 2000. pap. 29.95 (0-87745-681-X) U of Iowa Pr.

Alex, Lynn M. & Mallam, R. Clark. Cultures in Iowa: A Brief Study. (Illus.). 20p. 1995. pap. 1.50 (0-915992-81-7) Eastern National.

***Alex, Lynn Marie.** Iowa's Archaeological Past. LC 99-33566. (Bur Oak Ser.). (Illus.). 420p. 2000. text 49.95 (0-87745-680-1) U of Iowa Pr.

Alex, Marlee. Bible Heroes: Daniel. LC 97-146466. (Illus.). 64p. (J). (ps-k). 1996. 6.99 (1-57673-014-X, Gold n Honey) Zondervan.

— Bible Heroes 3. (Illus.). (J). (ps-3). 1998. 14.99 (1-57673-243-6) Zondervan.

Alex, Nicholas. New York Cops Talk Back: A Study of a Beleaguered Minority. LC 76-1852. 235p. reprint ed. pap. 72.90 (0-8357-9942-5, 201646000004) Bks Demand.

Alex, William. Dreams, the Unconscious & Analytical Therapy. 1971. pap. 3.00 (0-317-13542-2) C G Jung Frisco.

— When Old Gods Die. 1971. pap. 3.00 (0-317-13544-9) C G Jung Frisco.

Alex, William & Tatum, George B. Calvert Vaux: Architect & Planner. (Illus.). 288p. 1994. 100.00 (0-9640650-0-2) Ink NY.

Alexa, jt. auth. see Magnusson, Phillip C.

Alexakis, Alexander. Codex Parisinus Graecus 1115 & Its Archetype. LC 96-3603. (Dumbarton Oaks Studies: No. 34). 1996. 70.00 (0-88402-234-X, Dumbarton Rsch Lib) Dumbarton Oaks.

Alexander. American Public School Law. 4th ed. (Education Ser.). 850p. 1997. pap. 86.95 (0-314-20334-6) West Pub.

Alexander. American Public School Law. 5th ed. (Education Ser.). 2000. text 62.00 (0-534-57744-X) Wadsworth Pub.

***Alexander.** Bones. (Illus.). 224p. 2000. pap. 25.00 (0-8133-3806-9, Pub. by Westview) HarpC.

Alexander. Essay & Letter Writing. Date not set. pap. text. write for info. (0-582-52303-6, Pub. by Addison-Wesley) Longman.

— European Accounting Guide. 1994. text 34.00 (0-12-049899-5); text 98.00 (0-12-049900-2) Acad Pr.

Alexander. Experiences of Bereavement. 1997. pap. 12.95 (0-7459-3753-5, Pub. by Lion Pubng) Trafalgar.

Alexander. Facilities Management: Theory & Practice. LC 96-68681. (Illus.). 196p. (Orig.). (C). 1996. pap. 39.99 (0-419-20580-2, E & FN Spon) Routledge.

Alexander. Financial Market Data. text. write for info. (0-471-89975-5) Wiley.

Alexander. Financial Reporting. 5th ed. (ITBP Textbooks Ser.). 1999. pap. 24.99 (1-86152-488-9) Thomson Learn.

Alexander. First Book of Comprehension, Precision & Composition. 1997. pap. write for info. (0-582-52305-2) Addison-Wesley.

Alexander. Flights from Realism. 2000. text 14.95 (0-7131-6564-2) St Martin.

— Fundamentals of Electrical Circuits. LC 98-55323. 1999. 75.25 (0-256-25379-X) Glencoe.

***Alexander.** History 100. 2nd ed. 118p. 1998. pap. text, suppl. ed. 15.15 (0-536-01340-3) Pearson Custom.

Alexander. Hurst's The Heart, Vol. 1. 10th ed. 2000. write for info. (0-07-135694-0) McGraw.

— Hurst's The Heart, Vol. 2, Bk. 1. 10th ed. 2000. write for info. (0-07-135695-9) McGraw.

— Hurst's The Heart, Vol. 2, BK. 2. 10th ed. 2000. write for info. (0-07-135696-7) McGraw.

— Hurst's The Heart, Vol. 2, Set. 10th ed. 2000. write for info. (0-07-135693-2) McGraw.

— I Think You Think. Date not set. pap. text. write for info. (0-582-55510-8, Pub. by Addison-Wesley) Longman.

— K's First Case. 1992. pap. text. write for info. (0-582-07496-7, Pub. by Addison-Wesley) Longman.

— Learn Chess: A New Way for All. 2 vols., Set. 1988. pap. text 19.95 (0-08-032079-1, Pergamon Pr) Elsevier.

— El Libro de Alixandre. (Gesellschaft Fur Romanische Literatur Ser.: Vol. 10). xxviii, 333p. 1978. reprint ed. 72.00 (3-487-06543-6) G Olms Pubs.

— Longman Advanced Grammar: Reference & Practice. 1992. pap. text. write for info. (0-582-07978-0, Pub. by Addison-Wesley) Longman.

— Maine Jury Instruction Manual, Issue 3. 150p. 1999. ring bd. write for info. (0-327-01261-7, 8165714) LEXIS Pub.

***Alexander.** Nails. 1998. mass mkt. 6.95 (1-85626-292-8, Pub. by Cathie Kyle) Trafalgar.

— Normal Development of Functional Motor Skills. (C). 1998. pap. text 58.00 (0-12-784571-2) Acad Pr.

— On Aristotle's "On Sense Perception" LC 00-31558. 2000. write for info. (0-8014-3690-7) Cornell U Pr.

Alexander. To Anger the Devil. 174p. 1978. 8.50 (0-85978-034-1, Pub. by C W Daniel) Natl Bk Netwk.

— Vascular Access in Oncologic Therapy. (C). 1993. write for info. (0-318-70301-7) Lppncott W & W.

Alexander, et al. Family Property Laws - Wills, Trusts & Future Interests: Star Edition. 1991. pap. text 44.95 (0-88277-904-4) Foundation Pr.

Alexander, jt. auth. see Foner.

Alexander, jt. auth. see Noone.

Alexander, A. Biographical Sketches of the Founder & Principal Alumni of the Log College. 369p. 1985. reprint ed. lib. bdg. 69.00 (0-7812-0844-0) Rprt Serv.

— Letters to a Sex Therapist. 1990. pap. 21.00 (1-85461-000-7, Pub. by Northcote House) St Mut.

Alexander, A., ed. Foliar Fertilization. (Developments in Plant & Soil Sciences Ser.). 1986. text 234.00 (90-247-3288-3) Kluwer Academic.

Alexander, A., et al, eds. The Banks & Society. (C). 1989. 50.00 (0-85297-296-2, Pub. by Chartered Bank) St Mut.

Alexander, A., et al. A Landscape-Level Pronghorn Habitat Evaluation Model for Arizona. (Arizona Game & Fish Department Technical Report: No. 19). (Illus.). 50p. (Orig.). 1996. pap. 5.00 (0-917563-25-5) AZ Game & Fish.

— Pronghorn Home Ranges, Movements, & Habitat Selection in Central Arizona: Arizona Game & Fish Department Technical Report, No. 13. (Illus.). 80p. (Orig.). 1994. pap. 5.00 (0-917563-18-2) AZ Game & Fish.

Alexander, A. G., tr. see Makrakis, Apostolos.

Alexander, A. L., compiled by. Poems That Touch the Heart. enl. rev. ed. LC 56-11498. 425p. 1984. 19.95 (0-385-04401-1) Doubleday.

***Alexander, Adele.** Homelands & Waterways: The American Journey of the Bond Family, 1846-1926. 736p. 2000. pap. 16.00 (0-679-75871-2) Vin Bks.

Alexander, Adele L. Ambiguous Lives: Free Women of Color in Rural Georgia, 1789-1879. LC 91-10151. (Illus.). 304p. 1991. text 30.00 (1-55728-214-5) U of Ark Pr.

— Ambiguous Lives: Free Women of Color in Rural Georgia, 1789-1879. LC 91-10151. (Illus.). 304p. 1992. pap. 18.00 (1-55728-215-3) U of Ark Pr.

Alexander, Adele Logan. Homelands & Waterways: The American Journey of the Bond Family, 1846-1926. LC 98-43775. (Illus.). 720p. 1999. 30.00 (0-679-44228-6) Pantheon.

***Alexander, Agnes.** How to Use Hawaiian Fruit. (Illus.). 76p. 1999. reprint ed. pap. 7.95 (0-912180-53-6) Petroglyph.

Alexander, Alan A. & Muhlebach, Richard F. Operating Small Shopping Centers. LC 97-127182. 1997. write for info. (0-927547-71-6) Intl Coun Shop.

Alexander, Alan A. & Muhlebach, Richard F. Shopping Center Management. LC 91-40796. (Illus.). 424p. 1992. text 62.95 (0-944298-68-0, 752) Inst Real Estate.

Alexander, Alan A., jt. auth. see Muhlebach, Richard F.

Alexander, Albert G., tr. see Makrakis, Apostolos.

Alexander, Alex E. Bylina & Fairytale: The Origins of Russian Heroic Poetry. LC 72-94439. (Slavistic Printings & Reprintings Ser.: No. 281). 1973. 44.65 (90-279-2512-7) Mouton.

Alexander, Alison. Power Magic. (J). 1991. pap. 6.95 (0-671-74130-6) S&S Bks Yung.

Alexander, Alison, et al, eds. Media Economics: Theory & Practice. LC 92-26358. 416p. 1993. 89.95 (0-8058-0434-X); pap. 39.95 (0-8058-1307-1) L Erlbaum Assocs.

— Media Economics: Theory & Practice. 2nd ed. (LEA's Communication Ser.). 425p. 1997. write for info. (0-8058-1841-3); pap. write for info. (0-8058-1842-1) L Erlbaum Assocs.

Alexander, Alison & Hanson, Jarice, eds. Taking Sides: Clashing Views on Controversial Issues in Mass Media & Society. 3rd ed. LC 94-31766. (Illus.). 384p. (C). 1995. text 13.95 (1-56134-325-0, Dshkn McG-Hill) McGrw-H Hghr Educ.

— Taking Sides: Clashing Views on Controversial Issues in Mass Media & Society. 4th ed. (Illus.). 368p. (C). 1996. text 13.00 (0-697-35716-3, Dshkn McG-Hill) McGrw-H Hghr Educ.

Alexander, Alison, et al. Science Magic: Scientific Experiments for Young Children LC 86-12280. 45 p. 1986. 5.95 (0-13-795311-9) P-H.

Alexander, Alison, jt. ed. see Harris, Cheryl.

Alexander, Allan. Celtic Music for Guitar. 80p. 1997. pap. 22.95 incl. cd-rom (1-882146-57-3) A D G Prods.

***Alexander, Allan.** Celtic Music for Guitar, Vol. 2. 82p. 1999. pap. 22.95 incl. audio compact disk (1-882146-69-7) A D G Prods.

Alexander, Allison. Chaucer Pennsylvania. (C). pap. text 2.00 (0-393-10320-X) Norton.

Alexander, Amber. It's Me, Teddy! LC 95-10221. (Illus.). 32p. (J). (ps-3). 1995. 14.95 (0-88266-805-6, Garden Way Pub) Storey Bks.

Alexander, Amy. Fifty Black Women Who Changed America. LC 98-25237. (Illus.). 256p. 1998. 22.50 (1-55972-478-1, Birch Ln Pr) Carol Pub Group.

***Alexander, Amy, ed.** The Farrakhan Factor: African-American Writers on Leadership, Nationhood & Minister Louis Farrakhan. 320p. 1999. reprint ed. pap. text 15.00 (0-8021-3597-8, Grove) Grove-Atltic.

Alexander, Amy, jt. auth. see Poussaint, Alvin F.

Alexander, Andrea. Why Do Mice Celebrate Christmas? And Other Fun Questions of the Season. (Illus.). 64p. (Orig.). (J). (ps-5). 1991. pap. 13.95 (0-9628006-0-0) Zenon Pub.

Alexander, Anne. Thomas Hardy: The "Dream-Country" of His Fiction. (Critical Studies). 260p. 1987. 50.00 (0-389-20712-8, N8270) B&N Imports.

***Alexander, Anne.** Win the Fat War: 145 Real-Life Secrets to Weight-Loss Success. LC 99-59093. (Illus.). 224p. 2000. 15.95 (1-57954-113-5) Rodale Pr Inc.

Alexander, Anne, ed. Bibliography of Newfoundland, Vols. 1 & 2. 1449p. 1986. text 200.00 (0-8020-2402-5) U of Toronto Pr.

***Alexander, Anne, et al.** Win the Fat War Cookbook. 2001. 24.95 (1-57954-363-4) Rodale Pr Inc.

Alexander, Anthony F. College Apologetics: Proof of the Truth of the Catholic Faith. LC 91-65347. 246p. (C). 1994. reprint ed. pap. text 12.50 (0-89555-445-3, 1252) TAN Bks Pubs.

Alexander, Archibald. Evidence of the Authenticity, Inspiration & Canonical Authority of the Holy Scriptures. (Works of Reverend Archibald Alexander). 308p. reprint ed. lib. bdg. 49.00 (0-932051-73-1) Rprt Serv.

— Evidences of the Authenticity, Inspiration, & Canonical Authority of the Holy Scriptures. LC 70-38431. (Religion in America, Ser. 2). 314p. 1972. reprint ed. 25.95 (0-405-04052-0) Ayer.

— Feathers on the Moor. LC 67-22050. (Essay Index Reprint Ser.). 1977. 19.95 (0-8369-0145-2) Ayer.

— History of Colonization of the Western Coast of Africa. 2nd ed. LC 71-149861. (Black Heritage Library Collection). 1977. 36.95 (0-8369-8743-8) Ayer.

***Alexander, Archibald.** Thoughts on Religious Experience. 368p. 1998. pap. 15.99 (0-85151-757-9) Banner of Truth.

Alexander, Archibald, ed. see Tennent, Gilbert, et al.

***Alexander, Arthur M.** Hot on the Scent: A Visitor's Guide to the London of Sherlock Holmes. (Illus.). 288p. 1999. pap. 27.50 (1-899562-80-X, Calabash Pr) Ash-Tree.

***Alexander-Azlin, Mara Lee.** Beyond the Rainbow. LC 99-67519. 528p. 2000. pap. 22.95 (1-57921-257-3, 924-174, Pub. by WinePress Pub) BookWorld.

Alexander, B. Lost Victories: The Military Genius of Stonewall Jackson. 350p. 1996. 10.98 (0-7858-0722-5) Bk Sales Inc.

Alexander, Barbara E. Cassava Stew. (Nandi Bks.). 1992. 4.95 (0-938818-24-4) ECA Assoc.

Alexander, Ben. Out from Darkness. rev. ed. (Illus.). 224p. (Orig.). 1992. pap. 9.95 (0-9634071-0-4) Miranda Pr.

***Alexander, Ben.** Total Golf Binder. 2000. 69.95 (0-8094-9377-2) Time-Life.

Alexander-Bennett, Dawn & Pincus, Laura. Employment Law for Business. 2nd ed. LC 97-5652. 672p. (C). 1997. text 63.50 (0-256-22902-3, Irwn McGrw-H) McGrw-H Hghr Educ.

Alexander, Betsy. Path Through Deep Waters. Weinberger, Jane, ed. LC 98-75032. 350p. 1998. 10.00 (1-883650-51-8) Windswept Hse.

Alexander, Bevin. How Great Generals Win. LC 92-40518. 1993. 25.00 (0-393-03531-X) Norton.

— How Great Generals Win. 320p. 1995. reprint ed. pap. 12.50 (0-380-72436-7, Avon Bks) Morrow Avon.

***Alexander, Bevin.** How Hitler Could Have Won World War II: The Ten Fatal Errors That Led to Nazi Defeat. 352p. 2000. 25.00 (0-8129-3202-1) Crown Pub Group.

— Korea: First War We Lost: Revised Edition & Newly Restored Photos. 3rd rev. ed. (Illus.). 590p. 2000. pap. 19.95 (0-7818-0808-1) Hippocrene Bks.

Alexander, Bevin. Robert E. Lee's Civil War. LC 97-43148. (Illus.). 338p. 1998. 24.95 (1-55850-849-X) Adams Media.

— Robert E. Lee's Civil War. 1999. pap. 14.95 (1-58062-135-X) Adams Media.

— The Strange Connection: U. S. Intervention in China 1944-72, 34. LC 91-27239. (Contributions to the Study of World History Ser.: No. 34). 264p. 1992. 57.95 (0-313-28008-8, AXS/, Greenwood Pr) Greenwood.

Alexander, Bill. A Man's Book of the Spirit: Daily Meditations for a Mindful Life. 384p. (Orig.). 1994. pap. 10.00 (0-380-77175-6, Avon Bks) Morrow Avon.

***Alexander, Bob.** Math. 10th ed. 2000. text. write for info. (0-201-68484-5) Addison-Wesley.

Alexander, Bobby C. Televangelism Reconsidered: Ritual in Search for Human Community. LC 94-19987. (AAR Reflection & Theory in the Study of Religion Ser.: No. 68). 216p. 1994. 39.95 (1-55540-906-7, 010068); pap. 24.95 (1-55540-907-5, 010068) OUP.

— Victor Turner Revisited: Ritual As Social Change. (American Academy of Religion Academy Ser.). 202p. 1991. 24.95 (1-55540-600-9, 010174); pap. 15.95 (1-55540-601-7, 010174) OUP.

Alexander, Boyd. England's Wealthiest Son: A Study of William Beckford. LC 62-4094. (Illus.). 322p. reprint ed. pap. 99.90 (0-8357-6655-1, 203532400094) Bks Demand.

Alexander, Brandon. Flamingoes Overboard! (Full House Club Stephanie Ser.: Vol. 6). (J). (gr. 3-6). 1998. per. 3.99 (0-671-02124-9, Minstrel Bks) PB.

***Alexander, Brandon.** Kiss of Darkness. (Charmed Ser.: No. 2). 192p. (YA). (gr. 7-12). 2000. per. 4.99 (0-671-04163-0, Pocket Pulse) PB.

Alexander, Brian. Green Cathedrals: A Rain Forest Pilgrimage. (Illus.). 224p. 1995. 22.95 (1-55821-399-6) Lyons Pr.

Alexander, Brian, ed. Greece. (Travelers' Tales Guides Ser.). (Illus.). 400p. (Orig.). 1999. pap. 17.95 (1-885211-12-0) Trvlers Tale.

Alexander, Brian & Alexander, Cherry. What Do We Know about the Inuit? (What Do We Know about...? Ser.). (Illus.). 48p. (YA). (gr. 3 up). 1995. lib. bdg. 18.95 (0-87226-380-0, 63800B, P Bedrick Books) NTC Contemp Pub Co.

Alexander, Bruce. Blind Justice: A Sir John Fielding Mystery. 1995. mass mkt. 5.99 (0-425-15007-0) Berkley Pub.

— Blind Justice: A Sir John Fielding Mystery. large type ed. (Large Print Ser.). 576p. 1996. 25.99 (0-7089-3606-7) Ulverscroft.

***Alexander, Bruce.** The Color of Death. (Sir John Fielding Mystery Ser.). 288p. 2000. 23.95 (0-399-14648-2) Putnam Pub Group.

— Death of a Colonial: A Sir John Fielding Mystery. 2000. mass mkt. 6.50 (0-425-17702-5) Berkley Pub.

— Death of a Colonial: A Sir John Fielding Mystery. LC 99-48844. (G. K. Hall Core Ser.). 1999. 27.95 (0-7838-8823-6, G K Hall & Co) Mac Lib Ref.

Alexander, Bruce. Death of a Colonial: A Sir John Fielding Mystery. LC 99-20978. 288p. 1999. 23.95 (0-399-14564-8, G P Putnam) Peng Put Young Read.

— Jack, Knave & Fool: A Sir John Fielding Mystery. LC 98-15519. (Sir John Fielding Mystery Ser.). 288p. 1998. 22.95 (0-399-14419-6, G P Putnam) Peng Put Young Read.

***Alexander, Bruce.** Jack, Knave & Fool: A Sir John Fielding Mystery. large type ed. LC 98-53488. 1999. 27.95 (0-7862-1798-7) Thorndike Pr.

— Jack, Knave & Fool: A Sir John Fielding Mystery. 1999. reprint ed. mass mkt. 6.50 (0-425-17120-5, Prime Crime) Berkley Pub.

Alexander, Bruce. Murder in Grub Street: A Sir John Fielding Mystery. large type ed. (Ulverscroft Large Print Ser.). 608p. 1997. 27.50 (0-7089-3749-7) Ulverscroft.

— Murder in Grub Street: A Sir John Fielding Mystery. 320p. 1996. reprint ed. mass mkt. 5.99 (0-425-15550-1, Prime Crime) Berkley Pub.

— Person or Persons Unknown: A Sir John Fielding Mystery. (Sir John Fielding Mystery Ser.: Bk. 4). 336p. 1998. reprint ed. pap. 5.99 (0-425-16566-3, Prime Crime) Berkley Pub.

— Watery Grave. 320p. 1997. mass mkt. 5.99 (0-425-16036-X, Prime Crime) Berkley Pub.

— Watery Grave. large type ed. 544p. 1998. 29.99 (0-7089-3984-8) Ulverscroft.

Alexander, Bruce K. Peaceful Measures: Canada's Way Out of the "War on Drugs" 415p. 1990. text 50.00 (0-8020-2722-9); pap. text 20.95 (0-8020-6753-0) U of Toronto Pr.

Alexander, Bryan. The Vanishing Arctic. LC 97-178507. (Illus.). 192p. 1997. 35.00 (0-8160-3650-0) Facts on File.

Alexander, Bryan & Alexander, Cherry. An Eskimo Family. (Families the World Over Ser.). (Illus.). 32p. (J). (gr. 2-5). 1985. lib. bdg. 18.60 (0-8225-1656-X, Lerner Publctns) Lerner Pub.

— Inuit. LC 92-9894. (Threatened Cultures Ser.). (Illus.). 48p. (J). (gr. 5-6). 1992. lib. bdg. 24.26 (0-8114-2301-8) Raintree Steck-V.

Alexander, C. The Real Inner Secrets of Psychology: Creative Thought Power (1929) 200p. 1998. reprint ed. pap. 18.95 (0-7661-0412-5) Kessinger Pub.

— A Timeless Way of Building. 1978. pap. text 45.00 (0-19-502248-3) OUP.

***Alexander, C. & Simpkins, Annellen.** Simple Confucianism: A Guide to Living Virtuously. LC 99-48864. 160p. 2000. pap. 12.95 (0-8048-3177-7) Tuttle Pubng.

Alexander, C. & Simpkins, Annellen. Simple Taoism: A Guide to Living in Balance. LC 99-24271. 128p. 1999. pap. 12.95 (0-8048-3173-4) Tuttle Pubng.

— Simple Zen. LC 99-24270. 128p. 1999. pap. 12.95 (0-8048-3174-2) Tuttle Pubng.

Alexander, C., jt. auth. see Simpkins, Annellen M.

Alexander, C. H. Learn Chess Vol. 1: A New Way for All. 2nd ed. (Chess Ser.: No. 1). (Illus.). 104p. 1987. 19.90 (0-08-032067-8, Pergamon Pr) Elsevier.

***Alexander, Caitlind L.** Guide to HMO Billing. unabridged ed. Brown, Sharon E., ed. 135p. 1999. pap. write for info. (1-881159-28-0) Ins Career Dev.

Alexander, Caitlind L., jt. auth. see Insurance Career Development Center Staff.

Alexander, Caitlind L., ed. see Insurance Career Development Center Staff, et al.

Alexander, Carmela, jt. auth. see Kirk, Ruth.

Alexander, Carmen. Floating Around in the Middle. (Illus.). 30p. (J). (ps-5). 2000. pap. 10.00 (1-886383-76-6, Little Blue) Pride & Imprints.

— Rosemarie Returns to Her Garden. (Garden Stories Ser.). (Illus.). 30p. (J). (ps-4). 2000. pap. 10.00 (1-886383-68-5, Little Blue) Pride & Imprints.

— Rosemarie's Garden. (Garden Stories Ser.). (Illus.). 30p. (J). (ps-4). 2000. pap. 10.00 (1-886383-66-9, Little Blue) Pride & Imprints.

— Rosemarie's Roof Garden. (Garden Stories Ser.). (Illus.). 30p. (J). (ps-4). 2000. pap. 10.00 (1-886383-67-7, Little Blue) Pride & Imprints.

— Zoo: 1000 Miles. (Illus.). 30p. (J). (ps-5). 2000. pap. 10.00 (1-886383-57-X, Little Blue) Pride & Imprints.

Alexander, Carol. Rachel Carson, Writer & Scientist. (Illus.). (J). (gr. 1-4). 1995. pap. 4.95 (*0-8136-5738-5*); lib. bdg. 10.60 (*0-8136-5732-6*) Modern Curr.

***Alexander, Carol.** Risk Management & Analysis: Markets & Products. LC 98-15961. 360p. 1999. 95.00 (*0-471-97959-7*) Wiley.

Alexander, Carol. Risk Management & Analysis: Measuring & Modelling Financial Risk, Vol. 1. LC 98-24147. 304p. 1998. 95.00 (*0-471-97957-0*) Wiley.

Alexander, Caroline. The Endurance: Shackleton's Legendary Antarctic Expedition. LC 98-87214. (Illus.). 211p. 1998. 29.95 (*0-375-40403-1*) Knopf.

***Alexander, Caroline.** The Endurance: Shackleton's Legendary Antarctic Expedition. large type ed. LC 99-26901. (Nonfiction Ser.). 1999. 28.95 (*0-7838-8643-8*, G K Hall Lrg Type) Mac Lib Ref.

Alexander, Caroline. Mrs. Chippy's Last Expedition: The Newly Discovered Journal of Shackleton's Polar-Bound Cat. LC 97-15732. (Illus.). 176p. 1997. 16.00 (*0-06-017546-X*) HarpC.

— Mrs. Chippy's Last Expedition: The Remarkable Journal of Shackleton's Polar-Bound Cat. LC 97-15732. (Illus.). 176p. 1999. pap. 11.00 (*0-06-093261-9*) HarpC.

***Alexander, Caroline.** Mrs. Chippy's Last Expedition: The Remarkable Journal of Shackleton's Polar-Bound Cat. large type ed. LC 99-86698. (Illus.). (J). 2000. pap. 22.95 (*1-56895-847-1*) Wheeler Pub.

Alexander, Caroline. Now You Are Sara: A Memoir. Sandys-Wunsch, John, tr. LC 93-72362. 78p. 1993. pap. 9.95 (*0-914539-07-8*) Ben-Simon.

— One Dry Season: In the Footsteps of Mary Kingsley. LC 90-50188. (Vintage Departures Ser.). 304p. 1990. pap. 10.95 (*0-679-73189-X*) Vin Bks.

Alexander, Caroline, jt. auth. see Sheen, Joanna.

Alexander, Carrie. All Shook Up. (Temptation Ser.). 1996. per. 3.50 (*0-373-25698-1*, 1-25698-1) Harlequin Bks.

— The Amorous Heiress. 1997. per. 3.50 (*0-373-44028-6*, 1-44028-8) Harlequin Bks.

— Black Velvet: Blaze. (Temptation Ser.: Vol. 689). 1998. per. 3.75 (*0-373-25789-9*, 1-25789-8) Harlequin Bks.

— Black Velvet Valentines: Blaze. 1999. per. 3.75 (*0-373-25820-8*, Harlequin) Harlequin Bks.

— Fancy-Free. LC 95-6883. (Temptation Ser.). 217p. 1995. mass mkt. 3.25 (*0-373-25636-1*, 1-25636-1) Harlequin Bks.

— His Mistress. (Stolen Moments Ser.). 1993. pap. 1.99 (*0-373-83283-4*, 1-83283-1) Harlequin Bks.

— The Madcap Heiress. 1996. per. 3.50 (*0-373-44008-1*, 1-44008-0) Harlequin Bks.

— A Touch of Black Velvet: (Blaze) (Temptation Ser.: Vol. 704). 1998. per. 3.75 (*0-373-25804-6*, 1-25804-5) Harlequin Bks.

***Alexander, Carrie & Gabriel, Kristin.** The Bachelor Trap - Custom-Built Cowboy. (Duets Ser.: No. 25). 2000. mass mkt. 5.99 (*0-373-44091-X*) Harlequin Bks.

Alexander, Carrie, jt. auth. see Ireland, Liz.

Alexander, Carter. Some Present Aspects of the Work of Teachers' Voluntary Associations in the United States. (Columbia University. Teachers College. Contributions to Education Ser.: No. 36). reprint ed. 37.50 (*0-404-55036-3*) AMS Pr.

***Alexander, Catherine M. S. & Wells, Stanley, eds.** Shakespeare & Race. LC 99-89004. 240p. 2000. pap. write for info. (*0-521-77938-3*) Cambridge U Pr.

— Shakespeare & Race. LC 99-89004. (Illus.). 240p. 2000. write for info. (*0-521-77046-7*) Cambridge U Pr.

Alexander, Cecil F. All Things Bright & Beautiful. LC 91-28428. (Illus.). 32p. (J). (ps-2). 1992. 11.95 (*0-8249-8544-3*, Ideals Child) Hambleton-Hill.

***Alexander, Cecil Frances.** All Things Bright & Beautiful. (Illus.). 32p. 2000. 17.95 (*0-8192-1834-0*, 6257) Morehouse Pub.

Alexander, Charles. Arc of Light, Dark Matter. LC 92-80328. (Segue Bks.). (Orig.). 1992. pap. 8.00 (*0-937804-46-0*) Segue NYC.

— Hopeful Buildings. LC 90-1405. 176p. (Orig.). 1990. pap. 9.95 (*0-925904-03-1*) Chax Pr.

— A Journal of Treasured Momentu: My Weekly Lessons & Blessings. (Illus.). 126p. 1998. 12.00 (*0-9664645-0-8*) Alex-Zan.

***Alexander, Charles.** Knight Moves. (Illus.). 82p. 1999. pap. 6.95 (*0-945470-76-2*) Chess Ent.

***Alexander, Charles, ed.** Masters of Jazz Guitar: The Story of the Players & Their Music. (Illus.). 192p. 1999. 39.95 (*0-87930-592-4*) Miller Freeman.

Alexander, Charles, jt. auth. see Freeth, Nick.

Alexander, Charles, ed. see Higgins, Dick, et al.

Alexander, Charles C. Holding the Line: The Eisenhower Era, 1952-1961. LC 74-11714. 346p. reprint ed. pap. 107.30 (*0-7837-1744-X*, 205727700024) Bks Demand.

— John McGraw. LC 94-23951. (Illus.). 371p. Date not set. pap. 12.95 (*0-8032-5925-5*, Bison Books) U of Nebr Pr.

— The Ku Klux Klan in the Southwest. LC 95-15078. (Illus.). 320p. 1995. pap. 14.95 (*0-8061-2776-7*) U of Okla Pr.

— The Ku Klux Klan in the Southwest. LC 65-11831. 304p. reprint ed. 94.30 (*0-8357-9789-9*, 201609500098) Bks Demand.

— Our Game: An American Baseball History. (Illus.). 448p. 1995. pap. 14.95 (*0-8050-2094-2*, Owl) H Holt & Co.

— Our Game - An American Baseball History. (Illus.). 392p. 1997. 9.98 (*1-56731-130-X*, MJF Bks) Fine Comms.

— Rogers Hornsby: A Biography. 288p. 1995. 27.50 (*0-8050-2002-0*) H Holt & Co.

— Rogers Hornsby: A Biography. (Illus.). 384p. 1995. pap. 14.95 (*0-8050-4697-6*, Owl) H Holt & Co.

— Ty Cobb. LC 83-17409. (Illus.). 304p. 1985. pap. 14.95 (*0-19-503598-4*) OUP.

Alexander, Charles N., ed. Self-Recovery: Treating Addictions Using Transcendental Meditation & Maharishi Ayur-Veda. LC 94-3952. (Alcoholism Treatment Quarterly Ser.). (Illus.). 341p. 1995. pap. 24.95 (*1-56023-044-4*, Harrington Park); lib. bdg. 59.95 (*1-56024-454-2*) Haworth Pr.

Alexander, Charles N. & Langer, Ellen J., eds. Higher Stages of Human Development: Perspectives on Adult Growth. (Illus.). 416p. 1990. text 68.00 (*0-19-503483-X*) OUP.

Alexander, Charlotte. Monarch Notes on Dreiser's Sister Carrie. (Orig.). (C). 3.95 (*0-671-00662-2*, Arco) Macmillan Gen Ref.

— Monarch Notes on Emerson's Writings. (Orig.). (C). 3.95 (*0-671-00663-0*, Arco) Macmillan Gen Ref.

— Monarch Notes on Salinger's Franny & Zooey, Nine Stories. (Orig.). (C). 3.95 (*0-671-00866-8*, Arco) Macmillan Gen Ref.

— Monarch Notes on Thoreau's Walden & Other Writings. (Orig.). (C). 3.95 (*0-671-00695-9*, Arco) Macmillan Gen Ref.

Alexander, Charlotte. Tears of Rage. 1997. 24.00 (*0-671-00661-4*, PB Hardcover) PB.

Alexander, Charlotte A. Catcher in the Rye. 1976. 3.95 (*0-671-00691-6*, Arco) Macmillan Gen Ref.

— Monarch Notes Grapes of Wrath. (C). 3.95 (*0-671-00692-4*, Arco) Macmillan Gen Ref.

— Poetry of Emily Dickinson. 1965. 4.25 (*0-671-00780-7*, Arco) Macmillan Gen Ref.

Alexander, Cherry, jt. auth. see Alexander, Brian.

Alexander, Cherry, jt. auth. see Alexander, Bryan.

Alexander, Cheryl A. Mark of God Vol. 1: How to Get the Mark of God on Your Forehead. ix, 54p. 1997. pap. 6.99 (*0-9660632-9-5*) C A Alexander.

Alexander, Chip & Huffman, Dane. Tar Heel Trivia: Tantalizing Tidbits from a Basketball Powerhouse. Wilson, Jim, ed. LC 91-67942. (Illus.). 192p. (Orig.). 1991. pap. 9.95 (*1-880123-02-9*) VilCom Sports.

Alexander, Christie, ed. see D'Arezzo, Richard.

Alexander, Christine, ed. Bibliography of the Manuscripts of Charlotte Bronte. 205p. 1982. lib. bdg. 65.00 (*0-313-27665-X*) Greenwood.

Alexander, Christine & Sellars, Jane. The Art of the Brontes. (Illus.). 510p. (C). 1995. pap. text 36.95 (*0-521-43841-1*) Cambridge U Pr.

Alexander, Christine, ed. see Bronte, Charlotte.

Alexander, Christopher. Foreshadowing of Twenty-First Century Art: The Color & Geometry of Very Early Turkish Carpets. (Illus.). 352p. 1993. 150.00 (*0-19-520866-8*) OUP.

— The Oregon Experiment. (Illus.). 202p. 1975. 39.95 (*0-19-501824-9*) OUP.

— The Timeless Way of Building. (Illus.). 568p. 1979. 49.95 (*0-19-502402-8*) OUP.

Alexander, Christopher & Davis, Howard. The Production of Houses. LC 82-14097. (Center for Environmental Structure Ser.: Vol. 4). (Illus.). 383p. (C). 1985. 45.00 (*0-19-503223-3*) OUP.

Alexander, Christopher, et al. The Mary Rose Museum. LC 93-18221. (Illus.). 128p. 1995. 35.00 (*0-19-521017-4*) OUP.

— A New Theory of Urban Design. (Illus.). 272p. 1987. 45.00 (*0-19-503753-7*) OUP.

— A Pattern Language: Towns, Buildings, Construction. LC 74-22874. (Illus.). 1216p. 1977. 60.00 (*0-19-501919-9*) OUP.

***Alexander, Christopher F., Jr.** Bottleneck Highway, Sunrise Fizz. 65p. 1999. pap. 6.00 (*0-935931-89-9*) Iberian Pub.

Alexander, Christopher J. Gay & Lesbian Mental Health. 1998. pap. text 19.95 (*1-56023-936-0*, Harrington Park) Haworth Pr.

— Growth & Intimacy for Gay Men: A Workbook. (Illus.). 294p. (C). 1997. wbk. ed. 49.95 (*0-7890-0153-5*); pap., wbk. ed. 22.95 (*1-56023-901-8*, Harrington Park) Haworth Pr.

***Alexander, Christopher J.** Working with Gay Men & Lesbians in Private Psychotherapy Practice. 2000. pap. 19.95 (*1-56023-125-4*, Harrington Park) Haworth Pr.

Alexander, Christopher J., ed. Gay & Lesbian Mental Health: A Sourcebook for Practitioners. LC 95-43392. (Illus.). 277p. 1996. 49.95 (*1-56023-879-8*, Harrington Park) Haworth Pr.

— Working with Gay Men & Lesbians in Private Psychotherapy Practice. LC 98-48951. 107p. 1998. 29.95 (*0-7890-0693-6*) Haworth Pr.

Alexander, Christopher W. Notes on the Synthesis of Form. LC 64-13417. (Illus.). 216p. 1964. pap. text 16.50 (*0-674-62751-2*) HUP.

***Alexander, Claire.** The Asian 'Gang' Ethnicity, Identity, Masculinity. 192p. 2000. 65.00 (*1-85973-314-X*, Pub. by Berg Pubs); pap. 19.50 (*1-85973-319-0*, Pub. by Berg Pubs) NYU Pr.

Alexander, Claire E. The Art of Being Black: The Creation of Black Youth Identities. LC 96-225710. 224p. 1996. text 35.00 (*0-19-827982-5*) OUP.

Alexander, Clarence. The Law of Arrest: Criminal Law & Other Proceedings, 2 vols., Set. cvi, 2260p. 1949. lib. bdg. 78.00 (*0-89941-374-9*, 500210) W S Hein.

***Alexander, Clark, et al, eds.** Tidalities: Processes & Products. (Special Publications: Vol. 61). (Illus.). 172p. 1999. 121.50 (*1-56576-059-X*) SEPM.

Alexander, Claude V. Japanese Chin. (KW Ser.). (Illus.). 192p. 1990. 9.95 (*0-86622-575-7*, KW-205) TFH Pubns.

Alexander, Claudia B., jt. ed. see Partnow, Elaine.

Alexander, Clifton J. & Alexander, Sandy. Kick the Drug Habit: The Basic Guide. rev. ed. 134p. 1989. reprint ed. pap. 8.95 (*0-929658-00-0*) Antler Pub.

Alexander, Colin. Capturing Full-Trend Profits in the Commodity Futures Markets: Maximizing Reward & Minimizing Risk with the Wellspring System. 1992. 50.00 (*0-930233-50-6*) Windsor.

— Five Star Futures Trades: The Premier System for Trading the Biggest Market Moves. 171p. 1997. 55.00 (*0-930233-58-1*) Windsor.

***Alexander, Colin.** God's Adamantine Fate. LC 99-91011. 491p. 1999. 25.00 (*0-7388-0476-2*); pap. 18.00 (*0-7388-0477-0*) Xlibris Corp.

Alexander, Colin. Lady of Ice & Fire. 352p. 1996. reprint ed. mass mkt. 5.50 (*0-8439-4072-7*, Leisure Bks) Dorchester Pub Co.

— The Streetsmart Guide to Timing the Stock Market: When to Buy, Sell, & Sell Short. LC 99-18009. 368p. 1999. 29.95 (*0-07-134650-3*) McGraw.

Alexander Communications, Inc. Staff. A. R. 3: The Complete Annual Report & Corporate Image Planning Book. 300p. 1989. write for info. (*0-318-64726-5*) Macmillan.

— The Chicago Talent Sourcebook, No. 10. (Illus.). 600p. 1989. write for info. (*0-318-64727-3*) Macmillan.

Alexander, Consul. The Cobra Guide: Practical Solutions to Administration & Management. 256p. (C). 1996. text 50.00 (*0-7863-0537-1*, Irwn Prfssnl) McGraw-Hill Prof.

— Welfare Plan Guide: Practical Solutions to Administration & Management. 384p. (C). 1996. text 50.00 (*0-7863-0534-7*, Irwn Prfssnl) McGraw-Hill Prof.

Alexander Consulting Group Staff. The FMLA Guide: Practical Solutions to Administration & Management. LC 95-33566. (Illus.). 583p. (C). 1995. text 50.00 (*0-7863-0535-5*, Irwn Prfssnl) McGraw-Hill Prof.

— 1996 Quick Reference to ERISA Compliance. annual. 512p. 1996. pap. 125.00 (*1-56706-306-3*) Panel Pubs.

Alexander, Craig, jt. auth. see Sipski, Marca.

Alexander, Cristof, ed. see Omlor, Georg.

Alexander, Cuda. Got Your Back. 240p. 2000. pap. 12.95 (*0-312-24299-9*) St Martin.

Alexander, Cynthia. Digital Democracy: Policy & Politics in the Wired World. LC 99-177943. (Illus.). 256p. 1998. pap. text 26.50 (*0-19-541359-8*) OUP.

Alexander, Cynthia J., jt. auth. see McAllister, Mary L.

Alexander, D., ed. see Miller, Alan.

Alexander, D. E., et al, eds. Materials Modification & Synthesis by Ion Beam Processing. LC 97-811. (Materials Research Society Symposium Proceedings Ser.: No. 438). 727p. 1997. text 78.00 (*1-55899-342-8*) Materials Res.

Alexander, D. J., et al. A Study of Policy, Organisation & Provision in Community Education & Leisure & Recreation in Three Scottish Regions. 538p. (C). 1984. 60.00 (*0-7855-2391-X*, Pub. by Univ Nottingham) St Mut.

Alexander, D. S. Political History of the State of New York, 3 vols., Set. 1993. reprint ed. lib. bdg. 225.00 (*0-7812-5165-6*) Rprt Serv.

Alexander, D. Stanwood. The Alexanders of Maine. (Illus.). 129p. 1988. reprint ed. pap. 19.00 (*0-8328-0099-6*); reprint ed. lib. bdg. 29.00 (*0-8328-0098-8*) Higginson Bk Co.

Alexander, Dale. Arthritis & Common Sense. 256p. 1981. per. 11.00 (*0-671-42791-1*) S&S Trade Pap.

— Principles & Applications of Chemistry. 6th ed. 304p. (C). 1994. pap. text, spiral bd. 28.95 (*0-7872-0038-7*) Kendall-Hunt.

Alexander, Dana & Shea, Amy. Lasting Memories: A Guide to Writing Your Family History. 142p. (Orig.). 1996. pap., wbk. ed. 16.95 (*0-9653437-0-7*) Generations NC.

Alexander, Daniel. Intellectual Property & the Environment. (Environmental Law Ser.). 300p. 1996. 140.00 (*1-874698-95-3*, Pub. by Cameron May) Gaunt.

Alexander, Daniel, et al. State Aids & Public Enterprises. 300p. 1994. pap. text 193.00 (*0-406-00638-5*, UK, MICHIE) LEXIS Pub.

Alexander, Daniel C. Brief Calculus with Applications: In Business & the Social & Life Sciences. LC 95-94615. (Illus.). 805p. (C). 1996. text 49.95 (*0-943202-51-5*) H & H Pub.

Alexander, Daniel C. & Koeberlein, Geralyn M. Elementary Geometry for College Students 2nd ed. LC 98-71972. 1999. text 49.77 (*0-395-87055-0*) HM.

Alexander, Danielle, ed. Examiners Handbook Vol. I: Financial Condition. rev. ed. 826p. (C). 1998. ring bd. 100.00i (*0-89382-509-3*, EXF-ZU97) Nat Assn Insurance.

— Financial Condition Examiners Handbook. rev. ed. 826p. (C). 1999. ring bd. 100.00i (*0-89382-595-6*, EXF-ZM98) Nat Assn Insurance.

— Financial Condition Examiners Handbook. 21st ed. 83p. (C). 1997. ring bd. 100.00 (*0-89382-441-0*, EXF-ZM) Nat Assn Insurance.

— Guide to Compliance with State Audit Requirements. 3rd rev. ed. 704p. (C). 1998. ring bd. 75.00i (*0-89382-508-5*, CPA-ZU98) Nat Assn Insurance.

Alexander, Danny. Liner Notes: Soul Asylum. 128p. 1996. pap. 7.95 (*1-57297-122-3*) Blvd Books.

***Alexander, Darsie.** Body Language. 144p. 1999. 24.95 (*0-8109-6205-5*) Abrams.

Alexander, David. The Arts of War Vol. 1: Arms & Armour of the 7th to 19th Centuries. (Nassar D. Khalili Collection of Islamic Art: Vol. XXI). (Illus.). 240p. 1993. text 295.00 (*0-19-727618-0*) OUP.

— Bandit. 256p. (Orig.). 1994. mass mkt. 4.99 (*0-380-76860-7*, Avon Bks) Morrow Avon.

— Death Race. (Nomad Ser.: No. 116). 1992. per. 4.99 (*0-373-62116-7*) Harlequin Bks.

— Desert Fire. (Nomad Ser.). 1993. mass mkt. 4.99 (*0-373-62118-3*, 1-62118-4) Harlequin Bks.

— Fines & Restitution: Improvement Needed in How Offenders' Payment Schedules Are Determined. (Illus.) 63p. (C). 1999. pap. text 20.00 (*0-7881-7774-5*) DIANE Pub.

— How You Can Manipulate the Media: Guerrilla Methods to Get Your Story Covered by TV, Radio, & Newspapers. 112p. 1993. pap. 12.00 (*0-87364-729-7*) Paladin Pr.

— The Human Impact Reader: Readings & Case Studies. Goudie, Andrew, ed. LC 96-47638. (Readers in the Natural Environment Ser.). (Illus.). 448p. 1997. text 76.95 (*0-631-19979-9*); pap. text 31.95 (*0-631-19981-0*) Blackwell Pubs.

— My Real Name Is Lisa. 288p. 1996. 21.00 (*0-7867-0310-5*) Carroll & Graf.

— Natural Disasters Study Guide. 196p. (C). 1994. pap. text, spiral bd. 28.95 (*0-8403-9511-6*, 40951101) Kendall-Hunt.

— Nomad. 1992. per. 4.99 (*0-373-62115-9*, 1-62115-0) Harlequin Bks.

***Alexander, David.** Shadow Down. 2000. mass mkt. 6.99 (*0-425-17305-4*) Berkley Pub.

Alexander, David. Smart Bomb. (Nomad Ser.). 1993. mass mkt. 4.99 (*0-373-62117-5*, 1-62117-6) Harlequin Bks.

— Switchback. 256p. 1997. mass mkt. 5.99 (*0-380-79022-X*, Avon Bks) Morrow Avon.

***Alexander, David.** Tomorrow's Soldier: The Warriors, Weapons, & Tactics That Will Win America's Wars in the Twenty-First Century. 256p. 1999. mass mkt. 6.50 (*0-380-79502-7*, Avon Bks) Morrow Avon.

— 2000 Miller IAS Guide: Restatement & Analysis of International Accounting Standards. 600p. 2000. pap. 79.00 (*0-15-606978-4*) Harcourt.

Alexander, David. Zondervan Handbook to the Bible. LC 99-14821. 816p. 1999. 29.97 (*0-310-23095-0*) Zondervan.

Alexander, David, ed. 1998 European Accounting Guide. 2nd ed. 1998. pap. text 119.00 (*0-15-606261-5*) Harcourt Coll Pubs.

Alexander, David & Alexander, Pat. Nuevo Manual Biblico Ilustrado.Tr. of New Illustrated Bible Handbook. (SPA., Illus.). 1993. 29.99 (*0-8423-6289-4*, 490410) Editorial Unilit.

Alexander, David & Preisler, Jerome. Infosurfing Through the Net: How to Get On-Line Computer Services & Ride the Information Wave. 192p. (Orig.). 1995. mass mkt. 5.99 (*0-380-77764-9*, Avon Bks) Morrow Avon.

— The Internet Site Finder. (Orig.). 1996. mass mkt. 5.99 (*0-380-78269-3*, Avon Bks) Morrow Avon.

Alexander, David, jt. auth. see Alexander, Kern.

Alexander, David A., et al. Police Stress at Work. (Aberdeen University Press Bks.). 176p. 1991. pap. text 19.90 (*0-08-041199-1*, Pub. by Aberdeen U Pr) Macmillan.

Alexander, David A., jt. auth. see Eagles, John M.

Alexander, David C., jt. ed. see Pulat, B. Mustafa.

Alexander, David E. Black Motivation - Success Made Easy! You Must Read This, Vol. 1. (Illus.). 80p. (Orig.). 1988. pap. 11.00 (*0-685-29403-X*) Alexander Forney.

Alexander, David E. The Myths of the Lechuza. (Illus.). 78p. (Orig.). (J). Date not set. pap. 12.95 (*0-9623078-5-8*) Alexander Forney.

Alexander, David G. Atlantic Canada & Confederation: Essays in Canadian Political Economy. 176p. 1983. pap. 10.95 (*0-8020-6512-0*); text 27.50 (*0-8020-2487-4*) U of Toronto Pr.

Alexander, David J., ed. Newcastle Disease. (Developments in Veterinary Virology Ser.). (C). 1988. text 240.00 (*0-89838-392-7*) Kluwer Academic.

Alexander, David M. The Little Wide Mouth Gecko. (Illus.). (J). (ps-3). 1996. pap. 10.00 (*1-892455-00-5*) Desk Top KS.

Alexander, David P. & Williams, Pamela V. Health Care Fraud: Information-Sharing Proposals to Improve Enforcement Efforts. (Illus.). 96p. (Orig.). (C). 1996. pap. text 25.00 (*0-7881-3665-8*) DIANE Pub.

***Alexander, David T. & DeLorey, Thomas K.** Coin World Comprehensive Catalog & Encyclopedia of United States Coins. 592p. 1998. 17.00 (*0-944945-24-4*, Coin World) Amos Ohio.

Alexander, David T., ed. see Crestohl, Robert.

Alexander, David V. Arizona Frontier Military Place Names, 1846-1912. LC 98-60048. (Illus.). 184p. 1998. pap. 12.95 (*1-881325-25-3*) Yucca Tree Pr.

Alexander, De Alva S. Four Famous New Yorkers: The Political Careers of Cleveland, Platt, Hill, & Roosevelt; Forming Volume Four of "The Political History of the State of New York," 1882-1905. (BCL1 - United States Local History Ser.). 488p. 1991. reprint ed. text 99.00 (*0-7812-6271-2*) Rprt Serv.

Alexander, Dean C. Prospects of a U. S.-Chile Free Trade Agreement. (Nijhoff Law Specials Ser.). 164p. (C). 1994. pap. text 60.00 (*0-7923-2885-X*, Pub. by M Nijhoff) Kluwer Academic.

Alexander, Dean C., jt. auth. see Rubin, Seymour J.

***Alexander, Debbie.** Status of Education Reform in Public Elementary & Secondary Schools: Teachers' Perspectives. 94p. 1999. pap. 8.00 (*0-16-049879-1*) USGPO.

Alexander, Debra W. All My Dreams. 16p. (YA). (gr. 6-12). 1993. 3.95 (*1-56688-067-X*) Bur For At-Risk.

— All My Feelings. 23p. (J). (gr. k-5). 1992. 3.95 (*1-56688-055-6*) Bur For At-Risk.

— Don't Go. 16p. (J). (gr. k-5). 1992. 3.95 (*1-56688-057-2*) Bur For At-Risk.

— I Can't Remember. 16p. (J). (gr. k-5). 1992. 3.95 (*1-56688-059-9*) Bur For At-Risk.

— In This House Called Home. 24p. (YA). (gr. 6-12). 1993. 3.95 (*1-56688-065-3*) Bur For At-Risk.

— It Happened in Autumn. 24p. (YA). (gr. 6-12). 1993. 3.95 (*1-56688-069-6*) Bur For At-Risk.

— It Happened to Me. 24p. (J). (gr. k-5). 1992. 3.95 (*1-56688-058-0*) Bur For At-Risk.

— It's My Life. 24p. (YA). (gr. 6-12). 1993. 3.95 (*1-56688-066-1*) Bur For At-Risk.

— Something Bad Happened: A Story for Children Who Have Felt the Impact of Crime or Trauma. (Illus.). 16p. (J). (gr. k-5). 1992. pap. 3.95 (*1-56688-056-4*) Bur For At-Risk.

— The Way I Feel. 16p. (YA). (gr. 6-12). 1993. 3.95 (*1-56688-064-5*) Bur For At-Risk.

— When I Remember. 24p. (YA). (gr. 6-12). 1993. 3.95 (*1-56688-068-8*) Bur For At-Risk.

— The World I See. 24p. (J). (gr. k-5). 1992. 3.95 (*1-56688-054-8*) Bur For At-Risk.

***Alexander, Debra Whiting.** Children Changed by Trauma: A Healing Guide. 204p. 1999. pap. 13.95 (*1-57224-166-7*) New Harbinger.

Alexander, Dennis. Alfred's Basic Adult Duet Book: Level 1. (Alfred's Basic Adult Piano Course Ser.). 32p. 1986. pap. 5.95 (*0-7390-0780-7*, 2227) Alfred Pub.

— The Best of Dennis Alexander: A Special Collection of Six Early Intermediate Piano Solos, Bk. 2. 16p. 1995. pap. 5.50 (*0-7390-0362-3*, 14694) Alfred Pub.

— Bourree in D Minor. 4p. 1987. pap. 1.50 (*0-7390-0896-X*) Alfred Pub.

— Christmas Fantasy. 24p. 1992. pap. 5.95 (*0-7390-0575-8*, 6559) Alfred Pub.

— Christmas Silhouettes: 9 Intermediate to Late Intermediate Carol Arrangements for the Piano. 24p. 1990. pap. 5.95 (*0-7390-0383-6*, 6006) Alfred Pub.

— Dizzy Delight. 1999. pap. 2.50 (*0-7390-0304-6*, 18538) Alfred Pub.

— Dreamin' 4p. 1990. pap. 1.95 (*0-7390-0537-5*, 3636) Alfred Pub.

— Entrada in G Major. 4p. 1999. pap. 2.50 (*0-7390-0387-9*, 18528) Alfred Pub.

— Especially for Boys! 16p. 1998. pap. 5.50 (*0-7390-0397-6*, 18868) Alfred Pub.

— Especially for Girls. 16p. 1998. pap. 5.50 (*0-7390-0433-6*, 18867) Alfred Pub.

— Folk Song Portraits: Duets for Piano. 32p. 1989. pap. 6.95 (*0-7390-0527-8*, 364) Alfred Pub.

— God Rest Ye Merry, Gentlemen, Piano Duet. 8p. 1999. pap. 2.95 (*0-7390-0374-7*, 18979) Alfred Pub.

— Imperial Sonatina. (Alfred's Signature Ser.). 8p. 1997. pap. 2.95 (*0-7390-0792-0*, 17070) Alfred Pub.

— Just for You, Bk. 1. 32p. 1989. pap. 6.95 (*0-7390-0738-6*, 405) Alfred Pub.

— Just for You, Bk. 2. 32p. 1989. pap. 6.50 (*0-7390-0610-X*, 406) Alfred Pub.

Alexander, Dennis. The Magic of Music, Bk. 1. 24p. 1998. pap. 5.95 (*0-7390-0331-3*, 18110) Alfred Pub.

— The Magic of Music, Bk. 2. 24p. 1998. pap. 5.95 (*0-7390-0330-5*, 18111) Alfred Pub.

***Alexander, Dennis.** The Magic of Music: Book 3, Bk. 3. 24p. 1999. pap. 5.95 (*0-7390-0681-9*, 18112) Alfred Pub.

— Merry Christmas, Level 2. (Alfred's Basic Adult Piano Library). 32p. 1998. 6.95 (*0-7390-0573-1*, 18128) Alfred Pub.

— Peaceful Hearts: For the Right Hand Alone. 1999. mass mkt. 2.50 (*0-7390-0318-6*, 18995) Alfred Pub.

— Pranksters. 4p. 1990. pap. 1.95 (*0-7390-0875-7*, 3673) Alfred Pub.

— Showstoppers! 24p. 1994. pap. 5.50 (*0-7390-0860-9*, 11729) Alfred Pub.

— Silly Nilly Waltz. 4p. Date not set. pap. 2.50 (*0-7390-0721-1*, 19703) Alfred Pub.

— Splash of Color, Vol. 2. 16p. 1990. pap. 5.50 (*0-7390-0587-1*, 269) Alfred Pub.

— Twas the Night Before Christmas. 24p. 1993. 4.95 (*0-7390-0558-8*, 6683) Alfred Pub.

— With These Hands. 1999. 6.95 (*0-7390-0432-8*, 18555) Alfred Pub.

Alexander, Dennis, ed. Rossini/William Tell Overture. 4p. 1997. pap. 2.50 (*0-7390-0878-1*, 14342) Alfred Pub.

***Alexander, Dey, ed.** Philosophy in Cyberspace: A Guide to Philosophy-Related Resources on the Internet. 2nd ed. 404p. (Orig.). (C). 1998. pap. 25.00 (*1-889680-00-1*) Philos Document.

Alexander, Diane. Fitness in a Chair: For the Lazy, the Busy & the Movement-Impaired, Includes Aerobics. 2nd large type rev. ed. (Illus.). 60p. 1998. pap. 15.95 (*0-916329-01-1*) Dorleac-MacLeish.

— Playhouse. LC 84-70527. (Illus.). 237p. 1984. 19.95 (*0-916329-00-3*) Dorleac-MacLeish.

Alexander, Diane, ed. see Capon, Jack.

Alexander, Don. Bicyclist's Emergency Repair. (Illus.). 96p. (Orig.). 1986. pap. 5.95 (*0-939353-00-8*) Alexander & Alexander.

— Think to Win. (Illus.). 256p. 1994. pap. 19.95 (*0-8376-0070-7*) Bentley Pubs.

Alexander, Don & Ochowicz, Jim. Tour de France '86: The American Invasion. (Illus.). 192p. (Orig.). 1986. pap. 19.95 (*0-939353-01-6*) Alexander & Alexander.

Alexander, Don, jt. auth. see McSweeney, Phil.

Alexander, Don H. "Isn't That What We're Supposed to Believe?" Exploring Our Faith. 146p. 1998. pap. 14.95 (*1-885473-99-0*) Wood N Barnes.

Alexander, Don W. Rod of Iron: French Counterinsurgency Policy in Aragon During the Peninsular War. LC 84-5561. 260p. (C). 1985. 45.00 (*0-8420-2218-X*) Scholarly Res Inc.

Alexander, Donald G. Maine Jury Instruction Manual. 3rd ed. 95.00 (*0-327-12449-0*) LEXIS Pub.

Alexander, Donald G. Maine Jury Instruction Manual, 1990-1992. 2nd ed. 280p. 1993. ring bd., suppl. ed. 37.00 (*1-56257-250-4*, MICHIE) LEXIS Pub.

— Maine Jury Instruction Manual, 1990-1992. 2nd ed. 280p. 1994. spiral bd. 115.00 (*0-89442-108-5*, MICHIE) LEXIS Pub.

***Alexander, Donald L.** The Pursuit of Godliness: Sanctification in Christological Perspective. LC 99-34636. 240p. 1999. 52.00 (*0-7618-1451-5*); pap. 31.50 (*0-7618-1452-3*) U Pr of Amer.

Alexander, Donald L., ed. Telecommunications Policy: Have Regulators Dialed the Wrong Number? LC 97-9181. 184p. 1997. 57.95 (*0-275-95855-8*, Praeger Pubs) Greenwood.

Alexander, Donald L., jt. auth. see Sichel, Werner.

Alexander, Donald L., ed. see Ferguson, Sinclair B., et al.

Alexander, Doris. Creating Characters with Charles Dickens. 240p. 1991. 32.50 (*0-271-00725-7*) Pa St U Pr.

— Creating Literature Out of Life: The Making of Four Masterpieces. LC 95-43556. 1996. 45.00 (*0-271-01549-7*) Pa St U Pr.

— Eugene O'Neill's Creative Struggle: The Decisive Decade, 1924-1933. 384p. 1992. 40.00 (*0-271-00813-X*) Pa St U Pr.

Alexander, Dorothy & Strauss, Walter L., eds. The German Single-Leaf Woodcut, 1600-1700, 2 vols., Set. LC 76-22305. 828p. 1977. lib. bdg. 195.00 (*0-913870-05-6*) Abaris Bks.

Alexander, Dorsey, jt. auth. see Alexander, Joyce.

Alexander, Douglas W., ed. see State Bar of Texas Guide Committee.

Alexander, Drury B. The Sources of Classicism: Five Centuries of Architectural Books from the Collections of the Humanities Research Center. (Illus.). 1978. pap. 8.00 (*0-87959-084-X*) U of Tex H Ransom Ctr.

Alexander, E., III, et al, eds. Radiosurgery: Enhancement of Clinical Excellence. (Illus.). 112p. 1992. pap. 69.75 (*3-8055-5546-6*) S Karger.

Alexander, E. Curtis. Adam Clayton Powell, Jr. A Black Power Political Educator. LC 81-69171. (African American Educator Ser.: Vol. II). (Illus.). 174p. (Orig.). 1983. pap. 9.95 (*0-938818-03-1*) ECA Assoc.

— Adam Clayton Powell Jr. & the Harlem Renaissance. 1987. 3.95 (*0-938818-14-7*) ECA Assoc.

— Adam Clayton Powell, Jr. Speaks Out. 84p. 1990. pap. 8.95 (*0-938818-23-6*) ECA Assoc.

— African Foundations of Judaism & Christianity. LC 84-48679. (Alkelbulan Historical Research Society Monograph: No. 3). 84p. (Orig.). 1985. pap. 6.95 (*0-938818-08-2*) ECA Assoc.

— African Historical Religions: A Conceptual & Ethical Foundation for Western Religions. LC 83-83096. (Alkelbulan Historical Research Society Monograph: No. 2). (Illus.). 70p. 1984. pap. 6.95 (*0-938818-05-8*) ECA Assoc.

— Axioms & Quotations of Yosef ben-Jochannan. LC 80-70287. 118p. (Orig.). 1980. 10.95 (*0-938818-01-5*) ECA Assoc.

— Cheikh Anta Diop: An African Scientist. LC 84-81324. (Pan African Internationalist Handbook Ser.). 84p. (Orig.). 1984. pap. 6.95 (*0-938818-07-4*) ECA Assoc.

— Doc Ben Speaks Out. LC 89-81784. (Monograph Ser.: No. 1). 52p. 1982. pap. 5.95 (*0-938818-04-X*, Alkebulan Hist Res Soc) ECA Assoc.

— Elijah Muhammad on African American Education: A Guide for African & Black Studies Programs. LC 80-70878. (African American Educator Ser.: Vol. 1). (Illus.). 119p. (Orig.). 1981. pap. 9.95 (*0-938818-02-3*) ECA Assoc.

— Essays on the Black Family: Education, Religion & Mental Health. 1995. 12.95 (*0-938818-22-8*) ECA Assoc.

— A Methodology for Teaching the Culturally Particular African American Child: A Guide for Parents & Teachers. 1989. 3.95 (*0-938818-21-X*) ECA Assoc.

— Module Curriculum Guide: Reference Works of Yosef Ben-Jochannan. LC 89-81786. 35p. (Orig.). 1979. 3.95 (*0-938818-00-7*) ECA Assoc.

— Richard Allen: The First Exemplar of African American Education. LC 83-85051. (African American Educator Ser.: Vol. III). (Illus.). 174p. (Orig.). 1985. pap. 9.95 (*0-938818-06-6*) ECA Assoc.

Alexander, E. Curtis, ed. Cheikh Anta Diop: On Science, History & Technology. 85p. 1987. pap. 7.95 (*0-938818-10-4*) ECA Assoc.

— How to Publish & Market Your Own Book As an Independent Black Publisher. LC 84-48680. 100p. 1988. pap. 14.95 (*0-938818-09-0*) ECA Assoc.

— Who's Who in African Heritage Book Publishing. LC 87-82649. 160p. 1988. 21.95 (*0-938818-13-9*); pap. 11.95 (*0-938818-12-0*) ECA Assoc.

Alexander, E. Curtis, jt. auth. see Mwadilifu, Mwalimu I.

Alexander, E. R. Approaches to Planning: Introducing Current Planning Theories, Concepts & Issues. 136p. 1986. 35.00 (*2-88124-140-9*) Gordon & Breach.

Alexander, E. V., ed. see Turner, H. A.

Alexander, Earl, et al. My Dad Has HIV. (Illus.). 32p. (J). (gr. k-4). 1996. 14.95 (*0-925190-99-3*) Fairview Press.

Alexander, Eben, 3rd, et al, eds. Stereotactic Radiosurgery. (Illus.). 254p. 1993. text 110.00 (*0-07-001020-X*) McGraw-Hill HPD.

Alexander, Eben & Maciunas, Robert J. Advanced Neurosurgical Navigation. LC 98-21792. (Illus.). 624p. 1998. 199.00 (*0-86577-767-5*) Thieme Med Pubs.

Alexander, Edward. The Holocaust & the War of Ideas. LC 93-11119. 250p. (C). 1993. text 39.95 (*1-56000-122-4*) Transaction Pubs.

— Irving Howe Socialist, Critic, Jew: Jewish Literature & Culture. LC 97-27112. (Jewish Literature & Culture Ser.). 284p. 1998. 35.00 (*0-253-33364-4*) Ind U Pr.

— Isaac Bashevis Singer. (World Authors Ser.: No. 582). 168p. 1980. 28.95 (*0-8057-6424-0*) Macmillan.

— Isaac Bashevis Singer: A Study of the Short Fiction. (Twayne's Studies in Short Fiction: No. 18). 1990. 25.95 (*0-8057-8329-6*) Macmillan.

— The Jewish Idea & Its Enemies. 272p. (C). 1990. pap. 24.95 (*0-88738-873-6*) Transaction Pubs.

— The Jewish Wars: Reflections by One of the Belligerents. LC 95-21533. 221p. 1996. text 29.95 (*0-8093-2011-8*) S Ill U Pr.

— The Resonance of Dust: Essays on Holocaust Literature & Jewish Fate. LC 79-15515. 276p. 1979. reprint ed. pap. 85.60 (*0-608-00912-1*, 206170600011) Bks Demand.

— The Serpent & the Bees: A KGB Chronicle. 298p. 1990. 21.95 (*0-8191-7820-9*) U Pr of Amer.

Alexander, Edward, jt. ed. see Loewenberg, Robert J.

Alexander, Edward, ed. see Mill, John Stuart.

Alexander, Edward P. Military Memoirs of a Confederate: A Critical Narrative. (Illus.). 658p. 1993. reprint ed. pap. 17.95 (*0-306-80509-X*) Da Capo.

— The Museum in America: Innovators & Pioneers. LC 97-21127. (American Association for State & Local History Book Ser.). 224p. 1997. 62.00 (*0-7619-8946-3*); pap. 22.95 (*0-7619-8947-1*) AltaMira Pr.

— Museum Masters: Their Museums & Their Influence. LC 95-43139. (American Association for State & Local History Book Ser.). (Illus.). 440p. 1996. reprint ed. pap. 23.95 (*0-7619-9131-X*) AltaMira Pr.

— Museums in Motion: An Introduction to the History & Functions of Museums. LC 95-48343. (American Association for State & Local History Book Ser.). (Illus.). 320p. 1979. pap. 24.95 (*0-7619-9155-7*) AltaMira Pr.

— A Revolutionary Conservative: James Duane of New York. LC 78-38479. reprint ed. 20.00 (*0-404-00321-4*) AMS Pr.

Alexander, Edward P., ed. see Fontaine, John.

***Alexander, Edythe Louise.** Alexander's Care of the Patient in Surgery. 11th ed. LC 98-37345. 1248p. 1999. 68.00 (*0-323-00134-3*) Mosby Inc.

***Alexander, Elayne.** Venice, California. (Images of America Ser.). (Illus.). 128p. 1999. pap. 18.99 (*0-7385-0251-0*) Arcadia Publng.

Alexander, Elizabeth. Body of Life. 64p. (Orig.). 1996. pap. 10.95 (*1-882688-12-0*) Tia Chucha Pr.

— The Venus Hottentot. Rowell, Charles H., ed. (Callaloo Poetry Ser.). 52p. 1990. pap. 9.95 (*0-8139-1273-3*) U Pr of Va.

Alexander, Ellen. Chaska & the Golden Doll. LC 93-34691. (Illus.). 32p. (J). (ps-3). 1994. 14.45 (*1-55970-241-9*, Pub. by Arcade Pub Inc) Time Warner.

Alexander, Eric, ed. see Cunningham, Ian C. & Simpson-Wells, Hugh.

Alexander, Ernest. How Organizations Act Together: Interorganizational Coordination in Theory & Practice. 384p. 1995. text 75.00 (*2-88449-173-2*) Gordon & Breach.

— How Organizations Act Together: Interorganizational Coordination in Theory & Practice. 458p. 1995. pap. text 28.00 (*2-88449-174-0*) Gordon & Breach.

Alexander, Ernest R. Approaches to Planning: Introducing Current Planning Theories, Concepts & Issues. 2nd ed. ix, 173p. 1992. text 82.00 (*2-88124-511-0*); pap. text 36.00 (*2-88124-514-5*) Gordon & Breach.

ALexander, Ernest R. Effectiveness in Interorganizational Coordination: A Comparative Case Analysis. (Publications in Architecture & Urban Planning: No. R81-4). (Illus.). ii, 61p. 1981. 11.00 (*0-938744-15-1*) U of Wis Ctr Arch-Urban.

Alexander, Ernest R. & Judd, Lynne B. Coordinating the Organization of Library Services in Metropolitan Milwaukee. (Publications in Architecture & Urban Planning: No. R83-1). (Illus.). 97p. 1983. 12.00 (*0-938744-24-0*) U of Wis Ctr Arch-Urban.

Alexander, Ernest R., et al. Multiple-Objective Decision Making Methods for Transportation. (Publications in Architecture & Urban Planning: No. R85-3). (Illus.). iv, 85p. 1985. 11.00 (*0-938744-42-9*) U of Wis Ctr Arch-Urban.

Alexander, Eveline M. Cavalry Wife: The Diary of Eveline M. Alexander, 1866-1867. Myres, Sandra L., ed. LC 76-30611. (Illus.). 186p. (Orig.). 1988. pap. 14.95 (*0-89096-336-3*) Tex A&M Univ Pr.

Alexander, F. E. & Boyle, P., eds. Methods for Investigating Localized Clustering of Disease. LC 97-183624. (IARC Scientific Publications: No. 135). (Illus.). 264p. 1997. pap. text 89.50 (*92-832-2135-4*) OUP.

Alexander, F. M., jt. ed. see McGowan, Danny.

Alexander, F. Matthias. The Books of F. Matthias Alexander Vol. 1: Man's Supreme Inheritance; Constructive Conscious Control of the Individual; The Use of the Self; The Universal Constant in Living. (Illus.). 703p. 1997. reprint ed. 45.00 (*0-9658446-0-9*, 1) IRDEAT.

Alexander, Faith. Hills of My Heart. large type ed. (Linford Romance Library). 1991. pap. 16.99 (*0-7089-7059-1*) Ulverscroft.

Alexander, Felicia M. & Gannon, Jack R. Deaf Heritage Student Text & Workbook. (Illus.). 115p. (Orig.). 1984. pap. 11.95 (*0-913072-66-4*) Natl Assn Deaf.

Alexander, Flora. Contemporary Women Novelists. 128p. 1989. pap. 9.95 (*0-7131-6557-X*, A3854, Pub. by E A) Routldge.

Alexander, Floyce. Bottom Falling Out of the Dream. LC 76-55940. 86p. 1976. pap. 7.00 (*0-89924-010-0*) Lynx Hse.

— Memory of the Future. 41p. 1997. 6.00 (*1-890193-04-6*) Red Dragonfly.

— Red Deer. LC 79-26383. 75p. 1982. pap. 4.95 (*0-934332-21-5*) LEpervier Pr.

Alexander, Floyce, ed. see Randall, Margaret.

***Alexander, F.M.** Die Universelle Konstante Im Leben. iv, 250p. 1999. 72.25 (*3-8055-6826-6*) S Karger.

Alexander, Forsyth, jt. auth. see Bivins, John, Jr.

Alexander, Foscarina. The Aspiration Toward a Lost Natural Harmony in the Work of Three Italian Writers: Leopardi, Verga, & Moravia. LC 90-46357. (Studies in Italian Literature: Vol. 1). 136p. 1990. lib. bdg. 69.95 (*0-7734-9706-4*) E Mellen.

Alexander, Frances. Friends in Jesus. 1999. pap. text 9.99 (*1-84030-036-1*) Ambassador Prodns Ltd.

— Mother Goose on the Rio Grande. (Illus.). 96p. (J). (gr. 4 up). 1994. pap. 6.95 (*0-8442-7641-3*, Natl Textbk Co) NTC Contemp Pub Co.

— Mother Goose on the Rio Grande. LC 97-33333. (ENG & SPA., Illus.). 96p. 1997. pap. 7.95 (*0-8442-7642-1*, 76421) NTC Contemp Pub Co.

***Alexander, Frank.** Diamond Ball Games: Selected Dodge Ball Games, Variations, & New Games Played As Is or with Optional Diamond Rules! LC 99-179714. 40p. 1998. pap., teacher ed. 8.00 (*0-915256-47-9*, 105) Front Row.

Alexander, Frank. How to Make Your Own Trail Wines. 2nd ed. (Illus.). 32p. 1987. reprint ed. pap. 4.00 (*0-915256-23-1*) Front Row.

— Welcome to the New Tax-Free Economy: Taxes As We Know Them Are No Longer Necessary. 17p. (Orig.). 1992. pap. 4.00 (*0-915256-33-9*, Kokono) Front Row.

Alexander, Frank & Cuda, Heide Siegmund. Got Your Back: The Life of a Bodyguard in the Hardcore World of Gangsta Rap. LC 97-46984. (Illus.). 214p. 1998. 22.95 (*0-312-18111-6*) St Martin.

Alexander, Frank, ed. see Aycox, Frank.

Alexander, Frank, ed. see Capon, Jack.

Alexander, Frank, ed. see French, Ron & Horvat, Michael.

Alexander, Frank, ed. see Liebler, Scott.

Alexander, Frank, ed. see Smith, Garry L.

Alexander, Frank, ed. see Wood, Barbara L.

Alexander, Frank, ed. see Zion, Leela C.

Alexander, Frank J. In the Hours of Meditation. 101p. 1952. pap. 2.95 (*0-87481-162-7*) Vedanta Pr.

Alexander, Franz. Medical Value of Psychoanalysis. Chicago Institute for Psychoanalysis Staff, ed. LC 84-22475. (Classics in Psychoanalysis Monographs: No. 2). vi, 278p. 1985. 42.50 (*0-8236-3285-7*, BN03285) Intl Univs Pr.

— Psychosomatische Medizin: Grundlagen und Anwendungsgebiete. 4th rev. ed. (GER., Illus.). xvi, 244p. 1985. pap. text 44.65 (*3-11-010192-0*) De Gruyter.

Alexander, Franz, et al, eds. Psychoanalytic Pioneers. LC 94-41115. 1995. pap. 29.95 (*1-56000-815-6*) Transaction Pubs.

Alexander, Franz & Ross, Helen, eds. Impact of Freudian Psychiatry. x, 304p. 1961. pap. text 3.95 (*0-226-01355-3*, P62) U Ch Pr.

— The Impact of Freudian Psychiatry. LC 62-5413. (Phoenix Bks.: Pt. 62). 304p. reprint ed. pap. 94.30 (*0-608-09255-X*, 205405700002) Bks Demand.

— Twenty Years of Psychoanalysis. LC 77-93312. (Essay Index Reprint Ser.). 1977. 28.95 (*0-8369-1541-0*) Ayer.

Alexander, Franz G. & Selesnick, Sheldon T. The History of Psychiatry: An Evaluation of Psychiatric Thought & Practice from Prehistoric Times to the Present. LC 95-20598. 494p. 1995. pap. 60.00 (*1-56821-754-4*) Aronson.

Alexander, Fred. On Campus & Off: Reminiscences & Reflections of the First Professor of Modern History at the University of Western Australia 1916-1986. 29.95 (*0-85564-264-5*, Pub. by Univ of West Aust Pr) Intl Spec Bk.

Alexander, Frederick. Moving Frontiers, an American Theme & Its Application to Australian History. (History - United States Ser.). 48p. 1993. reprint ed. lib. bdg. 59.00 (*0-7812-4855-8*) Rprt Serv.

Alexander, Frederick H., jt. auth. see Sparks, A. Gilchrist, III.

Alexander, G. Medizin. 1983. 95.00 (*0-8288-1856-8*, M15409) Fr & Eur.

Alexander, G. Rumay. Domestic Violence: A Nursing Concern - 1 Hour. 2nd rev. ed. Rodriguez, M. Rosanna, ed. Johnson, Kathy, tr. (Illus.). 22p. 1998. pap. 12.95 (*1-57801-022-5*) Western Schls.

Alexander, G. Rumay & Rodriguez, M. Rosanna. Domestic Violence: A Nursing Concern - 3 Hour. Johnson, Kathy, tr. (Illus.). 46p. 1998. pap. 19.95 (*1-57801-021-7*) Western Schls.

Alexander, Gary. New Art International, No. 1. Sedley, Jeremy, ed. (Illus.). 124p. 1996. 39.95 (*0-9653228-0-7*); pap. 19.95 (*0-9653228-1-5*) Book Art Pr.

***Alexander, Gemma, ed.** The Mammoth Book of Heroic & Outrageous Women. (Mammoth Book Ser.). 512p. 1999. pap. text 10.95 (*0-7867-0695-3*) Carroll & Graf.

Alexander, Geoffrey. SQL 7 Database Design & Administration Exam Cram: Practice Tests. LC 99-43075. (Exam Cram Ser.). 1999. pap. text 29.99 (*1-57610-496-6*) Coriolis Grp.

Alexander, George & Penland, Ken. Bubishi: Martial Art Spirit. (Illus.). 201p. (Orig.). 1993. pap. 34.95 (*0-9631775-1-6*) Yamazato Pubns.

Alexander, George J. Honesty & Competition: False-Advertising Law & Policy under FTC Administration. LC 67-26213. 333p. reprint ed. pap. 103.30 (*0-608-15210-2*, 202740400055) Bks Demand.

— Writing a Living Will: Using a Durable Power-of-Attorney. LC 87-15816. 160p. 1987. pap. 12.95 (*0-275-92939-6*, B2939, Praeger Pubs) Greenwood.

— Writing a Living Will: Using a Durable Power-of-Attorney. LC 87-15816. 144p. 1987. 37.95 (*0-275-92801-2*, C2801, Praeger Pubs) Greenwood.

Alexander, George J., ed. International Perspectives on Aging. 308p. (C). 1992. lib. bdg. 124.50 (*0-7923-1691-6*) Kluwer Academic.

Alexander, George J. & Scheflin, Alan W. Law & Mental Disorder. LC 98-30548. 1224p. 1998. boxed set 85.00 (*0-89089-917-7*) Carolina Acad Pr.

Alexander, George P. Higher Education in India: Critical Issues & Trends. 200p. 1998. pap. text. write for info. (*0-9653688-8-2*) P & P Ent.

— New Americans: The Progress of Asian Indians in America. 128p. (Orig.). (C). 1997. pap. text 23.95 (*0-9653688-3-1*) P & P Ent.

Alexander, George W. Okinawa Island of Karate. 127p. 1992. pap. 29.95 (*0-9631775-0-8*) Yamazato Pubns.
— Worrior Jujitsu Training Manual. (Illus.). 187p. 1995. pap. 34.95 (*0-9631775-6-7*) Yamazato Pubns.

Alexander, Gerard L., jt. auth. see Kane, Joseph N.

Alexander, Gerda. Eutony: The Holistic Discovery of the Whole Person. LC 85-73009. (Illus.). 182p. (Orig.). 1986. pap. 10.95 (*0-9615659-0-X*) F Morrow.

Alexander, Gerda I. Fortis & Lenis in Germanic: Germanic Languages & Literature. (American University Studies: Germanic Languages & Literature: Ser. I, Vol. 18). 198p. (Orig.). (C). 1983. pap. text 20.80 (*0-8204-0028-9*) P Lang Pubng.

Alexander, Gilbert H. The Heart & Its Action: Roentgenkymographic Studies. LC 78-96979. (Illus.). 272p. 1971. 32.50 (*0-87527-001-8*) Green.

Alexander, Gordon J. Fundamentals of Investments. 3rd ed. LC 99-48069. 816p. (C). 2000. 90.67 (*0-13-292617-2*, Pub. by P-H) S&S Trade.

Alexander, Gordon J., et al. Fundamentals of Investments. 2nd ed. LC 92-20869. 896p. (C). 1993. 92.67 (*0-13-335449-0*) P-H.

Alexander, Gregory. Step-by-Step Watercolor Painting: A Complete Guide to Mastering Techniques with the Alexander Brothers. (Illus.). 160p. 1997. pap. text 16.95 (*0-8069-1333-9*) Sterling.

Alexander, Gregory, jt auth. see Darwish, Adel.

Alexander, Gregory S. Commodity & Property. LC 97-16784. 408p. 1997. 39.95 (*0-226-01353-7*) U Ch Pr.
— Commodity & Propriety: Competing Visions of Property in American Legal Thought, 1776-1970. 1999. pap. text 25.00 (*0-226-01354-5*) U Ch Pr.

Alexander, Gregory S. & Skapska, Grazyna, eds. A Fourth Way? Privatization, Property & the Emergence of New Market Economics. LC 93-1411. 320p. (C). 1993. pap. 23.99 (*0-415-90698-9*, A9559) Routledge.

Alexander, Guy. Silica & Me: The Career of an Industrial Chemist. LC 73-75723. (Chemistry in Action Ser.). 111p. 1973. pap. 8.95 (*0-8412-0162-5*) Am Chemical.

Alexander, Guy B. Chromatography: An Adventure in Graduate School. LC 77-8637. (Chemistry in Action Ser.). (Illus.). 175p. reprint ed. pap. 54.30 (*0-608-04346-X*, 206512600001) Bks Demand.

Alexander, H., jt. auth. see Brachet, Jean.

Alexander Hamilton Institute, Inc. Staff, Inc. The Legal Bermuda Triangle: Avoiding Employee Lawsuits When ADA, FMLA & WC Collide. LC 97-228939. (Executive Strategy Briefings Ser.). v, 102p. 1997. write for info. (*0-86604-350-0*) Hamilton Inst.

***Alexander, Hannah.** Sacred Trust. LC 99-6612. 352p. 1999. pap. 10.99 (*0-7642-2242-2*) Bethany Hse.
— Solemn Oath. LC 99-50972. 352p. 2000. pap. 10.99 (*0-7642-2348-8*) Bethany Hse.

Alexander, Hansen. Rare Integrity: The Biography of L. W. Payne, Jr., A Noble Texan. 50p. 1986. 35.00 (*0-932119-02-6*) Wind River Pr.

Alexander-Hanso. Taking Sides: Mass Media. 4th ed. 1996. 13.53 (*0-697-35741-4*, WCB McGr Hill) McGrw-H Hghr Educ.
— Taking Sides: Mass Media. 5th ed. 1998. pap. 18.44 (*0-697-39143-4*) McGraw.

Alexander-Harding, Pagan, ed. see Andrews, Ted.

Alexander-Harding, Pagyn, ed. see Andrews, Ted.

Alexander, Harriet S. American & British Poetry: A Guide to the Criticism, 1925-1978. Hendrick, George & Gerstenberger, Donna, eds. LC 83-24114. xii, 486p. 1984. text 70.00 (*0-8040-0848-5*) Swallow.
— American & British Poetry: A Guide to the Criticism, 1979-1990. LC 83-24114. 478p. (C). 1995. text 70.00 (*0-8040-0988-0*) Swallow.

Alexander, Harriet S., compiled by. English Language Criticism on the Foreign Novel, 1965-1975. LC 89-4430. 450p. (C). 1989. text 70.00 (*0-8040-0907-4*) Swallow.

Alexander, Hartley. Manito Masks: Dramatizations, with Music, of American Indian Spirit Legends. LC 77-94335. (One-Act Plays in Reprint Ser.). (Illus.). 1978. reprint ed. 25.00 (*0-8486-2031-3*) Roth Pub Inc.

***Alexander, Hartley B.** Latin-American Mythology. (LC History-America-E). 379p. 1999. reprint ed. lib. bdg. 89.00 (*0-7812-4292-4*) Rprt Serv.

Alexander, Hartley B. Nature & Human Nature: Essays Metaphysical & Historical. LC 75-3018. (Philosophy in America Ser.). reprint ed. 72.00 (*0-404-59011-X*) AMS Pr.
— The Problem of Metaphysics & the Meaning of Metaphysical Explanation. LC 72-38480. reprint ed. 29.50 (*0-404-00322-2*) AMS Pr.

***Alexander, Hartley B.** The World's Rim: Great Mysteries of the North American Indians. LC 99-22823. 1999. pap. text 8.95 (*0-486-40670-9*) Dover.

Alexander, Heather. Formally-Based Tools & Techniques for Human-Computer Dialogues. (Computers & Their Applications Ser.). 161p. 1987. text 47.95 (*0-470-20996-8*) P-H.
— Look Inside Your Brain. (Poke & Look Learning Ser.). (Illus.). 16p. (J). (ps-3). 1998. mass mkt. 9.99 (*0-448-41893-2*, G & D) Peng Put Young Read.

Alexander, Heather, jt. auth. see Baiul, Oksana.

Alexander, Helene. Fans. 1989. pap. 25.00 (*0-7478-0045-6*, Pub. by Shire Pubns) St Mut.

Alexander, Herbert & Wermer, John. Several Complex Variables & Banach Algebras. 3rd ed. LC 97-16661. (Graduate Texts in Mathematics Ser.). 304p. 1997. 49.00 (*0-387-98253-1*) Spr-Verlag.

Alexander, Herbert E. Financing Politics: Money, Elections, & Political Reform. 4th ed. 212p. 1992. pap. 24.95 (*0-87187-691-4*) Congr Quarterly.

Alexander, Herbert E., ed. Political Finance. LC 78-24439. (Sage Electoral Studies Yearbook: Vol. 5). (Illus.). 272p. reprint ed. pap. 84.40 (*0-608-10080-3*, 202186700026) Bks Demand.

Alexander, Herbert E. & Corrado, Anthony. Financing the 1992 Election. LC 95-3540. (American Political Institutions & Public Policy Ser.). (Illus.). 329p. (gr. 13). 1995. text 75.95 (*1-56324-437-3*); pap. text 32.95 (*1-56324-438-1*) M E Sharpe.

Alexander, Herbert E. & Lambert, Richard D., eds. Political Finance: Reform & Reality. LC 75-45503. (Annals Ser.: No. 425). 250p. 1976. pap. 18.00 (*0-87761-201-3*) Am Acad Pol Soc Sci.

Alexander, Holmes. Never Lose a War: Memoirs & Observations of a National Columnist. LC 83-18964. 158p. 1984. 14.95 (*0-8159-6223-1*) Devin.

Alexander, Holmes Moss. Aaron Burr the Proud Pretender. write for info. (*0-8371-7128-8*) Greenwood.

Alexander, Horace. Everyman's Struggle for Peace. LC 53-13146. (C). 1935. pap. 4.00 (*0-87574-074-X*) Pendle Hill.
— Gandhi Remembered. LC 71-84674. (Orig.). 1969. pap. 4.00 (*0-87574-165-7*) Pendle Hill.
— Quakerism in India. (C). 1945. pap. 4.00 (*0-87574-031-6*) Pendle Hill.

Alexander, Hubert G. The Language & Logic of Philosophy. 372p. (C). 1988. reprint ed. pap. text 31.00 (*0-8191-6966-8*) U Pr of Amer.

Alexander, Ian C. Office Location & Public Policy. LC 78-40206. (Topics in Applied Geography Ser.). 125p. reprint ed. pap. 38.80 (*0-608-12177-0*, 202527300043) Bks Demand.

Alexander, Ian J. The Foot: Examination & Diagnosis. 2nd ed. LC 96-40478. 1997. pap. text 32.00 (*0-443-07656-1*) Church.

Alexander, Irma. Wedding Music & Other Dissonance. 190p. 1997. pap. write for info. (*1-86106-565-5*, Pub. by Minerva Pr) Unity Dist.

Alexander, Irving E. Personology: Method & Content in Personality Assessment & Psychobiography. LC 89-36230. 294p. (Orig.). (C). 1990. text 54.95 (*0-8223-0996-3*); pap. text 19.95 (*0-8223-1020-1*) Duke.

Alexander, J. Model Engine Construction. 1986. reprint ed. pap. 15.95 (*0-917914-44-9*) Lindsay Pubns.

Alexander, J. A. Acts of the Apostles. (Banner of Truth Geneva Series Commentaries). 498p. 1991. reprint ed. 34.99 (*0-85151-309-3*) Banner of Truth.
— Alexander: Record of the Descendants of John Alexander of Lanarkshire, kScotland, & His Wife Margaret Glasson, Who Emigrated from Co. Armagh, Ireland, to Chester Co. PA. 220p. 1994. reprint ed. pap. 36.00 (*0-8328-4290-7*); reprint ed. lib. bdg. 46.00 (*0-8328-4289-3*) Higginson Bk Co.
— Real Estate Helpful Tips. 180p. 1992. write for info. (*0-9632254-0-5*) J A Alexander.

Alexander, J. A., jt. auth. see Bedell, Clyde B.

Alexander, J. B. Biographical Sketches of the Early Settlers of the Hopewell Section: And Reminiscences of the Pioneers & Their Descendants by Families, with Some Historical Facts Incidents. 104p. 1997. reprint ed. pap. 16.00 (*0-8328-6903-1*) Higginson Bk Co.
— History of Mecklenburg County: From 1740 to 1900. enl. rev. ed. (Illus.). 431p. 1997. reprint ed. lib. bdg. 46.00 (*0-8328-6905-8*) Higginson Bk Co.
— The History of Mecklenburg County, NC, 1740-1900. (Illus.). 458p. 1996. pap. 34.50 (*0-7884-0469-5*, A419) Heritage Bk.

Alexander, J. C., ed. Dynamical Systems. (Lecture Notes in Mathematics Ser.: Vol. 1342). vi, 726p. 1988. pap. 76.70 (*0-387-50174-6*) Spr-Verlag.

Alexander, J. C. & Harer, J. L., eds. Geometry & Topology. (Lecture Notes in Mathematics Ser.: Vol. 1167). vi, 292p. 1985. 42.95 (*0-387-16053-1*) Spr-Verlag.

Alexander, J. H., ed. see Scott, Sir Walter.

Alexander, J. Heywood. It Must Be Heard: The Musical Life of Cleveland, 1836-1918. (Illus.). 50p. 1981. pap. 8.95 (*0-911704-28-0*) Western Res.

Alexander, J. Heywood, ed. see Gombert, Nicolas, et al.

Alexander, J. J. G. The Master of Mary of Burgundy: A Book of Hours for Englebert of Nassau. LC 78-128576. 194p. 1993. 25.00 (*0-8076-1332-0*) Braziller.

Alexander, J. J. G., ed. The Master of Mary of Burgundy: A Book of Hours for Engelbert of Nassau. LC 78-128576. 194p. 1970. boxed set 45.00 (*0-8076-0578-6*) Braziller.

Alexander, J. L. Memorable Ceremonies & Poems: Including Material from "Along the Story Trail" 192p. 1993. pap. 6.50 (*0-88053-302-1*, S-109) Macoy Pub.

Alexander, J. M. & Gunasekera, J. S. Strength of Materials. (Mechanical Engineering Ser.). 450p. 1991. 99.95 (*0-13-853722-4*, 520701) P-H.

Alexander, J. M., et al. Engineering Processes: Engineering Materials, Vol. 2. LC 86-27426. (Mechanical Engineering Ser.). 365p. 1987. text 69.95 (*0-470-20960-7*) P-H.
— Manufacturing Technology: Engineering Materials, Vol. 1. (Mechanical Engineering Ser.). 238p. 1987. text 57.95 (*0-470-20815-5*) P-H.

Alexander, J. Neil. Waiting for the Coming: The Liturgical Meaning of Advent, Christmas & Epiphany. 95p. 1993. pap. 7.95 (*1-56929-011-3*, Pastoral Press) OR Catholic.

Alexander, J. Neil, ed. Time & Community: Studies in Liturgical History & Theology. (NPM Studies in Church Music & Liturgy). 468p. (Orig.). 1990. pap. 34.95 (*0-912405-66-X*, Pastoral Press) OR Catholic.

Alexander, J. Neil & Hatchett, Marion J. With Ever Joyful Hearts: Essays on Liturgy & Music : Honoring Marion J. Hatchett LC 99-17532. 1999. write for info. (*0-89869-321-7*) Church Pub Inc.

Alexander, J. O'Donel. Arthropods & Human Skin. (Illus.). 430p. 1984. 210.00 (*0-387-13235-X*) Spr-Verlag.

Alexander, J. R., ed. Visual Data Interpretation. 1992. 20.00 (*0-8194-0822-0*, 1668) SPIE.

Alexander, J. W. God Is Love: Communion Addresses. 368p. 1985. reprint ed. pap. 9.99 (*0-85151-459-6*) Banner of Truth.
— The Life of Archibald Alexander. 1992. 33.99 (*0-87377-931-2*) GAM Pubns.

***Alexander, J. W.** Remember Him. 2000. pap. 4.99 (*0-85151-790-0*) Banner of Truth.

Alexander, J. W. Thoughts on Preaching. 332p. 1975. 6.99 (*0-85151-210-0*) Banner of Truth.

Alexander, J. W., jt. auth. see Palmer, B. M.

Alexander, J. Wesley. Transplantation Tolerance Induction. (Medical Intelligence Unit Ser.). 275p. 1996. 99.00 (*1-57059-282-9*) Landes Bioscience.

Alexander, Jack. Rotonda: The Vision & the Reality, a Short History of a Florida Development. (Illus.). 224p. 1995. 14.95 (*1-881539-07-5*) Tabby Hse Bks.

Alexander, James. Abracadabra Violin, Bk. 2. 48p. (J). (gr. 2-3). 1998. pap. 7.95 (*0-7136-3727-7*, Pub. by A & C Blk) Midpt Trade.
— Client Care. 136p. 1993. pap. 25.00 (*1-85431-299-5*, Pub. by Blackstone Pr) Gaunt.

***Alexander, James.** Political Culture in Post-communist Russia: Formlessness & Recreation. LC 00-21164. 240p. 2000. text 65.00 (*0-312-23194-6*) St Martin.
— Readings in American Music. (C). pap. text. write for info. (*0-393-97411-1*) Norton.

Alexander, James A. & Lyons, Michael C. The Knowledge-Based Organization: Four Steps to Increasing Sales, Profits, & Market Share. 144p. 1994. text 25.00 (*0-7863-0353-0*, Irwn Prfssnl) McGraw-Hill Prof.

Alexander, James B. Early Babylonian Letters & Economic Texts. LC 78-63526. (Babylonian Inscriptions in the Collection of James B. Nies Ser.: 7). reprint ed. 45.00 (*0-404-60137-5*) AMS Pr.

Alexander, James E. Depression Kids: Shaping the Character of Our Lives. 260p. (Orig.). (YA). 1993. pap. 12.50 (*0-939965-07-0*) Macedon Prod.
— Historical Homes of Lincoln Terrace. (Illus.). 120p. 1993. pap. 9.95 (*0-939965-09-7*) Macedon Prod.
— Inchon to Wonsan: From the Deck of a Destroyer in the Korean War. LC 96-17785. (Illus.). 256p. 1996. 31.95 (*1-55750-022-3*) Naval Inst Pr.

***Alexander, James E., ed.** USS John A. Bole (DD-755) An Anecdotal History, 1945-1970. 272p. 2000. 25.00 (*0-939965-15-1*) Macedon Prod.

Alexander, James E., et al. Biology & Potential Impacts of Zebra Mussels in Large Rivers LC 97-208798. xx, 104p. 1997. write for info. (*0-89867-930-3*) Am Water Wks Assn.

Alexander, James E., jt. auth. see Berry, William A.

Alexander, James E., jt. auth. see Moore, Samuel T.

Alexander, James E., jt. auth. see Mulhausen, Harold L.

Alexander, James Edwin, jt. auth. see Berry, William A.

Alexander, James Edwin, jt. auth. see Burkett, William R.

Alexander, James I. Blue Coats, Black Skin: The Black Experience in the New York City Police Department Since 1891. LC 77-92716. 143p. reprint ed. pap. 44.40 (*0-8357-7330-2*, 205558200029) Bks Demand.

Alexander, James K., jt. auth. see Alpert, Martin A.

Alexander, James P. Internships in Communications. LC 95-7273. 216p. 1995. pap. text 19.95 (*0-8138-2231-9*); pap. text, teacher ed. write for info. (*0-8138-2232-7*) Iowa St U Pr.
— Programmed Journalism Editing. LC PN4785.A43. 183p. 1979. reprint ed. pap. 56.80 (*0-608-00302-6*, 206084800008) Bks Demand.

Alexander, James W. Consolation: Addresses to the Suffering People of God. 448p. 1992. reprint ed. 26.95 (*1-877611-53-0*) Soli Deo Gloria.
— Thoughts on Family Worship. 2nd rev. ed. Kistler, Don, ed. 154p. 1990. reprint ed. 18.95 (*1-57358-081-3*) Soli Deo Gloria.

***Alexander, Jane.** Command Performance: An Actress in the Theater of Politics. 304p. 2000. text 25.00 (*1-891620-06-1*) PublicAffairs NY.

Alexander, Jane. The Detox Plan: For Body, Mind & Spirit. LC 98-86035. (Illus.). 128p. 1998. pap. 16.95 (*1-885203-70-5*) Jrny Editions.

***Alexander, Jane.** Five-Minute Healer: Easy, Natural Ways to Look & Feel Better Fast. 160p. 2000. pap. 15.00 (*0-684-86945-4*, Fireside) S&S Trade Pap.

Alexander, Jane. Loveland. 288p. 1998. pap. 4.99 (*0-7860-0556-4*, Pinncle Kensgtn) Kensgtn Pub Corp.
— The Natural Year: A Seasonal Guide to Alternative Health & Beauty. 416p. 1999. pap. 13.50 (*0-380-73143-6*, Avon Bks) Morrow Avon.

***Alexander, Jane.** Spirit of the Home: How to Make Your Home a Sanctuary. (Illus.). 288p. 1998. 16.95 (*0-7225-3589-9*) Thorsons PA.
— Spirit of the Home: How to Make Your Home a Sanctuary. (Illus.). 192p. 2000. pap. write for info. (*0-8230-4901-9*) Watsn-Guptill.

Alexander, Jane, ed. see Alexander, Tom.

Alexander, Janet E. & Tate, Marsha A. Web Wisdom: How to Evaluate & Create Web Page Quality. LC 99-12314. 168p. 1999. 39.95 (*0-8058-3122-3*); pap. 16.50 (*0-8058-3123-1*) L Erlbaum Assocs.

Alexander, Jarda, ed. see Baker, Yaba.

***Alexander, Jason.** Empty Zone, Vol. 1. (Illus.). 96p. 1999. pap. 11.95 (*1-57989-025-3*) Sirius Ent.

Alexander, Jason. In Praise of the Common Man. LC 80-54489. 86p. (Orig.). 1980. pap. 9.95 (*0-931826-02-0*) Sitnalta Pr.
— Libertarians & the Fight Revolution. 122p. (Orig.). 1988. pap. 9.95 (*0-931826-03-9*) Sitnalta Pr.
— Why Johnny Can't Run, Swim, Pull, Dig, Slither, Etc. Porter, Deirdre J. G., ed. LC 78-58309. (Illus.). 206p. 1978. pap. text 9.95 (*0-931826-00-4*) Sitnalta Pr.

Alexander, Jean. Nurse in South America. large type ed. 320p. 1992. pap. 16.99 (*0-7089-7139-3*, Linford) Ulverscroft.

Alexander, Jean, tr. see Timofeev, Lev.

Alexander, Jeffrey. Fin de Siecle Social Theory: Relativism, Reduction & the Problem of Reason. 224p. (C). 1995. pap. 20.00 (*1-85984-091-4*, C0524, Pub. by Verso) Norton.

Alexander, Jeffrey A. Nursing Unit Organization: Its Effects on Staff Professionalism. Kalisch, Philip & Kalisch, Beatrice, eds. LC 82-13485. (Studies in Nursing Management: No. 4). 166p. 1982. reprint ed. pap. 51.50 (*0-8357-1369-5*, 207003800063) Bks Demand.

Alexander, Jeffrey C. Action & Its Environment: Toward a New Synthesis. 352p. 1988. text 57.50 (*0-231-06208-7*) Col U Pr.
— Action & Its Environment: Toward a New Synthesis. 352p. 1990. pap. text 25.50 (*0-231-06209-5*) Col U Pr.
— Twenty Lectures: Sociological Theory since World War II. LC 86-17106. 432p. 1988. pap. text 22.00 (*0-231-06211-7*) Col U Pr.

Alexander, Jeffrey C., ed. Neofunctionalism & After: Collected Readings. LC 97-8621. (Twentieth-Century Social Theory Ser.). 240p. 1997. text 62.95 (*1-55786-629-5*); pap. text 27.95 (*1-55786-630-9*) Blackwell Pubs.

Alexander, Jeffrey C., et al, eds. The Classical Tradition in Sociology: The American Tradition. 1664p. 1997. 750.00 (*0-7619-5325-6*) Sage.
— The Micro-Macro Link. 1987. pap. 19.95 (*0-520-06068-7*, Pub. by U CA Pr) Cal Prin Full Svc.

Alexander, Jeffrey C. & Colomy, Paul. Differentiation Theory: Problems & Prospects. 496p. 1990. text 57.50 (*0-231-06996-0*) Col U Pr.

Alexander, Jeffrey C. & Seidman, Steven, eds. Culture & Society: Contemporary Debates. 383p. (C). 1990. pap. text 21.95 (*0-521-35939-2*) Cambridge U Pr.

***Alexander, Jeffrey M.** Implementing a Physician Management Organization: A Guide to MSOs, PPMCs & MMCs. 166p. 1998. pap. 93.00 (*0-929156-55-2*) Atlantic Info Services Inc.

Alexander, Jennifer, jt. auth. see Davidson, Clifford.

Alexander, Jenny. Bullying: Practical & Easy-to-Follow Advice. LC 98-11292. (Your Child Ser.). 1998. pap. 9.95 (*1-86204-206-3*, Pub. by Element MA) Penguin Putnam.

***Alexander, Jenny.** Surfers Haunting for Beginners. 112p. 1998. pap. 7.95 (*0-14-037580-5*, Pub. by Pnguin Bks Ltd) Trafalgar.

***Alexander, Jesse.** Driven: The Motorsport Photographs of Jesse Alexander, 1952-1962. LC 00-22909. (Illus.). 2000. 22.95 (*0-8118-2851-4*) Chronicle Bks.

Alexander, Jessie L. & Hill, Phil. Looking Back. (Illus.). 160p. 1982. 24.95 (*0-686-45748-X*) At Speed Pr.

Alexander, Jim, jt. auth. see Hill, Nigel.

Alexander, Jo, et al, eds. Antenatal Care. 1994. pap. text 16.95 (*0-8020-7447-2*) U of Toronto Pr.
— Intrapartum Care. 1993. pap. text 16.95 (*0-8020-7451-0*) U of Toronto Pr.
— Postnatal Care. 1993. pap. text 17.95 (*0-8020-7452-9*) U of Toronto Pr.

***Alexander, Jocelyn, et al.** Violence & Memory: One Hundred Years in The 'Dark Forests' of Matabeleland. 2000. cd-rom. write for info. (*0-325-07032-6*) Greenwood.
— Violence & Memory: One Hundred Years in the 'Dark Forests' of Matabeleland. 2000. cd-rom. write for info. (*0-325-07033-4*) Greenwood.

Alexander, Joe. The Battle History of the U.S. Marines: A Fellowship of Valor. LC 99-12446. 432p. 1999. pap. 19.95 (*0-06-093109-4*) HarpC.

Alexander, John. Future War: Non-Lethal Weapons in Modern Warfare. 2nd ed. LC 98-19466. 272p. 1999. text 24.95 (*0-312-19416-1*) St Martin.
— Ghosts: Washington's Most Famous Ghost Stories. 160p. 1995. pap. 10.95 (*0-915168-07-3*) Wash Bk Trad.
— Ghosts! Washington Revisited: The Ghostlore of the Nation's Capital. LC 98-85936. 176p. 1998. pap. 14.95 (*0-7643-0653-7*) Schiffer.

Alexander, John, et al. ArcView/Avenue Programmer's Reference: Class Hierarchy Quick Reference & 101 Scripts. (C). 1995. pap. 54.95 (*1-56690-085-9*) Thomson Learn.
— Concepts & Models of Inorganic Chemistry. 3rd ed. 928p. 1994. text 109.95 (*0-471-62978-2*) Wiley.

Alexander, John, jt. auth. see Slade, Jim.

Alexander, John A. Champion of Faith (The Sermons of John Alexander Dowie) 1961. per. 5.25 (*0-89985-193-2*) Christ for the Nations.

***Alexander, John B.** Future War. (Illus.). 272p. 2000. pap. 14.95 (*0-312-26739-8*, St Martin Griffin) St Martin.

Alexander, John B., et al, eds. Security Systems & Nonlethal Technologies for Law Enforcement, Vol. 2934. LC 96-69894. 210p. 1997. 66.00 (*0-8194-2336-X*) SPIE.

Alexander, John B., et al. The Warrior's Edge. 240p. 1992. mass mkt. 4.99 (*0-380-71674-7*, Avon Bks) Morrow Avon.

***Alexander, John E.** A Record of the Descendants of John Alexander of Lanarkshire Scotland & His Wife, Margaret Glasson Who Emigrated from County Armagh, Ireland, to Chester County, Pennsylvania, A. D. 1736. 244p. 1999. (*0-7884-1221-3*, A420) Heritage Bk.

Alexander, John F. The Secular Squeeze: Reclaiming Christian Depth in a Shallow World. LC 93-18086. 307p. (Orig.). 1993. pap. 13.99 (*0-8308-1341-1*, 1341) InterVarsity.

Alexander, John H. Mosby's Men. 180p. 1987. reprint ed. 22.50 (*0-942211-15-4*) Olde Soldier Bks.
— The Works of John Henry Alexander, 1812-1867, Set. 1987. reprint ed. lib. bdg. 500.00 (*0-685-18580-X*) Rprt Serv.

A

An Asterisk (*) at the beginning of an entry indicates that the title is appearing for the first time.

A

Alexander, John H., ed. see Scott, Sir Walter.
Alexander, John K. The Selling of the Constitutional Convention: A History of News Coverage. 240p. (C). 1990. text 27.95 (*0-945612-15-X*) Madison Hse.
Alexander, John R. The New York Corporations: Legal Aspects of Organization & Operation. (Corporate Practice Ser.: No. 2-3). 1999. 95.00 (*1-55871-403-0*) BNA.
***Alexander, John R. & Lazell, James D.** Ribbon of Sand: The Amazing Convergence of the Ocean & the Outer Banks. LC 99-57677. (Chapel Hill Book Series). (Illus.). 255p. 2000. pap. 17.95 (*0-8078-4874-3*) U of NC Pr.
Alexander, John R., jt. auth. see Henn, Harry G.
Alexander, John T. Bubonic Plague in Early Modern Russia: Public Health & Urban Disaster. LC 79-3652. (Johns Hopkins University Studies in Historical & Political Science: Ser. 98, No. 1). (Illus.). 405p. reprint ed. pap. 125.60 (*0-7837-4783-7*, 204453900003) Bks Demand.
— Catherine the Great: Life & Legend. (Illus.). 456p. 1989. reprint ed. pap. text 18.95 (*0-19-506162-4*) OUP.
— Emperor of the Cossacks: Pugachev & the Frontier Jacguerie of 1773-1775. (Illus.). 248p. 1973. pap. 9.50 (*0-87291-045-8*) Coronado Pr.
Alexander, John T., ed. see Sugarbeet Congress Staff.
Alexander, John T., tr. see Anisimov, Evgenii V.
Alexander, John T., tr. see Platonov, Sergei F.
***Alexander, John W.** Criticism, Vol. 5. 2000. pap. 4.95 (*0-8308-6557-8*) InterVarsity.
Alexander, John W. Practical Criticism - Chinese Edition: Giving It & Taking It. Kao, Samuel E., tr. (CHI.). 19p. 1986. pap. 1.50 (*1-56582-015-0*) Christ Renew Min.
Alexander, John W., ed. The Journal of Bank Taxation. 185.00 (*0-685-69567-0*, JBT) Warren Gorham & Lamont.
***Alexander, John W. & Hayner, Stephen.** Criticism. 32p. 2000. 1.00 (*0-87784-057-1*) InterVarsity.
Alexander, John W., jt. auth. see Hartshorn, Truman A.
Alexander, Jon. American Personal Religious Accounts, 1600-1980: Toward an Inner History of America's Faiths. LC 83-21950. (Studies in American Religion: Vol. 8). 518p. 1983. lib. bdg. 119.95 (*0-88946-654-8*) E Mellen.
Alexander, Jon, ed. William Porcher DuBose: Selected Writings. (Sources of American Spirituality Ser.). 336p. 1988. 19.95 (*0-8091-0402-4*) Paulist Pr.
Alexander, Jon & Dimock, Giles, eds. Religion in Western Civilization since the Reformation: Select Readings. 184p. (C). 1983. pap. text 16.00 (*0-8191-3391-4*) U Pr of Amer.
Alexander, Jonah, jt. ed. see Rapoport, David C.
Alexander, Jonathan J. Medieval Illuminators & Their Methods of Work. LC 92-5576. (Illus.). 221p. 1994. pap. 30.00 (*0-300-06073-4*) Yale U Pr.
Alexander, Jonathan J., et al, compiled by. The Painted Page: Italian Renaissance Book Illumination 1450-1550. (Illus.). 198p. 1994. 85.00 (*3-7913-1385-1*, Pub. by Prestel) te Neues.
Alexander, Joseph A. Commentary on Isaiah. LC 92-16125. 1000p. 1992. reprint ed. pap. 30.99 (*0-8254-2137-3*, Kregel Class) Kregel.
— Commentary on Psalms. LC 89-2563. Orig. Title: The Psalms Translated & Explained. 576p. 1991. reprint ed. pap. 22.99 (*0-8254-2140-3*, Kregel Class) Kregel.
— Conquer with Your Seed: The War Is on to Captive Your Child. LC 97-69142. 82p. 1997. pap. write for info. (*1-57502-568-X*, PO1642) Morris Pubng.
— Doubt Reduces God to Your Size: Faith Magnifies God & Produces Results. LC 97-69141. 102p. 1997. pap. write for info. (*1-57502-569-8*, PO1643) Morris Pubng.
Alexander, Joseph H. Across the Reef: The Marine Assault of Tarawa. (Illus.). 52p. (Orig.). 1996. reprint ed. pap. text 20.00 (*0-7881-3538-4*) DIANE Pub.
— Closing In: Marines in the Seizure of Iwo Jima. (Illus.). 53p. 1996. reprint ed. pap. text 20.00 (*0-7881-3532-5*) DIANE Pub.
— The Final Campaign: Marines in the Victory on Okinawa. (Illus.). 53p. (Orig.). (C). 1996. pap. text 25.00 (*0-7881-3528-7*) DIANE Pub.
Alexander, Joseph H. Final Campaign: Marines in the Victory on Okinawa. 53p. 1996. pap. 5.00 (*0-16-061348-5*) USGPO.
Alexander, Joseph H. Storm Landings: Epic Amphibious Battles in the Central Pacific. LC 96-53479. (Illus.). 264p. 1997. 29.95 (*1-55750-032-0*) Naval Inst Pr.
— Utmost Savagery. 1997. mass mkt. 5.99 (*0-8041-1559-1*) Ivy Books.
— Utmost Savagery: The Three Days of Tarawa. LC 95-15534. (Illus.). 328p. 1995. 31.95 (*1-55750-031-2*) Naval Inst Pr.
Alexander, Joseph H. & Bartlett, Merrill L. Sea Soldiers in the Cold War: Amphibious Warfare, 1945-1991. LC 94-20845. (Illus.). 320p. 1994. 34.95 (*1-55750-055-X*) Naval Inst Pr.
Alexander, Joy, tr. see Niwano, Nikkyo.
Alexander, Joyce. Happy Bird Day. (Illus.). 1980. pap. 12.50 (*0-912020-18-0*) Turtles Quill.
— Whispers on the Wind: Poetry. 88p. 1999. pap. 8.00 (*1-57087-464-6*) Prof Pr NC.
Alexander, Joyce. Comfort Me with Apples: Dining in Literature. deluxe limited ed. 1993. pap. 15.00 (*0-937686-17-4*) Turtles Quill.
— A Flurry of Angels: Angels in Literature. deluxe limited ed. 1986. pap. 15.00 (*0-937686-13-1*) Turtles Quill.
— Messiah: Choruses from Handel's Messiah. deluxe limited ed. 24p. 1985. pap. 15.00 (*0-937686-10-7*) Turtles Quill.
— A Packet of Rhymes: Scottish & English Nursery Rhymes. deluxe limited ed. (J). 1989. pap. 15.00 (*0-937686-12-3*) Turtles Quill.
— Psalm 8. deluxe limited ed. 1991. pap. 15.00 (*0-937686-18-2*) Turtles Quill.
Alexander, Joyce. Psalm 104. deluxe limited ed. 32p. 1978. pap. 15.00 (*0-937686-27-1*) Turtles Quill.
Alexander, Joyce. The Sea: Excerpts from Herman Melville. 1970. pap. 12.50 (*0-912020-15-6*) Turtles Quill.
— Thaddeus. 1972. pap. 12.50 (*0-912020-20-2*) Turtles Quill.
Alexander, Joyce & Alexander, Dorsey. Chee & Ribbit. deluxe limited ed. 20p. 1995. bds. 20.00 (*0-614-14381-0*) Turtles Quill.
— Psalm 148, Etc. (Illus.). 1998. write for info. (*0-614-30683-3*) Turtles Quill.
***Alexander, Joyce W.** As Incense Rising. 72p. 2000. 8.00 (*1-57087-529-4*) Prof Pr NC.
Alexander, Judd H. In Defense of Garbage. LC 92-23977. 288p. 1993. 39.95 (*0-275-93627-9*, C3627, Praeger Pubs) Greenwood.
Alexander, Julia M., jt. auth. see Warner, Malcolm.
Alexander, Julie. Great Days: 50 Ways to Add Energy, Enthusiasm, & Enjoyment to Your Life. LC 97-93958. 181p. 1997. pap., mass mkt. 11.95 (*0-9659310-0-5*) Great Days.
***Alexander, Julie.** Making Life Count! 50 Ways to Great Days. 185p. 2000. pap. 11.95 (*0-9659310-1-3*, Pub. by Great Days) Herveys Bklink.
Alexander, June G. The Immigrant Church & Community: Pittsburgh's Slovak Catholics & Lutherans, 1880-1915. LC 86-30843. (Illus.). 198p. 1987. text 30.95 (*0-8229-3821-9*) U of Pittsburgh Pr.
Alexander, K. C. & Kumaran, K. P. Culture & Development: Cultural Patterns in Areas of Uneven Development. LC 92-14231. (Illus.). 203p. (C). 1992. 28.50 (*0-8039-9437-0*) Sage.
Alexander, K. C., et al. Tribals, Rehabilitation, & Development. (C). 1991. text 20.00 (*0-685-53666-1*, Pub. by Rawat Pubns) S Asia.
Alexander, K. L. & Watkins, J. C., eds. Spatial Stochastic Processes: A Festschrift in Honor of Ted Harris on His 70th Birthday. (Progress in Probability Ser.: No. 19). xii, 256p. 1991. 103.50 (*0-8176-3477-0*) Birkhauser.
Alexander, Kanjirathara C. The Process of Development of Societies. LC 94-4732. 1994. 32.00 (*0-8039-9171-1*) Sage.
Alexander, Karen. An Ancient Whisper. 275p. (Orig.). 1997. pap. 14.00 (*1-885733-36-4*) Windover Pr.
— A Gift from Daniel. LC 96-15438. 288p. (Orig.). 1996. pap. 12.00 (*0-399-52244-1*, Perigee Bks) Berkley Pub.
Alexander, Karen B., jt. auth. see Streicher, John P.
Alexander, Karl, et al. Time after Time. 1983. 5.50 (*0-87129-423-0*, T55) Dramatic Pub.
Alexander, Karl L. & Entwisle, Doris R. Achievement in the First Two Years of School: Patterns & Processes. (Monographs of the Society for Research in Child Development: No. 217 53.1). 166p. 1988. pap. text 15.00 (*0-226-01356-1*) U Ch Pr.
Alexander, Karl L., et al. On the Success of Failure: A Reassessment of the Effects of Retention in the Primary Grades. (Illus.). 284p. (C). 1995. text 54.95 (*0-521-41504-7*) Cambridge U Pr.
Alexander, Kate. Dawn. large type ed. 384p. 31.99 (*0-7089-9050-9*) Ulverscroft.
Alexander, Kate. Family Trees. large type ed. (Charnwood Large Print Ser.). 400p. 1997. 27.99 (*0-7089-8942-X*, Charnwood) Ulverscroft.
— The House of Hope. large type ed. (Charnwood Ser.). 528p. 1994. 27.99 (*0-7089-8752-4*, Charnwood) Ulverscroft.
— Songs of War. large type ed. 1988. 19.95 (*0-7089-8457-6*, Charnwood) Ulverscroft.
— Voices of Song. large type ed. (Ulverscroft Large Print Ser.). 624p. 1997. 27.99 (*0-7089-3584-2*) Ulverscroft.
Alexander, Katherina. A Stylistic Commentary on Phanocles & Related Texts. 168p. (Orig.). 1988. pap. 54.00 (*90-256-0885-X*, Pub. by AM Hakkert) BookLink Distributors.
Alexander, Kathryn. The Forever Husband. 256p. 1999. per. 4.50 (*0-373-87078-7*, Steeple Hill) Harlequin Bks.
***Alexander, Kathryn.** Heart of a Husband. (Love Inspired Ser.: Bk. 116). 2000. mass mkt. 4.50 (*0-373-87122-8*, 1-87122-7, Steeple Hill) Harlequin Bks.
Alexander, Kathryn. The Reluctant Bride. (Love Inspired Ser.: No. 18). 1998. per. 4.50 (*0-373-87018-3*, 1-87018-7) Harlequin Bks.
***Alexander, Kathryn.** Twin Wishes. 2000. per. 4.50 (*0-373-87102-3*) Harlequin Bks.
Alexander, Kathryn. A Wedding in the Family. (Love Inspired Ser.: Vol. 42). 1998. per. 4.50 (*0-373-87042-6*, 1-87042-7) Harlequin Bks.
Alexander, Kathy. Paradise Found: The Settlement of the Santa Catalina Mountains. (Illus.). (Orig.). 1991. pap. write for info. (*0-9628832-0-4*) Skunkworks.
Alexander, Kathy, jt. auth. see Collins, George J.
Alexander, Kay. Californian Catholicism. Hammond, Phillip, ed. (Religious Contours of California: Window to the World's Religions: Vol. I). 128p. (Orig.). 1993. pap. 9.95 (*1-56474-062-5*) Fithian Pr.
— Creative Learning Elementary Art Resources, Set 1: Clear. (Illus.). 83p. (J). (gr. k-3). 1989. teacher ed. 185.00 (*0-924509-01-5*, 5008) Crystal.
— Creative Learning Elementary Art Resources, Set 2: Clear. Hubbard, Loretta, ed. (Illus.). 1989. teacher ed. 185.00 (*0-924509-02-3*, 5009) Crystal.
Alexander, Kay & Day, Michael, eds. Discipline-Based Art Education: A Curriculum Sampler. LC 90-25233. (Illus.). 344p. 1991. ring bd. 15.00 (*0-89236-171-9*, Pub. by J P Getty Trust) OUP.
Alexander, Keith, jt. auth. see Barnes, Jim.
Alexander, Kenneth. Pharmaceutical Technology: Introduction to Pharmaceutical Systems II. (C). 1994. pap. text 15.00 (*1-57074-140-9*) Greyden Pr.
— Pharmaceutical Technology Lab Manual. 226p. (C). 1994. pap. text 15.00 (*1-57074-107-7*) Greyden Pr.
Alexander, Kenneth J., et al. The Economist in Business. LC 67-30476. vi, 199p. 1969. 37.50 (*0-678-06253-6*) Kelley.
Alexander, Kent. Legends of the Old West: Trailblazers, Desperadoes, Wranglers, & Yarn-Spinners. LC 94-8758. (Illus.). 120p. 1994. pap. 14.95 (*1-56799-109-2*, Friedman-Fairfax) M Friedman Pub Grp Inc.
Alexander, Kern, ed. Attracting & Compensating America's Teachers. LC 87-30830. (American Education Finance Association Ser.). 320p. 1988. text 35.00 (*0-88730-203-3*, HarpBusn) HarpInfo.
Alexander, Kern & Alexander, David. American Public School Law. 3rd ed. Hannan, ed. 880p. (C). 1992. mass mkt. 51.00 (*0-314-92952-5*) West Pub.
Alexander, Kern & Alexander, M. David. The Law of Schools, Students & Teachers in a Nutshell. 2nd ed. LC 94-48764. (Nutshell Ser.). 500p. (C). 1995. pap. 23.50 (*0-314-05882-6*) West Pub.
Alexander, Kern & Jordan, K. Forbis, eds. Educational Need in the Public Economy. LC 75-33898. (Illus.). 369p. reprint ed. pap. 114.40 (*0-7837-5089-7*, 204478700004) Bks Demand.
Alexander, Kern & Salmon, Richard G. Public School Finance in the U.S. LC 94-35294. 416p. 1995. 85.00 (*0-205-16631-8*) Allyn.
Alexander, Kern, jt. ed. see McKeown, Mary P.
Alexander, Kevin, ed. The Lippincott Manual of Primary Eye Care. (Illus.). 650p. (C). 1994. text 65.00 (*0-397-51109-4*, Lippnctt) Lppncott W & W.
Alexander, Kevin L., ed. The Lippincott Manual of Primary Eye Care. LC 94-24472. (Illus.). 576p. reprint ed. pap. 178.60 (*0-608-09718-7*, 206988400007) Bks Demand.
Alexander Kohut Memorial Foundation Staff. Jewish Studies in Memory of Israel Abrahams. Katz, Steven, ed. LC 79-7164. (Jewish Philosophy, Mysticism & History of Ideas Ser.). (Illus.). 1980. reprint ed. lib. bdg. 49.95 (*0-405-12274-8*) Ayer.
Alexander, Kwaime. The Flow: New Black Poetry in Motion. 1994. 10.00 (*0-938818-45-7*) ECA Assoc.
Alexander, Kwame. Just Us: Poems & Counter Poems, 1986-1995. (Blackwords Ser.: No. 1). 112p. 1995. pap. 9.95 (*1-888018-00-3*) Alexndr Pub.
— Kupenda: Black Love Poems. (Black Words Ser.). 112p. 1996. pap. 9.95 (*1-888018-06-2*) Alexndr Pub.
Alexander, Kwame, ed. see Datcher, Michael.
Alexander, Kwame, jt. ed. see Saloan, Kalamu Ya.
Alexander, Kyle. Bill Goldberg. LC 99-32899. (Illus.). 64p. 1999. 17.95 (*0-7910-5404-7*) Chelsea Hse.
— Bill Goldberg. LC 99-32899. (Wrestling Stars Ser.). (Illus.). 64p. (YA). (gr. 3 up). 1999. pap. 8.95 (*0-7910-5550-7*) Chelsea Hse.
— Story of the Wrestler They Call Sting. LC 99-34305. (Wrestling Stars Ser.). (Illus.). 64p. (YA). (gr. 3 up). 1999. pap. 8.95 (*0-7910-5551-5*) Chelsea Hse.
— The Story of the Wrestler They Call Sting. LC 99-34305. (Illus.). 64p. (YA). (gr. 3 up). 1999. 17.95 (*0-7910-5405-5*) Chelsea Hse.
***Alexander, Kyle.** Women of Pro Wrestling. (Pro Wrestling Legends Ser.). 2000. 17.95 (*0-7910-5839-5*) Chelsea Hse.
— Women of Pro Wrestling. LC 00-20731. (Pro Wrestling Legends Ser.). (Illus.). 2000. pap. 8.95 (*0-7910-5840-9*) Chelsea Hse.
— Wrestling's Most Punishing Finishing Moves. (Pro Wrestling Legends Ser.). (YA). 2000. 17.95 (*0-7910-5833-6*) Chelsea Hse.
— Wrestling's Most Punishing Finishing Moves. LC 00-20730. (Pro Wrestling Legends Ser.). (Illus.). (YA). 2000. pap. 8.95 (*0-7910-5834-4*) Chelsea Hse.
Alexander, L. G. The Essential English Grammar. LC 92-33523. 1993. pap. text. write for info. (*0-582-21869-1*) Longman.
— K's First Case. (American Structural Readers Ser.: Stage 2). (Illus.). 58p. (Orig.). 1989. pap. text 5.72 (*0-582-79815-9*, 75065) Longman.
— Longman English Grammar. 1989. pap. text 29.67 (*0-582-55892-1*, 78032) Longman.
— Questions & Answers in Marketing. (English As a Second Language Bk.). 1977. pap. text 4.95 (*0-582-55206-0*) Longman.
— Right Word Wrong Word. Date not set. pap. text. write for info. (*0-582-21860-8*, Pub. by Addison-Wesley) Longman.
Alexander, Lamar. The G.I. Bill for Children. 32p. 1992. pap. text 3.00 (*1-878802-15-1*) J M Ashbrook Ctr Pub Affairs.
— Lamar Alexander's Little Plaid Book. LC 98-18355. 160p. 1998. pap. 6.95 (*1-55853-579-9*) Rutledge Hill Pr.
— Six Months Off: An American Family's Australian Adventure. large type ed. (General Ser.). (Illus.). 504p. 1989. lib. bdg. 17.95 (*0-8161-4846-5*, G K Hall Lrg Type) Mac Lib Ref.
Alexander, Lamar, ed. see Schambra, William A., et al.
***Alexander, Larry.** Legal Rules & Legal Reasoning. LC 99-38741. (Collected Essays in Law Ser.). 275p. (C). 2000. text 101.95 (*0-7546-2004-2*) Ashgate Pub Co.
Alexander, Larry, ed. Constitutionalism: Philosophical Foundations. LC 97-32000. (Studies in Philosophy & Law). 332p. (C). 1998. text 54.95 (*0-521-48293-3*) Cambridge U Pr.
— Contract Law, 2 vols., I. (International Library of Essays in Law & Legal Theory). 1140p. (C). 1991. lib. bdg. 150.00 (*0-8147-0600-2*) NYU Pr.
— Contract Law, 2 vols., II. (International Library of Essays in Law & Legal Theory). 1140p. (C). 1991. lib. bdg. 150.00 (*0-8147-0601-0*) NYU Pr.
— Contract Law, 2 vols., Set. (International Library of Essays in Law & Legal Theory). 1140p. (C). 1991. lib. bdg. 250.00 (*0-8147-0602-9*) NYU Pr.
***Alexander, Larry, ed.** Freedom of Speech Vols. I & II: Foundations: Doctrine. LC 99-16906. (International Library of Essays in Law & Legal Theory). 1110p. 1999. text 175.95 (*1-84014-771-7*, Pub. by Ashgate Pub) Ashgate Pub Co.
Alexander, Larry L. Primary Care of the Posterior Segment. 2nd ed. (Illus.). 525p. (C). 1998. pap. text 125.00 (*0-8385-7970-1*, A7970-5, Apple Lange Med) McGraw.
Alexander, Larry L. & Horton, Paul. Whom Does the Constitution Command? A Conceptual Analysis with Practical Implications. 42. LC 87-32272. (Contributions in Legal Studies: No. 42). 181p. 1988. 52.95 (*0-313-26216-0*, AWC/, Greenwood Pr) Greenwood.
Alexander, Laurel. Career Networking: How to Develop the Right Contacts to Help You Throughout Your Working Life. (Jobs & Careers Ser.). 135p. 1997. pap. 19.95 (*1-85703-350-7*, Pub. by How To Bks) Trans-Atl Phila.
— Career Planning for Women: How to Make a Positive Impact on Your Working Life. (Jobs & Careers Ser.). 160p. 1996. pap. 19.95 (*1-85703-417-1*, Pub. by How To Bks) Trans-Atl Phila.
— Learning New Job Skills: How & Where to Obtain the Right Training to Help You Get on at Work. (Jobs & Careers Ser.). 127p. 1997. pap. 19.95 (*1-85703-375-2*, Pub. by How To Bks) Trans-Atl Phila.
— Surviving Redundancy: How to Take Charge of Yourself & Your Future. (Jobs & Careers Ser.). 160p. 1996. pap. 19.95 (*1-85703-187-3*, Pub. by How To Bks) Trans-Atl Phila.
Alexander, Leo. Medical Science under Dictatorship. 32p. (Orig.). 1996. pap. 4.00 (*0-930429-03-6*) Bibliographic Pr.
Alexander, Leroy E., jt. auth. see Klug, Harold P.
Alexander, Leslie B. & Kaye, Lenard W. Part-Time Employment for the Low-Income Elderly: Experiences from the Field. LC 96-35889. (Issues in Aging Ser.: Vol. 6). 204p. 1997. text 44.00 (*0-8153-1976-2*, SS1016) Garland.
Alexander, Lester, ed. see Satchidanada, Sri S.
Alexander, Lewis M., et al, eds. New Developments in Marine Science & Technology: Economic, Legal & Political Aspects of Change, 22nd Annual Conference Proceedings. 530p. 1989. 42.50 (*0-911189-20-3*) Law Sea Inst.
Alexander, Lewis M., jt. ed. see Charney, Jonathan I.
***Alexander, Linda.** Dorothy from Kansas Meets the Wizard of X. LC 99-61051. 276p. 1999. pap. write for info. (*1-58445-008-8*) Pulpless.
Alexander, Linda. Job Well Done. (Illus.). (J). (gr. 1-4). 1979. lib. bdg. 7.19 (*0-8313-0002-7*) Lantern.
— New Dimension in Women's Health. (Health Science Ser.). 104p. 1994. pap. 10.00 (*0-86720-981-X*) Jones & Bartlett.
— The Unpromised Land: The Struggle of Messianic Jews, Gary & Shirley Beresford. 207p. 1994. pap. 10.99 (*1-880226-56-1*) M J Pubs.
Alexander, Linda, et al. New Dimensions in Women's Health. 2nd ed. (Nursing Ser.). 1998. 50.00 (*0-7637-0552-7*) Jones & Bartlett.
Alexander, Linda L. & LaRosa, Judith H. New Dimensions in Women's Health. LC 93-50822. (Health Science Ser.). 464p. (C). 1994. 48.75 (*0-86720-777-9*) Jones & Bartlett.
Alexander, Linda Lewis & LaRosa, Judith H. New Dimensions in Women's Health. 2nd ed. (Illus.). 440p. (C). 1994. pap. text 51.25 (*0-7637-1083-0*) JB Pubns.
Alexander, Liza. Find the Seashell, No. 3. (Sesame Street Elmo's World Ser.). (Illus.). 32p. (J). 1999. pap. 3.25 (*0-679-89422-5*) ctwo design.
— Flutter by, Butterfly. LC 98-12693. (Elmo's World Ser.: Vol. 2). (J). 1998. pap. 3.25 (*0-679-88700-8*, Pub. by Random Bks Yng Read); lib. bdg. 8.99 (*0-679-98700-2*, Pub. by Random Bks Yng Read) Random.
— Giddy-Up. LC 98-13301. (Elmo's World Ser.: No. 1). (J). 1998. pap. 3.25 (*0-679-88697-4*, Pub. by Random Bks Yng Read) Random.
***Alexander, Liza.** It's Christmas. 2000. 1.99 (*0-375-80559-1*) Random Bks Yng Read.
Alexander, Liza. Remember When. (Elmo's World Ser.: No. 5). 1999. pap. 3.25 (*0-679-89424-1*, Pub. by Random Bks Yng Read) Random.
— Remember When. 3rd ed. (Elmo's World Ser.: No. 5). 1999. lib. bdg. 8.99 (*0-679-99424-6*, Pub. by Random Bks Yng Read) Random.
— Snuggle Up. (Elmo's World Ser.: No. 6). 1999. pap. 3.25 (*0-679-89425-X*, Pub. by Random Bks Yng Read); lib. bdg. 8.99 (*0-679-99425-4*, Pub. by Random Bks Yng Read) Random.
***Alexander, Liza.** Splish-Splashy Day. (Pictureback Ser.). 24p. (J). 2000. pap. 3.25 (*0-375-80437-4*, Pub. by Random Bks Yng Read) Random.
Alexander, Liza. Surprise, Mommy! LC 98-49494. (Elmo's World Ser.: No. 4). (J). 1999. pap. 3.25 (*0-679-89423-3*) Random.
— Surprise, Mommy! LC 98-49494. (Elmo's World Ser.). (J). 1999. lib. bdg. 8.99 (*0-679-99423-8*) Random.
— A Visit to the Sesame Street Museum. LC 87-1685. (Pictureback Ser.). (Illus.). 32p. (J). (gr. 3-6). 1987. pap. 3.25 (*0-394-88715-8*, Pub. by Random Bks Yng Read) Random.
— Winnie the Pooh & Valentines, Too. (Winnie the Pooh Ser.). 32p. (J). 1998. 12.95 (*0-7868-3217-7*, Pub. by Disney Pr) Time Warner.
***Alexander, Liza & Luke, David.** Bark, Spike, Bark! LC 97-44204. (Ready to Read: Vol. 4). (Illus.). 32p. (J). (gr. k-4). 1998. pap. 3.99 (*0-689-82129-8*) S&S Childrens.
Alexander, Lloyd. The Arkadians. 272p. (YA). (gr. 5 up). pap. 4.99 (*0-8072-1527-9*) Listening Lib.
Alexander, Lloyd. The Arkadians. LC 94-35025. 288p. (J). (gr. 5) 1995. 16.99 (*0-525-45415-2*, Dutton Child) Peng Put Young Read.

Alexander, Lloyd. The Arkadians. 1997. 10.09 (*0-606-11056-9*, Pub. by Turtleback) Demco.

Alexander, Lloyd. The Arkadians. (Illus.). 288p. (J). 1997. pap. 5.99 (*0-14-038073-6*) Viking Penguin.

— The Arkadians, 4. unabridged ed. (J). (gr. 5 up). 1998. audio 29.98 (*0-8072-8021-6*, YA969CX) Listening Lib.

Alexander, Lloyd. Beggar Queen. (J). 1985. 9.09 (*0-606-00255-3*, Pub. by Turtleback) Demco.

Alexander, Lloyd. The Beggar Queen. 256p. (YA). (gr. 6-12). 1985. mass mkt. 4.99 (*0-440-90548-6*, LLL BDD) BDD Bks Young Read.

— The Black Cauldron. LC 65-13868. (Chronicles of Prydain Ser.). 240p. (YA). (gr. 5-9). 1980. pap. 5.50 (*0-440-40649-8*, YB BDD) BDD Bks Young Read.

— The Black Cauldron. (Chronicles of Prydain Ser.). 220p. (J). 1980. mass mkt. 3.50 (*0-440-90649-0*, LLL BDD) BDD Bks Young Read.

***Alexander, Lloyd.** The Black Cauldron. (Chronicles of Prydain Ser.). 256p. (J). 1999. mass mkt. 2.99 (*0-440-22883-2*) Bantam.

Alexander, Lloyd. The Black Cauldron. LC 65-13868. (Chronicles of Prydain Ser.). 224p. (J). (gr. 4-6). 1995. 16.95 (*0-8050-0992-2*, Bks Young Read) H Holt & Co.

— The Black Cauldron. LC 98-40896. (Chronicles of Prydain Ser.). 190p. (J). (gr. 3-7). 1999. 18.95 (*0-8050-6131-2*) H Holt & Co.

— The Black Cauldron. (Classics Ser.). (Illus.). 96p. (J). 1994. 7.98 (*1-57082-035-X*, Pub. by Mouse Works) Time Warner.

— The Black Cauldron. (Chronicles of Prydain Ser.). (J). 1965. 10.09 (*0-606-02354-2*, Pub. by Turtleback) Demco.

— The Book of Three. (Chronicles of Prydain Ser.). 224p. (YA). (gr. 5-9). 1978. pap. 5.50 (*0-440-40702-8*, YB BDD) BDD Bks Young Read.

— The Book of Three. (Chronicles of Prydain Ser.). (J). 1995. 5.99 (*0-440-91069-2*) Dell.

— The Book of Three. LC 64-18250. (Chronicles of Prydain Ser.). 224p. (J). (gr. 4-6). 1995. 16.95 (*0-8050-0874-8*, Bks Young Read) H Holt & Co.

— The Book of Three. LC 98-40901. (Chronicles of Prydain Ser.). (J). (gr. 3-7). 1999. 18.95 (*0-8050-6132-0*) H Holt & Co.

— The Book of Three. (Chronicles of Prydain Ser.). (J). 1964. 10.09 (*0-606-02410-7*, Pub. by Turtleback) Demco.

— The Book of Three. large type ed. (Chronicles of Prydain Ser.). (J). 1995. pap. 59.00 (*0-614-09563-8*, L-34875-00) Am Printing Hse.

— The Castle of Llyr. LC no-na1155. (Chronicles of Prydain Ser.: Vol. 3). 208p. (J). (gr. 5-9). 1969. pap. 5.99 (*0-440-41125-4*, YB BDD) BDD Bks Young Read.

— The Castle of Llyr. LC 66-13461. (Chronicles of Prydain Ser.). 208p. (J). (gr. 4-6). 1995. 16.95 (*0-8050-1115-3*, Bks Young Read) H Holt & Co.

— The Castle of Llyr. LC 98-40897. (Chronicles of Prydain Ser.). 174p. (J). (gr. 3-7). 1999. 18.95 (*0-8050-6133-9*) H Holt & Co.

— The Castle of Llyr. (Chronicles of Prydain Ser.). (J). 1966. 10.09 (*0-606-02572-3*, Pub. by Turtleback) Demco.

***Alexander, Lloyd.** The Cat Who Wished to Be a Man. (Illus.). (J). 2000. pap. 4.99 (*0-14-130704-8*, PuffinBks) Peng Put Young Read.

Alexander, Lloyd. The Cat Who Wished to Be a Man. (J). 1973. 9.09 (*0-606-00337-1*, Pub. by Turtleback) Demco.

— Cat Who Wished to Be a Man. 112p. (J). (gr. 4-7). 1992. pap. 3.99 (*0-440-40580-7*) Dell.

Alexander, Lloyd. Cat Who Wished to Be a Man. 107p. pap. 3.99 (*0-8072-1505-8*) Listening Lib.

— Cat Who Wished to Be a Man. (Illus.). (J). 2000. 10.34 (*0-606-18393-0*) Turtleback.

— El Dorado Adventure. (Illus.). 176p. (J). (gr. 5-9). 2000. pap. 5.99 (*0-14-130463-4*, PuffinBks) Peng Put Young Read.

— Drackenberg Adventure. (J). 1988. 9.09 (*0-606-03238-X*, Pub. by Turtleback) Demco.

Alexander, Lloyd. The Drackenberg Adventure. 160p. (J). (gr. k-6). 1990. reprint ed. pap. 3.99 (*0-440-40296-4*) Dell.

— The El Dorado Adventure. 1988. write for info. (*0-440-80016-1*) Doubleday.

— First Two Lives of Lukas-Kasha. (Puffin Bks.). 224p. (J). 1998. pap. 4.99 (*0-14-130057-4*, PuffinBks) Peng Put Young Read.

***Alexander, Lloyd.** First Two Lives of Lukas-Kasha. (Puffin Novel Ser.). 1998. 10.09 (*0-606-13389-5*, Pub. by Turtleback) Demco.

Alexander, Lloyd. The Fortune-Tellers. (Illus.). (J). 1997. write for info. (*0-614-29287-5*, PuffinBks) Peng Put Young Read.

Alexander, Lloyd. The Fortune Tellers. (Picture Puffin Ser.). (J). 1997. 11.19 (*0-606-12293-1*, Pub. by Turtleback) Demco.

Alexander, Lloyd. The Fortune Tellers. (Illus.). 32p. (J). (ps-3). 1997. pap. 5.99 (*0-14-056233-8*) Viking Penguin.

— The Foundling: And Other Tales of Prydain. 128p. (J). (gr. 3-7). 1996. pap. 4.99 (*0-14-037825-1*, PuffinBks) Peng Put Young Read.

***Alexander, Lloyd.** The Foundling & Other Tales of Prydain. LC 98-42807. 98p. (J). (gr. 3-7). 1999. 17.95 (*0-8050-6130-4*) H Holt & Co.

Alexander, Lloyd. Gypsy Rizka. LC 98-41399. 144p. (YA). (gr. 3-7). 1999. 16.99 (*0-525-46121-3*, Dutton Child) Peng Put Young Read.

***Alexander, Lloyd.** Gypsy Rizka. (Illus.). 176p. (J). (gr. 5-9). 2000. pap. 4.99 (*0-14-130980-6*, PuffinBks) Peng Put Young Read.

Alexander, Lloyd. The High King. (Chronicles of Prydain Ser.). 304p. (J). (gr. 4-7). 1969. pap. 5.99 (*0-440-43574-9*, YB BDD) BDD Bks Young Read.

— The High King. (Chronicles of Prydain Ser.). 288p. (YA). (gr. 5-9). 1980. mass mkt. 3.99 (*0-440-93574-1*, LLL BDD) BDD Bks Young Read.

— The High King. LC 68-11833. (Chronicles of Prydain Ser.). 288p. (J). (gr. 4-6). 1995. 16.95 (*0-8050-1114-5*, Bks Young Read) H Holt & Co.

— The High King. LC 98-40900. (Chronicles of Prydain Ser.). 253p. (J). (gr. 3-7). 1999. 18.95 (*0-8050-6135-5*) H Holt & Co.

Alexander, Lloyd. The High King. (Chronicles of Prydain Ser.). (J). 1968. 10.09 (*0-606-03530-3*, Pub. by Turtleback) Demco.

Alexander, Lloyd. House Gobbaleen. 32p. (J). 1999. pap. 5.99 (*0-14-056504-3*, PuffinBks) Peng Put Young Read.

***Alexander, Lloyd.** How the Cat Swallowed Thunder. LC 00-24530. (Illus.). 40p. (J). (gr. k-4). 2000. 16.99 (*0-525-46449-2*, Dutton Child) Peng Put Young Read.

Alexander, Lloyd. Illyrian Adventure. (J). 1995. pap. 4.50 (*0-440-91042-0*) BDD Bks Young Read.

— Illyrian Adventure. (Illus.). 144p. (J). (gr. 5-9). 2000. pap. 5.99 (*0-14-130313-1*, PuffinBks) Peng Put Young Read.

— Illyrian Adventure. 1986. 9.99 (*0-606-02191-4*, Pub. by Turtleback) Demco.

— The Iron Ring. LC 96-29730. 256p. (J). 1997. 16.99 (*0-525-45597-3*) NAL.

***Alexander, Lloyd.** The Iron Ring, Class Set. unabridged ed. (J). 1998. boxed set 133.70 incl. audio (*0-7887-2555-6*, 46725) Recorded Bks.

— The Iron Ring, Homework Set. unabridged ed. 1998. boxed set 76.24 incl. audio (*0-7887-2251-4*, 40735) Recorded Bks.

Alexander, Lloyd. The Jedera Adventure. 160p. (J). 1990. pap. 4.50 (*0-440-40295-6*, YB BDD) BDD Bks Young Read.

— Jedera Adventure. (J). 1989. 9.60 (*0-606-04442-6*, Pub. by Turtleback) Demco.

***Alexander, Lloyd.** Marvelous Misadventures of Sebastian. (Illus.). 224p. (YA). (gr. 5-9). 2000. pap. 4.99 (*0-14-130816-8*, PuffinBks) Peng Put Young Read.

Alexander, Lloyd. The Philadelphia Adventure. 160p. (J). (gr. 4-7). 1992. pap. 3.99 (*0-440-40605-6*) Dell.

Alexander, Lloyd. Philadelphia Adventure. 1990. 9.09 (*0-606-00924-8*, Pub. by Turtleback) Demco.

Alexander, Lloyd. Remarkable Journey. 288p. (J). 1993. pap. 4.99 (*0-440-40890-3*) Dell.

— The Remarkable Journey of Prince Jen. LC 91-13720. 288p. (J). (gr. 5-10). 1991. 16.99 (*0-525-44826-8*, Dutton Child) Peng Put Young Read.

— The Remarkable Journey of Prince Jen. (J). 1991. 10.09 (*0-606-05986-5*, Pub. by Turtleback) Demco.

— Taran Wanderer. (Chronicles of Prydain Ser.). 272p. (J). (gr. k-6). 1969. pap. 5.99 (*0-440-48483-9*, YB BDD) BDD Bks Young Read.

— Taran Wanderer. LC 67-10230. (Chronicles of Prydain Ser.). 256p. (J). (gr. 4-6). 1995. 16.95 (*0-8050-1113-7*, Bks Young Read) H Holt & Co.

— Taran Wanderer. LC 98-40904. (Chronicles of Prydain Ser.). 222p. (J). (gr. 3-7). 1999. 18.95 (*0-8050-6134-7*) H Holt & Co.

— Taran Wanderer. (Chronicles of Prydain Ser.). (J). 1967. 10.09 (*0-606-00482-3*, Pub. by Turtleback) Demco.

— Time Cat: The Remarkable Journeys of Jason & Gareth. 206p. (J). (gr. 4-7). 1996. pap. 4.99 (*0-14-037827-8*, PuffinBks) Peng Put Young Read.

— Time Cat: The Remarkable Journeys of Jason & Gareth. LC 95-43015. 1996. 9.09 (*0-606-09972-7*, Pub. by Turtleback) Demco.

— Town Cats & Other Tales. 128p. (J). (gr. 3-7). 1998. pap. 4.99 (*0-14-130122-8*, PuffinBks) Peng Put Young Read.

— Westmark. 192p. (YA). (gr. 5-9). 1982. mass mkt. 4.50 (*0-440-99731-3*, LLL BDD) BDD Bks Young Read.

— Westmark. 1981. 9.60 (*0-606-00638-9*, Pub. by Turtleback) Demco.

— Wizard in a Tree. 144p. 1998. pap. 4.99 (*0-14-038801-X*) Viking Penguin.

— The Wizard in the Tree. (J). 1998. 9.60 (*0-606-13070-5*, Pub. by Turtleback) Demco.

Alexander, Lloyd, jt. auth. see Mouseworks Staff.

Alexander, Lloyd, tr. see Eluard, Paul.

Alexander, Lloyd, tr. see Sartre, Jean-Paul.

Alexander, Lorene, et al, eds. The Heritage of Pickens County, Alabama. (Heritage of Alabama Ser.: No. 54). (Illus.). 280p. 1999. 55.00 (*1-891647-30-X*) Herit Pub Consult.

Alexander, Lorraine, tr. see Barteve, Reine.

Alexander, Lorraine, tr. see Tansi, Sony L.

Alexander, Louis. Beyond the Facts: A Guide to the Art of Feature Writing. 2nd fac. ed. LC 82-1021. (Illus.). 330p. pap. 102.30 (*0-7837-7421-4*, 204721600006) Bks Demand.

Alexander, Loveday, ed. Images of Empire. (JSOTS Ser.: Vol. 122). 297p. (C). 1991. 85.00 (*1-85075-312-1*, Pub. by Sheffield Acad) CUP Services.

Alexander, Lydia. Wearing Purple. LC 98-24183. 224p. 1998. pap. 12.00 (*0-609-80174-0*, Crown) Crown Pub Group.

Alexander, Lyn. Make Doll Shoes: Workbook One, Vol. I. LC 90-179616. Vol. I. (Illus.). 40p. (C). 1985. pap. text 5.95 (*0-87588-335-4*) Hobby Hse.

— Make Doll Shoes: Workbook Two, Vol. II. Vol. II. (Illus.). 40p. (C). 1985. pap. text 5.95 (*0-87588-336-2*) Hobby Hse.

Alexander, Lynn. Pattern Designing for Dressmakers. (Illus.). 104p. 1998. pap. 14.95 (*0-87588-536-5*, 5553) Hobby Hse.

Alexander, Lynn M., jt. ed. see Winn, Sharon A.

Alexander, M. Where Does the Sky End, Grandpa? LC 90-36793. (Illus.). 32p. (J). (ps-3). 1992. 12.95 (*0-15-295603-4*, Harcourt Child Bks) Harcourt.

Alexander, M. David, jt. auth. see Alexander, Kern.

Alexander, M. E., jt. auth. see Fielding, P. M.

Alexander, M. Jacqui, et al, eds. Third Wave: Feminist Perspectives on Racism. 1997. pap. 19.95 (*0-913175-25-0*); lib. bdg. 39.95 (*0-913175-26-9*) Kitchen Table.

Alexander, M. Jacqui & Mohanty, Chandra T., eds. Feminist Genealogies, Colonial Legacies, Democratic Futures. (Thinking Gender Ser.). 352p. 1996. pap. 23.99 (*0-415-91212-1*) Routledge.

— Feminist Genealogies, Colonial Legacies, Democratic Futures. (Thinking Gender Ser.). 352p. (C). (gr. 13 up). 1996. 75.00 (*0-415-91211-3*) Routledge.

Alexander, M. S. Occupational Health & Safety Act Legislation Manual. 1995. ring bd. write for info. (*0-409-01063-4*, MICHIE) LEXIS Pub.

Alexander, Marc. Royal Murder LC 80-480087. 1978. 4.95 (*0-584-10446-4*) F Muller.

— To Anger the Devil. (Illus.). 210p. pap. 12.95 (*0-8464-4301-5*) Beekman Pubs.

Alexander, Margaret F., et al, eds. Nursing Practice: Hospital & Home; the Adult. LC 94-16626. 1995. pap. text 40.00 (*0-443-04338-8*) Church.

Alexander, Margaret W., jt. auth. see Biggers, John.

Alexander, Margo. College Algebra Workbook: Technology in the Classroom. 116p. (C). 1997. per. 27.95 (*0-7872-4316-7*, 41431601) Kendall-Hunt.

Alexander, Marianne. The Asteroid Midas (Were You Born to Be Rich?) (Illus.). 51p. 1997. pap. 5.00 (*1-888760-10-9*) Pandora Pubng.

— The Centaur Pholus. Creamer, Kitty, ed. (Illus.). 1996. 25.00 (*1-888760-01-X*) Pandora Pubng.

Alexander, Marianne, compiled by. The 1998 Asteroid Ephemeris - Zodiacal Order. annuals 300p. (Orig.). 1997. pap. write for info. (*1-888760-07-9*) Pandora Pubng.

— The 1998 Asteroid Ephemeris - Alphabetical Order. annuals 300p. 1997. pap. 25.00 (*1-888760-06-0*) Pandora Pubng.

***Alexander, Marianne, ed.** Asteroid Ephemeris. 372p. 1999. 25.00 (*1-888760-13-3*) Pandora Pubng.

***Alexander, Marianne, ed.** 2000 Asteroid Ephemeris - Alphabetical Order. 372p. 1999. pap. 25.00 (*1-888760-12-5*) Pandora Pubng.

Alexander, Marilyn B. & Preston, James. We Were Baptized Too: Claiming God's Grace for Lesbians & Gays. LC 95-46241. 176p. 1996. pap. 17.00 (*0-664-25628-7*) Westminster John Knox.

Alexander, Mark. Misdirection: The Secret to Successful Magic. unabridged ed. Fife, Bruce, ed. LC 98-49941. (Illus.). 64p. 1998. pap. 10.00 (*0-941599-36-1*, Pub. by Piccadilly Bks) Empire Pub Srvs.

Alexander, Martha. And My Mean Old Mother Will Be Sorry, Blackboard Bear. LC 98-14047. (Illus.). 32p. (J). (ps-1). 2000. 10.99 (*0-7636-0668-5*) Candlewick Pr.

— Blackboard Bear. LC 98-53913. (Illus.). 32p. (J). (ps-1). 1999. 12.99 (*0-7636-0667-7*) Candlewick Pr.

— La Bota de Lalo (Billy's Boot) Segovia, Francisco, tr. (SPA., Illus.). (J). 1993. 5.99 (*968-16-4200-7*, Pub. by Fondo) Continental Bk.

— Buenas Noches, Lola (Good Night, Lilly) Segovia, Francisco, tr. (SPA., Illus.). (J). 1993. 5.99 (*968-16-4202-3*, Pub. by Fondo) Continental Bk.

— How My Library Grew, By Dinah. (Illus.). 32p. (J). (gr. k-5). 1983. 18.00 (*0-8242-0679-7*) Wilson.

— Lola y Lalo (Lilly & Billy) Segovia, Francisco, tr. (SPA., Illus.). (J). 1993. 5.99 (*968-16-4201-5*, Pub. by Fondo) Continental Bk.

— Out, Out, Out. LC 68-15251. (Illus.). (J). (gr. k-3). 1968. lib. bdg. 6.95 (*0-685-01457-6*, Dial Yng Read) Peng Put Young Read.

— Poems & Prayers for the Very Young. (Illus.). (J). (ps-1). 1974. pap. 3.25 (*0-394-82705-8*, Pub. by Random Bks Yng Read) Random.

— Three Magic Flip Books. Incl. Magic Box. 1984. Magic Hat. 1984. Magic Picture. 1984. (Illus.). (J). (ps). 1984. 5.95 (*0-8037-0051-2*, 0578-170, Dial Yng Read) Peng Put Young Read.

— When a New Baby Comes. (Illus.). 1992. pap. 4.99 (*0-14-054723-1*) NAL.

— You're a Genius: Blackboard Bear. (J). 1997. 9.19 (*0-606-12850-6*, Pub. by Turtleback) Demco.

— You're a Genius, Blackboard Bear. LC 94-11060. (Illus.). (J). (ps-3). 1995. 12.95 (*1-56402-238-2*) Candlewick Pr.

— You're a Genius, Blackboard Bear. LC 94-11060. (Illus.). 32p. (J). (ps-1). 1997. reprint ed. pap. 3.99 (*0-7636-0366-X*) Candlewick Pr.

Alexander, Martha. A You're Adorable. LC 93-931. 22p. (J). (ps). 1998. bds. 6.99 (*0-7636-0674-X*) Candlewick Pr.

Alexander, Martha, jt. auth. see Ashforth, Camila.

***Alexander, Martha G.** I Sure Am Glad to See You, Blackboard Bear. 2nd ed. LC 00-29754. (Illus.). (J). 2001. write for info. (*0-7636-0669-3*) Candlewick Press.

Alexander, Martha G. When the New Baby Comes, I'm Moving Out. (J). 1979. 9.19 (*0-606-00648-6*, Pub. by Turtleback) Demco.

Alexander, Martin. Biodegradation & Bioremediation. 2nd ed. LC 98-89646. (Illus.). 14p. (C). 1999. text 59.95 (*0-12-049861-8*) Acad Pr.

— Introduction to Soil Microbiology. 2nd ed. LC 90-5047. 480p. (C). 1991. reprint ed. lib. bdg. 69.50 (*0-89464-512-9*) Krieger.

Alexander, Martin, ed. Biological Nitrogen Fixation: Ecology, Technology & Physiology. LC 83-3378. 258p. 1984. 75.00 (*0-306-41632-8*, Plenum Trade) Perseus Pubng.

Alexander, Martin S. The Republic in Danger: General Maurice Gamelin & the Politics of French Defence, 1933-1940. 587p. (C). 1993. text 95.00 (*0-521-37234-8*) Cambridge U Pr.

Alexander, Martin S., ed. French History since Napoleon. 432p. 1999. 75.00 (*0-340-67732-5*, Pub. by E A); pap. 24.95 (*0-340-67731-7*, Pub. by E A) OUP.

— Knowing Your Friends: Intelligence Inside Alliances & Coalitions from 1914 to the Cold War. LC 97-51346. (Studies in Intelligence). 336p. 1998. text 54.50 (*0-7146-4879-5*, Pub. by F Cass Pubs); pap. text 22.50 (*0-7146-4433-1*, Pub. by F Cass Pubs) Intl Spec Bk.

Alexander, Mary, jt. auth. see Hein, George E.

Alexander, Matthew. More Surrey Tales. 96p. 1987. 40.00 (*0-905392-61-2*) St Mut.

— Tales of Old Surrey. 96p. 1987. 30.00 (*0-905392-41-8*) St Mut.

Alexander, Maxine, et al, eds. American Heretic: Portrait of Jim Dombrowski, Artist & Activist. (Southern Exposure Ser.). (Illus.). 80p. (Orig.). (C). 1982. pap. 3.00 (*0-943810-71-X*) Inst Southern Studies.

— The Chinese: 100 Years in the South. (Southern Exposure Ser.). (Illus.). 64p. (Orig.). (C). 1984. pap. 4.00 (*0-943810-27-2*) Inst Southern Studies.

— Neighbors: "It Seems to Help Me Bear It Better When She Knows about It." (Southern Exposure Ser.). (Illus.). 72p. (Orig.). (C). 1983. pap. 3.00 (*0-943810-69-8*) Inst Southern Studies.

— Not No Easy Business: Interviews with Prostitutes. (Southern Exposure Ser.). (Illus.). 72p. (Orig.). (C). 1983. pap. 4.00 (*0-943810-68-X*) Inst Southern Studies.

— The Poisoning of Louisiana. (Southern Exposure Ser.). (Illus.). 72p. (Orig.). (C). 1984. pap. 4.00 (*0-943810-28-0*) Inst Southern Studies.

— Prevailing Voices: Stories of Triumph & Survival. (Southern Exposure Ser.). (Illus.). (Orig.). (C). 1982. pap. 3.00 (*0-943810-70-1*) Inst Southern Studies.

— The Smoke Ring: Politics & Tobacco in the Third World. (Southern Exposure Ser.). (Illus.). 64p. (Orig.). (C). 1984. pap. 4.00 (*0-943810-26-4*) Inst Southern Studies.

Alexander, Meena. Fault Lines. LC 92-4666. (Illus.). 240p. 1993. 35.00 (*1-55861-058-8*); pap. 12.95 (*1-55861-059-6*) Feminist Pr.

— Manhattan Music. rev. ed. LC 96-53344. (Illus.). 256p. (Orig.). 1997. reprint ed. pap. 14.95 (*1-56279-092-7*) Mercury Hse Inc.

— Nampally Road. LC 90-5849. 128p. 1991. 15.95 (*0-916515-82-6*); pap. 9.95 (*0-916515-90-7*) Mercury Hse Inc.

— Night Scene: The Garden. 32p. 1992. pap. 3.00 (*0-87376-074-3*) Red Dust.

— River & Bridge. 112p. 1996. pap. 11.95 (*0-920661-56-4*, Pub. by TSAR Pubns) LPC InBook.

— The Shock of Arrival: Reflections on Postcolonial Experience. 224p. 1996. 40.00 (*0-89608-546-5*) South End Pr.

— The Shock of Arrival: Reflections on Postcolonial Experience. LC 96-15058. 224p. 1996. pap. 15.00 (*0-89608-545-7*) South End Pr.

— Women in Romanticism: Mary Wollstonecraft, Dorothy Wordsworth, & Mary Shelley. 189p. (C). 1989. pap. 19.00 (*0-389-20885-X*); text 52.50 (*0-389-20884-1*) B&N Imports.

Alexander, Meg. His Lordship's Dilemma. (Historical Ser.: No. 7). 1998. pap. 4.99 (*0-373-30316-5*, 1-30316-3) Harlequin Bks.

— His Lordship's Dilemma. large type ed. (Mills & Boon Large Print Ser.). 350p. 1997. 23.99 (*0-263-15087-9*) Ulverscroft.

— The Last Enchantment. large type ed. 350p. 1995. 23.99 (*0-263-14423-2*) Ulverscroft.

— The Love Child. 1999. per. 4.99 (*0-373-30336-X*) Harlequin Bks.

***Alexander, Meg.** The Merry Gentleman. 1999. per. 4.99 (*0-373-30340-8*) Harlequin Bks.

Alexander, Meg. Miranda's Masquerade. large type ed. (Mills & Boon Large Print Ser.). 350p. 1997. 23.99 (*0-263-15239-1*, Pub. by Mills & Boon) Ulverscroft.

— The Sweet Cheat. large type ed. 350p. 1996. 23.99 (*0-263-14688-X*, Pub. by Mills & Boon) Ulverscroft.

Alexander, Melinda, jt. auth. see Hopkins, John A.

***Alexander, Meredith.** The It Girl's Guide to Video: Sex & Style on the Silver Screen. LC 99-25311. (Illus.). 128p. 1999. pap. 10.95 (*0-14-028594-6*) Studio Bks.

Alexander, Merle. God! You Are Incredible! LC 97-92680. 140p. 1997. pap. 12.95 (*0-9661171-0-7*) Majesty Publns.

Alexander, Michael. Az "En" Cimszavak a Vilaghoz es az Emberhez. Makkai, Adam, tr. from FRE. viii, 88p. (Orig.). 1987. pap. 18.00 (*0-933104-22-7*) Jupiter Pr.

— The Earlist English Poems: Third Revised Edition. 3rd rev. ed. (Illus.). 176p. 1991. pap. 11.95 (*0-14-044594-3*) Viking Penguin.

***Alexander, Michael.** A History of English Literature. LC 00-42201. (Foundations Ser.). (C). 2000. pap. write for info. (*0-333-67226-7*) St Martin.

— Net Security Your Digital Doberman: Sure-Fire Strategies for Wired Businesses. (Illus.). 282p. 1999. reprint ed. pap. text 25.00 (*0-7881-6538-0*) DIANE Pub.

Alexander, Michael. Old English Riddles: From the Exeter Book. 72p. 1984. pap. 14.95 (*0-85646-070-2*, Pub. by Anvil Press) Dufour.

***Alexander, Michael.** The Poetic Achievement of Ezra Pound. 256p. 1998. pap. 22.50 (*0-7486-0981-4*, Pub. by Edinburgh U Pr) Col U Pr.

Alexander, Michael, ed. Beowulf. 272p. (Orig.). 1995. pap. 12.95 (*0-14-043377-5*, Penguin Classics) Viking Penguin.

Alexander, Michael, et al, eds. St. Martin's Anthologies of English Literature, 5 vols., Set. 2985p. 1991. text 85.00 (*0-312-04474-7*) St Martin.

Alexander, Michael, tr. Beowulf. (Classics Ser.). 176p. (Orig.). 1973. pap. 8.95 (*0-14-044268-5*, Penguin Classics) Viking Penguin.

Alexander, Michael, ed. see Chaucer, Geoffrey.

Alexander, Michael A., jt. auth. see Molnar, Gabriella.

An Asterisk (*) at the beginning of an entry indicates that the title is appearing for the first time.

A

A

Alexander, Michael C. Trials in the Late Roman Republic, 149 B. C. to 50 B. C. (Phoenix Supplementary Volumes Ser.). 224p. 1990. text 47.50 (0-8020-5787-X) U of Toronto Pr.

Alexander, Michael O., jt. auth. see Griffin, Paul A.

Alexander, Michael V. The Growth of English Education, 1348-1648: A Social & Cultural History. LC 89-37531. 280p. 1990. lib. bdg. 45.00 (0-271-00687-0) Pa St U Pr.

— Three Crises in Early English History: Personalities & Politics During the Norman Conquest, the Reign of King John, & the Wars of the Roses. LC 98-8367. 288p. 1998. 56.00 (0-7618-1187-7); pap. 36.00 (0-7618-1188-5) U Pr of Amer.

Alexander, Michele & Long, Jeannie. How to Lose a Guy in 10 Days: The Universal Don'ts of Dating. LC 98-18348. (Illus.). 144p. 1998. pap. 6.99 (0-553-38007-9) Bantam.

Alexander, Milton J. A General Theory of Corporate Strategy & Business Policy. (Illus.). 196p. (C). 1994. 30.00 (0-912121-01-7) Univ Pubns AL.

Alexander-Moegerle, Gil. James Dobson's War on America. LC 96-50183. (Illus.). 306p. 1997. 25.95 (1-57392-122-X) Prometheus Bks.

Alexander, Morris. Israel & Me. (Illus.). 278p. 1977. 18.95 (0-87073-204-8) Schenkman Bks Inc.

Alexander-Mott, LeeAnn & Barry, D., eds. Understanding Eating Disorders: Anorexia Nervosa, Bulimia Nervosa, & Obesity. 275p. 1994. write for info. (1-56032-249-7) Taylor & Francis.

Alexander-Mott, LeeAnn & Lumsden, Barry D. Understanding Eating Disorders: Anorexia Nervosa, Bulimia Nervosa, & Obesity. LC 94-8719. 79.95 (1-56032-294-2); pap. 29.50 (1-56032-295-0) Taylor & Francis.

*Alexander, Myrna. After God's Heart: A Woman's Study on Loving & Obeying God from I Samuel. LC 99-58760. 160p. 2000. pap. 7.99 (1-57293-063-2) Discovery Hse Pubs.

Alexander, Myrna. With Him in Life's Struggles: A Woman's Study on the Faithfulness of God from Second Samuel. 128p. (Orig.). 1994. pap. 7.99 (0-929239-92-X) Discovery Hse Pubs.

— With Him in the Struggle: A Woman's Workshop on II Samuel. (Woman's Workshop Ser.). 128p. 1986. pap. 4.50 (0-310-37211-9, 10918P) Zondervan.

— A Woman of Wisdom: Lessons for Living from the Book of Proverbs. 128p. 1992. pap. 8.99 (0-929239-56-3) Discovery Hse Pubs.

— A Woman's Workshop on the Attributes of God: Behold Your God. 124p. 1978. mass mkt. 5.99 (0-310-37131-7, 10916P) Zondervan.

*Alexander, Nancy. Early Childhood Workshops That Work! The Essential Guide to Successful Training & Workshops. LC 00-35367. (Illus.). 392p. 2000. 29.95 (0-87659-215-9) Gryphon Hse.

Alexander, Nancy. Practicing Compassion for the Stranger. LC 86-63727. 1987. pap. 4.00 (0-87574-271-8) Pendle Hill.

Alexander, Nancy J. & Wentz, Anne C., eds. Idea to Product: The Process. 208p. 1996. 109.00 (0-387-94742-6) Spr-Verlag.

Alexander, Neville. Education & the Struggle for National Liberation in South Africa: Essays & Speeches by Neville Alexander, 1985-1989. LC 92-70643. 235p. 1992. reprint ed. 45.95 (0-86543-345-3); reprint ed. pap. 14.95 (0-86543-346-1) Africa World.

Alexander, Nicholas. International Retailing. LC 96-41659. 356p. 1997. pap. 58.95 (0-631-19722-2) Blackwell Pubs.

Alexander, Nicholas & Akehurst, Gary, eds. The Emergence of Modern Retailing, 1750-1950. LC 98-25283. 184p. 1999. 45.00 (0-7146-4922-8, Pub. by F Cass Pubs); pap. 22.50 (0-7146-4481-1, Pub. by F Cass Pubs) Intl Spec Bk.

Alexander, Nicholas, jt. ed. see Akehurst, Gary.

Alexander, Nina. Alison of Arabia. (Magic Attic Club Ser.). (Illus.). (J). (gr. 2-6). 1997. 12.95 (1-57513-087-4); pap. text 5.95 (1-57513-086-6) Magic Attic.

*Alexander, Nina. Alison Rides the Rapids. (Magic Attic Club Ser.). (Illus.). 75p. (J). (gr. 2-6). 1998. lib. bdg. 16.40 (1-57513-141-2) Magic Attic.

— Alison Rides the Rapids. Bodnar, Judit, ed. LC 98-27015. (Magic Attic Club Ser.). (Illus.). 80p. (J). (gr. 2-6). 1998. 12.95 (1-57513-122-6); pap. 5.95 (1-57513-121-8) Magic Attic.

Alexander, Nina. And the Winner Is.... (Full House Sisters Ser.: Vol. 3). 154p. (J). (gr. 1-5). 1999. per. 3.99 (0-671-04055-3) PB.

— April Fools! (Full House Michelle Ser.: Vol. 19). (J). (gr. 4-7). 1998. per. 3.99 (0-671-01729-2, Minstrel Bks) PB.

— The Case of the Haunted Camp. (New Adventures of Mary-Kate & Ashley Ser.). (Illus.). 85p. (J). (gr. 2-4). 1998. pap. 3.99 (0-590-29397-4) Scholastic Inc.

— The Case of the 202 Clues. (New Adventures of Mary-Kate & Ashley Ser.). (Illus.). 87p. (J). (gr. 2-4). 1998. pap. 3.99 (0-590-29307-9) Scholastic Inc.

— The Case of Thorn Mansion. (Adventures of Mary-Kate & Ashley Ser.). (J). (gr. 2-4). 1997. pap. 3.99 (0-590-88016-0) Scholastic Inc.

— He's the One. (Love Stories Ser.: N). 192p. (YA). (gr. 7-12). 1998. mass mkt. 3.99 (0-553-49250-0) BDD Bks Young Read.

*Alexander, Nina. Jane in a Land of Enchantment. (Magic Attic Club Ser.). (J). (gr. 2-6). 2001. 12.95 (1-57513-168-4); pap. 5.95 (1-57513-167-6) Magic Attic.

Alexander, Nina. Megan & the Borealis Butterfly. LC 98-50505. (Magic Attic Club Ser.). 80p. (J). (gr. 2-6). 1999. 5.95 (1-57513-152-8); 12.95 (1-57513-153-6) Magic Attic.

*Alexander, Nina. Megan & the Borealis Butterfly. (Magic Attic Club Ser.). 80p. (J). (gr. 2-6). 1999. lib. bdg. 16.40 (1-57513-154-4) Magic Attic.

— Playing for Keeps. (Love Stories Ser.). 192p. (YA). (gr. 7-12). 1999. mass mkt. 4.50 (0-553-49292-6) Bantam.

Alexander, Nina. Rose's Magic Touch. Korman, Susan, ed. LC 97-28008. (Magic Attic Club Ser.). (Illus.). 72p. (J). (gr. 2-6). 1997. 12.95 (1-57513-106-4) Magic Attic.

*Alexander, Nina. Tale of Two Alisons. (Magic Attic Club Ser.). (J). (gr. 2-6). 2001. 12.95 (1-57513-162-5); pap. 5.95 (1-57513-161-7) Magic Attic.

Alexander, Nina, jt. auth. see Scott, Kieran.

Alexander, Noble. I Will Die Free. LC 91-11308. 1991. pap. 9.99 (0-8163-1044-0) Pacific Pr Pub Assn.

Alexander, O. The St. John Genealogy: Descendants of Matthias of Dorchester, Massachusetts, 1634, of Windsor, Connecticut, 1640 (& Wethersfield & Norwalk) (Illus.). 639p. 1989. reprint ed. pap. 96.00 (0-8328-1107-6); reprint ed. lib. bdg. 104.00 (0-8328-1106-8) Higginson Bk Co.

Alexander of Aphrodisias. Ethical Problems. Sharples, R. W., tr. from GRE. (Ancient Commentators on Aristotle Ser.). 1990. text 47.50 (0-8014-2267-1) Cornell U Pr.

— On Aristotle's Metaphysics, No. 1. Dooley, W. E., tr. LC 88-47752. (Ancient Commentators on Aristotle Ser.). 192p. 1988. text 47.50 (0-8014-2235-3) Cornell U Pr.

— On Aristotle's "Metaphysics 5" Dooley, William E., tr. (Ancient Commentators on Aristotle Ser.). 232p. 1994. text 47.50 (0-8014-2969-2) Cornell U Pr.

— On Aristotle's "Metaphysics 4" Madigan, Arthur, tr. (Ancient Commentators on Aristotle Ser.). 208p. 1994. text 47.50 (0-8014-2977-3) Cornell U Pr.

— On Aristotle's Metaphysics 2&3. Dooley, William E. & Madigan, Arthur, trs. LC 91-41606. (Ancient Commentators on Aristotle Ser.). 224p. 1992. text 52.50 (0-8014-2740-1) Cornell U Pr.

— On Aristotle's "Meteorology 4" Lewis, Eric, tr. LC 95-37120. (Ancient Commentators on Aristotle Ser.). 1995. text 47.50 (0-8014-3225-1) Cornell U Pr.

— On Aristotle's "Prior Analytics", Vol. 1. Sorabji, Richard, ed. Mueller, Ian & Gould, Josiah, trs. LC 98-42203. (Ancient Commentators on Aristotle Ser.). 224p. 1998. 49.95 (0-8014-3618-4) Cornell U Pr.

— On Aristotle's "Prior Analytics", Vol. 2. Sorabji, Richard, ed. Mueller, Ian & Gould, Josiah, trs. (Ancient Commentators on Aristotle Ser.). 256p. 1998. 49.95 (0-8014-3617-6) Cornell U Pr.

— On Aristotle's "Prior Analytics 1. 1-7" Barnes, Jonathan et al, trs. from GRE. LC 91-55257. (Ancient Commentators on Aristotle Ser.). 272p. 1992. 49.95 (0-8014-2689-8) Cornell U Pr.

— Quaestiones 1.1 - 2.15. Sharples, R. W., tr. LC 91-21146. (Ancient Commentators on Aristotle Ser.). 192p. 1992. text 52.50 (0-8014-2714-2) Cornell U Pr.

— Quaestiones 2.16 - 3.15. Sharples, R. W., tr. (Ancient Commentators on Aristotle Ser.). 1994. text 45.00 (0-8014-3088-7) Cornell U Pr.

Alexander, OluFemi, ed. see Ray, Barbara L.

Alexander, Oscar W. Media in the 20th Century. (In the 20th Century Ser.). (Illus.). 192p. 1997. pap. 9.95 (0-912517-24-7) Bluewood Bks.

Alexander, P. Campaign Financing. 2000. 16.95 (0-19-504514-9) OUP.

— My Years with Indira Gandhi. (C). 1991. 18.00 (81-7094-087-7, Pub. by Vision) S Asia.

Alexander, P., et al, eds. A Laboratory Manual of Analytical Methods of Protein Chemistry (Including Polypeptides), Vols. 2-5. Incl. Vol. 3. Determination of the Size & Shape of Protein in Molecules. 1961. Vol. 4. Protein Analysis. 1965. write for info. (0-318-55172-1, Pub. by Pergamon Repr) Franklin.

Alexander, P. A. An Owner's Manual: For Becoming a Successful Human Being. 138p. 1996. per. 16.95 (0-7872-2225-9) Kendall-Hunt.

Alexander, P. C. Buddhism in Kerala. LC 78-72369. reprint ed. 37.50 (0-404-17215-6) AMS Pr.

— The Perils of Democracy. LC 95-901699. ix, 304p. 1995. 25.00 (81-7039-208-X, Pub. by Somaiya Publns) Nataraj Bks.

Alexander, Pagan, ed. see Andrews, Ted.

*Alexander, Pagyn. Dreamtime Magic. Haugen, Diane, ed. LC 00-100044. (Young Person's School of Magic & Mystery Ser.: Vol. 2). (Illus.). 224p. 2000. 17.95 (1-888767-38-3, Pub. by Dragonhawk Pubg) Partners Pubs Grp.

Alexander, Pamela. Commonwealth of Wings: An Ornithological Biography Based on the Life of John James Audubon. LC 90-50908. (Wesleyan Poetry Ser.). 72p. 1991. pap. 12.95 (0-8195-1193-5, Wesleyan Univ Pr); text 25.00 (0-8195-2191-4, Wesleyan Univ Pr) U Pr of New Eng.

— Inland. LC 96-51675. (Iowa Poetry Prize Ser.). 82p. (Orig.). 1997. pap. 10.95 (0-87745-582-1) U of Iowa Pr.

*Alexander, Pansy. Nail Art: The Nail Design Pack. 2000. pap. 19.95 (1-85868-825-6) Carlton Bks Ltd.

Alexander, Pat. Feast of Good Stories. 1997. 23.99 (0-7459-3853-1) Lion USA.

— God's Word for Me: Bible for Kids. (Illus.). 480p. (J). 1998. 14.99 (0-8054-1683-8) Broadman.

— Morning Has Broken: Stories & Poems for Easter. (Lion Book). 192p. (J). 1997. 15.99 (0-7459-3742-X, Lion) Chariot Victor.

— What a Wonderful World!: A Special Collection: Stories & Poems That Celebrate God's Creations, 1 vol. LC 98-51922. 1999. 19.99 (0-7459-4091-9) Lion USA.

Alexander, Pat, ed. The Lion Concise Bible Encyclopedia. large type ed. 716p. 1992. 29.95 (1-55905-103-5, Pub. by Clio Pr) HM.

— The Lion Encyclopedia of the Bible. 352p. 1978. 29.95 (0-88469-201-9) BMH Bks.

Alexander, Pat, jt. auth. see Alexander, David.

Alexander, Patricia A., ed. The Role of Knowledge in Learning & Instruction: A Special Issue of Educational Psychologist, Vol. 31, No. 2, 1996. 56p. 1996. pap. 20.00 (0-8058-9889-1) L Erlbaum Assocs.

Alexander, Patricia A., jt. ed. see Garner, Ruth.

*Alexander, Patrick H., ed. A Treasury of Humor. 464p. 2000. 24.95 (1-56563-457-8) Hendrickson MA.

*Alexander, Patrick H., et al, eds. The SBL Handbook of Style: For Ancient near Eastern, Biblical & Early Christian Studies. LC 99-46069. 280p. (C). 1999. 24.95 (1-56563-487-X) Hendrickson MA.

Alexander, Patrick H., ed. see Burgess, Stanley M. & McGee, Gary B.

Alexander, Patrick H., ed. see Carroll, John.

Alexander, Patrick H., ed. see Kurtz, John H.

Alexander, Patrick H., ed. see Pahl, John.

Alexander, Paul. Boulevard of Broken Dreams: The Life, Times & Legend of James Dean. (Illus.). 336p. 1997. pap. 13.95 (0-452-27840-6, Plume) Dutton Plume.

— Chains of Deceit. 224p. (Orig.). 1997. pap. text 9.95 (0-352-33206-9, Pub. by Virgin Bks) London Brdge.

— Empire. 1999. pap. 9.95 (0-14-012894-8, Viking); pap. 22.95 (0-670-83107-7) Viking Penguin.

*Alexander, Paul. The Final Restraint. 240p. 1999. mass mkt. 15.99 (0-352-33303-0) Virgin Pr.

— Rough Magic: A Biography of Sylvia Plath. LC 98-54914. (Illus.). 432p. 1999. reprint ed. mass mkt. 15.95 (0-306-80889-7, Pub. by Da Capo) HarpC.

Alexander, Paul. Salinger: A Biography. 352p. 1999. 24.95 (1-58063-080-4) Renaissance.

*Alexander, Paul. Salinger Biography. 352p. 2000. pap. 16.95 (1-58063-148-7) Renaissance.

Alexander, Paul. Sri Lankan Fisherman: Rural Capitalism & Peasant Society. 406p. (C). 1995. write for info. (0-614-06779-0) Sterling Pubs.

— Wrap Myself in a Rainbow Workbook. 100p. 1994. 9.95 (0-9642083-0-X) P Alexander.

Alexander, Paul B. Land Utilization in the Karst Region of Zgornja Pivka, Slovenia. LC 75-9151. 132p. 1967. 9.00 (0-686-28379-1) Studia Slovenica.

Alexander, Paul J. The Patriarch Nicephorus of Constantinople: Ecclesiastical Policy & Image Worship in the Byzantine Empire. LC 78-63177. (Heresies Ser.: No. II). reprint ed. 55.00 (0-404-16195-2) AMS Pr.

Alexander, Peter. Beginner's Guide to Computer Assisted Trading. LC 97-222573. (Illus.). 192p. 1997. pap. 29.95 (0-934380-37-6, 1116) Traders Pr.

*Alexander, Peter. Racializing Class Classifying. 1999. text 69.95 (0-312-22999-2) St Martin.

Alexander, Peter. Shakespeare's Life & Art. LC 78-25749. 247p. 1979. reprint ed. lib. bdg. 35.00 (0-313-20666-X, ALSA, Greenwood Pr) Greenwood.

*Alexander, Peter. Workers, War & the Origins of Apartheid: Labour & Politics in South Africa, 1939-48. LC 99-88370. 220p. 2000. text 44.95 (0-8214-1314-7, Ohio U Ctr Intl); pap. text 22.95 (0-8214-1315-5, Ohio U Ctr Intl) Ohio U Pr.

*Alexander, Peter, et al. Peter Alexander: In This Light. LC 98-40840. 1999. pap. 29.95 (0-917493-27-3) Orange Cnty Mus.

Alexander, Peter, jt. auth. see Weaton, Jack.

Alexander, Peter F. Alan Paton: A Biography. (Illus.). 536p. 1994. 35.00 (0-19-811237-8) OUP.

*Alexander, Peter F. Les Murray: A Life in Progress. (Illus.). 304p. 2000. 30.00 (0-374-11310-6) FS&G.

Alexander, Peter L. The Freshman Year. (C). 1988. pap. 39.95 (0-939067-15-3) Alexander Pub.

— How to Be Successful in Music Without Overpaying Your Dues. 105p. (C). 1987. pap. 19.95 (0-939067-04-8) Alexander Pub.

— How to Stay Booked a Year in Advance. 81p. (C). 1987. pap. 18.95 (0-939067-14-5) Alexander Pub.

— More Songwriting & Composing Techniques: Making Something Out of Nothing. (Illus.). 147p. (C). 1988. pap. text 19.95 (0-939067-80-3) Alexander Pub.

— Music Basics: An Easy to Understand Guide to Music Fundamentals. (Illus.). 114p. (C). 1988. pap. text 17.95 (0-939067-72-2) Alexander Pub.

Alexander, Peter L. & Rychner, Lorenz M. Korg DW 8000: Working Out with the Workhorse. (Illus.). 130p. (C). 1987. pap. text 19.95 (0-939067-25-0) Alexander Pub.

Alexander, Peter L., jt. auth. see Wheaton, Jack.

Alexander, Peter L., ed. see Burger, Jeff.

Alexander, Peter L., ed. see Carr, Beau & Rychner, Lorenz M.

Alexander, Peter L., ed. see Frankfurt, Scott & Rychner, Lorenz M.

Alexander, Peter L., ed. see Goetschius, Percy.

Alexander, Peter L., ed. see Goldfield, Paul, et al.

Alexander, Peter L., ed. see Maestas, Bobby.

Alexander, Peter L., ed. see Maestas, Bobby & Goldfield, Paul.

Alexander, Peter L., ed. see Rychner, Lorenz M.

Alexander, Peter L., ed. see Rychner, Lorenz M. & Mead, Charles.

Alexander, Peter L., ed. see Walker, Dan.

Alexander, Peter L., ed. see Walker, Dan & Verga, Jack.

Alexander, Philip. Hillel The Teacher Of Righteousness. 1999. pap. 8.95 (0-941037-75-4) D & F Scott.

Alexander, Philip & Vermes, Geza, eds. Qumran Cave 4 Vol. XIX: Serekh Ha-Yahad & Related Texts, 26. (Discoveries in the Judaean Desert Ser.: Vol. XXVI). (Illus.). 272p. 1998. text 120.00 (0-19-826981-1) OUP.

Alexander, Philip, tr. see Nowak, G. A.

Alexander, Philip S., ed. Textual Sources for the Study of Judaism. (Textual Sources for the Study of Religion Ser.). 208p. 1990. pap. text 17.95 (0-226-01297-2) U Ch Pr.

Alexander, Polly, jt. auth. see Choukas-Bradley, Melanie.

Alexander, R. McNeil. Optima for Animals. rev. ed. LC 96-12454. 1996. pap. 28.95 (0-691-02798-6, Pub. by Princeton U Pr) Cal Prin Full Svc.

Alexander, R. McNeill. Bones: The Unity of Form & Function. LC 94-3025. (Illus.). 224p. 1994. pap. 40.00 (0-02-583675-7, Maxwell Macmillan) Macmillan.

— The Dynamics of Dinosaurs & Other Extinct Giants. (Illus.). 224p. 1989. text 64.50 (0-231-06666-X) Col U Pr.

— Dynamics of Dinosaurs & Other Extinct Giants. 1991. pap. 17.50 (0-231-06667-8) Col U Pr.

— Energy for Animal Life. (Oxford Animal Biology Ser.). (Illus.). 176p. (C). 1999. text 75.00 (0-19-850053-X); pap. text 29.95 (0-19-850052-1) OUP.

— The Human Machine. LC 92-10517. (Illus.). 224p. (C). 1992. 41.00 (0-231-08066-2) Col U Pr.

Alexander, R. R. Paleozoic Epibionts. 116p. 1991. pap. text 108.00 (3-7186-5130-0, Harwood Acad Pubs) Gordon & Breach.

Alexander, R. S. Bonapartism & Revolutionary Tradition in France: The Federes of 1815. 336p. (C). 1991. text 69.95 (0-521-36112-5) Cambridge U Pr.

Alexander, R. Wayne, jt. ed. see Schlant, Robert C.

*Alexander, Raewyn. Concrete. LC 99-176362. 1998. write for info. (0-14-027377-8) Penguin Books.

Alexander, Ralph. Ezekiel. (Everyman's Bible Commentary Ser.). 160p. 1976. pap. 9.99 (0-8024-2026-5) Moody.

— Ezequiel. (Comentario Biblico Portavoz Ser.). Orig. Title: Ezekiel. (SPA.). 168p. 1979. pap. 6.99 (0-8254-1002-9, Edit Portavoz) Kregel.

— Physics Laboratory Manual. 3rd ed. 80p. (C). 1994. spiral bd. 16.95 (0-8403-9438-1) Kendall-Hunt.

Alexander, Randall C., jt. auth. see Greenswag, Louise R.

Alexander, Randall C., jt. ed. see Greenswag, Louise R.

Alexander, Randell C., jt. ed. see Greenswag, Louise R.

Alexander, Ray, jt. auth. see Yorke, Ivor.

Alexander, Rebecca. Alef Is Silent: A Hebrew Alphabet. (HEB., Illus.). 25p. (J). (gr. k-6). 1997. pap. 11.95 (0-9663356-0-0) Inksleeves.

Alexander, Richard, jt. auth. see Jones, Leo.

Alexander, Richard D. The Biology of Moral Systems. (Evolutionary Foundations of Human Behavior Ser.). 323p. (C). 1987. pap. text 27.95 (0-202-01174-7) Aldine de Gruyter.

Alexander, Richard D., jt. auth. see Otte, Daniel.

Alexander, Richard H. Vascular Access in the Cancer Patient. (Illus.). 256p. 1994. text 59.00 (0-397-51316-X) Lppncott W & W.

Alexander, Rinda J., jt. auth. see Wegner, Gail D.

*Alexander, Robert. The Anarchists in the Spanish Civil War, Vol. 2. 765p. 2000. pap. 34.50 (1-85756-412-X, Pub. by Janus Pubng) Paul & Co Pubs.

— The Anarchists in the Spanish Civil War, Vols. 1 709p. 2000. pap. 34.50 (1-85756-400-6, Pub. by Janus Pubng) Paul & Co Pubs.

Alexander, Robert. I Ain't Yo' Uncle: The New Jack Revisionist Uncle Tom's Cabin. 70p. 1996. pap. 5.60 (0-87129-647-0, I54) Dramatic Pub.

— Seeking God's Wisdom about Christian Homosexuality. 31p. 1993. write for info. (1-888258-00-4) Evangel Concern Wstrn.

— The Talking of Hands: Unpublished Writing by New Rivers Press Authors. LC 97-69844. 304p. 1998. pap. 19.95 (0-89823-199-X) New Rivers Pr.

— White Pine Sucker River: Collected Prose Poems. LC 91-61261. 82p. (Orig.). 1992. pap. 8.95 (0-89823-136-1) New Rivers Pr.

Alexander, Robert, et al, eds. The Party Train: A North American Collection of Prose Poetry. LC 95-69349. 400p. (Orig.). 1996. pap. 18.95 (0-89823-165-5) New Rivers Pr.

— The Talking of Hands: A Thirtieth Anniversary Celebration. LC 97-69844. 340p. 1998. 29.95 (0-89823-190-6) New Rivers Pr.

Alexander, Robert, et al. The Communist Tide in Latin America: A Selected Treatment. Herman, Donald L., ed. (Illus.). 215p. 1973. 10.00 (0-87959-072-6) U of Tex H Ransom Ctr.

*Alexander, Robert, et al. Plays from Woolly Mammoth. 1999. pap. 14.95 (0-88145-159-2) Broadway Play.

Alexander, Robert, jt. ed. see Elam, Harry J.

*Alexander, Robert C. Inventor of Stereo Sound: The Life & Works of Alan Dower Blumlein. LC 99-33677. 421p. 1999. text 56.95 (0-240-51577-3, Focal) Buttrwrth-Heinemann.

*Alexander, Robert Charles. Inventor of Stereo: The Life & Works of Alan Dower Blumlen. 448p. 2000. pap. 24.99 (0-240-51628-1, Focal) Buttrwrth-Heinemann.

Alexander, Robert J. The ABC Presidents: Conversations & Correspondence with the Presidents of Argentina, Brazil, & Chile. LC 92-3676. 336p. 1992. 65.00 (0-275-94110-8, C4110, Praeger Pubs) Greenwood.

— The Bolivarian Presidents: Conversations & Correspondence with Presidents of Bolivia, Peru, & Ecuador. LC 93-11892. 296p. 1994. 69.50 (0-275-94661-4, Praeger Pubs) Greenwood.

— Bolivia: Past, Present, & Future of Its Politics. Wesson, Robert, ed. LC 81-22661. (Politics in Latin America Ser.). 157p. 1982. 55.00 (0-275-90751-1, C0751, Praeger Pubs) Greenwood.

— International Maoism in the Developing World. LC 98-47813. 360p. 1999. 69.50 (0-275-96149-4, C6149, Praeger Pubs) Greenwood.

— International Trotskyism, 1929-1985: A Documented Analysis of the Movement. LC 90-38617. 1141p. 1991. text 178.00 (0-8223-0975-0) Duke.

— Presidents of Central America, Mexico, Cuba, & Hispaniola: Conversations & Correspondence. LC 95-6323. 280p. 1995. 65.00 (0-275-95278-9, Praeger Pubs) Greenwood.

— Presidents, Prime Ministers & Governors of the

An Asterisk (*) at the beginning of an entry indicates that the title is appearing for the first time.

English-Speaking Caribbean & Puerto Rico: Conversations & Correspondence. LC 96-33194. 304p. 1997. 69.50 (*0-275-95803-5*, Praeger Pubs) Greenwood.

— The Right Opposition: The Lovestoneites & the International Communist Opposition of the 1930's, 54. LC 80-1711. (Contributions in Political Science Ser.: No. 54). 342p. 1981. 59.95 (*0-313-22070-0*, AOP/, Greenwood Pr) Greenwood.

— Romulo Betancourt & the Transformation of Venezuela. LC 81-14684. 600p. (C). 1982. 49.95 (*0-87855-450-5*) Transaction Pubs.

— The Tragedy of Chile, 8. LC 77-91101. (Contributions in Political Science Ser.: No. 8). 509p. 1978. 79.50 (*0-313-20034-3*, ATC/, Greenwood Pr) Greenwood.

— Venezuela's Voice for Democracy: Conversations & Correspondence with Romulo Betancourt. LC 90-36176. 184p. 1990. 57.95 (*0-275-93728-3*, C3728, Praeger Pubs) Greenwood.

Alexander, Robert J., ed. Biographical Dictionary of Latin American & Caribbean Political Leaders. LC 87-17805. 519p. 1988. lib. bdg. 115.00 (*0-313-24353-0*, ADL/, Greenwood Pr) Greenwood.

— Political Parties of the Americas: Canada, Latin America, & the West Indies, 2 vols. LC 81-6952. (Greenwood Historical Encyclopedia of the World's Political Parties Ser.). (Illus.). 1274p. 1982. lib. bdg. 195.00 (*0-313-21474-3*, APA/) Greenwood.

— Political Parties of the Americas: Canada, Latin America, & the West Indies, 2 vols., Vol. 1. LC 81-6952. (Greenwood Historical Encyclopedia of the World's Political Parties Ser.). (Illus.). xxviii, 1274p. 1982. lib. bdg. 100.00 (*0-313-23753-0*, APA/01) Greenwood.

— Political Parties of the Americas: Canada, Latin America, & the West Indies, 2 vols., Vol. 2. LC 81-6952. (Greenwood Historical Encyclopedia of the World's Political Parties Ser.). (Illus.). xxviii, 1274p. 1982. lib. bdg. 100.00 (*0-313-23754-9*, APA/02) Greenwood.

Alexander, Robert L. The Architecture of Maximilian Godefrey. LC 74-6810. (Johns Hopkins Studies in Nineteenth-Century Architecture). (Illus.). 266p. reprint ed. pap. 82.50 (*0-8357-5725-0*, 202033100017) Bks Demand.

— The Sculpture & Sculptors of Yazilikaya. LC 84-40804. (Illus.). 168p. 1986. 39.50 (*0-87413-279-7*) U Delaware Pr.

Alexander, Robert R. Silvicultural Systems & Cutting Methods for Old-Growth Lodgepole Pine Forests in the Central & Southern Rocky Mountains. 40p. 1997. reprint ed. 11.00 (*0-89904-702-5*, Ecosystems Resrch); reprint ed. pap. 5.00 (*0-89904-703-3*, Ecosytems Resrch) Crumb Elbow Pub.

— Silvicultureal Systems & Cutting Methods for Old-Growth Spruce-Fir Forests in the Central & Southern Rocky Mountains. rev. ed. (Illus.). 40p. 1997. 11.00 (*0-89904-700-9*, Ecosytems Resrch); pap. 5.00 (*0-89904-701-7*, Ecosytems Resrch) Crumb Elbow Pub.

Alexander, Robert R., jt. auth. see Hess, Karl.

Alexander, Roberta, ed. Joining a Community of Readers: A Thematic Approach to Reading. LC 97-29538. (Illus.). 500p. (C). 1997. pap. text, student ed. 48.00 (*0-321-01181-3*) Addson-Wesley Educ.

***Alexander, Roberta & Lombardi, Jan.** A Community of Readers: A Thematic Approach to Reading. 2nd ed. LC 00-30497. 2001. write for info. (*0-321-04594-7*) Longman.

Alexander, Roberta & Lombardi, Jan. Joining a Community of Readers: A Thematic Approach to Reading. LC 97-29538. 1997. write for info. (*0-673-99610-7*) Longman.

Alexander, Roberta S. North Carolina Faces the Freedmen: Race Relations During Presidential Reconstruction, 1865-67. LC 84-28758. xvi, 238p. (C). 1985. text 38.95 (*0-8223-0628-X*) Duke.

Alexander-Roberts, Colleen. ADHD & Teens: A Parent's Guide to Making It Through the Tough Years. LC 95-23078. 208p. 1995. pap. 12.95 (*0-87833-899-3*) Taylor Pub.

— The ADHD Parenting Handbook: Practical Advice for Parents from Parents. 224p. 1994. pap. 12.95 (*0-87833-862-4*) Taylor Pub.

— The Essential Adoption Handbook. rev. ed. LC 93-7230. 256p. 1993. pap. 13.95 (*0-87833-840-3*) Taylor Pub.

Alexander-Roberts, Colleen. The Legal Adoption Guide: Safety Navigating the System. 208p. (Orig.). 1996. pap. 12.96 (*0-87833-933-7*) Taylor Pub.

Alexander-Roberts, Colleen & Snyder, Mark T. Does My Child Need a Therapist? LC 96-29588. 224p. (Orig.). 1997. pap. 12.95 (*0-87833-942-6*) Taylor Pub.

Alexander, Robin J. Growth & Decline. 1984. 57.95 (*0-275-91117-9*, C1117, Praeger Pubs) Greenwood.

Alexander, Rolf. Healing Power of the Mind: Practical Techniques for Health & Empowerment. LC 97-644. 128p. 1997. pap. 10.95 (*0-89281-729-1*, Heal Arts VT) Inner Tradit.

***Alexander, Rolf.** El Poder Curativo de la Mente (The Healing Power of the Mind) Practical Techniques for Health & Empowerment. (SPA.). 128p. 2000. pap. 10.95 (*0-89281-590-6*, Inner Trad Espanol) Inner Tradit.

Alexander, Ron. Metropolitan Diary: The Best of the New York Times Column. LC 97-7061. (Illus.). 256p. 1997. 20.00 (*0-688-14889-1*, Wm Morrow) Morrow Avon.

***Alexander, Ronald.** The Final Audit & Other Stories. LC 99-91653. 200p. 2000. pap. 12.95 (*0-9676003-1-6*) Hollyridge Pr.

Alexander, Ronald. Grand Prize. 1955. pap. 5.25 (*0-8222-0472-X*) Dramatists Play.

— Holiday for Lovers. 1957. pap. 5.25 (*0-8222-0525-4*) Dramatists Play.

— Nobody Loves an Albatross. 1964. pap. 5.25 (*0-8222-0830-X*) Dramatists Play.

— Time & Ginger. 1980. pap. 5.25 (*0-8222-1151-3*) Dramatists Play.

— Time Out for Ginger. 1953. pap. 3.25 (*0-8222-1152-1*) Dramatists Play.

Alexander, Ronald & Savino, Richard, eds. Francesca Caccini: The Secular Songs from Il Libro Primo delle Musiche, 1618. 128p. 1997. pap. 24.95 (*0-253-21139-5*) Ind U Pr.

Alexander, Ronald, et al. After I Fall: Collected Poems. 64p. (Orig.). 1991. pap. 8.95 (*0-941017-22-2*) Bombshelter Pr.

Alexander, Ronald G. Self, Supervenience & Personal Identity. LC 97-73210. (Avebury Series in Philosophy). 176p. 1997. text 64.95 (*1-85972-603-8*, Pub. by Ashgate Pub) Ashgate Pub Co.

Alexander, Ronald R. West Virginia Tech: A History. 2nd ed. LC 92-61982. (Illus.). 188p. 1992. text 14.95 (*0-929521-66-8*) Pictorial Hist.

***Alexander, Ronelle.** Intensive Bulgarian: A Textbook & Reference Grammar. LC 99-43697. (BUL., Illus.). 2000. 24.95 (*0-299-16744-5*) U of Wis Pr.

— Intensive Bulgarian Vol. 2: A Textbook & Reference Grammer. (BUL & ENG.). 2000. pap. 24.95 (*0-299-16754-2*) U of Wis Pr.

Alexander, Ronelle. The Structure of Vasko Popa's Poetry. (UCLA Slavic Studies: Vol. 14). (Illus.). 196p. 1987. 24.95 (*0-89357-149-0*) Slavica.

Alexander, Ronni. Putting the Earth First: Alternatives to Nuclear Security in Pacific Island States. LC 94-22585. 1994. 10.00 (*1-880309-09-2*) S M Matsunaga.

Alexander, Rosemary. Top Notch Teacher, No. 2. 1991. pap. 12.95 (*0-590-49122-9*) Scholastic Inc.

Alexander, Rosemary & Batsto, Karena. A Handbook for Garden Designers. (Illus.). 136p. (Orig.). 1996. pap. 19.95 (*0-7063-7476-2*, Pub. by WrLock) Sterling.

Alexander, Rosie. Folie a Deux: An Experience of One-to-One Therapy. 190p. (C). 1995. 45.00 (*1-85343-316-0*, Pub. by Free Assoc Bks) NYU Pr.

— Folie a Deux: An Experience of One-to-One Therapy. (C). 1995. pap. 24.95 (*1-85343-317-9*, Pub. by Free Assoc Bks) NYU Pr.

Alexander, Ross, jt. auth. see Steve, Darnall.

Alexander, Roy. Commonsense Time Management. (AMA Worksmart Ser.). 120p. (Orig.). 1992. pap. 10.95 (*0-8144-7791-7*) AMACOM.

— The Cruise of the Raider Wolf. (War & Warriors Ser.). 270p. 1991. 12.95 (*0-939482-36-3*, 0168, Noontide Pr) Legion Survival.

— Meet Your Planets: Fun with Astrology. LC 97-3512. (Illus.). 240p. (Orig.). 1997. pap. 12.95 (*1-56718-017-5*) Llewellyn Pubns.

Alexander, Roy & Millington, Andrew C. Vegetation Mapping: From Patch to Planet. LC 99-39850. 350p. 2000. 110.00 (*0-471-96592-8*) Wiley.

Alexander, Roy, jt. auth. see Roth, Charles B.

***Alexander, Rudolph, Jr.** Race & Justice. 137p. 2000. lib. bdg. 49.00 (*1-56072-809-4*) Nova Sci Pubs.

Alexander, Russell C. I Thought of It First. (Illus.). (Orig.). 1980. pap. write for info. (*1-877782-09-2*) MGM & Assocs.

Alexander, Ruth B. Number Jugglers: Math Game Book & Math Game Cards. LC 98-16542. 64p. 1998. pap. 12.95 (*0-7611-0882-3*) Workman Pub.

Alexander, Ruth M. The Girl Problem: Female Sexual Delinquency in New York, 1900-1930. (Illus.). 232p. 1995. text 39.95 (*0-8014-2821-1*) Cornell U Pr.

— The Girl Problem: Female Sexual Delinquency in New York, 1900-1930. (Illus.). 232p. (-k). 1998. pap. text 16.95 (*0-8014-8577-0*) Cornell U Pr.

Alexander, Ruth M., jt. auth. see Norton, Mary B.

Alexander, S. The Basis of Realism. (Studies in Philosophy: No. 4). 1972. reprint ed. pap. 39.95 (*0-8383-0110-X*) M S G Haskell Hse.

Alexander, S. L. Covering the Courts: A Handbook for Journalists. LC 98-47365. 200p. 1999. 49.00 (*0-7618-1296-2*); pap. 29.50 (*0-7618-1297-0*) U Pr of Amer.

Alexander, S. T. Adaptive Signal Processing. (Texts & Monographs in Computer Science). (Illus.). 185p. 1986. 79.95 (*0-387-96380-4*) Spr-Verlag.

Alexander, Sally. Becoming a Woman: And Other Essays in 19th & 20th Century Feminist History. 318p. (C). 1995. text 47.50 (*0-8147-0635-5*); pap. text 19.00 (*0-8147-0636-3*) NYU Pr.

***Alexander, Sally.** Do You Remember the Color Blue? The Questions Children Ask about Being Blind. LC 99-34130. (Illus.). 48p. (J). (gr. 4-7). 2000. 15.99 (*0-670-88043-4*, Viking Child) Peng Put Young Read.

Alexander, Sally. Women's Fabian Tracts. (Women's Source Library). 512p. 1989. 75.00 (*0-415-01244-9*) Routledge.

Alexander, Sally H. Taking Hold: My Journey into Blindness. LC 94-12302. 128p. (J). 1994. mass mkt. 14.95 (*0-02-700402-3*, Mac Bks Young Read) S&S Childrens.

Alexander, Samuel. Locke: 1908 Edition. (Key Texts Ser.). 102p. 1996. reprint ed. pap. 19.95 (*1-85506-181-3*) Bks Intl VA.

— Philosophical & Literary Pieces. LC 70-93313. (Essay Index Reprint Ser.). 1977. 26.95 (*0-8369-1269-1*) Ayer.

Alexander, Sandra, et al. The Freshman Year of Studies: A Guidebook. 140p. 1996. pap. text, per. 17.95 (*0-7872-2657-2*) Kendall-Hunt.

Alexander, Sandy. Franchising & You. (Illus.). 1970. pap. 5.95 (*0-87505-306-8*) Borden.

Alexander, Sandy, jt. auth. see Alexander, Clifton J.

Alexander, S.B. Optical Communication Receiver Design. (Telecommunications Ser.: No. 37). 328p. 1997. 48.00 (*0-85296-900-7*, TE037) INSPEC Inc.

Alexander, Scott. Advanced Rhinocerology. 21st ed. LC 81-51912. (Illus.). 128p. (Orig.). 1995. pap. 7.95 (*0-937382-01-9*) Rhinos Pr.

— Rhinoceros Success. 62nd ed. LC 80-51648. (Illus.). 123p. (Orig.). 1996. pap. 7.95 (*0-937382-00-0*) Rhinos Pr.

Alexander, Scott, ed. Salted with Fire: Unitarian Universalist Strategies for Sharing Faith & Growing Congregations. LC 94-40201. 272p. 1994. pap. 18.00 (*1-55896-289-1*, Skinner Hse Bks) Unitarian Univ.

Alexander, Scott & Karaszewski, Larry. Ed Wood. (Illus.). 160p. (Orig.). 1995. pap. 13.95 (*0-571-17568-6*) Faber & Faber.

— Man on the Moon: The Shooting Script. LC 99-51519. (Shooting Script Ser.). (Illus.). 224p. 1999. pap. 16.95 (*1-55704-400-7*, Pub. by Newmarket) Norton.

— The People vs. Larry Flynt: The Shooting Script. LC 96-31471. (Shooting Script Ser.). 1996. 24.95 (*1-55704-313-2*, Pub. by Newmarket) Norton.

— The People vs. Larry Flynt: The Shooting Script. LC 96-31471. (Illus.). 208p. 1996. pap. 15.95 (*1-55704-305-1*, Pub. by Newmarket) Norton.

Alexander, Scott R. Rhinocerotic Relativity. 15th ed. LC 83-60933. (Illus.). 120p. (Orig.). 1995. pap. 7.95 (*0-937382-02-7*) Rhinos Pr.

Alexander, Scott W. The Relational Pulpit: Closing the Gap Between Preacher & Pew. LC 93-15201. 1993. 14.00 (*1-55896-309-X*) Unitarian Univ.

Alexander, Scott W., ed. Everyday Spiritual Practice: Simple Pathways for Enriching Your Life. LC 98-50320. 272p. 1999. pap. 16.00 (*1-55896-375-8*, 5666, Skinner Hse Bks) Unitarian Univ.

— The Welcoming Congregation: Resources for Affirming Gay, Lesbian & Bisexual Persons. 164p. 1993. pap. 25.00 (*1-55896-190-9*) Unitarian Univ.

Alexander, Scott W., ed. see Blumenfeld, Warren J.

Alexander, Shana. The Astonishing Elephant. LC 99-50038. 304p. 2000. 25.95 (*0-679-45660-0*) Random.

— Happy Days: My Mother, My Father, My Sister & Me. LC 95-36398. (Illus.). 352p. 1995. 27.50 (*0-385-41815-9*) Doubleday.

***Alexander, Shana.** The Pizza Connection: Lawyers, Money, Drugs, Mafia. (Illus.). 442p. 1999. reprint ed. text 20.00 (*0-7881-6836-3*) DIANE Pub.

Alexander, Sharon, ed. see Samaniego, Fabian A., et al.

Alexander, Sharon K. From the Strawberry Patch. (Die-Cut Cookbooks Ser.: No. 1). (Illus.). 1982. pap. 12.95 (*0-9608126-0-1*) ABC Enterprises.

Alexander, Sharon K. & Fairbairn, Kay. All American Apple Cookbook. LC 82-70679. (Die-Cut Cookbooks Ser.: No. 2). (Illus.). 105p. 1982. pap. text 12.95 (*0-9608126-1-X*) ABC Enterprises.

Alexander, Sherry. The Home Day-Care Handbook: A Complete Guide for Establishing Your Own Day-Care Home. LC 86-27184. 197p. 1987. text 34.95 (*0-89885-344-3*, Kluwer Acad Hman Sci); pap. text 19.95 (*0-89885-365-6*, Kluwer Acad Hman Sci) Kluwer Academic.

Alexander, Shoshana. In Praise of Single Parents: Embracing the Challenge. 416p. 1994. pap. 13.95 (*0-395-66991-X*) HM.

— Women's Ventures, Women's Visions: 29 Inspiring Stories from Women Who Started Their Own Business. LC 97-22531. (Illus.). 217p. (Orig.). 1997. pap. 14.95 (*0-89594-823-0*) Crossing Pr.

Alexander, Shoshana, ed. see Marks, Carolyna.

***Alexander, Sibylle.** Told by the Peat Fire. (Storytelling Ser.). (Illus.). 128p. 1999. pap. write for info. (*1-869890-23-X*, Pub. by Hawthorn Press) Anthroposophic.

Alexander, Sidney. Marc Chagall: An Intimate Biography. (Illus.). 526p. 1994. pap. 16.95 (*1-56924-980-6*) Marlowe & Co.

Alexander, Sidney, ed. & tr. see Buonarroti, Michelangelo.

Alexander, Sidney, tr. see Guicciardini, Francesco.

Alexander, Sidney, tr. see Horace.

Alexander, Sidney S., et al. Five Monographs on Business Income. LC 73-84377. 1973. reprint ed. text 30.00 (*0-914348-00-0*) Scholars Bk.

Alexander, Sidney S., jt. ed. see Hammond, Paul Y.

***Alexander, Simone A. James.** Mother Imagery in the Novels of Afro-Caribbean Women. 224p. 2001. 32.50 (*0-8262-1309-X*) U of Mo Pr.

Alexander, Skye. Hidden Agenda. LC 97-93562. (Magical Mystery Ser.). 260p. (Orig.). 1997. pap. 9.95 (*0-9657717-4-1*) Mojo Pub.

***Alexander, Skye.** Magickal Astrology: Understanding Your Place in the Cosmos. 224p. 2000. pap. 12.99 (*1-56414-479-8*, New Page Bks) Career Pr Inc.

Alexander, Skye. Planets in Signs. Ren, Marah & Lockhart, Julie, eds. LC 87-63416. 272p. 1988. pap. 18.95 (*0-914918-79-6*, Whitford) Schiffer.

Alexander, Skye, ed. see Goldsmith, Martin.

Alexander, Skye, ed. see Morwyn.

Alexander, Skye, ed. see Scott, Gini G.

Alexander, Skye, ed. see Steiger, Brad.

Alexander, Stacy. Legal Education for the 21st Century. King, Donald B., ed. LC 98-38655. xxviii, 585p. 1999. 79.95 (*0-8377-0784-6*, 322350, Rothman) W S Hein.

Alexander, Stella. The Triple Myth. 1987. text 55.50 (*0-88033-122-4*, EE1224, Pub. by East Eur Monographs) Col U Pr.

Alexander, Stephanie, ed. see Delegorgue, Adulphe.

Alexander, Stephen, jt. ed. see Rossomando, Edward F.

Alexander, Stephen B. Optical Communication Receiver Design. LC 95-46526. (Tutorial Texts in Optical Engineering Ser.: Vol. TT22). 1996. pap. 48.00 (*0-8194-2023-9*) SPIE.

Alexander, Steven R. Patient Care Flow Chart. 4th ed. (Illus.). 608p. (C). 1988. text 59.95 (*1-878487-27-2*, 4301M) Practice Mgmt Info.

Alexander, Sue. Ellsworth & Millicent. LC 92-7705. (Illus.). 28p. (J). (gr. k up). 1993. 14.95 (*0-88708-247-5*, Picture Book Studio) S&S Childrens.

***Alexander, Sue.** One More Time, Mama. LC 98-47937. (Illus.). 32p. (J). (ps-k). 1999. 15.95 (*0-7614-5051-3*, Cav Child Bks) Marshall Cavendish.

Alexander, Sue. Small Plays for Special Days. LC 76-28424. (Illus.). 64p. (J). (ps-1). 1988. pap. 6.95 (*0-89919-798-1*, Clarion Bks) HM.

— Small Plays for Special Days. (J). 1988. 12.15 (*0-606-04397-7*, Pub. by Turtleback) Demco.

— There's More, Much More. LC 86-33632. (Illus.). 32p. (J). (ps-3). 1987. 12.95 (*0-15-200605-2*, Gulliver Bks) Harcourt.

— World Famous Muriel & the Magic Mystery. LC 89-22396. (Illus.). 32p. (J). (gr. k-3). 1990. lib. bdg. 12.89 (*0-690-04789-4*) HarpC Child Bks.

— World Famous Muriel & the Magic Mystery. LC 89-22396. (Illus.). 32p. (J). (gr. k-3). 1990. 12.95 (*0-690-04787-8*) HarpC Child Bks.

***Alexander, Susan.** Handmade Clay Crafts: Decorative Techniques & Projects. (Illus.). 2000. pap. 14.95 (*0-8069-4988-0*) Sterling.

Alexander, Susan. Winter Sunlight. large type ed. (Magna Large Print Ser.). 241p. 1998. 29.99 (*0-7505-1209-1*, Pub. by Mgna Lrg Print) Ulverscroft.

Alexander, Susan & Bogart, Taffnie. Charming Handmade Clay Crafts: Decorative Techniques & Projects. LC 98-3369. (Illus.). 128p. 1998. 27.95 (*0-8069-4284-3*) Sterling.

Alexander, Susan H., jt. auth. see Simon, Rita J.

Alexander, Susan R. The Diaries of John M. Miller of Westwood - Cincinnati Ohio: Excerpts from 1869-1870 & 1881-1894. LC 92-93448. (Illus.). 634p. 1993. 49.95 (*0-9633141-0-6*) S R Alexander.

Alexander, Susan V. Clean Water in Your Watershed: A Citizen's Guide to Watershed Protection. Reeder, Rachel, ed. (Illus.). 90p. (Orig.). 1993. pap. 19.95 (*1-880686-03-1*) Terrene Inst.

— Clean Water in Your Watershed: A Citizens Guide to Watershed Protection. (Illus.). 89p. 1996. reprint ed. pap. text 25.00 (*0-7881-3167-2*) DIANE Pub.

Alexander, Susie. Art for All Seasons: Kidworks. (Illus.). 160p. (J). (gr. 2 up). 1996. pap., wbk. ed. 14.95 (*1-55734-676-3*) Tchr Create Mat.

— Exploring Nature: Creative Kids. LC 98-61567. (Illus.). 160p. 1999. pap., teacher ed. 14.95 (*1-57690-362-1*, TCM2362) Tchr Create Mat.

Alexander, Susie. Learning Center Activities/Holidays. 80p. (J). (gr. k-2). 1997. pap. 9.95 (*1-57690-074-6*) Tchr Create Mat.

Alexander, Sy. The Tale of the Old Maypop Tree: A Southern Folktale. LC 96-92600. (E. Lee Harvey Collection). (Illus.). iv, 33p. (Orig.). (J). (ps-6). 1997. pap. write for info. (*0-9655726-3-3*) Proud Two-B Me.

Alexander, T. Desmond. Abraham in the Negev: A Source-Critical Investigation of Genesis 20:1-22:19. viii, 166p. 1997. reprint ed. pap. 25.00 (*0-85364-792-5*, Pub. by Paternoster Pub) OM Literature.

— From Paradise to the Promise Land. 227p. 1997. reprint ed. pap. 14.99 (*0-85364-647-3*, Pub. by Paternoster Pub) OM Literature.

— From Paradise to the Promised Land: An Introduction to the Main Themes of the Pentateuch. LC 97-44915. (Illus.). 230p. (C). 1998. pap. 14.99 (*0-8010-2174-X*) Baker Bks.

Alexander, T. G., jt. auth. see Woodruff, A. M.

Alexander, T. M. Beyond the Timberline: Trials & Triumphs of a Black Entrepreneur. 1997. pap. text 13.95 (*1-878647-39-3*) APU Pub Grp.

Alexander, Tania. A Little Russian Cookbook. 1997. 7.95 (*0-8118-1652-4*) Chronicle Bks.

Alexander, Tania & Jackson, Andy. The Fitkid Adventure Book: Health-Related Fitness for 5 to 14 Year Olds. (Illus.). 160p. 1995. pap. 17.95 (*1-85158-603-2*, Pub. by Mainstream Pubng) Trafalgar.

Alexander, Tania & Konova-Stone, Vera. A Little Russian Cookbook. (Little Bks.). (Illus.). 60p. 1990. 7.95 (*0-87701-794-8*) Chronicle Bks.

Alexander, Ted, jt. auth. see Biscoff, Joyce.

Alexander, Ted, jt. auth. see Marquez, Jay.

Alexander, Thea. How to Develop Your Macro Awareness. 48p. (Orig.). 1974. pap. 10.00 (*0-913080-05-5*) Macro Bks.

— How to Do Personal Evolution Tutoring. 48p. (Orig.). 1984. pap. 10.00 (*0-913080-10-1*) Macro Bks.

— How to Interpret Your Dreams from a Macro View. 48p. (Orig.). 1971. pap. 10.00 (*0-913080-07-1*) Macro Bks.

— How to Live a Macro Lifestyle. 64p. (Orig.). 1976. pap. 10.00 (*0-913080-06-3*) Macro Bks.

— The Institute for Macro Living Home Study Program, 3 vols. Incl. Vol. 1: 1-12: Macro Resource Person Training. 1984. 199.00 (*0-913080-13-6*); Vol. 3: 1-12: Personal Evolution Tutor Training. 1988. 199.00 (*0-913080-17-9*); Vol. 2: 1-12: Macro Practitioner Training. 1986. 199.00 (*0-913080-15-2*); 550.00 (*0-913080-21-7*) Macro Bks.

— The Institute for Macro Living Home Study Program Vols. 1-3: Complete Program. 1988. 550.00 (*0-614-10763-6*) Macro Bks.

— The Macro Study Guide & Workbook. 48p. (Orig.). 1984. pap., student ed., wbk. ed. 10.00 (*0-913080-11-X*) Macro Bks.

— The Macro Study Series, 7 vols., Set. 336p. (Orig.). 1984. pap. 44.95 (*0-913080-12-8*) Macro Bks.

— The Prophetess: Conversations with Rana. 48p. (Orig.). 1972. pap. 10.00 (*0-913080-08-X*) Macro Bks.

— Simultaneous Time: Twin Souls, Soul Mates, & Parallel Lives. 48p. (Orig.). 1982. pap. 10.00 (*0-913080-09-8*) Macro Bks.

— 2150 A. D. rev. ed. 352p. 1976. pap. 6.95 (*0-913080-04-7*) Macro Bks.

— 2150 A. D. The Macro Love Story. 281p. (Orig.). 1971. pap. 6.95 (*0-913080-03-9*) Macro Bks.

***Alexander, Theresa S.** Facing the Wolf: Inside the Process of Deep Feeling Therapy. 176p. 2000. reprint ed. 21.00 (*0-7881-9305-8*) DIANE Pub.

***Alexander, Therese, et al.** Rehabilitation Nursing Procedures Manual. 2nd ed. LC 99-10684. (Illus.). 400p. 1999. 60.00 (*0-07-048266-7*) McGraw-Hill HPD.

Alexander, Thomas B. Sectional Stress & Party Strength: A Study of Roll-Call Voting Patterns in the United States House of Representatives, 1836-1860. LC 67-21652. (Illus.). 326p. reprint ed. pap. 101.10 (*0-8357-3198-7*, 2039469000l2) Bks Demand.

— Thomas A. R. Nelson of East Tennessee. LC 56-63418. 224p. reprint ed. pap. 69.50 (*0-608-12312-9*, 202438300037) Bks Demand.

Alexander, Thomas B. & Beringer, Richard E. The Anatomy of the Confederate Congress: A Study of the Influences of Member Characteristics on Legislative Voting Behavior, 1861-1865. LC 76-138985. 447p. reprint ed. pap. 138.60 (*0-8357-3199-5*, 2039470000l2) Bks Demand.

Alexander, Thomas G. A Clash of Interests: Interior Department & Mountain West, 1863-96. LC 77-80144. (Illus.). xii, 256p. 1977. 4.95 (*0-8425-1480-5*, Friends of the Library) Brigham.

— Mormonism in Transition: A History of the Latter-Day Saints, 1890-1930. LC 96-4170. 396p. (C). 1996. pap. text 16.95 (*0-252-06578-6*) U of Ill Pr.

— Mormonism in Transition: A History of the Latter-day Saints, 1890-1930. LC 84-22164. (Illus.). 396p. 1986. text 24.95 (*0-252-01185-6*) U of Ill Pr.

— Things in Heaven & Earth: The Life & Times of Wilford Woodruff, a Mormon Prophet. LC 91-21223. (Illus.). 504p. 1993. pap. 18.95 (*1-56085-045-0*) Signature Bks.

— Utah, the Right Place: The Official Centennial History. (Illus.). 488p. 1996. pap. 29.95 (*0-87905-767-X*) Gibbs Smith Pub.

Alexander, Thomas G., ed. Great Basin Kingdom Revisited: Contemporary Perspectives. (Illus.). 160p. 1991. 19.95 (*0-87421-151-4*) Utah St U Pr.

Alexander, Thomas G., ed. see Grant, Ulysses S.

Alexander, Thomas M., jt. ed. see Hickman, Larry A.

Alexander, Tim. The Real Honky Tonk Piano. (Homespun Tapes Ser.). 1996. VHS 39.95 (*0-7935-6864-1*) H Leonard.

Alexander, Titus. Unravelling Global Apartheid: An Overview of World Politics. LC 96-27945. 288p. (C). 1996. 64.95 (*0-7456-1352-7*); pap. 27.95 (*0-7456-1353-5*) Blackwell Pubs.

***Alexander, Tom.** Best of Growing Edge Vol. 2: Popular Hydroponics & Gardening for Small Commercial Growers. Knutson, Amy, ed. & photos by by. (Best of Growing Edge Ser.: Vol. 2). (Illus.). 320p. 2000. pap. 24.97 (*0-944557-03-1*) New Moon Pub.

Alexander, Tom. Mountain Fever. Alexander, Jane, ed. LC 94-23589. (Illus.). 176p. 1995. 29.95 (*0-914875-26-4*) Bright Mtn Bks.

— Sinsemilla Tips: The Best Of. 3rd rev. ed. Coene, Trisha, ed. (Illus.). 288p. 1996. pap. 21.95 (*0-944557-02-3*) New Moon Pub.

Alexander, Tom & Parker, Don. Growing Edge, The Best of. (Illus.). 240p. (Orig.). 1994. pap. 19.95 (*0-944557-01-5*) New Moon Pub.

***Alexander-Travis, Pauline.** The Very Best Coaching & Study Course GRE CAT, GRE General Computer Adaptive Test. LC 99-70519. (Illus.). 1999. 20.95 (*0-87891-289-4*) Res & Educ.

***Alexander, Tricia.** Adjustment & Human Relations: A Lamp along the Way. LC 99-12587. 617p. 1999. pap. text 55.00 (*0-13-974395-2*) P-H.

***Alexander, Trisha.** A Baby for Rebecca. (Silhouette Ser.). 1999. 21.95 (*0-373-59593-X*) Harlequin Bks.

Alexander, Trisha. A Baby for Rebecca. 1996. per. 3.99 (*0-373-24070-8*, 1-24070-4) Silhouette.

— A Bride for John. (Special Edition Ser.). 1996. per. 3.99 (*0-373-24047-3*, 1-24047-2) Silhouette.

— A Bride for John. large type ed. (Silhouette Special Edition Ser.). 1999. 21.95 (*0-373-59394-5*) Harlequin Bks.

— Bride for Luke. (Special Ser.: Vol. 102). 1998. 21.95 (*0-373-59930-7*) Silhouette.

— A Bride for Luke (Three Brides & a Baby) 1996. per. 3.99 (*0-373-24024-4*, 1-24024-1) Silhouette.

***Alexander, Trisha.** Falling for an Older Man. (Special Edition Ser.). 2000. mass mkt. 4.50 (*0-373-24308-1*) Silhouette.

Alexander, Trisha. The Girl Next Door. (Special Edition Ser.). 1995. per. 3.75 (*0-373-09965-7*, 1-09965-4) Silhouette.

— Here Comes the Groom. (Special Edition Ser.). 1993. per. 3.50 (*0-373-09845-6*, 5-09845-4) Silhouette.

— Let's Make It Legal. 1994. per. 3.50 (*0-373-09924-X*, 1-09924-1) Harlequin Bks.

— A Mother for Jeffrey. 1998. mass mkt. 4.25 (*0-373-24211-5*, 1-24211-4) Silhouette.

— Mother of the Groom. 1993. mass mkt. 3.39 (*0-373-09801-4*, 5-09801-7) Silhouette.

— The Real Elizabeth Hollister. (Special Edition Ser.). 1995. per. 3.75 (*0-373-09940-1*, 1-09940-7) Silhouette.

— Say You Love Me. 1994. mass mkt. 3.50 (*0-373-09875-8*, 5-09875-1) Silhouette.

— Stop the Wedding! 1997. per. 3.99 (*0-373-24097-X*, 1-24097-7) Silhouette.

***Alexander, Trisha.** Stop the Wedding! large type ed. (Silhouette Romance Ser.). 2000. 22.95 (*0-373-59684-7*) Harlequin Bks.

Alexander, Trisha. Substitute Bride. (Special Edition Ser.: No. 1115). 1997. per. 3.99 (*0-373-24115-1*, 1-24115-7) Silhouette.

— This Child Is Mine. 1995. per. 3.75 (*0-373-09989-4*, 1-09989-4) Silhouette.

***Alexander, Trisha.** Wedding Bells & Mistletoe: Callahans & Kin. 1999. mass mkt. 4.25 (*0-373-24289-1*) Silhouette.

Alexander, Trisha. What Will the Children Think? (Special Edition Ser.). 1994. per. 3.50 (*0-373-09906-1*, 1-09906-8) Harlequin Bks.

— When Somebody Loves You. (Special Edition Ser.: No. 748). 1992. per. 3.39 (*0-373-09748-4*, 5-09748-0) Harlequin Bks.

— When Somebody Wants You. (Special Edition Ser.). 1993. per. 3.50 (*0-373-09822-7*, 5-09822-3) Silhouette.

— With This Wedding Ring. 1998. per. 4.25 (*0-373-24169-0*, 1-24169-4) Silhouette.

Alexander, Truman H. Loot. LC 79-39077. (Black Heritage Library Collection). 1977. reprint ed. 21.95 (*0-8369-9015-3*) Ayer.

Alexander, Valerie & Alexander, Valerie. Double Identity: How to Find the Best Person That is Within You. 119p. 1998. pap. 15.00 (*0-9667488-0-8*) Vel & Val.

Alexander, Valerie, jt. auth. see Alexander, Valerie.

Alexander, Van. First Chart. Haskell, Jimmie, ed. LC 70-182858. 112p. 1971. 14.95 incl. lp (*0-910468-01-X*) Criterion Mus.

Alexander, Vicente. World Alone. Hyde, Lewis & Unger, David, trs. (Illus.). 76p. 1982. 17.50 (*0-915778-41-6*) Penmaen Pr.

— World Alone. deluxe ed. Hyde, Lewis & Unger, David, trs. (Illus.). 76p. 1982. 150.00 (*0-915778-42-4*) Penmaen Pr.

Alexander, Victoria. Believe. 400p. 1998. mass mkt. 5.99 (*0-505-52267-5*, Love Spell) Dorchester Pub Co.

Alexander, Victoria. The Emperor's New Clothes. 368p. (Orig.). 1997. mass mkt. 5.50 (*0-505-52159-8*) Dorchester Pub Co.

— The Husband List. 384p. 2000. mass mkt. 5.99 (*0-380-80631-2*) Morrow Avon.

Alexander, Victoria. In the Wake of Suicide: Stories of the People Left Behind. LC 97-37016. 256p. 1998. pap. 22.95 (*0-7879-4052-6*) Jossey-Bass.

***Alexander, Victoria.** Paradise Bay. 400p. 1999. mass mkt. 5.99 (*0-505-52350-7*, Love Spell) Dorchester Pub Co.

— The Perfect Wife. 320p. (Orig.). 1996. mass mkt. 4.99 (*0-8439-4108-1*) Dorchester Pub Co.

Alexander, Victoria. Play It Again, Sam. 400p. (Orig.). 1998. mass mkt. 5.99 (*0-505-52247-0*, Love Spell) Dorchester Pub Co.

— A Taste of Australia: Bathers Pavilion Cookbook. (Illus.). 122p. 1995. 35.00 (*0-89815-756-0*) Ten Speed Pr.

***Alexander, Victoria.** The Wedding Bargain. LC 99-94460. 384p. 1999. mass mkt. 5.99 (*0-380-80629-0*, Avon Bks) Morrow Avon.

Alexander, Victoria, et al. The Cat's Meow. 400p. 1998. mass mkt. 5.99 (*0-505-52279-9*, Love Spell) Dorchester Pub Co.

— Santa Paws. 400p. (Orig.). 1997. mass mkt. 5.99 (*0-505-52235-7*, Love Spell) Dorchester Pub Co.

Alexander, Victoria D. Museums & Money: The Impact of Funding on Exhibitions, Scholarship, & Management. LC 95-49863. (IU Center on Philanthropy Series on Governance). 1996. 24.95 (*0-253-33205-2*) Ind U Pr.

Alexander, Victoria D. Museums & Money: The Impact of Funding on Exhibitions Scholarship & Management. (IU Center on Philanthropy Series in Governance). (Illus.). 204p. 1996. 27.95 (*0-253-33084-X*) Ind U Pr.

Alexander, Victoria N. Smoking Hopes. LC 95-19557. 208p. 1996. 22.00 (*1-877946-69-9*) Permanent Pr.

Alexander, Vincent C., jt. auth. see Barker, Robert A.

Alexander, Virginia W. Maury County, Tennessee, Deed, 1807-1817, Bks. A to F. 248p. 1981. reprint ed. 27.50 (*0-89308-185-X*) Southern Hist Pr.

Alexander, W. D., tr. see Remy, M. Jules.

Alexander, W. E. History of Winneshiek & Allamakee Counties. (Illus.). 739p. 1997. reprint ed. lib. bdg. 76.00 (*0-8328-6711-X*) Higginson Bk Co.

***Alexander, Wade F.** Aural Piano Tuning: The Basic Knowledge Necessary to Tune Pianos by Ear. (Illus.). vi, 64p. 2000. pap. text 25.00 (*0-9679858-0-3*) Greystone Pr NY.

Alexander, Walter S. Alexander. Sketch of Alexander Alexander, Who Emigrated from County Down, Ireland, in the Year 1770, & Settled in Cumberland County, PA, with a Genealogical Chart & Record of His Descendants. (Illus.). 79p. 1995. reprint ed. pap. 16.00 (*0-8328-4864-6*); reprint ed. lib. bdg. 26.00 (*0-8328-4863-8*) Higginson Bk Co.

Alexander, Wayne, et al, eds. Hurst's the Heart: Arteries & Veins. 9th ed. LC 97-19289. (Illus.). 2480p. 1997. text 130.00 (*0-07-057717-X*); text 145.00 (*0-07-912951-X*) McGraw-Hill HPD.

— Hurst's the Heart: Companion Handbook. 9th ed. LC 98-32437. (Illus.). 576p. 1998. pap. text 32.00 (*0-07-001024-2*) McGraw-Hill HPD.

***Alexander, Wes.** Stormfield. (Illus.). 100p. 2000. pap. 10.95 (*0-9662637-2-3*, Pub. by Stormfield Pr) Seven Hills Bk.

Alexander, Wesley, ed. see McCoy, Glenn.

Alexander, Will. Above the Human Nerve Domain. (Illus.). 72p. 1998. pap. 12.00 (*1-886350-81-7*) Pavement Saw.

— Asia & Haiti. (New American Poetry Ser.: No. 17). 144p. (Orig.). 1995. pap. 12.95 (*1-55713-189-9*) Sun & Moon CA.

— The Stratospheric Canticles. (Illus.). 80p. (Orig.). 1995. pap. 8.95 (*1-880766-08-6*) Pantograph Pr.

— Toward the Primeval Lightning Field. 120p. 1997. 10.50 (*1-882022-30-0*) O Bks.

Alexander, William. The Case of the Funny Money Man. LC 89-36358. (Clues Kids Ser.). (Illus.). 96p. (J). (gr. 4-7). 1997. pap. 3.95 (*0-8167-1693-5*) Troll Communs.

— The Case of the Gumball Bandits. LC 89-36558. (Clues Kids Ser.). (Illus.). 96p. (J). (gr. 4-7). 1997. pap. 3.95 (*0-8167-1697-8*) Troll Communs.

— Cool Water. LC 97-11891. 160p. 1997. pap. 12.00 (*1-57062-254-X*, Pub. by Shambhala Pubns) Random.

***Alexander, William.** Diabetic Retinopathy: A Guide For Primary Care Teams. Blackwell Science Incorporated, ed. (Illus.). 10p. 1998. pap. 26.95 (*0-632-05171-X*) Blackwell Sci.

Alexander, William. The Ghost of Shockly Manor. LC 89-36544. (Clues Kids Ser.). (Illus.). 96p. (J). (gr. 4-7). 1996. pap. 3.95 (*0-8167-1695-1*) Troll Communs.

— The History of Women from the Earliest Antiquity to the Present Time, 2 vols. LC 72-9610. reprint ed. 115.00 (*0-404-57401-7*) AMS Pr.

— The Laird of Drammochdyle & His Contemporaries: or Random Sketches Done in Outline with a Burnt Stick. Donaldson, William, ed. 184p. 1987. text 27.00 (*0-08-034520-4*, Pub. by Aberdeen U Pr); pap. text 19.90 (*0-08-034521-2*, Pub. by Aberdeen U Pr) Macmillan.

— Landscapes Wet-on-Wet. (Wet-on-Wet Ser.). (Illus.). 32p. 1995. pap. 6.95 (*1-56010-151-2*, HT252) W Foster Pub.

— The Magic of Oil Painting, No. 1. (How to Draw & Paint Ser.). (Illus.). 32p. 1989. pap. 6.95 (*0-929261-37-2*, HT162) W Foster Pub.

— The Magic of Oil Painting, No. 2. (How to Draw & Paint Ser.). (Illus.). 32p. 1989. pap. 6.95 (*0-929261-60-7*, HT208) W Foster Pub.

— The Tragedie of Darius. LC 72-6936. (English Experience Ser.: No. 293). 80p. 1971. reprint ed. 25.00 (*90-221-0293-9*) Walter J Johnson.

Alexander, William & Carter, I. Rural Life in Victorian Aberdeenshire. 176p. 1989. pap. 28.00 (*1-873644-06-X*, Pub. by Mercat Pr Bks) St Mut.

Alexander, William, jt. auth. see Hansen, Joan.

Alexander, William, jt. auth. see Shackelford, James F.

Alexander, William E. Systemic Bank Restructuring & Macroeconomic Policy. LC 97-26618. 1997. write for info. (*1-55775-665-1*) Intl Monetary.

Alexander, William E., et al, eds. The Adoption of Indirect Instruments of Monetary Policy. LC 95-19313. (Occasional Papers). 1995. write for info. (*1-55775-489-6*) Intl Monetary.

Alexander, William F. & Serfass, Richard W. Futuring Tools for Strategic Quality Planning in Education. LC 98-37412. 176p. 1999. 35.00 (*0-87389-442-1*, H1008) ASQ Qual Pr.

Alexander, William G. Alexander: Family Biographies of the Families of Alexander, Wilkinson, Sparr & Guthrie, with Sketches & Memorials. (Illus.). 180p. 1994. reprint ed. pap. 29.00 (*0-8328-4188-9*); reprint ed. lib. bdg. 39.00 (*0-8328-4187-0*) Higginson Bk Co.

Alexander, William M. State Leadership in Improving Instruction: A Study of the Leadership Service Function of State Education Departments, with Special Reference to Louisiana, Tennessee & Virginia. LC 71-176508. (Columbia University. Teachers College. Contributions to Education Ser.: No. 820). reprint ed. 37.50 (*0-404-55820-8*) AMS Pr.

Alexander, William M., jt. auth. see George, Paul S.

Alexander, William P., jt. auth. see Krauss, Bob.

Alexander, William R. Return of the Son: A Holy Contradiction. LC 98-92664. 52p. 1998. mass mkt. 7.95 (*0-9664132-0-2*, 01) Chldrn of God.

***Alexander, William R.** Return of the Son: A Holy Contradiction. 2nd ed. 52p. 1999. pap. 7.95 (*0-9664132-1-0*, 02) Chldrn of God.

Alexander-Williams, J., ed. Diseases of the Anus & Rectum. LC 76-182437. (Clinics in Gastroenterology Ser.: Vol. 4, No. 3). 216p. reprint ed. pap. 67.00 (*0-608-17925-6*, 201407300095) Bks Demand.

Alexander-Williams, John, jt. auth. see Brown, John S.

Alexander-Williams, John, jt. auth. see Kumar, Devinder.

Alexander, Wilma. Old Coach Road. 128p. (Orig.). (J). (gr. 3-6). 1990. pap. 5.95 (*0-7736-7305-9*) Stoddart Publ.

— Run for Your Life. 117p. (YA). (gr. 5-9). 1998. pap. 6.95 (*1-896184-46-4*) Roussan Pubs.

Alexander, Wilma E. And the Boats Go up & Down. 144p. (gr. 3-6). 1996. mass mkt. 4.95 (*0-7736-7344-X*) General Publishing Co.

Alexander, Wilma E. Queen's Silver. 125p. (gr. 3-6). 1996. mass mkt. 3.95 (*0-7736-7285-0*) General Publishing Co.

Alexander, Wilma J., et al. Word Processing: A Guide to Program Planning. 79p. 1984. 4.95 (*0-318-22248-5*, LT65) Ctr Educ Trng Employ.

Alexander, Winthrop. Dillingham: Genealogy of the Dillingham Family of New England. (Illus.). 311p. 1997. reprint ed. pap. 46.00 (*0-8328-8308-5*); reprint ed. lib. bdg. 56.00 (*0-8328-8307-7*) Higginson Bk Co.

Alexander, Y. & Pluchinsky, Dennis A. European Terrorism Today & Tomorrow. (Terrorism Library Bk.). 224p. 1991. 30.00 (*0-08-041070-7*, 4055M) Brasseys.

Alexander, Yona & Chertoff, Mordecai S., eds. Bibliography on Israel & Zionism. 1980. write for info. (*0-318-53298-0*) Herzl Pr.

Alexander, Yonah. Middle East Terrorism: Selected Group Profiles. (Illus.). 96p. (Orig.). (C). 1996. reprint ed. pap. text 35.00 (*0-7881-3515-5*) DIANE Pub.

Alexander, Yonah, ed. The Annual on Terrorism, 1986. 1987. pap. text 138.00 (*90-247-3608-0*) Kluwer Academic.

— The Annual on Terrorism, 1987. (C). 1989. lib. bdg. 189.00 (*90-247-3801-6*) Kluwer Academic.

— International Terrorism: Political & Legal Documents. 656p. (C). 1992. lib. bdg. 235.50 (*0-7923-1627-4*) Kluwer Academic.

— Middle East Terrorism: Current Threats & Future Prospects. LC 93-33931. 509p. 1994. 50.00 (*0-8161-7337-0*, G K Hall Lrg Type) Mac Lib Ref.

— Terrorism: An International Resource File: 1970-1979 Index. 389p. 1990. write for info. (*0-8357-2117-5*) Univ Microfilms.

— Terrorism: An International Resource File: 1970-1989 Bibliography. 241p. 1991. write for info. (*0-8357-2118-3*) Univ Microfilms.

— Terrorism: An International Resource File: 1980-1985 Index. 335p. 1989. 350.00 (*0-685-46002-9*) Univ Microfilms.

— Terrorism: An International Resource File: 1986 Index. 332p. 1987. 195.00 (*0-8357-0756-3*) Univ Microfilms.

— Terrorism: An International Resource File: 1987 Index. 177p. 1988. 195.00 (*0-8357-0800-4*) Univ Microfilms.

— Terrorism: An International Resource File: 1988 Index. 316p. 1989. 195.00 (*0-8357-0883-7*) Univ Microfilms.

— Terrorism: An International Resource File: 1989 Index. 158p. 1990. write for info. (*0-8357-0948-5*) Univ Microfilms.

— Terrorism: An International Resource File: 1990 Index. 185p. 1991. write for info. (*0-8357-2119-1*) Univ Microfilms.

Alexander, Yonah, et al, eds. Terrorism: Theory & Practice. (Special Studies in National & International Terrorism). 200p. 1979. text 44.00 (*0-89158-089-1*) Westview.

Alexander, Yonah & Ebinger, Charles K., eds. Political Terrorism & Energy: The Threat & the Response. LC 81-15695. 258p. 1982. 55.00 (*0-275-90750-3*, C0750, Praeger Pubs) Greenwood.

Alexander, Yonah & Foxman, Abraham H., eds. The Annual on Terrorism, 1988-1989. (C). 1990. lib. bdg. 129.50 (*0-7923-0757-7*) Kluwer Academic.

Alexander, Yonah & Friedlander, Robert A., eds. Self-Determination: National, Regional, & Global Dimensions. LC 80-65075. (Special Studies in National & International Terrorism). 1980. text 57.00 (*0-89158-090-5*) Westview.

Alexander, Yonah & Kittrie, Nicholas N., eds. Crescent & Star: Arab & Israeli Perspectives on the Middle East Conflict. LC 72-5797. (Studies in Modern Society: Political & Social Issues: No. 3). 37.50 (*0-404-10522-X*); pap. 14.00 (*0-404-10523-8*) AMS Pr.

Alexander, Yonah & Musch, Donald J. Terrorism: Documents of International & Local Control, 20 vols. LC 78-26126. 1979. 1490.00 (*0-379-00690-1*) Oceana.

Alexander, Yonah & Nanes, Allan. The United States & Iran: A Documentary History. LC 80-53318. 524p. 1980. pap. 24.95 (*0-313-27054-6*, P7054); lib. bdg. 95.00 (*0-313-27095-3*, U7095) Greenwood.

Alexander, Yonah & O'Day, Alan. The Irish Terrorism Experience. 240p. 1991. text 66.95 (*1-85521-210-2*, Pub. by Dartmth Pub) Ashgate Pub Co.

Alexander, Yonah & O'Day, Alan, eds. Ireland's Terrorist Dilemma. 1986. lib. bdg. 119.00 (*0-89838-912-7*) Kluwer Academic.

— Terrorism in Ireland. LC 83-3106. 277p. 1984. text 39.95 (*0-312-79260-3*) St Martin.

Alexander, Yonah & Pluchinsky, Dennis A., eds. Europe's Red Terrorists: The Fighting Communist Organizations. LC 92-26147. 258p. 1993. 49.50 (*0-7146-3488-3*, Pub. by F Cass Pubs); pap. 19.50 (*0-7146-4088-3*, Pub. by F Cass Pubs) Intl Spec Bk.

Alexander, Yonah & Sochor, Eugene, eds. Aerial Piracy & Aviation Security. (International Studies on Terrorism). 224p. 1990. lib. bdg. 99.00 (*0-7923-0932-4*) Kluwer Academic.

***Alexander, Yonah & Swetnam, Michael S., eds.** Cyberterrorism & Information Warfare. LC 99-75945. (Terrorism : Vols. 5-8). 2000p. 1999. 280.00 (*0-379-21415-6*) Oceana.

Alexander, Yonah, jt. ed. see Freedman, Lawrence Z.

Alexander, Yonah, ed. see Gleason, John M.

Alexander, Yonah, jt. ed. see O'Day, Alan.

Alexander, Yonah, jt. ed. see Rapoport, David C.

Alexander, Yonah, jt. ed. see Tavin, Eli.

Alexander, Zaia, tr. see Roubickova, Mandlova & Roubickova, Eva M.

***Alexander, Zhauna.** Amelia's Aquarium. (Illus.). 64p. (J). 1999. 21.95 (*1-895836-66-2*, Tesseract) Bk Collective.

Alexanderson, E. Pauline & Wagner, Harvey A., eds. Fermi: New Age for Nuclear Power. LC 78-67176. (ANS Monographs). (Illus.). 454p. 1979. 37.00 (*0-89448-017-0*, 690004) Am Nuclear Soc.

Alexanderson, Gerald, ed. The Polya Picture Album. 140p. 1987. 29.50 (*0-8176-3352-9*) Birkhauser.

Alexanderson, Gerald L., jt. auth. see Hillman, Abraham P.

Alexanderson, Gerald L., ed. see Boas, Ralph P., Jr.

Alexandersson, G. The Baltic Straits. 1982. lib. bdg. 75.50 (*90-247-2595-X*) Kluwer Academic.

Alexandersson, Olof. Living Water: Viktor Schauberger & the Secrets of Natural Energy. 6th ed. (Illus.). 160p. 1990. reprint ed. pap. write for info. (*0-946551-57-X*) ACCESS Pubs Network.

Alexandov, Mikhail. Uneasy Alliance: Relations Between Russia & Kazakhstan in the Post-Soviet Era, 1992-1997, 66. LC 98-45028. 344p. 1999. 65.00 (*0-313-30965-5*) Greenwood.

Alexandra. Last Diary of Tsaritsa Alexandra. Raskina, Alexandra & Khrustalev, Vladimir M., eds. Kozlov, Vladimir A., tr. LC 97-15675. (Illus.). 256p. 1997. 20.00 (*0-300-07212-0*) Yale U Pr.

***Alexandra, Anita.** Sex, Money, Power & Disease: Our Relationships to Healing. x, 250p. 1999. pap. 17.95 (*0-9676755-0-2*) Bonsai Pubng.

Alexandra, Bliss. Divorce - A New Yorker's Guide to Doing It Yourself. 2nd rev. ed. (Illus.). 216p. 1996. pap. 26.95 (*0-9631707-1-6*) Peoples Leg Guides.

Alexandra, John. Mephistopheles' Anvil: Forging a More Human Future. LC 96-33125. 350p. 1997. 24.95 (*1-889511-50-1*) Rose Harmony.

Alexandratos, Nikos, ed. European Agriculture: Policy Issues & Options to 2000. (Illus.). 224p. 1990. text 59.95 (*1-85293-119-1*, Pub. by P P Pubs) CRC Pr.

— World Agriculture: Towards 2010: An FAO Study. LC 94-43232. 514p. 1995. 270.00 (*0-471-95376-8*) Wiley.

An Asterisk (*) at the beginning of an entry indicates that the title is appearing for the first time.

***Alexandre-Bidon, Daniele & Lett, Didier.** Children in the Middle Ages. Gladding, Jody, tr. from FRE. LC 99-37711.Tr. of Enfants au Moyen Age. 176p. 2000. 30.00 (*0-268-02350-6*, Pub. by U of Notre Dame Pr) Chicago Distribution Ctr.

Alexandre, D. Y. Dynamique de la Regeneration Naturelle en Foret Dense de Cote-D'Ivoire (The Dynamics of Natural Regeneration in Dense Forest in Cote D'Ivoire) Strategies Ecologiques des Arbres de la Voute et Potentiels Floristiques (The Ecological Strategies of Canopy Trees & Floristic Potentials)Tr. of Dynamics of Natural Regeneration in Dense Forest in Cote D'Ivoire - The Ecological Strategies of Canopy Trees & Floristic Potentials. (FRE.). 102p. 1989. pap. 15.00 (*2-7099-0974-X*, Pub. by LInstitut Francais) Balogh.

Alexandre, Frederic, jt. ed. see Sun, Ron.

Alexandre, Laurien. Ideology, Government Broadcasting & Global Change. (Critical Studies in Communication & in the Cultural Industries). 192p. Date not set. pap. 45.00 (*0-8133-1938-2*) Westview.

— Voice of America: From Detente to Reagan Doctrine. Dervin, Brenda, ed. LC 88-10449. (Communication & Information Science Ser.). 224p. 1988. text 73.25 (*0-89391-465-7*) Ablx Pub.

Alexandre, Laurien, tr. see Gonzalez-Manet, Enrique.

Alexandre, Philippe, jt. ed. see Samuel-Scheyder, Monique.

Alexandre, Pierre, ed. French Perspectives in African Studies: A Collection of Translated Essays. LC 73-160402. (Illus.). 248p. reprint ed. pap. 76.90 (*0-8357-3209-6*, 205707900010) Bks Demand.

Alexandreia, Hermeias Von, see Von Alexandreia, Hermeias.

Alexandrescu, S., ed. Transformational Grammar & the Rumanian Language. 97p. (Orig.). 1977. pap. 12.00 (*90-316-0144-6*) J Benjamins Pubng Co.

Alexandrescu, Sorin, et al. Hemel en Aarde: Werelden van Verbeelding. (Illus.). 312p. 1991. pap. 29.00 (*90-272-2089-1*) J Benjamins Pubng Co.

Alexandrescu, Vlad. Le Paradoxe Chez Blaise Pascal. (Sciences pour la Communication Ser.: Vol. 49). (FRE.). 262p. 1997. 43.95 (*3-906754-72-3*, Pub. by P Lang) P Lang Pubng.

Alexandrescu, Yvonne, jt. auth. see Deletant, Denis.

Alexandrescu, Yvonne, jt. auth. see Deletant, Dennis.

Alexandrescu, Yvonnne, jt. auth. see Deletant, Dennis.

Alexandria, Vincent R. If Walls Could Talk: A Murder Detective Mystery. LC 98-75361. 181p. 1998. pap. 14.95 (*1-890622-56-7*) Leathers Pub.

Alexandria, Betty, pseud. Contigo (Poesias) LC 83-82881. (Coleccion Espejo de Paciencia). (SPA.). 63p. (Orig.). 1984. pap. 6.95 (*0-89729-346-0*) Ediciones.

Alexandria, Clement. Christ, the Educator. Wood, Simon P., tr. LC 66-20313. (Fathers of the Church Ser.: Vol. 23). 333p. 1954. reprint ed. pap. 103.30 (*0-7837-9142-9*, 204994200004) Bks Demand.

Alexandria, Dionysios Von, see Von Alexandria, Dionysios.

Alexandrian, Sarane. Dictionnaire de la Peinture Surrealiste: Dictionary of Surrealist Painting. (FRE.). 58p. 1973. 59.95 (*0-7859-0406-9*, M6601) Fr & Eur.

— Surrealist Art. (World of Art Ser.). (Illus.). (Orig.). 1985. pap. 14.95 (*0-500-20097-1*, Pub. by Thames Hudson) Norton.

Alexandridis, E. The Pupil. Telger, Terry C., tr. from GER. (Illus.). 115p. 1985. 105.00 (*0-387-96109-7*) Spr-Verlag.

Alexandridis, P. & Lindman, B., eds. Amphiphilic Block Copolymers. 1999. write for info. (*0-444-82441-3*) Elsevier.

Alexandrinus, Philo. Libellus de Opificio Mundi. Cohn, Leopold, ed. lviii, 108p. 1967. reprint ed. 32.00 (*0-318-70997-X*) G Olms Pubs.

Alexandris, Athina & Vaslamatzid, Grigoris. Countertransference: Theory, Technique, Teaching. 269p. 1993. pap. text 33.00 (*1-85575-028-7*, Pub. by H Karnac Bks Ltd) Other Pr LLC.

Alexandroff, Paul. Elementary Concepts of Topology. Farley, Alan E., tr. 57p. (C). 1961. pap. 3.95 (*0-486-60747-X*) Dover.

Alexandroff, Paul S. & Hopf, H. Topologie. LC 65-21833. (GER.). 25.00 (*0-8284-0197-7*) Chelsea Pub.

***Alexandrou.** Introduction to Fluid Mechanics. 800p. 2000. 81.00 (*0-13-801762-X*) P-H.

Alexandrou, jt. auth. see Beckett.

Alexandrou, Andreas N., jt. auth. see Papanastasiou, Tasos.

Alexandrov, A. D. A. D. Alexandrov: Selected Works. Part 1: Selected Scientific Papers, Vol. 4. Reshetnyak & Sutateladze, S. S., eds. (Classics of Soviet Mathematics Ser). 332p. 1996. text 96.00 (*2-88124-984-1*) Gordon & Breach.

Alexandrov, A. D. & Reshetnyak. General Theory of Irregular Curves. (C). 1989. text 223.00 (*90-277-2811-9*) Kluwer Academic.

Alexandrov, A. F., et al. Principles of Plasma Electrodynamics. (Electrophysics Ser.: Vol. 9). (Illus.). 510p. 1984. 102.95 (*0-387-12613-9*) Spr-Verlag.

Alexandrov, A. S. & Mott, Sir Nevill Francis. Polarons & Bipolarons. LC 96-146435. 300p. 1996. text 52.00 (*981-02-2298-X*) World Scientific Pub.

Alexandrov, A. S., jt. auth. see Mott, Sir Nevill Francis.

Alexandrov, A. S., jt. ed. see Mott, Sir Nevill Francis.

Alexandrov, B. G., ed. see GEF Black Sea Environmental Programme Staff.

Alexandrov, E. B., et al. Interference of Atomic State. LC 92-38510. (Springer Series on Atoms B Plus S Plasmas Ser.: No. 7). 1993. 141.95 (*0-387-53752-X*) Spr-Verlag.

Alexandrov, Natalia & Hussaini, M. Y., eds. Multidisciplinary Design & Optimization: State of the Art. LC 96-72047. (Proceedings in Applied Mathematics Ser.: No. 80). xvi, 455p. 1997. pap. 65.50 (*0-89871-359-5*, PR80) Soc Indus-Appl Math.

Alexandrov, P. Combinatorial Topology. unabridged ed. LC 98-7557. 654p. 1998. pap. 16.95 (*0-486-40179-0*) Dover.

Alexandrov, Paul S. Introduction to the Theory of Sets & Functions. write for info. (*0-685-07980-5*) Chelsea Pub.

Alexandrov, Stanimir A. Reservations in Unilateral Declarations Accepting the Compulsory Jurisdiction of the International Court of Justice. LC 94-35261. (Legal Aspects of Internatinal Organizations Ser.: Vol. 19). 1995. lib. bdg. 69.50 (*0-7923-3145-1*) Kluwer Academic.

Alexandrov, V. John. Affirmations of Wealth: 101 Secrets of Daily Success. LC 96-71011. 300p. (Orig.). 1997. pap. 19.95 (*1-886284-00-8*, Prof Dev Press) Chandler Hse.

Alexandrov, V. John. Your Spiritual Gold Mind: The Divine Guide to Financial Freedom. LC 99-96933. Date not set. 24.95 (*0-9676208-9-9*) Fearless Inc.

Alexandrov, V. V. & Gorsky, Nikolai D. From Humans to Computers: Cognition Through Visual Perception. (Series in Computer Science: Vol. 22). 212p. 1991. text 53.00 (*981-02-0298-9*); pap. text 28.00 (*981-02-0299-7*) World Scientific Pub.

— Image Representation & Processing: A Recursive Approach. LC 93-19677. (Mathematics & Its Applications Ser.: Vol. 261). 200p. (C). 1993. text 147.00 (*0-7923-2136-7*) Kluwer Academic.

Alexandrov, V. V. & Semenkov, A. I. Computer Simulation of Developing Structures in Nature, Society & Culture. (Series in Computer Science). 300p. 1997. text 68.00 (*981-02-1675-0*) World Scientific Pub.

Alexandrov, Vassil, et al. Recent Advances in Parallel Virtual Machine & Message Passing Interface: 5Th European Pvm Mpi User's Group Meeting, Liverpool, Uk, September 7-9, 1998, Vol. 149. LC 98-41661. (Lecture Notes in Computer Science). 1998. pap. 67.00 (*3-540-65041-5*) Spr-Verlag.

Alexandrov, Vladimir E. Andrei Bely: The Major Symbolist Fiction. (Russian Research Center Studies: No. 83). 256p. 1985. 34.00 (*0-674-03646-8*) HUP.

Alexandrov, Vladimir E., ed. The Garland Companion to Vladimir Nabakov. LC 94-37409. 848p. 1995. text 40.00 (*0-8153-0354-8*, H1474) Garland.

Alexandrov, Yu A. Fundamental Properties of the Neutron. Drozdova, T. F., tr. (Oxford Series on Neutron Scattering in Condensed Matter: No. 6). (Illus.). 224p. 1992. 75.00 (*0-19-851735-1*) OUP.

Alexandrova, A. Watercolours & Drawings of Russian & Soviet Artists in the Pushkin Fine Arts Museum. (ENG & RUS., Illus.). 1982. 65.00 (*0-7855-1683-2*) St Mut.

Alexandrova, Galina M., ed. see Open Linguistics Forum Staff.

Alexandrova, Vera. History of Soviet Literature. Ginsburg, Mirra, tr. from RUS. LC 70-156171. 369p. (C). 1971. reprint ed. lib. bdg. 37.50 (*0-8371-6114-2*, ALSL, Greenwood Pr) Greenwood.

Alexandrovna, Irina, ed. see Wilson, Art.

***Alexandrowicz, Alex & Wilson, David.** The Long Injustice: The Strange Story of Alex Alexandrowicz. 175p. 1999. pap. 36.00 (*1-872870-45-7*, Pub. by Waterside Pr) Gaunt.

Alexanian, Nubar, photos by. Where Music Comes From. LC 96-76476. (Illus.). 96p. 1996. 39.95 (*1-899235-06-X*, 620403, Pub. by Dewi Lewis) Dist Art Pubs.

Alexashenko, Sergei V., jt. auth. see Lbopez-Claros, Augusto.

Alexe, George. Diorame si Eseuri. (RUM.). 335p. (Orig.). 1997. pap. 14.99 (*0-9623183-2-9*) Moonfall Pr VA.

Alexe, George. Granita Dinspre Cer. 1991. pap. 10.00 (*0-9619930-5-7*) Moonfall Pr VA.

Alexeev, E. N., et al. Particles & Cosmology: Proceedings of the International School. 332p. 1994. text 106.00 (*981-02-1834-6*) World Scientific Pub.

Alexeev, E. N., ed. see Matveev, V. A., et al.

Alexeev, V. I. Rol' Cerkvi v Sozdanii Russkogo Gosudarstva: The Role of the Church in the Foundation of Russian Nation. 310p. 1990. write for info. (*0-9616413-7-1*) Multilingual.

Alexeev, Yuri, jt. auth. see Rapoport, Vitaly.

Alexeiev, Basil M. Chinese Gods of Wealth. (Illus.). 62p. 1989. pap. 8.95 (*9971-4-9184-2*) Heian Intl.

***Alexeyev, Vladimir.** Quantitative Analysis. 496p. 2000. pap. 37.50 (*0-89875-034-2*) U Pr Pacific.

Alexeyeva, Ludmilla & Goldberg, Paul. The Thaw Generation: Coming of Age in the Post-Stalin Era. LC 92-50913. (Russian & East European Studies: Vol. 19). (Illus.). 339p. 1993. reprint ed. text 16.95 (*0-8229-5911-9*) U of Pittsburgh Pr.

Alexeyeva, Natalia, ed. see Jelisavcic, Misha.

Alexeyeva, Natalia, ed. see Russian Info & Business Center, U. S. A. Staff.

Alexeyeva, Natalia, ed. see Russian Information & Business Center, Inc. Staff.

Alexiades, Miguel N. & Sheldon, Jennie W., eds. Selected Guidelines for Ethnobotanical Research: A Field Manual. (Advances in Economic Botany Ser.: No. 10). 306p. 1996. pap. text 22.95 (*0-89327-404-6*, AEB 10) NY Botanical.

Alexiades, V. & Solomon, Alan D. Mathematical Modeling of Melting & Freezing Processes. 275p. 1992. 57.95 (*1-56032-125-3*) Hemisp Pub.

***Alexiades, Vasilios & Siopsis, George.** Trends in Mathematical Physics: Proceedings of the Conference on Trends in Mathematical Physics, October 14-17, 1998, University of Tennessee, Knoxville. LC 99-30848. (Studies in Advanced Mathematics). 1999. write for info. (*0-8218-2006-0*) Am Math.

Alexiadou, Artemis. Adverb Placement: A Case Study in Antisymmetric Syntax. LC 97-38867. (Linguistik Aktuell - Linguistics Today Ser.: Vol. 18). x, 256p. 1997. lib. bdg. 65.00 (*1-55619-902-3*) J Benjamins Pubng Co.

***Alexiadou, Artemis, et al, eds.** The Syntax of Relative Clauses. LC 99-462049. (Linguistik Aktuell/Linguistics Today Ser.: Vol. 32). vi, 390p. 2000. 85.00 (*1-55619-916-3*) J Benjamins Pubng Co.

Alexiadou, Artemis & Hall, T. Allen, eds. Studies on Universal Grammar & Typological Variation. LC 96-37873. (Linguistik Actuel - Linguistics Today Ser.: Vol. 13). viii, 252p. 1997. lib. bdg. 78.00 (*1-55619-232-0*) J Benjamins Pubng Co.

Alexiadou, Artemis, et al. Studies in Greek Syntax. LC 98-39985. (Studies in Natural Language & Linguistic Theory). 1998. 119.00 (*0-7923-5290-4*) Kluwer Academic.

Alexiadou, Artemis, ed. see Daily, Mike.

Alexiadou, Artenis, jt. ed. see Wilder, Chris.

Alexiadou, Vefa. Festive Cuisine. (Illus.). 194p. 1996. 34.95 (*960-85018-9-X*) Howell Pr VA.

— Greek Cuisine. (Illus.). 160p. 1994. 24.95 (*960-85018-6-5*) Howell Pr VA.

— Greek Pastries & Desserts. (Illus.). 160p. 1994. 24.95 (*960-85018-7-3*) Howell Pr VA.

Alexie, Sherman. The Business of Fancydancing. LC 91-35048. 84p. 1992. 20.00 (*0-914610-00-7*) Hanging Loose.

— The Business of Fancydancing. 1992. pap. 12.00 (*0-914610-24-4*) Hanging Loose.

— First Indian on the Moon. 1993. 20.00 (*1-882413-03-2*); pap. 12.00 (*1-882413-02-4*) Hanging Loose.

— Indian Killer. LC 97-27448. 420p. 1998. reprint ed. mass mkt. 13.95 (*0-446-67370-6*, Pub. by Warner Bks) Little.

— The Lone Ranger & Tonto Fistfight in Heaven. LC 94-12378. 240p. 1998. pap. 13.00 (*0-06-097624-1*, Perennial) HarperTrade.

— The Man Who Loves Salmon. LC 98-197517. 36p. 1998. pap. 25.00 (*0-931659-39-6*) Limberlost Pr.

— The Man Who Loves Salmon. limited ed. LC 98-197517. 36p. 1998. 125.00 (*0-931659-40-X*) Limberlost Pr.

— Old Shirts & New Skins. LC 92-53282. (Native American Literature Ser.: No. 9). (Illus.). 100p. (Orig.). pap. 12.00 (*0-935626-36-0*) U Cal AISC.

***Alexie, Sherman.** One Stick Song. LC 99-58811. 2000. 25.00 (*1-882413-77-6*); pap. 15.00 (*1-882413-76-8*, Pub. by Hanging Loose) SPD-Small Pr Dist.

— Reservation Blues. 306p. 1996. reprint ed. mass mkt. 13.99 (*0-446-67235-1*, Pub. by Warner Bks) Little.

Alexie, Sherman. Smoke Signals. LC 98-21018. (J). 1998. pap. 10.45 (*0-7868-8392-8*, Pub. by Hyperion) Time Warner.

— The Summer of Black Widows. LC 96-9822. 144p. 1996. 22.00 (*1-882413-35-0*); pap. 13.50 (*1-882413-34-2*) Hanging Loose.

***Alexie, Sherman.** The Toughest Indian in the World. LC 99-86360. 240p. 2000. 24.00 (*0-87113-801-8*, Pub. by Grove-Atltic) Publishers Group.

Alexie, Sherman. Water Flowing Home. limited ed. (Orig.). 1995. 125.00 (*0-931659-26-4*) Limberlost Pr.

Alexier, Dony. Painting on Porcelain: Composition & Technique. (French Art & Craft Books). (Illus.). 80p. pap. 19.95 (*2-84415-001-2*, Pub. by Ulisse Editions) Penton Overseas.

Alexiev, Alex. Party-Military Relations in Eastern Europe: The Case of Romania. (CISA Working Papers: No. 15). 47p. (Orig.). 1979. pap. 15.00 (*0-86682-014-0*) Ctr Intl Relations.

Alexieva, et al. English-Bulgarian Conversational Dictionary. (BUL & ENG.). 244p. 1982. 19.95 (*0-8288-1597-6*, F34930) Fr & Eur.

Alexieva, Marguerite, tr. see Dzhagarov, Georgi.

Alexieva, Marguerite, tr. see Kirilov, Nikolai & Kirk, Frank, eds.

Alexieva, Marguerite, tr. see Panayotova, Dora.

Alexion, Margaret. After Antiquity: Greek Language, Myth, & Metaphor. (Myth & Poetics Ser.). (Illus.). 488p. 1998. 49.95 (*0-8014-3301-0*) Cornell U Pr.

Alexiou, Chris. Starting Small - Thinking Big: Practical Strategies for School Success. 200p. 1995. pap. 12.95 (*0-88962-579-4*) Mosaic.

Alexiou, M. & Lambropoulos, V., eds. The Text & Its Margins. LC 85-62596. 288p. 1985. 25.00 (*0-918618-30-4*); pap. 12.00 (*0-918618-29-0*) Pella Pub.

Alexis, Andre. Childhood. LC 98-13089. 256p. 1998. 23.00 (*0-8050-5981-4*) H Holt & Co.

— Childhood. 272p. 1999. pap. 13.00 (*0-8050-5982-2*, Owl) H Holt & Co.

— Despair. Date not set. pap. 14.00 (*0-8050-5980-6*, Owl) H Holt & Co.

— Despair: And Other Stories of Ottawa. LC 98-41602. 224p. 2000. 23.00 (*0-8050-5979-2*) H Holt & Co.

— The Fragments: A Commentary. Arnott, W. Geoffrey, ed. (Cambridge Classical Texts & Commentaries Ser.: No. 31). 907p. (C). 1996. text 180.00 (*0-521-55180-3*) Cambridge U Pr.

— Romanne und Erzahlungen, 3 bande. (GER.). 1996. write for info. (*3-487-10102-5*) G Olms Pubs.

Alexis, Jacques S. Compere General Soleil. (Imaginaire Ser.). (FRE.). 350p. 1985. pap. 15.95 (*2-07-028730-0*) Schoenhof.

***Alexis, Jacques S.** General Sun, My Brother. Coates, Carrol F., tr. 352p. 1999. 69.50 (*0-8139-1889-8*) U Pr of Va.

Alexis, Jacques S. General Sun, My Brother. Coates, Carrol F., tr. from FRE. & intro. by. LC 99-23064. (Illus.). 352p. 1999. pap. 19.95 (*0-8139-1890-1*) U Pr of Va.

— Romancero aux Etoiles: Choix de Vieux Chants Portugais. (Imaginaire Ser.). (FRE.). 271p. 1988. pap. 12.95 (*2-07-071229-X*) Schoenhof.

Alexis, Katina. Souls. Peters, Sally, ed. 304p. (Orig.). 1992. mass mkt. 4.99 (*0-671-67626-1*) PB.

Alexis, Kim. With a Little Luck. 1993. 20.00 (*0-671-70756-6*, Pocket Books) PB.

— With a Little Luck. Chelius, Jane, ed. 336p. 1994. mass mkt. 5.99 (*0-671-70757-4*, Pocket Star Bks) PB.

***Alexis, Kim & Denney, James D.** A Model for a Better Future. LC 98-31532. 224p. 1999. 16.99 (*0-7852-7456-1*) Nelson.

Alexis, Marcus, et al. Black Consumer Profiles: Food Purchasing in the Inner City. LC 80-622236. 97p. reprint ed. pap. 30.10 (*0-8357-7286-1*, 205635800060) Bks Demand.

Alexis, Michael N. & Sekeris, Constantin E., eds. Activation of Hormone & Growth Factor Receptors Molecular Mechanisms & Consequences: Proceedings of the NATO Advanced Research Workshop on "Molecular Mechanisms & Consequences of Activaton of Hormone & Growth Factor Receptors" Held in Nafplion, Greece, September 25-30, 1988. (C). 1989. text 202.50 (*0-7923-0573-6*) Kluwer Academic.

Alexis, Willibald. Romane und Erzahlungen: Daraus. Bernauer, Markus & Miller, Norbert, eds. (GER.). vi, 890p. 1996. reprint ed. 120.00 (*3-487-10106-8*) G Olms Pubs.

— Romane und Erzahlungen Band 5: Daraus. Bernauer, Markus & Miller, Norbert, eds. (GER.). xvi, 734p. 1999. reprint ed. 200.00 (*3-487-10109-2*, Pub. by G Olms Verlag) Lubrecht & Cramer.

Alexits, G. Approximation Theory Selected Papers: Selected Papers. (FRE & GER.). 298p. (C). 1983. 85.00 (*963-05-3204-2*, Pub. by Akade Kiado) St Mut.

Alexits, G. & Foldes, I. Convergence Problems of Orthogonal Series. LC 61-14566. (International Series of Monographs on Pure & Applied Mathematics: Vol. 20). 1961. 164.00 (*0-08-013811-X*, Pub. by Pergamon Repr) Franklin.

Alexopoulos, Christos, et al, eds. Proceedings, 1995 Winter Simulation Conference. LC 87-654182. 1463p. 1995. 210.00 (*0-7803-3018-8*, WSC-95) Soc Computer Sim.

Alexopoulos, Constantine J., et al. Introductory Mycology. 4th ed. LC 95-20699. 880p. 1995. text 102.95 (*0-471-52229-5*) Wiley.

Alexopoulos, George, jt. ed. see Murphy, Elaine.

Alexsandrowicz, D. R. Developmental Deviations & Personality: Theoretical Issues & Therapeutic Applications. xii, 126p. 1989. pap. text 62.00 (*2-88124-298-7*) Gordon & Breach.

***Alexseev, Mikhail A.** Ethnopolitical Identity, Economic Incentives & Regional Separatism in Post-Soviet Russia. LC 98-55180. 298p. 1999. text 49.95 (*0-312-21737-4*) St Martin.

Alexseev, Mikhail A. Without Warning: Threat Assessment, Intelligence & Global Struggle. LC 97-28936. 1997. text 45.00 (*0-312-17538-8*) St Martin.

Alexy, Trudi. The Mezuzah in the Madonnna's Foot: Marranso & Other Secret Jews--A Woman Discovers Her Spiritual Heritage. LC 94-18549. 320p. 1994. pap. 14.00 (*0-06-060340-2*, Pub. by Harper SF) HarpC.

***Alexzanderson, Gerald L.** The Random Walks of George Polya. LC 99-67969. (Spectrum Ser.). (Illus.). 320p. 2000. pap. 29.95 (*0-88385-528-3*) Math Assn.

Aleyev, Yu G. Nekton. (Illus.). 1977. text 191.50 (*90-6193-560-1*) Kluwer Academic.

Alf. Dictionnaire Commerciale.Tr. of Commercial Dictionary. (FRE.). 297p. 1979. pap. 59.95 (*0-8288-4791-6*, M9307) Fr & Eur.

Alf. Perfect Graphs. text. write for info. (*0-471-48970-0*) Wiley.

Alf. Romantiques Allemand, Vol. 2. (FRE.). 1977. 59.95 (*0-8288-5636-2*, M6119) Fr & Eur.

Alf, Evers. The Deer Jacker. (J). (gr. 1-7). Date not set. 14.99 (*0-614-19307-9*) OUP.

Alf, Martha, photos by. Martha Alf Vol. 1: Retrospective. LC 83-83032. (Illus.). 79p. (Orig.). 1984. pap. 16.00 (*0-911291-09-1*) Fellows Cont Art.

Alfa, Attahiru S. & Chakravarthy, Srinivas R., eds. Advances in Matrix Analytic Methods for Stochastic Models. (Illus.). 444p. (C). 1998. 95.00 (*0-9665847-0-8*) Ntble Pubns.

Alfa, Attahiru S., jt. ed. see Chakravarthy, Srinivas R.

Alfa, Caroline, et al. Experiments with Fission Yeast: A Laboratory Course Manual. (Illus.). 188p. (C). 1993. 39.00 (*0-87969-424-6*) Cold Spring Harbor.

Alfa Mdg. Corp. Staff, ed. see Georgeff, Milo.

Alfani, Mohamed. Vitalizing African Public Administration for Recovery & Development. Mutahaba, Gelase et al, eds. LC 91-46723. (Library of Management for Development). xiii, 119p. 1993. 30.00 (*1-56549-012-6*) Kumarian Pr.

Alfano, Joan. Heal with Your Heart: A New Vision for Holistic Nursing. (Illus.). 256p. (Orig.). 1996. pap. 11.95 (*1-885610-04-1*) European Amer.

Alfano, Peter, jt. auth. see Washington, MaliVai.

Alfano, R. R., ed. The Supercontinuum Laser Source. (Illus.). 440p. 1989. 139.95 (*0-387-96946-2*) Spr-Verlag.

Alfano, R. R. & Rothberg, L., eds. Photonics: Nonlinear Optics & Ultrafast Phenomena. 182p. (C). 1991. text 175.00 (*0-941743-93-4*) Nova Sci Pubs.

Alfano, Robert R., ed. Advances in Optical Biopsy & Optical Mammography. LC 97-39424. (Annals of the New York Academy of Sciences Ser.: No. 838). 205p. 1998. 90.00 (*1-57331-125-1*); pap. 90.00 (*1-57331-126-X*) NY Acad Sci.

— Optical Biopsy II, Vol. 3250. LC 98-227289. 226p. 1998. 69.00 (*0-8194-2689-X*) SPIE.

Alfano, Robert R., jt. ed. see Chance, Britton.

Alfano, Salvatore. Work of the Dividend Department. (Illus.). 208p. 1987. 29.95 (*0-13-965096-2*) NY Inst Finance.

Alfaro. Critical Thinking in Nursing: A Practical Approach. 2nd ed. Eoyang, Thomas, ed. LC 98-47454. (Illus.). 335p. (C). 1999. pap. text 24.95 (*0-7216-8277-4*, W B Saunders Co) Harcrt Hlth Sci Grp.

Alfaro-Alexander, Ana Maria. Hacia le Modernization de la Narrativa Peruana: El Grupo Pakrmo. LC 92-13337. (University of Texas Studies in Contemporary Spanish-American Fiction: Vol. 6). XVI, 256p. (C). 1993. text 48.95 (0-8204-1933-8) P Lang Pubng.

Alfaro, Angel G. Educacion y Cambio Social en Puerto Rico: Una Epoca Critica. 223p. (C). 1974. pap. 3.00 (0-8477-2715-7) U of PR Pr.

Alfaro, Antonio Gomez. The Great Gypsy Roud-Up: Spain-The General Imprisonment of Gypsies in 1749. (Gypsy Research Center Ser.).Tr. of Editorial Presencia Citano. 119p. 1993. pap. 17.95 (84-87347-12-6, Pub. by Univ of Herfordshire) Bold Strummer Ltd.

Alfaro, Aren, ed. see Brody, Marjorie.

Alfaro-Correa, Ana, jt. auth. see Lillie-Blanton, Marsha.

Alfaro, D. Virgil & Liggett, Peter. Vitreoretinal Surgery of the Injured Eye. LC 98-22167. 450p. 1998. text 145.00 (0-397-58428-8) Lppncott W & W.

Alfaro, E. J. & Delgado, A. J., eds. The Formation of the Milky Way. (Illus.). 376p. (C). 1995. text 80.00 (0-521-48177-5) Cambridge U Pr.

Alfaro, Juan. Introduccion a la Biblia: 101 Preguntas y Respuestas. LC 94-73014. (SPA.). 128p. 1995. pap. 6.95 (0-89243-790-1) Liguori Pubns.

— Manual para Proclamadores de la Palabra, 1999. (SPA.). 216p. 1998. pap. 12.00 (1-56854-219-4, SWL99) Liturgy Tr Pubns.

***Alfaro, Juan.** Spanish Workbook Lectors. (SPA & ENG.). 1999. pap. 10.00 (1-56854-288-7) Liturgy Tr Pubns.

Alfaro, Julian H., jt. auth. see Bomse, Marguerite D.

Alfaro-LeFevre, Rosalinda. Applying Nursing Process: A Step-by-Step Guide. 4th ed. LC 97-25194. 336p. 1997. pap. text 23.95 (0-397-55453-2) Lppncott W & W.

— Critical Thinking in Nursing: A Practical Approach. (Illus.). 1995. pap., teacher ed. write for info. (0-7216-5902-0, W B Saunders Co) Harcrt Hlth Sci Grp.

Alfaro-LeFevre, Rosalinda A. Critical Thinking in Nursing: A Practical Approach. LC 94-25233. 1995. pap. text 22.00 (0-7216-5897-0, W B Saunders Co) Harcrt Hlth Sci Grp.

Alfaro-Lefevre, Rosalinda A., et al. Drug Handbook: A Nursing Process Approach. 734p. (C). 1991. pap. 48.00 (0-201-09278-6) Addison-Wesley.

Alfaro, Luis, tr. see Wolverton, Terry & Weissman, Benjamin, eds.

Alfaro, M. Sanchez, jt. auth. see Hermoso, A. Gonzalez.

Alfaro Perez, Juan. Romantiques Allemands, Vol. 1. (ENG & SPA.). 478p. 1976. pap. 115.00 (0-8288-5614-1, S50094) Fr & Eur.

Alfaro, Ricardo J. Diccionario de Anglicismos. 2nd ed. (SPA.). 520p. 39.95 (0-7859-0420-4, S11836) Fr & Eur.

Alfasi, E., et al. Baba Sali. Dolinger, Leah, tr. from HEB. (Illus.). 224p. 1986. 16.95 (0-910818-65-7) Judaica Pr.

Alfasi, Yitzchok. Glimpses of Jewish Warsaw. LC 91-76035. 176p. 1992. 8.95 (1-56062-092-7); pap. 5.95 (1-56062-093-5) CIS Comm.

***Alfassi, Zeev B.** General Aspects of Free Radical Chemistry LC 98-42539. 574p. 1999. 325.00 (0-471-98760-3) Wiley.

Alfassi, Zeev B. Preconcentration Techniques for Trace Elements. 480p. 1991. lib. bdg. 239.00 (0-8493-5213-4, QD139) CRC Pr.

— S-Centered Radicals. LC 98-30282. (Chemistry of Free Radicals Ser.). 382p. 1999. 315.00 (0-471-98687-9) Wiley.

Alfassi, Zeev B., ed. Activation Analysis, I. 496p. 1990. lib. bdg. 165.95 (0-8493-4583-9, QD606) CRC Pr.

— Activation Analysis, II. 496p. 1990. lib. bdg. 153.00 (0-8493-4584-7, QD606) CRC Pr.

— Chemical Analysis by Nuclear Methods. LC 93-33546. 576p. 1994. 445.00 (0-471-93834-3) Wiley.

— Chemical Kinetics of Small Organic Radicals, Vol. I: General. 192p. 1988. 96.00 (0-8493-4362-3, QD471, CRC Reprint) Franklin.

— Chemical Kinetics of Small Organic Radicals, Vol. II: Reactions of Special Radicals. 256p. 1988. 121.00 (0-8493-4363-1, QD471, CRC Reprint) Franklin.

— Chemical Kinetics of Small Organic Radicals, Vol. III: Correlation & Calculation Methods. 240p. 1988. 125.00 (0-8493-4364-X, QD471, CRC Reprint) Franklin.

— Chemical Kinetics of Small Organic Radicals, Vol. IV: Reactions in Special Systems. 240p. 1988. 176.00 (0-8493-4365-8, QD471, CRC Reprint) Franklin.

— The Chemistry of Free Radicals: Peroxyl Radicals. LC 96-34040. 546p. 1997. 295.00 (0-471-97065-4) Wiley.

***Alfassi, Zeev B., ed.** The Chemistry of N-Centered Radicals. LC 98-231266. 728p. 1998. 425.00 (0-471-96186-8) Wiley.

Alfassi, Zeev B., ed. Determination of Trace Elements. LC 95-159534. 608p. 1994. 295.00 (3-527-28424-9, Wiley-VCH) Wiley.

***Alfassi, Zeev B., ed.** Instrumental Multi Element Chemical Analysis. LC 98-66852. (Illus.). 520p. 1998. write for info. (0-7514-0427-6) Kluwer Academic.

Alfassi, Zeev B. & Peisach, Max. Elemental Analysis by Particle Accelerators. 304p. 1991. lib. bdg. 229.00 (0-8493-6031-5, QD606) CRC Pr.

Alfassy, Leo. Blues Hanon. 1980. pap. 11.95 (0-8256-2224-7, AM27889) Music Sales.

— Boogie Woogie Hanon. 1980. pap. 11.95 (0-8256-2222-0, AM27400) Music Sales.

— Jazz Hanon. 1980. pap. 11.95 (0-8256-2223-9, AM27418) Music Sales.

— Original Piano Chord Finder. (Illus.). 40p. 1979. pap. 5.95 (0-8256-2389-8, AM24860) Music Sales.

Alfassy, Leo, ed. Baroque & Folk Tunes for Recorder. pap. 10.95 (0-86001-275-1, AM17948) Music Sales.

Alfau, Felipe. Chromos. LC 89-27250. 348p. 1990. 19.95 (0-916583-52-X) Dalkey Arch.

— Chromos. LC 89-27250. 352p. 1999. reprint ed. pap. 13.95 (1-56478-204-2) Dalkey Arch.

— Locos: A Comedy of Gestures. LC 88-14975. 224p. 1997. reprint ed. pap. 12.95 (1-56478-171-2) Dalkey Arch.

— Locos: A Comedy of Gestures. rev. ed. LC 88-14975. 206p. 1989. 19.95 (0-916583-30-9) Dalkey Arch.

— Sentimental Songs: La Poesia Cursi. Stavans, Ilan, tr. from SPA. & intro. by. LC 91-33545. 96p. 1992. 15.95 (0-916583-98-8); pap. 9.95 (0-916583-99-6) Dalkey Arch.

Alfaya, Javier. Una Luz En la Marisma. (J). (gr. 4-7). 1998. pap. text 11.95 (84-204-4806-0) Santillana.

Alfaya, Javier, tr. see Rodgers, Mary.

Alfeld, Louis E. Spotlight on Construction Productivity. 98.00 (0-317-59584-9) Constr Ind Pr.

Alferes, J. J., jt. ed. see Barahona, P.

Alferes, Jose J. & Pereira, Luis M. Reasoning with Logic Programming, Vol. 111. LC 96-27904. (Lecture Notes in Artificial Intelligence). 326p. 1996. pap. 44.50 (3-540-61488-5) Spr-Verlag.

Alferes, Jose J., et al. Logics in Artificial Intelligence: European Workshop, Jelia '96, Evora, Portugal, September 30-October 3, 1996, Proceedings. LC 96-33379. (Lecture Notes in Computer Science Ser.: Vol. 1126). 417p. 1996. 68.00 (3-540-61630-6) Spr-Verlag.

Alferi, Pierre. Natural Gaits. Swensen, Cole, tr. from FRE. (Sun & Moon Classics Ser.: Vol. 95). 56p. 1995. pap. 10.95 (1-55713-231-3) Sun & Moon CA.

Alferic. Aelfric's Catholoic Homilies: The First Series. Godden, Malcolm & Clemoes, Peter, eds. (Early English Text Society-Supplementary Ser.: Vol. 17). (Illus.). 584p. 1998. text 88.00 (0-19-722418-0) OUP.

Alferieff, Barbara E. One Life Through Many Facets. (ENG & RUS.). 182p. 1991. pap. write for info. (0-9660603-0-X) RE Pub.

Alferieff, M. E., tr. see Rabinovich, Semyon.

Alferieff, Michael, tr. see Pikin, S. A.

Alferirff, E. E., ed. Pisoma Tsarskoj Semji iz Zatotchenija. LC 73-91829.Tr. of Letters of the Tsar's Family from Captivity. (Illus.). 544p. 1974. 25.00 (0-317-29225-0) Holy Trinity.

Alfermann, A. W., jt. auth. see Verpoorte, R.

Alferov, Zh. I. Semiconductor Heterostructures. 1990. 104.00 (0-8493-7120-1, TK) CRC Pr.

Alferov, Zhores I., ed. Joint Soviet-American Workshop on the Physics of Semiconductor Lasers. LC 91-58537. (AIP Conference Proceedings Ser.: No. 240). 200p. 1992. 95.00 (0-88318-936-4) Am Inst Physics.

Alferov, Zhores I., et al, eds. Second International Conference on Optical Information Processing, Vol. 2969. 736p. 1996. 124.00 (0-8194-2375-0) SPIE.

Alfers, jt. auth. see Nash, Gary B.

Alfers, Kenneth G. Law & Order in the Capital City: A History of the Washington Police, 1800-1886, Vol. M5. 1976. 5.00 (1-888028-03-3) GWU Ctr WAS.

Alfert, M., ed. see Satir, Peter.

***Alfeyev, Hilarion.** St. Symeon, the New Theologian, & Orthodox Tradition. LC 99-55002. (Oxford Early Christian Studies). 300p. 2000. text. write for info. (0-19-827009-7) OUP.

Alfian, ed. see Chu, Godwin C.

Alfieri, Bruno, ed. see Klemantaski, Louis & Nixon, Chris.

Alfieri, Dino. Dictators Face to Face. Moore, David, tr. LC 78-755. (Illus.). 307p. 1978. reprint ed. lib. bdg. 65.00 (0-313-20285-0, ALDF, Greenwood Pr) Greenwood.

Alfieri, Rebecca, jt. auth. see Thorne, Allison.

Alfieri, Richard. Ricardo - Diary of a Matinee Idol. LC 89-34635. 256p. (Orig.). 1989. 18.95 (0-936784-65-2); pap. 9.95 (0-936784-66-0) J Daniel.

***Alfieri, RoseMarie.** Functional Training: Everyone's Guide to the New Fitness Revolution. 184p. 2001. pap. 17.95 (1-57826-063-9, Pub. by Hatherleigh) Norton.

Alfieri, Vittorio. The Prince & Letters. Corrigan, Beatrice & Molinaro, Julius A., trs. LC 75-185707. (Illus.). 214p. reprint ed. pap. 66.40 (0-608-10985-1, 201944400011) Bks Demand.

Alfin-Slater, R. B. & Kritchevsky, D. Cancer & Nutrition Vol. 7. (Human Nutrition Ser.). (Illus.). 508p. (C). 1991. text 110.00 (0-306-43425-3, Kluwer Plenum) Kluwer Academic.

— Nutrition & the Adult: Macronutrients, Vol. 3A. LC 79-25119. (Human Nutrition Ser.). (Illus.). 308p. (C). 1980. text 110.00 (0-306-40287-4, Kluwer Plenum) Kluwer Academic.

— Nutrition & the Adult Vol. 3B: Micronutrients. LC 79-25119. (Human Nutrition Ser.). (Illus.). 450p. (C). 1980. text 110.00 (0-306-40288-2, Kluwer Plenum) Kluwer Academic.

Alfino, Mark & Pierce, Linda. Information Ethics for Librarians. LC 97-29606. 174p. 1997. lib. bdg. 34.50 (0-7864-0376-4) McFarland & Co.

Alfino, Mark S., et al. McDonaldization Revisited: Critical Essays on Consumer Culture. LC 97-21852. 232p. 1998. 59.95 (0-275-95819-1, Praeger Pubs) Greenwood.

Alfino, Mark S., ed. see Wynyard, Robin.

***Alfiri, Bianca Maria.** Islamic Architecture of the Indian Subcontinent. (Illus.). 2000. 95.00 (3-8238-5443-7) V C Bertelsman.

Alfoeldi, Andreas & Alfoeldi, Elisabeth. Die Kontorniat-Medaillons. (Antike Muenzen und Geschnittene Steine Ser.: Vol. 6). (C). 1976. 226.95 (3-11-003484-0) De Gruyter.

Alfoeldi, Elisabeth, jt. auth. see Alfoeldi, Andreas.

Alfoeldy, Geza. Die Roemischen Inschriften von Tarraco, 2 vols. (Madrider Forschungen Ser.: Vol. 10). (GER.). (C). 1975. 246.15 (3-11-004403-X) De Gruyter.

Alfoeldy, Geza, ed. Corpus Inscriptionum Latinarum: Consilio et Auctoritate Academiae Scientiarum Berolinensis et Brandenburgensis Editum, Vol. VI, Pars VIII: Fasciculus Alter. (GER & LAT., Illus.). xxiv, 4666p. (Orig.). (C). 1996. pap. text 659.30 (3-11-015194-4) De Gruyter.

Alfoeldy, Geza, et al, eds. Corpus Inscriptionum Latinarum Vol. II, Part 14, Fascicle 1: Consilio et Auctoritate Academiae Scientiarum. 197p. (C). 1994. pap. text 398.50 (3-11-014304-6) De Gruyter.

Alfoldi, Andras. A Conflict of Ideas in the Late Roman Empire: The Clash Between the Senate & Valentinian I. Mattingly, Harold B., tr. LC 78-26781. 151p. 1979. reprint ed. lib. bdg. 49.75 (0-313-20836-0, ALCI, Greenwood Pr) Greenwood.

Alfoldi, Andreas. The Numbering of the Victories of the Emperor Gallienus & the Loyalty of His Legions. (Illus.). 1977. 4.75 (0-915018-28-4) Attic Bks.

Alfoldi, Andreas, et al. Die Kontorniat-Medaillons, Part 2. Deutsches Archalolgisches Institut Staff, ed. (Antike Muenzen und Geschnittene Steine Ser.: Vol. VI-2). (Illus.). xxiii, 358p. (C). 1990. lib. bdg. 267.70 (3-11-011905-6) De Gruyter.

Alfoldi, Laszlo, compiled by. East Central European Society & War, 1750-1920: Bibliography & Historiography. write for info. (0-318-60320-9) Brooklyn Coll Pr.

Alfoldy, Geza. Die Bauinschriften des Aquaduktes von Segovia und des Amphitheaters von Tarraco. (Madrider Forschungen Ser.: Vol. 19). (GER.). viii, 110p. (C). 1997. lib. bdg. 136.55 (3-11-014418-2) De Gruyter.

— Romische Heeresgeschichte: Beitrage, 1962-1985. (Mavors Roman Army Researches Ser.: Vol. III). (GER.). 587p. (C). 1987. 134.00 (90-70265-48-6, Pub. by Gieben) J Benjamins Pubng Co.

Alfonseca, Manuel. El Agua de la Vida. (Barco de Vapor Ser.).Tr. of Water of Life. 125p. 1998. pap. 6.50 (84-348-6024-4, Pub. by SM Ediciones) IBD Ltd.

***Alfonsi, Alice.** Anakin's Race for Freedom. LC 98-83058. (Star Wars). (Illus.). (J). (ps-3). 1999. pap. 3.99 (0-375-80027-1) Random Bks Yng Read.

Alfonsi, Alice. Eternal Love. 1998. mass mkt. 6.50 (0-515-12207-6, Jove) Berkley Pub.

— Eternal Sea. (Haunting Hearts Ser.). 352p. 1999. mass mkt. 5.99 (0-515-12434-6, Jove) Berkley Pub.

— Eternal Vows. 368p. 1997. mass mkt. 5.99 (0-515-12002-2, Jove) Berkley Pub.

— Godzilla vs. Gigan & the Smog Monster. LC 96-68785. (Pictureback Ser.). 24p. (J). (gr. 1-4). 1996. pap. 3.99 (0-679-88344-4, Pub. by Random Bks Yng Read) Random.

***Alfonsi, Alice.** Jedi Knights & Heroes. (Star Wars). (Illus.). 80p. (J). (ps-3). 2000. pap. 2.99 (0-375-80526-5, Pub. by Random Bks Yng Read) Random.

Alfonsi, Alice. Some Enchanted Evening. 352p. 1998. pap. 5.99 (0-515-12370-6, Jove) Berkley Pub.

Alfonsi, Alice & Scognamiglio, John, eds. Dark Seductions. 352p. 1993. mass mkt. 4.50 (0-8217-4331-7, Zebra Kensgtn) Kensgtn Pub Corp.

Alfonsi, Alice, ed. see Windham, Ryder.

Alfonsi, Ferando. Wall of Darkness.Tr. of Miro di Tenebra. 64p. 1980. pap. 7.50 (0-89304-599-3); pap. 7.50 (0-89304-598-5) Cross-Cultrl NY.

Alfonsi, Ferdinando P. Dictionary of Italian-American Poets. (American University Studies: Romance Languages & Literature: Ser. II, Vol. 112). 174p. (C). 1989. text 30.95 (0-8204-0916-2) P Lang Pubng.

Alfonso, Betty A. Manicuring: The Knowledge of Maintaining Beautiful Nails & Hands. Laborde Printers Staff, ed. (Illus.). 85p. (Orig.). 1992. pap. write for info. (0-9634492-0-6) Betty Bks.

Alfonso, Felipe B., jt. ed. see Korten, David C.

Alfonso, Harlaldo D. Community Power & Grassroots Democracy: The Transformation of Social Life. Kaufman, Michael, ed. LC 96-39524. 256p. 1997. text 22.50 (1-85649-488-8, Pub. by Zed Books) St Martin.

Alfonso, Haroldo Dilla, jt. auth. see Kaufman, Michael.

Alfonso, Lara Castilla. Busqueda Edicion Lujo. gif. ed. (SPA., Illus.). 183p. 1997. pap. text 29.98 (968-13-3072-2) Edit Diana.

— El Secreto. (SPA., Illus.). 135p. 1997. pap. text 9.98 (968-13-3066-8) Edit Diana.

Alfonso, Marbia M. Mudnoz Marbin Vs. the Bishops: An Approach to Church & State. LC 98-196013. xii, 210p. 1998. write for info. (1-881713-41-5) Pubns Intl Ltd.

Alfonso, Pablo. Cuba: El Dialogo Ignorado. (SPA.). 112p. (Orig.). 1993. pap. 10.00 (0-9631736-3-4) Ediciones Cambio.

— Los Fieles de Castro. 225p. 1991. pap. 20.00 (0-9631736-0-X) Ediciones Cambio.

Alfonso, Ralph. Ralph: Coffee, Jazz & Poetry. (Illus.). 128p. 1997. pap. 14.98 (0-934953-51-1) Water Row Pr.

Alfonso, Regina M. How Jesus Taught: The Methods & Techniques of the Master. LC 86-10812. (Illus.). 129p. (Orig.). 1986. pap. 6.95 (0-8189-0506-9) Alba.

Alfonso, Rudolfo. Just Poetry. LC 98-93921.Tr. of Justo Poesia. 156p. 1998. pap. 14.95 (0-7392-0001-1, PO2726) Morris Pubng.

Alfonso, Rui. One Good Man. write for info. (965-229-129-3, Pub. by Gefen Pub Hse) Gefen Bks.

Alfonso X. General Historia II, Vol. 1. (Illus.). lxvii, 477p. 1957. 25.00 (0-942260-01-5) Hispanic Seminary.

— General Historia II, Vol. 2. (Illus.). 417p. 1961. 25.00 (0-942260-02-3) Hispanic Seminary.

— Libro de las Cruzes. Kasten, Lloyd A. & Kiddle, Lawrence B., eds. (Illus.). xlviii, 173p. 1961. pap. 10.00 (0-942260-03-1) Hispanic Seminary.

Alford. Computer Systems Engineering Management. (Electrical Engineering & Electronics Ser.: Vol. 45). 392p. 1987. 150.00 (0-8247-7643-7) Dekker.

Alford, A. Gods of the New Millenium. mass mkt. 19.95 (0-340-69613-3, Pub. by Hodder & Stought Ltd) Trafalgar.

— Phoenix Solution. 1998. text 40.00 (0-340-69614-1, Pub. by Hodder & Stought Ltd) Trafalgar.

***Alford, Annie L.** The Four Seasons. 64p. 1999. pap. 8.00 (0-9676041-1-7) A L Alford.

— Teach Us to Pray. 128p. 1998. pap. 10.00 (0-9676041-0-9) A L Alford.

Alford, B. R., et al, eds. Electrophysiologic Evaluation in Otolaryngology. LC 97-985. (Advances in OtoRhinoLaryngology Ser.: Vol. 53, 1997). (Illus.). viii, 212p. 1997. 169.00 (3-8055-6427-9) S Karger.

Alford, B. W. BRITAIN WORLD ECON 1880. Briggs, Asa, ed. LC 95-5930. (Social & Economic History of England Ser.). 336p. (C). 1995. pap. text 31.88 (0-582-48676-9) Longman.

— British Economic Performance, 1945-1975. (New Studies in Economic & Social History: Vol. 4). 135p. (C). 1995. text 34.95 (0-521-55263-X); pap. text 10.95 (0-521-55790-9) Cambridge U Pr.

Alford, Brad A. & Beck, Aaron T. The Integrative Power of Cognitive Therapy. LC 96-47830. 197p. 1997. lib. bdg. 35.00 (1-57230-171-6, 0171) Guilford Pubns.

— The Integrative Power of Cognitive Therapy. 197p. 1998. pap. text 20.00 (1-57230-396-4) Guilford Pubns.

Alford, C. Ford. The Self in Social Theory: A Psychoanalytic Account of Its Construction in Plato, Hobbes, Locke, Rawls, & Rousseau. LC 90-39887. 237p. 1991. reprint ed. pap. 73.50 (0-608-07878-6, 205998500010) Bks Demand.

Alford, C. Fred. Group Psychology & Political Theory. LC 94-6774. 248p. 1994. 32.50 (0-300-05958-2) Yale U Pr.

— The Psychoanalytic Theory of Greek Tragedy. LC 92-13469. 240p. (C). 1992. 37.50 (0-300-05708-3) Yale U Pr.

— Science & the Revenge of Nature: Marcuse & Habermas. LC 85-627. x, 226p. 1985. 49.95 (0-8130-0817-4) U Press Fla.

***Alford, C. Fred.** Think No Evil: Korean Values in the Age of Globalization LC 99-30527. 1999. write for info. (0-8014-3666-4) Cornell U Pr.

***Alford, C Fred.** Think No Evil: Korean Values in The Age of Globalizaton. 1999. 32.50 (0-8014-3664-8) Cornell U Pr.

Alford, C. Fred. What Evil Means to Us. LC 97-10437. 200p. 1997. text 22.50 (0-8014-3430-0) Cornell U Pr.

Alford-Cooper, Finnegan. For Keeps: Marriages That Last a Lifetime. LC 97-38833. 232p. (C). (gr. 13). 1998. text 66.95 (0-7656-0122-2); pap. text 24.95 (0-7656-0123-0) M E Sharpe.

Alford, D., intro. Constitutional Crisis. 5.00 (0-8315-0072-7) Speller.

***Alford, D. V.** A Textbook of Agricultural Entomology. LC 99-34207. 1999. write for info. (0-632-05297-X) Blackwell Sci.

Alford, David V. A Color Atlas of Pests of Ornamental Trees, Shrubs & Flowers. 448p. 1995. text 119.95 (0-470-23494-6) Halsted Pr.

Alford, Delton L. Music in the Pentecostal Church. 113p. 1969. pap. 4.25 (0-87148-562-1) Pathway Pr.

Alford, Edna. The Garden of Elois Loon. 1986. text 16.95 (0-88982-082-1, Pub. by Oolichan Bks) Genl Dist Srvs.

— The Garden of Eloise Loon. 1986. pap. text 9.95 (0-88982-080-5, Pub. by Oolichan Bks) Genl Dist Srvs.

— A Sleep Full of Dreams. 1981. pap. text 16.95 (0-88982-031-7, Pub. by Oolichan Bks) Genl Dist Srvs.

— A Sleep Full of Dreams. 1993. pap. text 8.95 (0-88982-013-9, Pub. by Oolichan Bks) Genl Dist Srvs.

***Alford, Edna, et al, eds.** Rip-Rap. 264p. 1999. pap. 14.95 (0-920159-65-6) Banff Ctr.

Alford, Edna & Harris, Claire, eds. Kitchen Talk: Contemporary Women's Prose & Poetry. 304p. 1992. pap. 16.95 (0-88995-091-1, Pub. by Red Deer) Genl Dist Srvs.

Alford, Fred. Melainie Klein & Critical Social Theory: An Account of Politics, Art, & Reason Based on Her Psychoanalytic Theory. 256p. (C). 1989. 40.00 (0-300-04506-9) Yale U Pr.

Alford, George & Alford, Verna B. Ten Generations of Myers in America. 996p. 1996. write for info. (0-9654355-0-4) Fmly History.

Alford, George & Cullimore, Roy. Application of Heat & Chemicals in the Control of Biofouling Events in Wells. LC 98-31049. (Lewis Publishers' Sustainable Well Ser.). 150p. 1999. 79.95 (1-56670-385-9) Lewis Pubs.

Alford, Harold D. Procedures for School District Reorganization. LC 75-176509. (Columbia University. Teachers College. Contributions to Education Ser.: No. 852). reprint ed. 37.50 (0-404-55852-6) AMS Pr.

***Alford, Henry.** Big Kiss: One Actor's Desperate Attempt to Claw His Way to the Top. 240p. 2000. 19.95 (0-679-43873-4) Villard Books.

Alford, Henry. Municipal Bondage: One Man's Anxiety-Producing Adventures in the Big City. LC 95-1678. 256p. 1995. pap. 10.00 (1-57322-510-X, Riverhd Trade) Berkley Pub.

Alford, Jackie M. Peppermints in the Armoire. LC 97-94511. (Illus.). 160p. 1997. spiral bd. 19.95 (0-9660609-0-3) J M Alford.

Alford, James M. Employing Robotics in Small Manufacturing Firms: Strategic Implications. LC 87-3017. 202p. 1988. lib. bdg. 24.25 (0-89464-222-7) Krieger.

Alford, Jan. I Can't Believe I Have to Do This. LC 96-43543. 192p. (YA). (gr. 5 up). 1997. 16.95 (0-399-23130-7, G P Putnam) Peng Put Young Read.

***Alford, Jan.** I Can't Believe I Have to Do This. (J). 1999. pap. 5.99 (0-698-11785-9, PapStar) Peng Put Young Read.

Alford, Jan, jt. auth. see Sunny Sands Elementary School Students.

***Alford, Jane.** Victorian Fans & Posies in Cross Stitch. (Cross Stitch Ser.). (Illus.). 40p. 1999. pap. 6.95 (1-85391-759-1) Merehurst Ltd.

Alford, Jane, et al. Flowers in Cross Stitch. (Illus.). 160p. 1996. write for info. (1-57215-198-6) World Pubns.

An Asterisk (*) at the beginning of an entry indicates that the title is appearing for the first time.

Alford, Jeffrey & Duguid, Naomi. Flatbreads & Flavors: A Culinary Atlas. LC 94-30892. (Illus.). 356p. 1995. 30.00 (*0-688-11411-3*, Wm Morrow) Morrow Avon.

***Alford, Jeffrey & Duguid, Naomi.** Hot Sour Salty Sweet: A Culinary Journey Through Southeast Asia. LC 00-22092. 368p. 2000. 40.00 (*1-57965-114-3*) Artisan.

Alford, Jeffrey & Duguid, Naomi. Seductions of Rice: A Cookbook. LC 98-3951. (Illus.). 480p. 1998. 35.00 (*1-57965-113-5*, 85113) Artisan.

Alford, Jess, jt. auth. see Fritz, Edward C.

Alford, John. The Mountain Biker's Guide to O'ahu: Mauka Trails of Hawai'i. Clark, John, ed. (Illus.). 112p. (Orig.). 1995. pap. 12.95 (*0-9649843-0-X*) Ohana Pubng.

— Mountain Biking the Hawaiian Islands: Mauka to Makai. large type ed. LC 97-91699. (Illus.). 264p. (Orig.). 1997. pap. 15.95 (*0-9649843-1-8*) Ohana Pubng.

***Alford, John.** Mountain Biking the Hawaiian Islands: Mauka to Makai. 2nd ed. Clark, John, ed. LC 00-91396. (Illus.). 264p. (Orig.). 2000. pap. 15.95 (*0-9649843-2-6*) Ohana Pubng.

Alford, John A. Piers Plowman: A Glossary of Legal Diction. 202p. 1988. 75.00 (*0-85991-248-5*) Boydell & Brewer.

Alford, John A., ed. A Companion to Piers Plowman. (Illus.). 298p. 1988. pap. 18.95 (*0-520-06007-5*, ALFCOX, Pub. by U CA Pr) Cal Prin Full Svc.

— From Page to Performance: Essays in Early English Drama. LC 95-2384. 266p. 1995. 32.95 (*0-87013-379-9*) Mich St U Pr.

— Piers Plowman: A Guide to the Quotations. (Medieval & Renaissance Texts & Studies: Vol. 77). 176p. 1992. 18.00 (*0-86698-088-1*, MR77) MRTS.

Alford, John A., jt. ed. see Newhauser, Richard.

Alford, John A., jt. ed. see Schoonmaker, Donald.

Alford, Jonathan, ed. Sea Power & Influence: Old Issues & New Challenges. LC 80-67840. (Adelphi Library: Vol. 2). 224p. 1981. text 52.00 (*0-916672-72-7*) Rowman.

Alford, Judy. Collecting Crackle Glass. LC 96-72029. (Illus.). 160p. 1997. pap. 29.95 (*0-7643-0217-5*) Schiffer.

Alford, Katherine. Home Again, Home Again. (Illus.). 31p. (Orig.). (J). (gr. 2-7). 1996. pap. 12.00 (*0-9652438-0-X*) Little City.

A poignant & sophisticated little tale about a family living in the only-slightly-fictional college town of Phoebesville, Virginia, "not too far from the Atlantic Ocean, but not close enough to go there for a day." Dr. Quiddick is from the Upper Midwest, Mrs. Quiddick is from the Deep South, & they both pine sometimes for their childhood homes. Unlike their parents, the Quiddick children feel totally home in Phoebesville, & continue with happy detachment as their parents wrestle with a question more relevant today than ever before: Is Home where you come from? Or is Home where you are? HOME AGAIN, HOME AGAIN addresses this universal dilemma with humor & lighthearted poignancy, providing comfort & assurance to both children & adults, particularly those contemplating or recovering from a major move. Ms. Alford has a distinctively spare & amusing prose style. A professional freelance writer for 18 years, she is also a veteran of five cross-country moves with her four children & her husband, a professor at the University of Virginia. Whimsically illustrated by Anna Galloway, a student at Rhode Island School of Design. Contact: Little City Books, 1033 Locust Ave., Charlottesville, VA 22901; 800-373-5407 or 804-295-3577. *Publisher Paid Annotation.*

Alford, Kathy M., ed. see Clawson, Dell M.

Alford, Kenneth D. The Spoils of World War II: The American Military's Role in Stealing Europe's Treasures. LC 94-12608. (Illus.). 320p. 1994. 19.95 (*1-55972-237-1*, Birch Ln Pr) Carol Pub Group.

Alford, M. H. & Alford, V. L. Russian-English Scientific & Technical Dictionary, 2 vols. LC 73-88348. (ENG & RUS.). 1970. 637.00 (*0-08-012227-2*, Pub. by Pergamon Repr) Franklin.

Alford, Mack. Issue Driven System Engineering Managing the Design Iteration Process. (Systems Engineering Ser.). 1999. 69.95 (*0-8493-7835-4*, 7835) CRC Pr.

Alford, Marcus R. & Cohen, Marsha P. Jazz Danceology: Teaching & Choreographing Jazz Dance. 190p. 1992. pap. text 24.95 (*1-880716-00-3*) Dance Pr.

***Alford, Monty.** Winter Wise: Travel & Survival in Ice & Snow. (Illus.). 160p. 1999. pap. 14.95 (*1-895811-95-3*) Heritage Hse.

Alford, Mrs. Henry, ed. Life Journals & Letters of Henry Alford, 2 vols., Set. vii, 542p. reprint ed. 69.00 (*0-7812-0872-6*) Rprt Serv.

Alford, Neil M., ed. Growth & Processing of Electronic Materials. (Workshop Proceedings Ser.). (Illus.). 144p. 1998. 90.00 (*1-86125-072-X*, Pub. by Inst Materials) Ashgate Pub Co.

Alford, Neill H., Jr. & Dobris, Joel C. Teacher's Manual to Accompany Cases & Materials on Decedents' Estates & Trusts. 8th ed. (University Casebook Ser.). 229p. 1993. pap. text. write for info. (*1-56662-138-0*) Foundation Pr.

Alford, Norman. The Rhymers' Club: Poets of the Tragic Generation. 175p. 1996. pap. 17.95 (*0-312-16460-2*) St Martin.

Alford, Raye L. Genetics & Your Health: A Guide for the 21st Century Family. 288p. 1999. 29.95 (*0-9666748-2-0*, Pub. by Plexus Pub) IPG Chicago.

Alford, Raye Lynn. Genetics & Your Health: A Guide for the 21st Century Family. LC 98-31950. 270p. 1999. pap. 19.95 (*0-9666748-1-2*, Pub. by Plexus Pub) IPG Chicago.

***Alford, Rex E.** Songs of Sorrow. LC 98-91005. 1999. 15.95 (*0-533-13016-6*) Vantage.

Alford, Richard, ed. On the Word of Command: A Pictorial History of the Regimental Sergeant Major. 208p. (C). 1991. 135.00 (*0-946771-65-0*, Pub. by Spellmnt Pubs) St Mut.

Alford, Richard D. Naming & Identity: A Cross-Cultural Study of Personal Naming Practices. LC 86-80925. (Comparative Studies). 190p. 1988. pap. 20.00 (*0-87536-117-X*) HRAFP.

Alford, Ricker, jt. auth. see Meyers, Eric M.

Alford, Robbie M., jt. auth. see Morgan, Margie M.

Alford, Robert R. The Craft of Inquiry: Theories, Methods, Evidence. 176p. (C). 1998. text 50.00 (*0-19-511902-9*); pap. text 18.95 (*0-19-511903-7*) OUP.

— Health Care Politics: Ideological & Interest Group Barriers. LC 74-75611. 308p. Date not set. reprint ed. pap. 95.50 (*0-608-20980-5*, 205450800003) Bks Demand.

— Health Care Politics: Ideological & Interest Group Barriers to Reform. LC 74-75611. xiv, 294p. 1975. lib. bdg. 11.00 (*0-226-01379-0*) U Ch Pr.

— Health Care Politics: Ideological & Interest Group Barriers to Reform. LC 74-75611. 308p. reprint ed. pap. 95.50 (*0-608-09373-4*, 205411800004) Bks Demand.

— Party & Society: The Anglo-American Democracies. LC 72-9541. (Illus.). 396p. 1973. reprint ed. lib. bdg. 69.50 (*0-8371-6584-9*, ALPS, Greenwood Pr) Greenwood.

***Alford, Roger.** The City Burns at Night: Original Radio Script. 46p. 1999. pap. 10.00 (*0-9672822-0-9*) Lightning Bug.

Alford, Roger C., et al. One Hour Telecomputing. LC 84-9450. (C). 1985. pap. text 9.95 (*0-931543-01-0*) IM-Pr.

Alford, Ron. Auto Insurance Tricks & Repair Rip-Offs: A New & Different Kind of Owner's Manual. 5th rev. ed. 167p. (Orig.). 1999. pap. 14.95 (*0-924893-08-7*) Plan Pub.

— The Crime of the Century - Insurance: Everything You Need to Know Before You Buy Insurance. 114p. (Orig.). 1989. pap. 19.95 (*0-924893-00-1*) Plan Pub.

— How to Win the Insurance Claim Game: The Property Owner's Guide to Disaster Recovery & Claim Management. (Illus.). 120p. (Orig.). 1992. pap. text 12.95 (*0-924893-01-X*) Plan Pub.

Alford, Stephen. The Early Elizabethan Polity: William Cecil & the British Succession Crisis, 1558-1569. LC 97-32458. (Cambridge Studies in Early Modern British History). 288p. (C). 1998. text 59.95 (*0-521-62218-2*) Cambridge U Pr.

***Alford, Steve.** 50-Minute All-American Workout. 1999. pap. 35.95 incl. VHS Championship Bks & Vid Prodns.

Alford, Steve & Garrity, John. Playing for Knight: My Six Seasons with Coach Knight. 304p. 1990. pap. 9.95 (*0-671-72441-X*, Fireside) S&S Trade Pap.

Alford, Steve & Schilling, Ed. Basketball Guard Play. (Spalding Sports Library). (Illus.). 160p. (Orig.). 1995. pap. 12.95 (*1-57028-024-X*, 8024XH, Mstrs Pr) NTC Contemp Pub Co.

Alford, Terry. Prince among Slaves. (Illus.). 304p. 1986. pap. 14.95 (*0-19-504223-9*) OUP.

Alford, V. L., jt. auth. see Alford, M. H.

Alford, Verna B., jt. auth. see Alford, George.

Alford, Violet. Pyrenean Festivals: Calendar Customs, Music & Magic, Drama & Dance. LC 77-87730. 1977. reprint ed. 47.50 (*0-404-16577-X*) AMS Pr.

Alford, William P. To Steal a Book Is an Elegant Offense: Intellectual Property Law in Chinese Civilization. LC 94-15742. (Studies in East Asian Law). xiii , 222p. 1994. 39.50 (*0-8047-2270-6*) Stanford U Pr.

Alfred & Otte, James K. Alfred of Sareshel's Commentary on the Metheora of Aristotle: Critical Edition, Introduction, & Notes. LC 87-22334. (Studien und Texte Zur Geistesgeschichte des Mittelalters). 1911. pap. 36.50 (*90-04-08453-3*) Brill Academic Pubs.

Alfred, Audrey, et al. Ten Sisters: A True Story. 3rd ed. LC 96-77711. (Illus.). 297p. 1997. reprint ed. 24.95 (*1-878044-49-4*) Mayhaven Pub.

Alfred, B. M. Elements of Statistics for the Life & Social Science. (Texts in Statistics Ser.). (Illus.). xiii, 190p. 1987. 58.95 (*0-387-96500-9*) Spr-Verlag.

***Alfred, Eunice.** Prayer Changes Things. 200p. 1999. 15.00 (*0-9670227-1-1*) E Alfred.

Alfred, Gerald R. Heeding the Voices of Our Ancestors: Kahnawake Mohawk Politics & the Rise of Native Nationalism. LC 96-132074. (Illus.). 220p. 1995. pap. text 32.00 (*0-19-541138-2*) OUP.

Alfred, H. The Training & Use of Dental Auxiliary Personnel. (Public Health in Europe Ser.: No. 7). 70p. 1977. 9.00 (*92-9020-126-6*, 1320007) World Health.

Alfred, J. Tyrone & Cannon-Alfred, C. Medical Handbook for the Layman. 1969. 5.95 (*0-686-00411-6*) Alfred.

Alfred, Melba A. Right under Your Nose: A Novel. 94p. 1999. spiral bd. 9.95 (*0-9670845-4-7*) Annointed Wrtg.

Alfred P. Sloan Museum Staff, jt. ed. see Flint Journal Staff.

Alfred, Richard, et al. Core Indicators of Effectiveness for Community Colleges. 2nd ed. LC 99-217674. (Illus.). 40p. 1999. 16.00 (*0-87117-320-4*, 1432) Comm Coll Pr Am Assn Comm Coll.

Alfred, Richard L. & Carter, Patricia, eds. Changing Managerial Imperatives. LC 85-644753. (New Directions for Community Colleges Ser.: No. CC 84). 118p. (Orig.). 1994. pap. 22.00 (*1-55542-719-7*) Jossey-Bass.

Alfred, Richard L. & Hummel, Mary L. Instructional Dynamics in Two Year Postsecondary Institutions: Concepts, Trends, & Assessment Issues. 69p. 1987. 8.00 (*0-318-23413-0*, IN 318) Ctr Educ Trng Employ.

Alfred, Taiaiake. Peace, Power & Righteousness: An Indigenous Manifesto. LC 99-233319. 200p. 1999. pap. 19.95 (*0-19-541216-8*) OUP.

Alfred, Tennyson. Idylls of the King. Gray, J. M., ed. 376p. 1989. pap. 9.95 (*0-14-042253-6*, Penguin Classics) Viking Penguin.

Alfred the Great. Whole Works of Alfred the Great, 3 pts. in 2 vols. Giles, J. A., ed. LC 73-86832. reprint ed. 175.00 (*0-404-00380-X*) AMS Pr.

— The Works of Alfred the Great, 2 vols., Set. 1977. lib. bdg. 250.00 (*0-8490-2843-4*) Gordon Pr.

Alfred, William, et al, trs. Medieval Epics. LC 98-4488. 1998. 24.95 (*0-679-60301-8*) Modern Lib NY.

Alfredo, Gonzalez W. Dos y Dos Son Cinco y Otras 4 Comedias. LC 80-69553. (Coleccion Teatro). (SPA.). 255p. (Orig.). 1984. pap. 9.95 (*0-89729-276-6*) Ediciones.

Alfreds, Mike, jt. auth. see Wandor, Michelene.

Alfredson, James B. Jean Hugard. LC 97-9535. 1997. 20.00 (*0-916638-84-7*, D M Magic Bks) Meyerbooks.

— Newmann: The Pioneer Mentalist. (Illus.). 78p. 1989. 22.50 (*0-916638-42-1*, D M Magic Bks) Meyerbooks.

Alfredsson, Gudmundur & Eide, Asbjorn. The Universal Declaration of Human Rights: A Common Standard of Achievement. LC 99-13931. 1999. 237.00 (*90-411-1168-9*) Kluwer Law Intl.

***Alfredsson, Gudmundur & Ring, Rolf.** The Inspection Panel of the World Bank: A Different Complaints Procedure. LC 00-33066. (Raoul Wallenberg Institute Human Rights Guides Ser.). 2000. write for info. (*90-411-1390-8*) Kluwer Law Intl.

Alfredsson, Gudmundur & Tomasevski, Katarina. A Thematic Guide to Documents on Health & Human Rights: Global & Regional Standards Adopted by Intergovernmental Organizations, International Non-Governmental Organizations & Professional Associations. LC 98-7200. (Raoul Wallenberg Institute Human Rights Guides Ser.). 1998. write for info. (*90-411-1008-9*, Pub. by M Nijhoff) Kluwer Academic.

***Alfredsson, Gudmundur & Tomasevski, Katarina, eds.** A Thematic Guide to Documents on Health & Human Rights: Global & Regional Standards Adopted by Intergovernmental Organizations, International Non-Governmental Organizations & Professional Associations. (Raoul Wallenberg Institute Human Rights Guides Ser.: Vol. 2). 640p. 1998. 189.00 (*90-411-0544-1*) Kluwer Law Intl.

Alfredsson, Gudmundur & Tomasevski, Katarina, eds. A Thematic Guide to Documents on the Human Rights of Women: Global & Regional Standards Adopted by Intergovernmental Organizations, International Non-Governmental Organizations & Professional Associations. (Raoul Wallenberg Institute Human Rights Guides Ser.: Vol. 1). 448p. (C). 1995. lib. bdg. 151.00 (*90-411-0094-6*, Pub. by M Nijhoff) Kluwer Academic.

Alfredsson, P. H., jt. ed. see Johansson, A. V.

Alfrey, A. C., jt. auth. see Zatta, P. F.

Alfrey, Judith & Putnam, Tim. The Industrial Heritage: Managing Resources & Uses. (Heritage: Care-Preservation-Management Program Ser.). (Illus.). 344p. (C). (gr. 13). 1992. text 99.95 (*0-415-04068-X*, A7436) Routledge.

Alfrey, Shawn. The Sublime of Intense Sociability: Emily Dickinson, H. D. & Gertrude Stein. LC 99-20032. 184p. 2000. 34.50 (*0-8387-5402-3*) Bucknell U Pr.

Alfrey, Turner. Selected Papers of Turner Alfrey. Boyer, Raymond F. & Mark, Herman F., eds. LC 85-29344. (Illus.). 591p. reprint ed. pap. 183.30 (*0-7837-0603-0*, 204095100019) Bks Demand.

Alfriend, Bonnie. Secrets of the Superstars: Excellence in Selling New Homes. (Illus.). 319p. (Orig.). 1993. pap. text 24.95 (*0-9639500-0-2*) Alfriend & Assocs.

Alfriend, Bonnie & Tiller, Richard. New Home Sales Management: How to Build & Lead a Winning Team. 350p. (Orig.). 1996. pap. text 29.95 (*0-9639500-1-0*) Alfriend & Assocs.

Alfriend, K. Terry, et al, eds. AAS/AIAA Astrodynamics Conference, Aug. 14-17, 1995, Halifax, Nova Scotia, Canada, 2 vols., Set. LC 57-43769. (Advances in the Astronautical Sciences Ser.: Vol. 90). (Illus.). 2270p. 1996. 290.00 (*0-87703-407-9*, Am Astronaut Soc) Univelt Inc.

Alfriend, Kyle T., ed. Journal of Guidance, Control, & Dynamics, Vol. 19. 1996. 175.00 (*0-685-30530-9*, JGCD) AIAA.

Alfro-LeFevre, Rosalinda. Instructor's Manual for Critical Thinking in Nursing. 2nd ed. 95p. pap. text, teacher ed. write for info. (*0-7216-8278-2*, W B Saunders Co) Harcrt Hlth Sci Grp.

***Alfs, James.** Cooking with Ginger. (Illus.). 92p. 1999. pap. 11.95 (*0-9676207-0-8*) Regnig Mountain.

— Flash in the Pan. (Illus.). 90p. 1999. pap. 11.95 (*0-9676207-1-6*) Regnig Mountain.

Alfs, Matthew. Concepts of Father, Son, & Holy Spirit: A Classification & Description of the Trinitarian & Non-Trinitarian Theologies Existent Within Christendom. LC 83-63213. 104p. 1984. lib. bdg. 12.95 (*0-9612964-0-2*) Old Theology Bk Hse.

Alfsen, E. M. Compact Convex Sets & Boundary Integrals. LC 72-136352. (Ergebnisse der Mathematik und Ihrer Grenzgebiete Ser.: Vol. 57). (Illus.). 1971. 75.95 (*0-387-05090-6*) Spr-Verlag.

Alfsen, Erik M. & Shultz, Frederick W. Non-Commutative Spectral Theory for Affine Function Spaces on Convex Sets. LC 76-18309. (Memoirs Ser.: No. 6/172). 120p. 1976. pap. 22.00 (*0-8218-1872-4*, MEMO/6/172) Am Math.

Alft, E. C. Elgin: Days Gone By. LC 92-74380. (Illus.). 312p. 1992. 19.95 (*0-916445-37-2*) Crossroads Comm.

***Alfutov, N. A.** Stability of Elastic Structures. Balmont, V. & Evseev, E., trs. from RUS. LC 99-89581. (Foundations of Engineering Mechanics Ser.). (Illus.). ix, 337p. 2000. 99.00 (*3-540-65700-2*) Spr-Verlag.

Alfven, Hannes. Cosmic Plasma. 1981. text 106.00 (*90-277-1151-8*) Kluwer Academic.

— On the Origin of the Solar System. LC 72-9604. (International Series of Monographs on Physics). (Illus.). 194p. 1982. reprint ed. lib. bdg. 115.00 (*0-8371-6595-4*, AEALOS, Greenwood Pr) Greenwood.

Alfven, Hannes & Arrhenius, Gustaf. Structure & Evolutionary History of the Solar System. LC 75-29444. (Geophysics & Astrophysics Monographs: No. 5). xvi, 280p. 1975. pap. text 82.50 (*90-277-0660-3*); lib. bdg. 104.50 (*90-277-0611-5*) Kluwer Academic.

Alfving, Algert M., et al. Fun with Foods: A Recipe for Math & Science. (J). (gr. 5-9). 1987. 16.95 (*1-881431-07-X*, 1305) AIMS Educ Fnd.

Algaba, J., ed. Surgical & Prosthetic Voice Restoration after Total & Subtotal Laryngectomy: Proceedings of the 6th International Congress, San Sebastian, 29 September-1 October 1995. (International Congress Ser.: No. 1112). 432p. 1996. text 187.00 (*0-444-82345-X*, Excerpta Medica) Elsevier.

Algar, Ayla E. Classical Turkish Cooking: Traditional Turkish Food for the American Kitchen. 320p. 1999. pap. 15.00 (*0-06-093163-9*) HarpC.

— Classical Turkish Cooking: Traditional Turkish Food for the American Kitchen. LC 91-55096. 320p. 1991. 35.00 (*0-06-016317-8*) HarperTrade.

— The Complete Book of Turkish Cooking. LC 95-4555. 335p. 1996. 29.00 (*0-7103-0524-9*, Pub. by Kegan Paul Intl) Col U Pr.

— The Complete Book of Turkish Cooking. (Illus.). 336p. 1989. pap. 17.95 (*0-7103-0334-3*) Routledge.

Algar, H., tr. see Sayyid, Mujtaba L.

***Algar, Hamid.** Four Lectures on the Islamic Revolution of Iran. Orig. Title: The Roots of the Islamic Revolution. 150p. 2000. pap. 9.95 (*1-889999-25-3*) Islam Pubns Int.

— Four Lectures on the Islamic Revolution of Iran. rev. ed. Orig. Title: The Roots of the Islamic Revolution. 150p. 2000. 19.95 (*1-889999-27-X*) Islam Pubns Int.

— Imam Abu Hamid Ghazali: An Exponent of Islam in Its Totality. 52p. 2000. pap. 3.95 (*1-889999-15-6*) Islam Pubns Int.

Algar, Hamid. Jesus in the Qur'an. 56p. 1999. pap. 3.95 (*1-889999-09-1*) Islam Pubns Int.

— Sufism: Principles & Practice. 46p. 1999. pap. 3.95 (*1-889999-02-4*) Islam Pubns Int.

— The Sunna: Its Obligatory & Exemplary Aspects. 56p. (Orig.). 1999. pap. text 3.95 (*1-889999-01-6*) Islam Pubns Int.

— Surah Al-Fatihah: Foundation of the Qur'an. 52p. (Orig.). 1998. pap. text 3.50 (*1-889999-00-8*) Islam Pubns Int.

Algar, Hamid, tr. from PER. Constitution of the Islamic Republic of Iran. LC 80-19896. 94p. 1980. 9.95 (*0-933782-07-1*); pap. 3.95 (*0-933782-02-0*) Mizan Pr.

Algar, Hamid, ed. see Mutahhari, Ayatullah M.

Algar, Hamid, ed. see Shariati, Ali.

Algar, Hamid, tr. see Khomeini, Imam.

Algar, Hamid, tr. see Khumayni, Ruh A.

Algar, Hamid, tr. see Qutb, Sayyid.

Algar, Hamid, tr. see Razi, Najm A.

Algar, Hamid, tr. see Shariati, Ali.

Algar, J., jt. auth. see Clayton, R. J.

Algar, J., jt. ed. see Clayton, R. J.

Algar, V. S., et al, eds. Incompleteness & Uncertainty in Information Systems. LC 95-10003. (Workshops in Computing Ser.). (Illus.). 235p. 1994. 61.95 (*0-387-19897-0*) Spr-Verlag.

Algarin, Miguel. Action. LC 97-27602. 192p. 1997. per. 16.00 (*0-684-82611-9*) S&S Trade.

— Love Is Hard Work. 1997. 24.50 (*0-684-83999-7*) S&S Trade.

— Memorias de Loisaida. LC 97-2093. 128p. 1997. per. 13.00 (*0-684-82517-1*) S&S Trade.

— The Time Is Now. LC 83-72575. (ENG & SPA.). 86p. (Orig.). (C). 1985. pap. 7.00 (*0-934770-33-6*) Arte Publico.

Algarin, Miguel, ed. Aloud! Voices. 544p. 1995. pap. 14.95 (*0-8050-3257-6*) H Holt & Co.

— Aloud! Voices. (J). 1995. 30.00 (*0-8050-3275-4*) H Holt & Co.

Algarotti, Francesco. Saggio Sopra la Pittura (Livorno, 1763) fac. ed. (Documents of Art & Architectural History Ser.: Vol. 8). (ITA., Illus.). 1981. lib. bdg. 30.00 (*0-89371-206-X*) Broude Intl Edns.

Algarra, Luis A. Corazon y Pensamientos. 630p. (Orig.). 1989. pap. 15.00 (*0-685-28126-4*) L A A Algarra.

Algaze, G., et al. Town & Country in Southeastern Anatolia Vol. 2: The Stratigraphic Sequence at Kurban Hoyuk, 2 vols., Set. LC 90-61729. (Oriental Institute Publications: No. 110). (Illus.). 647p. 1990. 130.00 (*0-918986-65-6*) Orient Inst.

Algaze, Guillermo. The Uruk World System: The Dynamics of Early Mesopotamian Civilization. LC 92-27445. (Illus.). 174p. (C). 1993. 39.95 (*0-226-01381-2*) U Ch Pr.

Algazi, V. Ralph, et al, eds. Very High Resolution & Quality Imaging II, Vol. 3025. LC 97-175339. 194p. 1997. 59.00 (*0-8194-2436-6*) SPIE.

Algazi, V. Ralph & Tescher, Andrew G., eds. Very High Resolution & Quality Imaging III, Vol. 3308. 130p. 1998. 48.00 (*0-8194-2748-9*) SPIE.

A

Algebraic Methodology & Software Technology Staff, et al. Algebraic Methodology & Software Technology: 7th International Conference, AMST'98, Amazonia, Brazil, January 4-8, 1999: Proceedings. Goos, G. et al, eds. LC 98-53816. xi, 531p. 1999. pap. 75.00 (*3-540-65462-3*) Spr-Verlag.

Algeo, Ann M. The Courtroom As Forum: Homicide Trials by Dreiser, Wright, Capote, & Mailer. (Modern American Literature Ser.: Vol. 1). 164p. (C). 1996. text 41.95 (*0-8204-2733-0*) P Lang Pubng.

Algeo, John. Exercises in Contemporary English. 217p. (C). 1974. pap. text 25.00 (*0-15-512931-7*, Pub. by Harcourt Coll Pubs) Harcourt.

— On Defining the Proper Name. LC 73-9849. (University of Florida Humanities Monographs: No. 41). 102p. reprint ed. pap. 31.70 (*0-7837-0593-X*, 204094100019) Bks Demand.

— Problems of Origins & Development. 4th ed. (C). 1993. pap. text 37.00 (*0-15-500238-4*, Pub. by Harcourt Coll Pubs) Harcourt.

Algeo, John, ed. Fifty Years among the New Words: A Dictionary of Neologisms, 1941-1991. 267p. (C). 1991. text 64.95 (*0-521-41377-X*) Cambridge U Pr.

— Fifty Years among the New Words: A Dictionary of Neologisms, 1941-1991. 267p. (C). 1993. pap. text 25.95 (*0-521-44971-5*) Cambridge U Pr.

Algeo, John, jt. auth. see Pyles, Thomas.

Algeo, John, ed. see Pyles, Thomas.

Algeo, P. Problems in Organizational Development in English. 4th ed. (C). 1993. 81.00 (*0-15-501407-2*) Harcourt.

Algeo, Phillipa. Acid & Hallucinogens. (Understanding Drugs Ser.). 64p. (J). (gr. 5-7). 1990. lib. bdg. 20.80 (*0-531-10932-1*) Watts.

Alger, Abby L., tr. see Bentzon.

Alger, Abby L., tr. see De Solms, Marie T., pseud.

Alger, Chadwick F. Perceiving, Understanding & Coping with the World Relations of Everyday Life. Orig. Title: Internationaliation from Local Areas. 170p. (C). 1993. ring bd. 25.00 (*0-614-02999-6*) Amer Forum.

Alger, Chadwick F., ed. The Future of the United Nations System: Potential for the Twenty-First Century. LC 98-8997. 400p. 1998. pap. 29.95 (*92-808-0973-3*, Pub. by UN Univ Pr) Brookings.

Alger, Charles R. Alger Family Lines. 322p. (Orig.). 1994. pap. text 23.00 (*0-7884-0088-6*) Heritage Bk.

Alger, Dean. Megamedia: How Giant Corporations Dominate Mass Media, Distort Competition & Endanger Democracy. LC 98-21270. (Illus.). 256p. 1998. 27.95 (*0-8476-8389-3*) Rowman.

Alger, Dean E. The Media & Politics. 2nd ed. LC 95-20843. 532p. (C). 1995. pap. text 44.50 (*0-534-23694-4*) Harcourt.

Alger, Glenn M. Panic & Anxiety Attacks: Warning of a Physical Problem. 159p. (Orig.). 1990. pap. text 7.95 (*0-9626143-0-0*) Glendor Bks.

Alger, H. A., Jr. Erie Train Boy, No. 3. 171p. (YA). (gr. 5 up). 1996. reprint ed. pap. write for info. (*1-890050-00-8*) Carlisle Press.

Alger, Horatio, Jr. Abraham Lincoln, the Backwoods Boy. (Works of Horatio Alger Jr.). 1989. reprint ed. 75.00 (*0-7812-3550-2*) Rprt Serv.

— Adrift in New York. (Works of Horatio Alger Jr.). 1989. reprint ed. 75.00 (*0-685-58459-3*) Rprt Serv.

Alger, Horatio. Adrift in the City: Or, Oliver Conrad's Plucky Fight. 1976. reprint ed. lib. bdg. 25.95 (*0-88411-810-X*) Amereon Ltd.

Alger, Horatio, Jr. The Adventures of a New York Telegraph Boy. (Works of Horatio Alger Jr.). 1989. reprint ed. lib. bdg. 79.00 (*0-685-27609-0*) Rprt Serv.

— Andy Grant's Pluck. (Works of Horatio Alger Jr.). 1989. reprint ed. lib. bdg. 79.00 (*0-7812-3553-7*) Rprt Serv.

— Annie Graham: Or, The Young Lawyer's Fee & The Uncle's Return. (Gold Signature Ser.). (Illus.). 118p. 1987. 20.00 (*0-317-62761-9*) G K Westgard.

— The Backwoods Boy. (Works of Horatio Alger Jr.). 1989. reprint ed. lib. bdg. 79.00 (*0-7812-1713-X*) Rprt Serv.

— Ben Bruce. (Works of Horatio Alger Jr.). 1989. reprint ed. lib. bdg. 79.00 (*0-7812-3554-5*) Rprt Serv.

— Ben Logan's Triumph. (Works of Horatio Alger Jr.). 1989. reprint ed. lib. bdg. 79.00 (*0-7812-3555-3*) Rprt Serv.

— Bertha's Christmas Vision: An Autumn Sheaf. (Illus.). 248p. 1978. reprint ed. 24.00 (*0-686-35748-5*) G K Westgard.

— Bob Burton. (Works of Horatio Alger Jr.). 1989. reprint ed. lib. bdg. 79.00 (*0-7812-3556-1*) Rprt Serv.

— Both Sides of the Continent. (Works of Horatio Alger Jr.). 1989. reprint ed. lib. bdg. 79.00 (*0-7812-3557-X*) Rprt Serv.

Alger, Horatio. Brave & Bold. 1993. reprint ed. lib. bdg. 21.95 (*0-89968-450-5*) Buccaneer Bks.

— Brave & Bold: Or The Fortunes of a Factory Boy. 1976. reprint ed. lib. bdg. 25.95 (*0-88411-811-8*) Amereon Ltd.

Alger, Horatio, Jr. The Cash Boy. (Works of Horatio Alger Jr.). 1989. reprint ed. lib. bdg. 79.00 (*0-7812-3558-8*) Rprt Serv.

— Chester Rand. (Works of Horatio Alger Jr.). 1989. reprint ed. lib. bdg. 79.00 (*0-7812-3559-6*) Rprt Serv.

Alger, Horatio. Coming Back on Wall Street. LC 86-80419. (Illus.). 96p. 1986. pap. 12.00 (*0-87034-079-4*) Fraser Pub Co.

Alger, Horatio, Jr. Dan the Newsboy. (Works of Horatio Alger Jr.). 1989. reprint ed. lib. bdg. 79.00 (*0-7812-3560-X*) Rprt Serv.

Alger, Horatio. Dean Dunham: or The Waterford Mystery. 275p. 1974. reprint ed. lib. bdg. 23.95 (*0-88411-801-0*) Amereon Ltd.

Alger, Horatio, Jr. A Debt of Honor. (Works of Horatio Alger Jr.). 1989. reprint ed. lib. bdg. 79.00 (*0-7812-3561-8*) Rprt Serv.

— Digging for Gold. (Works of Horatio Alger Jr.). 1989. reprint ed. lib. bdg. 79.00 (*0-7812-3562-6*) Rprt Serv.

Alger, Horatio. Digging the Gold: A Story of California. 1976. reprint ed. lib. bdg. 25.95 (*0-88411-816-9*) Amereon Ltd.

— The Disagreeable Woman. 1976. lib. bdg. 16.95 (*0-88411-809-6*) Amereon Ltd.

Alger, Horatio, Jr. The Disagreeable Woman: A Social Mystery. 190p. 1978. reprint ed. 24.00 (*0-686-35752-3*) G K Westgard.

— Do & Dare. (Works of Horatio Alger Jr.). 1989. reprint ed. lib. bdg. 79.00 (*0-7812-3563-4*) Rprt Serv.

— Driven from Home. (Works of Horatio Alger Jr.). 1989. reprint ed. lib. bdg. 79.00 (*0-7812-3564-2*) Rprt Serv.

— The Eire Train Boy. (Works of Horatio Alger Jr.). 1989. reprint ed. lib. bdg. 79.00 (*0-7812-3565-0*) Rprt Serv.

Alger, Horatio. Erie Train Boy. 249p. 1974. reprint ed. lib. bdg. 23.95 (*0-88411-802-9*) Amereon Ltd.

— Erie Train Boy. 1993. reprint ed. lib. bdg. 19.95 (*0-89968-451-3*) Buccaneer Bks.

Alger, Horatio, Jr. The Errand Boy. (Works of Horatio Alger Jr.). 1989. reprint ed. lib. bdg. 79.00 (*0-7812-3566-9*) Rprt Serv.

— Falling in with Fortune. (Works of Horatio Alger Jr.). 1989. reprint ed. lib. bdg. 79.00 (*0-7812-3568-5*) Rprt Serv.

Alger, Horatio. Frank & Fearless. large type ed. 25.95 (*0-88411-803-7*) Amereon Ltd.

Alger, Horatio, Jr. Frank & Fearless. (Works of Horatio Alger Jr.). 1989. reprint ed. lib. bdg. 79.00 (*0-7812-3571-5*) Rprt Serv.

— Frank Hunters Peril. (Works of Horatio Alger Jr.). 1989. reprint ed. lib. bdg. 79.00 (*0-7812-3572-3*) Rprt Serv.

— From Canal Boy to President, the Boyhood & Manhood of James A. Garfield. (Works of Horatio Alger Jr.). 1989. reprint ed. lib. bdg. 79.00 (*0-7812-1711-3*) Rprt Serv.

— From Farm Boy to Senator: Being the History of the Boyhood & Manhood of Daniel Webster. (Works of Horatio Alger Jr.). 1989. reprint ed. lib. bdg. 79.00 (*0-7812-3573-1*) Rprt Serv.

Alger, Horatio. Getting Creamed on Wall Street. LC 85-70691. (Illus.). 60p. (Orig.). 1985. pap. 10.00 (*0-87034-075-1*) Fraser Pub Co.

Alger, Horatio, Jr. Grand'ther Baldwin's Thanksgiving with Other Ballads & Poems. 125p. 1978. reprint ed. 21.00 (*0-686-35750-7*) G K Westgard.

— Helen Ford. (Works of Horatio Alger Jr.). 1989. reprint ed. lib. bdg. 79.00 (*0-7812-1706-7*) Rprt Serv.

— Helping Himself. (Works of Horatio Alger Jr.). 1989. reprint ed. lib. bdg. 79.00 (*0-685-44743-X*) Rprt Serv.

— Hugo, the Deformed. (Illus.). 84p. 1978. 24.00 (*0-686-37019-8*) G K Westgard.

— Jack's Ward. (Works of Horatio Alger Jr.). 1989. reprint ed. lib. bdg. 79.00 (*0-7812-3576-6*) Rprt Serv.

Alger, Horatio. Jack's Ward: or The Boy Guardian. 1976. reprint ed. lib. bdg. 19.95 (*0-88411-817-7*) Amereon Ltd.

— Jed, the Poorhouse Boy. 1976. reprint ed. lib. bdg. 26.95 (*0-88411-814-2*) Amereon Ltd.

Alger, Horatio, Jr. Jed the Poorhouse Boy. (Works of Horatio Alger Jr.). 1989. reprint ed. lib. bdg. 79.00 (*0-7812-3577-4*) Rprt Serv.

— Joe the Hotel Boy. (Works of Horatio Alger Jr.). 1989. reprint ed. lib. bdg. 79.00 (*0-7812-3578-2*) Rprt Serv.

— Lesters Luck. (Works of Horatio Alger Jr.). 1989. reprint ed. lib. bdg. 79.00 (*0-685-44746-4*) Rprt Serv.

— Luke Walton. (Works of Horatio Alger Jr.). 1989. reprint ed. lib. bdg. 79.00 (*0-685-44745-6*) Rprt Serv.

Alger, Horatio. Luke Walton: or The Chicago Newsboy. 1976. reprint ed. lib. bdg. 25.95 (*0-88411-813-4*) Amereon Ltd.

Alger, Horatio, Jr. Making His Mark. (Illus.). 307p. 1979. reprint ed. 30.00 (*0-686-35753-1*) G K Westgard.

— Making His Mark. (Works of Horatio Alger Jr.). 1989. reprint ed. lib. bdg. 79.00 (*0-685-27600-7*) Rprt Serv.

— Making His Way. (Works of Horatio Alger Jr.). 1989. reprint ed. lib. bdg. 79.00 (*0-685-27579-5*) Rprt Serv.

— Making His Way: Frank Courtney's Struggle Upward. LC 74-15724. (Popular Culture in America Ser.). 290p. 1975. reprint ed. 26.95 (*0-405-06361-X*) Ayer.

Alger, Horatio. Mark Manning's Mission: or The Story of a Shoe Factory Boy. 268p. 1974. reprint ed. lib. bdg. 23.95 (*0-88411-804-5*) Amereon Ltd.

Alger, Horatio, Jr. Mark Mason's Victory. (Works of Horatio Alger Jr.). 1989. reprint ed. lib. bdg. 79.00 (*0-685-27577-9*) Rprt Serv.

— Ned Newton. (Works of Horatio Alger Jr.). 1989. reprint ed. lib. bdg. 79.00 (*0-685-27576-0*) Rprt Serv.

— Nelson the Newsboy. (Works of Horatio Alger Jr.). 1989. reprint ed. lib. bdg. 79.00 (*0-685-27575-2*) Rprt Serv.

— The New Schoolma'am: A Summer in North Sparta. 140p. 1976. reprint ed. 24.00 (*0-686-37020-1*) G K Westgard.

— Nothing to Do. (Works of Horatio Alger Jr.). 1989. reprint ed. lib. bdg. 79.00 (*0-685-27581-7*) Rprt Serv.

— Nothing to Do: A Tilt at Our Best Society. (Illus.). 45p. 1978. reprint ed. 18.00 (*0-686-37021-X*) G K Westgard.

— Number Ninety-One: The Adventures of a New York Telegraph Boy. (Illus.). 205p. 1977. reprint ed. 24.00 (*0-686-37022-8*) G K Westgard.

— The Odds Against Him. (Works of Horatio Alger Jr.). 1989. reprint ed. lib. bdg. 79.00 (*0-685-27580-9*) Rprt Serv.

— Only an Irish Boy. (Works of Horatio Alger Jr.). 1989. reprint ed. lib. bdg. 79.00 (*0-685-27578-7*) Rprt Serv.

— Out for Business. (Works of Horatio Alger Jr.). 1989. reprint ed. lib. bdg. 79.00 (*0-685-27566-3*) Rprt Serv.

— Paul Prescott's Charge. (Works of Horatio Alger Jr.). 1989. reprint ed. lib. bdg. 79.00 (*0-7812-1705-9*) Rprt Serv.

— Paul the Peddler. (Works of Horatio Alger Jr.). 1989. reprint ed. lib. bdg. 79.00 (*0-685-27568-X*) Rprt Serv.

— Paul the Peddler, or the Fortunes of a Young Street Merchant. large type ed. LC 98-89121. 280p. 1998. pap. 16.95 (*1-888725-02-8*) Sci & Human Pr.

— Phil the Fiddler. (Works of Horatio Alger Jr.). 1989. reprint ed. lib. bdg. 79.00 (*0-685-44741-3*) Rprt Serv.

Alger, Horatio. Phil the Fidler: or The Story of a Young Street Musician: Or, the Story of a Young Street Musician. 1976. reprint ed. lib. bdg. 22.95 (*0-88411-815-0*) Amereon Ltd.

Alger, Horatio, Jr. Ragged Dick. (YA). 1990. mass mkt. 5.95 (*0-451-52480-2*, Sig Classics) NAL.

— Ragged Dick. (Works of Horatio Alger Jr.). 1989. reprint ed. lib. bdg. 79.00 (*0-7812-1707-5*) Rprt Serv.

Alger, Horatio. Ragged Dick & Mark the Match Boy. (Orig.). 1998. per. 6.00 (*0-684-84290-4*) S&S Trade.

Alger, Horatio, Jr. Ragged Dick & Struggling Upward. (C). 1997. pap. text. write for info. (*0-321-02603-9*) Addson-Wesley Educ.

Alger, Horatio. Ralph Raymond's Heir. 125p. 1974. reprint ed. lib. bdg. 22.95 (*0-88411-805-3*) Amereon Ltd.

Alger, Horatio, Jr. Ralph Raymonds Heir. (Works of Horatio Alger Jr.). 1989. reprint ed. lib. bdg. 79.00 (*0-685-44742-1*) Rprt Serv.

— Randy of the River. (Works of Horatio Alger Jr.). 1989. reprint ed. lib. bdg. 79.00 (*0-685-27571-X*) Rprt Serv.

— Robert Coverdale's Struggle. (Works of Horatio Alger Jr.). 1989. reprint ed. lib. bdg. 79.00 (*0-7812-1714-8*) Rprt Serv.

— Robert Lawson: A Minister's Fortunes, a Story of New England. (Gold Signature Ser.). (Illus.). 120p. 1987. 20.00 (*0-317-59461-3*) G K Westgard.

— A Rolling Stone. (Works of Horatio Alger Jr.). 1989. reprint ed. lib. bdg. 79.00 (*0-685-27556-6*) Rprt Serv.

Alger, Horatio. Rolling Stone: or The Adventures of Wanderer. 294p. 1974. reprint ed. lib. bdg. 23.95 (*0-88411-806-1*) Amereon Ltd.

Alger, Horatio, Jr. Rough & Ready. (Works of Horatio Alger Jr.). 1989. reprint ed. lib. bdg. 79.00 (*0-685-27557-4*) Rprt Serv.

— Rufus & Rose. (Works of Horatio Alger Jr.). 1989. reprint ed. lib. bdg. 79.00 (*0-685-27561-2*) Rprt Serv.

— Ruperts Amition. (Works of Horatio Alger Jr.). 1989. reprint ed. lib. bdg. 79.00 (*0-685-27560-4*) Rprt Serv.

— Sam's Chance. (Works of Horatio Alger Jr.). 1989. reprint ed. lib. bdg. 79.00 (*0-685-27559-0*) Rprt Serv.

— Seeking His Choice. (Works of Horatio Alger Jr.). 1989. reprint ed. lib. bdg. 79.00 (*0-685-27558-2*) Rprt Serv.

— Shifting for Himself. (Works of Horatio Alger Jr.). 1989. reprint ed. lib. bdg. 79.00 (*0-685-27562-0*) Rprt Serv.

— Slow & Sure. (Works of Horatio Alger Jr.). 1989. reprint ed. lib. bdg. 79.00 (*0-685-27555-8*) Rprt Serv.

— The Store Boy. (Works of Horatio Alger Jr.). 1989. reprint ed. lib. bdg. 79.00 (*0-685-27554-X*) Rprt Serv.

— Strive & Succeed. (Works of Horatio Alger Jr.). 1989. reprint ed. lib. bdg. 79.00 (*0-685-27553-1*) Rprt Serv.

— Strong & Steady. (Works of Horatio Alger Jr.). 1989. reprint ed. lib. bdg. 79.00 (*0-685-44740-5*) Rprt Serv.

— Struggling Upward. fac. ed. (J). 1971. 6.95 (*0-87874-005-8*) Galloway.

— Struggling Upward. (Works of Horatio Alger Jr.). 1989. reprint ed. lib. bdg. 79.00 (*0-685-27564-7*) Rprt Serv.

— Struggling Upward: or Luke Larkin's Luck. 160p. 1984. reprint ed. pap. 5.95 (*0-486-24737-6*) Dover.

— Tattered Tom. (Works of Horatio Alger Jr.). 1989. reprint ed. lib. bdg. 79.00 (*0-7812-1710-5*) Rprt Serv.

— The Telegraph Boy. (Works of Horatio Alger Jr.). 1989. reprint ed. lib. bdg. 79.00 (*0-685-27551-5*) Rprt Serv.

— Timothy Crump's Ward: The New Years Loan & What Became of It. 188p. 1977. reprint ed. 30.00 (*0-686-37023-6*) G K Westgard.

— The Tin Box & What It Contained. (Works of Horatio Alger Jr.). 1989. reprint ed. lib. bdg. 79.00 (*0-685-27550-7*) Rprt Serv.

— Tom Brace Who He Was & How He Fared. (Works of Horatio Alger Jr.). 1989. reprint ed. lib. bdg. 79.00 (*0-685-27549-3*) Rprt Serv.

— Tom Temple's Career. (Works of Horatio Alger Jr.). 1989. reprint ed. lib. bdg. 79.00 (*0-685-27548-5*) Rprt Serv.

— Tom Thatcher's Fortune. (Works of Horatio Alger Jr.). 1989. reprint ed. lib. bdg. 79.00 (*0-685-27545-0*) Rprt Serv.

Alger, Horatio. Tom, the Bootblack: or The Road to Success. 1976. reprint ed. lib. bdg. 22.95 (*0-88411-812-6*) Amereon Ltd.

Alger, Horatio, Jr. Tom Tracey. (Works of Horatio Alger Jr.). 1989. reprint ed. lib. bdg. 79.00 (*0-685-27544-2*) Rprt Serv.

— Tom Tracy: The Trials of a New York Newsboy. (Illus.). 208p. 1978. reprint ed. 24.00 (*0-686-35749-3*) G K Westgard.

— Tom Turner's Legacy. (Works of Horatio Alger Jr.). 1989. reprint ed. lib. bdg. 79.00 (*0-685-27543-4*) Rprt Serv.

— Tony the Hero. (Works of Horatio Alger Jr.). 1989. reprint ed. lib. bdg. 79.00 (*0-685-27552-3*) Rprt Serv.

— Tony the Tramp. (Works of Horatio Alger Jr.). 1989. reprint ed. lib. bdg. 79.00 (*0-685-27542-6*) Rprt Serv.

Alger, Horatio. The Train Boy. 1975. reprint ed. lib. bdg. 23.95 (*0-88411-807-X*) Amereon Ltd.

Alger, Horatio, Jr. The Train Boy. (Works of Horatio Alger Jr.). 1989. reprint ed. lib. bdg. 79.00 (*0-685-27541-8*) Rprt Serv.

— Try & Trust. (Works of Horatio Alger Jr.). 1989. reprint ed. lib. bdg. 79.00 (*0-685-27540-X*) Rprt Serv.

— Wait & Win. (Works of Horatio Alger Jr.). 1989. reprint ed. lib. bdg. 79.00 (*0-7812-3619-3*) Rprt Serv.

— Wait & Win: The Story of Jack Drumond's Pluck. (Illus.). 279p. 1979. reprint ed. 30.00 (*0-686-35756-6*) G K Westgard.

— Walter Sherwoods Probation. (Works of Horatio Alger Jr.). 1989. reprint ed. lib. bdg. 79.00 (*0-7812-3620-7*) Rprt Serv.

— The Works of Horatio Alger Jr., Set. 1989. reprint ed. lib. bdg. 63.00 (*0-685-27536-1*) Rprt Serv.

— The World Before Him. (Works of Horatio Alger Jr.). 1989. reprint ed. lib. bdg. 79.00 (*0-7812-3621-5*) Rprt Serv.

— The Young Acrobat. (Works of Horatio Alger Jr.). 1989. reprint ed. lib. bdg. 79.00 (*0-7812-3622-3*) Rprt Serv.

— The Young Bank Messenger. (Works of Horatio Alger Jr.). 1989. reprint ed. lib. bdg. 79.00 (*0-7812-3623-1*) Rprt Serv.

— The Young Boatman of Pine Point. (Works of Horatio Alger Jr.). 1989. reprint ed. lib. bdg. 79.00 (*0-7812-3624-X*) Rprt Serv.

— The Young Book Agent. (Works of Horatio Alger Jr.). 1989. reprint ed. lib. bdg. 79.00 (*0-685-27530-2*) Rprt Serv.

— Young Captain Jack. (Works of Horatio Alger Jr.). 1989. reprint ed. lib. bdg. 79.00 (*0-7812-3626-6*) Rprt Serv.

Alger, Horatio. Young Captain Jack: or Son of a Soldier. 267p. 1974. reprint ed. lib. bdg. 23.95 (*0-88411-808-8*) Amereon Ltd.

Alger, Horatio, Jr. The Young Circus Rider. (Works of Horatio Alger Jr.). 1989. reprint ed. lib. bdg. 79.00 (*0-7812-3627-4*) Rprt Serv.

— The Young Miner. (Works of Horatio Alger Jr.). 1989. reprint ed. lib. bdg. 79.00 (*0-7812-3628-2*) Rprt Serv.

— The Young Musician. (Works of Horatio Alger Jr.). 1989. reprint ed. lib. bdg. 79.00 (*0-7812-3629-0*) Rprt Serv.

— The Young Patriots: Six Brave Boys in the Civil War. (Gold Signature Ser.). (Illus.). 154p. 1987. 24.00 (*0-685-43920-8*) G K Westgard.

— The Young Salesman. (Works of Horatio Alger Jr.). 1989. reprint ed. lib. bdg. 79.00 (*0-7812-3630-4*) Rprt Serv.

Alger, Horatio, Sr. & Sheaf, J. P., Jr. Addresses Delivered at the Semi-Centennial Celebration of the Dedication of the First Unitarian Church, South Natick (Massachusetts) November 20, 1878. (Illus.). 41p. 1977. reprint ed. pap. 6.00 (*0-686-35760-4*) G K Westgard.

Alger, Jeff. C++ for Real Programmers - KSO. 2nd rev. ed. LC 97-35352. (Illus.). 388p. 1998. pap. text 39.95 (*0-12-049942-8*) Acad Pr.

Alger, John G. Napoleon's British Visitors & Captives, 1801-1815. LC 71-113541. reprint ed. 42.50 (*0-404-00324-9*) AMS Pr.

— Paris in Seventeen Eighty-Nine to Seventeen Ninety-Four, Farewell Letters of Victims of the Guillotine. LC 78-113540. reprint ed. 57.50 (*0-404-00323-0*) AMS Pr.

Alger, John I. The Quest for Victory: The History of the Principles of War, 30. LC 81-13319. (Contributions in Military History Ser.: No. 30). 318p. 1982. 45.00 (*0-313-23322-5*, AMM/, Greenwood Pr) Greenwood.

Alger, Jr., Horatio. Ragged Dick & Struggling Upward. (American Library). 304p. (C). 1998. pap. 9.95 (*0-14-039033-2*) Addson-Wesley Educ.

Alger, Keith. The Political Economy of U. S. Trade Policy. LC 90-3611. (Foreign Economic Policy of the United States Ser.). 272p. 1990. reprint ed. text 10.00 (*0-8240-7467-X*) Garland.

Alger, Linda & Sanders, Priscilla. Good Health-Naturally! 20 Steps to Better Nutrition Using Natural Foods. LC 83-80405. 144p. 1983. pap. 10.98 (*0-88290-217-2*) Horizon Utah.

Alger, M. Polymer Science Dictionary. 544p. 1989. mass mkt. 175.95 (*1-85166-220-0*) Elsevier.

Alger, P. L., ed. Steinmetz: The Philosopher. viii, 188p. 1965. 70.00 (*0-677-65170-8*) Gordon & Breach.

Alger, Pat. Once in a Very Blue Moon: A Pat Alger Songbook. Okun, Milton, ed. 1994. pap. 16.95 (*0-89524-779-8*) Cherry Lane.

Alger, Phillip L. Induction Machines: Their Behavior & Uses. 2nd ed. LC 99-461716. xxi, 528p. 1995. pap. text 53.00 (*2-88449-199-6*) Gordon & Breach.

Alger, Raymond S. Electron Paramagnetic Resonance: Techniques & Applications. LC 67-20255. (Illus.). 602p. reprint ed. pap. 186.70 (*0-608-30855-2*, 201018000068) Bks Demand.

Alger, Russell A. The Spanish-American War. LC 78-146850. (Select Bibliographies Reprint Ser.). 1977. reprint ed. 36.95 (*0-8369-5617-6*) Ayer.

Alger, William R. Destiny of the Soul: Critical History of the Doctrine of a Future Life, 2 vols., Set. 10th ed. LC 68-19263. 1968. reprint ed. lib. bdg. 85.00 (*0-8371-0003-8*, ALDS) Greenwood.

— Destiny of the Soul: Critical History of the Doctrine of a Future Life, 2 vols., Vol. 1. 10th ed. LC 68-19263. 1968. reprint ed. lib. bdg. 55.00 (*0-313-21609-6*, ALDA) Greenwood.

— Destiny of the Soul: Critical History of the Doctrine of a Future Life, 2 vols., Vol. 2. 10th ed. LC 68-19263. 1968. reprint ed. lib. bdg. 55.00 (*0-313-21610-X*, ALDB) Greenwood.

— The Life of Edwin Forest, 2 vols., 1. LC 76-84505. 1972. 24.95 (*0-405-08199-5*, Pub. by Blom Pubns) Ayer.

— The Life of Edwin Forest, 2 vols., 2. LC 76-84505. 1972. 24.95 (*0-405-08200-2*, Pub. by Blom Pubns) Ayer.

— The Life of Edwin Forest, 2 vols., Set. LC 76-84505. 1972. 48.95 (*0-405-08198-7*, Pub. by Blom Pubns) Ayer.

Algera, Jen A. Performance Improvement Programmes in Europe: A Special Issue of the European Journal of Work & 1998. pap. 39.95 (*0-86377-777-5*, Pub. by Psychol Pr) Taylor & Francis.

Algeri, Salvatore J., et al. Microwaves Made Simple: The Workbook. LC 86-72681. (Artech House Microwave Library). 117p. reprint ed. pap. 36.30 (*0-7837-5846-4*, 204556500006) Bks Demand.

Algermissen, Jo A. Hometown Man. (Desire Ser.: No. 706). 1992. pap. 2.89 (*0-373-05706-7*, 5-05706-2) Harlequin Bks.

— I Do? (Yours Truly Ser.). 1996. per. 3.50 (*0-373-52020-4*, 1-52020-4) Silhouette.

An Asterisk (*) at the beginning of an entry indicates that the title is appearing for the first time.

Algermissen, Jo Ann. A Husband for Christmas. (Yours Truly Ser.). 1998. per. 3.50 (*0-373-52081-6*, 1-52081-6) Silhouette.

Algermissen, JoAnn. A Marry-Me Christmas. 1996. per. 3.50 (*0-373-52034-4*, 1-52034-5) Silhouette.

Algermissen, S. T. An Introduction to the Seismicity of the United States. 148p. 1983. pap. 12.00 (*0-943198-26-7*) Earthquake Eng.

Algert, Susan J., et al. Mexican-American Food Practices, Customs, & Holidays. 2nd ed. LC 98-20449. (Ethnic & Regional Food Practices Ser.). 1998. 10.00 (*0-88091-164-6*) Am Dietetic Assn.

Alghafis, Ali N. Universities in Saudi Arabia: Their Role in Science, Technology, & Development. 114p. (C). 1992. lib. bdg. 39.50 (*0-8191-8831-X*) U Pr of Amer.

Algie, Bob. How to Activate Your Web Site. LC 98-159767. 240p. 1997. 29.99 (*1-56276-527-2*, Ziff-Davis Pr) Que.

Algie, Bob. How to Activate Your Web Site. 240p. 1999. 29.99 (*1-56276-579-5*, Ziff-Davis Pr) Que.

Algie, Jimmie, jt. auth. see Hall, Anthony.

Algina, James, jt. auth. see Crocker, Linda.

Algom, Daniel, ed. Psychophysical Approaches to Cognition. LC 92-19503. (Advances in Psychology Ser.: Vol. 92). 628p. 1992. 192.00 (*0-444-88978-7*, North Holland) Elsevier.

Algonzzine, Kate. Time & Money. (Basic Skills Ser.). (Illus.). 32p. (J). (gr. k-1). 1998. pap. text 4.95 (*0-88724-466-1*, CD-2134) Carson-Dellos.

Algoo-Baksh, Stella. Austin C. Clarke. (Canadian Author Studies). 55p. 1997. pap. 9.95 (*1-55022-325-9*, Pub. by ECW) LPC InBook.

— Austin C. Clarke: A Biography. (Illus.). 234p. 1994. pap. 19.95 (*1-55022-218-X*, Pub. by ECW) LPC InBook.

Algosaibi, Ghazi. An Apartment Called Freedom. McLoughlin, Leslie, tr. from ARA. LC 96-669. 280p. 1996. 42.50 (*0-7103-0550-8*, Pub. by Kegan Paul Intl) Col U Pr.

— Seven. 280p. 1999. 24.95 (*0-86356-088-1*, Pub. by Saqi) Intl Spec Bk.

Algosaibi, Ghazi A. From the Orient & the Desert: Poems. LC 93-40620. (Illus.). 26p. 1994. pap. 17.00 (*0-7103-0478-1*) Routledge.

— The Gulf Crisis: An Attempt to Understand. LC 92-26232. 160p. 1993. 49.95 (*0-7103-0459-5*, B0085) Routledge.

Algosaibi, Ghazi A., ed. from ARA. Lyrics from Arabia. 2nd ed. Saleem, Qazi, tr. from ARA. LC 84-51201. (ARA, ENG & URD., Illus.). 108p. 1983. reprint ed. pap. 8.95 (*0-89410-447-0*, Three Contnts) L Rienner.

***Algotsson, Sharne.** African Style: Down to the Details. LC 99-86295. (Illus.). 176p. 2000. 32.50 (*0-609-60532-1*) C Potter.

Algotsson, Sharne & Davis, Denys. The Spirit of African Design. LC 95-12992. 176p. 1996. 35.00 (*0-517-59916-3*) C Potter.

Algoud, Albert & Garcia, Jose. Jeu de Dictionnaire, Mots Caches Langue Francaise. (FRE.). 1998. pap. 39.95 (*0-320-00366-3*) Fr & Eur.

Algoud, Henri, et al, texts. Authentic French Provincial Furniture from Provence, Normandy, & Brittany. LC 93-7055. (Illus.). 128p. 1993. pap. 12.95 (*0-486-27535-3*) Dover.

Algozzine, Bob. 50 Simple Ways to Make Teaching More Fun: If You're a Teacher You Gotta Have This Book! (Illus.). 158p. 1993. pap. text, teacher ed. 14.95 (*0-944584-93-4*, 50WAYS) Sopris.

— Handyman's Little Book of Wisdom. (Little Books of Wisdom Ser.). 160p. (Orig.). 1996. pap. 5.95 (*1-57034-046-3*) Globe Pequot.

— Teacher's Little Book of Wisdom. LC 95-15940. 160p. 1995. pap. 6.95 (*1-57034-017-X*) Globe Pequot.

***Algozzine, Bob.** Teacher's Little Book of Wisdom: Suggestions, Observations & Reminders for Teachers to Read. 2001. pap. 6.95 (*0-7627-0872-7*) Globe Pequot.

Algozzine, Bob & Ysseldyke, James E. Simple Ways to Make Teaching Math More Fun: Elementary School Edition. (Simple Ways Ser.). (Illus.). 88p. 1994. pap. text, teacher ed. 14.95 (*1-57035-028-0*, 50MATH) Sopris.

— Tactics for Improving Parenting Skills (TIPS) 210p. 1995. pap., teacher ed. 19.50 (*1-57035-035-3*, 77TIPS) Sopris.

Algozzine, Bob & Ysseldyke, Jim. Strategies & Tactics for Effective Instruction. 2nd ed. LC 98-118535. (Illus.). 268p. 1997. pap. text 29.50 (*1-57035-119-8*, C31STEI) Sopris.

Algozzine, Bob, et al. Behaviorally Disordered? Assessment for Identification & Instruction. 36p. 1991. pap. text 9.00 (*0-86586-198-6*, P339) Coun Exc Child.

Algozzine, Bob, ed. see Council for Exceptional Children Staff.

Algozzine, Bob, jt. ed. see Wood, Karen D.

Algozzine, Kate. Subtraction 0 to 10. (Basic Skills Ser.). (Illus.). 32p. (J). (gr. 1-2). 1997. pap. text 4.95 (*0-88724-390-8*, CD-2125) Carson-Dellos.

— Word Endings. (Basic Skills Ser.). (Illus.). 32p. (J). (gr. 1). 1997. pap. text 4.95 (*0-88724-404-1*, CD-2104) Carson-Dellos.

Algozzine, Robert. Problem Behavior Management: Educator's Resource Service. 2nd ed. LC 92-15097. ring bd. 154.00 (*0-8342-0333-2*, S53) Aspen Pub.

Algozzine, Robert & Obiakor, Festus E. Managing Problem Behaviors. 356p. (C). 1995. per. 50.95 (*0-7872-1250-4*, 41125001) Kendall-Hunt.

Algozzine, Robert, et al. Childhood Behavior Disorders: Applied Research & Educational Practice. 2nd ed. LC 91-8984. (Illus.). 550p. (C). 1997. pap. text 38.00 (*0-89079-719-6*, 8284) PRO-ED.

Algozzine, Robert, jt. auth. see Ysseldyke, James E.

Algozzini, Joseph. Lionel's Postwar Space & Military Trains. (Toy Train Reference Ser.: No. 2). (Illus.). 80p. (Orig.). 1996. pap. 16.95 (*0-89778-429-4*, 10-8075, Greenberg Books) Kalmbach.

Algozzini, Joseph P., ed. Lionel's Postwar F3's. (Toy Train Reference Ser.: No. 1). (Illus.). 80p. 1995. pap. 16.95 (*0-89778-398-0*, 10-7950, Greenberg Books) Kalmbach.

Algozzini, Joseph P., jt. auth. see Ambrose, Paul V.

Algra, K. A., et al, eds. Lucretius & His Intellectual Background. (Verhandelingen der Koninklijke Nederlandse Akademie van Wetenschappen, Afd. Letterkunde, Nieuwe Reeks Ser.: Vol. 172). 276p. 1997. pap. 51.50 (*0-444-85818-0*) Elsevier.

Algra, Keimpe, et al, eds. The Cambridge History of Hellenistic Philosophy. LC 98-36033. 916p. (C). 2000. text 135.00 (*0-521-25028-5*) Cambridge U Pr.

Algra, Keimpe, et al. Polyhistory: Studies in the History & Historiography of Ancient Philosophy. LC 96-30613. (Philosophia Antiqua Ser.). x, 438p. 1996. 161.00 (*90-04-10417-8*) Brill Academic Pubs.

Algra, Keimpe A. Concepts of Space in Greek Thought. LC 94-33784. (Philosphia Antiqua: 65). ix, 365p. 1994. 110.50 (*90-04-10172-1*) Brill Academic Pubs.

Algra, P. R., et al, eds. Diagnosis & Therapy of Spinal Tumors. LC 97-18905. (Medical Radiology). (Illus.). 250p. 1997. 169.00 (*3-540-58861-2*) Spr-Verlag.

Algranati, Israel D., jt. auth. see Goldemberg, Sarah M.

Algranati, Paula S. The Pediatric Patient: An Approach to History & Physical Examination. (Illus.). 232p. 1992. 32.00 (*0-683-00073-X*) Lppncott W & W.

Algren, Axel B., jt. auth. see Rowley, Frank B.

Algren, Nelson. America Eats. Schoonover, David E., ed. & frwd. by. LC 91-41109. (Iowa Szathmary Culinary Arts Ser.). (Illus.). 143p. 1992. 25.95 (*0-87745-361-6*) U of Iowa Pr.

— Chicago: City on the Make. LC 82-17974. vi, 106p. (C). 1987. pap. 10.00 (*0-226-01384-7*) U Ch Pr.

— L' Hommes au Bras d'Or. (FRE.). 544p. 1981. pap. 15.95 (*0-7859-1941-4*, 2070373207) Fr & Eur.

— The Last Carousel. LC 96-48583. 448p. 1997. pap. 14.95 (*1-888363-45-2*) Seven Stories.

— The Man with the Golden Arm. LC 89-71471. 348p. 1990. pap. 10.95 (*1-888363-18-5*) Seven Stories.

— The Man with the Golden Arm. 50th anniversary ed. Savage, William J., Jr. & Simon, Daniel, eds. LC 99-41331. (Illus.). 454p. 1999. text 35.00 (*1-58322-007-0*, Pub. by Seven Stories); pap. text 14.95 (*1-58322-008-9*, Pub. by Seven Stories) Publishers Group.

— The Neon Wilderness: 24 Short Stories. 1988. 23.95 (*0-8488-0415-5*) Amereon Ltd.

— The Neon Wilderness: 24 Short Stories. Simon, Dan, ed. LC 96-40151. 304p. 1997. reprint ed. pap. 10.95 (*1-888363-21-5*) Seven Stories.

— Never Come Morning. 1995. 5.60 (*0-87129-597-0*, N40) Dramatic Pub.

— Never Come Morning. LC 96-14829. 336p. 1987. reprint ed. pap. 10.95 (*1-888363-22-3*) Seven Stories.

— Nonconformity: Writing on Writing. Simon, Daniel, ed. & intro. by. LC 94-35205. 144p. 1996. 16.00 (*1-888363-05-3*) Seven Stories.

— Nonconformity: Writing on Writing. Simon, Daniel, ed. & afterword by by. 144p. 1997. pap. 9.95 (*1-888363-62-2*) Seven Stories.

— The Texas Stories of Nelson Algren. Drew, Bettina, ed. & intro. by. LC 95-12195. 208p. 1995. pap. 12.95 (*0-292-70468-2*); text 27.50 (*0-292-71577-3*) U of Tex Pr.

— A Walk on the Wild Side. 368p. 1998. pap. 13.00 (*0-374-52532-3*, Noonday) FS&G.

— A Walk on the Wild Side. (Classic Reprint Ser.). 368p. 1990. reprint ed. pap. 12.95 (*0-938410-80-6*, Thunders Mouth) Avalon NY.

— A Walk on the Wild Side. LC 78-509. 346p. 1978. reprint ed. lib. bdg. 52.50 (*0-313-20294-X*, ALWW, Greenwood Pr) Greenwood.

Alguire, Judith. Iced. LC 95-19138. 202p. 1995. pap. 10.95 (*0-934678-60-X*) New Victoria Pubs.

— Iced. 192p. write for info. (*0-88961-214-5*, Pub. by Womens Pr) LPC InBook.

Alhadeff, David A. Monopoly & Competition in Banking. Bruchey, Stuart, ed. LC 80-1129. (Rise of Commerical Banking Ser.). (Illus.). 1981. reprint ed. lib. bdg. 25.95 (*0-405-13629-3*) Ayer.

Alhadeff, Gina. The Sun at Midday: Tales of a Mediterranean Family. LC 96-26840. 240p. 1997. 4.99 (*0-679-41763-X*) Pantheon.

Alhadeff, Gini. The Sun at Midday: Tales of a Mediterranean Family. LC 97-16762. 240p. (Orig.). 1998. pap. 14.00 (*0-88001-578-0*) HarpC.

Alhaj A. Syed Abdul Latif. Islamic Cultural Studies. 140p. (Orig.). 1988. pap. 4.50 (*1-56744-306-0*) Kazi Pubns.

Alhaji Obaba Abdullahi Muhammad. Three Little Africans. (Illus.). 36p. (Orig.). (J). (gr. k-4). 1978. pap. 2.50 (*0-916157-00-8*) African Islam Miss Pubns.

Alhanati, Shelley & Kostoulas, Katina, eds. Primitive Mental States Vol. 1: Across the Lifespan, Vol. I. LC 10-901949. 296p. 1997. 52.00 (*1-56821-685-8*) Aronson.

Alhaq, Shuja. Forgotten Vision: A Study of Human Spirituality in the Light of the Islamic Tradition, Vol. 2. LC 97-902758. 1997. 38.00 (*81-259-0311-9*, Pub. by Vikas) S Asia.

Alhara, Herman. Basic Macrobiotics. 2nd rev. ed. Ferre, Carl, ed. 208p. 1998. pap. 12.95 (*0-918860-55-5*, 8240) G Ohsawa.

Alhara, T., ed. see Fletcher, L. S.

Alhara, T., jt. ed. see Fletcher, L. S.

Alhashim, Dhia D. & Robertson, James W. Accounting for Multinational Enterprises. LC 77-13732. (Key Issues Lecture Ser.). 1978. pap. write for info. (*0-672-97183-6*) Macmillan.

AlHashim, Dhia D., jt. auth. see Arpan, Jeffrey S.

Alhinc, J., tr. see Duvernoy, Henri M.

Alhir, Sinan Si. UML in a Nutshell. Oram, Andy, ed. (Illus.). 290p. 1998. pap. 24.95 (*1-56592-448-7*) OReilly & Assocs.

Alho, Kari. Financial Markets & Macroeconomic Policy in the Flow-of-Funds Framework. 193p. 1991. text 91.95 (*1-85628-111-6*, Pub. by Avebry) Ashgate Pub Co.

Alho, Kari, ed. The Economics & Policies of Integration - A Finnish Perspective. LC 96-36296. 228p. (C). 1995. lib. bdg. 118.00 (*0-7923-4265-8*) Kluwer Academic.

Alhsmith, Scott. The Complete Idiot's Guide to Planning the Perfect Vacation. 350p. 1995. 14.99 (*1-56761-531-7*, Alpha Ref) Macmillan Gen Ref.

Alhumaizi, Khalid. Surveying a Dynamical System: A Study of the Gray Scott Reaction in a Twophase Reactor. 1995. lib. bdg. 100.00 (*0-582-24688-1*, Pub. by Addison-Wesley) Longman.

Alhuwalia, S., jt. auth. see Ahluwalia, B. K.

***Ali.** Cold War in the High Himalayas. LC 99-32300. 286p. 1999. text 59.95 (*0-312-22693-4*) St Martin.

Ali & Smith. Trotsky for Beginners. (Documentary Comic Bks.). (Illus.). 1980. 6.95 (*0-906495-28-8*) Writers & Readers.

Ali, A. Ibn-As-Sikkit. 90p. 1985. pap. 3.50 (*1-56744-069-5*) Kazi Pubns.

— Status of Health in Nepal. (C). 1991. text 60.00 (*0-7855-0156-8*, Pub. by Ratna Pustak Bhandar) St Mut.

Ali, A., ed. Higgs Particle(s) Physics Issues & Experimental Searches in High-Energy Collisions. (Illus.). 478p. 1990. 135.00 (*0-306-43589-6*, Plenum Trade) Perseus Pubng.

— New Aspects of High-Energy Proton - Proton Collisions. (Ettore Majorana International Science Series, Life Sciences: Vol. 39). (Illus.). 446p. 1988. 120.00 (*0-306-43106-8*, Plenum Trade) Perseus Pubng.

Ali, A., et al, eds. Salamfestschrift: A Collection of Talks from the Conference on Highlights of Particle & Condensed Matter Physics. (Series in 20th Century Physics: Vol. 4). (Illus.). 628p. 1994. pap. 67.00 (*981-02-1422-7*) World Scientific Pub.

Ali, A. & Cifarelli, L. Heavy Flavours & High-Energy Collisions in the 1-100 TeV Range. LC 89-22891. (Ettore Majorana International Science Series, Life Sciences: Vol. 44). (Illus.). 628p. 1989. 145.00 (*0-306-43369-9*, Plenum Trade) Perseus Pubng.

Ali, A. & Hoodbhoy, P., eds. The MAB Beg Memorial Volume. 304p. (C). 1991. text 89.00 (*981-02-0714-X*) World Scientific Pub.

Ali, A., et al. Highlights of Particle & Condensed Matter Physics. 628p. 1994. text 137.00 (*981-02-1421-9*) World Scientific Pub.

Ali, A. F. Changing Social Stratification in Rural Bangladesh. (C). 1993. 22.00 (*81-7169-267-2*, Commonwealth) S Asia.

Ali, A. Yusuf, tr. The Holy Qur'an. (ARA & ENG.). 1862p. 1983. pap. 25.00 (*0-940368-31-5*, 3A); text 30.00 (*0-940368-32-3*, 3) Tahrike Tarsile Quran.

Ali, A. Yusuf, tr. see Ghazi, Abidullah & Quraishi-Ahmed, Huda, eds.

Ali, Aamir, ed. Environmental Protection of the Himalaya: A Mountaineers View. (C). 1994. text 14.00 (*81-7387-012-8*, Pub. by Indus Pub) S Asia.

ALI-ABA Committee on Continuing Professional Education Staff. ALI-ABA Report on the Survey of Bridge-the-Gap Programs. LC 85-71317. 78p. (Orig.). 1985. pap. 19.00 (*0-8318-0503-X*, B503) Am Law Inst.

— Continuing Legal Education for Professional Competence & Responsibility since Arden House II. LC 84-70340. 322p. 1984. pap. 7.00 (*0-8318-0427-0*, B427) Am Law Inst.

ALI-ABA Staff. ALI-ABA's Practice Checklist Manual on Advising Business Clients: Checklists, Forms, & Drafting Advice from "The Practical Lawyer," "The Practical Real Estate Lawyer," & The Practical Tax Lawyer" LC 97-75006. 244p. 1997. text 97.50 (*0-8318-1144-7*, F144) Am Law Inst.

***Ali, Abbas J.** Globalization of Business: Practice & Theory. LC 99-56499. (Illus.). 334p. (C). 2000. lib. bdg. 69.95 (*0-7890-0412-7*, Intl Busn Pr) Haworth Pr.

Ali, Abbas J., ed. How to Manage for International Competitiveness. LC 91-23645. (Illus.). 292p. 1992. pap. 39.95 (*1-56024-203-5*); lib. bdg. 79.95 (*1-56024-202-7*) Haworth Pr.

Ali, Abbas J., jt. ed. see Zahra, Shaker A.

Ali, Abdul. Arab Legacy to Humour Literature. LC 99-931520. 119 p. 1998. pap. 75.00 (*81-7533-085-6*, Pub. by Print Hse) St Mut.

— Islamic Dynasties of the Arab East: State & Civilization During the Later Medieval Times. 142p. 1996. pap. 175.00 (*81-7533-008-2*, Pub. by Print Hse) St Mut.

Ali, Abdul S. A Linguistic Study of the Development of Scientific Vocabulary in Standard Arabic. 200p. 1987. text 95.00 (*0-7103-0023-9*) Routledge.

Ali, Abdullah Y. The Meaning of the Glorious Quran, 2 vols., Set. 24.00 (*0-686-37146-1*) New World Press NY.

— The Meaning of the Holy Qur'an. 8th ed. LC 97-37495. (ARA.). 1824p. (Orig.). 1998. 21.95 (*0-915957-76-0*) Amana Corp.

— The Message of Islam. 127p. 1990. 7.95 (*81-7151-031-0*) Asia Bk Corp.

— Roman Transliteration of Part 29 of the Holy Qur'an (Arabic Text, Translation & Transliteration) Abuza'kuk, Ali R., ed. & intro. by. 128p. (Orig.). 1996. pap. text 3.00 (*1-881963-57-8*) Al-Saadawi Pubns.

— Roman Transliteration of the 30th Part of the Holy Qur'an: Arabic Text, Translation & Transliteration. Abuza'kuk, Ali R., ed. 128p. (Orig.). 1996. pap. text 2.50 (*1-881963-56-X*) Al-Saadawi Pubns.

Ali, Abdullah Y., comment. The Meaning of the Holy Qur'an. 9th rev. ed. LC 97-37495. 1824p. (Orig.). 1995. pap. 12.50 (*0-915957-77-9*) Amana Corp.

Ali, Abdullah Y., tr. The Meaning of the Holy Quran. 1800p. 1996. 95.00 (*0-614-21061-5*, 766) Kazi Pubns.

— Meaning of the Illustrious Quran. 990p. (Orig.). 1995. text 7.50 (*1-56744-507-1*) Kazi Pubns.

Ali, Abdullah Y., tr. The Story of Mary & Jesus from the Qur'an: Reprinted from the Meaning of the Holy Quran. LC 94-47660. 1995. pap. 3.00 (*0-915957-24-8*) amana pubns.

Ali, Abdullah Yusef, tr. The Meaning of the Holy Quran. 1824p. 1998. 14.95 (*0-915957-32-9*) amana pubns.

Ali, Abdullah Yusuf. A Cultural History of India During the British Period. LC 75-41006. reprint ed. 55.00 (*0-404-14723-2*) AMS Pr.

Ali, Abdullah Yusuf, tr. see Abuza'Kuk, Ali R.

Ali, Abid A., tr. see Qayyim, Ibn.

Ali, Agha S. The Country Without a Post Office: Poems. LC 96-38242. 96p. (C). 1997. 19.00 (*0-393-04057-7*) Norton.

— The Country Without a Post Office: Poems. 96p. 1998. pap. 11.00 (*0-393-31761-7*) Norton.

— The Half-Inch Himalayas. LC 86-9185. (Wesleyan New Poets Ser.). 64p. 1987. pap. 12.95 (*0-8195-1132-3*, Wesleyan Univ Pr) U Pr of New Eng.

— A Nostalgist's Map of America. 112p. 1992. pap. 9.95 (*0-393-30924-X*) Norton.

— Postcard from Kashmir. Barkan, Stanley H., ed. Azed, Jagan N., tr. (Review Chapbook Ser.: No. 23: Indian (Urdu) Poetry 1). (ENG & URD., Illus.). 32p. 1991. 15.00 (*0-89304-885-2*, CCC199); 15.00 (*0-89304-887-9*); pap. 5.00 (*0-89304-886-0*); pap. 5.00 (*0-89304-888-7*) Cross-Cultrl NY.

— A Walk Through the Yellow Pages. (Illus.). 32p. (Orig.). 1987. 20.00 (*0-933313-06-3*); pap. 4.50 (*0-933313-07-1*) SUN Gemini Pr.

***Ali, Agha Shahid, ed.** Ravishing DisUnities: Real Ghazals in English. 2000. 30.00 (*0-8195-6438-9*); pap. 14.95 (*0-8195-6437-0*) U Pr of New Eng.

Ali, Agha Shahid, et al. Gulf Coast Vol. 2: A Journal of Literature & Fine Arts. 11th ed. Burleson, Derick & Sher, Iva, eds. (Illus.). 144p. 1999. pap. 7.00 (*7-447-08746-7*) Gulf Cst TX.

Ali, Agha Shahid, tr. & intro. see Faiz, Faiz Ahmed.

Ali, Ahmed. Al-Qur'an: A Contemporary Translation. 576p. 1988. pap. 17.95 (*0-691-02046-9*, Pub. by Princeton U Pr); text 75.00 (*0-691-07329-5*, Pub. by Princeton U Pr) Cal Prin Full Svc.

— Twilight in Dehli. LC 93-45363. 224p. (Orig.). 1994. pap. 12.95 (*0-8112-1267-X*, NDP782, Pub. by New Directions) Norton.

Ali al Khuli, Muhammad. Dictionary of Applied Linguistics: Arabic. (ARA & ENG.). 179p. 1986. 35.00 (*0-86685-349-9*, LDL3499, Pub. by Librairie du Liban) Intl Bk Ctr.

— Dictionary of Theoretical Linguistics: English-Arabic with Arabic-English Glossary. (ARA & ENG.). 402p. 1982. 35.00 (*0-86685-306-5*, LDL3065, Pub. by Librairie du Liban) Intl Bk Ctr.

Ali al Mazru'i, Shaykh Al-Amin bin, see Al-Amin bin Ali al Mazru'i, Shaykh.

Ali, Alfred. Blackman Let Us Make Man in Our Image. 64p. (Orig.). (YA). 1995. reprint ed. pap. 5.95 (*0-9636025-2-7*) A Ali Lit Wrks.

— Blackman Let Us Make Man in Our Image. (Orig.). 1995. reprint ed. pap. 5.95 (*1-56411-136-9*) Untd Bros & Sis.

— The Blackman's Stolen Birthright (Money System) Blackman; I Make All Things New! A New Spiritual-Image. 136p. (Orig.). 1993. pap. 12.95 (*0-9636025-0-0*) A Ali Lit Wrks.

— The Resurrection of the Dead: Blackman Is Spiritually Dead. 59p. 1993. reprint ed. pap. 8.95 (*0-9636025-1-9*) A Ali Lit Wrks.

— 64 Years to Make a Negro: Willie Lynch Speech to the American Slave Owners in 1712. LC 94-73228. 190p. (Orig.). 1995. pap. 12.95 (*0-9636025-3-5*) A Ali Lit Wrks.

— 64 Years to Make a Negro Vol. 1, Pt. II: Including The Two Faces of Man. San Serif, Inc. Staff, ed. LC 96-96113. 256p. 1998. pap. 19.95 (*0-9636025-4-3*) A Ali Lit Wrks.

Ali, Almeen. Land-Locked States & International Law. (C). 1989. 16.00 (*81-7003-102-8*, Pub. by S Asia Pubs) S Asia.

— Land-Locked States & International Law: With Special Reference to the Role of Nepal. 238p. (C). 1989. 150.00 (*0-89771-088-6*, Pub. by Ratna Pustak Bhandar) St Mut.

Ali, Ameer. The Spirit of Islam. 1990. reprint ed. 18.50 (*81-85395-91-8*, Pub. by Low Price) S Asia.

Ali, Amina I. Ayub: The Patient. Cinquino, J. C., ed. (Prophets' Stories for Children from the Holy Qur'an Ser.: No. 12). (Illus.). 28p. (Orig.). (J). (gr. 4-6). 1996. write for info. (*1-881963-26-8*); pap. 2.50 (*1-881963-27-6*) Al-Saadawi Pubns.

— Dawud: The Warrior. Cinquino, J. C., ed. (Prophets' Stories for Children from the Holy Qur'an Ser.: No. 15). (Illus.). 28p. (Orig.). (J). (gr. 4-6). 1996. write for info. (*1-881963-32-2*); pap. 2.50 (*1-881963-33-0*) Al-Saadawi Pubns.

— Isa: The Healer. Cinquino, J. C., ed. (Prophets' Stories for Children from the Holy Qur'an Ser.: No. 20). (Illus.). 28p. (Orig.). (J). (gr. 4-6). 1996. write for info. (*1-881963-42-X*); pap. 2.50 (*1-881963-43-8*) Al-Saadawi Pubns.

— Muhammad: The Seal. Cinquino, J. C., ed. (Prophets' Stories for Children from the Holy Qur'an Ser.: No. 21). (Illus.). 28p. (Orig.). (J). (gr. 4-6). 1996. write for info. (*1-881963-44-6*); pap. 2.50 (*1-881963-45-4*) Al-Saadawi Pubns.

— Musa: The Spoken To. Cinquino, J. C., ed. (Prophets' Stories for Children from the Holy Qur'an Ser.: No. 13). (Illus.). 28p. (Orig.). (J). (gr. 4-6). 1996. write for info. (*1-881963-28-4*); pap. 2.50 (*1-881963-29-2*) Al-Saadawi Pubns.

— Shoayb: The Prophet of Madyan. Cinquino, J. C., ed. (Prophets' Stories for Children from the Holy Qur'an

A

An Asterisk (*) at the beginning of an entry indicates that the title is appearing for the first time.

A

Ser.: No. 11). (Illus.). 28p. (Orig.). (J). (gr. 4-6). 1996. write for info. (*1-881963-24-1*); pap. 2.50 (*1-881963-25-X*) Al-Saadawi Pubns.

— Sulayman: The Gifted. Cinquino, J. C., ed. (Prophets' Stories for Children from the Holy Qur'an Ser.: No. 16). (Illus.). 28p. (Orig.). (J). (gr. 4-6). 1996. write for info. (*1-881963-34-9*); pap. 2.50 (*1-881963-35-7*) Al-Saadawi Pubns.

— Yahya: The Forebearing Prophet. Cinquino, J. C., ed. (Prophets' Stories for Children from the Holy Qur'an Ser.: No. 19). (Illus.). 28p. (Orig.). (J). (gr. 4-6). 1996. write for info. (*1-881963-40-3*); pap. 2.50 (*1-881963-41-1*) Al-Saadawi Pubns.

— Yunus: The Repentant. Cinquino, J. C., ed. (Prophets' Stories for Children from the Holy Qur'an Ser.: No. 17). (Illus.). 28p. (Orig.). (J). (gr. 4-6). 1996. write for info. (*1-881963-36-5*); pap. 2.50 (*1-881963-37-3*) Al-Saadawi Pubns.

— Yusuf: The Honest. Cinquino, J. C., ed. (Prophets' Stories for Children from the Holy Qur'an Ser.: No. 10). (Illus.). 28p. (Orig.). (J). (gr. 4-6). 1996. write for info. (*1-881963-22-5*); pap. 2.50 (*1-881963-23-3*) Al-Saadawi Pubns.

— Zakaria: The Warshipper. Cinquino, J. C., ed. (Prophets' Stories for Children from the Holy Qur'an Ser.: No. 18). (Illus.). 28p. (Orig.). (J). (gr. 4-6). 1996. write for info. (*1-881963-38-1*); pap. 2.50 (*1-881963-39-X*) Al-Saadawi Pubns.

Ali, Amina I. & Cinquino, J. C. Harun: The Leader. (Prophets' Stories for Children from the Holy Qur'an Ser.: No. 14). (Illus.). 28p. (Orig.). (J). (gr. 4-6). 1996. write for info. (*1-881963-30-6*); pap. 2.50 (*1-881963-31-4*) Al-Saadawi Pubns.

Ali, Ansara. Polonia - i - Czlowiek, Ktory Zobaczyl Boga. rev. ed. Czyzycka, Magdalena, tr. from ENG. (POL., Illus.). 384p. 1995. 24.95 (*0-9636170-6-0*) Royal Rags.

— Polonia & the Man Who Saw God. deluxe ed. McRae, James J., ed. LC 94-43178. (ENG & POL., Illus.). 384p. 1995. 45.00 incl. audio (*0-9636170-8-7*) Royal Rags.

— Polonia & the Man Who Saw God. rev. ed. McRae, James J., ed. LC 94-43178. (Illus.). 384p. 1995. 24.95 (*0-9636170-5-2*) Royal Rags.

— The Sacred Adventures of a Taxi Driver. rev. ed. LC 93-8602. (Illus.). 544p. 1993. reprint ed. pap. 16.95 (*0-9636170-0-1*) Royal Rags.

— Thank You, Toronto & Happy Birthday. LC 93-60619. (Illus.). 96p. (Orig.). 1993. pap. 13.95 (*0-9636170-3-6*) Royal Rags.

Ali Anzaldua-Morales, Mohammad, tr. see Syed Mohammad Askari Jafery & Ali, Imam.

Ali, Asghar. Islam & Muslims: A Critical Reassessment. 1985. (C). 1988. 210.00 (*0-7855-4755-X*) St Mut.

Ali, Asghar, ed. Ethnic Conflicts in South Asia. (C). 1987. 21.00 (*81-202-0179-5*, Pub. by Ajanta) S Asia.

Ali, Assad. Happiness Without Death: Desert Hymns. 110p. 1996. pap. 9.00 (*0-614-21648-6*, 375) Kazi Pubns.

— Happiness Without Death: Desert Hymns. 96p. 1991. pap. 9.00 (*0-939660-39-3*) Threshold CA.

***Ali, Azra Asghar.** Emergence of Feminism among Indian Muslim Women, 1920-1947. 380p. 2000. 24.95 (*0-19-579152-5*) OUP.

Ali, B. Al-Salat in Quran. 270p. 1991. 45.00 (*1-56744-375-3*) Kazi Pubns.

— Hajjat-ul-Wada: Last Sermon. 1981. 3.00 (*1-56744-033-9*) Kazi Pubns.

Ali, B. Sheikh. Zakir Husain: Life & Times. 525p. (C). 1992. 40.00 (*0-7069-5924-8*, Pub. by Vikas) S Asia.

Ali, Carroll A. Survival & Liberation: Pastoral Theology in African American Context. LC 99-30856. 1999. pap. 19.99 (*0-8272-3443-0*) Chalice Pr.

Ali, Cynthia D., jt. auth. see Andrews, Sharon V.

Ali, Daud, ed. Invoking the Past: The Uses of History in South Asia. (Studies on South Asia). 384p. 2000. text 29.95 (*0-19-564978-8*) OUP.

Ali, E., et al, eds. Selected Papers of Abdus Salam. LC 94-2323. (Series on Twentieth Century Physics). 696p. 1994. pap. text 53.00 (*981-02-1663-7*) World Scientific Pub.

***Ali, Elvis, et al.** The All-in-One Guide to ADD & Hyperactivity. (Love Living Live Loving Ser.: Vol. 3). (Illus.). 392p. 2001. pap. 9.95 (*1-886508-29-1*, Ages Pubns) Adi Gaia Esalen.

— Natural Remedies & Supplements: All-in-One Guide to Vitamins, Minerals, Enzymes, Amino Acids, Fats, Herbs, Aromatherapy, Flower Remedies, Phytochemicals, Nuiraceuticals. LC 99-41819. 392p. 2000. pap. 9.95 (*1-886508-28-3*, Pub. by Adi Gaia Esalen) Genl Dist Srvs.

Ali, Elvis, et al. The Tea Tree Oil Bible: Your Essential Guide for Health & Home Uses. LC 98-3881. (Love Living & Live Loving & Health Ser.). 201p. 1999. pap. 7.95 (*1-886508-10-0*, Ages Pubns) Adi Gaia Esalen.

Ali Engineer, Asghar, ed. Kerala Muslims: Historical Perspective. (C). 1995. 22.50 (*0-8364-2911-7*, Pub. by Ajanta) S Asia.

Ali, F. & Ahmed, F. Divorce in Mohammedan Law: The Law of Triple Divorce. (C). 1990. 120.00 (*0-89771-147-5*) St Mut.

Ali, Fazal, et al. Wireless Communication IC's: Design Principles, Technologies, & Applications. (C). 2000. text 70.00 (*0-13-487100-6*) P-H.

Ali, G. Elfaki, et al. Energy Utilities & Institutions in Africa. Bhagavan, M. R., ed. (African Energy Policy Research Network Ser.). (Illus.). 224p. (C). 1996. pap. 25.00 (*1-85649-460-8*, Pub. by Zed Books) St Martin.

***Ali, Hana.** More Than a Hero: Muhammad Ali's Life Lessons Presented Through His Daughter's Eyes. LC 00-27422. (Illus.). 128p. 2000. 15.95 (*0-671-04236-X*, PB Hardcover) PB.

Ali, Hassan O., tr. see Doyle, Arthur Conan.

Ali, Hazrat, jt. auth. see Muhammad.

Ali, Husain Q. Apostate Son. unabridged ed. Green, Sharon, ed. (Illus.). 275p. (Orig.). 1998. pap. 14.95 (*0-9668914-0-6*, 1) Najiba Pub Co.

Ali, I., et al, eds. Chemical Mechanical Planarization in IC Device Manufacturing: 2nd International Symposium. LC 99-196375. (Proceedings Ser.: Vol. 98-7). (Illus.). 274p. 1998. 50.00 (*1-56677-201-X*) Electrochem Soc.

Ali, I. & Raghavan, S., eds. Chemical Mechanical Planarization in IC Device Manufacturing. LC 97-190838. (Proceedings Ser.: Vol. 96-22). (Illus.). 276p. 1997. 63.00 (*1-56677-172-2*) Electrochem Soc.

Ali Idris. Dongola: A Novel of Nubia. Theroux, Peter, tr. from ARA. LC 98-3151. 80p. 1999. 24.00 (*1-55728-531-4*); pap. 14.00 (*1-55728-532-2*) U of Ark Pr.

Ali, Ikram. History of the Punjab. (C). 1993. text 17.50 (*81-85557-00-4*, Pub. by Low Price) S Asia.

Ali, Imam, jt. auth. see Syed Mohammad Askari Jafery.

Ali, Imran. The Punjab under Imperialism, 1885-1947. LC 87-34466. 276p. 1988. reprint ed. pap. 85.60 (*0-608-02943-2*, 206400900008) Bks Demand.

Ali, Iqbal. Parents' Guide. 30p. 1996. pap. 2.50 (*0-614-21521-8*, 944) Kazi Pubns.

Ali, Jamil. Determination of the Coordinates of Positions for the Correction of Distances Between Cities. 1967. 24.95 (*0-8156-6007-3*, Pub. by Am U Beirut) Syracuse U Pr.

Ali, Javid, et al. Jane's U. S. Chemical Biological Defense Guidebook. LC 97-42837. 1997. 895.00 (*0-7106-1646-5*) Janes Info Group.

Ali, Juzar, et al. Pulmonary Pathophysiology. LC 98-7634. (Illus.). 347p. 1999. pap. text 43.50 (*0-07-062170-5*) McGraw-Hill HPD.

***Ali, Juzar, et al.** Radiology: Pre-Test Self Assessment & Review. (Illus.). 300p. 2000. Price not set. (*0-07-135959-1*) McGraw.

Ali, Kamil, jt. auth. see Stanton, Timothy.

Ali Khan, Haider. The Political Economy of Sanctions Against Apartheid. LC 89-34521. 120p. 1989. lib. bdg. 26.50 (*1-55587-145-3*) L Rienner.

Ali Khan Kirmani, Mir Hussain, see Kirmani, Mir Hussain Ali Khan.

Ali Khan, Mumtaz. Planning Processes & Muslim Responses to Rural Development in India. (C). 1993. 30.00 (*81-85565-25-2*, Pub. by Uppal Pub Hse) S Asia.

— Social Legislations & Civil Rights of Scheduled Castes in India. (C). 1993. 22.00 (*81-85565-26-0*, Pub. by Uppal Pub Hse) S Asia.

Ali, Lynda & Graham, Barbara. The Counselling Approach to Careers Guidance. LC 95-38972. (Illus.). 208p. (C). 1996. pap. 24.99 (*0-415-12173-6*) Routledge.

— The Counselling Approach to Careers Guidance. LC 95-38972. (Illus.). 208p. (C). 1996. 80.00 (*0-415-12172-8*) Routledge.

***Ali, Lynda & Graham, Barbara.** Moving on in Your Career: A Guide for Academics & Postgraduates. LC 99-44350. 168p. 2000. pap. write for info. (*0-415-17870-3*) Routledge.

Ali, M. Islam Reviewed. 2nd rev. ed. Skolfield, Ellis H., ed. 128p. (Orig.). 1999. pap. 6.95 (*0-9628139-7-4*) Fish Hse.

Ali, M., et al, eds. The Fourth International Conference on Industrial & Engineering Applications of Artificial Intelligence & Expert Systems - Proceedings: IEA - AIE, 91, 2 vols. 820p. (Orig.). (C). 1991. pap. 86.00 (*1-879921-00-6*) Univ TN Space.

Ali, M. A. Nervous Systems in Invertebrates. LC 87-25898. (NATO ASI Series A, Life Sciences: Vol. 141). (Illus.). 684p. 1987. 135.00 (*0-306-42770-2*, Plenum Trade) Perseus Pubng.

— Rhythms in Fishes. (NATO ASI Ser.: Vol. 236). (Illus.). 356p. (C). 1993. text 115.00 (*0-306-44318-X*, Kluwer Plenum) Kluwer Academic.

Ali, M. A., ed. Environmental Physiology of Fishes. LC 80-22156. (NATO ASI Series A, Life Sciences: Vol. 35). 734p. 1981. 135.00 (*0-306-40574-1*, Plenum Trade) Perseus Pubng.

Ali, M. A. & Klyne, M. A. Vision in Vertebrates. LC 85-12191. 282p. 1985. 79.50 (*0-306-42065-1*, Plenum Trade) Perseus Pubng.

Ali, M. Athar. The Apparatus of Empire: Appointments & Titles in the Mughal Empire, 1574-1658. 418p. 1985. 65.00 (*0-19-561500-X*) OUP.

— Mughal India: Studies in Polity, Ideas, Society & Culture. (Illus.), 392p. 1999. text 35.00 (*0-19-564860-9*) OUP.

Ali, M. Kassim Haji, see Haji Ali, M. Kassim.

Ali, M. Khalil & Ewer, Michael S. Cancer & the Cardiopulmonary System. fac. ed. LC 83-21089. (Illus.). 254p. pap. 78.80 (*0-7837-7214-9*, 204708400005) Bks Demand.

Ali, M. Mohamed. Ecological & Physiological Studies on the Alphalpha Ladybird. 199p. (C). 1979. 75.00 (*963-05-1702-7*, Pub. by Akade Kiado) St Mut.

Ali, Majid. The Butterfly & Life Span Nutrition. 419p. (Orig.). 1995. pap. 16.99 (*1-879131-01-3*) Inst of Prev Med.

— The Canary & Chronic Fatigue. 580p. 1995. pap. 20.00 (*1-879131-04-8*) Inst of Prev Med.

— The Cortical Monkey & Healing. 352p. 1995. pap. 14.99 (*1-879131-00-5*) Inst of Prev Med.

— The Ghoraa & Limbic Excercise. 355p. (Orig.). 1996. pap. 19.50 (*1-879131-02-1*) Inst of Prev Med.

— Healing, Miracles & the Bite of the Gray Dog. 550p. (Orig.). 1997. pap. 19.00 (*1-879131-11-0*) Inst of Prev Med.

— RDA: Rats, Drugs & Assumptions. (Illus.). 670p. 1995. pap. 21.00 (*1-879131-07-2*) Inst of Prev Med.

— What Do Lions Know about Stress? 500p. Date not set. pap. 20.00 (*1-879131-10-2*) Inst of Prev Med.

Ali, Masooma, tr. see Ansal, Jusum.

Ali, Maulana. A Manual of Hadith: The Traditions of the Prophet Muhammad. (ARA & ENG.). 424p. 1988. 45.00 (*0-7007-0110-9*, Pub. by Curzon Pr Ltd) Paul & Co Pubs.

Ali, Maulana M. The Antichrist & God & Magog. 72p. 1992. pap. 5.90 (*0-913321-04-4*) Ahmadiyya Anjuman.

— The Early Caliphate. 4th ed. Khan, Maulana M., tr. from URD. 214p. (Orig.). 1995. pap. 5.95 (*0-913321-27-3*) Ahmadiyya Anjuman.

— Holy Quran. 1987. pap. 16.00 (*0-913321-05-2*); lthr. 30.00 (*0-913321-11-7*) Ahmadiyya Anjuman.

— Introduction to the Study of Holy Quaran. 133p. (Orig.). 1992. 5.95 (*0-913321-06-0*) Ahmadiyya Anjuman.

— Living Thoughts of the Prophet Muhammad. 156p. (Orig.). 1992. pap. 5.95 (*0-913321-19-2*) Ahmadiyya Anjuman.

— Muhammad the Prophet. 7th ed. 208p. (Orig.). 1993. pap. 7.95 (*0-913321-07-9*) Ahmadiyya Anjuman.

— The New World Order. 4th ed. 86p. (Orig.). 1989. pap. 4.95 (*0-913221-33-3*) Ahmadiyya Anjuman.

Ali, Maulana Muhammad. Founder of the Ahmadiyya Movement. 1984. pap. 2.50 (*0-913321-64-8*) Ahmadiyya Anjuman.

— History & Doctrines of the Babi Movement. 2nd ed. 1997. pap. 4.95 (*0-913321-47-8*) Ahmadiyya Anjuman.

— History of the Prophets: As Narrated in the Holy Qur'an Compared with the Bible. 3rd ed. 1996. pap. 3.95 (*0-913321-14-1*) Ahmadiyya Anjuman.

— True Conception of the Ahmadiyya Movement. 1996. pap. 3.95 (*0-913321-28-1*) Ahmadiyya Anjuman.

Ali Mehmeti, Felix. Nonlinear Waves in Networks. LC 94-35239. (Mathematical Research Ser.: Vol. 80). 1994. pap. text 59.85 (*3-05-501640-8*, Pub. by Akademie Verlag) Wiley.

Ali, Mohamed. Ecological & Physiological Studies on the Alfalfa Ladybird. 1981. 90.00 (*0-569-08553-5*) St Mut.

Ali, Mohammad M. Medieval Islamic Pragmatics: Sunni Legal Theorists' Models of Texual Communication. 288p. 1998. 75.00 (*0-7007-1102-3*, Pub. by Curzon Pr Ltd) Paul & Co Pubs.

Ali, Mohammed. Ethnicity, Politics, & Society in Northeast Africa: Conflict & Social Change. 272p. (C). 1996. pap. text 29.50 (*0-7618-0283-5*); lib. bdg. 52.00 (*0-7618-0273-8*) U Pr of Amer.

— Telling Fortunes by Cards. Case, Carleton B., ed. 159p. 1997. reprint ed. spiral bd. 13.50 (*0-7873-1277-0*) Hlth Research.

Ali, Mohammed, et al, eds. Water Resources Policy for Asia: Proceeding of the Regional Symposium on Water Resources Policy in Agro-Socio-Economic Development, Dhaka, Bangladesh, 4-8 August 1985. 640p. (C). 1987. text 168.00 (*90-6191-684-4*, Pub. by A A Balkema) Ashgate Pub Co.

Ali, Moi. Copywriting. LC 97-214947. (CIN Practitioner Ser.). 256p. 1997. pap. text 32.95 (*0-7506-3510-X*) Buttrwrth-Heinemann.

Ali, Molana S. Masnavi Ravayeh. LC 89-16557. (ARA, FRE & PER.). 125p. (Orig.). 1990. pap. 15.00 (*0-8191-7676-1*) U Pr of Amer.

— The Secret Word. LC 88-39008. (ENG & PER.). 75p. (Orig.). 1989. pap. 12.00 (*0-8191-7331-2*) U Pr of Amer.

Ali, Moonis, jt. ed. see Forsyth, Graham F.

Ali Mourad, Suleiman, ed. see Al-Dimashqi, Ibn 'Asakir.

Ali, Muhammad & Richmond, Peter. Ali: Journey of a Holy Man. 1999. text 22.95 (*0-312-24653-6*) St Martin.

Ali, Muhsin J. Scheherazade in England: A Study of Nineteenth-Century English Criticism of the Arabian Nights. LC 80-53382. (Illus.). 193p. (Orig.). 1981. pap. 11.95 (*0-89410-247-8*, Three Contnts) L Rienner.

Ali, Mushin J. Scheherazade in England: A Study of Nineteenth-Century English Criticism of the Arabian Nights. Noss, Philip, ed. LC 80-53382. (Illus.). 193p. (Orig.). 1981. pap. 25.00 (*0-89410-246-X*, Three Contnts) L Rienner.

***Ali Nader Sh, Molana S.** Revelation: Elham. 60p. 1999. pap. 12.95 (*0-910735-64-6*, Pub. by MTO Printing & Pubn Ctr) ACCESS Pubs Network.

Ali, Naseem N., jt. auth. see Ali, S. Nazim.

***Ali-Olivas, Teresa.** Bible Bitches: Acknowledging the Reality about Women in the Old Testament. LC 99-91659. 171p. 2000. 25.00 (*0-7388-1164-5*); pap. 18.00 (*0-7388-1165-3*) Xlibris Corp.

Ali, Omar. Crisis in the Arabian Gulf: An Independent Iraqi View. LC 92-39281. 184p. 1993. 57.95 (*0-275-94158-2*, C4158, Praeger Pubs) Greenwood.

***Ali, Paul A. U.** Marshalling of Securities. 260p. 1999. text 160.00 (*0-19-826865-3*) OUP.

Ali, Quraysh, ed. & pref. see Gallery 37 Apprentice Artists Staff.

Ali, R. Southern Africa: An American Enigma. LC 85-31254. 239p. 1987. 59.95 (*0-275-92380-0*, C2380, Praeger Pubs) Greenwood.

Ali, R. M., et al. Computational Methods & Function Theory 1994: Proceedings of the Conference. 350p. 1995. text 106.00 (*981-02-2129-0*) World Scientific Pub.

Ali, Rabia & Lifschultz, Lawrence, eds. Why Bosnia? Writings on the Balkan War. 416p. (Orig.). 1993. 35.00 (*0-9630587-8-9*); pap. 19.95 (*0-9630587-9-7*) Pamphleteers.

Ali, Ridwan, et al. Sri Lanka's Rubber Industry: Succeeding in the Global Market. LC 97-26339. (World Bank Discussion Papers). 112p. 1997. pap. 22.00 (*0-8213-4004-2*) World Bank.

Ali Rob Sharif, Muhammed. Thermodynamics. (Test Yourself Ser.). 1997. pap. 12.95 (*0-614-27611-X*) NTC Contemp Pub Co.

Ali, S. The Spirit of Islam. 512p. 1987. 300.00 (*1-85077-179-0*, Pub. by Darf Pubs Ltd) St Mut.

— Teach Yourself Arabic. 1991. 9.50 (*0-935782-17-6*) Kazi Pubns.

Ali, S. A. Social & Economic Aspects of the Islam of Mohammad. LC 93-7498. 184p. 1993. 79.95 (*0-7734-9279-8*) E Mellen.

— The Spirit of Islam. 1991. 19.95 (*0-933511-62-0*) Kazi Pubns.

Ali, S. Ameer. Color & Learn the Names of the Family of Prophet Muhammad. 32p. (Orig.). (J). (ps). 1980. pap. 3.95 (*0-934905-13-4*) Kazi Pubns.

Ali, S. M. The Law of Interim Orders & Receivership. (C). 1988. 80.00 (*0-7855-3721-X*) St Mut.

Ali, S. M., ed. Marine Fisheries Economics & Development in India. LC 96-904824. 208p. 1996. pap. 163.00 (*81-7533-009-0*, Pub. by Print Hse) St Mut.

Ali, S. Mahmud. Cold War in the High Himalayas: The U. S. A., China & South Asia in the 1950s. 350p. (C). 1999. text 55.00 (*0-7007-1169-4*, Pub. by Curzon Pr Ltd) UH Pr.

— The Fearful State: Power, People & Internal War in South Asia. 272p. (C). 1993. text 65.00 (*1-85649-121-8*, Pub. by Zed Books); text 25.00 (*1-85649-122-6*, Pub. by Zed Books) St Martin.

Ali, S. Nazim & Ali, Naseem N. Information Sources on Islamic Banking & Economics 1980-1990. LC 94-1592. 350p. 1994. 93.50 (*0-7103-0486-2*) Routledge.

Ali, S. R. Izz-ad-Din al-Sulami. 1991. pap. 8.50 (*1-56744-109-2*) Kazi Pubns.

***Ali, S. T., et al, eds.** Trends in Quantum Mechanics. LC 99-88753. 400p. 1999. 88.00 (*981-02-4081-3*) World Scientific Pub.

***Ali, S. T., et al.** Coherent States, Wavelets & Their Generalizations. LC 99-39821. (Graduate Texts in Contemporary Physics Ser.). (Illus.). 350p. 1999. 79.95 (*0-387-98908-0*) Spr-Verlag.

Ali, S. T., et al. Quantization & Coherent States Methods - Proceedings of XI Workshop on Geometric Methods in Physics. 256p. 1993. text 121.00 (*981-02-1447-2*) World Scientific Pub.

Ali, S. T., tr. see Levy-Leblond, Jean-Marc & Balibar, F.

Ali, S. V. Hussain the Savior of Islam. LC 81-51900. 252p. 1981. pap. 6.00 (*0-940368-03-X*, 62A) Tahrike Tarsile Quran.

Ali, S. V., tr. see Revealed Book Staff.

Ali, Sabir. Environment & Resettlement Colonies of Delhi. (C). 1995. 18.50 (*81-241-0279-1*, Pub. by Har-Anand Pubns) S Asia.

— Modernising Urban India: An Essay in Environmental Sanitation. (C). 1994. 16.00 (*81-241-0116-7*, Pub. by Har-Anand Pubns) S Asia.

— Slums Within Slums. 1990. text 22.50 (*0-685-37407-6*, Pub. by Vikas) S Asia.

— Socio-Economic Status of Scavengers: A Study Sabir Ali. (C). 1994. 16.00 (*81-241-0184-1*, Pub. by Har-Anand Pubns) S Asia.

Ali, Salim. The Book of Indian Birds. 2nd rev. ed. LC 97-158425. (Illus.). 408p. (C). 1997. text 28.00 (*0-19-563731-3*) OUP.

Ali, Salim & Ripley, S. Dillon. Compact Handbook of the Birds of India & Pakistan: Together with Those of Bangladesh, Nepal, Bhutan, & Sri Lanka. 2nd ed. (Illus.). 884p. 1988. text 98.00 (*0-19-562063-1*) OUP.

— Cuckoo-Shrikes to Babaxes: Together with Those of Bagladesh, Nepal, Bhutan, & Sri Lanka, Vol. 6. 2nd ed. (Handbook of the Birds of India & Pakistan Ser.). (Illus.). 260p. 1996. text 39.95 (*0-19-562978-7*) OUP.

Ali, Salim & Ripley, S. Dillon. Handbook of the Birds of India & Pakistan: (Synopsis Nos. 435-665), Vol. 3: Stone Curlews to Owls. 2nd ed. (Illus.). 344p. 1982. text 42.50 (*0-19-561302-3*) OUP.

Ali, Salim & Ripley, S. Dillon. Handbook of the Birds of India & Pakistan: Together with Those of Bangladesh, Nepal, Bhutan & Sri Lanka, Vol. 5: Larks to the Grey Hypocolius. 2nd ed. (Illus.). 292p. 1987. text 39.95 (*0-19-561857-2*) OUP.

— Handbook of the Birds of India & Pakistan: Together with Those of Bangladesh, Nepal, Bhutan & Sri Lanka, Vol. 10. 2nd ed. (Illus.). 286p. 1999. text 55.00 (*0-19-563708-9*) OUP.

— Handbook of the Birds of India & Pakistan: Together with Those of Bangladesh, Nepal, Bhutan & Sri Lanka: Warblers to Redstarts, Vol. 8. 2nd ed. (Handbook of the Birds of India & Pakistan Ser.). (Illus.). 296p. 1997. text 40.00 (*0-19-563657-0*) OUP.

— Handbook of the Birds of India & Pakistan: Together with Those of Bangladesh, Nepal, Sikkim, Bhutan, & Sri Lanka; Robins to Wagtails, Vol. 9. 2nd ed. LC 99-176473. (Illus.). 328p. 1998. text 49.95 (*0-19-563695-3*) OUP.

— Handbook of the Birds of India & Pakistan Vol. 1: Synopsis 1-224. 2nd ed. (Illus.). 440p. 1979. text 45.00 (*0-19-561115-2*) OUP.

— Handbook of the Birds of India & Pakistan Vol. 2: (Synopsis Nos. 225-434) 2nd ed. (Illus.). 362p. 1981. text 45.00 (*0-19-561201-9*) OUP.

— Handbook of the Birds of India & Pakistan Vol. 4: (Synopsis Nos. 666-871), Vol. 4. 2nd ed. (Illus.). 284p. 1984. text 45.00 (*0-19-561551-4*) OUP.

— Handbook of the Birds of India & Pakistan Vol. 7: Together with Those of Bangladesh, Nepal, Bhutan, & Sri Lanka, Vol. 7. 2nd ed. (Illus.). 250p. (C). 1996. text 39.95 (*0-19-563590-6*) OUP.

— A Pictorial Guide to the Birds of the Indian Subcontinent. 2nd ed. LC 97-145281. (Illus.). 170p. 1996. text 28.00 (*0-19-563732-1*) OUP.

Ali-Shah, Omar. The Course of the Seeker. unabridged ed. LC 98-173071. 299p. 1997. pap. 25.00 (*2-909347-05-2*, Pub. by Tractus Bks) Tractus.

— The Rules or Secrets of the Naqshbandi Order. rev. unabridged ed. LC 98-61227. 350p. 1998. pap. 25.00 (*2-909347-09-5*, Pub. by Tractus Bks) Tractus.

— The Sufi Tradition in the West. 248p. pap. write for info. (*1-883816-00-9*) Alif Pub.

— Sufism As Therapy. unabridged ed. LC 98-120449. 256p. 1995. pap. 20.00 (*2-909347-03-6*, Pub. by Tractus Bks) Tractus.

— Sufism for Today. rev. unabridged ed. LC 98-120444. xix, 215p. 1993. pap. 14.00 (*2-909347-00-1*, Pub. by Tractus Bks) Tractus.

Ali Shah, Omar, tr. see Khayyam, Omar.

Ali-Shah, Omar, tr. see Sa'di.

Ali Shah, Sirdar I. Alone in Arabian Nights. rev. ed. 215p. 1992. 29.00 (*0-86304-063-2*, Pub. by Octagon Pr) ISHK.

Ali Shah, Sirdar Ikbal. Afghanistan of the Afghans. 272p. 1982. 19.00 (*0-900860-99-5*, Pub. by Octagon Pr) ISHK.

— Escape from Central Asia. 1980. 24.00 (*0-900860-78-2*, Pub. by Octagon Pr) ISHK.

— Lights of Asia. rev. unabridged ed. LC 98-61227. 320p. 1998. pap. 25.00 (*2-909347-10-9*, Pub. by Tractus Bks) Tractus.

— Muhammed: The Prophet. rev. unabridged ed. LC 98-118945. 285p. 1997. pap. 25.00 (*2-909347-04-4*, Pub. by Tractus Bks) Tractus.

— Selections from the Koran. LC 83-172424. 90p. 1980. 19.00 (*0-900860-85-5*, Pub. by Octagon Pr) ISHK.

— The Spirit of the East. 277p. 1973. pap. 11.00 (*0-900860-16-2*, Pub. by Octagon Pr) ISHK.

***Ali, Shaheen Sardar.** Equal Before Allah, Unequal Before Man? Negotiating Gender Hierarchies in Islam & International Law. LC 99-42867. 1999. 111.00 (*90-411-1268-5*) Kluwer Law Intl.

Ali, Shaheen Sardar & Rehman, Javaid. Indigenous Peoples & Ethnic Minorities of Pakistan: Constitutional & Legal Perspectives. (NIAS Monographs: Vol. 84). 192p. (C). 1999. text 52.00 (*0-7007-1159-7*, Pub. by Curzon Pr Ltd) UH Pr.

Ali, Shahrazad. Are You Still a Slave? 150p. (Orig.). 1994. pap. 10.00 (*0-933405-04-9*) Civilized Pubns.

— The Blackman's Guide to Understanding the Blackwoman. LC 90-1349. 200p. (Orig.). 1990. pap. 10.00 (*0-933405-01-4*) Civilized Pubns.

— The Blackwoman's Guide to Understanding the Blackman. LC 92-4982. 260p. (Orig.). 1992. pap. 12.00 (*0-933405-03-0*) Civilized Pubns.

— Day by Day. (Illus.). 20p. (Orig.). (J). (ps-12). 1996. pap. 4.00 (*0-933405-05-7*) Civilized Pubns.

— How Not to Eat Pork: Or Life Without the Pig. 4th ed. LC 85-70171. (Illus.). 104p. (Orig.). 1985. pap. 10.00 (*0-933405-00-6*) Civilized Pubns.

— Things Your Parents Should Have Told You: For Black Youth Born in the 1970's & 1980's. LC 98-26489. 150p. 1998. pap. 10.00 (*0-933405-07-3*) Civilized Pubns.

— Urban Survival for the Year 2000: How to Prepare for the Y2K Computer Problem in the Hood. (Illus.). 120p. 1999. pap. 10.00 (*0-933405-08-1*) Civilized Pubns.

Ali, Shanti S. & Ramchandani, R. R. India & the Western Indian Ocean States. 310p. 1981. 29.95 (*0-318-37238-X*) Asia Bk Corp.

Ali, Shanti S. & Ramchandani, R. R., eds. India & the Western Indian Ocean States: Towards Regional Cooperation in Development. 310p. 1981. 29.95 (*0-940500-85-X*, Pub. by Allied Pubs) Asia Bk Corp.

Ali, Sheikh R. The International Organizations & World Order Dictionary. LC 91-38953. (Clio Dictionaries in Political Science Ser.). 300p. 1991. lib. bdg. 50.00 (*0-87436-572-4*) ABC-CLIO.

— Oil, Turmoil, & Islam in the Middle East. LC 85-31254. 238p. 1986. 55.00 (*0-275-92135-2*, C2135, Praeger Pubs) Greenwood.

— The Peace & Nuclear War Dictionary. LC 89-14971. (Clio Dictionaries in Political Science Ser.). 350p. (C). 1989. lib. bdg. 49.00 (*0-87436-531-7*) ABC-CLIO.

Ali, Sheikh R., ed. Third World at the Crossroads. LC 88-28834. 232p. 1989. 55.00 (*0-275-93057-2*, C3057, Praeger Pubs) Greenwood.

Ali, Sheikh R. & Elliot, Jeffrey M. The Trilemma of World Oil Politics. LC 84-275. (Great Issues of the Day Ser.: No. 2). 152p. 1991. pap. 19.00 (*0-89370-268-4*) Millefleurs.

Ali, Sheikh R., jt. auth. see Elliot, Jeffrey M.

Ali, Showkat. Capital Flows, Saving, & Investment in the World Economy. rev. ed. LC 97-32975. (Financial Sector of the American Economy Ser.). 186p. 1998. text 46.00 (*0-8153-3073-1*) Garland.

***Ali, Suki, et al.** Global Feminist Politics: Identities in a Changing World. LC 99-54583. 2000. pap. write for info. (*0-415-21470-X*) Routledge.

Ali, Syed. Arabic for Beginners. (C). 1994. 6.75 (*81-85273-01-4*, Pub. by UBS Pubs Dist) S Asia.

***Ali, Syed.** Arabic for Beginners. 4th rev. ed. 204p. 2000. pap. 11.95 (*0-7818-0841-3*) Hippocrene Bks.

— Arabic for Beginners. 8th rev. ed. 1999. reprint ed. pap. 11.00 (*81-7476-216-7*, Pub. by UBS Pubs) S Asia.

— Let Us Converse in Arabic. 1998. pap. 11.50 (*81-7476-145-4*, Pub. by UBS Pubs) S Asia.

Ali, Syed & McRoy, Susan, eds. Representations for Multi-Modal Human-Computer Interaction: Papers from the AAAI Workshop. (Technical Reports: Vol. WS-98-09). (Illus.). 95p. 1998. spiral bd. 25.00 (*1-57735-062-6*) AAAI Pr.

Ali, Syed A. Quran: The Fundamental Law of Human Life, 5 vols. 1992. write for info. (*1-56744-459-8*) Kazi Pubns.

— Quran: The Fundamental Law of Human Life, Vol. 1. 385p. 1992. 29.95 (*1-56744-454-7*) Kazi Pubns.

— Quran: The Fundamental Law of Human Life, Vol. 2. 475p. 1992. 29.95 (*1-56744-455-5*) Kazi Pubns.

— Quran: The Fundamental Law of Human Life, Vol. 3. 522p. 1992. 29.95 (*1-56744-456-3*) Kazi Pubns.

— Quran: The Fundamental Law of Human Life, Vol. 4. 526p. 1992. 29.95 (*1-56744-457-1*) Kazi Pubns.

— Quran: The Fundamental Law of Human Life, Vol. 5. 505p. 1992. 29.95 (*1-56744-458-X*) Kazi Pubns.

— Quran - Fundamental Law of Human Life Vol. 1: Introduction. 386p. 1995. 29.95 (*1-56744-520-9*) Kazi Pubns.

— Quran - Fundamental Law of Human Life Vol. 2: Surah Fatiha - Surah Baqarah: 176. 348p. 1995. 29.95 (*1-56744-521-7*) Kazi Pubns.

— Quran - Fundamental Law of Human Life Vol. 3: Surah Baqarah: 177-273. 542p. 1995. 29.95 (*1-56744-522-5*) Kazi Pubns.

— Quran - Fundamental Law of Human Life Vol. 4: Surah Baqara: 274-Surah Nisa: 14. 548p. 1995. 29.95 (*1-56744-523-3*) Kazi Pubns.

— Quran - Fundamental Law of Human Life Vol. 5: Surah Nisa: 15-Surah Anam: 50. 526p. 1995. 29.95 (*1-56744-524-1*) Kazi Pubns.

— Quran - Fundamental Law of Human Life Vol. 6: Surah Anam: Si-Surah Ta Ubah: 129. 678p. 1995. 29.95 (*1-56744-525-X*) Kazi Pubns.

— Quran - Fundamental Law of Human Life Vol. 7: Surah Yunus-Surah Ibrahim. 446p. 1995. 29.95 (*1-56744-526-8*) Kazi Pubns.

— Quran - Fundamental Law of Human Life Vol. 8: Surah Hijr-Surah Hahf. 438p. 1995. 29.95 (*1-56744-527-6*) Kazi Pubns.

— Quran - Fundamental Law of Human Life Vol. 9: Surah Maryam-Surah Muminun. 497p. 1995. 29.95 (*1-56744-528-4*) Kazi Pubns.

— A Short History of Saracens. 1990. 19.95 (*0-933511-55-8*) Kazi Pubns.

Ali, Syed A., ed. Mahommedan Law, 2 vols. (C). 1985. 900.00 (*0-7855-6734-8*, Pub. by Himalayan Bks); 450.00 (*81-7002-013-1*, Pub. by Himalayan Bks); write for info. (*81-7002-012-3*, Pub. by Himalayan Bks) St Mut.

Ali, Syed A., jt. ed. see Bryant, M. Darrol.

Ali, Syed A., tr. see Imam, Zainul A.

***Ali, Syed F.** Neurochemistry of Drugs of Abuse: Cocaine, Ibogaine & Substituted Amphetamines. (Annals of the New York Academy of Science Ser.). 2000. pap. 24.95 (*0-8018-6546-8*) Johns Hopkins.

Ali, Syed F., ed. The Neurochemistry of Drugs of Abuse: Cocaine, Ibogaine, & Substituted Amphetamines. LC 98-3824. (Annals Ser.: Vol. 844). 362p. 1998. pap. 140.00 (*1-57331-146-4*) NY Acad Sci.

— The Neurochemistry of Drugs of Abuse: Cocaine, Ibogaine, & Substituted Amphetamines. LC 98-3824. (Annals of the New York Academy of Sciences Ser.: Vol. 844). 300p. 1998. 140.00 (*1-57331-145-6*) NY Acad Sci.

Ali, Syed F. & Takahashi, Yasuo. Cellular & Molecular Mechanisms of Drugs of Abuse: Cocaine, Ibogaine, & Substituted Amphetamines. LC 96-36646. (Annals of the New York Academy of Sciences Ser.: Vol. 801). 1996. 125.00 (*1-57331-036-0*) NY Acad Sci.

— Cellular & Molecular Mechanisms of Drugs of Abuse: Cocaine, Ibogaine & Substituted Amphetamines. LC 96-36646. (Annals of the New York Academy of Sciences Ser.). 1996. pap. 125.00 (*1-57331-037-9*) NY Acad Sci.

Ali, Syed Mubashir, jt. ed. see Khan, Bashir Ahmad.

Ali, Syed R. Digital Switching Systems: System Reliability & Analysis. LC 97-19408. 217p. 1997. 69.95 (*0-07-001069-2*) McGraw.

***Ali, Taisier M.** Civil Wars in Africa: Roots & Resolution. 322p. 1999. pap. 24.95 (*0-7735-1883-5*) McG-Queens Univ Pr.

Ali, Taisier M. & Matthews, Robert O., eds. Civil Wars in Africa: Roots & Resolution. (Illus.). 322p. 1999. text 60.00 (*0-7735-1777-4*) McG-Queens Univ Pr.

Ali, Tarig. 1968. LC 98-5657. 224p. 1998. 27.00 (*0-684-85360-4*) S&S Trade.

***Ali, Tariq.** The Book of Saladin: A Novel. 1999. pap. 15.00 (*1-85984-231-3*, Pub. by Verso) Norton.

Ali, Tariq. The Book of Saladin: A Novel. 280p. 2000. 23.00 (*1-85984-834-6*, Pub. by Verso) Norton.

— Fear of Mirrors. LC 98-165662. 240p. 1998. pap. 24.95 (*1-900850-10-9*, Pub. by Arcadia Bks) Dufour.

***Ali, Tariq.** Introducing Trotsky & Marxism. (Illus.). 176p. 2000. pap. 10.95 (*1-84046-155-1*) Totem Bks.

— Masters of the Universe? NATO's Balkan Crusade. Pinter, Harold et al, eds. 460p. 2000. 65.00 (*1-85984-752-8*, Pub. by Verso) Norton.

— Masters of the Universe: NATO's Balkan Crusade. Pinter, Harold et al, eds. 460p. 2000. pap. 20.00 (*1-85984-269-0*, Pub. by Verso) Norton.

Ali, Tariq. Shadows of the Pomegranate Tree. LC 93-37283. 242p. (gr. 13). 1993. pap. 15.00 (*0-86091-676-6*, Pub. by Verso) Norton.

***Ali, Tariq.** The Stone Woman: A Novel. (Islamic Quartet Ser.). 240p. 2000. 23.00 (*1-85984-764-1*, Pub. by Verso) Norton.

Ali, Tariq. Street Fighting Years: An Autobiography of the Sixties. (Citadel Underground Ser.). 288p. (Orig.). 1991. pap. 10.95 (*0-8065-1282-2*, Citadel Pr) Carol Pub Group.

Ali, Tariq, et al. Iranian Nights. 24p. 1989. pap. 10.95 (*1-85459-026-X*, Pub. by N Hern Bks) Theatre Comm.

Ali, Turan. Pretend Family Relationships: Testimonies of Lesbian & Gay Parents. (Sexual Politics Ser.). 192p. 1996. pap. 17.95 (*0-304-33150-3*) Continuum.

— We Are Family. (Sexual Politics Ser.). 256p. 1996. 69.95 (*0-304-33148-1*) Continuum.

***Ali, Wijdan.** Arab Islamic Art: From the Seventh to the Fifteenth Centuries. 176p. 1998. 29.50 (*977-424-476-1*, Pub. by Am Univ Cairo Pr) Col U Pr.

Ali, Wijdan. Modern Islamic Art: Development & Continuity. LC 97-24325. (Illus.). 224p. 1997. 59.95 (*0-8130-1526-X*) U Press Fla.

Ali, Will. The Three Levels of Our Rising. LC 90-86327. 134p. (Orig.). (C). 1991. pap. 12.95 (*1-879625-00-8*) Families Fam.

Ali, Yousuf. The Holy Quran with Arabic Text Commentary & Translation. 1992. 25.75 (*1-56744-046-0*) Kazi Pubns.

Ali, Yusef. The Holy Quran. (ARA & ENG.). 1754p. 1989. 20.00 (*0-86685-167-4*, AMA0335) Intl Bk Ctr.

Ali, Yusuf. The Holy Quran. LC 77-78098. 1915p. 10.00 (*0-89259-006-8*) Am Trust Pubns.

Ali, Zaki. Islam in the World. LC 74-180314. (Mid-East Studies). reprint ed. 57.50 (*0-404-56209-4*) AMS Pr.

Alia, Alyssa, jt. auth. see Snyder, Millie.

Alia, Emanuele E., et al, eds. Contractile Proteins in Muscle & Non-Muscle Cell Systems: Biochemistry, Physiology & Pathology. LC 85-12274. 752p. 1985. 135.00 (*0-275-91329-5*, C1329, Praeger Pubs) Greenwood.

***Alia, Valeria.** Uncovering the North: New, Media & Aboriginal People. (Illus.). 248p. 2000. pap. 22.95 (*0-7748-0707-5*) U of Wash Pr.

Aliabaci, M. H., et al. Localized Damage, Computer-Aided Assessment & Control Vol. 3: Advanced Computational Methods: First International Conference, 26-28 June 1990, Portsmouth, U. K. Brebbia, Carlos A. & Cartwright, D. J., eds. (Illus.). ix, 518p. 1990. 182.95 (*0-387-52716-8*) Spr-Verlag.

Aliabadi, M. H., ed. Dynamic Fracture Mechanics. LC 94-69711. (Computational Engineering Ser.). 328p. 1995. 150.00 (*1-56252-267-1*, 3439) Computational Mech MA.

— Fracture of Rock. LC 98-87994. (Advances in Fracture Mechanics Ser.: Vol. 5). 440p. 1999. 248.00 (*1-85312-542-3*, 5423) Computational Mech MA.

— Non-Linear Fracture & Damage Mechanics. (Advances in Fracture Mechanics Ser.: Vol. 4). 300p. 1998. 150.00 (*1-85312-508-3*, 5083, Pub. by WIT Pr) Computational Mech MA.

— Plate Bending Analysis with Boundary Elements. LC 97-67408. (Advances in Boundary Elements Ser.: Vol. 2). 368p. 1998. 148.00 (*1-85312-531-8*, 5318) Computational Mech MA.

— Thermo Mechanical Fatigue & Fracture. (Advances in Fracture Mechanics Ser.). 250p. 1998. 125.00 (*1-85312-549-0*) Computational Mech MA.

Aliabadi, M. H., et al, eds. Boundary Element Technology X. 248p. 1995. 146.00 (*1-85312-317-X*) Computational Mech MA.

Aliabadi, M. H., et al, eds. Computer Aided Assessment & Control of Localized Damage, 3 vols., Set. LC 90-61549. (Localized Damage Ser.: Vol. 1). 1990. 333.00 (*0-945824-53-X*) Computational Mech MA.

— Computer Aided Assessment & Control of Localized Damage Vol. 1: Fatigue & Fracture Mechanics. LC 90-61549. (Localized Damage Ser.: Vol. 1). 428p. 1990. 118.00 (*0-945824-49-1*) Computational Mech MA.

— Computer Aided Assessment & Control of Localized Damage Vol. 2: Non-Linear Behavior, Dynamics, Composite Materials & Industry. LC 90-61549. (Localized Damage Ser.: Vol. 1). 381p. 1990. 106.00 (*0-945824-51-3*) Computational Mech MA.

— Computer Aided Assessment & Control of Localized Damage Vol. 3: Advanced Computational Methods. LC 90-61549. (CAACOLD Ser.: Vol. 1). 528p. 1990. 146.00 (*0-945824-52-1*) Computational Mech MA.

— Computer Methods & Experimental Measurements for Surface Treatment Effects II. LC 95-67980. (Surface Treatment Ser.: Vol. 2). 320p. 1995. 152.00 (*1-56252-242-6*, 3188) Computational Mech MA.

— Localized Damage, Computer-Aided Assessment & Control: First International Conference, 26-28 June 1990, Portsmouth, U. K., 3 vols., Set. (Illus.). ix, 1307p. 1990. 526.95 (*0-387-52717-6*) Spr-Verlag.

— Localized Damage, Computer-Aided Assessment & Control Vol. 1: Fatigue & Fracture Mechanics: First International Conference, 26-28 June 1990, Portsmouth, U. K. (Illus.). ix, 418p. 1990. 182.95 (*0-387-52713-3*) Spr-Verlag.

— Localized Damage, Computer-Aided Assessment & Control Vol. 2: Non-Linear Behavior, Dynamics, Composite Materials & Industrial Applications: First International Conference, 26-28 June 1990, Portsmouth, U. K. (Illus.). ix, 371p. 1990. 182.95 (*0-387-52714-1*) Spr-Verlag.

— Localized Damage III: Computer Aided Assessment & Control. LC 94-70409. (Localized Damage Ser.: Vol. 3). 752p. 1994. 316.00 (*1-56252-186-1*, 2629) Computational Mech MA.

— Localized Damage II: Computer Aided Assessment & Control, 2 vols., Set. LC 92-70434. (Localized Damage Ser.: Vol. 2). 1354p. 1992. 459.00 (*1-56252-100-4*, 1711) Computational Mech MA.

Aliabadi, M. H. & Alessandri, C., eds. Contact Mechanics No. II: Computational Techniques. LC 95-68880. (Contact Mechanics Ser.: Vol. 2). 512p. 1995. 221.00 (*1-56252-250-7*, 3269) Computational Mech MA.

Aliabadi, M. H. & Alessandri, C., eds. Contact Mechanics II: Computational Techniques. 512p. 1995. 221.00 (*1-85312-326-9*) Computational Mech MA.

Aliabadi, M. H. & Brebbia, C. A., eds. Advances in Boundary Element Methods in Fracture Mechanics. 300p. 1992. 152.00 (*1-85312-102-9*) Computational Mech MA.

— Computational Techniques - Contact Mechanics. 536p. 1993. 172.00 (*1-85312-239-4*) Computational Mech MA.

Aliabadi, M. H. & Brebbia, Carlos A., eds. Advances in Boundary Element Methods for Fracture Mechanics. LC 92-70559. (Computational Engineering Ser.). 304p. 1993. 152.00 (*0-945824-85-8*) Computational Mech MA.

— Computer Methods & Experimental Measurements for Surface Treatment Effects. LC 92-75799. (Surface Treatment Ser.: Vol. 1). 400p. 1993. 163.00 (*1-56252-150-0*, 2262) Computational Mech MA.

— Surface Treatment III: Computer Methods & Experimental Measurements. LC 97-67016. 432p. 1997. 222.00 (*1-85312-469-9*, 4699) Computational Mech MA.

Aliabadi, M. H. & Kassab, A. J., eds. Coupled Field Problems. (Advances in Boundary Elements Ser.). 300p. 2000. 158.00 (*1-85312-554-7*, 5547, Pub. by WIT Pr) Computational Mech MA.

Aliabadi, M. H. & Rooke, D. P. Numerical Fracture Mechanics. 280p. 1991. 104.00 (*1-85312-057-X*) Computational Mech MA.

Aliabadi, M. H. & Rooke, D. P. Numerical Fracture Mechanics. LC 91-70200. 280p. (C). 1991. text 104.00 (*0-945824-39-4*, 057X) Computational Mech MA.

— Numerical Fracture Mechanics. (C). 1991. text 185.50 (*0-7923-1175-2*) Kluwer Academic.

Aliabadi, M. H. & Samartin, A., eds. Computational Methods in Contact Mechanics III. LC 97-67013. (Contact Mechanics Ser.: Vol. 3). 400p. 1997. 195.00 (*1-85312-468-0*, 4680) Computational Mech MA.

Aliabadi, M. H., jt. auth. see Portela, A.

Aliabadi, M. H., jt. ed. see Brebbia, C. A.

Aliabadi, M. H., jt. ed. see Brebbia, Carlos A.

Aliabadi, M. H., jt. ed. see Carpinteri, A.

Aliaga. Interactive Statistics. 1999. pap. text, student ed. 18.00 (*0-13-921776-2*) P-H.

Aliaga, Barbara. Learn to Type Fast: Completely New, Easy Method for Beginners. 4th ed. (Reference Ser.). 96p. 1988. reprint ed. pap. 12.95 (*0-88908-693-1*) Self-Counsel Pr.

Aliaga, J. L., jt. ed. see Proto, A. N.

Aliandro, H. Dicionario Portugues-Ingles.Tr. of Portuguese-English Dictionary. (ENG & POR.). 311p. 1980. pap. 12.95 (*0-8288-0490-7*, M9216) Fr & Eur.

— English-Portuguese Dictionary: Dicionario Ingles-Portugues. 2nd ed. (ENG & POR.). 343p. 1982. pap. 12.95 (*0-8288-0489-3*, M9215) Fr & Eur.

Alianza Staff. Diccionario de la Literatura, Vol. 2. Adell, tr. (SPA.). 864p. 1982. 95.00 (*0-8288-1575-5*, S29973) Fr & Eur.

Alibasah, Margaret M., tr. see Haasse, Hella S.

Alibasah, Margaret M., tr. see Mahieu, Vincent.

***Alibek, Ken W.** Biohazard: The Chilling True Story of the Largest Covert Biological Weapons Program in the World. 320p. 2000. pap. 12.95 (*0-385-33496-6*, Delta Trade) Dell.

Alibek, Ken W. & Handelman, Stephen. Biohazard: The Chilling True Story of the Largest Covert Biological Weapons Program in the World-Told from the Inside by the Man Who Ran It. LC UG447.8.A45 1999. 336p. 1999. 25.95 (*0-375-50231-9*) Random.

Aliber. Case Flexible Exchange. 1995. 32.00 (*0-226-01394-4*) U Ch Pr.

— Your Money & Life. 1996. pap. 16.95 (*0-226-01389-8*); lib. bdg. 38.00 (*0-226-01387-1*) U Ch Pr.

***Aliber, Robert Z.** The New International Money Game. 6th ed. LC 99-55593. 1999. pap. text 27.50 (*0-226-01397-9*) U Ch Pr.

— New International Money Game. 6th ed. 1999. lib. bdg. 50.00 (*0-226-01396-0*) U Ch Pr.

Aliber, Robert Z. Your Money & Your Life: Five Keys to the Puzzle. 250p. 1989. 19.95 (*1-55623-073-7*, Irwn Prfssnl) McGraw-Hill Prof.

Aliber, Robert Z., ed. International Finance, 2. 1200p. 1999. 400.00 (*1-85898-866-7*) E Elgar.

— National Monetary Policies & the Internation Financial System. LC 74-75610. (Midway Reprint Ser.). (Illus.). 339p. reprint ed. pap. 105.10 (*0-608-09374-2*, 205411900004) Bks Demand.

— National Monetary Policies & the International Finance System. LC 74-75610. (Midway Reprint Ser.). (Illus.). 339p. Date not set. reprint ed. pap. 105.10 (*0-608-20981-3*, 205450900003) Bks Demand.

Aliber, Robert Z. & Click, Reid W., eds. Readings in International Business: A Decision Approach. LC 92-21502. (Illus.). 347p. 1993. pap. text 27.50 (*0-262-51066-9*) MIT Pr.

Aliber, Robert Z., jt. ed. see Shultz, George P.

Alibertis, A., jt. auth. see Alibertis, C.

Alibertis, C. & Alibertis, A. The Wild Orchids of Crete. (Illus.). 176p. 1989. pap. 32.50 (*0-945345-41-0*) Lubrecht & Cramer.

Alibhai, Amir A. & International Labour Office Staff. Work. LC 90-120628. 99 p. 1989. write for info. (*92-2-106435-2*) Intl Labour Office.

Aliboni, Roberto. The Red Sea Region: Local Actors & the Superpowers. LC 84-24024. (Contemporary Issues in the Middle East Ser.). 200p. 1985. text 29.95 (*0-8156-2332-1*) Syracuse U Pr.

Aliboni, Roberto, ed. Southern European Security in the 1990s. LC 92-10508. 1992. text 59.00 (*1-85567-023-2*) St Martin.

Aliboni, Roberto, et al, eds. Security Challenges in the Mediterranean Region. LC 95-51117. 208p. 1996. 49.50 (*0-7146-4686-5*, Pub. by F Cass Pubs); pap. 22.50 (*0-7146-4220-7*, Pub. by F Cass Pubs) Intl Spec Bk.

***Alibrandi, Tom.** Hate Is My Neighbor: A True Story. 300p. 1999. pap. 14.95 (*0-9674044-0-1*) Stand Tgthr Pubs.

Alic, John A., et al. Beyond Spinoff: Military & Commercial Technologies in a Changing World. LC 91-36175. 448p. 1992. 35.00 (*0-87584-318-2*) Harvard Busn.

Alic, Margaret. Hypatia's Heritage: A History of Women in Science from Antiquity Through the 19th Century. LC 86-47501. (Illus.). 230p. (Orig.). 1986. pap. 15.50 (*0-8070-6731-8*) Beacon Pr.

Alice in Chains. Alice in Chains. 96p. 1996. otabind 19.95 (*0-7935-6373-9*) H Leonard.

Alice, Lynne, jt. ed. see Du Plessis, Rosemary.

***Alice, Mary & Downie, John.** Danger in Disguise. (J). 2000. pap. 6.95 (*1-896184-72-3*) Roussan Pubs.

Alice Shepherd Foundation Staff, jt. auth. see Schindler, Gustav.

A

Alice, Tiny. The Geek. 1995. mass mkt. 5.95 (*1-56333-341-4*) Masquerade.

Alicea, Gil C. & DeSena, Carmine. The Air Down Here: True Tales from a South Bronx Boyhood. LC 95-12962. (Illus.). 144p. 1995. 14.95 (*0-8118-1048-8*) Chronicle Bks.

***Alicea, Joseph M.** The Leadership Void: A Reality That's Not Beyond Repair. LC 99-91881. 2000. 25.00 (*0-7388-1364-8*); pap. 18.00 (*0-7388-1365-6*) Xlibris Corp.

Alicea, Marisa, jt. auth. see Friedman, Jennifer.

Alicia, Maria U. Poesias Para la Infancia. (SPA.). (ps-k). 1997. pap. text 9.98 (*968-409-940-1*) Edamex.

Alicino, Nick, ed. see Montgomery, Linda J.

Alicki, R. & Lendi, K. Quantum Dynamical Semigroups & Applications. (Lecture Notes in Physics Ser.: Vol. 286). viii, 196p. 1987. 34.95 (*0-387-18276-4*) Spr-Verlag.

Alico, Stella H. Benjamin Franklin-Martin Luther King Jr. (Pendulum Illustrated Biography Ser.). (Illus.). (J). (gr. 4-12). 1979. pap. text 2.95 (*0-88301-353-3*); student ed. 1.25 (*0-88301-377-0*) Pendulum Pr.

— Elvis Presley - The Beatles. (Pendulum Illustrated Biography Ser.). (Illus.). (J). (gr. 4-12). 1979. pap. text 2.95 (*0-88301-352-5*); student ed. 1.25 (*0-88301-376-2*) Pendulum Pr.

— Maria, Mota, & the Grandmother: A Novel. Ware, Laura, ed. LC 92-31237. (Illus.). 128p. (C). 1993. pap. 12.95 (*0-86534-190-7*) Sunstone Pr.

***Alid, Chadi, et al.** Foundations V. (Illus.). 104p. 1999. mass mkt. 2.00 (*1-888616-03-2*) Noel Grp.

Alidust, A., et al. What Is to Be Done: The Enlightened Thinkers & an Islamic Renaissance. Rajaee, Farhang, ed. & tr. by. from PER. 200p. 1987. 25.95 (*0-932625-04-5*); pap. text 11.95 (*0-932625-01-0*) Inst Res Islam.

Aliene. Berry Bears. 1997. 14.95 (*0-9623192-8-7*) Alaskakrafts Pub.

— Berry Bears. (J). 1997. pap. text 8.95 (*0-9623192-7-9*) Alaskakrafts Pub.

Alier, Juan M., jt. auth. see Guha, Ramachandra.

Alier, Verena M. Marriage, Class & Colour in Nineteenth-Century Cuba: A Study of Racial Attitudes & Sexual Values in a Slave Society. LC 73-82463. (Cambridge Latin American Studies: No. 17). 212p. reprint ed. pap. 60.50 (*0-608-16458-5*, 2026347) Bks Demand.

Aliermo, Pacita L. Touches of Grace. 1998. pap. write for info. (*1-58235-017-5*) Watermrk Pr.

Aliesan, Jody. Desperate for a Clearing. 37p. 1998. pap. 11.95 (*1-58249-002-3*) Grey Spider.

***Aliesan, Jody.** Loving in Time of War. 1999. pap. 13.00 (*0-911287-31-0*) Blue Begonia.

Aliesan, Jody & King, Julie. Soul Claiming. LC 75-23822. (Haystack Bks.). (Illus.). 76p. 1975. 6.00 (*0-913142-16-6*); pap. 3.50 (*0-913142-15-8*) Mulch Pr.

Aliev, Gefidar H. & Blair, Betty. Global Horizons: President Aliyev's Visit to the USA. LC 98-172202. 68p. 1997. write for info. (*0-9654388-1-3*) Azerbaijan Intl.

***Aliev, Y. M., et al.** Guided-Wave-Produced Plasmas. LC 99-58102. (Series in Atomic, Molecular, Optical & Plasma Physics Ser.: Vol. 24). (Illus.). 305p. 2000. 79.95 (*3-540-65273-6*) Spr-Verlag.

Alifanov, O. M. Inverse Heat Transfer Problems. Bergles, Arthur E. et al, eds. (International Series in Heat & Mass Transfer). 208p. 1995. 108.95 (*0-387-53679-5*) Spr-Verlag.

Alifanov, O. M., et al. Extreme Methods for Solving Ill-Posed Problems with Applications to Inverse Heat Transfer Problems. 306p. 1996. 77.50 (*1-56700-038-X*) Begell Hse.

Aliff, Gregory E., jt. auth. see Hahne, Robert L.

***Aliff, William.** Sonnets from the District. 1999. pap. write for info. (*1-58235-103-1*) Watermrk Pr.

Alifov, A. A. & Frolov, K. V. Interaction of Nonlinear Oscillating Systems. 1990. 260.00 (*0-89116-695-5*) Hemisp Pub.

Alig, Dorothy Stites, jt. auth. see Mailand, Harold F.

Alig, Joyce, ed. Mercer County Centennial Buildings. (Illus.). 46p. 1995. pap. 10.00 (*1-891095-08-0*, 5362-8) Mercer Cty Hist.

Alig, Joyce B. Brumm Heritage: Alsace, France to America. (Illus.). 680p. 1977. pap. 180.00 (*1-891095-00-5*, 5362-0) Mercer Cty Hist.

Alig, Joyce L. Celina, Ohio Sesquicentennial. (Illus.). 78p. 1984. pap. 5.00 (*1-891095-03-X*, 5362-3) Mercer Cty Hist.

— A History of Saint Henry, Ohio. (Illus.). vi, 200p. 1972. 25.00 (*1-891095-01-3*, 5362-1) Mercer Cty Hist.

— Mercer County, Ohio: The Five Courthouses, 1840-1998. (Illus.). 64p. 1998. pap. 10.00 (*1-891095-10-2*, 5362-10) Mercer Cty Hist.

— Ohio's Last Frontiersman: Connecticut Mariner Captain James Riley. (Illus.). viii, 432p. 1997. 39.95 (*1-891095-09-9*, 5362-9) Mercer Cty Hist.

— Saint Henry, Ohio Sesquicentennial, 1837-1987. (Illus.). 312p. 1987. 25.00 (*1-891095-04-8*, 5362-4) Mercer Cty Hist.

— Those Magnificent Big Barns in Mercer County of Western Ohio. (Illus.). xvi, 608p. 1993. 49.95 (*1-891095-07-2*, 5362-7) Mercer Cty Hist.

Alig, Joyce L., ed. Mercer County, Ohio History. (Illus.). 976p. 1980. 88.00 (*1-891095-02-1*, 5362-2) Mercer Cty Hist.

Alig, Joyce L. & Weber, Eugene, eds. Coldwater, Ohio at 150. (Illus.). 328p. 1988. 25.00 (*1-891095-05-6*, 5362-5) Mercer Cty Hist.

Alig, Joyce L., ed. see Shriver, Phillip, et al.

Alig, Leona T., compiled by. Index, 1830 Federal Population Census for Indiana. v, 245p. 1991. reprint ed. pap. 20.00 (*0-87195-074-X*) Ind Hist Soc.

***Aligheri, Dante.** The Inferno. Hollander, Robert & Hollander, Jean, trs. 620p. 2000. 35.00 (*0-385-49697-4*) Doubleday.

***Alighieri, Dante.** Cantos from Dante's Inferno. Schwerner, Armand, tr. 73p. 2000. pap. 13.95 (*1-883689-97-X*, Pub. by Talisman Hse) SPD-Small Pr Dist.

— Dante Alighieri's Divine Comedy: Purgatory: Verse Translation & Commentary, Vols. 3 & 4. Musa, Mark, tr. from ITA. (Masterpiece Editions Ser.). 696p. 2000. 89.95 (*0-253-33648-1*) Ind U Pr.

— Dante's Combined works: The Divine Comedy. May, Robin, ed. Longfellow, Henry Wadsworth, tr. from ITA. LC 00-104090. (Illus.). 649p. 2000. pap. 17.95 (*1-893774-24-4*, Allisone Pr) Star Rising.

— Divine Comedy: Selected Cantos. 2000. pap. 9.95 (*0-486-41127-3*) Dover.

— Inferno. (Bloom's Notes Ser.). 2000. pap. 4.95 (*0-7910-6018-7*) Chelsea Hse.

Alighieri, Dante. The Inferno of Dante: A New Verse Translation. Pinsky, Robert, tr. from ITA. LC 93-40169. (Illus.). 360p. 1994. text 40.00 (*0-374-17674-4*) FS&G.

***Alighieri, Dante.** Purgatorio: A New Verse Translation. Merwin, W. S., tr. from ITA. LC 99-40708. 368p. 2000. 30.00 (*0-375-40921-1*) Knopf.

Alighieri, Dante, jt. auth. see Privitera, Joseph Frederic.

Aligo, Richard J. Let's Do It: A Fundamental Guide to Slow-Pitch Softball. (Illus.). 194p. (Orig.). 1987. spiral bd. 14.95 (*0-9615760-7-3*) Nel-Mar Pub.

Alihan, Milla A. Social Ecology, a Critical Analysis. LC 64-24804. 267p. reprint ed. 55.50 (*0-8154-0008-X*) Cooper Sq.

Alijandra. Healing with the Rainbow Rays: The Art of Color Energy Therapy. (Illus.). 356p. 1995. pap. 18.95 (*0-9645766-0-0*) Alajandra-Rainbow.

Alikanov, J. Russian-Vietnamese Dictionary, 2 vols. 3rd ed. 1352p. (C). 1987. 220.00 (*0-7855-6491-8*, Pub. by Collets) St Mut.

Alikhan, A. M. Terrestrial Isopod Biology. (Crustacean Issues Ser.: Vol. 9). (Illus.). 220p. (C). 1995. text 110.00 (*90-5410-193-8*, Pub. by A A Balkema) Ashgate Pub Co.

Alikhan, Fatima, jt. ed. see Alam, Manzoor.

Alikhani, Alinaghi, ed. see Alam, Assadollah.

Aliki. Aliki's Americans. (J). 1998. pap. 9.99 (*0-689-81920-X*) S&S Childrens.

***Aliki.** All by Myself! LC 99-51672. 32p. (J). (ps-1). 2000. 14.95 (*0-06-028929-5*); lib. bdg. 14.89 (*0-06-028930-9*) HarpC Child Bks.

Aliki. At Mary Bloom's. rev. ed. LC 75-45482. (Illus.). 32p. (J). (gr. k-3). 1983. lib. bdg. 15.93 (*0-688-02481-5*, Grenwillow Bks) HarpC Child Bks.

— Best Friends Together Again. LC 94-12989. (Illus.). 32p. (J). (ps-3). 1995. 15.00 (*0-688-13753-9*, Grenwillow Bks) HarpC Child Bks.

Aliki. Best Friends Together Again. LC 94-12989. (Illus.). 32p. (J). (ps-3). 1995. 14.89 (*0-688-13754-7*, Grenwillow Bks) HarpC Child Bks.

Aliki. Christmas Tree Memories. LC 90-45575. (Illus.). 32p. (J). (ps-3). 1991. lib. bdg. 14.89 (*0-06-020008-1*) HarpC Child Bks.

— Christmas Tree Memories. LC 90-45575. (Trophy Picture Bk.). (Illus.). 32p. (J). (ps-3). 1994. pap. 5.95 (*0-06-443369-2*, HarpTrophy) HarpC Child Bks.

— Christmas Tree Memories. LC 90-45575. 1991. 11.15 (*0-606-06279-3*, Pub. by Turtleback) Demco.

— Communication. LC 91-48156. (Illus.). 32p. (J). (gr. k up). 1993. 14.00 (*0-688-10529-7*, Grenwillow Bks) HarpC Child Bks.

***Aliki.** Communication. 32p. (J). 1999. mass mkt. 4.95 (*0-688-17116-8*, Wm Morrow) Morrow Avon.

Aliki. Como Se Hace un Libro - How a Book Is Made. 1996. 10.95 (*84-261-2400-3*) Lectorum Pubns.

— Corn Is Maize: The Gift of the Indians. LC 75-6928. (Let's-Read-&-Find-Out Science Bks.). (Illus.). 40p. (J). (ps-3). 1976. lib. bdg. 15.89 (*0-690-00975-5*) HarpC Child Bks.

— Corn Is Maize: The Gift of the Indians. (Illus.). (J). 1982. pap. 3.79 (*0-690-04203-5*) HarpC Child Bks.

— Corn Is Maize: The Gift of the Indians. LC 75-6928. (Let's-Read-&-Find-Out Science Bks.). (Illus.). 40p. (J). (gr. k-3). 1986. pap. 4.95 (*0-06-445026-0*, HarpTrophy) HarpC Child Bks.

Aliki. Corn is Maize: The Gift of the Indians. (Let's Read-&-Find-Out Science Ser.). 1976. 10.15 (*0-606-09162-9*, Pub. by Turtleback) Demco.

Aliki. Digging Up Dinosaurs. LC 80-2250. (Let's-Read-&-Find-Out Science Bks.). (Illus.). 40p. (J). (gr. k-3). 1981. 12.95 (*0-690-04098-9*); lib. bdg. 12.89 (*0-690-04099-7*) HarpC Child Bks.

Aliki. Digging up Dinosaurs. (J). 1981. 10.15 (*0-606-03197-9*, Pub. by Turtleback) Demco.

Aliki. Digging Up Dinosaurs. rev. ed. LC 85-42979. (Trophy Let's Read-&-Find-Out Science Bk.). (Illus.). 32p. (J). (ps-3). 1988. pap. 4.95 (*0-06-445078-3*, HarpTrophy) HarpC Child Bks.

— Digging Up Dinosaurs. rev. ed. LC 87-29949. (Let's-Read-&-Find-Out Science Bks.). (Illus.). 32p. (J). (ps-3). 1988. lib. bdg. 15.89 (*0-690-04716-9*) HarpC Child Bks.

— Digging Up Dinosaurs Book & Tape. LC 85-42979. (Let's-Read-&-Find-Out Bk. & Cassette). 32p. (J). (ps-2). 1991. pap. 7.95 incl. audio (*1-55994-302-5*) HarperAudio.

— Dinosaur Bones. LC 85-48246. (Let's-Read-&-Find-Out Science Bks.). (Illus.). 32p. (J). (ps-3). 1988. lib. bdg. 14.89 (*0-690-04550-6*) HarpC Child Bks.

— Dinosaur Bones. LC 87-19626. (Trophy Let's-Read-&-Find-Out Bk.). (Illus.). 32p. (J). (gr. k-4). 1990. pap. 4.95 (*0-06-445077-5*, HarpTrophy) HarpC Child Bks.

Aliki. Dinosaur Bones. (Let's Read-&-Find-Out Science Ser.). (J). 1988. 10.15 (*0-606-03211-8*, Pub. by Turtleback) Demco.

Aliki. Los Dinosaurios Son Diferentes - Dinosaurs Are Different. 1996. 9.95 (*84-261-2753-3*) Lectorum Pubns.

— Dinosaurs Are Different. LC 84-45332. (Trophy Let's Read-&-Find-Out Science Bk.). (Illus.). 32p. (J). (ps-3). 1986. pap. 4.95 (*0-06-445056-2*, HarpTrophy) HarpC Child Bks.

Aliki. Dinosaurs Are Different. (Let's Read-&-Find-Out Science Ser.). (J). 1986. 10.15 (*0-606-03192-8*, Pub. by Turtleback) Demco.

Aliki. Dinosaurs Are Different Book & Tape. abr. ed. (J). (ps-3). 1990. 7.95 incl. audio (*1-55994-244-4*, TBC 2444) HarperAudio.

Aliki. Feelings. LC 84-4098. (Illus.). 32p. (J). (ps-3). 1984. 15.89 (*0-688-03832-8*, Grenwillow Bks) HarpC Child Bks.

Aliki. Feelings. LC 84-4098. (Illus.). 32p. (J). (ps up). 1984. 16.00 (*0-688-03831-X*, Grenwillow Bks) HarpC Child Bks.

— Feelings. LC 84-4098. (Illus.). 32p. (J). (ps-3). 1986. mass mkt. 4.95 (*0-688-06518-X*, Wm Morrow) Morrow Avon.

— Feelings. (J). 1984. 10.15 (*0-606-02480-8*, Pub. by Turtleback) Demco.

— Los Fosiles Nos Hablan Del Pasado - Fossils Tell of Long Ago. 1996. 9.95 (*84-261-2759-2*) Lectorum Pubns.

— Fossils Tell of Long Ago. LC 78-170999. (Let's-Read-&-Find-Out Science Bks.). (Illus.). 40p. (J). (gr. k-3). 1972. lib. bdg. 12.89 (*0-690-31379-9*) HarpC Child Bks.

— Fossils Tell of Long Ago. (Let's-Read-And-Find-Out Book Ser.). (J). 1990. 10.15 (*0-606-02136-1*, Pub. by Turtleback) Demco.

— Fossils Tell of Long Ago. rev. ed. LC 89-15468. (Let's-Read-&-Find-Out Science Bks.). (Illus.). 32p. (J). (gr. k-4). 1990. reprint ed. pap. 4.95 (*0-06-445093-7*, JS093, HarpTrophy) HarpC Child Bks.

— Fossils Tell of Long Ago. rev. ed. LC 89-17247. (Let's-Read-&-Find-Out Science Bks.). (Illus.). 32p. (J). (gr. k-4). 1990. 14.95 (*0-690-04844-0*); lib. bdg. 15.89 (*0-690-04829-7*) HarpC Child Bks.

— Go Tell Aunt Rhody. LC 96-163457. (Illus.). 40p. (J). (ps-3). 1996. mass mkt. 5.99 (*0-689-80765-1*) Aladdin.

— Go Tell Aunt Rhody. 1996. 11.19 (*0-606-09330-3*, Pub. by Turtleback) Demco.

— The Gods & Goddesses of Olympus. LC 93-17834. (Illus.). 48p. (J). (ps-3). 1994. 15.95 (*0-06-023530-6*) HarpC Child Bks.

— The Gods & Goddesses of Olympus. LC 93-17834. (Trophy Nonfiction Bk.). (Illus.). 48p. (J). (gr. 1 up). 1997. pap. 6.95 (*0-06-446189-0*, HarpTrophy) HarpC Child Bks.

— The Gods & Goddesses of Olympus. 1997. 11.15 (*0-606-11394-0*, Pub. by Turtleback) Demco.

— Green Grass & White Milk. (J). 1974. lib. bdg. 12.89 (*0-690-01119-9*) HarpC Child Bks.

— Hello! Good-Bye! LC 95-25090. (Illus.). 32p. (J). (ps-3). 1996. 15.00 (*0-688-14333-4*, Grenwillow Bks) HarpC Child Bks.

Aliki. Hello! Good-Bye! LC 95-25090. (Illus.). 32p. (J). (ps-3). 1996. 14.89 (*0-688-14334-2*, Grenwillow Bks) HarpC Child Bks.

Aliki. La Historia de Johnny Appleseed. 1992. 11.15 (*0-606-10438-0*, Pub. by Turtleback) Demco.

— La Historia de Johnny Appleseed (The Story of Johnny Appleseed) Mlawer, Teresa, tr. (Illus.). 32p. (J). (gr. k-2). 1992. 10.95 (*0-9625162-6-0*) Lectorum Pubns.

— La Historia de Johnny Appleseed (The Story of Johnny Appleseed) Mlawer, Teresa, tr. LC 49-125440. (SPA., Illus.). (J). (ps-3). 1995. pap. 5.95 (*1-880507-18-8*) Lectorum Pubns.

— How a Book Is Made. LC 85-48156. (Illus.). 32p. (J). (gr. 2 up). 1986. 14.95 (*0-690-04496-8*) HarpC Child Bks.

— How a Book Is Made. LC 85-48156. (Illus.). 32p. (J). (ps up). 1986. lib. bdg. 17.49 (*0-690-04498-4*) HarpC Child Bks.

— How a Book is Made. (J). 1988. 11.15 (*0-606-03818-3*, Pub. by Turtleback) Demco.

— How a Book Is Made. LC 85-48156. (Trophy Nonfiction Bk.). (Illus.). 32p. (J). (ps-3). 1988. reprint ed. pap. 6.95 (*0-06-446085-1*, HarpTrophy) HarpC Child Bks.

— The King's Day: Louis XIV of France. LC 88-38179. (Trophy Picture Bk.). (Illus.). 32p. (J). (gr. 2-6). 1991. pap. 4.95 (*0-06-443268-8*, HarpTrophy) HarpC Child Bks.

— La Leche: De la Vaca Al Envase (Milk: From Cow to Carton)Tr. of Milk: From Cow to Carton. 1996. 9.95 (*84-261-2757-6*) Lectorum Pubns.

— Manners. LC 89-34622. 32p. (J). (ps-3). 1990. 16.00 (*0-688-09198-9*, Grenwillow Bks) HarpC Child Bks.

Aliki. Manners. LC 89-34622. 32p. (J). (ps-3). 1990. 15.89 (*0-688-09199-7*, Grenwillow Bks) HarpC Child Bks.

Aliki. Manners. LC 92-43788. (Illus.). 40p. (J). (ps-3). 1997. mass mkt. 4.95 (*0-688-04579-0*, Wm Morrow) Morrow Avon.

— Manners. 1997. 10.15 (*0-606-11596-X*, Pub. by Turtleback) Demco.

— Marianthe's Story: Painted Words & Spoken Memories (Double Book), 2 bks. in 1. LC 97-36312. (Illus.). 64p. (J). (gr. k-3). 1998. 16.00 (*0-688-15661-4*, Grenwillow Bks) HarpC Child Bks.

***Aliki.** Marianthe's Story: Painted Words & Spoken Memories (Double Book), 2 bks. in 1. LC 97-36312. (Illus.). 64p. (J). (gr. k-3). 1998. 15.89 (*0-688-15662-2*, Grenwillow Bks) HarpC Child Bks.

Aliki. A Medieval Feast. LC 82-45923. (Illus.). 32p. (J). (gr. 2 up). 1983. lib. bdg. 15.89 (*0-690-04246-9*) HarpC Child Bks.

— Medieval Feast. LC 82-45923. (Illus.). 32p. (J). (gr. 2-6). 1983. 14.95 (*0-690-04245-0*) HarpC Child Bks.

Aliki. Medieval Feast. (J). 1986. 11.15 (*0-606-03251-7*, Pub. by Turtleback) Demco.

Aliki. A Medieval Feast. LC 82-45923. (Trophy Nonfiction Bk.). (Illus.). 32p. (J). (gr. 2 up). 1986. reprint ed. pap. 6.95 (*0-06-446050-9*, HarpTrophy) HarpC Child Bks.

— Mi Visita a los Dinosaurios (My Visit to the Dinosaurs) (SPA., Illus.). (ps-3). 1996. 9.95 (*84-261-2755-X*) Lectorum Pubns.

Aliki. Milk from Cow to Carton. (Let's Read-&-Find-Out Science Ser.). 1992. 10.15 (*0-606-09615-9*, Pub. by Turtleback) Demco.

Aliki. Milk from Cow to Carton. rev. ed. LC 91-23807. (Trophy Let's Read-&-Find-Out Science Bk.: Stage 2). (Illus.). 32p. (J). (ps-3). 1992. pap. 4.95 (*0-06-445111-9*, HarpTrophy) HarpC Child Bks.

Aliki. Mis Cinco Sentidos. (Let's Read-&-Find-Out Science Ser.).Tr. of My Five Senses. (SPA.). (J). 1995. 11.40 (*0-606-07873-8*) Turtleback.

Aliki. Modales - Manners. 1996. 10.95 (*84-261-2795-9*) Lectorum Pubns.

— Momias de Egipto - Mummies Are Made in Egypt. 1996. 10.95 (*84-261-2694-4*) Lectorum Pubns.

— Mummies Made in Egypt. LC 77-26603. (Illus.). 32p. (J). (gr. 2-6). 1979. lib. bdg. 15.89 (*0-690-03859-3*) HarpC Child Bks.

— Mummies Made in Egypt. LC 85-42746. (Trophy Nonfiction Bk.). (Illus.). 32p. (J). (gr. 2-6). 1985. pap. 6.95 (*0-06-446011-8*, HarpTrophy) HarpC Child Bks.

— Mummies Made in Egypt. 1985. 11.15 (*0-606-00342-8*, Pub. by Turtleback) Demco.

— My Feet. LC 89-49357. (Let's-Read-&-Find-Out Science Bks.). (Illus.). 32p. (J). (ps-1). 1990. lib. bdg. 16.89 (*0-690-04815-7*) HarpC Child Bks.

— My Feet. LC 89-49357. (Trophy Let's-Read-&-Find-Out Bk.). (Illus.). 32p. (J). (ps-1). 1992. pap. 5.95 (*0-06-445106-2*, HarpTrophy) HarpC Child Bks.

Aliki. My 5 Senses. (J). 1962. 12.89 (*0-690-56763-4*) HarpC Child Bks.

Aliki. My Five Senses. rev. ed. LC 88-35350. (Trophy Let's-Read-&-Find-Out Bk.). (Illus.). 32p. (J). (ps-1). 1989. pap. 4.95 (*0-06-445083-X*, HarpTrophy); lib. bdg. 15.89 (*0-690-04794-0*) HarpC Child Bks.

— My Five Senses. rev. ed. LC 88-853500. (Let's-Read-&-Find-Out Science Bks.). (Illus.). 32p. (J). (ps-3). 1989. 15.95 (*0-690-04792-4*) HarpC Child Bks.

— My Five Senses Big Book. rev. ed. LC 88-35350. (Let's-Read-&-Find-Out Science Bks.). (Illus.). 32p. (J). (ps-1). 1991. 21.95 (*0-06-020050-2*) HarpC Child Bks.

— My Five Senses (Spanish edition) Mis cinco sentitidos. Santacruz, Daniel, tr. LC 94-24656. (SPA., Illus.). 32p. (J). (ps-3). 1995. pap. 5.95 (*0-06-445138-0*, HarpTrophy) HarpC Child Bks.

— My Hands. LC 62-12810. (Let's-Read-&-Find-Out Science Bks.). (Illus.). 40p. (J). (gr. k-3). 1962. lib. bdg. 12.89 (*0-690-56834-7*) HarpC Child Bks.

— My Hands. rev. ed. LC 89-49158. (Let's-Read-&-Find-Out Science Bks.). (Illus.). 32p. (J). (ps-1). 1990. lib. bdg. 15.89 (*0-690-04880-7*) HarpC Child Bks.

— My Hands. rev. ed. LC 89-49158. (Trophy Let's-Read-&-Find-Out Bk.). (Illus.). 32p. (J). (ps-1). 1992. pap. 4.95 (*0-06-445096-1*, HarpTrophy) HarpC Child Bks.

— My Visit to the Aquarium. LC 92-18678. (Illus.). 40p. (J). (ps-3). 1993. 15.95 (*0-06-021458-9*); lib. bdg. 15.89 (*0-06-021459-7*) HarpC Child Bks.

— My Visit to the Aquarium. LC 92-18678. (Trophy Picture Bk.). (Illus.). 40p. (J). (ps-2). 1996. pap. 6.95 (*0-06-446186-6*, HarpTrophy) HarpC Child Bks.

— My Visit to the Aquarium. LC 92-18678. (J). 1993. 11.15 (*0-606-09657-4*, Pub. by Turtleback) Demco.

— My Visit to the Dinosaurs. LC 85-42748. (Trophy Let's-Read-&-Find-Out Bk.). (Illus.). 32p. (J). (ps-3). 1985. pap. 4.95 (*0-06-445020-1*, HarpTrophy) HarpC Child Bks.

— My Visit to the Dinosaurs. (Let's-Read-And-Find-Out Book Ser.). (J). 1985. 10.15 (*0-606-00343-6*, Pub. by Turtleback) Demco.

— My Visit to the Dinosaurs. rev. ed. LC 85-47538. (Let's-Read-&-Find-Out Science Bks.). (Illus.). Stage 2). (J). (ps-3). 1985. lib. bdg. 15.89 (*0-690-04423-2*) HarpC Child Bks.

— My Visit to the Dinosaurs Book & Tape. (J). 1990. pap. 7.95 incl. audio (*1-55994-247-9*) HarperAudio.

— My Visit to the Zoo. LC 96-9897. (Illus.). 40p. (J). (ps-3). 1997. 14.95 (*0-06-024939-0*) HarpC.

— My Visit to the Zoo. LC 96-9897. (Illus.). 40p. (J). (ps up). 1997. lib. bdg. 15.89 (*0-06-024943-9*) HarpC.

— My Visit to the Zoo. LC 96-9897. (Illus.). 40p. (YA). (ps-3). 1999. pap. 6.95 (*0-06-446217-X*, HarpTrophy) HarpC Child Bks.

— Story of Johnny Appleseed. LC 88-3145. (Illus.). 32p. (J). (ps-3). 1971. pap. 5.95 (*0-671-66746-7*) S&S Bks Yung.

— Story of Johnny Appleseed. 1963. 11.15 (*0-606-05030-2*, Pub. by Turtleback) Demco.

— The Story of William Penn. LC 93-26289. (Illus.). 32p. (Orig.). (J). 1994. mass mkt. 14.00 (*0-671-88558-8*) S&S Bks Yung.

— The Story of William Penn. LC 93-26289. (Orig.). (J). 1994. pap. 5.95 (*0-671-88646-0*, Half Moon Paper) S&S Childrens.

— Tabby: A Story in Pictures. LC 94-18523. (Illus.). 32p. (J). (ps-1). 1995. 13.95 (*0-06-024915-3*) HarpC.

— Those Summers. LC 95-1195. (Illus.). 40p. (J). (ps-3). 1996. 14.95 (*0-06-024937-4*) HarpC Child Bks.

— The Two of Them. LC 79-10161. 32p. (J). (ps-3). 1987. mass mkt. 4.95 (*0-688-07337-9*, Wm Morrow) Morrow Avon.

— Two of Them. (J). 1979. 10.15 (*0-606-04354-3*, Pub. by Turtleback) Demco.

An Asterisk (*) at the beginning of an entry indicates that the title is appearing for the first time.

— We Are Best Friends. LC 81-6549. (Illus.). 32p. (J). (gr. k-3). 1982. lib. bdg. 15.93 (*0-688-00823-2*, Grenwillow Bks) HarpC Child Bks.

— We Are Best Friends. LC 81-6549. (Illus.). 32p. (J). (ps-3). 1982. 17.00 (*0-688-00822-4*, Grenwillow Bks) HarpC Child Bks.

— We Are Best Friends. 1987. 10.15 (*0-606-03503-6*, Pub. by Turtleback) Demco.

Aliki. We Are Best Friends. LC 81-6549. (Illus.). 32p. (J). (ps-3). 1987. reprint ed. mass mkt. 5.95 (*0-688-07037-X*, Wm Morrow) Morrow Avon.

Aliki. A Weed Is a Flower: The Life of George Washington Carver. (Illus.). 32p. (J). (ps-3). 1988. pap. 14.00 (*0-671-66118-3*); pap. 5.95 (*0-671-66490-5*) S&S Bks Yung.

— Weed Is a Flower: The Life of George Washington Carver. (J). 1965. 11.15 (*0-606-03952-X*, Pub. by Turtleback) Demco.

— Welcome, Little Baby. LC 86-7648. (Illus.). 24p. (J). (gr. 2 up). 1987. 16.00 (*0-688-06810-3*, Grenwillow Bks) HarpC Child Bks.

— Welcome Little Baby: Miniature Edition. (Illus.). 24p. (J). (ps up). 1993. reprint ed. pap. 4.95 (*0-688-12665-0*, Wm Morrow) Morrow Avon.

— Wild & Woolly Mammoths. LC 94-48217. (Illus.). 32p. (J). (ps-3). 1995. 14.95 (*0-06-026276-1*) HarpC Child Bks.

— Wild & Woolly Mammoths: Revised ed. (Trophy Picture Bks.). (J). 1998. 11.15 (*0-606-13068-3*, Pub. by Turtleback) Demco.

— Wild & Woolly Mammoths: Revised Edition. LC 94-48217. (Trophy Picture Bk.). 32p. (J). (ps-3). 1998. pap. 6.95 (*0-06-446179-3*) HarpC Child Bks.

Aliki. William Shakespeare & the Globe. LC 98-7903. (Illus.). 48p. (J). (ps-3). 1999. 15.95 (*0-06-027820-X*) HarpC Child Bks.

— William Shakespeare & the Globe. LC 98-7903. (Illus.). 48p. (J). (ps-3). 1999. lib. bdg. 15.89 (*0-06-027821-8*) HarpC Child Bks.

***Aliki.** William Shakespeare & the Globe. LC 98-7903. (Illus.). 48p. (J). (gr. 4-7). 2000. pap. 6.95 (*0-06-443722-1*, HarpTrophy) HarpC Child Bks.

***Aliki.** Milk from Cow to Carton. (Illus.). (J). 1999. pap. 12.20 (*0-8335-9083-9*) Econo-Clad Bks.

Aliki, Susan. Ah, Music. 32p. pap. 5.95 (*0-06-446236-6*); lib. bdg. 15.89 (*0-06-028727-6*) HarpC.

— All by Myself! LC 99-51672. 32p. (ps-1). pap. 5.95 (*0-06-446253-6*) HarpC.

— Digging Up Dinosaurs. 33p. (J). (gr. 1-3). pap. 4.95 (*0-8072-1339-X*) Listening Lib.

— How a Book Is Made. (Illus.). (J). 1999. pap. 13.35 (*0-8335-2008-3*) Econo-Clad Bks.

— My 5 Senses. 1984. mass mkt. 4.95 (*0-06-445009-0*) HarpC.

— One Little Spoonful. 14p. pap. 5.95 (*0-694-01502-4*) HarpC.

Alim, Yusuf H. Al Maqasid al 'Ammah lil Shari'ah al Islamiyah: The General Objectives of Islamic Law. LC 91-3222. (Silsilat al Rasa'il al Jami'iyah Ser.: No. 5). (ARA.). 614p. (Orig.). 1991. 20.00 (*0-912463-83-X*); pap. 15.00 (*0-912463-84-8*) IIIT VA.

Alimaras, Peter. How to Change Your Mind: Using Modern Psychological Methods & the Wisdom of Edgar Cayce. LC 96-46154. 207p. (Orig.). 1997. pap. 12.95 (*0-87604-371-6*, 469) ARE Pr.

Alimayo, Chikuyo, pseud. A Garden on Cement. (Essays on Black America Ser.). (Illus.). 224p. 1973. 7.95 (*0-9606692-0-5*); pap. 3.95 (*0-9606692-1-3*) Eko Pubns.

— Once Around the Track. (Illus.). (YA). (gr. 9-12). 1974. 7.95 (*0-9606692-2-1*) Eko Pubns.

— Once around the Track. (Illus.). (YA). (gr. 9-12). 1974. pap. 3.95 (*0-9606692-3-X*) Eko Pubns.

***Alimbau, Jose Maria.** Vive Mejor Tu Vida. 1999. 20.95 (*84-08-03021-3*) Planeta Edit.

Alimonti, Joan M. Fifty-Two Sugar Free Desserts. Romano, Elizabeth, ed. 121p. (Orig.). 1989. pap. write for info. (*0-924753-00-5*) Quickline Pub.

Alin, Erika G. The United States & the 1958 Lebanon Crisis: American Intervention in the Middle East. LC 93-36101. 170p. (C). 1994. lib. bdg. 39.00 (*0-8191-9332-1*) U Pr of Amer.

Alinder, James, ed. Discovery & Recognition. LC 81-65401. (Untitled Ser.: No. 25). (Illus.). 56p. (Orig.). 1981. pap. 12.00 (*0-933286-24-4*) Frnds Photography.

Alinder, James, ed. see Giacomelli, Mario.

Alinder, James, ed. see Morris, Wright.

Alinder, James, ed. see Worth, Don D.

Alinder, Mary S. Ansel Adams: A Biography. (Illus.). 512p. 1998. pap. 17.95 (*0-8050-5835-4*, Owl) H Holt & Co.

Alinder, Mary S. & Stillman, Andrea G. Ansel Adams: Letters & Images, 1916-1984. (Illus.). 1990. pap. 29.95 (*0-8212-1788-7*, Pub. by Bulfinch Pr) Little.

Alinder, Mary S., jt. auth. see Adams, Ansel.

Alinder, Mary Street, jt. ed. see Stillman, Andrea G.

Alindogan-Medina, Noemi, tr. see Locke, Duane, et al.

Alings, Reinhard. Monument und Nation: Das Bild vom Nationalstaat im Medium Denkmal-zum Verhaeltnis Nation und Staat im Deutschen Kaiserreich 1871-1918. (Beitraege zur Kommunikationsgeschichte Ser.: Vol. 4). (GER., Illus.). xvi, 642p. (C). 1996. lib. bdg. 220.75 (*3-11-014985-0*) De Gruyter.

Alinhac, Serge. Blowup for Nonlinear Hyperbolic Equations. LC 95-2743. (Progress in Nonlinear Differential Equations & Their Applications Ser.: Vol. 17). 113p. 1995. 47.00 (*0-8176-3810-5*) Birkhauser.

— Blowup for Nonlinear Hyperbolic Equations. LC 95-2743. (Progress in Nonlinear Differential Equations & Their Applications Ser.: Vol. 17). 1995. write for info. (*3-7643-3810-5*) Birkhauser.

Alino, Ramon A. Unlocking Powerhouse. 408p. (C). 1992. pap. 39.95 (*1-882498-12-7*) Sftware Visions.

Alinsky, Saul. Reveille for Radicals. 1989. pap. 7.96 (*0-679-72112-6*) Vin Bks.

— Rules for Radicals. 1989. pap. 12.00 (*0-679-72113-4*) Vin Bks.

***Aliot, Etienne & Clementy, Jacques, eds.** Fighting Sudden Cardiac Death: A Worldwide Challenge. (Illus.). 600p. 2000. write for info. (*0-87993-460-3*) Futura Pub.

Aliot, Etienne & Lazzara, Ralph, eds. Ventricular Tachycardias. (Developments in Cardiovascular Medicine Ser.). 1987. lib. bdg. 230.50 (*0-89838-881-3*) Kluwer Academic.

Alioto, Angela. Straight to the Heart: Political Cantos. LC 97-65290. (Illus.). 272p. 1997. 22.95 (*0-9653524-2-0*) Russn Hill Pr.

Alioto, Anthony M. A History of Western Science. 2nd ed. 454p. 1992. pap. text 66.00 (*0-13-388513-5*) P-H.

Alioto, Joseph L., et al, eds. Teilhard de Chardin: In Quest of the Perfection of Man. LC 72-9596. 290p. 1973. 36.50 (*0-8386-1258-X*) Fairleigh Dickinson.

Aliotta, Antonio. The Idealistic Reaction Against Science. McCaskill, Agnes, tr. from ITA. LC 74-26246. (History, Philosophy & Sociology of Science Ser.). 1975. reprint ed. 41.95 (*0-405-06576-0*) Ayer.

Aliotta, Jerome J. The Puerto Ricans. 2nd ed. LC 95-10125. (Immigrant Experience Ser.). 120p. (YA). (gr. 5 up). 1995. lib. bdg. 19.95 (*0-7910-3360-0*) Chelsea Hse.

Aliotti, Shelley. My Pen Pal Scrapbook: An Educational Journey Through World Cultures. Tapscott, Diane, ed. LC 95-61366. (Illus.). 66p. (Orig.). (J). (gr. 3-8). 1995. pap. 19.95 (*0-9647396-0-7*) Wrld View CA.

Alippi, A., ed. Ultrasonic Signal Processing. 594p. (C). 1989. text 151.00 (*9971-5-0864-8*) World Scientific Pub.

Alippi, Adriano. Acoustic Sensing & Probing: Fourth Course of the International School on Physical Acoustics. 204p. 1992. text 121.00 (*981-02-0912-6*) World Scientific Pub.

Alippi, Adriano & Mayer, Walter G., eds. Ultrasonic Methods in Evaluation of Inhomogeneous Materials. (C). 1987. text 251.50 (*90-247-3490-8*) Kluwer Academic.

***Aliprantis, C. D. & Border, K.** Infinite Dimension Analysis: A Hitchhiker's Guide. 2nd enl. rev. ed. LC 99-39842. 650p. 1999. pap. 69.95 (*3-540-65854-8*) Spr-Verlag.

Aliprantis, C. D., ed. see Laslier, Jean-Francois.

Aliprantis, C. D., ed. see Moore, J. C.

Aliprantis, C. D., ed. see Moore, James C.

Aliprantis, Charalambos & Burkinshaw, Owen. Problems in Real Analysis. 2nd ed. LC 99-176757. (Illus.). vii, 403 p. (C). 1998. boxed set 59.95 incl. cd-rom (*0-12-050253-4*) Acad Pr.

Aliprantis, Charalambos D. Problems in Equilibrium Theory. LC 96-5034. (Illus.). 245p. 1996. text, student ed. 74.50 (*3-540-60753-6*) Spr-Verlag.

Aliprantis, Charalambos D., et al, eds. Positive Operators, Riesz Spaces, & Economics. (Studies in Economic Theory: Vol. 2). vii, 229p. 1991. 79.95 (*0-387-54658-8*) Spr-Verlag.

Aliprantis, Charalambos D. & Border, Kim C. Infinite Dimensional Analysis: A Hitchhiker's Guide. LC 94-31030. (Studies in Economic Theory: Vol. 4). 1994. write for info. (*3-540-58308-4*) Spr-Verlag.

— Infinite Dimensional Analysis: A Hitchhiker's Guide. LC 94-31030. (Studies in Economic Theory: Vol. 4). 1994. 107.95 (*0-387-58308-4*) Spr-Verlag.

Aliprantis, Charalambos D. & Burkinshaw, Owen. Principles of Real Analysis. 3rd ed. LC 98-3955. (Illus.). 415p. (C). 1998. boxed set 59.95 (*0-12-050257-7*) Acad Pr.

— Problems in Real Analysis: A Workbook with Solutions. 285p. 1990. text 52.00 (*0-12-050256-9*) Acad Pr.

Aliprantis, Charalambos D. & Chakrabarti, Subir Kumar. Games & Decision Making. LC 98-45396. (Illus.). 272p. (C). 1999. text 45.00 (*0-19-512609-2*) OUP.

— Solutions Manual for Games & Decision Making. 224p. (C). 1999. pap. text. write for info. (*0-19-513369-2*) OUP.

Aliprantis, Charalambos D., et al. Existence & Optimality of Competitive Equilibria. (Illus.). 284p. 1989. 87.95 (*0-387-50811-2*) Spr-Verlag.

— Existence & Optimality of Competitive Equilibria. (Illus.). xii, 284p. 1990. 53.95 (*0-387-52866-0*) Spr-Verlag.

Alireza, Marianne. At the Drop of a Veil. 1993. reprint ed. lib. bdg. 23.95 (*1-56849-013-5*) Buccaneer Bks.

***Alisanka, Eugenijus.** City of Ash. 2000. 44.95 (*0-8101-1783-5*); pap. text. write for info. (*0-8101-1784-3*) Northwestern U Pr.

Alisauskas, Arunas, ed. Romania. (C). 1998. 50.00 (*0-929851-36-6*) Am Assn Coll Registrars.

Aliseda-Llera, Atocha, et al, eds. Computing Natural Language: Context, Structure, & Processes. LC 97-43831. (Lecture Notes Ser.). 200p. (C). 1998. 59.95 (*1-57586-101-1*); pap. 22.95 (*1-57586-100-3*) CSLI.

Alisin, V., jt. auth. see Kragelsky, I. V.

Alisio, Giancarlo & Czmpofridano, Anna M., eds. Atlas of Naples. (Illus.). 150p. 1996. 175.00 (*1-56886-022-6*) Marsilio Pubs.

Alisjahbana, Takdir S. (Sutan Takdir). Language Planning for Modernization: The Case of Indonesian & Malaysian. (Contributions to the Sociology of Language Ser.: No. 14). 1976. pap. text 26.15 (*90-279-7712-7*) Mouton.

Alisky, Marvin. Historical Dictionary of Peru. LC 79-16488. (Latin American Historical Dictionaries Ser.: No. 20). 163p. 1979. 21.00 (*0-8108-1235-5*) Scarecrow.

Alisky, Marvin, jt. auth. see Briggs, Donald C.

Alison. Making Connections. (C). 1995. pap. 31.16 (*0-395-72044-3*) HM.

Alison, Archibald. Essays on the Nature & Principles of Taste. (Anglistica & Americana Ser.: No. 26). xiii, 415p. 1968. reprint ed. 105.00 (*0-685-66427-9*, 05102125) G Olms Pubs.

— History of Europe from the Commencement of the French Revolution to the Restoration of the Bourbons, 14 vols. 10th ed. LC 70-38482. reprint ed. 1043.00 (*0-404-00390-7*) AMS Pr.

Alison, Catherine, tr. see Grousset, Rene.

Alison, James. The Joy of Being Wrong: Original Sin Through Easter Eyes. LC 97-752. 240p. (Orig.). 1997. pap. 24.95 (*0-8245-1676-1*, Herdr & Herdr) Crossroad NY.

— Knowing Jesus. 128p. 1994. pap. 10.95 (*0-87243-202-5*) Templegate.

— Raising Abel: The Recovery of the Eschatological Imagination. LC 96-10684. 228p. (Orig.). 1996. pap. text 19.95 (*0-8245-1565-X*) Crossroad NY.

Alison, Jane, ed. Soundings: Cross Channel Photographic Mission. (Illus.). 108p. (C). 1994. pap. 29.95 (*0-9517427-5-2*, Pub. by Lund Humphries) Antique Collect.

***Alison, Lauren.** Backstreet Boys: Backstage Pass, A Photo Scrapbook. LC 98-235303. (Illus.). 48p. (gr. 4-9). 1998. pap. text 5.99 (*0-439-04531-2*) Scholastic Inc.

***Alison, Laurence J. & Canter, D. V.** Interviewing & Deception. 256p. 1999. 78.95 (*1-85521-380-X*) Ashgate Pub Co.

— Profiling Property Crimes. 70.95 (*1-84014-785-7*); 30.95 (*1-84014-787-3*) Ashgate Pub Co.

— Profiling Rape & Murder. 30.95 (*1-84014-495-5*); 70.95 (*1-85521-388-5*) Ashgate Pub Co.

***Alison, Laurence J. & Canter, David.** Assessing Accounts of Crime. LC 98-24989. (Offender Profiling Ser.). 400p. 1998. pap. 34.95 (*1-84014-491-2*, Pub. by Ashgate Pub) Ashgate Pub Co.

Alison, Laurence J., jt. ed. see Canter, David V.

Alison, Laurence J., jt. ed. see Canter, David.

Alison, M. R. & Sarraf, C. E. Apoptosis Factfile. (Illus.). 120p. 1998. 18.00 (*1-86094-111-7*, Pub. by Imperial College) World Scientific Pub.

Alison, Malcolm & Sarraf, Catherine. Understanding Cancer: From Basic Science to Clinical Practice. (Postgraduate Medical Science Ser.). (Illus.). 277p. (C). 1997. text 74.95 (*0-521-56154-X*) Cambridge U Pr.

— Understanding Cancer: From Basic Science to Clinical Practice. (Postgraduate Medical Science Ser.). (Illus.). 277p. (C). 1997. pap. text 29.95 (*0-521-56751-3*) Cambridge U Pr.

Alison, Marielle. How to Be a Bride & a Flower Girl, Too. (Illus.). 20p. (J). (ps-3). 1999. 14.95 (*0-689-82354-1*, 076714823549) S&S Childrens.

Alison, Olivia E., ed. see Talbott, Page.

Alison, Robert M. Breeding Biology & Behavior of the Oldsquaw (Clangula Hyemalis L.) 52p. 1975. 6.00 (*0-943610-18-4*) Am Ornithologists.

Alissandrakis, Costa E. & Schmieder, Brigitte, eds. Second Advances in Solar Physics Euroconference: Three-Dimensional Structure of Solar Active Regions. LC 98-74548. (Conference Series Proceedings: Vol. 155). 474p. 1998. 52.00 (*1-886733-75-9*) Astron Soc Pacific.

Alissi, Albert & Casper, Max, eds. Time As a Factor in Groupwork: Time-Limited Group Experiences. LC 85-7636. (Social Work with Groups Ser.: Vol. 8, No. 2). 160p. 1985. text 4.95 (*0-86656-409-8*); pap. text 2.95 (*0-86656-438-1*) Haworth Pr.

Alissi, Albert S. & Mergins, Catherine G. Voices from the Field: Group Work Responds. LC 96-52244. (Illus.). 181p. 1997. 49.95 (*0-7890-0138-1*) Haworth Pr.

Alister, Ian & Hauke, Christopher, eds. Contemporary Jungian Analysis: Post Jungian Perspectives from the Sap. LC 97-41078. (Illus.). 328p. (C). 1998. 80.00 (*0-415-14165-6*) Routledge.

— Contemporary Jungian Analysis: Postjungian Perspectives from the Sap. LC 97-41078. 272p. (C). 1998. pap. 25.99 (*0-415-14166-4*) Routledge.

Alistir, K. A. Disney's Aladdin Level 3: Genie School. LC 96-85663. (Disney's First Readers Ser.). (Illus.). 40p. (J). 1997. pap. 3.50 (*0-7868-4073-0*, Pub. by Disney Pr) Time Warner.

— My Ponies. LC 95-13238. (Hello Reader! Ser.: Level 2). (Illus.). (J). 1996. 3.50 (*0-590-25489-8*) Scholastic Inc.

Alistir, K. A. & McQueen, Lucinda. My Ponies. (Hello Reader! (Je Peux Lire!) Ser.). (FRE., Illus.). 32p. (J). 1996. pap. 5.99 (*0-590-16030-3*) Scholastic Inc.

Alive, Camila & Archibecque, Orlando. Serving Latino Communities: A How-to-Do-It Manual for Librarians. LC 97-49203. 253p. 1998. pap. 39.95 (*1-55570-276-7*) Neal-Schuman.

Alive Research Group Staff, compiled by. Encyclopedia of Natural Healing: The Authoritative Home Reference for Practical Self-Help. (Illus.). 1472p. 1997. 59.95 (*0-920470-75-0*) Alive Bks.

Aliverti, Ed, jt. auth. see Aliverti, Shirley.

Aliverti, Shirley & Aliverti, Ed. Once upon a Mat. 32p. 1993. pap. text 6.95 (*1-882336-03-8*) OK Bylines.

Alix. Sociology. 1995. student ed. 14.75 (*0-314-04775-1*) West Pub.

Alix, Ernest K. Sociology: An Everyday Life Approach. LC 94-30526. 624p. (C). 1995. 77.95 (*0-314-04435-3*) West Pub.

Alix, Jay. Financial Handbook for Bankruptcy Professionals: A Financial & Accounting Guide for Bankruptcy Judge's Attorneys & Accountants. 2nd ed. 864p. (C). 1996. text 89.95 (*0-314-08315-4*) West Pub.

Alix, Kathy. Master Your Disaster. 1997. pap. text 18.95 (*0-9646754-4-7*) Assure Yourself.

***Alizade, Alcira Miriam & Etchegoyen, R. Horacio.** Feminine Sensuality. 200p. 1999. pap. 31.50 (*1-85575-097-X*, Pub. by H Karnac Bks Ltd) Other Pr LLC.

Alizadeh, A., ed. see Kantor, Helene & Delougaz, P.

Alizadeh, Abbas. Prehistoric Settlement Patterns & Cultures in Susiana, Southwestern Iran: The Analysis of the F. G. L. Gremliza Survey Collection. (Technical Reports Ser.: No. 24). xiv, 176p. (Orig.). 1992. pap. 15.00 (*0-915703-29-7*) U Mich Mus Anthro.

Alizadeh, Ahmad, tr. see Ahmad, Jalal Al-e.

Aljalian, Arakel. St. Nerses Shnorhali: General Epistle. (Illus.). (Orig.). 1997. pap. text 15.00 (*1-885011-02-4*) St Nersess.

Aljian, George W. Purchasing Handbook. 3rd ed. 1152p. 1973. 59.95 (*0-07-001068-4*) McGraw.

Aljubouri, Alauddin H., jt. auth. see Khalili, Khalilullah.

Alkadra, Mohamad, jt. auth. see Miller, Hugh T.

Alkalay-Gut, Karen. Ignorant Armies LC 98-166080. (Jewish Writers Chapbook Ser.). 48 p. 1994. write for info. (*0-89304-488-1*) Cross-Cultrl NY.

— Mechitza. Barkan, Stanley H., ed. Megged, Eyal et al, trs. (Review Woman Writers Chapbook Ser.: No. 5).Tr. of Hebrew & Eng.. 48p. 1986. 15.00 (*0-89304-420-2*, CCC164); pap. 5.00 (*0-89304-421-0*) Cross-Cultrl NY.

— Mechitza: Mini. Barkan, Stanley H., ed. Megged, Eyal et al, trs. (Review Woman Writers Chapbook Ser.: No. 5).Tr. of Hebrew & Eng.. 48p. 1986. 15.00 (*0-89304-422-9*); pap. 5.00 (*0-89304-423-7*) Cross-Cultrl NY.

Alkalay-Gut, Karen & Barken, Stanley H. Israeli Writers. 1991. boxed set 50.00 (*0-685-49043-2*) Cross-Cultrl NY.

— Israeli Writers. limited ed. 1991. boxed set 75.00 (*0-89304-957-3*) Cross-Cultrl NY.

Alkalay, Karen. Making Love: Poems. 24p. 1980. 15.00 (*0-89304-062-2*); pap. 5.00 (*0-89304-063-0*) Cross-Cultrl NY.

Alkaley-Gut, Karen, ed. see Reich, Asher.

Alkali, Z. Stillborn Longman Africa. (Longman African Writers Ser.). (C). 1995. pap. 15.73 (*0-582-26432-4*) Addison-Wesley.

Alkalimat, Abdul. Black Power in Chicago: Harold Washington & the Crisis of the Black Middle Class: Mass Protest, Vol. 1. (Black Power in Chicago Ser.). 150p. 1987. 15.95 (*0-940103-10-9*); pap. 5.95 (*0-940103-11-7*) Twenty First Bks.

Alkalimat, Abdul, ed. Paradigms in Black Studies: Intellectual History, Cultural Meaning & Political Ideology. (Annual Theoretical Review in Afro-American Studies). 190p. (C). 1987. pap. 10.00 (*0-940103-03-6*); text 25.00 (*0-940103-02-8*) Twenty First Bks.

Alkalimat, Abdul, et al. Introduction to Afro-American Studies: A Peoples College Primer. 391p. (C). 1986. text 25.00 (*0-940103-01-X*); pap. text 12.95 (*0-940103-00-1*) Twenty First Bks.

Alkalimat, Abdul, jt. auth. see Johnson, David.

Alkalimat, Aboul. Malcolm X for Beginners. (Documentary Comic Bks.). (Illus.). 64p. (Orig.). 1990. pap. 4.95 (*0-86316-143-X*) Writers & Readers.

Alkan, A., et al, eds. Current Trends in Economics: Theory & Applications. LC 99-17743. (Studies in Economic Theory: Vol. 8). (Illus.). x, 546p. 1999. 119.00 (*3-540-65383-X*) Spr-Verlag.

***Alkan, Charles-Valenti.** Le Festin D'Esope & Other Works for Solo Piano. 1998. text 17.95 (*0-486-40066-2*) Dover.

Alkan, M. Ziya. Parasitology for the 21st Century. 1996. 104.25 (*0-85198-777-X*) C A B Intl.

Alkan, M. Ziya & Izcel, M. Ali, eds. Parasitology for the 21st Century: Keynote Papers from the VIII International Congress of Parasitology. (A CAB International Publication). (Illus.). 304p. 1996. text 105.00 (*0-85198-977-2*) OUP.

Alkana, Joseph. The Social Self: Hawthorne, Howells, William James, & Nineteenth-Century Psychology. LC 96-16404. 176p. 1996. text 29.95 (*0-8131-1971-5*) U Pr of Ky.

Alkana, Joseph, jt. ed. see Colatrella, Carol.

Alkebu-Lan, Horus M. The Journey to Truth: Fulfilling the Legacy of Black Nationalism. (Orig.). 1992. pap. text 10.00 (*0-9628788-1-2*) Alkebu-Lan & Assocs.

Alkebu-Lan, Horus M., et al. African-American Identity Crisis. 54p. (Orig.). 1991. pap. text 7.00 (*0-9628788-0-4*) Alkebu-Lan & Assocs.

Alkemade, Kim Van, see Van Alkemade, Kim.

Alkemi. Computer Security Manager. 200p. 1989. pap. 254.50 (*0-946395-48-9*, Pub. by Elsvr Adv Tech) Elsevier.

Alken, C. E., et al, eds. Encyclopedia of Urology, Vols. 28 5-7, 9, 11-13 & 15. Incl. Vol. 2. Physiology & Pathological Physiology. (Illus.). xx, 1009p. 1965. 336.00 (*0-387-03315-7*); Vol. 5, Pt. 1. Diagnostic Radiology. (Illus.). xii, 533p. 1962. 256.00 (*0-387-02846-3*); Vol. 6. Endoscopy. (Illus.). xxiv, 282p. 1959. 160.00 (*0-387-02419-0*); Vol. 7, Pt. 1. Malformations. (Illus.). xiv, 479p. 1968. 175.00 (*0-387-04165-6*); Vol. 9, Pt. 2. Inflammation Two: Specific Inflammations. (Illus.). xvi, 564p. 1959. 224.00 (*0-387-02420-4*); Vol. 11, Pt. 1. Organic Diseases. (Illus.). xiv, 286p. 1967. 152.00 (*0-387-03859-0*); Vol. 12. Functional Disturbances. (Illus.). xiv, 312p. 1960. 136.00 (*0-387-02551-0*); Vol. 13, Pt. 2. Operative Urology Two. (Illus.). 280p. 1970. 131.00 (*0-387-05142-2*); Vol. 15. Urology in Childhood. (Illus.). xvi, 353p. 1958. 144.00 (*0-387-02303-8*); Vol. 15, Supplement. Urology in Childhood. Williams, D. I. 1974. 118.00 (*0-387-06406-0*); write for info. (*0-318-55783-5*) Spr-Verlag.

Alken, Martha. The Healing Power of Forgiving. LC 97-4154. 144p. (Orig.). 1997. pap. 15.95 (*0-8245-1597-8*) Crossroad NY.

***Alker, David.** Fat Tuesday in WebWorld: The Handbook That Blows the Whistle on the World Wide Web. 1998. pap. 27.95 (*1-894104-00-5*) Burnt Tree.

Alker, G., jt. auth. see Doby, T.

Alker, Hayward, jt. ed. see Shapiro, Michael J.

Alker, Hayward R. Rediscoveries & Reformations: Humanistic Methodologies for International Studies. (Studies in International Relations: No. 41). 482p. (C). 1996. text 74.95 (*0-521-46130-8*) Cambridge U Pr.
— Rediscoveries & Reformations: Humanistic Methodologies for International Studies. (Studies in International Relations: No. 41). 482p. (C). 1996. pap. text 27.95 (*0-521-46695-4*) Cambridge U Pr.

Alkeseev, S. N., et al. Durability of Reinforced Concrete in Aggressive Media. (Russian Translation Ser.: No. 96). (ENG., Illus.). 394p. 1993. 85.00 (*90-5410-202-0*, Pub. by A A Balkema) Ashgate Pub Co.

Alkhafaji, Abbass & Biberman, Jerry, eds. Business Research Yearbook Vol. 4: Global Business Perspectives. 4th ed. 1000p. 1997. pap. write for info. (*0-614-22855-7*) Intl Academy of Busn Discip.

Alkhafaji, Abbass, jt. ed. see Biberman, Jerry.

Alkhafaji, Abbass F. Competitive Global Management: Principles & Strategies. LC 94-17214. (Illus.). 432p. (C). 1994. boxed set 62.95 (*1-884015-36-0*) St Lucie Pr.
— A Stakeholder Approach to Corporate Governance Managing in a Dynamic Environment. LC 88-32489. 302p. 1989. 72.95 (*0-89930-447-8*, ACA, Quorum Bks) Greenwood.

Alkhafaji, Abbass F., ed. Business Research Yearbook: Global Business Perspectives. 1146p. (Orig.). (C). 1994. pap. text 95.00 (*0-8191-9531-6*) U Pr of Amer.
— Business Research Yearbook: Global Business Perspectives, Vol. II, 1995. 994p. (Orig.). (C). 1995. pap. text 99.75 (*0-8191-9945-1*) U Pr of Amer.

Alkhafaji, Abbass F. & Biberman, Jerry, eds. Business Research Yearbook: Global Business Perspectives. (Publication of the International Academy of Business Diciplins Ser.). 976p. (Orig.). 1996. pap. text 125.00 (*0-7618-0340-8*) U Pr of Amer.
— Business Research Yearbook: Global Business Perspectives. (Publication of the International Academy of Business Diciplines Ser.: Vol. 3). 976p. (Orig.). 1996. 145.00 (*0-7618-0346-7*) U Pr of Amer.

Alkhairo, Wael. Speaking for Change: A Guide for Making Effective Friday Sermons (Khutbahs) LC 98-5355. 96p. 1998. pap. 5.95 (*0-915957-79-5*) amana pubns.

Alkharaji, Abbass F. Restructuring American Corporations: Causes, Effects & Implications. LC 90-32699. 208p. 1990. 59.95 (*0-89930-573-3*, ARK, Quorum Bks) Greenwood.

Alkhazraji, Khalid M. Immigrants & Cultural Adaptation in the American Workplace: A Study of Muslim Employees. rev. ed. LC 96-39499. (Studies in the History of American Labor). (Illus.). 168p. 1997. text 44.00 (*0-8153-2856-7*) Garland.

Alkidas, Alex C., ed. Vehicle Thermal Management. LC 93-87769. (Progress in Technology Ser.). 442p. 1994. 29.00 (*1-56091-502-1*, PT-46) Soc Auto Engineers.

Alkin, Glyn. Sound Recording & Reproduction. 1981. 19.95 (*0-240-51273-1*, Focal) Buttrwrth-Heinemann.
— Sound Recording & Reproduction. 3rd ed. LC 96-6731. (Media Manuals Ser.). 256p. 1997. pap. text 26.95 (*0-240-51467-X*, Focal) Buttrwrth-Heinemann.
— Sound Techniques for Video & TV. 2nd ed. 240p. 1989. pap. text 32.95 (*0-240-51277-4*, Focal) Buttrwrth-Heinemann.

Alkin, Marvin. Encyclopedia of Educational Research, Vol. 1. 6th ed. 1992. 110.00 (*0-02-896495-0*) Macmillan.

Alkin, Marvin C. Encyclopedia of Educational Research, Vol. 2. 6th ed. 1992. 110.00 (*0-02-896496-9*) Macmillan.
— Encyclopedia of Educational Research, Vol. 3. 6th ed. 1992. 110.00 (*0-02-896497-7*) Macmillan.
— Encyclopedia of Educational Research, Vol. 4. 6th ed. 1992. 110.00 (*0-02-896498-5*) Macmillan.

Alkin, Marvin C., ed. Debates on Evaluation. (Illus.). 288p. (C). 1990. 49.95 (*0-8039-3523-4*); pap. 23.95 (*0-8039-3524-2*) Sage.
— Debates on Evaluation. LC 90-8278. 302p. 1990. reprint ed. pap. 93.70 (*0-608-03001-5*, 206345100006) Bks Demand.

Alkin, Marvin C. & Jacobson, Phyllis. A Guide for Evaluation Decision Makers. LC 85-1805. (Illus.). 168p. (Orig.). 1985. reprint ed. pap. 52.10 (*0-608-01079-0*, 205938800001) Bks Demand.

Alkin, Marvin C. & Solmon, Lewis C., eds. The Costs of Evaluation. LC 83-2857. (Sage Focus Editions Ser.: No. 60). 199p. reprint ed. pap. 61.70 (*0-7837-1119-0*, 204164900022) Bks Demand.

Alkire, Durkwood. Tax Accounting, 2 vols. 1982. ring bd. 410.00 (*0-8205-1703-8*) Bender.

Alkire, Jan, jt. auth. see Thomas, Leo.

Alkire, R. C., et al, eds. Proceedings of the International Symposium on Electrochemical Processing of Tailored Materials, 2nd. LC 93-70057. (Proceedings Ser.: Vol. 93-12). 312p. 1993. 37.00 (*1-56677-027-0*) Electrochem Soc.

Alkire, Richard C., ed. see Kolb, Dieter M.

Alkire, Richard C., ed. see Symposium on Electrochemical Process & Plant Desig.

***Alkire, Tom.** There's More to Fishing Than Catching. (Illus.). 169p. 2000. 24.95 (*1-57188-206-5*); pap. 14.95 (*1-57188-205-7*) F Amato Pubns.

Alkire, William A. Lamotrek Atoll & Interisland Socioeconomic Ties. rev. ed. 190p. (C). 1989. reprint ed. pap. text 11.95 (*0-88133-399-9*) Waveland Pr.

Alkive, Arjay A. Whoever, Wherever You Are: For My Daughter, Adopted at Birth. 68p. 1997. pap. 10.95 (*1-57502-651-1*, PO1846) Morris Pubng.

Alkiviades, Alkis. Dotto & the Minotaur's Maze: An Interactive Connect-the-Dots Adventure. (Illus.). 48p. 1998. pap. 10.95 (*0-8109-2778-0*, Pub. by Abrams) Time Warner.

Alkofer, Reinhard & Reinhardt, Hugo. Chiral Quark Dynamics, Vol. VIII. Beiglbock, W. et al, eds. LC 95-24612. (Lecture Notes in Physics Ser.). 115p. 1995. 43.00 (*3-540-60137-6*) Spr-Verlag.

Alkon, Daniel L. Memory Traces in the Brain. (Illus.). 204p. 1987. pap. text 21.95 (*0-521-35867-1*) Cambridge U Pr.
— Memory Traces in the Brain. (Illus.). 208p. 1988. text 59.95 (*0-521-24735-7*) Cambridge U Pr.

Alkon, Daniel L. & Woody, Charles D., eds. Neural Mechanisms of Conditioning. (Illus.). 512p. (C). 1985. text 144.00 (*0-306-42041-4*, Kluwer Plenum) Kluwer Academic.

Alkon, Paul K. Origins of Futuristic Fiction. LC 86-25026. (Illus.). 354p. 1987. 35.00 (*0-8203-0932-X*) U of Ga Pr.
— Science Fiction Before 1900: Imagination Discovers Technology. (Twayne's Studies in Genre). 200p. 1994. 33.00 (*0-8057-0952-5*) Macmillan.
— Science Fiction Before 1900: Imagination Discovers Technology. 1995. pap. 14.95 (*0-8057-9237-6*, Hall Reference) Macmillan.

Alkon, Selig, jt. auth. see Colby, Marvelle S.

Alksne, Z. K. & Ikaunieks, Ya Y. Carbon Stars. rev. ed. Baumert, John H., ed. (Astronomy & Astrophysics Ser.: Vol. 11). Orig. Title: Uglerodnye Zvezdy. (Illus.). 192p. 1981. pap. 24.00 (*0-912918-16-0*, 0016) Pachart Pub Hse.

Alksne, Zenta, et al. Properties of Galactic Carbon Stars. Gallant, Christine A., tr. from RUS. (Orbit Ser.). (Illus.). 172p. (C). 1991. 48.50 (*0-89464-034-8*) Krieger.

Alkunchwar, Mehesh. Party. Marathi, Ashish R., tr. (C). 1989. 9.00 (*81-7046-035-2*, Pub. by Seagull Bks) S Asia.

All-Asia Consultation on Theological Education for. The Human & the Holy: Asian Perspectives in Christian Theology. Nacpil, Emerito P. & Elwood, Douglas J., eds. LC 80-14134. 384p. reprint ed. pap. 119.10 (*0-8357-4059-5*, 203674900005) Bks Demand.

All Childrens Hospital Foundation Staff. One Lump or Two. LC 88-24638. (Illus.). 1994. spiral bd. 19.95 (*0-87197-243-3*) Favorite Recipes.

All China Marketing Research Staff. ACMR China's Top One Hundred Thousand Companies, 1994. 4000p. (Orig.). 1994. pap. 290.00 (*0-9641047-6-8*) China Commun.

***All India Symposium on Veastu & Dash, Nilakanth.** Veastu, Astrology, & Architecture: Papers Presented At the First All India Symposium On Veastu, Bangalore, Held On June 3-4, 1995. LC 98-908844. ix, 238p. 1998. 100.00 (*81-208-1605-6*, Pub. by Motilal Bnarsidass) St Mut.

All India Symposium Staff. Physiology of Parasitism: Proceedings of the All India Symposium, Jabalpur, Feb. 24-27, 1978. Agarwal, G. P. & Bilgrami, K. S., eds. (Current Trends in Life Sciences Ser.: Vol. 7). vi, 478p. 1979. 50.00 (*0-88065-004-4*) Scholarly Pubns.

All Music Guide Staff & Erlewine, Michael. All Music Guide. 4th ed. 1504p. 1999. pap. 29.95 (*0-312-24287-5*) St Martin.

All Saints' Church Members & Jaffe, Morton S. Prepared for Us to Walk In. (Illus.). xvii, 168p. (Orig.). 1986. lib. bdg. 25.00 (*0-9617365-0-X*) M S Jaffe.

***All Saint's Episcopal Church Staff.** For They Shall Be Comforted: A Guide for Those Who Mourn a Loved One's Death & for Friends. 2nd ed. 48p. 1999. pap. 1.95 (*0-88028-216-9*) Forward Movement.

All Saints Episcopal Churchwomen Staff. La Bonne Cuisine: Cooking New Orleans Style. (Illus.). 337p. 1980. pap. 16.95 (*0-9606880-0-5*) ECS Inc.
— La Bonne Cuisine: Cooking New Orleans Style Lagniappe. 28p. 1986. pap. 3.00 (*0-9606880-1-3*) ECS Inc.

All Souls College Staff & International Commission of Jurists. Administrative Justice--Some Necessary Reforms: A Report of a JUSTICE-All Souls Committee. 492p. 1988. 115.00 (*0-19-825587-X*) OUP.

All the Seven Mighty Elohim Staff, contrib. by. The "I AM" Discourses. LC 95-9289. (Saint Germain Ser.: Vol. 14). 323p. 1995. 26.00 (*1-878891-61-8*) St Germain Press Inc.

All-Union Conference on Radiation Chemistry Staff. Radiation Chemistry of Aqueous Solutions: A Portion of Proceedings of the First All-Union Conference on Radiation Chemistry, 1st: 1957: Moscow. LC QD0601.A1. 80p. reprint ed. pap. 30.00 (*0-608-12991-7*, 202470800038) Bks Demand.
— Radiation Electrochemical Processes: A Portion of Proceedings of the First All-Union Conference on Radiation Chemistry ,1st: 1957: Moscow) LC QD0601.A1. 54p. reprint ed. pap. 30.00 (*0-608-12990-9*, 202470900038) Bks Demand.

Allaben, Frank. Ancestry of Howard Leander Crall: Monographs on the Crall, Haff, Beatty, & Other Families. (Illus.). 426p. 1989. reprint ed. pap. 66.50 (*0-8328-0437-1*); reprint ed. lib. bdg. 76.50 (*0-8328-0436-3*) Higginson Bk Co.

Allaby, Michael. Air: The Nature of Atmosphere & the Climate. (Elements Ser.). (Illus.). 208p. 1992. 35.00 (*0-8160-2525-8*) Facts on File.
— Basics of Environmental Science. (Illus.). 312p. (C). 1996. pap. 20.99 (*0-415-13019-0*) Routledge.

***Allaby, Michael.** Basics of Environmental Science. 2nd ed. LC 00-34466. 2000. pap. write for info. (*0-415-21176-X*) Routledge.

Allaby, Michael. Biology. (Collins Pocket Reference Ser.). 1996. pap. 10.00 (*0-00-470928-4*) Collins.
— Blizzards. LC 97-29898. (Dangerous Weather Ser.). 128p. 1997. 24.95 (*0-8160-3518-0*) Facts on File.
— A Chronology of Weather. LC 97-29898. (Dangerous Weather Ser.). 128p. 1998. 24.95 (*0-8160-3521-0*) Facts on File.
— Dictionary of the Environment. 2nd ed. 608p. 1984. 85.00 (*0-8288-1399-X*, M8686) Fr & Eur.
— Dictionary of the Environment. 3rd ed. 304p. (C). 1989. text 80.00 (*0-8147-0591-X*) NYU Pr.
— Dictionary of the Environment. 3rd ed. 304p. (C). 1990. pap. text 20.00 (*0-8147-0597-9*) NYU Pr.
— Dictionary of the Environment: Diccionario del Medio Ambiente. (SPA.). 421p. 1984. pap. 35.50 (*0-8288-1403-1*, S40721) Fr & Eur.

***Allaby, Michael.** Dorling Kindersley Guide to the Weather. LC 00-23803. (Illus.). 64p. (gr. 4-7). 2000. write for info. (*0-7894-6500-0*, Pub. by DK Pub Inc) Pub Resources Inc.

Allaby, Michael. Droughts. LC 97-9544. (Dangerous Weather Ser.). 128p. 1998. 24.95 (*0-8160-3519-9*) Facts on File.
— Fire: The Vital Source of Energy. LC 92-47224. (Elements Ser.). (Illus.). 208p. 1993. 35.00 (*0-8160-2714-5*) Facts on File.
— Floods. LC 97-18374. (Dangerous Weather Ser.). (Illus.). 128p. (YA). (gr. 6-12). 1998. 24.95 (*0-8160-3520-2*) Facts on File.
— How the Weather Works: 100 Ways Parents & Kids Can Share the Secrets of the Atmosphere. LC 94-43156. (Illus.). 224p. 1995. 24.00 (*0-89577-612-X*, Pub. by RD Assn) Penguin Putnam.
— How the Weather Works: 100 Ways Parents & Kids Can Share the Secrets of the Atmosphere. (Illus.). 192p. (J). (gr. 3-9). 1999. pap. text 16.95 (*0-7621-0234-9*, Pub. by RD Assn) Penguin Putnam.
— Hurricanes. LC 96-22475. (Dangerous Weather Ser.). 136p. (YA). (gr. 7 up). 1997. 24.95 (*0-8160-3516-4*) Facts on File.
— Inventing Tomorrow: How to Live in a Changing World LC 76-368057. 254 p. 1976. 4.95 (*0-340-19389-1*) St Martin.
— Temperate Forests. LC 98-23458. (Ecosystem Ser.). 1999. 45.00 (*0-8160-3678-0*) Facts on File.
— Water: Its Global Nature. (Elements Ser.). (Illus.). 208p. 1992. 35.00 (*0-8160-2526-6*) Facts on File.

Allaby, Michael, ed. A Dictionary of Ecology. 2nd ed. (Oxford Paperback Reference Ser.). (Illus.). 446p. (Orig.). 1999. pap. 15.95 (*0-19-280078-7*) OUP.
— A Dictionary of Plant Sciences. 2nd ed. (Oxford Paperback Reference Ser.). (Illus.). 516p. (Orig.). 1999. pap. 15.95 (*0-19-280077-9*) OUP.
— A Dictionary of Zoology. 2nd ed. (Oxford Paperback Reference Ser.). (Illus.). 606p. (Orig.). 1999. pap. 15.95 (*0-19-280076-0*) OUP.
— Ilustrated Dictionary of Science. rev. ed. (Illus.). 256p. 1995. 29.95 (*0-8160-3253-X*) Facts on File.

Allaby, Michael, et al, eds. A Dictionary of Earth Sciences. 2nd ed. LC 98-40309. (Oxford Paperback Reference Ser.). (Illus.). 631p. (Orig.). 1999. pap. 16.95 (*0-19-280079-5*) OUP.

Alladi, K., ed. Number Theory. (Lecture Notes in Mathematics Ser.: Vol. 1122). vii, 217p. 1985. 37.95 (*0-387-15222-9*) Spr-Verlag.
— Number Theory, Madras, 1987. (Lecture Notes in Mathematics Ser.: Vol. 1395). vii, 234p. 1989. 36.95 (*0-387-51595-X*) Spr-Verlag.

Alladin, Bilkiz. For Love of Begum. 1990. text 18.95 (*0-7069-5184-0*, Pub. by Vikas) S Asia.

***Alladin Paperbacks Staff.** Newbery Books a World of Award-winners Carton Pack. 1999. per. 215.28 (*0-689-00889-9*) Aladdin.

Alladina, Safder. Being Bilingual. 72p. 1995. pap. 15.00 (*1-85856-051-9*, Trentham Bks) Stylus Pub VA.

Alladina, Safder & Edwards, Viv, eds. Multilingualism in the British Isles, Vol. 1. LC 89-13672. (Longman Linguistics Library). 299p. 1991. reprint ed. pap. 92.70 (*0-608-03616-1*, 206444300001) Bks Demand.
— Multilingualism in the British Isles, Vol. 2. LC 89-13672. (Longman Linguistics Library). 290p. 1991. reprint ed. pap. 89.90 (*0-608-03617-X*, 206444300002) Bks Demand.

Allaerts, W. Involvement of Folliculo-Stellate Cells in Inhibitory Interactions in Rat Anterior Pituitary. (Acta Biomedica Lovaniensia Ser.: No. 11). 180p. (Orig.). 1989. pap. 49.50 (*90-6186-321-X*, Pub. by Leuven Univ) Coronet Bks.

Allah, Ahmad A. The Variant Readings of the Quran: A Critical Study of Their Historical & Linguistic Origins. (Academic Dissertations Ser.: Vol. 4). 1995. write for info. (*1-56564-230-9*); pap. write for info. (*1-56564-231-7*) IIIT VA.

Allah, Karim. Integration: Progress or Regret: Progress or Regret "Po Me" 64p. (Orig.). 1991. pap. text 6.50 (*0-9656639-0-6*) Menu Assocs.

Allahar, Anton. Class, Politics, & Sugar in Colonial Cuba. LC 90-22280. (Caribbean Studies: Vol. 2). 232p. 1990. lib. bdg. 89.95 (*0-88946-217-8*) E Mellen.

Allahar, Anton L., jt. auth. see Cote, James E.

Allahdadi, Firooz A., et al, eds. Small Spacecraft, Space Environments & Instrumentation Technologies, Vol. 3116. LC 98-191012. 284p. 1997. 59.00 (*0-8194-2538-9*) SPIE.

Allahdadi, Firooz A., jt. ed. see Maclay, Timothy D.

***Allahyari, Rebecca Anne.** Visions of Charity: Morality & the Politics of Homelessness. LC 99-48705. 296p. 2000. 45.00 (*0-520-22144-3*, Pub. by U CA Pr) Cal Prin Full Svc.
— Visions of Charity: Volunteer Workers & Moral Community. LC 99-48705. 296p. 2000. pap. 17.95 (*0-520-22145-1*, Pub. by U CA Pr) Cal Prin Full Svc.

Allain, Carol & Elwin, Rosamund, eds. Getting Wet: Tales of Lesbian Seductions. 174p. reprint ed. pap. 10.95 (*0-88961-170-X*, Pub. by Womens Pr) LPC InBook.

Allain, Louis J. Capital Investment Models of the Oil & Gas Industry: A Systems Approach. Bruchey, Stuart, ed. LC 78-22654. (Energy in the American Economy Ser.). (Illus.). 1979. lib. bdg. 46.95 (*0-405-11959-3*) Ayer.

Allain, Paul. Gardzienice: Polish Theatre in Transition. (Contemporary Theatre Studies). (Illus.). 196p. 1997. text 34.00 (*90-5702-105-6*, Harwood Acad Pubs); pap. text 16.00 (*90-5702-106-4*, Harwood Acad Pubs) Gordon & Breach.

Allain, Paul, jt. ed. see Gottlieb, Vera.

Allain, Violet A. & Pettus, Alvin M. Teaching Diverse Students: Preparing with Cases. LC 98-65077. (Fastback Ser.: No. 429). 50p. 1998. pap. 3.00 (*0-87367-629-7*, FB#429) Phi Delta Kappa.

Allaire. Basics of Finite Element Method. (West Engineering Ser.). 1985. pap., student ed. 12.95 (*0-534-95503-7*); text 66.95 (*0-534-95502-9*) PWS Pubs.

Allaire, AnnMarie. Ode to a Celtic King: Design an Heirloom of Your Own. (Illus.). 1998. pap. 10.00 (*0-9660393-2-7*) Rambling Hse.
— A Simple Sampler, But . . . Design an Heirloom of Your Own. (Illus.). 1997. pap. 8.00 (*0-9660393-1-9*) Rambling Hse.
— Victorian Sampler Stocking: Design an Heirloom of Your Own. (Illus.). 1997. pap. 19.95 (*0-9660393-0-0*) Rambling Hse.

Allaire, Anthony. Diary of Lieutenant Anthony Allaire of Fergusons Corps. LC 67-29025. (Eyewitness Accounts of the American Revolution Ser.). 1976. reprint ed. 16.95 (*0-405-01102-4*) Ayer.

Allaire, Barbara, jt. auth. see Zanzig, Thomas.

Allaire, Barbara, ed. see Ahlers, Julia & Wilt, Michael.

Allaire, Barbara, ed. see Koch, Carl, et al.

Allaire, Barbara, ed. see Lanave, Kevin.

Allaire, Barbara, ed. see Stoutzenberger, Joseph.

Allaire, Barbara, ed. see Toritto, Joseph.

Allaire, C., jt. auth. see Rigaud, M.

Allaire, Francois. Hockey Goaltending: For Young Players. (Illus.). 176p. (YA). 1997. pap. 19.95 (*1-55209-163-5*) Firefly Bks Ltd.

Allaire, Gloria. Andrea da Barberino & the Language of Chivalry. LC 97-8197. 224p. 1997. 49.95 (*0-8130-1528-6*) U Press Fla.

Allaire, Gloria, ed. Modern Retelling of Chivalric Texts. LC 98-22085. 256p. 1999. text 69.95 (*1-84014-612-5*, PN682.C53M63, Pub. by Ashgate Pub) Ashgate Pub Co.

Allaire, James & Broughton, Rosemary. Praying with Dorothy Day. Koch, Carl, ed. (Companions for the Journey Ser.). (Illus.). 128p. (Orig.). 1995. pap. 8.95 (*0-88489-306-5*) St Marys.

Allaire, Paul, ed. MAG, '95: Magnetic Bearings, Magnetic Drives & Dry Gas Seals International Conference. LC 95-61419. 380p. 1995. pap. text 89.95 (*1-56676-364-9*) Technomic.

Allaire, Paul E., ed. MAG, '93: Magnetic Bearings, Magnetic Drives & Dry Gas Seals International Conference & Exhibition. LC 93-60809. 275p. 1993. pap. text 79.95 (*1-56676-085-2*) Technomic.
— Proceedings of the Third International Symposium on Magnetic Bearings. LC 92-64061. 620p. 1992. text 89.95 (*0-87762-976-5*) Technomic.

Allaire, Paul E. & Trumper, David L., eds. Proceedings of the Sixth International Symposium on Magnetic Bearings. LC 98-86736. 760p. 1998. 189.95 (*1-56676-710-5*) Technomic.

Allais, Maurice, ed. Cardinalism: A Fundamental Approach. LC 93-8838. (Theory & Decision Library Series A). 320p. (C). 1994. lib. bdg. 186.50 (*0-7923-2398-X*, Pub. by Kluwer Academic) Kluwer Academic.

Allais, Maurice & Hagen, Ole, eds. Expected Utility Hypotheses & the Allais Paradox. (Theory & Decision Library: No. 21). 1979. lib. bdg. 321.50 (*90-277-0960-2*) Kluwer Academic.

Allal, Linda, et al, eds. L' Evaluation Formative dans un Enseignement Differencie: Actes du Colloque a l'Universite de Geneve (Mars 1978) 7th ed. (Exploration Ser.). (FRE.). 268p. 1995. 42.80 (*3-261-03954-X*) P Lang Pubng.

Allama Shibli Numani. Al-Faruq: Life of Umar the Great, Vol. 1. 350p. 1985. 14.50 (*1-56744-213-7*) Kazi Pubns.
— Al-Faruq: Life of Umar the Great, Vol. 2. 360p. (C). 1985. 14.50 (*1-56744-214-5*) Kazi Pubns.
— Sirat un-Nabi, 2 vol. set. M. Tayyib Bakhsh Budayuni, tr. 500p. (C). 1985. text 39.00 (*1-56744-376-1*) Kazi Pubns.

Allama Sir Abdullah Al-Mamun Al-Suhrawardy. The Sayings of Muhammad. LC 91-78174. (Wisdom of the East Ser.). 128p. 1992. reprint ed. 12.95 (*0-8048-1797-9*) Tuttle Pubng.

Allama Sir Abdullah al-Mamun alsuhrawardy. The Sayings of Muhammad. LC 79-52559. (Islam Ser.). 1980. reprint ed. lib. bdg. 17.95 (*0-8369-9266-0*) Ayer.

Allaman, Durward Bellmont & Henry, Richard John. The Allaman Heritage: The Descendants of Jacob Allemong & Anna Marie Balliet, & His Brother, Christian. LC 97-69899. (Illus.). 1997. write for info. (*0-89725-327-2*, Penobscot Pr) Picton Pr.

Allamandola, L. J. & Tielens, A. G., eds. Interstellar Dust: Proceedings of the 135th Symposium of the International Astronomical Union. (C). 1989. pap. text 80.00 (*0-7923-0449-7*); lib. bdg. 177.00 (*0-7923-0448-9*) Kluwer Academic.

Allamby, Michael. To the Best of My Knowledge & Belief. 156p. (Orig.). 1996. pap. 19.95 (*0-9651029-0-4*) Lemcas Bks.

Allameh Sayyed Mohammad Hosayn Tabatabai. Islamic Teachings: An Overview. Campbell, R. et al, trs. from PER. LC 88-62667. 200p. (Orig.). 1989. pap. 8.95 (*0-922817-00-6*) Mostazafan Foun.

Allami, Abul-Fazl. The A'in-i Akbari, 3 vols., Set. (C). 1989. 90.00 (*0-8364-2426-3*, Pub. by Usha) S Asia.

Allan. Clinical Coppler Ultrasound. 2000. text 50.00 (*0-443-05549-1*, W B Saunders Co) Harcrt Hlth Sci Grp.
— North Pakistan. 1999. text 49.95 (*0-312-12065-6*) St Martin.

Allan. Precision Time & GPS. text 125.00 (*0-471-38179-9*, Wiley Heyden) Wiley.

Allan. Rachel & the Tough Guy. large type ed. 1998. per. 3.50 (*0-373-15744-4*, Harlequin) Harlequin Bks.
— Satellite Microwave Remote Sensors. 1990. boxed set. write for info. (*0-318-68284-2*) P-H.

***Allan & Daniels.** Part-Time Workers 1999. 96p. 2000. pap. 29.99 (*0-8464-5124-7*) Beekman Pubs.

Allan, jt. auth. see Klooster.

***Allan, A. Grant.** Golfer's Dumb Moves: The Little Black Book on Golf Etiquette. McInnis, Carol, ed. LC 99-96837. 160p. 1999. 19.95 (*0-9671135-0-4*) Semiahmoo Pubg.

Allan, A. L. Practical Surveying & Computations. 2nd ed. LC 98-105135. (Illus.). 592p. 1997. pap. text 49.95 (*0-7506-3655-6*, Butterwrth Archit) Buttrwrth-Heinemann.

Allan, Alastair J. The Myth of Government Information. LC 91-105582. (Viewpoints in Library & Information Science: Vol. 6). 72p. reprint ed. pap. 30.00 (*0-608-20966-X*, 207183800002) Bks Demand.

Allan, Alice. An Intimate Look at Glenwood Springs Circa 1957. LC 98-232532. (Illus.). xii, 417p. 1998. pap. 24.95 (*0-9662980-0-4*) Old Timer Pubns.

Allan, Andrew, ed. see Adler, Arlene M. & Carlton, Richard R.

Allan, Andrew, ed. see Chabner, Davi-Ellen.

***Allan, Arthur L.** Maths for Map Makers. (Illus.). 320p. 1999. pap. text 50.00 (*0-7881-8121-1*) DIANE Pub.

***Allan, Barbara.** Developing Information & Library Staff Through Work-Based Learning: 101 Activities. 191p. 1999. 65.00 (*1-85604-281-2*, Pub. by Library Association) Bernan Associates.

Allan, Barbara. Guide to Information Sources in Alternative Therapy. 216p. 1988. text 57.95 (*0-566-05611-9*, Pub. by Gower) Ashgate Pub Co.

Allan, Barbara & Livesey, Brian. How To Use Biological Abstracts, Chemical Abstracts & Index Chemicus. 2nd ed. 114p. 1994. 65.95 (*0-566-07556-3*, Pub. by Gower) Ashgate Pub Co.

Allan, Barbara C., jt. auth. see Hodge, Barry S.

Allan, Bette. Sari. large type ed. (Linford Romance Library). 256p. 1994. pap. 16.99 (*0-7089-7517-8*, Linford) Ulverscroft.

Allan, C. B., et al. Less Common Metals in Proteins & Nucleic Acid Probes. Clarke, M. J., ed. LC 99-164802. (Structure & Bonding Ser.: Vol. 92). (Illus.). 170p. 1998. 139.00 (*3-540-63925-X*) Spr-Verlag.

Allan, C. J., jt. auth. see Jenkins, W. M. M.

Allan, Caroline, jt. ed. see Porter, Dan.

Allan, Clarissa, jt. auth. see Allan, Roy.

***Allan, Clarke.** The First Man to Be First Lady. 309p. 1999. pap. 17.95 (*0-7414-0157-6*) Buy Books.

Allan, D. G. William Shipley: Founder of the Royal Society of Arts. A Biography with Documents. 240p. 1968. 69.50 (*0-09-085700-3*) Elliots Bks.

Allan, D. G. & Schofield, R. E. Stephen Hales: Scientist & Philanthropist. 1980. 61.95 (*0-85967-482-7*, Pub. by Scolar Pr) Ashgate Pub Co.

Allan, D. J., ed. Plato: Republic I. (Bristol Greek Texts Ser.). (GRE.). 136p. 1993. pap. 20.95 (*1-85399-254-2*, Pub. by Brist Class Pr) Focus Pub-R Pullins.

Allan, D. J., ed. & tr. see Stenzel, Julius.

Allan, D. S. & Delair, J. B. Cataclysm: Compelling Evidence of a Cosmic Catastrophe in 9500 B. C. LC 97-20219. Orig. Title: When the Earth Nearly Died. 384p. (Orig.). 1997. reprint ed. pap. 20.00 (*1-879181-42-8*) Bear & Co.

Allan, Dave & Bevington, Adrian. From Doom to Boom: The Most Dramatic Decade in the Life of Middlesbrough FC. (Illus.). 192p. 1997. 39.95 (*1-85158-902-3*, Pub. by Mainstream Pubng) Trafalgar.

Allan, David. Birds of Prey of Southern, Central & East Africa. (Photographic Wildlife Pocket Guides Ser.). (Illus.). 144p. 1996. pap. 15.95 (*1-85368-903-3*, RCB-9033P, Pub. by New5 Holland) Chelsea Green Pub.

***Allan, David.** Ireland for Dummies. (For Dummies Ser.). 464p. 2000. pap. 19.99 (*0-7645-6199-5*) IDG Bks.

Allan, David. Virtue, Learning & the Enlightened Historian: Ideas of Scholarship & Society in Early Modern Scotland. 256p. 1993. pap. 35.00 (*0-7486-0438-3*, Pub. by Edinburgh U Pr) Col U Pr.

Allan, David & Brown, Vinson. An Illustrated Guide to Common Rocks & Their Minerals. rev. ed. LC 76-7372. (Illus.). 60p. (Orig.). 1976. pap. 4.95 (*0-87961-054-9*) Naturegraph.

Allan, David, ed. see Mallesons Stephen Jaques Staff.

Allan, David G. & O'Brien, Sinead. The Complete Idiot's Travel Guide to Ireland. (Complete Idiot's Travel Guide Ser.). (Illus.). 464p. 1999. pap. 16.95 (*0-02-863126-9*) Macmillan.

Allan, Diana & Allan, Ken. The Complete Saluki. (Book of the Breed). (Illus.). 160p. 1995. 24.95 (*0-948955-76-7*, Pub. by Ringpr Bks) Seven Hills Bk.

***Allan, Dick.** Sailing My Dream: A Voyage Around the World in a Small Sailing Boat. (Illus.). 323p. 1999. pap. 22.50 (*0-9533291-1-9*, Pub. by Longfellow Pubs) Trans-Atl Phila.

Allan, Doug, ed. Modern Method for Four Mallets. 208p. (YA). 1997. pap. text 19.95 (*0-7692-1228-X*, 0104B) Wrner Bros.

Allan, Elizabeth, jt. auth. see Watson, Adam.

Allan, Elizabeth, ed. see International Association of Business Communicator.

Allan, Eric. Every Puppy: Perfect Pet or Perfect Pest? LC 95-51851. 96p. 1996. 9.95 (*0-87605-474-2*) Howell Bks.

Allan, Francis C. The Mauser Parabellum. Koss, Joseph P., Jr., ed. (Illus.). 76p. (Orig.). 1985. pap. 14.95 (*0-9614814-0-4*) AK Enterprises.

***Allan, Francis C. & Goddard, Carl J.** The Japanese Naval Special Type 99 Rifles & Carbines: A Study of the Production History, Component Parts & Subassembly Method. P.Koss, Joseph, Jr., ed. (Illus.). 65p. 1999. 9.95 (*0-9614814-3-9*) AK Enterprises.

Allan, Francis C. & Masters, George R. Japanese Small Arms Ammunition. Koss, Joseph P., Jr., ed. (Illus.). 75p. 1987. pap. 14.95 (*0-9614814-1-2*) AK Enterprises.

Allan, Francis C. & Wakelam, Roger L. The Siamese Mauser. Koss, Joseph P., Jr., ed. (Illus.). 50p. 1987. pap. 7.95 (*0-9614814-2-0*) AK Enterprises.

Allan, G., et al, eds. Heterojunctions & Semiconductor Superlattices. (Illus.). viii, 253p. 1986. 123.95 (*0-387-16259-3*) Spr-Verlag.

Allan, George. The Importances of the Past: A Meditation on the Authority of Tradition. LC 85-2752. (SUNY Series in Philosophy). 260p. (C). 1985. text 21.50 (*0-88706-116-8*) State U NY Pr.

— Rethinking College Education. LC 97-11680. 240p. 1997. 29.95 (*0-7006-0842-7*) U Pr of KS.

Allan, George, ed. ACAD's Resource Handbook for Academic Deans. 1999. pap. 20.00 (*0-9668985-0-8*) Am Conf of Acad Deans.

Allan, Gordon. Fleet Street Around the Clock. 70p. 1997. pap. 5.95 (*1-898595-20-8*, Pub. by Sussex Acad Pr) Intl Spec Bk.

Allan, Graham. Family Life: Domestic Roles & Social Organization. 256p. 1990. pap. 32.95 (*0-631-14287-8*) Blackwell Pubs.

Allan, Graham. Kinship & Friendship in Modern Britain. (Oxford Modern Britain Ser.). (Illus.). 160p. 1996. text 24.95 (*0-19-878124-5*) OUP.

Allan, Graham. Kinship & Friendship in Modern Britain. (Illus.). 154p. 1996. pap. text 13.00 (*0-19-878125-3*) OUP.

***Allan, Graham & Crow, Graham.** Families, Households & Society. LC 00-34516. (Sociology for a Changing World Ser.). (Illus.). 2000. write for info. (*0-312-23848-7*) St Martin.

Allan, Graham, jt. ed. see Adams, Rebecca G.

Allan, Graham, jt. ed. see Skinner, Chris.

Allan, Graham G. & Robillard, Jean J., eds. Interactive Paper, Vol. 3227. LC 98-122034. 336p. 1997. 80.00 (*0-8194-2659-8*) SPIE.

Allan, H. H. Flora of New Zealand: Indigenous Dicots, Gymnosperms, Ferns & Fern Allies, Vol. I. 1961. 50.00 (*0-477-01056-3*, Pub. by Manaaki Whenua) Balogh.

Allan, Helen. Clinton Prison at Dannemora. (Illus.). 52p. 1987. pap. 7.95 (*1-890402-12-5*) Clinton Cnty Hist.

Allan, Helen, ed. Fire! The History of Firefighting in Clinton County, N. Y. (Illus.). 68p. 1991. pap. 9.95 (*1-890402-18-4*) Clinton Cnty Hist.

Allan, Herbert S. John Hancock, Patriot in Purple. (History - United States Ser.). 422p. 1993. reprint ed. lib. bdg. 99.00 (*0-7812-4878-7*) Rprt Serv.

***Allan, Ian & Caple, Jim.** Fantasy Football Index: 1999 Draft Guide. Taylor, Bruce, ed. (Illus.). 196p. 1999. pap. 5.99 (*1-928692-00-1*) Fantasy Index.

Allan, J. Book of Meditation for Everyday in Year. 366p. 1976. 14.95 (*0-318-36382-8*) Asia Bk Corp.

Allan, J., et al, eds. Computers in Railways VI. LC 99-208777. (Advances in Transport Ser.: Vol. 2). 1120p. 1998. 465.00 (*1-85312-598-9*, 5989, Pub. by WIT Pr) Computational Mech MA.

Allan, J., jt. auth. see Impey, M. Oliver.

Allan, J. A. Sahara. (C). 1980. text 15.50 (*0-906559-04-9*) Westview.

Allan, J. A., ed. Water, Peace & the Middle East: Negotiating Resources in the Jordan Basin. LC 95-62302. 250p. 1996. text 79.50 (*1-86064-055-9*, Pub. by I B T) St Martin.

Allan, J. A. & Mallat, Chibli, eds. Water in the Middle East: Legal, Political & Commercial Implications. 320p. 1995. text 79.50 (*1-85043-645-2*) I B T.

Allan, J. A., jt. ed. see Howell, P. P.

Allan, J. Mason. Introduction to the Kabbalah: With Special Reference to the Kabbalistic Elements in Freemasonry. 1994. pap. 4.95 (*1-55818-306-X*, Sure Fire) Holmes Pub.

Allan, J. P. Medieval & Post-Medieval Finds from Exeter, 1971-1980. (Illus.). 400p. 1993. text 80.00 (*0-85989-220-4*, Pub. by Univ Exeter Pr) Northwestern U Pr.

Allan, J. R. & Wiggins, W. D. Dolomite Reservoirs: Geochemical Techniques for Evaluating Origin & Distribution. (Continuing Education Course Note Ser.: No. 36). (Illus.). 170p. (Orig.). 1993. pap. 20.00 (*0-89181-185-0*, 906) AAPG.

Allan, J. W. & Roberts, Caroline, eds. Syria & Iran: Three Studies in Medieval Ceramics. (Oxford Studies in Islamic Art: No. IV). (Illus.). 248p. 1988. text 72.00 (*0-19-728007-2*) OUP.

Allan, J. W. & Roberts, Caroline, eds. Syria & Iran: Three Studies in Medieval Ceramics. (Oxford Studies in Islamic Art: No. IV). (Illus.). 248p. 1988. pap. text 59.00 (*0-19-728008-0*) OUP.

Allan, James. Islamic Ceramics. (Illus.). 80p. 1992. pap. 12.95 (*1-85444-001-2*, 001-2, Pub. by Ashmolean Mus) A Schwartz & Co.

— Islamic Ceramics. (Illus.). 80p. 1995. 19.95 (*1-85444-022-5*, 0012X, Pub. by Ashmolean Mus) A Schwartz & Co.

— A Sceptical Theory of Morality & Law. LC 97-29514. (Studies in Theoretical & Applied Ethics: Vol. 1). X, 277p. (C). 1998. text 51.95 (*0-8204-3891-X*) P Lang Pubng.

Allan, James, ed. Islamic Art in the Ashmolean Museum. 384p. 1996. 136.00 (*0-614-21581-1*, 1430) Kazi Pubns.

Allan, James A. Van, see Van Allan, James A., ed.

Allan, James H. Peacekeeping: Outspoken Observations by a Field Officer. LC 95-37754. (Praeger Series in War Studies). 224p. 1996. 59.95 (*0-275-95361-0*, Praeger Pubs) Greenwood.

***Allan, James W.** Islamic Metalwork: The Huhad Es-Said Collection. rev. ed. 128p. 1999. 90.00 (*0-85667-500-8*) P Wilson Serv.

Allan, James W. Islamic Metalwork: The Nuhad Es-Said Collection. (Illus.). 128p. 1982. text 115.00 (*0-85667-164-9*) Sothebys Pubns.

— Metalwork of the Islamic World. (Illus.). 128p. 1987. 95.00 (*0-85667-327-7*, Pub. by P Wilson) Scala Books.

Allan, James W., ed. Islamic Art in the Ashmolean Museum, Pt. I. (Oxford Studies in Islamic Art). (Illus.). 208p. 1996. text 85.00 (*0-19-728019-6*) OUP.

— Islamic Art in the Ashmolean Museum, Pt. II. (Oxford Studies in Islamic Art). (Illus.). 182p. 1996. text 85.00 (*0-19-728020-X*) OUP.

***Allan, Jane.** Establishing Phenomenal Rapport. 2000. boxed set 225.00 (*0-8464-5049-6*) Beekman Pubs.

Allan, Jane. Sharpen Your Team's Skills in Time Management. LC 96-46035. (Sharpen Your Team's Skills Ser.). 1998. pap. 19.95 (*0-07-709275-9*) McGraw.

Allan, Jay. Blocks. (My New Bk.). (Illus.). (J). (ps). 1993. pap. 5.95 (*0-9631798-1-0*) Silver Seahorse.

Allan, Jeanne. Charlotte's Cowboy. LC 96-553. 188p. 1995. per. 2.99 (*0-373-03384-2*) Harlequin Bks.

— The Cowboy Next Door: Back to the Ranch. (Romance Ser.). 1993. per. 2.99 (*0-373-03286-2*, 1-03286-1) Harlequin Bks.

— Do You Take This Cowboy? 1997. per. 3.25 (*0-373-03471-7*, 1-03471-9) Harlequin Bks.

— Do You Take This Cowboy? large type ed. 1997. per. 3.25 (*0-373-15717-7*) Harlequin Bks.

***Allan, Jeanne.** The Game Is Love. large type ed. 336p. 1999. 31.99 (*0-7505-1405-1*, Pub. by Mgna Lrg Print) Ulverscroft.

Allan, Jeanne. A Groom for Gwen: Guardian Angels. (Romance Ser.: Vol. 3524). 1998. per. 3.50 (*0-373-03524-1*, 1-03524-5) Harlequin Bks.

— A Groom for Gwen: Guardian Angels. large type ed. (Larger Print Ser.: Vol. 370). 1998. per. 3.50 (*0-373-15770-3*, 1-15770-0) Harlequin Bks.

— Un Mari Inoubliable. (Azur Ser.: No. 732). (FRE.). 1998. mass mkt. 3.50 (*0-373-34732-4*, 1-34732-7) Harlequin Bks.

— A Mistletoe Marriage. 1996. per. 3.25 (*0-373-03437-7*, 1-03437-0) Harlequin Bks.

— A Mistletoe Marriage. large type ed. (Hitched Ser.). 1996. per. 3.25 (*0-373-15683-9*) Harlequin Bks.

— Moving in with Adam. (Romance Ser.). 1996. per. 3.25 (*0-373-03408-3*, 1-03408-1) Silhouette.

— Needed: One Dad. 1997. per. 3.25 (*0-373-03456-3*, 1-03456-0) Harlequin Bks.

— Needed: One Dad. large type ed. 1997. per. 3.25 (*0-373-15702-9*, 1-15702-3) Harlequin Bks.

— One Bride Delivered. (Larger Print Ser.). 1999. per. 3.50 (*0-373-15814-9*, 1-15814-6) Harlequin Bks.

— One Bride Delivered. (Romance Ser.). 1999. per. 3.50 (*0-373-03568-3*, 1-03568-2) Harlequin Bks.

***Allan, Jeanne.** One Husband Needed. 2000. per. 3.50 (*0-373-15838-6*) Harlequin Bks.

— One Husband Needed. (Romance Ser.). 2000. mass mkt. 3.50 (*0-373-03592-6*) Harlequin Bks.

Allan, Jeanne. One Man to the Altar. (Romance Ser.: Bk. 3584). 187p. 2000. per. 3.50 (*0-373-03584-5*, 1-03584-9) Harlequin Bks.

***Allan, Jeanne.** One Mother Wanted: Hope Valley Brides. (Romance Ser.: No. 3576). 1999. per. 3.50 (*0-373-03576-4*, 1-03576-5) Harlequin Bks.

— One Mother Wanted: Hope Valley Brides. large type ed. (Larger Print Ser.: No. 422). 1999. per. 3.50 (*0-373-15822-X*, 1-15822-9) Harlequin Bks.

Allan, Jeanne. Rachel & the Tough Guy. (Romance Ser.: Vol. 3498). 1998. per. 3.50 (*0-373-03498-9*, 1-03498-2) Harlequin Bks.

— Rancher's Bride. (Romance Ser.: No. 175). 1992. per. 2.79 (*0-373-03175-0*, 1-03175-6) Harlequin Bks.

Allan, Jeff. Living with Adam. 1995. pap. 8.95 (*1-875243-16-X*) LPC InBook.

***Allan, Jerry.** The Horse & the Iron Ball: A Journey Through Time, Space & Technology. LC 00-8139. (Picture Bks.). (Illus.). 48p. (gr. 4-7). 2000. 16.95 (*0-8225-2158-X*, Lerner Publctns) Lerner Pub.

Allan, John. The Healing Energy of Love: A Personal Journal. LC 85-40770. (Illus.). 175p. (Orig.). 1999. pap. (*0-9643840-8-6*) Morning S P.

— How to be Better at Motivating People. (How to Be a Better...Ser.). 1996. pap. 15.95 (*0-7494-1913-X*) Kogan Page Ltd.

— The Kingdom of God. 1979. pap. 2.50 (*0-87516-286-X*) DeVorss.

— Living in the Presence of God: Love's Simple Path. LC 94-72771. (Illus.). 200p. (Orig.). 1995. pap. 12.00 (*0-9643840-7-8*) Morning S P.

— Twenty-Five Team Management Training Sessions. 464p. 1994. 341.95 (*0-566-07513-X*, Pub. by Gower) Ashgate Pub Co.

Allan, John, et al. Conversations in Spirit. LC 81-66244. 112p. (Orig.). 1981. pap. 5.50 (*0-87516-452-8*) DeVorss.

Allan, John A. B. Inscapes of the Child's World: Jungian Counseling in Schools & Clinics. LC 88-27831. (Illus.). 236p. (Orig.). 1988. pap. 19.50 (*0-88214-338-7*) Spring Pubns.

Allan, Johnnie. Memories - A Pictorial History of South Louisiana Music, 1912s-1990s Vols. 1 & 2: South Louisiana & East Texas Musicians. LC 95-76557. 330p. 1995. 36.00 (*0-9619335-4-2*); pap. 26.00 (*0-9619335-3-4*) Jadfel Pub.

Allan, Jonathan. My Cat. (Illus.). (J). 1999. pap. write for info. (*0-14-055272-3*) NAL.

Allan, Judith, jt. auth. see Lawless, Julia.

Allan, Julie. Actively Seeking Inclusion: Pupils with Special Needs in Mainstream Schools. LC 99-206495. (Studies in Inclusive Education Ser.). 160p. 1999. 79.95 (*0-7507-0737-2*, Falmer Pr); pap. 27.95 (*0-7507-0736-4*, Falmer Pr) Taylor & Francis.

Allan, Karen K. & Miller, Margery S. Purposeful Reading & Writing: Strategies in Context. 170p. (C). 1994. pap. text 50.00 (*0-15-501164-2*) Harcourt.

Allan, Karen K., jt. auth. see Miller, Margery S.

Allan, Keith. Linguistic Meaning, 2 vols., I. 1986. text 18.50 (*0-7102-0699-2*, Routledge Thoemms) Routledge.

— Linguistic Meaning, 2 vols., Vol. I. 400p. 1986. text 18.50 (*0-7100-9587-2*, Routledge Thoemms) Routledge.

— Linguistic Meaning, 2 vols., Vol. II. 400p. 1986. text 45.00 (*0-7102-0697-6*, Routledge Thoemms) Routledge.

Allan, Ken, jt. auth. see Allan, Diana.

Allan, Kenneth. The Meaning of Culture: Moving the Postmodern Critique Forward. LC 98-9941. 208p. 1998. 59.95 (*0-275-96124-9*, Praeger Pubs) Greenwood.

Allan, Lindsey D. Manual Fetal Echocardiology. 1986. text 89.00 (*0-85200-988-7*) Kluwer Academic.

Allan, Lois. Dennis Cunningham: Observation & Allegory. (Illus.). 24p. 1998. pap. 10.00 (*0-914435-29-9*) Marylhurst Art.

Allan, Lois, et al. Thomas Wood: 25 Years of Printmaking LC 98-88361. 48 p. 1998. write for info. (*0-938506-05-6*) Whatcom.

Allan, Margaret. The Doctor at Partridge Hill. large type ed. (Dales Large Print Ser.). 261p. 1997. pap. 18.99 (*1-85389-772-8*, Dales) Ulverscroft.

— Doctor David. large type ed. 256p. 1992. pap. 16.99 (*0-7089-7185-7*) Ulverscroft.

— Highland Doctor. large type ed. (Dales Large Print Ser.). 219p. 1997. pap. 18.99 (*1-85389-752-3*, Dales) Ulverscroft.

— The Last Mammoth. 400p. (Orig.). 1995. mass mkt. 4.99 (*0-451-18463-7*, Sig) NAL.

— The Man from Lamb Hill. large type ed. (Dales Large Print Ser.). 238p. 1996. pap. 18.99 (*1-85389-595-4*, Dales) Ulverscroft.

— The Song Is Ended. large type ed. (Dales Romance Ser.). 204p. 1993. pap. 18.99 (*1-85389-379-X*) Ulverscroft.

Allan, Margaret C. Women in Development: An Interpretive Essay. (C). 1990. pap. 30.00 (*0-7300-1200-X*, SSS338, Pub. by Deakin Univ) St Mut.

Allan, Martha, ed. & tr. see Muro, Ernest A.

Allan, Martin. This Powerful Rhyme: Passage Mostly from Shakespeare Translated into North-East Scots. 96p. 1990. pap. 21.00 (*1-898218-24-2*) St Mut.

***Allan, Max & Collins, Barbara.** Regeneration. 320p. 1999. mass mkt. 5.99 (*0-8439-4615-6*, Leisure Bks) Dorchester Pub Co.

Allan, Melinda. Hearst Marine Books Canoeing Basics. LC 93-37869. 1994. pap. 15.00 (*0-688-12476-3*, Wm Morrow) Morrow Avon.

Allan-Meyer, Kathleen. Little Bear's Big Adventure. LC 98-11239. (Illus.). 32p. (J). 1998. 5.49 (*1-57924-060-7*) Bob Jones Univ.

***Allan-Meyer, Kathleen.** Little Bear's Secret. LC 99-462161. (Illus.). (J). 2000. write for info. (*1-57924-358-4*) Bob Jones Univ.

— Little Bear's Surprise. LC 99-23596. (Illus.). 32p. (J). 1999. 5.49 (*1-57924-066-6*) Bob Jones Univ.

Allan, Morton. Morton Allan Directory of European Passenger Steamship Arrivals for the Years 1890 to 1930 at the Port of New York, & for the Years 1904 to 1926 at the Ports of New York, Philadelphia, Boston & Baltimore. LC 78-65163. 268p. 1998. reprint ed. 20.00 (*0-8063-0830-3*) Genealog Pub.

Allan, Mowbray. T. S. Eliot's Impersonal Theory of Poetry. LC 73-489. 189p. 1974. 29.50 (*0-8387-1311-4*) Bucknell U Pr.

Allan, Nancy, jt. auth. see Johnson, Randy.

Allan, Nancy P., jt. auth. see Johnson, Randy.

Allan, Nicholas. The Bird. LC 98-125044. 32p. (J). (ps-4). 1998. 7.95 (*0-385-32573-8*) Delacorte.

— Jesus' Christmas Party. 32p. (J). 1997. 8.95 (*0-385-32521-5*, DD Bks Yng Read) BDD Bks Young Read.

— Jesus' Christmas Party. (J). 1997. 7.95 (*0-614-29211-5*) Doubleday.

***Allan, Nicholas.** The Queen's Knickers. (J). 1998. pap. 6.95 (*0-09-928161-9*, Pub. by Random) Trafalgar.

Allan, Nigel J., ed. Mountains at Risk: Current Issues in Environmental Studies. (C). 1995. 38.00 (*81-7304-133-4*, Pub. by Manohar) S Asia.

Allan, Nigel J., et al, eds. Human Impact on Mountains. LC 86-31471. 308p. (C). 1992. pap. text 26.95 (*0-8476-7755-9*) Rowman.

Allan, P. B. Talking of Moths. 340p. 1943. 60.00 (*0-7855-0679-9*) St Mut.

Allan, Peta & Jolley, Moya, eds. The Curriculum in Nursing Education. 208p. (C). 1987. 25.00 (*0-7099-1462-8*, Pub. by C Helm) Routldge.

Allan, Pierre & Goldmann, Kjell, eds. The End of the Cold War: Evaluating Theories of International Realtions. LC 92-26090. 256p. (C). 1992. lib. bdg. 98.00 (*0-7923-1740-8*) Kluwer Academic.

Allan, Pierre & Schmidt, Christian, eds. Game Theory & International Relations: Preferences, Information, & Empirical Evidence. LC 93-50871. 232p. 1994. 95.00 (*1-85278-925-5*) E Elgar.

Allan, R., et al. El Nino Southern Oscillation & Climatic Variability. LC 97-160239. (Illus.). 414p. 1996. 110.00 incl. cd-rom (*0-643-05803-6*, Pub. by CSIRO) Accents Pubns.

Allan, R., jt. auth. see Billinton, R.

Allan, R., ed. see De Lacerda, Luiz D. & Salomons, W.

Allan, R. G. The Grain-Eating Birds of Sub-Saharan Africa: Identification, Biology & Management. 191p. 1997. pap. 125.00 (*0-85954-464-8*, Pub. by Nat Res Inst) St Mut.

Allan, R. G., et al, eds. Bias Issues in Teacher Certification Testing. 184p. 1988. 39.95 (*0-8058-0080-8*) L Erlbaum Assocs.

A

A

Allan, R. J. The Role of Particular Matter in the Fate of Contaminants in Aquatic Ecosystems LC 87-117742. (Scientific Ser.). vii, 128 p. 1986. write for info. (0-662-14762-6) Can7 Govern Pub.

Allan, R. J., et al, eds. High-Performance Computing. LC 98-46098. (Illus.). 592p. (C). 1999. text 130.00 (0-306-46034-3, Kluwer Plenum) Kluwer Academic.

Allan, R. J. & Roy, M. Lake Water Nutrient Chemistry & Chlorophyll A in Pasqua, Echo, Mission, Katepwa, Crooked & Round Lakes on the Qu'Appelle River, Saskatchewan LC 85-117001. (Scientific Ser.). (ENG & FRE.). v, 68 p. 1980. write for info. (0-662-10916-3) Can7 Govern Pub.

Allan, R. N. Inflammatory Bowel Diseases. 3rd ed. LC 97-5557. 1996. text 165.00 (0-443-05067-8) Church.

Allan, Richard G., et al. U. S. History, 5 vols., No. 2. Incl. Vol. 1. Modern America Takes Shape. 242p. 1981. 10.95 (0-86624-005-5, UU4); Vol. 2. Imperialism to Progressivism. 192p. 1981. 10.95 (0-86624-006-3, UU5); Vol. 3. War, Prosperity & Depression. 180p. 1981. 10.95 (0-86624-007-1, UU6); Vol. 4. Roosevelt Years of Depression & War. 184p. 1981. 10.95 (0-86624-008-X, UU7); Vol. 5. Cold War Years. 244p. 1981. 10.95 (0-86624-009-8, UU8); (Illus.). 1981. pap. text. write for info. (0-685-00760-X) Bilingual Ed Serv.

Allan, Robert & Scheidt, Stephen, eds. Heart & Mind: The Practice of Cardiac Psychology, A1412. LC 96-10543. 510p. 1996. 49.95 (1-55798-356-9) Am Psychol.

Allan, Robert F., et al. Collegefields: Youth from Delinquency to Freedom. 176p. (Orig.). 1981. text 25.00 (0-8290-0273-1); pap. text 12.95 (0-8290-0274-X) Irvington.

Allan, Robert N., et al, eds. Inflammatory Bowel Diseases. 2nd ed. (Illus.). 656p. 1990. text 129.00 (0-443-03819-8) Church.

Allan, Robert W., ed. Digital Cable Radio: The Tensions Between the Music Industry & the Broadcasting Industry. (Reports Presented at the Meeting of the International Association of Entertainment Lawyers MIDEM 1994, Cannes). 112p. 1994. pap. 95.00 (90-6215-418-2, Pub. by Maklu Uitgev) Gaunt.

Allan, Robin. Walt Disney & Europe: European Influences on the Animated Feature Films of Walt Disney. (Illus.). 300p. 1998. 49.95 (1-86462-040-4); pap. 24.95 (1-86462-041-2) Ind U Pr.

***Allan, Robin.** Walt Disney & Europe: European Influences on the Animated Feature Films of Walt Disney. LC 99-34700. 1999. 35.00 (0-253-21353-3) Ind U Pr.

Allan, Ronald C. & Ekonomon, Adam M., eds. Baldwin's Ohio Practice, Business Organizations Laws & Rules. 996p. 1996. pap. text 66.00 (0-8322-0637-7) Banks-Baldwin.

Allan, Ronald N., jt. auth. see Billinton, Roy.

Allan, Ross. Dog Obedience Training. (Illus.). 64p. 1997. 12.95 (0-7938-0149-4, WW-025) TFH Pubns.

Allan, Ross & American Society for the Prevention of Cruelty to. Dog Obedience Training: A Complete & Up-to-Date Guide. LC 97-4185. (Basic Domestic Pet Library). 76p. (J). (gr. 3 up). 1997. 19.95 (0-7910-4605-2) Chelsea Hse.

Allan, Roy & Allan, Clarissa. A Dog Owner's Guide to German Shepherd Dogs. (Illus.). 119p. 1995. 10.95 (1-56465-127-4, 16042) Tetra Pr.

— The Essential German Shepherd Dog. (Book of the Breed). (Illus.). 224p. 1994. 24.95 (0-948955-13-9, Pub. by Ringpr Bks) Seven Hills Bk.

Allan, S. J. How to Buy Foreclosure Properties on Shoestring. write for info. (0-934493-04-9) AlphaVideo Grp.

Allan, Sarah. The Shape of the Turtle: Myth, Art, & Cosmos in Early China. LC 90-30424. (SUNY Series in Chinese Philosophy & Culture). 230p. (C). 1991. pap. text 21.95 (0-7914-0460-9) State U NY Pr.

— The Shape of the Turtle: Myth, Art, & Cosmos in Early China. LC 90-30424. (SUNY Series in Chinese Philosophy & Culture). 230p. (C). 1991. text 64.50 (0-7914-0459-5) State U NY Pr.

— The Way of Water & Sprouts of Virtue. LC 96-36341. (SUNY Series in Chinese Philosophy & Culture). (Illus.). 181p. (C). 1997. text 53.50 (0-7914-3385-4); pap. text 17.95 (0-7914-3386-2) State U NY Pr.

Allan, Sean. The Plays of Heinrich von Kleist: Ideals & Illusions. (Studies in German). (Illus.). 333p. (C). 1996. text 64.95 (0-521-49511-3) Cambridge U Pr.

Allan, Sean & Sandford, John. DEFA Film: East German Cinema, 1946-1992. LC 97-41567. (Illus.). 328p. 1999. 59.95 (1-57181-943-6) Berghahn Bks.

Allan, Sean & Sandford, John, eds. DEFA Film: East German Cinema, 1946-1992. LC 97-41567. 328p. 1999. pap. 25.00 (1-57181-753-0) Berghahn Bks.

Allan, Stella. Arrow in the Dark. large type ed. (Ulverscroft Large Print Ser.). 448p. 1998. 29.99 (0-7089-3900-7) Ulverscroft.

— A Dead Giveaway. large type ed. (Ulverscroft Large Print Ser.). 416p. 1998. 29.99 (0-7089-3889-2) Ulverscroft.

***Allan, Stella.** A Mortal Affair. large type ed. 352p. 1999. 31.99 (0-7089-4081-1) Ulverscroft.

— No Marks for Trying. large type ed. 384p. 1999. 31.99 (0-7089-4093-5, Linford) Ulverscroft.

***Allan, Stuart.** Environmental Risks & the Media. LC 99-87826. 288p. 2000. pap. 24.99 (0-415-21447-5); text 75.00 (0-415-21446-7) Routledge.

Allan, Stuart. News Culture LC 99-19412. (Issues in Cultural & Media Studies). 1999. 24.95 (0-335-19915-1) OpUniv Pr.

***Allan, Stuart.** News Culture. 176p. 1999. pap. text 24.95 (0-335-19956-9) OpUniv Pr.

***Allan, Stuart, et al, eds.** Environmental Risks & the Media. (Illus.). 288p. 1999. 66.00 (1-85728-994-3, Pub. by UCL Pr Ltd); pap. 20.95 (1-85728-995-1, Pub. by UCL Pr Ltd) Taylor & Francis.

Allan, Stuart, jt. ed. see Adam, Barbara.

Allan, T. M. & Douglas, A. S. Seasonal Variation in Health & Diseases: With Sections on Effects of Weather & Temperature; a Bibliography. LC 94-14865. 496p. 1995. 150.00 (0-7201-2211-2) Continuum.

Allan, T. R. Law, Liberty, & Justice: The Legal Foundations of British Constitutionalism. LC 94-36743. 316p. 1995. pap. text 34.00 (0-19-825991-3) OUP.

Allan, Ted & Gordon, Sydney. The Scalpel & the Sword: The Story of Doctor Norman Bethune. rev. ed. LC 73-8059. 336p. 1974. reprint ed. pap. 10.00 (0-85345-302-0, Pub. by Monthly Rev) NYU Pr.

***Allan, Tony.** The Middle East Water Question: Hydropolitics & the Global Economy. 2000. text 59.50 (1-86064-582-8, Pub. by I B T) St Martin.

Allan, Tony. Pharaohs & Pyramids. (Time Travelers Bks.). (J). (gr. 4-9). 1977. pap. 6.95 (0-86020-084-1, Usborne) EDC.

— Robin Hood. (Library of Fantasy & Adventure). (Illus.). 79p. (J). (gr. 5 up). 1996. pap. 9.95 (0-7460-2063-5, Usborne) EDC.

— Tales of Real Haunting. (Usborne Reader's Library). (Illus.). 64p. (YA). (gr. 7 up). lib. bdg. 16.95 (1-58086-006-0, Usborne) EDC.

— Tales of Real Haunting. (Read Tales Ser.). (Illus.). 64p. (YA). (gr. 7-12). 1997. pap. 8.95 (0-7460-2359-6, Usborne) EDC.

— Tales of Robin Hood. (Library of Fantasy & Adventure). (Illus.). 96p. (J). (gr. 5 up). 1999. lib. bdg. 17.95 (0-88110-795-5, Usborne) EDC.

Allan, Tony & Warren, Andrew, eds. Deserts: The Encroaching Wilderness. LC 92-31992. (Illus.). 176p. 1993. 45.00 (0-19-520941-9) OUP.

Allan, Tony & Wingate, Philippa. Pharaohs & Pyramids. (Time Traveller Ser.). (Illus.). 32p. (J). (gr. 3-6). 1998. lib. bdg. 14.95 (0-88110-978-9, Usborne) EDC.

— Pharaohs & Pyramids. rev. ed. (Time Traveller Ser.). (Illus.). 32p. (J). (gr. 3-6). 1998. pap. 6.95 (0-7460-3069-X, Usborne) EDC.

Allan, Tuzyline J. Womanist & Feminist Aesthetics: A Comparative Review. LC 94-45726. 162p. (C). 1995. text 34.95 (0-8214-1109-8) Ohio U Pr.

— Womanist & Feminist Aesthetics: A Comparative Review. LC 94-45726. 162p. (C). 1996. reprint ed. pap. text 16.95 (0-8214-1152-7) Ohio U Pr.

— Women's Studies Quarterly Vol. 97, Nos. 3-4: Teaching African Literatures in a Global Literary Economy. 288p. 1997. pap. text 18.00 (1-55861-169-X) Feminist Pr.

***Allan, Vicky, contrib. by.** It's a Wild Life! Living with Animals. (J). 2000. pap. text 4.95 (1-902618-87-4, Pub. by Element Childrns) Penguin Putnam.

***Allan, Victoria J., ed.** Protein Localization by Fluorescence Microscopy: A Practical Approach. LC 99-37444. (The Practical Approach Ser.: No. 218). (Illus.). 256p. 2000. text 120.00 (0-19-963741-5); pap. text 55.00 (0-19-963740-7) OUP.

Allan, Walter. The Official History of the Melrose Sevens. (Illus.). 185p. 1995. 34.95 (1-85158-660-1, Pub. by Mainstream Pubng) Trafalgar.

Allan, Walter, jt. auth. see Anglim, Maryann.

Allan, Walter G. The Triad System. Silent Partners, Inc. Staff, ed. (Illus.). 21p. (Orig.). 1987. 295.00 incl. disk (0-9619483-0-2) W G Allan.

Allan, Wesley D., jt. auth. see Kashani, Javad H.

***Allan, William.** The Andromache & Euripidean Tragedy. LC 99-54337. (Oxford Classical Monographs). 250p. 2000. text 70.00 (0-19-815297-3) OUP.

Allan, William. History of Campaign of Gen. T. J. (Stonewall) Jackson in Shenandoah Valley of Virginia. (Illus.). 175p. 1975. reprint ed. 25.00 (0-89029-022-9) Morningside Bkshop.

— Stonewall Jackson, Robert E. Lee, & the Army of Northern Virginia, 1862. (Illus.). 755p. 1995. reprint ed. pap. 19.95 (0-306-80656-8) Da Capo.

Allan, William, et al. Transient Poet: William Allan Retrospective. 1993. write for info. (0-318-72127-9) Crocker Art Mus.

Allana, G. Eminent Muslim Freedom Fighters. (C). 1993. text 14.00 (81-85418-99-3, Pub. by Low Price) S Asia.

— Quaid-I-Azam Jinnah: The Story of a Nation. 550p. 1989. 39.00 (1-56744-361-3) Kazi Pubns.

Allanach, J., tr. see Mandel, Peter.

Allanach, Jack. Colour Me Healing: Colorpuncture: A New Medicine of Light. LC 97-25596. 1998. pap. 15.95 (1-86204-143-1, Pub. by Element MA) Penguin Putnam.

Allanbrook, Wye. Source Readings Vol. 5: Late 18th Century. rev. ed. LC 98-106574. (C). 1997. pap. text 48.00 (0-393-96698-4) Norton.

Allanbrook, Wye J. Rhythmic Gesture in Mozart: "Le Nozze Di Figaro" & "Don Giovanni" LC 83-9184. (Illus.). xii, 410p. 1986. pap. 15.95 (0-226-01404-5) U Ch Pr.

Allance of Artists Communites Staff. Artists Communities: A Directory of Residencies in the United States That Offer Time & Space for Creativity. 2nd ed. Snell, Tricia, ed. LC 99-58837. (Illus.). 220p. 2000. pap. 18.95 (1-58115-044-X) Allworth Pr.

Alland, Alexander, Jr The Human Imperative. LC 77-183227. 185p. (C). 1972. text 46.00 (0-231-03228-5) Col U Pr.

— Playing with Form: Children Draw in Six Countries. LC 82-25269. (Illus.). 224p. 1983. pap. text 23.50 (0-231-05609-5) Col U Pr.

Alland, Alexander, Jr. & Alland, Sonia. Crisis & Commitment: The Life History of a French Social Movement. (Library of Anthropology). 224p. 1994. text 53.00 (2-88124-641-9); pap. text 26.00 (2-88124-648-6) Gordon & Breach.

Alland, Alexander, jt. auth. see Codrescu, Andrei.

Alland, Alexander, Jr., ed. see Darwin, Charles.

Alland, Bronislawa. Memoirs of a Hidden Child During the Holocaust: My Life During the War. Alland, George, tr. from POL. LC 92-21427. (Illus.). 108p. 1992. text 59.95 (0-7734-9155-4) E Mellen.

Alland, George, tr. see Alland, Bronislawa.

Alland, Sonia, jt. auth. see Alland, Alexander, Jr.

Alland, Sonia, tr. see Bronsard, Marie.

Allane, Lee. Chinese Rugs: A Buyer's Guide. LC 92-80332. (Illus.). 144p. 1994. pap. 15.95 (0-500-27701-X, Pub. by Thames Hudson) Norton.

— Kilims: A Buyer's Guide. LC 95-60278. (Illus.). 144p. (Orig.). 1995. pap. 17.95 (0-500-27841-5, Pub. by Thames Hudson) Norton.

— Oriental Rugs: A Practical Guide. LC 88-50227. (Illus.). 146p. 1988. pap. 14.95 (0-500-27517-3, Pub. by Thames Hudson) Norton.

— Tribal Rugs: A Buyer's Guide. LC 96-60258. (Illus.). 144p. (Orig.). 1996. pap. 17.95 (0-500-27897-0, Pub. by Thames Hudson) Norton.

Allanson, B. R., ed. Lake Sibaya. (Monographiae Biologicae: No. 36). 1979. text 211.50 (90-6193-088-X) Kluwer Academic.

Allanson, B. R., et al. Inland Waters of Southern Africa: An Ecological Perspective. (C). 1990. text 309.50 (0-7923-0266-4) Kluwer Academic.

Allanson, Brian & Baird, Dan, eds. Estuaries of South Africa. LC 98-17406. (Illus.). 350p. (C). 1998. text 140.00 (0-521-58410-8) Cambridge U Pr.

Allanson, E. W., ed. Car Ownership Forecasting, Vol. 1. (Transportation Studies). 168p. 1982. text 173.00 (0-677-05690-7) Gordon & Breach.

Allara, David L. & Hawkins, Walter L., eds. Stabilization & Degradation of Polymers. LC 78-10600. (Advances in Chemistry Ser.: Vol. 169). 455p. 1978. reprint ed. pap. 141.10 (0-608-03866-0, 206431300008) Bks Demand.

Allara, Pamela. Exterior-Interior: Alice Neel. 72p. 1991. pap. 17.50 (1-880593-00-9) Tufts Univ Gallery.

Allara, Pamela. Pictures of People: Alice Neel's American Portrait Gallery. LC 97-18403. (Illus.). 358p. 1998. 45.00 (0-87451-837-7) U Pr of New Eng.

***Allara, Pamela.** Pictures of People: Alice Neel's American Portrait Gallery. LC 97-18403. (Illus.). 358p. 1998. 22.95 (1-58465-036-2) U Pr of New Eng.

Allard, Andrea & Wilson, Jeni. Gender Dimensions: Constructing Interpersonal Skills in the Classroom. (Illus.). 160p. 1995. pap. text, teacher ed. 17.00 (1-875327-34-7) E Curtain.

Allard, B., et al. Humic Substances in the Aquatic & Terrestrial Environment: Proceedings of an International Symposium held in Linkoping, Sweden, August 21-23, 1989. Bhattacharji, S. et al, eds. (Lecture Notes in Earth Sciences Ser.: Vol. 33). (Illus.). viii, 514p. 1991. 91.95 (0-387-53702-3) Spr-Verlag.

Allard, Bill. Safeguarding Our Children. LC 95-90961. 109p. (Orig.). 1996. pap. 7.95 (0-9649784-0-7) Utopia Bks.

Allard, C. Kenneth, et al. Seminar on Intelligence, Command, & Control: Guest Presentations, Spring 1991. McLaughlin, John, ed. (Illus.). 208p. (Orig.). 1993. pap. text. write for info. (1-879716-03-8, I-93-1) Ctr Info Policy.

Allard, Dean C., Jr. Spencer Fullerton Baird & the U. S. Fish Commission: A Study in the History of American Science. Sterling, Keir B., ed. LC 77-81138. (Biologists & Their World Ser.). 1978. lib. bdg. 36.95 (0-405-10738-2) Ayer.

Allard, Denise. Greece. LC 96-2612. (Postcards from Ser.). 32p. (J). (gr. 1-4). 1997. lib. bdg. 21.40 (0-8172-4022-5) Raintree Steck-V.

— India. LC 95-52955. (Postcards from Ser.). (J). 1996. lib. bdg. 21.40 (0-8172-4027-6) Raintree Steck-V.

***Allard, Denise.** India. (Postcards from... Ser.). (Illus.). 32p. (J). (gr. 2-4). 2000. pap. 4.95 (0-8172-6222-9) Raintree Steck-V.

Allard, Denise. Israel. LC 96-2610. (Postcards from Ser.). (J). 1997. lib. bdg. 21.40 (0-8172-4020-9) Raintree Steck-V.

— Israel. (Postcards from... Ser.). 1998. pap. 4.95 (0-8172-6218-0) Raintree Steck-V.

— Kenya. (Postcards from... Ser.). 1998. pap. 4.95 (0-8172-6219-9) Raintree Steck-V.

— Peru. LC 96-1451. (Postcards From Ser.). (Illus.). (J). 1997. lib. bdg. 21.40 (0-8172-4028-4) Raintree Steck-V.

— Pictures of the Past, 4 bks. Incl. Egyptians. LC 96-46378. 32p. (J). (gr. 2 up). 1997. lib. bdg. 21.27 (0-8368-1714-1); Greeks. LC 96-44372. 32p. (J). (gr. 2 up). 1997. lib. bdg. 21.27 (0-8368-1715-X); Romans. LC 96-46230. (Illus.). 32p. (J). (gr. 2 up). 1997. lib. bdg. 21.27 (0-8368-1716-8); Vikings. LC 96-46231. (Illus.). 32p. (J). (gr. 2 up). 1997. lib. bdg. 21.27 (0-8368-1717-6); (J). Set lib. bdg. 85.07 (0-8368-1713-3) Gareth Stevens Inc.

— Poland. LC 95-53804. (Postcards From Ser.). (J). 1996. lib. bdg. 21.40 (0-8172-4025-X) Raintree Steck-V.

***Allard, Denise.** United States. (Postcards from... Ser.). (Illus.). 32p. (J). (gr. 2-4). 2000. pap. 4.95 (0-8172-6220-2) Raintree Steck-V.

Allard, Denise. Vietnam. LC 96-255. (Postcards From Ser.). (J). 1997. lib. bdg. 21.40 (0-8172-4023-3) Raintree Steck-V.

— Vietnam. (Postcards from... Ser.). 1998. pap. 4.95 (0-8172-6221-0) Raintree Steck-V.

Allard, Denise M. & Thomas, Robert C., eds. Encyclopedia of Associations: Association Periodicals, 3 vols., Set. 1987. 205.00 (0-8103-2082-7) Gale.

— Encyclopedia of Associations Vol. 3: Association Periodicals. 500p. 1988. 85.00 (0-8103-2063-0) Gale.

Allard, Denise M., jt. auth. see Thomas, Robert C.

Allard, Emmy. Die Angriffe Gegen Descartes und Malebranche Im Journal De Trevoux 1701-1715. (Abhandlungen Zur Philosophie und Ihrer Geschichte Ser.: No. 43). viii, 58p. 1985. reprint ed. 20.00 (3-487-07611-X) G Olms Pubs.

Allard, Fran, jt. ed. see Starkes, Janet L.

Allard, Harry. Bumps in the Night. LC 96-3687. (Illus.). 48p. (J). 1996. 13.95 (0-385-32282-8); pap. 3.99 (0-440-41286-2) Delacorte.

— Bumps in the Night. LC 96-3687. (J). 1996. 9.19 (0-606-11175-1, Pub. by Turtleback) Demco.

— The Cactus Flower Bakery. LC 90-36565. (Illus.). 32p. (J). (ps-3). 1991. lib. bdg. 14.89 (0-06-020047-2) HarpC Child Bks.

— Cactus Flower Bakery. 1993. 11.15 (0-606-05179-1, Pub. by Turtleback) Demco.

— The E's a Party at Mona's Tonight. (Illus.). 32p. 1997. pap. 5.99 (0-440-41366-4) Dell.

— It's Nice to Have Wolf Around the House. 1977. 12.50 (0-385-11300-5) Doubleday.

— It's So Nice to Have a Wolf Around the House. (Illus.). 32p. (J). (ps-2). 1997. pap. 4.99 (0-440-41353-2, Yearling) BDD Bks Young Read.

Allard, Harry. It's So Nice to Have a Wolf Around the House. (J). 1997. 10.19 (0-606-11512-9, Pub. by Turtleback) Demco.

Allard, Harry. Miss Nelson Has a Field Day. (Miss Nelson Ser.). (Illus.). 32p. (J). (ps-3). 1985. 15.00 (0-395-36690-9) HM.

— Miss Nelson Has a Field Day. (Miss Nelson Ser.). (Illus.). 32p. (J). (ps-3). 1988. pap. 5.95 (0-395-48654-8, Sandpiper) HM.

— Miss Nelson Has a Field Day. (Carry-Along Book & Cassette Favorites Ser.). (Illus.). 1p. (J). (ps-3). 1989. pap. 9.95 incl. audio (0-395-52138-6, 480440) HM.

— Miss Nelson Has a Field Day. (Miss Nelson Ser.). (Illus.). (J). (ps-3). 1985. 11.15 (0-606-04276-8, Pub. by Turtleback) Demco.

— Miss Nelson Is Back. (Carry-Along Book & Cassette Favorites Ser.). (Illus.). 1p. (J). (ps-6). 1988. pap. 9.95 incl. audio (0-395-48872-9, 480436) HM.

— Miss Nelson Is Back. (Miss Nelson Ser.). (Illus.). (J). (ps-3). 1982. 10.15 (0-606-02538-3, Pub. by Turtleback) Demco.

— Miss Nelson Is Missing! (Miss Nelson Ser.). (SPA., Illus.). 32p. (J). (ps-3). 1998. 16.00 (0-395-90009-3) HM.

— Miss Nelson Is Missing! (Miss Nelson Ser.). (Illus.). (J). (ps-3). 1977. 10.15 (0-606-04400-0, Pub. by Turtleback) Demco.

— Miss Nelson Is Missing! unabridged ed. (Carry-Along Book & Cassette Favorites Ser.). 1p. (J). (gr. 4-8). 1993. pap. 9.95 incl. audio (0-395-66498-5, 480429) HM.

— Senorita Nelson Ha Desaparecido! 1998. 11.15 (0-606-13558-8, Pub. by Turtleback) Demco.

— La Senorita Nelson Ha Desaparecido. Canetti, Yanitzia, tr.Tr. of Miss Nelson is Missing. (SPA., Illus.). 32p. (J). (ps-3). 1998. pap. 5.95 (0-395-90008-5) HM.

— The Stupids Die. (J). 1981. 11.15 (0-606-00851-9, Pub. by Turtleback) Demco.

— The Stupids Have a Ball, 001. LC 77-27660. (Illus.). 32p. (J). (ps-3). 1978. 18.00 (0-395-26497-9) HM.

— The Stupids Have a Ball, 001. LC 77-27660. (Illus.). 32p. (J). (ps-3). 1984. pap. 5.95 (0-395-36169-9) HM.

— Stupids Have a Ball. (J). 1978. 11.15 (0-606-03207-X, Pub. by Turtleback) Demco.

— The Stupids Step Out, 001. LC 73-21698. (Illus.). 32p. (J). (gr. k-3). 1974. 16.00 (0-395-18513-0) HM.

— The Stupids Step Out, 001. LC 73-21698. (Illus.). 32p. (J). (ps-3). 1977. pap. 5.95 (0-395-25377-2) HM.

— The Stupids Step Out. (Book & Cassette Favorites Ser.). (Illus.). 1p. (J). (ps-3). 1989. pap. 9.95 incl. audio (0-395-52139-4, 490926, Clarion Bks) HM.

— Stupids Step Out. 1974. 11.15 (0-606-02283-X, Pub. by Turtleback) Demco.

— The Stupids Take Off. (Illus.). 32p. (J). (gr. k-3). 1993. pap. 5.95 (0-395-65743-1) HM.

— Stupids Take Off. (J). 1989. 11.15 (0-606-05628-9, Pub. by Turtleback) Demco.

— There's a Party at Mona's Tonight. 1997. pap. 5.99 (0-440-91191-5) Dell.

— There's a Party at Mona's Tonight. 1997. 11.19 (0-606-11976-0, Pub. by Turtleback) Demco.

Allard, Harry & Marshall, James. Miss Nelson Is Back. (Illus.). 32p. (J). (ps-3). 1982. 15.00 (0-395-32956-6) HM.

— Miss Nelson Is Back. (Miss Nelson Ser.). (Illus.). 32p. (J). (ps-3). 1986. pap. 5.95 (0-395-41668-X) HM.

— Miss Nelson Is Missing!, 001. (Miss Nelson Ser.). (Illus.). 32p. (J). (ps-3). 1977. 16.00 (0-395-25296-2) HM.

— Miss Nelson Is Missing!, 001. LC 76-55918. (Miss Nelson Ser.). (Illus.). 32p. (J). (ps-3). 1985. pap. 5.95 (0-395-40146-1) HM.

— The Stupids Die, 001. (Illus.). 32p. (J). (gr. k-3). 1981. 14.95 (0-395-30347-8) HM.

— The Stupids Die, 001. LC 80-27103. (Illus.). 32p. (J). (ps-3). 1985. pap. 5.95 (0-395-38364-1) HM.

— The Stupids Take Off. (Illus.). 32p. (J). (gr. k-3). 1989. 14.95 (0-395-50068-0) HM.

Allard, J. F. Propagation of Sound in Porous Media: Modelling Sound Absorbing Materials. (Illus.). 300p. (C). (gr. 13). 1994. text 94.95 (0-412-53470-3, Chap & Hall NY) Chapman & Hall.

Allard, James W., ed. see Bradley, F. H.

Allard, Jean-Louis. Le Mathematisme de Descartes. LC 65-53234. (Publications Seriees de l'Universite d'Ottawa: Vol. 68). (FRE.). 232p. 1963. reprint ed. pap. 72.00 (0-608-02188-1, 206285700003) Bks Demand.

Allard, K., tr. see Pape, Hansgeorg.

Allard, Kenneth. Command, Control & the Common Defense. 377p. 1996. per. 18.00 (0-16-053377-5) USGPO.

— Somalia Operations: Lessons Learned. (Illus.). 113p. 1997. reprint ed. pap. text 25.00 (0-7881-4662-9) DIANE Pub.

Allard, Kent. The Mad Chopper. 320p. 1998. pap. 5.99 (0-7860-0557-2, Pinncle Kensgtn) Kensgtn Pub Corp.

An Asterisk (*) at the beginning of an entry indicates that the title is appearing for the first time.

Allard, Lloyd. Lessons & Adventures in Sales. LC 93-8933. 296p. 1994. 17.95 (*1-56554-001-8*) Pelican.

— Selling. LC 91-12319. (Illus.). 176p. 1991. 16.95 (*0-88289-849-3*) Pelican.

— The Ultimate Selling Guide. 1999. pap. 12.95 (*1-56554-423-4*) Pelican.

Allard, Lucile E. A Study of the Leisure Activities of Certain Elementary School Teachers of Long Island. LC 70-176510. (Columbia University. Teachers College. Contributions to Education Ser.: No. 779). reprint ed. 37.50 (*0-404-55779-1*) AMS Pr.

Allard, M. June, jt. auth. see Harvey, Carol P.

Allard, Matsuo. Bird Day Afternoon. 32p. 1978. pap. 3.50 (*0-913719-06-4*, High Coo Pr) Brooks Books.

***Allard, Meredith.** My Brother's Battle: A Novel. LC 00-103987. 359p. 2000. 25.00 (*0-7388-2120-9*); pap. 18.00 (*0-7388-2121-7*) Xlibris Corp.

Allard, Michel, et al. Jeanne Calment: From Van Gogh's Time to Ours, 122 Extraordinary Years. large type ed. LC 98-53489. 1999. 25.95 (*0-7862-1777-4*) Thorndike Pr.

— 120 Years of Jeanne Calmunt. Coupland, Beth, tr. LC 98-31252. 175p. 1998. text 22.95 (*0-7167-3251-3*) W H Freeman.

Allard, Noel E. Speed: The Biography of Charles W. Holman. 2nd ed. LC 76-44068. (Illus.). 94p. 1986. reprint ed. pap. 13.95 (*0-911139-01-X*) Flying Bks.

Allard, Noel E. & Sandvick, Gerald N. Minnesota Aviation History, 1857-1945. (Illus.). 296p. 1993. 39.95 (*0-9637807-0-0*); pap. 29.95 (*0-9637807-1-9*) MAHB Pubng.

Allard, P., et al. Three-Dimensional Analysis of Human Locomotion. LC 97-11505. 424p. 1998. 169.95 (*0-471-96949-4*) Wiley.

Allard, Paul, et al, eds. Three-Dimensional Analysis of Human Movement. LC 93-37710. (Illus.). 384p. 1994. text 48.00 (*0-87322-623-2*, BALL0623) Human Kinetics.

Allard, William. Time at the Lake: A Minnesota Album. LC 97-21099. (Illus.). 1997. pap. 19.95 (*1-57025-133-9*) Pfeifer-Hamilton.

Allard, William A., photos by. A Time We Knew: Images of Yesterday in the Basque Homeland. LC 90-12259. (Basque Ser.). (Illus.). 120p. 1990. 34.95 (*0-87417-157-1*) U of Nev Pr.

Allard, William K. & Almgren, Frederick J., Jr., eds. Geometric Measure Theory & the Calculus of Variations. LC 85-18641. (Proceedings of Symposia in Pure Mathematics Ser.: Vol. 44). 464p. 1986. text 75.00 (*0-8218-1470-2*, PSPUM/44) Am Math.

Allardice, Bruce S. More Generals in Gray. LC 94-43870. (Illus.). 317p. 1995. 29.95 (*0-8071-1967-9*) La State U Pr.

Allardice, Pamela. A Fresh Look at Figs: Traditions, Myths & Mouth-Watering Recipes. (Illus.). 103p. 1994. 20.95 (*0-85572-225-8*, Pub. by Hill Content Pubng) Seven Hills Bk.

— Lavender. (Illus.). 86p. 1994. 18.95 (*0-85572-197-9*, Pub. by Hill Content Pubng) Seven Hills Bk.

— Myths, Gods & Fantasy: A Dictionary. 200p. (Orig.). 1991. lib. bdg. 40.00 (*0-87436-660-7*) ABC-CLIO.

***Allardice, Pamela.** Who Am I? (Illus.). 112p. 1999. 9.98 (*0-7651-1683-9*) Smithmark.

Allardice, R. W. A Simplified Dictionary of Modern Samoan. 228p. 1986. pap. text 29.00 (*0-908597-02-9*) UH Pr.

Allardt, Linda. The Names of the Survivors. LC 79-25878. 49p. 1979. 4.00 (*0-87886-108-4*, Greenfld Rev Pr) Greenfld Rev Lit.

Allardt, Linda, ed. see Emerson, Ralph Waldo.

Allardyce, Alexander, ed. see Ramsay, John.

Allardyce, Gilbert, jt. auth. see Berk, Eta F.

Allardyce, J., ed. Burnett: The Family of Burnett of Leys, with Collateral Branches. xxii, 367p. 1992. reprint ed. pap. 61.00 (*0-8328-2310-4*); reprint ed. lib. bdg. 71.00 (*0-8328-2309-0*) Higginson Bk Co.

Allardyce, Paula. Southern Folly. large type ed. 382p. 1982. 27.99 (*0-7089-0831-4*) Ulverscroft.

Allardyce, Robert, jt. auth. see Gollin, James.

Allars, M. Introduction to Australian Administrative Law. 366p. 1990. pap. 64.00 (*0-409-49547-6*, Austral, MICHIE) LEXIS Pub.

Allars, M. N. Administrative Law in Australia: Cases & Materials. 800p. 1996. pap. write for info. (*0-409-30245-7*, MICHIE) LEXIS Pub.

Allasio, John. National Competency Mathematics: A Worktext. rev. ed. 302p. 1994. pap. 10.95 (*0-937820-69-5*) WestSea Pub.

— National Competency Mathematics Answer Key. rev. ed. 20p. 1994. pap. 3.50 (*0-937820-70-9*) WestSea Pub.

Allasio, John, et al. RCT Mathematics Workbook. 2nd rev. ed. 182p. (YA). (gr. 8-12). 1995. pap. 9.50 (*0-937820-71-7*) WestSea Pub.

— RCT Mathematics Workbook Answer Key. 2nd rev. ed. 20p. (YA). (gr. 8-12). 1995. pap., teacher ed. 3.25 (*0-937820-72-5*) WestSea Pub.

— Sequential Math 1: A Workbook. 150p. (YA). (gr. 8-12). 1997. pap., wbk. ed. 9.50 (*0-937820-73-3*) WestSea Pub.

— Sequential Math 1 Answer Key. 20p. 1997. pap., teacher ed. 3.25 (*0-937820-74-1*) WestSea Pub.

— Sequential Math 3: A Workbook. 156p. (YA). (gr. 10-12). 1993. pap. 9.50 (*0-937820-67-9*) WestSea Pub.

— Sequential Math 3 Answer Key. 20p. (YA). (gr. 10-12). 1993. pap., teacher ed. 3.25 (*0-937820-68-7*) WestSea Pub.

— Sequential Math 2: A Workbook. 141p. (YA). (gr. 9-12). 1990. pap. 9.50 (*0-937820-65-2*) WestSea Pub.

— Sequential Math 2 Answer Key. 20p. (YA). (gr. 9-12). 1990. pap., teacher ed. 3.25 (*0-937820-66-0*) WestSea Pub.

Allason-Jones, L. & McKay, B. Coventina's Well. 112p. 1985. 27.00 (*0-946897-05-0*) David Brown.

***Allason, Rupert & Peake, Hayden B.** Encyclopedia of Treason & Treachery: Famous Cases of the Guilty & the Innocent. 2001. lib. bdg. 60.00 (*1-57607-113-8*) ABC-CLIO.

Allaun, Frank. Spreading the News: A Guide to Media Reform. 112p. 1988. 42.50 (*0-85124-488-2*, Pub. by Spkesman); pap. 21.50 (*0-85124-498-X*, Pub. by Spkesman) Coronet Bks.

Allaway, John. Exploring Human Behavior in Groups. 12p. 1971. pap. 6.00 (*0-9500029-4-1*, Pub. by Octagon Pr) ISHK.

Allbaugh. Plan Care Special Practice: Ambulatory Care. (Professional Reference - Nursing Ser.). 1994. pap. 20.95 (*0-8273-6121-1*) Delmar.

Allbaugh, Bonnie. Medical Nursing. Gettrust, Kathy V., ed. 620p. (C). 1993. pap. 33.50 (*0-8273-5947-0*) Delmar.

Allbaugh, Leland G. Crete: A Case Study of an Underdeveloped Area. LC 52-5849. 618p. reprint ed. pap. 191.60 (*0-608-30458-1*, 200002900025) Bks Demand.

Allbery, Debra. Walking Distance. LC 91-50111. (Poetry Ser.). 64p. (C). 1991. pap. 10.95 (*0-8229-5458-3*); text 19.95 (*0-8229-3687-9*) U of Pittsburgh Pr.

Allbeury, Ted. Aid & Comfort. large type ed. LC 98-17592. 337p. 1998. 25.95 (*0-7838-0175-0*) Mac Lib Ref.

— All Our Tomorrows. 304p. 1990. mass mkt. 4.95 (*0-445-40914-2*, Mysterious Paperbk) Warner Bks.

Allbeury, Ted. Berlin Exchange. 240p. 26.00 (*0-7278-5536-0*) Severn Hse.

Allbeury, Ted. A Choice of Enemies. large type ed. 384p. 1987. 16.95 (*0-7089-1567-1*) Ulverscroft.

— Deep Purple. 1990. 18.95 (*0-89296-401-4*) Mysterious Pr.

— Deep Purple. 1991. mass mkt. 4.95 (*0-445-40861-8*, Pub. by Warner Bks) Little.

— The Girl from Addis. 192p. 1995. reprint ed. 20.00 (*0-7278-4742-2*) Severn Hse.

— The Judas Factor. LC 84-172670. 201 p. 1984. write for info. (*0-450-06065-9*) New Eng Lib.

— The Judas Factor. 1989. mass mkt. 4.50 (*0-445-40691-7*, Mysterious Paperbk) Warner Bks.

— The Lantern Network. 208p. 1989. 17.95 (*0-89296-185-6*, Pub. by Mysterious Pr) Little.

— The Long Run. large type ed. LC 96-48664. 1997. lib. bdg. 22.95 (*0-7838-8041-3*, G K Hall Lrg Type) Mac Lib Ref.

— Mission Berlin. 1986. 15.95 (*0-8027-0892-7*) Walker & Co.

— Other Kinds of Treason. large type ed. (Adventure Suspense Ser.). 336p. 1992. 27.99 (*0-7089-8649-8*, Charnwood) Ulverscroft.

— Pay Any Price. large type ed. 1984. 13.95 (*0-7089-8204-2*, Charnwood) Ulverscroft.

***Allbeury, Ted.** The Reckoning. large type ed. LC 00-37439. 406p. 2000. 26.95 (*0-7862-2664-1*) Thorndike Pr.

Allbeury, Ted. The Seeds of Treason. 272p. 1987. 15.45 (*0-89296-181-3*, Pub. by Mysterious Pr) Little.

— The Seeds of Treason. 1988. mass mkt. 3.95 (*0-445-40709-3*, Mysterious Paperbk) Warner Bks.

***Allbeury, Ted.** Shadow of a Doubt. LC 99-12934. 1999. 25.95 (*0-7862-1906-8*) Thorndike Pr.

Allbeury, Ted. The Stalking Angel. LC 88-40065. 208p. 1988. 17.45 (*0-89296-184-8*, Pub. by Mysterious Pr) Little.

— A Time Without Shadows. 304p. 1992. mass mkt. 4.99 (*0-446-40090-4*, Pub. by Warner Bks) Little.

— A Time Without Shadows. large type ed. LC 91-8486. 516p. 1991. reprint ed. lib. bdg. 21.95 (*1-56054-158-X*) Thorndike Pr.

Allbright, Charles. Gravely the Mules Stopped Dancing. 176p. 1988. pap. 8.95 (*0-87483-062-1*) August Hse.

Allbritton, Cliff. Dare to Win! How to Live the American Dream! McGuirk, Stephanie, ed. LC 92-72950. (Illus.). 176p. 1992. 17.95 (*1-881834-00-X*) Atlas Crown.

— Personal Riches for Today's Singles. McGuirk, Stephanie, ed. (Orig.). 1992. pap. 6.95 (*1-881834-01-8*) Atlas Crown.

Allbut, R. London Rambles with Charles Dickens. LC 74-1229. (Studies in Dickens: No. 52). 1974. lib. bdg. 75.00 (*0-8383-1779-0*) M S G Haskell Hse.

— Rambles in Dickens' Land. LC 76-52947. (Studies in Dickens: No. 52). 1977. lib. bdg. 75.00 (*0-8383-2139-9*) M S G Haskell Hse.

Allbutt, T. C. Greek Medicine in Rome. LC 69-13230. 1972. reprint ed. 33.95 (*0-405-08201-0*, Pub. by Blom Pubns) Ayer.

Allbutt, Thomas C. The Historical Relations of Medicine & Surgery to the End of the 16th Century. LC 75-23672. reprint ed. 36.00 (*0-404-13225-1*) AMS Pr.

— Science & Medieval Thought. LC 75-23673. reprint ed. 29.50 (*0-404-13226-X*) AMS Pr.

Allcard, Clare. The Intricate Art of Living Afloat. (Illus.). 1990. 34.95 (*0-393-03334-1*) Norton.

— The Intricate Art of Living Afloat. (Illus.). 304p. (C). 1997. pap. 19.95 (*0-393-31596-7*) Norton.

Allchin, A. M. N. F. S. Grundtvig: An Introduction to His Life & Work. LC 98-107160. 336p. 1997. 39.95 (*87-7288-656-0*, Pub. by Aarhus Univ Pr) David Brown.

Allchin, A. M. & De Waal, Esther, eds. Daily Readings from Prayers & Praises in the Celtic Tradition. 96p. 1987. pap. 4.95 (*0-87243-151-7*) Templegate.

Allchin, A. M., ed. see St. Isaac of Syria.

Allchin, Bridget. South Asian Studies, Vol. 8. annuals (Illus.). 183p. 1992. pap. 45.00 (*0-614-21881-0*) David Brown.

Allchin, Bridget, ed. Living Traditions: Studies in the Ethnoarchaeology of South Asia. LC 94-907183. (Illus.). 391p. 1995. 49.50 (*81-204-0901-9*, Pub. by Oxbow Bks) David Brown.

— South Asian Studies, Vol. 2. annuals (Illus.). 86p. 1986. pap. 36.00 (*0-614-21887-X*) David Brown.

— South Asian Studies, Vol. 3. annuals (Illus.). 94p. 1987. pap. 36.00 (*0-614-21886-1*) David Brown.

— South Asian Studies, Vol. 4. annuals (Illus.). 147p. 1988. pap. 36.00 (*0-614-21885-3*) David Brown.

— South Asian Studies, Vol. 5. annuals (Illus.). 168p. 1989. pap. 36.00 (*0-614-21884-5*) David Brown.

— South Asian Studies, Vol. 6. annuals (Illus.). 265p. 1990. pap. 45.00 (*0-614-21883-7*) David Brown.

— South Asian Studies, Vol. 7. annuals (Illus.). 183p. 1991. pap. 45.00 (*0-614-21882-9*) David Brown.

— South Asian Studies, Vol. 9. annuals (Illus.). 179p. 1993. pap. 45.00 (*0-614-21880-2*) David Brown.

— South Asian Studies, Vol. 10. annuals (Illus.). 204p. 1994. pap. 45.00 (*0-614-21879-9*) David Brown.

— South Asian Studies, Vol. 11. annuals (Illus.). 187p. 1995. pap. 54.00 (*0-614-21878-0*) David Brown.

Allchin, Bridget & Allchin, Raymond. The Rise of Civilization in India & Pakistan. LC 82-1262. (World Archaeology Ser.). (Illus.). 392p. 1982. pap. text 42.95 (*0-521-28550-X*) Cambridge U Pr.

Allchin, Bridget, jt. ed. see Allchin, Raymond.

Allchin, F. R. & Chakrabarti, Dilip K., eds. A Source-Book of Indian Archaeology Vol. 2: Settlements, Technology & Trade. (C). 1997. 98.50 (*81-215-0465-1*, Pub. by M Manoharial) Coronet Bks.

Allchin, Raymond. The Archaeology of Early Historic South Asia: The Emergence of Cities & States. (Illus.). 389p. (C). 1995. text 80.00 (*0-521-37547-9*); pap. text 32.95 (*0-521-37695-5*) Cambridge U Pr.

Allchin, Raymond & Allchin, Bridget, eds. South Asian Archaeology, '95, 2 vols. LC 99-934371. 1995. 95.00 (*1-886106-82-7*) Science Pubs.

Allchin, Raymond, jt. auth. see Allchin, Bridget.

***Allcock, Debra.** Time Management. 96p. 2000. pap. 12.95 (*1-85835-539-7*, Pub. by Stylus Pub VA) LPC InBook.

Allcock, Debra. Your First Management Job: A Beginner's Guide. 1998. pap. 12.95 (*1-85835-592-3*, Indust Soc) Stylus Pub VA.

Allcock, Harry & Lampe, Frederick. Contemporary Polymer Chemistry. 2nd ed. LC 89-23092. 624p. 1990. 105.00 (*0-13-170549-0*) P-H.

Allcock, Harry R., ed. Inorganic Syntheses, Vol. 25. 300p. 1989. 110.00 (*0-471-61874-8*) Wiley.

***Allcock, John B.** Explaining Yugoslavia. LC 99-49369. 2000. pap. write for info. (*0-231-12055-9*) Col U Pr.

Allcock, John B., et al, eds. Yugoslavia in Transition: Choices & Constraints. 470p. 1992. 74.00 (*0-85496-609-9*) Berg Pubs.

***Allcock, John B. & Young, Antonia, eds.** Black Lambs & Grey Falcons: Women Travellers in the Balkans. (Illus.). 240p. 2000. 19.95 (*1-57181-807-3*) Berghahn Bks.

Allcock, John B. & Young, Antonia, eds. Black Lambs & Grey Falcons: Women Travellers in the Balkans. 2nd rev. ed. LC 99-34760. 224p. 1999. pap. 19.95 (*1-57181-744-1*) Berghahn Bks.

Allcock, John B., et al. Conflict in the Former Yugoslavia: An Encyclopedia. LC 98-41772. (Roots of Modern Conflict Ser.). 448p. 1998. lib. bdg. 65.00 (*0-87436-935-5*) ABC-CLIO.

***Allcock, Sheila, ed.** Information Sources in Development Studies. 300p. 1999. 75.00 (*1-85739-276-0*) Bowker-Saur.

***Allcorn, S. Robert.** Discovery. LC 99-177751. (New Jersey Practice Ser.). xxxix, 684 p. 1998. write for info. (*0-314-23851-4*) West Pub.

Allcorn, Seth. Anger in the Workplace: Understanding the Causes of Aggression & Violence. LC 94-16993. 152p. 1994. 57.95 (*0-89930-897-X*, Quorum Bks) Greenwood.

— Codependency in the Workplace: A Guide for Employee Assistance & Human Resource Professionals. LC 91-39807. 224p. 1992. 49.95 (*0-89930-644-6*, ACD, Quorum Bks) Greenwood.

— Working Together: Building Integrated Healthcare Organizations Through Improved Executive-Physician Collaboration. 225p. 1995. text 45.00 (*1-55738-614-5*, Irwn Prfssnl) McGraw-Hill Prof.

— Workplace Superstars in Resistant Organizations. LC 91-186. 216p. 1991. 55.00 (*0-89930-657-8*, AWE, Quorum Bks) Greenwood.

Allcorn, Seth & Diamond, Michael A. Managing People During Stressful Times: The Psychologically Defensive Workplace. LC 96-17925. 184p. 1997. 59.95 (*1-56720-082-6*, Quorum Bks) Greenwood.

Allcott, John V. The Campus at Chapel Hill: Two Hundred Years of Architecture. unabridged ed. (Illus.). xii, 108p. 1993. reprint ed. 17.95 (*0-940715-00-7*) Chapel Hill Hist.

— UNC Coloring Book. unabridged ed. (Illus.). 16p. (Orig.). (J). (gr. 1-3). 1993. pap. 2.00 (*0-940715-07-4*) Chapel Hill Hist.

Allcroft, Arthur. A History of Sicily, Four Hundred Ninety-One to Two Hundred Eighty-Nine B.C. 1977. lib. bdg. 250.00 (*0-8490-1986-9*) Gordon Pr.

***Allcroft, Britt.** A Better View for Gordon. 24p. (J). 2001. mass mkt. 3.25 (*0-375-81157-5*, Pub. by Random Bks Yng Read) Random.

— Magic Adventures of Mumfie. (Illus.). (J). 2000. 5.99 (*0-375-80097-2*, Pub. by Random Bks Yng Read) Random.

Allday, Christopher & Puppe, Volker. Cohomological Methods in Transformation Groups. (Studies in Advanced Mathematics: No. 32). 482p. (C). 1993. text 85.00 (*0-521-35022-0*) Cambridge U Pr.

Allday, J. Quarks, Leptons & the Big Bang. LC 97-49110. 1997. 98.00 (*0-7503-0461-8*) IOP Pub.

***Allday, Jonathan.** Apollo in Perspective: Spaceflight Then & Now. LC 99-46328. (Illus.). 320p. 1999. pap. 28.00 (*0-7503-0645-9*) IOP Pub.

Allday, Jonathan. Quarks, Leptons & the Big Bang. LC 97-49110. (Illus.). 315p. 1997. pap. 29.50 (*0-7503-0462-6*) IOP Pub.

Allday, R. K. An Agenda Discussed & in Focus. (C). 1989. text 30.00 (*0-902662-10-4*, Pub. by R K Pubns) St Mut.

— Manifesto for the Nation. (C). 1989. text 30.00 (*0-902662-00-7*, Pub. by R K Pubns) St Mut.

Alldis, Dominic. Classical Approach to Jazz Piano: Exploring Harmony. 240p. 2000. otabind 19.95 (*0-634-00177-9*) H Leonard.

Alldredge, Antoine D. Ssri Appl 6 Sigma Concpt. LC 92-25880. (Six Sigma Research Institute Ser.). 1992. pap. text 18.95 (*0-201-63435-X*) Addison-Wesley.

Alldridge, J. C. Ilse Aichinger. LC 74-92613. (Modern German Authors Texts & Contexts Ser.: Vol. 2). 1969. 13.95 (*0-8023-1235-7*) Dufour.

***Alldridge, Peter.** Relocating Criminal Law. LC 99-46649. (Applied Legal Philosophy Ser.). 272p. 2000. text 74.95 (*1-85521-268-4*, Pub. by Ashgate Pub) Ashgate Pub Co.

Alldridge, Peter, jt. auth. see Harpwood, Vivienne.

Alldrin, Loren. Home Studio Guide to Microphones. LC 97-73716. 1998. pap. 34.95 (*0-918371-22-8*, MixBooks) Intertec Pub.

Alldritt, Keith. Modernism in the Second World War: The Later Poetry of Ezra Pound, T. S. Eliot, Basil Bunting & Hugh MacDiarmid. 135p. (C). 1989. text 20.50 (*0-8204-0865-4*) P Lang Pubng.

Alle-Corliss, Lupe. Groupwork in Today's Agency Settings: A Lifespan Approach. 2002. 30.00 (*0-534-52769-8*) Wadsworth Pub.

Alle-Corliss, Lupe & Alle-Corliss, Randy. Human Service Agencies: An Orientation to Field Work. LC 97-15086. 271p. 1997. mass mkt. 45.95 (*0-534-34928-5*) Brooks-Cole.

Alle-Corliss, Randy, jt. auth. see Alle-Corliss, Lupe.

Alle, Sejon, ed. see Jones, Herbert L., Jr. & Patterson, Ella M.

Alle, Sejon, ed. see Patterson, Ella.

Alle, Sejon, ed. see Patterson, Ella M.

Alle, Sekpm, ed. see Patterson, Ella M.

Allebach, Jan P. Selected Papers on Halftone Imaging. LC 98-48545. (Milestone Ser.). 736p. 1999. 118.00 (*0-8194-3137-0*) SPIE.

Allebeck, Peter & Jansson, Bengt, eds. Ethics in Medicine: Individual Integrity vs. Demands of Society. LC 90-8229. (Karolinska Institute Nobel Conference Ser.). 240p. 1990. reprint ed. pap. 74.40 (*0-608-04664-7*, 206538500004) Bks Demand.

Allecorliss. Working in Human Service Agencies Practice Field. LC 98-30151. (Social Work Ser.). 469p. 1998. mass mkt. 43.95 (*0-534-34811-4*) Wadsworth Pub.

***Allee, Ann.** To Take a Stand: Alaskan Wilderness Adventure. (Illus.). 365p. 2000. pap. 16.95 (*0-929526-42-2*) Double B Pubns.

Allee, David J., et al, eds. Unified River Basin Management, Stage 2: Proceedings of a Symposium Held in Atlanta, Georgia, October 4-8, 1981. LC 82-72088. (Illus.). 510p. reprint ed. pap. 158.10 (*0-8357-3162-6*, 203942500012) Bks Demand.

Allee, Ernie, contrib. by. Your Favorite Hymns for Guitar, No. 1. 32p. 1964. 9.99 (*0-8341-9294-2*, MB-233) Lillenas.

Allee, John S. Product Liability. 550p. 1984. ring bd. 90.00 (*0-318-20280-8*, 00587) NY Law Pub.

Allee, Judith Waite, jt. auth. see Morgan, Melissa L.

Allee, Marjorie H. Jane's Island. (Illus.). 236p. (J). (gr. 6 up). 1988. reprint ed. 13.95 (*0-9611374-2-8*) Woods Hole Hist.

Allee, Mark A. Law & Local Society in Late Imperial China: Northern Taiwan in the Nineteenth Century. LC 94-30283. xii, 348p. 1994. 45.00 (*0-8047-2272-2*) Stanford U Pr.

Allee, Verna. The Knowledge Evolution: Expanding Organizational Intelligence. LC 96-48561. 224p. 1997. pap. 17.95 (*0-7506-9842-X*) Buttrwrth-Heinemann.

Allee, Warder C. Animal Aggregations, A Study in General Sociology. LC 75-41007. reprint ed. 37.50 (*0-404-14501-9*) AMS Pr.

— The Social Life of Animals. LC 75-41008. reprint ed. 52.50 (*0-404-14639-2*) AMS Pr.

Allegar, Daniel E., ed. see Southern Conference on Gerontology Staff.

Alleger, Daniel E., ed. Fertile Lands of Friendship: The Florida-Costa Rican Experiment in International Agricultural Cooperation. LC 62-20773. (Illus.). 326p. reprint ed. pap. 101.10 (*0-7837-5020-X*, 204468800004) Bks Demand.

Allegheny Trails Council, Boy Scouts of America & National Flag Foundation Staff. Broad Stripes & Bright Stars. LC 73-95742. (Illus.). 61p. 1996. reprint ed. 4.95 (*0-934021-05-8*) Natl Flag Foun.

Allego, Antonio. Telling Triple: Essays, Poems, & Stories. 136p. (Orig.). 1986. pap. 7.50 (*971-10-0281-7*, Pub. by New Day Pub) Cellar.

Allego, Antonio M. This Time Yesterday. 109p. (Orig.). 1983. pap. 7.50 (*971-10-0152-7*, Pub. by New Day Pub) Cellar.

Allego, Antonio M., jt. auth. see Reyes, Gracianus R.

Allegood, Thomas. The Handbook for Single Parents. 100p. (Orig.). 1997. pap. 9.95 (*1-57502-418-7*, PO1285) Morris Pubng.

***Allegra, Antonia.** Napa Valley: The Ultimate Winery Guide. 3rd rev. ed. LC 99-86937. (Illus.). 120p. 2000. pap. 19.95 (*0-8118-2858-1*) Chronicle Bks.

Allegra, Antonia & Gillette, Richard. Napa Valley: The Ultimate Winery Guide. LC 96-3063. 1997. pap. 19.95 (*0-8118-1544-7*) Chronicle Bks.

Allegra, C., et al, eds. Vasomotion & Flow Motion. (Progress in Applied Microcirculation Ser.: Vol. 20). (Illus.). viii, 88p. 1993. 85.25 (*3-8055-5750-7*) S Karger.

A

A

Allegra, C. & Bollinger, A., eds. Microvascular Therapeutic Advances in Venous Disorders Vol. 15, Suppl. 1: Journal: Int. J. Microcirc., 1995. (Journal Ser.: Vol. 15, Suppl. 1, 1995). (Illus.). iv, 56p. 1995. pap. 26.25 (3-8055-6253-5) S Karger.

Allegra, C. & Carlizza, A., eds. Proceedings Eighteenth European Conference Microcirculation, ESM, Rome, September 1994 No. 14, Supplement 1, No. 14. (International Journal of Microcirculation Ser.). (Illus.). iv, 262p. 1994. pap. 77.50 (3-8055-6035-4) S Karger.

Allegra, C. J., et al. Glossarium-Alternative Energy Sources, 2 vols. (DAN, DUT, ENG, FRE & GER.). 1218p. 1983. pap. 45.00 (0-8288-0709-4, M9560) Fr & Eur.

***Allegra, Donna.** Witness to the League of Blond Hip-Hop Dancers: A Novella & Short Stories. 248p. 2000. pap. 12.95 (1-55583-550-3, Pub. by Alyson Pubns) Consort Bk Sales.

Allegra, G. & Nahkosteen, J. A., eds. New Aspects in the Treatment of Pulmonary & Upper Airways Diseases. (Journal: Respiration: Vol. 51, Suppl. 1, 1987). iv, 68p. 1987. pap. 22.75 (3-8055-4592-4) S Karger.

Allegra, L. & Blasi, F. Chlamydia Pneumoniae Infection. 100p. 1995. pap. 46.00 (0-387-75007-X) Spr-Verlag.

***Allegra, L. & Blasi, F.** Mechanisms & Management of COPD Exacerbations. 100p. 1999. pap. 42.00 (88-470-0066-1, Pub. by Spr-Verlag) Spr-Verlag.

***Allegra, L. & Dal Negro, R.** Pneumological Aspects of Gastroesophageal Reflux. LC 99-24353. 190p. 1999. 89.00 (88-470-0049-1, Pub. by Spr-Verlag) Spr-Verlag.

Allegra, Luigi, et al, eds. Methods in Astmology. LC 93-14963. 1993. 174.00 (0-387-56428-4) Spr-Verlag.

Allegra, Luigi & Blasi, F. Chlamydia Pneumoniae Infection: The Lung & the Heart. LC 98-54981. 190p. 1999. pap. 99.00 (88-470-0047-5) Spr-Verlag.

Allegra, Luigi & Braga, Pier C., eds. Bronchial Mucology & Related Diseases. LC 90-9103. (Bronchial Mucology Ser.). (Illus.). 224p. 1990. reprint ed. pap. 69.50 (0-608-05831-9, 205979600007) Bks Demand.

Allegra, Luigi & Cogo, Annalisa, eds. High Altitude & Lung. (Respiration Ser.: Vol. 64, No. 6, 1997). (Illus.). 68p. 1997. pap. 50.50 (3-8055-6609-3) S Karger.

Allegra, Luigi, jt. ed. see Braga, Pier C.

Allegre, Claude. The Behavior of the Earth: Continental & Seafloor Mobility. LC 87-31102. (Illus.). 320p. 1988. 47.50 (0-674-06457-7) HUP.

— The Behavior of the Earth: Continental & Seafloor Mobility. (Illus.). 320p. 1990. pap. 20.50 (0-674-06458-5) HUP.

— From Stone to Star: A View of Modern Geology. Van Dam, Deborah K., tr. 248p. 1994. pap. 20.50 (0-674-83867-X) HUP.

— From Stone to Star: The Discovery of Interplanetary Geology. Van Dam, Deborah K., tr. from FRE. (Illus.). 288p. (C). 1992. 45.00 (0-674-83866-1) HUP.

Allegre-Papadacci, Marie C. Point de Croix. (FRE., Illus.). 192p. 1998. 34.00 (2-84229-045-3, DE19, Pub. by C Armand) Lacis Pubns.

Allegretti, Enzo V. Understanding & Using Symphony. (Microcomputing Ser.). 226p. (C). 1987. mass mkt. 25.50 (0-314-34640-6) West Pub.

— Understanding & Using Symphony. (Microcomputing Ser.). 226p. (C). 1987. pap. text, teacher ed. write for info. (0-314-34653-8) West Pub.

Allegretti, Joseph G. The Lawyer's Calling: Christian Faith & Legal Practice. 192p. 1996. pap. 12.95 (0-8091-3651-1, 3651-1) Paulist Pr.

***Allegretti, Joseph G.** Loving Your Job, Finding Your Passion: Work & the Spiritual Life. LC 99-87529. 208p. 2000. pap. 10.95 (0-8091-3939-1) Paulist Pr.

Allegretto, Michael. Blood Relative: A Jacob Lomax Mystery. 224p. 1992. text 20.00 (0-684-19409-0, Scribners Ref) Mac Lib Ref.

— Blood Stone. 272p. 1990. reprint ed. pap. 3.50 (0-380-71119-2, Avon Bks) Morrow Avon.

— The Dead of Winter. 256p. 1991. pap. 3.50 (0-380-71120-6, Avon Bks) Morrow Avon.

— The Night of Reunion. 288p. 1991. mass mkt. 4.99 (0-380-71442-6, Avon Bks) Morrow Avon.

— The Suitor: A Novel of Suspense. 256p. 1993. 19.00 (0-671-73644-2) S&S Trade.

Allegri. Callas by Callas. LC 98-14769. 168p. 1998. 35.00 (0-7893-0135-0, Pub. by Universe) St Martin.

Allegri, Francesca. Educational Services in Health Sciences Libraries. (Current Practice in Health Science Librarianship Ser.: Vol. 2). 196p. (C). 1995. 29.50 (0-8108-3004-3) Scarecrow.

***Allegri, Renzo.** Padre Pio: Man of Hope. LC 99-59678. 240p. 2000. pap. 10.99 (1-56955-138-3, Charis) Servant.

Allegri, Renzo. Teresa of the Poor: The Story of Her Life. 220p. 1998. pap. 10.99 (1-56955-100-6) Servant.

Allegri, Theodore H. The Artist's Model. LC 94-92441. 264p. (Orig.). 1994. pap. 6.99 (1-886382-00-X) Papillon Press.

Allegri, Theodore H., Sr. Handling & Management of Hazardous Wastes. 350p. 1985. 49.50 (0-412-00751-7, 9669, Chap & Hall NY) Chapman & Hall.

— Managing Warehouse & Distribution Operations. LC 93-17608. 336p. (C). 1993. text 79.95 (0-13-564618-9) P-H.

— Materials Handling: Principles & Practice. LC 91-35559. 542p. (C). 1992. reprint ed. 69.50 (0-89464-672-9) Krieger.

— Materials Management Handbook. (Illus.). 448p. 1991. 34.95 (0-8306-3513-0, 3513) McGraw-Hill Prof.

Allegri, Theodore H. Materials Management Handbook. 1991. 49.95 (0-07-157602-9) McGraw.

Allegrini, Ivo & De Santis, Franco, eds. Urban Air Pollution: Monitoring & Control Strategies. LC 95-48078. (NATO ASI Series, Partnership 2: Vol. 8). 477p. 1996. 219.00 (3-540-60707-2) Spr-Verlag.

Allegro, J. M. Qumran Cave 4 No. I. (Discoveries in the Judaean Desert Ser.: No. V). (Illus.). 160p. 1997. text 90.00 (0-19-826314-7) OUP.

Allegro, John. The Dead Sea Scrolls & the Christian Myth. rev. ed. LC 91-39558. (Illus.). 252p. (C). 1992. reprint ed. pap. 21.95 (0-87975-757-4) Prometheus Bks.

— Physician, Heal Thyself. LC 85-43081. 93p. 1985. 25.95 (0-87975-305-6) Prometheus Bks.

Alleine, Joseph. Sure Guide to Heaven. (Puritan Paperbacks Ser.). Orig. Title: Alarm to the Unconverted. 148p. 1995. pap. 4.99 (0-85151-081-7) Banner of Truth.

***Alleine, Joseph.** Wake Up & Live. 1998. pap. text 6.99 (0-946462-50-X) Grace Pubns Trust.

Alleine, Joseph. Wake up & Live. 112p. (Orig.). 1999. pap. text 6.99 (0-946462-55-0) Grace Pubns Trust.

Alleine, Richard. The World Conquered by the Faithful Christian. Kistler, Don, ed. LC 97-169837. 172p. 1997. 20.95 (1-57358-018-X) Soli Deo Gloria.

Allely, Steve. Encyclopedia of Native American Bows, Arrows & Quivers: Northeast, Southeast & Midwest. 1999. 29.95 (0-9645741-4-4) Bois dArc Pr.

— Encyclopedia of Native American Bows, Arrows & Quivers: Northeast, Southeast & Midwest. 1999. 29.95 (1-55821-992-7) Lyons Pr.

Allem, ed. see Balzac, Honore de.

Allem, ed. see De Musset, Alfred.

Allem, ed. see Musset, Alfred.

Allem, Maurice, jt. auth. see De Musset, Alfred.

Allem, Maurice, ed. see Balzac, Honore de.

Allem, Maurice, ed. see De Beaumarchais, Pierre-Augustin C.

Allem, Maurice, ed. see Hugo, Victor.

Allem, Maurice, ed. see Musset, Alfred.

Allem, Maurice, ed. see Musset, Alfred de.

Allem, Maurice, ed. see Sainte-Beuve, Charles-Augustin.

Allemagne, Henry & Grafton, Carol B. Antique Playing Cards: A Pictorial Treasury. LC 96-25991. (Illus.). 96p. 1996. pap. 11.95 (0-486-29265-7) Dover.

Alleman, Gayle Povia & American Association of Naturopathic Physicians Staff. Nature's Pharmacy: Your Guide to Healing Foods, Herbs, Supplements & Homeopathic Remedies. LC 98-66943. 384 p. 1998. write for info. (0-7853-2600-6) Pubns Intl Ltd.

Alleman, Bruce C. & Leeson, Andrea. In Situ & On-Site Bioremediation, Vol. 2. LC 97-7991. 686p. 1997. 82.50 (1-57477-027-6) Battelle.

— In Situ & On-Site Bioremediation, Vol. 3. LC 97-7991. 570p. 1997. 79.50 (1-57477-028-4) Battelle.

— In Situ & On-Site Bioremediation, Vol. 4. LC 97-7991. 658p. 1997. 82.50 (1-57477-029-2) Battelle.

— In Situ & On-Site Bioremediation, Vol. 5. LC 97-7991. 752p. 1997. 87.50 (1-57477-030-6) Battelle.

— In Situ & On-Site Bioremediation: Papers from the Fourth International In Situ & On-Site Bioremediation Symposium, New Orleans, April 28-May 1, 1997. LC 97-7991. 590p. 1997. 79.50 (1-57477-026-8) Battelle.

— In Situ Bioremediation of Petroleum Hydrocarbon & Other Organic Compounds. LC 99-23331. (Situ & On-Site Bioremediation Symposium Ser.). 576p. 1999. 75.00 (1-57477-076-4) Battelle.

— 1997 Bioremediation Symposium Proceedings Set, 5 vols. LC 97-7991. 1997. 349.50 (1-57477-031-4) Battelle.

***Alleman, Bruce C. & Leeson, Andrea, eds.** Bioreactor & Ex Situ Biological Treatment Technologies. LC 99-23338. (Situ & On-Site Bioremediation Symposium Ser.). 256p. 1999. 65.00 (1-57477-078-0) Battelle.

— Bioremediation of Metals & Inorganic Compounds. LC 99-23329. (Situ & On-Site Bioremediation Symposium Ser.). 184p. 1999. 55.00 (1-57477-077-2) Battelle.

— Bioremediation of Nitroaromatic & Haloaromatic Compounds. LC 99-23399. (Situ & On-Site Bioremediation Symposium Ser.). 278p. 1999. 65.00 (1-57477-080-2) Battelle.

— Bioremediation Technologies for Polycyclic Aromatic Hydrocarbon Compounds. LC 99-23398. (Situ & On-Site Bioremediation Symposium Ser.). 342p. 1999. 65.00 (1-57477-081-0) Battelle.

— Engineered Approaches for in Situ Bioremediation of Chlorinated Solvent Contamination. LC 99-23400. (Situ & On-Site Bioremediation Symposium Ser.). 336p. 1999. 65.00 (1-57477-075-6) Battelle.

— Natural Attenuation of Chlorinated Solvents, Petroleum Hydrocarbons & Other Organic Compounds. LC 99-23401. 378p. 1999. 65.00 (1-57477-074-8) Battelle.

— Phytoremediation & Innovative Strategies for Specialized Remedial Applications. LC 99-23328. (Situ & On-Site Bioremediation Symposium Ser.). 314p. 1999. 65.00 (1-57477-079-9) Battelle.

Alleman, Bruce C., jt. ed. see Leeson, Andrea.

Alleman, Francine, jt. auth. see Apostolou, Barbara.

Alleman, Gayle. Save Your Child from the Fat Epidemic: 7 Steps Every Parent Can Take to Ensure Healthy, Fit Children for Life. LC 99-48783. 272p. 1999. 22.00 (0-7615-2026-0) Prima Pub.

Alleman, James & Emmerson, Richard, eds. Perspectives on the Telephone Industry: The Challenge for the Future. 360p. 1989. text 45.00 (0-88730-376-5, HarpBusn) HarpInfo.

Alleman, James E., ed. Proceedings of the 52nd Purdue Industrial Waste Conference. (Illus.). 750p. (C). 1998. ring bd. 94.95 (1-57504-098-0) CRC Pr.

Alleman, Janet. Elementary Social Studies. (C). 1995. pap. text, student ed. 36.50 (0-15-502104-4, Pub. by Harcourt Coll Pubs) Harcourt.

Alleman, Richard. L. A. Man. 240p. (Orig.). 1990. mass mkt. 12.95 (0-446-38777-0, Pub. by Warner Bks) Little.

Alleman, Richard & Garrett, Peter. Therapist. 216p. 1989. 17.95 (0-8027-5747-2) Walker & Co.

Alleman, Roy V. Blizzard, 1949. Burnett, Betty, ed. (Illus.). 194p. (Orig.). 1991. pap. 10.95 (0-935284-88-5) Patrice Pr.

Alleman, Ted. Introduction to Computing in Criminal Justice. LC 95-50075. 182p. 1996. pap. text 64.00 (0-13-174525-5) P-H.

Alleman, Ted & Gido, Rosemary L. Turnstile Justice. LC 97-30516. 221p. 1997. pap. text 49.00 (0-13-301227-1) P-H.

Alleman, Ted, jt. auth. see Muraskin, Roslyn.

***Alleman, Thomas & Whiteside, Frances.** Introduction to Tort Law. 350p. (C). 2000. pap. text 37.50 (0-929563-54-9) Pearson Pubns.

Alleman, Tillie P. At Gettysburg, or What a Girl Saw & Heard of the Battle. (Illus.). 128p. 1994. reprint ed. 15.00 (1-879664-20-8) Stan Clark Military.

Allemand, Susan. Country Crossing, No. 3. (Illus.). 44p. Date not set. pap. 9.95 (1-57377-055-8, 01988402254) Easl Pubns.

***Allemand, Susan.** Pike Creek Primitives. (Illus.). 42p. 1999. pap. 10.95 (1-57377-072-8, 19884-2290) Easl Pubns.

Allemang, Elizabeth, et al. Midwives & Mothers: The Re-Emergence of Midwifery in Canada. 175p. Date not set. pap. 14.95 (0-929005-58-9, Pub. by Sec Story Pr) LPC InBook.

Allemann, Beda, jt. ed. see Koppen, Erwin.

Allemano, Marina, jt. auth. see Brogger, Suzanne.

Allen. Accounting for Success. 360p. 1993. 39.95 (0-07-103390-4) McGraw.

— Applied Calculus: Study Manual (Hardcover Book) 452p. (C). 1997. text, teacher ed. 34.00 (0-673-67549-1) Addison-Wesley.

— Biology: Critical Thinking. 1995. 75.93 (0-697-26882-9) McGraw.

— Biology: Critical Thinking Applications. 1995. teacher ed. 16.87 (0-697-22783-9) McGraw.

— Biology: Critical Thinking Workbook. 2nd ed. 1999. 7.74 (0-697-28544-8, WCB McGr Hill) McGrw-H Hghr Educ.

— Building Construction. 1998. pap. text, teacher ed. write for info. (0-471-34498-2) Wiley.

— Burning Sticks. 1991. pap. 8.95 (0-9624738-2-0) Six Lakes Arts.

— Buying a Business. 1986. lib. bdg. 81.50 (0-86010-570-9) Kluwer Academic.

***Allen.** By the Ages: Behavior & Development of Children Prebirth. 192p. 2000. pap. 15.95 (0-7668-2048-3) Delmar.

— Capital Markets. 2nd ed. 700p. (C). 2000. pap. text. write for info. (0-471-33182-1) Wiley.

Allen. Case Study: Critical Thinking. 2nd ed. 1999. wbk. ed. 11.74 (0-697-28545-6, WCB McGr Hill) McGrw-H Hghr Educ.

— Casenet-Microtone. (SWC-Management Ser.). 1997. mass mkt. 3.50 (0-538-88173-9) S-W Pub.

***Allen.** Chicken Licken: A Wickedly Funny Flap Book. 2000. 15.95 (0-385-40669-X, Pub. by Transworld Publishers Ltd) Trafalgar.

Allen. College Textbook Reading. (C). 1997. pap. text, teacher ed. 28.00 (0-15-503674-2) Harcourt Coll Pubs.

— College Textbook Reading 1997. annuals LC 97-76772. (C). 1997. pap. text 31.00 (0-15-503662-9, Pub. by Harcourt Coll Pubs) Harcourt.

— Construction Exercises 3rd ed. 1998. pap. text 32.95 (0-471-33344-1) Wiley.

— Correctness in America. 8th ed. 240p. 1997. pap. text, student ed. 23.60 (0-13-743527-4) P-H.

— Country Matters & Other Stories. 1992. pap. text. write for info. (0-17-556004-8) Addison-Wesley.

— Critical Thinking Case Study Workbook: Answer Key. 1995. 7.25 (0-697-29088-3, WCB McGr Hill) McGrw-H Hghr Educ.

— Developmental Profile Instructor's Guide: Prebirth Through Eight. 2nd ed. (Early Childhood Education Ser.). 32p. 1994. text, teacher ed. 14.95 (0-8273-5815-6) Delmar.

— DPG S/A of World Politics. 3rd ed. 1995. (1-56134-384-6, Dshkn McG-Hill) McGrw-H Hghr Educ.

— Effective Systems Strategy. 250p. 1991. pap. 53.33 (0-13-245515-3) P-H.

— Environment. 13th ed. 1994. 12.74 (1-56134-274-2) McGraw.

— Environment. 14th ed. 1995. 12.74 (1-56134-355-2) McGraw.

— Essential Elements for Strings: Violin, Bk. 1. 48p. 1994. pap. 4.95 (0-7935-3359-7, 04619001) H Leonard.

— Essentials of Managerial Accounting. 2nd ed. (SWC-Accounting). 1999. pap. 22.95 (0-87393-884-4) Dame Pubns.

— Exceptional Child: Inclusion in Early Childhood Education. 3rd ed. (Special Education Ser.). 80p. 1996. teacher ed. 16.00 (0-8273-6699-X, VNR) Wiley.

— Fire & Innocence. 1988. per. 3.50 (0-671-65878-6) PB.

— Fundamentals of Building Construction: The Architects' Studio Companion Set. 1312p. 1995. 99.00 (0-471-14524-6) Wiley.

— Global Strategy for Housing. (Illus.). 200p. (C). 1992. 120.00 (0-419-17840-6, E & FN Spon) Routledge.

— Growth/Management of Entrepreneur Businesses. LC 98-71973. 1998. text 52.17 (0-395-90670-9) HM.

— Guide to Karaoke Confidence. 1995. pap. text 8.95 (0-89724-609-8, EL03976) Wrner Bros.

Allen. Interpersonal Trauma text. write for info. (0-471-49102-0) Wiley.

Allen. Launching New Ventures. 1999. pap. 8.97 (0-395-91846-4) HM.

— Libya's Agricultural Growth. 1990. 48.50 (0-7146-2946-4, Pub. by F Cass Pubs) Intl Spec Bk.

— The Lost Ashlar. 1952. pap. 1.00 (0-88053-017-0, M066) Macoy Pub.

— Managerial Notes for Accounting. rev. ed. 1997. pap. 9.95 (0-87393-689-2) Dame Pubns.

— Marcus, Vol. 1. 1998. 6.99 (0-312-96623-7, Pub. by Tor Bks) St Martin.

***Allen.** Michael Schumacher - Quest For Red. 2000. 32.50 (1-85225-272-3, Pub. by Transworld Publishers Ltd) Trafalgar.

— Microtools: Integrated Software for WP, Spreadsheet & Data... (Computer Applications Ser.). 1990. pap. 25.75 (0-538-61440-4) Sth-Wstrn College.

— Personality Theories: Development, Growth & Diversity. 3rd ed. LC 99-18624. 518p. (C). 1999. 82.00 (0-205-28709-3, Macmillan Coll) P-H.

Allen. Politics of James Connolly. 256p. (C). 44.95 (0-7453-0394-3, Pub. by Pluto GBR); pap. 17.95 (0-7453-0473-7, Pub. by Pluto GBR) Stylus Pub VA.

— Portuguese Dictionary. (Reference Library). 1997. pap. 6.95 (1-85326-382-6, 3826WW, Pub. by Wrdsworth Edits) NTC Contemp Pub Co.

— Quaker Indictment, Vol. 4. (Quaker Mystery Ser.: 4). Date not set. mass mkt. 5.99 (0-312-96684-9, Pub. by Tor Bks) St Martin.

***Allen.** Quaker Witness. 2000. mass mkt. write for info. (0-312-97285-7) St Martin.

— Russian Embassies to the Georgian Kings, 1589-1605. 1998. 52.95 (0-521-01029-2) Ashgate Pub Co.

Allen. The Second Crucifixion. 24p. 1952. pap. 1.00 (0-88053-018-9, M067) Macoy Pub.

— Setting the Record Straight. 1999. text. write for info. (0-312-16703-2) St Martin.

— Spongiform Encephalopathies. 1993. text 107.00 (0-443-04928-9, W B Saunders Co) Harcrt Hlth Sci Grp.

— Star Crossed Renaissance. 35.00 (0-7146-1029-1, Pub. by F Cass Pubs) Intl Spec Bk.

— Student Atlas of Geography. 112p. 1999. pap. 14.69 (0-07-228568-0) McGraw.

— Train Robbery & Other Stories. 1993. pap. text. write for info. (0-17-556007-2) Addison-Wesley.

— The Wood Finisher's Handbook. (Sterling Publishing Co. Ser.). 1984. pap. 12.95 (0-8273-5383-9) Delmar.

Allen, et al, eds. Exploring Blue Highways: Literacy Reform, School Change & the Creation of Learning Communities. (Language & Literacy). 240p. (C). 1995. pap. text 18.95 (0-8077-3473-X) Tchrs Coll.

— Exploring Blue Highways: Literacy Reform, School Change & the Creation of Learning Communities. 240p. (C). 1995. text 41.00 (0-8077-3474-8) Tchrs Coll.

Allen & Chui. Elements of Calculus. 2nd ed. (Mathematics Ser.). 1989. student ed. 15.75 (0-534-09241-1) Brooks-Cole.

— Stdt Manual Elements Of Calculus. (Math). 1984. student ed. 11.25 (0-534-01189-6) Brooks-Cole.

Allen & Foulet. Paralleles. 1995. text, student ed. 71.00 incl. audio (0-13-337593-5) P-H.

Allen & Gilles. Essential Elements for String Bk. 1: Double Bass. 48p. 1994. pap. 4.95 (0-7935-4307-X, 04619004) H Leonard.

— Essential Elements for Strings, Bk. 1. 240p. 1994. teacher ed., spiral bd. 19.95 (0-7935-4309-6, 04619000) H Leonard.

— Essential Elements for Strings: Cello, Bk. 1. 48p. 1994. pap. 4.95 (0-7935-4305-3, 04619003) H Leonard.

— Essential Elements for Strings: Cello, Bk. 2. 48p. 1995. pap. 4.95 (0-7935-4299-5, 00862551) H Leonard.

— Essential Elements for Strings: Double Bass, Bk. 2. 48p. 1995. pap. 4.95 (0-7935-4300-2, 00862552) H Leonard.

— Essential Elements for Strings: Viola, Bk. 1. 48p. 1994. pap. 4.95 (0-7935-4306-1, 04619002) H Leonard.

— Essential Elements for Strings: Viola, Bk. 2. 48p. 1995. pap. 4.95 (0-7935-4298-7, 00862550) H Leonard.

— Essential Elements for Strings: Violin, Bk. 2. 48p. 1995. pap. 4.95 (0-7935-4297-9, 00862549) H Leonard.

— Essential Elements for Strings Bk. 1: Piano Accompaniment. 56p. 1995. pap. 8.95 (0-7935-4310-X, 04619005) H Leonard.

Allen & Kisailus, Edward C., eds. Glycoconjugates: Composition, Structure & Function. (Illus.). 696p. 1992. text 235.00 (0-8247-8431-6) Dekker.

Allen & Kuh. An Analytical Approach to Evidence. 1989. 52.00 (0-316-03414-2) Aspen Pub.

— Criminal Procedure: Supplement 1991. 1991. 8.95 (0-316-03457-6, Aspen Law & Bus) Aspen Pub.

— Federal Evidence: Supplement 1991. 1991. 20.95 (0-316-03452-5) Aspen Pub.

— Federal Rules of Evidence. 1989. 16.00 (0-316-03421-5) Aspen Pub.

— Supplement Constitutional Criminal Procedure. 1990. 14.00 (0-316-03451-7, Aspen Law & Bus) Aspen Pub.

Allen & Mukherjee. Women in India & Nepal. 1990. 100.00 (0-7855-0238-6, Pub. by Ratna Pustak Bhandar) St Mut.

Allen & Rotner. Changes. (J). 1998. pap. 4.95 (0-87628-168-4) Ctr Appl Res.

Allen & Saeger. General Biology: Lab Manual. 2nd ed. 352p. (C). 1998. spiral bd. 28.95 (0-7872-5091-0) Kendall-Hunt.

Allen & Schwartz. The Exceptional Child: Inclusion Early Childhood. 4th ed. (Early Childhood Education Ser.). (C). 2001. pap. text 39.95 (0-7668-0249-3) Delmar.

Allen & Seaton. Media of Conflict: War Reporting & Representations of Ethnic Violence. 256p. 1999. pap. 25.00 (1-85649-570-1); text 65.00 (1-85649-569-8) Zed Books.

Allen & Smith, Fouletier. Paralleles. 2nd ed. LC 99-42538. (FRE.). 544p. 1999. 58.00 (0-13-608464-8) S&S Trade.

Allen, et al. Global Education Handbook: Modules for Teaching Pre-School to Secondary School. (Illus.). 116p. (Orig.). 1996. pap. 7.50 (0-932288-91-X) Ctr Intl Ed U of MA.

— Pension Planning: Pensions, Profit-Sharing & Other Deferred Compensation Plans. 8th ed. LC 97-6226. 1997. 58.44 (0-256-13601-7, Irwn Prfssnl) McGraw-Hill Prof.

An Asterisk (*) at the beginning of an entry indicates that the title is appearing for the first time.

— Rails in the North Woods: Histories of Ten Adirondack Short Lines. (Illus.). 1999. pap. 21.95 (*0-925168-69-6*) North Country.

— Triploid Oysters: Hatchery Manual for Producing Triploid Oysters. 32p. 1989. pap. 8.00 (*0-295-77031-7*) U of Wash Pr.

Allen, jt. auth. see Attner.

Allen, jt. auth. see Hall.

Allen, jt. auth. see Klooster.

Allen, jt. auth. see Meyer, Earl C.

Allen, jt. auth. see Parsloe.

Allen, jt. auth. see Semmens, Lesley.

Allen, jt. auth. see Walker.

Allen, ed. see Hugo, Victor.

Allen, ed. see Laclos, Choderlos De.

Allen, ed. see Ruehl, Peter.

Allen, Gene & Jarman, Rick. Collaborative R&D: Manufacturing's New Tool. LC 98-53560. (National Association of Manufacturers Ser.). 336p. 1999. 58.95 (*0-471-31994-5*) Wiley.

Allen, Katy Z. James Meets the Prairie. LC 98-218316. (Cover-to-Cover Bks.). 56 p. 1997. write for info. (*0-7807-6688-1*, Covercraft) Perfection Learn.

Allen, Nancy K. Once upon a Dime: A Math Adventure. LC 99-11928. (Illus.). (J). 1999. 6.95 (*1-57091-161-4*) Charlesbridge Pub.

Allen, A. B., jt. ed. see Schwartz, M. William.

Allen, A. H. Design Data for Rectangular Beams & Slabs PART 1. 42p. (C). (gr. 13). 1998. pap. text 75.00 (*0-86310-029-5*, Pub. by Palladian) Scholium Intl.

— An Introduction to Prestressed Concrete. (Educational Ser.). (Illus.). 1978. pap. 35.00 (*0-7210-1090-3*, Pub. by C & CA) Scholium Intl.

Allen, A. H., jt. auth. see McMurtrie, Douglas C.

Allen, A. H., ed. see McMurtrie, Douglas C.

Allen, A. L. Allen. A Brief History of the Family of Nathan Allen & Mary Putnam, His Wife, Late of Ft. Plain, Montgomery County, NY, & of the Families of Reverend Aaron Putnam of Pomfret, CT, the Bulkeley, Prescott, Hall, Grosvenor, & Other Families with Which the Allen Family Were Connected. (Illus.). 132p. 1995. reprint ed. pap. 25.00 (*0-8328-4866-2*); reprint ed. lib. bdg. 35.00 (*0-8328-4865-4*) Higginson Bk Co.

— Arthritis, Rheumatism & Allied Disorders: How's Your Liver? Why Die of Cancer? 120p. 1996. reprint ed. spiral bd. 12.00 (*0-7873-0027-6*) Hlth Research.

Allen, A. M. A History of Verona. 1977. lib. bdg. 59.95 (*0-8490-2012-3*) Gordon Pr.

Allen, Abigail, jt. auth. see Crosby, Timothy.

Allen, Adela, tr. see Sierra, Judy & Kaminski, Robert.

Allen, Adrian, et al, eds. Mechanisms of Mucosal Protection in the Upper Gastrointestinal Tract. LC 83-19257. (Illus.). 416p. 1984. reprint ed. pap. 129.00 (*0-608-00654-8*, 206124200007) Bks Demand.

Allen, Adrianne T. Sheila's Show Biz Days. (Illus.). 64p. (Orig.). (J). (gr. k-6). 1993. pap. 5.95 (*1-56883-044-0*) Colonial Pr AL.

Allen, Al. Zinnias Grow on Either Side of the River. 320p. 1995. 19.95 (*0-943099-17-X*) M & M Pr.

Allen, Alastair, ed. Transputer Systems - Ongoing Research. LC 92-52507. (Transputer & Occam Engineering Ser.: Vol. 25). 274p. (gr. 12). 1992. 90.00 (*90-5199-085-5*, Pub. by IOS Pr) IOS Press.

Allen, Albert E. Mission Accomplished. LC 97-90878. 1998. pap. 12.95 (*0-533-12502-2*) Vantage.

Allen, Alexandra, jt. auth. see Arellano, Richard G.

Allen, Algernon R., jt. auth. see Annis, John R.

Allen, Alta K. Guseman. Abraham Guseman Descendants. (Illus.). 46p. 1997. reprint ed. pap. 9.00 (*0-8328-8870-2*); reprint ed. lib. bdg. 19.00 (*0-8328-8869-9*) Higginson Bk Co.

*__Allen, Amy.__ The Power of Feminist Theory. LC 98-41071. (Feminist Theory & Politics Ser.). 160p. 1998. text 59.00 (*0-8133-9072-9*, Pub. by Westview) HarpC.

— What Is It? (Illus.). 30p. (J). (ps-1). 2000. 9.95 (*1-887169-10-5*, Pub. by Wedding Solns) Natl Bk Netwk.

Allen, Amy, ed. Medical Device Industry Factbook. 3rd rev. ed. (Illus.). 190p. 1996. pap. 45.00 (*1-884551-02-5*) Canon Comns.

Allen, Ana M. The Beginner's Guide to Collecting Fine Art, African American Style. unabridged ed. Burroughs, Margaret T., ed. LC 98-91315. (Illus.). vii, 180p. 1998. pap. 15.00 (*0-9663094-0-5*, 1515) Positiv.

Allen, Andrew, jt. auth. see Ziethen, Karl-Heinz.

Allen, Andrew, ed. see Cameron, Michelle H.

Allen, Andrew, ed. see Campbell, Susan K.

Allen, Andrew, ed. see Culbreth, Luann & Kaut, Carolyn.

Allen, Andrew, ed. see Dowd, Steven B. & Tilson, Elwin R.

Allen, Andrew, ed. see Drose, Julia A.

Allen, Andrew, ed. see Kauffman, Timothy L.

Allen, Andrew, ed. see Kremkau, Frederick W.

Allen, Andrew, ed. see Labus, James B.

Allen, Andrew, ed. see Purtilo, Ruth.

Allen, Andrew, ed. see Snopek, Albert M.

Allen, Andrew, ed. see Tempkin, Betty B.

Allen, Andrew, ed. see Widmer, Ruth S. & Van Soelen, Kenneth W.

Allen, Andrew, jt. ed. see Yamani, Mai.

Allen, Anita L. Uneasy Access: Privacy for Women in a Free Society. (New Feminist Perspectives Ser.). 240p. (C). 1975. lib. bdg. 61.00 (*0-8476-7327-8*) Rowman.

— Uneasy Access: Privacy for Women in a Free Society. (New Feminist Perspectives Ser.). 240p. (C). 1988. pap. text 27.00 (*0-8476-7328-6*) Rowman.

Allen, Anita L. & Regan, Milton C., Jr., eds. Debating Democracy's Discontent: Essays on American Politics, Law, & Public Philosophy. LC 98-36852. 408p. 1999. 80.00 (*0-19-829484-0*) OUP.

— Debating Democracy's Discontent: Essays on American Politics, Law, & Public Philosophy. LC 98-36852. (Illus.). 408p. 1999. pap. 19.95 (*0-19-829496-4*) OUP.

Allen, Ann T. Feminism & Motherhood in Germany, 1800-1914. LC 90-21164. 275p. (C). 1991. text 45.00 (*0-8135-1686-2*) Rutgers U Pr.

Allen, Anne & Coley, Janis. Dance for All, Vol. 2. (Roehampton Teaching Studies Series - Entitlement for All Ser.: Vols. 2-3). 80p. 1995. pap. 21.95 (*1-85346-369-8*, Pub. by David Fulton) Taylor & Francis.

— Dance for All, Vol. 3. (Roehampton Teaching Studies Series - Entitlement for All Ser.: Vols. 2-3). 80p. 1995. pap. 21.95 (*1-85346-370-1*, Pub. by David Fulton) Taylor & Francis.

— Dance for All 1. LC 97-133457. (Entitlement for All Ser.). 76p. 1996. pap. text 24.95 (*1-85346-437-6*, Pub. by David Fulton) Taylor & Francis.

*__Allen, Anne Beiser.__ An Independent Woman: The Life of Lou Henry Hoover, 188. LC 99-462298. (Contributions in American History Ser.: Vol. 188). 2000. write for info. (*0-313-31466-7*) Greenwood.

Allen, Annette. Country of Light. LC 96-77330. (Illus.). 57p. 1996. pap. 10.00 (*1-880994-38-0*) Mt Olive Coll Pr.

Allen, Arnold O. Probability, Statistics & Queueing Theory: With Computer Science Applications. 3rd ed. 768p. 1997. write for info. (*0-12-051052-9*) Acad Pr.

— Probability, Statistics, & Queueing Theory with Computer Science Applications. 2nd ed. (Computer Science & Scientific Computing Ser.). 740p. 1990. text 51.00 (*0-12-051051-0*) Acad Pr.

— Queuing Theory. 3rd ed. 300p. 1998. write for info. (*0-12-051055-3*) Acad Pr.

Allen, Arthur W., III. Cross-Cultural Counseling: The Guidance Project & the Reluctant Seniors. (Teaching Cases in Cross-Cultural Education Ser.). 76p. (Orig.). (C). 1990. pap. text 7.50 (*1-877962-15-5*) Univ AK Ctr CCS.

Allen, Asa W. Genealogy of the Allen & Witter Families: Among the Early Settlers of This Continent & Their Descendants. (Illus.). 251p. 1988. reprint ed. pap. 37.50 (*0-8328-0105-4*); reprint ed. lib. bdg. 45.50 (*0-8328-0104-6*) Higginson Bk Co.

Allen Associates Staff. The New York Times American Studies Program, 3 pts. 64p. 1981. pap. text. write for info. (*0-912853-07-7*); write for info. (*0-912853-09-3*); write for info. (*0-912853-08-5*) NY Times.

Allen, B. Developing a Learning Organisation. (Financial Times Management Briefings Ser.). 1997. pap. 89.50 (*0-273-63254-X*, Pub. by F T P-H) Trans-Atl Phila.

Allen, B. C. Gazetteer of Bengal & North-East India. (C). 1993. reprint ed. 50.00 (*0-8364-2847-1*, Pub. by Mittal Pubs Dist) S Asia.

Allen, B. J., et al, eds. Progress in Neutron Capture Therapy for Cancer. (Illus.). 702p. (C). 1992. text 186.00 (*0-306-44104-7*, Kluwer Plenum) Kluwer Academic.

Allen, B. L. Basic Anatomy, A Laboratory Manual: The Human Skeleton - The Cat. 3rd ed. (Illus.). 204p. (C). 1986. pap., lab manual ed. 38.95 (*0-7167-1755-7*) W H Freeman.

Allen, B. R. Dermatology. (Brainscan MCQs Ser.). 110p. 1990. 21.95 (*0-387-19607-2*) Spr-Verlag.

Allen Baker, Mark. The Standard Guide to Collecting Autographs: A Reference & Value Guide. LC 98-87291. (Illus.). 608p. 1999. per. 24.95 (*0-87341-613-9*) Krause Pubns.

Allen, Barbara. Bible Stories Activities. (Illus.). (J). 1997. pap. text 2.29 (*0-7647-0069-3*) Schaffer Pubns.

— Falgoust: A History & Genealogy of the Falgoust & Falgout Families of France & Louisiana; 1555-1988. (Illus.). 600p. 1988. 30.00 (*0-9617559-1-1*) Oubres Bks.

— The Holistic Garden: A Simple Guide to a Safe, Fruitful, Ecologically-Balanced Landscape. Daniels, Elizabeth, ed. (Illus.). 135p. (Orig.). 1994. pap. 14.75 (*0-9635421-0-9*) Essent Sources.

— Homesteading the High Desert. LC 86-28125. (University of Utah Publications in the American West: No. 20). (Illus.). 203p. 1987. reprint ed. pap. 63.00 (*0-7837-8564-X*, 204937900011) Bks Demand.

— Reading for Understanding: Grade 1. (Illus.). (J). 1997. pap. text 2.29 (*0-7647-0094-4*) Schaffer Pubns.

— Remember the Flavors of Austin: A Restaurant Guide & Recipe Sampler. (Illus.). 37p. 1998. 5.99 (*0-9660872-1-6*) Bazaar Barbara.

— The Scottish Soldier. large type ed. 384p. 1988. 27.99 (*0-7089-1814-X*) Ulverscroft.

— Time Is a Lover. 288p. 1988. pap. 3.95 (*0-317-67262-2*) Bantam.

Allen, Barbara & Schlereth, Thomas J., eds. Sense of Place: American Regional Cultures. (Illus.). 224p. 1990. reprint ed. pap. text 18.00 (*0-8131-0817-9*) U Pr of Ky.

Allen, Barbara, ed. see Fiese, Bryan R.

Allen, Barbara, jt. ed. see Olson, Georgine N.

Allen, Barbara B. Astrogenesis: Secrets of the Playing Cards with Keys to Astrology. 160p. 1991. reprint ed. bds. 34.95 (*0-9627429-0-2*) M David Pub.

Allen, Barbara C., ed. see Patterson, William P.

Allen, Barry. Truth in Philosophy. LC 92-35722. 244p. 1993. text 37.95 (*0-674-91090-7*) HUP.

— Truth in Philosophy. 248p. 1995. pap. text 17.95 (*0-674-91091-5*, ALLTRX) HUP.

Allen, Beca L. A Woman's ABCs of Life: From Women Who Learned the Hard Way. 176p. (Orig.). 1994. pap. 6.95 (*0-915009-35-8*) World Leis Corp.

Allen, Bem P. Personality, Social, & Biological Perspectives on Personal Adjustment. 550p. (C). 1990. text 48.95 (*0-534-13020-8*) Brooks-Cole.

Allen, Bem P. & Potkay, Charles R. Adjective Generation Technique (AGT) Research & Applications. 500p. 1984. text 52.50 (*0-8290-0718-0*) Irvington.

Allen, Ben. Shop-Tested Router Techniques & Projects You Can Make: From the Editors of Wood Magazine. (Illus.). 96p. 1997. pap. 9.95 (*0-696-20743-5*) Meredith Bks.

— Shop-Tested Scrollsaw Techniques & Projects You Can Make: From the Editors of Wood Magazine. (Illus.). 96p. 1997. pap. 9.95 (*0-696-20741-9*) Meredith Bks.

— Shop-Tested Wookworking Tools You Can Make: From the Editors of Wood Magazine. (Illus.). 96p. 1997. pap. 9.95 (*0-696-20745-1*) Meredith Bks.

Allen, Ben, ed. Home Offices: Your Guide to Planning & Furnishing. LC 97-71332. (Illus.). 112p. (Orig.). 1997. pap. 12.95 (*0-696-20728-1*, Better Homes) Meredith Bks.

— How to Design & Build Fences & Gates. (Illus.). 96p. 1997. pap. 9.95 (*0-89721-320-3*, Ortho Bks) Meredith Bks.

— New Complete Guide to Home Repair & Improvement. 2nd ed. LC 97-71323. (Illus.). 600p. 1997. 34.95 (*0-696-20469-X*) Meredith Bks.

— Outdoor Projects 1-2-3. LC 97-71598. (Illus.). 480p. 1998. 34.95 (*0-696-20673-0*, Home Depot) Meredith Bks.

— Step-by-Step Basic Carpentry. LC 97-71326. (Illus.). 112p. 1997. pap. 12.95 (*0-696-20665-X*, Better Homes) Meredith Bks.

— Step-by-Step Masonry & Concrete. LC 97-71325. (Illus.). 112p. 1997. pap. 12.95 (*0-696-20666-8*, Better Homes) Meredith Bks.

Allen, Ben, ed. see Manley, Pamela J.

Allen, Ben T. Preventing Sexual Harassment On-Campus: Policies & Practices for Higher Education. 60p. 1995. 18.00 (*1-878240-40-4*) Coll & U Personnel.

*__Allen, Benedict.__ Edge of Blue Heaven: A Journey Through Mongolia. 256p. 1999. 31.95 (*0-563-38375-5*, BBC-Parkwest) Parkwest Pubns.

Allen, Benedict. Hunting the Gugu: In Search of the Lost Ape-Men of Sumatra LC 89-189396. 191p. 1989. write for info. (*0-333-45903-2*) Macmillan.

*__Allen, Benedict.__ More Great Railway Journeys. (Illus.). 224p. 2000. reprint ed. 27.00 (*0-7881-9411-9*) DIANE Pub.

Allen, Beth. Cozy Book of Tea Time Treats: Forty Bite-Size Desserts to Sweeten Your Day. (Cozy Bks.). (Illus.). 112p. 1996. boxed set 13.00 (*0-7615-0871-6*) Prima Pub.

— Life's Little Temptations: Forty Bite-Sized Desserts to Sweeten Your Day. LC 94-21796. (Illus.). 96p. 1994. 8.95 (*1-55958-587-0*) Prima Pub.

— Sensational Pies. LC 97-32726. 1998. 24.95 (*0-7621-0080-X*, Pub. by RD Assn) Penguin Putnam.

Allen, Beth, ed. Economics in a Changing World: Microeconomics, Vol. 2. 175p. 1997. text 79.95 (*0-312-15929-3*) St Martin.

Allen, Beth, ed. see Winquist, Alan H.

Allen, Beverly. Pier Paolo Pasolini: The Poetics of Heresy. (Illus.). 144p. (Orig.). 1982. pap. 56.50 (*0-915838-11-7*) Anma Libri.

— Rape Warfare: The Hidden Genocide in Bosnia-Herzegovina & Croatia. 208p. 1996. 19.95 (*0-8166-2818-1*) U of Minn Pr.

Allen, Beverly, et al, eds. The Defiant Muse: Italian Feminist Poems from the Middle Ages to the Present. LC 84-4841. (Defiant Muse Ser.). (ENG & ITA.). 151p. (Orig.). 1986. text 35.00 (*0-935312-48-X*); pap. text 11.95 (*0-935312-55-2*) Feminist Pr.

Allen, Beverly & Russo, Mary J. Revisioning Italy: National Identity & Global Culture. LC 97-20530. 1997. pap. 24.95 (*0-8166-2727-4*); text 62.95 (*0-8166-2726-6*) U of Minn Pr.

Allen, Beverly, tr. see Minghelli, Marina.

Allen, Bibb. Alabama Liability Insurance Handbook. LC 96-75624. 708p. 1996. 85.00 (*1-55834-319-9*, 60100, MICHIE) LEXIS Pub.

— Alabama Liability Insurance Handbook: 1998 Cumulative Supplement. LC 96-75624. 1998. 85.00 (*0-327-00112-7*, 60101-11) LEXIS Pub.

— Alabama Liability Insurance Handbook, 1999 Cumulative Supplement. 125p. 1999. 45.00 (*0-327-01148-3*, 6010112) LEXIS Pub.

Allen, Bill. Shadow Heart. 212p. 1998. spiral bd. 6.50 (*1-893687-02-3*) Yard Dog.

Allen, Bill & Dee, Davi, eds. Midnight Journeys. (Illus.). ii, 87p. 1995. pap. 9.95 (*1-893816-00-1*) Ozark Tri.

*__Allen, Bill, et al.__ Deja Doo. (Illus.). 78p. 1999. spiral bd. 5.00 (*1-893687-06-6*) Yard Dog.

Allen, Bill, et al. Effective Teacher Evaluation. LC 76-21433. (Mandala Series in Education). 39p. 1981. reprint ed. pap. 6.95 (*0-916250-20-2*) Irvington.

— Teacher Evaluation: A Color & Activity Book. LC 76-21433. (Mandala Series in Education). (Illus.). reprint ed. pap. 8.00 (*0-8290-2148-5*) Irvington.

Allen, Bill, jt. auth. see Hays, Dick.

Allen, Blair, et al. Septic System Owner's Manual. LC 98-28772. (Illus.). 192p. 2000. pap. 14.95 (*0-936070-20-X*) Shelter Pubns.

Allen, Blair H. Ashes Ashes All Fall Down. Carbone, Joyce, ed. 1997. pap. 4.95 (*1-878116-79-7*) JVC Bks.

— Trapped in a Cold War Travelogue LC 98-90884. 160p. 1998. write for info. (*1-884572-00-6*) Slashing Swords.

Allen, Bob. Come Walk With Me. LC 96-69087. 246p. (Orig.). 1997. pap. 18.95 (*1-57197-037-1*) Pentland Pr.

Allen, Bob. George Jones: The Life & Times of a Honky Tonk Legend. LC 94-20277. (Illus.). 320p. 1994. 19.95 (*1-55972-253-3*, Birch Ln Pr) Carol Pub Group.

— George Jones: The Life & Times of a Honky Tonk Legend. 1996. mass mkt. 6.99 (*0-312-95698-3*, Pub. by Tor Bks) St Martin.

— Guide to Collecting Cookbooks. 1995. pap. 14.95 (*0-89145-421-7*, 2081) Collector Bks.

Allen, Bob & Gilbert, Bill. The 500 Home Run Club: Baseball's Greatest Home Run Hitters from Aaron to Williams. (Illus.). 288p. 1999. 22.95 (*1-58261-031-2*) Sprts Pubng.

*__Allen, Bob & Gilbert, Bill.__ The 500 Home Run Club: Baseball's 16 Greatest Home Run Hitters from Babe Ruth to Mark McGuire. (Illus.). 2000. reprint ed. pap. 14.95 (*1-58261-289-7*) Sports Pub.

Allen, Bobbie. Classroom Guide to Suggested Activities & Projects. 112p. 19.95 (*0-915035-61-8*) Dawn Sign.

Allen, Bobbie, ed. see Eastman, Gil.

*__Allen, Boice-Terrel.__ The Daughters of a Mother. LC 00-190914. 2000. pap. 13.95 (*0-9701340-1-0*) rattlecat.

Allen-Bond, Jacquline. Business Calls. (Longman American Business English Skills Ser.). 1995. pap. text 9.92 (*0-582-08418-0*) Addison-Wesley.

Allen, Bonington & Gates, Henry Louis, Jr. More Great Railway Journeys. 224p. 1996. 29.95 (*0-563-38717-3*) MBI Pubg.

Allen, Bonnie J., jt. auth. see Walsdorf, John J.

Allen-Bradley, Janie, ed. see Ayres, Mary Jo.

Allen, Brian. Francis Hayman. LC 86-51284. (Illus.). 1987. 40.00 (*0-300-03915-8*) Yale U Pr.

Allen, Brian, ed. British Art Treasures from Russian Imperial Collections in the Hermitage. LC 96-60986. (Illus.). 320p. 1996. 75.00 (*0-300-06946-4*) Yale U Pr.

— Towards a Modern Art World. LC 94-61989. (Studies in British Art: No. 1). (Illus.). 240p. 1995. 45.00 (*0-300-06380-6*) Yale U Pr.

Allen, Brian, jt. auth. see Edelstein, T. J.

Allen, Brigid. Morrells of Oxford: The Family & Their Brewery, 1743-1993. (Illus.). 192p. 1994. pap. 17.95 (*0-7509-0634-0*, Pub. by Sutton Pub Ltd) Intl Pubs Mktg.

Allen, Brooke. The New York City Ballet's the Sleeping Beauty. (J). 1993. write for info. (*0-316-03459-2*) Little.

Allen, Bruce. Germany East: Dissent & Opposition. rev. ed. LC 91-71472. 191p. (Orig.). 1991. 47.99 (*0-921689-97-7*, Pub. by Black Rose); pap. 18.99 (*0-921689-96-9*, Pub. by Black Rose) Consort Bk Sales.

— Moss Flora of Central America Pt. 1: Sphagnaceae-Calymperaceae. (Monographs in Systematic Botany from the Missouri Botanical Garden: No. 49). (Illus.). 242p. 1994. 27.95 (*0-915279-26-6*) Miss Botan.

Allen, Bruce, ed. InfoMap Instructor's Guide. (Illus.). 75p. (Orig.). 1990. 39.95 incl. disk (*0-9606408-3-5*) Info Mgmt Pr.

*__Allen, Bruce, ed.__ Moss Flora of Central America Pt. 2: Pottiaceae-Orthotrichaceae. (Illus.). 2000. write for info. (*0-915279-87-8*) Miss Botan.

Allen, Bruce T. & Melnik, Arie. The Market for Electrical Generating Equipment. LC 73-620027. (MSU Public Utilities Papers: Vol. 1973). 91p. reprint ed. pap. 30.00 (*0-608-20488-9*, 207174000002) Bks Demand.

Allen, Bryan. Digital Wizardry: Creative Photoshop Techniques. LC 98-5974. (Illus.). 1998. pap. text 29.95 (*0-8174-3797-5*) Watsn-Guptill.

— The World of Phyllis Haylor & Ballroom Dancing. (Ballroom Dance Ser.). 1986. lib. bdg. 79.95 (*0-8490-3366-7*) Gordon Pr.

Allen, Bryan, ed. The World of Phyllis Haylor & Ballroom Dancing. (Ballroom Dance Ser.). 1985. lib. bdg. 79.95 (*0-87700-660-1*) Revisionist Pr.

Allen, Bryan, jt. auth. see Scrivener, Len.

Allen, Bryan, ed. see Scrivener, Len.

Allen, Bryce, ed. Evaluation of Public Services & Public Services Personnel: Proceedings of the 32nd Allerton Institute. 1991. 20.00 (*0-87845-086-6*) U of Ill Grad Sch.

— Information Tasks: Towards a User-Centered Approach to Information Systems. (Library & Information Science). (Illus.). 308p. 1996. text 45.00 (*0-12-051040-5*) Acad Pr.

Allen, Bryce L. & Weech, Terry L., eds. Critical Issues in Library Management: Organizing for Leadership & Decision-Making. (Occasional Papers: Vols. 198-199). 85p. (Orig.). 1995. pap. 15.00 (*0-614-10177-8*) U of Ill Grad Sch.

Allen, Bud & Bosta, Diana. Games Criminals Play: How You Can Profit by Knowing Them. LC 80-54225. 228p. 1981. reprint ed. 16.95 (*0-9605226-0-3*) Rae John.

— How to Be a Successful Trainer: Without Being Tarred & Feathered. 62p. 1981. vinyl bd. 8.95 (*0-9605226-8-9*) Rae John.

— Library of Lesson Plans: Courtroom Demeanor. 95p. 1982. vinyl bd. 39.95 (*0-939438-22-4*) Rae John.

— Library of Lesson Plans: Creative Thinking & Problem Solving. 80p. 1982. vinyl bd. 39.95 (*0-939438-19-4*) Rae John.

— Library of Lesson Plans: Forty Hour Orientation Package. 82p. 1981. vinyl bd. 39.95 (*0-9605226-4-6*) Rae John.

— Library of Lesson Plans: How Administrators & Victims Can Handle a Hostage Situation. 100p. 1982. ring bd. 49.95 (*0-939438-21-6*) Rae John.

— Library of Lesson Plans: How to Handle Classroom Disturbances. 64p. 1982. vinyl bd. 29.95 (*0-939438-20-8*) Rae John.

— Library of Lesson Plans: Rape Prevention-How to Avoid It & What to Do If You Can't. 41p. 1981. vinyl bd. 29.95 (*0-9605226-5-4*) Rae John.

— Library of Lesson Plans: Stress Management. 64p. 1981. vinyl bd. 49.95 (*0-939438-17-8*) Rae John.

— Library of Lesson Plans: Team Building & Listening Workshop. 90p. 1981. vinyl bd. 49.95 (*0-939438-16-X*) Rae John.

— Library of Lesson Plans: The Anatomy of a Set Up. 222p. 1981. ring bd. 59.95 (*0-939438-18-6*) Rae John.

— Library of Lesson Plans Vol. 1: Career Development. 285p. 1981. ring bd. 99.95 (*0-939438-02-X*) Rae John.

— Library of Lesson Plans Vol. 1, No. 1: Professionalism - What It Really Means. 50p. 1981. vinyl bd. 29.95 (*0-939438-00-3*) Rae John.

A

— Library of Lesson Plans Vol. 1, No. 2: Report Writing. 105p. 1981. 39.95 (*0-9605226-1-1*) Rae John.
— Library of Lesson Plans Vol. 1, No. 3: How to Take Promotional Examinations & Oral Interviews. 74p. 1981. vinyl bd. 29.95 (*0-9605226-3-8*) Rae John.
— Library of Lesson Plans Vol. 1, No. 4: How to Reduce Sick Leave. 57p. 1981. vinyl bd. 29.95 (*0-939438-01-1*) Rae John.
— Library of Lesson Plans Vol. 2: Supervision in Depth. 257p. 1981. ring bd. 99.95 (*0-939438-03-8*) Rae John.
— Library of Lesson Plans Vol. 2, No. 1: Basic Supervision. 73p. 1981. vinyl bd. 29.95 (*0-939438-09-7*) Rae John.
— Library of Lesson Plans Vol. 2, No. 2: Discretionary Decision Making. 61p. 1981. vinyl bd. 29.95 (*0-939438-10-0*) Rae John.
— Library of Lesson Plans Vol. 2, No. 3: Corrective Interviewing for Supervisors. 63p. 1981. vinyl bd. 29.95 (*0-939438-11-9*) Rae John.
— Library of Lesson Plans Vol. 2, No. 4: Human Relations. 67p. 1981. vinyl bd. 29.95 (*0-939438-12-7*) Rae John.
— Library of Lesson Plans Vol. 3: Improving Staff-Inmate Relations. 256p. 1981. ring bd. 99.95 (*0-939438-04-6*) Rae John.
— Library of Lesson Plans Vol. 3, No. 1: How to Recognize & Handle Disturbed Inmates. 41p. 1981. vinyl bd. 29.95 (*0-9605226-2-X*) Rae John.
— Library of Lesson Plans Vol. 3, No. 2: Counseling & Interviewing. 78p. 1981. vinyl bd. 29.95 (*0-939438-06-2*) Rae John.
— Library of Lesson Plans Vol. 3, No. 3: Staff-Inmate Relations. 82p. 1981. vinyl bd. 29.95 (*0-939438-07-0*) Rae John.
— Library of Lesson Plans Vol. 3, No. 4: Recognizing Signs of a Riot & What to Do about Them. 57p. 1981. vinyl bd. 29.95 (*0-939438-08-9*) Rae John.
— Library of Lesson Plans Vol. 4: Techniques of Custodial Functions. 227p. 1981. ring bd. 99.95 (*0-939438-05-4*) Rae John.
— Library of Lesson Plans Vol. 4, No. 1: Custodial Competence & Expectations. 79p. 1981. vinyl bd. 29.95 (*0-939438-13-5*) Rae John.
— Library of Lesson Plans Vol. 4, No. 2: Transportation of Prisoners & How to Build a Transportation Kit. 41p. 1981. vinyl bd. 29.95 (*0-9605226-6-2*) Rae John.
— Library of Lesson Plans Vol. 4, No. 3: What Most People Don't Know about Court Procedure. 42p. 1981. vinyl bd. 29.95 (*0-939438-14-3*) Rae John.
— Library of Lesson Plans Vol. 4, No. 4: Search Techniques. 67p. 1981. vinyl bd. 29.95 (*0-939438-15-1*) Rae John.
— Pure Gold. 87p. 1981. vinyl bd. 8.95 (*0-9605226-7-0*) Rae John.

Allen, C. G. A Manual of European Languages for Librarians. 2nd ed. LC 99-13806. 994p. 1999. 215.00 (*1-85739-241-8*) Bowker-Saur.

Allen, C. H., ed. Africa Bibliography 1993: Works on Africa Published During 1993. 448p. 1996. pap. 76.50 (*0-7486-0532-0*, Pub. by Edinburgh U Pr) Col U Pr.
— Africa Bibliography 1994: Works on Africa Published During 1994. 448p. 1996. pap. 76.50 (*0-7486-0854-0*, Pub. by Edinburgh U Pr) Col U Pr.

Allen, C. Leonard. The Cruciform Church: Becoming a Cross-Shaped People in a Secular World. 2nd ed. LC 89-82537. 191p. 1990. pap. 11.95 (*0-89112-098-X*) Abilene Christ U.
— Distant Voices: Discovering a Forgotten Past. 1993. pap. 11.95 (*0-89112-154-4*) Abilene Christ U.
— The Worldly Church: A Call for Biblical Renewal. 2nd ed. LC 87-81827. 116p. 1991. pap. 8.95 (*0-89112-150-1*) Abilene Christ U.

Allen, C. Leonard, jt. auth. see Hughes, Richard T.

Allen, C. M., et al. The Management of Acute Stroke. LC 88-23163. (Johns Hopkins Series in Contemporary Medicine & Public Health). (Illus.). 227p. 1988. reprint ed. pap. 70.40 (*0-608-05920-X*, 206625600008) Bks Demand.

Allen, C. Paul. Effective Structured Techniques: From Strategy to Case. 400p. (C). 1991. pap. text 47.00 (*0-13-155763-7*) P-H.

Allen, C. W. Astrophysical Quantities. 3rd ed. 310p. (C). 1976. text 80.00 (*0-485-11150-0*, Pub. by Athlone Pr) Humanities.

***Allen, C .W., et al.** Incorporate & Grow Rich! How to Cut Your Taxes 70& Protect Your Assets Forever. 2nd ed. 240p. 1999. pap. 49.99 (*0-9671871-0-9*) Sage Inter NV.

Allen, Cady H., jt. auth. see Rasooli, Jay M.

***Allen, Calvin H. & Rigsbee, W. Lynn, II.** Oman under Qaboos: From Coup to Constitution, 1970-1996. 272p. 2000. 57.50 (*0-7146-5001-3*, Pub. by F Cass Pubs) Intl Spec Bk.

Allen, Cameron. Guide to New Jersey Legal Bibliography & Legal History. (Illus.). xxv, 636p. 1984. reprint ed. 75.00 (*0-8377-0217-8*, Rothman) W S Hein.

Allen, Camille. A Partnership in Literacy: Teacher Education in an Urban School. LC 95-39274. 114p. 1996. pap. text 19.00 (*0-435-08859-9*, 08859) Heinemann.

Allen, Carl P., jt. auth. see Moriarity, Shane.

Allen, Carleton K. Democracy & the Individual. 109p. 1977. 13.95 (*0-8369-2933-0*) Ayer.

Allen, Carlton. Stories of Falling Toward Grace. LC 94-28529. 136p. 1994. pap. 12.00 (*1-880837-81-1*) Smyth & Helwys.

***Allen, Carmel.** Handbag: To Have & to Hold. 1999. 20.00 (*1-85868-769-1*, Pub. by Carlton Bks Ltd) Natl Bk Netwk.

Allen, Carol. Black Women Intellectuals: Strategies of Nation, Family, & Neighborhood in the Works of Pauline Hopkins, Jessie Fauset, & Marita Bonner. rev. ed. LC 97-38426. (Studies in African American History & Culture). 184p. 1998. text 45.00 (*0-8153-3112-6*) Garland.
— Earth: All about Earthquakes, Volacnoes, Glaciers, Oceans & More. (Illus.). 32p. (J). 1993. pap. 5.95 (*1-895688-06-X*, Pub. by Greey dePencier) Firefly Bks Ltd.
— Japan. (Illus.). 64p. (J). (gr. 4-8). 1992. student ed. 8.99 (*0-86653-684-1*, 1418) Good Apple.
— Provoking Feminisms. 264p. 1999. pap. 20.00 (*0-226-01439-8*); lib. bdg. 39.00 (*0-226-01437-1*) U Ch Pr.

Allen, Carol & Lustig, Herbert S. Tea with Demons: A True Story. Date not set. write for info. (*1-929760-10-8*); pap. write for info. (*1-929760-11-6*) Swan Multimedia.

Allen, Carol L., jt. auth. see Allen, James R.

Allen, Carol V. Nursing Process in Collaborative Practice. 2nd ed. LC 96-8018. 264p. (Orig.). (C). 1996. pap. text 26.95 (*0-8385-1467-7*, A1467-8) Appleton & Lange.

Allen, Carole. India. (Gifted Learning Ser.). 64p. teacher ed. 8.99 (*0-86653-739-2*, GA1454) Good Apple.
— Mexico. (Gifted Learning Ser.). 64p. 1995. teacher ed. 8.99 (*0-86653-854-2*, GA1536) Good Apple.

Allen, Carolyn. Following Djuna: Women Lovers & the Erotics of Loss. LC 95-23531. (Theories of Representation & Difference Ser.). 160p. (C). 1996. 35.00 (*0-253-33023-8*); pap. 13.95 (*0-253-21047-X*) Ind U Pr.

Allen, Caron & Watanabe, Natsumi. A Homestay in Japan: Nihon to no Deai, Intermediate Reader for Students of Japanese. LC 92-10662. (Illus.). 204p. 1992. pap. text 19.95 (*0-9628137-6-1*) Stone Bridge Pr.

Allen, Catherine. Century to Celebrate: A History of Woman's Missionary Union. (Illus.). 516p. 1987. pap. text 10.95 (*0-936625-16-3*, W874103) Womans Mission Union.
— Smart Cards: Seizing Strategic Business Opportunities. LC 96-41903. 312p. 1996. text 37.50 (*0-7863-1108-8*, Irwn Prfssnl) McGraw-Hill Prof.

Allen, Catherine B. The New Lottie Moon Story. 2nd ed. 320p. 1997. pap. text 12.95 (*1-56309-225-5*, W974118) Womans Mission Union.

Allen, Catherine J. The Hold Life Has: Coca & Cultural Identity in an Andean Community. LC 88-3965. (Series in Ethnographic Inquiry). (Illus.). 352p. (C). 1988. pap. text 17.95 (*0-87474-255-2*) Smithsonian.

Allen, Catherine J. & Garner, Nathan. Condor Qatay: Anthropology in Performance. (Illus.). 139p. (C). 1997. pap. text 10.95 (*0-88133-934-2*) Waveland Pr.

Allen, Chaney. I'm Black & I'm Sober: The Timeless Story of a Woman's Journey Back to Sanity. 2nd ed. LC 94-48160. 279p. (Orig.). pap. 11.95 (*1-56838-071-2*) Hazelden.

Allen, Charles. Notes of the Bacon-Shakespeare Question. 1973. 59.95 (*0-8490-0738-0*) Gordon Pr.
— Notes on the Bacon-Shakespeare Question. LC 75-113542. reprint ed. 52.50 (*0-404-00326-5*) AMS Pr.
— Plain Tales from the Raj: Images of British India in the 20th Century. LC 76-8693. (C). 1992. reprint ed. pap. text 10.00 (*0-8364-2835-8*, Pub. by Rupa) S Asia.
— Pocket Dictionary of Baritone Ukulele Chords. 1971. pap. 2.95 (*0-934286-21-3*) Kenyon.
— Pocket Dictionary of Mandolin Chords. 1971. pap. 2.95 (*0-934286-23-X*) Kenyon.
— Pocket Dictionary of Tenor Banjo Chords. 1971. pap. 2.95 (*0-934286-20-5*) Kenyon.
— Thunder & Lightning: The RAF in the Gulf War. xii, 165p. 1991. pap. 20.00 (*0-11-701625-X*, HM7728) Statnry Office.

Allen, Charles, jt. auth. see Ryder, George.

Allen, Charles D. American Book-Plates. (Illus.). 437p. 1972. 26.95 (*0-405-08202-9*) Ayer.

Allen, Charles E., jt. auth. see Harman, Thomas L.

Allen, Charles F. & Portis, Jonathan. The Comeback Kid: The Life & Career of Bill Clinton. (Illus.). 256p. 1992. 18.95 (*1-55972-154-5*, Birch Ln Pr) Carol Pub Group.

Allen, Charles L. All Things Are Possible Through Prayer: The Faith-Filled Guidebook That Can Change Your Life. LC 58-11022. 128p. (YA). (gr. 10). 1991. reprint ed. mass mkt. 3.99 (*0-8007-8000-0*, Spire) Revell.
— God's Psychiatry. LC 53-12523. 160p. (gr. 11). 1988. mass mkt. 3.99 (*0-8007-8015-9*, Spire) Revell.
— God's Psychiatry: Healing for the Troubled Heart & Spirit. LC 53-12523. 164p. (gr. 11). 1992. pap. 7.99 (*0-8007-5010-1*) Revell.
— Love Is Patient, Love Is Kind. LC 88-37589. 1989. 4.95 (*0-687-22812-3*) Abingdon.
— My Lord & My God. large type ed. (Large Print Inspirational Ser.). 80p. 1987. pap. 5.95 (*0-8027-2588-0*) Walker & Co.
— Siquiatria de Dios.Tr. of God's Psychiatry. 176p. 1975. 7.99 (*0-88113-280-2*) Caribe Betania.
— When You Graduate: Living a Life That Makes a Difference. deluxe ed. 64p. 1997. 6.99 (*0-88486-166-X*, Bristol Park Bks) Arrowood Pr.

Allen, Charles L. & Biggs, Mouzon. When You Graduate. rev. ed. LC 88-38571. 1989. 7.95 (*0-687-45043-8*) Abingdon.

Allen, Charles L. & Rice, Helen Steiner. When You Lose a Loved One/Life Is Forever. LC 59-5995. 132p. 1988. pap. 6.99 (*0-8007-5031-4*) Revell.

Allen, Charles Livingstone. Meet the Methodists: An Introduction to the United Methodist Church. LC 85-28794. 93p. 1986. pap. 4.95 (*0-687-24650-4*) Abingdon.
— Meet the Methodists: An Introduction to the United Methodist Church. 1998. pap. text 4.95 (*0-687-08232-3*) Abingdon.

Allen, Charles M. Grasses of Louisiana. 2nd ed. 320p. 1992. text 30.00 (*0-9633191-2-4*) CPH Preserv Soc.

Allen, Charles M., jt. auth. see Thomas, R. Dale.

Allen, Charles R., Jr. From Hitler to Uncle Sam: How American Intelligence Used Nazi War Criminals. 426p. write for info. (*0-318-61486-3*) Highgate Hse.
— Nazi War Criminals in America. LC 86-110559. 116p. 1985. 6.95 (*0-934215-00-6*) Highgate Hse.

Allen, Charles W. From Fort Laramie to Wounded Knee: In the West That Was. Jensen, Richard E., ed. LC 97-20276. (Illus.). xxvii, 296p. 1997. text 45.00 (*0-8032-1045-0*) U of Nebr Pr.

Allen, Charlotte. The Human Christ: The Misguided Search for the Historical Jesus. 1997. 28.00 (*0-02-874025-4*) Free Pr.
— The Human Christ: The Misguided Search for the Historical Jesus. LC 97-46463. 400p. 1998. 26.00 (*0-684-82725-5*) Free Pr.

Allen, Charlotte Vale. Acts of Kindness. 220p. 1998. reprint ed. pap. 20.00 (*1-892738-03-1*) Isld Nation.
— Acts of Kindness. 232p. 1998. reprint ed. 22.95 (*1-892738-18-X*, Pub. by Isld Nation) Brodart.
— Becoming. 1998. reprint ed. pap. 20.00 (*1-892738-09-0*) Isld Nation.
— Becoming. 224p. 1999. reprint ed. 22.95 (*1-892738-24-4*, Pub. by Isld Nation) Brodart.
— Becoming. 1994. reprint ed. 20.00 (*0-7278-4659-0*) Severn Hse.
— Claudia's Shadow. (Mira Bks.). 304p. 1996. per. 24.00 (*1-55166-245-0*, 1-66245-1, Mira Bks) Harlequin Bks.
— Claudia's Shadow. 1997. per. 5.99 (*1-55166-177-2*, 1-66177-6, Mira Bks) Harlequin Bks.
— Daddy's Girl. 272p. 1984. mass mkt. 6.99 (*0-425-11367-1*) Berkley Pub.

***Allen, Charlotte Vale.** Destinies. 318p. 1999. reprint ed. pap. 20.00 (*1-892738-25-2*) Isld Nation.
— Dream Train. 277p. 1999. reprint ed. pap. 20.00 (*1-892738-27-9*) Isld Nation.

Allen, Charlotte Vale. Dreaming in Color. 442p. 1995. per. 5.99 (*1-55166-030-X*, 1-66030-7, Mira Bks) Harlequin Bks.
— Dreaming in Color. large type ed. LC 93-6325. 1993. 23.95 (*1-56895-040-3*) Wheeler Pub.
— Gentle Stranger. 1998. reprint ed. pap. 20.00 (*1-892738-08-2*) Isld Nation.
— Gentle Stranger. 240p. 1999. reprint ed. 22.95 (*1-892738-23-6*, Pub. by Isld Nation) Brodart.
— Gifts of Love. 300p. 1998. reprint ed. pap. 20.00 (*0-9657437-5-6*) Isld Nation.
— Gifts of Love. 224p. 1998. reprint ed. 22.95 (*1-892738-10-4*, Pub. by Isld Nation) Brodart.
— Hidden Meanings. 1998. reprint ed. pap. 20.00 (*1-892738-07-4*) Isld Nation.
— Hidden Meanings. 272p. 1999. reprint ed. 23.95 (*1-892738-22-8*, Pub. by Isld Nation) Brodart.

***Allen, Charlotte Vale.** Illusions. 262p. 1999. reprint ed. pap. 20.00 (*1-892738-32-5*) Isld Nation.

Allen, Charlotte Vale. Intimate Friends. 1993. mass mkt. 5.99 (*0-8041-0665-7*) Ivy Books.

***Allen, Charlotte Vale.** Intimate Friends. 246p. 1999. reprint ed. pap. 20.00 (*1-892738-31-7*) Isld Nation.

Allen, Charlotte Vale. Julia's Sister. 240p. 1998. reprint ed. pap. 20.00 (*1-892738-01-5*) Isld Nation.
— Julia's Sister. 224p. 1998. reprint ed. 22.95 (*1-892738-16-3*, Pub. by Isld Nation) Brodart.

***Allen, Charlotte Vale.** Leftover Dreams. 592p. 1999. reprint ed. pap. 23.00 (*1-892738-29-5*) Isld Nation.

Allen, Charlotte Vale. Love Life. 272p. 1998. reprint ed. pap. 20.00 (*0-9657437-4-8*) Isld Nation.
— Matters of the Heart. 1998. reprint ed. pap. 22.00 (*1-892738-05-8*) Isld Nation.
— Matters of the Heart. 460p. 1999. reprint ed. 24.95 (*1-892738-20-1*, Pub. by Isld Nation) Brodart.
— Meet Me in Time. 400p. 1998. reprint ed. pap. 22.00 (*0-9657437-9-9*) Isld Nation.
— Meet Me in Time. 434p. 1998. reprint ed. 24.95 (*1-892738-14-7*, Pub. by Isld Nation) Brodart.
— Memories. 1998. reprint ed. pap. 20.00 (*1-892738-04-X*) Isld Nation.
— Memories. 336p. 1998. reprint ed. 23.95 (*1-892738-19-8*, Pub. by Isld Nation) Brodart.
— Mixed Emotions. 250p. 1998. pap. 20.00 (*0-9657437-8-0*) Isld Nation.
— Mixed Emotions. 1991. 19.00 (*0-7278-4159-9*) Severn Hse.
— Mixed Emotions. 260p. 1998. reprint ed. 22.95 (*1-892738-13-9*, Pub. by Isld Nation) Brodart.
— Moments of Meaning. 230p. 1998. reprint ed. pap. 20.00 (*1-892738-00-7*) Isld Nation.
— Moments of Meaning. 224p. 1998. reprint ed. 22.95 (*1-892738-15-5*, Pub. by Isld Nation) Brodart.
— Mood Indigo. 288p. 1997. 23.95 (*0-9657437-1-3*) Isld Nation.

***Allen, Charlotte Vale.** Mood Indigo. large type ed. 426p. 2000. lib. bdg. 27.95 (*1-58547-038-4*) Ctr Point Pubg.

Allen, Charlotte Vale. Night Magic. 1989. 18.95 (*0-689-11884-8*) Atheneum Yung Read.
— Night Magic. 288p. 1989. 22.95 (*0-385-25212-9*) Doubleday.

***Allen, Charlotte Vale.** Night Magic. 2nd ed. 274p. 1998. reprint ed. pap. 20.00 (*0-9657437-3-X*) Isld Nation.

Allen, Charlotte Vale. Painted Lives. large type ed. (General Ser.). 470p. 1991. lib. bdg. 20.95 (*0-8161-5180-6*, G K Hall Lrg Type) Mac Lib Ref.

***Allen, Charlotte Vale.** Painted Lives. 266p. 1999. reprint ed. pap. 20.00 (*1-892738-33-3*) Isld Nation.

Allen, Charlotte Vale. Perfect Fools. 230p. 1998. pap. 20.00 (*0-9657437-7-2*) Isld Nation.
— Perfect Fools. 224p. 1998. reprint ed. 22.95 (*1-892738-12-0*, Pub. by Isld Nation) Brodart.
— Pieces of Dreams. 1998. reprint ed. pap. 20.00 (*1-892738-06-6*) Isld Nation.
— Pieces of Dreams. 314p. 1999. reprint ed. 23.95 (*1-892738-21-X*, Pub. by Isld Nation) Brodart.

Allen, Charlotte Vale. Promises. 369p. 1980. reprint ed. pap. 20.00 (*1-892738-26-0*) Isld Nation.

Allen, Charlotte Vale. Running Away. 1996. pap. text 5.50 (*1-55166-150-0*, 1-66150-3, Mira Bks) Harlequin Bks.
— Somebody's Baby. LC 95-22162. 304p. 1995. 19.95 (*1-55166-124-1*, Mira Bks) Harlequin Bks.
— Somebody's Baby. (Mira Bks.). 1996. mass mkt. 5.99 (*0-614-08421-0*, 1-66067-9, Mira Bks); per. 5.99 (*1-55166-067-9*, Mira Bks) Harlequin Bks.
— Sweeter Music. 200p. 1998. reprint ed. pap. 20.00 (*1-892738-02-3*) Isld Nation.
— Sweeter Music. 224p. 1998. reprint ed. 22.95 (*1-892738-17-1*, Pub. by Isld Nation) Brodart.
— Sweeter Music. 1994. reprint ed. lib. bdg. 19.00 (*0-7278-4595-0*) Severn Hse.
— Times of Triumph. 1998. reprint ed. pap. 20.00 (*0-9657437-6-4*) Isld Nation.
— Times of Triumph. 398p. 1998. reprint ed. 24.95 (*1-892738-11-2*, Pub. by Isld Nation) Brodart.

***Allen, Charlotte Vale.** Time/Steps. 546p. 1999. reprint ed. pap. 23.00 (*1-892738-30-9*) Isld Nation.

Allen, Charlotte Vale, see Marlowe, Katharine, pseud.

Allen, Chester. Badlands Showdown. large type ed. (Linford Western Library). 240p. 1987. pap. 8.95 (*0-7089-6348-X*, Linford) Ulverscroft.
— Farming Comes of Age: The Remarkable Photographs of J. C. Allen & Son. Strode, William, ed. (Illus.). 160p. 1994. 24.95 (*1-56469-024-5*) Harmony Hse Pub.

Allen, Chris. The Foreplay Gourmet: Over One Hundred Outrageous Recipes for Making Love. 128p. 1995. 19.95 (*0-9636454-3-9*) Creat Fire.
— The Foreplay Gourmet Vol. II: Over One Hundred More Outrageous Recipes for Making Love. 128p. 1997. 19.95 (*0-9636454-4-7*) Creat Fire.

Allen, Chris. 1001 Sex Secret Every Ma. LC 94-23333. 352p. 1995. pap. 8.00 (*0-380-72483-9*, Avon Bks) Morrow Avon.
— 1001 Sex Secret Every Wo. LC 94-32316. 352p. 1995. pap. 8.00 (*0-380-72484-7*, Avon Bks) Morrow Avon.

Allen, Chris. One Thousand One Sex Secrets Every Man Should Know. 340p. (Orig.). 1993. pap. 14.95 (*0-9636454-0-4*) Creat Fire.
— One Thousand One Sex Secrets Every Woman Should Know. 340p. (Orig.). 1993. pap. 14.95 (*0-9636454-1-2*) Creat Fire.
— One Thousand One Sex Secrets Set: 1001 Sex Secrets Every Man Should Know; 1001 Sex Secrets Every Woman Should Know, 2 vols., Set. 680p. 1993. pap. 24.95 (*0-9636454-2-0*) Creat Fire.

Allen, Chris & John, Deborah R., eds. Advances in Consumer Research: Proceedings of the 1993 Conference, Vol. 21. 608p. 1994. 59.00 (*0-915552-32-9*) Assn Consumer Res.

Allen, Chris & Radu, Michael. Benin & the Congo. 220p. 1992. 49.00 (*0-86187-481-1*, Pub. by P P Pubs) Cassell & Continuum.
— Benin & the Congo. (Marxist Regimes Ser.). 220p. 1992. pap. 17.50 (*0-86187-482-X*) St Martin.

Allen, Chris & Williams, Gavin, eds. Sub-Saharan Africa. LC 81-16902. (Sociology of "Developing Societies" Ser.). 240p. 1982. pap. 14.00 (*0-85345-598-8*, Pub. by Monthly Rev) NYU Pr.

Allen, Chris, jt. auth. see Kurtz, Edwin B.

Allen, Chris, ed. see Rison, Robert.

Allen, Chris, tr. see Caulfield, Carlota.

Allen, Christina G. Christina's African Adventure. 1924. lib. bdg. write for info. (*0-688-17827-8*, Wm Morrow) Morrow Avon.

***Allen, Christine, ed.** Skills for Life: Information Literacy for Grades K-6. 2nd ed. (Professional Growth Ser.). (Illus.). 227p. 1999. pap. 39.95 (*0-938865-83-8*) Linworth Pub.

***Allen, Christine & Anderson, Mary Alice, eds.** Skills for Life: Information Literacy for Grades 7-12. 2nd ed. (Professional Growth Ser.). (Illus.). 237p. 1999. pap. 39.95 (*0-938865-84-6*) Linworth Pub.

***Allen, Christine & Varner, Collin.** Gardens of Vancouver. 2000. 36.95 (*1-55192-288-6*) Raincoast Bk.

Allen, Christopher. Art in Australia: From Colorization to Postmodernism. LC 96-61173. (World of Art Ser.). (Illus.). 224p. (Orig.). 1997. pap. 14.95 (*0-500-20301-6*, Pub. by Thames Hudson) Norton.
— Evidence. 2nd ed. (Questions & Answers Ser.). 278p. 1996. 18.00 (*1-85941-267-X*, Pub. by Cavendish Pubng) Gaunt.
— The Law of Evidence in Victorian England. LC 96-49926. (Cambridge Studies in English Legal History). 222p. (C). 1997. text 59.95 (*0-521-58418-3*) Cambridge U Pr.

***Allen, Christopher.** Oracle8 Certified Professional Financial Applications Consultant Exam Guide. 1072p. 2000. 99.99 (*0-07-212358-3*) McGraw.

Allen, Christopher. Practical Guide to Evidence. xlii, 395p. 1998. pap. 38.00 (*1-85941-316-1*, Pub. by Cavendish Pubng) Gaunt.
— Sourcebook on Evidence. (Sourcebook Ser.). 750p. 1996. pap. 44.00 (*1-85941-110-X*, Pub. by Cavendish Pubng) Gaunt.

Allen, Christopher & Allen, Kimberly. A Butler's Life: Scenes from the Other Side of the Silver Salver. LC 94-24937. 192p. 1996. 18.95 (*0-913720-95-X*) Beil.

Allen, Christopher, et al. Case Preparation, 1998-99. 3rd ed. (Inns of Court School of Law Ser.). 335p. 1998. pap. 42.00 (*1-85431-771-7*) Gaunt.
— Case Preparation, 1997/98. 2nd ed. (Inns of Court School of Law Ser.). 335p. 1997. pap. 40.00 (*1-85431-673-7*, Pub. by Blackstone Pr) Gaunt.

Allen, Christopher, jt. auth. see Eades, J. S.

Allen, Christopher J., jt. auth. see Allen, Cynthia L.

Allen, Christopher S. Transformation of the German Political Party System: Institutional Crisis or Democratic Renewal? LC 99-13734. 288p. 1999. 69.95 (*1-57181-127-3*) Berghahn Bks.

Allen, Chuck. Oklahoma Celebrity Cookbook. Wyett, Stacey, ed. 160p. 1991. 14.95 (*0-9631825-0-1*) Exec Coffee Srv.

Allen, Cindi N. Take a Bite Out of Ryme: Poetry Unit. (J). Date not set. teacher ed. 6.95 (*0-910857-62-8*, 062-8AP) Educ Impress.

Allen, Claudia. Ripe Conditions. LC 95-145824. 1994. 5.60 (*0-87129-485-0*, R56) Dramatic Pub.

— Winter. 54p. 1996. pap. 5.60 (*0-87129-634-9*, W77) Dramatic Pub.

Allen, Claudia, et al. Understanding Cognitive Performance Modes: Version 1.3. 1997. pap. 35.00 (*0-9654111-0-9*) Allen Conf.

Allen, Claudia K. Structures of the Cognitive Performance Modes. Bertrand, James O., ed. (Illus.). 120p. 1999. pap. 35.00 (*0-9654111-3-3*) Allen Conf.

Allen, Claudia K., et al. Occupational Therapy Treatment Goals for the Physically & Cognitively Disabled. 350p. (C). 1992. pap. text 58.00 (*0-910317-72-0*) Am Occup Therapy.

Allen, Cliff & Kania, Deborah. Web Catalog Cookbook. LC 97-9529. (Illus.). 412p. 1997. pap., pap. text 44.99 incl. cd-rom (*0-471-18331-8*) Wiley.

Allen, Cliff, et al. Internet World's Guide to One-to-One Web Marketing. LC 97-48813. 400p. 1998. pap. 29.99 (*0-471-25166-6*) Wiley.

Allen, Clifford. The Sexual Perversions & Abnormalities: A Study in the Psychology of Paraphilia. LC 78-27783. 346p. 1979. reprint ed. lib. bdg. 69.50 (*0-313-20627-9*, ALSP, Greenwood Pr) Greenwood.

Allen, Clifford G., Jr. & Davis, Murt. How to Buy Life Insurance & Live to Enjoy It: A Shocking Expose of Insurance Industry Lies, Frauds & Abuses & How to Beat Them. 116p. (Orig.). 1994. pap. 29.00 (*0-9637850-0-1*) Equity Pr PA.

Allen, Colin, et al, eds. Nature's Purposes: Analyses of Function & Design in Biology. LC 97-29290. 576p. 1998. 60.00 (*0-262-01168-9*, Bradford Bks) MIT Pr.

— Nature's Purposes: Analysis of Function & Design in Biology. LC 97-29290. (Illus.). 576p. 1998. pap. text 30.00 (*0-262-51097-9*, Bradford Bks) MIT Pr.

Allen, Colin & Bekoff, Marc. Species of Mind: The Philosophy & Biology of Cognitive Ethology. LC 97-3263. (Illus.). 232p. 1997. 35.00 (*0-262-01163-8*, Bradford Bks) MIT Pr.

— Species of Mind: The Philosophy & Biology of Cognitive Ethology. LC 97-3263. (Illus.). 232p. 1999. reprint ed. pap. 18.50 (*0-262-51108-8*, Bradford Bks) MIT Pr.

Allen, Colin, et al. Logic Primer. LC 92-11314. 171p. (C). 1992. pap. text 15.00 (*0-262-51065-0*, Bradford Bks) MIT Pr.

Allen, Colin, jt. auth. see Cummins, Denise D.

Allen, Connie J., jt. auth. see Allen, Gerald R.

***Allen, Conrad.** Murder on the Lusitania. 2000. mass mkt. 5.99 (*0-312-97571-6*) St Martin.

— Murder on the Mauretania. 2000. 23.75 (*0-312-24116-X*) St Martin.

***Allen, Constance.** Bert's Beautiful Sights. (Illus.). 10p. (J). 2000. 3.99 (*0-375-80484-6*, Pub. by Random Bks Yng Read) Random.

— Elmo's Christmas Colors. LC 99-46963. (Sesame Street Pop-up Ser.). (Illus.). 24p. (J). (ps). 2000. 4.99 (*0-375-80371-8*) Random.

— Elmo's Mother Goose. (Big Bird's Favorite Bird Bks.). 12p. 2000. 4.99 (*0-375-80541-9*, Pub. by Random Bks Yng Read) Random.

— Ernie Follows His Nose. (Illus.). 10p. (J). 2000. 3.99 (*0-375-80485-4*) Random Bks Yng Read.

— Grover's Guide to Good Manners. (J). 2001. mass mkt. 4.99 (*0-375-81209-1*, Pub. by Random Bks Yng Read) Random.

Allen, Constance. Merry Christmas Everybody. (ps-3). 1999. pap. 3.25 (*0-375-80370-X*, Pub. by Random Bks Yng Read) Random.

Allen, Constance M. Romance of a Mystic Ring (1906) 204p. 1998. reprint ed. pap. 17.95 (*0-7661-0538-5*) Kessinger Pub.

***Allen, Corey.** Arranging in the Digital World: Techniques for Arranging Popular Music Using Today's Electronic & Digital Instruments. 88p. 2000. per. 19.95 incl. disk (*0-634-00634-7*) H Leonard.

Allen County Police Officers Association Staff, compiled by. Kids Talk to Kids. (Annual Essay Contest Ser.). 75p. (Orig.). (YA). (gr. 6-12). 1990. pap. write for info. (*0-9614659-6-4*) Cuchullain Pubns.

— Kids Talk to Kids. 75p. (Orig.). (YA). (gr. 6-12). 1991. pap. write for info. (*0-9614659-7-2*) Cuchullain Pubns.

Allen, Craig. Eating Out in Barcelona & Caytalunya: A Personal Guide to over 75 Local Restaurants. LC 94-5658. (Illus.). 192p. 1994. pap. 13.95 (*1-56656-151-5*) Interlink Pub.

— Eisenhower & the Mass Media: Peace, Prosperity, & Prime-Time TV. LC 92-35615. (Illus.). xii, 260p. (C). 1993. 55.00 (*0-8078-2080-6*); pap. 19.95 (*0-8078-4409-8*) U of NC Pr.

Allen, Craig M. Women & Men Who Sexually Abuse Children: A Comparative Analysis. Bear, Euan, ed. LC 92-60133. 80p. 1991. reprint ed. pap. 17.50 (*1-884444-09-1*) Safer Soc.

Allen, Cynthia L. Case-Marking & Reanalysis: Grammatical Relations from Old to Early Modern English. (Illus.). 528p. 1995. text 95.00 (*0-19-824096-1*) OUP.

— Case-Marking & Reanalysis: Grammatical Relations from Old to Early Modern English. (Illus.). 528p. 1999. pap. text 35.00 (*0-19-823867-3*) OUP.

***Allen, Cynthia L. & Allen, Christopher J.** Antique Lighting of the Nineteenth Century, 3 vols. (Illus.). 400p. 1999. pap. 85.00 (*1-929638-01-9*) Antique Light.

— Antique Lighting of the Nineteenth Century: The Lighting Fixtures of Mitchell Vance & Company, New York, NY, Vol. 3. (Illus.). 1999. pap. 25.00 (*1-929638-04-3*) Antique Light.

— Antique Lighting of the Nineteenth Century: The Lighting Fixtures of W. C. Vosburgh Company, Brooklyn NY, Vol. 2. (Illus.). 1999. pap. 25.00 (*1-929638-03-5*) Antique Light.

— Antique Lighting of the Nineteenth Century: The Lighting Fixtures of C. H. McKenney & Co., Boston, Massachusetts, Vol. 1. (Illus.). 1999. pap. 35.00 (*1-929638-02-7*) Antique Light.

Allen, D. Dancing Tales & Other Fishy Jingles. (Shorey Historical Ser.). 95p. reprint ed. pap. 10.00 (*0-8466-0287-3*, S287) Shoreys Bkstore.

— Family Justice: A Structure for the Family Court. (C). 1989. 39.00 (*0-903534-68-1*, Pub. by Brit Ag for Adopt & Fost) St Mut.

— Indians of the Northwest Coast. (Illus.). 32p. pap. 4.95 (*0-919654-82-7*) Hancock House.

— Totem Poles of the Northwest. (Illus.). 32p. pap. 4.95 (*0-919654-83-5*) Hancock House.

Allen, D. C., jt. auth. see Hamilton, P.

Allen, D. G., jt. auth. see Heintz, A. Peter.

Allen, D. H. & Lagoudas, D. C., eds. Damage Mechanics in Composites. (AMD Series, Vol. 150: AD: Vol. 32). 336p. 1992. 65.00 (*0-7918-1108-5*, G00752) ASME.

Allen, D. H. & Voyiadjis, George Z., eds. Damage & Interfacial Debonding in Composites. LC 96-227542. (Studies in Applied Mechanics: Vol. 44). 284p. Date not set. text 163.75 (*0-444-82338-7*) Elsevier.

Allen, D. J. An Annotated List of Diseases, Pathogens & Associated Fungi of the Common Bean (Phaseolus Vulgaris) in Eastern & Southern Africa. (Phytopathological Paper Ser.: No. 34). 32p. 1995. pap. 34.50 (*0-85198-938-1*) C A B Intl.

— The Pathology of Tropical Food Legumes: Disease Resistance in Crop Improvement. LC 82-20301. (Illus.). 431p. reprint ed. pap. 133.70 (*0-8357-4396-9*, 205233900007) Bks Demand.

Allen, D. J. & Lenne, J. M., eds. The Pathology of Food & Pasture Legumes. LC 97-15283. (A CAB International Publication). (Illus.). 776p. (C). 1998. text 175.00 (*0-85199-166-1*) OUP.

Allen, D. K., jt. auth. see Holyoak, J. H.

Allen, D. M. Deciphering Motivation in Psychotherapy. LC 91-2458. (Critical Issues in Psychiatry Ser.). (Illus.). 200p. (C). 1991. text 45.00 (*0-306-43790-2*, Kluwer Plenum) Kluwer Academic.

Allen, D. Ronald. The Stars of His Coming. (Illus.). 122p. 1997. pap. 10.95 (*0-9635272-2-3*, BK101) Pillar TX.

Allen, D. W. & Walker, B. J. Organophosphorous Chemistry, Vol. 25. (Specialist Periodical Reports). 350p. 1994. 310.00 (*0-85186-390-6*, R6390) CRC Pr.

— Organophosphorus Chemistry, Vol. 24. 432p. 1993. 310.00 (*0-85186-320-5*, R6320) CRC Pr.

***Allen Daley, Patrick.** Most Riveting Read Alouds of All Time! Build Comprehension, Listening & Higher-Order Thinking. 1999. pap. 14.95 (*0-439-04759-5*) Scholastic.

Allen, Dan. The Dandelion House & Scenes from Love's Cafe. 1995. pap. 8.99 (*0-8341-9437-6*, MP-768) Nazarene.

Allen, Dan. Don't Die on the Mountain. 2nd ed. LC 97-95034. (Illus.). viii, 214p. 1998. pap. 12.00 (*0-9662690-0-4*) Diapensia Pr.

Allen, Dana G. A Handbook of Veterinary Drugs. 678p. 1993. text 47.95 (*0-397-51265-1*) Lppncott W & W.

— A Handbook of Veterinary Drugs. 2nd ed. LC 98-9454. 688p. 1998. pap. text 45.95 (*0-397-58435-0*) Lppncott W & W.

Allen, Dana G. & Pringle, John K. A Handbook of Veterinary Drugs. 2nd ed. 688p. 1998. pap. text. write for info. (*0-7817-1443-5*) Lppncott W & W.

Allen, Danice. Arms of a Stranger. 384p. (Orig.). 1995. mass mkt. 4.50 (*0-380-77726-6*, Avon Bks) Morrow Avon.

— Perfect Gentleman. 1997. mass mkt. 5.50 (*0-380-78151-4*, Avon Bks) Morrow Avon.

— Remember Me. 384p. (Orig.). 1996. mass mkt. 4.99 (*0-380-78150-6*, Avon Bks) Morrow Avon.

Allen, Daniel G. Allen. Genealogy of the Allen Family (Of Prudence Island, RI) 154p. 1997. reprint ed. pap. 24.00 (*0-8328-7233-4*); reprint ed. lib. bdg. 34.00 (*0-8328-7232-6*) Higginson Bk Co.

Allen, Daniel K. On Macintosh Programming: Advanced Techniques. 512p. 1989. pap. text 24.95 (*0-201-51737-X*) Addison-Wesley.

***Allen, Danielle S.** The Politics of Punishing in Democratic Athens. LC 99-34848. 371p. 1999. 39.50 (*0-691-05869-5*, Pub. by Princeton U Pr) Cal Prin Full Svc.

Allen, Darina. The Festive Food of Ireland. LC 92-85180. (Illus.). 62p. 1994. pap. 7.95 (*1-879373-35-1*) Roberts Rinehart.

— Festive Food of Ireland. (Illus.). 63p. 1993. 13.95 (*1-879373-37-8*) Roberts Rinehart.

— Simply Delicious. (Illus.). 78p. (Orig.). 1989. pap. 15.95 (*0-7171-1687-5*, Pub. by Gill & MacMill) Irish Bks Media.

— Simply Delicious Fish. (Illus.). 100p. (Orig.). 1991. pap. 15.95 (*0-7171-1822-3*, Pub. by Gill & MacMill) Irish Bks Media.

— Simply Delicious Food for Families & Friends. (Simply Delicious Ser.). (Illus.). 108p. 1993. pap. 15.95 (*0-7171-2060-0*, Pub. by Gill & MacMill) Irish Bks Media.

— Simply Delicious Irish Christmas. LC 98-34444. (Illus.). 100p. 1998. pap. 14.95 (*1-56554-408-0*) Pelican.

— Simply Delicious Meals in Minutes. (Simply Delicious Ser.). (Illus.). 90p. (Orig.). 1996. pap. 15.95 (*0-7171-2375-8*, Pub. by Gill & MacMill) Irish Bks Media.

— Simply Delicious 2. (Illus.). 91p. (Orig.). 1990. pap. 15.95 (*0-7171-1770-7*, Pub. by Gill & MacMill) Irish Bks Media.

— Simply Delicious Versatile Vegetables. (Simply Delicious Ser.). (Illus.). 144p. (Orig.). 1994. pap. 15.95 (*0-7171-2152-6*, Pub. by Gill & MacMill) Irish Bks Media.

Allen, Dave. In Your Own Voice: A Manual for Public Speakers. 2nd ed. 70p. 1989. pap. text 9.95 (*0-89641-185-0*) American Pr.

Allen, David. Air: All about Cyclones, Rainbows, Clouds, Ozone & More. (Illus.). 32p. (J). 1993. pap. 5.95 (*1-895688-08-6*, Pub. by Owl Bks) Firefly Bks Ltd.

— Assessing Student Learning: From Grading to Understanding. LC 98-16982. (Series on School Reform). 1998. 51.00 (*0-8077-3754-2*); pap. 23.95 (*0-8077-3753-4*) Tchrs Coll.

***Allen, David.** The Collection of Short Stories. Loftise, Gary, ed. 201p. (J). 2000. pap. text 12.95 (*0-9642120-1-3*) Chiffon Pubs.

Allen, David. Common Foreign Security. 144p. 1999. pap. 19.00 (*0-582-30492-X*) Addison-Wesley.

— Fear of Strangers: And Its Consequences. 224p. (Orig.). 1993. pap. 13.50 (*0-937884-14-6*, Bennington Bks) Hystry Mystry.

— Geography 110 Workbook. 84p. (C). 1998. pap. text 18.95 (*0-7872-5681-1*, 41568101) Kendall-Hunt.

***Allen, David.** Ipswich Borough Archives, 1255-1835: A Catalogue. (Suffolk Records Society Ser.). (Illus.). 758p. 2000. 75.00 (*0-85115-772-6*, Suffolk Records Soc) Boydell & Brewer.

Allen, David. Kenai Pathways. (Illus.). 44p. 1995. pap. 4.95 (*0-930931-14-9*) Alaska Natural.

***Allen, David.** Peaceful Edge: Staying Stress Free & Productive in a World of Too Much to Do. 192p. 2001. text 24.95 (*0-670-88906-7*, Viking) Viking Penguin.

— Performing Chekhov. LC 99-31944. 280p. (C). 1999. pap. 24.99 (*0-415-18935-7*) Routledge.

— Stanislavski for Beginners. 1999. pap. text 11.00 (*0-86316-268-1*) Writers & Readers.

Allen, David & Evans, Jan, compiled by. Double Happiness, Two Lives in China. 347p. 1995. per. 17.50 (*0-614-24790-X*) Tesseract SD.

Allen, David C. Succeeding on Your Own Terms. 145p. 1998. 20.00 (*0-9665267-0-8*) Excel Pr NC.

Allen, David F., ed. The Cocaine Crisis. LC 86-30518. 270p. 1987. 65.00 (*0-306-42482-7*, Plenum Trade) Perseus Pubng.

Allen, David G. In English Ways: The Movement of Societies & the Transferal of English Local Law & Custom to Massachusetts Bay in the Seventeenth Century. LC 80-13198. 334p. reprint ed. pap. 103.60 (*0-7837-0286-8*, 204060700018) Bks Demand.

Allen, David G., et al, eds. Critique, Resistance, & Action: Working Papers in the Politics of Nursing. LC 92-48677. 208p. (C). 1992. pap. text 24.95 (*0-88737-563-4*) Natl League Nurse.

Allen, David G. & Hall, David, eds. Seventeenth-Century New England. xx, 340p. 1984. text 40.00 (*0-8139-1048-X*) U Pr of Va.

Allen, David G. & McDermott, Kathleen. Accounting for Success: A History of Price Waterhouse in America, 1890-1990. LC 92-15492. 400p. 1993. 35.00 (*0-87584-328-X*) Harvard Busn.

Allen, David G. & White, Robert A., eds. Subjects on the World's Stage: Essays on British Literature of the Middle Ages & the Renaissance. LC 94-42534. (Illus.). 320p. 1995. 43.50 (*0-87413-544-3*) U Delaware Pr.

— Traditions & Innovations: Essays on British Literature of the Middle Ages & the Renaissance. LC 88-40599. (Illus.). 272p. 1990. 39.50 (*0-685-32622-5*) Bucknell U Pr.

— Traditions & Innovations: Essays on British Literature of the Middle Ages & the Renaissance. LC 88-40599. (Illus.). 272p. 1990. 39.50 (*0-685-31211-9*) Susquehanna U Pr.

— Traditions & Innovations: Essays on British Literature of the Middle Ages & the Renaissance. LC 88-40599. (Illus.). 272p. 1990. 39.50 (*0-685-31249-6*) U Delaware Pr.

— The Work of Dissimilitude: Essays from the 6th Citadel Conference on Medieval & Renaissance Literature. LC 90-51011. (Illus.). 296p. 1992. 42.50 (*0-87413-435-8*) U Delaware Pr.

Allen, David G., ed. see Adams, John Q.

Allen, David G., jt. ed. see Lee, John A.

Allen, David H. & Haisler, Walter E. Introduction to Aerospace Structural Analysis. LC 84-13194. (Illus.). 528p. 1985. text 106.95 (*0-471-88839-7*) Wiley.

Allen, David J. Sussex. (Country Guide Ser.: No. 4). (Illus.). 120p. pap. 12.50 (*0-7478-0272-6*, Pub. by Shire Pubns) Parkwest Pubns.

Allen, David J. & Imrie, Patrick R. Discovering the North Downs Way. (Orig.). 1989. pap. 25.00 (*0-85263-884-1*, Pub. by Shire Pubns) St Mut.

Allen, David M. Accommodation & Cleaning Services Vol. 1: Operations. (Illus.). 312p. (Orig.). 1999. pap. 39.00 (*0-7487-0290-3*, Pub. by S Thornes Pubs) Trans-Atl Phila.

— Accommodation & Cleaning Services Vol. 2: Management, Vol.2. (Illus.). 128p. (Orig.). 1999. pap. 39.00 (*0-7487-0331-4*, Pub. by S Thornes Pubs) Trans-Atl Phila.

— Family Systems Approach to Individual Psychotherapy. LC 94-70369. 392p. 1995. pap. 60.00 (*1-56821-246-1*) Aronson.

— Unifying Individual & Family Therapies. LC 87-46328. (Jossey-Bass Social & Behavioral Science Ser.). 389p. reprint ed. pap. 120.60 (*0-7837-6531-2*, 204564300007) Bks Demand.

Allen, David N. & Levine, Victor. Nurturing Advanced Technology Enterprises: Emerging Issues in State & Local Economic Development Policy. LC 86-9411. 285p. 1986. 49.95 (*0-275-92136-0*, C2136, Praeger Pubs) Greenwood.

Allen, David S. & Jensen, Robert, eds. Freeing the First Amendment: Critical Perspectives on Freedom of Expression. 288p. (C). 1995. text 55.00 (*0-8147-0637-1*); pap. text 19.50 (*0-8147-0638-X*) NYU Pr.

Allen, David T. & Rosselot, Kirsten S. Pollution Prevention for Chemical Processes. LC 96-8438. 456p. 1996. 79.95 (*0-471-11587-8*) Wiley.

— Pollution Prevention for Chemical Processes: A Handbook with Solved Problems from the Refining & Chemical Processing Industries. (Illus.). 144p. (Orig.). (C). 1994. pap. text 40.00 (*0-7881-1407-7*) DIANE Pub.

Allen, David T., ed. see Setac Organization Staff & Setac Foundation for Environmental Education Staff.

Allen, David W., jt. auth. see Cull, Helen A.

Allen, David Y. Long Island (NY) Maps & Their Makers. LC 98-187438. 1997. 23.95 (*0-8488-1804-0*) Amereon Ltd.

***Allen, Davina.** The Changing Shape of Nursing Practice: The Role of Nurses in the Hospital Division of Labour. LC 00-30822. 2000. pap. write for info. (*0-415-21649-4*) Routledge.

Allen, Debbie. Brothers of the Knight. Sherry, Toby, ed. LC 98-53361. (Illus.). 40p. (J). (gr. k-4). 1999. 15.99 (*0-8037-2488-8*, Dial Yng Read) Peng Put Young Read.

— Trade Secrets of Retail Stars. Design & Type Staff, ed. 120p. (Orig.). 1996. pap. 19.95 (*0-9650965-4-8*) Image Dynamics.

Allen, Deborah. Puffins. LC 98-17172. (Let's Investigate Ser.). (Illus.). 32p. (YA). (gr. 2 up). 1999. lib. bdg. 19.95 (*0-88682-610-1*, Creat Educ) Creative Co.

Allen, Deborah E. Thinking Toward Solutions: Problem-Based Learning Activities for General Biology. Duch, Barbara J., ed. (Illus.). 128p. (C). 1998. pap. text 15.00 (*0-03-025033-1*, Pub. by Harcourt Coll Pubs) Harcourt.

Allen, Deborah I., jt. auth. see Bowman, Marjorie A.

Allen, Dell K. & Mortensen, Kay S. Metallurgy & Materials Science: Laboratory Manual. LC TN0669.A44. 224p. reprint ed. pap. 69.50 (*0-608-11135-X*, 201157800079) Bks Demand.

Allen, Denise. Roman Glass in Britain. (Archaeology Ser.: No. 76). (Illus.). 64p. 1999. pap. 10.50 (*0-7478-0373-0*, Pub. by Shire Pubns) Parkwest Pubns.

Allen, Dennis & Allen, Nan. The Door: A Resurrection Celebration. 1995. pap. 6.99 (*0-8341-9410-4*, ME-47) Nazarene.

***Allen, Dennis & Allen, Nan.** Kingdom Quest: The Ultimate Challenge. 1999. write for info. (*0-8341-9997-1*) Lillenas.

Allen, Dennis & Allen, Nan. Mr. Funfiddle's Christmas: Singer's Activity Book. 1995. pap. 3.99 (*0-8341-9308-6*, MC-92) Nazarene.

Allen, Dennis, et al. Positive I. D. 60p. 1987. 6.99 (*0-8341-9160-1*, MB-580) Lillenas.

Allen, Dennis, jt. auth. see Allen, Nan.

Allen, Dennis, jt. auth. see Bolton, Martha.

Allen, Dennis W. Sexuality in Victorian Fiction. LC 93-16225. (Project for Discourse & Theory Ser.: Vol. 15). 182p. 1994. pap. 13.95 (*0-8061-2583-7*) U of Okla Pr.

Allen, Derek. Economic Evaluation of Projects. 3rd ed. 194p. 1991. 40.00 (*0-85295-266-X*, 9CH17) Gulf Pub.

— Handbook of International Company Structures in the Major Industrial & Trading Countries of the World. 96p. 1995. 17.95 (*0-572-01521-6*, Pub. by Foulsham UK) Assoc Pubs Grp.

— Italy. LC 95-30687. (Country Fact Files Ser.). (J). 1996. lib. bdg. 24.26 (*0-8114-6196-3*) Raintree Steck-V.

Allen, Desmond W. Arkansas Confederate Pension Applications from Calhoun, Dallas, Ouachita, & Union Counties. 1991. pap. 10.00 (*0-941765-66-0*) Arkansas Res.

— Arkansas Confederate Pension Applications from Eastern Arkansas: Arkansas, Chicot, Clay, Craighead, Crittenden, Cross, Desha, Greene, Lee, Mississippi, Monroe, Phillips, Poinsett & St. Francis Counties. 50p. 1991. pap. 10.00 (*0-941765-57-1*) Arkansas Res.

— Arkansas Confederate Soldiers Series, 3 vols., Set. 1990. pap. 68.00 (*0-941765-70-9*) Arkansas Res.

— Arkansas' Mexican War Soldiers. 135p. 1988. pap. 18.00 (*0-941765-38-5*) Arkansas Res.

— Arkansas' Spanish-American War Soldiers. (Illus.). 273p. 1988. pap. 24.00 (*0-941765-32-6*) Arkansas Res.

— Arkansas Township Digest: Minor Civil Divisions, 1820-1990. (Illus.). 1994. pap. 32.00 (*0-941765-92-X*) Arkansas Res.

— Arkansas Union Soldiers Pension Application Index. LC 87-71975. 182p. 1987. pap. 20.00 (*0-941765-14-8*) Arkansas Res.

— Camp Pike, Arkansas, Index to Soldiers' Naturalizations, 1918. 134p. 1988. pap. 18.00 (*0-941765-39-3*) Arkansas Res.

— First Arkansas Confederate Mounted Rifles. (Illus.). 104p. 1988. pap. 16.00 (*0-941765-34-2*) Arkansas Res.

— First Arkansas Union Cavalry. (Arkansas Union Regiment Ser.). 148p. 1987. pap. 17.00 (*0-941765-16-4*) Arkansas Res.

— First Arkansas Union Infantry. (Arkansas Union Regiment Ser.). 104p. 1987. pap. 15.00 (*0-941765-20-2*) Arkansas Res.

— First Steps in Genealogy. LC 98-34129. 128p. 1998. pap. 14.99 (*1-55870-489-2*, Betrwy Bks) F & W Pubns Inc.

— The Fourteenth Arkansas Confederate Infantry. (Illus.). 58p. 1988. pap. 16.00 (*0-941765-29-6*) Arkansas Res.

— Fourth Arkansas Union Cavalry. (Arkansas Union Regiment Ser.). 120p. 1988. pap. 15.00 (*0-941765-19-9*) Arkansas Res.

— Index to Arkansas Confederate Pension Applications. 324p. 1991. pap. 37.00 (*0-941765-54-7*) Arkansas Res.

A

A

— Index to Arkansas Confederate Soldiers, Vol. I, A-G. (Arkansas Confederate Soldiers Ser.). (Illus.). 230p. 1990. pap. 24.00 (*0-941765-51-2*) Arkansas Res.

— Index to Arkansas Confederate Soldiers, Vol. II, H-O. (Arkansas Confederate Soldiers Ser.). (Illus.). 211p. 1990. pap. 24.00 (*0-941765-52-0*) Arkansas Res.

— Index to Arkansas Confederate Soldiers, Vol. III, P-Z. (Arkansas Confederate Soldiers Ser.). (Illus.). 212p. 1990. pap. 24.00 (*0-941765-53-9*) Arkansas Res.

— Index to the Sharp County Record Newspaper, Evening Shade, Arkansas, 1877-1883. 2nd ed. (Illus.). 113p. 1993. pap. 20.00 (*0-941765-87-3*) Arkansas Res.

— Izard County, Arkansas, Tax Records, 1829-1866. 2nd ed. 178p. 1993. pap. 22.00 (*0-941765-88-1*) Arkansas Res.

***Allen, Desmond W.** Masonic Death Records from the Grand Lodge of Arkansas, 1941-1990. 315p. (Orig.). 1999. pap. 39.00 (*1-56546-153-3*) Arkansas Res.

Allen, Desmond W. Second Arkansas Union Cavalry. (Arkansas Union Regiment Ser.). 122p. 1987. pap. 15.00 (*0-941765-17-2*) Arkansas Res.

— Second Arkansas Union Infantry. (Arkansas Union Regiment Ser.). 81p. 1987. pap. 15.00 (*0-941765-21-0*) Arkansas Res.

— The Seventh Arkansas Confederate Infantry. (Illus.). 52p. 1988. pap. 14.00 (*0-941765-28-8*) Arkansas Res.

— Third Arkansas Union Cavalry. (Arkansas Union Regiment Ser.). 118p. 1987. pap. 15.00 (*0-941765-18-0*) Arkansas Res.

— Thirty-Eighth Arkansas Confederate Infantry. (Illus.). 73p. 1988. pap. 16.00 (*0-941765-37-7*) Arkansas Res.

— The Twenty-Seventh Arkansas Confederate Infantry. LC 87-70001. 101p. 1987. pap. 14.00 (*0-941765-10-5*) Arkansas Res.

— Where to Write for Confederate Pensions. 50p. 1998. pap. 5.95 (*1-56546-124-X*) Arkansas Res.

— Where to Write for County Maps. 3rd ed. 50p. 1998. pap. 5.95 (*1-56546-123-1*) Arkansas Res.

Allen, Desmond W., compiled by. Arkansas' Damned Yankees: An Index to Union Soldiers in Arkansas Regiments. 220p. 1987. pap. 22.00 (*0-941765-12-1*) Arkansas Res.

Allen, Desmond W., ed. Arkansas Death Record Index, 1914-1923. 572p. (Orig.). 1996. pap. 49.50 (*1-56546-078-2*) Arkansas Res.

— Arkansas Death Record Index, 1924-1933. 610p. 1997. pap. 49.50 (*1-56546-094-4*) Arkansas Res.

— Arkansas Death Record Index, 1934-1940. 475p. (Orig.). 1996. pap. 49.50 (*1-56546-086-3*) Arkansas Res.

— Central Arkansas Death Record Index, 1914-1923: Garland, Grant, Hot Spring, Lonoke, Perry, Prairie, Pulaski, & Saline Counties. 128p. (Orig.). 1996. pap. 18.00 (*1-56546-085-5*) Arkansas Res.

— Central Arkansas Death Record Index, 1924-1933: Garland, Grant, Hot Spring, Lonoke, Perry, Prairie, Pulaski, & Saline Counties. 135p. 1997. pap. 18.00 (*1-56546-119-3*) Arkansas Res.

— Central Arkansas Death Record Index, 1934-1940: Garland, Grant, Hot Spring, Lonoke, Perry, Prairie, Pulaski, & Saline Counties. 94p. (Orig.). 1996. pap. 16.00 (*1-56546-093-6*) Arkansas Res.

— Early Lawrence County, Arkansas, Records 1817-1830. 52p. (Orig.). 1995. pap. text 15.00 (*1-56546-071-5*) Arkansas Res.

— Eastern Arkansas Death Record Index, 1914-1923: Clay, Craighead, Crittenden, Cross, Greene, Lee, Mississippi, Monroe, Phillips, Poinsett, & St. Francis Counties. 109p. (Orig.). 1996. pap. 16.00 (*1-56546-079-0*) Arkansas Res.

— Eastern Arkansas Death Record Index, 1924-1933: Clay, Craighead, Crittenden, Cross, Greene, Lee, Mississippi, Monroe, Phillips, Poinsett, & St. Francis Counties. 153p. 1997. pap. 20.00 (*1-56546-113-4*) Arkansas Res.

— Eastern Arkansas Death Record Index, 1934-1940: Clay, Craighead, Crittenden, Cross, Greene, Lee, Mississippi, Monroe, Phillips, Poinsett & St. Francis Counties. 99p. (Orig.). 1996. pap. 16.00 (*1-56546-087-1*) Arkansas Res.

— Faulkner County, Arkansas Personal Property Tax Book, 1890. 56p. 1984. pap. 10.00 (*0-941765-00-8*) Arkansas Res.

— Fulton County, Arkansas, Tax Records, 1849-1868. 104p. 1987. pap. 15.00 (*0-941765-26-1*) Arkansas Res.

— Index to the Tract Books for Fulton County, Arkansas. 83p. 1986. pap. 14.00 (*0-941765-08-3*) Arkansas Res.

— Index to the Tract Books for Izard & Stone Counties in Arkansas. 77p. 1984. pap. 14.00 (*0-941765-01-6*) Arkansas Res.

— Index to the Tract Books for Polk County, Arkansas. 70p. 1985. pap. 14.00 (*0-941765-02-4*) Arkansas Res.

— Little Rock, Arkansas, National Cemetery Burial Roster. 214p. (Orig.). 1997. pap. 28.00 (*1-56546-102-9*) Arkansas Res.

— Marion County, Arkansas, Tax Records, 1841-1866. 179p. 1988. pap. 19.50 (*0-941765-35-0*) Arkansas Res.

— North Central Arkansas Death Record Index, 1914-1923: Baxter, Cleburne, Conway, Faulkner, Fulton, Independence, Izard, Jackson, Lawrence, Randolph, Sharp, Stone, Van Buren, White, & Woodruff Counties. 74p. (Orig.). 1996. pap. 16.00 (*1-56546-080-4*) Arkansas Res.

— North Central Arkansas Death Record Index, 1924-1933: Baxter, Cleburne, Conway, Faulkner, Fulton, Independence, Izard, Jackson, Lawrence, Randolph, Sharp, Stone, Van Buren, White & Woodruff Counties. 84p. 1997. pap. 16.00 (*1-56546-114-2*) Arkansas Res.

— North Central Arkansas Death Record Index, 1934-1940: Baxter, Cleburne, Conway, Faulkner, Fulton, Independence, Izard, Jackson, Lawrence, Randolph, Sharp, Stone, Van Buren, White & Woodruff Counties. 55p. (Orig.). 1996. pap. 15.00 (*1-56546-088-X*) Arkansas Res.

— Northwestern Arkansas Death Record Index, 1914-1923: Benton, Boone, Carroll, Madison, Marion, Newton, Searcy, & Washington Counties. 53p. (Orig.). 1996. pap. 15.00 (*1-56546-081-2*) Arkansas Res.

— Northwestern Arkansas Death Record Index, 1924-1933: Benton, Boone, Carroll, Madison, Marion, Newton, Searcy, & Washington Counties. 52p. 1997. pap. 15.00 (*1-56546-115-0*) Arkansas Res.

— Northwestern Arkansas Death Record Index, 1934-1940: Benton, Boone, Carroll, Madison, Marion, Newton, Searcy, & Washington Counties. 50p. (Orig.). 1996. pap. 15.00 (*1-56546-089-8*) Arkansas Res.

— Pence Funeral Home, Conway, Arkansas, 1881-1904, Vol. I. LC 86-60930. 154p. 1986. pap. 18.00 (*0-941765-06-7*) Arkansas Res.

— Pence Funeral Home, Conway, Arkansas, 1904-1926, Vol. II. 212p. 1986. pap. 22.00 (*0-941765-07-5*) Arkansas Res.

— Southeastern Arkansas Death Record Index, 1914-1923: Arkansas, Ashley, Bradley, Chicot, Cleveland, Desha, Drew, Jefferson, & Lincoln Counties. 54p. (Orig.). 1996. pap. 15.00 (*1-56546-083-9*) Arkansas Res.

— Southeastern Arkansas Death Record Index, 1924-1933: Arkansas, Ashley, Bradley, Chicot, Cleveland, Desha, Drew, Jefferson, & Lincoln Counties. 74p. 1997. pap. 16.00 (*1-56546-117-7*) Arkansas Res.

— Southeastern Arkansas Death Record Index, 1934-1940: Arkansas, Ashley, Bradley, Chicot, Cleveland, Desha, Drew, Jefferson, & Lincoln Counties. 52p. (Orig.). 1996. pap. 15.00 (*1-56546-091-X*) Arkansas Res.

— Southwestern Arkansas Death Record Index, 1914-1923: Calhoun, Clark, Columbia, Dallas, Hempstead, Howard, Lafayette, Little River, Miller, Nevada, Ouachita, Pike, Sevier, & Union Counties. 72p. (Orig.). 1996. pap. 16.00 (*1-56546-084-7*) Arkansas Res.

— Southwestern Arkansas Death Record Index, 1924-1933: Calhoun, Clark, Columbia, Dallas, Hempstead, Howard, Lafayette, Little River, Miller, Nevada, Ouachita, Pike, Sevier, & Union Counties. 92p. 1997. pap. 16.00 (*1-56546-118-5*) Arkansas Res.

— Southwestern Arkansas Death Record Index, 1934-1940: Calhoun, Clark, Columbia, Dallas, Hempstead, Howard, Lafayette, Little River, Miller, Nevada, Ouachita, Pike, Sevier, & Union Counties. 61p. (Orig.). 1996. pap. 15.00 (*1-56546-092-8*) Arkansas Res.

— Western Arkansas Death Record Index, 1914-1923: Crawford, Franklin, Johnson, Logan, Montgomery, Polk, Pope, Scott, Sebastian, & Yell Counties. 61p. (Orig.). 1996. pap. 15.00 (*1-56546-082-0*) Arkansas Res.

— Western Arkansas Death Record Index, 1924-1933: Crawford, Franklin, Johnson, Logan, Montgomery, Polk, Pope, Scott, Sebastian, & Yell Counties. 72p. 1997. pap. 16.00 (*1-56546-116-9*) Arkansas Res.

— Western Arkansas Death Record Index, 1934-1940: Crawford, Franklin, Johnson, Logan, Montgomery, Polk, Pope, Scott, Sebastian, & Yell Counties. 50p. (Orig.). 1996. pap. 15.00 (*1-56546-090-1*) Arkansas Res.

— Woodruff County, Arkansas, Loose Probate Records, 1862-1900. 107p. 1999. pap. 18.00 (*1-56546-137-1*) Arkansas Res.

Allen, Desmond W. & Billingsley, Carolyn E. Beginner's Guide to Family History Research. 3rd ed. 112p. 1997. pap. 7.95 (*1-56546-101-0*) Arkansas Res.

— Social Security Applications: A Genealogical Resource. rev. ed. (Illus.). 18p. 1995. pap. 5.95 (*1-56546-069-3*) Arkansas Res.

Allen, Desmond W. & McLane, Bobbie J. Arkansas Land Patents: Arkansas, Chicot, & Desha Counties (Granted Through 30 June 1908) (County Ser.). (Illus.). 126p. (Orig.). 1991. pap. 16.00 (*1-56546-001-4*) Arkansas Res.

— Arkansas Land Patents: Ashley County (Granted Through 30 June 1908) (County Ser.). (Illus.). 89p. (Orig.). 1991. pap. 14.00 (*1-56546-003-0*) Arkansas Res.

— Arkansas Land Patents: Baxter County (Granted Through 30 June 1908) (County Ser.). (Illus.). 80p. (Orig.). 1991. pap. 14.00 (*1-56546-004-9*) Arkansas Res.

— Arkansas Land Patents: Benton County (Granted Through 30 June 1908) (County Ser.). (Illus.). 156p. (Orig.). 1991. pap. 18.00 (*1-56546-005-7*) Arkansas Res.

— Arkansas Land Patents: Boone County (Granted Through 30 June 1908) (County Ser.). (Illus.). 116p. (Orig.). 1991. pap. 16.00 (*1-56546-006-5*) Arkansas Res.

— Arkansas Land Patents: Bradley County (Granted Through 30 June 1908) (County Ser.). (Illus.). 97p. (Orig.). 1991. pap. 14.00 (*1-56546-007-3*) Arkansas Res.

— Arkansas Land Patents: Calhoun County (Granted through 30 June 1908) (County Ser.). (Illus.). 79p. (Orig.). 1991. pap. 14.00 (*1-56546-008-1*) Arkansas Res.

— Arkansas Land Patents: Carroll County (Granted through 30 June 1908) (County Ser.). (Illus.). 116p. (Orig.). 1991. pap. 16.00 (*1-56546-009-X*) Arkansas Res.

— Arkansas Land Patents: Clark County (Granted through 30 June 1908) (County Ser.). (Illus.). 83p. (Orig.). 1991. pap. 14.00 (*1-56546-010-3*) Arkansas Res.

— Arkansas Land Patents: Cleburne County (Granted through 30 June 1908) (County Ser.). (Illus.). 78p. (Orig.). 1991. pap. 14.00 (*1-56546-011-1*) Arkansas Res.

— Arkansas Land Patents: Cleveland County (Granted through 30 June 1908) (County Ser.). (Illus.). 72p. (Orig.). 1991. pap. 14.00 (*1-56546-012-X*) Arkansas Res.

— Arkansas Land Patents: Columbia County (Granted through 30 June 1908) (County Ser.). (Illus.). 115p. (Orig.). 1991. pap. 16.00 (*1-56546-013-8*) Arkansas Res.

— Arkansas Land Patents: Conway, Faulkner, & Perry Counties (Granted through 30 June 1908) (County Ser.). (Illus.). 142p. (Orig.). 1991. pap. 18.00 (*1-56546-014-6*) Arkansas Res.

— Arkansas Land Patents: Crawford County (Granted Through 30 June 1908) (County Ser.). (Illus.). 68p. (Orig.). 1991. pap. 14.00 (*1-56546-015-4*) Arkansas Res.

— Arkansas Land Patents: Dallas County (Granted through 30 June 1908) (County Ser.). (Illus.). 57p. (Orig.). 1991. pap. 14.00 (*1-56546-016-2*) Arkansas Res.

— Arkansas Land Patents; Drew County (Granted through 30 June 1908. (County Ser.). (Illus.). 90p. (Orig.). 1991. pap. 14.00 (*1-56546-017-0*) Arkansas Res.

— Arkansas Land Patents: Eastern Arkansas Counties (Granted Through 30 June 1908) (County Ser.). (Illus.). 234p. (Orig.). 1991. pap. 24.00 (*1-56546-002-2*) Arkansas Res.

— Arkansas Land Patents: Franklin County (Granted through 30 June 1908) (County Ser.). (Illus.). 73p. (Orig.). 1991. pap. 14.00 (*1-56546-018-9*) Arkansas Res.

— Arkansas Land Patents: Fulton County (Granted through 30 June 1908) (County Ser.). (Illus.). 99p. (Orig.). 1991. pap. 14.00 (*1-56546-019-7*) Arkansas Res.

— Arkansas Land Patents: Garland County (Granted through 30 June 1908) (County Ser.). (Illus.). 99p. (Orig.). 1991. pap. 14.00 (*1-56546-020-0*) Arkansas Res.

— Arkansas Land Patents: Grant & Saline Counties (Granted through 30 June 1908) (County Ser.). (Illus.). 128p. (Orig.). 1991. pap. 16.00 (*1-56546-021-9*) Arkansas Res.

— Arkansas Land Patents: Hempstead County (Granted through 30 June 1908) (County Ser.). (Illus.). 91p. (Orig.). 1991. pap. 14.00 (*1-56546-022-7*) Arkansas Res.

— Arkansas Land Patents: Hot Spring County (Granted through 30 June 1908) (County Ser.). (Illus.). 62p. (Orig.). 1991. pap. 14.00 (*1-56546-023-5*) Arkansas Res.

— Arkansas Land Patents: Howard County (Granted through 30 June 1908) (County Ser.). (Illus.). 102p. (Orig.). 1991. pap. 14.00 (*1-56546-024-3*) Arkansas Res.

— Arkansas Land Patents: Independence County (Granted through 30 June 1908) (County Ser.). (Illus.). 111p. (Orig.). 1991. pap. 14.00 (*1-56546-025-1*) Arkansas Res.

— Arkansas Land Patents: Izard County (Granted through 30 June 1908) (County Ser.). (Illus.). 108p. (Orig.). 1991. pap. 14.00 (*1-56546-026-X*) Arkansas Res.

— Arkansas Land Patents: Jackson, Lawrence, & Woodruff Counties (Granted through 30 June 1908) (County Ser.). (Illus.). 81p. (Orig.). 1991. pap. 14.00 (*1-56546-027-8*) Arkansas Res.

— Arkansas Land Patents: Jefferson County (Granted through 30 June 1908) (County Ser.). (Illus.). 80p. (Orig.). 1991. pap. 14.00 (*1-56546-028-6*) Arkansas Res.

— Arkansas Land Patents: Johnson County (Granted through 30 June 1908) (County Ser.). (Illus.). 72p. (Orig.). 1991. pap. 14.00 (*1-56546-029-4*) Arkansas Res.

— Arkansas Land Patents: Lafayette County (Granted through 30 June 1908) (County Ser.). (Illus.). 73p. (Orig.). 1991. pap. 14.00 (*1-56546-030-8*) Arkansas Res.

— Arkansas Land Patents: Lincoln County (Granted through 30 June 1908) (County Ser.). (Illus.). 64p. (Orig.). 1991. pap. 14.00 (*1-56546-031-6*) Arkansas Res.

— Arkansas Land Patents: Little River County (Granted through 30 June 1908) (County Ser.). (Illus.). 66p. (Orig.). 1991. pap. 14.00 (*1-56546-032-4*) Arkansas Res.

— Arkansas Land Patents: Logan County (Granted through 30 June 1908) (County Ser.). (Illus.). 91p. (Orig.). 1991. pap. 14.00 (*1-56546-033-2*) Arkansas Res.

— Arkansas Land Patents: Lonoke & Prairie Counties (Granted through 30 June 1908) (County Ser.). (Illus.). 75p. (Orig.). 1991. pap. 14.00 (*1-56546-034-0*) Arkansas Res.

— Arkansas Land Patents: Madison County (Granted through 30 June 1908) (County Ser.). (Illus.). 151p. (Orig.). 1991. pap. 18.00 (*1-56546-035-9*) Arkansas Res.

— Arkansas Land Patents: Marion County (Granted through 30 June 1908) (County Ser.). (Illus.). 107p. (Orig.). 1991. pap. 14.00 (*1-56546-036-7*) Arkansas Res.

— Arkansas Land Patents: Miller County (Granted through 30 June 1908) (County Ser.). (Illus.). 63p. (Orig.). 1991. pap. 14.00 (*1-56546-037-5*) Arkansas Res.

— Arkansas Land Patents: Montgomery County (Granted through 30 June 1908) (County Ser.). (Illus.). 73p. (Orig.). 1991. pap. 14.00 (*1-56546-038-3*) Arkansas Res.

— Arkansas Land Patents: Nevada County (Granted through 30 June 1908) (County Ser.). (Illus.). 81p. (Orig.). 1991. pap. 14.00 (*1-56546-039-1*) Arkansas Res.

— Arkansas Land Patents: Newton County (Granted through 30 June 1908) (County Ser.). (Illus.). 99p. (Orig.). 1991. pap. 14.00 (*1-56546-040-5*) Arkansas Res.

— Arkansas Land Patents: Ouachita County (Granted through 30 June 1908) (County Ser.). (Illus.). 101p. (Orig.). 1991. pap. 14.00 (*1-56546-041-3*) Arkansas Res.

— Arkansas Land Patents: Pike County (Granted through 30 June 1908) (County Ser.). (Illus.). 85p. (Orig.). 1991. pap. 14.00 (*1-56546-042-1*) Arkansas Res.

— Arkansas Land Patents: Polk County (Granted through 30 June 1908) (County Ser.). (Illus.). 95p. (Orig.). 1991. pap. 14.00 (*1-56546-043-X*) Arkansas Res.

— Arkansas Land Patents: Pope County (Granted through 30 June 1908) (County Ser.). (Illus.). 83p. (Orig.). 1991. pap. 14.00 (*1-56546-044-8*) Arkansas Res.

— Arkansas Land Patents: Pulaski County (Granted through 30 June 1908) (County Ser.). (Illus.). 82p. (Orig.). 1991. pap. 14.00 (*1-56546-045-6*) Arkansas Res.

— Arkansas Land Patents: Randolph County (Granted through 30 June 1908) (County Ser.). (Illus.). 84p. (Orig.). 1991. pap. 14.00 (*1-56546-046-4*) Arkansas Res.

— Arkansas Land Patents: Scott County (Granted through 30 June 1908) (County Ser.). (Illus.). 77p. (Orig.). 1991. pap. 14.00 (*1-56546-047-2*) Arkansas Res.

— Arkansas Land Patents: Searcy County (Granted through 30 June 1908) (County Ser.). (Illus.). 87p. (Orig.). 1991. pap. 14.00 (*1-56546-048-0*) Arkansas Res.

— Arkansas Land Patents: Sebastian County (Granted through 30 June 1908) (County Ser.). (Illus.). 80p. (Orig.). 1991. pap. 14.00 (*1-56546-049-9*) Arkansas Res.

— Arkansas Land Patents: Sevier County (Granted through 30 June 1908) (County Ser.). (Illus.). 88p. (Orig.). 1991. pap. 14.00 (*1-56546-050-2*) Arkansas Res.

— Arkansas Land Patents: Sharp County (Granted through 30 June 1908) (County Ser.). (Illus.). 97p. (Orig.). 1991. pap. 14.00 (*1-56546-051-0*) Arkansas Res.

— Arkansas Land Patents: Stone County (Granted through 30 June 1908) (County Ser.). (Illus.). 75p. (Orig.). 1991. pap. 14.00 (*1-56546-052-9*) Arkansas Res.

— Arkansas Land Patents: Union County (Granted through 30 June 1908) (County Ser.). (Illus.). 140p. (Orig.). 1991. pap. 18.00 (*1-56546-053-7*) Arkansas Res.

— Arkansas Land Patents: Van Buren County (Granted through 30 June 1908) (County Ser.). (Illus.). 83p. (Orig.). 1991. pap. 14.00 (*1-56546-054-5*) Arkansas Res.

— Arkansas Land Patents: Washington County (Granted through 30 June 1908) (County Ser.). (Illus.). 199p. (Orig.). 1991. pap. 22.00 (*1-56546-055-3*) Arkansas Res.

— Arkansas Land Patents: White County (Granted through 30 June 1908) (County Ser.). (Illus.). 77p. (Orig.). 1991. pap. 14.00 (*1-56546-056-1*) Arkansas Res.

— Arkansas Land Patents: Yell County (Granted through 30 June 1908) (County Ser.). (Illus.). 85p. (Orig.). 1991. pap. 14.00 (*1-56546-057-X*) Arkansas Res.

Allen, Desmond W. & Vanaman, Henryetta W., eds. Fulton County, Arkansas, Folks, 1890-1894. LC 87-70493. 137p. 1987. pap. 18.00 (*0-941765-11-3*) Arkansas Res.

Allen, Desmond W., et al. Guide to Faulkner County, Arkansas, Loose Probate Packets, 1873-1917. 57p. 1985. pap. 10.00 (*0-941765-03-2*) Arkansas Res.

Allen, Desmond W., jt. auth. see Billingsley, Carolyn E.

Allen, Desmond W., jt. auth. see McLane, Bobbie J.

Allen, Desmond W., ed. see Craig, Marion S.

Allen, Desmond W., ed. see North, S. N.

Allen, Desmond W., ed. see Turnbo, Silas C.

***Allen, Desmond Walls.** Arkansas Death Record Index, 1941-1948. 701p. 1999. pap. 59.50 (*1-56546-154-1*) Arkansas Res.

— Arkansas Donation Lands, 1871-1875. 210p. 2000. pap. 28.00 (*1-56546-171-1*) Arkansas Res.

***Allen, Desmond Walls, compiled by.** Central Arkansas Death Record Index, 1941-1948: Garland, Grant, Hot Spring, Lonoke, Perry, Prairie, Pulaski, & Saline Counties. 207p. 1999. pap. 28.00 (*1-56546-155-X*) Arkansas Res.

— Eastern Arkansas Death Record Index, 1941-1948: Clay, Craighead, Crittenden, Cross, Greene, Lee, Mississippi, Monroe, Phillips, Poinsett, & St. Francis Counties. 161p. 1999. pap. 24.00 (*1-56546-158-4*) Arkansas Res.

— North Central Arkansas Death Record Index, 1941-1948: Baxter, Cleburne, Conway, Faulkner, Fulton, Independence, Izard, Jackson, Lawrence, Randolph, Sharp, Stone, Van Buren, White, & Woodruff Counties. 97p. 1999. pap. 18.00 (*1-56546-161-4*) Arkansas Res.

— Northwestern Arkansas Death Record Index, 1941-1948: Benton, Boone, Carroll, Madison, Marion, Newton, Searcy, & Washington Counties. 72p. 1999. pap. 16.00 (*1-56546-160-6*) Arkansas Res.

— Southeastern Arkansas Death Record Index, 1941-1948: Arkansas, Ashley, Bradley, Chicot, Cleveland, Desha, Drew, Jefferson, & Lincoln Counties. 99p. 1999. pap. 18.00 (*1-56546-159-2*) Arkansas Res.

— Southwestern Arkansas Death Record Index, 1941-1948: Calhoun, Clark, Columbia, Dallas, Hempstead, Howard, Lafayette, Little River, Miller, Nevada, Onachita, Pike, Sevier, & Union Counties. 116p. 1999. pap. 21.00 (*1-56546-156-8*) Arkansas Res.

— Western Arkansas Death Record Index, 1941-1948: Crawford, Franklin, Johnson, Logan, Montgomery, Polk, Pope, Scott, Sebastian, & Yell Counties. 93p. 1999. pap. 18.00 (*1-56546-157-6*) Arkansas Res.

Allen, Devere. Allen. Descendants of William Allin of Prudence Island, Rhode Island, b. 1640 (England), Emigr. to Rhode Island ca. 1660. 338p. 1995. reprint ed. pap. 53.00 (*0-8328-4558-2*); reprint ed. lib. bdg. 63.00 (*0-8328-4557-4*) Higginson Bk Co.

— The Fight for Peace. LC 79-137525. (Peace Movement in America Ser.). xi, 740p. 1972. reprint ed. lib. bdg. 65.95 (*0-89198-052-0*) Ozer.

Allen, Devere, ed. Adventurous Americans. LC 71-156604. (Essay Index Reprint Ser.). 1977. reprint ed. 28.95 (*0-8369-2264-6*) Ayer.

— Pacifism in the Modern World. LC 72-137526. (Peace Movement in America Ser.). xvii, 278p. 1972. reprint ed. lib. bdg. 35.95 (*0-89198-053-9*) Ozer.

Allen, Diana. Gourmet: The Quick & Easy Way. 3rd ed. (Illus.). 148p. 1992. reprint ed. pap. 10.95 (*0-9636263-0-2*) D Allen Ent.

Allen, Diane & Frederick, Larry. In Pictures Arches & Canyonlands: The Continuing Story. LC 93-77021. (Illus.). 48p. (Orig.). 1993. pap. 7.95 (*0-88714-078-5*) KC Pubns.

— In Pictures Arches & Canyonlands: The Continuing Story. Morales, Brigitte, tr. (GER., Illus.). 48p. (Orig.). 1993. pap. 8.95 (*0-88714-701-1*) KC Pubns.

— In Pictures Arches & Canyonlands: The Continuing Story. La Bras, Yvon, tr. (FRE., Illus.). 48p. (Orig.). 1993. pap. 8.95 (*0-88714-702-X*) KC Pubns.

— In Pictures Arches & Canyonlands: The Continuing Story. Petzinger, Saori, tr. (JPN., Illus.). 48p. (Orig.). 1996. pap. 8.95 (*0-88714-703-8*) KC Pubns.

***Allen, Diane & Frederick, Larry.** In Pictures Arches & Canyonlands: The Continuing Story. Comollo, Adriano, tr. from ENG. LC 93-77021. (ITA., Illus.). 48p. 1999. pap. 8.95 (*0-88714-833-6*) KC Pubns.

Allen, Diane D. & Piersma, Mary L. Developing Thematic Units: Process & Product. LC 94-17953. 240p. (C). 1994. mass mkt. 52.95 (*0-8273-6321-4*) Delmar.

Allen, Diane M., jt. auth. see Bowman, Ann G.

Allen, Dick. Crash! 1989. write for info. (*0-318-64980-2*) HM.

— Flight & Pursuit: Poems. LC 87-3242. 63p. reprint ed. pap. 30.00 (*0-608-09826-4*, 206999400007) Bks Demand.

— Ode to the Cold War: Poems New & Selected. LC 96-25051. 160p. (Orig.). 1997. 25.00 (*0-9641151-9-0*); pap. 14.95 (*1-889330-00-0*) Sarabande Bks.

— Overnight in the Guest House of the Mystic: Poems. LC 83-25620. 59p. 1984. reprint ed. pap. 30.00 (*0-608-00860-5*, 206165100010) Bks Demand.

Allen, Diogenes. Christian Belief in a Postmodern World: The Full Wealth of Conviction. 240p. (Orig.). 1989. pap. 22.95 (*0-8042-0625-2*) Westminster John Knox.

— Love: Christian Romance, Marriage, Friendship. 2nd ed. 168p. (Orig.). 1997. reprint ed. pap. write for info. (*0-9653625-1-5*) Caroline Pr.

— Path of Perfect Love. rev. ed. LC 92-3122. Orig. Title: Finding Our Father. 113p. 1992. pap. 9.95 (*1-56101-057-X*) Cowley Pubns.

— Philosophy for Understanding Theology. LC 84-48510. 252p. 1985. pap. 24.95 (*0-8042-0688-0*) Westminster John Knox.

— Spiritual Theology: The Theology of Yesterday for Spiritual Help Today. LC 97-623. 170p. 1997. pap. 11.95 (*1-56101-130-4*) Cowley Pubns.

Allen, Diogenes & Springsted, Eric O. Spirit, Nature, & Community: Issues in the Thought of Simone Weil. LC 93-36973. (SUNY Series, Simone Weil Studies). 241p. (C). 1994. pap. text 19.95 (*0-7914-2018-3*) State U NY Pr.

— Spirit, Nature, & Community: Issues in the Thought of Simone Weil. LC 93-36973. (SUNY Series, Simone Weil Studies). 241p. (C). 1994. text 59.50 (*0-7914-2017-5*) State U NY Pr.

— Spirituality & Theology: Essays in Honor of Diogenes Allen. LC 97-44672. 176p. (Orig.). 1998. pap. 19.95 (*0-664-25741-0*) Westminster John Knox.

Allen, Diogenes & Springsted, Eric O., eds. Primary Readings in Philosophy for Understanding Theology. 336p. (Orig.). 1997. pap. 24.95 (*0-664-25208-7*) Westminster John Knox.

Allen, Diogenis. Temptation. 3rd ed. Orig. Title: Between Two Worlds. xi, 155p. 1996. reprint ed. pap. 9.95 (*0-9653625-0-7*) Caroline Pr.

Allen, Dodie & Andre, Bruce. Cowboys of Santa Cruz County. Beronius, George, ed. (Illus.). 68p. 1996. 27.50 (*0-9655525-1-9*) C Allen Photo.

Allen, Don A. & Davis, Lanny J. Allen & Davis on Computer Contracting: A User's Guide with Forms & Strategies. 2nd ed. 1380p. 1992. ring bd. 210.00 (*0-13-038365-1*) Aspen Law.

Allen, Don C. Doubt's Boundless Sea. 1979. 28.95 (*0-405-10577-0*) Ayer.

— The Harmonious Vision: Studies in Milton's Poetry. enl. ed. LC 79-117254. 166p. 1970. 34.00 (*0-8018-1191-0*) Johns Hopkins.

— The Legend of Noah: Renaissance Rationalism in Art, Science, & Letters. fac. ed. LC 49-49065. (Illus.). 243p. 1949. reprint ed. pap. 75.40 (*0-7837-8067-2*, 204782000008) Bks Demand.

— Mysteriously Meant: The Rediscovery of Pagan Symbolism & Allegorical Interpretation in the Renaissance. LC 77-105363. 366p. reprint ed. 113.50 (*0-8357-9279-X*, 201516000092) Bks Demand.

Allen, Don C., ed. A Celebration of Poets. LC 67-18376. 253p. reprint ed. pap. 78.50 (*0-608-15133-5*, 202307800032) Bks Demand.

— The Moment of Poetry. LC 80-17079. (Percy Graeme Turnbull Memorial Lectures on Poetry, 1958). 135p. 1980. reprint ed. lib. bdg. 49.50 (*0-313-22406-4*, ALMP, Greenwood Pr) Greenwood.

Allen, Donald. The New American Poetry, 1945-1960. 470p. 1999. pap. 16.95 (*0-520-20953-2*, Pub. by U CA Pr) Cal Prin Full Svc.

Allen, Donald & Butterick, George F., eds. The Postmoderns: The New American Poetry Revisited. rev. ed. LC 79-52054. 448p. 1982. pap. 14.95 (*0-8021-5035-7*, Grove) Grove-Atltic.

Allen, Donald & Guy, Rebecca. Conversation Analysis: The Sociology of Talk. (Janua Linguarum, Ser. Minor: No. 200). 284p. 1978. pap. text 41.55 (*90-279-3002-3*) Mouton.

Allen, Donald, ed. see Dorn, Edward.

Allen, Donald, ed. see Ginsberg, Allen.

Allen, Donald, ed. see Kerouac, Jack.

Allen, Donald, ed. see O'Hara, Frank.

Allen, Donald, ed. see Spicer, Jack.

Allen, Donald, ed. see Welch, Lew.

Allen, Donald, jt. ed. see Whalen, Philip.

Allen, Donald, ed. & intro. see Welch, Lew.

Allen, Donald E., jt. auth. see Arafat, Ibtihaj S.

Allen, Donald M., ed. see Garcia Lorca, Federico.

Allen, Donald M., tr. see Ionesco, Eugene.

Allen, Donna. The Media Technology Road to Democracy & Equality. (Toward a Radical Restructuring of the Communication Media Ser.: Vol. 5). (Illus.). 28p. (Orig.). 1995. pap. 5.00 (*0-930470-17-6*) Womens Inst Free Press.

— Media Without Democracy & What to Do about It. 1991. 5.00 (*0-930470-15-X*) Womens Inst Free Press.

***Allen, Donna.** Murray Family History: 200 Years in Fayette County, PA. (Illus.). 65p. 1999. pap. 15.00 (*0-9658079-1-6*) Donna Allen.

Allen, Donna. My Say: One Woman's Slightly Skewed Perception of Life. (Illus.). 80p. 1997. pap. 9.95 (*0-9658079-0-8*) Donna Allen.

Allen, Donna, et al. Women Transforming Communications: Global Perspectives. LC 96-4467. 420p. 1996. 62.00 (*0-8039-7266-0*); pap. 28.95 (*0-8039-7267-9*) Sage.

Allen, Donna, jt. auth. see Allen, Lee.

Allen, Doris. Creative Keyboard for Adult Beginners. 2nd ed. 304p. (C). 1992. spiral bd. 37.95 (*0-8403-8130-1*) Kendall-Hunt.

Allen, Dorothea. Science Demonstrations for the Elementary Classroom. 288p. (C). 1988. pap. text 27.95 (*0-13-794652-X*, Parker Publishing Co) P-H.

Allen, Dorothy J. & Fahey, Brian M. Being Human in Sport. LC 76-39966. 188p. reprint ed. pap. 58.30 (*0-8357-7118-0*, 205618400055) Bks Demand.

Allen, Dorothy S. Plaster Art: Step-by-Step. Cole, Tom, ed. LC 80-70317. (Illus.). 172p. (Orig.). 1981. pap. 12.95 (*0-9605204-0-6*) Dots Pubns.

Allen, Doug. Best of Steven. LC 98-21421. 96p. 1998. 22.95 (*0-87816-624-6*) Kitchen Sink.

— The best of Steven. LC 98-21421. 96p. 1998. pap. 12.95 (*0-87816-616-5*) Kitchen Sink.

Allen, Douglas. Structure & Creativity in Religion. (Religion & Reason Ser.: No. 14). 1978. 53.85 (*90-279-7594-9*) Mouton.

Allen, Douglas, ed. Religion & Political Conflict in South Asia: India, Pakistan, & Sri Lanka, 34. LC 91-45627. (Contributions to the Study of Religion Ser.: No. 34). 240p. 1992. 59.95 (*0-313-27309-X*, ARP, Greenwood Pr) Greenwood.

Allen, Douglas & Berger, Adriana. Myth & Religion in Mircea Eliade. LC 98-30209. (Theorists of Myth Ser.: Vol. 11). 386p. 1998. 75.00 (*0-8240-3720-0*, H1168) Garland.

Allen, Douglas, Jr., jt. auth. see Gordon, Brad J.

Allen, Douglas, jt. auth. see Moore, James N.

Allen, Douglas, ed. see Malhotra, Ashok.

Allen, Douglas C. Principles of Forest Entomology. LC 84-8509. (Illus.). 224p. 1984. student ed. 18.95 (*0-8156-2318-6*) Syracuse U Pr.

Allen, Douglas C. & Coufal, James E. Introduction to Forest Entomology: A Training Manual for Forest Technicians. LC 84-8510. (Illus.). 168p. reprint ed. pap. 52.10 (*0-8357-8628-5*, 203505100092) Bks Demand.

Allen, Durward L. Wolves of Minong: Isle Royale's Wild Community. LC 93-8192. (Ann Arbor Paperbacks Ser.). 528p. (C). 1993. pap. 19.95 (*0-472-08237-X*, 08237) U of Mich Pr.

***Allen, Dwight.** The Green Suit. LC 00-36243. 288p. 2000. 22.95 (*1-56512-274-7*) Algonquin Bks.

Allen, Dwight, ed. Baha'i Daybook: Passages for Deepening & Meditation. rev. ed. 374p. 1996. pap. 7.95 (*0-87743-154-X*) Bahai.

Allen, Dwight W. Schools for a New Century: A Conservative Approach to Radical School Reform. LC 91-39815. 200p. 1992. 49.95 (*0-275-93649-X*, C3649, Praeger Pubs) Greenwood.

Allen, E., et al. The Architect's Studio Companion: Technical Guidlines for Preliminary Design; & Architectural Detailing. 764p. 1992. 110.00 (*0-471-30305-4*) Wiley.

Allen, E. Anthony. Caring for the Whole Person. 100p. 1996. pap. 9.95 (*0-912552-93-X*) MARC.

Allen, E. Anthony, et al. Health, Healing & Transformation. 109p. 1991. pap. 3.95 (*0-912552-74-3*) MARC.

Allen, E. M. America's Story As Told in Postage Stamps. 1975. 250.00 (*0-87968-381-3*) Gordon Pr.

Allen, E. Ross, jt. auth. see Neill, Wilfred T.

Allen, E. W. Memorial of Joseph & Lucy Clark Allen. (Illus.). 246p. 1988. reprint ed. pap. 37.00 (*0-8328-0109-7*); reprint ed. lib. bdg. 45.00 (*0-8328-0108-9*) Higginson Bk Co.

Allen, Earl E. Debt: How to Get Out-& Stay Out-God's Way. 81p. (Orig.). 1989. pap. text. write for info. (*1-878766-00-7*); audio. write for info. (*1-878766-03-1*) Miracle TX.

— Debt: How to Get Out-& Stay Out-God's Way. (Illus.). (Orig.). 1990. write for info. incl. audio (*1-878766-05-8*) Miracle TX.

— Debt: How to Get Out-& Stay Out-God's Way, Set. (Illus.). (Orig.). 1990. pap. text. write for info. (*1-878766-02-3*) Miracle TX.

— The Get Out of Debt Workbook: A Supplement to Debt. (Illus.). (Orig.). 1989. write for info. (*1-878766-01-5*) Miracle TX.

Allen, Echo. The Actor's Common Sense Guide to La-La Land: Survival Tips for Pilot Season. Waters, Lisa, ed. 78p. 1997. pap. 29.95 (*1-57502-577-9*, P01664) Reign Intl.

Allen, Ed H., jt. auth. see Firth, Henry.

Allen, Edith B. 100 Bible Games. (Game & Party Bks.). 90p. (YA). (gr. 10 up). 1967. pap. 5.99 (*0-8010-0033-5*) Baker Bks.

Allen, Edward. Architectural Detailing: Function, Constructability, Aesthetics. LC 92-19378. (Illus.). 296p. 1992. 80.00 (*0-471-54792-1*) Wiley.

— Fundamentals of Building Construction: Materials & Methods. 3rd ed. LC 98-8019. (Illus.). 864p. 1998. 89.95 (*0-471-18349-0*) Wiley.

— Mustang Sally. 1994. pap. 9.95 (*0-393-31156-2*) Norton.

— Shaping Structures: Statics. LC 96-37609. 416p. 1997. 75.00 (*0-471-16968-4*) Wiley.

— Stone Shelters. (Illus.). 222p. 1971. pap. text 13.50 (*0-262-51010-3*) MIT Pr.

— Straight Through the Night. LC 88-26707. 270p. 1989. 17.95 (*0-939149-19-2*) Soho Press.

— Straight Through the Night. 1990. pap. 9.95 (*0-939149-36-2*) Soho Press.

Allen, Edward & Iano, Joseph. The Architect's Studio Companion: Rules of Thumb for Preliminary Design. 2nd ed. LC 95-16412. 496p. 1995. 75.00 (*0-471-04069-X*) Wiley.

Allen, Edward, jt. auth. see Zalewski, Waclaw.

Allen, Edward B. Early American Wall Paintings, 1710-1850. LC 77-77694. (Library of American Art). 1971. reprint ed. lib. bdg. 35.00 (*0-306-71332-2*) Da Capo.

— How Buildings Work: The Natural Order of Architecture. 2nd ed. (Illus.). 256p. 1995. 39.95 (*0-19-509100-0*) OUP.

Allen, Edward D. & Valette, Rebecca M. Classroom Techniques: Foreign Languages & English As a Second Language. (Illus.). 418p. (C). 1994. reprint ed. pap. text 21.95 (*0-88133-809-5*) Waveland Pr.

Allen, Edward F. The Complete Dream Book. rev. ed. 288p. 1985. mass mkt. 5.99 (*0-446-34105-3*, Pub. by Warner Bks) Little.

Allen, Edward H. Hands on Fiction. 162p. (C). 1995. pap. text, wbk. ed. 22.00 (*0-13-238882-0*) P-H.

Allen, Edward J. Merchants of Menace - The Mafia: A Study of Organized Crime. (Illus.). 344p. 1962. pap. 41.95 (*0-398-06004-5*) C C Thomas.

— Merchants of Menace - The Mafia: A Study of Organized Crime. fac. ed. (Illus.). 344p. 1962. 55.95 (*0-398-04187-3*) C C Thomas.

— The Second United Order among the Mormons. LC 73-38483. (Columbia University. Studies in the Social Sciences: No. 419). reprint ed. 20.00 (*0-404-51419-7*) AMS Pr.

Allen, Edward S. Freedom in Iowa: The Role of the Iowa Civil Liberties Union. LC 76-47009. 196p. reprint ed. pap. 60.80 (*0-8357-6754-X*, 203541100095) Bks Demand.

Allen, Eleanor. Ghost Dog. (Illus.). (J). 1998. pap. 3.50 (*0-590-16369-8*) Scholastic Inc.

***Allen, Eleanor.** Ghost Dog. 1998. 8.60 (*0-606-13421-2*, Pub. by Turtleback) Demco.

Allen, Eleanor. Home Sweet Home: A History of Housework. (Junior Reference Ser.). (Illus.). 64p. (J). (gr. 6 up). 1979. 14.95 (*0-7136-1927-9*) Dufour.

— Victorian Children. (Junior Reference Ser.). (Illus.) 64p. (J). (gr. 6 up). 1988. 15.95 (*0-7136-1324-6*) Dufour.

— Wartime Children, 1939-1945. (Junior Reference Ser.). (Illus.). 64p. (J). (gr. 6 up). 1983. 14.95 (*0-7136-1503-6*) Dufour.

— Wash & Brush Up. (Junior Reference Ser.). (Illus.). 64p. (J). (gr. 7 up). 1984. 14.95 (*0-7136-1639-3*) Dufour.

Allen, Elizabeth, et al, eds. The Case Books of John Hunter, FRS. (Illus.). 699p. 1993. 148.00 (*1-85070-542-5*) Prthnon Pub.

Allen, Elizabeth, ed. see Allen, James A.

Allen, Elizabeth, ed. see Reznicek, E. K.

Allen, Elizabeth, ed. see Townsend, Richard P. & Ward, Roger.

Allen, Elizabeth C. Beyond Realism: Turgenev's Poetics of Secular Salvation. LC 91-19405. 288p. 1992. 39.50 (*0-8047-1873-3*) Stanford U Pr.

Allen, Elizabeth C. & Morson, Gary S., eds. Freedom & Responsibility in Russian Literature: Essays in Honor of Robert Louis Jackson. (Studies in Russian Literature & Theory; Yale Russian & East European Publications: no. 12). 280p. 1994. 35.00 (*0-8101-1146-2*) Northwestern U Pr.

Allen, Elizabeth C., ed. & tr. see Turgenev, Ivan Sergeevich.

Allen, Elizabeth E. Bright Destiny. 1990. mass mkt. 4.95 (*0-446-35339-6*, Pub. by Warner Bks) Little.

— Freedom Fire. 1986. mass mkt. 3.95 (*0-446-30253-8*, Pub. by Warner Bks) Little.

— Rebel. 1985. mass mkt. 3.95 (*0-446-32551-1*, Pub by Warner Bks) Little.

— To Fortune Born. 352p. 1988. mass mkt. 4.50 (*0-446-35174-1*, Pub. by Warner Bks) Little.

Allen, Elizabeth L. & Mohr, Donald D. Affordable Justice: How to Settle Any Dispute, Including Divorce, Out of Court. 2nd ed. LC 98-225599. (Illus.). 216p. 1998. 19.95 (*0-9655876-6-5*) West Coast Pr.

Allen, Ellen G. Japanese Flower Arrangement: A Complete Primer. LC 62-21731. (Illus.). 86p. 1991. pap. 9.95 (*0-8048-1687-5*) Tuttle Pubng.

Allen, Elsa G. The History of American Ornithology Before Audubon. (Illus.). 1979. reprint ed. 45.00 (*0-934626-00-6*) W G Arader.

Allen, Elsie. Pomo Basketmaking: A Supreme Art for the Weaver. Brown, Vinson, ed. (Illus.). 67p. 1972. pap. 6.95 (*0-87961-016-6*) Naturegraph.

— Your Credit Your Car Your Choice. 48p. 1992. student ed. write for info. (*1-882783-49-2*) Auto-Know Cnslting.

Allen, Eric. Ride to Revenge. (Orig.). 1979. mass mkt. 1.95 (*0-89083-551-9*, Zebra Kensgtn) Kensgtn Pub Corp.

Allen, Esther, tr. see Borges, Jorge Luis.

Allen, Esther, tr. see Castellanos, Rosario.

Allen, Esther, tr. see Cendrars, Blaise.

Allen, Esther, tr. see Darrieussecq, Marie.

Allen, Esther, tr. see de Zegher, Catherine M. & Vicona, Cecilia.

Allen, Esther, tr. see Paternosto, Cesar.

Allen, Esther, tr. see Verbitsky, Horacio.

Allen, Esther, tr. see Villaurrutia, Xavier & Paz, Octavio.

Allen, Esther, tr. & afterword by see Castellanos, Rosario.

Allen, Esther, tr. & afterword by see Le, Linda.

***Allen, Esther M.** Muffinology et. Cetera. (Illus.). 72p. 1999. pap. text 6.95 (*0-932855-31-8*) Winner Enter.

Allen, Ethan. Baseball Play & Strategy. 3rd ed. LC 81-17177. 458p. (C). 1982. lib. bdg. 19.95 (*0-89874-450-4*) Krieger.

— Ethan Allen & His Kin: Correspondence, 1772-1819 - A Selected Edition, 2 vols. Duffy, John J., ed. LC 98-5557. (Illus.). 889p. 1998. 100.00 (*0-87451-858-X*) U Pr of New Eng.

***Allen, Ethan.** A Narrative of Colonel Ethan Allen's Captivity. Arch, Stephen Carl, ed. LC 99-74752. (Emergent Texts in American Literature Ser.). 73p. (C). 2000. pap. text 6.95 (*1-58390-009-8*, Copley Editions) Copley Pub.

Allen, Ethan. Narrative of Ethan Allen. 124p. 1987. reprint ed. pap. 8.95 (*1-55709-127-7*) Applewood.

Allen, Ethan & Allen, Ira. Collected Works, 3 vols., Set. LC 91-77183. 1992. 96.00 (*1-56541-210-9*) Chalidze.

Allen, Ethan P. 911 until Help Arrives. 304p. (C). 1994. pap. text, spiral bd., vinyl bd. 25.95 (*0-8403-9204-4*) Kendall-Hunt.

Allen, Ethel K., jt. auth. see Allen, O. N.

Allen, Eugenie. The Best Ever Kids' Book of Lists. 128p. (Orig.). (YA). 1991. pap. 2.95 (*0-380-76357-5*, Avon Bks) Morrow Avon.

Allen, Evelyn W. Baffles the Bunny Presents: My First Crossword Puzzles. (Illus.). 50p. (Orig.). (J). (gr. 2). 1995. pap. 5.95 (*0-9651123-0-6*) E W Allen.

Allen, Everett S. Children of the Light: The Rise & Fall of New Bedford Whaling & the Death of the Arctic Fleet. (Illus.). 302p. 1998. pap. text 10.00 (*0-7881-5284-X*) DIANE Pub.

— Children of the Light: The Rise & Fall of New Bedford Whaling & the Death of the Arctic Fleet. 320p. 1983. reprint ed. pap. 9.95 (*0-940160-23-4*) Parnassus Imprints.

Allen, Everett T., Jr., et al. Pension Planning: Pensions, Profit-Sharing, & Other Deferred Compensation Plans. 7th ed. 448p. (C). 1992. text 69.75 (*0-256-08296-0*, Irwn McGrw-H) McGrw-H Hghr Educ.

Allen, Evlyn. Figuring It Out: Diet & Exercise for a Lovelier You. LC 77-74493. (Illus.). 85p. 1977. pap. 5.98 (*0-88290-078-1*) Horizon Utah.

Allen, F. A., jt. auth. see Brace, Arthur William.

Allen, F. R., et al, eds. The Management of Risk to Society from Potential Accidents: The Main Report of the UKAEA Working Group on the Risks to Society from Potential Major Accidents: With an Executive Summary. LC 92-26262. 176p. 1992. ring bd. 183.95 (*1-85166-892-6*, Chap & Hall CRC) CRC Pr.

Allen, Fal, jt. auth. see Cantwell, Dick.

Allen, Farrow, jt. auth. see Stewart, Dick.

***Allen, Faye Wolfe.** The Third Testament. LC 99-93615. 1999. 22.95 (*0-533-13085-9*) Vantage.

Allen, Felicity. Health Psychology: Theory & Practice. LC 98-219960. (Illus.). 368p. 1998. pap. 45.00 (*1-86448-659-7*, Pub. by Allen & Unwin Pty) Paul & Co Pubs.

***Allen, Felicity.** Jefferson Davis, Unconquerable Heart. LC 99-39915. 832p. 1999. 34.95 (*0-8262-1219-0*) U of Mo Pr.

Allen, Frances, jt. auth. see Malley, Barbara.

Allen, Francis A. Borderland of Criminal Justice: Essays in Law & Criminology. LC 64-24972. xii, 140p. 1964. lib. bdg. 10.00 (*0-226-01416-9*) U Ch Pr.

— Borderland of Criminal Justice: Essays in Law & Criminology. LC 64-24972. xii, 140p. 1974. pap. text 2.45 (*0-226-01417-7*) U Ch Pr.

— The Borderland of Criminal Justice: Essays in Law & Criminology. LC 64-24972. 148p. reprint ed. pap. 45.90 (*0-608-09375-0*, 205412000004) Bks Demand.

— The Crimes of Politics: Political Dimensions of Criminal Justice. LC 73-93506. 119p. reprint ed. pap. 36.90 (*0-7837-5932-0*, 204573100007) Bks Demand.

— The Habits of Legality: Criminal Justice & the Rule of the Law. (Studies in Crime & Public Policy). 168p. 1996. text 45.00 (*0-19-510088-3*) OUP.

Allen, Francis H., ed. see Thoreau, Henry David.

Allen, Francis J. The Concrete Battleship: Fort Drum, El Fraile Island, Manila Bay. LC 88-90957. (Illus.). 52p. (Orig.). (C). 1989. pap. 8.95 (*0-929521-06-4*) Pictorial Hist.

Allen, Frank K., et al. The Golfer's Bible. rev. ed. 112p. 1989. pap. 12.95 (*0-385-24102-X*) Doubleday.

Allen, Franklin & Gale, Douglas. Financial Innovation & Risk Sharing. LC 93-51058. (Illus.). 352p. 1994. 48.50 (*0-262-01141-7*) MIT Pr.

***Allen, Franklin & Gate, Douglas.** Comparing Financial Systems. LC 99-30173. (Illus.). 584p. 1999. 55.00 (*0-262-01177-8*) MIT Pr.

Allen, Franklin W. Breaking the Barriers: A History of Church/Mission Relationships in the Philippines. 146p. (C). 1990. pap. 6.95 (*9971-972-91-3*) OMF Bks.

Allen, Fraser H. & Seba, Richard D. Economics of Worldwide Pet Production. 563p. 1993. 69.50 (*0-930972-17-1*) Oil & Gas.

Allen, Fred. Much Ado about Me. 402p. reprint ed. lib. bdg. 27.95 (*0-88411-291-8*) Amereon Ltd.

Allen, Frederick. Atlanta Rising: The Invention of an International City 1946-1996. LC 95-82237. (Illus.). 240p. 1996. 20.00 (*1-56352-296-9*) Longstreet.

— Secret Formula. 544p. 1995. pap. 16.00 (*0-88730-751-5*, HarpBusn) HarpInfo.

— Secret Formula: How Brilliant Marketing & Relentless Salesmanship Made Coca-Cola the Best-Know Product in the World. LC 94-10397. (Illus.). 320p. 1994. 25.00 (*0-88730-672-1*, HarpBusn) HarpInfo.

— Secret Formula: How Brilliant Marketing & Salesmanship Made Coca-Cola the Best Known Product in the World. (Illus.). 500p. 1999. reprint ed. text 25.00 (*0-7881-6153-9*) DIANE Pub.

Allen, Frederick L. Big Chance. 288p. Date not set. 23.95 (*0-8488-2563-2*) Amereon Ltd.

— The Big Change: America Transforms Itself: 1900-1950. LC 92-11261. 322p. (C). 1992. pap. 24.95 (*1-56000-639-0*) Transaction Pubs.

— Only Yesterday. LC 56-13462. 320p. 1942. pap. 8.00 (*0-06-080004-6*, P4, Perennial) HarperTrade.

— Only Yesterday: An Informal History of the 1920s. LC 97-19930. (Investment Classics Ser.). 285p. 1997. 21.95 (*0-471-18952-9*) Wiley.

— Since Yesterday. 304p. Date not set. 23.95 (*0-8488-2564-0*) Amereon Ltd.

— Since Yesterday: The 1930s in America. LC 86-45060. 400p. 1986. reprint ed. pap. 14.00 (*0-06-091322-3*, PL1322, Perennial) HarperTrade.

***Allen, Frederick Lewis.** Only Yesterday: An Informal History of the 1920s. LC 00-28345. 352p. 2000. pap. 13.00 (*0-06-095665-8*, Perennial) HarperTrade.

Allen, Frederick S. Zurich: The 1820's to the 1870's - A Study in Modernization. (Illus.). 146p. (Orig.). (C). 1986. pap. text 19.50 (*0-8191-5512-8*) U Pr of Amer.

A

Allen, G. Sequencing of Proteins & Peptides. 2nd ed. (Laboratory Techniques in Biochemistry & Molecular Biology Ser.: Vol. 9). 426p. 1989. pap. 62.00 (*0-444-81021-8*) Elsevier.

Allen, G. C. Appointment in Japan: Memories of Sixty Years. (Illus.). 196p. (C). 1983. text 35.00 (*0-485-11237-X*, Pub. by Athlone Pr) Humanities.

— Modern Japan & Its Problems. 2nd ed. LC 89-18575. 180p. (C). 1990. reprint ed. text 70.00 (*0-485-11310-4*, Pub. by Athlone Pr) Humanities.

Allen, G. D., et al. Elements Of Calculus. LC 82-12874. (Math). 512p. (C). 1983. mass mkt. 34.50 (*0-534-01188-8*) Brooks-Cole.

Allen, G. M., jt. auth. see Tozzer, Alfred M.

Allen, Gardner W. A Naval History of the American Revolution, 2 vols., Set. (Illus.). 752p. 1995. reprint ed. lib. bdg. 79.95 (*0-8328-4503-5*) Higginson Bk Co.

— Our Naval War with France. (BCL1 - U. S. History Ser.). 323p. 1992. reprint ed. lib. bdg. 89.00 (*0-7812-6139-2*) Rprt Serv.

Allen, Garland A., jt. auth. see Baker, Jeffrey J.

Allen, Garland E., jt. auth. see Baker, Jeffrey J.

Allen, Garrison. Baseball Cat. Vol. 4. 336p. 1998. mass mkt. 5.99 (*1-57566-309-0*) Kensgtn Pub Corp.

— Baseball Cat, No. 4. LC 96-80072. 304p. 1997. 18.95 (*1-57566-183-7*, Knsington) Kensgtn Pub Corp.

— Desert Cat. 304p. 1994. mass mkt. 3.99 (*0-8217-4503-4*, Zebra Kensgtn) Kensgtn Pub Corp.

— Dinosaur Cat. LC 97-75386. Vol. 5. 336p. 1998. 12.00 (*1-57566-304-X*, Knsington) Kensgtn Pub Corp.

— Dinosaur Cat. (Big Mike Mystery Ser.). 336p. 1999. mass mkt. 5.99 (*1-57566-426-7*) Kensgtn Pub Corp.

— Movie Cat. LC 98-67618. 304p. 1999. text 20.00 (*1-57566-413-5*) Kensgtn Pub Corp.

— Royal Cat: A Big Mike Mystery. Vol. 2. 304p. 1996. mass mkt. 4.99 (*1-57566-045-8*) Kensgtn Pub Corp.

— Stable Cat. 304p. 1997. mass mkt. 5.50 (*1-57566-188-8*, Knsington) Kensgtn Pub Corp.

Allen, Garth. Education at Risk. LC 97-179495. (Cassell Education Ser.). 130p. 1997. 89.50 (*0-304-33834-6*, LB2822, Pub. by Cassell) LPC InBook.

Allen, Gary. Kissinger: The Secret Side of the Secretary of State. 1976. 12.00 (*0-89245-003-7*) Devin.

— Kissinger: The Secret Side of the Secretary of State. 1994. reprint ed. lib. bdg. 24.95 (*1-56849-369-X*) Buccaneer Bks.

— The Missionary Who Forgot His Name. (Illus.). 145p. (Orig.). 1994. pap. 8.00 (*1-882775-06-6*) Selva Edit.

— None Dare Call It Conspiracy. 22.95 (*0-8488-1232-8*) Amereon Ltd.

— None Dare Call It Conspiracy. 142p. 1990. reprint ed. 27.95 (*0-89966-661-2*) Buccaneer Bks.

Allen, Gary. None Dare Call It Conspiracy. unabridged ed. 141p. 1971. reprint ed. pap. 10.00 (*0-945001-29-0*) GSG & Assocs.

Allen, Gary. The Resource Guide for Food Writers. 304p. 1999. pap. 19.99 (*0-415-92250-X*) Routledge.

— The Rockefeller File. 1994. reprint ed. lib. bdg. 27.95 (*1-56849-368-1*) Buccaneer Bks.

***Allen, Gary, et al.** Proceedings of the 25th Annual International Congress on Veterinary Acupuncture. (Illus.). 240p. 1999. spiral bd. 30.00 (*0-9616627-0-0*) Intl Vet Acup.

Allen, Gay. American Prosody. (BCL1-PS American Literature Ser.). 342p. 1993. reprint ed. lib. bdg. 89.00 (*0-7812-6582-7*) Rprt Serv.

Allen, Gay W. A Reader's Guide to Walt Whitman. LC 97-21258. xiii, 234p. 1997. pap. 16.95 (*0-8156-0488-2*) Syracuse U Pr.

— The Solitary Singer: A Critical Biography of Walt Whitman. LC 84-16462. (Illus.). 642p. reprint ed. pap. 199.10 (*0-608-08825-0*, 206946400004) Bks Demand.

— The Solitary Singer: A Critical Biography of Walt Whitman. LC 84-16462. (Illus.). xx, 616p. 1985. reprint ed. pap. 15.95 (*0-226-01435-5*) U Ch Pr.

— Walt Whitman. rev. ed. LC 68-30926. (Illus.). 252p. reprint ed. pap. 78.20 (*0-7837-3614-2*, 204348000009) Bks Demand.

— Walt Whitman Handbook. (University Classics Ser.). 560p. reprint ed. spiral bd. 59.50 (*0-87532-050-3*) Hendricks House.

— William James. LC 79-629874. (University of Minnesota Pamphlets on American Writers Ser.: No. 88). 48p. (Orig.). reprint ed. pap. 30.00 (*0-7837-2902-2*, 205755300006) Bks Demand.

Allen, Gay W. & Folsom, Ed, eds. Walt Whitman & the World. LC 95-479. 480p. 1995. text 49.95 (*0-87745-497-3*); pap. text 22.95 (*0-87745-498-1*) U of Iowa Pr.

Allen, Gemmy. Management 136 - 1370. (Orig.). (C). 1995. pap. 24.19 (*1-56870-179-9*) RonJon Pub.

— Management 7371 - 7372. (Orig.). (C). 1995. pap. text 30.43 (*1-56870-222-1*) RonJon Pub.

— Marketing 2370: Principles of Marketing. (C). 1995. 21.03 (*1-56870-200-0*) RonJon Pub.

***Allen, Gemmy.** Supervision. 1999. pap. text 35.10 (*1-56870-354-6*) RonJon Pub.

Allen, Geoffrey. Comprehensive Polymer Science: Plus Two Supplements, 7 vols. 1996. 3034.00 (*0-08-042681-6*, Pergamon Pr) Elsevier.

***Allen, Geoffrey.** The Gun Ringer. 1998. pap. 24.95 (*1-875998-39-X*, Pub. by Central Queensland) Accents Pubns.

Allen, Geoffrey. Proteins Vol. 1: Principles of Protein Structure. 360p. 1997. 128.50 (*1-55938-671-1*) Jai Pr.

Allen, Geoffrey, ed. Proteins: Applications of Proteins, Vol. 15. Date not set. 128.50 (*1-55938-685-1*) Jai Pr.

— Proteins: Cell Surface Proteins, Vol. 11. Date not set. 128.50 (*1-55938-681-9*) Jai Pr.

— Proteins: Major Non-Immune System Proteins of Blood Plasma, Vol. 5. Date not set. 128.50 (*1-55938-675-4*) Jai Pr.

— Proteins: Major Structural Proteins, Vol. 7. Date not set. 128.50 (*1-55938-677-0*) Jai Pr.

— Proteins: Nucleic Acid Binding Proteins, Vol. 13. Date not set. 128.50 (*1-55938-683-5*) Jai Pr.

— Proteins: Physical & Chemical Properties of, Vol. 2. 1999. 128.50 (*1-55938-672-X*) Jai Pr.

— Proteins: Plasma Membrane Transport Proteins, Vol. 10. Date not set. 128.50 (*1-55938-680-0*) Jai Pr.

— Proteins: Protein & the Immune System, Vol. 4. Date not set. 128.50 (*1-55938-674-6*) Jai Pr.

— Proteins: Protein Growth Factors & Cytokines, Vol. 6. Date not set. 128.50 (*1-55938-676-2*) Jai Pr.

— Proteins: Protein Synthesis & Degradation, Vol. 3. Date not set. 128.50 (*1-55938-673-8*) Jai Pr.

— Proteins: Protein Toxins & Defense Proteins, Vol. 14. Date not set. 128.50 (*1-55938-684-3*) Jai Pr.

— Proteins: Proteins in Oxidative Metabolism, Vol. 12. Date not set. 128.50 (*1-55938-682-7*) Jai Pr.

— Proteins: Proteins of the Cytoskeleton & Cell Motility, Vol. 9. Date not set. 128.50 (*1-55938-679-7*) Jai Pr.

— Proteins: Soluble Proteins of the Cytoplasm, Vol. 8. Date not set. 128.50 (*1-55938-678-9*) Jai Pr.

Allen, Geoffrey & Bevington, J. C. Comprehensive Polymer Science: The Synthesis, Characterization, Reactions & Applications of Polymers, 7 vols., Set. (Illus.). 5367p. 1988. 3120.00 (*0-08-032515-7*, Pergamon Pr) Elsevier.

Allen, Geoffrey & Bevington, J. C., eds. Chain Polymerization I. (Comprehensive Polymer Science Ser.: Vol. 3). (Illus.). 897p. 1990. 585.00 (*0-08-036207-9*, Pergamon Pr) Elsevier.

— Chain Polymerization II. (Comprehensive Polymer Science Ser.: Vol. 4). (Illus.). 602p. 1990. 375.00 (*0-08-036208-7*, Pergamon Pr) Elsevier.

— Polymer Reactions. (Comprehensive Polymer Science Ser.: Vol. 6). (Illus.). 664p. 1990. 440.00 (*0-08-036210-9*, Pergamon Pr) Elsevier.

— Speciality Polymers & Polymer Processing. (Comprehensive Polymer Science Ser.: Vol. 7). (Illus.). 685p. 1990. 440.00 (*0-08-036211-7*, Pergamon Pr) Elsevier.

— Step Polymerization. (Comprehensive Polymer Science Ser.: Vol. 5). (Illus.). 753p. 1990. 480.00 (*0-08-036209-5*, Pergamon Pr) Elsevier.

Allen, Geoffrey & Petrie, S. E., eds. Physical Structure of the Amorphous State. LC 76-53665. 312p. reprint ed. pap. 96.80 (*0-608-16967-6*, 202710500054) Bks Demand.

Allen, George. Daily Management of Manufactured Home Landlease Communities. McCarty, Susan, ed. (Monograph Ser.: No. 3). 30p. 1993. 25.00 (*1-878350-03-X*) PMN Pub.

— Development, Sale & Purchase of Manufactured Home Landlease Communities. McCarty, Susan, ed. (Monograph Ser.: No. 2). 30p. 1993. 25.00 (*1-878350-02-1*) PMN Pub.

— Industry Associations Directory for the Manufactured Housing Industry. 40p. 1999. 50.00 (*1-878350-13-7*) PMN Pub.

***Allen, George.** Introduction to Manufactured Housing: Monograph V. 25p. 1999. pap. 25.00 (*1-878350-10-2*) PMN Pub.

— Manufactured Home Community Management. 3rd rev. ed. 242p. 1998. pap. 60.00 (*1-878350-07-2*) PMN Pub.

Allen, George. The Mental Game (The Inner Game of Bowling) LC 83-50980. (Illus.). 192p. 1983. pap. 12.95 (*0-933554-18-4*) Tech-Ed Pub.

— Real Estate & Property Management. McCarty, Susan, ed. (Monograph Ser.: No. 1). 30p. (C). 1993. 25.00 (*1-878350-01-3*) PMN Pub.

— Real Estate Brokers Directory for the Manufactured-Home Community Industry. 5p. 1999. 100.00 (*1-878350-11-0*) PMN Pub.

— Upper Management Related Reports & Directories. McCarty, Susan, ed. (Monograph Ser.: No. 4). 30p. (C). 1993. 25.00 (*1-878350-04-8*) PMN Pub.

— Vendor Resources Directory for the Manufactured Home Community Industry. 22p. 1999. 25.00 (*1-878350-12-9*) PMN Pub.

Allen, George, tr. Book of the Dead: or Going Forth by Day: Ideas of the Ancient Egyptians Concerning the Hereafter As Expressed in Their Own Terms. LC 74-10338. (Studies in Ancient Oriental Civilization: No. 37). 306p. 1974. pap. text 24.00 (*0-226-62410-2*) U Ch Pr.

Allen, George & Rada, Alejandro. The Role of Biological Control in Pest Management. LC SB0975.A44. 184p. 1984. reprint ed. pap. 57.10 (*0-608-01994-1*, 206265000003) Bks Demand.

Allen, George & Ritger, Dick. The Complete Guide to Bowling Principles: The Encyclopedia of Principles. LC 81-85284. (Encyclopedia of Bowling Instruction Ser.: Vol. 1). (Illus.). 280p. 1982. 17.95 (*0-933554-00-1*); pap. 12.95 (*0-933554-01-X*) Tech-Ed Pub.

— The Complete Guide to Bowling Strikes: The Encyclopedia of Strikes. LC 80-53200. (Encyclopedia of Bowling Instruction Ser.: Vol. 2). (Illus.). 222p. (C). 1981. 17.95 (*0-933554-02-8*); pap. 12.95 (*0-933554-03-6*) Tech-Ed Pub.

— Encyclopedia of Bowling Instruction, 3 vols., Set. 1982. 34.95 (*0-933554-14-1*) Tech-Ed Pub.

Allen, George, et al. Development, Marketing & Operation of Manufactured Home Communities. 400p. (C). 1993. text 80.00 (*0-471-59519-5*) PMN Pub.

***Allen, George, et al.** Development, Marketing & Operation of Manufactured Home Communities. 2nd rev. ed. (Illus.). 500p. 2001. text 80.00 (*1-878350-16-1*) PMN Pub.

Allen, George, et al. How to Find, Buy, Manage & Sell a Manufactured Home Community. LC 96-18386. 544p. 1996. text 80.00 (*0-471-13587-9*) PMN Pub.

Allen, George, jt. auth. see Bigelow, Stephen J.

Allen, George, jt. auth. see Ritger, Dick.

Allen, George, ed. see Jackson, Chrissy.

Allen, George B. Fraud Identification Handbook: Fraud Avoidance Through Knowledge, 1. LC 98-92302. 1998. pap. text 22.95 (*0-9669160-0-X*) Preventive Pr.

Allen, George C. Japanese Industry: Its Recent Development & Present Condition. LC 75-30093. (Institute of Pacific Relations Ser.). reprint ed. 32.50 (*0-404-59501-4*) AMS Pr.

— Japan's Economic Recovery. LC 85-30542. (Illus.). 226p. 1986. reprint ed. lib. bdg. 65.00 (*0-313-25039-1*, ALJE, Greenwood Pr) Greenwood.

— The Structure of Industry in Britain: A Study in Economic Change. 3rd ed. LC 66-70817. 281p. reprint ed. pap. 87.20 (*0-608-12213-0*, 202526300043) Bks Demand.

Allen, George C. & Donnithorne, Audrey G. Western Enterprise in Far Eastern Economic Development, China & Japan. LC 54-1323. 291p. reprint ed. pap. 90.30 (*0-608-13722-7*, 205525400011) Bks Demand.

Allen, George H. & Pacelli, Joseph G. George Allen's Guide to Special Teams. LC 89-37574. (Illus.). 240p. (Orig.). 1990. pap. 19.95 (*0-88011-370-7*, PALL0370) Human Kinetics.

Allen, George P. A History & Genealogical Record of the Alling-Allens of New Haven, Conn., the Descendants of Roger Alling, First, & John Alling, Sr., from 1639. (Illus.). 317p. 1988. reprint ed. pap. 47.50 (*0-8328-0113-5*); reprint ed. lib. bdg. 55.50 (*0-8328-0112-7*) Higginson Bk Co.

Allen, George P., jt. auth. see Posamentier, Henry W.

Allen, George R. The Graduate Students' Guide to Theses & Dissertations: A Practical Manual for Writing & Research. LC 73-3774. 122p. reprint ed. pap. 37.90 (*0-8357-4786-7*, 203772300009) Bks Demand.

— History of William H. Allen, Bookseller, 1918-1997. (Illus.). 36p. 1997. pap. 10.00 (*1-884718-71-X*, 49711) Oak Knoll.

— Unforgettable Strategies for Success. 96p. (Orig.). 1987. pap. 6.95 (*0-933554-50-8*) Tech-Ed Pub.

Allen, George W. Allen History & Genealogy. 120p. 1997. reprint ed. pap. 19.00 (*0-8328-7229-6*); reprint ed. lib. bdg. 29.00 (*0-8328-7228-8*) Higginson Bk Co.

Allen, Gerald. Marine Life of the Pacific & Indian Oceans: A Periplus Nature Guide. 1997. pap. 19.95 (*0-614-27433-8*) Periplus.

Allen, Gerald, text. Tropical Marine Life. (Illus.). 64p. 1997. 9.95 (*962-593-157-0*) Tuttle Pubng.

Allen, Gerald R. Cockatiel Handbook. 256p. 1981. 19.95 (*0-87666-956-9*, PS-741) TFH Pubns.

— Marine Life of the Pacific & Indian Oceans. (Illus.). 96p. 1997. pap. 19.95 (*962-593-016-7*, Periplus Eds) Tuttle Pubng.

— Rainbowfishes: In Nature & in the Aquarium. (Illus.). 182p. 28.95 (*1-56465-149-5*, 16468) Tetra Pr.

Allen, Gerald R. & Allen, Connie J. All about Cockatiels. (Illus.). 1980. 11.95 (*0-87666-955-0*, PS-746) TFH Pubns.

Allen, Gerald R. & Robertson, D. R. Fishes of the Tropical Eastern Pacific. (Illus.). 332p. (C). 1994. text 75.00 (*0-8248-1675-7*) UH Pr.

Allen, Gerald R. & Werner, Timothy B., eds. A Rapid Biodiversity Assessment of the Coral Reefs of Milne Bay, Papua New Guinea. (RAP Working Papers: No. 11). (Illus.). 75p. (C). 1998. pap. text 19.95 (*1-881173-54-2*) Conser Intl.

Allen, Gerald R., jt. auth. see Fautin, Daphne G.

Allen, Gilbert. Commandments at Eleven. LC 94-6556. 64p. (Orig.). 1994. pap. write for info. (*0-914061-46-1*) Orchises Pr.

— In Everything: Poems Nineteen Seventy-Two to Nineteen Seventy-Nine. LC 81-82661. 75p. (YA). (gr. 9-12). 1982. per. 5.00 (*0-916418-37-5*) Lotus.

— Second Chances. LC 90-48742. 80p. (Orig.). 1991. pap. 10.00 (*0-914061-20-8*) Orchises Pr.

Allen, Ginny, et al. Oregon Painters, the First Hundred Years (1859-1959) Index & Biographical Dictionary. LC 99-23461. 341p. 1999. 40.00 (*0-87595-271-2*) Oregon Hist.

Allen, Glen. Colorado Poetry: And Thoughts of Yesteryear. 86p. (Orig.). 1989. pap. 4.95 (*0-9622131-0-1*) McKee Bks.

Allen, Gloria L. Deposition Questions: English & Spanish. (ENG & SPA.). 365p. 1995. ring bd. 69.00 (*0-913875-20-1*, 5201) Lawyers & Judges.

Allen, Gloria S. & Tuckhorn, Nancy G. A Maryland Album: Quiltmaking Traditions, 1634-1934. LC 95-2387. (Illus.). 224p. 1995. 34.95 (*1-55853-341-9*) Rutledge Hill Pr.

Allen, Glover M. Extinct & Vanishing Mammals of the Western Hemisphere: With the Marine Species of All Oceans. LC 72-85661. (Illus.). xv, 620p. 1973. reprint ed. lib. bdg. 73.50 (*0-8154-0433-6*) Cooper Sq.

Allen-Goad, Pamela, ed. see Nelson, Julia.

Allen, Grace M., tr. see Bidder, Hans.

Allen, Graham. Harold Bloom: Poetics of Conflict. 240p. (C). 1994. pap. text 26.50 (*0-13-302274-9*) P-H.

— Intertextuality. LC 99-55504. (New Critical Idiom Ser.). 1999. 50.00 (*0-415-17474-0*); pap. 12.99 (*0-415-17475-9*) Routledge.

Allen, Grant. An African Millionaire: Episodes in the Life of the Illustrious Colonel Clay. LC 75-32732. (Literature of Mystery & Detection Ser.). (Illus.). 1976. reprint ed. 26.95 (*0-405-07862-5*) Ayer.

— An African Millionaire: Episodes in the Life of the Illustrious Colonel Clay. 336p. 1980. reprint ed. pap. 6.95 (*0-486-23992-6*) Dover.

— The British Barbarians. LC 74-15943. (Science Fiction Ser.). (Illus.). 226p. 1975. reprint ed. 19.95 (*0-405-06272-9*) Ayer.

— The Evolution of the Idea of God. 1977. lib. bdg. 59.95 (*0-8490-1796-3*) Gordon Pr.

— The Evolution of the Idea of God. 157p. 1996. reprint ed. spiral bd. 15.50 (*0-7873-0022-5*) Hlth Research.

— The Evolution of the Idea of God: An Inquiry into the Origins of Religion. 157p. 1998. reprint ed. spiral bd. 24.00 (*1-885395-91-4*) Book Tree.

— Falling in Love: With Other Essays on More Exact Branches of Science. LC 72-3357. (Essay Index Reprint Ser.). 1977. reprint ed. 23.95 (*0-8369-2884-9*) Ayer.

— The Woman Who Did. Wintle, Sarah & Trotter, David, eds. (Oxford Popular Fiction Ser.). 288p. 1995. pap. 8.95 (*0-19-282312-4*) OUP.

Allen, Greg, et al. Too Much Light Makes the Baby Go Blind. 126p. 1993. pap. 8.95 (*1-56850-031-9*) Chicago Plays.

Allen, H. & Starr, Tomas B. Hierarchy: Perspectives for Ecological Complexity. LC 81-22010. (Illus.). 326p. reprint ed. pap. 101.10 (*0-608-09256-8*, 205405800002) Bks Demand.

Allen, H. C. & Hill, C. P., eds. British Essays in American History. LC 82-20916. 348p. (C). 1983. reprint ed. lib. bdg. 69.50 (*0-313-23789-1*, ALBE, Greenwood Pr) Greenwood.

Allen, H. G. Analysis & Design of Structural Sandwich Panels. 1969. 142.00 (*0-08-012870-X*, Pub. by Pergamon Repr) Franklin.

Allen, H. J., jt. ed. see Wilbur, J. B.

Allen, H. L. & Taylor, M. P. Charts & Fundamentals in the Foreign Exchange Market. LC HG3851.. (Bank of England. Discussion Papers: No. 40). 58p. reprint ed. pap. 30.00 (*0-7837-6658-0*, 204626900011) Bks Demand.

Allen, H. M., ed. see Erasmus, Desiderius.

Allen, H. Warner, jt. auth. see Bentley, E. C.

Allen, Hank, ed. The Tool Shed Treasury: The Best Articles on Antique Tool Collecting from Crafts. LC 96-85178. (Illus.). 176p. (Orig.). 1996. pap. 18.50 (*1-879335-71-9*) Astragal Pr.

***Allen, Hariett.** Dear Santa Claus. (Illus.). 32p. (J). (ps-5). 2000. 16.95 (*1-57102-171-X*, Ideals Child) Hambleton-Hill.

Allen, Harold. Cosmic Perspective. Charles, Rodney & Dunn, Sharon, eds. LC 97-66215. 275 p. 1998. 21.95 (*1-887472-23-1*) Sunstar Pubng.

Allen, Harold B. Semantic Confusion: A Report from Atlas Files. (Publications of the American Dialect Society: No. 33). 24p. 1960. pap. 2.50 (*0-8173-0669-2*) U of Ala Pr.

— A Survey of the Teaching of English to Non-English Speakers in the United States. Cordasco, Francesco, ed. LC 77-90403. (Bilingual-Bicultural Education in the U. S. Ser.). 1978. reprint ed. lib. bdg. 23.95 (*0-405-11072-3*) Ayer.

Allen, Harold B., compiled by. Linguistics & English Linguistics. 2nd ed. LC 75-42974. (Goldentree Bibliographies Series in Language & Literature). (C). 1977. pap. text 16.95 (*0-88295-558-6*) Harlan Davidson.

Allen, Harold B., et al. Minor Dialect Areas of the Upper Midwest; A Tentative Bibliography of Kentuch Speech; The Language of Jazz Musicians. (Publications of the American Dialect Society; No. 30). 48p. 1958. pap. 4.80 (*0-8173-0630-7*) U of Ala Pr.

Allen, Harold E. & Linn, Michael D. Dialect & Language Variation. 1986. pap. text 59.95 (*0-12-051130-4*) Acad Pr.

Allen, Harold J., jt ed. see Wilbur, James B.

Allen, Harold W. The Eternal Universe. LC 89-92234. (Illus.). 180p. (Orig.). (C). 1989. pap. 10.95 (*0-9624555-0-4*) Perspective Bks.

— The Eternal Universe. 2nd rev. ed. LC 90-91699. (Illus.). 183p. (Orig.). 1990. pap. 14.95 (*0-9624555-1-2*) Perspective Bks.

— The Face on Mars. Charles, Rodney, ed. LC 97-65711. 240p. 1997. pap. 12.95 (*1-887472-27-4*) Sunstar Pubng.

***Allen, Harold W. G.** Lunar Encounter: Science Fiction with a Sojourn into Cosmology & Philosophy. LC 00-190493. 232p. 2000. pap. 12.95 (*0-9624555-2-0*) Perspective Bks.

Allen, Harper. The Man That Got Away. (Intrigue Ser.). 1998. per. 3.99 (*0-373-22468-0*, 1-22468-2) Harlequin Bks.

— Twice Tempted. (Intrigue Ser.: Bk. 547). 2000. per. 3.99 (*0-373-22547-4*, 1-22547-3) Harlequin Bks.

Allen, Harry E. & Simonsen, Clifford E. Corrections in America. (Illus.). 768p. (C). 1994. teacher ed. write for info. (*0-318-72450-2*) Macmillan.

— Corrections in America: An Introduction. 8th ed. LC 96-49655. 656p. 1997. 83.00 (*0-13-598038-0*) P-H.

— Terrorism & Justice: An Introduction. LC 99-15762. (Illus.). 344p. (C). 1999. pap. text 47.00 (*0-02-301731-7*, Macmillan Coll) P-H.

Allen, Harry E., et al. Probation & Parole in America. LC 85-10093. 336p. (C). 1985. 35.00 (*0-02-900440-3*) Free Pr.

Allen, Harry E., jt. auth. see Latessa, Edward J.

Allen, Harry S. & Volgyes, Ivan, eds. Israel, the Middle East, & U. S. Interests. LC 82-22357. 190p. 1983. 45.00 (*0-275-90934-4*, C0934, Praeger Pubs) Greenwood.

Allen, Harvey A., et al. Teaching & Learning in the Middle Level School. LC 92-31113. 464p. (C). 1993. 93.00 (*0-675-21347-9*, Merrill Coll) P-H.

Allen, Hayward. Great Blue Heron. LC 91-2400. 176p. 1991. pap. 16.95 (*1-55971-094-2*, NorthWord Pr) Creat Pub Intl.

Allen, Heather. Leaving a Shadow. 75p. 1996. pap. 12.00 (*1-55659-113-6*) Copper Canyon.

An Asterisk (*) at the beginning of an entry indicates that the title is appearing for the first time.

Allen, Heather L. Weaving Contemporary Rag Rugs: New Designs & Traditional Techniques. LC 97-19740. 128p. 1998. 24.95 (*1-887374-39-6*, Pub. by Lark Books) Random.

Allen, Helen, et al. Exchange Rate Equations. LC HG1703.. (Bank of England. Discussion Papers. Technical Ser.: No. 39). 16p. reprint ed. pap. 30.00 (*0-7837-4399-8*, 204413900012) Bks Demand.

Allen, Helena G. The Betrayal of Liliuokalani: Last Queen of Hawaii, 1838-1917. 432p. 1991. reprint ed. mass mkt. 7.95 (*0-935180-89-3*) Mutual Pub HI.

— Kalakaua, Renaissance King. 320p. 1995. mass mkt. 6.95 (*1-56647-059-5*) Mutual Pub HI.

— Sanford Ballard Dole: Hawaii's Only President, 1844-1926. LC 87-72591. (Illus.). 304p. 1988. 24.95 (*0-87062-184-X*) A H Clark.

***Allen, Henriette L.** Reading Skills Competency Tests: Competency Tests for Basic Reading Skills. LC 98-51643. (Illus.). 123p. 1999. spiral bd. 29.95 (*0-13-021325-X*) P-H.

— Ready-to-Use Vocabulary, Word Analysis & Comprehension Activities. LC 96-18332. (Reading Skills Activities Library). (Illus.). (J). (gr. 4). 1998. spiral bd. 28.95 (*0-87628-481-0*) Ctr Appl Res.

— Ready-to-Use Vocabulary, Word Analysis & Comprehension Activities. LC 96-18332. (Reading Skills Activities Library). (Illus.). (J). (gr. 5). 1998. spiral bd. 28.95 (*0-87628-480-2*) Ctr Appl Res.

— Ready-to-Use Vocabulary, Word Analysis & Comprehension Activities. (Reading Skills Activities Library). (Illus.). (J). (gr. 6). 1998. spiral bd. 28.95 (*0-87628-479-9*) Ctr Appl Res.

Allen, Henriette L., et al. Ready-to-Use Reading & Study Skills Mastery Activities: Secondary Level. LC 96-26401. 1996. spiral bd. 28.95 (*0-87628-593-0*) Ctr Appl Res.

— Ready-to-Use Vocabulary, Word Analysis & Comprehension Activities: First Grade Reading Level. LC 96-18332. (Reading Skills Activities Library). 1996. spiral bd. 28.95 (*0-87628-932-4*) Ctr Appl Res.

— Ready-to-Use Vocabulary, Word Analysis & Comprehension Activities: Second Grade Reading Level. LC 96-18332. (Reading Skills Activities Library). 256p. 1996. spiral bd. 28.95 (*0-87628-933-2*) Ctr Appl Res.

— Ready-to-Use Vocabulary, Word Analysis & Comprehension Activities: Third Grade Reading Level. LC 96-18332. (Reading Skills Activities Library). 256p. 1996. spiral bd. 28.95 (*0-87628-934-0*) Ctr Appl Res.

Allen, Henry. Fool's Mercy. 8.95 (*0-931848-62-8*) Dryad Pr.

— Glare & Other Poems. 24p. 1993. pap. 6.95 (*0-931848-81-4*) Dryad Pr.

— Toward the Morning. 464p. Date not set. 29.95 (*0-8488-2200-5*) Amereon Ltd.

***Allen, Henry.** What It Felt Like: Living in the American Century. LC 00-24239. 176p. 2000. 20.00 (*0-375-42063-0*) Pantheon.

Allen, Henry E. Turkish Transformation: A Study in Social & Religious Development. LC 68-57588. (Illus.). 251p. 1969. reprint ed. lib. bdg. 35.00 (*0-8371-0284-7*, ALTT, Greenwood Pr) Greenwood.

Allen, Henry J. & Gompers, Samuel. Party of the Third Part: The Story of the Kansas Industrial Relations Court. LC 74-156401. (American Labor Ser., No. 2). 1971. reprint ed. 23.95 (*0-405-02911-X*) Ayer.

Allen, Henry S. Going Too Far Enough: American Culture at Century's End. 224p. 1994. 21.00 (*1-56098-367-1*) Smithsonian.

Allen, Henry T. Atnatanas: Natives of Copper River, Alaska. (Shorey Indian Ser.). 14p. 1970. reprint ed. pap. 10.00 (*0-8466-4015-5*) Shoreys Bkstore.

Allen, Henry Wilson, see Fisher, Clay Henry Will, pseud.

Allen, Henry Wilson, see Henry, Will, pseud.

Allen, Herbert E. Metals in Groundwater. (Illus.). 464p. 1993. lib. bdg. 75.00 (*0-87371-277-3*, L277) Lewis Pubs.

Allen, Herbert E., ed. Metal Contaminated Aquatic Sediments. 350p. (C). 1996. ring bd. 84.95 (*1-57504-010-7*) CRC Pr.

Allen, Herbert E., et al, eds. Metal Speciation & Contamination of Soil. 384p. 1994. lib. bdg. 75.00 (*0-87371-697-3*, L697) Lewis Pubs.

— Metals in Surface Waters. LC 97-33660. (Illus.). 300p. 1997. ring bd. 64.95 (*1-57504-087-5*) CRC Pr.

Allen, Herbert E., jt. ed. see Kramer, James R.

Allen, Herbert F. A Study of the Comedies of Richard Brome, Especially as Representative of Dramatic Decadence. (BCL1-PR English Literature Ser.). 61p. 1992. reprint ed. lib. bdg. 59.00 (*0-7812-7238-6*) Rprt Serv.

Allen, Hervey. Action at Aquila. 1993. reprint ed. lib. bdg. 89.00 (*0-7812-5420-5*) Rprt Serv.

— Israfel: The Life & Times of Edgar Alan Poe, 2 vols., Set. 1993. reprint ed. lib. bdg. 180.00 (*0-7812-5419-1*) Rprt Serv.

— Wampum & Old Gold. LC 70-144716. (Yale Series of Younger Poets: No. 9). reprint ed. 18.00 (*0-404-53809-6*) AMS Pr.

Allen, Horace N. Korean Tales. LC 78-67682. (Folktale Ser.). reprint ed. 42.50 (*0-404-16053-0*) AMS Pr.

Allen, Howard W. Poindexter of Washington: A Study in Progressive Politics. LC 80-20123. 352p. 1981. 36.95 (*0-8093-0952-1*) S Ill U Pr.

Allen, Howard W. & Lacey, Vincent A., eds. Illinois Elections, 1818-1990: Candidates & County Returns for President, Governor, Senate, & House of Representatives. LC 91-24792. 560p. (C). 1992. 67.00 (*0-8093-1735-4*) S Ill U Pr.

***Allen, Hubert A., Jr.** Breakfast with Kamuzu. 128p. 2001. pap. 13.95 (*0-9641694-4-4*) H Allen & Assocs.

Allen, Hubert A. The Petroglyph Calendar: An Archaeoastronomy Adventure. LC 98-92855. (Illus.). 160p. (Orig.). 1998. pap. 18.95 (*0-9641694-5-2*) H Allen & Assocs.

Allen, Hubert A., Jr. Shadows on the Wall: A Story of Malawi Africa. LC 90-980887. (Illus.). 56p. (YA). (gr. 4-12). 1988. mass mkt. write for info. (*0-9641694-3-6*) H Allen & Assocs.

Allen, Hubert A., Jr., jt. auth. see Helitzer-Allen, Deborah L.

Allen, Hubert J. & Newbigin, Lesslie. Roland Allen: Pioneer, Priest, & Prophet. 248p. (Orig.). 1995. pap. 10.95 (*0-88028-157-X*, 1305) Forward Movement.

Allen, Hubert R. The Gravity Connection. LC 96-91041. 1997. pap. 10.95 (*0-533-12260-0*) Vantage.

Allen, Hugh. The House of Goodyear: A Story of Rubber & of Modern Business. LC 75-41745. (Companies & Men: Business Enterprises in America Ser.). (Illus.). 1976. reprint ed. 47.95 (*0-405-08063-8*) Ayer.

— The Kenya Ceramic Jiko: A Manual for Stovemakers. (Illus.). 192p. 1991. pap. 25.00 (*1-85339-083-6*, Pub. by Intermed Tech) Stylus Pub VA.

Allen, Hugh, jt. auth. see Bielenberg, Carl.

Allen, Hugh D., et al. Moss & Adams' Heart Disease in Infants, Children & Adolescents: Including the Fetus & Young Adult. 6th ed. Orig. Title: Adams' Heart Disease in Infants, Children, & Adolescents. 1,472p. text 259.00 (*0-683-30742-8*) Lppncott W & W.

Allen, Hugh D., et al. Workbook in Pediatric Echocardiography. LC 76-57460. 291p. reprint ed. pap. 90.30 (*0-608-15902-6*, 203083700071) Bks Demand.

Allen, Ira, jt. auth. see Allen, Ethan.

***Allen, Irene.** Celebrate Austin Vol. 11: And the Texas Hill Country. rev. ed. (Illus.). 128p. 1999. 7.95 (*1-893524-02-7*) Celeb Pubns.

Allen, Irene. Quaker Indictment: An Elizabeth Elliot Mystery. LC 97-31615. 256p. 1997. text 21.95 (*0-312-16970-1*) St Martin.

— Quaker Testimony, Vol. 1. (Elizabeth Elliot Mystery Ser.). 1998. mass mkt. 5.99 (*0-312-96424-2*) St Martin.

Allen, Irving L. The Language of Ethnic Conflict. LC 82-9610. 168p. 1983. pap. text 20.00 (*0-231-05557-9*) Col U Pr.

— Unkind Words: Ethnic Labeling from Redskin to WASP. LC 90-32392. 152p. 1990. 45.00 (*0-89789-217-8*, H217, Bergin & Garvey); pap. 15.95 (*0-89789-220-8*, G220, Bergin & Garvey) Greenwood.

***Allen, Isabel.** Structure As Design. (Illus.). 160p. 1999. 40.00 (*1-56496-604-6*) Rockport Pubs.

Allen, J. As a Man Thinketh. 1987. 8.95 (*0-933062-22-2*) R H Sommer.

Allen, J. Diary. mass mkt. 6.95 (*0-7472-5171-1*, Pub. by Headline Bk Pub) Trafalgar.

— Journal. mass mkt. 6.95 (*0-7472-5092-8*, Pub. by Headline Bk Pub) Trafalgar.

Allen, J. The Workwoman's Guide. LC 86-28550. 315p. 1986. reprint ed. pap. 29.95 (*0-904983-02-1*) OPUS Pubns.

Allen, J. & Voges, R., eds. Synthesis & Applications of Isotopically Labelled Compounds 1994: 1994 Proceedings of the Fifth International Symposium, Strasburg, France, 20-24 June 1994. 956p. 1995. 540.00 (*0-471-95143-9*) Wiley.

Allen, J. A. C Is for Cajun Coloring Book. 8th ed. 1993. pap. 2.65 (*0-87511-652-3*) Claitors.

— Cajun Hidden Word Puzzle. 1983. pap. 2.95 (*0-87511-644-2*) Claitors.

Allen, J. B. The Medicine Keepers. 93p. 1997. pap. 20.00 (*1-888609-04-4*) Grey Hrse Pr.

Allen, J. B., jt. auth. see Segal, J. A.

Allen, J. B., ed. see Fletcher, Harvey.

Allen, J. C., jt. auth. see Hudson, N. G.

Allen, J. Dean. California Criminal Law Case Finder. LC 96-68462. 1996. 100.00 (*1-55834-359-8*, 80194-10, MICHIE) LEXIS Pub.

Allen, J. Edward. The Basics of Winning Blackjack. 2nd ed. LC 92-72054. (Illus.). 64p. 1992. mass mkt. 4.95 (*0-940685-24-8*, Gambling Res) Cardoza Pub.

— Basics of Winning Caribbean Stud Poker & Let It Ride. LC 96-85048. (Illus.). 64p. 1996. mass mkt. 4.95 (*0-940685-65-5*) Cardoza Pub.

— The Basics of Winning Craps. rev. ed. LC 98-71030. (Basics of Winning Ser.). (Illus.). 64p. 1999. mass mkt. 4.95 (*1-58042-003-6*) Cardoza Pub.

— The Basics of Winning Keno. rev. ed. LC 97-67122. (Illus.). 64p. 1997. mass mkt. 4.95 (*0-940685-83-3*) Cardoza Pub.

— The Basics of Winning Poker. 2nd ed. LC 92-72051. (Illus.). 64p. 1992. mass mkt. 4.95 (*0-940685-29-9*, Gambling Res) Cardoza Pub.

— Basics of Winning Roulette. 3rd rev. ed. LC 98-71035. (Basics of Winning Ser.). 64p. 1998. mass mkt. 4.95 (*1-58042-004-4*) Cardoza Pub.

— The Basics of Winning Slots. rev. ed. LC 97-67123. (Illus.). 64p. 1997. mass mkt. 4.95 (*0-940685-82-5*) Cardoza Pub.

— Basics of Winning Video Poker. LC 97-94819. 64p. 1998. mass mkt. 4.95 (*0-940685-97-3*) Cardoza Pub.

— Beat the Odds. 4th ed. LC 93-70983. (Illus.). 320p. 1993. reprint ed. pap. 7.95 (*0-940685-41-8*) Cardoza Pub.

— Winning Craps for the Serious Player. 2nd ed. LC 96-71756. (Illus.). 240p. 1997. pap. 14.95 (*0-940685-74-4*) Cardoza Pub.

Allen, J. Garrott, ed. The Physiology & Treatment of Peptic Ulcer. LC 59-10421. 246p. reprint ed. pap. 76.30 (*0-608-12489-3*, 202410900035) Bks Demand.

Allen, J. H. Judah's Sceptre & Joseph's Birthright. 4th ed. 436p. 1997. reprint ed. pap. 23.00 (*0-7873-0028-4*) Hlth Research.

Allen, J. H. & Greenough, J. B. New Latin Grammar. Kittredge, George L. et al, eds. (College Classical Ser.). 490p. 1992. lib. bdg. 37.50 (*0-89241-001-9*) Caratzas.

— New Latin Grammar. Kittredge, George L. et al, eds. (College Classical Ser.). 490p. 1995. pap. 22.50 (*0-89241-331-X*) Caratzas.

Allen, J. H. D. Portuguese Word-Formation with Suffixes. (LD Ser.: No. 33). 1941. 25.00 (*0-527-00779-X*) Periodicals Srv.

Allen, J. J. The Man in the Red Velvet Dress: Inside the World of Cross Dressing. (Illus.). 288p. 1996. 21.95 (*1-55972-338-6*, Birch Ln Pr) Carol Pub Group.

***Allen, J. J.** Posing & Lighting Techniques for Studio Portrait Photography. (Illus.). 120p. 2000. pap. 29.95 (*1-58428-031-X*, Pub. by Amherst Media) IPG Chicago.

***Allen, J. M.** Atlantis: The Andes Solution. LC 98-29449. (Illus.). 188p. 1999. text 26.95 (*0-312-21923-7*) St Martin.

Allen, J. M., et al, eds. Celebrating Age. 208p. 1996. 66.95 (*1-85628-589-8*, Pub. by Avebry) Ashgate Pub Co.

Allen, J. M., ed. see ASM International Staff.

Allen, J. Michael & Allen, James B. HCO World Hist From. LC 92-53296. (College Outline Ser.). (Illus.). 480p. 1993. pap. 17.00 (*0-06-467138-0*, Harper Ref) HarpC.

Allen, J. P., ed. see Chomsky, Noam.

Allen, J. R. Experiments in Physical Sedimentology. 64p. (Orig.). 1985. pap. text 19.95 (*0-04-551066-0*) Routledge.

***Allen, J. R. L.** Principles of Physical Sedimentology. 272p. 2000. reprint ed. pap. 74.95 (*1-930665-10-5*) Blackburn Pr.

Allen, J. Romilly. Celtic Art in Pagan & Christian Times. 1977. lib. bdg. 69.95 (*0-8490-1589-8*) Gordon Pr.

***Allen, J. Romilly.** Celtic Art in Pagan & Christian Times. (Illus.). 315p. 1999. reprint ed. pap. text 20.00 (*0-7881-6577-1*) DIANE Pub.

Allen, J. Thomas, Jr., jt. auth. see Abernathy, Kenneth.

Allen, J. Timothy. Mothers Around the Manger. LC 98-17456. 128p. 1998. pap. 12.00 (*1-57312-186-X*) Smyth & Helwys.

— Seasons in the Year: Poems, Prayers, Praise, & Prose. LC 93-18733. 192p. 1993. pap. 14.00 (*1-880837-22-6*) Smyth & Helwys.

— When the Season Is Dry: A Promise & a Wilderness. 160p. 1995. pap. 14.00 (*1-57312-010-3*) Smyth & Helwys.

Allen, J. W., et al, eds. A Poem Concerning the Death of the Prophet Muhammad - Utendi Wa Kutawafu Nabii. LC 91-32526. (Studies in African Literature: Vol. 6). (Illus.). 172p. 1991. lib. bdg. 79.95 (*0-7734-9705-6*) E Mellen.

Allen, J. W., tr. see Bakari, Mtoro B.

***Allen, J. Wayde.** Nist Microwave Power Standards in Waveguide. 50p. 1999. per. 4.50 (*0-16-056931-1*) USGPO.

Allen, Jack. Marilyn by Moonlight. (Illus.). 1996. 50.00 (*0-614-20389-9*, Barclay House) Zinn Pub Grp.

— Marilyn by Moonlight: A Remembrance in Rare Photos. LC 96-19148. 1996. 50.00 (*0-935016-45-7*) Zinn Pub Grp.

***Allen, Jack M., Jr.** Four Play: Four Key Plays That Make a Winning Marriage. 75p. 2000. pap. 9.99 (*1-58695-008-8*) HeartSpring Media.

Allen, Jackie, jt. auth. see Peerce, Donna.

Allen, Jackie M., ed. School Counseling: New Perspectives & Practices. 192p. 1998. text 15.00 (*1-56109-081-C*, EC 231) CAPS Inc.

***Allen, Jacqueline C.** A Toy Train Story: The Remarkable History of M. T. H. Electric Trains. (Illus.). 356p. 2000. 49.95 (*0-615-11526-8*) MTH.

***Allen, Jamerson C.** Working with Independent Contractors, Leased Workers & Outsourcing: Action Guide, Winter, 2000. Brown, Wendy L., ed. 88p. 2000. 58.00 (*0-7626-0395-X*, BU-11772) Cont Ed Bar-CA.

Allen, James. Above Life's Turmoil. 163p. 1993. pap. 15.00 (*0-89540-203-3*, SB-203) Sun Pub.

— Achieving Profitability with a Medical Office System. (Illus.). 150p. 1993. ring bd. 59.95 (*0-07-600633-6*, ME101) Practice Mgmt Info.

— All These Things Added. 192p. 1983. pap. 15.00 (*0-89540-129-0*, SB-129) Sun Pub.

— As a Man Thinketh. 1981. pap. 3.50 (*0-87516-000-X*) DeVorss.

— As a Man Thinketh. 64p. 1989. 1.95 (*0-929896-05-X*) MindArt Pub.

— As a Man Thinketh. (Family Inspirational Library). 72p. 1959. 5.95 (*0-399-12829-8*, G P Putnam) Peng Put Young Read.

— As a Man Thinketh. 1948. 7.99 (*0-88088-037-6*) Peter Pauper.

— As a Man Thinketh. 88p. 1983. pap. 4.50 (*0-89540-136-3*, SB-136) Sun Pub.

— As a Man Thinketh. 160p. 6.99 (*0-529-05908-8*, F12); im. lthr. 3.99 (*0-529-05906-1*, D6) World Publng.

— As a Man Thinketh, Vol. 2. Fedor, James H., ed. 148p 1988. pap. 7.95 (*0-929896-00-9*) MindArt Pub.

— As a Man Thinketh Mini Edition. 1999. 4.95 (*0-8362-7897-6*) Andrews & McMeel.

— As I Think. Christensen, Art W., ed. 62p. 1991. 8.95 (*0-87516-636-9*) DeVorss.

— As You Think. 2nd ed. Allen, Marc, ed. LC 98-15084C. 96p. 1998. reprint ed. pap. 9.95 (*1-57731-074-8*) New Wrld Lib.

— As You Think, So Shall You Become. Nolan, Mark, ed. & pref. by. 90p. (Orig.). 1994. pap. 12.95 (*1-881754-68-5*) Dolphin Pubng.

— As You Thinketh, 1. 2nd ed. Powell, Judith L. et al, eds. LC 88-12347. (Shores Beyond Time Ser.). 104p. 1988. pap. text 12.95 (*1-56087-147-4*) Top Mtn Pub.

— Basketball: Play Like a Pro. (Be the Best Ser.). (J). 1990. 8.15 (*0-606-04613-5*, Pub. by Turtleback) Demco.

— Byways of Blessedness. 202p. 1992. pap. 20.00 (*0-89540-202-5*, SB-202) Sun Pub.

— Directory of U. S. Colleges & Universities Offering a Curriculum in LTC Administration & State Board Licensure Requirements for LTC Administrators. 233p. 1997. pap. 34.00 (*0-9635064-2-0*) Nat Assn Bds Exam.

— The Divine Companion. 152p. 1997. pap. 15.00 (*0-89540-329-3*, SB-329) Sun Pub.

— Eight Pillars of Prosperity. 233p. 1992. pap. 20.00 (*0-89540-201-7*, SB-201) Sun Pub.

— Entering the Kingdom. 82p. 1993. pap. 8.00 (*0-89540-226-2*, SB-226) Sun Pub.

— Entering the Kingdom. 98p. 1996. reprint ed. spiral bd. 10.00 (*0-7873-0023-3*) Hlth Research.

— Entering the Kingdom. 98p. 1996. reprint ed. pap. 7.95 (*1-56459-906-X*) Kessinger Pub.

— The Wisdom of James Allen: 5 Classic Works combined into One. Zubko, Andy, ed. (Radiant Life Ser.). 384p. (Orig.). 1997. pap. 7.95 (*1-889606-00-6*) Radiant Summit.

— Football, Play Like a Pro. LC 89-38633. (Be the Best! Ser.). (Illus.). 64p. (J). (gr. 4-8). 1990. lib. bdg. 15.85 (*0-8167-1929-2*) Troll Communs.

— Football, Play Like a Pro. LC 89-38633. (Be the Best! Ser.). (Illus.). 64p. (J). (gr. 4-8). 1997. pap. 3.95 (*0-8167-1930-6*) Troll Communs.

— Foundation Stones to Happiness & Success. 53p. 1997. pap. 5.50 (*0-89540-327-7*, SB-327) Sun Pub.

— From Passion to Peace. 64p. 1981. pap. 5.50 (*0-89540-077-4*, SB-077) Sun Pub.

— From Poverty to Power. 184p. 1980. pap. 17.00 (*0-89540-061-8*, SB-061) Sun Pub.

— From Poverty to Power: Or the Realization of Prosperity & Peace (1906) 202p. 1996. reprint ed. pap. 16.95 (*1-56459-907-8*) Kessinger Pub.

— From Poverty to Power: The Realization of Prosperity & Peace. 200p. 1996. reprint ed. spiral bd. 17.00 (*0-7873-0025-X*) Hlth Research.

— The Heavenly Life. 84p. 1993. pap. 8.00 (*0-89540-227-0*, SB-227) Sun Pub.

— A Journey with Jesus: Stations of the Cross for School Children. 40p. (Orig.). 1995. pap. 2.95 (*0-8146-2306-9*, Liturg Pr Bks) Liturgical Pr.

— Light on Life's Difficulties. 137p. 1992. pap. 14.00 (*0-89540-217-3*, SB-217) Sun Pub.

— Man: King of Mind, Body & Circumstance. 55p. 1992. pap. 6.00 (*0-89540-212-2*, SB-212) Sun Pub.

— The Mastery of Destiny. 120p. 1992. pap. 12.00 (*0-89540-209-2*, SB-209) Sun Pub.

— The Mastery of Destiny. 120p. 1998. reprint ed. pap. 10.00 (*0-7873-0024-1*) Hlth Research.

— The Mastery of Destiny, 1909. 120p. 1996. reprint ed. pap. 9.00 (*1-56459-850-0*) Kessinger Pub.

— Meditations - A Year Book. 366p. 1992. pap. 30.00 (*0-89540-192-4*, SB-192) Sun Pub.

— Men & Systems. 149p. 1997. pap. 15.00 (*0-89540-326-9*, SB-326) Sun Pub.

— Morning & Evening Thoughts. 71p. 1983. pap. 7.00 (*0-89540-137-1*, SB-137) Sun Pub.

— Natural Language Understanding. 550p. (C). 1988. text 59.25 (*0-8053-0330-8*) Benjamin-Cummings.

— Natural Language Understanding. 2nd ed. (C). 1994. 62.81 (*0-8053-0334-0*) Benjamin-Cummings.

— Out from the Heart. 54p. 1992. pap. 6.00 (*0-89540-228-9*, SB-228) Sun Pub.

— The Path of Prosperity. 88p. 1998. pap. 8.00 (*0-89540-403-6*, SB-403) Sun Pub.

— The Path of Prosperity. 88p. 1996. reprint ed. spiral bd. 10.00 (*0-7873-0026-8*) Hlth Research.

— The Path of Prosperity, 1907. 88p. 1996. reprint ed. pap. 9.50 (*1-56459-851-9*) Kessinger Pub.

— The Shining Gateway. 58p. 1997. pap. 6.00 (*0-89540-328-5*, SB-328) Sun Pub.

— Tape Natrl Lang Understanding. 550p. (C). 1988. audio 64.75 (*0-8053-0332-4*) Benjamin-Cummings.

— Through the Gate of Good. 66p. 1992. pap. 6.00 (*0-89540-216-5*, SB-216) Sun Pub.

— The Way of Peace. 113p. 1992. pap. 10.00 (*0-89540-229-7*, SB-229) Sun Pub.

***Allen, James, ed.** Without Sanctuary: Lynching Photography in America. (Illus.). 209p. 2000. 60.00 (*0-944092-69-1*) Twin Palms Pub.

Allen, James, et al, eds. Proceedings of the 1st International Conference on Principles of Knowledge Representation & Reasoning. (Representation & Reasoning Ser.). 520p. (C). 1989. pap. text 39.95 (*1-55860-032-9*) Morgan Kaufmann.

— Proceedings of the 2nd International Conference on Principles of Knowledge Representation & Reasoning. (Representation & Reasoning Ser.). 602p. (C). 1991. pap. text 44.95 (*1-55860-165-1*) Morgan Kaufmann.

— Readings in Planning. 1990. pap. text 54.95 (*1-55860-130-9*) Morgan Kaufmann.

Allen, James & Hulst, Dorothy. As a Woman Thinketh. 62p. 1982. pap. 5.95 (*0-87516-483-8*) DeVorss.

Allen, James & Powell, Tag. From Poverty to Power: The Pathway to Prosperity & Peace. rev. ed. Nguyen, Alina et al, eds. LC 91-28159. (Illus.). 144p. 1994. pap. 9.95 (*1-56087-018-4*) Top Mtn Pub.

Allen, James, et al. Reasoning about Plans. Brachman, Ronald J., ed. (Representation & Reasoning Ser.). 500p. 1991. text 54.95 (*1-55860-137-6*) Morgan Kaufmann.

— The Royal Women of Amarna. LC 96-34517. (Illus.). 144p. 1996. 45.00 (*0-8109-6504-6*, Pub. by Abrams) Time Warner.

Allen, James, jt. auth. see Success, D. L.

Allen, James, ed. see Karimov, Islam.

Allen, James A. The Audiovisual Handbook: How to Save Money on AV Rentals. Simon, Gary & Allen, Elizabeth, eds. (Illus.). 216p. (Orig.). 1993. pap. 39.95 (*0-9634718-0-5*) Allen Media.

— Studies in Innovation in the Steel & Chemical Industries. LC 68-583. x, 246p. 1967. lib. bdg. 39.50 (0-678-06790-2) Kelley.

Allen, James B. Selected Poems & New. 76p. (Orig.). 1993. pap. 12.00 (0-9635033-0-8) Salt Creek Pr.

Allen, James B. & Leonard, Glen M. The Story of the Latter-Day Saints. 2nd enl. rev. ed. LC 92-33934. (Illus.). xiv, 802p. 1993. 25.00 (0-87579-565-X) Deseret Bk.

Allen, James B. & Welch, John W. Coming to Zion. LC 97-21140. (BYU Studies Monographs). 1997. pap. 14.95 (0-8425-2341-3, BYU Studies) Brigham.

Allen, James B., et al. Hearts Turned to the Fathers: A History of the Genealogical Society of Utah, 1894-1994. LC 95-5504. (BYU Studies). 392p. 1995. 19.95 (0-8425-2327-8, Friends of the Library) Brigham.

***Allen, James B., et al.** Studies in Mormon History, 1830-1997: An Indexed Bibliography. LC 99-46135. 2000. 100.00 (0-252-02565-2) U of Ill Pr.

Allen, James B., jt. auth. see Allen, J. Michael.

Allen, James B., jt. auth. see Luecke, Gerald.

Allen, James C. Lend Your Way to Wealth: Private Lending in Real Estate. 1990. pap. 14.95 (0-8306-9019-0) McGraw-Hill Prof.

— Lending Opportunities in Real Estate: A High-Profit Strategy for Every Inventor. (Illus.). 192p. 1988. 24.95 (0-8306-1819-8, 30019H) McGraw-Hill Prof.

Allen, James De Vere, see De Vere Allen, James.

***Allen, James E.** Assisted Living Administration: The Knowledge Base. LC 99-25081. 640p. 1999. 72.95 (0-8261-1253-6) Springer Pub.

Allen, James E. The Licensing Exam Review Guide in Nursing Home Administration: 1000 Test Questions in the Nation Examination Format on the 1996 Domains of Practice. 3rd ed. LC 96-47701. 208p. 1997. 34.95 (0-8261-5922-2) Springer Pub.

— Long Term Care Facility Resident Assessment Instrument: User's Manual. LC 97-3056. 496p. 1997. 42.95 (0-8261-9900-3) Springer Pub.

***Allen, James E.** The National Exam & Self-Study Guide for Assisted Living Administration: The Knowledge Base. LC 00-22374. 2000. pap. write for info. (0-8261-1354-0) Springer Pub.

Allen, James E. Nursing Home Administration. 3rd ed. LC 96-33640. (Illus.). 632p. 1997. 69.95 (0-8261-5392-5) Springer Pub.

— Nursing Home Federal Requirements & Guidelines to Surveyors. 3rd ed. LC 96-48423. 312p. 1997. 44.95 (0-8261-8122-8) Springer Pub.

***Allen, James E.** Nursing Home Requirements & Guidelines to Surveyors. 4th ed. LC 99-55521. 440p. 2000. pap. 46.95 (0-8261-8123-6) Springer Pub.

Allen, James E. & Bender, Deborah. Managing Teenage Pregnancy: Access to Abortion, Contraception & Sex Education. LC 79-89009. 300p. 1980. 69.50 (0-275-90444-X, C0444, Praeger Pubs) Greenwood.

Allen, James E., jt. auth. see Courtney, Susan J.

Allen, James E., ed. see Sorenson & Rock Staff, et al.

Allen, James H. May's Manual of the Diseases of the Eye. LC 74-10746. 442p. 1974. reprint ed. 48.50 (0-88275-190-5) Krieger.

Allen, James L. Aftermath. (Principle Works of James Lane Allen). 1989. reprint ed. lib. bdg. 79.00 (0-7812-1730-X) Rprt Serv.

— The Alabaster Box. (Principle Works of James Lane Allen). 1989. reprint ed. lib. bdg. 79.00 (0-7812-1744-X) Rprt Serv.

— Blue-Grass Region of Kentucky: And Other Kentucky Articles. LC 74-39712. (Essay Index Reprint Ser.). 1977. reprint ed. 28.95 (0-8369-2734-6) Ayer.

— The Blue Grass Region of Kentucky & Other Kentucky Articles. (Principle Works of James Lane Allen). 1989. reprint ed. lib. bdg. 90.00 (0-7812-1727-X) Rprt Serv.

— The Bride of Mistletoe. (Principle Works of James Lane Allen). 1989. reprint ed. lib. bdg. 90.00 (0-7812-1736-9) Rprt Serv.

— A Cathedral Singer. (Principle Works of James Lane Allen). 1989. reprint ed. lib. bdg. 79.00 (0-7812-1741-5) Rprt Serv.

— Choir Invisible. 1897. 7.00 (0-403-00000-9) Scholarly.

— The Choir Invisible. LC 73-86169. reprint ed. 22.50 (0-404-00327-3) AMS Pr.

— The Choir Invisible. (Principle Works of James Lane Allen). 1989. reprint ed. lib. bdg. 79.00 (0-7812-1732-6) Rprt Serv.

— The Doctors Christmas Eve. (Principle Works of James Lane Allen). 1989. reprint ed. lib. bdg. 90.00 (0-7812-1737-7) Rprt Serv.

— The Emblems of Fidelity. (Principle Works of James Lane Allen). 1989. reprint ed. lib. bdg. 79.00 (0-7812-1743-1) Rprt Serv.

— Flute & Violin. (Principle Works of James Lane Allen). 1989. reprint ed. lib. bdg. 90.00 (0-7812-1726-1) Rprt Serv.

— Flute & Violin & Other Kentucky Tales & Romances. LC 78-98555. (Short Story Index Reprint Ser.). 1977. 18.95 (0-8369-3129-7) Ayer.

— The Heroine in Bronze. (Principle Works of James Lane Allen). 1989. reprint ed. lib. bdg. 90.00 (0-7812-1738-5) Rprt Serv.

— John Gray. (Principle Works of James Lane Allen). 1989. reprint ed. lib. bdg. 90.00 (0-7812-1728-8) Rprt Serv.

— A Kentucky Cardinal. LC 68-20002. (Americans in Fiction Ser.). (Illus.). 138p. reprint ed. pap. text 7.50 (0-89197-818-6); reprint ed. lib. bdg. 16.50 (0-8398-0056-8) Irvington.

— A Kentucky Cardinal. (Principle Works of James Lane Allen). 1989. reprint ed. lib. bdg. 79.00 (0-7812-1729-6) Rprt Serv.

— A Kentucky Cardinal, Aftermath, & Other Selected Works. Bottorff, William K., ed. (Masterworks of Literature Ser.). 1967. 16.95 (0-8084-0200-5); pap. 13.95 (0-8084-0201-3) NCUP.

— A Kentucky Warbler. (Principle Works of James Lane Allen). 1989. reprint ed. lib. bdg. 79.00 (0-7812-1742-3) Rprt Serv.

— Landmark. LC 70-110177. (Short Story Index Reprint Ser.). 1977. 18.95 (0-8369-3328-1) Ayer.

— The Landmark. (Principle Works of James Lane Allen). 1989. reprint ed. lib. bdg. 79.00 (0-685-44737-5) Rprt Serv.

— The Last Christmas Tree. (Principle Works of James Lane Allen). 1989. reprint ed. lib. bdg. 79.00 (0-7812-1739-3) Rprt Serv.

— Mettle of the Pasture. LC 74-94468. reprint ed. 31.50 (0-404-00328-1) AMS Pr.

— Mettle of the Pasture. LC 03-15441. 1969. reprint ed. 13.00 (0-403-00137-4) Scholarly.

— The Mettle of the Pasture. (Principle Works of James Lane Allen). 1989. reprint ed. lib. bdg. 79.00 (0-7812-1735-0) Rprt Serv.

— The Reign of Law: A Tale of the Kentucky Hemp Fields. LC 77-164556. (American Fiction Reprint Ser.). 1977. reprint ed. 34.95 (0-8369-7032-2) Ayer.

— The Reign of Law: A Tale of the Kentucky Hemp Fields. (Principle Works of James Lane Allen). 1989. reprint ed. lib. bdg. 79.00 (0-7812-1734-2) Rprt Serv.

— Summer in Arcady. (Principle Works of James Lane Allen). 1989. reprint ed. lib. bdg. 79.00 (0-7812-1731-8) Rprt Serv.

— The Sword of Youth. (Principle Works of James Lane Allen). 1989. reprint ed. lib. bdg. 79.00 (0-7812-1740-7) Rprt Serv.

— Two Gentlemen of Kentucky. (Principle Works of James Lane Allen). 1989. reprint ed. lib. bdg. 79.00 (0-7812-1733-4) Rprt Serv.

— The Works of James Allen, 1849-1925, Set. 1987. reprint ed. lib. bdg. 500.00 (0-685-18585-0) Rprt Serv.

Allen, James L. & Medley, Max W. Microwave Circuit Design Using Programmable Calculators. LC 80-17806. (Artech House Microwave Library). (Illus.). 304p. reprint ed. pap. 94.30 (0-8357-4186-9, 203696400006) Bks Demand.

Allen, James L. & Peddy, Carolyn P. Amplitude Variation with Offset: Gulf Coast Case Studies. LC 93-6249. (Geophysical Developments Ser.: No. 4). 111p. 1993. 66.00 (1-56080-063-1, 124A) Soc Expl Geophys.

***Allen, James Lane.** The Choir Invisible. 252p. 2000. pap. 9.95 (0-594-00261-3) Eightn Hundrd.

— The Sword of Youth. 252p. 2000. pap. 9.95 (0-594-04320-4) Eightn Hundrd.

***Allen, James P.** Middle Egyptian: An Introduction to the Language & Culture of Hieroglyphs. (Illus.). 524p. (C). 1999. 74.95 (0-521-65312-6); pap. 29.95 (0-521-77483-7) Cambridge U Pr.

Allen, James P. & Turner, Eugene. The Ethnic Quilt: Population Diversity in Southern California. unabridged ed. (Illus.). x, 300p. (Orig.). 1997. 49.95 (0-9656966-1-8); pap. 29.95 (0-9656966-0-X) Ctr Geographical Studies.

Allen, James R. & Allen, Carol L. Ready! Set!! Goals!!! unabridged ed. (Illus.). 250p. 1997. wbk. ed. write for info. (0-9657365-0-4, Life Goals) Goals Pub.

Allen, James R., et al. PPC's 1120 Deskbook, 2 vols. Incl. Vol. 1. 1997. ring bd. 150.00 (0-7646-0311-6); Vol. 2. 1997. ring bd. 150.00 (0-7646-0312-4); Set ring bd. 150.00 (0-7646-0041-9); Set ring bd. 150.00 (0-7646-0310-8) Prctnrs Pub Co.

Allen, James S. In the Public Eye: A History of Reading in Modern France, 1800-1940. (Illus.). 325p. 1991. text 52.50 (0-691-03162-2, Pub. by Princeton U Pr) Cal Prin Full Svc.

— The Neutrino. LC 57-5464. 178p. 1958. reprint ed. pap. 55.20 (0-608-02870-3, 206393400007) Bks Demand.

— The Philippine Left on the Eve of World War II. 2nd ed. LC 92-4722. (Studies in Marxism: Vol. 29). 167p. 1993. 32.95 (0-930656-67-9); pap. 14.95 (0-930656-68-7) MEP Pubns.

— Poignant Relations: Three Modern French Women LC 99-28341. 2000. write for info. (0-8018-6204-3) Johns Hopkins.

— Popular French Romanticism: Authors, Readers, & Books in the 19th Century. LC 80-27129. (Illus.). 307p. 1981. reprint ed. pap. 95.20 (0-608-07588-4, 205990300010) Bks Demand.

— Reconstruction: The Battle for Democracy, 1865-1876. LC 37-34604. (History of the American People Ser.). (Illus.). 256p. reprint ed. pap. 79.40 (0-8357-3513-3, 203424800089) Bks Demand.

— The Romance of Commerce & Culture: Capitalism, Modernism & the Chicago-Aspen Crusade for Cultural Reform. LC 83-4816. xvi, 352p. 1983. 33.00 (0-226-01458-4) U Ch Pr.

— The Romance of Commerce & Culture: Capitalism, Modernism & the Chicago-Aspen Crusade for Cultural Reform. LC 83-4816. xvi, 350p. 1986. pap. text 17.00 (0-226-01459-2) U Ch Pr.

— The Romance of Commerce & Culture: Capitalism, Modernism, & the Chicago-Aspen Crusade for Cultural Reform. LC 83-4816. (Illus.). 352p. reprint ed. pap. 109.20 (0-608-08040-3, 206900500002) Bks Demand.

Allen, James S., ed. see Breton, Genevieve.

Allen, James S., ed. see Lenin, Vladimir Il'ich.

Allen, James T. The First Year of Greek. LC 93-16311. 1994. 32.95 (0-89863-172-6) Star Pub CA.

— Greek Theatre of the Fifth Century Before Christ. LC 68-2221. (Studies in Drama: No. 39). (C). 1969. reprint ed. lib. bdg. 75.00 (0-8383-0647-0) M S G Haskell Hse.

Allen, James T. & Italie, Gabriel. A Concordance to Euripides. (GER.). xii, 686p. 1954. write for info. (0-318-70529-X) G Olms Pubs.

Allen, James Van, see Skromme, Arnold B. & Van Allen, James.

Allen, James W. Nishapur: Metalwork from the Early Islamic Period. (Illus.). 120p. 1981. 19.95 (0-87099-271-6, 0-8109-6464-3) Metro Mus Art.

Allen, James W., et al, eds. Biology of Mammalian Germ-Cell Mutagenesis. (Banbury Reports: No. 34). (Illus.). 350p. 1990. 95.00 (0-87969-234-0) Cold Spring Harbor.

Allen, Jamey D. Five Artists - Five Directions: Working in Polymer Clay. (Illus.). 64p. 1995. pap. 15.95 (0-9620543-8-0) Flower Valley Pr.

Allen, Jamie. Red Star Rising. LC 97-202887. 350p. 1997. pap. text 24.95 (981-00-8083-2) Buttrwrth-Heinemann.

Allen, Jan, jt. auth. see Catron, Carol E.

Allen, Jane A., ed. see Day, Holliday D.

Allen, Jane E. & Allen, Roger B. Flashing Oars: Rowing on the Schuylkill. (Illus.). 45p. (Orig.). 1985. pap. 1.50 (0-913346-11-X) Indep Seaport.

Allen, Jane H., jt. auth. see Allen, Janet L.

Allen, Jane I. Residencies for Artists. Papparella, Michael, ed. (Art Calendar Guide Ser.). 41p. 1999. pap. 9.95 (0-945388-13-6) Art Calendar.

Allen, Janet. It's Never Too Late: Leading Adolescents to Lifelong Literacy. LC 94-41022. 218p. 1995. pap. text 23.00 (0-435-08839-4, 08839) Heinemann.

— Words, Words, Words: Teaching Vocabulary in Grades 4-12. LC 98-53589. 140p. 1999. pap. 17.50 (1-57110-085-7) Stenhse Pubs.

***Allen, Janet.** Yellow Brick Roads: Shared & Guided Paths to Independent Reading 4-12. Stratton, Philippa, ed. 2000. pap. text, teacher ed. write for info. (1-57110-319-8) Stenhse Pubs.

Allen, Janet & Gonzalez, Kyle. There's Room for Me Here: Literacy Workshop in the Middle School. LC 97-30613. (Illus.). 256p. 1997. pap. text 20.00 (1-57110-042-3) Stenhse Pubs.

Allen, Janet, ed. see Allen, Maury.

Allen, Janet K. Working Model Design. (C). 1995. pap. text. write for info. (0-201-83265-8) Addison-Wesley.

***Allen, Janet K., et al, eds.** ISSS 1999 Proceedings of the 43rd Annual Conference of the International Society for the Systems Sciences. 1250p. 1999. 60.00 incl. cd-rom (0-9664183-2-8) Intl Soc Sys Sciences.

Allen, Janet L. & Allen, Jane H. Around the Oak Table: Family Recipes & Old Maxims. 312p. 1997. pap. 14.95 (0-9654630-1-X); boxed set 24.95 (0-9654630-0-1) Quality Hill.

Allen, Janet V. Out from Madness. (Illus.). 133p. (Orig.). 1993. pap. 10.00 (1-885193-04-1) Good Samaritan.

Allen, Janis. I Saw What You Did & I Know Who You Are: Bloopers, Blunders & Success Stories on Giving & Receiving Recognition. 2nd ed. 219p. 1990. reprint ed. pap. 18.95 (0-937100-04-8) Perf Manage.

Allen, Janis & McCarthy, Michael. You Made My Day: Co-Worker Recognition & Relationships. LC 99-30508. 144p. 2000. pap. 9.95 (0-86730-787-0) Lebhar Friedman.

Allen, Jay, tr. see Mengin, Robert.

***Allen, Jean.** Hurricanes. LC 00-21414. (Natural Disasters Ser.). (Illus.). 48p. (YA). (gr. 5 up). 2000. lib. bdg. 21.26 (0-7368-0587-7, Capstone Bks) Capstone Pr.

— Tornadoes. LC 00-21319. (Natural Disasters Ser.). (Illus.). 48p. (YA). (gr. 5 up). 2000. lib. bdg. 21.26 (0-7368-0588-5, Capstone Bks) Capstone Pr.

Allen, Jeanne. Designer's Guide to Color 3. (Designers Guide Ser.: No. 3). (Illus.). 120p. (Orig.). 1986. 19.95 (0-87701-415-9); pap. 12.95 (0-87701-408-6) Chronicle Bks.

— Showing Your Colors: A Designer's Guide to Coordinating Your Wardrobe. LC 86-2656. (Designers Guide Ser.). (Illus.). 134p. (Orig.). 1986. pap. 10.95 (0-87701-381-0) Chronicle Bks.

Allen, Jeanne & Dale, Angela. The School Reform Handbook: How to Improve Your Schools. LC 95-68282. 166p. (Orig.). 1995. 9.95 (0-9646028-0-6) Ctr Educ Reform.

Allen, Jeanne, jt. ed. see Clancy, Patricia.

Allen, Jeff. Quickstart to Social Dancing: An Easy to Follow Guide for Beginners-Gets You on the Dance Floor & Compliments Your Dance Lessons. 2nd rev. ed. LC 96-93013. (Quickstart Ser.: No. 1). (Illus.). 127p. 1997. pap. 19.95 (0-9654423-1-4) Q Q S Publns.

***Allen, Jeff.** Quickstart to Swing: An Easy-to-Follow Guide for Swing Dancing - Beginner Through Teaching Level. LC 00-190078. (Quickstart to Social Dancing Program Ser.: Vol. 3). (Illus.). 216p. 2000. pap. 21.95 (0-9654423-3-0) Q Q S Publns.

Allen, Jeff. Quickstart to Tango: An Easy-to-Follow Guide for Beginners to Passion & Drama on the Dance Floor. LC 97-91693. (Quickstart Ser.: Vol. 2). (Illus.). 130p. (Orig.). 1997. pap. 19.95 (0-9654423-2-2) Q Q S Publns.

Allen, Jeff, ed. see Rails-to-Trails Conservancy Staff.

Allen, Jeffery R. Harbors & Spirits. LC 97-23788. 164p. (Orig.). 1999. pap. 14.95 incl. audio compact disk (1-55921-208-X) Moyer Bell.

Allen, Jeffery R., et al. Private, No. 6. (Illus.). 163p. 1991. pap. 7.00 (1-881377-01-6) Private Lives.

Allen, Jeffner. Lesbian Philosophy: Explorations. (Series in Lesbian & Feminist Theory). 120p. (Orig.). 1986. pap. 9.95 (0-934903-86-7) Inst Lesbian.

— Reverberations: Across the Shimmering CASCADAS. LC 93-31711. (Series in Feminist Philosophy). 204p. (C). 1994. pap. text 14.95 (0-7914-1898-7) State U NY Pr.

— Reverberations: Across the Shimmering CASCADAS. LC 93-31711. (SUNY Series in Feminist Philosophy). 204p. (C). 1994. text 44.50 (0-7914-1897-9) State U NY Pr.

— Sinousities: Lesbian Poetic Politics. LC 95-22357. (Illus.). 200p. 1996. 35.00 (0-253-33022-X); pap. 15.95 (0-253-21046-1) Ind U Pr.

Allen, Jeffner, ed. Lesbian Philosophies & Cultures. LC 90-9554. (SUNY Series in Feminist Philosophy). 410p. (C). 1990. text 44.50 (0-7914-0383-1); pap. text 16.95 (0-7914-0384-X) State U NY Pr.

Allen, Jeffner & Young, Iris M., eds. The Thinking Muse: Feminism & Modern French Philosophy. LC 88-45388. 224p. 1989. 34.95 (0-253-35980-5); pap. 12.95 (0-253-20502-6, MB 502) Ind U Pr.

Allen, Jeffrey. Guide to Karaoke Confidence. 1995. pap. text 8.95 (0-7604-0007-5, EL03976) Wrner Bros.

***Allen, Jeffrey.** Secrets of Singing Female Voice. 2000. pap. 44.95 (0-7692-7805-1) Wrner Bros.

Allen, Jeffrey. Secrets of Singing Male Voice. 1994. pap. text 44.95 incl. audio compact disk (0-910957-76-2, EL03806MCD) Wrner Bros.

***Allen, Jeffrey.** Secrets of Singing Male Voice: Low & High. 1999. pap. text 44.95 (0-7692-7804-3) Warner Bks.

Allen, Jeffrey G. The Career Trap: Breaking Through the 10-Year Barrier to Get the Job You Really Want. 192p. 1995. pap. 16.95 (0-8144-7823-9) AMACOM.

Allen, Jeffrey G. The Complete Q & A Job Interview Book. 2nd ed. LC 96-48797. 240p. (Orig.). 1997. pap. 14.95 (0-471-18094-7) Wiley.

— The Complete Q & A Job Interview Book. 3rd ed. 223p. (Orig.). 1997. pap. 14.95 (0-471-39145-X) Wiley.

Allen, Jeffrey G. Complying with the ADA: A Small Business Guide to Hiring & Employing the Disabled. LC 92-34801. (Small Business Editions Ser.). 210p. 1993. 79.95 (0-471-59049-5) Wiley.

— How to Turn an Interview into a Job. 112p. 1986. per. 9.00 (0-671-62134-3) S&S Trade Pap.

— The Interactive Interviewing Technique. 1995. wbk. ed. 69.95 incl. audio (0-9649242-0-X) Career Mgmt Inst.

— Jeff Allen's Best! The Resume. 144p. 1990. pap. 12.95 (0-471-52536-7) Wiley.

— The Resume Makeover: The Resume Writing Guide That Includes Personalized Feedback. LC 94-34133. 288p. 1995. pap. 14.95 (0-471-04624-8) Wiley.

— Successful Job Search Strategies for the Disabled: Understanding the ADA. 229p. 1994. 85.00 (0-471-59234-X) Wiley.

Allen, Jeffrey L. Secrets of Singing: Female Edition. Feldstein, Sandy, ed. (Illus.). 388p. (Orig.). (C). 1994. 44.95 incl. disk (0-910957-77-0, EL03806FCD) Wrner Bros.

***Allen, Jeffrey Renard.** Rails under My Back. LC 99-38696. 576p. 2000. 25.00 (0-374-24626-2) FS&G.

Allen, Jeffrey S. & Klein, Roger J. Ready . . . Set . . . R. E. L. A. X. A Research Base Program of Relaxation, Learning & Self Esteem for Children. LC 93-90702. (Illus.). 205p. (Orig.). (J). (ps-8). 1996. pap. 23.95 (0-9636027-0-5) Allen & Klein.

Allen, Jelisaveta S., et al, eds. To Hellenikon, Studies in Honor of Speros Vryonis, Jr. Vol. II: Byzantinoslavica, Armeniaca, Islamica, the Balkans, & Modern Greece. 479p. 1993. lib. bdg. 75.00 (0-89241-513-4) Caratzas.

Allen, Jennifer. Fifth Quarter: The Scrimmage of a Football Coach's Daughter. 256p. 2000. 23.95 (0-679-45202-8) Random.

Allen, Jennifer Q., jt. auth. see Christianson, Robbin C.

Allen, Jennifer Q., jt. ed. see Smith, L. Dennis.

Allen, Jennifer Quay, jt. ed. see Smith, L. Dennis.

Allen, Jerrold P., jt. auth. see Smith, Perry M.

Allen, Jerry C. Conrad Veidt: From Caligari to Casablanca. 2nd ed. LC 92-39569. 362p. 1993. 18.50 (0-940168-27-8) Boxwood.

Allen, Jessica. Quotable Men of the Twentieth Century. LC 99-36934. 272p. 1999. 20.00 (0-688-16285-1, Wm Morrow) Morrow Avon.

Allen, Jessica, ed. see Ventura, Jesse.

Allen, Jessie & Pifer, Alan, eds. Women on the Front Lines: Meeting the Challenge of an Aging America. LC 92-34290. 280p. (C). 1993. lib. bdg. 24.50 (0-87766-574-5) Urban Inst.

Allen, Jim. Acts, James. Vol. 9. 332p. 1996. 24.99 (0-946351-35-X, Pub. by John Ritchie) Loizeaux.

***Allen, Jim.** Chevy & GMC Truck: Performance Handbook. (Illus.). 160p. 2000. pap. 21.95 (0-7603-0798-9, 130122AP, Pub. by MBI Pubg) Motorbooks Intl.

Allen, Jim. Epistles of Peter, John, Jude. Vol. 5. 338p. 1996. 24.99 (0-946351-09-0, Pub. by John Ritchie) Loizeaux.

— Illustrated Buyers Guide Jeep, New Edition: Jeep, New Edition. LC 99-14926. 224p. 1999. pap. 17.95 (0-7603-0299-5) MBI Pubg.

— Illustrated Classic 4 X 4 Buyers Guide. LC 97-41447. (Illus.). 192p. 1997. pap. 17.95 (0-7603-0340-1) MBI Pubg.

— Jeep 4x4 Performance Handbook. LC 98-35041. (Performance Handbook Ser.). (Illus.). 192p. 1998. pap. 21.95 (0-7603-0470-X) Motorbooks Intl.

— Matthew, Mark. Vol. 2. 588p. 1996. 24.99 (0-946351-02-3, Pub. by John Ritchie) Loizeaux.

— No Title. Robeson, Jerry, ed. (Illus.). 1998. pap. write for info. (1-891879-01-4) Shiloh Pub.

— Perdition: A Play in Two Acts. (C). 1996. 29.95 (0-86372-099-4); pap. 10.95 (0-86372-100-1) LPC InBook.

Allen, Jim, ed. see Howe, Carrol B.

Allen, Jimmy. Burden of a Secret: A Story of Truth & Mercy in the Face of AIDS. 256p. 1995. 20.00 (0-345-40091-7, Moorings) Ballantine Pub Grp.

— Burden of a Secret: A Story of Truth & Mercy in the Face of AIDS. 256p. 1996. pap. 10.99 (0-345-40789-X, Moorings) Ballantine Pub Grp.

Allen, Jo. Writing in the Workplace. LC 97-40070. 524p. (C). 1997. pap. text 57.00 (0-205-17373-X) P-H.

An Asterisk (*) at the beginning of an entry indicates that the title is appearing for the first time.

— Writing in the Workplace: Examination Copy. 640p. (C). 1997. pap. text. write for info. (*0-205-27688-1*, T7688-9) Allyn.

Allen, Jo A., jt. auth. see Kissman, Kris.

Allen, Jo A., jt. auth. see Neidhardt, Elizabeth R.

Allen, Jo Ann, et al. Men in Therapy: The Challenge of Change. (Family Therapy Ser.). 284p. 1991. reprint ed. pap. text 18.95 (*0-89862-485-1*) Guilford Pubns.

Allen, Jo Ann, jt. auth. see Neidhardt, Elizabeth R.

Allen, Jo Beth, ed. Class Actions: Teaching for Social Justice in Elementary & Middle School. LC 98-55471. 10. 192p. 1999. text 44.00 (*0-8077-3857-3*) Tchrs Coll.

Allen, Jo Harvey. Cheek to Cheek: Poems & Excerpts From Interviews. Robertson, Kirk, ed. (Windriver Ser.). (Illus.). 64p. (Orig.). (C). 1983. pap. 6.00 (*0-916918-22-X*); pap. text 25.00 (*0-916918-23-8*) Duck Down.

Allen, Joan D., jt. auth. see Allen, Paul M.

Allen, JoBeth. Class Actions: Teaching for Social Justice in Elementary & Middle School LC 98-55471. (Practitioner Inquiry Ser.). 192p. 1999. pap. text 19.95 (*0-8077-3856-5*) Tchrs Coll.

Allen, JoBeth & Mason, Jana M., eds. Risk Makers, Risk Takers, Risk Breakers: Reducing the Risks for Young Literacy Learners. LC 88-27400. 351p. (Orig.). (C). 1989. pap. 25.00 (*0-435-08483-6*, 08483) Heinemann.

Allen, JoBeth, et al. Engaging Children: Community & Chaos in the Lives of Young Literacy Learners. LC 93-14853. 288p. (C). 1993. pap. text 25.00 (*0-435-08767-3*, 08767) Heinemann.

Allen, JoCindee & Rice, Joe. Heart Dance. (Illus.). 64p. (Orig.). 1986. pap. 12.50 (*0-685-16998-7*) Workshop Pubns.

Allen, Joel A. The American Bisons Living & Extinct. LC 73-17790. (Natural Sciences in America Ser.). (Illus.). 295p. 1974. reprint ed. 23.95 (*0-405-05701-6*) Ayer.

— History of the North American Pinnipeds: A Monograph of the Walruses, Sea-Lions, Sea-Bears & Seals of North America. LC 73-17792. (Natural Sciences in America Ser.). (Illus.). 806p. 1974. reprint ed. 58.95 (*0-405-05702-4*) Ayer.

Allen, John. Annual Editions: Environment, 97-98. 16th ed. 256p. (C). 1997. text. write for info. (*0-697-37266-9*) Brown & Benchmark.

— Christmas Gifts, Christmas Voices. 76p. 1996. pap. 7.95 (*0-9654115-0-8*, EC9604) Echo Canyon.

— DPG Student Atlas of World Politics. 2nd ed. LC 93-73029. 112p. (C). 1993. text 11.74 (*1-56134-229-7*, Dshkn McG-Hill) McGrw-H Hghr Educ.

Allen, John. Dushkin Student Atlas of Environmental Issues. 1997. teacher ed. 1.49 (*0-697-36521-2*, WCB McGr Hill) McGrw-H Hghr Educ.

Allen, John. Environment: 1996-1997. annuals 15th ed. 256p. (C). 1996. text. write for info. (*0-697-31581-9*) Brown & Benchmark.

— Fabulous Fairisle: A Complete Guide to Traditional Patterns & Classic Styles. (Illus.). 128p. (Orig.). 1991. pap. 16.95 (*0-312-06113-7*) St Martin.

— John Allen's Treasury of Machine Knitting Stitches. 1993. pap. 16.95 (*0-7063-9910-2*, Pub. by WrLock) Sterling.

— Porsche 956, 962 LC 87-82838. (Motoring Bks.). 158p. 1988. write for info. (*0-85429-642-5*) GT Foulis.

— Succeed: A Handbook on Structuring Managerial Thought. (Illus.). 64p. 1986. pap. 8.00 (*0-907791-04-2*) Synerg CA.

***Allen, John.** Unsettling Cities. LC 98-37560. 1999. write for info. (*0-415-20071-7*); pap. write for info. (*0-415-20072-5*) Routledge.

Allen, John & Gartz, Jochen. Some Recent Notes & Observations on the Occurrence & Use of Enthnogenic Fungi in Third World Countries. (Ethnomycological Journal Sacred Mushroom Ser.: No. 6). (Illus.). 50p. 1998. pap. 10.00 (*1-58214-028-6*) Mltilingl Bks.

Allen, John & Hamnett, Chris, eds. A Shrinking World? (Shape of the World Ser.: Vol. 2). (Illus.). 272p. (C). 1996. text 57.95 (*0-19-874186-3*); pap. text 24.95 (*0-19-874187-1*) OUP.

Allen, John & Jackson, Robert M. Environment Annual Editions 1996 & 1997. annuals (C). 1996. text. write for info. (*0-697-38699-6*) Brown & Benchmark.

Allen, John & Massey, Doreen B. The Economy in Question LC 88-61870. (Restructuring Britain Ser.). x, 277p. 1988. write for info. (*0-8039-8168-6*) Sage.

Allen, John & McDowell, Linda. Landlords & Property: Social Relations in the Private Rented Sector. (Cambridge Human Geography Ser.). 224p. (C). 1989. text 59.95 (*0-521-36028-5*) Cambridge U Pr.

Allen, John & Nelson, Mark. Space Biospheres. LC 86-33226. 96p. (C). 1987. reprint ed. lib. bdg. 12.95 (*0-89464-011-9*) Krieger.

Allen, John, et al. Cataclysms on the Columbia. (Illus.). 221p. 1991. pap. 14.95 (*0-88192-215-3*) Timber.

— Geography Matters! A Reader. Massey, Doreen et al, eds. (Illus.). 224p. 1985. text 64.95 (*0-521-26887-7*) Cambridge U Pr.

— Geography Matters! A Reader. Massey, Doreen et al, eds. (Illus.). 224p. 1985. pap. text 21.95 (*0-521-31708-8*) Cambridge U Pr.

— Re-Thinking the Region: Spaces of Neo-Liberalism. LC 97-13458. (Illus.). 176p. (C). 1998. 75.00 (*0-415-16821-X*); pap. 25.99 (*0-415-16822-8*) Routledge.

Allen, John, jt. auth. see Evertz, Gabriele.

Allen, John, jt. ed. see Massey, Doreen.

Allen, John A. Teonanacatl: Ancient & Contemporary Names of MesoAmerica & Other Regions. (Ethnomycological Journal Sacred Mushroom Ser.: No. 3). (Illus.). 48p. 1998. pap. 10.00 (*1-58214-025-1*) Mltilingl Bks.

Allen, John B. From Skisport to Skiing: One Hundred Years of an American Sport, 1840-1940. LC 93-9224. (Illus.). 248p. 1993. lib. bdg. 30.00 (*0-87023-844-2*) U of Mass Pr.

— From Skisport to Skiing: One Hundred Years of an American Sport, 1840-1940. LC 93-9224. (Illus.). 248p. 1996. pap. 16.95 (*1-55849-047-7*) U of Mass Pr.

— New England Skiing. (Images of America Ser.). 1999. pap. 16.99 (*0-7524-0494-6*) Arcadia Publng.

Allen, John D. Divine Freedom: The Greatest Freedom Is Now Yours. LC 98-94055. 332p. 1998. pap. 16.50 (*0-9669211-0-0*) Golden Pearl.

Allen, John E. Bin Rock & Dump Rock: Recollections of a Geologist with Ten Years of Non-Geological Essays. LC 96-46450. 1996. pap. write for info. (*0-9633919-3-3*) Hells Canyon.

Allen, John E., jt. auth. see Bishop, Ellen M.

Allen, John H. Allen. Brief History of the Allen Family in America. 28p. 1997. reprint ed. pap. 6.00 (*0-8328-7235-0*); reprint ed. lib. bdg. 16.00 (*0-8328-7234-2*) Higginson Bk Co.

— Judah's Sceptre & Joseph's Birthright. 1946. 8.00 (*0-685-08809-X*) Destiny.

Allen, John J. Don Quixote: Hero or Fool?, Pt. II. LC 71-625420. (University of Florida Humanities Monographs: No. 46). vii, 118p. 1979. pap. 14.95 (*0-8130-0630-9*) U Press Fla.

— Don Quixote Pt. 1: Hero or Fool: A Study in Narrative Technique. LC 71-625420. (University of Florida Humanities Monographs: No. 29). 96p. reprint ed. pap. 30.00 (*0-7837-5034-X*, 204470700004) Bks Demand.

— The Reconstruction of a Spanish Golden Age Playhouse: El Corral del Principe (1583-1744) LC 83-1241. (Illus.). xii, 129p. 1984. 49.95 (*0-8130-0755-0*) U Press Fla.

***Allen, John L., Jr.** Cardinal Ratzinger: The Vatican's Enforcer of the Faith. 336p. 2000. 24.95 (*0-8264-1265-3*) Continuum.

Allen, John L. Environment, 98-99. 17th ed. (Annual Ser.). (Illus.). 240p. 1998. pap. text 12.25 (*0-697-41790-5*, Dshkn McG-Hill) McGrw-H Hghr Educ.

— Jedediah Smith & the Mountain Men of the American West. Goetzmann, William H., ed. (World Explorers Ser.). (Illus.). 120p. (YA). (gr. 5 up). 1991. lib. bdg. 19.95 (*0-7910-1319-7*) Chelsea Hse.

— Lewis & Clark & the Image of the American Northwest. Orig. Title: Passage Through the Garden. (Illus.). 448p. 1998. reprint ed. pap. 12.95 (*0-486-26914-0*) Dover.

— Passage Through the Garden: Lewis & Clark & the Image of the American Northwest. LC 74-14512. 440p. reprint ed. pap. 136.40 (*0-608-13450-3*, 202277300029) Bks Demand.

Allen, John L., ed. North American Exploration Vol. 1: A New World Disclosed. LC 96-33025. (Illus.). xvii, 540p. 1997. text 85.00 (*0-8032-1015-9*) U of Nebr Pr.

— North American Exploration Vol. 2: A Continent Defined. LC 96-33025. (Illus.). ix, 474p. 1997. text 85.00 (*0-8032-1023-X*) U of Nebr Pr.

— North American Exploration Vol. 3: A Continent Comprehended. LC 96-33025. (Illus.). xiii, 656p. 1997. text 85.00 (*0-8032-1043-4*) U of Nebr Pr.

Allen, John P. & Columbus, Megan, eds. Assessing Alcohol Problems: A Guide for Clinicians & Researchers. (Illus.). 575p. (Orig.). (C). 1997. pap. text 75.00 (*0-7881-3829-4*) DIANE Pub.

Allen, John P., jt. ed. see Fertig, Joanne B.

Allen, John P., jt. ed. see Litten, Raye Z.

Allen, John R. Principles of Physical Sedimentology. (Illus.). 400p. (C). 1985. text 60.00 (*0-04-551095-4*); pap. text 39.95 (*0-04-551096-2*) Routledge.

Allen, John R., jt. auth. see Kennedy, Ken.

Allen, John S. GT 40 - the Legend Lives On. (Osprey Colour Library). (Illus.). 128p. 1995. pap. 18.95 (*1-85532-524-1*, Pub. by Ospry) Motorbooks Intl.

Allen, John S., tr. see Blauert, Jens.

Allen, John S., tr. see Cremer, Lothar.

***Allen, John Terry.** Let My People Know: A Manual for Understanding the Black Presence in the Bible. (Illus.). 80p. 2000. pap. 9.95 (*0-936369-76-0*) Son-Rise Pubns.

Allen, John W. Magic Mushrooms of the Pacific Northwest. (Ethnomycological Journals Sacred Mushroom Studies: No. 4). (Illus.). 1996. pap. 12.00 (*1-58214-026-X*) Mltilingl Bks.

— Maria Sabina: Saint Mother of the Mushrooms. 28p. 1997. pap. 7.00 (*0-9631518-9-4*) Mltilingl Bks.

— Wassen's First Voyage: The Rediscovery of Entheogenic Mushrooms. (Ethnomycological Journals Sacred Mushroom Ser.: No. 2). 30p. 1998. pap. 7.00 (*1-58214-027-8*) Mltilingl Bks.

Allen, John W., et al. The Foundations of Free Enterprise. 24p. 1979. 1.00 (*0-86599-004-2*) PERC.

— Strategic Directions in Supermarket Deli-Prepared Foods. (Illus.). 98p. (Orig.). (C). 1992. pap. text 20.00 (*1-56806-001-7*) DIANE Pub.

Allen, John W., jt. auth. see Seccombe, Thomas.

***Allen, Jon G.** Coping with Trauma: A Guide to Self-Understanding. 385p. 1999. pap. 17.00 (*0-88048-996-0*, 8996) Am Psychiatric.

Allen, Jon G. & Collins, Dean T., eds. Contemporary Treatment of Psychosis: Healing Relationships in the "Decade of the Brain" LC 96-5658. 128p. 1996. pap. 25.00 (*1-56821-873-7*) Aronson.

***Allen, Jon L.** Not for Attribution: A Treasury of Public Relations - Public Affairs Anecdotes. LC 99-91546. 1999. 25.00 (*0-7388-0870-9*); pap. 18.00 (*0-7388-0871-7*) Xlibris Corp.

Allen, Jon L. Texas on Stamps. LC 96-14898. (Illus.). 128p. (Orig.). 1996. pap. 14.95 (*0-87565-164-X*) Tex Christian.

Allen, Jonathan. A Bad Case of Animal Nonsense: Featuring the Animal Alphabet, Poems, I Know an Old Lady, Rhyming Animals. LC 97-24265. (Illus.). 64p. (J). (ps-2). 1998. pap. 10.95 (*1-56792-083-7*) Godine.

— Chicken Licken: A Wickedly Funny Flap Book. LC 98-87317. (Illus.). 20p. (J). 1999. pap. 6.00 (*0-15-202175-2*) Harcourt.

***Allen, Jonathan.** Don't Wake the Baby! LC 98-53931. (Illus.). 18p. (J). 2000. 19.99 (*0-7636-0891-2*, Pub. by Candlewick Pr) Penguin Putnam.

Allen, Jonathan. Mucky Moose. (Illus.). 32p. (J). (ps-3). 1996. per. 5.95 (*0-689-80651-5*) Aladdin.

— Mucky Moose. LC 90-6363. (J). 1996. 11.15 (*0-606-09643-4*, Pub. by Turtleback) Demco.

Allen, Jonathan & Thomson, Leighton F., eds. Advanced Research in VLSI: Proceedings of the Fifth MIT Conference. 400p. 1988. 47.50 (*0-262-01100-X*) MIT Pr.

Allen, Jonathan, jt. auth. see Lear, Edward.

Allen, Joseph. Battles of the British Navy, 2 vols, Set. 1977. lib. bdg. 250.00 (*0-8490-1480-8*) Gordon Pr.

— Genealogical Sketches of the Allen Family of Medfield: With an Account of the Golden Wedding of Ellis & Lucy Allen; Also of Gershom & Abigail (Allen) Adams. (Illus.). 88p. 1988. reprint ed. pap. 15.00 (*0-8328-0101-1*); reprint ed. lib. bdg. 23.00 (*0-8328-0100-3*) Higginson Bk Co.

— Mikey Goes Whale Watching. Trout, M. D., ed. (Illus.). 50p. (Orig.). (J). (gr. 1-5). 1986. pap. 8.95 (*0-917071-04-2*); lib. bdg. 13.50 (*0-917071-05-0*) Ocean Allen Pub.

— The Mystery of Fidelity. 121p. 1984. pap. 9.95 (*0-916586-59-6*, Pub. by Holy Cross Orthodox) BookWorld.

— Widowed Priest: Crisis in Ministry. 176p. 1994. pap. 9.95 (*1-880971-01-1*) Light&Life Pub Co MN.

Allen, Joseph & Astor, Bart. 10 Minute Guide to Choosing a College. LC 95-26767. 144p. 1995. 10.95 (*0-02-860615-9*) Macmillan.

Allen, Joseph, ed. see Saliba, Philip.

Allen, Joseph D. & Pittenger, David J. Statistics Tutor: Tutorial & Computational Software for the Behavioral Sciences. 215p. 1991. pap. text 19.50 (*0-471-57142-3*) Wiley.

***Allen, Joseph D. & Pittenger, David J.** Statistics Tutor: Tutorial & Computational Software for the Behavioral Sciences. 2nd ed. 192p. 1999. pap. 40.95 incl. cd-rom (*0-471-17092-5*) Wiley.

Allen, Joseph H. Our Liberal Movement in Theology: Chiefly As Shown in Recollections of the History of Unitarianism in New England. 3rd ed. LC 73-38432. (Religion in America, Ser. 2). 230p. 1972. reprint ed. 23.95 (*0-405-04053-9*) Ayer.

— The Works of Joseph Henry Allen, 1820-1980, Set. 1987. reprint ed. lib. bdg. 500.00 (*0-685-18586-9*) Rprt Serv.

***Allen, Joseph J.** Inner Way: Toward a Rebirth of Eastern Christian Spiritual Direction. LC 99-39977. 1999. pap. write for info. (*1-885652-34-8*) Holy Cross Orthodox.

Allen, Joseph J. The Ministry of the Church: Image of Pastoral Care. LC 86-22037. 232p. (Orig.). 1986. pap. 11.95 (*0-88141-044-6*) St Vladimirs.

***Allen, Joseph J.** Vested in Grace: Marriage & Priesthood in the Christian East. LC 00-44823. 2000. pap. write for info. (*1-885652-43-7*) Holy Cross Orthodox.

Allen, Joseph J., ed. Orthodox Synthesis: The Unity of Theological Thought. LC 81-5674. 231p. (Orig.). 1981. pap. 10.95 (*0-913836-84-2*) St Vladimirs.

Allen, Joseph J., jt. auth. see Saliba, Philip.

Allen, Joseph L. Love & Conflict: A Covenantal Model of Christian Ethics. 336p. (C). 1995. reprint ed. pap. text 28.50 (*0-8191-9763-7*) U Pr of Amer.

***Allen, Joseph L.** War: A Primer for Christians. 72p. 2000. pap. 5.95 (*0-87074-451-8*) SMU Press.

Allen, Joseph R. In the Voice of Others: Chinese Music Bureau Poetry. LC 92-1185. (Michigan Monographs in Chinese Studies: No. 63). 293p. 1992. text 45.00 (*0-89264-096-0*); pap. text 25.00 (*0-89264-097-9*) Ctr Chinese Studies.

Allen, Joseph R., ed. The Book of Songs. rev. ed. Waley, Arthur, tr. from CHI. LC 87-7440. 416p. 1996. pap. 14.00 (*0-8021-3477-7*, Grove) Grove-Atltic.

Allen, Joseph R., tr. & comment see Yang Mu.

Allen, Joy, jt. auth. see Beaumont, Karen.

Allen, Joy, jt. illus. see Hood, Susan.

Allen, Joyce. Teaching Reading: Easy As A B C. Date not set. ring bd. 10.00 (*0-9667329-0-1*) J Allen.

Allen, Judd R., et al. The Culture Change Planner. 16p. 1998. pap. text 9.95 (*0-941703-15-0*) Healthyculture.

Allen, Judith. Rose Scott: Vision & Revision in Feminism, 1880-1925. (Illus.). 342p. 1994. text 55.00 (*0-19-554846-9*) OUP.

Allen, Judith A. Sex & Secrets: Crimes Involving Australian Women since 1880. (Illus.). 302p. 1990. pap. 32.00 (*0-19-554839-6*) OUP.

Allen, Judith C., ed. Consumer's Guide to Doctoral Degree Programs in Nursing. 165p. 1990. 15.95 (*0-88737-455-7*) Natl League Nurse.

Allen, Judson B. The Ethical Poetic of the Later Middle Ages: A Decorum of Convenient Distinction. LC 82-146615. 347p. reprint ed. pap. 107.60 (*0-8357-4719-0*, 203763400009) Bks Demand.

— The Friar As Critic: Literary Attitudes in the Later Middle Ages. LC 77-123037. 188p. reprint ed. pap. 58.30 (*0-7837-6194-5*, 204591600009) Bks Demand.

Allen, Judson B. & Moritz, Theresa A. A Distinction of Stories: The Medieval Unity of Chaucer's Fair Chain of Narratives for Canterbury. LC 80-26629. 270p. 1981. reprint ed. pap. 83.70 (*0-608-04443-1*, 206497500012) Bks Demand.

Allen, Judy. Anthology for the Earth. LC 97-674. (Illus.). 96p. (J). (gr. 5 up). 1998. 21.99 (*0-7636-0301-5*) Candlewick Pr.

***Allen, Judy.** Backyard Books: Are you a Butterfly? LC 99-45777. (Backyard Bks.). (Illus.). 32p. (J). 2000. 8.95 (*0-7534-5240-5*) LKC.

— Backyard Books: Are You a Spider? (Illus.). 32p. (J). 2000. 9.95 (*0-7534-5243-X*) LKC.

Allen, Judy. Cultural Awareness for Children. pap. 32.00 (*0-201-28731-5*) Addison-Wesley.

Allen, Judy. Eagle. LC 93-28541. 1996. 11.19 (*0-606-10175-6*, Pub. by Turtleback) Demco.

Allen, Judy. Eagle. LC 93-28541. (Illus.). 32p. (J). (ps-3). 1996. reprint ed. pap. 5.99 (*1-56402-952-2*) Candlewick Pr.

— Elephant. LC 92-54407. (Illus.). 1995. pap. 4.99 (*1-56402-438-5*) Candlewick Pr.

***Allen, Judy.** Event Planning: The Ultimate Guide to Successful Meetings, Corporate Events, Fundraising Galas. 288p. 2000. 29.95 (*0-471-64412-9*) Wiley.

Allen, Judy. Guide to Stamps & Stamp Collecting. (Hobby Guides Ser.). (Illus.). 32p. (YA). (gr. 5 up). 1989. pap. 6.95 (*0-86020-548-7*, Usborne) EDC.

— Panda. (J). 1993. 10.19 (*0-606-07990-4*) Turtleback.

— Seal. LC 93-3642. (Illus.). 32p. (J). (ps up). 1994. 14.95 (*1-56402-145-9*) Candlewick Pr.

Allen, Judy. Seal. LC 93-3642. 1996. 11.19 (*0-606-10299-X*, Pub. by Turtleback) Demco.

Allen, Judy. Tiger. 1992. 10.19 (*0-606-06059-6*, Pub. by Turtleback) Demco.

— Whale. LC 92-53019. (Illus.). 32p. (J). (ps up). 1993. 15.95 (*1-56402-160-2*) Candlewick Pr.

Allen, Judy. Whale. 1993. 10.19 (*0-606-06862-7*, Pub. by Turtleback) Demco.

Allen, Judy. What is a Wall, After All? (Read & Wonder Ser.). 1995. 11.19 (*0-606-08364-2*, Pub. by Turtleback) Demco.

***Allen, Judy & Brock, Susan A.** Healthcare Communication Using Personality Type: Patients Are Different! LC 99-55354. 2000. pap. write for info. (*0-415-21374-6*) Routledge.

***Allen, Judy & Humphries, Tudor.** Are You a Ladybug? LC 99-42381. (Up the Garden Path Ser.). (Illus.). 32p. (J). 2000. 8.95 (*0-7534-5241-3*, Kingfisher) LKC.

— Are You a Snail? LC 99-42382. (Up the Garden Path Ser.). (Illus.). 32p. (J). 2000. 8.95 (*0-7534-5242-1*, Kingfisher) LKC.

Allen, Judy & Kneen, Deborah. Fabulous Folk Art Gifts for under $20.00. LC 96-161503. (Illus.). 96p. 1996. pap. 14.95 (*1-86351-169-5*, Pub. by Sally Milner) Sterling.

Allen, Judy E. The Five Stages of Getting Well. 221p. (Orig.). 1993. pap. 14.95 (*0-9627954-0-2*) LifeTime OR.

Allen, Julia. Forty Word Yellowstone Series, 4 bks., Set. (Illus.). (J). (gr. k-3). 1994. 39.80 (*0-89868-238-X*, Read Res) ARO Pub.

— My First Animal Ride. (My First Ser.). (Illus.). (J). (gr. k-3). 1987. 9.95 (*0-89868-179-0*); pap. 3.95 (*0-89868-180-4*) ARO Pub.

— My First Camping Trip. (My First Ser.). (Illus.). (J). (gr. k-3). 1987. 9.95 (*0-89868-181-2*); pap. 3.95 (*0-89868-182-0*) ARO Pub.

— My First Camping Trip: Big Big Book. (My First Ser.). (Illus.). (J). (gr. k-3). 1987. 22.00 (*0-614-24513-3*) ARO Pub.

— My First Cold. (My First Thirty Word Book Ser.). (Illus.). (J). (gr. k-3). 1994. pap. 3.95 (*0-89868-232-0*, Read Res); lib. bdg. 9.95 (*0-89868-224-X*, Read Res) ARO Pub.

— My First Dentist Visit. (My First Ser.). (Illus.). (J). (gr. k-3). 1987. 9.95 (*0-89868-185-5*); pap. 3.95 (*0-89868-186-3*) ARO Pub.

— My First Doctor Visit. (My First Ser.). (Illus.). (J). (gr. k-3). 1987. 9.95 (*0-89868-187-1*); pap. 3.95 (*0-89868-188-X*) ARO Pub.

— My First Garden. (My First Thirty Word Books Ser.). (Illus.). (J). (gr. k-3). 1994. pap. 3.95 (*0-89868-221-5*, Read Res); lib. bdg. 9.95 (*0-89868-220-7*, Read Res) ARO Pub.

— My First Grade. (My First Thirty Word Book Ser.). (Illus.). (J). (gr. k-3). 1994. pap. 3.95 (*0-89868-223-1*, Read Res); lib. bdg. 9.95 (*0-89868-222-3*, Read Res) ARO Pub.

— My First Job. (My First Ser.). (Illus.). (J). (gr. k-3). 1987. 3.95 (*0-89868-183-9*); pap. 9.95 (*0-89868-184-7*) ARO Pub.

— My First Party. (My First Thirty Word Book Ser.). (Illus.). (J). (gr. k-3). 1994. pap. 3.95 (*0-89868-234-7*, Read Res); lib. bdg. 9.95 (*0-89868-233-9*, Read Res) ARO Pub.

— My First Phone Call. (My First Ser.). (Illus.). (J). (gr. k-3). 1987. 9.95 (*0-89868-189-8*); pap. 3.95 (*0-89868-190-1*) ARO Pub.

— Sixty Word Grand Canyon Series, 6 bks., Set. (Illus.). (J). (gr. k-3). 1994. pap. 23.70 (*0-89868-240-1*, Read Res) ARO Pub.

— Thirty Word My First Series, 6 bks. (Illus.). (J). (gr. k-3). 1987. 59.70 (*0-89868-236-3*); pap. 27.30 (*0-89868-237-1*) ARO Pub.

Allen, Julius W. Tenderness & Turmoil: Letters Between a Mother & Daughter During World War I. LC 98-39705. 286p. 1998. pap. 14.95 (*0-929765-62-1*) Seven Locks Pr.

Allen, June, compiled by. Our Town: Discover Ketchikan. (Illus.). 100p. 1998. pap. 4.95 (*0-9634438-1-X*) Hist Ketchikan.

Allen, June & Charles, Patricia, eds. Spirit! Historic Ketchikan, Alaska. 148p. (Orig.). pap. 12.95 (*0-9634438-0-1*) Hist Ketchikan.

Allen, K., jt. ed. see Tomlinson, Dylan.

Allen, K. Eileen. The Exceptional Child: Mainstreaming in Early Childhood Education. 2nd ed. LC 91-3984. 320p. 1992. pap. 34.95 (*0-8273-3691-8*) Delmar.

— The Exceptional Child: Mainstreaming in Early Childhood Education. 2nd ed. 320p. 1992. pap., teacher ed. 10.50 (*0-8273-3692-6*) Delmar.

A

An Asterisk (*) at the beginning of an entry indicates that the title is appearing for the first time.

Allen, K. Eileen & Marotz, Lynn R. Developmental Profiles: Pre-Birth Through Eight. 2nd ed. LC 93-45861. 184p. (C). 1994. mass mkt. 35.95 (*0-8273-5814-8*) Delmar.

Allen, K. Eileen & Schwartz, Ilene S. The Exceptional Child: Inclusion in Early Childhood Education. 3rd rev. ed. LC 95-19167. 416p. (C). 1995. mass mkt. 54.95 (*0-8273-6698-1*) Delmar.

Allen, K. Eilleen. Developmental Profiles: Birth to Six. (Early Childhood Education Ser.). 1989. pap. 23.00 (*0-8273-3355-2*) Delmar.

Allen, K. Radway. Conservation & Management of Whales. LC 79-90505. (Washington Sea Grant Ser.). (Illus.). 120p. 1980. 15.00 (*0-295-95706-9*) U of Wash Pr.

***Allen, Karen.** Pearl City Control Theory. 310p. 1999. pap. 13.00 (*0-9671784-0-1*) Cabbages & Kings.

***Allen, Karen, et al.** Health Insurance Coverage for the Self Employed with No Employees in the U.S., 1993: Data from the National Employer Health Insurance Survey LC 99-25356. (DHHS Publication Ser.). 1999. write for info. (*0-8406-0554-4*) Natl Ctr Health Stats.

Allen, Karen, et al. Nursing Care of the Addicted Client. LC 95-50020. 384p. 1996. pap. text 36.95 (*0-397-55204-1*) Lppncott W & W.

Allen, Karen, jt. auth. see Scottoline, Lisa.

Allen, Karen K. & Miller, Margery S. Reading the Newspaper: Advanced Level. 160p. (Orig.). (YA). (gr. 9-12). 1989. pap. text 14.96 (*0-89061-500-4*, Jamestwn Pub) NTC Contemp Pub Co.

Allen, Karen M. The Human-Animal Bond: An Annotated Bibliography. LC 85-1916. 256p. 1985. 26.50 (*0-8108-1792-6*) Scarecrow.

— Women's Health Across the Lifespan: A Comprehensive Perspective. LC 96-22832. (Illus.). 544p. 1996. pap. text 38.95 (*0-397-55216-5*) Lppncott W & W.

Allen, Kate. Give My Secrets Back: An Alison Kaine Mystery. LC 94-38403. 200p. (Orig.). 1995. pap. 9.95 (*0-934678-64-2*) New Victoria Pubs.

— I Knew You Would Call. LC 95-19140. 202p. (Orig.). 1995. pap. 10.95 (*0-934678-70-7*) New Victoria Pubs.

— Just a Little Lie: An Alison Kaine Mystery. LC 98-27388. (Alison Kaine Mystery Ser.: Vol. 4). 224p. 1998. pap. 12.95 (*0-934678-94-4*) New Victoria Pubs.

— The Legend of the Whistle Pig Wrangler. LC 95-79690. (Illus.). 32p. (J). (ps-4). 1996. 14.95 (*1-887218-00-9*) Kumquat Pr.

— Li'l Miss Fuss Budget. (Illus.). 21p. (J). (gr. k-6). 1996. 14.95 (*1-887218-02-5*) Kumquat Pr.

— The Lizard Who Followed Me Home. (Illus.). 32p. (J). (ps-4). 1995. 14.95 (*1-887218-01-7*) Kumquat Pr.

— Takes One to Know One: An Alison Kaine Mystery. LC 96-8841. 200p. (Orig.). 1996. pap. 10.95 (*0-934678-74-X*) New Victoria Pubs.

Allen, Kate. Tell Me What You Like: An Alison Kaine Mystery. LC 92-47054. (Orig.). 1993. pap. 11.95 (*0-934678-48-0*) New Victoria Pubs.

Allen, Kate, jt. auth. see Ingulsrud, John E.

Allen, Katherine R. Single Women - Family Ties: Life Histories of Older Women. (New Perspectives on Family Ser.). 152p. (C). 1989. text 48.00 (*0-8039-2804-1*); pap. text 22.95 (*0-8039-2805-X*) Sage.

— Single Women - Family Ties: Life Histories of Older Women. LC 89-6383. (New Perspectives on Family Ser.). 152p. 1989. reprint ed. pap. 47.20 (*0-608-02765-0*, 206383100007) Bks Demand.

Allen, Katherine R., jt. auth. see Baber, Kristine M.

***Allen, Kathleen.** Ebusiness Technology Kit for Dummies. (For Dummies Ser.). 384p. 2000. pap. 24.99 (*0-7645-5261-9*) IDG Bks.

***Allen, Kathleen & Economy, Peter.** Complete MBA for Dummies. (For Dummies Ser.). 432p. 2000. pap. 19.99 (*0-7645-5204-X*) IDG Bks.

Allen, Kathleen, jt. auth. see Price, Courtney H.

Allen, Kathleen, ed. see Miller, Bob.

***Allen, Kathleen E. & Cherrey, Cynthia.** Systemic Leadership: Enriching the Meaning of Our Work. 152p. 2000. 54.00 (*1-883485-19-3*, Pub. by Am Coll Personnel); pap. 24.50 (*1-883485-20-7*, Pub. by Am Coll Personnel) U Pr of Amer.

Allen, Kathleen M., et al, eds. Interpreting Space: GIS & Archaeology. 350p. 1990. 99.00 (*0-85066-824-7*, Pub. by Tay Francis Ltd) Taylor & Francis.

Allen, Kathleen R. Computer Office Setup That Really Works! Computerization for Business. Engel, Peter H., ed. (Office Depot's Small Business Solutions Ser.). (Illus.). 128p. (Orig.). 1995. pap. 13.95 (*1-886111-23-5*) Affinity CA.

— Launching New Ventures: An Entrepreneurial Approach. 2nd ed. LC 98-71974. 1998. text 59.96 (*0-395-91845-6*) HM.

— NYT Growing & Managing a Business: 25 Keys to Building Your Company. LC 99-37755. 104p. 1999. pap. 12.95 (*0-86730-774-9*) Lebhar Friedman.

— Office Design That Really Works. (Small Business Solutions Ser.). (Illus.). 128p. 1995. pap. 13.95 (*0-8442-2999-7*, NTC Business Bks) NTC Contemp Pub Co.

— Time & Information Management That Really Works! Organization for the '90s. Engel, Peter H., ed. (Office Depot's Small Business Solutions Ser.). (Illus.). 128p. (Orig.). 1995. pap. 13.95 (*1-886111-22-7*) Affinity CA.

Allen, Kathleen R. & Engel, Peter H. Office Design That Really Works! Design for the 90s. (Office Depot's Small Business Solutions Ser.). (Illus.). 128p. (Orig.). 1995. pap. 13.95 (*1-886111-21-9*) Affinity CA.

Allen, Kathleen R., jt. auth. see Meyer, Earl C.

Allen, Kathy O. Karmic Networking. 76p. 1998. pap. write for info. (*1-57502-947-2*, PO2607) Morris Pubng.

Allen, Kay. Boundary Breaking. 392p. (C). 1995. pap. text, per. 36.95 (*0-7872-0274-6*) Kendall-Hunt.

Allen, Keith & Ferrari, Anthony M. 101 of the World's Most Effective Pick-Up Lines. Huijgen, Matthew, ed. (Illus.). 128p. (Orig.). 1997. pap. 9.95 (*0-9634641-2-4*) Ace Co & Assocs.

Allen, Ken. Dart Grammar Workbook No. 2, Vol. 2. 2nd ed. 304p. 1996. pap. text, wbk. ed. 31.53 (*0-13-518788-5*) P-H.

— Ken Allen's Guide to Upland Bird Hunting: A Complete Guide to Grouse Woodcock & Pheasant Hunting in New England. LC 86-21789. (Illus.). 172p. (Orig.). 1986. pap. 8.95 (*0-89621-126-6*) Nrth Country Pr.

Allen, Kenneth B. Enhancing Competitiveness in the Information Age: Strategies & Tactics for Special Librarians & Information Professionals. 64p. 1997. pap. text 29.00 (*0-87111-476-3*) SLA.

Allen, Kenneth W., et al. China's Air Force Enters the 21st Century. LC 95-17782. 275p. (Orig.). 1995. pap. text 15.00 (*0-8330-1648-2*, MR-580-AF) Rand Corp.

Allen, Kerry J. How Can I: Except Some Man Should Guide Me. 86p. (Orig.). 1997. pap. 8.00 (*1-57502-399-7*, PO1239) Morris Pubng.

***Allen, Kevin.** August Jaeger: Portrait of Nimrod : A Life in Letters & Other Writings. LC 00-23684. 2000. write for info. (*1-85928-366-7*) Ashgate Pub Co.

— Crunch: Big Hitters, Shot Blockers, & Bone Crushers: A History of Fighting in the NHL. 1999. 22.95 (*1-57243-303-5*) Triumph Bks.

Allen, Kevin. There Zin H A. LC 99-70480. 224p. 1999. 19.95 (*0-9671490-0-2*) One Lighthse Pr.

— U. S. A. Hockey: The Celebration of a Great Tradition. 192p. 1997. 35.00 (*1-57243-236-5*) Triumph Bks.

Allen, Kevin, jt. auth. see Hull, Brett.

Allen, Kevin K. After the Lovin' A Book for Women. vii, 123p. 1998. pap. 10.95 (*0-9668011-0-5*) Brennan Lane Pubns.

Allen, Kieran. Fianna Fail & Irish Labour: 1926 to the Present. LC 96-50123. 240p. 1997. pap. 49.95 (*0-7453-0865-1*, Pub. by Pluto GBR); pap. 17.95 (*0-7453-0866-X*, Pub. by Pluto GBR) Stylus Pub VA.

Allen, Kimberly, jt. auth. see Allen, Christopher.

Allen, Kimberly B. Wedding Wonders: Tales & Traditions, Customs & Curiosities. Caton, Patrick, ed. LC 96-76132. 168p. 1996. 5.95 (*1-56245-264-9*) Great Quotations.

Allen, Kirkland, jt. auth. see Allen, Minerva.

Allen, Kring. The Paradox of Preaching. (Illus.). 104p. (Orig.). 1986. pap. 9.95 (*1-55630-018-2*) Brentwood Comm.

Allen, Kristen, ed. Agricultural Policies in a New Decade. LC 89-43667. 356p. 1990. pap. 29.95 (*0-915707-54-3*) Resources Future.

Allen, Kristen & Macmillan, Katie, eds. United States - Canadian Agricultural Trade Challenges: Developing Common Approaches - Proceedings of a Symposium Held at Spring Hill Conference Center, Wayzata, Minnesota, July 22-24, 1987, Cosponsored by National Center for Food & Agricultural Policy at Resources for the Future & C. D. Howe Institute. LC 88-10299. 230p. reprint ed. pap. 71.30 (*0-8357-3283-5*, 203950600013) Bks Demand.

Allen, L. Franklin Half Dollars. (Illus.). 1981. pap. 10.00 (*0-932106-04-8*) S J Durst.

Allen, L., et al. Nutrient Regulation During Pregnancy, Lactation & Infant Growth. LC 94-6848. (Advances in Experimental Medicine & Biology Ser.: Vol. 352). (Illus.). 308p. (C). 1994. text 89.50 (*0-306-44719-3*, Kluwer Plenum) Kluwer Academic.

Allen, L. David. The Prince & the Pauper Notes. (Cliffs Notes Ser.). 80p. (Orig.). (C). 1980. pap. text 4.95 (*0-8220-1096-8*, Cliff) IDG Bks.

Allen, L. David & Roberts, James L. A Connecticut Yankee in King Arthur's Court: Notes. (Cliffs Notes Ser.). 64p. (Orig.). (gr. 9-12). 1982. pap. 4.95 (*0-8220-0324-4*, Cliff) IDG Bks.

Allen, L. David & Thompson, Frank H., Jr. Animal Farm: Notes. (Cliffs Notes Ser.). 64p. 1967. pap. 4.95 (*0-8220-0174-8*, Cliff) IDG Bks.

Allen, L. H., et al. Advances in Carbon Dioxide Effects Research. LC 97-71150. (ASA Special Publications: Vol. 61). 228p. 1997. 36.00 (*0-89118-133-4*) Am Soc Agron.

Allen, La Rue, jt. auth. see Rickel, Annette U.

Allen, Larry. The ABC-CLIO World History Companion to Capitalism. LC 98-3908. 404p. 1998. lib. bdg. 65.00 (*0-87436-944-4*) ABC-CLIO.

— Historical Encyclopedia of Money. LC 99-38048. 328p. (YA). (gr. 10 up). 1999. lib. bdg. 75.00 (*1-57607-037-9*) ABC-CLIO.

Allen, Laura. Clever Letters: Fun Ways to Wiggle Your Words. LC 97-12893. (American Girl Library Ser.). (Illus.). 96p. (Orig.). (J). (gr. 3-7). 1997. pap. text 9.95 (*1-56247-528-2*, Amer Girl Library) Pleasant Co.

— Mr. Henry. (J). 1924. write for info. (*0-688-16653-9*); lib. bdg. write for info. (*0-688-16654-7*) Lothrop.

***Allen, Laura & Tilley, Debbie.** The Quiz Book: Clues to You & Your Friends, Too! LC 99-17482. 1999. pap. text 6.95 (*1-56247-750-1*) Pleasant Co.

Allen, Laura J. Rollo & Tweedy & the Ghost at Dougal Castle. (I Can Read Bks.). (Illus.). (J). (ps-3). 1996. pap. 8.95 incl. digital audio (*0-694-70053-3*) HarpC.

— Rollo & Tweedy & the Ghost at Dougal Castle. (I Can Read Bks.). (Illus.). 64p. (J). (gr. 1-3). 1992. lib. bdg. 15.89 (*0-06-020107-X*) HarpC Child Bks.

— Rollo & Tweedy & the Ghost at Dougal Castle. (I Can Read Bks.). (Illus.). 64p. (J). (gr. 1-3). 1994. pap. 3.95 (*0-06-444182-2*, HarpTrophy) HarpC Child Bks.

Allen, Laura J. Rollo & Tweedy & the Ghost at Dougal Castle. (I Can Read Bks.). (J). (gr. 1-3). 1994. 8.95 (*0-606-06703-5*, Pub. by Turtleback) Demco.

Allen, Laura J. Where Is Freddy? LC 85-45275. (I Can Read Bks.). (Illus.). 64p. (J). (ps-3). 1986. 11.95 (*0-06-020098-7*) HarpC Child Bks.

***Allen, Laurence.** On the Road Again; The Best Years of Our Lives: Three Plays. 180p. 2000. pap. 19.95 (*1-85411-265-1*, Pub. by Seren Bks) Dufour.

Allen, Laurence R., jt. auth. see Kraus, Richard.

Allen, Laurie. Comedy Duo Scenes for Teens. (Encore Scene Book Ser.). (YA). 1998. pap. 8.95 (*1-57514-022-5*, 5021) Encore Perform Pub.

Allen, Layman E. The Meditation Game: Strategy. 1976. pap. 2.00 (*0-911624-41-4*) Wffn Proof.

— Real Numbers: Arithmetic. 1966. 3.00 (*0-911624-04-X*) Wffn Proof.

Allen, Layman E. & Ross, Joan. IMP (Instructional Math Play) Kits: Individual Solitare Kits. 1971. 20.00 (*0-911624-18-X*) Wffn Proof.

Allen, Layman E., et al. On-Words: The Game of Word Structures. 1978. 25.00 (*0-911624-40-6*) Wffn Proof.

Allen, Laymen, jt. auth. see University of Houston Editorial Staff.

Allen, Lee. Cooperstown Corner. 181p. pap. 10.00 (*0-910137-41-2*) Soc Am Baseball Res.

***Allen, Lee.** The Hole in My Vision: Watching My Own Age-Related Macular Degeneration. Folk, James C. & Thompson, H. Stanley, eds. (Illus.). 96p. 2000. 100.00 (*1-57216-085-3*); pap. 49.95 (*1-57216-084-5*) Penfield.

Allen, Lee. Hot Stove League. 24.95 (*0-8488-1494-0*) Amereon Ltd.

***Allen, Lee.** The Hot Stove League: Raking the Embers of Baseball's Golden Age. 224p. 2000. pap. 12.95 (*1-892129-44-2*) Total Sprts.

Allen, Lee & Allen, Donna. The Special Guest. 96p. 1996. 12.95 (*1-57566-120-9*, Knsington); 8.95 (*1-57566-117-9*, Knsington) Kensgtn Pub Corp.

Allen, Lee, ed. see Rommel, Erwin.

Allen, Lee M. & Saeger, Richard T. Georgia State Politics: The Constitutional Foundation. 3rd ed. 278p. (C). per. write for info. (*0-7872-6738-4*) Kendall-Hunt.

Allen, Leonard. Discovering Our Roots: Ancestry of the Churches of Christ. LC 87-72685. 200p. 1988. pap. 10.95 (*0-89112-006-8*) Abilene Christ U.

Allen, Lesette. Elana's Destiny. (Orig.). 1997. mass mkt. 5.95 (*0-352-33218-2*, Pub. by BLA4) London Brdge.

Allen, Leslie. Ezekiel 1-19. (Biblical Commentary Ser.: Vol. 28). 29.99 (*0-8499-0830-2*) Word Pub.

— Ezekiel 20-48. (Biblical Commentary Ser.: Vol. 29). 29.99 (*0-8499-0228-2*) Word Pub.

— Hosea-Malachi: Commentary. (Bible Study Commentaries Ser.). 1987. pap. 4.95 (*0-87508-163-0*) Chr Lit.

— Two Hour Applique. 1999. pap. 14.95 (*0-8069-8667-0*) Sterling.

— Two-Hour Applique: Over 200 Original Designs. LC 95-49198. (Illus.). 128p. 1996. 24.95 (*0-8069-4277-0*) Sterling.

Allen, Leslie, et al. Exploring America's Historic Places. LC 97-18669. 1997. write for info. (*0-7922-4232-7*) Natl Geog.

— Exploring America's Historic Places. LC 97-18669. 1998. 16.00 (*0-7922-3652-1*) Natl Geog.

Allen, Leslie C. I, II Chronicles. (Communicator's Commentary Ser.: Vol. 10). 445p. 25.99 (*0-8499-0415-3*); pap. 14.99 (*0-8499-3549-0*) Word Pub.

— Joel, Obadiah, Jonah & Micah. (New International Commentary on the Old Testament Ser.). 427p. 1976. 36.00 (*0-8028-2531-1*) Eerdmans.

— Psalms 101-150. (Biblical Commentary Ser.: Vol. 21). 1983. 29.99 (*0-8499-0220-7*) Word Pub.

Allen, Lew. Guide to Renewing Your School: Lessons from the League. 1999. pap. 28.95 (*0-7879-4691-5*) Jossey-Bass.

Allen, Lew & Lunsford, Barbara. How to Form Networks for School Renewal. LC 95-5355. 1995. pap. 8.95 (*0-87120-242-5*) ASCD.

***Allen, Lillian.** Psychic Unrest. 112p. 2000. pap. 9.99 (*1-895837-55-3*) Insomniac.

Allen, Lillian. Why Me? (Illus.). 24p. (J). pap. 4.95 (*1-895248-02-7*, Pub. by Womens Pr) LPC InBook.

— Women Do This Every Day: Selected Poems of Lillian Allen. (Not a Luxury Poetry Ser.). 144p. pap. 10.95 (*0-88961-192-0*, Pub. by Womens Pr) LPC InBook.

Allen, Lily L. Personality: Its Cultivation & Power & How to Attain. 170p. 1992. pap. 15.00 (*0-89540-218-1*, SB-218) Sun Pub.

Allen, Linda. Capital Markets & Institutions: A Global View. LC 96-48795. 800p. 1997. text 96.95 (*0-471-13049-4*) Wiley.

***Allen, Linda.** Decking the Halls: The Folklore & Traditions of Christmas Plants. (Illus.). 95p. 2000. 12.95 (*1-57223-383-4*) Willow Creek Pr.

Allen, Linda, et al. Selling Successfully in Mexico: Proven Strategies for Market Research, Advertising, Direct Marketing & Trade Show Exhibiting. 228p. 1997. spiral bd. 29.00 (*1-893323-09-9*) WorldTrade Exec.

Allen, Linda L. An Oven Heated by the Baker: On Fire for the Lord! 110p. 1998. pap. 11.95 (*1-892878-00-3*) You Deserve It.

Allen, Lisa M., jt. ed. see Rimmer, Peter J.

Allen, Lisette. Ace of Hearts. LC 97-144987. (Black Lace Ser.). 288p. (Orig.). 1996. mass mkt. 5.95 (*0-352-33059-7*, Pub. by Virgin Bks) London Brdge.

— The Amulet. (Black Lace Ser.). 1995. mass mkt. 5.95 (*0-352-33019-8*, Pub. by Virgin Bks) London Brdge.

— Elena's Conquest. (Black Lace Ser.). 1994. mass mkt. 5.95 (*0-352-32950-5*, Pub. by Virgin Bks) London Brdge.

— Nadya's Quest. 256p. (Orig.). 1997. mass mkt. 5.95 (*0-352-33135-6*, Pub. by BLA4) London Brdge.

— Nicole's Revenge. (Black Lace Ser.). 1995. mass mkt. 5.95 (*0-352-32984-X*, Pub. by Virgin Bks) London Brdge.

***Allen, Lisette.** Risky Business. (Black Lace Ser.). 1998. mass mkt. 6.95 (*0-352-33280-8*, Pub. by BLA4) London Brdge.

Allen, Lochie J. & Kinney, Edward C., eds. Proceedings of the Bio-Engineering Symposium for Fish Culture. LC 80-68383. 307p. 1981. text 28.00 (*0-913235-25-3*, 530.08) Am Fisheries Soc.

Allen, Lois R., ed. Review of Research in Nursing Education, Vol. V. (C). 1992. pap. text 9.95 (*0-88737-542-1*, 15-2448) Natl League Nurse.

Allen, Lori & Voss, Dan. Ethics in Technical Communication: Shades of Gray. LC 96-26312. 410p. 1997. pap. 44.99 (*0-471-15328-1*) Wiley.

Allen, Loring. Venezuelan Economic Development: A Politico-Economic Analysis. Altman, Edward I. & Walter, Ingo I., eds. LC 76-10395. (Contemporary Studies in Economic & Financial Analysis: Vol. 7). 325p. 1977. 78.50 (*0-89232-011-7*) Jai Pr.

Allen, Louis. The End of the War in Asia. (Illus.). 1976. 34.95 (*0-8464-0043-X*) Beekman Pubs.

— Singapore, 1941-1942. LC 92-20935. 351p. 1993. text 47.50 (*0-7146-3473-5*, Pub. by F Cass Pubs) Intl Spec Bk.

— Singapore, 1941-1942. Frankland, Noble & Dowling, Christopher, eds. LC 79-52236. (Politics & Strategy of the Second World War Ser.). 343p. 1979. 27.50 (*0-87413-160-X*) U Delaware Pr.

Allen, Louise. Bisexual Imaginary: Representation, Identity & Desire. 1997. pap. text 15.95 (*0-304-33745-5*) Continuum.

— Lesbian Idol: Martina, K. D. & the Consumption of Lesbian Masculinity. LC 97-224836. (Sexual Politics Ser.). 184p. 1997. pap. text 18.95 (*0-304-33819-2*) Continuum.

— Lesbian Idol: Martina, K. D. & the Consumption of Lesbian Masculinity. LC 97-224836. (Sexual Politics Ser.). 1997. 69.95 (*0-304-33818-4*) Continuum.

Allen, Loyd. Gift Quest: A Search for Spiritual Gifts. Nelson, Becky, ed. 38p. (Orig.). (YA). (gr. 7-12). 1994. pap. text 4.95 (*1-56309-099-6*, C946102, Wrld Changers Res) Womans Mission Union.

***Allen, Loyd V., Jr.** Allen's Compounded Formulations: The U. S. Pharmacist Collection, 1995 to 1998. LC 99-47778. 141p. 1999. pap. text 49.00 (*0-917330-99-4*) Am Pharm Assn.

Allen, Loyd V., Jr. The Art, Science & Technology of Pharmaceutical Compounding. LC 98-25173. (Illus.). 319p. 1998. text 70.00 (*0-917330-88-9*) Am Pharm Assn.

Allen, Lyle. Mutual Funds: Your Key to Sound Financial Planning. 144p. (Orig.). 1994. pap. 10.00 (*0-380-77690-1*, Avon Bks) Morrow Avon.

— Protect Your Money: Strategies for a Worry Free Retirement. 192p. 2000. pap. 17.95 (*1-58501-000-6*) CeShore Pubg.

Allen, Lynn. AutoCAD Inside & Out: The Best of Lynn Allen from Cadence Magazine. (Illus.). 261p. 1997. pap. 29.95 (*0-87930-517-7*) Miller Freeman.

Allen, Lynn, ed. Active Older Adults: Ideas for Action. LC 98-35639. (Illus.). 208p. 1999. 19.00 (*0-7360-0128-X*, BALL0128) Human Kinetics.

— Physical Activity Ideas for Action: Elementary Level. LC 96-32497. 152p. (Orig.). 1996. pap. text 16.00 (*0-88011-554-8*, BALL0554) Human Kinetics.

— Physical Activity Ideas for Action: Secondary Level. LC 96-32474. 200p. (Orig.). 1996. pap. text 16.00 (*0-88011-555-6*, BALL0555) Human Kinetics.

Allen, Lynne & McGibbon, Phyllis. The Best of Printmaking: An International Collection. (Illus.). 160p. 1997. 27.99 (*1-56496-371-3*, Quarry Bks) Rockport Pubs.

Allen, M. Anglia: Perfect & Popular. (Illus.). 144p. 1997. 24.95 (*0-947981-07-1*, Pub. by Motor Racing) Motorbooks Intl.

— Evaluation of Educational Programmes in Nursing. 67p. 1977. 12.00 (*92-4-156054-1*) World Health.

— Marvellous Moths of Nepal. (C). 1991. 60.00 (*0-7855-0194-0*, Pub. by Ratna Pustak Bhandar) St Mut.

— Women in India & Nepal. (C). 1991. text 75.00 (*0-7855-0165-7*, Pub. by Ratna Pustak Bhandar) St Mut.

Allen, M., ed. Computer Modelling of New Materials: A Special Issue of the Journal Molecular Simulation. 208p. 1989. pap. text 350.00 (*2-88124-728-8*) Gordon & Breach.

Allen, M., et al. Conexiones Electricas - Electrical Connections. (ENG & SPA.). (J). (gr. 4-9). 1994. 16.95 (*1-881431-37-1*, 1437) AIMS Educ Fnd.

— Critters: K-6 Life Science Activities. (J). (gr. k-6). 1989. 16.95 (*1-881431-23-1*, 1208) AIMS Educ Fnd.

— Electrical Connections. (Magnetism & Electricity Ser.). (J). (gr. 4-9). 1991. 16.95 (*1-881431-28-2*, 1212) AIMS Educ Fnd.

— Water Precious Water: A Collection of Elementary Water Activities. (J). (gr. 2-6). 1988. 16.95 (*1-881431-22-3*, 1301) AIMS Educ Fnd.

Allen, M. B., III, et al. Multiphase Flow in Porous Media. (Lecture Notes in Engineering Ser.: Vol. 34). 310p. 1988. 101.95 (*0-387-96731-1*) Spr-Verlag.

Allen, M. D. The Medievalism of Lawrence of Arabia. LC 88-43433. 224p. 1991. lib. bdg. 32.50 (*0-271-00673-0*) Pa St U Pr.

Allen, M. J. Plato's 3rd Eye: Studies in Marsilio Metaphysics & Its Sources. (Collected Studies: Vol. CS483). 350p. 1995. 113.95 (*0-86078-472-X*, Pub. by Variorum) Ashgate Pub Co.

Allen, M. J., et al, eds. Charge & Field Effects in Biosystems, Vol. 2. LC 89-26551. (Illus.). 400p. 1989. 120.00 (*0-306-43401-6*, Plenum Trade) Perseus Pubng.

— Charge & Field Effects in Biosystems - 3. x, 502p. 1991. 97.00 (*0-8176-3564-5*) Birkhauser.

— Sir Philip Sidney's Achievements. LC 89-45860. (Studies in the Renaissance: No. 28). 1990. 42.50 (*0-404-62298-4*) AMS Pr.

Allen, M. J., et al. Sentencing Law & Practice in Northern Ireland. 3rd ed. LC 98-182632. xli, 401 p. 1998. write for info. *(0-85389-721-2)* Queens U Belfast.

Allen, M. P. & Tildesley, D. J. Computer Simulation of Liquids. (Illus.). 404p. 1989. pap. text 65.00 *(0-19-855645-4)* OUP.

Allen, M. P. & Tildesley, D. J., eds. Computer Simulation in Chemical Physics. LC 93-17086. (NATO Advanced Study Institutes Series C, Mathematical & Physical Sciences: Vol. 397). 1993. text 303.50 *(0-7923-2283-5)* Kluwer Academic.

Allen, M. Ray. Between the Thorns: Windcarver Songs of Appalachia. Adams, Joseph D., ed. LC 91-61028. xii, 68p. (Orig.). 1991. pap. 5.00 *(1-880016-06-0)* Road Pubs.

***Allen, M. Ray.** Beyond Star Bottom & Other Poems: Poems on Mental & Physical Journies Colored by an Appalachian Heritage. Taylor, Kendrick B. & Searle, Helen W., eds. 96p. 2000. pap. 9.95 *(0-9664709-4-X)* Mountain Empire.

Allen, Madelene. Reunion: The Search for My Birth Family. 224p. 1992. 24.95 *(0-7737-2588-1)* Genl Dist Srvs.

Allen, Madelene F. Wake of the Invercauld: Shipwrecked in the Sub-Antarctic: A Great-Granddaughter's Pilgrimage. (Illus.). 256p. 1997. 45.00 *(0-7735-1688-3,* Pub. by McG-Queens Univ Pr) CUP Services.

Allen, Maragret. Dr. Maggie's Phonics Resource Guide, No. 2925. Kupperstein, Joel, ed. (Dr. Maggie's Phonics Readers Ser.). (Illus.). 160p. (J). (ps-1). 1999. pap. 16.98 *(1-57471-530-5)* Creat Teach Pr.

Allen, Marc. Visionary Business: An Entrepreneur's Guide to Success. LC 95-33675. 192p. 1996. 16.95 *(1-880032-46-5)* New Wrld Lib.

— Visionary Business: An Entrepreneur's Guide to Success. LC 95-33675. 192p. 1997. pap. 12.95 *(1-57731-019-5)* New Wrld Lib.

— A Visionary Life: Conversations on Personal & Planetary Evolution. LC 97-39586. 208p. 1998. pap. 12.95 *(1-57731-021-7)* New Wrld Lib.

Allen, Marc, jt. auth. see Fisher, Mark.

Allen, Marc, ed. see Allen, James.

Allen, Marc, ed. see McDonald, John.

Allen, Marc, ed. see Regardie, Israel.

***Allen, Marcus.** Strength of the Heart: Marcus Allen's Life Little Playbooks. LC 99-21801. 48p. 1999. 14.95 *(0-7407-0017-0)* Andrews & McMeel.

Allen, Marcus & Stowers, Carl. Marcus Allen. LC 97-16522. (Illus.). 352p. 1997. text 24.95 *(0-312-16924-8)* St Martin.

***Allen, Marcus & Stowers, Carleton.** Marcus. LC 99-41905. 430p. 1999. 29.95 *(1-56000-457-6)* Transaction Pubs.

Allen, Marcus T., jt. auth. see Floyd, Charles F.

Allen, Margaret. The ABC Bags, No. 2908. Kupperstein, Joel, ed. (Dr. Maggie's Phonics Readers Ser.). (Illus.). 16p. (J). (ps-1). 1999. pap. 2.99 *(1-57471-583-6)* Creat Teach Pr.

— Barney Bear's Party, Vol. 2920. Kupperstein, Joel, ed. (Dr. Maggie's Phonics Readers Ser.). (Illus.). 16p. (J). 1999. pap. 2.99 *(1-57471-595-X)* Creat Teach Pr.

— Cat & Dog at the Circus, Vol. 2922. Kupperstein, Joel, ed. (Dr. Maggie's Phonics Readers Ser.). (Illus.). 16p. (J). 1999. pap. 2.99 *(1-57471-597-6)* Creat Teach Pr.

— Click, Click, No. 2907. Kupperstein, Joel, ed. (Dr. Maggie's Phonics Readers Ser.). (Illus.). 16p. (J). (ps-1). 1999. pap. 2.99 *(1-57471-582-8)* Creat Teach Pr.

— Dave & Jane's Band, Vol. 2912. Kupperstein, Joel, ed. (Dr. Maggie's Phonics Readers Ser.). (Illus.). 16p. (J). 1999. pap. 2.99 *(1-57471-587-9)* Creat Teach Pr.

— Direct Marketing. 1997. pap. text 19.95 *(0-7494-2052-9)* Kogan Page Ltd.

— Dr. Maggie's Play & Discover Language, Vol. 2349. Bruno, Janet, ed. (Illus.). 72p. (J). (ps-1). 1998. pap. 12.98 *(1-57471-361-2)* Creat Teach Pr.

— Dr. Maggie's Play & Discover Math, Vol. 2348. Corker, Joanne, ed. (Illus.). 72p. (J). (ps-1). 1998. pap. 12.98 *(1-57471-360-4)* Creat Teach Pr.

— Dr. Maggie's Play & Discover Phonics, Vol. 2346. Corker, Joanne, ed. (Illus.). 72p. (J). (ps-2). 1998. pap. 12.98 *(1-57471-358-2)* Creat Teach Pr.

— Dr. Maggie's Play & Discover Science, Vol. 2347. Corker, Joanne, ed. (Illus.). 72p. (J). (ps-1). 1998. pap. 12.98 *(1-57471-359-0)* Creat Teach Pr.

— Dr. Maggie's Play & Discover Special Me, Vol. 2350. Corcker, Joanne, ed. (Illus.). 72p. (J). (ps-2). 1998. pap. 12.98 *(1-57471-362-0)* Creat Teach Pr.

— Draw & Share, No. 2910. Kupperstein, Joel, ed. (Dr. Maggie's Phonics Readers Ser.). (Illus.). 16p. (J). (ps-1). 1999. pap. 2.99 *(1-57471-585-2)* Creat Teach Pr.

— Hap & Cap, No. 2902. Kupperstein, Joel, ed. (Dr. Maggie's Phonics Readers Ser.). (Illus.). 16p. (J). (ps-1). 1999. pap. 2.99 *(1-57471-562-3)* Creat Teach Pr.

— I Spy, No. 2901. Kupperstein, Joel, ed. (Dr. Maggie's Phonics Readers Ser.). (Illus.). 16p. (J). (ps-1). 1999. pap. 2.99 *(1-57471-561-5)* Creat Teach Pr.

— Jet It, Get It, No. 2906. Kupperstein, Joel, ed. (Dr. Maggie's Phonics Readers Ser.). (Illus.). 16p. (J). (ps-1). 1999. pap. 2.99 *(1-57471-566-6)* Creat Teach Pr.

***Allen, Margaret.** Jo Jo in Outer Space, Vol. 2923. Kupperstein, Joel, ed. (Dr. Maggie's Phonics Readers Ser.). (Illus.). 16p. (J). 1999. pap. 2.99 *(1-57471-598-4)* Creat Teach Pr.

Allen, Margaret. The Little Green Man Visits Pine Cone Grove, Vol. 2915. Kupperstein, Joel, ed. (Dr. Maggie's Phonics Readers Ser.). (Illus.). 16p. (J). (ps-2). 1999. pap. 2.99 *(1-57471-590-9)* Creat Teach Pr.

— Mr. Noisy at the Dude Ranch, Vol. 2916. Kupperstein, Joel, ed. (Dr. Maggie's Phonics Readers Ser.). (Illus.). 16p. (J). (ps). 1999. pap. 2.99 *(1-57471-591-7)* Creat Teach Pr.

— Out to Gumball Pond, Vol. 2918. Kupperstein, Joel, ed. (Dr. Maggie's Phonics Readers Ser.). (Illus.). 16p. (J). 1999. pap. 2.99 *(1-57471-593-3)* Creat Teach Pr.

— Pete's Street Beat, Vol. 2913. Kupperstein, Joel, ed. (Dr. Maggie's Phonics Readers Ser.). (Illus.). 16p. (J). 1999. pap. 2.99 *(1-57471-588-7)* Creat Teach Pr.

***Allen, Margaret.** Phonics Games Vol. 2954: 22 Reproducible Games for Playful Phonics Practice. Kupperstein, Joel, ed. (Dr. Maggie's Phonics Ser.). 48p. 1999. pap. text 5.98 *(1-57471-632-8,* 2954) Creat Teach Pr.

— Phonics Learning Centers Vol. 2956: 42 Independent Activities for Hands-On Phonics Review. Kupperstein, Joel, ed. (Dr. Maggie's Phonics Ser.). 48p. 1999. pap. text 5.98 *(1-57471-630-1,* 2956) Creat Teach Pr.

— Phonics Make & Take Activity Books Vol. 2955: 24 Mini-Books for Take-Home Phonics Fun. Kupperstein, Joel, ed. (Dr. Maggie's Phonics Ser.). 48p. 1999. pap. text 5.98 *(1-57471-631-X)* Creat Teach Pr.

Allen, Margaret. Pom - Pom's Big Win, No. 2904. Kupperstein, Joel, ed. (Dr. Maggie's Phonics Readers Ser.). (Illus.). 16p. (J). (ps-1). 1999. pap. 2.99 *(1-57471-564-X)* Creat Teach Pr.

— Pug's Hugs, No. 2905. Kupperstein, Joel, ed. (Dr. Maggie's Phonics Readers Ser.). (Illus.). 16p. (J). (ps-1). 1999. pap. 2.99 *(1-57471-565-8)* Creat Teach Pr.

— The Rainy Day Band, Vol. 2921. Kupperstein, Joel, ed. (Dr. Maggie's Phonics Readers Ser.). (Illus.). 16p. (J). 1999. pap. 2.99 *(1-57471-596-8)* Creat Teach Pr.

— Riddle & Rhyme with Apron Annie, Vol. 2924. Kuppastein, Joel, ed. (Dr. Maggie's Phonics Readers Ser.). (Illus.). 16p. (J). (ps-1). 1999. pap. 2.99 *(1-57471-599-2)* Creat Teach Pr.

— Sad Sam & Blue Sue, Vol. 2917. Kupperstein, Joel, ed. (Dr. Maggie's Phonics Readers Ser.). 16p. (J). 1999. pap. 2.99 *(1-57471-592-5)* Creat Teach Pr.

— Sing - Song Sid, No. 2909. Kupperstein, Joel, ed. (Dr. Maggie's Phonics Readers Ser.). (Illus.). 16p. (J). (ps-1). 1999. pap. 2.99 *(1-57471-584-4)* Creat Teach Pr.

— Sister of the Sky. 384p. 1999. mass mkt. 6.99 *(0-451-19040-8,* Onyx) NAL.

— Splish, Splash, Vol. 2919. Kupperstein, Joel, ed. (Dr. Maggie's Phonics Readers Ser.). (Illus.). 16p. (J). 1999. pap. 2.99 *(1-57471-594-1)* Creat Teach Pr.

— Top Job, Mom!, No. 2903. Kupperstein, Joel, ed. (Dr. Maggie's Phonics Readers Ser.). (Illus.). 16p. (J). (ps-1). 1999. pap. 2.99 *(1-57471-563-1)* Creat Teach Pr.

— Truck Tricks, Vol. 2911. Kupperstein, Joel, ed. (Dr. Maggie's Phonics Readers Ser.). (Illus.). 16p. (J). 1999. pap. 2.99 *(1-57471-586-0)* Creat Teach Pr.

— Twice As Nice, Vol. 2914. Kupperstein, Joel, ed. (Dr. Maggie's Phonics Readers Ser.). (Illus.). 16p. (J). 1999. pap. 2.99 *(1-57471-589-5)* Creat Teach Pr.

Allen, Margaret Day & Hamilton, Ladd. Lewiston Country: An Armchair History LC 90-60181. vi, 253p. 1990. write for info. *(0-9626050-0-X)* Nez Perce Cnty Hist Soc.

Allen, Margaret P. No Road Maps. LC 93-70617. 1993. 11.95 *(0-8158-0493-8)* Chris Mass.

— Ornament in Indian Architecture. LC 89-40766. (Illus.). 504p. 1992. 65.00 *(0-87413-399-8)* U Delaware Pr.

Allen, Margerie G. The Fire Inside. LC 96-78380. (Illus.). 133p. 1997. pap. 20.00 *(1-880994-43-7)* Mt Olive Coll Pr.

Allen, Marguerite De Huszar. The Faust Legend: Popular Formula & Modern Novel. (Germanic Studies in America: Vol. 53). 178p. (C). 1985. text 16.50 *(0-8204-0210-9)* P Lang Pubng.

Allen, Maria F. Portuguese in Three Months. LC 98-48003. (Hugo Ser.). 256p. 1999. pap. 14.95 *(0-7894-4429-1)* DK Pub Inc.

Allen, Maria Fernanda. Hugo Portuguese in Three Months: Simplified Language Course. LC 98-48003. (Hugo Ser.). (POR & ENG.). 1999. 29.95 *(0-7894-4438-0)* DK Pub Inc.

Allen, Marie & Marks, Shelly. Miscarriage: Women Sharing from the Heart. LC 92-22852. 272p. 1993. pap. 17.95 *(0-471-54834-0)* Wiley.

Allen, Marion, ed. Wills of the Archdeaconry of Suffolk, 1620-24. (Suffolk Records Society Ser.: No. 31). 1989. 45.00 *(0-85115-530-8)* Boydell & Brewer.

Allen, Marion E., ed. Wills of the Archdeaconry of Suffolk, 1625-6. (Suffolk Records Society Ser.: Vol. 37). (Illus.). 298p. (C). 1995. 45.00 *(0-85115-644-4)* Boydell & Brewer.

Allen, Marjorie N. Changes. 1995. 10.15 *(0-606-07358-2,* Pub. by Turtleback) Demco.

— 100 Years of Children's Books in America: Decade by Decade. LC 95-34104. 352p. 1996. 35.00 *(0-8160-3044-8)* Facts on File.

— What Are Little Girls Made Of? A Guide to Female Role Models in Children's Literature. LC 98-8148. 1999. 28.95 *(0-8160-3673-X,* Checkmark) Facts on File.

— What Are Little Girls Made Of? Guide to Female Role Models in Children's Books. LC 98-8148. (J). 1998. 15.95 *(0-8160-3694-2)* Facts on File.

Allen, Marjorie N. & Rotner, Shelley. Changes. LC 90-6601. (Illus.). 32p. (J). (ps-1). 1991. mass mkt. 14.00 *(0-02-700252-7,* Mac Bks Young Read) S&S Childrens.

Allen, Mark. Chrysalis: A Journey into the New Spiritual America. (Illus.). 180p. 1997. pap. 9.95 *(0-89496-011-3)* Ross Bks.

***Allen, Mark.** Healing One Day at a Time. 384p. 1999. pap. 9.95 *(2-921556-91-X,* Pub. by Modus Viv) ACCESS Pubs Network.

— Love One Day at a Time. 384p. 1998. pap. 9.95 *(2-921556-58-8)* Modus Viv.

— One Day at a Time, Box Set. 1152p. 1999. boxed set 19.95 *(2-921556-92-8,* Pub. by Modus Viv) ACCESS Pubs Network.

— Superiors 2: Pleasures of the Flesh. 144p. 2000. pap. 20.95 *(1-55634-422-8,* Pub. by S Jackson Games) BookWorld.

Allen, Mark & Babbitt, Bob. Mark Allen's Total Triathlete. (Illus.). 176p. (Orig.). 1988. pap. 12.95 *(0-8092-4589-2,* 458920, Contemporary Bks) NTC Contemp Pub Co.

Allen, Mark & Gonzalez, Jean. Working with DOS 5.0. 280p. 1993. pap. 44.67 *(0-13-962465-1)* P-H.

— Working with DOS 5.0. 1992. write for info. *(0-318-69571-5)* Prentice ESL.

— Working with Dos 6.0. 448p. 1994. pap. 43.33 *(0-13-101460-9)* P-H.

Allen, Mark, et al. Diagnostic Medical Sonography: Echocardiography. 2nd ed. LC 98-10883. 652p. 1998. text 110.00 *(0-397-55262-9)* Lppncott W & W.

— Workouts for Working People: How You Can Get in Great Shape While Staying Employed. LC 99-38824. 175p. 2000. pap. 19.95 *(0-375-75270-6)* Random.

Allen, Mark, jt. auth. see Fisher, John H.

Allen, Marlene B. Running with the Tide: Time, Like Tide, Will Not Wait for Dreams. LC 97-93345. (Illus.). 398p. 1998. pap. 16.95 *(0-9656839-0-7)* Gimcrack.

Allen, Marshall, et al. The Time Is at Hand: The Rosicrucian Nature of Goethe's Fairy Tale of the Green Snake & the Beautiful Lily & the Mystery Dramas of Rudolf Steiner. LC 95-46451. (Illus.). 192p. (Orig.). 1996. pap. 24.95 *(0-88010-400-7)* Anthroposophic.

Allen, Martha M. Georgetown's Yesteryears, IV: The Way It Was. LC 87-1196. (Georgetown's Yesteryears Sesquicentennial Ser.). (Illus.). xii, 133p. (Orig.). 1987. 20.00 *(0-936149-07-8)*; pap. 8.00 *(0-936149-06-X)* Georgetown Herit.

— Georgetown's Yesteryears, Vol. II: The People Remember. LC 85-24936. (Georgetown's Yesteryears Sesquicentennial Ser.). (Illus.). xvi, 158p. (Orig.). 1985. 20.00 *(0-936149-02-7)*; pap. 8.00 *(0-936149-01-9)* Georgetown Herit.

Allen, Martha M., ed. Georgetown's Yesteryears, III: A Special Place. LC 87-11986. (Georgetown's Yesteryears Sesquicentennial Ser.). (Illus.). xvi, 151p. 1987. 20.00 *(0-936149-05-1)*; pap. 8.00 *(0-936149-04-3)* Georgetown Herit.

Allen, Martha M., ed. Georgetown's Yesteryears, I: Reaching for the Gold Ring. (Georgetown's Yesteryears Sesquicentennial Ser.). (Illus.). 86p. (Orig.). 1985. pap. 5.00 *(0-936149-00-0)* Georgetown Herit.

Allen, Marty. Let's Play Ball. (Illus.). 32p. (J). (ps-6). 1999. text 14.99 *(0-9672972-0-6)* Kids Bks Pub.

Allen, Marva, ed. see Van Peebles, Melvin.

Allen, Marvin & Robinson, Jo. Angry Men, Passive Men: Understanding the Roots of Men's Anger & How to Move Beyond It. Orig. Title: In the Company of Men. 256p. 1994. reprint ed. pap. 11.00 *(0-449-90811-9,* Columbine) Fawcett.

Allen, Mary. Animals in American Literature. LC 82-17369. 224p. 1983. text 24.95 *(0-252-00975-4)* U of Ill Pr.

— The Necessary Blankness: Women in Major American Fiction of the Sixties. LC 75-38780. 226p. 1976. text 24.95 *(0-252-00519-8)* U of Ill Pr.

— The Rooms of Heaven: A Story of Love, Death, Grief & the Afterlife. LC 98-43129. 330p. 1999. 24.00 *(0-679-45460-8)* Knopf.

— The Rooms of Heaven: A Story of Love, Death, Grief & the Afterlife. 1999. pap. 13.00 *(0-679-77656-7)* Vin Bks.

Allen, Mary C., ed. Favorite Love Stories in Large Print. large type ed. (Anthologies Ser.). 400p. 1991. 23.95 *(0-8161-5002-8,* G K Hall Lrg Type) Mac Lib Ref.

— Great Ghost Stories in Large Print. large type ed. (General Ser.). 408p. 1988. lib. bdg. 21.95 *(0-8161-4423-0,* G K Hall Lrg Type) Mac Lib Ref.

Allen, Mary E. Tales of Adventure & Discovery. (Illus.). 80p. (Orig.). (J). (gr. 1-5). 1996. pap. 9.95 *(0-9651675-0-X)* MEA Prods.

— When We Become the Parent to Our Parents. (Illus.). 80p. 1998. pap. 9.95 *(0-9651675-1-8)* MEA Prods.

Allen, Mary J. Introduction to Psychological Research. LC 93-84981. 267p. (C). 1994. pap. text 32.50 *(0-87581-378-X,* IPR) F E Peacock Pubs.

Allen, Mary J. & Yen, Wendy M. Introduction to Measurement Theory. LC 78-25821. 810p. (C). 1979. mass mkt. 40.00 *(0-8185-0283-5)* Brooks-Cole.

Allen, Mary M., ed. see International Science & Technology, Inc. Staff.

Allen, Mary S. Pioneer Policewomen. Heyneman, Julie H., ed. LC 71-156001. reprint ed. 36.50 *(0-404-09100-8)* AMS Pr.

Allen, Matthew. Military Helicopter Doctrines of the Major Powers, 1945-1992: Making Decisions about Air-Land Warfare, 137. LC 92-30230. (Contributions in Military Studies Ser.: No. 137). 328p. 1993. 69.50 *(0-313-28522-5,* AMY, Greenwood Pr) Greenwood.

— Undermining the Japanese Miracle: Work & Conflict in a Japanese Coalmining Community. (Illus.). 308p. (C). 1994. text 59.95 *(0-521-45009-8)* Cambridge U Pr.

Allen, Matthew, jt. auth. see Borkowski, Gary L.

Allen, Maureen, et al. Primarily Bears: A Collection of Elementary Activities. (J). (gr. k-6). 1987. 16.95 *(1-881431-15-0,* 1207) AIMS Educ Fnd.

***Allen, Maury.** China Spy: The Story of Hugh Francis Redmond: His Country above All Else. Allen, Janet, ed. LC 97-95325. (Illus.). 188p. 1998. 19.95 *(0-9663322-0-2)* Gazette Pr.

— House of Heroes & Other Stories. 2000. text 24.95 *(0-312-26175-6)* St Martin.

Allen, Maury. Memories of the Mick. LC 96-54060. (Illus.). 208p. 1997. 29.95 *(0-87833-973-6)* Taylor Pub.

***Allen, Max.** Crush: The New Australian Wine Book. (Illus.). 240p. 2000. 30.00 *(1-84000-324-3,* Pub. by Mitchell Beazley) Antique Collect.

Allen, Max, et al. New World of Wine. (Illus.). 160p. 1998. 29.95 *(1-85732-520-6,* Pub. by Mitchell Beazley) Antique Collect.

Allen, Mayme & Kelsch, Janine. Challenging Word Games. LC 98-116197. (Illus.). 96p. 1997. pap. 5.95 *(0-8069-9854-7)* Sterling.

— 101 Word Games: A Wide Variety of Games for Puzzlers Who Love a Challenge. LC 90-19740. (Illus.). 128p. 1991. pap. 5.95 *(0-8069-8234-9)* Sterling.

Allen, Mckinley. How to Get into a Relationship & Keep the Fire Burning. 49p. (Orig.). (YA). (gr. 9 up). 1993. pap. 5.95 *(1-886415-06-4)* Special Books.

Allen-Meares, Paula. Social Work with Children & Adolescents. 1994. write for info. *(0-614-32039-9)* Longman.

— Social Work with Children & Adolescents. 352p. (C). 1995. pap. text 45.94 *(0-8013-0211-0)* Longman.

Allen-Meares, Paula & Shapiro, Constance H., eds. Adolescent Sexuality: New Challenges for Social Work. LC 89-1668. (Journal of Social Work & Human Sexuality: Vol. 8, No. 1). (Illus.). 178p. 1989. text 49.95 *(0-86656-901-4)* Haworth Pr.

Allen-Meares, Paula & Shore, David, eds. Adolescent Sexualities: Overviews & Principles of Intervention. LC 86-228200. (Journal of Social Work & Human Sexuality: Vol. 5, No. 1). 114p. 1986. text 49.95 *(0-86656-569-8)* Haworth Pr.

Allen-Meares, Paula, et al. Social Work Services in Schools. 3rd ed. LC 98-55957. 354p. (C). 1999. 54.00 *(0-205-29147-3,* Longwood Div) Allyn.

Allen, Melanie, jt. auth. see Fry, William F.

Allen, Merlin W. A Revision of the Marine Nematodes of the Superfamily Draconematoidea Filipjev, 1918 (Nematoda: Draconematina) LC 77-83108. (University of California Publications in Social Welfare: No. 109). (Illus.). 141p. reprint ed. pap. 43.80 *(0-608-10284-9,* 203157900075) Bks Demand.

***Allen, Merrill J.** Forensic Aspects of Vision & Highway Safety. 2nd ed. LC 00-35233. 2000. write for info. *(1-930056-03-6)* Lawyers & Judges.

Allen, Merrill J., et al. Forensic Aspects of Vision & Highway Safety. LC 96-46149. 475p. 1996. 75.00 *(0-913875-24-4,* 5244-N) Lawyers & Judges.

Allen-Mersh, T. G. Surgical Oncology. (Illus.). 480p. 1995. text 90.00 *(0-412-48940-6,* Pub. by E A) OUP.

***Allen-Meyer, Glenn.** Nameless Organizational Change: No-Hype, Low-Resistance Corporate Transformation. LC 99-91251. (Illus.). 224p. 2000. 24.95 *(0-9675079-0-1)* Talwood Craig Pubng.

Allen, Michael. The American Cocker Book. (Illus.). 528p. 1989. text 24.95 *(0-9623515-0-4)* Amer Cocker Mag.

— Anthropology of Nepal: People, Problems & Processes. 1994. pap. 128.00 *(0-7855-0407-9,* Pub. by Ratna Pustak Bhandar) St Mut.

***Allen, Michael.** Family Secrets: D.W. Griffith's Feature Films. 1999. 65.00 *(0-85170-744-0)* Ind U Pr.

Allen, Michael. Go on ... Dance! 133p. 1995. pap. 24.95 *(0-9649633-0-2)* Dbletime Pubns.

— How to Have It All. 427p. (Orig.). 1997. pap. 22.95 *(1-884350-58-5)* Alpha Pubng.

— How to Make It in Musicals: The Insider's Guide to a Career As a Singer-Dancer. LC 99-49420. (Illus.). 256p. 1999. pap. 18.95 *(0-8230-8815-4)* Watsn-Guptill.

— Proven Health Tips Encyclopedia. 433p. (Orig.). 1997. pap. 18.95 *(0-9638596-6-8)* Amer Pubng.

— Rodeo Cowboys in the North American Imagination. LC 98-22963. (History & Humanities Ser.). (Illus.). 248p. 1998. 29.95 *(0-87417-315-9)* U of Nev Pr.

***Allen, Michael.** Saints of the Church: A Teacher's Guide to the Vision Books. 144p. 2000. pap. 14.95 *(0-89870-783-8,* Pub. by Ignatius Pr) Midpt Trade.

Allen, Michael. Seamus Heaney. LC 96-27424. 224p. 1997. pap. 17.95 *(0-312-16503-X)* St Martin.

Allen, Michael, ed. Seamus Heaney. LC 96-27424. 224p. 1997. text 39.95 *(0-312-16502-1)* St Martin.

— The Web Journal of Current Legal Issues: 1995 Yearbook. 365p. 1995. pap. 74.00 *(1-85431-515-3,* Pub. by Blackstone Pr) Gaunt.

— The Web Journal of Current Legal Issues: 1996 Yearbook. 282p. 1997. pap. 80.00 *(1-85431-690-7,* Pub. by Blackstone Pr) Gaunt.

Allen, Michael & Thompson, Brian. Cases & Materials on Constitutional & Administrative Law. 4th ed. 765p. 1996. 44.00 *(1-85431-554-4,* Pub. by Blackstone Pr) Gaunt.

— Cases & Materials on Constitutional & Administrative Law. 5th ed. 827p. 1998. pap. 48.00 *(1-85431-846-2)* Gaunt.

Allen, Michael & Wilcox, Angela, eds. Critical Approaches to Anglo-Irish Literature. (Irish Literary Studies: No. 29). 1988. 59.00 *(0-389-20790-X,* N8348) B&N Imports.

Allen, Michael, et al. Cases & Materials on Constitutional & Administrative Law. 3rd ed. 704p. 1994. pap. 42.00 *(1-85431-328-2,* Pub. by Blackstone Pr) Gaunt.

Allen, Michael, ed. & illus. see Beauchamp, Richard G.

Allen, Michael, ed. & photos by see Allen, Thelma E.

Allen, Michael F. The Ecology of Mycorrhizae. (Cambridge Studies in Ecology). (Illus.). 196p. (C). 1991. pap. text 33.95 *(0-521-33553-1)* Cambridge U Pr.

Allen, Michael G. & Stevens, Robert L. Middle Grades Social Studies: Teaching & Learning for Active & Responsible Citizenship. 2nd ed. LC 97-15612. 180p. (C). 1997. pap. text 30.00 *(0-205-27118-9)* Allyn.

Allen, Michael I., tr. see Riche, Pierre.

Allen, Michael J. Nuptial Arithmetic: Marsilio Ficino's Commentary on the Fatal Number in Book VIII of Plato's Republic. LC 92-26074. 1994. 60.00 *(0-520-08143-9,* Pub. by U CA Pr) Cal Prin Full Svc.

— Textbook on Criminal Law. 3rd ed. 468p. 1993. 48.00 *(1-85431-447-5,* Pub. by Blackstone Pr) Gaunt.

A

— Textbook on Criminal Law. 4th ed. LC 98-132076. 457p. 1997. pap. 38.00 (*1-85431-655-9*, Pub. by Blackstone Pr) Gaunt.

*__Allen, Michael J.__ Textbook on Criminal Law. 5th ed. 479p. 1999. 31.00 (*1-85431-893-4*, Pub. by Blackstone Pr) Gaunt.

Allen, Michael J., ed. & tr. see Ficino, Marsilio.

Allen, Michael L., tr. see Galanin, M. D., ed.

Allen, Michael P. Understanding Regression Analysis. LC 97-20373. 228p. (C). 1997. 42.50 (*0-306-45648-6*, Plenum Trade) Perseus Pubng.

*__Allen, Michael S.__ Business Portfolio Management: Valuation, Risk Assessment & EVA Strategies. LC 99-46189. (Financial Management Ser.). 256p. 2000. 39.95 (*0-471-37640-X*) Wiley.

Allen, Michael S. Night Parents. (Cleveland Poets Ser.: No. 42). 28p. (Orig.). 1988. pap. 4.00 (*0-914946-64-1*) Cleveland St Univ Poetry Ctr.

Allen, Mike. Travelin' Light. LC 95-94875. (Orig.). pap. 10.00 (*0-9648689-0-3*) Lght Lines Pr.

Allen, Mike & Hodgkinson, Robert. Buying a Business. 2nd ed. 208p. 1989. lib. bdg. 98.00 (*1-85333-277-1*, Pub. by Graham & Trotman) Kluwer Academic.

Allen, Mike & Preiss, Raymond W., eds. Persuasion: Advances Through Meta-Analysis. LC 98-11061. (Communication Ser.). 304p. (C). 1998. pap. 26.50 (*1-57273-067-6*); text 62.50 (*1-57273-066-8*) Hampton Pr NJ.

Allen, Milton F. Acupinch Cramp Relief...in Seconds. (Illus.). 64p. 1981. pap. 1.95 (*0-9607456-0-2*) Acupinch.

Allen, Minerva & Allen, Kirkland. The Effectual Fervent Prayer. Coke, Andrea, ed. 95p. (Orig.). (YA). (gr. 10). 1997. pap. 8.95 (*1-889448-02-8*) NBN Publishers Group.

Allen, Miriam M., ed. Love, Groucho: Letters from Groucho Marx to His Daughter Miriam. unabridged ed. (Illus.). 241p. 1993. pap. 14.95 (*0-571-19809-0*) Faber & Faber.

Allen, Missy. Dangerous Insects. (Encyclopedia of Danger Ser.). (J). 1992. 15.15 (*0-606-05223-2*, Pub. by Turtleback) Demco.

*__Allen, Missy & Peissel, Michel.__ Dangerous Mammals: The Encyclopedia of Danger. (Illus.). 119p. (YA). (gr. 6-8). 2000. 20.00 (*0-7881-9239-6*) DIANE Pub.

Allen, Missy, jt. auth. see Peissel, Michel.

Allen, Mitch. Hands-On Java Beans. LC 97-66155. 480p. 1997. per. 40.00 (*0-7615-1047-8*) Prima Pub.

Allen, Mitch, jt. auth. see Kraut, Carolyn.

Allen, Mitchell, jt. auth. see Smedley, Christine S.

*__Allen-Morotz.__ Developmental Profiles: Pre-Birth Through Eight. 3rd ed. LC 98-26634. 208p. (C). 1998. pap. text 39.95 (*0-8273-8605-2*) Delmar.

Allen, Morse S. Satire of John Marston. LC 65-26460. (Studies in Drama: No. 39). 1969. reprint ed. lib. bdg. 75.00 (*0-8383-0500-8*) M S G Haskell Hse.

Allen Murphey, Edith Van, see Van Allen Murphey, Edith.

Allen, Murray E., ed. Musculoskeletal Pain Emanating from the Head & Neck: Current Concepts in Diagnosis, Management, & Cost Containment. LC 96-31753. (Journal of Musculoskeletal Pain: Vol. 4, No. 4). 202p. (C). 1996. 34.95 (*0-7890-0005-9*) Haworth Pr.

Allen, Myron B., III & Isaacson, Eli L. Numerical Analysis for Applied Science. LC 97-16688. (Pure & Applied Mathematics: A Wiley-Interscience Series of Texts, Monographs & Tracts). 492p. 1997. 84.95 (*0-471-55266-6*) Wiley.

Allen, Myrtle. The Ballymaloe Cookbook. (Illus.). 203p. (Orig.). 1984. reprint ed. pap. 17.95 (*0-7171-1339-6*, Pub. by Gill & MacMill) Irish Bks Media.

*__Allen, Myrtle.__ Myrtle Allen's Cooking at Ballymaloe House. 2000. 27.50 (*1-58479-042-3*) Stewart Tabori & Chang.

Allen, N., et al, eds. The City Gardener's Cookbook: Totally Fresh, Mostly Vegetarian, Decidedly Delicious Recipes from Seattle's P-Patches. LC 93-42640. (Illus.). 256p. (Orig.). 1994. pap. 14.95 (*0-912365-99-4*) Sasquatch Bks.

Allen, N. J., et al, eds. Oxford University Papers on India, Vol. 1, Pt. 1. (Illus.). 160p. 1987. 19.95 (*0-19-561860-2*) OUP.

Allen, N. J., et al. On Durkheim's Elementary Forms of Religious Life. LC 97-29595. (Studies in Social & Political Thought). 240p. (C). 1998. 85.00 (*0-415-16286-6*) Routledge.

Allen, N. J., jt. ed. see James, Wendy.

Allen, Nan & Allen, Dennis. Case of the Missing Christmas. (J). 1988. audio 10.99 (*0-685-68522-5*, TA-9095C) Lillenas.

— I.M.A.G.E. A Youth Musical about Who We Really Are. 1998. pap. 6.99 (*0-8341-9778-2*) Nazarene.

Allen, Nan, jt. auth. see Allen, Dennis.

Allen, Nancy. Fair Seafarer: A Honeymoon Adventure with the Merchant Marine. LC 97-22081. (Illus.). 224p. 1997. 21.95 (*1-882593-20-0*) Bridge Wrks.

— Homicide: Perspectives on Prevention. LC 79-11841. 192p. 1980. pap. text 18.95 (*0-87705-412-6*, Kluwer Acad Hman Sci) Kluwer Academic.

Allen, Nancy & Carringer, Robert. An Annotated Catalog of Unpublished Film & Television Scripts in the University of Illinois Library at Urban-Champaign. LC 83-5110. (Robert B. Downs Publication Fund: No. 7). 125p. 1983. pap. 10.00 (*0-87845-069-6*) U of Ill Grad Sch.

Allen, Nancy & Oldham, Lea Leever. Expand Your Time Use Potential. 1987. 2.00 (*0-942923-00-6*) NETWIC.

Allen, Nancy, ed. see Couch, Nena.

*__Allen, Nancy Campbell.__ Love Beyond Time: A Novel. LC 99-36448. 1999. pap. 12.95 (*1-57734-540-1*, 01114344) Covenant Comms.

— Sky Full of Ribbons: A Novel. LC 99-36448. 2000. write for info. (*1-57734-605-X*) Covenant Comms.

— A Time for the Heart. LC 00-43050. 2000. write for info. (*1-57734-678-5*) Covenant Comms.

*__Allen, Nancy L.__ NAEP 1996 Technical Report. 860p. 1999. per. 65.00 (*0-16-050094-X*) USGPO.

— Technical Report of the NAEP 1996 State Assessment Program in Mathematics. LC 97-212886. 538p. 1997. pap. 32.00 (*0-16-049225-4*) USGPO.

— Technical Report of the NAEP 1996 State Assessment Program in Science. LC 98-130274. 390p. 1998. pap. 22.00 (*0-16-049391-9*) USGPO.

Allen, Nancy M. Not So Trivial for Science & Social Studies. 200p. (Orig.). (J). (gr. 2). 1996. pap. 15.95 (*0-913956-95-3*) EBSCO.

— Not So Trivial for Science & Social Studies. 200p. (Orig.). (J). (gr. 3). 1996. pap. 15.95 (*0-913956-96-1*) EBSCO.

— Not So Trivial for Science & Social Studies. 400p. (Orig.). (J). (gr. 4). 1996. pap. 19.95 (*0-913956-97-X*) EBSCO.

— Not So Trivial for Science & Social Studies. 500p. (Orig.). (J). (gr. 5). 1996. pap. 19.95 (*0-913956-98-8*) EBSCO.

— Not So Trivial for Science & Social Studies. 600p. (Orig.). (J). (gr. 6). 1996. pap. 19.95 (*0-913956-99-6*) EBSCO.

— Word Force for Science & Social Studies. (Illus.). 171p. (Orig.). (J). (gr. 2). 1996. pap. 19.95 (*0-913956-90-2*) EBSCO.

— Word Force for Science & Social Studies. (Illus.). 153p. (Orig.). (J). (gr. 3). 1996. pap. 19.95 (*0-913956-91-0*) EBSCO.

— Word Force for Science & Social Studies. (Illus.). 188p. (Orig.). (J). (gr. 4). 1996. pap. 19.95 (*0-913956-92-9*) EBSCO.

— Word Force for Science & Social Studies. (Illus.). 198p. (Orig.). (J). (gr. 5). 1996. pap. 19.95 (*0-913956-93-7*) EBSCO.

— Word Force for Science & Social Studies. (Illus.). 233p. (Orig.). (J). (gr. 6). 1996. pap. 19.95 (*0-913956-94-5*) EBSCO.

Allen, Naomi, ed. see Trotsky, Leon.

Allen, Natalie J., jt. auth. see Meyer, John P.

Allen, Neal. Network Maintenance & Troubleshooting Guide. Good, Joan, ed. LC 97-60196. (Illus.). 176p. (Orig.). 1997. pap. text 29.95 (*0-9638650-1-3*) Fluke.

Allen, Ned B. Sources of John Dryden's Comedies. LC 67-21718. 316p. 1967. reprint ed. 60.00 (*0-87752-002-X*) Gordian.

Allen, Nick. Making Sense of the Children Act: A Guide for the Social & Welfare Services. LC 97-38899. 298p. 1998. pap. 54.95 (*0-471-97831-0*) Wiley.

Allen, Nick, et al, eds. Fundraising on the Internet: Recruiting & Renewing Donors Online. (Illus.). 168p. 1997. pap. 24.95 (*0-9624891-8-2*) Strathmoor Pr.

Allen, Nick & Allen, Rosie. 101 Ways to Your Wife's/Husband's Heart. 128p. 1995. pap. 5.99 (*0-7852-7788-9*) Nelson.

Allen, Noel L. North Carolina Unfair Business Practice. 702p. 95.00 (*0-327-01933-6*) LEXIS Pub.

Allen, Noel L. North Carolina Unfair Business Practice. LC 95-78586. 702p. 1995. 95.00 (*1-55834-250-8*, 60095, MICHIE) LEXIS Pub.

— North Carolina Unfair Business Practice, 1998 Cumulative Supplement. 200p. 1998. suppl. ed. 42.00 (*0-327-00397-9*, 6009612) LEXIS Pub.

Allen, Noris S. & Reese, William D. Calymperaceae, Leucophanaceae. (Flora Neotropica Monographs: No. 58-59). (Illus.). 113p. 1993. pap. 17.50 (*0-89327-372-4*) NY Botanical.

Allen, Norm R., Jr., ed. African-American Humanism: An Anthology. LC 91-3642. 286p. (Orig.). (C). 1991. pap. 20.95 (*0-87975-658-6*) Prometheus Bks.

Allen, Norma B., jt. auth. see Cooper, Patricia J.

Allen, Norman. Current Trends in Polymer Photochemistry. 400p. 1995. 120.00 (*0-13-138785-5*) P-H.

Allen, Norman, jt. auth. see Tellado, Marta L.

Allen, O. Jane & Deming, Lynn H., eds. Publications Management: Essays for Professional Communicators. LC 94-14936. (Baywood's Technical Communications Ser.). 258p. 1994. pap. 29.22 (*0-89503-164-7*); text 38.95 (*0-89503-163-9*) Baywood Pub.

Allen, O. N. & Allen, Ethel K. The Leguminosae: A Source Book of Characteristics, Uses & Nodulation. LC 80-5104. (Illus.). 878p. 1981. 75.00 (*0-299-08400-0*) U of Wis Pr.

Allen, O. P. Allen Memorial: Descendants of Samuel Allen of Windsor Ct., 1640-1907. (Illus.). 301p. 1990. reprint ed. pap. 39.50 (*0-8328-1433-4*); reprint ed. lib. bdg. 49.50 (*0-8328-1432-6*) Higginson Bk Co.

Allen, O. Wesley, Jr. Good News from Tinyville: Stories of Hope & Heart. LC 99-21268. 160p. 1999. pap. 14.99 (*0-8272-1242-9*, 984043, Pub. by Chalice Pr) Abingdon.

*__Allen, O. Wesley, Jr.__ Reading the Synoptic Gospels: Basic Methods for Interpreting Matthew, Mark & Luke. LC 99-49162. 160p. 2000. pap. 14.99 (*0-8272-3219-5*) Chalice Pr.

*__Allen, Oliver E.__ Tales of Old Tribeca: An Illustrated History of New York's Triangle Below Canal. Glassman, Carl, ed. (Illus.). 128p. 1999. 28.95 (*0-9674336-0-6*) Tribeca Trib Inc.

Allen, Oliver E. The Tiger: The Rise & Fall of Tammany Hall. (Illus.). 1993. 24.95 (*0-201-62463-X*) Addison-Wesley.

Allen, Oliver E. & Bubel, Nancy. Step-by-Step Gardening Techniques Illustrated. LC 95-22047. (Illus.). 224p. (Orig.). 1996. 22.95 (*0-88266-912-5*, 912-5, Garden Way Pub) Storey Bks.

Allen, Ollie J. "Jim" Allen: His Memoirs. LC 97-77477. (Illus.). xviii, 68p. 1998. pap. 9.95 (*1-56167-398-6*) Am Literary Pr.

Allen, Orphia J. Barbara Pym: Writing a Life. LC 94-18867. 1994. 37.00 (*0-8108-2875-8*) Scarecrow.

Allen, Orrin P. Descendants of Nicholas Cady, of Watertown, Mass., 1645-1910. (Illus.). 546p. 1989. reprint ed. pap. 69.50 (*0-8328-0361-8*); reprint ed. lib. bdg. 79.50 (*0-8328-0360-X*) Higginson Bk Co.

Allen, Owen. The Effective Manager: Handling Change & Priorities the Specific Action Way. LC 87-63534. (Illus.). 110p. (C). 1988. text 25.00 (*0-932569-02-1*) Specific Action.

— Management Power the Specific Action Way: A Short Course in Management Logic. LC 84-52618. (Illus.). 112p. (C). 1988. reprint ed. text 25.00 (*0-932569-00-5*) Specific Action.

— Personality Power the Specific Action Way: A Complete Course in Management Styles. LC 87-63535. (Illus.). 110p. (C). 1988. text 25.00 (*0-932569-01-3*) Specific Action.

Allen, P. A. Earth Surface Processes. LC 96-39095. (Illus.). 448p. 1997. pap. 57.00 (*0-632-03507-2*) Blackwell Sci.

Allen, P. G., et al. Bioeconomics of Aquaculture. (Developments in Aquaculture & Fisheries Science Ser.: Vol. 13). 352p. 1984. 201.50 (*0-444-42301-X*, I-102-84) Elsevier.

Allen, P. S. The Age of Erasmus: Lectures Delivered in the Universities of Oxford & London. 303p. 1997. pap. 25.00 (*1-57910-084-8*) Wipf & Stock.

— Erasmus' Services to Learning. 1974. lib. bdg. 59.95 (*0-8490-0123-4*) Gordon Pr.

— Erasmus' Services to Learning. (Studies in Philosophy: No. 40). 1972. reprint ed. pap. 39.95 (*0-8383-0111-8*) M S G Haskell Hse.

Allen, P. S., ed. see Erasmus, Desiderius.

Allen, Pamela. Belinda. LC 93-168286. 1996. 10.19 (*0-606-09064-9*, Pub. by Turtleback) Demco.

Allen, Pamela. Free Space: A Perspective on the Small Group in Women's Liberation. LC 72-49893. (Illus.). 64p. (Orig.). 1970. pap. 4.25 (*0-87810-006-7*) Times Change.

Allen, Pamela. Who Sank the Boat? LC 82-19832. 1996. 11.44 (*0-606-10067-9*) Turtleback.

Allen, Pat & DeRuiter, Gerald L. Backpacking in Michigan. 2nd ed. LC 88-27753. (Illus.). 200p. 1989. pap. 17.95 (*0-472-06386-3*, 06386) U of Mich Pr.

Allen, Pat, ed. see Gale, Jack L.

Allen, Pat B. Art Is a Way of Knowing. 1995. pap. 15.00 (*1-57062-078-4*, Pub. by Shambhala Pubns) Random.

Allen, Patricia. Among the Heavens: The Human Side of Spaceflight. (Illus.). 200p. (Orig.). 1989. write for info. (*0-9622456-0-7*, 001); pap. write for info. (*0-9622456-1-5*) HFSI Inc.

— Food for the Future: Conditions & Contradictions of Sustainability. 344p. (Orig.). 1993. pap. 90.00 (*0-471-58082-1*) Wiley.

Allen, Patricia. Metepenagiag: New Brunswick's Oldest Village. (Illus.). 41p. 1994. pap. 9.95 (*0-86492-139-X*, Pub. by Goose Ln Edits) Genl Dist Srvs.

Allen, Patricia & Harmon, Sandra. Getting to 'i Do' 272p. 1995. pap. 12.50 (*0-380-71815-4*, Avon Bks) Morrow Avon.

— Staying Married . . . And Loving It! How to Get What You Want from Your Man Without Asking. LC 96-53066. 272p. 1997. 23.00 (*0-688-05291-6*, Wm Morrow) Morrow Avon.

Allen, Patrick. Romantic Georgia: More Than 300 Things to Do for Southern Lovers. 160p. 1999. pap. 10.95 (*1-892514-13-3*) Hill St Pr.

*__Allen, Patrick.__ Special Operations Aviation: The Men & Machines of the Elite Units. LC 99-30754. (Illus.). 128p. 1999. pap. 26.95 (*0-7603-0763-6*, Pub. by MBI Pubg) Motorbooks Intl.

Allen, Patrick, ed. Literary Nashville. LC 99-37701. 320p. 1999. pap. 16.95 (*1-892514-11-7*) Hill St Pr.

— Literary Savannah. 296p. 1998. pap. 16.95 (*1-892514-01-X*) Hill St Pr.

*__Allen, Patrick, ed.__ Literary Washington, D. C. LC 99-88137. 320p. 2000. pap. 16.95 (*1-892514-63-X*) Hill St Pr.

Allen, Patrick, jt. auth. see Weaver, Dexter.

Allen, Patrick, jt. ed. see Long, Judy.

Allen, Patrick, ed. see Stern, H. H.

Allen, Patrick D. Modeling Global Positioning System Effects in the TLC/NLC Model. LC 94-20919. 1994. pap. 13.00 (*0-8330-1559-1*, MR-393-AF/A) Rand Corp.

Allen, Patrick D. & Noehrenberg, Peter C. U. S. Dependence on Strategic Materials from Southern African Nations. LC 92-15871. 1992. pap. 7.50 (*0-8330-1252-5*, R-4165-OSD) Rand Corp.

Allen, Patsy, jt. auth. see Allen, Tom.

Allen, Paul. American Crawl. LC 96-49504. 73p. (Orig.). 1997. pap. 10.95 (*1-57441-027-X*) UNTX Pr.

— A History of the American Revolution, 2 vols., Vol. 1. LC 72-10761. (American Revolutionary Ser.). 612p. reprint ed. lib. bdg. 58.00 (*0-8290-0369-X*) Irvington.

— A History of the American Revolution, 2 vols., Vol. 2. LC 72-10761. (American Revolutionary Ser.). 528p. reprint ed. lib. bdg. 58.00 (*0-686-96756-9*) Irvington.

— The Life of Charles Brockden Brown. LC 75-25800. 424p. 1975. lib. bdg. 75.00 (*0-8201-1160-0*) Schol Facsimiles.

*__Allen, Paul.__ Realizing Ebusiness with Components. 336p. 2000. pap. text 39.95 (*0-201-67520-X*) Addison-Wesley.

Allen, Paul. The Works of Paul Allen, 1775-1826, Set. 1987. reprint ed. lib. bdg. 500.00 (*0-685-18587-7*) Rprt Serv.

Allen, Paul & Frost, Stuart. Component-Based Development for Enterprise System: Applying the Select Perspective. LC 98-138007. (Managing Object Technology Ser.: Vol. 12). 496p. 1998. pap. text 44.95 (*0-521-64999-4*) Cambridge U Pr.

*__Allen, Paul C.__ Philip III & the Pax Hispanica, 1598-1621: The Failure of Grand Strategy. LC 99-40557. (Historical Publications). (Illus.). 333p. 2000. 35.00 (*0-300-07682-7*) Yale U Pr.

Allen, Paul H. Reengineering the Bank: A Blueprint for Survival & Success. LC 94-205311. 225p. 1994. text 40.00 (*1-55738-715-X*, Irwn Prfssnl) McGraw-Hill Prof.

— Reengineering the Bank: A Blueprint for Survival & Success. LC 97-1289. 240p. 1997. per. 24.95 (*0-7863-1111-8*, Irwn Prfssnl) McGraw-Hill Prof.

Allen, Paul M. Vladimir Soloviev: Russian Mystic. LC 72-81592. (Illus.). 544p. 1978. lib. bdg. 15.95 (*0-8334-0709-0*, Spir Sci Lib) Garber Comm.

Allen, Paul M. & Allen, Joan D. Fingal's Cave, the Poems of Ossian & Celtic Christianity. LC 94-43197. (Illus.). 252p. 1999. 24.95 (*0-8264-1144-4*) Continuum.

*__Allen, Paul M. & Allen, Joan D.__ Francis of Assisi's Canticle of the Creatures: A Modern Spiritual Path. (Illus.). 1999. pap. 14.95 (*0-8264-1185-1*) Continuum.

Allen, Paul M. & Merezhkovsky, Dmitri S. Atlantis-Europe: The Secret of the West. LC 71-157506. 456p. 1989. reprint ed. pap. 16.95 (*0-89345-243-2*, Steinerbks) Garber Comm.

Allen, Paul M. & Ris Allen, Joan de. Francis of Assisi's Canticle of the Creatures: A New Spiritual Path. (Illus.). 120p. 1996. 18.95 (*0-8264-0876-1*) Continuum.

Allen, Paul M., jt. auth. see LePlongeon, Augustus.

Allen, Paul M., jt. auth. see Steiner, Rudolf.

Allen, Paul M., ed. see Steiner, Rudolf.

Allen, Paul R. Informix: Client/Server Application Development. LC 96-47947. (McGraw Hill Series on Client/Server Computing). (Illus.). 576p. 1996. pap. 49.95 (*0-07-913056-9*) McGraw.

Allen, Paul R. & Bambara, Joseph. Informix Universal Data Option. LC 98-17832. 853p. 1998. pap. 59.99 (*0-07-913697-4*) McGraw.

Allen, Paul R., et al. Informix: Client/Server Application Development. (Illus.). 452p. 1997. pap. text 45.00 (*0-07-005996-9*) McGraw.

Allen, Paula. Social Work Practice with Children & Adolescents. (C). 1995. pap. text. write for info. (*0-8013-1477-1*) Addison-Wesley.

Allen, Paula, et al. Columbus & Beyond: Views from Native Americans. Jorgen, Randolph, ed. LC 91-67396. (Orig.). 1992. pap. 7.95 (*1-877856-06-1*) SW Pks Mnmts.

Allen, Paula Gunn. Grandmothers of the Light: A Medicine Woman's Sourcebook. (Illus.). 272p. 1992. pap. 14.00 (*0-8070-8103-5*) Beacon Pr.

— Life Is a Fatal Disease: Selected Poems, 1964-94. 224p. (Orig.). 1997. pap. 16.95 (*0-931122-85-6*) West End.

— Off the Reservation: Reflections on Boundary-Busting, Border-Crossing Loose Cannons. Hooks, Tisha, ed. LC 98-21247. 272p. 1998. 25.00 (*0-8070-4640-X*) Beacon Pr.

— Off the Reservation: Reflections on Boundary-Busting, Border-Crossing Loose Canons. LC 98-21247. 272p. 1999. pap. 17.00 (*0-8070-4641-8*) Beacon Pr.

— The Sacred Hoop: Recovering the Feminine in American Indian Traditions. rev. ed. LC 92-6332. 336p. 1992. pap. 15.00 (*0-8070-4617-5*) Beacon Pr.

— Skins & Bones. 69p. (Orig.). 1988. pap. 8.95 (*0-931122-50-3*) West End.

— The Woman Who Owned the Shadows. LC 94-5839. 225p. (Orig.). 1983. pap. 10.95 (*1-879960-18-4*) Aunt Lute Bks.

Allen, Paula Gunn, ed. Song of the Turtle: American Indian Literature, 1974-1994. 1996. 25.00 (*0-614-96849-6*) One Wrld.

— The Song of the Turtle Vol. 2: American Indian Literature, 1974-1994. 352p. 1996. 25.00 (*0-345-37525-4*) One Wrld.

— Spider Woman's Granddaughters: Traditional Tales & Contemporary Writing by Native American Women. 256p. 1990. pap. 12.50 (*0-449-90508-X*, Columbine) Fawcett.

— Studies in American Indian Literature: Critical Essays & Course Designs. LC 82-12516. (MLA Commission on the Literatures & Languages of America Ser.). xiv, 384p. 1983. pap. 19.75 (*0-87352-355-5*, B104P) Modern Lang.

Allen, Paula Gunn & Smith, Patricia C. As Long as the Rivers Flow: The Stories of Nine Native Americans. LC 95-47642. 176p. (J). (gr. 4-7). 1996. 15.95 (*0-590-47869-9*) Scholastic Inc.

Allen, Paula Gunn, ed. see Dunn, Carolyn.

*__Allen, Paula Smith.__ Metamorphosis & the Emergence of the Feminine: A Motif of "Difference" in Women's Writing. LC 98-30528. (Studies on Themes & Motifs in Literature: Vol. 45). 192p. 1999. 46.95 (*0-8204-4122-8*) P Lang Pubng.

Allen, Pauline, jt. auth. see Mayer, Wendy.

Allen, Pauline, tr. see Grillmeier, Aloys & Hainthaler, Theresia.

Allen, Penelope J. Leaves from the Family Tree. 372p. 1982. 45.00 (*0-89308-227-9*) Southern Hist Pr.

— Tennessee Soldiers in the Revolution: A Roster of Soldiers Living During the Revolutionary War in the Counties of Washington & Sullivan. LC 75-970. 71p. 1996. reprint ed. pap. 7.50 (*0-8063-0666-1*) Genealog Pub.

Allen, Penny. The Face of the Deep: Healing Body & Soul. (Illus.). 1998. pap. 19.95 (*1-86163-040-9*) Holmes Pub.

*__Allen, Peter.__ Bunnies, Crocodiles & Me: Stories of Baby Beginnings. Bonfante-Warren, Alexandra, tr. LC 99-72238. (Illus.). 78p. (J). (gr. 2 up). 1999. 14.95 (*0-8109-4105-8*, Pub. by Abrams) Time Warner.

— Interesting Times: Life in Uganda under Idi Amin. (Illus.). 568p. 2000. 34.95 (*1-85776-468-4*, Pub. by Book Guild Ltd) Trans-Atl Phila.

Allen, Peter. Small & Medium-Sized Restaurant Chains. 250p. 1987. 1250.00 (*0-941285-10-3*) FIND-SVP.

— Understanding Ear Infections. (Illus.). 28p. (C). 1993. reprint ed. pap. 24.95 (*0-9622326-1-0*) The Davis Ctr.

An Asterisk (*) at the beginning of an entry indicates that the title is appearing for the first time.

Allen, Peter, ed. The Affluent Market. 2nd ed. 250p. 1987. pap. 995.00 (*0-941285-00-6*) FIND-SVP.
— Ambulatory Care Clinics. 200p. 1989. pap. 1495.00 (*0-941285-42-1*) FIND-SVP.
— Animal Health Products. 1989. pap. 995.00 (*0-317-01801-9*) FIND-SVP.
— Artificial Intelligence: A Market Assessment. 200p. 1984. pap. 1250.00 (*0-931634-44-X*) FIND-SVP.
— The Automotive Aftermarket. 250p. 1987. 995.00 (*0-317-66677-0*) FIND-SVP.
— Bottled Water Market. 204p. 1988. pap. 1295.00 (*0-941285-39-1*) FIND-SVP.
— Breakfast Breads. 200p. 1989. pap. 1295.00 (*0-941285-45-6*) FIND-SVP.
— Cardiovascular Therapy & Drug Market. 300p. 1988. pap. 1495.00 (*0-941285-38-3*) FIND-SVP.
— The Changing Pasta Market. 2nd ed. 218p. 1983. pap. 985.00 (*0-931634-32-6*) FIND-SVP.
— The Cheese Market. 245p. 1985. pap. text 295.00 (*0-931634-55-5*) FIND-SVP.
— The Cheese Market. 246p. 1988. pap. 1295.00 (*0-941285-36-7*) FIND-SVP.
— Conductive Plastics. 240p. 1984. pap. 295.00 (*0-931634-43-1*) FIND-SVP.
— The Cracker Market. 100p. 1989. pap. 795.00 (*0-318-41828-2*) FIND-SVP.
— Diagnosis Related Groups. 200p. 1984. pap. 995.00 (*0-931634-38-5*) FIND-SVP.
— Electronic Data Interchange in the Healthcare Industry. 150p. 1989. pap. 995.00 (*0-317-01804-3*) FIND-SVP.
— Emerging Trends in Physician's Office Diagnostic Testing. 150p. 1985. pap. text 1475.00 (*0-931634-61-X*) FIND-SVP.
— The Factory Automation Industry. 2nd ed. 250p. 1987. pap. text 1750.00 (*0-941285-06-5*) FIND-SVP.
— The Fascimile Market. 200p. 1987. 1450.00 (*0-941285-12-X*) FIND-SVP.
— Free-Standing & Office-Based Ambulatory Care: Surgicenters, Emergency Clinics, Occupational Clinics, & Office-Based Surgery. 2nd ed. 208p. 1984. pap. 795.00 (*0-931634-33-4*) FIND-SVP.
— Fresh Produce: High Margin Opportunities in a Dynamic Market. 280p. 1987. pap. 1250.00 (*0-318-23703-2*) FIND-SVP.
— Frozen Novelties. 300p. 1987. pap. 1250.00 (*0-941285-02-2*) FIND-SVP.
— Fruit Juices. 135p. 1989. pap. 1950.00 (*0-317-01802-7*) FIND-SVP.
— Hazardous Waste Market. 2nd ed. 250p. 1986. pap. 995.00 (*0-931634-72-5*) FIND-SVP.
— Healthy Snacks. 200p. 1987. pap. 1250.00 (*0-941285-11-1*) FIND-SVP.
— High Technology Industrial Ceramics: 1987 Edition. 480p. 1987. 1450.00 (*0-317-66676-2*) FIND-SVP.
— The Home Do-It-Yourself Market. 200p. 1988. 995.00 (*0-941285-16-2*) FIND-SVP.
— Home Health Care Products & Services, 1987. 500p. 1987. pap. 1475.00 (*0-941285-03-0*) FIND-SVP.
— The Ice Cream Market. 223p. 1988. 1295.00 (*0-941285-20-0*) FIND-SVP.
— Imported Beer Market. (Illus.). 242p. 1985. pap. 295.00 (*0-931634-57-1*) FIND-SVP.
— The Imported Beer Market: Strategic Issues. 188p. (Orig.). 1982. pap. 225.00 (*0-931634-19-9*) FIND-SVP.
— Integration of the Home Audio & Video Equipment Industries. 300p. 1985. pap. text 295.00 (*0-931634-58-X*) FIND-SVP.
— The Long-Term Care Industry. 200p. 1989. pap. 1795.00 (*0-317-01805-1*) FIND-SVP.
— The Market for Children's Toys & Games. 222p. 1985. pap. 295.00 (*0-931634-49-0*) FIND-SVP.
— The Market for Collectible Dolls. 248p. 1985. pap. text 295.00 (*0-931634-53-9*) FIND-SVP.
— The Market for Fresh Produce. 200p. 1989. pap. 1295.00 (*0-318-41824-X*) FIND-SVP.
— The Market for Fruit & Vegetable Juices. 340p. 1986. pap. text 1250.00 (*0-318-18886-4*) FIND-SVP.
— Market for Gourmet Coffees & Teas. 157p. 1988. pap. 495.00 (*0-941285-33-2*) FIND-SVP.
— The Market for Home Textiles. 100p. 1989. pap. 695.00 (*0-317-01800-0*) FIND-SVP.
— Market for Industrial Adhesives. 193p. 1988. 1795.00 (*0-941285-35-9*) FIND-SVP.
— The Market for Lasers in Medicine. 239p. 1989. pap. 1495.00 (*0-941285-49-9*) FIND-SVP.
— The Market for Lifestyle & Ready-to-Assemble Furniture. 125p. 1989. pap. 695.00 (*0-941285-47-2*) FIND-SVP.
— The Market for Office Furniture & Equipment. 200p. 1989. pap. 1495.00 (*0-318-41825-8*) FIND-SVP.
— The Market for Physical Fitness & Exercise Equipment. 250p. 1987. pap. 1250.00 (*0-931634-74-1*) FIND-SVP.
— The Market for Rugs & Carpeting. 120p. 1989. pap. 695.00 (*0-941285-58-8*) FIND-SVP.
— The Market for Salted Snacks. 200p. 1987. pap. 1250.00 (*0-941285-04-9*) FIND-SVP.
— Markets & Innovations in Wound Care. 200p. 1989. pap. 1795.00 (*0-318-41827-4*) FIND-SVP.
— Markets for Home Security & Energy Management Systems. 158p. 1988. 1495.00 (*0-941285-34-0*) FIND-SVP.
— The Maturity Market. 222p. 1988. pap. 995.00 (*0-941285-28-6*) FIND-SVP.
— The Maturity Market: Americans 55 & Over. 200p. 1985. pap. 995.00 (*0-931634-47-4*) FIND-SVP.
— Medical Prosthetic Devices & Artificial Organs. 279p. 1983. pap. 295.00 (*0-931634-35-0*) FIND-SVP.
— Men's Grooming Market. 220p. 1987. pap. 995.00 (*0-941285-08-1*) FIND-SVP.
— Meter Reading Equipment. 200p. 1988. pap. 1795.00 (*0-941285-25-1*) FIND-SVP.
— Microcomputer Software Distribution. 180p. 1984. pap. 295.00 (*0-931634-34-2*) FIND-SVP.
— The Microwave Cooking Market. 200p. 1986. pap. 1250.00 (*0-931634-67-9*) FIND-SVP.
— Microwaveable Foods Market. 188p. 1988. pap. 1295.00 (*0-941285-31-6*) FIND-SVP.
— Monoclonal Antibodies. 300p. 1988. pap. 1795.00 (*0-941285-26-X*) FIND-SVP.
— The Motion Picture Industry. 200p. 1982. pap. 985.00 (*0-931634-24-5*) FIND-SVP.
— Municipal Waste. 1989. pap. 1795.00 (*0-317-01803-5*) FIND-SVP.
— The New Baby Boom. 234p. 1988. 995.00 (*0-941285-21-9*) FIND-SVP.
— Non-Store Retailing. 250p. 1989. pap. 1495.00 (*0-941285-50-2*) FIND-SVP.
— The Noninstitutional Senior Market for Healthcare Products & Services. 2nd ed. 250p. 1984. pap. 295.00 (*0-931634-46-6*) FIND-SVP.
— Office Supplies Market. 200p. 1989. pap. 995.00 (*0-941285-53-7*) FIND-SVP.
— Pasta Market. 198p. 1988. pap. 1295.00 (*0-941285-40-5*) FIND-SVP.
— Personal Care Appliances. 200p. 1988. pap. 1295.00 (*0-941285-32-4*) FIND-SVP.
— Premium Adult Desserts. 250p. 1988. 1295.00 (*0-941285-18-9*) FIND-SVP.
— Prepared Frozen Foods. 232p. 1987. pap. 1250.00 (*0-941285-05-7*) FIND-SVP.
— Processed Foods Packaging. 200p. 1986. pap. 985.00 (*0-685-09455-3*) FIND-SVP.
— The Retail Banking Revolution. 200p. 1985. pap. text 295.00 (*0-931634-60-1*) FIND-SVP.
— A Review of Pediatric Over-the-Counter Drugs. 25p. 1989. pap. 250.00 (*0-941285-41-3*) FIND-SVP.
— The Roofing Industry. 314p. 1982. pap. 295.00 (*0-931634-23-7*) FIND-SVP.
— RX & OTC Cough & Cold Products. 206p. 1985. pap. text 2955.00 (*0-931634-51-2*) FIND-SVP.
— The Sauces & Gravies Market. 200p. 1988. 995.00 (*0-941285-19-7*) FIND-SVP.
— The Semiconductor Industry. 310p. 1984. pap. 295.00 (*0-931634-40-7*) FIND-SVP.
— Shelf-Stable & Refrigerated Microwaveable Meals. 149p. 1988. pap. 795.00 (*0-941285-37-5*) FIND-SVP.
— The Small Appliance Industry. 400p. (Orig.). 1983. pap. 295.00 (*0-931634-30-X*) FIND-SVP.
— Specialty Retailing: Markets & Strategies for the 1990s. 250p. 1987. 995.00 (*0-941285-15-4*) FIND-SVP.
— The Status of Aquaculture in the U. S. 300p. (Orig.). 1981. pap. 795.00 (*0-931634-21-0*) FIND-SVP.
— Superalloys. 295p. 1984. pap. 295.00 (*0-931634-37-7*) FIND-SVP.
— The Superpremium Ice Cream Market. 270p. 1989. pap. 1295.00 (*0-941285-44-8*) FIND-SVP.
— Time-Temperature Indicators. 200p. 1988. 1750.00 (*0-941285-17-0*) FIND-SVP.
— Tofu Consumer Awareness & Purchasing Patterns. 87p. (Orig.). 1981. pap. 750.00 (*0-931634-20-2*) FIND-SVP.
— The U. S. Bottled Water Market. 3rd ed. 300p. 1986. pap. 1250.00 (*0-931634-31-8*) FIND-SVP.
— The U. S. Fish Industry. 299p. (Orig.). 1982. pap. 1095.00 (*0-931634-22-9*) FIND-SVP.
— The U. S. Hispanic Market. 260p. 1984. pap. 295.00 (*0-931634-48-2*) FIND-SVP.
— Water Pollution Control Equipment & Services. 228p. 1989. pap. 1795.00 (*0-941285-51-0*) FIND-SVP.
— The Water Purification Market. 300p. 1987. pap. 1250.00 (*0-941285-09-X*) FIND-SVP.
— The Wine Cooler Market. 200p. 1985. pap. text 295.00 (*0-931634-18-0*) FIND-SVP.
— The World Market for High Technology Industrial Ceramics. 351p. 1985. pap. 295.00 (*0-931634-29-6*) FIND-SVP.
— Yogurt Market. 100p. 1989. pap. 795.00 (*0-941285-43-X*) FIND-SVP.

Allen, Peter J. & Davies, Stan. International Directory of Man-Made Fibre Producers: Europe, North America, Japan. 120p. (C). 1991. text 90.00 (*1-870812-36-0*, Pub. by Textile Inst) St Mut.

Allen, Peter K. Robotic Object Recognition Using Vision & Touch. (C). 1987. text 84.00 (*0-89838-245-9*) Kluwer Academic.

Allen, Peter L. The Art of Love: Amatory Fiction from Ovid to the Romance of the Rose. LC 92-21610. (Middle Ages Ser.). 200p. (C). 1992. text 27.95 (*0-8122-3188-0*) U of Pa Pr.

***Allen, Peter Lewis.** The Wages of Sin: Sex & Disease, Past & Present. LC 99-48603. (Illus.). 200p. 2000. 25.00 (*0-226-01460-6*) U Ch Pr.

Allen, Peter M. Cities & Regions As Self-Organizing Systems: Model of Complexity, Vol. 1. (Environmental Problems & Social Dynamics Ser.). 267p. 1997. text 59.00 (*90-5699-070-5*); pap. text 23.00 (*90-5699-071-3*) Gordon & Breach.
— Vladimir Soloviev: Russian Mystic. LC 72-81592. (Illus.). 544p. 1978. pap. 10.95 (*0-8334-1750-9*, Steinerbks) Garber Comm.

Allen Petrick, Jane. Beyond Time Management: Life Balancing Connections. 2nd ed. LC 98-87566. 100p. 1998. pap. 14.95 (*0-9664670-2-7*) ID Publ.

Allen, Petula, jt. auth. see Slater, Ann.

Allen, Philip. Electronics. (C). 1996. text. write for info. (*0-201-51528-8*) Addison-Wesley.

Allen, Philip A. & Bashore, Theodore R., eds. Age Differences in Word & Language Processing. LC 95-30483. (Advances in Psychology Ser.: Vol. 110). 466p. 1995. 152.50 (*0-444-81766-2*) Elsevier.

Allen, Phillip. The Atlas of Atlases: The Map Maker's Vision of the World. (Illus.). 160p. 1992. 60.00 (*0-8109-3918-5*) Abrams.

Allen, Phillip E. & Holberg, Douglas R. CMOS Analog Circuit Design. (Oxford Series in Electrical & Computer Engineering). (Illus.). 720p. 1996. text 89.95 (*0-19-510720-9*) OUP.

Allen, Phyllis, jt. auth. see Mullins, William.

Allen, Phyllis Sloan, et al. Beginnings of Interior Environment. 8th ed. LC 99-36535. (Illus.). 385p. (C). 1999. 64.00 (*0-13-083290-1*) P-H.

Allen, Phyllis W., jt. auth. see Britts, Maurice W.

Allen, Pinney L., et al. Georgia Limited Liability Company Forms & Practice Manual. LC 95-31404. 504p. 1995. ring bd. 219.90 (*1-57400-005-5*) Data Trace Pubng.

Allen, Pokey. Pokey: The Good Fight. LC 97-71515. (Illus.). 200p. 1997. pap. 14.95 (*0-9658911-0-0*) Bootleg Bks.

Allen, Polly R. The ECU: Birth of a New Currency. (Occasional Paper Ser.: No. 20). 67p. 1986. pap. 10.00 (*1-56708-019-7*) Grp of Thirty.

Allen, Polly Reynolds, jt. auth. see Stein, Jerome L.

Allen, Polly W. Building Domestic Liberty: Charlotte Perkins Gilman's Architectural Feminism. LC 87-35311. (Illus.). 208p. (C). 1988. pap. 16.95 (*0-87023-628-8*) U of Mass Pr.

Allen, Prudence. The Concept of Woman: The Aristotelian Revolution, 750 B. C.-A. D. 1250. LC 96-9102. 637p. 1997. pap. 35.00 (*0-8028-4270-4*) Eerdmans.

Allen, R. Praise: A Matter of Life & Breath. Chan, Silas, tr. (CHI.). 204p. 1982. pap. write for info. (*0-941598-04-7*) Living Spring Pubns.

Allen, R. & Kuh. Constitutional Criminal Procedure. 2nd ed. 1991. 51.00 (*0-316-03398-7*, Aspen Law & Bus) Aspen Pub.

Allen, R., et al. Voices of the Americas: Traditional Music & Dance from North, South, & Central America, & the Caribbean. Allen, Ray, ed. LC 87-51358. (Orig.). (C). 1988. pap. 5.00 (*0-945017-00-6*) World Mus Inst.

Allen, R. A., jt. auth. see Grace, J.

Allen, R. C. How to Build a Fortune in Commodities. 1983. 25.00 (*0-930233-12-3*) Windsor.
— The Professional Trading System. (Illus.). 97p. 1982. pap. 45.00 (*0-930233-21-2*, Pub. by Windsor) Natl Bk Netwk.
— The Secret of Success. LC 98-84752. 176p. 1998. reprint ed. pap. 10.00 (*0-937539-29-5*) Executive Bks.

Allen, R. E. The Dialogues of Plato, Vol. 1. LC 84-17349. Vol. 1. 352p. (C). 1989. pap. 20.00 (*0-300-04488-7*) Yale U Pr.
— The Dialogues of Plato Vol. 3: Ion, Hippias Minor, Laches, Protagoras. LC 84-17349. 248p. 1996. 42.50 (*0-300-06343-1*) Yale U Pr.

Allen, R. E. The Oxford Writers' Dictionary. 448p. 1990. pap. 11.95 (*0-19-282669-7*) OUP.

Allen, R. E., tr. The Dialogues of Plato Vol. II: The Symposium. 192p. (C). 1993. pap. 15.00 (*0-300-05699-0*) Yale U Pr.
— Ion, Hippias Minor, Laches, Protagoras. (Dialogues of Plato Ser.: Vol. 3). 248p. 1998. pap. 18.00 (*0-300-07438-7*) Yale U Pr.
— Plato's Parmenides. rev. ed. (Dialogues of Plato Ser.: Vol. 4). 384p. 1997. pap. 18.00 (*0-300-07729-7*) Yale U Pr.

Allen, R. E., tr. & comment see Plato.

***Allen, R. G. & United Nations Food & Agriculture Organization Staff.** Crop Evapotranspiration: Guidelines for Computing Crop Water Requirements. LC 99-230093. (Illus.). 1998. 35.00 (*92-5-104219-5*, Pub. by FAO) Bernan Associates.

Allen, R. H., et al. Part-Time Farming in the Southeast. LC 74-165677. (Research Monographs: Vol. 9). 1971. reprint ed. lib. bdg. 42.50 (*0-306-70341-6*) Da Capo.

Allen, R. I. & Stewart, Ian, eds. Estimating & Projecting Input-Output Coefficients. (Illus.). xviii, 104p. 1975. lib. bdg. 69.50 (*0-678-08071-2*) Kelley.

Allen, R. L. Hand-Book of Saratoga & Strangers' Guide. (Illus.). 131p. 1997. reprint ed. pap. 17.50 (*0-8328-6223-1*) Higginson Bk Co.

Allen, R. T. Beyond Liberalism. LC 98-23204. 266p. 1998. text 39.95 (*1-56000-355-3*) Transaction Pubs.
— The Education of Autonomous Man. 110p. 1992. 61.95 (*1-85628-381-X*, Pub. by Avebry) Ashgate Pub Co.
— The Structure of Value. (Avebury Series in Philosophy). 170p. 1993. 66.95 (*1-85628-458-1*, Pub. by Avebry) Ashgate Pub Co.
— Transcendence & Immanence in the Philosophy of Michael Polanyi & Christian Theism. LC 92-30293. (Rutherford Studies in Contemporary Theology: Vol. 5). 204p. 1992. text 89.95 (*0-7734-1635-8*) E Mellen.

Allen, R. T., et al, eds. The Repair of Concrete Structures. 2nd ed. LC 93-135425. 212p. 1993. 144.95 (*0-7514-0086-6*, Pub. by B Acad & Prof) Routldge.

Allen, Rae, ed. see Sulkin, S. E.

Allen, Ralph. Common Saltwater Fishes of Southwest Florida. (Florida Sea Grant Bulletin Ser.: No. 25). 48p. 1993. write for info. (*0-912747-06-4*) FL Sea Grant Coll.

Allen, Ralph, tr. see Goldoni, Carlo.

Allen, Ralph G., ed. The Best Burlesque Sketches: As Adapted for Sugar Babies & Other Entertainments. LC 94-34272. (Illus.). 352p. 1994. pap. 12.95 (*1-55783-189-0*) Applause Theatre Bk Pubs.

Allen, Ralph G., jt. auth. see Gassner, John.

Allen, Ralph H., Jr. Flight of a Wandering Sparrow. rev. ed. LC 87-63410. 141p. 1987. pap. 5.95 (*0-945277-01-6*) New Creation Bks.
— A Man Called Sparrow. (Illus.). 157p. (Orig.). 1997. pap. 5.95 (*0-945277-02-4*) New Creation Bks.
— Sparrow's Song. LC 87-63404. 115p. 1990. reprint ed. pap. 4.95 (*0-945277-00-8*) New Creation Bks.

Allen, Ralph O., ed. Archaeological Chemistry IV: Developed from a Symposium Sponsored by the Division of History of Chemistry at the 193rd Meeting of the American Chemical Society, Denver, CO, April 5-10, 1987. LC 88-7953. (Advances in Chemistry Ser.: No. 220). (Illus.). 524p. 1989. reprint ed. pap. 162.50 (*0-608-06788-1*, 206698500009) Bks Demand.
— Archaeological Chemistry IV. LC 88-7953. (Advances in Chemistry Ser.: No. 220). vii, 524p. 1988. 89.95 (*0-8412-1449-2*) Am Chemical.

Allen, Rand L., et al. A Comprehensive Guide to the Federal Acquisition Streamlining Act: Complying with FASA. rev. ed. 1995. ring bd. 310.00 (*1-56726-045-4*, B5880) Mgmt Concepts.

Allen, Randall & Bohannon, Keith S., eds. Campaigning with "Old Stonewall" Confederate Captain Ujanirtus Allen's Letters to His Wife. LC 97-50293. (Illus.). 352p. 1998. 34.95 (*0-8071-2256-4*) La State U Pr.

Allen, Ray. Singing in the Spirit: African-American Sacred Quartets in New York City. LC 91-16943. (Publications of the American Folklore Society, Bibliographical & Special Ser.). (Illus.). 296p. (Orig.). (C). 1991. text 39.95 (*0-8122-3050-7*); pap. text 16.95 (*0-8122-1331-9*) U of Pa Pr.

Allen, Ray, et al. Island Sounds in the Global City: Caribbean Popular Music & Identity in New York. LC 97-81777. (I. S. A. M. Special Publications: No. 4). (Illus.). 185p. 1998. pap. 17.95 (*0-9661472-0-0*) NY Folklore.

Allen, Ray, ed. see Allen, R., et al.

Allen, Raye V. Gordon Conway: Fashioning a New Woman. LC 96-45862. (American Studies). (Illus.). 368p. 1997. 65.00 (*0-292-70459-3*); pap. 34.95 (*0-292-70470-4*) U of Tex Pr.

Allen, Raymond F. Allen. The Allens, from William (1602-79) of Manchester, England, & Salem & Manchester, Mass., in the Direct Line Through Nathaniel of Beverly, Mass. & Sedgwick, Me., to Lt. Raymond Frederick Allen, Jr., b. 1931m. 121p. 1997. reprint ed. pap. 19.50 (*0-8328-7243-1*); reprint ed. lib. bdg. 29.50 (*0-8328-7242-3*) Higginson Bk Co.

Allen, Rebecca. Native Americans at Mission Santa Cruz, 1791-1834: Interpreting the Archaeological Record. LC 98-36326. (Perspectives in California Archaeology Ser.: No. 5). (Illus.). 1998. pap. text 25.00 (*0-917956-92-3*) UCLA Arch.

Allen, Rebecca, jt. auth. see Brody, J. J.

Allen, Reginald E. Greek Philosophy: Tales to Aristotle. 2nd ed. LC 84-26067. 432p. 1985. pap. 12.95 (*0-02-900660-0*) Free Pr.
— Greek Philosophy: Tales to Aristotle. 3rd rev. ed. LC 84-26067. 1991. pap. 17.95 (*0-02-900495-0*) Free Pr.
— Socrates & Legal Obligation. LC 80-18193. 162p. 1980. reprint ed. pap. 50.30 (*0-7837-2981-2*, 205747300006) Bks Demand.

Allen, Renata & Bodall, Howard, contrib. by. The Witch & the Magic Mountain. 65p. 1991. pap. 5.95 (*0-87129-061-8*, W70) Dramatic Pub.

Allen, Richard. CADD Desktop Tutor: Release 14 Update for AutoCAD. 2nd unabridged ed. Meyers, Ron, ed. Angelini, Mike, tr. (Illus.). 175p. 1997. wbk. ed. 249.00 incl. cd-rom (*1-891502-09-3*, R14UPDA97) Tech Learn Co.
— A Collection of Hymns & Spiritual Songs from Various Authors. LC 98-208266. lvi, 112 p. 1987. write for info. (*0-929386-06-X*) AMEC Sunday Schl Union.
— Complete Richard Allen, Vol. 1. 288p. (Orig.). 1992. pap. 16.95 (*0-9518497-1-9*, Pub. by S T Pubng) AK Pr Dist.
— Complete Richard Allen, Vol. 2. 288p. (Orig.). 1992. pap. 16.95 (*0-9518497-5-1*, Pub. by S T Pubng) AK Pr Dist.
— Complete Richard Allen, Vol. 3. 288p. (Orig.). 1992. pap. 16.95 (*0-9518497-7-8*, Pub. by S T Pubng) AK Pr Dist.
— Complete Richard Allen, Vol. 4. 272p. (Orig.). 1994. pap. 16.95 (*1-898927-15-4*, Pub. by S T Pubng) AK Pr Dist.
— The Complete Richard Allen, Vol. 5. 1996. pap. 16.95 (*1-898927-30-8*, Pub. by S T Pubng) AK Pr Dist.
— The Complete Richard Allen, Vol. 6. 288p. 1997. pap. 14.95 (*0-614-28384-1*, Pub. by S T Pubng) AK Pr Dist.

***Allen, Richard.** The Concept of the Self: A Study of Black Identity. (African American Life Ser.). (Illus.). 240p. 2001. 34.95 (*0-8143-2898-9*) Wayne St U Pr.

Allen, Richard. David Hartley on Human Nature. LC 99-17961. (SUNY Series in the Philosophy of Psychology). 480p. (C). 1999. text 73.50 (*0-7914-4233-0*) State U NY Pr.

Allen, RIchard. The Moving Pageant: A Literary Sourcebook on London Street-Life, 1700-1914. LC 97-38277. (Illus.). 264p. (C). 1998. 75.00 (*0-415-15307-7*) Routledge.

Allen, Richard. The Moving Pageant: A Literary Sourcebook on London Street-Life, 1700-1914. LC 97-38277. 249p. (C). 1998. pap. 24.99 (*0-415-15308-5*) Routledge.
— Projecting Illusion: Film Spectatorship & the Impression of Reallity. (Cambridge Studies in Film). (Illus.). 188p. 1997. pap. text 17.95 (*0-521-58715-8*) Cambridge U Pr.

***Allen, Richard.** Shimmering Spokes: One Australian's 16,000 KM Odyssey. (Illus.). 368p. 2000. pap. 14.95 (*1-86436-521-8*, Pub. by New Holland) BHB Intl.

Allen, Richard. The Social Passion: Religion & Social Reform in Canada 1914-1928. 416p. 1990. pap. text 20.95 (*0-8020-6199-0*) U of Toronto Pr.
— The Social Passion: Religion & Social Reform in Canada, 1914-1928. LC 71-151352. (Illus.). 412p. reprint ed. pap. 127.80 (*0-8357-8325-1*, 203401800088) Bks Demand.

Allen, Richard, compiled by. Crime Movie Posters. (Illustrated History of Movies Through Posters Ser.: Vol. 5). (Illus.). 76p. 1997. 50.00 (*1-887893-20-2*); pap. 20.00 (*1-887893-19-9*) B Hershenson.

An Asterisk (*) at the beginning of an entry indicates that the title is appearing for the first time.

***Allen, Richard & Gonzales, S. Ishii, eds.** Alfred Hitchcock Centenary Essays. (British Film Institute Ser.). 1999. 65.00 (*0-85170-735-1*); pap. 22.95 (*0-85170-736-X*) Ind U Pr.

Allen, Richard & Hershenson, Bruce, compiled by. Horror Movie Posters. (Illustrated History of Movies Through Posters Ser.: Vol. 7). (Illus.). 80p. 1998. 50.00 (*1-887893-26-1*); pap. 20.00 (*1-887893-25-3*) B Hershenson.

Allen, Richard & Martz, Laura. Mechanical Desktop 2.0/3.0: Surface Modeling - Student Manual. 2nd unabridged ed. (Illus.). 200p. 1998. pap. text 75.00 incl. disk (*1-891502-27-1*, MDT20SUR) Tech Learn Co.

Allen, Richard & Smith, Murray, eds. Film Theory & Philosophy: Aesthetics & the Analytical Tradition. LC 97-12930. 486p. 1998. text 75.00 (*0-19-815921-8*) OUP.

***Allen, Richard & Smith, Murray, eds.** Film Theory & Philosophy: Aesthetics & the Analytical Tradition. (Illus.). 474p. 1999. pap. 29.95 (*0-19-815988-9*) OUP.

Allen, Richard, et al. Fundamentals of Numerical Computing. LC 96-22074. 288p. 1996. text 89.95 (*0-471-16363-5*) Wiley.

Allen, Richard, jt. auth. see Haney, Gloria.

Allen, Richard, jt. auth. see Jones, Absalom.

Allen, Richard, jt. auth. see Martz, Laura.

Allen, Richard, jt. auth. see Rebello, Stephen.

Allen, Richard, jt. auth. see Trivedi, Harish.

Allen, Richard, ed. see Banthin, Richard.

Allen, Richard, ed. see Farricielli, Susan.

Allen, Richard, ed. see Farricielli, Susan, et al.

Allen, Richard, jt. ed. see Hershenson, Bruce.

Allen, Richard, ed. see Martz, Laura.

Allen, Richard, ed. see Martz, Laura, et al.

Allen, Richard, ed. see Meyers, Ron & Kane, Bill.

Allen, Richard B. Slaves, Freedmen & Indentured Laborers in Colonial Mauritius. (African Studies: Vol. 99). (Illus.). 225p. (C). 1999. 64.95 (*0-521-64125-X*) Cambridge U Pr.

Allen, Richard B., ed. Atlantic Fishermans Handbook. (Illus.). 482p. (Orig.). 1982. pap. 9.00 (*0-9608932-0-2*) Fisheries Comm.

— Defense Counsel Teaching Manual: The ABC's of Defense. (IADC In-House Defense Lawyer Training Program Ser.). 238p. (Orig.). 1990. pap. write for info. (*0-9621989-1-9*) IADC IL.

Allen, Richard B., jt. ed. see Montgomery, C. Barry.

Allen, Richard B., jt. ed. see Waicukauski, Ronald J.

Allen, Richard C. David Hartley on Human Nature. LC 99-17961. (SUNY Series in the Philosophy of Psychology). 469p. (C). 1999. pap. text 24.95 (*0-7914-4234-9*) State U NY Pr.

Allen, Richard C. & Ferster, Elyce Z., eds. Readings in Law & Psychiatry. LC 74-24384. 848p. reprint ed. pap. 200.00 (*0-608-30180-9*, 200440700041) Bks Demand.

Allen, Richard C., et al. Massachusetts Nonprofit Organizations, 1998 Supplement. Marx, Frederic J., ed. LC 97-76388. 1998. ring bd. 145.00 (*1-57589-081-X*, 97-04.41-BK) Mass CLE.

Allen, Richard C., ed. see Baviello, Mary A., et al.

Allen, Richard C., ed. see Hutton, Cynthia A. & Gould, Robert N.

Allen, Richard D. & Chapman, Jeremy. A Manual of Renal Transplantation. (Illus.). 320p. 1994. pap. text 49.95 (*0-340-55154-2*, Pub. by E A) OUP.

Allen, Richard E., tr. see Konrad, George.

Allen, Richard G. Management of Irrigation & Drainage Systems. LC 93-5107. 1216p. 1993. 99.00 (*0-87262-919-8*) Am Soc Civil Eng.

Allen, Richard G., et al, eds. Lysimeters for Evapotranspiration & Environmental Measurements. LC 91-21900. 456p. 1991. pap. text 41.00 (*0-87262-813-2*) Am Soc Civil Eng.

Allen, Richard G., et al. American Government, 3 vols. Incl. Vol. 1. Origins of American Government & Citizenship: Political Parties & Elections. 156p. 1981. 9.95 (*0-86624-035-7*, US0); Vol. 2. Birth of Our Nation-Congress & the Laws-The President & His Cabinet. 256p. 1981. 9.95 (*0-86624-036-5*, US1); Vol. 3. Courts & Liberty: The World at Our Doorstep. 174p. 1981. 9.95 (*0-86624-037-3*, US2); (Illus.). 1981. Set pap. text 10.95 (*0-86624-012-8*) Bilingual Ed Serv.

— U. S. History, 4 vols., No. 1. Incl. Vol. 1. America - Its Discovery, Independence & Early Problems. 290p. 1981. 10.95 (*0-86624-001-2*, UT1); Vol. 2. Strengthening the New Nation. 270p. 1981. 10.95 (*0-86624-002-0*, UT2); Vol. 3. Republic Expands. 192p. 1981. 10.95 (*0-86624-003-9*, UT3); Vol. 4. Expansion, Destruction & Reconstruction. 156p. 1981. 10.95 (*0-86624-004-7*, UT4); (Illus.). 1981. pap. text. write for info. (*0-318-51083-9*) Bilingual Ed Serv.

Allen, Richard H. Star Names: Their Lore & Meaning. 1990. 23.50 (*0-8446-1527-7*) Peter Smith.

— Star Names: Their Lore & Meaning. rev. ed. 563p. 1963. pap. 10.95 (*0-486-21079-0*) Dover.

***Allen, Richard J.** Parashah Plays: For Children of All Ages. LC 00-101923. 275p. (J). (gr. k-6). 2000. pap. 11.95 (*0-86705-047-0*) A R E Pub.

Allen, Richard K. Dispute Avoidance & Resolution for Consulting Engineers. LC 93-43314. 81p. 1993. 22.00 (*0-87262-903-1*) Am Soc Civil Eng.

Allen, Richard L. & Martz, Laura. Cimlogic Toolbox Professional 14.X. unabridged ed. (Illus.). 175p. 1998. pap. text 75.00 incl. disk (*1-891502-34-4*) Tech Learn Co.

— Cimlogic Toolbox Sheetmetal 14.X. 2nd unabridged ed. (Illus.). 175p. 1998. pap. text 75.00 incl. disk (*1-891502-35-2*, CTP14X) Tech Learn Co.

— Mechanical Desktop 3.0: Surface Modeling - Student Manual. 2nd large type unabridged ed. (Illus.). 200p. 1998. pap. text 95.00 (*1-891502-33-6*, MDT30SUR) Tech Learn Co.

— Mechanical Desktop 3.0 Update - Student Manual. 2nd large type unabridged ed. (Illus.). 200p. 1998. pap. text 75.00 (*1-891502-30-1*, MDT30UPD) Tech Learn Co.

— Mechanical Desktop 2.0: Assembly Modeling - Instructor Manual. 2nd large type unabridged ed. (Illus.). 300p. 1998. pap. text 95.00 (*1-891502-28-X*, MDT20SOLI) Tech Learn Co.

— Mechanical 3.0: Assembly Modeling - Student Manual. 2nd unabridged ed. (Illus.). 200p. 1998. pap. text 95.00 (*1-891502-32-8*, MDT30ASM) Tech Learn Co.

Allen, Richard L., et al. Mechanical Desktop 2.0 Update. 2nd unabridged ed. (Illus.). 200p. 1998. pap. text 75.00 incl. disk (*1-891502-21-2*, MDT20UPD) Tech Learn Co.

Allen, Richard L., ed. see Farricrelli, Susan, et al.

Allen, Richard L., ed. see Martz, Laura.

Allen, Richard S. The Northrop Story, 1929-1939. LC 90-7094. (Illus.). 178p. 1993. 29.95 (*0-88740-585-1*) Schiffer.

— Revolution in the Sky: The Lockheed's of Aviation's Golden Age. LC 88-9839. (Illus.). 256p. 1993. 37.50 (*0-88740-584-3*) Schiffer.

***Allen, Ricky.** Bone of My Bone & Flesh of My Flesh. 134p. 1999. pap. 10.00 (*0-7392-0269-3*, PO3352) Morris Pubng.

Allen, Roach Van, see Van Allen, Roach.

Allen, Rob. Managing Electronic Documents As Assets. 41p. 1997. 100.00 (*0-89258-344-4*, C142) Assn Inform & Image Mgmt.

Allen, Rob, jt. auth. see Gillum, Perry.

Allen, Rob, jt. auth. see Gillum, Perry E.

Allen, Robert. Blues & Ballads. LC 75-302484. 103p. 1974. 3.95 (*0-87886-047-9*, Greenfld Rev Pr) Greenfld Rev Lit.

— Creating Wealth. rev. ed. 304p. 1986. per. 12.00 (*0-671-62100-9*) S&S Trade Pap.

— Daniel Webster: Defender of the Union. (Sower Ser.). (Illus.). 159p. (YA). (gr. 5-9). 1989. pap. 7.99 (*0-88062-156-7*) Mott Media.

— A June Night in the Late Cenozoic. 164p. 1995. text 12.95 (*0-88982-141-0*, Pub. by Oolichan Bks) Genl Dist Srvs.

— Mensa: Know Yourself. 1995. 7.98 (*0-7858-0426-9*) Bk Sales Inc.

— Mensa: New Number Puzzles. 128p. 1997. pap. text 7.98 (*0-7858-0810-8*) Bk Sales Inc.

— Mensa: New Word Puzzles. 128p. 1997. pap. text 7.98 (*0-7858-0809-4*) Bk Sales Inc.

***Allen, Robert.** Mensa: Number Puzzles for Kids. (Mensa Ser.). (Illus.). 224p. (J). (gr. 4-7). 2000. mass mkt. 4.50 (*0-439-10841-1*) Scholastic Inc.

Allen, Robert. Mensa: Riddles & Conundrums. 1995. 7.98 (*0-7858-0425-0*) Bk Sales Inc.

— Mensa Challenge Your IQ. (Mensa Word Games for Kids Ser.). 1999. pap. text 9.95 (*1-85868-311-4*, Pub. by Carlton Bks Ltd) Natl Bk Netwk.

— Mensa Number Puzzles. (Mensa Word Games for Kids Ser.). 1999. pap. text 9.95 (*1-85868-309-2*, Pub. by Carlton Bks Ltd) Natl Bk Netwk.

— Mensa Riddles & Conundrums. (Mensa Word Games for Kids Ser.). 1999. pap. text 9.95 (*1-85868-310-6*, Pub. by Carlton Bks Ltd) Natl Bk Netwk.

— Mensa Word Games for Kids, Vol. 1. LC 94-228344. 128p. (J). (gr. 4-7). 1994. pap. 9.95 (*1-55958-593-5*) Prima Pub.

— Mensa Word Puzzles. (Mensa Word Games for Kids Ser.). 1999. pap. text 9.95 (*1-85868-308-4*, Pub. by Carlton Bks Ltd) Natl Bk Netwk.

***Allen, Robert.** Mind Mazes for Kids. (Mensa Ser.). (Illus.). 224p. (J). (gr. 4-7). 2000. mass mkt. 4.50 (*0-439-10843-8*) Scholastic Inc.

Allen, Robert. No Risk Real Estate, Vol. 1. 39.95 (*0-911505-19-9*) Lifecraft.

— Official Scrabble Quiz Game Book. (Illus.). 128p. 1997. pap. text 9.95 (*0-8065-1945-2*, Citadel Pr) Carol Pub Group.

— The Official Scrabble Quiz Game Book, Vol. 2. (Illus.). 128p. 1999. pap. 14.95 (*1-85868-522-2*, Pub. by Carlton Bks Ltd) Natl Bk Netwk.

— Protein Staining & Identification Techniques. Budowle, Bruce, ed. LC 99-39668. (Molecular Laboratory Methods Ser.). (Illus.). 120p. 1999. 44.95 (*1-881299-08-2*) Eaton Pub Co.

— Reluctant Reformers: The Impact of Racism on American Social Reform Movements. LC 73-85495. 1974. pap. 12.95 (*0-88258-026-4*) Howard U Pr.

***Allen, Robert.** Secret Codes for Kids. (Mensa Ser.). (Illus.). 224p. (J). (gr. 4-7). 2000. mass mkt. 4.50 (*0-439-10842-X*) Scholastic Inc.

— 2000 Import Performance Directory. 324p. 2000. pap. 10.95 (*0-9668418-1-6*, 130088AE, Pub. by A Marketing) Motorbooks Intl.

Allen, Robert. Waste Not, Want Not. 1991. 20.00 (*1-85383-095-X*, Pub. by Escan Pubns) Island Pr.

— William Jennings Bryan: Golden-Tongued Orator. (Sower Ser.). (Illus.). 166p. (YA). (gr. 5-9). 1992. pap. 7.99 (*0-88062-160-5*) Mott Media.

***Allen, Robert.** Word Puzzles for Kids. (Mensa Ser.). (Illus.). 224p. (J). (gr. 4-7). 2000. mass mkt. 4.50 (*0-439-10840-3*) Scholastic Inc.

Allen, Robert. The Write Book for Christian Families. LC 93-37031. 144p. 1993. pap. 9.95 (*0-89084-723-1*, 078014) Bob Jones Univ.

Allen, Robert & McCarthy, Peter. Mechanics of the Spine. 1999. pap. 55.00 (*0-7506-2455-8*) Buttrwrth-Heinemann.

***Allen, Robert & Skitt, Carolyn.** Mensa All-Color Puzzle Book Vol. 1: Hundreds of Puzzles to Challenge You. (Illus.). (J). 2000. pap. 19.95 (*1-55209-498-7*) Firefly Bks Ltd.

— Mensa All-Color Puzzle Book Vol. 2: Challenge Your Mind with over 400 Full-Color Puzzles. (Illus.). (J). 2000. pap. 19.95 (*1-55209-500-2*) Firefly Bks Ltd.

Allen, Robert, et al. Credit Based Systems as Vehicles for Change in Universities & Colleges. (Managing Innovation & Change Ser.). 192p. 1995. pap. 29.95 (*0-7494-1244-5*, Kogan Pg Educ) Stylus Pub VA.

Allen, Robert, jt. auth. see Boyd, Herb.

Allen, Robert, jt. auth. see Theadore, Louis.

Allen, Robert, jt. auth. see Theodore, Louis.

Allen, Robert, ed. see Martin, James & Keaveny, Timothy J.

Allen, Robert A. Billy Sunday: Homerun to Heaven. Rock, Louise, ed. (Sower Ser.). (Illus.). 160p. (J). (gr. 5-9). 1985. pap. 7.99 (*0-88062-125-7*) Mott Media.

— The Christian Orchestra: And Other Plays for Church. (Christian Theatre Ser.). 40p. (Orig.). 1995. pap. 8.95 (*1-57514-107-8*) Encore Perform Pub.

— Don't Give up the Script! Writing Original Sketches for the Church. Wray, Rhonda, ed. LC 96-47744. (Illus.). 176p. (Orig.). 1997. pap. 12.95 (*1-56608-028-2*, B204) Meriwether Pub.

— Prince of Peace. 60p. 1995. pap. 4.00 (*1-57514-140-X*, 1076) Encore Perform Pub.

Allen, Robert A. & Rosenbluth, Gideon, eds. False Promises: The Failure of Conservative Economics. 264p. 1992. pap. 13.50 (*0-921586-20-5*, Pub. by New Star Bks) Genl Dist Srvs.

— Restraining the Economy: Social Credit Economics Policies for B. C. in the Eighties. 266p. 1986. pap. 14.95 (*0-919573-61-4*, Pub. by New Star Bks) Genl Dist Srvs.

Allen, Robert A., jt. ed. see Hawkins, Joyce M.

Allen, Robert C. Enclosure & the Yeoman: The Agricultural Development of the South Midlands, 1450-1850. 392p. 1992. 85.00 (*0-19-828296-6*) OUP.

— Horrible Prettiness: Burlesque & American Culture. LC 90-48608. (Cultural Studies of the United States). (Illus.). xvi, 366p. (C). 1991. 49.95 (*0-8078-1960-3*); pap. 18.95 (*0-8078-4316-4*) U of NC Pr.

— Speaking of Soap Operas. LC 84-21894. x, 245p. (C). 1985. pap. 17.95 (*0-8078-4129-3*) U of NC Pr.

— Vaudeville & Film. Jowett, Garth S., ed. LC 79-6667. (Dissertations on Film, 1980 Ser.). 1980. lib. bdg. 26.95 (*0-405-12901-7*) Ayer.

Allen, Robert C., ed. Channels of Discourse, Reassembled: Television & Contemporary Criticism. 2nd ed. LC 91-50784. (Illus.). xiii, 420p. (C). 1992. pap. 18.95 (*0-8078-4374-1*) U of NC Pr.

— To Be Continued: Soap Operas & Global Media Cultures. LC 94-11394. (Comedia Ser.). (Illus.). 408p. (C). 1995. pap. 22.99 (*0-415-11007-6*, C0004) Routledge.

— To Be Continued: Soap Operas & Global Media Cultures. LC 94-11394. (Comedia Ser.). (Illus.). 408p. (C). (gr. 13). 1995. 75.00 (*0-415-11006-8*, C0001) Routledge.

Allen, Robert C. & Budowle, Bruce. Gel Electrophoresis of Proteins & Nucleic Acids: Selected Techniques. LC 94-12072. xvi, 352p. (C). 1994. lib. bdg. 106.15 (*3-11-013896-4*) De Gruyter.

Allen, Robert C. & Gomery, Douglas. Film History: Theory & Practice. 248p. (C). 1985. pap. 44.06 (*0-07-554871-2*) McGraw.

Allen, Robert C., ed. see Suskind, Robert M.

Allen, Robert D. Biology: A Critical Thinking Approach. 320p. (C). 1995. text 49.75 (*0-697-14749-5*, WCB McGr Hill) McGrw-H Hghr Educ.

— Biology: A Critical Thinking Approach. 184p. (C). 1995. text, teacher ed. write for info. (*0-697-28134-5*, WCB McGr Hill) McGrw-H Hghr Educ.

— Biology: A Critical Thinking Approach. 80p. (C). 1995. text, student ed. 10.00 (*0-697-27526-4*, WCB McGr Hill) McGrw-H Hghr Educ.

— Critical Thinking Case. 2nd ed. 184p. (C). 1995. text, wbk. ed. write for info. (*0-697-34250-6*, WCB McGr Hill) McGrw-H Hghr Educ.

Allen, Robert D. & Stroup, David J. Teaching Critical Thinking Skills in Biology. 1993. 5.00 (*0-941212-13-0*) Natl Assn Bio Tchrs.

Allen, Robert D. & Williams, Vicki S. Physics: For Scientists & Engineers - Instructor's Resource Manual. 4th ed. 2000. teacher ed. write for info. (*1-57259-516-7*) Worth.

Allen, Robert D. & Wolfe, Thomas E., eds. The Real Estate Almanac. LC 80-12417. (Real Estate For Professional Practitioners Ser.). 468p. reprint ed. pap. 145.10 (*0-608-11587-8*, 205541300021) Bks Demand.

Allen, Robert D., jt. auth. see Stroup, David J.

***Allen, Robert E.** The First Battalion of the 28th Marines on Iwo Jima: A Day-by-Day History from Personal Accounts & Official Reports, with Complete Muster Rolls. LC 99-16751. (Illus.). 470p. 1999. boxed set 65.00 (*0-7864-0560-0*) McFarland & Co.

Allen, Robert E. & Keaveny, Timothy J. Contemporary Labor Relations. 672p. 1983. text. write for info. (*0-201-00047-4*) Addison-Wesley.

— Contemporary Labor Relations. 2nd ed. (Illus.). 736p. (C). 1988. text 54.95 (*0-201-10083-5*) Addison-Wesley.

Allen, Robert F. The Going-On Problem: Wittgenstein on Guidance. LC 94-11509. (American University Studies, Series V, Philosophy: Vol. 153). 1994. write for info. (*0-8204-2236-3*) P Lang Pubng.

— Love, Peace, & Other Major Issues: Selected Poems. 113p. (Orig.). 1991. pap. 9.95 (*0-941703-09-6*) Healthyculture.

— A Program for Personal & Cultural Change: Modules on Smoking, Nutrition, Weight Control, Physical Fitness, & Stress, 5 vols. (Illus.). 60p. (C). 1981. reprint ed. pap. 8.95 (*0-941703-03-7*) Healthyculture.

— A Program for Personal & Cultural Change on Nutrition. LC 81-17569. (Illus.). 40p. (C). 1990. reprint ed. pap., student ed. 8.95 (*0-941703-07-X*) Healthyculture.

— A Program for Personal & Cultural Change on Physical Fitness. LC 81-15029. (C). 1990. reprint ed. pap., student ed. 8.95 (*0-941703-08-8*) Healthyculture.

— A Program for Personal Change on Smoking. LC 81-15025. (Illus.). 40p. (C). 1990. reprint ed. pap., student ed. 8.95 (*0-941703-04-5*) Healthyculture.

— A Program for Personal Change on Stress Resolution. LC 81-15041. (Illus.). 40p. (C). 1990. reprint ed. pap., student ed. 8.95 (*0-941703-05-3*) Healthyculture.

— A Program for Personal Change on Weight Control. LC 81-15026. 40p. 1990. reprint ed. pap., student ed. 8.95 (*0-941703-06-1*) Healthyculture.

Allen, Robert F. & Linde, Shirley. Lifegain: The Exciting New Program That Will Change Your Health & Your Life. 248p. 1981. 16.95 (*0-941703-02-9*) Healthyculture.

Allen, Robert F., et al. The Organizational Unconscious: How to Create the Corporate Culture You Want & Need. 2nd ed. 229p. 1987. reprint ed. pap. 8.95 (*0-941703-00-2*) Healthyculture.

Allen, Robert F., jt. auth. see Harris, Sara.

***Allen, Robert G.** Multiple Streams of Income. LC 99-58145. (Illus.). 300p. 2000. text 24.95 (*0-471-38180-2*, Wiley Heyden) Wiley.

Allen, Robert G. Nothing Down: Dynamic New High-Profit, Low-Risk Strategies for Building Real Estate Wealth in the '90s - The New Revised Edition for the All-Time Bestselling Real Estate Book. 368p. 1990. 23.50 (*0-671-72558-0*) S&S Trade.

Allen, Robert G., jt. auth. see Guerriero, Janice M.

Allen, Robert H. Simple Annals: 200 Years of an American Family. LC 96-45312. 208p. 1997. 22.00 (*1-56858-090-8*) FWEW.

Allen, Robert H., ed. Expert Systems for Civil Engineers: Knowledge Representation. 304p. 1992. pap. text 32.00 (*0-87262-892-2*) Am Soc Civil Eng.

Allen, Robert L. Black Awakening in Capitalist America. LC 90-80153. 305p. (C). 1990. 29.95 (*0-86543-172-8*); pap. 9.95 (*0-86543-157-4*) Africa World.

— Opening Doors: The Life & Work of Joseph Schumpeter, 2 vols., Set. (C). 1990. pap. 44.95 (*1-56000-720-6*) Transaction Pubs.

— Opening Doors: The Life & Work of Joseph Schumpeter, 2 vols., Vol. 1: Europe. 335p. (C). 1993. pap. 24.95 (*1-56000-716-8*) Transaction Pubs.

— Opening Doors: The Life & Work of Joseph Schumpeter, 2 vols., Vol. 2: America. 340p. (C). 1990. pap. 24.95 (*1-56000-717-6*) Transaction Pubs.

Allen, Robert L. Port Chicago Mutiny. 224p. 1993. reprint ed. pap. 9.95 (*1-56743-010-4*, Amistad) HarperTrade.

Allen, Robert L. Verb System of Present-Day American English. 2nd ed. (Janua Linguarum, Series Practica: No. 24). (Orig.). 1982. pap. text 34.65 (*90-279-0643-2*) Mouton.

— The Wings of Icarus, Vol. 1. Fifield, Robert S., ed. v, 121p. (Orig.). 1996. pap. 12.95 (*0-9655100-0-X*) R L Allen.

Allen, Robert L. & Egger, Rowland. Middle Eastern Economic Relations with the Soviet Union, Eastern Europe, & Mainland China. LC 85-14822. 128p. 1985. reprint ed. lib. bdg. 59.50 (*0-313-23535-X*, ALMI, Greenwood Pr) Greenwood.

Allen, Robert L., jt. auth. see Brown, Lee.

Allen, Robert M. Elements of Rorschach Interpretation, with an Extended Bibliography. LC 54-6098. (Illus.). 242p. reprint ed. pap. 75.10 (*0-608-11344-1*, 201042400070) Bks Demand.

— Student's Rorschach Manual: An Introduction to Administering, Scoring & Interpreting Researcher's Psychodiagnostic Inkblot Test. rev. ed. LC 77-14710. xii, 361p. 1978. 52.50 (*0-8236-6201-2*) Intl Univs Pr.

Allen, Robert P. Roseate Spoonbill. (Illus.). 1990. 12.50 (*0-8446-1528-5*) Peter Smith.

Allen, Robert R., ed. see Erasmus, Desiderius.

Allen, Robert R., ed. see Greene, Donald J.

Allen, Robert S., ed. Our Fair City. LC 73-19124. (Politics & People Ser.). 396p. 1974. reprint ed. 29.95 (*0-405-05851-9*) Ayer.

Allen, Robert S., jt. auth. see Pearson, Drew.

Allen, Robert T., jt. auth. see Robison, Henry W.

Allen, Robert V. Russia Looks at America: The View to 1917. LC 88-600001. 322p. 1988. 20.00 (*0-8444-0593-0*, 030-001-00128) Lib Congress.

Allen, Robert W., ed. Standards for Paternity Testing Laboratories. 3rd ed. 1998. pap. text 55.00 (*1-56395-096-0*) Am Assn Blood.

Allen, Robert W. & AuBuchon, James P., eds. Molecular Genetics in Diagnosis & Research. LC 95-35428. (Illus.). 161p. (C). 1995. 45.00 (*1-56395-044-8*) Am Assn Blood.

Allen, Roberta. Amazon Dream. (Illus.). 192p. (Orig.). 1993. pap. 10.95 (*0-87286-270-4*) City Lights.

— Certain People & Other Stories. LC 96-17291. (Coffee-to-Go Short-Short Story Ser.). 128p. (Orig.). 1997. pap. 10.95 (*1-56689-052-7*) Coffee Hse.

— The Daughter. 118p. Date not set. 8.00 (*0-936756-86-1*) Autonomedia.

***Allen, Roberta.** The Dreaming Girl: A Novel. LC 99-89049. 2000. 12.95 (*1-891305-51-4*) Painted Leaf.

Allen, Roberta. Fast Fiction. LC 97-10956. 208p. 1997. 18.99 (*1-884910-27-0*, Story Press) F & W Pubns Inc.

***Allen, Roberta.** The Traveling Woman: A Novel. LC 99-86963. 2000. write for info. (*1-891305-52-2*) Painted Leaf.

Allen, Roberta & Mascolini, Marcia. Process of Writing. 144p. (C). 1996. pap. text 30.40 (*0-13-182114-8*) P-H.

Allen, Robin. Hidden Memories. 1999. mass mkt. 5.99 (*0-345-43257-6*) Ballantine Pub Grp.

Allen, Robin, ed. see Feynman, Richard Phillips.

Allen, Robin H. Hidden Memories. LC 97-220316. 368p. 1997. pap. 10.95 (*1-885478-16-X*, Pub. by Genesis Press) BookWorld.

Allen, Robin W., ed. see Feynman, Richard Phillips.

***Allen, Rocelia J.** Discovery Deck. 60p. 2000. pap. 8.00 (*0-8059-5011-7*) Dorrance.

Allen, Rodger Van, see Miller, Merle & Cogley, John.
Allen, Rodger Van, see Cogley, John.
Allen, Rodney. Threshold of Terror: The Last Hours of the Monarchy in the French Revolution. 1999. 34.95 (*0-7509-2030-0*, Pub. by Sutton Publng) Intl Pubs Mktg.
Allen, Rodney F., jt. auth. see Massialas, Byron G.
Allen, Roger. The Arabic Literary Heritage: The Development of Its Genres & Criticism. LC 97-27113. 475p. (C). 1998. text 95.00 (*0-521-48066-3*) Cambridge U Pr.
***Allen, Roger.** An Introduction to Arabic Literature. 282p. (C). 2000. text Price not set. (*0-521-77230-3*); pap. text Price not set. (*0-521-77657-0*) Cambridge U Pr.
Allen, Roger, ed. Critical Perspectives on Yusuf Idris. LC 92-35320. (Critical Perspectives Ser.: Vol. 43). 180p. 1994. pap. 16.00 (*0-89410-672-4*, Three Contnts) L Rienner.
Allen, Roger, et al, eds. Arabic Literature: Then & Now. (Nimrod Ser.). (Illus.). 149p. (C). 1981. pap. text 5.50 (*0-942374-07-X*) Art & Human Council Tulsa.
Allen, Roger, jt. ed. see Jayyusi, Salma K.
Allen, Roger, tr. see Mahfouz, Naguib.
Allen, Roger B. Common Sense Discipline: What to Say & Do When Children Misbehave. (Illus.). 86p. (Orig.). 1984. pap. 4.95 (*0-916979-00-8*) Common Sen Pubns.
Allen, Roger B., jt. auth. see Allen, Jane E.
Allen, Roger B., jt. auth. see Popkin, Susan A.
Allen, Roger E. Pooh on Management. 192p. 1999. pap. 9.95 (*0-452-27336-6*, Plume) Dutton Plume.
— Pooh on Problem Solving. 164p. 1999. pap. 9.95 (*0-452-27526-1*, Plume) Dutton Plume.
— Winnie-the-Pooh on Management: In Which a Very Important Bear & His Friends Are Introduced to a Very Important Subject. (Illus.). 192p. 1994. 18.95 (*0-525-93898-2*, Dutt) Dutton Plume.
Allen, Roger E. & Allen, Stephen D. Winnie-the-Pooh on Problem Solving: In Which Pooh, Piglet, & Friends Explore How to Solve Problems So You Can Too. LC 95-17641. 1995. write for info. (*0-614-07806-7*) NAL.
Allen, Roger MacBride. Allies & Aliens. 726p. 1995. mass mkt. 5.99 (*0-671-87658-9*) Baen Bks.
Allen, Roger MacBride. Ambush at Corellia. (Star Wars: Bk. 1). (YA). (gr. 5 up). mass mkt. 5.99 (*0-614-32220-0*) Bantam.
Allen, Roger MacBride. Ambush at Corellia. (Star Wars: Bk. 1). (YA). (gr. 5 up). 1995. 11.09 (*0-606-08197-6*, Pub. by Turtleback) Demco.
— Ambush at Corellia, Vol. I. LC 00-4217. (Star Wars: Bk. 1). 320p. (YA). (gr. 5 up). 1995. mass mkt. 5.99 (*0-553-29803-8*, Spectra) Bantam.
— The Arabic Novel: An Historical & Critical Introduction. LC 82-3235. 183p. 1982. reprint ed. pap. 56.80 (*0-608-06943-4*, 206715100009) Bks Demand.
— Assault at Selonia. (Star Wars: Bk. 2). (YA). (gr. 5 up). 1995. 11.09 (*0-606-08198-4*, Pub. by Turtleback) Demco.
— Assault at Selonia, Set. abr. ed. (Star Wars: Bk. 2). (YA). (gr. 5 up). 1995. audio 16.99 (*0-553-47203-8*) BDD Aud Pub.
— Assault at Selonia, Vol. II. LC 00-3728. (Star Wars: Bk. 2). 320p. (YA). (gr. 5 up). 1995. mass mkt. 5.99 (*0-553-29805-4*, Spectra) Bantam.
***Allen, Roger MacBride.** David Brin's Out of Time: The Game of Worlds. LC 98-94860. (Out of Time Ser.: No. 3). 256p. (YA). (gr. 7 up). 1999. mass mkt. 4.99 (*0-380-79969-3*, Avon Bks) Morrow Avon.
— The Depths of Time. LC 99-40436. 420p. 2000. pap. 13.95 (*0-553-37811-2*, Spectra) Bantam.
Allen, Roger MacBride. Isaac Asimov's Inferno. (Caliban Ser.: Bk. 2). 320p. 1994. pap. 12.00 (*0-441-00023-1*) Ace Bks.
— Isaac Asimov's Inferno. (Caliban Trilogy Ser.). 1998. mass mkt. 5.99 (*0-441-00514-4*) Ace Bks.
— Isaac Asimov's Utopia. LC 96-219770. 320p. 1996. pap. 13.00 (*0-441-00245-5*) Ace Bks.
— Isaac Asimov's Utopia. 368p. 1999. reprint ed. mass mkt. 6.50 (*0-441-00471-7*) Ace Bks.
— Ring of Charon. 512p. 1990. mass mkt. 4.95 (*0-8125-3014-4*, Pub. by Tor Bks) St Martin.
— The Shattered Sphere. 416p. 1995. mass mkt. 5.99 (*0-8125-3016-0*, Pub. by Tor Bks) St Martin.
— Showdown at Centerpoint. (Star Wars: Bk. 3). 336p. (YA). (gr. 5 up). 1995. mass mkt. 5.99 (*0-553-29806-2*, Spectra) Bantam.
Allen, Roger MacBride. Showdown at Centerpoint. (Star Wars: Bk. 3). (YA). (gr. 5 up). 1995. 11.09 (*0-606-09891-7*, Pub. by Turtleback) Demco.
Allen, Roger MacBride & Kotani, Eric. Supernova. 352p. (Orig.). 1991. mass mkt. 4.50 (*0-380-76060-6*, Avon Bks) Morrow Avon.
Allen, Roger MacBride, jt. auth. see Asimov, Isaac.
Allen, Roger P. Scripts & Strategies in Hypnotherapy. 162p. 1997. pap. 24.95 (*1-899836-08-X*, Pub. by Crown Hse) LPC Group.
Allen, Roland. The Compulsion of the Spirit: A Roland Allen Reader. Paton, David & Long, Charles H., eds. LC 83-14006. 158p. reprint ed. pap. 49.00 (*0-608-14507-6*, 202533800043) Bks Demand.
— Missionary Methods: St. Paul's or Ours? 184p. 1962. pap. 12.00 (*0-8028-1001-2*) Eerdmans.
Allen, Roland. The Spontaneous Expansion of the Church: And the Causes That Kinder It. 170p. 1997. pap. 18.00 (*1-57910-198-4*) Wipf & Stock.
Allen, Roland. The Spontaneous Expansion of the Church: And the Causes That Kinder It. 158p. 1994. reprint ed. pap. 15.00 (*1-881266-10-9*) Fuller Seminary.
Allen, Roland E. Relativity, Particle Physics & Cosmology: Proceedings of the Richard Arnowitt Fest Texas , USA. 350p. 1999. 78.00 (*981-02-3794-4*) World Scientific Pub.
Allen, Ron. I Want My Body Back. 64p. (Orig.). 1996. pap. text 10.00 (*1-56439-054-3*) Ridgeway.
— Who Were Shake-speare? The Ultimate Who-Dun-It. LC 97-69058. 208p. 1998. pap. 14.95 (*1-891083-00-7*) Silverado CA.
Allen, Ronald & Kuhns, Richard. Constitutional Criminal Procedure: An Examination of the Fourth, Fifth & Sixth Amendments & Related Areas. LC 84-80836. (C). 1985. 39.00 (*0-316-03415-0*) Aspen Pub.
Allen, Ronald B. The Majesty of Man: The Dignity of Being Human. rev. ed. LC 98-15296. 218p. 1998. pap. text 11.99 (*0-8254-2139-X*) Kregel.
Allen, Ronald Barclay. And I Will Praise Him: A Guide to Worship in the Psalms. LC 99-18853. 1999. 12.99 (*0-8254-2011-3*) Kregel.
Allen, Ronald J. Constitutional Crime Procedure. 3rd ed. 1568p. 1995. 60.00 (*0-316-03476-2*) Aspen Pub.
— Contemporary Biblical Interpretation for Preaching. 160p. 1984. pap. 12.00 (*0-8170-1002-5*) Judson.
— Interpreting the Gospel: An Introduction to Preaching. 304p. 1998. pap. 24.99 (*0-8272-1619-X*) Chalice Pr.
— Our Eyes Can Be Opened: Preaching the Miracle Stories of the Synoptic Gospels Today. LC 81-43679. 146p. (C). 1983. pap. text 17.00 (*0-8191-2671-3*) U Pr of Amer.
***Allen, Ronald J.** Preaching Luke - Acts. 2000. pap. 16.99 (*0-8272-2965-8*) Chalice Pr.
Allen, Ronald J. Preaching the Topical Sermon. 176p. (Orig.). 1992. pap. 17.95 (*0-664-25306-7*) Westminster John Knox.
— The Teaching Sermon. (Teaching Sermon Ser.). 160p. (Orig.). 1995. pap. 12.95 (*0-687-37522-3*) Abingdon.
Allen, Ronald J., ed. Patterns of Preaching: A Sermon Sampler. 272p. 1998. pap. 22.99 (*0-8272-2953-4*) Chalice Pr.
Allen, Ronald J. & Bartholomew, Gilbert L. Preaching Verse by Verse. LC 99-47265. 160p. 1999. pap. 14.95 (*0-664-25804-2*) Westminster John Knox.
Allen, Ronald J., et al. Arthritis of the Hip & Knee: The Active Person's Guide to Taking Charge. LC 97-15388. (Illus.). 256p. 1997. pap. 14.95 (*1-56145-149-5*) Peachtree Pubs.
— Constitutional Criminal Procedure: An Examination of the Fourth, Fifth, & Sixth Amendments, & Related Areas. 1568p. 1995. teacher ed. write for info. (*0-316-03771-0*, 37710) Aspen Law.
Allen, Ronald J., et al. Constitutional Criminal Procedure: An Examination of the Fourth, Fifth, & Sixth Amendments, & Related Areas: With Teacher's Manual. 3rd ed. 1568p. 1995. teacher ed. write for info. (*0-7355-0634-5*, 06345) Panel Pubs.
Allen, Ronald J., et al. Evidence: Text, Cases & Problems. 2nd ed. LC 97-17186. 1250p. 1997. boxed set 59.00 (*1-56706-556-2*) Aspen Law.
— Theology for Preaching: Authority, Truth & Knowledge of God in a Postmodern Ethos. LC 97-7471. 176p. 1997. pap. 14.95 (*0-687-01717-3*) Abingdon.
Allen, Ronald J., jt. auth. see Holbert, John C.
Allen, Ronald J., jt. auth. see Williamson, Clark M.
Allen, Ronald J., ed. see Brown-Taylor, Barbara.
Allen, Ronald J., ed. see Farmer, David A.
Allen, Ronald J., jt. ed. see Greenhaw, David M.
Allen, Ronald J., ed. see Watley, William D.
Allen, Rosamund, ed. see Wace & Lawman.
Allen, Rosamund S., ed. Richard Rolle: The English Writings. (Classics of Western Spirituality Ser.: Vol. 59). 256p. 1988. 16.95 (*0-8091-0401-6*); pap. 12.95 (*0-8091-3008-4*) Paulist Pr.
Allen, Rosie, jt. auth. see Allen, Nick.
Allen, Roy E. Cybor & Gaia: The New World Order. (Illus.). 290p. (Orig.). 1997. pap. 23.00 (*0-9659158-0-8*) Global Outlook.
***Allen, Roy E.** Financial Crises & Recession in the Global Economy. 2nd ed. LC 99-21908. 212p. 1999. 90.00 (*1-84064-087-1*) E Elgar.
Allen, Roy F. Literary Life in German Expressionism & the Berlin Circles. LC 82-4762. (Studies in the Fine Arts: The Avant-Garde: No. 25). (Illus.). 414p. reprint ed. pap. 128.40 (*0-8357-1315-6*, 207060100005) Bks Demand.
Allen, Roy G. Macro Economic Theory. LC 67-12508. (C). 1969. reprint ed. pap. text 10.50 (*0-312-50330-X*) St Martin.
Allen, Ruby, ed. see Czimbal, Bob & Zadikov, Maggie.
Allen, Rupert C. Psyche & Symbol in the Theater of Federico Garcia Lorca: Perlimplin, Verma, Blood Wedding. LC 74-4285. 234p. reprint ed. pap. 72.60 (*0-8357-7721-9*, 203607800002) Bks Demand.
— Symbolic Experience: A Study of Poems by Pedro Salinas. LC 81-10307. 190p. 1982. reprint ed. pap. 58.90 (*0-608-01659-4*, 206231400002) Bks Demand.
— The Symbolic World of Federico Garcia Lorca. LC 72-80890. 1972. 20.00 (*0-8263-0245-9*) Lib Soc Sci.
Allen, Russell N. Virginia Search & Seizure for Law Enforcement Officers. 110p. pap. 19.95 (*0-87526-551-0*) Gould.
Allen-Russell, Shelle, jt. auth. see Teacher Created Materials Staff.
Allen, Ruth. Children's Book Prizes: An Evaluation & History of Major Awards for Children's Books in the English-Speaking World. LC 97-39918. (Illus.). 250p. 1998. text 86.95 (*1-85928-237-7*, Pub. by Ashgate Pub) Ashgate Pub Co.
***Allen, Ruth, ed.** The Heritage of Marengo County, Alabama. (Heritage of Alabama Ser.: Vol. 46). 320p. 2000. 60.00 (*1-891647-58-X*) Herit Pub Consult.
***Allen, S.** Lives of the Indian Princes. 1998. pap. 163.00 (*81-86982-05-1*, Pub. by Business Pubns) St Mut.
Allen, S. Manager's Guide to Audiovisuals. 1979. text 13.95 (*0-07-001093-5*) McGraw.
— Nobel Lectures in Literature 1968-1980. 208p. 1994. text 40.00 (*981-02-1174-0*); pap. text 21.00 (*981-02-1175-9*) World Scientific Pub.
— Nobel Lectures in Literature 1981-1990. 176p. 1994. text 40.00 (*981-02-1176-7*); pap. text 21.00 (*981-02-1177-5*) World Scientific Pub.
— Svensk Ordbok (Swedish Dictionary) (SWE.). 1513p. 1986. 195.00 (*0-8288-2071-6*, F60690) Fr & Eur
Allen, S., ed. Of Thoughts & Words: The Relation Between Language & Mind. LC 96-130659. 308p. 1995. 78.00 (*1-86094-005-6*) World Scientific Pub.
— Of Thoughts & Words: The Relation Between Language & Mind, Proceedings of Nobel Symposium 92, Stockholm, Sweden 8 - 12 August 1994. 310p. 1996. text 78.00 (*981-02-2446-X*, GAIXnRa-P2918) World Scientific Pub.
Allen, S., jt. ed. see Miles, Edward L.
Allen, S. C. & Brocklehurst, J. C. Medicine in Old Age. 4th ed. LC 97-37958. (C). 1998. pap. text 29.95 (*0-443-05778-8*) Church.
Allen, S. C., et al. Case Studies in Medicine for the Elderly. 1987. pap. text 73.50 (*0-85200-698-5*) Kluwer Academic.
Allen, S. Carol & Harwin, Cary C. The Complete Business Guide for a Profitable Internet, BBS, or Online Service. 400p. (Orig.). 1995. pap. 49.97 (*1-884078-20-6*) InfoLink.
— How to Successfully Run a BBS for Profit. LC 93-79734. 304p. (Orig.). 1993. pap. 49.95 (*1-884078-19-2*) InfoLink.
Allen, Sam. The Art of Shaker Chairmaking. 1998. write for info. (*0-8069-9653-6*) Sterling.
— Cabinetry Basics. LC 91-12939. (Basics Ser.). (Illus.). 128p. 1991. pap. 10.95 (*0-8069-8290-X*) Sterling.
— Classic Finishing Techniques. (Illus.). 128p. 1995. pap. 14.95 (*0-8069-0513-1*) Sterling.
— Finishing Basics. LC 92-21004. (Illus.). 128p. 1992. pap. 10.95 (*0-8069-7228-9*) Sterling.
— Finishing Workbench Shop Reference. 1998. write for info. (*0-8069-9997-7*) Sterling.
— Joinery Basics. LC 91-41312. (Illus.). 128p. 1992. pap. 10.95 (*0-8069-7234-3*) Sterling.
— Making Cabinets & Built-Ins: Techniques & Plans. Ornitz, Laurel, ed. LC 86-5997. (Illus.). 384p. (Orig.). 1985. pap. 19.95 (*0-8069-6330-1*) Sterling.
— Making Workbenches: Planning, Building, Outfitting. LC 95-4875. (Illus.). 160p. 1995. pap. 14.95 (*0-8069-0535-2*) Sterling.
— Plane Basics. LC 93-24609. (Basics Ser.). (Illus.). 128p. 1993. pap. 10.95 (*0-8069-8804-5*) Sterling.
— The Wood Finisher's Handbook. LC 84-8557. (Illus.). 160p. (Orig.). 1984. pap. 14.95 (*0-8069-7914-3*) Sterling.
— Wood Joiner's Handbook. LC 89-26189. (Illus.). 288p. (Orig.). 1990. pap. 14.95 (*0-8069-6999-7*) Sterling.
Allen, Sam R., jt. ed. see Stevenson, Peter E.
Allen, Samuel. Every Round & Other Poems. LC 87-80159. 159p. (Orig.). (YA). (gr. 9-12). 1987. pap. 9.00 (*0-916418-65-0*) Lotus.
Allen, Samuel M. & Thomas, Edwin L. Structure of Materials. LC 98-35188. 464p. 1999. text 109.95 (*0-471-00082-5*) Wiley.
Allen, Sandra & Dlugokinski, Eric. Ben's Secret. 28p. (J). (gr. k-6). 1992. pap. 9.95 (*1-882801-00-8*) Feelings Factory.
Allen, Sarah. Cats. LC 95-43797. (Pocket Gem Ser.). (Illus.). 64p. (J). (gr. 1 up). 1996. 3.95 (*0-8120-6591-3*) Barron.
— The Kingfisher Children's Encyclopedia. LC 97-47595. (Illus.). 500p. (J). (gr. 3-9). 1998. 39.95 (*0-7534-5154-4*) LKC.
Allen, Scott & Craven, John P., eds. Alternatives in Deepsea Mining. (Law of the Sea Workshop Ser.: No. W5). 1979. 4.00 (*0-911189-01-7*) Law Sea Inst.
Allen, Scott D., ed. see Wootan, Fred C.
Allen, Shanley E. M. Aspects of Argument Structure Acquisition in Inuktitut. LC 96-38627. (Language Acquisition & Language Disorders Ser.: Vol. 13). xv , 244p. 1996. lib. bdg. 79.00 (*1-55619-776-4*) J Benjamins Pubng Co.
Allen, Sharon, ed. see Mills-Thornton, Serena G.
Allen, Sharon B., et al. Life & Health Insurance Marketing. 2nd ed. LC 97-72887. 733p. text 65.95 (*1-57974-008-1*, Pub. by Life Office) PBD Inc.
Allen, Sheila & Truman, Carole, eds. Women in Business: Perspectives on Women Entrepreneurs. LC 92-44130 224p. (C). 1993. pap. 29.95 (*0-415-06312-4*) Thomson Learn.
— Women in Business: Perspectives on Women Entrepreneurs. LC 92-44130. (Social Analysis Ser.). 240p. (C). (gr. 13). 1993. pap. 71.95 (*0-415-06311-6*) Thomson Learn.
Allen, Sheila & Wolkowitz, Carol. Homeworking: Myths & Realities LC 88-215585. (Women in Society Ser.). x, 225 p. 1987. write for info. (*0-333-42363-1*) Macmillan Ed.
Allen, Sheila, jt. auth. see Leonard, Diana.
Allen, Sheila R. The Helpful Ghost. large type ed. LC 90-28926. 337p. 1991. reprint ed. lib. bdg. 18.95 (*1-56054-147-4*) Thorndike Pr.
— The Meddlesome Ghost. 285p. 1989. 18.95 (*0-8027-1083-2*) Walker & Co.
— The Meddlesome Ghost. large type ed. 348p. 1991. reprint ed. lib. bdg. 18.95 (*1-56054-116-4*) Thorndike Pr.
— The Passionate Ghost. large type ed. 325p. 1991. reprint ed. lib. bdg. 18.95 (*1-56054-187-3*) Thorndike Pr.
— The Passionate Ghost Bk. IV: The Lovers of Steadford Abbey, Bk. IV. 224p. 1991. 19.95 (*0-8027-1158-8*) Walker & Co.
— The Reluctant Ghost. (Lovers of Steadford Abbey Ser.). 252p. 1989. 18.95 (*0-8027-1057-3*) Walker & Co.
Allen, Shelley J., jt. ed. see Dawbarn, David.
Allen, Sherhonda, ed. see Brooks, John R. & Wiant, Harry V., Jr.
Allen, Sherilyn. The Official Book of the Neapolitan Mastiff, AKC Rank No. 48. (Illus.). 320p. 1996. 69.95 (*0-7938-2083-9*, TS255) TFH Pubns.
***Allen, Shirley.** Forbidden Love. large type ed. 192p. 2000. pap. 18.99 (*0-7089-5634-3*, Linford) Ulverscroft.
— Impossible Love. 200p. 2000. 18.99 (*0-7089-5658-0*) Ulverscroft.
Allen, Shirley. Race for Love. large type ed. (Ulverscroft Large Print Ser.). 544p. 1997. 27.99 (*0-7089-3767-5*) Ulverscroft.
Allen, Shirley. To Love in Vain. large type ed. 224p. pap. 18.99 (*0-7089-5406-5*) Ulverscroft.
— Voyage into Peril. large type ed. 208p. pap. 18.99 (*0-7089-5436-7*) Ulverscroft.
Allen-Shore, Lena. Rendezvous with Love. (With Love to Life Ser.). 118p. (C). 1988. pap. write for info. (*0-922351-01-5*) L Allen-Shore.
— Thinking of Rembrandt And... Life: On the Canvas of Your Soul. (Illus.). 104p. (C). 1988. pap. write for info. (*0-922351-00-7*) L Allen-Shore.
Allen, Simon, et al. UK Business in Europe: A Statistical Comparison. LC 99-236058. (Illus.). 1995. write for info. (*0-11-620722-1*) Statnry Office.
Allen, Simona A., ed. see Murphy, E. Louise.
Allen-Smith, Joyce E., jt. ed. see Stewart, James B.
Allen, Stan. Points + Lines: Diagrams & Projects for the City. LC 98-38817. (Illus.). 144p. 1999. pap. 35.00 (*1-56898-155-4*) Princeton Arch.
Allen, Stan, contrib. by. Practice: Architecture, Technique & Representation. (Illus.). 170p. 1999. text 22.00 (*90-5701-032-1*, 810593); pap. text 18.00 (*90-5701-072-0*, 810594) Gordon & Breach.
Allen, Stan, ed. Colossal Urbanism. (Illus.). 96p. Date not set. pap. write for info. (*1-883584-12-4*) CUGSA.
Allen, Stan, jt. auth. see Meier, Richard.
Allen, Standish K., Jr., et al. Triploid Oysters: Hatchery Manual for Producing Triploid Oysters. 32p. 1989. VHS 250.00 (*0-295-77034-1*) U of Wash Pr.
Allen, Stephanie & Zeiger, Carolyn A. Doing It All Isn't Everything: A Woman's Guide to Harmony & Empowerment. 1993. 19.95 (*0-9632788-1-9*); pap. 12.95 (*0-9632788-0-0*) New Perspect.
Allen, Stephanie W. Creating Your Own Funeral or Memorial Service: A Workbook. (Illus.). 144p. 1998. pap., wbk. ed. 16.95 (*0-9644207-2-4*) KiteShade Pubng.
***Allen, Stephanie West.** The Sexual Harassment Prevention Workshop. (Trainer's Workshop Ser.: Vol. 3). 300p. 2000. 35.00 (*0-8144-7051-3*) AMACOM.
Allen, Stephanie West, see West Allen, Stephanie.
Allen, Stephen D. Reality: Drugs & Guns--No-Win Solutions. LC 92-64322. 126p. (J). (gr. k-8). 1992. pap. 14.95 (*0-9634084-7-X*) S D A Pub.
Allen, Stephen D., jt. auth. see Allen, Roger E.
Allen, Steve. The Bug & the Slug in the Rug. LC 95-78159. (Illus.). 44p. (J). 1995. 16.95 (*1-880851-17-2*) Greene Bark Pr.
— But Seriously... Steve Allen Speaks His Mind. LC 96-24257. 392p. 1996. 24.95 (*1-57392-090-8*) Prometheus Bks.
— Canyoneering: The San Rafael Swell. LC 91-24599. (Illus.). 320p. (Orig.). (C). 1992. pap. 16.95 (*0-87480-372-1*) U of Utah Pr.
— Canyoneering 3: Loop Hikes in Utah's Escalante. 3rd ed. LC 97-24495. 386p. 1997. pap. text 21.95 (*0-87480-545-7*) U of Utah Pr.
— Canyoneering 2: Technical Loop Hikes in Southern Utah. LC 94-31739. (Illus.). 248p. (Orig.). 1995. pap. 19.95 (*0-87480-467-1*) U of Utah Pr.
— Die Laughing. LC 97-72052. 304p. 1998. 21.00 (*1-57566-241-8*, Knsington) Kensgtn Pub Corp.
— Die Laughing. 288p. 1999. mass mkt. 5.99 (*1-57566-380-5*) Kensgtn Pub Corp.
***Allen, Steve.** Domain. 2001. write for info. (*0-312-87476-6*, Pub. by Forge NYC) St Martin.
Allen, Steve. Dumbth: And Eighty-One Ways to Make Americans Smarter. LC 89-10647. 359p. 1989. 25.95 (*0-87975-539-3*) Prometheus Bks.
— Dumbth: And Eighty-One Ways to Make Americans Smarter. LC 89-10647. 359p. (C). 1991. reprint ed. pap. 17.95 (*0-87975-650-0*) Prometheus Bks.
— Dumbth: The Lost Art of Thinking. 2nd rev. ed. LC 98-29615. 445p. 1998. pap. 18.95 (*1-57392-237-4*) Prometheus Bks.
— Hi-Ho, Steverino! large type ed. 477p. 1992. reprint ed. lib. bdg. 18.95 (*1-56054-521-6*) Thorndike Pr.
— Hi Ho Steverino: My Adventure in the Wonderful Wacky World of TV. 308p. 1994. pap. 12.95 (*1-56980-010-3*) Barricade Bks.
— Hi-Ho, Steverino: My Adventures in the Wonderful Wacky World of Television. LC 91-40755. 308p. 1992. 19.95 (*0-942637-55-0*) Barricade Bks.
— How to Be Funny: Discovering the Comic You. LC 97-51191. 306p. 1998. pap. text 17.95 (*1-57392-206-4*) Prometheus Bks.
— The Hustler's Handbook: How to Play Pool for Fun & Profit. LC 93-84911. (Illus.). 268p. (Orig.). 1993. 29.95 (*1-883824-02-8*); pap. 19.95 (*1-883824-03-6*) Premier GA.
— Make'em Laugh. LC 92-20700. (Illus.). 339p. 1993. 25.95 (*0-87975-837-6*) Prometheus Bks.
— The Man Who Turned Back the Clock & Other Short Stories. LC 95-20054. 348p. 1995. 25.95 (*1-57392-002-9*) Prometheus Bks.
— Meeting of Minds, 4 vols., Vol. 1. LC 89-62786. 191p. 1989. pap. 17.95 (*0-87975-550-4*) Prometheus Bks.
— Meeting of Minds, 4 vols., Vol. 2. LC 89-62786. 255p. 1989. pap. 17.95 (*0-87975-565-2*) Prometheus Bks.
— Meeting of Minds, 4 vols., Vol. 3. LC 89-62786. 185p. 1989. pap. 17.95 (*0-87975-566-0*) Prometheus Bks.
— Meeting of Minds, 4 vols., Vol. 4. LC 89-62786. 174p. 1989. pap. 17.95 (*0-87975-567-9*) Prometheus Bks.

A

— Meeting of Minds: The Television Scripts, 4 vols., Set. 805p. 1989. pap. 59.95 (0-87975-561-X) Prometheus Bks.

— More Steve Allen on the Bible, Religion & Morality, Bk. II. LC 92-41364. 452p. 1993. 27.95 (0-87975-736-1) Prometheus Bks.

— Murder in Hawaii. LC 98-66231. 320p. 1999. 22.00 (1-57566-375-9) Kensgtn Pub Corp.

***Allen, Steve.** Murder in Hawaii. 2000. mass mkt. 5.99 (1-57566-529-8, Knsington) Kensgtn Pub Corp.

Allen, Steve. Murder in Hollywood. write for info. (0-318-62729-9, Zebra Kensgtn) Kensgtn Pub Corp.

— Murder in Manhattan. 352p. 1991. mass mkt. 4.95 (0-8217-3440-7, Zebra Kensgtn) Kensgtn Pub Corp.

— Murder on the Atlantic. 288p. 1995. 19.95 (0-8217-5062-3, Zebra Kensgtn) Kensgtn Pub Corp.

— Murder on the Atlantic. 304p. 1996. mass mkt. 5.99 (1-57566-097-0, Knsington) Kensgtn Pub Corp.

— Murder on the Glitter Box. 352p. 1998. mass mkt. 5.99 (1-57566-245-0, Knsington) Kensgtn Pub Corp.

— Reflections. LC 94-11257. 326p. (Orig.). (C). 1994. 25.95 (0-87975-904-6) Prometheus Bks.

— Ripoff: A Report on Moral Collapse & Corruption in America. 1979. 9.95 (0-8184-0249-0) Carol Pub Group.

— Steve Allen on the Bible Bks. 1-2: Religion & Morality, 2 vols. LC 90-39954. 938p. 1992. 48.95 (0-87975-738-8) Prometheus Bks.

— Steve Allen on the Bible, Religion & Morality. LC 90-39954. 464p. (C). 1990. 26.95 (0-87975-638-1) Prometheus Bks.

***Allen, Steve.** Steve Allen's Songs: 100 Lyrics with Commentary. LC 99-42567. (Illus.). 160p. 1999. boxed set 33.00 (0-7864-0736-0) McFarland & Co.

Allen, Steve. The Wake. 107p. 1996. pap. 5.60 (0-87129-719-1, M80) Dramatic Pub.

— Wake up to Murder. LC 96-76489. 256p. 1996. 19.95 (1-57566-090-3, Knsington) Kensgtn Pub Corp.

— Wake up to Murder. 384p. 1997. mass mkt. 5.99 (1-57566-236-1, Knsington) Kensgtn Pub Corp.

Allen, Steven. Girls on the Tenth Floor & Other Stories. LC 78-128718. (Short Story Index Reprint Ser.). 1977. 17.95 (0-8369-3608-6) Ayer.

Allen, Steven, jt. auth. see Kleinstein, Arnold.

Allen, Steven J. Violation of Trust: Whatever Happened to the Social Security Trust Funds. LC 95-74711. 144p. 1995. mass mkt. 2.95 (0-9648635-0-2) Srs Coalition.

Allen, Steven W. Do-It-Yourself Living Trust Plan: For a Married Couple. 58p. 1990. student ed. 395.00 (1-879033-00-3) Legal Awareness.

— Do-It-Yourself Living Trust Plan: For a Single Person. 45p. 1990. student ed. 395.00 (1-879033-01-1) Legal Awareness.

Allen, Stewart. Status of the Interior Columbia Basin: Summary of Scientific Findings. Quigley, Tom, ed. (Illus.). 146p. 1998. reprint ed. pap. text 35.00 (0-7881-3809-X) DIANE Pub.

Allen, Stewart E., ed. Chemical Analysis of Ecological Materials. 2nd ed. (Illus.). 384p. (C). 1989. text 149.95 (0-632-01742-2) Blackwell Sci.

Allen, Stewart L. The Devil's Cup: Coffee, the Driving Force in History. LC 99-39137. 256p. 1999. 25.00 (1-56947-174-6) Soho Press.

Allen, Stuart. Trigg in Tibet. 66p. 1993. pap. 6.95 (1-55939-016-6) Snow Lion Pubns.

Allen, Sture. Text Processing: Text Analysis & Generation. (Data Linguistica Ser.). 653p. (Orig.). 1982. pap. text 85.00 (91-22-00594-3) Coronet Bks.

Allen, Sture, ed. Possible Worlds in Humanities, Arts, & Sciences: Proceedings of Nobel Symposium 65. (Research in Text Theory Ser.: Vol. 14). x, 453p. (C). 1989. lib. bdg. 150.00 (3-11-011220-5) De Gruyter.

— The Situation of High-Quality Literature: Papers Presented at the Swedish Academy Nobel Jubilee Symposium, Stockholm, 1991. 150p. (Orig.). 1993. pap. 45.00 (91-22-01567-1) Coronet Bks.

— Translation of Poetry & Poetic Prose: Proceedings of the Nobel Symposium 110 Stockholm, Sweden 23 - 29 August 1998. 300p. 1999. 56.00 (981-02-3922-X) World Scientific Pub.

Allen, Sue. Victorian Bookbindings: A Pictorial Survey. rev. ed. LC 76-7420. 58p. 1976. lib. bdg. 34.00 (0-226-68787-2) U Ch Pr.

Allen, Sue A. How to Use Leg Wraps, Bandages & Boots: Supportive Leg Care for Your Horse. McKinney, Betty J., ed. LC 96-962. (Illus.). 112p. (Orig.). 1996. pap. 11.95 (0-931866-72-3) Alpine Pubns.

Allen, Susan & Mor, Vincent, eds. Living in the Community with Disability: Service Needs, Use, & Systems. LC 97-47018. (Illus.). 352p. 1998. 58.95 (0-8261-1168-8) Springer Pub.

Allen, Susan D. Coronary Angioplasty. Holloran, Colleen A., ed. (Illus.). 32p. 1992. pap. text 2.85 (0-916999-12-2) HERC Inc.

Allen, Susan D. & Holloran, Colleen A. Reconnecting. (Illus.). 32p. 1991. pap. text 2.75 (0-916999-11-4) HERC Inc.

Allen, Susan D., et al. The Puzzle of Heart Failure - Putting the Pieces Together: For Heart Failure Patients. (Illus.). 64p. 1991. pap. text 3.25 (0-916999-09-2) HERC Inc.

— Your Valves: Channels to a Healthy Heart: For Valve Disease & Valve Surgery Patients. (Illus.). 64p. 1991. pap. text 3.25 (0-916999-10-6) HERC Inc.

Allen, Susan D., jt. auth. see Dietitians in College & University Food Service St.

Allen, Susan D., jt. auth. see Egan, Maureen.

Allen, Susan D., ed. see Gibson, Nancy, et al.

Allen, Susan D., ed. see Markey, Barb & Hunt, Tad.

Allen, Susan D., ed. see Okerlund, Twila.

Allen, Susan E. & Birdwhistell, Terry L., eds. The Frontier Nursing Service Oral History Project: An Annotated Guide. LC 85-51419. (University of Kentucky Libraries Occasional Papers: No. 9). (Illus.). 125p. (Orig.). 1987. pap. 15.00 (0-917519-05-1) U of KY Libs.

Allen, Susan G. & Serwatka, Thomas S. Auditory Perception Test for the Hearing Impaired. 35p. 1994. pap. 13.95 (0-931421-29-2); pap. 26.95 (0-931421-38-1) Psychol Educ Pubns.

Allen, Susan H. Finding the Walls of Troy: Frank Calvert & Heinrich Schliemann at Hisarlik. LC 98-13101. 486p. 1999. 35.00 (0-520-20868-4, Pub. by U CA Pr) Cal Prin Full Svc.

Allen, Susan L., ed. Media Anthropology: Informing Global Citizens. LC 93-17649. 208p. 1993. 55.00 (0-89789-342-5, Bergin & Garvey) Greenwood.

Allen, Suzan W. & Talbot, Karen H. Preparing Preschoolers: An Easy-to-Use Nursery School Program with Lesson Plans & Teaching Aids for Parents & Professionals. LC 80-83029. 150p. (Orig.). 1981. pap. 15.98 (0-88290-160-5, 2047) Horizon Utah.

— Projects for Preschoolers: A Super Fun Collection of Games, Crafts & Guided Activities for Young Children. 72p. (Orig.). 1981. pap. 19.98 (0-88290-161-3, 2048) Horizon Utah.

— Teaching Preschoolers: Preparing Preschoolers, Projects for Preschoolers, 2 bks., Set. 1994. pap. 33.98 (0-88290-463-9) Horizon Utah.

Allen, T. Pharaohs & Pyramids. (Time Travelers Bks.). (J). (gr. 4-9). 1977. lib. bdg. 14.95 (0-88110-103-6, Usborne) EDC.

— Program Power I: How It Was, What Happened, What It's Like Now. 104p. 1994. pap. 6.00 (0-317-05543-7, 93-90586) Tenavision.

Allen, T., jt. auth. see Polmer, N.

Allen, T., ed. see Particle Size Analysis Conference Staff.

Allen, T. D. Writing to Create Ourselves: New Approaches for Teachers, Students, & Writers. LC 82-1878. 255p. 1982. 22.95 (0-8061-1768-0) U of Okla Pr.

Allen, T. Diener, jt. auth. see Autry, Gloria D.

Allen, T. E., ed. Oil Spill Chemical Dispersants: Research, Experience, & Recommendations - STP 840. 448p. 1984. 54.00 (0-8031-0400-6, STP840) ASTM.

Allen, T. Earl, jt. auth. see Miller, David K.

Allen, T. F. & Starr, Thomas B. Hierarchy: Perspectives for Ecological Complexity. LC 81-22010. (Illus.). 328p. 1997. pap. text 16.00 (0-226-01432-0) U Ch Pr.

Allen, T. F., ed. see Allen, Timothy F. & Hoekstra, Thomas W.

Allen, T. G. An Iron Age & Romano-British Enclosed Settlement at Watkins Farm, Oxon. (Windrush Valley Ser.: Vol. 1). (Illus.). 130p. 1990. pap. 20.00 (0-947816-80-1, Pub. by Oxford Univ Comm Arch) David Brown.

— Lithics & Landscape: Archaeological Discoveries on the Thames Water Pipeline at Gatehampton Farm, Goring, Oxfordshire. (Thames Valley Ser.: Vol. 7). (Illus.). 140p. 1995. pap. 32.00 (0-947816-85-2, Pub. by Oxford Univ Comm Arch) David Brown.

— A Medieval Grange of Abingdon Abbey at Dean Court Farm, Cumnor, Oxford. (Illus.). 218p. 1995. pap. 23.50 (0-946897-91-3, Pub. by Oxbow Bks) David Brown.

Allen, T. G. & Robinson, M. A. The Prehistoric Landscape & Iron Age Enclosed Settlement at Mingies Ditch, Hardwick-with-Yelford, Oxfordshire. (Windrush Valley Ser.: Vol. 2). (Illus.). 250p. 1993. pap. 50.00 (0-947816-82-8, Pub. by Oxford Univ Comm Arch) David Brown.

Allen, T. G., et al. Excavations at Roughground Farm, Lechlade, Gloucestershire: A Prehistoric & Roman Landscape. (Cotswold Water Park Ser.: Vol. 1). (Illus.). 208p. 1993. pap. 43.00 (0-947816-83-6, Pub. by Oxford Univ Comm Arch) David Brown.

Allen, T. Harrell. Lee's Last Major General: Bryan Grimes of North Carolina. (Illus.). 352p. 1998. 24.95 (1-882810-23-6) Savas Pub.

— New Methods in Social Science Research: Policy Sciences & Futures Research. LC 76-12840. (Praeger Special Studies). 176p. 1978. 42.95 (0-275-90282-X, C0282, Praeger Pubs) Greenwood.

Allen, T. Harrell, jt. auth. see Nager, Norman R.

Allen, T. Jeff, et al, eds. Sodium-Calcium Exchange. (Illus.). 344p. 1989. text 89.50 (0-19-854735-8) OUP.

Allen, T. R. A Penny for a Rembrandt: A Journal of a Pilgrimage to Assisi, the Holy Land, Rome & the Vatican. 202p. 1999. 9.00 (0-9672704-0-5) T R Allen.

Allen, T. W., ed. Opera, 5 vols. Incl. Vol. 1. Iliad, I-XII. 3rd ed. Monroe, D. B. 298p. 1920. text 23.00 (0-19-814528-4); Vol. 2. Iliad, XIII-XXIV. 3rd ed. Monroe, D. B., ed. 314p. 1920. text 24.95 (0-19-814529-2); Vol. 3. Odyssey, I-XII. 2nd ed. Monroe, D. B., ed. 242p. 1922. text 22.00 (0-19-814531-4); Vol. 4. Odyssey, XIII-XXIV. 2nd ed. Monroe, D. B., ed. 228p. 1922. text 22.00 (0-19-814532-2); Vol. 5. Hymns, Etc. Monroe, D. B., ed. 294p. 1922. text 27.00 (0-19-814534-9); (Oxford Classical Texts Ser.). (C). write for info. (0-318-54864-X) OUP.

Allen, T. W., et al, eds. Homeric Hymns. cxv, 471p. 1980. reprint ed. 78.00 (90-256-0820-5, Pub. by AM Hakkert) BookLink Distributors.

Allen, T. W., ed. see Homer.

Allen, Ted, jt. auth. see Omelianuk, Scott.

Allen, Terence. Particle Size Measurement. 4th ed. (Illus.). 736p. 1990. mass mkt. 182.95 (0-412-35070-X, A4396) Chapman & Hall.

Allen, Terese. Fresh Market Wisconsin: Good Food, Good Folks & Good Fun at Community Celebrations. LC 93-70423. 176p. 1993. pap. 14.95 (0-942495-26-8) Palmer Pubns Inc.

— Hometown Flavor: A Cook's Tour of Wisconsin's Butcher Shops, Bakeries, Cheese Factories & Other Speciality Markets. LC 98-8212. (Illus.). 180p. 1998. pap. 18.95 (1-879483-42-4) Prairie Oak Pr.

— Wisconsin Food Festivals: Good Food, Good Folks & Good Fun at Community Celebrations. LC 95-17345. (Illus.). 184p. 1995. pap. 15.95 (0-942495-45-4) Palmer Pubns Inc.

Allen, Terese, ed. Home Cooked Culture: Wisconsin Through Recipes. (Illus.). 110p. 1998. pap. 14.95 (0-9667012-0-8) Wisconsin Art.

Allen, Terry. Five Essays on Islamic Art. (Illus.). x, 189p. 1988. pap. 35.00 (0-944940-00-5) Solipsist Pr.

— Terry Allen: A Simple Story (Juarez) LC 92-85535. (Illus.). 80p. (Orig.). 1991. pap. 20.00 (1-881390-02-0) OSU Wexner Ctr.

Allen, Terry & Hickey, Dave. Big Witness (Living in Wishes) Terry Allen. (Illus.). 56p. 1989. pap. 9.00 (0-930495-05-5) San Fran Art Inst.

Allen, Terry, et al. Ohio. LC 86-25063. 24p. (Orig.). 1986. pap. 5.00 (0-932706-11-8) WSU Art Gallrs.

Allen, Thelma E. Recipes from Sweet Yesterday, Vol. 1. Allen, Michael, ed. & photos by by. (Illus.). 200p. 1993. mass mkt. 15.00 (0-9668322-0-5) Sweet Yesterday.

— Recipes from Sweet Yesterday, Vol. 2. Allen, Michael, ed. & photos by by. (Illus.). 200p. 1995. mass mkt. 15.00 (0-9668322-1-3) Sweet Yesterday.

— Recipes from Sweet Yesterday, Vol. 3. Allen, Michael, ed. & photos by by. (Illus.). 200p. 1998. mass mkt. 15.00 (0-9668322-2-1) Sweet Yesterday.

Allen, Theodore W. The Invention of the White Race: Racial Oppression & Social Control. (Haymarket Ser.: Vol. 1). 260p. (C). 1994. pap. 22.00 (0-86091-660-X, B2505, Pub. by Verso) Norton.

— The Invention of the White Race Vol. 2: The Origins of Racial Oppression in Anglo-America. 1997. pap. 22.00 (1-85984-076-0, Pub. by Verso) Norton.

***Allen, Theresa C.** Mama Said, "Get in the House" Embracing the Wisdom of Mama & God. Brooks, Pamela, ed. LC 99-98137. xi, 129p. 2000. pap. 13.00 (0-9676710-0-0) Allens Ink.

— Times Past: A 31-Day Devotional of Psalms, Poetry, Power, Prayer & Praise. Brooks, Pamela, ed. 70p. 2000. write for info. (0-9676710-1-9) Allens Ink.

Allen, Thomas. Integration Is Genocide. LC 96-95226. iv, 92p. (Orig.). 1997. pap. 8.00 (0-9656663-0-1) T C Allen.

— New Song & Dance from the Central Pacific: Creating & Performing the Fatele of Tokelau in the Islands & in New Zealand. (Dance & Music Ser.: No. 9). 180p. 1996. 54.00 (0-945193-77-7) Pendragon NY.

***Allen, Thomas.** The Right to Property in Commonwealth Constitutions. LC 99-19518. (Cambridge Studies in International & Comparative Law: No. 11). 280p. (C). 2000. 69.95 (0-521-58377-2) Cambridge U Pr.

Allen, Thomas B. America from Space. (Illus.). 160p. 1998. 29.95 (1-55209-280-1) Firefly Bks Ltd.

— The Blue & the Gray with National Geographic Guide to the "Civil War National Battlefield Park" Bendavid-Val, Leah & Harrell, Mary Ann, eds. (Illus.). 320p. 1992. 41.95 (0-87044-877-3) Natl Geog.

— The Blue & the Gray with National Geographic Guide to the "Civil War National Battlefield Park" Bendavid-Val, Leah & Harrell, Mary Ann, eds. LC 92-13567. (Illus.). 320p. 1993. 40.00 (0-87044-876-5) Natl Geog.

— Code-Name Downfall: The Invasion of Japan, November 1, 1945. 1995. 25.00 (0-671-88628-2) S&S Trade.

***Allen, Thomas B.** Offerings at the Wall: Artifacts from the Vietnam Veterans Memorial Collection. (Illus.). 287p. 1999. reprint ed. pap. text 25.00 (0-7881-6384-1) DIANE Pub.

— Offerings at the Wall: Artifacts from the Vietnam Veterans Memorial Collection. (Illus.). 288p. 2000. reprint ed. text 40.00 (0-7881-9180-2) DIANE Pub.

Allen, Thomas B. The Shark Almanac: A Fully Illustrated Natural History of Sharks, Skates & Rays. LC 98-38524. (Illus.). 274p. 1999. 35.00 (1-55821-582-4) Lyons Pr.

***Allen, Thomas B.** Shark Attacks: Their Causes & Avoidance. (Illus.). 2001. 24.95 (1-58574-174-4) Lyons Pr.

— The Washington Monument: It Stands for All. (Illus.). 224p. 1999. 24.95 (1-56331-931-4, Pub. by Discovery) Random.

— The Washington Monument: It Stands for All. LC 00-25608. (Illus.). 172p. 2000. 29.95 (1-56331-921-7) Discovery.

— The Washington Monument: It Stands for All. LC 00-25608. (Illus.). 2000. write for info. (1-56331-788-5) Discovery.

Allen, Thomas B. & Hyman, Charles O., eds. We Americans: Celebrating a Nation Its People & Its Past. LC 99-31275. 336p. 1999. per. 39.50 (0-7922-7005-3) Natl Geog.

Allen, Thomas B. & Polmar, Norman. Code-Name Downfall: The Secret Plan to Invade Japan & Why Truman Dropped the Bomb. (Illus.). 320p. 1995. 25.00 (0-684-80406-9) S&S Trade.

Allen, Thomas B., jt. auth. see Cohen, William S.

Allen, Thomas B., jt. auth. see Polmar, Norman.

Allen, Thomas C. Adam to Abraham: The Early History of Man. LC 98-92753. vi, 234p. 1998. pap. 12.95 (0-9656663-1-X) T C Allen.

***Allen, Thomas C.** Species of Men: A Polygenetic Hypothesis. LC 99-94487. 389p. 1999. pap. 15.95 (0-9656663-2-8) T C Allen.

Allen, Thomas E. Young Deaf Adults & the Transition from High School to Postsecondary Careers. (Illus.). 70p. (Orig.). (C). 1995. pap. text 20.00 (0-7881-2362-9) DIANE Pub.

Allen, Thomas J. The Butterflies of West Virginia & Their Caterpillars. LC 97-4637. (Illus.). 346p. 1997. pap. 22.95 (0-8229-5657-8) U of Pittsburgh Pr.

— Managing the Flow of Technology: Technology Transfer & the Dissemination of Technological Information Within the R & D Organization. 336p. 1984. pap. text 23.00 (0-262-51027-8) MIT Pr.

Allen, Thomas J. & Morton, Michael S., eds. Information Technology & the Corporation of the 1990s: Research Studies. (Illus.). 544p. 1994. text 60.00 (0-19-506806-8) OUP.

Allen, Thomas O. & Roberts, Alan P. Production Operations, 2 vols., Set. 720p. 1993. 120.00 (0-930972-18-X) Oil & Gas.

— Production Operations, Vol. 1. 4th ed. 374p. 1993. 64.00 (0-930972-19-8) Oil & Gas.

— Production Operations, Vol. 2. 4th ed. 346p. 1993. 64.00 (0-930972-20-1) Oil & Gas.

Allen, Thomas W. The ASEAN Report, 2 vols. Wain, Barry, ed. Incl. Vol. 1. Comparative Assessment of the ASEAN Countries. 1980. Vol. 2. Evolution & Programs of ASEAN: The Asian Wall Street Journal. 1980. (Illus.). 414p. 1980. Set pap. 125.00 (0-295-95740-9, 80-110683) U of Wash Pr.

— The Homeric Catalogue of Ships. (Illus.). xi, 191p. write for info. (0-318-70851-5) G Olms Pubs.

Allen-Thompson, Pam, jt. ed. see Dodds, Dinah.

Allen, Tim. Anesthesia & Analgesia for Companion & Laboratory Animals: Bibliography January 1989-January 1995. 98p. (Orig.). (C). 1995. pap. text 25.00 (0-7881-1969-9) DIANE Pub.

— Animal Welfare Legislation, Regulations, & Guidelines: Bibliography. January 1990-January 1995. 57p. (Orig.). (C). 1995. pap. text 25.00 (0-7881-1970-2) DIANE Pub.

— Don't Stand Too Close to a Naked Man. LC 94-28625. (Illus.). 224p. (J). 1994. 19.95 (0-7868-6134-7, Pub. by Hyperion) Time Warner.

— Don't Stand Too Close to a Naked Man. (Illus.). 272p. (J). 1995. reprint ed. mass mkt. 6.50 (0-7868-8902-0, Pub. by Hyperion) Time Warner.

— Ethical & Moral Issues Relating to Animals: A Bibliography. 53p. (Orig.). (C). 1994. pap. text 30.00 (0-7881-0650-3) DIANE Pub.

— I'm Not Really Here. LC 96-36959. 255p. (J). 1996. 21.95 (0-7868-6257-2, Pub. by Hyperion) Time Warner.

— I'm Not Really Here. LC 96-36959. 304p. (J). 1997. reprint ed. mass mkt. 6.99 (0-7868-8932-2, Pub. by Hyperion) Time Warner.

— In Search of Cool Ground: War, Flight & Homecoming in Northeast Africa. LC 96-16119. 350p. 1996. 79.95 (0-86543-524-3); pap. 21.95 (0-86543-525-1) Africa World.

Allen, Tim, ed. Anesthesia & Analgesia for Companion & Laboratory Animals: A Bibliography--January 1988-January 1994. 81p. (Orig.). (C). 1994. pap. text 40.00 (0-7881-1074-8) DIANE Pub.

***Allen, Tim & Eade, John, eds.** Divide Europeans. LC 99-27525. 360p. 1999. 117.00 (90-411-1213-8) Kluwer Law Intl.

Allen, Tim & Morsink, Hubert, eds. When Refugees Go Home: African Experiences. 400p. (C). 1994. 59.95 (0-86543-432-8); pap. 18.95 (0-86543-433-6) Africa World.

***Allen, Tim & Thomas, Alan, eds.** Poverty & Development: Into the 21st Century. (Illus.). 460p. 2000. pap. 29.95 (0-19-877626-8) OUP.

Allen, Tim & Thomas, Alan, eds. Poverty & Development in the Nineteen Nineties. 432p. 1992. 65.00 (0-19-877330-7) OUP.

— Poverty & Development in the Nineteen Nineties. (Illus.). 432p. 1992. pap. text 24.00 (0-19-877331-5) OUP.

Allen, Tim, jt. auth. see Skelton, Tracey.

Allen, Timothy F. & Hoekstra, Thomas W. Toward a Unified Ecology. 400p. 1991. text 70.00 (0-231-06918-9) Col U Pr.

— Toward a Unified Ecology. Allen, T. F. & Roberts, David W., eds. (Complexity in Ecological Systems Ser.). 384p. 1993. pap. 35.50 (0-231-06919-7) Col U Pr.

Allen, Timothy F., jt. auth. see Ahl, Valerie.

Allen, Tom. A Closer Look at Dr. Laura: A Spiritual Perspective. LC 99-216015. 314p. 1999. 19.99 (0-88965-159-0, Pub. by Horizon Books) Chr Pubns.

***Allen, Tom.** Hope for Hurting Parents: When Grown Children Make Bad Choices. 20p. 1999. pap. 1.59 (0-87509-850-9) Chr Pubns.

Allen, Tom. Let Him That Is Without Sin . . . 1998. pap. 1.59 (0-87509-748-0) Chr Pubns.

— Spiritual Leadership Begins at Home. (Contemporary Christian Living Ser.). 19p. (Orig.). 1991. pap. 1.59 (0-87509-463-5) Chr Pubns.

— Ten Foolish Things Christians Do to Stunt Their Growth. LC 96-84983. 1996. pap. 10.99 (0-87509-674-3) Chr Pubns.

— What to Expect Now That You're a Christian: The Pleasures & Pressures of the Faith. 208p. 1999. pap. text 9.99 (0-87509-774-X) Chr Pubns.

***Allen, Tom.** With No Remorse: Murder & Mayhem in our Schools - A Biblical Response. 294p. 1999. pap. 11.99 (0-88965-183-3, Pub. by Horizon Books) Chr Pubns.

Allen, Tom & Allen, Patsy. Captain Scruffy. (Illus.). 32p. (J). (ps-1). 1993. 15.95 (0-460-88104-3, Pub. by J M Dent & Sons) Trafalgar.

— Zizz Cleans Up. (Illus.). 32p. (J). (ps). 1993. 15.95 (0-460-88102-7, Pub. by J M Dent & Sons) Trafalgar.

Allen, Tom, jt. auth. see Abernethy, Kenneth.

Allen, Tom, jt. auth. see Gorton, Dennis L.

Allen, Tom, jt. auth. see Johnson, David.

Allen, Tracey J. & Harmon, Jacque L. APOK Space Explorers. LC 98-9034. (Illus.). 64p. (J). (gr. 1-6). 1999. pap. text 14.95 (0-9664107-0-X) APOK Kreations.

Allen, Tracy. Geography of the Non-Western World: An Introductory. 102p. (C). 1996. pap. text, per., lab manual ed. 10.95 (0-7872-2020-5) Kendall-Hunt.

An Asterisk (*) at the beginning of an entry indicates that the title is appearing for the first time.

***Allen, Traudi.** Cross-Currents in Contemporary Australian Art. (Illus.). 176p. 2000. text 65.00 (*90-5703-511-1*) Craftsman House.

Allen, Traudi. John Perceval. (Illus.). 224p. 1992. pap. 39.95 (*0-522-84495-2*, Pub. by Melbourne Univ Pr) Paul & Co Pubs.

— Roar! Art Collective. (Illus.). 144p. 1995. text 26.00 (*976-8097-82-5*) Gordon & Breach.

Allen, Trevor. The Storm Passed By: Ireland, 1941-42. 197p. 1996. 29.50 (*0-7165-2616-6*, Pub. by F Cass Pubs) Intl Spec Bk.

***Allen, Tricia.** Texas Weather. 318p. 2000. 14.95 (*1-929976-00-3*, Pub. by Top Pubns) Herveys Bklink.

Allen, Valerie. Chaucer. LC 96-24892. 240p. 1997. text 39.95 (*0-312-16259-6*) St Martin.

— The Night Thief. LC 89-28459. (Illus.). 32p. (J). (ps-3). 1990. 14.95 (*0-88289-774-8*) Pelican.

Allen, Vera, ed. see Larsen, Phyllis.

Allen, Vernelle B. Basic Principles of Christian Counseling. 175p. 1994. pap. write for info. (*1-885984-08-1*) Wings of Healing.

— Echoes from a Mountain: Welcome to My World. 65p. 1994. pap. write for info. (*1-885984-12-X*) Wings of Healing.

— From Ape? From Adam? 90p. 1994. pap. write for info. (*1-885984-03-0*) Wings of Healing.

— Living the "High" Life: God's Way? Man's Way? 226p. 1994. pap. write for info. (*1-885984-09-X*) Wings of Healing.

— The Making of Plowshares. 77p. (Orig.). 1994. pap. write for info. (*1-885984-14-6*) Wings of Healing.

— On Wings of Healing. 90p. 1995. pap. write for info. (*1-885984-06-5*) Wings of Healing.

— Out of Egypt, Out of Bondage. 80p. 1995. pap. write for info. (*1-885984-07-3*) Wings of Healing.

— Parents Aren't Perfect. 110p. 1994. pap. write for info. (*1-885984-01-4*) Wings of Healing.

— Poems Are for Children: Welcome to My World. 78p. (J). 1994. pap. write for info. (*1-885984-10-3*) Wings of Healing.

— Rainbows & Butterflies: Welcome to My World. 1994. pap. write for info. (*1-885984-13-8*) Wings of Healing.

— That Woman in Proverbs. 95p. 1994. pap. write for info. (*1-885984-11-1*) Wings of Healing.

— The Three "R's" of Calvary. 85p. 1994. pap. write for info. (*1-885984-05-7*) Wings of Healing.

— When Giants Fall. 70p. pap. write for info. (*1-885984-02-2*) Wings of Healing.

— When It Hurts to Say Good-Bye: Welcome to My World. 48p. 1994. pap. write for info. (*1-885984-00-6*) Wings of Healing.

— Where the Law Stopped & Grace Began. 170p. 1994. pap. text. write for info. (*1-885984-04-9*) Wings of Healing.

Allen, Vernon & Kuhn, Glenda P. A Caddie: A Servant of Golf. Palmer, George W., ed. 157p. 1995. pap. 9.95 (*0-9643029-4-2*) SpritSBo.

Allen, Vernon L. & Scheibe, Karl E., eds. The Social Context of Conduct: Psychological Writings of Theodore R. Sarbin. LC 82-473. 273p. 1982. 65.00 (*0-275-90752-X*, C0752, Praeger Pubs) Greenwood.

***Allen, Vicki L.** For Molly. 370p. 1999. 24.95 (*0-9674880-3-6*) Magnol Pub.

— For Molly. 370p. 2000. pap. write for info. (*0-9674880-4-4*) Magnol Pub.

Allen, Victor L. Social Analysis: A Marxist Critique & Alternative. LC 75-327627. 338p. reprint ed. pap. 104.80 (*0-608-30708-4*, 201004900074) Bks Demand.

Allen, Virginia. Mountain Biking to Natural Arches. Moore, Chris & Anderson, Frank, eds. (Illus.). 70p. 2001. mass mkt. 7.95 (*1-891858-07-6*, 4011) Arch Hunter Bks.

— My Fifty Favorite Arches. (Illus.). 88p. 1998. pap. 6.95 (*1-891858-02-5*, 4010) Arch Hunter Bks.

***Allen, Virginia.** Reflections. 2000. write for info. (*1-58235-576-2*) Watermrk Pr.

Allen, Virginia F. Crossword Puzzles to Help You Learn to Spell. 64p. 1991. 4.95 (*0-940723-07-7*) SIIS.

— Reading for Life: A First Book for Adults & Their Tutors. 288p. (Orig.). 1987. pap. text 18.50 (*0-940723-00-X*) SIIS.

— The Sounds of American English: A Handbook for English As a Second Language. 33p. 1989. teacher ed. 5.00 (*0-940723-06-9*) SIIS.

— Techniques in Teaching Vocabulary. (Teaching Techniques in English as a Second or Foreign Language Ser.). (Illus.). 144p. (Orig.). (C). 1983. pap. text 13.50 (*0-19-434130-5*) OUP.

Allen, Virginia F. & Forman, Sidney. English As a Second Language: A Comprehensive Bibliography. Cordasco, Francesco, ed. LC 77-90404. (Bilingual-Bicultural Education in the U. S. Ser.). 1978. reprint ed. lib. bdg. 28.95 (*0-405-11073-1*) Ayer.

Allen, Virginia F. & Quan, Cao. The Sounds of American English: A Handbook for English as a Foreign Language, English-Vietnamese Edition. 49p. 1986. teacher ed. 8.95 (*0-940723-04-2*) SIIS.

Allen, Virginia G., jt. ed. see Rigg, Pat.

Allen, Virginia M. The Femme Fatale: Erotic Icon. LC 82-62834. xviii, 258p. 1983. 25.00 (*0-87875-267-6*) Whitston Pub.

Allen, Virginia P. Before the Pattern: An Idea Book for Drawing Garment Designs. 1975. pap. 2.95 (*0-686-11167-2*) Spinning Spool.

— Beyond the Pattern: A Guide to Creative Sewing & Design with Knit Fabrics. LC 73-91225. 1973. pap. 9.95 (*0-686-09884-6*); lib. bdg. 15.95 (*0-686-09885-4*) Spinning Spool.

Allen, Vivien. Hall Caine: Portrait of a Victorian Romancer. 350p. 1997. pap. 23.95 (*1-85075-809-3*, Pub. by Sheffield Acad) CUP Services.

***Allen, Vivien, ed.** Dear Mr. Rossetti: The Letters of Dante Gabriel Rossetti & Hall Caine, 1878-1881. 350p. 2000. 55.00 (*1-84127-049-0*, Pub. by Sheffield Acad); pap. 25.00 (*1-84127-050-4*, Pub. by Sheffield Acad) CUP Services.

Allen, W. A. The Sheepeaters. 1989. boxed set 15.95 (*0-87770-464-3*) Ye Galleon.

Allen, W. B., et al, eds. The Essential Antifederalist. LC 85-5303. 292p. (Orig.). 1985. pap. 17.50 (*0-8191-4632-3*); lib. bdg. 52.00 (*0-8191-4631-5*) U Pr of Amer.

***Allen, W. B. & Cloonan, Kevin A.** The Federalist Papers: A Commentary : "The Baton Rouge Lectures" (Masterworks in the Western Tradition Ser.: Vol. 3). 440p. 2000. pap. text 34.95 (*0-8204-3756-5*) P Lang Pubng.

Allen, W. C. Annals of Haywood County, 1808-1935: Historical, Sociological, Biographical & Genealogical. (Illus.). 632p. 1997. reprint ed. lib. bdg. 66.50 (*0-8328-6901-5*) Higginson Bk Co.

— History of Halifax County. (Illus.). 235p. 1997. reprint ed. lib. bdg. 29.00 (*0-8328-6900-7*) Higginson Bk Co.

Allen, W. E., ed. see Finney, Charles G.

Allen, W. Edward, jt. auth. see England, C. W.

Allen, W. Gordon. Enigma Fantastique. 194p. 1996. reprint ed. pap. 19.50 (*0-7873-0021-7*) Hlth Research.

Allen, W. Gore. Renaissance in the North. LC 79-111810. (Essay Index Reprint Ser.). 1977. 20.95 (*0-8369-1590-9*) Ayer.

Allen, W. S., ed. Longman Structural Readers, Stage 6. (English As a Second Language Bk.). 1981. pap. 4.25 (*0-685-03098-9*) Longman.

Allen, W. Sidney. Sandhi: The Theoretical, Phonetic, & Historical Bases of Word-Junction in Sanskrit. (Janua Linguarum, Series Minor: No. 17). 1972. reprint ed. pap. text 24.65 (*90-279-2360-4*) Mouton.

— Vox Latina: A Guide to the Pronunciation of Classical Latin. (Illus.). 152p. (C). 1989. pap. text 16.95 (*0-521-37936-9*) Cambridge U Pr.

Allen, Wallace W. A Design for News. LC 81-2022. (Illus.). 1981. spiral bd. 10.95 (*0-932272-04-5*) Minneapolis Tribune.

Allen, Walter. All in a Lifetime. 1988. 22.95 (*0-8488-0416-3*) Amereon Ltd.

***Allen, Walter.** Bellemere. 2000. 19.95 (*0-9673439-5-X*) InSync Commn.

Allen, Walter. Governor Chamberlain's Administration in South Carolina: A Chapter of Reconstruction in the Southern States. LC 73-95060. (Select Bibliographies Reprint Ser.). 1977. 42.95 (*0-8369-5062-3*) Ayer.

Allen, Walter, jt. auth. see Farley, Reynolds.

Allen, Walter C., ed. Serial Publications in Large Libraries. LC 74-629637. (Allerton Park Institute Ser.: No. 16). 194p. 1970. 10.00 (*0-87845-011-4*) U of Ill Grad Sch.

Allen, Walter C. & Delzell, Robert F., eds. Ideals & Standards: The History of the University of Illinois Graduate School of Library & Information Science, 1893-1993. 1992. 25.00 (*0-87845-089-0*) U of Ill Grad Sch.

Allen, Walter G., Jr. When You Least Expect Me. LC 98-71832. (Illus.). 80p. 1998. pap. 7.00 (*0-9665008-0-6*) Gathering-USA.

Allen, Walter P. Easy Crossword Puzzles for People Learning English. 1956. pap. 2.50 (*0-87789-026-9*) ELS Educ Servs.

— More Easy Crossword Puzzles for People Learning English. 1970. pap. 2.50 (*0-87789-031-5*) ELS Educ Servs.

Allen, Walter R., et al, eds. Black American Families, 1965 to 1984: A Classified, Selectively Annotated Bibliography, 16. LC 86-14959. (Bibliographies & Indexes in Afro-American & African Studies: No. 16). 511p. 1986. lib. bdg. 65.00 (*0-313-25613-6*, ALB/) Greenwood.

Allen, Walter R., et al, eds. College in Black & White: African American Students in Predominantly White & in Historically Black Public Universities. LC 90-32306. (SUNY Series, Frontiers of Education). 322p. (C). 1991. text 24.50 (*0-7914-0485-4*) State U NY Pr.

Allen, Walter R., jt. auth. see Farley, Reynolds.

Allen, Ward. Translating for King James: Notes Made by a Translator of King James's Bible. LC 69-17535. 164p. 1993. reprint ed. pap. 19.95 (*0-8265-1246-1*) Vanderbilt U Pr.

Allen, Ward S. & Jacobs, Edward C. The Coming of the King James Gospels: A Collation of the Translators' Work-in-Progress. 448p. 1995. pap. 36.00 (*1-55728-345-1*); text 58.00 (*1-55728-327-3*) U of Ark Pr.

Allen, Warren D. Our Marching Civilization. LC 77-25408. (Music Reprint Ser.). 1978. reprint ed. lib. bdg. 23.50 (*0-306-77568-9*) Da Capo.

Allen, Warren W. Accounting Tutorial: A Transaction Analysis. 2nd ed. (BA - Accounting - First Year Ser.). 1988. pap. 9.95 (*0-538-02790-8*) S-W Pub.

— Advanced Automated Accounting - DOS. 3rd ed. (Accounting Advanced Ser.). 1994. mass mkt. 30.95 (*0-538-62317-9*) S-W Pub.

— Advanced Automated Accounting - Working Papers. 3rd ed. (BE - Accounting Advanced Ser.). 1994. pap., wbk. ed. 9.95 (*0-538-62319-5*) S-W Pub.

— Advanced Automated Accounting, Mac. 3rd ed. (BE - Accounting Advanced Ser.). 1995. 96.95 (*0-538-62324-1*); mass mkt. 30.95 (*0-538-62318-7*) S-W Pub.

— Automated Acccounting for Windows. 5th ed. (BA - Accounting - First Year Ser.). 1996. 79.95 (*0-538-63966-0*) S-W Pub.

— Automated Accounting for Windows. 5th ed. (BA - Accounting - First Year Ser.). 1995. pap. 37.95 (*0-538-63961-X*) S-W Pub.

— Automated Accounting for Windows, Enrichment Activities. 5th ed. (BA - Accounting - First Year Ser.). 1995. pap. 8.95 (*0-538-64163-0*) S-W Pub.

— Automated Accounting for Windows, Working Papers. 5th ed. (BA - Accounting - First Year Ser.). 1995. pap. 9.95 (*0-538-64190-8*) S-W Pub.

— Computerized Payroll Procedures. 2nd ed. (BA - Accounting - First Year Ser.). 1988. mass mkt. 16.95 (*0-538-60038-1*) S-W Pub.

— Microtools. 3rd ed. (DF - Computer Applications Ser.). 1993. mass mkt. 30.95 (*0-538-61656-3*) S-W Pub.

— Microtools: Integrated Software for Word. (DF - Computer Applications Ser.). 1988. mass mkt. 25.95 (*0-538-10160-1*) S-W Pub.

— Microtools Reference Handbook. (DF - Computer Applications Ser.). 1988. mass mkt. 11.95 (*0-538-10167-9*) S-W Pub.

— Theory of Dividends. (FB - Introduction to Finance Ser.). (C). 2001. mass mkt. 62.95 (*0-538-80270-7*) S-W Pub.

Allen, Warren W. & Klooster, Dale H. Microtools: Integrated Software for Word Processing, Spreadsheet, & Database. large type ed. 1991. 80.50 (*0-614-09877-7*, L-85812-00) Am Printing Hse.

Allen, Warren W., jt. auth. see Klooster, Dale H.

Allen, Warren W., jt. auth. see Oguinn.

Allen, Wendy & Foultier-Smith, Nicole. Paralleles: Commuication et Culture. (Illus.). 542p. (C). 1994. text 61.00 (*0-13-249889-8*) P-H.

Allen, Wendy L. & Terrell, Ronald L. Field Validation of the Environmental Conditioning System. (SHRP Ser.: No. A-396). 194p. (Orig.). (C). 1994. pap. text 15.00 (*0-309-05811-2*, PA396) SHRP.

Allen Wheeler, Wendy. Path Through the Fire: A Cancer Story. (Illus.). x, 90p. 1998. pap. 18.00 (*0-9666778-0-3*) W Wheeler.

Allen White, Donald. Maryland Real Estate: Practice & Law. 9th ed. LC 98-33295. 1999. pap. 14.95 (*0-7931-3181-2*) Dearborn.

Allen, Whitney, ed. see Dunn, Cynthia & Chadwick, Gary.

Allen, Whitney, ed. see Getz, Kenneth.

Allen, Will W., ed. Banneker: The Afro-American Astronomer. LC 77-168504. (Black Heritage Library Collection). reprint ed. 10.00 (*0-8369-8858-2*) Ayer.

Allen, Will W. & Murray, Daniel A. Banneker the Afro-American Astronomer. Date not set. pap. 15.95 (*0-88143-145-1*) Ayer.

Allen, Willard A. Know Your Car. 3rd ed. LC 73-85126. (Illus.). 199p. reprint ed. pap. 61.70 (*0-8357-4288-1*, 203708700007) Bks Demand.

Allen, William. Accounts of Shipwrecks & Other Disasters. (Works of William Allen). 1989. reprint ed. lib. bdg. 90.00 (*0-7812-1767-9*) Rprt Serv.

— American Biographical & Historical Dictionary. (Works of William Allen). 1989. reprint ed. lib. bdg. 99.00 (*0-7812-1766-0*) Rprt Serv.

— A Book of Christian Sonnets. (Works of William Allen). 1989. reprint ed. lib. bdg. 90.00 (*0-7812-1773-3*) Rprt Serv.

— Envelope Design for Buildings. LC 97-26280. 288p. 1997. 89.95 (*0-7506-2854-5*) Buttrwrth-Heinemann.

— Execution of Justice in England. Kingdon, Robert M., ed. Incl. True, Sincere & Modest Defense of English Catholics. (Documents Ser.). 38.50 (*0-918016-41-X*) Folger Bks.

***Allen, William.** Green Phoenix: Restoring the Tropical Forests of Guanacaste, Costa Rica. (Illus.). 336p. 2001. 30.00 (*0-19-510893-0*) OUP.

Allen, William. Junius Unmasked. (Works of William Allen). 1989. reprint ed. lib. bdg. 79.00 (*0-7812-1768-7*) Rprt Serv.

— Lectures for Young Men. (Works of William Allen). 1989. lib. bdg. 79.00 (*0-7812-1769-5*) Rprt Serv.

— Loners & Dreamers: The Cosmic Voyage of a Literary Outlaw. 500p. 2000. 26.00 (*0-9672117-1-9*) Wolfhawk Bks.

— Memoir of John Codman D. D. (Works of William Allen). 1989. reprint ed. lib. bdg. 79.00 (*0-7812-1771-7*) Rprt Serv.

— Poems of the Nazareth & the Cross. (Works of William Allen). 1989. reprint ed. lib. bdg. 79.00 (*0-7812-1774-1*) Rprt Serv.

— Psalms & Hymns for Public Worship. (Works of William Allen). 1989. reprint ed. lib. bdg. 79.00 (*0-7812-1770-9*) Rprt Serv.

Allen, William. Sand Dreams. 254p. mass mkt. 4.99 (*1-55197-002-3*) Picasso Publ.

Allen, William. Sevastopol: On Photographs of War. LC 97-20264. (Illus.). vi, 90p. 1997. pap. 13.00 (*1-879378-29-9*) Xenos Riverside.

— The Works of William Allen, 1784-1868, Set. 1987. reprint ed. lib. bdg. 500.00 (*0-685-18589-3*) Rprt Serv.

— Wunnissoo. (Works of William Allen). 1989. reprint ed. lib. bdg. 79.00 (*0-685-44734-0*) Rprt Serv.

Allen, William & Taylor, Sue H. Aransas: The Life of a Texas Coastal County. LC 97-14504. 1997. pap. 24.95 (*1-57168-166-3*, Eakin Pr) Sunbelt Media.

Allen, William, et al. Orientation & Mobility Teaching Manual. 2nd ed. 120p. (C). 1997. pap. text 24.00 (*1-890786-04-7*) Visions-Srvs.

Allen, William, jt. auth. see Wienbroer, Diana R.

Allen, William, ed. see Ames, Fisher.

Allen, William A., et al. How Drugs Can Affect Your Life: The Effects of Drugs on Safety & Well-Being - With Special Emphasis on Prevention of Drug Use. 3rd ed (Illus.). 294p. (C). 1992. pap., spiral bd. 44.95 (*0-398-05762-1*) C C Thomas.

Allen, William A., jt. auth. see Wagner, Glendolin D.

Allen, William B. Let the Advice Be Good: A Defense of Madison's Democratic Nationalism. LC 93-1608. 76p. (Orig.). (C). 1993. pap. text 18.50 (*0-8191-9155-8*); lib. bdg. 39.50 (*0-8191-9154-X*) U Pr of Amer.

Allen, William B., ed. & compiled by see Washington, George.

Allen, William C. In the Greatest Solemn Dignity: The Capitol's Four Cornerstones. 47p. 1995. pap. 4.00 (*0-16-063261-7*) USGPO.

Allen, William C. In the Greatest Solemn Dignity: The Capitol's Four Cornerstones. LC 94-47080. (Senate Document Ser.: No. 103-28). 47p. 1995. pap. 3.50 (*0-614-32198-0*, 052-071-01085-8) USGPO.

Allen, William F., et al, eds. Slave Songs of the United States. 176p. 1998. pap. text 6.95 (*0-486-28573-1*) Dover.

— Slave Songs of the United States. 1960. 16.50 (*0-8446-1411-4*) Peter Smith.

— Slave Songs of the United States. LC 72-138330. (Black Heritage Library Collection). 1980. reprint ed. 25.95 (*0-8369-8722-5*) Ayer.

Allen, William F., et al. Slave Songs of the United States. LC 95-81112. 168p. 1996. reprint ed. pap. 9.95 (*1-55709-434-9*) Applewood.

Allen, William G. American Prejudice Against Color. LC 75-82165. (Anti-Slavery Crusade in America Ser.). 1970. reprint ed. 21.95 (*0-405-00603-9*) Ayer.

— Overlords & Olympians. 182p. 1996. reprint ed. spiral bd. 21.50 (*0-7873-0029-2*) Hlth Research.

— Wheatley, Banneker & Horton. 1977. 14.95 (*0-88143-148-6*) Ayer.

— Wheatley, Banneker & Horton. LC 77-133145. (Black Heritage Library Collection). 1977. reprint ed. 7.00 (*0-8369-8657-1*) Ayer.

Allen, William K. Historical Reflections: The Community & the Afro-American Pioneer Physicians of Columbus, Ohio. LC 89-85838. (Illus.). 60p. 1990. 17.00 (*0-9624897-0-0*) W K Allen.

Allen, William R. The Midnight Economist. 1996. pap. text 24.95 (*0-913878-57-X*) T Horton & Dghts.

— The Midnight Economist: Meditations on Truth & Public Policy. LC 89-11242. 300p. (C). 1989. pap. 19.95 (*1-55815-055-2*) ICS Pr.

Allen, William R., ed. Conversations with Kurt Vonnegut. LC 88-13968. (Literary Conversations Ser.). 328p. 1988. pap. 18.00 (*0-87805-358-1*) U Pr of Miss.

Allen, William R., ed. see Bringhurst, Newell G.

Allen, William S. The Nazi Seizure of Power: The Experience of a Single German Town, 1922-1945. rev. ed. 388p. 1965. pap. 16.95 (*0-531-05633-3*) Watts.

— A Study in Latin Prognosis. LC 70-176513. (Columbia University. Teachers College. Contributions to Education Ser.: No. 135). reprint ed. 37.50 (*0-404-55135-1*) AMS Pr.

Allen, Willis M., Jr., jt. auth. see Villard, Henry Serrano.

Allen, Wilma L. Set for Life: The Only Complete Guide to Retirement Living in New Hampshire. LC 93-60807. 75p. 1993. pap. 9.95 (*0-9637690-0-6*) Wellington Allen Grp.

Allen, Woody. Four Films of Woody Allen. 448p. 1982. pap. 20.00 (*0-394-71229-3*) Random.

— Getting Even. 128p. 1978. pap. 9.00 (*0-394-72640-5*, V-640) Vin Bks.

— Side Effects. 1988. 21.95 (*0-8488-0365-5*) Amereon Ltd.

— Side Effects. 160p. 1986. mass mkt. 5.99 (*0-345-34335-2*) Ballantine Pub Grp.

— Without Feathers. 224p. 1986. mass mkt. 5.99 (*0-345-33697-6*) Ballantine Pub Grp.

— Woody Allen on Woody Allen: In Conversation with Stig Bjorkman. Bjorkman, Stig, ed. LC 94-26866. (Illus.). 288p. 1995. pap. 12.00 (*0-8021-3425-4*, Grove) Grove-Atltic.

Allen, Yvonne. Spelling - Rules - Tools. 1993. 4.95 (*1-55708-239-1*, R343) McDonald Pub Co.

— Vocabulary. 1982. 4.95 (*1-55708-234-0*, R245) McDonald Pub Co.

Allen, Yvonne, as told by. Spelling - Word Ele. 1981. 4.95 (*1-55708-238-3*, R341) McDonald Pub Co.

Allen, Yvonne, ed. Vocabulary. 1979. 4.95 (*1-55708-173-5*, R259) McDonald Pub Co.

Allen, Yvonne, ed. see Leschen, Ann & Witcher, Marie.

Allen, Yvonne, ed. see Leschen, Ann, et al.

Allen, Yvonne, ed. see Witcher, Marie.

Allen, Zachariah. The Practical Tourist: or Sketches of the State of the Useful Arts, & of Society, Scenery in Great Britain, France & Holland, 2 vols. LC 73-38258. (Evolution of Capitalism Ser.). 896p. 1972. reprint ed. 57.95 (*0-405-04111-X*) Ayer.

Allen, Zita. Black Women Leaders of the Civil Rights Movement. LC 96-26134. (African-American Experience Ser.). 160p. (YA). (gr. 9-12). 1996. lib. bdg. 24.00 (*0-531-11271-3*) Watts.

Allenbaugh, Eric. Wake-Up Calls: You Don't Have to Sleepwalk Through Your Life, Love, Or Career! 288p. 1992. 18.95 (*0-9631194-1-9*) Discov Pubns.

— Wake-Up Calls: You Don't Have to Sleepwalk Through Your Life, Love, or Career. 288p. 1994. pap. 12.00 (*0-671-88707-6*, Fireside) S&S Trade Pap.

Allenbaugh, Kay. Chocolate for a Lovers Heart: Soul Soothing Stories that Celebrate the Power of Love. LC 98-31935. 208p. 1999. pap. 11.00 (*0-684-86298-0*) S&S Trade.

— Chocolate for a Mother's Heart: Inspiring Stories that Celebrate the Spirit of Motherhood. LC 99-19543. 195p. 1999. pap. 11.00 (*0-684-86299-5*, Fireside) S&S Trade Pap.

***Allenbaugh, Kay.** Chocolate for a Teen's Soul: Life Changing Stories for Young Women about Growing Wise & Growing Strong. LC 00-29366. 224p. 2000. pap. 12.00 (*0-684-87081-9*, Fireside) S&S Trade Pap.

— Chocolate for a Woman's Blessing: 77 Heartwarming Stories of Gratitude That Celebrate the Good Things in Life. 2001. pap. 12.00 (0-7432-0308-9, Fireside) S&S Trade Pap.

Allenbaugh, Kay. Chocolate for a Woman's Heart: 77 Stories of Love, Kindness & Compassion to Nourish Your Soul & Sweeten Your Dreams. LC 98-3080. 272p. (YA). 1998. per. 11.00 (0-684-84896-1) S&S Trade Pap.

*__Allenbaugh, Kay.__ Chocolate for a Woman's Heart & Soul. 507p. 2000. reprint ed. text 20.00 (0-7881-9238-8) DIANE Pub.

— Chocolate for a Woman's Soul: Stories to Feed Your Spirit & Warm Your Heart. 1997. audio 12.00 (0-671-57964-9) S&S Audio.

Allenbaugh, Kay. Chocolate for a Woman's Soul: 77 Stories Feed Your Spirit & Warm Your Heart. LC 96-51676. 256p. 1997. per. 11.00 (0-684-83217-8) S&S Trade Pap.

— Chocolate for a Woman's Spirit: 77 Stories of Inspiration to Lift Your Heart & Sooth Your Soul. LC 99-41727. 204p. 1999. per. 12.00 (0-684-84897-X, Fireside) S&S Trade Pap.

*__Allenbaugh, Kay.__ Chocolate par el Corazon de la Mujer: 77 Relatos de Amor, Bondad y Compasion para Nutrir su Alm. (SPA.). 2000. pap. 12.00 (0-684-87084-3, Fireside) S&S Trade Pap.

— Chocolate para el Alma de la Mujer: 77 Relatos Para Nutrir su Espiritu y Recomfortar su Corazon. (SPA.). 288p. 2000. pap. 12.00 (0-684-87083-5, Fireside) S&S Trade Pap.

Allenbraugh, Kay. Chocolate for a Woman's Heart & Soul: Stories of Love, Courage & Compassion to Nourish Your Spirit & Sweeten Your Dreams. LC 98-40620. 512p. 1998. pap. 20.00 (0-684-85785-5) S&S Trade.

Allenby, B. R., jt. auth. see Graedel, T. E.

*__Allenby, Braden R.__ Industrial Ecology: Policy Framework & Implementation. LC 98-7300. 320p. (C). 1998. pap. 62.00 (0-13-921180-2) P-H.

Allenby, Braden R., ed. see National Academy of Engineering Staff.

Allenby, R. Numbers & Proofs. (An Arnold Publication). (Illus.). x288p. 1998. pap. text 24.95 (0-340-67653-1, Pub. by E A) OUP.

Allenby, R. B. Linear Algebra. (Modular Mathematics Ser.). 227p. 1995. pap. 17.95 (0-340-61044-1, Pub. by E A) Routldge.

— Rings, Fields & Groups: An Introduction to Abstract Algebra. 2nd ed. (An Arnold Publication). (Illus.). 416p. 1991. pap. 35.00 (0-340-54440-6, A6424, Pub. by E A) OUP.

Allende, Gladys. Precious Memories. 160p. 1997. pap. 13.00 (0-8059-4217-3) Dorrance.

*__Allende, Isabel.__ Afrodita: Cuentos, Recetas y Otros Afrodisiacos. LC 97-31618. 328p. 1998. 26.00 (0-06-017591-5, HarperFlamingo) HarpC.

Allende, Isabel. Afrodita: Cuentos, Recetas y Otros Afrodisiacos. LC 97-31618. (SPA., Illus.). 328p. 1998. pap. 18.00 (0-06-093008-X) HarpC.

— Aphrodite: A Memoir of the Senses. Sayers Peden, Margaret, tr. from SPA. LC 97-40274. Orig. Title: Afrodita. 320p. 1998. 26.00 (0-06-017590-7, HarperFlamingo) HarpC.

— Aphrodite: A Memoir of the Senses. Peden, Margaret Sayers, tr. from SPA. Orig. Title: Afrodita. (Illus.). 320p. 1999. pap. 16.00 (0-06-093017-9) HarpC.

— Aphrodite: A Memoir of the Senses. large type ed. Peden, Margaret Sayers, tr. LC 98-24626. Orig. Title: Afrodita. 1998. 27.95 (0-7838-0310-9, G K Hall Lrg Type) Mac Lib Ref.

— La Casa de los Espiritus. LC 95-7172.Tr. of House of the Spirits. (SPA.). 464p. 1995. pap. 13.00 (0-06-095130-3, Harp PBks) HarpC.

— Conversations with Isabel Allende. Rodden, John, ed. & tr. by. from SPA. Invernizzi, Virginia, tr. from SPA. LC 99-6138. 461p. (YA). 1999. 50.00 (0-292-77092-8); pap. 24.95 (0-292-77093-6) U of Tex Pr.

— Cuentos de Eva Luna. LC 95-6472. (SPA.). 256p. 1995. pap. 13.00 (0-06-095131-1, Harp PBks) HarpC.

— Cuentos de Eva Luna. 4th ed. (SPA.). 256p. 1991. pap. 24.95 (0-7859-5019-2) Fr & Eur.

*__Allende, Isabel.__ Daughter of Fortune: A Novel. Peden, Margaret Sayers, tr. from SPA. LC 99-26021. 416p. 1999. 26.00 (0-06-019491-X) HarpC.

— Daughter of Fortune: A Novel. Peden, Margaret Sayers, tr. from SPA. 400p. 2000. pap. 14.00 (0-06-093275-9, Perennial) HarperTrade.

Allende, Isabel. De Amor y de Sombra.Tr. of Love & Shadows. (SPA.). 281p. 1985. pap. 10.50 (84-01-38034-0, 3028) Ediciones Norte.

— De Amor y de Sombra. LC 95-7173.Tr. of Love & Shadows. (SPA.). 272p. 1995. pap. 12.00 (0-06-095129-X, Harp PBks) HarpC.

— De Amor y de Sombra. 5th ed.Tr. of Love & Shadows. (SPA.). 288p. 1991. pap. 9.95 (0-7859-5023-0) Fr & Eur.

— Eva Luna. 320p. 1989. mass mkt. 7.99 (0-553-28058-9) Bantam.

— Eva Luna. (SPA.). 282p. 1987. pap. 14.00 (84-01-38110-X, 3037) Ediciones Norte.

— Eva Luna. (SPA.). 304p. 1991. pap. 12.95 (0-7859-5020-6) Fr & Eur.

— Eva Luna. large type ed. Peden, Margaret Sayers, tr. (General Ser.). 439p. 1990. lib. bdg. 19.95 (0-8161-4834-1, G K Hall Lrg Type) Mac Lib Ref.

— Eva Luna Spanish Language Edition. LC 95-7170. (SPA.). 288p. 1995. pap. 12.00 (0-06-095128-1, Harp PBks) HarpC.

*__Allende, Isabel.__ Hija de la Fortuna. 2nd ed. 1999. 24.95 (84-01-01210-4) Plaza.

Allende, Isabel. Hija De La Fortuna: Novela. Peden, Margaret Sayers, tr. (SPA.). 432p. 1999. 26.00 (0-06-019492-8) HarpC.

*__Allende, Isabel.__ Hija De La Fortuna: Novela. 432p. 2000. pap. 14.00 (0-06-093276-7, Perennial) HarperTrade.

Allende, Isabel. The House of the Spirits. Bogin, Magda, tr. Orig. Title: La casa de los espiritus. 448p. 1986. mass mkt. 7.99 (0-553-27391-4, Bantam Classics) Bantam.

— The House of the Spirits. Bogin, Magda, tr. LC 84-48516. Orig. Title: La casa de los espiritus. 400p. 1985. 29.95 (0-394-53907-9) Knopf.

— The Infinite Plan: Novel, A. Peden, Margaret Sayers, tr. 400p. 1994. reprint ed. pap. 14.00 (0-06-092498-5, Perennial) HarperTrade.

— Of Love & Shadows. Peden, Margaret Sayers, tr. from SPA. Orig. Title: De amor y de sombra. 1987. 25.00 (0-394-54962-7) Knopf.

— Of Love & Shadows. Peden, Margaret Sayers, tr. from SPA. LC 86-46164. Orig. Title: De amor y de sombra. 1988. 11.60 (0-606-03879-5, Pub. by Turtleback) Demco.

— Paula. LC 95-2452. 336p. 1996. pap. 14.00 (0-06-092721-6) HarpC.

— Paula. large type ed. Peden, Margaret Sayers, tr. from SPA. LC 95-16376. 539p. 1995. 26.95 (0-7838-1373-2, G K Hall Lrg Type) Mac Lib Ref.

— Paula SPA. (SPA.). 368p. 1996. pap. 13.00 (0-06-092720-8, Perennial) HarperTrade.

— El Plan Infinito. LC 95-7171.Tr. of Infinite Plan. (SPA.). 336p. 1995. pap. 13.00 (0-06-095127-3, Harp PBks) HarpC.

*__Allende, Isabel.__ The Stories of Eva Luna. 352p. 1999. 25.50 (0-684-87359-1) S&S Trade.

Allende, Isabel. The Stories of Eva Luna. large type ed. Peden, Margaret Sayers, tr. 1991. lib. bdg. 20.95 (0-8161-5253-5, G K Hall Lrg Type) Mac Lib Ref.

— The Stories of Eve Luna. 384p. 1992. mass mkt. 7.99 (0-553-57535-X) Bantam.

Allende, Isabel & Peden, Margaret Sayers. Of Love & Shadows. Orig. Title: De amor y de sombra. 304p. 1988. mass mkt. 7.99 (0-553-27360-4) Bantam.

Allende, Isabel, et al. Diez Cuentos de Eva Luna: Con Guia de Comprension y Repaso de Gramatica. Taggart, Kenneth M. & Woods, Richard D., eds. (SPA.). 256p. (C). 1994. pap. 29.38 (0-07-001356-X) McGraw.

Allende, Lester N., et al. Claves Psicologicas en Nuestra America, Vision Puertorriquena. (Editorial Homines Ser.). (SPA.). 300p. 1991. pap. text 20.00 (0-9623590-3-3) Libros-Ediciones.

Allender, Allen. Shake My Sillies Out. LC 87-750478. (Raffi Songs to Read Ser.). 32p. (J). (ps-2). 1990. pap. 5.99 (0-517-56647-8, Pub. by Crown Bks Yng Read) Random.

Allender, Dan & Longman, Tremper. Bold Purpose. LC 98-19883. 1998. pap. 16.97 (0-8423-5351-8) Tyndale Hse.

Allender, Dan, jt. auth. see Crabb, Larry.

Allender, Dan B. Corazon Herido.Tr. of Wounded Heart. (SPA.). 266p. 1995. 10.99 (0-88113-144-X, B031-144X) Caribe Betania.

*__Allender, Dan B.__ The Healing Path: How the Hurst in Your Past Can Lead You to a More Abundant Life. 272p. 2000. pap. 12.95 (1-57856-391-7) Waterbrook Pr.

Allender, Dan B. The Healing Path: How the Hurts in Your Past Can Lead You to a More Abundant Life. LC 98-50556. 272p. 1999. 19.95 (1-57856-109-4) Waterbrook Pr.

— The Healing Path Study Guide: How the Hurts in Your Past Can Lead You to a More Abundant Life. 96p. 1999. pap., student ed. 6.95 (1-57856-156-6) Waterbrook Pr.

— The Wounded Heart: Hope for Adult Victims of Sexual Abuse. LC 90-61684. 264p. (Orig.). 1990. pap. 15.00 (0-89109-289-7) NavPress.

— Wounded Heart Workbook: A Companion Workbook for Personal or Group Use. 192p. 1992. pap., wbk. ed. 17.00 (0-89109-665-5) NavPress.

Allender, Dan B. & Longman, Tremper. Bold Love: The Courageous Practice of Life's Ultimate Influence. LC 92-60188. 320p. 1992. pap. 14.00 (0-89109-703-1) NavPress.

— Intimate Allies. 388p. 1997. 10.99 (0-8423-1824-0) Tyndale Hse.

Allender, Dan B., jt. auth. see Crabb, Larry.

Allender, Dan B., jt. auth. see Crabb, Lawrence J., Jr.

Allender, Jerome S. Imagery in Teaching & Learning: An Autobiography of Research in Four World Views. LC 90-45472. 264p. 1991. 55.00 (0-275-93638-4, C3638, Praeger Pubs) Greenwood.

Allender, Judith & Rector, Cherie. Readings in Gerontological Nursing. LC 97-33646. 688p. 1998. pap. text 29.95 (0-7817-9201-0) Lppncott W & W.

Allender, Judith, jt. auth. see Nasrawi, Christina.

Allender, Judith A. Community & Home Health Nursing. LC 97-19138. (Lippincott's Review Ser.). 400p. 1997. pap. text 21.95 (0-397-55456-7) Lppncott W & W.

Allender, Judith A., jt. auth. see Nasrawi, Christina Wu.

Allender, Judith A., jt. auth. see Spradley, Barbara W.

Allender, Julie A. End of My Rope: Gender Cooperation Model. (Illus.). 200p. (Orig.). 1995. 10.00 (0-9647278-5-4) J A Allender.

Allender, Stephen. Report Writing. (C). 1991. pap. 60.00 (0-85171-095-6, Pub. by IPM Hse) St Mut.

Allendoerfer, Carl B., ed. Differential Geometry: Proceedings of the 3rd Symposium in Pure Mathematics of the American Mathematical Society, Held at the University of Arizona, February 18-19, 1960 in Tucson, AZ with the Support of the National Science Foundation. LC 62-5289. (Proceedings of Symposia in Pure Mathematics Ser.: No. 3). 210p. reprint ed. pap. 65.10 (0-608-02659-X, 205255400004) Bks Demand.

Allendoerfer, Carl B., ed. see Pure Mathematics Symposium Staff.

*__Allendorf, Cole.__ Conservation & the Genetics of Populations. (Biology Ser.). 2001. text 60.00 (0-534-37716-5) Brooks-Cole.

Allendorf, M. D., et al, eds. Chemical Vapor Deposition: CVD XIV & EUROCVD 11. (Proceedings Ser.: Vol. 97-25). 1652p. 1997. 107.00 (1-56677-178-1) Electrochem Soc.

*__Allendorf, M. D., et al, eds.__ Fundamental Gas-Phase & Surface Chemistry of Vapor-Phase Materials Synthesis. LC 99-62428. 486p. 1999. 97.00 (1-56677-217-6, PV 98-23) Electrochem Soc.

Allenmark, Stig G. Chromatographic Emanitio-Separation. (Analytical Chemistry Ser.). 232p. 1988. text 67.95 (0-470-21080-X) P-H.

Allenov, M. M. Alexander Andreyevich Ivanov. 204p. 1980. 35.00 (0-7855-0684-5) St Mut.

Allenson, Michael, jt. auth. see Seligson, Michelle.

Allensworth, Carl. The Simple Truth. 1963. pap. 3.25 (0-8222-1029-0) Dramatists Play.

Allensworth, Carl & Allensworth, Dorothy. Interurban. 1964. pap. 5.25 (0-8222-0573-4) Dramatists Play.

Allensworth, Dorothy, jt. auth. see Allensworth, Carl.

Allensworth, Wayne. The Russian Question: Nationalism, Modernization, & Post-Communist Russia. LC 98-24157. 368p. 1998. 69.00 (0-8476-9002-4) Rowman.

— The Russian Question: Nationalism, Modernization & Post-Communist Russia. LC 98-24157. 368p. 1998. pap. 23.95 (0-8476-9003-2) Rowman.

Allentuch, Harriet R. Madame de Sevigne: A Portrait in Letters. LC 78-16378. 219p. 1978. reprint ed. lib. bdg. 59.50 (0-313-20537-X, ALMS, Greenwood Pr) Greenwood.

Allenworth, Don T. City Planning Politics. LC 80-134. 273p. 1980. 59.95 (0-275-90445-8, C0445, Praeger Pubs) Greenwood.

Aller, Doris, jt. auth. see Aller, Paul.

Aller, L. Methods for Determining the Location of Abandoned Wells. 130p. 1984. 19.50 (1-56034-031-2, T034) Natl Grnd Water.

Aller, Lawrence H. Atoms, Stars, & Nebulae. 3rd ed. (Illus.). 380p. (C). 1991. pap. text 39.95 (0-521-31040-7) Cambridge U Pr.

— Atoms, Stars, & Nebulae. 3rd ed. (Illus.). 380p. (C). 1991. text 105.00 (0-521-32512-9) Cambridge U Pr.

— Physics of Therman Gaseous Nebulae: Physical Processes in Gaseous Nebulae. 1984. lib. bdg. 133.00 (90-277-1814-8) Kluwer Academic.

Aller, Lawrence H., jt. ed. see Middlehurst, Barbara M.

Aller, Paul & Aller, Doris. Build Your Own Adobe. LC NA7165.A4. (Illus.). 120p. 1946. reprint ed. pap. 30.00 (0-7837-1222-7, 204175300023) Bks Demand.

Aller, Susan B. Emma & the Night Dogs. LC 96-32823. (Illus.). 32p. (J). (gr. 1-4). 1997. lib. bdg. 14.95 (0-8075-1993-6) A Whitman.

— J. M. Barrie: The Magic Behind Peter Pan. LC 94-5452. (Lerner Biography Ser.). (Illus.). 128p. (J). (gr. 5 up). 1994. lib. bdg. 23.93 (0-8225-4918-2, Lerner Publctns) Lerner Pub.

Allerdyce, Alexander, ed. see Ramsay, John.

Allergy & Asthma Network/Mothers of Asthma, Inc. S. Consumer Update on Asthma. 64p. 1995. 7.95 (0-7872-1016-1) Kendall-Hunt.

Allerhand, Michael. Knowledge Based Speech Pattern. 1988. text 39.95 (0-07-001404-3) McGraw.

Allers, Rudolf. Forming Character in Adolescents. 192p. 1998. reprint ed. 19.95 (0-912141-67-0) Roman Cath Bks.

— Practical Psychology in Character Development. abr. ed. 190p. 1999. reprint ed. 22.95 (0-912141-72-7) Roman Cath Bks.

— What's Wrong with Freud. 262p. 1998. reprint ed. 19.95 (0-912141-66-2) Roman Cath Bks.

Allerson, Sharon, jt. auth. see Kirn, Elaine.

Allert, Beate, ed. Languages of Visuality: Crossings Between Science, Art, Politics, & Literature. LC 95-45568. (Kritik Ser.). (Illus.). 284p. (C). 1996. 39.95 (0-8143-2540-8); pap. 19.95 (0-8143-2607-2) Wayne St U Pr.

Allert, Charlene. Women's Health Issues: HP 570 Course Study Guide. 180p. (C). 1992. write for info. (0-933195-21-4) CA College Health Sci.

Allert, Kathy. American Indian Girl & Boy Paper Dolls in Full Color. 81st ed. (Illus.). (J). (gr. k-3). 1992. pap. 2.95 (0-486-27116-1) Dover.

— French Folk Costumes Paper Dolls. (Illus.). 1991. pap. 3.95 (0-486-26847-0) Dover.

*__Allert, Kathy.__ German Girl & Boy Paper Dolls. (J). 1999. spiral bd. 3.50 (0-486-40573-7) Dover.

Allert, Kathy. Italian Girl & Boy Paper Dolls in Full Color. (Illus.). (J). (gr. k-3). 1993. pap. 3.50 (0-486-27461-6) Dover.

— Japanese Girl & Boy Paper Dolls. (Illus.). 1991. pap. 2.95 (0-486-26680-X) Dover.

Allert, Kathy. Little Plains Indian Girl. (Little Activity Bks.). (Illus.). (J). 1995. pap. 1.00 (0-486-28427-1) Dover.

Allert, Kathy. Little Southwest Indian Girl Paper Doll. 80th ed. (Illus.). (J). (gr. k-3). 1994. pap. 1.00 (0-486-27927-8) Dover.

Allert, Kathy. Little Woodlands Indian Girl. (Little Activity Bks.). (Illus.). (J). 1994. pap. 1.00 (0-486-28165-5) Dover.

Allert, Kathy. Mexican Girl & Boy Paper Dolls. (Illus.). (J). (gr. k-3). 1992. pap. 3.50 (0-486-27229-X) Dover.

Allert, Kathy. Northeastern Indian Girl. (Little Activity Bks.). (Illus.). (J). 1996. pap. 1.00 (0-486-28977-X) Dover.

— Russian Girl & Boy Paper Dolls. (Illus.). (J). 1999. pap. 3.95 (0-486-40809-4) Dover.

Allert, Kathy. Scandinavian Girl & Boy Paper Dolls. (Illus.). (J). (gr. 4-7). 1993. pap. 3.50 (0-486-27684-8) Dover.

Allert, Kathy. Southwest Indian Boy. (Little Activity Bks.). (Illus.). (J). 1995. pap. 1.00 (0-486-28796-3) Dover.

Allert, Kathy. Spanish Girl & Boy Paper Dolls. (Illus.). (J). (gr. k-3). 1993. pap. 2.95 (0-486-27499-3) Dover.

— Traditional Folk Costumes Paper Dolls. (Illus.). 1984. pap. 4.95 (0-486-24571-3) Dover.

Allert, Tilman. Die Familie: Fallstudien zur Unverwustlichkeit einer Lebensform. 320p. 1997. pap. 38.70 (3-11-014860-9) De Gruyter.

Allerton, George. Ten Memorable People of Western Electric at 555 Union Blvd, (Allentown, PA.) 30p. (Orig.). 1997. pap. 1.00 (0-945620-06-3) Associated Specialties.

Allerton, George L. A Gift from Grandma: "Our Family" As Grandma Remembers. (Illus.). 128p. 1990. pap. 8.95 (0-945620-02-0) Associated Specialties.

— Our Family History & Records. (Illus.). 352p. 1988. pap. 13.95 (0-945620-00-4); ring bd. 19.95 (0-945620-01-2) Associated Specialties.

Allerton, Jay. Bomber's Moon. large type ed. (Linford Romance Library). 272p. 1986. pap. 6.95 (0-7089-6225-4, Linford) Ulverscroft.

— The Laurel Path. large type ed. 1991. 27.99 (0-7089-2420-4) Ulverscroft.

Allerton, Mark. Hindi in Three Months. LC 98-31748. (Hugo's Simplified Language Course Ser.). 144p. 1999. pap. 14.95 (0-7894-4427-5) DK Pub Inc.

— Hugo Hindi in Three Months: Simplified Language Course. LC 98-31748. (Hugo Ser.). (HIN & ENG.). 1999. 24.95 incl. audio (0-7894-4436-4, D K Ink) DK Pub Inc.

Allerton Park Institute Staff. Organizing the Library's Support: Donors, Volunteers, Friends. Krummel, Donald W., ed. LC 80-14772. 125p. reprint ed. pap. 38.80 (0-7837-1234-0, 204137100020) Bks Demand.

Allerton, W. S. & Currier, Horace T. History of the Allerton Family in the United States, 1585 to 1885, & a Genealogy of the Descendants of Issac Allerton. (Illus.). 149p. 1988. reprint ed. pap. 30.00 (0-8328-0111-9); reprint ed. lib. bdg. 38.00 (0-8328-0110-0) Higginson Bk Co.

Alles, Anthony, jt. auth. see Minoli, Daniel.

Alles, Gregory D. The Iliad, the Ramayana, & the Work of Religion: Failed Persuasion & Religious Mystification. (Hermeneutics, Studies in the History of Religions). 200p. (C). 1994. 37.50 (0-271-01319-2); pap. 18.95 (0-271-01320-6) Pa St U Pr.

Alles, Gregory D., jt. ed. see Ellwood, Robert S.

Alles, Gregory D., ed. see Otto, Rudolf.

Alles, Gregory D., ed. see Wach, Joachim.

Allesandra, Tony, et al. Be Your Own Sales Manager: Strategies & Tactics for Managing Your Accounts, Your Territory, & Yourself. 262p. 1990. per. 13.00 (0-671-76175-7) Simon & Schuster.

Allesch, Jurgen. Consulting in Innovation: Practice, Methods & Perspectives. 360p. 1991. 150.00 (0-444-88370-3) Elsevier.

Allesch, Jurgen, ed. Regional Development in Europe: Recent Initiatives & Experiences - Proceedings of the Fourth International Conference on Science Parks & Innovation Centres Held in Berlin, Nov. 12-13, 1987. xiv, 368p. (C). 1989. lib. bdg. 111.55 (3-11-011815-7) De Gruyter.

Allesch, Jurgen, jt. ed. see Ewers, Hans-Jurgen.

Allessie, Maurits A. & Fromer, Martin, eds. Atrial & Ventricular Fibrillation: Mechanisms & Device Therapy. LC 96-29416. (Bakken Research Center Ser.: Vol. 9). (Illus.). 448p. 1996. 98.00 (0-87993-650-9) Futura Pub.

Allett, John. New Liberalism: The Political Economy of J. A. Hobson. LC 82-136586. 287p. reprint ed. pap. 89.00 (0-8357-8247-6, 203398300088) Bks Demand.

Alletz, Pons-Augustin. Dictionnaire Theologique Portatif. (FRE.). viii, 679p. reprint ed. write for info. (0-318-71995-9) G Olms Pubs.

Alleva, Enrico, ed. Behavioural Brain Research in Naturalistic & Semi-Naturalistic Settings: Proceedings of the NATO Advanced Study Institute: Possibilities & Perspectives, Acquafredda di Maratea, Italy, September 10-20, 1994. (NATO ASI Series D). 488p. (C). 1995. text 230.00 (0-7923-3570-8) Kluwer Academic.

Allevato, Claudio & Williams, David. Acoustic Emission Nondestructive Evaluation of Yankee Dryers. Corboy, W. G., ed. LC 92-23971. 1992. 87.00 (0-89852-301-X, 0101R208) TAPPI.

Allevato, Diane. Sausage Patty. (J). 1998. per. 3.99 (0-9644062-1-7) Animal Place.

Alley. United Nations in Southeast Asia & the South Pacific. LC 98-4423. 256p. 1998. text 65.00 (0-312-21470-7) St Martin.

Alley, Alyson B. & Restrepo, Tanya E. Doggie Diary: Our Years Together. (Illus.). 66p. 1997. 15.95 (0-9659756-0-6) Happy Tails.

Alley, Brian. A+ Certification Test Prep. LC 98-85728. 1998. pap. 24.99 (1-56205-892-4) New Riders Pub.

Alley, David. Sky: All about Planets, Stars, Galaxies, Eclipses & More. (Illus.). 32p. (J). 1993. pap. 5.95 (1-895688-04-3, Pub. by Greey dePencier) Firefly Bks Ltd.

Alley, David L. December 7, 1941, a Different Path. LC 95-70515. 215p. 1995. pap. 17.95 (1-882194-16-0) TN Valley Pub.

*__Alley, E. Roberts.__ Water Quality Control Handbook. (Illus.). 1008p. 2000. 125.00 (0-07-001413-2) McGraw.

Alley, E. Roberts, et al. Air Quality Control Handbook. LC 98-9163. (Illus.). 1008p. 1998. text 99.95 (0-07-001411-6) McGraw-Hill Prof.

Alley, Elizabeth & Williams, Mark. In the Same Room: Conversations with New Zealand Writers. (Illus.). 322p. 1992. 19.95 (1-86940-072-0, Pub. by Auckland Univ) Paul & Co Pubs.

Alley, F. C., jt. auth. see Cooper, C. David.

Alley, Gene. Alley Ancestors. (Illus.). 918p. 1997. 80.00 (*0-944619-46-0*) Gregath Pub Co.

Alley, Henry. The Lattice. LC 85-20102. 287p. 1986. 19.95 (*0-918056-03-9*) Ariadne Pr.

— The Quest for Anonymity: The Novels of George Eliot. LC 96-29628. 184p. 1997. 33.50 (*0-87413-621-0*) U Delaware Pr.

— Through Glass. LC 79-21296. (American Land Ser.: Vol. 1). 191p. (Orig.). 1979. pap. 7.95 (*0-916078-07-8*) Iris Pr.

— Umbrella of Glass. LC 88-11729. 170p. 1988. 14.95 (*0-932576-61-3*) Breitenbush Bks.

Alley, J. Mark. The Violent Years: The Founding of a Kansas Town. LC 92-73893. (Illus.). 108p. (Orig.). 1992. pap. 12.95 (*0-9627947-6-7*) Hearth KS.

Alley, John R., Jr., jt. auth. see Arrington, Leonard J.

Alley, Joseph W. Williamson: Alden Williamson Genealogy: Genealogical Record of Alden Williamson's Family in Pike, Martin, Floyd, Johnson, Lawrence & Boyd Counties in Ky., & Mingo, Wayne, Logan, Lincoln, Cabell & Wyoming Cos. in W.V. (Illus.). 254p. 1996. reprint ed. pap. 39.00 (*0-8328-5595-2*); reprint ed. lib. bdg. 49.00 (*0-8328-5594-4*) Higginson Bk Co.

Alley, Joseph W. & Bowne. History of Sonoma County, CA: Including Its Geology, Topography, Mountains, Valleys & Street, Together with a Full & Particular Record of the Spanish Grants, Its Early History & Settlements...Seperate Histories of Each Township...& Biographical Sketches of Early & Prominent Settlers. 709p. 1996. reprint ed. lib. bdg. 75.00 (*0-8328-5185-X*) Higginson Bk Co.

Alley, Ken. Awkward Christian Soldiers: Comic Relief from the Back Pew. LC 97-43536. 96p. 1998. 7.99 (*0-87788-024-7*, H Shaw Pubs) Waterbrook Pr.

— Once upon a Pew: More Fun Than Having the Preacher Over! LC 95-69412. 209p. (Orig.). 1995. pap. 10.95 (*0-9645085-0-8*) Prtnrshp Bk Servs.

***Alley, Lynn.** Lost Arts: A Celebration of Culinary Traditions. rev. ed. 176p. 2000. pap. 12.95 (*1-58008-176-2*) Ten Speed Pr.

Alley, Mark, ed. see Frear, Jon S.

***Alley, Michael.** The Craft of Editing: A Guide for Managers, Scientists & Engineers. LC 99-56072. (Illus.). 160p. 2000. pap. 19.95 (*0-387-98964-1*) Spr-Verlag.

Alley, Michael. The Craft of Scientific Writing. 3rd ed. LC 96-15207. 282p. 1996. pap. text 24.95 (*0-387-94766-3*) Spr-Verlag.

Alley, Peter. Resedit Complete Bk Dsk. 576p. 1991. pap. text 32.95 (*0-201-55075-X*) Addison-Wesley.

Alley, Peter & Strange, Carolyn. Resedit Complete. 2nd ed. 448p. 1993. pap. text 36.95 (*0-201-62686-1*) Addison-Wesley.

Alley, R., et al. Avenues of Sedimentation of Carbonate Skeletal Sands in Rice Bay, San Salvador, Bahamas. (Occasional Papers - 1986: No. 2). 14p. 1986. pap. text 1.50 (*0-935909-21-4*) Bahamian.

Alley, R. W. Take Charge of Your Life Therapy. Engelhardt, Lisa, ed. LC 94-70290. 88p. 1995. pap. 4.95 (*0-87029-271-4*) Abbey.

Alley, R. W. Old MacDonald Had a Farm. (Pudgy Pal Board Bks.). 18p. (J). (ps up). 1991. bds. 3.99 (*0-448-40106-1*, G & D) Peng Put Young Read.

— The Teeny Tiny Woman. LC 86-485. (Step into Reading Ser.: A Step 1 Book). 32p. (J). (ps-1). 1986. lib. bdg. 11.99 (*0-394-98320-3*, Pub. by Random Bks Yng Read) Random.

— The Teeny Tiny Woman. LC 86-485. (Step into Reading Ser.: A Step 1 Book). 32p. (J). (ps-3). 1986. pap. 3.99 (*0-394-88320-9*, Pub. by Random Bks Yng Read) Random.

Alley, R. W., jt. illus. see Pulver, Robin.

Alley, Reuben E. History of the University of Richmond: 1830-1971. LC 76-54906. 286p. 1977. text 30.00 (*0-8139-0700-4*) U Pr of Va.

Alley, Reuben E., jt. auth. see Smith, Kenneth C.

Alley, Richard. Rocking the Parks. 184p. (C). 1998. spiral bd. 22.95 (*0-7872-5706-0*, 41570602) Kendall-Hunt.

— Rocking the Parks: Geological Stories of the National Parks. 184p. (C). 1998. spiral bd. 20.95 (*0-7872-5447-9*, 41544701) Kendall-Hunt.

***Alley, Richard B.** The Two-Mile Time Machine: Ice Cores, Abrupt Climate Change, & Our Future. LC 00-36730. (Illus.). 240p. 2000. 24.95 (*0-691-00493-5*) Princeton U Pr.

Alley, Richard E. & Graham, Earl K. Planet Earth: GeoScience Twenty. 176p. (C). 1996. spiral bd. 16.01 (*0-7872-2007-8*) Kendall-Hunt.

Alley, Rick. The Talking Book of July: Poems. LC 97-19394. 62p. 1997. 23.00 (*0-910055-34-3*); pap. 12.00 (*0-910055-35-1*) East Wash Univ.

Alley, Robert. Advanced Lake Fly-Fishing: The Skillful Tuber. (Illus.). 120p. (Orig.). 1991. 29.95 (*0-936608-98-6*); pap. 14.95 (*0-936608-97-8*) F Amato Pubns.

— School Prayer: The Court, the Congress & the First Amendment. LC 93-38940. 273p. 1994. 28.95 (*0-87975-843-0*) Prometheus Bks.

Alley, Robert H. 40 Best Trout Flies. (Illus.). 68p. (Orig.). 1996. pap. 8.95 (*1-57188-084-4*) F Amato Pubns.

Alley, Robert S. The Supreme Court on Church & State. (Illus.). 464p. 1988. pap. text 28.95 (*0-19-505029-0*) OUP.

— Without a Prayer: Religious Expression in Public Schools. LC 96-27812. 277p. 1996. 26.95 (*1-57392-097-5*) Prometheus Bks.

Alley, Robert S., ed. The Constitution & Religion: Leading Supreme Court Cases on Church & State. 450p. 1999. 74.95 (*1-57392-704-X*); pap. 24.95 (*1-57392-703-1*) Prometheus Bks.

— James Madison on Religious Liberty. LC 85-62743. 338p. (C). 1985. reprint ed. pap. 25.95 (*0-87975-537-7*) Prometheus Bks.

Alley, Robert S., jt. ed. see Rose, Brian G.

Alley, Roderic. New Zealand & the Pacific. (Replica Edition Ser.). (Illus.). 300p. (C). 1983. pap. text 1.75 (*0-86531-929-4*, Pub. by Westview) HarpC.

Alley, S. David, jt. auth. see Haaland, Ole.

***Alley, Sarah.** Bicycling America's National Parks: Arizona & New Mexico: The Best Road & Trail Rides from the Grand Canyon to Carlsbad Caverns. 2000. pap. 17.95 (*0-88150-481-5*, Pub. by Countryman) Norton.

***Alley, Sarah Bennett.** Bicycling America's National Parks: Utah & Colorado: The Best Road & Trail Rides from Canyonlands to Rocky Mountain National Park. LC 99-58158. 2000. pap. 17.95 (*0-88150-426-2*, Pub. by Countryman) Norton.

Alley, Thomas R., ed. Social & Applied Aspects of Perceiving Faces. (Wm Mace Ser.). 304p. 1988. text 89.95 (*0-8058-0163-4*) L Erlbaum Assocs.

Alley, Walter, jt. auth. see Billiet, Walter E.

Alley, William M., ed. Regional Ground Water Quality. 640p. 1993. text 114.95 (*0-442-00937-2*, VNR) Wiley.

Alley, William M., ed. Regional Ground-Water Quality. (Industrial Health & Safety Ser.). 634p. 1993. 160.00 (*0-471-28453-X*, VNR) Wiley.

Alleyn, Edward. Alleyn Papers: A Collection of Original Documents Illustrative of the Life & Times of Edward Alleyn & of the Early English Stage. LC 79-113543. reprint ed. 37.50 (*0-404-00329-X*) AMS Pr.

***Alleyn, F.** Dark Obsession. 224p. 1998. pap. 15.99 (*0-352-33281-6*) Virgin Pr.

Alleyn, Fredrica. The Bracelet. (Black Lace Ser.). 300p. 1997. mass mkt. 5.95 (*0-352-33110-0*, Pub. by Virgin Bks) London Brdge.

— Cassandra's Conflict. (Black Lace Ser.). 1995. mass mkt. 5.95 (*0-352-32859-2*, Pub. by Virgin Bks) London Brdge.

— Dark Obsession. (Black Lace Ser.). 1995. mass mkt. 5.95 (*0-352-33026-0*, Pub. by Virgin Bks) London Brdge.

— Dramatic Affairs. (Black Lace Ser.). 1998. mass mkt. 6.95 (*0-352-33289-1*, Pub. by BLA4) London Brdge.

— The Gallery. 256p. (Orig.). 1997. mass mkt. 5.95 (*0-352-33148-8*, Pub. by BLA4) London Brdge.

***Alleyn, Susanne.** A Far Better Rest: Novel. LC 99-87103. 360p. 2000. 25.00 (*1-56947-197-5*) Soho Press.

Alleyne, Cargill H., Jr. & Barrow, Daniel L. Neurosurgery Board Review: Questions & Answers for Self-Assessment. 2nd ed. LC 96-29700. (Illus.). 254p. 1997. pap. 39.95 (*0-86577-706-3*) Thieme Med Pubs.

Alleyne, Imekada J. African Roots in Britain. 1994. pap. 4.95 (*0-86543-425-5*) Africa World.

Alleyne, M., jt. auth. see Nash, Rose.

Alleyne, Mark D. International Power & International Communication. 200p. 1995. text 55.00 (*0-312-12534-8*) St Martin.

— News Revolution: Political & Economic Decisions about Global Information. 252p. 1996. pap. 19.95 (*0-312-16498-X*); text 45.00 (*0-312-15894-7*) St Martin.

Alleyne, Mervyn C. Roots of Jamaican Culture. 196p. 1989. text 29.95 (*0-7453-0245-9*); pap. text 15.95 (*0-7453-0369-2*) Routledge.

Alleyne, Michael H. Nationhood from the Schoolbag: A Historical Analysis of the Development of Secondary Education in Trinidad & Tobago. LC 95-50786. (Coleccion INTERAMER Ser.: No. 63). 1995. write for info. (*0-8270-3591-8*) OAS.

Alleyne, Sonia, ed. Starlog Entertainment Presents: Belle's Book of Lingerie. 1999. pap. 4.99 (*0-934551-65-0*) Starlog Grp Inc.

Alleyne, Vanessa. There Were Times When I Thought I Was Crazy: A Black Woman's Story of Incest. LC 97-114052. 176p. 1997. pap. 13.95 (*1-896705-08-1*) Sister Vis Pr.

***Allfrey, Brian G.** Delirious: A Collection of Poems for Kids 8- 88. large type ed. (Illus.). 116p. (J). (gr. 2-12). 1999. 17.95 (*0-9674403-0-0*) Delirious Pubg.

Allfrey, Phyllis S. The Orchid House. LC 96-20720. 250p. (C). 1996. pap. 16.95 (*0-8135-2332-X*) Rutgers U Pr.

— The Orchid House. large type ed. 320p. 1992. 22.95 (*1-85089-599-6*) Transaction Pubs.

Allgaier, April L., jt. auth. see Allgaier, Wayne.

Allgaier, Michael W., et al, eds. ASNT Nondestructive Testing Handbook, Vol. 8: Visual & Optical Testing. LC 93-521. 380p. 1993. 121.25 (*0-931403-05-7*, 133) Am Soc Nondestructive.

Allgaier, Wayne & Allgaier, April L. Leaves, Roots & Branches: The John Allgaier Family of Kankakee, Illinois. 198p. 1992. 35.00 (*0-9635551-0-3*) Robin Pr MA.

Allgeier, Albert R. & Allgeier, Elizabeth R. Sexual Interactions. 4th ed. 800p. (C). 1995. text 63.96 (*0-669-33337-9*) HM Trade Div.

Allgeier, Albert R., jt. auth. see Allgeier, Elizabeth R.

Allgeier, Elizabeth R. & Allgeier, Albert R. Sexual Interactions. 3rd ed. LC 90-83168. 720p. (C). 1991. text 63.96 (*0-669-24320-5*); teacher ed. 2.66 (*0-669-24322-1*); student ed. 22.36 (*0-669-24321-3*) HM Trade Div.

Allgeier, Elizabeth R., jt. auth. see Allgeier, Albert R.

Allgeier, Elizabeth R., jt. auth. see Winters, Deborah M.

***Allghower, Frank & Zheng, Alex.** Nonlinear Model Predictive Control. LC 00-23622. (Progress in Systems & Control Theory Ser.). 2000. write for info. (*0-8176-6297-9*) Birkhauser.

***Allghower, Frank & Zheng, Alex, eds.** Nonlinear Model Predictive Control. (Progress in Systems & Control Theory Ser.: Vol. 26). 488p. 2000. 109.00 (*3-7643-6297-9*, Pub. by Birkhauser) Spr-Verlag.

Allgoewer, M., et al, eds. Progress in Surgery, 2 vols., 11. (Illus.). 1972. 57.50 (*3-8055-1379-8*) S Karger.

— Progress in Surgery, 2 vols., 12. (Illus.). 1973. 85.25 (*3-8055-1617-7*) S Karger.

— Progress in Surgery, Vol. 10. (Illus.). x, 132p. 1971. 48.00 (*3-8055-1285-6*) S Karger.

— Progress in Surgery, Vol. 13. 300p. 1974. 121.00 (*3-8055-1741-6*) S Karger.

— Progress in Surgery, Vol. 14. x, 192p. 1975. 80.00 (*3-8055-2181-2*) S Karger.

Allgood, Dave & Allgood, Stephanie. Merry Bear Book of Dreams: A Book to Read & Color. 2nd ed. (Illus.). 36p. (J). (ps-3). 1985. pap. 2.95 (*0-933103-00-X*) Merry Bears.

Allgood, J. H., et al. Mexico: The Fertilizer Industry. (Technical Bulletin Ser.: No. T-16). (Illus.). 60p. (Orig.). 1979. pap. 4.00 (*0-88090-015-6*) Intl Fertilizer.

Allgood, J. R. & Swihart, G. R. Design of Flexural Members for Static & Blast Loading. LC 76-92268. (American Concrete Institute Monographs: No. 5). 175p. reprint ed. pap. 54.30 (*0-608-16783-5*, 205617000053) Bks Demand.

Allgood, Myralyn F., ed. & tr. see Bonifaz, Oscar.

Allgood, Stephanie, jt. auth. see Allgood, Dave.

***Allgor, Catherine.** Parlor Politics: In Which the Ladies of Washington Help Build a City & a Government. 352p. 2000. 29.95 (*0-8139-1998-3*) U Pr of Va.

Allgower, E., et al, eds. Bifurcation & Symmetry: Cross Influence Between Mathematics & Applications. LC 92-11639. (International Series of Numerical Mathematics: Vols. 104). 336p. 1992. 122.00 (*0-8176-2739-1*, Pub. by Birkhauser) Princeton Arch.

Allgower, E. & Georg, K. Numerical Continuation Methods: An Introduction. Graham, R. L. et al, eds. (Computational Mathematics Ser.: Vol. 13). (Illus.). xiv, 388p. 1990. 123.95 (*0-387-12760-7*) Spr-Verlag.

Allgower, Eugene A. & Georg, Kurt, eds. Computational Solution of Nonlinear Systems of Equations. LC 90-27. (LAM Ser.: Vol. 26). 762p. 1990. text 235.00 (*0-8218-1131-2*, LAM/26) Am Math.

Allgower, Eugene L., et al, eds. Exploiting Symmetry in Applied & Numerical Analysis: AMS-SIAM Summer Seminar in Applied Mathematics, July 26-August 1, 1992, Colorado State University. LC 93-30491. (Lectures in Applied Mathematics: Vol. 29). 459p. 1993. pap. 58.00 (*0-8218-1134-7*, LAM/29) Am Math.

Allgower, M., et al, eds. ASIF - Technique for Internal Fixation of Fractures. 1975. 348.00 (*0-387-92105-2*) Spr-Verlag.

Allgower, M. & Arder, F., eds. State of the Art of Surgery, Nineteen Seventy-Nine to Nineteen Eighty. 116p. 1980. 18.95 (*0-387-10136-5*) Spr-Verlag.

Alli, Antero. The Akashic Record Player: A Non-Stop Geomantic Conspiracy. LC 88-83350. 160p. (Orig.). 1988. pap. 12.95 (*0-941404-91-9*) New Falcon Pubns.

— Angel Tech: A Modern Shaman's Guide to Reality Selection. 2nd ed. LC 86-82908. 292p. (Orig.). 1991. pap. 12.95 (*1-56184-009-2*) New Falcon Pubns.

Alli, B. O., et al. Report of the National Workshop on Child Labour in Ethiopia. LC 97-980762. ii, 106 p. 1996. write for info. (*92-2-110152-5*) Intl Labour Office.

Alli, B. O., et al. Report on the National Workshop on Child Labour Policy & Action Programme for Ethiopia. LC 97-980722. ii, 54 p. 1996. write for info. (*92-2-110503-2*) Intl Labour Office.

***Alli, Benjamin.** Fundamental Principles of Occupational Health & Safety. 112p. 2000. pap. 14.95 (*92-2-110869-4*, Pub. by ILO) ILO Pubns Ctr.

Alli, Warisu O., jt. auth. see Beckett, Paul.

Allia, P., et al, eds. Fundamental & Applicative Aspects of Disordered Magnetism. 260p. (C). 1989. text 89.00 (*9971-5-0579-7*) World Scientific Pub.

Alliance Book Company Staff. Sophy I. 1999. pap. text 9.99 (*0-89804-600-9*) Alliance Bk Co.

***Alliance Book Company Staff.** Sophy I. 1999. pap. text 9.99 (*0-89804-603-3*) Alliance Bk Co.

Alliance Book Company Staff. Sophy II. 1999. pap. text 9.99 (*0-89804-601-7*) Alliance Bk Co.

— Sophy III. 1999. pap. text 9.99 (*0-89804-602-5*) Alliance Bk Co.

Alliance for CME Staff. The Alliance for Continuing Medical Education: The First Twenty Years. 120p. 1996. pap. text, per. 17.95 (*0-7872-2041-8*) Kendall-Hunt.

***Alliance for Safe Driving (U.S.).** License to Drive in New York. LC 99-37573. 2000. 41.95 (*0-7668-0307-4*) Delmar.

***Alliance for Safe Driving (U.S.), contrib. by.** License to Drive in Arizona. LC 99-32336. 2000. pap. 41.95 (*0-7668-0306-6*) Delmar.

***Alliance for Safe Driving Staff.** Illinois. (Career Education - License to Drive Ser.). 2002. write for info. (*0-7668-2370-9*) Delmar.

— License to Drive. 560p. 41.95 (*0-7668-1351-7*, Pub. by Delmar) Thomson Learn.

Alliance for Safe Driving Staff. License to Drive. LC 98-38549. 1999. 33.95 (*0-7668-0302-3*) Delmar.

***Alliance for Safe Driving Staff.** License to Drive. 2000. pap., wbk. ed. 11.21 (*0-7668-2812-3*) Delmar.

— License to Drive: California. LC 99-37572. (Career Education Ser.). 520p. 2000. 17.95 (*0-7668-0311-2*) Delmar.

— License to Drive: Florida. (Career Education Ser.). 2002. 31.50 (*0-7668-2368-7*) Delmar.

— License to Drive: Mississippi. (Career Education Ser.). 2000. 31.50 (*0-7668-2287-7*) Delmar.

— License to Drive: New Mexico. (Career Education Ser.). 2001. 31.50 (*0-7668-2285-0*) Delmar.

— License to Drive: Ohio. (Career Education Ser.). 2000. pap. 17.95 (*0-7668-0309-0*) Delmar.

— License to Drive: Texas. (Career Education Ser.). 2000. pap. 17.95 (*0-7668-0310-4*) Delmar.

— License to Drive-Massachusetts State Specific Text. (Career Education Ser.). 2000. pap. 24.50 (*0-7668-2022-X*) Delmar.

— Michigan. (Career Education - License to Drive Ser.). 2001. 31.50 (*0-7668-2372-5*) Delmar.

— Nevada. (Career Education - Licence to Drive Ser.). 2000. 31.50 (*0-7668-2374-1*) Delmar.

— North Carolina. (Career Education - License to Drive Ser.). 2002. 31.50 (*0-7668-2376-8*); 10.50 (*0-7668-2377-6*) Delmar.

— Pennsylvania. (Career Education - License to Drive Ser.). 2001. 31.50 (*0-7668-2378-4*) Delmar.

— South Carolina. (Career Education - License to Drive Ser.). 2002. 31.50 (*0-7668-2380-6*) Delmar.

— Tennessee. (Career Education - License to Drive Ser.). 2001. 31.50 (*0-7668-2382-2*) Delmar.

— Wisconsin. (Career Education - License to Drive Ser.). 2001. 31.50 (*0-7668-2384-9*) Delmar.

Alliance for the Arts Staff. Kids Culture Catalog: A Cultural Guide to New York City for Kids, Families, & Schools. 2nd ed. LC 98-17205. (Illus.). 224p. (J). (gr. k up). 1998. pap. 12.95 (*0-8109-2799-3*, Pub. by Abrams) Time Warner.

— Kids' Culture Catalog: A Teacher & Parent's Guide to Education Programs of NYC'S Cultural Resources. Jones, Patricia & Kass, Abby, eds. LC 87-72495. (Illus.). 196p. (Orig.). 1987. pap. 7.95 (*0-912443-02-2*) Alliance Arts.

Alliance for the Arts Staff, et al. New York City Culture Catalog: A Guide to New York City's Museums, Concert Halls, Theaters, Zoos, Botanical Gardens, Historic Houses & Libraries. LC 93-34782. (Illus.). 224p. 1994. pap. 12.95 (*0-8109-2578-8*, Pub. by Abrams) Time Warner.

Alliance of American Insurers Staff. Handbook of Hazardous Materials. 248p. 1983. pap. text 16.00 (*1-887271-17-1*) Alliance Am Insurers.

— Handbook of Organic Industrial Solvents. 132p. 1987. pap. text 12.00 (*1-887271-13-9*) Alliance Am Insurers.

— Occupational Safety & Health: A Directory of State Approaches. 110p. 1993. pap. text 35.00 (*1-887271-09-0*) Alliance Am Insurers.

— Policy Kit: A Collection of Sample Insurance Forms, 1995-1996. 546p. 1995. pap. text 22.95 (*1-887271-19-8*) Alliance Am Insurers.

Alliance of Artists' Communities Staff. Artists' Communities: A Directory of Residencies in the United States That Offer Time & Space for Creativity. LC 96-84643. (Illus.). 192p. (Orig.). 1996. pap. 16.95 (*1-880559-65-X*) Allworth Pr.

***Alliance Staff.** 1999 Alliance for Children & Families Directory of Member Organizations. 1999. pap. 365.00 (*0-87304-317-0*) Manticore Pubs.

Allianz Versicherungs-AG Staff & Muenchner Rueckversicherungs-Gesellschaft Staff, eds. Handbook of Loss Prevention. Cahn-Speyer, P., tr. from GER. 1978. 69.95 (*0-387-07822-3*) Spr-Verlag.

***Alliata, Zorina.** Return to Shambala. 92p. 1999. pap. 10.95 (*0-7414-0328-5*) Buy Books.

Alliband, Terry. Catalysts of Development: Voluntary Agencies in India. fac. ed. LC 82-83155. (Kumarian Press Library of Management for Development). 128p. (Orig.). 1994. pap. 39.70 (*0-7837-7572-5*, 204732500007) Bks Demand.

Allibert, M. Life of St. Benedict. LC 70-168505. (Black Heritage Library Collection). 1977. reprint ed. 25.95 (*0-8369-8859-0*) Ayer.

Allibone, Jill. George Devey Architect, 1820-1886. LC 91-189598. 1997. 11.95 (*0-7188-2785-6*, Lutterworth-Parkwest) Parkwest Pubns.

Allibone, Jill & Evans, David. The Inns of Court. (Illus.). 160p. 1996. 70.00 (*0-9521773-1-5*, Pub. by Black Dog Pubg) RAM Publications.

Allibone, Samuel A. An Alphabetical Index to the New Testament. (Principle Works of Samuel Austin Allibone). 1989. reprint ed. lib. bdg. 99.00 (*0-7812-1785-7*) Rprt Serv.

— Critical Dictionary of English Literature & British & American Authors, 3 vols. 1972. 300.00 (*0-87968-965-X*) Gordon Pr.

— A Critical Dictionary of English Literature & British & American Authors, 6 vols., Set. (Principle Works of Samuel Austin Allibone). 1989. reprint ed. lib. bdg. 540.00 (*0-7812-1784-9*) Rprt Serv.

— Great Authors of All Ages. (Principle Works of Samuel Austin Allibone). 1989. reprint ed. lib. bdg. 70.00 (*0-7812-1789-X*) Rprt Serv.

— Poetical Quotations from Chaucer to Tennyson. 1972. 59.95 (*0-8490-0855-7*) Gordon Pr.

— Poetical Quotations from Chaucer to Tennyson. (Principle Works of Samuel Austin Allibone). 1989. reprint ed. lib. bdg. 79.00 (*0-7812-1787-3*) Rprt Serv.

— Prose Quotations from Socrates to Macaulay. 1972. 59.95 (*0-8490-0902-2*) Gordon Pr.

— Prose Quotations from Socrates to Macaulay. (Principle Works of Samuel Austin Allibone). 1989. reprint ed. lib. bdg. 79.00 (*0-7812-1788-1*) Rprt Serv.

— The Union Bible Companion. (Principle Works of Samuel Austin Allibone). 1989. reprint ed. lib. bdg. 79.00 (*0-7812-1786-5*) Rprt Serv.

— The Works of Samuel Austin Allibone, 1816-1889, Set. 1987. reprint ed. lib. bdg. 1000.00 (*0-685-18590-7*) Rprt Serv.

Allica, Greer. Meditation Workbook. 116p. 1994. pap. 22.00 (*0-86012-193-3*, Pub. by Srch Pr) St Mut.

Allie, Glen, jt. auth. see Edgerton, Leslie.

Allied Chemical Corporation Staff & Mastroianni, M. J. New Working Fluids for Gas-Fired Cycle Heat Pumps. 104p. 1975. pap. 4.50 (*0-318-12658-3*, M50077) Am Gas Assn.

Allies, Jabez. On the Ancient British, Roman & Saxon Antiquities & Folk-Lore of Worcestershire. 2nd ed. Dorson, Richard M., ed. LC 77-70577. (International Folklore Ser.). (Illus.). 1977. reprint ed. lib. bdg. 42.95 (*0-405-10078-7*) Ayer.

A

Allies, Mary H. Three Catholic Reformers of the Fifteenth Century. LC 73-38755. (Essay Index Reprint Ser.). 1977. reprint ed. 16.95 (*0-8369-2633-1*) Ayer.

Allies, Mary H., tr. see Joannes, Damascenus.

Alliev, M. K. Hematology Reviews Vol. 3, Pt. 4: Clinical Disorders of the System Regulating the Aggregate State of Blood & Methods for Their Management, Vol. 3. (Soviet Medical Reviews Ser.: Section C). v, 111p. 1990. text 121.00 (*3-7186-4960-8*, Harwood Acad Pubs) Gordon & Breach.

Alliez, Eric. Capital Times: Tales from the Conquest of Time. Van Den Abbeele, Georges, tr. (Theory out of Bounds Ser.: Vol. 6). 344p. 1995. pap. 24.95 (*0-8166-2260-4*); text 62.95 (*0-8166-2259-0*) U of Minn Pr.

Alligood, Kathleen, et al. Chaotic Dynamical Systems. LC 95-51304. (Textbooks in Mathematical Sciences Ser.). 1996. write for info. (*0-614-95889-X*) Spr-Verlag.

Alligood, Martha R. & Marriner-Tomey, Ann, eds. Nursing Theory: Utilization & Application. (Illus.). 256p. (C). (gr. 13). 1996. pap. text 35.00 (*0-8151-0812-5*, 27759) Mosby Inc.

Alligood, Martha R., jt. auth. see Marriner-Tomey, Ann.

Allin, Cephas D. Annexation, Preferential Trade & Reciprocity: An Outline of the Canadian Annexation Movement of 1849-50, with Special Reference to the Questions of Preferential Trade & Reciprocity. (BCL1 - History - Canada Ser.). 398p. 1991. reprint ed. text 89.00 (*0-7812-6356-5*) Rprt Serv.

Allin, Craig & Coyne, Mark, eds. Natural Resources, 3 vols. LC 97-43364. (Illus.). 978p. 1998. lib. bdg. 315.00 (*0-89356-912-7*) Salem Pr.

Allin, Craig W. The Politics of Wilderness Preservation, 64. LC 81-6234. (Contributions in Political Science Ser.: No. 64). 304p. 1982. 65.00 (*0-313-21458-1*, ALP/, Greenwood Pr) Greenwood.

Allin, Craig W., ed. International Handbook of National Parks & Nature Reserves. LC 89-26039. 560p. 1990. lib. bdg. 115.00 (*0-313-24902-4*, AIN/, Greenwood Pr) Greenwood.

***Allin, Craig W. & McClenaghan, Robert.** Encyclopedia of Environmental Issues. LC 99-46373. 2000. write for info. (*0-89356-995-X*); write for info. (*0-89356-996-8*); write for info. (*0-89356-997-6*) Salem Pr.

Allin, Dana H. Cold War Illusions: America, Europe & Soviet Power, 1969-1989. LC 94-28776. 277p. 1995. text 45.00 (*0-312-12374-4*) St Martin.

— Cold War Illusions: America, Europe & Soviet Power, 1969-1989. 277p. 1998. pap. 18.95 (*0-312-17296-6*) St Martin.

Allin, Joan E., jt. auth. see Hodge, William C.

Allin, Lawrence C. The United States Naval Institute, Intellectual Forum of the New Navy, 1873-1889. 381p. (Orig.). 1978. pap. 47.95 (*0-89126-066-8*) MA-AH Pub.

Allin, Michael. Zarafa: A Giraffe's True Story, from Deep Africa to the Heart of Paris. 224p. 1999. pap. 9.95 (*0-385-33411-7*, Delta Trade) Dell.

Allin, Richard. The Southern Legislative Dictionary. LC 97-199908. (Illus.). 36p. 1983. pap. 3.95 (*0-914546-50-3*) Rose Pub.

Alling, Abigail & Nelson, Mark. Life under Glass: The Inside Story of Biosphere 2. (Illus.). 272p. 1993. pap. 16.95 (*1-882428-07-2*) Synerg CA.

Alling, C., et al. Alcohol, Cell Membranes & Signal Transduction in Brain. (Illus.). 334p. (C). 1993. text 105.00 (*0-306-44583-2*, Kluwer Plenum) Kluwer Academic.

Alling, Charles C., III, et al, eds. Impacted Teeth. LC 92-49774. (Illus.). 512p. 1993. text 110.00 (*0-7216-2968-7*, W B Saunders Co) Harcrt Hlth Sci Grp.

Alling, Charles C., 3rd, jt. ed. see Catone, Guy A.

***Alling, Norman L. & Ribenboim, Paulo.** Collected Papers of Norman Alling. LC 98-231653. (Illus.). 1998. write for info. (*0-88911-796-9*) Queens U Inst Intergov.

Alling, Robert B. Babson & Allied Families in America. (Illus.). 77p. 1997. reprint ed. pap. 14.50 (*0-8328-7313-6*); reprint ed. lib. bdg. 24.50 (*0-8328-7312-8*) Higginson Bk Co.

Alling, Roger, Jr., pref. More Sermons That Work: Prize Winning Sermons 1992 with Addresses & Sermons from a Conference for Preachers. 142p. (Orig.). 1992. pap. 4.00 (*0-88028-135-9*, 1186) Forward Movement.

Alling, Roger, pref. Sermons That Work IV. 128p. (Orig.). 1994. pap. 4.95 (*0-88028-153-7*, 1283) Forward Movement.

— Sermons That Work III: Prize Winning Sermons & Addresses, 1993. 136p. (Orig.). 1993. pap. 4.95 (*0-88028-144-8*, 1226) Forward Movement.

***Alling, Roger & Schlafer, David J.** Sermons that Work X. 144p. 2001. 12.95 (*0-8192-1818-9*, 6126) Morehouse Pub.

Alling, Roger & Schlafer, David J., eds. Preaching As the Art of Sacred Conversation. 144p. 1997. pap. 10.95 (*0-8192-1699-2*) Morehouse Pub.

— Preaching Through the Year of Mark: Sermons That Work VIII. LC 99-28155. 144p. 1997. pap. 9.95 (*0-8192-1761-1*, 2504) Morehouse Pub.

— Sermons That Work V: Distinctive Dimensions in Anglican Preaching. 128p. (Orig.). 1995. pap. 6.95 (*0-88028-167-7*, 1342) Forward Movement.

Alling, Roger, jt. auth. see Schlafer, David J.

Allinger, Glenn D., et al. Mathematics Projects Handbook. 4th ed. LC 99-32453. 93p. 1999. pap. 13.95 (*0-87353-472-7*) NCTM.

Allinger, Norman L., et al. Organic Chemistry. 2nd ed. LC 75-18431. 1976. text 77.95 (*0-87901-050-9*) Worth.

— Organic Chemistry. 2nd ed. LC 75-18431. 1976. pap. text, student ed. 14.95 (*0-87901-078-9*) Worth.

Allinger, Norman L., jt. ed. see Burkert, Ulrich.

Allinger, Norman L., jt. ed. see Eliel, Ernest L.

Allingham. Rational Choice. LC 99-21114. (Illus.). 1999. text 65.00 (*0-312-22446-X*) St Martin.

Allingham, G. E. Growing up in Khacki: The Life of a Military Brat. 350p. 1998. pap. 12.95 (*1-884570-83-6*) Research Triangle.

Allingham, Helen & Williams, E. Baumer, eds. Letters to William Allingham. LC 70-148739. reprint ed. 42.50 (*0-404-00343-5*) AMS Pr.

Allingham, Margery. The Allingham Case-Book. 224p. 1998. lib. bdg. 21.95 (*1-56723-000-8*) Yestermorrow.

— The Allingham Case-Book. 2nd ed. 240p. 1992. mass mkt. 3.95 (*0-88184-889-1*) Carroll & Graf.

***Allingham, Margery.** The Black Dudley Murder. 224p. 2000. mass mkt. 5.95 (*0-7867-0754-2*, Pub. by Carroll & Graf) Publishers Group.

Allingham, Margery. The Black Dudley Murder. 224p. 1988. mass mkt. 3.99 (*0-380-70575-3*, Avon Bks) Morrow Avon.

— The Black Dudley Murder. 227p. 1998. lib. bdg. 22.95 (*1-56723-001-6*) Yestermorrow.

— The Black Dudley Murder. 1994. reprint ed. lib. bdg. 27.95 (*1-56849-252-9*) Buccaneer Bks.

— Black Plumes. 1994. lib. bdg. 18.95 (*1-56849-458-0*) Buccaneer Bks.

— Black Plumes. 192p. 1995. mass mkt. 3.95 (*0-7867-0290-7*) Carroll & Graf.

— Black Plumes. 1998. lib. bdg. 23.95 (*1-56723-002-4*) Yestermorrow.

— Cargo of Eagles. 206p. 1998. lib. bdg. 21.95 (*1-56723-003-2*) Yestermorrow.

— Cargo of Eagles. 224p. 1990. reprint ed. mass mkt. 3.99 (*0-380-70576-1*, Avon Bks) Morrow Avon.

***Allingham, Margery.** The Case of the Late Pig. LC 98-51894. 165 p. 1999. write for info. (*0-7540-3641-3*) Chivers N Amer.

Allingham, Margery. The Case of the Late Pig. 160p. 1989. pap. 3.50 (*0-380-70577-X*, Avon Bks) Morrow Avon.

— The Case of the Late Pig. LC 98-51894. 1999. pap. text 19.95 (*0-7838-8507-5*) Thorndike Pr.

— The China Governess. 272p. 1990. mass mkt. 4.50 (*0-380-70578-8*, Avon Bks) Morrow Avon.

— The China Governess. 224p. 1998. lib. bdg. 21.95 (*1-56723-004-0*) Yestermorrow.

— Coroner's Pidgin. 1998. lib. bdg. 22.95 (*1-56723-005-9*) Yestermorrow.

— Dancers in Mourning. 272p. 1996. mass mkt. 4.95 (*0-7867-0384-9*) Carroll & Graf.

— Dancers in Mourning. 1998. lib. bdg. 22.95 (*1-56723-006-7*) Yestermorrow.

— Deadly Duo. 1998. lib. bdg. 19.95 (*1-56723-007-5*) Yestermorrow.

— Deadly Duo. 1993. reprint ed. lib. bdg. 15.95 (*0-89968-452-1*) Buccaneer Bks.

— Deady Duo. 208p. 1996. mass mkt. 4.50 (*0-7867-0335-0*) Carroll & Graf.

— Death of a Ghost. 192p. 1997. mass mkt. 4.95 (*0-7867-0441-1*) Carroll & Graf.

— Death of a Ghost. 175p. 1998. lib. bdg. 19.95 (*1-56723-008-3*) Yestermorrow.

— Death of a Ghost. 175p. 1993. reprint ed. 16.95 (*0-89190-195-7*) Amereon Ltd.

— Death of a Ghost. 1993. reprint ed. lib. bdg. 15.95 (*0-89968-453-X*) Buccaneer Bks.

— The Estate of the Beckoning Lady. 256p. 1990. mass mkt. 3.99 (*0-380-70574-5*, Avon Bks) Morrow Avon.

— The Estate of the Beckoning Lady. 1998. lib. bdg. 22.95 (*1-56723-009-1*) Yestermorrow.

— Fashion in Shrouds. 280p. 1995. mass mkt. 4.95 (*0-7867-0224-9*) Carroll & Graf.

— Fashion in Shrouds. 1998. lib. bdg. 22.95 (*1-56723-010-5*) Yestermorrow.

— Fashion in Shrouds. 1993. reprint ed. lib. bdg. 18.95 (*0-89968-454-8*) Buccaneer Bks.

***Allingham, Margery.** The Fear Sign. 240p. 2000. mass mkt. 5.95 (*0-7867-0755-0*, Pub. by Carroll & Graf) Publishers Group.

Allingham, Margery. The Fear Sign. 240p. 1989. pap. 3.95 (*0-380-70571-0*, Avon Bks) Morrow Avon.

— The Fear Sign. 1998. lib. bdg. 20.95 (*1-56723-011-3*) Yestermorrow.

— Flowers for the Judge: An Albert Campion Mystery. 248p. 1995. mass mkt. 4.50 (*0-7867-0291-5*) Carroll & Graf.

— Flowers for the Judge: An Albert Campion Mystery. large type ed. LC 91-46195. 396p. 1992. lib. bdg. 19.95 (*1-56054-325-6*) Thorndike Pr.

— The Gyrth Chalice Mystery. 256p. 1989. mass mkt. 3.99 (*0-380-70572-9*, Avon Bks) Morrow Avon.

***Allingham, Margery.** Look to the Lady. large type unabridged ed. 2000. 26.95 (*0-7531-6101-X*, 16101X, Pub. by ISIS Lrg Prnt) ISIS Pub.

Allingham, Margery. The Margery Allingham Omnibus. Incl. Crime at Black Dudley. 1983. Look to the Lady. 1983. Mystery Mile. 1983. 592p. 1983. Set pap. 7.95 (*0-14-006058-8*, Penguin Bks) Viking Penguin.

— The Mind Readers. 272p. 1990. pap. 3.95 (*0-380-70570-2*, Avon Bks) Morrow Avon.

— The Mind Readers. 286p. 1998. lib. bdg. 23.95 (*1-56723-012-1*) Yestermorrow.

— Mr. Campion & Others. 272p. 1991. pap. 3.95 (*0-380-70579-6*, Avon Bks) Morrow Avon.

— Mr. Campion's Lucky Day & Other Stories. 240p. 1992. mass mkt. 3.95 (*0-88184-890-5*) Carroll & Graf.

— More Work for the Undertaker. 272p. 1989. pap. 3.95 (*0-380-70573-7*, Avon Bks) Morrow Avon.

— More Work for the Undertaker. 253p. 1998. lib. bdg. 22.95 (*1-56723-013-X*) Yestermorrow.

— Mystery Mile. 250p. 1994. 4.50 (*0-7867-0168-4*) Carroll & Graf.

— Mystery Mile. 264p. 1998. lib. bdg. 25.95 (*1-56723-014-8*) Yestermorrow.

— No Love Lost. 176p. 1991. mass mkt. 3.95 (*0-88184-723-2*) Carroll & Graf.

— No Love Lost. 176p. 1998. lib. bdg. 20.95 (*1-56723-015-6*) Yestermorrow.

— The Oaken Heart. large type ed. 368p. 1991. 21.95 (*1-85089-344-6*, Pub. by ISIS Lrg Prnt) Transaction Pubs.

— The Patient at Peacock's Hall. 20.95 (*0-89190-165-5*) Amereon Ltd.

***Allingham, Margery.** The Patient at Peacocks Hall. large type ed. 172p. 2000. pap. 20.95 (*0-7838-8966-6*) Mac Lib Ref.

Allingham, Margery. Pearls Before Swine. 224p. 1996. mass mkt. 4.95 (*0-7867-0338-5*) Carroll & Graf.

— Pearls Before Swine. 240p. 1998. lib. bdg. 21.95 (*1-56723-016-4*) Yestermorrow.

— Pearls Before Swine. 192p. reprint ed. lib. bdg. 18.95 (*0-89190-196-5*, Rivercity Pr) Amereon Ltd.

— Police at the Funeral. 232p. 1994. mass mkt. 3.95 (*0-7867-0169-2*) Carroll & Graf.

— Police at the Funeral. 1998. lib. bdg. 21.95 (*1-56723-017-2*) Yestermorrow.

— The Return of Mr. Campion: Uncollected Stories. Morpurgo, J. E., ed. & intro. by. 192p. 1991. pap. 3.95 (*0-380-71448-5*, Avon Bks) Morrow Avon.

— Safer Than Love. 17.95 (*0-89190-166-3*) Amereon Ltd.

***Allingham, Margery.** Safer Than Love. LC 00-31899. 2000. write for info. (*0-7838-9096-6*, G K Hall & Co) Mac Lib Ref.

Allingham, Margery. Sweet Danger. 256p. 1988. mass mkt. 5.95 (*0-14-008779-6*, Penguin Bks) Viking Penguin.

— Take Two at Bedtime. Date not set. lib. bdg. 20.95 (*0-8488-1951-9*) Amereon Ltd.

— Tether's End: An Albert Campion Mystery. 208p. 1996. mass mkt. 4.95 (*0-7867-0383-0*) Carroll & Graf.

— Tether's End: An Albert Campion Mystery. 216p. 1998. lib. bdg. 20.95 (*1-56723-018-0*) Yestermorrow.

— Tether's End: An Albert Campion Mystery. 176p. reprint ed. lib. bdg. 16.95 (*0-89190-197-3*, Rivercity Pr) Amereon Ltd.

— The Tiger in the Smoke. 21.95 (*0-89190-198-1*) Amereon Ltd.

— The Tiger in the Smoke. 1994. lib. bdg. 17.95 (*1-56849-459-9*) Buccaneer Bks.

***Allingham, Margery.** The Tiger in the Smoke. 232p. 2000. mass mkt. 5.95 (*0-7867-0719-4*) Carroll & Graf.

Allingham, Margery. Traitor's Purse. 224p. 1997. mass mkt. 4.95 (*0-7867-0447-0*) Carroll & Graf.

— Traitor's Purse. 176p. 1998. lib. bdg. 19.95 (*1-56723-019-9*) Yestermorrow.

— Traitor's Purse. large type ed. LC 91-41613. 333p. 1992. reprint ed. lib. bdg. 25.95 (*1-56054-324-8*) Thorndike Pr.

— Traitor's Purse. 176p. reprint ed. lib. bdg. 16.95 (*0-89190-199-X*, Rivercity Pr) Amereon Ltd.

— Traitor's Purse. 1994. reprint ed. lib. bdg. 24.95 (*1-56849-251-0*) Buccaneer Bks.

— The White Cottage Mystery. 139p. 1990. mass mkt. 3.50 (*0-88184-666-X*) Carroll & Graf.

Allingham, Margery & Carter, Youngman. Mr. Campion's Farthing. 191p. 1990. mass mkt. 3.95 (*0-88184-667-8*) Carroll & Graf.

— Mr. Campion's Quarry. 240p. 1991. mass mkt. 3.95 (*0-88184-724-0*) Carroll & Graf.

Allingham, Michael. Unconscious Contracts: A Psychoanalytic Theory of Society. 176p. 1988. text 45.00 (*0-7102-0996-7*, Routledge Thoemms) Routledge.

Allingham, Ruth. Glimpses of the Past: Oral Histories from Naselle. (Illus.). 208p. 1998. pap. 24.95 (*0-9665655-0-9*) Pcfc Cty Hist.

Allingham, William. Ballad Book. LC 76-76931. (Granger Index Reprint Ser.). 1977. 21.95 (*0-8369-6000-9*) Ayer.

— Fifty Modern Poems. LC 74-148740. reprint ed. 34.50 (*0-404-00344-3*) AMS Pr.

— Laurence Bloomfield in Ireland: A Modern Poem. LC 71-148742. reprint ed. 39.50 (*0-404-00346-X*) AMS Pr.

— Poems. LC 78-148741. reprint ed. 20.00 (*0-404-00345-1*) AMS Pr.

— Songs, Ballads, & Stories. LC 75-148743. reprint ed. 41.50 (*0-404-00347-8*) AMS Pr.

Allington, Maynard, II. The Court of Blue Shadows: A Novel. LC 94-20236. 288p. 1995. 22.95 (*0-02-881104-6*) Brasseys.

Allington, Maynard. The Fox in the Field: A WWII Novel of India. LC 93-17964. (World War II Commemorative Ser.). 224p. 1994. 19.95 (*0-02-881085-6*) Brasseys.

— The Grey Wolf. 256p. (Orig.). 1995. reprint ed. pap. 17.95 (*1-57488-042-X*) Brasseys.

Allington, Peter & Greenhill, Basil. The First Atlantic Liners: Seamanship in the Age of Paddle Wheel, Sail & Screw. (Illus.). 176p. 1997. 55.00 (*0-85177-668-X*, Pub. by Brasseys) Brasseys.

Allington, Richard & Walmsley, Sean, eds. No Quick Fix: Rethinking Literacy Programs in America's Elementary Schools. (Language & Literacy Ser.). 288p. (C). 1995. text 44.00 (*0-8077-3389-X*); pap. text 20.95 (*0-8077-3388-1*) Tchrs Coll.

Allington, Richard L. Senses: Feeling. (J). 1990. pap. text 6.95 (*0-8172-2478-5*) Raintree Steck-V.

Allington, Richard L., ed. Teaching Struggling Readers: Articles from "The Reading Teacher" LC 97-36583. 1998. pap. text 29.95 (*0-87207-183-9*) Intl Reading.

Allington, Richard L. & Cunningham, Patricia M. Schools That Work. LC 95-15798. (Illus.). 224p. (C). 1997. pap. text 28.00 (*0-673-99881-9*) Addson-Wesley Educ.

Allington, Richard L., et al. You Have Seen Our Faces: Stories about America. large type ed. 1993. 39.50 (*0-614-09864-5*, L-78685-00) Am Printing Hse.

Allington, Robert, ed. see Galichenko, Nicholas.

Allinson. Understanding Patent Law. 28.95 (*1-85521-706-6*); 70.95 (*1-85521-811-9*) Ashgate Pub Co.

Allinson, A. R., ed. The War Diary of the Emperor Frederick III, 1870-1871. LC 77-114529. (Illus.). 355p. 1971. reprint ed. lib. bdg. 45.00 (*0-8371-4824-3*, FRWD, Greenwood Pr) Greenwood.

Allinson, A. R., tr. see Frederick III.

Allinson, A. R., tr. see Michelet, Jules.

Allinson, Alfred, tr. see France, Anatole, pseud.

Allinson, Anne C. Children of the Way. LC 74-103490. (Short Story Index Reprint Ser.). 1977. 19.95 (*0-8369-3232-3*) Ayer.

— Selected Essays. LC 68-55836. (Essay Index Reprint Ser.). 1977. 20.95 (*0-8369-0146-0*) Ayer.

Allinson, Edward P. & Penrose, Boies. The City Government of Philadelphia. LC 78-63768. (Johns Hopkins University. Studies in the Social Sciences. Thirtieth Ser. 1912: 1-2). reprint ed. 37.50 (*0-404-61035-8*) AMS Pr.

Allinson, Frank G., tr. see Menander.

***Allinson, Gary D.** The Columbia Guide to Modern Japanese History. LC 99-10678. (Guides to Asian History Ser.). 259p. 1999. 45.00 (*0-231-11144-4*) Col U Pr.

Allinson, Gary D. Japanese Urbanism: Industry & Politics in Kariya, 1872-1972. LC 74-84141. 292p. reprint ed. pap. 90.60 (*0-7837-4839-6*, 204448600003) Bks Demand.

— Japan's Postwar History. LC 96-38163. (Illus.). 224p. 1996. text 39.95 (*0-8014-3312-6*); pap. text 14.95 (*0-8014-8372-7*) Cornell U Pr.

Allinson, Gary D. & Sone, Yasunori, eds. Political Dynamics in Contemporary Japan. LC 92-56777. (Illus.). 336p. 1993. text 49.95 (*0-8014-2852-1*); pap. text 17.95 (*0-8014-8096-5*) Cornell U Pr.

Allinson, Kenneth. The Wild Card of Design: A Perspective on Architecture in a Project Management Environment. 2nd ed. (Illus.). 458p. 1993. pap. text 39.95 (*0-7506-2329-2*) Buttrwrth-Heinemann.

Allinson, Kenneth, jt. auth. see Thornton, Victoria.

***Allinson, Mark.** Contemporary Germany. LC 99-54271. (Contemporary Europe Ser.). (ENG & GER.). 2000. write for info. (*0-582-35714-4*) Longman.

— Politics & Popular Opinion in East Germany, 1945-1968. LC 99-43348. 1999. 74.95 (*0-7190-5554-7*) Manchester Univ Pr.

— A Spanish Labyrinth: The Films of Pedro Almodovar. (Illus.). 208p. 2000. pap. 18.95 (*1-86064-507-0*, Pub. by I B T) St Martin.

Allinson, Richard S., ed. Cumulative Index to Volumes 1-17 (1968-1985) of Criminal Justice Abstracts. 414p. 1989. text 125.00 (*0-9606960-5-9*, Criminal Justice) Willow Tree NY.

Allinson, Robert E. Chuang-Tzu for Spiritual Transformation: An Analysis of the Inner Chapters. LC 88-19974. (SUNY Series in Philosophy). 203p. (C). 1989. text 24.50 (*0-88706-967-3*) State U NY Pr.

Allinson, Robert E., ed. Understanding the Chinese Mind: The Philosophical Roots. 328p. 1989. 29.95 (*0-685-47313-9*) OUP.

— Understanding the Chinese Mind: The Philosophical Roots. 322p. 1990. reprint ed. pap. text 18.95 (*0-19-585022-X*) OUP.

Allinson, Russel R. Drug Abuse: Why It Happens & How to Prevent It. LC 84-7369. 130p. (Orig.). 1984. pap. 9.95 (*0-9612990-1-0*) Valley Publishing.

Allinson, Sidney. The Bantams: The Untold Story of World War I. (Illus.). 300p. 1994. pap. 12.95 (*0-88962-190-X*) Mosaic.

— Jeremy Kane: A Canadian Historical Adventure Novel of the 1837. LC 98-87510. 325p. 1998. 25.00 (*0-7388-0101-1*); pap. 15.00 (*0-7388-0102-X*) Xlibris Corp.

Allinson, Stephen P. Debt Recovery. 2nd ed. (Practice Notes Ser.). 102p. 1993. pap. write for info. (*0-85121-088-0*, Pub. by Cavendish Pubng) Gaunt.

Allio, Robert J. The Practical Strategist. 1990. pap. text 16.95 (*0-88730-399-4*, HarpBusn) HarpInfo.

— The Practical Strategist: Business & Corporate Strategy for the 1990s. 240p. 1988. text 32.95 (*0-88730-319-6*, HarpBusn) HarpInfo.

Allio, Robert J. & Pennington, Malcolm W., eds. Corporate Planning: Techniques & Applications. LC 78-25803. 446p. reprint ed. pap. 138.30 (*0-608-12908-9*, 202353700033) Bks Demand.

Allion, J., ed. see Maritain, Jacques & Maritain, Raissa.

Allion, J., ed. see Maritan, Jacques & Maritain, Raissa.

Allione, Tsultrim. Places She Lives. 1999. pap. 21.95 (*0-670-84762-3*) Viking Penguin.

***Allione, Tsultrim.** Women of Wisdom. LC 00-9126. 268p. 2000. pap. 16.95 (*1-55939-141-3*) Snow Lion Pubns.

***Alliot, Hector.** Bibliography of Arizona. 1999. reprint ed. 75.00 (*1-57898-185-9*) Martino Pubng.

Alliot, J. M., et al, eds. Artificial Evolution: European Conference, AE 95, Brest, France, September 4-6, 1995. LC 96-13937. (Lecture Notes in Computer Science Ser.: Vol. 1063). 396p. 1996. pap. 68.00 (*3-540-61108-8*) Spr-Verlag.

Allioux, Alain, jt. auth. see Giono, Jean.

Allis, Charles. Allis Genealogy. (Illus.). 32p. 1997. reprint ed. pap. 6.50 (*0-8328-7245-8*); reprint ed. lib. bdg. 16.50 (*0-8328-7244-X*) Higginson Bk Co.

Allis, Horatio D. Allis. Genealogy of William Allis of Hatfield, Mass. & Descendants, 1630-1919. (Illus.). 237p. 1997. reprint ed. pap. 36.50 (*0-8328-7247-4*); reprint ed. lib. bdg. 46.50 (*0-8328-7246-6*) Higginson Bk Co.

Allis, James B., jt. auth. see Bell, Albert A., Jr.

Allis, Lee, et al. Inside Macromedia Director 6 with Lingo. LC 97-8061. 1008p. 1997. 55.00 (*1-56205-728-6*) New Riders Pub.

Allis, Marguerite. Not Without Peril. 414p. 1989. reprint ed. 18.95 (*0-9622471-0-3*) Old Fort Four.

Allis, Oswald T. God Spake by Moses: An Exposition of the Pentatench. LC 58-59922. 1951. pap. 7.99 (*0-87552-103-7*) P & R Pubng.
Allison. Computers: Tools Productivity. (C). 1986. pap. text 26.50 (*0-03-070437-5*) Harcourt Coll Pubs.
— Cultural Attraction & Cultural Distribution. LC 99-35481. 321p. 1999. pap. text 35.00 (*0-13-737818-1*) P-H.
Allison. Electrical Controls. 162p. 1997. 25.00 (*0-89606-339-9*, 306) Am Assn Voc Materials.
— Guide to Herbs for Horses. 2000. pap. 8.95 (*0-85131-646-8*, Pub. by J A Allen) Trafalgar.
Allison. SAPT Gastroenterology. 2nd ed. 1996. pap. 15.95 (*0-7234-2589-2*) Wolfe Pubng AZ.
— Textual Encounters. (C). Date not set. pap. text, teacher ed. 15.00 (*0-15-502858-8*) Harcourt Coll Pubs.
— Textual Encounters. (C). 1999. text 57.00 (*0-15-502857-X*) Harcourt Coll Pubs.
Allison, et al. Paramedic Skills & Equipment. (Illus.). 352p. 1991. 24.95 (*0-685-54092-8*) Mosby Inc.
Allison, jt. auth. see Bates, Ernest S.
Allison, jt. auth. see Pounder.
***Allison, Desmond M.** Text in Education & Society. LC 98-474023. 1998. pap. 24.00 (*9971-69-222-8*) Sngapore Univ Pr.
Allison, A. F. & Rogers, D. M. The Contemporary Printed Literature of the English Counter-Reformation Between 1558 & 1640, Vol. I. 291p. 1989. text 139.95 (*0-85967-640-4*, Pub. by Scolar Pr) Ashgate Pub Co.
— The Contemporary Printed Literature of the English Counter-Reformation Between 1558 & 1640: Works in English, Vol. 2. 286p. 1994. 139.95 (*0-85967-852-0*, Pub. by Scolar Pr) Ashgate Pub Co.
Allison, Alcott. The White Stone: A Mystical Novel from Early Ireland. LC 92-17296. 155p. (Orig.). 1992. pap. 8.95 (*0-9620507-2-5*) Cosmic Concepts Pr.
Allison, Alexander W., et al. Masterpieces of the Drama. 6th rev. ed. LC 90-43954. 1056p. (C). 1990. pap. text 72.00 (*0-02-301975-1*, Macmillan Coll) P-H.
Allison, Alexandra. Outstanding Child Care with a Professional Nanny. 38p. (Orig.). pap. 29.99 (*1-878235-24-9*) Taylor Pub MI.
— Romance: A Tradition Lost. rev. ed. 90p. (Orig.). 1990. pap. 29.99 (*1-878235-01-X*) Taylor Pub MI.
Allison, Alida. Isaac Bashevis Singer: Children's Stories & Childhood Memoirs. (Twayne's United States Authors Ser.: Vol. 661). 176p. (J). 1996. 32.00 (*0-8057-9226-0*, Twyne) Mac Lib Ref.
***Allison, Alida, ed.** Russell Hoban/Forty Years: Essays on His Writings for Children. (Reference Library of the Humanities). 275p. 2000. pap. 18.95 (*0-8153-3799-X*) Garland.
Allison, Alida, ed. see Berkus, Rusty.
***Allison, Amy.** Antonio Bandaras. (Latinos in the Limelight Ser.). (Illus.). 2000. 17.95 (*0-7910-6102-7*) Chelsea Hse.
— Germany. LC 00-29072. (Dropping in on Ser.). (Illus.). 2001. write for info. (*1-55916-284-8*) Rourke Bk Co.
— Roger Williams. (Colonial Leaders Ser.). 2000. 18.95 (*0-7910-5964-2*) Chelsea Hse.
— Shakespeare's Globe. LC 99-27313. (Building History Ser.). (Illus.). 96p. (YA). (gr. 8-12). 2000. lib. bdg. 23.70 (*1-56006-526-5*) Lucent Bks.
Allison, Andrew M., et al. The Real Benjamin Franklin. LC 82-70110. (American Classic Ser.). (Illus.). xx, 504p. 1982. 16.95 (*0-88080-000-3*); pap. 13.95 (*0-88080-001-1*) Natl Ctr Constit.
— The Real Thomas Jefferson. 2nd ed. LC 83-17404. (American Classic Ser.). (Illus.). 709p. 1983. 17.95 (*0-88080-005-4*); pap. 14.95 (*0-88080-006-2*) Natl Ctr Constit.
Allison, Andrew M., jt. auth. see Parry, Jay A.
Allison, Anita, et al. Bluebonnet Trail Cookbook. LC 95-94609. 317p. 1995. 17.95 (*0-9647290-0-8*) JAM Pubs.
Allison, Anne. Nightwork: Sexuality, Pleasure & Corporate Masculinity in a Tokyo Hostess Club. LC 93-34877. 228p. 1994. pap. text 15.00 (*0-226-01487-8*) U Ch Pr.
— Nightwork: Sexuality, Pleasure & Corporate Masculinity in a Tokyo Hostess Club. LC 93-34877. 228p. 1996. lib. bdg. 37.00 (*0-226-01485-1*) U Ch Pr.
— Permitted & Prohibited Desires: Mothers, Comics, & Censorship in Japan. LC 99-16356. 225p. 2000. pap. 16.95 (*0-520-21990-2*, Pub. by U CA Pr) Cal Prin Full Svc.
Allison, Anthony. Hear These Voices: Youth at the Edge of the Millennium. LC 98-38464. (Illus.). (YA). (gr. 6 up). 1999. 22.99 (*0-525-45353-9*) NAL.
Allison, Anthony C., jt. ed. see Gregoriadis, Gregory.
Allison, Beverly. Effie. (J). 1999. pap. 19.95 (*0-590-72989-6*) Scholastic Inc.
***Allison, Brian.** Titus at the Gates of Syon. LC 99-487839. 1999. write for info. (*0-7541-0572-5*, Pub. by Minerva Pr) Unity Dist.
Allison, Bruce N. & Cliff, Gerald H., eds. Representations of Groups: Annual Seminar, June 10-24, 1994, Banff, Alberta, Canada. LC 95-32961. (Canadian Mathematical Society, Conference Proceedings Ser.: Vol. 16). 385p. 1995. pap. 110.00 (*0-8218-0311-5*, CMSAMS/16) Am Math.
Allison, C. Three Hundred Sixty-Five Days of Gardening. 416p. 1995. 17.95 (*0-06-017032-8*) HarperTrade.
Allison, C. FitzSimons. The Cruelty of Heresy: An Affirmation of Christian Orthodoxy. LC 93-39541. 200p. 1994. pap. 14.95 (*0-8192-1513-9*) Morehouse Pub.
— Fear, Love & Worship. 1983. 4.95 (*0-8164-2020-3*, SP17) Harper SF.
Allison, Caroline, jt. auth. see Clark, John.
***Allison, Carrie & Starr, Stacey.** Pointing Toward Home & Song of Yasuka: Poems. 71p. 1999. pap. 10.00 (*0-910479-07-0*) Mid-America Pr.
Allison, Carrie C., ed. see Mariano, Thomas.
Allison, Charlene J., et al. Winds of Change: Women in Northwest Commercial Fishing. LC 89-16422. (Illus.). 232p. 1989. pap. 25.00 (*0-295-96840-0*) U of Wash Pr.
Allison, Charles D. C & C++ Code Capsules: A Prescription for Your Software Ailments. LC 98-10622. 570p. (C). 1997. pap. text 39.95 incl. disk (*0-13-591785-9*) P-H.
***Allison, Charles Elmer.** History of Yonkers from the Earliest Times to 1896: Including an Elaborate Description of Its Aborigines. fac. ed. 454p. 2000. reprint ed. 49.00 (*0-7404-2612-5*) Higginson Bk Co.
Allison, Cherri, ed. see Doyle, Edith M.
Allison, Cherri, ed. see Gallo, Jon J., et al.
Allison, Cherri, ed. see Harris, L. Randolph, et al.
Allison, Cherri, ed. see House, Susan T. & Pone, Daniel A.
Allison, Cherri, ed. see Janin, Susan Y., et al.
Allison, Cherri N., ed. see Depper, Estelle M. & Bannon, Alexander L.
Allison, Christine. 365 Bedtime Stories. LC 98-9894. (Illus.). 448p. 1998. 21.95 (*0-7679-0096-0*) Broadway BDD.
Allison, Christine, ed. Kurdish Culture & Identity. 192p. (C). 1996. text 62.50 (*1-85649-329-6*, Pub. by Zed Books) St Martin.
Allison, Christine & Ringold, Dena. Labor Markets in Transition in Central & Eastern Europe 1989-1995. LC 96-37183. (Technical Papers: No. 352). 80p. 1996. pap. 22.00 (*0-8213-3834-X*) World Bank.
Allison, Christine, jt. auth. see Allison, Wick.
Allison, Christine, jt. auth. see Bentz, Rick.
***Allison, Clinton B.** Kellie McGarrh's Hangin' in Tough: Mildred E. Doyle, School Superintendent. LC 99-47661. (History of Schools & Schooling Ser.: Vol. 3). 160p. (C). 2000. pap. text 29.95 (*0-8204-3744-1*) P Lang Pubng.
Allison, Clinton B. Present & Past: Essays for Teachers in the History of Education. (Counterpoints Ser.: Vol. 6). 232p. (C). 1995. pap. text 29.95 (*0-8204-1780-7*) P Lang Pubng.
Allison, Courtney D., et al. Bank Investment Products Deskbook. Smith, Brian W. & Mayer, Brown & Platt Staff, eds. 608p. 1995. 165.00 (*0-7913-2468-0*) Warren Gorham & Lamont.
Allison, D. V., ed. see Cockburn, J. & Mitchell, A.
***Allison, Dale C., Jr.** The Intertextual Jesus: Scripture in Q. 288p. 2000. pap. 28.00 (*1-56338-329-2*) TPI PA.
Allison, Dale C., Jr. Jesus of Nazareth: Millenarian Prophet. LC 98-21602. 272p. 1998. 20.00 (*0-8006-3144-7*, 1-3144, Fortress Pr) Augsburg Fortress.
— The Jesus Tradition in Q. LC 97-12416. 256p. 1997. 27.00 (*1-56338-207-5*) TPI PA.
— The New Moses: A Matthean Typology. LC 93-18735. 304p. 1994. 30.00 (*0-8006-2699-0*, 1-2699, Fortress Pr) Augsburg Fortress.
Allison, Dale C. Sermon on the Mount: Inspiring the Moral Imagination. LC 99-11108. 1999. pap. text 17.95 (*0-8245-1791-1*) Crossroad NY.
Allison, Dale C., Jr. The Silence of Angels. LC 95-35121. 144p. (Orig.). (C). 1995. pap. 15.00 (*1-56338-131-1*) TPI PA.
Allison, Dale C., jt. auth. see Davies, W. D.
***Allison, David.** Ultimate Code Book 2000. (Official Strategy Guides Ser.). (Illus.). (YA). 2000. pap. 14.99 (*0-7615-2738-9*) Prima Pub.
***Allison, David B.** Reading the New Nietzsche: An Approach to His Principal Works. 224p. 2000. 67.50 (*0-8476-8979-4*) Rowman.
— Reading the New Nietzsche: An Approach to His Principal Works. 244p. 2000. pap. 21.95 (*0-8476-8980-8*, Pub. by Rowman) Natl Bk Netwk.
Allison, David B., ed. Bright Barkley & the Adventures of the Squigglies. (Bright Barkley Ser.). (Illus.). 40p. (Orig.). (J). (ps up). pap. text 3.95 (*0-614-06981-5*) Bilingual Block.
— Handbook of Assessment Methods for Eating Behaviors & Weight Related Problems: Measures, Theory & Research. 550p. 1994. 75.00 (*0-8039-4791-7*) Sage.
— The New Nietzsche: Contemporary Styles of Interpretation. 302p. 1985. reprint ed. pap. text 19.50 (*0-262-51034-0*) MIT Pr.
Allison, David B., et al, eds. Psychosis & Sexual Identity: Toward a Post-Analytic View of the Schreber Case. LC 87-10077. (SUNY Series, Intersections: Philosophy & Critical Theory). (Illus.). 343p. 1988. pap. text 24.95 (*0-88706-617-8*) State U NY Pr.
— Sade & the Narratives of Transgression. (Studies in French: No. 52). 287p. (C). 1995. text 64.95 (*0-521-44415-2*) Cambridge U Pr.
Allison, David B. & Pi-Sunyer, Xavier F., eds. Obesity Treatment: Establishing Goals, Improving Outcomes & Reviewing the Research Agenda: Proceedings of a NATO ARW Held in New York City, June 2-5, 1993. (NATO ASI Ser.: Vol. 278). (Illus.). 290p. (C). 1995. text 95.00 (*0-306-45115-8*, Kluwer Plenum) Kluwer Academic.
Allison, David B. & Roberts, Mark S. Disordered Mother or Disordered Diagnosis? Munchausen by Proxy Syndrome. LC 98-34172. 336p. 1998. 39.95 (*0-88163-290-2*) Analytic Pr.
Allison, David B., tr. see Derrida, Jacques.
***Allison, Desmond.** Language Testing & Evaluation: An Introductory Course. 265p. 1999. pap. text 35.00 (*9971-69-226-0*, Pub. by Sngapore Univ Pr) Coronet Bks.
Allison, Diane. Jesus' Little Parables of the Kingdom. 32p. (J). (ps-2). 1998. 16.95 (*0-87510-327-8*) Writings of Mary Baker.
— Pets, People, & Prayer: For Pet Lovers of All Ages. LC 97-224304. 48p. 1997. pap. 11.95 (*0-87510-326-X*, G61360) Writings of Mary Baker.
Allison, Donald L., ed. see Coburn, J. Osborn.
Allison, Dorothy. Bastard Out of Carolina. 320p. 1996. pap. 12.95 (*0-452-27864-3*, Plume) Dutton Plume.
— Bastard Out of Carolina. LC 91-34607. 320p. 1998. pap. 12.95 (*0-452-26957-1*) Dutton Plume.
— Bastard Out of Carolina. (C). 1997. pap. text. write for info. (*0-8013-3146-3*) Longman.
— Cavedweller. 434p. 1999. pap. 13.95 (*0-452-27969-0*, Plume) Dutton Plume.
— Cavedweller. LC 97-43860. 448p. 1998. 24.95 (*0-525-94167-3*) NAL.
— Cavedweller. large type ed. LC 98-4367. 639p. 1998. 26.95 (*0-7862-1503-8*) Thorndike Pr.
***Allison, Dorothy.** Cavedweller Reader's Group Guide. 1998. pap. write for info. (*0-525-94434-6*, Dutton Child) Peng Put Young Read.
Allison, Dorothy. Skin: Talking about Sex, Class & Literature. LC 94-15071. 208p. 1994. pap. 14.95 (*1-56341-044-3*); lib. bdg. 28.95 (*1-56341-045-1*) Firebrand Bks.
— Trash. LC 88-30175. 176p. 1988. pap. 12.95 (*0-932379-51-6*); lib. bdg. 24.95 (*0-932379-52-4*) Firebrand Bks.
— Two or Three Things I Know for Sure. 96p. 1996. pap. 9.95 (*0-452-27340-4*, Plume) Dutton Plume.
— Two or Three Things I Know for Sure. LC 95-17752. (Illus.). 96p. 1995. 14.95 (*0-525-93921-0*) NAL.
— The Women Who Hate Me: Poetry, 1980-1990. LC 91-311. 72p. (Orig.). 1991. pap. 8.95 (*0-932379-98-2*); lib. bdg. 18.95 (*0-932379-99-0*) Firebrand Bks.
Allison, Drew & Devet, Donald. The Foam Book: An Easy Guide to Building Polyfoam Puppets. (Illus.). 116p. 1997. pap. 14.95 (*0-9678575-1-1*) Grey Seal.
— The Foam Book: An Easy Guide to Building Polyfoam Puppets. (Illus.). 115p. 2000. pap. write for info. (*0-9678575-0-3*) Grey Seal.
Allison, Elizabeth K. Kelly. Early Southwest Virginia Families of Kelly, Smyth, Buchanan, Clark & Related Families of Edmonson, Keys, Beattie, Ryburn, McDonald. (Illus.). 135p. 1997. reprint ed. pap. 21.00 (*0-8328-9395-1*); reprint ed. lib. bdg. 31.00 (*0-8328-9394-3*) Higginson Bk Co.
Allison, Elliot, et al. Monadnock Sightings: Birds of Dublin, N. H. (Including Gerald H. Thayer's List of 1909) LC 79-13478. (Illus.). (Orig.). 1979. pap. 10.00 (*0-87233-051-6*) Bauhan.
Allison, F. C., jt. auth. see Klaften, E. Berthold.
Allison, G. Mini English - Thai - English Dictionary. (ENG & THA.). 460p. 1979. pap. 16.95 (*0-8288-4820-3*, M9900) Fr & Eur.
Allison, G. Burgess. The Lawyer's Quick Guide to Microsoft Internet Explorer. LC 97-74005. 1998. pap. 49.95 (*1-57073-510-7*) Amer Bar Assn.
— The Lawyer's Quick Guide to Netscape Navigator. LC 97-71798. 1998. pap. 49.95 (*1-57073-429-1*) Amer Bar Assn.
Allison-Garrett. Academic Job Digest: International Supplement. Garrett, W. E., ed. 60p. (Orig.). 1990. pap. text 29.99 (*1-878235-02-8*) Taylor Pub MI.
— Academic Job Digest: Tired of the Corp World? 91p. (Orig.). 1990. pap. 29.99 (*1-878235-10-9*) Taylor Pub MI.
— California Job Journal. 91p. 1990. pap. 29.99 (*1-878235-04-4*) Taylor Pub MI.
— How to Find a Nanny. 70p. (Orig.). 1990. pap. text 29.99 (*1-878235-00-1*) Taylor Pub MI.
— Wrongfully Terminated. 40p. (Orig.). 1990. pap. text 29.99 (*1-878235-03-6*) Taylor Pub MI.
Allison, Gary D. Constitutional Law: Adaptable to Courses Utilizing Materials by Gunther. LC 87-115705. (Legalines Ser.). 397p. 14.50 (*0-685-18647-4*) Harcourt.
Allison Gas Turbine Division of General Motors Sta. Research & Development of Proton-Exchange-Membrane (PEM) Fuel Cell System for Transportation Applications: Fuel Cell Infrastructure & Commercialization Study. (Fuel Cell Information Ser.: Vol. XIII). (Illus.). 187p. 1997. lib. bdg. 155.00 (*0-89934-339-2*, BT971) Bus Tech Bks.
Allison, Gordon H. Easy Thai: An Introduction to the Thai Language. LC 69-12085. (THA.). 106p. (Orig.). 1969. pap. 12.95 (*0-8048-0159-2*) Tuttle Pubng.
Allison, Graham T. Conceptual Models & the Cuban Missile Crisis. (Reprint Series in Political Science). (C). 1991. reprint ed. pap. text 2.30 (*0-8290-2617-7*, P-422) Irvington.
Allison, Graham T., ed. Rethinking America's Security: Beyond Cold War to New World Order. (Illus.). 320p. (C). 1992. pap. text 18.25 (*0-393-96218-0*) Norton.
Allison, Graham T., et al, eds. A Primer for the Nuclear Age. (Occasional Papers: No. 6). 152p. (C). 1990. pap. text 21.00 (*0-8191-7701-6*); lib. bdg. 40.00 (*0-8191-7700-8*) U Pr of Amer.
— Windows of Opportunity: From Cold Wave to Peaceful Competition in U. S. - Soviet Relations. 356p. 1989. pap. text 17.95 (*0-88730-379-X*, HarpBusn) HarpInfo.
Allison, Graham T. & Nicolaidis, Kalypso, eds. The Greek Paradox: Promise Versus Performance. LC 96-46473 (CSIA Studies in International Security). (Illus.). 208p. 1997. pap. text 16.50 (*0-262-51092-8*) MIT Pr.
Allison, Graham T., et al. Avoiding Nuclear Anarchy: Containing the Threat of Loose Russian Nuclear Weapons & Fissile Material. LC 95-25376. (CSIA Studies in International Security: No. 12). (Illus.). 104p. 1996. pap. text 17.50 (*0-262-51088-X*) MIT Pr.
Allison, Graham T., jt. auth. see Power, Samantha.
***Allison, Grahman, ed.** The Essence of Decision: Explaining Cuban Missile. 2nd ed. LC 98-36413. 440p. (C). 1999. pap. text 19.69 (*0-321-01349-2*) Addson-Wesley Educ.
Allison, Gregory S., pref. 1999-2000 Finance Calendar of Duties for City & County Officials. 1999. pap. 6.00 (*1-56011-357-X*) Institute Government.
Allison, H. J., jt. auth. see Camp, Charles L.
Allison, Heather. Counterfeit Cowgirl: Back to the Ranch. (Romance Ser.). 1994. per. 2.99 (*0-373-03309-5*, 1-03309-1); per. 2.99 (*0-373-15555-7*) Harlequin Bks.
— Haunted Spouse. (Romance Ser.). 1993. per. 2.99 (*0-373-03284-6*, 1-03284-6) Harlequin Bks.
— His Cinderella Bride. 1997. per. 3.25 (*0-373-15712-6*) Harlequin Bks.
— His Cinderella Bride. (Romance Ser.: No. 3466). 1997. per. 3.25 (*0-373-03466-0*, 1-03466-9) Harlequin Bks.
— Ivy's League. (Romance Ser.). 1993. mass mkt. 2.99 (*0-373-03269-2*, 1-03269-7) Harlequin Bks.
— Marry in Haste: Whirlwind Weddings. (Romance Ser.: No. 3487). 1998. per. 3.25 (*0-373-03487-3*, 1-03487-5) Harlequin Bks.
— Marry in Haste: Whirlwind Weddings. large type ed. 1998. per. 3.25 (*0-373-15733-9*) Harlequin Bks.
— Marry Me. (Romance Ser.). 1997. per. 3.25 (*0-373-03445-8*, 1-03445-3) Harlequin Bks.
— Marry Me. large type ed. 1997. per. 3.25 (*0-373-15691-X*, Harlequin) Harlequin Bks.
— The Santa Sleuth: (Kids & Kisses Christmas) (Romance Ser.). 1994. per. 2.99 (*0-373-03341-9*, 1-03341-4) Harlequin Bks.
— Temporary Texan. (Romance Ser.). 1996. per. 3.25 (*0-373-03421-0*, 1-03421-4) Harlequin Bks.
— Undercover Lover (Sealed with a Kiss) LC 96-554. 186p. 1995. mass mkt. 2.99 (*0-373-03386-9*) Harlequin Bks.
Allison, Henry E. Idealism & Freedom: Essays on Kant's Theoretical & Practical Philosophy. 239p. (C). 1996. text 59.95 (*0-521-48295-X*); pap. text 20.95 (*0-521-48337-9*) Cambridge U Pr.
— Kant's Theory of Freedom. 316p. (C). 1990. pap. text 24.95 (*0-521-38708-6*) Cambridge U Pr.
— Kant's Transcendental Idealism: An Interpretation & Defense. LC 85-5756. 390p. 1986. pap. 20.00 (*0-300-03629-9*, Y-567) Yale U Pr.
Allison, Henry E., ed. see Kant, Immanuel.
Allison, Horatio. Design of Low- & Medium-Rise Steel Buildings. 48p. 1991. 20.00 (*1-56424-028-2*, D805) Am Inst Steel Construct.
Allison, I. M., ed. Experimental Mechanics: Advances in Design, Testing & Analysis, Proceedings of the 11th International Conference, Oxford, 24-28 August, 1998, 2 vols. 1450p. (C). 1998. text 159.00 (*90-5809-014-0*, Pub. by A A Balkema) Ashgate Pub Co.
Allison, Ira S. Geology of Pluvial Lake Chewaucan, Lake County, Oregon. LC 81-22415. (Illus.). 80p. (C). 1982. pap. 12.95 (*0-87071-069-9*) Oreg St U Pr.
Allison, J. Delivered at Home. (Illus.). 192p. (Orig.). 1996. pap. 47.75 (*1-56593-352-4*, 0676) Singular Publishing.
Allison, J. M., ed. Concerning the Education of a Prince: Correspondence of the Princess of Nassau-Saarbruck 13 June - 15 November 1758. 1941. 49.50 (*0-686-51358-4*) Elliots Bks.
***Allison, J. W. F.** A Continental Distinction in the Common Law: A Historical & Comparative Perspective on English Public Law. LC 99-58635. 2000. write for info. (*0-19-829865-X*) OUP.
Allison, Jackson E., et al. Advanced Life Support Skills. (Illus.). 304p. (C). (gr. 13). 1993. pap. text 21.95 (*0-8016-7426-3*, 00200) Mosby Inc.
Allison, James. Behavioral Economics. LC 83-8058. 223p. 1983. 49.95 (*0-275-90935-2*, C0935, Praeger Pubs) Greenwood.
— Water in the Garden. (Illus.). 160p. 1991. 31.95 (*3-89356-042-4*, 16051) Tetra Pr.
— Water in the Garden: A Complete Guide to the Design & Installation of Ponds, Fountains, Streams, & Waterfalls. (Illus.). 160p. 1991. 32.50 (*0-8212-1839-5*, Pub. by Bulfinch Pr) Little.
***Allison, James E.** Quick Help with Troublesome Words & Phrases. LC 00-41357. 2001. write for info. (*0-7641-1633-9*) Barron.
Allison, Jenene J. Revealing Difference: The Fiction of Isabelle de Charriere. LC 94-48885. 176p. 1995. 33.50 (*0-87413-566-4*) U Delaware Pr.
Allison, Joe. Spades & Pruning Hooks: A Guide to Christian Devotional Resources. unabridged ed. 240p. 1998. pap. 14.95 (*1-891314-00-9*, 14009, Pub. by Jordan IN) BookWorld.
— Swords & Whetstones: A Guide to Christian Bible Study Resources. unabridged ed. Orig. Title: Bible Study Resource Guide. 208p. 1999. pap. 14.95 (*1-891314-01-7*, 14017, Pub. by Jordan IN) BookWorld.
Allison, Joe, jt. auth. see Hines, Samuel G.
Allison, Joe, ed. see Foggs, Edward L.
Allison, Joel, et al. The Interpretation of Psychological Tests. LC 66-41476. 342p. 1968. 38.95 (*0-89116-326-3*) Hemisp Pub.
Allison, John. A Continental Distinction in the Common Law: An Historical & Comparative Perspective on English Public Law. 286p. 1996. text 70.00 (*0-19-825877-1*) OUP.
— Dropped Stitches in Tennessee History: Little Known Facts in the Earliest History of Tennessee. (Illus.). 208p. 1991. reprint ed. 14.95 (*0-932807-52-6*) Overmountain Pr.
— Edward Elgar: Sacred Music. 160p. 1995. 32.00 (*1-85411-119-1*); pap. 16.95 (*1-85411-118-3*) Dufour.
— Pocket Companion To Opera: Including More Than 150 Works. 1999. pap. 9.95 (*1-85732-253-3*) Mitchell Beazley.
Allison, John, ed. Notable Men of Tennessee, Personal & Genealogical, with Portraits, 2 vols., Set. (Illus.). 667p. 1995. reprint ed. lib. bdg. 71.50 (*0-8328-4723-2*) Higginson Bk Co.
Allison, John E., jt. ed. see Larsen, James M.
Allison, John R. The Legal Environment of Business. LC 92-70971. 1993. 13.50 (*0-685-75613-0*) Dryden Pr.

A

An Asterisk (*) at the beginning of an entry indicates that the title is appearing for the first time.

Allison, John R. & Prentice, Robert A. The Legal Environment of Business. 4th ed. 798p. (C). 1993. 13.50 (*0-318-70110-3*); 17.75 (*0-03-098059-3*); 17.75 (*0-03-098058-5*) Dryden Pr.

Allison, John R. & Thomas, Dennis L., eds. Telecommunications Deregulation: Market Power & Cost Allocation Issues, 2. LC 90-32725. 304p. 1990. 62.95 (*0-89930-572-5*, ATA, Quorum Bks) Greenwood.

Allison, Jonathan. Patrick Kavanagh: A Reference Guide. LC 96-29255. 1996. 45.00 (*0-8161-7286-2*, G K Hall & Co) Mac Lib Ref.

Allison, Jonathan, ed. Yeats's Political Identities: Selected Essays. LC 95-50287. 368p. (C). 1996. text 49.50 (*0-472-10445-4*, 10445) U of Mich Pr.

Allison, Joseph D., ed. see Bangs, Carl.

Allison, Joseph D., ed. see Massey, James E.

Allison, Joseph D., ed. see Wesley, John.

Allison, Julie A. & Wrightman, Lawrence S. Rape: The Misunderstood Crime. LC 93-14800. 307p. (C). 1993. text 56.00 (*0-8039-3706-7*); pap. text 26.00 (*0-8039-3707-5*) Sage.

Allison, June W. Power & Preparedness in Thucydides. LC 88-46115. (American Journal of Philology Monographs: No. 5). 192p. 1989. text 30.00 (*0-8018-3821-5*) Johns Hopkins.

— Word & Concept in Thucydides. LC 97-16847. (APA American Classical Studies Ser.). 278p. 1997. 27.95 (*0-7885-0363-4*, 400441) OUP.

Allison, June W., ed. Conflict, Antithesis & the Ancient Historian. LC 89-70904. 225p. reprint ed. pap. 69.80 (*0-608-09652-0*, 206976700006) Bks Demand.

Allison, K. J., ed. A History of the County of York: East Riding, Vol. V. (Victoria History of the Counties of England Ser.). (Illus.). 208p. 1984. 149.00 (*0-19-722760-0*) OUP.

— Victoria History of the Counties of England: York East Riding, Vol. 4. (Illus.). 1979. 125.00 (*0-19-722752-X*) OUP.

Allison, K. W. & Child, John. Liverworts of New Zealand. 304p. 1996. 29.95 (*0-908569-05-X*, Pub. by Univ Otago Pr) Intl Spec Bk.

Allison, Karen H. The Vegetarian Compass: New Directions in Vegetarian Cooking. LC 97-46897. 416p. (gr. 8). 1998. 29.95 (*0-316-03843-1*) Little.

Allison, Karen J. A View from the Islands: The Samal of Tawi-tawi. LC 81-85309. (International Museum of Cultures Publications: No. 15). 50p. (Orig.). 1984. pap. 6.90 (*0-88312-168-9*) S I L Intl.

Allison, Kathleen Cahill, jt. auth. see American Medical Association.

Allison, Keith & Day, Chris. A Guide to Poisonous Plants. 1997. pap. 30.00 (*0-85131-698-0*, Pub. by J A Allen) Trafalgar.

— The Holistic Management of Dogs. (Illus.). 168p. 1999. 32.50 (*0-85131-693-X*, Pub. by J A Allen) Trafalgar.

Allison, Keith & Day, Christopher. A Guide to Alternative Therapies for Horses. 1996. pap. 30.00 (*0-85131-665-4*, Pub. by J A Allen) Trafalgar.

— A Guide to Herbs for Horses. 1995. pap. 35.00 (*0-85131-635-2*, Pub. by J A Allen) Trafalgar.

— The Holistic Management of Horses. 224p. 1996. 95.00 (*0-85131-623-9*, Pub. by J A Allen) Trafalgar.

Allison, L. A Practical Introduction to Denotational Semantics. (Cambridge Computer Science Texts Ser.: No. 23). (Illus.). 144p. 1987. pap. text 21.95 (*0-521-31423-2*) Cambridge U Pr.

Allison, Leslie Minturn. Mildred Minturn: A Biography. (Illus.). 192p. pap. 13.95 (*0-9698752-3-1*) Sh1oreline.

Allison, Lewis L. Keeping up Your Spirits Therapy. LC 90-75415. 1991. pap. 4.95 (*0-87029-242-0*) Abbey.

Allison-Lewis, Linda. Kentucky's Best: Fifty Years of Great Recipes. LC 98-39155. 256p. 1998. 19.95 (*0-8131-2069-1*) U Pr of Ky.

Allison, Libby, et al. Grading in the Post-Process Classroom: From Theory to Practice. LC 97-28934. 1997. pap. 24.00 (*0-86709-437-0*, Pub. by Boynton Cook Pubs) Heinemann.

Allison, Lincoln. Ecology & Utility: The Philosophical Dilemmas of Planetary Management. LC 91-33641. 240p. 1992. 32.50 (*0-8386-3490-7*) Fairleigh Dickinson.

***Allison, Lincoln.** Taking Sport Seriously. 1999. pap. text 17.95 (*3-89124-479-7*) Perseus Pubng.

Allison, Lincoln, ed. The Changing Politics of Sport. LC 92-26931. 1993. text 29.95 (*0-7190-3671-2*, Pub. by Manchester Univ Pr) St Martin.

— The Utilitarian Response: The Contemporary Viability of Utilitarian Political Philosophy. (Modern Politics Ser.: Vol. 24). 218p. (C). 1990. text 45.00 (*0-8039-8273-9*) Sage.

Allison, Linda. Blood & Guts. (Brown Paper School Bks.). (Illus.). 127p. (J). (gr. 5-12). 1976. pap. 12.95 (*0-316-03443-6*) Little.

Allison, Linda. Blood & Guts: A Working Guide to Your Own Insides. (Brown Paper School Bks.). (J). 1976. 17.05 (*0-606-04022-6*, Pub. by Turtleback) Demco.

Allison, Linda. Gee, Wiz! How to Mix Art & Science, or, the Art of Thinking Scientifically. (Brown Paper School Bks.). (J). 1983. 18.05 (*0-606-04018-8*, Pub. by Turtleback) Demco.

— The Sierra Club Summer Book. (Illus.). 160p. (J). (gr. 3-7). 1989. pap. 7.95 (*0-316-03433-9*) Little.

— Table-Top Science: Intermediate. (Illus.). 96p. (Orig.). (J). (gr. 3-6). 1997. pap. 11.95 (*1-57612-019-8*, MM2051) Monday Morning Bks.

— Table-Top Science: Primary. (Illus.). 96p. (Orig.). (J). (gr. 1-3). 1997. pap. 11.95 (*1-57612-018-X*, MM2050) Monday Morning Bks.

— Trash Artists Workshop. LC 80-84184. (Crafts Workshop Ser.). (J). (gr. 3-8). 1981. pap. 9.99 (*0-8224-9780-8*) Fearon Teacher Aids.

Allison, Linda & Ferguson, Tom. Stethoscope Book & Kit. (J). (gr. 2-7). 1991. pap. 12.90 (*0-201-57096-3*) HarperTrade.

Allison, Linda, et al. Earthquakes. LC 88-81209. (Science in Action Learning Ser.). 18 p. 1987. write for info. (*0-929201-02-7*) Kay Productions.

Allison, Liz. Davey Allison: A Celebration of Life. (Illus.). 144p. 1995. 34.95 (*1-57427-044-3*) Howell Pr VA.

Allison, Lora. Celebration: Banners, Dance, & Holiness in Worship. rev. ed. LC 87-83390. (Illus.). 148p. (C). 1995. pap. 16.95 (*0-9631284-2-6*) Celebrat Minist.

— Flaming Purpose: A People of Fire. Walters, Elinor M., ed. (Illus.). 200p. (Orig.). (C). 1995. pap. 9.95 (*0-9631284-3-4*) Celebrat Minist.

— Overcomer. 96p. (Orig.). 1993. pap. 8.99 (*1-56043-098-2*) Destiny Image.

— The Overcomers Are Coming Forth! 90p. (Orig.). 1991. pap. 5.95 (*0-9631284-1-8*) Celebrat Minist.

Allison, Loren K. Employee Selection: A Legal Perspective. 60p. (C). 1996. 20.00 (*0-939900-44-0*) Soc Human Resc Mgmt.

Allison, Lynda. Goodbye, Granny Dix. LC 90-29320. 171p. (Orig.). 1991. pap. 3.99 (*0-932581-82-X*) Word Aflame.

Allison, M. Lee, ed. A Preliminary Assessment of Energy & Mineral Resources Within the Grand Staircase-Escalante National Monument. LC QE168.A322. (Circular of the Utah Geological Survey Ser.: Vol. 93). (Illus.). 36p. 1997. pap. 4.00 (*1-55791-601-2*, C-93) Utah Geological Survey.

***Allison, Maggie & Heathcote, Owen, eds.** Forty Years of the Fifth French Republic: Actions, Dialogues & Discourses. LC 99-41310. 387p. (C). 1999. pap. 58.95 (*0-8204-4620-3*) P Lang Pubng.

Allison, Margaret. Indiscretion. 1996. mass mkt. 5.99 (*0-671-56328-9*) PB.

— The Last Curve. 383p. 1999. mass mkt. 6.50 (*0-671-56326-2*) PB.

— Promise Me. 1997. per. 5.99 (*0-671-56327-0*) PB.

Allison, Marian, ed. see Flores, Bettina R.

Allison, Mark, ed. see Dake, Finis J., Sr.

Allison, Martha B. & Lieberman, Barbara B. The Road from Home Cookbook: A Collection of Old-Fashioned Recipes, Many Adapted to Present Day Low-Fat, Low-Cholesterol, & Vegetarian Tastes. (Illus.). 110p. (Orig.). 1996. pap. 12.95 (*0-9655826-0-4*, 1891-96) MCB Partnership.

Allison, Mary A. & Kelly, Susanne. The Complexity Advantage: How the Science of Complexity Can Help Your Business Achieve Peak Performance. LC 98-47604. 240p. 1998. 24.95 (*0-07-001400-0*) McGraw.

Allison, Mary B. Doctor Mary in Arabia: Memoirs. Shaw, Sandra, ed. LC 93-31393. 1994. 42.50 (*0-292-70454-2*); pap. 19.95 (*0-292-70456-9*) U of Tex Pr.

Allison, Mike. The Problem Buster's Guide. 208p. 1996. pap. 26.95 (*0-566-07761-2*, Pub. by Gower) Ashgate Pub Co.

***Allison, Mike & Browning, Peter.** Works MGs: The Illustrated History of Works MGs in Record-Breaking, Trials, Races & Rallies. (Illus.). 248p. 2000. 39.95 (*1-85960-603-2*, 129531AE, Pub. by J H Haynes & Co) Motorbooks Intl.

Allison, Nan & Beck, Carol. Full & Fulfilled: The Science of Eating to Your Soul's Satisfaction, No. I. 172p. 1998. pap. 12.95 (*0-9659117-9-9*) A&B Books.

Allison, Nancy. The Illustrated Encyclopedia of Body-Mind Disciplines. LC 98-24969. (Illus.). 600p. 1998. pap. 12.95 (*0-8239-2546-3*) Rosen Group.

Allison, Norman E. No Flight. unabridged ed. 156p. 1998. pap. 13.95 (*1-892896-25-7*) Buy Books.

Allison, P. A. & Briggs, D. E. Taphonomy: Releasing the Data Locked in the Fossil Record. (Topics in Geobiology Ser.: Vol. 9). (Illus.). 546p. (C). 1991. text 125.00 (*0-306-43876-3*, Kluwer Plenum) Kluwer Academic.

Allison, P. A., jt. ed. see Bosence, D. W.

Allison, Pamela C. & Barrett, Kate R. Elementary Physical Education. LC 99-59612. 332p. (C). 2000. pap. text 51.00 (*0-205-17509-0*, Macmillan Coll) P-H.

Allison, Patricia. Hooked-But Not Helpless: Kicking Nicotine Addiction. 3rd ed. 1999. pap. text. write for info. (*0-9623683-7-7*) BridgeCity Bks.

— Stop Smoking with Patricia Allison: A Personal Program for Treating Nicotine Addiction. 1998. 124.95 incl. audio (*0-9668836-0-8*) Natl Ctr Addict.

Allison, Patricia & Yost, Jack. Hooked - But Not Hopeless: Kicking Nicotine Addiction. (Illus.). 192p. 1996. pap. 14.95 (*0-9623683-3-4*) BridgeCity Bks.

Allison, Paul D. Event History Analysis: Regression for Longitudinal Event Data. (Quantitative Applications in the Social Sciences Ser.: Vol. 46). 96p. (Orig.). (C). 1984. pap. text 10.95 (*0-8039-2055-5*) Sage.

— Multiple Regression: A Primer. LC 98-40066. (Pine Forge Press Series in Research Methods & Statistics). 1999. pap. 19.95 (*0-7619-8533-6*) Sage.

— Processes of Stratification in Science. Zuckerman, Harriet & Merton, Robert K., eds. LC 80-13567. (Dissertations on Sociology Ser.). 1980. lib. bdg. 25.95 (*0-405-12946-7*) Ayer.

— Survival Analysis Using the SAS System, a Practical Guide. LC 96-172979. 304p. (C). 1998. pap. 37.95 (*1-55544-279-X*, BR55233) SAS Publ.

***Allison, Penelope M.** Archaeology of Household Activities: Dwelling in the Past. 1999. write for info. (*0-415-18052-X*) Routledge.

Allison, Peter B., ed. Labor, Worklife & Industrial Relations: Sources of Information. LC 84-4539. (Behavioral & Social Sciences Librarian Ser.: Vol. 3, No. 3). 128p. 1984. text 39.95 (*0-86656-317-2*) Haworth Pr.

Allison, R. J., jt. auth. see Thomas, D. G.

Allison, Ralph & Schwarz, Ted. Minds in Many Pieces: Revealing the Spiritual Side of Multiple Personality Disorder. 2nd rev. ed. LC 98-96785. 220p. 1999. pap. 29.95 (*0-9668949-0-1*) CIE Publ.

Allison, Richard. Please Die I Want a Promotion: How to Maximize Employee Contribution & Flexibility. 216p. (Orig.). 1996. pap. 17.95 (*1-57502-139-0*) Morris Pubng.

***Allison, Richard C. & Coe, Jack J., Jr.** Protecting Against the Expropriation Risk in Investing Abroad. 520p. 1999. ring bd. 245.00 (*1-57823-001-2*) Juris Pubng.

Allison, Robert J. Australia. (Country Fact Files Ser.). (J). 1996. lib. bdg. 24.26 (*0-8114-5642-0*) Raintree Steck-V.

***Allison, Robert J.** Crescent Obscured: The United States & the Muslim World. (Illus.). 1999. pap. text 17.00 (*0-226-01490-8*) U Ch Pr.

— Development of a Nation, (1783-1815), Vol. 4. (American Eras Ser.). 400p. 1997. 85.00 (*0-7876-1481-5*, GML00198-110780) Gale.

Allison, Robert J., ed. World War II. (History in Dispute Ser.). 323p. 1999. 110.00 (*1-55862-396-5*) St James Pr.

Allison, Rosemary. The Pillow. (Kids of Canada Ser.). (Illus.). 32p. (J). 1979. 5.95 (*0-88862-245-7*, Pub. by J Lorimer) Formac Dist Ltd.

Allison, Rosemary, tr. see Duchesne, Christiane.

Allison, Roy. The Soviet Union & the Strategy of Non-Alignment in the Third World. 304p. (C). 1989. text 59.95 (*0-521-35511-7*) Cambridge U Pr.

Allison, Roy, ed. Challenges for the Former Soviet South. LC 95-4438. (Post-Soviet Business Forum Ser.). 365p. (C). 1995. pap. 19.95 (*0-8157-0321-X*) Brookings.

— Radical Reform in Soviet Defense Policy: Selected Papers from the Fourth World Congress for Soviet & East European Studies, Harrogate, 1990. LC 91-36102. 256p. 1992. text 69.95 (*0-312-07545-6*) St Martin.

Allison, Roy & Bluth, Christoph, eds. Security Dilemmas in Russia & Eurasia. 368p. 1997. 49.95 (*1-86203-026-X*, Pub. by Royal Inst Intl Affairs); pap. 19.95 (*1-86203-016-2*, Pub. by Royal Inst Intl Affairs) Brookings.

Allison, Sarah E. & Renpenning, Kathie M. Nursing Administration in the 21st Century. LC 98-25382. 1998. 48.00 (*0-7619-1455-2*); pap. 22.50 (*0-7619-1456-0*) Sage.

Allison, Sheila. Song of David. (Great Big Bks.). (Illus.). 16p. (J). (gr. k-1). 1995. pap. 14.95 (*0-687-07065-1*) Abingdon.

Allison, Shelia. A Song of David: Leader's Guide. (J). (gr. k-1). 1.50 (*0-687-05367-6*) Abingdon.

Allison, Sonia. Chinese Regional Specialties. 1994. 9.95 (*0-572-01765-0*, Pub. by W Foulsham) Trans-Atl Phila.

— Chocolate. 1994. 9.95 (*0-572-01823-1*, Pub. by W Foulsham) Trans-Atl Phila.

— Classic 1000 Microwave Recipes. 1999. pap. text 9.95 (*0-572-01945-9*) Trans-Atl Phila.

— Desserts. 1994. 9.95 (*0-572-01660-3*, Pub. by W Foulsham) Trans-Atl Phila.

— Herbs for Cooking. 64p. 1994. 9.95 (*0-572-01858-4*, Pub. by W Foulsham) Trans-Atl Phila.

— The Indian Restaurant Menu Recipes. (Illus.). 192p. (Orig.). 1996. pap. 22.50 (*0-572-01703-0*, Pub. by W Foulsham) Trans-Atl Phila.

Allison, Sonia, ed. Grills & Barbecues. (Gourmet Cookshelf Ser.). (Illus.). 64p. 1993. 13.95 (*0-572-01704-9*, Pub. by W Foulsham) Trans-Atl Phila.

Allison, Sonia, ed. see Rudatis, Renato.

Allison, Stacy. Many Mountains to Climb: Lessons on the True Meaning of Success from the First American Woman to Top Mt. Everest. LC 99-38520. 270p. 1999. pap. 15.95 (*1-58151-011-X*) BookPartners.

Allison, Stacy & Carl, Peter. Beyond The Limits: A Woman's Triumph on Everest: U . K . Edition. 1994. write for info. (*0-316-90768-5*) Little.

***Allison, Stacy & Carlin, Peter.** Beyond the Limits: A Woman's Triumph on Everest. 2nd rev. ed. LC 99-39762. 273p. 1999. pap. 15.95 (*1-58151-056-X*) BookPartners.

Allison, Stephen, jt. auth. see Saari.

Allison, Stephen, jt. auth. see Saari, Peggy.

Allison, Terry L., jt. ed. see Curry, Renee R.

Allison, Thomas. English Religious Life in the Eighth Century As Illustrated by Contemporary Letters. LC 70-136409. reprint ed. 20.00 (*0-404-00348-6*) AMS Pr.

Allison, Virginia, jt. auth. see Grimm, Gary.

Allison, W. H. Inventory of Unpublished Material for American Religion History in Protestant Church Archives & Other Repositories. (CIG Ser.: Vol. 3). 1910. 30.00 (*0-527-00683-1*) Periodicals Srv.

Allison, Wick. Condemned to Repeat. LC 98-5536. 224p. 1998. 18.00 (*0-670-85951-6*) Viking Penguin.

Allison, Wick & Allison, Christine. That's in the Bible? The Ultimate Learn-As-You Play Bible Quizbook. LC 94-6690. 1994. 16.95 (*0-385-31097-8*) Delacorte.

Allison, William. American Diplomats in Russia: Case Studies in Orphan Diplomacy, 1916-1919. LC 96-49809. (Praeger Studies in Diplomacy & Strategic Thought). 208p. 1997. 62.95 (*0-275-95863-9*, Praeger Pubs) Greenwood.

Allison, William H. & Barnes, W. W. Baptist Ecclesiology: An Original Anthology. Gaustad, Edwin S., ed. LC 79-52582. (Baptist Tradition Ser.). 1980. lib. bdg. 23.95 (*0-405-12449-X*) Ayer.

Allison, William W. Profitable Risk Control: The Winning Edge. 197p. 1986. 14.95 (*0-939874-71-7*) ASSE.

Allison, Winn O. Beacon Small-Group Bible Studies: Jeremiah, Lamentations: God's Unfailing Love. Wolf, Earl C., ed. 96p. (Orig.). 1986. pap. text 4.99 (*0-8341-1106-3*) Beacon Hill.

***Alliss.** Sunday Telegraph Golf Course: Guide 13. 1998. pap. 17.95 (*0-00-218832-5*, Pub. by HarpC) Trafalgar.

Alliss, Peter & Hobbs, Michael. The Open: The British Open Golf Championship since the War LC 84-136343. 256p. 1984. write for info. (*0-00-217175-9*) Collins SF.

Allister, Ray. Friese-Greene: Close-Up of an Inventor. LC 71-169339. (Arno Press Cinema Program Ser.). (Illus.). 212p. 1972. reprint ed. 19.95 (*0-405-03908-5*) Ayer.

Alliston. James Fenimore Cooper. 1999. write for info. (*0-201-40939-9*) Addison-Wesley.

Alliston, April. Virtue's Faults, or, Women's Correspondences in Eighteenth-Century Fiction. 1996. 39.50 (*0-8047-2660-4*) Stanford U Pr.

Alliston, April, jt. auth. see Lee, Sophia.

Alliston, April, jt. auth. see Schirmeister, Pamela.

Alliston, April, ed. see Lee, Sophia.

Alliston, Eleanor. Island Affair. large type ed. 352p. 1988. 27.99 (*0-7089-1860-3*) Ulverscroft.

Alliston, John. Destroyer Man. large type ed. (Illus.). 1991. 27.99 (*0-7089-2421-2*) Ulverscroft.

Allitt, John S. Donizetti: In the Light of Romanticism & the Teaching of John Simon Mayr. (Illus.). 304p. 1992. pap. 29.95 (*1-85230-299-2*, Pub. by Element MA) Penguin Putnam.

Allitt, Patrick. Catholic Converts: British & American Intellectuals Turn to Rome. LC 96-29989. 352p. 1996. text 35.00 (*0-8014-2996-X*) Cornell U Pr.

***Allitt, Patrick.** Catholic Converts: British & American Intellectuals Turn to Rome. 2000. pap. text 18.95 (*0-8014-8663-7*) Cornell U Pr.

Allitt, Patrick. Catholic Intellectuals & Conservative Politics in America, 1950-1985. 336p. 1995. pap. text 16.95 (*0-8014-8300-X*) Cornell U Pr.

Allix, Charles. Carriage Clocks: Their History & Development. (Illus.). 496p. 1974. 89.50 (*0-902028-25-1*) Antique Collect.

Allix, Peter. The Ecclesiastical History of the Ancient Churches of Piedmont & of the Albigenses. 1989. reprint ed. 32.00 (*0-685-25291-4*) Church History.

Allman, Angelo. JK2000. 28p. 1998. pap. 9.95 (*1-885206-64-X*) Cader Pubng.

Allman, Barbara. ABC Dot-to-Dot: Activity Book. (J). 1997. pap. text 2.29 (*0-7647-0252-1*) Schaffer Pubns.

— Bible Dot-to-Dot: Coloring Book. (Illus.). (J). 1997. pap. text 2.29 (*0-7647-0066-9*) Schaffer Pubns.

— Children's Pew Activities. 1997. pap. text 3.95 (*0-7647-0071-5*) Schaffer Pubns.

— Getting Ready to Read. (Illus.). (J). 1997. pap. text 2.29 (*0-7647-0093-6*) Schaffer Pubns.

— Her Piano Sang: A Story about Clara Schumann. LC 96-18217. (Creative Minds Bks.). (Illus.). (J). 1996. lib. bdg. 19.95 (*1-57505-012-9*, Carolrhoda) Lerner Pub.

— Jesus & Me Dot-to-Dot: Activity Book. (J). 1997. pap. text 2.29 (*0-7647-0250-5*) Schaffer Pubns.

— Language Arts Puzzles & Games. (Gifted & Talented Ser.). (Illus.). 64p. (J). (gr. k-1). 1999. pap. 4.95 (*0-7373-0206-2*, Pub. by Lowell Hse) NTC Contemp Pub Co.

— Noah's Ark Dot-to-Dot: Activity Book. (J). 1997. pap. text 2.29 (*0-7647-0249-1*) Schaffer Pubns.

— Numbers Dot-to-Dot: Activity Book. (J). 1997. pap. text 2.29 (*0-7647-0251-3*) Schaffer Pubns.

***Allman, Barbara.** A World in Focus: Central & South America. (Illus.). 80p. 2000. pap. 11.95 (*1-56711-347-8*) Blackbirch.

***Allman, Barbara & Haas, Shelly O.** Dance of the Swan: A Story about Anna Pavlova. LC 00-9614. (Creative Minds Biography Ser.). (Illus.). (YA). 2000. write for info. (*1-57505-463-9*, Carolrhoda) Lerner Pub.

Allman, C. B. Lewis Wetzel, Indian Fighter. rev. ed. (Illus.). 1961. 16.95 (*0-8159-6107-3*) Devin.

— The Life & Times of Lewis Wetzel. (Illus.). 244p. (Orig.). 1995. reprint ed. pap. text 18.00 (*0-7884-0204-8*) Heritage Bk.

Allman, Eileen, ed. see Burks-Shiver, Jacqueline.

Allman, Eileen J. Jacobean Revenge Tragedy & the Politics of Virtue. LC 99-18960. 216p. 1999. 36.50 (*0-87413-698-9*) U Delaware Pr.

Allman, Eric, jt. auth. see Costales, Bryan.

Allman, Gary L. & Stinson, Michael C. FrontPage 97 Web Designer's Guide. LC 96-36320. (Web Construction Kits Ser.). (Illus.). 600p. 1997. 39.99 (*1-57169-045-X*) Sams.

Allman, George J. Greek Geometry from Thales to Euclid. LC 75-13250. (History of Ideas in Ancient Greece Ser.). 1979. reprint ed. 25.95 (*0-405-07287-2*) Ayer.

***Allman, Jean B. & Tashjian, Victoria.** I Will Not Eat Stone: A Women's History of Colonial Asante. 275p. 2000. 24.00 (*0-325-07000-8*); write for info. (*0-325-07001-6*) Greenwood.

Allman, Jean M. The Quills of the Porcupine: Asante Nationalism in an Emergent Ghana. LC 92-45198. (Illus.). 352p. (Orig.). (C). 1993. 60.00 (*0-299-13760-0*); pap. 24.95 (*0-299-13764-3*) U of Wis Pr.

Allman, John. Clio's Children. LC 84-22659. 96p. 1985. 16.95 (*0-8112-0935-0*, Pub. by New Directions); pap. 7.95 (*0-8112-0936-9*, NDP590, Pub. by New Directions) Norton.

— Curve Away from Stillness: Science Poems. LC 88-22791. 96p. (Orig.). 1989. pap. 7.95 (*0-8112-1081-2*, NDP667, Pub. by New Directions) Norton.

— Descending Fire & Other Stories. LC 94-6746. 176p. 1994. 19.95 (*0-8112-1274-2*, Pub. by New Directions) Norton.

***Allman, John.** Evolving Brains. (Illus.). 240p. 2000. pap. text 22.95 (*0-7167-6038-X*) W H Freeman.

Allman, John. Inhabited World: New & Selected Poems 1970-1995. LC 95-25075. 160p. 1995. pap. 14.95 (*0-9648056-0-X*) W Stevens Soc.

— Scenarios for a Mixed Landscape. LC 86-2421. 80p. (Orig.). 1986. pap. 7.95 (*0-8112-0989-X*, NDP619, Pub. by New Directions) Norton.

Allman, Joyce. Basic Speech Communication: Student Workbook. 1998. text, student ed., wbk. ed. 10.87 (*1-56870-311-2*) RonJon Pub.

Allman, Kevin. Hot Shot. LC 97-17825. 256p. 1998. text 22.95 (*0-312-16866-7*) St Martin.

Allman, M. V. Laser-Beam Interactions with Materials. (Materials Science Ser.: Vol. 2). (Illus.). 240p. 1987. 58.00 (*0-387-17568-7*) Spr-Verlag.

Allman, Mark C., jt. auth. see Bond, Victor R.

Allman, Paul, et al. Word Play: Six Hundred Words You Need to Know, Set. 1995. pap. 19.95 incl. audio (*0-8120-8319-9*) Barron.

Allman, Paula. Adult Development: An Overview of Recent Research. (C). 1986. reprint ed. 35.00 (*0-902031-46-5*, Pub. by Univ Nottingham) St Mut.

— Revolutionary Social Transformation: Democratic Hopes, Political Possibilities & Critical Education. LC 99-14843. 184p. 1999. 49.95 (*0-89789-667-X*, Bergin & Garvey) Greenwood.

Allman, Richard M., jt. auth. see Clair, Jeffrey M.

Allman, Richard M., jt. ed. see Clair, Jeffrey M.

Allman, Ros & Trenkel, Susan. Back to Baby Basics. (Illus.). 155p. 1999. pap. 12.00 (*0-627-01937-4*, Pub. by J L Van Schaik) BHB Intl.

Allman, Ruth C. Canaan Valley & the Black Bear. (Illus.). 1976. reprint ed. pap. 12.00 (*0-87012-220-7*) McClain. A history of Canaan Valley since its early settlement to the present time with over 80 pictures. Also, true stories & pictures of the black bear, very much a native. The author has lived in the valley all of her life. Third Printing, 1981. *Publisher Paid Annotation.*

Allman, S. Audean, et al. Curriculum Development: A Reflection of Programmatic Trends. (Illus.). 231p. 1980. pap. text 16.95 (*0-89641-049-8*) American Pr.

— Environmental Education: A Promise for the Future. 196p. 1982. pap. text 14.95 (*0-89641-085-4*) American Pr.

Allman, Sheldon & Pickett, Bob. Frankenstein Unbound - Another Monster Musical. 75p. 1995. pap. 5.95 (*0-87129-600-4*, F08) Dramatic Pub.

— I'm Sorry the Bridge Is Out, You'll Have to Spend the Night - Musical. 1988. 5.95 (*0-87129-484-2*, I01) Dramatic Pub.

Allman, William F. The Stone Age Present: How Evolution Has Shaped Modern Life-From Sex, Violence, & Language to Emotions, Morals, & Communities. 288p. 1994. 23.00 (*0-671-89226-6*) S&S Trade.

Allman, William F., jt. ed. see Schrier, Eric W.

Allmand, Christopher. Henry V. LC 92-29108. (English Monarchs Ser.: Vol. 10). 1993. 50.00 (*0-520-08293-1*, Pub. by U CA Pr) Cal Prin Full Svc.

— The Hundred Years War: England & France at War 1300-c.1450. (Cambridge Medieval Textbooks Ser.). (Illus.). 224p. (C). 1988. pap. text 17.95 (*0-521-31923-4*) Cambridge U Pr.

Allmand, Christopher, ed. The New Cambridge Medieval History c. 1415-c. 1500, Vol. 7. (Illus.). 1000p. (C). 1998. text 95.00 (*0-521-38296-3*) Cambridge U Pr.

— Power, Culture & Religion in France, 1350-1550. (Illus.). 178p. 1989. 75.00 (*0-85115-514-6*) Boydell & Brewer.

— Society at War Vol. 5: The Experience of England & France During the Hundred Years War. LC 98-24326. (Warfare in History Ser.). 256p. 1998. 63.00 (*0-85115-672-X*) Boydell & Brewer.

Allmann, et al. Grammatik-Verstehen 7/8. Klasse, Uben, Beherrschen. (GER.). 182p. 21.00 (*3-580-64170-0*) Langenscheidt.

Allmen, Diane. Postcards. 1991. pap. 9.95 (*0-87637-802-5*) Hse Collectbls.

Allmen, Jean-Jacques Von, see Von Allmen, Jean-Jacques, ed.

Allmen, Martin Von, see Von Allmen, Martin.

Allmen, Tania Von, see Von Allmen, Tania.

Allmendinger. Planning Beyond 2000. LC 98-49776. 318p. (C). 1999. 99.00 (*0-471-98441-8*); pap. 39.95 (*0-471-98442-6*) Wiley.

Allmendinger, Blake. Ten Most Wanted: The New Western Literature. LC 97-37577. (Illus.). 224p. 1998. pap. 18.99 (*0-415-91463-9*) Routledge.

— Ten Most Wanted: The New Western Literature. LC 97-37577. (Illus.). 224p. (C). 1998. 75.00 (*0-415-91462-0*) Routledge.

Allmendinger, Blake, jt. auth. see Matsumoto, Valerie J.

Allmendinger, David, ed. Incidents of My Life: Edmund Ruffin's Autobiographical Essays. (Illus.). 274p. 1990. text 45.00 (*0-8139-1279-2*) U Pr of Va.

Allmendinger, E. Eugene, ed. Submersible Vehicle Systems Design. (Illus.). 425p. 1990. 75.00 (*0-614-06721-9*) Soc Naval Arch.

***Allmendinger, Philip.** Introduction to Planning Practice. LC 99-40030. 400p. 2000. pap. text 34.95 (*0-471-98522-8*) Wiley.

— Introduction to Planning Practice. LC 99-40030. 400p. 2000. text 85.00 (*0-471-98521-X*) Wiley.

— Planning in Post Modern Times. LC 00-37779. (RTPI Library). 2000. pap. write for info. (*0-415-23423-9*) Routledge.

Allmendinger, Philip. Thatcherism & Planning: The Case of Simplified Planning Zones. LC 97-70889. (Illus.). 208p. 1997. text 59.95 (*1-85972-671-2*, Pub. by Ashgate Pub) Ashgate Pub Co.

Allmendinger, Philip & Thomas, Huw. Urban Planning & the British New Right. LC 97-39629. (Illus.). 304p. (C). 1998. 85.00 (*0-415-15462-6*) Routledge.

— Urban Planning & the British New Right. LC 97-39629. 287p. (C). 1998. pap. 27.95 (*0-415-15463-4*) Routledge.

Allmers, Nancy M. Appleton & Lange's Review for the Surgical Technology Examination. 4th rev. ed. LC 96-19661. 216p. (C). 1998. pap. 34.95 (*0-8385-0270-9*, A0270-7, Apple Lange Med) McGraw.

Allmon, W. D. Bulletins of American Paleontology Vol. 99: Review of the Bullia Group (Gastropoda: Nassariidae), with Comments on Its Evolution, Biogeography, & Phylogeny, Vol. 335. 179p. 1990. 45.00 (*0-87710-417-4*) Paleo Res.

Allmon, Warren. Prehistoric Ocean Discovery Kit: An Explorer's Kit. (Illus.). 64p. (J). (gr. 4-7). 1996. 18.95 (*1-56138-593-X*) Running Pr.

***Allmon, Warren & Bottjer, David J., eds.** Evolutionary Paleoecology: The Ecological Context of Macroevolutionary Change. 320p. 2000. text 45.00 (*0-231-10994-6*); pap. text 25.00 (*0-231-10995-4*) Col U Pr.

Allmon, Warren D., jt. ed. see Ross, Robert M.

Allmond, Bayard W., et al. The Family Is the Patient: Using Family Interviews in Children's Medical Care. LC 98-33474. 362p. 1998. pap. 25.00 (*0-683-30288-4*) Lppncott W & W.

Allnatt, Alan & Lidiard, Alan. Atomic Transport in Solids. (Illus.). 596p. (C). 1994. text 145.00 (*0-521-37514-2*) Cambridge U Pr.

Allnatt, John. Transmitted-Picture Assessment. LC 82-21895. (Illus.). 319p. reprint ed. pap. 98.90 (*0-8357-3572-9*, 203421000089) Bks Demand.

Allnutt, Frank. The Christian's New Heart. (Illus.). 124p. 1997. pap. 12.00 (*0-934374-03-1*) Allnutt Pub.

— The Christian's New Heart. 2nd enl. ed. (Illus.). 75p. 1999. pap. 12.00 (*0-934374-04-X*) Allnutt Pub.

— A Closer Look at Close Encounters. 2nd enl. rev. ed. 84p. 1999. pap. 12.00 (*0-934374-09-0*) Allnutt Pub.

— Cry of the Wounded Soldier. 124p. 1997. pap. 7.99 (*0-934374-00-7*) Allnutt Pub.

— Unlocking the Mystery of the Force. rev. ed. LC 83-72138. 208p. 1983. reprint ed. pap. 2.95 (*0-934374-02-3*) Allnutt Pub.

***Allnutt, Frank.** Unlocking the Mystery of the Force. 5th rev. ed. 192p. 1999. pap. 9.99 (*0-934374-11-2*) Allnutt Pub.

Allnutt, Frank, jt. ed. see Galvin, John.

Allnutt, Gillian. Blackthorn. 64p. 1994. pap. 14.95 (*1-85224-270-1*, Pub. by Bloodaxe Bks) Dufour.

— Nantucket & the Angel. LC 97-171760. 64p. 1997. pap. 15.95 (*1-85224-382-1*, Pub. by Bloodaxe Bks) Dufour.

Allnutt, Robin M. Miami Sourcebook: For Millennium's End. (Illus.). 144p. (Orig.). 1995. pap. 15.00 (*0-9628748-8-4*) Chameleon Eclectic.

Allocca, John A. Clinical Nutrition for the Balanced Body. (Illus.). 398p. 1997. pap. text 60.00 (*0-9659987-1-1*) Allocca Tech.

— Essential Nutrition. 2nd rev. ed. (Illus.). 223p. 1997. pap. text 19.95 (*0-9659987-0-3*) Allocca Tech.

Allock, Donald. WordPerfect & Running with Fortran 90. (C). 1997. pap. text. write for info. (*0-201-42783-4*) Addison-Wesley.

Alloin, D. M. & Mariotti, Jean-Marie, eds. Diffraction-Limited Imaging with Very Large Telescopes. (C). 1989. text 213.50 (*0-7923-0192-7*) Kluwer Academic.

Alloin, D. M., jt. auth. see Mariotti, J. M.

Alloin, Danielle M. & Mariotti, Jean-Marie, eds. Adaptive Optics for Astronomy: Proceedings of the NATO Advanced Study Institute on Adaptive Optics for Astronomy Cargese, Corse, France, June 29-July 9, 1993. LC 94-4222. (NATO Advanced Study Institutes Series C, Mathematical & Physical Sciences: Vol. 423). 356p. 1994. text 188.50 (*0-7923-2748-9*) Kluwer Academic.

Allon, Dafna, tr. see Ringelblum, Emmanuel.

Allor. In Private Practices. (C). Date not set. text. write for info. (*0-415-00133-1*) Routledge.

— In Private Practices. (C). (gr. 13). Date not set. write for info. (*0-415-00132-3*) Routledge.

Allor, David J. The Planning Commissioners Guide. LC 83-62938. (Illus.). 186p. 1984. pap. 24.95 (*0-918286-30-1*, Planners Press) Am Plan Assn.

Allora. English Assamese Dictionary. (ASM & ENG.). 1992. reprint ed. 24.95 (*0-8288-8415-3*) Fr & Eur.

— English Assamese Pocket Dictionary. (ASM & ENG.). 1992. reprint ed. 9.95 (*0-8288-8416-1*) Fr & Eur.

— Nepali - English Dictionary. (ENG & NEP.). 1992. reprint ed. 14.95 (*0-8288-8417-X*) Fr & Eur.

Allot, A. & Woodman, Gordon R., eds. People's Law & State Law: The Bellagio Papers. viii, 354p. 1985. pap. 84.30 (*90-6765-100-1*); pap. 90.75 (*3-11-013108-0*) Mouton.

Allot, Robert. England's Parnassus: Or, the Choysest Flowers of Our Modern Poets. LC 72-167. (English Experience Ser.: No. 216). 510p. 1970. reprint ed. 85.00 (*90-221-0216-5*) Walter J Johnson.

— Wits Theatre of the World. LC 70-17131. (English Experience Ser.: No. 359). 560p. 1971. reprint ed. 51.00 (*90-221-0359-5*) Walter J Johnson.

Allott, ed. see Boursault.

Allott, Angela M., jt. ed. see Bromley, David W.

Allott, Anna J. Inked Over, Ripped Out: Burmese Storytellers & the Censors. 85p. 1993. 5.00 (*0-934638-12-8*) PEN Am Ctr.

Allott, Antony N. Essays in African Law, with Special Reference to the Law of Ghana. LC 74-30925. 323p. 1975. reprint ed. lib. bdg. 22.50 (*0-8371-7885-1*, ALAL, Greenwood Pr) Greenwood.

Allott, Miriam, ed. Essays on Shelley. LC 81-12885. (English Texts & Studies). 304p. 1982. 44.00 (*0-389-20127-8*, 06903) B&N Imports.

— Keats: Complete Poems. (Longman Annotated English Poets Ser.). (Illus.). (C). 1996. pap. 61.00 (*0-582-48457-X*) Longman.

Allott, Miriam, ed. see Arnold, Matthew.

Allott, P. Eunomia: A New Order for a New World. (Illus.). 456p. 1991. 35.00 (*0-19-825599-3*) OUP.

Allott, Stephen. Alcuin of York: The Life & Letters of the Saxon Scholar, AD 732 to 804. (C). 1988. 68.00 (*1-85072-021-5*, Pub. by W Sessions) St Mut.

***Allott, Stephen.** Alcuin of York (c.732-804 AD) 1999. pap. 21.00 (*0-900657-21-9*, Pub. by W Sessions) St Mut.

Allott, Stephen. Friends in York. 1999. pap. 21.00 (*0-900657-40-5*, Pub. by W Sessions) St Mut.

— John Wilhelm Rowntree. 1999. pap. 24.00 (*1-85072-137-8*, Pub. by W Sessions) St Mut.

— Lindley Murray (1745-1826) 1999. pap. 21.00 (*1-85072-088-6*, Pub. by W Sessions) St Mut.

***Allott, Stephen.** Meanings - Biblical Commentaries. 1999. pap. 23.00 (*1-85072-155-6*, Pub. by W Sessions) St Mut.

Allouache, Merzak. Bab El-Oued. Brewer, Angela M., tr. LC 98-38470. 134p. 1998. lib. bdg. 32.00 (*0-89410-859-X*, Three Contnts) L Rienner.

Allouache, Merzak & Naqvi, Tahira. Bab El-Oued. Brewer, Angela M., tr. LC 98-38470. 150p. 1998. pap. 13.95 (*0-89410-860-3*, Three Contnts) L Rienner.

Allouba, Esmat, tr. see Al-Ramlyn, Lenin.

Allouche, Adel. Mamluk Economics: A Study & Translation of Al-Maqrizi's Igathah. 176p. (C). 1994. 35.00 (*0-87480-431-0*) U of Utah Pr.

Allouche, Jose & Pogorel, Gerard, eds. Technology Management & Corporate Strategies: A Tricontinental Perspective. 368p. 1995. text 142.50 (*0-444-82173-2*, North Holland) Elsevier.

Alloula, Malek. The Colonial Harem. Godzich, Myrna & Godzich, Wlad, trs. from FRE. LC 85-16527. (Theory & History of Literature Ser.: Vol. 21). (Illus.). 135p. (Orig.). 1986. pap. 19.95 (*0-8166-1384-2*) U of Minn Pr.

Alloway & Graham. Sniffy the Virtual Rat Pro. 1999. pap. text 20.25 (*0-534-35865-9*) Thomson Learn.

***Alloway, Alonda.** Souls Sold. 78p. 1999. pap. 10.00 (*0-9673825-0-5*) Abysmal Pubg.

Alloway, Brian J. Heavy Metals in Soils: Their Origins, Chemical Behaviour & Bioavailability. 339p. 1990. text 224.00 (*0-470-21598-4*, 900129) Halsted Pr.

Alloway, Catherine S., ed. The Book Stops Here: New Directions for Bookmobile Service. LC 90-32198. (Illus.). 394p. 1992. 45.00 (*0-8108-2251-2*) Scarecrow.

Alloway, David. El Camino Del Rio - The River Road, FM170. (Illus.). 52p. (Orig.). 1996. pap. 4.00 (*1-885696-08-6*) TX Prks & Wldlife.

***Alloway, David.** Desert Survival Skills. (Illus.). 288p. 2000. 40.00 (*0-292-70491-7*); pap. 21.95 (*0-292-70492-5*) U of Tex Pr.

Alloway, David N. Minorities & the American City. LC 79-124683. 124p. 1970. pap. 13.50 (*0-685-45320-0*) St Aedans Pr & Bk.

Alloway, David N., jt. auth. see Cordasco, Francesco.

Alloway, J. Evans & Weisbrodt, Jerry. A Better Reason: A Handbook for Critical Thinking, Reading Comprehension & Test Mastery. LC 88-146057. 160p. 1988. student ed. 8.95 (*0-945623-00-3*) ESI Pubns.

Alloway, K., jt. auth. see Pritchard, T.

Alloway, Lawrence. Network: Art & the Complex Present. Kuspit, Donald, ed. LC 83-24201. (Contemporary American Art Critics Ser.: No. 1). 324p. reprint ed. 100.50 (*0-8357-1519-1*, 207061700007) Bks Demand.

— Roy Lichtenstein. LC 83-2788. (Modern Masters Ser.). (Illus.). 128p. 1983. 35.00 (*0-89659-330-4*); pap. 14.95 (*0-89659-331-2*) Abbeville Pr.

Alloway, Lawrence & Demetrion, James T. Art in Western Europe: The Postwar Years. LC 78-66783. (Illus.). 120p. 1978. pap. 12.00 (*0-614-31046-6*) Edmundson.

Alloway, Lawrence & MacNaughton, Mary D. Adolph Gottlieb: A Retrospective. LC 81-65351. (Illus.). 176p. 1995. 50.00 (*1-55595-124-4*); 35.00 (*1-55595-125-2*) Hudson Hills.

Alloway, Lawrence, et al. Urban Encounters: Art Architecture Audience. (Illus.). 64p. (Orig.). 1980. pap. 15.00 (*0-88454-055-3*) U of Pa Contemp Art.

Alloway Publishing Staff. The Burns Federation: Song Book. (C). 1989. pap. text 40.00 (*0-902320-10-6*, Pub. by Alloway Pub) St Mut.

— Complete Letters & Complete Poetical Works of Robert Burns, 2 vols. 1980. 150.00 (*0-907526-69-1*, Pub. by Alloway Publ); 300.00 (*0-907526-70-5*, Pub. by Alloway Publ) St Mut.

— Historical Aspects of Newmilns. 1980. 60.00 (*0-907526-44-6*, Pub. by Alloway Publ) St Mut.

Alloy. Abnormal Psych. Text. 7th ed. 1996. 65.25 (*0-07-844964-2*) McGraw.

— Abnormal Psychology Casebook. 7th ed. 1995. 63.00 (*0-07-911861-5*) McGraw.

Alloy, Jan L., ed. see Pettinelli, Vincent D.

Alloy, L. B., jt. auth. see O'Hara, M. W.

Alloy, Lauren B. Cognitive Processes in Depression. LC 87-8696. (Illus.). 400p. 1988. reprint ed. pap. 124.00 (*0-608-07874-3*, 205988400010) Bks Demand.

Alloy, Lauren B. & Acocella, Joan R. Abnormal Psychology: Current Perspectives. 7th ed. (C). 1995. pap., student ed. 18.75 (*0-07-006629-9*) McGraw.

Alloy, Lauren B., et al. Abnormal Psychology: Current Perspectives. 7th ed. (C). 1996. text 65.25 (*0-07-844963-4*) McGraw.

— Abnormal Psychology: Current Perspectives. 7th rev. ed. LC 95-16246. 1996. text. write for info. (*0-07-006615-9*) McGraw.

— Abnormal Psychology: Current Perspectives. 8th ed. LC 98-4014. 1998. write for info. (*0-07-115653-4*) McGraw.

— Abnormal Psychology: Current Perspectives. 8th ed. LC 98-4014. 1998. 74.25 (*0-07-292838-7*) McGraw.

***Alloy Publishers Staff.** Do It Yourself Beauty. (Illus.). (YA). 2000. pap. 5.99 (*0-14-130918-0*, AlloyBks) Peng Put Young Read.

— Slam. (Illus.). (YA). 2000. pap. 5.99 (*0-14-130919-9*, AlloyBks) Peng Put Young Read.

***Alloy Publishers Staff & Shaw, Tucker.** Any Advice? (Illus.). (YA). 2000. pap. 5.99 (*0-14-130921-0*, AlloyBks) Peng Put Young Read.

— Dreams: Explore the You That You Can't Control. (Illus.). (YA). 2000. pap. 5.99 (*0-14-130920-2*, AlloyBks) Peng Put Young Read.

Alloyd Corporation Staff. Coating of Copper Wire for Severe Environment Electrical Insulation. 56p. 1962. 8.40 (*0-317-34499-4*, 19) Intl Copper.

Allphin, Clela. Women in the Plays of Henrik Ibsen. 1974. lib. bdg. 250.00 (*0-87700-211-8*) Revisionist Pr.

Allphin-Hoggatt, Clela. The Writing Cycle. 2nd rev. ed. LC 86-26093. 300p. (C). 1991. pap. text. write for info. (*0-935732-27-6*) Roxbury Pub Co.

Allphin, N. W. Visions Unveiled or the Revelation Explained. 298p. 1985. 8.95 (*0-933672-89-6*, C-2098) Star Bible.

***Allport, Dave.** First Contact Evangelism. 140p. 1999. pap. 10.00 (*0-9675818-0-X*) BASIC Coll.

Allport, Floyd H. Institutional Behaviour: Essays. LC 71-90460. 526p. 1969. reprint ed. lib. bdg. 79.50 (*0-8371-2145-0*, ALIB, Greenwood Pr) Greenwood.

Allport, Gordon W. ABCs of Scapegoating. 40p. 4.50 (*0-88464-028-0*) ADL.

— Becoming: Basic Considerations for a Psychology of Personality. LC 55-5975. (Terry Lectures Ser.). (C). 1960. pap. 11.00 (*0-300-00002-2*, Y20) Yale U Pr.

— The Nature of Personality: Selected Papers. LC 74-2795. 220p. 1975. reprint ed. lib. bdg. 65.00 (*0-8371-7432-5*, ALNP, Greenwood Pr) Greenwood.

— The Nature of Prejudice. 1979. pap. 17.00 (*0-201-00179-9*) Addison-Wesley.

Allport, Gordon W., ed. Letters from Jenny. LC 65-18327. (Illus.). 238p. (Orig.). (C). 1965. pap. 7.95 (*0-15-650700-5*, Harvest Bks) Harcourt.

Allport, Gordon W., et al, eds. Cultural Groups & Human Relations: Conference on Educational Problems of Special Cultural Groups--Teachers College, Columbia University, 1949. LC 77-117772. (Essay Index Reprint Ser.). 1977. 20.95 (*0-8369-1792-8*) Ayer.

Allport, Gordon W., et al. Study of Values. 3rd ed. teacher ed. 14.64 (*0-395-08460-1*); teacher ed. 2.40 (*0-395-08466-0*) HM.

Allport, Gordon W., jt. auth. see Cantril, Hadley.

Allport, Gordon W., ed. see James, William.

Allport, Richard. Heal Your Cat the Natural Way. (Illus.). 128p. 1997. 21.95 (*0-87605-615-X*) Howell Bks.

— Homeopathy for Cats: Healing Your Pet the Natural Way. 128p. 1999. pap. 17.95 (*0-89087-940-0*) Celestial Arts.

— Homeopathy for Dogs: Healing Your Pet the Natural Way. 128p. 1999. pap. 17.95 (*0-89087-939-7*) Celestial Arts.

***Allport, Richard.** The Illustrated Encyclopedia of Natural Healthcare for Pets: Therapies, Nutrition, Exercise. (Illus.). 2001. 35.00 (*1-86204-722-7*) Element MA.

Allport, Susan. A Natural History of Parenting. LC 97-32812. 256p. 1998. pap. 13.00 (*0-609-80182-1*, Crown) Crown Pub Group.

— The Nature of Food: Exploring the Roots of Our Ingestible World - From Foraging to Hunting to Haute Cuisine. LC 99-46244. 288p. 2000. 23.00 (*0-609-60149-0*) Harmony Bks.

— Sermons in Stone. 208p. 1994. pap. 13.95 (*0-393-31202-X*) Norton.

Allred, B. W., ed. see Potomac Corral of the Westerners Staff.

Allred, Carol G. Positive Action Family Kit. (Illus.). 372p. 1995. spiral bd. 54.95 (*1-57160-012-4*); ring bd. 59.95 (*1-57160-078-7*) Positive Action.

— Positive Actions for Living: A Guide for Learning Parent, Family, Community & Personal Positive Actions. LC 95-72954. (Illus.). 381p. 1996. pap. 49.95 (*1-57160-082-5*); pap., wbk. ed. 4.00 (*1-57160-090-6*); pap. text 44.95 (*1-57160-087-6*) Positive Action.

***Allred, Garth.** Unlocking the Powers of Faith. 1999. pap. 13.95 (*1-57734-500-2*, 01114514) Covenant Comms.

Allred, Gordon. The Companion. 1992. pap. 7.95 (*0-88494-832-3*) Bookcraft Inc.

— Dori the Mallard. (Illus.). (J). (gr. 5 up). 1968. 8.95 (*0-8392-3052-4*) Astor-Honor.

— Hungry Journey. 160p. 1973. pap. 2.50 (*0-89036-000-6*) Liahona Pub Trust.

— Old Crackfoot. (Illus.). (J). (gr. 5 up). 1965. 8.95 (*0-8392-3051-6*) Astor-Honor.

Allred, H. & Hobdell, M. H. The Planning & Development of Educational Programmes for Personnel in Oral Health. (WHO Offset Publications: No. 93). 101p. 1986. pap. text 16.00 (*92-4-170093-9*, 1120093) World Health.

Allred, Jacki & Olsen, Claudia. Where Can We Turn? A Parent's Guide to Evaluating Treatment Programs for Troubled Youth. 48p. 1995. pap. 4.99 (*1-56684-092-9*) Evans Bk Dist.

Allred, Janice. God the Mother & Other Theological Essays. LC 96-18402. 282p. (Orig.). 1998. 24.95 (*1-56085-086-8*) Signature Bks.

Allred, Jeannette A. Lamentations & Ecstasies of the Soul. Vogt, Robert M. & Diaz, Mildred, eds. (Books That Touch). Date not set. pap. 8.95 (*0-9659765-9-9*) Vonet Pub.

Allred, Joanne. Whetstone. 24p. 1996. pap. 7.00 (*1-886226-01-6*) Flume Pr.

Allred, John, jt. auth. see Gallagher, Charlotte.

Allred, Michael D. Madman, No. 1. (Illus.). 48p. (J). (gr. 4 up). 1994. reprint ed. pap. 3.95 (*0-87816-275-5*) Kitchen Sink.

— Madman Adventures, No. 3. (Illus.). 48p. 1993. pap. 2.95 (*1-56862-026-8*) Kitchen Sink.

— Madman Adventures Collection. Amara, Philip, ed. (Illus.). 112p. (YA). 1994. pap. 14.95 (*0-87816-314-X*) Kitchen Sink.

A

— The Oddity Odyssey. (Madman Adventures Ser.). (Illus.). 144p. (YA). 1994. pap. 12.95 (*0-87816-315-8*) Kitchen Sink.

Allred, Michael W. You Might Be a Mormon If... LC 98-28156. 1998. pap. 10.95 (*1-57734-285-2*, 01113410) Covenant Comms.

Allred, Mike. Red Rocket 7. (Illus.). 208p. (YA). (gr. 7 up). 1998. pap. 29.95 (*1-56971-347-2*) Dark Horse Comics.

— Superman/Madman Hullabaloo! (Illus.). 1998. pap. text 8.95 (*1-56971-301-4*) Dark Horse Comics.

Allred, O. M. Automotive Window Engraving for Fun & Profit. (Illus.). 32p. 1986. pap. 12.95 (*0-936035-00-5*) O M Allred.

— The Real Estate Professional's Signage Advertising Guidebook. LC 89-91590. (Illus.). 85p. (Orig.). 1989. pap. 26.00 (*0-936035-06-4*) O M Allred.

Allred, Roger C. & Allred, Russell S. The Family Business: Power Tools for Survival, Success & Succession. LC 97-215287. 208p. 1997. pap. 12.00 (*0-425-15773-3*) Berkley Pub.

Allred, Ron E., ed. see International SAMPE Electronics Conference Staff.

Allred, Ruel A. Spelling Trends, Contest, & Methods. (What Research Says to the Teacher Ser.). 1987. pap. 3.95 (*0-8106-1062-0*) NEA.

Allred, Russell S., jt. auth. see Allred, Roger C.

Allred, Stephen. Employment Law: A Guide for North Carolina Public Employers. 3rd ed. LC 99-462509. (C). 1999. pap. text 35.00 (*1-56011-351-0*, 99.06) Institute Government.

— Hospital As Employer. rev. ed. (Hospital Law in North Carolina Ser.). 36p. 1992. pap. 10.50 (*1-56011-224-7*, 85.03P) Institute Government.

— A Legal Guide to Public Employee Free Speech in North Carolina. 2nd ed. 58p. (C). 1995. pap. text 12.00 (*1-56011-239-5*) Institute Government.

Allred, Tamera S. On the Homefront: A Woman's Reflections on Hearth & Heart. (Illus.). 206p. 1992. pap. text 12.95 (*0-9635429-0-7*) Homefront Prods.

Allred, Terri & Burns, Gary. Stop! Just for Kids: For Kids with Sexual Touching Problems by Kids with Sexual Touching Problems. LC 98-208921. (Illus.). 160p. (Orig.). (J). (gr. 4). 1997. pap. 15.00 (*1-884444-37-7*) Safer Soc.

Allred, V. Dean. Oil Shale Processing Technology. LC 81-65818. (Illus.). 240p. 1982. 60.00 (*0-86563-001-1*) Ctr Prof Adv.

Allred, Wayne. A Complete Guide to Effective Excuses. (Illus.). 106p. 1993. pap. 5.95 (*1-885027-05-2*) Willow T Bks.

— The Disgusted Driver's Handbook: Instructions for Surviving on Roads Infested with Idiots. (Illus.). 95p. 1998. pap. 5.95 (*1-885027-09-5*) Willow T Bks.

— Geezerhood, What to Expect Now You Are As Old As Dirt. (Illus.). 1996. reprint ed. pap. 5.95 (*1-885027-06-0*) Willow T Bks.

— How to Confuse the Idiots in Your Life: Learn How To: Baffle Clueless Questioners, Entertain Your Friends, Get Enjoyment from Your Own Idiots. (Illus.). 104p. 1999. pap. 5.95 (*1-885027-10-9*) Willow T Bks.

— How to Cope When You Are Surrounded by Idiots: Or If You Are One. rev. ed. LC 95-91062. (Illus.). 107p. 1994. pap. 5.95 (*1-885027-03-6*) Willow T Bks.

— The Outhouse Book: Readin' That's Probably Not Ready for Indoor Plumbing. (Illus.). 101p. 1997. pap. 5.95 (*1-885027-07-9*) Willow T Bks.

— There Are Some Things Worse Than Being over Forth. (Illus.). 24p. (Orig.). 1993. reprint ed. pap. 2.95 (*1-885027-00-1*) Willow T Bks.

— Whenever Your Attitude Stinks, Read This: Another Trendy Book to Make You Feel OK When Your Life Is a Complete Disaster. (Illus.). 97p. 1997. pap. 5.95 (*1-885027-08-7*) Willow T Bks.

— Yes, Even You Can Be a Country Person. LC 95-91060. (Illus.). 124p. (Orig.). 1995. reprint ed. pap. 5.95 (*1-885027-04-4*) Willow T Bks.

***Allrich, Karri.** Recipes from a Vegetarian Goddess: Delectable Feasts Through the Seasons. LC 99-462300. (Illus.). 200p. 2000. pap. 17.95 (*1-56718-016-7*) Llewellyn Pubns.

Allrich, Louise. Olga De Amaral: Tapestries from the Moonbasket. (Illus.). 12p. 1989. write for info. (*0-318-66602-2*) Allrich Gallery.

Allrich, Steve. Oil Painting for the Serious Beginner: Basic Lessons in Becoming a Good Painter. (Illus.). 144p. 1996. pap. text 19.95 (*0-8230-3269-8*) Watsn-Guptill.

Allrich, Ted. The On-Line Investor: Busing Your Personal Computer to Find & Invest in the Most Profitable Stocks. 2nd ed. LC 99-462634. 256p. 1999. pap. 15.95 (*0-312-20808-1*, St Martins Paperbacks) St Martin.

— Online Investor. LC 96-43900. 272p. 1996. pap. 15.95 (*0-312-15183-7*) St Martin.

— Win Big Think Small. 1999. pap. 22.95 (*0-525-93975-X*) Viking Penguin.

Allsebrook, Mary. Born to Rebel: The Life of Harriet Boyd Hawes. (Illus.). 236p. 1992. 25.00 (*0-946897-40-9*, Pub. by Oxbow Bks) David Brown.

— Prototypes of Peacemaking: The First Forty Years of the U. N. 1987. 45.00 (*0-912289-72-4*) St James Pr.

Allsen. Fitness for Life. 6th ed. 1996. 10.00 (*0-697-24653-1*, WCB McGr Hill) McGrw-H Hghr Educ.

Allsen, Philip E. Fitness for Life. 7th ed. 2000. pap. text 18.00 (*0-697-29672-5*) McGraw.

— Strength Training: Beginners, Body Builders & Athletes. 192p. (C). 1996. per. 15.95 (*0-7872-1837-5*) Kendall-Hunt.

Allsen, Philip E. & Witbeck, Alan R. Racquetball. 6th ed. LC 95-80431. 128p. (C). 1996. text 9.60 (*0-697-25627-8*) Brown & Benchmark.

Allsen, Philip E., et al. Fitness for Life: An Individualized Approach. 5th ed. 272p. (C). 1992. text. write for info. (*0-697-10061-8*) Brown & Benchmark.

— Fitness for Life: An Individualized Approach. 6th ed. LC 96-85930. 272p. (C). 1996. text 20.00 (*0-697-23329-4*) Brown & Benchmark.

Allsen, Thomas T. Commodity & Exchange in the Mongol Empire: A Cultural History of Islamic Textiles. (Studies in Islamic Civilization). 154p. (C). 1997. text 49.95 (*0-521-58301-2*) Cambridge U Pr.

Allshouse, Jane E., jt. auth. see Frazao, Elizabeth.

Allsobrook, David I. Liszt: My Travelling Circus Life. LC 91-3578. (Music in Georgian & Victorian Society Ser.). (Illus.). 272p. (C). 1991. 36.95 (*0-8093-1785-0*) S Ill U Pr.

Allsop, D. F. Cannons. (Land Warfare: Brassey's New Battlefield Weapons & Technology Ser.). (Illus.). 140p. (Orig.). (C). 1995. pap. 25.00 (*1-85753-104-3*, Pub. by Brasseys) Brasseys.

— Small Arms & Machine Guns. (Brassey's Land Warfare Ser.). 360p. 1998. 39.95 (*1-85753-250-3*, Pub. by Brasseys) Brasseys.

Allsop, Derek, et al. Brassey's Essential Guide to Military Small Arms: Design Principles & Operating Methods. LC 96-48906. (Illus.). 336p. 1997. 75.00 (*1-85753-107-8*, Pub. by Brasseys) Brasseys.

Allsop, Derick. The Game of Their Lives: Voices of the Football People. (Illus.). 192p. 1996. 34.95 (*1-85158-800-0*, Pub. by Mainstream Pubng) Trafalgar.

— Reliving the Dream: The Triumph & the Tears of Manchester United's 1968 European Cup Heroes. (Illus.). 192p. 1998. pap. 22.95 (*1-84018-056-0*, Pub. by Mainstream Pubng) Trafalgar.

Allsop, Fred W. History of the Arkansas Press for a Hundred Years. (Illus.). 688p. 1978. reprint ed. 25.00 (*0-89308-073-X*) Southern Hist Pr.

Allsop, J. Regulating Medical Work: Formal & Informal Controls. (Health Services Management Ser.). 224p. 1996. 112.95 (*0-335-19405-2*); pap. 31.95 (*0-335-19404-4*) OpUniv Pr.

Allsop, Judith. Health Policy & the NHS. 2nd ed. LC 94-28346. (Social Policy in Britain Ser.). 1995. write for info. (*0-582-04279-8*) Longman.

***Allsop, Nicola Hines & Allsop, Rodney.** Alexandria: A Story of Love, Friendship & Forgiveness. ix, 122p. (YA). 2000. pap. text 14.99 (*0-9679475-0-2*) Rallsop Pubng.

Allsop, Peter. Arcangelo Corelli: "New Orpheus of Our Times" LC 98-7973. (Oxford Monographs on Music). (Illus.). 280p. 1999. text 75.00 (*0-19-816562-5*) OUP.

Allsop, Rodney, jt. auth. see Allsop, Nicola Hines.

Allsop, Terry. Mentoring for Science Teachers. Benson, Ann, ed. LC 96-23677. 128p. 1996. pap. 27.95 (*0-335-19514-8*) OpUniv Pr.

Allsop, Terry & Benson, Ann. Mentoring for Science Teachers. LC 96-23677. 128p. 1996. 88.95 (*0-335-19515-6*) OpUniv Pr.

Allsopp, Bruce. Spirit of Europe: A Subliminal History. (Illus.). 256p. 1997. 46.50 (*1-85776-168-5*, Pub. by Book Guild Ltd) Trans-Atl Phila.

Allsopp, C. E., jt. auth. see Thompson, R. C.

Allsopp, D., et al, eds. Microbial Diversity & Ecosystem Function. (Illus.). 400p. 1995. text 120.00 (*0-85198-898-9*) OUP.

***Allsopp, David.** The Bluffer's Guide to Skiing: Bluff Your Way in Skiing. (Bluffer's Guides Ser.). 64p. 1999. pap. 5.95 (*1-902825-62-4*) Oval Bks.

Allsopp, Fred W. Albert Pike: A Biography. 370p. 1992. reprint ed. pap. 29.95 (*1-56459-134-4*) Kessinger Pub.

Allsopp, Jeannette, jt. ed. see Allsopp, Richard.

***Allsopp, Michael E.** Christian Ethics & the New Catechism. LC 99-27302. 1999. write for info. (*0-940866-80-3*) U Scranton Pr.

Allsopp, Michael E. & Burke, Ronald R., eds. John Henry Newman: Theology & Reform. LC 92-21667. 304p. 1992. text 20.00 (*0-8153-0384-X*, H01475) Garland.

Allsopp, Michael E. & Downes, David A. Saving Beauty: Further Studies in Hopkins. LC 93-41179. (Origins of Modernism Ser.). 368p. 1994. text 30.00 (*0-8153-0834-5*, H1587) Garland.

Allsopp, Michael E. & O'Keefe, John J. Veritatis Splendor: American Responses. (Illus.). 240p. (Orig.). 1995. pap. 19.95 (*1-55612-760-X*) Sheed & Ward WI.

Allsopp, Michael E. & Sundermeier, Michael W., eds. Gerard Manley Hopkins (1844-1889) New Essays on His Life, Writing & Place in English Literature. LC 89-9309. (Studies in British Literature: Vol. 1). 260p. 1988. lib. bdg. 49.95 (*0-88946-928-8*) E Mellen.

Allsopp, Richard. The Dictionary of Caribbean English Usage. LC 97-108598. 776p. (C). 1996. text 38.00 (*0-19-866152-5*) OUP.

***Allsopp, Richard & Allsopp, Jeannette, eds.** Dictionary of Caribbean English Usage: With a French & Spanish Supplement. 697p. 2000. reprint ed. 30.00 (*0-7881-9418-6*) DIANE Pub.

Allsopp, Vicky. Understanding Economics. LC 95-11819. 464p. (C). 1995. pap. 29.99 (*0-415-09133-0*) Routledge.

— Understanding Economics. LC 95-11819. 464p. (C). (gr. 13). 1995. 100.00 (*0-415-09132-2*) Routledge.

***Allsport Photographic Agency Staff.** Visions of Wimbledon. (Illus.). 2000. 29.95 (*0-233-99868-3*, Pub. by Andre Deutsch) Trafalgar.

Allsport Staff. Visions of Allsport. (Illus.). 144p. 2000. 35.00 (*0-7893-0223-3*, Pub. by Universe) St Martin.

— Visions of Tennis. 1996. 24.95 (*1-899163-25-5*) Cimino Pub Grp.

***Allstetter, William, ed.** Science & Technology Almanac, 2000. (Illus.). 464p. 2000. pap. 65.00 (*1-57356-286-6*) Oryx Pr.

***Allstetter, William & Schuyler, Tami.** The Cutting Edge: An Encyclopedia of Advanced Technologies. LC 99-215056. (Illus.). 368p. 2000. text 75.00 (*0-19-512899-0*) OUP.

Allston, Aaron. The Complete Fighter's HandBook. 2nd ed. 1989. 19.95 (*0-88038-779-3*, Pub. by TSR Inc) Random.

— The Complete Ninja's Handbook. 1995. 20.00 (*0-7869-0159-4*, Pub. by TSR Inc) Random.

— Doc Sidhe. 352p. 1995. mass mkt. 5.99 (*0-671-87662-7*) Baen Bks.

— Double Jeopardy: Car Wars, No. 4. 224p. (Orig.). 1994. mass mkt. 4.99 (*0-8125-3463-8*, Pub. by Tor Bks) St Martin.

— Iron Fist. (Star Wars: No. 6). 336p. (J). (gr. 3-7). 1998. mass mkt. 5.99 (*0-553-57897-9*, Spectra) Bantam.

— Solo Command. (Star Wars: No. 7). 352p. (J). (gr. 3-7). 1999. mass mkt. 5.99 (*0-553-57900-2*) Bantam.

— Star Wars. (Star Wars Ser.). 1999. mass mkt. 5.99 (*0-553-58125-2*) Bantam.

— Starfighters of Adumar. (Star Wars: X-Wing (Numbered) Ser.: No. 9). 291p. (J). (gr. 3-7). 1999. mass mkt. 5.99 (*0-553-57418-3*) Bantam.

— ULTIMA Underworld Clue Book: Mysteries of the Abyss. (Illus.). 64p. (Orig.). 1992. pap. 14.95 (*0-929373-08-1*) Origin Syst.

— Wraith Squadron. (Star Wars: No. 5). 432p. (J). (gr. 3-7). 1998. mass mkt. 5.99 (*0-553-57894-4*, Spectra) Bantam.

Allston, Aaron, jt. auth. see Lisle, Holly.

Allston, Frank J. Con-glom-er-ate: A Case Study of IC Industries under William Johnson. (Illus.). 336p. (C). 1991. 24.95 (*0-9632709-0-7*) Illumina Concepts.

Allston, Washington. Autobiographical Works of Washington Allston. LC 91-4433. 336p. 1991. reprint ed. 50.00 (*0-8201-1450-2*) Schol Facsimiles.

— Lectures on Art, & Poems, 1850, & Monaldi, 1841. LC 67-10124. 646p. 1967. 75.00 (*0-8201-1001-9*) Schol Facsimiles.

— Lectures on Art-Poems. LC 75-171379. (Library of American Art). 1972. reprint ed. lib. bdg. 49.50 (*0-306-70414-5*) Da Capo.

— The Works of Washington Allston, 1779-1843, Set. 1987. reprint ed. lib. bdg. 600.00 (*0-685-18591-5*) Rprt Serv.

Allswang, Benzion. The Final Resolution: Combating Anti-Jewish Hostility. 1988. 18.95 (*0-87306-455-0*) Feldheim.

Allswang, John M. Bosses, Machines, & Urban Voters. rev. ed. LC 85-24042. 192p. 1986. reprint ed. pap. text 14.95 (*0-8018-3312-4*) Johns Hopkins.

***Allswang, John M.** Initiative & Referendum in California, 1898-1998. LC 99-44068. 365p. 2000. 60.00 (*0-8047-3811-4*) Stanford U Pr.

— Initiative & Referendum in California, 1898-1998. LC 99-44068. 365p. 2000. pap. 24.95 (*0-8047-3821-1*) Stanford U Pr.

Allswang, John M. The Political Behavior of Chicago's Ethnic Groups, 1918-1932. LC 80-837. (American Ethnic Groups Ser.). 1981. lib. bdg. 35.95 (*0-405-13401-0*) Ayer.

Allswede, Jerry L., ed. see Technical Association of the Pulp & Paper Industry.

Allsworth-Jones, P. The Szeletian: And the Transition from Middle to Upper Paleolithic in Central Europe. 448p. 1986. 135.00 (*0-19-813401-0*) OUP.

Allt, Peter, ed. see Yeats, William Butler.

Allton, Don. You & Your Voice Are One: A Renegade Voice Teacher Speaks Out. Allton, Mary K., ed. (Illus.). 157p. (Orig.). 1991. pap. text 14.95 (*0-9625217-1-X*) M E K A.

Allton, Mary K. Color Your World Like a Rainbow. 96p. (Orig.). (C). 1989. pap. 8.95 (*0-9625217-0-1*) M E K A.

— Whimsy with Words. (Illus.). 68p. (Orig.). (YA). (gr. 7 up). 1996. pap. 8.00 (*0-9625217-2-8*) M E K A.

Allton, Mary K., ed. see Allton, Don.

Alluisi, Earl A. & Fleishman, Edwin A., eds. Stress & Performance Effectiveness Vol. 3: Stress & Performance Effectiveness. (Human Performance & Productivity Ser.). 288p. 1982. text 69.95 (*0-89859-091-4*) L Erlbaum Assocs.

Allum, Dianne J., ed. Cochlear Implant Rehabilitation in Children & Adults. LC 96-218443. (Illus.). 342p. (Orig.). 1996. pap. 55.00 (*1-56593-794-5*, 1550) Singular Publishing.

Allum, Faith T. Respite. (Illus.). 48p. (Orig.). 1985. pap. 3.00 (*0-9613349-2-4*) F T Allum.

— Seasons & Love. (Illus.). 44p. (Orig.). 1984. pap. 3.00 (*0-9613349-1-6*) F T Allum.

— White Water, Pebbles & Love. (Illus.). 48p. (Orig.). 1984. pap. 3.00 (*0-9613349-0-8*) F T Allum.

Allum, J. H., et al, eds. Natural & Artificial Control of Hearing & Balance. LC 93-11042. (Progress in Brain Research Ser.: Vol. 97). 452p. 1993. 273.50 (*0-444-81252-0*) Elsevier.

Allum, P. A. Italy: Republic Without Government? LC 73-20230. (Comparative Modern Government Ser.). (Illus.). 267p. (C). 1974. pap. text 14.00 (*0-393-09302-6*) Norton.

— Politics & Society in Post-War Naples. LC 75-174259. 426p. reprint ed. pap. 121.50 (*0-608-12327-7*, 2024408) Bks Demand.

Allum, Percy. State & Society in Europe. (Illus.). 619p. (C). 1995. text 70.95 (*0-7456-0409-9*); pap. text 31.95 (*0-7456-0410-2*) Blackwell Pubs.

Allum, W. L., jt. auth. see Fielding, J. W.

Allums, Betty, ed. see Allums, Charles.

Allums, Betty, ed. see Eastman, Samuel.

Allums, Betty, ed. see Innerarity, Al.

Allums, Betty, ed. see Lane, Michael.

Allums, Charles. Du Berry & His Crops. Majette, Baji & Allums, Betty, eds. 119p. (Orig.). 1985. 8.00 (*0-932211-01-1*) BA Cross Ctrl.

— Our Time Has Come. Allums, Betty, ed. LC 89-91703. 85p. (Orig.). 1989. pap. 9.00 (*0-685-39071-3*) BA Cross Ctrl.

— Sing a New Song. Allums, Betty, ed. (Illus.). 135p. (Orig.). 1984. pap. 8.75 (*0-932211-00-3*) BA Cross Ctrl.

Allums, Larry. Fairhope, 1894-1994: A Pictorial History. LC 94-9449. 1994. write for info. (*0-89865-896-9*) Donning Co.

Allums, Larry, ed. The Epic Cosmos. LC 92-31772. (Studies in Genre). 378p. (Orig.). (C). 1992. pap. 19.95 (*0-911005-22-6*) Dallas Inst Pubns.

Allured, Allen R., ed. see MC Pub. Co. Staff.

Allured, Michael. McCutcheon's Emulsifiers & Detergent: International Edition. rev. ed. LC 82-644576. 308p. 1998. pap. 72.00 (*0-944254-56-X*) MC Pub Co NJ.

— McCutcheon's Emulsifiers & Detergents: North American Edition. 330p. 1998. pap. 72.00 (*0-944254-55-1*) MC Pub Co NJ.

— McCutcheon's Emulsifiers & Detergents: North American Edition & International Edition. rev. ed. 588p. 1998. 176.00 (*0-944254-57-8*) MC Pub Co NJ.

— McCutcheon's Functional Materials: International Edition. LC 82-644577. 132p. 1998. pap. 61.00 (*0-944254-59-4*) MC Pub Co NJ.

— McCutcheon's Functional Materials: North American Edition. rev. ed. LC 82-644577. 354p. 1998. pap. 72.00 (*0-944254-58-6*) MC Pub Co NJ.

Allured, Michael, ed. McCutcheon's Emulsifiers & Detergents: North American Edition. 330p. 1997. pap. 72.00 (*0-944254-48-9*) MC Pub Co NJ.

Allured, Michael, ed. see MC Pub. Co. Staff.

Alluvial Staff. No Ka Oi. 1996. 39.95 (*0-9652009-0-6*) Alluvial Ent.

— No Ka Oi. 1996. 75.00 (*0-9652009-7-3*) Alluvial Ent.

— Provocateur, 6 Vols. 1996. pap. text 125.00 (*0-9652009-6-5*) Alluvial Ent.

Allvine, Fred C. Marketing: Principles & Practices. 868p. (C). 1987. text 66.00 (*0-15-555101-9*) Dryden Pr.

Allvine, Fred C. & Patterson, James M. Competition, Ltd: The Marketing of Gasoline. LC 70-180491. 344p. reprint ed. pap. 106.70 (*0-608-13652-2*, 205519700011) Bks Demand.

— Highway Robbery: An Analysis of the Gasoline Crisis. LC 74-1598. (Illus.). 273p. reprint ed. 84.70 (*0-8357-9216-1*, 201760600007) Bks Demand.

Allwein, Gerard, et al, eds. Formalizing Reasoning with Visual & Diagrammatic Representations: Papers from the AAAI Fall Symposium. (Technical Reports: Vol. FS-98-04). (Illus.). 112p. 1998. spiral bd. 25.00 (*1-57735-078-2*) AAAI Pr.

Allwein, Gerard & Barwise, Jon, eds. Logical Reasoning with Diagrams. (Studies in Logic & Computation: No. 6). (Illus.). 288p. 1996. text 55.00 (*0-19-510427-7*) OUP.

Allwood, C. W. & Gagiano, C. A., eds. Handbook of Psychiatry for Primary Care. LC 98-146717. (Medical Handbook Ser.). (Illus.). 336p. 1998. pap. 32.50 (*0-19-571182-3*) OUP.

Allwood, Gill. French Feminisms: Gender & Violence in Contemporary Theory. LC 99-203826. (Gender, Change & Society Ser.). 1999. pap. text 24.95 (*1-85728-803-3*) Taylor & Francis.

— French Feminisms: Gender & Violence in Contemporary Theory. LC 99-203826. (Gender, Change & Society Ser.). 169p. 1999. 75.00 (*1-85728-802-5*) UCL Pr Ltd.

***Allwood, Gill & Wadia, Khursheed.** Women & Politics in France, 1958-2000. LC 00-36632. (Illus.). 2000. pap. write for info. (*0-415-18493-2*) Routledge.

Allwood, J., et al, eds. Logic in Linguistics. LC 76-46855. (Cambridge Textbooks in Linguistics Ser.). (Illus.). 200p. 1977. pap. text 20.95 (*0-521-29174-7*) Cambridge U Pr.

Allwood, Jens & Gardenfors, Peter, eds. Cognitive Semantics: Meaning & Cognition. LC 98-44717. (Pragmatics & Beyond New Ser.: Vol. 55). x, 201p. 1999. pap. 24.95 (*1-55619-818-3*) J Benjamins Pubng Co.

***Allwood, Jens & Gardenfors, Peter, eds.** Cognitive Semantics: Meaning & Cognition. LC 98-44717. (Pragmatics & Beyond New Ser.: Vol. 55). x, 201p. 1999. 00.00 (*1-55619-817-5*) J Benjamins Pubng Co.

Allwood, Jens & Hjelmquist, Erland, eds. Foregrounding Background: Papers from the First Meeting of the European Psycholinguistics Association. 248p. (Orig.). 1985. pap. text 50.00 (*91-578-0145-2*) Coronet Bks.

Allwood, M. C. & Wright, Patricia. The Cytotoxics Handbook. 3rd ed. LC 96-53119. 1997. write for info. (*1-85775-141-8*, Radcliffe Med Pr) Scovill Paterson.

Allwood, Martin S., tr. see Aurell, Tage.

Allwood, Michael, et al, eds. The Cytotoxics Handbook. (Illus.). 400p. 1997. 115.00 (*0-917330-83-8*, T-276, Pub. by Radcliff Med) Am Pharm Assn.

Allwood, Michael & Wright, Patricia, eds. The Cytotoxics Handbook. 2nd ed. 1993. 74.95 (*1-870905-04-0*, Radcliffe Med Pr) Scovill Paterson.

Allwood, R. J. Techniques & Applications of Expert Systems in the Construction Industry. 1989. text 49.95 (*0-470-21389-2*) P-H.

Allwood, Rodney. Common-Sense Principles for Managers & Supervisors: Pearls of Wisdom Suitable for Framing. (Illus.). 184p. 1996. pap. text 8.95 (*0-9652443-0-X*) Profitabilty Res.

Allworth, Edward, ed. Central Asia: One Hundred Thirty Years of Russian Dominance, a Historical Overview. 3rd ed. LC 94-18395. (Central Asia Book Ser.). (Illus.). 672p. 1994. text 68.50 (*0-8223-1554-8*); pap. text 26.95 (*0-8223-1521-1*) Duke.

— Ethnic Russia in the U. S. S. R. The Dilemma of Dominance. LC 79-22959. (Policy Studies). 270p. 1980. 100.00 (*0-08-023700-2*, Pergamon Pr) Elsevier.

— Soviet Nationality Problems. LC 77-166211. (Illus.). 296p. 1971. text 64.50 (*0-231-03493-8*) Col U Pr.

An Asterisk (*) at the beginning of an entry indicates that the title is appearing for the first time.

— The Tatars of Crimea: Their Struggle for Survival. LC 87-33186. (Central Asia Book Ser.). (Illus.). xv, 396p. (C). 1988. text 62.95 (*0-8223-0758-8*) Duke.

Allworth, Edward, tr. see Sinasi, Ibrahim.

Allworth, Edward A. The Modern Uzbeks: From the Fourteenth Century to the Present, a Cultural History. (Publication Series: Studies of Nationalities in the U. S. S. R.: No. 373). 410p. 1990. pap. 24.95 (*0-8179-8732-0*) Hoover Inst Pr.

Allworth, Edward A., ed. The Tatars of Crimea: Return to the Homeland. 2nd enl. rev. ed. LC 97-19110. (Central Asia Book Ser.). (Illus.). ix, 380p. 1998. lib. bdg. 59.95 (*0-8223-1985-3*) Duke.

— The Tatars of Crimea: Return to the Homeland. 2nd expanded rev. ed. LC 97-19110. (Central Asia Book Ser.). (Illus.). ix, 380p. 1998. pap. text 19.95 (*0-8223-1994-2*) Duke.

Allworth, Louise M. Battle Ground, in & Around: A Pictorial Drama of Early Northwest Pioneer Life. 2nd ed. LC 75-43292. (Illus.). 400p. 1984. reprint ed. 30.00 (*0-9613899-0-7*) Write Stuff.

Allworth, S. T. & Zobel, R. N. Introduction to Real-Time Software Design. 2nd ed. 1990. pap. 38.00 (*0-387-91307-6*) Spr-Verlag.

Allworthy, A. W. The Petition Against God: The Full Story Behind RM-2493. LC 75-43375. (Illus.). 150p. 1976. pap. 3.95 (*0-917320-07-7*) Mho & Mho.

Allwright, A. D. & Oliver, O. Contracting for Goods & Services. 194p. (C). 1986. 110.00 (*0-7855-5748-2*, Pub. by Inst Pur & Supply) St Mut.

Allwright, A. D. & Oliver, R. W. Contracting for Goods & Services. 194p. (C). 1988. 60.00 (*0-7855-3775-9*, Pub. by Inst Pur & Supply) St Mut.

— Contracting for Goods & Services. 194p. (C). 1989. 90.00 (*0-7855-4640-5*, Pub. by Inst Pur & Supply) St Mut.

Allwright, A. D., jt. auth. see Oliver, R. W.

Allwright, Richard & Bailey, Kathleen M. Focus on the Language Classroom: An Introduction to Classroom Research for Language Teachers. (New Directions in Language Teaching Ser.). 270p. (C). 1991. pap. text 20.95 (*0-521-26909-1*) Cambridge U Pr.

— Focus on the Language Classroom: An Introduction to Classroom Research for Language Teachers. (New Directions in Language Teaching Ser.). 270p. (C). 1991. text 54.95 (*0-521-26279-8*) Cambridge U Pr.

Allyn. AIDS. 1996. text 49.50 (*0-205-26852-8*) Allyn.

— Education 1996. 1996. pap. text. write for info. (*0-205-26438-7*) Allyn.

Allyn. Humanities Titles 96. 1996. pap. text. write for info. (*0-205-26446-8*) Allyn.

Allyn. Math Analysis in Business & Economy. 1999. text 12.32 (*0-205-13780-6*) P-H.

Allyn. Playing the Game. 1996. text 49.50 (*0-205-26868-4*) Allyn.

— Psyched. 1.2 World Psy. 1996. text 24.95 (*0-205-26173-6*) Allyn.

— Social Science Titles 96. 1996. pap. text. write for info. (*0-205-26451-4*) Allyn.

Allyn. Sociology. 3rd ed. 1996. pap. text. write for info. (*0-205-26865-X*) Allyn.

— Using & Documenting Electricity. 1995. pap. text 4.00 (*0-205-19578-4*) Allyn.

Allyn & Bacon. Chemistry Molecular Model. 1p. 1986. 33.00 (*0-205-10345-6*) Addison-Wesley.

Allyn & Bacon Editorial Staff. General Education Case Series. (C). 1996. pap. text 40.00 (*0-205-18551-7*) Allyn.

***Allyn & Bacon Incorporate Staff.** Curriculum Planning: New Approach. 7th ed. LC 99-17383. 548p. (C). 1999. pap. text 68.00 (*0-205-30710-8*) Allyn.

***Allyn & Bacon Incorporated Staff.** Graduate Students on Teaching Writing. LC 99-32224. 290p. (C). 1999. pap. text 29.00 (*0-205-30696-9*) Allyn.

***Allyn & Bacon Incorporated Staff, ed.** Applying Sociology. (C). 2001. text 24.00 (*0-205-30616-0*) Allyn.

Allyn & Bacon Incorporated Staff, ed. Contemporary Health Communications. 2000. 30.67 (*0-205-30777-9*, Longwood Div) Allyn.

— Contemporary Social Problems & Careers in Sociology. 4th ed. (C). 1998. text 50.00 (*0-205-30445-1*) Allyn.

— Criminology. 7th ed. 624p. (C). 2000. 64.00 (*0-205-30775-2*) Allyn.

***Allyn & Bacon Incorporated Staff, ed.** Effective Practices for Diverse Classrooms. (C). 2000. text 49.00 (*0-205-30628-4*) Allyn.

— A Family. 9th ed. 304p. (C). 1999. write for info. (*0-205-30761-2*) Allyn.

— Four In One: Thinking, Reading, Writing & Researching. (C). 1999. text. write for info. (*0-205-30266-1*) Allyn.

— Grammar in the Classroom. 2nd ed. (C). 2000. text 59.00 (*0-205-30655-1*) Allyn.

— Group Counseling. (C). 2000. text 53.00 (*0-205-30630-6*) Allyn.

Allyn & Bacon Incorporated Staff, ed. Health & Culture. (C). 2001. 37.33 (*0-205-30764-7*) Allyn.

***Allyn & Bacon Incorporated Staff, ed.** Health Care Policy. (C). 2000. text 34.67 (*0-205-30672-1*) Allyn.

— Human Relations & Educational Leadership. (C). 2001. text 64.00 (*0-205-30631-4*) Allyn.

Allyn & Bacon Incorporated Staff, ed. Human Service Agencies: An Orientation to Field Work. (C). 2001. 26.67 (*0-205-30762-0*, Longwood Div) Allyn.

***Allyn & Bacon Incorporated Staff, ed.** In Conflict & Order. 9th ed. 608p. (C). 2000. text 46.00 (*0-205-30644-6*) Allyn.

— An Introduction to Group Work Practice. 4th ed. LC 99-87491. 560p. 2000. 56.00 (*0-205-30763-9*) Allyn.

Allyn & Bacon Incorporated Staff, ed. An Introduction to Human Services: Policy & Practice. 4th ed. (C). 1999. write for info. (*0-205-30758-2*) Allyn.

***Allyn & Bacon Incorporated Staff, ed.** Introduction to Teaching Students with High Incidence Disabilities. (C). 2000. text 57.33 (*0-205-30632-2*) Allyn.

— Lower Level Reading Skills. 2000. 34.00 (*0-205-30755-8*) Allyn.

Allyn & Bacon Incorporated Staff, ed. Modern Educational Measurement. 3rd ed. 128p. (C). 1999. write for info. (*0-205-30757-4*) Allyn.

— The Natural Speaker. 3rd ed. 48p. (C). 1999. write for info. (*0-205-30759-0*) Allyn.

— Psychology. 7th ed. (C). 1999. write for info. (*0-205-30737-X*) Allyn.

— Radio Broadcasting Industry. 256p. 2000. pap. text 33.00 (*0-205-30791-4*) Allyn.

***Allyn & Bacon Incorporated Staff, ed.** Readings in the Psychology of Gender. 2000. 32.00 (*0-205-30594-6*) Allyn.

Allyn & Bacon Incorporated Staff, ed. Social Problems. 8th ed. 608p. 1999. write for info. (*0-205-30786-8*); write for info. (*0-205-30787-6*); pap. 20.00 (*0-205-30784-1*) Allyn.

— Social Problems. 8th ed. 176p. 2000. write for info. (*0-205-30785-X*) Allyn.

— Social Psychology. 9th ed. 1999. write for info. (*0-205-30788-4*) Allyn.

— Social Security. LC 99-50146. (English Workers & the Coming of the Welfare Ser.). 160p. 2000. pap. 20.00 (*0-205-30790-6*) Allyn.

***Allyn & Bacon Incorporated Staff, ed.** Social Studies for Children. 12th ed. 1999. write for info. (*0-205-30730-2*) Allyn.

— Sociological Social Psychology. (C). 2000. text 58.67 (*0-205-30666-7*) Allyn.

— Sociology: Concepts & Applications in a Diverse World. 5th ed. 544p. (C). 2000. pap. text 35.00 (*0-205-30596-2*) Allyn.

— The Stereotypical World of Sociology, Vol. 1. 1998. VHS 21.95 (*0-205-29897-4*) Allyn.

— Supporting African-American Children. 2000. 40.00 (*0-205-30651-9*) Allyn.

— Teachers, Computers & Curriculum. 3rd ed. 1999. write for info. (*0-205-30729-9*) Allyn.

— Teaching Elementary Language Arts. 6th ed. 112p. 1999. write for info. (*0-205-30723-X*) Allyn.

Allyn & Bacon Incorporated Staff, ed. Teaching in America. 2nd ed. (C). 1999. write for info. (*0-205-30731-0*) Allyn.

— Technical Writing. 4th ed. (C). 1999. write for info. (*0-205-30724-8*) Allyn.

— Ten Things Every College Student Should Know. 64p. (C). 1999. write for info. (*0-205-30769-8*) Allyn.

— Testing! Testing! What Every Parent Should Know about School Tests. LC 99-37785. 289p. 1999. pap. 18.99 (*0-205-30595-4*) Allyn.

***Allyn & Bacon Incorporated Staff, ed.** Whole Writing Teacher. (C). 2000. 33.00 (*0-205-30576-8*) Allyn.

— The World of Psychology. (C). 1998. text. write for info. (*0-205-30617-9*) Allyn.

Allyn & Bacon Staff. Human Sexuality. 4th ed. (C). 1999. student ed. 15.00 (*0-205-30553-9*) Allyn.

***Allyn & Bacon Staff.** Total Health: Achieving Your Personal Best Telecourse (20- 1999. pap. text 2120.00 (*0-205-29139-2*) Allyn.

Allyn & Bacon Staff. Volleyball. 64p. (C). 1998. pap. text 10.00 (*0-536-01255-5*) Pearson Custom.

Allyn & Bacon Staff, ed. Attaining Competence for School Administrators. LC 99-46206. 227p. (C). 1999. pap. text 30.00 (*0-205-30613-6*) Allyn.

— Literacy Development in the Early Years: Helping Children Read & Write. 4th ed. LC 00-20251. 400p. (C). 2000. pap. text 48.00 (*0-205-30589-X*) Allyn.

Allyn, Bruce & Findlay, Esther B. Your Rugged Constitution. 3rd ed. (Illus.). 296p. (C). 1969. 35.00 (*0-8047-0405-8*) Stanford U Pr.

Allyn, Bruce J., et al, eds. Back to the Brink: Proceedings of the Moscow Conference on the Cuban Missile Crisis, January 27-28, 1989. (Occasional Papers: No. 9). 248p. (Orig.). (C). 1992. lib. bdg. 48.50 (*0-8191-7923-X*) U Pr of Amer.

Allyn, Charles. The Battle of Groton Heights: A Collection of Narratives, Official Reports, Records, Etc., of the Storming of Ft. Griswold. (Illus.). 399p. 1992. reprint ed. lib. bdg. 42.50 (*0-8328-6526-5*) Higginson Bk Co.

Allyn, Charles, ed. Florida Fishes. LC 82-84138. 80p. 1982. pap. 3.95 (*0-8200-0122-8*) Great Outdoors.

Allyn, David. Make Love, Not War: The Sexual Revolution: An Unfettered History. 2000. write for info. (*0-316-03916-0*) Little.

***Allyn, David.** Make Love, Not War: The Sexual Revolution: An Unfettered History. LC 99-33784. (Illus.). 432p. (gr. 8). 2000. 26.95 (*0-316-03930-6*) Little.

Allyn, Doug. All Creatures Dark & Dangerous: The Dr. David Westbrook Stories. 200p. 1999. 30.00 (*1-885941-31-5*); pap. 16.00 (*1-885941-32-3*) Crippen & Landru.

— Black Water, Vol. 1. 1997. mass mkt. 5.99 (*0-312-96150-2*) St Martin.

— A Dance in Deep Water: A Mitch Mitchell Mystery. LC 97-17822. 256p. 1997. text 22.95 (*0-312-16807-1*) St Martin.

— Icewater Mansions. 1996. mass mkt. 5.50 (*0-312-95764-5*, Pub. by Tor Bks) St Martin.

Allyn, E. G. Bua Luang Compact Transliterated Thai-English Dictionary. Chaiyana, Samorn, ed. 396p. 1998. pap. 14.95 (*0-942777-18-2*) Floating Lotus.

— The Bua Luang Compact WYSIWYS English-Thai Dictionary. 349p. (Orig.). 1994. pap. 12.95 (*0-942777-13-1*) Floating Lotus.

***Allyn, E. G.** The Men of Thailand: Thailand's Culture & Gay Subculture for Travelers. 7th ed. Chaiyana, Samorn, ed. (Illus.). 524p. 1999. pap. 23.95 (*0-942777-30-1*) Floating Lotus.

Allyn, E. G. Thai Phrase Handbook: What You See Is What You Say. Inpradith, Somboon & Benchamat, Nukul, eds. LC 91-76316. (Illus.). 304p. (Orig.). (C). 1993. pap. 14.95 (*0-942777-04-2*) Floating Lotus.

Allyn, E. G., ed. The Dove Coos II: Gay Experiences by the Men of Thailand. Jonathon, David, tr. 175p. (Orig.). 1993. reprint ed. pap. 14.00 (*0-942777-09-3*) Floating Lotus.

Allyn, Edward. How to Start a Mail Order Business. 1987. 20.00 (*0-318-24038-6*) Allyn Air.

— Mold Design I: For Plastic Injection. (Illus.). 69p. (C). 1987. student ed. 15.00 (*0-9619068-6-3*) Allyn Air.

Allyn, Elizabeth P., et al. A Guide to Historic Houses in Ohio Open to the Public. 2nd rev. ed. LC 84-62235. (Illus.). 112p. (Orig.). 1996. pap. 10.50 (*0-9650831-0-1*) Nat Soc Colnal Dames.

Allyn, G. Abnormal Psychology. (C). 1997. write for info. (*0-205-27966-X*, Macmillan Coll) P-H.

Allyn, Jan, contrib. by. Handbook of Landscape Palms. (Illus.). 70p. (Orig.). 1995. pap. 6.95 (*0-8200-0412-X*) Great Outdoors.

Allyn, John. Forty-Seven Ronin Story. LC 70-121274. (Illus.). 240p. 1970. pap. 9.95 (*0-8048-0196-7*) Tuttle Pubng.

Allyn, Joyce, ed. see Anderson, Robert.

Allyn, Nancy E. The Right to Vote. LC 86-16480. (Milestone Documents in the National Archives Ser.). 26p. 1988. pap. text 0.50 (*0-911333-51-7*, 200108) National Archives & Recs.

Allyn, Nancy E., compiled by. Broadsides & Posters from the National Archives. LC 86-743. (Illus.). 32p. 1986. pap. text 2.50 (*0-911333-37-1*, 200049) National Archives & Recs.

Allyn, Oliver. Dreams of a Landlocked Boatman: Adventures on the Connecticut River. LC 98-9161. 1998. pap. 15.00 (*1-880158-18-3*) J N Townsend.

Allyn, Rube. How to Cook Your Catch. 80p. (Orig.). 1963. pap. 3.95 (*0-8200-0801-X*) Great Outdoors.

Allyn, Stan. The Day the Sun Didn't Rise. LC 91-73404. (Illus.). 128p. 1991. pap. 10.00 (*0-8323-0487-5*) Binford Mort.

— Heave To! You'll Drown Yourselves! 3rd ed. LC 82-72425. (Illus.). 160p. 1992. pap. 10.00 (*0-8323-0409-3*) Binford Mort.

— Top Deck Twenty! Best West Coast Sea Stories! LC 89-60951. (Illus.). 160p. (Orig.). 1989. pap. 10.00 (*0-8323-0469-7*) Binford Mort.

Allyne, Kerry. Beneath Wimmera Skies. large type ed. 272p. 1993. 27.99 (*0-7505-0553-2*, Pub. by Mgna Lrg Print) Ulverscroft.

— Carpentaria Moon. large type ed. 269p. 1993. 27.99 (*0-7505-0441-2*, Pub. by Mgna Lrg Print) Ulverscroft.

— Disastrous Encounters. large type ed. (Magna Large Print Ser.). 1994. 27.99 (*0-7505-0669-5*, Pub. by Mgna Lrg Print) Ulverscroft.

— Return to Wallaby Creek. large type ed. (Magna Romance Ser.). 266p. 1992. 27.99 (*0-7505-0413-7*) Ulverscroft.

Allyson, Margaret, ed. see Sheats, Cliff & Greenwood-Robinson, Maggie.

Allyson, Trudy E. Lumbar Vertebrae & Injuries: Medical Subject Analysis with Reference Bibliography. LC 85-48091. 150p. 1987. 47.50 (*0-88164-454-4*); pap. 44.50 (*0-88164-455-2*) ABBE Pubs Assn.

Allyson, Wendy, ed. see Gudger, S. I.

Alm, Alvin L. & Weiner, Robert, eds. Oil Shock: Policy Response & Implementation. LC 83-22459. 256p. 1984. text 32.00 (*0-88410-900-3*, HarpBusn) HarpInfo.

Alm, Andy, jt. auth. see Rohwedder, W. J.

Alm, Goran. Great Royal Palaces of Sweden: Vasa to Bernadotte. 1998. 75.00 (*0-935748-99-7*) Scala Books.

Alm, Irene. Catalog of Venetian Librettos at the University of California, Los Angeles. LC 92-24457. (UC Publications in Catalogs & Bibliographies: Vol. 9). 1992. 150.00 (*0-520-09762-9*, Pub. by U CA Pr) Cal Prin Full Svc.

Alm, Kristie. Turkey: The Perfect Food for Every Occasion! 1993. pap. 3.99 (*0-425-14092-X*) Berkley Pub.

***Alm, Leslie R.** Crossing Borders, Crossing Boundaries: The Role of Scientists in the U.S. Acid Rain Debate. LC 99-88624. 160p. 2000. 55.00 (*0-275-96916-9*, Praeger Pubs) Greenwood.

Alm, Richard, jt. auth. see Cox, W. Michael.

Almaas, A. H. Diamond Heart Bk. 1: Elements of the Real in Man. LC 86-71832. 247p. (Orig.). 1989. pap. 12.00 (*0-936713-01-1*) Diamond Bks CA.

— Diamond Heart Bk. 2: The Freedom to Be. LC 88-51949. 211p. (Orig.). 1989. pap. 12.00 (*0-936713-04-6*) Diamond Bks CA.

— Diamond Heart Bk. 3: Being & the Meaning of Life. LC 90-81060. 211p. (Orig.). 1990. pap. 12.00 (*0-936713-05-4*) Diamond Bks CA.

— Diamond Heart Bk. 4: Indestructible Innocence. LC 97-68082. 370p. (Orig.). 1997. pap. 14.00 (*0-936713-11-9*) Diamond Bks CA.

— Essence with the Elixir of Enlightenment: The Diamond Approach to Inner Realization, 2 vols. in 1. LC 97-43966. 272p. 1998. pap. 14.95 (*1-57863-044-4*) Weiser.

***Almaas, A. H.** Facets of Unity: The Enneagram of Holy Ideas. 316p. 1999. pap. 18.00 (*0-936713-14-3*) Diamond Bks CA.

Almaas, A. H. Heart Dweller. 32p. 1996. 6.50 (*0-936713-13-5*) Diamond Bks CA.

— Luminous Night's Journey: An Autobiographical Fragment. LC 96-84412. 131p. 1995. pap. 14.00 (*0-936713-08-9*, 11300) Diamond Bks CA.

— The Pearl Beyond Price: Integration of Personality into Being: An Object Relations Approach. LC 87-51720. (Diamond Mind Ser.: Bk. 2). 506p. 1988. pap. 19.50 (*0-936713-02-X*) Diamond Bks CA.

— The Point of Existence: Transformations of Narcissism in Self-Realization. LC 96-84403. 602p. 1996. pap. 21.50 (*0-936713-09-7*) Diamond Bks CA.

— The Void: A Psychodynamic Investigation of the Relationship Between Mind & Space. 2nd ed. LC 85-82559. (Diamond Mind Ser.: Bk. 1). 160p. (Orig.). 1986. pap. 14.00 (*0-936713-06-2*) Diamond Bks CA.

— Work on the Superego. Maitri, Sandra, ed. 20p. 1992. 4.00 (*0-936713-07-0*) Diamond Bks CA.

Almaas, Ingerid Helsing. Vienna. (Architecture in Context Ser.). (ENG, FRE & GER., Illus.). 80p. 1997. pap. 9.95 (*3-89508-270-8*, 810087) Konemann.

— Vienna: A Guide to Recent Architecture. LC 98-148403. 320 p. 1995. write for info. (*1-899858-02-4*) Ellipsis.

— Vienna: Architecture Guide. (Architecture Guides Ser.). (Illus.). 320p. 1997. pap. 5.95 (*3-89508-279-1*) Konemann.

ALMACA Staff. Continuum of Services. pap. 5.00 (*0-318-22971-4*) EAPA.

— Standards for Employee Assistance Programs. pap. 20.00 (*0-318-22967-6*) EAPA.

ALMACA Staff & Atlantic-Richfield Company Staff. A Guide for Supervisors. pap. 3.00 (*0-318-22968-4*) EAPA.

Almack, John C., ed. Modern School Administration. LC 78-121445. (Essay Index Reprint Ser.). 1977. 23.95 (*0-8369-1902-5*) Ayer.

Almada, Carlos, jt. auth. see Medeiros, Flavio Henrique.

Almada, Jose L., et al, eds. Coastlines of Mexico. LC 93-14142. (Coastlines of the World Ser.). 176p. 1993. 23.00 (*0-87262-963-5*) Am Soc Civil Eng.

Almadari, F. Cold Dorwn-Draughts. 1995. pap. 60.00 (*0-86022-401-5*, Pub. by Build Servs Info Assn) St Mut.

Almade, Frank D. Just Wages for Church Employees. LC 93-17331. (American University Studies, VII, Theology & Religion: Vol. 153). XIV, 202p. (C). 1994. text 39.95 (*0-8204-2126-X*) P Lang Pubng.

Almagno, Romano S. & Harkins, Conrad L. Studies Honoring Ignatius Charles Brady, Friar Minor. (Theology Ser.). 496p. 1976. pap. 25.00 (*1-57659-029-1*) Franciscan Inst.

Almagor, Gila. Under the Domim Tree. Schenker, Hillel, tr. LC 95-3356. 176p. (J). (gr. 7 up). 1995. 15.00 (*0-671-89020-4*) S&S Bks Yung.

Almagor, Uri. Pastoral Partners: Affinity & Bond Partnership among the Dassanetch of South-West Ethiopia. LC 78-4128. 258p. 1978. 49.50 (*0-8419-0384-0*, Africana) Holmes & Meier.

Almagor, Uri, jt. ed. see Maybury-Lewis, David.

Almagro, Bertha, compiled by. Early American Medical Imprints, 1668-1820: Subject, Name, & Format Index to the Microfilm Collection. 23p. (C). 1981. pap. text 55.00 (*0-89235-027-X*) Primary Srce Media.

Almagro, M., ed. see Menendez Pidal, Ramon.

Almagro, Martin, et al. Historia de Espana No. 1: Espana Primitiva: La Historia Preromana, Vol. 3. 852p. 1992. 189.50 (*84-239-4803-X*) Elliots Bks.

— Historia de Espana Vol. 2: Espana Primitiva: La Protohistoria. 720p. 1992. 189.50 (*84-239-4802-1*) Elliots Bks.

Almaguer, Tomas. Racial Fault Lines: The Historical Origins of White Supremacy in California. LC 93-42513. 1994. pap. 17.95 (*0-520-08947-2*, Pub. by U CA Pr) Cal Prin Full Svc.

Alman, Brian. Thin Meditations: Weight-loss for the Mind & Body. 200p. (Orig.). 1995. teacher ed. 19.95 (*0-9644867-5-X*); pap. 19.95 (*0-9644867-3-3*); text 19.95 (*0-9644867-2-5*); pap. text 19.95 (*0-9644867-4-1*); lib. bdg. 19.95 (*0-9644867-1-7*) Longevity Educ.

— Thin Meditations: Weight-loss for the Mind & Body. 200p. (Orig.). 1995. 22.95 (*0-9644867-0-9*) Longevity Educ.

Alman, Brian M. & Lambrou, Peter T. Self-Hypnosis: The Complete Manual for Health & Self-Change. 2nd ed. LC 91-29007. (Illus.). 304p. 1991. pap. 22.95 (*0-87630-650-4*) Brunner-Mazel.

Alman, David. World Full of Strangers. LC 74-29040. (Labor Movement in Fiction & Non-Fiction Ser.). reprint ed. 49.50 (*0-404-58521-3*) AMS Pr.

Alman, Isadora. Sex Information, May I Help You? LC 92-6939. Orig. Title: Aural Sex & Verbal Intercourse. 176p. (Orig.). (YA). (gr. 11 up). 1992. pap. 9.50 (*0-940208-14-8*) Down There Pr.

Almand, J. D. Frustration Road. LC 90-43992. 1990. pap. 14.95 (*0-87949-323-2*) Ashley Bks.

Almand, L. Davis. Home Security for Single People: A Basic Guide to Secure Living. 160p. (C). 1995. pap. 12.95 (*1-886094-07-1*) Chicago Spectrum.

Almand, Warren, et al. CLAST - College Level Academic Skills Test. (Illus.). 570p. 1999. pap. text 18.95 (*0-87891-933-3*) Res & Educ.

Almaney, A. J. Strategic Management: A Framework for Decision Making & Problem Solving. 370p. (C). 1992. pap. text 31.95 (*1-879215-04-7*) Sheffield WI.

— Strategic Management: The Process of Gaining a Competitive Advantage. 3rd ed. 443p. 1997. pap. 34.80 (*0-87563-801-5*) Stipes.

Almansa, Andres De, see De Almansa, Andres.

Almansa, Isabel P. Como Leer a Juan Ramon Jimenez. 45.50 (*0-685-69530-1*) Scripta.

Almanza, Barbara, ed. Foodservice Planning: Layout, design, & Equipment. 4th ed. LC 99-31236. (Illus.). 532p. (C). 1999. 75.00 (*0-13-096446-8*) P-H.

Almanza, Estella, jt. auth. see Baca, Leonard M.

Almanza, Francisco G., tr. see Baker, R. A.

Almanzar, Jose A. El Sabor de lo Prohibido: Antologia Personal. (Caribbean Collection). 1993. pap. 11.50 (*0-8477-0188-3*) U of PR Pr.

Almaraz, ed. Texas: A History of Five Centuries. (C). 1999. pap. text, student ed. write for info. (0-321-01228-3) Addison-Wesley.

Almaraz, Felix D., Jr. The San Antonio Missions & Their System of Land Tenure. (Illus.). 118p. 1989. 19.95 (0-292-74653-9) U of Tex Pr.

Almaraz, Felix D., ed. The Mexican Borderlands. (Illus.). 116p. 1985. pap. 15.00 (0-89745-066-3) Sunflower U Pr.

Almaraz, Felix D., Jr., et al. Borderlands: The Heritage of the Lower Rio Grande Through the Art of Jose Cisneros. Nirenberg, Jackie, ed. (Illus.). 159p. 1998. write for info. (1-888594-03-9) Hidalgo Cty Hist Mus.

Almaraz, Humberto. Santa Will Love My Tree (Play Format) (Illus.). 12p. (Orig.). (J). (ps-3). 1982. pap. 5.00 incl. lp (0-9616528-1-0) Alpha Beto Music.

— Santa Will Love My Tree (Story Format) 12p. (Orig.). (J). (ps-2). 1982. pap. 5.00 incl. lp (0-9616528-0-2) Alpha Beto Music.

***Almarez, Felix D.** Knight Without Armor: Carlos Eduardo Castaneda, 1896-1958. LC 99-24693. 1999. 39.95 (0-89096-890-X) Tex A&M Univ Pr.

Almario, Lyn, ed. see O'Boyle, Lily G. & Alejandro, Reynaldo.

Almarode, Jay. Multi-User Smalltalk. (Management Briefings Ser.). 51p. 1996. 85.00 (1-884842-68-2, QA76) SIGS Bks & Multimedia.

Almasi, David, jt. auth. see Ridenour, David A.

Almasi, George S. & Gottlieb, Allan. Highly Parallel Computing. (Illus.). 600p. (C). 1989. text 56.95 (0-8053-0177-1) Benjamin-Cummings.

Almasi, George S. & Gottlieb, Allan. Highly Parallel Computing: Solutions Manual. 2nd ed. student ed. write for info. (0-8053-0445-2) Benjamin-Cummings.

Almasi, Janice F., jt. ed. see Gambrell, Linda B.

Almasi, Miklos. The Philosophy of Appearances. 294p. (C). 1989. 150.00 (963-05-4554-3, Pub. by Akade Kiado) St Mut.

— The Philosophy of Appearances. 300p. (C). 1989. text 171.00 (90-277-2150-5, D Reidel) Kluwer Academic.

Almassy, Stephen E., jt. auth. see Burrill, G. Steven.

Almayrac, G., tr. see Bouisson, Maurice.

Almazan, Vincent, tr. see Rohlfs, Gerhard.

Almbladh, Karin. Studies in the Book of Jonah. (Studia Semitica Upsaliensia: No. 7). 54p. (Orig.). 1986. pap. text 25.00 (91-554-1535-0, Pub. by Uppsala Univ Acta Univ Uppsaliensis) Coronet Bks.

Almdal, Preben. Aspects of European Integration: A View of the European Community & the Nordic Countries. 108p. (Orig.). 1986. pap. text 30.00 (87-7492-578-4, Pub. by Odense Universitets Forlag) Coronet Bks.

Almeda, Frank & Pringle, Catherine M., eds. Tropical Rainforests: Diversity & Conservation. LC 88-70979. (Memoirs of the California Academy of Sciences Ser.: No. 12). (Illus.). 1988. 30.00 (0-940228-19-X) Calif Acad Sci.

Almeder, Robert. Harmless Naturalism: The Limits of Science & the Nature of Philosophy. LC 97-53307. 240p. 1998. 52.95 (0-8126-9379-5); pap. 24.95 (0-8126-9380-9) Open Court.

Almeder, Robert. Human Happiness & Morality: A Brief Introduction to Ethics. LC 99-48053. 210p. 2000. pap. 18.95 (1-57392-760-0) Prometheus Bks.

***Almeder, Robert.** Human Happiness & Morality: A Brief Introduction to Ethics. LC 99-48053. 210p. 2000. 49.95 (1-57392-759-7) Prometheus Bks.

Almeder, Robert, jt. auth. see Humber, James M.

Almeder, Robert E., jt. ed. see Humber, James M.

Almeder, Robert F. Blind Realism: An Essay on Human Knowledge & Natural Science. 288p. (C). 1991. text 52.00 (0-8476-7709-5) Rowman.

— Blind Realism: An Essay on Human Knowledge & Natural Science. 288p. 1996. pap. text 23.95 (0-8476-8280-3) Rowman.

Almeder, Robert F. & Humber, James M., eds. Quantitative Risk Assessment. LC 84-640015. (Biomedical Ethics Reviews Ser.: No. 1986). 278p. 1987. 49.50 (0-89603-056-3) Humana.

Almeder, Robert F., jt. auth. see Fetzer, James H.

Almeder, Robert F., jt. ed. see Humber, James M.

Almedia, Rhea V. Expansions of Feminist Family Theory Through Diversity. 1994. pap. 19.95 (1-56023-063-0, Harrington Park) Haworth Pr.

Almedom, Astier M., et al. Hygiene Evaluation Procedures. 130p. 1997. pap. 10.00 (0-9635522-8-7, Pub. by Int Nutrit Fnd) Stylus Pub VA.

Almeida, A. Betamio De, see De Almeida, A. Betamio, ed.

Almeida, A. T. De, see De Almeida, A. T.

Almeida, A. T. De, see Casals, A. & De Almeida, A. T., eds.

Almeida, Abraao De, see De Almeida, Abraao.

Almeida, Alvaro, jt. auth. see Sperandeo, Victor.

Almeida, Anibal T. De, see De Almeida, Anibal T., ed.

Almeida, Anibaltde, et al. Energy Efficiency Improvements in Electric Motors & Drives. LC 97-22628. x, 511p. 1997. text. write for info. (3-540-63068-6) Spr-Verlag.

Almeida, Anna L. Ozorio De, see Ozorio de Almeida, Anna L.

Almeida, Antonio de. Thematic Catalogue of the Works of Jacques Offenbach, 2 vol. set. (Illus.). 1168p. 2000. 265.00 (0-19-315267-3) OUP.

Almeida, Arthur A., et al. The Vincent Thomas Bridge: San Pedro's "Golden Gate" (Illus.). 48p. (Orig.). 1988. pap. 3.00 (0-9611556-2-0) San Pedro Hist.

Almeida, Bira. Capoeira - A Brazilian Art Form: History, Philosophy, & Practice. LC 86-8553. (Illus.). 224p. 1986. pap. 14.95 (0-938190-29-6) North Atlantic.

***Almeida, Bira.** Capoeira Training Manual. 200p. 2001. pap. 18.95 (1-55643-364-6) North Atlantic.

Almeida, Darcy F. De, see De Almeida, Darcy F., ed.

***Almeida, Diane M.** The Esperpento Tradition in the Works of Rambon del Valle Inclban & Luis Budnuel. LC 00-41885. (Spanish Studies). (Illus.). 2000. write for info. (0-7734-7693-8) E Mellen.

Almeida, Hermione De, see De Almeida, Hermione.

Almeida, Irene M., ed. & intro. see Silka, Henry P.

Almeida, J., et al, eds. Lattices, Semigroups & Universal Algebra. (Illus.). 350p. (C). 1990. text 132.00 (0-306-43412-1, Kluwer Plenum) Kluwer Academic.

Almeida, J. & Atanasiu, P. Manual for Rapid Laboratory Viral Diagnosis. (WHO Offset Publications: No. 47). 48p. 1979. 4.00 (92-4-170047-5) World Health.

Almeida, J., jt. auth. see Pangborn, M.

Almeida, Jorge. Finite Semigroups & Universal Algebra. LC 94-27352. 532p. 1995. text 86.00 (981-02-1895-8) World Scientific Pub.

***Almeida, Laurindo.** Albeniz for Acoustic Guitar - Laurindo Almeida. 80p. 1999. pap. 14.95 (0-7866-3413-8, 97041) Mel Bay.

— Brazilian Refections: Intermediate-Advanced Level. 40p. 1996. pap. 19.95 incl. audio compact disk (0-7866-2101-X, 95984BCD) Mel Bay.

Almeida, Laurindo. Guitar Tutor. 9.95 (0-910468-03-6) Criterion Mus.

Almeida, Laurindo. Praise Every Morning: Intermediate-Advanced Level. 40p. 1996. pap. 19.95 incl. audio compact disk (0-7866-2100-1, 95983BCD) Mel Bay.

Almeida, Luis F. Cadena Y, see Cadena y Almeida, Luis F.

Almeida, Marcio, ed. Recent Developments in Soil & Pavement Mechanics: Proceedings of the International Symposium, Rio de Janeiro, Brazil, 25-27 June 1997. (Illus.). 512p. (C). 1997. text 123.00 (90-5410-885-1, Pub. by A A Balkema) Ashgate Pub Co.

Almeida, Margarite & Cavello, James. Katsuyuki Suzuki: Circus Magic. (Illus.). 28p. 1996. pap. 28.00 (0-9655834-0-6) Westwood Gallery.

Almeida, Miguel V. De, see De Almeida, Miguel V.

Almeida, O. F. & Shippenberg, T. S., eds. Neurobiology of Opioids. (Illus.). xxii, 456p. 1991. 182.95 (0-387-50835-X) Spr-Verlag.

Almeida, Onesimo T. L (U. S. A.) Landia: A De'Cima Ilha. 293p. 1987. pap. 10.00 (0-318-41700-6) Gavea-Brown.

Almeida, Onesimo T., ed. Jose Rodrigues Migueis: Lisbon in Manhattan. LC 83-83071. 216p. (Orig.). 1984. pap. 7.50 (0-943722-10-1) Gavea-Brown.

— The Sea Within. Monteiro, George, tr. from POR. LC 83-80877. (Illus.). 115p. (Orig.). 1983. pap. 3.50 (0-943722-09-8) Gavea-Brown.

***Almeida, Oscar D.** Microlaparascopy. 119p. 2000. 149.95 (0-471-34574-1) Wiley.

Almeida Prado, Bento L. De, see De Almeida Prado, Bento L.

***Almeida, Rhea V.** Transformations of Gender & Race: Family & Developmental Perspectives. LC 98-48952. 1998. write for info. (0-7890-0673-1) Haworth Pr.

Almeida, Rhea V., ed. Expansions of Feminist Family Theory Through Diversity. LC 94-175. (Journals of Feminist Family Therapy). (Illus.). 134p. (C). 1994. lib. bdg. 39.95 (1-56024-667-7) Haworth Pr.

— Transformations of Gender & Race: Family & Developmental Perspectives. 155p. 1999. 34.95 (0-7890-0655-3) Haworth Pr.

Almeida, Rui M. Halide Glasses for Infrared Fiberoptics. 1987. text 233.00 (90-247-3480-0) Kluwer Academic.

Almeida, S. A. S., jt. auth. see Fontes, F. Lima.

Almeida, S. M. Flora of the Savantwadi, 2 vols., Set, Vols. 1 & 2. (C). 1990. text 300.00 (81-85046-87-5, Pub. by Scientific Pubs) St Mut.

Almeida, Sherri-Lynne A., et al. Clinical Delegation in the Emergency Care Setting. (Regional Conference Ser.). (Illus.). Date not set. ring bd. 475.00 (0-935890-23-8) Emerg Nurses IL.

Almeida, T. Jaguar Hunting in the Matto-Grosso & Bolivia: With Notes on Other Game. 2nd ed. LC 92-130647. (Illus.). 313p. 1990. 35.00 (0-940143-21-6) Safari Pr.

Almeida-Val, V. M. De, see Val, A. L. & De Almeida-Val, V. M.

Almeida, W. F., jt. ed. see De Castro, A. F.

***Almekinder, Connie & De Boef, Walter.** Encouraging Diversity. 368p. 2000. pap. 25.00 (1-85339-510-2, Pub. by Intermed Tech) Stylus Pub VA.

***Almekinders, Conny & Louwaars, Niels.** Farmers' Seed Production: A New Handbook. 240p. 1999. pap. 29.95 (1-85339-466-1, Pub. by Intermed Tech) Stylus Pub VA.

Almekinders, Geert J. Foreign Exchange Intervention: Theory & Evidence. LC 95-6824. 240p. 1995. 95.00 (1-85898-263-4) E Elgar.

Almekinders, Louis C. Soft Tissue Injuries in Sports Medicine. 288p. 1995. pap. 54.95 (0-86542-382-2) Blackwell Sci.

Almeleh, Fiona. Plants & Flowers of the Desert. (Butterfly Bks.). 32p. (J). (gr. 3-5). 1985. 8.95 (0-86685-446-0) Intl Bk Ctr.

Almen, J. O. Durability of Automobile Gears. (Technical Papers: Vol. P122). (Illus.). 38p. 1935. pap. text 30.00 (1-55589-240-X) AGMA.

— Factors Influencing the Durability of Automobile Transmission Gears. (Technical Papers: Vol. P147). (Illus.). 25p. 1937. pap. text 30.00 (1-55589-243-4) AGMA.

— Facts & Fallacies of Stress Determination. (Technical Papers: Vol. P225). (Illus.). 27p. 1941. pap. text 30.00 (1-55589-270-1) AGMA.

— Improving the Fatigue Strength of Machine Parts. (Technical Papers: Vol. P233). (Illus.). 28p. 1943. pap. text 30.00 (1-55589-294-9) AGMA.

— Supplement to Factors Influencing the Durability of Automobile Transmission Gears. (Technical Papers: Vol. P164). (Illus.). 21p. 1937. pap. text 30.00 (1-55589-244-2) AGMA.

— Surface Deterioration of Gear Teeth. (Technical Papers: Vol. P219.02). (Illus.). 32p. 1948. pap. text 30.00 (1-55589-247-7) AGMA.

Almen, Lowell G. One Great Cloud of Witnesses: You & Your Congregation in the Evangelical Lutheran Church in America. LC 97-19707. 1997. 8.99 (0-8066-3622-X, 10-362210) Augsburg Fortress.

Almena, Fernando. El Bandido Carahigo. (Punto Infantil Ser.). (SPA.). (J). 1989. 10.60 (0-606-05253-4, Pub. by Turtleback) Demco.

— Pocachicha. 4th ed. (Punto Juvenil Ser.). (SPA.). (J). 1988. 10.05 (0-606-05551-7, Pub. by Turtleback) Demco.

Almenas, K. & Lee, R. Nuclear Engineering: An Introduction, Set. (Illus.). 568p. 1992. 118.95 incl. 5.25 hd (0-387-53960-3) Spr-Verlag.

***Almer, Ennis C.** Statistical Tricks & Traps: An Illustrated Guide to the Misuses of Statistics. (Illus.). 64p. (C). 1999. pap. text 11.95 (1-884585-23-X) Pyrczak Pub.

***Almere, Kay.** Encyclopedia of Mesoamerican Mythology. 2000. lib. bdg. 65.00 (0-87436-999-1) ABC-CLIO.

***Almes, Rosita.** Let Me Help You with Your Business: How I Made a Fortune by Following These Three Steps Motivation, Marketing, Management. LC 00-90140. 210p. 2000. pap. write for info. (0-9679083-0-2) Brand Wayn Pubns.

Almeyda, Gloria. Dinero que Cuenta: Servicios Financieros el Alcance de la Mujer Microempresaria.Tr. of Money Matters - Reaching Women Microentrepreneurs with Financial Services. (SPA.). 190p. 1997. pap. text 15.00 (1-886938-16-4) IADB.

— Money Matters: Reaching Women Microentrepreneurs with Financial Services.Tr. of Dinero que Cuenta - Servicios Financieros al Alcance de la Mujer Microempresaria. 190p. 1997. pap. text 15.00 (1-886938-15-6) IADB.

Almgren. Financial Mathematics. (Mathematics Ser.). 2002. 55.00 (0-534-36470-5) Brooks-Cole.

Almgren, F. J., Jr. Existence & Regularity Almost Everywhere of Solutions to Elliptic Variational Problems with Constraints. LC 75-41603. (Memoirs Ser.: No. 4/165). 199p. 1976. pap. 23.00 (0-8218-1865-1, MEMO/4/165) Am Math.

Almgren, Frederick J., Jr. Selected Works of Frederick J. Almgren, Jr. Taylor, Jean E., ed. LC 99-13039. 586p. 1999. 105.00 (0-8218-1067-7) Am Math.

Almgren, Frederick J., Jr., jt. ed. see Allard, William K.

Almgren, Gunnar, et al, eds. Improvement of Mine Productivity & Overall Economy by Modern Technology: 13th World Mining Congress, Stockholm, 31 May - 5 June 1987, 2 vols., Set. 995p. (C). 1987. text 336.00 (90-6191-701-8, Pub. by A A Balkema) Ashgate Pub Co.

— Mine Mechanization & Automation: Proceedings of the Second International Symposium on Mine Mechanization & Automation, Lulea, Sweden 7-10 June 1993. (Illus.). 827p. (C). 1993. text 181.00 (90-5410-314-0, Pub. by A A Balkema) Ashgate Pub Co.

Almgren, Gunnar, et al. Amelioration de la Productivite & Reduction Globale des Couts dans l'Industrie Miniere Grace a la Technologie Moderne. 645p. 1987. pap. 207.00 (90-6191-744-1, Pub. by A A Balkema) Ashgate Pub Co.

Almich, Anita & Almich, Dan. When Are We Going to Get There? A Guide to Help Travelers Answer That Question. (Illus.). 100p. (Orig.). 1997. pap. 11.95 (0-9650570-1-1) Evergreen Creations.

Almich, Dan. Cranberries &... LC 95-96075. 140p. (Orig.). 1995. pap. 11.95 (0-9650570-0-3) Evergreen Creations.

Almich, Dan, jt. auth. see Almich, Anita.

Almira, Jacques. La Fuite a Constantinople ou la Vie du Comte de Bonneval. (FRE.). 478p. 1988. pap. 17.95 (0-7859-2089-7, 2070379450) Fr & Eur.

— Le Voyage a Naucratis. (FRE.). 552p. 1990. pap. 21.95 (0-7859-2148-6, 2070382834) Fr & Eur.

Almirall, Jose R. & Furton, Kenneth G. Forensic Science Explained: Guide for Understanding the Use of Science I. 1999. 39.95 (0-8493-8123-1) CRC Pr.

Almirall, Leon V. Caninees & Coyotes. deluxe ed. (Illus.). 176p. 1995. 30.00 (0-614-04525-8) Donald R Hoflin.

Almirante, Jose. Diccionario Militar, 2 vols., Set. (SPA.). 700p. 1988. pap. 55.00 (0-7859-6497-5, 847823005X); pap. 105.00 (0-7859-6315-4, 8478230033) Fr & Eur.

— Diccionario Militar, Vol. 1. (SPA.). 600p. 1988. pap. 55.00 (0-7859-6316-2, 8478230041) Fr & Eur.

Almirol, Edwin B. Ethnic Identity & Social Negotiation: A Study of a Filipino Community in California. LC 83-45347. (Immigrant Communities & Ethnic Minorities in the U. S. & Canada Ser.: No. 10). 1985. 47.50 (0-404-19401-X) AMS Pr.

Almodovar, Antonio & Cardoso, Luis. History of Portuguese Economic Thought. LC 98-149947. (History of Economic Thought Ser.). 152p. (C). 1998. 75.00 (0-415-17887-8) Routledge.

Almodovar, Norma J. Cop to Call Girl. 360p. 1994. mass mkt. 5.50 (0-380-72304-2, Avon Bks) Morrow Avon.

Almodovar, Pedro. The Flower of My Secret. Bush, Peter, tr. LC 96-164178. (Illus.). (Orig.). 1997. pap. 13.95 (0-571-17870-7) Faber & Faber.

Almog, Joseph, et al, eds. Themes from Kaplan. (Illus.). 624p. 1989. text 65.00 (0-19-505217-X) OUP.

***Almog, Oz.** The Sabra: The Creation of the New Jew. Watzman, Haim, tr. (Illus.). 352p. 2000. 35.00 (0-520-21642-3, Pub. by U CA Pr) Cal Prin Full Svc.

Almog, Ruth. Death in the Rain: A Novel. Bilu, Dalya, tr. LC 91-61530. 216p. 1993. pap. 12.95 (1-878610-09-0) Red Crane Bks.

Almog, Shmuel, et al, eds. Zionism & Religion. LC 98-22925. (Tauber Institute Ser.: No. 30). 366p. 1998. text 50.00 (0-87451-882-2) U Pr of New Eng.

Almog, Shumel. Nationalism & Antisemitism in Modern Europe, 1815-1945. (Studies in Antisemitism). (Illus.). 186p. 1990. 59.95 (0-08-037254-6, Prgamon Press) Buttrwrth-Heinemann.

Almogi, Yosef. Total Commitment. LC 81-70146. (Illus.). 320p. 1982. 20.00 (0-8453-4749-7, Cornwall Bks) Assoc Univ Prs.

Almohar, Ariel, tr. see Gorbachev, Valeri.

Almoli, Solomon B. Dream Interpretation from Classical Jewish Sources. Elman, Yaakov, tr. from ENG. LC 98-12315. 1998. 22.95 (0-88125-533-5) Ktav.

Almon, Bert. Earth Prime. LC 94-156395. 96p. 1994. pap. 11.95 (0-919626-69-6, Pub. by Brick Bks) Genl Dist Srvs.

— Taking Possession. 1976. 6.85 (0-941490-17-3) Solo Pr.

— William Humphrey, Destroyer of Myths. LC 97-39058. (Texas Writers Ser.: No. 6). 462p. 1998. 23.00 (1-57441-044-X) UNTX Pr.

Almon, Clopper. Craft of Economic Modeling. 2nd ed. 312p. (C). 1990. text 38.60 (0-536-57784-6) Pearson Custom.

Almon, Clopper. A Study Companion to an Outline of Esoteric Science. LC 99-185479. 96p. 1998. pap. 10.95 (0-88010-453-8, 3011) Anthroposophic.

Almon, Harold, ed. After Your/My Accident: Harold Almon's Guide to: A Plan for "Just in Case" rev. ed. 50p. 1996. spiral bd. 12.95 (0-917921-00-3) Bee At Ease Pr.

— Business Hospitality Protocols: Harold Almon's Guide to: Giving Back & Saying Thank You. rev. ed. 80p. 1997. spiral bd. 19.95 (0-917921-05-4) Bee At Ease Pr.

— Business Social Protocols: Harold Almon's Guide to: Things One Business Man Will Tell Another. rev. ed. 100p. 1996. spiral bd. 19.95 (0-917921-16-X) Bee At Ease Pr.

— Creative Table Setting: Harold Almon's Guide to: Creatively Setting & Seating Your Table. rev. ed. 85p. 1996. spiral bd. 19.95 (0-917921-23-2) Bee At Ease Pr.

— Executive Dining Protocols: Harold Almon's Guide to: Being Excruciatingly Fork Literate & Considerate. rev. ed. 95p. 1996. spiral bd. 19.95 (0-917921-24-0) Bee At Ease Pr.

— Flawless Dining Service: Harold Almon's Guide to: Dining Service Flawlessly Provided. rev. ed. (Illus.). 102p. (Orig.). 1998. spiral bd. 29.95 (0-917921-11-9) Bee At Ease Pr.

— Life's Little Talks: Harold Almon's Guide to: Insightful Things Someone Meant to Tell You When You Think You Have Had It. rev. ed. 55p. 1996. spiral bd. 12.95 (0-917921-14-3) Bee At Ease Pr.

— Male Care Matters: Harold Almon's Guide to: Things Someone Will Tell a Son. rev. ed. (Illus.). 93p. 1996. spiral bd. 19.95 (0-917921-12-7) Bee At Ease Pr.

Almon, John, ed. A Collection of Papers Relative to the Dispute Between Great Britain & America, 1764-1775. LC 70-146272. (Era of the American Revolution Ser.). 1971. reprint ed. lib. bdg. 39.50 (0-306-70127-8) Da Capo.

Almon, Russell. Kid Can't Miss. 224p. (YA). 1992. pap. 3.50 (0-380-76261-7, Avon Bks) Morrow Avon.

Almond, Angela. Get It Taped: Recording & Using Audio Cassettes in Church. (C). 1989. 25.00 (0-9510086-3-3, Pub. by Jay Bks) St Mut.

Almond, Barbara & Almond, Richard. The Therapeutic Narrative: Fictional Relationships & the Process of Psychological Change. LC 96-550. 224p. 1996. 65.00 (0-275-95362-9, Praeger Pubs); write for info. (0-614-13022-0, Praeger Pubs); pap. 21.95 (0-275-95579-6, Praeger Pubs) Greenwood.

Almond, Brenda. Educational Thought: An Introduction. (Modern Revivals in Philosophy Ser.). 112p. 1993. text 39.95 (0-7512-0264-9, Pub. by Gregg Revivals) Ashgate Pub Co.

— Exploring Ethics: A Travelers Tale. LC 97-37182. 288p. 1998. 57.95 (0-631-19952-7); pap. 24.95 (0-631-19953-5) Blackwell Pubs.

— Exploring Philosophy: The Philosophical Quest. 2nd ed. 256p. (C). 1995. pap. text 24.95 (0-631-19485-1) Blackwell Pubs.

Almond, Brenda, ed. AIDS, a Moral Issue: The Ethical, Legal, & Social Aspects. 2nd ed. 224p. 1997. pap. 17.95 (0-312-16153-0) St Martin.

Almond, Brenda, ed. Introducing Applied Ethics: A Guide to the Current Debates. 320p. (C). 1995. 61.95 (0-631-19389-8); pap. 26.95 (0-631-19391-X) Blackwell Pubs.

Almond, D. C., et al, eds. Industrial Raw Materials of the Arabian Gulf & Their Utilization: Proceedings of the First Conference on Indigenous Raw Materials & Their Utilization in the Gulf Region. 288p. 1992. 135.00 (0-7103-0376-9, A4531) Routledge.

— Industrial Raw Materials of the Arabian Gulf & Their Utilization: Proceedings of the First Conference on Indigenous Raw Materials & Their Utilization in the Gulf Region. (Illus.). 540p. 1994. 127.50 (0-7103-0769-1) Routledge.

— Raw Materials of the Arabian Gulf & Their Utilisation: Proceedings of the First Conference on Indigenous Raw Materials & Their Utilisation in the Gulf Region. 288p. 1990. 135.00 (0-7103-0333-5, A4531) Routledge.

Almond, D. C., jt. auth. see Ahmed, F.

***Almond, David.** Heaven Eyes. (YA). 2001. mass mkt. (0-385-32770-6) BDD Bks Young Read.

— Kit's Wilderness. LC 99-34332. 240p. (YA). (gr. 6-9). 2000. 15.95 (0-385-32665-3) Delacorte.

— Skellig. (Illus.). 192p. (J). (gr. 4-7). 2000. pap. 4.99 (0-440-41602-7, Yearling) BDD Bks Young Read.

— Skellig. (J). 1999. 16.95 (0-7540-6066-7) Chivers N Amer.

An Asterisk (*) at the beginning of an entry indicates that the title is appearing for the first time.

Almond, David. Skellig. LC 98-23121. 192p. (YA). (gr. 3-7). 1999. 15.95 (*0-385-32653-X*) Delacorte.

Almond, Denise L., ed. see Huck, Daniel F. & Sauber, Kirk A.

Almond, Gabriel Abraham. The American People & Foreign Policy. 2nd ed. LC 77-7019. 269p. 1977. reprint ed. lib. bdg. 35.00 (*0-8371-9617-5*, ALAM, Greenwood Pr) Greenwood.

— Comparative Politics Today. 7th ed. (C). 2000. pap. text Price not set. (*0-321-00318-7*) Addison-Wesley.

— A Discipline Divided: Schools & Sects in Political Science. 320p. (C). 1989. text 52.00 (*0-8039-3301-0*); pap. text 25.00 (*0-8039-3302-9*) Sage.

— Plutocracy & Politics in New York City. LC 97-27164. (Urban Policy Challenges Ser.). 288p. (C). 1997. pap. 28.00 (*0-8133-9983-1*, Pub. by Westview) HarpC.

***Almond, Gabriel Abraham, ed.** Comparative Politics Today. 7th ed. LC 99-52270. 800p. (C). 1999. pap. text 63.00 (*0-321-01858-3*) Addison-Wesley Educ.

Almond, Gabriel Abraham, ed. Comparative Politics Today: A World View. 6th ed. (C). 1995. teacher ed. write for info. (*0-673-54309-9*) Addison-Wesley Educ.

Almond, Gabriel Abraham, ed. Comparative Politics Today: A World View. 6th ed. (C). 1997. 71.00 (*0-673-54312-9*, GoodYrBooks) Addison-Wesley Educ.

— Comparative Politics Today: A World View. 7th ed. (C). 2000. (*0-321-06937-4*) Benjamin-Cummings.

Almond, Gabriel Abraham & Coleman, James S., eds. The Politics of the Developing Areas. LC 60-9763. 608p. reprint ed. pap. 188.50 (*0-8357-2929-X*, 203916700011) Bks Demand.

Almond, Gabriel Abraham & Powell, G. Bingham. Comparative Politics Today: A World View. 5th ed. (C). 1991. text 55.50 (*0-673-52029-3*) Addson-Wesley Educ.

Almond, Gabriel Abraham & Powell, G. Bingham, Jr., eds. Comparative Politics Today. 6th ed. LC 95-39648. 656p. (C). 1997. pap. text 69.00 (*0-673-52474-4*) Addson-Wesley Educ.

Almond, Gabriel Abraham & Verba, Sidney. The Civic Culture: Political Attitudes & Democracy in Five Nations. LC 63-12666. 576p. reprint ed. pap. 178.60 (*0-8357-3844-2*, 203657700004) Bks Demand.

— Civic Culture Study, 1959-1960. 1974. write for info. (*0-89138-065-5*) ICPSR.

Almond, Gabriel Abraham & Verba, Sidney, eds. The Civic Culture Revisited. 422p. (C). 1989. reprint ed. text 52.00 (*0-8039-3559-5*) Sage.

Almond, Gabriel Abraham, et al. Comparative Politics. 2nd ed. LC 95-45451. 288p. (C). 1997. pap. text 36.93 (*0-673-52480-9*) Addison-Wesley Educ.

— Comparative Politics: A Theoretical Framework. 194p. (C). 1997. pap. text 28.00 (*0-673-52282-2*) Addison-Wesley Educ.

Almond, Glen, et al. The Swine AI Book: A Field & Laboratory Technicians' Guide to Artificial Insemination in Swine. Cronje, Ruth, ed. (Illus.). 108p. (Orig.). (C). 1994. 19.95 (*0-9640737-0-6*) Swine AI Pubns.

— The Swine AI Book: A Field & Laboratory Technicians Guide to Artificial Insemination in Swine. 2nd rev. ed. (SPA., Illus.). 120p. (C). 1997. pap. text 25.00 (*0-9640737-1-4*) Swine AI Pubns.

— The Swine Inseminators' Handbook. (Illus.). 80p. (Orig.). (C). 1997. pap. text 15.00 (*0-9640737-2-2*) Swine AI Pubns.

Almond, Harold. The Stories of a West Virginia Doctor. LC 97-93910. 120p. 1997. pap. 8.00 (*0-87012-583-4*) McClain.
Join general practitioner, Doctor Harold Almond as he recounts his most entertaining & heartwarming tales of his life as a West Virginia doctor. These easy-to-read stories are sure to enlighten & humor any reader. ***Publisher Paid Annotation.***

***Almond, Harry H. & Burger, James A., eds.** The History & Future of Warfare: Selections from the Professional Readings in Military Strategy Published by the Strategic Studies Institute of the U. S. Army War College. LC 99-47838. 950p. 1999. 185.00 (*90-411-9462-2*) Kluwer Law Intl.

Almond, Harry J. Iraqi Statesman: A Portrait of Mohammad Fadhel Jamali. (Illus.). 192p. (Orig.). 1993. pap. 19.95 (*1-85239-509-5*) Grosvenor USA.

***Almond, Jocelyn.** An Egyptian Book of Shadows: Eight Seasonal Rites for Egyptian Paganism. 2000. 19.95 (*0-7225-3893-6*) Thorsons PA.

Almond, Johnny R. Pray As You Go: A Travel Guide for Prayerful Living. 369p. 1998. pap. 12.95 (*1-57087-383-6*) Prof Pr NC.

Almond, Jordan. Dictionary of Word Origins: A History of the Words Expressions & Cliches We Use. 288p. 1995. pap. 12.95 (*0-8065-1713-1*, Citadel Pr) Carol Pub Group.

Almond, Joseph P., Sr. Plumbers' Handbook. 6th ed. LC 82-1342. 1982. write for info. (*0-672-23370-3*) Macmillan.

Almond, Joseph P. Plumber's Handbook. 8th ed. 368p. 1991. pap. 15.95 (*0-02-501570-2*) Macmillan.

— The Plumbers Maintenance/Troubleshooting Pocket Manual. 9th ed. 352p. 1997. 16.95 (*0-02-861501-8*, Aude IN) IDG Bks.

Almond, L., ed. National Curriculum for Physical Education. 256p. 1991. pap. 49.95 (*0-419-17070-7*, A6275, E & FN Spon) Routledge.

Almond, Larry H., jt. auth. see Davis-Almond, L. A.

Almond, Marc. Angel of Death in the Adonis Lounge. 1995. per. 7.95 (*0-85449-079-5*, Pub. by Gay Mens Pr) LPC InBook.

Almond, Marc. Beautiful Twisted Night. pap. 18.00 (*1-84166-023-X*, Pub. by Ellipsis) Norton.

Almond, Mark. Europe's Backyard War: The War in the Balkans. LC 95-176983. xix, 437 p. 1994. write for info. (*0-7493-1659-4*) Mndrin.

— National Pacifism Germany's New Temptation. (C). 1991. 35.00 (*0-907967-26-4*, Pub. by Inst Euro Def & Strat) St Mut.

— Retreat to Moscow? Gorbachev & the East. (C). 1990. 35.00 (*0-907967-21-3*, Pub. by Inst Euro Def & Strat) St Mut.

Almond, Mark, ed. Decline Without Fall: Romania under Ceausescu. (C). 1988. 35.00 (*0-907967-96-5*, Pub. by Inst Euro Def & Strat) St Mut.

Almond, Peter. Aviation: The Early Years: The Hutton Getty Picture Collection. (ENG, FRE & GER., Illus.). 360p. 1998. 29.95 (*3-89508-682-7*, 810113) Konemann.

Almond, Peter E., jt. ed. see Gagliardi, Raymond A.

***Almond, Peter R., et al.** Protocol for Clinical Reference Dosimetry of High-Energy Photon & Electron Beams No. 67: Report of the AAPM Radiation Therapy Committee TG No. 51. 22p. 2000. pap. text. write for info. (*1-888340-25-8*) AAPM.

Almond, Philip C. Adam & Eve in Seventeenth-Century Thought. LC 99-10370. 288p. 1999. 54.95 (*0-521-66076-9*) Cambridge U Pr.

— The British Discovery of Buddhism. 196p. 1988. text 59.95 (*0-521-35503-6*) Cambridge U Pr.

— Heaven & Hell in Enlightenment England. (Illus.). 232p. (C). 1994. text 64.95 (*0-521-45371-2*) Cambridge U Pr.

— Mystical Experience & Religious Doctrine: An Investigation of the Study of Mysticism in World Religions. (Religion & Reason Ser.: No. 26). 197p. 1982. text 52.35 (*90-279-3160-7*) Mouton.

— Rudolf Otto: An Introduction to His Philosophical Theology. LC 83-19865. (Studies in Religion). 182p. reprint ed. pap. 56.50 (*0-7837-2450-0*, 204259900005) Bks Demand.

Almond, R. Graphical Relief Models. 1992. text. write for info. (*0-442-01223-3*) Chapman & Hall.

Almond, Richard. The Healing Community: Dynamics of the Therapeutic Milieu. LC 73-17733. 464p. 1974. 40.00 (*0-87668-111-9*) Aronson.

Almond, Richard, jt. auth. see Almond, Barbara.

Almond, Russell G. Graphical Belief Models: Algorithms & Examples. LC 94-24208. (Illus.). 427p. (gr. 13). 1995. ring bd. 74.95 (*0-412-06661-0*, Chap & Hall CRC) CRC Pr.

Almonte, Paul & Desmond, Theresa. Street Gangs. LC 93-25330. (Update Ser.). (J). 1994. pap. 4.95 (*0-382-24758-2*, Crstwood Hse) Silver Burdett Pr.

Almorza, D., jt. ed. see Ramos, H. M.

Almoster Ferreira, M. A., ed. Ionic Processes in the Gas Phase. 1983. text 176.50 (*90-277-1688-9*) Kluwer Academic.

***Almovist, C. J. L.** Queen's Tiara. 2000. pap. 15.95 (*1-900850-51-6*) Arcadia Bks.

Almquist, Alan. Human Sexuality. LC 95-214607. 560p. (C). 1995. pap., per. write for info. (*0-7872-0524-9*); text, student ed. write for info. (*0-7872-0525-7*) Kendall-Hunt.

— Human Sexuality Pak, Set. 608p. (C). 1995. pap. text 65.95 (*0-7872-0523-0*, 41052301) Kendall-Hunt.

Almquist, Alan J. & Manyak, Anne, eds. Milestones in Human Evolution. (Illus.). 274p. (C). 1993. pap. text 16.95 (*0-88133-736-6*) Waveland Pr.

Almquist, Alan J., jt. auth. see Boaz, Noel T.

Almquist, Alan J., jt. auth. see Heizer, Robert F.

Almquist, Bo & Dorson, Richard M., eds. Hereditas: Essays & Studies Presented to Professor Seamus O Duilearga. LC 80-737. (Folklore of the World Ser.). (Illus.). 1981. reprint ed. lib. bdg. 49.95 (*0-405-13301-4*) Ayer.

Almquist, Ebbe. Lighthouses & Harbors, Vol. 1. 1999. 19.99 (*0-7858-1102-8*) Bk Sales Inc.

***Almquist, Ed.** Hot Rod Pioneers: The Creators of the Fastest Sport on Wheels. LC 00-36527. (Illus.). 400p. 2000. 39.00 (*0-7680-0232-X*, R-228) Soc Auto Engineers.

Almquist, L. Arden. Debtor Unashamed: The Road to Mission Is a Two-Way Street. (Orig.). 1993. pap. 12.95 (*0-910452-76-8*) Covenant.

Almquist, Leann G. Joseph Alsop & American Foreign Policy: The Journalist As Advocate. 226p. (C). 1993. lib. bdg. 48.50 (*0-8191-9095-0*) U Pr of Amer.

Almquist, Norma. Traveling Light: Poems. 64p. (Orig.). 1997. pap. 9.00 (*1-56474-192-3*) Fithian Pr.

Almquist, Norma, ed. see Towner, Annemarie E.

Almquist, S., jt. auth. see Link, Frances R.

Almquist, Sharon G. Sound Recordings & the Library. (Occasional Papers: No. 179). 1987. pap. 2.50 (*0-685-34542-4*) U of Ill Grad Sch.

Almquist, Sharon G., compiled by. Opera Singers Mediagraphy: Concerts, Recitals & Feature Films, 73. LC 98-41642. (Music Reference Collection: Vol. 73). 392p. 1999. lib. bdg. 79.50 (*0-313-29592-1*, Greenwood Pr) Greenwood.

Almquist, Sharon G., ed. Opera Mediagraphy: Video Recordings & Motion Pictures, 40. LC 93-28491. (Music Reference Collection: No. 40). 288p. 1993. lib. bdg. 65.00 (*0-313-28490-3*, Greenwood Pr) Greenwood.

Almqvist & Wiksell, eds. The Nobel Prizes, 1986: Presentations, Biographies & Lectures. (Illus.). 344p. 1987. 74.50 (*91-85848-11-5*) Coronet Bks.

Almqvist, Birgitta. Approaching the Culture of Toys in Swedish Child Care: A Literature Survey & a Toy Inventory. (Uppsala Studies in Education: No. 54). 175p. (Orig.). 1994. pap. 42.50 (*91-554-3260-3*) Coronet Bks.

Almqvist, Carl Jonas Love. The Queen's Diadem. Sandstroem, Yvonne, tr. (SCAND Ser.). 250p. 1992. 50.00 (*1-879751-00-3*) Camden Hse.

Almqvist, Carl Jonas Love. Sara Videbeck - The Chapel. Benson, Adolph B., tr. from SWE. LC 77-185449. (Library of Scandinavian Literature). 1972. lib. bdg. 6.75 (*0-8057-3354-X*) Irvington.

Almqvist, Jane H. Mountmellick Work: Irish White Embroidery. 2nd ed. 80p. 1996. pap. 15.95 (*0-85105-512-5*, Pub. by Smyth) Dufour.

Al'muhamedov, M. I., et al. Stability & Dynamic Systems. (Translations Ser.: Series 1, Vol. 5). 510p. 1962. pap. 38.00 (*0-8218-1605-5*, TRANS1/5) Am Math.

Almust, Ajay S. Lohia the Rebel Gandhian. LC 98-901558. xiii, 256p. 1998. 27.00 (*81-7099-633-3*, Pub. by Mittal Pubs Dist) Nataraj Bks.

AlMuttaqi, Ali H., tr. see Al-Jilani, Shaikh A.

Almy, Amy B. At Christmas Time the World Grows Young. LC 70-116926. (Short Story Index Reprint Ser.). 1977. 16.95 (*0-8369-3428-8*) Ayer.

***Almy, Gary L.** How Christian Is Christian Counseling? The Dangerous Secular Influences That Keep Us from Caring for Souls. LC 99-54975. 352p. 1999. pap. 24.00 (*1-58134-135-0*) Crossway Bks.

Almy, Gerald. Freshwater Fishing in Virginia. (Illus.). 96p. 1995. 9.95 (*1-885937-04-0*, Virginia Heritage) Casco Commns.

Almy, Marion A. & Luer, George M. Guide to the Prehistory of Historic Spanish Point in Southwest Florida. 2nd rev. ed. Orig. Title: Spanish Point: The Guide to Prehistory. (Illus.). 41p. 1987. pap. 3.00 (*0-9660576-0-0*) Gulf Coast Herit.

Almy, Millie C. Children's Experiences Prior to First Grade & Success in Beginning Reading. LC 71-176516. (Columbia University. Teachers College. Contributions to Education Ser.: No. 954). reprint ed. 37.50 (*0-404-55954-9*) AMS Pr.

Almy, Millie C. & Genishi, Celia. Ways of Studying Children: An Observation Manual for Early Childhood Teachers. 2nd ed. LC 79-13881. 215p. 1979. pap. text 17.95 (*0-8077-2551-X*) Tchrs Coll.

Almy, Millie C., et al. Studying School Children in Uganda: Four Reports of Exploratory Research. LC 74-122548. 85p. reprint ed. 30.00 (*0-8357-9607-8*, 201776300008) Bks Demand.

— Young Children's Thinking: Studies of Some Aspects of Piaget's Theory. LC 66-16091. (Illus.). 168p. reprint ed. pap. 52.10 (*0-608-11266-6*, 201317600086) Bks Demand.

Almy, Virginia. Sevier County, Tennessee Buyer's Guide for Houses or Land. Baldwin, Juanitta, ed. 230p. (Orig.). 1996. pap. 15.00 (*1-880308-06-1*) Suntop.

Almy, Virginia & Baldwin, Juanitta. Oh Henry - Here Comes a U-Haul! LC 97-13855. (Illus.). 112p. (Orig.). 1997. pap. 15.00 (*1-880308-08-8*) Suntop.

Alnaes, Karsten. Boy from Duck River: A Norwegian Adventure Tale. Ingebritsen, Runa, tr. Tr. of Even 1814. (Illus.). 104p. 1995. 18.95 (*0-87839-102-9*); pap. 9.95 (*0-87839-101-0*) North Star.

Alnasrawi, Abbas. Arab Nationalism, Oil, & the Political Economy of Dependency, 120. LC 90-25225. (Contributions in Economics & Economic History Ser.: No. 120). 232p. 1991. 59.95 (*0-313-27610-2*, AAQ, Greenwood Pr) Greenwood.

— Arab Oil & United States Energy Requirements. (Monographs: No. 16). 88p. (Orig.). 1982. pap. 5.95 (*0-937694-52-5*) Assn Arab-Amer U Grads.

— The Economy of Iraq: Oil, Wars, Destruction of Development & Prospects, 1950-2010, 154. LC 93-37510. (Contributions in Economics & Economic History Ser.: No. 154). 208p. 1994. 62.95 (*0-313-29186-1*, Greenwood Pr) Greenwood.

— OPEC in a Changing World Economy. LC 84-7196. 202p. 1985. reprint ed. pap. 62.70 (*0-608-04074-6*, 206480600011) Bks Demand.

Alnasrawi, Abbas & Rubenberg, Cheryl, eds. Consistency of U. S. Foreign Policy: The Gulf War & the Iran-Contra Affair. (Monographs: No. 23). 155p. (Orig.). 1989. pap. 10.95 (*0-937694-81-9*) Assn Arab-Amer U Grads.

Alner, Jonathan, ed. see Chan, Stephen.

Alnor, William M. UFO Cults & the New Millennium. LC 98-5609. 208p. 1999. pap. 14.99 (*0-8010-5791-4*) Baker Bks.

— UFOs in the New Age: Extraterrestrial Messages & the Truth of Scripture. LC 92-482. (Christian Research Institute Ser.). 296p. (gr. 10). 1992. pap. 12.99 (*0-8010-0226-5*) Baker Bks.

Aloan, Clarie A. Respiratory Care of the Newborn & Child. 2nd ed. LC 96-39478. 544p. 1997. pap. text 42.00 (*0-397-54925-3*) Lppncott W & W.

Alobaidi, Joseph. Le Commentaire des Psaumes par le Qaraite Salmon Ben Yeruham Psaumes 1-10: Introduction, Edition, Traduction. (Bible dans l'Histoire Ser.: Vol. 1). (FRE.). 508p. 1996. 60.95 (*3-906754-29-4*, Pub. by P Lang) P Lang Pubng.

Alobaidi, Joseph, ed. The Messiah in Isaiah 53: The Commentaries of Saadia Gaon, Salmon ben Yeruham & Yefet ben Eli on Is 52:13-53:12, No. 2. (Bible dans l'Historie: Vol. 2). 211p. 1998. 31.95 (*3-906760-54-5*) P Lang Pubng.

— The Messiah in Isaiah 53: The Commentaries of Saadia Gaon, Salmon Ben Yeruham & Yefet Ben Eli on Is 52:13-53:12 - Edition & Translation. LC 98-28590. (Bible dans l'Historie Ser.: Vol. 2). 211p. (C). 1998. pap. 31.95 (*0-8204-4201-1*) P Lang Pubng.

Alock, Norman Z., jt. auth. see CPRI Researchers Staff.

Aloes, Paul D. Polyurethanes: Index of New Information with Authors, Subjects & References. 150p. 1996. 47.50 (*0-7883-1270-7*); pap. 44.50 (*0-7883-1271-5*) ABBE Pubs Assn.

— Polyurethanes: Index of New Information with Authors, Subjects & References. rev. ed. 155p. 1998. 47.50 (*0-7883-1986-8*); pap. 44.50 (*0-7883-1987-6*) ABBE Pubs Assn.

Aloff, Mindy. Night Lights. Gale, Vi, ed. LC 79-84510. (First Bk.). (Illus.). 1979. pap. 5.00 (*0-915986-14-0*) Prescott St Pr.

— Night Lights. limited ed. Gale, Vi, ed. LC 79-84510. (First Bk.). (Illus.). 1979. 20.00 (*0-915986-13-2*) Prescott St Pr.

Aloff, Mindy & Cohen, Marty. On the Nile. 4p. 1978. pap. 1.00 (*0-932264-23-9*) Trask Hse Bks.

Alofsin, Anthony. The Final Decade: Architectural Issues for the 1990s & Beyond, Vol. 7. (Illus.). 128p. 1992. 22.00 (*0-8478-5553-8*) Ctr for Amer Archit.

— Frank Lloyd Wright: The Lost Years, 1910-1922: A Study of Influence. (Illus.). 456p. 1993. 55.00 (*0-226-01366-9*) U Ch Pr.

— Frank Lloyd Wright - The Lost Years, 1910-1922: A Study of Influence. (Illus.). 416p. (gr. 2). 1998. pap. 35.00 (*0-226-01504-1*) U Ch Pr.

***Alofsin, Anthony.** Limits of Sayable. 1998. 50.00 (*0-226-01506-8*) U Ch Pr.

Alofsin, Anthony, ed. Frank Lloyd Wright: An Index to the Taliesin Correspondence, 5 vols., Set. LC 88-11201. 4572p. 1988. text 300.00 (*0-8240-4029-5*) Garland.

— Frank Lloyd Wright: Europe & Beyond. LC 99-10128. 295p. 1999. 50.00 (*0-520-21116-2*, Pub. by U CA Pr) Cal Prin Full Svc.

Alofsin, Anthony & Mugerauer, Robert. Dwelling: Social Life, Buildings, & the Spaces Between Them, Vol. 8. (Illus.). 101p. 1993. 22.00 (*0-292-71163-8*) Ctr for Amer Archit.

Alofsin, Anthony, jt. auth. see Speck, Larwrence W.

Alofsin, Dorothy. America's Triumph: Stories of American Jewish Heroes. LC 72-148205. (Biography Index Reprint Ser.). 1977. 24.95 (*0-8369-8052-2*) Ayer.

Alogoskoufis, George, et al, eds. External Constraints on Macroeconomic Policy: The European Experience. (Illus.). 406p. (C). 1991. text 69.95 (*0-521-40527-0*) Cambridge U Pr.

Alogoskoutis, George, et al. Europe's Unemployment Problem: A Monitoring European Integration Report. LC 96-145723. 147p. (C). 1995. pap. 14.95 (*1-898128-14-6*, Pub. by Ctr Econ Policy Res) Brookings.

Aloi. General Zoology. 11th ed. 2000. pap., student ed. 18.74 (*0-07-290976-5*) McGraw.

Aloia, John F. Osteoporosis: A Guide to Prevention & Treatment. LC 88-13819. (Illus.). 248p. (Orig.). 1989. reprint ed. pap. 76.90 (*0-608-06461-0*, 206729900009) Bks Demand.

Aloian, David, ed. College in a Yard, II. (Alumni Association Ser.). (Illus.). 215p. 1986. 14.50 (*0-674-14151-2*) HUP.

Aloimonos, Yiannis, ed. Active Perception. (Computer Vision Ser.). 304p. 1993. text 59.95 (*0-8058-1290-3*) L Erlbaum Assocs.

— Visual Navigation: From Biological Systems to Unmanned Ground Vehicles. LC 96-18717. (Computer Vision Ser.). 432p. (C). 1996. text 99.95 (*0-8058-2050-7*) L Erlbaum Assocs.

Aloise, Gene. Nuclear Nonproliferation: Implementation of the U. S. - North Korean Agreed Framework on Nuclear Issues. (Illus.). 66p. (C). 1998. pap. text 20.00 (*0-7881-3858-8*) DIANE Pub.

Aloisi, Patricia. Instant Drug Index 1998. 1998. spiral bd. 29.95 (*0-632-04331-8*) Blackwell Sci.

***Aloisi, Patricia.** Instant Drug Index 1999. LC 99-217807. 1999. spiral bd. 29.95 (*0-632-04447-0*) Blackwell Sci.

Aloisi, Patricia. Instant Drug Index, 1997. 1996. spiral bd. 29.95 (*0-632-04302-4*) Blackwell Sci.

***Aloisi, Patricia.** Instant Drug Index 2000. 2000. spiral bd. 29.95 (*0-632-04523-X*) Blackwell Sci.

Aloisi, Ralph M. Principles of Immunology & Immunodiagnostics. LC 87-31150. 248p. reprint ed. pap. 76.90 (*0-7837-2689-9*, 204306700006) Bks Demand.

Aloj, Totaro E., et al. Advances in Age Pigments Research, Vol. 64. (Advances in the Biosciences Ser.). (Illus.). 430p. 1987. 94.00 (*0-08-035721-0*, Pergamon Pr) Elsevier.

Alok, S. K. Family Welfare Planning: The Indian Experience. (C). 1992. 28.00 (*81-210-0296-6*, Pub. by Inter-India Pubns) S Asia.

Alokeranjan, Dasgupta. Roots in the Void: Baul Songs of Bengal. 1983. 5.00 (*0-8364-0972-8*, Pub. by KP Bagchi) S Asia.

Alomar, O. & Wiedenmann, R. N., eds. Zoophytophagous Heteroptera: Implications for Life History & IPM. (Thomas Say Publications in Entomology). 202p. 1996. pap. 35.00 (*0-938522-58-2*, ESATSP8) Entomol Soc.

***Alomari.** Cyrano Version of Oracle 8 & Unix Performance Tuning. (C). 1999. pap. 24.00 (*0-13-087509-0*) P-H.

Alomari, Ahmed. Oracle & Unix Performance Tuning. LC 97-13114. 288p. (C). 1997. pap. text 44.95 (*0-13-849167-4*) P-H.

— Oracle & Unix Performance Tuning. 2nd ed. LC 98-22873. 352p. 1998. pap. text 39.99 (*0-13-907676-X*) P-H.

— Oracle DBA Reference Library. (C). 1997. pap. text 119.95 incl. cd-rom (*0-13-894742-2*) P-H.

***Alomari, Ahmed.** Oracle 8i & UNIX Performance Tuning. (PTR Oracle Ser.). (Illus.). 450p. 2000. pap. 49.99 (*0-13-018706-2*) P-H.

***Alomari, Mohammed.** The Secrecy of Evil: The Qabala & Its Followers: The Knights Templars, Illuminati, Freemasonry & Other Secret Societies from Early to Modern Times. (Illus.). 111p. (Orig.). 1999. pap. 17.95 (*0-9673559-0-7*) Azimuth Sys.

Alomes, Stephen. When London Calls: The Expatriation of Australian Creative Artists to Britain. LC 99-35912. (Illus.). 272p. 2000. 64.95 (*0-521-62031-7*) Cambridge U Pr.

— When London Calls: The Expatriation of Australian Creative Artists to Britain. LC 93-35912. (Illus.). 272p. 2000. pap. 22.95 (*0-521-62978-0*) Cambridge U Pr.

A

Alon, Gedaliah. The Jews in Their Land in the Talmudic Age. Levi, Gershon, ed. & tr. by. from HEB. LC 88-23495. 840p. 1989. pap. 24.95 (0-674-47495-3) HUP.

***Alon, Ilan.** The Internationalization of United States Franchizing Systems. LC 99-36253. 1999. write for info. (0-8153-3387-0) Garland.

Alon, Nahi, jt. auth. see Omer, Haim.

Alon, Noga & Spencer, Joel H. The Probabilistic Method. LC 91-13119. (Interscience Series in Discrete Mathematics). 272p. 1991. 99.95 (0-471-53588-5) Wiley.

***Alon, Noga & Spencer, Joel H.** The Probabilistic Method. 2nd ed. 320p. 2000. 84.95 (0-471-37046-0) Wiley.

Alon, Ruthy. Mindful Spontaneity: Lessons in the Feldenkrais Method. 300p. (Orig.). (C). 1995. pap. 22.95 (1-55643-185-6) North Atlantic.

— Mindful Spontaneity: Moving in Tune with Nature: Lessons in the Feldenkrais Method. 284p. (Orig.). 1990. pap. write for info. (1-85327-050-4, Pub. by Prism Pr) Assoc Pubs Grp.

Alon, Uri & Chan, James C., eds. Phosphate in Pediatric Health & Disease. 352p. 1993. lib. bdg. 219.00 (0-8493-6785-9, RJ399, CRC Reprint) Franklin.

Alon, Uri & DeSanto, N. G., eds. Pediatric Hypertension. (Child Nephrology & Urology Journal: Vol. 12, No. 2-3, 1992). (Illus.). 112p. 1992. pap. 55.75 (3-8055-5608-X) S Karger.

Aloneftis, A. Stochastic Adaptive Control Results & Simulation. (Lecture Notes in Control & Information Sciences: Vol. 98). xii, 120p. 1987. 31.95 (0-387-18055-9) Spr-Verlag.

Alongi, Anthony, et al. A Portable Action Lab for Creating Quality: Student Projects for Health Careers. (Illus.). 50p. 1997. pap. 25.00 (1-887410-91-0) Jobs for Future.

Alongi, D. M. Coastal Ecosystem Processes. LC 97-36262. (Marine Science Ser.). 448p. 1997. boxed set 94.95 (0-8493-8426-5) CRC Pr.

Alongi, Daniel & Robertson, Alistair, eds. Tropical Mangrove Ecosystems. (Coastal & Estuarine Studies: Vol. 41). 1993. 37.00 (0-87590-255-3) Am Geophysical.

Alongi, Maria R. & Grant, Robert P. FrancoAmerican Security Cooperation: From Principle to Practice. (Symposium Report Ser.). 60p. (Orig.). 1995. pap. 13.95 (0-9629930-5-0) US CREST.

Aloni, Nimrod. Beyond Nihilism: Nietzsche As Edifying Philosopher. 216p. (C). 1992. lib. bdg. 44.00 (0-8191-8431-4) U Pr of Amer.

Aloni, Yosef, ed. Molecular Aspects of Papovaviruses. (Developments in Molecular Virology Ser.). (C). 1987. text 159.00 (0-89838-971-2) Kluwer Academic.

Alonig, Edwin. Poems, a Life Primer. 150p. 10.00 (0-685-53107-4) Soft Teach Inc.

Alonimo, Cesar. Dispersos. LC 90-83714. (Coleccion Espejo de Paciencia). (SPA.). 77p. 1991. pap. 8.95 (0-89729-578-1) Ediciones.

— Dispersos. 2nd rev. ed. LC 94-94604. 80p. 1994. write for info. (0-9642694-0-6) C Alonimo.

— Espejos. (SPA.). 80p. 1994. write for info. (0-9642694-1-4) C Alonimo.

Alonso. Guia Rapida Lotus 1-2-3. 2nd ed.Tr. of Spanish Guide to Lotus 1-2-3. (SPA.). 1991. 10.95 (0-7859-3692-0, 8428317437) Fr & Eur.

— Physics. 2nd ed. (World Student Ser.: Bk. 2). (C). 1983. pap. text 15.33 (0-201-00162-4) Addison-Wesley.

— Thread of Blood (H&E) Colonialism, Revolution, & Gender on Mexico's Northern Frontier. LC 95-32475. (Hegemony & Experience Ser.). (Illus.). 303p. 1995. 46.00 (0-8165-1511-5) U of Ariz Pr.

Alonso, Ana M. Thread of Blood: Colonialism, Revolution, & Gender on Mexico's Northern Frontier. LC 95-32475. (Hegemony & Experience Ser.). 1995. pap. 19.95 (0-8165-1574-3) U of Ariz Pr.

Alonso, Andres R. & Cox, Sarah. Virginia's Roanoke Valley: Heart of the Blue Ridge. (Illus.). 200p. 1999. 35.00 (0-9670545-1-6) Foto Vision.

Alonso, Andres R. & Smith, Mike. Martinsville Speedway, Half-Mile of Thunder. (Illus.). 160p. 1999. 29.95 (0-9670545-0-8) Foto Vision.

Alonso, Anne & Swiller, Hillel I., eds. Group Therapy in Clinical Practice. LC 92-10416. 581p. 1993. text 61.95 (0-88048-323-7, 8323) Am Psychiatric.

Alonso, Carlos. Augustinian Law & Charism: The Life & Work of Clement of Osimo. Rotelle, John E., ed. Fellowes, Audrey, tr. from SPA. LC 88-70366. (Augustinian Ser.). (Illus.). 72p. 1988. pap. 4.95 (0-941491-17-X) Augustinian Pr.

Alonso, Carlos J. The Burden of Modernity: The Rhetoric of Cultural Discourse in Spanish America. 240p. 1998. text 39.95 (0-19-511863-4) OUP.

— The Spanish American Regional Novel: Modernity & Autochthony. (Cambridge Studies in Latin American & Iberian Literature: No. 2). 224p. (C). 1990. text 69.95 (0-521-37210-0) Cambridge U Pr.

Alonso, Carlos J., ed. Julio Cortazar: New Readings. LC 97-24282. (Studies in Latin American & Iberian Literature: Vol. 13). (Illus.). 224p. (C). 1998. 69.95 (0-521-45210-4) Cambridge U Pr.

Alonso, Claudia Pazos, see Pazos Alonso, Claudia, ed.

Alonso Cortes, Narciso, ed. see De Persia, Juan.

Alonso, Damaso. Diccionario Medieval Espanol, Vol. 1. (SPA.). 176p. 1991. pap. 12.95 (0-7859-5143-1) Fr & Eur.

— Diccionario Medieval Espanol, Vol. 2. 3rd ed. (SPA.). 216p. 1991. pap. 12.95 (0-7859-5144-X) Fr & Eur.

— Estudios Linguisticos Peninsulares, Vol. 1. (SPA.). 706p. 1993. pap. 150.00 (84-249-3453-9) Elliots Bks.

— Estudios y Ensayos sobre Literatura: Primera Parte - Desde Los Origenes Romanicos Hasta Finales Del Siglo XVI, Vol. 2. (SPA.). 1090p. 1993. pap. 150.00 (84-249-3455-5) Elliots Bks.

— Estudios y Ensayos sobre Literatura: Segunda Parte - Finales del Diglo XVI y Siglo XVII, Vol. 3. (SPA.). 1008p. 1993. pap. 150.00 (84-249-3462-8) Elliots Bks.

— Estudios y Ensayos sobre Literatura: Tercera Parte - Ensayos Sobre Literatura Contemporanea, Vol. 4. (SPA., Illus.). 1010p. 1993. pap. 150.00 (84-249-3477-6) Elliots Bks.

— Gongora y El Gongorismo, Vol. II. (SPA., Illus.). 720p. 1993. pap. 150.00 (84-249-0262-9) Elliots Bks.

— Gongora y El Gongorismo, Vol. 7, III. (SPA.). 890p. 1993. pap. 150.00 (84-249-0968-2) Elliots Bks.

— Gongora y El Gongorismo, Vols. 1 & 5. (SPA., Illus.). 792p. 1993. pap. 150.00 (84-249-3502-0) Elliots Bks.

— Hijos de la Ina: Children of Wrath. Rivers, Elias L., ed. & tr. by. from SPA. LC 77-119107. 183p. reprint ed. pap. 56.80 (0-608-14601-3, 202582100045) Bks Demand.

— Hijos de la Ira. Rubio, Fanny, ed. (Nueva Austral Ser.: Vol. 134). (SPA.). 1991. pap. text 24.95 (84-239-1934-X) Elliots Bks.

— Obras Completas de Damaso Alonso: Comentarios de Textos, Vol. 8. (SPA.). 732p. 1993. pap. 150.00 (84-249-1012-5) Elliots Bks.

— Oscura Noticia - Hombre y Dios. Chicharro Chamorro, Antonio, ed. (Nueva Austral Ser.: No. 247). (SPA.). 1991. pap. text 24.95 (84-239-7247-X) Elliots Bks.

— Poesia Espanola y Otros Estudios, Vol. 9. (SPA.). 706p. 1993. pap. 150.00 (84-249-1408-2) Elliots Bks.

— Poesia y Prosa Literaria Vol. X: Obras Completas. (SPA.). 1994. pap. 150.00 (0-614-00241-9) Elliots Bks.

Alonso de Santos, Jose L. El Album Familiar: Bajarse Al Moro. Amoros, Andres, ed. (Nueva Austral Ser.: No. 260). (SPA.). 1993. pap. text 24.95 (84-239-7260-7) Elliots Bks.

— Hostages in the Barrio. Halsey, Martha T., ed. Zatlin, Phyllis, tr. from SPA. LC 96-62017. (Contemporary Spanish Plays Ser.: Vol. 12).Tr. of Estanquera de Vallecas. (Illus.). 80p. 1997. pap. 8.00 (1-888463-02-3) Estreno.

Alonso, Deana & Zaslow, Brandon. Entre Mundos. LC 95-25069. (SPA.). 258p. (C). 1995. pap. text 45.33 (0-13-148347-1) P-H.

Alonso, E. E. & Delage, P. Unsaturated Soils, Vol. 1. 500p. 1995. 91.00 (90-5410-584-4) Ashgate Pub Co.

— Unsaturated Soils, Vol. 2. 500p. 1995. 91.00 (90-5410-585-2) Ashgate Pub Co.

— Unsaturated Soils, Vol. 3. 1997. 91.00 (90-5410-586-0) Ashgate Pub Co.

Alonso, E. E. & Delage, P., eds. Unsaturated Soils: Proceedings: International Conference (1st: 1995: Paris, France), 3 vols., Set. (Illus.). 1500p. (C). 1997. 246.00 (90-5410-583-6, Pub. by A A Balkema) Ashgate Pub Co.

Alonso, Eutimio. Cana Roja. LC 80-65446. (SPA.). 348p. (Orig.). 1982. pap. 14.95 (0-89729-251-0) Ediciones.

Alonso, Fernando. El Arbol de los Suenos.Tr. of Dream Trees. (Orig.). (J). (gr. 4-7). 1998. pap. text 9.95 (84-204-4802-8) Santillana.

— El Arbol Que No Tenia Hojas (The Tree Without Leaves) (Superbks./Superlibros). (SPA.). (J). (gr. k-1). pap. 6.95 (0-88272-469-X); pap. 6.95 (0-88272-470-3) Santillana.

— El Arbol Que No Tenia Hojas (The Tree Without Leaves), Big Book. (Superbks./Superlibros). (SPA.). (J). (gr. k-1). 21.95 (0-88272-459-2); 21.95 (0-88272-460-6) Santillana.

— Celiana y la Ciudad Sumergida (Celiana & the Enchanted City) (Superbks./Superlibros). (J). (gr. k-1). pap. 6.95 (0-88272-495-9) Santillana.

— Celiana y la Ciudad Sumergida (Celiana & the Enchanted City) (Superbks./Superlibros). (SPA.). (J). (gr. k-1). 1989. pap. 6.95 (0-88272-493-2) Santillana.

— Celiana y la Ciudad Sumergida (Celiana & the Enchanted City), Big Book. (Superbks./Superlibros). (SPA.). (J). (gr. k-1). 1989. 21.95 (0-88272-492-4); 21.95 (0-88272-494-0) Santillana.

— The Elf & the Robot (El Duende y el Robot) (Illus.). 91p. (J). (gr. 3-5). 1998. 8.95 (84-392-8108-0) Gaviota Pr.

— La Estatua y el Jardincito (The Statue & the Little Garden) (Superbks./Superlibros). (SPA.). (J). (gr. k-1). 1989. pap. 6.95 (0-88272-507-6); pap. 6.95 (0-88272-509-2) Santillana.

— La Estatua y el Jardincito (The Statue & the Little Garden), Big Book. (Superbks./Superlibros). (SPA.). (J). (gr. k-1). 1989. 21.95 (0-88272-506-8); 21.95 (0-88272-508-4) Santillana.

— Las Estrellas y la Princesa Liwayway (Princess Liwayway & the Stars) (Superbks./Superlibros). (SPA.). (J). (gr. k-1). 1989. pap. 6.95 (0-88272-497-5); pap. 6.95 (0-88272-499-1) Santillana.

— Las Estrellas y la Princesa Liwayway (Princess Liwayway & the Stars), Big Book. (Superbks./Superlibros). (SPA.). (J). (gr. k-1). 1989. 21.95 (0-88272-496-7); 21.95 (0-88272-498-3) Santillana.

— Las Fantasias de la Lechera (A Milkmaid's Daydreams) (Superbks./Superlibros). (SPA.). (J). (gr. k-1). pap. 6.95 (0-88272-473-8); pap. 6.95 (0-88272-474-6) Santillana.

— Las Fantasias de la Lechera (A Milkmaid's Daydreams), Big Book. (Superbks./Superlibros). (SPA.). (J). (gr. k-1). 21.95 (0-88272-463-0); 21.95 (0-88272-464-9) Santillana.

— El Hombrecillo de Papel. 1996. 8.95 (84-392-8728-3) Lectorum Pubns.

***Alonso, Fernando.** El Hombrecito Vestido de Gris y Otros Cuentos. 1999. pap. text 14.95 (84-204-4765-X) Alfaguara Ediciones.

Alonso, Fernando. The Little Red Hen (La Gallina Paulina) (Illus.). 26p. (J). (gr. k-2). 1989. 6.95 (0-88272-468-1) Santillana.

— El Mandarin y Los Pajaros (The Mandarin's Birds) (Superbks./Superlibros). (SPA.). (J). (gr. k-1). 1989. pap. 6.95 (0-88272-503-3); pap. 6.95 (0-88272-505-X) Santillana.

— El Mandarin y Los Pajaros (The Mandarin's Birds), Big Book. (Superbks./Superlibros). (SPA.). (J). (gr. k-1). 1989. 21.95 (0-88272-502-5); 21.95 (0-88272-504-1) Santillana.

— La Vista de la Primavera (Spring & the Forgotten City) (Superbks./Superlibros). (SPA.). (J). (gr. k-1). 1989. pap. 6.95 (0-88272-511-4) Santillana.

— La Vista de la Primavera (Spring & the Forgotten City), Big Book. (Superbks./Superlibros). (SPA.). (J). (gr. k-1). 1989. 21.95 (0-88272-510-6); 21.95 (0-88272-512-2) Santillana.

***Alonso, Fernando, et al.** Amigos (Friends) (Superbooks (Superlibros) Ser.). (ENG & SPA.). (J). (gr. k-12). 1998. 21.95 (0-88272-568-8) Santillana.

Alonso, Fernando, et al. La Vista de la Primavera (Spring & the Forgotten City) Little Book. (Superbooks (Superlibros) Ser.). 1998. 6.95 (0-88272-513-0) Santillana.

Alonso, Harriet H. Peace As a Women's Issue: A History of the U. S. Movement for World Peace & Women's Rights. (Studies on Peace & Conflict Resolution). (Illus.). 360p. 1993. pap. text 19.95 (0-8156-0269-3) Syracuse U Pr.

— The Women's Peace Union & the Outlawry of War, 1921-1942. LC 96-33216. (Contemporary Issues in the Middle East Ser.). xxvii, 224p. 1996. reprint ed. pap. 19.95 (0-8156-0417-3, ALWPP) Syracuse U Pr.

Alonso, Irma T. De, see De Alonso, Irma T., ed.

Alonso, Irma Tirado De, see Tirado de Alonso, Irma, ed.

Alonso, J. M. Althea. LC 76-2875. 1976. 15.95 (0-914590-24-3); pap. 6.95 (0-914590-25-1) Fiction Coll.

Alonso, Joaquin M. The Secret of Fatima Fact & Legend. Dominican Nuns of the Perpetual Rosary, tr. from SPA. LC 79-13182. (Illus.). 1990. reprint ed. 11.95 (0-911218-14-9); reprint ed. pap. 5.95 (0-911218-15-7) Ravengate Pr.

Alonso, Juan. Killing the Mandarin. 320p. 1995. 21.95 (1-56131-062-X, NAB) I R Dee.

Alonso, Julio A. & March, Norman H. Electrons in Metals & Alloys. 603p. 1989. text 151.00 (0-12-053620-X) Acad Pr.

Alonso, Karen. Korematsu vs. United States: Japanese-American Internment Camps. LC 97-29582. (Landmark Supreme Court Cases Ser.). (Illus.). 128p. (YA). (gr. 6 up). 1998. lib. bdg. 20.95 (0-89490-966-5) Enslow Pubs.

***Alonso, Karen.** Loving v. Virginia: Interracial Marriage. LC 99-50541. (Landmark Supreme Court Cases Ser.). (Illus.). 112p. (YA). (gr. 6 up). 2000. lib. bdg. 20.95 (0-7660-1338-3) Enslow Pubs.

Alonso, Karen. Schenck vs. United States: Restrictions on Free Speech. LC 98-34010. (Landmark Supreme Court Cases Ser.). 128p. (YA). (gr. 6 up). 1999. lib. bdg. 20.95 (0-7660-1089-9) Enslow Pubs.

Alonso, Laurent & Schott, Rene. Random Generation of Trees: Random Generators in Computer Science. LC 94-39286. 208p. (C). 1994. text 133.50 (0-7923-9528-X) Kluwer Academic.

Alonso, Liwayway, tr. see Mosel, Arlene.

Alonso, Liwayway, tr. see Ness, Evaline.

Alonso, Lou. Student Teaching Guide for Blind & Visually Impaired University Students: Adapted Methods & Procedures. braille ed. LC 86-7979. 52p. 1987. 14.95 (0-89128-183-5) Am Foun Blind.

— Student Teaching Guide for Blind & Visually Impaired University Students: Adapted Methods & Procedures. large type ed. LC 86-7979. 52p. 1987. pap. 14.95 (0-89128-142-8) Am Foun Blind.

Alonso, Lou, ed. see Raynor, Sherry & Drouillard, Richard.

Alonso, Luis R. La Estrella Que Cayo Una Noche en el Mar. LC 95-61210. (Coleccion Caniqui). (SPA.). 229p. (Orig.). 1995. pap. 18.00 (0-89729-780-6) Ediciones.

Alonso, Manuel. Extrano, Muy Extrano. 1998. pap. text 9.95 (84-204-4906-7) Santillana.

— El Gibaro: An English Translation, 2 vols. in 1. (Studies in Puerto Rican History, Literature & Culture). 1980. lib. bdg. 495.00 (0-8490-2926-0) Gordon Pr.

— El Jibaro. (Clasicos Ser.). (SPA.). 292p. 1996. pap. write for info. (0-929441-89-3) Pubns Puertorriquenas.

Alonso, Marcello. Physics. 1138p. (C). 1992. pap. text 65.00 (0-201-56518-8) Addison-Wesley.

Alonso, Marcelo. Fisica. (SPA.). 992p. (C). 1995. pap. text 32.00 (0-201-62565-2) Addison-Wesley.

Alonso, Marcelo, ed. Organization & Change in Complex Systems. 278p. 1989. 34.95 (0-89226-059-9) Paragon Hse.

Alonso, Marcelo & Finn, Edward J. Fundamental University Physics, 2 vols. 2nd ed. Incl. Vol. 1. Mechanics. 1980. text 14.36 (0-201-00076-8); Vol. 2. Fields & Waves. 2nd ed. (C). 1983. text 21.33 (0-201-00077-6); (C). write for info. (0-318-50140-6) Addison-Wesley.

Alonso, Martin. Diccionario del Espanol Moderno: Dictionary of Modern Spanish. 5th ed. (SPA.). 1100p. 1978. 125.00 (0-8288-4898-X, S12229) Fr & Eur.

Alonso, Martin. Diccionario Medieval Espanol, 2 vols. (SPA.). 1632p. 1986. 295.00 (0-7859-9575-7) Fr & Eur.

Alonso, Miguel E. The Art of Problem Solving in Organic Chemistry. LC 86-13349. 336p. 1987. 99.95 (0-471-84784-4) Wiley.

Alonso-Nunez, J. M. The Ages of Rome. 28p. (C). 1982. pap. 10.00 (90-70265-84-2, Pub. by Gieben) J Benjamins Pubng Co.

***Alonso, Paula.** Between Revolution & the Ballot Box: The Origins of the Argentine Radical Party. (Cambridge Latin American Studies: No. 86). (Illus.). 272p. (C). 2000. 49.95 (0-521-77185-4) Cambridge U Pr.

Alonso, Peter. Physics. (World Student Ser.: Bk. 3). (C). 1969. pap. text 14.33 (0-201-00262-0) Addison-Wesley.

— Physics. rev. ed. (C). 1996. pap. text. write for info. (0-201-40349-8) Addison-Wesley.

Alonso, Santiago G., jt. auth. see Falero, J. Eugenio.

Alonso-Schokel, Luis. The Eucharist. (C). 1988. 39.00 (0-7855-3219-6, Pub. by St Paul Pubns) St Mut.

Alonso Schokel, Luis. A Manual of Hermeneutics. (Biblical Seminar Ser.: Vol. 54). 181p. 1998. pap. 28.50 (1-85075-850-6, Pub. by Sheffield Acad) CUP Services.

Alonso, Sergio L., et al, eds. La Antropologia Fisica en Mexico: Estudios Sobre la Poblacion Antigua y Contemporanea. (SPA., Illus.). 426p. 1996. pap. 32.00 (968-36-5631-5, UN46, Pub. by Instit de Invest) UPLAAP.

***Alonso Tarrio, Leovigildo, et al.** Studies in Duality on Noetherian Formal Schemes & Non-Noetherian Ordinary Schemes. LC 99-42685. (Contemporary Mathematics Ser.). 126p. 1999. 33.00 (0-8218-1942-9) Am Math.

Alonso, William. Location & Land Use: Toward a General Theory of Land Rent. LC 63-17193. (Publications of the Joint Center for Urban Studies of the Massachusetts Institute of Technology & Harvard University). 219p. reprint ed. pap. 67.90 (0-7837-2215-X, 205730500004) Bks Demand.

Alonso, William, ed. Population in an Interacting World. LC 86-20133. (Illus.). 296p. 1987. 49.95 (0-674-69008-7) HUP.

Alonso, William & Starr, Paul, eds. The Politics of Numbers. LC 86-10060. (Population of the United States in the 1980s: A Census Monograph Ser.). 480p. 1989. pap. 18.50 (0-87154-016-9) Russell Sage.

Alonto, Zafrullah M. & Magdaong-Manginsay, Edna G. Ang Hanging Di-Namamatay: Nobelang Pangkasaysayan. (TAG.). 178p. (Orig.). 1993. pap. 12.50 (971-10-0470-4, Pub. by New Day Pub) Cellar.

Alonzo. Tejano Legacy: Rancheros & Settlers in South Texas, 1734-1900. LC 97-34454. xii, 357p. 1998. pap. 22.50 (0-8263-1897-5) Univ of New Mexico Schl.

***Alonzo, Anne-Marie.** Desire Alone. Nelson, Lucille, tr. (Illus.). 70p. 1999. pap. text. write for info. (0-88961-238-2) Womans Pr.

Alonzo, Anne-Marie. Lead Blues. 48p. 1990. pap. 5.00 (0-920717-43-8) Guernica Editions.

Alonzo, August N. Time Alterations: An Astonishing Phenomenon of Natural Law with Applications Ranging from Health Maintenance to the Eradication of Terminal Illness, 6 vols., I. Word for Word, Inc. Staff, ed. LC 89-50550. 147p. (Orig.). (C). 1989. write for info. (0-9622698-0-8) Taqua Pub.

— Time Alterations: An Astonishing Phenomenon of Natural Law with Applications Ranging from Health Maintenance to the Eradication of Terminal Illness, 6 vols., II. Word for Word, Inc. Staff, ed. LC 89-50550. 147p. (Orig.). (C). 1989. write for info. (0-9622698-1-6) Taqua Pub.

— Time Alterations: An Astonishing Phenomenon of Natural Law with Applications Ranging from Health Maintenance to the Eradication of Terminal Illness, 6 vols., III. Word for Word, Inc. Staff, ed. LC 89-50550. 147p. (Orig.). (C). 1989. write for info. (0-9622698-3-2) Taqua Pub.

— Time Alterations: An Astonishing Phenomenon of Natural Law with Applications Ranging from Health Maintenance to the Eradication of Terminal Illness, 6 vols., IV. Word for Word, Inc. Staff, ed. LC 89-50550. 147p. (Orig.). (C). 1989. write for info. (0-9622698-4-0) Taqua Pub.

— Time Alterations: An Astonishing Phenomenon of Natural Law with Applications Ranging from Health Maintenance to the Eradication of Terminal Illness, 6 vols., Set. Word for Word, Inc. Staff, ed. LC 89-50550. 147p. (Orig.). (C). 1989. pap. 39.95 (0-9622698-9-1) Taqua Pub.

— Time Alterations: An Astonishing Phenomenon of Natural Law with Applications Ranging from Health Maintenance to the Eradication of Terminal Illness, 6 vols., V. Word for Word, Inc. Staff, ed. LC 89-50550. 147p. (Orig.). (C). 1989. write for info. (0-9622698-6-7) Taqua Pub.

— Time Alterations: An Astonishing Phenomenon of Natural Law with Applications Ranging from Health Maintenance to the Eradication of Terminal Illness, 6 vols., VI. Word for Word, Inc. Staff, ed. LC 89-50550. 147p. (Orig.). (C). 1989. write for info. (0-9622698-7-5) Taqua Pub.

— Time Alterations: An Option to Live. Wohlstadter, Barbara, ed. LC 90-70502. (Illus.). 125p. (Orig.). 1990. pap. 9.95 (0-9622698-2-4) Taqua Pub.

Alonzo, Gisela P. Distant Fever. 231p. 1984. 6.95 (0-89697-172-4) Intl Univ Pr.

Alonzo, R. Gregory. Say Yes to Success. ii, 114p. 1996. pap. 10.00 (0-9651822-0-7) Candu.

Alonzo, Ray. Simple Acts of Kindness: Simple Inspiration & Ideas to Bring Delight & Goodness to Others. Orig. Title: Just Because. 160p. 1997. pap. 5.99 (1-57757-025-1) Honor Bks.

***Alonzo, Ray.** Simple Acts of Kindness for Kids: Little Ways to Make a Big Difference. (Illus.). (J). 2000. pap. 6.99 (1-57757-765-5) Trade Life.

Alonzo, Robert J. Electrical Safety for Petroleum Facilities. LC 97-34224. (Illus.). 188p. 1997. text 89.95 (1-885581-08-4, 4359) ASSE.

Alonzo, Roy S. UPS Guide to Owning & Managing a Bar or Tavern. 250p. 1994. pap. 15.95 (0-936894-67-9, 610058-01) Dearborn.

— The Upstart Guide to Owning & Managing a Restaurant. 224p. 1995. pap. 15.95 (0-936894-89-X, 6100-85-01) Dearborn.

***Alonzo, Tamara.** Just Imagine... What If There Were No Black People in the World! (Illus.). 20p. (J). (gr. 3-8). 1999. pap. 7.97 (0-9673627-0-9) Good Stuff CA.

An Asterisk (*) at the beginning of an entry indicates that the title is appearing for the first time.

Alosh, M. Mahdi. Advanced Arabic I Student Manual: Arabic Composition. (ARA & ENG.). 74p. 1992. student ed. 9.50 (*0-87415-220-8*, 870) Foreign Lang.

Alosh, M. Mahdi. Intermediate Arabic Three: A Reading Course. audio 10.00 (*0-87415-218-6*, 86B) Foreign Lang.

Alosh, Mahdi. Advanced Arabic I - Arabic Composition. (Introductory Course for Teaching Modern Standard Arabic to Speakers of Other Languages Ser.). (ARA., Illus.). 74p. (C). 1991. student ed., ring bd. 10.00 (*0-87415-219-4*, 87) Foreign Lang.

— Advanced Arabic II - Living Arabic. (Introductory Course for Teaching Modern Standard Arabic to Speakers of Other Languages Ser.). 83p. 1991. teacher ed. 9.50 (*0-87415-222-4*, 880) Foreign Lang.

— Advanced Arabic II - Living Arabic. (Introductory Course for Teaching Modern Standard Arabic to Speakers of Other Languages Ser.). (ARA., Illus.). 83p. (C). 1991. student ed., ring bd. 10.00 (*0-87415-221-6*, 88) Foreign Lang.

***Alosh, Mahdi.** Advanced Arabic Selections for Reading & Writing. 128p. (C). 1999. pap. 10.00 (*0-87415-338-7*) Foreign Lang.

— Ahlan Wa-Sahlan: Li-ta0alum Al-0arabeiyah Warzeifeiyan Lil-Mubtadi.ein, 10 vols. LC 99-36606. (Yale Language Ser.). (ARA.). 616p. 2000. 44.95 (*0-300-05854-3*) Yale U Pr.

Alosh, Mahdi. Elementary Arabic Pt. 3: Ahlan wa Sahlan, Student Manual. rev. ed. (Introductory Course for Teaching Modern Standard Arabic to Speakers of Other Languages Ser.). (ARA., Illus.). 146p. (C). 1991. student ed., ring bd. 14.00 (*0-87415-208-9*, 830) Foreign Lang.

— Intermediate Arabic Pt. 1: Our Living Language. rev. ed. (Introductory Course for Teaching Modern Standard Arabic to Speakers of Other Languages Ser.). (ARA., Illus.). 162p. (C). 1992. student ed. 15.00 (*0-87415-211-9*, 840) Foreign Lang.

— Intermediate Arabic Pt. 2: Our Living Language. (Introductory Course for Teaching Modern Standard Arabic to Speakers of Other Languages Ser.). (ARA., Illus.). 184p. (C). 1992. reprint ed. student ed., spiral bd. 17.00 (*0-87415-213-5*, 85) Foreign Lang.

— Intermediate Arabic Pt. 3: A Reading Course. rev. ed. (Introductory Course for Teaching Modern Standard Arabic to Speakers of Other Languages Ser.). (ARA., Illus.). 108p. (C). 1991. student ed., spiral bd. 12.00 (*0-87415-216-X*, 86) Foreign Lang.

— Learner, Text & Context in Foreign Language Acquisition: An Arabic Perspective. LC 97-35861. (Pathways to Advanced Skills Ser.: Vol. 4). 1997. 26.95 (*0-87415-333-6*, PA04) Foreign Lang.

Alotaibi, Muhammad, et al. Original People, 4 bks., Set II, Reading Level 5. (Illus.). 288p. (J). (gr. 4-8). 1989. 50.00 (*0-685-58809-2*) Rourke Corp.

— Original People, 4 bks., Set II, Reading Level 5. (Illus.). 288p. (J). (gr. 4-8). 1989. lib. bdg. 66.68 (*0-86625-269-X*) Rourke Pubns.

Alotta, Amy L. George Washington Never Slept Here: Stories Behind the Street Names of Washington, D. C. (Illus.). 176p. 1993. pap. 14.95 (*0-929387-82-1*) Bonus Books.

Alotta, Robert I. Mermaids, Monasteries, Cherokees & Custer: The Stories Behind Philadelphia Street Names. (Illus.). 267p. (Orig.). 1990. pap. 14.95 (*0-933893-90-6*) Bonus Books.

Alouf, J. E., et al, eds. Bacterial Protein Toxins. (Fems Symposia Ser.). 1984. text 83.00 (*0-12-053080-5*) Acad Pr.

Alouf, J. E. & Freer, J. H., eds. Sourcebook of Bacterial Protein Toxins. (Illus.). 518p. 1991. text 104.00 (*0-12-053078-3*) Acad Pr.

Alouf, Joseph E. The Comprehensive Sourcebook of Bacterial Protein Toxins. 2nd ed. LC 99-62163. (Illus.). 704p. 1999. 159.95 (*0-12-053075-9*) Acad Pr.

Alouini, Mohamed-Slim, jt. auth. see Simon, Marvin K.

Aloysius. A Healer's Herbal: Recipes for Medicinal Herbs & Weeds. LC 98-21854. Orig. Title: Comfort to the Sick. 448p. 1998. pap. 19.95 (*1-57863-106-8*) Weiser.

Aloysius, G. Nationalism Without a Nation in India. 278p. 1998. text 22.95 (*0-19-564104-3*) OUP.

— Nationalism Without a Nation in India. 280p. (J). 1999. pap. 13.95 (*0-19-564653-3*) OUP.

Alp, Esen E., jt. auth. see Wynter, Clive.

***Alpar, Emin Kaya & Gosling, Peter, eds.** Trauma: A Scientific Basis for Care. (An Arnold Publication). (Illus.). 400p. 1999. text 98.50 (*0-340-70093-9*, Pub. by E A) OUP.

Alpatov, M. Artistic Problems of the Italian Renaissance. 286p. 1976. 83.00 (*0-7855-0693-4*) St Mut.

Alpatov, V. M., ed. Early Russian Icon Painting. 332p. (C). 1984. 415.00 (*0-569-08854-2*) St Mut.

Alpatow, Michael. Die Dresdner Galerie: Alte Meister. 2nd rev. ed. (GER., Illus.). 370p. 1995. text 31.00 (*3-364-00015-8*) Gordon & Breach.

Alpaugh, Craig. Bad for Business. LC 90-52520. (Orig.). 1985. pap. 5.00 (*0-88734-307-4*) Players Pr.

— Bless Me, Father. 1974. 5.50 (*0-87129-307-2*, B25) Dramatic Pub.

— Filthy Habit: Playscript. LC 91-51079. (Orig.). 1985. pap. 5.00 (*0-88734-311-2*) Players Pr.

— The Neighborhood Crime Watch. 1995. 5.50 (*0-87129-481-8*, N26) Dramatic Pub.

— The Only Thing. 81p. 1996. pap. 5.50 (*0-87129-661-6*, O57) Dramatic Pub.

— Rough Night at the North Pole. 36p. 1989. pap. 3.50 (*0-87129-607-1*, R40) Dramatic Pub.

— Snatch a Falling Star. 62p. 1991. pap. 5.50 (*0-87129-025-1*, S93) Dramatic Pub.

Alpaugh, David. Counterpoint. 96p. 1994. pap. 11.95 (*0-934257-55-8*) Story Line.

Alpaugh, David, ed. Times Ten: An Anthology of Northern California Poets. unabridged ed. (Select Poets Ser.: No. 1). (Illus.). 190p. 1997. pap. 10.00 (*1-891298-00-3*) Small Poetry.

Alpay, Daniel. Schur Functions, Operator Colligations, & Reproducing Kernel Pontryagin Spaces. LC 97-17908. (Operator Theory, Advances, & Applications Ser.). 1997. write for info. (*0-8176-5763-0*) Birkhauser.

Alpay, Daniel, et al. Schur Functions, Operator Colligations, & Reproducing Kernel Pontryagin Spaces. LC 97-17908. (Operator Theory Ser.: No. 96). 248p. 1997. 110.00 (*3-7643-5763-0*) Birkhauser.

Alpay, Mete H. How to Make an "A" in Freshman Chemistry Laboratory for the First-Year Student. (Illus.). 325p. (C). pap. text 17.95 (*0-9634134-0-6*) Home Ed Systs.

Alpen, Edward L. Radiation Biophysics. 2nd ed. LC 97-74421. (Illus.). 484p. 1997. text 69.95 (*0-12-053085-6*) Morgan Kaufmann.

Alpen, Edward L., et al, eds. Population Exposure from the Nuclear Fuel Cycle. 370p. 1988. text 110.00 (*2-88124-278-2*) Gordon & Breach.

Alpen, Ernest Van, see Van Alpen, Ernest.

***Alper, Alan.** Official Best of the Web Shopping Guide. 2000. 19.95 (*0-7615-2834-2*) Prima Pub.

Alper, Allen M., ed. Phase Diagrams in Advanced Ceramics. (Treatise on Materials Science & Technology Ser.). (Illus.). 237p. 1995. text 95.00 (*0-12-341834-8*) Acad Pr.

Alper, Ann F. A Brief Green History of Planet Earth. 112p. (Orig.). (YA). (gr. 7-9). 1995. pap. 6.95 (*1-57515-079-4*) PPI Pubng.

Alper, Ann Fitzpatrick, see Fitzpatrick Alper, Ann.

Alper, Benedict S. Love & Politics in Wartime: Letters to My Wife, 1943-45. Scott, Joan W., ed. 248p. 1992. 26.50 (*0-252-01877-X*) U of Ill Pr.

Alper, Bob. A Rabbi Confesses. (Illus.). 112p. (Orig.). 1995. pap. 9.95 (*1-888016-18-3*) Finkstrom Prods.

Alper, Frank. Exploring Atlantis, No. I. 2nd ed. (Illus.). 157p. 1990. reprint ed. pap. 11.95 (*0-929365-01-1*) Adamis Intl.

— Exploring Atlantis, No. II. 2nd ed. (Illus.). 158p. 1990. reprint ed. pap. 11.95 (*0-929365-02-X*) Adamis Intl.

Alper, Gerald. Blind Alleys: Obstacles along the Road to Intimacy. LC 97-22580. 156p. 1997. 34.95 (*1-57309-198-7*); pap. 14.95 (*1-57309-197-9*) Intl Scholars.

— Control Games: Avoiding Intimacy on the Singles Scene. LC 95-49764. 1996. 40.00 (*1-56821-729-3*) Aronson.

— The Dark Side of the Analytic Moon: A Memoir of Life in a Training Institute. 174p. 1997. 34.95 (*1-57309-017-4*); pap. 19.95 (*1-57309-016-6*) Intl Scholars.

— Minding the Other's Mind: The Factor of Control & Dominance in Contemporary Relationships. LC 96-39510. 124p. 1997. 39.95 (*1-57309-101-4*); pap. 24.95 (*1-57309-100-6*) Intl Scholars.

— Narcissistic Giving: A Study of People Who Cheat in Relationships. LC 94-28831. 130p. 1996. 44.95 (*1-883255-81-3*); pap. 24.95 (*1-883255-80-5*) Intl Scholars.

— Portrait of the Artist As a Young Patient: Psychodynamic Studies of the Creative Personality. LC 97-30453. 260p. 1997. pap. 19.95 (*1-57309-203-7*) Intl Scholars.

— Power Games: Why Winners Win & Losers Lose. 153p. 1999. pap. 24.95 (*1-57309-397-1*) Intl Scholars.

— Power Plays: Their Uses & Abuses in Human Relations. LC 97-51293. 294p. 1998. 34.95 (*1-57309-267-3*); pap. 16.95 (*1-57309-259-2*) Intl Scholars.

— The Puppeteers: Studies of Obsessive Control. LC 94-33056. 224p. 1994. 19.95 (*0-88064-160-6*) Fromm Intl Pub.

— The Puppeteers: Studies of Obsessive Control. LC 98-24869. 228p. 1998. pap. 19.95 (*1-57309-316-5*) Intl Scholars.

— The Singles Scene: A Psychoanalytic Study of the Breakdown of Intimacy. LC 93-6446. 128p. 1995. 37.95 (*1-883255-15-5*) Intl Scholars.

— Singles Scene: A Psychoanalytical Study of the Breakdown of Intimacy. LC 93-6446. 1995. pap. 14.95 (*1-883255-14-7*) Intl Scholars.

Alper, Harvey P., ed. Mantra. LC 87-6489. (SUNY Series in Religious Studies). 343p. (C). 1988. pap. text 21.95 (*0-88706-599-6*) State U NY Pr.

— Understanding Mantras. LC 87-6481. (SUNY Series in Religious Studies). 530p. (C). 1989. text 34.50 (*0-88706-598-8*) State U NY Pr.

Alper, Janice P., ed. Learning Together: A Source Book on Jewish Family Education. LC 87-70964. 477p. 1987. pap. text 22.50 (*0-86705-020-9*) A R E Pub.

Alper, Janis & Grishaver, Joel Lurie. Mah la'Asot: What Should I Do?: A Book of Ethical Problems & Jewish Responses. (Illus.). 64p. (Orig.). (J). (gr. 4-8). 1992. pap. text 5.50 (*0-933873-69-7*) Torah Aura.

Alper, Joseph & Nelson, Gordon L. Polymeric Materials: Chemistry for the Future. LC 89-293. (Other Technical Bks.). (Illus.). 103p. (C). 1989. text 29.95 (*0-8412-1622-3*, Pub. by Am Chemical); pap. text 17.95 (*0-8412-1613-4*, Pub. by Am Chemical) OUP.

Alper, Lisa & Krause, Michael. Las Vegas Casino Employment Guide. (Illus.). 95p. (Orig.). 1994. pap. 12.95 (*0-9641012-0-3*) Jordan Pubng.

***Alper, Matthew.** The "God" Part of the Brain: A Scientific Interpretation of Human Spirituality & God. 4th rev. ed. 181p. 2000. pap. 11.95 (*0-9660367-0-0*) Rogue Pr NY.

Alper, Neil O., et al. Artists in the Work Force: Employment & Earnings, 1970 to 1990. LC 96-9596. (National Endowment for the Arts Research Division Report Ser.: No. 37). 150p. 1996. pap. 13.95 (*0-929765-48-6*) Seven Locks Pr.

Alper, Neil O., jt. auth. see Hellman, Daryl A.

Alper, Robert A. Life Doesn't Get Any Better Than This: The Holiness of Little Daily Dramas. LC 96-12887. 224p. (Orig.). 1996. pap. 12.00 (*0-89243-932-7*, Liguori Triumph) Liguori Pubns.

Alper, Sandra, et al. Inclusion: Are We Abandoning or Helping Students? Herman, Jerry J. & Herman, Janice L., eds. LC 95-15806. (Practicing Administrator's Leadership Ser.). 88p. 1995. pap. 14.95 (*0-8039-6249-5*) Corwin Pr.

Alper, Sandra K., et al, eds. Families of Students with Disabilities: Consultation & Advocacy. LC 93-6854. 368p. 1993. pap. text 48.00 (*0-205-14038-6*) Allyn

***Alper, Sandra K., et al.** Alternate Assessment of Students with Disabilities in Inclusive Settings. LC 00-30609. 288p. 2000. pap. text 61.00 (*0-205-30615-2*) Allyn

Alper, Sandra K., jt. auth. see Ryndak, Diane L.

Alper, Steven M. Next! Auditioning for the Musical Theatre. LC 95-19090. 105p. 1995. pap. 12.95 (*0-435-08686-3*, 08686) Heinemann.

Alperi, Victor. Los Suenos de un Portugues y Otras Historias. LC 95-67274. (SPA.). 101p. 1995. pap. 20.00 (*0-89295-082-X*) Society Sp & Sp-Am.

Alperin, Barry J. & McCririe, Philip G. Industry in Crisis: Reengineering Your Appraisal Career. 362p. 1996. pap. 59.95 (*1-56842-050-1*) Marshall & Swift.

Alperin, Diane E., jt. auth. see Richie, Nicholas D.

Alperin-Hochman, Marlene. The Doll Hospital Directory: A National Directory of Doll Repair & Restoration Services in the United States. 2nd rev. ed. Resnick-Gallo, Laurie, ed. (Illus.). 144p. 1998. pap. 29.95 (*0-9611774-6-2*, DHD2) Ultimate Coll.

— Living with Dolls: Tips & Advice from the Professionals, Vol. I. Resnick-Gallo, Laurie, ed. Date not set. pap. write for info. (*0-9611774-7-0*) Ultimate Coll.

Alperin, Howard J. & Chase, Roland F. Consumer Law Sales Practices & Credit Regulation 1993 Pocket Parts: To Accompany the Bound Volume, 2 vols., 1. 270p. 1993. write for info. (*0-314-01870-0*) West Pub.

— Consumer Law Sales Practices & Credit Regulation 1993 Pocket Parts: To Accompany the Bound Volume, 2 vols., 2. 270p. 1993. write for info. (*0-314-01871-9*) West Pub.

— Consumer Law, Volume 1, Sales practices & Credit Regulation, Sections 1 to 340. (Practice Ser.). 331p. 1986. text. write for info. (*0-314-23203-6*) West Pub

Alperin, J. L. Local Representation Theory: Modular Representations As an Introduction to the Local Representation Theory of Finite Groups. (Cambridge Studies in Advanced Mathematics: No. 11). 188p. (C). 1993. pap. text 26.95 (*0-521-44926-X*) Cambridge U Pr.

Alperin, J. L. & Bell, Rowen B. Groups & Representations. LC 95-17160. (Graduate Texts in Mathematics Ser.: No. 165). 208p. 1995. 59.95 (*0-387-94525-3*) Spr-Verlag.

— Groups & Representations. LC 95-17160. (Graduate Texts in Mathematics Ser.: Vol. 162). 194p. 1995. 27.95 (*0-387-94526-1*) Spr-Verlag.

Alperin, Melissa & Miner, Kathleen. Using Epi Info: A Step by Step Guide. Thacker, Netha, ed. (Illus.). 424p. (Orig.). 1997. pap. text 49.95 (*1-57931-010-9*) ToucanEd Pubns.

Alperin, R. C., ed. Arboreal Group Theory: Proceedings of a Workshop Held September 13-16, 1988. (Mathematical Sciences Research Institute Publications: Vol. 19). (Illus.). 384p. 1991. 65.95 (*0-387-97518-7*) Spr-Verlag.

Alperin, Richard J., jt. auth. see Hamilton, John M.

Alperin, Richard M. & Phillips, David G., eds. The Impact of Managed Care on the Practice of Psychotherapy: Innovations, Implementation, & Controversy. LC 96-41932. 256p. 1996. 31.95 (*0-87630-830-2*) Brunner-Mazel.

Alpern, Andrew. Historic Manhattan Apartment Houses. LC 95-22141. (Illus.). 96p. (Orig.). 1996. pap. text 8.95 (*0-486-28872-2*) Dover.

— Luxury Apartment Houses of Manhattan: An Illustrated History. LC 92-26286. (Illus.). 192p. (Orig.). 1993. pap. 12.95 (*0-486-27370-9*) Dover.

— New York's Fabulous Luxury Apartments: With Original Floor Plans from the Dakota, River House, Olympic Tower & Other Great Buildings. (Illus.). 176p. 1987. reprint ed. pap. 10.95 (*0-486-25318-X*) Dover.

— 101 Questions about Copyright Law. LC 98-41538. 80p. 1998. pap. 2.95 (*0-486-40448-X*) Dover.

Alpern, Andrew & Durst, Seymour. New York's Architectural Holdouts. unabridged ed. LC 96-45227. (Illus.). 172p. 1997. reprint ed. pap. text 12.95 (*0-486-29425-0*) Dover.

Alpern, Hymen, jt. auth. see Martel, Jose.

Alpern, Kenneth D., ed. The Ethics of Reproductive Technology. 376p. (C). 1992. pap. text 27.95 (*0-19-507435-1*) OUP.

Alpern, Laura. ILO Manual for Labour Information Centres. iii, 110p. (Orig.). 1991. pap. 15.75 (*92-2-107095-6*) Intl Labour Office.

Alpern, Lynne & Blumenfeld, Esther. Oh Lord, I Sound Just Like Mama. (Illus.). 120p. 1986. pap. 6.95 (*0-931948-93-2*) Peachtree Pubs.

Alpern, Lynne, jt. auth. see Blumenfeld, Esther.

Alpern, Merry. Dirty Windows. 112p. 35.00 (*1-881616-58-4*) Dist Art Pubs.

— Shopping. (Illus.). 160p. 1999. 39.95 (*3-908247-15-2*, Pub. by Scalo Pubs) Dist Art Pubs.

Alpern, Mildred. Longman's Guide to the Advanced Placement Examination in European History. 1993. pap. text 26.80 (*0-8013-0943-3*) Longman.

Alpern, Sara. Freda Kirchwey: A Woman of the Nation. (Illus.). 331p. 1987. 43.00 (*0-674-31828-5*) HUP.

Alpern, Sara, et al, eds. The Challenge of Feminist Biography: Writing the Lives of Modern American Women. (Women in American History Ser.). (Illus.). 224p. (C). 1992. text 44.95 (*0-252-01926-1*); pap. text 14.95 (*0-252-06292-2*) U of Ill Pr.

Alpern, Stanley B. Amazons of Black Sparta: The Women's Regiment of Dahomey. LC 97-51832. 280p. 1998. pap. 18.95 (*0-8147-0678-9*); text 55.00 (*0-8147-0677-0*) NYU Pr.

Alperovits, Yosef Y. Ohr Hatfilla, Vol. 1. (HEB.). 397p. 20.00 (*0-8266-5226-3*) Kehot Pubn Soc.

— Ohr Hatfilla, Vol. 2. (HEB.). 525p. 20.00 (*0-8266-5227-1*) Kehot Pubn Soc.

— Ohr Hatfilla, Vol. 3. (HEB.). 395p. 1992. 20.00 (*0-8266-5228-X*) Kehot Pubn Soc.

— Ohr Hatfilla, Vol. 4. (HEB.). 633p. 1994. 25.00 (*0-8266-5229-8*) Kehot Pubn Soc.

Alperovitz, Gar. Atomic Diplomacy: Hiroshima & Potsdam; The Use of the Atomic Bomb & the American Confrontation with Soviet Power. 2nd expanded ed. 414p. (C). 1994. 54.95 (*0-7453-0948-8*, Pub. by Pluto GBR); pap. 24.95 (*0-7453-0947-X*, Pub. by Pluto GBR) Stylus Pub VA.

Alperovitz, Gar. The Decision to Use the Atomic Bomb. 1996. pap. 16.00 (*0-679-76285-X*) Vin Bks.

Alperovitz, Gar. The Decision to Use the Atomic Bomb & the Architecture of an American Myth. 847p. 1998. text 35.00 (*0-7881-5919-4*) DIANE Pub.

— The Decision to Use the Atomic Bomb & the Architecture of an American Myth. LC 95-8778. 688p. 1995. 32.50 (*0-679-44331-2*) Knopf.

Alpers, Adam. The Acadian Matrix. 136p. 1999. pap. 13.00 (*0-8059-4608-X*) Dorrance.

— Change Your Room. LC 99-11936. 1999. 14.95 (*0-7894-3956-5*) DK Pub Inc.

Alpers, Charles N. & Blowes, David W., eds. Environmental Geochemistry of Sulfide Oxidation: Developed from a Symposium Sponsored by the Division of Geochemistry at the 204th National Meeting of the American Chemical Society, Washington DC; August 23-28,1992. LC 93-39250. (ACS Symposium Ser.: No. 550). 752p. 1994. text 150.00 (*0-8412-2772-1*, Pub. by Am Chemical) OUP.

Alpers, David H. Manual Nutritional International Edition. 2nd ed. 1988. 15.95 (*0-316-03514-9*) Little.

— Manual Nutritional Therapeutics: Asia. 2nd ed. 1988. 10.95 (*0-316-03517-3*) Little.

— Manual of Nutritional Therapeutics. 3rd ed. (Spiral Manual Ser.). 624p. 1995. spiral bd. 38.00 (*0-316-03524-6*) Lppncott W & W.

Alpers, David H. & Wittenberg, Stephen M. Clinician's Companion: A Study Guide for Effective & Humane Patient Care. (Illus.). 224p. 1986. 29.95 (*0-316-03511-4*, Little Brwn Med Div) Lppncott W & W.

Alpers, David H., jt. ed. see Tadataka Yamada.

Alpers, Edward A. & Fontaine, Pierre-Michel, eds. Walter Rodney, Revolutionary & Scholar: A Tribute. 200p. (Orig.). 1982. pap. 10.00 (*0-918456-08-6*, Crossroads) African Studies Assn.

Alpers-Golz, Roswitha. Der Begriff Skopos in der Stoa und Seine Vorgeschichte. (Spudasmata Ser.: Bd. VIII). (GER.). vi, 272p. 1976. 50.00 (*3-487-05933-9*) G Olms Pubs.

Alpers, Jody. Cowboy's Christmas. (Illus.). 24p. (Orig.). (J). (gr. k-6). 1996. pap. 6.95 (*0-9640533-1-4*) Libros de Ninos.

— T Is for Tortilla: A Southwestern Alphabet Book. (Illus.). 30p. (J). (gr. k-6). 1993. pap. 6.95 (*0-9640533-0-6*) Libros de Ninos.

Alpers, Leonard, jt. auth. see Kuhn, Dolores.

Alpers, Lynne, jt. auth. see Blumenfeld, Esther.

Alpers, Michael. Das Nachrepublikanische Finanzsystem: Fiscus und Fisci in der Fruehen Kaiserzeit. (Untersuchungen zur Antiken Literatur und Geschichte Ser.: No. 45). (GER.). 359p. (C). 1995. lib. bdg. 152.30 (*3-11-014562-6*) De Gruyter.

Alpers, Michael P., jt. ed. see Attenborough, Robert D.

Alpers, Paul J. What Is Pastoral? 1997. pap. text 14.95 (*0-226-01517-3*) U Ch Pr.

— What Is Pastoral? LC 95-35356. 448p. (C). 1997. 34.95 (*0-226-01516-5*) U Ch Pr.

Alpers, Svetlana. The Art of Describing: Dutch Art in the Seventeenth Century. LC 82-6969. (Illus.). 316p. (C). 1983. lib. bdg. 51.00 (*0-226-01512-2*) U Ch Pr.

— The Art of Describing: Dutch Art in the Seventeenth Century. LC 82-6969. (Illus.). 302p. (C). 1984. pap. text 24.95 (*0-226-01513-0*) U Ch Pr.

— The Making of Rubens. LC 94-30637. (Illus.). 186p. 1995. 40.00 (*0-300-06010-6*) Yale U Pr.

— The Making of Rubens. (Illus.). 186p. 1996. pap. 25.00 (*0-300-06744-5*) Yale U Pr.

— Rembrandt's Enterprise: The Studio & the Market. LC 87-16161. (Illus.). 308p. 1990. pap. 24.95 (*0-226-01518-1*) U Ch Pr.

— Rembrandt's Enterprise: The Studio & the Market. (Illus.). 308p. 1997. 35.95 (*0-226-01514-9*) U Ch Pr.

— Tiepolo & the Pictorial Intelligence. (Illus.). 192p. 1996. pap. 30.00 (*0-300-06817-4*) Yale U Pr.

Alpers, Svetlana & Baxandall, Michael. Tiepolo & the Pictorial Intelligence. LC 94-13926. (Illus.). 192p. 1994. 60.00 (*0-300-05978-7*) Yale U Pr.

Alpers, Von Christian. The Commercial Real Estate Market in the U. S. (ENG & GER.). 1997. 30.00 (*0-86640-061-3*) German Am Chamber.

Alperson, Myra. Building the Corporate Community Development Team. (Report Ser.: No. 1205-98-RR). (Illus.). 58p. 1998. pap. text 100.00 (*0-8237-0654-0*) Conference Bd.

***Alperson, Myra.** Dim Sum, Bagels, & Grits: A Sourcebook for Multicultural Families. 304p. 2001. pap. 15.00 (*0-374-52611-7*) FS&G.

Alperson, Myra. Foundations for a New Democracy: Corporate Social Investment in South Africa. 239p. (Orig.). 1995. pap. text 17.95 (*0-86975-463-7*, Pub. by Ravan Pr) Ohio U Pr.

— The International Adoption Handbook: How to Make Foreign Adoption Work for You. LC 96-39053. 224p. 1997. pap. 14.95 (*0-8050-4579-1*) H Holt & Co.

Alperson, Philip. Musical Worlds: New Directions in the Philosophy of Music. LC 97-33027. 1998. pap. 14.95 (*0-271-01769-4*) Pa St U Pr.

Alperson, Philip A., ed. The Philosophy of the Visual Arts. (Illus.). 640p. (C). 1992. pap. text 46.00 (*0-19-505975-1*) OUP.

— What Is Music? An Introduction to the Philosophy of Music. LC 93-41866. (C). 1994. reprint ed. pap. text 20.00 (*0-271-01318-4*) Pa St U Pr.

Alpert. Cardiology for the Primary Care Physician. 2nd ed. (C). 1998. 95.00 (*0-8385-1563-0*, Apple Lange Med) McGraw.

Alpert. Emile Durkheim & His Sociology. 248p. 1993. 63.95 (*0-7512-0129-4*) Ashgate Pub Co.

Alpert, Arlena. The Communication Resource Workbook: For Creative Customer Care. (Illus.). 90p. 1998. spiral bd. 20.00 (*1-891076-11-6*) Gemini Press.

Alpert, Arlene. Moving Without Madness: A Guide to Handling the Stress & Emotions of Moving. (Illus.). ix, 150p. 1997. pap. 14.95 (*1-891076-00-0*) Gemini Press.

— Traveling Beyond Life's Roadblocks: Creating a Life of Choice. (Illus.). 2000. pap. 15.00 (*1-891076-12-4*) Gemini Press.

Alpert, Augusta. The Solving of Problem-Situations by Preschool Children. LC 74-176514. (Columbia University. Teachers College. Contributions to Education Ser.: No. 323). reprint ed. 37.50 (*0-404-55323-0*) AMS Pr.

***Alpert, Barbara.** Child of My Heart: A Celebration of Adoption. 192p. (Orig.). 1999. pap. 12.00 (*0-425-16901-4*) Berkley Pub.

Alpert, Barbara. No Friend Like a Sister: A Celebration in Words & Memories. LC 97-104871. 192p. 1996. pap. 11.00 (*0-425-15531-5*) Berkley Pub.

Alpert, Barbara & Holbrook, Gail. Bride's Little Instruction Book. (Illus.). 96p. 1995. pap. 4.99 (*0-7860-0149-6*, Pinncle Kensgtn) Kensgtn Pub Corp.

***Alpert, Barbara & Holbrook, Gail.** The Bride's Little Instruction Book. 96p. 2000. mass mkt. 5.99 (*0-7860-1360-5*) Kensgtn Pub Corp.

Alpert, Barbara, jt. auth. see Lund, JoAnna M.

Alpert, Barbara, jt. auth. see Lund, Joanna M.

Alpert, Barbara, jt. auth. see Lund, JoAnna M.

Alpert, Barbara, jt. auth. see Lund, Joanna M.

Alpert, Barbara, jt. auth. see Lund, JoAnne M.

Alpert, Barbara, jt. auth. see Matthews, Scott.

Alpert, Bill. Castle Garden. 1996. pap. 21.95 (*1-877946-99-0*) Permanent Pr.

Alpert, Carl, tr. see Cohen, Asher, ed.

Alpert, Cathryn. Rocket City. 1996. pap. 12.00 (*0-679-77016-X*) Vin Bks.

Alpert, Eugene. Conventional Wisdom: A Television Viewer's Guide to the 1992 National Political Conventions. 36p. 1992. pap. 6.95 (*1-881846-00-8*) C-Span.

Alpert, Geoffrey & Dunham, Roger. The Force Factor: Measuring Police Use of Force Relative to Suspect Resistance. LC 97-69037. 32p. 1997. pap. 5.50 (*1-878734-52-0*) Police Exec Res.

Alpert, Geoffrey P., ed. Legal Rights of Prisoners. LC 80-17241. (Sage Criminal Justice System Annuals Ser.: No. 14). 280p. reprint ed. pap. 86.80 (*0-8357-8466-5*, 203473400091) Bks Demand.

Alpert, Geoffrey P. & Dunham, Roger. Police Use of Force: A Statistical Analysis of the Metro-Dade Police Department. LC 95-71262. (Police Research & Evaluation Ser.: Vol. 1). 44p. (Orig.). 1995. pap. text 6.50 (*1-878734-38-5*) Police Exec Res.

Alpert, Geoffrey P. & Dunham, Roger G. Police Pursuit Driving: Controlling Responses to Emergency Situations, 27. LC 89-23247. (Contributions in Criminology & Penology Ser.: No. 27). 200p. 1990. 52.95 (*0-313-27261-1*, ALC/, Greenwood Pr) Greenwood.

— Policing Multi-Ethnic Neighborhoods: The Miami Study & Findings for Law Enforcement in the United States, 20. LC 88-3112. (Contributions in Criminology & Penology Ser.: No. 20). 176p. 1988. 42.95 (*0-313-26290-X*, ATP/) Greenwood.

— Policing Urban America. 3rd rev. ed. LC 97-205587. (Illus.). 312p. (C). 1996. pap. text 17.95 (*0-88133-917-2*) Waveland Pr.

Alpert, Geoffrey P. & Fridell, Lorie. Police Vehicles & Firearms: Instruments of Deadly Force. 167p. (C). 1992. pap. text 13.95 (*0-88133-613-0*) Waveland Pr.

Alpert, Geoffrey P., jt. ed. see Dunham, Roger G.

Alpert, Geoffrey P., jt. ed. see Haas, Kenneth C.

Alpert, Geoffry & Piquero, Alex. Community Policing: Contemporary Readings. LC 99-185364. (Illus.). 458p. (C). 1998. pap. text 23.95 (*0-88133-981-4*) Waveland Pr.

Alpert, George. Paintings. (Illus.). 85p. 1987. 50.00 (*0-941737-00-4*) Paradise Hse.

— Taos Pueblo. LC 83-63106. (Illus.). 160p. 1984. 60.00 (*0-87358-350-7*) Paradise Hse.

Alpert, George, et al. A Second Chance to Live: The Suicide Syndrome. LC 75-20452. (Photography Ser.). (Illus.). 90p. 1976. pap. 6.95 (*0-306-80023-3*) Da Capo.

Alpert, Gerri. Bike Abroad: 439 Organized Trips with 70 Companies in 49 Countries. Owen, Suzanne, ed. (Trip Finders Ser.). (Illus.). 221p. (Orig.). 1995. pap. 29.95 (*1-885150-00-8*) New Voyager.

Alpert, Hollis. Fellini: A Life. LC 98-164883. (Illus.). 337p. 1995. pap. 12.95 (*1-56924-954-7*) Marlowe & Co.

Al'pert, I. L. Radio Wave Propagation & the Ionosphere. LC 61-17727. 404p. reprint ed. pap. 125.30 (*0-608-10304-7*, 202065600018) Bks Demand.

Al'pert, Iakov L. Waves & Satellites in the Near-Earth Plasma. Barbour, Julian B., tr. from RUS. LC 74-19475. (Studies in Soviet Science). (Illus.). 206p. 1974. reprint ed. pap. 63.90 (*0-608-05556-5*, 206602400006) Bks Demand.

Alpert, J. S., ed. Recent Advances in the Management of Patients with Acute Myocardial Infarction. (Journal: Cardiology: Vol. 76, No. 2). (Illus.). 92p. 1989. pap. 55.75 (*3-8055-5038-3*) S Karger.

Alpert, J. S., et al, eds. Progressi Nella Ricerca e Nella Terapia Con Nitrati - Advances in Nitrate Research & Therapy Pt. 1. (Journal: Cardiology: Vol. 84, Suppl. 1, 1994). (Illus.). iv, 72p. 1994. pap. 23.50 (*3-8055-5893-7*) S Karger.

Alpert, J. S., jt. ed. see Becker, R. C.

Alpert, J. S., jt. ed. see Rezakovic, D.

Alpert, Jane. Growing up Underground. 1990. pap. 12.95 (*0-8065-1196-6*, Citadel Pr) Carol Pub Group.

Alpert, Janice. I Always Start My Diet on Monday: A Unique Program to Permanently Conquer Emotional Overeating. unabridged ed. 208p. (Orig.). 1997. pap. 13.95 (*0-9655023-0-9*) Pearl Pub IL.

Alpert, Jonathan A. Florida Real Estate: Florida Practice Systems Library Selection. LC 81-85397. 1982. 230.00 (*0-318-11930-7*) West Group.

— Florida Real Estate: Florida Practice Systems Library Selection. 1991. suppl. ed. 76.00 (*0-317-03265-8*) West Group.

Alpert, Joseph S. Cardiology for the Primary Care Physician. 2nd ed. LC 97-41983. 1997. write for info. (*1-57340-115-3*) Current Med.

— The Heart Attack Handbook: A Commonsense Guide to Treatment, Recovery & Staying Well. 2nd ed. 180p. 1985. mass mkt. 6.95 (*0-316-03506-8*) Little.

— Manual CRDV Asia, No. 3. 1988. 10.95 (*0-316-03521-1*) Little.

— Physiopathology of the Cardiovascular System. 348p. 1984. 31.95 (*0-316-03504-1*, Little Brwn Med Div) Lppncott W & W.

Alpert, Joseph S., ed. Cardiology for the Primary Care Physician. (Illus.). 384p. 1996. text 95.00 (*1-57340-024-6*) Current Med.

Alpert, Joseph S. & Francis, Gary S. Handbook of Coronary Care. 5th ed. LC 92-48484. 288p. 1993. pap. text 36.00 (*0-316-03526-2*) Lppncott W & W.

Alpert, Joseph S. & Francis, Gary S. Handbook of Coronary Care. 6th ed. 240p. pap. text 37.95 (*0-7817-1958-5*) Lppncott W & W.

Alpert, Joseph S. & Rippe, James M. Manual of Cardiovascular Diagnosis & Therapy. 2nd ed. (Spiral Manual Ser.). 426p. 1985. spiral bd. 21.00 (*0-316-03510-6*, Little Brwn Med Div) Lppncott W & W.

— Manual of Cardiovascular Diagnosis & Therapy. 4th ed. LC 95-24885. 416p. 1996. spiral bd. 39.00 (*0-316-03531-9*) Lppncott W & W.

***Alpert, Joseph S., et al.** Valvular Heart Disease 3rd ed. LC 99-16809. 1999. write for info. (*0-7817-2310-8*) Lppncott W & W.

Alpert, Joseph S., jt. auth. see Dalen, James E.

Alpert, Joseph S., jt. ed. see Francis, Gary S.

Alpert, Judith L., ed. Psychoanalysis & Women: Contemporary Reappraisals. 360p. 1994. reprint ed. pap. 29.95 (*0-88163-191-4*) Analytic Pr.

— Sexual Abuse Recalled: Treating Trauma in the Era of the Recovered Memory Debate. 440p. 1995. 50.00 (*1-56821-363-8*) Aronson.

Alpert, Judith L., et al. Psychological Consultation in Educational Settings. LC 82-8995. (Jossey-Bass Social & Behavioral Science Ser.). 359p. reprint ed. pap. 111.30 (*0-8357-4796-4*, 203773300009) Bks Demand.

Alpert, Judith L., et al. Psychological Consultation in Educational Settings: Casebook for Working with Administrators, Teachers, Students. LC 94-45754. 362p. 1995. pap. 40.00 (*1-56821-485-5*) Aronson.

Alpert, June & Harrison, Michael A. Enlightened Eating for Better Health. 2nd ed. 104p. 1989. reprint ed. pap. text 14.50 (*0-940429-05-5*) M B Glass Assocs.

Alpert, Lou. Dancing with the Shadows in My Room. (Illus.). 32p. (J). (ps-3). 1991. 12.95 (*1-879085-06-2*, Whispering Coyote) Charlesbridge Pub.

— Emma & the Magic Dance. (Illus.). 32p. (J). (ps-3). 1991. boxed set 12.95 (*1-879085-01-1*, Whispering Coyote) Charlesbridge Pub.

— Emma Giggled. (Illus.). 32p. (J). (ps-3). 1991. boxed set 12.95 (*1-879085-02-X*, Whispering Coyote) Charlesbridge Pub.

— Emma Lights up the Sky. (Illus.). 32p. (J). (ps-3). 1991. boxed set 12.95 (*1-879085-03-8*, Whispering Coyote) Charlesbridge Pub.

— Emma Swings. (Illus.). 32p. (J). (ps-3). 1991. boxed set 12.95 (*1-879085-04-6*, Whispering Coyote) Charlesbridge Pub.

— Emma's Turn to Dance. (Illus.). 32p. (J). (ps-3). 1991. boxed set 12.95 (*1-879085-00-3*, Whispering Coyote) Charlesbridge Pub.

— The Man in the Moon & His Flying Balloon. (Illus.). 32p. (J). (ps-8). 1991. lib. bdg. 12.95 (*1-879085-05-4*, Whispering Coyote) Charlesbridge Pub.

— Max & the Great Blueness. LC 92-23313. (Illus.). 32p. (J). (ps-3). 1993. 13.95 (*1-879085-38-0*, Whispering Coyote) Charlesbridge Pub.

— You & Your Dad. LC 91-44412. (Illus.). 32p. (J). (ps-2). 1992. 14.95 (*1-879085-36-4*, Whispering Coyote) Charlesbridge Pub.

— You & Your Dad. (J). (ps-2). 1998. pap. 5.95 (*1-58089-004-0*, Whispering Coyote) Charlesbridge Pub.

Alpert, M. E., et al. Chemical & Radionuclide Food Contamination. (Illus.). 220p. (C). 1973. text 29.50 (*0-8422-7091-4*) Irvington.

Alpert, Mark. Eccentric Muscle Training in Sports & Orthopaedics. 2nd ed. LC 95-7871. 1995. text 39.00 (*0-443-08987-6*) Church.

Alpert, Martin A. Cardiac Arrhythmias: A Bedside Guide to Diagnosis & Treatment. LC 79-28272. (Illus.). 303p. reprint ed. pap. 94.00 (*0-8357-6763-9*, 203542400095) Bks Demand.

Alpert, Martin A. & Alexander, James K. The Heart & Lung in Obesity. LC 97-30470. (Illus.). 264p. 1998. 81.00 (*0-87993-685-1*) Futura Pub.

Alpert, Merna J. The Chronically Disabled Elderly in Society, 24. LC 93-39351. (Contributions to the Study of Aging Ser.: Vol. 24). 160p. 1994. 55.00 (*0-313-29109-8*, Greenwood Pr) Greenwood.

Alpert, Michael. New International History of the Spanish Civil War. 304p. 1998. pap. 19.95 (*0-312-21043-4*) St Martin.

***Alpert, Michael.** A Night-Sea Journey. 381p. 2000. pap. 14.95 (*0-913006-72-6*) Puckerbrush.

Alpert, Nachum. Destruction of Slonim Jewry: The Story of the Jews During the Holocaust. Rosenfeld, Max, ed. & tr. by. from YID. LC 90-81303. (Illus.). 400p. 1990. 23.95 (*0-89604-136-0*, Holocaust Library) US Holocaust.

Alpert, Nancy L. Religion & Psychology: A Medical Subject Analysis & Research Index with Bibliography. LC 83-71657. 150p. 1985. 47.50 (*0-88164-034-4*); pap. 44.50 (*0-88164-035-2*) ABBE Pubs Assn.

Alpert, Norman R., ed. Myocardial Hypertrophy & Failure. fac. ed. LC 83-3407. (Perspectives in Cardiovascular Research Ser.: No. 7). (Illus.). 720p. pap. 200.00 (*0-7837-7414-1*, 204720900006) Bks Demand.

***Alpert, Rebecca T.** Like Bread on the Seder Plate: Jewish Lesbians & the Transformation of Tradition. (Between Men - Between Women Ser.). 225p. 1998. pap. 16.50 (*0-231-09661-5*) Col U Pr.

Alpert, Rebecca T. Like Bread on the Seder Plate: Lesbian Transformation of Jewish Texts. LC 96-43411. (Between Men - Between Women Ser.). 224p. 1997. 26.00 (*0-231-09660-7*) Col U Pr.

***Alpert, Rebecca T., ed.** Voices of the Religious Left: A Contemporary Sourcebook. LC 99-37972. 304p. 2000. pap. 27.95 (*1-56639-757-X*) Temple U Pr.

— Voices of the Religious Left: A Contemporary Sourcebook. LC 99-37972. 304p. (C). 2000. 84.50 (*1-56639-756-1*) Temple U Pr.

***Alpert, Rebecca T. & Staub, Jacob J.** Exploring Judaism: A Reconstructionist Approach. 2nd rev. ed. LC 00-190796. xviii, 185p. 2000. pap. 14.95 (*0-935457-50-X*) Reconstructionist Pr.

***Alpert, Reuven.** Caught in the Crack: Encouters with the Jewish-Muslims of Turkey--A Spiritual Travelogue. 2000. write for info. (*0-7657-6161-0*) Aronson.

Alpert, Reuven. God's Middlemen: A Habad Retrospective (Stories of Mythical Rabbis) LC 97-29964. (Illus.). 184p. 1997. 17.95 (*1-883991-17-X*) Whte Cloud Pr.

Alpert, Richard, et al, eds. Assessing Basic Academic Skills in Higher Education: The Texas Approach. 288p. (C). 1988. text 69.95 (*0-8058-0336-X*) L Erlbaum Assocs.

Alpert, Sandra F. The Bully Busting Series: A Trilogy. (Illus.). (Orig.). (J). (gr. k-5). 1996. pap. 6.99 (*1-884931-03-0*) Global Commit.

— Commitment: Select Sculptures by Annette S. Friedman. (Illus.). 16p. 1994. pap. 5.00 (*1-884931-00-6*) Global Commit.

— Horrible Howard: The Bully & Coward. (Bully Busting Trilogy Ser.: Bk. 1). (Illus.). (Orig.). (J). (gr. k-5). Date not set. pap. write for info. (*1-884931-02-2*) Global Commit.

Alpert, Sherman. Design Patterns Smalltalk Companion. LC 97-48513. 464p. (C). 1998. 39.95 (*0-201-18462-1*) Addison-Wesley.

Alpert, Stanley L. Gertrude & the Printed Page. LC 98-93483. 1998. 23.00 (*1-892666-00-6*) Alperts Bookery.

— Mohop Mogande. LC 98-93481. 460p. 1998. 27.00 (*1-892666-03-0*) Alperts Bookery.

— A Roomful of Paradox. LC 98-93482. 1998. 27.00 (*1-892666-01-4*) Alperts Bookery.

— The Swan Song Pentad. LC 98-93484. 1998. 23.00 (*1-892666-02-2*) Alperts Bookery.

Alpert, Stuart W. What to Do until Enlightenment: Healing Ourselves ... Healing the Earth. Tick, Edward, ed. (Frontiers in Psychotherapy Ser.). 168p. (C). 1991. pap. 39.50 (*0-89391-804-0*); text 73.25 (*0-89391-805-9*) Ablx Pub.

Alpert, Toni. Celebrating Cultural Diversity - Primary: A Study Guide. Friedland, J. & Kessler, R., eds. (Novel-Ties Ser.). (J). (gr. 1-3). 1993. pap. text, student ed. 20.95 (*1-56982-037-6*) Lrn Links.

Alpert, William T. The Minimum Wage in the Restaurant Industry. LC 86-8111. 175p. 1986. 55.00 (*0-275-92085-2*, C2085, Praeger Pubs) Greenwood.

***Alpert, William T. & Woodbury, Stephen A., eds.** Employee Benefits, Labor Costs & Labor Markets in Canada & the United States. LC 00-31999. 500p. 2000. 46.00 (*0-88099-206-9*); pap. 29.00 (*0-88099-205-0*) W E Upjohn.

Alpert, William T., jt. ed. see Sanders, Sol W.

***Alpert, Yakov L.** Making Waves: Stories from My Life. LC 00-35918. (Illus.). 288p. 2000. 30.00 (*0-300-07821-8*) Yale U Pr.

Alpha Architecture Committee Staff, et al. Alpha Architecture Reference Manual. 3rd ed. LC 98-155189. 952p. 1998. pap. text 56.95 (*1-55558-202-8*) Buttrwrth-Heinemann.

***Alpha Books Staff.** Complete Idiot's Guide to Intermediate Spanish. (Complete Idiot's Guides (Lifestyle) Ser.). (SPA.). 408p. 2000. pap. 16.95 (*0-02-863924-3*, Alpha Ref) Macmillan Gen Ref.

— The Complete Idiot's Guide to Tax Write Offs. (Complete Idiot's Guides Ser.). 384p. 1998. pap. text 16.95 (*0-02-862684-2*) Macmillan Gen Ref.

Alpha Books Staff. Complete Idiot's Pocket Guide to Word for Windows 6.0: New Edition. 114p. 1993. 5.99 (*1-56761-368-3*, Alpha Ref) Macmillan Gen Ref.

— Moving to Chicago. LC 96-680495. 208p. 1996. 14.95 (*0-02-861281-7*) IDG Bks.

— Moving to Los Angeles. 208p. 1996. 14.95 (*0-02-861280-9*) IDG Bks.

— Moving to New York. 208p. 1996. pap. text 14.95 (*0-02-861279-5*) IDG Bks.

— Moving to Washington D. C. 208p. 1996. 14.95 (*0-02-861282-5*) IDG Bks.

— Online Investing. (Teach Yourself in 1 Day). 468p. 1999. pap. 18.95 (*0-02-863618-X*) Macmillan.

— Personal Finance. (Teach Yourself ...in 24 Hours Ser.). 480p. 2000. pap. 19.99 (*0-02-863619-8*) Macmillan Gen Ref.

***Alpha Books Staff.** Teach Yourself French in 1 Day. (Teach Yourself Ser.). 468p. 1999. pap. 18.95 (*0-02-863617-1*, Alpha Ref) Macmillan Gen Ref.

— Teach Yourself Spanish in 1 Day. (Teach Yourself Ser.). 528p. 2000. pap. 17.99 (*0-02-863616-3*, Alpha Ref) Macmillan Gen Ref.

Alpha Development Group Staff. The Big Basics Book of Microsoft Office. (Illus.). 589p. 1995. 19.99 (*1-56761-623-2*, Alpha Ref) Macmillan Gen Ref.

— The Big Basics Book of PCs. (Illus.). 598p. (Orig.). 1995. 19.99 (*1-56761-624-0*, Alpha Ref) Macmillan Gen Ref.

— The Big Basics Book of Windows 3.1. (Illus.). 600p. (Orig.). 1995. pap. 19.99 (*1-56761-625-9*, Alpha Ref) Macmillan Gen Ref.

***Alpha Development Group Staff.** The Complete Idiot's Gudie to Sunken Ships & Treasures. 352p. 1999. pap. text 16.95 (*0-02-863231-1*, Pub. by Macmillan Gen Ref) S&S Trade.

Alpha Development Group Staff. The Complete Idiot's Guide to a Happy Healthy Heart. LC 98-86098. 352p. 1998. pap. text 16.95 (*0-02-862393-2*) Macmillan Gen Ref.

***Alpha Development Group Staff.** The Complete Idiot's Guide to Creative Workplace. 352p. 1999. pap. 16.95 (*0-02-863371-7*, Alpha Ref) Macmillan Gen Ref.

Alpha Development Group Staff. The Complete Idiot's Guide to Dinosaurs. LC 98-85974. 352p. 1998. pap. text 17.95 (*0-02-862390-8*) Macmillan Gen Ref.

***Alpha Development Group Staff.** The Complete Idiot's Guide to Einstein's Universe. 384p. 1999. pap. text 16.95 (*0-02-863180-3*, Pub. by Macmillan) S&S Trade.

Alpha Development Group Staff. The Complete Idiot's Guide to Handling Difficult Employees. (Complete Idiot's Guide Ser.). (Illus.). 368p. 2000. pap. 18.95 (*0-02-863370-9*, Pub. by Macmillan) S&S Trade.

***Alpha Development Group Staff.** The Complete Idiot's Guide to Herbal Remedies. 400p. 1999. pap. text 16.95 (*0-02-863372-5*, Pub. by Macmillan Gen Ref) S&S Trade.

Alpha Development Group Staff. Complete Idiot's Guide to Investing for Women. 352p. 1998. 16.95 (*0-02-862942-6*) Macmillan Gen Ref.

— The Complete Idiot's Guide to Jewish History & Culture. (Complete Idiot's Guides Ser.). 1998. pap. text 16.95 (*0-02-862711-3*) Macmillan Gen Ref.

— Complete Idiot's Guide to Learning American Sign Language. LC 98-85701. (Illus.). 352p. 1998. pap. text 16.95 (*0-02-862388-6*) Macmillan Gen Ref.

— Complete Idiot's Guide to Learning Italian on Your Own. LC 98-84951. (Complete Idiot's Guide Ser.). (Illus.). 456p. 1998. pap. 16.95 (*0-02-862125-5*) Macmillan Gen Ref.

***Alpha Development Group Staff.** The Complete Idiot's Guide to Managing. (Complete Idiot's Guides). 1998. pap. text 16.95 (*0-02-862744-X*) Macmillan.

Alpha Development Group Staff. The Complete Idiot's Guide to Office Politics. LC 98-85128. 352p. 1998. pap. text 16.95 (*0-02-862397-5*) Macmillan Gen Ref.

***Alpha Development Group Staff.** The Complete Idiot's Guide to Photography Like a Pro. 2nd ed. 400p. 1999. pap. text 16.95 (*0-02-863636-8*) Macmillan.

— The Complete Idiot's Guide to Scrapbooking. 432p. 1999. pap. text 16.95 (*0-02-863640-6*) Macmillan.

Alpha Development Group Staff. The Complete Idiot's Guide to Searching for Extra-Terrestrials. LC 98-85119. (Illus.). 352p. 1998. pap. text 16.95 (*0-02-862387-8*) Macmillan Gen Ref.

— Complete Idiot's Guide to Self-Esteem. 352p. 1998. pap. 16.95 (*0-02-862930-2*) Macmillan Gen Ref.

— The Complete Idiot's Guide to Successful Business Habits. 352p. 1998. pap. text 17.95 (*0-02-862396-7*) Macmillan.

***Alpha Development Group Staff.** Motivating People. 368p. 1999. pap. text 16.95 (*0-02-863200-1*, Pub. by Macmillan) S&S Trade.

Alpha Development Group Staff. The Pocket Idiot's Guide to Spanish Phrases. LC 99-60218. (Pocket Idiot's Guides Ser.). (Illus.). 242p. 1998. pap. 9.95 (*0-02-862703-2*) Macmillan Gen Ref.

Alpha Development Group Staff & O'Hara, Shelley. The Complete Idiot's Guide to Buying & Repairing PCs. 2nd ed. (Illus.). 400p. 1995. 16.99 (*1-56761-583-X*, Alpha Ref) Macmillan Gen Ref.

Alpha Development Group Staff & Rosanoff, Nancy. Making Money Through Intuition. (Complete Idiot's Guide Ser.). (Illus.). 371p. 1999. pap. 17.95 (*0-02-862740-7*) Macmillan Gen Ref.

Alpha Development Group Staff & Shafran, Andy. The Complete Idiot's Guide to CompuServe. (Illus.). 350p. (Orig.). 1995. 21.99 (*1-56761-607-0*, Alpha Ref) Macmillan Gen Ref.

Alpha Institute Staff & Ryder, Brent G. The Alpha Book on Cancer & Living: For Patients, Family, & Friends. rev. ed. LC 93-71332. (Illus.). 448p. 1993. reprint ed. pap. 16.95 (*0-9632360-1-6*) Alpha Inst.

Alpha Lifespan Staff. Road Rage in the Kitchen: Woman-to-Woman Secrets for Permanent Weight Loss! (Illus.). 315p. 1999. pap. 19.95 (*1-886246-10-6*) Alpha LifeSpan.

***Alpha Omega Publishing Staff.** Horizons Math Kindergarten, 2 bks. (Illus.). (J). 2000. pap. 65.00 (*0-7403-0313-9*) Alpha AZ.

— Horizons Math Kindergarten, Bk. 1. (Illus.). (J). 2000. pap. 12.50 (*0-7403-0309-0*) Alpha AZ.

— Horizons Math Kindergarten, Bk. 2. (Illus.). (J). 2000. pap. 12.50 (*0-7403-0310-4*) Alpha AZ.

— Lifepac Gold Mathematics Grade 6: Boxed Set Includes Everything for Both Teacher & Student. (Illus.). 1996. boxed set 44.98 (*0-86717-084-0*) Alpha AZ.

— Science, Grade 3, 1. (Lifepac Ser.). 1998. 46.95 (*0-86717-238-X*, Alpha Omega) Domhan Bks.

— Switched-On Schoolhouse, 5 vols. (Illus.). (J). 2000. pap. 259.95 (*0-7403-0227-2*) Alpha AZ.

Alpha Omicron Pi Fraternity Staff. Celebrate the Century: History of Alpha Omicron Pi Fraternity. (Illus.). Date not set. 45.00 (*0-9657120-0-1*) Alpha Omic Pi.

Alpha Publishing Corporation, Staff. Money Power. 1995. pap. 12.95 (*1-884350-53-4*) Alpha Pub CA.

Alpha Pyramis Research Division Staff. Advertising Catering & Other Businesses Creatively with Rhyming Recipes, Menu Rhymes, Greetings: Includes Site Licensing Forms & Fee. (Recipe & Recipe Recitals Ser.). 1993. ring bd. 179.00 (*0-913597-79-1*) Prosperity & Profits.

— Advertising Fashions with Poetry. 38p. 1994. ring bd. 19.95 (*0-913597-60-0*) Prosperity & Profits.

— Advertising Recycled Clothing Fashions with Poetry. 70p. 1994. ring bd. 32.95 (*0-913597-61-9*) Prosperity & Profits.

— Alchemy: A Reference. rev. ed. 50p. 1998. pap. 12.95 (*0-913597-40-6*) Prosperity & Profits.

— Alfreda's Recipe Ingredient Substitution Cookbook. 50p. 1985. ring bd. 19.95 (*0-913597-87-2*) Prosperity & Profits.

— Almost Sugar & Not Quite Butter - Alternative Sugar & Butter Reference. 1989. pap. 8.95 (*0-913597-02-3*) Prosperity & Profits.

— Ancient Egypt - Rhyming Stories. 50p. 1990. pap. 17.95 (*0-913597-39-2*) Prosperity & Profits.

— Be Somebody, Be Yourself: Greetings for the Fax Machine, Etc. 50p. 1992. ring bd. 24.95 (*0-913597-37-6*) Prosperity & Profits.

— Bread Pudding: Fifty & More Delicious Ways to Make Bread Pudding. rev. ed. LC 98-128362. (Illus.). 70p. 1992. ring bd. 21.95 (*0-913597-16-3*) Prosperity & Profits.

— Business Start-up Fees: An International Report. 100p. 1983. ring bd. 119.95 (*0-913597-01-5*) Prosperity & Profits.

— Carob: Recipe Ingredient Substitution Cookbook. 1984. ring bd. 19.95 (*0-317-00781-5*) Prosperity & Profits.

— Catering Services: Creative Suggestion Pages. rev. ed. 1992. ring bd. 29.95 (*0-913597-89-9*) Prosperity & Profits.

— Clip Art Flower Designs for Programs, Announcements, Invitations, Etc. (Illus.). 62p. (Orig.). 1992. ring bd. 26.95 (*0-913597-30-9*) Prosperity & Profits.

— Craft Person's Notebook. 1992. student ed., ring bd. 19.95 (*0-913597-83-X*) Prosperity & Profits.

— Dear Departed: Poetry for the Occasion. 20p. 1984. pap. text 7.95 (*0-913597-67-8*) Prosperity & Profits.

— Energized Color Clip Art Book. LC 83-90742. 60p. 1993. ring bd. 325.00 (*0-913597-00-7*) Prosperity & Profits.

— Family Business, Small Business Ideas for Advertising, Marketing & How To. rev. ed. 16p. 1993. ring bd. 49.95 (*0-913597-92-9*) Prosperity & Profits.

— Fundraiser's Directory of Ideas, Phone Scripts, Recycling, Tours, Food Fairs & More. 100p. 1993. 59.95 (*0-913597-27-9*) Prosperity & Profits.

— Gift Basket Idea Encyclopaedia. rev. ed. 86p. 1993. ring bd. 32.95 (*0-913597-13-9*) Prosperity & Profits.

— Gourmet Food Poems & Recipes, Appetizing Ideas: Book One. rev. ed. 13p. 1996. ring bd. 21.95 (*0-913597-62-7*) Prosperity & Profits.

— Greeting Cards & Letter Designs to Duplicate & Use. (Illus.). 60p. (Orig.). 1992. ring bd. 26.95 (*0-913597-33-3*) Prosperity & Profits.

— Herbal Poetry Book of Medicinal Uses, Bk. 1. 11p. 1992. pap. text 7.95 (*0-913597-54-6*) Prosperity & Profits.

— Home Exchanges, Vacation Time Sharing, Bed & Breakfast Organizations: A How to Find or Locate Workbook. 200p. 1991. ring bd. 24.95 (*0-913597-04-X*) Prosperity & Profits.

— Honey Yes: Honey Use Poetry. (Alphabet Poem Ser.). 6p. 1984. pap. text 7.00 (*0-913597-44-9*) Prosperity & Profits.

— I Am, I Am, I Am: A Poetry Book. 60p. 1984. pap. 6.00 (*0-913597-63-5*) Prosperity & Profits.

— Incorporating Fees: A Researchers Self Help Workbook. 60p. 1983. ring bd. 32.95 (*0-913597-05-8*) Prosperity & Profits.

— Kid's Rhymes-Stories, Games & More. 75p. 1991. teacher ed., ring bd. 21.95 (*0-913597-93-7*) Prosperity & Profits.

— Make It Tasty Spice Blend & Food Business Cookbook. (Illus.). 78p. (C). 1993. ring bd. 49.95 (*0-913597-09-0*) Prosperity & Profits.

— The Multi-Charity Benefit Greeting Card Concept. rev. ed. (Illus.). 68p. 1992. student ed., ring bd. 19.95 (*0-913597-58-9*) Prosperity & Profits.

— Natural & Hot Springs: An Index & Travel Planners Workbook. rev. ed. (Illus.). 70p. 1995. pap. text, wbk. ed. 25.95 (*0-913597-07-4*) Prosperity & Profits.

— New Age Consciousness & Awareness Poetry, Bk. 1. 15p. 1985. pap. 7.95 (*0-913597-59-7*) Prosperity & Profits.

— Non-Bank Safe Deposit Boxes: An International Directory. rev. ed. 215p. 1997. ring bd. 32.95 (*0-913597-08-2*) Prosperity & Profits.

— Potpourri Making Easy & Simple Workbook. (Illus.). 75p. (Orig.). 1992. ring bd., wbk. ed. 24.95 (*0-913597-28-7*) Prosperity & Profits.

— Recycling Simulation Activity Sessions, Vol. 1. 60p. 1984. ring bd. 29.95 (*0-913597-57-0*) Prosperity & Profits.

— Rhyming Pattern Reference One. 8p. 1984. ring bd. 26.95 (*0-913597-46-5*) Prosperity & Profits.

— Rhyming Recipe & Cookbook, Vol. 1. 21p. 1984. ring bd. 27.95 (*0-913597-50-3*) Prosperity & Profits.

— Seeds As Food Use: A Workbook, 1. 1984. ring bd. 25.95 (*0-913597-70-8*) Prosperity & Profits.

— Self Storage Units or Warehouses: An International Report. 300p. 1983. ring bd. 52.95 (*0-913597-12-0*) Prosperity & Profits.

— Small Business Services Possibilities. 38p. 1948. ring bd. 49.95 (*0-913597-45-7*) Prosperity & Profits.

— Story Time Stories That Rhyme Vol. 1: Fish Convention, Rainbow, Miss Divine Sunshine & Others. 106p. (J). (gr. 4-12). 1992. ring bd. 27.95 (*0-913597-99-6*) Prosperity & Profits.

— Vinegar Use Poetry Pages. 30p. 1984. pap. text 6.50 (*0-913597-66-X*) Prosperity & Profits.

Alpha Pyramis Research Division Staff, ed. Kids Rhyme Word Mapping Treasure Hunt Collection. (Illus.). 60p. (Orig.). 1991. teacher ed., ring bd. 19.95 (*0-913597-85-6*) Prosperity & Profits.

Alpha Research & Development, Inc. Staff. Investigation of Adhesives for Use with Copper Hydrolytic & Thermal Stability. 53p. 1966. 7.95 (*0-317-34531-1*, 79) Intl Copper.

Alpha Research Division Staff. The Complete Idiot's Guide to Protecting Yourself From. 350p. 1995. 16.99 (*1-56761-602-X*, Alpha Ref) Macmillan Gen Ref.

— The Complete Idiot's Guide to 1-2-3 for Windows 95. (Illus.). 375p. 1995. 19.99 (*0-7897-0374-2*, Alpha Ref) Macmillan Gen Ref.

— Dictionnaire Encyclopedique Alpha, 6 vols. (FRE.). 1983. 1295.00 (*0-7859-8050-4*, 2-8270-0295-7) Fr & Eur.

— Ten Minute Guide to Excel for Windows 95. (Illus.). 178p. 1995. 12.99 (*0-7897-0373-4*, Alpha Ref) Macmillan Gen Ref.

Alpha Sigma Alpha Staff. Narcissus. 1987. 14.95 (*0-9616651-0-6*) Alpha Sigma Alpha.

Alphandery, Paul. Les Idees Morales Chez les Heterodoxes Latins Au Debut Du Xiiie Siecle. LC 78-63184. (Heresies of the Early Christian & Medieval Era Ser.: Second Ser.). reprint ed. 42.50 (*0-404-16198-7*) AMS Pr.

Alpharetta, Georgia, jt. auth. see Twing, J. W.

Alphei, Cord. Die Hildesheimer Michaeliskirche Im Wiederaufbau, 1945-1960. (GER.). 80p. 1993. 29.80 (*3-487-09812-1*) G Olms Pubs.

Alphen, Corry Van, see Van Alphen, Corry.

Alpher, Barry. Yir-Yoront Lexicon: Sketch & Dictionary of an Australian Language. LC 91-32572. (Trends in Linguistics, Documentation Ser.: No. 6). xii, 795p. (C). 1991. lib. bdg. 229.25 (*3-11-012682-6*) Mouton.

Alpher, Joseph, ed. Encyclopedia of Jewish History: Events & Eras of the Jewish People. (Illus.). 288p. 1986. 40.00 (*0-8160-1220-2*) Facts on File.

— Nationalism & Modernity: A Mediterranean Perspective. LC 86-11222. 151p. 1986. 49.95 (*0-275-92137-9*, C2137, Praeger Pubs) Greenwood.

***Alpher, Ralph A. & Herman, Robert.** Genesis of the Big Bang. (Illus.). 256p. 2000. 29.95 (*0-19-511182-6*) OUP.

Alpheus, A. Complete Hypnotism, Mesmerism, Mind Reading & Spiritualism. 217p. 1996. reprint ed. pap. 17.00 (*0-7873-0030-6*) Hlth Research.

— Hypnotism: Method, Application & Use. 1991. lib. bdg. 75.00 (*0-8490-5042-1*) Gordon Pr.

— Were You Born under a Lucky Star? 217p. 1996. reprint ed. spiral bd. 16.00 (*0-7873-0031-4*) Hlth Research.

Alphey, L. DNA Sequencing. LC 97-20709. (Introduction to Biotechniques Ser.). (Illus.). 176p. 1997. text 34.95 (*0-387-91509-5*) Spr-Verlag.

Alphin. Dinosaur Hunter. 64p. (J). Date not set. 14.95 (*0-06-028303-3*); lib. bdg. 14.89 (*0-06-028304-1*) HarpC Child Bks.

— The Dinosaur Hunter. 64p. (J). Date not set. pap. 3.95 (*0-06-444256-X*) HarpC Child Bks.

Alphin, Arthur B., et al. Any Shot You Want: The A-Square Rifle & Handloading Manual. (Illus.). 626p. (Orig.). 1996. pap. text 39.95 (*0-9643683-1-5*) Bluegrass Bks.

Alphin, Elaine M. A Bear for Miguel. LC 94-36723. (I Can Read Bks.). (Illus.). 64p. (J). (gr. 2-4). 1997. pap. 3.95 (*0-06-444234-9*, HarpTrophy) HarpC Child Bks.

— A Bear for Miguel. (I Can Read Bks.). (J). (gr. 2-4). 1997. 8.95 (*0-606-11098-4*, Pub. by Turtleback) Demco.

— The Ghost Cadet. 88p. (J). (gr. 4-6). 1995. 14.95 (*0-8050-1614-7*, Bks Young Read) H Holt & Co.

— Ghost Cadet. 192p. (J). (gr. 4-7). 1992. pap. 3.99 (*0-590-45244-4*, Apple Paperbacks) Scholastic Inc.

— Irons. LC 97-10539. (Household History Ser.). (J). (gr. 5 up). 1997. lib. bdg. 22.60 (*1-57505-238-5*, Carolrhoda) Lerner Pub.

— Toasters. LC 97-34328. (Household History Ser.). 48p. (J). (gr. 3-6). 1998. 22.60 (*1-57505-243-1*, Carolrhoda) Lerner Pub.

— Tournament of Time. LC 94-96624. 125p. (Orig.). (J). (gr. 4-6). 1994. pap., per. 3.95 (*0-9643683-0-7*) Bluegrass Bks.

— Vacuum Cleaners. LC 96-36457. (Household History Ser.). 48p. (J). 1997. 16.95 (*1-57505-018-8*, Carolrhoda) Lerner Pub.

***Alphin, Elaine Marie.** Counterfeit Son. LC 00-8168. (Illus.). 256p. (J). (gr. 8-12). 2000. 17.00 (*0-15-202645-2*, Harcourt Child Bks) Harcourt.

Alphin, Elaine Marie. Ghost Cadet. 1991. 9.09 (*0-606-00878-0*, Pub. by Turtleback) Demco.

***Alphin, Elaine Marie.** Siege Ghost. 1999. text 15.95 (*0-8050-6158-4*) St Martin.

— Telephones. LC 99-50528. (Household History Ser.). (J). 2000. write for info. (*1-57505-432-9*, Carolrhoda) Lerner Pub.

— Write for Kids: Colorful Characters. (Illus.). 208p. (gs up). 2000. pap. 16.99 (*0-89879-985-6*, Wrtrs Digest Bks) F & W Pubns Inc.

Alphin, Fronca, et al. Winning Nutrition for Athletes. (Illus.). 27p. 1997. pap. 14.95 (*0-9665624-0-2*) Duke Univ Sport Perf.

Alphonse, Ephraim S. Guaymi Grammar & Dictionary with Some Ethnological Notes. (Bureau of American Ethnology Bulletins Ser.). 128p. 1995. lib. bdg. 79.00 (*0-7812-4162-6*) Rprt Serv.

Alphonso, Gina, jt. auth. see Gray, Adele.

Alphonso, Patrick M. Game Fanatic's Guide to PC Cheats. LC 97-93745. 224p. 1997. mass mkt. 5.99 (*0-380-79603-1*, Avon Bks) Morrow Avon.

Alphonsus, Mary. St. Rose of Lima. LC 81-86444. 304p. 1993. reprint ed. pap. 15.00 (*0-89555-172-1*) TAN Bks Pubs.

Alpi, Deborah Lazaroff. Robert Siodmak: A Biography, with Critical Analyses of His Films Noirs & a Filmography of All His Works. LC 98-16267. (Illus.). 420p. 1998. lib. bdg. 58.50 (*0-7864-0489-2*) McFarland & Co.

Alpiar, Hal. Doctor Business: How to Boost Practice Growth & Strengthen Long-Term Relationships. Rogers, Gregg, ed. LC 94-3563. (Illus.). 232p. 1994. 39.95 (*1-57066-003-4*, ME056) Practice Mgmt Info.

— Doctor Shopping: How to Choose the Right Doctor for You & Your Family. Rogers, Gregg, ed. LC 96-10783. 250p. (Orig.). 1996. pap. 12.95 (*1-885987-01-3*, ME069, Health Info Pr) Practice Mgmt Info.

Alpine Enterprises Staff. The Occult Technology of Power. 62p. (Orig.). 1974. pap. text 8.00 (*1-55950-009-3*) Loompanics.

Alpiner, Jerome G. & McCarthy, Patricia A. Rehabilitative Audiology: Children & Adults. 2nd ed. (Illus.). 544p. 1993. 49.00 (*0-683-00078-0*) Lppncott W & W.

***Alpiner, Jerome G. & McCarthy, Patricia A., eds.** Rehabilitation Audiology: Children & Adults. 3rd ed. LC 99-32657. 690p. 1999. 56.00 (*0-683-30652-9*) Lppncott W & W.

Alpini, D. & Cesarini, N. Whiplash Injuries & Disequilibrium: Diagnosis & Treatment. (Illus.). 220p. 1996. 125.00 (*3-540-75015-0*) Spr-Verlag.

Alpizar, Samuel. Manual de la Vida (Manual of the Life) (SPA., Illus.). 16p. (Orig.). 1993. pap. 5.00 (*0-9655165-0-4*) S Alpizar.

— Manual of Life. 18p. 1998. pap. 5.00 (*0-9655165-1-2*) S Alpizar.

***Alplin, Richard & Montchamp, Joseph.** Dictionary of Contemporary France. (Illus.). 500p. 1999. lib. bdg. 65.00 (*1-57958-115-3*) Fitzroy Dearborn.

Alpoge, Atila & Dacier, Liz. Putting Citizens First: The Portuguese Experience in Administrative Reform. (Public Management Occasional Papers: No. 13). 164p. (Orig.). 1996. pap. 24.00 (*92-64-15332-2*, 42-96-63-1) OECD.

Alport, David. Sticky Remote Pocket Gay Video Guide. 1998. pap. 11.95 (*0-9663146-0-3*) OLS Pub.

Alport, David, jt. auth. see Kolber-Stuart, Billy.

Alport, Rita, tr. see Parker-Fairbanks, Dixie, et al.

Alquie, Ferdinand, ed. see Descartes, Rene.

Alquier, Claude. Dictionnaire Encyclopedique Economique et Social. 2nd ed. (FRE.). 1990. write for info. (*0-7859-7955-7*, 2-7178-1834-0) Fr & Eur.

Alquin, Hubert. The Antiphony. 196p. 1983. pap. 3.95 (*0-7736-7053-X*) Genl Dist Srvs.

Alrawi, Karim. A Gift of Glory. 128p. 1998. pap. 10.95 (*0-9668157-0-X*) MBPAC Pr.

***Alrawi, Karim.** The Girl Who Lost Her Smile. LC 99-462308. (Illus.). 32p. (J). (ps-3). 2000. 16.95 (*1-890817-17-1*, Pub. by Winslow Pr) Publishers Group.

Alreck, Pamela L. & Settle, Robert B. The Survey Research Handbook. LC 84-71129. 350p. 1984. text 52.50 (*0-87094-529-7*, Irwn Prfssnl) McGraw-Hill Prof.

— The Survey Research Handbook. 2nd ed. LC 94-7619. (Marketing Ser.). 470p. (C). 1994. text 39.00 (*0-256-10321-6*, Irwn McGrw-H) McGrw-H Hghr Educ.

Alreck, Pamela L. & Settle, Robert G. The Survey Research Handbook: Guidelines & Strategies for Conducting a Survey. 2nd ed. 496p. 1994. text 50.00 (*0-7863-0358-1*, Irwn Prfssnl) McGraw-Hill Prof.

***Alred, Geof, et al.** The Mentoring Pocketbook. 112p. 2000. pap. 8.95 (*1-57922-006-1*) Stylus Pub VA.

***Alred, Gerald J.** Business Writer's Handbook. 6th ed. 720p. 2000. text 39.95 (*0-312-25494-6*) St Martin.

Alred, Gerald J. St. Martin's Bibliography of Business & Technical Communication: A Resource for Teachers. LC 96-69583. 164p. 1997. pap. text 13.95 (*0-312-13314-6*) St Martin.

Alred, Gerald J., et al. Business & Technical Writing: An Annotated Bibliography of Books, 1880-1980. LC 80-29211. 249p. 1981. 21.00 (*0-8108-1397-1*) Scarecrow.

***Alred, Gerald J., et al.** Handbook of Technical Writing. LC 99-62313. (Illus.). 720p. 2000. text 39.95 (*0-312-25496-2*) St Martin.

Alred, Gerald J., et al. The Professional Writer: A Guide for Advanced Technical Writing. LC 90-71628. 426p. (Orig.). (C). 1991. pap. text 46.95 (*0-312-00248-3*) St Martin.

Alrich, Peggy. Orchids on Stamps. (Illus.). 88p. 1991. pap. 9.00 (*0-935991-12-3*) Am Topical Assn.

Alroth, Brita. Greek Gods & Figurines: Aspects of the Anthropomorphic Dedications. (Uppsala Studies in Ancient Mediterranean & Near Eastern Civilizations: No. 18). (Illus.). 120p. (Orig.). 1989. pap. 36.50 (*91-554-2367-1*) Coronet Bks.

— Opuscula Atheniensia XVII. (Acta Instituti Atheniensis Regni Sueciae Ser.: Vol. XXXVII). (Illus.). 238p. 1988. pap. 97.50 (*91-7916-000-X*, Pub. by P Astroms) Coronet Bks.

Alroth, Brita, ed. Opuscula Romana XV. (Acta Instituti Romani Regni Sueciae, Series in 4 Degrees: Vol. XLII). (Illus.). 120p. 1985. pap. 87.50 (*91-7042-099-8*, Pub. by P Astroms) Coronet Bks.

— Opuscula Romana XVII. (Acta Instituti Romani Regni Sueciae, Series in 4 Degrees: Vol. XLVI). (Illus.). 247p. 1989. pap. 97.50 (*91-7042-135-8*, Pub. by P Astroms) Coronet Bks.

— Opuscula Romana XVI. (Acta Instituti Romani Regni Sueciae, Series in 4 Degrees: Vol. XLIV). (Illus.). 166p. 1987. pap. 92.50 (*91-7042-120-X*, Pub. by P Astroms) Coronet Bks.

Alroth, Brita & Acta Instituti Atheniensis Staff, eds. Opuscula Atheniensia XVI. (Acta Instituti Atheniensis Regni Sueciae Ser.: Vol. XXXIV). (Illus.). 130p. (Orig.). 1986. pap. 57.50 (*91-85086-80-0*, Pub. by P Astroms) Coronet Bks.

Alroth, Brita, jt. ed. see Linders, Tullia.

Als, Hilton. David Salle: Bears/Interiors. Monk, Robert, ed. (Illus.). 20p. 1999. 30.00 (*1-880154-28-5*) Gagosian Gallery.

***Als, Hilton.** The Group. 192p. 2000. text 23.00 (*0-374-21037-3*) FS&G.

Als, Hilton. The Women. 200p. 1996. 21.00 (*0-374-29205-1*) FS&G.

— The Women. 160p. 1998. pap. text 11.00 (*0-374-52529-3*, Noonday) FS&G.

Als, Hilton, et al, contrib. by. Our Town: Images & Stories from the Museum of the City of New York. LC 97-20742. (Illus.). 224p. 1997. 39.95 (*0-8109-3698-4*, Pub. by Abrams) Time Warner.

Als, Hilton & Museum of the City of New York Staff. Our Town: Images & Stories from the Museum of the City of New York. LC 97-20742. 1997. pap. write for info. (*0-910961-09-3*) Abrams.

Alsaffar, Adnan M., ed. Fiftieth Anniversary of the Hydraulics Division, 1938-1988. LC 90-40326. 160p. 1990. pap. text 5.00 (*0-87262-770-5*) Am Soc Civil Eng.

Alsager, Dale. The Incredible Gang Ranch. (Illus.). 448p. (Orig.). 1990. pap. 19.95 (*0-88839-211-7*) Hancock House.

Alsager, Judy. Gang Ranch: The Real Story. 288p. 1994. pap. 19.95 (*0-88839-275-3*) Hancock House.

Alsaker, Francoise D. & Flammer, August. The Adolescent Experience in Twelve Nations: European & American Adolescents in the Nineties. LC 98-11809. (Research Monographs in Adolescence). 192p. 1998. 45.00 (*0-8058-2552-5*) L Erlbaum Assocs.

Alsaker, Rasmus. Cause & Cure of All Disease. 8p. 1996. reprint ed. spiral bd. 8.00 (*0-7873-1278-9*) Hlth Research.

Alsayyad, Nezar. Cities & Caliphs: On the Genesis of Arab Muslim Urbanism, 26. LC 90-19913. (Contributions to the Study of World History Ser.: No. 26). 208p. 1991. 55.00 (*0-313-27791-5*, ASC/, Greenwood Pr) Greenwood.

— Forms of Dominance: On the Architecture & Urbanism of the Colonial Enterprise. 366p. 1992. 74.95 (*1-85628-236-8*, Pub. by Avebry) Ashgate Pub Co.

***Alsayyad, Nezar, ed.** Hybrid Urbanism: Identity Discourse & the Built Environment. 2001. write for info. (*0-275-96612-7*) Greenwood.

Alsayyad, Nezar, jt. ed. see Bourdier, Jean-Paul.

Alsberg, Carl L. Combination in the American Bread-Baking Industry: With Some Observations on the Mergers of 1924-25. LC 73-1987. (Big Business; Economic Power in a Free Society Ser.). 1973. reprint ed. 12.95 (*0-405-05071-2*) Ayer.

Alsbury, Alison, ed. see Maw, Nigel G., et al.

Alschech, Josef, jt. auth. see Jerusalmi, Isaac.

Alscher, Ruth G. Antioxidants in Higher Plants. 192p. 1993. lib. bdg. 169.00 (*0-8493-6328-4*, QK898) CRC Pr.

***Alschuler, Albert W.** Blowing Out the Moral Lights Around Us: The Life, Work & Legacy of Oliver Wendell Holmes. LC 00-8279. 1999. 30.00 (*0-226-01520-3*) U Ch Pr.

Alschuler, Alfred S. Developing Achievement Motivation in Adolescents: Education for Human Growth. LC 72-84336. 330p. 1973. 39.95 (*0-87778-037-4*) Educ Tech Pubns.

Alschuler, Joan N. The Guardian ad Litem Handbook. 2nd ed. LC 97-29359. 545p. 1997. ring bd. 115.00 incl. disk (*0-945574-97-5*) State Bar WI.

Alschuler, Lawrence R., et al, eds. Dependent Agricultural Development & Agrarian Reform in Latin America. LC 81-171788. (Social Sciences Studies 12, Institute for International Cooperation: Vol. 2). 198p. 1981. reprint ed. pap. 61.40 (*0-608-02180-6*, 206284900004) Bks Demand.

Alschuler, Lawrence R., et al. Developpement Agricole Dependant & Mouvements Paysans en Amerique Latine. LC HD1790.5.D48. (Cahiers des Sciences Sociales 11, Livres & Monographies de l'Institut de Cooperation Internationale: Vol. 1). (FRE.). 230p. 1981. reprint ed. pap. 71.30 (*0-608-02197-0*, 206286700004) Bks Demand.

Alschuler, Mari. The Nightmare of Falling Teeth. 20p. 1998. pap. 7.95 (*0-944754-54-6*) Pudding Hse Pubns.

***Alsdorf, Debbie.** Living Love. LC 00-27251. 2000. 7.99 (*0-7814-3383-5*) Cook Communs Minist.

— Steadfast Love. LC 00-27263. 2000. 7.99 (*0-7814-3384-3*) Cook Communs Minist.

A

An Asterisk (*) at the beginning of an entry indicates that the title is appearing for the first time.

A

***Alsdurf, James.** Eating Disorders, 5 vols. 1999. pap. 4.95 (*0-8308-6591-8*) InterVarsity.

***Alsdurf, James & Alsdurf, Phyllis.** Battered into Submission: The Tragedy of Wife Abuse in the Christian Home. 166p. (Orig.). 1998. pap. 17.00 (*1-57910-199-2*) Wipf & Stock.

Alsdurf, Phyllis, jt. auth. see Alsdurf, James.

Alseda, L., et al. Combinatorial Dynamics & Entrophy in Dimensions One. (Advanced Series in Nonlinear Dynamics). 344p. 1993. text 74.00 (*981-02-1344-1*) World Scientific Pub.

***Alseda, Lluis, et al.** Combinatorial Dynamics & Entropy in Dimension One, Vol. 5. 2nd ed. 350p. 2000. 76.00 (*981-02-4053-8*) World Scientific Pub.

***Alsen, Eberhard, ed.** The New Romanticism: American Fiction since 1950. 380p. 2000. 85.00 (*0-8153-3547-4*); pap. 29.95 (*0-8153-3548-2*) Garland.

Alsever, Robert N. & Gotlin, Ronald W. Handbook of Endocrine Tests in Adults & Children. 2nd ed. LC 78-53201. 260p. reprint ed. pap. 80.60 (*0-608-18270-2*, 203299800082) Bks Demand.

Alsford, Denis B. Match Holders: 100 Years of Ingenuity. LC 94-65852. (Illus.). 160p. 1994. pap. 29.95 (*0-88740-633-5*) Schiffer.

Alsford, Stephen, ed. The Meta Incognita Project: Contributions to Field Studies. (Mercury Ser.: Directorate No. 6). (Illus.). 228p. 1993. pap. 19.95 (*0-660-14010-1*, Pub. by CN Mus Civilization) U of Wash Pr.

Alsford, Stephen, jt. auth. see MacDonald, George F.

Alshag, N., jt. auth. see Yallouz, Itshak.

Alshalabi, Firyal M. Summer 1990. LC 99-94911. 138 p. 1999. pap. text 6.99 (*0-9669988-0-4*) Aunt Straw.

Alsharhan, A. S., et al, eds. Quaternary Deserts & Climatic Change: Proceedings of an International Conference, Al Ain, 9-11 December 1995. LC 99-496401. (Illus.). 636p. (C). 1998. text 104.00 (*90-5410-597-6*, Pub. by A A Balkema) Ashgate Pub Co.

Alsharhan, A. S. & Nairn, A. E. Sedimentary Basins & Petroleum Geology of the Middle East. LC 97-48322. 978p. 1997. 284.50 (*0-444-82465-0*) Elsevier.

Alshawi, Hiyan, ed. The Core Language Engine. (Bradford Books-MITP-ACL Series Natural Language Processing). (Illus.). 280p. 1992. 39.95 (*0-262-01126-3*) MIT Pr.

Alsheimer, Charles J. Hunting Whitetails by the Moon. Durkin, Patrick, ed. LC 99-63748. 256p. 1999. pap. 19.95 (*0-87341-813-1*) Krause Pubns.

— Whitetail: The Ultimate Challenge. LC 95-76857. (Illus.). 223p. 1995. pap. 14.95 (*0-87341-338-5*, WVC01) Krause Pubns.

— Whitetail Behavior Through the Seasons. LC 96-76703. 208p. 1996. 34.95 (*0-87341-449-7*) Krause Pubns.

Alsheimer, Charles J. & Watkins, Larry C. A Guide to Adirondack Deer Hunting. LC 87-71882. (Illus.). 221p. (Orig.). 1987. 49.95 (*0-944076-00-9*); pap. 13.95 (*0-944076-01-7*) Beaver Creek.

Alsheler, Joseph. The Rifleman of the Ohio. 432p. 1981. reprint ed. lib. bdg. 35.95 (*0-89968-226-X*, Lghtyr Pr) Buccaneer Bks.

Alshich, Moshe. A Harvest of Majesty: The Book of Ruth. Shahar, Ravi, tr. (The Alshich Tanach Ser.). 416p. 1992. 25.95 (*1-58330-036-8*) Feldheim.

— Solace Amidst the Ashes. Shahar, Ravi, tr. 328p. 1993. 23.95 (*1-58330-127-5*) Feldheim.

Alsina, Alex. The Role of Argument Structure in Grammar: Evidence from Romance. 320p. (C). 1996. 69.95 (*1-57586-035-X*); pap. 25.95 (*1-57586-034-1*) CSLI.

Alsina, Alex, et al, eds. Complex Predicates. (Lecture Notes Ser.). (Illus.). 350p. (C). 1997. 64.95 (*1-57586-047-3*); pap. 23.95 (*1-57586-046-5*) CSLI.

Alsina, C., et al, eds. Iteration Theory (ECIT 87) European Conference. 480p. 1989. text 130.00 (*981-02-0041-2*) World Scientific Pub.

Alsina, Claudi. Vocabulari Catala de Matematica Basica. 4th ed. (CAT.). 48p. 1976. pap. 8.95 (*0-7859-5081-8*) Fr & Eur.

Alsina, Jose. Los Grandes Periodos De la Cultura Griega. (Nueva Austral Ser.: No. 54). (SPA.). 1991. pap. text 24.95 (*84-239-1854-8*) Elliots Bks.

— Teoria Literaria Griega. (SPA.). 618p. 1993. 150.00 (*84-249-1457-0*) Elliots Bks.

Alsina, Ramon, jt. auth. see Perez, Jose.

Alsing, Ingrid. Lexikon Landwirtschaft. 2nd ed. (GER.). 703p. 1993. 225.00 (*0-7859-8333-3*, 3406135613) Fr & Eur.

Alsip, Barbara W., et al. Operation Provide Comfort: Review of U. S. Air Force Investigation of Black Hawk Fratricide Incident. (Illus.). 56p. (C). 1998. pap. text 20.00 (*0-7881-7548-3*) DIANE Pub.

Alsmeyer, D. & Atkins, A. G., eds. Guide to Science & Technology in the Asia Pacific Area: A Reference Guide. LC 79-310835. 548p. reprint ed. pap. 169.90 (*0-608-17058-5*, 202771700056) Bks Demand.

Alsmeyer, Marie B. Six Years after D-Day: Cycling Through Europe. LC 94-48004. 176p. (Orig.). 1995. pap. 14.95 (*0-929398-82-3*) UNTX Pr.

Alsobrook, David. Claves Biblicas para Vivir Libre de Temor Itodos los Dias de Su Vida! (SPA.). 44p. (Orig.). 1996. pap. write for info. (*1-885630-41-7*) HLM Producciones.

***Alsobrook, David.** Jesus Christ, M.D., 1vol. 1999. pap. text 6.95 (*0-89228-146-4*) Impact Christian.

— Understanding the Accuser. 120p. 1999. pap. text 10.99 (*1-85240-238-5*) SOV5.

Alsobrook, David. What Christians Should Know about How to Pray Effectively for Your Lost Loved Ones. (What Christian Should Know Ser.). 48p. 1999. pap. 5.99 (*1-85240-224-5*) SOV5.

Alsobrook, Rosalyn. Emerald Storm. 496p. 1986. mass mkt. 3.95 (*0-8217-1874-6*, Zebra Kensgtn) Kensgtn Pub Corp.

— For the Love of Pete. (Seascape Romance Ser.: Vol. 4). 1997. mass mkt. 5.99 (*0-312-96136-7*) St Martin.

— Love's Image. 288p. 1996. mass mkt. 4.99 (*0-8217-5332-0*, Zebra Kensgtn) Kensgtn Pub Corp.

— One Heart. 384p. 1997. mass mkt. 5.50 (*0-8217-5599-4*, Zebra Kensgtn) Kensgtn Pub Corp.

— The Perfect Stranger, Vol. 2. (Seascape Romance Ser.). 1996. mass mkt. 5.99 (*0-312-95875-7*) St Martin.

— Tomorrow's Treasures. (Seascape Ser.). 330p. 1997. mass mkt. 5.99 (*0-312-96394-7*, St Martins Paperbacks) St Martin.

Alsoffar, Adnan, jt. ed. see Holly, Forrest M.

Alson, Peter. Confessions of an Ivy League Bookie: A True Tale of Love & the Vig. Date not set. 22.00 (*0-614-13897-3*, Crown) Crown Pub Group.

Alsop, A. & Ryan, S. Making the Most of Fieldwork Education: A Practical Approach. LC 96-84232. (Illus.). 240p. (Orig.). (C). 1996. pap. text 45.00 (*1-56593-439-3*, 1108) Singular Publishing.

Alsop, Dave, jt. ed. see Mitchell, David.

Alsop, David, jt. auth. see Mitchell, David.

Alsop, Derek & Walsh. The Practice of Reading. LC 98-49468. 1999. pap. 21.95 (*0-312-22157-6*) St Martin.

Alsop, Fred J., III. Backyard Birds: A Complete Guide to Attracting, Identifying, & Photographing Birds in Your Southern Backyard. LC 97-39806. (Southern Birdwatchers Ser.). (Illus.). 176p. 1998. pap. text 16.95 (*1-57587-068-1*) Crane Hill AL.

— Birds of the Smokies. Kemp, Steve, ed. (Natural History Handbook Ser.). (Illus.). 168p. (Orig.). 1991. pap. 10.95 (*0-937207-05-5*) GSMNH.

Alsop, Fred J., III, photos by. Birds of Land Between the Lakes. LC 91-76141. (Miscellaneous Publication Ser.: No. 5). (Illus.). 234p. 1991. 7.00 (*1-880617-00-5*) APSU Ctr Fld Bio.

Alsop, G. I., et al, eds. Salt Tectonics. (Geological Society Special Publication Ser.: No. 100). 320p. 1995. 110.00 (*1-897799-44-6*, 343, Pub. by Geol Soc Pub Hse) AAPG.

Alsop, George & Mereness, Newton D. Character of the Province of Maryland. LC 74-39491. (Select Bibliographies Reprint Ser.). 1977. reprint ed. 12.95 (*0-8369-9900-2*) Ayer.

Alsop, J. D., jt. auth. see Hair, P. E.

Alsop, Joseph & Gelatt, Roland. F. D. R. LC 97-52742. 1998. 14.99 (*0-517-20296-4*) Random Hse Value.

***Alsop, Marcus.** Western Sadhus & Sannyasins in India. 150p. 2000. pap. 14.95 (*0-934252-50-5*, Pub. by Hohm Pr) SCB Distributors.

Alsop, Peter. Take Me with You! (J). 1988. 9.95 (*0-8256-1116-4*) Moose Schl Records.

Alsop, Peter, et al. In the Hospital. 64p. (J). (gr. k-6). 1989. pap. 15.00 (*1-877942-00-6*, MS503) Moose Schl Records.

— The Stayin' over Songbook. (J). 1994. 11.00 (*1-877942-01-4*) Moose Schl Records.

***Alsop, Rachel.** A Reversal of Fortunes? Women, Work & Change in East Germany. LC HD6150.5.A47 2000. (Illus.). 176p. 2000. 39.95 (*1-57181-965-7*); pap. 17.50 (*1-57181-771-9*) Berghahn Bks.

Alsop, Richard. The Echo with Other Poems. LC 70-104403. 357p. reprint ed. lib. bdg. 37.50 (*0-8398-0057-6*) Irvington.

— The Works of Richard Alsop, 1761-1815, Set. 1987. reprint ed. lib. bdg. 500.00 (*0-685-18592-3*) Rprt Serv.

Alsop, Richard, et al. The Echo, with Other Poems. 357p. 1987. pap. text 9.95 (*0-8290-2107-8*) Irvington.

Alsop, Ronald J., ed. see Wall Street Journal Editors.

Alsop, Susan M. Yankees at the Court. 1987. pap. 4.95 (*0-685-18039-5*) PB.

— Yankees at the Court: The First Americans in Paris. LC 81-43284. 1982. 17.95 (*0-385-15635-9*) Doubleday.

Alsop, Ted J. Principles of Physical Geography: An Introduction to Natural Phenomena. 384p. (C). 1993. per. 38.95 (*0-8403-8777-6*) Kendall-Hunt.

Alspach, Jen, jt. auth. see Alspach, Ted.

Alspach, Jennifer. Illustrator 7 Complete. LC 96-80330. 590p. 1997. 45.00 (*1-56830-364-5*) Hayden.

— Photoshop & Illustrator Synergy. LC 97-78213. (Illus.). 288p. 1998. pap. 49.99 (*0-7645-3134-4*) IDG Bks.

Alspach, Jennifer, jt. auth. see Alspach, Ted.

Alspach, JoAnn, et al. Critical Care Nursing Handbook. Joyce, Joan M., ed. (Allied Health Professions Monograph). (Illus.). 269p. (C). 1983. 35.00 (*0-87527-318-1*) Green.

Alspach, JoAnn G. The Educational Process in Nursing Staff Development. LC 94-20732. 1994. write for info. (*0-8016-0060-X*) Mosby Inc.

Alspach, Joann G., jt. auth. see Shade, Bruce R.

Alspach, JoAnn G., ed. see Harvey, Maurene A.

Alspach, JoAnn Grif. The Educational Process in Nursing Staff Development: Applications to Critical. 2nd ed. (Illus.). 340p. (C). (gr. 13). 1994. text 51.95 (*0-8016-7422-0*, 00060) Mosby Inc.

Alspach, Loretta H., jt. auth. see Alspach, Philip H.

Alspach, Philip H. & Alspach, Loretta H. Swiss - Bernese Oberland: A Summer Guide with Specific Trips to the Mountains, Lakes & Villages. LC 92-71079. 104p. 1992. pap. 16.95 (*0-9632235-3-4*) Intercon CA.

Alspach, Russell K. Irish Poetry, from the English Invasion to 1798. 2nd rev. ed. LC 75-28807. reprint ed. 24.50 (*0-404-13800-4*) AMS Pr.

Alspach, Russell K., ed. see Yeats, William Butler.

Alspach, Sandra. The Communication Web: An Introduction to Human Communication Processes. 456p. (C). 1996. pap. text, per. 53.95 (*0-7872-1781-6*, 41178101) Kendall-Hunt.

Alspach, Ted. Acrobat 3 for Macintosh & Windows: Visual QuickStart Guide. LC 97-182540. 208p. (C). 1997. pap. text 16.95 (*0-201-68848-4*) Peachpit Pr.

— The Complete Idiot's Guide to Pagemaker. (Illus.). 375p. (Orig.). 1995. pap. 19.99 (*0-7897-0377-7*) Que.

— The Complete Idiot's Guide to PhotoShop. 384p. 1994. 24.95 (*1-56761-527-9*, Alpha Ref) Macmillan Gen Ref.

— The Complete Idiot's Guide to QuarkXPress. (Illus.). 357p. (Orig.). 1994. 19.95 (*1-56761-519-8*, Alpha Ref) Macmillan Gen Ref.

— Illustrator Effects Magic. 1997. 39.99 (*1-56830-383-1*) Hayden.

— Illustrator 8 Bible. LC T385.A46616 1999. 816p. 1998. pap. 49.99 (*0-7645-3269-3*) IDG Bks.

— Illustrator 7 Bible. LC 97-70956. (Illus.). 1000p. 1997. pap. 49.99 (*0-7645-4027-0*) IDG Bks.

— Illustrator 7 Studio Secrets. LC 97-70953. (Illus.). 336p. 1998. pap. 49.99 (*0-7645-4026-2*) IDG Bks.

***Alspach, Ted.** Illustrator "X" Bible. (Illus.). 1000p. 2000. pap. 39.99 (*0-7645-3429-7*) IDG Bks.

— Illustrator "X" for Dummies. (For Dummies Ser.). (Illus.). 384p. 2000. pap. 19.99 (*0-7645-0668-4*) IDG Bks.

Alspach, Ted. MacWorld Illustrator 5.0/5.5 Bible. LC 94-75905. 650p. 1994. pap. 39.95 (*1-56884-097-7*) IDG Bks.

Alspach, Ted. MacWorld Illustrator 6 Bible. 2nd ed. (Illus.). 850p. 1996. pap. 39.99 (*1-56884-494-8*) IDG Bks.

Alspach, Ted. PageMaker 6.5 for Macintosh: Visual QuickStart Guide. LC 97-222189. 304p. (C). 1997. pap. text 18.95 (*0-201-69649-5*, Pub. by Peachpit Pr) Addison-Wesley.

— PageMaker 6.5 for Windows: Visual QuickStart Guide. LC 97-226315. 304p. (C). 1997. pap. text 18.95 (*0-201-69650-9*, Pub. by Peachpit Pr) Addison-Wesley.

***Alspach, Ted.** Pagemaker 6.5 Plus for Windows: Visual Quickstart Guide. 2nd ed. LC 99-461830. 320p. (C). 1999. pap. text 18.99 (*0-201-35460-8*) Peachpit Pr.

— PDF with Acrobat 4: Visual QuickStart Guide. 208p. (C). 1999. pap. text 17.99 (*0-201-35461-6*) Peachpit Pr.

***Alspach, Ted & Alspach, Jen.** PhotoDeluxe Home Edition 4 for Windows: Visual QuickStart Guide. 2nd ed. 224p. (C). 2000. pap. 17.99 (*0-201-35479-9*) Adobe Pr.

Alspach, Ted & Alspach, Jen. PhotoDeluxe Two for Windows & Macintosh: Visual QuickStart Guide. LC 98-132816. 208p. (C). 1997. pap. text 16.95 (*0-201-69670-3*) Addison-Wesley.

Alspach, Ted & Alspach, Jennifer. Conan TK 4. 352p. 1995. pap. 7.99 (*0-614-03871-5*) Tor Bks.

Alspach, Tim. On Solid Ground: The Christian Basics. LC 97-61854. 128p. 1997. pap. 9.99 (*1-57921-052-X*) WinePress Pub.

Alspach, Timothy. On Solid Ground: The Christian Basics. (Illus.). 86p. (Orig.). 1996. pap. 5.00 (*1-57502-361-X*) Morris Pubng.

Alspaugh, Leann D. & Yevtushenko, Yevgeny. Ancel E. Nunn. (Illus.). (Orig.). 1996. write for info. (*0-9653006-0-9*, 713-523-4300) G Wurzer Gall.

***Alspaugh, M. A.** Bulk Material Handling by Conveyor Belt III. LC 99-88995. (Illus.). 2000. pap. write for info. (*0-87335-198-3*) SMM&E Inc.

Alspaugh, M. A. & Bailey, R. O., eds. Native Sulfur: Developments in Geology & Exploration. LC 95-73103. (Illus.). 150p. (Orig.). 1996. pap. 49.00 (*0-87335-113-4*, 138-X) SMM&E Inc.

Alspaugh, Mark, ed. Bulk Material Handling by Conveyor Belt II. 288p. 1998. pap. 54.00 (*0-87335-157-6*, 157-6) SMM&E Inc.

Alspaugh, Mark A. & Bailey, Richard O., eds. Bulk Material Handling by Conveyor Belt. LC 95-73103. (Illus.). 150p. (Orig.). 1996. pap. 49.00 (*0-87335-138-X*, 138-X) SMM&E Inc.

Alspector, Josh, et al, eds. Proceedings of the International Workshop on Applications of Neural Networks to Telecommunications, Vol. 2. (Neural Networks: The INNS Series of Texts, Monographs, & Proceedings). 320p. 1993. text 79.95 (*0-8058-1560-0*) L Erlbaum Assocs.

— Proceedings of the International Workshop on Applications of Neural Networks to Telecommunications, Vol. 2. 384p. 1995. text 79.95 (*0-8058-2084-1*) L Erlbaum Assocs.

Alspector, Joshua, et al, eds. Proceedings of the International Workshop on Applications of Neural Networks to Telecommunications 3. LC 97-13153. 296p. 1997. 79.95 (*0-8058-2900-8*) L Erlbaum Assocs.

Alsted, Johann H. Templum Musicum: or The Musical Synopsis. fac. ed. (Monuments of Music & Music Literature in Facsimile Ser., Series II: Vol. 35). 1967. lib. bdg. 32.50 (*0-8450-2235-0*) Broude.

Alstedt, Johann H. Clavis Artis Lullianae. (GER.). vii, 182p. 1983. reprint ed. write for info. (*3-487-07309-9*) G Olms Pubs.

Alster, Bendt. Proverbs of Ancient Sumer: The World's Earliest Proverb Collections, 2 vols., Set. LC 97-37014. 970p. 1996. 90.00 (*1-883053-20-X*) CDL Pr.

Alster, Tina S. Manual of Cutaneous Laser Techniques. LC 96-37985. 200p. 1997. text 116.00 (*0-397-58429-6*) Lppncott W & W.

***Alster, Tina S.** Manual of Cutaneous Laser Techniques. 2nd ed. LC 99-43217. 259p. 1999. write for info. (*0-7817-1960-7*, Lippnctt) Lppncott W & W.

Alster, Tina S. & Apfelberg, David B. Cosmetic Laser Surgery: A Practitioner's Guide. 2nd ed. LC 98-3394. (Illus.). 393p. 1998. 235.00 (*0-471-25270-0*) Wiley.

Alster, Tina S. & Preston, Lydia. The Essential Guide to Cosmetic Laser Surgery. (Illus.). 200p. (Orig.). 1997. pap. 16.00 (*1-887110-09-7*) Allian Pubng.

Alsterda, Grayce H. A Branch with Twigs from John Spencer of Rhode Island. (Illus.). 181p. 1987. pap. text 25.00 (*0-9617035-1-2*) G H Alsterda.

— William Card Seventeen Ten to Seventeen Eighty-Five with Ancestors & Some Descendants. LC 86-174208. (Illus.). 66p. 1986. pap. text 11.00 (*0-9617035-0-4*) G H Alsterda.

Alstete, Jeffrey W. Benchmarking in Higher Education: Adapting Best Practices to Improve Quality. Fife, Jonathan D., ed. LC 96-78397. (ASHE-ERIC Higher Education Reports: Vol. 95-5). (Illus.). 100p. (Orig.). 1996. pap. 24.00 (*1-878380-69-9*) GWU Grad Schl E&HD.

Alstine, Julie Van, see McLean, Candi.

Alston. Fundamentals of Physical Science. 1998. 30.00 (*0-07-230880-X*) McGraw.

Alston & Mills. Cpsm Lml Anatomy & Physiol. 1998. pap. text 8.74 (*0-07-230121-X*) McGraw.

Alston, jt. auth. see Coombs.

Alston, Andrew. Garrow & Alston: Law of Wills & Administration. 5th ed. 709p. 1984. boxed set 99.00 (*0-409-60130-6*, NZ, MICHIE) LEXIS Pub.

— Residential Tenancies. 2nd ed. 126p. 1993. pap. 63.00 (*0-409-78969-0*, NZ, MICHIE) LEXIS Pub.

Alston, Clarence E. Reclaiming Our Youth. 80p. (Orig.). (YA). 1998. pap. 7.95 (*1-883928-20-6*) Longwood.

Alston, Dallas E., jt. ed. see Hargreaves, John A.

Alston, Dana, ed. see Bullard, Robert, et al.

Alston, David. Encounters Evelyn Williams. (Illus.). 40p. 1997. pap. 14.95 (*0-901673-53-6*, Pub. by Art Bks Intl) Partners Pubs Grp.

— Ross & Cromarty: A Historical Guide. 1999. pap. text 15.95 (*1-874744-48-3*, Pub. by Birlinn Ltd) Dufour.

Alston, David, jt. auth. see Curtis, Tony.

Alston, Denise A. Recruiting Minority Classroom Teachers: A National Challenge. 40p. (Orig.). 1988. pap. text 7.50 (*1-55877-007-0*) Natl Governor.

Alston, E. Cookies. Date not set. 12.50 (*0-06-016994-X*) HarperTrade.

Alston, Edith. Let's Visit a Space Camp. LC 89-34373. (Let's Visit Ser.). (Illus.). 32p. (J). (gr. 2-4). 1990. pap. text 3.50 (*0-8167-1744-3*); lib. bdg. 15.35 (*0-8167-1743-5*) Troll Communs.

Alston, Elizabeth. Biscuits & Scones: 72 Recipes - From Breakfast Biscuits to Homey Desserts. LC 87-29110. (Illus.). 96p. 1988. 12.00 (*0-517-56345-2*) C Potter.

— Elizabeth Alston's Best Baking: 80 Recipes for Angel Food Cakes, Chiffon Cakes, Coffee Cakes, Pound Cakes. LC 99-40942. 208p. 2000. pap. 15.00 (*0-06-095329-2*, Perennial) HarperTrade.

— Muffins: Sixty Sweet & Savory Recipes from Old Favorites to New. 96p. 1984. 11.00 (*0-517-55587-5*) C Potter.

***Alston, Elizabeth.** Wedding Cakes. (Illus.). 2001. 30.00 (*0-609-60389-2*, Pub. by Crown Pub Group) Random House.

Alston, Emerson. Moccasins. LC 99-64517. 128p. (YA). (gr. 8-12). 2000. pap. 7.95 (*1-56315-220-7*, Pub. by SterlingHse) Natl Bk Netwk.

Alston, Ervin M. Instructional Resources for Teachers Exploring West Africa Vol. 1: A Young Person's Guide to Understanding African History & Culture. 41p. 1997. pap., teacher ed. 20.00 (*0-9655385-1-6*) Softly Pubns.

Alston, Eugenia. Growing up Chimpanzee. LC 74-12307. (Illus.). 32p. (J). (gr. 1-4). 1975. 11.95 (*0-690-00015-4*) HarpC Child Bks.

Alston, Farnum K., jt. auth. see Bryson, John M.

Alston, Frances K. Caring for Other People's Children: A Complete Guide to Family Day Care. LC 92-17036. (Early Childhood Education Ser.). (Illus.). 320p. (C). 1992. pap. 19.95 (*0-8077-3218-4*) Tchrs Coll.

Alston, George G. & Vanacore, Connie. The Winning Edge: Show Ring Secrets. (Illus.). 176p. 1992. 25.95 (*0-87605-834-9*) Howell Bks.

***Alston, Giles & King, Anthony.** From the Moon to Mars: The Politics of Space. (Illus.). 192p. (C). 2000. pap. text. write for info. (*1-889119-27-X*, Chatham House Pub) Seven Bridges.

Alston, Harvey, jt. auth. see Best, Inc. Staff.

Alston, J. B. Yoruba Drama in English: Interpretation & Production. LC 88-34185. (Studies in African Literature). 192p. 1989. lib. bdg. 79.95 (*0-88946-726-9*) E Mellen.

Alston, Jacquelyn G. Comparative Nationalism: Definitions, Interpretations, & the Black American & British West African Experience to 1947. 2nd ed. LC 85-80588. 283p. (Orig.). 1985. pap. 10.95 (*0-9614733-6-3*) Hist Dimensions.

Alston, Jon P. The American Samurai: Blending American & Japanese Managerial Practice. (Studies in Organization: No. 6). (Illus.). xii, 370p. 1985. 80.80 (*3-11-010619-1*); pap. 29.95 (*3-11-012034-8*) De Gruyter.

— The Intelligent Businessman's Guide to Japan. LC 89-51725. 152p. (Orig.). 1990. pap. 12.95 (*0-8048-1633-6*) Tuttle Pubng.

— The Social Dimensions of International Business: An Annotated Bibliography, 12. LC 92-29466. (Bibliographies & Indexes in Economics & Economic History Ser.: No. 12). 336p. 1992. lib. bdg. 75.00 (*0-313-28029-0*, ACR, Greenwood Pr) Greenwood.

Alston, Jon P. & He, Yongxin. Business Guide to Modern China. LC 96-46475. (International Business Ser.). 191p. 1997. 29.95 (*0-87013-423-X*) Mich St U Pr.

***Alston, Julian M.** A Meta-Analysis of the Rates of Return to Agricultural R & D: Ex Pede Herculem? LC 00-40733. 2000. pap. write for info. (*0-89629-116-2*) Intl Pubs Co.

Alston, Julian M. Paying for Agricultural Productivity. LC 99-17315. (International Food Policy Research Institute Ser.). (Illus.). 304p. 1999. pap. 21.50 (*0-8018-6278-7*) Johns Hopkins.

Alston, Julian M.., et al, eds. Science under Scarcity: Principles & Practice for Agricultural Research Evaluation & Priority Setting. LC 99-181580. (CABI Publishing Ser.). 624p. 1998. pap. text 45.00 (*0-85199-299-4*) OUP.

An Asterisk (*) at the beginning of an entry indicates that the title is appearing for the first time.

Alston, Julian M. & Pardey, Philip G. Making Science Pay: Economics of Agricultural R & D Policy. (Studies in Agricultural Policy). 324p. 1995. 29.95 (*0-8447-3900-6*) Am Enterprise.

Alston, Julian M., et al. Paying for Agricultural Productivity. LC 99-17315. (International Food Policy Research Institute Ser.). (Illus.). 315p. 1999. 59.95 (*0-8018-6185-3*) Johns Hopkins.

***Alston, Lee, et al.** Titles, Conflict & Land Use: The Development of Property Rights & Land Reform on the Brazilian Amazon Frontier. LC 98-58060. (Economics, Cognition & Society Ser.). (Illus.). 248p. 1999. text 49.50 (*0-472-11006-3*, 11006) U of Mich Pr.

Alston, Lee, jt. auth. see Pope, David.

Alston, Lee J., et al, eds. Empirical Studies in Institutional Change. (Political Economy of Institutions & Decisions Ser.). (Illus.). 371p. (C). 1996. text 64.95 (*0-521-55313-X*) Cambridge U Pr.

— Empirical Studies in Institutional Change. (Political Economy of Institutions & Decisions Ser.). (Illus.). 371p. (C). 1996. pap. text 22.95 (*0-521-55743-7*) Cambridge U Pr.

Alston, Lee J. & Ferrie, Joseph P. Southern Paternalism & the Rise of the American Welfare State: Economics, Politics, & Institutions, 1865-1965. LC 97-52779. (Political Economy of Institutions & Decisions Ser.). (Illus.). 192p. (C). 1998. text 49.95 (*0-521-62210-7*) Cambridge U Pr.

Alston, Linda D. What Every Female Should Know (Especially Teenagers) 32p. 1993. pap. write for info. (*0-9636803-1-5*) Eagles Eye.

Alston, Liviu L., ed. High-Voltage Technology. LC TK0153.A48. (United Kingdom Atomic Energy Authority, Harwell Post-Graduate Ser.). (Illus.). 426p. reprint ed. pap. 132.10 (*0-608-30051-9*, 205195200016) Bks Demand.

Alston, Margaret. Women on the Land: The Hidden Heart of Rural Australia. 1995. pap. 22.95 (*0-86840-382-2*, Pub. by New South Wales Univ Pr) Intl Spec Bk.

Alston, Margaret & Bowles, Wendy. Research for Social Workers: An Introduction to Methods. LC 99-179993. (Studies in Society Ser.). 320p. 1998. pap. 29.95 (*1-86448-517-5*, Pub. by Allen & Unwin Pty) Paul & Co Pubs.

Alston, Nelson G. Sonnets in the Name of Love. Avent, Barbara P., ed. (Illus.). 64p. (Orig.). (YA). 1993. pap. 10.95 (*0-9632202-2-5*) Alpha Bk N Pr.

— A Time for Glory . . . And Hate: The American Civil Rights Movement. Hayden, Murial, ed. (Illus.). 96p. (Orig.). 1993. pap. 8.95 (*0-9632202-0-9*) Alpha Bk N Pr.

Alston, Nelson G., ed. see Avent, Barbara P.

Alston, Pat, ed. see Adams, Andrew.

Alston, Philip. Development & the Rule of Law: Prevention Verses Cure as a Human Rights Strategy. LC K 3240.4.A48. 131p. reprint ed. pap. 40.70 (*0-8357-6645-4*, 203531200094) Bks Demand.

***Alston, Philip.** The EU & Human Rights. LC 99-28822. 976p. 2000. text 135.00 (*0-19-829806-4*); pap. text 55.00 (*0-19-829809-9*) OUP.

Alston, Philip. Promoting Human Rights Through Bills of Rights: Comparative Perspectives. LC 97-19746. 584p. 2000. text 95.00 (*0-19-825822-4*) OUP.

Alston, Philip, ed. Human Rights Laws. 500p. (C). 1996. lib. bdg. 150.00 (*0-8147-0613-4*) NYU Pr.

***Alston, Philip, ed.** People's Rights: The State of the Art. (Collected Courses of the Academy of European Law: Volume 9). 280p. 2000. text 72.00 (*0-19-829875-7*) OUP.

Alston, Philip, ed. The United Nations & Human Rights: A Critical Appraisal. 784p. 1995. pap. text 45.00 (*0-19-826001-6*) OUP.

Alston, Philip, et al, eds. Children, Rights, & the Law. 282p. 1992. pap. text 38.00 (*0-19-825776-7*) OUP.

Alston, Philip & Chiam, Madelaine, eds. Treaty-Making & Australia: Globalisation Versus Sovereignty? 309p. 1995. pap. 29.95 (*1-86287-195-7*, Pub. by Federation Pr) Gaunt.

***Alston, Philip & Crawford, James, eds.** The Future of U. N. Human Rights Treaty Monitoring. LC 99-34665. (Illus.). 504p. (C). 2000. 85.00 (*0-521-64195-0*); pap. 29.95 (*0-521-64574-3*) Cambridge U Pr.

Alston, Philip & Tomasevski, Katarina. The Right to Food. 1984. lib. bdg. 89.50 (*90-247-3087-2*) Kluwer Academic.

Alston, Philip, jt. auth. see Steiner, Henry.

Alston, Philip, jt. ed. see Bustelo, Mara R.

Alston, R. C. Books with Manuscript. (Manuscript Studies). 616p. 1994. 120.00 (*0-7123-0329-4*, Pub. by B23tish Library) U of Toronto Pr.

— A Checklist of Women Writers, 1801-1900: Fiction, Verse, Drama. 530p. 1991. 70.00 (*0-8161-7295-1*, Hall Reference) Macmillan.

Alston, R. C., ed. Order & Connexion: Studies in Bibliography & Book History - Selected Papers from the Munby Seminar, Cambridge, July, 1994. LC 96-42403. (Illus.). 224p. 1997. 75.00 (*0-85991-506-9*) Boydell & Brewer.

Alston, R. C. & Hill, B. S., compiled by. Books Printed on Vellum in the Collections of the British Library. 208p. 1996. 60.00 (*0-7123-0433-9*, Pub. by B23tish Library) U of Toronto Pr.

Alston, R. C. & Jannetta, M. J. Bibliography, Machine Readable Cataloguing & the Estc / LC 80-468576. 246p. 1978. write for info. (*0-904654-17-6*) Br Library Bd.

Alston, Rebecca. The Autobiography of John Brown. LC 93-94297. 73p. 1996. 10.95 (*0-533-10981-7*) Vantage.

Alston, Regina. My Book. Mason, Mary J., ed. (Illus.). 10p. (J). (ps-6). 1997. pap., spiral bd. 8.00 (*1-890864-02-1*) Breath of Life.

Alston, Richard. Aspects of Roman History, A.D. 14-117. LC 97-24205. 368p. (C). 1998. pap. 19.99 (*0-415-13237-1*) Routledge.

— Aspects of Roman History, A.D. 14-117. LC 97-24205. (Illus.). 368p. (C). 1998. 65.00 (*0-415-13236-3*) Routledge.

— Soldier & Society in Roman Egypt: A Social History. LC 95-13204. (Illus.). 272p. (C). (gr. 13). 1995. 90.00 (*0-415-12270-8*) Routledge.

— Soldier & Society in Roman Egypt: Social History. (Illus.). 272p. (C). 1998. pap. 25.99 (*0-415-18606-4*) Routledge.

Alston, Richard M. Commercial Irrigation Enterprise: The Fear of Water Monopoly & the Genesis of Market Distortion in the Nineteenth Century American West. LC 77-14752. (Dissertations in American Economic History Ser.). 1977. 30.95 (*0-405-11025-1*) Ayer.

Alston, Robert, ed. see Omar, Adisa M.

Alston, Sandra, jt. auth. see Fleming, Patricia.

Alston, Schandra K. Thompkinsel, see Thompkinsel Alston, Schandra K.

Alston, Sharon M. Schemes & Truth. 32p. 1989. write for info. (*0-8062-3587-X*) Macmillan.

Alston, Theodore A., jt. auth. see D'Ambra, Michael.

Alston, Tom, jt. auth. see Weinstein, Jerry.

Alston, Toni M., et al, eds. Dream Reader: Psychoanalytic Articles on Dreams. LC 93-17645. xviii, 772p. 1993. 115.00 (*0-8236-1452-2*) Intl Univs Pr.

Alston, W. G. The Developmental Challenge Course. (Illus.). 110p. 1985. pap. 14.95 (*0-932392-23-7*) Mouvement Pubns.

Alston, W. P., tr. see Husserl, Edmund.

Alston, Wallace M., Jr., ed. see Gillespie, Thomas W.

Alston, William P. Divine Nature & Human Language: Essays in Philosophical Theology. LC 89-898. 288p. 1989. pap. text 18.95 (*0-8014-9545-8*) Cornell U Pr.

— Epistemic Justification: Essays in the Theory of Knowledge. LC 89-42865. 352p. 1989. 49.95 (*0-8014-2257-4*) Cornell U Pr.

***Alston, William P.** Illocutionary Acts & Sentence Meaning. LC 99-52786. 2000. 48.50 (*0-8014-3669-9*) Cornell U Pr.

Alston, William P. Perceiving God: The Epistemology of Religious Experience. LC 91-55068. 336p. 1993. text 47.50 (*0-8014-2597-2*); pap. text 17.95 (*0-8014-8155-4*) Cornell U Pr.

— A Realist Conception of Truth. 296p. 1996. pap. text 17.95 (*0-8014-8410-3*) Cornell U Pr.

— The Reliability of Sense Perception. LC 92-54964. 1993. text 32.50 (*0-8014-2862-9*) Cornell U Pr.

Alston, William P. The Reliability of Sense Perception. LC 92-54964. 160p. 1996. pap. text 12.95 (*0-8014-8101-5*) Cornell U Pr.

Alston, Y. R., jt. ed. see Coombs, J.

Alstott, Anne, jt. auth. see Ackerman, Bruce A.

Alstrom, T., jt. ed. see Grasbeck, R.

Alstyne, Richard Van, see Van Alstyne, Richard.

Alstyne, Richard W. Van, see Van Alstyne, Richard W.

Alstyne, W. Scott Van, see Van Alstyne, W. Scott, Jr.

***Alsum, Cris.** Who Am I to Judge? (Christian Character Development Ser.). 2000. pap. text 6.99 (*0-7644-2131-X*) Group Pub.

***Alsup, Dan.** Driftboats: A Complete Guide. (Illus.). 86p. 2000. pap. 19.95 (*1-57188-189-1*, DRB) F Amato Pubns.

Alsup, Phillip. Games-in-a-Box Book: The Ultimate Games Resource. LC 99-167513. 127p. 1998. pap. text 12.95 (*0-7673-3016-1*, Convntn Pr) LifeWay Christian.

Alsuwaiyel, M. H. Algorithms: Design Techniques & Analysis. 1999. 97.00 (*981-02-3740-5*) World Scientific Pub.

Alswang, Hope, jt. auth. see Peirce, Donald C.

Alsworth, MaryDean. Gleanings from Alta California. LC 80-68882. 139p. (Orig.). 1980. pap. 22.00 (*0-939052-00-8*) Dean Pubns.

— More Gleanings from Alta California. LC 82-72383. 146p. (Orig.). 1982. pap. 22.00 (*0-939052-01-6*) Dean Pubns.

Alszeghy, Zoltan & Flick, Maurizio. Introductory Theology. 1983. pap. 14.95 (*0-87193-198-2*) Dimension Bks.

Alt, A. Tilo. Theodor Storm. LC 72-2793. (Twayne's World Authors Ser.). 157p. (C). 1973. text 20.95 (*0-8290-1757-7*) Irvington.

Alt, Albrecht. Essays on Old Testament History & Religion. (Biblical Seminar Ser.: Vol. 9). 274p. 1989. pap. 19.95 (*1-85075-204-4*, Pub. by Sheffield Acad) CUP Services.

Alt, Albrecht, jt. ed. see Dalman, Gustav.

***Alt, Arthur T. & Bernhard, Julia.** Arnold Zweig Sein Werk Im Kontext Der Deutschsprachigen Exilliteratur: Akten des IV. Internationalen Arnold-Zweig-Symposiums Durham, N. C. 1996. 261p. 1999. 69.95 (*3-906760-78-2*) P Lang Pubng.

***Alt, Betty & Wells, Sandra.** Wicked Women: Black Widows, Child Killers, & Other Women in Crime. 192p. 2000. pap. 18.00 (*1-58160-078-X*) Paladin Pr.

Alt, Betty S. & Stone, Bonnie D. Campfollowing: Adventures of the Military Wife. LC 90-24999. 176p. 1991. 55.00 (*0-275-93721-6*, C3721, Praeger Pubs); pap. 17.95 (*0-275-93722-4*, B3722, Praeger Pubs) Greenwood.

***Alt, David.** Glacial Lake Missoula & Its Humongous Floods. (Illus.). 184p. 2000. pap. 16.00 (*0-87842-415-6*) Mountain Pr.

Alt, David & Hyndman, Donald W. Northwest Exposures: A Geologic Story of the Northwest. LC 95-37140. 456p. 1995. pap. text 24.00 (*0-87842-323-0*) Mountain Pr.

— Roadside Geology of Idaho. LC 89-36471. (Roadside Geology Ser.). (Illus.). 403p. 1989. pap. 18.00 (*0-87842-219-6*) Mountain Pr.

— Roadside Geology of Montana. LC 86-17954. (Roadside Geology Ser.). (Illus.). 435p. 1986. pap. 18.00 (*0-87842-202-1*) Mountain Pr.

— Roadside Geology of Northern California. LC 74-81834. (Roadside Geology Ser.). (Illus.). 256p. 1975. pap. 5.00 (*0-87842-055-X*) Mountain Pr.

— Roadside Geology of Oregon. LC 77-25841. (Roadside Geology Ser.). (Illus.). 278p. 1978. reprint ed. pap. 15.00 (*0-87842-063-0*) Mountain Pr.

— Roadside Geology of Washington. LC 84-8409. (Roadside Geology Ser.). (Illus.). 320p. (Orig.). 1984. pap. 18.00 (*0-87842-160-2*) Mountain Pr.

Alt, David, ed. see Chronic, Halka.

Alt, David, ed. see Eversman, Sharon & Carr, Mary.

Alt, David, ed. see Harris, Stephen L.

Alt, David, ed. see Van Diver, Bradford B.

***Alt, David D. & Hyndman, Donald W.** Roadside Geology of Northern & Central California. LC 99-48554. 2000. pap. 20.00 (*0-87842-409-1*) Mountain Pr.

Alt, E. U., et al, eds. Implantable Cardioverter - Defibrillator. (Illus.). 256p. 1992. 89.00 (*0-387-53927-1*) Spr-Verlag.

— Rate Adaptive Cardiac Pacing. LC 92-48249. (Illus.). 352p. 1993. 114.00 (*0-387-54051-2*) Spr-Verlag.

Alt, Edith, jt. auth. see Alt, Herschel.

Alt, Frederick W., et al, eds. Nuclear Oncogenes. (Illus.). 194p. (Orig.). 1987. pap. text 30.00 (*0-87969-305-3*) Cold Spring Harbor.

Alt, Friedrich, jt. ed. see Zereini, Fathi.

Alt, Herschel & Alt, Edith. Russia's Children: A First Report on Child Welfare in the Soviet Union. LC 75-18353. 240p. 1975. reprint ed. lib. bdg. 59.50 (*0-8371-8330-8*, ALRC, Greenwood Pr) Greenwood.

Alt, James E. & Shepsle, Kenneth A., eds. Perspectives on Positive Political Economy. (Political Economy of Institutions & Decisions Ser.). (Illus.). 278p. (C). 1990. text 69.95 (*0-521-39221-7*); pap. text 21.95 (*0-521-39851-7*) Cambridge U Pr.

***Alt, James E., et al.** Competition & Cooperation: Conversations with Nobelists about Economics & Political Science. LC 99-25812. 336p. 1999. 39.95 (*0-87154-010-X*) Russell Sage.

Alt, Jeannette, jt. auth. see Stolte, H.

***Alt, Jeff.** A Walk for Sunshine: A 2,160-Mile Expedition for Charity on the Appalachian Trail. (Illus.). 2000. pap. 14.95 (*0-9679482-0-7*) Dreams Shared.

Alt, K. W., et al, eds. Dental Anthropology: Fundamentals, Limits & Prospects. LC 98-37799. (Illus.). 450p. 1998. text 89.95 (*3-211-82974-1*) Spr-Verlag.

Alt, Ruth R. & Kirkland, Mary L. Steps to Composition: A Pre-Composition Workbook for Students of English As a Second Language. 321p. 1973. pap. 7.95 (*0-87840-175-X*) Georgetown U Pr.

***Alt, Susan J., ed.** A Day of Fun: For Twins & More! (Illus.). 16p. (J). 1999. pap. 5.95 (*1-891846-09-4*) Busn Word.

— Hugs & Kisses: For Twins, Triplets & More! (Illus.). 16p. (J). 1999. pap. 5.95 (*1-891846-12-4*) Busn Word.

— Summer & Fall: For Twins & More! (Illus.). 16p. (J). 1999. pap. 5.95 (*1-891846-11-6*) Busn Word.

Alt, Susan J., ed. The Twinship Sourcebook: Your Guide to Understanding Multiples. 3rd ed. LC 93-60586. 270p. 1997. pap. 14.95 (*0-9636745-4-4*) Busn Word.

***Alt, Susan J., ed.** Winter & Spring: For Twins & More! (Illus.). 16p. (J). 1999. pap. 5.95 (*1-891846-10-8*) Busn Word.

***Alt, Susan J., et al, eds.** Toddler Twins: Twinship Sourcebook2: Practical Parenting During the Toddler Years. LC 00-101148. 200p. 2000. pap. 14.95 (*1-891846-14-0*) Busn Word.

***Alt-Trans Cleveland Staff.** Car-Free in Cleveland. (Illus.). iv, 108p. 2000. pap. 6.95 (*0-9663999-1-9*) EcoCity Clvlnd.

Alt, W., et al, eds. Biological Motion: Proceedings of a Workshop Held in Konigswinter, Germany, March 15-19, 1989. (Lecture Notes in Biomathematics Ser.: Vol. 89). x, 604p. 1991. 114.95 (*0-387-53520-9*) Spr-Verlag.

— Dynamics of Cell & Tissue Motion. LC 97-39810. (Mathematics & Biosciences in Interaction Ser.). xvi, 336p. 1997. 69.50 (*3-7643-5781-9*) Birkhauser.

Alt, W., et al. Dynamics of Cell & Tissue Motion. LC 97-39810. (Mathematics & Biosciences in Interaction Ser.). 1997. write for info. (*0-8176-5781-9*) Birkhauser.

Alta. Momma: A Start on All the Untold Stories. LC 74-79105. 77 p. (Orig.). (J). 1974. write for info. (*0-87810-528-X*) Times Change.

— Momma: A Start on All the Untold Stories. LC 74-79105. (Illus.). 80p. (Orig.). 1974. pap. 4.50 (*0-87810-028-8*) Times Change.

Alta, C. Allah Created Everything. (Illus.). 28p. (J). (gr. 1-3). 1995. 14.95 (*1-884187-09-9*) AMICA Pub Hse.

— Allah Created Everything. Khokhar, Rafiah, ed. LC 94-71172. (Illus.). 28p. (J). (ps-2). 1995. 14.95 (*1-884187-04-8*) AMICA Pub Hse.

ALTA Staff, jt. auth. see ACSM Staff.

***Altaba-Artal, Dolors.** Aphra Behn's English Feminism: Wit & Satire. LC 99-32201. 232p. 1999. 39.50 (*1-57591-029-2*) Susquehanna U Pr.

Altabe, David F. Spanish & Portuguese Jewry Before & after 1492. 168p. (Orig.). 1993. pap. 11.95 (*0-87203-139-X*) Hermon.

Altabe, David F., et al. Studies on Turkish-Jewish History: Political & Social Relations, Literature & Linguistics: The Quincentennial Papers. LC 96-12191. 1996. pap. 29.95 (*0-87203-146-2*) Hermon.

Altaf, Zafar. Entrepreneurship in the Third World: Risk & Uncertainty in Industry in Pakistan. 240p. 1988. lib. bdg. 52.50 (*0-7099-0574-2*) Routledge.

Altalib, Hisham. Training Guide for Islamic Workers. 3rd ed. LC 91-12896. (Human Development Ser.: No. 1). (Illus.). 397p. 1993. pap. 25.00 (*1-56564-120-5*) IIIT VA.

Altamiranda, Daniel, jt. ed. see Foster, David W.

Altamirano, Fernando. Metodo de Estenotipia en Espanol Compatible con el Uso de Computadoras. (SPA.). (Orig.). (C). 1990. pap. write for info. (*0-318-66797-5*) Stenograph Corp.

Altamirano, Ignacio. El Zarco. (SPA.). pap. 7.95 (*968-432-264-X*, Pub. by Porrua) Continental Bk.

Altamirano-Piolle, Maria E. Jose Maria Valasco, 1840-1912: A National Homage, 2 vols., Set. (Illus.). 556p. 1994. pap. 65.00 (*0-8263-1609-3*) U of NM Pr.

Altamirano, Teofilo, et al. Migrants, Regional Identities & Latin American Cities. LC 97-3401. (Society for Latin American Anthropology Publication Ser.). 1997. write for info. (*0-913167-79-7*) Am Anthro Assn.

Altamuro, Vincent J. & Clarkson, Sandra P. Exploring with Pattern Blocks. (J). (ps-3). 1995. pap. 9.50 (*0-201-48029-8*) Addison-Wesley.

— Exploring with Pattern Blocks. 64p. 1989. pap. text 9.50 (*0-938587-09-9*) Cuisenaire.

Altan, Taylan, ed. The North American Metalworking Research Conference, May 17-19, 1976: Proceedings. LC 76-6005. (Illus.). 494p. reprint ed. pap. 153.20 (*0-608-17820-9*, 203248300079) Bks Demand.

Altan, Taylan, et al. Metal Forming: Fundamentals & Applications. (Illus.). 353p. 1983. 98.00 (*0-87170-167-7*, 6435) ASM.

Altarejos-Espinosa, Eva L. To a Patient Named Nick: A Different Kind of Story of a Nurse & an AIDS Patient. LC 95-71609. 152p. 1998. 14.95 (*0-9648529-0-X*) Carelife Pubng.

Altarelli, Guido. The Development of Perturbative QCD. LC 95-122859. 400p. 1994. text 99.00 (*981-02-1702-1*); pap. text 61.00 (*981-02-1703-X*) World Scientific Pub.

Altarelli, Guido, jt. auth. see Diella, L.

Altarriba, Jeanette, ed. Cognition & Culture: A Cross-Cultural Approach to Cognitive Psychology. LC 93-36251. (Advances in Psychology Ser.: Vol. 103). 420p. 1993. 159.00 (*0-444-89639-2*, North Holland) Elsevier.

Altbach, Edith H., et al, eds. German Feminism: Readings in Politics & Literature. LC 83-17849. 389p. (C). 1984. pap. text 24.95 (*0-87395-841-1*) State U NY Pr.

Altbach, P. G., jt. auth. see Boli, J.

Altbach, P. G., jt. auth. see Eisemon, Thomas O.

Altbach, P. G., jt. auth. see Tarrow, N. Bernstein.

Altbach, Philip, ed. International Higher Education: An Encyclopedia, 2 vols. LC 90-46952. 1175p. 1991. text 60.00 (*0-8240-4847-4*, SS506) Garland.

Altbach, Philip, et al. Academic Supermarkets: A Critical Case Study of a Multiversity. LC 71-173853. (Jossey-Bass Higher Education Ser.). 390p. reprint ed. 120.90 (*0-8357-9294-3*, 201379100087) Bks Demand.

Altbach, Philip, ed. see Duryea, E. D.

Altbach, Philip, ed. see Dziech, Billie W. & Hawkins, Michael W.

Altbach, Philip, ed. see Tillet, Anthony & Lesser, Barry.

Altbach, Philip, ed. see Youn, Ted I.

Altbach, Philip G. Comparative Higher Education: Knowledge, the University, & Development. LC 97-49237. (Contemporary Studies in Social & Policy Issues in Education). 1998. 73.25 (*1-56750-380-2*); pap. 24.95 (*1-56750-381-0*) Ablx Pub.

— Higher Education in the Third World: Themes & Variations. 2nd rev. ed. LC 86-72987. 260p. 1988. pap. text 12.95 (*0-89891-036-6*) Advent Bks Div.

— The Knowledge Context: Comparative Perspectives on the Distribution of Knowledge. LC 86-19167. 203p. (C). 1987. text 65.50 (*0-88706-444-2*); pap. text 21.95 (*0-88706-445-0*) State U NY Pr.

— The Muse of Modernity: Essays on Culture as Development in Africa. LC 97-167780. 1997. pap. text 19.95 (*0-86543-561-8*) Africa World.

— Student Political Activism: An International Reference Handbook. LC 88-34719. 519p. 1989. lib. bdg. 105.00 (*0-313-26016-8*, ASQ, Greenwood Pr) Greenwood.

— Student Politics in America: A Historical Analysis. LC 97-597. (Foundations of Higher Education Ser.). 277p. 1997. pap. text 24.95 (*1-56000-944-6*) Transaction Pubs.

***Altbach, Philip G., ed.** Private Prometheus: Private Higher Education & Development In the 21st Century, 77. LC 99-16142. Vol. 77. 248p. 1999. 65.00 (*0-313-31248-6*) Greenwood.

Altbach, Philip G., ed. Publishing & Development in the Third World. 442p. 1992. 90.00 (*1-873836-40-6*, Pub. by H Zell Pubs) Seven Hills Bk.

Altbach, Philip G., et al, eds. Comparative Education. LC 89-17524. ix, 533p. (C). 1989. reprint ed. pap. text 18.95 (*0-89891-038-2*) Advent Bks Div.

— Excellence in Education. LC 85-61565. 290p. (C). 1985. pap. 23.95 (*0-87975-301-3*) Prometheus Bks.

— Higher Education in American Society. 3rd ed. LC 94-26224. (Frontiers of Education Ser.). 384p. (C). 1994. pap. 24.95 (*0-87975-905-4*) Prometheus Bks.

— Publishing in the Third World: Knowledge & Development. LC 84-27920. 240p. (C). 1985. text 35.00 (*0-435-08006-7*, 08006) Heinemann.

— Textbooks in American Society: Politics, Policy, & Pedagogy. LC 90-43397. (SUNY Series, Frontiers in Education). 261p. (C). 1991. pap. text 24.95 (*0-7914-0670-9*) State U NY Pr.

Altbach, Philip G. & Choi, Hyaeweol. Bibliography on Publishing & Book Development in the Third World, 1980-1993. LC 93-34124. (Bellagio Studies in Publishing: No. 3). 156p. 1993. pap. 39.50 (*1-56750-085-4*); text 73.25 (*1-56750-084-6*) Ablx Pub.

Altbach, Philip G. & Eng Thye Jason Tan, compiled by. Programs & Centers in Comparative & International Education: An International Inventory. LC 94-13234. (Special Studies in Comparative Education: No. 34). 1994. 15.00 (*0-937033-57-X*) Grad Schl of Educ.

Altbach, Philip G. & Hassan, Salah M., eds. The Muse of Modernity: Essays on Culture As Development in Africa. LC 97-167780. 248p. 69.95 (*0-86543-560-X*) Africa World.

A

Altbach, Philip G. & Hoshino, Edith S., eds. International Book Publishing: An Encyclopedia. 1996. lib. bdg. 125.00 (*1-884964-16-8*) Fitzroy Dearborn.

— International Book Publishing: An Encyclopedia. LC 94-10027. (Reference Library of the Humanities: Vol. 1562). 768p. 1995. text 40.00 (*0-8153-0786-1*, H1562) Garland.

Altbach, Philip G. & Kelly, Gail P. Textbooks in the Third World: Policy, Content & Context. LC 88-21825. 284p. 1988. text 54.00 (*0-8240-4294-8*) Garland.

Altbach, Philip G. & Kelly, Gail P., eds. New Approaches to Comparative Education. LC 85-24523. vi, 342p. (C). 1986. pap. text 20.50 (*0-226-01526-2*); lib. bdg. 40.00 (*0-226-01525-4*) U Ch Pr.

Altbach, Philip G. & Lambert, Richard D., eds. The Academic Profession. LC 80-65242. (Annals of the American Academy of Political & Social Science Ser.: No. 448). 1980. 28.00 (*0-87761-248-X*); pap. 18.00 (*0-87761-249-8*) Am Acad Pol Soc Sci.

Altbach, Philip G. & Lomotey, Kofi, eds. The Racial Crisis in American Higher Education. LC 90-33700. (SUNY Series, Frontiers in Education). 275p. (C). 1991. pap. text 24.95 (*0-7914-0521-4*) State U NY Pr.

Altbach, Philip G. & Rathgeber, Eva-Maria. Publishing in the Third World: Trend Report & Bibliography. LC 80-20146. 186p. 1980. 55.00 (*0-275-90446-6*, C0446, Praeger Pubs) Greenwood.

Altbach, Philip G. & Selvaratnam, Viswanathan. From Dependence to Autonomy. (C). 1989. lib. bdg. 171.00 (*90-247-3777-X*) Kluwer Academic.

Altbach, Philip G. & Teferra, Damtew. Knowledge Dissemination in Africa: The Role of Scholarly Journals. LC 97-30158. (Studies in Publishing). 1997. write for info. (*0-9646078-3-2*) Bellagio Pub.

— Publishing & Development: A Book of Readings. LC 97-43609. (Studies in Publishing). 1997. 20.00 (*0-09-640784-0*) Bellagio Pub.

— Publishing in African Languages: Challenges & Prospects. LC 99-10511. (Bellagio Studies in Publishing ; 10 Ser.). 1999. write for info. (*0-9646078-5-9*) Bellagio Pub.

Altbach, Philip G., et al. American Higher Education in the Twenty-First Century: Social, Political, & Economic Challenges. LC 98-3331. 440p. 1998. 52.00 (*0-8018-5888-7*) Johns Hopkins.

***Altbach, Philip G., et al.** American Higher Education in the Twenty-First Century: Social, Political, & Economic Challenges. LC 98-3331. 440p. 1998. pap. 24.95 (*0-8018-5889-5*) Johns Hopkins.

Altbach, Philip G., et al. Education in South Asia: A Bibliography. 372p. 1987. 49.95 (*81-7036-050-1*) Asia Bk Corp.

— Education in South Asia: A Select Annotated Bibliography. LC 86-29548. (Reference Books in International Education: Vol. 3). 376p. 1987. text 77.00 (*0-8240-8453-5*) Garland.

— Research on Foreign Students & International Study: An Overview & Bibliography. LC 85-3372. 416p. 1985. 65.00 (*0-275-90052-5*, C0052, Praeger Pubs) Greenwood.

— Scientific Development & Higher Education: The Case of Newly Industrializing Nations. LC 88-38101. 396p. 1989. 75.00 (*0-275-93264-8*, C3264, Praeger Pubs) Greenwood.

Altbach, Philip G., jt. auth. see Ben-David, Joseph.

Altbach, Philip G., ed. see Carnegie Foundation for the Advancement of Teachin.

Altbach, Philip G., jt. ed. see Chitnis, Suma.

Altbach, Philip G., jt. ed. see Cummings, William K.

Altbach, Philip G., ed. see Eisemon, Thomas O.

Altbach, Philip G., ed. see Johnstone, D. Bruce.

Altbach, Philip G., jt. ed. see Morsy, Zaghloul.

Altbach, Philip G., jt. ed. see Morsy, Zhagloul.

Altbauer, Moshe & Lunt, Horace G., eds. An Early Slavonic Psalter from Rus' Vol. 1: Phoreproduction. LC 78-59967. (Harvard Ukrainian Studies). 189p. 1979. 7.50 (*0-674-22310-1*) HUP.

***Altcappenberg, Hein-Thomas Schulze, et al.** Sandro Botticelli: The Picture Cycle for Dante's Divine Comedy. (Illus.). 360p. 2000. 75.00 (*0-8109-6633-6*, Pub. by Abrams) Time Warner.

Altcheck, A., et al, eds. The Uterus: Pathology, Diagnosis & Management. (Clinical Perspectives in Obstetrics & Gynecology Ser.). (Illus.). 504p. 1991. 140.00 (*0-387-97422-9*) Spr-Verlag.

Altcheck, A. & Deligdisch, L. Ovarian Disorders: Pathology, Diganosis & Management. (Illus.). 512p. 1996. 119.95 (*0-89640-263-0*) Igaku-Shoin.

Altchek, David W. Shoulder: A Method of Evaluation & Assessment. 160p. 1995. 55.00 (*0-07-001284-9*) McGraw.

Altea, Rosemary. The Eagle & the Rose: A Remarkable True Story. 1996. pap. write for info. (*0-446-67213-0*) Warner Bks.

— The Eagle & the Rose: A Remarkable True Story. LC 94-42252. 320p. 1996. reprint ed. mass mkt. 6.99 (*0-446-60364-3*, Pub. by Warner Bks) Little.

Altea, Rosemary. Give the Gift of Healing: A Concise Guide to Spiritual Healing. 112p. 1997. pap. 20.00 (*0-688-15511-1*, Wm Morrow) Morrow Avon.

Altea, Rosemary. Give the Gift of Healing: A Concise Guide to Spiritual Healing. LC 97-11531. (Illus.). 110p. 1997. pap. 20.00 (*0-614-30561-6*, Wm Morrow) Morrow Avon.

— Proud Spirit. limited ed. 288p. 1997. 75.00 (*0-688-15510-3*, Wm Morrow) Morrow Avon.

— Proud Spirit: Lessons, Insights & Healing from "The Voice of the Spirit World" LC 96-40333. 288p. 1997. 19.95 (*0-688-14998-7*, Wm Morrow) Morrow Avon.

— Proud Spirit: Lessons, Insights & Healing From 'the Voice Of The Spirit World' LC 96-40333. 288p. 1998. pap. 10.00 (*0-688-16067-0*, Wm Morrow) Morrow Avon.

***Altea, Rosemary.** You Own the Power: Stories & Exercises to Inspire & Unleash the Force Within. LC 99-16820. 336p. 2000. 25.00 (*0-688-15276-7*) Morrow Avon.

***Altea, Samantha Jane.** All Things Dead & Dying. 2001. write for info. (*0-688-17002-1*, Wm Morrow) Morrow Avon.

***Altegoer, Diana B.** Reckoning Words: Baconian Science & the Construction of Truth in English Renaissance Culture. LC 99-55050. (Illus.). 216p. 2000. 38.50 (*0-8386-3825-2*) Fairleigh Dickinson.

Altein, Leib, ed. see Schneerson, Menachem M.

Altekar, A. S. The Position of Women in Hindu Civilization. 384p. 1978. 17.95 (*0-318-37082-4*) Asia Bk Corp.

Altekar, A. S., jt. auth. see Majumdar, R. C.

Altemeyer, Bob. The Authoritarian Specter. LC 97-15548. (Illus.). 384p. 1996. 41.50 (*0-674-05305-2*) HUP.

Altemeyer, Bob & Hunsberger, Bruce. Amazing Conversions: Why Some Turn to Faith & Others Abandon Religion. LC 97-3301. 268p. 1997. 29.95 (*1-57392-147-5*) Prometheus Bks.

Altemoeller, E. M. Fragespiele. (GER.). 112p. (C). 1987. pap. text 31.75 (*3-12-550810-X*, Pub. by Klett Edition) Intl Bk Import.

Altemoller, Frank. Handel und Umwelt Im Recht der Welthandelsorganisation WTO: Umweltrelevante Streitfalle in der Spruchpraxis Zu Artikel III und XX GATT. (Europaische Hochschulschriften Ser.: Reihe 3, Vol. 2361). XXXV, 417p. 1998. pap. 73.95 (*3-631-33261-0*) P Lang Pubng.

Altemose, Charlene. Lo Que Usted Debe Saber Sobre el Catecismo de la Iglesia Catolica. LC 94-78007. (SPA.). 64p. (Orig.). 1994. pap. 1.95 (*0-89243-695-6*) Liguori Pubns.

— Lo Que Usted Debe Saber Sobre los Sacramentos. LC 95-80150. (SPA.). 64p. 1995. pap. 3.95 (*0-89243-857-6*) Liguori Pubns.

***Altemose, Charlene.** The RCIA & You: Welcoming New Catholics. (Illus.). 32p. 1999. pap. 4.95 (*0-7648-0402-2*) Liguori Pubns.

Altemose, Charlene. What You Should Know about Angels. LC 95-40228. 80p. (Orig.). 1996. pap. 4.95 (*0-89243-906-8*) Liguori Pubns.

— What You Should Know about Mary. LC 97-74320. (Illus.). 80p. 1998. pap. 4.95 (*0-7648-0162-7*) Liguori Pubns.

— What You Should Know about the Catechism of the Catholic Church. LC 93-79929. 64p. (Orig.). 1994. pap. 1.95 (*0-89243-647-6*) Liguori Pubns.

Altemose, Charlene. What You Should Know about the Mass. LC 92-72595. (Illus.). 64p. 1992. pap. text 3.95 (*0-89243-462-7*) Liguori Pubns.

— What You Should Know about the RCIA. 48p. 1999. pap. 4.95 (*0-7648-0401-4*) Liguori Pubns.

Altemose, Charlene. What You Should Know about the Sacraments. LC 94-75243. 64p. 1994. pap. 4.95 (*0-89243-629-8*) Liguori Pubns.

— What You Should Know about the Saints. LC 96-78938. 80p. 1997. pap. 4.95 (*0-7648-0047-7*) Liguori Pubns.

— Why Do Catholics...? A Guide to Catholic Belief & Practice. LC 89-7429. 1990. pap. 10.75 (*0-697-02690-6*, WCB McGr Hill) McGrw-H Hghr Educ.

Alten. Audio in Media. 3rd ed. (Radio/TV/Film Ser.). 1990. text. write for info. (*0-534-12135-7*) Wadsworth Pub.

Alten, M., et al. Mathias J. Alten: Journey of an American Painter. LC 98-71838. 175 p. 1998. write for info. (*0-942159-22-5*) Grnd Rpds Art Mus.

Alten, Bruce Von, see Von Alten, Bruce.

Alten, Florian Von, see Von Alten, Florian.

Alten, Stanley R. Audio & Media. 3rd ed. 1990. mass mkt. 45.95 (*0-534-12132-2*) Brooks-Cole.

— Audio in Media. 2nd ed. 612p. (C). 1986. pap. write for info. (*0-534-06156-7*) Wadsworth Pub.

— Audio in Media. 3rd ed. 644p. (C). 1990. pap. 38.50 (*0-534-12134-9*) Wadsworth Pub.

— Audio in Media. 5th ed. LC 98-2866. (Radio/TV/Film Ser.). 1998. pap. 82.95 (*0-534-54801-6*) Wadsworth Pub.

— Audio in Media: The Recording Studio. LC 95-34591. (C). 1995. pap. 65.95 (*0-534-26064-0*) Wadsworth Pub.

Alten, Steve. Meg: A Novel of Deep Terror. 352p. 1997. mass mkt. 6.99 (*0-553-84016-9*) Bantam.

— Meg: A Novel of Deep Terror. 352p. 1998. reprint ed. mass mkt. 6.50 (*0-553-57910-X*) Bantam.

— The Trench. 304p. 1999. text 23.95 (*1-57566-430-5*) Kensgtn Pub Corp.

***Alten, Steve.** Trench. 352p. 2000. mass mkt. 6.99 (*0-7860-1114-9*, Pinncle Kensgtn) Kensgtn Pub Corp.

Alten, T., et al, eds. Challenges of the 21st Century: Proceedings of the World Tunneling Congress '99, Olso, Norway, 31 May - 3 June 1999, 2 vols. (Illus.). 980p. 1999. 150.00 (*90-5809-063-9*, Pub. by A A Balkema) Ashgate Pub Co.

Altena, I. Van Regteren, see Van Regteren Altena, I.

***Altenbach, Hans-Josef, et al, eds.** Creep & Damage in Materials & Structures. (CISM International Centre for Mechanical Sciences Ser.: 399). ix, 348p. 2000. pap. (*3-211-83321-8*) Spr-Verlag.

Altenbach, J. Scott. Locomotor Morphology of the Vampire Bat, Desmodus Rotundus. (ASM Special Publications: No. 6). (Illus.). vi, 137p. 1979. 12.00 (*0-943612-05-5*) Am Soc Mammalogists.

Altenbaugh, Richard J. Education for Struggle: The American Labor Colleges of the 1920's & 1930's. 304p. 1990. 49.95 (*0-87722-680-6*) Temple U Pr.

***Altenbaugh, Richard J., ed.** Historical Dictionary of American Education. LC 98-51632. 520p. 1999. lib. bdg. 95.00 (*0-313-28590-X*) Greenwood.

Altenbaugh, Richard J., ed. The Teacher's Voice: A History of Teaching in Twentieth Century America. 227p. 1992. pap. 29.95 (*1-85000-961-9*, Falmer Pr) Taylor & Francis.

Altenbaugh, Richard J., et al. Caring for Kids: A Critical Study of Urban School Leavers. LC 95-7252. 1995. 85.00 (*0-7507-0192-7*, Falmer Pr) Taylor & Francis.

— Caring for Kids: A Critical Study of Urban School Leavers. LC 95-7252. 215p. 1995. pap. 27.95 (*0-7507-0193-5*, Falmer Pr) Taylor & Francis.

Altenberg, Bengt, jt. ed. see Aijmer, Karin.

Altenberg, G. A. & Ubaldi, V. Dizionario Italiano-Tedesco, Tedesco-Italian: Italian-German, German-Italian Dictionary. deluxe ed. (GER & ITA.). 395p. 1979. 9.95 (*0-8288-4733-9*, M9176) Fr & Eur.

Altenberg, Henry E. Holisitc Medicine: A Meeting of East & West. 192p. 1998. pap. 19.95 (*0-87040-902-6*) Japan Pubns USA.

— Holistic Medicine: A Meeting of Easy & West. (Illus.). 192p. (Orig.). 1992. pap. 22.00 (*0-87040-876-3*) Japan Pubns USA.

Altenbernd, Lynn & Lewis, Leslie L. A Handbook for the Study of Drama. LC 88-33321. 96p. (C). 1989. reprint ed. pap. text 20.00 (*0-8191-7264-2*) U Pr of Amer.

Altenburg, J. Ernst. Trumpeters' & Kettledrummers' Art (1795) Tarr, Edward H., tr. from GER. LC 74-4026. (Illus.). 168p. 1974. 15.00 (*0-914282-01-8*) Brass Pr.

Altenburg, Johann E. Versuch Einer Anleitung zur Heroisch-Musikalischen Trompeter und Pauker-Kunst. fac. ed. (Monuments of Music & Music Literature in Facsimile Ser., Series II: Vol. 36). 1966. lib. bdg. 45.00 (*0-8450-2236-9*) Broude.

Altenburg, Tom, jt. auth. see Miller, Steve.

Altenburger, Roland. Anredeverhalten in China Um 1750: Soziolinguistische Untersuchungen Am Roman "Rulin Waishi" (Schweizer Asiatische Studien Ser.: No. 27). 358p. 1997. 52.95 (*3-906757-14-5*, Pub. by P Lang) P Lang Pubng.

Altenburger, Rolf, ed. see Schwab, Arnold, et al.

ALTENER Programme Staff, jt. auth. see European Commission.

Altengarten, James S. & Molyneaux, Gary A. The History, Philosophy & Methodology of Geography: A Bibliography Selected for Education & Research, No. 957. 1976. 5.50 (*0-686-20385-2*, Sage Prdcls Pr) Sage.

Altenhofen. Excel. (C). 1990. text. write for info. (*0-201-52278-0*) Addison-Wesley.

— MS-DOS. (C). 1990. text. write for info. (*0-201-52277-2*) Addison-Wesley.

— Oracle. (C). 1990. text. write for info. (*0-201-52276-4*) Addison-Wesley.

— Word Perfect. (C). 1990. text. write for info. (*0-201-52274-8*) Addison-Wesley.

Altenhuber-Sallaberger. Le Francais Actif Cassette, No. 1B. 120p. student ed., wbk. ed. 11.95 incl. audio (*0-88729-801-X*) Langenscheidt.

Altenkamper, Henner & Eldenburg, Matthias. Color Atlas of Venous Disease. De Groot, Walter P., tr. LC 93-31254. 112p. 1994. text 79.95 (*0-397-51395-X*) Lppncott W & W.

***Altenkirch, T., et al, eds.** Types for Proofs & Programs: International Workshop, TYPES '98, Kloster Irsee, Germany, March 27-31, 1998, Selected Papers. LC 99-49081. (Lecture Notes in Computer Science Ser.: Vol. 1657). viii, 207p. 1999. pap. 45.00 (*3-540-66537-4*) Spr-Verlag.

Altenpohl, D. G., et al. Materials in World Perspective. (Materials Research & Engineering Ser.: Vol. 1). (Illus.). 208p. 1980. 51.95 (*0-387-10037-7*) Spr-Verlag.

Altenpohl, Dietrich G., ed. Aluminum: Technology, Applications, & Environment. LC 97-75874. (Illus.). 500p. 1998. 95.00 (*0-87339-406-2*, 4062) Minerals Metals.

Altensteig, Johann & Tytz, Johann. Lexicon Theologicum Quo Tanquam Clave Theologicae Fores Aperiuntur et Omnium Fere Terminorum et Obsciorum Vocum, Quae es Theologicae Studiosos Facile Remorantur, Etymologiae, Ambiguitates, Defitiones, Etc. (LAT.). xvi, 994p. 1974. reprint ed. lib. bdg. 320.00 (*3-487-04903-1*) G Olms Pubs.

Altenstetter, Christa & Bjorkman, James W., eds. Health Policy Reform, National Variations & Globalization. LC 96-10820. (Advances in Political Science Ser.). 405p. 1997. text 65.00 (*0-312-16101-8*) St Martin.

Altenstetter, Christa & Haywood, Stuart C., eds. From Rhetoric to Reality: Comparative Health Policy & the New Right. LC 90-44165. 366p. 1991. text 65.00 (*0-312-05343-6*) St Martin.

Altenstetter, Christa, jt. ed. see Bjorkman, James W.

Altepeter, Thomas S., jt. auth. see Breen, Michael J.

***Alter.** German Quest & Structure, 1800-1900. (Illus.). 192p. 2000. pap. text 24.95 (*0-340-54017-6*, Pub. by E A) OUP.

Alter. Out of Third Reich: Refugee Historians in Postwar Britian. 250p. 1998. text 59.50 (*1-86064-189-X*, Pub. by I B T) St Martin.

Alter, Anna. Don't Eat a Mouse with a Spoon. (J). Date not set. 15.95 (*0-688-17882-0*, Grenwillow Bks); lib. bdg. 15.89 (*0-688-17883-9*, Grenwillow Bks) HarpC Child Bks.

— The Three Little Kittens. 2001. text 15.95 (*0-8050-6471-0*) H Holt & Co.

Alter, Blanche P., jt. auth. see Young, Neal S.

Alter, Catherine & Evens, Wayne. Evaluating Your Practice: A Guide to Self-Assessment. LC 90-9467. (Social Work Ser.: Vol. 18). 208p. 1990. 33.95 (*0-8261-6960-0*) Springer Pub.

Alter, Catherine & Hage, Jerald. Organizations Working Together: Coordination in Interorganizational Networks. (Library of Social Research: Vol. 191). (Illus.). 240p. (C). 1992. 59.95 (*0-8039-4826-3*); pap. 26.00 (*0-8039-4827-1*) Sage.

Alter, G., et al. Catalogue of Star Clusters & Associations. 76p. (C). 1970. 171.00 (*963-05-5555-7*, Pub. by Akade Kiado) St Mut.

— Catalogue of Star Clusters & Associations. 76p. 1970. 45.00 (*0-569-08810-0*) St Mut.

Alter, Gary J., jt. auth. see Ehrlich, Richard M.

Alter, George. Family & the Female Life Course: The Women of Verviers, Belgium, 1849-1880. LC 87-40360. (Life Course Studies). (Illus.). 240p. (C). 1988. pap. text 24.95 (*0-299-11204-7*) U of Wis Pr.

Alter-Gilbert, Gilbert. Pipe Dreams: An Anthology of Drug Experiences in Literature. 1998. pap. text 16.00 (*1-57650-088-8*) Hi Jinx Pr.

Alter-Gilbert, Gilbert, ed. Life & Limb: Selected Tales of Peril, Predicament, & Dire Distress. LC 96-76623. 224p. 1997. pap. 16.00 (*1-57650-047-0*) Hi Jinx Pr.

Alter-Gilbert, Gilbert, tr. see Asturias, Miguel Angel.

Alter-Gilbert, Gilbert, tr. see Huidobro, Vicente.

Alter-Gilbert, Gilbert, tr. see Lugones, Leopoldo.

Alter, H. Materials Recovery from Municipal Waste: Unit Operations in Practice. (Illus.). 280p. 1983. text 155.00 (*0-8247-7134-6*) Dekker.

Alter, Harvey. The Greatly Growing Garbage Problem. (Illus.). 50p. 1988. pap. 33.00 (*0-89834-107-8*, 0113) US Chamber DC.

Alter, Harvey & Dunn, J. J. Solid Waste Conversion to Energy: Current European & U. S. Practice. LC 80-14138. (Pollution Engineering & Technology Ser.: Vol. 11). (Illus.). 180p. reprint ed. pap. 55.80 (*0-608-08908-7*, 206954300005) Bks Demand.

Alter, Henry C. Of Messages & Media: Teaching & Learning by Public Television. (Notes & Essays Ser.: No. 58). (C). 1968. pap. text 2.00 (*0-87060-022-2*, NES 58) Syracuse U Cont Ed.

Alter, Iska. The Good Man's Dilemma: Social Criticism in the Fiction of Bernard Malamud. LC 79-8836. (Studies in Modern Literature: No. 5). 1981. 29.50 (*0-404-18038-8*) AMS Pr.

Alter, J. Cecil. Jim Bridger. (Illus.). xii, 358p. 1979. reprint ed. pap. 15.95 (*0-8061-1509-2*) U of Okla Pr.

Alter, Jane, jt. auth. see Alter, Robert M.

Alter, Jean. A Sociosemiotic Theory of Theatre. LC 90-41885. 296p. (C). 1990. text 39.95 (*0-8122-3054-X*) U of Pa Pr.

Alter, Jonathan. Two Faces of Mr. Clinton. 224p. 1999. text 23.00 (*1-891620-26-6*) PublicAffairs NY.

Alter, Jonathan B., jt. auth. see Freedman, Warren.

Alter, Joseph D., jt. auth. see Dreher, Barbara B.

***Alter, Joseph S.** Gandhi's Body: Sex, Diet & the Politics of Nationalism. 2000. write for info. (*0-8122-3556-8*) U of Pa Pr.

— Knowing Dil Das: Stories of a Himalayan Hunter. LC 99-32283. (Contemporary Ethnography Ser.). 1999. 17.50 (*0-8122-1712-8*) U of Pa Pr.

Alter, Joseph S. The Wrestler's Body: Identity & Ideology in North India. (C). 1992. 55.00 (*0-520-07697-4*, Pub. by U CA Pr) Cal Prin Full Svc.

Alter, Judith. Rodeos: The Greatest Show on Dirt. LC 96-12143. (First Books-Performances & Entertainment Ser.). 64p. (J). 1996. lib. bdg. 22.00 (*0-531-20245-3*) Watts.

— Rodeos: The Greatest Show on Dirt. (First Bks.). 64p. (J). 1997. pap. 6.95 (*0-531-15816-0*) Watts.

— Women of the Old West. LC 88-34549. (First Bks.). (Illus.). 64p. (J). (gr. 3-5). 1989. lib. bdg. 22.00 (*0-531-10756-6*) Watts.

Alter, Judith B. Dance-Based Dance Theory: From Borrowed Models to Dance-Based Experience. 2nd ed. LC 96-47029. (New Studies in Aesthetics: Vol. 7). 196p. (C). 1996. pap. text 29.95 (*0-8204-3705-0*) P Lang Pubng.

— Dancing & Mixed Media: Early Twentieth Century Modern Dance Theory in Text & Photography. 2nd ed. (New Studies in Aesthetics: Vol. 17). XIV, 225p. (C). 1996. pap. text 32.95 (*0-8204-3459-0*) P Lang Pubng.

Alter, Judith M. Luke & the Van Zandt County War. LC 84-101. (Chaparral Bks.). (Illus.). 132p. (J). (gr. 4 up). 1984. 10.95 (*0-912646-88-8*) Tex Christian.

Alter, Judy. After Pa Was Shot. LC 89-12176. (Illus.). 192p. (Orig.). (J). (gr. 3-10). 1991. reprint ed. pap. 5.95 (*0-936650-12-5*, Pub. by E C Temple) Sunbelt Media.

— Amusement Parks: Roller Coasters, Ferris Wheels, & Cotton Candy. LC 97-3809. (First Book Ser.). (J). (gr. 4-6). 1997. 22.00 (*0-531-20304-2*) Watts.

— A Ballad for Sallie. 288p. 1998. reprint ed. mass mkt. 4.50 (*0-8439-4365-3*, Leisure Bks) Dorchester Pub Co.

— Beauty Pageants: Tiaras, Roses, & Runways. LC 96-41100. (First Bk.). (J). (gr. 4-6). 1997. lib. bdg. 22.00 (*0-531-20253-4*) Watts.

— Beauty Pageants: Tiaras, Roses & Runways. (J). (gr. 4-6). 1997. pap. text 6.95 (*0-531-15874-8*) Watts.

— Callie Shaw, Stable Boy: A Novel. LC 96-8490. 192p. (YA). (gr. 5-9). 1996. 15.95 (*1-57168-092-6*, Eakin Pr) Sunbelt Media.

***Alter, Judy.** Christopher Reeve: Triumph over Tragedy. (Book Report Biographies Ser.). (Illus.). (YA). 2000. pap. 6.95 (*0-531-16455-1*) Watts.

— Christopher Reeve: Triumph over Tragedy. LC 99-87463. (Book Report Biography Ser.). (Illus.). 2000. 22.00 (*0-531-11674-3*) Watts.

Alter, Judy. Cissie Palmer: Putting Wealth to Work. LC 97-43216. (Community Builders Ser.). (Illus.). 43p. (J). (gr. 3-5). 1998. 23.00 (*0-516-20972-8*) Childrens.

— Cissie Palmer: Putting Wealth to Work. LC 97-43216. (Community Builders Ser.). (Illus.). 48p. (J). (gr. 3-5). 1999. pap. text 6.95 (*0-516-26345-5*) Childrens.

— Dorothy Johnson. LC 80-70458. (Western Writers Ser.: No. 44). (Illus.). 47p. (Orig.). 1980. pap. 4.95 (*0-88430-068-4*) Boise St U W Writ Ser.

— Extraordinary Women of the American West. 1999. lib. bdg. 16.95 (*0-516-26465-6*) Childrens.

— Extraordinary Women of the American West. LC 98-5812. (Extraordinary People Ser.). (J). (gr. 6). 1999. 37.00 (*0-516-20974-4*) Childrens.

An Asterisk (*) at the beginning of an entry indicates that the title is appearing for the first time.

— Jeanne Williams. LC 91-55032. (Western Writers Ser.: No. 98). (Illus.). 54p. 1991. 4.95 (*0-88430-097-8*) Boise St U W Writ Ser.

— Katie & the Recluse. LC 90-23695. 176p. (J). (gr. 3-10). 1991. reprint ed. pap. 5.95 (*0-936650-13-3*, Pub. by E C Temple) Sunbelt Media.

— Maggie & a Horse Named Devildust. LC 88-22815. (Illus.). 160p. (J). (gr. 3-10). 1989. pap. 5.95 (*0-936650-08-7*, Pub. by E C Temple) Sunbelt Media.

— Maggie & Devildust Ridin' High. LC 89-2683. (Illus.). 160p. (Orig.). (J). (gr. 3-10). 1990. pap. 5.95 (*0-936650-10-9*, Pub. by E C Temple) Sunbelt Media.

— Maggie & the Search for Devildust. LC 88-8019. (Illus.). 160p. (J). (gr. 3-10). 1989. pap. 5.95 (*0-936650-09-5*, Pub. by E C Temple) Sunbelt Media.

***Alter, Judy.** Mapping the American West. LC 00-23533. (Illus.). (J). 2001. write for info. (*0-516-21599-X*) Childrens.

Alter, Judy. Mattie. 192p. 1997. reprint ed. mass mkt. 3.99 (*0-8439-4156-1*) Dorchester Pub Co.

— Meet Me at the Fair! Country, State, & World's Fairs & Expositions. LC 97-5700. (First Book Ser.). 64p. (J). 1997. lib. bdg. 22.00 (*0-531-20307-7*) Watts.

— Sam Houston: A Leader for Texas. LC 97-25199. (Community Builders Ser.). 48p. (J). 1998. 23.00 (*0-516-20834-9*) Childrens.

— Sam Houston: A Leader for Texas. DeCapua, Sarah, ed. (Community Builders Ser.). (Illus.). 48p. (J). 1998. pap. 6.95 (*0-516-26331-5*) Childrens.

— The Santa Fe Trail. LC 97-32710. (Community of Freedom Ser.). (J). 1998. 19.50 (*0-516-21145-5*) Childrens.

— The Santa Fe Trail. LC 97-32710. (Cornerstones to Freedom Ser.). (Illus.). 32p. (J). (gr. 4-6). 1999. pap. text 5.95 (*0-516-26396-X*) Childrens.

— Stewart Edward White. LC 75-7011. (Western Writers Ser.: No. 18). (Illus.). 48p. (Orig.). 1975. pap. 4.95 (*0-88430-017-X*) Boise St U W Writ Ser.

— Stretch & Strengthen. 1986. pap. 9.95 (*0-685-11807-X*) HM.

— Stretch & Strengthen: A Safe, Comprehensive Exercise Program to Balance Your Muscle Strength. 240p. 1992. pap. 16.00 (*0-395-52808-9*) HM.

— Thistle Hill: The History & the House. LC 87-10251. (Illus.). 88p. (Orig.). 1988. pap. 5.95 (*0-87565-074-0*) Tex Christian.

— Vaudeville: The Birth of Show Business. (First Bks.). 64p. (J). 1998. lib. bdg. 22.00 (*0-531-20358-1*) Watts.

— Wild West Shows: Rough Riders & Sure Shots. LC 96-41099. (First Bks.). (J). 1997. lib. bdg. 22.00 (*0-531-20274-7*) Watts.

— Wild West Shows: Rough Riders & Sure Shots. LC 96-41099. (J). 1997. pap. text 6.95 (*0-531-15875-6*) Watts.

Alter, Judy & Row, A. T., eds. Unbridled Spirits: Short Fiction about Women in the Old West. LC 93-14335. 392p. (C). 1994. pap. 17.95 (*0-87565-124-0*) Tex Christian.

Alter, Michael J. Science of Flexibility. 2nd ed. LC 95-50410. (Illus.). 392p. 1996. text 42.00 (*0-87322-977-0*, BALT0977) Human Kinetics.

— Sport Stretch. 2nd ed. LC 97-14591. (Illus.). 232p. 1997. pap. 15.95 (*0-88011-823-7*, PALT0823) Human Kinetics.

— Why the Torah Begins with the Letter Beit. LC 97-35823. 1998. 40.00 (*0-7657-9992-8*) Aronson.

Alter, Michael J., ed. What Is the Purpose of Creation? A Jewish Anthology. LC 90-48734. 346p. 1996. pap. 30.00 (*1-56821-515-0*) Aronson.

Alter, Michel. The French Law of Business Contracts: General Principles. Levasseur, Alain A., tr. from FRE. 131p. (Orig.). 1986. pap. text 11.00 (*0-940448-12-2*) LSU Law Pubns.

Alter, Milton, jt. ed. see Gorelick, Philip B.

Alter, Nora M. Vietnam Protest Theatre: The Television War on Stage. LC 95-32287. (Drama & Performance Studies). 256p. (Orig.). 1996. 29.95 (*0-253-33032-7*) Ind U Pr.

***Alter, Orly & Yamamoto, Yoshihisa.** Quantum Theory of Measurement of a Single System. LC 99-59408. 160p. 2000. text 74.95 (*0-471-28308-8*) Wiley.

Alter, Peggy & Solomon, Sharon. Modeling Chocolate Made Easy: A Decorating Guide. 44p. 1995. pap. text 4.95 (*0-9648004-0-3*) Confection Art.

***Alter, Peter.** The German Question & Europe: A History. (An Arnold Publication). 192p. 2000. text 72.00 (*0-340-74153-8*, Pub. by E A) OUP.

Alter, Peter. Nationalism. 176p. 1989. pap. 12.95 (*0-7131-6519-7*, Pub. by E A) Routldge.

— Nationalism. 2nd ed. LC 94-223681. 160p. 1995. pap. text 18.95 (*0-340-60061-6*, B3542, Pub. by E A) OUP.

Alter, Reinhard & Monteath, Peter, eds. Rewriting the German Past: History & Identity in the New Germany. LC 96-49082. 304p. (C). 1997. pap. 18.50 (*0-391-04026-X*); text 60.00 (*0-391-04025-1*) Humanities.

Alter, Richard C. The Tired Tourist's Concise Guide to Florence. rev. ed. (Illus.). 1978. pap. 3.00 (*0-89726-000-7*) Foldabook Pub.

— The Tired Tourist's Concise Guide to London. LC 78-55944. (Illus.). 1978. pap. 3.00 (*0-89726-002-3*) Foldabook Pub.

— The Tired Tourist's Concise Guide to Paris. LC 78-75278. (Illus.). 1979. pap. 3.00 (*0-89726-005-8*) Foldabook Pub.

— The Tired Tourist's Concise Guide to Rome. LC 79-57049. (Illus.). 1980. pap. 3.00 (*0-89726-031-7*) Foldabook Pub.

***Alter, Robert.** Canon & Creativity: Modern Writing & the Authority of Scripture. LC 00-35168. 192p. 2000. 18.50 (*0-300-08424-2*) Yale U Pr.

Alter, Robert. The David Story: A Translation with Commentary of 1 & 2 Samuel. LC 99-21116. 448p. 1999. 30.00 (*0-393-04803-9*) Norton.

***Alter, Robert.** The David Story: A Translation with Commentary of 1 & 2 Samuel. 448p. 2000. reprint ed. pap. 15.95 (*0-393-32077-4*) Norton.

Alter, Robert. Genesis: Translation & Commentary. 384p. 1997. pap. 14.95 (*0-393-31670-X*) Norton.

— King Solomon's Cat. Date not set. 13.00 (*0-06-098749-9*) HarpC.

— Motives for Fiction. LC 83-10829. 248p. 1984. 35.95 (*0-674-58762-6*) HUP.

— Necessary Angels: Tradition & Modernity in Kafka, Benjamin, & Scholem. LC 90-46478. 160p. 1991. text 22.00 (*0-674-60663-9*, ALTNEC) HUP.

— The Pleasure of Reading in an Ideological Age. 256p. 1996. pap. 13.00 (*0-393-31499-5*) Norton.

— The World of Biblical Literature. LC 91-55462. 240p. 1993. reprint ed. pap. 16.00 (*0-465-09256-X*, Pub. by Basic) HarpC.

Alter, Robert, ed. Modern Hebrew Literature. LC 75-9928. (Library of Jewish Studies). 384p. 1975. pap. text 19.95 (*0-87441-235-8*) Behrman.

Alter, Robert, tr. Genesis: Translation & Commentary. 324p. 1996. 25.00 (*0-393-03981-1*) Norton.

Alter, Robert & Cosman, Carol. A Lion for Love: A Critical Biography of Stendhal. 304p. 1986. pap. 17.00 (*0-674-53575-8*) HUP.

Alter, Robert & Kermode, Frank, eds. The Literary Guide to the Bible. 704p. 1990. pap. text 17.95 (*0-674-87531-1*) Belknap Pr.

— The Literary Guide to the Bible. LC 86-32172. (Illus.). 688p. 1987. text 52.95 (*0-674-87530-3*) HUP.

Alter, Robert M. & Alter, Jane. The Transformative Power of Crisis: Our Journey to Psychological Healing & Spiritual Awakening. LC 99-45054. 304p. 2000. 25.00 (*0-06-039276-2*, ReganBks) HarperTrade.

Alter, Ruth. The Painted Rocks. (Illus.). 35p. (Orig.). (J). (gr. 3-8). 1996. pap. 8.95 (*0-9653725-0-2*) San Dieguito Riv.

Alter, Stephen. All the Way to Heaven: An American Boyhood in the Himalayas. LC 97-40677. 288p. 1998. 25.00 (*0-8050-5158-9*) H Holt & Co.

***Alter, Stephen.** From Amritsar to Lahore: A Journey Across the India-Pakistan Border. 2000. 24.95 (*0-8122-3565-7*) U of Pa Pr.

— From Amritsar to Lahore: A Journey Across the India-Pakistan Border. LC 00-33800. (Illus.). 2000. 24.95 (*0-8122-1743-8*) U of Pa Pr.

Alter, Stephen. Inside India. (Illus.). 126p. (C). 1988. 495.00 (*81-7002-001-8*, Pub. by Himalayan Bks) St Mut.

Alter, Stephen, ed. Post-Colonial Discourse in South Asia. (Asian Studies: Vol. 18). (Illus.). 643p. 1999. pap. 20.00 (*977-424-486-9*, Pub. by Am Univ Cairo Pr) Col U Pr.

Alter, Stephen G. Darwinism & the Linguistic Image: Language, Race, & Natural Theology in the Nineteenth Century. LC 98-14270. (New Studies in American Intellectual & Cultural History). 227p. 1998. 39.00 (*0-8018-5882-8*) Johns Hopkins.

Alter, Steven. Information Systems: A Management Perspective. 2nd rev. ed. 1996. 14.06 (*0-8053-2330-9*) Benjamin-Cummings.

— Information Systems: A Management Perspective. 3rd ed. LC 98-36555. 541p. (C). 1998. 87.00 (*0-201-35109-9*, Prentice Hall) P-H.

Alter, Steven L. Decision Support Systems: Current Practice & Continuing Challenges. LC 78-67960. 1979. text 47.50 (*0-201-00193-4*) Addison-Wesley.

— Information Systems. (Illus.). 752p. (C). 1991. text 67.00 (*0-201-51030-8*) Addison-Wesley.

— Information Systems & Spreadsheet & Database Cases for Information Systems Bundle. (C). 1992. 66.00 (*0-201-51503-2*) Addison-Wesley.

Alter, Stewart. Truth Well Told: McCann-Erickson & the Pioneering of Global Advertising. 320p. 1994. write for info. (*0-9642622-0-7*) McCann Erickson.

Alteras, Isaac. Eisenhower & Israel: United States-Israeli Relations, 1953-1960. LC 92-44703. (Illus.). 408p. 1993. 49.95 (*0-8130-1205-8*); pap. 19.95 (*0-8130-1206-6*) U Press Fla.

Alterbaum, Irene, jt. auth. see Buck, Joyce.

Altergott, Karen, ed. Daily Life in Later Life: Comparative Perspectives. LC 88-3245. (Sage Focus Editions Ser.: No. 99). 252p. reprint ed. pap. 78.20 (*0-7837-6593-2*, 204615700011) Bks Demand.

— One World, Many Families. 81p. (Orig.). (C). 1993. pap. 21.95 (*0-916174-38-7*) Natl Coun Family.

Altergott, W. & Henneke, E., eds. Characterization of Advanced Materials. (Illus.). 200p. (C). 1991. 95.00 (*0-306-43837-2*, Plenum Trade) Perseus Pubng.

Alteri, Nicholas D., Jr., et al. Basic Skills for Chemistry. 8th rev. ed. 224p. (C). (gr. 11 up). 1987. reprint ed. pap. text 17.95 (*0-940139-02-2*) Consortium RI.

Alteriis, Martin de, see De Alteriis, Martin.

Alterman, Arthur I., ed. Substance Abuse & Psychopathology. (Applied Clinical Psychology Ser.). 412p. 1985. 80.00 (*0-306-41849-5*, Plenum Trade) Perseus Pubng.

Alterman, Eric. As We Remember Zion: Israel & the Liberal Imagination. 1999. write for info. (*0-7868-6170-3*) Hyperion.

— It Ain't No Sin to Be Glad Your're Alive: The Promise of Bruce Springsteen. LC 99-38539. (Illus.). 224p. (gr. 8). 1999. 20.00 (*0-316-03885-7*) Little.

— Lying in State. 2000. write for info. (*0-316-03888-1*) Little.

***Alterman, Eric.** Sound & Fury: The Making of the Washington Punditocracy. LC 99-42030. 336p. 2000. pap. text 17.95 (*0-8014-8639-4*) Cornell Pr.

Alterman, Eric. Who Speaks for America? Why Democracy Matters in Foreign Policy. LC 98-30148. 224p. 1998. text 25.00 (*0-8014-3574-9*) Cornell U Pr.

Alterman, Glenn. Creating Your Own Monologue. LC 99-89558. 208p. 1999. pap. 14.95 (*1-58115-038-5*) Allworth Pr.

— Promoting Your Acting Career. LC 98-70412. 224p. 1998. pap. 18.95 (*1-880559-97-8*) Allworth Pr.

— Street Talk: Character Monologues for Actors. (Monologue Audition Ser.). 112p. 1991. pap. 8.95 (*0-9622722-5-6*) Smith & Kraus.

— Two-Minute Monologs: Original Audition Scenes for Professional Actors. Zapel, Theodore O., ed. LC 98-3956. 144p. 1998. pap. 14.95 (*1-56608-038-X*, 3219) Meriwether Pub.

— 2 Minutes & Under: Character Monologues for Actors. (Monologue Audition Ser.). 100p. 1993. pap. 9.95 (*1-880399-49-0*) Smith & Kraus.

— Uptown: Character Monologues for Actors. LC 92-37750. (Monologue Audition Ser.). 86p. 1992. pap. 8.95 (*1-880399-08-3*) Smith & Kraus.

Alterman, Glenn, ed. The Job Book I: 100 Acting Jobs for Actors. LC 94-46978. 224p. 1995. pap. 11.95 (*1-880399-81-4*) Smith & Kraus.

— The Job Book II: 100 Day Jobs for Actors. (Career Development Ser.). 128p. 1995. pap. 11.95 (*1-880399-99-7*) Smith & Kraus.

— What to Give Your Agent for Christmas & 100 Other Tips for the Working Actor. 128p. 1995. pap. 8.95 (*1-880399-57-1*) Smith & Kraus.

Alterman, Ina B., et al, eds. Seismotectonics of the Central California Coast Ranges. LC 94-28189. (Special Papers: Vol. 292). 1994. pap. 50.25 (*0-8137-2292-6*) Geol Soc.

Alterman, Irwin M. Michigan Antitrust Digest. 190p. 1975. ring bd., suppl. ed. 55.00 (*0-685-38200-1*, 75-005) U MI Law CLE.

— Michigan Antitrust Digest: 1989 Supplement. 190p. 1989. suppl. ed. 12.00 (*0-685-47523-9*) U MI Law CLE.

— Michigan Antitrust Digest: 1990 Supplement. 190p. 1990. suppl. ed. 15.00 (*0-685-58875-0*) U MI Law CLE.

— Michigan Antitrust Digest: 1992 Supplement. 190p. 1992. suppl. ed. 18.00 (*0-685-58876-9*) U MI Law CLE.

— Plain & Accurate Style in Court Papers. 179p. 1987. text 37.00 (*0-8318-0563-3*, B563) Am Law Inst.

Alterman, Jon B. New Media, New Politics? Fun Satellite Television to the Internet Arab World. LC 98-44198. (Policy Paper Ser.: No. 48). 1998. pap. 19.95 (*0-944029-28-0*) Wash Inst NEP.

Alterman, Jon B., ed. Sadat & His Legacy: Egypt & the World, 1977-1997. LC 98-14803. 218p. 1998. pap. 19.95 (*0-944029-74-4*) Wash Inst NEP.

Alterman, L., et al. Creatures of the Dark: The Nocturna Prosimians. (Illus.). 586p. 1996. 135.00 (*0-306-45183-2*, Kluwer Plenum) Kluwer Academic.

Alterman, Rachelle. Evaluating Linkage & Beyond: The New Method for Supply of Affordable Housing & Its Impact. LC HT0167.. 76p. reprint ed. pap. 30.00 (*0-7837-3869-2*, 204370000010) Bks Demand.

Alterman, Rachelle & Cars, Goran, eds. Neighbourhood Regeneration: An International Evaluation. 240p. 1991. text 110.00 (*0-7201-2073-X*) Continuum.

Alterman, Seymour. How to Control Diabetes. 1997. mass mkt. 6.99 (*0-345-42158-2*) Ballantine Pub Grp.

***Alterman, Seymour.** How to Prevent, Control & Cure Diabetes. Kullman, Donald, ed. 224p. 2000. 24.95 (*0-88391-019-5*) F Fell Pubs Inc.

***Alterman, Seymour L.** How to Control Diabetes: A Complete Guide & Meal Planner to Live a Longer, Healthier & Happier Life. Kullman, Donald A., ed. (Illus.). 266p. 2000. reprint ed. pap. text 15.00 (*0-7881-6897-5*) DIANE Pub.

Alternative Defense Commission. Defense Without the Bomb. 320p. 1983. pap. 29.95 (*0-8002-3080-9*) Taylor & Francis.

Alternative Medicine Digest Editors, jt. auth. see Goldberg, Burton.

Alternative Medicine Editors, jt. auth. see Goldberg, Burton.

Alternative Medicine Research Staff. Vermont Holistic Health Directory. 35p. (C). 1996. pap. 20.00 (*1-893553-00-0*) AMRITA Pr.

Alternative Museum Staff. Artists of Conscience I: Sixteen Years of Social & Political Commentary. LC 91-76403. 72p. 1992. pap. text 15.00 (*0-932075-36-3*) Alternative Mus.

— Artists of Conscience II. LC 92-71124. 64p. 1992. pap. text 15.00 (*0-932075-37-1*) Alternative Mus.

— Belfast-Beirut: A Tale of Two Cities. LC 89-82083. (Illus.). (Orig.). (C). 1990. pap. 8.00 (*0-932075-28-2*) Alternative Mus.

— Beyond Aesthetics: Artists of Conscience. LC 90-55615. (Illus.). (Orig.). 1991. pap. 10.00 (*0-932075-33-9*) Alternative Mus.

— Despo Magoni: Recent Paintings. LC 86-70055. (Illus.). 1986. pap. 3.00 (*0-932075-08-8*) Alternative Mus.

— Dia de los Muertos, No. 3: Homelessness. LC 90-55614. (Orig.). 1990. pap. 10.00 (*0-932075-32-0*) Alternative Mus.

— Emilio Cruz: Recent Paintings & Drawings. LC 84-73546. (Illus.). (Orig.). 1985. pap. text 4.00 (*0-932075-00-2*) Alternative Mus.

— Endangered Species: Ecological Commentaries. LC 87-70146. (Illus.). (Orig.). 1987. pap. 6.00 (*0-932075-14-2*) Alternative Mus.

— Foreign Affairs: Conflicts in the Global Village. LC 88-70646. 1988. pap. 15.00 (*0-932075-21-5*) Alternative Mus.

— George Dyens: Big Bang II. LC 88-71673. (Illus.). 1988. pap. 4.00 (*0-932075-22-3*) Alternative Mus.

— Gerda Myer Bernstein. 1995. pap. text 7.00 (*0-932075-42-8*) Alternative Mus.

— Gustavo Ramos Rivera: Recent Abstract Painting. LC 88-70179. 1988. 4.00 (*0-932075-20-7*) Alternative Mus.

— Keith Morrison: Recent Painting. LC 90-80546. (Illus.). (Orig.). 1990. pap. 4.00 (*0-932075-29-0*) Alternative Mus.

— Luminosity. LC 86-71975. (Illus.). (Orig.). 1986. pap. 5.00 (*0-932075-11-8*) Alternative Mus.

— Michiko Itatani. LC 85-73084. (Illus.). 1985. pap. 5.00 (*0-932075-04-5*) Alternative Mus.

— Mon Reve: A Visual Record of Haiti since the Departure of the Duvaliers. LC 89-81813. (Illus.). (C). 1989. pap. 12.00 (*0-932075-27-4*) Alternative Mus.

— Occupation & Resistance: American Impressions of the Intifada. LC 90-80547. (Illus.). 80p. (Orig.). 1990. pap. 15.00 (*0-932075-30-4*) Alternative Mus.

— Peter Dean: A Retrospective. LC 90-55616. (Orig.). 1990. pap. 6.00 (*0-932075-31-2*) Alternative Mus.

— The Robert Blackburn Workshop. LC 88-71297. (Orig.). 1988. pap. 6.00 (*0-932075-18-5*) Alternative Mus.

— Southern Exposure: Not a Regional Exhibition. LC 85-71155. (Illus.). 56p. (Orig.). (C). 1985. pap. text 8.00 (*0-932075-02-9*) Alternative Mus.

— Syncretism: The Art of the 21st Century. LC 90-86368. (Orig.). 1991. pap. text 8.00 (*0-932075-35-5*) Alternative Mus.

— Theater of the Object, 1958-1972: Reconstruction, Re-Creation, Reconsideration. LC 89-84275. (Illus.). 1989. pap. 7.00 (*0-932075-26-6*) Alternative Mus.

Alternatives for Simple Living Staff. The Alternative Wedding Book: Create a Beautiful Wedding That Reflects Your Values & Doesn't Cost the Earth. 128p. 1997. pap. 11.95 (*1-55145-081-X*) NStone Publ.

— Simplify & Celebrate: Embracing the Soul of Christmas. (Illus.). 208p. 1997. pap. 15.95 (*1-896836-14-3*) NStone Publ.

— Treasury of Celebrations: Create Celebrations That Reflect Your Values & Don't Cost the Earth. LC 96-910435. 288p. 1996. pap. 19.95 (*1-55145-088-7*) NStone Publ.

Alterovitz, S. A., jt. auth. see Pouch, J. J.

Alterovitz, S. A., jt. ed. see Pouch, J. J.

***Alterowitz, Ralph J.** Lovin' Ain't Over: The Couple's Guide to Better Sex after Prostate Disease. 2000. pap. write for info. (*1-883257-03-4*) Hlth Edu Lit.

***Alterra, Aaron.** The Caregiver: A Life with Alzheimer's. 224p. 2000. pap. 14.00 (*1-58642-007-0*, Pub. by Steerforth Pr) Publishers Group.

Alterra, Aarron. The Caregiver: A Life with Alzheimer's. LC 99-16480. 200p. 1999. 21.00 (*1-883642-62-0*) Steerforth Pr.

Alters. Biology: Understanding Life. 2nd ed. 1996. text (*0-8151-0858-3*) Mosby Inc.

— Biology Today. 1993. 29.37 (*0-697-40326-2*, WCB McGr Hill) McGrw-H Hghr Educ.

— Biology Today. 1993. lab manual ed. 29.37 (*0-697-40356-4*, WCB McGr Hill) McGrw-H Hghr Educ.

— Biology Understanding Life. 2nd ed. 1996. (*0-8151-0829-X*) Mosby Inc.

— Concepts for Healthy Living. LC 97-44581. 1997. pap. 43.25 (*0-534-35405-X*) Brooks-Cole.

— Concepts for Healthy Living. 1998. mass mkt., student ed. 16.00 (*0-534-35407-6*) Brooks-Cole.

— Concepts for Healthy Living with InfoTrac. (Health Sciences Ser.). 1998. 39.50 incl. cd-rom (*0-534-36329-6*) Brooks-Cole.

— Contemporary Health. (Health Sciences Ser.). Date not set. 39.50 (*0-314-12517-5*) Brooks-Cole.

— Essential Concepts for Healthy Living. (Health Sciences Ser.). 1998. 8.00 (*0-534-35783-0*) Brooks-Cole.

— Essential Concepts for Healthy Living with InfoTrac. (Health Sciences Ser.). 1998. 30.00 incl. cd-rom (*0-534-36376-8*) Brooks-Cole.

***Alters, Brian & Alters, Sandra.** Handbook on Teaching Evolution: A Practitioner's Guide. (Illus.). 192p. (C). 2000. pap. text 18.75 (*0-7637-1118-7*) JB Pubns.

Alters Jamison, Cheryl & Jamison, Bill. Born to Grill: An American Celebration. LC 98-11608. (Illus.). 512p. 1998. 27.95 (*1-55832-111-X*) Harvard Common Pr.

***Alters, Sandra.** Biology: Understanding Life 3rd ed. LC 99-29957. 1999. write for info. (*0-7637-0837-2*) Jones & Bartlett.

Alters, Sandra & Schiff, Wendy. Essential Concepts for Healthy Living. LC 97-52730. 1998. pap. 32.75 (*0-534-35732-6*) Brooks-Cole.

Alters, Sandra, jt. auth. see Alters, Brian.

Alters, Sandra M. & Dennehy, Cad. Biology - Understanding Life. 2nd ed. 672p. (C). 1996. text, student ed. 23.12 (*0-8151-0837-0*, WCB McGr Hill) McGrw-H Hghr Educ.

Alters, Sandra M., et al. Biology Today, 1. 514p. (C). 1993. text. write for info. (*0-8151-3845-8*, WCB McGr Hill) McGrw-H Hghr Educ.

***Alters, Sandy.** Biology: Understanding Life. 3rd ed. (Illus.). (C). 1999. pap. text, teacher ed. write for info. (*0-7637-1215-9*); pap. text, student ed. 24.00 (*0-7637-1216-7*) JB Pubns.

— Human Biology. 2nd ed. (Illus.). 608p. (C). 2000. text 55.00 (*0-7637-0836-4*) JB Pubns.

Alterton, Margaret. Origins of Poe's Critical Theory. (BCL1-PS American Literature Ser.). 191p. 1992. reprint ed. lib. bdg. 69.00 (*0-7812-6833-8*) Rprt Serv.

Alterwein, Roy A. Young Again! (Illus.). 308p. (Orig.). 1994. pap. 11.95 (*0-9640992-0-9*) Med Hlth Pub.

Altes, A. Korthals & N. K. C. A. In't Veld Staff. The Forgotten Battle: Overloon & the Maas Salient 1944-45. 272p. 1997. 80.00 (*1-873376-43-X*, Pub. by Spellmnt Pubs) St Mut.

Altes, H. Twenty-Six Selected Studies for Flute. 100p. 1986. per. 11.95 (*0-7935-5422-5*) H Leonard.

Altes, Harvey C., et al. Manhunt: The Book. LC 98-66795. (Illus.). 452p. 1998. pap. write for info. (*0-9664959-1-8*) TFA Publishing.

Altes, Steve. Little Book of Bad Business Advice. LC 97-170092. 1997. mass mkt. 6.99 (*0-312-96223-1*) St Martin.

Altet, Xavier B., ed. Art & Architecture of Spain. LC 98-70883. (Illus.). 576p. (gr. 8). 1998. 125.00 (*0-8212-2456-5*) Little.

Altfeld, E. Milton. The Jews' Struggle for Religious & Civil Liberty in Maryland. LC 78-99859. (Civil Liberties in American History Ser.). 1970. reprint ed. lib. bdg. 29.50 (*0-306-71859-6*) Da Capo.

— The Jews' Struggle for Religious & Civil Liberty in Maryland. (Illus.). 211p. 1997. reprint ed. pap. 22.50 (*0-8328-7109-5*) Higginson Bk Co.

Altfelder, Klaus. Lexikon der Unternehmensfuehrung. (GER.). 1973. 85.00 (*0-8288-6307-5*, M7219) Fr & Eur.

Altgeld, John P. Live Questions: Including Our Penal Machinery & Its Victims. LC 79-156003. (Foundations of Criminal Justice Ser.). reprint ed. 31.50 (*0-404-09103-2*) AMS Pr.

— The Mind & Spirit of John Peter Altgeld. Christman, Henry M., ed. LC 70-128200. (Essay Index Reprint Ser.). 1977. 18.95 (*0-8369-1860-6*) Ayer.

— The Mind & Spirit of John Peter Altgeld: Selected Writings & Addresses. Christman, Henry M., ed. LC 70-128200. (Essay Index Reprint Ser.). 185p. reprint ed. lib. bdg. 17.00 (*0-8290-0801-2*) Irvington.

— Reasons for Pardoning the Haymarket Anarchists. LC 86-80035. 80p. 1986. reprint ed. pap. 7.00 (*0-88286-124-7*) C H Kerr.

Altgelt & Gouw. Chromatography in Petroleum Analysis. (Chromatographic Science Ser.: Vol. 11). (Illus.). 512p. 1979. text 225.00 (*0-8247-6790-X*) Dekker.

Altgelt, Klaus H. & Boduszynski, Micczyslaw H., eds. Composition & Analysis of Heavy Petroleum Fractions. (Chemical Industries Ser.: Vol. 54). (Illus.). 512p. 1993. text 215.00 (*0-8247-8946-6*) Dekker.

Altgelt, Klaus H., ed. see American Chemical Society Symposium on Gel Permeat.

Altgilbers, Larry L., et al. Magnetocumulative Generators. LC 99-13257. (High Pressure Shock Compression of Condensed Matter Ser.). 500p. 1999. 99.00 (*0-387-98786-X*) Spr-Verlag.

Alth, Charlotte & Alth, Max. Constructing & Maintaining Your Well & Septic System. (Illus.). 240p. 1984. 19.95 (*0-8306-0654-8*, 1654); pap. 13.95 (*0-8306-1654-3*) McGraw-Hill Prof.

Alth, M. Sharpening Hand Tools. 1983. pap. 2.95 (*0-88266-280-5*, Storey Pub) Storey Bks.

Alth, Mac, et al. Wells & Septic Systems. 2nd ed. 272p. 1991. pap. 18.95 (*0-07-157779-3*) McGraw.

Alth, Max. Do-It-Yourself Plumbing. LC 87-42815. (Illus.). 316p. (Orig.). 1987. pap. 12.95 (*0-8069-6514-2*) Sterling.

— Wells & Septic Systems. 2nd ed. 272p. 1991. 25.95 (*0-8306-2137-7*) McGraw-Hill Prof.

— Wells & Septic Systems. 2nd ed. (Illus.). 272p. 1991. pap. 18.95 (*0-8306-2136-9*) McGraw-Hill Prof.

Alth, Max, jt. auth. see Alth, Charlotte.

Altham, J. E. & Harrison, Ross, eds. World, Mind & Ethics: Essays on the Ethical Philosophy of Bernard Williams. 237p. (C). 1995. text 59.95 (*0-521-36024-2*) Cambridge U Pr.

***Altham, Keith.** No More Mr. Nice Guy: World's Top Entertainment Publicist Tells his Superstar Clients Exactly What He Thinks of Them. (Illus.). 308p. 2000. 14.95 (*1-85782-373-7*) Blake Publng.

Althaus, Anne-Marie. A Touch of Sepia. LC 93-26299. (Illus.). (J). 1994. 4.25 (*0-383-03781-6*) SRA McGraw.

Althaus, Frank, tr. see Kostenevich, Albert Grigor'evich & Gosudarstvennyi Ermitazh.

Althaus, Hans, et al. Lexikon der Germanistischen Linguistik: Lexicon of German Linguistics. 2nd ed. (GER.). 870p. 1980. 195.00 (*0-8288-1965-3*, M7256) Fr & Eur.

Althaus, Hans J., jt. ed. see Mog, Paul.

Althaus, Hans P. Die Cambridger Loewenfabel von 1382: Untersuchung und Edition eines defektiven Textes. (Quellen und Forschungen zur Sprach und Kulturgeschichte der Germanischen Voelker). (Illus.). 238p. (C). 1971. 140.00 (*3-11-003939-7*) De Gruyter.

***Althaus, Horst.** Hegel. 2000. 29.95 (*0-7456-1781-6*, Pub. by Polity Pr) Blackwell Pubs.

Althaus, Keith. Rival Heavens. (Provincetown Poets Ser.: No. 1). (Illus.). 64p. 1993. 35.00 (*0-944854-07-9*); pap. 10.00 (*0-944854-06-0*) Provincetown Arts.

Althaus, Paul. Theology of Martin Luther. Schultz, Robert C., tr. from GER. LC 66-17345. 464p. 1966. pap. 25.00 (*0-8006-1855-6*, 1-1855, Fortress Pr) Augsburg Fortress.

Althaus, Thomas. Apigrammatisches Barock. (Quellen und Forschungen zur Literatur und Kulturgeschichte: Vol. 9(243)). (GER.). xi, 394p. 1996. lib. bdg. 131.85 (*3-11-015433-1*) De Gruyter.

***Althaus, Thomas.** Sprachlichkeit. Zur Thematik und Zu Den Schriften von Helmut Arntzen: Vortrage und Wurdigungen. 96p. 1999. 26.95 (*3-631-34699-9*) P Lang Pubng.

Althauser, Doug. You Can Free Yourself from Alcohol & Drugs: Work a Program That Keeps You in Charge. LC 98-66699. 192p. 1998. pap. 13.95 (*1-57224-118-7*) New Harbinger.

Althauser, Robert & Wallace, Michael, eds. Research in Social Stratification & Mobility, Vol. 2. 350p. 1983. 73.25 (*0-89232-302-7*) Jai Pr.

— Research in Social Stratification & Mobility, Vol. 3. 224p. 1984. 73.25 (*0-89232-331-0*) Jai Pr.

— Research in Social Stratification & Mobility, Vol. 4. 296p. 1985. 73.25 (*0-89232-563-1*) Jai Pr.

— Research in Social Stratification & Mobility, Vol. 5. 371p. 1986. 73.25 (*0-89232-660-3*) Jai Pr.

— Research in Social Stratification & Mobility, Vol. 6. 285p. 1987. 73.25 (*0-89232-717-0*) Jai Pr.

— Research in Social Stratification & Mobility, Vol. 7. 352p. 1989. 78.50 (*0-89232-897-5*) Jai Pr.

— Research in Social Stratification & Mobility, Vol. 8. 352p. 1990. 73.25 (*1-55938-019-5*) Jai Pr.

— Research in Social Stratification & Mobility, Vol. 9. 375p. 1991. 73.25 (*1-55938-205-8*) Jai Pr.

— Research in Social Stratification & Mobility, Vol. 10. 336p. 1991. 73.25 (*1-55938-403-4*) Jai Pr.

— Research in Social Stratification & Mobility, Vol. 11. 347p. 1993. 73.25 (*1-55938-491-3*) Jai Pr.

— Research in Social Stratification & Mobility, Vol. 12. 400p. 1993. 73.25 (*1-55938-542-1*) Jai Pr.

— Research in Social Stratification & Mobility, Vol. 14. 1995. 73.25 (*1-55938-892-7*) Jai Pr.

— Research in Social Stratification & Mobility: An Annual Compilation of Research, Vol. 1. 319p. 1981. 78.50 (*0-89232-067-2*) Jai Pr.

Althea. Be Careful. (Dinosaur Ser.). (Illus.). (J). 1988. pap. 2.95 (*0-85122-751-1*) Parkwest Pubns.

— Colours of Things. (Dinosaur Ser.). (Illus.). (J). 1982. pap. 2.95 (*0-85122-742-2*) Parkwest Pubns.

— Crossing Roads. (Dinosaur Ser.). (Illus.). (J). pap. 2.95 (*0-85122-725-2*) Parkwest Pubns.

— How Do Things Grow? LC 90-10923. (First Science Ser.). (Illus.). 32p. (J). (gr. k-3). 1991. lib. bdg. 17.25 (*0-8167-2118-1*) Troll Communs.

— How Do Things Grow? LC 90-10923. (First Science Ser.). (Illus.). 32p. (J). (gr. k-3). 1997. pap. 3.95 (*0-8167-2119-X*) Troll Communs.

— If You Were a Gerbil. (Dinosaur Ser.). (Illus.). (J). 1988. pap. 2.95 (*0-85122-708-2*) Parkwest Pubns.

— Opposites of Things. (Dinosaur Ser.). (Illus.). (J). 1982. pap. 2.95 (*0-85122-714-7*) Parkwest Pubns.

— Shapes of Things. (Dinosaur Ser.). (Illus.). (J). 1986. pap. 2.95 (*0-85122-749-X*) Parkwest Pubns.

— Sizes of Things. (Dinosaur Ser.). (Illus.). (J). 1987. pap. 2.95 (*0-85122-687-6*) Parkwest Pubns.

— Speed of Things. (Dinosaur Ser.). (Illus.). (J). 1988. pap. 2.95 (*0-85122-730-9*) Parkwest Pubns.

— Trees & Leaves. LC 89-20308. (Nature Club Ser.). (Illus.). 32p. (J). (gr. 3-6). 1990. pap. 4.95 (*0-8167-1968-3*) Troll Communs.

— What Makes Things Move? LC 90-10924. (First Science Ser.). (Illus.). 32p. (J). (gr. k-3). 1991. lib. bdg. 17.25 (*0-8167-2124-6*) Troll Communs.

— What Makes Things Move? LC 90-10924. (First Science Ser.). (Illus.). 32p. (J). (gr. k-3). 1997. pap. 3.95 (*0-8167-2125-4*) Troll Communs.

— When Uncle Bob Dies. (Dinosaur Ser.). (Illus.). (J). pap. 2.95 (*0-85122-727-9*) Parkwest Pubns.

Altheide, David L. An Ecology of Communication: Cultural Formats of Control. 257p. 1995. pap. text 25.95 (*0-202-30533-3*); lib. bdg. 46.95 (*0-202-30532-5*) Aldine de Gruyter.

— Qualitative Media Analysis. LC 95-41796. (Qualitative Research Methods Ser.: Vol. 38). 112p. 1996. 24.00 (*0-7619-0198-1*); pap. 10.50 (*0-7619-0199-X*) Sage.

Altheide, David L. & Snow, Robert P. Media Worlds in the Postjournalism Era. (Communication & Social Order Ser.). 287p. 1991. pap. text 26.95 (*0-202-30377-2*); lib. bdg. 51.95 (*0-202-30376-4*) Aldine de Gruyter.

Altheim, Franz & Stiehl, Ruth. Christentum am Roten Meer, Vol. 1. (C). 1971. 346.15 (*3-11-003790-4*) De Gruyter.

— Christentum am Roten Meer, Vol. 2. (C). 1973. 346.15 (*3-11-003791-2*) De Gruyter.

— Geschichte Mittelasiens im Altertum. (GER., Illus.). (C). 1970. 326.95 (*3-11-002677-5*) De Gruyter.

Althen, Gary. American Ways: A Guide for Foreigners in the United States. LC 87-46023. 192p. (Orig.). 1988. pap. text 16.95 (*0-933662-68-8*) Intercult Pr.

— The Handbook of Foreign Student Advising. rev. ed. LC 95-3433. 296p. (C). 1995. pap. text 21.95 (*1-877864-34-X*) Intercult Pr.

Althen, Gary, ed. Learning Across Cultures. 200p. 1994. pap. 19.00 (*0-912207-67-1*) NAFSA Washington.

Alther, Lisa. Five Minutes in Heaven. 1996. pap. 12.95 (*0-452-27613-6*, Plume) Dutton Plume.

— Kinflicks. LC 95-47910. 1996. pap. 13.95 (*0-452-27677-2*, Plume) Dutton Plume.

— Other Women. 1996. pap. 13.95 (*0-452-27678-0*, Plume) Dutton Plume.

Altherr, Ilse. Blackwork Companion. (Illus.). 90p. 1999. pap. text 29.50 (*0-9624090-1-4*) I Altherr.

— Mastering the Art of Pulled Thread Embroidery. (Illus.). 132p. (Orig.). 1989. reprint ed. spiral bd. 24.50 (*0-9624090-0-6*) I Altherr.

Altherr, Thomas L., ed. Procreation or Pleasure? Sexual Attitudes in American History. LC 83-12. 180p. (C). 1983. pap. text 12.75 (*0-89874-609-4*) Krieger.

Altherr, Thomas L., et al. America's History: Test Bank, Vol. 1. 3rd ed. 1997. write for info. (*1-57259-219-2*) Worth.

— America's History: Test Bank, Vol. 2. 3rd ed. 1997. write for info. (*1-57259-220-6*) Worth.

— Sports in North America: A Documentary History. LC 92-171131. 1992. 134.72 (*0-87569-188-9*) Academic Intl.

Althoen, Steven C. & Bumcrot, Robert J. Matrix Methods in Finite Mathematics: An Introduction with Applications to Business & Industry. 350p. (C). 1976. text 40.50 (*0-393-09192-9*) Norton.

Althoen, Steven C., jt. auth. see Frank, Harry.

***Althofer, Heinz.** Kunst und Umwelt Umwelt und Kunst. 2000. 48.95 (*3-631-35707-9*) P Lang Pubng.

Althoff. Choice Wellness. 3rd ed. (C). 1996. pap. text, lab manual ed. 27.00 (*0-13-777939-9*) P-H.

— Choices in Wellness for Life. 3rd ed. 312p. (C). 1996. pap. text 40.00 (*0-13-777921-6*) P-H.

***Althoff, Claire J., et al.** Who Gets Grandma's Yellow Pie Plate: A Guide to Passing on Personal Possessions. LC 99-60715. (Illus.). 95p. 1999. pap. 12.50 (*1-888440-08-2*) U MN Ext Serv.

Althoff, Doug. The Winchester Company, 1924. (Illus.). 112p. 1995. text. write for info. (*1-886094-05-5*) Chicago Spectrum.

***Althoff, Gerd, et al, eds.** Medieval Concepts of the Past: Ritual, Memory, Historiography. (Publications of the German Historical Institute, Washington, D. C.). (Illus.). 328p. 2000. write for info. (*0-521-78066-7*) Cambridge U Pr.

***Althoff, K. D., et al, eds.** Case-Based Reasoning Research & Development: Third International Conference on Case-Based Reasoning, ICCBR-99, Seeon Monastery, Germany, July 27-30, 1999, Proceedings. LC 99-37087. (Lecture Notes in Artificial Intelligence Ser.: Vol. 1650). xii, 598p. 1999. pap. 91.00 (*3-540-66237-5*) Spr-Verlag.

Althoff, K. D., et al, eds. Topics in Case-Based Reasoning, Vol. 837. (Lecture Notes in Artificial Intelligence Ser.). 471p. 1994. 65.95 (*0-387-58330-0*) Spr-Verlag.

Althoff, K. H. & Meyer, W., eds. High Energy Spin Physics Conference Report, Vol. 1: Proceedings of the International Symposium, 9th, Bonn, FRG, September 6-15, 1990. (Illus.). xv, 651p. 1991. 114.95 (*0-387-54127-6*) Spr-Verlag.

Althoff, Karl F. The Magna Carta of the Christian Church. Grimm, Werner, tr. from GER. 19p. 1982. pap. 3.00 (*0-919924-15-8*, Pub. by Steiner Book Centre) Anthroposophic.

Althoff, Philip, jt. ed. see Leachman, Robert B.

Althoff, Phillip & Rush, Michael. Introduction to Political Sociology. LC 77-180276. 1972. pap. 4.95 (*0-672-61311-5*, Bobbs) Macmillan.

Althoff, William F. Sky Ships: A History of the Airship in the United States Navy. LC 94-14873. (Illus.). 304p. 1998. reprint ed. pap. 24.95 (*0-935553-32-0*) Pacifica Military.

Altholz, Josef L. Anatomy of a Controversy: The Debate over "Essays & Reviews" 208p. 1994. 74.95 (*1-85928-040-4*, Pub. by Scolar Pr) Ashgate Pub Co.

— Churches in the Nineteenth Century. LC 66-30446. (Orig.). (C). 1967. write for info. (*0-672-51130-4*, Bobbs); pap. 6.95 (*0-672-60682-8*, Bobbs) Macmillan.

— The Religious Press in Britain, 1760-1900, 22. LC 89-1956. (Contributions to the Study of Religion Ser.: No. 22). 225p. 1989. 59.95 (*0-313-25738-8*, AHW, Greenwood Pr) Greenwood.

— Type Right! 2128 HD. 1980. pap. 17.20 (*0-02-830710-0*) S&S Trade.

Altholz, Josef L., ed. The Mind & Art of Victorian England. LC 75-22686. 254p. reprint ed. pap. 78.80 (*0-7837-2980-4*, 205747400006) Bks Demand.

***Altholz, Josef L., ed.** Selected Documents in Irish History. LC 99-46033. 160p. 2000. text 59.95 (*0-7656-0541-4*) M E Sharpe.

— Selected Documents in Irish History. 160p. 2000. reprint ed. pap. text 19.95 (*0-7656-0542-2*) M E Sharpe.

Altholz, Josef L., ed. see Acton, John E.

***Althoumlfer, Ingo, et al.** Numbers, Information & Complexity. 672p. 2000. 155.00 (*0-7923-7765-6*) Kluwer Academic.

Althouse, A. D., et al. Modern Refrigeration & Air Conditioning. LC 87-57. (Illus.). 1199p. 1996. text 55.96 (*1-56637-300-X*) Goodheart.

***Althouse, Andrew D., et al.** Modern Refrigeration & Air Conditioning. LC 99-89117. 2000. write for info. (*1-56637-724-2*) Goodheart.

Althouse, Andrew D., et al. Modern Welding: Complete Coverage of the Welding Field in One Easy-to-Use Volume! LC 99-17784. 779p. 2000. 53.28 (*1-56637-605-X*) Goodheart.

Althouse, Jay. Copyright: The Complete Guide for Music Educators, 2nd Edition. 2nd rev. ed. 144p. (Orig.). 1997. pap. 10.95 (*0-939139-07-3*, 02-101) Music In Action.

Althouse, Jay. Copyright Guide. 2nd ed. 144p. 1990. pap. 10.95 (*0-7390-0753-X*, 02-101) Alfred Pub.

Althouse, Jay. The Sacred Trumpet Soloist. 1999. pap. 27.95 incl. audio compact disk (*0-7390-0034-9*, 18925); pap. 14.95 (*0-7390-0033-0*, 18923) Alfred Pub.

— Sunday Savers for SAB Choirs. 1999. pap. 4.95 (*0-7390-0036-5*, 18914) Alfred Pub.

Althouse, Jay, ed. Folk Songs for Solo Singers, Medium High Voice, Bk. 2. 1996. pap. 9.95 (*0-88284-810-0*); pap. 9.95 (*0-88284-811-9*) Alfred Pub.

Althouse, Jay, et al, eds. Ready to Sing Folk Songs. (Ready to Sing... Ser.). 64p. Date not set. pap. 14.95 (*0-7390-0225-2*, 17173); pap. 24.95 incl. audio compact disk (*0-7390-0226-0*, 17175) Alfred Pub.

Althouse, Jay & Albrecht, Sally K. I Sing, You Sing. 1999. pap. 34.95 incl. audio compact disk (*0-7390-0084-5*, 18725); pap. 14.95 (*0-7390-0085-3*, 18723) Alfred Pub.

Althouse, Jay, et al. Carols for Two. 1996. pap. 20.95 incl. audio compact disk (*0-88284-997-2*, 16021) Alfred Pub.

Althouse, Jay, et al. Christmas for Solo Singers/Medium High. 1995. pap. 9.95 (*0-7390-0008-X*, 11676) Alfred Pub.

Althouse, Jay, et al. Christmas for Solo Singers/Medium High. 1995. pap. 20.90 incl. audio compact disk (*0-7390-0009-8*, 11684) Alfred Pub.

Althouse, Jay, et al. Christmas for Solo Singers/Medium Low. 1995. pap. 9.95 (*0-7390-0054-3*, 11677) Alfred Pub.

Althouse, Jay, et al. Christmas for Solo Singers/Medium Low. 1995. pap. 20.90 incl. audio compact disk (*0-7390-0055-1*, 11685) Alfred Pub.

— The Christmas Soloist, Medium High Voice. 1992. pap. 9.95 (*0-88284-999-9*, 3385) Alfred Pub.

— Christmas Soloist, the Medium High. 1997. pap. 20.90 incl. audio compact disk (*0-7390-0001-2*, 16412) Alfred Pub.

— Folk Songs for Solo Singers, Medium-High, Bk. 1. 1993. pap. 9.95 (*0-88284-872-0*, 4952) Alfred Pub.

Althouse, Jay, et al. Folk Songs for Solo Singers, Medium-Low, Bk. 1. 1996. pap. 20.90 incl. audio compact disk (*0-88284-877-1*, 16634) Alfred Pub.

Althouse, Jay, et al. Folk Songs for Solo Singers, Medium-Low, Bk.1. 1993. pap. 9.95 (*0-88284-875-5*, 4953) Alfred Pub.

— Folk Songs for Solo Singers/Medium High, Vol. 2. 1996. pap. 20.90 incl. audio compact disk (*0-7390-0023-3*, 16304) Alfred Pub.

— Folk Songs for Solo Singers/Medium Low, Vol. 2. 64p. 1996. pap. 20.90 incl. audio compact disk (*0-7390-0244-9*, 16305) Alfred Pub.

Althouse, Jay, et al. Spirituals for Solo Singers/Medium High. 64p. 1994. pap. 9.95 (*0-7390-0058-6*, 11696) Alfred Pub.

— Spirituals for Solo Singers/Medium High. 1997. pap. 20.90 incl. audio compact disk (*0-7390-0059-4*, 16915) Alfred Pub.

— Spirituals for Solo Singers/Medium Low. 64p. 1994. pap. 9.95 (*0-7390-0057-8*, 11698) Alfred Pub.

— Spirituals for Solo Singers/Medium Low. 1997. pap. 20.90 incl. audio compact disk (*0-7390-0056-X*, 16916) Alfred Pub.

Althouse, Jay, jt. auth. see Albrecht, Sally.

Althouse, Jay, jt. auth. see Albrecht, Sally K.

Althouse, Jay, jt. auth. see Robinson, Russell.

Althouse, John, et al. Auto Air Conditioning Technology. (Illus.). 255p. 1991. text 34.64 (*0-87006-815-6*) Goodheart.

Althouse, Jonathan, jt. auth. see Surbrook, Truman.

Althouse, Larry & Althouse, Valere. What You Need Is What You've Got: Rediscovering, Developing & Using Your Inner Resources. LC 88-13100. 208p. 1989. pap. 9.95 (*0-87728-691-4*) Weiser.

Althouse, Mark L., jt. ed. see Leonelli, Joseph.

***Althouse, R. Brad, et al.** Get 'Em on Task: A Computer Signaling Program to Teach Attending & Self-Management Skills. 40p. 1999. 29.50 incl. cd-rom (*1-57035-197-X*, 113GET) Sopris.

Althouse, Ralph, et al. Chemicals & Industrial Processes Associated with Cancer in Humans: IARC Monographs, Volumes 1 to 20. Report of an IARC Ad Hoc Working Group Which Met in Lyon, 15-17 January 1979 to Advise the Director, IARC, on Chemicals Carcinogenic for Humans. LC 82-110863. (IARC Monographs. Supplement: No. 1). 85p. reprint ed. pap. 30.00 (*0-8357-6465-6*, 203583600097) Bks Demand.

Althouse, Rochelle B. Work-Related Lung Disease Surveillance Report (1994) (Illus.). 149p. (C). 1997. reprint ed. pap. text 40.00 (*0-7881-3336-5*) DIANE Pub.

***Althouse, Rochelle B.** Work-Related Lung Disease Surveillance Report 1999. 5th ed. (Illus.). 224p. 2000. pap. text 40.00 (*0-7881-8869-0*) DIANE Pub.

Althouse, Rochelle B., ed. Work-Related Lung Disease Surveillance Report (1996) 4th ed. (Illus.). 482p. (C). 1997. pap. text 50.00 (*0-7881-3742-5*) DIANE Pub.

Althouse, Ronald C., jt. auth. see Brooks, Dana D.

Althouse, Ronald C., jt. ed. see Brooks, Dana D.

Althouse, Rosemary. Investigating Mathematics with Young Children. 192p. (C). 1994. pap. text 19.95 (*0-8077-3349-0*) Tchrs Coll.

— Investigating Science Experiences with Young Children. 208p. (Orig.). 1988. pap. text 19.95 (*0-8077-2912-4*) Tchrs Coll.

— The Young Child: Learning with Understanding. LC 81-4600. (Illus.). 283p. 1981. reprint ed. pap. 87.80 (*0-7837-8944-0*, 204965500002) Bks Demand.

Althouse, Rosemary & Main, Cecil. Science Experiences for Young Children: Air. LC 74-23257. (Illus.). 38p. 1975. reprint ed. pap. 30.00 (*0-608-00845-1*, 206163600010) Bks Demand.

— Science Experiences for Young Children: As We Grow. LC 74-23257. (Illus.). 40p. 1975. reprint ed. pap. 30.00 (*0-608-00850-8*, 206164100010) Bks Demand.

— Science Experiences for Young Children: Colors. LC 74-23257. (Illus.). 49p. 1975. reprint ed. pap. 30.00 (*0-608-00851-6*, 206164200010) Bks Demand.

— Science Experiences for Young Children: Food. LC 74-23257. (Illus.). 37p. 1975. reprint ed. pap. 30.00 (*0-608-00849-4*, 206164000010) Bks Demand.

— Science Experiences for Young Children: Magnets. LC 74-23257. (Illus.). 57p. 1975. reprint ed. pap. 30.00 (*0-608-00846-X*, 206163700010) Bks Demand.

— Science Experiences for Young Children: Pets. LC 74-23257. (Illus.). 45p. 1975. pap. 30.00 (*0-608-00852-4*, 206164300010) Bks Demand.

— Science Experiences for Young Children: Seeds. LC 74-23257. (Illus.). 38p. 1975. reprint ed. pap. 30.00 (*0-608-00853-2*, 206164400010) Bks Demand.

— Science Experiences for Young Children: Senses. LC 74-23257. (Illus.). 41p. 1975. reprint ed. pap. 30.00 (*0-608-00844-3*, 206163500010) Bks Demand.

— Science Experiences for Young Children: Water. LC 74-23257. (Illus.). 39p. 1975. reprint ed. pap. 30.00 (*0-608-00847-8*, 206163800010) Bks Demand.

— Science Experiences for Young Children: Wheels. LC 74-23257. (Illus.). 29p. 1975. reprint ed. pap. 30.00 (*0-608-00848-6*, 206163900010) Bks Demand.

Althouse, Valere, jt. auth. see Althouse, Larry.

Althurian Society Staff. Law of the Way (1911) 262p. 1998. reprint ed. pap. 15.95 (*0-7661-0674-8*) Kessinger Pub.

Althusius, Johannes. Politica. Carney, Frederick S., tr. & abr. by. LC 94-30586. (Liberty Classics Ser.). Orig. Title: Politica Methodice Digesta. lxii, 240p. 1995. 19.50 (*0-86597-114-5*); pap. 7.50 (*0-86597-115-3*) Liberty Fund.

An Asterisk (*) at the beginning of an entry indicates that the title is appearing for the first time.

— Politica Methodice Digesta of Johannes Althusius. Mayer, J. P., ed. LC 78-67326. (European Political Thought Ser.). 1979. reprint ed. lib. bdg. 42.95 (*0-405-11673-X*) Ayer.

Althusser, Louis. For Marx. rev. ed. (C). 1996. pap. 17.00 (*1-85984-146-5*, Pub. by Verso) Norton.

— The Future Lasts Forever: A Memoir. 384p. 1995. pap. 14.95 (*1-56584-278-2*, Pub. by New Press NY) Norton.

— Lenin & Philosophy & Other Essays. Brewster, Ben, tr. from FRE. LC 78-178710. 256p. 1972. pap. 16.00 (*0-85345-213-X*, Pub. by Monthly Rev) NYU Pr.

— Machiavelli & Us. LC 99-13811. 1999. 30.00 (*1-85984-711-0*, Pub. by Verso) Norton.

***Althusser, Louis.** Machiavelli & Us. Matherson, Francois, ed. Elliott, Gregory, tr. 160p. 2001. pap. 19.00 (*1-85984-282-8*, Pub. by Verso) Norton.

Althusser, Louis. Reading Capital. 2nd ed. 1998. pap. 19.00 (*1-85984-164-3*, Pub. by Verso) Norton.

— The Spectre of Hegel: Early Writings. Goshgarian, G. M., tr. LC 96-50054. 1997. pap. 20.00 (*1-85984-099-X*, Pub. by Verso) Norton.

— Writings on Psychoanalysis: Freud & Lacan. 208p. 1996. 31.00 (*0-231-10168-6*) Col U Pr.

— Writings on Psychoanalysis: Freud & Lacan. 1999. pap. 16.50 (*0-231-10169-4*) Col U Pr.

Altick, Richard D. The English Common Reader: A Social History of the Mass Reading Public, 1800-1900. LC 68-54599. (Midway Reprint Ser.). 439p. reprint ed. pap. 136.10 (*0-608-09257-6*, 205405900002) Bks Demand.

— The English Common Reader: A Social History of the Mass Reading Public, 1800-1900. LC 57-6975. (Midway Reprint Ser.). x, 440p. 1983. reprint ed. pap. text 20.00 (*0-226-01540-8*) U Ch Pr.

— The English Common Reader: A Social History of the Mass Reading Public, 1800-1900. 2nd ed. LC 98-19581. 468p. 1998. text 52.50 (*0-8142-0793-6*, ALTENG); pap. text 19.95 (*0-8142-0794-4*, ALTENX) Ohio St U Pr.

— Of a Place & a Time: Remembering Lancaster. LC 90-29296. (Illus.). 184p. (C). 1991. lib. bdg. 25.00 (*0-208-02321-6*, Archon Bks) Shoe String.

— The Presence of the Present: Topics of the Day in the Victorian Novel. LC 90-34806. (Studies in Victorian Life & Literature). 854p. 1991. text 65.00 (*0-8142-0518-6*) Ohio St U Pr.

— Punch: The Lively Youth of a British Institution, 1841-1851. LC 96-32091. (Studies in Victorian Life & Literature). 1997. text 62.50 (*0-8142-0710-3*) Ohio St U Pr.

— The Scholar Adventurers. LC 87-11064. 338p. 1987. reprint ed. pap. text 23.95 (*0-8142-0435-X*) Ohio St U Pr.

— The Shows of London. LC 77-2755. 576p. 1978. 50.00 (*0-674-80731-6*) Belknap Pr.

— Victorian People & Ideas. (Illus.). 338p. (C). 1974. pap. text 16.75 (*0-393-09376-X*) Norton.

Altick, Richard D. & Fenstermaker, John J. The Art of Literary Research. 4th ed. (C). 1992. text 46.00 (*0-393-96240-7*) Norton.

Altick, Richard D. & Wright, Andrew H. Selective Bibliography for the Study of English & American Literature. 5th ed. LC 74-2642. xii, 168p. 1975. write for info. (*0-02-302100-4*) Glencoe.

Altick, Richard D., ed. see Carlyle, Thomas.

***Altidor, Raoul.** Koule Midi. Eloi, Rodney S., ed. (Koleksyon Feliks Moriso-Lewa Ser.). 69p. 1999. 10.00 (*1-58437-000-9*) Edit Memo.

Altier, William J. The Thinking Manager's Toolbox: Five Processes for Effective Problem Solving. LC 99-28357. (Illus.). 240p. 1999. 25.00 (*0-19-513196-7*) OUP.

Altieri, Charles. Act & Quality: A Theory of Literary Meaning & Humanistic Understanding. LC 81-2147. 352p. 1981. pap. 19.95 (*0-87023-428-5*) U of Mass Pr.

Altieri, Charles. Enlarging the Temple: New Directions in American Poetry During the 1960's. LC 77-89773. 256p. 1979. 34.50 (*0-8387-2127-3*); pap. 17.95 (*0-8387-5012-5*) Bucknell U Pr.

— Painterly Abstraction in Modernist American Poetry: Infinite Incantations of Ourselves. (Cambridge Studies in American Literature & Culture: No. 37). 537p. (C). 1990. text 80.00 (*0-521-33085-8*) Cambridge U Pr.

— Postmodernisms Now: Essays on Contemporaneity in the Arts. LC 98-17143. (Literature & Philosophy Ser.). 1998. 50.00 (*0-271-01803-8*) Pa St U Pr.

— Postmodernisms Now: Essays on Contemporaneity in the Arts. LC 98-17143. (Literature & Philosophy Ser.). (Illus.). 304p. 1998. pap. 22.50 (*0-271-01804-6*) Pa St U Pr.

Altieri, Charles, ed. Painterly Abstraction in Modernist American Poetry: The Contemporaneity of Modernism. LC 94-30713. (Literature & Philosophy Ser.). (Illus.). 544p. 1995. pap. 22.50 (*0-271-01419-9*) Pa St U Pr.

Altieri, Charles F. Modern Poetry. LC 76-4656. (Goldentree Bibliographies Series in Language & Literature). (C). 1980. pap. text 14.95 (*0-88295-550-0*) Harlan Davidson.

Altieri, Daniel, jt. auth. see Cooney, Eleanor.

Altieri, Dario C. The Coagulation-Inflammation Interface: Coagulation Assembly on Leukocytes. LC 97-9703. (Molecular Biology Intelligence Unit Ser.). 1997. 99.00 (*1-57059-504-6*) Landes Bioscience.

Altieri, James. Spearheaders: A Personal History of Darby's Rangers. LC 79-18951. 1979. reprint ed. 25.95 (*0-89201-061-4*) Zenger Pub.

Altieri, Joanne. The Theatre of Praise: The Panegyric Tradition in Seventeenth-Century English Drama. LC 84-40479. 240p. 1986. 40.00 (*0-87413-275-4*) U Delaware Pr.

Altieri, Miguel A. Agroecology: The Science of Sustainable Agriculture. 2nd ed. 448p. (C). 1995. pap. 28.00 (*0-8133-1718-5*, Pub. by Westview) HarpC.

— Biodiversity & Pest Management in Agroecosystems. LC 92-22613. (Illus.). 189p. 1994. lib. bdg. 49.95 (*1-56022-037-6*) Haworth Pr.

Altieri, Miguel A. & Hecht, Susanna B., eds. Agroecology & Small Farm Development. 336p. 1990. lib. bdg. 89.95 (*0-8493-4885-4*, SB) CRC Pr.

Altieri, Miguel A. & Liebman, Matthew Z., eds. Weed Management in Agroecosystems Ecological Approaches: Ecological Approaches, 2 vols., Vol. I. LC 87-25619. 192p. 1988. 204.00 (*0-8493-6816-2*, SB611, CRC Reprint) Franklin.

Altieri, V. J., jt. auth. see American Gas Association Committee on Revision of.

Altiner, Y. Analytical Surface Deformation Theory: For Detection of the Earth's Crust Movements. LC 99-23784. (Illus.). 110p. 1999. 62.00 (*3-540-65820-3*) Spr-Verlag.

Alting, J. H., jt. auth. see Buning, W. De Cock.

Alting, Leo. Manufacturing Engineering Processes. 2nd expanded rev. ed. (Manufacturing Engineering & Materials Processing Ser.: Vol. 40). (Illus.). 512p. 1993. text 69.75 (*0-8247-9129-0*) Dekker.

Alting Von Gesau, Frans A. & Pelkmans, Jacques, eds. National Economic Security: Perceptions, Threats, & Policies. 253p. 1983. pap. 24.95 (*0-87855-946-9*) Transaction Pubs.

Alting Von Geusau, Frans A. Uncertain Detente. 310p. 1979. lib. bdg. 105.50 (*90-286-0818-4*) Kluwer Academic.

Alting von Geusau, Frans A. M., see von Geusau, Frans A. M. Alting.

Altink, Sietske. Stolen Lives: Trading Women into Sex & Slavery. 1996. pap. text 17.95 (*1-56023-885-2*) Haworth Pr.

***Altintas, Yusuf.** Manufacturing Automation: Metal Cutting Mechanics, Machine Tool Vibrations & CNC Design. (Illus.). 304p. (C). 2000. 90.00 (*0-521-65029-1*); pap. 39.95 (*0-521-65973-6*) Cambridge U Pr.

Altiok, Tayfur. Performance Analysis of Manufacturing Systems. LC 96-14273. (Series in Operations Research). 355p. 1996. 49.95 (*0-387-94773-6*) Spr-Verlag.

Altizer, A. B. Self & Symbolism in the Poetry of Michelangelo, John Donne & Agrippa d'Aubigne. (Archives Internationales D'Histoire des Idees Ser.: No. 10). 117p. 1973. pap. text 69.50 (*90-247-1551-2*, Pub. by M Nijhoff) Kluwer Academic.

Altizer, Anne W., compiled by. Seeking Major Gifts: How Fifty-Seven Institutions Do It. 166p. 1992. pap. 15.00 (*0-89964-287-X*, 28402) Coun Adv & Supp Ed.

Altizer, Nell. The Man Who Died En Route. LC 88-7581. 72p. 1989. 17.50 (*0-87023-645-8*) U of Mass Pr.

Altizer, Thomas J. The Contemporary Jesus. LC 96-39269. 224p. (C). 1997. text 59.50 (*0-7914-3375-7*); pap. text 19.95 (*0-7914-3376-5*) State U NY Pr.

— The Descent into Hell: A Study of the Radical Reversal of the Christian Consciousness. 222p. 1984. 9.95 (*0-8164-1194-8*) Harper SF.

— History as Apocalypse. LC 84-16289. 265p. (C). 1985. pap. text 24.95 (*0-88706-014-5*) State U NY Pr.

— Mircea Eliade & the Dialectic of the Sacred. LC 73-15398. 219p. 1975. reprint ed. lib. bdg. 35.00 (*0-8371-7196-2*, ALME, Greenwood Pr) Greenwood.

— The Self-Embodiment of God. LC 87-13365. (Brown Classics in Judaica Ser.). 114p. 1987. reprint ed. pap. text 18.00 (*0-8191-6467-4*) U Pr of Amer.

— Total Presence: The Language of Jesus & the Language of Today. 128p. 1984. 11.95 (*0-8164-0461-5*) Harper SF.

***Altizer, Thomas J. J.** Living the Death of God: A Theological Memoir. 220p. 2000. 22.00 (*1-58177-067-7*) Barrytown Ltd.

— The New Apocalypse: The Radical Christian Vision of William Blake. LC 00-35845. (Series in Philosophical & Cultural Studies in Religion). 2000. write for info. (*1-888570-56-3*) Davies Grp.

Altland, Millard, jt. auth. see Cornell, William A.

Altmaier, Elizabeth M. & Meyer, Merle E. Applied Specialties in Psychology. 500p. 1985. text 39.95 (*0-89859-714-5*) L Erlbaum Assocs.

— Applied Specialties in Psychology. 600p. (C). 1985. text. write for info. (*0-07-554880-1*) McGraw.

Altmaier, Elizabeth M., jt. auth. see Ross, Randall R.

Altman. Allergy in Primary Care. (C). 1999. text. write for info. (*0-7216-8166-2*, W B Saunders Co) Harcrt Hlth Sci Grp.

***Altman.** Arguing about Law: An Introduction to Legal Philosophy. 2nd ed. (Philosophy Ser.). (C). 2000. text 26.50 (*0-534-54352-9*) Wadsworth Pub.

— Lunch at the Zoo. LC 00-22430. (Illus.). 80p. (gr. 2-5). 1999. text 15.95 (*0-8050-6070-7*) St Martin.

Altman. Matt Damon & Ben Affleck: On & Off Screen. LC 98-73303. (Illus.). 128p. (J). (gr. 3 up). 1998. pap. 4.50 (*0-06-107145-5*) HarpC.

Altman & Chemers. Culture & Environment. 1979. pap. text 11.25 (*0-8185-0348-3*) Brooks-Cole.

Altman, A. Agricultural Biotechnology. LC 97-38712. (Books in Soils, Plants, & the Environment Ser.). (Illus.). 792p. 1997. text 195.00 (*0-8247-9439-7*) Dekker.

Altman, Adelaide. Professor Pishposh & the Robots. (Illus.). 48p. (J). (ps-2). 1988. 12.95 (*0-933905-05-X*); pap. 9.95 (*0-933905-16-5*) Claycomb Pr.

Altman, Alexandria. John Carpenter Speaks Out: Experiences about Roswell, Bermuda Triangle, UFO's Extra Terrestrial Life. (It's Time Ser.). 1998. pap. text 9.95 (*1-885640-39-0*) Intl Netwrk.

Altman, Allen & Swift, Bryon. Checklist of the Birds of South America. 3rd rev. ed. LC 89-90962. (Illus.). 84p. 1993. pap. 6.50 (*0-9622559-2-0*) A Altman & B Swift.

Altman, Amry & Caddy, John, eds. Rural Arts Collaborations. (Illus.). 193p. (Orig.). 1994. pap. 10.00 (*0-927663-22-8*) COMPAS.

Altman, Andrew. Arguing about Law: An Introduction to Legal Philosophy. LC 95-14658. 250p. 1995. pap. 23.50 (*0-534-22032-0*) Wadsworth Pub.

Altman, Andrew, jt. ed. see Sellers, Mortimer.

Altman, Ann & Gonzales-Serva, Marilyn. How to Murder Your Husband. 160p. 1998. pap. 9.95 (*1-57566-252-3*, Knsington) Kensgtn Pub Corp.

Altman, Arie & Waisel, Yoav, eds. Biology of Root Formation & Development: Proceedings of the Second International Symposium Held in Jerusalem, Israel, June 23-28, 1996. LC 97-31141. (Basic Life Sciences Ser.: Vol. 65). (Illus.). 390p. 1998. 150.00 (*0-306-45706-7*, Kluwer Plenum) Kluwer Academic.

Altman, Arnold & Schwartz, Allen D. Malignant Diseases of Infancy, Childhood & Adolescence. 2nd ed. (Major Problems in Clinical Pediatrics Ser.: Vol. 18). 1983. text 160.00 (*0-7216-1211-3*, W B Saunders Co) Harcrt Hlth Sci Grp.

Altman, B. N., jt. ed. see Altman, H. J.

Altman, Billy. Laughter's Gentle Soul: The Life of Robert Benchley. (Illus.). 384p. (C). 1997. 30.00 (*0-393-03833-5*) Norton.

Altman, Brian A., ed. & illus. see Larson, Mary.

Altman, C. & Suchy, K. Reciprocity, Spatial Mapping & Time Reversal in Electromagnetics. (C). 1991. text 180.50 (*0-7923-1339-9*) Kluwer Academic.

Altman, Carole. You Can Be Your Own Sex Therapist. reprint ed. pap. 12.95 (*0-9657527-9-8*) Casper Pubng.

Altman, Charles. The Video Connection: Integrating Video into Language Teaching. (C). 1988. pap. text 18.76 (*0-395-48143-0*) HM.

Altman, Chris. Catfishing. LC 91-91473. (Complete Angler's Library). 247p. 1992. write for info. (*0-914697-44-7*) N Amer Outdoor Grp.

Altman, Cindy L., ed. see Gatton, T. Harry.

Altman, David. Liquid Propellant Rockets. LC 60-12048. (Princeton Aeronautical Paperbacks Ser.: No. 1). 197p. reprint ed. pap. 61.10 (*0-8357-6192-4*, 205682300090) Bks Demand.

Altman, David G., et al. Public Health Advocacy: Creating Community Change to Improve Health. (Illus.). 150p. (Orig.). 1994. pap. 24.00 (*1-879552-12-4*) SCRDP.

Altman, David W. & Watanabe, Kazuo N., eds. Plant Biotechnology Transfer to Developing Countries. (Biotechnology Intelligence Unit Ser.). (Illus.). 300p. 1995. text 74.00 (*0-12-054505-5*) Acad Pr.

Altman, Dennis. Homosexual: Oppression & Liberation. LC 93-18284. 320p. (C). 1993. reprint ed. text 45.00 (*0-8147-0623-1*); reprint ed. pap. text 16.50 (*0-8147-0624-X*) NYU Pr.

— Power & Community: Organizational & Cultural Responses to AIDS. LC 94-5754. 1994. 69.95 (*0-7484-0193-8*); pap. 24.95 (*0-7484-0194-6*) Taylor & Francis.

Altman, Devra L. A Manual for Small & Medium-Sized Law Libraries. LC 76-372536. (Research Contributions of the American Bar Foundation Ser.: 1976, No. 2). 35p. reprint ed. pap. 30.00 (*0-608-12377-3*, 205212900038) Bks Demand.

Altman, DG, told to. Constrained Markov Decision Processes. 256p. 1999. lib. bdg. 69.95 (*0-8493-0382-6*, Chap & Hall CRC) CRC Pr.

Altman, Diana. Hollywood East: Louis B. Mayer & the Origins of the Studio System. (Illus.). 288p. 1992. 19.95 (*1-55972-140-5*, Birch Ln Pr) Carol Pub Group.

***Altman, Don.** Art of the Inner Meal: Eating As a Spiritual Path. LC 99-14672. 224p. 1999. 20.00 (*0-06-251635-3*) HarpC.

Altman, Don. 201 Unique Ways to Make Your Wedding Special. 2nd expanded rev. ed. Hammers, Maryanne, ed. LC 97-15175. (Illus.). 144p. 1997. pap. 9.95 (*0-9639161-4-9*) Moon Lake Media.

Altman, Don B. Digital Frontier Job & Opportunity Finder. (Illus.). 256p. (Orig.). 1996. pap. 19.95 (*0-9639161-1-4*) Moon Lake Media.

Altman, Donald E. Contingency Table Analysis in Geographic Research: A Bibliographic Essay, No. 898. 1975. 6.00 (*0-686-20371-2*, Sage Prdcls Pr) Sage.

Altman, Douglas. For Guys. (Looking Good Ser.: Set II). 32p. (J). 1989. lib. bdg. 19.93 (*0-86625-284-3*) Rourke Pubns.

Altman, Douglas, jt. ed. see Chalmers, Iain.

***Altman, Douglas A., et al, eds.** Statistics with Confidence. 2nd ed. 240p. 2000. pap. text 34.95 (*0-7279-1375-1*, Pub. by BMJ Pub) Login Brothers Bk Co.

Altman, Edward, jt. ed. see Vanderhoof, Irwin T.

Altman, Edward I. Corporate Financial Distress & Bankruptcy: A Complete Guide to Predicting & Avoiding Distress & Profiting from Bankruptcy. 2nd ed. LC 92-26897. 384p. 1993. 99.95 (*0-471-55253-4*) Wiley.

— Distressed Securities: Analyzing & Evaluating Market Potential & Investment Risk. (Institutional Investor Publications). 225p. 1991. text 60.00 (*1-55738-189-5*, Irwn Prfssnl) McGraw-Hill Prof.

— Handbook of Corporate Finance. LC 86-15978. (Professional Banking & Finance Ser.). 928p. 1986. 170.00 (*0-471-81957-3*) Wiley.

Altman, Edward I., ed. The High Yield Debt Market: Investment Performance & Economic Impact. 208p. 1990. 55.00 (*1-55623-235-7*, Irwn Prfssnl) McGraw-Hill Prof.

Altman, Edward I., et al, eds. Efficiency in the Municipal Bond Market: The Use of Tax Exempt Financing for Private Purposes. LC 80-82481. (Contemporary Studies in Economic & Financial Analysis: Vol. 30). 300p. 1981. 78.50 (*0-89232-168-7*) Jai Pr.

— Innovations in Bond Portfolio Management: Immunization & Duration Analysis. LC 82-81206. (Contemporary Studies in Economic & Financial Analysis: Vol. 41). 363p. 1983. 78.50 (*0-89232-320-5*) Jai Pr.

Altman, Edward I. & Kao, Duen L. Corporate Bond Rating Drift: An Examination of Rating Agency Credit Quality Changes over Time. (Orig.). 1991. pap. text 20.00 (*0-943205-12-3*) RFICFA.

Altman, Edward I. & Nammacher, Scott A. Investment in Junk Bonds: Inside the High Yield Debt Market. LC 86-15979. (Professional Banking & Finance Ser.). 257p. 1987. 24.95 (*0-471-84886-7*) Wiley.

Altman, Edward I. & Vanderhood, Irwin T. The Strategic Dynamics of the Insurance Industry: Asset & Liability Management Issues. 416p. 1996. text 75.00 (*0-7863-0463-4*, Irwn Prfssnl) McGraw-Hill Prof.

Altman, Edward I. & Vanderhoof, Irwin T. The Financial Dynamics of the Insurance Industry. LC 94-27616. 528p. 1994. text 65.00 (*1-55623-634-4*, Irwn Prfssnl) McGraw-Hill Prof.

Altman, Edward I. & Walter, Ingo I., eds. Contemporary Studies in Economic & Financial Analysis Vol. 42, Pt. A: Problems in Financing Small Business. 1984. 78.50 (*0-89232-390-6*) Jai Pr.

— Contemporary Studies in Economic & Financial Analysis Vol. 42, Pt. B: Sources of Financing for Small Business. 1983. 78.50 (*0-89232-391-4*) Jai Pr.

Altman, Edward I., et al. Application of Classification Techniques in Business, Banking & Finance. Walter, Ingo I., ed. LC 76-5759. (Contemporary Studies in Economic & Financial Analysis: Vol. 3). 440p. 1981. 78.50 (*0-89232-004-4*) Jai Pr.

Altman, Edward I., ed. see Ahlers, David M.

Altman, Edward I., ed. see Ahmad, Jaleel.

Altman, Edward I., ed. see Allen, Loring.

Altman, Edward I., ed. see Balabkins, Nicholas.

Altman, Edward I., ed. see Bierwag, G. O.

Altman, Edward I., ed. see Dreyer, Jacob S.

Altman, Edward I., ed. see Fewings, David R.

Altman, Edward I., ed. see Ghatak, Subrata.

Altman, Edward I., ed. see Gladwin, Thomas N.

Altman, Edward I., ed. see Hallwood, Paul.

Altman, Edward I., ed. see Hunt, Lacy H., 2nd.

Altman, Edward I., ed. see Kobrin, Stephen J.

Altman, Edward I., ed. see Levich, Richard M.

Altman, Edward I., ed. see Newfarmer, Richard.

Altman, Edward I., ed. see Oldfield, George S., Jr.

Altman, Edward I., ed. see Parry, Thomas G.

Altman, Edward I., ed. see Pastre, Olivier.

Altman, Edward I., ed. see Plaut, Steven E.

Altman, Edward I., ed. see Roxburgh, Nigel.

Altman, Edward I., ed. see Schwartz, Robert A. & Bloch, Ernest.

Altman, Edward I., ed. see Siebert, Horst, et al.

Altman, Edward I., ed. see Sinkey, Joseph F., Jr.

Altman, Edward I., ed. see Stapleton, Richard C. & Subrahmanyam, M. G.

Altman, Edward I., ed. see Thompson, John K.

Altman, Edward I., ed. see Uri, Noel D.

Altman, Edward I., ed. see Walker, William B.

Altman, Ellen, jt. auth. see Hernon, Peter.

Altman, Ellyn. Talk with Me: Giving the Gift of Language & Emotional Health to the Hearing-Impaired Child. LC 87-72929. 222p. (Orig.). 1988. pap. text 22.95 (*0-88200-163-9*) Alexander Graham.

Altman, Forrest. A Dog's Life: The Autobiography of Rusty the Ready (That Good Old Red-Haired River Dog) large type ed. LC 97-91035. (Illus.). 261p. (YA). (gr. 3-12). 1997. pap. 15.00 (*0-9652081-1-7*) Star Sq Pr.

***Altman, Forrest.** 26 Wilderness Adventures: Afoot & Afloat. Westerfield, Renee, ed. LC 99-96636. (Illus.). 220p. 1999. pap. 20.00 (*0-9652081-2-5*) Star Sq Pr.

Altman, Gail S. Beethoven: A Man of His Word: Undisclosed Evidence for His Immortal Beloved. LC 95-79083. 448p. 1996. 24.95 (*1-888071-01-X*) Anubian Pr.

— Beethoven: A Man of His Word: Undisclosed Evidence for His Immortal Beloved. LC 95-79083. (Illus.). 429p. 1996. pap. 17.95 (*1-888071-00-1*) Anubian Pr.

— Fatal Links: The Curious Deaths of Beethoven & the Two Napoleons. (Illus.). 228p. 1999. pap. 15.95 (*1-888071-02-8*) Anubian Pr.

Altman, Gaylene, jt. auth. see Delmar.

Altman, H. J., ed. Alzheimer's Disease: Problems, Prospects, & Perspectives. LC 87-15374. (Illus.). 412p. 1987. 95.00 (*0-306-42662-5*, Plenum Trade) Perseus Pubng.

Altman, H. J. & Altman, B. N., eds. Alzheimer's & Parkinson's Diseases: Recent Advances in Research & Clinical Management. (Illus.). 628p. (C). 198.00 (*0-306-43482-2*, Kluwer Plenum) Kluwer Academic.

— Alzheimer's & Parkinson's Diseases: Recent Advances in Research & Clinical Management. LC 90-7241. (Illus.). 604p. 1990. 145.00 (*0-306-83482-0*, Plenum Trade) Perseus Pubng.

Altman, I. & Christensen, K. Environment & Behavior Studies: Emergence of Intellectual Traditions. LC 90-7098. (Human Behavior & Environment: Advances in Theory & Research Ser.: Vol. 11). (Illus.). 392p. (C). 1990. 80.00 (*0-306-43468-7*, Plenum Trade) Perseus Pubng.

Altman, I. & Churchman, A. Women & the Environment. (Human Behavior & Environment Ser.: Vol. 13). (Illus.). 340p. (C). 1994. 54.50 (*0-306-44680-4*, Plenum Trade) Perseus Pubng.

Altman, I. & Low, S. M. Place Attachment. (Human Behavior & Environment: Advances in Theory & Research Ser.: Vol. 12). (Illus.). 336p. (C). 1992. 54.50 (*0-306-44071-7*, Kluwer Plenum) Kluwer Academic.

Altman, I. & Wohlwill, J. Elderly People & the Environment. (Human Behavior & Environment Ser.: Vol. 7). (Illus.). 362p. (C). 1984. 70.00 (*0-306-41429-5*, Plenum Trade) Perseus Pubng.

A

Altman, I. & Wohlwill, J. F. Behavior & the Natural Environment. LC 83-7285. (Human Behavior & Environment Ser.: Vol. 6). (Illus.). 362p. (C). 1983. 75.00 (*0-306-41099-0*, Plenum Trade) Perseus Pubng.

— Environment & Culture. LC 76-382942. (Human Behavior & Environment Ser.). (Illus.). 368p. (C). 1980. 80.00 (*0-306-40367-6*, Plenum Trade) Perseus Pubng.

— Home Environments. LC 85-12272. (Human Behavior & Environment Ser.: Vol. 8). (Illus.). 362p. (C). 1985. 70.00 (*0-306-41976-9*, Plenum Trade) Perseus Pubng.

— Neighborhood & Community Environments. LC 87-11276. (Human Behavior & Environment Ser.: Vol. 9). (Illus.). 320p. (C). 1987. 65.00 (*0-306-42513-0*, Plenum Trade) Perseus Pubng.

Altman, I. & Zube, E. H. Public Places & Spaces. (Human Behavior & Environment Ser.: Vol. 10). (Illus.). 334p. (C). 1989. 60.00 (*0-306-43079-7*, Plenum Trade) Perseus Pubng.

Altman, Ida. Emigrants & Society: Extremadura & Spanish America in the Sixteenth Century. 315p. (C). 1989. 55.00 (*0-520-06494-1*, Pub. by U CA Pr) Cal Prin Full Svc.

***Altman, Ida.** Transatlantic Ties in the Spanish Empire. LC 99-47891. 2000. 45.00 (*0-8047-3663-4*) Stanford U Pr.

Altman, Ida. A Word Dig. 48p. (J). (gr. 3-7). 1994. pap. text 2.95 (*0-9644604-0-8*) Strother Publ.

Altman, Ida, jt. ed. see Lockhart, James.

Altman, Ira. The Concept of Intelligence: A Philosophical Analysis. LC 97-9741. 104p. 1997. 36.50 (*0-7618-0736-5*); pap. 17.50 (*0-7618-0737-3*) U Pr of Amer.

***Altman, Ira.** Lectures in Philosophy: A Beginner's Guide to the Logic of Discourse & Disputation. 102p. 2000. pap. text 11.00i (*1-891877-07-0*) Sheron Ent.

Altman, Irving, et al. Investment Recovery. LC 76-26926. (AMA Management Briefing Ser.). 44p. reprint ed. pap. 30.00 (*0-608-13618-2*, 205130400094) Bks Demand.

Altman, Irwin. The Environment & Social Behavior. 256p. 1981. reprint ed. pap. text 15.95 (*0-8290-0639-7*) Irvington.

Altman, Irwin, et al, eds. Transportation & Behavior. LC 76-382942. (Human Behavior & Environment Ser.: Vol. 5). 304p. (C). 1982. 65.00 (*0-306-40773-6*, Plenum Trade) Perseus Pubng.

Altman, Irwin & Chemers, Martin M. Culture & Environment. (Environment & Behavior Ser.: No. 2). (Illus.). 337p. 1984. pap. text 27.95 (*0-521-31970-6*) Cambridge U Pr.

Altman, Irwin & Ginat, Joseph. Polygamous Families in Contemporary Society. (Illus.). 527p. (C). 1996. pap. text 27.95 (*0-521-56731-9*) Cambridge U Pr.

— Polygamous Families in Contemporary Society. (Illus.). 527p. (C). 1996. text 69.95 (*0-521-56169-8*) Cambridge U Pr.

Altman, Irwin, jt. ed. see Stokols, Daniel.

Altman, Irwin, ed. see Zube, Ervin H.

Altman, J. & Bayer, S. Development of the Cranial Nerve Ganglia & Related Nuclei in the Rat. (Advances in Anatomy, Embryology & Cell Biology Ser.: Vol. 74). (Illus.). 100p. 1982. 39.95 (*0-387-11337-1*) Spr-Verlag.

Altman, Jack. Pesticide Interactions in Crop Production. 592p. 1993. boxed set 229.00 (*0-8493-6339-X*, SB951) CRC Pr.

Altman, Jack, jt. auth. see Rumney, Laurence.

***Altman, Joan, et al.** Eye of the Storm: Essays in the Aftermath. Rickert, Ellen, ed. 228p. 2000. 19.95 (*1-928556-06-X*) Coastal NC.

***Altman, John.** A Gathering of Spies. LC 99-462174. (Illus.). 336p. 2000. 24.95 (*0-399-14641-5*) Putnam Pub Group.

Altman, Joseph. Organic Foundations of Animal Behavior. LC 65-18350. (Illus.). 1966. text 39.50 (*0-03-052230-7*) Irvington.

Altman, Joseph & Bayer, Shirley. Atlas of Prenatal Rat Brain Development. (Illus.). 664p. 1994. boxed set 152.95 (*0-8493-8993-3*) CRC Pr.

Altman, Joseph & Bayer, Shirley A. Development of the Cerebellar System: In Relation to Its Evolution, Structure & Functions. LC 96-28715. (Illus.). 800p. 1996. boxed set 179.95 (*0-8493-9490-2*) CRC Pr.

Altman, Joseph, jt. auth. see Bayer, Shirley A.

Altman, Joyce & Goldberg, Sue. Dear Bronx Zoo. (J). (gr. 4-7). 1992. pap. 3.50 (*0-380-71649-6*, Avon Bks) Morrow Avon.

Altman, Laurie. Jazz Moments, Bk. 1. 24p. 1994. pap. text 5.95 (*0-87487-577-3*) Summy-Birchard.

— Jazz Moments, Bk. 2. 24p. 1994. pap. text 5.95 (*0-87487-578-1*) Summy-Birchard.

Altman, Lawrence K. Who Goes First? The Story of Self-Experimentation in Medicine. LC 97-42122. 454p. 1998. pap. 17.95 (*0-520-21281-9*, Pub. by U CA Pr) Cal Prin Full Svc.

Altman, Leon L. The Dream in Psychoanalysis. rev. ed. LC 75-13572. 280p. (Orig.). 1975. 42.50 (*0-8236-1431-X*) Intl Univs Pr.

***Altman, Linda.** The Legend of Freedom Hill. (Illus.). 32p. (J). (ps-5). 2000. 15.95 (*1-58430-003-5*, Pub. by Lee & Low Bks) Publishers Group.

Altman, Linda, ed. see Bass, Maureen.

Altman, Linda J. Amelia's Road. LC 92-59982. (Illus.). 32p. (J). (ps-5). 1993. 15.95 (*1-880000-04-0*) Lee & Low Bks.

— Amelia's Road. LC 92-59982. (Illus.). 32p. (J). (gr. k-5). 1995. pap. 6.95 (*1-880000-27-X*) Lee & Low Bks.

— The California Gold Rush in American History. LC 96-54262. (In American History Ser.). (Illus.). (YA). (gr. 5 up). 1997. lib. bdg. 20.95 (*0-89490-878-2*) Enslow Pubs.

— El Camino de Amelia. Santacruz, Daniel M., tr. LC 93-38627. (SPA., Illus.). 32p. (J). (ps-5). 1994. 15.95 (*1-880000-07-5*); pap. 6.95 (*1-880000-10-5*) Lee & Low Bks.

— The Creation of Israel. LC 97-46033. (World History Ser.). (YA). 1998. 22.45 (*1-56006-288-6*) Lucent Bks.

***Altman, Linda J.** Death: An Introduction to Medical-Ethical Dilemmas. LC 99-32714. (Issues in Focus Ser.). (Illus.). 112p. (gr. 6 up). 2000. lib. bdg. 20.95 (*0-7660-1246-8*) Enslow Pubs.

Altman, Linda J. Decade That Roared. LC 97-8727. (History & Social Studies). 112p. (YA). (gr. 7 up). 1997. 21.40 (*0-8050-4133-8*) TFC Bks NY.

— Forever Outsiders: Jews & History from Ancient Times to August 1935. Shulman, William, ed. LC 96-48179. (Holocaust Ser.). (Illus.). 80p. (YA). (gr. 7 up). 1997. lib. bdg. 19.45 (*1-56711-200-5*) Blackbirch.

— Genocide: The Systematic Killing of a People. LC 95-6941. (Issues in Focus Ser.). (Illus.). 112p. (YA). (gr. 6 up). 1995. lib. bdg. 20.95 (*0-89490-664-X*) Enslow Pubs.

— The Holocaust Ghettos. LC 97-37638. (Holocaust Remembered Ser.). (Illus.). 128p. (YA). (gr. 6 up). 1998. lib. bdg. 20.95 (*0-89490-994-0*) Enslow Pubs.

— The Holocaust, Hitler & Nazi Germany. LC 98-54629. (Holocaust Remembered Ser.). (Illus.). 112p. (YA). (gr. 6 up). 1999. lib. bdg. 20.95 (*0-7660-1230-1*) Enslow Pubs.

— Life on an Israeli Kibbutz. (Way People Live Ser.). (Illus.). 112p. (J). (gr. 5-12). 1996. lib. bdg. 22.45 (*1-56006-328-9*) Lucent Bks.

— Mr. Darwin's Voyage. (People in Focus Ser.). (Illus.). (YA). (gr. 5 up). 1995. pap. 7.95 (*0-382-24962-3*, Dillon Silver Burdett) Silver Burdett Pr.

Altman, Linda J. Mr. Darwin's Voyage. LC 94-27367. (J). (gr. 1-8). 1995. 13.95 (*0-87518-609-2*, Dillon Silver Burdett) Silver Burdett Pr.

Altman, Linda J. Nobody Wants Annie. (Sundown Fiction Collection). (Illus.). (J). (gr. 3). 1993. 3.95 (*0-88336-209-0*) New Readers.

— Plague & Pestilence: A History of Infectious Disease. LC 98-12677. (Issues in Focus Ser.). (Illus.). 128p. (YA). (gr. 6-12). 1998. lib. bdg. 20.95 (*0-89490-957-6*) Enslow Pubs.

— The Pullman Strike of 1894: Turning Point for American Labor. (Spotlight on American History Ser.). (Illus.). 64p. (J). (gr. 4-6). 1994. lib. bdg. 21.90 (*1-56294-346-4*) Millbrook Pr.

— Slavery & Abolition in American History. LC 99-19885. (In American History Ser.). (Illus.). 128p. (YA). (gr. 5 up). 1999. lib. bdg. 20.95 (*0-7660-1124-0*) Enslow Pubs.

— Small Dogs. LC 97-40463. (Perfect Pets Ser.). (J). 1999. lib. bdg. 22.79 (*0-7614-0795-2*) Marshall Cavendish.

— Women Inventors. LC 96-20460. (American Profiles Ser.). (Illus.). 144p. (J). (gr. 5-12). 1997. 19.95 (*0-8160-3385-4*) Facts on File.

***Altman, Linda Jacobs.** Alzheimer's Disease. LC 00-9237. (Diseases & Disorders Ser.). (Illus.). (J). 2000. write for info. (*1-56006-695-4*) Lucent Bks.

— Amelia's Road. 1993. 12.15 (*0-606-08913-6*, Pub. by Turtleback) Demco.

— Arkansas, 5 vols. , Set. LC 98-43959. (Celebrate the States Ser.). (Illus.). 144p. (J). (gr. 4-7). 2000. lib. bdg. 35.64 (*0-7614-0672-7*, Benchmark NY) Marshall Cavendish.

— Big Dogs. Mavrikis, Peter, ed. LC 99-49674. (Perfect Pets Ser.). (Illus.). 32p. (J). (gr. 1-4). 2001. lib. bdg. 22.79 (*0-7614-1101-1*, Benchmark NY) Marshall Cavendish.

— El Camino De Amelia. 1993. 11.15 (*0-606-08918-7*, Pub. by Turtleback) Demco.

— Parrots. Mavrikis, Peter, ed. LC 99-49672. (Perfect Pets Ser.). (Illus.). 32p. (J). (gr. 1-4). 2001. lib. bdg. 22.79 (*0-7614-1102-X*, Benchmark NY) Marshall Cavendish.

Altman, Louis & Callman, Rudolf. Callmann Unfair Competition, Trademarks & Monopolies: 1981-1989, 9 vols., Set. 4th ed. LC 81-7639. (IP Ser.). 1981. ring bd. 1195.00 (*0-685-24625-6*) West Group.

Altman, M. Dicionario Tecnico Contabil - Portugues-Ingles, Ingles-Portugues: Portuguese-English, English-Portuguese Techncal Accounting Dictionary. (ENG & POR.). 126p. 1990. pap. 35.00 (*0-8288-4017-2*, M9355) Fr & Eur.

Altman, Marjorie & Crocker, Ruth, eds. Social Groupwork & Alcoholism. LC 82-2998. (Social Work with Groups Ser.: Vol. 5, No. 1). 92p. 1982. text 39.95 (*0-917724-94-1*) Haworth Pr.

— Social Groupwork & Alcoholism. LC 82-2998. (Social Work with Groups Ser.: Vol. 5, No. 1). 92p. 1985. pap. text 14.95 (*0-86656-439-X*) Haworth Pr.

Altman, Mark A. Trek Navigator: The Ultimate Guide to the Entire Trek Saga. LC 97-17888. 304p. 1998. pap. 13.95 (*0-316-03812-1*) Little.

Altman, Mark A., jt. auth. see Gross, Edward.

Altman, Mark A., jt. auth. see Gross, Edward A.

Altman, Mary A. & Weil, Robert I. How to Manage Your Law Office. 1973. ring bd. 215.00 (*0-8205-1356-3*) Bender.

Altman, Maya, et al. How Do I Pay for My Long Term Health Care. (Illus.). 120p. 1988. pap. 12.95 (*0-9620825-0-3*) Berkeley Planning Assocs.

Altman, Mieczyslaw. Contractors & Contractor Directions Theory & Applications: A New Approach to Solving Equations. LC 77-21442. (Lecture Notes in Pure & Applied Mathematics Ser.: Vol. 32). 304p. reprint ed. pap. 94.30 (*0-608-08909-5*, 206954400005) Bks Demand.

— A Theory of Optimization & Optimal Control for Nonlinear Evolution & Singular Operator Equations. 292p. (C). 1990. text 48.00 (*981-02-0326-8*) World Scientific Pub.

Altman, Mike, jt. auth. see Green, Larry.

Altman, Mike, ed. see Hogan, Chuck.

Altman, Millys N. Racing in Her Blood. LC 79-3018. (YA). (gr. 7 up). 1980. lib. bdg. 12.89 (*0-397-31895-2*) HarpC Child Bks.

Altman, Morris. Human Agency & Material Welfare: Revisions in Microeconomics & Their Implications for Public Policy. LC 96-41255. (Illus.). 152p. (C). 1996. lib. bdg. 97.00 (*0-7923-9818-1*) Kluwer Academic.

Altman, Moses S. The Undying Swan: Selected Poems in Russian. Mamantov, Ilya A., ed. LC PG3476.A395N. (RUS.). 254p. reprint ed. pap. 78.80 (*0-8357-7065-6*, 200898100086) Bks Demand.

Altman, N., et al, eds. Technology & Work in German Industry. 432p. (C). 1992. pap. 81.95 (*0-415-07926-8*, A7403) Thomson Learn.

Altman, Nathaniel. The Deva Handbook: How to Work with Nature's Subtle Energies. (Illus.). 192p. 1995. pap. 12.95 (*0-89281-552-3*, Destiny Bks) Inner Tradit.

***Altman, Nathaniel.** Healing Springs: The Ultimate Guide to Taking the Waters. (Illus.). 320p. 2000. pap. 18.95 (*0-89281-836-0*) Inner Tradit.

— The Little Giant Encyclopedia of Meditations & Blessings. LC 99-44618. (Illus.). 512p. 2000. pap. 9.95 (*0-8069-6517-7*) Sterling.

Altman, Nathaniel. The Little Giant Encyclopedia of Names. 512p. (J). 1999. 9.95 (*0-8069-9840-7*) Sterling.

— The Little Giant Encyclopedia of Palmistry. rev. ed. LC 98-44562. (Little Giant Ser.). (Illus.). 1999. pap. 9.95 (*0-8069-6161-9*) Sterling.

— Oxygen Healing Therapies: For Optimum Health & Vitality. expanded rev. ed. LC 98-23505. 296p. 1998. pap. 14.95 (*0-89281-793-3*, Heal Arts VT) Inner Tradit.

— The Palmistry Workbook. (Workbook Ser.). (Illus.). 160p. 1984. pap. 14.95 (*0-85030-352-4*) Sterling.

— Sacred Trees. LC 93-28182. (Illus.). 288p. (Orig.). 1994. pap. 16.00 (*0-87156-470-X*, Pub. by Sierra) Random.

***Altman, Nathaniel.** Sacred Trees: Spirituality, Wisdom & Well-Being. 2000. pap. 14.95 (*0-8069-7809-0*) Sterling.

Altman, Nathaniel. Terapias de Oxigeno.Tr. of Oxygen Healing Therapies. (ENG & SPA., Illus.). 1995. pap. 12.95 (*0-89281-472-1*) Inner Tradit.

Altman, Nathaniel, jt. auth. see Epstein, Donald M.

Altman, Nathaniel, jt. auth. see Rosa, Jose.

Altman, Neil. The Analyst in the Inner City: Race, Class & Culture Through a Psychoanalytic Lens. (Relational Perspectives Book Ser.: Vol. 3). 188p. 1995. 36.00 (*0-88163-173-6*) Analytic Pr.

Altman, P. & Katz, D. Inbred & Genetically Defined Strains of Laboratory Animals Pt. 1: Mouse & Rat. LC 78-73555. (Biological Handbks.: Vol. 3: 1). 1979. reprint ed. 193.00 (*0-08-030073-1*, Pub. by Pergamon Repr) Franklin.

Altman, Patricia & West, Caroline. Threads of Identity: Maya Costume of the 1960s in Highland Guatemala. LC 92-72523. (Illus.). 192p. (C). 1992. 45.00 (*0-930741-23-4*); pap. 27.00 (*0-930741-24-2*) UCLA Fowler Mus.

Altman, Patrick, jt. auth. see Green, Nancy L.

Altman, Paul M., jt. auth. see Lubaroff, Martin I.

Altman, Paula, ed. Energy Education Resources: Kindergarten Through 12th Grade (1996) (Illus.). 104p. (Orig.). (C). 1996. pap. text 20.00 (*0-7881-3033-1*) DIANE Pub.

***Altman, Paula, ed.** Energy Education Resources: Kindergarten Through 12th Grade (1998) 102p. (C). 1999. pap. text 15.00 (*0-7881-8233-1*) DIANE Pub.

Altman, Penny, jt. auth. see Friedman, Ronald J.

Altman, Ralph. Availability for Work: A Study in Unemployment Compensation. LC 68-8935. (Illus.). 350p. 1969. reprint ed. lib. bdg. 69.50 (*0-8371-0004-6*, ALAW, Greenwood Pr) Greenwood.

Altman, Rebecca Bridges. PowerPoint 2000/98 for Windows & Macintosh: Visual QuickStart Guide. 250p. 1999. pap. text 17.99 (*0-201-35441-1*) Peachpit Pr.

Altman, Reuben, jt. auth. see Prehm, Herbert J.

Altman, Richard M. Creating Investor Demand for Company Stock: A Guide for Financial Managers. LC 86-25566. 413p. 1988. 79.50 (*0-89930-173-8*, ACI/, Quorum Bks) Greenwood.

— Investor Response to Management Decisions: A Research-Based Analysis of Actions & Effects. LC 90-8874. 392p. 1992. 69.50 (*0-89930-448-6*, AIR/, Quorum Bks) Greenwood.

Altman, Rick. The American Film Musical. LC 86-45473. (Illus.). 400p. 1987. 59.95 (*0-253-30413-X*); pap. 24.95 (*0-253-20514-X*, MB 514) Ind U Pr.

— The American Film Musical. LC 86-45473. (Illus.). 396p. Date not set. reprint ed. pap. 122.80 (*0-608-20577-X*, 2054492) Bks Demand.

— Film Genre. LC 99-229768. (Distributed for the British Film Institute Ser.). 272p. 1999. pap. 22.50 (*0-85170-717-3*, Pub. by British Film Inst) Ind U Pr.

— Film/Genre. LC 99-229768. (Distributed for the British Film Institute Ser.). 272p. 1999. text 65.00 (*0-85170-718-1*, Pub. by British Film Inst) Ind U Pr.

— Mastering CorelDraw 8. 4th ed. LC 97-81023. 960p. 1998. pap. text 49.99 (*0-7821-2208-6*) Sybex.

***Altman, Rick.** Mastering CorelDraw 9. (Mastering Ser.). 944p. 1999. 39.99 (*0-7821-2520-4*) Sybex.

Altman, Rick. Sound Theory - Sound Practice. 256p. (C). 1992. pap. 19.99 (*0-415-90457-9*) Routledge.

Altman, Rick, ed. Genre: The Musical. (BFI Readers in Film Ser.). 180p. 1983. pap. 13.95 (*0-7100-0817-1*, Routledge Thoemms) Routledge.

Altman, Robert. The Quintessential Cat. 1996. pap. text 14.95 (*0-02-861446-1*) Macmillan.

Altman, Robert. Ready to Wear - Pret-a-Porter. (Illus.). 190p. (J). 1995. pap. 19.45 (*0-7868-8103-8*, Pub. by Hyperion) Time Warner.

Altman, Robert B. & Forbes, Neil A., eds. Self-Assessment Color Review of Avian Medicine. (Illus.). 192p. 1998. pap. 34.95 (*0-8138-2339-0*) Iowa St U Pr.

Altman, Robert B., et al. Avian Medicine & Surgery. Valkoff, Sandra, ed. 720p. 1996. text 99.00 (*0-7216-5446-0*, W B Saunders Co) Harcrt Hlth Sci Grp.

***Altman, Roberta.** Jump, Wiggle, Twirl & Giggle: 25 Easy & Irresistible Movement Activities That Teach Early Concentration. (Illus.). (J). 2000. pap. 14.95 (*0-590-01972-4*) Scholastic Inc.

Altman, Roberta. The Prostate Answer Book. 176p. (Orig.). 1993. mass mkt. 5.50 (*0-446-36408-8*, Pub. by Warner Bks) Little.

— The Quintessential Cat: A Connoisseur's Guide to the Cat in History, Art, Literature, Legend. LC 94-14095. (Illus.). 304p. 1994. 27.50 (*0-671-85008-3*) Macmillan.

— Waking up, Fighting Back: The Politics of Breast Cancer. 1996. 23.95 (*0-614-97048-2*) Little.

Altman, Roberta & Sarg, Michael J. The Cancer Dictionary. (Illus.). 360p. 1994. reprint ed. pap. 16.95 (*0-8160-3027-8*) Facts on File.

***Altman, Roberta & Sarg, Michael J.** Cancer Dictionary. rev. ed. LC 99-21201. (Illus.). 400p. 1999. text 40.00 (*0-8160-3953-4*, Checkmark); pap. text 19.95 (*0-8160-3954-2*, Checkmark) Facts on File.

Altman, Russ, ed. Proceedings of the Second International Conference on Intelligent Systems for Molecular Biology. (Illus.). 408p. (Orig.). 1995. pap. text 45.00 (*0-929280-68-7*) AAAI Pr.

Altman, Russ B. Biocomputing '99: Proceedings of the Pacific Symposium. (Computer Science Ser.). 1999. 118.00 (*981-02-3624-7*) World Scientific Pub.

Altman, Russ B., et al, eds. Biocomputing '98: Proceedings of the Pacific Symposium Maui, Hawaii, U. S. A. 4-9 January, 1998. 600p. 1998. 138.00 (*981-02-3278-0*) World Scientific Pub.

Altman, Samuel P., ed. Orbital Hodograph Analysis. (Science & Technology Ser.: Vol. 3). 150p. 1965. 20.00 (*0-87703-031-6*, Am Astronaut Soc) Univelt Inc.

Altman, Sandra. Enlightenment: Step-by-Step. 1996. write for info. (*1-880546-08-6*) Miracles Pr.

— Illumination: A Journey in the Light. Neff, Joanna, ed. 180p. (Orig.). 1994. pap. 12.95 (*1-880546-07-8*) Miracles Pr.

— Revelation: A Call to Awaken. Neff, Joanna, ed. 272p. (Orig.). 1991. pap. 15.95 (*1-880546-05-1*) Miracles Pr.

***Altman-Sauer, Lydian, et al.** Twenty Questions Nonprofits Often Ask about Working with Local Government. (C). 2000. pap. write for info. (*1-56011-379-0*) Institute Government.

Altman, Seymour, jt. auth. see Altman, Violet.

Altman, Sheldon. Acupuncture for Animals. 300p. 25.00 (*0-317-31551-X*) Chans Corp.

Altman, Sheryl. Way Too Much Information: A Fanatic's Guide to Dawson's Creek. 128p. (YA). (gr. 5 up). 1998. pap. 4.50 (*0-06-107137-4*) HarpC Child Bks.

Altman, Sig. Comic Image of the Jew: Explorations of a Pop Culture Phenomenon. LC 71-146161. 234p. 1975. 29.50 (*0-8386-7869-6*) Fairleigh Dickinson.

Altman, Stephen E. Equal Employment Opportunity: Rising Trends in EEO Complaint Caseloads in the Federal Sector. (Illus.). 65p. (C). 1999. text 20.00 (*0-7881-7741-9*) DIANE Pub.

***Altman, Stephen E., ed.** Alternative Dispute Resolution (ADR) Employers' Experiences with ADR in the Workplace. 81p. (C). 1999. pap. text 20.00 (*0-7881-4087-6*) DIANE Pub.

***Altman, Steven.** The Touch. 2000. 14.00 (*0-7434-0715-6*, Pub. by ibooks) S&S Trade.

Altman, Stuart. Regulating Managed Care: Theory, Practice, & Future Options. LC 99-24496. (Jossey-Bass Health Ser.). 400p. 1999. text 45.95 (*0-7879-4783-0*) Jossey-Bass.

Altman, Stuart H., et al, eds. The Future U. S. Healthcare System: Who Will Care for the Poor & Uninsured? LC 97-23221. 426p. 1997. pap. text 50.00 (*1-56793-067-0*, PUSHS-1009) Health Admin Pr.

Altman, Stuart H. & Reinhardt, Uwe E., eds. Strategic Choices for a Changing Health Care System. LC 96-2630. (Baxter Health Policy Review Ser.: Vol. 2). 413p. 1996. 54.00 (*1-56793-040-9*, 0975) Health Admin Pr.

Altman, Susan. The Encyclopedia of African-American Heritage. LC 96-15459. 320p. (J). (gr. 5-12). 40.00 (*0-8160-3289-0*) Facts on File.

— The Encyclopedia of African-American Heritage. (Illus.). 320p. (J). (gr. 5-12). 1998. reprint ed. pap. 18.95 (*0-8160-3824-4*) Facts on File.

***Altman, Susan.** Encyclopedia of African-American Heritage. 2nd ed. (Illus.). 352p. 2000. 40.00 (*0-8160-4125-3*) Facts on File.

Altman, Susan. Extraordinary Black Americans from Colonial to Contemporary Times. LC 88-11977. (Extraordinary People Ser.). (Illus.). 240p. (J). (gr. 6 up). 1989. lib. bdg. 37.00 (*0-516-00581-2*) Childrens.

— Extraordinary Black Americans from Colonial to Contemporary Times. (Extraordinary People Ser.). (Illus.). 208p. (YA). (gr. 6 up). 1993. pap. 16.95 (*0-516-40581-0*) Childrens.

Altman, Tim, jt. auth. see McAllister, Dawson.

Altman, Tracy A. FDA & USDA Nutrition Labeling Guide: Decision Diagrams, Checklists, & Regulations. LC 98-85935. 480p. 1998. 99.95 (*1-56676-706-7*) Technomic.

Altman, Violet & Altman, Seymour. The Book of Buffalo Pottery. rev. ed. LC 70-75071. (Illus.). 192p. 1987. 27.50 (*0-88740-088-4*) Schiffer.

Altman, Walter Forrest. The Dan River Book: Odyssey, Epic, Guide. 4th ed. LC 96-203994. (Illus.). 320p. 1998. pap. 20.00 (*0-9652081-0-9*) Star Sq Pr.

Altmann, Alexander. Essays in Jewish Intellectual History. LC 80-54471. 334p. reprint ed. pap. 103.60 (*0-608-09586-9*, 205438800005) Bks Demand.

— The Meaning of Jewish Existence: Theological Essays, 1930-1939. Ivry, Alfred L., ed. Ehrlich, Edith & Ehrlich,

An Asterisk (*) at the beginning of an entry indicates that the title is appearing for the first time.

Leonard H., trs. from GER. LC 90-28748. (Tauber Institute Ser.: No. 12). 219p. 1991. text 45.00 (*0-87451-554-8*) U Pr of New Eng.

— Moses Mendelssohn: A Biographical Study. (Illus.). 914p. 1998. pap. 34.95 (*1-874774-53-6*, Pub. by Littman Lib) Intl Spec Bk.

— Studies in Religious Philosophy & Mysticism. (New Reprints in Essay & General Literature Index Ser.). 1977. reprint ed. 26.95 (*0-518-10194-0*) Ayer.

Altmann, Alexander, ed. Jewish Medieval & Renaissance Studies. LC 67-13250. (Philip W. Lown Institute of Advanced Judaic Studies, Brandeis University, Studies & Texts: No. 4). 392p. reprint ed. pap. 121.60 (*0-7837-2216-8*, 205730600004) Bks Demand.

Altmann, Anna E., jt. auth. see De Vos, Gail.

Altmann, Barbara K. The Love Debate Poems of Christine de Pizan. LC 97-43642. 336p. 1998. 49.95 (*0-8130-1578-2*) U Press Fla.

Altmann, Edward & Hallesky, George J. Sentence Analysis with Technical Examples. 222p. (C). 1995. text 27.00 (*0-536-58694-2*) Pearson Custom.

Altmann, Gabriel & Koch, Walter A., eds. Systems: New Paradigms for the Human Sciences. LC 98-12728. 781p. 1998. 153.00 (*3-11-015619-9*) De Gruyter.

Altmann, Gerry T. The Ascent of Babel: An Exploration of Language, Mind & Understanding. LC 97-10427. (Illus.). 270p. (C). 1997. 27.50 (*0-19-852378-5*) OUP.

— Cognitive Models of Speech Processing: Psycholinguistic & Computational Perspectives on the Lexicon. 892p. 1998. 49.95 (*0-86377-975-1*) Taylor & Francis.

Altmann, Gerry T., ed. Cognitive Models of Speech Processing: Psycholinguistic & Computational Perspectives. (Series ACL-MIT in Natural Language Processing). 552p. 1995. pap. text 26.50 (*0-262-51084-7*, Bradford Bks) MIT Pr.

Altmann, Gerry T. M. The Ascent of Babel: An Exploration of Language, Mind, & Understanding. (Illus.). 272p. 1999. pap. text 17.95 (*0-19-852377-7*) OUP.

Altmann, Jeanne. Baboon Mothers & Infants. LC 79-21568. (Illus.). 256p. 1980. 34.95 (*0-674-05856-9*) HUP.

— Baboon Mothers & Infants. LC 79-21568. (Illus.). 256p. 1981. pap. 15.95 (*0-674-05857-7*) HUP.

Altmann, Jurgen, ed. Verification at Vienna: Monitoring Reductions of Conventional Armed Forces. xiii, 396p. 1992. text 88.00 (*2-88124-539-0*) Gordon & Breach.

Altmann, Jurgen, et al, eds. Verification after the Cold War: Broadening the Process. LC 95-101531. 400p. 1994. pap. 49.50 (*90-5383-291-2*, Pub. by VU Univ Pr) Paul & Co Pubs.

Altmann, M. R. Portuguese & English Accounting Dictionary (Diccionario Tecnico Contabile) (ENG & POR.). 126p. 1987. reprint ed. pap. 35.00 (*85-224-0254-X*, M9355) Fr & Eur.

Altmann, Patricia & Luciano, Lisa. Ready-to-Use Literature Activities: With Techniques & Ideas for Using Video in the Classroom. 264p. 1988. pap. text 27.95 (*0-87628-779-8*) Ctr Appl Res.

— Ready to Use Literature Activities for Grades 7-12 with Techniques & Ideas for Using Video in the Classroom. 264p. 1988. pap., student ed. 24.95 (*0-685-22934-3*) P-H.

Altmann, Scott, tr. see Roques, Henri.

Altmann, Simon L. Band Theory of Metals. (C). 1970. 121.00 (*0-08-015602-9*, Pub. by Pergamon Repr) Franklin.

— Band Theory of Solids: An Introduction from the Point of View of Symmetry. (Illus.). 300p. 1994. reprint ed. pap. text 45.00 (*0-19-855866-X*) OUP.

Altmann, Simon L. Icons & Symmetries. (Illus.). 116p. 1992. text 45.00 (*0-19-855599-7*) OUP.

Altmann, Simon L. & Herzig, Peter. Point-Group Theory Tables. (Illus.). 716p. 1994. text 145.00 (*0-19-855226-2*) OUP.

Altmann, Stuart A. Foraging for Survival. LC 97-45726. 609p. 1998. 70.00 (*0-226-01595-5*) U Ch Pr.

— Foraging for Survival: Yearling Baboons in Africa. LC 97-45726. 610p. 2000. pap. text 40.00 (*0-226-01596-3*) U Ch Pr.

Altmann, Stuart A., ed. Social Communication among Primates. LC 65-25120. (Midway Reprint Ser.). (Illus.). xiv, 392p. (C). 1982. pap. text 18.00 (*0-226-01597-1*) U Ch Pr.

— Social Communication among Primates. LC 65-25120. (Illus.). 406p. reprint ed. pap. 125.90 (*0-608-09258-4*, 205406000002) Bks Demand.

Altmann, Walter. Die Romischen Grabaltare der Kaiserzeit. LC 75-10626. (Ancient Religion & Mythology Ser.). (GER., Illus.). 1976. reprint ed. 22.95 (*0-405-07002-0*) Ayer.

Altmann, Wilhelm, ed. see Haydn, Joseph.

Altmansberger, Harold N. & Wallace, Marc J., Jr. Designing a Goalsharing Program Vol. 43: An Approach to Rewarding Employees for Achieving Business Goals. (Building Blocks Ser.). (Illus.). 1998. pap. 24.95 (*1-57963-050-2*, A0243) Am Compensation.

Altmeyer, A. P., jt. auth. see Bucksch, Herbert.

Altmeyer, Arthur J. The Formative Years of Social Security. LC 66-11801. 332p. 1966. reprint ed. pap. 103.00 (*0-608-01932-1*, 206258700003) Bks Demand.

Altmeyer, P., et al, eds. Ultrasound in Dermatology. (Illus.). 544p. 1992. 272.00 (*0-387-53750-3*) Spr-Verlag.

Altmeyer, P., et al. Wound Healing & Skin Physiology. LC 94-29175. 1995. 178.00 (*0-387-56124-2*) Spr-Verlag.

Altmeyer, Peter, et al, eds. Skin Cancer & UV-Radiation. LC 97-10068. (Illus.). 1300p. 1997. text 225.00 (*3-540-62723-5*) Spr-Verlag.

Altner, Manfred. Hermynia Zur Muhlen: Eine Biographie. 1997. 33.95 (*3-906756-07-6*, Pub. by P Lang) P Lang Pubng.

Altner, Patricia. Vampire Readings: An Annotated Bibliography. (Illus.). 144p. 1998. pap. 19.50 (*0-8108-3504-5*) Scarecrow.

Alto, Marta, jt. auth. see Palmer, Pati.

***Altobello, Brian.** In the Shadows Furious: The Brutal Battle for New Georgia. (Illus.). 400p. 2000. 29.95 (*0-89141-717-6*) Presidio Pr.

Altobello, Patricia & Pierce, Deirdre. Literary Sands of Key West. (Literary Cities Ser.). (Illus.). 80p. (Orig.). 1996. pap. 8.95 (*1-57359-004-5*, Starrhill Press) Black Belt Communs.

Altoff, Gerard T. Amongst My Best Men: African-Americans & the War of 1812. LC 95-69728. (Illus.). 201p. (Orig.). 1996. pap. 12.95 (*1-887794-02-6*) Perry Grp.

— Deep Water Sailors - Shallow Water Soldiers: Manning the United States Fleet on Lake Erie - 1813. LC 92-83902. (Illus.). 203p. 1993. pap. 10.95 (*1-887794-01-8*) Perry Grp.

— Oliver Hazard Perry & the Battle of Lake Erie. (Illus.). 38p. 1990. pap. 2.50 (*1-887794-00-X*) Perry Grp.

Altoff, Gerard T., jt. auth. see Skaggs, David C.

Altoff, Gerard T., jt. auth. see Skaggs, David Curtis.

***Altom, Tim.** Programming with Python. 1999. pap. 34.99 (*0-7615-2334-0*) Prima Pub.

Altoma, Salih J. Problems of Diglossia in Arabic: A Comparative Study of Classical & Iraqi Arabic. LC 69-11663. (Middle Eastern Monographs: No. 21). 177p. (C). 1969. pap. 4.50 (*0-674-70775-3*) HUP.

Altomare, Francesco & Campiti, Michele. Korovkin-Type Approximation Theory & Its Applications. LC 94-16853. (Studies in Mathematics: Vol. 17). xi, 672p. 1994. 157.95 (*3-11-014178-7*) De Gruyter.

Altomare, Mary, jt. auth. see Naijrass, Brian.

Alton, et al, eds. Ovidii, Nasonis: Fastorum Libri Sex. (LAT.). 1997. pap. 29.95 (*3-8154-1568-3*, T1568, Pub. by B G Teubner) U of Mich Pr.

Alton, Albert. In God's Hands. Garfield Publications Staff, ed. (Illus.). 272p. (Orig.). 1984. pap. 5.95 (*0-9609856-1-1*) Garfield Pubns.

Alton, Bruce S., ed. Religions & Languages: A Colloquium. LC 91-18280. (Toronto Studies in Religion: Vol. 13). XII, 165p. 1991. 39.95 (*0-8204-1695-9*) P Lang Pubng.

Alton, Connie & Greene, Woody. Computer Concepts. (Illus.). 50p. 1997. pap. text 7.00 (*1-887281-52-5*) Labyrinth CA.

***Alton, David.** Citizen Virtues. 1999. 29.95 (*0-00-274019-2*, Pub. by HarpC) Trafalgar.

Alton, G. G. & Jones, Lois M. Laboratory Techniques in Brucellosis. 2nd ed. (Monographs: No. 55). (ENG, FRE, RUS & SPA., Illus.). 92p. 1975. pap. text 35.00 (*92-4-140055-2*, 1140055) World Health.

Alton, H. Moving Pictures: Trigger Pictures to Help Children Talk about Moves in There Life. 1987. 50.00 (*0-903534-73-8*, Pub. by Brit Ag for Adopt & Fost) St Mut.

Alton, Jay. Thunder Hawk. LC 97-200188. (Illus.). 218p. (J). (ps-12). 1997. pap. 13.95 (*0-912382-34-1*) Black Letter.

Alton, John. Living Qigong: The Chinese Way to Good Health & Long Life. LC 96-47018. (Illus.). 192p. 1997. pap. 19.95 (*1-57062-106-3*, Pub. by Shambhala Pubns) Random.

— Painting with Light. LC 93-41275. 1994. 60.00 (*0-520-08630-9*, Pub. by U CA Pr); pap. 24.95 (*0-520-08949-9*, Pub. by U CA Pr) Cal Prin Full Svc.

Alton, L., jt. auth. see Gorodner, B.

Alton, Robert. Violin & Cello Building & Repairing. 1988. reprint ed. lib. bdg. 59.00 (*0-7812-0517-4*) Rprt Serv.

— Violin & Cello Building & Repairing. 1976. reprint ed. lib. bdg. 59.00 (*0-403-03758-1*) Scholarly.

Alton, Tim. Electricity for Heating, Ventilation & Air. LC 97-24649. 691p. (C). 1997. 105.00 (*0-13-524893-0*) P-H.

Alton, Walter G., Jr. Malpractice: A Trial Lawyer's Advice for Physicians. 1977. 21.50 (*0-316-03500-9*, Little Brwn Med Div) Lppncott W & W.

Altoon, Ronald A. International Shopping Center Architecture: Details, Concepts, & Projects. (Illus.). 192p. 1996. 69.95 (*0-934590-81-8*) Visual Refer.

***Altopp, David.** Coach Quotes for Baseball. 135p. 2000. pap. 9.95 (*1-57167-428-4*) Coaches Choice.

***Altorki, Soraya & Cole, Donald.** Beddouin, Settlers, & Holiday-Makers: Egypt's Changing Northwest Coast. LC 98-961187. 256p. 1998. pap. 19.50 (*977-424-484-2*, Pub. by Am Univ Cairo Pr) Col U Pr.

Altorki, Soraya & El-Solh, Camillia F., eds. Arab Women in the Field: Studying Your Own Society. 200p. 1988. 45.00 (*0-8156-2449-2*); pap. 19.95 (*0-8156-2450-6*) Syracuse U Pr.

Altorki, Soraya, jt. auth. see Nelson, Cynthia.

Altose, M. D. & Kawakami, Y., eds. Control of Breathing in Health & Disease. LC 99-32707. (Lung Biology in Health & Disease Ser.). (Illus.). 800p. 1999. text 225.00 (*0-8247-9854-6*) Dekker.

Altounyan, R. E., ed, see Asthma & Chronic Bronchitis in Children & Their Pr.

Altounyan, Taqui. Chimes from a Wooden Bell. 200p. 1991. text 39.50 (*1-85043-239-2*, Pub. by I B T) St Martin.

— Chimes from a Wooden Bell: A Hundred Years in the Life of a Euro-Armenian Family. 1991. 21.95 (*0-685-40073-5*, Pub. by I B T) St Martin.

Altov, H., jt. auth. see Altshuller, G.

Altov, Henry. The Art of Inventing: How to Invent & How to Solve Technical Problems. Shulyak, Lev, tr. from RUS. LC 93-60989. (Illus.). 170p. (Orig.). 1994. 40.00 (*0-9640740-1-X*) Tech Innovat.

Altreuter, Gregory. The Death Collection. (Illus.). 24p. 1982. pap. 3.00 (*0-911627-04-9*) Neither-Nor Pr.

— Dog Shoots Owner, Then Kills Self. (Illus.). 10p. 1981. pap. 2.45 (*0-911627-02-2*) Neither-Nor Pr.

Altria, Kevin D., ed. Capillary Electrophoresis Guidebook: Principles, Operation & Applications. LC 96-20891. (Methods in Molecular Biology Ser.: No. 52). 384p. 1995. 79.50 (*0-89603-315-5*, QD79) Humana.

Altrichter, Herbert. Images of Educational Changes. LC 99-44710. 1998. pap. text 28.95 (*0-335-20188-1*) Taylor & Francis.

— Images of Educational Changes. LC 99-44710. 192p. 2000. 85.00 (*0-335-20189-X*) Taylor & Francis.

Altrichter, Herbert, et al. Teachers Investigate Their Work: An Introduction to the Methods of Action Research. LC 92-45851. (Investigating Schooling Ser.). (Illus.). 256p. (C). 1993. pap. 24.99 (*0-415-09357-0*, B2451) Routledge.

— Windows: Research & Evaluation on a Distance Education Course. 177p. (C). 1991. pap. 68.00 (*0-7300-1347-2*, IDE806, Pub. by Deakin Univ) St Mut.

Altringham, John D. Bats: Biology & Behaviour. (Illus.). 272p. 1998. reprint ed. pap. text 34.95 (*0-19-850322-9*) OUP.

Altringham, Ron, jt. auth. see Watson, Alasdair.

Altripp, Michael. Die Prothesis und Ihre Bildausstattung in Byzanz Unter Besonderer Berucksichtigung der Denkmaler Griechenlands. Schreiner, Peter, ed. (Studien und Texte Zur Byzantinistik Ser.: Vol. 4). (Illus.). XII, 334p. 1998. pap. 67.95 (*3-631-32382-4*) P Lang Pubng.

Altrocchi, Julia & Cooley, Julia. Wolves Against the Moon. 1994. pap. 16.95 (*0-912382-32-5*) Black Letter.

Altrocchi, Rudolph, tr. see Sommi-Picenardi, Girolamo.

Altrock, Chris. The Cross: Saved by the Shame of It All. LC 98-3459. 1998. pap. 9.99 (*0-89900-805-4*) College Pr Pub.

Altrock, Constantin Von, see Von Altrock, Constantin.

Altrock, Constatin von, see Von Altrock, Constatin.

Altschiller, Donald. Hate Crimes: A Reference Handbook. LC 98-50275. (Contemporary World Issues Ser.). 204p. 1999. lib. bdg. 45.00 (*0-87436-937-1*) ABC-CLIO.

Altschiller, Donald, ed. Affirmative Action. (Reference Shelf Ser.: Vol. 63, No. 3). 168p. 1991. pap. 25.00 (*0-8242-0813-7*) Wilson.

— China at the Crossroads. LC 94-9187. (Reference Shelf Ser.: Vol. 66, No. 3). 1994. pap. 25.00 (*0-8242-0854-4*) Wilson.

— The Information Revolution. LC 95-23641. (Reference Shelf Ser.: Vol. 67, No. 5). 1995. pap. 25.00 (*0-8242-0872-2*) Wilson.

— Political Change in Southeast Asia, Vol. 61, No. 5. (Reference Shelf Ser.). 220p. (C). 1989. pap. 25.00 (*0-8242-0784-X*) Wilson.

— The United Nations' Role in World Affairs: A Renewed Role in World Affairs. LC 93-21142. (Reference Shelf Ser.: Vol. 65, No. 2). 1993. pap. 25.00 (*0-8242-0841-2*) Wilson.

Altschud, James W., jt. auth. see Witkin, Belle R.

Altschul, Aaron M. Low-Calorie Foods Handbook. (Food Science & Technology Ser.: Vol. 56). (Illus.). 608p. 1993. text 225.00 (*0-8247-8812-5*) Dekker.

Altschul, Aaron M., jt. auth. see American Chemical Society Evaluation of World Reso.

Altschul, B. J. Cracker Cookin' & Other Favorites: Cookbook & Restaurant Guide to Florida's Best Eateries, What to See in Florida. (Famous Florida! Ser.). (Illus.). 306p. 1989. pap. 16.95 (*0-942084-07-1*) SeaSide Pub.

Altschul, B. J., jt. auth. see LaFray, Joyce.

Altschul, B. J., ed. see LaFray, Joyce & Kushnir, Millie.

Altschul, Carlos, tr. see Cardenal, Ernesto.

Altschul, Donald S. Legal Limericks. (Illus.). 96p. (Orig.). 1993. pap. 7.95 (*1-882278-05-4*) Survival Series.

Altschul, Jeffrey, et al. Cultural Resources Investigations in the Mojave River Forks Reservoir, San Bernardino County, California. (Statistical Research Technical Ser.: No. 2). (Illus.). 94p. 1985. spiral bd. 7.50 (*1-879442-01-9*) Stats Res.

— Man & Settlement in the Upper Santa Ana River Drainage: A Cultural Resources Overview. (Statistical Research Technical Ser.: No. 1). (Illus.). 137p. 1984. spiral bd. 10.00 (*1-879442-00-0*) Stats Res.

— Man & Settlement in the Upper Santa Ana River Drainage: A Cultural Resources Overview. fac. ed. (Illus.). 144p. 1984. reprint ed. pap. text 15.63 (*1-55567-566-2*) Coyote Press.

***Altschul, Jeffrey H.** Islanders & Mainlanders: Prehistoric Context for the Southern California Coast & Channel Islands. 200p. 2000. pap. text 18.95 (*1-879442-92-2*) Stats Res.

Altschul, Jeffrey H. Prehistoric Adaptation to a Desert Spring Environment: Archaeological Investigations of Surprise Spring, San Bernardino County, California. (Statistical Research Technical Ser.: No. 27). (Illus.). 189p. 1990. per. 13.50 (*1-879442-25-6*) Stats Res.

Altschul, Jeffrey H. & Fairley, Helen C. Man, Models, & Management: An Overview of the Arizona Strip & the Management of Its Cultural Resources. 400p. 1989. write for info. (*0-318-70191-X*) US BLM.

Altschul, Jeffrey H. & Jones, Bruce A. A Cultural Resources Sample Survey of Operations Zones, Barry M. Goldwater Range, Marine Corps Air Station, Yuma, Arizona. (Statistical Research Technical Ser.: No. 24). (Illus.). 70p. 1989. spiral bd. 10.00 (*1-879442-23-X*) Stats Res.

Altschul, Jeffrey H. & Lindsay, Sylvia, eds. On the Bajada: Archaeological Studies at Davis-Monthan Air Force Base, Tucson, Arizona. (Statistical Research Technical Ser.: No. 41). (Illus.). 249p. (Orig.). (C). 1993. pap. text, per. 22.50 (*1-879442-40-X*) Stats Res.

Altschul, Jeffrey H. & Ros, Martin R. A Block Clustering Approach to the Definition of Site Classes & an Examination of the Relationship Between Data Recording Strategies & Intrasite Spatial Analysis. fac. ed. (Statistical Research (Tucson, Arizona) Technical Ser.: Nos. 3 & 4). (Illus.). 182p. 1985. reprint ed. pap. text 19.38 (*1-55567-568-9*) Coyote Press.

Altschul, Jeffrey H. & Rose, Martin R. A Block Clustering Approach to the Definition of Site Classes & an Examination of the Relationship Between Data Recording Strategies & Intrasite Spatial Analysis. (Statistical Research Technical Ser.: Nos. 3 & 4). (Illus.). 160p. 1985. spiral bd. 12.50 (*1-879442-02-7*) Stats Res.

Altschul, Jeffrey H. & Shelley, Steven D. Class II Cultural Resources Survey for the Gila Land Disposal Project, Yuma County, Arizona. (Statistical Research Technical Ser.: No. 8). 38p. 1987. spiral bd. 5.00 (*1-879442-48-5*) Stats Res.

— Cultural Resources Inventory of Eight Titan Missile Silos in the Greater Tucson Area, Pima County, Arizona. (Statistical Research Technical Ser.: No. 12). 18p. 1987. spiral bd. 2.00 (*1-879442-49-3*) Stats Res.

— Data Recovery along Route N-13, Navajo Indian Reservation Pt. I: Research Design. (Statistical Research Technical Ser.: No. 16). 215p. 1988. spiral bd. 17.50 (*1-879442-14-0*) Stats Res.

— Research Design: Data Recovery along Route N13, Navajo Indian Reservation. fac. ed. (Statistical Research (Tucson, Arizona) Technical Ser.: No. 16). (Illus.). 227p. 1988. reprint ed. pap. text 24.38 (*1-55567-571-9*) Coyote Press.

— Yamisevul: An Archaeological Treatment Plan & Testing Report for CA-RIV-269, Riverside County, California. fac. ed. (Statistical Research (Tucson, Arizona) Technical Ser.: No. 9). (Illus.). 186p. 1987. reprint ed. pap. text 20.00 (*1-55567-569-7*) Coyote Press.

Altschul, Jeffrey H., et al. The Antelope Hill Project Pt. 1: A Class III Archaeological Survey & Treatment Plan of the Wellton - Mohawk Irrigation & Drainage District Quarry at Antelope Hill, Yuma County, Arizona. (Statistical Research Technical Ser.: Vol. 60). (Illus.). 64p. (Orig.). 1996. spiral bd. 7.50 (*1-879442-57-4*) Stats Res.

— Cultural Resources Investigations in the Mojave River Forks Reservoir, San Bernardino County, California. fac. ed. (Statistical Research (Tucson, Arizona) Technical Ser.: No. 2). (Illus.). 102p. 1985. reprint ed. pap. text 11.56 (*1-55567-567-0*) Coyote Press.

— The Deep Creek Site (CA-SBr-176) A Late Prehistoric Base Camp in the Mojave River Forks Region, San Bernardino County, California. (Statistical Research Technical Ser.: No. 22). (Illus.). 98p. 1989. per. 12.50 (*1-879442-20-5*) Stats Res.

— The Garden Canyon Project: Studies at Two Rockshelters at Fort Huachuca, Southeastern Arizona. (Statistical Research Technical Ser.: No. 39). (Illus.). 156p. 1993. per. 18.50 (*1-879442-37-X*) Stats Res.

— Life in the Ballona: Archaeological Investigations at the Admiralty Site (CA-LAn-47) & the Channel Gateway Site (CA-LAn-1596-H) (Statistical Research Technical Ser.: No. 33). (Illus.). 452p. 1992. per. 32.50 (*1-879442-31-0*) Stats Res.

— The Playa Vista Archaeological & Historical Project Vol. 1: Research Design. (Statistical Research Technical Ser.: No. 29). (Illus.). 219p. 1991. spiral bd. 25.00 (*1-879442-27-2*) Stats Res.

— Research Design: Cultural Resources Inventory Program for the Marine Corps Air Ground Combat Center, Twentynine Palms, California. (Statistical Research Technical Ser.: No. 17). 55p. 1989. spiral bd. 6.00 (*1-879442-15-9*) Stats Res.

— Research Design: Cultural Resources Inventory Program for the Marine Corps Air Ground Combat Center, Twentynine Palms, California. fac. ed. (Statistical Research (Tucson, Arizona) Technical Ser.: No. 17). (Illus.). 59p. 1989. reprint ed. pap. text 7.19 (*1-55567-572-7*) Coyote Press.

Altschul, Jeffrey H., jt. auth. see Deaver, William L.

Altschul, Jeffrey H., jt. auth. see Shelley, Steven D.

Altschul, Jeffrey H., jt. auth. see Swanson, Mark T.

Altschul, Jeffrey H., jt. ed. see Ezzo, Joseph A.

Altschul, Jeffrey H., jt. ed. see Shelley, Steven D.

Altschul, Michael. Anglo-Norman England: Ten Sixty-Six to Eleven Fifty-Four. LC 78-80816. (Conference on British Studies, Bibliographical Handbooks). 92p. reprint ed. pap. 26.30 (*0-8357-5481-2*, 2022432) Bks Demand.

— A Baronial Family in Medieval England: The Clares, 1217-1314. LC 78-64244. (Johns Hopkins University. Studies in the Social Sciences. Thirtieth Ser. 1912: 2). reprint ed. 27.00 (*0-404-61349-7*) AMS Pr.

— A Baronial Family in Medieval England: The Clares, 1217-1314. LC 65-22947. (Johns Hopkins University Studies in Historical & Political Science: Series 83, No. 2). 352p. reprint ed. pap. 109.20 (*0-8357-5969-5*, 200492600048) Bks Demand.

Altschul, Monique, tr. see Cardenal, Ernesto.

Altschul, Pamela, ed. see Lofland, Donald J.

Altschul, Siri V. Drugs & Foods from Little Known Plants: Notes in Harvard University Herbaria. LC 72-85145. 518p. 1973. 55.50 (*0-674-21676-8*) HUP.

Altschul, Sol, ed. Childhood Bereavement & Its Aftermath. (Chicago Institute for Psychoanalysis Emotions & Behavior Monograph Ser.: No. 8). 1988. 67.50 (*0-8236-0772-0*) Intl Univs Pr.

Altschuld, James W. & Engle, Molly, eds. The Preparation of Professional Evaluators: Issues, Perspectives, & Programs. LC 85-644749. (New Directions for Evaluation Ser.: No. PE 62). 97p. (Orig.). 1994. pap. 22.00 (*0-7879-9968-7*) Jossey-Bass.

Altschuld, Ruth & Haworth, Robert. Advances in Organ Biology Vol. 4, Pts. A & B: Heart Metabolism in Failure, 2 pts., Vol. 4. 1998. 257.00 (*0-7623-0389-1*) Jai Pr.

Altschule, Mark D. Essays on the Rise & Decline of Bedside Medicine. (Illus.). 458p. 1988. text 32.50 (*0-8121-1226-1*) Lppncott W & W.

A

— What Medicine Is About: Using Its Past to Improve Its Future. (Countway Library Associates Historical Publication: No. 3). 100p. 1975. 7.95 (*0-686-15547-5*) F A Countway.

Altschule, Mark D., jt. auth. see Beecher, Henry K.

Altschule, Mark D., jt. auth. see Valeri, C. Robert.

Altschuler, Bruce. Making It New: The Avant Garde in Exhibition. LC 93-34281. (Illus.). 288p. 1994. 49.50 (*0-8109-3637-2*, Pub. by Abrams) Time Warner.

Altschuler, Bruce E. Keeping a Finger on the Public Pulse: Private Polling & Presidential Elections, 72. LC 81-6965. (Contributions in Political Science Ser.: No. 72). (Illus.). 197p. 1982. 52.95 (*0-313-23046-3*, AKF/, Greenwood Pr) Greenwood.

— LBJ & the Polls. 160p. 1990. 24.95 (*0-8130-0996-0*) U Press Fla.

— Running in Place: A Campaign Journal. LC 95-21336. 1999. pap. text 24.95 (*0-8304-1439-8*) Thomson Learn.

Altschuler, Bruce E. & Sgroi, Ceka A. Understanding Law in Our Changing Society. 2nd ed. LC 95-44488. 527p. 1995. pap. text 48.00 (*0-13-449019-3*) P-H.

Altschuler, D. R., et al, eds. Cosmology & Elementary Particles: Proceedings of the 2nd Winter School of Physics. 400p. (C). 1992. text 114.00 (*981-02-0808-1*) World Scientific Pub.

Altschuler, D. R., jt. ed. see Nieves, J. F.

Altschuler, David M. & Armstrong, Troy L. Intensive Aftercare for High-Risk Juveniles: An Assessment. (Illus.). 195p. 1998. pap. text 35.00 (*0-7881-7357-X*) DIANE Pub.

Altschuler, Eric L. Bachanalia: The Essential Listener's Guide to Bach's "Well-Tempered Clavier" 254p. 1998. text 23.00 (*0-7881-5801-5*) DIANE Pub.

Altschuler, Glenn C. Andrew D. White-Educator, Historian, Diplomat. LC 78-58065. (Illus.). 296p. 1978. text 45.00 (*0-8014-1156-4*) Cornell U Pr.

— Better Than Second Best: Love & Work in the Life of Helen Magill. LC 89-5041. (Women in American History Ser.). (Illus.). 200p. 1990. text 29.95 (*0-252-01669-6*) U of Ill Pr.

— Race, Ethnicity & Class in American Social Thought, 1865-1919. Eisenstadt, A. S. & Franklin, John H., eds. LC 81-173970. (American History Ser.). 168p. (C). 1982. pap. text 11.95 (*0-88295-808-9*) Harlan Davidson.

Altschuler, Glenn C. & Grossvogel, David I. Changing Channels: America in TV Guide. (Illus.). 232p. 1992. 21.95 (*0-252-01779-X*) U of Ill Pr.

Altschuler, Mark. Your Passport to Making It Abroad. pap. 5.00 (*0-8315-0133-2*) Speller.

Altschuler, MD, et al, eds. Radiation Therapy Physics. LC 94-25784. 1994. write for info. (*3-540-55430-0*) Spr-Verlag.

Altschuler, Richard, ed. The Living Legacy of Marx Durkheim & Weber: Applications & Analyses of Classical Sociological Theory by Modern Social Scientists. LC 97-78374. (Living Legacy Ser.: Vol. 1). 624p. 1998. pap. text 39.95 (*1-884092-54-3*) R Altschuler.

Altschuler, Richard A., et al, eds. Neurobiology of Hearing: The Central Auditory System. LC 87-42836. (Neurobiology of Hearing Ser.). (Illus.). 507p. 1991. reprint ed. pap. 157.20 (*0-608-07238-9*, 206746300009) Bks Demand.

— Neurobiology of Hearing: The Cochlea. LC 86-22116. 506p. 1986. reprint ed. pap. 156.90 (*0-608-04681-7*, 206540200004) Bks Demand.

Altschuler, Stephen. Hidden Walks in the Bay Area: Pathways, Essays & Yesterdays. LC 90-70115. (Illus.). 180p. 1991. pap. 9.95 (*0-934136-43-2*) Good Life.

Altschuler, Steven & Ludwig, Stephen, eds. Pediatrics at a Glance. LC 97-41516. 450p. (C). 1998. pap. 49.95 (*0-8385-8142-0*, A-8142-0, Apple Lange Med) McGraw.

Altschuler, Steven M. & Liacouras, Christopher A. Clinical Pediatric Gastroenterology. LC 97-47601. (Illus.). 704p. (C). 1998. text 85.00 (*0-443-05542-4*) Church.

Altschull, J. Herbert. Agents of Power. LC 83-14906. (Annenberg-Longman Communication Bks.). 320p. (C). 1984. text 35.95 (*0-582-28417-1*, 71451) Longman.

Altschull, J. Herbert. From Milton To McLuhan. 384p. (C). 1990. pap. 57.00 (*0-582-28562-3*, 71590) Longman.

Altsheler, Joseph. Candidate. Date not set. lib. bdg. 25.95 (*0-8488-2122-X*) Amereon Ltd.

— Herald of the West. Date not set. lib. bdg. 25.95 (*0-8488-2119-X*) Amereon Ltd.

— Last Rebel. Date not set. lib. bdg. 25.95 (*0-8488-2123-8*) Amereon Ltd.

— My Captive. Date not set. lib. bdg. 25.95 (*0-8488-2124-6*) Amereon Ltd.

— The Sun of Saratoga. Date not set. lib. bdg. 25.95 (*0-8488-2121-1*) Amereon Ltd.

Altsheler, Joseph A. After the Battle. rev. ed. (Read-Along Radio Dramas Ser.). (J). (gr. 6-10). 1987. reprint ed. ring bd. 38.00 (*1-878298-20-8*) Balance Pub.

— Apache Gold. 1976. reprint ed. lib. bdg. 27.95 (*0-88411-941-6*) Amereon Ltd.

— Apache Gold. 1990. reprint ed. lib. bdg. 22.95 (*0-89968-455-6*) Buccaneer Bks.

— Before the Dawn. 22.95 (*0-8488-1234-4*) Amereon Ltd.

— Before the Dawn. 1976. lib. bdg. 21.95 (*0-89968-000-3*, Lghtyr Pr) Buccaneer Bks.

— Before the Dawn: A Story of the Fall of Richmond. Date not set. lib. bdg. 39.95 (*0-8488-1233-6*, 208) Amereon Ltd.

— Border Watch. 26.95 (*0-685-71959-6*) Amereon Ltd.

— Border Watch. 1976. lib. bdg. 31.95 (*0-89968-001-1*, Lghtyr Pr) Buccaneer Bks.

— The Eyes of the Woods. 25.95 (*0-8488-1235-2*) Amereon Ltd.

— The Eyes of the Woods. 1976. lib. bdg. 31.95 (*0-89968-145-X*, Lghtyr Pr) Buccaneer Bks.

— The Eyes of the Woods. (Young Trailer Ser.). 319p. 1984. reprint ed. lib. bdg. 31.95 (*0-89968-244-8*) Buccaneer Bks.

— The Forest of Swords. 1993. reprint ed. lib. bdg. 21.95 (*0-89968-573-0*) Buccaneer Bks.

— Forest Rangers. 25.95 (*0-8488-1236-0*) Amereon Ltd.

— The Forest Runners. 1976. lib. bdg. 29.95 (*0-89968-002-X*, Lghtyr Pr) Buccaneer Bks.

— Free Rangers. 26.95 (*0-8488-1237-9*) Amereon Ltd.

— Free Rangers. 350p. 1981. reprint ed. lib. bdg. 35.95 (*0-89968-225-1*, Lghtyr Pr) Buccaneer Bks.

— The Great Sioux Trail. 25.95 (*0-89190-825-0*) Amereon Ltd.

— The Great Sioux Trail. 1990. reprint ed. lib. bdg. 21.95 (*0-89968-457-2*) Buccaneer Bks.

— The Guns of Bull Run. 1976. reprint ed. lib. bdg. 25.95 (*0-88411-942-4*) Amereon Ltd.

— The Guns of Bull Run. 1990. reprint ed. lib. bdg. 21.95 (*0-89968-458-0*) Buccaneer Bks.

— The Guns of Europe. Date not set. lib. bdg. 39.95 (*0-8488-1860-1*, 204) Amereon Ltd.

— The Guns of Europe. 1993. reprint ed. lib. bdg. 21.95 (*0-89968-572-2*) Buccaneer Bks.

— The Guns of Shiloh. 1976. reprint ed. lib. bdg. 25.95 (*0-88411-943-2*) Amereon Ltd.

— The Guns of Shiloh. 1990. reprint ed. lib. bdg. 21.95 (*0-89968-459-9*) Buccaneer Bks.

— Guthrie of the Times: A Story of Success. Date not set. lib. bdg. 39.95 (*0-8488-1861-X*, 205) Amereon Ltd.

— Horseman of the Plains. 1976. reprint ed. lib. bdg. 27.95 (*0-88411-946-7*) Amereon Ltd.

— The Horsemen of the Plains. 1990. reprint ed. lib. bdg. 23.95 (*0-89968-460-2*) Buccaneer Bks.

— The Hosts of the Air. 1990. reprint ed. lib. bdg. 20.95 (*0-89968-461-0*) Buccaneer Bks.

— The Hosts of the Air: The Story of a Quest in the Great War. 327p. reprint ed. lib. bdg. 25.95 (*0-88411-947-5*) Amereon Ltd.

— Hunters of the Hills. 26.95 (*0-8488-0904-1*) Amereon Ltd.

— The Hunters of the Hills. 1990. reprint ed. lib. bdg. 22.95 (*0-89968-462-9*) Buccaneer Bks.

— In Circling Camps. 28.95 (*0-8488-0715-4*) Amereon Ltd.

— In Hostile Red. 1976. lib. bdg. 15.80 (*0-89968-003-8*, Lghtyr Pr) Buccaneer Bks.

— In Hostile Red: A Romance of the Monmouth Campaign. Date not set. lib. bdg. 39.95 (*0-8488-1238-7*, 209) Amereon Ltd.

— The Keepers of the Trail. 324p. 1992. reprint ed. lib. bdg. 35.95 (*0-89966-932-8*) Buccaneer Bks.

— The Keepers of the Trail: A Story of the Great Woods. 323p. reprint ed. lib. bdg. 24.95 (*0-88411-948-3*) Amereon Ltd.

— Kentucky Frontiersmen: The Adventures of Henry Ware, Hunter & Border Fighter. rev. ed. Kenton, Nathaniel, ed. LC 88-50581. (Kentucky Frontiersmen Ser.: Vol. 1). (Illus.). 256p. (J). (gr. 5-10). 1988. 16.95 (*0-929146-01-8*) Voyageur Pub.

— The Lords of the Wild. 24.95 (*0-8488-0905-X*) Amereon Ltd.

— The Lords of the Wild. 1993. reprint ed. lib. bdg. 21.95 (*0-89968-563-3*) Buccaneer Bks.

— The Lost Hunters. 1990. reprint ed. lib. bdg. 20.95 (*0-89968-463-7*) Buccaneer Bks.

— The Lost Hunters: A Story of Wild Man & Great Beasts. 311p. reprint ed. lib. bdg. 27.95 (*0-88411-949-1*) Amereon Ltd.

— The Masters of the Peaks. 1990. reprint ed. lib. bdg. 20.95 (*0-89968-464-5*) Buccaneer Bks.

— The Masters of the Peaks: A Story of the Great North Woods. 311p. reprint ed. lib. bdg. 24.95 (*0-88411-938-6*) Amereon Ltd.

— The Quest of the Four. 1990. reprint ed. lib. bdg. 19.95 (*0-89968-465-3*) Buccaneer Bks.

— The Quest of the Four: A Story of the Comanches & Buena Vista. 386p. reprint ed. lib. bdg. 27.95 (*0-88411-939-4*) Amereon Ltd.

— The Rifleman of the Ohio. 25.95 (*0-8488-1239-5*) Amereon Ltd.

— The Rock of Chickamauga. 25.95 (*0-8488-0071-0*) Amereon Ltd.

— The Rock of Chickamauga. 1993. reprint ed. lib. bdg. 21.95 (*0-89968-567-6*) Buccaneer Bks.

— Rulers of the Lakes. 25.95 (*0-8488-0906-8*) Amereon Ltd.

— The Rulers of the Lakes. 1993. reprint ed. lib. bdg. 21.95 (*0-89968-565-X*) Buccaneer Bks.

— The Scouts of Stonewall. 1976. lib. bdg. 19.95 (*0-89968-004-6*, Lghtyr Pr) Buccaneer Bks.

— The Scouts of Stonewall. 1990. reprint ed. lib. bdg. 21.95 (*0-89968-466-1*) Buccaneer Bks.

— The Scouts of Stonewall: The Story of the Great Valley Campaign. (Joseph A. Altsheler Civil War Ser.). 1985. 25.95 (*0-8488-0070-2*) Amereon Ltd.

— Scouts of the Valley. 26.95 (*0-8488-1241-7*) Amereon Ltd.

— Scouts of the Valley. 345p. 1981. reprint ed. lib. bdg. 35.95 (*0-89968-227-8*, Lghtyr Pr) Buccaneer Bks.

— Shades of the Wilderness. 1990. reprint ed. lib. bdg. 21.95 (*0-89968-467-X*) Buccaneer Bks.

— Shades of the Wilderness: A Story of Lee's Great Stand. 312p. reprint ed. lib. bdg. 25.95 (*0-88411-940-8*) Amereon Ltd.

— The Shadow of the North. 357p. 1976. reprint ed. lib. bdg. 23.95 (*0-88411-944-0*) Amereon Ltd.

— The Shadow of the North. 1990. reprint ed. lib. bdg. 19.95 (*0-89968-468-8*) Buccaneer Bks.

— A Soldier of Manhattan. Date not set. lib. bdg. 39.95 (*0-8488-1863-6*, 207) Amereon Ltd.

— The Star of Gettysburg. 1976. reprint ed. lib. bdg. 26.95 (*0-88411-945-9*) Amereon Ltd.

— The Star of Gettysburg. 1990. reprint ed. lib. bdg. 22.95 (*0-89968-469-6*) Buccaneer Bks.

— The Sun of Quebec. 25.95 (*0-8488-0907-6*) Amereon Ltd.

— The Sun of Quebec. 1993. reprint ed. lib. bdg. 21.95 (*0-89968-564-1*) Buccaneer Bks.

— The Sword of Antietam. 1993. reprint ed. lib. bdg. 21.95 (*0-89968-566-8*) Buccaneer Bks.

— The Sword of Antietam: The Story of the Nation's Crisis. (Joseph A. Altsheler Civil War Ser.). 1985. 27.95 (*0-89190-986-9*) Amereon Ltd.

— The Texan Scouts. 26.95 (*0-8488-0730-8*) Amereon Ltd.

— The Texan Scouts. (Texan Ser.). 1985. 21.95 (*0-8488-0202-0*) Amereon Ltd.

— The Texan Scouts. 1993. reprint ed. lib. bdg. 21.95 (*0-89968-569-2*) Buccaneer Bks.

— The Texan Star. 26.95 (*0-8488-0729-4*) Amereon Ltd.

— The Texan Star. (Texan Ser.). 1985. 21.95 (*0-8488-0201-2*) Amereon Ltd.

— The Texan Star. 1993. reprint ed. lib. bdg. 21.95 (*0-89968-570-6*) Buccaneer Bks.

— The Texan Triumph. 24.95 (*0-8488-0731-6*) Amereon Ltd.

— The Texan Triumph. (Texan Ser.). 1985. 21.95 (*0-8488-0203-9*) Amereon Ltd.

— The Texan Triumph. 1993. reprint ed. lib. bdg. 21.95 (*0-89968-571-4*) Buccaneer Bks.

— The Tree of Appomattox. 1993. reprint ed. lib. bdg. 21.95 (*0-89968-568-4*) Buccaneer Bks.

— The Tree of Appomattox: A Story of the Civil War's Close. (Joseph A. Altsheler Civil War Ser.). 1985. 23.95 (*0-8488-0073-7*) Amereon Ltd.

— The Wilderness Road: A Romance of St. Clair's Defeat & Wayne's Victory. Date not set. lib. bdg. 39.95 (*0-8488-1862-8*, 206) Amereon Ltd.

— The Young Trailers. 25.95 (*0-89190-824-2*) Amereon Ltd.

— The Young Trailers. 1976. lib. bdg. 31.95 (*0-89968-005-4*, Lghtyr Pr) Buccaneer Bks.

Altshool, Elsa. When Ragtime Was Young & Grandma Did the Cooking. Eberhardt, Mary, ed. (Illus.). 206p. (Orig.). 1993. pap. 10.00 (*0-9633372-0-3*) Centurys End.

Altshuler, Alan, et al. The Future of the Automobile: The Report of MIT's International Automobile Program. 336p. 1986. reprint ed. pap. text 15.50 (*0-262-51038-3*) MIT Pr.

Altshuler, Alan, ed. see National Research Council Staff.

Altshuler, Alan A., ed. Transportation & Communication Policy. (C). 1977. pap. 15.00 (*0-918592-22-4*) Pol Studies.

Altshuler, Alan A. & Behn, Robert D., eds. Innovation in American Government: Challenges, Opportunities, & Dilemmas. LC 97-21096. 394p. 1997. 42.95 (*0-8157-0358-9*) Brookings.

— Innovation in American Government: Challenges, Opportunities, & Dilemmas. LC 97-21096. 394p. 1997. pap. 18.95 (*0-8157-0357-0*) Brookings.

Altshuler, Alan A., et al. Regulation for Revenue: The Political Economy of Land Use Exactions. 175p. (C). 1993. 34.95 (*0-8157-0356-2*); pap. 14.95 (*0-8157-0355-4*) Brookings.

Altshuler, B. L., et al, eds. Mesoscopic Phenomena in Solids. (Modern Problems in Condensed Matter Sciences Ser.: Vol. 30). xx, 556p. 1991. 311.50 (*0-444-88454-8*, North Holland) Elsevier.

Altshuler, Bob. The Chef's Helper. LC 84-730283. 1984. student ed. 7.00 (*0-8064-0403-5*, 926) Bergwall.

Altshuler, Bruce. The Avant-Garde in Exhibition: New Art in the 20th Century. LC 97-34726. 288p. 1998. 24.95 (*0-520-21192-8*, Pub. by U CA Pr) Cal Prin Full Svc.

— Isamu Noguchi. LC 93-36608. (Modern Masters Ser.: Vol. 16). (Illus.). 128p. 1994. 35.00 (*1-55859-754-9*); pap. 14.95 (*1-55859-755-7*) Abbeville Pr.

Altshuler, Bruce, jt. auth. see Obrist, Hans-Ulrich.

Altshuler, Constance W. Cavalry Yellow & Infantry Blue: Army Officers in Arizona Between 1851 & 1886. 418p. (C). 1996. 45.00 (*0-910037-28-0*) AZ Hist Soc.

Altshuler, David A. Hitler's War Against the Jews. 1995. pap., teacher ed. 14.95 (*0-87441-298-6*) Behrman.

— Hitler's War Against the Jews - The Holocaust: A Young Reader's Version of the War Against the Jews: 1933-1945 by Lucy Dawidowicz. LC 78-5418. (Illus.). 1978. pap. 9.95 (*0-87441-222-6*) Behrman.

Altshuler, David A., ed. see Rossel, Seymour.

Altshuler General Svc. Staff, compiled by. Lawson-Chester Genealogy. 50p. 1994. reprint ed. pap. 10.00 (*0-8328-4126-9*) Higginson Bk Co.

Altshuler, Gregory B., et al, eds. Laser Applications in Medicine & Dentistry. (Europto Ser.: Vol. 2922). 472p. 1996. 110.00 (*0-8194-2324-6*) SPIE.

— Medical Applications of Lasers in Dermatology, Cardiology, Gynecology, Ophthalmology & Dentistry II, LC 98-145664. (Europto Ser.: Vol. 3192). 306p. 1997. 99.00 (*0-8194-2624-5*) SPIE.

Altshuler, Kenneth Z., jt. ed. see Rush, John.

Altshuler, Mordechai. Soviet Jewry since the Second World War: Population & Social Structure, 5. LC 86-12139. (Studies in Population & Urban Demography: No. 5). (Illus.). 296p. 1987. 59.95 (*0-313-24494-4*, ASO/, Greenwood Pr) Greenwood.

Altshuler, Thelma C., jt. auth. see Janaro, Richard P.

Altshuller, G. & Altov, H. And Suddenly the Inventor Appeared: TRIZ, the Theory of Inventive Problem Solving. Shulyak, Lev, tr. 171p. 1996. pap. write for info. (*0-9640740-2-8*) GOAL-QPC.

***Altshuller, G., et al.** Tools of Classical TRIZ. 266p. 1999. 75.00 (*1-928747-02-7*) Ideation Intl.

Altshuller, G. S. Creativity As an Exact Science. (Studies in Cybernetics: Vol. 5). xii, 320p. 1984. text 179.00 (*0-677-21230-5*) Gordon & Breach.

Altshuller, Genrich, et al. 40 Principles: Triz Keys to Innovation. LC 97-80921. (Tools Ser.). 135p. 1998. write for info. (*0-9640740-3-6*) Tech Innovat.

Altshuller, Mark & Dryzhakova, Elena. Put' Otrecheniya. LC 85-24728. (RUS.). 350p. 1985. pap. 16.50 (*0-938920-53-7*) Hermitage Pubs.

Altstadt, Audrey L. The Azerbaijani Turks: Power & Identity under Russian Rule. (Publication Ser.: No. 410). (Illus.). 334p. (C). 1992. text 38.95 (*0-8179-9181-6*); pap. text 18.95 (*0-8179-9182-4*) Hoover Inst Pr.

Altstatt & Ferrand. Putting It Together. 2nd ed. 200p. (C). 1998. spiral bd. 24.80 (*0-536-01192-3*) S&S Trade.

Altstatt, Jeanne & Handy, Judith. Putting It Together. 170p. (C). 1996. text 28.20 (*0-536-59681-6*) Pearson Custom.

***Altstein, Howard & McRoy, Ruth G.** Does Family Preservation Serve a Child's Best Interests? LC 00-26363. (Controversies in Public Policy Ser.). 152p. 2000. pap. 17.95 (*0-87840-787-1*); text 45.00 (*0-87840-786-3*) Georgetown U Pr.

Altstein, Howard & Simon, Rita J., eds. Intercountry Adoptions: A Multinational Perspective. LC 90-7380. 216p. 1990. 55.00 (*0-275-93287-7*, C3287, Praeger Pubs) Greenwood.

Altstein, Howard, jt. auth. see Simon, Rita J.

Altug, Sumru & Labadie, Pamela. Dynamic Choice & Asset Markets. (Illus.). 374p. 1994. text 54.95 (*0-12-055455-0*) Acad Pr.

Altug, Ziya & Hoffman, Janet L. Manual of Clinical Exercise Testing, Prescription & Rehabilitation. Martin, Jerome L., ed. (Illus.). 384p. (C). 1993. pap. text 37.95 (*0-8385-0241-5*, A0241-8) Appleton & Lange.

Altukhov, Yu. P. Population Genetics: Diversity & Stability. xiii, 352p. 1990. text 305.00 (*3-7186-4984-5*, Harwood Acad Pubs) Gordon & Breach.

Altum, Bernard. Der Vogel und Sein Leben. Sterling, Keir B., ed. LC 77-81082. (Biologists & Their World Ser.). (GER.). 1978. reprint ed. lib. bdg. 19.95 (*0-405-10652-1*) Ayer.

Altunin, V. V., ed. Thermophysical Properties of Freons, Vol. 1. Ghojel, Jamil I., tr. from RUS. (National Standard Reference Data Service of the U. S. S. R.: A Series of Property Tables). 200p. 1987. 235.00 (*0-89116-600-9*) Hemisp Pub.

— Thermophysical Properties of Freons, Vol. 2. Ghojel, Jamil I., tr. from RUS. (National Standard Reference Data Service of the U. S. S. R.: A Series of Property Tables). 243p. 1987. 235.00 (*0-89116-601-7*) Hemisp Pub.

Altura, B. M., ed. Ionic Regulation of the Microcirculation. (Advances in Microcirculation Ser.: Vol. 11). (Illus.). x, 174p. 1982. 129.75 (*3-8055-3429-9*) S Karger.

— Magnesium, Stress & the Cardiovascular System. (Journal: Magnesium: Vol. 5, No. 3-4, 1986). (Illus.). 120p. 1986. pap. 55.00 (*3-8055-4355-7*) S Karger.

— Vascular Endothelium & Basement Membranes. (Advances in Microcirculation Ser.: Vol. 9). (Illus.). 1979. 53.25 (*3-8055-3054-4*) S Karger.

Altura, B. M., et al, eds. Magnesium in Cellular Processes & Medicine. iv, 244p. 1987. 172.25 (*3-8055-4369-7*) S Karger.

Altura, B. M. & Altura, Bella T., eds. Dietary Minerals & Cardiovascular Disease. (Journal: Magnesium: Vol. 1, No. 3-6). (Illus.). vi, 188p. 1983. pap. 113.25 (*3-8055-3682-8*) S Karger.

Altura, B. M. & Halevy, S., eds. Cardiovascular Actions of Anesthetics & Drugs Used in Anesthesia, Set: Vols. 1 & 2. (Illus.). xx, 570p. 1987. 352.75 (*3-8055-4159-7*) S Karger.

— Cardiovascular Actions of Anesthetics & Drugs Used in Anesthesia: Basic Aspects, Vol. 1. (Illus.). viii, 268p. 1986. 169.75 (*3-8055-4157-0*) S Karger.

— Regional Blood Flow & Clinical Considerations. (Cardiovascular Actions of Anesthetics & Drugs Used in Anesthesia Ser.: Vol. 2). (Illus.). viii, 296p. 1987. 187.00 (*3-8055-4158-9*) S Karger.

Altura, B. M. & Kruck, F., eds. Interactions of Magnesium & Potassium on Cardiac & Vascular Smooth Muscle. (Journal: Magnesium: Vol. 3, No. 4-6, 1984). (Illus.). iv, 192p. 1985. pap. 75.75 (*3-8055-4149-X*) S Karger.

Altura, B. M., jt. ed. see Durlach, J.

Altura, Bella T., jt. ed. see Altura, B. M.

Altus-Buller, Martha, jt. auth. see Whittenburg, Gerald E.

Altvater, Elmar, jt. ed. see Prunskiene, Kazimiera.

Altvater, Elmara, et al, eds. The Poverty of Nations: A Guide to the Debt Crisis from Argentina to Zaire. Bond, Terry, tr. from GER. LC 90-46692. (Illus.). 272p. (C). 1991. pap. 19.95 (*0-86232-949-3*, Pub. by Zed Books); text 55.00 (*0-86232-948-5*, Pub. by Zed Books) St Martin.

Altvater, Elmara & Lithuanian European Institute Staff. Transformation, Cooperation, & Conversion: Proceedings of the NATO Advanced Research Workshop on Scientific & Technical Cooperation of the Baltic States in the New Europe & the Conversion of Their Industry, Vilnius, Lithuania, June 5-8, 1995. Prunskiene, Kazimiera, ed. LC 96-30326. (NATO ASI Series, Partnership SubSeries 4: Science & Technology Policy). 168p. (C). 1996. lib. bdg. 110.50 (*0-7923-4178-3*) Kluwer Academic.

***Altwegg, K.** Composition & Origin of Cometary Materials. LC 99-89295. (Space Sciences Series of ISSI). 2000. write for info. (*0-7923-6154-7*) Kluwer Academic.

Altwein, J. E., et al, eds. Incidental Carcinoma of the Prostate. (Illus.). 312p. 1991. 97.95 (*0-387-53225-0*) Spr-Verlag.

Altwein, J. E. & Denis, L. J., eds. Finasteride, MSD: Innovation in the Management of Benign Prostatic Hyperplasia. (Journal: European Urology: Vol. 25, Suppl. 1, 1994). (Illus.). iv, 36p. 1993. pap. 17.50 (*3-8055-5914-3*) S Karger.

Altwein, J. E. & Kirby, R. S., eds. Treating the Whole Patient: BPH & Beyond. (Journal Ser.: Vol. 29, Suppl. 1, 1996). (Illus.). iv, 52p. 1996. pap. 21.75 (*3-8055-6295-0*) S Karger.

Altwein, J. E., jt. ed. see Jacobi, G. H.

Altwein, J. E., jt. ed. see Sommerkamp, H.

An Asterisk (*) at the beginning of an entry indicates that the title is appearing for the first time.

Alty, A. & Mason, T. Seclusion & Mental Health. 208p. 1994. 35.95 (*1-56593-303-6*, 0627) Singular Publishing.

Alty, J. L., et al, eds. People & Computers VIII: Proceedings of the HCI '93 Conference. (British Computer Society Conference Ser.: No. 7). (Illus.). 502p. (C). 1994. pap. text 80.00 (*0-521-46633-4*) Cambridge U Pr.

Alty, Jim L., jt. auth. see Coombs, M. J.

Alty, Jim L., jt. ed. see Weir, George.

Aluise, J. J. The Physician as Manager. 2nd ed. (Illus.). xvi, 260p. 1986. 80.00 (*0-387-96381-2*) Spr-Verlag.

***Aluisio, Frank V., et al.** Orthopaedics. 2nd ed. LC 97-41655. (House Officer Ser.). (Illus.). 300p. 1998. write for info. (*0-683-18213-7*) Lppncott W & W.

Aluja, Martin & Liedo, Pablo, eds. Fruit Flies: Biology & Management. LC 92-25589. (Illus.). 528p. 1992. 92.95 (*0-387-97905-0*) Spr-Verlag.

***Aluja, Martin & Norrbom, Allen L.** Fruit Flies (Tephritidae) LC 99-45290. 944p. 1999. write for info. (*0-8493-1275-2*) CRC Pr.

Aluka. Contemporary Physical Science. 1999. pap. 68.44 (*0-07-229109-5*) McGraw.

Aluka, I. J. Physical Science: A Laboratory Approach. 200p. 1996. spiral bd. 31.95 (*0-8403-5371-5*) Kendall-Hunt.

Aluko, Olajide & Shaw, Timothy M., eds. Southern Africa in the 1980s. 320p. 1985. text 60.00 (*0-04-320169-5*) Routledge.

Alulis, Joseph & Sullivan, Vickie, eds. Shakespeare's Political Pageant: Essays in Politics & Literature. 304p. 1996. pap. text 24.95 (*0-8476-8290-0*); lib. bdg. 64.50 (*0-8476-8289-7*) Rowman.

Alulis, Joseph, jt. ed. see Lawler, Peter A.

Aluma, John, et al. Settlement in Forest Reserves, Game Reserves & National Parks in Uganda: A Study of Social, Economic, & Tenure Factors Affecting Land Use & Deforestation in Mabira Forest Reserve, Kibale Forest Reserve & Kibale Game Reserve/Corridor. (Research Paper Ser.: Vol. 98). (Illus.). xiv, 64p. (C). 1989. pap. 7.00 (*0-934519-08-0*, RP98) U of Wis Land.

Alumni & Athletes from F.S.U. Staff. Seminole Fan Fare. LC 96-85437. (Illus.). 255p. 1996. 19.95 (*0-9652228-0-2*) Extra Pt Club.

Alumni of William & Mary Staff. William & Mary by the Sea: Cookbook. LC 97-73499. (Illus.). 190p. (Orig.). 1997. pap. 16.93 (*0-9615670-7-4*) Soc Alu Wm.

Alumulhim, Mohamed B. Middle East Oil: A Redistribution of Values Arising from the Oil Industry. 352p. (C). 1991. lib. bdg. 62.00 (*0-8191-8179-X*) U Pr of Amer.

Alund, Aleksandra, jt. auth. see Schieup, Carl-Ulrik.

Alur, R., et al, eds. Hybrid Systems III: Verification & Control. LC 96-16989. (Lecture Notes in Computer Science Ser.: Vol. 1066). 618p. 1996. pap. 94.00 (*3-540-61155-X*) Spr-Verlag.

Alur, R. & Henzinger, T. A., eds. Computer Aided Verification: 8th International Conference, CAV '96, New Brunswick, NJ, July 31-August 3, 1996. (Lecture Notes in Computer Science Ser.). 472p. 1996. pap. 75.00 (*3-540-61474-5*) Spr-Verlag.

Aluri, Rao & Riggs, Donald E., eds. Expert Systems in Libraries. LC 90-263. 352p. (C). 1990. text 73.25 (*0-89391-589-0*) Ablx Pub.

***Alurista.** As Our Barrio Turns... Who the Yoke B On? (Illus.). 2000. pap. 12.00 (*0-9660773-3-4*) Calaca Pr.

Alurista. Et Tu...Raza? 80p. (Orig.). 1996. pap. 9.00 (*0-927534-48-7*) Biling Rev-Pr.

— Return: Poems Collected & New. LC 81-68424. (ENG & SPA.). 176p. 1982. reprint ed. pap. 15.00 (*0-916950-24-7*) Biling Rev-Pr.

— Tremble Purple: Seven Poems. (Illus.). 29p. (Orig.). (C). 1986. pap. 3.00 (*0-945308-00-0*) Getting Together Pubns.

— Z Eros. LC 94-32330. (Orig.). 1994. pap. 9.00 (*0-927534-45-2*) Biling Rev-Pr.

Alurkar, S. K. Solar & Interplanetary Disturbances. LC 96-49790. (Astronomy & Astrophysics Ser.). 1997. write for info. (*981-02-2925-9*) World Scientific Pub.

Alurralde, Carlos. A Statement of the Laws of Argentina in Matters Affecting Business. 1976. lib. bdg. 134.95 (*0-8490-2666-0*) Gordon Pr.

Alusi, Barbara M. My Home - The Home of Many. LC 86-80685. (Illus.). 128p. 1986. 17.00 (*0-934188-20-3*) Evans Pubns.

Alustiza, Mary. The Basque Table: A Cookbook by Mary Alustiza - Basque Lore - Customs - Vignettes, Treasured Recipes of the Alustiza Family. (Illus.). 232p. 1996. 24.95 (*0-9653699-0-0*) Azitsula Bks.

Alva, Walter & Donnan, Christopher B. Royal Tombs of Sipan. LC 93-26536. (Illus.). 234p. 1995. pap. 35.00 (*0-930741-30-7*, Pub. by UCLA Fowler Mus) U CA Pr.

— Tumbas Reales de Sipan. LC 93-72310. (Illus.). 234p. 1995. 50.00 (*0-930741-31-5*, Pub. by UCLA Fowler Mus); pap. 35.00 (*0-930741-32-3*, Pub. by UCLA Fowler Mus) U CA Pr.

Alva, Walter, jt. auth. see Longhena, Maria.

Alvager, Torsten K., jt. auth. see Beach, David P.

Alvan, Bond. Memoir of the Rev. Pliny Fisk: Late Missionary to Palestine. Davis, Moshe, ed. LC 77-70683. (America & the Holy Land Ser.). 1977. reprint ed. lib. bdg. 36.95 (*0-405-10230-5*) Ayer.

Alvar Aalto Archive Staff. The Architectural Drawings of Alvar Aalto, 1917-1939 Vol. 6: Aalto's Own Home in Helsinki, Finnish Pavilion at the 1937 World's Fair in Paris, & Other Buildings & Projects, 1932-1937. LC 93-27504. (Illus.). 424p. 1994. text 220.00 (*0-8153-0595-8*) Garland.

— The Architectural Drawings of Alvar Aalto, 1917-1939 Vol. 6: Aalto's Own Home in Helsinki, Finnish Pavilion at the 1937 World's Fair in Paris, & Other Buildings & Projects, 1932-1937, 2 vols., 8. LC 93-27504. (Illus.). 512p. 1994. text 220.00 (*0-8153-0597-4*) Garland.

Alvar Aalto Foundation Staff. The Architectural Drawings of Alvar Aalto, 1917-1939, Vol. 1: Buildings & Projects, 1917-1926. LC 93-27504. (Illus.). 560p. 1993. text 220.00 (*0-8153-0590-7*) Garland.

— The Architectural Drawings of Alvar Aalto, 1917-1939, Vol. 2: Muurame Church, Southwestern Finland Agric. LC 93-27504. (Illus.). 408p. 1993. text 220.00 (*0-8153-0591-5*) Garland.

— The Architectural Drawings of Alvar Aalto, 1917-1939, Vol. 3: Viipuri City Library, Turun Sanomat Buildi. LC 93-27504. (Illus.). 464p. 1993. text 220.00 (*0-8153-0592-3*) Garland.

— The Architectural Drawings of Alvar Aalto, 1917-1939, Vol. 4: Paimio Tuberculosis Sanatorium, City of Tu. LC 93-27504. (Illus.). 392p. 1994. text 220.00 (*0-8153-0593-1*) Garland.

— The Architectural Drawings of Alvar Aalto, 1917-1939, Vol. 5: Helsinki Stadium, Zagreb Central Hospital. LC 93-27504. (Illus.). 424p. 1994. text 220.00 (*0-8153-0594-X*) Garland.

Alvar, Ezquerra M. Diccionario Actual de la Lengua Espana Vox. (SPA.). 1696p. 1995. 95.00 (*0-7859-6152-6*, 8471531747) Fr & Eur.

Alvar Ezquerra, Manuel. Oxford Duden German & Spanish Dictionary: Oxford Duden Bildworterbuch Deutsch und Spanisch. (GER & SPA.). 860p. 1985. 75.00 (*0-8288-0347-1*, F19220) Fr & Eur.

Alvar, Manuel. Estudios Lexicos: Primera Serie. (Dialect Ser.: No. 6). (Illus.). vi, 216p. 1984. 17.50 (*0-942260-31-7*) Hispanic Seminary.

— Estudios Lexicos: Segunda Serie. (Dialect Ser.: No. 12). iv, 160p. 1992. 15.00 (*0-940639-72-6*) Hispanic Seminary.

— Juan Ramon Jimenez y la Palabra Poetica. LC 84-25635. (UPREX, Estudios Literarios Ser.: No. 70). 155p. 1986. 5.00 (*0-8477-0070-4*) U of PR Pr.

Alvar, Manuel, ed. see Machado, Antonio.

Alvarado, Adalberto. El Pensamiento Martiano: Diccionario. 2nd ed. Garcia, Lucia & Ghazi, Maggie, eds. 376p. 1994. pap. text 14.95 (*0-9641506-0-3*) Edit Interamerica.

Alvarado, Alfredo, jt. auth. see Bornemisza, Elmer.

Alvarado, Ana M. Anecdotas Cubanas: Leyenda y Folclore. LC 96-86849. (Coleccion Caniqui). (SPA.). 85p. (Orig.). 1996. pap. 9.95 (*0-89729-819-5*) Ediciones.

— En Torno a la Cubania: Aproximaciones a la Idiosincrasia Cubana. LC 98-87602. (Coleccion Cuba y sus Jueces). (SPA., Illus.). 144p. (Orig.). 1998. pap. 13.00 (*0-89729-882-9*) Ediciones.

Alvarado, Ana M., ed. see Tierno, Susan F.

Alvarado, Ana M., tr. see Castle, Kathryn.

Alvarado, Ana M., tr. see Rogers, Karen.

Alvarado, Ana M., tr. see Rogers, Karen M.

Alvarado, Ana M., tr. see Tierno, Susan F.

Alvarado, Ana M., tr. see Tierno, Susan F., et al.

Alvarado, Carol. Harry's Last Wish: A Story about Forever. 32p. (J). 1999. pap. 19.95 incl. audio (*0-944963-20-X*) Glastonbury CA.

Alvarado, Cecelia. In Our Own Way: How Anti-Bias Work Shapes Our Lives. LC 99-27080. 1999. pap. text 19.95 (*1-884834-50-7*) Redleaf Pr.

Alvarado, Jose & Creedy, John. Population Ageing, Migration & Social Expenditure. LC 97-37218. 208p. (C). 1998. 75.00 (*1-85898-724-5*) E Elgar.

Alvarado, Lisa. Reclamo/Reclamation. 2nd rev. ed. (Illus.). 46p. 1994. pap. 9.00 (*0-9648506-0-5*) La Onda Negra.

Alvarado, Manuel & Boyd-Barrett, Oliver. Media Education: An Introduction. (Illus.). 464p. 1992. pap. 35.00 (*0-85170-295-3*, Pub. by British Film Inst) Ind U Pr.

Alvarado, Manuel & Collins, Richard, eds. Slan. 1993. reprint ed. lib. bdg. 18.95 (*0-89968-380-0*, Lghtyr Pr) Buccaneer Bks.

Alvarado, Manuel & Stewart, John. Made for Television: Euston Films Limited. 228p. (Orig.). (C). 1988. pap. text 11.95 (*0-685-63002-1*, A0159) Heinemann.

Alvarado, Manuel & Thompson, John O., eds. The Media Reader. (Illus.). 376p. 1990. 45.00 (*0-85170-258-9*, Pub. by British Film Inst); pap. 22.95 (*0-85170-259-7*, Pub. by British Film Inst) Ind U Pr.

***Alvarado, Manuel, et al.** Representation & Photography: A Screen Education Reader. LC 00-34519. (Illus.). 2000. pap. write for info. (*0-312-23851-7*) St Martin.

***Alvarado, Minerva.** Treasured Memories. 2000. pap. write for info. (*1-58235-413-8*) Watermrk Pr.

Alvarado, N. & Banks, Cicely. Progresa Con las Matematicas. (SPA., Illus.). 448p. (J). (gr. 8-9). 1994. text, student ed. 48.00 (*0-9624192-0-6*) N Bacchus.

Alvarado, Noemi, jt. auth. see Banks, Cicely.

Alvarado, Rafael A. Just Because I'm Black. 349p. mass mkt. 5.99 (*1-896329-02-0*) Picasso Publ.

— The Miracle of the Red Roses. LC 99-91867. 2000. 25.00 (*0-7388-1348-6*); pap. 18.00 (*0-7388-1349-4*) Xlibris Corp.

Alvarado, Sergio J. Understanding Editorial Text: A Computer Model of Argument Comprehension. (C). 1990. text 113.50 (*0-7923-9123-3*) Kluwer Academic.

Alvarenga, Marisol, tr. see Tula, Maria Teresa.

Alvarenga, Oneyda. Musica Popular Brasileira. 1976. lib. bdg. 59.95 (*0-8490-2308-4*) Gordon Pr.

Alvares, Claude. Science, Development & Violence: The Revolt Against Modernity. (Oxford India Paperbacks Ser.). 200p. 1995. pap. 7.95 (*0-19-563281-8*) OUP.

Alvares, Claude, ed. Another Revolution Fails: A Study of India's Operation Flood Project. 1986. 24.00 (*0-8364-1523-X*, Pub. by Ajanta) S Asia.

Alvarez. Principles of Money, Banking & Finance. 7th ed. (C). 1990. text 17.00 (*0-465-06354-3*) Basic.

Alvarez, A. ADA: The Design Choice: Proceedings of the Ada-Europe International Conference, Madrid 1989. (Ada Companion Ser.). (Illus.). 288p. (C). 1990. text 80.00 (*0-521-38130-4*) Cambridge U Pr.

— Night. (Illus.). 224p. 1996. pap. 13.00 (*0-393-31434-0*, Norton Paperbks) Norton.

— Savage God: A Study of Suicide. 1990. pap. 9.95 (*0-393-30657-7*) Norton.

— Stewards of Excellence: Studies in Modern English & American Poets. LC 70-159035. 191p. (C). 1971. reprint ed. 50.00 (*0-87752-152-2*) Gordian.

***Alvarez, A.** Where Did It All Go Right: A Memoir. 352p. 2000. 25.00 (*0-688-18003-5*, Wm Morrow) Morrow Avon.

Alvarez, A., et al. Progress of Continental Law in the 19th Century. Register, L. B., tr. (Continental Legal History Ser.: Vol. 11). (Illus.). xlix, 558p. 1969. reprint ed. 85.00 (*0-8377-1900-3*, Rothman) W S Hein.

Alvarez, A., ed. see Sterne, Laurence.

Alvarez, A. R., ed. BICMOS Technology & Applications. 2nd ed. LC 93-14295. (International Series in Engineering & Computer Science, VLSI, Computer Architecture, & Digital Screen Processing). 424p. (C). 1993. text 141.50 (*0-7923-9384-8*) Kluwer Academic.

Alvarez, Albert, ed. see Bahr, Donald M.

***Alvarez, Alejandro G. & Carnegie Endowment for International Peace Staff.** International Law & Related Subjects from the Point of View of the American Continent: A Report on Lectures Delivered in the Universities of the United States, 1916-1918, under the Auspices of the Carnegie Endowment or International Peace, Including a Comparative Study of the Universities of Latin America & the United States. LC 99-46127. 2000. write for info. (*1-57588-588-3*) W S Hein.

Alvarez-Altman, Grace & Burelbach, Frederick M., eds. Names in Literature: Essays from Literary Onomastics Studies. LC 87-18916. 248p. (Orig.). (C). 1988. pap. text 24.00 (*0-8191-6610-3*); lib. bdg. 47.50 (*0-8191-6609-X*) U Pr of Amer.

Alvarez, Anne. Autism & Personality: Findings from the Tavistock Autism Workshop. LC 98-43904. 1999. pap. 29.99 (*0-415-14602-X*) Routledge.

***Alvarez, Anne.** Autistic Child as a Person. LC 98-43904. 1999. write for info. (*0-415-14601-1*) Routledge.

Alvarez, Anne. Live Company: Psychoanalytic Therapy with Autistic, Abused & Borderline Psychotic Children. LC 91-40447. 264p. (C). 1992. pap. 24.99 (*0-415-06097-4*, Pub. by Tavistock) Routldge.

Alvarez, Anthony R., ed. BICMOS Technology & Applications. (C). 1989. text 118.50 (*0-7923-9033-4*) Kluwer Academic.

***Alvarez, Bachman.** Murder American Style. (Criminal Justice Ser.). 2001. 25.00 (*0-534-53470-8*) Wadsworth Pub.

Alvarez, Belinda, et al. A Revision of Axinellidae (Porifera; Demospongiae) of the Central West Atlantic Region: A Collection of Papers of the Symposium, Atlantic City, NJ, 1956. LC 98-16422. (Smithsonian Contributions to Zoology Ser.: No. 598). (Illus.). 51p. reprint ed. pap. 30.00 (*0-608-10642-9*, 207126400009) Bks Demand.

Alvarez, Benjamin & Gomez, Hernando, eds. Laying the Foundation: The Institutions of Knowledg in Developing Countries. LC 95-173153. 224p. 1994. pap. 17.50 (*0-88936-684-5*, IDRC6845, Pub. by IDRC Bks) Stylus Pub VA.

Alvarez-Bolado, G. & Swanson, L. W. Developmental Brain Maps: Structure of the Embryonic Rat Brain. LC 96-15900. 160p. 1996. 224.00 (*0-444-81903-7*) Elsevier.

Alvarez-Borland, Isabel. Discontinuidad y Ruptura en Guillermo Cabrera Infante. LC 82-84325. 144p. 1983. pap. text 10.00 (*0-935318-09-7*) Edins Hispamerica.

Alvarez Bravo, Armando. Las Cien Mejores Poesias Cubanas. Date not set. pap. write for info. (*0-89729-685-0*) Ediciones.

— Los Diez Libros Fundamentales de la Historia de Cuba. (SPA.). Date not set. pap. write for info. (*0-89729-684-2*) Ediciones.

Alvarez, Carlos M. Understanding Ethnic Identities: A Psychocontextual. Kincheloe, Joe & Steinberg, Shirley R., eds. (Critical Education Practice Ser.). 200p. Date not set. text 30.00 (*0-8153-1646-1*); pap. text 18.95 (*0-8153-2328-X*) Garland.

Alvarez, Carmelo. People of Hope: The Protestant Movement in Central America. 1990. pap. 3.95 (*0-377-00212-7*) Friendship Pr.

Alvarez, Catalina. Antojitos Mexicanos. 1996. pap. text 7.98 (*968-403-922-0*) Selector.

Alvarez, Celia, et al. Speech & Ways of Speaking in a Bilingual Puerto Rican Community. 232p. (Orig.). 1988. pap. 10.00 (*1-878483-12-9*) Hunter Coll CEP.

Alvarez-Cobelas, M. & International Association of Phytoplankton Taxonom. Phytoplankton & Trophic Gradients, Vol. 129. LC 98-24597. (Developments in Hydrobiology Ser.). 372p. 1998. write for info. (*0-7923-5171-1*) Kluwer Academic.

***Alvarez, Corwyn.** The Conversion. 120p. 2000. 15.95 (*1-56167-567-9*) Noble Hse MD.

Alvarez, Cristina. Diccionario Etnolinguistico del Idioma Maya Yucateco Colonial Vol. III: Aprovechamiento de los Recursos Naturales. (SPA.). 660p. 1997. pap. 34.50 (*968-36-3145-2*, UN053, Pub. by Instit de Invest) UPLAAP.

Alvarez, Cynthia. Babe: Home Sweet Home. LC 97-40800. (J). 1998. lib. bdg. 11.99 (*0-679-98967-6*, Pub. by Random Bks Yng Read) Random.

— Big Slammu: A Coloring Book. (Happy House Coloring Ser.). (J). 1996. pap. 0.55 (*0-679-88000-3*, Pub. by Random Bks Yng Read) Random.

— Fuzzytail Farm. (Illus.). 22p. (J). 1996. 3.99 (*0-679-87202-7*) Random.

— Reindeer Baby. LC 94-69484. 22p. (J). 1995. 3.99 (*0-679-87123-3*) Random.

— Rescue Mission. 1996. 10.00 (*0-679-85854-7*) Random.

— Stop That Volcano. (Illus.). (J). 1996. pap. 3.25 (*0-679-87613-8*, Pub. by Random Bks Yng Read) Random.

— Street Sharks: Mutant Mania! (Street Sharks Storybooks Ser.). (J). (ps-2). 1996. pap. 4.99 (*0-614-15725-0*) Random.

— Streex: A Coloring Book. (Happy House Coloring Ser.). (J). 1996. pap. 0.55 (*0-679-87999-4*, Pub. by Random Bks Yng Read) Random.

Alvarez, David. Allied & Axis Signals Intelligence in World War II. LC 99-23171. (Studies in Intelligence Ser.). 248p. 1999. 49.00 (*0-7146-4958-9*) Intl Spec Bk.

— Allied & Axis Signals Intelligence in World War II. LC 99-23171. (Studies in Intelligence Ser.). 248p. 1999. pap. 24.50 (*0-7146-8019-2*) Intl Spec Bk.

Alvarez, David, jt. ed. see Guarneri, Carl J.

***Alvarez, David J.** Secret Messages: Codebreaking & American Diplomacy, 1930-1945. LC 99-49798. (Modern War Studies). (Illus.). 304p. 2000. text 35.00 (*0-7006-1013-8*) U Pr of KS.

Alvarez, David J. & Graham, Robert A. Nothing Sacred: Nazi Espionage Against the Vatican, 1939-1945. LC 97-11657. (Studies in Intelligence). 190p. 1997. 52.50 (*0-7146-4744-6*, Pub. by F Cass Pubs); pap. 24.50 (*0-7146-4302-5*, Pub. by F Cass Pubs) Intl Spec Bk.

Alvarez de Ulloa, Leonor, jt. auth. see Ulloa, Justo.

Alvarez del Real, Maria E. Banderas y Escudos del Mundo (Flags & Coat of Arms of the World) (SPA., Illus.). 272p. (Orig.). 1986. pap. 7.50 (*0-944499-17-1*) Editorial Amer.

Alvarez del Real, Maria E., ed. Aprenda a Redactar Correctamente: Everything You Need to Know As It Relates to Your Business, Writing Technique.. Language... (SPA., Illus.). 320p. (Orig.). 1987. pap. 3.50 (*0-944499-01-5*) Editorial Amer.

— Cocina Latino Americana. (SPA., Illus.). 304p. (Orig.). (YA). 1988. pap. 4.50 (*0-944499-44-9*) Editorial Amer.

— Como Escribir Cartas De Amor. (SPA., Illus.). 288p. (Orig.). (YA). 1988. pap. 4.00 (*0-944499-38-4*) Editorial Amer.

— Diccionario Escolar. 2nd ed. LC 83-80787. (SPA., Illus.). 228p. (J). (gr. 2). 1986. pap. 3.75 (*0-944499-13-9*) Editorial Amer.

— Diccionario Moderno. 10th rev. ed. (SPA.). 640p. (C). pap. 4.50 (*0-944499-99-6*) Editorial Amer.

— Diccionario para Crucigramas. (SPA.). 384p. (Orig.). 1986. pap. 4.00 (*0-944499-15-5*) Editorial Amer.

— Doce Mil Minibiografias. 2nd ed. LC 81-72104. (SPA., Illus.). 800p. pap. 6.00 (*0-944499-12-0*) Editorial Amer.

— Encyclopedia Medica de la Mujer. 4th ed. LC 81-72100. (SPA., Illus.). 528p. 1988. pap. 4.95 (*0-944499-29-5*) Editorial Amer.

— Frases Celebres De Todos los Tiempos. (SPA., Illus.). 336p. (Orig.). (YA). 1988. pap. 4.00 (*0-944499-40-6*) Editorial Amer.

— Medicamentos Indigenas. (SPA., Illus.). 448p. 1988. pap. 4.00 (*0-944499-42-2*) Editorial Amer.

— Las Novelas Mas Famosas Del Mundo. (SPA., Illus.). 400p. (Orig.). (C). 1991. pap. 4.95 (*1-56259-001-4*) Editorial Amer.

— Pensando en Su Nino. 5th ed. LC 81-71533. (SPA., Illus.). 448p. 1985. pap. 5.95 (*0-944499-09-0*) Editorial Amer.

— Recordando Sus Vidas Pasadas. (SPA., Illus.). 288p. (Orig.). 1991. pap. 4.95 (*1-56259-000-6*) Editorial Amer.

Alvarez del Real, Maria E., ed. see Editorial America, S. A. Staff.

Alvarez-Detrell, Felicia G. Balseros: Historia Oral del Exodo Cubano del '94 - Oral History of the Cuban Exodus of '94. (ENG & SPA.). 187p. 1997. pap. 16.00 (*0-89729-828-4*) Ediciones.

Alvarez-Detrell, Tamara & Paulson, Michael G., eds. The Traveler in the Life & Works of George Sand. LC 93-60502. x, 168p. 1993. 45.00 (*0-87875-441-5*) Whitston Pub.

Alvarez-Detrell, Tamara, jt. auth. see Paulson, Michael G.

Alvarez, E., et al, eds. Theoretical Physics: Cosmology & Particle Physics: Proceedings of the 17th International GIFT Seminar, Peniscola, Spain, 2-7 June, 1986. 300p. 1987. pap. 54.00 (*9971-5-0314-X*) World Scientific Pub.

— Theoretical Physics: Cosmology & Particle Physics: Proceedings of the 17th International GIFT Seminar, Pensacola, Spain, 2-7 June, 1986. 300p. 1987. text 117.00 (*9971-5-0259-3*) World Scientific Pub.

Alvarez, Elena, tr. see Maguire, Daniel C. & Maguire, Marjorie R.

Alvarez, Ernesto. Manuel Zeno Gandia: Estetica & Sociedad. LC 86-16082. 253p. 1987. pap. 12.00 (*0-8477-3520-6*) U of PR Pr.

Alvarez-Estrada, R. F., et al, eds. Models of Hadron Structure Based on Quantum Chromodynamics. (Lecture Notes in Physics Ser.: Vol. 259). vi, 294p. 1986. 40.95 (*0-387-16795-1*) Spr-Verlag.

Alvarez, Felipe. Guerrilla Women. 64p. 1996. pap. 4.95 (*1-885901-20-8*) Presbyters Peartree.

Alvarez, Fernando. Regimiento Contra la Peste: Biblioteca Nacional de Madrid I-51. Purificacion Zabia, Maria, ed. (Medieval Spanish Medical Texts Ser.: No. 18). (SPA.). 6p. 1987. 10.00 incl. fiche (*0-940639-14-9*) Hispanic Seminary.

Alvarez, Fernando M., ed. Teatros y Vida Teatral en Badajoz, 1601-1699. (Fuentes Para la Historia del Teatro en Espana, Series C: Vol. 27). (SPA.). 325p. 1997. 53.00 (*1-85566-054-7*, Pub. by Tamesis Bks Ltd) Boydell & Brewer.

Alvarez-Gaume, L., et al, eds. Superstrings 1987: Proceedings of the Trieste Spring School on Superstrings, 1987. 432p. (Orig.). (C). 1988. pap. 44.00 (*9971-5-0518-5*, MPH-P549S); text 102.00 (*9971-5-0297-6*, MPH-P549) World Scientific Pub.

Alvarez-Gaume, L., tr. see Galindo, A. & Pascual, P.

A

Alvarez, Gloria. Desert Kiss. (Encanto Ser.). 384p. 1999. mass mkt. 5.99 (0-7860-0668-4) Kensgtn Pub Corp.

***Alvarez, Gloria.** Winning Isabel/Isabel Mi Amor. (Encanto Ser.). 384p. 2000. mass mkt. 5.99 (0-7860-1059-2, Pinncle Kensgtn) Kensgtn Pub Corp.

Alvarez-Gonzalez, Rafael. ADP-Ribosylation Reactions: From Bacterial Pathogenesis to Cancer. LC 98-29792. (Developments in Molecular & Cellular Biochemistry Ser.). 1998. write for info. (0-7923-8235-8) Kluwer Academic.

***Alvarez, Graig J., et al.** Practice Guide for Conducting Extra-Territorial Discovery for Use in U. S. Litigation. 2nd expanded rev. ed. 130p. 1999. 42.50 (0-327-01593-4, 6995010) LEXIS Pub.

Alvarez, Griselda. Sonetos Terminales (Terminal Songs) (SPA.). 161p. 1997. 13.99 (968-16-5321-1, Pub. by Fondo) Continental Bk.

Alvarez, Guy & Practising Law Institute Staff. What the Small Office Practitioner Must Know about Legal Resources & Client Development on the Internet. LC 98-137675. 192 p. 1997. write for info. (0-87224-355-9) PLI.

Alvarez-Hesse, Gloria. La Cronica Sarracina: Estudio de los Elementos Novelescos y Caballerescos. LC 89-32490. (American University Studies: Romance Languages & Literature: Ser. II, Vol. 124). 200p. (C). 1990. text 39.50 (0-8204-0984-7) P Lang Pubng.

Alvarez, Hiram. Dogs from Illusion. 199p. 1994. pap. 11.95 (0-9624536-5-X) Chusma Hse.

Alvarez, I., et al. Atomic & Molecular Physics: Proceedings of 4th U. S.-Mexico Workshop. 500p. 1995. text 108.00 (981-02-2370-6) World Scientific Pub.

Alvarez, Ines, tr. see Berenstain, Stan & Berenstain, Jan.

Alvarez, Ines, tr. see De Cuenca, Pilar.

Alvarez, Ines, tr. see Eastman, P. D.

Alvarez, J. G. & Touchstone, J. C. Practical Manual on Lipid Analysis I: Fatty Acids. 104p. 1991. student ed. 29.95 (0-945537-02-6) Norell Pr.

Alvarez, Jose, et al. Living in Paris. LC 96-37994. (Illus.). 256p. 1997. 50.00 (2-08-013621-6, Pub. by Flammarion) Abbeville Pr.

***Alvarez, Jose E.** The Betrothed of Death: The Spanish Foreign Legion During the RIF Rebellion, 1920-1927, 40. LC 99-55222. (Contributions in Comparative Colonial Studies: Vol. 40). 2000. write for info. (0-313-30697-4, Greenwood Pr) Greenwood.

Alvarez, Jose E. The Unofficial Guide to Transformers, 1980s-1990s. (Illus.). 160p. 1999. pap. 29.95 (0-7643-0927-7) Schiffer.

Alvarez, Jose L. Diffusion & Consumption of Business Knowledge. LC 97-19226. 1997. text 65.00 (0-312-17666-X) St Martin.

Alvarez, Jose M. Cuentos y Cronicas Cubanas. LC 89-84624. (Coleccion Caniqui). (SPA.). 157p. (Orig.). 1991. pap. 15.00 (0-89729-539-0) Ediciones.

Alvarez, Josefina. All about Cuban Cooking. 2nd rev. ed. Earley, Joseph, ed. LC 92-90187.Tr. of Todo Acerca de la Couida Cubana. (SPA & ENG.). 162p. 1999. reprint ed. spiral bd. 14.95 (0-9632503-0-2) AACC Pubs.

Alvarez, Juan. Chocolate, Chipmunks, & Canoes: An American Indian Words Coloring Book. LC 90-60331. (Illus.). 32p. (J). (gr. 1-3). 1991. pap. 3.95 (1-878610-03-1) Red Crane Bks.

— Jose Rabbit's Southwest Adventures: An ABC Coloring Book with Spanish Words. (Illus.). 32p. (Orig.). (J). (gr. 1-3). 1990. pap. 3.95 (1-878610-00-7) Red Crane Bks.

Alvarez, Juan M. Feng Shui: La Armonia del Vivir. rev. ed. (SPA., Illus.). 220p. (Orig.). 1998. pap. write for info. (1-892231-00-X, 0301) Fairy Ring.

— Feng Shui, the Harmony of Life: The Harmony of Life. (Illus.). 230p. 1998. pap. 18.00 (1-892231-01-8) Fairy Ring.

— Feng Shui, the Mystical Meaning. (Illus.). 235p. 1999. pap. 21.50 (1-892231-04-2, Pub. by Fairy Ring) ACCESS Pubs Network.

Alvarez, Julia. En el Tiempo de las Mariposas. Costa Picazo, Rolando, tr. (SPA.). 1998. pap. 13.95 (0-452-27996-8, Plume) Dutton Plume.

— Homecoming: New & Collected Poems. 128p. 1996. pap. 12.95 (0-452-27567-9, Plume) Dutton Plume.

— How the Garcia Girls Lost Their Accents. 308p. (YA). (gr. 10 up). 1999. 17.95 (0-945575-57-2, 71557) Algonquin Bks.

— How the Garcia Girls Lost Their Accents. (Contemporary Fiction Ser.). 304p. 1992. pap. 12.95 (0-452-26806-0) Dutton Plume.

***Alvarez, Julia.** In the Name of Salome. LC 00-25818. 368p. 2000. 23.95 (1-56512-276-3, 72276) Algonquin Bks.

Alvarez, Julia. In the Time of the Butterflies: A Novel. LC 94-15004. 344p. 1999. 21.95 (1-56512-038-8, 72038) Algonquin Bks.

— In the Time of the Butterflies: A Novel. LC 95-8091. 325p. 1995. pap. 12.95 (0-452-27442-7, Plume) Dutton Plume.

— The Other Side. Orig. Title: El Otro Lado. 176p. 1996. pap. 10.95 (0-452-27341-2, Plume) Dutton Plume.

— The Secret Footprints. LC 99-42217. 2000. 16.95 (0-679-89309-1) Knopf.

— The Secret Footprints. LC 99-42217. (Illus.). 40p. (ps up). 2000. lib. bdg. 18.99 (0-679-99309-6) Knopf.

— Something to Declare: Essays. LC 98-20994. 312p. 1999. 20.95 (1-56512-193-7, 72193) Algonquin Bks.

***Alvarez, Julia.** Something to Declare: Essays. 320p. 1999. pap. 13.95 (0-452-28067-2, Plume) Dutton Plume.

— Tia Lola Stories. (J). 2001. 15.95 (0-375-80215-0, Pub. by Random Bks Yng Read); lib. bdg. 17.99 (0-375-90215-5) Random Bks Yng Read.

Alvarez, Julia. Yo! LC 96-24611. 350p. 1999. 18.95 (1-56512-157-0, 72157) Algonquin Bks.

— Yo! LC 97-39937. 320p. 1997. pap. 12.95 (0-452-27918-6, Plume) Dutton Plume.

***Alvarez, Julia.** Yo! (SPA.). 1999. pap. 16.95 (0-452-28140-7) NAL.

Alvarez, Julie, jt. auth. see Eichner, Bill.

Alvarez, Kathleen H. Williams & Wilkins' Dental Hygiene Handbook. LC 97-41381. 625p. 1998. pap. 29.95 (0-683-30089-X) Lppncott W & W.

Alvarez, Kenneth C. Twilight of the Panther: Biology, Bureaucracy & Failure in an Endangered Species Program. 502p. 1993. pap. 19.95 (0-9635656-0-5) Myakka River.

Alvarez-Koki, Francisco. Entre Dos Aguas. (SPA.). 104p. 1995. pap. 6.00 (1-884912-03-6) Latino Pr.

Alvarez-Leefmans, F. J. & Russell, J. M. Chloride Channels & Carriers in Nerve, Muscle & Glial Cells. (Illus.). 444p. (C). 1990. text 125.00 (0-306-43426-1, Kluwer Plenum) Kluwer Academic.

Alvarez, Louis. The New Orleans Bicycle Book. (Illus.). 168p. (Orig.). 1984. pap. 5.95 (0-9614451-0-6) Little Nemo Pr.

Alvarez, Luis M., tr. see Evans, Tony.

Alvarez, Luis M., tr. see Swindoll, Charles R.

Alvarez, Lupe & Pujol, Ernesto, contrib. by. 1990s Art from Cuba: A National Residency & Exhibition Program. (Illus.). 55p. 1997. pap. 10.00 (1-883967-07-4) Art in General.

Alvarez, Lynne. Lynne Alvarez Vol. 1: Collected Plays, Vol. I. LC 98-24129. (Contemporary Playwrights Ser.). 320p. 1998. pap. 19.95 (1-57525-146-9) Smith & Kraus.

Alvarez, M. F., ed. see Menendez Pidal, Ramon.

Alvarez, Maria D. & Murray, Gerald F. Haitian Migrant Children in the United States. Fetterman, David M., ed. (Studies in Education & Culture). 250p. Date not set. text 37.50 (0-8153-1167-2) Garland.

Alvarez, Maria V., jt. auth. see Norman, Jill.

Alvarez, Mark. The Baseball Research Journal. 1997. pap. 9.95 (0-910137-70-6) Soc Am Baseball Res.

— The Baseball Research Journal, No. 22. 1993. pap. 7.95 (0-910137-54-4) Soc Am Baseball Res.

— The Home Office Book: How to Set up an Efficient Personal Workspace in the Computer Age. (Illus.). 304p. 1990. 24.95 (0-9625427-8-4); pap. 14.95 (0-9625427-9-2) Goodwood Pr.

— The National Pastime, No. 13. 1993. pap. 7.95 (0-910137-52-8) Soc Am Baseball Res.

— The National Pastime, 1994, No. 14. 1994. pap. 9.95 (0-910137-56-0) Soc Am Baseball Res.

Alvarez, Mark, ed. The Baseball Research Journal, No. 24. Date not set. per. 9.95 (0-910137-63-3) Soc Am Baseball Res.

— The Baseball Research Journal No. 23. per. 9.95 (0-910137-57-9) Soc Am Baseball Res.

— The Baseball Research Journal, 1992. 112p. 1992. pap. 7.95 (0-910137-50-1) Soc Am Baseball Res.

— The Baseball Research Journal, 1996, No. 24. (Illus.). 144p. 1996. pap. 9.95 (0-910137-66-8) Soc Am Baseball Res.

— The National Pastime, No. 15. 1995. pap. 9.95 (0-910137-62-5) LPC InBook.

— The National Pastime, No. 16. 1996. pap. 9.95 (0-910137-64-1) Soc Am Baseball Res.

***Alvarez, Mark, ed.** The National Pastime Vol. 19: A Review of Baseball History. (Illus.). 116p. 1999. pap. 12.00 (0-910137-77-3, Pub. by Soc Am Baseball Res) U of Nebr Pr.

Alvarez, Mark, ed. The National Pastime, 1997, Vol. 17. 1997. pap. 9.95 (0-910137-68-4) Soc Am Baseball Res.

Alvarez, Mark, jt. auth. see Cleveland, Will.

Alvarez, Max J. Index to Motion Pictures Reviewed by Variety, 1907-1980. LC 81-23236. 520p. 1982. 47.50 (0-8108-1515-X) Scarecrow.

Alvarez Nazario, Manuel. Arqueologia Linguistica. (SPA.). 1996. pap. 9.95 (0-8477-0229-4) U of PR Pr.

— El Influjo Indigena En el Espanol De Puerto Rico. LC 76-1826. (Coleccion Mente y Palabra). (SPA.). vi, 216p. (Orig.). 1977. 5.00 (0-8477-0526-9) U of PR Pr.

Alvarez, Nicolas E. Agua De Fuego. LC 90-84744. (Coleccion Espejo de Paciencia). (SPA.). 60p. (Orig.). 1991. pap. 9.00 (0-89729-583-8) Ediciones.

— Analisis Arquetipico, Mitico y Simbolico de Pedro Paramo. LC 83-80471. (SPA.). 139p. (Orig.). 1983. pap. 12.00 (0-89729-330-4) Ediciones.

— Discurso e Historia en la Obra Narrativa de Jorge Luis Borges. LC 98-60868. (SPA.). 258p. 1998. pap. 30.00 (0-89295-092-7) Society Sp & Sp-Am.

Alvarez, Norma, ed. see Mikkelson, Holly M.

Alvarez, O., et al, eds. Random Surfaces & Quantum Gravity. (NATO ASI Ser.: Vol. 262). (Illus.). 416p. (C). 1991. text 156.00 (0-306-43939-5, Kluwer Plenum) Kluwer Academic.

Alvarez, Octavio. The Celestial Brides: A Study in Mythology & Archaeology. LC 77-91208. (Illus.). 1978. 30.00 (0-9601520-0-8) H Reichner.

Alvarez-Ossorio, Jose R. & Goedegebuure, Ben G., eds. New Worlds in Information & Documentation: Proceedings of the Forty-Sixth Conference & Congress Held in Madrid, Spain, 22-29 October, 1992. LC 94-10009. 506p. 1994. 126.75 (0-444-81891-X) Elsevier.

***Alvarez, Paul & Auchter, Norma.** Salon Violin Gems Piano Accompaniment. 120p. 1999. pap. 15.95 (0-7866-5111-3, 98643) Mel Bay.

Alvarez, Paul H., jt. ed. see Voros, Gerald J.

Alvarez Quintero, Joaquin, jt. auth. see Alvarez Quintero, Serafin.

Alvarez Quintero, Serafin & Alvarez Quintero, Joaquin. A Sunny Morning. unabridged ed. Landes, William-Alan, ed. Floyd, Lucretia X., tr. from SPA. LC 97-31005. 55p. (Orig.). 1997. pap. 6.00 (0-88734-394-5) Players Pr.

Alvarez, R. Michael. Information & Elections. LC 98-30391. (Michigan Studies in Political Analysis). 288p. 1998. pap. text 19.95 (0-472-08575-1, 08575) U of Mich Pr.

***Alvarez, Rafael.** Hometown Boy: The Hoodle Patrol & Other Curiosities of Baltimore. 336p. 1999. pap. 13.95 (1-893116-01-8) Baltimore Sun.

— Orlo & Leini. LC 99-87708. (Illus.). 176p. 2000. pap. 14.95 (1-891521-07-1) Woodholme Hse.

Alvarez, Robert R., Jr. Familia: Migration & Adaptation in Baja & Alta California, 1880-1975. (Illus.). 230p. 1991. pap. 16.95 (0-520-07389-4, Pub. by U CA Pr) Cal Prin Full Svc.

Alvarez, Robert S. Library Boss: Thoughts on Library Personnel. 322p. 1987. 19.95 (0-9618247-0-0) Admin Digest Pr.

— Library Log: The Diary of a Public Library Director. 388p. 1991. 22.95 (0-9618247-2-7) Admin Digest Pr.

Alvarez, Roberto, tr. see Rhee, Jhoon.

Alvarez, Rodolfo & Lutterman, Kenneth G. Discrimination in Organizations: Using Social Indicators to Manage Social Change. LC 78-62567. (Jossey-Bass Social & Behavioral Science Ser.). 453p. reprint ed. pap. 140.50 (0-608-16867-X, 202774400056) Bks Demand.

Alvarez, Roman & Vidal, M. Carmen, eds. Translation, Power, Subversion. LC 95-50708. (Topics in Translation Ser.: Vol. 8). 160p. 1996. 69.00 (1-85359-351-6, Pub. by Multilingual Matters); pap. 24.95 (1-85359-350-8, Pub. by Multilingual Matters) Taylor & Francis.

Alvarez, Ronald A. & Kline, Susan C. A Family Album: The American Family in Literature & History. large type ed. National Council on the Aging Staff, ed. (Large Print Inspirational Ser.). (Illus.). 1988. pap. 10.95 (0-8027-2626-7) Walker & Co.

— The Remembered Past, 1914-1945. large type ed. National Council on the Aging Staff, ed. (Large Print Inspirational Ser.). (Illus.). 1988. pap. 11.95 (0-8027-2627-5) Walker & Co.

Alvarez, Rosario. La Iconografia Musical Latinoamericana en el Renaciento y en el Barroco - Latin American Musical Iconography in the Renaissance & in the Baroque Period: Su Importancia y Pautas para su Estudio - Its Importance & Guidelines for Its Study. LC 92-47115. (Coleccion Interamer Ser.: No. 26). (ENG & SPA.). 1993. write for info. (0-8270-3177-7) OAS.

Alvarez, Ruth M., ed. see O'Neill, Eugene.

Alvarez, Ruth M., ed. see Porter, Katherine Anne.

Alvarez-Sandoval, Emanuel. The Contrast Between Buddha & Christ: A Comparative Study. 126p. 1993. pap. text 12.50 (1-883286-01-8) ERCO.

— El Contraste Entre Buddha y Cristo: Un Estudio Comparativo. (SPA.). 118p. 1992. pap. text 12.50 (1-883286-00-X) ERCO.

Alvarez, Santiago V. Recalling the Revolution: Memoirs of a Filipino General. Malay, Paula C., tr. LC 92-71216. 280p. (Orig.). (C). 1992. pap. 14.95 (1-881261-05-0) U Wisc Ctr SE Asian.

Alvarez, Servando, et al, eds. Architecture & Urban Space. 872p. (C). 1991. lib. bdg. 355.50 (0-7923-1418-2) Kluwer Academic.

Alvarez, Sonia E., et al, eds. Cultures of Politics/Politics of Cultures: Revisioning Latin American Social Movements. LC 97-43513. 480p. (C). 1998. pap. text 32.00 (0-8133-3072-6, Pub. by Westview) HarpC.

— Cultures of Politics/Politics of Cultures: Revisioning Latin American Social Movements. LC 97-43513. 480p. (C). 1998. text 85.00 (0-8133-3071-8, Pub. by Westview) HarpC.

Alvarez, Sonia E., jt. ed. see Escobar, Arturo.

Alvarez, Thomas, ed. The Prayers of Teresa of Avila. 5th ed. 136p. 1990. pap. 9.95 (1-56548-065-1) New City.

Alvarez, Tom. How to Create Action, Fantasy & Adventure Comics. LC 96-4305. (Illus.). 144p. 1996. 24.99 (0-89134-661-9, North Lght Bks) F & W Pubns Inc.

Alvarez, Tom & Morga, Michael. Master of Magic: Shadows of Time. Payne, Michael, ed. (Illus.). 350p. (Orig.). (YA). (gr. 9-12). 1998. pap. text 6.95 (1-880852-00-4) Magical Pub FL.

Alvarez, Tony. Undercover Operations Survival in Narcotics Investigations. LC 93-13542. 130p. 1993. pap. 23.95 (0-398-06005-3) C C Thomas.

— Undercover Operations Survival in Narcotics Investigations. LC 93-13542. 130p. (C). 1993. text 34.95 (0-398-05871-7) C C Thomas.

Alvarez, Victoriano S. Episodios Nacionales Mexicanos (Mexican National Episodes), Vol. II. (SPA., Illus.). 615p. 1984. 14.99 (968-16-1758-4, Pub. by Fondo) Continental Bk.

— Episodios Nacionales Mexicanos (Mexican National Episodes), Vol. III. (SPA., Illus.). 448p. 1984. 14.99 (968-16-1759-2, Pub. by Fondo) Continental Bk.

— Episodios Nacionales Mexicanos (Mexican National Episodes), Vol. VI. (SPA., Illus.). 581p. 1984. 14.99 (968-16-1762-2, Pub. by Fondo) Continental Bk.

— Episodios Nacionles Mexicanos (Mexican National Episodes), Vol. IV. (SPA., Illus.). 757p. 1984. 14.99 (968-16-1760-6, Pub. by Fondo) Continental Bk.

Alvarez, Victoriano S., told to. Episodios Nacionales Mexicanos (Mexican National Episodes), Vol. V. (SPA., Illus.). 741p. 1984. 14.99 (968-16-1761-4, Pub. by Fondo) Continental Bk.

Alvarez, Walter. T. Rex & the Crater of Doom. LC 96-49208. 200p. 1997. 24.95 (0-691-01630-5, Pub. by Princeton U Pr) Cal Prin Full Svc.

— T. Rex & the Crater of Doom. LC 98-9369. 208p. 1998. pap. 13.00 (0-375-70210-5) Vin Bks.

Alvarez, Walter C. Alvarez on Alvarez. LC 76-47216. (Illus.). 160p. (Orig.). 1977. pap. 6.95 (0-89407-005-3) Strawberry Hill.

Alvaro, Albert M., ed. see Santos, Elsie S.

Alvaro, Corrado. Revolt in Aspromonte: Novel. Frenaye, Frances, tr. from ITA. LC 62-12393. 128p. 1988. reprint ed. pap. 1.35 (0-8112-0002-7, NDP119, Pub. by New Directions) Norton.

Alvaro, Corrado, et al. Plays for a New Theatre: Long Night of Medea, Methusalem or the Eternal Bourgeois, Assault upon Charles Sumner, Wax Museum, Knackery for All. LC 66-17821. 288p. 1966. 7.50 (0-8112-0245-3, Pub. by New Directions) Norton.

Alvaro, D., ed. Vanishing Bile Duct Syndrome - Pathophysiology & Treatment. (Falk Symposium Ser.). 272p. (C). 1997. text 127.00 (0-7923-8721-X) Kluwer Academic.

Alvaro, J. Gonzalez. Espasa Escolar. 4th ed. (SPA., Illus.). 1040p. 1994. 44.95 (84-239-6670-4) Elliots Bks.

Alvarsson, Jan-Ake. The Mataco of the Gran Chaco: An Ethnographic Account of Change & Continuity in Mataco Socio-Economic Organization (Bolivia) (Uppsala Studies in Cultural Anthropology: No. 11). (Illus.). 314p. (Orig.). 1988. pap. 50.00 (91-554-2251-9, Pub. by Uppsala Univ Acta Univ Upsaliensis) Coronet Bks.

Alvazzi Del Frate, Anna, jt. ed. see Zvekic, Ugljesa.

Alvear, Jose. Web Developer.Com Guide to Streaming Multimedia. LC 97-48761. 448p. 1998. pap. text 44.99 incl. cd-rom (0-471-24822-3) Wiley.

Alvelo, Wilfredo. El Aire y Otras Mentiras. (SPA.). 42p. (Orig.). 1989. pap. 6.00 (0-9623552-0-8) Ed Arcas.

— De-Abismos y De-Lirios. (SPA., Illus.). 64p. 1999. pap. 8.95 (1-882573-13-7, Zinnia Bks) Serena Bay.

Alveng, Dag, photos by. Layers of Light. (Illus.). 126p. 1995. pap. 65.00 (82-7384-471-4) Dist Art Pubs.

Alver, Manuel. Pasos de un Peregrino, Tras las Huellas de Espana. (Nueva Austral Ser.: No. 230). (SPA.). 1991. pap. text 24.95 (84-239-7230-5) Elliots Bks.

Alvera, Pier L. Giordano. (Portraits of Greatness Ser.). (ENG & ITA., Illus.). 80p. 1986. pap. 12.50 (0-918367-08-5) Elite.

Alvera, Pierluigi. Giordano. (Portraits of Greatness Ser.). (Illus.). 65p. (Orig.). 1986. pap. 12.50 (0-918367-07-7) Elite.

Alvera, Pierluigi & Spada, Marco, eds. Rossini. Rosenthal, Raymond, tr. from ITA. (Portraits of Greatness Ser.). (ENG & ITA., Illus.). 87p. 1987. 17.50 (0-918367-11-5); pap. 12.50 (0-918367-21-2) Elite.

Alveres, C. Homo-Feber: Technology & Culture in India, China & the West. 275p. 1979. 16.95 (0-318-37332-7) Asia Bk Corp.

Alverga, Alex P. De, see De Alverga, Alex P.

Alvermann, Donna, et al. Branching Out. large type ed. 1995. 13.50 (0-614-09564-6, L-34779-00) Am Printing Hse.

— Rolling down the River. large type ed. 1995. 9.50 (0-614-09607-3, L-34796-00) Am Printing Hse.

Alvermann, Donna E., et al, eds. Reconceptualizing the Literacies in Adolescents' Lives. LC 97-31059. 400p. 1998. pap. 39.95 (0-8058-2560-6) L Erlbaum Assocs.

— Reconceptualizing the Literacies in Adolescents' Lives. LC 97-31059. 432p. 1998. write for info. (0-8058-2559-2) L Erlbaum Assocs.

— Research Within Reach: Secondary School Reading: A Research Guided Response to Concerns of Reading Educators. LC 87-3928. 200p. reprint ed. pap. 62.00 (0-7837-1236-7, 204137300020) Bks Demand.

Alvermann, Donna E. & Phelps, Stephen F. Content Reading & Literacy: Succeeding in Today's Diverse Classrooms. 2nd ed. LC 97-2055. 384p. 1997. 74.00 (0-205-27011-5) Allyn.

— Content Reading & Literacy: Succeeding in Today's Diverse Classrooms. 2nd ed. 144p. (C). 1997. text, teacher ed. write for info. (0-205-27503-6, T7503-0) Allyn.

Alvermann, Donna E., et al. Popular Culture in the Classroom: Teaching & Researching Critical Media Literacy. LC 98-54821. (Literacy Studies Ser.). 1999. pap. 21.95 (0-87207-245-2, 245) Intl Reading.

— Using Discussion to Promote Reading Comprehension. LC 87-3107. 74p. reprint ed. pap. 30.00 (0-7837-6200-3, 204592200009) Bks Demand.

Alvermann, Donna E., jt. ed. see Santa, Carol M.

Alvermann, Klaus. Power & Grace: The Working Horse. LC 89-27969. (Illus.). 144p. 1990. 35.00 (0-87701-723-9) Chronicle Bks.

Alvermann-Ronge, Friederike. To Write in Defence of the Legal Constitution. 222p. write for info. (3-487-09692-7) G Olms Pubs.

Alvernaz, Bill, jt. auth. see Norton, Peter.

Alverno. Mathematical Connections Revised. 2nd ed. 280p. (C). 1999. 39.00 (0-536-02295-X) Pearson Custom.

Alverno College. Basic College Mathematics. 2nd ed. 420p. 1999. pap. text 39.50 (0-536-02333-6) Pearson Custom.

Alverson, Dayton L., jt. ed. see Pruter, A. T.

Alverson, Hoyt. Semantics & Experience: Universal Metaphors of Time in English, Mandarin, Hindi, & Sesotho. LC 93-40748. (Parallax). 1994. 29.95 (0-8018-4811-3) Johns Hopkins.

Alverson, Marianne. Under African Sun. LC 86-16474. (Illus.). 250p. (C). 1987. 19.95 (0-226-01623-4) U Ch Pr.

— Under African Sun. LC 86-16474. (Illus.). 256p. (C). 1997. pap. 12.95 (0-226-01624-2) U Ch Pr.

— Under African Sun. LC 86-16474. (Illus.). 249p. reprint ed. pap. 77.20 (0-608-09259-2, 205406100002) Bks Demand.

Alverson, William, et al. Wild Forests: Conservation Biology & Public Policy. LC 94-8950. 1994. text 55.00 (1-55963-187-2); pap. text 30.00 (1-55963-188-0) Island Pr.

***Alves.** World Economic Geography. 438p. 1999. pap. text 36.00 (0-536-02795-1) Pearson Custom.

An Asterisk (*) at the beginning of an entry indicates that the title is appearing for the first time.

Alves, A. S. Discrete Models of Fluid Dynamics: Advances in Mathematics for Applied Science, Vol. 2. LC 91-3670. 272p. 1991. text 89.00 (*981-02-0521-X*) World Scientific Pub.

Alves, Abel A. Brutality & Benevolence: Human Ethnology, Culture & the Birth of Mexico, 8. LC 95-51382. (Contributions in Latin American Studies: Vol. 8). 264p. 1996. 65.00 (*0-313-29982-X*, Greenwood Pr) Greenwood.

Alves, Antonio C., et al, eds. Frontiers of Laser Spectroscopy of Gases. (C). 1988. text 260.00 (*90-277-2748-1*) Kluwer Academic.

***Alves, Beth, et al.** Discover Your Prayer Gifting. 2000. pap. 11.99 (*0-8307-2644-6*, Regal Bks) Gospel Lght.

Alves, Dora. New Perspectives for U. S.-Asia Pacific Security Strategy: The 1991 Pacific Symposium. (Illus.). 197p. (Orig.). (C). 1994. pap. text 40.00 (*0-7881-1232-5*) DIANE Pub.

Alves, Dora, ed. Change, Interdependence & Security in the Pacific Basin: The 1990 Pacific Symposium. (Illus.). 395p. (Orig.). (C). 1994. pap. text 45.00 (*0-7881-1116-7*) DIANE Pub.

— Cooperative Security in the Pacific Basin: The 1988 Pacific Symposium. 346p. (Orig.). (C). 1995. pap. text 40.00 (*0-7881-2149-9*) DIANE Pub.

— The Maori & the Crown: An Indigenous People's Struggle for Self-Determination, 68. LC 98-50236. (Contributions to the Study of World History Ser.: Vol. 68). 216p. 1999. 55.00 (*0-313-31058-0*) Greenwood.

Alves, Elizabeth. The Mighty Warrior: A Guide to Effective Prayer. 216p. 1998. pap. 10.99 (*0-8307-2333-1*) Gospel Lght.

***Alves-Foss, J., et al, eds.** Formal Syntax & Semantics of Java. LC 99-35369. (Lecture Notes in Computer Science Ser.: Vol. 1523). ix, 404p. 1999. pap. 49.00 (*3-540-66158-1*) Spr-Verlag.

Alves, Gregory, jt. auth. see Tarrazo, Manuel.

Alves, Jeffrey R. How to Break into the Film Business: The Production Assistant Handbook. LC 91-52900. (Illus.). 112p. (Orig.). 1991. pap. 15.00 (*0-88734-616-2*) Players Pr.

Alves, Joseph T. Confidentiality in Social Work. LC 84-721. 268p. (C). 1984. reprint ed. lib. bdg. 65.00 (*0-313-24459-6*, ALCO, Greenwood Pr) Greenwood.

Alves, Maria H. State & Opposition in Military Brazil. (Latin American Monographs: No. 63). 368p. 1988. reprint ed. pap. 12.95 (*0-292-77617-9*) U of Tex Pr.

Alves, Mark, ed. Papers from the Third Annual Meeting of the Southeast Asian Linguistics Society (1993) 249p. (Orig.). 1995. pap. text 19.95 (*1-881044-12-2*) ASU Prog SE Asian.

Alves, Mary E. & Kelley, Patrick. Saint Francis of Assisi: Gentle Revolutionary. rev. ed. LC 99-24380. (Encounter the Saints Ser.: No. 4). 114p. (J). (gr. 5-9). 1999. pap. write for info. (*0-8198-7030-7*) Pauline Bks.

Alves, Michael, jt. auth. see Sargent, Sam.

Alves, Michael J., jt. auth. see Cassidy, Daniel J.

Alves, Miriam. Onfim Nos...Finally Us... Escritoras Negras Brasileviras Contemporaneas - Contemporary Black Brazilian Women Writers. Durham, Carolyn R., tr. (Illus.). 260p. 1995. 35.00 (*0-89410-789-5*, Three Contnts); pap. 16.00 (*0-89410-790-9*, Three Contnts) L Rienner.

Alves, P. Gasparini & Hoffman, Kerstin. The Transfer of Sensitive Technologies & the Future of Control Regimes. 139p. 1997. 35.00 (*92-1-100744-5*) UN.

Alves, Pericles G., ed. Building Confidence in Outer Space Activities: CSBMs & Earth-to-Space Monitoring. (UNIDIR Ser.). (Illus.). 388p. 1996. text 91.95 (*1-85521-630-2*, Pub. by Dartmth Pub) Ashgate Pub Co.

Alves, Pericles G., ed. Increasing Access to Information Technology for International Security: Forging Cooperation among Research Institutes. 210p. 1997. 55.00 (*92-1-100759-3*) UN.

Alves, Pericles G. & Cipollone, Diana B., eds. Curbing Illicit Trafficking in Small Arms & Sensitive Technologies: An Action-Oriented Agenda. 260p. 1998. pap. 25.00 (*92-9045-127-0*) UN.

Alves, Robert. Sketches of a History of Literature. LC 67-18714. 320p. 1967. reprint ed. 50.00 (*0-8201-1002-7*) Schol Facsimiles.

Alves, Rubem A. Protestantism & Repression: A Brazilian Case Study. Wright, Jamie, ed. Drury, John, tr. LC 82-3594.Tr. of Protestantismo e repressao. 255p. (Orig.). reprint ed. pap. 79.10 (*0-8357-8359-4*, 203484300091) Bks Demand.

Alves, Rudolf. Integrierte Fuhrung & Imitationsmanagement in Filialsystemen des Handels: Ein Beitrag zur Anwendung der Ergebnisse Empirischer Erfolgsforschung. (GER., Illus.). XXV, 314p. 1996. 57.95 (*3-631-30804-3*) P Lang Pubng.

Alves, Vicki L., ed. see Zerbe, Richard M.

***Alves, Vladimir Castro, ed.** Integrated Circuits & Systems Design: Proceedings of the 12th Symposium Natal, Brazil, 1999. LC 99-66115. 250p. 1999. 115.00 (*0-7695-0387-X*) IEEE Comp Soc.

Alvesson, Mats. Communication, Power & Organization. expanded rev. ed. LC 96-6132. (De Gruyter Studies in Organization: No. 72).Tr. of Kommunikation, Makt, Organisation. xii, 225p. (C). 1996. text 62.95 (*3-11-014622-3*); pap. text 29.95 (*3-11-014897-8*) De Gruyter.

— Management of Knowledge-Intensive Companies. (De Gruyter Studies in Organization: Vol. 61). x, 367p. (C). 1995. lib. bdg. 79.95 (*3-11-012865-9*) De Gruyter.

— Organization Theory & Technocratic Consciousness: Rationality, Ideology, & Quality of Work. (Studies in Organization: No. 8). x, 286p. 1987. lib. bdg. 74.95 (*3-11-010574-8*) De Gruyter.

Alvesson, Mats & Breg, Per O. Corporate Culture & Organizational Symbolism: An Overview. (Studies in Organization: No. 34). xii, 258p. (C). 1992. pap. text 25.95 (*3-11-013607-4*); lib. bdg. 59.95 (*3-11-012154-9*) De Gruyter.

Alvesson, Mats & Willmott, Hugh. Critical Management Studies. (Illus.). 272p. (C). 1992. text 59.95 (*0-8039-8454-5*); pap. text 24.95 (*0-8039-8455-3*) Sage.

— Making Sense of Management: A Critical Introduction. LC 96-68525. 272p. 1996. 79.95 (*0-8039-8388-3*); pap. 27.50 (*0-8039-8389-1*) Sage.

Alvesson, Mats, jt. auth. see Billing, Yvonne D.

***Alvestad, Kathryn Anderson.** Developing Parent & Community Understanding of Performance-Based Assessment. LC 00-28777. 2000. write for info. (*1-930556-02-0*) Eye On Educ.

Alvestrand, Harald. X.400 Use of Extended Character Sets. 18p. (Orig.). (C). 1995. pap. text 25.00 (*0-7881-1954-0*) DIANE Pub.

Alvey, Ada, ed. In Search of St. James-Cornwall to Compestella: A Mediaeval Pilgrimage. (C). 1989. 105.00 (*1-85022-050-6*, Pub. by Dyllansow Truran); 85.00 (*1-85022-045-X*, Pub. by Dyllansow Truran) St Mut.

Alvey, C. George & Johnson, Marceda. Essentials of Math with Business Applications. 5th ed. 403p. 1995. text, wbk. ed. 24.59 (*0-02-805380-X*) Glencoe.

Alvey, Edward. History of Mary Washington College, 1908-1972. LC 73-92624. 698p. reprint ed. pap. 200.00 (*0-608-16272-8*, 202716600054) Bks Demand.

Alvey, G. C. & Rosenberg, R. Robert. Business Math. 3rd ed. 1984. text 11.56 (*0-07-053823-9*) McGraw.

Alvey, Gerald. Kentucky Folklore. (New Books for New Readers). 64p. 1989. pap. 5.95 (*0-8131-0902-7*) U Pr of Ky.

Alvey, N. G., et al. Genstat Manual Release 4.03. 1980. 23.80 (*0-317-52192-6*, Pub. by Numer Algo) Princeton Bk Co.

— Genstat Manual Release 4.04a. 1983. 42.00 (*0-317-52197-7*, Pub. by Numer Algo) Princeton Bk Co.

Alvey, R. Gerald, ed. Kentucky Bluegrass Country. LC 91-48029. (Folklife in the South Ser.). (Illus.). 1992. pap. 16.95 (*0-87805-544-4*) U Pr of Miss.

Alvi, Dana I. & Benis, Leslie. Kuvasz: AKC Rank #109. (Rare Breed Ser.). (Illus.). 96p. 1997. 19.95 (*0-7938-0758-1*, RX-108) TFH Pubns.

Alvi, Effraim. The Amador Study on Aging, Nutrition, & Stress. LC 84-51500. (Illus.). 116p. 1984. pap. 39.95 (*0-918493-02-1*) Sierra Pub Co.

Alvi, Imtiaz. The Informal Sector in Urban Economy: Low Income Housing in Lahore. LC 97-930474. (Illus.). 1997. write for info. (*0-19-577664-X*) OUP.

Alvi, Jonell, jt. auth. see Ornsby, Tim.

Alvi, Moniza. A Bowl of Warm Air. 56p. (C). 1996. pap. 11.95 (*0-19-282520-8*) OUP.

Alvi, Sajida, ed. Urdu for Children, Vol. 1. 58p. 1997. pap. 14.95 (*0-7735-1620-4*, Pub. by McG-Queens Univ Pr) CUP Services.

— Urdu for Children, Vol. 2, Bk.1 44p. 1997. pap. 14.95 (*0-7735-1621-2*, Pub. by McG-Queens Univ Pr) CUP Services.

— Urdu for Children, Book One, Bk. 1. 174p. 1997. pap., teacher ed. 24.95 (*0-7735-1622-0*, Pub. by McG-Queens Univ Pr); pap., wbk. ed. 8.95 (*0-7735-1623-9*, Pub. by McG-Queens Univ Pr) CUP Services.

Alvi, Sajida S., ed. Urdu for Children, Bk. 1. (Canadian Urdu Language Textbook Ser.). (J). (ps-1). 1997. pap. 19.95 incl. audio (*0-7735-1624-7*, PK1973, Pub. by McG-Queens Univ Pr) CUP Services.

Alvi, Sajida S., tr. from PER. Advice on the Art of Governance (Mau'izah-i Jahangiri) of Muhammad Baqir Najm-i Sani: An Indo-Islamic Mirror for Princes. LC 88-16342. (SUNY Series in Near Eastern Studies). (ENG & PER.). 215p. (C). 1989. pap. text 24.95 (*0-88706-919-3*) State U NY Pr.

***Alvi, Shahid.** Youth & the Canadian Criminal Justice System LC 99-43544. 1999. pap. 30.95 (*0-87084-891-7*) Anderson Pub Co.

Alviar, J. Jose. Klesis: The Theology of the Christian Vocation According to Origen. 228p. 1993. text 45.00 (*1-85182-104-X*, Pub. by Four Cts Pr) Intl Spec Bk.

***Alvig, Mark R. & Petracek, Thomas M.** A Practical Guide to Successful Estate Planning: Iowa, Minnesota, North Dakota, South Dakota, Wisconsin. (User-Friendly Financial Ser.). (Illus.). 148p. 2000. pap. 18.95 (*1-58007-021-3*, Pub. by Specialty Pr) Voyageur Pr.

Alvin, Andrea, jt. auth. see Alvin, John.

Alvin, Dave. Any Rough Times Are Now Behind You: Selected Poems & Writings 1979-1995. LC 97-130529. 162p. (Orig.). 1995. pap. 12.00 (*1-884615-09-0*) Incommcdo San Diego.

— Crazy Ones. 150p. 1999. pap. text 12.00 (*1-888277-05-X*, Pub. by Incommcdo San Diego) Consort Bk Sales.

Alvin, J. Doubly Gross Jokes. 1986. pap. 3.50 (*0-8217-3980-8*) NAL.

Alvin, John & Alvin, Andrea. Simba's Pride. LC 99-161339. 96p. (J). 1998. 7.99 (*1-57082-876-8*, Pub. by Mouse Works) Time Warner.

Alvin, Juliette & Warwick, Auriel. Music Therapy for the Autistic Child. 2nd ed. (Illus.). 164p. 1992. pap. text 22.00 (*0-19-816276-6*) OUP.

Alvin, Julius. Agonizingly Gross Jokes. 1991. mass mkt. 3.50 (*0-8217-3648-5*, Zebra Kensgtn) Kensgtn Pub Corp.

— Awesomely Gross Jokes. 160p. 1991. mass mkt. 3.50 (*0-8217-3613-2*, Zebra Kensgtn) Kensgtn Pub Corp.

— Best of Gross Jokes, No. I. 160p. 1996. mass mkt. 4.99 (*0-8217-5469-6*, Zebra Kensgtn) Kensgtn Pub Corp.

— The Best of Gross Jokes II. 144p. 1997. mass mkt. 4.99 (*0-8217-5602-8*, Zebra Kensgtn) Kensgtn Pub Corp.

— The Big Book of Gross Jokes. LC 98-177855. 224p. 1997. pap. 8.00 (*1-57566-235-3*, Knsington) Kensgtn Pub Corp.

— Bigger Book of Gross Jokes. LC 99-204382. 192p. 1998. pap. 9.00 (*1-57566-362-7*) Kensgtn Pub Corp.

— Brutally Gross Jokes, Vol. XXVI. 160p. 1998. pap. 4.99 (*0-8217-5884-5*, Zebra Kensgtn) Kensgtn Pub Corp.

— Double Gross Jokes. 1986. mass mkt. 2.50 (*0-8217-1945-9*, Zebra Kensgtn) Kensgtn Pub Corp.

***Alvin, Julius.** Fiendishly Gross Jokes, Vol. XXX. 2000. mass mkt. 4.99 (*0-8217-6526-4*, Zebra Kensgtn) Kensgtn Pub Corp.

Alvin, Julius. Fresh Gross Jokes, Vol. 7. 1989. mass mkt. 2.95 (*0-8217-2624-2*, Zebra Kensgtn) Kensgtn Pub Corp.

— Frightfully Gross Jokes, Vol. 3. 1999. mass mkt. 4.99 (*0-8217-6347-4*, Zebra Kensgtn) Kensgtn Pub Corp.

— Gross Jokes. 1991. mass mkt. 3.50 (*0-8217-3620-5*, Zebra Kensgtn) Kensgtn Pub Corp.

— Gross Jokes Vol. IX: Astonishingly Gross Jokes. 1990. mass mkt. 2.95 (*0-685-39024-1*, Zebra Kensgtn) Kensgtn Pub Corp.

***Alvin, Julius.** Grossest Jokes of the Century, Vol. 1 1999. pap. 9.00 (*1-57566-531-X*, Knsington) Kensgtn Pub Corp.

— Hilariously Gross Jokes. 1999. mass mkt. 4.99 (*0-8217-6285-0*, Zebra Kensgtn) Kensgtn Pub Corp.

Alvin, Julius. Infinitely Gross Jokes, Vol. 18. 160p. 1994. mass mkt. 3.99 (*0-8217-4785-1*, Zebra Kensgtn) Kensgtn Pub Corp.

— Insanely Gross Jokes, No. 25. 160p. 1997. mass mkt. 4.99 (*0-8217-5682-6*, Zebra Kensgtn) Kensgtn Pub Corp.

— Intensely Gross Jokes, Vol. XIII. 160p. 1993. mass mkt. 3.50 (*0-8217-4168-3*, Zebra Kensgtn) Kensgtn Pub Corp.

— Obnoxiously Gross Jokes. 128p. 1999. mass mkt. 4.99 (*0-8217-6177-3*, Zebra Kensgtn) Kensgtn Pub Corp.

***Alvin, Julius.** Offensively Gross Jokes. 2000. mass mkt. 4.99 (*0-8217-6644-9*, Zebra Kensgtn) Kensgtn Pub Corp.

Alvin, Julius. Outrageously Gross Jokes XXVI. 160p. 1997. mass mkt. 4.99 (*0-8217-5784-9*, Zebra Kensgtn) Kensgtn Pub Corp.

— Savagely Gross Jokes. 1995. mass mkt. 4.50 (*0-8217-5149-2*, Zebra Kensgtn) Kensgtn Pub Corp.

— Terribly Gross Jokes, Vol. XIX. 160p. 1995. mass mkt. 3.50 (*0-8217-4873-4*, Zebra Kensgtn) Kensgtn Pub Corp.

— Totally Gross Jokes. 1991. mass mkt. 3.50 (*0-8217-3622-1*, Zebra Kensgtn) Kensgtn Pub Corp.

— Unbearably Gross Jokes, Vol. XXII. 160p. 1996. mass mkt. 4.99 (*0-8217-5264-2*, Zebra Kensgtn) Kensgtn Pub Corp.

— Unbelievably Gross Jokes, Vol. XXVII. 160p. 1998. pap. 4.99 (*0-8217-5950-7*, Zebra Kensgtn) Kensgtn Pub Corp.

— Unspeakably Gross Jokes. (Gross Jokes Ser.: No. 20). 160p. 1995. mass mkt. 3.99 (*0-8217-5009-7*, Zebra Kensgtn) Kensgtn Pub Corp.

— Wildly Gross Jokes. 144p. 1996. mass mkt. 4.99 (*0-8217-5350-9*, Zebra Kensgtn) Kensgtn Pub Corp.

Alvin, Mitzi. Evidence to the Contrary. 80p. (Orig.). 1998. pap. 12.95 (*0-911051-97-X*) Plain View.

Alvin, Pam, jt. auth. see Conlin, Ross.

Alvin, Raymond. Get a Grip New York Bk. 2: How to Complain Effectively & Get Satisfaction. 2nd enl. expanded rev. ed. LC 97-159842. Orig. Title: The NYC Get a Grip Gripe Book. (Illus.). 364p. (Orig.). 1997. pap. 12.95 (*0-9644961-3-5*) Streetbeat.

— The New York City Get-a-Grip Gripe Book: Raising Hell & Getting Satisfaction with the 51 Most Maddening Hassles, Vol. 1. (Illus.). 256p. (Orig.). 1995. pap. 10.95 (*0-9644961-2-7*) Streetbeat.

Alvin S. White Studio Staff. Bambi Looks for His Forest Friends. LC 91-73808. (Surprise Lift-the-Flap Bk.). 18p. (J). (ps-k). 1992. 9.95 (*1-56282-074-5*, Pub. by Disney Pr) Little.

Alvin, Vernon C. How to Slay the Monster in Your Mortgage. Alvin, Virginia M., ed. LC 85-51507. (Illus.). 52p. (Orig.). 1985. pap. 6.95 (*0-935247-00-9*) Vervir.

Alvin, Virginia M., ed. see Alvin, Vernon C.

Alvine, Lynne & Cullum, Linda. Breaking the Cycle: Gender, Literacy & Learning. LC 99-15379. 1999. pap. text 18.00 (*0-86709-490-7*, Pub. by Boynton Cook Pubs) Heinemann.

Alvino, A. Progress in Elliptic & Parabolic Partial Differential Equations. (Pitman Research Notes in Mathematics Ser.). 1995. lib. bdg. 55.95 (*0-582-25970-3*) Longman.

Alvino, Angelo, et al, eds. Partial Differential Equations of Elliptic Type. (Symposia Mathematica Ser.: No. 35). 233p. (C). 1994. text 69.95 (*0-521-46048-4*) Cambridge U Pr.

Alvino, Barbara M., ed. & photos by see Fagnelli, Ernesto.

Alvino, James & Gifted Children Newsletter Staff. Parents Guide to Raising a Gifted Child: Recognizing & Development of Your Child's Potential. 1985. 21.95 (*0-316-03727-3*) Little.

Alvino, James, jt. auth. see Gifted Children Monthly Editors.

Alvino, Kathleen M., ed. Strategic Planning: A Human Resource Tool for Higher Education. LC 95-70889. 121p. (Orig.). 1995. pap. 30.00 (*1-878240-46-3*) Coll & U Personnel.

— Strategic Planning: A Human Resource Tool for Higher Education. (Orig.). 1996. 30.00 (*0-614-96413-X*) Coll & U Personnel.

Alvis, Joel L., Jr. Religion & Race: Southern Presbyterians, 1946-1983. LC 93-23923. 208p. (Orig.). 1994. pap. text 19.95 (*0-8173-0701-X*) U of Ala Pr.

Alvis, John. Divine Purpose & Heroic Response in Homer & Virgil: The Political Plan of Zeus. 320p. 1995. pap. text 27.95 (*0-8476-8015-0*); lib. bdg. 77.00 (*0-8476-8014-2*) Rowman.

Alvis, John E. Shakespeare's Understanding of Honor. LC 89-61997. 282p. 1990. lib. bdg. 34.95 (*0-89089-382-9*) Carolina Acad Pr.

***Alvis, John E. & West, Thomas G., eds.** Shakespeare as Political Thinker. 2000. 24.95 (*1-882926-50-1*) ISI Books.

Alvisi, A. Essential Diafora Italian-Spanish, Spanish-Italian Dictionary: Diccionario Esencial Diafora Italiano-Espanol-Italiano. (ITA & SPA.). 425p. 1982. 24.95 (*0-8288-0376-5*, S40510) Fr & Eur.

Alvisi, C. & Hill, C. R., eds. Investigative Ultrasonology. 200p. 1981. pap. 55.00 (*0-8464-1221-7*) Beekman Pubs.

Alvord, Clarence W. The Illinois Country, 1673-1818. LC 86-19350. (Sesquicentennial History of Illinois Ser.). (Illus.). 572p. 1987. reprint ed. text 29.95 (*0-252-01337-9*) U of Ill Pr.

Alvord, Clarence W. & Bidgood, Lee. The First Explorations of the Trans-Allegheny Region by the Virginians, 1650-1674. (Illus.). 275p. 1996. reprint ed. pap. 24.00 (*0-8063-4611-6*, 9028) Clearfield Co.

Alvord, Douglas. Sarah's Boat: A Young Girl Learns the Art of Sailing. LC 93-37971. (Illus.). 48p. (J). (gr. 3-6). 1994. 16.95 (*0-88448-117-4*) Tilbury Hse.

***Alvord, Katie.** Divorce Your Car! Ending the Love Affair with the Automobile. (Illus.). 320p. 2000. pap. 17.95 (*0-86571-408-8*, Pub. by New Soc Pubs) Consort Bk Sales.

***Alvord, Lori Arviso & Van Pelt, Elizabeth Cohen.** The Scalpel & the Silver Bear: The First Navajo Woman Surgeon Combines Western Medicine & Traditional Healing. 224p. 2000. pap. 12.95 (*0-553-37800-7*, Spectra) Bantam.

Alvord, Lori Arviso & Van Pelt, Elizabeth Cohen. The Scalpel & the Silver Bear: The First Navajo Women Surgeon Combines Western Medicine & Traditional Healing. LC 99-12331. 240p. 1999. 23.95 (*0-553-10012-2*) Bantam.

Alvord, R., jt. illus. see Greenfield, N. S.

Alvord, Samuel M. Descendants of Alexander Alvord, of Windsor, Conn., & Northampton, Mass. (Illus.). 823p. 1988. reprint ed. pap. 103.00 (*0-8328-0117-8*); reprint ed. lib. bdg. 113.00 (*0-8328-0116-X*) Higginson Bk Co.

***Alvrez, Alicia.** The Ladies Room Reader: The Ultimate Women's Trivia Book. LC 00-9566. 2000. write for info. (*1-57324-557-7*) Conari Press.

Alvrez, Alicia, ed. Bedtime: 365 Nightly Readings for Passion & Romance. 224p. 1999. pap. 13.95 (*1-57324-184-9*) Conari Press.

Alvstam, Claes G., ed. Manufacturing & Services Vol. 15. (National Atlas of Sweden Ser.). (Illus.). 176p. 1998. text 99.50 (*91-87760-34-7*) Coronet Bks.

Alvy, Harvey B. & Robbins, Pamela. If I Only Knew . . . Success Strategies for Navigating the Principalship. LC 97-45423. (One-Off Ser.). 224p. 1998. 61.95 (*0-8039-6643-1*); pap. 27.95 (*0-8039-6644-X*) Corwin Pr.

Alvy, Harvey B., jt. auth. see Robbins, Pam.

Alvy, Harvey B., jt. auth. see Robbins, Pamela.

Alvy, Kerby T. Parent Training Today: A Social Necessity. LC 94-70800. 377p. (Orig.). 1994. pap. 19.95 (*1-884984-06-1*) Ctr Improve Chld.

Alvy, Kirby T. Black Parenting: Strategies for Training. 260p. 1992. reprint ed. pap. 19.95 (*0-8290-2636-3*) Irvington.

Alwall, N., ed. see International Congress of Nephrology, 4th, Stockho.

Alwan. Statistical Process Control. LC 99-27679. 768p. 1999. 85.00 (*0-256-11939-2*) McGraw.

Alwan, Mohamed. Algeria Before the United Nations. 1959. 8.95 (*0-8315-0064-6*) Speller.

Alwani, Taha J. The Ethics of Disagreement in Islam. Al Shaikh-Ali, A. S., ed. Hamid, AbdulWahid, tr. LC 92-39110. (Issues of Islamic Thought Ser.: No. 5). 158p. (Orig.). 1993. 15.00 (*1-56564-117-5*); pap. 7.50 (*1-56564-118-3*) IIIT VA.

— Islah al Fikr al Islami Bayna al Qudarat wa al 'Aqabat (Reform of the Islamic Intellectual Discourse Between Abilities & Obstacles: A Working Paper) LC 91-27987. (Silsilat Islamiyat al Ma'rifah Ser.: No. 9). 98p. (Orig.). 1991. pap. 5.00 (*0-685-70432-7*) IIIT VA.

— Khawatir fi al Azmah al Fikriyah wa al Ma'zaq al Hadari lil Ummah al Islamiyah: (Thoughts on the Intellectual Crisis & the Civilizational Predicament of the Muslim Ummah) (Silsilat Rasa'il Islamiyat al Ma'rifah Ser.: No. 1). (ARA.). 24p. (Orig.). 1989. pap. 2.00 (*1-56564-160-4*) IIIT VA.

— Outlines of a Cultural Strategy. LC 95-195124. (Occasional Papers: No. 1). 32p. 1989. pap. 4.00 (*0-912463-58-9*) IIIT VA.

— Source Methodology in Islamic Jurisprudence: Usul al Fiqh al Islami. 2nd rev. ed. DeLorenzo, Yusuf G. & Al Shaikh-Ali, A. S., trs. from ARA. LC 90-26084. (Research Monographs: No. 1). 112p. (Orig.). 1993. pap. 5.00 (*0-685-70283-9*) IIIT VA.

Alwani, Taha J., jt. auth. see Bishri, Tariq A.

Alward, Cleo M. Thomas "Old Tom" Higgins, 1790-1836, Illinois Mounted Ranger, War of 1812: Research of Higgins & Related Families. LC 97-72837. (Illus.). xxiii, 190p. 1997. pap. 16.50 (*0-9658670-0-5*) C M Alward.

Alward, Debra, ed. see Dulac, Gerry & Parascenzo, Marino.

Alward, Edgar C. Estate Records Planning Guide. rev. ed. (Illus.). 65p. (Orig.). 1996. pap. 12.95 (*1-880836-10-6*) Pine Isl Pr.

— Memories Are Made of This. (Illus.). 140p. (Orig.). 1995. pap. 22.00 (*1-880836-08-4*) Pine Isl Pr.

An Asterisk (*) at the beginning of an entry indicates that the title is appearing for the first time.

A

— Memories Are Made of This. 2nd rev. ed. (Odyssey of a Teacher Ser.). (Illus.). 258p. (Orig.). 1998. 89.00 (*1-891016-28-8*) Esparto Pr.

— Research Paper, Step-by-Step. 4th rev. ed. Orig. Title: Easing the Agony of the Research Paper. (Illus.). 182p. (YA). (gr. 7 up). 1996. pap. text, wbk. ed. 28.00 (*1-880836-11-4*) Pine Isl Pr.

— Research Paper, Step-by-Step: Simplified Method of Learning the Research Process. rev. ed. Orig. Title: Research Paper, Step-by-Step. 198p. 1996. pap. text 35.00 (*1-880836-16-5*) Pine Isl Pr.

— Research Paper, Step-by-Step: Simplified Method of Learning the Research Process. 5th rev. ed. Orig. Title: Research Paper, Step-by-Step. (Illus.). 155p. 1998. pap., wbk. ed. 35.00 (*1-891016-26-1*) Esparto Pr.

Alward, Edgar C. & Alward, Jean A. Punctuation Plain & Simple. LC 96-51152. (In Plain English Ser.). 192p. (Orig.). 1997. pap. 11.99 (*1-56414-274-4*) Career Pr Inc.

Alward, Edgar C. & Dale, E. Up Your Punctuation! An Almost Non-Grammatical Approach to Punctuation. 112p. (Orig.). (YA). (gr. 9-12). 1988. pap. 12.95 (*0-9620092-0-2*) Pine Isl Pr.

Alward, Edgar C. & Murphy, Kathleen, eds. Voices from Paradise. (Illus.). 116p. (Orig.). 1990. 35.00 (*0-9620092-2-9*); pap. 15.00 (*0-685-47512-3*) Pine Isl Pr.

Alward, Edgar C., ed. see Clark, Nan.

Alward, Edgar C., ed. see Cyr, Ruth N.

Alward, Edgar C., ed. see Ludwig, Ray & Morrison, Ivy.

Alward, Edgar C., ed. see Masure, Myrle T.

Alward, Edgar C., ed. see Vickery, Roy B.

Alward, Edward T. Martorell's Tirant lo Blanch: A Program for Military & Social Reform in Fifteenth-Century Christendom. LC 85-2916. (North Carolina Studies in the Romance Languages & Literatures: No. 225). 224p. reprint ed. pap. 69.50 (*0-608-20065-4*, 207133700011) Bks Demand.

Alward, Emily, et al, eds. The Magic Within: An Anthology. LC 94-60709. 208p. 1994. pap. 9.95 (*0-9641438-9-5*) WorldEdge Pr.

Alward, Gregory, jt. auth. see Case, Pamela.

Alward, Jean A., jt. auth. see Alward, Edgar C.

Alward, Ruth R. Nurse's Guide to Marketing. (Home Care Aide Ser.). 1990. pap. 43.45 (*0-8273-4203-9*) Delmar.

Alward, Ruth R. & Monk, Timothy H. The Nurse's Shift Work Handbook. (Illus.). 147p. (Orig.). (C). 1993. pap. text 21.95 (*1-55810-087-3*, NP-82) Am Nurses Pub.

***Alward, Wallace L. M.** The Requisites in Ophthalmology: Glaucoma. (Illus.). 350p. (C). 1999. text. write for info. (*0-323-00106-8*) Mosby Inc.

Alway, Frank, ed. Used Prices Guide Copier Blue Book: Fall 1998. 247p. 1998. pap. 59.00 (*1-58156-041-9*) Asay Pub.

Alway, Joan. Critical Theory & Political Possibilities: Conceptions of Emancipatory Politics in the Works of Horkheimer, Adorno, Marcuse & Habermas, 111. LC 94-29849. 184p. 1995. 55.00 (*0-313-29317-1*, Greenwood Pr) Greenwood.

Alway, Peter. The Art of Scale Model Rocketry. (Illus.). 96p. (Orig.). 1994. pap. text 15.00 (*0-9627876-3-9*) Saturn Pr MI.

— Retro Rockets: Experimental Rockets, 1926-1941. (Illus.). 96p. 1996. 18.00 (*0-9627876-6-3*) Saturn Pr MI.

***Alway, Peter.** Rockets of the World. 3rd rev. ed. (Illus.). 384p. 1999. 35.00 (*0-9627876-7-1*, Pub. by Saturn Pr MI) Partners Bk Dist.

Alweil, Judi. Ribbon Knits. LC 97-47034. (Illus.). 112p. 1998. pap. 21.95 (*1-56158-244-1*, 070371) Taunton.

Alwes, Karla. Imagination Transformed: The Evolution of the Female Character in Keats's Poetry. LC 92-23190. 224p. (C). 1993. 29.95 (*0-8093-1835-0*) S Ill U Pr.

Alwi Bin Alhady. Malay Customs & Traditions. LC 77-87477. (Illus.). reprint ed. 42.50 (*0-404-16789-6*) AMS Pr.

Alwin, Duane F., et al. Political Attitudes over the Life Span: The Bennington Women after 50 Years. LC 91-50319. (Life Course Studies). (Illus.). 352p. 1992. pap. 22.95 (*0-299-13014-2*) U of Wis Pr.

Alwin-Hill, Raymond & Stevenson, Robert Louis. Treasure Island. LC 91-52607. 64p. (Orig.). (YA). 1991. pap. 6.00 (*0-88734-412-7*) Players Pr.

Alwin, John A. Montana Portrait: The Land & Its People. LC 93-9396. (Montana Geographic Ser.: No. 17). (Illus.). 160p. (Orig.). 1993. pap. 9.95 (*1-56037-008-4*) Am Wrld Geog.

Alwin, Lawrence F. A Guide to Measure the Performance of Information Systems. 91p. (Orig.). (C). 1992. pap. text 25.00 (*1-56806-060-2*) DIANE Pub.

— Tough Choices - Finding Ways to Balance Criminal Justice Policy & Criminal Justice Dollars: A Review of Management Controls at the Texas Department of Criminal Justice. (Illus.). 60p. (Orig.). (C). 1994. pap. text 20.00 (*0-7881-0218-4*) DIANE Pub.

Alwin, Robert, jt. auth. see Hackworth, Robert.

Alwin, Robert H. & Hackworth, Robert D. Interactive Beginning Algebra. LC 97-72104. Orig. Title: Algebra Programmed - Part 1. 400p. (Orig.). 1997. pap. text 45.95 (*0-943202-63-9*) H & H Pub.

— Interactive Elementary Algebra. LC 97-71129. 555p. (Orig.). 1997. pap. text 45.95 (*0-943202-62-0*) H & H Pub.

— Interactive Intermediate Algebra. LC 97-72390. Orig. Title: Algebra Programmed - Part 3. 680p. (Orig.). 1997. pap. text 51.95 (*0-943202-64-7*) H & H Pub.

Alwin, Robert H., jt. auth. see Hackworth, Robert.

Alwitt, Linda F. & Donley, Thomas. Marketing & the Poor. (Illus.). 320p. 1996. 46.00 (*0-8039-7211-3*); pap. 19.95 (*0-8039-7212-1*) Sage.

Alwitt, Linda F. & Mitchell, Andrew A., eds. Psychological Processes & Advertising Effects: Theory, Research, & Applications. 320p. 1991. pap. 34.00 (*0-89859-515-0*) L Erlbaum Assocs.

Alwitt, Robert S. Oxide-Electrolyte Interfaces: Proceedings of Symposium Papers Held at the 142nd Meeting of the Society. LC 73-75171. 310p. reprint ed. pap. 96.10 (*0-608-10058-7*, 205182000008) Bks Demand.

Alwitt, Robert S., ed. see Symposium on Aluminum Surface Treatment Technology.

Alwood, Edward. Straight News: Gays, Lesbians, & the News Media. LC 96-526. (Between Men - Between Women Ser.). (Illus.). 386p. 1996. 31.50 (*0-231-08436-6*) Col U Pr.

— Straight News: Gays, Lesbians, & the News Media. (Illus.). 386p. 1998. pap. 18.50 (*0-231-08437-4*) Col U Pr.

Alworth, E. Paul, jt. ed. see Hayden, Donald E.

Alxander, Lloyd, tr. see Eluard, Paul.

Aly, Ahmad A. Economic Cooperation in Africa: In Search of Direction. LC 94-18823. 147p. 1994. lib. bdg. 40.00 (*1-55587-525-4*) L Rienner.

Aly, Bower, ed. see Hamilton, Alexander.

Aly, Goetz. Endloesung: Voelkerverschiebung und der Mord an den Europaeischen Juden. (GER.). 448p. 1995. 43.25 (*3-10-000411-6*, Pub. by S Fischer) Intl Bk Import.

Aly, Gotz. Final Solution: Nazi Population Policy & the Murder of the European Jews. LC 98-36599. 314p. 1999. pap. text 19.95 (*0-340-67758-9*, Pub. by E A) OUP.

***Aly, Gotz.** Final Solution: Nazi Population Policy & the Murder of the European Jews. LC 98-36599. 1999. text 75.00 (*0-340-67757-0*, Pub. by E A) OUP.

Aly, Gotz, et al. Cleansing the Fatherland: Nazi Medicine & Racial Hygiene. Cooper, Belinda, tr. LC 93-42564. 1994. pap. 16.95 (*0-8018-4824-5*) Johns Hopkins.

Aly, Ibrahim. Readings in Management Accounting. 432p. (C). 1995. pap. text, per. 53.95 (*0-7872-0315-7*, 41031501) Kendall-Hunt.

Aly, Lucile. John G. Neihardt. LC 76-45135. (Western Writers Ser.: No. 25). 48p. 1976. pap. 4.95 (*0-88430-024-2*) Boise St U W Writ Ser.

Aly, Osman M., jt. auth. see Faust, Samuel D.

Aly, Raza & Maibach, Howard. Atlas of Infections of the Skin. Fletcher, Judy, ed. LC 98-74079. (Illus.). 352p. (C). 1999. text 170.00 (*0-443-05587-4*) Church.

Aly, Raza & Shinefield, Henry R. Bacterial Interference. 192p. 1982. 102.95 (*0-8493-6285-7*, QR99, CRC Reprint) Franklin.

Alyea. Arm Chair Chemistry. (Illus.). 1990. teacher ed. write for info. (*1-877991-16-3*, AP4272); student ed. write for info. (*1-877991-15-5*, AP1801) Flinn Scientific.

Alyea, Elmer C. & Meek, Devon W., eds. Catalytic Aspects of Metal Phosphine Complexes. LC 81-12903. (Advances in Chemistry Ser.: No. 196). 1982. 76.95 (*0-8412-0601-5*) Am Chemical.

— Catalytic Aspects of Metal Phosphine Complexes. LC 81-12903. (Advances in Chemistry Ser.: Vol. 196). 431p. 1982. reprint ed. pap. 133.70 (*0-608-03509-2*, 206422800008) Bks Demand.

Alyea, Lisa A. & Hoglund, David E., eds. Human Detection & Positive Identification Vol. 2932: Methods & Technologies. LC 96-69895. 200p. 1997. 56.00 (*0-8194-2334-3*) SPIE.

Alyea, Paul E. & Blanche, R. Fairhope, 1894-1954: The Story of a Single Tax Colony. LC 76-42716. (Communal Societies in America Ser.). reprint ed. 37.50 (*0-404-60051-4*) AMS Pr.

Alyett, Robert, ed. Translations of the Carnival Comedies of Hans Sachs, 1494-1576. LC 94-17946. (Studies in German Language & Literature: Vol. 16). (Illus.). 217p. 1995. text 89.95 (*0-7734-1342-1*) E Mellen.

***Alyn, Glen.** Huckleberry Minh: A Walk Through Dreamland. 115p. 1999. pap. 15.00 (*1-877603-61-9*) Pecan Grove.

Alyoshin, Samuil. Theme & Variations. Glenny, Michael, tr. from RUS. 1979. pap. 5.60 (*0-87129-128-2*, T83) Dramatic Pub.

Alzaga, Florinda. La Avellaneda: Intensidad y Vanguardia. LC 96-86801. (Coleccion Polymita Ser.). (SPA., Illus.). 414p. 1997. pap. 29.00 (*0-89729-818-7*) Ediciones.

Alzaga, Florinda, ed. see Gomez de Avellaneda, Gertrudis.

***Alzamora, Stella M., et al.** Minimally Processed Fruits & Vegetables: Fundamental Aspects & Applications. LC 00-38113. (Illus.). 2000. write for info. (*0-8342-1672-8*) Aspen Pub.

Alzate, Beatriz, jt. ed. see Pineda, Roberto.

Alzermant, M. & Aleskerov, F. T. Theory of Choice. LC 97-105721. (Studies in Mathematical & Managerial Economics: Vol. 38). 324p. 1995. 145.75 (*0-444-82210-0*, North Holland) Elsevier.

Alzola, Concepcion T. Habla Tradicional de Cuba: Refranero Familiar. LC 87-71297. 128p. (Orig.). 1987. pap. 15.00 (*0-943503-01-9*) ASHAM.

Alzona, Encarnacion. Some French Contemporary Opinions of the Russian Revolution of 1905. LC 70-158244. (Columbia University. Studies in the Social Sciences: No. 228). reprint ed. 20.00 (*0-404-51228-3*) AMS Pr.

Alzueta, Miquel, jt. auth. see Miralles, Francesc.

Am Esch, J. Schulte & Kochs, E., eds. Central Nervous System Monitoring in Anesthesia & Intensive Care. LC 94-2610. 1993. 106.00 (*0-387-57134-5*) Spr-Verlag.

Am-Fem Company Staff. International Directory of Amateur Female Fighting. 1987. pap. 30.00 (*0-317-56930-9*) AM-FEM Co.

Am, I. The Goddess Speaks. (God's Words for the New Millennium Ser.: Vol. 7). (Illus.). Date not set. pap. 19.95 (*1-892177-52-8*, Lightning Source) Heaven Earth.

— I Am: Autobiography of a Goddess. Date not set. 59.95 (*1-892177-09-9*, Lightning Source); pap. 19.95 (*1-892177-10-2*, Lightning Source) Heaven Earth.

— Jesus Christ's Words for the New Millennium. (God's Words for the New Millennium Ser.: Vol. 8). (Illus.). Date not set. 59.95 (*1-892177-07-2*, Lightning Source); pap. 19.95 (*1-892177-08-0*, Lightning Source) Heaven Earth.

— Miracle Cures for the New Millennium. (God's Words for the New Millennium Ser.: Vol. 9). (Illus.). Date not set. pap. 19.95 (*1-892177-59-5*, Lightning Source) Heaven Earth.

— The Sex Diet. Date not set. pap. 19.95 (*1-892177-57-9*, Lightning Source); mass mkt. write for info. (*1-892177-58-7*, Lightning Source) Heaven Earth.

— The Silicone Survival Handbook: How to Get Well from Silicone Poisoning Caused by Breast Implants. Date not set. pap. 19.95 (*1-892177-51-X*, Lightning Source) Heaven Earth.

Am Rhyn, Otto H. Mysteria: History of the Secret Doctrines & Mystic Rites of Ancient Religions & Medieval & Modern Secret Orders. 245p. 1996. reprint ed. pap. 19.95 (*1-56459-606-0*) Kessinger Pub.

***AMA Counsel on Ethics Staff, ed.** Code of Medical Ethics: Current Opinions with Annotations 2000-2001. (Illus.). 2000. pap. 37.95 (*1-57947-077-7*) AMA.

***AMA Staff.** The American Medical Association Essential Guide to Asthma. 2000. reprint ed. per. 6.99 (*0-7434-0357-6*) PB.

— The American Medical Association Essential Guide to Depression. 2000. reprint ed. per. 6.99 (*0-7434-0359-2*) PB.

— The American Medical Association Essential Guide to Hypertension. 2000. reprint ed. per. 6.99 (*0-7434-0360-6*) PB.

— The American Medical Association Essential Guide to Menopause. 2000. reprint ed. per. 6.99 (*0-7434-0358-4*) PB.

— Guides to the Evaluation of Permanent Impairment. 5th ed. 2000. 139.00 (*1-57947-085-8*) AMA.

— Medicolegal Forms with Legal Analysis: Documenting Issues in the Patient-Physician Relationship. 2nd ed. 224p. 1999. pap. text 44.95 (*0-89970-905-2*) AMA.

***AMA Staff, ed.** Physician Socioeconomic Statistics Text 2000-2001. (Illus.). 2000. pap. 495.00 (*1-57947-088-2*) AMA.

AMA Winter Educators' Conference Staff. AMA Winter Educators' Conference, 1986: Marketing Education: Knowledge Development, Dissemination, & Utilization. Guiltinan, Joseph P. & Achabal, Dale, eds. LC 86-17263. (American Marketing Association, Proceedings Ser.). (Illus.). 239p. 1986. reprint ed. pap. 74.10 (*0-7837-9761-3*, 206048900005) Bks Demand.

— Research Methods & Casual Modeling in Marketing: AMA Winter Educators' Conference, 1983. Darden, William R. et al, eds. LC 83-3713. (American Marketing Association, Proceedings Ser.). (Illus.). 288p. reprint ed. pap. 89.30 (*0-7837-2495-0*, 204266000005) Bks Demand.

Amaa-Ra, Solara A. Invoking Your Celestial Guardians. rev. ed. (Illus.). 64p. 1990. reprint ed. pap. text 10.00 (*1-878246-01-1*) Star-Borne.

Amaan, Markus-Christia. Tunable Laser Diodes. LC 98-28218. 1998. 105.00 (*0-89006-963-8*) Artech Hse.

Amabile, George. Rumours of Paradise - Rumours of War: Poems. 144p. 1995. pap. 13.99 (*0-7710-0736-1*) McCland & Stewart.

Amabile, Rick. Inside Indy Car Racing, Vol. 2. Taylor, Jill, ed. (Illus.). 90p. 1992. pap. 13.95 (*0-9622382-4-4*) AM Cars.

— Inside Indy Car Racing, Vol. 3. (Illus.). 100p. 1992. pap. 13.95 (*0-9622382-3-6*) AM Cars.

— Inside Indy Car Racing 1991, Vol. 2. Taylor, Jill, ed. (Illus.). 88p. (Orig.). (C). 1991. pap. text 13.95 (*0-9622382-2-8*) AM Cars.

Amabile, Teresa M. Creativity in Context: Update to the Social Psychology of Creativity. (C). 1996. pap. 25.00 (*0-8133-3034-3*, Pub. by Westview) HarpC.

— Growing up Creative: Nurturing a Lifetime of Creativity. (Illus.). 1992. reprint ed. pap. 14.95 (*0-930222-89-X*) Creat Educ Found.

Amabile, Teresa M. & Gryskiewicz, Stanley S. Creativity in the R&D Laboratory. (Technical Reports: No. 130G). 34p. 1987. pap. 12.00 (*0-912879-28-9*) Ctr Creat Leader.

Amabile, Teresa M., jt. auth. see Hennessey, Beth A.

Amacher & Ulbrich. Principles of Economics. 3rd ed. (Thomson Executive Press Ser.). 1986. 13.25 (*0-538-27169-8*); mass mkt., student ed. 12.50 (*0-538-08691-2*) S-W Pub.

Amacher, A. Loren. Pediatric Head Injuries Handbook. (Illus.). 138p. 1988. pap. 24.50 (*0-87527-337-8*) Green.

Amacher, Ethel S., jt. auth. see Eaddy, Virginia B.

Amacher, Gregory S., jt. ed. see Hyde, William F.

Amacher, M. C., jt. auth. see Selim, H. M.

Amacher, Peter. Freud's Neurological Education & Its Influence on Psychoanalytic Theory. LC 65-19461. (Psychological Issues Monographs: No. 16, Vol. 4, No. 4). 93p. (Orig.). 1966. 27.50 (*0-8236-2040-9*) Intl Univs Pr.

Amacher, Richard E. Edward Albee. rev. ed. (United States Authors Ser.: No. 141). 240p. 1982. 26.95 (*0-8057-7349-5*) Macmillan.

Amacher, Richard E. & Lange, Victor, eds. New Perspectives in German Literary Criticism: A Collection of Essays. LC 78-12472. 496p. reprint ed. pap. 153.80 (*0-8357-2777-7*, 203990300014) Bks Demand.

Amacher, Ryan C. Patient Care in Neurosurgery, No. 3. 3rd ed. 1990. 45.00 (*0-316-03640-4*, Little Brwn Med Div) Lppncott W & W.

Amacher, Ryan C., et al, eds. Challenges to a Liberal International Economic Order. LC 79-11687. 504p. reprint ed. pap. 156.30 (*0-8357-4445-0*, 203728200008) Bks Demand.

Amacher, Ryan C. & Ulbrich, Holley H. Microeconomic Principles & Policy. 6th ed. LC 94-17223. (C). 1994. mass mkt. 72.95 (*0-538-83850-7*) S-W Pub.

— Principles Of Economics. 3rd ed. (Thomson Executive Press). 1985. mass mkt. 35.25 (*0-538-08671-8*, H67) S-W Pub.

— Principles Of Economics Macro. 3rd ed. (Thomson Executive Press). 1986. mass mkt. 24.50 (*0-538-08690-4*, H69) S-W Pub.

— Principles Of Economics Micro. 3rd ed. (Thomson Executive Press). 1986. mass mkt. 24.50 (*0-538-08681-5*, H68) S-W Pub.

Amacher, Ryan C., jt. ed. see Meiners, Roger E.

Amacom Staff, ed. see Shultz, Susan F.

Amada, Gerald. Coping with the Disruptive College Student: A Practical Model. LC 93-34165. 124p. 1994. pap. 18.95 (*0-912557-16-8*) Coll Admin Pubns.

— A Guide to Psychotherapy. 1997. pap. 11.00 (*0-345-42010-1*) Ballantine Pub Grp.

— A Guide to Psychotherapy: A Comprehensive Guide That Demystifies Psychotherapy. (Orig.). 1995. mass mkt. 5.99 (*0-345-38185-8*) Ballantine Pub Grp.

— The Mystified Fortune-Teller & Other Tales from Psychotherapy. LC 97-34255. 216p. 1998. 24.95 (*1-56833-099-5*) Madison Bks UPA.

— The Power of Negative Thinking: Coming to Terms with Our Forbidden Emotions. LC 98-54369. 260p. 1999. 24.95 (*1-56833-125-8*) Madison Bks UPA.

Amada, Gerald, ed. Mental Health on the Community College Campus. 2nd ed. 152p. (Orig.). (C). 1985. pap. text 20.00 (*0-8191-4915-2*); lib. bdg. 47.50 (*0-8191-4914-4*) U Pr of Amer.

Amada, Gerald & Smith, Michael C. Coping with Misconduct in the College Classroom: A Practical Model. LC 98-33175. (Higher Education Administration Ser.). 1999. 18.95 (*0-912557-23-0*) Coll Admin Pubns.

Amadahy, Zainab. The Moons of Palmares. LC 98-154430. 224p. 1998. pap. write for info. (*1-896705-22-7*) Sister Vis Pr.

Amadei, B., et al. Rock Mechanics for Industry: Proceedings of the 37th Rock Mechanics Symposium, Vail, Colorado, U. S. A, 6-9 June, 1999, 2 vols. 1300p. (C). 1999. text 150.00 (*90-5809-052-3*, Pub. by A A Balkema) Ashgate Pub Co.

Amadei, Bernard, jt. ed. see Kane, William F.

Amadei-Pulice, Maria Alicia. Calderon y el Barroco: Exaltacion y Engano de los Sentidos. LC 90-42421. (Purdue University Monographs in Romance Languages: Vol. 31). (SPA., Illus.). xii, 258p. 1990. 83.00 (*1-55619-073-5*); pap. 27.95 (*1-55619-074-3*) J Benjamins Pubng Co.

Amaden-Crawford, Connie. Block Theory & Master Pattern Review. (Illus.). 11p. 1998. pap. text 9.75 (*0-9649516-3-0*) Fashion Patterns.

— Customizing the Bodice & Blouse Master Patterns. (Illus.). 25p. 1998. pap. text 18.95 (*0-9649516-2-2*) Fashion Patterns.

— Fashion Your Own Pants Simple Way. 67p. (C). 1994. pap. 15.75 (*0-9649516-0-6*) Fashion Patterns.

— Fashion Your Own Skirts the Simple Way. 117p. (C). 1995. spiral bd. 24.75 (*0-9649516-1-4*) Fashion Patterns.

Amadeo, Douglas, ed. see Griffin, James B.

Amadeo, Edward J. Institutions, Inflation & Unemployment. 200p. 1994. 80.00 (*1-85278-682-5*) E Elgar.

— Keyne's Principles of Effective Demand. (New Directions in Modern Economics Ser.). 208p. 1989. text 80.00 (*1-85278-148-3*) E Elgar.

Amadeo, Edward J. & Horton, Susan. Labour Productivity & Flexibility. LC 97-12037. 256p. 1997. text 69.95 (*0-312-17522-1*) St Martin.

Amadeo, Edward J., jt. auth. see Dutt, Amitava K.

Amadeus of Lausanne, jt. auth. see Bernard of Clairvaux.

Amadi, Elechi. The Concubine. (African Writers Ser.). 222p. (C). 1966. pap. 9.95 (*0-435-90556-2*, 90556) Heinemann.

— Estrangement. (African Writers Ser.). 244p. (Orig.). (C). 1986. pap. 7.95 (*0-435-90564-3*, 90564) Heinemann.

Amadi, Elechi. The Great Ponds. (African Writers Ser.). 192p. (C). 1970. pap. 10.95 (*0-435-90044-7*, 90044) Heinemann.

Amadi, L. O. Dictionary of Nigerian History: From Aba to Zazzau. 386p. 1998. 74.95 (*1-57309-207-X*); pap. 54.95 (*1-57309-206-1*) Intl Scholars.

Amadie, Jimmy. Harmonic Foundation for Jazz & Popular Music. LC 81-670040. 168p. (Orig.). (C). 1981. pap. text 24.95 (*0-9613035-0-6*) Thornton Pubns.

— Jazz Improvement: How to Play It & Teach It. LC 90-71929. 158p. 1991. spiral bd. 25.00 (*0-9613035-1-4*) Thornton Pubns.

***Amadife, Emmanuel N.** Pre-Theories & Theories of Foreign Policy-Making. LC 99-13537. 192p. 1999. 35.00 (*0-7618-1364-0*) U Pr of Amer.

Amadio. 2000 Year Book of Hand Surgery. (Illus.). 350p. 2000. text 80.00 (*0-8151-0165-1*, 25766) Mosby Inc.

Amadio, Jill, jt. auth. see Vallee, Eleanor.

Amadio, Nadine. John Coburn: Paintings. (Illus.). 208p. 1990. text 42.00 (*0-947131-20-5*) Gordon & Breach.

Amadio, Peter C. 1998 Year Book of Hand Surgery. (Illus.). 464p. (C). (gr. 13). 1998. text 80.00 (*0-8151-0163-5*, 25764) Mosby Inc.

Amadio, Peter C., ed. see Year Book of Hand Surgery Staff.

Amadio, Roberto M. & Curien, Pierre-Louis. Domains & Lambda Calculi. LC 98-212250. (Tracts in Theoretical Computer Science Ser.: No. 46). 550p. (C). 1998. text 74.95 (*0-521-62277-8*) Cambridge U Pr.

Amadio, William. Systems Development: A Practical Approach. 500p. (C). 1988. text 24.00 (*0-394-39232-9*) Mitchell Pub.

***Amadiume, Ifi.** Daughters of the Goddess Daughters. LC 99-54578. 2000. pap. 27.50 (*1-85649-806-9*) St Martin.

An Asterisk (*) at the beginning of an entry indicates that the title is appearing for the first time.

— Daughters of the Goddess Daughters of Imperialsim. LC 99-54578. 2000. text 69.95 (*1-85649-805-0*) St Martin.

Amadiume, Ifi. Male Daughters, Female Husbands: Gender & Sex in an African Society. (C). 1987. pap. 22.50 (*0-86232-595-1*, Pub. by St Martin) St Martin.

— Male Daughters, Female Husbands: Gender & Sex in an African Society. (C). 1987. text 49.95 (*0-86232-594-3*, Pub. by Zed Books) St Martin.

***Amadiume, Ifi.** Politics of Memory: Truth, Healing & Social Justice. LC 99-87433. 2000. pap. 22.50 (*1-85649-843-3*) Zed Books.

***Amadiume, Lfi.** Politics of Memory. LC 99-87433. 2000. text 65.00 (*1-85649-842-5*, Pub. by Zed Books) St Martin.

Amado, Adrian. Disparate Regional Development in Brazil: A Monetary Production Approach. LC 97-73376. 384p. 1997. text 78.95 (*1-85972-631-3*, Pub. by Ashgate Pub) Ashgate Pub Co.

Amado, Angela N., ed. Friendships & Community Connections Between People with & Without Disabilities. LC 92-47436. 416p. 1993. pap. 33.95 (*1-55766-121-9*) P H Brookes.

Amado, Elisa. Barrilete: A Kite for the Day of the Dead. LC 99-932006. (Illus.). 32p. (J). (ps-3). 1999. 15.95 (*0-88899-366-8*) Grndwd Bks.

— Barrilete: A Kite For The Day Of The Dead. (SPA., Illus.). 32p. (ps-3). 1999. pap. 6.95 (*0-88899-381-1*) Grndwd Bks.

— Un Barrilete: Para el Dia de los Muertos. (SPA., Illus.). 32p. (J). (ps-3). 1999. pap. 15.95 (*0-88899-367-6*) Grndwd Bks.

Amado, Jorge. Bahia de Tous les Saints. (FRE.). 1981. pap. 11.95 (*0-7859-1936-8*, 2070372995) Fr & Eur.

— Captains of the Sands. Rabassa, Gregory, tr. from POR. Orig. Title: Capitaes da areia. 256p. 1988. pap. 7.95 (*0-380-89718-0*, Avon Bks) Morrow Avon.

— Les Chemins de la Faim. (FRE.). 437p. 1991. pap. 21.95 (*0-7859-2156-7*, 2070383326) Fr & Eur.

Amado, Jorge. Dona Flor & Her Two Hu. De Onis, Harriet, tr. from POR. 1977. mass mkt. 6.99 (*0-380-01796-2*, 60044-7, Avon Bks) Morrow Avon.

Amado, Jorge. Dona Flor & Her Two Husbands. De Onis, Harriet, tr. from POR. Orig. Title: Dona Flor e seus dois maridos. 1998. pap. 6.99 (*0-380-35402-0*, Avon Bks) Morrow Avon.

Amado, Jorge. Gabriela, Clove & Cinnamon. Taylor, James L. & Grossman, William R., trs. from POR. Orig. Title: Gabriela, cravo e canela, cronica de uma cidade do interior; romance. 512p. 1982. mass mkt. 6.99 (*0-380-01205-7*, Avon Bks) Morrow Avon.

Amado, Jorge. Gabriela, Clove & Cinnamon. Taylor, James L. & Grossman, William R., trs. from POR. Orig. Title: Gabriela, cravo e canela, cronica de uma cidade do interior; romance. 1988. pap. 12.50 (*0-380-75470-3*, Avon Bks) Morrow Avon.

Amado, Jorge. The Golden Harvest. Landers, Clifford E., tr. from POR. Orig. Title: Sao jorge dos ilheus. 368p. (Orig.). 1992. pap. 12.50 (*0-380-76100-9*, Avon Bks) Morrow Avon.

Amado, Jorge. Home Is the Sailor: The Whole Truth Concerning the Redoubtful Adventures of Captain Vasco Moscoso de Arago, Master Mariner. De Onis, Harriet, tr. from POR. Orig. Title: A completa verdade sobre as discutidas aventuras do Comandante Vesco Moscoso de Arag?o, capit?o de longo curso. (J). 1988. pap. 7.95 (*0-380-45187-5*, Avon Bks) Morrow Avon.

— Home Is the Sailor: The Whole Truth Concerning the Redoubtful Adventures of Captain Vasco Moscoso de Arago, Master Mariner. De Onis, Harriet, tr. from POR. Orig. Title: A completa verdade sobre as discutidas aventuras do Comandante Vesco Moscoso de Arag?o, capit?o de longo curso. 256p. 1988. pap. 7.95 (*0-380-75474-6*, Avon Bks) Morrow Avon.

Amado, Jorge. Jubiaba. Neves, Margaret A., tr. from POR. 304p. 1984. mass mkt. 4.50 (*0-380-88567-0*, Avon Bks) Morrow Avon.

— Jubiaba. Neves, Margaret A., tr. from POR. 304p. 1989. pap. 7.95 (*0-380-75479-7*, Avon Bks) Morrow Avon.

Amado, Jorge. Pen, Sword & Camisole: A Fable to Kindle a Hope. Lane, Helen R., tr. from POR. Orig. Title: Farda, fardao, camisola de dormir. 1989. pap. 7.95 (*0-380-75480-0*, Avon Bks) Morrow Avon.

— Sea of Death. Rabassa, Gregory, tr. from POR. Orig. Title: Mar morto. 288p. 1989. pap. 7.95 (*0-380-75478-9*, Avon Bks) Morrow Avon.

Amado, Jorge. Shepherds of the Night. De Onis, Harriet, tr. from POR. Orig. Title: Pastores da noite. 384p. 1988. pap. 7.95 (*0-380-75471-1*, Avon Bks) Morrow Avon.

Amado, Jorge. Suor. Orig. Title: Suor. (FRE.). 189p. 1991. pap. 10.95 (*0-7859-2177-X*, 2070384268) Fr & Eur.

— Tereza Batista: Home from the Wars. Merello, Barbara S., tr. 576p. 1988. pap. 9.95 (*0-380-75468-1*, Avon Bks) Morrow Avon.

— Les Terres au Bout du Monde. Orig. Title: Terras do sem fim. (FRE.). 379p. 1991. pap. 18.95 (*0-7859-2241-5*, 207038425X) Fr & Eur.

— Tieta, the Goat Girl: Or the Return of the Prodigal Daughter: Melodramatic Serial Novel in 5 Sensational Episodes, with a Touching Epilogue, Thrills & Suspense! Merello, Barbara S., tr. from POR. Orig. Title: Tieta do Agreste, pastora de cabras. 688p. 1988. pap. 9.95 (*0-380-75477-0*, Avon Bks) Morrow Avon.

— The Two Deaths of Quincas Wateryell: A Tall Tale. Orig. Title: A morte e a morte de Quincas Berro Dagua. 112p. 1988. pap. 5.95 (*0-380-75476-2*, Avon Bks) Morrow Avon.

Amado, Jorge. The Violent Land. Putnam, Samuel, tr. from POR. Orig. Title: Terras do sem fim. 288p. 1988. pap. 10.00 (*0-380-75475-4*, Avon Bks) Morrow Avon.

Amado, Jorge. War of the Saints. Rabassa, Gregory, tr. from POR. LC 93-5310.Tr. of Sumico da Santa. 368p. 1995. pap. 14.95 (*0-553-37440-0*) Bantam.

Amadon Corporation Staff, ed. Le Livre D'Urantia. (FRE.). 1783p. 1961. 52.00 (*0-942430-00-X*) Amadon.

Amadon, George F. Rise of the Ironclads. LC 88-60845. (Illus.). 80p. 1988. pap. 9.95 (*0-933126-90-5*) Pictorial Hist.

***Amador, Adela.** Southwest Flavor: Adela Amador's Tales from the Kitchen. (Illus.). 150p. 2000. spiral bd. 9.95 (*0-937206-61-X*, Pub. by New Mexico Mag) U of NM Pr.

Amador, Adela. Undercurrents: New Mexico Stories, Then & Now. LC 98-93739. (Illus.). 176p. 1999. pap. 12.00 (*0-938513-27-3*) Amador Pubs.

Amador De Los Rios, Jose. Historia Critica de la Literatura Espanola, 7 vols., Set. cliv, 4201p. 1970. reprint ed. 625.00 (*0-318-71612-7*) G Olms Pubs.

— Historica Critica de la Literatura Espanola, 7 vols., set. (SPA.). 4201p. 1993. 500.00 (*84-249-1924-6*) Elliots Bks.

Amador, Dora. La Sonrisa Disidente: Itinerario de una Conversion. LC 98-85304. (Coleccion Cuba y sus Jueces). (SPA.). 267p. 1998. pap. 15.00 (*0-89729-871-3*, 871-3) Ediciones.

Amador, E. M. Diccionario Manual Aleman-Espanol, Spanisch-Deutsch. 17th ed. (GER & SPA.). 936p. 1977. 14.95 (*0-8288-5352-5*, S50382) Fr & Eur.

— Diccionario Manual Amador Aleman-Espanol,Espanol-Aleman. (GER & SPA.). 1400p. 1988. 89.95 (*0-7859-0882-X*, S50385) Fr & Eur.

— Diccionario Manual Amador Ingles-Espanol, Espanol-Ingles. (ENG & SPA.). 944p. 35.00 (*0-7859-0953-2*, S-50395) Fr & Eur.

— English-Spanish, Spanish-English Dictionary: Diccionario Ingles-Espanol-Ingles, 2 vols. rev. ed. (ENG & SPA.). 1400p. 1983. 175.00 (*0-8288-0733-7*, S2789) Fr & Eur.

— French-Spanish, Spanish-French Dictionary: Diccionario Frances-Espanol-Frances, 2 vols. (FRE & SPA.). 2000p. 1983. 150.00 (*0-8288-0735-3*, S2792) Fr & Eur.

— German-Spanish, Spanish-German Dictionary: Diccionario Aleman-Espanol-Aleman, Vol. 2. (GER & SPA.). 1635p. 1983. 175.00 (*0-8288-0348-X*, S12381) Fr & Eur.

— Spanish-Italian, Italian-Spanish Dictionary: Diccionario Italiano-Espanol-Italiano, Vol. 2. 1550p. 1983. 150.00 (*0-8288-0377-3*, S12383) Fr & Eur.

Amador, Emilio M. Diccionario Aleman-Espanol, Espanol-Aleman, 2 vols. (GER & SPA.). 1991. 87.50 (*0-685-68144-0*) Fr & Eur.

— Diccionario Aleman-Espanol, Espanol-Aleman, 2 vols., Set. (GER & SPA.). 2096p. 1991. 150.00 (*0-7859-5891-6*, 8430311130) Fr & Eur.

— Diccionario Aleman-Espanol, Espanol-Aleman, 2 vols., Vol. 1. (GER & SPA.). 1056p. 1991. 75.00 (*0-7859-3352-2*, 8430311149) Fr & Eur.

— Diccionario Aleman-Espanol, Espanol-Aleman, 2 vols., Vol. 2. (GER & SPA.). 1040p. 1991. 75.00 (*0-7859-3353-0*, 8430311157) Fr & Eur.

— Diccionario Italiano-Espanol y Espanol-Italiano, 2 vols., Set. (ITA & SPA.). 1984p. 1988. 150.00 (*0-7859-5884-3*, 8430310762) Fr & Eur.

— Diccionario Italiano-Espanol y Espanol-Italiano, Vol. 1. (ITA & SPA.). 1040p. 1988. pap. 75.00 (*0-7859-5885-1*, 8430310770) Fr & Eur.

Amador, J. D. Academic Constraints in Rhetorical Criticism of the New Testament: An Introduction to a Rhetoric of Power. LC 99-179286. (JSNTS Ser.: Vol. 174). 354p. 1999. 85.00 (*1-85075-923-5*, Pub. by Sheffield Acad) CUP Services.

Amador, Mark E., jt. auth. see Fox, Robert W.

Amador, Xavier F. & David, Anthony S., eds. Insight & Psychosis. LC 96-18781. (Illus.). 384p. 1998. text 60.00 (*0-19-508497-7*) OUP.

Amador, Xavier F. & Kiersky, Judith. Being Single in a Couples' World: How to Be Happy on Your Own & Stay Open to Love! LC 97-44090. 240p. 1998. 23.50 (*0-684-84349-8*) Free Pr.

— Being Single in a Couples' World: How to Be Happy Single While Looking for Love. 240p. 1999. pap. 12.00 (*0-684-85235-7*, Fireside) S&S Trade Pap.

Amador, Xavier F., jt. auth. see Rosen, Laura E.

Amador, Zeneida A. Exits & Entrances: Personal Essays. 353p. (C). 1992. pap. 14.75 (*971-10-0487-9*, Pub. by New Day Pub) Cellar.

Amadou, Robert. Bibliographie Generals Des Ecrits De Louis-Claude de Saint-Martin, Vol. IV. 300p. write for info. (*0-318-71425-6*) G Olms Pubs.

— Calendrier De la Vie et Des Ecrits De Louis-Claude de Saint-Martin, Vol. III. 350p. write for info. (*0-318-71424-8*) G Olms Pubs.

— Etudes Sur Louis-Claude de Saint-Martin, Vol. V. 300p. write for info. (*0-318-71426-4*) G Olms Pubs.

— Recueils des Notes Theosophiques, Vol. VII. write for info. (*0-318-71428-0*) G Olms Pubs.

Amadou, Robert, ed. La Correspondence Ine, Vol. XI. 330p. write for info. incl. 3.5 hd (*0-318-71422-1*) G Olms Pubs.

Amadou, Robert, intro. Oeuvres Completes Vol. 5: De l'Espret des Choses (1800) Controverse Avec Garat (1801), 2 vols., 1. 856p. 1990. reprint ed. write for info. (*3-487-09345-6*) G Olms Pubs.

— Oeuvres Completes Vol. 5: De l'Espret des Choses (1800) Controverse Avec Garat (1801), 2 vols., 2. 856p. 1990. reprint ed. write for info. (*3-487-09346-4*) G Olms Pubs.

Amadou, Robert & Joly, Alice. De l'Agent Inconnu Au Philosophie Inconnu, Vol. VI. 262p. reprint ed. write for info. (*0-318-71427-2*) G Olms Pubs.

Amadou, Robert, ed. see De Loos, Onesime-Henri & Chaumette, Pierre G.

Amadou, Robert, ed. see De Saint-Martin, Louis-Claude.

Amadou, Robert, ed. see Matter, Jacques.

Amadou, Robert, ed. see Moreau, Louis & Franck, Adolphe.

Amadou, Robert, ed. see Saint-Martin, Louis-Claude D.

Amadou, Robert, ed. see Teder, pseud & Czerny, Zigmund.

***Amadouny, Vartan.** Jordan. 2nd rev. ed. Vol. 55. 1999. lib. bdg. 83.00 (*1-85109-308-7*) ABC-CLIO.

Amaducci, S. Asbestos: Directory of Unpublished Studies. 1982. text 148.50 (*90-277-1414-2*) Kluwer Academic.

Amaducci, S., ed. Asbestos: Directory of Research & Documentation Centres. 1982. text 171.00 (*90-277-1415-0*) Kluwer Academic.

— Asbestos: Directory of Unpublished Studies. 2nd ec. 222p. 1987. mass mkt. 77.95 (*1-85166-073-9*) Elsevier.

***Amaducci, Sandro.** Dictionary of Definitions of EU Regulated Products: Dictionary & CD-ROM. 480p. 1999. 180.00 incl. cd-rom (*90-411-9677-3*) Kluwer Law Intl.

Amahan, Ali, jt. auth. see Khatibi, Abdelkebir.

Amajani, Babak J., jt. auth. see Barzelay, Michael.

Amaker, Norman C. Civil Rights & the Reagan Administration. 1988. 29.95 (*0-87766-452-8*); pap. 25.00 (*0-87766-451-X*) U Pr of Amer.

Amaladass, Anand, ed. Philosophy & Human Development. 333p. 1986. 19.95 (*0-318-37037-9*) Asia Bk Corp.

Amaladoss, Michael. Life in Freedom: Liberation Theologies from Asia. LC 96-29694. 196p. (Orig.). 1997. pap. 24.00 (*1-57075-124-2*) Orbis Bks.

— Making All Things New: Dialogue, Pluralism, & Evangelization. LC 90-40483. 216p. 1990. reprint ed. pap. 67.00 (*0-7837-9847-4*, 206057600005) Bks Demand.

Amalberti, Rene R., jt. ed. see Sarter, Nadine.

Amaldi, E. & Ghirardi, G., eds. Science in Europe. 230p. (C). 1989. text 108.00 (*9971-5-0842-7*) World Scientific Pub.

Amaldi, E., et al. Electroproduction at Low Energy & Hadron Form Factors. (Tracts in Modern Physics Ser.: Vol. 83). (Illus.). 1979. 47.95 (*0-387-08998-5*) Spr-Verlag.

Amaldi, U., et al. Advances in Hadron Therapy: Proceedings of the 2nd International Symposium on Hadrontherapy, PSI & CERN, Switzerland, 9-13 September, 1996. Vol. 1144. LC 97-41613. (International Congress Ser.). 547p. 1997. 247.00 (*0-444-82782-X*) Elsevier.

Amaldi, Ugo & Larrson, Borje, eds. Hadrontherapy in Oncology: Proceedings of the First International Symposium on Hadrontherapy, Como, Italy, October 1993. LC 94-36767. (International Congress Ser.: No. 1077). 782p. 1994. 314.00 (*0-444-81918-5*) Elsevier.

Amalfitano, John L., jt. auth. see Jones, Thomas H.

Amalgamated Clothing Workers of America, et al. Records of the Amalgamated Clothing Workers of America. LC 92-3417. (The C.I.O. & Industrial Unionism in America Ser.). 61p. 1989. write for info. (*1-55655-141-X*) U Pubns Amer.

Amalric, F. & Banuri, T., eds. People, the Environment & Responsibility: Case Studies from Rural Pakistan. LC 95-18100. (Illus.). 116p. 1995. 62.00 (*1-85070-652-2*) Prthnon Pub.

Amalric, P., ed. see International Symposium on Fluorescein Angiography.

Amalrik, Andrei. Nose! Nose? No-Se & Other Plays. Weissbort, Daniel, tr. from RUS. & intro. by. LC 72-90507. 228p. (Orig.). 1973. pap. 2.95 (*0-15-667350-9*, Harvest Bks) Harcourt.

Amalsad, Meher D. Bread for the Head. (Illus.). 112p. (Orig.). 1997. pap. 5.95 (*0-87573-038-8*) Jain Pub Co.

— Gifts That Lift, Shift & Uplift: Words You Share with People Who Care. LC 96-96132. (Orig.). 1997. disk 24.95 (*1-888912-03-0*) Brainmstrs.

— Gifts That Lift, Shift & Uplift: Words You Share with People Who Care. 2nd rev. ed. LC 96-96132. 121p. (Orig.). 1996. pap. 7.00 (*1-888912-02-2*) Brainmstrs.

— Gifts that Lifts, Shifts, & Uplifts: Words You Can Share with People Who Care. LC 96-96132. 121p. (Orig.) 1996. pap. 7.00 (*1-888912-00-6*) Brainmstrs.

Aman, Alfred C., Jr. Administrative Law & Process. LC 93-21398. (C). 1993. 55.00 (*0-8205-0007-0*) Bender.

— Administrative Law in a Global Era. LC 91-33216. 224p. 1992. text 37.50 (*0-8014-2372-4*) Cornell U Pr.

Aman, Alfred C., Jr. & Mayton, William T. Administrative Law. LC 93-21398. (Hornbook Ser.). 917p. (C). 1992. 41.50 (*0-314-00584-6*) West Pub.

Aman, Anders. Architecture & Ideology in Eastern Europe During the Stalin Era: An Aspect of Cold War History. (American History Foundation Ser.). (Illus.). 356p. 1992. 42.00 (*0-262-01130-1*) MIT Pr.

Aman, Catherine. Scottish Americans. (Peoples of North America Ser.). (Illus.). 128p. (YA). (gr. 5 up). 1990. 19.95 (*1-55546-132-8*) Chelsea Hse.

Aman, Michael G. Working Bibliography on Behavioral & Emotional Disorders & Assessment Instruments in Mental Retardation. 40p. (Orig.). (C). 1996. pap. text 20.00 (*0-7881-2739-X*) DIANE Pub.

Aman, Michael G. & Singh, N. N., eds. Psychopharmacology of the Developmental Disabilities. (Disorders of Human Learning, Behavior, & Communication Ser.). (Illus.). 235p. 1988. 96.95 (*0-387-96679-X*) Spr-Verlag.

Aman, Michael G., et al. Antianxiety Medicines: Medicines for People with Too Much Worry. (Project MED Ser.). (Illus.). (J). (gr. 2 up). 1999. pap. write for info. (*0-9658966-6-8*, 6) OSU Nisonger.

***Aman, Michael G., et al.** Anticonvulsant Medicines: Medicines for People with Epilepsy. large type ed. (Project MED Ser.). (YA). (gr. 2 up). 2000. pap. write for info. (*0-9658966-7-6*) OSU Nisonger.

Aman, Michael G., et al. Antidepressant Medicines: An Easy-to-Read Guide for People Taking Medicine. (Project Med). (Illus.). 1999. pap. text. write for info. (*0-9658966-3-3*, 4) OSU Nisonger.

— Antimanic Medicines: Medicines for People with Mood Problems. (Project MED Ser.). (Illus.). (J). (gr. 2 up). 1999. pap. write for info. (*0-9658966-5-X*, 5) OSU Nisonger.

— Antipsychotic Medicines: An Easy-to-Read Guide for People Taking Medicine. (Project Med). (Illus.). 1999. pap. text. write for info. (*0-9658966-2-5*, 3) OSU Nisonger.

— Patients' Rights & Responsibilities: An Easy-to-Read Guide for People Taking Medicine. (Project Med). (Illus.). 1999. pap. text. write for info. (*0-9658966-1-7*, 1) OSU Nisonger.

— Stimulant Medicines: An Easy-to-Read Guide for People Taking Medicine. (Project Med). (Illus.). 1999. pap. text. write for info. (*0-9658966-4-1*, 7) OSU Nisonger.

Aman, Michael G., jt. ed. see Reiss, Steven.

Aman, Michael G., jt. ed. see Werry, John S.

Aman, Mohammed M., et al, eds. Trends in Urban Library Management: Proceedings of the Urban Library Management Institute Held in October, 1988 at the University of Wisconsin-Milwaukee. LC 89-10285. 180p. 1989. 27.50 (*0-8108-2245-8*) Scarecrow.

Aman, Reinhold. Hillary Clinton's Pen Pal: A Guide to Life & Lingo in Federal Prison. 96p. (Orig.). 1996. pap. 9.95 (*0-916500-14-4*) Maledicta.

Aman, Reinhold, ed. How Do They Do It? A Collection of Wordplays Revealing the Sexual Proclivities of Man & Beast. 64p. 1983. pap. 5.00 (*0-916500-09-8*) Maledicta.

— Maledicta 8 (1984-85) The International Journal of Verbal Aggression. LC 77-649633. (Maledicta: International Journal of Verbal Aggression Ser.: Vol. 8). (Illus.). 320p. 1985. pap. 25.00 (*0-916500-28-4*) Maledicta.

— Maledicta 11 (1990-95) The International Journal of Verbal Aggression. LC 77-649633. (Illus.). 160p. 1995. pap. 12.50 (*0-916500-31-4*) Maledicta.

— Maledicta 4, (1980) The International Journal of Verbal Aggression. LC 77-649633. (Maledicta: International Journal of Verbal Aggression Ser.: Vol. 4, No. 1 & 2). (Illus.). 320p. 1980. pap. 25.00 (*0-916500-55-1*) Maledicta.

— Maledicta 14 (2000) The International Journal of Verbal Aggression. LC 77-649633. (Illus.). 160p. 2000. pap. 15.00 (*0-916500-34-9*) Maledicta.

— Maledicta 9 (1986-87) Lillian Mermin Feinsilver Festschrift. LC 77-649633. (Maledicta: International Journal of Verbal Aggression Ser.: Vol. 9). (Illus.). 320p. 1988. pap. 25.00 (*0-916500-29-2*) Maledicta.

— Maledicta 10, (1988-1989) The International Journal of Verbal Aggression. LC 77-649633. (Illus.). 320p. 1990. pap. 25.00 (*0-916500-30-6*) Maledicta.

— Maledicta 5, (1981) Elias Petropoulos Festschrift. LC 77-649633. (Maledicta: International Journal of Verbal Aggression Ser.: Vol. 5, Nos. 1 & 2). (Illus.). 352p. (C). 1982. pap. 25.00 (*0-916500-25-X*) Maledicta.

— Maledicta 7, (1983) Peter Tamony Festschrift. LC 77-649633. (Maledicta: International Journal of Verbal Aggression Ser.: Vol. 7). (Illus.). 320p. 1984. pap. 25.00 (*0-916500-27-6*) Maledicta.

— Maledicta 1, (1977) G. Legman Festschrift. LC 76-649633. (Maledicta: International Journal of Verbal Aggression: Vol. 1 No. 1 & 2). (C). 1978. pap. 25.00 (*0-916500-50-0*) Maledicta.

— Maledicta 6, (1982) The International Journal of Verbal Aggression. LC 77-649633. (Maledicta: International Journal of Verbal Aggression Ser.: Vol. 6, Nos. 1 & 2). (Illus.). 320p. 1983. pap. 25.00 (*0-916500-26-8*) Maledicta.

— Maledicta 13 (1997-99) The International Journal of Verbal Aggression. LC 77-649633. (Illus.). 160p. 2000. pap. 15.00 (*0-916500-33-0*) Maledicta.

— Maledicta 3 (1979) Ernest Borneman Festschrift. LC 77-649633. (Maledicta: International Journal of Verbal Aggression Ser.: Vol. 3). (Illus.). 1979. reprint ed. pap. 25.00 (*0-916500-48-9*) Maledicta.

— Maledicta 12 (1996) The International Journal of Verbal Aggression. (Illus.). 160p. (Orig.). 1996. pap. 12.50 (*0-916500-32-2*) Maledicta.

— Maledicta 2 (1978) The International Journal of Verbal Aggression. LC 77-649633. (Maledicta: International Journal of Verbal Aggression Ser.: Vol. 2, No. 1-2). (Illus.). (C). 1979. pap. 25.00 (*0-916500-52-7*) Maledicta.

— Opus Maledictorum: Insults, Curses, Slurs, & Other Bad Words from Around the World. 350p. (Orig.). 1996. pap. 14.95 (*1-56924-836-2*) Marlowe & Co.

— Talking Dirty: A Bawdy Compendium of Colorful Language, Humourous Insults & Wicked Jokes. 222p. 1994. pap. 11.95 (*0-7867-0164-1*) Carroll & Graf.

Aman, Reinhold, ed. see Raeithel, Gert.

Amana Heritage Society. Guten Appetite from Amana Kitchens: The Amana Heritage Society Cookbook Old & New Recipes. 1996. 15.50 (*1-57216-061-6*) Penfield.

Amanat, Abbas. Cities & Trade: Consul Abbott on the Economy of Iran, 1847-1866. 256p. 1984. 29.00 (*0-86372-006-4*) Evergreen Dist.

***Amanat, Abbas.** History of the Babi Insurrection of Mazandaran In 1848-1849. (PER., Illus.). 1999. text (*90-04-11363-0*) Brill Academic Pubs.

Amanat, Abbas. The Pivot of the Universe: Nasir al-Din Shah & the Iranian Monarchy, 1831-1896. 1998. 45.00 (*0-934211-51-5*) Mage Pubs Inc.

— The Pivot of the Universe: Nasir al-Din Shah & the Iranian Monarchy, 1831-1896. LC 95-50481. (Illus.). 532p. (C). 1997. 50.00 (*0-520-08321-0*, Pub. by U CA Pr) Cal Prin Full Svc.

— Resurrection & Renewal: The Making of the Babi Movement in Iran, 1844-1850. LC 88-47716. 528p. 1989. text 59.95 (*0-8014-2098-9*) Cornell U Pr.

Amanat, Abbas, ed. see Wills, C. J.

A

An Asterisk (*) at the beginning of an entry indicates that the title is appearing for the first time.

Amanat, Ebrahim & Beck, Jean. The Troubled Adolescent: A Practical Guide. Hacke, Gregory, ed. 432p. 1994. pap. text 35.00 (0-912791-93-4, Ishiyaku EuroAmerica) Med Dent Media.

*Amand, Mulk Raj. Untouchable. (Nick Hern Bks.). 2000. pap. 14.95 (1-85459-446-X) Theatre Comm.

Amandry, Pierre. La Mantique Apollinienne a Delphes: Essai sur le Fonctionnement de L'Oracle. LC 75-10627. (Ancient Religion & Mythology Ser.). (FRE., Illus.). 1976. reprint ed. 25.95 (0-405-07003-9) Ayer.

Amann, Anton, et al, eds. Fractals, Quasicrystals, Chaos, Knots & Algebraic Quantum Mechanics. (C). 1988. text 173.50 (90-277-2750-3) Kluwer Academic.

Amann, Anton H., jt. auth. see Osborne, David W.

Amann, Charles A., ed. see Symposium on Combustion Modeling in Reciprocating.

Amann, Dick. Become a Certified Paralegal for $99.95. LC 76-52041. (Illus.). 250p. 1977. ring bd. 99.95 (0-685-42307-7) Prog Studies.

— How to Make the Purchased Part Cycle Work to Your Company's Advantage. LC 76-52041. (Illus.). 250p. 1977. ring bd. 49.95 (0-917194-03-9) Prog Studies.

— The Lead Poisoning of America's School Children: An Action Plan. 150p. (Orig.). 1991. text 99.50 (0-917194-21-7) Prog Studies.

— Silent Sky: Aviation's War on the American Public. 200p. 1991. 99.95 (0-917194-19-5) Prog Studies.

Amann, Dick & Smith, Dick. Forgotten Women of Computer History. Whitson, Dick, ed. (Illus.). 1978. pap. 49.95 (0-917194-09-8) Prog Studies.

*Amann, Edmund. Economic Liberalization & Industrial Performance in Brazil. (Queen Elizabeth House Series in Development Studies). (Illus.). 320p. 2000. text 80.00 (0-19-829612-6) OUP.

Amann, Enne, jt. tr. see Amann, Peter.

Amann, Enne, tr. see Bisilliat, Jeanne, et al.

Amann, Eric. Cicada Voices: Selected Haiku of Eric Amann, 1966-1979. 64p. (Orig.). 1983. pap. 10.00 (0-913719-25-0, High Coo Pr) Brooks Books.

Amann, H., et al, eds. Progress in Partial Differential Equations: Pont-A-Mousson 1997. 208p. 1998. ring bd. 55.95 (0-582-31708-8, LM1708, Chap & Hall CRC) CRC Pr.

— Progress in Partial Differential Equations Vol. 2: Pont-A-Mousson. 224p. 1998. ring bd. 55.95 (0-582-31709-6, LM1709, Chap & Hall CRC) CRC Pr.

Amann, H., et al. Topics in Nonlinear Analysis: The Herbert Amann Anniversary Volume. LC 98-47312. (Progress in Nonlinear Differential Equations & Their Applications Ser.). 1998. write for info. (0-8176-6016-X) Birkhauser.

Amann, H., ed. see Tondeur, Philippe H.

Amann, Herbert. Gewoehnliche Differentialgleichungen. 497p. 1983. 60.80 (3-11-009573-4) De Gruyter.

— Linear & Quasilinear Parabolic Problems Vol. 1: Abstract Linear Theory. LC 95-7400. (Monographs in Mathematics: Vol. 89). 376p. 1995. 119.00 (0-8176-5114-4) Birkhauser.

— Ordinary Differential Equations: An Introduction to Nonlinear Analysis. Metzen, Gerhard, tr. (Studies in Mathematics: Vol. 13). (Illus.). xiii, 458p. (C). 1990. lib. bdg. 84.95 (3-11-011515-8) De Gruyter.

*Amann, Herbert. Topics in Nonlinear Analysis: The Herbert Amann Anniversary Volume. LC 98-47312. (Progress in Nonlinear Differential Equations & Their Applications). 1998. write for info. (3-7643-6016-X) Birkhauser.

Amann, Peter & Amann, Enne, trs. No Tears for Mao. 279p. 1995. 22.95 (0-89733-410-8) Academy Chi Pubs.

Amann, Peter, tr. see Bisilliat, Jeanne, et al.

Amann, Ronald & Cooper, Julian, eds. Industrial Innovation in the Soviet Union. LC 81-70484. 528p. 1982. 75.00 (0-300-02772-9) Yale U Pr.

Amann, Rupert P. & Siedel, George E., Jr., eds. Prospects for Sexing Mammalian Sperm. LC 82-70138. (Illus.). 306p. reprint ed. pap. 94.90 (0-7837-0549-2, 204088300019) Bks Demand.

Amann, Sandra, et al. The Fine Art Collector's Guide Vol. 1: To Securing, Preserving & Conserving Works of Art Including Tax Planning. LC 95-73310. (Illus.). 102p. (Orig.). 1996. pap. write for info. (0-9651046-0-5) Nordstern Ins.

*Amann, Wolfgang. Stadte- und Siedlungsbau in Wien, 1945-1958. iv, 226p. 1999. 37.95 (3-631-34464-3) P Lang Pubng.

Amano, Ikuo. Education & Examination in Modern Japan. 240p. 1990. 39.50 (0-86008-448-5, Pub. by U of Tokyo) Col U Pr.

Amano, Koji. Host Range & Geographical Distribution of the Powdery Mildew Fungi. 741p. 1987. 110.00 (4-7622-9486-1, Pub. by Busn Ctr Acad) Intl Spec Bk.

Amano, R. S., et al, eds. Heat Transfer in Turbulent Flows - 1993. (HTD Ser.: Vol. 246). 172p. 1993. 45.00 (0-7918-1159-X, G00803) ASME.

Amano, Takashi. Aquarium Plant Paradise. (Illus.). 64p. 12.95 (0-7938-0518-X) TFH Pubns.

Amano, Talsashi. Natural Aquarium World, Bk. 1. (Illus.). 192p. 1993. 35.95 (0-7938-0089-7, TS206) TFH Pubns.

— Nature Aquarium World, Bk. 2. 162p. 1996. 39.95 (0-7938-2077-4, TS-284) TFH Pubns.

— Nature Aquarium World, Bk. 3. 1996. 29.95 (0-7938-2078-2, TS-285) TFH Pubns.

Amano, Yu. Karl Barths Ethik der Versohnungslehre: Ihre Theologische Rezeption in Japan und Ihre Bedeutung Fur die Kirchlich-Gesellschaftliche Situation in Japan. (Europaische Hochschulschriften Ser.: Reihe 23, Bd. 518). (GER.). V, 268p. 1994. 49.95 (3-631-47801-1) P Lang Pubng.

Amanolahi, Sekandar & Thackston, Wheeler M., eds. Tales from Luristan. (Harvard Iranian Ser.). (Illus.). 276p. 1987. pap. 19.95 (0-674-86780-7) HUP.

Amanor, Kojo S. Global Restructuring & Land Rights in Ghana: Forest Food Chains, Timber & Rural Livelihoods. LC 99-212247. 185p. 1999. pap. 21.95 (91-7106-437-0) Transaction Pubs.

— The New Frontier: The Response of Farmers to Land Degradation: A West African Study. (Illus.). 244p. (C). 1994. text 65.00 (1-85649-241-9, Pub. by Zed Books) St Martin.

Amans, Jean-Louis, jt. auth. see Grangeat, Pierre.

Amant, J. A., ed. Desert Tortoise Council Symposium, 1976. 15.00 (0-318-23139-5) Desert Tortoise Coun.

Amant, Kristi, ed. see Arrants, Cheryl & Asbjornsen, Jan.

Amantea, Carlos. The Lourdes of Arizona. 150p. 1989. 17.95 (0-917320-30-1); pap. 10.95 (0-917320-11-5) Mho & Mho.

Amantea, Carlos A. The Blob That Ate Oaxaca & Other Travel Tales. LC 91-19828. 457p. 1992. pap. 12.95 (0-917320-32-8) Mho & Mho.

Amanuddin, Syed. Creativity & Reception: Toward a Theory of Third World Criticism. (American University Studies: General Literature: Ser. XIX, Vol. 12). X, 202p. (C). 1988. text 32.60 (0-8204-0623-6) P Lang Pubng.

Amanzeh, Augustine A. Festival of African Animals. (Illus.). 10p. (YA). (gr. 3-12). 1997. 8.00 (1-890606-01-4) A A Amanzeh.

— A Guide to Mental Hospital Visitation: The Mental Hospital Handbook. unabridged ed. 64p. (Orig.). 1996. 10.00 (0-614-30082-7) A A Amanzeh.

— Let's Go to Africa & Nigeria: A Poetic Profile. 70p. (Orig.). 1998. pap. 9.00 (1-890606-04-9) A A Amanzeh.

— When Children Can Be Children: Adults Must Help. unabridged ed. (Illus.). 15p. (YA). (gr. 8-12). 1997. 8.00 (1-890606-02-2) A A Amanzeh.

— When the Gods Shoot. unabridged ed. 50p. (Orig.). 1997. pap. 12.00 (1-890606-03-0) A A Amanzeh.

Amar, Akhil Reed. The Bill of Rights: Creation & Reconstruction. LC 97-38370. 432p. 1998. 35.00 (0-300-07379-8) Yale U Pr.

*Amar, Akhil Reed. The Bill of Rights: Creation & Reconstruction. LC 97-38370. (Illus.). 432p. 2000. pap. 17.95 (0-300-08277-0) Yale U Pr.

Amar, Akhil R. Constitution & Criminal Procedure: First Principles. LC 96-21079. 288p. 1997. 35.00 (0-300-06678-3) Yale U Pr.

— The Constitution & Criminal Procedure: First Principles. 288p. 1998. pap. 16.00 (0-300-07488-3) Yale U Pr.

Amar, Akhil R. & Hirsch, Alan. For the People: What the Constitution Really Says About Your Rights. LC 97-38241. 304p. 1998. 25.50 (0-684-82694-1) Free Pr.

Amar, Ben M., et al, eds. Growth & Form: Nonlinear Aspects. (NATO ASI Ser.: Vol. 276). (Illus.). 512p. (C). 1992. text 174.00 (0-306-44046-6, Kluwer Plenum) Kluwer Academic.

Amar, E., et al, eds. Analyse Complexe. (Lecture Notes in Mathematics Ser.: Vol. 1094). ix, 185p. 1984. 34.95 (0-387-13886-2) Spr-Verlag.

Amar, Joseph P., tr. see St. Ephrem the Syrian.

Amar, Jules. The Human Motor. (Physical Education Reprint Ser.). (Illus.). 1972. reprint ed. lib. bdg. 32.50 (0-697-00060-5) Irvington.

Amara, H. A. & Founou-Tchuigoua, B., eds. African Agriculture: The Critical Choices. LC 89-35869. (UNU Studies in African Political Economy: Vol. 6). 320p. (C). 1990. pap. 19.95 (0-86232-799-7, Pub. by Zed Books); text 55.00 (0-86232-798-9, Pub. by Zed Books) St Martin.

Amara, Mark S. & Neff, George E. Geological Road Trips in Grant County, Washington. Zak, Aleta, ed. LC 96-83503. (Illus.). 104p. (Orig.). 1996. pap. 14.95 (0-9649545-0-8) Adam East Mus.

*Amara, Muhammad Hasan. Politics & Sociolinguistic Reflexes: Palestinian Border Villages. LC 99-22264. (Studies in Bilingualism: Vol. 19). xx, 261p. 1999. 79.00 (1-55619-950-3) J Benjamins Pubng Co.

Amara, Philip, ed. see Allred, Michael D.

Amara, Philip, ed. see Chelsea, David.

Amara, Philip, ed. see Conner, Jeff.

Amara, Philip, ed. see Moore, Alan.

Amara, Philip, ed. see Schreiner, Dave.

Amara, Philip, ed. see Steffan, Dan, et al.

Amara, Philip, ed. see Wrightson, Bernie.

Amara, Phillip. Species: Human Race. 1997. pap. text 11.95 (1-56971-219-0) Dark Horse Comics.

Amara, Roy C. Toward Understanding the Social Impact of Computers. 136p. 1974. 10.50 (0-318-14427-1, R29) Inst Future.

*Amara, Roy C., et al. Health & Health Care 2010: The Forecast, the Challenge. LC 99-88438. 2000. write for info. (0-7879-5348-2) Jossey-Bass.

Amara, Roy C., et al. Industrial Robot Outlook. 26p. 1985. 6.00 (0-318-19206-3, R-62) Inst Future.

Amaral, Alberto C. Do, see Do Amaral, Alberto C.

Amaral, Aracy A. & Herkenhoff, Paulo. UltraModern: The Art of Contemporary Brazil. (Illus.). 128p. 1993. 34.95 (0-318-70269-X); pap. text 21.95 (0-940979-24-1) Natl Museum Women.

Amaral, David. Lusophone African Liberators: The University Years. (Graduate Student Papers Competition). 20p. (Orig.). 1979. pap. text 2.00 (0-941934-27-6) Indiana Africa.

Amaral, David F. & Gulbrand, Jennifer. Aromantic Notes: Recipes for Romantic Dining. 49p. 1997. pap. 12.95 (0-9662261-0-0) Global Note Mus.

*Amaral, G. Pajama Sam. (Illus.). 112p. (J). (ps-2). 2000. pap. 2.99 (1-57064-949-9, 73116, Humongous Bks) Lyrick Pub.

*Amaral, Gayla. Babies & Barney: Hooray for Daddies! LC 00-105003. (J). (ps). 2000. 5.95 (1-58668-053-6) Lyrick Studios.

— Barney on the Go! A Treasury of "Go to" Books. LC 00-100348. (Barney's Go to Ser.). (Illus.). 164p. (J). (ps-2). 2000. 10.95 (1-57064-732-1, 97983) Lyrick Pub.

— Barney's Color Train Readalong. LC 00-102608. (Illus.). 24p. (J). (ps-k). 2000. pap. 6.95 (1-57064-713-5, 97964) Lyrick Pub.

Amaral, Gayla. Barney's Star Light, Star Bright. LC 99-66253. (Barney Ser.). (Illus.). 20p. (J). (ps-k). 2000. 5.95 (1-57064-708-9, Barney Publ) Lyrick Pub.

*Amaral, Gayla. I Can Learn with Barney. LC 00-105002. 68p. (J). (ps). 2001. 5.95 (1-58668-048-X) Lyrick Pub.

*Amaral, Gayla, ed. Barney, Let's Discover. (Illus.). 32p. (J). (ps). 2001. 0.99 (1-58668-134-6) Lyrick Studios.

— Barney Let's Pretend. (Illus.). 32p. (J). (ps). 2001. 0.99 (1-58668-133-8) Lyrick Studios.

— Barney's Favorite Easter Stories. LC 00-105013. (Illus.). 48p. (J). (ps). 2001. 4.95 (1-58668-072-2) Lyrick Studios.

— Barney's I Love Animals. (Illus.). 112p. (J). (ps). 2001. 2.99 (1-58668-131-1) Lyrick Studios.

— Barney's I Love Nursery Rhymes! (Illus.). 64p. (J). (ps). 2001. 1.99 (1-58668-132-X) Lyrick Studios.

Amaral, Gayla, jt. auth. see Kearns, Kimberly.

Amaral, Geraldine & Cunningham, Nancy B. Tarot Celebrations: Honoring the Inner Voice. (Illus.). 312p. pap. 16.95 (1-57281-105-6, BK176) US Games Syst.

Amaral, Geraldine & Cunningham, Nancy B. Tarot Celebrations: Honoring the Inner Voice. LC 97-18744. (Illus.). 336p. 1997. pap. 16.95 (1-57863-014-2) Weiser.

Amaral, Grant. Idaho--the Whitewater State: A Guidebook. Andrews, Laura, ed. (Illus.). 314p. (Orig.). 1995. reprint ed. pap. 19.95 (0-9622344-0-0) Watershed Bks.

Amaral, Joao F. Do, see Do Amaral, Joao F.

Amaral, John, jt. auth. see Frank, Dave.

Amaral, Michel. Officer Safety Vol. 6: Tactics for Survival. 6th rev. ed. (Illus.). 248p. 1998. reprint ed. pap. text 29.95 (0-9645535-1-1) IPAT.

Amaral, Michel E. Officer Safety: Tactics for Survival. 5th ed. (Illus.). 180p. 1996. 24.95 (0-9645535-0-3) IPAT.

Amaral, Mike, jt. auth. see Payton, George T.

Amaral, P. V., ed. see Sellars, Wilfrid.

*Amaral, Ricardo C. Jose Bonifacio de Andrada e Silva: The Greatest Man in Brazilian History. LC 99-91805. 2000. 25.00 (0-7388-1286-2); pap. 18.00 (0-7388-1287-0) Xlibris Corp.

Amaral, Samuel. The Rise of Capitalism on the Pampas: The Estancias of Buenos Aires, 1785-1870. LC 96-53311. (Latin American Studies: Vol. 83). (Illus.). 400p. (C). 1998. 59.95 (0-521-57248-7) Cambridge U Pr.

Amarante, Hector. La Novela Dominicana en N. Y. (SPA.). 122p. 1998. pap. 8.00 (0-938693-12-3) Maya Pubns.

Amaranth, Lee A. Communicating in Sign. LC 97-51145. (Illus.). 176p. 1998. pap. 12.00 (0-684-83520-7, Fireside) S&S Trade Pap.

Amarasinghe, Upali. Dryden & the Pope in the Early Nineteenth Century: A Study of Changing Literary Taste, 1800-1830. LC 62-52188. 256p. reprint ed. pap. 73.00 (0-608-13567-4, 2022433) Bks Demand.

Amarat, Hasan. Ibn An-Nafis Kompendium Uber die Wissenschaft Von Den Grundlagen des Hadit. (Arabistische Texte und Studien: Vol. 1). (Illus.). 219p. 1986. 32.00 (3-487-07821-X) G Olms Pubs.

*Amarell, Uwe. Dissertationes Botanicae, Vol. 325. (Illus.). 246p. 2000. pap. 65.00 (3-443-64237-3, Pub. by Gebruder Borntraeger) Balogh.

Amarendra, Dr. Poverty, Rural Development & Public Policy. 1998. 30.00 (81-7629-097-1) Deep & Deep Pubns.

Amargies. Vaccination Against Brucellosis in Ruminants Using Inactivated H38 Vaccine. (C). 1987. 12.50 (0-317-66877-3, Pub. by Oxford IBH) S Asia.

Amari & Freeman. Neural Networks & Chaos. Szu, Harold, ed. (INNS Series of Texts, Monographs, & Proceedings). 300p. 1993. write for info. (0-8058-1501-5) L Erlbaum Assocs.

Amari, S. Speech Hearing & Neural Networks Models. LC 94-77518. 200p. (gr. 12). 1995. 74.00 (90-5199-178-9) IOS Press.

Amari, S. & Kasabov, N., eds. Brain-Like Computing & Intelligent Information Systems. 400p. 1998. 79.00 (981-3083-58-1) Spr-Verlag.

Amari, S., et al. Differential Geometry in Statistical Inference. LC 87-82603. (IMS Lecture Notes - Monographs: Vol. 10). iv, 232p. 1988. pap. 25.00 (0-940600-12-9) Inst Math.

Amari, S., jt. ed. see Arbib, Michael A.

Amari, S. I., et al, eds. Progress in Neural Information Processing Set: Proceedings of the International Conference on Neural Information Processing (ICONIP '96), Hong Kong, 2 vols. (Illus.). 700p. 1997. pap. 102.00 (981-3083-05-0) Spr-Verlag.

Amari, Shunichi & Asian Pacific Neural Network Assembly Staff. Progress in Neural Information Processing: ICONIP'96: Proceedings of the International Conference on Neural Information Processing, Hong Kong, 24-27 September 1996. LC 96-27442. 1997. 59.95 (981-3083-04-2); pap. 59.95 (981-3083-03-4) Spr-Verlag.

Amari, Suad. Cooking the Lebanese Way. (Easy Menu Ethnic Cookbooks Ser.). (Illus.). 48p. (J). (gr. 5 up). 1986. lib. bdg. 19.93 (0-8225-0913-X, Lerner Publctns) Lerner Pub.

*Amarillas, Susan. Molly's Hero. (Historical Ser.: Bk. 518). 2000. per. 4.99 (0-373-29118-3, 1-29118-6) Harlequin Bks.

Amarillas, Susan. Scanlin's Law. 1995. per. 4.50 (0-373-28883-2) Harlequin Bks.

— Silver & Steel. LC 95-16516. (Historical Ser.). 296p. 1994. per. 3.99 (0-373-28833-6, 1-28833-6) Harlequin Bks.

— Wild Card. 1997. per. 4.99 (0-373-28988-X, 1-28988-3) Harlequin Bks.

— Wyoming Renegade. (Historical Ser.). 1997. per. 4.99 (0-373-28951-0, 1-28951-1) Harlequin Bks.

Amarillo Genealogical Society Staff, ed. Texas Panhandle Forefathers, Vol. I. (Illus.). 387p. 1983. reprint ed. text 30.00 (0-88107-011-4) Curtis Media.

Amaringo, Pablo, jt. auth. see Luna, Luis E.

*Amarloui, M. Stor Persisk-Norsk Ordbok. (PER & NOR.). 1004p. 1998. 275.00 (0-320-02253-6) Fr & Eur.

Amarloui, Mano. Norsk - Persisk Ordbok. (NOR & PER.). 784p. 1992. 350.00 (0-7859-3667-X, 8200029751) Fr & Eur.

Amarnath, Panbdit. Living Idioms in Hindustani Music: A Dictionary of Terms & Terminology. (C). 1995. 18.00 (81-7223-104-0, Pub. by Indus Pub) S Asia.

Amarnick, Claude. Dr. Amarnick's Mind over Matter Pain Relief Program. LC 95-81679. 204p. 1995. 24.95 (1-880539-37-3); pap. 9.95 (1-880539-36-5) Garrett FL.

— Don't Put Me in a Nursing Home! LC 96-77342. 182p. (Orig.). 1996. pap. 13.95 (1-880539-38-1) Garrett FL.

Amaro, Juan & Culpepper, John. Americans - Mexicans Folk Wisdom. (Illus.). 38p. (Orig.). (C). 1994. pap., student ed. write for info. (0-9624186-2-5) Warm Days Retirement.

Amaro, Juan & Elder, Cindy. Dichos, Retranes y Opiniones. Culpepper, John, ed. & illus. by. (ENG & SPA.). 40p. (Orig.). (C). 1989. pap. write for info. (0-9624186-1-7) Warm Days Retirement.

Amarosa, Richard, ed. see Semrock, Ralph.

Amaru, Tuppacc, III. Mental Aerobics: Self Power. Chekwas, Sam, ed. 160p. (Orig.). 1997. pap. 11.00 (1-885778-26-0) Seaburn.

Amaryan, L. S. Soft Soil Properties & Testing Methods. Zeidler, Ryszard B., ed. (Selected Translations of Russian Geotechnical Literature Ser.). (Illus.). 192p. (C). 1993. text 91.00 (90-5410-134-2, Pub. by A A Balkema) Ashgate Pub Co.

Amasino, R. M. Cellular Communication in Plants. LC 93-10041. (Illus.). 200p. (C). 1993. text 85.00 (0-306-44415-1, Kluwer Plenum) Kluwer Academic.

Amastae, Jon, ed. see Linguistic Symposium on Romance Languages Staff.

Amat, Carlos Gomez, see Gomez Amat, Carlos.

Amat, Gilbert, et al. Rotation-Vibration of Polyatomic Molecules: Higher Order Energies & Frequencies of Spectral Transitions. LC 71-152569. 447p. reprint ed. pap. 138.60 (0-608-17026-7, 202711500054) Bks Demand.

Amat, Oriol, jt. auth. see Blake, John.

Amat, Salvador R. Defectos y Alteraciones de los Frutos Citricos en su Comercializacion. 2nd ed. (SPA., Illus.). 155p. 1988. pap. 35.00 (84-404-3207-0, Pub. by S R Amat) FL Sci Source.

Amata, E. Paul & Jensen, Maryanne G. Help! I Don't Know Where to Start! A Guide to Getting Started as a Massachusetts Lawyer. LC 98-88591. 264p. 1998. write for info. (1-57589-103-4) Mass CLE.

*Amat'Al-Quddus, Majida, compiled by. Coming to Islam: A Muslim Anthology Vol. I: Shahada - (Declaration of Faith Testimonials) 2nd ed. (Illus.). 264p. 1999. reprint ed. 49.95 (0-932974-95-3, 27943); reprint ed. pap. 29.95 (0-932974-99-6, 27943) River Garden.

— Coming to Islam: A Muslim Anthology Vol. II: Shahada - (Declaration of Faith Testimonials) (Illus.). 264p. 2000. 49.95 (0-932974-94-5, 27942); pap. 29.95 (0-932974-98-8, 27942) River Garden.

— Coming to Islam: A Muslim Anthology Vol. III: Polygyny. (Illus.). 200p. 2001. pap. 29.95 (0-932974-96-1, 27945) River Garden.

— Coming to Islam: A Muslim Anthology Vol. V: Hajj - Pilgrimage of a Lifetime. (Illus.). 264p. 2001. 49.95 (0-932974-89-9, 27944); pap. 29.95 (0-932974-90-2, 27944) River Garden.

*Amatayakul, Margret. The Role of Health Information Managers in CPR Projects: A Practical Guide. (Illus.). 292p. 1999. pap. text 55.00 (1-58426-032-7, AB102699) Am Hlth Info.

Amatayakul, Margret, et al. 1999 Comprehensive Guide to Electronic Medical Records. 549p. 1999. pap. write for info. (1-57987-108-9) Faulkner & Gray.

Amate, E. A., jt. ed. see Kottke, Frederic J.

*Amate, Roberto Cobas. Wilfredo Lam: Obra Grafica. 2000. pap. 19.95 (0-89013-377-8) Museum NM Pr.

Amatea, Ellen S., jt. auth. see Brown, Norman M.

Amateau, Maurice F., ed. see Metallurgical Society of AIME Staff.

*Amateis, Carole & Amateis-Marsh, Melissa. Benjamin Bean: Planting, Growing, Harvesting. (Illus.). 42p. (YA). 2000. pap. write for info. (0-7392-0505-6, PO4148) Morris Pubng.

Amateis-Marsh, Melissa, jt. auth. see Amateis, Carole.

*Amatenstein, Sherry. Q & A Dating Book. 240p. 2000. pap. 10.95 (1-58062-274-7) Adams Media.

Amateur Athletic Foundation Staff. AAF-CIF Track & Field Coaches Manual. (Illus.). 223p. (C). 1994. pap. 34.95 (0-685-72202-3) Amateur Ath LA.

Amateur Swimming Association Staff. Swimming. (Know the Sport Ser.). (Illus.). 48p. 1997. pap. 5.95 (0-8117-2835-8) Stackpole.

Amati, Daniele, jt. ed. see Ellis, John.

Amati-Mehler, Jacqueline, et al, eds. The Babel of the Unconscious: Mother Tongue & Foreign Languages in the Psychoanalytic Dimension. 322p. 1993. 50.00 (0-8236-0530-2) Intl Univs Pr.

*Amato. Literature Express Level 4. (C). 2002. text 32.50 (0-8384-0174-0) Heinle & Heinle.

Amato. Literature Express Level 4: Assessment. 2002. pap. 32.50 (0-8384-0169-4) Heinle & Heinle.

— Literature Express Level 4: Text. 2002. pap. text 30.00 (0-8384-0165-1) Heinle & Heinle.

A

A

Amberger, J Christopher. Secret History of the Sword. 1999. pap. text 19.95 (*1-892515-04-0*) Multi-Media Comms.

***Ambergis, Lenore.** The Erotic Soul: A Pillow Book. (Illus.). 74p. 1999. pap. 7.95 (*0-9666649-1-4*) Full Moon CT.

Amberhill, Bevan. The Bloody Man. 244p. 15.95 (*1-55128-007-8*, Pub. by Mercury Bk) LPC InBook.

***Amberiadis, Kostas, et al, eds.** In-Line Characterization, Yield Reliability & Failure Analyses in Microelectronic Manufacturing. (Europto Ser.: Vol. 3743). 352p. 1999. pap. text 84.00 (*0-8194-3223-7*) SPIE.

Amberlain, Robert. Arcanos Negros de Hitler. Cruz, Rosa Ana Dominguez, tr. (Illus.). 349p. 1997. pap. 30.00 (*968-890-179-2*) Edivision Comp.

Amberley, John R. An Analysis of Religious Belief. LC 76-161318. (Atheist Viewpoint Ser.). 745p. 1972. reprint ed. 45.95 (*0-405-03621-3*) Ayer.

Amberry, Tom & Reed, Philip. Free Throw: Art & Mechanics of the Free Throw by the World's Greatest Free Throw Shooter. LC 96-15790. (Illus.). 144p. 1996. pap. 10.95 (*0-06-273434-2*) HarpC.

Ambers, Henry J. The Dirigible & the Future. rev. ed. LC 81-69805. 70p. 1981. pap. 10.00 (*0-9600874-1-9*) Edelweiss Pr.

— The Unfinished Building. LC 74-19535. 400p. 1974. 19.95 (*0-9600874-2-7*) Edelweiss Pr.

— The Waltzer. LC 76-114002. 320p. 1970. 19.95 (*0-9600874-4-3*) Edelweiss Pr.

***Amberson, Cynthia.** Meditative Moments: Imageries & Journeys for Your Inner Self & Your Soul. Chadwick, Gloria, ed. LC 00-130513. 110p. 2000. pap. 11.95 (*1-883717-18-3*) Myst Mndscapes.

Amberson, Joanne. Hikes to Waterfalls in Shenandoah National Park. (Illus.). 24p. 1997. pap. 2.00 (*0-931606-20-9*) Shenandoah Nat Assn.

Amberson, Max L. & Anderson, B. H. Learning Through Experience in Agricultural Industry. 1978. text 16.96 (*0-07-000851-5*) McGraw.

Amberson, Max L., ed. see Bishop, Douglas D.

Amberson, Max L., ed. see Peterson, Paul, et al.

Amberson, Max L., ed. see Shinn, Glen C. & Weston, Curtis.

Amberson, Max L., ed. see Stewart, Robert.

Ambert, Alba. Porque Hay Silencio. (Pioneer Ser.).Tr. of Perfect Silence. 208p. 1998. pap. 11.95 (*1-55885-250-6*) Arte Publico.

Ambert, Alba N. The Eighth Continent & Other Stories. LC 97-22169. 160p. 1997. pap. 12.95 (*1-55885-217-4*) Arte Publico.

— A Perfect Silence. LC 94-29360. 199p. 1995. 9.95 (*1-55885-125-9*) Arte Publico.

Ambert, Alba N. & Melendez, Sarah E. Bilingual Education: A Sourcebook. LC 86-23125. 356p. reprint ed. pap. 110.40 (*0-7837-2178-1*, 204251600004) Bks Demand.

Ambert, Anne-Marie. The Effect of Children on Parents. LC 91-8366. 312p. 1992. pap. 24.95 (*1-56024-118-7*); lib. bdg. 49.95 (*1-56024-117-9*) Haworth Pr.

***Ambert, Anne-Marie.** The Effect of Children on Parents. 2nd ed. LC 00-33536. 2000. write for info. (*0-7890-0855-6*, Haworth Clinical) Haworth Pr.

Ambert, Anne-Marie. Ex-Spouses & New Spouses Vol. 7: A Study of Relationships. LC 89-15220. (Contemporary Studies in Sociology: Vol. 7). 213p. 1989. 78.50 (*1-55938-064-0*) Jai Pr.

***Ambert, Anne-Marie.** Families in the New Millennium. 560p. 2000. (*0-321-05048-7*) Addison-Wesley.

Ambert, Anne-Marie. Parents, Children, & Adolescents: Interactive Relationships & Development in Context. LC 96-24646. 398p. (C). 1997. 59.95 (*0-7890-6034-5*) Haworth Pr.

— Parents, Children, & Adolescents: Interactive Relationships & Development in Context, Incl. instr's. manual. LC 96-24646. 398p. (C). 1997. pap. 24.95 (*0-7890-0181-0*) Haworth Pr.

— The Web of Poverty: Psychosocial Perspectives. LC 97-14968. (Illus.). 296p. 1997. 49.95 (*0-7890-0231-0*); pap. 24.95 (*0-7890-0232-9*) Haworth Pr.

Ambert, Jay. Blackbird Singing. LC 98-21182. 1998. 23.95 (*0-312-86554-6*, Pub. by Forge NYC) St Martin.

Ambery, Jean. On Suicide: A Discourse on Voluntary Death. Barlow, John D., tr. from GER. LC 98-53904. 160p. 1999. 19.95 (*0-253-33563-9*) Ind U Pr.

Ambewadikar, R. M., jt. auth. see Borkar, V. V.

***Ambikanander, Swami.** Principles of Breathwork: The Only Introduction You'll Ever Need. (Illus.). 160p. 1999. pap. 11.00 (*0-7225-3830-8*) Thorsons PA.

Ambinder, Richard F. & Glaser, Sally L., eds. Epstein-Barr Virus & Malignancy. 500p. 1999. 125.00 (*0-89603-701-0*) Humana.

***Ambjorn, Jan, et al, eds.** Strong & Electroweak Matter '98. 420p. 1999. 94.00 (*981-02-4031-7*) World Scientific Pub.

Ambjorn, Jan, et al. The Geometry of Dynamical Triangulations. Beiglbsck, W. et al, eds. LC 97-35967. (Lecture Notes in Physics Ser.). viii, 197p. 1997. 49.95 (*3-540-63330-8*) Spr-Verlag.

— Quantum Geometry: A Statistical Field Theory Approach. (Cambridge Monographs on Mathematical Physics). 377p. 1997. text 105.00 (*0-521-46167-7*) Cambridge U Pr.

Amble, Becky L., compiled by. Love, from Grandma Gift Book: Words of Wisdom & Hope from Grandmothers Around the World. 144p. 1995. pap. 9.99 (*1-881830-23-3*, DS18386) Garborgs.

— Prayers from Grandma Gift Book. (Illus.). 96p. 1998. 12.99 (*1-58375-421-0*) Garborgs.

Amble, Rebecca. Love, from Grandma: Words of Wisdom & Hope from America's Grandmothers. (Illus.). 144p. (Orig.). 1994. pap. 10.95 (*0-9643203-0-4*) Future Focus.

— Marketing Your Start-Up Business: A Step-by-Step Guide. 152p. (Orig.). 1994. pap. text. write for info. (*0-9643203-1-2*) Future Focus.

Ambler. Waiting. 1991. 75.00 (*0-89296-457-X*, Pub. by Mysterious Pr) Little.

Ambler, A. P., et al, eds. Economics of Design & Test for Electronic Circuits & Systems. LC 92-21721. 250p. 1993. 42.00 (*0-13-224767-4*, Pub. by Tavistock-E Horwood) Routldge.

Ambler, Charles, jt. ed. see Crush, Jonathan.

Ambler, Charles H. History of Transportation in the Ohio Valley. 1993. reprint ed. lib. bdg. 89.00 (*0-7812-5335-7*) Rprt Serv.

— Thomas Ritchie: A Study in Virginia Politics. (Law, Politics & History Ser.). 1970. reprint ed. lib. bdg. 39.50 (*0-306-70092-1*) Da Capo.

Ambler, Effie. Russian Journalism & Politics, 1861-1881: The Career of Aleksei S. Suvorin. LC 72-173671. 239p. reprint ed. pap. 74.10 (*0-608-17737-7*, 203203200077) Bks Demand.

Ambler, Eric. Background to Danger. 280p. 1990. mass mkt. 3.95 (*0-88184-611-2*) Carroll & Graf.

— Cause for Alarm. 264p. 1990. mass mkt. 3.95 (*0-88184-664-3*) Carroll & Graf.

— Cause for Alarm. 246p. reprint ed. lib. bdg. 22.95 (*0-89190-466-2*, Rivercity Pr) Amereon Ltd.

— A Coffin for Dimitrios. LC 96-35453. 216p. 1996. pap. 8.95 (*0-7867-0364-4*) Carroll & Graf.

— A Coffin for Dimitrios. 214p. reprint ed. lib. bdg. 22.95 (*0-89190-461-1*, Rivercity Pr) Amereon Ltd.

— A Coffin for Dimitrios. 1990. reprint ed. lib. bdg. 18.95 (*0-89968-471-8*) Buccaneer Bks.

— The Dark Frontier. Date not set. pap. text. write for info. (*0-17-556892-8*) Addison-Wesley.

— The Dark Frontier. 304p. 1990. 18.95 (*0-89296-413-8*) Mysterious Pr.

— The Dark Frontier. 1991. mass mkt. 5.95 (*0-446-40001-7*, Pub. by Warner Bks) Little.

— Epitaph for a Spy. 256p. 1991. pap. 3.95 (*0-88184-716-X*) Carroll & Graf.

— Epitaph for a Spy. 201p. reprint ed. lib. bdg. 22.95 (*0-89190-462-X*, Rivercity Pr) Amereon Ltd.

— Epitaph for a Spy. 1990. reprint ed. lib. bdg. 18.95 (*0-89968-472-6*) Buccaneer Bks.

— Eric Ambler: Classic Tales of Espionage & Suspense. 1992. 9.98 (*0-88365-805-4*) Galahad Bks.

Ambler, Eric. Espionage: Three Great Spy Novels: A Collection Consisting of a Coffin for Dimitros. 1995. 11.98 (*0-88365-908-5*) Galahad Bks.

Ambler, Eric. Here Lies: An Autobiography. 233 p. 1988. pap. 8.95 (*0-89296-940-7*) Mysterious Pr.

— Here Lies: An Autobiography. LC 85-221232. 234 p. 1985. write for info. (*0-297-78588-5*) Weidenfeld & Nicolson.

— Journey into Fear. 1988. 22.95 (*0-8488-0191-1*) Amereon Ltd.

— Journey into Fear. 254p. 1990. mass mkt. 3.95 (*0-88184-665-1*) Carroll & Graf.

— Judgement on Deltchev. 229p. reprint ed. lib. bdg. 22.95 (*0-89190-463-8*, Rivercity Pr) Amereon Ltd.

— Judgment on Deltchev. 240p. 1991. mass mkt. 3.95 (*0-88184-766-6*) Carroll & Graf.

— The Levanter. 24.95 (*0-88411-296-9*) Amereon Ltd.

— The Light of Day. 224p. 1992. pap. 3.95 (*0-88184-836-0*) Carroll & Graf.

— The Light of Day. 215p. reprint ed. lib. bdg. 21.95 (*0-89190-464-6*, Rivercity Pr) Amereon Ltd.

— Passage of Arms. 224p. 1992. mass mkt. 3.95 (*0-88184-837-9*) Carroll & Graf.

— The Schirmer Inheritance. 208p. 1991. mass mkt. 3.95 (*0-88184-767-4*) Carroll & Graf.

— Siege of the Villa Lipp. 24.95 (*0-89190-465-4*) Amereon Ltd.

— State of Siege. 160p. 1991. pap. 3.95 (*0-88184-717-8*) Carroll & Graf.

— Waiting for Orders. 1991. 18.45 (*0-89296-241-0*, Pub. by Mysterious Pr) Little.

— Waiting for Orders. 144p. 1992. mass mkt. 4.99 (*0-446-40093-9*, Pub. by Warner Bks) Little.

Ambler, J. Richard. Caldwell Village. LC 68-28353. (Utah Anthropological Papers: No. 84). 1966. 30.00 (*0-404-60684-9*) AMS Pr.

Ambler, J. Richard & Olson, Alan P. Salvage Archaeology in the Cow Springs Area, 1960. (Technical Ser.). 57p. 1977. pap. 7.95 (*0-685-14718-5*, TS-15) Mus Northern Ariz.

Ambler, John S., ed. The French Welfare State: Surviving Social & Ideological Change. 320p. (C). 1993. pap. text 19.50 (*0-8147-0626-6*) NYU Pr.

Ambler, Louise T. Benjamin Franklin: A Perspective. (Illus.). 148p. 1975. pap. 4.95 (*0-916724-18-2*, 4182) Harvard Art Mus.

— Early Science at Harvard: Innovators & Their Instruments, 1765-1865. (Illus.). 92p. 1969. pap. 4.95 (*0-916724-15-8*) Harvard Art Mus.

Ambler, Mark & Marrow, John. Priorities for Environmental Expenditures in Industry: Eastern Europe & the Former Soviet Union. LC 97-35148. (Report for the Environmental Action Programme for Central & Eastern Europe Ser.). 265p. 1998. pap. 22.00 (*0-8213-4086-7*, 14086) World Bank.

***Ambler, Scott, ed.** The Unified Process Construction Phase: Best Practices in Implementing the UP. (Illus.). 400p. 2000. pap. 34.95 (*1-929629-01-X*) C M P Books.

— The Unified Process Elaboration Phase: Best Practices in Implementing the UP. (Illus.). 304p. 2000. pap. 34.95 (*1-929629-05-2*) C M P Books.

***Ambler, Scott & Constantine, Larry, eds.** The Unified Process Inception Phase: Best Practices in Implementing the UP. 400p. 2000. pap. 34.95 (*1-929629-10-9*, Pub. by C M P Books) Publishers Group.

Ambler, Scott W. Building Object Applications That Work: Your Step-by-Step Handbook for Developing Robust Systems with Object Technology. LC 98-144638. (Managing Object Technology Ser.: No. 9). 512p. (C). 1998. pap. 39.95 (*0-521-64826-2*) Cambridge U Pr.

— More Process Patterns: Delivering Large-Scale Systems Using Object Technology. LC 98-45451. (Managing Object Technology Ser.: No. 19). 416p. (C). 1999. 44.95 (*0-521-65262-6*) Cambridge U Pr.

***Ambler, Scott W.** The Object Primer: The Application Developer's Guide to Object-Orientation. (Managing Object Technology Ser.: No. 3). 250p. 2000. pap. 39.95 (*0-521-78519-7*) Cambridge U Pr.

Ambler, Scott W. Process Patterns: Building Large-Scale Systems Using Object Technology Series. LC 99-160053. (Managing Object Technology Ser.: No. 15). 300p. (C). 1998. 39.95 (*0-521-64568-9*) Cambridge U Pr.

Ambler, Scott W., jt. auth. see Sigs Books Staff.

Ambler, Tim. Financial Times Guide to Marketing: An A-Z of Tools, Terms & Techniques. (Illus.). 256p. (Orig.). 1995. pap. text 15.95 (*0-273-62032-0*) F T P-H.

***Ambler, Tim.** Marketing Metrics. 256p. 2000. pap. 29.00 (*0-273-64248-0*) F T P H.

— Silk Route to International Marketing. 288p. 2000. 30.00 (*0-273-64203-0*) F T P H.

***Ambler, Tim & Witzel, Morgen.** Doing Business in Greater China. LC 99-86052. 2000. pap. write for info. (*0-415-22329-6*) Routledge.

Ambler, Wayne S. Garden Harvest Cookbook: Growing & Cooking Vegetables. LC 97-148482. (Illus.). 192p. 1997. write for info. (*0-7853-1587-X*) Pubns Intl Ltd.

— Treasury of Gardening LC 98-128759. 576 p. 1997. write for info. (*0-7853-2254-X*) Pubns Intl Ltd.

Ambos-Spies, Klaus, et al, eds. Complexity Theory: Current Research. 321p. (C). 1993. text 31.95 (*0-521-44220-6*) Cambridge U Pr.

— Recursion Theory Week: Proceedings of a Conference Held in Oberwolfach, FRG March 19-29, 1989. (Lecture Notes in Mathematics Ser.: Vol. 1432). (Illus.). vi, 393p. 1990. pap. 50.00 (*0-387-52772-9*) Spr-Verlag.

Ambramoff. Kingdom Animalia: Acoelomates, Vol. 1. Date not set. 1.50 (*0-7167-9120-X*) W H Freeman.

— Kingdom Animalia: Phyla Hemich, Vol. 1. Date not set. 1.50 (*0-7167-9121-8*) W H Freeman.

Ambrams, Richard. Electroconvulsive Therapy. 3rd ed. LC 96-36870. (Illus.). 392p. 1997. text 59.50 (*0-19-510944-9*) OUP.

Ambraseys, N. N., et al. The Seismicity of Egypt, Arabia & the Red Sea: A Historical Review. (Illus.). 201p. (C). 1995. text 100.00 (*0-521-39120-2*) Cambridge U Pr.

Ambre, Ago, tr. see Toots, Villu.

***Ambrecht, John W., et al.** Handling Postmortem Trust Administration: A Checklist - Action Guide, Summer 1999. Gerber, Mary, ed. 80p. 1998. ring bd. 58.00 (*0-7626-0363-1*, ES-11903) Cont Ed Bar-CA.

Ambree, A., jt. auth. see Desai, Santosh N.

Ambrester, Marcus L., jt. auth. see Strause, Glynis H.

Ambrieno, Robert. Project Management. (Illus.). 300p. 1997. lib. bdg. 295.00 (*1-890299-06-5*) Gov Technology.

Ambriere, Madeleine. Dictionnaire du XIXe Siecle Europeen, 1800-1900. 1424p. 1997. 395.00 (*0-7859-9581-1*) Fr & Eur.

Ambriola, V. & Tortora, G. Advances in Software Engineering & Knowledge Engineering. (Series on Software Engineering & Knowledge). 180p. 1993. text 53.00 (*981-02-1594-0*) World Scientific Pub.

***Ambro, Darrell.** Solaris 7 System Administrator Exam Cram. 2000. pap. text 34.99 (*1-57610-547-4*) Coriolis Grp.

AmBroc, Charles, ed. see Metzker, Mary.

Ambrogi, Donna M. & Gerard, Lenore. Autonomy of Nursing Home Residents: A Study of California Admission Agreements. 125p. 1986. write for info. (*0-318-64283-2*, 41,825) NCLS Inc.

Ambrogi, Robert J., et al. The Internet Guide for Massachusetts Lawyers. LC 97-70629. (Illus.). 272p. 1997. pap. text 55.00 (*1-57589-068-2*, 97-11.07-BK) Mass CLE.

Ambroise-Thomas, P. & Petersen, E. L. Congenital Toxoplasmosis: Scientific Background, Clinical Management & Control. (Illus.). 300p. 1999. pap. 159.00 (*2-287-59664-X*, Pub. by Spl France Editions) Spr-Verlag.

Ambron, Joanna, jt. auth. see Stanley, Linda.

Ambros, Veronika. Pavel Kohout und die Metamorphosen Des Sozialistischen Realismus. LC 92-39109. (Russian & East European Studies in Aesthetics & the Philosophy of Culture: Vol. 3). 190p. 1993. text 48.95 (*0-8204-2015-8*) P Lang Pubng.

Ambrosch, W. D., et al, eds. The Intelligent Network. (Illus.). xiv, 294p. 1989. pap. 61.00 (*0-387-50897-X*) Spr-Verlag.

Ambrose. Happy Way to Numbers. 1987. pap., teacher ed. 25.25 (*0-03-006472-4*) Harcourt Schl Pubs.

— Hexameron, Paradise, & Cain & Abel. Savage, John J., tr. LC 77-81354. (Fathers of the Church Ser.: Vol. 42). 461p. reprint ed. pap. 143.00 (*0-7837-9148-8*, 204994800004) Bks Demand.

— Letters, 1-91. LC 67-28583. (Fathers of the Church Ser.: Vol. 26). 515p. 1954. 36.95 (*0-8132-0026-1*) Cath U Pr.

— Reading Group Guide. 1997. pap. write for info. (*0-684-00454-2*, Touchstone) S&S Trade Pap.

— Seven Exegetical Works. McHugh, Michael P., tr. LC 71-157660. (Fathers of the Church Ser.: Vol. 65). 494p. 1972. reprint ed. pap. 153.20 (*0-7837-9201-8*, 204995100004) Bks Demand.

Ambrose. Simplified Engineering. 9th ed. text, teacher ed. write for info. (*0-471-37920-4*) Wiley.

Ambrose, A., jt. auth. see Lazerowitz, M.

Ambrose, Alice, ed. G. E. Moore: Lectures on Metaphysics, 1934-1935. LC 91-34228. 249p. (C). 1992. text 53.95 (*0-8204-1673-8*) P Lang Pubng.

Ambrose, Alice & Lazerowitz, Morris, eds. Ludwig Wittgenstein: Philosophy & Language. (Wittgenstein Studies). 325p. 1996. pap. 27.00 (*1-85506-488-X*) Bks Intl VA.

Ambrose, Alice, jt. auth. see Lazerowitz, Morris.

Ambrose, Alice, ed. see Wittgenstein, Ludwig Josef Johann.

Ambrose, Alison. Discovering English Watercolours. 1989. pap. 25.00 (*0-85263-902-3*, Pub. by Shire Pubns) St Mut.

Ambrose, Andy & Roth, Darlene. Metropolitan Frontiers: A Short History of Atlanta. LC 95-82239. (Illus.). 226p. 1996. pap. 14.95 (*1-56352-284-5*) Longstreet.

Ambrose, Ann. Microsoft Word for Windows: Tutorial/Applications. (WP - Word Processing Concepts Ser.). (C). 1994. mass mkt. 16.95 (*0-538-70948-0*) S-W Pub.

— William Wright, Candidate: A Wordperfect Simulation. (TA - Typing/Keyboarding Ser.). 1992. mass mkt. 10.00 (*0-538-61368-8*) S-W Pub.

Ambrose, Ann P. The Candidate: Employee's Guide & Reference Manual. LC 97-39433. 1998. pap. 16.95 (*0-538-68391-0*) S-W Pub.

— Hotel Regal Crown, Washington, D. C. Employees Guide & Procedures Manual. 2nd ed. LC 93-27112. 1994. 22.95 (*0-538-62400-0*) S-W Pub.

Ambrose, Ann P. & Jones, Dorothy L. SBI (Small Business Institute) Advanced Simulation: Corel, WordPerfect Microsoft. LC 97-32091. 1998. pap. 16.95 (*0-538-68387-2*) S-W Pub.

Ambrose, Betty. Fear Doesn't Live Here Anymore: My Personal Summary. 50p. (Orig.). 1996. pap. 7.00 (*1-57502-322-9*, D01087) Morris Pubng.

Ambrose, Bonnie A. The Little Bodice Construction Book: A Workbook on Period Bodices. LC 98-114660. (Illus.). 56p. (Orig.). 1995. pap. 7.95 (*0-89676-131-2*, Costume & Fashion Pr) QSMG Ltd.

— The Little Corset Construction Book: A Workbook on Period Underwear. (Little Costume Workbook Ser.). (Illus.). 52p. (Orig.). 1997. pap. 7.95 (*0-89676-130-4*, Costume & Fashion Pr) QSMG Ltd.

— The Little Hatmaking Book: A Workbook on Turn-of-the-Century Hats, Vol. 1. LC 94-50778. 1994. pap. 7.95 (*0-89676-126-6*, Costume & Fashion Pr) QSMG Ltd.

Ambrose, Bonnie H. Introduction to Costuming. (Illus.). 54p. 1997. teacher ed. 20.95 (*0-9664341-1-0*) Costme Wkshp.

— Introduction to Costuming. (Illus.). 54p. (YA). (gr. 10-12). 1997. wbk. ed. 18.95 (*0-9664341-0-2*) Costme Wkshp.

Ambrose, Brendalyn P. Democratization & the Protection of Human Rights in Africa: Probems & Prospects. LC 95-3335. 240p. 1995. 59.95 (*0-275-95143-X*, Praeger Pubs) Greenwood.

Ambrose, Christine, ed. see Murphy, Edmond & Geety, Harry.

Ambrose, Christine, ed. see Rossi, Doug.

***Ambrose, Craig.** A Picture Book & Price Guide to Antique American Quilts. large type ed. (Illus.). 200p. 2000. pap. text 25.00 (*0-9679834-0-1*) C Ambrose.

Ambrose, David. Mother of God. large type ed. 496p. 1997. 34.50 (*0-7089-8936-5*) Ulverscroft.

— Superstition. LC 98-13710. 368p. 1998. 24.00 (*0-446-52344-5*, Pub. by Warner Bks) Little.

— Superstition. 432p. 1999. mass mkt. 6.99 (*0-446-60782-7*, Pub. by Warner Bks) Little.

Ambrose, David P. The Man Who Turned into Himself: A Novel. LC 95-16220. 208p. 1995. pap. 10.00 (*0-312-13119-4*) St Martin.

Ambrose, Delorese. Leadership: The Journey Inward. 128p. 1995. pap. text, per. 17.95 (*0-7872-0973-2*) Kendall-Hunt.

Ambrose, Douglas. Henry Hughes & Proslavery Thought in the Old South. LC 96-30214. 240p. 1996. text 45.00 (*0-8071-2080-4*) La State U Pr.

Ambrose, Dunston P. Assassin Bugs Sect. VII: Phylogeny. (Illus.). 310p. 1998. 92.00 (*1-57808-030-4*) Science Pubs.

Ambrose, E. J. The Nature & Origin of the Biological World. 190p. 1982. text 78.95 (*0-470-27513-8*); pap. text 38.95 (*0-470-27514-6*) P-H.

Ambrose, E. K. Ambrose's Chronology of World Rulers & Leaders. 378p. 1996. pap. 22.95 (*0-9639502-3-1*) Hist Enter.

Ambrose, Glover. How to Have a Garage Sale. 2nd ed. 11p. 1995. reprint ed. pap. 2.00 (*0-9679834-1-X*) C Ambrose.

Ambrose, Greg. Shark Bites: True Stories of Survival. LC 97-156041. (Illus.). 144p. (Orig.). (J). (gr. 3-7). 1996. pap. 9.95 (*1-57306-054-2*) Bess Pr.

— Surfer's Guide to Hawaii: Hawaii Gets All the Breaks. LC 91-70850. (Illus.). 160p. 1991. pap. 11.95 (*0-935848-90-8*) Bess Pr.

— Travel Smart: Hawaii. 2nd rev. ed. 240p. 1998. pap. 14.95 (*1-56261-410-X*, Travel Smart) Avalon Travel.

Ambrose, Greg, jt. auth. see Hall, Sandra K.

Ambrose, Harrison W., 3rd & Ambrose, Katharine P. A Handbook of Biological Investigation. 5th ed. 202p. 1995. pap. text 21.95 (*0-88725-216-8*) Hunter Textbks.

***Ambrose, Harrison W., 3rd & Ambrose, Katherine Peckham.** A Handbook of Biological Investigation. 6th ed. (Illus.). 220p. 2000. pap. text 24.95 (*0-88725-266-4*) Hunter Textbks.

Ambrose, Henrietta, jt. auth. see Morris, Ann.

Ambrose, Henry B. I Found Atlantis: And Antlantean Migrations. Hickey, Jaet, ed. 504p. 1993. per. 29.95 (*0-9638627-1-5*) Success Systs.

— I Found Atlantis: Atlantean Migrations. Hickey, Janet, ed. 500p. 1994. 34.95 (*0-9638627-0-7*) Success Systs.

An Asterisk (*) at the beginning of an entry indicates that the title is appearing for the first time.

Ambrose, Isaac. The Christian Warrior. 150p. 1997. 18.95 (*1-57358-017-1*) Soli Deo Gloria.
— Looking unto Jesus. 1994. 34.99 (*0-87377-998-3*) GAM Pubns.
***Ambrose, James.** Simplified Engineering for Architects & Builders. 9th ed. 96p. 2000. pap., student ed. 29.95 (*0-471-37919-0*) Wiley.
Ambrose, James. Simplified Engineering for Builders & Architects. 9th ed. LC 99-39543. 736p. 2000. text 75.00 (*0-471-32191-5*) Wiley.
Ambrose, James & Vergun, Dimitry. Design for Earthquakes. LC 98-29972. 384p. 1999. 59.95 (*0-471-24188-1*) Wiley.
— Simplified Building Design for Wind & Earthquake Forces. LC 94-30569. (Parker-Ambrose Simplified Design Guides Ser.). (Illus.). 368p. 1997. pap. 59.95 (*0-471-19211-2*) Wiley.
Ambrose, James, jt. auth. see Parker, Harry.
Ambrose, James E. Building Construction. 192p. (gr. 13). 1990. text 60.95 (*0-442-20755-7*) Chapman & Hall.
— Building Construction: Interior Systems. (Illus.). 208p. (C). (gr. 13). 1991. text 67.95 (*0-442-00292-0*) Chapman & Hall.
— Building Construction: Service Systems. (Illus.). 160p. (gr. 13). 1992. text 60.95 (*0-442-00294-7*) Chapman & Hall.
— Building Construction: Site & Below-Grade Systems. 156p. (gr. 13). 1991. text 60.95 (*0-442-00293-9*) Chapman & Hall.
— Building Construction & Design. 403p. (gr. 13). 1992. text 60.95 (*0-442-00719-1*) Chapman & Hall.
— Building Structures. 2nd ed. LC 92-16362. 720p. 1993. 99.00 (*0-471-54060-9*) Wiley.
— Construction Revisited: An Illustrated Guide to Construction Details of the Early 20th Century. LC 92-27286. 250p. 1993. 110.00 (*0-471-59130-0*) Wiley.
— Design of Building Trusses. 448p. 1994. 79.00 (*0-471-55842-7*) Wiley.
— Simplified Design of Building Foundations. 2nd ed. LC 88-17221. (Parker Simplified Design Guides Ser.). 256p. 1988. 75.00 (*0-471-85898-6*) Wiley.
— Simplified Design of Building Structures. 2nd ed. LC 90-27415. 280p. (C). 1993. reprint ed. lib. bdg. 42.50 (*0-89464-574-9*) Krieger.
— Simplified Design of Building Structures. 3rd ed. LC 95-16411. (Parker-Ambrose Simplified Design Guides Ser.). 288p. 1995. 79.00 (*0-471-03744-3*) Wiley.
— Simplified Design of Masonry Structures. LC 90-46401. 204p. 1997. pap. 59.95 (*0-471-17988-4*) Wiley.
— Simplified Engineering for Architects & Builders. 8th ed. (Parker-Ambrose Simplified Design Guides Ser.). 112p. 1993. pap., student ed. 29.95 (*0-471-58860-1*) Wiley.
Ambrose, James E. & Brandow, Peter. Simplified Site Design. LC 91-26269. (Parker Simplified Design Guides Ser.). 216p. 1992. 69.95 (*0-471-53029-8*) Wiley.
Ambrose, James E. & Ollswang, Jeffrey E. Simplified Design for Building Sound Control. LC 94-23802. 161p. 1995. 69.95 (*0-471-56908-9*) Wiley.
Ambrose, James E. & Parker, Harry. Simplified Design of Concrete Stuctures. 7th ed. LC 96-23740. (Parker-Ambrose Simplified Design Guides Ser.). 376p. 1996. 79.00 (*0-471-13918-1*) Wiley.
— Simplified Design of Steel Structures. LC 97-51. (Parker-Ambrose Simplified Design Guides Ser.). (Illus.). 464p. 1997. 69.95 (*0-471-16574-3*) Wiley.
Ambrose, James E. & Vergun, Dimitry. Design for Lateral Forces. LC 86-28929. 336p. 1987. 80.00 (*0-471-84889-1*) Wiley.
— Seismic Design of Buildings. LC 90-26564. 304p. (C). 1993. reprint ed. lib. bdg. 48.50 (*0-89464-583-8*) Krieger.
— Simplified Building Design for Wind & Earthquake Forces. 3rd ed. LC 94-30569. (Parker-Ambrose Simplified Design Guides Ser.). 368p. 1995. 79.00 (*0-471-30958-3*) Wiley.
Ambrose, James E., jt. auth. see Parker, Harry.
Ambrose, Jamie. Willa Cather: Writing at the Frontier. LC 87-29969. (Women's Ser.). 188p. 1989. 24.95 (*0-85496-152-6*) Berg Pubs.
— Willa Cather: Writing at the Frontier. (Women's Ser.). 188p. 1992. pap. 17.50 (*0-85496-668-4*) Berg Pubs.
Ambrose, Jeanne. Syntaxe Comparative Francais-Anglais. (FRE.). 123p. 29.50 (*0-916379-42-6*) Scripta.
***Ambrose, Jennifer.** Claire Danes. (Illus.). 160p. 2000. pap. 15.95 (*1-55022-402-6*, Pub. by ECW) LPC InBook.
Ambrose, John W., Jr. Euripides' Hecuba. (Greek Commentaries Ser.). 104p. (Orig.). (C). 1981. pap. text 6.00 (*0-929524-08-X*) Bryn Mawr Commentaries.
Ambrose, John W., Jr. & Wooley, Allan D. Euripides' Helen. (Greek Commentaries Ser.). 160p. (C). 1992. pap. text 8.00 (*0-929524-75-6*) Bryn Mawr Commentaries.
Ambrose, Katharine P., jt. auth. see Ambrose, Harrison W., 3rd.
Ambrose, Katherine Peckham, jt. auth. see Ambrose, Harrison W., 3rd.
Ambrose, Kevin E. Great Blizzards of New York City: A Photographic History of New York City's Most Memorable Winter Storms. (Illus.). 120p. 1994. 26.95 (*0-9639502-1-5*) Hist Enter.
Ambrose, Kevin L. Blizzards & Snowstorms of Washington, D. C. A Photographic History of Washington's Most Memorable Winter Storms. (Illus.). 120p. 1993. 19.95 (*0-9639502-0-7*) Hist Enter.
Ambrose, Martha & Bunting, Eleanor E. Grammar Connection: Guidelines for Clast Success. 320p. (C). 1993. per. 31.95 (*0-8403-8934-5*) Kendall-Hunt.
Ambrose, Michael & Manachino, Albert J. Paper Purgatory. (Illus.). 20p. (Orig.). 1990. pap. 2.50 (*0-9634181-2-2*) Argo Pr.

Ambrose of Milan. On Virginity. Callam, Daniel, tr. (Translation Ser.). 65p. 1996. pap. 8.00 (*0-920669-06-9*, Pub. by Peregrina Pubng) Cistercian Pubns.
Ambrose, Paul V. Greenberg's Guide to Lionel Trains, 1945-1969 Vol. III: Cataloged Sets. 2nd rev. ed. Carp, Roger, ed. 208p. 1998. pap. 44.95 (*0-89778-449-9*, 10-8120, Kalmbach Books) Kalmbach.
— Greenberg's Guide to Lionel Trains, 1945-1969, Vol. I. 9th ed. (Illus.). 272p. 1996. pap. 39.95 (*0-89778-503-7*, 10-7795, Greenberg Books) Kalmbach.
Ambrose, Paul V. & Algozzini, Joseph P. Greenberg's Guide to Lionel Trains, 1945-1969 Vol. IV: Uncatalogued Sets. Morey, Barbara, ed. 128p. 1992. text 39.95 (*0-89778-287-9*, 10-7600HB, Greenberg Books); pap. text 29.95 (*0-89778-282-8*, Greenberg Books) Kalmbach.
Ambrose, Paul V. & Lovelock, Harold J. Greenberg's Guide to Lionel Trains, 1945-1969 Vol. VII: Selected Variations. (Illus.). 160p. 1995. pap. 44.95 (*0-89778-361-1*, 10-7910, Greenberg Books) Kalmbach.
Ambrose, Paul V. & Lovelock, Harry. Greenberg's Guide to Lionel Trains, 1945-1969 Vol. V: Rare & Unusual. 160p. 1993. pap. 39.95 (*0-89778-377-8*, 10-7530, Greenberg Books) Kalmbach.
— Greenberg's Guide to Lionel Trains, 1945-1969 Vol. V: Rare & Unusual, Vol. 6. 160p. 1993. text 49.95 (*0-89778-328-X*, 10-7530, Greenberg Books) Kalmbach.
Ambrose, Peele. Hampton Roads University: An Executive's Assistant Simulation. LC 96-46632. (KU - Office Procedures Ser.). 1998. pap. 24.95 (*0-538-71597-9*) S-W Pub.
Ambrose, Peter. Fossil Butte National Monument: Along the Shores of Time. (Illus.). Date not set. pap. 4.95 (*0-9651504-4-5*) Dinosaur Nature.
— Urban Process & Power. LC 93-44565. (Illus.). 240p. (C). 1994. pap. 25.99 (*0-415-00851-4*, B3829) Routledge.
— Urban Process & Power. LC 93-44565. (Illus.). 264p. (C). (gr. 13). 1994. 85.00 (*0-415-00850-6*, B3825) Routledge.
— Whatever Happened to Planning? 224p. 1987. text 59.50 (*0-416-37100-0*, 1121) Routledge.
Ambrose, Peter, et al. Surviving Divorce: Men Beyond Marriage. LC 82-22217. 206p. 1983. text 40.50 (*0-86598-122-1*) Rowman.
Ambrose, R. Aphrodisia. mass mkt. 6.95 (*0-7472-4920-2*, Pub. by Headline Bk Pub) Trafalgar.
— Honey Trap. mass mkt. 6.95 (*0-7472-5169-X*) Headline Bk Pub.
— Out of Control. mass mkt. 6.95 (*0-7472-5168-1*) Headline Bk Pub.
— Please Tease Me. mass mkt. 6.95 (*0-7472-5472-9*, Pub. by Headline Bk Pub) Trafalgar.
— Queen of the Night. 1997. mass mkt. 6.95 (*0-7472-5719-1*, Pub. by Headline Bk Pub) Trafalgar.
***Ambrose, S. & Katzenberg, Mary Anne.** Biogeochemical Approaches in Paleodietary Analysis. LC 00-42334. (Advances in Archaeological & Museum Science Ser.). 2000. write for info. (*0-306-46457-8*) Plenum.
Ambrose, Stephen, jt. ed. see Brinkley, Douglas.
Ambrose, Stephen E. Americans at War. LC 97-18689. 240p. 1997. 28.00 (*1-57806-026-5*) U Pr of Miss.
***Ambrose, Stephen E.** Americans at War. 252p. 1998. reprint ed. pap. 14.00 (*0-425-16510-8*) Berkley Pub.
Ambrose, Stephen E. Band of Brothers: E Company, 506th Regiment, 101st Airborne from Normandy to Hitler's Eagle's Nest. (Illus.). 336p. 1993. per. 14.00 (*0-671-86736-9*) S&S Trade Pap.
— Citizen Soldiers: The U. S. Army from the Normandy Beaches to the Bulge to the Surrender of Germany, June 7, 1944 - May 7, 1945. LC 97-23876. (Illus.). 512p. 1997. 27.50 (*0-684-81525-7*) S&S Trade.
— Citizen Soldiers: The U. S. Army from the Normandy Beaches to the Bulge to the Surrender of Germany, June 7, 1944 - May 7, 1945. large type ed. LC 98-6684. (Large Print Bks.). 783p. 1998. 28.95 (*0-7838-0174-2*) Mac Lib Ref.
— Citizen Soldiers: The U. S. Army from the Normandy Beaches to the Bulge to the Surrender of Germany, June 7, 1944-May 7, 1945. (Illus.). 512p. 1999. text 27.00 (*0-7881-6050-8*) DIANE Pub.
***Ambrose, Stephen E.** Citizen Soldiers: The U. S. Army from the Normandy Beaches to the Bulge to the Surrender of Germany, June 7, 1944-May 7, 1945. (Illus.). 528p. 1998. per. 16.00 (*0-684-84801-5*, Touchstone) S&S Trade Pap.
— Comrades: Brothers, Fathers, Heroes, Sons, Pals. LC 99-27400. (Illus.). 139p. 1999. 21.00 (*0-684-86718-4*) S&S Trade.
— Comrades: Brothers, Fathers, Heroes, Sons, Pals. 144p. 2000. pap. 11.00 (*0-7432-0074-8*, Touchstone) S&S Trade Pap.
— Comrades: Brothers, Fathers, Heroes, Sons, Pals. LC 99-46167. 1999. write for info. (*1-56895-777-7*) Wheeler Pub.
Ambrose, Stephen E. Crazy Horse & Custer: The Parallel Lives of Two American Warriors. (Illus.). 560p. 1996. pap. 15.95 (*0-385-47966-2*, Anchor NY) Doubleday.
— D - Day: June 6, 1944. (Illus.). 656p. 1994. 29.50 (*0-671-67334-3*) S&S Trade.
— D Day: June 6, 1944: The Climactic Battle of World War II. 656p. 1995. per. 17.00 (*0-684-80137-X*, Touchstone) S&S Trade Pap.
Ambrose, Stephen E. D-Day: June 6, 1944: The Climactic Battle of WWII, Set. unabridged ed. 1994. audio 25.00 (*0-671-89478-1*, 692179, Pub. by S&S Audio) Lndmrk Audiobks.
Ambrose, Stephen E. D-Day, June 6, 1944: The Climactic Battle of World War II. LC 93-40353. (Illus.). 656p. 1994. pap. 16.00 (*0-671-88403-4*) S&S Trade.
— D-Day, June 6, 1944: The Climactic Battle of World War II. large type ed. LC 98-47714. (Illus.). 962p. 1999. 30.00 (*0-7838-8469-9*, G K Hall Lrg Type) Mac Lib Ref.

***Ambrose, Stephen E.** Duty, Honor, Country: A History of West Point. LC 99-39408. 375p. 1999. pap. 16.95 (*0-8018-6293-0*) Johns Hopkins.
Ambrose, Stephen E. Duty, Honor, Country: A History of West Point. LC 66-14372. 375p. reprint ed. pap. 116.30 (*0-608-14277-8*, 201568400095) Bks Demand.
— Eisenhower: Soldier & President. (Illus.). 640p. 199_. per. 17.00 (*0-671-74758-4*, Touchstone) S&S Trade Pap.
***Ambrose, Stephen E.** Eisenhower & Berlin, 1945: The Decision to Halt at the Elbe. 120p. 2000. pap. text 12.95 (*0-393-32010-3*) Norton.
Ambrose, Stephen E. Halleck: Lincoln's Chief of Staff. LC 61-11740. 248p. (C). 1996. pap. 12.95 (*0-8071-2071-5*) La State U Pr.
— Ike's Spies: Eisenhower & the Espionage Establishment. LC 99-48550. 385p. 1999. reprint ed. pap. 18.00 (*1-57806-207-1*) U Pr of Miss.
— Nixon: The Education of a Politician, 1913-1962. 1988. pap. 18.00 (*0-671-65722-4*, Touchstone) S&S Trade Pap.
***Ambrose, Stephen E.** Nothing Like It in the World: The Men Who Built the Transcontinental Railroad 1865-1869. (Illus.). 416p. 2000. 28.00 (*0-684-84609-8*) S&S Trade.
— Nothing Like It in the World: The Men Who Built the Transcontinental Railroad 1865-1869. large type ed. 416p. 2000. 28.00 (*0-7432-0430-1*) S&S Trade.
Ambrose, Stephen E. Pegasus Bridge: June 6, 1944. (Illus.). 400p. 1988. pap. 11.00 (*0-671-67156-1*, Touchstone) S&S Trade Pap.
— The Supreme Commander: The War Years of Dwight D. Eisenhower. LC 99-43264. 732p. 1999. reprint ed. pap. 20.00 (*1-57806-206-3*) U Pr of Miss.
— Undaunted Courage: Meriwether Lewis, Thomas Jefferson & the Opening of the American West. 528p. 1997. per. 16.00 (*0-684-82697-6*, Touchstone) S&S Trade Pap.
— Upton & the Army. LC 64-21590. (Illus.). 190p. (C). 1993. pap. 12.95 (*0-8071-1850-8*) La State U Pr.
— The Victors: Eisenhower & His Boys: The Men of World War II. LC 98-37808. (Illus.). 400p. 1998. 27.50 (*0-684-85628-X*) S&S Trade.
***Ambrose, Stephen E.** The Victors: Eisenhower & His Boys: The Men of World War II. 400p. 1999. per. 16.00 (*0-684-85629-8*) S&S Trade Pap.
Ambrose, Stephen E. The Victors: Eisenhower & His Boys: The Men of World War II. LC 99-10603. 1999. 26.95 (*1-56895-636-3*) Wheeler Pub.
Ambrose, Stephen E., ed. Institutions in Modern America: Innovation in Structure & Process. LC 67-16043. (Johns Hopkins University Ser.: 1966). 157p. reprint ed. pap. 48.70 (*0-608-18657-0*, 202582200046) Bks Demand.
— A Wisconsin Boy in Dixie: Civil War Letters of James K. Newton. LC 94-24104. (Illus.). 214p. 1995. pap. 12.95 (*0-299-02484-9*) U of Wis Pr.
Ambrose, Stephen E. & Abell, Sam. Lewis & Clark: Voyage of Discovery. LC 98-20061. 1998. denim. write for info. (*0-7922-7155-6*); denim 41.95 (*0-7922-7085-1*) Natl Geog.
Ambrose, Stephen E. & Brinkley, Douglas. Rise to Globalism: American Foreign Policy since 1938. 8th rev. ed. LC 90-44958. xiv, 464p. (Orig.). (C). 1998. pap. 14.95 (*0-14-026831-6*) Addson-Wesley Educ.
Ambrose, Stephen E. & Immerman, Richard H. Milton S. Eisenhower: Educational Statesman. LC 83-4. (Illus.). 351p. 1983. reprint ed. pap. 108.90 (*0-608-05921-8*, 206625700008) Bks Demand.
Ambrose, Stephen E., jt. ed. see Bischof, Gunter.
Ambrose, Susan A., et al. Journeys of Women in Science & Engineering: No Universal Constants. LC 96-50415. (Labor & Social Change Ser.). (Illus.). 512p. (C). 2000. 84.50 (*1-56639-527-5*) Temple U Pr.
***Ambrose, Susan A., et al.** Journeys of Women in Science & Engineering: No Universal Constants. (Labor & Social Change Ser.). (Illus.). 512p. (C). 2000. pap. 27.95 (*1-56639-528-3*) Temple U Pr.
Ambrose, Susan A., jt. auth. see Davidson, Cliff I.
Ambrose, Tim & Paine, Crispin. Museum Basics. (Heritage: Care-Preservation-Management Program Ser.). (Illus.). 336p. (C). 1993. pap. 32.99 (*0-415-05770-1*, A7853) Routledge.
— Museum Basics. (Heritage: Care-Preservation-Management Program Ser.). (Illus.). 196p. (C). (gr. 13). 1993. text 79.95 (*0-415-05769-8*, A7849) Routledge.
Ambrose, Z. Philip. Euripides' Heraclidae. (Greek Commentaries Ser.). 86p. (Orig.). (C). 1990. pap. text 6.00 (*0-929524-68-3*) Bryn Mawr Commentaries.
Ambrosetti, A., et al, eds. Nonlinear Functional Analysis & Applications to Differential Equations: Proceedings of the 2nd School ICTP, Trieste, Italy 21 April-9th May, 1997. 400p. 1998. 84.00 (*981-02-3470-8*) World Scientific Pub.
Ambrosetti, Antonio & Chang, K. C., eds. Variational Methods in Nonlinear Analysis. LC 93-45010. 292p. 1995. text 116.00 (*2-88124-937-X*) Gordon & Breach.
Ambrosetti, Antonio & Dell'Antonio, G. F., eds. Variational & Local Methods in the Study of Hamiltonian Systems: Proceedings of the Workshop: International Centre for Theoretical Physics, Trieste, Italy, 24-28 October, 1995. LC 95-37192. 224p. 1995. write for info. (*981-02-2490-7*) World Scientific Pub.
Ambrosetti, Antonio & Prodi, Giovanni. A Primer of Nonlinear Analysis. (Studies in Advanced Mathematics: No. 34). (Illus.). 179p. (C). 1995. pap. text 25.95 (*0-521-48573-8*) Cambridge U Pr.
Ambrosetti, Antonio & Zelati, Vittorio C. Periodic Solutions of Singular Lagrangian Systems. LC 93-24376. (Progress in Nonlinear Differential Equations & Their Applications Ser.: No. 10). xii, 157 p. 1993. 54.50 (*0-8176-3655-2*) Birkhauser.
Ambrosetti, Ronald. Eric Ambler. LC 94-7612. (Twayne's English Authors Ser.: No. 507). 192p. 1994. 32.00 (*0-8057-8369-5*, Twyne) Mac Lib Ref.
Ambrosetti, Ronald J., jt. ed. see Browne, Ray B.

Ambrosi, Alain, jt. ed. see Thede, Nancy.
Ambrosi, Hans & Stewart, Kerry B. A Traveller's Wine Guide to Germany. LC 96-45977. (Traveller's Wine Guides Ser.). (Illus.). 144p. 1998. pap. 17.95 (*1-56656-223-6*) Interlink Pub.
Ambrosia, Angela, jt. auth. see Carey, Patrick.
Ambrosiani, Bjorn, jt. auth. see Clarke, Helen.
Ambrosiano, Nancy & Harcourt, Mary. Complete Plans for Building Horsebarns Big & Small. 2nd ed. 1997. 39.95 (*0-914327-61-5*) Breakthrgh NY.
Ambrosini, Michelle, jt. auth. see Morretta, Teresa M.
Ambrosini, Richard O. Conrad's Fiction As Critical Discourse. 267p. (C). 1991. text 69.95 (*0-521-40349-9*) Cambridge U Pr.
Ambrosino, Salvatore V. Seams of a Woman's Soul. 2nd ed. Leone, Jacqueline, ed. 76p. 1999. reprint ed. pap. 7.95 (*0-9662561-1-5*) Camb Pub Co.
— The Swelling Tide. (Illus.). xi, 500p. 1997. pap. 39.95 (*0-9662561-0-7*) Camb Pub Co.
Ambrosio. Digital Systems. 7th ed. 1997. pap. text, student ed. 36.20 (*0-13-833708-X*) P-H.
Ambrosio, jt. auth. see Deloach.
Ambrosio, Francis J., ed. The Question of Christian: Philosophy Today. (Perspectives in Continental Philosophy Ser.: Vol. 9). 300p. 1999. 35.00 (*0-8232-1981-X*, Pub. by Fordham) BookMasters.
— The Question of Christian: Philosophy Today. (Perspectives in Continental Philosophy Ser.: Vol. 9). 300p. 1999. pap. 17.50 (*0-8232-1982-8*, Pub. by Fordham) BookMasters.
Ambrosio, Joe. Rock Rhythms for the Young. 24p. 1984. pap. 5.95 (*0-938170-06-6*) Wimbledon Music.
Ambrosio, Jorge A., et al. Crashworthiness of Transportation Systems: Structural Impact & Occupant Protection: Proceedings of the NATO Advanced Study Institute on Crashworthiness of Transportation Systems, Troia, Portugal, July 7-19, 1997. LC 97-7527. (NATO ASI Series). 631p. 1997. text 378.00 (*0-7923-4487-1*) Kluwer Academic.
Ambrosio, Jorge A.C., jt. ed. see Pereira, Manuel F.
Ambrosio, L., et al. Calculus of Variations & Partial Differential Equations: Topics on Geometrical Evolution Problems & Degree Theory. Buttazzo, G. et al, eds. LC 98-54672. (Universitext Ser.). iv, 375p. 1999. pap. 64.00 (*3-540-64803-8*) Spr-Verlag.
***Ambrosio, Luigi, et al.** Functions of Bounded Variation & Free Discontinuity Problems. LC 99-46602. (Oxford Mathematical Monographs). (Illus.). 464p. 2000. text 95.00 (*0-19-850245-1*) OUP.
Ambrosio, Nora. Learning about Dance: An Introduction to Dance As an Art Form & Entertainment. 2nd ed. 274p. (C). per. 24.95 (*0-7872-6421-0*) Kendall-Hunt.
Ambrosio, Nora. Learning about Dance: An Introduction to Dance As an Art Form & Entertainment. 2nd ed. LC 97-205459. 192p. 1997. pap. text, per. 27.95 (*0-7872-3422-2*, 41342201) Kendall-Hunt.
Ambrosio, Thomas, jt. auth. see Beck, Robert J.
Ambrosios, Hieromonk, jt. auth. see Chrysostomos, Archimandrite.
Ambrosius. Concerning the Mysteries. 1977. pap. 1.25 (*0-89981-013-6*) Eastern Orthodox.
Ambrosius, Edgar E. Mechanical Measurement & Instrumentation. LC 66-21850. (Illus.). 594p. reprint ed. pap. 184.20 (*0-608-11702-1*, 201303700083) Bks Demand.
Ambrosius, Gerald & Hubbard, William H. Social & Economic History of the Twentieth-Century Europe. LC 89-1750. (Illus.). 416p. 1989. 56.00 (*0-674-81340-5*); pap. 25.95 (*0-674-81341-3*) HUP.
Ambrosius, Lloyd E. Wilsonian Statecraft: Theory & Practice of Liberal Internationalism During World War One. LC 91-4766. (America in the Modern World Ser.). 170p. (C). 1991. 45.00 (*0-8420-2393-3*) Scholarly Res Inc.
— Woodrow Wilson & the American Diplomatic Tradition: The Treaty Fight in Perspective. 341p. (C). 1990. pap. text 20.95 (*0-521-38585-7*) Cambridge U Pr.
Ambrosius, Lloyd E., ed. A Crisis of Republicanism: American Politics in the Civil War Era. LC 89-38372. (Illus.). 148p. 1990. reprint ed. pap. 45.90 (*0-7837-8858-4*, 204956800001) Bks Demand.
***Ambrosius, Mark R.** Baseball Umpires Guidebook Vol. I: Mechanics for a Crew of Two Officials. 3rd rev. ed. Topp, Bill, ed. (Illus.). 166p. 2000. pap. text 32.95 (*1-58208-014-3*, Referee Books) Ref Enterps.
Ambrosius, Mark R. Baseball Umpires' Guidebook Vol. II: Communications & Mechanics. Ehret, Scott, ed. (Illus.). 169p. 1995. pap. 32.95 (*0-9660209-4-4*) Ref Enterps.
Ambrosoli, Mauro. The Wild & the Sown: Agriculture & Botany in Western Europe, 1350-1850. Salvatorelli, Mary, tr. LC 96-300. (Past & Present Publications). (Illus.). 487p. (C). 1997. text 69.95 (*0-521-46509-5*) Cambridge U Pr.
Ambrosy, Markus, et al, eds. Divinum et Humanum: Gunter R. Schmidt zum 60. Geburtstag: Religions-Padagogische Herausforderungen in Vergangenheit und Gegenwart. (GER., Illus.). 322p. 1996. 57.95 (*3-631-30051-4*) P Lang Pubng.
Ambroz, Oton. Realignment of World Power, 1. LC 73-149631. 744p. 1972. 13.95 (*0-8315-0114-6*) Speller.
— Realignment of World Power, 2. LC 73-149631. 744p. 1972. 13.95 (*0-8315-0115-4*) Speller.
***Ambroziak, Brian M. & Ambroziak, Jeffrey R.** Infinite Perspectives: Two Thousand Years of Three-Dimensional Mapmaking - Includes 3-D Glasses. LC 99-30923. (Illus.). 116p. 1999. 75.00 (*1-56898-195-3*) Princeton Arch.
Ambroziak, Jeffrey R., jt. auth. see Ambroziak, Brian M.
Ambrozic, Aloysius M. The Hidden Kingdom: A Redactional-Critical Study of the References to the Kingdom of God in Mark's Gospel. Fitzmyer, Joseph A.,

A

A

ed. LC 72-89100. (Catholic Biblical Quarterly Monographs: No. 2). xi, 280p. 1972. pap. 9.00 (*0-915170-01-9*) Catholic Bibl Assn.

Ambrozie, Calin-Grigore & Vasilescu, Florian-Horia. Banach Space Complexes. LC 95-30318. (Mathematics & Its Applications Ser.: Vol. 334). 212p. (C). 1995. text 118.00 (*0-7923-3630-5*) Kluwer Academic.

Ambrus, Glenys, jt. auth. see Ambrus, Victor G.

Ambrus, J. L., ed. Pentoxifylline, Pharmacological & Clinical Research. 35.00 (*0-915340-06-2*) PJD Pubns.

Ambrus, J. L., et al, eds. Advances in Some Aspects of Osteoporosis. 1985. pap. 35.00 (*0-915340-13-5*) PJD Pubns.

Ambrus, Julian L., ed. Hematologic Reviews, 3 Vols., Vol. 1. LC 68-54162. 298p. reprint ed. pap. 92.40 (*0-608-16564-6*, 202780700001) Bks Demand.

— Hematologic Reviews, 3 Vols., Vol. 2. LC 68-54162. 299p. reprint ed. pap. 92.70 (*0-608-16565-4*, 202780700002) Bks Demand.

— Hematologic Reviews, 3 Vols., Vol. 3. LC 68-54162. 438p. reprint ed. pap. 135.80 (*0-608-16566-2*, 202780700003) Bks Demand.

Ambrus-Lakatos, Lorand, ed. see Anderson, Ronald W., et al.

Ambrus-Lakatos, Lorand, ed. see Von Hagen, Jurgen, et al.

Ambrus, Victor. Drawing Animals. (Illus.). 120p. 1998. 24.99 (*0-89134-929-4*, North Lght Bks) F & W Pubns Inc.

— How to Draw the Human Figures. (Illus.). 120p. 1998. 24.99 (*0-89134-930-8*, North Lght Bks) F & W Pubns Inc.

— One, Two... Where's the Shoe? 1998. 14.95 (*0-86315-261-9*, Pub. by Floris Bks) Anthroposophic.

Ambrus, Victor. Favorite Fairy Tales Told in France. LC 93-29665. 96p. (J). (gr. 4-7). 1994. mass mkt. 5.95 (*0-688-12596-4*, Wm Morrow) Morrow Avon.

— Horse Stories. LC 93-29422. (Story Library). 260p. (Orig.). (J). (gr. 1 up). 1994. pap. 7.95 (*1-85697-966-0*) LKC.

*__Ambrus, Victor.__ The Iliad. 96p. (J). 2000. 22.95 (*0-7534-5330-4*); pap. 15.95 (*0-7534-5321-5*) LKC.

Ambrus, Victor. Thundering Hooves: A Collection of Horse Stories. (Story Library). 260p. (J). (gr. 1 up). 1996. pap. 7.95 (*1-85697-675-0*) LKC.

— A Treasury of Stories from Around the World. LC 92-43153. (Treasury of Stories Ser.). 160p. (J). (ps-4). 1993. pap. 6.95 (*1-85697-932-6*) LKC.

Ambrus, Victor G. The Canterbury Tales. LC 85-60147. 128p. 1985. 14.95 (*1-56288-259-7*) Checkerboard.

— King Arthur. (Oxford Illustrated Classics Ser.). 96p. (YA). 1999. pap. 12.95 (*0-19-274177-2*) OUP.

— Ways of Drawing Hands: A Guide to Expanding Your Visual Awareness. 64p. 1998. reprint ed. text 13.00 (*0-7881-5226-2*) DIANE Pub.

Ambrus, Victor G. & Ambrus, Glenys. Santa Claus Snowed Under. (Illus.). 32p. (J). 1995. (*0-19-279941-X*) OUP.

Ambruster, Lynda. Practice Using MS-DOS 6.2 Wkbk. LC 93-86967. 262p. 1994. 27.99 (*1-56529-674-5*) Que.

Ambry, Margaret. Consumer Power: How Americans Spend. 400p. 1992. pap. 27.50 (*1-55738-411-8*, Irwn Prfssnl) McGraw-Hill Prof.

*__Ambuehl, James.__ Correlated Contents: Fan Mythos Number 1. Price, Robert M., ed. & intro. by. (Illus.). 96p. 1998. pap. 7.95 (*0-9659433-2-1*) Mythos Bks.

Ambuel, David, jt. ed. see Amin Razavi, Mehdi.

Ambuel, J. Philip & Ambuel, Louise. Letters via Chinook: Life in Montana in the 20s & 30s. (Illus.). xiv, 219p. (Orig.). 1996. pap. 10.00 (*0-9652972-0-9*) J & L Ambuel.

Ambuel, Louise, jt. auth. see Ambuel, J. Philip.

Ambulando, Solvitur. In the Hudson Highlands. (Illus.). 320p. 1977. reprint ed. 16.95 (*0-915850-08-7*) Walking News Inc.

Ambulator, Alice V. Collected Writings of Alice. 214p. (Orig.). 1995. pap. text 10.00 (*0-9639719-2-1*) Lambs Fold Ranch.

Ambulatory ECG Monitoring, First National Conferen. Proceedings. Jacobsen, Nancy K. & Yarnall, Stephen R., eds. (Illus.). 150p. 1976. 16.50 (*0-917054-08-3*) Med Communications.

Amburgey. Introduction to Employment Law. (Paralegal Ser.). (C). 2001. pap. 39.00 (*0-8273-8454-8*) Delmar.

Amburgey, Terry & Dacin, Tina. Evolutionary Development of Credit Unions. 44p. 1993. pap. 100.00 (*1-880572-07-9*) Filene Res.

Amburgy, Patricia M., et al, eds. The History of Art Education: Proceedings from the Penn State Conference (1989) 301p. (C). 1992. pap. text 25.00 (*0-937652-63-6*, 226) Natl Art Ed.

Amburn, Ellis. Buddy Holly: Biography. 432p. 1996. pap. 16.95 (*0-312-14557-8*) St Martin.

— Dark Star: The Roy Orbison Story. 352p. 1990. 18.95 (*0-8184-0518-X*) Carol Pub Group.

*__Amburn, Ellis.__ The Most Beautiful Woman in the World: The Obsessions, Passions & Courage of Elizabeth Taylor. 304p. 2000. 25.00 (*0-06-019376-X*, Cliff Street) HarperTrade.

— The Most Beautiful Woman in the World: The Obsessions, Passions & Courage of Elizabeth Taylor. large type ed. (Illus.). 656p. 2000. pap. 25.00 (*0-06-019719-6*) HarpC.

Amburn, Ellis. Mother Courage. 2000. mass mkt. 6.99 (*0-06-101408-7*) HarpC.

Amburn, Ellis. Pearl: The Obsessions & Passions of Janis Joplin. 384p. 1993. mass mkt. 13.95 (*0-446-39506-4*, Pub. by Warner Bks) Little.

Amburn, Ellis. Subterranean Kerouac: The Hidden Life of Jack Kerouac. LC 98-14324. 448p. 1998. text 27.95 (*0-312-14531-4*) St Martin.

— Subterranean Kerouac: The Hidden Life of Jack Kerouac. 448p. 1999. pap. 16.95 (*0-312-20677-1*) St Martin.

AMC Books Staff, ed. AMC Guide to Mount Desert Island & Acadia National Park. 5th ed. LC 92-47221. (Trail Guide Ser.). (Illus.). 168p. 1993. pap. 12.95 (*1-878239-22-8*) AMC Books.

AMC Press Staff. ACM/SIGCHI Conference Proceedings. 450p. (C). 1997. pap. text 51.95 (*0-201-32229-3*) Addison-Wesley.

Amchan, Arthur J. Heroes, Martyrs, & Survivors of the Civil War: The Generation That Fought the War & Its Legacy. LC 90-85281. (Illus.). 353p. (Orig.). 1991. pap. 18.95 (*0-9617132-2-4*) Amchan Pubns.

— The Kaiser's Senator: Robert M. LaFollette's Alleged Disloyalty During World War I. LC 93-91074. (Illus.). 205p. (Orig.). 1994. pap. 14.95 (*0-9617132-3-2*) Amchan Pubns.

— The Most Famous Soldier in America: Nelson A. Miles, 1839-1925. (Illus.). 214p. 1989. pap. 14.95 (*0-9617132-1-6*) Amchan Pubns.

— The Slower Runner's Guide. (Illus.). 62p. (Orig.). 1985. pap. 5.95 (*0-9617132-0-8*) Amchan Pubns.

Amchin, Jess. Psychiatric Diagnosis: A Biopsychosocial Approach Using DSM-III-R. LC 90-874. (Illus.). 218p. 1991. reprint ed. pap. 67.60 (*0-608-06652-4*, 206684900009) Bks Demand.

Amcotts, Peter M. The Best Laid Plans: A 20th Century Odyssey on Four Continents, a First Hand View, an Autobiography. unabridged ed. LC 97-93254. (Illus.). 350p. (Orig.). 1997. pap. 24.95 (*0-9657629-9-8*) Intl Res & Dev.

Amdahl, Kenn. Land of Debris & the Home of Alfredo: A Novel. 1997. pap. 14.00 (*0-9627815-8-4*) Clearwater Pub.

— There Are No Electrons: Electronics for Earthlings. 330p. (Orig.). (C). 1991. pap. 12.95 (*0-9627815-9-2*) Clearwater Pub.

Amdahl, Kenn & Loats, Jim. Algebra Unplugged. 1995. pap. text 14.95 (*0-9627815-7-6*) Clearwater Pub.

Amdam, Rolv P. & Lange, Even, eds. Crossing the Borders. (Studies in Norwegian Business History). 176p. 1995. pap. 21.00 (*82-00-02496-2*) Scandnvan Univ Pr.

Amde, Amde M., jt. ed. see Colville, James.

Amdur, Kathryn E. Syndicalist Legacy: Trade Unions & Politics in Two French Cities in the Era of World War I. LC 86-1633. (Working Class in American History Ser.). 496p. 1986. text 44.95 (*0-252-01238-0*) U of Ill Pr.

Amdur, Melissa. Anthony Quinn: Mexican-American Actor. (Hispanics of Achievement Ser.). (Illus.). 120p. (YA). (gr. 5 up). 1993. lib. bdg. 19.95 (*0-7910-1251-4*) Chelsea Hse.

Amdur, Richard. Linda Ronstadt: Mexican-American Singer. (Hispanics of Achievement Ser.). (Illus.). 120p. (YA). (gr. 5 up). 1994. lib. bdg. 19.95 (*0-7910-1781-8*) Chelsea Hse.

— Toxic Materials. (Earth at Risk Ser.). (Illus.). 128p. (J). (gr. 5 up). 1993. lib. bdg. 19.95 (*0-7910-1574-2*) Chelsea Hse.

Amdursky, Robert S. & Gillette, Clayton P. Municipal Debt Finance Law: Theory & Practice. 544p. 1992. boxed set 155.00 (*0-316-31430-7*, Aspen Law & Bus) Aspen Pub.

Ameche, Carol. As We Wait in Joyful Hope. 1999. pap. text 8.95 (*1-57918-111-2*) Queenship Pub.

— Bands of Love. 1999. pap. text 8.95 (*1-57918-109-0*) Queenship Pub.

Ameche, Carol, jt. auth. see Hammonds, Harriet.

Ameche, Carol, jt. auth. see Hammons, Harriet.

Ameche, Yvonne. Broad Shoulders & Tight Ends. 1997. pap. text 14.95 (*1-888170-02-6*) Advent Quest.

Ameche, Yvonne K. & Braatz, Geraldine A. Broad Shoulders & Tight Ends. (Illus.). (Orig.). 1995. pap. 14.95 (*0-9640964-0-4*) Fair Catch.

*__Amed.__ Organizations & People. 1999. pap. 113.95 (*0-566-08188-1*) Ashgate Pub Co.

Amedee-Jones, Lesline. On the Inside. 32p. (Orig.). 1994. pap. 10.00 (*1-886094-00-4*) Chicago Spectrum.

Amedeo, Douglas & Golledge, Reginald G. An Introduction to Scientific Reasoning in Geography. LC 84-9656. 448p. (C). 1986. reprint ed. lib. bdg. 42.50 (*0-89874-764-3*) Krieger.

Amedick, Deborah. A Cat Named Wellington: His Lessons for Christmas. (Animal Ser.). (Illus.). 36p. (J). (ps-1). 1998. pap. 4.95 (*1-891210-79-3*, CNWXM1) Bartlett Pub.

— A Cat Named Wellington: His Lessons for Life. LC 98-72107. (Animal Ser.). (Illus.). 52p. (J). (ps-1). 1998. pap. 6.95 (*1-891210-87-4*, CNW01) Bartlett Pub.

Amedroz, H. F., tr. see Miskawayh, Ibn, et al.

Ameen, Farooq, ed. Contemporary Architecture. LC 97-900349. 1997. 59.00 (*81-85026-35-1*, Pub. by Marg Publns) Art Media Resources.

Ameen, Joyce. My Baby Daddy: Another Baby - No Husband. (Illus.). 100p. 1998. pap. text 7.95 (*0-9664325-0-9*) Four Malse.

Ameen, M. S., ed. Fractography: Fracture Topography As a Tool in Fracture Mechanics & Stress Analysis. (Geological Society Special Publication Ser.: No. 92). (Illus.). 248p. 1995. 93.00 (*1-897799-32-2*, 334, Pub. by Geol Soc Pub Hse) AAPG.

Ameen, M. S., jt. ed. see Cosgrove, J. W.

*__Ameerally, Phillip.__ Lo Esencial en Anatomia. (C). 1998. text 14.09 (*84-8174-363-1*) Mosby Inc.

*__Amegbleame, Simon A. & Teko-Agbo, Ambroise, texts.__ Les Femmes dans le Processus Litteraire au Togo. 250p. 1999. 38.95 (*3-906763-85-4*, Pub. by P Lang) P Lang Pubng.

Ameil, Rick. Cooking with the Stars. LC 99-30376. 144p. 1999. pap. text 12.95 (*0-7641-1114-0*) Barron.

*__Ameis, Jerry A. & Ebenezer, Jazlin V.__ Mathematics on the Internet: A Resource for K-12 Teachers. LC 99-14010. 129p. 1999. pap. 15.00 (*0-13-011061-2*) P-H.

Ameiss, Bill & Graver, Jane. Love, Sex & God. (Learning about Sex Ser.: Bk. 5). 128p. (YA). (gr. 9 up). 1988. pap. 8.99 (*0-570-03556-2*, 14-2105) Concordia.

Amelang, James S. The Flight of Icarus: Artisan Autobiography in Early Modern Europe. LC 98-23284. 512p. 1998. 60.00 (*0-8047-3340-6*) Stanford U Pr.

— Honored Citizens of Barcelona: Patrician Culture & Class Relations, 1490-1714. LC 85-43205. (Illus.). 288p. reprint ed. pap. 89.30 (*0-608-06305-3*, 206666700008) Bks Demand.

Amelar, Chris. The Guitar F/X Cookbook. 56p. 1997. otabind 14.95 incl. audio compact disk (*0-7935-6509-X*, HL0695080) H Leonard.

— Stand Alone '80s Rock. (Handy Guide Ser.). 1995. pap. 12.95 incl. audio compact disk (*0-7390-0020-9*, 14185) Alfred Pub.

— Stand Alone Rock. (Alfred's Handy Guide). 32p. (YA). 1992. reprint ed. pap. 9.95 (*0-88284-544-6*, 4430) Alfred Pub.

Amelin, B., jt. auth. see Pinkevich, A.

Amelinckx, S., ed. Electron Microscopy: Principles & Fundamentals. 528p. 1997. 535.00 (*3-527-29479-1*) Wiley.

Amelinckx, S., et al, eds. Handbook of Microscopy: Applications in Materials Science, Solid-State Physics & Chemistry, 3 vols. Incl. Vol. 1, Methods. Methods I. Van Tendeloo, Gustaaf, ed. LC 97-145430. (Illus.). 550p. 1996. 535.00 (*3-527-29280-2*, Wiley-VCH); Vol. 2, Methods II. Methods II. Van Tendeloo, G., ed. LC 97-145430. 550p. 1996. 535.00 (*3-527-29473-2*); Vol. 3, Applications. Applications. Van Tendeloo, Gustaaf, ed. LC 97-145430. (Illus.). 550p. 1996. 535.00 (*3-527-29293-4*, Wiley-VCH); 1101p. 1996. 1425.00 (*3-527-29444-9*, Wiley-VCH) Wiley.

Ameling, W., ed. First European Simulation Congress: ESC 83. (Informatik-Fachberichte Ser.: Vol. 71). 653p. 1983. 55.00 (*0-387-12723-2*) Spr-Verlag.

Ameling, Walter. Herodes Atticus, Bd. I: Biographie & Bd. II: Inschriftenkatalog. (GER.). xxvi, 423p. 1983. 95.00 (*0-318-70430-7*) G Olms Pubs.

— Herodes Atticus, 2 vols., Set. (Subsidia Epigraphica Ser.: Vol. XI). (GER.). xxvi, 423p. 1983. 95.00 (*3-487-07375-7*) G Olms Pubs.

Amelio, Gil F. & Simon, William. Profit from Experience: The National Semiconductor Story of Transformation Management. LC 97-25041. 352p. 1997. per. 14.00 (*0-684-83702-1*, Touchstone) S&S Trade Pap.

Amelio, Gil F. & Simon, William L. On the Firing Line: My 500 Days at Apple. 298p. 1999. pap. 15.00 (*0-88730-919-4*, HarpBusn) HarpInfo.

Amelio, Gil F. & Simon, William L. Profit from Experience: The National Semiconductor Story of Transformation Management. (Industrial Engineering Ser.). 312p. 1995. 26.95 (*0-471-28704-0*, VNR) Wiley.

Amelio, Gil F., et al. Profit from Experience: The National Semiconductor Story of Transformation Management. LC 95-35688. (Industrial Engineering Ser.). 312p. 1995. 26.95 (*0-442-02055-4*, VNR) Wiley.

Amelio, Lucio, et al. Joseph Beuys: Arena-Where Would I Have Got If I Had Been Intelligent! Cooke, Lynne & Kelly, Karen, eds. LC 93-73428. (GER., Illus.). 294p. 1994. 60.00 (*0-944521-30-4*) Dia Ctr Arts.

Amell, Alma. Rosa Montero's Odyssey. 126p. (Orig.). (C). 1994. lib. bdg. 37.00 (*0-8191-9353-4*) U Pr of Amer.

Amell, Alma, tr. see Rojas, Carlos.

Amell, Samuel. The Contemporary Spanish Novel: An Annotated, Critical Bibliography, 1936-1994, 50. LC 95-36085. (Bibliographies & Indexes in World Literature Ser.: No. 50). 288p. 1996. lib. bdg. 79.50 (*0-313-24784-6*, Greenwood Pr) Greenwood.

Amell, Samuel, ed. Literature, the Arts & Democracy: Spain in the '80s. LC 88-46146. 144p. 1990. 32.50 (*0-8386-3373-0*) Fairleigh Dickinson.

Amelung, Arthur & Janicke, Oskar. Ortnit und die Wolfdietriche. (Deutsches Heldenbuch Ser.: Band 1). (GER.). lxxii, 302p. 1968. write for info. (*3-296-17103-7*, Pub. by Weidmann) Lubrecht & Cramer.

— Ortnit und die Wolfdietriche. (Deutsches Heldenbuch Ser.: Band 2). (GER.). l, 352p. 1968. write for info. (*3-296-17104-5*, Pub. by Weidmann) Lubrecht & Cramer.

Amelung, Torsten. Globaler Umweltschutz als Verteilungsproblem im Nord-Sud-Konflikt: Ursachen und Losungsmoglichkeiten Dargestellt am Beispiel der Rodung Tropischer Regenwalder. (GER., Illus.). 307p. 1996. pap. 51.95 (*3-631-30350-5*) P Lang Pubng.

Amelung, Walther, ed. Die Sculpturen des Vaticanischen Museums Band I Text. Band II Text. Fotomechanischer Nachdruck in Einem Band Mit Einem Neuen Vorwort Von Bernard Andreae. (GER.). (C). 1995. lib. bdg. 453.85 (*3-11-014767-X*) De Gruyter.

Amelunxen, C. A. Fotografie Nach der Fotografie. (GER., Illus.). 324p. 1995. text 71.00 (*3-364-00361-0*, Verlag Kunst) Gordon & Breach.

Amembal, Deane & Associates Staff. Leasing Training Self-Study Workbook. 1995. 295.00 (*1-85564-379-0*, Pub. by Euromoney) Am Educ Systs.

Amembal, Sudhir. Lease Securitization: Securitizing Lease Receivables in the 1990s. Halladay, Shawn D., ed. LC 93-71547. (Illus.). 200p. (Orig.). pap. 45.00 (*0-945988-07-9*) Amembal & Halladay.

Amembal, Sudhir P. & Halladay, Shawn D. Accounting for Equipment Leases: A Complete Guide. (Illus.). 500p. 1991. 115.00 (*0-945988-03-6*) Amembal & Halladay.

Amembal, Sudhir P., et al. The Handbook of Equipment Leasing. 824p. 85.00 (*0-945988-00-1*) Amembal & Halladay.

— Leasing Applications Handbook for the HP-12C. (Illus.). 300p. 1991. student ed. 49.95 (*0-945988-02-8*) Amembal & Halladay.

— Leasing Applications Handbook for the HP-17B. (Illus.). 335p. 1991. text, student ed. 49.95 (*0-945988-01-X*) Amembal & Halladay.

Amembal, Sudhir P., jt. auth. see Isom, Terry A.

Amemiya, Takeshi. Advanced Econometrics. (Illus.). 576p. 1985. 55.00 (*0-674-00560-0*) HUP.

— Introduction to Statistics & Econometrics. LC 93-3777. 384p. 1993. 45.00 (*0-674-46225-4*) HUP.

— Studies in Econometric Theory: The Collected Essays of Takeshi Amemiya. (Economists of the Twentieth Century Ser.). 496p. 1994. 120.00 (*1-85278-797-X*) E Elgar.

Amen, Antony. Teenagers Guide to A. D. D. Understanding & Treating Attention Disorders Through the Teenage Years. 208p. 1996. pap. text 29.95 (*1-886554-05-6*) MindWrks.

Amen, Carol. Changing Problems into Challenges. (Uplook Ser.). 1972. pap. 0.99 (*0-8163-0068-2*, 03109-6) Pacific Pr Pub Assn.

Amen, Constancio. Christian Faith vs. Unbelief. 1987. pap. 6.95 (*0-9618383-0-2*) GN Inc.

— Questions on Christian Faith. 1988. pap. 7.95 (*0-9618383-2-9*) GN Inc.

*__Amen, Daniel.__ Healing ADD from the Inside Out. 432p. 2001. 24.95 (*0-399-14644-X*) Putnam Pub Group.

Amen, Daniel G. Change Your Brain, Change Your Life: The Breakthrough Program for Conquering Anxiety, Depression, Obsessiveness, Anger & Impulsiveness. LC 99-20343. (Illus.). 368p. 1999. pap. 15.00 (*0-8129-2998-5*, Times Bks) Crown Pub Group.

— Don't Shoot Yourself in the Foot. 352p. (Orig.). 1992. mass mkt. 12.99 (*0-446-39373-8*, Pub. by Warner Bks) Little.

— Images into the Mind: A Radical New Look at Understanding & Changing Behavior. (Illus.). 252p. 1995. pap. text 49.95 (*1-886554-01-3*) MindWrks.

— Mind Coach: How to Teach Children & Teenagers to Think Positive & Feel Good. (Illus.). 40p. (Orig.). 1997. pap. 19.95 (*1-886554-07-2*) MindWrks.

— New Skills for Frazzled Parents: The Instruction Manual That Should Come with Your Child. 129p. 2000. pap. 29.95 (*1-886554-02-1*, 499-005, Pub. by MindWrks) BookWorld.

— Two Minutes a Day for a Life of Love. 1996. mass mkt. 5.99 (*0-312-95869-2*) St Martin.

— Windows into the A. D. D. Mind: Understanding & Treating Attention Deficit Disorder. 1996. 39.95 (*1-886544-00-X*) Suma Ching Hai Intl.

— Windows into the A. D. D. Mind: Understanding & Treating Attention Deficit Disorders, Childhood Through Adulthood. 238p. 1996. 39.95 (*1-886554-00-5*) MindWrks.

— Windows into the A. D. D. Mind: Understanding & Treating Attention Deficit Disorders in the Everyday Lives of Children, Adolescents & Teenagers. rev. ed. (Illus.). 238p. 1997. pap. 29.95 (*1-886554-08-0*) MindWrks.

— You Don't Have to Hurt: Attention Deficit Disorder in Intimate Relationships. 184p. (Orig.). 1997. pap. 29.95 (*1-886554-06-4*) MindWrks.

Amen, Michael M. American Foreign Policy in Greece 1944-1949: Economic, Military & Institutional Aspects. (European University Studies: Political Science: Ser. 31, Vol. 13). XXI, 310p. 1978. 57.00 (*3-261-02436-4*) P Lang Pubng.

Amen, Nur A. The Ankh: African Origin of Electromagnetism. 4th rev. ed. LC 99-20623. (Illus.). 144p. 2000. reprint ed. pap. 10.95 (*1-886433-12-7*) A&B Bks.

*__Amen, Nur A.__ The Ankh: African Origin of Electromagnetism. 4th rev. ed. (Illus.). 144p. 2000. reprint ed. 21.95 (*1-886433-11-9*) A&B Bks.

Amen Ra. Sexual Ecstasy from Ancient Wisdom. LC 93-93602. (Illus.). 60p. (Orig.). 1993. pap. 15.95 (*0-943217-03-2*) Summum.

Amen, Ra U. An Afrocentric Guide to a Spiritual Union. (Illus.). 129p. (Orig.). 1992. pap. 9.95 (*1-877662-07-0*) Kamit Pubns.

Amend. Experimental Chemistry: A Lm T/A Gen Org. 2nd ed. (C). 1993. pap. text, lab manual ed. 40.50 (*0-03-097560-3*) Harcourt Coll Pubs.

— General Organic Chemistry & Biology. 2nd ed. (C). 1993. pap. text, teacher ed. 32.00 (*0-03-029014-7*) Harcourt Coll Pubs.

— STU COMP GEN ORG&BIO2E&ORG&BIO. 2nd ed. (C). 1993. pap. text, student ed. 31.50 (*0-03-029017-1*) Harcourt Coll Pubs.

Amend, Andrew & Washburn, Matt. The College Financial Aid Video Program: A Step-by-Step Guide of Getting More Money Out of the Financial Aid System. (Illus.). 51p. 1996. spiral bd. 29.95 incl. VHS (*0-9654983-8-7*) A&W Pub KS.

Amend, Bill. At Least This Place Sells T-Shirts. LC 96-84102. (Foxtrot Collection). (Illus.). 128p. (Orig.). 1996. pap. 9.95 (*0-8362-2120-6*) Andrews & McMeel.

— Black Bart Says Draw. (Illus.). 128p. (Orig.). 1991. pap. 9.95 (*0-8362-1869-8*) Andrews & McMeel.

— Bury My Heart at Fun-Fun Mountain. (Foxtrot Collection). (Illus.). 128p. 1993. pap. 8.95 (*0-8362-1706-3*) Andrews & McMeel.

*__Amend, Bill.__ Camp Foxtrot: A FoxTrot Treasury. LC 98-85335. (Illus.). 256p. 1998. pap. 12.95 (*0-8362-6747-8*) Andrews & McMeel.

Amend, Bill. Come Closer, Roger, There's a Mosquito on Your Nose: A Foxtrot Collection. LC 97-71626. (Illus.). 128p. (Orig.). 1997. pap. 9.95 (*0-8362-3656-4*) Andrews & McMeel.

— Eight Yards, Down & Out. (Foxtrot Collection). (Illus.). 128p. 1992. pap. 8.95 (*0-8362-1884-1*) Andrews & McMeel.

— Enormously FoxTrot: A Foxtrot Treasury. (Illus.). 256p. 1994. pap. 14.95 (*0-8362-1759-4*) Andrews & McMeel.

— FoxTrot. (Illus.). 128p. (Orig.). 1989. pap. 9.95 (*0-8362-1856-6*) Andrews & McMeel.

— FoxTrot: En Masse, a Fox Trot Treasury. (Illus.). 256p. (Orig.). 1992. pap. 12.95 (*0-8362-1897-3*) Andrews & McMeel.

— FoxTrot: The Works. (Illus.). 256p. (Orig.). 1990. pap. 12.95 (*0-8362-1848-5*) Andrews & McMeel.

— FoxTrot Beyond a Doubt: A FoxTrot Treasury. LC 96-97239. (Illus.). 256p. (Orig.). 1997. pap. 12.95 (*0-8362-2694-1*) Andrews & McMeel.

***Amend, Bill.** Foxtrot Treasury. (Illus.). 252p. 2000. pap. 14.95 (*0-7407-0532-6*) Andrews & McMeel.

Amend, Bill. "I'm Flying, Jack...I Mean, Roger" A FoxTrot Collection. 128p. 1999. pap. 9.95 (*0-7407-0004-9*) Andrews & McMeel.

— May the Force Be with Us, Please. (Illus.). 128p. 1994. pap. 9.95 (*0-8362-1741-1*) Andrews & McMeel.

— Pass the Loot: A Fox Trot Collection. (Illus.). 128p. (Orig.). 1990. pap. 9.95 (*0-8362-1815-9*) Andrews & McMeel.

— The Return of the Lone Iguana: A Fox Trot Collection. LC 95-81037. (Illus.). 128p. (Orig.). (YA). 1996. pap. 9.95 (*0-8362-1027-1*) Andrews & McMeel.

— Say Hello to Cactus Flats: A Fox Trot Collection. (Illus.). 128p. (Orig.). 1993. pap. 8.95 (*0-8362-1720-9*) Andrews & McMeel.

***Amend, Bill.** Sincerely Foxtrot: A Foxtrot Treasury. (Illus.). 2000. pap. 74.75 (*0-7407-1286-1*) Andrews & McMeel.

Amend, Bill. Take Us to Your Mall: A FoxTrot Collection. (Illus.). 128p. 1995. pap. 8.95 (*0-8362-1780-2*) Andrews & McMeel.

***Amend, Bill.** Think iFruity. (Foxtrot Collection). 128p. 2000. pap. 9.95 (*0-7407-0454-0*) Andrews & McMeel.

Amend, Bill. Welcome to Jassorassic Park: A Foxtrot Collection. 127 p. 1998. pap. text 9.95 (*0-8362-5183-0*) Andrews & McMeel.

— Wildly FoxTrot: A Fox Trot Treasury. (Illus.). 256p. 1995. pap. 12.95 (*0-8362-0416-6*) Andrews & McMeel.

***Amend, James M.** Patent Law: A Primer for Federal District Court Judges. 93p. 1999. pap. 10.00 (*0-9677776-0-7*, BCLT-99-A-1) BCLT Pr.

Amend, John R. General, Organic & Biological Chemistry. 2nd ed. (C). 1993. text 91.00 (*0-03-029012-0*) Harcourt Coll Pubs.

— Measurement: The Basic Science. LC 96-178718. (Chemistry Ser.). 104p. (Orig.). 1997. pap. 13.75 (*0-7637-0187-4*) Jones & Bartlett.

Amend, Karen K. & Ruiz, Mary S. Achieving Compatibility with Handwriting Analysis, Vol. II: Exploring Your Sexual Relationships, Vol. II. 1992. pap. 17.95 (*0-87877-169-7*) Newcastle Pub.

Amend, Karen S., jt. auth. see Ruiz, Mary S.

Amend, Robert H. & Schrader, Michael A. Media for Business. (Illus.). 258p. 1991. 44.95 (*0-86729-264-4*, Focal) Buttrwrth-Heinemann.

***Amende, Coral.** Country Confidential: The Lowdown on the High Living, Heartbreaking & Hell-Raising of Country Music's Biggest Stars. LC 99-24341. 256p. 1999. pap. 12.95 (*0-452-28119-9*, Plume) Dutton Plume.

Amende, Coral. Legends in Their Own Time: A Popular Biographical Dictionary. 378p. 1998. pap. text 14.00 (*0-7881-5746-9*) DIANE Pub.

— Random House Famous Name Finder: Concise Biographies of over 10,000 Legendary People Indexed Four Ways: Last Name, First Name, Nickname, Spouse's Name. LC 99-29776. 383p. 1999. pap. 14.00 (*0-375-70602-X*) Random Ref & Info.

***Amende, Coral.** Rock Confidential: A Backstage Pass to the Outrageous World of Rock 'n' Roll. 320p. 2000. pap. 13.95 (*0-452-28157-1*, Plume) Dutton Plume.

Amendola, Aniello, ed. Advanced Seminar on Common Cause Failure Analysis in Probabilistic Safety Assessment. (C). 1989. text 207.50 (*0-7923-0268-0*) Kluwer Academic.

Amendola, Aniello & Keller, Alfred Z. Reliability Data Bases. (C). 1987. text 206.50 (*90-277-2549-7*) Kluwer Academic.

Amendola, Aniello & Saiz de Bustamante, Amalio, eds. Reliability Engineering. (C). 1988. text 282.00 (*90-277-2762-7*) Kluwer Academic.

Amendola, Anunziato, ed. Athletic Injuries of the Foot & Ankle. 432p. Date not set. text 70.00 (*0-07-001219-9*) McGraw-Hill HPD.

Amendola, Aurelio, photos by. Michelangelo: The Pieta. (Illus.). 208p. 1999. boxed set 65.00 (*88-8118-108-8*, Pub. by Skira IT) Abbeville Pr.

***Amendola, Aurelio & Contardi, Bruno.** St. Peter's. (Illus.). 192p. 1999. 60.00 (*3-8238-0542-8*) te Neues.

Amendola, Joseph. Baker's Manual. 4th ed. 276p. 1993. pap. 32.95 (*0-442-00997-6*, VNR) Wiley.

Amendola, Joseph. The Bakers' Manual. 4th ed. 288p. 1992. pap. 39.95 (*0-471-28467-X*, VNR) Wiley.

— Ice Carving Made Easy. 2nd ed. 128p. 1994. pap. 39.95 (*0-471-28570-6*, VNR) Wiley.

Amendola, Joseph. Ice Carving Made Easy. 2nd ed. (Illus.). 114p. 1994. pap. 34.95 (*0-442-01507-0*, VNR) Wiley.

— Understanding Baking. 2nd ed. (Illus.). 300p. 1992. pap. 29.95 (*0-442-00967-4*, VNR) Wiley.

Amendola, Joseph & Lundberg, Donald. Understanding Baking. 2nd ed. 299p. 1992. pap. 39.95 (*0-471-28457-2*, VNR) Wiley.

Amendola, Karen L. Assessing Law Enforcement Ethics: A Summary Report Based on the Study Conducted with the Oregon Department of State Police. 40p. (Orig.). 1996. pap. 10.00 (*1-884614-10-8*) Police Found.

Amendola, Mario & Gaffard, Jean-Luc. Out of Equilibrium. (Illus.). 296p. 1998. text 65.00 (*0-19-829380-1*) OUP.

Amendola, Sandra L., jt. auth. see Heppel, Monica L.

Amendt, Bob, jt. auth. see Ziegler, Bert.

Ameniya, Mako, tr. see Sazama, Jenny.

Amenkhienan, Felix E. Accounting in Developing Countries: A Framework for Standard Setting. LC 85-20892. (Research for Business Decisions Ser.: No. 82). (Illus.). 113p. reprint ed. pap. 35.10 (*0-8357-1717-8*, 207035600088) Bks Demand.

Amenoff, Gregory. Sky Below: 18 Paintings by Gregory Amenoff. LC 97-19467. (Illus.). 48p. 1997. 39.95 (*1-889097-06-3*) Hard Pr MA.

Amenomori, Takayoshi & Yamamoto, Tadashi. The Nonprofit Sector in Japan. LC 97-48660. (John Hopkins Nonprofit Sector Ser.). 208p. 1998. 39.95 (*0-7190-5385-4*, Pub. by Manchester Univ Pr) St Martin.

Ament, jt. auth. see Reiff.

***Ament, Pat.** Climbing Everest: A Meditation on Mountaineering & the Spirit of Adventure. (Illus.). 176p. 2000. 17.95 (*0-07-136445-5*) McGraw.

Ament, Pat. High Endeavors. (Illus.). 200p. 1991. pap. 12.95 (*1-879415-00-3*) Mtn n Air Bks.

— John Gill: Master of Rock. LC 98-23874. (Climbing Classics Ser.). (Illus.). 224p. 1998. pap. 17.95 (*0-8117-2853-6*) Stackpole.

— Reflections on Being the Best Climber in the World. 88p. 1999. pap. 10.95 (*0-9648606-4-3*) Two Lights.

— Royal Robbins: Spirit of the Age. LC 97-25724. (Illus.). 304p. 1998. pap. 19.95 (*0-8117-2913-3*) Stackpole.

Amenta. Histology: From Normal Microanatomy to Pathology. 7th ed. (Illus.). 690p. 1997. text 39.00 (*88-299-1195-X*, Pub. by Piccin Nuova) Gordon & Breach.

***Amenta, Edwin.** Bold Relief: Institutional Politics & the Orgins of Modern American Social Policy. (Studies in American Politics). 2000. pap. text 19.95 (*0-691-05068-6*, Pub. by Princeton U Pr) Cal Prin Full Svc.

Amenta, Edwin. Bold Relief: Institutional Politics & the Origins of Modern American Social Policy. LC 97-24509. (Studies in American Politics). 360p. 1998. text 39.50 (*0-691-01712-3*, Pub. by Princeton U Pr) Cal Prin Full Svc.

Amenta, Francesco. Peripheral Dopamine Pathophysiology. LC 89-7255. 408p. 1990. 205.00 (*0-8493-6949-5*, RC409, CRC Reprint) Franklin.

Amenta, Francesco, ed. Aging of the Autonomic Nervous System. 368p. 1993. lib. bdg. 225.00 (*0-8493-6981-9*, QP368) CRC Pr.

Amenta, Madalon O., ed. AIDS & the Hospice Community. LC 91-20825. (Hospice Journal Ser.). (Illus.). 190p. 1991. pap. text 17.95 (*1-56023-011-8*, Harrington Park); lib. bdg. 54.95 (*1-56024-184-5*, Harrington Park) Haworth Pr.

Amenta, Madalon O., jt. ed. see Gallagher-Allred, Charlette R.

Amenta, P. S. Histology: From Normal Microanatomy to Pathology. 6th ed. 660p. (C). 1991. text 42.00 (*1-57235-000-8*) Piccin Nuova.

Amer. Management of Information. Date not set. text. write for info. (*0-03-006379-5*) Harcourt Coll Pubs.

— Paradigms & Programs. 96p. 1990. 15.95 (*0-02-897009-8*) Macmillan.

Amer, A. A. Responsible Driving. 1992. 43.72 (*0-02-635945-6*) Glencoe.

— Responsible Driving Checklist. 1992. 18.00 (*0-02-635952-9*) Glencoe.

***Amer, Amin A. M. A.** The Gateway of Ramesses IX in the Temple of Amun at Karnak. (Illus.). 45p. 1999. pap. 48.00 (*0-85668-711-1*, Pub. by Aris & Phillips) David Brown.

Amer, Elizabeth, jt. auth. see Mungall, Constance.

Amer Institute of Accountants Staff. Accountants' Index, 1920, 2 vols. Brief, Richard P., ed. (Foundations of Accounting Ser.: No. 24). 1578p. 1988. reprint ed. text 30.00 (*0-8240-6140-3*) Garland.

Amer, Ramses. The United Nations & Foreign Military Interventions: A Comparative Study of the Application of the Charter. 2nd ed. 314p. (Orig.). 1994. pap. 68.00 (*91-90610-27-X*, Pub. by Uppsala Universitet) Coronet Bks.

Amer, Ramses, jt. auth. see Thayer, Carlyle A.

Amer. Sleep Disorders Assn. Staff. The International Classification of Sleep Disorders: Diagnostic & Coding Manual. rev. ed. 1997. write for info. (*0-9657220-0-7*); pap. write for info. (*0-9657220-1-5*) Am Sleep Disorders.

Amer. Soc. of Naval Engineers Staff. Naval Engineering & American Sea Power. 2nd ed. 528p. 1998. 49.95 (*0-7872-4838-X*) Kendall-Hunt.

Amer. Symphony Orchestra League Staff. The Gold Book, 1997-98: A Sourcebook of Successful & Creative Orchestra Fundraising, Education, Ticket Sales & Service Projects. 174p. 1997. 47.00 (*0-614-28548-8*) Am Symphony Orch.

Amer. Textbk. Council Staff. History Textbooks: A Standard & Guide. LC 94-70447. 64p. 1994. pap. 10.00 (*0-9640064-0-5*) Am Textbk Coun.

Amer, Yeldez G., et al, eds. Vacuum Design of Synchrotron Light Sources: AIP Conference Proceedings, No. 236. LC 91-55527. (American Vacuum Society Ser.: No. 12). (Illus.). 448p. 1991. lib. bdg. 85.00 (*0-88318-873-2*) Am Inst Physics.

Amerasekera, A. & Najim, F. Failure Mechanisms in Semiconductor Devices. 2nd ed. LC 96-49978. 358p. 1997. 95.00 (*0-471-95482-9*) Wiley.

Amerasekera, Ajith, et al. ESD in Silicon Integrated Circuits. (Design & Measurement in Electronic Engineering Ser.). 224p. 1996. 165.00 (*0-471-95481-0*) Wiley.

Amerasinghe, C. F. Case-Law of the World Bank Administrative Tribunal: An Analytical Digest, Vol. III. 240p. 1998. text 145.00 (*0-19-826576-X*) OUP.

— Case-Law of the World Bank Administrative Tribunal Vol. 2: An Analytical Digest. 274p. 1993. text 85.00 (*0-19-825819-4*) OUP.

— Documents on International Administrative Tribunals. 224p. 1989. 90.00 (*0-19-825636-1*) OUP.

— The Law of the International Civil Service: International Administrative Tribunals, Vol. 1. 2nd ed. 726p. 1994. text 160.00 (*0-19-825879-8*) OUP.

— The Law of the International Civil Service: International Administrative Tribunals, Vol. 2. 2nd ed. (Illus.). 582p. 1994. text 210.00 (*0-19-825880-1*) OUP.

— Local Remedies in International Law. 438p. (C). 1990. 230.00 (*0-949009-79-2*, Pub. by Grotius Pubns Ltd) St Mut.

— Principles of the Institutional Law of International Organizations. (Cambridge Studies in International & Comparative Law). 549p. (C). 1996. text 95.00 (*0-521-56254-6*) Cambridge U Pr.

American Red Cross Staff. Professional Rescuer. 2nd ed. (C). (gr. 13). 1997. write for info. (*0-8151-1253-X*) Mosby Inc.

Amerding, Carl E. The Old Testament & Criticism. (Biblical & Theological Classics Library: Vol. 20). vii, 134p. 1997. reprint ed. pap. 9.99 (*0-85364-812-3*, Pub. by Paternoster Pub) OM Literature.

Amerding, Carl E. & Gasque, W. Ward, eds. A Guide to Biblical Prophecy. 288p. 1989. pap. 14.95 (*0-943575-11-7*) Hendrickson MA.

***Ameredes, Harry.** Fantastic Book of Canes, Pipes & Walking Sticks: A Sketchbook of Designs for Collectors, Woodcarvers & Artists. 2nd ed. (Illus.). 128p. 2000. pap. 12.95 (*1-56523-130-9*, Pub. by Fox Chapel Pub) IPG Chicago.

Amereon Ltd. Staff, ed. see Nolan, William F.

***Ameri, Anan, et al.** Arab American Encyclopedia. LC 99-37499. 260p. (J). 1999. text 42.00 (*0-7876-2952-9*, UXL) Gale.

Ameri, Houshang. Politics of Staffing the United Nations Secretariat, Vol. 8. (Major Concepts in Politics & Political Theory Ser.). XX, 604p. (C). 1996. 74.95 (*0-8204-2810-8*) P Lang Pubng.

Ameri, Sussan M. Die Deutschnationale Sprachbewegung im Wilhelminischen Reich. LC 89-27009. (German Life & Civilization Ser.). (GER.). IX, 287p. (C). 1991. text 48.00 (*0-8204-1119-1*) P Lang Pubng.

Ameria, Alberto, et al, eds. Tubulo-Interstitial Nephropathies. (Developments in Nephrology Ser.). (C). 1991. text 163.50 (*0-7923-1200-7*) Kluwer Academic.

America Association for Vocational Institute Mater, jt. auth. see Henderson.

***America Baseball Staff.** Baseball America's 2000 Directory: The Complete Pocket Baseball Guide. (Illus.). 344p. 2000. pap. text 13.95 (*0-945164-14-9*) Baseball Amer.

America Film Institute Staff. American Film Institute Catalog: Within Our Gates - Ethnicity in American Feature Films, 1911-1960. Gevinson, Alan, ed. LC 97-16620. 1571p. 1997. 175.00 (*0-520-20964-8*, Pub. by U CA Pr) Cal Prin Full Svc.

America Insurance Assoc. Staff. Source Book of Health Insurance Data, 1997-1998. 216p. 1998. pap. text 35.00 (*1-879143-45-3*) Health Ins Assn Am.

America, Millard. How to Get Rid of a Telemarketer. LC 95-83149. (Illus.). 96p. (Orig.). 1995. pap. 7.00 (*1-887317-01-5*) Bad Dog Pr.

America, P., ed. Parallel Database Systems: Proceedings of PRISMA Workshop, Noordwijk, the Netherlands, September 24-26, 1990. (Lecture Notes in Computer Science Ser.: Vol. 503). viii, 433p. 1991. 44.95 (*0-387-54132-2*) Spr-Verlag.

America, P., et al, eds. ECOOP, 1991: Proceedings of the European Conference on Object-Oriented Programming, Geneva, Switzerland, July 15-19, 1991. (Lecture Notes in Computer Science Ser.: Vol. 512). x, 396p. 1991. 44.95 (*0-387-54262-0*) Spr-Verlag.

America Pulpwood Association Staff. Chain Saw Manual. 2nd ed. 100p. 1988. pap. text 16.25 (*0-8134-2776-2*) Interstate.

America, Richard F. Paying the Social Debt: What White America Owes Black America. LC 93-2861. 160p. 1993. 57.95 (*0-275-94450-6*, C4450, Praeger Pubs) Greenwood.

— Philanthropy & Economic Development, 162. LC 94-30933. (Contributions in Economics & Economic History Ser.: Vol. 162). 248p. 1995. 62.95 (*0-313-28809-7*, Greenwood Pr) Greenwood.

— Soul in Management: How African-American Managers Thrive in the Competitive Corporate Environment. 256p. 1997. pap. text 13.95 (*0-8065-1946-0*, Citadel Pr) Carol Pub Group.

America, Richard F., ed. The Wealth of Races: The Present Value of Benefits from Past Injustices, 132. LC 89-25728. (Contributions in Afro-American & African Studies: No. 132). 240p. 1990. 55.00 (*0-313-25753-1*, ARR/, Greenwood Pr) Greenwood.

America, Richard F. & Anderson, Bernard E. Soul in Management: How African-American Managers Can Succeed in a White Business Environment. LC 95-50092. 256p. 1996. 19.95 (*1-55972-353-X*, Birch Ln Pr) Carol Pub Group.

America Taschen Saff. Architecture Assortment. 1999. pap. text 24.99 (*0-676-58830-1*) Hse Collectbls.

American. Brighter Child: Muppet Workbook, Sound Patterns, More Phonics. 1993. pap., student ed. 2.25 (*1-56189-284-X*) Amer Educ Pub.

— Genre Favorites for Young Adult. Estes, Sally, ed. 1994. pap. 7.95 (*0-8389-5755-2*) ALA.

***American Institute of Aeronautics & Astronautics Staff.** Guide to Global Aerosol Models LC 99-36696. 1999. write for info. (*1-56347-348-8*) AIAA.

— Guide to Modeling Earth's Trapped Radiation Environment LC 99-35575. 1999. write for info. (*1-56347-349-6*) AIAA.

— Special Project Report. LC 99-29067. 1999. write for info. (*1-56347-351-8*) AIAA.

— Special Project Report. LC 99-42015. 1999. write for info. (*1-56347-362-3*) AIAA.

***American Institute of Aeronautics & Astronautics Staff & Atmospheric & Space Environments Committee on Standards.** Guide to Reference & Standard Ionosphere Models. LC 99-23533. 64p. 1999. pap. 39.95 (*1-56347-347-X*) AIAA.

American & Barr, Linda. Brighter Child Grade Six: Spelling & Writing. 1994. pap. 2.25 (*1-56189-136-3*) Amer Educ Pub.

American & Branstetter, Kacy. Brighter Child Grade Four: Reading. 1994. pap. 2.25 (*1-56189-125-8*) Amer Educ Pub.

American & British Committee for the International. The New Testament in Greek: The Gospel According to St. Luke, Vol. 3, Pt. 1. (New Testament in Greek Ser.). 314p. 1984. text 160.00 (*0-19-826167-5*) OUP.

American & British Committees of the Int. Greek Ne, ed. Codex Bezae: Studies from the Lunel Colloquium, June 1994. (New Testament Tools & Studies: Vol. 22). xxx, 383p. 1996. 139.50 (*90-04-10393-7*) Brill Academic Pubs.

American & World Geographic Staff. Albuquerque: Where the World Celebrates Ballooning. 1997. 29.95 (*1-56037-114-5*); pap. text 15.95 (*1-56037-113-7*) Am Wrld Geog.

American Academy for Jewish Research Staff. Facets of Medieval Judaism: Proceedings. (Jewish People; History, Religion, Literature Ser.). 1978. 21.95 (*0-405-05262-6*) Ayer.

American Academy in Rome Staff. American Academy in Rome. Incl. 264p. 1956. 30.50. 193p. 1957. 24.50. 224p. 1917. 19.00. (Illus.). 280p. 1980. 30.50 (Memoirs Ser.: No. 1). (Illus.). 172p. 1917. 30.50 (*0-318-12311-8*) Am Acad Rome.

— Memoirs of the American Academy in Rome, Vols. 3-22, & 26. LC DG0065.. 241p. reprint ed. pap. 74.80 (*0-608-16090-3*, 202673300002) Bks Demand.

***American Academy in Rome Staff.** Memoirs of the American Academy in Rome 1997, Vol. 42. Bell, Malcolm, Jr., ed. (Illus.). 254p. (C). 1999. text 55.00 (*1-879549-06-9*) Am Acad Rome.

— Memoirs of the American Academy in Rome (1998), Vol. 43. Bell, Malcolm, Jr., ed. (Illus.). 254p. (C). text 55.00 (*1-879549-07-7*) Am Acad Rome.

American Academy in Rome Staff, jt. auth. see Boyden, Martha.

American Academy of Allergies, Asthma & Immunology, jt. auth. see FastMark Editorial Staff.

American Academy of Ambulatory Care Nursing Staff, jt. auth. see American Nurses Association Staff.

American Academy of Arts & Letters Staff. Academy Papers. LC 70-117749. (Essay Index Reprint Ser.). 1977. 21.95 (*0-8369-1641-7*) Ayer.

— Commemorative Tributes of the Academy, 1905-1941. LC 68-20286. (Essay Index Reprint Ser.). 1977. 23.95 (*0-8369-0147-9*) Ayer.

— Four Addresses in Commemoration of the Twentieth Anniversary of the Founding of the Academy, No. 54. LC 67-22068. (Essay Index Reprint Ser.). 1977. 15.95 (*0-8369-0148-7*) Ayer.

— Proceedings of the American Academy of Arts & Letters. 1996. 15.00 (*0-915974-41-X*) Am Acad Arts.

— Proceedings of the American Academy of Arts & Letters, Vol. 46. 1997. 15.00 (*0-915974-40-1*) Am Acad Arts.

— Proceedings of the American Academy of Arts & Letters, Vol. 47. 1997. 15.00 (*0-915974-42-8*) Am Acad Arts.

— Proceedings of the American Academy of Arts & Letters, Vol. 48. 1998. 15.00 (*0-915974-43-6*) Am Acad Arts.

American Academy of Arts & Sciences Staff. Science & the Modern Mind: A Symposium. Holton, Gerald, ed. LC 70-167304. (Essay Index Reprint Ser.). 1977. reprint ed. 15.95 (*0-8369-2446-0*) Ayer.

American Academy of Arts & Sciences Staff, jt. auth. see American Institute of Physics Staff.

American Academy of Arts & Sciences Staff, jt. auth. see GAAC Staff.

American Academy of Cardiovascular & Pulmonary Reh. Guidelines for Pulmonary Rehabilitation Programs. 2nd rev. ed. LC 97-46467. (Illus.). 264p. 1998. pap. text 35.00 (*0-88011-863-6*, BAAC0863) Human Kinetics.

***American Academy of Child & Adolescence Staff & Pruitt, David.** Your Child: Emotional, Behavioral, & Cognitive Development from Birth Through Preadolescence, 496p. 2000. pap. 15.00 (*0-06-273730-9*, HarpRes) HarpInfo.

American Academy of Child & Adolescent Psychiatry Staff & American Psychiatric Association Staff. Criteria for Short-Term Treatment of Acute Psychiatric Illness. LC 99-183946. 46p. 1998. pap. text 26.00 (*0-89042-412-8*, 2412) Am Psychiatric.

American Academy of Child & Adolescent Psychiatry Staff, jt. auth. see Pruitt, David B.

American Academy of Craniomandibular Disorders Staff. Craniomandibular Disorders: Guidelines for Evaluation, Diagnosis, & Management. McNeill, Charles, ed. 54p. 1990. pap. text 18.00 (*0-86715-227-3*) Quint Pub Co.

American Academy of Dermatology Staff. Dermatology Teaching File Vol. II: Gross & Microscopic Presentations. Hood, Antoinette F., ed. (C). 1995. write for info. (*0-8151-0082-5*) Mosby Inc.

American Academy of Dermatology Staff, ed. Physician's Reference Guide to Medical Literature, Dermatology: A Compendium of Medical Books, Abstracts of Journal Articles, Educational Software, Audio & Video Cassettes. 1995. write for info. (*0-614-06028-1*) Prof & Tech Pub.

American Academy of Dermatology Staff & Pearson, Tom. Mini-Consults in Dermatology: Gross & Microscopic Symposium, Vol. III. (gr. 13). 1996. text 169.00 (*0-8151-1552-0*) Mosby Inc.

***American Academy of Environmental Engineers Staff.** Guide for Administrator's & Faculty to Abet Accreditation in Environmental Engineering. 2nd ed. Anderson, William, ed. LC 99-26197. 190p. (C). 1999. 75.00 (*1-883767-29-6*) Am Acad Environ.

American Academy Of Facial Plastic And Reconstructive Surgery Staff. Developing, Marketing & Managing Your Facial Plastic Surgery Practice: Resource Manual. LC 98-35897. 1998. write for info. (*0-9651231-2-X*) Am Acad Facial.

— The Face Book: A Consumer's Guide to Facial Plastic Surgery. Hill, T. Susan, ed. LC 97-33558. (Illus.). 144p. 1997. pap. 29.95 (*0-9651231-1-1*) Am Acad Facial.

American Academy of Family Physicians Foundation S, jt. auth. see FastMark Editorial Staff.

American Academy Of Family Physicians Staff & Preparticipation Physical Evaluation Task Force. Preparticipation Physical Evaluation. 2nd ed. LC 96-27879. 1996. text 29.95 (*0-07-001627-5*) McGraw.

American Academy of Family Physicians Staff & Society of Teachers of Family Medicine Staff. Fellowship Directory for Family Physicians, 2000. 1998. 10.00 (*0-685-72365-8*) Soc Tchrs Fam Med.

American Academy of Family Physicians Staff, jt. auth. see Dial, Lanyard K.

American Academy of Family Physicians Staff, jt. auth. see Zuber, Thomas J.

American Academy of Healthcare Attorneys of the Am. Legal Issues & the Integrated Delivery System: An Executive Guide. Randall, Deborah A., ed. LC 96-8090. 104p. 1996. pap. 40.00 (*1-55648-159-4*, 118119) AHPI.

American Academy of Nursing Staff. HIV/AIDS Nursing Care Summit Proceedings: Nursing Care Summit Proceedings. Holzemer, William L. & Portillo, Carmen F., eds. 272p. (Orig.). 1994. pap. 22.50 (*1-55810-102-0*, G-186) Am Nurses Pub.

American Academy of Nursing Staff, jt. auth. see Epstein, Paul R.

American Academy of Optometry, jt. auth. see Optical Society of America Staff.

American Academy of Orofacial Pain Staff. Orofacial Pain: Guidelines for Assessment, Classification, & Management. Okeson, Jeffrey P., ed. LC 96-4651. (Illus.), 300p. 1996. pap. text 28.00 (*0-86715-312-1*) Quint Pub Co.

American Academy of Orthopaedic Surgeons Staff. Atlas of Orthotics Assistive Devices. 3rd ed. (Illus.). 720p. (C). (gr. 13). 1996. text 134.00 (*0-8151-0052-3*, 25689) Mosby Inc.

— Complete Global Service Data for Orthopaedic Surgery. LC 98-176765. xv, 1433 p. 1997. write for info. (*0-89203-182-4*) Amer Acad Ortho Surg.

***American Academy of Orthopaedic Surgeons Staff.** Emergency Care & Transportation of the Sick & Injured. 7th ed. (Illus.). 328p. (C). 1999. pap. text, student ed. 29.25 (*0-7637-1026-1*) JB Pubns.

— EMT-Basic Field Care: A Case-Based Approach. (Illus.). 96p. (C). 1998. pap. text 18.75 (*0-7637-0880-1*) JB Pubns.

— EMTB. 6th rev. ed. (Illus.). 784p. (C). 1998. pap. text 52.00 (*0-7637-0803-8*) JB Pubns.

— EMTB. 7th ed. (Illus.). (C). 1998. pap. text 10.00 (*0-7637-0906-9*) JB Pubns.

— EMTB. 7th ed. (Illus.). 992p. (C). 1999. text 55.00 (*0-7637-1044-X*); text, teacher ed. 77.50 (*0-7637-1070-9*) JB Pubns.

— EMTB Supplements Folder. 7th ed. (Illus.). (C). 1999. pap. text, suppl. ed. write for info. (*0-7637-1143-8*) JB Pubns.

— EMTB Cyberclass. 7th ed. (Illus.). (C). 1999. pap. text 66.50 (*0-7637-1104-7*) JB Pubns.

American Academy of Orthopaedic Surgeons Staff. Maine Probate Series, 3 vols., Set. 5th rev. ed. 1991. ring bd. 195.00 (*0-614-05891-0*, MICHIE) LEXIS Pub.

— Orthopaedic Knowledge Update: Shoulder & Elbow. Norris, Tom R., ed. LC 97-43921. (OKU Specialty Ser.). (Illus.). 424p. 1997. pap. 115.00 (*0-89203-170-0*) Amer Acad Ortho Surg.

***American Academy of Orthopaedic Surgeons Staff.** Professional Rescuer CPR Instructor's Manual. (Illus.). 40p. (C). 1998. pap. text, teacher ed. 20.00 (*0-7637-0889-5*) JB Pubns.

— SSG- EMTB. 7th ed. (Illus.). 448p. (C). 1999. pap. text, student ed. 29.25 (*0-7637-0804-6*) JB Pubns.

American Academy of Orthopaedic Surgeons Staff, ed. Post-Graduate Orthopaedic Fellowships, 1996. 370p. 1996. pap. 35.00 (*0-89203-149-2*) Amer Acad Ortho Surg.

American Academy of Orthopaedic Surgeons Staff, jt. auth. see American Academy of Pediatrics Staff.

American Academy of Orthopaedic Surgeons Staff, jt. ed. see Betz, Randal R.

American Academy of Pediatirics Staff. American Academy of Pediatrics Guide. 1997. 125.00 (*0-676-53162-8*) Villard Books.

American Academy of Pediatrics Staff. Adolescent Medicine Residency Training Resources. 238p. 1995. ring bd. 34.95 (*0-910761-74-4*) Am Acad Pediat.

***American Academy of Pediatrics Staff.** American Academy of Pediatrics Guide to Your Child's Nutrition: Making Peace at the Table & Building Healthy Eating Habits for Life. (Illus.). 256p. 1999. pap. 19.95 (*0-375-75487-3*) Villard Books.

American Academy of Pediatrics Staff. American Academy of Pediatrics Guide to Your Child's Symptoms. 256p. 1998. pap. 18.95 (*0-375-75257-9*) Villard Books.

— Annotated Bibliography of Pediatric Cardiology. 188p. 1994. pap. 29.95 (*0-910761-55-8*) Am Acad Pediat.

— Assessment of Sexual Maturity Stages in Girls. 15p. 1995. pap. 24.95 (*0-910761-95-7*) Am Acad Pediat.

— Caring for Your Baby & Young Child: Birth to Age 5. rev. ed. Shelov, Steven P. et al, eds. (American Academy of Pediatrics Ser.). (Illus.). 736p. 1998. pap. 17.95 (*0-553-37962-3*) Bantam.

— Child Health Services & Pediatric Education: Report of the Committee for the Study of Child Health Services. LC 74-1661. (Children & Youth Ser.). 304p. 1974. reprint ed. 26.95 (*0-405-05943-4*) Ayer.

— The Classification of Child & Adolescent Mental Diagnoses in Primary Care. Wolrarch, Mark L., ed. LC 95-75817. 368p. 1996. pap. 39.95 (*0-910761-71-X*) Am Acad Pediat.

— Coding for Pediatrics: A Manual for Documentation & Reimbursement. 4th ed. Jacobsen, A. D. et al, eds. LC 98-71822. 163 p. 1998. write for info. (*1-58110-012-4*) Am Acad Pediat.

— Computers in the Primary Care Office. 3rd ed. LC 95-75174. 248p. 1995. spiral bd. 54.95 (*0-910761-70-1*) Am Acad Pediat.

— Drugs of Pediatric Emergencies. 54p. 1998. pap. 12.95 (*1-58110-014-0*) Am Acad Pediat.

— Emergency Medical Services for Children: The Role of the Primary Care Provider. 266p. 1992. pap. 44.95 (*0-910761-37-X*) Am Acad Pediat.

— Government Affairs Handbook. LC 98-70032. 172p. 1998. pap. 40.00 (*1-58110-004-3*) Am Acad Pediat.

— Guide for Starting a Medical Office. 1997. pap. text 44.95 (*0-910761-86-8*) Coker Publishing.

***American Academy of Pediatrics Staff.** Guide to Your Child's Sleep: Birth Through Adolescence. COHEN, GEORGE J., ed. LC 99-27284. 224p. 1999. pap. 12.95 (*0-679-76981-1*) Villard Books.

American Academy of Pediatrics Staff. Guidelines for Air & Ground Transport of Neonatal & Pediatric Patients. 153p. 1993. pap. 24.95 (*0-910761-44-2*) Am Acad Pediat.

— Guidelines for Health Supervision III, Cue Cards. 3rd ed. LC 96-79630. 257p. 1997. pap. 44.95 (*0-910761-83-3*) Am Acad Pediat.

— Handbook of Common Poisonings in Children. 3rd ed. LC 94-71471. 280p. 1994. pap. 44.95 (*0-910761-58-2*) Am Acad Pediat.

— Health in Day Care: A Manual for Health Professionals. 243p. 1987. pap. 42.95 (*0-910761-13-2*) Am Acad Pediat.

— Managed Care & Children with Special Health Care Needs. 197p. 1997. pap. 29.95 (*0-910761-80-9*) Am Acad Pediat.

— Maryland Vehicle Law: 1993 Edition. 25.00 (*0-614-05893-7*, MICHIE) LEXIS Pub.

— Medical Liability for Pediatricians. 5th ed. 176p. 1995. pap. 49.95 (*0-910761-72-8*) Am Acad Pediat.

— 1997 Report of the Committee on Infectious Diseases. 24th ed. 764p. 1997. pap. 84.95 (*0-910761-85-X*) Am Acad Pediat.

— Pediatric Nutrition Handbook. 4th ed. LC 98-70031. 833p. 1998. pap. 69.95 (*1-58110-005-1*) Am Acad Pediat.

— Pediatric Procedural Terminology - PPT. 3rd ed. 184p. 1995. pap. 34.95 (*0-910761-67-1*) Am Acad Pediat.

— A Pediatrician's Guide to Managed Care. 270p. 1995. ring bd. 49.95 (*0-910761-62-0*) Am Acad Pediat.

— Policy Reference Guide of the American Academy of Pediatrics: A Comprehensive Guide to AAP Statements Issued Through December 1997. 11th ed. 1998. pap. 79.95 (*0-910761-98-1*) Am Acad Pediat.

— Practice Parameters from the American Academy of Pediatrics: A Compilation of Evidence-Based Guidelines for Pediatric Practice. 396p. 1997. pap. 39.95 (*0-910761-78-7*) Am Acad Pediat.

— Practicing Adolescent Medicine: A Collection of Resources. LC 94-70994. 362p. 1994. pap. 44.95 (*0-910761-56-6*) Am Acad Pediat.

— School Health: Policy & Practice. 5th ed. 428p. 1993. pap. 44.95 (*0-910761-42-6*) Am Acad Pediat.

— Selecting a Pediatric Residency: An Employment Guide. 110p. 1993. pap. 20.00 (*0-910761-47-7*) Am Acad Pediat.

— Sports Medicine: Health Care for Young Athletes. 2nd ed. 328p. 1991. pap. 42.95 (*0-910761-28-0*) Am Acad Pediat.

— Substance Abuse: A Self Teaching Guide for Health Professionals. 193p. 1988. pap. 44.95 (*0-910761-20-5*) Am Acad Pediat.

— Your Baby's First Year. rev. ed. Shelov, Steven P., ed. LC 99-163038. 618p. 1998. mass mkt. 6.99 (*0-553-57904-5*) Bantam.

American Academy of Pediatrics Staff & American Academy of Orthopaedic Surgeons Staff. Essentials of Musculoskeletal Care. Snider, Robert K., ed. LC 98-117881. (Illus.). 686p. 1997. 100.00 (*0-89203-162-X*) Amer Acad Ortho Surg.

American Academy of Pediatrics Staff & American College of Emergency Physicians Staff. APLS: The Pediatric Emergency Medicine Course. 2nd ed. 280p. 1993. pap. 79.95 (*0-910761-45-0*) Am Acad Pediat.

American Academy of Pediatrics Staff & American College of Obstetricians & Gynecologists. Guidelines for Perinatal Care. 4th ed. LC 97-19319. 472p. 1997. 60.00 (*0-915473-35-6*) Am Coll Obstetric.

American Academy of Pediatrics Staff & American Heart Association Staff. Instructor's Manual for Neonatal Resuscitation. rev. ed. 212p. 1995. ring bd. 35.00 (*0-910761-64-7*) Am Acad Pediat.

— Pediatric Advanced Life Support, 1997-99. Chameides, Leon & Hazinski, Mary Fran, eds. LC 99-179983. (Emergency Cardiovascular Care Programs Ser.). (Illus.). 150p. 1997. pap. 25.00 (*0-87493-619-5*) Am Heart.

— Textbook of Neonatal Resuscitation. 2nd ed. 376p. 1994. spiral bd. 30.00 (*0-910761-61-2*) Am Acad Pediat.

— Textbook of Pediatric Basic Life Support. LC 99-179982. (Illus.). 120p. 1997. pap. text. write for info. (*0-87493-620-9*) Am Heart.

— Texto de Reanimacion Neonatal. (SPA.). 376p. 1997. pap. 30.00 (*0-910761-88-4*) Am Acad Pediat.

American Academy of Pediatrics Staff & American Public Health Association Staff. Caring for Our Children: National Health & Safety Performance Standards - Guidelines for Out-of-Home Child Care Programs. 410p. 1992. pap. 34.95 (*0-87553-205-5*) Am Acad Pediat.

American Academy of Pediatrics Staff & Kempe, C. Henry, National Center on Child Abuse. The Visual Diagnosis of Child Physical Abuse. 1994. student ed., ring bd. 149.95 (*0-910761-46-9*) Am Acad Pediat.

American Academy of Pediatrics Staff & Machtinger, Edward. Spanish for Pediatric Medicine: A Practical Communication Guide. LC 97-71403. (SPA.). 219p. 1997. spiral bd. 34.95 (*0-910761-84-1*) Am Acad Pediat.

American Academy of Pediatrics Staff, Section on C. A Guide to Reference & Resources in Child Abuse & Neglect. 2nd ed. LC 97-74709. 292p. 1998. pap. 34.95 (*0-910761-93-0*) Am Acad Pediat.

American Academy of Periodontology. Glossary of Periodontic Terms 1992. 52p. 1992. pap. 35.00 (*0-9624699-3-9*) Amer Acad Periodontology.

American Academy of Periodontology Staff. Q & A on Reporting Periodontal Services. 32p. 1992. pap. 25.00 (*0-9624699-4-7*) Amer Acad Periodontology.

— The World Workshop in Clinical Periodontics - Proceedings. 260p. 1989. 65.00 (*0-9624699-1-2*) Amer Acad Periodontology.

American Academy of Physical Education, Meeting (5. The Cutting Edge in Physical Education & Exercise Science Research: Fifty-Eighth Annual Meeting, Cincinnati, Ohio, April 7-8, 1986. Safrit, Margaret J. & Eckert, Helen M., eds. LC 87-129579. (American Academy of Physical Education Papers: No. 20). (Illus.). 136p. 1987. reprint ed. pap. 42.20 (*0-608-07104-8*, 206733100009) Bks Demand.

— The Cutting Edge in Physical Education & Exercise Science Research: 58th Annual Meeting, Cincinnati, OH, April 7-8, 1986. Safrit, Margaret J. & Eckert, Helen M., eds. LC 87-129579. (American Academy of Physical Education Papers: Vol. 20). (Illus.). 136p. reprint ed. pap. 42.20 (*0-608-20843-4*, 207194200003) Bks Demand.

American Academy of Physical Education Staff. Exercise & Health: Fifty-Fourth Annual Meeting, Minneapolis, Minnesota, April 6-7, 1983. LC 84-194051. (American Academy of Physical Education Papers: No. 17). (Illus.). 159p. 1984. reprint ed. pap. 49.30 (*0-608-07110-2*, 206733700009) Bks Demand.

American Academy of Political & Social Science. Adjusting to Scarcity: Proceedings of the American Academy of Political & Social Science, 79th. Lambert, Richard D. & Wolfgang, Marvin E., eds. LC 74-29624. (Annals Ser.: No. 420). 250p. 1975. pap. 18.00 (*0-87761-191-2*) Am Acad Pol Soc Sci.

— The Police & the Crime Problem. Sellin, Thorsten D., ed. reprint ed. 42.50 (*0-404-09145-8*) AMS Pr.

American Academy of Political & Social Science Sta. America's Race Problems. LC 72-95419. (Studies in Black History & Culture: No. 54). 1970. reprint ed. lib. bdg. 58.95 (*0-8383-0959-3*) M S G Haskell Hse.

— The Environment & the Quality of Life: A World View: Proceedings of the American Academy of Political & Social Science, Annual Meeting, 83rd. Wolfgang, Marvin E. & Ginsberg, Ralph B., eds. LC 79-50266. (Annals Ser.: No. 444). 1979. 28.00 (*0-87761-240-4*); pap. 18.00 (*0-87761-241-2*) Am Acad Pol Soc Sci.

— Negro's Progress in Fifty Years. LC 71-92737. 266p. 1969. reprint ed. lib. bdg. 59.50 (*0-8371-2187-6*, NEP&) Greenwood.

— Reform in Administration of Justice. LC 79-156961. (Foundations of Criminal Justice Ser.). reprint ed. 34.50 (*0-404-09101-6*) AMS Pr.

American Academy of Political & Social Science Sta, ed. Annals of the American Academy of Political & Social Science. LC 76-112556. (Literature of Cinema Ser.). 1970. reprint ed. 27.95 (*0-405-01601-8*) Ayer.

American Academy of Political & Social Science Sta & Greene, Lee S., eds. City Bosses & Political Machines. LC 72-14147. (Essay Index Reprint Ser.). 1977. reprint ed. 21.95 (*0-518-10000-6*) Ayer.

American Academy of Political & Social Science Sta & Reynolds, Harry W. Intergovernmental Relations in the United States. 1978. 19.95 (*0-405-10497-9*, 10329) Ayer.

American Academy of Religion, Academic Study of Re. The Academic Study of Religion: 1975 Proceedings & Public Schools Religion-Studies: 1975 Proceedings - American Academy of Religion Annual Meeting, 1975. Preprinted Papers for the Academic Study of Religion Section, Compiled by Anne Carr, & the Public Schools Religion-Studies Group, Compiled by Nicholas Piediscalzi. LC 75-26653. 141p. reprint ed. pap. 43.80 (*0-7837-5402-7*, 204516600005) Bks Demand.

American Academy of Religion, Committee on the Sta. Guide to the Perplexing: A Survival Manual for Women in Religious Studies. LC 92-38549. (American Academy of Religion, Individual Volumes Ser.: No. 2). 106p. 1992. pap. 14.95 (*1-55540-803-6*, 01 08 02) OUP.

American Academy of Religion Staff. Abstracts, 1988: American Academy of Religion, Society of Biblical Literature. LC 90-640164. (Illus.). 377p. reprint ed. pap. 116.90 (*0-608-08680-0*, 206920300003) Bks Demand.

— Abstracts, 1985: American Academy of Religion, Society of Biblical Literature. Richards, Kent H. & Wiggins, James B., eds. LC 90-640164. 256p. reprint ed. pap. 79.40 (*0-608-08836-6*, 206947500004) Bks Demand.

— Abstracts, 1984: American Academy of Religion, Society of Biblical Literature. Richards, Kent H. & Wiggins, James B., eds. LC 90-640164. 284p. reprint ed. pap. 88.10 (*0-608-08835-8*, 206947400004) Bks Demand.

— Abstracts, 1986: American Academy of Religion, Society of Biblical Literature. Richards, Kent H. & Wiggins, James B., eds. LC 90-640164. 273p. reprint ed. pap. 84.70 (*0-608-08837-4*, 206947600004) Bks Demand.

— The HarperCollins Dictionary of Religion. Smith, Jonathan et al, eds. LC 95-37024. (Illus.). 1200p. 1995. 47.50 (*0-06-067515-2*, Pub. by Harper SF) HarpC.

— Philosophy of Religion & Theology, 1975: Proceedings for the Section on Philosophy of Religion & Theology, American Academy of Religion, Annual Meeting, 1975. McClendon, James W., Jr., ed. LC 75-26618. 233p. reprint ed. pap. 72.30 (*0-608-08840-4*, 206947900004) Bks Demand.

American Accounting Association Staff. Accounting & Reporting Standards for Corporate Financial Statements & Preceding Statements & Supplements. 64p. 1957. 2.00 (*0-86539-006-1*) Am Accounting.

American Admiralty Bureau Staff. American Admiralty Bureau's American Vessel Traffic Systems. 98p. (C). 1997. pap. 19.95 (*1-879778-66-1*, BK-0724) Marine Educ.

American Air Mail Society, jt. auth. see Heifetz, Murray.

American Air Mail Society Staff. The Air Mails of Canada & Newfoundland: A Volume in the Sixth Edition of the American Air Mail Catalogue. LC 97-74087. (Illus.). 1997. write for info. (*0-939429-17-9*) Am Air Mail.

American Air Mail Society Staff, ed. American Air Mail Catalogue, 5 vols. 2138p. 1981. 12.50 (*0-685-67497-5*) Am Air Mail.

— American Air Mail Catalogue, 5 vols., 1. 2138p. 1981. write for info. (*0-939429-04-7*) Am Air Mail.

— American Air Mail Catalogue, 5 vols., 2. 2138p. 1981. 18.00 (*0-939429-05-5*) Am Air Mail.

— American Air Mail Catalogue, 5 vols., 3. 2138p. 1981. write for info. (*0-939429-06-3*) Am Air Mail.

— American Air Mail Catalogue, 5 vols., 5. 2138p. 1981. 18.00 (*0-939429-08-X*) Am Air Mail.

— Ellington-Zwisler Pocket Mail Catalog, Vol. II. 180p. 1973. 10.00 (*0-939429-11-X*); 8.00 (*0-318-12361-4*) Am Air Mail.

American Alliance for Health, Physical Education,. Best of Challenge, 3 vols. Incl. Vol. 1. Articles from the Dec. 1965 Through May-June 1970 Issues. pap. 4.95 (*0-88314-032-2*, 245-25124); Vol. 2. Articles from the Sept.-Oct. 1970 Through May-June 1973 Issues. American Alliance for Health, Physical Education,, ed. pap. 4.95 (*0-88314-033-0*, 245-25562); Vol. 3. Articles from the Sept. 73 Through May 76 Issues. American Alliance for Health, Physical Education,, ed. pap. 4.95 (*0-88314-034-9*); pap. write for info. (*0-318-50146-5*) AAHPERD.

— Children's Dance. rev. ed. 1981. pap. 8.50 (*0-88314-041-1*) AAHPERD.

— Health Education Teaching Ideas: Secondary. 1992. pap. 15.00 (*0-88314-529-4*) AAHPERD.

American Alliance for Health, Physical Education, Recreation & Dance Staff, jt. auth. see Physical Best (Program) Staff.

American Alliance for Theatre & Education Staff. A Model Drama - Theatre Curriculum: Philosophy, Goals & Objectives. 106p. (Orig.). 1987. pap. text 12.50 (*0-87602-027-9*) Anchorage.

American Aluminum Company Staff. Melting & Casting Aluminum. (Illus.). 180p. 1993. reprint ed. pap. 14.95 (*1-57002-078-7*) Univ Publng Hse.

American Animal Hospital Association Staff. Cardiac Disease in the Dog & Cat: A Diagnostic Handbook. 220p. 1986. 17.95 (*0-9616498-0-1*) Am Animal Hosp Assoc.

— Scientific Proceedings of the Annual Meeting of the American Animal Hospital Association. 467p. 1984. 9.50 (*0-9616498-7-9*) Am Animal Hosp Assoc.

— Scientific Proceedings of the Annual Meeting of the American Animal Hospital Association, 1981. 408p. 1981. 9.50 (*0-685-43407-9*) Am Animal Hosp Assoc.

American Anthropological Association Staff. Explorations in Anthropology & Theology. Salamone, Frank A. & Adams, Walter R., eds. LC 96-49252. 298p. 1997. 57.50 (*0-7618-0660-1*); pap. 32.50 (*0-7618-0661-X*) U Pr of Amer.

American Anti-Slavery Society Staff. Anti-Slavery History of the John Brown Year: Being the Twenty-Seventh Report of the American Anti-Slavery Society. LC 70-82169. (Anti-Slavery Crusade in America Ser.). 1974. reprint ed. 18.95 (*0-405-00604-7*) Ayer.

— Legion of Liberty & Force of Truth, Containing the Thoughts, Words, & Deeds of Some Prominent Apostles, Champions, & Martyrs. LC 71-82199. (Anti-Slavery Crusade in America Ser.). (Illus.). 1970. reprint ed. 18.95 (*0-405-00605-5*) Ayer.

— Proceedings of the American Anti-Slavery Society at Its Third Decade. LC 79-82166. (Anti-Slavery Crusade in America Ser.). 1970. reprint ed. 11.95 (*0-405-00606-3*) Ayer.

American Antiquarian Society Staff. American Women's Diaries: From the Collection of the American Antiquarian Society. LC 89-892145. 1984. write for info. (*0-918414-14-8*) Readex Bks.

An Asterisk (*) at the beginning of an entry indicates that the title is appearing for the first time.

— The Collections & Programs of the American Antiquarian Society: A 175th-Anniversary Guide. (Illus.). 194p. 1987. pap. text 12.50 (*0-912296-93-3*) Am Antiquarian.

American Arbitration Association Staff. The Alternative Dispute Resolution Practice Guide. 400p. 1993. ring bd. write for info. (*0-8403-9146-3*) Kendall-Hunt.

— Survey of International Arbitration Sites. 3rd ed. LC 84-81526. 175p. 1993. reprint ed. pap. 15.00 (*0-943001-09-9*) Am Arbitration.

American Arbitration Association Staff, ed. Arbitration & the Law. 1994. 50.00 (*0-929179-97-8*) Juris Pubng.

American Arbitration Association Staff & Shepard's Mcgraw-Hill Staff. Insurance ADR Manual. 503p. 1993. 85.00 (*0-685-72811-0*) Am Arbitration.

American Architectural Foundation Staff. Energy Design for Architects. LC 88-24542. 369p. 1988. pap. text 59.00 (*0-88173-074-2*) Fairmont Pr.

American Association of Naturopathic Physicians Staff, jt. auth. see Alleman, Gayle Povia.

American Assembly Staff. Alcoholism & Related Problems: Issues for the American Public. LC 84-13451. 226p. reprint ed. pap. 70.10 (*0-8357-5301-8*, 202985900066) Bks Demand.

— Arms Control. LC 75-117750. (Essay Index Reprint Ser.). 1977. 20.95 (*0-8369-1780-4*) Ayer.

— Arms Control: Issues for the Public. LC 61-14148. (Illus.). 223p. reprint ed. pap. 69.20 (*0-8357-3825-6*, 203654700004) Bks Demand.

— Cultural Affairs & Foreign Relations. LC 63-10670. (Spectrum Bks.). 192p. reprint ed. pap. 59.60 (*0-608-17918-3*, 202797600057) Bks Demand.

— Disorders in Higher Education. LC 79-9350. (Spectrum Bks.). 224p. reprint ed. pap. 69.50 (*0-608-17926-4*, 202797700057) Bks Demand.

— Economic Security for Americans. LC 72-111811. (Essay Index Reprint Ser.). 1977. 28.95 (*0-8369-1640-9*) Ayer.

— The Economy & the President: Nineteen Hundred Eighty & Beyond. LC 80-17443. (Spectrum Bks.: Vol. S-AA-51). 192p. reprint ed. pap. 59.60 (*0-608-16976-5*, 205625500056) Bks Demand.

— Ethnic Relations in America. Liebman, Lance M., ed. LC 82-552. 192p. reprint ed. pap. 59.60 (*0-608-14047-3*, 202797800057) Bks Demand.

— The Farm & the City: Rivals or Allies? LC 80-19998. (Spectrum Bks.). (Illus.). 192p. reprint ed. pap. 59.60 (*0-608-17943-4*, 202797900057) Bks Demand.

— Financial Services: The Changing Institutions & Government Policy. LC 83-13995. 299p. reprint ed. pap. 92.70 (*0-608-18815-8*, 202986100066) Bks Demand.

— The Future of American Political Parties: The Challenge of Governance. LC 82-13182. 191p. reprint ed. pap. 59.30 (*0-608-17957-4*, 202798000057) Bks Demand.

— Global Companies: The Political Economy of World Business. Ball, George W., ed. LC 75-5557. 192p. reprint ed. pap. 59.60 (*0-608-13157-1*, 201539700094) Bks Demand.

— Mexico & the United States. LC 81-5171. 208p. reprint ed. pap. 64.50 (*0-608-16983-8*, 205625400056) Bks Demand.

— Military Service in the United States. Scowcroft, Brent, ed. LC 81-22744. (Illus.). 245p. reprint ed. pap. 76.00 (*0-608-18004-1*, 202798100057) Bks Demand.

— The Nuclear Power Controversy. Murphy, Arthur W., ed. LC 76-40017. 192p. reprint ed. pap. 59.60 (*0-608-11007-8*, 201539800093) Bks Demand.

— On Understanding Art Museums. LC 74-34015. 224p. reprint ed. pap. 69.50 (*0-608-18816-6*, 202986300066) Bks Demand.

— Outer Space: Prospects for Man & Society. rev. ed. Bloomfield, Lincoln P., ed. LC 72-3391. (Essay Index Reprint Ser.). 1977. reprint ed. 19.95 (*0-8369-2886-5*) Ayer.

— Outer Space Prospects for Man & Society. Bloomfield, Lincoln P., ed. LC 62-9281. (Illus.). 220p. reprint ed. pap. 68.20 (*0-608-18392-X*, 202986400066) Bks Demand.

— The Performing Arts & American Society. LC 78-1404. 224p. reprint ed. pap. 69.50 (*0-608-18393-8*, 202986500066) Bks Demand.

— Public Workers & Public Unions. Zagoria, Sam, ed. LC 75-38793. (Spectrum Bks.). 192p. reprint ed. pap. 59.60 (*0-608-16968-4*, 205625700056) Bks Demand.

— Regrowing the American Economy. LC 83-3171. 191p. reprint ed. pap. 59.30 (*0-608-18817-4*, 202986600066) Bks Demand.

— Running the American Corporation. LC 78-16922. (Spectrum Bks.). 196p. reprint ed. pap. 60.80 (*0-608-18040-8*, 202798200057) Bks Demand.

— Secretary of State. LC 73-133511. (Select Bibliographies Reprint Ser.). 1977. 19.95 (*0-8369-5543-9*) Ayer.

— U. S. Monetary Policy. rev. ed. Jacoby, Neil H., ed. LC 79-164586. (Select Bibliographies Reprint Ser.). 1977. reprint ed. 20.95 (*0-8369-5702-4*) Ayer.

— The United States & Africa. LC 75-117751. (Essay Index Reprint Ser.). 1977. 21.95 (*0-8369-1781-2*) Ayer.

— The United States & Africa. rev. ed. Goldschmidt, Walter, ed. LC 63-20154. 316p. reprint ed. pap. 98.00 (*0-608-18818-2*, 202986800066) Bks Demand.

— The United States & Eastern Europe. Byrnes, Robert F., ed. LC 67-23502. (Illus.). 191p. reprint ed. pap. 59.30 (*0-608-18819-0*, 202986900066) Bks Demand.

— The United States & the Far East. Thorp, Willard L., ed. LC 62-12831. 192p. reprint ed. pap. 59.60 (*0-608-30671-1*, 205084000060) Bks Demand.

— The United States & the Middle East. LC 64-14027. 192p. reprint ed. pap. 59.60 (*0-608-17439-4*, 202987000066) Bks Demand.

— The United States & the Philippines. Golay, Frank H., ed. LC 66-22802. 192p. reprint ed. pap. 59.60 (*0-608-17440-8*, 202987100066) Bks Demand.

— United States Monetary Policy. rev. ed. Jacoby, Neil H., ed. LC 64-7956. (Illus.). 255p. reprint ed. pap. 79.10 (*0-608-17441-6*, 202987200066) Bks Demand.

— Youth Employment & Public Policy. LC 79-27022. (Spectrum Bks.). 175p. reprint ed. pap. 54.30 (*0-608-16973-0*, 205625600056) Bks Demand.

American Assembly Staff & Stevens, G. G. The United States & the Middle East. (New Reprints in Essay & General Literature Index Ser.). 1977. reprint ed. 22.95 (*0-518-10195-9*, 10195) Ayer.

American Assn. of Veterinary Lab. Diagnosticians,. Culture Methods for the Detection of Animal Salmonellosis & Arizonosis: A Manual. LC 75-32022. 95p. 1976. reprint ed. pap. 30.00 (*0-608-00064-7*, 206083000006) Bks Demand.

American Assoc. of Law Libraries, State, Court & Cty. Law Libraries Special Interest Sect. Staff, et al, compiled by. Sourcebook for Law Library Governing Boards & Committees. LC 93-26593. (AALL Publications Ser.: No. 45). xvi, 430p. 1994. ring bd. 70.00 (*0-8377-9291-6*, Rothman) W S Hein.

American Assocation for Artificial Intelligence Staff, ed. National Conference on Artificial Intelligence: Proceedings, 18 August, 1983. (Illus.). 368p. 1983. pap. text 45.00 (*0-262-51052-9*) AAAI Pr.

American Association for Artificial Intelligence S. National Conference on Artificial Intelligence: Proceedings, 18-20 August 1982. (Illus.). 456p. 1982. pap. text 45.00 (*0-262-51051-0*) AAAI Pr.

— National Conference on Artificial Intelligence: Proceedings, 18-21 August, 1980. (Illus.). 339p. 1980. pap. text 40.00 (*0-262-51050-2*) AAAI Pr.

— National Conference on Artificial Intelligence: Proceedings, 6-10 August, 1984. (Illus.). 386p. 1984. pap. text 45.00 (*0-262-51053-7*) AAAI Pr.

American Association for Artificial Intelligence S, ed. AAAI - 91: Proceedings of the Ninth National Conference on Artificial Intelligence, 2 vols., Set. (AAAI Press Ser.). (Illus.). 900p. 1991. pap. text 75.00 (*0-262-51059-6*) MIT Pr.

American Association for Artificial Intelligence Staff. AAAI 99: Proceedings of the Sixteenth National Conference on Artificial Intelligence. LC 99-461779. (AAAI Press Ser.). (Illus.). 1200p. 1999. pap. text 85.00 (*0-262-51106-1*) MIT Pr.

— National Conference on Artificial Intelligence: Proceedings, August 1987, 2 vols. (Illus.). 1986. pap. text 55.00 (*0-262-51055-3*) AAAI Pr.

American Association for Artificial Intelligence Staff, ed. AAAI - 94: Proceedings of the Twelfth National Conference on Artificial Intelligence. 1994. pap. text 93.50 (*0-262-51078-2*) MIT Pr.

American Association for Critical Care Nurses Staff. AACN Procedure Manual for Critical Care. 3rd ed. Boggs, Rochelle L. & Wooldridge-King, Maribeth, eds. (Illus.). 984p. 1993. pap. text 65.00 (*0-7216-3073-1*, W B Saunders Co) Harcrt Hlth Sci Grp.

American Association for Gifted Children Staff. The Gifted Child. Witty, Paul A., ed. LC 79-148630. 338p. 1972. reprint ed. lib. bdg. 35.00 (*0-8371-6002-2*, AAGC, Greenwood Pr) Greenwood.

American Association for International Aging Staff & Hansan Group Staff. 365 Ways: Retirees' Resource Guide for Productive Lifestyles. Kerschner, Helen K. & Hansan, John E., eds. LC 96-28187. 240p. 1996. 35.00 (*0-313-30196-4*, Greenwood Pr) Greenwood.

American Association for Medical Transcription Sta, ed. Introductory Module. (Exploring Transcription Practices Ser.). 60p. (C). 1993. pap., student ed. 495.00 incl. digital audio (*0-935229-16-7*) Am Assoc Med.

American Association for Medical Transcription Sta, ed. Mini-Module, No. MS1: Skillbuilding in Medicine-Surgery. (Exploring Transcription Practices Ser.). 16p. (C). 1993. text, student ed. 30.00 incl. audio (*0-935229-18-3*) Am Assoc Med.

— Mini-Module, No. MS3: Skillbuilding in Medicine-Surgery. (Exploring Transcription Practices Ser.). 16p. (C). 1995. text, student ed. 30.00 incl. audio (*0-935229-26-4*) Am Assoc Med.

— Mini-Module, No. R1: Skillbuilding in Radiology. (Exploring Transcription Practices Ser.). 16p. (C). 1993. student ed. 30.00 incl. audio (*0-935229-19-1*) Am Assoc Med.

— Mini-Module, No. R2: Skillbuilding in Radiology. (Exploring Transcription Practices Ser.). 16p. (C). 1994. text, student ed. 30.00 incl. audio (*0-935229-24-8*) Am Assoc Med.

American Association for Medical Transcription Staff. Introductory Module Handbook. (Exploring Transcription Practices Ser.). 60p. (C). 1993. pap. text, student ed. 50.00 incl. audio (*0-935229-17-5*) Am Assoc Med.

American Association for Medical Transcription Staff, ed. General Surgery Module. 2nd ed. (Exploring Transcription Practices Ser.). 93p. (C). 1996. wbk. ed. 225.00 incl. audio (*0-935229-29-9*) Am Assoc Med.

American Association for Nude Recreation. The North American Guide to Nude Recreation. 19th ed. 198p. 1997. pap. text 24.95 (*1-882033-06-X*) AANR.

American Association for Nude Staff. North American Guide to Nude Recreation: The Most Comprehensive Listing of Nude Recreation Resorts & Clubs. 20th ed. 224p. 1999. pap. 24.95 (*1-882033-08-6*) AANR.

American Association for Pediatric Ophthalmology &, jt. ed. see Lennerstrand, Gunnar.

American Association for the Advancement of Science Staff. Aging, Some Social & Biological Aspects: Proceedings of the American Association for the Advancement of Science, Symposia presented at the Chicago Meeting. Shock, Nathan W., ed. LC 73-167305. (Essay Index Reprint Ser.). 1977. reprint ed. 36.95 (*0-8369-2735-4*) Ayer.

— American Association for the Advancement of Science: Caribbean Studies, a Symposium. Rubin, Vera, ed. LC 84-45529. (American Ethnological Society Monographs: No. 34). 1988. reprint ed. 22.50 (*0-404-62933-4*) AMS Pr.

— Astronomical Photoelectric Photometry. Wood, Frank B., ed. LC 53-12745. 149p. reprint ed. pap. 46.20 (*0-8357-5823-0*, 200020400025) Bks Demand.

— Benchmarks for Science Literacy. (Illus.). 448p. 1994. pap. 26.50 (*0-19-508986-3*) OUP.

— Benchmarks for Science Literacy: Science for All Americans Set. 1994. pap. 35.00 (*0-19-509110-8*) OUP.

— Blueprints for Reform. LC 97-24503. 1997. write for info. (*0-87168-608-2*) AAAS.

— Blueprints for Reform: Science, Mathematics & Technology Education. LC 98-13962. (Illus.). 320p. 1998. pap. 17.95 (*0-19-512427-8*) OUP.

— Boston Studies in the Philosophy of Science, Vol. 11: Proceedings of the American Association for the Advancement of Science, Section L, 1949. Seeger, R. J. & Cohen, R. S., eds. LC 73-83555. (Synthese Library: No. 58). 554p. 1974. pap. text 101.50 (*90-277-0276-0*, D Reidel); lib. bdg. 165.00 (*90-277-0390-6*, D Reidel) Kluwer Academic.

— Designs for Science Literacy. LC 99-38299. (Illus.). 256p. 2000. pap. 24.95 (*0-19-513278-5*) OUP.

— Global Effects of Environmental Pollution: Proceedings of the American Association for the Advancement of Science Symposium, Dallas, December 1968. Singer, S. Fred, ed. LC 78-118129. 218p. 1970. text 95.50 (*90-277-0151-2*) Kluwer Academic.

— Ground Level Climatology: A Symposium Presented at the Berkeley Meeting of the American Association for the Advancement of Science. Shaw, Robert H., ed. LC 67-29427. (American Association for the Advancement of Science Publication Ser.: No. 86). 407p. reprint ed. pap. 126.20 (*0-608-30190-6*, 201516800092) Bks Demand.

— Guatemala: Case Reports, 1980-1985. LC JL1496. (AAAS Publication: No. 86-8). 91p. reprint ed. pap. 30.00 (*0-608-15672-8*, 203198300077) Bks Demand.

— Industrial Science, Present & Future. Christman, Ruth C. & Bonnell, Allen T., eds. LC 70-90598. (Essay Index Reprint Ser.). 1977. 19.95 (*0-8369-1201-2*) Ayer.

***American Association for the Advancement of Science Staff.** Middle Grades Mathematics Textbooks: A Benchmarks Based Evaluation. LC 99-54400. 1999. write for info. (*0-87168-635-X*) AAAS.

American Association for the Advancement of Science Staff. Present State of Physics: Proceedings of the American Advancement of Science, New York, 1949. Brackett, Frederick S., ed. LC 75-99617. (Essay Index Reprint Ser.). 1977. 30.95 (*0-8369-1542-9*) Ayer.

— Resources for Science Literacy: Professional Development. LC 96-49376. (Illus.). 144p. 1997. pap. text 49.95 incl. audio compact disk (*0-19-510875-6*) OUP.

— Science & Security: The Future of Arms Control. Wander, W. James et al, eds. LC Q 0181.A1A68. (AAAS Publication: No. 86-16). 229p. reprint ed. pap. 71.00 (*0-8357-6435-4*, 203580600097) Bks Demand.

— Systems of Units, National & International Aspects: A Symposium Organized by Section M on Engineering. Kayan, Carl F., ed. LC 59-15335. (American Association for the Advancement of Science Publication Ser.: No. 57). 307p. reprint ed. pap. 95.20 (*0-608-13038-9*, 201517000094) Bks Demand.

American Association for the Advancement of Slavic Studies Staff & University of Illinois at Urbana-Champaign Staff. The American Bibliography of Slavic & East European Studies for 1993. 630p. (C). (gr. 13). 1996. text 116.95 (*1-56324-750-X*) M E Sharpe.

— The American Bibliography of Slavic & East European Studies for 1994. 728p. 1999. text 157.95 (*1-56324-751-8*) M E Sharpe.

American Association for the International Commiss. Human Rights & U. S. Foreign Policy: The First Decade, 1973-1983. LC 84-305. 1984. 20.00 (*0-916265-00-5*) Am Assn Intl Comm Jurists.

American Association for the Study & Cure of Inebr. Proceedings of the American Association for the Study & Cure of Inebriates: 1870 to 1875. Grob, Gerald N., ed. LC 80-1271. (Addiction in America Ser.). 1981. lib. bdg. 49.95 (*0-405-13565-3*) Ayer.

American Association for the Study & Cure of Inebriety. The Disease of Inebriety from Alcohol, Opium & Other Narcotic Drugs: Its Etiology, Pathology Treatment & Medico-Legal Relations. Grob, Gerald N., ed. LC 80-1210. (Addiction in America Ser.). 1981. reprint ed. lib. bdg. 38.95 (*0-405-13566-1*) Ayer.

American Association for the Study & Prevention of Infant Mortality. Transactions: Proceedings of the American Association for the Study & Prevention of Infant Mortality Meeting, 1st, New Haven, 1909. LC 74-1663. (Children & Youth Ser.). 356p. 1974. reprint ed. 29.95 (*0-405-05944-2*) Ayer.

American Association Homes for the Aging Staff. Aging in Place: Supporting the Frail Elderly in Residential Environments. 352p. (C). 1990. 36.66 (*0-673-24945-X*) Addson-Wesley Educ.

American Association of Anatomists, Cajal Club Mee. Neuromorphological Plasticity: Proceedings of the Symposium, Dallas, Texas, April 1972. Bernstein, J. & Goodman, D. C., eds. (Brain, Behavior & Evolution Ser.: Vol. 8, Nos. 1-2). (Illus.). 164p. 1973. reprint ed. 42.50 (*3-8055-1703-3*) S Karger.

American Association of Blood Banks, jt. auth. see Triulzi, Darrell.

American Association of Cardiovascular & Pulmonary Rehabilitation Staff. Guidelines for Cardiac Rehabilitation & Secondary Prevention Programs. 3rd rev. ed. LC 98-40336. (Illus.). 294p. 1998. pap. text 35.00 (*0-88011-817-2*) Human Kinetics.

American Association of Colleges for Teacher Educa. Multicultural Teacher Education, Vol. 1. LC 80-80105. 224p. reprint ed. pap. 69.50 (*0-7837-2596-5*, 204275900001) Bks Demand.

American Association of Colleges of Nursing Staff. Building a Database for Nursing Education Enrollment Management. 175p. 1989. 18.00 (*0-922148-03-1*) AACN.

— Guide to Schools of Nursing in Four-Year Colleges & Universities: Baccalaureate & Graduate Programs in the United States, Its Territories & Canada. (Ace-Macmillan Series on Higher Education). 736p. 1987. write for info. (*0-317-59321-8*) Macmillan.

— Successful Enrollment Management: A Workbook for Nursing Education Recruitment Professionals. Redman, Barbara K., ed. 250p. (Orig.). 1989. student ed. 35.00 (*0-922148-01-5*) AACN.

American Association of Collegiate Registrars & Ad. AACRAO Strategic Enrollment Management Casebook: Cases from the Field. Dolence, Michael G., ed. LC 95-13756. 187p. 1996. 40.00 (*0-929851-38-2*) Am Assn Coll Registrars.

— The AACRAO Survey of Grading Policies in Member Institutions: A Report. LC LB2368.A44. 44p. 1971. reprint ed. pap. 30.00 (*0-8357-5002-7*, 202407800036) Bks Demand.

— Academic Record & Transcript Guide. LC LB2341.. 24p. reprint ed. pap. 30.00 (*0-8357-5031-0*, 202407700036) Bks Demand.

— Certification of Students under Veterans Laws: Information for Certifying Officials & Other Advisors of Veterans, Their Dependents or Survivors & Service Persons. LC UB0357.A4. (Illus.). 94p. reprint ed. pap. 30.00 (*0-8357-7531-3*, 203624100001) Bks Demand.

— Definitions of Terms for Admissions & Records. LC LB2351.2.D43. (AACRAO Handbook, 1980: Data & Definitions Ser.). 82p. reprint ed. pap. 30.00 (*0-8357-3112-X*, 203936900012) Bks Demand.

— Guide for International Admissions & Evaluation Officers: A Project of the Committee on Admissions, Evaluation & Placement - International Education. LC LB2341.G85. 431p. reprint ed. pap. 133.70 (*0-8357-3113-8*, 203937000012) Bks Demand.

— The Registrar's Guide to Facilities Planning & Management. LC LB2341.A43. 61p. reprint ed. pap. 30.00 (*0-608-12615-2*, 202407400036) Bks Demand.

— Retention of Records: A Guide for Retention & Disposal of Student Records. LC LB2341.A52. 67p. reprint ed. pap. 30.00 (*0-608-12612-8*, 202407300036) Bks Demand.

— Survey of the Management & Utilization of Electronics Data Processing Systems in Admission, Records, & Registration, 1969-70. LC LB2341.A42. 139p. reprint ed. pap. 43.10 (*0-608-12621-7*, 202407600036) Bks Demand.

American Association of Collegiate Registrars & Ad, ed. Retention of Records: Guide for Retention & Disposal of Student Records. LC 98-8595. 37p. 1998. reprint ed. pap. 17.00 (*1-57858-018-8*, 1243) Am Assn Coll Registrars.

American Association of Collegiate Registrars & Ad, jt. auth. see Task Force for the Academic Record & Transcript Gu.

American Association of Community & Junior College. Small-Rural Community Colleges: Report of the Commission on Small and-or Rural Community Colleges. LC 88-152947. (Illus.). 70p. reprint ed. pap. 30.00 (*0-7837-2481-0*, 204263700005) Bks Demand.

American Association of Community Colleges Staff. Core Issues in Community Colleges. LC LB2328.. (Studies in Transfer, Remedial, Workforce, Future Trends). 95p. reprint ed. pap. 30.00 (*0-608-08033-0*, 206799800001) Bks Demand.

— Teleconferencing Resources at U. S. Community Colleges. 400p. 1997. pap. 195.00 (*0-87117-304-2*, 1401) Comm Coll Pr Am Assn Comm Coll.

American Association of Critical-Care Nurses Staff. Acute Care Nurse Practitioner: Clinical Reference & Certification Review. Eoyang, Thomas, ed. LC 98-4059. (Illus.). 1088p. (C). 1998. text 65.00 (*0-7216-7311-2*, W B Saunders Co) Harcrt Hlth Sci Grp.

— The Clinical Nurse Specialist Role in Critical Care. Gawlinski, Anna & Kern, Leslie S., eds. LC 93-30391. (Illus.). 335p. 1994. text 55.00 (*0-7216-3715-9*, W B Saunders Co) Harcrt Hlth Sci Grp.

— Core Curriculum for Pediatric Critical Care Nursing. Slota, Margaret C., ed. (Illus.). 830p. 1997. pap. text 45.00 (*0-7216-6114-9*, W B Saunders Co) Harcrt Hlth Sci Grp.

— Critical Care Procedures Performance Evaluation. LC 94-13892. (Illus.). 187p. 1994. text 74.00 (*0-7216-5441-X*, W B Saunders Co) Harcrt Hlth Sci Grp.

American Association of Critical Care Nurses Staff. Educator's Supplement: Critical Care. 80p. 1995. pap. text, per. 19.95 (*0-7872-0476-5*) Kendall-Hunt.

American Association of Diabetes Educators Staff, jt. auth. see Betschart, Anne.

***American Association of Drilli Staff.** Shale Shaker Handbook: Techniques & Technology for Improving Solids Control Management. LC 99-13067. 300p. 1999. pap. text 65.00 (*0-88415-948-5*) Gulf Pub.

A

American Association of Equine Practitioners Staff. Proceedings of the Fortieth Annual Convention of the American Association of Equine Practitioners, Held in Vancouver, British Columbia, December 4-7, 1994. Bakhaus, Rebecca P., ed. LC 79-2671. 212p. 1994. reprint ed. pap. 65.80 (0-608-01731-0, 206238800002) Bks Demand.

— Proceedings of the Forty-First Annual Convention of the American Association of Equine Practitioners, Held in Lexington, Kentucky, December 3-6, 1995. Zinninger, Susan E., ed. LC 79-2671. 298p. 1995. reprint ed. pap. 92.40 (0-608-01732-9, 206238900002) Bks Demand.

— Proceedings of the 44th Annual Convention of the American Association of Equine Practitioners, Baltimore, MD, December 6-9, 1998, Vol. YN, 1998. LC 79-2671. (Illus.). 328p. reprint ed. pap. 101.70 (0-608-20237-1, 207149600044) Bks Demand.

— Proceedings of the Thirty-Ninth Annual Convention of the American Association of Equine Practitioners, Held in San Antonio, Texas, December 5-8, 1993. LC 79-2671. 310p. 1993. reprint ed. pap. 96.10 (0-608-01730-2, 206238700002) Bks Demand.

American Association of Homes for the Aging Staff. AAHA Directory of Members, 1995. rev. ed. LC 78-641009. 214p. (Orig.). 1986. pap. text 50.00 (0-943774-31-4) Am Assn Homes.

American Association of Individual Investors Staff. The Individual Investor's Guide to Computerized Investing. 15th ed. (Illus.). 350p. 1998. pap. 24.95 (1-883328-03-9) Am Assn Indiv Investors.

— The Individual Investor's Guide to Computerized Investing, 1998. 14th rev. ed. (Illus.). 250p. 1997. pap. 24.95 (1-883328-01-2) Am Assn Indiv Investors.

***American Association of Individual Investors Staff.** The Individual Investor's Guide to Computerized Investing 2000. 16th rev. ed. 350p. 1999. pap. text 24.95 (1-883328-05-5) Am Assn Indiv Investors.

American Association of Individual Investors Staff. The Individual Investor's Guide to Low-Load Mutual Funds. 17th rev. ed. 950p. 1998. pap. 24.95 (1-883328-02-0) NTC Contemp Pub Co.

— The Individual Investor's Guide to Low-Load Mutual Funds 1999. 18th rev. ed. LC 95-75595. 1020p. 1999. pap. 24.95 (1-883328-04-7) Am Assn Indiv Investors.

***American Association of Individual Investors Staff.** The Individual Investor's Guide to Low-Load Mutual Funds, 2000. 19th rev. ed. LC 95-75595. 1020p. 2000. pap. 24.95 (1-883328-06-3) Am Assn Indiv Investors.

American Association of Laboratory Animal Science. Environmental Variables in Animal Experimentation: Proceedings of the American Association fo Laboratory Animal Science, New Jersey, 1970. Magalhaes, Hulda, ed. LC 72-3526. (Illus.). 146p. 1974. 15.00 (0-8387-1231-2) Bucknell U Pr.

American Association of Law Librarians Staff & Dyer, Susan K. Manual of Procedures for Private Law Libraries: 1984 Supplement. LC 84-11589. (AALL Publications: No. 21). ix, 130p. 1984. 18.50 (0-317-00875-7) Am Assn Law Libs.

American Association of Law Libraries Staff. Contemporary Practice of Public International Law. Schaffer, Ellen G. & Snyder, Randall J., eds. LC 97-8608. 297p. 1997. text 85.00 (0-379-21374-5) Oceana.

***American Association of Law Libraries Staff.** Index to Legal Periodicals. 1998. reprint ed. 575.00 (1-57588-439-9) W S Hein.

American Association of Law Libraries Staff. Introduction to Foreign Legal Systems. Danner, Richard A. & Bernal, Marie L., eds. 423p. 1994. text 85.00 (0-379-21350-8) Oceana.

— Introduction to International Business Law: Legal Transactions in a Global Economy. Seer, Gitelle & Smolka-Day, Maria I., eds. LC 96-24868. 295p. 1996. text 85.00 (0-379-21364-8) Oceana.

— Introduction to International Organizations. Louis-Jacques, Lyonette & Korman, Jeanne S., eds. LC 95-21251. 620p. 1996. text 85.00 (0-379-21351-6) Oceana.

— Law Librarianship: Historical Perspectives. Gasaway, Laura N. & Chiorazzi, Michael G., eds. LC 96-9121. (AAAL Publications: No. 52). xxi, 664p. 1996. 75.00 (0-8377-0149-X, Rothman) W S Hein.

— Library of Congress Classification: Class J Political Science, 1995 Edition Cumulative Schedule & Index. 1995th ed. LC 96-28994. (AALL Publications: No. 54). xiii, 884p. 1996. ring bd. 110.00 (0-8377-9327-0, Rothman) W S Hein.

American Association of Law Libraries Staff, jt. auth. see Dershem, Larry D.

American Association of Legal Nurses Staff, ed. Legal Nurse Consulting: Principles & Practice. LC 97-50089. 800p. 1997. boxed set 75.00 (1-57444-123-X, SL123X) St Lucie Pr.

American Association of Medical Assistants Staff. Health Care Law & Ethics. rev. ed. v, 320p. 1995. pap. 20.00 (0-942732-02-2) Am Med Assts.

— Workbook to Accompany "Health Care Law & Ethics" v, 130p. 1995. student ed. 20.00 (0-942732-03-0) Am Med Assts.

***American Association of Museums Staff.** The AAM Guide to Museum Giving: A Directory of Giving Opportunities at Museums Across the United States. (Illus.). 145p. 1999. pap. 10.00 (0-931201-62-4) Am Assn Mus.

— Code of Ethics for Museums. 16p. 1999. pap. 6.00 (0-931201-65-9) Am Assn Mus.

American Association of Museums Staff. Museums Count. Grogg, Ann, ed. LC 93-51504. 112p. 1993. pap. 30.00 (0-931201-17-9) Am Assn Mus.

— Official Museum Directory. 28th ed. 1997. 219.00 (0-87217-958-3) Natl Register.

American Association Of Museums Staff. Official Museum Directory. 28th ed. 1998. pap. text 292.00 (0-87217-960-5) Natl Register.

American Association of Museums Staff. A Statistical Survey of Museums in the United States & Canada. LC 75-21957. (America in Two Centuries Ser.). 1976. reprint ed. 16.95 (0-405-07735-1) Ayer.

American Association of Neurological Surgeons Staff. Neurosurgical Operative Atlas, Vol. 1-8. 1500p. 500.00 (0-683-07234-X) Am Assn Neuro.

American Association of Occupational Health Nurses. AAOHN - Core Curriculum for Occupational Health Nursing. Eoyang, Thomas, ed. LC 97-7112. 288p. 1997. pap. text 51.50 (0-7216-6904-2, W B Saunders Co) Harcrt Hlth Sci Grp.

American Association of Petroleum Geologists Staff. Depositional Environments in Carbonate Rocks: A Symposium. Friedman, Gerald M., ed. LC QE0471.15.C3. (Society of Economic Paleontologists & Mineralogists, Special Publication Ser.: Special Publication No. 4). 217p. reprint ed. pap. 67.30 (0-608-16620-0, 202665500050) Bks Demand.

— Possible Future Oil Provinces of the United States & Canada: Proceedings of the American Association of Petroleum Geologists, 26th, Houston, 1941. Levorsen, Arville I., ed. LC 41-23448. 160p. reprint ed. pap. 49.60 (0-608-13920-3, 202374400033) Bks Demand.

American Association of School Administrators Staf. Creating Quality Schools. 34p. 1992. pap. 2.50 (0-87652-176-6, 21-00191) Am Assn Sch Admin.

— Healthy Kids for the Year 2000: An Action Plan for Schools. 1993. 2.50 (0-87652-157-X, 021-00306) Am Assn Sch Admin.

— How Our Investment in Education Pays Off. 24p. 1994. pap. 2.50 (0-87652-191-X, 21-00431) Am Assn Sch Admin.

— Improving Student Achievement. LC 92-73478. (Orig.). 1993. pap. 12.95 (0-87652-175-8, 21-00308) Am Assn Sch Admin.

— Keeping Spirits High: Renewing Our Commitment to Education. 32p. 1993. pap. 2.50 (0-87652-198-7) Am Assn Sch Admin.

— Local School Councils . . . Where We Stand. 12p. 1994. pap. 2.50 (0-87652-209-6, 21-00441) Am Assn Sch Admin.

— Making Sense of Testing & Assessment. 28p. 1993. pap. 2.50 (0-87652-190-1) Am Assn Sch Admin.

— The Nongraded Primary: Making Schools Fit Children. 28p. 1992. pap. 2.50 (0-87652-184-7, 21-00192) Am Assn Sch Admin.

— Quality Goes to School: Readings in Total Quality Management in Education. 1993. pap. 24.95 (0-87652-204-5, 21-00425) Am Assn Sch Admin.

— Roles & Relationships: School Boards & Superintendents. 1994. 3.50 (0-87652-208-8, 021-00439) Am Assn Sch Admin.

— Speaking & Writing Skills for Educators. LC 92-74902. (Orig.). 1993. pap. 2.50 (0-87652-182-0, 21-00240) Am Assn Sch Admin.

American Association of School Administrators Staf & Glass, Tom. The Study of the American School Superintendency, 1992: America's Education Leaders in a Time of Reform. 103p. 1992. pap. 25.00 (0-87652-177-4, 21-00189) Am Assn Sch Admin.

American Association of School Librarians Staff. Information Power: Guidelines for School Library Media Programs. LC 88-3480. 144p. 1988. pap. text 15.00 (0-8389-3352-1) ALA.

— Media Programs: District & School. LC 74-32316. 136p. reprint ed. pap. 42.20 (0-7837-5918-5, 204571700007) Bks Demand.

— Realization: The Final Report of the Knapp School Libraries Project. Sullivan, Peggy, ed. LC 68-29658. 410p. reprint ed. pap. 127.10 (0-608-13217-9, 202421600035) Bks Demand.

American Association of School Librarians Staff & Association for Educational Communications Governm. Information Literacy Standards for Student Learning: Linking the Library Media Program to the Content Areas. LC 98-23314. 64p. 1998. pap. 20.00 (0-8389-3471-4) ALA.

— Information Power: Building Partnerships for Learning. LC 98-23291. 206p. 1998. pap. 35.00 (0-8389-3470-6) ALA.

American Association of State Colleges & Universit. Minorities in Public Higher Education: At a Turning Point. LC 87-17554. 72p. (Orig.). (C). 1988. pap. text 13.00 (0-88044-083-X); lib. bdg. 25.50 (0-88044-093-7) AASCU Press.

— Policies & Practice: A Focus on Higher Education Retention. LC 97-35812. 1997. write for info. (0-88044-136-4) AASCU Press.

American Association of Teachers of French. Bilingual Education & FES: Keeping the Child in Focus. LC LC3725.A5. 77p. (Orig.). pap. 30.00 (0-608-05581-6, 206604100006) Bks Demand.

— Fles: U. S. A. Success Stories. LC LB1578.A47. 95p. 1972. pap. 30.00 (0-608-05584-0, 206604400006) Bks Demand.

— FLES & Bilingual Education: Getting the Word Out. LC PC2068.U7A5. 83p. (Orig.). 1974. pap. 30.00 (0-608-05582-4, 206604200006) Bks Demand.

— Foreign Language Teaching Techniques in FLES & Bilingual Settings: A Report by the FLES Committee of the American Association of Teachers of French. LC PB0035.A6. 196p. 1973. pap. 60.80 (0-608-05583-2, 206604300006) Bks Demand.

American Association of Teachers of French, et al. Acquiring Cross-Cultural Competence: Four Stages for Students of French. Singerman, Alan J., ed. LC 96-175571. 144p. (C). 1996. pap. 27.50 (0-8442-1784-0, VF1784-0) NTC Contemp Pub Co.

American Association of Teachers of French Staff, jt. auth. see Lipton, Gladys C.

American Association of Textile Chemists & Coloris. Color Measurement Principles & the Textile Industry, 1995. (Symposium Papers). 1995. 60.00 (0-685-57399-0) AATCC.

— Technical Manual, 1998. LC 54-34349. 429p. 1996. write for info. (0-685-57400-8) AATCC.

American Association of University Instructors in. Proceedings of the American Association of University Instructors in Accounting, 3 vols. Brief, Richard P., ed. LC 80-1468. (Dimensions of Accounting Theory & Practice Ser.). 1980. lib. bdg. 125.95 (0-405-13498-3) Ayer.

American Association of University Women Staff. Gaining a Foothold: Women's Transitions Through Work & College. LC 99-15622. 1999. write for info. (1-879922-22-3) Am Assoc U Women.

— Gender Gaps: Where Schools Still Fail Our Children. 144p. 1999. pap. text 13.95 (1-56924-665-3) Marlowe & Co.

American Association of University Women Staff, et al. Girls in the Middle: Working to Succeed in School. LC 96-24677. 1996. 14.95 (1-879922-15-0) Am Assoc U Women.

American Association of University Women Staff, jt. auth. see Haag, Pamela.

American Association of Zoological Parks & Aquariu, et al. Manual of Federal Wildlife Regulations, 2 vols. 1985. 200.00 (0-317-01290-8) Am Assoc Z Pk.

American Association on Artificial Intelligence St, jt. ed. see Shrobe, Howard.

American Association on Mental Retardation Staff. Shaping Our Destiny: A Consumer's Guide to Quality Community Services for People with Developmental Disabilities & Their Families. LC 98-9713. 1998. pap. write for info. (0-940898-54-3) Am Assn Mental.

American Association On Mental Retardation Staff, ed. Shaping Our Destiny: A Provider's Guide to Quality Community Services for People with Developmental Disabilities & Their Families. LC 98-9765. 1998. pap. write for info. (0-940898-53-5) Am Assn Mental.

American Association on Mental Retardation Staff, jt. auth. see Demchak, Maryann.

American Association Physics Teachers Staff, jt. auth. see American Institute Physics Staff.

American AstroAnalysts Institute. Astroanalysis. Incl. Sagittarius. 1983. 8.95 (0-448-12564-1); 360p. 1977. Set pap. 8.95 (0-685-01830-X, G & D) Peng Put Young Read.

***American Astroanalysts Institute Staff.** Aquarius: Your Personal Horoscope. rev. ed. (Astroanalysis Ser.). 2000. pap. 12.95 (0-425-17568-5) Berkley Pub.

— Aries: Your Personal Horoscope. rev. ed. (Astroanalysis Ser.). 2000. pap. 12.95 (0-425-17558-8) Berkley Pub.

American Astroanalysts Institute Staff. Astroanalysis: Taurus. 256p. 1988. pap. 12.95 (0-425-11207-1) Berkley Pub.

***American Astroanalysts Institute Staff.** Cancer: Your Personal Horoscope. rev. ed. (Astroanalysis Ser.). 2000. pap. 12.95 (0-425-17561-8) Berkley Pub.

— Capricorn: Your Personal Horoscope. rev. ed. (Astroanalysis Ser.). 2000. pap. 12.95 (0-425-17567-7) Berkley Pub.

— Gemini: Your Personal Horoscope. rev. ed. (Astroanalysis Ser.). 2000. pap. 12.95 (0-425-17560-X) Berkley Pub.

— Leo: Your Personal Horoscope. rev. ed. (Astroanalysis Ser.). 2000. pap. 12.95 (0-425-17562-6) Berkley Pub.

— Libra: Your Personal Horoscope. rev. ed. (Astroanalysis Ser.). 2000. pap. 12.95 (0-425-17564-2) Berkley Pub.

— Pisces: Your Personal Horoscope. rev. ed. (Astroanalysis Ser.). 2000. pap. 12.95 (0-425-17569-3) Berkley Pub.

— Sagittarius: Your Personal Horoscope. rev. ed. (Astroanalysis Ser.). 2000. pap. 12.95 (0-425-17566-9) Berkley Pub.

— Scorpio: Your Personal Horoscope. rev. ed. (Astroanalysis Ser.). 2000. pap. 12.95 (0-425-17565-0) Berkley Pub.

— Taurus: Your Personal Horoscope. rev. ed. (Astroanalysis Ser.). 2000. pap. 12.95 (0-425-17559-6) Berkley Pub.

— Virgo: Your Personal Horoscope. rev. ed. (Astroanalysis Ser.). 2000. pap. 12.95 (0-425-17563-4) Berkley Pub.

American Astroanalysts Institute Staff & Vedral, Joyce L. Astroanalysis: Capricorn. 256p. 1988. pap. 12.95 (0-425-11215-2) Berkley Pub.

American Astronautical Society Staff. Post Apollo Space Exploration, 2 Vols, Pt. II. (Advances in the Astronautical Sciences Ser.: Vol. 20). 1966. 35.00 (0-87703-023-5) Univelt Inc.

American Audio Prose Library Staff. So Long, See You Tomorrow. Date not set. 27.00 (1-55644-422-2) Am Audio Prose.

***American Autobobile Association Staff.** Responsible Driving. 1999. pap. 63.00 (0-02-653382-0) Glencoe.

— Responsible Driving, 1997. 1997. teacher ed. 47.51 (0-02-653351-0); teacher ed., student ed. 12.33 (0-02-653364-2) Glencoe.

American Automobile Assiciation. AAA Britain Bed & Breakfast. 700p. 1999. pap. 16.95 (1-56251-276-5) AAA.

American Automobile Association Staff. AAA Caribbean Travel Book. 302p. 1999. pap. 15.00 (1-56251-283-8) AAA.

— AAA Europe Road Atlas. 128p. 1999. 19.95 (1-56251-278-1, Pub. by AAA) S&S Trade.

***American Automobile Association Staff.** AAA France Bed & Breakfast. 300p. 1999. pap. 16.95 (1-56251-277-3) AAA.

American Automobile Association Staff. AAA France Road Atlas. 144p. 1999. pap. 19.95 (1-56251-275-7, Pub. by AAA) S&S Trade.

***American Automobile Association Staff.** AAA New Car & Truck Buyer's Guide. (Illus.). 2000. pap. 14.95 (1-56251-318-4) AAA.

American Automobile Association Staff. AAA Road Atlas, 1988. 1987. pap. 5.95 (0-317-66546-4) Random.

— AAA Travel Guide to Europe. 568p. 1987. pap. 8.95 (0-317-63131-4) Random.

— Guide to the Best Wineries in North America. 1993. pap. write for info. (1-56251-096-7) AAA.

— A Photo Journey to Central Florida. (Illus.). 472p. 1992. per. 12.95 (1-56251-013-4) S&S Trade.

— A Photo Journey to New York City. (Illus.). 472p. 1992. per. 12.95 (1-56251-012-6) S&S Trade.

— A Photo Journey to San Francisco. (Illus.). 472p. 1992. per. 12.95 (1-56251-014-2) S&S Trade.

— A Photo Journey to Washington, D.C. (Illus.). 472p. 1992. per. 12.95 (1-56251-011-8) S&S Trade.

— Sportsmanlike Driving. 7th ed. (J). 1975. text 25.24 (0-07-001292-X) McGraw.

— Sportsmanlike Driving. 8th rev. ed. Cranford, Carolyn E., ed. (Illus.). (gr. 10-12). 1980. text 22.56 (0-07-001330-6); pap. text 14.80 (0-07-001331-4) McGraw.

— Sportsmanlike Driving. 9th ed. 352p. (J). (gr. 9-12). 1987. text 22.16 (0-07-001338-1) McGraw.

— Sportsmanlike Driving. 9th ed. 352p. (YA). (gr. 9-12). 1987. pap. text, wbk. ed. 21.09 (0-07-001339-X) McGraw.

American Automobile Manufacturers Association, Inc & Bruce, Robert. Automobiles of America. 5th rev. ed. (Illus.). 170p. 1996. pap. 19.95 (1-880524-21-X) Cars & Parts.

American Automoblie Association Staff. AAA Guide to North American Bed & Breakfasts, Country Inns & Historical Lodgings. (Illus.). 750p. 1999. pap. text 21.95 (1-56251-290-0) AAA.

American Ballet Theater Staff. The American Ballet Theatre: A Twenty-Five-Year Retrospective. LC 99-21800. 176p. 1999. pap. 24.95 (0-7407-0018-9) Andrews & McMeel.

***American Ballet Theater Staff.** The American Ballet Theatre: A Twenty-Five-Year Retrospective. LC 99-21800. 176p. 1999. 39.95 (0-7407-0019-7) Andrews & McMeel.

American Banker Bond Buyer Staff. American Bankers Association Key to Routing Numbers: Currently Assigned Routing Numbers of All Eligible Financial Institutions. 1990. 69.00 (1-56310-003-7) Amer Bank Bond Buyer.

— The Rand McNally Bankers Directory, 3 vols. 2nd ed. 1990. 245.00 (1-56310-002-9) Amer Bank Bond Buyer.

— The Rand McNally Bankers Directory, 3 vols., 3. 1990. write for info. (1-56310-001-0) Amer Bank Bond Buyer.

— The Rand McNally Bankers Directory, 3 vols., Vols. 1 & 2. 1990. write for info. (1-56310-000-2) Amer Bank Bond Buyer.

— The Rand McNally Credit Union Directory. 1990. 115.00 (1-56310-004-5) Amer Bank Bond Buyer.

American Bankers Association Staff. Banking Terminology. 3rd rev. ed. Nielsen, James F., ed. 409p. 1989. pap. text 40.00 (0-89982-360-2) Am Bankers.

— The Evolution of Bank Call Centers: A Focus on Profitability. 66p. (Orig.). 1996. pap. text 170.00 (0-89982-005-0) Am Bankers.

— The Retention of Bank Records. rev. ed. 223p. 1990. 95.00 (0-685-57996-4) Am Bankers.

— Securities Processing. 2nd rev. ed. Buzzell, Allyn C., ed. (Illus.). 651p. (C). 1989. text 70.00 (0-89982-359-9) Am Bankers.

American Bankers Association Staff & O'Connor, William J. EFT: Regulation E Comprehensive Compliance Manual. LC 82-227487. (Illus.). 200p. 1989. 253.00 incl. disk (0-685-57854-2) Am Bankers.

American Bankers Association Staff, et al. Internet Sources for Bankers: A Selective Guide to Web Sites, 1997. 76p. 1977. pap. text 17.50 (0-89982-052-2) Am Bankers.

American Bankers Association Staff, jt. auth. see Hooks, Jon A.

American Bantam Car Company Staff. Bantam Model BRC Jeep, 1941 Prototype: TM-10-1205. Post, Dan R., ed. LC 75-185932. (Illus.). 128p. 1971. pap. 12.95 (0-911160-44-2) Post Group.

American Bar Asociation Staff, jt. auth. see Haig, Robert L.

American Bar Assn. Staff, jt. auth. see Tigar, Michael E.

American Bar Association. A Comprehensive Analysis of Current Consumption Tax Proposals: A Report of the ABA Section of Taxation, Tax Systems Task Force. LC 98-116973. vii, 292 p. 1997. write for info. (1-57073-527-1) Amer Bar Assn.

— Guide to Fixed-Price Supply Subcontract Terms & Conditions: A Project of the Federal Subcontracting Committee, Section of Public Contract Law, American Bar Association. 2nd ed. LC 98-164960. 197 p. 1998. write for info. (1-57073-575-1) Amer Bar Assn.

— Teaching & Learning Professionalism: Symposium Proceedings, October 2-4, 1996, Oak Brook, Illinois. LC 97-207829. v, 149 p. 1997. write for info. (1-57073-500-X) Amer Bar Assn.

American Bar Association, jt. auth. see Branham, Lynn S.

American Bar Association, Chicago, State and Local Government Law Section, jt. auth. see Ross, Mary Massaron.

American Bar Association, Commission on Election L. Election Communications & The Campaign of 1992. 190p. 1984. pap. 10.00 (0-89707-143-3, 357-0008) Amer Bar Assn.

— Provisions of State Codes of Professional Responsibility Governing Lawyer Advertising & Solicitation. 417p. 1990. pap. 75.00 (0-89707-595-1, 406-0011) Amer Bar Assn.

An Asterisk (*) at the beginning of an entry indicates that the title is appearing for the first time.

American Bar Association, Criminal Justice Staff. An Emerging Judicial Role in Family Court. 40p. 1986. pap. 7.50 (*0-318-36241-4*, 509-0236) Amer Bar Assn.
— Sample Pleadings for Use in Juvenile Deliquency Proceedings. 55p. 1986. pap. 7.50 (*0-318-36209-0*, 509-0027) Amer Bar Assn.
American Bar Association, Division of Communicatio. How to Choose & Use a Lawyer. 1981. pap. 0.50 (*0-318-36230-9*, 317-0029) Amer Bar Assn.
American Bar Association, Family Law Staff. Divorce & Family Mediation. LC 86-80203. 46p. 1986. pap. 22.95 (*0-318-36124-8*, 513-0022) Amer Bar Assn.
American Bar Association, General Practice Staff. Design & Construction Contracts: Representing the Owner. LC 87-70921. 219p. 1987. pap. 39.95 (*0-89707-289-8*, 515-0067) Amer Bar Assn.
— Military Motions. LC 86-72226. 27p. 1986. pap. 14.95 (*0-89707-269-3*, 515-0063) Amer Bar Assn.
American Bar Association, Lawyers Conference Task. Caseflow Management in the Trial Court: Now & for the Future. LC 87-73074. 95p. 1987. pap. 2.50 (*0-89707-328-2*, 410-0009) Amer Bar Assn.
— Defeating Delay: Developing & Implementing a Court Delay Reduction Program: Based Upon the American Bar Association's Court Delay Reduction Standards. LC 86-70015. xiv, 200p. 1986. pap. 17.50 (*0-89707-218-9*, 410-0006) Amer Bar Assn.
American Bar Association, Litigation Staff. The Promised Land: And Other Courthouse Adventures. LC 87-70688. 176p. 1987. pap. 14.50 (*0-89707-300-2*, 531-0054) Amer Bar Assn.
American Bar Association, Natural Resources Law St. Drafting Standard Form Farmout Agreements. LC 86-72566. 62p. 1986. pap. 29.95 (*0-89707-273-1*, 535-0007) Amer Bar Assn.
— Joint Operating Agreement. LC 86-72949. 220p. 1986. pap. 29.95 (*0-89707-279-0*, 535-0008) Amer Bar Assn.
— Offshore Bidding Agreements: Tailoring the Right One for Your Company. LC 86-72950. 44p. 1986. pap. 39.95 (*0-89707-280-4*, 535-0010) Amer Bar Assn.
— Railroad Land Grants. LC 87-70130. 121p. 1987. pap. 29.95 (*0-89707-284-7*, 535-0011) Amer Bar Assn.
American Bar Association, Professional Education P & Geltzer, Robert L. Guidelines for a Corporate Law Department Manual. LC 88-70202. 54p. (Orig.). 1988. pap. 35.00 (*0-89707-023-2*, 549-0077) Amer Bar Assn.
American Bar Association, Public Contract Law Sect. Architect Engineer Liability: A Growth Period. 45p. 1985. pap. 20.00 (*0-89707-170-0*, 539-0043) Amer Bar Assn.
American Bar Association, Public Education Staff. The American Lawyer: When & How to Use One. 36p. 1993. pap. 2.50 (*0-89707-848-9*, 235-0021) Amer Bar Assn.
— Law in the Workplace. 80p. 1987. pap. 2.50 (*0-318-36200-7*, 235-0015) Amer Bar Assn.
American Bar Association, Science & Technology Sta. Software Contract Forms: 1987 Collection. LC 87-70985. 1081p. 1987. pap. 37.50 (*0-89707-303-7*, 545-0006) Amer Bar Assn.
American Bar Association, Section of Antitrust Law & Loftis, James R. Antitrust Law Developments. 3rd ed. LC 92-71591. 1700p. 1992. 215.00 (*0-89707-638-9*, 503-0210) Amer Bar Assn.
American Bar Association. Section of Antitrust Law & Pasahow, Lynn H. Vertical Restrictions upon Buyers Limiting Purchases of Goods from Others. LC 82-72695. xii, 99p. 1982. pap. 20.00 (*0-89707-081-X*, 503-0043) Amer Bar Assn.
American Bar Association, Section of Taxation Staf. ABA Sales & Use Tax Desk Book, 1993-94 Edition. Young, D. Michael & Piper, John T., eds. 1994. 240.00 (*1-57073-096-2*) ABA Prof Educ Pubns.
American Bar Association, Special Committee on Dis & Shapo, Marshall S. Towards a Jurisprudence of Injury: The Continuing Creation of a System of Substantive Justice in American Tort Law: Report to the American Bar Association. LC 85-112535. 996p. 1984. 55.00 (*0-685-10475-3*, 486-0001) Amer Bar Assn.
American Bar Association Staff. The ABA Guide to Consumer Law. LC 96-21617. 1997. pap. 13.00 (*0-8129-2347-2*, Times Bks) Crown Pub Group.
American Bar Association Staff. The ABA Guide to Family Law. 192p. 1996. pap. 13.00 (*0-8129-2791-5*) Random.
— ABA Guide to Wills & Estates. 1995. pap. 12.00 (*0-8129-2349-9*, Times Bks) Crown Pub Group.
*__American Bar Association Staff.__ ABA Law Series, Vol. 3. 2000. pap. write for info. (*0-679-74208-5*, Times Bks) Crown Pub Group.
American Bar Association Staff. ABA Standards for Criminal Justice, 4 vols., 1. 2nd ed. LC 79-91936. 1980. 80.00 (*0-316-03710-9*, Aspen Law & Bus) Aspen Pub.
— ABA Standards for Criminal Justice, 4 vols., 2. 2nd ed. LC 79-91936. 1980. 80.00 (*0-316-03711-7*) Aspen Pub.
— ABA Standards for Criminal Justice, 4 vols., 3. 2nd ed. LC 79-91936. 1980. 80.00 (*0-316-03712-5*) Aspen Pub.
— ABA Standards for Criminal Justice, 4 vols., 4. 2nd ed. LC 79-91936. 1980. 80.00 (*0-316-03713-3*) Aspen Pub.
— ABA Standards for Criminal Justice, 4 vols., Set. 2nd ed. LC 79-91936. 1980. ring bd. 325.00 (*0-316-03709-5*, Aspen Law & Bus) Aspen Pub.
— ABA Standards for Criminal Justice, Chapter 7, Mental Health. LC 86-2067. 528p. 1986. 50.00 (*0-316-03725-7*) Aspen Pub.
— Administrative Law Review, 1949-1996, 49 vols. 1949. 2147.50 (*0-8377-9000-X*, Rothman) W S Hein.
— American Bar Association Approved Law Schools. LC 97-70077. 464p. 1997. pap. 19.95 (*0-02-861757-6*) Macmillan.
— The American Bar Association Legal Guide for Americans Over Fifty: Everything You & Your Children Need to Know about Retirement, Health & Long-Term Care, Workplace Discrimination, & Social Security. LC 97-22270. 272p. 1998. pap. 13.00 (*0-8129-2937-3*, Times Bks) Crown Pub Group.
— American Bar Association Legal Guide for Small Business: Everything a Small-Business Person Must Know, from Start-Up to Employment Laws to Financing & Selling a Business. LC 99-86498. 288p. 2000. pap. 15.00 (*0-8129-3015-0*, Times Bks) Crown Pub Group.
— Annotations to Surplus Lines Statutes. 3rd ed. LC 98-54741. 1999. write for info. (*1-57073-649-9*) Amer Bar Assn.
*__American Bar Association Staff.__ Business Law for Fun ... Just for Fun. LC 99-38794. 1999. pap. write for info. (*1-57073-695-2*) Amer Bar Assn.
— The Collected TriBar Legal Opinion Reports, 1979-1998. LC 99-20276. 1999. write for info. (*1-57073-625-1*) Amer Bar Assn.
American Bar Association Staff. A Commerical Lawyer's Take on the Electronic Purse: An Analysis of Commercial Law Issues Associated with Stored-Value Cards. LC 98-34519. 1998. pap. write for info. (*1-57073-488-7*) Amer Bar Assn.
— Cost Accounting for Law Firms. LC 83-73344. 59p. 1984. pap. 29.95 (*0-89707-127-1*, 511-0088) Amer Bar Assn.
— The Directory of Minority Judges of the United States. 2nd ed. LC 97-207426. xv, 283p. 1997. write for info. (*1-57073-472-0*) Amer Bar Assn.
— Documenting the Attorney-Client Relationship: Law Firm Policies on Engagement, Termination & Declination. LC 98-52163. 1999. pap. 44.95 (*1-57073-529-8*) Amer Bar Assn.
— Flying Solo: A Survival Guide for the Solo Lawyer. 2nd ed. LC 84-70863. 362p. 1994. pap. 69.95 (*0-89707-922-1*, 511-0328) Amer Bar Assn.
*__American Bar Association Staff.__ Handbook for the Conduct of Shareholders' Meetings. LC 00-25234. 2000. pap. write for info. (*1-57073-778-9*) Amer Bar Assn.
American Bar Association Staff. Interlocking Directorates under Section Eight of the Clayton Act. LC 84-72063. 67p. 1984. pap. 20.00 (*0-89707-151-4*, 503-0057) Amer Bar Assn.
— Justice for a Generation. LC 85-70533. 502p. 1985. pap. 10.00 (*0-89707-171-9*, 168-0002) Amer Bar Assn.
— Legal Status of Prisoners. 106p. 1983. 30.00 (*0-316-03720-6*); pap. 10.00 (*0-316-03722-2*) Aspen Pub.
— Manual of Class Action Notice Forms. LC 79-50160. 320p. 1979. pap. 10.00 (*0-685-07097-2*, 5030023) Amer Bar Assn.
— Model Business Corporation Act: Official Text with Official Comments & Statutory Cross-References. 3rd ed. LC 98-13878. 1998. 395.00 (*1-57073-424-0*) Amer Bar Assn.
— Model Business Corporation Act Annotated, 1984: Professional Corporation Supplement: Close Corporation Supplement. 3rd ed. LC 98-14871. 1998. 150.00 (*1-57073-555-7*); 150.00 (*1-57073-556-5*); 150.00 (*1-57073-558-1*); 150.00 (*1-57073-559-X*) Amer Bar Assn.
— Model Business Corporation Act Annotated, 1984: Professional Corporation Supplement: Close Corporation Supplement. 3rd ed. LC 98-14871. 1998. 150.00 (*1-57073-557-3*) Amer Bar Assn.
— Model Code of Professional Responsibility & Code of Judicial Conduct: As Amended August, 1980. LC 83-202790. v, 71p. 1982. pap. 12.95 (*0-685-08534-1*, 561-0010) Amer Bar Assn.
— Model Jury Instructions for Business Tort Litigation: A Project of the Business Torts Litigation Committee, Subcommittee on Jury Instructions, Section of Litigation. 3rd ed. LC 96-19560. 1996. pap. write for info. (*1-57073-336-8*) Amer Bar Assn.
— Model Positive Pay Services Agreement & Commentary. LC 99-34479. 1999. write for info. (*1-57073-691-X*) Amer Bar Assn.
— "No Comment" Can Be a Comment, or, How to Handle Reporters (gently!) A Lawyer's Guide to the Press. LC 95-126982. (Young Lawyers Desktop Reference Guide Ser.). v, 13 p. 1994. write for info. (*1-57073-085-7*) Amer Bar Assn.
— Official American Bar Association Guide to Approved Law Schools: 1999 Edition. 480p. 1998. pap. 21.95 (*0-02-862192-1*, Pub. by Macmillan) S&S Trade.
*__American Bar Association Staff.__ Official American Bar Association Guide to Approved Law Schools: 2000 Edition. Kurt Snyder, ed. (ABA Approved Law Schools Ser.). (Illus.). 480p. 1999. pap. 21.95 (*0-02-862824-1*, Arc) IDG Bks.
— Official American Bar Association Guide to Approved Law Schools 2001. 400p. 2000. pap. 21.95 (*0-7645-6231-2*) IDG Bks.
American Bar Association Staff. Reference Handbook on the Comprehensive General Liability Policy: Coverage Provisions, Exclusions, & Other Litigation Issues. LC 95-77230. 297p. 1995. pap. 79.95 (*1-57073-209-4*, 519-0249) Amer Bar Assn.
— Section of Corporation, Banking & Business Law: Proceedings, 1939-1950. 1939. mic. film 2240.00 (*0-318-57396-2*) W S Hein.
— Section of Corporation, Banking & Business Law: Proceedings, 1939-1950, Set. 1939. 110.00 (*0-686-89499-5*) W S Hein.
— Section of Criminal Law: Proceedings, 1955-1963, Set. 1955. 95.00 (*0-686-89500-2*) W S Hein.
— Section of Criminal Law: Program & Committee Reports, 1932-1955, Set. 1955. 42.50 (*0-8377-9015-8*, Rothman) W S Hein.
— Section of International & Comparative Law: Proceedings, 1942-1965, 23 vols. 1942. mic. film 42.50 (*0-318-57398-9*) W S Hein.
— Section of International & Comparative Law: Proceedings, 1942-1965, 23 vols., Set. 1942. 350.00 (*0-8377-9006-9*, Rothman) W S Hein.
— Section of Municipal Law: Proceedings, 1935, Set. 1935. 25.00 (*0-8377-9201-0*, Rothman) W S Hein.
— Section of Patent, Trademark & Copyright Law: Committee Reports, 1961-1990, Set. 1930. 700.00 (*0-8377-9008-5*) W S Hein.
— Section of Patent, Trademark & Copyright Law: Proceedings, 1935-1990, 48 vols., Set. 1935. 665.00 (*0-8377-9007-7*, Rothman) W S Hein.
— Section of Public Utility Law: Program & Committee Reports, 1933, Set. 1977. 25.00 (*0-685-42623-8*) W S Hein.
— Section of Real Property Probate & Trust Law: Proceedings, 1938-1965, 28 vols., Set. 1938. 525.00 (*0-686-89519-3*) W S Hein.
— Section of Taxation: Proceedings, 1940-1946, 7 vols., Set. 1940. ring bd. 25.00 (*0-8377-9215-0*, Rothman) W S Hein.
— Serving Two Masters: The Law of Lawyer Disqualification. 54p. 1984. 7.95 (*0-89707-149-2*, 515-0022) Amer Bar Assn.
— Term Loan Handbook. 3rd ed. 268p. 1983. write for info. (*0-318-65471-7*, H4285X) P-H.
— The TIPS Index of Papers: An Index of Papers Prepared for the ABA Tort & Insurance Practice Section & Presented at Its Meetings & Through Its Publications. LC 85-243283. (Book about ... Ser.). 176p. 1985. pap. 5.00 (*0-89707-178-6*, 519-0041) Amer Bar Assn
— The Use of Economists in Antitrust Litigation. LC 84-71278. 81p. 1984. pap. 35.00 (*0-89707-145-X*, 503-0054) Amer Bar Assn.
— You & the Law. (Illus.). 608p. 1993. 19.98 (*0-88176-663-1*, 4004700) Pubns Intl Ltd.
— You & the Law. 2nd rev. ed. (Illus.). 608p. 1994. 25.00 (*0-8129-2361-8*) Random.
American Bar Association Staff, contrib. by. Guidelines for the Approval of Legal Assistant Education Programs (Effective September 1, 1997) ABA Guidelines for Legal Assistant Programs. LC 97-204864. 40p. 1997. pap. 5.00 (*1-57073-463-1*, 423-0037) Amer Bar Assn.
— The Railway Labor Act: 1999 Cumulative Supplement. 261p. 1999. pap., suppl. ed. 145.00 (*1-57018-13[illegible]-4*, 1131) BNA Books.
American Bar Association Staff & Center for Professional Responsibility Staff. Model Rules of Professional Conduct. LC 93-73874. viii, 165p. 1994. write for info. (*0-89707-933-7*) Amer Bar Assn.
— Model Rules of Professional Conduct. LC 97-80168. viii, 153 p. 1997. write for info. (*1-57073-511-5*) Amer Bar Assn.
American Bar Association Staff & Conference on the Federal Election Commission. The Federal Election Commission: Conference Highlights, Washington, D.C., March 1982. LC 82-72032. 8p. 1982. pap. 2.00 (*0-685-06815-3*, 357-0007) Amer Bar Assn.
American Bar Association Staff & Cox, Henry B. War, Foreign Affairs & Constitutional Power, 1829-1901. LC 76-15392. 440p. 1984. pap. 35.00 (*0-88410-956-[illegible]*, HarpBusn) HarpInfo.
American Bar Association Staff & Soper, Steven P. Restoring Bipartisanship in Foreign Affairs. 74p. 1985. pap. 5.00 (*0-89707-208-1*, 355-0011) Amer Bar Assn.
American Bar Association Staff & Weil, Manges. Reorganizing Failing Businesses: A Comprehensive Review & Analysis of Financial Restructuring & Business Reorganization. LC 98-47352. 1998. pap. write for info. (*1-57073-634-0*, ABA Corp Banking) Amer Bar Assn.
American Bar Association Staff, et al. Criminal Justice Standards Bench Book for Special Court Judges. LC 82-72587. v, 66p. 1982. pap. 5.00 (*0-89707-085-2*, 482-0002) Amer Bar Assn.
American Bar Association Staff, jt. auth. see ABA Center for Pro Bono Staff.
American Bar Association Staff, jt. auth. see Baldwin, Ben G.
American Bar Association Staff, jt. auth. see Becker, Mary.
American Bar Association Staff, jt. auth. see Bordon, David E.
American Bar Association Staff, jt. auth. see Brill, Ralph L.
American Bar Association Staff, jt. auth. see Cain, George H.
American Bar Association Staff, jt. auth. see Choper, Jesse H.
American Bar Association Staff, jt. auth. see Clore, Duncan L.
American Bar Association Staff, jt. auth. see Collins, Thomas J.
American Bar Association Staff, jt. auth. see Denger, Michael L.
American Bar Association Staff, jt. auth. see Featherstone, Thomas M.
American Bar Association Staff, jt. auth. see Gallagher, Edward G.
American Bar Association Staff, jt. auth. see Gerrard, Michael.
American Bar Association Staff, jt. auth. see Goode, M. Jane.
American Bar Association Staff, jt. auth. see Gosdin, James L.
American Bar Association Staff, jt. auth. see Gumpert, David E.
American Bar Association Staff, jt. auth. see Judge Advocate General's Staff.
American Bar Association Staff, jt. auth. see Kain, Cole S.
American Bar Association Staff, jt. auth. see Leitner, David L.
American Bar Association Staff, jt. auth. see Lockwood, Carol E.
American Bar Association Staff, jt. auth. see Lovell, Russell A., Jr.
American Bar Association Staff, jt. auth. see Luneburg, William V.
American Bar Association Staff, jt. auth. see Rice, Larry.
American Bar Association Staff, jt. auth. see Simpson, Reagan W.
American Bar Association Staff, jt. auth. see TIPS Property Insurance Law Committee.
American Bar Association Staff, jt. auth. see Walkowiak, Vincent S.
American Bar Association Staff, ed. see Grossman, Barry L. & Hoffman, Gary M.
American Bar Association Staff, ed. see Notestine, Kerry E.
American Bar Association Staff, Banking & Business Law , jt. auth. see Haynesworth, Harry J.
American Bar Association, Standing Commission on L. Congress, the President, & Foreign Policy. 1984. pap. 7.50 (*0-89707-163-8*) Amer Bar Assn.
— The Media & Government Leaks. 32p. 1984. pap. 3.00 (*0-89707-157-3*, 355-0007) Amer Bar Assn.
American Bar Association, Standing Commission on L & American Bar Association, Standing Committee on En. National Security & the First Amendment. LC 84-7106. 34p. 1984. pap. 3.00 (*0-89707-142-5*, 355-0002) Amer Bar Assn.
American Bar Association Standing Commission on La. Law & National Security: Access to Strategic Resources. 162p. 1986. pap. 7.00 (*0-318-36441-7*, 355-0014) Amer Bar Assn.
— Legal Assistants Update, Vol. 5. LC 80-647738. 180p. 1986. pap. 6.00 (*0-89707-260-X*, 423-0021) Amer Bar Assn.
American Bar Association, Standing Committee on En. Common Boundary-Common Problems: The Environmental Consequences of Energy Production. LC 82-70885. 116p. 1982. pap. 10.00 (*0-318-36242-2*, 359-0008) Amer Bar Assn.
— Gideon Undone: The Crisis in Indigent Defense Funding. 18p. 1983. pap. 3.00 (*0-89707-116-6*, 419-0002) Amer Bar Assn.
— Law & Security in Outer Space. 182p. 1983. pap. 3.00 (*0-685-10018-9*, 355-0003) Amer Bar Assn.
— The Private Assumption of Previously Public Responsibilities: The Expanding Role of Private Institutions in Public Environmental Decision-Making. LC 86-72459. 37p. 1986. pap. 15.00 (*0-89707-270-7*, 359-0015) Amer Bar Assn.
American Bar Association, Standing Committee on En, jt. auth. see American Bar Association, Standing Commission on L.
American Bar Association. Standing Committee on La, jt. auth. see American Bar Association. Working Group on Intelli.
American Bar Association, Tort & Insurance Practic. The Bond Default Manual. 2nd ed. LC 95-76558. 632p. 1995. pap. 84.95 (*1-57073-169-1*, 519-0163) Amer Bar Assn.
— CGL Reporter, Vol. 9. 298p. 1997. ring bd. 208.00 (*1-886813-30-2*) Intl Risk Mgt.
— CGL Reporter: Binder 8. 1996. 208.00 (*1-886813-24-8*) Intl Risk Mgt.
— Damages Recoverable in Maritime Matters. LC 83-73103. 153p. 1984. pap. 37.00 (*0-89707-126-3*, 519-0037) Amer Bar Assn.
— Pollution & Contamination: How Will Property Insurers Respond? LC 87-70246. 192p. 1987. pap. 29.95 (*0-89707-285-5*, 519-0067) Amer Bar Assn.
— Surety Law Topical Index. LC 87-62071. 608p. 1993. pap. 64.95 (*0-89707-320-7*, 519-0225) Amer Bar Assn.
American Bar Association, Tort & Insurance Practic, jt. auth. see Madole, Juanita M.
American Bar Association Urban, State & Local Government Law Sect. Annotations to the Model Procurement Code for State & Local Governments. LC 92-80969. 144p. 1996. pap. 84.95 (*0-89707-780-6*, 533-0061) Amer Bar Assn.
— The Impact of Zoning on Group Homes for the Mentally Disabled: A National Survey. LC 86-72525. 44p. 1986. pap. 12.95 (*0-89707-272-3*, 533-0026) Amer Bar Assn.
American Bar Association. Working Group on Intelli & American Bar Association. Standing Committee on La. Oversight & Accountability of the U. S. Intelligence Agencies: An Evaluation. LC 86-132506. iii, 119p. 1985. pap. 5.00 (*0-89707-213-8*, 355-0010) Amer Bar Assn.
American Bar Association, Young Lawyers Division S. Directory of In-House Training Providers. 30p. 1988. pap. 5.00 (*0-685-21542-3*, 549-0070) Amer Bar Assn.
American Bar Foundation Staff. Annotated Code of Professional Responsibility. LC 79-55893. xxii, 478p. 1979. 30.00 (*0-910058-95-4*, 304720); pap. 20.00 (*0-910058-96-2*, 304720) W S Hein.
— International Directory of Bar Associations. 4th ed. LC 80-71013. xi, 49p. 1983. pap. 20.00 (*0-910059-02-0*, 304840) W S Hein.
— Legal Expense Insurance: The European Experience in Financing Legal Services. LC 75-996. ix, 117p. 1975. pap. 25.00 (*0-910058-69-5*, 765-0016-01) W S Hein.
— The Legal Profession in the United States, 2 vols. in 1. (American Bar Foundation Publication Ser.). (RUS.). 1985. pap. 25.00 (*0-910058-21-0*, 304910) W S Hein.
— The Legal Profession in the United States. 3rd ed. LC 85-72996. (American Bar Foundation Publication Ser.). ix, 79p. 1985. pap. 22.00 (*0-910059-08-X*, 304910) W S Hein.

A

— Legal Service Plans: Approaches to Regulation. Pfennigstorf, Werner & Kimball, Spencer L., eds. LC 77-87182. xxiv, 662p. 1977. 35.00 (*0-910058-86-5*, 765-0018-01) W S Hein.
— List & Index to the Proceedings in Star Chamber for the Reign of James I (1603-1625) in the Public Record Office, London: Class STAC8, 3 vols., Set. Barnes, Thomas G., ed. LC 75-542. (American Bar Foundation Publication Ser.). 2312p. 1975. 135.00 (*0-910058-68-7*, 304950) W S Hein.
— Sample Incorporating Indenture. 18p. 1965. pap. 1.00 (*0-910058-27-X*) Am Bar Foun.

American Bar Foundation Staff & Curran, Barbara A. The Legal Needs of the Public: The Final Report of a National Survey. LC 77-85325. (American Bar Foundation Publication Ser.). xxxvi, 382p. 1977. 38.50 (*0-910058-82-2*, 304900) W S Hein.

American Bar Foundation Staff, et al. Overcoming Legal Uncertainties about Use of Solar Energy Systems. LC 77-95217. (American Bar Foundation Publications). viii, 80p. 1978. pap. 20.00 (*0-910058-89-X*, 305000) W S Hein.

American Bar Foundation Staff, jt. auth. see Nimmer, Raymond T.

American Bartenders' Association Staff. Cocktailing.... The American Bartenders' Association Complete Guide of Professional Cocktailing. Starcevic, James P., ed. 11p. (Orig.). 1986. pap. text 2.95 (*0-916689-85-9*) Am Bartenders.

American Bartenders' Association Staff & Starcevic, James P. The Great Drinks Book. 48p. (Orig.). 1986. pap. 5.95 (*0-916689-86-7*) Am Bartenders.
— The Mocktail Alcohol-Free Cocktails Guide. 28p. (Orig.). 1988. pap. text 5.95 (*0-916689-87-5*) Am Bartenders.

American Bed & Breakfast Association Staff. Inspected, Rated & Approved. (Illus.). 346p. 1994. pap. 16.95 (*0-934473-26-9*) Am Bed & Breakfast.
— Inspected, Rated & Approved: Bed & Breakfasts & Country Inns. 1993. pap. 14.95 (*0-934473-21-8*) Am Bed & Breakfast.
— Inspected, Rated & Approved: Bed & Breakfasts & Country Inns, 1994. 1993. pap. 14.95 (*0-934473-25-0*) Am Bed & Breakfast.
— A Treasury of Bed & Breakfast. 2nd ed. Sonke, Sarah W., ed. (Illus.). 201p. 1986. pap. 14.95 (*0-934473-01-3*) Am Bed & Breakfast.
— A Treasury of Bed & Breakfast. 2nd rev. ed. 201p. 1986. pap. 14.95 (*0-915765-23-3*) Am Bed & Breakfast.
— A Treasury of Bed & Breakfast. 3rd rev. ed. 189p. 1987. pap. 14.95 (*0-317-91103-1*) Am Bed & Breakfast.

American Belgian Tervuren Club Staff. The Complete Belgian Tervuren. (Illus.). 256p. 1990. 25.95 (*0-87605-051-8*) Howell Bks.

***American Bible Society Staff.** Be the Best You Can Be, 5 vols. 2000. pap. text 3.50 (*5-550-02412-8*) Nairi.
— Bible for Outreach. 1999. pap. text 3.05 (*5-550-00737-1*) Nairi.
— Children of Color Storybook Bible. (Illus.). (J). 2000. 9.95 (*5-550-02393-8*) Nairi.
— Extreme Faith Youth Bible. (YA). 2000. pap. text 3.25 (*1-58516-066-0*) Am Bible.
— Few Who Dared to Trust God. 2000. pap. text 11.75 (*5-550-02389-X*); pap. text 11.75 (*5-550-02390-3*) Nairi.
— For Families under Stress, 5 vols. 2000. pap. text 3.50 (*5-550-02414-4*) Nairi.
— The Gospel According to St. John. 2000. pap. text 2.95 (*1-58516-083-0*) Am Bible.
— The Gospel According to St. Luke. 2000. pap. text 2.95 (*1-58516-086-5*) Am Bible.
— The Gospel According to St. Matthew. 2000. pap. text 2.95 (*1-58516-084-9*) Am Bible.
— Holy Bible. 1674p. 2000. pap. text 9.95 (*1-58516-021-0*) Am Bible.
— Holy Bible. 1999. 7.25 (*5-550-00735-5*); pap. text 3.05 (*5-550-00736-3*) Nairi.
— Holy Bible. 1999. pap. 3.05 (*1-58516-080-6*) Am Bible.
— Illustrated New Testament. (Illus.). 2000. pap. text 6.15 (*1-58516-036-9*) Am Bible.
— Learning Bible. (Illus.). 2000. pap. text 34.95 (*1-58516-025-3*) Am Bible.
— Life & Teachings of Jesus of Nazareth: Includes the Four Gospels, Acts, Psalms & Proverbs. 672p. 2000. pap. text 2.95 (*1-58516-095-4*) Am Bible.
— Making of a Bible. 2000. pap. 4.95 (*5-550-01012-7*) Nairi.
— Ruth A Creative Bible Study Guide. 2000. pap. 3.95 (*1-58516-000-8*) Am Bible.
— Spanish Gospel of John - Pocketsize - Reina Valera Version. 1999. 2.99 (*1-58516-037-7*) Am Bible.
— Word for Life, 5 vols. 2000. pap. text 3.50 (*5-550-02415-2*) Nairi.
— Your Young Christian's First Bible. (Illus.). 1551p. (J). (gr. 2-9). 2000. pap. text 10.25 (*1-58516-076-8*) Am Bible.

American Bible Society Staff, tr. see Hoffman, Elizabeth, ed.

American Bible Society Staff, tr. see Lysik, David A., ed.

American Bioethics Advisory Commission. Ban Human Cloning: Report of the American Bioethics Advisory Commission. (Illus.). 77p. 1997. pap. 15.00 (*1-890712-26-4*, EG9) Amer Life League.

American Biographical Institute Staff. Two Thousand Notable Americans. LC 81-71697. xiiii, 552 p. 1983. write for info. (*0-934544-23-9*) Am Biog Inst.

American Bird Conservancy Staff, jt. auth. see Griggs, Jack.

American Birding Association, Checklist Committee. ABA Checklist: Birds of the Continental United States & Canada. 5th ed. LC 96-84448. 128p. 1996. pap. 10.00 (*1-878788-32-9*) Amer Birding Assn.

American Birding Association Staff & USDA Forest Service Staff. Birdfinding in Forty National Forests & Grasslands. Boyle, William J., Jr. & Wauer, Roland H., eds. LC 94-7047. (Illus.). 186p. (Orig.). 1996. pap. 14.95 (*1-878788-29-9*, 025) Amer Birding Assn.

American Board of Certified Managed Care Providers. Managed Behavioral Healthcare: Provider Training & Development. D'Alessandro, Alex, ed. LC 92-48824. 1992. pap. 95.00 (*0-935255-77-X*) Of Course Pubns.

American Board of Medical Specialities Staff, jt. ed. see Marquis Who's Who Staff.

American Boiler Manufacturers Association Staff. The American Boiler Industry: A Century of Innovation. Axtman, William H. et al, eds. LC 88-70632. (Illus.). 240p. 1988. 37.50 (*0-9620057-0-3*) Amer Boiler.
— Handbook of Power, Utility & Boiler Terms & Phrases. 6th ed. 160p. 1992. 64.95 (*0-87814-385-8*) PennWell Bks.

American Book Collector Magazine Staff, compiled by. Directory of Specialized American Bookdealers, 1984-1985. 2nd ed. xiv, 344p. 1984. lib. bdg. 35.00 (*0-89679-012-6*) Moretus Pr.

American Book Collector Magazine Staff, ed. Directory of Specialized American Bookdealers. 3rd ed. 520p. 1987. 47.50 (*0-89679-013-4*) Moretus Pr.
— Directory of Specialized American Bookdealers, 1981-1982. 1981. 19.95 (*0-89679-005-3*) Moretus Pr.

American Booksellers Association Staff. American Booksellers Association: 1995 Membership Directory. 372p. (Orig.). 1995. pap. 100.00 (*1-879556-17-0*) ABA.
— Booksellers Make a Difference: Selected Proceedings of the 1994 Convention of the American Booksellers Association. 72p. (Orig.). 1994. pap. 10.00 (*1-879556-13-8*) ABA.

American BookWorks Corporation Staff. Tell Me Doctor: About Prenatal Care. (Illus.). 96p. (Orig.). 1989. pap. 4.95 (*0-317-94000-7*) Amer Bookworks.

American Bookworks Corporation Staff. Tell Me Doctor: About Prenatal Care. 1991. pap. 4.95 (*0-9622813-0-1*) Amer Bookworks.

American Bookworks Staff & Peterson's Guides Staff. Peterson's ACT English Flash. Moscowitz, Mark, ed. LC 97-11301. (Peterson's Guides Ser.). 208p. (Orig.). (YA). 1997. pap. 8.95 (*1-56079-767-3*) Petersons.
— Peterson's ACT Math Flash. Moscowitz, Mark, ed. LC 97-12094. (Peterson's Guides Ser.). 208p. (Orig.). (YA). 1997. pap. 8.95 (*1-56079-766-5*) Petersons.
— Peterson's Panic Plan for the ACT. Moscowitz, Mark, ed. LC 97-19985. (Peterson's Guides Ser.). 256p. (Orig.). (YA). 1997. pap. 9.95 (*1-56079-769-X*) Petersons.

American Brain Tumors Association Staff. A Primer of Brain Tumors. 7th ed. (Illus.). 132p. 1998. pap. write for info. (*0-944093-52-3*) Am Brain Tumor.

American Brokerage Consultants Staff. 1996 Survey Reports on Bank Retail Investment Services. (1996 Bank Representative Compensaion Survey Ser.: Vol. 2). Date not set. write for info. (*0-89982-021-2*) Am Bankers.
— 1996 Survey Reports on Bank Retail Investment Services. (1996 Banker's Report Card on Ihino-Party Marketing Companies Ser.: Vol. 3). Date not set. write for info. (*0-89982-022-0*) Am Bankers.
— 1996 Survey Reports on Bank Retail Investment Services. (1996 Bankers' Report Card on Mutual Fund Companies Ser.: Vol. 4). Date not set. write for info. (*0-89982-023-9*) Am Bankers.
— 1996 Survey Reports on Bank Retail Investment Services. (Nineteen Ninety-Six Bankers' Report Card on Proprietary Mutual Funds Ser.: Vol. 7). 1975. 17.50 (*0-89982-051-4*) Am Bankers.
— 1996 Survey Reports on Bank Retail Investment Services. (Nineteen Ninety-Six Bankers' Report Card on Variable Annuity Vendors Ser.: Vol. 6). 1976. 17.50 (*0-89982-050-6*) Am Bankers.
— 1996 Survey Reports on Bank Retail Investment Services. (Nineteen Ninety-Six Bankers' Report Card on Fixed Annuity Vendors Ser.: Vol. 5). 1978. 30.00 (*0-89982-024-7*) Am Bankers.
— 1996 Survey Reports on Bank Retail Investment Services. (1996 National Survey of Bank Retail Investment Services Ser.: Vol. 1). 1997. write for info. (*0-89982-020-4*) Am Bankers.

American Bureau of Metal Statistics, Inc. Staff. ABMS Non-Ferrous Metal Data Publication. 1989. write for info. (*0-910064-23-7*) Am Bur Metal.

***American Business Directories Staff.** Alabama Business Directory, 1999-2000. 1632p. 1999. boxed set 450.00 incl. cd-rom (*0-7687-0139-2*, 1043-7924) Am Busn Direct.
— Alabama State Credit Directory, 2000 Edition. rev. ed. 384p. 1999. boxed set 145.00 incl. cd-rom (*0-7687-0289-5*) Am Busn Direct.
— Alaska/Hawaii/Nevada State Credit Directory, 2000 Edition. rev. ed. 384p. 1999. boxed set 115.00 incl. cd-rom (*0-7687-0290-9*) Am Busn Direct.
— Alberta Business Directory, 1999-2000. 1264p. 1999. boxed set 495.00 incl. cd-rom (*0-7687-0185-6*, 1203-5149) Am Busn Direct.
— American Big Businesses Directory, 2000 Edition. rev. ed. 9712p. 1999. boxed set 695.00 incl. cd-rom (*0-7687-0205-4*) Am Busn Direct.
— American Manufacturers Directory, 2000 Edition. rev. ed. 3520p. 1999. boxed set 695.00 incl. cd-rom (*0-7687-0206-2*) Am Busn Direct.
— Arizona Business Directory, 2000 Edition. rev. ed. 1568p. 1999. boxed set 450.00 incl. cd-rom (*0-7687-0166-X*) Am Busn Direct.
— Arizona State Credit Directory, 2000 Edition. rev. ed. 384p. 1999. boxed set 145.00 incl. cd-rom (*0-7687-0291-7*) Am Busn Direct.
— Arkansas Business Directory, 1999-2000. rev. ed. 1120p. 1999. boxed set 450.00 incl. cd-rom (*0-7687-0154-6*) Am Busn Direct.
— Arkansas/Mississippi State Credit Directory, 2000 Edition. rev. ed. 496p. 1999. boxed set 145.00 incl. cd-rom (*0-7687-0292-5*) Am Busn Direct.
— Atlantic Provinces Business Directory, 2000 Edition. rev. ed. 1008p. 1999. boxed set 395.00 incl. cd-rom (*0-7687-0188-0*) Am Busn Direct.
— British Columbia Business Directory, 1999-2000. 1680p. 1999. boxed set 495.00 incl. cd-rom (*0-7687-0184-8*, 1203-5165) Am Busn Direct.
— California Business Directory, 1999-2000. 10896p. 1999. boxed set 520.00 incl. cd-rom (*0-7687-0140-6*) Am Busn Direct.
— California State Credit Directory, 2000 Edition. rev. ed. 2976p. 1999. boxed set 195.00 incl. cd-rom (*0-7687-0293-3*) Am Busn Direct.
— Chicago Area Business Directory, 1999-2000. rev. ed. 2752p. 1999. boxed set 415.00 incl. cd-rom (*0-7687-0161-9*) Am Busn Direct.
— Colorado Business Directory, 1999-2000. 1840p. 1999. boxed set 520.00 incl. cd-rom (*0-7687-0145-7*, 1048-7204) Am Busn Direct.
— Colorado State Credit Directory, 2000 Edition. rev. ed. 464p. 1999. boxed set 165.00 incl. cd-rom (*0-7687-0294-1*) Am Busn Direct.
— Connecticut Business Directory, 2000 Edition. rev. ed. 1504p. 1999. boxed set 450.00 incl. cd-rom (*0-7687-0177-5*) Am Busn Direct.
— Connecticut Business Directory 2001. 2000. 425.00 (*0-7687-0264-X*) Am Busn Direct.
— Connecticut/Rhode Island State Credit Directory, 2000 Edition. rev. ed. 448p. 1999. boxed set 145.00 incl. cd-rom (*0-7687-0295-X*) Am Busn Direct.
— Delaware Business Directory, 1999-2000. rev. ed. 432p. 1999. boxed set 375.00 incl. cd-rom (*0-7687-0155-4*) Am Busn Direct.
— Delaware/District of Columbia/West Virginia State Credit Directory, 2000 Edition. rev. ed. 384p. 1999. boxed set 145.00 incl. cd-rom (*0-7687-0296-8*) Am Busn Direct.
— Denver Metro Business Directory, 1999-2000. rev. ed. 3568p. 1999. boxed set 495.00 incl. cd-rom (*0-7687-0196-1*) Am Busn Direct.
— Downstate Illinois Business Directory, 1999-2000. rev. ed. 1680p. 1999. boxed set 415.00 incl. cd-rom (*0-7687-0162-7*) Am Busn Direct.

American Business Directories Staff. Entrepreneurs Business Directory, 1999-2000. 4416p. 1999. boxed set 595.00 (*0-7687-0202-X*) Am Busn Direct.

***American Business Directories Staff.** Florida Business Directory, 1999-2000. 5584p. 1999. boxed set 520.00 incl. cd-rom (*0-7687-0135-X*, 1048-7093) Am Busn Direct.
— Florida State Credit Directory, 2000 Edition. rev. ed. 1520p. 1999. boxed set 195.00 incl. cd-rom (*0-7687-0297-6*) Am Busn Direct.
— Georgia Business Directory, 1999-2000. rev. ed. 2704p. 1999. boxed set 520.00 incl. cd-rom (*0-7687-0149-X*) Am Busn Direct.
— Georgia Business Directory 2000-01. 2000. 495.00 (*0-7687-0234-8*) Am Busn Direct.
— Georgia State Credit Directory, 2000 Edition. rev. ed. 688p. 1999. boxed set 175.00 incl. cd-rom (*0-7687-0298-4*) Am Busn Direct.
— Hawaii Business Directory, 2000 Edition. rev. ed. 624p. 1999. boxed set 375.00 incl. cd-rom (*0-7687-0178-3*) Am Busn Direct.
— Hillsborough County Business Directory, 1999-2000. 1728p. 1999. boxed set 450.00 (*0-7687-0194-5*) Am Busn Direct.
— Idaho Business Directory, 1999-2000. rev. ed. 704p. 1999. boxed set 375.00 incl. cd-rom (*0-7687-0150-3*) Am Busn Direct.
— Idaho/Montana/Wyoming State Credit Directory, 2000 Edition. rev. ed. 352p. 1999. boxed set 115.00 incl. cd-rom (*0-7687-0299-2*) Am Busn Direct.
— Illinois Business Directory, 1999-2000. 4432p. 1999. boxed set 520.00 incl. cd-rom (*0-7687-0160-0*) Am Busn Direct.

American Business Directories Staff. Illinois Business Directory 1997-1998, 3 vols. rev. ed. Incl. Chicago Area Business Directory, 1997-98. rev. ed. 2624p. 1997. boxed set 495.00 (*1-56105-950-1*); Downstate Illinois Business Directory, 1997-1998. rev. ed. 1584p. 1997. boxed set 465.00 (*1-56105-951-X*); 695.00 (*1-56105-949-8*) Am Busn Direct.

***American Business Directories Staff.** Illinois State Credit Directory, 2000 Edition. rev. ed. 1136p. 1999. boxed set 195.00 incl. cd-rom (*0-7687-0300-X*) Am Busn Direct.
— Indiana Business Directory, 1999-2000. 2128p. 1999. boxed set 520.00 incl. cd-rom (*0-7687-0143-0*, 1048-7255) Am Busn Direct.
— Indiana State Credit Directory, 2000 Edition. rev. ed. 512p. 1999. boxed set 165.00 incl. cd-rom (*0-7687-0301-8*) Am Busn Direct.
— Iowa Business Directory, 1999-2000. 1328p. 1999. boxed set 450.00 incl. cd-rom (*0-7687-0146-5*, 1048-7263) Am Busn Direct.
— Iowa/Kansas State Credit Directory, 2000 Edition. rev. ed. 592p. 1999. boxed set 145.00 incl. cd-rom (*0-7687-0302-6*) Am Busn Direct.
— Kansas City Metro Business Directory, 2000 Edition. rev. ed. 2976p. 1999. boxed set 495.00 incl. cd-rom (*0-7687-0200-3*) Am Busn Direct.
— Kentucky Business Directory, 1999-2000. rev. ed. 1424p. 1999. boxed set 450.00 incl. cd-rom (*0-7687-0163-5*) Am Busn Direct.
— Kentucky/South Carolina State Credit Directory, 2000 Edition. rev. ed. 720p. 1999. boxed set 145.00 incl. cd-rom (*0-7687-0303-4*) Am Busn Direct.
— Louisiana Business Directory, 2000 Edition. rev. ed. 1680p. 1999. boxed set 520.00 incl. cd-rom (*0-7687-0173-2*) Am Busn Direct.
— Louisiana State Credit Directory, 2000 Edition. rev. ed. 400p. 1999. boxed set 165.00 incl. cd-rom (*0-7687-0304-2*) Am Busn Direct.
— Maine Business Directory, 1999. 704p. 1999. boxed set 375.00 incl. cd-rom (*0-7687-0131-7*, 1048-7115) Am Busn Direct.
— Maine/New Hampshire/Vermont State Credit Directory, 2000 Edition. rev. ed. 384p. 1999. boxed set 115.00 incl. cd-rom (*0-7687-0305-0*) Am Busn Direct.
— Manitoba Business Directory, 1999-2000. rev. ed. 544p. 1999. boxed set 395.00 incl. cd-rom (*0-7687-0186-4*) Am Busn Direct.
— Maryland Business Directory, 1999-2000. rev. ed. 1744p. 1999. boxed set 520.00 incl. cd-rom (*0-7687-0156-2*) Am Busn Direct.
— Maryland State Credit Directory, 2000 Edition. rev. ed. 464p. 1999. boxed set 145.00 incl. cd-rom (*0-7687-0306-9*) Am Busn Direct.
— Massachusetts Business Directory, 1999-2000. rev. ed. 2496p. 1999. boxed set 520.00 incl. cd-rom (*0-7687-0164-3*) Am Busn Direct.
— Massachusetts State Credit Directory, 2000 Edition. rev. ed. 640p. 1999. boxed set 175.00 incl. cd-rom (*0-7687-0307-7*) Am Busn Direct.
— Michigan Business Directory, 1999-2000. 3520p. 1999. boxed set 520.00 incl. cd-rom (*0-7687-0136-8*, 1047-1790) Am Busn Direct.
— Michigan State Credit Directory, 2000 Edition. rev. ed. 880p. 1999. boxed set 175.00 incl. cd-rom (*0-7687-0308-5*) Am Busn Direct.
— Minneapolis Metro Business Directory, 1999-2000. rev. ed. 2896p. 1999. boxed set 495.00 incl. cd-rom (*0-7687-0199-6*) Am Busn Direct.
— Minnesota Business Directory, 1999-2000. rev. ed. 1920p. 1999. boxed set 520.00 incl. cd-rom (*0-7687-0157-0*) Am Busn Direct.
— Minnesota State Credit Directory, 2000 Edition. rev. ed. 464p. 1999. boxed set 165.00 incl. cd-rom (*0-7687-0309-3*) Am Busn Direct.
— Missouri Business Directory, 1999-2000. 2176p. 1999. boxed set 520.00 incl. cd-rom (*0-7687-0147-3*, 1048-7301) Am Busn Direct.
— Missouri State Credit Directory, 2000 Edition. rev. ed. 528p. 1999. boxed set 175.00 incl. cd-rom (*0-7687-0310-7*) Am Busn Direct.
— Montana Business Directory, 1999-2000. rev. ed. 624p. 1999. boxed set 375.00 incl. cd-rom (*0-7687-0151-1*) Am Busn Direct.
— Nebraska Business Directory, 2000 Edition. rev. ed. 880p. 1999. boxed set 415.00 incl. cd-rom (*0-7687-0174-0*) Am Busn Direct.
— Nebraska/North Dakota/South Dakota State Credit Directory, 2000 Edition. rev. ed. 384p. 1999. boxed set 125.00 incl. cd-rom (*0-7687-0311-5*) Am Busn Direct.
— Nevada Business Directory, 1999-2000. rev. ed. 752p. 1999. boxed set 375.00 incl. cd-rom (*0-7687-0158-9*) Am Busn Direct.
— New Hampshire Business Directory, 1999-2000. 688p. 1999. boxed set 375.00 incl. cd-rom (*0-7687-0144-9*, 1048-714X) Am Busn Direct.
— New Jersey Business Directory, 1999. 2992p. 1999. boxed set 520.00 incl. cd-rom (*0-7687-0132-5*, 1048-7158) Am Busn Direct.
— New Jersey State Credit Directory, 2000 Edition. rev. ed. 784p. 1999. boxed set 175.00 incl. cd-rom (*0-7687-0312-3*) Am Busn Direct.
— New Mexico Business Directory, 1999-2000. rev. ed. 816p. 1999. boxed set 375.00 incl. cd-rom (*0-7687-0152-X*) Am Busn Direct.
— New Mexico/Utah State Credit Directory, 2000 Edition. rev. ed. 368p. 1999. boxed set 115.00 incl. cd-rom (*0-7687-0313-1*) Am Busn Direct.
— New York Business Directory, 2000 Edition. rev. ed. 6160p. 1999. boxed set 520.00 incl. cd-rom (*0-7687-0167-8*) Am Busn Direct.

American Business Directories Staff. New York Business Directory 1998. Incl. New York Metro Business Directory, 1998. rev. ed. 3648p. 1997. boxed set 595.00 (*1-56105-957-9*); Upstate New York Business Directory, 1998. rev. ed. 2384p. 1997. boxed set 465.00 (*1-56105-958-7*); 795.00 (*1-56105-956-0*) Am Busn Direct.

***American Business Directories Staff.** New York Metro Business Directory, 2000 Edition. rev. ed. 3680p. 1999. boxed set 415.00 incl. cd-rom (*0-7687-0168-6*) Am Busn Direct.
— New York State Credit Directory, 2000 Edition. rev. ed. 1664p. 1999. boxed set 195.00 incl. cd-rom (*0-7687-0314-X*) Am Busn Direct.

American Business Directories Staff. 1997 Credit Reference Directory, 12 vols. Incl. Pacific Region. rev. ed. 3456p. 1997. 325.00 (*1-56105-910-2*); 1997. 1295.00 (*1-56105-906-4*) Am Busn Direct.

***American Business Directories Staff.** North Carolina Business Directory, 1999-2000. 2848p. 1999. boxed set 520.00 incl. cd-rom (*0-7687-0137-6*, 1046-9060) Am Busn Direct.
— North Carolina State Credit Directory, 2000 Edition. rev. ed. 736p. 1999. boxed set 175.00 incl. cd-rom (*0-7687-0315-8*) Am Busn Direct.
— North Dakota Business Directory, 2000 Edition. rev. ed. 480p. 1999. boxed set 375.00 (*0-7687-0170-8*) Am Busn Direct.
— Northern California Business Directory, 1999-2000. 4704p. 1999. boxed set 415.00 incl. cd-rom (*0-7687-0141-4*, 1063-4177) Am Busn Direct.

— North/West Texas Business Directory, 1999-2000. rev. ed. 3456p. 1999. boxed set 415.00 incl. cd-rom (*0-7687-0207-0*) Am Busn Direct.
— Ohio Business Directory, 2000 Edition. rev. ed. 4208p. 1999. boxed set 520.00 incl. cd-rom (*0-7687-0179-1*) Am Busn Direct.
— Ohio Business Directory 2001. 2000. 495.00 (*0-7687-0266-6*) Am Busn Direct.
— Ohio State Credit Directory, 2000 Edition. rev. ed. 1040p. 1999. boxed set 175.00 incl. cd-rom (*0-7687-0316-6*) Am Busn Direct.
— Oklahoma State Credit Directory, 2000 Edition. rev. ed. 1999. boxed set 145.00 incl. cd-rom (*0-7687-0317-4*) Am Busn Direct.
— Omaha-Lincoln Area Business Directory, 1999. 1824p. 1999. boxed set 495.00 (*0-7687-0192-9*) Am Busn Direct.
— Omaha/Lincoln Business Directory 2000. 2000. 495.00 (*0-7687-0279-8*) Am Busn Direct.
American Business Directories Staff. Ontario Business Directory, 1999. 3856p. 1999. boxed set 595.00 incl. cd-rom (*0-7687-0182-1*, 1203-5246) Am Busn Direct.
***American Business Directories Staff.** Oregon Business Directory, 1999-2000. 1520p. 1999. boxed set 450.00 incl. cd-rom (*0-7687-0148-1*, 1047-8809) Am Busn Direct.
— Oregon State Credit Directory, 2000 Edition. rev. ed. 368p. 1999. boxed set 145.00 incl. cd-rom (*0-7687-0318-2*) Am Busn Direct.
— Orlando Metro Business Directory, 1999-2000. rev. ed. 3328p. 1999. boxed set 495.00 incl. cd-rom (*0-7687-0197-X*) Am Busn Direct.
— Pennsylvania Business Directory, 2000 Edition. rev. ed. 4528p. 1999. boxed set 520.00 incl. cd-rom (*0-7687-0180-5*) Am Busn Direct.
— Pennsylvania State Credit Directory, 2000 Edition. rev. ed. 1120p. 1999. boxed set 175.00 incl. cd-rom (*0-7687-0319-0*) Am Busn Direct.
— Physicians & Surgeons Directory, 2000 Edition. rev. ed. 2920p. 1999. boxed set 695.00 incl. cd-rom (*0-7687-0203-8*) Am Busn Direct.
— Quebec Business Directory, 2000 Edition. rev. ed. 2656p. 1999. boxed set 495.00 incl. cd-rom (*0-7687-0187-2*) Am Busn Direct.
American Business Directories Staff. St. Paul Metro Business Directory, 1999-2000. 1552p. 1999. boxed set 395.00 (*0-7687-0195-3*) Am Busn Direct.
— Saskatchewan Business Directory, 1999-2000. 544p. 1999. boxed set 395.00 incl. cd-rom (*0-7687-0183-X*, 1203-5238) Am Busn Direct.
***American Business Directories Staff.** South Carolina Business Directory, 1999. 1520p. 1999. boxed set 450.00 incl. cd-rom (*0-7687-0133-3*, 1046-0934) Am Busn Direct.
— South Dakota Business Directory, 1999. 496p. 1999. boxed set 375.00 incl. cd-rom (*0-7687-0134-1*, 1048-7409) Am Busn Direct.
— Southern California Business Directory, 1999-2000. 6192p. 1999. boxed set 415.00 incl. cd-rom (*0-7687-0142-2*, 1061-2181) Am Busn Direct.
— South/Gulf Coast Texas Business Directory, 1999-2000. rev. ed. 3440p. 1999. boxed set 415.00 incl. cd-rom (*0-7687-0208-9*) Am Busn Direct.
— Tacoma/Olympia Metro Business Directory, 1999-2000. rev. ed. 1744p. 1999. boxed set 395.00 incl. cd-rom (*0-7687-0198-8*) Am Busn Direct.
— Tennessee Business Directory, 1999-2000. rev. ed. 2032p. 1999. boxed set 520.00 incl. cd-rom (*0-7687-0153-8*) Am Busn Direct.
— Tennessee Business Directory 2000-01. 2000. 495.00 (*0-7687-0238-0*) Am Busn Direct.
— Tennessee State Credit Directory, 2000 Edition. rev. ed. 512p. 1999. boxed set 165.00 incl. cd-rom (*0-7687-0320-4*) Am Busn Direct.
— Texas Business Directory, 1999-2000. rev. ed. 6896p. 1999. boxed set 520.00 incl. cd-rom (*0-7687-0159-7*) Am Busn Direct.
— Texas State Credit Directory, 2000 Edition. rev. ed. 1872p. 1999. boxed set 195.00 incl. cd-rom (*0-7687-0321-2*) Am Busn Direct.
— Upstate New York Business Directory, 2000 Edition. rev. ed. 2480p. 1999. boxed set 415.00 incl. cd-rom (*0-7687-0169-4*) Am Busn Direct.
— Utah Business Directory, 1999-2000. 880p. 1999. boxed set 375.00 incl. cd-rom (*0-7687-0138-4*, 1048-7417) Am Busn Direct.
— Virginia Business Dirctory 2000-01. 2000. 495.00 (*0-7687-0252-6*) Am Busn Direct.
— Virginia Business Directory, 1999-2000. rev. ed. 2352p. 1999. boxed set 520.00 incl. cd-rom (*0-7687-0165-1*) Am Busn Direct.
— Virginia State Credit Directory, 2000 Edition. rev. ed. 608p. 1999. boxed set 165.00 incl. cd-rom (*0-7687-0322-0*) Am Busn Direct.
— Washington Business Directory, 2000 Edition. rev. ed. 2256p. 1999. boxed set 520.00 incl. cd-rom (*0-7687-0175-9*) Am Busn Direct.
— Washington, D. C. Area Business Directory, 2000 Edition. rev. ed. 1440p. 1999. boxed set 450.00 incl. cd-rom (*0-7687-0172-4*) Am Busn Direct.
— Washington State Credit Directory, 2000 Edition. rev. ed. 560p. 1999. boxed set 165.00 incl. cd-rom (*0-7687-0323-9*) Am Busn Direct.
— West Virginia Business Directory, 2000 Edition. rev. ed. 736p. 1999. boxed set 375.00 incl. cd-rom (*0-7687-0176-7*) Am Busn Direct.
American Business Directories Staff. Willamette Valley Business Directory, 1999-2000. 1616p. 1999. boxed set 395.00 (*0-7687-0193-7*) Am Busn Direct.
***American Business Directories Staff.** Wisconsin Business Directory, 2000 Edition. rev. ed. 2304p. 1999. boxed set 520.00 incl. cd-rom (*0-7687-0181-3*) Am Busn Direct.
— Wisconsin State Credit Directory, 2000 Edition. rev. ed. 528p. 1999. boxed set 165.00 incl. cd-rom (*0-7687-0324-7*) Am Busn Direct.
— Wyoming Business Directory, 2000 Edition. rev. ed. 432p. 1999. boxed set 375.00 incl. cd-rom (*0-7687-0171-6*) Am Busn Direct.
— Wyoming Business Directory 2001. 2000. 350.00 (*0-7687-0258-5*) Am Busn Direct.
***American Business Directories Staff, et al.** Alabama Business Directory (2000-20001) 1,632p. 2000. boxed set 450.00 incl. cd-rom (*0-7687-0224-0*) Am Busn Direct.
— Alaska Business Directory (2000) 512p. 2000. boxed set 375.00 incl. cd-rom (*0-7687-0210-0*) Am Busn Direct.
— Alberta Business Directory (2000-2001) 1,264p. 2000. boxed set 495.00 incl. cd-rom (*0-7687-0272-0*) Am Busn Direct.
— British Columbia Business Directory (2000-2001) 1,680p. 2000. boxed set 495.00 incl. cd-rom (*0-7687-0271-2*) Am Busn Direct.
— California Business Directory (2000-2001) 10,896p. 2000. 520.00 incl. cd-rom (*0-7687-0225-9*) Am Busn Direct.
— Colorado Business Directory (2000-2001) 1,840p. 2000. boxed set 520.00 incl. cd-rom (*0-7687-0230-5*) Am Busn Direct.
— Colorado Front Range Business Directory (2000) 2,928p. 2000. boxed set 395.00 incl. cd-rom (*0-7687-0278-X*) Am Busn Direct.
— Entrepreneurs Business Directory 2000-2001. 4,416p. 2000. boxed set 595.00 incl. cd-rom (*0-7687-0325-5*) Am Busn Direct.
— Florida Business Directory (2000-2001) 5,584p. 2000. boxed set 520.00 incl. cd-rom (*0-7687-0220-8*) Am Busn Direct.
— Hillsborough County Business Directory (2000-2001) 1,728p. 2000. boxed set 450.00 incl. cd-rom (*0-7687-0281-X*) Am Busn Direct.
— Indiana Business Directory (2000-2001) 2,128p. 2000. boxed set 520.00 incl. cd-rom (*0-7687-0228-3*) Am Busn Direct.
— Iowa Business Directory (2000-2001) 1,328p. 2000. boxed set 450.00 incl. cd-rom (*0-7687-0231-3*) Am Busn Direct.
— Kansas Business Directory (2000) 1,248p. 2000. boxed set 450.00 incl. cd-rom (*0-7687-0213-5*) Am Busn Direct.
— Maine Business Directory (2000) 704p. 2000. boxed set 375.00 incl. cd-rom (*0-7687-0216-X*) Am Busn Direct.
— Michigan Business Directory (2000-2001) 3,250p. 2000. boxed set 520,00 incl. cd-rom (*0-7687-0221-6*) Am Busn Direct.
— Mississippi Business Directory (2000) 1,088p. 2000. boxed set 415.00 incl. cd-rom (*0-7687-0211-9*) Am Busn Direct.
— Missouri Business Directory (2000-2001) 2,176p. 2000. boxed set 520.00 incl. cd-rom (*0-7687-0232-1*) Am Busn Direct.
— New Hampshire Business Directory (2000-2001) 688p. 2000. boxed set 375.00 incl. cd-rom (*0-7687-0229-1*) Am Busn Direct.
— New Jersey Business Directory (2000) 2,992p. 2000. boxed set 520.00 incl. cd-rom (*0-7687-0217-8*) Am Busn Direct.
— North Carolina Business Directory (2000-2001) 2,848p. 2000. boxed set 520.00 incl. cd-rom (*0-7687-0222-4*) Am Busn Direct.
— Northern California Business Directory (2000-2001) 4,704p. 2000. boxed set 415.00 incl. cd-rom (*0-7687-0226-7*) Am Busn Direct.
— Oklahoma Business Directory (2000) 1,504p. 2000. boxed set 450.00 incl. cd-rom (*0-7687-0214-3*) Am Busn Direct.
— Ontario Business Directory (2000) 3,856p. 2000. boxed set 595.00 incl. cd-rom (*0-7687-0269-0*) Am Busn Direct.
— Oregon Business Directory (2000-2001) 1,520p. 2000. boxed set 450.00 incl. cd-rom (*0-7687-0233-X*) Am Busn Direct.
— Pinellas County Business Directory (2000) 1,680p. 2000. boxed set 450.00 incl. cd-rom (*0-7687-0276-3*) Am Busn Direct.
— Portland Metro Business Directory (2000-2001) 3,568p. 2000. boxed set 550.00 incl. cd-rom (*0-7687-0201-1*) Am Busn Direct.
— Rhode Island Business Directory (2000) 560p. 2000. boxed set 375.00 incl. cd-rom (*0-7687-0212-7*) Am Busn Direct.
— St Paul Metro Business Directory (2000-2001) 1,552p. 2000. boxed set 395.00 incl. cd-rom (*0-7687-0282-8*) Am Busn Direct.
— Saskatchewan Business Directory (2000-2001) 544p. 2000. boxed set 395.00 incl. cd-rom (*0-7687-0270-4*) Am Busn Direct.
— Seattle Metro Business Directory (2000) 4,160p. 2000. boxed set 550.00 incl. cd-rom (*0-7687-0277-1*) Am Busn Direct.
— South Carolina Business Directory (2000) 1,520p. 2000. boxed set 450.00 incl. cd-rom (*0-7687-0218-6*) Am Busn Direct.
— South Dakota Business Directory (2000) 496p. 2000. boxed set 375.00 incl. cd-rom (*0-7687-0219-4*) Am Busn Direct.
— Southern California Business Directory (2000-2001) 6,192p. 2000. 415.00 incl. cd-rom (*0-7687-0227-5*) Am Busn Direct.
— Utah Business Directory (200-2001) 880p. 2000. boxed set 375.00 incl. cd-rom (*0-7687-0223-2*) Am Busn Direct.
— Vermont Business Directory (2000) 448p. 2000. boxed set 375.00 incl. cd-rom (*0-7687-0215-1*) Am Busn Direct.
***American Business Directory Staff.** Big Businesses Directory 2001. 2000. 595.00 (*0-7687-0328-X*) Am Busn Direct.
— Delaware Business Directory 2000-2001. 2000. 350.00 (*0-7687-0240-2*) Am Busn Direct.
— Manufacturers Directory 2001. 2000. 595.00 (*0-7687-0327-1*) Am Busn Direct.
— Physicians/Surgeons Directory 2001. 2000. 595.00 (*0-7687-0326-3*) Am Busn Direct.
***American Business Directory Staff, ed.** U. S. Business Directory. (Illus.). 2000. 795.00 (*0-7687-0204-6*) Am Busn Direct.
— Willamette Valley Business 2000-2001. (Illus.). 2000. 395.00 (*0-7687-0280-1*) Am Busn Direct.
American Business Womens Association Staff. Working Woman's Quick Cookbook. LC 96-85127. (Illus.). 1996. 15.95 (*0-9652588-0-7*) Am Busn Womens.
***American Camping Association.** Stories for the Campfire. 2nd ed. Hanson, Bob & Roemmich, Bill, eds. LC 99-59509. (Illus.). 112p. 2000. spiral bd. 9.95 (*0-87603-169-6*, Pub. by Am Camping) IPG Chicago.
— 2000 Guide to ACA-Accredited Camps. (Illus.). 240p. 2000. pap. 10.95 (*0-87603-166-1*, Pub. by Am Camping) IPG Chicago.
American Camping Association Staff. Accreditation Standards for Camp Programs & Services: 1998 Edition. rev. ed. LC 98-41821. Orig. Title: Camp Standards with Interpretations for the Accreditation of Organized Camps. 260p. 1998. pap., per. 42.95 (*0-87603-159-9*) Am Camping.
— Camp Boating: Programmed Curriculum Guidelines. LC 93-30281. 96p. 1993. pap. 19.95 (*0-87603-136-X*) Am Camping.
— Health Record Log. 88p. 1994. spiral bd. 9.95 (*0-87603-141-6*) Am Camping.
— Marketing & Communications Strategies: An Action Plan for Camps. 124p. 1991. pap. 250.00 (*0-87603-130-0*) Am Camping.
— Standards Organizer: Written Documentation Organizer for ACA Accreditation. rev. ed. Orig. Title: Standards Organizer for Day & Resident Camps. (Illus.). 33?p. 1998. ring bd. 42.95 (*0-87603-163-7*) Am Camping.
American Canal Society Staff. The Canals of New York State: 1995 Edition. (Illus.). 1995. 7.00 (*0-933788-82-7*) Am Canal & Transport.
American Canal Society Staff & Wyld, Lionel D. The Erie Canal: A Bibliography. LC 78-112128. (Orig.). 1978. pap. 2.50 (*0-685-46266-8*) CSNY.
***American Cancer Society.** American Cancer Society Assortment, 3. 1999. pap. text 14.95 (*0-676-58492-6*) Random.
— American Cancer Society Quick & Healthy Cookbook. (Illus.). 1999. pap. 14.95 (*0-944235-18-2*) Am Cancer NY.
American Cancer Society. Cancer Source Book for Nurses. 7th ed. LC 96-29088. (Nursing Ser.). 496p. 1996. pap. 32.50 (*0-7637-0242-0*) Jones & Bartlett.
— High Country Cooking in Colorado. 192p. 1981. pap. 5.00 (*0-686-31478-6*) Am Cancer Colo.
— I Love New York Cooking from Other Lands. 192p. 1981. pap. 5.00 (*0-686-31485-9*) Am Cancer Syracuse.
***American Cancer Society.** Kids' First Cookbook: Delicious - Nutritious Treats to Make Yourself! LC 99-52304. (Illus.). (J). 1999. 13.95 (*0-944235-19-0*) Am Cancer NY.
American Cancer Society. Look What's Cooking Now: Minnesota Heritage Cookbook, Vol. II. Zelickson, Sue, ed. (Illus.). 176p. (Orig.). 1985. pap. 10.00 (*0-9602796-1-X*) Am Cancer Minn.
— Seasonal Samplings. 192p. 1981. pap. 6.00 (*0-686-31482-4*) Am Cancer Mich.
— A Slice of the Big Apple. 192p. 1982. pap. 6.00 (*0-686-31486-7*) Am Cancer Forest Hills.
— Stop Smoking Program Guide. 184p. write for info. (*0-318-62025-1*, 5003) Am Cancer NY.
American Cancer Society, Arkansas Division, Inc. S. Arkansas Heritage: Recipes Past & Present. LC 92-32004. 1992. pap. write for info. (*0-87197-356-1*) Favorite Recipes.
American Cancer Society, CT Division, Inc. Staff. Connecticut Cooks II. (Illus.). 318p. 1985. 9.95 (*0-9608732-9-5*) ACS CT Div.
American Cancer Society, Inc. Staff. Tiger Lily - A Minor Miracle. (Illus.). 1997. pap. 9.95 (*0-9661975-0-X*) Tiger Lily.
***American Cancer Society, Inc. Staff, ed.** American Cancer Society Guide to Complementary & Alternative Cancer Methods. 464p. 2000. 32.95 (*0-944235-29-8*) Am Cancer NY.
— American Cancer Society Guide to Complementary & Alternative Cancer Methods. (Illus.). 464p. 2000. pap. 24.95 (*0-944235-24-7*) Am Cancer NY.
— A Breast Cancer Journey: Your Personal Guidebook. 304p. 2000. pap. text 18.95 (*0-944235-28-X*) Am Cancer NY.
American Cancer Society, Minnesota Div. Staff. Minnesota Heritage Cookbook I: Hand-Me-Down Recipes, No. I. LC 93-71690. (Illus.). 1993. spiral bd. 15.95 (*0-87197-374-X*) Favorite Recipes.
— Minnesota Heritage Cookbook II: Look What's Cooking Now!, No. II. LC 93-71761. (Illus.). 1993. spiral bd. 15.95 (*0-87197-375-8*) Favorite Recipes.
American Cancer Society Staff. The American Cancer Society Prostate Cancer: Resource for Patients & Their Families. rev. ed. LC 99-230190. (Illus.). 336p. 1999. pap. 14.95 (*0-375-75319-2*) Villard Books.
American Cancer Society Staff, jt. auth. see Silverman, Sol.
American Cancer Society Staff & Volunteers. Simply Nutritious. 180p. 1988. 5.00 (*0-317-01470-6*) Am Cancer Syracuse.
American Canoe Association Staff. Introduction to Paddling: Canoeing Basics for Lakes & Rivers. LC 97-212343. (Illus.). 32p. (Orig.). 1996. pap. 5.95 (*0-89732-202-9*) Menasha Ridge.
American Cartographic Association Staff. Choosing a World Map: Attributes, Distortions, Aspects. 15p. 1988. pap. 12.00 (*0-614-06090-7*, C168) Am Congrs Survey.
— Mapping the Map Projection to the Need. 28p. 1991. pap. 20.00 (*0-614-06089-3*, C170) Am Congrs Survey.
— Which Map Is Best? Projections for World Maps. 14p. 1988. pap. 12.00 (*0-614-06091-5*, C167) Am Congrs Survey.
American Catholic Historic Association Staff. Catholic Philosophy of History, Vol. 3. LC 67-23190. (Essay Index Reprint Ser.). 1977. 18.95 (*0-8369-0285-8*) Ayer.
American Catholic Missionary Staff. The First American Catholic Missionary Congress: Proceedings of the American Catholic Missionary, 1st, Chicago, 1908. 1978. 56.95 (*0-405-10837-0*, 11844) Ayer.
American Catholic Press Staff. How to Use the Psalm Tones. 1987. pap. 1.25 (*0-915866-14-5*) Am Cath Pr.
American Center for Design Staff. 100 Show 19: The Nineteenth Annual of the American Center for Design. (Illus.). 176p. 1997. 35.00 (*2-88046-337-8*, Rotovision) Watsn-Guptill.
American Ceramic Society Staff. Ancient Technology to Modern Science. Kingery, W. D., ed. LC 85-6134. (Ceramics & Civilization Ser.: Vol. 1). (Illus.). 353p. reprint ed. pap. 109.50 (*0-8357-3195-2*, 203946600012) Bks Demand.
— Cements Research Progress, 1977: A Survey of the Scientific Literature on Cements, Published During 1977 Prepared by Members of the Cements Division of the American Ceramic Society. Young, J. Francis, ed. LC 77-642098. 396p. 1978. reprint ed. pap. 122.80 (*0-608-00724-2*, 206149900009) Bks Demand.
American Ceramic Society Staff. Environmental Issues & the Management of Waste, Vol. 1. 1992. 140.00 (*90-5410-080-X*) Ashgate Pub Co.
— Environmental Issues & the Management of Waste, Vol. 2. 1992. 140.00 (*90-5410-081-8*, Pub. by A A Balkema) Ashgate Pub Co.
American Ceramic Society Staff. Phase Equilibria Diagrams: Phase Diagrams for Ceramists: Annual 93. Mchale, Anna E., ed. LC 93-658073. 235p. 1993. reprint ed. pap. 72.90 (*0-608-00725-0*, 206150000009) Bks Demand.
— Proceedings of Unified International Technical Conference on Refractories: Fifth Biennial Worldwide Congress: Refractories, A Worldwide Technology. LC 97-31094. 1997. 245.00 (*1-57498-048-3*, G033) Am Ceramic.
American Cetacean Society Staff. Field Guide to the Orca. (Sasquatch Field Guide Ser.). (Illus.). 50p. (Orig.). 1990. pap. 6.95 (*0-912365-37-4*) Sasquatch Bks.
American Chain Association Staff. Chains for Power Transmission & Material Handling: Design & Applications Handbook. (Mechanical Engineering Ser.: Vol. 18). (Illus.). 376p. 1982. text 165.00 (*0-8247-1701-5*) Dekker.
— Chains for Power Transmission & Material Handling: Design & Applications Handbook. LC 82-17971. (Mechanical Engineering Ser.: No. 18). (Illus.). 371p. reprint ed. pap. 115.10 (*0-7837-0803-3*, 204111800019) Bks Demand.
American Chamber of Commerce in Japan Staff. A Consumer's Guide to Prices in Japan. 100p. 1996. pap. 12.95 (*4-915682-05-6*) Tuttle Pubng.
— Finding a Home in Tokyo. 64p. (Orig.). 1996. pap. 12.95 (*4-915682-06-4*) Tuttle Pubng.
— A Guide to Doing Business in Japan. 232p. (Orig.). 1996. pap. 18.00 (*4-915682-07-2*) Tuttle Pubng.
— Making Trade Talks Work: Lessons from Recent History. 188p. 1997. pap. 30.00 (*4-915682-08-0*) Tuttle Pubng.
— Setting up an Office in Japan. (Illus.). 198p. (Orig.). 1994. pap. 28.00 (*0-8048-3009-6*) Tuttle Pubng.
American Chemical Society, Division of Fuel Chemis. Research with Argonne Premium Coal Samples, Gasification Mechanisms, New Materials Derived from Hydrocarbon Fuels, Novel Analytical Techniques for Fossil Fuels, Posters - General & SCI-MIX: Preprints of Papers Presented at the 202nd ACS National Meeting, New York, NY, August 25-30, 1991. LC TP0318.. (Preprints of Papers: Vol. 36, No. 3, 1990). 563p. reprint ed. pap. 174.60 (*0-7837-1009-7*, 204132100020) Bks Demand.
American Chemical Soc. Chemistry in Context. 1993. 170.31 (*0-697-21950-X*, WCB McGr Hill) McGrw-H Hghr Educ.
— Chemistry in Context. 1994. teacher ed. 10.74 (*0-697-24892-5*, WCB McGr Hill) McGrw-H Hghr Educ.
American Chemical Society (ACS) Staff. Chemcom: Chemistry in the Community. 2nd ed. 464p. (C). 1996. pap. text, teacher ed. 69.90 (*0-8403-5506-8*) Kendall-Hunt.
American Chemical Society (ACS) Staff, jt. auth. see Urbansky, Edward Todd.
American Chemical Society, Analytical Methods in t. Analytical Methods in the Food Industry: A Collection of the Papers of the Symposium, San Francisco, 1949. LC 50-12845. (American Chemical Society Advances in Chemistry Ser.: No. 3). (Illus.). 77p. reprint ed. pap. 30.00 (*0-8357-5458-8*, 201156200080) Bks Demand.
American Chemical Society, Chemistry & Public Affa. Chemistry & the Food System: A Study. LC 80-11194. (Illus.). 156p. 1980. reprint ed. pap. 48.40 (*0-608-04348-6*, 206512800001) Bks Demand.

A

American Chemical Society, Div. of Organic Chemistry & Industrial & Engineering Chemistry Staff. System of Nomenclature for Terpene Hydrocarbons: Acyclics, Monocyclics, Bicyclics. LC 55-4170. (American Chemical Society Advances in Chemistry Ser.: No. 14). 110p. reprint ed. pap. 34.10 (*0-608-30965-6*, 205018300080) Bks Demand.

American Chemical Society, Division of Agricultura. Gibberellins - A Collection of Papers: Comprising the Symposium on Gibberellins, Presented Before the Division of Agricultural & Food Chemistry at the 138th National Meeting of the American Chemical Society, New York, NY, September 1960. LC 61-11135. (Advances in Chemistry Ser.: No. 28). (Illus.). 173p. 1961. reprint ed. pap. 53.70 (*0-608-03269-7*, 206377800007) Bks Demand.

— Molecular Modeling: From Virtual Tools to Real Problems. Kumosinski, Thomas F. & Liebman, Michael N., eds. LC 94-38705. (Symposium Ser.: No. 576). (Illus.). 530p. 1994. text 125.95 (*0-8412-3042-0*, Pub. by Am Chemical) OUP.

— Natural Pest Control Agents: A Symposium. LC 66-22355. (Advances in Chemistry Ser.: No. 53). (Illus.). 152p. 1966. reprint ed. pap. 47.20 (*0-608-03271-9*, 206379000007) Bks Demand.

— Use of Sugars & Other Carbohydrates in the Food Industry: A Collection of Papers. LC 55-4135. (Advances in Chemistry Ser.: No. 12). (Illus.). 146p. 1955. reprint ed. pap. 45.30 (*0-608-03266-2*, 206378500007) Bks Demand.

American Chemical Society, Division of Fuel Chemis. Applications of Oil Chemistry in Exploration & Production: Past, Present & Future; Value-Added Products from Hydrocarbon Streams; On-Line Analytical Techniques for Fuel Processing - Characterization; General Papers - Preprints of Symposia Presented at the 215th ACS National Meeting, March 29-April 2, 1998, Dallas, TX. LC TP0315.. (American Chemical Society, Division of Fuel Chemistry, Preprints of Papers: Vol. 43, No. 2). (Illus.). 164p. reprint ed. pap. 50.90 (*0-608-09010-7*, 206964500005) Bks Demand.

— Bioprocessing for Environmental Benefits, Hydro-, Hydrous-, & Thermal Pyrolysis, Processing & Product Selectivity of Synthetic Fuels, Upgrading Strategies, General Papers & Mass Transfer in Coal Conversion Processes, Developments in Clean Coal Technology: Preprints of Papers Presented at the 204th ACS National Meeting, Washington, DC, August 23-28, 1992. LC TP0315.. (Preprints of Papers: Vol. 37, No. 4). 499p. reprint ed. pap. 154.70 (*0-7837-3204-X*, 204319800007) Bks Demand.

— Chemistry & Geochemistry of Oil Shales: Preprints of Papers Presented at Seattle, Washington, March 20-25, 1983. LC QE0516.. (American Chemical Society Division of Fuel Chemistry, Preprints of Papers Ser.: Vol. 28, No. 3). 251p. reprint ed. pap. 77.90 (*0-608-13784-7*, 202032000016) Bks Demand.

— Chemistry of Low Rank Coals: Supercritical Phenomena. LC TP0321.. (American Chemical Society, Division of Fuel Chemistry, Preprints of Papers: Vol. 28, No. 4). 424p. 1983. reprint ed. pap. 131.50 (*0-608-08127-2*, 202176700023) Bks Demand.

— Chemistry of Mineral Matter & Ash in Coal. LC TP0325.A63. (American Chemistry Society, Division of Fuel Chemistry Preprints of Papers: Vol. 29, No. 4). 370p. 1984. reprint ed. pap. 114.70 (*0-608-08128-0*, 202416300035) Bks Demand.

— Chromatography of Coal Derived Products: General Papers. LC TP0953.C57. (Preprints of Papers-American Chemical Society, Division of Fuel Chemistry Ser.: vol. 26, no. 2). 204p. reprint ed. pap. 63.30 (*0-608-16250-7*, 201504700098) Bks Demand.

— Co-utilization of Coal & Waste Materials: C1 Chemistry: Preprints of Papers Presented at the 209th ACS National Meeting, Anaheim, CA, April 2-7, 1995. LC TP0325.. (Preprints of Papers: Vol. 40, No. 1). 218p. 1995. reprint ed. pap. 67.60 (*0-7837-9208-5*, 204995800004) Bks Demand.

— Coal Gasification Chemistry: Flash Hydrogenation of Coal; Pyrolysis Reactions of Coal; Government Role in Fuel R & D; Henry H. Storch Award Symposium (&) General Papers Presented at Washington, D. C., September 10-14, 1979. LC TP0315.. (Preprints of Papers: Vol. 24, No. 3). 308p. reprint ed. pap. 95.50 (*0-608-14429-0*, 205182400008) Bks Demand.

— Combustion Chemistry, Clean Energy from Waste & Coal, Catalyst Selectivity for Fuel Processing: Preprints of Papers Presented at the 202nd ACS National Meeting, New York, NY, August 25-30, 1991. LC TP0318.. (Preprints of Papers: Vol. 36, No. 4). 582p. reprint ed. pap. 180.50 (*0-7837-1010-0*, 204132000020) Bks Demand.

— Environmental Control in Synfuels Processes: Catalytic Reactions Involving Synthesis Gas. LC TP0698.A4. (Preprints of Papers: Vol. 25, No. 2). 216p. reprint ed. pap. 67.00 (*0-608-13478-3*, 201212200095) Bks Demand.

— Environmental Science of Fossil Fuels, General Papers: Presented at Miami Beach, FL, April 28-May 3, 1985. LC TP0319.. (American Chemical Society Division of Fuel Chemistry, Preprints of Papers Ser.: No. 30, No. 2). 385p. reprint ed. pap. 119.40 (*0-608-13340-X*, 202556300044) Bks Demand.

— Feedstock Recycling of Waste Polymers: Impact of Trace Elements & Ash Composition in Fuel Utilization, Boiler Performance, & Combusion Byproduct Properties: Preprints of Symposia Presented at the 214th ACS National Meeting, Las Vegas, NV, September 8-11, 1997. LC 71-17970. (American Chemical Society, Division of Fuel Chemistry, Preprints of Papers: Vol. 42, No. 4). 210p. 1997. reprint ed. pap. 65.10 (*0-608-07542-6*, 206776000009) Bks Demand.

— Fundamentals of Gas-Carbon Reactions, Chemistry & Characterization of Coal Macerals, General Papers, Coal to Liquid Products, General Papers, Chemistry & Characterization of Fossil Fuels: Preprints of Papers Presented at Seattle, Washington, March 20-25, 1983. LC TP0321.. (American Chemical Society, Division of Fuel Chemistry, Preprints of Papers: Vol. 28, No. 1). 220p. reprint ed. pap. 68.20 (*0-608-14466-5*, 202026500016) Bks Demand.

— General Papers, Air Toxics & Coal, Technologies for the Utilization - Disposal of Waste Materials, Catalytic Conversion of Polycyclic Aromatic Hydrocarbons, SOx-NOx, Membership Directory: Preprints of Papers Presented at the 210th ACS National Meeting, Chicago, IL, August 20-25, 1995. LC TP0318.. (American Chemical Society, Division of Fuel Chemistry, Preprints of Papers: Vol. 40, No. 4). 377p. 1995. reprint ed. pap. 116.90 (*0-608-00538-X*, 206141700008) Bks Demand.

— Iron Based Catalysts for Coal Liquefaction: Hazardous Air Pollutants from Fossil Fuel Conversion; General Papers; Preprints of Papers Presented at the 205th ACS National Meeting Denver, CO, March 28-April 2, 1993. LC TP0315.. (Reprints of Papers: Vol. 38, No. 1). (Illus.). 383p. reprint ed. pap. 118.80 (*0-7837-4669-5*, 204441300001) Bks Demand.

— New Analytical Methods for Characterizing Fossil Fuels & Derived Products, Direct Coal Liquefaction, Biomass Fuels: Preprints of Papers Presented at the 210th ACS National Meeting, Chicago, IL, August 20-25, 1995. LC TP0318.. (American Chemical Society, Division of Fuel Chemistry, Preprints of Papers: Vol. 40, No. 3). 392p. 1995. reprint ed. pap. 121.60 (*0-608-00537-1*, 206141600008) Bks Demand.

— New Applications of Analytical Techniques to Fossil Fuels: General Papers Presented at New York, April 13-18, 1986. LC TP0319.. (American Chemical Society Division of Fuel Chemistry, Preprints of Papers Ser.: Vol. 31, No. 1). 346p. reprint ed. pap. 107.30 (*0-608-18380-6*, 202729900055) Bks Demand.

— Oil Shale, Tar Sands, & Related Materials: General Papers: Storch Award Symposium: Preprints of Papers Presented at San Francisco, California, August 24-29, 1980. LC TP0315.A4. (Preprints of Papers: Vol. 25, No. 3). 298p. reprint ed. pap. 92.40 (*0-608-13474-0*, 201327900094) Bks Demand.

— Oxygenates As Fuel Additives: Clean Coal Technology; CNG, LNG, & LPG Use As Alternative Fuels; Trace Element Geochemistry of Coal & Related Fuels; Thermal Decomposition & Gasification Mechanisms; General Papers; Preprints of Papers Presented at the 207th ACS National Meeting, San Diego, CA, March 13-17, 1994. LC TP0315.. (Preprints of Papers: Vol. 39, No. 2). 374p. reprint ed. pap. 116.00 (*0-7837-6800-1*, 204663200003) Bks Demand.

— Pedagogical Symposium on Global Climate Change, Analytical Techniques for Characterizing Coal & Coal Conversion Products, Chemistry of Asphalt & Asphalt-Aggregate Mixes: Preprints of Papers Presented at the 204th ACS National Meeting, Washington, DC, August 23-28, 1992. LC TP0315.. (Preprints of Papers: Vol. 37, No. 3). 548p. reprint ed. pap. 169.90 (*0-7837-3203-1*, 204319700007) Bks Demand.

— Physical Methods for Fossil Fuels Characterization, Coal Gasification, Pyrolysis & Biomass: Presented at Miami Beach, FL, April 28-May 3, 1985, Vol. 7. LC TP0321.. (American Chemical Society Division of Fuel Chemistry, Preprints of Papers Ser.: Vol. 30, No. 1). 435p. reprint ed. pap. 134.90 (*0-608-13336-1*, 202556400044) Bks Demand.

— Production, Analysis & Upgrading of Oils from Biomass. LC TP0324.P7. (Preprints of Papers: Vol. 32, No. 2). (Illus.). 334p. reprint ed. pap. 103.60 (*0-608-18396-2*, 202998800067) Bks Demand.

— Seventy-Fifth Anniversary of the Fuel Chemistry Division: Stability & Oxidation Chemistry of Fuels; Combustion Chemistry of Traditional & Non-Traditional Fuels - Preprints of Symposia Presented at the 215th ACS National Meeting, March 29-April 2, 1998, Dallas, TX. LC TP0315.. (American Chemical Society, Division of Fuel Chemistry, Preprints of Papers: Vol. 43, No. 1). (Illus.). 227p. reprint ed. pap. 70.40 (*0-608-09009-3*, 206964400005) Bks Demand.

— Status of Coal Research: Combustion Chemistry & Soot Formation; Storch Award Symposium on Coal Maceral Characterizations & Separation; SO2 & NOx Removal Techniques; Preprints of Papers Presented at the 207th ACS National Meeting, San Diego, CA, March 13-17, 1994. LC TP0315.. (Preprints of Papers: Vol. 39, No. 1). 280p. reprint ed. pap. 86.80 (*0-7837-6801-X*, 204663300003) Bks Demand.

— Storch Award, Conversion of FGD Residues & Utility Fly Ash to Marketable Products, Ash Chemistry: Phase Relationships in Ashes & Slags; General Papers. Preprints of Papers Presented at the 211th ACS National Meeting, Held in New Orleans, Louisiana, March 24-28, 1996. LC TP0318.. (American Chemical Society, Division of Fuel Chemistry, Preprints of Papers: Vol. 41, No. 2). 258p. 1996. reprint ed. pap. 80.00 (*0-608-01767-1*, 206242500003) Bks Demand.

— Storch Award, General Papers, Materials & Chemicals Synthesis from Fossil Fuels & Biomass, Advanced Power Generation, Ultrafine Particle Catalysis: Preprints of Papers Presented at the 209th ACS National Meeting, Anaheim, CA, April 2-7, 1995. LC TP0315.. (Preprints of Papers: Vol. 40, No. 2). 199p. 1995. reprint ed. pap. 61.70 (*0-7837-9209-3*, 204995900004) Bks Demand.

— Storch Award Symposium: Alternate Uses for Fossil Fuels; Coal Dissolution - Low Severity Liquefaction; Catalysts of Flue Gas Cleanup Processes: Preprints of Papers Presented at the 205th ACS National Meeting, Denver, CO, March 28-April 2, 1993. LC TP0315. (Preprints of Papers: Vol. 38, No. 2). 423p. reprint ed. pap. 131.20 (*0-7837-4670-9*, 204441400002) Bks Demand.

— Thermal Analytical Techniques: Gasification Mechanisms; Production & Use of Carbon-Based Materials for Environmental Cleanup; Preprints of Papers Presented at the 211th ACS National Meeting, Held in New Orleans, Louisiana, March 24-28, 1996. LC TP0318.. (American Chemical Society, Division of Fuel Chemistry, Preprints of Papers: Vol. 41, No. 1). 527p. 1996. reprint ed. pap. 163.40 (*0-608-01766-3*, 206242400003) Bks Demand.

American Chemical Society, Division of Fuel Chemistry Staff. Production & Use of Carbon-Based Materials for Environmental Cleanup: Microscopic Studies of Coal & Carbon: The Chemistry of Carbon in Coal Fly Ash Formation, Control & Utilization; Modified Asphalts; General Papers; Preprints of Papers Presented at the 216th ACS National Meeting, August 22-27, 1998, Boston, MA. LC 71-17970. (American Chemical Society, Division of Fuel Chemistry, Preprints of Papers: Vol. 43, No. 4). 398p. 1998. reprint ed. pap. 123.40 (*0-608-10663-1*, 207126800009) Bks Demand.

American Chemical Society, Division of Inorganic C. Mechanistic Bioinorganic Chemistry. Thorp, H. Holden & Pecoraro, Vincent L., eds. LC 95-15128. (Advances in Chemistry Ser.: Vol. 246). (Illus.). 400p. 1995. text 120.00 (*0-8412-3062-5*, Pub. by Am Chemical) OUP.

American Chemical Society, Division of Petroleum Chemistry Staff. Origin & Refining of Petroleum. LC 73-164409. (Advances in Chemistry Ser.: No. 103). (Illus.). 240p. 1971. reprint ed. pap. 74.40 (*0-608-03276-X*, 206379400007) Bks Demand.

American Chemical Society, Division of Polymeric M. Flow-Induced Structure in Polymers. Nakatani, Alan I. & Dadmun, Mark D., eds. LC 95-16754. (ACS Symposium Ser.: No. 597). (Illus.). 378p. 1995. text 110.00 (*0-8412-3230-X*, Pub. by Am Chemical) OUP.

American Chemical Society Division of Polymeric Ma, et al. Hyphenated Techniques in Polymer Characterization: Thermal-Spectroscopic & Other Methods. Provder, Theodore et al, eds. LC 94-38926. (Symposium Ser.: No. 581). (Illus.). 200p. 1994. text 57.95 (*0-8412-3057-9*, Pub. by Am Chemical) OUP.

American Chemical Society, Division of the History. Kekule Centennial. LC 66-30726. (Advances in Chemistry Ser.: No. 61). (Illus.). 206p. 1966. reprint ed. pap. 63.90 (*0-608-03272-7*, 206379100007) Bks Demand.

American Chemical Society, Division of Water, Air,. Nonequilibrium Systems in Natural Water Chemistry. LC 76-170252. (Advances in Chemistry Ser.: No. 106). (Illus.). 352p. 1971. reprint ed. pap. 109.20 (*0-608-03277-8*, 206379500007) Bks Demand.

American Chemical Society, Divison of Fuel Chemist. Degradative Processes of Fuels in the Environment: Carbons for Advanced Energy & Environmental Applications; Fuels, Emissions, & Toxicity; New Analytical Techniques in Fuel Chemistry: Preprints of Symposia Presented at the 214th ACS National Meeting, Las Vegas, NV, September 8-11, 1997. LC 71-17970. (American Chemical Society, Division of Fuel Chemistry, Preprints of Papers: Vol. 42, No. 3). 196p. 1997. reprint ed. pap. 60.80 (*0-608-07541-8*, 206775900009) Bks Demand.

— Fuels for the Year 2000 & Beyond: Novel Upgrading Techniques in Fuel Processing: New Technology/ Development for Energy Storage; Reactor & Reaction Modeling; General Papers: Preprints of Papers Presented at the 216th ACS National Meeting, August 22-27, 1998, Boston MA. LC 71-17970. (American Chemical Society, Division of Fuel Chemistry, Preprints of Papers: Vol. 43, No. 3). (Illus.). 444p. reprint ed. pap. 137.70 (*0-608-10664-X*, 207126900009) Bks Demand.

American Chemical Society Evaluation of World Reso & Altschul, Aaron M. World Protein Resources: Proceedings of the American Chemical Society Evaluation of World Resources Symposium, Atlantic City, 1965. LC 66-28666. (American Chemical Society Advances in Chemistry Ser.: No. 57). 303p. reprint ed. pap. 94.00 (*0-608-10846-4*, 205018500078) Bks Demand.

American Chemical Society, International Developme. Cellulose Chemistry & Technology: A Symposium Sponsored by the Cellulose, Paper, & Textile Division at the Meeting of American Chemical Society, 171st, New York, N. Y., April 5-9, 1976. Arthur, Jett C., Jr., ed. LC 77-6649. (American Chemical Society Symposium Ser.: No. 48). (Illus.). 406p. reprint ed. pap. 125.90 (*0-608-11646-7*, 201523500093) Bks Demand.

American Chemical Society, Non-Stoichiometric Comp. Nonstoichiometric Compounds: A Symposium Sponsored by the Division of Inorganic Chemistry at the 141st Meeting of the American Chemical Society, Washington, D.C., 1962. LC 63-16562. (Advances in Chemistry Ser.: 39). 261p. reprint ed. pap. 81.00 (*0-608-14816-4*, 202563100045) Bks Demand.

American Chemical Society, Physical Functions of H. Physical Functions of Hydrocolloids: A Collection of Papers of the Symposium, Atlantic City, NJ, 1956. LC 62-3026. (American Chemical Society Advances in Chemistry Ser.: No. 25). 107p. reprint ed. pap. 33.20 (*0-608-30689-4*, 205018400080) Bks Demand.

American Chemical Society Staff. Addition & Condensation Polymerization Proceses: A Symposium Sponsored by the Division of Industrial & Engineering Chemistry at the 155th Meeting of the American Chemical Society, San Francisco, CA, April 1-5, 1968 - Norbert A. J. Platzer, Symposium Chairman. LC 78-102896. (Advances in Chemistry Ser.: No. 91). (Illus.). 789p. 1969. reprint ed. pap. 200.00 (*0-608-06765-2*, 206696200009) Bks Demand.

— Adsorption from Aqueous Solution: A Symposium Co-Sponsored by the Division of Water, Air, & Waste Chemistry & the Division of Colloid & Surface Chemistry at the 154th Meeting of the American Chemical Society, Chicago, IL, Sept. 14-15, 1967. LC 68-59407. (Advances in Chemistry Ser.: No. 79). (Illus.). 222p. 1968. reprint ed. pap. 68.90 (*0-608-06814-4*, 206701100009) Bks Demand.

— Advanced Propellant Chemistry: A Symposium. LC 66-22356. (Advances in Chemistry Ser.: Vol. 54). (Illus.). 300p. reprint ed. pap. 93.00 (*0-8357-5131-7*, 205225700080) Bks Demand.

— Agricultural Applications of Petroleum Products: A Collection of Papers Comprising the Symposium on Agricultural Applications of Petroleum Products, Presented Before the Divisions of Agricultural & Food Chemistry & Petroleum Chemistry at the 118th Meeting of the American Chemical Society, Chicago, IL, September 1951. LC 54-1575. (Advances in Chemistry Ser.: Vol. 7). (Illus.). 108p. 1952. reprint ed. pap. 33.50 (*0-608-06912-4*, 206712000009) Bks Demand.

— Anaerobic Biological Treatment Processes: A Symposium Sponsored by the Division of Water, Air, & Waste Chemistry at the 159th Meeting of the American Chemical Society, Houston, TX, February 26, 1970 - Frederick G. Pohland, Symposium Chairman. LC 74-176092. (Advances in Chemistry Ser.: No. 105). (Illus.). 206p. 1971. reprint ed. pap. 63.90 (*0-608-06768-7*, 206696500009) Bks Demand.

— Azeotropic Data, Vol. 2. LC 52-3085. (Advances in Chemistry Ser.: Vol. 35). (Illus.). 106p. 1962. reprint ed. pap. 32.90 (*0-608-07553-1*, 205265300002) Bks Demand.

— Azeotropic Data: Tables of Azeotropes & Nonazeotropes. LC 52-3085. (Advances in Chemistry Ser.: Vol. 6). (Illus.). 332p. 1952. reprint ed. pap. 103.00 (*0-608-06913-2*, 206712100009) Bks Demand.

— Bioinorganic Chemistry: A Symposium Co-Sponsored by the Division(s) of Inorganic Chemistry of the American Chemical Society & the Chemical Institute of Canada at Virginia Polytechnic Institute & State University, Blacksburg, VA, June 22-25, 1970 - Raymond Dessy, John Dillard & Larry Taylor, Symposium Co-Chairman. LC 70-153666. (Advances in Chemistry Ser.: No. 100). (Illus.). 446p. 1971. reprint ed. pap. 138.30 (*0-608-06767-9*, 206696400009) Bks Demand.

— Cellulases & Their Applications: A Symposium Sponsored by the Division of Cellulose, Wood, & Fiber Chemistry at the 156th Meeting of the American Chemical Society, Atlantic City, NJ September 11-12, 1968 - George J. Hajny & Elwyn T. Reese, Symposium Co-Chairman. LC 73-108269. (Advances in Chemistry Ser.: No. 95). (Illus.). 480p. 1969. reprint ed. pap. 148.80 (*0-608-06760-1*, 206695700009) Bks Demand.

*__American Chemical Society Staff.__ ChemCom. 2000. pap. text. write for info. (*0-7167-3551-2*) W H Freeman.

American Chemical Society Staff. ChemCom: Chemistry in the Community; A Project of the American Chemical. 3rd ed. LC 96-79934. 643p. 1998. 47.90 (*0-7872-0560-5*) Kendall-Hunt.

*__American Chemical Society Staff.__ Chemcom Core. 4th ed. 2000. pap. text. write for info. (*0-7167-3890-2*) W H Freeman.

American Chemical Society Staff. Chemical Marketing: The Challenges of the Seventies: A Symposium Sponsored by the Division of Chemical Marketing & Economics at the 156th Meeting of the American Chemical Society, Atlantic City, NJ, Sept. 9-11, 1968. LC 68-57115. (Advances in Chemistry Ser.: No. 83). (Illus.). 207p. 1968. reprint ed. pap. 64.20 (*0-608-06815-2*, 206701200009) Bks Demand.

— Chemical Nomenclature: A Collection of Papers Comprising the Symposium on Chemical Nomenclature, Presented Before the Division of Chemical Literature at the 120th Meeting--Diamond Jubilee--of the American Chemical Society, New York, NY, September 1951. LC 53-3165. (Advances in Chemistry Ser.: Vol. 8). (Illus.). 116p. reprint ed. pap. 36.00 (*0-608-06911-6*, 206711900009) Bks Demand.

— Chemical Reactions in Electrical Discharges: A Symposium Co-Sponsored by the Division of Fuel Chemistry & the Division of Physical Chemistry at the 153rd Meeting of the American Chemical Society, Miami Beach, FL, April 11-13, 1967. LC 70-76951. (Advances in Chemistry Ser.: No. 80). (Illus.). 526p. 1969. reprint ed. pap. 163.10 (*0-608-06802-0*, 206699900009) Bks Demand.

*__American Chemical Society Staff.__ Chemistry in a Biological Context. 2000. text. write for info. (*0-7167-3126-6*) W H Freeman.

— Chemistry In Context. 3rd ed. LC 99-40273. 1999. 50.74 (*0-697-36024-5*) McGraw.

American Chemical Society Staff. Chemistry in Context: Applying Chemistry to Society. 432p. (C). 1993. text, student ed. write for info. (*0-697-21951-8*, WCB McGr Hill) McGrw-H Hghr Educ.

— Chemistry in Context: Applying Chemistry to Society. 432p. (C). 1993. text. write for info. (*0-697-21948-8*, WCB McGr Hill) McGrw-H Hghr Educ.

— Chemistry in Context: Applying Chemistry to Society. (C). 1994. text, student ed. write for info. (*0-697-27732-1*, WCB McGr Hill) McGrw-H Hghr Educ.

*__American Chemical Society Staff.__ Chemistry in the Community. 2000. pap. text. write for info. (*0-7167-3916-X*); pap. text, wbk. ed. write for info. (*0-7167-3917-8*) W H Freeman.

American Chemical Society Staff. Contact Angle, Wettability, & Adhesion: The Kendall Award Symposium Honoring William A. Zisman, Sponsored by the Division of Colloid & Surface Chemistry at the

144th Meeting of the American Chemical Society, Los Angeles, CA, April 2-3, 1963. LC 63-14481. (Advances in Chemistry Ser.: Vol. 43). (Illus.). 401p. reprint ed. pap. 124.40 (*0-608-06918-3*, 206712600009) Bks Demand.

— Deoxy Sugars: A Symposium Co-Sponsored by the Division of Carbohydrate Chemistry & the Division of Microbial Chemistry & Technology at the 152nd Meeting of the American Chemical Society, New York, NY, Sept. 13-14, 1966. LC 68-8968. (Advances in Chemistry Ser.: No. 74). (Illus.). 269p. 1968. reprint ed. pap. 83.40 (*0-608-06806-3*, 206700300009) Bks Demand.

— Dietary Chemicals vs. Dental Caries: Based on a Symposium on Dietary Chemicals in Relation to Dental Caries, Sponsored by the Agricultural & Food Chemistry Division at the 1966 Winter Meeting of the American Chemical Society, Phoenix, AZ, January18, 1966 - Robert s. Harris, Symposium Chairman. LC 71-142197. (Advances in Chemistry Ser.: No. 94). (Illus.). 192p. 1970. reprint ed. pap. 59.60 (*0-608-06763-6*, 206696000009) Bks Demand.

— Drug Discovery: Science & Development in a Changing Society - Two Symposia Sponsored by the Division of Medicinal Chemistry at the 160th Meeting of the American Chemical Society, Chicago, IL, September 15-16, 1970 - Barry Bloom & Glenn E. Ullyot, Symposia Chairmen. LC 70-184206. (Advances in Chemistry Ser.: No. 108). (Illus.). 304p. 1971. reprint ed. pap. 94.30 (*0-608-06770-9*, 206696700009) Bks Demand.

— Engineering Plastics & Their Commercial Development: A Symposium Co-Sponsored by the Division of Chemical Marketing & Economics & the Division of Polymer Chemistry at the 157th Meeting of the American Chemical Society, Minneapolis, MN, April 15-16, 1969 - George F. Foy, Symposium Chairman. LC 78-102896. (Advances in Chemistry Ser.: No. 96). (Illus.). 138p. 1969. reprint ed. pap. 42.80 (*0-608-06761-X*, 206695800009) Bks Demand.

— Epoxy Resins: A Symposium Sponsored by the Division of Organic Coatings & Plastics Chemistry at the 155th Meeting of the American Chemical Society, San Francisco, CA, April 3-4, 1968. LC 70-113408. (Advances in Chemistry Ser.: No. 92). (Illus.). 240p. 1970. reprint ed. pap. 74.40 (*0-608-06812-8*, 206700900009) Bks Demand.

— Equilibrium Concepts in Natural Water Systems: A Symposium Sponsored by the Division of Water, Air, & Waste Chemistry at the 151st Meeting of the American Chemical Society, Pittsburgh, PA, March 23-24, 1966. LC 67-27366. (Advances in Chemistry Ser.: No. 67). (Illus.). 352p. 1967. reprint ed. pap. 109.20 (*0-608-06793-8*, 206699000009) Bks Demand.

— Extractive & Azeotropic Distillation: Based on Papers Presented at Two Symposia Sponsored by the Division of Industrial & Engineering Chemistry of the American Chemical Society at the 160th Meeting, Chicago, Ill., Sept. 17, 1970, & the 163rd Meeting, Boston, Mass., April 14, 1972. LC 72-92811. (Advances in Chemistry Ser.: No. 115). 188p. reprint ed. pap. 58.30 (*0-608-17748-2*, 205224600070) Bks Demand.

— Fate of Organic Pesticides in the Aquatic Environment: A Symposium Sponsored by the Division of Pesticide Chemistry at the 161st Meeting of the American Chemical Society, Los Angeles, CA, March 29-31, 1971. LC 72-87028. (Advances in Chemistry Ser.: No. 111). (Illus.). 288p. 1972. reprint ed. pap. 89.30 (*0-608-06778-4*, 206697500009) Bks Demand.

— Fire Retardant Paints: A Collection of Papers Comprising the Symposium on Fire Retardant Paints, Presented Before the Division of Paint, Plastics, & Printing Ink Chemistry at the 123rd Meeting of the American Chemical Society, Los Angeles, CA, March 1953. LC 55-215. (Advances in Chemistry Ser.: Vol. 9). (Illus.). 95p. 1954. reprint ed. pap. 30.00 (*0-608-06910-8*, 206711800009) Bks Demand.

— Flavor Chemistry: A Symposium Sponsored by the Division of Agricultural & Food Chemistry at the 149th Meeting of the American Chemical Society, Detroit, Mich., April 6-7, 1965. LC 66-27216. (Advances in Chemistry Ser.: No. 56). (Illus.). 288p. reprint ed. pap. 89.30 (*0-7837-6756-0*, 204638500011) Bks Demand.

— Flavor-Food Interactions: Developed from a Symposium Sponsored by the Division of Agricultural & Food Chemistry at the 208th National Meeting of the American Chemical Society, Washington, DC. August 21-25, 1994, Vol. 633. McGorrin, Robert J. & Leland, Jane V., eds. LC 96-20197. (ACS Symposium Ser.: No. 633). (Illus.). 248p. 1996. text 95.00 (*0-8412-3409-4*, Pub. by Am Chemical) OUP.

— Fuel Cell Systems: Symposia Sponsored by the Division of Fuel Chemistry at the 145th & 146th Meetings of the American Chemical Society, New York, NY, Sept. 12-13, 1963 & Philadelphia, PA, April 6-7, 1964. LC 65-16399. (Advances in Chemistry Ser.: Vol. 47). (Illus.). 373p. 1965. reprint ed. pap. 115.70 (*0-608-06921-3*, 206712900009) Bks Demand.

— Fuel Cell Systems II: Fifth Biennial Fuel Cell Symposium Sponsored by the Division of Fuel Chemistry at the 154th Meeting of the American Chemical Society, Chicago, IL, September 12-14, 1967 - Bernard S. Baker, Symposium Chairman. LC 76-99924. (Advances in Chemistry Ser.: No. 90). (Illus.). 456p. 1969. reprint ed. pap. 141.40 (*0-608-06764-4*, 206696100009) Bks Demand.

— Fuel Gasification: A Symposium Sponsored by the Division of Fuel Chemistry at the 152nd Meeting of the American Chemical Society, New York, NY, September 12-13, 1966. LC 67-31495. (Advances in Chemistry Ser.: No. 69). (Illus.). 286p. 1967. reprint ed. pap. 88.70 (*0-608-06795-4*, 206699200009) Bks Demand.

American Chemical Society Staff. Fuels & Chemicals from Biomass, Vol. 666. Saha, Badal C. & Woodward, Jonathan, eds. LC 97-6914. (ACS Symposium Ser.: No. 666). (Illus.). 368p. 1997. text 125.00 (*0-8412-3508-2*, Pub. by Am Chemical) OUP.

American Chemical Society Staff. Fumigants: Environmental Behavior, Exposure, & Analysis, Vol. 652. Seiber, James N. et al, eds. LC 96-44112. (ACS Symposium Ser.: No. 652). (Illus.). 228p. 1996. text 105.00 (*0-8412-3475-2*, Pub. by Am Chemical) OUP.

— Highly Excited Molecules: Relaxation, Reaction, & Structure, Vol. 678. Mullin, Amy S. et al, eds. LC 97-34824. (Symposium Ser.). 344p. 1997. text 110.95 (*0-8412-3534-1*, Pub. by Am Chemical) OUP.

— Homogeneous Catalysis: Industrial Applications & Implications: A Symposium Sponsored by the Division of Industrial & Engineering Chemistry at the 152nd Meeting of the American Chemical Society, New York, NY, Sept. 13-14. LC 68-24578. (Advances in Chemistry Ser.: No. 70). (Illus.). 293p. 1968. reprint ed. pap. 90.90 (*0-608-06796-2*, 206699300009) Bks Demand.

— Interaction of Liquids at Solid Substrates: A Symposium Sponsored by the Division of Organic Coatings & Plastics Chemistry at the 154th Meeting of the American Chemical Society, Chicago, IL, Sept. 11-12, 1966. LC 68-59406. (Advances in Chemistry Ser.: No. 87). (Illus.). 222p. 1968. reprint ed. pap. 68.90 (*0-608-06818-7*, 206701500009) Bks Demand.

— Ion-Molecule Reactions in the Gas Phase: A Symposium Sponsored by the Division of Physical Chemistry at the 152nd Meeting of the American Chemical Society, New York, NY, Sept. 12-13, 1966, Pierre J. Ausloos, Symposium Chairman. LC 66-28609. (Advances in Chemistry Ser.: Vol. 58). (Illus.). 344p. 1966. reprint ed. pap. 106.70 (*0-608-07552-3*, 205265200009) Bks Demand.

— Irradiation of Polymers: A Symposium Sponsored by the Division of Industrial & Engineering Chemistry at the 151st Meeting of the American Chemical Society, Pittsburgh, PA, March 29-30, 1966. LC 67-27365. (Advances in Chemistry Ser.: No. 66). 287p. 1967. reprint ed. pap. 89.00 (*0-608-06798-9*, 206699500009) Bks Demand.

— Isotope Effects in Chemical Processes: Based on a Symposium Sponsored by the Division of Nuclear Chemistry & Technology at the 153rd Meeting of the American Chemical Society, Miami Beach, FL, April 11, 1967. LC 71-84867. (Advances in Chemistry Ser.: No. 89). (Illus.). 288p. 1969. reprint ed. pap. 89.30 (*0-608-06755-5*, 206695200009) Bks Demand.

— A Key to Pharmaceutical & Medicinal Chemistry Literature: A Collection of Papers Comprising Two Symposia of One Day Each Presented Before the Divisions of Chemical Literature & Medicinal Chemistry at the 124th & 126th National Meetings of the American Chemical Society, Chicago, September 1953 & September 1954. LC 56-4453. (Advances in Chemistry Ser.: Vol. 16). (Illus.). 258p. 1956. reprint ed. pap. 80.00 (*0-608-06907-8*, 206711500009) Bks Demand.

— Lanthanide/Actinide Chemistry: A Symposium Co-Sponsored by the Division of Inorganic Chemistry & the Division of Nuclear Chemistry & Technology at the 152nd Meeting of the American Chemical Society, New York, NY, Sept. 13-14, 1966. LC 67-31656. (Advances in Chemistry Ser.: No. 71). (Illus.). 371p. 1967. reprint ed. pap. 115.10 (*0-608-06803-9*, 206700000009) Bks Demand.

— Lignin Structure & Reactions: A Symposium Sponsored by the Division of Cellulose, Wood, & Fiber Chemistry at the 150th Meeting of the American Chemical Society, Atlantic City, NJ, Sept. 13-14, 1965. LC 66-28847. (Advances in Chemistry Ser.: Vol. 59). (Illus.). 283p. 1966. reprint ed. pap. 87.80 (*0-608-06914-0*, 206712200009) Bks Demand.

— Liquid-Crystalline Polymer Systems: Technological Advances. Isayev, Avraam I. et al, eds. LC 96-20169. (ACS Symposium Ser.: No. 632). (Illus.). 432p. 1996. text 130.00 (*0-8412-3408-6*, Pub. by Am Chemical) OUP.

— Literature of Chemical Technology: Based on Papers Presented at Two Symposia Sponsored by the Division of Chemical Literature of the American chemical Society at the 143rd Meeting, Cincinnati, OH, Jan. 13-14, 1963, & the 145th Meeting, New York, Sept. 9-13, 1963. LC 68-59481. (Advances in Chemistry Ser.: No. 78). 742p. 1968. reprint ed. pap. 200.00 (*0-608-06810-1*, 206700700009) Bks Demand.

— Literature of the Combustion of Petroleum: A Collection of Papers Presented at the Symposium on the Literature of the Combustion of Petroleum Held by the Division of Chemical Literature & the Division of Petroleum Chemistry at the 129th National Meeting of the American Chemical Society in Dallas, TX, April 1956. LC 59-627. (Advances in Chemistry Ser.: Vol. 20). (Illus.). 299p. 1958. reprint ed. pap. 92.70 (*0-608-06903-5*, 206711100009) Bks Demand.

— Literature Resources for Chemical Process Industries: A Collection of Papers Comprising Five Symposia & Thirteen General Papers Presented Before the Division of Chemical Literature at Several Recent National Meetings of the American Chemical Society. LC 54-4626. (Advances in Chemistry Ser.: Vol. 10). (Illus.). 588p. 1954. reprint ed. pap. 182.30 (*0-608-06909-4*, 206711700009) Bks Demand.

— Mass Spectrometry in Inorganic Chemistry: A Symposium Sponsored by the Division of Inorganic Chemistry at the 152nd Meeting of the American Chemical Society, New York, NY, Sept. 15-16, 1966. LC 68-25995. (Advances in Chemistry Ser.: No. 72). (Illus.). 337p. 1968. reprint ed. pap. 104.50 (*0-608-06804-7*, 206700100009) Bks Demand.

— Molecular Association in Biological & Related Systems: A Symposium Sponsored by the Division of Colloid & Surface Chemistry at the 153rd Meeting of the American Chemical Society, Miami Beach, FL, April 13-14, 1967. LC 68-59079. (Advances in Chemistry Ser.: No. 84). (Illus.). 318p. 1968. reprint ed. pap. 98.60 (*0-608-06816-0*, 206701300009) Bks Demand.

— Molecular Modeling of Nucleic Acids. Leontis, Neocles B. et al, eds. LC 97-42151. (ACS Symposoium Ser.: No. 682). 450p. 1997. text 135.00 (*0-8412-3541-4*, Pub. by Am Chemical) OUP.

— Molecular Modification in Drug Design: A Symposium Sponsored by the Division of Medicinal Chemistry at the 145th Meeting of the American Chemical Society, New York, NY, Sept. 9-10, 1963. LC 64-22278. (Advances in Chemistry Ser.: Vol. 45). (Illus.). 236p. 1964. reprint ed. pap. 73.20 (*0-608-06923-X*, 206713100009) Bks Demand.

— The Mossbauer Effect & Its Application in Chemistry: A Symposium Organized by Carl W. Seidel for Nuclear Science & Engineering Corp., Pittsburgh, PA. Held in New York, NY, September 12, 1966. LC 67-31407. (Advances in Chemistry Ser.: No. 68). (Illus.). 188p. 1967. reprint ed. pap. 58.30 (*0-608-06794-6*, 206699100009) Bks Demand.

— Multicomponent Polymer Systems: A Symposium Co-Sponsored by the Division of Industrial & Engineering Chemistry, the Division of Polymer Chemistry, & the Division of Cellulose, Wood, & Fiber Chemistry at the 159th Meeting of the American Chemical Society, Houston, TX, February 23-26, 1970 - Norbert A. J. Platzer, Symposium Chairman. LC 70-159768. (Advances in Chemistry Ser.: No. 99). (Illus.). 616p. 1971. reprint ed. pap. 191.00 (*0-608-06759-8*, 206695600009) Bks Demand.

— Natural Plant Hydrocolloids: A Collection of Papers Comprising the Symposium of Natural Plant Hydrocolloids, Presented Before the Divisions of Colloid Chemistry & Agricultural & Food Chemistry at the 122nd Meeting of the American Chemical Society, Atlantic City, NJ, September 1952. LC 55-367. (Advances in Chemistry Ser.: Vol. 11). (Illus.). 107p. 1954. reprint ed. pap. 33.20 (*0-608-06908-6*, 206711600009) Bks Demand.

— New Approaches to Pest Control & Eradication: A Symposium Sponsored by the Pesticides Subdivision of the Division of Agricultural & Food Chemistry at the 142nd Meeting. Hall, Stanley A., ed. LC 63-19396. (American Chemical Society Advances in Chemistry Ser.: No. 41). 86p. reprint ed. pap. 30.00 (*0-608-30177-9*, 201953000013) Bks Demand.

— Nonmilitary Defense: Chemical & Biological Defenses in Perspective: A Collection of Papers Comprising the Symposium on Nonmilitary Defense, Presented Before the Division of Industrial & Engineering Chemistry, in Participation with the Special Board Committee on Civil Defense, at the 137th Meeting of the American Chemical Society, Cleveland, OH, April 1960. LC 60-50429. (Advances in Chemistry Ser.: Vol. 26). (Illus.). 108p. 1960. reprint ed. pap. 33.50 (*0-608-06895-0*, 206710300009) Bks Demand.

— Ordered Fluids & Liquid Crystals: A Symposium Sponsored by the Division of Colloid & Surface Chemistry at the 150th Meeting of the American Chemical Society, Atlantic City, NJ, September 14-15, 1965. LC 67-19831. (Advances in Chemistry Ser.: No. 63). (Illus.). 342p. 1967. reprint ed. pap. 106.10 (*0-608-06797-0*, 206699400009) Bks Demand.

— Organic Pesticides in the Environment: A Symposium Co-Sponsored by the Division of Water, Air, & Waste Chemistry & the Pesticide Subdivision of the Division of Agricultural & Food Chemistry at the 150th Meeting of the American Chemical Society, Atlantic City, NJ, Sept. 13-15, 1965. LC 66-30613. (Advances in Chemistry Ser.: No. 60). (Illus.). 319p. 1966. reprint ed. pap. 98.90 (*0-608-06799-7*, 206699600009) Bks Demand.

— Patents for Chemical Inventions: Symposia Sponsored by the Division of Chemical Literature & the Division of Industrial & Engineering Chemistry, at the 145th Meeting of the American Chemical Society, New York, NY, September 9 & 13, 1963. LC 64-24274. (Advances in Chemistry Ser.: Vol. 46). 125p. 1964. reprint ed. pap. 38.80 (*0-608-06922-1*, 206713000009) Bks Demand.

— Pesticidal Formulations Research: Physical & Colloidal Chemical Aspects: A Symposium Co-Sponsored by the Division of Agricultural & Food Chemistry & the Division of Colloid & Surface Chemistry at the 153rd National Meeting, Miami Beach, FL, April 13-14, 1967. LC 74-81252. (Advances in Chemistry Ser.: No. 86). (Illus.). 222p. 1969. reprint ed. pap. 68.90 (*0-608-06817-9*, 206701400009) Bks Demand.

— Pesticides Identification at the Residue Level: A Symposium Sponsored by the Division of Pesticide Chemistry of the American Chemical Society at the Joint Conference of the Chemical Society of Canada & the American Chemical Society at Toronto, Ontario Canada, May 26-27, 1970 - Francis J. Biros, Symposium Chairman. LC 70-164408. (Advances in Chemistry Ser.: No. 104). (Illus.). 192p. 1971. reprint ed. pap. 59.60 (*0-608-06769-5*, 206696600009) Bks Demand.

— Pesticides in Tropical Agriculture: A Collection of Papers Comprising the Symposium on Pesticides in Tropical Agriculture, Presented Before the Division of Agricultural & Food Chemistry at the 126th Meeting of the American Chemical Society, New York, NY, September 1954. LC 55-4179. (Advances in Chemistry Ser.: Vol. 13). (Illus.). 106p. 1955. reprint ed. pap. 32.90 (*0-608-06905-1*, 206711300009) Bks Demand.

— Phytochemicals for Pest Control, Vol. 658. Hedin, Paul A. et al, eds. LC 96-52457. (Symposium Ser.: No. 658). (Illus.). 356p. 1997. text 115.00 (*0-8412-3488-4*, Pub. by Am Chemical) OUP.

— Plasticization & Plasticizer Processes: A Symposium Sponsored by the Division of Industrial & Engineering Chemistry at the 147th Meeting of the American Chemical Society, Philadelphia, PA, April 6-7, 1964. LC 65-23931. (Advances in Chemistry Ser.: Vol. 48). (Illus.). 210p. 1965. reprint ed. pap. 65.10 (*0-608-06920-5*, 206712800009) Bks Demand.

— Platium Group Metals & Compounds: A Symposium Sponsored by the Division of Inorganic Chemistry at the 158th Meeting of the American Chemical Society, New York, NY, September 8-9, 1969. LC 76-152755. (Advances in Chemistry Ser.: No. 98). (Illus.). 173p. 1971. reprint ed. pap. 53.70 (*0-608-06758-X*, 206695500009) Bks Demand.

— Polymeric Foams: Science & Technology. Khemani, Kishan C., ed. LC 97-8468. (ACS Symposium Ser.: No. 669). (Illus.). 236p. 1997. text 105.00 (*0-8412-3516-3*, Pub. by Am Chemical) OUP.

— Process Measurement & Control. 280p. 1989. 455.00 incl. audio (*0-685-25943-9*, A8); student ed. 42.00 (*0-685-25944-7*) Am Chemical.

— Quimica en la Sociedad. (SPA.). 592p. (C). 1997. pap. text 32.00 (*0-201-62581-4*) Addison-Wesley.

— Radionuclides in the Environment: A Symposium Sponsored by the Division of Nuclear Chemistry & Technology at the 155th Meeting of the American Chemical Society, San Francisco, CA, April 1-3, 1968 - E. C. Freiling, Symposium Chairman. LC 74-112987. (Advances in Chemistry Ser.: No. 93). (Illus.). 541p. 1970. reprint ed. pap. 167.80 (*0-608-06762-8*, 206695900009) Bks Demand.

— Reagent Chemicals: American Chemical Society Specifications, Official from April 1, 1993. 8th ed. LC 92-44959. (Illus.). 820p. 1993. text 157.95 (*0-8412-2502-8*, Pub. by Am Chemical) OUP.

***American Chemical Society Staff.** Reagent Chemicals: American Chemical Society Specifications, Official from January 1, 2000. 9th ed. LC 99-38870. (An American Chemical Society Publication). (Illus.). 768p. 1999. 165.00 (*0-8412-3671-2*) OUP.

American Chemical Society Staff. Refining Petroleum for Chemicals: A Symposium Co-Sponsored by the Division of Petroleum Chemistry & the Division of Industrial & Engineering Chemistry at the 158th Meeting of the American Chemical Society, New York, NY, September 10-12, 1969 - L. J. Spillane & H. P. Leftin, Symposium Co-Chairmen. LC 76-140417. (Advances in Chemistry Ser.: No. 97). (Illus.). 303p. 1970. reprint ed. pap. 94.00 (*0-608-06766-0*, 206696300009) Bks Demand.

— Regenerative EMF Cells: A Symposium Co-Sponsored by the Division of Industrial & Engineering Chemistry & the Division of Fuel Chemistry at the 149th Meeting of the American Chemical Society, Detroit, MI, April 8-9, 1965. LC 67-25567. (Advances in Chemistry Ser.: No. 64). (Illus.). 317p. 1967. reprint ed. pap. 98.30 (*0-608-06800-4*, 206699700009) Bks Demand.

— Saline Water Conversion: A Collection of Papers Comprising the Symposium on Saline Water Conversion, Presented Before the Division of Water & Waste Chemistry at the 137th National Meeting of the American Chemical Society, Cleveland, Ohio, April, 1960. LC 60-53480. (Advances in Chemistry Ser.: Vol. 27). (Illus.). reprint ed. pap. 78.20 (*0-608-07564-7*, 2066223) Bks Demand.

— Saline Water Conversion II: Based on Symposia Sponsored by the Division of Water & Waste Chemistry at the 139th & 141st Meetings of the American Chemical Society, March 27, 1961 & March 27-8, 1962. LC 60-53480. (Advances in Chemistry Ser.: No. 38). (Illus.). 210p. reprint ed. pap. 65.10 (*0-608-06894-2*, 206710200002) Bks Demand.

***American Chemical Society Staff.** Science in a Technical World: Carbonated Beverages. LC 99-48024. 2000. pap. text 15.95 (*0-7167-3788-4*) W H Freeman.

— Science in a Technical World: Drug Discovery. 2001. pap. text 15.95 (*0-7167-4044-3*) W H Freeman.

— Science in a Technical World: Food Safety. 2001. pap. text 15.95 (*0-7167-4041-9*) W H Freeman.

— Science in a Technical World: Plant & Tissue Culture. LC 99-57584. 2000. pap. text. write for info. (*0-7167-3786-8*) W H Freeman.

— Science in a Technical World: Pulp & Paper. LC 99-57583. 2000. pap. text. write for info. (*0-7167-3787-6*) W H Freeman.

— Science in the Technical World: Criminal Forensics. 2001. pap. text 15.95 (*0-7167-4030-3*) W H Freeman.

— Science in the Technical World: Medical Technology. 2001. pap. text 15.95 (*0-7167-4033-8*) W H Freeman.

— Science in the Technical World: Petroleum Refine. 2001. pap. text 15.95 (*0-7167-4038-9*) W H Freeman.

— Science Technology World: Paint. 2000. pap. text. write for info. (*0-7167-3783-3*) W H Freeman.

— Science Technology World: Polymers. LC 99-57141. 2000. pap. text 15.95 (*0-7167-3784-1*) W H Freeman.

— Science Technology World: Water Treatment. LC 99-87174. 2000. pap. text. write for info. (*0-7167-3785-X*) W H Freeman.

American Chemical Society Staff. Searching the Chemical Literature: A Collection of the Papers Presented at the Symposium on Searching the Chemical Literature Held by the Division of Chemical Literature of the American Chemical Society at the 117th National Meeting in Detroit, April 16 to 21, 1950. LC 51-3553. (Advances in Chemistry Ser.: Vol. 4). (Illus.). 188p. reprint ed. pap. 58.30 (*0-608-06900-0*, 206710800009) Bks Demand.

— Searching the Chemical Literature: Based on Papers Presented by the Division of Chemical Literature & the Division of Chemical Education of the American Chemical Society at National Meetings from 1947 to 1956. rev. ed. LC 61-11330. (Advances in Chemistry Ser.: No. 30). (Illus.). 348p. reprint ed. pap. 107.90 (*0-608-06893-4*, 206710100009) Bks Demand.

— Solid Surfaces & the Gas-Solid Interface: Papers

A

Presented at the Kendall Award Symposium Honoring Stephen Brunauer, Division of Colloid & Surface Chemistry, 139th Meeting of the American Chemical Society, St. Louis, MO, March 1961. LC 61-18397. (Advances in Chemistry Ser.: Vol. 33). (Illus.). 389p. reprint ed. pap. 120.60 (*0-608-06928-0*, 206713600009) Bks Demand.

— Spices: Flavor Chemistry & Antioxidant Properties, Vol. 660. Risch, Sara J. & Ho, Chi-Tang, eds. LC 96-52322. (Symposium Ser.: No. 660). (Illus.). 264p. 1997. text 105.00 (*0-8412-3495-7*, Pub. by Am Chemical) OUP.

— Stabilization of Polymers & Stabilizer Processes: A Symposium Sponsored by the Division of Industrial & Engineering Chemistry at the 153rd Meeting of the American Chemical Society, Miami Beach, FL, April 11-13, 1967. LC 68-59459. (Advances in Chemistry Ser.: No. 85). (Illus.). 350p. reprint ed. pap. 108.50 (*0-608-06809-8*, 206700600009) Bks Demand.

American Chemical Society Staff. Substructure Searching of Computer-Readable Cas 8ci Chemical Nomenclature Files: Based on Nomenclature Used in the 8th Collective Index to Chemical Abstracts, 1967-1971. LC 73-84537. 88p. 1973. write for info. (*0-8412-0182-X*) Am Chemical.

American Chemical Society Staff. Sulfur Research Trends: The Third Annual Mardi Gras Symposium Sponsored by the Louisiana Section of the American Chemical Society at Loyola University, New Orleans, LA, February 18-19, 1971 - David J. Miller, T. K. Wiewiorowski, Symposium Chairmen. LC 72-77163. (Advances in Chemistry Ser.: No. 110). (Illus.). 241p. reprint ed. pap. 74.80 (*0-608-06771-7*, 206696800009) Bks Demand.

— Technology for Waterborne Coatings. Glass, J. Edward, ed. LC 97-5741. (Symposium Ser.: No. 663). (Illus.). 290p. 1997. text 115.00 (*0-8412-3501-5*, Pub. by Am Chemical) OUP.

— Thermodynamic Properties of the Elements. Industrial & Engineering Chemistry Staff, ed. LC QD0466.T45. (Advances in Chemistry Ser.: No. 18). 240p. 1956. reprint ed. pap. 74.40 (*0-608-03267-0*, 206378600007) Bks Demand.

— Trace Inorganics in Water: A Symposium Sponsored by the Division of Water, Air & Waste Chemistry at the 153rd Meeting of the American Chemical Society, Miami Beach, FL, April 10-13, 1967. LC 68-25996. (Advances in Chemistry Ser.: No. 73). (Illus.). 406p. 1968. reprint ed. pap. 125.90 (*0-608-06805-5*, 206700200009) Bks Demand.

— Training of Literature Chemists: A Collection of Papers Comprising the Symposium on Training of Literature Chemists, Presented Before the Division of Chemical Education & the Division of Chemical Literature at the 127th National Meeting of the American Chemical Society, Cincinnati, OH, March 1955. LC 56-4451. (Advances in Chemistry Ser.: Vol. 17). (Illus.). 48p. 1956. reprint ed. pap. 30.00 (*0-608-06906-X*, 206711400009) Bks Demand.

American Chemical Society Staff. Vocabulary Guide for Keyword Subject Index. LC 75-157653. 1971. write for info. (*0-8412-0116-1*) Am Chemical.

American Chemical Society Staff. Werner Centennial: A Symposium Co-Sponsored by the Division of Inorganic Chemistry & the Division of the History of Chemistry at the 152nd Meeting of the American Chemical Society, New York, NY, Sept. 12-16, 1966. LC 67-17811. (Advances in Chemistry Ser.: No. 62). (Illus.). 671p. 1967. reprint ed. pap. 200.00 (*0-608-06819-5*, 206701600009) Bks Demand.

— Wine: Nutritional & Therapeutic Benefits. Watkins, Tom R., ed. LC 96-52456. (Symposium Ser.: Vol. 661). (Illus.). 296p. 1997. text 95.00 (*0-8412-3497-3*, Pub. by Am Chemical) OUP.

American Chemical Society Staff, et al. Toughened Plastics II: Novel Approaches in Science & Engineering. Riew, C. Keith & Kinloch, Anthony J., eds. LC 96-38478. (Advances in Chemistry Ser.: Vol. 252). 400p. 1996. text 150.00 (*0-8412-3151-6*) OUP.

American Chemical Society Staff, jt. auth. see Fitzgerald, John J.

American Chemical Society Staff, jt. auth. see Fourkas, John T.

American Chemical Society Staff, jt. auth. see Voress, Louise.

American Chemical Society Symposium on Chemical &. Protein Nutritional Quality of Foods & Feeds: Proceedings, 2 pts., Pt. 1. Friedman, Mendel, ed. LC 74-335459. (Nutrition & Clinical Nutrition Ser.: No. 1). (Illus.). 648p. reprint ed. pap. 200.00 (*0-7837-0637-5*, 204098100001) Bks Demand.

— Protein Nutritional Quality of Foods & Feeds: Proceedings, 2 pts., Pt. 2. Friedman, Mendel, ed. LC 74-33549. (Nutrition & Clinical Nutrition Ser.: No. 1). (Illus.). 696p. reprint ed. pap. 200.00 (*0-7837-0638-3*, 204098100002) Bks Demand.

American Chemical Society Symposium on Gel Permeat. Gel Permeation Chromatography: Proceedings. Altgelt, Klaus H. & Segal, Leon, eds. LC 78-154609. 668p. reprint ed. pap. 200.00 (*0-608-16440-2*, 202675400052) Bks Demand.

American Chemical Society Symposium on Permselecti. Permselective Membranes: Selected Papers. Rogers, C. E., ed. LC 77-163051. (Illus.). 222p. reprint ed. pap. 68.90 (*0-7837-0900-5*, 204120500019) Bks Demand.

American Chemical Society Symposium on Reflectance. Modern Aspects of Reflectance Spectroscopy: Proceedings. Wendlandt, Wesley W., ed. LC 68-19188. (Illus.). 264p. 1968. reprint ed. pap. 81.90 (*0-608-05478-X*, 206594700006) Bks Demand.

American Chemical Society Task Force on Laboratory. Laboratory Waste Management: A Guidebook. LC 93-45546. 250p. 1994. text 36.95 (*0-8412-2735-7*, Pub. by Am Chemical); pap. text 28.00 (*0-8412-2849-3*, Pub. by Am Chemical) OUP.

***American Chemistry Society.** Science in the Technical World: Semiconductor. 2001. pap. text 15.95 (*0-7167-4036-2*) W H Freeman.

American Civil Liberties Union Staff, jt. auth. see Human Rights Watch Staff.

American Civil Liberties Union Staff, jt. auth. see Primer, Ben.

American Classical League Committee on Writing Acr, jt. auth. see Sebesta, Judith L.

American Club Staff. Masterpiece Recipes of the American Club. (Illus.). 208p. 1993. write for info. (*0-9635933-1-5*); pap. 24.95 (*0-9635933-0-7*) Kohler Co.

American Coaching Effectiveness Program Staff. ACEP Level 1: Self-Study Manual. 1987. pap. text 17.00 (*0-87322-095-1*, ACEP5700) Human Kinetics.

— Rookie Coaches Baseball Guide. LC 94-27660. (Illus.). 80p. reprint ed. pap. 30.00 (*0-608-20813-2*, 207191200003) Bks Demand.

— Rookie Coaches Basketball Guide. LC 90-40062. (Illus.). 80p. reprint ed. pap. 30.00 (*0-608-20811-6*, 207191000003) Bks Demand.

— Rookie Coaches Football Guide. LC 94-27663. (Illus.). 80p. reprint ed. pap. 30.00 (*0-608-20815-9*, 2071914) Bks Demand.

— Rookie Coaches Ski Racing Guide. LC 93-11877. (Illus.). 73p. 1994. reprint ed. pap. 30.00 (*0-608-04280-3*, 206505900012) Bks Demand.

— Rookie Coaches Softball Guide. LC 91-42386. (Illus.). 80p. reprint ed. pap. 30.00 (*0-608-20814-0*, 207191300003) Bks Demand.

— Rookie Coaches Tennis Guide. LC 90-22335. (Illus.). 80p. (Orig.). reprint ed. pap. 30.00 (*0-608-20812-4*, 207191100003) Bks Demand.

— Rookie Coaches Volleyball Guide. LC 94-31696. (Illus.). 80p. reprint ed. pap. 30.00 (*0-608-20816-7*, 207191500003) Bks Demand.

American Coaching Effectiveness Program Staff & U. S. A. Wrestling Staff. Rookie Coaches Wrestling Guide. LC 91-20203. 72p. 1991. pap. 9.95 (*0-88011-421-5*, ACEP0402) Human Kinetics.

American College Faculty Staff. The IRS Restructuring & Reform Act of 1998 (Supplement to Financial Planning 2000) 20p. (C). 1998. pap. text. write for info. (*1-57996-009-X*) Amer College.

— Taxpayer Relief Act of 1997, The American College's Guide for Financial Services Professionals. LC 97-76836. 61p. (C). 1997. pap. text 15.00 (*1-57996-000-6*) Amer College.

***American College Faculty Staff, ed.** Readings in Wealth Accumulation Planning. 10th ed. LC 99-72568. 530p. 1999. text 46.00 (*1-57996-014-6*) Amer College.

American College of Cardiology Staff. ACCSAP - Adult Clinical Cardiology Self Assessment Program. Lewis, Richard P., ed. LC 93-70707. (Illus.). 300p. 1993. text 395.00 (*1-882764-01-3*) Am Coll Cardiology.

— Procedure Coding for Cardiologists: The American College of Cardiology Guide to CPT-4. 100p. 1992. pap. text 55.00 (*1-882764-00-5*) Am Coll Cardiology.

American College of Chest Physicians Staff, ed. see Irwin, R. S., et al.

American College of Chest Physicians Staff, ed. see Prakash.

American College of Chest Physicians Staff, ed. see Prakash, et al.

American College of Chest Physicians Staff, ed. see Weg, John G., et al.

American College of Emergency Physicians, Ohio Chapter Staff, ed. see Dietrich, Ann Marie & Shaner, Steven.

American College of Emergency Physicians Staff. Continuous Quality Improvement in EMS. 1992. 80.00 (*0-07-000210-X*) McGraw.

— Emergency Medicine Risk Management: A Comprehensive Review. 1991. 132.00 (*0-07-000214-2*) McGraw.

— The EMT. (Illus.). 688p. (gr. 13). 1999. text 38.95 (*0-8151-0100-7*, 24559) Mosby Inc.

— Managing the Emergency Department: A Team Approach. 1992. 120.00 (*0-07-000209-6*) McGraw.

— Paramedic. LC 97-21620. (Illus.). 896p. (gr. 13). 1997. text 49.95 (*0-8016-6361-X*, 06361) Mosby Inc.

American College of Emergency Physicians Staff. Paramedic Field Care: A Complaint-Based Approach. Pons, Peter T. & Cason, Debra, eds. 1997. wbk. ed. write for info. (*0-8016-6425-X*) Mosby Inc.

— Paramedic Field Care: A Complaint Based Approach. Pons, Peter T. & Cason, Debra, eds. 1998. teacher ed. write for info. (*0-8151-0088-4*) Mosby Inc.

American College of Emergency Physicians Staff. Principles of EMS Systems. 2nd ed. 1994. 95.00 (*0-07-000213-4*) McGraw.

— Vital Link. 2nd ed. 99p. (gr. 13). 1994. 65.00 (*0-8151-0064-7*) Mosby Inc.

— Vital Link Vol. 2: With CEH Packet, Vol. 2. 1994. suppl. ed. 65.00 (*0-07-000212-6*) McGraw.

— Vital Link I. (gr. 13). 1994. 65.00 (*0-8151-0063-9*) Mosby Inc.

***American College of Emergency Physicians Staff & Krohmer, Jon.** The EMT: A Case-Based Approach. 352p. 1998. teacher ed. write for info. (*0-8151-0101-5*) Mosby Inc.

American College of Emergency Physicians Staff, jt. auth. see American Academy of Pediatrics Staff.

American College of Foot Surgeons Staff. Complications in Foot Surgery: Prevention & Management. LC 75-28130. 253p. reprint ed. pap. 78.50 (*0-608-14443-6*, 205186700012) Bks Demand.

American College of Legal Medicine. Legal Medicine. 4th ed. LC 97-43320. (Illus.). 688p. (C). (gr. 13). 1998. text 145.00 (*0-8151-3669-2*, 31390) Mosby Inc.

American College of Mechano-Therapy Staff. Textbook of Chiropractic. 96p. 1996. reprint ed. spiral bd. 12.00 (*0-7873-0032-2*) Hlth Research.

American College of Mechano Therapy Staff. Textbook of Osteopathy. 96p. 1996. reprint ed. pap. 12.00 (*0-7873-1155-3*) Hlth Research.

American College of Nurse-Midwives Staff & Jacobs, Sandra. Having Your Baby with a Nurse-Midwife: Everything You Need to Know to Make an Informed Decision. LC 92-36373. 304p. 1993. pap. 10.45 (*1-56282-860-6*, Pub. by Hyperion) Time Warner.

American College of Obstetricians & Gynecologists. Litigation Assistant: A Guide for the Defendant Physician. LC 86-25856. 1986. 12.00 (*0-915473-07-0*) Am Coll Obstetric.

— Litigation Assistant: A Guide for the Defendant Physician. 2nd ed. LC 98-14138. 1998. 19.00 (*0-915473-45-3*) Am Coll Obstetric.

— Planning for Pregnancy, Birth, & Beyond. LC 95-6754. Orig. Title: ACOG Guide to Planning for Pregnancy, Birth, & Beyond. 323p. 1995. 12.95 (*0-915473-27-5*) Am Coll Obstetric.

— Planning for Pregnancy, Birth, & Beyond. rev. ed. Orig. Title: ACOG Guide to Planning for Pregnancy, Birth, & Beyond. 1997. mass mkt. 6.99 (*0-451-19175-7*, Sig) NAL.

— Precis: An Update in Obstetrics & Gynecology. 2nd ed. LC 99-15357. 1999. write for info. (*0-915473-51-8*) Am Coll Obstetric.

— Precis, Gynecology: An Update in Obstetrics & Gynecology. LC 97-52566. 1998. pap. write for info. (*0-915473-41-0*) American College of Emergency Physicians.

— Precis, Obstetrics: An Update in Obstetrics & Gynecology. LC 97-52567. 1998. pap. write for info. (*0-915473-40-2*) American College of Emergency Physicians.

— Precis, Oncology: An Update in Obstetrics & Gynceology. LC 97-51748. 1998. pap. write for info. (*0-915473-42-9*, A2841) American College of Emergency Physicians.

— Precis, Primary & Preventive Care: An Update in Obstetrics & Gynecology. Dunn, Leo J., ed. LC 97-52069. 230p. 1998. pap. 45.00 (*0-915473-39-9*) American College of Emergency Physicians.

— Precis, Reproductive Endocrinology: An Update in Obstetrics & Gynecology. LC 97-51260. 1998. 39.00 (*0-915473-43-7*) Am Coll Obstetric.

American College of Obstetricians & Gynecologists, jt. auth. see American Academy of Pediatrics Staff.

American College of Obstetricians & Gynecologists Staff. Quality Assessment & Improvement in Obstetrics & Gynecology. LC 94-1230. 113p. 1994. 40.00 (*0-915473-19-4*) Am Coll Obstetric.

***American College of Obstetricians and Gynecologists.** Encyclopedia of Women's Health & Wellness. LC 00-29971. 2000. pap. write for info. (*0-915473-60-7*) Am Coll Obstetric.

— Planning for Pregnancy, Birth, & Beyond. 3rd ed. LC 99-58049. 2000. write for info. (*0-915473-56-9*) Am Coll Obstetric.

American College of Obstetrics & Gynecology. Precis: An Update in Obstetrics & Gynecology. 1978. text 27.50 (*0-07-001134-6*) McGraw.

American College of Physicians Staff & Kitchens, Lloyd W. American College of Physicians Ethics Manual. 4th ed. LC 98-15901. 1998. 10.00 (*0-943126-67-3*) Amer Coll Phys.

American College of Physicians Task Force on Adult. Guide for Adult Immunization. 3rd ed. LC 94-3075. 240p. 1994. pap. 24.00 (*0-943126-23-1*) Amer Coll Phys.

American College of Preventive Medicine Staff, ed. see Hasselbring, Bobbie, et al.

American College of Radiology Staff, jt. auth. see Dunnick, N. Reed.

American College of Rheumatology, Glossary Committ. Dictionary of the Rheumatic Diseases: Health Status Measurement, Vol. III. 80p. (C). 1988. pap. text. write for info. (*0-911059-03-2*) Cntct Assocs Intl.

American College of Sports Medicine Educational Ma. ACSM Clinical Track Certification Study Guide, 1997. 48p. 1997. pap., student ed. 13.95 (*0-683-30354-6*) Lppncott W & W.

— ACSM Clinical Track Certification Study Guide, 1998. LC 98-145935. iii, 48 p. 1998. pap. 13.95 (*0-683-30600-6*) Lppncott W & W.

— Health & Fitness Study Guide, 1997. 59p. 1997. student ed. 13.95 (*0-683-30353-8*) Lppncott W & W.

American College of Sports Medicine Health, Fitnes. ACSM Health & Fitness Track Certification Study Guide, 1998. 59p. 1998. pap. 13.95 (*0-683-30601-4*) Lppncott W & W.

American College of Sports Medicine Staff. ACSM Clinical Track Certification Study Guide, 2000. 48p. pap. text 14.95 (*0-7817-2526-7*) Lppncott W & W.

— ACSM Health/Fitness Track Certification Study Guide, 2000. 80p. pap. text 14.95 (*0-7817-2527-5*) Lppncott W & W.

— ACSM 2000 Clinical Track Certification Study Kit. pap. text. write for info. (*0-7817-2816-9*) Lppncott W & W.

— ACSM 2000 Health/Fitness Track Certification Study Kit. pap. text. write for info. (*0-7817-2815-0*) Lppncott W & W.

American College of Sports Medicine Staff. ACSM's Exercise Management for Persons with Chronic Diseases & Disabilities. Durstine, J. Larry, ed. LC 96-48817. 280p. 1997. text 42.00 (*0-87322-798-0*, BACS0798) Human Kinetics.

American College of Sports Medicine Staff. ACSM's Guidelines for Clinical Exercise Physiology: Exercise Testing & Prescription for Special Populations. 400p. pap. text. write for info. (*0-7817-2348-5*) Lppncott W & W.

— ACSM's Guidelines for Exercise Testing & Prescription. 6th ed. 392p. pap. text 29.95 (*0-683-30355-4*) Lppncott W & W.

American College of Sports Medicine Staff. ACSM's Health/Fitness Facility Standards & Guidelines. 2nd rev. ed. Tharrett, Stephen J. & Peterson, James A., eds. LC 97-10276. (Illus.). 224p. 1997. text 39.00 (*0-87322-957-6*, BACS0957) Am Coll Sports Med.

American College of Sports Medicine Staff. ACSM's Resources for Clinical Exercise Physiology for Special Populations. 650p. pap. text. write for info. (*0-7817-2347-7*) Lppncott W & W.

American College of Sports Medicine Staff. American College of Sports Medicine 40th Anniversary Lectures. anniversary limited ed. LC 94-71614. (Illus.). 120p. (Orig.). 1994. pap. 10.00 (*1-885377-00-2*) Am Coll Sports Med.

— Exercise & Sport Sciences Reviews (ESSR), Vol. 26. annuals LC 98-23508. 1998. 60.00 (*0-683-18346-X*) Lppncott W & W.

American College of Sports Medicine Staff, ed. ACSM Clinical Track Certification 1999. 48p. pap. text, student ed. 14.95 (*0-683-30799-1*) Lppncott W & W.

— Acsm Health & Fitness Track Certification 1999. 72p. pap. text, student ed. 14.95 (*0-683-30798-3*) Lppncott W & W.

American College of Sports Medicine Staff, et al. ACSM's Resource Manual for Guidelines for Exercise Testing & Prescription. 3rd ed. LC 97-50181. (Illus.). 608p. 1998. 49.95 (*0-683-00026-8*) Lppncott W & W.

American College of Sports Medicine Staff, jt. auth. see Mahler, Donald A.

American College of Surgeons, Committee on the Imp. Resource for Optimal Care of the Injured Patient, 1993. rev. ed. LC 93-11972. (Illus.). 1993. pap. text 12.00 (*1-880696-03-7*) Am Coll Surgeons.

American College of Surgeons Committee on Trauma S. Advanced Trauma Life Support Course. rev. ed. (Illus.). 1997. student ed. 50.00 (*1-880696-10-X*) Am Coll Surgeons.

— Advanced Trauma Life Support Course. rev. ed. (Illus.). 1998. teacher ed. 50.00 (*1-880696-09-6*) Am Coll Surgeons.

American College of Surgeons Staff. Advanced Trauma Life Support Course. (Illus.). (Orig.). 1994. student ed. write for info. (*1-880696-06-1*) Am Coll Surgeons.

— Advanced Trauma Life Support Course. (SPA., Illus.). (Orig.). 1994. student ed. write for info. (*1-880696-05-3*) Am Coll Surgeons.

— A List of Fellows, 1913. ix, 187p. reprint ed. 39.00 (*0-932051-29-4*) Rprt Serv.

American College of Surgeons Staff, jt. auth. see Nora, Paul F.

American College of Veterinary Ophthalmologists, G. Ocular Disorders Proven or Suspected to Be Hereditary in Dogs. (Illus.). 296p. (Orig.). 1992. pap. text 10.00 (*0-9635163-0-2*) Canine Eye Reg.

American College Staff. Guidelines in Assessing Risk Tolerance. 40p. (C). 1994. pap. text 40.00 (*0-943590-56-6*) Amer College.

— Personal Financial Fact Finding. LC 92-70340. 100p. (Orig.). (C). 1992. pap. text 42.95 (*0-943590-36-1*) Amer College.

— Readings & Applications in Ethics for Field Managers. LC 94-74178. 75p. (Orig.). 1995. pap. text 9.95 (*0-943590-65-5*) Amer College.

American College Testing Program Staff. Study Power Leader's Guide. (Study Power Ser.). 99p. (Orig.). (YA). (gr. 7 up). 1987. teacher ed. 4.00 (*0-937734-63-2*) ACT.

— Study Power, Managing Time & Environment. 30p. (Orig.). (YA). (gr. 7 up). 1987. student ed. 1.00 (*0-937734-65-9*) ACT.

— Study Power, Preparing for Tests. 14p. (Orig.). (YA). (gr. 7 up). 1987. student ed. 1.00 (*0-937734-69-1*) ACT.

— Study Power, Reading Textbooks. 21p. (Orig.). (YA). (gr. 7 up). 1987. student ed. 1.00 (*0-937734-66-7*) ACT.

— Study Power Student Workbook Set. (Orig.). (YA). (gr. 7 up). 1987. student ed. 5.00 (*0-937734-64-0*) ACT.

— Study Power, Taking Class Notes. 22p. (Orig.). (YA). (gr. 7 up). 1987. pap. text, student ed. 1.00 (*0-937734-67-5*) ACT.

— Study Power, Taking Tests. (Study Power Ser.). 13p. (Orig.). (YA). (gr. 7 up). 1987. student ed. 1.00 (*0-937734-70-5*) ACT.

— Study Power, Using Resources. (Study Power Ser.). 14p. (Orig.). (YA). (gr. 7 up). 1987. pap. text, student ed. 1.00 (*0-937734-68-3*) ACT.

American Colortype Co., Staff. Cut & Assemble Paper Dollhouse Furniture. 81st ed. (J). 1981. pap. 5.95 (*0-486-24150-5*) Dover.

American Commitments National Panel Staff. American Pluralism & the College Curriculum: Higher Education in a Diverse Democracy. LC 95-80684. (American Commitments Ser.: Vol. 3). 44p. 1995. pap. 10.00 (*0-911696-65-2*) Assn Am Coll.

— The Drama of Diversity & Democracy Vol. 1: Higher Education & American Commitments. LC 95-80683. (American Commitments Ser.: Vol. 2). (Illus.). 44p. 1995. pap. 10.00 (*0-911696-64-4*) Assn Am Coll.

— Liberal Learning & the Arts of Connection for the New Academy. LC 95-80685. (American Commitments Ser.: Vol. 2). 41p. 1995. pap. 10.00 (*0-911696-66-0*) Assn Am Coll.

***American Compensation Association Staff.** Calculate This! Formula Book. (Guidebook Ser.). 1999. 29.95 (*1-57963-070-7*) Am Compensation.

— Conducting an Audit of Direct Compensation Program, Vol. 48. (Building Blocks Ser.). (Illus.). 1999. pap. 24.95 (*1-57963-068-5*) Am Compensation.

— Conducting an Audit of the International Assignment Management Program, Vol. 49. (Building Blocks Ser.). (Illus.). 1999. pap. 24.95 (*1-57963-069-3*) Am Compensation.
— Glossary of Compensation & Benefit Terms. LC 99-207354. (Illus.). 1999. pap. 24.95 (*1-57963-067-7*) Am Compensation.
— Measuring Team Performance Vol. 47: A Seven Step Guide to Team Success. (Building Blocks Ser.). (Illus.). 1999. pap. 24.95 (*1-57963-063-4*) Am Compensation.
— Out of the Vortex Finding Order in Merger & Acquisition Chaos. (Building Blocks Ser.). (Illus.). 1998. pap. 39.95 (*1-57963-062-6*) Am Compensation.
American Compensation Association Staff. Report on the 1998-1999 Total Salary Increase Budget Survey. (Illus.). 1998. 95.00 (*1-57963-058-8*) Am Compensation.
***American Compensation Association Staff.** Strategic Outsourcing of Benefits Administration Vol. 46: A Framework for Creating Successful Outsourcing Solutions. (Building Blocks Ser.). (Illus.). 1998. pap. 24.95 (*1-57963-060-X*) Am Compensation.
— Understanding & Influencing the Federal Legislative & Regulatory Process: A Guide for Compensation & Benefits Professionals. (Building Blocks Ser.). (Illus.). 1998. pap. 24.95 (*1-57963-061-8*) Am Compensation.
American Compensation Association Staff & American Management Association Staff, contrib. by. Salary Survey Guidebook: Finding & Evaluating Compensation & Benefit Data. (Illus.). 1998. pap. 95.00 (*1-57963-056-1*) Am Compensation.
American Concrete Institute Deflections of Structu. Deflections of Concrete Structures: Proceedings of the American Concrete Institute Symposium, San Francisco, 1974. LC 73-94365. (American Concrete Institute Publication: No. SP-43). (Illus.). 643p. reprint ed. pap. 199.40 (*0-608-18565-5*, 200378600033) Bks Demand.
American Concrete Institute Staff. Abeles Symposium: Fatigue of Concrete. LC 73-92588. (American Concrete Institute Publication: SP-41). (Illus.). 358p. reprint ed. pap. 111.00 (*0-8357-5004-3*, 201334000086) Bks Demand.
— Accelerated Strength Testing. LC 78-58275. (ACI Publication: No. SP-56). (Illus.). 327p. 1978. reprint ed. pap. 101.40 (*0-7837-5221-0*, 204495200005) Bks Demand.
— Analysis of Structural Systems for Torsion. LC 72-96325. (ACI Publication: Vol. SP-35). 446p. reprint ed. pap. 138.30 (*0-8357-5437-5*, 203082500070) Bks Demand.
— Behavior of Concrete under Temperature Extremes. LC 73-85854. (American Concrete Institute Publication: No. SP-39). (Illus.). 214p. reprint ed. pap. 66.40 (*0-8357-7109-1*, 200429600040) Bks Demand.
— Bibliography on Pre-stressed Concrete. 2nd ed. LC TA0440.A4. (American Concrete Institute Bibliography Ser.: No. 1). 106p. reprint ed. pap. 32.90 (*0-8357-3596-6*, 200425400039) Bks Demand.
— Commentary on Building Code Requirements for Reinforced Concrete (ACI 318-63) Report of ACI Committee 318, Standard Building Code. LC 65-6942. (American Concrete Institute Publication: No. SP-10). 100p. reprint ed. pap. 31.00 (*0-608-10916-9*, 200235100012) Bks Demand.
— Concrete Bridge Design: Papers Presented to the First International Symposium on Concrete Bridge Design, Toronto, 1967. LC 68-54701. (American Concrete Institute Publication: SP-23). (Illus.). 831p. reprint ed. pap. 200.00 (*0-608-10955-X*, 200307900018) Bks Demand.
— Concrete Design: United States & European Practices. LC 78-72044. (American Concrete Institute Publication: No. SP-59). (Illus.). 352p. reprint ed. pap. 109.20 (*0-608-18587-6*, 202276200029) Bks Demand.
— Concrete for Nuclear Reactors, 3 vols., 1. LC 72-81007. (American Concrete Institute Publication: No. SP-34). (Illus.). 648p. 1972. reprint ed. pap. 200.00 (*0-608-08150-7*, 201230100082) Bks Demand.
— Concrete for Nuclear Reactors, 3 vols., 2. LC 72-81007. (American Concrete Institute Publication: No. SP-34). (Illus.). 541p. 1972. reprint ed. pap. 167.80 (*0-608-08151-5*, 201230100083) Bks Demand.
— Concrete for Nuclear Reactors, 3 vols., 3. LC 72-81007. (American Concrete Institute Publication: No. SP-34). (Illus.). 569p. 1972. reprint ed. pap. 176.40 (*0-608-08152-3*, 201230100084) Bks Demand.
— Corrosion of Metals in Concrete. LC 75-9405. (ACI Publication: No. SP-49). (Illus.). 142p. reprint ed. pap. 44.10 (*0-7837-5219-9*, 204495000005) Bks Demand.
— Designing for Effects of Creep, Shrinkage, Temperature in Concrete Structures. LC 78-156591. (American Concrete Institute Publication: No. SP-27). (Illus.). 438p. reprint ed. pap. 135.80 (*0-608-18581-7*, 200449200047) Bks Demand.
— Durability of Concrete. LC 74-33723. (ACI Publication: No. SP-47). (Illus.). 391p. reprint ed. pap. 121.30 (*0-608-17927-2*, 202796000057) Bks Demand.
— Earthquake Effects on Reinforced Concrete Structures: U. S. - Japan Research. LC 84-72963. (American Concrete Institute Publication: No. SP-84). (Illus.). 436p. reprint ed. pap. 135.20 (*0-7837-6671-8*, 204628700011) Bks Demand.
— Foundations for Equipment & Machinery. LC 82-83638. (Publication Ser.: No. SP-78). 288p. reprint ed. pap. 89.30 (*0-7837-2182-X*, 204252000004) Bks Demand.
— History of Concrete, Thirty B. C. to 1926 A. D. Annotated. fac. ed. LC 82-204682. (ACI Bibliography Ser.: No. 14). 116p. 1994. pap. 36.00 (*0-7837-7701-9*, 204745800007) Bks Demand.
— Impact of Computers on the Practice of Structural Engineering in Concrete. LC 72-78494. (American Concrete Institute Publication: SP-33). (Illus.). 320p. reprint ed. pap. 99.20 (*0-608-11121-X*, 201230000082) Bks Demand.
— Industrialization in Concrete Building Construction. LC 75-1803. (ACI Publication: No. SP-48). (Illus.). 237p. reprint ed. pap. 73.50 (*0-7837-5218-0*, 204494900005) Bks Demand.
— Models for Concrete Structures. LC 79-103139. (American Concrete Institute Publication: SP-24). (Illus.). 503p. reprint ed. pap. 156.00 (*0-608-10959-2*, 202276000029) Bks Demand.
— Monolithic Refractories. Lankard, David R., ed. LC 82-72101. (ACI Publication: No. SP-74). (Illus.). 162p. reprint ed. pap. 50.30 (*0-7837-5222-9*, 204495400005) Bks Demand.
— Permeability of Concrete. Whiting, David & Walitt, Arthur, eds. LC 88-71000. (ACI Publication: No. SP-108). (Illus.). 231p. reprint ed. pap. 71.70 (*0-7837-5223-7*, 204495500005) Bks Demand.
— Polymers in Concrete. LC 73-86176. (American Concrete Institute Publication: No. SP-40). (Illus.). 368p. reprint ed. pap. 114.10 (*0-608-18574-4*, 200429400040) Bks Demand.
— Polymers in Concrete: International Symposium. LC 78-73077. (American Concrete Institute Publication: SP-58). 426p. reprint ed. pap. 132.10 (*0-608-13002-8*, 202508200042) Bks Demand.
— Proportioning Concrete Mixes. LC 74-18167. (ACI Publication: No. SP-46). (Illus.). 519p. reprint ed. pap. 160.90 (*0-7837-5217-2*, 204494800005) Bks Demand.
— Realism in the Application of ACI Standard 214-65. LC 73-75845. (Publication Ser.: No. SP-37). 223p. reprint ed. pap. 69.20 (*0-7837-2181-1*, 204251900004) Bks Demand.
— Reinforced Concrete Columns. LC 75-8454. (American Concrete Institute Publication: SP-50). (Illus.). 320p. reprint ed. pap. 99.20 (*0-608-10960-6*, 202276100029) Bks Demand.
— Reinforced Concrete Design Handbook: Working Stress Method in Accordance with ACI 318-63. 3rd ed. LC 65-16807. (American Concrete Institute Publication: Vol. SP-3). 271p. 1965. reprint ed. pap. 84.10 (*0-608-02421-X*, 206306400004) Bks Demand.
— Reinforced Concrete Structures Subjected to Wind & Earthquake Forces. LC 80-66852. (American Concrete Institute Publication: No. SP-63). (Illus.). 632p. reprint ed. pap. 196.00 (*0-7837-6670-X*, 204628600011) Bks Demand.
— Response of Multistory Concrete Structures to Lateral Forces. LC 72-93775. (American Concrete Institute Publication: SP-36). (Illus.). 320p. reprint ed. pap. 99.20 (*0-608-11570-3*, 200235200012) Bks Demand.
— Roadways & Airport Pavements. LC 75-10374. (American Concrete Institute Publication: SP-51). (Illus.). 291p. reprint ed. pap. 90.30 (*0-608-10949-5*, 201759300007) Bks Demand.
— Shear in Reinforced Concrete, 1. LC 73-94112. (American Concrete Institute Publication: SP-42). (Illus.). 433p. 1974. reprint ed. pap. 134.30 (*0-608-08374-7*, 200429500040) Bks Demand.
— Shear in Reinforced Concrete, 2. LC 73-94112. (American Concrete Institute Publication: SP-42). (Illus.). 524p. 1974. reprint ed. pap. 162.50 (*0-608-18595-7*, 200429500041) Bks Demand.
— Torsion in Concrete, 1784-1974: Annotated - Prepared by ACI Committee 438, Torsion; E. L. Kemp, Chairman. LC 78-103744. (ACI Bibliography Ser.: No. 12). 150p. reprint ed. pap. 46.50 (*0-7837-5213-X*, 204494400005) Bks Demand.
American Concrete Institute Staff & American Society of Civil Engineers Staff. Building Code Requirements for Masonry Structures (ACI 530-92 - ASCE 5-92 - TMS 402-92), Specifications for Masonry Structures (ACI 530.1-92 - ASCE 6-92 - TMS 602-92) Commentary on Building Code Requirements for Masonry Structures (ACI 530-92 - ASCE 5-92 - TMS 402-92), Commentary on Specifications for Masonry Structures (ACI 530.1-92 - ASCE 6-92 - TMS 602-92) LC 92-33528. 88p. 1992. 8.00 (*0-87262-928-7*) Am Soc Civil Eng.
— Specifications for Masonry Structures (ACI 530.1- 92 - ASCE 6-92 - TMS 602-92), Detroit, Mich. LC 92-33527. 16p. 1992. 21.00 (*0-87262-929-5*) Am Soc Civil Eng.
American Concrete Institute Staff & Jenny, Daniel P. Lightweight Concrete. LC 71-162468. (American Concrete Institute Publication: SP-29). (Illus.). 333p. reprint ed. pap. 103.30 (*0-608-11604-1*, 200308000018) Bks Demand.
American Concrete International Staff. Design of Concrete Beams for Torsion. 100p. 1997. pap. 20.00 (*0-89312-175-4*, EB106D) Portland Cement.
American Conference of Governmental Industrial Hygenists Staff. Ergonomic Interventions to Prevent Musculoskeletal Injuries in Industry. (Illus.). 216p. 1987. lib. bdg. 84.95 (*0-87371-103-3*, L103) Lewis Pubs.
— Exposure Assessment for Epidemiology & Hazard Control. 336p. 1990. lib. bdg. 95.00 (*0-87371-197-1*, L197) Lewis Pubs.
— Hazard Assessment & Control Technology in Semiconductor Manufacturing. (Industrial Hygiene Science Ser.). (Illus.). 322p. 1989. lib. bdg. 89.95 (*0-87371-132-7*, L132) Lewis Pubs.
American Conference on Coal Science (1964: Univers. Coal Science: The American Conference on Coal Science Sponsored by the Pennsylvania State University with the Division of Fuel Chemistry of the American Chemical Society, the Geological Society of America, & the Organic Geochemistry Group of the Geochemical Society, Held at Pennsylvania State University, University Park, PA, June 23-26, 1964. LC 66-25071. (Advances in Chemistry Ser.: Vol. 55). (Illus.). 755p. 1966. reprint ed. pap. 200.00 (*0-608-06916-7*, 206712400009) Bks Demand.
American Conference Staff. Industrial Ventilation - Metric: A Manual of Deconineal Practice. 23rd ed. (Illus.). 512p. 1998. text 69.00 (*1-882417-22-4*, 2092M) Am Conf Govt Indus Hygienist.
— Threshold Limit Values & Biological Exposure Indices, 1998. 184p. 1998. spiral bd. 19.50 (*1-882417-23-2*, 0028) Am Conf Govt Indus Hygienist.
American Conscious, Inc., Staff, ed. see Hill, Anderson C., II.
American Consulting Engineers Council Staff. ACEC Membership Directory, 1990-91. 550p. 1988. 140.00 (*0-318-41580-1*) Am Consul Eng.
***American Correctional Assoc. Staff, ed.** From AIDS to the Internet: Correctional Realities. LC 98-55315. 232p. 1999. pap. 23.95 (*1-56991-110-X*) Am Correctional.
American Correctional Assoc. Staff, ed. State of Corrections: 1998 Conference Proceedings. 250p. 1999. pap. 25.00 (*1-56991-099-5*) Am Correctional.
American Correctional Association. Standards for Adult Correctional Institutions. 3rd ed. 199p. (Orig.). 1990. pap. 43.00 (*0-929310-26-8*, 303R) Am Correctional.
***American Correctional Association.** Supervision: A Handbook of Success. rev. ed. LC 99-177284. 134p. 1998. pap. 17.95 (*1-56991-089-8*) Am Correctional.
American Correctional Association. Working with Manipulative Inmates Correspondence Course, 2 vols., Set. (Orig.). 1992. pap. 60.00 (*0-929310-81-0*, 176) Am Correctional.
— Working with Special Needs Offenders Course, 3 vols. 1992. pap. 70.00 (*0-929310-68-3*, 175) Am Correctional.
American Correctional Association & Commission on Accreditation for Corrections Staff. Standards for Juvenile Community Residential Facilities. 3rd ed. 112p. 1994. pap. 28.00 (*1-56991-004-9*, 338) Am Correctional.
— Standards for Juvenile Day Treatment Programs. 240p. (Orig.). 1993. pap. 28.00 (*0-929310-99-3*, 336) Am Correctional.
— Standards for Juvenile Detention Facilities. 3rd ed. 147p. 1991. pap. 29.00 (*0-929310-52-7*, 334) Am Correctional.
American Correctional Association & Halasz, Ida M. Attitude: Your Key to Success. rev. ed. LC 99-177278. (Illus.). 104p. 1998. pap. 17.95 (*1-56991-084-7*, 145) Am Correctional.
— Diversity: Communicating Effectively. rev. ed. LC 99-177272. (Illus.). 124p. 1998. pap. 17.95 (*1-56991-085-5*, 146) Am Correctional.
American Correctional Association, ed. see Commission on Accreditation for Corrections Staff & Hutton Scott D.
American Correctional Association & Commission on. Certification Standards for Food Service Programs. 79p. 1989. pap. 23.00 (*0-929310-06-3*, 383) Am Correctional.
— Standards for Small Jail Facilities. 89p. (Orig.). 1989. pap. 23.00 (*0-929310-04-7*, 382) Am Correctional.
— Standards for the Administration of Correctional Agencies. 2nd ed. 172p. 1993. pap. text 28.00 (*0-929310-79-9*, 335) Am Correctional.
American Correctional Association Staff. Behavior Management Correspondence Course, Vol. 1. 266p. 1994. pap. 60.00 (*0-929310-82-9*, 160) Am Correctional.
— Causes, Preventive Measures, & Methods of Controlling Riots & Disturbances in Correctional Institutions. 4th rev. ed. (Illus.). 85p. 1995. pap. 24.00 (*0-929310-23-3*, 132) Am Correctional.
— Conflict: Managing It Effectively. rev. ed. LC 99-177283. 98p. 1998. pap. 17.95 (*1-56991-088-X*) Am Correctional.
— Correctional Facility Law Libraries: An A to Z Resource Guide. rev. ed. 146p. 1991. pap. 16.00 (*0-929310-55-1*, 203) Am Correctional.
— Correctional Issues: Community Corrections. LC 96-21018. 131p. 1996. pap. 15.95 (*1-56991-045-6*) Am Correctional.
— Correctional Issues: Juvenile Justice Programs & Trends. LC 96-24874. 100p. 1996. pap. 15.95 (*1-56991-047-2*) Am Correctional.
— Correctional Mid-Management Skills Correspondence Course, 2 vols., Set. Rosetti, Rosalie & Geiman, Diane, eds. (Orig.). 1988. pap. 70.00 (*0-942974-94-8*, 168) Am Correctional.
— Correctional Officer I Correspondence Course, Bks. I-IV. 3rd rev. ed. 572p. 1997. pap. 70.00 (*1-56991-060-X*) Am Correctional.
American Correctional Association Staff. Correctional Officer II Correspondence Course: Includes Final Test, 4 vols. 2nd rev. ed. Geiman, Diane & Flannery, Denise, eds. (Illus.). 1997. pap. 70.00 (*1-56991-061-8*) Am Correctional.
American Correctional Association Staff. Feedback: Giving It, Receiving It. rev. ed. LC 99-177282. 108p. 1998. pap. 17.95 (*1-56991-087-1*) Am Correctional.
— Legal Issues for Correctional Staff Correspondence Course, 2 vols. rev. ed. Capitol Communication Systems, Inc. Staff, ed. & illus. by. LC 96-116620. 321p. 1999. pap. 70.00 (*1-56991-107-X*) Am Correctional.
— Legal Issues for Probation & Parole Officers Correspondence Course, 2 bks., Set. Rosetti, Rosalie & Geiman, Diane, eds. (Illus.). 1988. pap. 70.00 (*0-929310-03-9*, 169) Am Correctional.
— Listening Skills: Are You Hearing the Real Message? rev. ed. LC 99-175542. (Illus.). 96p. 1998. pap. 17.95 (*1-56991-086-3*, 144) Am Correctional.
— Policies & Procedures: Adult Local Detention Facilities. 428p. 1992. pap. 60.00 (*0-929310-71-3*, 325) Am Correctional.
— Policies & Procedures: Juvenile Community Residential Facilities. 145p. (Orig.). 1990. 28.00 (*0-929310-30-6*) Am Correctional.
— Policies & Procedures: Juvenile Detention Facilities. 206p. (Orig.). 1992. pap. text 27.00 (*0-929310-61-6*, 458) Am Correctional.
— Reclaiming Offender Accountability: Intermediate Sanctions for Probation & Parole Violators. Rhine, Edward E., ed. 114p. 1993. pap. 21.00 (*0-929310-59-4*, 499) Am Correctional.
— Record of Staff Visits to Restricted Units. rev. ed. 196p. 1991. pap. 24.95 (*0-929310-50-0*, 431) Am Correctional.
— Report Writing--Self-Instructional Course, Bks. I & II, Incl. Test. rev. ed. 442p. 1999. pap. 70.00 (*1-56991-106-1*) Am Correctional.
— Standards for Correctional Training Academies. 136p. (Orig.). 1993. pap. text 28.00 (*0-929310-94-2*, 324) Am Correctional.
— Suicide Prevention in Custody Course: Correspondence Course, No. 1, plus test. rev. ed. LC 98-219065. 194p. 1998. pap. 45.00 (*1-56991-062-6*, 190, 190T) Am Correctional.
— Supervising Young Offenders Correspondence Course, No. I, II & test. LC 98-219062. (Illus.). 132p. 1998. pap. 70.00 (*1-56991-090-1*, 131) Am Correctional.
— Vital Statistics in Corrections. 100p. 1998. pap. 29.95 (*1-56991-073-1*, 633) Am Correctional.
American Correctional Association Staff, ed. Current Concepts in Correctional Leadership. 40p. 1998. pap. 15.95 (*1-56991-091-X*, 133) Am Correctional.
— 1997-1999 National Juvenile Detention Directory. 258p. 1997. pap. 50.00 (*1-56991-072-3*, 628) Am Correctional.
American Correctional Association Staff & Association of Specialized and Cooperative Library Agencies, American Library Asssociation. Library Standards for Adult Correctional Institutions, 1992. 47p. 1992. 15.00 (*0-8389-7583-6*) ASCLA.
American Correctional Association Staff & Commission on Accreditation for Corrections Staff. Standards for Adult Correctional Boot Camp Programs. 169p. 1995. pap. 30.00 (*1-56991-019-7*) Am Correctional.
— Standards for Adult Parole Authorities. 2nd ed. 53p. 1981. pap. 12.00 (*0-942974-28-X*, 301) Am Correctional.
— Standards for Adult Probation & Parole Field Services. 3rd rev. ed. LC 99-181995. (Illus.). 92p. 1998. pap. 19.95 (*1-56991-094-4*) Am Correctional.
— Standards for Correctional Industries. 26p. 1981. 14.00 (*0-942974-39-5*, 306) Am Correctional.
— Standards for Electronic Monitoring Programs. 178p. 1995. 30.00 (*1-56991-022-7*, 291) Am Correctional.
— Standards for Juvenile Correctional Boot Camp Programs. 155p. 1995. 28.00 (*1-56991-018-9*, 293) Am Correctional.
— Standards for Juvenile Training Schools. 3rd ed. 160p. 1991. pap. 28.00 (*0-929310-44-6*, 307) Am Correctional.
— Standards for Small Juvenile Detention Facilities. 131p. 1991. 28.00 (*0-929310-60-8*, 320) Am Correctional.
American Correctional Association Staff, jt. auth. see Witke, Leonard R.
American Correctional Association Staff, ed. see Sisson, John W., Jr.
American Correctional Food Service Association Sta. Correctional Food Service Correspondence Course, 2 vols. rev. ed. 1996. pap. 70.00 (*1-56991-015-4*) Am Correctional.
American Council for Headache Education Staff, et al. Migraine: The Complete Guide. LC 93-27843. 304p. 1994. pap. 12.95 (*0-440-50458-9*) Dell.
American Council for Nationalities Service, et al. Records of the American Council for Nationalities Service, 1921-1971: Microfilmed from the Holdings of the Immigration History Research Center, University of Minnesota, Twin Cities. LC 90-12762. (Research Collections in American Immigration). 26p. 1989. write for info. (*1-55655-063-4*) U Pubns Amer.
***American Council of Learned Societies.** American National Biography. Garraty, John A. & Carnes, Mark C., eds. LC 98-20826. 1998. write for info. (*0-19-512780-3*) OUP.
American Council of Learned Societies. Dictionary of American Biography Comprehensive Index Updated Through Supplement 10, Supp. 10. LC 96-3081. 1091p. 1996. 120.00 (*0-684-80482-4*) Macmillan.
— Studies in the History of Culture. LC 70-86728. (Essay Index Reprint Ser.). 1977. 28.95 (*0-8369-1170-9*) Ayer.
American Council of Learned Societies, ed. The Comprehensive Index to Dictionary of American Biography. 1990. 95.00 (*0-684-19114-8*) S&S Trade.
— Concise Dictionary of Scientific Biography. 784p. 1981. 95.00 (*0-684-16650-X*, Scribners Ref) Mac Lib Ref.
American Council of Learned Societies, ed. see Diamandouros, Nikiforos P. & Gunther, Richard.
American Council of Teachers of Russian Staff. Cultural Handbook to the New Independent States. 54p. 1994. pap. text 7.95 (*0-9643332-1-X*) ACIE.
American Council on Education, Higher Education Pa, jt. auth. see Association of Governing Boards.
American Council on Education Staff. Community College Fact Book. (ACE-Oryx Series on Higher Education). (Illus.). 192p. 1988. 31.95 (*0-02-900941-3*) Free Pr.
— Free Press. 7th ed. 1992. lib. bdg. 49.95 (*0-02-900937-5*) Free Pr.
— The Guide to the Evaluation of Educational Experiences in the Armed Services, 1988, 4 vols., Set. 1988. text 75.00 (*0-02-900035-1*) Free Pr.
— The National Guide to Educational Credit for Training Programs, 1988. 639p. (C). 1988. text 39.95 (*0-02-900021-1*) Free Pr.
— The 1996 Guide to the Evaluation of Educational Experiences in the Armed Forces, 3 vols. Incl. Vol. 2: Navy. 624p. 1996. pap. 35.00 (*1-57356-056-1*); 1996. Set pap. 85.00 (*1-57356-054-5*) Oryx Pr.
***American Council on Education Staff, ed.** The National Guide to Educational Credit for Training Programs, 2000. 10th ed. (Ace/Oryx Series on Higher Education). 1200p. 2000. pap. 90.00 (*1-57356-281-5*) Oryx Pr.

A

An Asterisk (*) at the beginning of an entry indicates that the title is appearing for the first time.

— 1999-2000 Accredited Institutions of Post-Secondary Education. 24th ed. (Ace-Oryx Series on Higher Education). 736p. 2000. pap. 59.95 (1-57356-282-3) Oryx Pr.

— The 2000 Guide to the Evaluation of Educational Experiences in the Armed Services, 3 vols. (Ace/Oryx Series on Higher Education). 1888p. 2000. pap. 90.00 (1-57356-273-4) Oryx Pr.

American Council on Education Staff & Bauer, David G. The Complete Grants Sourcebook for Higher Education. 2nd ed. 608p. 1985. 85.00 (0-02-901950-8, 2019) Free Pr.

***American Council on Exercise Staff.** Group Fitness Instructor Manual: ACE's Resource for Fitness Professionals. (Illus.). 300p. 2000. text 34.95 (1-890720-01-1) Am Coun Exer.

American Council on Exercise Staff, ed. see Bricker, Kathryn.

American Council on Exercise Staff, ed. see Carrico, Mara.

American Council on Exercise Staff, ed. see Lewis-McCormick, Irene.

American Council on Exercise Staff, ed. see Rochford, Tim.

American Council on Exercise Staff, ed. see Siebert, Richard.

American Council on Science & Health Staff. Cigarettes: What the Warning Label Doesn't Tell You. LC 97-22232. 190p. 1997. pap. text 16.95 (1-57392-158-0) Prometheus Bks.

American Council Staff. Credited Institute of Post. 2nd ed. 1988. pap. 27.50 (0-02-913980-5) Free Pr.

American Council Staff, et al. LaFayette's Encyclopedia of American Non Traditional Higher Education, 3 vols., Set. 3rd ed. (Illus.). 498p. 1991. 80.00 (0-685-30550-3) ACUPAE.

American Councils for International Education Staff. Cultural Orientation Handbook for U. S. Exchanges with the Russian Federation. Choate, Lisa A. & Davidson, Dan E., eds. 40p. 1997. pap. text 8.95 (0-9643332-8-7) ACIE.

American Crystallographic Association Staff. Motion in Molecules: Calculation of Crystal Packing & Non-Bonded Forces. (American Crystallographic Association Program & Abstracts Ser. 2: Vol.12, No. 1). 58p. 1984. pap. 10.00 (0-317-05920-3) Polycrystal Bk Serv.

— Small Angle Scattering: Perspectives in Crystallography at Atomic Resolution. (American Crystallographic Association Program & Abstracts Ser. 2). 1983. pap. 10.00 (0-686-45047-7) Polycrystal Bk Serv.

— Thirty-Second Annual Denver X-Ray Conference: Summer Meeting, Snowmass, CO. (American Crystallographic Association Program & Abstracts Ser. 2: Vol. 11, No. 2). 72p. 1983. pap. 10.00 (0-317-03259-3) Polycrystal Bk Serv.

American Cultural Exchange, Language School Staff & Criminale, Ulrike. Springboard to French: Introduction to the French Language. (Springboard Ser.). (FRE., Illus.). 32p. (J). (gr. k-4). 1991. 14.95 incl. audio (0-86717-821-3) Alpha AZ.

— Springboard to German: Introduction to the German Language. (Springboard Ser.). (GER., Illus.). 32p. (J). (gr. k-4). 1991. 14.95 (0-86717-824-8) Alpha AZ.

— Springboard to Spanish: Introduction to the Spanish Language. (Springboard Ser.). (SPA., Illus.). (J). (gr. k-4). 1991. 14.95 (0-86717-827-2) Alpha AZ.

American Cusanus Society Staff. Nicolas of Cusa on Christ & the Church: Essays in Memory of Chandler McCuskey Brooks. Christianson, Gerald & Izicki, Thomas M., eds. LC 96-5099. (Studies in the History of Christian Thought, 0081-8607: No. 71). xviii, 362p. 1996. 139.00 (90-04-10519-0) Brill Academic Pubs.

***American Dairy Science Association Staff.** Dairy Management Practices, Housing, & Cattle Health. (ADSA Scientific Reader Ser.). (Illus.). 220p. 2000. pap. 40.00 (1-884706-02-9) Fed Animal Sci.

— Mastitis Control & Milk Quality. (ADSA Scientific Reader Ser.). (Illus.). 260p. (C). 2000. 40.00 (1-884706-03-7) Fed Animal Sci.

American Dental Association, Bureau of Library & I. Index to Dental Literature. 1981. 125.00 (0-686-77270-9) Am Dental.

— Index to Dental Literature. annuals 1981. 100.00 (0-934510-11-3) Am Dental.

American Dental Hygienists' Association Staff & Block Drug Company. Office Emergency Procedures. 1979. 20.00 (0-318-19096-6) Am Dental Hygienists.

— Patient Assessment. 1980. 30.00 (0-318-19097-4) Am Dental Hygienists.

American Diabetes Association. The American Diabetes Association Complete Guide to Diabetes. 446p. 1997. pap. text 19.95 (0-945448-91-0, 4809-01) Am Diabetes.

— The American Diabetes Association Complete Guide to Diabetes. 480p. 1997. mass mkt. 6.99 (0-553-57826-X) Bantam.

— The American Diabetes Association Complete Guide to Diabetes. 2nd ed. LC 99-49617. 454p. 1999. pap. 23.95 (1-58040-038-8, 00388Q, Pub. by Am Diabetes) NTC Contemp Pub Co.

— American Diabetes Association Guide to Diabetes Coding. LC 98-52396. 1999. 0.00 (1-58040-034-5) Am Diabetes.

— Brand-Name Diabetic Meals in Minutes. LC 97-7677. (Illus.). 200p. (Orig.). 1997. pap. 12.95 (0-945448-76-7, 4620-01, Pub. by Am Diabetes) NTC Contemp Pub Co.

— Classic Cooking. rev. ed. LC 98-191570. (Month of Meals Ser.). Orig. Title: Month of Meals. (Illus.). 64p. 1998. pap. 14.95 (1-58040-014-0, 00140Q, Pub. by Am Diabetes) NTC Contemp Pub Co.

— The Complete Quick & Hearty Diabetic Cookbook. LC 97-46530. (Illus.). 256p. 1998. pap. 12.95 (1-58040-002-7, 00027Q, Pub. by Am Diabetes) NTC Contemp Pub Co.

— Dear Diabetes Advisor. LC 97-10397. (Illus.). 120p. (Orig.). 1997. pap. 11.95 (0-945448-83-X, 4813-01, Pub. by Am Diabetes) NTC Contemp Pub Co.

— Diabetes: 1996 Vital Statistics. 112p. 1995. pap. 19.95 (0-945448-43-0, 5702-01) Am Diabetes.

— Diabetes A to Z: What You Need to Know about Diabetes - Simply Put. 3rd ed. LC 97-30806. (Illus.). 202p. 1997. pap. 11.95 (0-945448-95-3, 4801-01) Am Diabetes.

***American Diabetes Association.** Diabetes A to Z: What You Need to Know about Diabetes - Simply Put Treatment & Self Care. 4th ed. LC 99-46249. 202p. 2000. pap. 14.95 (1-58040-035-3, 00353Q, Pub. by Am Diabetes) NTC Contemp Pub Co.

American Diabetes Association. Diabetes A to Z: What You Need to Know about Diabetes-Simply Put. 3rd ed. LC 97-30806. 202p. 1998. pap. 11.95 (0-945448-96-1, 4801-01) Am Diabetes.

— Direct & Indirect Costs of Diabetes in the United States in 1992. 32p. 1993. pap. 19.95 (0-945448-32-5, 5701-01) Am Diabetes.

— Ethnic Delights. (Month of Meals Ser.). 64p. 1998. pap. 14.95 (1-58040-015-9, 00159Q, Pub. by Am Diabetes) NTC Contemp Pub Co.

— Family Cookbook. LC 80-16722. 391p. 1980. 12.95 (0-87619-891-4) P-H.

— Family Cookbook, Vol. III. 400p. 1987. 23.00 (0-13-004145-9) Am Dietetic Assn.

— Maximizing the Role of Nutrition in Diabetes Management. 64p. 1994. pap. 24.95 (0-945448-42-2, 5607-01) Am Diabetes.

— Meals on the Go: Meals in Minutes. rev. ed. (Month of Meals Ser.). Orig. Title: Month of Meals 3. (Illus.). 64p. 1998. pap. 14.95 (1-58040-016-7, 00167Q, Pub. by Am Diabetes) NTC Contemp Pub Co.

— Medical Management of Pregnancy Complicated by Diabetes. 2nd ed. 136p. 1995. pap. 39.95 (0-945448-44-9, 5401-01) Am Diabetes.

— Old-Time Favorites. (Month of Meals Ser.). 64p. 1998. pap. 14.95 (1-58040-017-5, 00175Q, Pub. by Am Diabetes) NTC Contemp Pub Co.

— Therapy for Diabetes Mellitus & Related Disorders. 2nd ed. 384p. 1994. pap. 34.50 (0-945448-38-4, PMTDRD2) Am Diabetes.

— Type 2 Diabetes: Your Healthy Living Guide. 2nd ed. LC 96-54838. 280p. 1997. pap. 16.95 (0-945448-79-1, 00791Q, Pub. by Am Diabetes) NTC Contemp Pub Co.

— Vegetarian Pleasures: Vegetarian Pleasures. rev. ed. LC 98-191568. (Month of Meals Ser.). Orig. Title: Month of Meals 5. (Illus.). 64p. 1998. pap. 14.95 (1-58040-018-3, 00183Q, Pub. by Am Diabetes) NTC Contemp Pub Co.

— Winning with Diabetes. LC 97-49112. 160p. 1998. pap. 12.95 (0-945448-97-X, 00979Q, Pub. by Am Diabetes) NTC Contemp Pub Co.

American Diabetes Association & American Dietetic Association Staff. Exchange Lists for Meal Planning. rev. ed. (Illus.). 32p. 1995. pap. write for info. (0-945448-09-0, 5601) Am Diabetes.

— Exchange Lists for Weight Management. (Illus.). 31p. 1995. pap. write for info. (0-945448-17-1, 5603) Am Diabetes.

— The Official Pocket Guide to Diabetic Exchanges. LC 97-41452. (Illus.). 64p. 1997. pap. 5.95 (1-58040-003-5, 00035Q, Pub. by Am Diabetes) NTC Contemp Pub Co.

***American Diabetes Association & American Dietic Association Staff.** New Family Cookbook for People with Diabetes. LC 99-27030. 544p. 1999. pap. 27.50 (0-684-82660-7) Simon & Schuster.

American Diabetes Association, jt. auth. see American Dietetic Association Staff.

American Diabetes Association, jt. auth. see FastMark Editorial Staff.

American Diabetes Association Staff. The American Diabetes Association Complete Guide to Diabetes. LC 96-19104. 446p. 1996. 29.95 (0-945448-64-3, 4808-01) Am Diabetes.

— Diabetes & Pregnancy: What to Expect. 3rd ed. (Illus.). 72p. 1996. pap. 9.95 (0-945448-05-8, 4903-01, Pub. by Am Diabetes) NTC Contemp Pub Co.

— Diabetes Education Goals. LC 95-10032. (Practical Approaches in Diabetes Care Ser.). 1995. pap. 24.95 (0-945448-49-X, 5502-01) Am Diabetes.

— Gestational Diabetes. 3rd ed. 80p. 1997. pap. 9.95 (0-945448-90-2, 4902-01, Pub. by Am Diabetes) NTC Contemp Pub Co.

— The Health Professional's Guide to Diabetes & Exercise. LC 95-31497. (Illus.). 352p. 1995. pap. 49.95 (0-945448-52-X) Am Diabetes.

— How to Cook for People with Diabetes. LC 96-48837. 152p. 1996. pap. 11.95 (0-945448-68-6, 4616-01, Pub. by Am Diabetes) NTC Contemp Pub Co.

— Magic Menus. LC 96-42081. 256p. 1996. pap. 14.95 (0-945448-72-4, 4707-01, Pub. by Am Diabetes) NTC Contemp Pub Co.

— Type 2 Diabetes: Your Healthy Living Guide. LC 92-17906. (Illus.). 248p. 1996. pap. 24.95 (0-945448-27-9) Am Diabetes.

***American Diabetes Association Staff.** Type 2 Diabetes: Your Healthy Living Guide. 2nd ed. 2000. 16.95 (1-58040-060-4) Am Diabetes.

***American Diabetes Association Staff, ed.** ADA Complete Guide to Diabetes. 2nd ed. (Illus.). 2000. mass mkt. 6.99 (0-553-58300-X) Bantam.

American Diabetes Association Staff, ed. Life with Diabetes: A Series of Teaching Outlines. LC 97-22986. (Illus.). 683p. 1997. 75.00 (0-945448-80-5, 5507-01) Am Diabetes.

American Diabetes Association Staff, jt. auth. see Johnson, Patricia D.

American Diabetic Association & American Diatetic Association. The American Diabetes Association/The American Dietetic Association Family Cookbook, Vol. II. rev. ed. (Illus.). 448p. 1987. 23.00 (0-671-76131-5) S&S Trade.

— The American Diabetes Association/The American Dietetic Association Family Cookbook: With Microwave Adaption, Vol. III. 416p. 1987. 23.00 (0-671-76133-1) S&S Trade.

American Dialect Society Staff, jt. auth. see Bronstein, Arthur J.

American Dietetic Association, jt. auth. see American Diabetic Association.

American Diatetic Association Staff. The American Dietetic Association Family Cookbook. 1989. 9.98 (0-13-024980-7) P-H.

— The American Dietetic Asssociation Family Cookbook: The American Tradition, Vol. 4. (Illus.). 416p. 1991. 22.50 (0-671-76695-3) S&S Trade.

American Diet Association Staff. The Essential Guide to Nutrition & the Foods We Eat. LC 98-41937. 240p. 1999. pap. 15.95 (0-06-273346-X, Perennial) HarperTrade.

American Dietetic Association, Dietetic Association. Cut The Fat ! 224p. 1996. pap. 7.50 (0-06-273487-3) HarpC.

American Dietetic Association, Sports & Cardiovasc. Cardiovascular Disease: Nutrition for Prevention & Treatment. Kris-Etherton, Penny M., ed. LC 90-1031. (Illus.). 349p. (Orig.). 1990. pap. text 42.00 (0-88091-078-X, 0104) Am Dietetic Assn.

American Dietetic Association Staff. Accreditation - Approval Manual for Dietetic Education Programs. 2nd ed. LC 87-71110. 132p. (Orig.). 1991. pap. 28.45 (0-88091-031-3) Am Dietetic Assn.

— Being Vegetarian. 144p. 1996. pap. 5.95 (1-56561-093-8) Wiley.

— Calcium in Your Life. LC 98-231828. 168p. (Orig.). 1997. pap. 5.95 (1-56561-117-9) Wiley.

— Carbohydrates: What You Need to Know, 6 Vols. 1998. pap. 41.70 (1-56561-144-6) Wiley.

***American Dietetic Association Staff.** Carbohydrates: What You Need to Know. LC 98-230635. 96p. 1998. pap. 6.95 (1-56561-143-8); pap. 8.95 (0-471-34670-5) Wiley.

American Dietetic Association Staff. Food Allergies: Up-to-Date Tips from the World's Foremost Nutrition Experts. LC 98-230650. 112p. (Orig.). 1998. pap. 6.95 (1-56561-128-4) Wiley.

— Food Folklore: Tales & Truths about What We Eat. LC 98-231233. 96p. 1998. pap. 6.95 (1-56561-168-3) Wiley.

***American Dietetic Association Staff.** Food Folklore: Tales & Truths about What We Eat. 96p. 1998. pap. 6.95 (0-471-34716-7) Wiley.

American Dietetic Association Staff. Handbook of Clinical Dietetics. LC 80-11317. 480p. 1981. 65.00 (0-300-02256-5) Yale U Pr.

— Licensing Guidebook for Nutrition Professionals, 1990. LC 90-130121. 75p. 1990. reprint ed. pap. 30.00 (0-608-03029-5, 206348000006) Bks Demand.

— Medical Nutrition Therapy Across the Continuum of Care. 200p. 1997. ring bd. 80.00 incl. VHS, disk (0-88091-149-2) Am Dietetic Assn.

— Monthly Nutrition Companion: Up-to-Date Tips from the World's Foremost Nutrition Experts. LC 98-231231. 224p. 1997. pap. 6.95 (1-56561-099-7) Wiley.

American Dietetic Association Staff. Monthly Nutrition Companion: Up-to-Date Tips from the World's Foremost Nutrition Experts. 208p. 1997. pap. 10.95 (0-471-34688-8) Wiley.

American Dietetic Association Staff. Nutrition & Health Campaign for Women Slide Set & Script Narratives. 66p. 1994. ring bd. 45.95 incl. sl. (0-88091-141-7) Am Dietetic Assn.

— Nutrition for a Healthy Pregnancy, 6 Vols. 1998. pap. 41.70 (1-56561-161-6) Wiley.

— Pediatric Manual of Clinical Dietetics. LC 97-33561. 1997. write for info. (0-88091-160-3) Am Dietetic Assn.

— Pregnancy Nutrition: Good Health for You & Your Baby. 96p. 1998. pap. 8.95 (0-471-34697-7) Wiley.

— Productivity Management for Nutrition Care. LC RA0975.5.D5. 61p. 1986. reprint ed. pap. 30.00 (0-608-03562-9, 205256000009) Bks Demand.

— Reimbursement & Insurance Coverage for Nutrition Services. LC 91-26128. 207p. 1991. reprint ed. pap. 64.20 (0-608-03030-9, 206348100006) Bks Demand.

— Role Delineation for Registered Dietitians & Entry-Level Dietetic Technicians. 311p. 1990. pap. 38.50 (0-88091-079-8, 0303) Am Dietetic Assn.

— Role Delineation Study for Entry-Level Registered Dietitians, Entry-Level Dietetic Technicians, & Beyond-Entry-Level Registered Dietitians Technical Report, 3 vols. 1989. ring bd. 125.00 (0-88091-080-1, 0301); 58.00 (0-318-68899-9); 33.00 (0-318-68900-6); 46.00 (0-318-68901-4) Am Dietetic Assn.

— Safe Food for You & Your Family. 160p. 1996. pap. 5.95 (1-56561-094-6) Wiley.

American Dietetic Association Staff. Safe Food for You & Your Family. (Nutrition Now Ser.). 160p. 1996. pap. 5.95 (0-471-34699-3) Wiley.

American Dietetic Association Staff. Skim the Fat. 224p. 1995. pap. 10.95 (1-56561-062-8) Wiley.

American Dietetic Association Staff. Skim the Fat: A Practical & Up-to-Date Food Guide. 224p. 1995. pap. 10.95 (0-471-34703-5) Wiley.

American Dietetic Association Staff. Snacking Habits: Up to Date Advice from the World's Foremost Nutrition Experts. LC 98-231228. 112p. (Orig.). 1997. pap. 6.95 (1-56561-122-5) Wiley.

— Vitamins, Minerals, & Dietary Supplements. LC 99-190489. 112p. 1998. pap. 6.95 (1-56561-170-5) Wiley.

***American Dietetic Association Staff.** Vitamins, Minerals, & Dietary Supplements. 112p. 1998. pap. 6.95 (0-471-34749-3) Wiley.

American Dietetic Association Staff. Vitamins, Minerals, & Food Supplements Nutrition. 1996. pap. text 5.95 (1-56561-092-X) Wiley.

American Dietetic Association Staff & American Diabetes Association. Family Cookbook, Vol. 1. rev. ed. LC 87-42674. 392p. 1987. 23.00 (0-13-024901-7, 0840) Am Dietetic Assn.

— Family Cookbook, Vol. 2. rev. ed. LC 87-42674. 448p. 1987. 23.00 (0-685-51757-8, 0841) Am Dietetic Assn.

American Dietetic Association Staff & Office of Disease Prevention & Health Promotion St. Worksite Nutrition: A Guide to Planning, Implementation, & Evaluation. 2nd ed. LC 93-6120. 1993. 12.00 (0-88091-126-3) Am Dietetic Assn.

American Dietetic Association Staff, et al. Preparation of Formula for Infants: Guidelines for Health Care Facilities. LC 91-26127. 1991. pap. 10.95 (0-88091-089-5, 0164) Am Dietetic Assn.

American Dietetic Association Staff, jt. auth. see American Diabetes Association.

American Dietetic Association Staff, jt. auth. see Balagopal, Padmini.

American Dietetic Association Staff, jt. auth. see Hess, Mary Abbott.

American Dietetic Association Staff, jt. auth. see Higgins, Catherine.

American Dietetic Association Staff, jt. auth. see Rosenbloom, Christine.

***American Dietetic Staff.** Cut the Fat. 1998. pap. 8.50 (0-06-273681-7) HarpC.

American Dietic Association Staff, jt. auth. see American Diabetes Association.

American Economic Association Staff, compiled by. Readings in Business Cycle Theory. LC 76-29403. (BCL Ser.). 736p. reprint ed. 41.50 (0-404-15330-5) AMS Pr.

— Readings in the Theory of Income Distribution. LC 76-29414. (BCL Ser. II). reprint ed. 52.50 (0-404-15332-1) AMS Pr.

American Economic Association Staff, ed. Readings in the Social Control of Industry. LC 72-14175. (Essay Index Reprint Ser.). 1977. reprint ed. 30.95 (0-518-10001-4) Ayer.

American Education. A Basic Skills Curriculum Beginners Bible. 1997. pap. text 10.95 (1-56189-476-1) Amer Educ Pub.

— Complete Book at Science, Grades 3 & 4. 352p. 1999. pap. text 14.95 (1-56189-502-4) Amer Educ Pub.

— Complete Book of Science, Grades 1 & 2, 1. 1999. pap. text 14.95 (1-56189-501-6) Amer Educ Pub.

— Learn at Home, Grade K. 1999. pap. text 29.95 (1-56189-508-3) Amer Educ Pub.

— Learn at Home, Grade 1. 1999. pap. text 29.95 (1-56189-509-1) Amer Educ Pub.

— Learn at Home, Grade 2. 1999. pap. text 29.95 (1-56189-510-5) Amer Educ Pub.

— Learn at Home, Grade 3. 1999. pap. text 29.95 (1-56189-511-3) Amer Educ Pub.

— Learn at Home, Grade 4. 1999. pap. text 29.95 (1-56189-512-1) Amer Educ Pub.

— Learn at Home, Grade 5. 1999. pap. text 29.95 (1-56189-513-X) Amer Educ Pub.

— Learn at Home, Grade 6. 1999. pap. text 29.95 (1-56189-514-8) Amer Educ Pub.

***American Education Publishers Staff.** Alphabet Wookbook. (Beginners Bible Ser.). 2000. pap. 14.95 (1-56189-617-9) Amer Educ Pub.

American Education Publishers Staff. Brighter Child Grade Five: Reading Comprehension. 1994. pap. 2.25 (1-56189-145-2) Amer Educ Pub.

— Brighter Child Grade Four: Reading Comprehension. 1994. pap. 2.25 (1-56189-144-4) Amer Educ Pub.

— Brighter Child Grade Six: Reading Comprehension. 1994. pap. 2.25 (1-56189-146-0) Amer Educ Pub.

***American Education Publishers Staff, ed.** Complete Book of Animals. (Complete Bks.). (Illus.). 352p. 2000. pap. 14.95 (1-56189-544-X) Amer Educ Pub.

American Education Publishing. Complete Book of Time & Money. 352p. (J). (gr. k-3). 1998. pap. text 14.95 (1-56189-500-8) Amer Educ Pub.

American Education Publishing Staff. Addition. (Brighter Child Ser.). (Illus.). (J). 1993. pap. text 3.49 (1-56189-287-4) Amer Educ Pub.

— Alphabet with Stencils. (J). (ps-3). 1993. 3.49 (1-56189-291-2) Amer Educ Pub.

American Education Publishing Staff. Brighter Child: English. (J). (gr. 4). 1994. pap. text 2.25 (1-56189-128-2) Amer Educ Pub.

— Brighter Child: Reading. 1994. pap. 2.25 (1-56189-126-6) Amer Educ Pub.

— Brighter Child: Reading Comprehension. (J). (gr. 2). 1994. pap. 2.25 (1-56189-142-8) Amer Educ Pub.

— Brighter Child: Spelling & Writing. 1994. pap. 2.25 (1-56189-131-2) Amer Educ Pub.

— Brighter Child Grade Four: Spelling & Writing. 1994. pap. text 2.25 (1-56189-134-7) Amer Educ Pub.

— Brighter Child Grade One Reading Comprehension. 1994. pap. text 2.25 (1-56189-141-X) Amer Educ Pub.

— Complete Book of Alphabet & Numbers. 352p. 1998. pap. text 14.95 (1-56189-499-0) Amer Educ Pub.

— Complete Book of Map & Geography Skills. 352p. 1998. pap. text 14.95 (1-56189-503-2) Amer Educ Pub.

***American Education Publishing Staff.** Complete Book of Reading & Writing. (Complete Bks.). (Illus.). 352p. (J). (gr. 3-8). 2000. pap. 14.95 (1-56189-585-7) Amer Educ Pub.

An Asterisk (*) at the beginning of an entry indicates that the title is appearing for the first time.

— Division. (Brighter Child Ser.). (Illus.). (J). 1994. pap. text 3.49 (*1-56189-274-2*) Amer Educ Pub.

American Education Publishing Staff. Enrichment Gifted Math-Reading Grades 1-2. (J). (gr. 1-2). 1997. pap. text 12.95 (*1-56189-451-6*) Amer Educ Pub.

— Enrichment Gifted Math-Reading Grades 3-4. (J). (gr. 3-4). 1997. pap. text 12.95 (*1-56189-452-4*) Amer Educ Pub.

— Enrichment Gifted Math-Reading Grades 5-6. (J). (gr. 5-6). 1997. pap. text 12.95 (*1-56189-453-2*) Amer Educ Pub.

— Kindergarten Caps & Small Letters. (Beginners Bible Ser.). (J). 1997. pap. text 2.25 (*1-56189-471-0*) Amer Educ Pub.

— Kindergarten English & Phonics. (Beginners Bible Ser.). (J). 1997. pap. text 2.25 (*1-56189-472-9*) Amer Educ Pub.

American Education Publishing Staff. Muppet Multiplication Flash Cards. (Brighter Child Ser.). (Illus.). (J). 1993. pap. text 3.49 (*1-56189-289-0*) Amer Educ Pub.

American Education Publishing Staff. Muppet Workbook, Beginning Sounds, Phonics. (Brighter Child Ser.). 1993. pap. text 2.25 (*1-56189-282-3*) Amer Educ Pub.

— Muppet Workbook, Letters, Capital & Small. (Brighter Child Ser.). 1993. pap. text 2.25 (*1-56189-281-5*) Amer Educ Pub.

— Muppet Workbook, Same & Different. (Brighter Child Ser.). 1993. pap. text 2.25 (*1-56189-283-1*) Amer Educ Pub.

— Muppet Workbook, Sorting & Ordering. (Brighter Child Ser.). 1993. pap. text 2.25 (*1-56189-286-6*) Amer Educ Pub.

— Muppet Workbook, Thinking Skills. (Brighter Child Ser.). 1993. pap. text 2.25 (*1-56189-285-8*) Amer Educ Pub.

American Education Publishing Staff. Numbers & Counting. (Brighter Child Ser.). (Illus.). (J). 1993. pap. text 3.49 (*1-56189-293-9*) Amer Educ Pub.

American Education Publishing Staff. Phonics: Grade K. (J). (ps-3). 1994. pap., student ed. 3.25 (*1-56189-357-9*) Amer Educ Pub.

— Phonics: Grade 1. (J). (ps-3). 1994. pap. 3.25 (*1-56189-358-7*) Amer Educ Pub.

— Phonics: Grade 2. (J). (ps-3). 1994. pap. 3.25 (*1-56189-359-5*) Amer Educ Pub.

American Education Publishing Staff. Phonics with Stencils. (Brighter Child Ser.). (J). (ps-3). 1993. 3.49 (*1-56189-290-4*) Amer Educ Pub.

American Education Publishing Staff. Preschool Alphabet. (Beginners Bible Ser.). (J). 1997. pap. text 2.25 (*1-56189-469-9*) Amer Educ Pub.

— Preschool Colors & Shapes. (Beginners Bible Ser.). (J). 1997. pap. text 2.25 (*1-56189-468-0*) Amer Educ Pub.

— Preschool Numbers. (Beginners Bible Ser.). (J). 1997. pap. text 2.25 (*1-56189-470-2*) Amer Educ Pub.

American Education Publishing Staff. Subtraction. (Brighter Child Ser.). (Illus.). (J). 1993. pap. text 3.49 (*1-56189-288-2*) Amer Educ Pub.

***American Education Publishing Staff, ed.** Complete Book of Arts & Crafts. (Complete Bks.). (Illus.). 256p. 2000. pap. 14.95 (*1-56189-586-5*) Amer Educ Pub.

— Complete Book of Brain Teasers. (Complete Bks.). (Illus.). 352p. 2000. pap. 14.95 (*1-56189-548-2*) Amer Educ Pub.

— Complete Book of Math Games. (Complete Bks.). (Illus.). 352p. 2000. pap. 14.95 (*1-56189-549-0*) Amer Educ Pub.

— Complete Book of Presidents. (Complete Bks.). (Illus.). 352p. 2000. pap. 14.95 (*1-56189-547-4*) Amer Educ Pub.

— Complete Book of Reading & Writing. (Complete Bks.). (Illus.). 352p. (J). (gr. 1-9). 2000. pap. 14.95 (*1-56189-584-9*) Amer Educ Pub.

— Complete Book of Travel Games. (Complete Bks.). (Illus.). 352p. 2000. pap. 14.95 (*1-56189-546-6*) Amer Educ Pub.

American Education Research Association. Encyclopedia of Educational Research, 4 vols. 7th ed. 2001. 375.00 (*0-02-864945-1*) Mac Lib Ref.

— Encyclopedia of Educational Research, Vol. 1. 7th ed. 2001. 110.00 (*0-02-864941-9*) Mac Lib Ref.

— Encyclopedia of Educational Research, Vol. 2. 7th ed. 2001. 110.00 (*0-02-864942-7*) Mac Lib Ref.

— Encyclopedia of Educational Research, Vol. 3. 7th ed. 2001. 110.00 (*0-02-864943-5*) Mac Lib Ref.

— Encyclopedia of Educational Research, Vol. 4. 7th ed. 2001. 110.00 (*0-02-864944-3*) Mac Lib Ref.

American Education Staff. Kindergarten Math. (Beginners Bible Ser.). (J). 1997. pap. text 2.25 (*1-56189-473-7*) Amer Educ Pub.

American Educational Research Association Staff. Handbook of Research on Curriculum. 1088p. 1992. 75.00 (*0-02-900385-7*) Free Pr.

American END Society Committee, jt. auth. see American Journal of EEG Technology Staff.

American Enterprise Institute for Public Policy Re. Contemporary Economic Problems, 1978. LC 78-14962. 368p. reprint ed. pap. 114.10 (*0-8357-4456-6*, 203729400008) Bks Demand.

— Contemporary Economic Problems, 1979. LC HC0106.7.A2. 448p. reprint ed. pap. 138.90 (*0-8357-4457-4*, 203729500008) Bks Demand.

— Contemporary Economic Problems, 1980. LC HC0106.7.C67. (Illus.). 352p. reprint ed. pap. 109.20 (*0-8357-4458-2*, 203729600008) Bks Demand.

— The Economics of Crime & Punishment: A Conference. LC 73-86979. (Illus.). 242p. reprint ed. pap. 75.10 (*0-8357-4469-8*, 203731300008) Bks Demand.

— Essays in Contemporary Economic Problems: Demand, Productivity & Population. LC HC0106.8.E88. (Contemporary Economic Problems Ser.: No. 1981-1982). (Illus.). 364p. reprint ed. pap. 112.90 (*0-8357-4474-4*, 203732100008) Bks Demand.

— Essays in Contemporary Economic Problems: Disinflation. LC HG0455.E87. 336p. reprint ed. pap. 104.20 (*0-8357-4766-2*, 203770300009) Bks Demand.

— How Can Our Physical Environment Best Be Controlled & Developed? LC TD0180.A44. (American Enterprise Institute for Public Policy Research. High School Debate Ser.). 125p. reprint ed. pap. 38.80 (*0-608-10903-7*, 201708700006) Bks Demand.

American Enterprise Institute for Public Policy Re, jt. auth. see Hausman, Jerry A.

American Ethnological Society Staff. American Ethnological Society Monographs, 1940-1972. 1988. write for info. (*0-404-62900-8*) AMS Pr.

— American Ethnological Society Proceedings, 1957-1972, 16 vols. 1988. write for info. (*0-404-62650-5*) AMS Pr.

— Publications of the American Ethnological Society, Vols. 1-22. write for info. (*0-404-58150-1*) AMS Pr.

— Symposium on Community Studies in Anthropology: American Ethnological Society Proceedings, 1963. LC 84-45550. 1988. reprint ed. pap. 35.00 (*0-404-62657-2*) AMS Pr.

American Express Publisher Staff, ed. Quick from Scratch. LC 98-2721. 1998. 25.95 (*0-916103-45-5*) Am Express Food.

***American Express Staff.** MMDI Amex Tax Guide. 96p. 1999. pap. 3.50 (*0-06-105912-9*) HarpC.

American Express Tax & Business Staff. The American Express 1999 Tax Guide. 816p. 2000. pap. 14.95 (*0-88730-961-5*, HarpBusn) HarpInfo.

— American Express Tax Guide 1997. 1997. 13.50 (*0-614-19913-1*, HarpBusn) HarpInfo.

American Family Records Association Staff. AFRA Member Directory & Ancestral Surname Registry, Vol. 2. Baldwin, Betty C. & Karns, Kermit B., eds. 40p. 1985. pap. 5.00 (*0-913233-03-X*) AFRA.

— AFRA Member Directory & Ancestral Surname Registry, 1984, Vol. 1. Baker, Shirley R. & Karns, Kermit B., eds. 57p. 1984. pap. 5.00 (*0-913233-02-1*) AFRA.

— AFRA Member Directory & Ancestral Surname Registry, 1990, Vol. 6. Baldwin, Betty C. & Baldwin, Ben S., eds. 41p. 1990. pap. 5.00 (*0-913233-16-1*) AFRA.

— AFRA Pedigree Tables, 1990, Vol. I. Karns, Kermit B., ed. 56p. 1990. pap. 5.00 (*0-913233-17-X*) AFRA.

American Family Records Association Staff, et al. AFRA Member Directory & Ancestral Surname Registry, Vol. 3. 29p. 1986. pap. 5.00 (*0-913233-05-6*) AFRA.

— AFRA Member Directory & Ancestral Surname Registry, Vol. 5. 20p. 1988. pap. 5.00 (*0-913233-13-7*) AFRA.

American Federation of Arts Staff. Cultural Resources of Boston. (Orig.). 1965. 10.00 (*0-8079-0030-3*); pap. 5.00 (*0-8079-0031-1*) October.

— New Chinese Landscape. (Illus.). (Orig.). 1966. pap. 4.00 (*0-8079-0093-1*) October.

— Thirty-Third Biennial Exhibition of Art, Venice, 1966. (Illus.). 1966. 5.00 (*0-8079-0123-7*); pap. 2.00 (*0-8079-0124-5*) October.

American Federation of Arts Staff & Hapgood, Susan. Neo-Dada: Redefining Art, 1958-1962. LC 94-7388. (Illus.). 160p. 1994. 42.50 (*0-87663-629-6*, Pub. by Universe) St Martin.

American Federation of Labor Staff. American Federation of Labor: History, Encyclopedia, Reference Book, 3 vols., Set. Roberts, William C. & Erb, Mary, eds. LC 77-3562. 1977. lib. bdg. 295.00 (*0-8371-9568-3*, AFLH) Greenwood.

— American Federation of Labor: History, Encyclopedia, Reference Book, 3 vols., Vol. 1. Roberts, William C. & Erb, Mary, eds. LC 77-3562. 1977. lib. bdg. 55.00 (*0-8371-9569-1*, AFLI) Greenwood.

— American Federation of Labor: History, Encyclopedia, Reference Book, 3 vols., Vol. 2. Roberts, William C. & Erb, Mary, eds. LC 77-3562. 1977. lib. bdg. 55.00 (*0-8371-9570-5*, AFLJ) Greenwood.

— American Federation of Labor: History, Encyclopedia, Reference Book, 3 vols., Vol. 3. Roberts, William C. & Erb, Mary, eds. LC 77-3562. 1977. lib. bdg. 75.00 (*0-8371-9571-3*, AFLK) Greenwood.

— American Federation of Labor: History, Encyclopedia, Reference Book, 3 vols., Vol. 4. Roberts, William C. & Erb, Mary, eds. LC 77-3562. 1977. lib. bdg. 85.00 (*0-8371-9572-1*, AFLL) Greenwood.

— American Federation of Labor: History, Encyclopedia, Reference Book, 3 vols., Vol. 5. Roberts, William C. & Erb, Mary, eds. LC 77-3562. 1977. lib. bdg. 65.00 (*0-8371-9598-5*, AFLM) Greenwood.

American Federation of Labor Staff, et al. The American Federation of Labor Records: The Samuel Gompers Era, 1877-1937. LC 86-893468. (Research Collections in Labor Studies). 1985. write for info. (*0-89093-895-4*) U Pubns Amer.

American Feed Manufacturers Association, jt. auth. see American Feed Manufacturers Association Staff.

American Feed Manufacturers Association Staff. Feed Manufacturing Technology. Pfost, Harry, ed. 1976. 50.00 (*0-686-00374-8*) AG Pr.

American Feed Manufacturers Association Staff & American Feed Manufacturers Association. Managing Truck Fleet Operations. 196p. 1983. 35.00 (*0-318-12576-5*, 024) Am Feed Industry.

American Film Institute Staff. American Film Institute Catalog: Feature Films, 1921-1930. LC 96-45734. 2600p. 1997. 325.00 (*0-520-20969-9*, Pub. by U CA Pr) Cal Prin Full Svc.

— American Film Institute Catalog: Feature Films, 1961-1970. LC 96-45734. 2148p. 1997. 325.00 (*0-520-20970-2*, Pub. by U CA Pr) Cal Prin Full Svc.

— The American Film Institute Catalog of Motion Pictures Produced in the United States: Feature Films, 1911-1920, 2 vols. 1504p. 1989. 195.00 (*0-520-06301-5*, Pub. by U CA Pr) Cal Prin Full Svc.

— The American Film Institute Catalog of Motion Pictures Produced in the United States: Film Beginnings 1893-1910; A Work in Progress, 2 vols. 1790p. 1995. 205.00 (*0-8108-3021-3*) Scarecrow.

American Film Institute Staff & Mitchell, Carolyn B. American Film Institute Catalog of Motion Pictures Produced in the United States: Feature Films 1931-1940, 3 vols. 1993. 225.00 (*0-520-07908-6*, Pub. by U CA Pr) Cal Prin Full Svc.

American Financial Directories Staff. MoneyFind BookWare: Directory of Scholarships. 512p. 1994. pap. 29.95 incl. disk (*1-883609-06-2*) Am Finan.

— MoneyFind BookWare: Directory of Small Business Investors. 1994. pap. write for info. incl. disk (*1-883609-00-3*) Am Finan.

American Fisheries Society Northeastern Division S. Acid Rain - Fisheries. Johnson, R. E., ed. LC 82-74271. 357p. 1982. text 30.00 (*0-913235-26-1*, 530.07C) Am Fisheries Soc.

American Fishing & Tackle Manufacturer's Associati. Sport Fishing & Aquatic Resources Handbook: Student Manual, AK Version. 112p. 1991. pap. text, per. 3.50 (*0-8403-6930-1*) Kendall-Hunt.

— Sport Fishing & Aquatic Resources Handbook: Student Manual, CT Version. 112p. 1991. pap. text, per. 3.50 (*0-8403-6932-8*) Kendall-Hunt.

— Sport Fishing & Aquatic Resources Handbook: Student Manual, NM Version. 112p. 1991. pap. text, per. 3.50 (*0-8403-6935-2*) Kendall-Hunt.

— Sport Fishing & Aquatic Resources Handbook: Student Manual, WA Version. 120p. 1991. pap. text, per. 3.50 (*0-8403-6929-8*) Kendall-Hunt.

American Floral Services, Inc. Staff. PFD Manual. Morley, Jim, ed. (SPA.). 80p. (C). 1994. text. write for info. (*0-944074-03-0*) AFS Education.

American Floral Services Staff. PFD Manual. Morley, Jim, ed. (POR.). 80p. (C). 1994. text. write for info. (*0-944074-04-9*) AFS Education.

— PFD Sympathy Design Manual. Morley, Jim, ed. (Illus.). 104p. 1995. text 29.95 (*0-944074-05-7*) AFS Education.

***American Football Coaches Association.** Offensive Football Strategies. LC 99-47997. (Illus.). 336p. 1999. pap. 22.95 (*0-7360-0139-5*) Human Kinetics.

American Football Coaches Association Staff. AFCA's Defensive Football Drills. LC 96-8061. (Illus.). 168p. (Orig.). 1996. pap. 15.95 (*0-88011-476-2*, PAFC0476) Human Kinetics.

— AFCA's Offensive Football Drills. LC 97-26550. (Illus.). 184p. 1997. pap. 15.95 (*0-88011-526-2*, PAFC0526) Human Kinetics.

***American Football Coaches Association Staff.** Defensive Football Strategies. LC 00-39597. (Illus.). 312p. 2000. pap. 22.95 (*0-7360-0142-5*) Human Kinetics.

American Football Coaches Association Staff. Football Coaching Strategies. LC 95-8140. 216p. (Orig.). 1995. pap. 18.95 (*0-87322-869-3*, PAFC0869) Human Kinetics.

American Foreign Policy Council Staff. Modernizing Foreign Assistance: Resource Management As an Instrument of Foreign Policy. LC 91-46992. 160p. 1992. 47.95 (*0-275-94224-4*, C4224, Praeger Pubs) Greenwood.

American Forestry Association Staff. Trees Every Boy & Girl Should Know. (J). (gr. 1-6). 4.50 (*0-686-26729-X*, 31) Am Forests.

American Forestry Association Staff, et al, eds. Shading Our Cities: A Resource Guide for Urban & Community Forests. LC 89-15453. 329p. 1989. text 40.00 (*0-933280-96-3*); pap. text 24.95 (*0-933280-95-5*) Island Pr.

American Foundation for the Blind. How to Integrate the Aging Person Who Is Visually Handicapped into Community Senior Programs. LC HV1597.5. 32p. reprint ed. pap. 30.00 (*0-608-16869-6*, 202734900055) Bks Demand.

— An Introduction to Working with the Aging Person Who is Visually Handicapped. LC 74-193162. 59p. reprint ed. pap. 30.00 (*0-608-16874-2*, 202735000055) Bks Demand.

American Foundation for the Blind & Graham, Milton D. Eight Hundred Fifty-One Blinded Veterans: A Success Story. LC 68-5051. 350p. reprint ed. pap. 108.50 (*0-608-16545-X*, 202734100055) Bks Demand.

American Foundation for the Blind Staff. The Future of Work for Disabled People: Employment & the New Technology. LC 86-3447. 120p. reprint ed. pap. 37.20 (*0-7837-2761-5*, 204314800006) Bks Demand.

— Sources of Products for Blind & Visually Impaired Persons. LC 92-159159. 59p. reprint ed. pap. 30.00 (*0-7837-5188-5*, 204492200004) Bks Demand.

American Foundrymen Society Staff. Cupola Hand Book. 5th ed. 688p. 1984. 90.00 (*0-317-32613-9*, FC8401) Am Foundrymen.

American-French Genealogical Society Staff. Baptisms & Marriages of Our Lady of Good Help Catholic Church, Mapleville, RI, 1905-1995. vii, 298p. 1995. spiral bd. 30.00 (*1-929920-38-5*) American French.

— Baptisms, Marriages & Burials of Sacred Heart Catholic Church, West Thompson, CT, 1879-1990. x, 234p. 1995. spiral bd. 30.00 (*1-929920-37-7*) American French.

— Baptisms of Holy Family Catholic Church, Woonsocket, RI, 1902-1991. viii, 716p. 1999. spiral bd. 40.00 (*1-929920-39-3*) American French.

— Baptisms of Notre Dame Catholic Church, Central Falls, RI, 1873-1988, 2 vols. 1995. spiral bd. 50.00 (*1-929920-20-2*) American French.

— Baptisms of Precious Blood Catholic Church, Woonsocket, RI, 1870-1995, 3 vols. 1998. spiral bd 60.00 (*1-929920-40-7*) American French.

— Baptisms of Saint Anne Catholic Church, Fall River, Massachusetts, 1869-1996, 4 vols. 1999. spiral bd. 120.00 (*1-929920-42-3*) American French.

— Baptisms of St. John the Baptist Catholic Church, Pawtucket, RI, 1884-1988. vii, 765p. 1996. spiral bd. 40.00 (*1-929920-15-6*) American French.

— Baptisms of St. John the Baptist Catholic Church, West Warwick, RI, 1873-1989, 2 vols. 1992. spiral bd. 60.00 (*1-929920-24-5*) American French.

— Baptisms of St. Joseph Catholic Church, Pascoag, RI, 1893-1991. iv, 349p. 1993. spiral bd. 35.00 (*1-929920-21-0*) American French.

— Baptisms of St. Joseph Catholic Church, North Grosvenordale, CT, 1872-1990, 2 vols. 1995. spiral bd. 45.00 (*1-929920-22-9*) American French.

— Baptisms of St. Joseph Catholic Church: Attleboro, Massachusetts (1905-1986) vii, 367p. 2000. spiral bd. 35.00 (*1-929920-58-X*) American French.

— Baptisms of St. Matthew Catholic Church, Central Falls, RI, 1906-1988. viii, 592p. 1999. spiral bd. 38.00 (*1-929920-23-7*) American French.

— Births Recorded in the Town Reports of Peterboro, NH, 1887-1951. vi, 454p. 1995. spiral bd. 35.00 (*1-929920-34-2*) American French.

— Births Recorded in the Town Reports of Swansea, MA, 1879-1973. vii, 359p. 1994. spiral bd. 35.00 (*1-929920-35-0*) American French.

— Burials from the Menard Funeral Home, Woonsocket, RI, 1970-1990. iv, 272p. 1991. spiral bd. 25.00 (*1-929920-03-2*) American French.

— Burials of Courchesne Funeral Home, Worcester, MA, 1930-1988. vi, 268p. 2000. spiral bd. 30.00 (*1-929920-63-6*) American French.

— Burials of Holy Family Catholic Church, Woonsocket, RI, 1902-1987. vii, 702p. 1999. spiral bd. 40.00 (*1-929920-65-2*) American French.

— Burials of St. Joseph Catholic Church: Attleboro, Massachusetts (1905-1986) vii, 239p. 2000. spiral bd. 25.00 (*1-929920-59-8*) American French.

— Burials of St. Matthew Catholic Church, Central Falls, RI, 1906-1988. vii, 466p. 1999. spiral bd. 35.00 (*1-929920-55-5*) American French.

— Burials of the Alfred Roy & Sons Funeral Home, Worcester, MA, 1904-1994, 2 vols. 1995. spiral bd. 50.00 (*1-929920-54-7*) American French.

— Burials of the Auclair Funer Home, Fall River, MA, 1944-1992. vi, 416p. 1995. spiral bd. 30.00 (*1-929920-49-0*) American French.

— Burials of the Egidio Dipardo & Sons Funeral Home, Woonsocket, RI, 1926-1995. vii, 680p. 1998. spiral bd. 35.00 (*1-929920-51-2*) American French.

— Burials of the Gilman-Valade Funeral Homes, Putnam & North Grosvenordale, CT, 1920-1969. viii, 563p. 1993. spiral bd. 35.00 (*1-929920-06-7*) American French.

— Burials of the Gilman-Valde Funeral Homes, Putnam & North Grosvenordale, CT, 1970-1990. vii, 458p. 1995. spiral bd. 30.00 (*1-929920-07-5*) American French.

— Burials of the Hickey-Grenier Funeral Home, Brockton, MA, 1911-1987. v, 410p. 1993. spiral bd. 35.00 (*1-929920-47-4*) American French.

— Burials of the Joseph Lavzon & Sons Funeral Home, Woonsocket, RI, 1911-1988. vi, 624p. 1996. spiral bd. 35.00 (*1-929920-48-2*) American French.

— Burials of the Lamoureux Funeral Home, New Bedford, MA, 1930-1980. vi, 304p. 1994. spiral bd. 25.00 (*1-929920-26-1*) American French.

— Burials of the Menoche Funeral Home, Woonsocket, RI, 1955-1984. vi, 236p. 1997. spiral bd. 25.00 (*1-929920-05-9*) American French.

— Elmwood Memoria/Meunier's Funer Service, Burlington, VT 1934-1990. vii, 330p. 1992. spiral bd. 30.00 (*1-929920-46-6*) American French.

— Franco-American Marriages of New Bedford, MA (1865-1920) viii, 478p. 1986. per. 40.00 (*1-929920-14-8*) American French.

— Je Me Souviens la Cuisine de la Grandmere (I Remember Grandmother's Kitchen), 2 vols. 1981. spiral bd. 13.00 (*1-929920-43-1*) American French.

— Je Me Souviens la Cuisine de la Grandmere (I Remember Grandmother's Kitchen), Vol. I. viii, 227p. 1981. spiral bd. 7.95 (*1-929920-44-X*) American French.

— Je Me Souviens la Cuisine de la Grandmere (I Remember Grandmother's Kitchen), Vol. II. v, 252p. 1996. spiral bd. 7.95 (*1-929920-45-8*) American French.

— Marriages & Baptisms of St. Michael Catholic Church, Swansea, MA (Ocean Grove) 1922-1995. vi, 49p. 1996. spiral bd. 30.00 (*1-929920-36-9*) American French.

— Marriages of Blessed Sacrament Catholic Church, Fall River, MA, 1892-1995. vii, 204p. 1996. spiral bd. 30.00 (*1-929920-18-0*) American French.

— Marriages of Precious Blood Catholic Church, Woonsocket, RI, 1870-1995: Indexed by Men & Women, 2 vols. 1998. spiral bd. 60.00 (*1-929920-29-6*) American French.

— Marriages of Sacred Heart Catholic Church, North Attleboro, MA, 1904-1990. vii, 242p. 1993. spiral bd. 35.00 (*1-929920-19-9*) American French.

— Marriages of St. Ambrose Catholic Church, Albion, RI, 1905-1986. viii, 59p. 1999. spiral bd. 12.50 (*1-929920-30-X*) American French.

— Marriages of Saint Anne Catholic Church, Fall River, Massachusetts, 1869-1996, 2 vols. 1999. spiral bd. 70.00 (*1-929920-41-5*) American French.

— Marriages of St. Cecilia's Catholic Church, Pawtucket, RI (1910-1996) iv, 398p. 1987. per. 35.00 (*1-929920-11-3*) American French.

— Marriages of St. Jean-Baptiste Catholic Church: Fall River, Massachusetts (1901-1996) viii, 300p. 2000. spiral bd. 35.00 (*1-929920-57-1*) American French.

A

— Marriages of St. John the Baptist Catholic Church, West Warwick, RI (ARCTIC) 1873-1980, 2 vols. 1987. per. 50.00 (*1-929920-10-5*) American French.

— Marriages of St. John the Evangelist Catholic Church, Slatersville, RI, 1872-1986. x, 310p. 1988. per. 28.50 (*1-929920-13-X*) American French.

— Marriages of St. Joseph Catholic Church, Pascoag, RI, 1893-1991. vii, 276p. 1993. spiral bd. 35.00 (*1-929920-56-3*) American French.

— Marriages of St. Joseph's Catholic Church, Ashton, RI, 1872-1986. x, 246p. 1988. per. 24.00 (*1-929920-01-6*) American French.

— Marriages of St. Joseph's Catholic Church, Attleboro, MA, 1905-1986. viii, 232p. 1988. per. 22.50 (*1-929920-02-4*) American French.

— Marriages of St. Joseph's Catholic Church, Natick, RI, 1875-1989. viii, 410p. 1993. spiral bd. 40.00 (*1-929920-53-9*) American French.

— Marriages of St. Matthew Catholic Church, Central Falls, RI, 1906-1988. vii, 466p. 1999. spiral bd. 40.00 (*1-929920-28-8*) American French.

— Marriages of St. Matthew's Catholic Church, Fall River, MA, 1888-1986. x, 309p. 1987. per. 27.00 (*1-929920-00-8*) American French.

— Marriages of St. Stephen's Catholic Church, Attleboro, MA (Dodgeville) 1880-1986. vi, 225p. 1988. per. 19.95 (*1-929920-12-1*) American French.

— Marriages of St. Theresa Catholic Church, Blackstone, MA, Jul 1929-Jun 1987. viii, 132p. 1987. spiral bd. 15.00 (*1-929920-31-8*) American French.

— Marriages of St. Theresa Catholic Church, Nasonville, RI, 1923-1986. vii, 65p. 1993. spiral bd. 15.00 (*1-929920-32-6*) American French.

— Marriages Recorded in the Town of Blackstone, MA, 1845-1900. vii, 601p. 1994. spiral bd. 35.00 (*1-929920-52-0*) American French.

— Marriages Recorded in the Town Reports of Peterboro, NH, 1887-1948. vii, 559p. 1995. spiral bd. 35.00 (*1-929920-33-4*) American French.

American-French Genealogical Society Staff & Burkhart, Janice. Baptisms of St. Cecilia's Catholic Church, Pawtucket, RI, 1910-1988. ix, 466p. 1988. spiral bd. 35.00 (*1-929920-17-2*) American French.

— Baptisms of St. James Catholic Church, Manville, RI, 1860-1991. viii, 706p. 1994. spiral bd. 40.00 (*1-929920-16-4*) American French.

— Burials of St. Joseph Catholic Church, North Grosvenordale, CT, 1872-1990. vii, 576p. 1995. spiral bd. 35.00 (*1-929920-08-3*) American French.

— Burials of the Potuin Funeral Home, West Warwick, RI, 1893-1960, 2 vols. (Illus.). 1994. spiral bd. 50.00 (*1-929920-04-0*) American French.

— Burials of the Potuin Funeral Home, West Warwick, RI, 1960-1995. v, 376p. 1996. spiral bd. 25.00 (*1-929920-27-X*) American French.

American Friends Service Committee Staff. The Sun Never Sets: Confronting the Network of Foreign U. S. Military Bases. Gerson, Joseph & Birchard, Bruce, eds. 390p. 1991. 40.00 (*0-89608-400-0*); pap. 16.00 (*0-89608-399-3*) South End Pr.

American Fuchsia Society Staff, ed. Checklist of Fuchsias Registered, 1973-1983. (Illus.). 91p. 1983. 1.00 (*0-9613167-0-5*) Am Fuchsia.

— Fuchsia Culture. (Illus.). 160p. 1984. 9.95 (*0-9613167-1-3*) Am Fuchsia.

— Fuchsia Judging School Manual & AFS Judging Rules. rev. ed. 63p. 1986. 4.00 (*0-9613167-2-1*) Am Fuchsia.

American Garden Guides Staff. American Garden Guides: Rose Gardening. 1995. pap. 25.00 (*0-679-75830-5*) Pantheon.

American Gas Association Committee on Revision of & Altieri, V. J. Gas Analysis & Testing of Gaseous Materials. 567p. 1945. 5.00 (*0-318-12626-5*, X51145) Am Gas Assn.

American Gas Association, GAMA Joint Customer Serv. Fundamentals of Electricity. 82p. 1974. pap. 2.00 (*0-318-12620-6*, XH0175) Am Gas Assn.

— Fundamentals of Gas Appliances. 63p. 1976. pap. 2.00 (*0-318-12623-0*, XH1076) Am Gas Assn.

— Fundamentals of Gas Combustion. 85p. 1973. pap. 2.00 (*0-318-12624-9*, XH0373) Am Gas Assn.

American Gas Association Operating Section Compres. Compressor Station Operations. Parker, Robert L., ed. LC 85-70460. (Gas Engineering & Operating Practices Ser.). (Illus.). 304p. (C). 1985. 25.00 (*0-87257-000-2*, XY0185) Am Gas Assn.

— Corrosion Control & System Protection. Parker, Robert L., ed. (Gas Engineering & Operating Services Ser.). 276p. 1986. 30.00 (*0-87257-001-0*) Am Gas Assn.

— Operating Section Proceedings: Index: 1950-1969. 90p. 1970. pap. 3.00 (*0-318-12640-0*, X50070) Am Gas Assn.

American Gas Association, Pipeline Research Commit, Jr. & Hardy, H. Reginald. A Study to Evaluate the Stability of Underground Gas Storage Reservoirs. 404p. 1972. 10.00 (*0-318-12710-5*, L19724) Am Gas Assn.

American Gas Association, Pipeline Research Commit, et al. Branch Connections: Data for Design. 181p. 1957. pap. 2.50 (*0-318-12591-9*, L00300) Am Gas Assn.

— Noise Abatement at Gas Pipeline Installations: Physiological, Psychological & Legal Aspects of Noise, Vol. I. 58p. 1959. pap. 1.50 (*0-318-12660-5*, L00210) Am Gas Assn.

— Threshold Pressure in Gas Storage. 309p. 1971. 6.00 (*0-318-12724-5*, L20170) Am Gas Assn.

American Gas Association Pipeline Research Committ. AC Effects on Transmission Pipelines. 58p. 1978. pap. 20.00 (*0-318-12581-1*, L51278) Am Gas Assn.

— Field Validation of Atmospheric Dispersion Models for Natural Gas Compressor Stations. 100p. 1980. pap. 20.00 (*0-318-12615-X*, L51387) Am Gas Assn.

— Manual for the Determination of Supercompressibility Factors of Natural Gas. 407p. 1963. pap. 12.00 (*0-318-12650-8*, L00340) Am Gas Assn.

American Gas Association Pipeline Research Committ, et al. Earth Current Effects on Buried Pipelines: Analysis of Ohio & Vancouver Field Tests. 54p. 1968. pap. 2.50 (*0-318-12599-4*, L30510) Am Gas Assn.

— Research on the Properties of Line Pipe: Summary Report. 135p. 1962. pap. 3.00 (*0-318-12691-5*, L00290) Am Gas Assn.

— Retrograde Condensation in Natural Gas Pipelines. 512p. 1975. 12.00 (*0-318-12698-2*, L22277) Am Gas Assn.

American Gas Association. Policy Evaluation & Anal. New Technologies for Gas Energy Supply & Efficient Use, 1983 Update. (Illus.). 43p. write for info. (*0-318-57841-7*) Am Gas Assn.

American Gas Association Research Committee, et al. New Concepts in Underground Storage of Natural Gas. 342p. 1966. 7.50 (*0-318-12657-5*, L00400) Am Gas Assn.

American Gas Association Staff. Gas Appliance Service Manual 1: Range Manual 1992 Supplement. 2nd ed. 352p. 1992. pap. text 75.00 (*0-8403-8352-5*) Kendall-Hunt.

— Gas Engineers Handbook. Segeler, C. George, ed. LC 65-17328. (Illus.). 1550p. 1965. 125.00 (*0-8311-3011-3*) Indus Pr.

— Glossary for the Gas Industry. rev. ed. 83p. 1975. pap. 3.50 (*0-318-12635-4*, F50000) Am Gas Assn.

— A Guide to Natural Gas Cooling. Itteilag, Richard L., ed. LC 93-17395. 164p. 1993. 74.00 (*0-88173-133-1*) Fairmont Pr.

— Methane: A Critical Assessment of Sources, Technologies, & Economics. LC 83-15007. (Series of Special Reports: No. 8). 218p. reprint ed. pap. 67.60 (*0-7837-0681-2*, 204101400019) Bks Demand.

— Natural Gas Applications for Air Pollution Control. Hay, Nelson, ed. LC 85-45879. 359p. 1986. text 58.00 (*0-88173-013-0*) Fairmont Pr.

— Regulation of the Gas Industry, 5 vols., Set. 1981. ring bd. 980.00 (*0-8205-1311-3*) Bender.

American Gas Association Staff & Hay, Nelson E., eds. Guide to Natural Gas Cogeneration. 2nd ed. (Illus.). 543p. 1991. 68.00 (*0-88173-125-0*, 0261) Fairmont Pr.

American Gas Association Staff & Payne, F. William. Guide to New Natural Gas Utilization Technologies. LC 83-49499. 300p. 1984. text 45.00 (*0-915586-94-0*) Fairmont Pr.

American Gas Association, Transient Flow Committee, et al. Transient Flow in Natural Gas Transmission Systems. 273p. 1964. 5.00 (*0-318-12725-3*, L20030) Am Gas Assn.

American Gas Association Transmission Measurement. A. G. A. Gas Measurement Manual, Pts. 12-13. rev. ed. 100p. 1978. pap. 7.00 (*0-318-12579-X*, XQO278) Am Gas Assn.

American Genealogical Lending Library Staff. A Key to the United States Federal Census, 1880. 65p. 1988. pap. 5.95 (*0-917890-70-1*) Herit Quest.

— United States Census Key, 1850, 1860 & 1870. 193p. 1987. pap. 14.95 (*0-932022-32-4*) Herit Quest.

American Genealogical Research Institute Staff. How to Trace Your Family Tree. LC 73-88881. 208p. 1975. mass mkt. 6.95 (*0-385-09885-5*) Doubleday.

American Geographic Publishing Staff. Minnesota: A Photographic Celebration. (Illus.). 96p. (Orig.). 1989. pap. 14.95 (*0-938314-76-9*) Am Wrld Geog.

American Geographical Society Library, New York St. Research Catalogue of the American Geographical Society: First Supplement, 2 pts. Incl. Pt. 1. Regional Catalogue., 2 vols. 1972. 300.00 (*0-8161-0999-0*, G K Hall & Co); Pt. 2. Tropical Catalogue., 2 vols. 1987. 335.00 (*0-8161-1522-2*, G K Hall & Co); Suppl. 2. Tropical Catalogue. 1978. 330.00 (*0-8161-0081-0*, G K Hall & Co); write for info. (*0-318-52348-5*, G K Hall & Co) Mac Lib Ref.

American Geographical Society Library, New York St, ed. Author, Title, Subject & Geographic Catalogs of the Glaciology Collection, Department of Exploration & Field Research, 3 vols, Set. 1971. 345.00 (*0-8161-0922-2*, G K Hall & Co) Mac Lib Ref.

American Geographical Society of New York Staff. New England's Prospect, 1933. Adams, James T. et al, eds. LC 78-111763. reprint ed. 49.50 (*0-404-00354-0*) AMS Pr.

— Oriental Explorations & Studies, 6 vols., Set. reprint ed. 438.00 (*0-404-60230-4*) AMS Pr.

— Pioneer Settlement. LC 74-90599. (Essay Index Reprint Ser.). 1977. 34.95 (*0-8369-1241-1*) Ayer.

American Geological Institute Staff. Bibliography & Index of Colorado Geology, 1875 to 1975. (Bulletin Ser.: No. 37). 488p. 1976. 7.50 (*1-884216-02-1*); pap. 3.50 (*1-884216-03-X*) Colo Geol Survey.

— Bibliography & Index of Colorado Geology, 1981-1982. (Information Ser.: No. 19). 111p. (Orig.). 1983. pap. 2.00 (*1-884216-17-X*) Colo Geol Survey.

— Bibliography & Index of Colorado Geology, 1983. (Information Ser.: No. 21). 127p. (Orig.). 1983. pap. 5.00 (*1-884216-18-8*) Colo Geol Survey.

— Bibliography & Index of Colorado Geology, 1984-1989. (Information Ser.: No. 30). 584p. (Orig.). 1990. pap. 12.00 (*1-884216-22-6*) Colo Geol Survey.

— Dictionary of Geological Terms. 3rd rev. ed. LC 82-45315. (Illus.). 576p. 1976. pap. 15.95 (*0-385-18101-9*, Anchor NY) Doubleday.

— Physical Geology. 5th ed. 285p. 1999. pap. text, lab manual ed. 48.00 incl. audio compact disk (*0-13-011630-0*) P-H.

American Geological Institute Staff, et al. Physical Geology. 560p. 1995. pap. 38.95 (*0-8016-7872-2*) Mosby Inc.

American Geological Institute Staff, jt. auth. see U. S. Bureau of Mines Staff.

American Geological Society Staff. Russian-English Geological Dictionary. (ENG & RUS.). 559p. 1993. reprint ed. lib. bdg. 49.95 (*0-7859-3711-0*) Fr & Eur.

American Geology Institute Staff. Envrionmental Geology. 2001. teacher ed. 29.00 (*0-697-28799-8*, WCB McGr Hill) McGrw-H Hghr Educ.

American Geophysical Union Staff. Eutrophication in a Coastal Marine Ecosystem. Richardson, Katherine & Jurgensen, Bo B., eds. LC 96-29236. (Coastal & Estuarine Studies: Vol. 52). 272p. 1996. 55.00 (*0-87590-266-9*) Am Geophysical.

— Sedimentation & Stratigraphy of Carbonate Rock Sequences. LC 89-15053. 1989. write for info. (*0-87590-689-3*) Am Geophysical.

American Geophysical Union Staff, jt. auth. see Maul, George A.

American Girl Library, jt. auth. see Whitney, Brooks.

American Group Publishing Staff. X Windows 4 98 - The Other Win98! Why Get Just Software When You Can Have a Whole NEW Computer $498.00: Available 2 CD-ROM's with X-Windows-4-98 NTAGS Linux O/S, Netscape 4, Real Audio Player, with Caldera 1.3 O/S & Netware 4.1 for Linux. 200p. 1998. mass mkt. 29.95 (*1-891950-09-6*, 1891950096) Amer Group Pub.

American Group Staff. The Children's Intro Book to Linux, DOS, & Windows Computers & Education on the Internet: Safe, Secure & Free Software Use of an Old PC for Your Kids!: Includes CD-ROM with Red Hat 5.2 Based Mandrake Linux O/S, Netscape, Real Audio Player, & Instructions on How to Install It for Auxillary Use by Your Child. (Illus.). 160p. (Orig.). 1999. mass mkt. 27.95 incl. cd-rom (*1-891950-14-2*, Pub. by Amer Group Pub) Koen Bk Distributors.

American Gunsmith Editors, ed. Choosing & Using Gunsmithing Tools, Pt. I. (American Gunsmith Library). (Illus.). 200p. 1998. reprint ed. 26.95 (*1-879620-50-2*) Belvoir Pubns.

— Choosing & Using Gunsmithing Tools, Pt. II. (American Gunsmith Library). (Illus.). 200p. 1998. reprint ed. 26.95 (*1-879620-51-0*) Belvoir Pubns.

— Gunsmithing the Handgun: The Shooters Guide to Fit, Function & Repair. (American Gunsmith Library: Vol. II). (Illus.). 304p. 1997. reprint ed. 26.95 (*1-879620-47-2*) Belvoir Pubns.

— Gunsmithing the Rifle: Fixes & Upgrades for the Precision Shooter. (American Gunsmith Library: Vol. III). (Illus.). 254p. 1998. reprint ed. 26.95 (*1-879620-48-0*) Belvoir Pubns.

— Gunsmithing the Shotgun: Tips & Techniques. (American Gunsmith Library: Vol. IV). (Illus.). 200p. 1998. reprint ed. 26.95 (*1-879620-49-9*) Belvoir Pubns.

— Shoot Where You Aim! The Gunsmith's Secrets to Accurizing Any Firearm. (American Gunsmith Library). (Illus.). 233p. 1997. reprint ed. 26.95 (*1-879620-52-9*) Belvoir Pubns.

American Gunsmith Editors Staff. Practical Gunsmithing. LC 96-83883. (Illus.). 256p. 1996. pap. 19.95 (*0-87349-187-4*, PG, DBI Bks) Krause Pubns.

American Health Foundation Staff, et al. Know Your Body Teacher's Guide: Grade 5. 512p. 1996. teacher ed., ring bd. 65.00 (*0-7872-0799-3*) Kendall-Hunt.

— Know Your Body Teacher's Guide: Grade 6. 464p. 1995. teacher ed. 65.00 (*0-7872-0801-9*) Kendall-Hunt.

American Health Network Staff. Anchors Health Network Resource Book. 100p. (Orig.). 1995. pap. 10.50 (*0-9634399-9-5*) Funmakers.

American Health Research Institute Staff. Acetaminophen: Index of New Information with Authors & Subjects. rev. ed. 1996. 47.50 (*0-7883-0840-8*); pap. 44.50 (*0-7883-0841-6*) ABBE Pubs Assn.

— Africa - Multi-National Cultures, Progress, Stagnations, Crises & HIV: Index of New Information, 2 vols. Incl. Vol. 1, A-L. (Illus.). 170p. 1998. pap. 44.50 (*0-7883-1679-6*); Vol. 2, M-Z. (Illus.). 180p. 1998. pap. 44.50 (*0-7883-1681-8*); 89.00 (*0-7883-1677-X*) ABBE Pubs Assn.

— Africa--Multi-National Cultures, Progress, Stagnations, Crises & HIV: Index of New Information, 2 vols. Incl. Vol. 1, A-L. (Illus.). 170p. 1998. 47.50 (*0-7883-1678-8*); Vol. 2, M-Z. (Illus.). 180p. 1998. 47.50 (*0-7883-1680-X*); 95.00 (*0-7883-1676-1*) ABBE Pubs Assn.

— Anthropology of Minority Groups: Index of New Information with Authors & Subjects. rev. ed. LC 94-24771. 151p. 1994. 47.50 (*0-7883-0268-X*); pap. 44.50 (*0-7883-0269-8*) ABBE Pubs Assn.

— Anti-Oxidants: Index of National & International Research Developments with Authors, Subjects & Bibliography. 180p. 1993. 47.50 (*1-55914-778-4*); pap. 44.50 (*1-55914-779-2*) ABBE Pubs Assn.

— Anti-Oxidants & Effects on Longevity: Index of New Information with Authors, Subjects, & Bibliography. rev. ed. LC 94-35129. 171p. 1994. 47.50 (*0-7883-0266-3*); pap. 44.50 (*0-7883-0267-1*) ABBE Pubs Assn.

— Anti-Oxidants & Toxicity Research Studies: Index of New Information with Authors, Subjects & Bibliography. 180p. 1993. 47.50 (*1-55914-782-2*); pap. 44.50 (*1-55914-783-0*) ABBE Pubs Assn.

— Birth Defects - Including Drug, Diet & Chemical - Induced: Index of New Information for Reference & Research. (Illus.). 150p. 1997. 47.50 (*0-7883-1062-3*); pap. 44.50 (*0-7883-1063-1*) ABBE Pubs Assn.

— Blacks & Their Bio-Medical History: Index of Modern Authors & Subjects with Guide for Rapid Research. LC 90-56302. 160p. 1991. 47.50 (*1-55914-404-1*); pap. 44.50 (*1-55914-405-X*) ABBE Pubs Assn.

— Blacks & Their Bio-Medical History: Index of Modern Authors & Subjects with Guide for Rapid Research. 155p. 1997. 47.50 (*0-7883-1570-6*); pap. 44.50 (*0-7883-1571-4*) ABBE Pubs Assn.

— Cancer & Carcinogens in Your Environment at Home, Work & Recreation. LC 95-17724. 150p. 1995. write for info. (*0-7883-0748-7*); pap. write for info. (*0-7883-0749-5*) ABBE Pubs Assn.

— Carcinogens: Index of Modern Information. LC 88-47988. 150p. 1990. 47.50 (*1-55914-196-4*); pap. 44.50 (*1-55914-197-2*) ABBE Pubs Assn.

— Carpal Tunnel Syndrome - Causes, Symptoms, Diagnosis, Treatments & Surgery: Index of New Information Including Complications. rev. ed. LC 96-3127. 131p. 1996. 47.50 (*0-7883-1102-6*); pap. 44.50 (*0-7883-1103-4*) ABBE Pubs Assn.

— Clothing, Fire Retardants & Fire-Proofing Agents: Index & Reference Book of New Information. 150p. 1996. 47.50 (*0-7883-0848-3*); pap. 44.50 (*0-7883-0849-1*) ABBE Pubs Assn.

— Cocaine & Its Damaging Influences: Index of Modern Authors & Subjects with Guide for Rapid Research. LC 94-34580. 1994. 47.50 (*0-7883-0256-6*) ABBE Pubs Assn.

— Cocaine & Its Damaging Influences: Index of Modern Authors & Subjects with Guide for Rapid Research. LC 94-34580. 1994. pap. 44.50 (*0-7883-0257-4*) ABBE Pubs Assn.

— Crime Investigations with Forensic Sciences: Index of New Information with Authors & Subjects. LC 95-16450. 1995. write for info. (*0-7883-0432-1*); pap. 44.50 (*0-7883-0433-X*) ABBE Pubs Assn.

— Crime Victims--Assault Types, Violence Variations, Injuries & Forensics: Index of New Information. 160p. 1997. 47.50 (*0-7883-1700-8*); pap. 44.50 (*0-7883-1701-6*) ABBE Pubs Assn.

— Decision Making in Health Sciences: Medical Analysis Index with Reference Bibliography. LC 85-48752. 150p. 1987. 47.50 (*0-88164-378-5*); pap. 44.50 (*0-88164-379-3*) ABBE Pubs Assn.

— Drug Addiction, Substance Abuse & Narcotic Dependence: Index of New Information with Authors, Subjects, Research Categories & References. rev. ed. 145p. 1997. 47.50 (*0-7883-1436-X*); pap. 44.50 (*0-7883-1437-8*) ABBE Pubs Assn.

— Efficiency & Performance in Health Sciences: Medical Analysis Index with Reference Bibliography. rev. ed. LC 94-34918. 131p. 1994. 47.50 (*0-7883-0360-0*); pap. 44.50 (*0-7883-0361-9*) ABBE Pubs Assn.

— Fetal Alcohol Syndrome the Man-Made Disease for Babies & Children: Index of New Information. 160p. 1998. 47.50 (*0-7883-1900-0*); pap. 44.50 (*0-7883-1901-9*) ABBE Pubs Assn.

— Fluoxetine (Prozac, Fluoxetine HCl) Index of New Information with Authors & Subjects. LC 92-54234. 150p. 1992. 47.50 (*1-55914-616-8*); pap. 44.50 (*1-55914-617-6*) ABBE Pubs Assn.

— Governments & Agencies: Index of Activities & Information. LC 88-47565. 150p. 1990. 47.50 (*1-55914-204-9*); pap. 47.50 (*1-55914-205-7*) ABBE Pubs Assn.

— Health Care Reform: Specifics, Economics & Legislative Actions & Philosophy of Health Care: Index of Progress, 1994-1995. 322p. 1995. 47.50 (*0-7883-0650-2*); pap. 44.50 (*0-7883-0651-0*) ABBE Pubs Assn.

— Health Hazards - Skin Problems & Disorders Caused by Employment Sites & Occupational Diversity: Index of New Information with Authors, Subjects, & References. LC 96-12482. 1996. 47.50 (*0-7883-1044-5*); pap. 44.50 (*0-7883-1045-3*) ABBE Pubs Assn.

— Health Programs - Scope, Strategies, Criticisms & Practices: Index of New Information. LC 95-18253. 153p. 1995. 47.50 (*0-7883-0694-4*); pap. 44.50 (*0-7883-0695-2*) ABBE Pubs Assn.

— Health Scientists' Bible of Bibliography with Index of Authors & Subjects. rev. ed. 193p. 1995. 47.50 (*0-7883-0626-X*); pap. 44.50 (*0-7883-0627-8*) ABBE Pubs Assn.

— Hemorrhoids: Index of New Information with Authors & Subjects. LC 92-54211. 180p. 1992. 47.50 (*1-55914-574-9*); pap. 44.50 (*1-55914-575-7*) ABBE Pubs Assn.

— Human Abnormalities Caused by Chemicals, Drugs & Substances: Index of New Information with References. rev. ed. 157p. 1998. 47.50 (*0-7883-1894-2*); pap. 44.50 (*0-7883-1895-0*) ABBE Pubs Assn.

— Insurance & Economic Values of Life: Index of Modern Authors & Subjects with Guide for Rapid Research. LC 90-56287. 160p. 1991. 47.50 (*1-55914-386-X*); pap. 44.50 (*1-55914-387-8*) ABBE Pubs Assn.

— Insurance & Economic Values of Life: Index of Modern Authors & Subjects with Guide for Rapid Research. 1997. 47.50 (*0-7883-1536-6*); pap. 44.50 (*0-7883-1537-4*) ABBE Pubs Assn.

— Intelligence: International Survey with Research Subject Index & Bibliography. Bartone, John C., ed. LC 82-72014. 115p. 1982. 37.50 (*0-941864-44-8*); pap. 34.50 (*0-941864-45-6*) ABBE Pubs Assn.

— Intestinal Inflammation (Colitis, Enteritis, Crohn's Disease)--Treatment & Therapy: Index of New Information. 157p. 1997. 47.50 (*0-7883-1602-8*); pap. 44.50 (*0-7883-1603-6*) ABBE Pubs Assn.

— Jews & Ethnic Factors: Health Science Research Index with Bibliography. LC 88-47581. 150p. 1988. 47.50 (*0-88164-704-7*); pap. 44.50 (*0-88164-705-5*) ABBE Pubs Assn.

— Medical & Scientific Reports & Research on Efficiency & Performance in the Health Sciences. 180p. 1993. 47.50 (*1-55914-870-5*); pap. 44.50 (*1-55914-871-3*) ABBE Pubs Assn.

— Medical Dangers to Health & Energy in Our Drinking Water in the United States: Index of New Information. 150p. 1994. 47.50 (*0-7883-0070-9*); pap. 44.50 (*0-7883-0071-7*) ABBE Pubs Assn.

— Medical Decisions & "Advance Directives" Index of New

A

Information Including "Do-Not-Resuscitate" Orders, Accuracy of Judgments & Legal Aspects. rev. ed. (Illus.). 189p. 1997. 47.50 (*0-7883-0674-X*); pap. 44.50 (*0-7883-0673-1*) ABBE Pubs Assn.

— Medical Devices & Equipment - Design, Supplies, Failures, Control, Contaminations & Alarms: Index & Research Bible. 160p. 1995. 47.50 (*0-7883-0220-5*); pap. 44.50 (*0-7883-0221-3*) ABBE Pubs Assn.

— Medical Effects of Free Radicals: Index of New Information with Authors & Subjects. LC 95-16341. 1995. 47.50 (*0-7883-0775-4*); pap. write for info. (*0-7883-0776-2*) ABBE Pubs Assn.

— Medical Ethics & Health Sciences: Research Subject Analysis with Reference Bibliography. LC 85-48094. 150p. 1987. 47.50 (*0-88164-460-9*); pap. 44.50 (*0-88164-461-7*) ABBE Pubs Assn.

— Medical Libraries - Roles, Services & Challenges: Index of Modern Authors & Subjects with Guide for Rapid Research. LC 90-56303. 160p. 1991. 47.50 (*1-55914-402-5*); pap. 44.50 (*1-55914-403-3*) ABBE Pubs Assn.

— Medical Psychology of Adolescents: Index of New Information. rev. ed. 165p. 1998. 47.50 (*0-7883-1956-6*); pap. 44.50 (*0-7883-1957-4*) ABBE Pubs Assn.

— Medical Psychology of Crime - Including Patients. 150p. 1996. 47.50 (*0-7883-0918-8*); pap. 44.50 (*0-7883-0919-6*) ABBE Pubs Assn.

— Medical Research of Sexual Partners: Index of New Information. 150p. 1996. 47.50 (*0-7883-0914-5*); pap. 44.50 (*0-7883-0915-3*) ABBE Pubs Assn.

— Medical Research on Students: A Subject Analysis with Bibliography. LC 84-45736. 150p. 1987. 47.50 (*0-88164-250-9*); pap. 44.50 (*0-88164-251-7*) ABBE Pubs Assn.

— Medical Studies of Aggression: Index of New Information. 150p. 1996. 47.50 (*0-7883-0922-6*); pap. 44.50 (*0-7883-0923-4*) ABBE Pubs Assn.

— Medical Studies of Gunshot Wounds: Index of New Information with Authors, Subjects & References. 150p. 1996. 47.50 (*0-7883-0926-9*); pap. 44.50 (*0-7883-0927-7*) ABBE Pubs Assn.

— Medical Studies of Human Cadavers - Normal & Diseased: Index of New Information. 150p. 1996. 47.50 (*0-7883-0978-1*); pap. 44.50 (*0-7883-0979-X*) ABBE Pubs Assn.

— Medical Studies of Violence: Index of New Information. 150p. 1996. 47.50 (*0-7883-0920-X*); pap. 44.50 (*0-7883-0921-8*) ABBE Pubs Assn.

— Medical Subject Analysis of a Selected Bibliography Concerning General Counseling. rev. ed. Bartone, John C., ed. LC 94-34597. 161p. 1994. 47.50 (*0-7883-0238-8*); pap. 44.50 (*0-7883-0239-6*) ABBE Pubs Assn.

— Medical Uses of Anti-Oxidants for Cancer Prevention: Index of New Information with Authors, Subjects & Bibliography. LC 95-16102. 1995. 47.50 (*0-7883-0470-4*); pap. 44.50 (*0-7883-0471-2*) ABBE Pubs Assn.

— Mental & Intelligence Tests: Medical Subject Analysis with Research Bibliography. LC 84-45652. 150p. 1985. 37.50 (*0-88164-226-6*); pap. 34.50 (*0-88164-227-4*) ABBE Pubs Assn.

— Mental Health Services--Status, Trends & Practices: Index of New Information. 160p. 1998. 47.50 (*0-7883-1652-4*); pap. 44.50 (*0-7883-1653-2*) ABBE Pubs Assn.

— Milk & Milk Research: Medical & Scientific Index with Reference Bibliography. LC 88-47595. 150p. 1988. 47.50 (*0-88164-746-2*); pap. 44.50 (*0-88164-747-0*) ABBE Pubs Assn.

— Noise & Adverse Effects on Health: Medical Subject Analysis with Reference Bibliography. LC 85-48089. 150p. 1987. 47.50 (*0-88164-450-1*); pap. 44.50 (*0-88164-451-X*) ABBE Pubs Assn.

— Nuclear Warfare: Science & Medical Subject Analysis with Reference Bibliography. LC 85-48095. 150p. 1987. 47.50 (*0-88164-462-5*); pap. 44.50 (*0-88164-463-3*) ABBE Pubs Assn.

— Organ Donations & Procurements: Index of Authors & Subjects. 180p. 1993. 47.50 (*1-55914-936-1*); pap. 44.50 (*1-55914-937-X*) ABBE Pubs Assn.

— Petroleum & Medicine: Scientific Subject Index with Research Bibliography. LC 88-47604. 150p. 1988. 47.50 (*0-88164-742-X*); pap. 44.50 (*0-88164-743-8*) ABBE Pubs Assn.

***American Health Research Institute Staff.** Phenytoin (Dilantin, Diphenylhydantoin) - Therapy & Clinical Uses: Index of New Information with Authors, Subjects & References. rev. ed. 150p. 1999. 47.50 (*0-7883-2182-X*); pap. 44.50 (*0-7883-2183-8*) ABBE Pubs Assn.

American Health Research Institute Staff. Phenytoin (Dilantin, Diphenylhydantoin) & Its Adverse Effects in the Human Body. LC 89-18673. 201p. 1990. 47.50 (*1-55914-120-4*); pap. 44.50 (*1-55914-121-2*) ABBE Pubs Assn.

— Prozac (Fluoxetine) - Side Effects & Harmful Reactions: New Information with Authors & Subjects. rev. ed. 1994. 47.50 (*0-7883-0172-1*); pap. 44.50 (*0-7883-0173-X*) ABBE Pubs Assn.

— Psycho-Physiological Disorders: General & Medical Research Subject Directory with Bibliography. Bartone, John C., ed. LC 82-72012. 236p. 1982. 47.50 (*0-941864-40-5*); pap. 44.50 (*0-941864-41-3*) ABBE Pubs Assn.

— Rape Victims, Offenders, Treatment & Jurisprudence: Medical Subject Analysis & Research Guide. Bartone, John C., ed. LC 83-45537. 140p. 1984. 47.50 (*0-88164-122-7*); pap. 44.50 (*0-88164-123-5*) ABBE Pubs Assn.

— Refugees--Health, Disease, Demographics, Dissidents, PTSD, Wounded & Survivors: Index of New Information. 160p. 1998. 47.50 (*0-7883-1654-0*); pap. 44.50 (*0-7883-1655-9*) ABBE Pubs Assn.

— Religion & the HIV-AIDS Community: Index of New Information with Authors & Subjects. rev. ed. LC 94-34806. 109p. 1994. 47.50 (*0-7883-0448-8*); pap. 44.50 (*0-7883-0449-6*) ABBE Pubs Assn.

— Research--World Developments in Health, Science, Life & Work: Index of New Information. 160p. 1997. 47.50 (*0-7883-1722-9*); pap. 44.50 (*0-7883-1723-7*) ABBE Pubs Assn.

— Saccharin & Its Health Risk Controversy: Index of New Information. 160p. Date not set. 47.50 (*0-7883-1860-8*); pap. 44.50 (*0-7883-1861-6*) ABBE Pubs Assn.

— Sex Disorders: Medical Subject Analysis & Research Guidebook with Bibliography. Bartone, John C., ed. LC 84-45866. 150p. 1987. 47.50 (*0-88164-288-6*); pap. 44.50 (*0-88164-289-4*) ABBE Pubs Assn.

— Sexology Encyclopedia Vol. 1: Sex & Intercourse Research: Index & Reference Books of New Information. Bartone, John C., ed. (Illus.). 175p. 1996. pap. 39.95 (*0-7883-0851-3*) ABBE Pubs Assn.

— Sexology Encyclopedia Vol. 1: Sex & Intercourse Research: Index & Reference Books of New Information, 25 vols., Set. Bartone, John C., ed. (Illus.). 175p. 1996. 49.95 (*0-7883-0850-5*) ABBE Pubs Assn.

— Sexology Encyclopedia Vol. 11: Sex Disorders: Sex Disorders: Index & Reference Books of New Information. Bartone, John C., ed. (Illus.). 153p. 1996. pap. 39.95 (*0-7883-0871-8*) ABBE Pubs Assn.

— Sexology Encyclopedia Vol. 11: Sex Disorders: Sex Disorders: Index & Reference Books of New Information, 25 vols., Set. Bartone, John C., ed. (Illus.). 153p. 1996. 49.95 (*0-7883-0870-X*) ABBE Pubs Assn.

— Sexology Encyclopedia Vol. 15: Sex Behavior: Index & Reference Books of New Information. Bartone, John C., ed. (Illus.). 153p. 1996. 49.95 (*0-7883-0878-5*); pap. 39.95 (*0-7883-0879-3*) ABBE Pubs Assn.

— Technology Assessments: Index of New Information with Authors, Subjects, & Bibliography. LC 94-30989. 1994. write for info. (*0-7883-0412-7*); pap. write for info. (*0-7883-0413-5*) ABBE Pubs Assn.

— Technology Assessments in Health Sciences. 150p. 1990. 47.50 (*1-55914-110-7*); pap. 44.50 (*1-55914-111-5*) ABBE Pubs Assn.

— Therapeutic Uses of Antioxidants for Health Improvements: Index of New Information with Authors, Subjects, & Bibliography. LC 95-16388. 1995. write for info. (*0-7883-0468-2*); pap. write for info. (*0-7883-0469-0*) ABBE Pubs Assn.

— Therapy Made Easy with Computer Assistance: Index of New Information with Authors & Subjects. rev. ed. 149p. 1994. 47.50 (*0-7883-0398-8*); pap. 44.50 (*0-7883-0399-6*) ABBE Pubs Assn.

— Tissue Donations in Health, Disease & Post-Mortem Gifts: Index of Authors & Subjects. 180p. 1993. 47.50 (*1-55914-932-9*); pap. 44.50 (*1-55914-933-7*) ABBE Pubs Assn.

— Tretinoin - Actions, Harmful Reactions, & Variations in Therapy: Index of New Information with Authors, Subjects, & References. rev. ed. LC 96-3122. 151p. 1996. 47.50 (*0-7883-1046-1*); pap. 44.50 (*0-7883-1047-X*) ABBE Pubs Assn.

— Veterans: Index of Problems, Cases & Outcomes - Before, During & After Wars. LC 90-56249. 220p. 1991. 47.50 (*1-55914-260-X*); pap. 44.50 (*1-55914-261-8*) ABBE Pubs Assn.

— Weather, Health & Biomedicine: Subject Analysis Index with Research Bibliography. LC 85-47846. 150p. 1987. 47.50 (*0-88164-354-8*); pap. 44.50 (*0-88164-355-6*) ABBE Pubs Assn.

— Women & Women's Rights: A Medical, Psychological & International Subject Survey with Research Index & Bibliography. Bartone, John C., ed. LC 83-70089. 146p. 1984. 47.50 (*0-941864-98-7*); pap. 44.50 (*0-941864-99-5*) ABBE Pubs Assn.

— Women's Health Services: Index of New Information with Authors & Subjects. LC 92-54209. 150p. 1992. 47.50 (*1-55914-570-6*); pap. 44.50 (*1-55914-571-4*) ABBE Pubs Assn.

***American Heart Association Staff.** AHA around the World Cookbook. 2000. pap. 17.00 (*0-8129-3307-9*) Random.

— Aha Cakes, Cookies & Dessert. 2000. pap. write for info. (*0-8129-3335-4*) Random.

American Heart Association Staff. AHA Low Fat. 1995. pap. write for info. (*0-8129-2786-9*) Random.

— American Heart Association Around The World Cookbook. 1996. 25.00 (*0-8129-2344-8*, Times Bks) Crown Pub Group.

— American Heart Association Clip Strip Program. 1995. pap. 29.94 (*0-8129-2669-2*, Times Bks) Crown Pub Group.

— American Heart Association Cookbook. 5th rev. ed. (Illus.). 1993. pap. 17.00 (*0-8129-2282-4*, Times Bks) Crown Pub Group.

— American Heart Association Cookbook, No. 5. 5th ed. (Heart Care Titles Ser.). 1994. mass mkt. 6.99 (*0-345-39488-7*) Ballantine Pub Grp.

— American Heart Association Family Guide to Stroke: Treatment, Recovery & Prevention. (Illus.). 320p. 1996. pap. 15.00 (*0-8129-2721-4*, Times Bks) Crown Pub Group.

— The American Heart Association Guide to Eating Well & Living. Date not set. write for info. (*0-8129-2730-3*, Times Bks) Crown Pub Group.

— The American Heart Association Guide to Heart Attack Treatment: The Most up to Date Information on Treatment Recovery Prevention. 320p. 1998. pap. 15.00 (*0-8129-2978-0*, Times Bks) Crown Pub Group.

— The American Heart Association Kids' Cookbook. LC 92-56800. (Illus.). 128p. (J). (gr. 4 up). 1993. 16.00 (*0-8129-1930-0*, Times Bks) Crown Pub Group.

***American Heart Association Staff.** American Heart Association Low-Fat & Luscious Desserts: Cakes, Cookies, Pies & Other Temptations. (Illus.). 256p. 2000. 21.00 (*0-8129-3336-2*) Random.

American Heart Association Staff. The American Heart Association Low-Fat, Low Cholesterol Cookbook: Heart-Healthy, Easy-to-Make Recipes that Taste Great. 2nd ed. LC 97-17099. (Illus.). 352p. 1997. 25.95 (*0-8129-2684-6*, Times Bks) Crown Pub Group.

***American Heart Association Staff.** American Heart Association Meals in Minutes: Over 200 All-New Quick & Easy Low-Fat Recipes. LC 99-52989. (Illus.). 288p. 2000. 26.95 (*0-8129-3332-X*, Times Bks) Crown Pub Group.

American Heart Association Staff. The American Heart Association Not Quite Vegetarian Cookbook. 1998. write for info. (*0-8129-2952-7*, Times Bks) Crown Pub Group.

— The American Heart Association Quick & Easy Cookbook. LC 94-19973. (Illus.). 1995. 25.95 (*0-8129-2251-4*) Random.

— American Heart Association 365 Ways to Get Out the Fat. LC 97-28430. 128p. 1997. pap. 4.99 (*0-8129-6385-7*, Times Bks) Crown Pub Group.

— The American Heart Association's Fitting in Fitness. LC 96-49730. 173p. 1997. pap. 4.99 (*0-8129-2911-X*, Times Bks) Crown Pub Group.

— Get Out the Fat: An Easy-to-Follow Program for Trimming the Fat from Your Diet. 1996. pap. 4.99 (*0-8129-2747-8*) Random.

— The American Heart Association's Your Heart: An Owner's Manual. LC 94-45518. 384p. 1995. text 27.95 (*0-13-359324-X*) P-H.

— Be Like the Animals: HeartPower! Student Reader-Level K-2. (HeartPower! American Heart Association Schoolsite Program Ser.). (Illus.). 48p. (J). (gr. k-2). 1996. pap. write for info. (*0-87493-303-X*) Am Heart.

— Big News Straight from the Heart: HeartPower! Big Book. (HeartPower! American Heart Association Schoolsite Program Ser.). (Illus.). 16p. (J). (ps-2). 1996. pap. write for info. (*0-87493-301-3*) Am Heart.

— Brand Name Fat & Cholesterol Counter. 2nd rev. ed. LC 95-7027. 400p. 1995. pap. 5.99 (*0-8129-2367-7*, Times Bks) Crown Pub Group.

— Cakes, Cookies & Desserts. 1999. write for info. (*0-8129-2957-8*, Times Bks) Crown Pub Group.

***American Heart Association Staff.** CPT, 2000. (C). 1999. ring bd. 60.00 (*1-57947-019-X*) Thomson Learn.

American Heart Association Staff. La Gran Noticia! Directo desde el Corazon: HeartPower! Big Book. (HeartPower! American Heart Association Schoolsite Program Ser.). (SPA., Illus.). 16p. (J). (ps-2). 1996. pap. write for info. (*0-87493-309-9*) Am Heart.

— The Healthy Heart Walking Book: The American Heart Association Walking Program. (Illus.). 192p. 1995. 14.95 (*0-02-860447-4*, Pub. by Macmillan) S&S Trade.

— HeartPower! A Teacher Resource Book. (HeartPower! American Heart Association Schoolsite Program Ser.). (Illus.). 104p. 1996. pap. write for info. (*0-87493-304-8*); pap. write for info. (*0-87493-306-4*); pap. write for info. (*0-87493-308-0*); pap., teacher ed. write for info. (*0-87493-300-5*) Am Heart.

— HeartPower! A Teacher Resource Book. (HeartPower! American Heart Association Schoolsite Program Ser.). (Illus.). 104p. (J). (gr. k-2). 1996. pap. write for info. (*0-87493-302-1*) Am Heart.

— Living Well, Staying Well: The Ultimate Guide to Help Prevent Heart Disease & Cancer. 336p. 1998. pap. 14.00 (*0-8129-3067-3*, Times Bks) Crown Pub Group.

— The New American Heart Association Cookbook. 6th rev. ed. LC 99-462584. (Illus.). 698p. 1999. 30.00 (*0-8129-2954-3*, Times Bks) Crown Pub Group.

— Quick & Easy Cookbook. 1999. write for info. (*0-8129-2955-1*, Times Bks) Crown Pub Group.

— The Smoking Yokadokas Level 6-8: HeartPower! Student Reader. (HeartPower! American Heart Association Schoolsite Program Ser.). (Illus.). 48p. (J). (gr. 1-3). 1996. pap. write for info. (*0-87493-307-2*) Am Heart.

— Textbook of Advanced Cardiac Life Support. Cummins, Richard O., ed. LC 98-203719. (Illus.). 348p. 1994. pap. text. write for info. (*0-87493-626-8*) Am Heart.

— Who Invented Running? Level 3-5: HeartPower! Student Reader. (HeartPower! American Heart Association Schoolsite Program Ser.). (Illus.). 32p. 1996. pap. write for info. (*0-87493-305-6*) Am Heart.

— Your Heart: American Heart Association's Complete Guide to Heart Health. 432p. 1996. per. 6.99 (*0-671-53081-X*) PB.

American Heart Association Staff, jt. auth. see American Academy of Pediatrics Staff.

American Heart Associstion Staff. American Heart Association Quick & Easy Cookbook: More Than 200 Healthful Recipes You Can Make in Minutes. 288p. 1998. pap. 17.00 (*0-8129-3011-8*, Times Bks) Crown Pub Group.

American Hemerocallis Society Staff. Daylilies: The Beginner's Handbook. Gatlin, Frances L., ed. (Illus.). 80p. 1991. pap. text 6.00 (*0-9631072-0-8*) Am Hemerocallis.

American Heraldic Society Staff. King. Genealogy of the King Family. 199p. 1997. reprint ed. pap. 29.50 (*0-8328-9427-3*); reprint ed. lib. bdg. 39.50 (*0-8328-9426-5*) Higginson Bk Co.

American Heritage Dictionaries Editors. American Heritage Children's Dictionary. LC 98-21414. (Illus.). 864p. (J). (gr. 3-6). 1998. 17.00 (*0-395-85739-2*) HM.

— American Heritage Dictionary. large type ed. LC 98-8702. 384p. 1998. 15.00 (*0-395-92932-6*) HM.

— Roget's II Thesaurus. large type ed. LC 98-8701. 264p. 1998. 15.00 (*0-395-92933-4*) HM.

American Heritage Dictionaries Editors, ed. Compact American Dictionary of Computer Words: An A to Z Guide to Hardware, Software & Cyberspace. LC 98-19870. (Illus.). 324p. 1998. pap. text 12.00 (*0-395-90214-2*, AHD & Ref) HM.

— Compact American Heritage Dictionary: A Concise Dictionary of American English. LC 98-13749. 201p. 1998. 10.00 (*0-395-90212-6*) HM.

— Compact American Medical Dictionary: A Concise & Up-To-Date Guide to Medical Terms. LC 98-20456. (Illus.). 506p. 1998. pap. text 12.00 (*0-395-88409-8*, AHD & Ref) HM.

— Compact American Thesaurus: An Easy-To-Use Guide for Choosing the Right Word. LC 98-13757. 516p. 1998. 10.00 (*0-395-90213-4*) HM.

American Heritage Dictionaries Staff, ed. The American Heritage Dictionary of Geography: Places & Peoples of the World. LC 97-10624. (Illus.). 458p. (YA). (gr. 5 up). 1997. 22.00 (*0-395-86448-8*) HM.

— Dictionary of Computer Words: An A to Z Guide for Today's Computers. rev. ed. LC 95-1175. (Illus.). 352p. 1995. pap. 11.95 (*0-395-72834-7*) HM.

American Heritage Dictionary. Word Desk Set III, 3 vols. 20102p. 1996. boxed set 19.00 (*0-395-75694-4*) HM.

American Heritage Dictionary Editors. American Heritage First Dictionary. LC 98-215999. (Illus.). 377p. (J). (gr. 1-3). 1998. 15.00 (*0-395-90210-X*) American Heritage Inc.

— American Heritage Picture Dictionary. (Illus.). 144p. (J). (ps-1). 1998. 12.00 (*0-395-90215-0*) HM.

— American Heritage Student Dictionary. (Illus.). 1120p. (J). (gr. 6-9). 1998. 18.00 (*0-395-90211-8*) HM.

— Diccionario Ingles. (SPA.). 1982. 9.95 (*0-395-31254-X*); pap. 12.00 (*0-395-31255-8*) HM.

— The Professional Secretary's Handbook. 3rd ed. LC 95-12835. (Illus.). 592p. 1995. 18.95 (*0-395-69621-6*, AHD & Ref) HM.

— Roget's II: The New Thesaurus, 4 vols. 3rd large type ed. 1306p. 326.50 (*0-614-20562-X*, L-38172-00 APHB) Am Printing Hse.

American Heritage Dictionary Editors. Word Mysteries & Histories: From Quiche to Humble Pie, 001. LC 86-10455. (Illus.). 304p. 1987. pap. 9.95 (*0-395-40264-6*) HM.

American Heritage Editors. Compact American Spanish Dictionary: Spanish-English/English-Spanish. LC 99-11861. (ENG & SPA.). 616p. 1999. 14.00 (*0-395-96215-3*) HM.

***American Heritage Magazine Editorial Staff.** American Heritage. LC 99-462173. 2000. 35.00 (*0-8129-3249-8*, Times Bks) Crown Pub Group.

***American Heritage Magazine Staff.** American Heritage Great Minds of History. (Illus.). 2000. pap. text 15.95 (*0-471-39022-4*) Wiley.

American Heritage Publishing Staff. American Heritage Dictionary. 1989. 11.60 (*0-606-02011-X*, Pub. by Turtleback) Demco.

American Heritage Staff. The American Heritage Children's Dictionary. (Illus.). (J). (gr. 3-8). 1995. 26.00 incl. cd-rom (*0-395-73580-7*) HM.

— The American Heritage College Dictionary. 3rd ed. 1664p. 1993. 24.00 (*0-395-67161-2*) HM.

— American Heritage Dictionary. 1987. mass mkt. 5.99 (*0-440-80000-5*) Dell.

— American Heritage Dictionary. 3rd ed. LC 00-1368. (Illus.). 960p. 1994. pap. 12.95 (*0-385-31254-7*, Delta Trade) Dell.

— American Heritage Dictionary: College Edition. 3rd ed. 960p. (C). 1994. pap. 5.95 (*0-395-69956-8*) HM.

— The American Heritage Dictionary of the English Language. 3rd ed. (Illus.). 2184p. 1992. 50.00 (*0-395-44895-6*) HM.

— American Heritage Essential Reference Set, 3 vols. 1994. boxed set 17.00 (*0-395-71811-2*) HM.

— Good Beginnings How Can I Get There. LC 97-71039. (Illus.). 4p. (J). 1997. bds. 3.95 (*0-395-87493-9*) HM.

— Good Beginnings How Do I Feel. LC 97-71036. (Illus.). 4p. (J). 1997. bds. 3.95 (*0-395-85908-5*) HM.

— Good Beginnings What Color Is It. LC 97-71037. (Illus.). 4p. (J). 1997. bds. 3.95 (*0-395-85909-3*) HM.

— Good Beginnings Where Can I Go. LC 97-71038. (Illus.). 4p. (J). 1997. bds. 3.95 (*0-395-87492-0*) HM.

— Historical Houses of America. pap. 6.95 (*0-686-60941-7*, 24711-5, Fireside) S&S Trade Pap.

American Historic Inns Incorporated Staff, jt. auth. see Sakach, Deborah.

American Historical Association Staff. War As a Social Institution: The Historian's Perspective. Clarkson, Jessie D. & Cochran, Thomas C., eds. LC 73-38408. reprint ed. 22.50 (*0-404-01575-1*) AMS Pr.

American Historical Association Staff, jt. auth. see Foner, Eric.

American Historical Association Staff, jt. auth. see Seip, Terry L.

American Historical Association Staff, ed. see American Jewish Historical Society Staff, et al.

American Historical Foundation Staff, ed. M-1911A1 Automatic Pistol: Proud American Legend. (Illus.). (Orig.). 1985. pap. 8.95 (*0-933489-03-X*) Amer Hist Found.

American Historical Foundation Staff, ed. see Stack, Richard L.

American Historical Society of Germans from Russia. Lieblings-Lieder Unserer Vorvater. (Illus.). 215p. 1982. pap. 14.50 (*0-914222-06-6*) Am Hist Soc Ger.

***American Historical Society Staff.** Schlegel's German-American Families in the U. S. Genealogical & Biographical, New York Edition. 796p. 2000. 85.00 (*0-7404-0034-7*) Higginson Bk Co.

American History Workshop Staff & Constitution Works Staff. "By Americans for Americans" 3rd ed. 198p. (YA). (gr. 5-12). 1996. reprint ed. pap. text, teacher ed. 10.00 (*1-930158-06-8*) Constitution Wrks.
— "By Americans for Americans" 4th ed. 100p. (YA). (gr. 5-12). 1997. reprint ed. pap. text, teacher ed. write for info. (*1-930158-05-X*) Constitution Wrks.
— Denver Dispatch vs. United States. 7th ed. 68p. (YA). (gr. 5-12). 1996. reprint ed. pap. text, teacher ed. 10.00 (*1-930158-00-9*) Constitution Wrks.
— Denver Dispatch vs. United States, Level 1. 8th ed. (Illus.). 88p. (YA). (gr. 5-12). 1997. reprint ed. pap. text, student ed. 10.00 (*1-930158-02-5*) Constitution Wrks.
— Denver Dispatch vs. United States, Level 2. 8th ed. (Illus.). 92p. (YA). (gr. 5-12). 1997. reprint ed. pap. text, student ed., wbk. ed. 10.00 (*1-930158-01-7*) Constitution Wrks.
— El Despacho de Denver vs. Estados Unidos. 5th ed. Orig. Title: Denver Dispatch vs. United States. (SPA., Illus.). 92p. (YA). (gr. 5-12). 1996. reprint ed. pap. text, student ed. 10.00 (*1-930158-14-9*) Constitution Wrks.
— The Fourteenth Amendment & Equal Protection of the Laws. 7th ed. 62p. (YA). (gr. 5-12). 1996. reprint ed. pap. text, teacher ed. 10.00 (*1-930158-03-3*) Constitution Wrks.
— The Fourteenth Amendment & Equal Protection of the Laws. 8th ed. 94p. (YA). (gr. 5-12). 1997. reprint ed. pap. text, student ed., wbk. ed. 10.00 (*1-930158-04-1*) Constitution Wrks.
— SpeakOut! vs. United States. 58p. (YA). (gr. 5-12). 1997. pap. text, teacher ed. 10.00 (*1-930158-07-6*) Constitution Wrks.
— SpeakOut! vs. United States. (Illus.). 96p. (YA). (gr. 5-12). 1997. pap. text, student ed., wbk. ed. 10.00 (*1-930158-08-4*) Constitution Wrks.

American Home Economics Association Staff. Textile Handbook. 5th ed. LC 74-31289. 127p. reprint ed. pap. 39.40 (*0-7837-4785-3*, 204454100003) Bks Demand.

American Homebrewers Association Staff. Zymurgy: The Best Articles & Advice from America's #1 Home Brewing Magazine. Papazian, Charlie, ed. LC 97-49055. 416p. 1998. pap. 13.00 (*0-380-79399-7*, Avon Bks) Morrow Avon.

American Homebrewers Association Staff, compiled by. Winners Circle: 10 Years of Award-Winning Homebrew Recipes. (Illus.). 199p. 1989. pap. 11.95 (*0-937381-14-4*) Brewers Pubns.

American Homeowners Foundation Staff. Home Buyer's Plan. 84p. 1994. pap. 8.95 (*0-940313-02-2*) Am Home Found.
— Home Investor's Plan. 92p. 1994. reprint ed. pap. 8.95 (*0-940313-01-4*) Am Home Found.
— How to Sell Your Home Fast! (Illus.). 142p. (Orig.). 1995. pap. 12.95 (*0-940313-08-1*) Am Home Found.

American Honey Institute Staff & Iowa Honey Producers Association Staff. Old Favorite Honey Recipes & Honey Recipes Book, 2 bks. in 1. (Illus.). 96p. (Orig.). 1988. pap. 5.95 (*0-916638-17-0*) Meyerbooks.

American Horse Shows Association Staff. Dressage Illustrated, Level 1. Legend Enterprises Staff, ed. & photos by by. (Illus.). 12p. 1998. pap. 14.00 (*1-893878-01-5*) Legend Ents.
— Dressage Illustrated, Level 2. Legend Enterprises Staff, ed. & photos by by. (Illus.). 12p. 1998. pap. 14.00 (*1-893878-02-3*) Legend Ents.
— Dressage Illustrated, Level 3. Legend Enterprises Staff, ed. & photos by by. (Illus.). 12p. 1998. pap. 14.00 (*1-893878-03-1*) Legend Ents.
— Dressage Illustrated, Level 4. Legend Enterprises Staff, ed. & photos by by. (Illus.). 12p. 1998. pap. 14.00 (*1-893878-04-X*) Legend Ents.
— Dressage Illustrated, Level 5. Legend Enterprises Staff, ed. & photos by by. (Illus.). 12p. 1994. pap. 14.00 (*1-893878-05-8*) Legend Ents.
— Dressage Illustrated: Training Level, 1998 Edition. (Illus.). 16p. 1998. pap. 14.00 (*1-893878-00-7*) Legend Ents.

***American Horticultural Society Staff.** American Horticultural Society: Pests & Diseases. Greenwood, Pippa et al, eds. LC 99-48249. (Illus.). 224p. 2000. 34.95 (*0-7894-5074-7*, D K Ink) DK Pub Inc.

American Horticultural Society Staff, jt. auth. see DK Publishing Staff.

American Horticultural Society Staff, jt. auth. see Heriteau, Jacqueline.

American Hospital Association. AHA Guide to the Health Care Field. 1997. pap. 275.00 (*0-87258-717-7*) AHPI.
— Basic Guide to Hospital Public Relations 2nd ed. LC 83-21354. vi, 96 p. 1984. write for info. (*0-87258-422-4*) Am Hospital.
— Estimated Useful Lives of Depreciable Hospital Assets. LC 84-2879. v, 5 p. 1983. 12.50 (*0-939450-18-6*) AHPI.

American Hospital Association Staff. AHA Guide to Health Care Field. 1996. 1996. pap. text 250.00 (*0-87258-706-1*) Am Hospital.

***American Hospital Association Staff.** AHA Guide to the Health Care Field 1999-2000. (Illus.). 1999. pap. text 372.00 (*0-87258-749-5*) Am Hospital.

American Hospital Association Staff. AHA Hospital Stat: Emerging Trends in Hospitals: 1995-1996 Edition. (Illus.). 178p. (Orig.). 1996. pap. 95.00 (*0-87258-682-0*) Am Hospital.
— Catalog of the Library of the American Hospital Association, Asa S. Bacon Memorial Library, Chicago, 5 vols, Set. 1976. 610.00 (*0-8161-1210-X*, G K Hall & Co) Mac Lib Ref.
— Community Benefit & Tax-Exempt Status: A Self-Assessment Guide for Hospitals. 100p. (Orig.). 1988. 40.00 (*0-87258-498-4*, 001800) Am Hospital.
— Cumulative Index of Hospital Literature: 1950-1954. Incl. 1955-1959. 460p. 1960. boxed set 45.00 (*0-87258-329-5*, AHA-121002); 1950-1954. 540p. 1955. 45.00 (*0-87258-328-7*, AHA-121001); write for info. (*0-318-50490-1*) Am Hospital.
— Estimated Useful Lives of Depreciable Hospital Assets. LC 83-8767. 1983. write for info. (*0-87258-409-7*) Am Hospital.
— Hospital Literature Index: 1992 Annual Cumulative. 604p. 1993. 260.00 (*0-87258-598-0*, 121480) Am Hospital.
— Hospital Literature Index: 1993 Cumulative Annual. 600p. 1993. 290.00 (*0-87258-656-1*, 121490) Am Hospital.
— Hospital Statistics, 1999 ed. 1998. pap. text 200.00 (*0-87258-746-0*) Am Hospital.
— Maintenance Management for Medical Equipment. (Illus.). 270p. (Orig.). 1994. pap. 100.00 (*0-685-72235-X*, 055855) Am Hospital.
— Management of HIV Infection in the Hospital. 3rd rev. ed. LC 89-34355. Orig. Title: A Hospitalwide Approach to AIDS. 58p. 1988. pap. 15.00 (*0-87258-501-8*, 094642) Am Hospital.
— Mapping Your Risk Management Course in Ambulatory Care. (Illus.). 52p. (Orig.). 1995. pap. 20.00 (*0-87258-694-4*) Am Hospital.
— Mapping Your Risk Management Course in Home Health Care. (Illus.). 32p. (Orig.). 1995. pap. 20.00 (*0-87258-701-0*) Am Hospital.
— Mapping Your Risk Management Course in Integrated Delivery Networks. (Illus.). 40p. (Orig.). 1995. pap. 20.00 (*0-87258-697-9*) Am Hospital.
— Mapping Your Risk Management Course in Stand-Alone Hospitals. (Illus.). 50p. (Orig.). 1996. pap. 20.00 (*0-87258-702-9*) Am Hospital.
— MediTrends, 1995-1996. 3rd ed. 100p. 1995. pap. 75.00 (*0-87258-708-8*, 012010) Am Hospital.
— Nursing Licensure Guidelines, 1999 Ed. 1999. pap. text 65.00 (*1-887617-62-0*) St Bart Pr Ltd.
— A Prelude to Strategic Planning: Making Your Organization & Community Fit for Success. (Illus.). 52p. (Orig.). 1989. pap. 35.00 (*0-87258-521-2*, 184206) Am Hospital.
— Quality Resource Packet for Trustees. 78p. (Orig.). 1992. pap. 100.00 (*0-87258-629-4*, 196300) Am Hospital.
— Smoking & Hospitals Are a Bad Match! (Illus.). 47p. 1988. 35.00 (*0-87258-517-4*, 166901) Am Hospital.
— Strategic Planning Workbook. (Illus.). 114p. 1989. 60.00 (*0-87258-520-4*, 184205) Am Hospital.
— Values in Conflict: Resolving Ethical Issues in Health Care. 2nd ed. 120p. (Orig.). 1994. pap. 29.00 (*0-87258-668-5*, 025002) Am Hospital.
— The Volunteer Services Department in a Health Care Institution. 2nd rev. ed. LC 88-37456. 56p. 1988. pap. 14.00 (*0-87258-493-3*, 202166) Am Hospital.

American Hospital Association Staff, et al. The Guide to Governance for Hospital Trustees. (Illus.). 110p. (Orig.). 1990. pap. 54.95 (*0-87258-546-8*, 196600) Am Hospital.
— Integrated Health Care 100 Directory. LC 97-52243. Date not set. 595.00 (*1-55648-234-5*) AHPI.

American Hospital Association Staff, jt. auth. see Wolgin, Francie.

American Hospital Pub Staff. 100 Faces of Health Care. 1999. pap. text 66.00 (*1-55648-276-0*) AHPI.

American Hotel & Motel Association Staff. Hospitality Environments: Innovative Architectural & Interior Design. (Illus.). 208p. 1997. text 59.95 (*0-07-001300-4*) McGraw.

American Humane Association, Children's Division Staff. Child Welfare Services Enhancement Grant: Family Center Initiative Project Report. (Illus.). ii, 134p. 1996. pap. text 15.00 (*0-930915-13-5*, CFC01) Am Humane Assn.
— Child Welfare Services Enhancement Grant: Universal Home Visitation Project Report & Implementation Guide. (Illus.). iii, 222p. 1996. pap. text 15.00 (*0-930915-14-3*, CHV01) Am Humane Assn.
— Guidebook for the Visual Assessment of Physical Child Abuse. (Illus.). 57p. 1996. pap. text 95.00 incl. VHS (*0-930915-12-7*, CAV100) Am Humane Assn.
— Tribal-State Relationships in Child Welfare. LC 98-101408. 61p. 1997. pap. text 8.50 (*0-930915-18-6*, CIBTS02) Am Humane Assn.

American Humane Association, Children's Division Staff, ed. Child Welfare Workload Analysis & Resource Management: Warm Workshop & Practitioner's Meeting - Resource Manual. (Illus.). viii, 276p. 1993. ring bd. 40.00 (*0-930915-16-X*, CWM01) Am Humane Assn.

***American Humane Association, Children's Division Staff, ed.** 5th National Roundtable on Managed Care in Child Welfare Services: Summary of Proceedings. (Illus.). 2000. pap. write for info. (*0-930915-34-8*) Am Humane Assn.

American Humane Association, Children's Division Staff, ed. Fifth National Roundtable on Outcome Measures in Child Welfare Services. LC 98-227307. (Illus.). 150p. 1997. pap. text 25.00 (*0-930915-19-4*, COM05) Am Humane Assn.

***American Humane Association, Children's Division Staff, ed.** First National Roundtable on Implementing the Adoption & Safe Families Act: Summary of Proceedings. (Illus.). 175p. 2000. pap. 25.00 (*0-930915-32-1*) Am Humane Assn.

American Humane Association, Children's Division Staff, ed. First National Roundtable on Managed Care in Child Welfare Services: Keeping the Focus on Kids: Outcomes, Ethics & Partnerships in a Managed Care Environment: Summary of Proceedings. (Illus.). iv, 91p. 1997. pap. text 25.00 (*0-930915-07-0*, CMC01) Am Humane Assn.
— First National Roundtable on Outcome Measures in Child Welfare Services: Summary of Proceedings. (Illus.). iii, 266p. 1993. pap. text 20.00 (*0-930915-05-4*, COM01) Am Humane Assn.
— Fourth National Roundtable on Outcome Measures in Child Welfare Services: Summary of Proceedings. (Illus.). iii, 146p. 1997. pap. text 25.00 (*0-930915-06-2*, COM04) Am Humane Assn.
— Helping in Child Protective Services: A Competency-Based Casework Handbook. (Illus.). xii, 412p. 1991. pap. text 25.00 (*0-930915-09-7*, CHP01) Am Humane Assn.
— 1997 National Roundtables on Family Group Decision Making: Summary of Proceedings. LC 99-183360. (Illus.). 1998. pap. text 25.00 (*0-930915-21-6*, CFGD02) Am Humane Assn.
— Second National Roundtable on Managed Care in Child Welfare Services: Keeping the Focus on Kids: Summary of Proceedings. LC 99-183373. (Illus.). v, 109p. 1997. pap. text 25.00 (*0-930915-10-0*, CMC02) Am Humane Assn.
— Second National Roundtable on Outcome Measures in Child Welfare Services: Summary of Proceedings. (Illus.). vi, 130p. 1995. pap. text 20.00 (*0-930915-04-6*, COM02) Am Humane Assn.
— Selected Annotated Readings on Outcome Measures in Child Welfare Services. (Illus.). ii, 35p. 1993. pap. text 7.50 (*0-930915-11-9*, COM01A) Am Humane Assn.
— Sixth National Roundtable on Outcome Measures in Child Welfare Services: Summary of Proceedings. (Illus.). 1998. pap. text 25.00 (*0-930915-22-4*, COM06) Am Humane Assn.
— Third National Roundtable on Managed Care in Child Welfare Services: Summary of Proceedings. LC 99-183602. (Illus.). 1998. pap. text 25.00 (*0-930915-23-2*, CMC03) Am Humane Assn.
— Third National Roundtable on Outcome Measures in Child Welfare Services: Summary of Proceedings. (Illus.). iii, 99p. 1996. pap. text 25.00 (*0-930915-03-8*, COM03) Am Humane Assn.

***American Humane Association, Children's Division Staff, ed.** 13th National Roundtable on Child Protective Services Risk Assessment: Summary of Proceedings. (Illus.). 2000. pap. write for info. (*0-930915-33-X*) Am Humane Assn.

American Humane Association, Children's Division Staff, ed. 12th National Roundtable on CPS Risk Assessment: Summary of Proceedings. (Illus.). 1999. pap. text 25.00 (*0-930915-25-9*) Am Humane Assn.

American Humane Association Staff. Innovations for Children's Services for the 21st Century: Family Group Decision Making & Patch. LC 97-215784. (Illus.). 1997. pap. text 27.00 (*0-930915-17-8*, CFGD01) Am Humane Assn.

***American Humane Association Staff, ed.** Fourth National Roundtable on Managed Care in Child Welfare Services: Summary of Proceedings. (Illus.). 1999. pap. 25.00 (*0-930915-28-3*) Am Humane Assn.

American Humane Association Staff, ed. 1999 National Roundtable on Family Group Decision Making & International Conference: Summary of Proceedings. (Illus.). 2000. pap. 25.00 (*0-930915-31-3*) Am Humane Assn.
— Seventh National Roundtable on Outcome Measures in Child Welfare Services: Summary of Proceedings. (Illus.). 2000. pap. 25.00 (*0-930915-30-5*) Am Humane Assn.

American Humane Association Staff. First National Roundtable on Innovative Community-Based Partnerships: Summary of Proceedings. 94p. 1999. pap. 15.00 (*0-930915-26-7*) Am Humane Assn.
— 1998 National Roundtable on Family Group Decision Making: Summary of Proceedings. 90p. 1999. pap. 25.00 (*0-930915-27-5*) Am Humane Assn.

American Illustration Staff. American Illustration. 17th ed. (Illus.). 1998. 55.00 (*0-688-16493-5*, Wm Morrow) Morrow Avon.
— American Photography. 14th ed. (Illus.). 1998. 55.00 (*0-688-16478-1*, Wm Morrow) Morrow Avon.

American Immigration Center Ser. Marriage Visa Kit: Obtaining US Residency for Alien Spouse. (Do-It-Yourself Immigration Ser.). 40p. 1998. pap. 69.00 (*0-9663425-3-4*) Amer Immig Ctr.

American Immigration Center Staff. Family Relations Visa Package: Obtaining US Residency for Alien Relative. (Do-It-Yourself Immigration Ser.). 50p. 1998. pap. 65.00 (*0-9663425-8-5*) Amer Immig Ctr.
— Fiance Visa Package: Obtaining an Entry Visa for an Alien Fiance (K-1) (Do-it-Yourself Immigration Ser.). 52p. 1998. pap. 65.00 (*0-9663425-2-6*) Amer Immig Ctr.
— H-1B Visa Package: Temporary Employment in the USA. (Do-It-Yourself Immigration Ser.). 34p. 1998. pap. 65.00 (*0-9663425-5-0*) Amer Immig Ctr.
— Priority Workers Visa Package. (Do-it-Yourself Immigration Ser.). 52p. 1998. pap. 69.00 (*0-9663425-4-2*) Amer Immig Ctr.
— Student Visa Package: F-1 Temporary U. S. Study Visa. (Do-It-Yourself Immigration Ser.). 31p. 1998. pap. 39.00 (*0-9663425-1-8*) Amer Immig Ctr.

***American Immigration Network Staff.** How to Apply for & Obtain a K-1 Finace Visa: The Complete Do It Yourself U. S. Immigration Kit. (Complete Do It Yourself U. S. Immigration Ser.). 2000. pap. text 49.95 (*1-893960-01-3*) Amer Immig Network.
— How to Apply for & Obtain the H-1B Visa: Temporary Work Visa for Professionals. (Complete Do It Yourself U. S. Immigration Ser.). 2000. 49.95 (*1-893960-00-5*) Amer Immig Network.

American Indian Lawyer Training Program, Inc., Sta. They Are Young Once but Indian Forever: A Summary & Analysis of Investigative Hearings on Indian Child Welfare, April 1980. Myers, Joseph A., ed. & frwd. by. (Illus.). 207p. (Orig.). (C). 1981. pap. 6.00 (*0-939890-00-3*) Am Indian LTP.

American Indian Lawyer Training Program, Inc., Sta & American Indian Resources Institute Staff. Indian Tribes as Sovereign Governments: A Sourcebook on Federal-Tribal History, Law, & Policy. Miklas, Christine L., ed. 156p. (Orig.). (C). 1991. pap. text 12.50 (*0-939890-07-0*, AIRI) Am Indian LTP.

American Indian Lawyer Training Program Staff. Indian Water Policy in a Changing Environment: Perspectives on Indian Water Rights. (Illus.). 163p. (Orig.). (C). 1982. pap. text 6.00 (*0-939890-05-4*) Am Indian LTP.

American Indian Resources Institute Staff. Tribal Water Management Handbook. (Illus.). 208p. (Orig.). (C). 1988. pap. text 24.00 (*0-939890-08-9*) Am Indian LTP.

American Indian Resources Institute Staff, jt. auth. see American Indian Lawyer Training Program, Inc., Sta.

American Industrial Hygiene Association. Occupational Health & Safety Management System: An AIHA Guidance Document. LC 96-231697. 31 p. 1996. write for info. (*0-932627-74-9*) Am Indus Hygiene.
— Welding Health & Safety Resource Manual. 40p. 1984. 22.00 (*0-932627-17-X*) Am Indus Hygiene.

American Industrial Hygiene Association, jt. auth. see Dotter, Earl.

American Industrial Hygiene Association Staff. American Industrial Association Journal Cumulative Index, 1940-1957, Vol. I. 88p. 1988. 30.00 (*0-932627-04-8*) Am Indus Hygiene.
— American Industrial Hygiene Association Journal Cumulative Index, 1958-1973, Vol. II. 144p. 1975. 30.00 (*0-932627-05-6*) Am Indus Hygiene.
— American Industrial Hygiene Association Journal Cumulative Index, 1974-1983, Vol. III. 115p. 1984. 30.00 (*0-932627-06-4*) Am Indus Hygiene.
— Arc Welding & Your Health: A Handbook of Health Information for Welding. 16p. 1984. 15.00 (*0-932627-00-5*) Am Indus Hygiene.
— Biohazards Reference Manual. 160p. 1985. 35.00 (*0-932627-19-6*) Am Indus Hygiene.
— Hygienic Guides Series, Set. (Guide Ser.). 12.50 (*0-317-56141-3*) Am Indus Hygiene.
— Quality Assurance Manual for Industrial Hygiene Chemistry. 74p. 1988. 40.00 (*0-932627-32-3*) Am Indus Hygiene.

American Insect Projects Inc. Staff. American Beetles. 1200p. 1999. 150.00 (*0-8493-1925-0*) CRC Pr.

American Inst. of Certified Public Accountants Sta. Financial Management Seminar for Not-for-Profit Organizations. fac. ed. LC HF5686.C2. 100p. 1990. reprint ed. pap. 31.00 (*0-7837-8212-8*, 204797100009) Bks Demand.
— Strategic Thrusts for the Future: Report of the Strategic Planning Committee. fac. ed. LC HF5627.. 174p. 1988. reprint ed. pap. 54.00 (*0-7837-8213-6*, 204797200009) Bks Demand.

American Institute of Architecture Staff. Environmental Resource Guide. Ep. 1999. cd-rom 125.00 (*0-471-34618-7*) Wiley.

American Institue of Certified Public Accountants. AICPA Technical Practice Aids: As of June 1, 1997. Miceli, Michael A., ed. 1364p. reprint ed. pap. 180.00 (*0-7837-1056-9*, 2041536) Bks Demand.
— AICPA Technical Practice Aids: Technical Information Service Inquiries & Replies: Statements of Position, Accounting Standards Division: Practice Bulletins: as of June 1, 1988. Miceli, Michael A., ed. LC HF5616.U5A55. (Illus.). 1234p. reprint ed. pap. 200.00 (*0-8357-6416-8*, 203578400097) Bks Demand.
— Checklists & Illustrative Financial Statements for Life Insurance Companies: December 1992 Edition. Moliterno, Steven, ed. LC 91-657702. (Financial Accounting & Reporting Practice Aid Ser.). 113p. reprint ed. pap. 35.10 (*0-7837-6786-2*, 204661800003) Bks Demand.

American Institue of Physics Staff. Physics of High Energy Particle Accelerators: Fermilab School. Month, M. et al, eds. LC 82-72421. (AIP Conference Proceedings Ser.: No. 87). 960p. 1982. lib. bdg. 48.00 (*0-88318-186-X*) Am Inst Physics.

American Institute for Cancer Research Staff. Diet & Breast Cancer. (Advances in Experimental Medicine & Biology Ser.: Vol. 364). (Illus.). 200p. (C). 1994. text 79.50 (*0-306-44895-5*, Kluwer Plenum) Kluwer Academic.

American Institute for Cancer Research Staff, ed. Diet & Cancer: Molecular Mechanisms of Interactions. LC 95-17694. (Advances in Experimental Medicine & Biology Ser.: Vol. 375). 236p. 1995. 89.50 (*0-306-45067-4*, Kluwer Plenum) Kluwer Academic.
— Dietary Fat & Cancer: Genetic & Molecular Interactions. LC 97-4389. (Advances in Experimental Medicine & Biology Ser.: Vol. 422). (Illus.). 268p. (C). 1997. text 107.00 (*0-306-45683-4*, Kluwer Plenum) Kluwer Academic.

American Institute for Certified Public Accountant. Disclosure Checklists & Illustrative Financial Statements for Banks: January, 1989. Kelly, J. Byrne, ed. LC 89-648499. (Financial Accounting & Reporting Practice Aid Ser.). 85p. reprint ed. pap. 30.00 (*0-8357-4107-9*, 203687300005) Bks Demand.

***American Institute for CPCU Staff.** Code of Professional Ethics of the American Institute for CPCU. 6th ed. Wiening, Eric A., ed. LC 99-73211. 177p. (C). 1999. text 10.00 (*0-89463-089-X*, 104) Am Inst FCPCU.

American Institute for CPCU Staff. The CPCU Handbook of Insurance Policies. 3rd ed. LC 98-71626. 474p. 1998. pap. text 16.00 (*0-89463-080-6*, 9) Am Inst FCPCU.

American Institute for Economic Research Staff. The A-Z Vocabulary for Investors. rev. ed. (Economic Education Bulletin Ser.: No. 7). 131p. 1997. pap. 7.00 (*0-913610-02-X*) Am Inst Econ Res.

An Asterisk (*) at the beginning of an entry indicates that the title is appearing for the first time.

American Institute for Preventive Medicine (AIPM). Staying Well. LC 93-34773. (For Your Information Ser.). 1993. 8.95 (*1-56420-027-2*); audio 16.00 (*1-56420-028-0*) New Readers.

American Institute for Preventive Medicine Staff. Aging with Confidence. LC 93-40576. (For Your Information Ser.). 1993. 8.95 (*1-56420-017-5*); audio 16.00 (*1-56420-018-3*) New Readers.

— Managing Stress. LC 93-40575. (For Your Information Ser.). 1993. 8.95 (*1-56420-025-6*); audio 16.00 (*1-56420-026-4*) New Readers.

— The Safe, Self-Confident Child. LC 93-40577. (For Your Information Ser.). 1993. 8.95 (*1-56420-033-7*); audio 16.00 (*1-56420-034-5*) New Readers.

American Institute for Preventive Medicine Staff & Powell, Don R. Health at Home: Your Complete Guide to Symptoms, Solutions, & Self-Care. LC 97-169384. (Illus.). 384p. (Orig.). 1996. pap. 15.95 (*0-9635612-8-6*) Am Inst Prevent.

— HealthyLife Self-Care Guide. 96p. 1997. pap. 4.95 (*0-9635612-2-7*) Am Inst Prevent.

American Institute for Preventive Medicine Staff, jt. auth. see Powell, Don R.

American Institute for Research. Science Success for Students with Disabilities. (YA). 1993. pap. text 18.50 (*0-201-81939-2*) Addison-Wesley.

American Institute of Aeronautics & Astronautics S. AIAA-AAS Astrodynamics Conference: A Collection of Technical Papers, Scottsdale, AZ, August 1-3, 1994. LC 94-25999. 1994. pap. 260.00 (*1-56347-090-X*, CP9411) AIAA.

— AIAA Aerodynamic Decelerator Systems Technology Conference: Proceedings, 11th. 1991. pap. 120.00 (*1-56347-139-6*, CP912) AIAA.

— AIAA Aerospace Design Engineers Guide. 3rd ed. LC 92-29652. 294p. 1993. 49.95 (*1-56347-045-4*, 45-4) AIAA.

— AIAA Aerospace Design Engineers Guide. 4th ed. LC 98-34952. 10-79p. 1998. pap. write for info. (*1-56347-283-X*) AIAA.

— AIAA Applied Aerodynamics Conference: Proceedings, 10th. 1992. 240.00 (*1-56347-171-X*, CP926) AIAA.

— AIAA Applied Aerodynamics Conference: Proceedings, 9th. 9th ed. 1991. pap. 190.00 (*1-56347-141-8*, CP918) AIAA.

— AIAA-ASME-ASCE-AHS-ASC 35th Structures, Structural Dynamics & Materials Conference: April 18-20, 1994, Hilton Head, South Carolina, 5 Vols. LC 94-13439. 350p. 1994. pap. 350.00 (*1-56347-101-9*, CP942(890)) AIAA.

— AIAA Atmospheric Flight Mechanics Conference. 1991. pap. 160.00 (*1-56347-173-6*, CP916) AIAA.

— AIAA Atmospheric Flight Mechanics Conference. 617p. 1993. pap. 240.00 (*1-56347-143-4*, CP936) AIAA.

— AIAA Atmospheric Flight Mechanics Conference: Proceedings. (Orig.). 1985. pap. 85.00 (*1-56347-142-6*, CP857) AIAA.

— AIAA Atmospheric Flight Mechanics Conference: Proceedings. (Orig.). 1992. pap. 220.00 (*1-56347-144-2*, CP929) AIAA.

— AIAA Atmospheric Flight Mechanics Conference: Proceedings, 11th. 1984. pap. 50.00 (*1-56347-145-0*, CP849) AIAA.

— AIAA Communication Satellite Systems Conference: Proceedings, 11th. 1986. pap. 100.00 (*0-317-43145-5*, CP862) AIAA.

— AIAA Computers in Aerospace: Proceedings, 6th. 1987. pap. 90.00 (*1-56347-148-5*, CP8710) AIAA.

— AIAA Computing in Aerospace: Proceedings, 9th. 1993. pap. 370.00 (*1-56347-149-3*, CP939) AIAA.

— AIAA Dynamics Specialist Conference: April 21-22, 1994, Hilton Head, South Carolina, 1 Vol. LC 94-13442. 65p. 1994. pap. 160.00 (*1-56347-103-5*, CP943(890)) AIAA.

— AIAA Dynamics Specialist Conference: Proceedings. 1992. pap. 210.00 (*1-56347-159-0*, CP923) AIAA.

— AIAA Flight Simulation Technologies Conference. 1987. 75.00 (*1-56347-152-3*, CP877) AIAA.

— AIAA Flight Simulation Technologies Conference: Proceedings. 1992. pap. 130.00 (*1-56347-200-7*, CP9211) AIAA.

— AIAA Flight Simulation Technologies Conference: Proceedings. 347p. 1993. pap. 130.00 (*1-56347-151-5*, CP937) AIAA.

— AIAA Guidance & Control Conference: Proceedings. 1991. 290.00 (*1-56347-153-1*, CP915) AIAA.

— AIAA Guide for Berthing - Docking - Grasping Interfaces for Serviceable Spacecraft: Standard. 32p. 1992. pap. 29.95 (*1-56347-052-7*, G-056-92) AIAA.

— AIAA Guide for Human Performance Measurements: Standard. 156p. 1992. pap. 79.95 (*1-56347-026-8*, G-035-92) AIAA.

— AIAA Guide for Implementing Software Development Files Conforming to DoD-Std-2167A: Standard. 16p. 1991. pap. 24.95 (*0-930403-81-9*, G-009-91) AIAA.

— AIAA Guide for Reusable Software: Assessment Criteria for Aerospace Applications: Standard. 28p. 1993. pap. 24.95 (*1-56347-049-7*, G-010-93) AIAA.

— AIAA Guide for the Preparation of Operational Concept Documents: Standard. LC 92-46902. 1993. pap. 29.95 (*1-56347-050-0*, G-043-92) AIAA.

— AIAA Guide for the Verification & Validation of Computational Fluid Dynamics Simulations. LC 98-8138. 1998. write for info. (*1-56347-285-6*) AIAA.

— AIAA Guide for Utility Connector Interfaces for Serviceable Spacecraft. 42p. (Orig.). 1995. pap. 29.95 (*1-56347-134-5*, G-072-95) AIAA.

— AIAA Guide to Design for On-Orbit Spacecraft Servicing. 400p. 1991. pap. 39.95 (*1-56347-028-4*, G-042-91) AIAA.

— AIAA Guide to Standard & Reference Atmosphere Models: Standard. 80p. 1990. pap. 79.95 (*0-930403-84-3*, G-003-90) AIAA.

— AIAA International Balloon Technology Conference: Proceedings. 1991. pap. 144.00 (*1-56347-155-8*, CP919) AIAA.

— AIAA Lighter-Than-Air Systems Technology Conference: Proceedings. 104p. 1993. pap. 120.00 (*1-56347-156-6*, CP938) AIAA.

— AIAA Lighter-Than-Air Technology Conference. 1991. pap. 100.00 (*1-56347-157-4*, CP913) AIAA.

— AIAA Lighter-Than-Air Technology Conference: Proceedings, 8th. 1987. pap. 75.00 (*1-56347-158-2*, CP879) AIAA.

— AIAA Materials Specialist Conference - Coating Technology for Aerospace Systems: Proceedings. 1992. pap. 210.00 (*0-685-59650-8*, CP924) AIAA.

— AIAA Recommended Practice Part 1: Astrodynamics-Concepts, Terms & Symbols. 56p. 1994. pap. text 29.95 (*1-56347-098-5*, R-064-94(890)) AIAA.

— AIAA Recommended Practice for Atmospheric & Space Flight Vehicle Coordinate Systems: Standard. 65p. 1991. pap. 44.95 (*0-930403-82-7*, R-004-92) AIAA.

— AIAA Recommended Practice for Human-Computer Interfaces for Space Systems Operations: Standard. 32p. 1991. pap. 49.95 (*0-930403-93-2*, R-023-91) AIAA.

— AIAA Recommended Practice for Reporting Earth-to-Orbit Mission Profiles: Standard. 1993. pap. 14.95 (*1-56347-053-5*, R-060-93) AIAA.

— AIAA Recommended Practice for Software Reliability: Standard. 76p. 1992. pap. 49.95 (*1-56347-024-1*, R-013-92) AIAA.

— AIAA Recommended Practice for Space Operations & Support Documentation: Standard. LC 93-28271. 20p. 1993. pap. 24.95 (*1-56347-070-5*, R-024-93) AIAA.

— AIAA Recommended Practice for Spacecraft System Design in SI Units. 8p. 1991. pap. 14.95 (*0-930403-87-8*, R-021-91) AIAA.

— AIAA Special Report: Contemporary Models of the Orbital Environment. 112p. 1994. pap. text 39.95 (*1-56347-108-6*, SP-069-94(890)) AIAA.

— AIAA Special Report: Future of Aerospace: Standard. 36p. 1990. pap. 14.95 (*0-930403-88-6*, SP-039-90) AIAA.

— AIAA Special Report: Guidance, Navigation & Control Information Interface Standards. 200p. 1994. pap. text 24.95 (*1-56347-109-4*, SP-073-94(890)) AIAA.

— AIAA Special Report: Orbital Debris Mitigation: Technical, Legal, & Economic Aspects. (Illus.). 50p. 1992. pap. 29.95 (*1-56347-023-3*, SP-016-92) AIAA.

— AIAA Special Report: Standardization for Commercial Space Transportation Operations: Standard. 40p. 1993. 24.95 (*1-56347-076-4*, SP-063-93) AIAA.

— AIAA Special Report: Strategic Issues in Aerospace Standardization. 80p. 1994. pap. text 14.95 (*1-56347-110-8*, SP-074-94(890)) AIAA.

— AIAA Standard for Aerodynamic Decelerator Drawings. 54p. 1991. pap. 49.95 (*0-930403-94-0*, S-017-91) AIAA.

— AIAA Standard Terminology for Space Structures. 32p. 1991. pap. 24.95 (*0-930403-83-5*, S-001-91) AIAA.

— AIAA Standard Vocabulary for Space Automation & Robotics. 220p. (Orig.). 1995. pap. write for info. (*1-56347-132-9*, S-066-95) AIAA.

— AIAA Structures, Structural Dynamics & Materials Conference: Proceedings, 28th, 1987, 2 vols., Set. 1987. pap. 200.00 (*1-56347-160-4*, CP872) AIAA.

— AIAA Structures, Sturctural Dynamics & Materials Conference: Proceedings, 32nd. 1991. pap. 245.00 (*1-56347-161-2*, CP911) AIAA.

— AIAA/USAF/NASA/ISSMO Symposium on Multidisciplinary Analysis & Optimization: A Collection of Technical Papers, September 7-9, 1994, Panama City Beach, FL. LC 94-34446. 1994. pap. 340.00 (*1-56347-097-7*, CP9413) AIAA.

— Computing in Aerospace: A Collection of Technical Papers. LC 95-7861. 1995. write for info. (*1-56347-119-1*) AIAA.

— Computing in Aerospace: A Collection of Technical Papers, Vol. VI. LC 95-7861. 1995. 90.00 (*0-614-16777-9*, CP8710) AIAA.

— Computing in Aerospace: A Collection of Technical Papers, Vol. VII. LC 95-7861. 1995. 130.00 (*0-614-16778-7*, CP8910) AIAA.

— Computing in Aerospace: A Collection of Technical Papers, Vol. IX. LC 95-7861. 1995. 370.00 (*0-614-16779-5*, CP939) AIAA.

— Computing in Aerospace: A Collection of Technical Papers, Vol. X. LC 95-7861. 1995. 250.00 (*0-614-16780-9*, CP951) AIAA.

— Guidance, Navigation & Control Conference, Proceedings Held August, 1997 at New Orleans, Louisiana. 1997. pap. 350.00 (*1-56347-234-1*, CP9710(9991)) AIAA.

— Recommended Practice for Parts Management. LC 96-29532. 1997. pap. 29.95 (*1-56347-199-X*) AIAA.

American Institute of Aeronautics & Astronautics S & American National Standards Institute. Recommended Practice for Human-Computer Interface for Space System Operations. LC 96-46443. 1997. write for info. (*1-56347-206-6*) AIAA.

American Institute of Aeronautics & Astronautics S & American National Standards Institute Staff. Guide to Reference & Standard Atmosphere Models. LC 96-47636. 1997. pap. write for info. (*1-56347-195-7*) AIAA.

***American Institute of Aeronautics & Astronautics Staff.** Assessment of Experimental Uncertainty with Application to Wind Tunnel Testing. LC 99-41147. 1999. write for info. (*1-56347-364-X*) AIAA.

— Space Systems - Metallic Pressure Vessels, Pressurized Structures & Pressure Components. LC 99-41144. 1999. write for info. (*1-56347-365-8*) AIAA.

***American Institute of Aeronautics & Astronautics Staff & American National Standards Institute Staff.** Guide to Human Performance Measurements. LC 00-40175. (Illus.). 2000. write for info. (*1-56347-451-4*) AIAA.

American Institute of Aeronautics & Astronautics Staff, jt. auth. see American National Standards Institute Staff.

American Institute of Architects Academy of Archit & U. S. Department of Health & Human Services Editor. Guidelines for Design & Construction of Hospital & Health Care Facilities: 1996-97. (Illus.). 146p. 1996. pap. 60.00 (*1-55835-151-5*, J189-96) AIA Press.

American Institute of Architects, Chicago Chapter. AIAA - RAES Aerodynamic Decelerator Systems Technology Conference & Seminar: Proceedings. 1993. pap. 184.00 (*1-56347-137-X*, CP932) AIAA.

— AIAA - USAF - NASA - OAI Symposium on Multidisciplinary Analysis & Optimization: Proceedings. 1992. pap. 300.00 (*0-685-63115-X*, CP9213) AIAA.

American Institute of Architects, Long Island Chap & Society for the Preservation of Long Island Anticu. AIA Architectural Guide to Nassau & Suffolk Counies, Long Island. (Illus.). 176p. (Orig.). 1998. pap. 14.95 (*0-486-26946-9*) Dover.

American Institute of Architects Staff. Accessible Design: Periodical Bibliography. LC 91-46168. 1992. write for info. (*1-56635-001-8*) AIA Lib Arch.

— Environmental Resource Guide. LC 95-49568. 880p. 1996. 225.00 (*0-471-14043-0*) Wiley.

— Health Facilities Review, 1992-93. (Illus.). 176p. 1993. pap. 20.00 (*1-55835-090-X*) AIA Press.

American Institute of Architects Staff, et al. Guidelines for Planning & Design of Biomedical Research Laboratory Facilities. (Illus.). 100p. 1999. pap. 50.00 (*1-879304-95-3*) AIA DC.

American Institute of Architects Staff, jt. auth. see Fuller, Larry Paul.

American Institute of Banking Staff, ed. see Mayall, Donald.

American Institute of Biological Sciences. American Institute of Biological Sciences: Membership Directory & Handbook, 1986-1987. Chambers, Charles M., ed. 230p. (Orig.). 1986. pap. text 5.00 (*0-936829-00-1*) Am Inst Bio Sci.

***American Institute of Certificate Staff.** AICPA's Uniform CPA Exam 2000. 432p. 1999. pap. text 60.00 (*0-02-863546-9*, Arco) Macmillan Gen Ref.

American Institute of Certified Public Accountants. Accountants' Index: Thirtieth Supplement, January-December 1981, 2 vols., 1. Pierce, Linda C., ed. LC 21-10690. reprint ed. pap. 160.00 (*0-8357-5047-7*, 2025781) Bks Demand.

— Accountants' Index: Thirtieth Supplement, January-December 1981, 2 vols., 2. Pierce, Linda C., ed. LC 21-10690. 889p. reprint ed. pap. 180.00 (*0-8357-5048-5*) Bks Demand.

— Accountants' Index: Thirty-First Supplement, January-December 1982, 2 vols., 1. Pierce, Linda C., ed. LC 21-10690. reprint ed. pap. 160.00 (*0-8357-5049-3*, 2025782) Bks Demand.

— Accountants' Index: Thirty-First Supplement, January-December 1982, 2 vols., 2. Pierce, Linda C., ed. LC 21-10690. 874p. reprint ed. pap. 180.00 (*0-8357-5050-7*) Bks Demand.

— Accountants' Index: Thirty-Second Supplement, January-December 1983, 2 Vols., 1. Pierce, Linda C., ed. LC 21-10690. 709p. reprint ed. pap. 200.00 (*0-8357-5051-5*, 202757900001) Bks Demand.

— Accountants' Index: Thirty-Second Supplement, January-December 1983, 2 Vols., 2. Pierce, Linda C., ed. LC 21-10690. 767p. reprint ed. pap. 200.00 (*0-8357-5052-3*, 202757900002) Bks Demand.

— Accountants' Index: Twentieth Supplement, January 1971 to December 1971 (Inclusive) LC 21-10690. 925p. reprint ed. pap. 200.00 (*0-8357-5053-1*, 202375100033) Bks Demand.

— Accountants' Index: Twenty-Eighth Supplement, January-December 1979, 2 vols., 1. Kubat, Jane & Pierce, Linda C., eds. reprint ed. pap. 160.00 (*0-8357-5054-X*, 2025779) Bks Demand.

— Accountants' Index: Twenty-Eighth Supplement, January-December 1979, 2 vols., 2. Kubat, Jane & Pierce, Linda C., eds. 781p. reprint ed. pap. 180.00 (*0-8357-5055-8*) Bks Demand.

— Accountants' Index: Twenty-Fifth Supplement, January-December, 1976. Kubat, Jane, ed. LC 21-10690. 1188p. reprint ed. pap. 200.00 (*0-8357-5056-6*, 202375500033) Bks Demand.

— Accountants' Index: Twenty-Fourth Supplement, January-December 1975. Kubat, Jane, ed. LC 21-10690. 1115p. reprint ed. pap. 200.00 (*0-8357-5057-4*, 202375400033) Bks Demand.

— Accountants' Index: Twenty-Second Supplement, January-December 1973. Hegge, Karen L., ed. LC 21-10690. 1022p. reprint ed. pap. 180.00 (*0-8357-5058-2*, 2023752) Bks Demand.

— Accountants' Index: Twenty-Seventh Supplement, January-December 1978, 2 vols., 1. Kubat, Jane, ed. reprint ed. pap. 160.00 (*0-8357-5059-0*, 2025778) Bks Demand.

— Accountants' Index: Twenty-Seventh Supplement, January-December 1978, 2 vols., 2. Kubat, Jane, ed. 801p. reprint ed. pap. 180.00 (*0-8357-5060-4*) Bks Demand.

— Accountants' Index: Twenty-Sixth Supplement, January-December, 1977, 2 Vols., 1. Kubat, Jane, ed. LC 21-10690. reprint ed. pap. 160.00 (*0-8357-5061-2*, 2023756) Bks Demand.

— Accountants' Index: Twenty-Sixth Supplement, January-December, 1977, 2 Vols., 2. Kubat, Jane, ed. LC 21-10690. reprint ed. pap. 160.00 (*0-8357-5062-0*) Bks Demand.

— Accountants' Index: Twenty-Third Supplement, January-December 1974. Simmons, Karen H., ed. LC 21-10690. 1250p. reprint ed. pap. 200.00 (*0-8357-5063-9*, 202375300033) Bks Demand.

— Accountants' Index Master List of Subject Headings, 1988. LC 89-643886. 758p. reprint ed. pap. 200.00 (*0-8357-4118-4*, 203690400005) Bks Demand.

— Accounting & Financial Reporting by State & Local Governments: An Experiment. LC 81-186653. 65p. reprint ed. pap. 30.00 (*0-8357-6419-2*, 203578600097) Bks Demand.

— Accounting by Agricultural Producers & Agricultural Cooperatives. LC HF5686.A3A6. 81p. reprint ed. pap. 30.00 (*0-8357-5064-7*, 202396000034) Bks Demand.

— Accounting for Employee Capital Accumulation Plans. LC HF5549.5.I5A. (Issues Paper). 207p. reprint ed. pap. 64.20 (*0-7837-0276-0*, 204058900017) Bks Demand.

— Accounting for Installment Lending Activities of Finance Companies. LC HF5686.C495.. (Issues Paper). 91p. reprint ed. pap. 30.00 (*0-7837-0274-4*, 204058300017) Bks Demand.

— Accounting Practice: Selected Questions & Unofficial Answers Indexed to Content Specification Outline. Blum, James D. & Dexter, David S., eds. LC 84-160638. 267p. reprint ed. pap. 82.80 (*0-8357-5068-X*, 202509300042) Bks Demand.

— The Accounting Profession in Argentina: By Coopers & Lybrand, Argentina, Harteneck, Lopez & Cia. LC 87-150526. (Professional Accounting in Foreign Countries Ser.). 136p. 1989. reprint ed. pap. 42.20 (*0-608-00519-3*, 206139600008) Bks Demand.

— The Accounting Profession in Belgium: By Jeffreys Henry International, Paneth, Haber & Zimmerman, U. S. A., Riske & Co., Belgium. LC 87-150526. (Professional Accounting in Foreign Countries Ser.). 88p. 1992. reprint ed. pap. 30.00 (*0-608-00518-5*, 206139500008) Bks Demand.

— The Accounting Profession in Hong Kong. 2nd rev. ed. LC 87-150526. (Professional Accounting in Foreign Countries Ser.). 97p. 1993. reprint ed. pap. 30.10 (*0-608-03193-3*, 206367200005) Bks Demand.

— The Accounting Profession in Japan. LC HF5616.J3A33. (Professional Accounting in Foreign Countries Ser.). 87p. 1988. reprint ed. pap. 30.00 (*0-7837-3035-7*, 204289300006) Bks Demand.

— The Accounting Profession in Japan. 2nd rev. ed. LC 87-150526. (Professional Accounting in Foreign Countries Ser.). 83p. 1992. reprint ed. pap. 30.00 (*0-608-03196-8*, 206367500005) Bks Demand.

— The Accounting Profession in Mexico. 2nd rev. ed. LC 87-150526. (Professional Accounting in Foreign Countries Ser.). 83p. 1992. reprint ed. pap. 30.00 (*0-608-03197-6*, 206367600005) Bks Demand.

— The Accounting Profession in the Netherlands. LC HF5616.N4. (Professional Accounting in Foreign Countries Ser.). 96p. reprint ed. pap. 30.00 (*0-7837-1055-0*, 204153500021) Bks Demand.

— The Accounting Responses to Changing Prices: Experimentation with Four Models, by Task Force on Conceptual Framework for Accounting & Reporting, AICPA. LC HF5657.A684. 237p. reprint ed. pap. 73.50 (*0-8357-5071-X*, 202757400055) Bks Demand.

— Accounting Theory: Selected Questions & Unofficial Answers Indexed to Content Specification Outline. Blum, James D. & Rhuda, Charles A., eds. LC 84-160551. 111p. reprint ed. pap. 34.50 (*0-8357-5072-8*, 202509400042) Bks Demand.

— Accounting Trends & Techniques: 46th Annual Cumulative Survey of the Accounting Aspects of the Annual Reports of 600 Industrial & Merchandising Corporations to Which Are Added Excerpts...the Reports Analyzed Are Those with Fiscal Years Ended Not Later Than February 2, 1992. 46th ed. Shohet, Jack & Rikert, Richard, eds. LC 48-2517. 536p. 1992. pap. 166.20 (*0-7837-8534-8*, 204934700010) Bks Demand.

— Accounting Trends & Techniques: 47th Annual Cumulative Survey of the Accounting Aspects of the Annual Reports of 600 Industrial & Merchandising Corporations to Which Are Added Excerpts...the Reports Analyzed Are Those with Fiscal Years Ended Not Later Than January 31, 1993. 47th ed. Shohet, Jack & Rikert, Richard, eds. LC 48-2517. 600p. 1993. pap. 186.00 (*0-7837-8535-6*, 204934800010) Bks Demand.

— AICPA Audit & Accounting Manual: As of June 1, 1990. Huntley, Linda J., ed. LC HF5667.A55. (Nonauthoritative Practice Aids Ser.). 1150p. reprint ed. pap. 200.00 (*0-7837-1057-7*, 204153700021) Bks Demand.

— AICPA Audit & Accounting Manual: As of June 1, 1992. Polin, Gail K., ed. LC HF5667.A437. (Nonauthoritative Practice Aids Ser.). 1357p. reprint ed. pap. 200.00 (*0-7837-6641-6*, 204624800011) Bks Demand.

— AICPA Audit & Accounting Manual: Nonauthoritative Practice Aids: As of June 1, 1991. Huntley, Linda J., ed. LC 89-159088. 1373p. reprint ed. pap. 200.00 (*0-7837-4641-5*, 204436500002) Bks Demand.

— AICPA Directory of Accounting Education, 1992-93. Anspacher, Stephen J. & Romeo, Leticia B., eds. LC 93-642349. 982p. reprint ed. pap. 200.00 (*0-7837-6635-1*, 204622700011) Bks Demand.

— AICPA Financial Statement Preparation Manual: Nonauthoritative Practice Aids, As of March 1, 1990. Tursi, Michael A., ed. LC HF5681.B2. 666p. reprint ed. pap. 200.00 (*0-7837-1059-3*, 204155200021) Bks Demand.

— AICPA Financial Statement Preparation Manual: Nonauthoritative Practice Aids, As of March 1, 1991. Tursi, Michael A., ed. LC HF5686.B2F56. 868p. 1991. pap. 200.00 (*0-7837-8654-9*, 204935000010) Bks Demand.

— AICPA Industry Audit Guide: Audits of Airlines with Conforming Changes As of May 1, 1992. 88p. 1992. pap. 24.00 (*0-685-67098-8*, 4759) CCH INC.

A

— AICPA Professional Standards: As of June 1, 1988, Vol. 1. LC HF5667.A43. 941p. reprint ed. pap. 200.00 (*0-8357-6417-6*, 203578500001) Bks Demand.
— AICPA Professional Standards: As of June 1, 1988, Vol. 2. LC HF5667.A43. 972p. reprint ed. pap. 200.00 (*0-8357-6418-4*, 203578500002) Bks Demand.
— AICPA Professional Standards: As of June 1, 1990, Vol. 1. LC 86-643417. 884p. reprint ed. pap. 200.00 (*0-7837-1053-4*, 204153400001) Bks Demand.
— AICPA Professional Standards: As of June 1, 1990, Vol. 2. LC 86-643417. 1090p. reprint ed. pap. 200.00 (*0-7837-1054-2*, 204153400002) Bks Demand.
— AICPA Professional Standards: As of June 1, 1991, 2 vols., Vol. 1. LC HF5667.A55. 788p. (Orig.). reprint ed. pap. 200.00 (*0-7837-4855-8*, 204417000001) Bks Demand.
— AICPA Professional Standards: As of June 1, 1991, 2 vols., Vol. 2. LC HF5667.A55. 1210p. (Orig.). reprint ed. pap. 200.00 (*0-7837-4856-6*, 204417000002) Bks Demand.
— AICPA Professional Standards: As of June 1, 1992, Vol. 1. LC HF5616.U5A54. 848p. reprint ed. pap. 200.00 (*0-7837-6633-5*, 204622600001) Bks Demand.
— AICPA Professional Standards: As of June 1, 1992, Vol. 2. LC HF5616.U5A54. 1211p. reprint ed. pap. 200.00 (*0-7837-6634-3*, 204622600002) Bks Demand.
— AICPA Professional Standards: As of June 1, 1993, Vol. 1. LC Hf5667.A44. 644p. 1993. pap. 199.70 (*0-7837-8485-6*, 204928800001) Bks Demand.
— AICPA Professional Standards: As of June 1, 1993, Vol. 2. LC HF5667.A44. 846p. 1993. pap. 200.00 (*0-7837-8486-4*, 204928800002) Bks Demand.
— AICPA Professional Standards: Code of Conduct Bylaws; as of June 1, 1990. LC HF5667.A55. 262p. pap. 81.30 (*0-7837-1921-3*, 204212900001) Bks Demand.
— AICPA Quality Review Program Manual. LC 89-182240. 294p. reprint ed. pap. 91.20 (*0-7837-0085-7*, 204034700016) Bks Demand.
— AICPA Quality Review Program Manual: As of January 1, 1990. LC HF5657.A35. 412p. pap. 127.80 (*0-7837-0073-3*, 204032200016) Bks Demand.
— AICPA Quality Review Program Manual: As of January 1, 1991. LC 89-182240. 427p. reprint ed. pap. 132.40 (*0-7837-4640-7*, 204436400002) Bks Demand.
— AICPA Quality Review Program Manual: As of June 1, 1992. LC 89-182240. 527p. reprint ed. pap. 163.40 (*0-7837-6636-X*, 204622800011) Bks Demand.
— AICPA Technical Practice Aids: Technical Information Service, Inquiries & Replies; Statements of Position, Accounting Standards Division, Auditing Standards Division; Practice Bulletins, As of June 1, 1993. Shohet, Jack, ed. LC HF5616.U5A58. 1856p. 1993. pap. 200.00 (*0-7837-8484-8*, 204928700010) Bks Demand.
— AICPA Technical Practice Aids, As of June 1, 1992: Technical Information Service Inquiries & Replies. Polin, Gail K., ed. LC HF5616.U5A58. 1494p. reprint ed. pap. 200.00 (*0-7837-6638-6*, 204624500011) Bks Demand.
— AICPA Uniform CPA Exam 1995. 1995. 37.50 (*0-671-89921-X*) S&S Trade.
— AICPA Uniform CPA Examination: 1988 Edition. 688p. (Orig.). 1988. pap. 27.95 (*0-318-36106-X*) P-H.
— AICPA Vest-Pocket Accounting & Auditing Reference, 1992. Kappel, Arthur R., ed. LC 91-3561. 303p. reprint ed. pap. 94.00 (*0-7837-5352-7*, 204511300005) Bks Demand.
— AICPA Vest-Pocket Accounting & Auditing Reference, 1993. Kappel, Arthur R., ed. LC 94-643059. 325p. 1993. pap. 100.80 (*0-7837-8469-4*, 204927400010) Bks Demand.
— AICPA's Uniform CPA Exam, 1999 Edition. 720p. 1998. pap. 60.00 (*0-02-862688-5*, Arc) IDG Bks.
— The AICPA's Uniform CPA Exam, 1994. 1994. pap. 37.50 (*0-671-88311-9*, Arco) Macmillan Gen Ref.
— The AICPA's Uniform CPA Exam, 1995. 704p. 1994. 40.00 (*0-02-860020-7*) Macmillan.
— The AICPA's Uniform CPA Exam, 1996. 704p. 1995. 49.95 (*0-02-860583-7*) Macmillan.
— An Analysis of Earnings & Profits with Recommendations, Taxation of Corporate Distribution & Adjustments Subcommittee, Earnings & Profits Task Force. LC 78-109540. 210p. reprint ed. pap. 65.10 (*0-8357-5426-X*, 202757300055) Bks Demand.
— Audit & Accounting Guide: Audits of Finance Companies. annuals 2nd ed. 117p. 1996. pap. 33.00 (*0-87051-003-7*) Am Inst CPA.
— Audit Approaches for a Computerized Inventory System. LC HF5681.S8A93. (Computer Services Guidelines Ser.). (Illus.). 70p. reprint ed. pap. 30.00 (*0-8357-4260-1*, 203705600007) Bks Demand.
— Audit Planning. 3rd ed. LC 89-6695. (Technical Information for Practitioners Ser.: No. 2). 80p. reprint ed. pap. 30.00 (*0-7837-6629-7*, 204621700011) Bks Demand.
— Auditing: Selected Questions & Unofficial Answers Indexed to Content Specification Outline. Blum, James D., ed. LC HF5667.A93. 110p. reprint ed. pap. 34.10 (*0-8357-5873-7*, 202509600042) Bks Demand.
— Auditing in Common Computer Environments. LC 94-41127. (Auditing Procedure Studies). 1995. 31.50 (*0-87051-161-0*) Am Inst CPA.
— Auditors' Use of Microcomputers. LC HF5679.A83. (Auditing Procedure Study Ser.). 59p. 1986. pap. 30.00 (*0-7837-8487-2*, 204928900010) Bks Demand.
— Audits of Agricultural Producers & Agricultural Cooperatives: Including Statements of Position Issued by the Accounting Standards Division - Includes Audit Risk Alerts: Agribusiness Industry Developments - 1991. LC HF5686.A36A4. (Audit & Accounting Guide Ser.). 175p. reprint ed. pap. 54.30 (*0-7837-3736-X*, 204341000009) Bks Demand.
— Audits of Agricultural Producers & Agricultural Cooperatives: With Conforming Changes As of May 1, 1992. LC HF5686.A36A9. (Audit & Accounting Guide Ser.). 140p. reprint ed. pap. 43.40 (*0-7837-6648-3*, 204625500011) Bks Demand.
— Audits of Agricultural Producers & Agricultural Cooperatives: With Conforming Changes As of May 1, 1993. fac. ed. LC HF5686.A36A4. (Audit & Accounting Guide Ser.). 142p. 1993. pap. 44.10 (*0-7837-8233-0*, 204799700009) Bks Demand.
— Audits of Airlines. LC 81-186979. (Industry Audit Guide Ser.). 97p. reprint ed. pap. 30.10 (*0-8357-8032-5*, 203408700087) Bks Demand.
— Audits of Airlines: Including Statement of Position Issued by the Accounting Standards Division - Includes Audit Risk Alerts: Airline Industry Developments - 1991. 2nd ed. LC HF5686.. (Industry Audit Guide Ser.). 120p. reprint ed. pap. 37.20 (*0-7837-3737-8*, 204341100009) Bks Demand.
— Audits of Airlines: With Conforming Changes As of May 1, 1992. LC HF5686.A38A8. (Industry Audit Guide Ser.). 83p. reprint ed. pap. 30.00 (*0-7837-6655-6*, 204626300011) Bks Demand.
— Audits of Airlines: With Conforming Changes As of May 1, 1993. fac. ed. LC HF5686.A38A4. (Industry Audit Guide Ser.). 87p. 1993. pap. 30.00 (*0-7837-8237-3*, 204900100009) Bks Demand.
— Audits of Banks: Prepared by the Banking Committee. LC 83-134099. 206p. reprint ed. pap. 63.90 (*0-8357-5875-3*, 202396900034) Bks Demand.
— Audits of Banks: With Conforming Changes As of May 1, 1992. LC HG1707.5.A83. (Industry Audit Guide Ser.). 234p. reprint ed. pap. 72.60 (*0-7837-6645-9*, 204625200011) Bks Demand.
— Audits of Brokers & Dealers in Securities. 2nd ed. LC HF5686.B65A4. 245p. reprint ed. pap. 76.00 (*0-8357-5876-1*, 202509100042) Bks Demand.
— Audits of Brokers & Dealers in Securities: With Conforming Changes As of May 1, 1992. LC HF5686.B65A4. (Audit & Accounting Guide Ser.). 179p. reprint ed. pap. 55.50 (*0-7837-6657-2*, 204626800011) Bks Demand.
— Audits of Casinos: With Conforming Changes As of May, 1, 1993. fac. ed. LC HF5686.G23G3. (Audit & Accounting Guide Ser.). (Illus.). 81p. 1993. pap. 30.00 (*0-7837-8234-9*, 204799800009) Bks Demand.
— Audits of Casinos. Includes - Audit Risk Alerts: Casino Industry Developments-1991: Update to AICPA Audit & Accounting Guide, Audits of Casinos. LC HF5686.G23A9. (Audit & Accounting Guide Ser.). 94p. reprint ed. pap. 30.00 (*0-7837-4581-8*, 204416900003) Bks Demand.
— Audits of Certain Nonprofit Organizations: As of December 31, 1990. LC HF5686.N56A4. (AICPA Audit & Accounting Guide Ser.). 190p. reprint ed. pap. 58.90 (*0-7837-3556-1*, 204339300009) Bks Demand.
— Audits of Certain Nonprofit Organizations: With Conforming Changes As of May 1, 1992. LC HF5686.N56A5. (Audit & Accounting Guide Ser.). 161p. reprint ed. pap. 50.00 (*0-7837-6647-5*, 204625400011) Bks Demand.
— Audits of Certain Nonprofit Organizations: With Conforming Changes As of May 1, 1993. LC HF5686.N56A4. (Audit & Accounting Guide Ser.). 327p. 1993. pap. 101.40 (*0-7837-8471-6*, 204927600010) Bks Demand.
— Audits of Colleges & Universities: Including Statement of Position Issued by the Accounting Standards Division. 2nd ed. LC LB2342.A66. (Industry Audit Guide Ser.). 143p. reprint ed. pap. 44.40 (*0-7837-3552-9*, 204338900009) Bks Demand.
— Audits of Credit Unions: As of December 1, 1992. LC HG2037.A46. (Audit & Accounting Guide Ser.). 176p. 1992. reprint ed. pap. 54.60 (*0-608-00520-7*, 206139700008) Bks Demand.
— Audits of Employee Benefit Plans: As of March 31, 1991. LC 91-21605. (AICPA Audit & Accounting Guide Ser.). 265p. reprint ed. pap. 82.20 (*0-7837-3553-7*, 204339000009) Bks Demand.
— Audits of Entities with Oil & Gas Producing Activities: Includes: Audit Risk Alerts - Oil & Gas Producers Industry Developments - 1991. LC HF5686.P3A93. (Audit & Accounting Guide Ser.). 152p. reprint ed. pap. 47.20 (*0-7837-3735-1*, 204340900009) Bks Demand.
— Audits of Entities with Oil & Gas Producing Activities: Proposed Audit & Accounting Guide, April 25, 1984. LC HF5686.O4. (Exposure Draft Ser.). 101p. 1984. reprint ed. pap. 31.40 (*0-8357-5877-X*, 202510200042) Bks Demand.
— Audits of Entities with Oil & Gas Producing Activities: With Conforming Changes As of May 1, 1992. LC HF5686.P3A43. (Audit & Accounting Guide Ser.). 112p. reprint ed. pap. 34.80 (*0-7837-6653-X*, 204626000011) Bks Demand.
— Audits of Entities with Oil & Gas Producing Activities, with Conforming Changes As of May 1, 1993. fac. ed. LC HF5686.P3A43. (Audit & Accounting Guide Ser.). 112p. 1993. pap. 34.80 (*0-7837-8230-6*, 204799100009) Bks Demand.
— Audits of Federal Financial Assistance to State & Local Governmental Units: Proposed Audit Guide, 1984. LC HF5657.. 122p. reprint ed. pap. 37.90 (*0-8357-5878-8*, 202508700042) Bks Demand.
— Audits of Federal Government Contractors: With Conforming Changes As of May 1, 1992. LC HF5686.P923A. (Audit & Accounting Guide Ser.). 185p. reprint ed. pap. 57.40 (*0-7837-6649-1*, 204625600011) Bks Demand.
— Audits of Finance Companies. LC HF5686.C495. (Industry Audit Guide Ser.). 131p. reprint ed. pap. 40.70 (*0-8357-5879-6*, 203314800084) Bks Demand.
— Audits of Finance Companies: (Including Independent & Captive Financing Activities of Other Companies) with Conforming Changes As of May 1, 1993. LC HF5686.C495A. (Audit & Accounting Guide Ser.). 118p. 1993. pap. 36.60 (*0-7837-8470-8*, 204927500010) Bks Demand.
— Audits of Finance Companies: With Conforming Changes As of May 1, 1992. LC HF5686.C495A. (Audit & Accounting Guide Ser.). 116p. reprint ed. pap. 36.00 (*0-7837-6652-1*, 204625900011) Bks Demand.
— Audits of Government Contractors: Including Statement of Position Issued by the Accounting Standards Division. 2nd ed. LC HF5686.P923. 140p. reprint ed. pap. 43.40 (*0-7837-0277-9*, 204059800017) Bks Demand.
— Audits of Investment Companies: As of December 31, 1990. LC HF5686.I58A9. (AICPA Audit & Accounting Guide Ser.). 188p. reprint ed. pap. 58.30 (*0-7837-4580-X*, 204416800003) Bks Demand.
— Audits of Investment Companies: Proposed Audit & Accounting Guide, 1985. LC HF5686.I58A4. (Exposure Draft Ser.). 186p. reprint ed. pap. 57.70 (*0-8357-5880-X*, 202508800042) Bks Demand.
— Audits of Investment Companies: With Conforming Changes As of May 1, 1992. LC HF5686.I58A4. (Audit & Accounting Guide Ser.). 200p. reprint ed. pap. 62.00 (*0-7837-6643-2*, 204625000011) Bks Demand.
— Audits of Investment Companies: With Conforming Changes As of May 1, 1993. LC HF5686.I58A4. (Audit & Accounting Guide Ser.). 264p. 1993. reprint ed. pap. 81.90 (*0-608-00523-1*, 206140100008) Bks Demand.
— Audits of Not-for-Profit Organizations Receiving Federal Awards: Amendment to AICPA Audit & Accounting Guides, Audits of Providers of Health Care Services, Audits of Voluntary Health & Welfare Organizations, Audits of Colleges & Universities, & Audits of Certain Nonprofit Organizations. LC 94-232762. (AICPA - Statement of Position Ser.: No. 92-9). 211p. 1992. reprint ed. pap. 65.50 (*0-608-03190-9*, 206364500007) Bks Demand.
— Audits of Property & Liability Insurance Companies: As of December 31, 1990. LC HG8077.A9312. (AICPA Audit & Accounting Guide Ser.). 176p. reprint ed. pap. 54.60 (*0-7837-3555-3*, 204339200009) Bks Demand.
— Audits of Property & Liability Insurance Companies: With Conforming Changes As of May 1, 1992. LC HG8077.A93. (Audit & Accounting Guide Ser.). 204p. reprint ed. pap. 63.30 (*0-7837-6642-4*, 204624900011) Bks Demand.
— Audits of Providers of Health Care Services: As of December 31, 1990. LC HF5665.H7A55. (AICPA Audit & Accounting Guide Ser.). 276p. reprint ed. pap. 85.60 (*0-7837-3558-8*, 204339500009) Bks Demand.
— Audits of Providers of Health Care Services: Proposal Audit & Accounting Guide. LC HF5686.H7E9. (Exposure Draft Ser.). 185p. reprint ed. pap. 57.40 (*0-8357-8033-3*, 203409200087) Bks Demand.
— Audits of Providers of Health Care Services: With Conforming Changes As of May 1, 1992. LC HF5686.H7A54. (Audit & Accounting Guide Ser.). 249p. reprint ed. pap. 77.20 (*0-7837-6651-3*, 204625800011) Bks Demand.
— Audits of Savings Institutions: As of August 31, 1991: Audit Risk Alerts: Savings Institutions Industry Developments, 1991. LC HF5686.B8A5. (AICPA Audit & Accounting Guide Ser.). 343p. reprint ed. pap. 106.40 (*0-7837-3559-6*, 204339600009) Bks Demand.
— Audits of Savings Institutions: With Conforming Changes As of May 1, 1992. LC HF5686.B8S27. (Audit & Accounting Guide Ser.). 303p. reprint ed. pap. 94.00 (*0-7837-6650-5*, 204625700011) Bks Demand.
— Audits of Savings Institutions: With Conforming Changes As of May 1, 1993. LC HF5665.B8A54. (Audit & Accounting Guide Ser.). 307p. 1993. pap. 95.20 (*0-7837-8473-2*, 204927800010) Bks Demand.
— Audits of Savings Institutions, with Conforming Changes As of May 1, 1994. LC 95-649751. (Audit & Accounting Guide Ser.). 303p. 1994. reprint ed. pap. 94.00 (*0-608-03191-7*, 206364600007) Bks Demand.
— Audits of Small Businesses. LC 85-171942. (Auditing Procedure Study Ser.). (Illus.). 108p. reprint ed. pap. 33.50 (*0-8357-5881-8*, 203314700084) Bks Demand.
— Audits of State & Local Governmental Units: Proposed Audit & Accounting Guide, May 17, 1993. LC HJ9816.A9. (Exposure Draft Ser.). 202p. reprint ed. pap. 62.70 (*0-7837-6700-5*, 204632500011) Bks Demand.
— Audits of State & Local Governmental Units: With Conforming Changes As of May 1, 1992. LC HJ9816.A53. (Audit & Accounting Guide Ser.). 291p. reprint ed. pap. 90.30 (*0-7837-6656-4*, 204626700011) Bks Demand.
— Audits of State & Local Governmental Units, with Conforming Changes As of May 1, 1993. LC HF5665.L63A5. (Audit & Accounting Guide Ser.). 400p. 1993. reprint ed. pap. 124.00 (*0-608-00524-X*, 206140200008) Bks Demand.
— Audits of State & Local Governmental Units, 1994. LC 95-649736. (Audit & Accounting Guide Ser.). 458p. 1994. reprint ed. pap. 142.00 (*0-608-03195-X*, 206367400005) Bks Demand.
— Audits of Stock Life Insurance Companies: Including Statements of Position Issued by Auditing Standards Division, & Statement of Financial Accounting Standards Issued by the Financial Accounting Standards Board. LC HG8848.A44. 266p. reprint ed. pap. 82.50 (*0-7837-0076-8*, 204032500016) Bks Demand.
— Audits of Stock Life Insurance Companies: With Conforming Changes As of May 1, 1992. LC HG8848.A5. (Industry Audit Guide Ser.). 216p. reprint ed. pap. 67.00 (*0-7837-6654-8*, 204626100011) Bks Demand.
— Audits of Stock Life Insurance Companies: With Conforming Changes As of May 1, 1993. LC 95-43495. (Industry Audit Guide Ser.). 216p. 1993. reprint ed. pap. 67.00 (*0-608-00521-5*, 206139800008) Bks Demand.
— Audits of Voluntary Health & Welfare Organizations: As of December 31, 1990. LC HF5668.A43. (AICPA Industry Audit Guide Ser.). 94p. reprint ed. pap. 30.00 (*0-7837-3554-5*, 204339100009) Bks Demand.
— Audits of Voluntary Health & Welfare Organizations: With Conforming Changes As of May 1, 1992. LC HF5686.C3A45. (Industry Audit Guide Ser.). 63p. reprint ed. pap. 30.00 (*0-7837-6646-7*, 204625300011) Bks Demand.
— Audits of Voluntary Health & Welfare Organizations: With Conforming Changes As of May 1, 1993. LC HF5686.C3A5. (Industry Audit Guide Ser.). 223p. 1993. pap. 69.20 (*0-7837-8474-0*, 204927900010) Bks Demand.
— Automation of the Tax Practice of the '90s. LC HF5681.T3A47. 116p. 1991. pap. 36.00 (*0-7837-8477-5*, 204928200010) Bks Demand.
— Business Information Guide. LC 85-118541. (Illus.). 135p. reprint ed. pap. 41.90 (*0-8357-4596-1*, 203752800008) Bks Demand.
— Business Law: Selected Questions & Unofficial Answers Indexed to Content Specification Outline. Blum, James D. & Goldstein, Mark S., eds. LC 84-189048. 151p. reprint ed. pap. 46.90 (*0-8357-7496-1*, 202509500042) Bks Demand.
— Checklist Supplement & Illustrative Financial Statements for Construction Contractors: August 1992 Edition. Safran, Martin S., ed. LC 91-656163. (Financial Accounting & Reporting Practice Aid Ser.). 40p. reprint ed. pap. 30.00 (*0-7837-6792-7*, 204662400003) Bks Demand.
— Checklists & Illustrative Financial Statements for Agricultural Cooperatives: March 1993 Edition. Rikert, Richard, ed. LC 93-42103. (Financial Accounting & Reporting Practice Aid Ser.). 115p. reprint ed. pap. 35.70 (*0-7837-6793-5*, 204662500003) Bks Demand.
— Checklists & Illustrative Financial Statements for Banks. Selden, Neil, ed. LC 91-660138. (Financial Accounting & Reporting Practice Aid Ser.). 102p. reprint ed. pap. 31.70 (*0-7837-5353-5*, 204511400005) Bks Demand.
— Checklists & Illustrative Financial Statements for Banks: October 1992 Edition. Selden, Neil, ed. LC 91-660138. (Financial Accounting & Reporting Practice Aid Ser.). 116p. reprint ed. pap. 36.00 (*0-7837-6789-7*, 204662100003) Bks Demand.
— Checklists & Illustrative Financial Statements for Colleges & Universities: July 1991 Edition. LC 90-35497. (Financial Accounting & Reporting Practice Aid Ser.). 90p. reprint ed. pap. 30.00 (*0-7837-6640-8*, 204624700011) Bks Demand.
— Checklists & Illustrative Financial Statements for Common Interest Realty Associations: June 1992 Edition. Polin, Gail K., ed. LC 94-643136. (Financial Accounting & Reporting Practice Aid Ser.). 76p. reprint ed. pap. 30.00 (*0-7837-6794-3*, 204662600003) Bks Demand.
— Checklists & Illustrative Financial Statements for Corporations: October 1992 Edition. LC 91-660069. (Financial Accounting & Reporting Practice Aid Ser.). 121p. reprint ed. pap. 37.60 (*0-7837-6791-9*, 204662300003) Bks Demand.
— Checklists & Illustrative Financial Statements for Credit Unions: November 1992 Edition. Kappel, Arthur R., ed. LC 91-656164. (Financial Accounting & Reporting Practice Aid Ser.). 83p. reprint ed. pap. 30.00 (*0-7837-6790-0*, 204662200003) Bks Demand.
— Checklists & Illustrative Financial Statements for Credit Unions: September 1991 Edition. Kappel, Arthur R., ed. LC 91-656164. (Financial Accounting & Reporting Practice Aid Ser.). 63p. reprint ed. pap. 30.00 (*0-7837-5499-X*, 204526400005) Bks Demand.
— Checklists & Illustrative Financial Statements for Defined Benefit Pension Plans, April 1992 Edition. fac. ed. Kappel, Arthur R., ed. LC 96-640692. (Financial Accounting & Reporting Practice Aid Ser.). 53p. 1992. reprint ed. pap. 30.00 (*0-7837-8218-7*, 204797700009) Bks Demand.
— Checklists & Illustrative Financial Statements for Employee Health & Welfare Benefit Plans, May 1992 Edition. LC 92-19067. (Financial Accounting & Reporting Practice Aid Ser.). 60p. 1993. pap. 30.00 (*0-7837-8537-2*, 204935100010) Bks Demand.
— Checklists & Illustrative Financial Statements for Finance Companies: November 1992 Edition. Tursi, Michael A., ed. LC 91-656162. (Financial Accounting & Reporting Practice Aid Ser.). 88p. reprint ed. pap. 30.00 (*0-7837-6787-0*, 204661900003) Bks Demand.
— Checklists & Illustrative Financial Statements for Finance Companies, January 1992. Tursi, Michael A., ed. LC 91-656162. (Financial Accounting & Reporting Practice Aid Ser.). 86p. reprint ed. pap. 30.00 (*0-7837-5351-9*, 204511200005) Bks Demand.
— Checklists & Illustrative Financial Statements for Health Care Providers: May 1993 Edition. Safran, Martin S., ed. LC 91-19501. (Financial Accounting & Reporting Practice Aid Ser.). 140p. reprint ed. pap. 43.40 (*0-7837-6788-9*, 204662000003) Bks Demand.
— Checklists & Illustrative Financial Statements for Life Insurance Companies. fac. ed. Reilly, Rosemary M., ed. LC 91-657702. (Financial Accounting & Reporting Practice Aid Ser.). 99p. 1992. pap. 30.70 (*0-7837-8248-9*, 204901100009) Bks Demand.
— Checklists & Illustrative Financial Statements for Nonprofit Organizations: November 1990. LC 91-649899. (Financial Accounting & Reporting Practice Aid Ser.). (Illus.). 131p. reprint ed. pap. 40.70 (*0-7837-4639-3*, 204436300002) Bks Demand.
— Checklists & Illustrative Financial Statements for Not-for-Profit Organizations, May 1993 Edition. Levitin,

Moshe S., ed. LC 91-649899. (Financial Accounting & Reporting Practice Aid Ser.). 126p. 1993. pap. 39.10 (*0-7837-8479-1*, 204928400010) Bks Demand.

— Checklists & Illustrative Financial Statements for Property & Liability Insurance Companies: April 1992 Edition. Reilly, Rosemary M., ed. LC 92-37374. (Financial Accounting & Reporting Practice Aid Ser.). 102p. reprint ed. pap. 31.70 (*0-7837-5497-3*, 204526200005) Bks Demand.

— Checklists & Illustrative Financial Statements for Savings Institutions: January 1993 Edition. Selden, Neil, ed. LC 92-37422. (Financial Accounting & Reporting Practice Aid Ser.). 121p. reprint ed. pap. 37.60 (*0-7837-6795-1*, 204662700003) Bks Demand.

— Checklists & Illustrative Financial Statements for Savings Institutions: May 1992 Edition. Selden, Neil, ed. LC 92-37422. (Financial Accounting & Reporting Practice Aid Ser.). 125p. reprint ed. pap. 38.80 (*0-7837-5498-1*, 204526300005) Bks Demand.

— Checklists & Illustrative Financial Statements for State & Local Governmental Units: April 1992 Edition. Cornwall, Susan, ed. LC 91-94264. (Financial Accounting & Reporting Practice Aid Ser.). 208p. reprint ed. pap. 64.50 (*0-7837-6639-4*, 204624600011) Bks Demand.

— Checklists & Illustrative Financial Statements for State & Local Governmental Units, June 1993 Edition. Levitin, Moshe S., ed. LC 91-94264. (Financial Accounting & Reporting Practice Aid Ser.). 165p. 1993. pap. 51.20 (*0-7837-8478-3*, 204928300010) Bks Demand.

— Checklists & Illustrative Financial Statements for Stock Life Insurance Companies: November 1990. LC 91-657702. (Financial Accounting & Reporting Practice Aid Ser.). (Illus.). 102p. reprint ed. pap. 31.70 (*0-7837-4638-5*, 204436200002) Bks Demand.

— Codification of Statements of Auditing Standards, Numbers 1 to 47. LC HF5667.A494. 813p. reprint ed. pap. 200.00 (*0-608-13004-4*, 202508600042) Bks Demand.

— Codification of Statements of Standards for Accounting & Review Services: Numbers 1 to 7, As of January 1, 1994. LC HF5616.U5A43. 104p. 1994. reprint ed. pap. 32.30 (*0-608-00516-9*, 206133700008) Bks Demand.

— Codification of Statements on Auditing Standards, No. 1-49. LC HF5667.A55. 879p. reprint ed. 200.00 (*0-608-16872-6*, 202756900055) Bks Demand.

— Codification of Statements on Auditing Standards: Including Statement on Financial Forecasts & Projections & Statements on Standards for Attestation Engagements, Numbers 1 to 7, 1993. LC 95-640326. 842p. 1983. pap. 200.00 (*0-7837-8259-4*, 204903700009) Bks Demand.

— Codification of Statements on Auditing Standards (Including Statement on Financial Forecasts & Projections & Statements on Standards for Attestation Engagements) 1989, No. 1-63, 1990. LC HF5667.A556. 942p. pap. 200.00 (*0-7837-0279-5*, 204060000017) Bks Demand.

— Codification of Statements on Auditing Standards (Including Statement on Financial Forecasts & Projections & Statements on Standards for Attestation Engagements) 1989, Nos. 1-62. LC HF5667.A55. 878p. reprint ed. pap. 200.00 (*0-8357-4111-7*, 203688200005) Bks Demand.

— Codification of Statements on Standards for Accounting & Review Services: Nos. 1-5. LC HF5616.U5A53. 94p. reprint ed. pap. 30.00 (*0-608-13006-0*, 202509200042) Bks Demand.

— Codification of Statements on Standards for Accounting & Review Services: Numbers One to Six As of January 1, 1992. fac. ed. LC HF5616.U5A4. 104p. 1992. pap. 32.30 (*0-7837-8648-4*, 204901700009) Bks Demand.

— Codification of Statements on Standards for Accounting & Review Services: Numbers 1 to 7, As of January 1, 1995. LC 95-644360. 104p. 1995. reprint ed. pap. 32.30 (*0-608-03192-5*, 206364800007) Bks Demand.

— Codification of Statements on Standards for Accounting & Review Services, As of January 1, 1989, Nos. 1-6. LC HF5616.U5. 93p. reprint ed. pap. 30.00 (*0-8357-4112-5*, 203688300005) Bks Demand.

— Codification of Statements on Standards for Accounting & Review Services, Numbers 1-7, As of January 1, 1993. fac. ed. LC HF5616.U5A43. 104p. 1993. pap. 32.30 (*0-7837-8257-8*, 204903400009) Bks Demand.

— Codification of Statements on Standards for Attestation Engagements: As of January 1, 1989. LC 95-640617. 116p. reprint ed. pap. 36.00 (*0-8357-4113-3*, 203688400005) Bks Demand.

— Codification of Statements on Standards for Attestation Engagements: As of January 1, 1990. LC 95-640617. 122p. reprint ed. pap. 37.90 (*0-7837-1061-5*, 204155600021) Bks Demand.

— Codification of Statements on Standards for Attestation Engagements: Numbers 1 to 3, As of January 1, 1995. LC 95-640617. 176p. 1995. reprint ed. pap. 54.60 (*0-608-03189-5*, 206364400007) Bks Demand.

— Codification of Statements on Standards for Attestation Engagements, As of January 1, 1992. LC 95-640617. 124p. 1992. pap. 38.50 (*0-7837-8258-6*, 204903500009) Bks Demand.

— Codification of Statements on Standards for Attestation Engagements, As of January 1, 1993. fac. ed. LC 95-640617. 124p. 1993. pap. 38.50 (*0-7837-8649-2*, 204901800009) Bks Demand.

— Common Interest Reality Associations: With Conforming Changes As of May 1, 1993 - Conforming Interest Reality Associations Task Force, AICPA. LC HF5686.H63A4. (Audit & Accounting Guide Ser.). 113p. 1993. pap. 35.10 (*0-7837-8488-0*, 204929000010) Bks Demand.

— Common Interest Realty Associations: As of August 31, 1991. fac. ed. LC HF5686.H63C6. (AICPA Audit & Accounting Guide Ser.). 97p. 1991. reprint ed. pap. 30.10 (*0-7837-8647-6*, 204901600009) Bks Demand.

— Compliance Auditing Applicable to Governmental Entities & Other Recipients of Governmental Financial Assistance. fac. ed. LC HF5667.A54. (Statement on Auditing Standards Ser.: No. 63). 73p. 1989. reprint ed. pap. 30.00 (*0-7837-8251-9*, 204901900009) Bks Demand.

— Compliance with Federal Election Campaign Requirements: A Guide for Candidates. 4th ed. LC 83-208707. (Illus.). 224p. reprint ed. pap. 69.50 (*0-8357-4116-8*, 203689700005) Bks Demand.

— Confirmation of Accounts Receivable: Auditing Procedure Study. LC 96-564. 1996. 31.50 (*0-87051-177-7*) Am Inst CPA.

— Construction Contractors: As of December 31, 1990. LC TH0425.C66X. (AICPA Audit & Accounting Guide Ser.). 181p. reprint ed. pap. 56.20 (*0-7837-3557-X*, 204339400009) Bks Demand.

— Construction Contractors: With Conforming Changes As of May 1, 1992. LC HF5686.B7A7. (Audit & Accounting Guide Ser.). 183p. reprint ed. pap. 56.80 (*0-7837-6644-0*, 204625100011) Bks Demand.

— Construction Contractors: With Conforming Changes As of May 1, 1993. LC HF5686.B7A43. (Audit & Accounting Guide Ser.). 181p. 1993. pap. 56.20 (*0-7837-8472-4*, 204927700010) Bks Demand.

— Digest of State Accountancy Laws & State Board Regulations, 1987-1988. LC KF2910.1.Z95. 113p. pap. 35.10 (*0-8357-6903-8*, 203796100009) Bks Demand.

— Digest of State Accountancy Laws & State Board Regulations, 1992. LC 78-643269. 154p. 1992. pap. 47.80 (*0-7837-8536-4*, 204934900010) Bks Demand.

— Digest of State Accounting Laws & State Board Regulations 1996. 144p. 1996. pap. text 29.50 (*0-87051-086-X*) Am Inst CPA.

— Disclosure Checklists & Illustrative Financial Statements for Corporations. Tursi, Michael A., ed. LC 89-29254. (Financial Accounting & Reporting Practice Aid Ser.). 110p. reprint ed. pap. 34.10 (*0-7837-1058-5*, 204153800021) Bks Demand.

— Disclosure Checklists & Illustrative Financial Statements for Corporations: Winter 1988. Tursi, Michael A., ed. LC 89-29254. (Financial Accounting & Reporting Practice Aid Ser.). 118p. reprint ed. pap. 36.60 (*0-8357-4108-7*, 203687400005) Bks Demand.

— Disclosure Checklists & Illustrative Financial Statements for Credit Unions: Winter 1988. Kelly, J. Byrne, ed. LC 89-29255. (Financial Accounting & Reporting Practice Aid Ser.). 54p. reprint ed. pap. 30.00 (*0-8357-4106-0*, 203687200005) Bks Demand.

— Disclosure Checklists & Illustrative Financial Statements for Nonprofit Organizations: January, 1989. Miceli, Michael A., ed. LC 89-648512. 95p. reprint ed. pap. 30.00 (*0-8357-4109-5*, 203687500005) Bks Demand.

— Disclosure Checklists & Illustrative Financial Statements for Savings & Loan Associations: January, 1989. Kelly, J. Byrne, ed. LC 89-648456. (Financial Accounting & Reporting Practice Aid Ser.). 83p. reprint ed. pap. 30.00 (*0-8357-4105-2*, 203687100005) Bks Demand.

— Disclosure Checklists & Illustrative Financial Statements for State & Local Governmental Units: Winter 1988. Cornwall, Susan, ed. LC 89-29257. (Financial Accounting & Reporting Practice Aid Ser.). 132p. reprint ed. pap. 41.00 (*0-8357-4110-9*, 203687700005) Bks Demand.

— Executive Information Systems. LC 93-39335. 1993. 22.00 (*0-87051-144-0*) Am Inst CPA.

— Firm on Firm Review Directory, January 1993: A Directory of Private Companies Practice Section Member Firms That Have Expressed An Interest in Conducting Peer Reviews & Quality Reviews. fac. ed. LC 89-646808. 269p. 1993. pap. 83.40 (*0-7837-8255-1*, 204902300009) Bks Demand.

— Guidance for an Experiment on Reporting Current Value Information for Real Estate. LC HF5686.R3. 50p. reprint ed. pap. 30.00 (*0-608-13008-7*, 202510300042) Bks Demand.

— Guide for Prospective Financial Statements. fac. ed. LC HF5681.B2G84. 242p. 1992. reprint ed. pap. 75.10 (*0-7837-8646-8*, 204901500009) Bks Demand.

— Index to Accounting & Auditing Technical Pronouncements, As of December 1, 1991. fac. ed. Monaghan, Margaret et al, eds. LC 78-648377. 1010p. 1992. pap. 200.00 (*0-7837-8249-7*, 204901400009) Bks Demand.

— Index to Accounting & Auditing Technical Pronouncements As of December 1, 1992. fac. ed. Wolfteich, Lois, ed. LC 78-648377. 1092p. 1993. reprint ed. pap. 200.00 (*0-7837-8256-X*, 204902600009) Bks Demand.

— Index to Accounting & Auditing Technical Pronouncements As of December 1, 1994. 17th ed. Wolfteich, Lois, ed. LC 78-648377. 1322p. 1995. reprint ed. pap. 200.00 (*0-608-03194-1*, 206367300005) Bks Demand.

— International Accounting & Auditing Standards, As of October 1, 1988. LC 89-109949. 512p. reprint ed. pap. 158.80 (*0-8357-4258-X*, 203704900007) Bks Demand.

— International Accounting & Auditing Standards, As of October 1, 1989. LC 89-109949. 600p. reprint ed. pap. 186.00 (*0-7837-1052-6*, 204153300021) Bks Demand.

— Local Government Audit & Accounting Manual As of March 1, 1991. Cornwall, Susan et al, eds. LC HJ9777.A3L63. (Nonauthoritative Practice Aid Ser.). 432p. reprint ed. pap. 134.00 (*0-7837-3733-5*, 204339900009) Bks Demand.

— Local Governmental Accounting Trends & Techniques, 1988. Cornwall, Susan, ed. LC 88-26313. 236p. reprint ed. pap. 73.20 (*0-8357-4117-6*, 203689900005) Bks Demand.

— Local Governmental Audit & Accounting Manual As of March 1, 1992. Cornwall, Susan, ed. LC HJ9777.A3L63. (Nonauthoritative Practice Aids Ser.). 521p. reprint ed. pap. 161.60 (*0-7837-6628-9*, 204621500011) Bks Demand.

— Manual for State Legislative Programs - Prepared by the State Legislation Committee, American Institute of Certified Public Accountants. 2nd ed. LC 82-199346. 59p. reprint ed. pap. 30.00 (*0-7837-0080-6*, 204033800016) Bks Demand.

— The Measurement of Corporate Social Performance: Determining the Impact of Business Actions on Areas of Social Concern - Issued by the Committee on Social Measurement, AICPA. LC HF5343.A54. 365p. reprint ed. pap. 113.20 (*0-608-17997-3*, 202657500050) Bks Demand.

— Operating a Successful Accounting Practice: A Collection of Material from the Journal of Accountancy Practitioners Forum. Rea, Richard C., ed. LC 79-117870. 336p. reprint ed. pap. 104.20 (*0-608-15097-5*, 202577300046) Bks Demand.

— Peer Review Manual, Pt. 1. 4th ed. LC 86-217293. 187p. reprint ed. pap. 58.00 (*0-7837-0086-5*, 204035300001) Bks Demand.

— Peer Review Manual, Pt. 2: Instructions & Checklists. LC 86-217293. 475p. reprint ed. pap. 147.30 (*0-7837-0087-3*, 204035300002) Bks Demand.

— Peer Review Manual: Instructions & Checklists - American Institute of Certified Public Accountants, Division for CPA Firms, SEC Practice Section. 5th rev. ed. LC 87-108519. 432p. pap. 134.00 (*0-7837-0084-9*, 204034600016) Bks Demand.

— Personal Financial Planning: The Team Approach. LC 87-142958. (Management Advisory Services Practice Aids, Small Business Consulting Practice Aid Ser. Vol. 7). 144p. 1987. reprint ed. pap. 44.70 (*0-608-00517-7*, 206135000008) Bks Demand.

— Personal Financial Planning Manual: Nonauthoritative Explanations & Illustrations as of August 1, 1988, 2 vols., Vol. 1. LC HG0179.. 451p. reprint ed. pap. 139.90 (*0-8357-6901-1*, 203796000001) Bks Demand.

— Personal Financial Planning Manual: Nonauthoritative Explanations & Illustrations as of August 1, 1988, 2 vols., Vol. 2. LC HG0179.. 252p. reprint ed. pap. 78.20 (*0-8357-6902-X*, 203796000002) Bks Demand.

— Proposed Audit & Accounting Guide Audits of Employee Benefit Plans. 3rd rev. ed. LC HD7105.4.A9. (Exposure Draft Ser.). 227p. pap. 70.40 (*0-7837-0072-5*, 204032100016) Bks Demand.

— Proposed Audit & Accounting Guide for Consideration of the Internal Control Structure in a Financial Statement Audit: August 21, 1989. LC HF5667.. (Exposure Draft Ser.). 229p. reprint ed. pap. 71.00 (*0-8357-4259-8*, 203705100007) Bks Demand.

— Proposed Uniform Accountancy Act, December 2, 1990. LC KF1357.. 72p. reprint ed. pap. 30.00 (*0-7837-1051-8*, 204152800021) Bks Demand.

— Recommended Tax Law Changes. LC 82-165275. 105p. reprint ed. pap. 32.60 (*0-608-16898-X*, 202757500055) Bks Demand.

— Report of the Task Force on the Quality of Audits of Governmental Units. LC 87-149765. 80p. reprint ed. pap. 30.00 (*0-8357-4592-9*, 203752300008) Bks Demand.

— Report on Corporate State Tax Administrative Uniformity. LC 90-810. 58p. 1990. pap. 30.00 (*0-7837-8476-7*, 204928100010) Bks Demand.

— Restructuring Professional Standards to Achieve Professional Excellence in a Changing Environment: Report of the Special Committee on Standards of Professional Conduct for Certified Public Accountants. LC HF5616.U5.A5. 72p. reprint ed. pap. 30.00 (*0-7837-0079-2*, 204033600016) Bks Demand.

— Review of the Structure & Operations of the SEC Practice Section: Report of the SECPS Review Committee. LC HF5616.U5A58. 86p. reprint ed. pap. 30.00 (*0-608-13007-9*, 202509700042) Bks Demand.

— Savings & Loan Associations: An AICPA Audit & Accounting Guide. 4th rev. ed. LC 87-161844. 246p. reprint ed. pap. 76.30 (*0-7837-1922-1*, 204213000001) Bks Demand.

— Selected Readings for CPAs in Industry: July-December 1989, Vol. 1. LC 91-641527. 169p. pap. 52.40 (*0-7837-0074-1*, 204032300001) Bks Demand.

— Selected Readings for CPAs in Industry: July-December 1989, Vol. 2. LC 91-641527. 174p. pap. 54.00 (*0-7837-0075-X*, 204032300002) Bks Demand.

— Selected Readings for CPAs in Industry, January-June 1990, Vol. 1. LC 91-641527. 155p. reprint ed. pap. 48.10 (*0-7837-6631-9*, 204622200001) Bks Demand.

— Selected Readings for CPAs in Industry, January-June 1990, Vol. 2. LC 91-641527. 159p. reprint ed. pap. 49.30 (*0-7837-6632-7*, 204622200002) Bks Demand.

— Supervision, Review, & Report Processing. LC 90-1075. (Technical Information for Practitioners Ser.: No. 5). 89p. reprint ed. pap. 30.00 (*0-7837-6627-0*, 204621400011) Bks Demand.

— Tax Practice Guides & Checklists, 1993. LC KF6320.T39. 386p. 1993. pap. 119.70 (*0-7837-8475-9*, 204928000010) Bks Demand.

— Tax Practice Guides & Checklists, 1990. LC KF6300.. 330p. reprint ed. pap. 102.30 (*0-7837-1923-X*, 204213400001) Bks Demand.

— Tax Practice Guides & Checklists, 1991. LC KF6320.T39. 310p. reprint ed. pap. 96.10 (*0-7837-6698-X*, 204632200011) Bks Demand.

— Tax Practice Guides & Checklists, 1992. LC KF6320.T39. 338p. reprint ed. pap. 104.80 (*0-7837-6699-8*, 204632300011) Bks Demand.

— Understanding Audits & the Auditor's Report: A Guide for Financial Statement Users. 2nd ed. LC 96-31406. 1996. write for info. (*0-87051-180-7*) Am Inst CPA.

— Uniform CPA Examination: May 1982 to November 1983: Questions. LC HF5661.. 256p. reprint ed. pap. 79.40 (*0-8357-6422-2*, 203579000001) Bks Demand.

— Uniform CPA Examination: May 1985-May 1989: Selected Questions & Unofficial Answers. Indexed to Content Specification Outlines: Accounting Practice, Accounting Theory, Auditing, Business Law. Examinations Division Staff, ed. LC HF5661.A55. 645p. pap. 200.00 (*0-7837-0275-2*, 204058600017) Bks Demand.

— Updated Illustrations of Management's Discussion & Analysis of Financial Condition & Results of Operations: A Survey of the Application of Recently Amended Rules 14a-3 & 14c-3 of the Securities & Exchange Act of 1934 in Annual Reports to Shareholders. Goodman, Hortense & Lorensen, Leonard, eds. LC HF5681.B2G65. (Financial Report Survey Ser.: No. 26). 93p. reprint ed. pap. 30.00 (*0-7837-3734-3*, 204340000009) Bks Demand.

American Institute of Certified Public Accountants, contrib. by. Information Security. LC 94-35671. 1994. 18.75 (*0-87051-160-2*) Am Inst CPA.

American Institute of Certified Public Accountants, ed. Uniform CPA Examination, May 1984-May 1988: Selected Questions & Unofficial Answers: Indexed to Content Specification Outlines. LC HF5661.U63. 642p. reprint ed. pap. 199.10 (*0-8357-3041-7*, 203929600012) Bks Demand.

American Institute of Certified Public Accountants & Federal Election Campaign Guide Task Force Staff. Compliance with Federal Election Campaign Requirements: A Guide for Candidates. 5th ed. LC 83-208707. 216p. 1990. 52.50 (*0-87051-073-8*) Am Inst CPA.

American Institute of Certified Public Accountants & Forster, Pannell K. The Accounting Profession in Australia. LC 87-150526. (Professional Accounting in Foreign Countries Ser.). 120p. 1990. reprint ed. pap. 37.20 (*0-608-00522-3*, 206139900008) Bks Demand.

American Institute of Certified Public Accountants & Tursi, Michael A. Checklists & Illustrative Financial Statements for Corporations: October 1991 Edition. LC 91-660069. (Financial Accounting & Reporting Practice Aid Ser.). 115p. 1991. reprint ed. pap. 35.70 (*0-7837-5496-5*, 204526100005) Bks Demand.

American Institute of Certified Public Accountants, et al. Checklists & Illustrative Financial Statements for Health Care Providers. LC 91-19501. (Financial Accounting & Reporting Practice Aid Ser.). 118p. reprint ed. pap. 36.60 (*0-7837-6630-0*, 204621800011) Bks Demand.

— Local Government Audit & Accounting Manual As of March 1, 1990. Cornwall, Susan, ed. LC HJ9777.. (Nonauthoritative Practice Aid Ser.). 432p. reprint ed. pap. 134.00 (*0-7837-1381-9*, 204155300021) Bks Demand.

American Institute Of Certified Public Accountants, jt. auth. see Association for Accounting Marketing Staff.

American Institute of Certified Public Accountants, jt. auth. see Friedig, Randi M.

American Institute of Certified Public Accountants Staff. AICPA Peer Review Program Manual as of March 1, 1996. LC 96-221680. 708p. Date not set. reprint ed. pap. 200.00 (*0-608-20778-0*, 207187700003) Bks Demand.

— AICPA Professional Standards, as of June 1, 1997 ol. 1: U. S. Auditing Standards, Attestation Standards. LC 86-643417. 993p. reprint ed. pap. 200.00 (*0-608-20799-3*, 207189800001) Bks Demand.

— AICPA Professional Standards, as of June 1, 1997 Vol. 2: Accounting & Review Services, Code of Professional Conduct, Bylaws, International Accounting, International Auditing, Consulting Services, Quality Control, Peer Review, Tax Practice, Personal Financial Planning, Continuing Professional Education. LC 86-643417. 1514p. reprint ed. pap. 200.00 (*0-608-20800-0*, 207189800002) Bks Demand.

— AICPA Technical Practice Aids: Technical Information Service Inquiries & Replies Statements of Position, Accounting Standards Division, Auditing Standards, Auditing Standards Division, Practice Bulletins as of June 1, 1997. LC 96-644513. 1548p. Date not set. reprint ed. pap. 200.00 (*0-608-20763-2*, 207186200003) Bks Demand.

— Audit Risk Alert, 1996/97: General Update on Auditing & Accounting Matters. LC HF5667.6.A55. (Audit Risk Alerts Ser.). 43p. Date not set. reprint ed. pap. 30.00 (*0-608-20761-6*, 207186000003) Bks Demand.

***American Institute of Certified Public Accountants Staff.** Audit Sampling. rev. ed. LC 99-32359. (Auditing Practice Release Ser.). 130p. 1999. pap. 31.50 (*0-87051-270-6*, 021061) Am Inst CPA.

American Institute of Certified Public Accountants Staff. Audits of Agricultural Producers & Agricultural Cooperatives: With Conforming Changes as of May 1, 1997. LC 96-649816. (AICPA Audit & Accounting Guide Ser.). 154p. Date not set. reprint ed. pap. 47.80 (*0-608-20796-9*, 207189500003) Bks Demand.

— Audits of Airlines: With Confronting Changes as of May 1, 1997. LC 96-649814. 102p. Date not set. reprint ed. pap. 31.70 (*0-608-20771-3*, 207187000003) Bks Demand.

— Audits of Casinos: With Conforming Changes as of May 1, 1997. LC 95-649746. (AICPA Audit & Accounting Guide Ser.). 89p. reprint ed. pap. 30.00 (*0-608-20798-5*, 207189700003) Bks Demand.

— Audits of Certain Nonprofit Organizations with Conforming Changes as of May 1, 1994. LC 96-649764. (AICPA Audit & Accounting Guide Ser.). 331p. Date not set. reprint ed. pap. 102.70 (*0-608-20766-7*, 207186500003) Bks Demand.

— Audits of Credit Unions: With Conforming Changes as of

May 1, 1996. LC 96-649813. (AICPA Audit & Accounting Guide Ser.). 195p. reprint ed. pap. 60.50 (*0-608-20870-1*, 207196900003) Bks Demand.

— Audits of Credit Unions: With Conforming Changes as of May 1, 1997. LC HG2037.A93. (AICPA Audit & Accounting Guide Ser.). 197p. Date not set. reprint ed. pap. 61.10 (*0-608-20747-0*, 207184600003) Bks Demand.

— Audits of Entities with Oil & Gas Producing Activities: With Conforming Changes as of May 1, 1997. LC 95-646901. (AICPA Audit & Accounting Guide Ser.). 130p. Date not set. reprint ed. pap. 40.30 (*0-608-20774-8*, 207187300003) Bks Demand.

— Audits of Federal Government Contractors: With Conforming Changes as of May 1, 1997. LC 96-641409. (AICPA Audit & Accounting Guide Ser.). 191p. Date not set. reprint ed. pap. 59.30 (*0-608-20795-0*, 207189400003) Bks Demand.

— Audits of Finance Companies: Including Independent & Captive Fincancing Activities of Other Companies, with Conforming Changes as of May 1, 1997. LC 95-649728. (AICPA Audit & Accounting Guide Ser.). 128p. Date not set. reprint ed. pap. 39.70 (*0-608-20790-X*, 207188900003) Bks Demand.

— Audits of Investment Companies: With Conforming Changes as of May 1, 1997. LC 96-649820. (AICPA Audit & Accounting Guide Ser.). 298p. Date not set. reprint ed. pap. 92.40 (*0-608-20749-7*, 207184800002) Bks Demand.

— Audits of Property & Liability Insurance Companies: With Conforming Changes as of May 1, 1997. LC 96-649769. (AICPA Audit & Accounting Guide Ser.). 290p. Date not set. reprint ed. pap. 89.90 (*0-608-20777-2*, 207187600003) Bks Demand.

— Banks & Savings Institutions: With Conforming Changes as of May 1, 1997. LC 96-34400. (AICPA Audit & Accounting Guide Ser.). 394p. Date not set. reprint ed. pap. 122.20 (*0-608-20748-9*, 207184700002) Bks Demand.

— Banks & Savings Institutions Industry Developments, 1996/97. LC 95-640175. (Audit Risk Alerts Ser.). 34p. reprint ed. pap. 30.00 (*0-608-20804-3*, 207190300003) Bks Demand.

— Board of Examiners Uniform CPA Examination: 1996 Annual Report. LC HF5601.A815. 47p. Date not set. reprint ed. pap. 30.00 (*0-608-20765-9*, 207186400003) Bks Demand.

— Brokers & Dealers in Securities: As of April 1, 1997. LC 97-48356. (AICPA Audit & Accounting Guide Ser.). 272p. Date not set. reprint ed. pap. 84.40 (*0-608-20792-6*, 207189100003) Bks Demand.

— Checklist Supplement & Illustrative Financial Statements for Investment Companies. LC 99-102009. (Financial Accounting & Reporting Practice Aid Ser.). 35p. Date not set. reprint ed. pap. 30.00 (*0-608-20794-2*, 207189300003) Bks Demand.

— Checklist Supplement & Illustrative Financial Statements for Real Estate Ventures. LC 97-643294. (A Financial Accounting & Reporting Practice Aid Ser.). 35p. Date not set. reprint ed. pap. 30.00 (*0-608-20791-8*, 207189000003) Bks Demand.

— Checklists & Illustrative Financial Statements for Banks & Saving Institutions. LC 99-100852. (A Financial Accounting & Reporting Practice Aid Ser.). 96p. Date not set. reprint ed. pap. 30.00 (*0-608-20784-5*, 207188300003) Bks Demand.

— Checklists & Illustrative Financial Statements for Common Interest Realty Associations. LC 94-643136. (A Financial Accounting & Reporting Practice Aid Ser.). 67p. Date not set. reprint ed. pap. 30.00 (*0-608-20753-5*, 207185200003) Bks Demand.

— Checklists & Illustrative Financial Statements for Corporations. LC 91-660069. (A Financial Accounting & Reporting Practice Aid Ser.). 93p. Date not set. reprint ed. pap. 30.00 (*0-608-20786-1*, 207188500003) Bks Demand.

— Checklists & Illustrative Financial Statements for Health Care Organizations. LC 92-19067. (A Financial Accounting & Reporting Practice Aid Ser.). 119p. Date not set. reprint ed. pap. 36.90 (*0-608-20755-1*, 207185400003) Bks Demand.

— Checklists & Illustrative Financial statements for Life Insurance Companies. LC 91-657702. (A Financial Accounting & Reporting Practice Aid Ser.). 93p. Date not set. reprint ed. pap. 30.00 (*0-608-20785-3*, 207188400003) Bks Demand.

— Checklists & Illustrative Financial Statements for Non-for-Profit Organizations. LC 91-649899. (A Financial Accounting & Reporting Practice Aid Ser.). 75p. Date not set. reprint ed. pap. 30.00 (*0-608-20750-0*, 207184900002) Bks Demand.

— Checklists & Illustrative Financial Statements for Poverty & Liability Insurance Companies. LC 95-640612. (Financial Accounting & Reporting Practice Aid Ser.). 85p. Date not set. reprint ed. pap. 30.00 (*0-608-20793-4*, 207189200003) Bks Demand.

— Codification of Statements on Standards for Accounting & Review Services, Vol. 1-7. LC 95-644360. 108p. Date not set. reprint ed. pap. 33.50 (*0-608-20769-1*, 207186800003) Bks Demand.

— Common Interest Realty Associations: With Conforming Changes as of May 1, 1997. LC 96-649817. 117p. Date not set. reprint ed. pap. 36.30 (*0-608-20773-X*, 207187200003) Bks Demand.

— Common Interest Realty Associations Industry Developments: 1995/96. LC 93-33355. (Audit Risk Alerts Ser.). 22p. Date not set. reprint ed. pap. 30.00 (*0-608-20787-X*, 207188600003) Bks Demand.

— Construction Contractors Industry Developments, 1996/97. LC 93-642462. (Audit Risk Alerts Ser.). 33p. reprint ed. pap. 30.00 (*0-608-20805-1*, 207190400003) Bks Demand.

— Credit Union Industry Developments, 1996/97. LC 93-642431. (Audit Risk Alerts Ser.). 28p. Date not set. reprint ed. pap. 30.00 (*0-608-20776-4*, 207187500003) Bks Demand.

— Digest of State Accountancy Laws & State Board Regulations. LC 78-643269. 169p. Date not set. reprint ed. pap. 52.40 (*0-608-20754-3*, 207185300003) Bks Demand.

— FDIC Improvement Act Implementation Issues: Update to AICPA Industry Audit Guide, Audits of Banks & AICPA Audit & Accounting guide, Audits of Savings Institutions. LC KF1023.29.F3. (Audit Risk Alerts Ser.). 59p. Date not set. reprint ed. pap. 30.00 (*0-608-20788-8*, 207188700003) Bks Demand.

— Firm-on-Firm Review Directory, January 1997: A Directory of Private Companies Practice Section Member Firms That Have Expressed an Interest in Conducting Peer Reviews. LC 89-646808. 204p. Date not set. reprint ed. pap. 63.30 (*0-608-20767-5*, 207186600003) Bks Demand.

— Health Care Industry Developments, 1996/97. LC 93-642386. (Audit Risk Alerts Ser.). 35p. Date not set. reprint ed. pap. 30.00 (*0-608-20762-4*, 207186100003) Bks Demand.

— Health Care Organizations: With Conforming Changes as of May 1, 1997. LC HF5601.A778. (AICPA Audit & Accounting Guide Ser.). 252p. reprint ed. pap. 78.20 (*0-608-20797-7*, 207189600003) Bks Demand.

— Implementing the Expectation Gap Auditing Standards. LC HF5667.I46. (Reprinted from the Journal of Accountancy Ser.). 63p. Date not set. reprint ed. pap. 30.00 (*0-608-20752-7*, 207185100003) Bks Demand.

— Information for Canadian Chartered Accountant CPA Candidates. 3rd ed. LC HF5661.I468. 36p. reprint ed. pap. 30.00 (*0-608-20802-7*, 207190100003) Bks Demand.

— Information for International Uniform CPA Qualification Examination Candidates. LC HF5661.. 42p. reprint ed. pap. 30.00 (*0-608-20974-0*, 207186900003) Bks Demand.

— Information for Uniform CPA Examination Candidates. 13th ed. LC 97-648368. 102p. Date not set. reprint ed. pap. 31.70 (*0-608-20775-6*, 207187400003) Bks Demand.

— Insurance Industry Developments, 1996/97. LC 96-649773. (Audit Risk Alerts Ser.). 39p. Date not set. reprint ed. pap. 30.00 (*0-608-20789-6*, 207188800003) Bks Demand.

— Investment Companies Industry Developments, 1996/97. LC 93-642387. (Audit Risk Alerts Ser.). 27p. reprint ed. pap. 30.00 (*0-608-20806-X*, 207190500003) Bks Demand.

— MAP Selected Readings, 1996. LC 86-655896. 575p. Date not set. reprint ed. pap. 178.30 (*0-608-20764-0*, 207186300003) Bks Demand.

— Not-for-Profit Organizations: With Conforming Changes as of May 1, 1997. LC 96-34724. 389p. Date not set. reprint ed. pap. 120.60 (*0-608-20772-1*, 207187100003) Bks Demand.

— Peer Review Program Materials. LC HF5616.U5A58. 372p. Date not set. reprint ed. pap. 115.40 (*0-608-20779-9*, 207187800003) Bks Demand.

— Real Estate Industry Developments, 1996/97. LC 95-641038. (Audit Risk Alerts Ser.). 38p. Date not set. reprint ed. pap. 30.00 (*0-608-20759-4*, 207185800003) Bks Demand.

— Report of the Special Advisory Committee on Internal Accounting Control. LC HF5667.A547. 60p. Date not set. reprint ed. pap. 30.00 (*0-608-20758-6*, 207185700003) Bks Demand.

— Report of the Special Task Force on Audits of Repurchase Securities Transactions. LC 86-118663. 39p. Date not set. reprint ed. pap. 30.00 (*0-608-20760-8*, 207185900003) Bks Demand.

— Retail Industry Developments, 1996/97. LC 98-640198. (Audit Risk Alerts Ser.). 34p. reprint ed. pap. 30.00 (*0-608-20803-5*, 207190200003) Bks Demand.

— Securities Industry Developments, 1996/97. LC 93-642416. (Audit Risk Alerts Ser.). 32p. reprint ed. pap. 30.00 (*0-608-20801-9*, 207190000003) Bks Demand.

— Tax Practice Guides & Checklists: AICPA Tax Division. LC KF6320.T39. 395p. Date not set. reprint ed. pap. 122.50 (*0-608-20751-9*, 207185000003) Bks Demand.

— Tax Practice Guides & Checklists: AICPA Tax Division, 1997 Edition. LC KF6320.T39. 490p. reprint ed. pap. 151.90 (*0-608-20871-X*, 207197000003) Bks Demand.

***American Institute of Certified Public Accountants Staff.** Understanding Audits & the Auditor's Report: A Guide for Financial Statement Users. 3rd ed. LC 00-30610. 2000. write for info. (*0-87051-307-9*) Am Inst CPA.

American Institute of Certified Public Accountants Staff. Uniform CPA Examination: May 1989 Questions & Unofficial Answers. LC 84-640994. 93p. Date not set. reprint ed. pap. 30.00 (*0-608-20780-2*, 207187900003) Bks Demand.

— Uniform CPA Examination: November 1989 Questions & Unoffical Answers. LC 84-640994. 95p. Date not set. reprint ed. pap. 30.00 (*0-608-20782-9*, 207188100003) Bks Demand.

— Uniform CPA Examination: November 1990 Questions & Unoffical Answers. LC 84-640994. 99p. Date not set. reprint ed. pap. 30.70 (*0-608-20781-0*, 207188000003) Bks Demand.

— Uniform CPA Examination: November 1991 Questions & Unoffical Answers. LC 84-640994. 99p. Date not set. reprint ed. pap. 30.70 (*0-608-20783-7*, 207188200003) Bks Demand.

American Institute of Certified Public Accountants Staff & Dodds, J. Terry. Solo Practice: An Owners' Manual for Success. LC 98-33283. 250p. 1999. 59.95 (*0-87051-243-9*, No. 090463) Am Inst CPA.

American Institute of Certofied Public Accountants, contrib. by. The AICPA's Uniform CPA Exam, 1997. 97th ed. 1996. 49.95 (*0-02-861191-8*) Macmillan.

American Institute of Chemical Engineers Annual Me. Guidelines for Integrating Process Safety Management, Environment, Safety, Health & Quality. LC 96-31457. 173p. 1996. 120.00 (*0-8169-0683-1*) Am Inst Chem Eng.

— Guidelines for Process Safety Documentation. LC 94-22854. 1994. 120.00 (*0-8169-0625-4*, G-27) Am Inst Chem Eng.

***American Institute of Chemical Engineers Annual Me.** Guidelines for Process Safety in Batch Reaction Systems. LC 99-51662. 1999. write for info. (*0-8169-0780-3*) Am Inst Chem Eng.

American Institute of Chemical Engineers Annual Me. Guidelines for Use of Vapor Cloud Dispersion Models. 2nd ed. LC 96-26950. 271p. 1996. 140.00 (*0-8169-0702-1*) Am Inst Chem Eng.

— Twenty-Five Years of Chemical Engineering Progress. Kirkpatrick, S. D., ed. LC 68-55837. (Essay Index Reprint Ser.). 1977. 23.95 (*0-8369-0149-5*) Ayer.

***American Institute of Chemical Engineers Staff.** Guidelines for Process Safety in Outsourced Manufacturing Operations. LC 00-40166. 2000. write for info. (*0-8169-0812-5*) Am Inst Chem Eng.

American Institute of CPA Staff. AICPA 1998. 704p. 1997. 60.00 (*0-02-861927-7*) Macmillan.

American Institute of CPAs Staff. Analytical Procedures. LC 98-18515. (Auditing Procedure Studies). 56p. 1998. pap. 31.50 (*0-87051-204-8*, 021063) Am Inst CPA.

American Institute of Graphic Arts Staff. AIGA Professional Practices in Graphic Design. Crawford, Tad, ed. 320p. 1998. pap. 24.95 (*1-880559-89-7*) Allworth Pr.

American Institute of Graphic Staff. Graphic Design U. S. A: The Annual of the American Institute of Graphic Arts. 1998. 59.95 (*0-8230-7232-0*) Watsn-Guptill.

American Institute of Law & Criminology Staff. Journal of the American Institute of Law & Criminology. LC 71-154571. (Police in America Ser.). 1971. reprint ed. 18.95 (*0-405-03361-3*) Ayer.

American Institute of Maintenance Staff, Jr. The Contract Cleaner Companion. LC 79-55158. 162p. 1982. pap. 42.95 (*0-9609052-0-0*) Natl Trade.

— Floor Care Guide. 149p. 1982. pap. 16.95 (*0-9609052-1-9*) Natl Trade.

— Selection & Care of Cleaning Equipment. 86p. 1982. pap. 9.95 (*0-9609052-3-5*) Natl Trade.

American Institute of Physics. Causality & Physical Theories, No. 16. Rolnick, William B., ed. LC 73-93420. (Conference Proceedings Ser.). 177p. 1974. 12.00 (*0-88318-115-0*) Am Inst Physics.

— Experimental Meson Spectroscopy 1974: Proceedings of the AIP Conference, Boston 1974, No. 21. Garelick, David A., ed. LC 74-82628. (AIP Conference Proceedings Ser.). 452p. 1974. 19.00 (*0-88318-120-7*) Am Inst Physics.

— Experiments on High Energy Particle Collisions-1973: Proceedings of Conference, No. 12. Panvini, R. S., ed. LC 73-81705. 419p. 1973. 15.00 (*0-88318-111-8*) Am Inst Physics.

— Feedback & Dynamic Control of Plasmas: Princeton, NJ, 1970, No. 1. Chu, T. K. & Hendel, H. W., eds. LC 70-141596. (AIP Conference Proceedings Ser.). 364p. 1970. 14.00 (*0-88318-100-2*) Am Inst Physics.

— High Energy Collisions-1973: Proceedings, No. 15. Quigg, Chris, ed. LC 73-92324. 314p. 1973. 13.75 (*0-88318-114-2*) Am Inst Physics.

— Laser Techniques for Extreme Ultraviolet Spectroscopy: Boulder, 1982. McIlrath, T. J. & Freeman, R. R., eds. LC 82-73205. (AIP Conference Proceedings Ser.: No. 90). 497p. 1982. lib. bdg. 37.00 (*0-88318-189-4*) Am Inst Physics.

— Magnetism & Magnetic Materials: Chicago, 1971, 2 pts. Graham, C. D., Jr. & Rhyne, J. J., eds. LC 59-2468. (AIP Conference Proceedings Ser.: No. 5). 1573p. 1972. 22.00 (*0-88318-104-5*) Am Inst Physics.

— Magnetism & Magnetic Materials: Denver, Co., 1972, 2 pts. Graham, C. D., Jr. & Rhyne, J. J., eds. LC 72-623469. (AIP Conference Proceedings Ser.: No. 10). 1714p. 1973. 24.00 (*0-88318-109-6*) Am Inst Physics.

— Magnetism & Magnetic Materials: Proceedings, 1973, 2 pts. Graham, C. D., Jr. & Rhyne, J. J., eds. LC 52-2468. (AIP Conference Proceedings Ser.: No. 18). 1974. 25.00 (*0-88318-117-7*) Am Inst Physics.

— Mathematical Methods in Hydrodynamics & Integrability in Dynamical Systems: La Jolla Institute, 1981. Tabor, Michael & Treve, Yvain M., eds. LC 82-72462. (AIP Conference Proceedings Ser.: No. 88). 352p. 1982. lib. bdg. 34.00 (*0-88318-187-8*) Am Inst Physics.

— Momentum Wave Functions: Adelaide, Australia, 1982. Weigold, Erich, ed. LC 82-72375. (AIP Conference Proceedings Ser.: No. 86). 345p. 1982. lib. bdg. 34.00 (*0-88318-185-1*) Am Inst Physics.

— Neutrinos, 1974: Philadelphia, Pa., 1974, No. 22. Baltay, Charles, ed. LC 74-82413. (AIP Conference Proceedings Ser.). 1974. 16.00 (*0-88318-121-5*) Am Inst Physics.

— Neutron Scattering: Argonne National Laboratory, 1981. Faber, John, Jr., ed. LC 82-73094. (AIP Conference Proceedings Ser.: No. 89). 397p. 1982. lib. bdg. 35.50 (*0-88318-188-6*) Am Inst Physics.

— Particle Physics, 1971: Univ. of California, Irvine, Dec., 1971, No. 6. Bander, M. et al, eds. LC 72-81239. (AIP Conference Proceedings Ser.). 185p. 1972. 11.00 (*0-88318-105-3*) Am Inst Physics.

— Physics in the Steel Industry: APS-AISI, Lehigh University, 1981. Schwerer, Fred C., ed. LC 82-72033. (AIP Conference Proceedings Ser.: No. 84). 409p. 1982. lib. bdg. 36.00 (*0-88318-183-5*) Am Inst Physics.

— Pi-Pi Scattering, 1973, No. 13. Williams, D. K. & Hagopian, V., eds. LC 73-81704. (AIP Conference Proceedings Ser.). 361p. 1973. 14.00 (*0-88318-112-6*) Am Inst Physics.

— Proton-Antiproton Collider Physics: Madison, Wisconsin, 1982. Barger, V. et al, eds. LC 82-72141. (AIP Conference Proceedings Ser.: No. 85). 676p. 1982. lib. bdg. 42.00 (*0-88318-184-3*) Am Inst Physics.

— Structure & Excitation of Amorphous Solids: Proceedings of the AIP International Conference, Williamsburg, 1976. Lucovsky, G. & Galeener, F. L., eds. LC 76-22279. (AIP Conference Proceedings Ser.: No. 31). 1976. 19.50 (*0-88318-130-4*) Am Inst Physics.

— Superconductivity in D & F-Band Metals: Proceedings of the Conference, Univ. of Rochester, 1971, No. 4. Douglass, D. H., ed. LC 74-188879. (AIP Conference Proceedings Ser.). 375p. 1972. 14.00 (*0-88318-103-7*) Am Inst Physics.

— Thermal Expansion: Proceedings, No. 17. Taylor, R. E. & Denman, G. L., eds. LC 73-94415. 1974. pap. 14.00 (*0-88318-116-9*) Am Inst Physics.

— Thermal Expansion, 1971: Proceedings of the Conference, Corning, NY, 1971, No. 3. Graham, M. G. & Hagy, H. E., eds. LC 72-76970. (AIP Conference Proceedings Ser.). 311p. 1972. 13.00 (*0-88318-102-9*) Am Inst Physics.

— Topics in Statistical Mechanics & Biophysics-A Memorial to Julius L. Jackson, No. 27. Piccirelli, R. A., ed. LC 75-36309. (AIP Conference Proceedings Ser.). 209p. 1976. 17.00 (*0-88318-126-6*) Am Inst Physics.

American Institute of Physics Staff. AIP Directory of Organizations with Physics, Astronomy & Geophysics Staff. 1997. pap. text 50.00 (*1-56396-665-4*) Am Inst Physics.

— Cyclotrons 1972: Proceedings of the Conference, Univ. of British Columbia, Vancouver, 1972, No. 9. Burgerson, J. J. & Strathdee, A., eds. LC 72-92798. (Conference Proceedings Ser.). 836p. 1972. 19.00 (*0-88318-108-8*) Am Inst Physics.

— Directory of Physics & Astronomy Staff, 1990-1991. 402p. 1990. 60.00 (*0-88318-809-0*) Am Inst Physics.

— Experimental Meson Spectroscopy 1972: Proceedings of the Conference, Philadelphia, Pa., April 1972, No. 8. Kwan-Wu Lai & Rosenfeld, Arthur H., eds. LC 72-88226. (AIP Conference Proceedings Ser.). (Illus.). 489p. 1972. 14.00 (*0-88318-107-X*) Am Inst Physics.

— Graduate Programs, 1995-1995: In Physics, Astronomy, & Related Fields. 1994. 45.00 (*1-56396-395-7*) Am Inst Physics.

— Instructions to Authors & Volume Editors for the Preparation of AIP Book Manuscript. LC 95-35413. 1995. write for info. (*1-56396-529-1*) Am Inst Physics.

— 1997-98 Graduate Programs of Physis, Astronomy & Related Fields. 1997. pap. 48.00 (*1-56396-771-5*) Am Inst Physics.

— Temperature: Its Measurement & Control in Science & Industry, Pt. 3 Biology & Medicine. Herzfeld, Charles M., ed. LC 62-19138. 696p. 1972. reprint ed. 49.50 (*0-88275-058-5*, (K)VN) Krieger.

— Temperature: Its Measurement & Control in Science & Industry, Vol. 3, Pt. 2: Applied Methods & Instruments. Herzfeld, Charles M., ed. LC 62-19138. 1108p. 1972. reprint ed. 79.50 (*0-88275-059-3*, (K)VN) Krieger.

American Institute of Physics Staff, ed. 1999 Graduate Programs in Physics, Astronomy, & Related Fields. 962p. 1998. pap. 50.00 (*1-56396-822-3*) Am Inst Physics.

***American Institute of Physics Staff, ed.** 2000 Graduate Programs in Physics, Astronomy & Related Fields. 962p. 1999. pap. 50.00 (*1-56396-887-8*, Pub. by Am Inst Physics) Spr-Verlag.

American Institute of Physics Staff & American Academy of Arts & Sciences Staff. Exploring the History of Nuclear Physics: Proceedings of the AIP & American Academy of Arts & Sciences Joint Conference, Brookline, Mass., 1967 & 1969, No. 7. LC 72-81883. (Illus.). 271p. 1972. 13.00 (*0-88318-106-1*) Am Inst Physics.

American Institute of Physics Staff & Warnow, Joan N. Images of Einstein: A Catalog. 3rd rev. ed. (Illus.). 80p. 1990. pap. 15.00 (*0-88318-248-3*) Am Inst Physics.

American Institute of Timber Construction Staff. Timber Construction Manual. 4th ed. 928p. 1994. 130.00 (*0-471-30970-2*) Wiley.

American Institute Physics Staff & American Association Physics Teachers Staff. Powerful Ideas in Physical Science. (Illus.). 1200p. 1996. teacher ed. 500.00 (*0-917853-66-0*) Am Assn Physics.

American Institutes of Architects, Chicago Chapter. AIAA 1991 Earth Observations Directory: A Worldwide Listing of Government Institutions & Related Groups. 172p. (Orig.). 1990. pap. 39.95 (*0-930403-80-0*, SP-012-90) AIAA.

***American Institution for Cancer Research Staff.** Stopping Cancer Before It Starts: American Institute for Cancer Research's Program for Cancer Prevention. 336p. 2000. pap. 16.95 (*0-312-25467-9*) St Martin.

American Intellectual Property Law Association Sta. An Overview of Intellectual Property: An Original Anthology. LC 76-43205. (Illus.). 1977. reprint ed. lib. bdg. 26.95 (*0-405-09876-6*) Ayer.

American Iris Society Staff. Basic Iris Culture. (Illus.). 1982. 1.25 (*0-9601242-3-3*) Am Iris.

American Italian Historical Association. Conference, et al. Shades of Black & White: Conflict & Collaboration Between Two Communities : Selected Essays from the 30th Annual Conference of the American Italian Historical Society, 13-15 November 1997, Cleveland, Ohio. LC 99-12671. 1997. 19.95 (*0-934675-43-0*) Am Italian.

— Shades of Black & White: Conflict & Collaboration Between Two Communities : Selected Essays from the

An Asterisk (*) at the beginning of an entry indicates that the title is appearing for the first time.

30th Annual Conference of the American Italian Historical Society, 13-15 November 1997, Cleveland, Ohio. LC 99-12671. 1999. write for info. (0-934675-44-9) Am Italian.
— A Tavola: Food, Tradition & Community among Italian Americans ; Selected Essays from the 29th Annual Conference of the American Italian Historical Association, November 1996, Pittsburgh, Pennslyvania. LC 98-49792. 1996. 19.95 (0-934675-41-4) Am Italian.
— A Tavola: Food, Tradition & Community among Italian Americans ; Selected Essays from the 29th Annual Conference of the American Italian Historical Association, November 1996, Pittsburgh, Pennslyvania. LC 98-49792. 1998. write for info. (0-934675-42-2) Am Italian.

American Jewish Archives Staff. Manuscript Catalog of the American Jewish Archives. 1971. 505.00 (0-8161-1430-7, G K Hall & Co) Mac Lib Ref.
— Manuscript Catalog of the American Jewish Archives, Supplement 1. 1978. suppl. ed. 175.00 (0-8161-1436-6, G K Hall & Co) Mac Lib Ref.

American Jewish Committee. The Jewish Communities of Nazi-Occupied Europe. 400p. 1982. reprint ed. 49.50 (0-86527-337-5) Fertig.
— The Jews in Nazi Germany. x, 177p. 1982. reprint ed. 35.00 (0-86527-110-0) Fertig.

American Jewish Historical Society Staff. American Jewish Desk Reference: The Ultimate One-Volume Reference to the Jewish Experience in America. LC 99-37154. 642p. (YA). (gr. 6 up). 1999. 39.95 (0-375-40243-8) Random Ref & Info.
— An Index to Publications of the American Jewish Historical Society, Set, Vols. 21-50 (1931-1961) 460p. 1996. 100.00 (0-926019-76-7) Carlson Pub.
— An Index to Publications of the American Jewish Historical Society, Vols. 51-80 (1961-1991) 700p. 1996. 150.00 (0-926019-77-5) Carlson Pub.

American Jewish Historical Society Staff & Herzl, Theodor Foundation in New York City Staff. Early History of Zionism in America: Proceedings of the American Jewish Historical Society & Theodor Herzl Foundation Conference, New York City, Dec. 26-27, 1955. LC 77-70725. (America & the Holy Land Ser.). 1977. reprint ed. lib. bdg. 29.95 (0-405-10268-2) Ayer.

American Jewish Historical Society Staff, et al. The Palestine Question in American History. American Historical Association Staff, ed. 1978. 17.95 (0-405-11521-0) Ayer.

American Joint Committee on Cancer. Manual for Staging of Cancer. 2nd ed. Beahrs, Oliver H. & Myers, Max H., eds. (Illus.). 220p. 1983. text 19.50 (0-397-50594-9, 65-07594, Lippnctt) Lppncott W & W.

American Journal of EEG Technology Staff. EEG Electrodes, Application & Infection Control. (Illus.). iv, 174p. 1995. per. 25.00 (1-57797-005-5) ASET.
— EEG Recording Techniques & Instrumentation. (Illus.). iv, 190p. 1995. per. 25.00 (1-57797-003-9) ASET.

American Journal of EEG Technology Staff & American END Society Committee. EEG Montages & Polarity. (Illus.). iv, 174p. 1996. per. 25.00 (1-57797-002-0) ASET.
— Long Term Monitoring for Epilepsy. (Illus.). iv, 178p. 1995. per. 24.00 (1-57797-004-7) ASET.

American Journal of END Technology Staff. Drugs & Their Effects on Neurodiagnostics. rev. ed. LC 99-188506. (Illus.). 1997. per. 25.00 (1-57797-010-1) ASET.
— EEG Activation & Artifacts. (Illus.). 1996. per. 25.00 (1-57797-006-3) ASET.
— EEG Clinical Correlations, 3 vols. Incl. Vol. I. Epilepsy. (Illus.). 1996. per. 28.00 (1-57797-028-4); Vol. II. Infectious, Vascular & Structural Disorders. (Illus.). 1998. per. 28.00 (1-57797-029-2); Vol. III. Coma, Cerebral Death, Psychiatry & Geriatrics. (Illus.). 1998. per. 25.00 (1-57797-030-6); Set pap. 75.00 (1-57797-027-6) ASET.
— EEG Patterns & Normal Variants. (Illus.). 1996. spiral bd. 28.00 (1-57797-011-X) ASET.
— Intraoperative Monitoring, 2 vols. Incl. Vol. 1. Evoked Potentials. 2nd rev. ed. American END Society Committee. (Illus.). iv, 254p. 1996. per. 28.00 (1-57797-025-X); Vol. 2. EEG. (Illus.). iv, 160p. 1996. per. 28.00 (1-57797-026-8); 1996. Set per. 52.00 (1-57797-024-1) ASET.
— Neonatal EEG. (Illus.). 1998. per. 28.00 (1-57797-008-X) ASET.
— Nerve Conduction Studies for the Technologist. 1999. spiral bd. 25.00 (1-57797-007-1) ASET.
— Pediatric EEG. (Illus.). 1998. per. 28.00 (1-57797-009-8) ASET.

American Journal of Nursing, New York Staff. Catalog of the Sophia F. Palmer Memorial Library, 2 vols., Set. 1973. 240.00 (0-8161-1066-2, G K Hall & Co) Mac Lib Ref.

American Judicature Society Staff, jt. auth. see Boatright, Robert G.

American Kennel Club, Staff. AKC Complete Dog Book. 19th ed. LC 97-46178. 1997. 32.95 (0-87605-047-X, Pub. by Macmillan) S&S Trade.

American Kennel Club Staff. The American Kennel Club Dog Care & Training. (Illus.). 214p. 1991. per. 11.50 (0-87605-405-X) Howell Bks.
— The Complete Dog Book for Kids. (J). 1996. 34.95 (0-87605-458-0); pap. 22.95 (0-87605-460-2) Howell Bks.

American Kurdish Information Network (AKIN) Staff & Human Rights Alliance (HRA) Staff, eds. Free Leyla Zana! (Illus.). 125p. (Orig.). 1997. write for info. (0-9658604-5-0) Amer Kurd Info.

American Kurdish Information Network Staff & Human Rights Alliance Staff, eds. The Fast for Peace in Kurdistan & the Freedom of Leyla Zara. (Illus.). 145p. 1998. pap. write for info. (0-9658604-9-3) Amer Kurd Info.

American Land Title Association Staff. Mortgage Banking & Title Insurance. 60p. (C). 1996. pap. 45.00 (1-57599-009-1, Real Est Fin Pr) Mortgage Bankers.

American Law Institute. Restatement of the Law, Second: Complete Set & Individual Topics. LC 65-5788. 1999. 5014.50 (0-317-01987-2) Bisel Co.

American Law Institute Ser. American Law Institute, Restatement of the Law, Second, Property - Donative Transfers, Vol. 4. 2nd ed. 500p. (C). 1992. text. write for info. (0-314-94409-5) West Pub.

American Law Institute Staff. American Law Institute, Restatement of the Law, Second, Torts 2d Appendix Volume 310-402 (July 1984-June 1991) 577p. (C). 1992. text. write for info. (0-314-01271-0) West Pub.
— Complex Litigation: Statutory Recommendations & Analysis with Reporter's Study: a Model System for State-to-State Transfer & Consolidation. LC 94-72046. xxx, 592p. 1994. 115.00 (0-8318-5472-3, 5472) Am Law Inst.
— Principles of Corporate Governance: Analysis & Recommendations, 2 vols. Greenwald, Mike, ed. LC 93-31619. liv, 477p. 1994. text 135.00 (0-314-02630-4, 5463) Am Law Inst.
— Principles of Corporate Governance: Analysis & Recommendations, 2 vols., Vol. 1. Greenwald, Mike, ed. LC 93-31619. liv, 432p. 1994. text 135.00 (0-314-02629-0, 5463) West Pub.
— Restatement of the Law, Second, Agency: Appendix, Vol. 7. xxv, 686p. 1994. 67.00 (0-314-02811-0, 5434) West Pub.
— Restatement of the Law, Third: Suretyship & Guaranty. LC 96-14635. xx, 361p. (C). 1996. 72.00 (0-314-09422-9, 5542) Am Law Inst.
— Restatement of the Law Third, Property--Mortgages: Official Text. LC 97-33191. xvi, 743p. (C). 1997. 89.75 (0-314-22626-5, 6076) West Pub.
— Unfair Competition, Student Edition, Restatement of the Law. 683p. 1996. reprint ed. pap. text, student ed. write for info. (0-314-20581-0) West Pub.

American Lawyer Staff, jt. ed. see Court TV Staff.

American Legion, National Americanism Commission. Isms: A Review of Alien Isms, Revolutionary Communism, & Their Active Sympathizers in the United States. 2nd ed. Grob, Gerald N., ed. LC 76-46092. (Anti-Movements in America Ser.). (Illus.). 1977. reprint ed. 24.95 (0-405-09965-7) Ayer.

American Legislative Exchange Council Staff & Butcher, James. Source Book of American State Legislation, 1985-1986. LC 82-642083. 1985. 10.00 (0-317-37050-2) Am Legislative.

American Library Assn. Staff. ALA's Guide to Best Reading 1998. 64p. 1998. pap. 29.95 (0-8389-7948-3) ALA.

***American Library Association.** Banned Books 1999 Resource Guide: Free People Read Freely. 180p. 1999. pap. 25.00 (0-8389-8011-2) American Library Association National Library.

American Library Association. Banned Books Resource Guide, 1997. LC 88-65970. 1997. pap. text 26.00 (0-8389-7886-X) Tate Gallery.
— Guide for Training Collection Development Librarians: Subcommittee on Guide for Training Collection Development Librarians; Stafffing & Organization of Collection Development Evaluation Committee. LC 96-24552. (Collection Management & Development Guides). 61p. 1996. 15.00 (0-8389-3463-3) ALA.
— Smart Training: Library Personnel. 1997. 40.00 (0-8389-7934-3) American Library Association National Library.

American Library Association, Committee on Catalog. Guidelines for Using AACR2, Chapter 9 for Cataloging Microcomputer Software. fac. ed. LC 84-11168. 36p. 1994. pap. 30.00 (0-7837-7309-9, 204723600007) Bks Demand.

American Library Association Committee, on Intelle. Freedom of Communication: Proceedings of the American Library Association, Committee on Intellectual Freedom, 1st Conference, New York, 1952. Dix, William & Bixler, Paul, eds. LC 71-104989. (Essay Index Reprint Ser.). 1977. 20.95 (0-8369-1439-2) Ayer.

American Library Association, Evaluation of Refere. The Reference Assessment Manual. LC 97-168023. 384p. 1995. pap. 35.00 (0-87650-344-X) Pierian.

American Library Association Library Instruction R. Information for a New Age: Redefining the Librarian. xiii, 192p. 1995. lib. bdg. 26.50 (1-56308-278-0) Libs Unl.

American Library Association Reference & Subscript, ed. Reference & Subscription Books Reviews, 4 vols. Incl. 1981-1982. 169p. 1982. (0-8389-0380-0); 1982-1983. 120p. 1983. (0-8389-3291-6); 10.00 (0-318-59490-0) ALA.

American Library Association Resources & Technical. ALA Filing Rules. LC 80-22186. 59p. 1980. pap. 15.00 (0-8389-3255-X) ALA.

American Library Association Staff. The ALA Yearbook: A Review of Library Events, 1982, Vol. 8, 1983. LC 76-647548. (Illus.). 380p. 1983. reprint ed. pap. 117.80 (0-7837-9673-0, 206039700008) Bks Demand.
— ALA Yearbook of Library & Information Services: A Review of Library Events, 1989, Vol. 15, 1990. LC 76-647548. (Illus.). 343p. 1990. reprint ed. pap. 106.40 (0-7837-9674-9, 206040200015) Bks Demand.
— American Library Association Index to General Literature, 3 vols., Set. Incl. Vol. 1. Basic Volume. LC 79-143240. 1970. 90.00 (0-87650-017-3); Vol. 2. Supplement. LC 79-143240. 1970. 39.50 (0-87650-018-1); Vol. 3. Author Index. 1972. 39.50 (0-87650-019-X); LC 79-143240. 1977. 155.00 (0-685-24375-3) Pierian.
— The Arbuthnot Lectures, 1970-1979: With a Biographical Sketch of May Hill Arbuthnot. fac. ed. LC 79-26095. 213p. 1994. pap. 66.10 (0-7837-7312-9, 204723900007) Bks Demand.
— Censorship Litigation & the Schools: Proceedings of a Colloquium Held January 1981. LC 82-24458. 173p. reprint ed. pap. 53.70 (0-7837-5973-8, 204577500007) Bks Demand.
— Curriculum Alternatives: Experiments in School Library Media Education. LC 74-12070. 253p. reprint ed. pap. 78.50 (0-608-12424-9, 202426100035) Bks Demand.
— Directory of Outreach Services in Public Libraries. LC Z 0716.A5. 640p. reprint ed. pap. 198.40 (0-608-12583-0, 202394400034) Bks Demand.
— 50 Years of Notable Books. viii, 192p. 1996. pap. 15.95 (0-8389-7836-3) ALA.

***American Library Association Staff.** Guidelines on Subject Access to Individual Works of Fiction, Drama, Etc. 2nd ed. LC 00-41597. 2000. write for info. (0-8389-3503-6) ALA.

American Library Association Staff. An Index to General Literature: The ALA Index. LC 72-165612. (Essay Index Reprint Ser.). 1977. 48.95 (0-8369-2382-0) Ayer.
— Information Freedom & Censorship: World Report 1991. LC 90-29177. 487p. 1991. pap. 151.00 (0-7837-9684-6, 206041300005) Bks Demand.
— Intellectual Freedom Manual. 4th ed. LC 92-10699. (Illus.). 319p. 1992. reprint ed. pap. 98.90 (0-608-01738-8, 206239600002) Bks Demand.
— Job & Career Information Centers for Public Libraries: A Step-by-Step Manual. LC 85-13519. (Public Library Reporter: No. 21). 56p. reprint ed. pap. 30.00 (0-7837-5919-3, 204571800007) Bks Demand.
— Library Buildings: Innovation for Changing Needs. fac. ed. LC 73-39011. 303p. 1994. pap. 94.00 (0-7837-7311-0, 204723800007) Bks Demand.
— Library Effectiveness: A State of the Art: Papers from a 1980 ALA Preconference, 1980. LC Z 0665. 423p. reprint ed. pap. 131.20 (0-608-12587-3, 202394900034) Bks Demand.
— Library Personnel Policies. 1990. 30.00 (0-8389-7463-6) ALA.
— Newberry & Caldecott Awards: A Guide to the Medal & Honor Books, 1998 Edition. LC 93-648805. (Newberry & Caldecott Awards Ser.). 160p. 1999. pap. text 17.00 (0-8389-3495-1) ALA.
— Notable Children's Books, 1940-1959: Prepared by the Book Re-Evaluation Committee. LC 66-24177. 47p. reprint ed. pap. 30.00 (0-608-12796-5, 202421300035) Bks Demand.
— Notable Children's Books, 1940-1970. LC 77-641. 94p. reprint ed. pap. 30.00 (0-7837-5965-7, 204576600007) Bks Demand.
— Notable Children's Books, 1971-75. LC 81-65981. (Illus.). 48p. 1981. reprint ed. pap. 30.00 (0-7837-9676-5, 206040400005) Bks Demand.
— Personnel Organization & Procedure: A Manual Suggested for Use in Public Libraries. 2nd ed. LC 68-21023. 59p. reprint ed. pap. 30.00 (0-608-12794-9, 202421400035) Bks Demand.
— Public Library Data, 1995. 1996. 60.00 (0-8389-7784-7) ALA.
— Research on Adolescence for Youth Service: An Annotated Bibliography on Adolescent Development, Educational Needs, & Media, 1978-1980. Hodges, Gerald G. & Bradburn, Frances B., eds. LC 83-25785. 160p. reprint ed. pap. 49.60 (0-7837-5956-8, 204575600007) Bks Demand.

American Library Association Staff. Serials Automation for Acquisition & Inventory Control: Papers from the Institute, Milwaukee, September 4-5, 1980. Potter, William G. & Sirkin, Arlene F., eds. LC 81-10798. 191p. reprint ed. pap. 59.30 (0-7837-5958-4, 204575800007) Bks Demand.

American Library Association Staff, ed. Catalog of "A. L. A." Library: 5000 Volumes for a Popular Library Selected by the American Library Association & Shown at the World's Columbian Exposition. LC 98-12959. xx, 592p. 1998. reprint ed. 85.00 (0-9631902-3-7) Canonymous.

American Library Association Staff, et al. Alternative Publishers of Books in North America: American Library Association, Social Responsibilities Round Table, Alternatives in Print Task Force. 3rd enl. rev. ed. 120p. 1997. pap. 20.00 (0-9640119-5-6) Crises Press.

American Library Association Staff, jt. auth. see Joint Steering Committee for Revision of AACR2.

American Library Association Staff, jt. auth. see McCook, Kathleen D.

American Library Association Staff, jt. auth. see Young Adults Library Services Association Staff.

American Library Association, Young Adult Services. African Encounter: A Selected Bibliography of Books, Films, & Other Materials for Promoting an Understanding of Africa among Young Adults. LC 63-22444. 80p. reprint ed. pap. 30.00 (0-8357-5231-3 200178200006) Bks Demand.

American Library Association's Social Responsibili. The Coretta Scott King Awards Book: From Vision to Reality. Smith, Henrietta, ed. LC 97-204892. (Illus.). 130p. (Orig.). 1994. pap. text 28.00 (0-8389-3441-2) ALA.

American Library Association,Taft Group Staff. The Big Book of Library Grant Money, 1998 to 1999. 1500p. 1998. 235.00 (0-8389-0739-3) ALA.

American Library Trustee Association, et al. Determining Your Public Library's Future Size: A Needs Asessment & Planning Model. LC 95-44499. (Illus.). 155p. 1996. pap. 30.00 (0-8389-0671-0, 0671-0-2045) ALA.

American Lung Association Staff. American Lung Association's Family Guide to Asthma & Allergies. LC 96-53497. (Illus.). 256p. 1998. pap. 13.95 (0-316-03815-6, Back Bay) Little.

American Lung Association Staff, jt. auth. see Edelman, Norman.

American Machinist & Automated Manufacturing Magaz, ed. Practical Ideas . . . for Metalworking Operations, Tooling, & Maintenance. (Illus.). 330p. 1988. reprint ed. 32.50 (0-932905-05-6) Penton Pub.

American Machinist Staff. Practical Ideas. (Illus.). 116p. 1998. pap. 22.95 (0-932905-13-7) Penton Pub.

American Management Association. Leadership Development. 112p. 1998. pap. 250.00 (0-8144-7975-8) AMACOM.

American Management Association, Research Developm. Managing Industrial Energy Conservation. LC 77-22251. (American Management Associations' Management Briefing Ser.). (Illus.). 61p. reprint ed. pap. 30.00 (0-608-11715-3, 205020000078) Bks Demand.
— New Products, New Profits: Company Experiences in New Product Planning. Marting, Elizabeth, ed. LC 64-12772. 303p. reprint ed. pap. 94.00 (0-608-12964-X, 202391900034) Bks Demand.

American Management Association Staff. The AMA Style Guide for Business Writing. 240p. 1996. 29.95 (0-8144-0297-6) AMACOM.
— The Creative Edge: How Companies Support Creativity & Innovation. LC 95-14142. 1995. write for info. (0-8144-6712-1) AMACOM.
— Performance Appraisal Challenge. (The Challenge Ser.). 1998. 49.95 (0-8144-1203-3) AMACOM.
— Write for Results. 124p. 1998. pap. text 49.95 (1-890003-00-X) AMACOM.

American Management Association Staff, jt. auth. see Luthans, Fred.

American Management Association Staff, jt. auth. see Saratoga Institute Staff.

American Management Association Staff, jt. auth. see Weeks, Melvyn J.

American Management Association Staff, jt. contrib. by see American Compensation Association Staff.

American Management Associations, Research & Devel. Achieving Full Value from R & D Dollars. LC 62-3195. (American Management Associations Management Reports: No. 69). 109p. reprint ed. pap. 33.80 (0-8357-5074-4, 200032400025) Bks Demand.

***American Map Company Staff.** Shanghai: World-City Map 1:15,000. (Illus.). 1998. pap. 9.95 (0-8416-1003-7) Am Map.

American Map Corp. Staff. Atlas of Business Control of U. S. 1993. 29.95 (0-8416-9704-3) Am Map.
— Scholastic World Atlas, No. 9552. (J). (gr. 7-9). 1993. pap. 3.95 (0-8416-9552-0) Am Map.
— Student Atlas of the Bible. (Series 9500). (Illus.). 1994. 6.95 (0-8416-9559-8) Am Map.
— Students Indexed World Atlas, No. 695512. (Illus.). (gr. 7-12). 1983. pap. 2.95 (0-8416-9551-2) Am Map.
— Student's Notebook Atlas. LC 94-675161. 1998. pap. 2.99 (0-8416-9608-X) Am Map.
— U. S. Zip Codes Atlas. 1994. pap. 29.95 (0-8416-9607-1, 696071) Am Map.

American Map Corp. Staff, ed. Atlas Mundial. (SPA., Illus.). (J). (gr. 7-12). 1992. pap. 2.95 (0-8416-9555-5, 695555) Am Map.

American Map Corporation. Quick & Easy World Atlas. 48p. 5.95 (0-8416-9553-9, 695539) Am Map.

American Map Corporation Staff. Chicagoland Atlas. 1998. 39.95 (0-8416-9223-8) Am Map.
— City to City Atlas 1999, 1. 1998. pap. text 17.95 (0-8416-9229-7) Am Map.
— Family World Atlas. 1994. 34.95 (0-8416-2025-3) Am Map.
— Great World Atlas. 4th ed. (Illus.). 1994. 59.95 (0-8416-2005-9, 620059) Am Map.

***American Map Publishing Staff.** New Orleans. 3rd ed. (Insight Guides - USA Ser.). 1999. pap. 21.95 (0-88729-029-9) Langenscheidt.

American Map Publishing Staff. 1999 Full Size U. S. Road Atlas. 1998. pap. 10.95 (0-8416-2386-4) Am Map.
— 1999 Truckers Atlas. 1998. pap. 19.95 (0-8416-9228-9) Am Map.
— 1999 U. S. Road Atlas. 1998. pap. 7.95 (0-8416-9227-0) Am Map.

***American Map Publishing Staff.** Portugal. 3rd ed. 1999. pap. 21.95 (0-88729-026-4) Langenscheidt.
— Thailand. 1999. pap. 7.95 (0-8416-2068-7) Langenscheidt.
— Venice. LC 98-689878. 1999. pap. text 7.95 (0-8416-2036-9) Am Map.

American Map Staff. Atlas of Human Anatomy, No. 614466. (Illus.). 1985. pap. 2.50 (0-8416-1446-6) Am Map.
— Full-Size U. S. Road Atlas. (Insight Guides Ser.). 1998. pap. 10.95 (0-8416-2382-1) Am Map.
— Schick Anatomy Atlas. 1999. pap. text 19.95 (0-8416-1450-4) Am Map.
— Spain & Portugal Travel Atlas. 2nd ed. 72 p. 1990. pap. write for info. (0-8416-2055-5) Am Map.
— Trucker's Atlas. (Insight Guides Ser.). 1998. pap. 19.95 (0-8416-9216-5) Am Map.

American Maps Staff. South America. (Insight Guides Ser.). 1998. 23.95 (0-88729-128-7) Langenscheidt.

American Marketing & Publishing Co. Staff, ed. How to Prosper Through Word Power. 64p. (Orig.). 1991. pap. 1.50 (0-9628406-0-2) Chrstian Pub Netwrk.

American Marketing Association. A Basic Bibliography on Marketing Research, 1974. 3rd ed. Cousineau, Alain et al, eds. LC 74-187908. (American Marketing Association Bibliography Ser.: No. 2). 309p. reprint ed. pap. 95.80 (0-8357-5973-3, 202666700051) Bks Demand.

An Asterisk (*) at the beginning of an entry indicates that the title is appearing for the first time.

— Marketing Doctoral Dissertation Abstracts, 1979. LC HF5415.M2977. (American Marketing Association Bibliography Ser.: No. 34). 162p. reprint ed. pap. 50.30 (*0-608-16297-3*, 202667000051) Bks Demand.

— Marketing Doctoral Dissertation Abstracts, 1980. Greer, Thomas, ed. LC Z 7164.M18A5. (American Marketing Association Bibliography Ser.: No. 39). 209p. reprint ed. pap. 64.80 (*0-608-16300-7*, 202667100051) Bks Demand.

American Marketing Association Staff. AMA Educators' Proceedings, 1983. Murphy, Patrick E. et al, eds. LC 83-4623. (American Marketing Association, Proceedings Ser.: No. 49). (Illus.). 476p. reprint ed. pap. 147.60 (*0-8357-4761-1*, 203768800009) Bks Demand.

— AMA Educators' Proceedings, 1984. Belk, Russell W. et al, eds. LC 84-9240. (American Marketing Association, Proceedings Ser.: No. 50). 447p. reprint ed. pap. 138.60 (*0-8357-4762-X*, 203768900009) Bks Demand.

— AMA Educators' Proceedings, 1988: Efficiency & Effectiveness in Marketing. LC 86-643031. (American Marketing Association Proceedings Ser.: No. 54). (Illus.). 350p. 1988. reprint ed. pap. 108.50 (*0-608-04081-9*, 206481300011) Bks Demand.

— Changing Values & Social Trends: How Do Organizations React? Presented Jointly by the Market Research Society & the American Marketing Association, June 1974, Oxford, England. LC HF5415.C474. 224p. reprint ed. pap. 69.50 (*0-608-12629-2*, 201159300079) Bks Demand.

— Marketing Theory & Practice: 1989 AMA Winter Educators' Conference. Childers, Terry L. et al, eds. LC 89-272. (American Marketing Association Proceedings Ser.). (Illus.). 408p. 1989. reprint ed. pap. 126.50 (*0-608-04082-7*, 206481400011) Bks Demand.

— Proceedings of the 1990 AMA Microcomputers in Marketing Education Conference: March 31-April 2, 1990, New Orleans, Louisiana. Berman, Barry et al, eds. LC 90-189871. (Illus.). 265p. 1990. reprint ed. pap. 82.20 (*0-608-04084-3*, 206481600011) Bks Demand.

— Research Frontiers in Marketing: Dialogues & Directions: 1978 Educator's Proceedings. Jain, Subhash C., ed. LC 78-8596. (American Marketing Association, Proceedings Ser.: 43). 455p. reprint ed. pap. 141.10 (*0-608-14605-6*, 202336400032) Bks Demand.

— Review of Marketing, 1987. Houston, Michael J., ed. LC 78-649100. 515p. 1987. reprint ed. pap. 159.70 (*0-7837-9765-6*, 206049300005) Bks Demand.

American Marketing Association Staff, ed. Marketing Masters. LC 91-32691. 278p. (Orig.). 1991. pap. 24.95 (*0-87757-219-4*) Am Mktg.

American Marketing Association Staff & Weidenbaum, Murray L. The Military Market in the United States. LC 63-4878. 57p. reprint ed. pap. 30.00 (*0-608-30676-2*, 200217300011) Bks Demand.

American Marketing Association Staff, jt. auth. see Abrams, Bill.

American Marketing Association Staff, jt. auth. see Kania, Deborah.

American Marketing Association Staff, jt. auth. see Parmerlee, David.

American Mathematical Society. Reviews in Number Theory, 1984-96: As Printed in Mathematical Reviews. LC 97-38703. 4294p. 1997. pap. 325.00 (*0-8218-0848-6*); pap. 42.00 (*0-8218-0931-8*) Am Math.

American Mathematical Society Special Session Staf. Ordered Fields & Real Algebraic Geometry. Dubois, D. W. & Recio, T., eds. LC 82-3951. (Contemporary Mathematics Ser.: No. 8). 368p. 1982. reprint ed. pap. 114.10 (*0-608-03973-X*, 205256500012) Bks Demand.

American Mathematical Society Staff. Author Index of Mathematical Reviews, 1960-64, 2 pts. LC 42-4221. 661p. 1978. pap. 368.00 (*0-8218-0026-4*, MREVIN 60/64) Am Math.

— Differential Equations. LC QA0003.A5716. (American Mathematical Society. Translations Ser.: Vol. 4). 479p. reprint ed. pap. 148.50 (*0-7837-1795-4*, 204199600001) Bks Demand.

— Differential Geometry & Calculus of Variations. LC QA0003.A5716. (American Mathematical Society Ser.: Vol. 6). (Illus.). 515p. reprint ed. pap. 159.70 (*0-608-09252-5*, 205275600006) Bks Demand.

— Eight Papers on Algebra & Number Theory. LC 51-5559. (American Mathematical Society. Translations Ser.: Vol. 4). 243p. reprint ed. pap. 75.40 (*0-7837-3398-4*, 204335700008) Bks Demand.

— Eleven Papers on Topology. LC 51-5559. (American Mathematical Society. Translations Ser.: Vol. 78). (Illus.). 257p. reprint ed. pap. 79.70 (*0-7837-1794-6*, 204199500001) Bks Demand.

— Eleven Papers on Topology, Function Theory & Differential Equations. LC 51-5559. (American Mathematical Society Translations Ser.: Ser. 2, Vol. 1). (Illus.). 308p. reprint ed. pap. 95.50 (*0-608-09618-0*, 205277600007) Bks Demand.

— Functional Analysis & Measure Theory. fac. ed. LC QA0003.A5716. (American Mathematical Society, Translations Ser.: Series 1, Vol. 10). 554p. 1962. reprint ed. pap. 171.80 (*0-608-01006-5*, 206186400012) Bks Demand.

— Lie Algebras & Lie Groups: Five Papers Prepared in Connection with the First Summer Mathematical Institute. LC 52-42839. (American Mathematical Society: No. 14). 61p. 1972. reprint ed. pap. 30.00 (*0-608-03971-3*, 205256300011) Bks Demand.

— Lie Groups. LC QA0003.A5716. (American Mathematical Society: No. 9). (Illus.). 545p. 1962. reprint ed. pap. 169.00 (*0-608-03970-5*, 205256200011) Bks Demand.

— Norbert Wiener, 1894-1964. 145p. 1988. pap. 30.00 (*0-8218-0030-2*, NW) Am Math.

— Number Theory & Operator Theory. fac. ed. LC QA0003.A4. (Translations Ser.: Vol. 13, No. 2). 350p. 1960. reprint ed. pap. 108.50 (*0-7837-8297-7*, 204908300013) Bks Demand.

— Probability & Physical Problems. LC 77-9609. (American Mathematical Society Ser.: Vol. 11). (Illus.). 401p. reprint ed. pap. 124.40 (*0-608-09198-7*, 205270200003) Bks Demand.

— Problems of Elastic Stability & Vibrations. Komkov, Vadim, ed. LC 81-12833. (Contemporary Mathematics Ser.: Vol. 4). (Illus.). 147p. reprint ed. pap. 45.60 (*0-608-09609-1*, 205276700007) Bks Demand.

— Reviews in Number Theory, 1984-96: As Printed in Mathematical Reviews. LC 97-38703. 1055p. 1997. pap. 107.00 (*0-8218-0932-6*); pap. 42.00 (*0-8218-0933-4*) Am Math.

— Reviews in Number Theory, 1984-96: As Printed in Mathematical Reviews. LC 97-38703. 606p. 1997. pap. 62.00 (*0-8218-0935-0*); pap. 78.00 (*0-8218-0936-9*); pap. 102.00 (*0-8218-0937-7*) Am Math.

— Series & Approximation. LC 72-185271. (American Mathematical Society Translations Ser.: Series 1, Vol. 3). (Illus.). 395p. reprint ed. pap. 122.50 (*0-608-09617-2*, 205277500007) Bks Demand.

— Space Mathematics. Rosser, J. B., ed. LC 66-20435. (Lectures in Applied Mathematics: Vol. 5). 296p. 1966. reprint ed. pap. 57.00 (*0-8218-1105-3*, LAM-5) Am Math.

— Space Mathematics, Pt. 2. Rosser, J. B., ed. LC 66-20435. (Lectures in Applied Mathematics: Vol. 7). 315p. 1966. text 49.00 (*0-8218-1107-X*, LAM-7) Am Math.

— Topology & Topological Algebra. LC QA0003.A5716. (American Mathematical Society Ser.: Series 1, 8). 467p. 1968. pap. 144.80 (*0-608-05172-1*, 205259300001) Bks Demand.

— Transactions of the Moscow Mathematical Society. LC 65-4713. 390p. reprint ed. pap. 120.90 (*0-7837-1793-8*, 204199400001) Bks Demand.

— Twelve Papers on Logic & Differential Equations. LC 51-5559. (American Mathematical Society Translations Ser.: Ser. 2, Vol. 29). 385p. reprint ed. pap. 119.40 (*0-608-09620-2*, 205277800007) Bks Demand.

— Twenty Volume Author Index of Mathematical Reviews, 1940-59, 2 pts. LC 42-4221. 2201p. 1980. 466.00 (*0-8218-0024-8*, MREVIN 40/59) Am Math.

— Two Papers on Homotopy Theory of Continuous Mappings. LC 51-5559. (American Mathematical Society Translations Ser.: Ser. 2, Vol. 7). 325p. reprint ed. pap. 100.80 (*0-608-09619-9*, 205277700007) Bks Demand.

American Mathematical Society Staff, et al. Fifteen Papers on Series & Functions of Complex Variables. LC 51-5559. (American Mathematical Society Ser.: Series 2, No. 43). 324p. reprint ed. pap. 100.50 (*0-608-20155-3*, 205280000011) Bks Demand.

— Twelve Papers on Algebra, Algebraic Geometry & Topology. LC QA0001.A482. (American Mathematical Society: Vol. 84). 279p. 1969. reprint ed. pap. 86.50 (*0-608-09600-8*, 205275800007) Bks Demand.

— Twelve Papers on Analysis & Applied Mathematics. LC 51-5559. (American Mathematical Society Translations Ser.: Series 2, Vol. 35). 367p. reprint ed. pap. 113.80 (*0-608-09599-0*, 205275700007) Bks Demand.

American Mathematical Society Staff, jt. auth. see Ewing, John.

American Mathematical Society Staff, jt. auth. see Society for Industrial & Applied Mathematics Staff.

American Matron. The Maternal Physician: A Treatise on the Nurture & Management of Infants from the Birth until Two Years Old Being the Result of Sixteen Years' Experience in the Nursery. 2nd ed. LC 70-180581. (Medicine & Society in America Ser.). 294p. 1972. reprint ed. 20.95 (*0-405-03958-1*) Ayer.

American Medical Association. The AMA Family Medical Guide. 29.95 (*0-317-65276-1*) Random.

— The AMA Handbook of First Aid & Emergency Care. LC 99-14152. 2000. pap. 16.95 (*0-375-75486-5*) Random Hse Chldrns.

— The American Medical Association Encyclopedia of Medicine. 1989. 45.00 (*0-394-56528-2*) Random.

— The American Medical Association Family Medical Guide. rev. ed. LC 86-17659. (Illus.). 832p. 1987. 35.00 (*0-394-55582-1*) Random.

— The American Medical Association Family Medical Guide. 3rd ed. 37.50 (*0-614-19673-6*, OP290494WE) AMA.

— The American Medical Association Guide to Prescription & Over-the-Counter Drugs. 25.00 (*0-614-19672-8*, OP290590WE) AMA.

— American Medical Association Guide to Your Family's Symptoms. 1992. pap. 15.00 (*0-8129-2037-6*, Times Bks) Crown Pub Group.

— The American Medical Association Guide to Your Family's Symptoms. pap. 15.00 (*0-614-19671-X*, OP953794WE) AMA.

— The American Medical Association Handbook of First Aid & Emergency Care. 70p. 8.95 (*0-614-19674-4*, OP290390WE) AMA.

— American Medical Association Pocket Guide to Emergency First Aid. LC 92-56798. 96p. 1993. pap. 4.99 (*0-679-74672-2*) Random.

— Assessing the Value of the Medical Practice: The Physician's Handbook for Measuring & Maximizing Practice Value. (Practice Success Ser.). 1996. pap. 44.95 (*0-89970-787-4*, OP315196WE) AMA.

— A Benchmark Study on Physicians' Use of the World Wide Web. 1999. 2800.00 (*0-89970-935-4*) AMA.

— Buying, Selling, & Owning the Medical Practice: The Physician's Handbook to Ownership Options. (Practice Success Ser.). 1996. pap. 44.95 (*0-89970-788-2*, OP315396WE) AMA.

— Caring for the Country: A History & Celebration of the First 150 Years of the American Medical Association. 1997. 49.95 (*0-375-50000-6*) Random.

— Code Medical Ethics: Current Opinions with Annotations. 1998. 34.95 (*0-89970-960-5*) AMA.

— Complete Guide to Your Children's Health. LC 98-6970. 640p. 1998. 39.95 (*0-679-45776-3*) Random.

***American Medical Association.** Council of Judicial & Ethical Affairs: Reports on Managed Care. 1998. pap. text 32.95 (*0-89970-963-X*) AMA.

— CPT, Professional Edition 2000. (C). 1999. 54.00 (*1-57947-018-1*) Thomson Learn.

— CPT, 2000. 640p. (C). 1999. pap. 47.95 (*1-57947-016-5*) Thomson Learn.

American Medical Association. CPT, 1999. (C). 1999. write for info. (*0-89970-940-0*) Thomson Learn.

— Electronic Data Interchange: The Physicians' Guide. pap. 29.95 (*0-89970-764-5*, OP205996WE) AMA.

— Encyclopedia Medica del Hogar. 1991. text 60.00 (*0-07-104016-1*) McGraw.

— Evaluating & Negotiating Compensation Arrangements: Understanding the Process & Ensuring You. (Career Development Ser.). 1998. pap. text 39.95 (*0-89970-894-3*) AMA.

— Graduate Medical Education Directory, 1999-2000. 1999. 64.95 (*0-89970-984-2*) AMA.

— A Guide to Forming Physician-Directed Managed Care Networks. 1995. 48.95 (*0-89970-730-0*, OP601595WE) AMA.

— The Guides Casebook: Cases to Accompany Guides to the Evaluation of Permanent Impairment. 4th ed. 1999. 59.95 (*0-89970-970-2*) AMA.

— Guides to the Evaluation of Permanent Impairment. 4th ed. 1993. 89.95 (*0-89970-553-7*, A4226) AMA.

— The Health Care Almanac: A Resource Guide to the Medical Field. (Illus.). 410p. 1999. pap. 29.95 (*0-89970-707-6*, OP311795WE) AMA.

American Medical Association. Health Care Almanac: Every Person's Guide to the Thoughtful & Practical Sides of Medicine. 1997. 27.95 (*0-89970-900-1*) AMA.

American Medical Association. Health Care Fraud & Abuse: A Physician's Guide to Compliance. 224p. 2000. pap. 59.95 (*0-89970-978-8*, OP083599) AMA.

— Health Professions Career & Education Directory. 28th ed. 1997. pap. text 60.00 (*0-89970-834-X*) AMA.

— Health Professions Education Directory. 1999. 54.95 (*0-89970-987-7*) AMA.

— Home Medical Advisor: The New Self Help Guide to Symptoms, Diseases & Medical Emergencies. 320p. 1988. 24.95 (*0-394-56523-1*) Random.

— ICD-9, 1999. 1998. per. 66.95 (*0-89970-952-4*) AMA.

— Implementing a Physican Organization. LC 98-147772. 72p. 1996. pap. 68.95 (*0-89970-733-5*, OP601695WE) AMA.

— Integration Strategies for the Medical Practice: The Physician's Handbook to Integration Alternatives. (Practice Success Ser.). 1996. pap. 44.95 (*0-89970-789-0*, OP315096WE) AMA.

— Managing Managed Care in the Medical Practice: The Physician's Handbook for Success & Survival. (Practice Success Ser.). 1996. pap. 44.95 (*0-89970-757-2*, OP701095WE) AMA.

— Mastering the Reimbursement Process. 2nd ed. 200p. 1999. pap. 49.95 (*0-89970-762-9*, OP080095WE) AMA.

— Medical Group Practices in the U. S., 1999 Edition. 1999. 99.95 (*0-89970-958-3*) AMA.

— Medicare RBRVS: The Physicians' Guide, 1997 Edition. rev. ed. 496p. 1997. pap. 59.95 (*0-89970-860-9*, OP059697WE) AMA.

— Personnel Management in the Medical Practice: The Physician's Handbook for Successful Management. (Practice Success Ser.). 1996. pap. 44.95 (*0-89970-756-4*, OP700995WE) AMA.

— The Physician's Guide to Internet Explorer. 1999. 29.95 (*0-89970-934-6*) AMA.

— Physician's Socioeconomic Statistics, 1999-2000 Edition. 1999. 495.00 (*0-89970-974-5*) AMA.

— Planning for a Successful Career Transition: The Physician's Guide to Managing Career Change. (Illus.). 65p. 1999. pap. 27.95 (*0-89970-980-X*, OP208299) AMA.

— Starting a Medical Practice: The Physician's Handbook for Successful Start-Up. (Practice Success Ser.). 1996. pap. 44.95 (*0-89970-786-6*, OP315296WE) AMA.

American Medical Association, ed. CPT: Timesaver, 1998. annuals rev. ed. 550p. 1998. ring bd. 57.95 (*1-57066-076-X*, 9806) Practice Mgmt Info.

— CPT, 1998. deluxe rev. ed. 550p. 1998. text 57.95 (*1-57066-077-8*, 9804); spiral bd. 52.95 (*1-57066-075-1*, 9801) Practice Mgmt Info.

— CPT 1999 Coder's Choice. rev. ed. 1998. pap. text 54.95 (*1-57066-095-6*, 9901) Practice Mgmt Info.

— CPT 1999 Deluxe. rev. ed. 1998. 57.95 (*1-57066-097-2*, 9904) Practice Mgmt Info.

— CPT 1999 Timesaver Binder. rev. ed. 1998. ring bd. 57.95 (*1-57066-096-4*, 9903) Practice Mgmt Info.

***American Medical Association, ed.** CPT 2000 Coder's Choice. (Illus.). 1999. pap. text 54.95 (*1-57066-156-1*, 20001) Practice Mgmt Info.

— CPT 2000 Codes on Disk. 1999. pap. text 149.95 incl. disk (*1-57066-159-6*, 20008) Practice Mgmt Info.

— CPT 2000 Deluxe. 1999. text 59.95 (*1-57066-158-8*, 20004) Practice Mgmt Info.

— CPT 2000 TimeSaver Binder. 1999. ring bd. 59.95 (*1-57066-160-X*, 20003) Practice Mgmt Info.

American Medical Association, ed. CPT 1998 Codes on Disk. annuals rev. ed. 550p. 1998. pap. 129.95 incl. disk (*1-57066-078-6*, 9808) Practice Mgmt Info.

***American Medical Association, ed.** CPT 2000. 1999. 54.95 (*1-57066-157-X*, 20002) Practice Mgmt Info.

American Medical Association, ed. Outcomes Research Resource Guide, 97-98: A Survey of Current Activities. 1998. pap. 49.95 (*0-89970-907-9*) AMA.

American Medical Association & Allison, Kathleen Cahill. Complete Guide to Women's Health. Slupik, Ramona I., ed. LC 96-33738. 768p. 1996. 39.95 (*0-679-43122-5*) Random.

American Medical Association & Iverson, Cheryl. Manual of Style: A Guide for Authors & Editors. 9th ed. LC 97-19246. 660p. 1997. 34.95 (*0-683-40206-4*) Lppncott W & W.

American Medical Association & Melek, Jacques. Cancer & All You Need to Know to Avoid It. (Illus.). 500p. (Orig.). 1984. pap. text 24.95 (*0-685-09133-3*, Sunbright Bks) J Melek.

— Cancer-Birth Control Pills: Cause & Effect, Relationship, Benefits vs. Risks. (Illus.). 500p. (Orig.). 1984. pap. 19.85 (*0-685-09135-X*, Sunbright Bks) J Melek.

American Medical Association, jt. auth. see Epner, Janet E. Gans.

American Medical Association, jt. auth. see Gorey, Thomas M.

American Medical Association, Committee on Medicolegal Aspects Staff. Alcohol & the Impaired Driver: A Manual on the Medicolegal Aspects of Chemical Tests for Intoxication with Supplement on Breath-Alcohol Tests. LC 75-183674. (Illus.). 292p. reprint ed. pap. 90.60 (*0-8357-5299-2*, 203032500068) Bks Demand.

American Medical Association Department of Drugs S. Drug Evaluations. 6th ed. 1770p. 1986. text 68.00 (*0-03-012647-9*, W B Saunders Co) Harcrt Hlth Sci Grp.

***American Medical Association Judicial Council Staff.** CPT, 2000. 640p. (C). 1999. ring bd. 51.95 (*1-57947-017-3*) Thomson Learn.

***American Medical Association Staff.** Alternative Medicine: An Objective Assessment. (Illus.). 656p. 1999. lib. bdg. 75.00 (*1-57947-002-5*) AMA.

— CPT 2000 Changes: An Insider's View. (Coding Ser.). (Illus.). 450p. 2000. pap. text 49.95 (*1-57947-091-2*) AMA.

— Graduate Medical Education Directory 2000-2001. 2000. pap. text 70.00 (*1-57947-060-2*) AMA.

— The Handbook of Physician Health: The Essential Guide to Understanding the Health Care Needs of Physicians. (Illus.). 225p. 2000. 54.00 (*1-57947-004-1*) AMA.

— Health Professions Career & Education Directory. 450p. 2000. pap. text 60.00 (*1-57947-063-7*) AMA.

— 1999 CPT. (Medical Assisting Ser.). (C). 1999. pap. (*0-89970-941-9*) Delmar.

— Principles of CPT Coding. (Coding Ser.). (Illus.). 325p. 1999. pap. 49.95 (*0-89970-996-6*) AMA.

American Medical Association Staff, ed. AMA Drug Evaluations Annual 1994. 2400p. 1994. 98.95 (*0-89970-602-9*, 932347) US Pharmacopeia.

— Council of Judicial & Ethical Affairs Reports on End-Of-Life Care. 1998. pap. 32.95 (*0-89970-962-1*) AMA.

***American Medical Association Staff, ed.** Medicare RBRVS: The Physician's Guide, 1999 Manual. 464p. 1999. pap. 64.00 (*0-89970-967-2*) Aspen Pub.

— 1999 HCPCS. 1998. pap. 44.00 (*0-89970-950-8*) Aspen Pub.

American Medical Sales School, Inc. Staff. The 1994 Dallas, Fort Worth Medical Directory. rev. ed. Huggins, Diane, ed. & intro. by. (Illus.). 737p. 1994. 42.50 (*1-882328-02-7*) Am Med Sales.

— U. S. A. Medical Directories: Dallas - Fort Worth, 1995-96 Issue. rev. ed. Huggins, Diane, ed. & intro. by. (Illus.). 410p. 1995. 42.50 (*1-882328-03-5*) Am Med Sales.

***American Medical Womens Assocation Staff, et al.** Womens Complete Wellness Book: American Medical Women's Association. (Illus.). 38.99p. 2000. pap. 24.95 (*0-312-25472-5*) St Martin.

American Medical Women's Association Staff. The Complete Family Health Book. 2000. text 35.00 (*1-58238-019-8*, Whitman Coin) St Martin.

American Mensa Limited Staff, jt. auth. see Ryan, Steve.

American Mercury Staff. American Mercury Reader. (BCL1-PS American Literature Ser.). 378p. 1993. reprint ed. lib. bdg. 89.00 (*0-7812-6597-5*) Rprt Serv.

— The American Mercury Reader: A Selection of Distinguished Articles. Spivak, Lawrence E. & Angoff, Charles, eds. LC 75-41009. (BCL Ser.: No. II). reprint ed. 37.50 (*0-404-14765-8*) AMS Pr.

— Readings from the American Mercury. Knight, G. C., ed. LC 68-16902. (Essay Index Reprint Ser.). 1977. 20.95 (*0-8369-0150-9*) Ayer.

American Meteorological Society, Boston Staff. Cumulated Bibliography & Index to Meteorological & Geoastrophysical Abstracts: 1950-1969. 1972. 960.00 (*0-8161-0183-3*, G K Hall & Co) Mac Lib Ref.

American Micro Systems Staff. MOS Integrated Circuits: Theory, Fabrication, Design & Systems Applications. Penny, William M. & Lau, Lillian, eds. LC 79-1039. 494p. 1979. reprint ed. 49.50 (*0-88275-897-7*) Krieger.

American Mosquito Control Association Staff. Ground Equipment & Insecticides for Mosquito Control: Bulletin Number Two. rev. ed. 101p. 1968. 2.00 (*0-318-12860-8*) Am Mosquito.

— Manual for Mosquito Rearing & Experimental Techniques No. 5: Bulletin. 105p. 1970. 3.50 (*0-318-12862-4*) Am Mosquito.

American Motorcyclist Association Staff. 1996 AMA Superbike Series Media Guide. Lawrence, Larry, ed. (Illus.). 306p. (Orig.). 1996. pap. 18.95 (*0-9649722-1-2*) D Bull.

American Museum of Natural History Staff, ed. Research Catalog of the Library of the American Museum of Natural History: Authors, 13 vols. 1977. 1515.00 (*0-8161-0064-0*, G K Hall & Co) Mac Lib Ref.

An Asterisk (*) at the beginning of an entry indicates that the title is appearing for the first time.

American National Metric Council, Consumer Liaison. Metric Reference for Consumers. 565p. 1990. pap. text 2.50 (*3-504-40005-6*) Am Natl.

American National Metric Council, Educational Mate. Metric Guide for Educational Materials: A Handbook for Teachers, Writers & Publishers. 1977. pap. text 3.00 (*0-916148-09-2*) Am Natl.

American National Metric Council Staff. Managing Metrication in Business & Industry. LC 75-45846. (Illus.). 215p. reprint ed. pap. 66.70 (*0-7837-0966-8*, 204127100019) Bks Demand.

American National Red Cross. Adapted Aquatics. 1977. pap. 3.95 (*0-385-12611-5*) Doubleday.

American National Red Cross Staff. American Red Cross HIV/AIDS Facts Book. LC 98-230746. vii, 284 p. 1998. write for info. (*0-86536-216-5*) Am Nat Red Cross.

American National Red Cross Symposium Staff. Development of Plasma Derivatives for Clinical Use: Proceedings of the American Red Cross Symposium, Washington, October 1971 - Journal: Vox Sanguinis, Vol. 23, Nos. 1 & 2. Jamieson, G. A., ed. (Illus.). 1972. pap. 46.75 (*3-8055-1483-2*) S Karger.

American National Standards Committee. National Electrical Safety Code, ANSI C2-1990. rev. ed. (Illus.). 432p. 1989. pap. 38.00 (*1-55937-011-4*, SH12641) IEEE Standards.

American National Standards Committee on Library W, jt. auth. see Council of National Library & Information Associat.

American National Standards Institute, jt. auth. see American Institute of Aeronautics & Astronautics S.

American National Standards Institute, jt. auth. see IEEE Power Engineering Society Staff.

American National Standards Institute Staff. Information Retrieval: Information Retrieval Application Service Definition & Protocol Specification for Open Systems Interconnection. rev. ed. 40p. (C). 1993. pap. 40.00 (*0-88738-934-1*) Transaction Pubs.

***American National Standards Institute Staff & American Institute of Aeronautics & Astronautics Staff.** American National Standard Guide to Human Performance Measurements. LC 99-89292. 2000. pap. write for info. (*1-56347-389-5*) AIAA.

American National Standards Institute Staff, jt. auth. see American Institute of Aeronautics & Astronautics S.

American National Standards Institute Staff, jt. auth. see American Institute of Aeronautics & Astronautics Staff.

American National Standards Institute Staff, jt. auth. see Clapp, Allen L.

American Negro Academy Staff. American Negro Academy Occasional Papers Nos. 1-22. LC 77-94134. (American Negro: His History & Literature. Series 3). 1970. 24.95 (*0-405-01913-0*) Ayer.

American Neurological Association, Committee for t. Eugenical Sterilization. Grob, Gerald N., ed. LC 78-22556. (Historical Issues in Mental Health Ser.). (Illus.). 1980. reprint ed. lib. bdg. 18.95 (*0-405-11910-0*) Ayer.

American Nuclear Society. American Nuclear Society Standards. 786p. 1974. 113.00 (*0-89448-200-9*, 250003) Am Nuclear Soc.

American Nuclear Society Staff & American Society of Civil Engineers Staff. High Level Radioactive Waste Management: Proceedings of the Fifth Annual International Conference, Las Vegas, NV, May 22-26, 1994, 4 vols. 3000p. 1994. 371.00 (*0-7844-0022-9*) Am Soc Civil Eng.

American Nuclear Society Staff, et al. Decommissioning, Decontamination & Reutilization: Worldwide Experience - DD&R, What Does It Mean. White, M. G. et al, eds. LC 97-16076. xv, 288p. 1997. 60.00 (*0-89448-622-5*) Am Nuclear Soc.

American Nuclear Society Staff, jt. auth. see American Society of Civil Engineers Staff.

American Nuclear Society Staff, jt. contrib. by see American Society of Civil Engineers Staff.

American Numismatic Society New York Staff. Dictionary & Auction Catalogues of the Library of the American Numismatic Society, New York, Set. 1970. 685.00 (*0-8161-1489-7*, G K Hall & Co) Mac Lib Ref.

American Numismatic Society Staff. Auction Catalog of the American Numismatic Society, New York. 1970. 160.00 (*0-8161-1426-9*, G K Hall & Co) Mac Lib Ref.

— Dictionary & Auction Catalogues of the Library of the American Numismatic Society, Supplement 2. 1973. suppl. ed. 160.00 (*0-8161-1427-7*, G K Hall & Co) Mac Lib Ref.

— Dictionary & Auction Catalogues of the Library of the American Numismatic Society, Supplement 3. 1983. suppl. ed. 260.00 (*0-8161-1375-0*, G K Hall & Co) Mac Lib Ref.

— Sylloge Nummorum Graecorum: The Collection of the American, Lucania, Pt. 2. LC 61-19327. (Illus.). 79p. reprint ed. pap. 30.00 (*0-7837-6971-7*, 203746000002) Bks Demand.

American Numismatic Society Staff, jt. auth. see Stahl, Alan M.

American Nurses Association Staff. American Nurses Association Model Practice Act. 64p. 1996. pap. 16.95 (*1-55810-128-4*, NP-110) Am Nurses Pub.

— Continuous Quality Improvement in Nursing. Dienemann, Jacqueline, ed. & intro. by. LC 92-17870. 144p. (C). 1992. pap. 14.95 (*1-55810-075-X*, NP-80, Am Nurses Fnd) Am Nurses Pub.

— Culturally Competent Assessment for Family Violence. LC 98-6511. 1998. pap. 18.95 (*1-55810-140-3*) Am Nurses Pub.

— Guidelines on Reporting Incompetent, Unethical or Illegal Practices. 13p. 1994. pap. 12.95 (*0-614-02735-7*, NP-91) Am Nurses Pub.

American Nurses' Association Staff. Implementing Nursing's Report Card: A Study of RN Staffing, Length of Stay & Patient Outcomes. LC 97-9524. 1997. pap. 15.95 (*1-55810-134-9*) Am Nurses Pub.

American Nurses Association Staff. Managing Genetic Information: Implications for Nursing Practice. 60p. 1995. pap. text 14.95 (*1-55810-111-X*, NP-102) Am Nurses Pub.

— Nursing Care Report Card for Acute Care. 1995. pap. text 34.95 (*1-55810-112-8*, NP-101) Am Nurses Pub.

— Principles for Nurse Staffing with Annotated Bibliography. LC 99-19077. 56p. 1999. pap. 19.95 (*1-55810-144-6*, 9902AB) Am Nurses Pub.

— Psychiatric Mental Health Nursing Psychopharmacology Project. 88p. (Orig.). 1994. pap. text 25.95 (*1-55810-104-7*, PMH-13) Am Nurses Pub.

— Registered Professional Nurses & Unlicensed Assistive Personnel. 2nd ed. LC 97-147045. 96p. (Orig.). 1996. 16.95 (*1-55810-132-2*, NP-89A) Am Nurses Pub.

— Scope of Practice for Nursing Informatics. 15p. 1994. pap. 8.95 (*0-614-02736-5*, NP-90) Am Nurses Pub.

— A Statement on the Scope & Standards of Psychiatric-Mental Health Clinical Nursing Practice. 47p. (C). 1994. text 14.95 (*1-55810-098-9*, PMH-12) Am Nurses Pub.

— Utilization of Agency for Health Care Policy & Research Guidelines. 1994. 14.95 (*0-614-02744-6*, NP-99) Am Nurses Pub.

American Nurses Association Staff & American Academy of Ambulatory Care Nursing Staff. Nursing in Ambulatory Care: The Future Is Here. LC 97-145420. 54p. 1997. 18.95 (*1-55810-135-7*, ST-2) Am Nurses Pub.

American Nurses Association Staff & Oncology Nursing Society Staff. Statement on the Scope & Standards on Oncology Nursing Practice. LC 96-2450. 50p. 1996. pap. 14.95 (*1-55810-121-7*, MS-23) Am Nurses Pub.

American Nurses Association Staff & Research in Marketing, Incorporated Staff. The Acute Care Nurse in Transition. LC 96-20009. 72p. 1996. pap. 19.95 (*1-55810-127-6*, EC-152) Am Nurses Pub.

American Nurses Association Staff & Respiratory Nursing Society Staff. Statement on the Scope & Standards of Respiratory Nursing Practice. 20p. 1994. pap. 14.95 (*0-614-02738-1*, NP-96) Am Nurses Pub.

American Nurses Association Staff & Society of Otorhinolaryngology Staff. Statement on the Scope & Standards of Otorhinolaryngology Clinical Nursing Practice. 20p. 1994. pap. 14.95 (*0-614-02739-X*, NP-95) Am Nurses Pub.

American Nurses Association Staff, et al. Nursing Quality Indicators: Definitions & Implications. LC 96-19465. 88p. 1996. pap. 29.95 (*1-55810-125-X*, NP-108, Am Nurses Fnd) Am Nurses Pub.

American Nurses Association Staff, jt. auth. see Marion, Lucy N.

American Occupational Therapy Association Staff. Guidelines for Occupational Therapy Practice in Home Health. LC 95-171546. 150p. (C). 1995. pap. text 25.00 (*1-56900-023-9*) Am Occup Therapy.

— The Occupational Therapy Manager. rev. ed. Bair, Jeanette, ed. 685p. (C). 1996. pap. text 55.00 (*0-910317-76-3*) Am Occup Therapy.

American Occupational Therapy Association Staff, jt. auth. see Larson, K. Oscar.

American Organization of Nurse Executives Staff. The Business of Nursing. LC 95-47785. 1996. pap. 40.00 (*1-55648-151-9*, 154153) AHPI.

— The Managed Care Challenge for Nurse Executives. LC 96-24117. (AONE Leadership Ser.). (Illus.). 124p. (Orig.). 1996. pap. 40.00 (*1-55648-164-0*, 154154) AHPI.

— Market-Driven Nursing: Developing & Marketing Patient Care Services. LC 98-45912. (AONE Leadership Ser.). 172p. 1999. 36.00 (*1-55648-247-7*) AHPI.

— Patient As Partner: The Cornerstone of Community Health Improvement. LC 97-1280. (AONE Leadership Ser.: Vol. 3). 100p. 1997. pap. text 32.00 (*1-55648-200-0*, 054100) AHPI.

American Organization of Nurse Executives Staff, jt. auth. see Donahue, M. Patricia.

American Organization of Nurse Staff, jt. auth. see Weaver, Diana Jane.

American Ornithologists' Union Staff. Checklist of North American Birds: The Species of Birds of North America from the Arctic Through Panama, Including the West Indies & Hawaiian Islands. 7th ed. LC 99-162265. 829 p. 1998. 49.95 (*1-891276-00-X*) Allen Pr.

American Ornithologists' Union Staff, ed. see Mengel, Robert M.

American Orthopaedic Association Staff. Osteonecrosis: Etiology, Diagnosis, & Treatment. Urbaniak, James R. & Jones, John P., Jr., eds. LC 97-41931. (Illus.). 453p. 1997. 120.00 (*0-89203-174-3*) Amer Acad Ortho Surg.

American Orthopaedic Foot & Ankle Society Staff, jt. auth. see Mizel, Mark S.

American Orthopaedic Society for Sports Medicine S. The Athletic Female. Pearl, Arthur J., ed. LC 92-27038. (Illus.). 328p. 1993. text 42.00 (*0-87322-410-8*, BPEA0410) Human Kinetics.

American Outdoor Safety League Staff. Boater's Safety Handbook. Brown, Robert, ed. (Illus.). 52p. 1982. pap. 3.50 (*0-89886-072-5*) Mountaineers.

— Emergency Survival Handbook. 48p. 1979. 3.50 (*0-89886-052-0*) Mountaineers.

American Paper Institute, Inc. Staff, ed. see Text & Cover Paper Manufacturers of American Paper.

American Peace Corps Volunteers Staff, compiled by. Himalayan Gourmet: (Recipes Using Mostly Locally Available Materials) 298p. (C). 1985. 55.00 (*0-89771-093-2*, Pub. by Ratna Pustak Bhandar) St Mut.

American Peace Society Staff, ed. Prize Essays on a Congress of Nations: For the Adjustment of International Disputes, & for the Promotion of Universal Peace Without Resort to Arms. LC 98-13864. xii, 706p. 1998. reprint ed. 95.00 (*0-9631902-6-1*) Canonymous.

***American Peptide Symposium Staff, et al.** Peptides for the New Millennium: Proceedings of the 16th American Peptide Symposium, June 16-July 1, 1999, Minneapolis, Minnesota, U. S. A. LC 00-41098. 2000. write for info. (*0-7923-6445-7*) Kluwer Academic.

American Petroleum Institute Staff. Energy in America: Progress & Potential. LC 81-12706. (Illus.). 40p. 1985. pap. text. write for info. (*0-89364-042-5*) Am Petroleum.

— Manual of Petroleum Measurement Standards. LC 80-67080. (Chapter 11.1 -- Volume Correction Factors Ser.: Vol. II). (Illus.). 592p. 1980. 90.00 (*0-89364-023-9*, 852-27015) Am Petroleum.

— Manual of Petroleum Measurement Standards. LC 80-67080. (Chapter 11.1 -- Volume Correction Factors Ser.: Vol. III). (Illus.). 563p. 1980. 90.00 (*0-89364-024-7*, 852-27032) Am Petroleum.

— Manual of Petroleum Measurement Standards. LC 80-67080. (Chapter 11.1 -- Volume Correction Factors Ser.: Vol. IV). (Illus.). 878p. 1980. 90.00 (*0-89364-025-5*, 852-27045) Am Petroleum.

— Manual of Petroleum Measurement Standards. LC 80-67080. (Chapter 11.1 -- Volume Correction Factors Ser.: Vol. IX). (Illus.). 587p. 1980. 90.00 (*0-89364-032-8*, 852-27130) Am Petroleum.

— Manual of Petroleum Measurement Standards. LC 80-67080. (Chapter 11.1 -- Volume Correction Factors Ser.: Vol. V). (Illus.). 812p. 1980. 90.00 (*0-89364-026-3*, 852-27060) Am Petroleum.

— Manual of Petroleum Measurement Standards. LC 80-67080. (Chapter 11.1 -- Volume Correction Factors Ser.: Vol. VI). (Illus.). 563p. 1980. 90.00 (*0-89364-027-1*, 852-27085) Am Petroleum.

— Manual of Petroleum Measurement Standards. LC 80-67080. (Chapter 11.1 -- Volume Correction Factors Ser.: Vol. VII). (Illus.). 958p. 1980. 90.00 (*0-89364-029-8*, 852-27100) Am Petroleum.

— Manual of Petroleum Measurement Standards. (Chapter 11.1 -- Volume Correction Factors Ser.: Vol. VIII). (Illus.). 881p. 1980. 90.00 (*0-89364-030-1*, 852-27115) Am Petroleum.

— Manual of Petroleum Measurement Standards. LC 80-67080. (Chapter 11.1 -- Volume Correction Factors Ser.: Vol. X). (Illus.). 420p. 1980. 90.00 (*0-89364-033-6*, 852-27145) Am Petroleum.

American Pharmaceutical Association Staff. Tableting Specification Manual. 4th ed. Young, Linda, ed. LC 95-179739. (Illus.). 128p. 1995. spiral bd. 125.00 (*0-917330-67-6*) Am Pharm Assn.

— Your Guide to Non-Prescription Drugs. (Illus.). 500p. write for info. (*0-8290-1580-9*) Irvington.

American Pharmaceutical Association Staff, jt. ed. see Peirce, Andrea.

American Philisophical Association Staff, jt. auth. see Hull, Richard T.

American Philosophical Association Staff, jt. auth. see Hull, Richard T.

American Philosophical Society Staff. Year Book. LC 39-2034. 1997. pap. 20.00 (*0-87169-991-5*, YRBK-1996) Am Philos.

American Philosophical Society Staff, jt. auth. see Bearn, Alexander G.

American Philosophical Society Staff, jt. auth. see Carter, Edward Carlos.

American Philosophical Society Staff, jt. auth. see Jefferson, Thomas.

American Philosophical Society Staff, ed. see Library Staff, et al.

American Physical Society Conference, New York Cit. Materials Technology: Proceedings. Chynoweth, A. G. & Walsh, W. M., eds. LC 76-27967. (AIP Conference Proceedings Ser.: No. 32). 1976. 18.00 (*0-88318-131-2*) Am Inst Physics.

American Physical Society Staff, et al. The Minneapolis Meeting, DPF 96: Twin Cities Campus, University of Minnesota, Minneapolis, U. S. A., 10-15 August, 1996. LC 98-14015. 1998. 168.00 (*981-02-3969-6*) World Scientific Pub.

American Physical Society Staff, jt. auth. see International Quantum Electronics Conference Staff.

***American Physiological Society, ed.** Graduate Study in Psychology 2000. 568p. 2000. pap. 21.95 (*1-55798-660-6*) Am Psychol.

American Physiological Society & Gerard, R. W. Mirror to Physiology: A Self-Survey of Physiological Science. LC 58-10348. 384p. reprint ed. pap. 119.10 (*0-608-16745-2*, 202639400049) Bks Demand.

American Phytopathological Society Staff, jt. auth. see Baudoin, A. B. A. M.

American Poetry & Literacy Project Staff. 101 Great American Poems: An Anthology. LC 97-51163. (Thrift Editions Ser.). 96p. 1998. pap. 1.00 (*0-486-40158-8*) Dover.

American Poetry & Literacy Staff. Songs for the Open Road: Poems of Travel & Adventure. LC 98-49683. 80p. 1999. pap. text 1.00 (*0-486-40646-6*) Dover.

American Political Network, Inc. Staff & LTV Corporation Staff. The Almanac of 1988 Presidential Politics. Maloney, Gary, ed. (Illus.). 164p. (Orig.). 1989. pap. 12.95 (*0-9621971-0-6*) APN Inc.

American Political Science Association Staff, ed. Biographical Directory 1988. rev. ed. 607p. (C). 1988. pap. text 12.00 (*0-915654-81-4*) Am Political.

American Political Science Association Staff & Committee on American Legislatures. American State Legislatures. LC 73-92294. 294p. 1970. reprint ed. lib. bdg. 65.00 (*0-8371-2434-4*, AMSL, Greenwood Pr) Greenwood.

American Political Science Association Staff, jt. auth. see Maltzman, Forrest.

American Production & Inventory Control Society, I, ed. Just-in-Time Student Guide. rev. ed. (Illus.). 1992. 37.00 (*1-55822-069-0*) Am Prod & Inventory.

American Production & Inventory Control Society St. Aerospace & Defense Symposium Proceedings. 237p. 1991. 25.00 (*1-55822-034-8*) Am Prod & Inventory.

— Aerospace & Defense Symposium Proceedings: Improving the Process: The Smart Challenge. 225p. 1992. 25.00 (*1-55822-090-9*) Am Prod & Inventory.

— Aerospace & Defense Symposium Proceedings: Molding a New World. 208p. 1993. 25.00 (*1-55822-101-8*) Am Prod & Inventory.

— Customers & Products Reprints. 138p. 1992. 23.00 (*1-55822-032-1*) Am Prod & Inventory.

— Integrated Enterprise Management Reprints. 152p. 1992. 23.00 (*1-55822-097-6*) Am Prod & Inventory.

— Inventory Management Instructor Guide Kit. 1994. 600.00 (*1-55822-066-6*) Am Prod & Inventory.

— Inventory Management Reprints. LC 86-70610. 213p. 1993. pap. 21.00 (*1-55822-037-2*) Am Prod & Inventory.

— Inventory Management Student Guide. 1991. 37.00 (*1-55822-067-4*) Am Prod & Inventory.

— Logistics Reprints. 207p. 1993. 23.00 (*1-55822-031-3*) Am Prod & Inventory.

— Manufacturing Processes Reprints. 199p. 1993. 23.00 (*1-55822-080-1*) Am Prod & Inventory.

— Master Planning Instructor Guide Kit. 1994. 600.00 (*1-55822-072-0*) Am Prod & Inventory.

— Master Planning Student Guide. 1994. 37.00 (*1-55822-073-9*) Am Prod & Inventory.

— Material & Capacity Requirements Planning Student Guide. 1993. 37.00 (*1-55822-077-1*) Am Prod & Inventory.

— Process Industry Specific Industry Software Requirements Guide. 64p. 1991. 15.00 (*1-55822-079-8*) Am Prod & Inventory.

— Process Industry Symposium: Dynamic Performance Through Innovation. 122p. 1991. 25.00 (*1-55822-049-6*) Am Prod & Inventory.

— Process Industry Symposium: Dynamic Performance Through Innovation. 115p. 1992. 25.00 (*1-55822-092-5*) Am Prod & Inventory.

— Process Industry Symposium: Forum for Change. 88p. 1993. 25.00 (*1-55822-102-6*) Am Prod & Inventory.

— Production Activity Control Instructor Guide Kit. 1991. 600.00 (*1-55822-070-4*) Am Prod & Inventory.

— Production Activity Control Student Guide. 1991. 37.00 (*1-55822-071-2*) Am Prod & Inventory.

— Remanufacturing Proceedings: Doing It Better the Second Time. 122p. 1992. 25.00 (*1-55822-098-4*) Am Prod & Inventory.

— Remanufacturing Proceedings: Real Solutions from Real People. 152p. 1993. 25.00 (*1-55822-103-4*) Am Prod & Inventory.

— Remanufacturing Proceedings: Regenerating Resources Through Repair & Remanufacturing. 43p. 1991. 25.00 (*1-55822-082-8*) Am Prod & Inventory.

— Remanufacturing Resource Book. 392p. 1996. 15.00 (*1-55822-100-X*) Am Prod & Inventory.

— Repetitive Manufacturing Group Reprints: Crucial Issues. 216p. 1992. 16.50 (*1-55822-093-3*) Am Prod & Inventory.

— Small Manufacturing Reprints: Tools for the Small Manufacturer. 110p. 1992. 16.50 (*1-55822-089-5*) Am Prod & Inventory.

— Systems & Technologies Instructor Guide Kit. 1995. 600.00 (*1-55822-074-7*) Am Prod & Inventory.

— Systems & Technologies Reprints. LC 98-153903. 239p. 1995. 21.00 (*1-55822-041-0*) Am Prod & Inventory.

— Systems & Technologies Student Guide. 1995. 37.00 (*1-55822-075-5*) Am Prod & Inventory.

American Production & Inventory Control Society St, ed. Bar Coding Reprints. LC 83-70845. 127p. 1983. pap. 10.00 (*0-935406-25-5*) Am Prod & Inventory.

— Facing the Challenge: Report of 1994 Remanufacturing Symposium & Technical Exhibit. 66p. (Orig.). 1994. pap. 25.00 (*1-55822-110-7*) Am Prod & Inventory.

— Material & Capacity Requirements Planning Reprints. LC 86-70024. 332p. 1993. pap. 21.00 (*1-55822-042-9*) Am Prod & Inventory.

— Service Parts Seminar Proceedings, 1983. LC 83-72512. 90p. 1983. pap. 5.00 (*0-935406-31-X*, 40631) Am Prod & Inventory.

— Zero Inventories Seminar Proceedings: September 1983. LC 83-72511. 82p. 1983. pap. 5.00 (*0-935406-32-8*, 40632) Am Prod & Inventory.

American Production & Inventory Control Society St & Langthorp, Herb. Aerospace & Defense Specific Industry Group Resource Book. 166p. 1992. 14.00 (*1-55822-091-7*) Am Prod & Inventory.

American Production & Inventory Control Society St & Rodwell, Dorothy. Focused Study Group Manual. 75p. 1991. 18.00 (*1-55822-081-X*) Am Prod & Inventory.

American Production & Inventory Control Society St, jt. auth. see SVC SIG Staff.

American Production & Inventory Control Society St, ed. see Burnham, John M.

American Production & Inventory Control Society St, ed. see Duin, Spencer, et al.

American Productivity & Quality Center Staff. Benchmarking Management Guide. (Illus.). 255p. 1993. 40.00 (*1-56327-045-5*) Productivity Inc.

American Prosecutors Research Institute Staff. Prior Conviction in DUI Prosecutions: A Prosecutor's Guide to Prove Out-of-State DUI - DWI Convictions. 620p. 1998. pap. write for info. (*0-327-00228-X*, 61442-10) LEXIS Pub.

An Asterisk (*) at the beginning of an entry indicates that the title is appearing for the first time.

American Prospect Researchers Association Staff. The American Prospector: Contemporary Issues in Prospect Research. 176p. 1991. 26.95 (*0-930807-19-7*, 600229) Fund Raising.

American Psychiatric Assoc. Staff, ed. Handbook of Psychiatric Practice in the Juvenile Court. LC 91-23403. 198p. 1992. pap. text 12.95 (*0-89042-233-8*, 2233) Am Psychiatric.

American Psychiatric Assocation Staff. The Psychiatrist's Guide to Capitation & Risk-Based Contracting. LC 97-12762. 114p. 1997. pap. text 27.00 incl. disk (*0-89042-453-5*, 2453) Am Psychiatric.

— The Psychiatrist's Guide to Managed Care Contracting. LC 97-12315. 96p. 1997. pap. text 27.00 (*0-89042-454-3*, 2454) Am Psychiatric.

— The Psychiatrist's Guide to Practice Management. LC 97-8762. 104p. 1997. pap. text 27.00 (*0-89042-451-9*, 2451) Am Psychiatric.

— Public Mental Health: A Changing System in an Era of Managed Care. LC 97-11029. 74p. 1997. pap. text 26.00 (*0-89042-452-7*, 2452) Am Psychiatric.

American Psychiatric Association, Commission on Ps. Psychotherapy Research: Methodological & Efficacy Issues. LC 82-8763. 277p. reprint ed. pap. 85.90 (*0-8357-7796-0*, 203615800002) Bks Demand.

American Psychiatric Association, Department of Ed. Directory of Psychiatry Residency Training Programs. 7th ed. 752p. 1997. pap. text 31.00 (*0-89042-708-9*, 2708) Am Psychiatric.

American Psychiatric Association, Ethics Committee. Opinions of the Ethics Committee on the Principles of Medical Ethics: With Annotations Especially Applicable to Psychiatry. LC RC0455.2.E8. 58p. 1993. reprint ed. pap. 30.00 (*0-608-02019-2*, 206267500003) Bks Demand.

American Psychiatric Association Ethics Committee. The Principles of Medical Ethics with Annotations Especially Applicable to Psychiatry: 1998 Edition. 38p. 1998. pap. text 3.00 (*0-89042-140-4*, 2140) Am Psychiatric.

American Psychiatric Association Office of Researc. Research Funding & Resource Manual: Mental Health & Addictive Disorders. Pincus, Harold A., ed. 432p. 1995. pap. text 56.00 (*0-89042-216-8*, 2216) Am Psychiatric.

American Psychiatric Association Staff. American Psychiatric Association Practice Guideline for Major Depressive Disorder in Adults. 51p. 1993. pap. text 24.50 (*0-89042-301-6*, 2301) Am Psychiatric.

— American Psychiatric Association Practice Guideline for the Treatment of Patients with Alzheimer's Disease. 1997. pap. text 24.50 (*0-89042-310-5*, 2310) Am Psychiatric.

***American Psychiatric Association Staff.** American Psychiatric Association Practice Guideline for the Treatment of Patients with Depressive Disorder. 2nd ed. 100p. 2000. pap. 24.50 (*0-89042-316-4*) Am Psychiatric.

— American Psychiatric Association Practice Guideline for the Treatment of Patients with Eating Disorders. 2nd ed. 84p. 2000. pap. 24.50 (*0-89042-314-8*) Am Psychiatric.

American Psychiatric Association Staff. American Psychiatric Association Practice Guideline for the Treatment of Patients with Nicotine Dependence. 80p. 1996. pap. text 24.50 (*0-89042-308-3*, 2308) Am Psychiatric.

— American Psychiatric Association Practice Guideline for the Treatment of Patients with Panic Disorder. 80p. 1998. pap. text 24.50 (*0-89042-311-3*, 2311) Am Psychiatric.

— American Psychiatric Association Practice Guideline for the Treatment of Patients with Schizophrenia. LC 97-152812. 145p. 1997. pap. text 24.50 (*0-89042-309-1*, 2309) Am Psychiatric.

— American Psychiatric Association Practice Guideline for the Treatment of Patients with Substance Use Disorders: Alcohol, Cocaine, Opioids. 126p. 1995. pap. text 24.50 (*0-89042-303-2*, 2303) Am Psychiatric.

***American Psychiatric Association Staff.** American Psychiatric Association Practice Guidelines for the Treatment of Psychiatric Disorders: Compendium 2000. 768p. 2000. 64.95 (*0-89042-312-1*) Am Psychiatric.

— American Psychiatric Association Practice Guidelines for the Treatment of Psychiatric Disorders: Compendium 2000. 768p. 2000. pap. write for info. (*0-89042-315-6*) Amer Psych Assn.

American Psychiatric Association Staff. The American Psychiatric Association's Psychiatric Glossary. LC 84-473. 152p. reprint ed. pap. 47.20 (*0-8357-7805-3*, 203617500002) Bks Demand.

— Continuing Medical Education Syllabus & Scientific Proceedings in Summary Form: The One Hundred & Fortieth Annual Meeting of the American Psychiatric Association, Chicago, IL, May 9-14, 1987. LC RC0327.A485. 327p. reprint ed. pap. 101.40 (*0-8357-7795-2*, 203615600002) Bks Demand.

— Continuing Medical Education Syllabus & Scientific Proceedings in Summary Form: The One Hundred & Thirty-Fifth Annual Meeting of the American Psychiatric Association, Toronto, Canada, May 15-21, 1982. LC RC0327.. 351p. reprint ed. pap. 108.90 (*0-8357-3036-0*, 203928400011) Bks Demand.

— Continuing Medical Education Syllabus & Scientific Proceedings in Summary Form: The One Hundred & Thirty-Ninth Annual Meeting of the American Psychiatric Association, Washington, DC, May 10-16, 1986. LC RC0327.A485. 321p. reprint ed. pap. 99.60 (*0-8357-7794-4*, 203615500002) Bks Demand.

— Dangerous Sex Offenders: A Task Force Report of The American Psychiatric Association. LC 98-50587. 1999. 29.95 (*0-89042-280-X*, 2280) Am Psychiatric.

— Desk Reference to the Diagnostic Criteria from DSM-IV, No. IV. (DSM-IV: New Diagnostic Issues Ser.). 358p. 1994. pap. 26.50 (*0-89042-064-5*, 2064) Am Psychiatric.

***American Psychiatric Association Staff.** Desk Reference to the Diagnostic Criteria from DSM-IV: Text Revision 2000. rev. ed. 496p. 2000. pap. 26.50 (*0-89042-027-0*) Am Psychiatric.

American Psychiatric Association Staff. Diagnostic & Statistical Manual of Mental Disorders. 3rd ed. LC 79-55868. 506p. reprint ed. pap. 156.90 (*0-8357-3037-9*, 203928500011) Bks Demand.

— Diagnostic & Statistical Manual of Mental Disorders: DSM-IV. 4th ed. LC 94-6304. (Diagnostic & Statistical Manual of Mental Disorders (DSM) Ser.). 886p. 1994. pap. 49.95 (*0-89042-062-9*, 2062) Am Psychiatric.

— Diagnostic & Statistical Manual of Mental Disorders: DSM-IV. 4th ed. LC 94-6304. (Diagnostic & Statistical Manual of Mental Disorders (DSM) Ser.). 886p. 1994. 64.95 (*0-89042-061-0*, 2061) Am Psychiatric.

— Diagnostic & Statistical Manual of Mental Disorders: Primary Care Version (DSM-IV-PC) 4th ed. 208p. 1995. pap. text 29.50 (*0-89042-407-1*, 2407); spiral bd. 42.50 (*0-89042-406-3*, 2406) Am Psychiatric.

— Diagnostic & Statistical Manual of Mental Disorders: Primary Care Version-International Version (DSM-IV-PC, International Version) 4th ed. LC 95-49850. 252p. 1996. pap. text 29.50 (*0-89042-408-X*, 2408) Am Psychiatric.

***American Psychiatric Association Staff.** Diagnostic & Statistical Manual of Mental Disorders, DSM-IV: Text Revision 2000. 4th ed. 1000p. 2000. 64.95 (*0-89042-024-6*); pap. 49.95 (*0-89042-025-4*) Am Psychiatric.

American Psychiatric Association Staff. DSM-IV Sourcebook, Vol. 1. 768p. 1994. pap. text 78.00 (*0-89042-070-X*, 2070) Am Psychiatric.

— DSM-IV Sourcebook, Vol. 2. 1184p. 1995. text 129.00 (*0-89042-069-6*, 2069); pap. text 78.00 (*0-89042-071-8*, 2071) Am Psychiatric.

— DSM-IV Sourcebook, Vol. 3. 912p. 1997. text 129.00 (*0-89042-073-4*, 2073); pap. text 78.00 (*0-89042-074-2*, 2074) Am Psychiatric.

— Economic Fact Book for Psychiatry. LC RA0790.6. (Illus.). 149p. reprint ed. pap. 46.20 (*0-8357-3039-5*, 203928800011) Bks Demand.

— Economic Fact Book for Psychiatry. 2nd ed. LC 87-933. (Illus.). 199p. 1987. reprint ed. pap. 61.70 (*0-608-06663-X*, 206686000009) Bks Demand.

— An Economic Survival Manual for Private Practice Psychiatrists. LC 85-7377. (Private Practice Monograph Ser.). 144p. reprint ed. pap. 44.70 (*0-8357-2808-0*, 203622200011) Bks Demand.

***American Psychiatric Association Staff.** Handbook of Psychiatric Measures. 816p. 2000. 79.95 (*0-89042-415-2*) Am Psychiatric.

American Psychiatric Association Staff. The Homeless Mentally Ill: A Task Force Report. Lamb, H. Richard, ed. LC 84-16916. 340p. 1984. reprint ed. pap. 105.40 (*0-7837-2090-4*, 204236600004) Bks Demand.

— An International Psychiatric Directory. 80p. 1993. pap. 35.00 (*0-89042-248-6*, 2248) Am Psychiatric.

— Issues in Forensic Psychiatry: Insanity Defense, Hospitalization of Adults, Model Civil Commitment Law, Sentencing Process, Child Custody Consultation. LC 84-191829. 261p. reprint ed. pap. 81.00 (*0-8357-7808-8*, 203618000002) Bks Demand.

***American Psychiatric Association Staff.** Manual of Nursing Home Practice for Psychiatrists. LC 99-48771. 2000. write for info. (*0-89042-283-4*) Amer Psych Assn.

American Psychiatric Association Staff. The Principles of Medical Ethics: With Annotations Especially Applicable to Psychiatry. LC 95-179629. 33p. 1993. reprint ed. pap. 30.00 (*0-608-02020-6*, 206267600003) Bks Demand.

***American Psychiatric Association Staff.** Psychiatric Self-Assessment & Review (PSA-R) 1999. pap. 225.00 (*0-89042-285-0*) Am Psychiatric.

American Psychiatric Association Staff. Psychiatric Services for Addicted Patients: A Task Force Report of the American Psychiatric Association. 144p. 1995. text 9.95 (*0-89042-276-1*, 2276) Am Psychiatric.

***American Psychiatric Association Staff.** Psychiatric Services in Jails & Prisons. 2nd ed. 96p. 2000. pap. 19.00 (*0-89042-287-7*) Am Psychiatric.

American Psychiatric Association Staff. The Psychiatrist's Managed Care Primer. LC 97-11404. 111p. 1997. pap. text 26.00 (*0-89042-450-0*, 2450) Am Psychiatric.

***American Psychiatric Association Staff.** Quick Reference to the Diagnostic Criteria from DSM-IV: Text Revision 2000. 496p. 2000. pap. 23.00 (*0-89042-026-2*) Am Psychiatric.

American Psychiatric Association Staff. Tardive Dyskinesia: Report of the American Psychiatric Association Task Force on Late Neurological Effects of Antipsychotic Drugs. LC 80-137799. (Task Force Report: No. 18). 211p. reprint ed. pap. 65.50 (*0-8357-2805-6*, 203616900011) Bks Demand.

— Task Force Report on Clinician Safety, No. 33. LC 93-10489. 35p. 1993. pap. text 3.00 (*0-89042-244-3*, 2244) Am Psychiatric.

American Psychiatric Association Staff, ed. American Psychiatric Association Practice Guideline for the Treatment of Patients with Bipolar Disorder. 88p. 1995. pap. text 24.50 (*0-89042-302-4*, 2302) Am Psychiatric.

American Psychiatric Association Staff, et al. American Psychiatric Association Capitation Handbook: Actuarially Determined Capitation Rates for Mental Health Benefits. 112p. 1995. pap. text 37.00 (*0-89042-277-X*, 2277) Am Psychiatric.

— DSM-IV KSO Coding Update, 1996: (1996 Edition - Includes ICD-9-CM Codes Effective October 1, 1996) LC 96-38257. 72p. 1996. 10.00 (*0-89042-409-8*, 2409) Am Psychiatric.

American Psychiatric Association Staff, jt. auth. see American Academy of Child & Adolescent Psychiatry Staff.

American Psychiatric Association Staff, Task Force. Psychosocial Aspects of Nuclear Developments: Report. LC 82-71902. (American Psychiatric Association Tasl Fprce Report Ser.: No. 20). 105p. reprint ed. pap. 32.60 (*0-8357-7802-9*, 203617100002) Bks Demand.

— A Typology of Community Residential Services: Report. LC 82-24467. (American Psychiatric Association Task Force Report Ser.: No. 21). 97p. reprint ed. pap. 30.10 (*0-8357-7803-7*, 203617200002) Bks Demand.

American Psychiatric Association, Task Force on Bi. Electroconvulsive Therapy: Report. LC 78-69521. (American Psychiatric Association Task Force Report Ser.: No. 14). 214p. reprint ed. pap. 66.40 (*0-8357-7800-2*, 203616800002) Bks Demand.

American Psychiatric Association, Task Force on Biofeedback. Biofeedback: Report. LC 80-66989. (American Psychiatric Association Task Force Report Ser.: No. 19). 125p. reprint ed. pap. 38.80 (*0-8357-7801-0*, 203617000002) Bks Demand.

American Psychiatric Association Task Force Staff. Benzodiazepine Dependence, Toxicity, & Abuse. LC 90-571. 116p. 1990. text 19.95 (*0-89042-228-1*, 2228) Am Psychiatric.

— Ethnic Minority Elderly: Task Force Report of the American Psychiatric Association. LC 93-27940. 192p. 1993. text 11.95 (*0-89042-247-8*, 2247) Am Psychiatric.

***American Psychiatric Nursing Association Staff.** Advanced Practice Nursing in Psychiatric & Mental Health Care. Shea, Carol A. et al, eds. LC 99-29231. 704p. (C). 1999. text. write for info. (*0-323-00352-4*) Mosby Inc.

American Psychoanalytic Association, Committee on. Cumulative Index of the Journal of the American Psychoanalytic Association: 1953-1974, Vols. 1-22. LC 75-37247. 1975. 102.00 (*0-8236-1111-6*); pap. 102.00 (*0-8236-1110-8*) Intl Univs Pr.

American Psychological Association. Conditioning & Learning: Teachers Handbook & Duplication Masters. (Human Behavior Curriculum Project Ser.). (gr. 9-12). 1981. 9.95 (*0-8077-2624-9*) Tchrs Coll.

— Graduate Study in Psychology: 1998 with 1999 Addendum. 728p. 2000. pap. text 21.95 (*1-55798-589-8*) Am Psychol.

American Psychological Association Directorate wit. Financing Your Practice: Using Business Planning & Financial Management to Your Advantage. (Practitioner's Toolbox Ser.). 1996. 29.95 (*1-55798-361-5*) Am Psychol.

American Psychological Association, Office of Rural Health Staff, ed. Caring for the Rural Community: An Interdisciplinary Curriculum. LC 94-49194. 76p. 1995. pap. 14.95 (*1-55798-288-0*) Am Psychol.

American Psychological Association Practice Direct. Marketing Your Practice: Creating Opportunities for Success. (APA Practitioner's Toolbox Ser.). 82p. 1996. pap. 29.95 (*1-55798-358-5*) Am Psychol.

— Organizing Your Practice Through Automation: Managing Information & Data. (APA Practitioner's Toolbox Ser.). 72p. 1996. pap. 29.95 (*1-55798-359-3*) Am Psychol.

— Practicing Psychology in Hospitals & Other Health Care Facilities. LC 97-51278. (Illus.). 156p. 1998. pap. 29.95 (*1-55798-491-3*) Am Psychol.

American Psychological Association Practice Direct & Coopers & Lybrand, L. L. P. Staff. Developing an Integrated Delivery System: Organizing a Seamless System of Care. LC 96-4648. (APA Practitioner's Toolbox Ser.). 1996. pap. 29.95 (*1-55798-350-X*) Am Psychol.

American Psychological Association Practice Direct & Coopers & Lybrand Staff. Building a Group Practice: Creating a Shared Vision for Success. (APA Practitioner's Toolbox Ser.). 1995. pap. 29.95 (*1-55798-318-6*) Am Psychol.

— Contracting with Organizaed Delivery Systems: Selecting, Evaluating & Negotiating Contracts. LC 95-43415. (Practitioner's Toolbox Ser.). 1995. pap. 29.95 (*1-55798-348-8*) Am Psychol.

American Psychological Association Practice Direct, et al. Contracting on a Capitated Basis: Managing Risk for Your Practice. LC 96-23681. (Practitioners Toolbox Ser.). 94p. 1996. pap. 29.95 (*1-55798-362-3*) Am Psychol.

American Psychological Association Practice Direct, jt. auth. see Yenney, Sharon L.

American Psychological Association Staff. Activities Handbook, Teaching a Psychology of People Vol. 1: Resources for Gender & Sociocultural Awareness. 7th ed. 244p. (C). 1994. text. write for info. (*0-697-27870-0*) Brown & Benchmark.

— Activities Handbook, Teaching a Psychology of People Vol. 2: Resources for Gender & Sociocultural Awareness. 7th ed. 245p. (C). 1994. text. write for info. (*0-697-27871-9*) Brown & Benchmark.

***American Psychological Association Staff.** Apa: Style Helper 2.0: Software for New Writers in The Behavioral Sciences. 1999. sl. 39.95 (*1-55798-622-3*) Am Psychol.

American Psychological Association Staff. Blacks in the United States: Abstracts of the Psychological & Behavioral Literature, 1987-1995. Keita, Gwendolyn P. & Peterson, Anne, eds. LC 96-36788. (Bibliographies in Psychology Ser.). 305p. 1996. pap. text 19.95 (*1-55798-406-9*) Am Psychol.

— Changing Attitudes: Student Booklet. (Human Behavior Curriculum Project Ser.). 64p. (Orig.). (gr. 9-12). 1981. pap. text 3.95 (*0-8077-2621-4*) Tchrs Coll.

— Changing Attitudes: Teachers Handbook & Duplication Masters. (Human Behavior Curriculum Project Ser.). 50p. (Orig.). (gr. 9-12). 1981. 9.95 (*0-8077-2622-2*) Tchrs Coll.

— Conditioning & Learning: Student Booklet. (Human Behavior Curriculum Project Ser.). 64p. (gr. 9-12). 1981. pap. text 3.95 (*0-8077-2623-0*) Tchrs Coll.

— Education & Training Beyond the Doctoral Degree: Proceedings of the American Psychological Association National Conference on Postdoctoral Education & Training in Psychology. LC 95-5399. 299p. (Orig.). 1995. pap. text 29.95 (*0-8236-8036-3*) Intl Univs Pr.

— Getting In: A Step-by-Step Plan for Gaining Admission to Graduate School in Psychology. LC 93-33069. (Illus.). 221p. 1993. pap. text 14.95 (*1-55798-219-8*) Am Psychol.

— International Opportunities for Advanced Training & Research in Psychology. Werber, Morton & Nicholas, Phoebe O., eds. LC 66-28054. 405p. reprint ed. pap. 125.60 (*0-7837-0487-9*, 204081100018) Bks Demand.

— Journals in Psychology: A Resource Listing for Authors. 5th ed. 257p. 1997. pap. 20.00 (*1-55798-438-7*) Am Psychol.

— Language & Communication: Student Booklet. (Human Behavior Curriculum Peoject Ser.). 60p. (Orig.). (gr. 9-12). 1981. pap. text 3.95 (*0-8077-2625-7*) Tchrs Coll.

— Language & Communication: Teachers Handbook & Duplication Masters. (Human Behavior Curriculum Project Ser.). (Orig.). (gr. 9-12). 1981. pap. 9.95 (*0-8077-2626-5*) Tchrs Coll.

***American Psychological Association Staff.** Manual de Estilo de Publicaciones de la American Psychological Association. 480p. 1998. pap. 21.95 (*968-426-793-2*) Am Psychol.

American Psychological Association Staff. Natural Behavior in Humans & Animals. (Human Behavior Curriculum Project Ser.). 55p. (Orig.). 1981. teacher ed. 9.95 (*0-8077-2614-1*); pap. text 3.95 (*0-8077-2613-3*) Tchrs Coll.

— 1998 APA Membership Register. 1998. 35.00 (*1-55798-502-2*) Am Psychol.

— Psychology & Mental Health: A Report of the Institute on Education & Training for Psychological Contributions to Mental Health, Held at Stanford University in August, 1955. Strother, Charles R., ed. LC 57-11124. 160p. reprint ed. pap. 49.60 (*0-7837-0488-7*, 204081200018) Bks Demand.

— Psychology & National Health Insurance: A Sourcebook. Kiesler, Charles A. et al, eds. LC 79-19251. 659p. reprint ed. pap. 200.00 (*0-7837-0489-5*, 204081300018) Bks Demand.

— Psychology & the Problems of Society. Korten, Frances F. et al, eds. LC 72-115967. 471p. reprint ed. pap. 146.10 (*0-7837-0491-7*, 204081500018) Bks Demand.

— PsycINFO User Manual. (Illus.). 351p. 1992. ring bd. 45.00 (*1-55798-164-7*) Am Psychol.

— Publication Manual of the American Psychological Association. 4th ed. LC 94-11498. 368p. 1994. text 31.95 (*1-55798-243-0*, 420-0041); pap. text 21.95 (*1-55798-241-4*, 4200040) Am Psychol.

— Report. Woodworth, R. S., ed. (Psychology Monographs General & Applied: Vol. 13). 1974. reprint ed. pap. 55.00 (*0-8115-1412-9*) Periodicals Srv.

— School Life & Organizational Psychology. (Human Behavior Curriculum Project Ser.). 64p. (Orig.). 1981. teacher ed. 9.95 (*0-8077-2618-4*); pap. text 3.95 (*0-8077-2617-6*) Tchrs Coll.

— Social Influences on Behavior: Student Booklet. (Human Behavior Curriculum Project Ser.). 80p. (Orig.). (gr. 9-12). 1981. pap. text 3.95 (*0-8077-2619-2*) Tchrs Coll.

— Social Influences on Behavior: Teachers Handbook. (Human Behavior Curriculum Project Ser.). 48p. (Orig.). (gr. 9-12). 1981. pap. 9.95 (*0-8077-2620-6*) Tchrs Coll.

— Standards for Educational & Psychological Tests Prepared by a Joint Committee of the American Psychological Association, American Educational Research Association & National Council on Measurement in Education. LC 74-75734. 78p. reprint ed. pap. 30.00 (*0-7837-0495-X*, 204081900018) Bks Demand.

— Studying Personality: Student Booklet. (Human Behavior Curriculum Project Ser.). 75p. (Orig.). (gr. 9-12). 1981. pap. text 3.95 (*0-8077-2627-3*) Tchrs Coll.

— Studying Personality: Teachers Manual & Duplication Masters. (Human Behavior Curriculum Project Ser.). (Orig.). (gr. 9-12). 1981. pap. 9.95 (*0-8077-2628-1*) Tchrs Coll.

— Teaching a Psychology of People: Resources for Gender & Sociocultural Awareness. 7th ed. 220p. (C). 1994. text. write for info. (*0-697-27869-7*) Brown & Benchmark.

— Teaching a Psychology of People Vol. 3: Resources for Gender & Sociocultural Awareness. 7th ed. 384p. (C). 1994. text. write for info. (*0-697-27872-7*) Brown & Benchmark.

***American Psychological Association Staff, ed.** Videos in Psychology: A Resource Directory. LC 00-27618. 200p. 2000. pap. text 14.95 (*1-55798-709-2*, 431-0560) Am Psychol.

American Psychological Association Staff & McDermott, Will & Emery Staff. Models for Multidisciplinary Arrangements: A State-by-State Review of Options. LC 96-27361. (APA Practitioner's Toolbox Ser.). 135p. 1996. 29.95 (*1-55798-363-1*) Am Psychol.

American Psychological Association Staff, et al. States of Consciousness. (Human Behavior Curriculum Project Ser.). 55p. 1981. teacher ed. 9.95 (*0-8077-2616-8*); pap. text 3.95 (*0-8077-2615-X*) Tchrs Coll.

American Psychological Association, Women & Health & Organizations for Professional Women Staff. A Women's Mental Health Agenda. Russo, Nancy F., ed. LC 85-72729. 99p. (Orig.). 1985. pap. 10.00 (*0-912704-44-6*) Am Psychol.

American Psychopathological Assn. Staff. Contemporary Sexual Behavior: Critical Issues in the 1970s. Zubin, Joseph & Money, John, eds. LC 72-4013. (Publications of the American Psychopathological Association: No. 28). (Illus.). 496p. 1973. reprint ed. pap. 153.80 (*0-608-04046-0*, 206478200011) Bks Demand.

An Asterisk (*) at the beginning of an entry indicates that the title is appearing for the first time.

American Psychopathological Association Staff. Evaluation of Psychological Therapies: Psychotherapies, Behavior Therapies, Drug Therapies, & Their Interactions: Proceedings of the Sixty-Fourth Annual Meeting. Spitzer, Robert L. & Klein, Donald F., eds. LC 75-11360. 334p. 1976. reprint ed. pap. 103.60 (*0-608-15158-0*, 202587600046) Bks Demand.

— Genetic Research in Psychiatry: Proceedings of the Sixty-Third Annual Meeting of the American Psychopathological Association. Fieve, Ronald R. et al, eds. LC 74-24394. (Illus.). 320p. 1975. reprint ed. pap. 99.20 (*0-608-05960-9*, 206629700008) Bks Demand.

— Mental Disorders in the Community - Progress & Challenge: Proceedings of the 75th Annual Meeting of the American Psychopathological Association, New York City, February 28-March 2, 1985. Barrett, James E. & Rose, Robert M., eds. LC 86-14311. 393p. 1986. reprint ed. pap. 121.90 (*0-608-07579-5*, 205989400010) Bks Demand.

— Psychopathology & Psychopharmacology: Proceedings of the Sixty-Second Annual Meeting. Cole, Jonathan O. et al, eds. LC 72-12347. 312p. reprint ed. pap. 96.80 (*0-608-14755-9*, 202309100032) Bks Demand.

— Trends of Mental Disease. Grob, Gerald N., ed. LC 78-22547. (Historical Issues in Mental Health Ser.). (Illus.). 1980. reprint ed. lib. bdg. 17.95 (*0-405-11901-1*) Ayer.

American Psychosomatic Society Staff. Toward an Integrated Medicine: Classics from Psychosomatic Medicine 1959 - 1979. 358p. 1995. text 16.50 (*0-88048-727-5*, 8727) Am Psychiatric.

American Public Health Association, Jails & Prison. Standards for Health Services in Correctional Institutions. 2nd ed. Dubler, Nancy N., ed. LC 86-14078. 160p. 1986. 15.00 (*0-87553-143-1*) Am Pub Health.

American Public Health Association Staff, et al, eds. Mental Disorders, Suicide. LC 74-186673. (Vital & Health Statistics Monographs, American Public Health Association). (Illus.). 331p. 1972. 41.00 (*0-674-56735-8*) HUP.

American Public Health Association Staff, et al. Selected Physical & Chemical Standard Methods for Students. 674p. 1990. 60.00 (*0-87553-144-X*) Am Pub Health.

American Public Health Association Staff, jt. auth. see American Academy of Pediatrics Staff.

American Public Power Association Staff, et al. The Public's First Right to Generally Generated Power: An Analysis of the Preference Clause. LC 85-243014. 38p. 1985. 10.00 (*0-317-01241-X*) APPA.

American Public Works Association Staff. For the Public Works Professional's Bookshelf. (Management Ser.: No. 2). 38p. 1987. pap. text 7.00 (*0-917084-52-7*) Am Public Works.

— History of Public Works in the United States, 1776-1976. LC 76-11513. (C). 1976. 20.00 (*0-917084-03-9*) Am Public Works.

— Managing Snow Removal & Ice Control Programs: A Practical Guide to the How, When, Where & Why of Effective Public Works Practices. (Special Reports: No. 42). (Illus.). 168p. (Orig.). 1974. pap. text 25.00 (*0-917084-25-X*) Am Public Works.

— Microcomputers in Public Works. rev. ed. (Special Reports: No. 53). 600p. 1987. ring bd. 75.00 (*0-917084-54-3*) Am Public Works.

— Public Works Communication Manual. 128p. (Orig.). 1984. pap. text 35.00 (*0-917084-04-7*) Am Public Works.

— Public Works Today: A Profile of Local Service Organizations & Managers. (Special Reports: No. 57). 86p. (Orig.). 1990. pap. text 65.00 (*0-917084-16-0*) Am Public Works.

— Street Cleaning Practice. 3rd ed. (Illus.). (C). 1978. text 28.00 (*0-917084-27-6*) Am Public Works.

— Urban Stormwater Management. (Special Reports: No. 49). (Illus.). 312p. (Orig.). 1981. pap. text 45.00 (*0-917084-41-1*) Am Public Works.

American Public Works Association Staff, et al. Hot-Mix Asphalt Paving Handbook. LC 91-74090. (Illus.). 240p. (Orig.). 1991. pap. text 35.00 (*0-917084-51-9*) Am Public Works.

American Public Works Association, Street Sanitati. Street Cleaning Practice. 2nd ed. LC TD0817.A53. (American Public Works Association Research Foundation Projects Ser.: No. 105). 440p. reprint ed. pap. 136.40 (*0-608-10839-1*, 201593600004) Bks Demand.

American Public Works Association, Water Resources. A Study of Nationwide Costs to Implement Municipal Stormwater Best Management Practices: Final Report. (Illus.). 105p. (Orig.). 1992. pap. text 20.00 (*0-917084-19-5*) Am Public Works.

American Publishing Editors. The Most Valuable Book Ever Published. 2nd rev. ed. 244p. 1997. pap. 16.95 (*0-9638596-5-X*) Amer Pubng.

American Publishing, Inc., Staff. Foods That Heal. (Orig.). 1995. pap. 12.95 (*0-9638596-3-3*) Alpha Pub CA.

***American Publishing Staff.** Sydney. 3rd ed. (Insight City Guides-Foreign Ser.). (Illus.). 1999. pap. text 21.95 (*0-88729-066-3*) Langenscheidt.

American Quaternary Association. Processes & Environments of Glacial Margins. 173p. 1986. 10.00 (*0-318-22004-0*) Am Quaternary Assn.

American Quaternary Association. Biennial Meeting,. Character & Timing of Rapid Environmental & Climatic Changes: Abstracts. 188p. 1982. 10.00 (*0-318-16892-8*) Am Quaternary Assn.

American Quaternary Association Staff. Climatic Changes from Fourteen Thousand to Nine Thousand Years Ago: Proceedings of the American Quaternary Association, Biennial Meeting, 1st, 1970. 167p. 1970. 10.00 (*0-318-13126-9*) Am Quaternary Assn.

American Quilter's Society Appraisal Certification. Protecting Your Quilts: A Guide for Quilt Owners. rev. ed. LC 96-214672. 32p. 1998. 6.95 (*0-89145-965-0*, No. 4779) Collector Bks.

***American Quilter's Society Staff.** Storm at Sea: New Quilts from an Old Favorite. Smith, Barbara, ed. LC 00-38070. (Illus.). 96p. 2000. pap. 19.95 (*1-57432-741-0*, Am Quilters Soc) Collector Bks.

American Radio Relay League, jt. auth. see Briggs, Jeff.

American Radio Relay League Staff. The ARRL Handbook for Radio Amateurs, 1999. 1200p. 1998. pap. 32.00 (*0-87259-181-6*) Am Radio.

***American Radio Relay League Staff.** The ARRL Handbook for Radio Amateurs 2000. 77th ed. 1200p. 1999. pap. 32.00 (*0-87259-183-2*, Pub. by Am Radio) ACCESS Pubs Network.

American Radio Relay League Staff. The ARRL RFI Book: Practical Cures for Radio Frequency Interference. LC 98-221242. 320p. 1998. pap. 20.00 (*0-87259-683-4*) Am Radio.

American Red Cross-Boys & Girls Clubs Staff. Act Smart. (gr. 13). 1995. 6.00 (*0-8151-0918-0*) Mosby Inc.

American Red Cross Staff. American Red Cross Adult CPR. LC 92-583. 96p. (C). (gr. 13). 1992. pap. text 9.70 (*0-8016-7062-4*) Mosby Inc.

— American Red Cross Babysitter's Handbook. LC 98-11145. (J). 1998. 9.75 (*0-8151-3685-4*) Mosby Inc.

— American Red Cross Basic HIV/AIDS Fundamentals. LC 98-230754. ix, 304p. 1997. teacher ed. write for info. (*0-86536-217-3*) Am Nat Red Cross.

— American Red Cross Child Story Activity Book. 20p. (J). (ps-3). 1992. pap. text 43.00 (*0-8016-6509-4*) Mosby Inc.

— American Red Cross Community CPR. 124p. (C). (gr. 13). 1992. pap. text 12.50 (*0-8016-7066-7*) Mosby Inc.

— American Red Cross Community First Aid & Safety. 240p. (gr. 13). 1992. pap. text 13.50 (*0-8016-7064-0*) Mosby Inc.

— American Red Cross Community First Aid & Safety. 256p. (C). (gr. 13). 1994. pap. text 13.50 (*0-8016-7538-3*) Mosby Inc.

— American Red Cross Oxygen Administration. 24p. (gr. 13). 1993. pap. text 50.00 (*0-8016-7276-7*) Mosby Inc.

— American Red Cross Preventing Disease Transmissions. 24p. (C). (gr. 13). 1993. pap. text 31.25 (*0-8016-7272-4*) Mosby Inc.

— American Red Cross Standard First Aid. 231p. (gr. 13). 1992. pap. text 13.50 (*0-8016-7065-9*) Mosby Inc.

— American Red Cross until Help Arrives Booklet. LC 92-39673. 16p. (gr. 13). 1992. pap. text 18.75 (*0-8016-7063-2*) Mosby Inc.

— American Red Cross until Help Arrives Booklet. (SPA.). 16p. (gr. 13). 1993. pap. text 18.75 (*0-8016-7756-4*) Mosby Inc.

— Aquactic Safety. (C). (gr. 13). 1992. 3.95 (*0-8016-7686-X*) Mosby Inc.

— Aquatic Examiner Program Chapter Handbook. (gr. 13). 1994. 5.00 (*0-8151-0275-5*) Mosby Inc.

— ARC Foundations for Caregiving Textbook. 512p. (gr. 13). 1993. pap. text 22.50 (*0-8016-6515-9*) Mosby Inc.

— Automated External Defibrillation. LC 98-14957. 1998. 40.00 (*0-323-00439-3*) Mosby Inc.

— Basic Lifeguard Textbook. 336p. (C). (gr. 13). 1994. pap. text 20.00 (*0-8016-7555-3*) Mosby Inc.

— Basic Water Rescue. 64p. (gr. 13). 1997. pap. text 4.75 (*0-8151-7955-3*) Mosby Inc.

— Canoeing-Kayaking. 1995. 16.90 (*0-86536-020-0*) Mosby Inc.

— Childcare: Development. 1995. pap. text, wbk. ed. 5.95 (*0-86536-184-3*) Mosby Inc.

— Childcare: Health & Safety Units. 1995. pap. text, wbk. ed. 8.25 (*0-86536-183-5*) Mosby Inc.

— Community CPR. LC 92-584. 1993. 6.50 (*0-685-61104-3*) Mosby Inc.

— Community Water Safety. 1994. 5.50 (*0-685-65130-4*) Mosby Inc.

— Community Water Safety. 96p. (C). (gr. 13). 1994. pap. text 10.00 (*0-8016-7550-2*) Mosby Inc.

— Community Water Safety. (C). (gr. 13). 1996. pap. text 10.00 (*0-8151-0925-3*) Mosby Inc.

— CPR for the Professional Rescuer. LC 92-41664. (Illus.). 1993. write for info. (*0-8016-0706-X*) Mosby Inc.

— Emergency Response. rev. ed. (C). (gr. 13). 1997. pap. text 5.00 (*0-8151-2635-2*, 31634) Mosby Inc.

— Emergency Response. 2nd ed. LC 96-41118. (gr. 13). 1996. pap. text 32.00 (*0-8151-1260-2*) Mosby Inc.

— Emergency Response Instructor's Notebook. 1993. 85.00 (*0-8016-9015-3*) Mosby Inc.

— First Aid: Responding to Emergencies. 2nd ed. (gr. 13). 1996. 45.00 (*0-8151-0956-3*); pap. text 4.50 (*0-8151-0957-1*) Mosby Inc.

— First Aid: Responding to Emergencies Instructor's. 1991. 250.00 (*0-8016-9029-3*); 6.25 (*0-8016-9023-4*) Mosby Inc.

— First Aid: Responding to Emergencies Instructor's. (gr. 13). 1991. disk 250.00 (*0-8016-9030-7*) Mosby Inc.

— First Aid Fast. (Illus.). 84p. (gr. 13). 1994. pap. text 5.00 (*0-8151-0258-5*) Mosby Inc.

— First Aid Fast. (gr. 13). 1996. pap. text 5.00 (*0-8151-0908-3*) Mosby Inc.

— First Aid When Help Is Delayed. LC 96-7932. 1996. write for info. (*0-8151-1576-8*) Mosby Inc.

— Foundations for Care Giving. 1993. 24.95 (*0-8016-8105-7*) Mosby Inc.

American Red Cross Staff. Foundations for Caregiving Instructor's Manual. 544p. 1993. write for info. (*0-8151-0013-2*) Mosby Inc.

American Red Cross Staff. Foundations for Caregiving Skills Book. 288p. 1993. pap. text 12.50 (*0-8016-6514-0*) Mosby Inc.

— The Game Plan: Strategies for Marketing Success. (gr. 13). 1996. 6.55 (*0-8151-1365-X*) Mosby Inc.

— Healthy Pregnancy-Healthy Baby. 208p. 1995. pap. text, wbk. ed. 8.75 (*0-86536-196-7*) Mosby Inc.

— Infant & Child CPR. LC 92-582. 94p. (gr. 13). 1992. pap. text 9.70 (*0-8016-7061-6*) Mosby Inc.

American Red Cross Staff. Lifeguarding Instructor's Manual. (Illus.). 656p. 1994. write for info. (*0-8016-7553-7*) Mosby Inc.

American Red Cross Staff. Lifesaving First Aid for Children: A Quick-Reference Guide. 2nd rev. ed. Preniszni, Dan, ed. (Illus.). 1998. write for info. (*0-9665371-1-4*) Laerdal Med Corp.

— Pet First Aid: Cats & Dogs. (gr. 13). 1997. 10.00 (*0-8151-2318-3*) Mosby Inc.

— Professional Lifeguard Textbook. 96p. (C). (gr. 13). 1994. pap. text 10.00 (*0-8016-7554-5*) Mosby Inc.

— Professional Rescuer. 2nd ed. (C). (gr. 13). 1997. teacher ed. write for info. (*0-8151-1254-8*) Mosby Inc.

— Professional Rescuer: Instructor-Trainer Guide. 2nd ed. (C). (gr. 13). 1997. teacher ed. write for info. (*0-8151-1255-6*) Mosby Inc.

— Responding to Emergencies. 2nd ed. (gr. 13). 1996. pap. text 25.00 (*0-8151-0351-4*) Mosby Inc.

— Small Craft Safety. 96p. (gr. 13). 1997. pap. text 8.00 (*0-8151-7956-1*) Mosby Inc.

— Sport Safety Training. (Illus.). 192p. (C). (gr. 13). 1997. spiral bd. 12.50 (*0-8151-0983-0*, 29435) Mosby Inc.

— Sport Safety Training Course Text Package. (C). (gr. 13). 1997. pap. text 15.75 (*0-8151-0998-9*, 29483) Mosby Inc.

— Start Sailing Right. 1997. 14.95 (*0-86536-144-4*) Mosby Inc.

— Swimming & Diving. rev. ed. 368p. (gr. 13). 1995. pap. text 21.00 (*0-8151-0595-9*) Mosby Inc.

— Swimming Public Brochure. (gr. 13). 1996. write for info. (*0-8151-0969-5*) Mosby Inc.

— Water Safety. 176p. (gr. 13). 1995. teacher ed. 3.50 (*0-8151-0810-9*) Mosby Inc.

— Water Safety Instructor's Candidate Kit. rev. ed. (gr. 13). 1995. 46.00 (*0-8151-0598-3*) Mosby Inc.

— Water Safety Instructor's Manual. 1977. 10.00 (*0-8016-7549-9*) Mosby Inc.

— Water Safety Instructor's Manual. 336p. (gr. 13). 1995. pap. text, teacher ed. 12.40 (*0-8151-0596-7*) Mosby Inc.

American Red Cross Staff & Handal, Kathleen A. The American Red Cross First Aid & Safety Handbook. 320p. 1992. pap. 17.95 (*0-316-73646-5*, Back Bay) Little.

American Red Cross Staff, tr. see Garehime, Ed.

American Refugee Committee, jt. auth. see Physicians for Human Rights Staff.

American Registry of Pathology Staff & Armed Forces Institute of Pathology Staff. Selected Cases in General & Systemic Pathology. (C). 1991. 250.00 incl. disk (*1-56815-000-8*) Mosby Inc.

American Rescue Dog Association Staff. Search & Rescue Dogs: Training Methods. (Illus.). 256p. 1991. 24.95 (*0-87605-733-4*) Howell Bks.

American Rights & Responsibilities Committee of the American Bar Association Staff, jt. auth. see Employee Rights & Responsibilities Committee of the American Bar Association Staff.

***American Rose Society.** Ultimate Rose. LC 99-86577. 2000. 19.95 (*0-7894-5206-5*) DK Pub Inc.

American Rose Society, jt. auth. see Abler, Elizabeth.

American Safety Video Publishers. Pass! ACLS No. II: Case-Based Scenarios. 96p. 1998. 29.95 incl. VHS (*0-8151-0915-6*, A1057) Mosby Inc.

— Pass ACLS! No. III: Skills Based. 2nd ed. 1998. 29.95 incl. VHS (*0-8151-0940-7*, A8681) Mosby Inc.

— Pass EMT-Basic: New Curriculum. 1996. 32.95 (*0-8151-0883-4*, S2046) Mosby Inc.

American Safety Video Publishers, Inc. Staff. Pals Plus Instructor's Guide. 96p. 1993. teacher ed. 39.95 (*0-8016-7761-0*) Mosby Inc.

— Pass ACLS Booklet. 1993. 9.95 (*0-8016-7985-0*) Mosby Inc.

American Safety Video Publishers Staff. EZ ECG's. (Illus.). 96p. 1994. write for info. (*0-8151-0033-7*) Mosby Inc.

American Safety Video Publishers Staff. Learning ECGS, Videotape Series: Instructor's Manual. 1993. teacher ed. write for info. (*0-8016-8095-6*) Mosby Inc.

— Pass CPR! (Illus.). 96p. 1993. pap. text 9.95 (*0-8151-0036-1*) Mosby Inc.

American Sailing Association Staff. Cruising Fundamentals. 160p. 1992. pap. 18.95 (*0-87742-334-2*) Intl Marine.

American Sailing Association Staff, jt. auth. see White, Rick.

American Scandinavian Foundation Staff. Index Nordicus: A Cumulative Index to English-Language Periodicals on Scandinavian Studies. 1980. 210.00 (*0-8161-0080-2*, G K Hall & Co) Mac Lib Ref.

American School Band Directors Association Staff. The New ASBDA Curriculum Guide: A Reference Book for School Band Directors. Proctor, Thom, ed. LC 98-101975. 224p. (Orig.). 1997. pap. text 24.95 (*1-57623-997-7*, EL9737) Wrner Bros.

American School Health Association Staff, et al. The National Adolescent Student Health Survey. (Illus.). 178p. (Orig.). 1989. pap. 5.00 (*0-88314-453-0*, A4530) AAHPERD.

American School of Classical Studies at Athens Sta. Studies in Athenian Architecture, Sculpture & Topography: In Honor of Homer A. Thompson. LC 81-14994. (Hesperia Supplement Ser.: No. 20). (Illus.). xii, 191p. 1982. pap. 15.00 (*0-87661-520-5*) Am Sch Athens.

— Studies in Attic Epigraphy, History & Topography: In Honor of Eugene Vanderpool. LC 81-12876. (Hesperia Supplement Ser.: No. 19). (Illus.). xii, 207p. 1982. pap. 15.00 (*0-87661-519-1*) Am Sch Athens.

American School of Classical Studies Staff. Catalogue of the Gennadius Library, American School of Classical Studies, Athens. 1970. 795.00 (*0-8161-1498-6*, G K Hall & Co) Mac Lib Ref.

— Catalogue of the Gennadius Library, American School of Classical Studies, Athens, Supplement 1. 1973. suppl. ed. 160.00 (*0-8161-1499-4*, G K Hall & Co) Mac Lib Ref.

American Schools of Oriental Research Staff. Sardis, Idalion & Tell el-Handaquq North. DeMaleissye-Melun, Judith & Dever, William G., eds. LC 96-41756. (Annual of the American Schools of Oriental Research Ser.: Vol. 53). (Illus.). 154p. (C). 1994. 51.00 (*0-7885-0315-4*, Pub. by Am Sch Orient Res) David Brown.

American Schools of Oriental Research Staff, jt. auth. see Charlesworth, James H.

American Scientific Affiliation Staff. Contemporary Issues in Science & Christian Faith: An Annotated Bibliography. 130p. 1992. pap. text 10.00 (*1-881479-01-3*) Am Sci Affil.

American Self-Help Clearinghouse Staff. The Self-Help Sourcebook: Your Guide to Community & Online Support Groups. 6th rev. ed. White, Barbara J. & Madara, Edward J., eds. LC 97-75663. Orig. Title: The Self-Help Sourcebook: Finding & Forming Mutual Aid Self-Help Groups. 348p. 1997. pap. 10.00 (*0-9634322-7-3*) St Clares Hlth.

American Showcase Inc. Staff. Conceptual People & Photography. (Illus.). 1998. pap. 28.00 (*1-882202-19-8*) NY Gold.

— Conceptual People Photography 12, 12. (Conceptual People Photography Ser.). 1999. pap. text 28.00 (*1-882202-22-8*) NY Gold.

— Conceptual Still Life Photography. (Illus.). 1998. pap. 25.00 (*1-882202-20-1*) NY Gold.

— Conceptual Still Life Photography 12. (Conceptual Still Life Photography Ser.). 1999. pap. text 25.00 (*1-882202-23-6*) NY Gold.

— Creative Options 2: For Business & Annual Reports. (Illus.). 230p. 1996. pap. text 37.50 (*0-8230-6517-0*) Watsn-Guptill.

— Direct Stock. 1998. pap. 49.00 (*0-9633977-5-3*) Direct Stock.

***American Showcase Inc. Staff.** Direct Stock 8, 8. (Direct Stock Ser.). 1999. pap. text 49.00 (*0-9633977-6-1*) Direct Stock.

American Showcase Inc. Staff. New Media Showcase: The Digital Sourcebook, No. 6. (Illus.). 266p. 1996. pap. text 29.95 (*0-8230-6516-2*) Watsn-Guptill.

***American Showcase Inc. Staff.** New Media Showcase 8: The Digital Sourcebook, 1. 1998. pap. text 29.95 (*1-887165-24-X*) Am Showcase.

American Showcase Inc. Staff. Showcase Stock: Premier Illustration. 1998. pap. text 21.95 (*1-887165-22-3*) Am Showcase.

American Social History Project Staff. Freedom's Unfinished Revolution: The Civil War & Reconstruction. Foner, Eric, ed. (Illus.). 256p. (Orig.). 1996. pap. 19.95 (*1-56584-198-0*, Pub. by New Press NY) Norton.

***American Social History Project Staff.** Who Built America, Vols. 2. 2000. pap. 30.95 (*1-57259-303-2*) St Martin.

American Society Civil Engineers Staff. Flood-Runoff Analysis. LC 96-20785. (U.S. Army Corps of Engineers Adapted Technical Engineering & Design Guides Ser.). 192p. 1996. 48.00 (*0-7844-0187-X*) Am Soc Civil Eng.

American Society for Eighteenth-Century Studies St. Studies in Eighteenth-Century Culture, Vol. 25. Conger, Sydny M. & Hayes, Julie C., eds. LC 75-648277. (Illus.). 336p. reprint ed. pap. 104.20 (*0-608-08803-X*, 206944200025) Bks Demand.

American Society for Engineering Education Staff. ASEE Membership Handbook, 1994. 250p. (Orig.). 1993. pap. write for info. (*0-87823-132-3*) Am Soc Eng Ed.

— Directory of Engineering & Engineering Technology Undergraduate Programs, 1993. (Illus.). 1993. pap. 49.95 (*0-87823-143-9*) Am Soc Eng Ed.

— Directory of Engineering & Engineering Technology Undergraduate Programs, 1994. (Illus.). 1994. pap. 49.95 (*0-87823-147-1*) Am Soc Eng Ed.

— Directory of Engineering Graduate Studies & Research, 1993. (Illus.). (C). 1993. pap. 69.95 (*0-87823-146-3*) Am Soc Eng Ed.

American Society for Healthcare Central Service Pe. Training Manual for Central Service Technicians. LC 86-3332. (Illus.). 278p. 1986. pap. text 70.00 (*0-87258-442-9*, 031802) Am Hospital.

— Training Manual for Central Service Technicians: Instructor's Manual. (Illus.). 94p. (Orig.). 1991. pap. text 35.00 (*0-87258-615-4*, 031084) Am Hospital.

— Training Manual for Central Service Technicians: Workbook. (Illus.). 173p. (C). 1994. 35.00 (*0-87258-678-2*, 031803) Am Hospital.

American Society for Healthcare Education & Traini. Competency Assessment: Allied Health. Ulschak, Francis L. & Hayman, Barbara A., eds. (Illus.). 208p. (Orig.). 1994. pap. 125.00 (*0-87258-661-8*, 049855) Am Hospital.

— Competency Assessment: Challenges & Opportunities for Health Care Educators. 258p. (Orig.). 1992. pap. 130.00 (*0-87258-582-4*, 049906) Am Hospital.

American Society for Healthcare Risk Management St. Risk Management Handbook for Health Care Organizations. 2nd rev. ed. Carroll, Roberta, ed. LC 97-10917. (Illus.). 610p. 1997. text 95.00 (*1-55648-185-3*, 178159) AHPI.

A

American Society for Industrial Security Staff, ed. Security Abstracts: Article Summaries from Security Management 1989-1994. (Reference Ser.). (Orig.). Date not set. pap. write for info. (*1-887056-03-3*) Am Soc Indus Secur.

— Violence in the Workplace: A Survey of Published Literature 1989-1994. (Reference Ser.). iv, 52p. (Orig.). 1994. pap. 48.00 (*1-887056-02-5*) Am Soc Indus Secur.

American Society for Industrial Security Staff, jt. ed. see Information Resources Center Staff.

American Society for Information Science Staff, jt. auth. see Milstead, Jessica L.

American Society for Materials & Testing Staff. Low-Temperature Pumpability Characteristics of Engine Oils in Full-Scale Engines - DS 57. 104p. 1975. pap. 16.00 (*0-8031-0392-1*, DS57) ASTM.

American Society for Metals Staff. Aluminum Transformation Technology & Applications, 1981: Proceedings of the Second International Symposium. Pampillo, C. A., ed. LC 82-70649. (Materials-Metalworking Technology Ser.). 676p. reprint ed. pap. 200.00 (*0-8357-5338-7*, 202699600053) Bks Demand.

— ASM Metal Reference Book: A Handbook of Data about Metals & Metalworking. LC 81-20670. 434p. reprint ed. pap. 134.60 (*0-8357-5792-7*, 202704600053) Bks Demand.

— Atlas of Microstructures of Industrial Alloys. Lyman, Taylor, ed. LC 72-171167. (Metals Handbook Ser.: Vol. 7, 8th ed.). (Illus.). 381p. reprint ed. pap. 118.20 (*0-7837-1865-9*, 204206600001) Bks Demand.

— Carburizing & Carbonitriding. LC 76-55702. 233p. reprint ed. pap. 72.30 (*0-608-12108-8*, 202514500042) Bks Demand.

— Case Histories in Failure Analysis. LC 79-9124. (Illus.). 439p. reprint ed. pap. 136.10 (*0-7837-1858-6*, 204205900001) Bks Demand.

— Casting Design Handbook: Prepared from the Contributions of 18 Committees (Sponsored by the United States Air Force & the American Society for Metals) LC 62-53240. (Illus.). 344p. reprint ed. pap. 106.70 (*0-608-11595-9*, 201321600083) Bks Demand.

— Control of Distortion & Residual Stress in Weldments: Proceedings of an International Conference. Saperstein, Z. Phillip, ed. LC 77-13326. (Materials-Metalworking Technology Ser.). 93p. reprint ed. pap. 30.00 (*0-608-11870-2*, 202305900031) Bks Demand.

— Corrosion. Coburn, Seymour K., ed. LC 83-7371. (Source Bks.). (Illus.). 452p. reprint ed. pap. 140.20 (*0-7837-1860-8*, 204206100001) Bks Demand.

— Cutting Tool Materials: Proceedings of an International Conference : 15-17 Sept, 1980 Kentucky. LC 81-3505. (Materials-Metalworking Technology Ser.). 447p. reprint ed. pap. 138.60 (*0-608-17233-2*, 202698400053) Bks Demand.

— Diffusion: Papers Presented at a Seminar of the American Society for Metals, October 14 & 15, 1972. LC 73-88315. 383p. reprint ed. pap. 118.80 (*0-608-16163-2*, 201947900013) Bks Demand.

— Duplex Stainless Steels. Lula, R. A., ed. LC 83-71074. (Conference Proceedings - American Society for Metals Ser.). (Illus.). 811p. reprint ed. pap. 200.00 (*0-8357-6098-7*, 203431100089) Bks Demand.

— Efficient Materials & Coatings: Proceedings of the American Society for Metals Highway & Off-Highway Vehicles Activity Sessions Materials & Processing Congress, 13-15 November 1979 Chicago, IL. LC 81-3440. (Materials-Metalworking Technology Ser.). 200p. reprint ed. pap. 62.00 (*0-608-16398-8*, 202703400053) Bks Demand.

— Fabrication of Composite Materials. Schwartz, Mel M., ed. LC 84-73363. (Illus.). 416p. reprint ed. pap. 129.00 (*0-7837-1863-2*, 204206400001) Bks Demand.

— Ferritic Steels for High-Temperature Applications: Proceedings of an ASM International Conference on Production, Fabrication, Properties & Application of Ferritic Steels for High-Temperature Applications, Warren, PA, 1981. Khare, Ashok K., ed. LC 82-73608. (Illus.). 344p. reprint ed. pap. 106.70 (*0-608-15945-X*, 203306000083) Bks Demand.

— Fracture & Failure: Analyses, Mechanisms & Applications: Proceedings of the American Society for Metals Fracture & Failure Sessions at the 1980 Western Metal & Tool Exposition & Conference, 17-20 March, 1980, Los Angeles, CA. Tung, Paul P. et al, eds. LC 81-66629. (Materials-Metalworking Technology Ser.). 191p. reprint ed. pap. 59.30 (*0-608-16485-2*, 202704000053) Bks Demand.

— Heat Treating. LC 81-12692. (Metals Handbook Ser.: Vol. 4). 848p. reprint ed. pap. 200.00 (*0-7837-2775-5*, 204316600006) Bks Demand.

— High-Temperature Property Data: Ferrous Alloys. Rothman, M. F., ed. LC 88-133105. 556p. reprint ed. pap. 172.40 (*0-7837-2762-3*, 204315300006) Bks Demand.

— Hydrogen Damage: A Discriminative Selection of Outstanding Articles & Papers from the Scientific Literature. Beachem, Cedric D., ed. LC 77-14966. 422p. reprint ed. pap. 130.90 (*0-608-12738-8*, 202434600036) Bks Demand.

— Hydrogen in Metals: Proceedings of an International Conference on the Effects of Hydrogen on Materials Properties & Selection & Structural Design, Seven Springs Conference Center, Champion, PA, 23-27 September, 1973. Bernstein, I. M. & Thompson, Anthony W., eds. LC 73-86455. (Materials-Metalworking Technology Ser.: No. 2). 775p. reprint ed. pap. 200.00 (*0-608-17143-3*, 205219500056) Bks Demand.

— Influence of Metallurgy on Hole Making Operations: Drilling, Reaming, Tapping & Others. LC 77-13357. (Materials-Metalworking Technology Ser.). (Illus.). 216p. reprint ed. pap. 67.00 (*0-608-10757-3*, 201949100013) Bks Demand.

— Influence of Metallurgy on Machinability: An International Symposium, Proceedings. LC 75-29683. (Materials-Metalworking Technology Ser.: No. 7). (Illus.). 480p. reprint ed. pap. 148.80 (*0-608-10752-2*, 201947700013) Bks Demand.

— The Inhomogeneity of Plastic Deformation: Papers Presented at a Seminar of the American Society for Metals. LC 72-95850. 328p. reprint ed. pap. 101.70 (*0-608-11276-3*, 201948400013) Bks Demand.

— Interface Migration & Control of Microstructure: Proceedings of an International Symposium Held in Conjunction with ASM's Metals Congress & TMS-AIME Fall Meeting, Detroit, MI, USA, 17-21 September 1984. Pande, C. S. et al, eds. LC 86-70299. (Illus.). 212p. reprint ed. pap. 65.80 (*0-8357-4096-X*, 203686200005) Bks Demand.

— Materials Engineering in the Arctic: Proceedings of an International Conference, St. Jovite, Quebec, Canada, Sept. 27 - Oct. 1, 1976. LC 77-4214. (Illus.). 343p. reprint ed. pap. 106.40 (*0-608-30313-5*, 201949900013) Bks Demand.

— Materials in Nuclear Energy: Proceedings of an International Conference, Huntsville, Ontario, Canada, 29 September - 2 October 1982. LC 83-71303. 280p. reprint ed. 86.80 (*0-608-17156-5*, 202698900053) Bks Demand.

— The Metallurgical Evolution of Stainless Steels: A Discriminative Selection of Outstanding Articles & Papers from the Scientific Literature. Pickering, F. B., ed. LC 79-12994. 487p. reprint ed. pap. 151.00 (*0-608-13094-X*, 201949500013) Bks Demand.

— Metals Handbook Comprehensive Index. LC 85-62432. 557p. reprint ed. pap. 172.70 (*0-8357-6209-2*, 203430700089) Bks Demand.

— NDE of Microstructure for Process Control: Proceedings of a Symposium - Sponsored by the Materials Testing & Quality Control Division, Nondestructive Testing Committee of ASM at the ASM Metals Congress, Detroit, MI, September 18-19, 1984. Wadley, H. N., ed. LC 85-73216. (Illus.). 212p. reprint ed. pap. 65.80 (*0-8357-4098-6*, 203686400005) Bks Demand.

— New Developments in Stainless Steel Technology: Conference Proceedings. Lula, R. A., ed. LC 85-72035. (Illus.). 399p. reprint ed. pap. 123.70 (*0-8357-6234-3*, 203432000089) Bks Demand.

— New Trends in Materials Processing: Papers Presented at a Seminar of the American Society for Metals, October 19-20, 1974. LC 75-42155. (Illus.). 371p. reprint ed. pap. 115.10 (*0-608-11708-0*, 201947600013) Bks Demand.

— Nondestructive Evaluation in the Nuclear Industry: An International Conference, 13-15 February, 1978, Salt Lake City, Utah, Proceedings. Natesh, R., ed. LC 78-25552. (Materials-Metalworking Technology Ser.). (Illus.). 536p. reprint ed. pap. 166.20 (*0-608-10729-8*, 201948800013) Bks Demand.

— Nondestructive Evaluation in the Nuclear Industry: Proceedings of the Third International Conference. LC 81-67225. (Materials-Metalworking Technology Ser.). 695p. reprint ed. 200.00 (*0-608-17149-2*, 202698600053) Bks Demand.

— Nondestructive Inspection & Quality Control. Boyer, Howard E., ed. LC 76-382089. (Illus.). 465p. reprint ed. pap. 144.20 (*0-7837-1857-8*, 204205800001) Bks Demand.

— Phase Transformations & Related Phenomena in Steels: Papers Presented at the E. C. Bain Seminar of the American Society for Metals. LC 72-95849. 98p. reprint ed. pap. 30.40 (*0-608-13091-5*, 201949600013) Bks Demand.

— Polymeric Materials: Relationships Between Structure & Mechanical Behavior: Papers Presented at a Seminar of the American Society for Metals. LC 74-20127. 626p. reprint ed. pap. 194.10 (*0-608-10143-5*, 201549400094) Bks Demand.

— Prevention of Structural Failures: The Role of NDT, Fracture Mechanics & Failure Analysis: Proceedings of Two Annual Forums, 19-22 June, 1977 & 14-16 June 1976, Tarpon Springs, Florida. LC 78-15388. (Materials-Metalworking Technology Ser.). (Illus.). 360p. reprint ed. pap. 111.60 (*0-608-10738-7*, 201948900013) Bks Demand.

— Process Modeling - Fundamentals & Applications to Metals: Proceedings of American Society for Metals Process Modelling Sessions. LC 80-12489. (Material-Metalworking Technology Ser.). 456p. reprint ed. 141.40 (*0-608-17141-7*, 202698500053) Bks Demand.

— Production to near Net Shape: Source Book: A Collection of Outstanding Articles from the Technical Literature. Van Tyne, C.J & Avitzur, B., eds. LC 82-73611. (Illus.). 413p. reprint ed. pap. 128.10 (*0-608-18679-1*, 203307700083) Bks Demand.

— The Properties & Performance of Materials in the Coal Gasification Environment: Proceedings of a Conference Held 8-10 September 1980, Pittsburgh, PA - Sponsored by the Gas Research Institute... et al. Hill, V. L. & Black, Herbert L., eds. LC 81-67327. (Materials-Metalworking Technology Ser.). 831p. reprint ed. pap. 200.00 (*0-608-16500-X*, 202704100053) Bks Demand.

— Properties & Selection: Irons & Steels. LC 78-14934. (Metals Handbook Ser.: No. 1). 818p. reprint ed. pap. 200.00 (*0-7837-2771-2*, 204316200006) Bks Demand.

— Properties & Selection: Nonferrous Alloys & Pure Metals. LC 79-21644. (Metals Handbook Ser.: Vol. 2). 871p. reprint ed. pap. 200.00 (*0-7837-2773-9*, 204316400006) Bks Demand.

— Properties & Selection: Stainless Steels, Tool Materials & Special-Purpose Metals. LC 80-26336. (Metals Handbook Ser.: Vol. 3). 900p. reprint ed. pap. 200.00 (*0-7837-2774-7*, 204316500006) Bks Demand.

— Residual Stress for Designers & Metallurgists: Proceedings of a Conference Held 9-10 April 1980, Chicago, IL. Vande Walle, Larry J., ed. LC 81-4876. (Materials-Metalworking Technology Ser.). 255p. reprint ed. pap. 79.10 (*0-608-16372-4*, 202703300053) Bks Demand.

— Source Book on Applications of the Laser in Metalworking: A Comprehensive Collection of Outstanding Articles from the Periodical & Reference Literature. Metzbower, Edward A., ed. LC 81-52317. (ASM Engineering Bookshelf Ser.). (Illus.). 399p. reprint ed. pap. 123.70 (*0-8357-3542-7*, 203431500089) Bks Demand.

— Source Book on Brazing & Brazing Technology: A Comprehensive Collection of Outstanding Articles from the Periodical & Reference Literature. LC 80-17457. 440p. reprint ed. pap. 136.40 (*0-608-16574-3*, 202705000053) Bks Demand.

— Source Book on Cold Forming: A Discriminative Selection of Outstanding Articles from the Periodical Literature. LC 75-6855. (American Society for Metals. Engineering Bookshelf Ser.). (Illus.). 375p. reprint ed. pap. 116.30 (*0-608-11713-7*, 201950100013) Bks Demand.

— Source Book on Copper & Copper Alloys: A Comprehensive Collection of Outstanding Articles from the Periodical & Reference Literature. LC 79-21667. 424p. reprint ed. pap. 131.50 (*0-608-16532-8*, 202704500053) Bks Demand.

— Source Book on Ductile Iron: A Discriminative Selection of Outstanding Articles from the Periodical & Reference Literature. Rauch, A. H., ed. LC 77-9278. (ASM Engineering Bookshelf Ser.). 400p. reprint ed. pap. 124.00 (*0-608-13088-5*, 201950000013) Bks Demand.

— Source Book on Electron Beam & Laser Welding: A Comprehensive Collection of Outstanding Articles from the Periodical & Reference Literature. Schwartz, Melvin M., ed. LC 81-109899. (ASM Engineering Bookshelf Ser.). (Illus.). 408p. reprint ed. pap. 126.50 (*0-8357-3543-5*, 203431600089) Bks Demand.

— Source Book on Gear Design, Technology & Performance: A Comprehensive Collection of Outstanding Articles from the Periodical & Reference Literature. LC 79-27246. 429p. reprint ed. pap. 133.00 (*0-608-17876-4*, 203271500080) Bks Demand.

— Source Book on Heat Treating: A Discriminative Selection of Outstanding Articles from the Literature Periodicals. LC 75-25598. (ASM Engineering Bookshelf Ser.: Vol. 1: Materials & Processes). (Illus.). 398p. reprint ed. pap. 123.40 (*0-608-10692-5*, 205190400013) Bks Demand.

— Source Book on Industrial Alloy & Engineering Data: A Comprehensive Collection of Alloy & Engineering Data in Tabular & Graphical Form. LC 77-28985. 483p. reprint ed. pap. 149.80 (*0-608-12736-1*, 202434700036) Bks Demand.

— Source Book on Innovative Welding Processes: A Comprehensive Collection of Outstanding Articles from the Periodical & Reference Literature. Schwartz, Melvin M., ed. LC 81-3535. (ASM Engineering Bookshelf Ser.). (Illus.). 384p. reprint ed. pap. 119.10 (*0-8357-3544-3*, 203431400089) Bks Demand.

— Source Book on Materials Selection: A Discriminative Selection of Outstanding Articles from the Periodical & Reference Literature. Gunie, Russell B., ed. LC 77-1347. 487p. reprint ed. pap. 151.00 (*0-608-16541-7*, 202704700002) Bks Demand.

— Source Book on Nitriding: A Discriminative Selection of Outstanding Articles from the Periodical & Reference Literature. LC 79-23934. 328p. reprint ed. pap. 101.70 (*0-608-16550-6*, 202704800053) Bks Demand.

— Source Book on Powder Metallurgy: A Comprehensive Collection of Oustanding Articles from the Periodical & Reference Literature. Bradbury, Samuel, ed. LC 78-24466. 439p. reprint ed. pap. 136.10 (*0-608-12733-7*, 202434800036) Bks Demand.

— Source Book on Selection & Fabrication of Aluminum Alloys: A Comprehensive Collection of Outstanding Articles from the Industrial & Reference Literature. LC 78-18869. 480p. reprint ed. pap. 148.80 (*0-608-16524-7*, 202704400053) Bks Demand.

— Source Book on Wear Control Technology: A Comprehensive Collection of Outstanding Articles from the Periodical & Reference Literature. Rigney, David A. & Glaeser, W. A., eds. LC 78-12162. (ASM Engineering Bookshelf Ser.). 464p. reprint ed. pap. 143.90 (*0-608-12731-0*, 202434900036) Bks Demand.

— Specialized Cleaning, Finishing & Coating Processes: Proceedings of a Conference Held February 5-6, 1980, Los Angeles, California. LC 81-2755. (Materials-Metalworking Technology Ser.). 424p. reprint ed. pap. 131.50 (*0-608-12729-9*, 202435000036) Bks Demand.

— Superalloys. Donachie, Matthew J., Jr., ed. LC 83-71812. (Source Bks.). (Illus.). 424p. reprint ed. pap. 131.50 (*0-7837-1862-4*, 204206300001) Bks Demand.

— Technological Impact of Surfaces: Relationship to Forming, Welding, & Painting: Proceedings of a Conference, 14-15 April 1981, Dearborn, MI. LC 81-69527. (Materials-Metalworking Technology Ser.). (Illus.). 367p. reprint ed. pap. 113.80 (*0-608-16007-5*, 203308500083) Bks Demand.

— Unusual Techniques & New Applications of Metallography Vol. 1: Papers Taken from the Metallography Symposia Held at the ASM Metals Congress, St. Louis, Missouri, 27 October 1982 & Philadelphia, Pennsylvania, 4-5 October 1983. LC 85-71946. (Illus.). 149p. 1985. reprint ed. pap. 46.20 (*0-608-10384-5*, 203308600001) Bks Demand.

— Unusual Techniques & New Applications of Metallography Vol. 2: Papers Taken from the Metallography Symposia Held at the ASM Metals Congress, St. Louis, Missouri, 27 October 1982 & Philadelphia, Pennsylvania, 4-5 October 1983. LC 85-71946. (Illus.). 171p. 1986. reprint ed. pap. 53.10 (*0-608-10385-3*, 203308600002) Bks Demand.

— Wear & Fracture Prevention: Proceedings of a Conference Held May 21-22, 1980, Peoria, Illinois. LC 81-67226. (Materials-Metalworking Technology Ser.). 319p. reprint ed. pap. 98.90 (*0-608-12727-2*, 202435100037) Bks Demand.

— Welding & Brazing of Carbon Steels, Bk. 3: Resistance Welding. Davis, Charles A., ed. LC 76-44372. 151p. 1976. reprint ed. pap. 46.90 (*0-608-08530-8*, 205214700003) Bks Demand.

— Welding & Brazing of Carbon Steels, Bk. 4: Gas Welding & Brazing. Davis, Charles A., ed. LC 76-44372. 172p. reprint ed. pap. 53.40 (*0-608-12399-4*, 205214700004) Bks Demand.

— Welding of HSLA Structural Steels: Proceedings of an International Conference. Rothwell, A. B. & Gray, J. Malcolm, eds. LC 78-18220. (Materials Metalworking Technology Ser.). 805p. reprint ed. pap. 200.00 (*0-608-13102-4*, 201949000013) Bks Demand.

American Society for Metals Staff & Ashbrook, R. L. Rapid Solidification Technology. LC 82-74298. (Source Bks.). (Illus.). 448p. 1983. reprint ed. pap. 138.90 (*0-7837-1861-6*, 204206200001) Bks Demand.

American Society for Metals Staff & Kortesoja, Victor A. Properties & Selection of Tool Materials. LC 75-26829. 320p. reprint ed. pap. 99.20 (*0-608-13111-3*, 201948300013) Bks Demand.

American Society for Metals Staff & Periodical Publication Department Staff, compiled by. Source Book on Stainless Steels: A Discriminative Selection of Outstanding Articles from the Periodical & Reference Literature. LC 76-867. (AMS Engineering Bookshelf Ser.). (Illus.). 416p. reprint ed. pap. 129.00 (*0-608-30710-6*, 201949700013) Bks Demand.

American Society for Metals Staff, et al. Failure Analysis: The British Engine Technical Reports. LC 81-68626. (Illus.). 510p. reprint ed. pap. 158.10 (*0-7837-1872-1*, 203305800083) Bks Demand.

— Materials to Supply the Energy Demand: Proceedings of an International Conference. Hawbolt, E. B. & Mitchell, A., eds. LC 81-66630. 918p. reprint ed. pap. 200.00 (*0-608-17187-5*, 202699500053) Bks Demand.

American Society for Microbiology Staff. Bacteriophage T4. Matthews, Christopher K. et al, eds. LC 83-11945. (Illus.). 420p. reprint ed. pap. 130.20 (*0-8357-7510-0*, 203600200097) Bks Demand.

— Frontiers in Microbiology: A Collection of Minireviews from the Journal of Microbiology. Walker, Graham C. & Kaiser, Dale, eds. LC 92-38223. (Illus.). 154p. reprint ed. pap. 47.80 (*0-608-10417-5*, 206991600008) Bks Demand.

— Legionella: Proceedings of the 2nd International Symposium. Thornsberry, Clyde et al, eds. LC 83-21499. (Illus.). 385p. reprint ed. pap. 119.40 (*0-8357-7511-9*, 203600300097) Bks Demand.

— Manual of Methods for General Bacteriology. Gerhardt, Philipp, ed. LC 80-22275. (Illus.). 536p. reprint ed. pap. 166.20 (*0-8357-7509-7*, 203600100097) Bks Demand.

— The Pathogenic Neisseriae: Proceedings of the 4th International Symposium, Asilomar, California, 21-25 October 1984. Schoolnik, Gary K. et al, eds. LC 85-20108. 659p. reprint ed. pap. 200.00 (*0-7837-4044-1*, 204387400011) Bks Demand.

— Virus Attachment & Entry into Cells: Proceedings of an ASM Conference Held in Philadelphia, Pennsylvania, 10-13 April 1985. Crowell, Richard L. & Lonberg-Holm, Karl, eds. LC 85-28731. 224p. reprint ed. pap. 69.50 (*0-7837-4039-5*, 204386900011) Bks Demand.

American Society for Microbiology Staff, et al. Manual of Clinical Laboratory Immunology. 3rd ed. Rose, Noel R., ed. LC 85-26675. 1026p. reprint ed. pap. 200.00 (*0-7837-4037-9*, 204386700011) Bks Demand.

— Manual of Clinical Microbiology. Lennette, Edwin H., ed. LC 84-28304. 1165p. reprint ed. pap. 200.00 (*0-7837-4036-0*, 204386600011) Bks Demand.

American Society for Nondestructive Testing (ASNT). ASNT Level III Study Guide: Eddy Current Method. (Illus.). 72p. (Orig.). (C). 1983. pap. 39.00 (*0-931403-80-4*, 2257) Am Soc Nondestructive.

— ASNT Level III Study Guide: Magnetic Particle Method. (Illus.). 84p. (Orig.). (C). 1980. pap. 39.00 (*0-931403-78-2*, 2253) Am Soc Nondestructive.

— ASNT Level III Study Guide: Radiography Method. (Illus.). 92p. (C). 1988. pap. 53.50 (*0-931403-81-2*, 2259) Am Soc Nondestructive.

— ASNT Nondestructive Testing Handbook, Vol. I. McMaster, Robert C., ed. (Illus.). 451p. 1959. 70.00 (*0-931403-53-7*, 101) Am Soc Nondestructive.

— ASNT Training Program: Liquid Penetrant Method (Instructor Package) (Illus.). 219p. (C). 1979. 189.25 (*0-931403-63-4*, 544) Am Soc Nondestructive.

— ASNT Training Program: Liquid Penetrant Method (Student Package) (Illus.). 219p. (C). 1979. 55.50 (*0-931403-62-6*, 543) Am Soc Nondestructive.

— ASNT Training Program: Magnetic Particle Method (Student Package) (Illus.). 91p. (Orig.). 1979. pap. 64.50 (*0-931403-60-X*, 438) Am Soc Nondestructive.

— ASNT Training Program: Radiography Method (Instructor Package) (Illus.). 451p. (C). 1980. 264.75 (*0-931403-57-X*, 231) Am Soc Nondestructive.

— ASNT Training Program: Radiography Method (Student Package) (Illus.). 451p. (C). 1980. 72.50 (*0-931403-56-1*, 230) Am Soc Nondestructive.

— Directory of Educational Institutions Offering Courses in Nondestructive Testing. 7p. (Orig.). 1991. pap. 4.50 (*0-931403-84-7*, 114) Am Soc Nondestructive.

— Mass Spectrometer Testing HM. (Illus.). 51p. (Orig.). (C). 1996. pap. 31.25 (*0-931403-40-5*, 2033M) Am Soc Nondestructive.
— Materials Evaluation 50 Year Index. 392p. (Orig.). 1994. pap. 59.00 (*1-57117-006-5*) Am Soc Nondestructive.
— Proceedings of the Third International Symposium on Acoustic Emission from Composite Materials (AECM-3) July 17-21, 1989, Paris, France: July 17-21, 1989, Paris, France. (Illus.). 441p. (Orig.). (C). 1989. pap. 31.00 (*0-931403-88-X*, 770) Am Soc Nondestructive.
— Question & Answer Book A: Radiographic Test Method, Levels I, II & III. (Illus.). 74p. (Orig.). (C). 1996. pap. 31.25 (*0-931403-45-6*, 2026) Am Soc Nondestructive.
— Question & Answer Book B: Magnetic Particle Method, Levels I-III. (Illus.). 43p. (Orig.). 1994. pap. 31.25 (*0-931403-11-1*, 2027) Am Soc Nondestructive.
— Question & Answer Book C: Ultrasonic Test Method, Levels I-III. (Illus.). 55p. (Orig.). 1994. pap. 31.25 (*0-931403-46-4*, 2028) Am Soc Nondestructive.
— Question & Answer Book D: Liquid Penetrant Method, Levels I, II & III. 45p. (C). 1996. pap. 31.25 (*0-931403-10-3*, 2029) Am Soc Nondestructive.
— Question & Answer Book E: Eddy Current Test Method, Levels I, II, III & Flux Leakage Methods, Levels I, II & III. (Illus.). 56p. (C). 1995. pap. 31.25 (*0-931403-16-2*, 2030) Am Soc Nondestructive.
— Question & Answer Book F: Neutron Radiographic Test Method, Level I, II, & III. 40p. (Orig.). 1994. pap. 31.25 (*0-931403-14-6*, 2031) Am Soc Nondestructive.
— Question & Answer Book HH: Halogen Diode Detector Leak Testing, Levels I, II, III. (Illus.). 24p. (Orig.). (C). 1995. pap. 31.25 (*0-931403-73-1*, 2033H) Am Soc Nondestructive.
— Question & Answer Book HP: Pressure Change Measurement Testing. (Illus.). 33p. (Orig.). 1994. pap. 31.25 (*0-931403-39-1*, 2033P) Am Soc Nondestructive.
— Recommended Practice No. SNT-TC-1A, 1988 Edition. 1989. 41.60 (*0-931403-50-2*, 2045) Am Soc Nondestructive.

American Society for Phenomenology Fine Arts Staff, jt. auth. see Kronegger, Marlies.

American Society for Political & Legal Philosophy. Authority, 1. Freidrich, Carl J., ed. LC 81-7114. (Nomos One Ser.). 234p. 1982. reprint ed. lib. bdg. 35.00 (*0-313-23185-0*, AMAU, Greenwood Pr) Greenwood.

American Society for Public Administration Staff. Spatial Dimensions of Development Administration: American Society for Public Administration. LC 75-161358. (Comparative Administration Group Ser.). 288p. reprint ed. pap. 89.30 (*0-608-15081-9*, 202620100048) Bks Demand.

American Society for Quality Staff. ISO 9000 For Small Business. 1996. pap. 58.00 (*92-67-10238-9*) ISO.
— The Product Recall Planning Guide. 2nd ed. LC 99-17454. xvii, 84p. 1999. write for info. (*0-87389-457-X*) ASQ Qual Pr.

American Society for Surgery of the Hand Staff. The Hand: Examination & Diagnosis. 2nd ed. LC 82-4140. 129p. reprint ed. pap. 40.00 (*0-8357-4654-2*, 203758600008) Bks Demand.
— The Hand: Examination & Diagnosis. 3rd ed. (Illus.). 136p. 1990. pap. text 24.95 (*0-443-08715-6*) Church.
— The Hand: Primary Care of Common Problems. 2nd ed. (Illus.). 173p. 1990. pap. text 24.95 (*0-443-08584-6*) Church.

American Society for Surgery of the Hand Staff, ed. Hand Surgery Update. (Illus.). 454p. 1996. pap. 115.00 (*0-89203-150-6*) Amer Acad Ortho Surg.

American Society for Surgery of the Hand Staff, jt. auth. see Light, Terry R.

American Society for Testing & Materials Staff. Annual Book of ASTM Standards, 1996, Vols. 1-15. LC 83-641658. (Illus.). 798p. reprint ed. pap. 200.00 (*0-608-09159-6*, 206929000004) Bks Demand.
— Annual Book of ASTM Standards, 1983, Vols. 1-15. LC 40-10712. 1090p. pap. 200.00 (*0-8357-5614-9*, 202547200044) Bks Demand.
— Annual Book of ASTM Standards, 1987, 15 vols., Vols. 1-15. LC 83-641658. (Illus.). 1161p. reprint ed. pap. 200.00 (*0-608-16098-9*, 203435900090) Bks Demand.
— Annual Book of ASTM Standards, 1988, Vols. 1-15. LC 83-641658. (Illus.). 855p. reprint ed. pap. 200.00 (*0-8357-4085-4*, 203678500005) Bks Demand.
— Annual Book of ASTM Standards, 1990, Vols. 1-15. LC 83-641658. 942p. 1990. reprint ed. pap. 200.00 (*0-7837-1974-4*, 204217900002) Bks Demand.
— Annual Book of ASTM Standards, 1991, Vols. 1-15. LC 83-641658. 676p. 1991. reprint ed. pap. 200.00 (*0-7837-4482-X*, 204419000001) Bks Demand.
— Annual Book of ASTM Standards, 1993, Vols. 1-15. LC 83-641658. (Illus.). pap. 180.00 (*0-7837-8958-0*, 2049671) Bks Demand.
— Annual Book of ASTM Standards, 1994, Vols. 1-15. LC 83-641658. (Illus.). 1196p. reprint ed. pap. 200.00 (*0-608-01646-2*, 206223100002) Bks Demand.
— Annual Book of ASTM Standards, 1995, Vols. 1-15. LC 83-641658. (Illus.). 1272p. 1995. pap. 200.00 (*0-608-05655-3*, 206610900006) Bks Demand.
— Application of Advanced & Nuclear Physics to Testing Materials. LC 65-19687. (American Society for Testing & Materials Special Technical Publication Ser.: Special Technical Publication, No. 373). 141p. reprint ed. pap. 43.80 (*0-8357-5658-0*, 200073900040) Bks Demand.
— Applications of Modern Metallographic Techniques. LC 78-114749. (American Society for Testing & Materials Special Technical Publication Ser.: No. 480). 280p. reprint ed. pap. 86.80 (*0-8357-5669-6*, 201659400002) Bks Demand.
— Aspects of Lubricant Oxidation: A Symposium. Stadmiller, W. H. & Smith, Andrew N., eds. LC 86-22314. (ASTM Special Technical Publication: No. 916). 88p. reprint ed. pap. 30.00 (*0-7837-4798-5*, 204483900003) Bks Demand.
— ASTM & Other Specifications & Classifications for Petroleum Products & Lubricants: Fuels & Oils, Bituminous Materials, Solvents. LC 89-6452. 505p. reprint ed. pap. 156.60 (*0-7837-5979-7*, 204578300007) Bks Demand.
— ASTM Fire Test Standards. 3rd ed. LC 90-34084. (Illus.). 904p. reprint ed. pap. 200.00 (*0-7837-6055-8*, 204586800008) Bks Demand.
— ASTM Specifications for Carbon & Alloy Steel Plates for Pressure Vessels: (Excluding Corrosion Resisting Steel Plates) LC TA0492.P7A64. 186p. reprint ed. pap. 57.70 (*0-8357-6029-4*, 203443400089) Bks Demand.
— ASTM Specifications for Structural Steel. LC TA0404.5.A42. 234p. reprint ed. pap. 72.60 (*0-8357-5812-5*, 202399100035) Bks Demand.

***American Society for Testing & Materials Staff.** ASTM Standard Test Methods on Total Organ [i.e. Organic] Carbon in Water. LC 99-16725. 1999. write for info. (*0-8031-2723-5*) ASTM.

American Society for Testing & Materials Staff. ASTM Standards for Maintenance Repair & Operations in the Chemical Process Industry. 2nd ed. LC 96-44770. 1996. 125.50 (*0-8031-1827-9*, CHEMPRD) ASTM.
— ASTM Standards in Building Codes: Specifications, Test Methods, Practices, Classifications, Terminology, 4 vols., Vol. 1. 28th ed. LC 83-641658. 1850p. reprint ed. pap. 200.00 (*0-7837-4880-9*, 204483400001) Bks Demand.
— ASTM Standards in Building Codes: Specifications, Test Methods, Practices, Classifications, Terminology, 4 vols., Vol. 2. 28th ed. LC 83-641658. 1955p. reprint ed. pap. 200.00 (*0-7837-4881-7*, 204483400002) Bks Demand.
— ASTM Standards in Building Codes: Specifications, Test Methods, Practices, Classifications, Terminology, 4 vols., Vol. 3. 28th ed. LC 83-641658. 1950p. reprint ed. pap. 200.00 (*0-7837-4882-5*, 204483400003) Bks Demand.
— ASTM Standards in Building Codes: Specifications, Test Methods, Practices, Classifications, Terminology, 4 vols., Vol. 4. 28th ed. LC 83-641658. 1792p. reprint ed. pap. 200.00 (*0-7837-4883-3*, 204483400004) Bks Demand.
— ASTM Standards on Building Economics. LC 90-295. (Illus.). 68p. 1990. reprint ed. pap. 30.00 (*0-7837-4704-7*, 204485100003) Bks Demand.
— ASTM Standards on Chromatography: Gas Chromatography, Liquid Chromatography, Thin-Layer Chromatography, Steric Exclusion Chromatography. LC 40-10712. 772p. reprint ed. pap. 200.00 (*0-8357-5815-X*, 202916300058) Bks Demand.
— ASTM Standards on Color & Appearance Measurement. 2nd ed. LC 83-641658. 359p. 1987. reprint ed. pap. 111.30 (*0-7837-4705-5*, 204484500003) Bks Demand.

***American Society for Testing & Materials Staff.** ASTM Standards on Design, Planning & Reporting of Ground Water & Vadose Zone Investigations. 2nd ed. LC 99-35329. 1999. write for info. (*0-8031-2719-7*) ASTM.

American Society for Testing & Materials Staff. ASTM Standards on Electrical Protective Equipment for Workers. 8th ed. LC 91-22201. 140p. reprint ed. pap. 43.40 (*0-7837-5980-0*, 204578400007) Bks Demand.
— ASTM Standards on Fasteners. LC 78-108362. 336p. reprint ed. pap. 104.20 (*0-8357-5816-8*, 201550900094) Bks Demand.
— ASTM Standards on Gaskets. 3rd ed. LC 83-641658. 107p. reprint ed. pap. 33.20 (*0-8357-5817-6*, 203194600077) Bks Demand.
— ASTM Standards on Geosynthetics. LC 91-148. (Illus.). 111p. reprint ed. pap. 34.50 (*0-7837-6095-7*, 205914100007) Bks Demand.
— ASTM Standards on Geosynthetics. 3rd ed. LC 92-46796. (Illus.). 138p. 1993. reprint ed. pap. 42.80 (*0-608-01627-6*, 206221200002) Bks Demand.
— ASTM Standards on Ground Water & Vadose Zone Investigations. LC 92-16915. (Illus.). 174p. reprint ed. pap. 54.00 (*0-7837-6293-3*, 204600800010) Bks Demand.

***American Society for Testing & Materials Staff.** Astm Standards on Ground Water & Vadose Zone Investigations: Drilling, Sampling, Geophysical Logging, Well Installation & Decommissioning. 2nd ed. LC 99-36979. 1999. write for info. (*0-8031-2718-9*) ASTM.

American Society for Testing & Materials Staff. ASTM Standards on Lead in & Around Buildings. LC 98-27928. 226p. 1998. pap. 79.00 (*0-8031-2590-9*, LEAD1) ASTM.
— ASTM Standards on Manufactured Carbon & Graphite Products, 1981. LC TP0245.C4A5. (Illus.). 94p. reprint ed. pap. 30.00 (*0-8357-6877-5*, 205231700095) Bks Demand.
— ASTM Standards on Masonry. LC 89-18301. 200p. 1990. reprint ed. pap. 62.00 (*0-7837-4797-7*, 204483800003) Bks Demand.
— ASTM Standards on Materials & Environmental Microbiology. LC 87-27054. (Illus.). 313p. reprint ed. pap. 97.10 (*0-7837-4786-1*, 204482300003) Bks Demand.
— ASTM Standards on Soil Compaction. LC 91-36474. 179p. reprint ed. pap. 55.50 (*0-7837-5978-9*, 204578200007) Bks Demand.
— ASTM Standards on Technical Aspects of Products Liability Litigation. LC 83-641658. 18p. reprint ed. pap. 30.00 (*0-8357-5818-4*, 203194500077) Bks Demand.
— ASTM Standards Related to Materials, Systems & Testing for Roofing & Waterproofing. LC 99-34576. 1999. write for info. (*0-8031-2716-2*) ASTM.
— ASTM Standards Related to Ready Mixed Concrete. LC 98-2736. 178p. 1998. 49.00 (*0-8031-2587-9*, CONCRETE) ASTM.
— ASTM Standards Related to Stitches & Seams. LC 98-3269. 1998. 45.00 (*0-8031-2588-7*, STITCHES) ASTM.
— ASTM Viscosity Index Calculated from Kinematic Viscosity. LC 65-24834. No. DS 39a. 959p. reprint ed. pap. 200.00 (*0-8357-5819-2*, 201995200015) Bks Demand.
— Basic Principles of Sensory Evaluation: Sponsored by Committee E-18 on Sensory Evaluation of Materials & Products. LC 68-15548. (ASTM Special Technical Publication: No. 433). (Illus.). 112p. reprint ed. pap. 34.80 (*0-7837-4417-X*, 204416100012) Bks Demand.
— Cleaning Stainless Steel: A Symposium. LC 73-80188. (American Society for Testing & Materials Special Technical Publication Ser.: 538). (Illus.). 238p. reprint ed. pap. 73.80 (*0-608-11469-3*, 200906800072) Bks Demand.
— Compaction of Soils. LC 65-18214. (American Society for Testing & Materials Special Technical Publication Ser.: Special Technical Publication, No. 377). 141p. reprint ed. pap. 43.80 (*0-608-11599-1*, 200073400040) Bks Demand.
— Compilation & Index of Trade Names, Specifications & Producers of Stainless Alloys & Superalloys. LC 72-91409. (ASTM Data Ser.: Vol. DS45A). 57p. reprint ed. pap. 25.00 (*0-608-31719-5*, 2019652) Bks Demand.
— Composite Materials: Fatigue & Fracture: A Symposium, Vol. 1. LC 86-3509. (ASTM Special Technical Publication: No. 907). (Illus.). 404p. reprint ed. pap. 125.30 (*0-7837-4788-8*, 204482500001) Bks Demand.
— Composite Materials: Testing & Design (4th Conference)-a Conference Sponsored by ASTM, Valley Forge, Pa., 3-4 May 1976. LC 76-40796. (American Society for Testing & Materials Special Technical Publication Ser.: No. 617). 540p. reprint ed. pap. 167.40 (*0-608-14115-1*, 202429500036) Bks Demand.
— Corrosion of Metals under Thermal Insulation: A Symposium Sponsored by ASTM Committees C-16 on Thermal Insulation. Pollock, Warren I. & Barnhart, Jack M., eds. LC 85-10616. (ASTM Special Technical Publication: No. 880). (Illus.). 250p. reprint ed. pap. 77.50 (*0-7837-6360-3*, 204607200010) Bks Demand.
— Cyclic Stress-Strain Behavior: Analysis, Experimentation & Failure Prediction Symposium Sponsored by ASTM Committee E-9 Bal Harbour, FL. LC TA0401.3.C92. (ASTM Special Technical Publication: 519). 289p. reprint ed. pap. 89.60 (*0-608-15317-6*, 205633200060) Bks Demand.
— Definitions for Asbestos & Other Health-Related Silicates: A Symposium. Levadie, Benjamin, ed. LC 83-72557. (ASTM Special Technical Publication Ser.: No. 834). (Illus.). 221p. reprint ed. pap. 68.60 (*0-7837-4790-X*, 204482700003) Bks Demand.
— Determination of Nonmetallic Compounds in Steel: A Symposium. LC 66-12290. (American Society for Testing & Materials Special Technical Publication Ser.: No. 393). 103p. reprint ed. pap. 32.00 (*0-608-10768-9*, 200096700050) Bks Demand.
— Directory of Testing Laboratories, Commercial-Institutional. LC 82-71209. (ASTM Special Technical Publication: No. 333E). 194p. reprint ed. pap. 60.20 (*0-8357-6822-8*, 203550400095) Bks Demand.
— Directory of Testing Laboratories, 1988. LC TA0416.. 266p. reprint ed. pap. 82.50 (*0-8357-6821-X*, 203550300095) Bks Demand.
— Directory of Testing Laboratories, 1991. LC 88-659052. 374p. reprint ed. pap. 116.00 (*0-7837-4796-9*, 204483700003) Bks Demand.
— Effects of High-Energy Radiation on Inorganic Substances: A Symposium. LC 66-21923. (American Society for Testing & Materials Special Technical Publication Ser.: No. 400). 176p. reprint ed. pap. 54.60 (*0-608-10775-1*, 200093700050) Bks Demand.
— Electron Fractography: A Symposium Presented At the 70th Annual Meeting, American Society for Testing & Materials, Boston, Mass., 25-30 June 1967. LC 68-15547. (ASTM Special Technical Publication: No. 436). 236p. reprint ed. pap. 73.20 (*0-608-14332-4*, 201659300002) Bks Demand.
— Erosion by Cavitation or Impingement: A Symposium. LC 67-12411. (American Society for Testing & Materials Special Technical Publication Ser.: No. 408). 292p. reprint ed. pap. 90.60 (*0-608-11763-3*, 200097500051) Bks Demand.
— Evaluation of Relative Density & Its Role in Geotechnical Projects Involving Cohesionless Soils. Selig, E. T. & Ladd, R. S., eds. LC 72-90704. (ASTM Special Technical Publication: No. 523). 516p. reprint ed. pap. 160.00 (*0-608-12577-6*, 202398900035) Bks Demand.
— Fatigue Crack Propagation. LC 67-14532. (Special Technical Publication: No. 415). 552p. reprint ed. pap. 171.20 (*0-608-11766-8*, 200112500063) Bks Demand.
— Fatigue of Compacted Bituminous Aggregate Mixtures: A Symposium Presented at the Seventy-Fourth Annual Meeting, ASTM, Atlantic City, NJ, 27 June-2 July 1971. LC 70-189383. (ASTM Special Technical Publication: No. 508). (Illus.). 179p. reprint ed. pap. 55.50 (*0-608-17944-2*, 202916200058) Bks Demand.
— Fifty Years of Progress in Metallographic Techniques. LC 67-26105. (American Society for Testing & Materials Special Technical Publication Ser.: 430). 415p. reprint ed. pap. 128.70 (*0-608-11162-7*, 200087600049) Bks Demand.
— Fire Risk Assessment: A Symposium. Castino, G. T. & Harmathy, Tibor Z., eds. LC 81-68807. (ASTM Special Technical Publication: No. 762). 111p. reprint ed. pap. 34.50 (*0-608-12578-4*, 202399000035) Bks Demand.
— First Supplement to Molecular Formula List of Compounds, Names, & References to Published Infrared Spectra: Indexed by the Wyanadotte-ASTM (Kuentzel) Punched-Card Index. LC Z 7144.S7A53. (ASTM Special Technical Publication: No. 331-A). 116p. pap. 36.00 (*0-608-15554-3*, 205638100062) Bks Demand.
— Flow & Fracture of Metals & Alloys in Nuclear Environments. LC 65-16810. No. 380. 477p. reprint ed. pap. 136.00 (*0-317-08035-0*, 2000740) Bks Demand.
— Fracture Toughness Testing & Its Applications: A Symposium Presented at the Sixty-Seventh Annual Meeting , American Society for Testing & Materials, Chicago, Ill., 1964. LC 65-16811. No. 381. 423p. reprint ed. pap. 120.60 (*0-317-08197-7*, 2015506) Bks Demand.
— Galvanic & Pitting Corrosion - Field & Laboratory Studies: Two Symposia Presented at the 1974 Materials Engineering Congress, ASTM, Detroit, MI., 22-23 Oct. 1974. LC 75-2510. (ASTM Special Technical Publication: No. 576). 318p. reprint ed. pap. 98.60 (*0-608-15789-9*, 203102700073) Bks Demand.
— Handbook of Vapor Degreasing. LC 76-1382. (ASTM Special Technical Publication: No. 310A). 63p. reprint ed. pap. 30.00 (*0-608-12574-1*, 202398600035) Bks Demand.
— Hot Corrosion Problems Associated with Gas Turbines. LC 67-17473. (American Society for Testing & Materials Special Technical Publication Ser.: No. 421).. 303p. reprint ed. pap. 94.00 (*0-608-11563-0*, 200112300063) Bks Demand.
— Hydraulic System Cleanliness: A Symposium Presented At the 73rd Annual Meeting American Society for Testing & Materials, Toronto, Ont., Canada, 21-26 June 1970. LC 70-151113. (American Society for Testing & Materials Special Technical Publication Ser.: No. 491). 89p. reprint ed. pap. 30.00 (*0-608-14116-X*, 202429400036) Bks Demand.
— Hydrogen Embrittlement Testing: A Symposium Presented at the Seventy-Fifth Annual Meeting, American Society for Testing & Materials, Los Angeles, CA, 25-30 June 1972. LC 73-87352. (Illus.). 280p. reprint ed. pap. 86.80 (*0-7837-0985-4*, 204129100019) Bks Demand.
— The Influence of State of Stress on Low-Cycle Fatigue of Structural Materials: A Literature Survey & Interpretive Report. LC 73-90274. (ASTM Special Technical Publication: No. 549). (Illus.). 52p. reprint ed. pap. 30.00 (*0-7837-5976-2*, 204578000007) Bks Demand.
— Instrumentation for Monitoring Air Quality: A Symposium. LC 74-76066. (ASTM Special Technical Publication: No. 555). 200p. reprint ed. pap. 62.00 (*0-608-17777-6*, 205656600074) Bks Demand.

***American Society for Testing & Materials Staff.** ISO/IEC Selected Standards for Testing Plastics. 2nd ed. LC 99-46703. 1999. write for info. (*0-8031-2726-X*) ASTM.

American Society for Testing & Materials Staff. Laser Induced Damage in Optical Materials, 1976: Proceedings of a Symposium. Glass, Alexander J. & Guenther, Arthur H., eds. LC 76-600074. (ASTM Special Technical Publication: No. 622). 412p. reprint ed. pap. 127.80 (*0-608-13150-4*, 201551000094) Bks Demand.
— Low Cycle Fatigue: A Symposium. LC 87-23714. 1306p. reprint ed. pap. 200.00 (*0-7837-5975-4*, 204577900007) Bks Demand.
— Manual of Industrial Corrosion Standards & Control. Cocks, F. H., ed. LC 73-75375. (ASTM Special Technical Publication: No. 534). 308p. reprint ed. pap. 95.50 (*0-608-15315-X*, 205633100060) Bks Demand.
— Manual on Hydrocarbon Analysis. Drews, A. W., ed. LC 88-37542. (ASTM Data Ser.: MNL 3). (Illus.). 854p. reprint ed. pap. 200.00 (*0-7837-4794-2*, 204483500003) Bks Demand.
— Manual on Industrial Water & Industrial Waste Water. 2nd ed. LC 67-4371. 148-I. 1007p. reprint ed. pap. 180.00 (*0-317-10882-4*, 2000636) Bks Demand.
— Manual on Low Cycle Fatigue Testing. LC 70-97730. (ASTM Special Technical Publication: No. 465). 210p. reprint ed. pap. 65.10 (*0-608-12575-X*, 202398700035) Bks Demand.
— Manual on Sensory Testing Methods. LC 68-15545. (ASTM Special Technical Publication: No. 434). 84p. reprint ed. pap. 30.00 (*0-7837-4702-0*, 204484900003) Bks Demand.
— Manual on Test Sieving Methods: Guidelines for Establishing Sieve Analysis Procedures. LC 69-17122. (ASTM Special Technical Publication: No. 447A). 49p. reprint ed. pap. 30.00 (*0-608-16278-7*, 202666500051) Bks Demand.
— Manual on the Use of Thermocouples in Temperature Measurement. 3rd ed. LC 80-69066. (ASTM Special Technical Publication: Vol. 470B). (Illus.). 276p. 1981. reprint ed. pap. 85.60 (*0-7837-8943-2*, 204965400002) Bks Demand.
— Manual on Water. 4th ed. Hamilton, C. E., ed. LC 78-51579. (ASTM Special Technical Publication: No. 442A). 480p. reprint ed. pap. 148.80 (*0-7837-6484-7*, 204651100001) Bks Demand.
— Mass Spectrometric Characterization of Shale Oils. LC 86-1203. (ASTM Special Technical Publication: No. 902). (Illus.). 155p. reprint ed. pap. 48.10 (*0-7837-5977-0*, 204578100007) Bks Demand.
— Measurement of Dielectric Properties under Space Conditions. LC 67-17472. No. 420. 106p. reprint ed. pap. 30.30 (*0-317-08047-4*, 2001119) Bks Demand.
— The Microstructure of Bronze Sinterings. LC 62-20903. (American Society for Testing & Materials Special Technical Publication Ser.: Special Technical Publication, No. 323). 11p. reprint ed. pap. 30.00 (*0-608-11478-2*, 200013000025) Bks Demand.
— Orientation Effects in the Mechanical Behavior of Anisotropic Structural Materials. LC 66-29104. (American Society for Testing & Materials Special Technical Publication Ser.: Special Technical Publication, No. 405). 97p. reprint ed. pap. 30.10 (*0-608-11589-4*, 200070300039) Bks Demand.

A

— Paint Testing Manual: Physical & Chemical Examination of Paints, Varnishes, Lacquers & Colors. 13th ed. Sward, G. G., ed. LC 75-186850. (ASTM Special Technical Publication: No. 500). 612p. reprint ed. pap. 189.80 (*0-608-12023-5*, 202283500030) Bks Demand.
— Papers on Industrial Water & Industrial Waste. LC 63-12705. (American Society for Testing & Materials Special Technical Publication Ser.: No. 337). 77p. reprint ed. pap. 30.00 (*0-608-10791-3*, 200014300025) Bks Demand.
— Performance Testing of Shipping Containers - Sponsored by ASTM Committee D-10 on Packaging. LC 83-641658. 244p. reprint ed. pap. 75.70 (*0-608-15556-X*, 205638400064) Bks Demand.
— Physical Constants of Hydrocarbons CO to CON. LC 79-170766. (ASTM Data Ser.: No. DS 4A). 76p. reprint ed. pap. 30.00 (*0-8357-4126-5*, 205706100005) Bks Demand.
— Plane Strain Crack Toughness: Testing of High Strength Metallic Materials. LC 66-29517. No. 410. 136p. reprint ed. pap. 38.80 (*0-317-08331-7*, 2051707) Bks Demand.
— Progress in Flaw Growth & Fracture Toughness Testing: Proceedings of the 1972 National Symposium on Fracture Mechanics, Philadelphia, PA, 28-30, 1972. LC 73-76198. (American Society for Testing & Materials Special Technical Publication Ser.: No. 536). 501p. reprint ed. pap. 155.40 (*0-608-11427-8*, 202254600028) Bks Demand.
— Radiation Effects in Electronics. LC 65-18216. No. 384. 243p. reprint ed. pap. 69.30 (*0-317-08042-3*, 2000743) Bks Demand.
— Recent Advances in Composites in the United States & Japan: A Symposium. Vinson, Jack R. & Taya, Minoru, eds. LC 85-6119. (ASTM Special Technical Publication: No. 864). (Illus.). 739p. reprint ed. pap. 200.00 (*0-7837-4787-X*, 204482400003) Bks Demand.
— Sealant Technology in Glazing Systems: A Symposium. LC 77-83433. (ASTM Special Technical Publication: 638). 116p. reprint ed. pap. 36.00 (*0-608-12040-5*, 202251600030) Bks Demand.
— Selected ASTM Standards for Fence Materials & Products. 4th ed. LC 88-22152. 178p. 1988. reprint ed. pap. 55.20 (*0-8357-2582-0*, 204027600015) Bks Demand.
— Selected ASTM Standards on Packaging. LC 40-10712. (Illus.). 239p. 1984. reprint ed. pap. 74.10 (*0-608-15590-X*, 202966000062) Bks Demand.
— Selected ASTM Standards on Packaging. 2nd ed. LC TS0195.6.S46. (Illus.). 223p. 1987. reprint ed. pap. 69.20 (*0-8357-3058-1*, 203931400011) Bks Demand.
— Skid Resistance of Highway Pavements. LC 72-97870. (American Society for Testing & Materials Special Technical Publication Ser.: No. 530). 165p. reprint ed. pap. 51.20 (*0-608-11716-1*, 201643800004) Bks Demand.
— Some Fundamentals of Analytical Chemistry: A Symposium Presented at the Seventy-Sixth Annual Meeting, American Society for Testing & Materials. LC 74-81159. (American Society for Testing & Materials Special Technical Publication Ser.: No. 564). (Illus.). 87p. reprint ed. pap. 30.00 (*0-608-30006-3*, 201550700094) Bks Demand.
— Space Radiation Effects. LC 64-14650. (American Society for Testing & Materials Special Technical Publication Ser.: Special Technical Publication, No. 363). 165p. reprint ed. pap. 51.20 (*0-608-11758-7*, 200075300040) Bks Demand.
— Special Procedures for Testing Soil & Rock for Engineering Purposes. 5th ed. LC 70-114701. (ASTM Special Technical Publication: No. 479). 641p. reprint ed. pap. 198.80 (*0-608-15312-5*, 205632900060) Bks Demand.
— Specifications for Carbon & Alloy-Steel Plates for Pressure Vessels. LC TS0283.. 186p. reprint ed. pap. 57.70 (*0-608-13631-X*, 201912500011) Bks Demand.
— Standard Practice for Use of the International System of Units (SI) The Modernized Metric System. LC QC0094.S72. (ASTM Data Ser.: E 380-91a). 37p. reprint ed. pap. 30.00 (*0-7837-4703-9*, 204485000003) Bks Demand.

***American Society for Testing & Materials Staff.** Standards on Indoor Air Quality. LC 99-48393. 1999. write for info. (*0-8031-2728-6*) ASTM.

American Society for Testing & Materials Staff. Steel Forgings, Vol. 2. Nisbett, Edward G. & Melilli, Albert S., eds. LC 97-26639. (STP 1259 Ser.). (Illus.). 375p. 1997. text 69.00 (*0-8031-2423-6*, STP1259) ASTM.
— Stress Corrosion Cracking: The Slow Strain-Rate Technique, a Symposium. Ugiansky, Gilbert M. & Payer, J. H., eds. LC 78-68418. (ASTM Special Technical Publication: No. 665). (Illus.). 452p. pap. 117.50 (*0-608-17401-7*, 2056403) Bks Demand.
— Stress Corrosion Cracking - The Slow Strain-Rate Technique. Uglansky, Gilbert M. & Payer, J. H., eds. LC 78-68418. (ASTM Special Technical Publication: No. 665). (Illus.). 452p. 1979. reprint ed. pap. 140.20 (*0-608-10337-3*, 203550900095) Bks Demand.
— Stress Corrosion Testing. LC 67-20038. (American Society for Testing & Materials Special Technical Publication Ser.: Special Technical Publication, No. 425). 388p. reprint ed. pap. 120.30 (*0-608-11772-2*, 200114400064) Bks Demand.
— Structural Fatigue in Aircraft. LC 66-28344. No. 404. 207p. reprint ed. pap. 59.00 (*0-317-09263-4*, 2001130) Bks Demand.
— Structure & Properties of Ultrahigh-Strength Steels. LC 65-19686. (American Society for Testing & Materials Special Technical Publication Ser.: Special Technical Publication, No. 370). 227p. reprint ed. pap. 70.40 (*0-608-11755-2*, 200074100040) Bks Demand.
— Symposium on Cleaning & Materials Processing for Electronics & Space Apparatus. LC 63-15794. No. 342. 273p. reprint ed. pap. 77.90 (*0-317-08016-4*, 2000138) Bks Demand.
— Symposium on Dynamic Behavior of Materials. LC 63-20729. (American Society for Testing & Materials Special Technical Publication Ser.: No. 336). 323p. reprint ed. pap. 100.20 (*0-608-11522-3*, 200014400025) Bks Demand.
— Symposium on Fatigue Tests of Aircraft Structures: Low-Cycle, Full-Scale, & Helicopters. LC 63-15793. No. 338. 279p. reprint ed. pap. 79.60 (*0-317-09223-5*, 2000142) Bks Demand.
— Symposium on Lubricants for Automotive Equipment. LC 63-15729. No. 334. 259p. reprint ed. pap. 73.90 (*0-317-09152-2*, 2000122) Bks Demand.
— Symposium on Materials for Aircraft, Missiles, & Space Vehicles. LC 63-20730. 345. 149p. reprint ed. pap. 42.50 (*0-317-09214-6*, 2000136) Bks Demand.
— Symposium on Radiation Effects on Metals & Neutron Dosimetry. LC 63-12698. (American Society for Testing & Materials Special Technical Publication Ser.: Special Technical Publication, No. 341). 415p. reprint ed. pap. 128.70 (*0-608-11532-0*, 200013900025) Bks Demand.
— Symposium on Recent Developments in Nondestructive Testing of Missiles & Rockets. No. 350. 121p. reprint ed. pap. 34.50 (*0-317-09141-7*, 2000116) Bks Demand.
— Symposium on Spectrochemical Analysis for Trace Elements. LC 58-3176. (American Society for Testing & Materials Special Technical Publication Ser.: No. 221). 85p. reprint ed. pap. 30.00 (*0-608-10787-5*, 200011200028) Bks Demand.
— Symposium on Spectroscopy. LC 60-9523. No. 269. 251p. reprint ed. pap. 71.60 (*0-317-09560-9*, 2000106) Bks Demand.
— Symposium on Standards for Filament-Wound Reinforced Plastics. LC 62-22246. (American Society for Testing & Materials Special Technical Publication Ser.: Special Technical Publication, No. 327). 336p. reprint ed. pap. 104.20 (*0-608-11474-X*, 200012000025) Bks Demand.
— Symposium on Stress-Strain-Time-Temperature Relationships in Materials. LC 62-22248. (American Society for Testing & Materials Special Technical Publication Ser.: Special Publication, No. 325). 135p. reprint ed. pap. 41.90 (*0-608-11510-X*, 200013300025) Bks Demand.
— Symposium on the Chemical & Physical Effects of High-Energy Radiation on Inorganic Substances. LC 64-14646. (American Society for Testing & Materials Special Technical Publication Ser.: No. 359). 119p. reprint ed. pap. 36.90 (*0-608-10777-8*, 200074800040) Bks Demand.
— Techniques of Electron Microscopy, Diffraction, & Microprobe Analysis. No. 372. 95p. reprint ed. pap. 27.10 (*0-317-09550-1*, 2000730) Bks Demand.
— Temper Embrittlement of Alloy Steels: A Symposium Presented at the Seventy-Fourth Annual Meeting, American Society for Testing & Materials. LC 73-185535. (American Society for Testing & Materials Special Technical Publication Ser.: No. 499). 141p. reprint ed. pap. 43.80 (*0-608-11178-3*, 201550400094) Bks Demand.
— Testing for Prediction of Material Performance in Structures & Components: A Symposium. Presented at the Annual Meeting, American Society & Materials. LC 72-79572. No.515. 319p. reprint ed. pap. 91.00 (*0-317-08194-2*, 2015505) Bks Demand.
— Testing of Peats & Organic Soils: A Symposium - Sponsored by ASTM Committee D-18 on Soil & Rock, Toronto, Canada, 23 June 1982. Jarrett, P. M., ed. LC 83-70259. (ASTM Special Technical Publication: No. 820). (Illus.). 249p. reprint ed. pap. 77.20 (*0-8357-3565-6*, 203426900089) Bks Demand.
— Testing Techniques for Rock Mechanics. LC 66-24783. (American Society for Testing & Materials Special Technical Publication Ser.: Special Technical Publication, No. 402). 304p. reprint ed. pap. 94.30 (*0-608-11768-4*, 200112900063) Bks Demand.
— Underwater Soil Sampling, Testing, & Construction Control: A Symposium Presented at the Seventy-Fourth Annual Meeting, American Society for Testing & Materials, Atlantic City, 1971. LC 77-185536. (ASTM Special Technical Publication: 501). 247p. reprint ed. pap. 76.60 (*0-608-12576-8*, 202398800035) Bks Demand.
— Unified Numbering System for Metals & Alloys: And Cross Index of Chemically-Similar Specification - A Joint Activity of the Society of Automotive Engineers, American Society for Testing & Materials. LC 77-89064. (American Society for Testing & Materials Special Technical Publication Ser.: No. DS-56A). 288p. reprint ed. pap. 89.30 (*0-608-14114-3*, 202429600036) Bks Demand.
— Unified Numbering System Covered by UNS Numbers, July, 1974. LC 75-309848. 186p. reprint ed. pap. 57.70 (*0-608-11777-3*, 202152500022) Bks Demand.
— Water Quality Criteria. LC 67-14533. (American Society for Testing & Materials Special Technical Publication Ser.: 416). 127p. reprint ed. pap. 39.40 (*0-608-11561-4*, 200070700039) Bks Demand.
— X-Ray & Optical Emission Analysis of High-Temperature Alloys: A Symposium. LC 65-18213. (American Society for Testing & Materials Special Technical Publication Ser.: No. 376). 52p. reprint ed. pap. 30.00 (*0-608-10783-2*, 200085100048) Bks Demand.

American Society for Testing & Materials Staff & ASTM Committee D-10 on Packaging Staff. Selected Standards on Packaging 5th ed. LC 99-22712. 1999. write for info. (*0-8031-2713-8*) ASTM.

American Society for Testing & Materials Staff & ASTM Special Technical Publication Staff, Jr. Bearing Steels: Into the 21st Century. Hoo, Joseph J. & Green, Williard B., eds. LC 98-6575. (STP Ser.: Vol. 1327). (Illus.). 525p. 1998. text 89.00 (*0-8031-2421-X*, STP1327) ASTM.

***American Society for Testing & Materials Staff & ASTM Subcommittee D20.96 on Environmentally Degradable Plastics Staff.** Standards Pertaining to the Biodegradability & Compostability of Plastics. LC 99-35158. 1999. write for info. (*0-8031-2720-0*) ASTM.

American Society for Testing & Materials Staff & National Association of Corrosion Engineers Staff. ASTM & NACE Standards Related to Underground Storage Tanks. LC 98-44343. 171p. 1998. write for info. (*0-8031-2596-8*) ASTM.

American Society for Testing & Materials Staff & Society of Automotive Engineers Staff. Metals & Alloys in the Unified Numbering System: With A Description of the System & a Cross Index of Chemically Similar Specifications a Joint Activity of the Society of Automotive Engineers, & ASTM. 3rd ed. LC 84-108328. (ASTM Data Ser.: No. 56B). 364p. reprint ed. pap. 112.90 (*0-608-15328-1*, 205633400060) Bks Demand.

American Society for Testing & Materials Staff & Wilson, M. A. Nondestructive Rapid Identification of Metals & Alloys by Spot Test. LC 73-90275. 550. 60p. reprint ed. pap. 25.00 (*0-317-08730-4*, 2006068) Bks Demand.

American Society for Testing & Materials Staff, et al. ASTM Standards on Masonry. 3rd ed. LC 96-54485. 1997. write for info. (*0-8031-1832-5*, MASONRY97) ASTM.
— Exterior Insulation Finish Systems (EIFS) Materials, Properties & Performance, STP 1269. 2nd ed. Nelson, Peter E. & Kroll, Richard E., eds. LC 96-45102. (STP Ser.). (Illus.). 215p. 1996. text 49.00 (*0-8031-2040-0*, STP1269) ASTM.
— Fatigue at Elevated Temperatures. Carden, A. E., ed. LC 73-76958. (American Society for Testing & Materials Special Technical Publication Ser.: 520). (Illus.). 811p. reprint ed. pap. 200.00 (*0-608-11650-5*, 200640800058) Bks Demand.

American Society for Testing & Materials Staff, jt. auth. see Raymond, Louis.

American Society for Testing & Materials Staff, jt. auth. see Staub, Hal.

American Society for Testing Materials Staff. ASTM Painting Inspection Standards for Field or Shop Applications. LC 94-21809. 1994. 54.00 (*0-8031-1797-3*, FIELD) ASTM.
— ASTM Standards on Environmental Sampling. 2nd ed. LC 97-15930. 1997. write for info. (*0-8031-1835-X*, ENVSAMP) ASTM.
— ASTM Standards Related to the Phase II Environmental Site Assessment Process. LC 97-42558. 1998. 99.00 (*0-8031-1848-1*, PHASE2) ASTM.

American Society for the Defense of Tradition, Fam. The Whole Truth about SWAPO: Idealistic Christians & Heroes of Freedom & Justice? or Instruments of International Communist Aggression? LC 84-71115. (Illus.). 66p. (Orig.). (C). 1984. pap. 2.50 (*1-877905-23-2*) Am Soc Defense TFP.

American Society for the Prevention of Cruelty to. Big Cats, Little Cats. (Illus.). 48p. (Orig.). (J). (gr. k-4). 1991. 4.95 (*1-879326-09-4*) Living Planet Pr.

American Society for the Prevention of Cruelty to, jt. auth. see Allan, Ross.

American Society for the Prevention of Cruelty to, jt. auth. see Coborn, John.

American Society for the Prevention of Cruelty to, jt. auth. see Deply, Karl-Herbert.

American Society for the Prevention of Cruelty to, jt. auth. see Field, Mary.

American Society for the Prevention of Cruelty to, jt. auth. see Gardner, J. R.

American Society for the Prevention of Cruelty to, jt. auth. see Gerstenfeld, Sheldon L.

American Society for the Prevention of Cruelty to, jt. auth. see Glass, Spencer.

American Society for the Prevention of Cruelty to, jt. auth. see Kelsey-Wood, Dennis.

American Society for the Prevention of Cruelty to, jt. auth. see Nelson, Chris.

American Society for the Prevention of Cruelty to, jt. auth. see Ovechka, Greg.

American Society for the Prevention of Cruelty to, jt. auth. see Radford, Elaine.

American Society for the Prevention of Cruelty to, jt. auth. see Richards, James R.

American Society for the Prevention of Cruelty to, jt. auth. see Schmidt, Horst.

American Society for the Prevention of Cruelty to, jt. auth. see Smith, J. E.

American Society for the Prevention of Cruelty to, jt. auth. see Smith, R. M.

American Society for the Prevention of Cruelty to, jt. auth. see Van Den Nieuwenhuizen, A.

American Society for Training & Development (ASTD). Quality of Work Life: Perspectives for Business & the Public Sector. Skrovan, Daniel J., ed. 208p. 1983. text. write for info. (*0-201-07755-8*) Addison-Wesley.

American Society for Training & Development Staff. Developing High-Performance Work Teams: Fourteen Case Studies from the Real World of Training. Jones, Steven D. et al, eds. LC 97-78237. (In Action Ser.). 265 p. 1998. pap. 50.00 (*1-56286-079-8*) Am Soc Train & Devel.

American Society for Training & Development Staff, jt. auth. see Alden, Jay.

American Society for Training & Development Staff, jt. auth. see Stadius, Ruth.

American Society for Training and Development Staff. Implementing Evaluation Systems & Processes. Phillips, Jack J., ed. LC 98-74118. (In Action Ser.). 306p. 1998. pap. 50.00 (*1-56286-101-8*) Am Soc Train & Devel.
— Managing the Small Training Staff: Twelve Case Studies from the Real World of Training. McCoy, Carol Prescott & Phillips, Jack J., eds. LC 98-70301. (In Action Ser.). 227 p. 1998. pap. 50.00 (*1-56286-082-8*) Am Soc Train & Devel.

American Society of African Culture Staff. Pan-Africanism Reconsidered. LC 76-3618. 376p. 1976. reprint ed. lib. bdg. 35.00 (*0-8371-8792-3*, ASPA, Greenwood Pr) Greenwood.

American Society of Agricultural Engineers. Drainage Design & Management: Proceedings of the Fifth National Drainage Symposium. LC 87-72844. 440p. 1987. pap. 55.25 (*0-916150-88-7*, P0787) Am Soc Ag Eng.
— John Deere Tractors, 1918 to 1994. rev. ed. LC 87-70256. 86p. (Orig.). 1994. pap. 14.95 (*0-916150-84-4*) Am Soc Ag Eng.
— Latest Developments in Livestock Housing: Proceedings of the Second Technical Section of the CIGR. LC 87-71042. 417p. 1987. pap. 51.00 (*0-916150-87-9*, P0687) Am Soc Ag Eng.

American Society of Agricultural Engineers, compiled by. Microirrigation: A Compilation of Technical Papers. (Illus.). 363p. 1995. pap. 39.50 (*0-929355-63-6*, M0395) Am Soc Ag Eng.

American Society of Agronomy. Division A-6, et al. Replenishing Soil Fertility in Africa: Proceedings of an International Sysmposium Cosponsored by Divisions A-6 (International Agronomy) & S-4 (Soil Fertility & Plant Nutrition), & the International Center for Research in Agroforestry, Held at the 88th Annual Meetings of the American Society of Agronomy & the Soil Science Society of America, Indianapolis, Indiana, 6 November 1996. LC 97-77363. (Illus.). 1997. write for info. (*0-89118-829-0*) Soil Sci Soc Am.

American Society of Appraisers Staff. Appraisal of Farmland: Use-Value Assessment Laws & Property Taxation, No. 8. LC 78-74140. (Monographs). 1979. pap. 5.00 (*0-937828-17-3*) Am Soc Appraisers.

American Society of Architectural Perspectivists S. Architecture in Perspective Vol. 10: 10th Annual International Competition of Architectural Illustration. 144p. 1996. 29.99 (*1-56496-249-0*) Rockport Pubs.
— Architecture in Perspective Six: A Competitive Exhibition of Architectural Delineation. (Illus.). 76p. 1992. pap. 20.00 (*0-442-30889-2*, VNR) Wiley.

American Society of Association Executives Staff. Achieving Excellence in Governance. (Illus.). 76p. 1996. pap. 27.00 (*0-88034-109-2*) Am Soc Assn Execs.

American Society of Association Executives Staff. Achieving Goals. rev. ed. 5p. 1985. pap. text 3.30 (*0-88034-013-4*) Am Soc Assn Execs.
— Assess Your Strengths & Weaknesses: A Workbook for Evaluating Your Association. 70p. (Orig.). 1988. pap. 24.95 (*0-88034-011-8*) Am Soc Assn Execs.
— Association Educator's Toolkit: Your Guide to Developing, Implementing, & Evaluating Association Education Programs. 297p. 1995. pap. 71.95 (*0-88034-101-7*) Am Soc Assn Execs.
— Association Operating Ratio Report. 10th ed. 96p. 1997. pap. 165.00 (*0-88034-128-9*) Am Soc Assn Execs.
— Association Technology Trends, 1997. 175p. 1997. pap. 115.00 (*0-88034-132-7*) Am Soc Assn Execs.
— Attracting, Organizing & Keeping Members. Butler, Wilford A., ed. 188p. (Orig.). 1989. pap. 55.00 (*0-88034-032-0*) Am Soc Assn Execs.
— Finding the Right Format. 404p. 1990. pap. text 38.00 (*0-88034-043-6*) Am Soc Assn Execs.
— HR Quick Forms: A Sourcebook for Association Professionals: User Guide. LC 96-32843. 1996. 125.00 (*0-88034-107-6*) Am Soc Assn Execs.
— Letter Idea Book. 3rd ed. 246p. (Orig.). 1989. pap. 75.00 (*0-88034-034-7*) Am Soc Assn Execs.
— Policies & Procedures in Association Management, 1996. 210p. 1996. pap. 125.00 (*0-88034-108-4*) Am Soc Assn Execs.

American Society of Association Executives Staff & Norris, Donald N. Getting Your Association Hooked on Quality: A How-To Guide & Workbook for CEOs, Volunteers & Staff. (Illus.). ix, 66p. 1993. pap. 66.00 (*0-88034-074-6*) Am Soc Assn Execs.

American Society of Association Executives Staff & Svevo-Cianci, Kimberly A. Associations & the Global Marketplace. 353p. 1995. pap. 55.00 (*0-88034-092-4*) Am Soc Assn Execs.

***American Society of Association Executives Staff, et al.** Facing The Future: A Report on the Trends & Issues Affecting Associations. LC 98-54235. (Illus.). xviii, 130p. 1998. pap. 42.00 (*0-88034-150-5*) Am Soc Assn Execs.

American Society of Association Executives Staff, jt. auth. see Cox, John B.

American Society of Association Executives Staff, jt. auth. see DeLizia, James.

American Society of Association Executives Staff, jt. auth. see Schlegel, John F.

American Society of Brewing Chemists Society Staff. Methods of Analysis of the American Society of Brewing Chemists. 8th rev. ed. LC 92-72143. 586p. 1992. ring bd. 460.00 (*1-881696-01-4*) Am Brewing Chems.

American Society of Civil Engineers. Bearing Capacity of Soils. LC 94-243. (Technical Engineering & Design Guides As Adapted from the U. S. Army Corps of Engineers Ser.: No. 7). 152p. 1994. pap. 35.00 (*0-87262-997-X*, ASCE Press) Am Soc Civil Eng.

An Asterisk (*) at the beginning of an entry indicates that the title is appearing for the first time.

— Earthquake-Actuated Automatic Gas Shutoff Devices. LC 98-41629. (ASCE Standard Ser.). 11p. 1998. 24.00 (*0-7844-0354-6*) Am Soc Civil Eng.

***American Society of Civil Engineers.** Standard Practice for Direct Design of Precast Concrete Box Sections for Jacking in Trenchless Construction. LC 00-40590. (Illus.). 2000. write for info. (*0-7844-0497-6*) Am Soc Civil Eng.

American Society of Civil Engineers, Aero-Space Tr. Space Age Facilities: Papers, Specialty Conference, Cocoa Beach, Fl., November 17-19, 1965. LC 68-23. 398p. reprint ed. pap. 123.40 (*0-608-11602-5*, 200490800047) Bks Demand.

American Society of Civil Engineers, Civil Enginee. High Performance Construction Materials: An Essential National Program for America & Its Infrastructure, 3 vols., Vol. 1: Executive Report. LC 92-45823. 30p. 1993. 43.00 (*0-87262-938-4*) Am Soc Civil Eng.

— High Performance Construction Materials: An Essential National Program for America & Its Infrastructure, 3 vols., Vol. 2: Technical Report. LC 92-45823. 58p. 1993. 107.00 (*0-87262-939-2*) Am Soc Civil Eng.

— High Performance Construction Materials: An Essential National Program for America & Its Infrastructure, 3 vols., Vol. 3: Appendix. LC 92-45823. 1993. write for info. (*0-87262-940-6*) Am Soc Civil Eng.

American Society of Civil Engineers, Committee on. Guide to Employment Conditions for Civil Engineers. 4th ed. LC 94-34407. (Manuals & Reports on Engineering Practice Ser.: Vol. 55). 32p. 1994. 13.00 (*0-7844-0057-1*) Am Soc Civil Eng.

— Hydraulic Design of Reversible Flow Trashracks. LC 93-16936. 130p. 1993. 17.00 (*0-87262-948-1*) Am Soc Civil Eng.

— Hyogo-Ken Nanbu Earthquake of January 17, 1995. Werner, Stuart D. & Dickenson, Stephen E., eds. LC 96-6207. 120p. 1996. pap. 25.00 (*0-7844-0161-6*) Am Soc Civil Eng.

American Society of Civil Engineers, Engineering M. The Relation of Engineering Mechanics Research to the Practice of Civil Engineering: Engineering Mechanics Division Specialty Conference, Washington, D.C., October 12-14, 1966. LC 67-1660. (Illus.). 867p. reprint ed. pap. 200.00 (*0-608-11623-8*, 200490400047) Bks Demand.

American Society of Civil Engineers, Environmental. Radiation Energy Treatment of Water, Wastewater, & Sludge: A State-of-the-Art Report. LC 92-20609. 64p. 1992. pap. text 13.00 (*0-87262-901-5*) Am Soc Civil Eng.

American Society of Civil Engineers, Geotechnical. Serviceability of Earth Retaining Structures: Proceedings of Sessions Sponsored by the Geotechnical Engnering Division of the American Society of Civil Engineers in Conjunction with the ASCE National Convention in Atlanta, Georgia, October 9-13,1994. Finno, Richard J., ed. LC 94-23244. (Geotechnical Special Publications: Vol. 42). 164p. 1994. 22.00 (*0-7844-0051-2*) Am Soc Civil Eng.

American Society of Civil Engineers Geotechnical E. Fracture Mechanics Applied to Geotechnical Engineering: Proceedings of Sessions Sponsored by the Geotechnical Engineering Division of the American Society of Civil Engineers in Conjunctions with the ASCE National Convention in Atlanta, Georgia, October 9-13, 1994. Vallejo, Luis E. & Liang, Robert Y., eds. LC 94-23245. (Geotechnical Special Publications: Vol. 43). 168p. 1994. 26.00 (*0-7844-0056-3*) Am Soc Civil Eng.

— Ground Failures under Seismic Conditions: Proceedings of the Sessions Sponsored by the Geotechnical Engineering Division of the American Civil Engineers in Conjunction with the ASCE National Convention in Atlanta, Georgia, October 9-13, 1994. Prakash, Shamsher & Dakoulas, Panos, eds. LC 94-23246. (Geotechnical Special Publications: Vol. 44). 268p. 1994. 33.00 (*0-7844-0055-5*) Am Soc Civil Eng.

American Society of Civil Engineers, Hydraulics Di. Fundamentals & Advancements in Hydraulic Measurements & Experimentation: Proceedings of the Symposium Sponsored by the Hydraulics Division of the American Society of Civil Engineers, in Cooperation with the Environmental Engineering Division, et al, of the American Society of Civil Engineers. Pugh, Clifford A., ed. LC 94-26048. 552p. 1994. 55.00 (*0-7844-0036-9*) Am Soc Civil Eng.

— Perception, 2001: A Report on Defining the Role of Geo-Engineering in the 21st Century. LC 94-22285. 48p. 1994. 5.00 (*0-7844-0042-3*) Am Soc Civil Eng.

American Society of Civil Engineers, Irrigation &. Age of Changing Priorities for Land & Water: Irrigation & Drainage Division Specialty Conference, Spokane, Washington, September 26-28, 1972. LC 73-155132. 492p. reprint ed. pap. 152.60 (*0-8357-5251-8*, 200786600067) Bks Demand.

— Environmental Aspects of Irrigation & Drainage: Proceedings of Specialty Conference, July 21-23, 1976. LC TC0809.E5. 749p. reprint ed. pap. 200.00 (*0-608-11496-0*, 201645700004) Bks Demand.

American Society of Civil Engineers, Materials Eng. Infrastructure - New Materials & Methods of Repair: Proceedings of the Third Materials Engineering Conference, San Diego, California, November 13-16, 1994. Basham, Kim D., ed. LC 94-24420. 1268p. 1994. 118.00 (*0-7844-0063-6*) Am Soc Civil Eng.

American Society of Civil Engineers, Power Divisio. Electric Power Today & Tomorrow: Conference Papers, Power Division Specialty Conference, Denver, Colorado, August 18-20, 1965. LC 65-6824. 892p. reprint ed. pap. 200.00 (*0-608-11029-9*, 200490500047) Bks Demand.

American Society of Civil Engineers, Special Commi. Letter Symbols & Glossary for Hydraulics: With Special Reference to Irrigation Hydraulics. LC 42-233. (American Society of Civil Engineers Manuals of Engineering Practice Ser.: No. 11). 42p. reprint ed. pap. 30.00 (*0-608-14328-6*, 205200000027) Bks Demand.

American Society of Civil Engineers Staff. Agricultural & Urban Considerations in Irrigation & Drainage: Selected Papers from Specialty Conference, Fort Collins, Colorado, April 22-24. LC TC0803.S6. 808p. reprint ed. pap. 200.00 (*0-8357-5265-8*, 202252000027) Bks Demand.

— Airport Terminal Facilities: ASCE-AOCI Specialty Conference, Houston, Texas. LC TL0725.A4. 335p. reprint ed. pap. 103.90 (*0-8357-5287-9*, 200490900048) Bks Demand.

— Airports: Challenges of the Future. LC 76-371620. 219p. reprint ed. pap. 67.90 (*0-8357-5288-7*, 201011900073) Bks Demand.

— Analysis & Design of Retaining Structures Against Earthquakes: Proceedings of Sessions Sponsored by the Soil Dynamics Committee of the ASCE Geotechnical Engineering Division in Conjunction with the ASCE Convention in Washington, D. C., November 10-14, 1996. Prakash, Shamsher, ed. LC 96-44715. (Geotechnical Special Publications). 88p. 1996. 23.00 (*0-7844-0206-X*) American Society of Geolinguistics.

— Automated People Mover Standards. LC 96-49993. 32p. 1996. pap. text 39.00 (*0-7844-0193-4*) Am Soc Civil Eng.

— Automated People Movers No. II: New Links for Land Use - Automated People Mover Opportunities for Major Activity Centers: Proceedings of the Second International Conference, Miami, Florida, March 13-15, 1989. Bondada, Murthy V. et al, eds. LC 89-17833. 1062p. reprint ed. pap. 200.00 (*0-7837-1473-4*, 205716800020) Bks Demand.

— Award-Winning ASCE Papers in Geotechnical Engineering, 1950-1959: Papers, Discussions, & Closures from ASCE Proceedings, & the Journal of the Soil Mechanics & Foundations Division. LC 77-369726. (Illus.). 819p. reprint ed. pap. 200.00 (*0-8357-5934-2*, 203003800067) Bks Demand.

— Coastal Engineering: Proceedings of 10th Conference, Tokyo, Japan, September, 1966, Vol. 1. LC TC0203.5. 805p. reprint ed. pap. 200.00 (*0-608-08148-5*, 201954500001) Bks Demand.

— Coastal Engineering: Proceedings of 10th Conference, Tokyo, Japan, September, 1966, Vol. 2. LC TC0203.5. 766p. 1967. reprint ed. pap. 200.00 (*0-608-18518-3*, 201954500002) Bks Demand.

— Coastal Structures '79: A Specialty Conference on the Design, Construction Maintenance, & Performance of Port & Coastal Structures, March 14-16, 1979, Alexandria, VA: A Symposium, Vol. 1. LC 79-106948. 648p. 1979. reprint ed. pap. 200.00 (*0-608-08146-9*, 202315900001) Bks Demand.

— Coastal Structures '79: A Specialty Conference on the Design, Construction Maintenance, & Performance of Port & Coastal Structures, March 14-16, 1979, Alexandria, VA: A Symposium, Vol. 2. LC 79-106948. 577p. 1979. reprint ed. pap. 178.90 (*0-608-08147-7*, 202315900002) Bks Demand.

— Computing in Civil Engineering: Conference. LC TA0345.. (Illus.). 863p. reprint ed. pap. 200.00 (*0-608-30738-6*, 201954400013) Bks Demand.

— Construction Congress V: Managing Engineered Construction in Expanding Global Markets: Proceedings of the Congress, Minneapolis, Minnesota, October 5-7, 1997. Anderson, Stuart D., ed. LC 97-31096. (Illus.). 1080p. 1997. pap. text 85.00 (*0-7844-0290-6*, 40290-6) Am Soc Civil Eng.

— Converting Existing Hydro-Electric Dams & Reservoirs into Pumped Storage Facilities: Engineering Foundation Conference, Franklin Pierce College, Rindge, NH, August 18-23, 1974. LC 75-323056. (Illus.). 612p. 1975. reprint ed. pap. 189.80 (*0-608-04429-6*, 205966500012) Bks Demand.

***American Society of Civil Engineers Staff.** Conveyance of Residuals from Water & Wastewater Treatment. LC 99-59471. (Manuals & Reports on Engineering Practice). 2000. write for info. (*0-7844-0438-0*) Am Soc Civil Eng.

American Society of Civil Engineers Staff. Current Geotechnical Practice in Mine Waste Disposal: Papers Collected by the Committee on Embankment Dams & Slopes of the Geotechnical Engineering Division. LC 79-106963. 266p. reprint ed. pap. 82.50 (*0-608-11775-7*, 201954200013) Bks Demand.

— Degradation of Natural Building Stone: Proceedings of 2 Sessions by the Rock Mechanics Committee of the Geo-Institute of the American Society of Civil Engineers in Conjunction with the ASCE Convention in Minneapolis, Minnesota, October 5-8, 1997. Labuz, J. F., ed. LC 97-36205. (Geotechnical Special Publication Ser.: Vol. 72). (Illus.). 140p. 1997. pap. text 21.00 (*0-7844-0279-5*, 40279-5) Am Soc Civil Eng.

— Design & Construction of Steel Chimney Liners. LC 80-475728. 226p. reprint ed. pap. 70.10 (*0-608-13964-5*, 202501700040) Bks Demand.

— Design of Blast Resistant Buildings in Petrochemical Facilities. LC 97-20895. 280p. 1997. 40.00 (*0-7844-0265-5*) Am Soc Civil Eng.

— Design of Guyed Transmission Structures. LC 97-26968. (ASCE Manuals & Reports on Engineering Practice: No. 91). 96p. 1997. 28.00 (*0-7844-0284-1*) Am Soc Civil Eng.

— Design of Hydraulic Steel Structures: Technical Engineering & Design Guide As Adapted from U. S. Army Corps of Engineers. LC 96-45929. (Technical Engineering & Design Guides as Adapted from the U. S. Army Corps of Engineers Ser.: No. 22). 56p. 1997. 24.00 (*0-7844-0212-4*) Am Soc Civil Eng.

— Design of Latticed Steel Transmission Structures. LC 98-41267. (ASCE Standard Ser.). 43p. 1998. 42.00 (*0-7844-0324-4*) Am Soc Civil Eng.

— Design of Water Intake Structures for Fish Protection. LC 81-70988. (Illus.). 175p. 1982. reprint ed. pap. 54.30 (*0-608-17890-X*, 205667300080) Bks Demand.

— Dewatering: Avoiding Its Unwanted Side Effects. Powers, J. Patrick, ed. LC 85-70483. (Illus.). 84p. reprint ed. pap. 30.00 (*0-8357-8676-5*, 205683300091) Bks Demand.

— Earthquake Engineering & Soil Dynamics: Proceedings of the ASCE Geotechnical Engineering Division Specialty Conference, June 19-21, 1978, Pasadena, CA, 3 vols., 1. LC 79-112252. 578p. 1978. reprint ed. pap. 179.20 (*0-608-08173-6*, 202562900001) Bks Demand.

— Earthquake Engineering & Soil Dynamics: Proceedings of the ASCE Geotechnical Engineering Division Specialty Conference, June 19-21, 1978, Pasadena, CA, 3 vols., 2. LC 79-112252. 586p. 1978. reprint ed. pap. 181.70 (*0-608-08174-4*, 202562900002) Bks Demand.

— Earthquake Engineering & Soil Dynamics: Proceedings of the ASCE Geotechnical Engineering Division Specialty Conference, June 19-21, 1978, Pasadena, CA, 3 vols., 3. LC 79-112252. 473p. 1978. reprint ed. pap. 146.70 (*0-608-08175-2*, 202562900003) Bks Demand.

— Engineering & Contracting Procedure for Foundations: Responsibilities of the Contracting Parties. LC 42-229. (American Society of Civil Engineers Manuals of Engineering Practice Ser.: No. 8). 26p. reprint ed. pap. 30.00 (*0-608-30379-8*, 201645000004) Bks Demand.

***American Society of Civil Engineers Staff.** Environmental Site Characterization & Remediation Design Guidance. LC 99-32028. (Manuals & Reports on Engineering Practice). 144p. 1999. 40.00 (*0-7844-0439-9*) Am Soc Civil Eng.

American Society of Civil Engineers Staff. Environmental Site Investigation Guidance Manual. (ASCE Manual & Report on Engineering Practice: Vol. 83). 160p. 1995. 29.00 (*0-7844-0096-2*) Am Soc Civil Eng.

— Flexural Mechanics of Reinforced Concrete: Proceedings of the International Symposium, Miami, Fla., Nov. 10-12, 1964. LC 66-402. (Illus.). 603p. reprint ed. pap. 187.00 (*0-608-11582-7*, 200278800015) Bks Demand.

— The Glossary of the Mapping Sciences. LC 94-30078. 594p. 1994. 80.00 (*1-57083-011-8*, 5021) ASP & RS.

— The Glossary of the Mapping Sciences. LC 94-30078. 592p. 1994. 87.00 (*0-7844-0050-4*) Am Soc Civil Eng.

American Society Of Civil Engineers Staff. Guide to Improved Earthquake Performance of Electric Power Systems. LC 99-20666. (ASCE Manuals & Reports on Engineering Practice Ser.). 368p. 1999. 98.00 (*0-7844-0414-3*) Am Soc Civil Eng.

American Society of Civil Engineers Staff. Guidelines for Inspection & Monitoring of In-Service Penstocks. LC 98-35900. 256p. 1998. 42.00 (*0-7844-0378-3*) Am Soc Civil Eng.

— Guidelines for Retirement of Dams & Hydroelectric Facilities. LC 97-24340. 248p. 1997. 22.00 (*0-7844-0270-1*) Am Soc Civil Eng.

— Guidelines for Seismic Evaluation & Design of Petrochemical Facilities. LC 97-20918. 288p. 1997. 40.00 (*0-7844-0264-7*) Am Soc Civil Eng.

— Guidelines of Engineering Practice for Braced & Tied-Back Excavations. LC 97-36244. (Geotechnical Special Publication Ser.: Vol. 74). (Illus.). 160p. 1997. pap. text 18.00 (*0-7844-0293-0*, 40293-0) Am Soc Civil Eng.

— Hydrology Handbook. 2nd ed. LC 96-41049. (ASCE Manual & Report on Engineering Practice). 832p. 1996. 175.00 (*0-7844-0138-1*) Am Soc Civil Eng.

— In Situ Measurement of Soil Properties: Proceedings of the American Society of Civil Engineers Specialty Conference, North Carolina State University, 1975, Vol. 1. LC TA0710.A73. 560p. reprint ed. pap. 173.60 (*0-608-14682-X*, 205204500001) Bks Demand.

— In Situ Measurement of Soil Properties: Proceedings of the American Society of Civil Engineers Specialty Conference, North Carolina State University, 1975, Vol. 2. LC TA0710.A73. 397p. reprint ed. pap. 123.10 (*0-608-14683-8*, 205204500002) Bks Demand.

— In-Situ Remediation of the Geoenvironment: Proceedings of the Conference Sponsored by the Geo-Institute & the Environmental Engineering Division of the American Society of Civil Engineers, Minneapolis, Minnesota, October 5-8, 1997. Evans, Jeffrey C., ed. LC 97-36206. (Geotechnical Special Publication Ser.). (Illus.). 608p. 1997. pap. text 52.00 (*0-7844-0278-7*, 40278-7) Am Soc Civil Eng.

— Independent Project Peer Review. LC 98-41266. 1998. write for info. (*0-7844-0356-2*) Am Soc Civil Eng.

— Manhole Inspection & Rehabilitation. LC 97-26967. (ASCE Manuals & Reports on Engineering Practice: Vol. 92). (Illus.). 96p. 1997. 39.00 (*0-7844-0285-X*, 40285-X) Am Soc Civil Eng.

— Materials for the New Millennium: Proceedings of the Fourth Materials Engineering Conference, Washington D. C., November 10-14, 1996, 2 vols. Chong, K. P., ed. LC 96-44714. 1776p. 1996. 175.00 (*0-7844-0210-8*) Am Soc Civil Eng.

— Measurement of Oxygen Transfer in Clean Water. 2nd ed. LC 93-9407. 56p. 1993. 34.00 (*0-87262-885-X*) Am Soc Civil Eng.

— Mechanical Connections in Wood Structures. (Manuals & Reports on Engineering Practice: Vol. 84). 248p. 1995. 43.00 (*0-7844-0110-1*) Am Soc Civil Eng.

— Minimum Design Loads for Buildings & Other Structures. LC 94-3854. 134p. 1994. pap. 44.00 (*0-87262-904-X*) N K Gregg.

— Modeling of Flood Propagation over Initially Dry Areas: Proceedings of the Specialty Conference Held in Milan, Italy at ENEL-DSR-CRIS, 29 June - 1 July 1994. Molinaro, Paolo & Natale, Luigi, eds. LC 94-19397. 384p. 1994. 31.00 (*0-7844-0035-0*) Am Soc Civil Eng.

***American Society of Civil Engineers Staff.** Navstar Global Positioning System Surveying. LC 99-41148. (Technical Engineering & Design Guides Ser.). 2000. write for info. (*0-7844-0353-8*) Am Soc Civil Eng.

American Society of Civil Engineers Staff. Pipeline: Materials & Design. Schrock, B. Jay, ed. LC 84-71894. 79p. 1984. reprint ed. pap. 30.00 (*0-608-00801-X*, 205935000011) Bks Demand.

— Pipeline Crossings. LC 96-8562. (Manuals & Reports on Engineering Practice Ser.). 144p. 1996. 39.00 (*0-7844-0183-7*) Am Soc Civil Eng.

— Pipeline Crossings: Proceedings of the Specialty Conference, Burlington, Vermont, June 16-19, 1996. LC 96-19475. 520p. 1996. 54.00 (*0-7844-0180-2*) Am Soc Civil Eng.

— Placement & Improvement of Soil to Support Structures: Specialty Conference Held at Cambridge, MA, August 26-28, 1968. LC 72-185397. (Illus.). 446p. reprint ed. pap. 138.30 (*0-608-30749-1*, 201953500013) Bks Demand.

— Quality Assurance: A National Commitment: Proceedings of the Conference, Minneapolis, Minnesota, October 5-8, 1997. Niyargikar, Rao & Reinhart, Debra, eds. LC 97-36203. (Illus.). 280p. 1997. pap. text 29.00 (*0-7844-0292-2*, 40292-2) Am Soc Civil Eng.

— Reinforced Concrete Floor Slabs: Research & Design. LC TA0683.5.S6A. (Reinforced Concrete Research Council Bulletin Ser.: No. 20). 215p. reprint ed. pap. 66.70 (*0-608-13078-8*, 201954300013) Bks Demand.

***American Society of Civil Engineers Staff.** Seismic Analysis of Safety-Related Nuclear Structures & Commentary. LC 99-51970. 1999. write for info. (*0-7844-0433-X*) Am Soc Civil Eng.

American Society of Civil Engineers Staff. Seismic Guidelines for Ports. Werner, Stuart D., ed. LC 98-10619. (Technical Council on Lifeline Earthquake Engineering Monograph Ser.). 376p. 1998. pap. 69.00 (*0-7844-0327-9*) Am Soc Civil Eng.

— Selling Effectively to the Civil Engineering Market. 16p. 1991. 11.00 (*0-87262-835-3*) Am Soc Civil Eng.

— Social & Ecological Aspects of Irrigation & Drainage: Selected Papers. LC 75-30807. 381p. reprint ed. pap. 118.20 (*0-608-11597-5*, 200786500067) Bks Demand.

— Soil Improvement: History, Capabilities & Outlook: Report by the Committee on Placement & Improvement of Soils of the Geotechnical Engineering Division of the American Society of Civil Engineers. LC 78-104862. (Illus.). 186p. reprint ed. pap. 57.70 (*0-608-30737-8*, 201954900013) Bks Demand.

— Specification for Structural Steel Beams with Web Openings. LC 98-41258. (ASCE Standard Ser.). 32p. 1998. 35.00 (*0-7844-0300-7*) Am Soc Civil Eng.

— Standard for Load Resistance Factor Design (LRFD) for Engineered Wood Construction: ASCE-16-95. 125p. 1996. 39.00 (*0-7844-0041-5*) Am Soc Civil Eng.

— Standard for the Structural Design of Composite Slabs. LC 94-3855. (ASCE Standard Ser.). 100p. 1994. 48.00 (*0-87262-954-6*) Am Soc Civil Eng.

— Standard Guidelines for In-Process Oxygen Transfer Testing. LC 97-8344. 64p. 1997. 39.00 (*0-7844-0114-4*) Am Soc Civil Eng.

— Standard Guidelines for the Design & Installation of Pile Foundations. LC 96-30072. 40p. 1997. 28.00 (*0-7844-0219-1*) Am Soc Civil Eng.

— Standard Guidelines for the Design of Urban Subsurface Drainage. LC 94-3853. 72p. 1994. 30.00 (*0-87262-996-1*) Am Soc Civil Eng.

***American Society of Civil Engineers Staff.** Standard Practice for Direct Design of Buried Precast Concrete Box Sections. LC 00-38955. (ASCE Standard Ser.). (Illus.). 2000. write for info. (*0-7844-0472-0*) Am Soc Civil Eng.

— Standard Practice for Direct Design of Buried Precast Concrete Pipe Using Standard Installations (SIDD) LC 00-38952. (ASCE Standards Ser.). (Illus.). 2000. write for info. (*0-7844-0471-2*) Am Soc Civil Eng.

— Standard Practice for Direct Design of Precast Concrete Pipe for Jacking in Trenchless Construction. LC 00-33177. (ASCE Standard Ser.). (Illus.). 2000. write for info. (*0-7844-0496-8*) Am Soc Civil Eng.

American Society of Civil Engineers Staff. Standard Practice for Shotcrete Vol. 11: Technical Engineering & Design Guides As Adapted from the U. S. Army Corps of Engineers. LC 95-11427. (Technical Engineering & Design Guides As Adapted from the U. S. Army Corps of Engineers Ser.: No. 11). 72p. 1995. pap. 26.00 (*0-7844-0068-7*) Am Soc Civil Eng.

— State-of-the-Art Report on Air-Supported Structures. LC 79-125997. (Illus.). 103p. reprint ed. pap. 32.00 (*0-608-11557-6*, 201955600013) Bks Demand.

— Structural Design of Closure Structures for Local Flood Protection Projects. LC 96-45930. (Technical Engineering & Design Guides As Adapted from the U. S. Army Corps of Engineers: No. 21). 128p. 1997. 32.00 (*0-7844-0211-6*) Am Soc Civil Eng.

— Structural Failures: Modes, Causes, Responsibilities. LC TA0630.A8. (Illus.). 111p. reprint ed. pap. 34.50 (*0-608-30745-9*, 201953900013) Bks Demand.

***American Society of Civil Engineers Staff.** Topographic Surveying. LC 99-49722. (Technical Engineering & Design Guides as Adapted from the U. S. Army Corps of Engineers Ser.). 1999. write for info. (*0-7844-0374-0*) Am Soc Civil Eng.

American Society of Civil Engineers Staff. Urban Subsurface Drainage. LC 98-25673. (Manuals & Reports on Engineering Practice). 188p. 1998. 42.00 (*0-7844-0323-6*) Am Soc Civil Eng.

— Water Systems Seventy-Nine: Proceedings of the ASCE

A

Water Resources Planning & Management Division Specialty Conference, University of Houston, Hilton Hotel Center, February 25-28, 1979. LC 79-105513. 237p. reprint ed. pap. 73.50 (*0-608-11512-6*, 201954800013) Bks Demand.

— Wind Loads & Anchor Bolt Design for Petrochemical Facilities. LC 97-20890. 160p. 1997. 30.00 (*0-7844-0262-0*) Am Soc Civil Eng.

— Wind Tunnel Testing of Buildings & Structures. LC 98-44103. (Manuals & Reports on Engineering Practice). 232p. 1998. 59.00 (*0-7844-0319-8*) Am Soc Civil Eng.

— Wood Engineering in the 21st Century: Research Needs & Goals: Proceedings of the Workshop Offered in Conjunction with the SEI ASCE Structures Congress XV, Portland, Oregon, 16 April 1997. Fridley, Kenneth J., ed. LC 97-31342. 168p. 1998. pap. 28.00 (*0-7844-0295-7*) Am Soc Civil Eng.

American Society of Civil Engineers Staff, compiled by. Assessment of Resources & Needs in Highway Technology Education. 227p. 1975. pap. 3.00 (*0-87262-117-0*) Am Soc Civil Eng.

— Bicycle Transportation: A Civil Engineer's Notebook for Bicycle Facilities. LC 80-70171. 193p. 1980. pap. 15.00 (*0-87262-260-6*) Am Soc Civil Eng.

— Case Studies of Applied Advanced Data Collection & Management. LC 80-65303. 416p. 1980. pap. 35.00 (*0-87262-037-9*) Am Soc Civil Eng.

— Coastal Engineering: 1976, 4 vols., Set. 2242p. 1977. pap. 15.00 (*0-87262-083-2*) Am Soc Civil Eng.

— Conservation & Utilization of Water & Energy Resources. 541p. 1979. pap. 6.00 (*0-87262-189-8*) Am Soc Civil Eng.

— Contribution of Irrigation & Drainage to the World Food Supply. 430p. 1975. pap. 5.00 (*0-87262-114-6*) Am Soc Civil Eng.

— Cumulative Index to ASCE Publications, 1960-1969. 928p. 1970. 7.00 (*0-87262-232-0*) Am Soc Civil Eng.

— Cumulative Index to ASCE Publications, 1970-1974. 1066p. 1974. 7.00 (*0-87262-233-9*) Am Soc Civil Eng.

— The Current State of Knowledge of Lifeline Earthquake Engineering. 486p. 1977. pap. 5.00 (*0-87262-086-7*) Am Soc Civil Eng.

— Dynamic Planning for Environmental Quality in the 1980's. 281p. 1978. pap. 5.00 (*0-87262-098-0*) Am Soc Civil Eng.

— Effective Project Management Techniques. 83p. 1973. pap. 3.00 (*0-87262-058-1*) Am Soc Civil Eng.

— Environmental Effects of Large Dams. 229p. 1978. pap. 3.00 (*0-87262-125-1*) Am Soc Civil Eng.

— Environmental Impact. 399p. 1973. pap. 18.00 (*0-87262-063-8*) Am Soc Civil Eng.

— Environmental Impacts of International Civil Engineering Projects & Practices. 263p. 1978. pap. 5.00 (*0-87262-129-4*) Am Soc Civil Eng.

— Evaluation, Maintenance & Upgrading of Wood Structures: A Guide & Commentary. LC 82-72779. 434p. 1982. pap. 15.00 (*0-87262-317-3*) Am Soc Civil Eng.

— Fatigue Life of Prestressed Concrete Beams. 96p. 1977. pap. 3.00 (*0-87262-094-8*) Am Soc Civil Eng.

— A Guide to Urban Arterial Systems. LC 81-69231. 368p. 1981. pap. 26.00 (*0-87262-280-0*) Am Soc Civil Eng.

— International Air Transportation Conference. 420p. 1977. pap. 5.00 (*0-87262-093-X*) Am Soc Civil Eng.

— International Air Transportation Conference, 2 vols., Set. 834p. 1979. pap. 9.00 (*0-87262-201-0*) Am Soc Civil Eng.

— International Seminar on Probabilistic & Extreme Load Design of Nuclear Plant Facilities. 454p. 1979. pap. 5.00 (*0-87262-146-4*) Am Soc Civil Eng.

— Is Water Quality Enhancement Feasible? 137p. 1970. pap. 3.00 (*0-87262-025-5*) Am Soc Civil Eng.

— Management of Engineering of Control Systems for Water Pipelines. 141p. 1978. pap. 5.00 (*0-87262-132-4*) Am Soc Civil Eng.

— Need for National Policy for the Use of Underground Space. 238p. 1973. pap. 5.00 (*0-87262-102-2*) Am Soc Civil Eng.

— Nuclear Facilities Siting. LC 82-73507. 64p. 1982. pap. 14.00 (*0-87262-344-0*) Am Soc Civil Eng.

— Nuclear Waste Management. LC 82-73506. 52p. 1982. pap. 3.00 (*0-87262-343-2*) Am Soc Civil Eng.

— Predicting & Designing for Natural & Man-Made Hazards. 297p. 1979. pap. 6.00 (*0-87262-187-1*) Am Soc Civil Eng.

— Quality System in Construction. 210p. 1974. pap. 3.00 (*0-87262-073-5*) Am Soc Civil Eng.

— Readings in Cost Engineering. 730p. 1979. pap. 8.00 (*0-87262-147-2*) Am Soc Civil Eng.

— Reaeration Research. 376p. 1979. pap. 5.00 (*0-87262-142-1*) Am Soc Civil Eng.

— Reducing Risk & Liability Through Better Specifications & Inspection. LC 82-70874. 165p. 1982. pap. 5.00 (*0-87262-301-7*) Am Soc Civil Eng.

— Solid Waste Research & Development Needs for Emerging Coal Technologies: ASCE-PRC-EPRI Workshop Proceedings. 268p. 1979. pap. 5.00 (*0-87262-199-5*) Am Soc Civil Eng.

— Stability of Structures under Static & Dynamic Loads. 820p. 1977. pap. 6.00 (*0-87262-095-6*) Am Soc Civil Eng.

— Transactions of the American Society of Civil Engineers, Vol. 144. 791p. 1980. 9.00 (*0-87262-236-3*) Am Soc Civil Eng.

— Transactions of the American Society of Civil Engineers, Vol. 146. 1056p. 1982. 9.00 (*0-87262-309-2*) Am Soc Civil Eng.

— Transportation & Energy. 456p. 1978. pap. 5.00 (*0-87262-135-9*) Am Soc Civil Eng.

American Society of Civil Engineers Staff, contrib. by. ASCE Salary Survey, 1993. 72p. 1993. 5.00 (*0-87262-893-0*) Am Soc Civil Eng.

American Society of Civil Engineers Staff, ed. Computing in Civil Engineering: Proceedings of the Third Congress Held in Conjunction with A. E. C. Systems '96, Anaheim, California, June 17-19, 1996. LC 96-19480. 1108p. 1996. 103.00 (*0-7844-0182-9*) Am Soc Civil Eng.

American Society of Civil Engineers Staff, et al, eds. Glossary: Water & Wastewater Control Engineering. 3rd ed. LC 80-70933. 398p. 1981. 30.00 (*0-87262-262-2*) Am Soc Civil Eng.

American Society of Civil Engineers Staff & American Nuclear Society Staff. High Level Radioactive Waste Management: Proceedings of the International Topical Meeting, Las Vegas, 1990, 2 vols., Set. LC 90-375. 1457p. 1990. pap. text 209.00 (*0-87262-751-9*) Am Soc Civil Eng.

American Society of Civil Engineers Staff & American Nuclear Society Staff, contrib. by. High Level Radioactive Waste Management: Proceedings of the Sixth Annual International Conference, Las Vegas, NV, April 30-May 5, 1995. 810p. 1995. pap. 120.00 (*0-7844-0082-2*) Am Soc Civil Eng.

American Society of Civil Engineers Staff & American Water Works Association Staff. Management of Water Treatment Plant Residuals. LC 96-19472. (Asce Manuals & Reports of Engineering Practice). 320p. 1996. 70.00 (*0-7844-0181-0*) Am Soc Civil Eng.

American Society of Civil Engineers Staff & McKee, Brian J. Historic American Covered Bridges. (Illus.). 160p. 1997. 39.95 (*0-19-521335-1*) OUP.

American Society of Civil Engineers Staff & UNESCO/IHP-IV Project M-4.3. Staff. Sustainability Criteria for Water Resource Systems. LC 98-2739. 280p. 1998. 49.00 (*0-7844-0331-7*) Am Soc Civil Eng.

American Society of Civil Engineers Staff & Water Pollution Control Federation Staff, eds. Gravity Sanitary Sewer Design & Construction. LC 81-69182. (Manual & Report on Engineering Practice Ser.: No. 60). 291p. 1982. 38.00 (*0-87262-313-0*) Am Soc Civil Eng.

American Society of Civil Engineers Staff, et al. Probabilistic Mechanics & Structural Reliability: Proceedings of the Seventh Specialty Conference: Worcester Polytechnic Institute, Worcester, Massachusetts, USA, August 7-9, 1996. Frangopol, Dan M. & Grigoriu, Mircea D., eds. LC 96-22148. 1024p. 1996. 87.00 (*0-7844-0184-5*) American Society of Geolinguistics.

American Society of Civil Engineers Staff, jt. auth. see Ahmed, Nazeer.

American Society of Civil Engineers Staff, jt. auth. see American Concrete Institute Staff.

American Society of Civil Engineers Staff, jt. auth. see American Nuclear Society Staff.

American Society of Civil Engineers Staff, jt. auth. see Ansari, Farhad.

American Society Of Civil Engineers Staff, jt. auth. see Benz, Stephen M.

American Society of Civil Engineers Staff, jt. auth. see Burt, C. M.

American Society of Civil Engineers Staff, jt. auth. see Chini, Abdol R.

American Society of Civil Engineers Staff, jt. auth. see Conference on Robotics for Challenging Environment.

American Society of Civil Engineers Staff, jt. auth. see Cotton, Maureen K.

American Society of Civil Engineers Staff, jt. auth. see Cuoco, Daniel A.

American Society of Civil Engineers Staff, jt. auth. see Day, Nicholas B.

American Society of Civil Engineers Staff, jt. auth. see Finno, Richard J.

American Society of Civil Engineers Staff, jt. auth. see Johnson, Stewart W.

American Society of Civil Engineers Staff, jt. auth. see Lambrechts, James R.

American Society of Civil Engineers Staff, jt. auth. see Maji, Arup.

American Society of Civil Engineers Staff, jt. auth. see Matheson, Gordon.

American Society of Civil Engineers Staff, jt. auth. see Sale, Dwight B.

American Society of Civil Engineers Staff, jt. auth. see Smith, John W.

American Society of Civil Engineers Staff, jt. auth. see Stone, William C.

American Society of Civil Engineers Staff, jt. auth. see Structural Engineering Institute Staff.

American Society of Civil Engineers Staff, jt. auth. see Tommelein, Iris D.

American Society of Civil Engineers Staff, jt. auth. see Water Environment Federation Staff.

American Society of Civil Engineers Staff, jt. contrib. by see American Water Works Association Staff.

American Society of Civil Engineers Staff, jt. ed. see Tan, Chia K.

American Society of Civil Engineers, Surveying Eng. Engineering Surveying Manual. (C). 1985. 275.00 (*81-85046-46-8*, Pub. by Scientific) St Mut.

American Society of Civil Engineers, Task Committe. Planning & Design Guidelines for Small Craft Harbor. rev. ed. LC 94-20810. (Manuals & Reports on Engineering Practice Ser.: No. 50). 296p. 1994. 54.00 (*0-7844-0033-4*) Am Soc Civil Eng.

— Steel Penstocks. LC 93-13346. (Manual & Report on Engineering Practice Ser.: No. 79). 464p. 1993. 53.00 (*0-87262-951-1*) Am Soc Civil Eng.

American Society of Civil Engineers, Task Committe, et al. Urban Drainage Rehabilitation Programs & Techniques: Selected Papers on Urban Drainage Rehabilitation from 1988-1993 Water Resources Planning & Management Division Conference Sessions. LC 94-5426. 240p. 1994. 27.00 (*0-7844-0038-5*) Am Soc Civil Eng.

American Society of Civil Engineers Task Committee. Tensioned Fabric Structures: A Practical Introduction. Shaeffer, R. E., ed. LC 96-11376. 120p. 1996. 25.00 (*0-7844-0156-X*) Am Soc Civil Eng.

American Society of Civil Engineers, Urban Transpo. Transportation Planning & Air Quality II: Proceedings of the National Conference, Sheraton Tara Hotel & Resort, Denver, Massachusetts, May 24-26, 1993. Wholley, Thomas F., ed. LC 94-5431. 216p. 1994. 27.00 (*0-87262-914-7*) Am Soc Civil Eng.

American Society Of Clinical Pathologists. Handbook of Clinical Pathology. 2nd ed. LC 99-24739. 1999. 60.00 (*0-89189-376-8*) Am Soc Clinical.

American Society of Composers, Authors & Publisher. ASCAP Copyright Law Symposium, No. 38. 320p. 1992. text 57.50 (*0-231-07606-1*) Col U Pr.

— ASCAP Copyright Law Symposium, No. 39. 320p. 1992. text 57.50 (*0-231-07608-8*) Col U Pr.

American Society of Consultant Pharmacists Staff, intro. Pharmacy Legislation & Regulations, 1992. rev. ed. 134p. 1992. pap. text 43.00 (*0-934322-09-0*) Am Soc Consult Phar.

American Society of Corporate Secretaries Staff. Assisting Insiders with Federal Securities Law Compliance: A Guide for the Corporate Secretary. write for info. (*0-318-61652-1*) Am Soc Corp Sec.

American Society of Heating, Refrigerating & Air-C. Heat & Cold: Mastering the Great Indoors. (Illus.). 352p. (C). 1995. text. write for info. (*1-883793-05-X*) Wolfe Pubng.

American Society of Indexers Staff. Starting an Indexing Business. LC 93-40013. 1994. 30.00 (*0-936547-20-0*) Am Soc Index.

— Subheadings: A Matter of Opinion. LC 95-8853. 1995. 15.00 (*0-936547-30-8*) Am Soc Index.

American Society of International Law & Nederlands, ed. Contemporary International Law Issues - Sharing Pan-European & American Perspectives: Proceedings of the Joint Conference 1991 of the American Society of International Law & Nederlandse Vereniging voor International Recht. 276p. (C). 1992. pap. text 43.50 (*0-7923-1681-9*) Kluwer Academic.

American Society of International Law Staff. Basic Documents of International Economic Law, 2 vols., Set. Zamora, Stephen & Brand, Ronald A., eds. 1990. 100.00 (*0-685-66959-9*); 100.00 (*0-685-67167-4*, 5124) CCH INC.

— International Law & the Middle East Crisis: A Symposium. LC 58-1485. (Tulane Studies in Political Science: No. 4). 97p. Date not set. reprint ed. pap. 30.10 (*0-608-20660-1*, 207209700003) Bks Demand.

American Society of International Law Staff, ed. Contemporary International Law Issues - Opportunities at a Time of Momentous Change: Proceedings of the Second Joint Conference Held in the Hague, The Netherlands, July 22-24, 1993. 433p. (C). 1994. pap. text 63.00 (*0-7923-2831-0*) Kluwer Academic.

American Society of International Law Staff, ed. see Jessup, Philip C.

American Society of Legislative Clerks & Secretari. Inside the Legislative Process. 175p. 1996. 30.00 (*1-55516-901-5*, 7148) Natl Conf State Legis.

— Mason's Manual of Legislative Procedure. rev. ed. 677p. 1989. reprint ed. 40.00 (*1-55516-729-2*, 7120) Natl Conf State Legis.

American Society of Magazine Photographers Staff. Assignment Photography. Halsey, David, ed. 40p. 1991. pap. 14.00 (*0-9605474-0-1*) Am Soc Media.

American Society of Mammalogists Staff. The Smithsonian Book of North American Mammals. Wilson, Don E. & Ruff, Sue, eds. LC 98-43375. (Illus.). 750p. 1999. pap. 75.00 (*1-56098-845-2*) Smithsonian.

American Society of Mechanical Engineers, Rubber & Plastic Division Staff. Symposium on Graphite Fiber Composites: An Integrated Approach to Their Development & Use Presented at ASME Winter Meeting, Pittsburgh, PA, Nov. 1967. LC 67-31228. 77p. reprint ed. pap. 30.00 (*0-608-30435-2*, 201230300082) Bks Demand.

American Society of Mechanical Engineers Staff. Advanced Aluminum & Titanium Structures: Presented at the Winter Annual Meeting of the American Society of Mechanical Engineers, Washington, D.C., November 15-20, 1981. Goodman, J. W., ed. LC 81-69003. (AD Ser.: No. 02). (Illus.). 49p. reprint ed. pap. 30.00 (*0-8357-2905-2*, 203914200011) Bks Demand.

— Advances in Aerospace Structures & Materials, 1982: Presented at the Winter Annual Meeting of the American Society of Mechanical Engineers, Phoenix, AZ, November 14-19, 1982. Laurenson, Robert M. & Yuceoglu, Umur, eds. LC 81-69004. (AD Ser.: No. 03). (Illus.). 146p. reprint ed. pap. 45.30 (*0-8357-2904-4*, 203914100011) Bks Demand.

— Advances in Bioengineering, 1976: Presented at the Winter Meeting of the American Society of Mechanical Engineers, New York, N. Y., Dec. 5-10, 1976. Smith, Charles R., ed. LC TA0164.A3819. (Illus.). 48p. reprint ed. pap. 30.00 (*0-8357-5141-4*, 201686700007) Bks Demand.

— Advances in Bioengineering, 1979: Papers Presented at the Winter Annual Meeting of the American Society of Mechanical Engineers, New York, New York, December 2-7, 1979. Wells, Michael K., ed. LC 74-81161. (Illus.). 197p. reprint ed. pap. 61.10 (*0-8357-2857-9*, 203909200010) Bks Demand.

— Advances in Bioengineering, 1981: Presented at the Winter Annual Meeting of the American Society of Mechanical Engineers, Washington, D.C., November 15-20, 1981. Viano, David C., ed. LC 74-81161. (Illus.). 240p. reprint ed. pap. 74.40 (*0-8357-2826-9*, 203906200010) Bks Demand.

— Advances in Bioengineering, 1982: Presented at the Winter Annual Meeting of the American Society of Mechanical Engineers, Phoenix, Arizona, November 14-19, 1982. Thibault, Lawrence, ed. LC 74-81161. (Illus.). 186p. reprint ed. pap. 57.70 (*0-8357-2816-1*, 203905500010) Bks Demand.

— Advances in Bioengineering, 1983: Presented at the Winter Annual Meeting of the American Society of Mechanical Engineers, Boston, MA, November 13-18, 1983. Bartel, Donald L., ed. LC 74-81161. 162p. reprint ed. pap. 50.30 (*0-8357-8690-0*, 203365500087) Bks Demand.

— Advances in Bioengineering, 1993: Presented at the ASME Winter Annual Meeting, New Orleans, Louisiana, November 28-December 3, 1993. Tarbell, John M., ed. LC 74-81161. (BED Ser.: Vol. 26). 672p. 1993. reprint ed. pap. 200.00 (*0-608-00290-9*, 205931800008) Bks Demand.

— Advances in Composite Materials & Structures: Presented at the Winter Annual Meeting of the American Society of Mechanical Engineers, Anaheim, California, December 10-12, 1986. Wang, S. S. & Rajapakse, Y. D., eds. LC 88-46223. (AMD Ser.: Vol. 82). 164p. 1989. reprint ed. pap. 50.90 (*0-608-00287-9*, 205931500008) Bks Demand.

— Advances in Reliability & Stress Analysis: Presented at the ASME Winter Annual Meeting, San Francisco, CA, December, 1978. Burns, John J., Jr., ed. LC 79-50208. 258p. reprint ed. pap. 80.00 (*0-8357-5183-X*, 205630800056) Bks Demand.

— Analysis Techniques in Acoustics: Presented at the Winter Annual Meeting of the American Society of Mechanical Engineers, San Francisco, California, December 10-15, 1989. LC 89-46299. (NCA Ser.: Vol. 7). 78p. 1989. reprint ed. pap. 30.00 (*0-608-00288-7*, 205931600008) Bks Demand.

— Applications of Numerical Methods to Forming Processes: Papers Presented at the Winter Annual Meeting of the American Society of Mechanical Engineers, San Francisco, CA, December 10-15, 1978. Armen, Harry & Jones, R. F., Jr., eds. LC 78-59882. (AMD Ser.: Vol. 28). (Illus.). 211p. reprint ed. pap. 65.50 (*0-8357-5671-8*, 203270200080) Bks Demand.

— Behavior of Superheater Alloys in High Temperature, High Pressure Steam. Lien, George E., ed. LC 68-19905. (Illus.). 119p. reprint ed. pap. 36.90 (*0-8357-7110-5*, 201688600005) Bks Demand.

— Biomechanics Symposium, 1979: Presented at the Joint ASME-CSME Applied Mechanics, Fluids Engineering, & Bioengineering Conference, Niagara. Van Buskirk, William C., ed. LC 79-113524. (AMD Ser.: Vol. 32). (Illus.). 243p. reprint ed. pap. 75.40 (*0-8357-2858-7*, 203909300010) Bks Demand.

— Case Studies in Computer Control: Presented at the Winter Annual Meeting of ASME, San Francisco, CA, December 10-15, 1978. Al-Shaikh, Al & Auslander, D. M., eds. LC 78-68110. 93p. reprint ed. pap. 30.00 (*0-8357-8709-5*, 203363800087) Bks Demand.

— Cavitation State of Knowledge: Discussions Presented at the ASME Fluids Engineering & Applied Mechanics Conference, Northwestern University, Evanston, Illinois, June 16-18, 1969. Robertson, J. M. & Wislicenus, G. F., eds. LC 73-173121. 50p. reprint ed. pap. 30.00 (*0-608-14323-5*, 201685300007) Bks Demand.

— The Characterization of Carbon Dioxide Absorbing Agents for Life Support Equipment: Presented at the Winter Annual Meeting of the American Society of Mechanical Engineers, Phoenix, Arizona, November 14-19, 1982. Nuckols, Marshall L. & Smith, Karen A., eds. LC 82-73176. (OED Ser.: Vol. 10). (Illus.). 214p. reprint ed. pap. 66.40 (*0-8357-2835-8*, 203907100010) Bks Demand.

— Coal Fouling & Slagging Parameters - Prepared by the ASME Research Committee on Corrosion & Deposits from Combustion Gases. Winegartner, E. C., ed. LC 75-323265. 42p. reprint ed. pap. 30.00 (*0-608-17903-5*, 201491900094) Bks Demand.

— Cogeneration District Heating Applications: Papers Presented at the Winter Annual Meeting of the American Society of Mechanical Engineers, San Francisco, California, December 10-15, 1978. Oliker, Ishai, ed. LC 78-68082. (Illus.). 49p. reprint ed. pap. 30.00 (*0-8357-2869-2*, 203910500011) Bks Demand.

— Combustion Fundamentals for Waste Incineration. LC 74-19743. 224p. reprint ed. pap. 69.50 (*0-608-13178-4*, 202418200035) Bks Demand.

— Compact Heat Exchangers - History, Technological Advancement & Mechanical Design Problems: Presented at the Winter Annual Meeting of the American Society of Mechanical Engineers, Chicago, Illinois, November 16-21, 1980, & the 24th Annual International Gas Turbine Conference & First ASME Solar Energy Conference, San Diego, California, March 11-15, 1979. McDonald, C. F. et al, eds. LC 80-69189. (HTD Ser.: Vol. 10). 197p. reprint ed. pap. 61.10 (*0-7837-1446-7*, 205242100017) Bks Demand.

— Computational Methods for Infinite Domain Mediastructure Interaction: Presented at the Winter Annual Meeting of the American Society of Mechanical Engineers, Washington, D.C., November 15-20, 1981. Kalinowski, Anthony J., ed. LC 81-69005. (AMD Ser.: Vol. 46). (Illus.). 234p. reprint ed. pap. 72.60 (*0-8357-2865-X*, 203910100011) Bks Demand.

— Computational Techniques for Interface Problems: Presented at the Winter Annual Meeting of the American Society of Mechanical Engineers, San Francisco, California, December 10-15, 1978. Park, K. C. &

Gartling, D. K., eds. LC 78-59883. (AMD Ser.: Vol. 30). (Illus.). 189p. reprint ed. pap. 58.60 (*0-8357-2871-4*, 203910700011) Bks Demand.

— Computer Analysis of Large-Scale Structures: Presented at the Winter Annual Meeting of the American Society of Mechanical Engineers, Washington, D.C., November 15-20, 1981. Park, K. C. & Jones, R. F., Jr., eds. LC 81-69006. (AMD Ser.: Vol. 49). (Illus.). 108p. reprint ed. pap. 33.50 (*0-8357-2911-7*, 203914800011) Bks Demand.

— Computer Applications in Manufacturing Systems: Planning, Control, & Robots: Papers Presented at the Winter Annual Meeting of the American Society of Mechanical Engineers, Chicago, Illinois, November 16-21, 1980. DeVries, W. R., ed. LC 80-69150. (PED Ser.: Vol. 2). 106p. reprint ed. pap. 32.90 (*0-608-15360-5*, 205637100061) Bks Demand.

— Computer Technology in Fusion Energy Research: Presented at the Winter Annual Meeting of the American Society of Mechanical Engineers, San Francisco, California, December 10-15, 1978. Akin, John E. & Gray, W. Harvey, eds. LC 78-59895. (PVP Ser.: No. 031). (Illus.). 123p. reprint ed. pap. 38.20 (*0-8357-2873-0*, 203910900011) Bks Demand.

— Computers in Flow Predictions & Fluid Dynamics Experiments. Ghia, K. N. et al, eds. LC 81-69010. 242p. reprint ed. pap. 75.10 (*0-608-11877-X*, 202314700032) Bks Demand.

— Computing in Applied Mechanics: Presented at the Winter Annual Meeting of the ASME, New York City, December 5-10, 1976. LC 76-28858. Vol. 18. 186p. reprint ed. pap. 53.10 (*0-317-26614-4*, 2024186) Bks Demand.

— Computing Methods in Geophysical Mechanics: Papers Presented at the Winter Annual Meeting of the American Society of Mechanical Engineers, Atlanta, Georgia, November 27-December 2, 1977. Shaw, R. P., ed. LC 77-87327. (Illus.). 208p. reprint ed. pap. 64.50 (*0-8357-2898-6*, 203913400011) Bks Demand.

— Constitutive Equations in Viscoplasticity: Phenomenological & Physical Aspects. Valanis, K. C., ed. LC TA0418.14.A5. (AMD Ser.: Vol. 21). 86p. reprint ed. pap. 30.00 (*0-8357-2887-0*, 203912300011) Bks Demand.

— Control of Manufacturing Processes & Robotic Systems: Presented at the Winter Annual Meeting of ASME, Boston, MA, November 13-18, 1983. Hardt, David E. & Book, Wayne J., eds. LC 83-72724. (Illus.). 290p. reprint ed. pap. 89.90 (*0-608-17567-6*, 203055900069) Bks Demand.

— Cooling Tower Plume Modeling & Drift Measurement: A Review of the State-of-the-Art. LC 75-21277. (Illus.). 180p. reprint ed. pap. 55.80 (*0-8357-2872-2*, 203910800011) Bks Demand.

— Deep Ocean Mining: Presented at the Winter Annual Meeting of the American Society of Mechanical Engineers, New York, New York, December 2-7, 1979. Flipse, John E., ed. LC 79-54436. (OED Ser.: Vol. 8). (Illus.). 79p. reprint ed. pap. 30.00 (*0-8357-2859-5*, 203909400010) Bks Demand.

— Deepwater Mooring & Drilling: Presented at the Winter Annual Meeting of the American Society of Mechanical Engineers, New York, New York, December 2-7, 1979. Lou, Y. K., ed. LC 79-54437. (OED Ser.: Vol. 7). (Illus.). 209p. reprint ed. pap. 64.80 (*0-8357-2860-9*, 203909500011) Bks Demand.

— Diagnosing Machinery Health: Presented at the Winter Annual Meeting of the American Society of Mechanical Engineers, San Francisco, California, December 10-15, 1978. Dill, J. F. & Petrovic, W. K., eds. LC 78-59891. 68p. reprint ed. pap. 30.00 (*0-608-11730-7*, 201539400094) Bks Demand.

— Differential Games: Theory & Applications. LC 74-128583. 147p. reprint ed. pap. 45.60 (*0-608-30981-8*, 201331200085) Bks Demand.

— Disposal of Industrial Wastes by Combustion, Vol. 2. LC 73-63622. 57p. reprint ed. pap. 30.00 (*0-608-11583-5*, 200613400061) Bks Demand.

— Drilling Technology, 1994: Presented at the Energy-Sources Technology Conference, New Orleans, LA, January 23-26, 1994. Vozniak, John P., ed. LC 85-70237. (PED Ser.: Vol. 56). 280p. 1994. reprint ed. pap. 86.80 (*0-608-00282-8*, 205931000007) Bks Demand.

— Ductility & Toughness Considerations in Elevated Temperature Service: Presented at the Winter Annual Meeting of the American Society of Mechanical Engineers, San Francisco, California, December 10-15, 1978. Smith, George V., ed. LC 78-60046. (MPC Ser.: No. 8). (Illus.). 416p. reprint ed. pap. 129.00 (*0-8357-2900-1*, 203913600011) Bks Demand.

— Dynamics of Structured Solids. Hermann, George, ed. LC 68-58743. 114p. reprint ed. pap. 35.40 (*0-608-30979-6*, 201680700005) Bks Demand.

— Earthquake Ground Motion & Its Effects on Structures: Presented at the Winter Annual Meeting of the American Society of Mechanical Engineers, Phoenix, Arizona, November 14-19, 1982. Datta, S. K., ed. LC 82-73177. (AMD Ser.: Vol. 53). (Illus.). 208p. reprint ed. pap. 64.50 (*0-8357-2907-9*, 203914400011) Bks Demand.

— Effects of Melting & Processing Variables on the Mechanical Properties of Steel: Presented at the Winter Annual Meeting of the American Society of Mechanical Engineers, Atlanta, Georgia, November 27-December 2, 1977; Sponsored by the Metal Properties Council, Inc. the Materials Division, ASME. Smith, George V., ed. LC 77-87326. (Illus.). 349p. reprint ed. pap. 108.20 (*0-608-17565-X*, 203055100069) Bks Demand.

— Emerging Technologies in Aerospace Structures, Design, Structural Dynamics, & Materials: Presented at the Aerospace Conference, Century 2--Emerging Technology Conferences, San Francisco, California, August 13-15, 1980. Vinson, Jack R., ed. LC 80-66037. (Illus.). 334p. reprint ed. pap. 103.60 (*0-8357-2908-7*, 203914500011) Bks Demand.

— Energy Conservation in Building Heating & Air Conditioning Systems. Gopal, R. et al, eds. LC 78-60047. 109p. reprint ed. pap. 33.80 (*0-608-11876-1*, 202314600032) Bks Demand.

— Engine Design, Operation, & Control Using Computer Systems: Presented at the Eleventh Annual Fall Technical Conference of the ASME Internal Combustion Engine Division, Dearborn, MI, October 15-18, 1989. Harrington, D. L., ed. LC 89-46161. (ICE Ser.: Vol. 9). 224p. 1989. reprint ed. pap. 69.50 (*0-608-00284-4*, 205931200007) Bks Demand.

— Engineering Computer Software: Verification, Qualification, Certification; Symposium. Presentations from ASME First National Congress on Pressure Vessels & Piping, San Francisco, CA, May 1971. Berman, Irwin, ed. LC 73-173859. 130p. 1971. reprint ed. pap. 40.30 (*0-608-08203-1*, 201682800005) Bks Demand.

— Enhanced Recovery & Rotating Equipment - A Workbook for Petroleum Engineers: Presented at the 1980 Petroleum Mechanical Engineering Conference, Denver, Colorado, September 14-16, 1980. Thayer, K. B., ed. LC 80-68344. (Illus.). 83p. reprint ed. pap. 30.00 (*0-8357-2891-9*, 203912700011) Bks Demand.

— Environmental Effects of Thermal Discharges: The Elements in Formulating a Rational Public Policy. LC 77-139496. 50p. reprint ed. pap. 30.00 (*0-608-11757-9*, 201691000005) Bks Demand.

— Fatigue, Creep, & Pressure Vessels for Elevated Temperature Service: Presented at the Winter Annual Meeting of the American Society of Mechanical Engineers, Washington, D.C., November 15-20, 1981. Lawton, Carl W. & Seeley, R. Rodger, eds. LC 81-69252. (MPC Ser.: No. 17). (Illus.). 212p. reprint ed. pap. 65.80 (*0-8357-2882-X*, 203911900011) Bks Demand.

— Fatigue Life Technology: Presented at the 22nd Annual International Gas Turbine Conference, Philadelphia, Pa., March 27-31, 1977. Cruse, T. A. & Gallagher, J. P., eds. LC 77-70040. 122p. reprint ed. pap. 37.90 (*0-608-14392-8*, 201935000011) Bks Demand.

— Finite Elasticity: Presented at the Winter Annual Meeting of American Society of Mechanical Engineerings, Atlanta, Georgia, 1977. Rivlin, R. S., ed. LC 77-89014. (American Society of Mechanical Engineers, Applied Mechanics Division Ser.: AMD; Vol. 27). 158p. reprint ed. pap. 49.00 (*0-608-11850-8*, 202093400020) Bks Demand.

— Finite Element Methods for Convection Dominated Flows: Presented at the Winter Annual Meeting of the American Society of Mechanical Engineers, New York, NY, December 2-7, 1979. Hughes, T. J., ed. LC 79-54426. (AMD Ser.: No. 34). 232p. reprint ed. pap. 72.00 (*0-608-16897-1*, 205630700056) Bks Demand.

— Flow in Primary, Non-Rotating Passages in Turbomachines: Presented at the Winter Annual Meeting of the American Society of Mechanical Engineerings, New York, New York, December 2-7, 1979. Herring, H. J. et al, eds. LC 79-54429. 194p. reprint ed. pap. 60.20 (*0-8357-8717-6*, 203363200087) Bks Demand.

— Flow-Induced Heat Exchanger Tube Vibration - 1980: Presented at the Winter Annual Meeting of the American Society of Mechanical Engineers, Chicago, Illinois, November 16-21, 1980. Chenoweth, James M. & Stenner, John R., eds. LC 80-69188. (HTD Ser.: Vol. 9). (Illus.). 71p. reprint ed. pap. 30.00 (*0-8357-2833-1*, 203906900010) Bks Demand.

— Flows in Internal Combustion Engines: Presented at the Winter Annual Meeting of the American Society of Mechanical Engineers, Phoenix, Arizona, November 14-19, 1982. Uzkan, Teoman, ed. LC 82-73181. 117p. reprint ed. pap. 33.40 (*0-8357-2735-1*, 2039843) Bks Demand.

— Fluid Flow & Heat Transfer over Rod or Tube Bundles: Presented at the Winter Annual Meeting of the American Society of Mechanical Engineers, New York, New York, December 2-7, 1979. Yao, S. C. & Pfund, P. A., eds. LC 79-54431. 244p. reprint ed. pap. 75.70 (*0-8357-8718-4*, 203363100087) Bks Demand.

— Fluid Jet Control Devices: Papers Presented at the Winter Annual Meeting of the ASME New York, 1962. Brown, Forbes T., ed. LC 63-433. 96p. reprint ed. pap. 30.00 (*0-608-11657-2*, 201029300068) Bks Demand.

— Fluid Mechanics in the Petroleum Industry: Papers Presented at the Winter Annual Meeting of ASME, Houston, TX, November 30-December 5, 1975. Dalton, Charles & Denizen, Early, eds. LC 75-8346. 75p. reprint ed. pap. 30.00 (*0-608-30630-4*, 201683100005) Bks Demand.

— Fluid Mechanics of Combustion: Papers Presented at Joint Fluids Engineering & CSME Conference, Montreal, Quebec, May 13-15, 1974. Dussourd, J. L. & Lehmann, R., eds. LC 74-78505. 273p. reprint ed. pap. 84.70 (*0-608-30858-7*, 205171800005) Bks Demand.

— Fluid Transmission Line Dynamics: Presented at the Winter Annual Meeting of the American Society of Mechanical Engineers, Washington, D.C., November 15-20, 1981. Franke, M. E. & Drzewiecki, T. M., eds. LC 81-69009. (Illus.). 128p. reprint ed. pap. 39.70 (*0-8357-2849-8*, 203908400010) Bks Demand.

— Fuel-Coolant Interactions: Presented at the Winter Annual Meeting of the American Society of Mechanical Engineers, Washington, D.C., November 15-20, 1981. Corradini, M. L. & Bishop, A. A., eds. LC 81-69013. (HTD Ser.: Vol. 19). (Illus.). 119p. reprint ed. pap. 36.90 (*0-8357-2832-3*, 203906800010) Bks Demand.

— Gas Turbine Combustion & Fuels Technology: Presented at the Winter Annual Meeting of the American Society of Mechanical Engineers, Atlanta, Georgia, November 27-December 2, 1977. Bastress, E. Karl, ed. LC 77-87997. 79p. reprint ed. pap. 30.00 (*0-608-15364-8*, 205637300061) Bks Demand.

— The Generation of Isochronous Stress-Strain Curves: Papers Presented at the Winter Annual Meeting of ASME, New York, NY, November 26-30, 1972. LC 72-93459. (Illus.). 91p. reprint ed. pap. 30.00 (*0-608-30373-9*, 201682100005) Bks Demand.

— The Guide to Hydropower Mechanical Design. (Illus.). 400p. 1996. 125.00 (*0-9651765-0-9*) HCI Publns.

— Heat Transfer in Fire & Combustion Systems, 1993: Presented at the 29th National Heat Transfer Conference, Atlanta, GA, August 8-11, 1993. Farouk, Bakhtier et al, eds. LC 93-236136. (HTD Ser.: Vol. 270). 283p. 1993. reprint ed. pap. 87.80 (*0-608-00281-X*, 205930900007) Bks Demand.

— Heat Transfer in Low Reynolds Number Flow. Brown, George A. & Moszynski, Jerzy R., eds. LC 70-180676. 75p. reprint ed. pap. 30.00 (*0-608-30864-1*, 201012600068) Bks Demand.

— Heat Transfer in Nuclear Waste Disposal: Presented at the Winter Annual Meeting of the American Society of Mechanical Engineers, Chicago, Illinois, November 16-21, 1980. Kulacki, Frank A. & Lyczkowski, Robert W., eds. LC 80-69190. (HTD Ser.: Vol. 11). (Illus.). 118p. reprint ed. pap. 36.60 (*0-8357-2831-5*, 203906700010) Bks Demand.

— Heat Transfer in Ocean Thermal Energy Conversion (OTEC) Systems: Presented at the Winter Annual Meeting of the ASME, Chicago, Illinois, November 16-21, 1980. Owens, William L., ed. LC 80-69191. (HTD Ser.: Vol. 12). 78p. reprint ed. pap. 30.00 (*0-8357-8724-9*, 203363300087) Bks Demand.

— Heat Transfer in Porous Media: Presented at the Winter Annual Meeting of the American Society of Mechanical Engineers, Phoenix, Arizona, November 14-19, 1982. Beck, J. V. & Yao, L. S., eds. LC 82-73167. (HTD Ser.: Vol. 22). (Illus.). 116p. reprint ed. pap. 36.00 (*0-8357-2864-1*, 203910000011) Bks Demand.

— Heat Transfer in Rod Bundles: Papers Presented at the Winter Annual Meeting of the American Society of Mechanical Engineers, New York, December 3, 1968. LC 68-58742. 176p. reprint ed. pap. 54.60 (*0-608-11842-7*, 201132600078) Bks Demand.

— Heat Transfer in Solar Energy Systems: Presented at the Winter Annual Meeting of the American Society of Mechanical Engineers, Atlanta, Georgia, Nov. 27-Dec. 2, 1977. Howell, J. R. & Min, T., eds. LC 77-89012. 141p. reprint ed. pap. 43.80 (*0-608-30873-0*, 205173000003) Bks Demand.

— High Energy Rate Fabrication: Presented at the Winter Annual Meeting of the American Society of Mechanical Engineers, Phoenix, Arizona, November 14-19, 1982. LC 82-73415. (PVP Ser.: Vol. 70). (Illus.). 88p. reprint ed. pap. 30.00 (*0-8357-2834-X*, 203907000010) Bks Demand.

— Highway Collision Reconstruction: Presented at the Winter Annual Meeting of ASME, Chicago, Illinois, November 16-21, 1980. Moffatt, Edward A. & Moffatt, Charles C., eds. LC 80-69198. (Illus.). 125p. reprint ed. pap. 38.80 (*0-608-17566-8*, 203055200069) Bks Demand.

— Hyperbaric Diving Systems & Thermal Protection: Presented at the Winter Annual Meeting of ASME, San Francisco, CA, December 10-15, 1978. Johnson, Charles E. et al, eds. LC 78-68077. (QED Ser.: Vol. 6). 155p. reprint ed. pap. 48.10 (*0-8357-8725-7*, 203364000087) Bks Demand.

— Indexes to Nineteen-Eighty Publications. LC TJ0001.A5. (Transactions of American Society of Mechanical Engineers Ser.: Vol. 103). 221p. reprint ed. pap. 68.60 (*0-608-10780-8*, 201691600007) Bks Demand.

— Inelastic Behavior of Composite Materials: Papers Presented at 1975 ASME Winter Annual Meeting, Houston, TX, November 30-December 5, 1975. Herakovich, Carl T., ed. LC 75-8348. (AMD Ser.: Vol. 13). 220p. reprint ed. pap. 68.20 (*0-8357-8728-1*, 203364500087) Bks Demand.

— Interactive Computer Graphics in Engineering: Presented at the Winter Annual Meeting of the American Society of Mechanical Engineers, New York, N. Y., December 5-10, 1976. Hulbert, L. E., ed. LC 77-77033. 84p. reprint ed. pap. 30.00 (*0-608-30555-3*, 205132800096) Bks Demand.

— Interactive Fluid-Structural Dynamic Problems in Power Engineering: Presented at the Joint Conference of the Pressure Vessels & Piping, Materials, Nuclear Engineering, Solar Energy Divisions, Denver, Colorado, June 21-25, 1981. Moody, Frederick J. & Au-Yang, M. K., eds. LC 80-71107. (PVP Ser.: Vol. 46). (Illus.). 183p. 1981. reprint ed. pap. 56.80 (*0-8357-2842-0*, 203907700010) Bks Demand.

— Isolation of Mechanical Vibration, Impact & Noise: A Colloquium Presented at the ASME Design Engineering Technical Conference, Cincinnati, Ohio, Sept., 1973. Snowdon, John C. & Ungar, Eric E., eds. LC 73-84652. (ASME Applied Mechanics Division Ser.: Vol. 1). 276p. reprint ed. pap. 85.60 (*0-608-30845-5*, 205153600086) Bks Demand.

— Loss Prevention of Rotating Machinery: Papers Presented at ASME Petroleum Division Conference, Houston, Texas, September 1971. LC 71-187881. 58p. reprint ed. pap. 30.00 (*0-608-11681-5*, 201132800078) Bks Demand.

— Manual on Cutting of Metals, with Single-Point Tools. 2nd ed. LC 53-1487. 560p. reprint ed. pap. 173.60 (*0-608-11620-3*, 200472300046) Bks Demand.

— Manufacturing Solutions Based on Engineering Sciences: Presented at the Winter Annual Meeting of the American Society of Mechanical Engineers, Washington, D.C., November 15-20, 1981. Kops, L., ed. LC 81-69018. (PED Ser.: Vol. 3). (Illus.). 213p. reprint ed. pap. 66.10 (*0-8357-2827-7*, 203906300010) Bks Demand.

— Marine Propulsion: Presented at the Winter Annual Meeting of the ASME, New York, NY, December 5-10, 1976. Sladky, J., ed. LC 76-28850. (American Society of Mechanical Engineers, Applied Mechanics Division Ser.: Vol. 2). (Illus.). 235p. reprint ed. pap. 72.90 (*0-608-10776-X*, 201681500005) Bks Demand.

— Material-Environment Interactions in Structural & Pressure Containment Service: Papers Presented at the Winter Annual Meeting of the American Society of Mechanical Engineers, Chicago, Illinois, November 16-21, 1980. Smith, George V., ed. LC 80-69194. (MPC Ser.: No. 15). (Illus.). 166p. reprint ed. pap. 51.50 (*0-8357-2879-X*, 203911600011) Bks Demand.

— Materials of Construction of Fluid Machinery & Their Relationship to Design & Performance: Presented at the Winter Annual Meeting of the American Society of Mechanical Engineers, Washington, D.C., November 15-20, 1981. Cherry, R. C. et al, eds. LC 81-69017. (Illus.). 111p. reprint ed. pap. 34.50 (*0-8357-2863-3*, 203909900011) Bks Demand.

— Measurement & Control for Batch Manufacturing: Presented at the Winter Annual Meeting of the American Society of Mechanical Engineers, Phoenix, Arizona, November 14-19, 1982. Hardt, D. E., ed. LC 82-73180. (Illus.). 201p. reprint ed. pap. 62.40 (*0-8357-2856-0*, 203909100010) Bks Demand.

— Measurement in Polyphase Flows: Papers Presented at the Winter Annual Meeting of the American Society of Mechanical Engineers, San Francisco, California, December 10-15, 1978. Stock, David E., ed. LC 78-68328. 131p. reprint ed. pap. 40.70 (*0-608-30896-X*, 205171200005) Bks Demand.

— Measurements in Polyphase Flows, 1982: Presented at the 1982 AIAA-ASME Joint Fluids, Plasma, Thermophysics & Heat Transfer Conference, St. Louis, Missouri, June 7-11, 1982. Heidrick, T. R. & Patel, B. R., eds. LC 78-68328. (Illus.). 135p. reprint ed. pap. 41.90 (*0-8357-2847-1*, 203908200010) Bks Demand.

— Measurements of the Impacts of Materials Substitution: A Case Study in the Automobile Industry: Presented at the Winter Annual Meeting of ASME, San Francisco, CA, December 10-15, 1978. Bleloch, Andrew L., ed. LC 78-59892. 72p. reprint ed. pap. 30.00 (*0-8357-8737-0*, 203363900087) Bks Demand.

— Mechanics of Bimodulus Materials: Presented at the ASME Winter Annual Meeting, New York, New York, December 2-7, 1979. Bert, Charles W., ed. LC 79-54427. (AMD Ser.: Vol. 33). (Illus.). 93p. reprint ed. pap. 30.00 (*0-8357-2853-6*, 203908800010) Bks Demand.

— Mechanics of Superconducting Structures: Presented at the Winter Annual Meeting of the American Society of Mechanical Engineers, Chicago, IL, November 16-21, 1980. Moon, Francis C., ed. LC 80-69184. (AMD Ser.: Vol. 41). (Illus.). 143p. reprint ed. pap. 44.40 (*0-8357-2910-9*, 203914700011) Bks Demand.

— Metallic Bellows & Expansion Joints: Presented at the Joint Conference of the Pressure Vessels & Piping, Materials, Nuclear Engineering, Solar Energy Divisions, Denver, CO, 1. Brown, S. J. et al, eds. LC 81-65236. (PVP Ser.: No. 51). (Illus.). 160p. pap. 49.60 (*0-608-15567-5*, 205639600001) Bks Demand.

— Modal Testing & Model Refinement: Presented by the Winter Annual Meeting of the American Society of Mechanical Engineers, Boston, Massachusetts, November 13-18, 1983. Chu, David F., ed. LC 83-72721. (AMD Ser.: Vol. 59). 165p. pap. 51.20 (*0-7837-0207-8*, 204050300017) Bks Demand.

— Modeling, Simulation, Testing & Measurements for Solar Energy Systems: Presented at the Winter Annual Meeting of ASME, San Francisco, CA., December 10-15, 1978. Nash, J. M. & Smok, J. T., eds. LC 78-67977. 107p. reprint ed. pap. 33.20 (*0-608-12625-X*, 202418300035) Bks Demand.

— Nonlinear Numerical Analysis of Reinforced Concrete: Presented at the Winter Annual Meeting of the American Society of Mechanical Engineers, Phoenix, Arizona, November 14-19, 1982. Schwer, Leonard E., ed. LC 82-73178. (Illus.). 129p. reprint ed. pap. 40.00 (*0-8357-2850-1*, 203908500010) Bks Demand.

— Numerical Modeling of Manufacturing Processes: Presented at the Winter Annual Meeting of the American Society of Mechanical Engineers, Atlanta, Georgia, November 27-December 2, 1977. Jones, R. F., Jr. et al, eds. LC 77-87324. (Illus.). 188p. reprint ed. pap. 58.30 (*0-8357-2851-X*, 203908600010) Bks Demand.

— Particulate Laden Flows in Turbomachinery: Presented at 1982 AIAA-ASME Joint Fluids, Plasma, Thermophysics, & Heat Transfer Conference, St. Louis, Missouri, June 7-11, 1982. Tabakoff, W. et al, eds. LC 82-71170. (Illus.). 156p. reprint ed. pap. 48.40 (*0-8357-2846-3*, 203908100010) Bks Demand.

— Peaking Power Generation: Presented at the Winter Annual Meeting of the American Society of Mechanical Engineers, Chicago, Illinois, November 16-21, 1980. Miliaras, E. S., ed. LC 80-69795. (Illus.). 58p. reprint ed. pap. 30.00 (*0-8357-2888-9*, 203912400011) Bks Demand.

— Performance Characteristics of Hydraulic Turbines & Pumps: Presented at the Winter Annual Meeting of ASME, Boston, MA, November 13-18, 1983. Swift, Walter L. et al, eds. LC 83-72716. (FED Ser.: Vol. 6). 214p. reprint ed. pap. 66.40 (*0-8357-8747-8*, 203365600087) Bks Demand.

— Performance of Pressure Vessels with Clad & Overlayed Stainless Steel Linings: Presented at the Joint Conference of the Pressure Vessels & Piping, Materials, Nuclear Engineering, Solar Energy Divisions, Denver, Colorado, June 21-25, 1981. Sluzalis, L. I. & Dempsey, P. E., eds. LC 81-69253. (MPC Ser.: No. 16). (Illus.). 77p. reprint ed. pap. 30.00 (*0-8357-2881-1*, 203911800011) Bks Demand.

— Present Status & Research Needs in Energy Recovery

from Wastes: Proceedings of the 1976 Conference Presented at Hueston Woods State Park, Oxford, Ohio, September 19-24, 1976. Matula, Richard A., ed. LC 77-151398. (Illus.). 452p. reprint ed. pap. 140.20 (*0-8357-2876-5*, 203911200011) Bks Demand.

— Pressure Vessels: A Workbook for Engineers. Hicks, E. J., ed. LC 81-111549. 58p. reprint ed. pap. 30.00 (*0-608-14291-3*, 201737200007) Bks Demand.

— Progress in Engineering Optimization, 1981: Presented at the ASME Design Engineering Technical Conferences, Hartford, Connecticut, September 20-23, 1981. Mayne, R. W. & Ragsdell, K. M., eds. LC 81-68332. (Illus.). 157p. reprint ed. pap. 48.70 (*0-8357-2837-4*, 203907300010) Bks Demand.

— Properties of Steel Weldments for Elevated Temperature Pressure Containment Applications: Presented at the Winter Annual Meeting of the American Society of Mechanical Engineers, San Francisco, California, December 10-15, 1978. Smith, George V., ed. LC 78-60045. (MPC Ser.: No. 9). (Illus.). 211p. reprint ed. pap. 65.50 (*0-8357-2899-4*, 203913500011) Bks Demand.

— PTFE Seals in Reciprocating Compressors: Manual of Material Selection, Design & Operating Practices. LC 74-32657. 90p. reprint ed. pap. 30.00 (*0-608-11747-1*, 201682400005) Bks Demand.

— Rail Transportation Proceedings, 1973: Papers & Discussions from Joint ASME-IEEE Railroad Conference, St. Louis, Missouri, April 11-12, 1973, Winter Annual Meeting of the ASME, New York, NY, November 26-30, 1972. LC 72-139216. 277p. reprint ed. pap. 85.90 (*0-8357-8754-0*, 203362500087) Bks Demand.

— Reliability Design for Vibroacoustic Environments: Papers Presented at the Winter Annual Meeting of the American Society of Mechanical Engineers, New York, NY, November 17-21, 1974. Kana, Daniel D. & Butler, Thomas G., eds. LC 74-81164. (Illus.). 193p. reprint ed. pap. 59.90 (*0-608-17872-1*, 203270400080) Bks Demand.

— Report on Diesel & Gas Engines Power Costs, 1974: Data for 1972 & Previous Years. LC TK1191.A4. 33p. reprint ed. pap. 30.00 (*0-608-30762-9*, 201331800086) Bks Demand.

— Research Needs Report: Energy Conversion Research. LC 77-367323. 137p. reprint ed. pap. 42.50 (*0-8357-8758-3*, 203363500087) Bks Demand.

— Risers, Arctic Design Criteria, Equipment Reliability in Hydrocarbon Processing: A Workbook for Engineers, Presented at 37th Petroleum Mechanical Engineering Workshop & Conference, September 13-15, 1981, Dallas, Texas. Kozik, Thomas J., ed. LC 81-186405. 250p. reprint ed. pap. 77.50 (*0-608-14390-1*, 201935100011) Bks Demand.

— Robotics Research & Advanced Application: Presented at the Winter Annual Meeting of ASME, Phoenix, Arizona, November 14-19,1982. Book, Wayne J., ed. LC 82-73173. 293p. reprint ed. pap. 90.90 (*0-608-12623-3*, 202418400035) Bks Demand.

— The Role of Nucleation in Boiling & Cavitation: Symposium Presented at Joint Fluids Engineering, Heat Transfer & Lubrication Conference, Detroit, Michigan, May 26-27, 1970. LC QC0304.R64. 23p. reprint ed. pap. 30.00 (*0-608-10158-3*, 201687700006) Bks Demand.

— Scaling in Two-Phase Flows: Presented at the Winter Annual Meeting of the American Society of Mechanical Engineers, Chicago, Illinois, November 16-21, 1980. Saha, P. & Farukhi, Nayeem M., eds. LC 80-69193. (HTD Ser.: Vol. 14). (Illus.). 59p. reprint ed. pap. 30.00 (*0-8357-2817-X*, 203905600010) Bks Demand.

— Shuttle Propulsion Systems: Presented at the Winter Annual Meeting of the American Society of Mechanical Engineers, Phoenix, Arizona, November 14-19, 1982. Robinson, John W., ed. LC 82-73179. (AD Ser.: No. 05). (Illus.). 93p. reprint ed. pap. 30.00 (*0-8357-2906-0*, 203914300011) Bks Demand.

— Singular Perturbations: Order Reduction in Control System Design. LC 72-87029. 68p. reprint ed. pap. 30.00 (*0-608-30405-0*, 201230400082) Bks Demand.

— Small Hydro-Power Fluid Machinery: Presented at the Winter Annual Meeting of the American Society of Mechanical Engineers, Chicago, Illinois, November 16-21, 1980. Webb, D. R. & Papadakis, C. N., eds. LC 80-68343. 116p. reprint ed. pap. 36.00 (*0-8357-6996-8*, 203904900010) Bks Demand.

— Solar Engineering, 1993: Presented at the ASME International Solar Energy Conference, Washington, D. C., April 4-9, 1993. Kirkpatrick, Allan & Worek, William, eds. LC 93-155719. 548p. 1993. reprint ed. pap. 169.90 (*0-608-00283-6*, 205931100007) Bks Demand.

— Solid Earth Geophysics & Geotechnology: Presented at the Winter Annual Meeting of the American Society of Mechanical Engineers, Chicago, Illinois, November 16-21, 1980. Nemat-Nasser, S., ed. LC 78-59886. (AMD Ser.: Vol. 42). (Illus.). 95p. reprint ed. pap. 30.00 (*0-8357-2848-X*, 203908300010) Bks Demand.

— Stochastic Problems in Control. LC 68-8579. 124p. reprint ed. pap. 38.50 (*0-608-30973-7*, 201648400004) Bks Demand.

— Stochastic Processes in Dynamical Problems. LC 71-105935. 121p. reprint ed. pap. 37.60 (*0-608-13167-9*, 202418000035) Bks Demand.

— Structural Materials for Service at Elevated Temperatures in Nuclear Power Generation: Symposium November 30 - December 3, 1975. Schaefer, Adolph O., ed. LC 81-52553. 368p. reprint ed. pap. 114.10 (*0-608-09449-8*, 205424900005) Bks Demand.

— Surface Mechanics: Papers Presented at a Symposium Held November 16-21, 1969, at the ASME Winter Annual Meeting in Los Angeles. Ling, Frederick F., ed. LC 72-101588. 188p. reprint ed. pap. 58.30 (*0-608-14971-3*, 202596600047) Bks Demand.

— Surface Roughness Effects in Hydrodynamic & Mixed Lubrication: Presented at the Winter Annual Meeting of the American Society of Mechanical Engineers, Chicago, Illinois, November 16-21, 1980. Rohde, S. M. & Cheng, H. S., eds. LC 80-69179. (Illus.). 217p. reprint ed. pap. 67.30 (*0-8357-2830-7*, 203906600010) Bks Demand.

— Survey of Nucleonic Heat Transfer Research & Development. LC 72-185848. Vol. 1. 44p. reprint ed. pap. 25.00 (*0-317-09936-1*, 2016900) Bks Demand.

— Survival of Mechanical Systems in Transient Environments: Presented at the Winter Annual Meeting of the American Society of Mechanical Engineers, New York, December 2-7, 1979. Geers, Thomas L. & Tong, Pin, eds. LC 79-54424. (AMD Ser.: Vol. 36). (Illus.). 195p. reprint ed. pap. 60.50 (*0-8357-2854-4*, 203908900010) Bks Demand.

— Symposium on Measurement in Unsteady Flow: Presented at the ASME Hydraulic Division Conference, Worcester, Mass., May 21-23, 1962. LC 63-2546. 118p. reprint ed. pap. 36.60 (*0-608-11721-8*, 205044000081) Bks Demand.

— Symposium on Two & One Fourth Chrome One Molybdenum Steel in Pressure Vessels & Piping: Held as Part of the 25th Annual Petroleum- Engineering Conference, & The Second Annual Pressure Vessels & Piping Conference, September 16-17, 1970, Denver, CO. Schaefer, Adolph O., ed. LC 75-28161. 216p. reprint ed. pap. 67.00 (*0-608-17868-3*, 203269900080) Bks Demand.

— Thermal Problems in Biotechnology: Presented at the Winter Annual Meeting of ASME, New York, NY, December 3, 1968. LC 68-58741. (Illus.). 132p. reprint ed. pap. 41.00 (*0-608-30393-3*, 201682200005) Bks Demand.

— Thermomechanical Behavior of High-Temperature Composites: Presented at the Winter Annual Meeting of the American Society of Mechanical Engineers, Phoenix, Arizona, November 14-19, 1982. Jortner, Julius, ed. LC 82-73182. (AD Ser.: No. 04). (Illus.). 128p. reprint ed. pap. 39.70 (*0-8357-2909-5*, 203914600011) Bks Demand.

— Thermophysical Properties: Proceedings of the Fourth Symposium, University of Maryland, College Park, Maryland, 1968. Moszynski, Jerzy R., ed. LC 59-1391. 486p. reprint ed. pap. 150.70 (*0-608-14347-2*, 205192300014) Bks Demand.

— Towards the Factory of the Future: Emergence of the Computerized Factory & Its Impact on Society: Presented at the Winter Annual Meeting of the ASME, Chicago, Illinois, November 16-21, 1980. Kops, L., ed. LC 80-69197. (PED Ser.: Vol. 1). 120p. pap. 37.20 (*0-608-15561-6*, 205638900064) Bks Demand.

— Turbomachinery Developments in Steam & Gas Turbines: Presented at the Winter Annual Meeting of the American Society of Mechanical Engineers, Atlanta, Georgia, November 27-December 2, 1977. Steltz, W. G., ed. LC 77-88002. (Illus.). 104p. reprint ed. pap. 32.30 (*0-608-11709-9*, 201332100085) Bks Demand.

— Use of Computers in Managing Material Property Data: Presented at the Winter Annual Meeting of the American Society of Mechanical Engineers, Chicago, Illinois, November 16-21, 1980. Graham, James A., ed. LC 80-69196. (MPC Ser.: No. 14). (Illus.). 72p. reprint ed. pap. 30.00 (*0-8357-2902-8*, 203913800011) Bks Demand.

— Vibration & Behavior of Composite Structures: Presented at the Winter Annual Meeting of the American Society of Mechanical Engineers, San Francisco, California, December 10-15, 1989. Mei, C. et al, eds. LC 89-46375. (AD Ser.: Vol. 14). 79p. 1989. reprint ed. pap. 30.00 (*0-608-00291-7*, 205931900008) Bks Demand.

American Society of Mechanical Engineers Staff & Uzkan, Teoman. New Developments in Engine Design & Combustion. LC 98-73768. 1998. write for info. (*0-7918-1581-1*) ASME Pr.

American Society of Mechanical Engineers Staff, et al. Flow Studies in Air & Water Pollution: Presented at the Joint Meeting of the Fluids Engineering Division & the Applied Mechanics Division, Georgia Institute of Technology, Atlanta, GA, June, 1973. Arndt, Roger E., ed. LC 73-80154. 232p. reprint ed. pap. 72.00 (*0-608-11754-4*, 201683900005) Bks Demand.

American Society of Mechanical Engineers Staff, jt. auth. see International Material Management Society Staff.

American Society of Media Photographers Staff. ASMP Professional Business Practices in Photography. 5th rev. ed. LC 97-72046. (Illus.). 416p. 1997. pap. 24.95 (*0-927629-14-3*) Allworth Pr.

American Society of Media Photographers Staff & Weisgrau, Richard. Formalizing Agreements. Skinner, Peter, ed. 32p. 1995. pap. write for info. (*0-9605474-3-6*) Am Soc Media.

American Society of Metals Staff. Source Book on Maraging Steels: A Comprehensive Collection of Outstanding Articles from the Periodical & Reference Literature. LC 79-13743. (AMS Engineering Bookshelf Ser.). (Illus.). 400p. reprint ed. pap. 124.00 (*0-608-30699-1*, 201949300013) Bks Demand.

American Society of Newspaper Editors. ASNE Proceedings: Proceedings of the Convention of the American Society of Newspaper Editors, San Francisco, 1987. 1989. 25.00 (*0-318-33452-6*) Am Soc News.

— Newsroom Management Handbook. 1985. 15.00 (*0-318-33451-8*) Am Soc News.

American Society of Notaries Staff. New Jersey Notary Handbook. 3rd ed. LC 72-97800. 90p. 1997. pap. 9.95 (*0-318-13197-8*) Am Soc Notaries.

American Society of Notaries Staff, et al. Manual for Notaries Public of Virginia. LC 82-72541. (Illus.). viii, 83p. 1982. 9.95 (*0-317-00824-2*) Am Soc Notaries.

American Society of Pediatric Neurosurgery, ed. Concepts in Pediatric Neurosurgery, No. 1. (Illus.). x, 238p. 1982. 165.25 (*3-8055-2904-X*) S Karger.

— Concepts in Pediatric Neurosurgery, No. 2. (Illus.). x, 222p. 1982. 165.25 (*3-8055-3454-X*) S Karger.

American Society of PeriAnesthesia Nurses Staff. Ambulatory Surgical Nursing Core Curriculum. Connor, Maura, ed. LC 98-34732. (Illus.). 635p. (C). 1998. pap. text 47.00 (*0-7216-6522-5*, W B Saunders Co) Harcrt Hlth Sci Grp.

— Core Curriculum for Perianesthesia Nursing Practice. 4th ed. Connor, Maura, ed. LC 98-28129. (Illus.). 600p. 1998. pap. text. write for info. (*0-7216-7896-3*, W B Saunders Co) Harcrt Hlth Sci Grp.

American Society of Post Anesthesia Nurses Staff. Certification Review for Perianesthesia Nursing. 3rd ed. Carlson, Kathy, ed. LC 95-36450. (Illus.). 379p. 1995. pap. text 33.00 (*0-7216-4492-9*, W B Saunders Co) Harcrt Hlth Sci Grp.

American Society of Tool & Manufacturing Engineers. Non-Traditional Machining Processes. Springborn, R. K., ed. LC 67-17078. (American Society of Tool & Manufacturing Engineers Manufacturing Data Ser.). 190p. reprint ed. pap. 58.90 (*0-608-11724-2*, 205119800085) Bks Demand.

— Pneumatic Controls for Industrial Application: A Practical & Comprehensive Presentation of Pneumatic Control System Fundamentals, Control Devices, Associated Facilities, & Application Circuitry for Manual, Semiautomatic, & Automatic Industrial Operations. Wilson, Frank W., ed. LC 65-13379. (Manufacturing Data Ser.). 174p. reprint ed. pap. 54.00 (*0-608-13149-0*, 202417800035) Bks Demand.

American Sociological Association Staff. American Sociological Association Style Guide. viii, 38p. (Orig.). 1996. pap. 10.00 (*0-912764-27-9*) Am Sociological.

American Sociological Society Staff. The Family. LC 78-169370. (Family in America Ser.). 226p. 1976. reprint ed. 23.95 (*0-405-03846-1*) Ayer.

— Social Problems - Social Processes: Selected Papers from the Proceedings of the American Sociological Society, 1932. Bogardus, Emory S., ed. LC 67-23173. (Essay Index Reprint Ser.). 1977. 19.95 (*0-8369-0151-7*) Ayer.

American Speech - Language Hearing Association Sta. Guidelines for Audiologic Screening. LC 98-114043. 1997. spiral bd. 10.00 (*0-910329-96-6*, 0112060) Am Speech Lang Hearing.

American Speech-Language-Hearing Association Staff. ASHA Desk Reference, 4 vols. 1997. ring bd. 85.00 (*1-58041-003-0*, 0111972) Am Speech Lang Hearing.

— Technology 2000: Clinical Applications For Speech-language Pathology. LC 98-161891. 93p. 1997. write for info. (*1-58041-002-2*) Am Speech Lang Hearing.

American Speech-Language-Hearing Association Staff, et al. Gender & Health Issues: A Resource Handbook. 250p. 1996. pap. 23.00 (*0-910329-87-7*, 0112014) Am Speech Lang Hearing.

American Speech-Language-Hearing Foundation Staff. The First Yes: Poems about Communicating. Goldberg, Barbara, ed. LC 96-36752. (Orig.). 1997. pap. 16.50 (*0-931848-92-X*) Dryad Pr.

American Spiritualist Assembly Directors, ed. see Rizer, Arden C., Jr.

American Sport Education Program Staff. Coaching Principles Course Instructor Guide. 4th ed. 152p. 1996. teacher ed., ring bd. 69.00 (*0-88011-618-8*, ACEP0008) Human Kinetics.

— Coaching Youth Baseball. 2nd ed. LC 95-35124. (Coaching Youth Sport Ser.). (Illus.). 152p. (Orig.). 1996. pap. 12.95 (*0-87322-965-7*, ACEP0424) Human Kinetics.

— Coaching Youth Basketball. 2nd rev. ed. LC 95-14388. (Coaching Youth Sport Ser.). (Illus.). 141p. 1995. pap. 12.95 (*0-87322-892-8*, ACEP0421) Human Kinetics.

— Coaching Youth Football. 2nd ed. LC 96-31306. (Coaching Youth Sport Ser.). (Illus.). 176p. 1996. pap. 12.95 (*0-88011-539-4*, ACEP0426) Human Kinetics.

— Coaching Youth Hockey. LC 95-34844. (Coaching Youth Sport Ser.). 184p. 1995. pap. 12.95 (*0-87322-964-9*, ACEP0431) Human Kinetics.

— Coaching Youth Lacrosse. LC 96-41428. (Coaching Youth Sport Ser.). (Illus.). 256p. 1997. pap. 13.95 (*0-88011-627-7*, ACEP0432) Human Kinetics.

— Coaching Youth Soccer. 2nd ed. LC 95-2206. (Coaching Youth Sport Ser.). (Illus.). 160p. 1995. pap. 12.95 (*0-87322-831-6*, ACEP0420) Human Kinetics.

— Coaching Youth Softball. 2nd rev. ed. LC 95-35123. (Coaching Youth Sport Ser.). (Illus.). 152p. 1995. pap. 12.95 (*0-87322-967-3*, ACEP0425) Human Kinetics.

— Coaching Youth Tennis. 2nd rev. ed. LC 97-52260. (Illus.). 152p. 1998. pap. 12.95 (*0-87322-966-5*, ACEP0423, Amer Sport Educ) Human Kinetics.

— Coaching Youth Volleyball. 2nd rev. ed. LC 96-3039. (Coaching Youth Sport Ser.). (Illus.). 168p. 1996. pap. 12.95 (*0-88011-540-8*, ACEP0427) Human Kinetics.

— Event Management for Sport Directors: American Sport Education Program. LC 95-21941. (Illus.). 144p. 1995. spiral bd. 22.00 (*0-87322-968-1*, ACEP0320) Human Kinetics.

— Rookie Coaches Soccer Guide. LC 90-28000. (Illus.). 80p. reprint ed. pap. 30.00 (*0-608-20810-8*, 207190900003) Bks Demand.

— Sport Parent. LC 94-3914. (Illus.). 96p. 1994. pap. text 8.95 (*0-87322-696-8*, ACEP0452) Human Kinetics.

— Sport Parent Facilitator Manual. (Illus.). 1998. pap. text, teacher ed. 69.00 incl. VHS (*0-87322-799-9*, ACEP0457) Human Kinetics.

— SportParent Survival Guide: The Thinking Parent's Guide to Not Just Surviving Youth Sport-but Thriving in It! (Illus.). 16p. 1994. pap. text 10.00 (*0-87322-697-6*, ACEP0453) Human Kinetics.

American Sport Education Program Staff & Leonard, John. Rookie Coaches Swimming Guide. LC 94-27661. (Illus.). 80p. (Orig.). 1994. pap. 9.95 (*0-87322-645-3*, ACEP0410) Human Kinetics.

American Sport Education Program Staff & National Federation Interscholastic Coaches Educat. Citizenship Through Sports Clinic Instructor Guide. (Illus.). 106p. 1998. teacher ed., student ed., spiral bd. 69.00 (*0-88011-984-5*, ACEP0014) Human Kinetics.

— Citizenship Through Sports Clinic Study Guide. (Illus.). 14p. 1998. pap. text, student ed. 40.00 (*0-88011-990-X*, ACEP0019) Human Kinetics.

American Standard, Inc. Staff. Expendable Cores for Copper Alloy Die Casting. 49p. 1970. 7.35 (*0-317-34524-9*, 132) Intl Copper.

***American Statistical Association Staff.** Exploring Statistics in the Elementary Grades, Bk. 1. (Illus.). 152p. (J). 1998. 15.95 (*1-57232-344-2*) Seymour Pubns.

American Steamship Company Staff. How to Make a Steamship Float & Other Great Lakes Recipes. (Illus.). 135p. (Orig.). 1984. spiral bd. 10.95 (*0-937360-04-X*) Harbor Hse MI.

— How to Make a Steamship Float & Other Great Lakes Recipes. (Orig.). 1996. pap. 10.95 (*0-937360-05-8*) Harbor Hse MI.

American String Teachers Association Staff. Sforzando! Music Medicine for String Players. Mischakoff, Anne, ed. 1985. pap. text 10.95 (*0-89917-462-0*) Am String Tchrs.

American String Teachers Association Staff, jt. auth. see Music Educators Staff.

American Studies Association Staff. American Perspectives: The National Self-Image in the Twentieth Century. Spiller, Robert E. & Larrabee, Eric, eds. LC 61-8841. (Library of Congress Series in American Civilization). 228p. 1961. reprint ed. pap. 70.70 (*0-7837-1727-X*, 205725700024) Bks Demand.

American Studies Symposium Staff. GLI/Italiani Negli Stati Uniti (Italians in the United States) Proceedings of the American Studies Symposium, 3rd, University of Florence, May 27-29, 1969. LC 74-17932. (Italian American Experience Ser.). (Illus.). 1975. reprint ed. 41.95 (*0-405-06404-7*) Ayer.

American Sunday-School Union of Philadelphia Staff. Am I a Child of God? unabridged ed. (Children's Heritage Ser.). (Illus.). 64p. (J). (gr. 4-6). 1995. pap. 4.75 (*1-58339-108-8*, D8) Triangle Press.

American Symphony Orchestra League Staff. Americanizing the American Orchestra: Report of the National Task Force for the American Orchestra, an Initiative for Change. 250p. 1993. student ed. 25.00 (*1-883807-00-X*) Am Symphony Orch.

— The Gold Book, 1998-99: A Sourcebook of Successful & Creative Orchestra Fund-Raising, Education, Ticket Sales, & Service Projects. 196p. 1998. 30.00 (*1-883807-06-9*) Am Symphony Orch.

— The Gold Book, 1997-98: A Sourcebook of Successful & Creative Orchestra Fund-Raising, Education, Ticket Sales, & Service Projects. 163p. 1997. 33.00 (*1-883807-05-0*) Am Symphony Orch.

American Technical Publishers Staff. Practical Math. 3rd ed. LC 94-6617. 352p. 1994. pap. 22.96 (*0-8269-2244-9*) Am Technical.

American Telephone & Telegraph Staff. UNIX-R System V Programmer's Guide. (Illus.). 848p. 1987. pap. text 34.95 (*0-317-58031-0*) P-H.

American Temperance Society Staff. Permanent Temperance Documents of the American Temperance Society. LC 77-38433. (Religion in America, Ser. 2). 566p. 1972. reprint ed. 42.95 (*0-405-04054-7*) Ayer.

American Textile History Museum Staff & Hawthorne, Catherine B. And So to Sleep: Jacquard Coverlets from the Hawthorne Collection (Exhibit Catalogue, May 2-July 31, 1999) LC 99-62086. (Illus.). 47p. 1999. pap. 19.50 (*0-937474-14-2*) Am Textile Hist.

American TFP Staff. The Womb Becomes a Tomb: Are We Sacrificing to Moloch? (Illus.). 90p. (Orig.). 1992. pap. 5.95 (*1-877905-26-7*) Am Soc Defense TFP.

American TFP Staff, ed. see Study Commission of the American TFP Staff.

American Theatre Wing Staff. The Tony Award: A Complete Listing of Winners & Nominees with a History of the American Theatre Wing. LC 94-36644. 176p. 1994. pap. 14.95 (*0-435-08658-8*, 08658) Heinemann.

American Topical Association Carto-Philatelists-Ma. Map Stamps of the World. (Illus.). 39p. (Orig.). 1982. pap. 7.00 (*0-614-25041-2*) Am Topical Assn.

American Topical Association Staff, jt. auth. see Dodson, Larry.

American Tourister Staff. Durable Zippered Book/bible Cover: Burgandy Poly/nylon for Paperback. 1997. 22.00 (*1-889273-23-6*) Talbot Mktg Grp.

American Tourister Staff. Durable Zippered Book/Bible Cover; Tapestry Fabric: Paisley Pattern for Paperback. 1998. 13.00 (*1-889273-45-7*) Talbot Mktg Grp.

American Tract Society Staff. The American Tract Society Documents, Eighteen Twenty-Four to Nineteen Twenty-Five. LC 74-38434. (Religion in America, Ser. 2). 484p. 1972. reprint ed. 31.95 (*0-405-04055-5*) Ayer.

— Enormity of the Slave-Trade. LC 77-133153. (Black Heritage Library Collection). 1977. 18.95 (*0-8369-8708-X*) Ayer.

American Trade Union Delegation to the Soviet Unio. Soviet Russia in the Second Decade. Chase, Stuart et al, eds. LC 72-8432. (Select Bibliographies Reprint Ser.). 1977. reprint ed. 20.95 (*0-8369-6961-8*) Ayer.

American Training Association Staff. Standards for the Practice of Therapeutic Recreation & Self Assessment Guide. 32p. (Orig.). 1993. pap. text 18.75 (*1-889435-02-3*) Am Therapeutic.

American Trucking Assn. Staff, ed. Managing Fatigue in Transportation. 176p. 1997. pap. text 75.00 (*0-86587-589-8*, 589) Gov Insts.

American Trucking Association, National Accounting & American Trucking Association, National Freight Cl. Motor Carrier Credit & Collection Practices Manual. rev. ed. 400p. 1992. pap. 155.00 (*0-88711-143-2*) Am Trucking Assns.

American Trucking Association National Accounting. ATA Accounting Service for Motor Carriers. 550p. 1996. ring bd. 155.00 (*0-88711-303-6*) Am Trucking Assns.

***American Trucking Association National Accounting.** Managing Your Independent Contract Fleet Survey: A Nationwide Survey of Trucking Companies Utilizing Owner-Operators. 37p. 1999. pap. text 95.00 (*0-88711-375-3*) Am Trucking Assns.

American Trucking Association National Accounting. NAFC State Tax Guide. 1100p. 1988. ring bd. 395.00 (*0-88711-021-5*) Am Trucking Assns.

American Trucking Association, National Freight Cl. Profitable Trucking. 161p. 1994. pap. text 12.95 (*0-88711-267-6*) Am Trucking Assns.

American Trucking Association, National Freight Cl, jt. auth. see American Trucking Association, National Accounting.

***American Trucking Association, Safety Department S.** Facts for Drivers. 550p. 1999. ring bd. 2.99 (*0-88711-374-5*) Am Trucking Assns.

American Trucking Association Sales & Marketing Co, jt. auth. see Clowdis, Charles W., Jr.

American Trucking Association Staff. ATA Trucking Salaried Employees Compensation Study, 1997, 2 vols. 529p. 1997. 450.00 (*0-88711-383-4*) Am Trucking Assns.

— Motor Carrier Technology Directory. 88p. 1999. pap. text 45.00 (*0-88711-398-2*) Am Trucking Assns.

— Trucksource: Soures of Trucking Industry Information. Covington-Jones, Barbara & Dluzynski, Janice, eds. 388p. 1999. pap. text 60.00 (*0-88711-367-2*) Am Trucking Assns.

***American Trucking Association, Trucking Informatio.** Motor Carrier Annual Report. (Financial & Operating Statistics Ser.). 548p. 1999. pap. text 400.00 (*0-88711-376-1*) Am Trucking Assns.

***American Trucking Associations National Accounting.** NAFC Sales Tax Service. 300p. 1999. ring bd. 215.00 (*0-88711-396-6*) Am Trucking Assns.

American Trucking Associations National Accounting. Risk Management Manual for Motor Carriers. 468p. 1986. ring bd. 175.00 (*0-88711-078-9*) Am Trucking Assns.

***American Trucking Associations National Accounting.** Risk Management Manual for Motor Carriers. 1998. ring bd. 195.00 (*0-88711-393-1*) Am Trucking Assns.

***American Trucking Associations Staff.** Guidelines for Loss Prevention: Physical Security in Motor Carrier Terminals. 40p. 1998. pap. 10.50 (*0-88711-395-8*) Am Trucking Assns.

American Trust Publications, ed. see Al-Faruqi, Llamya.

American Trust Publications, ed. see Mir, Mustansir.

American Trust Publications, ed. see Simpson, Juwairiah J.

American Unitarian Association Staff. From Servitude to Service. Cremin, Lawrence A. & Barnard, Frederick A., eds. LC 74-101402. (American Education: Its Men, Ideas, & Institutions. Series 1). 1975. reprint ed. 26.95 (*0-405-01382-5*) Ayer.

American Urological Association Allied Staff. AUAA (American Urological Association Allied) Urologic Nursing: Principles & Practice. Karlowicz, Karen A., ed. LC 92-49388. (Illus.). 736p. 1994. text 91.50 (*0-7216-2731-5*, W B Saunders Co) Harcrt Hlth Sci Grp.

American Urological Association Staff. History of Urology, 2 vols. Ballanger, Edgard G. et al, eds. LC 75-23674. reprint ed. 90.00 (*0-404-13300-2*) AMS Pr.

American Vacuum Society, Education Committee Staff. Experimental Vacuum Science & Technology. LC 72-97485. (Illus.). 288p. reprint ed. pap. 89.30 (*0-7837-0730-4*, 204105400019) Bks Demand.

***American Veterinary Association Staff.** Veterinary Medical School Admission Requirements in the United States & Canada 1999: 1999 Edition for 2000 Matriculation, Vol. 1. 1999. pap. 16.50 (*1-55753-168-4*) Purdue U Pr.

American Volleyball Coaches Association Staff. The Best of Coaching Volleyball Bk. 1: The Basic Elements of the Game. Asher, Kinda, ed. (Illus.). 176p. (Orig.). 1996. pap. 14.95 (*1-57028-083-5*, 80835H, Mstrs Pr) NTC Contemp Pub Co.

— The Best of Coaching Volleyball Bk. 2: The Advanced Elements of the Game. Asher, Kinda, ed. (Illus.). 176p. (Orig.). 1996. pap. 14.95 (*1-57028-084-3*, 80843H, Mstrs Pr) NTC Contemp Pub Co.

— Coaching Volleyball. rev. ed. LC 97-2296. Orig. Title: AVCA Handbook. (Illus.). 352p. 1997. pap. 19.95 (*1-57028-124-6*, 81246H, Mstrs Pr) NTC Contemp Pub Co.

American Water Resources Association, Annual Confe. Advances in the Development & Use of Models in Water Resources: Proceedings, November 5-10, 1995, Houston, TX. Cleveland, Theodore G., ed. LC 95-80551. (American Water Resources Association Technical Publication Ser.: Vol. TPS-95-3). 332p. 1995. reprint ed. pap. 103.00 (*0-608-02438-4*, 206308100004) Bks Demand.

American Water Resources Association, Conference (. Water Management in Urban Areas: Proceedings, November 5-10, 1995, Houston, TX. Loethen, Mark L., ed. LC 95-80552. (American Water Resources Association Technical Publication Ser.: Vol. TPS-95-4). 363p. 1995. reprint ed. pap. 103.50 (*0-608-02439-2*, 2063082) Bks Demand.

American Water Resources Association, Conference (23rd: 1987: Salt Lake City, UT) Staff. Aquifers of the Western Mountain Area: Regional Aquifer Systems of the United States: Papers Presented at 23rd Annual AWRA Conference & Symposium, November 1-6, 1987, Salt Lake City, UT. McLean, John S. & Johnson, A. Ivan, eds. LC GB1199.3.M6A. (AWRA Monograph: Vol. 14). 233p. reprint ed. pap. 72.30 (*0-608-02441-4*, 206308400004) Bks Demand.

American Water Resources Association, Conference (24th: 1998: Milwaukee, WI) Staff. Aquifers of the Midwestern Area: Regional Aquifer Systems of the United States: Papers Presented at the 14th Annual AWRA Conference & Symposium, November 6-11, 1988, Milwaukee, WI. Swain, L. A. & Johnson, A. Ivan, eds. LC GB1199.3.M53. (AWRA Monograph: Vol. 13). 251p. reprint ed. pap. 77.90 (*0-608-02442-2*, 206308500004) Bks Demand.

American Water Resources Association, Spring Symposium Staff. Water in the 21st Century: Conservation, Demand & Supply - Proceedings of the American Water Resources Association, Annual Spring Symposium, April 23-26, 1995, Salt Lake City, UT. Austin, Lloyd H. et al, eds. LC 94-70722. (American Water Resources Association Technical Publication Ser.: Vol. 95-1). (Illus.). 760p. reprint ed. pap. 200.00 (*0-608-09839-6*, 207080900007) Bks Demand.

American Water Resources Association Staff. Aquifers of the Far West: Papers Presented at AWRA Symposium on Water Supply & Water Reuse: 1992 & Beyond, June 2-6, 1991, San Diego, CA. Prince, Keith R. & Johnson, A. Ivan, eds. LC GB1199.3.M6. (AWRA Monograph: Vol. 16). (Illus.). 131p. reprint ed. pap. 40.70 (*0-7837-9227-1*, 204997800004) Bks Demand.

— Aquifers of the Southern & Eastern States: Papers Presented at AWRA 27th Annual Conference & Symposium, September 8-13, 1991, New Orleans, LA. Hotchkiss, William R. & Johnson, A. Ivan, eds. LC GB1199.3.M6. (AWRA Monograph: Vol. 17). (Illus.). 119p. reprint ed. pap. 36.90 (*0-7837-9228-X*, 204997900004) Bks Demand.

— GIS & Water Resources: Proceedings, AWRA Annual Symposium. Hallam, Cheryl A. et al, eds. LC 96-86079. (American Water Resources Association Technical Publication Ser.: No. TPS-96-3). (Illus.). 492p. 1996. reprint ed. pap. 152.60 (*0-608-04279-X*, 206503200012) Bks Demand.

— Managing Water Resources During Global Change: AWRA 28 Annual Conference & Symposium, an International Conference, Reno, NV, November 1-5, 1992. Herrmann, Raymond, ed. LC 92-74227. (American Water Resources Association Technical Publication Ser.: Vol. TPS-92-4). (Illus.). 874p. 1992. reprint ed. pap. 200.00 (*0-7837-9224-7*, 204997500004) Bks Demand.

— New York City Water Supply Studies - Watershed Restoration, Management: American Water Resources Association, Symposium Proceedings. McDonnell, Jeffrey J. et al, eds. LC 96-85384. (American Water Resources Association Technical Publication Ser.: No. TPS-96-2). (Illus.). 192p. 1996. reprint ed. pap. 59.60 (*0-608-04278-1*, 206503100012) Bks Demand.

— Options for Reaching Water Quality Goals: Proceedings of a Symposium Held in Washington, D. C. at the Twentieth Annual Conference of the American Water Resources Association - Co-Sponsored by Tennessee Valley Authority. Schad, Theodore M., ed. LC 85-71658. (American Water Resources Association Technical Publication Ser.: No. TPS 84-2). (Illus.). 225p. reprint ed. pap. 69.80 (*0-7837-5566-X*, 204534100005) Bks Demand.

— Proceedings of the Fourth American Water Resources Conference Held November 18-22, 1968, Commodore Hotel, New York, New York. Cohen, Philip & Francisco, Martha N., eds. LC HD1694.A5C6. (American Water Resources Association Proceedings Ser.: No. 6). 793p. reprint ed. pap. 200.00 (*0-608-13802-9*, 201781100008) Bks Demand.

— Regional Aquifer Systems of the United States, Aquifers of the Atlantic & Gulf Coastal Plain: Papers Presented at 22nd Annual AWRA Conference & Symposium, November 9-14, 1986, Atlanta GA. Vecchioli, John & Johnson, A. Ivan, eds. LC GB1018.A5. (AWRA Monograph Ser.: No. 9). 179p. reprint ed. pap. 55.50 (*0-8357-4078-1*, 203676800005) Bks Demand.

— Southwest Alluvial Basins of Arizona: Papers Presented at 21st Annual AWRA Conference & Symposium, August 11-16, 1985, Tucson, AZ. Anderson, T. W. & Johnson, A. Ivan, eds. LC GB1001.. (AWRA Monograph Series Regional Aquifer Systems of the United States: No. 7). (Illus.). 120p. 1986. reprint ed. pap. 37.20 (*0-7837-9596-3*, 206035300005) Bks Demand.

— Surface & Ground Water Quality: Pollution Prevention, Remediation, & the Great Lakes. Jennings, Aaron A. & Spangenberg, N. Earl, eds. LC 90-85959. (American Water Resources Association Technical Publication Ser.: Vol. TPS-91-1). (Illus.). 284p. (Orig.). 1991. reprint ed. pap. 88.10 (*0-7837-9221-2*, 204997200004) Bks Demand.

— Symposia on Water Resources Education, a Lifetime of Learning: Changing Roles in Water Resources Management & Policy. LC 93-71755. (American Water Resources Association Technical Publication Ser.: Vol. TPS-93-2). (Illus.). 732p. 1993. reprint ed. pap. 200.00 (*0-7837-9225-5*, 204997600004) Bks Demand.

— Transferring Models to Users: Proceedings of the Symposium Held November 4-8, 1990, at the Hyatt Regency Denver, Denver, Colorado. Janes, Eric B. & Hotchkiss, William R., eds. LC 90-84161. (American Water Resources Association Technical Publication Ser.: Vol. TPS-90-3). (Illus.). 416p. 1990. reprint ed. pap. 129.00 (*0-7837-9219-0*, 204997000004) Bks Demand.

— Water Management of River Systems: 27 Annual Conference & Resource Development of the Lower Mississippi River, Symposium Proceedings, New Orleans, LA, September 8-13, 1991. Dhamotharan, Dhamo, ed. LC 91-75128. (American Water Resources Association Technical Publication Ser.: Vol. TPS-91-3). 504p. 1991. reprint ed. pap. 156.30 (*0-7837-9223-9*, 204997400004) Bks Demand.

— Watershed Restoration Management: Physical, Chemical, & Biological Considerations: American Water Resources Association, Symposium Proceedings. McDonnell, Jeffrey J. et al, eds. LC 96-85383. (American Water Resources Association Technical Publication Ser.: No. TPS-96-1). (Illus.). 534p. 1996. reprint ed. pap. 165.60 (*0-608-04277-3*, 206503000012) Bks Demand.

— Wetlands: Concerns & Successes: Proceedings of the Symposium Held September 17-22, 1989, Tampa, FL. Fisk, David W., ed. LC 89-84352. (American Water Resources Association Technical Publication Ser.: Vol. TPS-89-3). (Illus.). 582p. 1989. reprint ed. pap. 180.50 (*0-7837-9218-2*, 204996900004) Bks Demand.

American Water Resources Association Staff, jt. auth. see Whipple, William.

American Water Resources Association, Summer Sympo. Effects of Human-Induced Changes on Hydrologic Systems: Proceedings, Annual Summer Symposium of the American Water Resources Association, June 26-29, 1994, Jackson Hole, WY. Marston, Richard A. & Hasfurther, Victor R., eds. LC 94-70721. 1202p. 1994. reprint ed. pap. 200.00 (*0-608-02437-6*, 206308000004) Bks Demand.

American Water Works Association. Computer Conference & Austin, Tex. Proceedings: 1997 Computer Conference : April 13-16, 1997, Austin, Texas) LC 97-172018. (Illus.). 1997. write for info. (*0-89867-898-6*) Am Water Wks Assn.

American Water Works Association Research Foundati & DVGS-Technologiezentrum Wasser Staff. Internal Corrosion of Water Distribution Systems. 2nd ed. LC 95-53857. 586p. 1996. 265.00 (*0-89867-759-9*, 90508) Am Water Wks Assn.

American Water Works Association Research Foundati, et al. Water Treatment Membrane Processes: A Joint Project by Three of the Worlds Largest Agencies. LC 96-17666. 320p. 1996. 84.95 (*0-07-001559-7*) McGraw.

American Water Works Association Staff. Construction Contract Administration. LC 96-42131. (Manual of Water Supply Practices Ser.: No. M47). (Illus.). 149p. 1996. pap. 98.00 (*0-89867-871-4*, 30047) Am Water Wks Assn.

***American Water Works Association Staff.** Design & Construction of Small Water Systems: An Awwa Small Systems Resource Book. 2nd ed. LC 99-30568. 1999. write for info. (*0-89867-999-0*) Am Water Wks Assn.

American Water Works Association Staff. Distribution System Requirements for Fire Protection. 3rd ed. LC 97-36649. (AWWA Manual Ser.). 1997. write for info. (*0-89867-935-4*) Am Water Wrks.

***American Water Works Association Staff.** Principles of Water Rates, Fees & Charges. LC 00-36212. (Manual of Water Supply Practices Ser.). 2000. write for info. (*1-58321-070-9*) Am Water Wks Assn.

American Water Works Association Staff. Simplified Procedures for Water Examination. 4th ed. LC 97-25864. (AWWA Manual Ser.: No. M12). 1997. 60.00 (*0-89867-914-1*, 30012) Am Water Wks Assn.

— Steel Water-Storage Tanks. LC 98-41256. (Manual Ser.). 145p. 1998. 98.00 (*0-89867-977-X*) Am Water Wks Assn.

***American Water Works Association Staff.** Water Audits & Leak Detection. 2nd ed. LC 99-52127. (Illus.). 1999. write for info. (*1-58321-018-0*) Am Water Wks Assn.

— Water Meters--Selection, Installation, Testing & Maintenance. 4th ed. LC 99-44930. (Manual Ser.). 1999. write for info. (*1-58321-017-2*) Am Water Wks Assn.

— Water Quality & Treatment: A Handbook Of Community Water Supplies. 5th ed. LC 99-49136. (Illus.). 1248p. 1999. 125.00 (*0-07-001659-3*) McGraw.

— Water Rate Structures & Pricing. 2nd ed. LC 99-35852. (Manual Ser.). 1999. write for info. (*1-58321-000-8*) Am Water Wks Assn.

American Water Works Association Staff. Water Utility Capital Financing. 2nd ed. LC 98-16938. 1998. 45.00 (*0-89867-957-5*) Am Water Wks Assn.

American Water Works Association Staff, contrib. by. Under the Microscope: Examining Microbes In Groundwater : the 1996 Goundwater Foundation Symposium Proceedings : Sept. 5 & 6, 1996, Boston, Mass. LC 97-221320. xi, 176p. 1997. write for info. (*0-89867-895-1*) Am Water Wks Assn.

American Water Works Association Staff, ed. Reverse Osmosis & Nanofiltration. LC 98-45001. (AWWA Manual Ser.). 1998. write for info. (*0-89867-978-8*) Am Water Wks Assn.

American Water Works Association Staff & American Society of Civil Engineers Staff, contrib. by. Water Treatment Plant Design. 3rd ed. LC 97-26057. (Illus.). 806p. 1997. text 115.00 (*0-07-001643-7*) Am Soc Civil Eng.

American Water Works Association Staff, jt. auth. see American Society of Civil Engineers Staff.

American Water Works Association Staff, jt. auth. see Kirmeyer, Gregory J.

***American Welding Society Staff.** Safety & Health Fact Sheets. 2nd ed. LC 99-184237. 1998. write for info. (*0-87171-582-1*) Am Welding.

American Welding Society Staff, ed. Hazleton Laboratories, Toxicity of Welding Fume in Rats (TWFR) (Illus.). 186p. 1987. pap. 100.00 (*0-87171-273-3*); 36.00 (*0-685-67543-2*) Am Welding.

American Yoga Association Staff & Christensen, Alice. 20 Minute Yoga Workouts. 160p. 1995. pap. 14.00 (*0-345-38845-3*) Ballantine Pub Grp.

American Yoga Association Staff, jt. auth. see Christensen, Alice.

Americana Club Staff. American Studies in Honor of William Kenneth Boyd. Jackson, D. K., ed. LC 68-20295. (Essay Index Reprint Ser.). 1977. 23.95 (*0-8369-0395-1*) Ayer.

Americanists Staff. Indian Tribes of Aboriginal America: Proceedings of the International Congress of Americanists, 29th. Tax, Sol, ed. (Illus.). 410p. 1967. reprint ed. 64.50 (*0-8154-0233-3*) Cooper Sq.

America's Bar Review Staff. Outline Constitutional Law. (C). 1995. pap. text 12.95 (*1-879563-21-5*) Lexicon CA.

— Outline Contracts. (C). 1995. pap. text 12.95 (*1-879563-22-3*) Lexicon CA.

— Outline Criminal Law. (C). 1995. pap. text 9.95 (*1-879563-23-1*) Lexicon CA.

— Outline Criminal Procedure. (C). 1995. pap. text 9.95 (*1-879563-24-X*) Lexicon CA.

— Outline Evidence. (C). 1995. pap. text 12.95 (*1-879563-25-8*) Lexicon CA.

— Outline Property. (C). 1995. pap. text 12.95 (*1-879563-26-6*) Lexicon CA.

— Outline Torts. (C). 1995. pap. text 9.95 (*1-879563-27-4*) Lexicon CA.

— Practice Essay Exams. (C). 1992. pap. text 16.95 (*1-879563-28-2*) Lexicon CA.

— Practice Performance Tests. (C). 1992. pap. text 34.95 (*1-879563-29-0*) Lexicon CA.

Americas Watch Staff. Argentina: Truth & Partial Justice in Argentina: An Update. 100p. (Orig.). 1991. pap. 7.00 (*0-929692-91-8*, Am Watch) Hum Rts Watch.

— Carnage Again: Preliminary Report on Violations of the Laws of War by Both Sides in the November 1989 Offensive in El Salvador. 50p. 1989. 7.00 (*0-929692-86-1*, Am Watch) Hum Rts Watch.

— Chile: Human Rights & the Plebiscite. 256p. (Orig.). 1988. pap. 15.00 (*0-938579-64-9*) Hum Rts Watch.

— Chile in Transition: Human Rights since the Plebiscite. 98p. 1989. 7.00 (*0-929692-36-5*, Am Watch) Hum Rts Watch.

— Cuba - Human Rights in Cuba: The Need to Sustain the Pressure. 120p. (Orig.). 1989. pap. 10.00 (*0-929692-12-8*, Am Watch) Hum Rts Watch.

— The Drug War in Colombia: The Neglected Tragedy of Political Violence. 136p. 1990. pap. 12.00 (*0-929692-48-9*, Am Watch) Hum Rts Watch.

— El Salvador & Human Rights: The Challenge of Reform. 150p. 1991. pap. 5.00 (*0-929692-90-X*, Am Watch) Hum Rts Watch.

— Harvesting Oppression: Forced Haitian Labor in the Dominican Sugar Industry. LC 90-82959. 70p. 1990. 7.00 (*0-929692-60-8*, Am Watch) Hum Rts Watch.

— In the Army's Hands: Human Rights in Haiti on the Eve of the Elections. LC 90-86195. 72p. 1990. 7.00 (*0-929692-80-2*, Am Watch) Hum Rts Watch.

— The Killings in Colombia. 128p. 1989. pap. 7.00 (*0-929692-18-7*, Am Watch) Hum Rts Watch.

— The Killings in Northern Nicaragua. 72p. 1989. 6.00 (*0-929692-37-3*, Am Watch) Hum Rts Watch.

— The Laws of War & the Conduct of the Panama Invasion. 30p. 1990. 6.00 (*0-929692-44-6*, Am Watch) Hum Rts Watch.

— Messengers of Death: Human Rights in Guatemala, November 1988 to February 1990. 86p. 1990. pap. 10.00 (*0-929692-43-8*, Am Watch) Hum Rts Watch.

— Mexico - Human Rights in Mexico: A Policy of Impunity. LC 90-82958. 96p. (Orig.). 1990. pap. 7.00 (*0-929692-62-4*, Am Watch) Hum Rts Watch.

— The New Year's Day Killings of the Nuns in Nicaragua: A Report on an Investigation. 40p. 1990. 5.00 (*0-929692-92-6*, Am Watch) Hum Rts Watch.

— Prison Conditions in Jamaica. LC 90-82156. (Prison Conditions Ser.). 56p. 1990. pap. 7.00 (*0-929692-57-8*, Am Watch) Hum Rts Watch.

— Prison Conditions in Mexico. LC 90-84348. (Prison Conditions Ser.). 60p. 1991. pap. 7.00 (*0-929692-71-3*, Am Watch) Hum Rts Watch.

— Reverting to Despotism: Human Rights in Haiti. 156p. 1990. 10.00 (*0-929692-55-1*, Am Watch) Hum Rts Watch.

— Violation of Fair Trial Guarantees by the FMLN's Ad Hoc Courts: El Salvador. 24p. 1990. 5.00 (*0-929692-82-9*, Am Watch) Hum Rts Watch.

— A Year of Reckoning: El Salvador a Decade after the Assassination of Archbishop Romero. 200p. 1990. pap. 15.00 (*0-929692-50-0*, Am Watch) Hum Rts Watch.

Americas Watch Staff & Physicians for Human Rights Staff. Guatemala: Getting Away with Murder. (Illus.). 128p. (Orig.). 1991. pap. 10.00 (*1-56432-024-3*) Hum Rts Watch.

Americas Watch Staff, jt. auth. see Human Rights Watch Staff.

Amerika, Mark. The Kafka Chronicles: A Novel. (Black Ice Books Ser.). 189p. 1993. pap. 9.00 (*0-932511-54-6*) Fiction Coll.

— Sexual Blood. 187p. 1995. pap. 9.00 (*1-57366-000-0*) Fiction Coll.

— Sexual Blood. 1995. pap. write for info. (*0-573-66000-X*) French.

Amerika, Mark & Olsen, Lance, eds. In Memorium to Postmodernism: Essays on the Avant-Pop. 212p. 1996. pap. 20.00 (*1-879691-32-9*) SDSU Press.

Amerikaner. My Silly Book of ABCs. (J). 1994. pap. 3.95 (*0-382-24677-2*) Silver Burdett Pr.

A

An Asterisk (*) at the beginning of an entry indicates that the title is appearing for the first time.

A

Amerikaner, Phyllis. Career Cutouts: Clever & Creative Activities for Kids to "Picture" Themselves in 75 Different Careers. Clark Editorial & Design Staff, ed. (Illus.). 96p. (Orig.). (J). (ps-3). 1997. pap. 10.95 (0-88160-294-9, LW364) Learning Wks.

— Design a Paper Doll You. (Illus.). (J). 1996. pap. 6.95 (0-88160-293-0, LW363) Learning Wks.

— The Jewish Paper Doll Book: Celebrating Special Days Throughout the Jewish Year. Clark Editorial & Design Staff, ed. (Illus.). 56p. (J). (gr. k-7). 1998. pap. 9.95 (0-88160-306-6, LW375) Learning Wks.

— Middle School Language Challenge. (Middle School Ser.). (Illus.). 128p. (J). (gr. 5-8). 1994. pap. 9.95 (0-88160-272-8, LW1011) Learning Wks.

— Millennium Paper Doll Book. 1998. pap. 9.95 (0-88160-319-8) Learning Wks.

— Paper Doll Christmas: Holiday Fun for Creative Kids. Clark Editorial & Design Staff, ed. (Illus.). 56p. (J). (gr. k-7). 1998. pap. 9.95 (0-88160-304-X, LW373) Learning Wks.

— Paper Doll Party. (Illus.). 56p. (Orig.). (J). (gr. 1-5). 1996. pap. 10.95 (0-88160-291-4, LW361) Learning Wks.

Amerikaner, Susan. Gifted & Talented. (Illus.). 96p. (J). (gr. k-1). 1992. pap. 4.95 (1-56565-021-2, 00212W, Pub. by Lowell Hse) NTC Contemp Pub Co.

— Gifted & Talented Language Arts. (Illus.). 96p. (J). 1992. pap. 4.95 (0-929923-85-5, 00855W, Pub. by Lowell Hse) NTC Contemp Pub Co.

— Gifted & Talented Language Arts. (Illus.). 96p. (J). 1993. pap. 4.95 (1-56565-064-6, 00646W, Pub. by Lowell Hse) NTC Contemp Pub Co.

— Gifted & Talented Reading Workbook. (Illus.). 96p. (J). (ps-1). 1992. pap. 4.95 (0-929923-83-9, 00839W, Pub. by Lowell Hse) NTC Contemp Pub Co.

— Gifted & Talented Reading Workbook. (Illus.). 96p. (J). (gr. 1-3). 1993. pap. 4.95 (1-56565-040-9, 00409W, Pub. by Lowell Hse) NTC Contemp Pub Co.

— My Silly Book of ABCs. Brook, Bonnie, ed. (Silly Me Ser.). (Illus.). 32p. (J). (ps-1). 1989. pap. 3.95 (0-382-24672-1); lib. bdg. 6.95 (0-671-68363-2) Silver Burdett Pr.

— My Silly Book of Colors. Brook, Bonnie, ed. (Silly Me Ser.). (Illus.). 32p. (J). (ps-1). 1989. pap. 3.95 (0-382-24674-8); lib. bdg. 6.95 (0-671-68364-0) Silver Burdett Pr.

— My Silly Book of Colors. (Silly Me Ser.). (SPA.). 32p. (J). 1994. pap. 3.95 (0-382-24679-9) Silver Burdett Pr.

— My Silly Book of Counting. Brook, Bonnie, ed. (Silly Me Ser.). (Illus.). 32p. (J). (ps-1). 1989. pap. 3.95 (0-382-24673-X); lib. bdg. 6.95 (0-671-68365-9) Silver Burdett Pr.

— My Silly Book of Counting. (Silly Me Ser.). (SPA., Illus.). 32p. (J). 1994. pap. 3.95 (0-382-24678-0) Silver Burdett Pr.

— My Silly Book of Opposites. Brook, Bonnie, ed. (Silly Me Ser.). (Illus.). 32p. (J). (ps-1). 1989. pap. 3.95 (0-382-24675-6); lib. bdg. 6.95 (0-671-68366-7) Silver Burdett Pr.

— My Silly Book of Opposites. (Silly Me Ser.). (SPA., Illus.). 32p. (J). 1994. pap. 3.95 (0-382-24680-2) Silver Burdett Pr.

— One Hundred & One Things to Do to Develop Your Child's Gifts & Talents, Vol. 1. 1989. mass mkt. 5.95 (0-8125-9497-5, Pub. by Tor Bks) St Martin.

— Question & Answer Book for Ages Four to Six. LC 95-43319. (Gifted & Talented Ser.). 64p. (J). (ps-3). 1995. pap. 5.95 (1-56565-349-1, 03491W, Pub. by Lowell Hse) NTC Contemp Pub Co.

— Question & Answer Book for Ages Six to Eight. LC 95-43318. (Gifted & Talented Ser.). 64p. (J). (ps-3). 1995. pap. 5.95 (1-56565-351-3, 03513W, Pub. by Lowell Hse) NTC Contemp Pub Co.

***Amerikaner, Susan.** Questions & Answers. (Illus.). (J). 2000. pap. 9.95 (0-7373-0512-6) Lowell Hse Juvenile.

***Amerikaner, Susan, et al.** Gifted & Talented Questions & Answers. (Gifted & Talented Ser.). (Illus.). 192p. (J). (ps-1). 2000. pap. 9.95 (0-7373-0344-1, 03441W, Pub. by Lowell Hse Juvenile) NTC Contemp Pub Co.

***Ameriks, Karl.** Kant & the Fate of Autonomy: Problems in the Appropriation of the Critical Philosophy. (Modern European Philosophy Ser.). 368p. (C). 2000. text 54.95 (0-521-78101-9); pap. text 19.95 (0-521-78614-2) Cambridge U Pr.

— Kant's Theory of Mind: An Analysis of the Paralogisms of Pure Reason. expanded ed. 372p. 2000. text 65.00 (0-19-823896-7) OUP.

***Ameriks, Karl, ed.** Cambridge Companion to German Idealism. (Cambridge Companions to Philosophy Ser.). 336p. (C). 2000. Price not set. (0-521-65178-6); pap. Price not set. (0-521-65695-8) Cambridge U Pr.

Ameriks, Karl & Sturma, Dieter, eds. The Modern Subject: Conceptions of the Self in Classical German Philosophy. LC 95-4244. (SUNY Series in Contemporary Continental Philosophy). 252p. (C). 1995. text 49.50 (0-7914-2753-6); pap. text 17.95 (0-7914-2754-4) State U NY Pr.

Ameriks, Karl, ed. & tr. see Kant, Immanuel.

Ameriks, Karl, tr. see Husserl, Edmund.

Amerine, M. A. & Borg, Axel E. A Bibliography on Grapes, Wines, Other Alcoholic Beverages, & Temperance Published in the United States Before 1901. LC 96-20782. (University of California Publications in Geological Sciences Ser.). 1996. 55.00 (0-520-09805-6, Pub. by U CA Pr) Cal Prin Full Svc.

Amerine, Maynard A., ed. Wine Production Technology in the United States. LC 80-28041. (Symposium Ser.: No. 145). 1981. 29.95 (0-8412-0596-5); pap. 21.95 (0-8412-0602-3) Am Chemical.

— Wine Production Technology in the United States. LC 80-28041. (ACS Symposium Ser.: No. 145). (Illus.). 240p. 1981. reprint ed. pap. 74.40 (0-608-03231-X, 206375000007) Bks Demand.

Amerine, Maynard A. & Roessler, Edward B. Wines: Their Sensory Evaluation. 2nd enl. rev. ed. LC 83-1539. (Illus.). 432p. (C). 1983. text 26.40 (0-7167-1479-5) W H Freeman.

Amerine, Maynard A. & Singleton, Vernon L. Wine: An Introduction. rev. ed. LC 75-46031. 1978. pap. 18.95 (0-520-03202-0, Pub. by U CA Pr) Cal Prin Full Svc.

Amerine, Maynard A., jt. auth. see Ough, C. S.

Amerine, Maynard A., jt. auth. see Stewart, George F.

Ameringer, Carl F. State Medical Boards & the Politics of Public Protection. LC 98-21738. 272p. 1998. 39.95 (0-8018-5987-5) Johns Hopkins.

Ameringer, Charles D. The Caribbean Legion: Patriots, Politicians, Soldiers of Fortune, 1946-1950. LC 94-39178. 184p. 1995. 45.00 (0-271-01451-2); pap. 18.95 (0-271-01452-0) Pa St U Pr.

***Ameringer, Charles D.** Cuban Democratic Experience: The Autentico Years, 1944-1952. LC 99-87367. (Illus.). 240p. 2000. 49.95 (0-8130-1755-6) U Press Fla.

Ameringer, Charles D. Democracy in Costa Rica. LC 82-9065. 138p. 1982. 31.95 (0-275-90753-8, C0753, Praeger Pubs) Greenwood.

Ameringer, Charles D., ed. Political Parties of the Americas, 1980s to 1990s: Canada, Latin America, & the West Indies. LC 92-3032. 696p. 1992. lib. bdg. 115.00 (0-313-27418-5, AAP/, Greenwood Pr) Greenwood.

Ameringer, Oscar. If You Don't Weaken. (American Autobiography Ser.). 476p. 1995. reprint ed. lib. bdg. 99.00 (0-7812-8442-2) Rprt Serv.

— If You Don't Weaken: The Autobiography of Oscar Ameringer. 2nd ed. LC 83-47830. (Illus.). 525p. 1983. reprint ed. pap. 18.95 (0-8061-1790-7) U of Okla Pr.

Amerio, Alberto, et al, eds. Drugs, Systemic Diseases, & the Kidney. (Illus.). 418p. 1989. 105.00 (0-306-43219-6, Plenum Trade) Perseus Pubng.

Amerio, Romano. Iota Unum: A Study of Changes in the Catholic Church in the Twentieth Century. Parsons, John P., tr. from ITA. LC 97-180013. 786p. 1997. reprint ed. pap. 24.95 (0-9639032-1-7) Sarto Hse.

***Ameritonia Staff.** Marathon Love. Holmes, Sarah, ed. 215p. 2000. pap. write for info. (0-9701345-0-9) Ameritonia Inspir.

***Amerlinck, Mari-Jose, ed.** Architectural Anthropology. 2001. write for info. (0-89789-683-1, Bergin & Garvey) Greenwood.

Amerman, Daniel R. Mortgage Securities: The High-Yield Alternative to CDs - The Low Risk Alternative to Stocks. 300p. 1993. text 32.50 (1-55738-477-0, Irwn Prfssnl) McGraw-Hill Prof.

***Amernic, Jerry & Nyp, Gary.** Canada's Technology Triangle: An Economic Celebration. LC 99-31722. (Illus.). 152p. 1999. write for info. (1-885352-91-3) Community Comm.

Amernic, Jerry & Tefft, Maryanne, eds. Markham: Shaping a Destiny. LC 98-38584. (Illus.). 160p. 1998. 39.00 (1-885352-78-6) Community Comm.

Amernick. Patent Law for the Non-Lawyer. 2nd ed. (Illus.). 220p. 1994. text 62.95 (0-412-99171-3, Chap & Hall NY) Chapman & Hall.

Amero, Jeanne. Apple Recipes. 36p. (Orig.). 1983. pap. 2.75 (0-940844-14-1) Wellspring.

Amero, Richard, jt. auth. see Hudson, Andrew.

Amerom, H. W. Van, see Van Amerom, H. W.

Amerongen, J. B. Van. Actor in Dickens. LC 70-91891. (Illus.). 1972. 26.95 (0-405-08204-5) Ayer.

Amerongen, J. B. Van, see Van Amerongen, J. B.

Amerongen, Jerry Van, see Van Amerongen, Jerry.

Ameros, Andres. Luces de Candilejas, los Espectaculos en Espana, 1898-1936. (Nueva Austral Ser.: No. 196). (SPA.). 1991. pap. text 24.95 (84-239-1996-X) Elliots Bks.

Amersfoort, M. R. Phased - Array Wavelength Demultiplenes & Their Integration with Photodetectors. 108p. 1994. pap. 57.50 (90-407-1041-4, Pub. by Delft U Pr) Coronet Bks.

Amerson, Andrew, ed. see Adamson, Bruce Campbell.

Amerson, Price. Roland Petersen: A Retrospective Exhibition. (Illus.). 44p. 1989. pap. 20.00 (0-8150-0016-2) Wittenborn Art.

Amerson, Robert. How Democracy Triumphed over Dictatorship: Public Diplomacy in Venezuela. 256p. 1995. pap. 27.50 (1-879383-42-X) Am Univ Pr.

— How Democracy Triumphed over Dictatorship: Public Diplomacy in Venezuela. 256p. (C). 1995. lib. bdg. 71.50 (1-879383-33-0) Am Univ Pr.

Amerson, Robert C. From the Hidewood: Memories of a Dakota Neighborhood. LC 96-6356. (Midwest Reflections Ser.). xiv, 364p. 1996. 32.00 (0-87351-333-9); pap. 17.95 (0-87351-334-7) Minn Hist.

Amerson, Susan, ed. see Adamson, Bruce Campbell.

Amert, Susan. In a Shattered Mirror: The Later Poetry of Anna Akhmatova. LC 91-29985. 288p. (C). 1992. 39.50 (0-8047-1982-9) Stanford U Pr.

Amery, A. Hypertensive Cardiovascular Disease. 1982. text 482.00 (90-247-2534-8) Kluwer Academic.

Amery, Colin. Architecture, Industry, & Innovation: The Work of Nicholas Grimshaw & Partners. LC 96-140963. (Illus.). 256p. (C). 1995. 69.95 (0-7148-2923-4, Pub. by Phaidon Press) Phaidon Pr.

***Amery, Colin.** Architecture, Industry & Innovation: The Work of Nicholas Grimshaw & Partners, 1965-1988. (Illus.). 256p. 2000. pap. 29.95 (0-7148-3934-5) Phaidon Pr.

Amery, Colin. Four London Architects: Chipperfield, Mather, Parry, Stanton & Williams. (Illus.). 48p. (Orig.). 1988. pap. text 17.50 (0-262-51043-X) MIT Pr.

— Period Houses & Their Details. (Illus.). 211p. 1978. pap. text 29.95 (0-7506-0795-5) Buttrwrth-Heinemann.

Amery, Colin & Runciman, Rosy. Glyndebourne: Building a Vision. LC 94-60274. (Orig.). 1994. pap. 24.95 (0-500-27754-0, Pub. by Thames Hudson) Norton.

Amery, Colin, et al. The Pritzker Architecture Prize: The First Twenty Years. LC 98-41323. (Illus.). 208p. 1999. 49.50 (0-8109-4371-9, Pub. by Abrams) Time Warner.

Amery, Francis, ed. & tr. see Lorrain, Jean.

Amery, H. At the Zoo. (What's Happening? Ser.). (Illus.). 16p. (J). (ps-3). 1984. pap. 4.50 (0-7460-1542-9, Usborne) EDC.

— Barn on Fire. (Farmyard Tales Ser.). (Illus.). 16p. (J). (ps up). 1989. pap. 3.95 (0-7460-0471-0, Usborne) EDC.

— Children's Songbook. 1989. pap. 9.95 (0-7460-0264-5, Usborne) EDC.

Amery, H. Kitten's Day Out. (Farmyard Tales Ser.). (Illus.). 16p. (J). (ps-3). 1992. pap. 4.95 (0-7460-1415-5) EDC.

Amery, H. The Naughty Sheep. (Farmyard Tales Ser.). (Illus.). 16p. (J). (ps up). 1989. pap. 3.95 (0-7460-0470-2, Usborne) EDC.

— New Pony. (Farmyard Tales Ser.). (Illus.). 64p. (J). (ps up). 1993. pap. 3.95 (0-7460-1414-7) EDC.

— Pig Gets Lost. (Farmyard Tales Ser.). (Illus.). 16p. (J). (ps up). 1992. pap. 4.95 (0-7460-0590-3) EDC.

— Pig Gets Stuck. (Farmyard Tales Ser.). (Illus.). 16p. (J). (ps). 1989. lib. bdg. 11.95 (0-88110-374-8, Usborne) EDC.

— Pig Gets Stuck. (Farmyard Tales Ser.). (Illus.). 16p. (J). (ps-3). 1989. pap. 3.95 (0-7460-0469-9, Usborne) EDC.

— The Runaway Tractor. (Farmyard Tales Ser.). (Illus.). 16p. (J). (ps up). 1989. pap. text 3.95 (0-7460-0472-9, Usborne) EDC.

— Scarecrow's Secret. (Farmyard Tales Ser.). (Illus.). 16p. (J). (ps up). 1992. pap. 3.95 (0-7460-0584-9) EDC.

Amery, H. Silly Sheepdog. (Farmyard Tales Ser.). (Illus.). 16p. (J). (ps-3). 1992. pap. 3.95 (0-7460-1412-0) EDC.

Amery, H., compiled by. Animal Poems. (Poetry Bks.). (Illus.). 32p. (J). (gr. 2-6). 1990. pap. 6.95 (0-7460-0442-7, Usborne) EDC.

— Christmas Carols. (Songbook Ser.). (Illus.). 64p. (J). (ps up). 1990. pap. 9.95 (0-7460-0432-X, Usborne) EDC.

Amery, H. & Cartwright, S. First One Hundred Words French Sticker Book. (First Hundred Words Ser.). (Illus.). 32p. (J). (ps up). 1994. pap. 7.95 (0-7460-2117-8, Usborne) EDC.

Amery, H. & Cartwright, Stephen. Where's Rusty? (Farmyard Tales Flap Bks.). (Illus.). 16p. (J). 1999. 15.95 (1-58086-149-0) EDC.

Amery, H. & DiBello, P. The First Thousand Words in Italian. (Picture Word Bks.). (Illus.). 64p. (J). (ps-7). 1983. 12.95 (0-86020-768-4) EDC.

Amery, Heather. At the Seaside. (What's Happening? Ser.). (Illus.). 20p. (J). (ps up). 1985. pap. 4.50 (0-7460-1540-2, Usborne) EDC.

***Amery, Heather.** Book of Bible Stories. gif. ed. (Bible Tales Readers Ser.). (Illus.). 200p. (J). (ps up). 2000. 24.95 (0-7460-4145-4, Usborne) EDC.

Amery, Heather. Camping Out. (Farmyard Tales Ser.). (Illus.). 16p. (J). (ps-1). 1995. pap. 3.95 (0-7460-2046-5, Usborne) EDC.

— Children's Songbook. (Songbook Ser.). 64p. (J). (ps-3). 1998. 18.95 (1-58086-151-2, Usborne) EDC.

— Christmas Carols. rev. ed. (Songbooks Ser.). (Illus.). 64p. (Orig.). (J). (ps up). 1997. pap. 9.95 (0-7460-3134-3, Usborne) EDC.

— Daniel & the Lions. (Bible Tales Ser.). (Illus.). 16p. (Orig.). (J). (ps-k). 1997. pap. 4.50 (0-7460-2965-9, Usborne) EDC.

— Daniel & the Lions. (Bible Tales Ser.). (Illus.). 16p. (Orig.). (J). (ps up). 1997. lib. bdg. 12.95 (0-88110-925-8, Usborne) EDC.

— Farmyard Tales Alphabet Book. (Farmyard Tales Ser.). (Illus.). 32p. (J). (ps-3). 1998. 10.95 (0-7460-3014-2, Usborne) EDC.

***Amery, Heather.** Farmyard Tales Christmas Flap Book. (Farmyard Tales Ser.). (Illus.). 24p. (YA). (ps up). 2000. pap. 9.95 (0-7460-4138-1, Usborne) EDC.

Amery, Heather. Farmyard Tales Pop-Up Carousel Book. (Farmyard Tales Pop-Up Ser.). (Illus.). 8p. (J). (ps-k). 1999. 17.95 (0-7460-3335-4, Usborne) EDC.

— First Hundred Words in French. (First Hundred Words Ser.). (FRE & ENG.). (ps up). 1988. 8.95 (0-7460-0364-1) EDC.

— First Hundred Words in French. (First Hundred Words Ser.). 32p. (ps up). 1999. lib. bdg. 16.95 (0-88110-323-3) EDC.

— First Hundred Words in Spanish. (First Hundred Words Ser.). (ps up). 1988. 8.95 (0-7460-0366-8) EDC.

— First Hundred Words in Spanish. (First Hundred Words Ser.). 32p. (ps up). 1999. lib. bdg. 16.95 (0-88110-325-X) EDC.

— First Hundred Words Spanish Sticker Book. (First Hundred Words Ser.). (SPA & ENG., Illus.). 38p. (J). (ps-3). 1995. pap. 7.95 (0-7460-2152-6, Usborne) EDC.

— First Story Book. 1989. 14.96 (0-88110-386-1) EDC.

— First Story Book. (First Stories Ser.). 1989. 12.95 (0-7460-0258-0, Usborne) EDC.

— First Thousand Words in French Sticker Book. (Picture Word Bks.). (FRE & ENG., Illus.). 70p. (J). (ps-7). 1998. pap. 9.95 (0-7460-3007-X, Usborne) EDC.

— First Thousand Words in German. rev. ed. (Picture Word Bks.). (GER, FRE & ENG., Illus.). 50p. (J). (ps-7). 1979. 12.95 (0-7460-2307-3) EDC.

— First Thousand Words in Hebrew. (First Thousand Words Ser.). (Illus.). 62p. (J). (ps-7). 1985. 12.95 (0-86020-863-X, Usborne) EDC.

— First Thousand Words in Spanish. (Picture Word Bks.). (Illus.). 50p. (J). (ps-7). 1979. 11.95 (0-86020-277-1); 12.95 (0-7460-2309-X, Usborne) EDC.

— First Thousand Words in Spanish Pack. (J). 1994. 19.95 incl. digital audio (0-88110-686-0) EDC.

— First Thousand Words Sticker Book. (Picture Word Bks.). (Illus.). 70p. (J). (ps-7). 1998. pap. 9.95 (0-7460-3006-1, Usborne) EDC.

— The Good Samaritan. (Bible Tales Ser.). (Illus.). 16p. (J). (ps-k). 1998. lib. bdg. 12.95 (1-58086-124-5, Usborne) EDC.

— The Good Samaritan. (Bible Tales Ser.). (Illus.). 16p. (J). (ps up). 1998. 4.50 (0-7460-2969-1, Usborne) EDC.

***Amery, Heather.** Greek Myths for Young Children. (Illus.). 128p. (ps-3). 2000. lib. bdg. 26.95 (1-58086-261-6) EDC.

Amery, Heather. Grumpy Goat Sticker Book. (Farmyard Tales Sticker Storybook Ser.). (Illus.). 18p. (Orig.). (J). (ps up). 1997. pap. 6.95 (0-7460-2996-9, Usborne) EDC.

— Jonah & the Whale. (Bible Tales Ser.). (Illus.). 16p. (J). (ps-k). 1997. pap. 4.50 (0-7460-2745-1, Usborne) EDC.

— Jonah & the Whale. (Illus.). 16p. (J). (ps up). 1997. lib. bdg. 12.95 (0-88110-885-5, Usborne) EDC.

— Joseph & His Amazing Coat. Tyler, Jenny, ed. (Bible Tales Ser.). (Illus.). 16p. (Orig.). (J). (ps-k). 1997. pap. 4.50 (0-7460-2747-8, Usborne) EDC.

— Joseph & His Amazing Coat. Tyler, Jenny, ed. (Bible Tales Ser.). (Illus.). 16p. (Orig.). (J). (ps up). 1997. lib. bdg. 12.95 (0-88110-931-2, Usborne) EDC.

— Little Dragon. (Castle Tales Ser.). (Illus.). 16p. (J). (ps-3). 1996. pap. 4.50 (0-7460-2508-4, Usborne); lib. bdg. 12.95 (0-88110-868-5, Usborne) EDC.

— Moses in the Bulrushes. Tyler, Jenny, ed. (Bible Tales Ser.). (Illus.). 16p. (Orig.). (J). (ps-k). 1997. pap. 4.50 (0-7460-2743-5, Usborne) EDC.

— Moses in the Bulrushes. Tyler, Jenny, ed. (Bible Tales Ser.). (Illus.). 16p. (Orig.). (J). (ps up). 1997. lib. bdg. 12.95 (0-88110-936-3, Usborne) EDC.

— Noah's Ark. (Bible Tales Ser.). (Illus.). 16p. (J). (ps-k). 1997. pap. 4.50 (0-7460-2741-9, Usborne) EDC.

— Noah's Ark. (Bible Tales Ser.). (Illus.). 16p. (J). (ps up). 1997. lib. bdg. 12.95 (0-88110-886-3, Usborne) EDC.

— Noah's Ark: Rainbow of Promise. (Usborne Kid Kits Ser.). (Illus.). (J). (ps up). 1997. 13.95 (0-88110-952-5, Usborne) EDC.

— The Old Steam Train. (Farmyard Tales Readers Ser.). (Illus.). 16p. 1999. pap. text 4.95 (0-7460-3336-2, Usborne) EDC.

— Old Testament: A Collection of Bible Stories. (Children's Bible Ser.). (Illus.). 72p. 1999. text 15.95 (0-7460-3457-1, Usborne) EDC.

— On the Farm. (What's Happening? Ser.). (Illus.). 20p. (J). (ps-3). 1984. pap. text 4.50 (0-7460-1538-0, Usborne) EDC.

***Amery, Heather.** Los Panes y los Peces (Loaves & Fishes) (Bible Tales Readers Ser.). (Illus.). 16p. (J). (ps up). 1999. 6.95 (0-7460-3650-7, Usborne) EDC.

Amery, Heather. Princess & the Pig. (Castle Tales Ser.). (Illus.). 16p. (J). (ps-3). 1996. pap. 4.50 (0-7460-2510-6, Usborne) EDC.

— Prodigal Son. (Bible Tales Readers Ser.). (Illus.). 16p. 1999. pap. text 4.50 (0-7460-2971-3, Usborne) EDC.

— Prodigal Son. (Illus.). 16p. (J). (ps-3). 1999. 12.95 (1-58086-176-8) EDC.

— Royal Broomstick. (Castle Tales Ser.). (Illus.). 16p. (J). (ps-3). 1996. pap. 4.50 (0-7460-2512-2, Usborne); lib. bdg. 12.95 (0-88110-867-7, Usborne) EDC.

— Rusty's Train Ride. (Farmyard Tales Readers Ser.). (Illus.). 16p. 1999. pap. text 4.95 (0-7460-3462-8, Usborne) EDC.

— Silly Sheepdog Sticker Book. (Farmyard Tales Sticker Storybook Ser.). (Illus.). 18p. (Orig.). (J). (ps up). 1997. pap. 6.95 (0-7460-2995-0, Usborne) EDC.

— The Snow Storm. (Farmyard Tales Ser.). (Illus.). 16p. (J). (ps up). 4.95 (0-7460-2042-2, Usborne) EDC.

— The Story of Jesus. (Bible Tales Readers Ser.). (Illus.). 96p. (J). (ps-3). 1999. text 19.95 (0-7460-3467-9, Usborne) EDC.

— Surprise Visitors. (Farmyard Tales Ser.). (Illus.). 16p. (J). (ps up). 1994. pap. 4.95 (0-7460-2044-9, Usborne) EDC.

— Tournament. (Castle Tales Ser.). (Illus.). 16p. (J). (ps-3). 1996. pap. 4.50 (0-7460-2514-9, Usborne); lib. bdg. 12.95 (0-88110-866-9, Usborne) EDC.

— Tractor in Trouble. (Farmyard Tales Ser.). (Illus.). 16p. (J). (ps up). 1992. pap. 3.95 (0-7460-0588-1) EDC.

***Amery, Heather.** La Tunica de Jose (Joseph & His Amazing Coat) (Bible Tales Readers Ser.). (SPA., Illus.). 16p. (J). (ps-3). 1999. 6.95 (0-7460-3649-3, Usborne) EDC.

Amery, Heather. The Usborne Children's Bible. (J). (ps-4). 1998. 19.95 (0-7460-3043-6, Usborne) EDC.

— The Usborne Children's Songbook. 2nd rev. ed. (Songbooks Ser.). (Illus.). 64p. (J). (ps-3). 1998. pap. 10.95 (0-7460-2981-0, Usborne) EDC.

— Where's Curly? (Farmyard Tales Ser.). (Illus.). 16p. (J). (ps-k). 1998. pap. 7.95 (0-7460-3011-8, Usborne) EDC.

— Where's Curly? (Usborne Farmyard Tales Flap Bks.). (Illus.). 16p. (J). (ps up). 1998. lib. bdg. 15.95 (1-58086-150-4, Usborne) EDC.

— Where's Rusty? (Farmyard Tales Ser.). (Illus.). 16p. (J). (ps-k). 1998. pap. 7.95 (0-7460-3010-X, Usborne) EDC.

— Where's Woolly? (Farmyard Tales Flap Books Ser.). (Illus.). 16p. (J). (ps-2). 1998. text 7.95 (0-7460-3012-6, Usborne); lib. bdg. 15.95 (1-58086-127-X, Usborne) EDC.

— Woolly Stops the Train. (Farmyard Tales Readers Ser.). (Illus.). 16p. 1999. pap. text 4.95 (0-7460-3468-7, Usborne) EDC.

Amery, Heather, ed. El Arca de Noe/Noah's Ark. (Bible Tales Readers Ser.). (Illus.). 16p. (J). (ps up). 1999. pap. 6.95 (0-7460-3430-X, Usborne) EDC.

— Bible Stories from the Old Testament. (Bible Tales Readers Ser.). (Illus.). 96p. (J). (ps-k). 1999. 19.95 (0-7460-3453-9, Usborne) EDC.

***Amery, Heather, ed.** La Biblia para Ninos - Children's Bible. (SPA., Illus.). 144p. (J). (ps-3). 2000. pap. 19.95 (0-7460-3674-4, Pub. by Usbrne Pbng UK) EDC.

An Asterisk (*) at the beginning of an entry indicates that the title is appearing for the first time.

Amery, Heather, ed. Camping Out Sticker Book. (Farmyard Tales Sticker Bks.: Vol. 12). (Illus.). 18p. (J). (ps-3). 1999. text 6.95 (*0-7460-3517-9*, Usborne) EDC.

*__Amery, Heather, ed.__ Dolly & the Train. (Farmyard Tales Readers Ser.). (Illus.). 16p. (J). (ps-3). 2000. pap. 4.95 (*0-7460-3470-9*) Usbrne Pbng UK.

Amery, Heather, ed. The Easter Story. (Bible Tales Readers Ser.). (Illus.). 16p. (J). (ps-k). 1999. pap. 4.50 (*0-7460-3358-3*, Usborne) EDC.

*__Amery, Heather, ed.__ The Easter Story. (Bible Tales Readers Ser.). (Illus.). 16p. (J). (ps-k). 1999. lib. bdg. 12.95 (*1-58086-170-9*, Usborne) EDC.

— Farmyard Tales Storybook. (Illus.). 128p. (J). (ps-3). 2000. 19.95 (*0-7460-3715-5*, Pub. by Usbrne Pbng UK) EDC.

— Greek Myths for Young Children. (Illus.). 128p. (J). (ps-3). 2000. 18.95 (*0-7460-3725-2*, Pub. by Usbrne Pbng UK) EDC.

Amery, Heather, ed. Loaves & Fishes. (Bible Tales Readers Ser.). (Illus.). 16p. (J). (ps-k). 1999. pap. 4.50 (*0-7460-2967-5*, Usborne) EDC.

*__Amery, Heather, ed.__ Loaves & Fishes. (Bible Tales Readers Ser.). (Illus.). 16p. (J). (ps-k). 1999. lib. bdg. 12.95 (*1-58086-160-1*, Usborne) EDC.

Amery, Heather, ed. Market Day Sticker Book. (Farmyard Tales Sticker Bks.). (Illus.). 18p. (J). (ps-3). 1999. text 6.95 (*0-7460-3516-0*, Usborne) EDC.

— La Navidad/Christmas Story. (Bible Tales Readers Ser.). (Illus.). 16p. (J). (ps up). 1999. 6.95 (*0-7460-3431-8*, Usborne) EDC.

— Pig Gets Lost Sticker Book. (Farmyard Tales Sticker Bks.: Vol. 9). (Illus.). 18p. (J). (ps-3). 1999. text 6.95 (*0-7460-3514-4*, Usborne) EDC.

*__Amery, Heather, ed.__ Pig Gets Stuck Book. (Big Bks.). (Illus.). 16p. (J). (ps up). 1999. pap. text 14.95 (*0-7460-3488-1*, Usborne) EDC.

— The Runaway Tractor. (Big Bks.). (Illus.). 16p. (J). (ps-3). 1999. pap. text 14.95 (*0-7460-3489-X*, Usborne) EDC.

Amery, Heather, ed. Runaway Tractor Sticker Book. (Farmyard Tales Sticker Bks.). (Illus.). 18p. (J). (ps-3). 1999. text 6.95 (*0-7460-3515-2*, Usborne) EDC.

— Starting to Count. (Sticker Learning Bks.). (Illus.). 18p. (J). (ps-3). 1999. pap. text 6.95 (*0-7460-3406-7*, Usborne) EDC.

*__Amery, Heather, ed.__ Train Stories. (Farmyard Tales Readers Ser.). (Illus.). 16p. (J). (ps-3). 2000. 12.95 (*0-7460-3473-3*, Pub. by Usbrne Pbng UK) EDC.

Amery, Heather, retold by. David & Goliath. (Bible Tales Ser.). (Illus.). 16p. (J). (ps-k). 1998. pap. 4.50 (*0-7460-2963-2*, Usborne) EDC.

— David & Goliath. (Bible Tales Ser.). (Illus.). 16p. (J). (ps up). 1998. lib. bdg. 12.95 (*0-88110-991-6*, Usborne) EDC.

Amery, Heather & Cartwright, S. First Hundred Words in German. (First Hundred Words Ser.). (GER., Illus.). 32p. (J). (ps-3). 1988. pap. 8.95 (*0-7460-0365-X*, Usborne) EDC.

— First Hundred Words in German. (First Hundred Words Ser.). (GER., Illus.). 32p. (J). (ps up). 1999. lib. bdg. 16.95 (*0-88110-324-1*, Usborne) EDC.

— First One Hundred Words Sticker Book. (First Hundred Words Ser.). (Illus.). 32p. (J). (ps up). 1994. pap. 7.95 (*0-7460-2116-X*, Usborne) EDC.

Amery, Heather & Cartwright, Stephen. The First Hundred Words. (Illus.). 32p. (J). (ps up). 1988. 8.95 (*0-7460-0186-X*); lib. bdg. 16.95 (*0-88110-322-5*) EDC.

— The Usborne First Thousand Words in Japanese. (Illus.). 47p. (J). (ps-7). lib. bdg. 20.95 (*0-88110-817-0*) EDC.

Amery, Heather & Kirilenko, Katrina. The First Thousand Words in Russian. (Picture Word Bks.). (Illus.). 64p. (J). (ps-7). 1983. 12.95 (*0-86020-769-2*) EDC.

Amery, Heather & Vanage, P. Rome & Romans. (Time Travelers Bks.). (J). (gr. 4-9). 1976. pap. 6.95 (*0-86020-070-1*, Usborne); lib. bdg. 14.95 (*0-88110-101-X*, Usborne) EDC.

*__Amery, Heather & Vangas, Patricia, eds.__ Rome & Romans Big Books. (Big Bks.). (Illus.). 16p. (J). (ps-3). 1999. text 14.95 (*0-7460-3491-1*, Usborne) EDC.

Amery, Heather, et al. First Thousand Words in English. (Picture Word Bks.). (FRE, GER & SPA., Illus.). 64p. (J). (ps-7). 1979. 12.95 (*0-7460-2303-0*, Usborne) EDC.

— The First Thousand Words in Hebrew. (Illus.). 47p. (J). (ps-7). lib. bdg. 20.95 (*0-88110-573-2*) EDC.

— The First Thousand Words in Italian. (Illus.). 47p. (J). (ps-7). 1998. lib. bdg. 20.95 (*0-88110-579-1*) EDC.

— Rome & Romans. (Time Traveller Ser.). (Illus.). 32p. (J). (gr. 3-6). 1998. lib. bdg. 14.95 (*0-88110-977-0*, Usborne) EDC.

— Rome & Romans. rev. ed. (Time Traveller Ser.). (Illus.). 32p. (J). (gr. 3-6). 1998. pap. 6.95 (*0-7460-3071-1*, Usborne) EDC.

Amery, Heather, jt. auth. see Cartwright, Stephen.

Amery, Heather, jt. auth. see Lewis, Jan.

Amery, Heather, jt. auth. see Usborne Publishing Ltd. Staff.

*__Amery, Hussein A. & Wolf, Aaron T.__ Water in the Middle East. LC 99-30146. (Illus.). 336p. 1999. 45.00 (*0-292-70494-1*); pap. 24.95 (*0-292-70495-X*) U of Tex Pr.

Amery, Jean. At the Mind's Limits: Contemplations by a Survivor on Auschwitz & Its Realities. Rosenfeld, Sidney & Rosenfeld, Stella P., trs. LC 80-7682. (Indiana-Holocaust Museum Reprint Ser.). 128p. 1980. 17.50 (*0-253-17724-3*) Ind U Pr.

— At the Mind's Limits: Contemplations by a Survivor on Auschwitz & Its Realities. Rosenfeld, Sidney & Rosenfeld, Stella P., trs. LC 80-7682. (Indiana-Holocaust Museum Reprint Ser.). 128p. 1998. pap. 10.95 (*0-253-21173-5*) Ind U Pr.

— On Aging: Revolt & Resignation. Barlow, John D., tr. LC 93-41804. 160p. 1994. 19.95 (*0-253-30675-2*) Ind U Pr.

Amery, Jean, et al. Diccionario Manual Amador Aleman-Espanol, Espanol-Aleman. 9th ed. (GER & SPA.). 839p. 1977. 275.00 (*0-7859-6911-X*, 3411012714) Fr & Eur.

Amery, Leopold S. The Forward View. LC 75-179500. (Select Bibliographies Reprint Ser.). 1977. reprint ed. 26.95 (*0-8369-6629-5*) Ayer.

Ames. Small Business Management. Date not set. pap. text, teacher ed. write for info. (*0-314-71074-4*) West Pub.

Ames, A. The Behaviour of Captive Polar Bears. 67p. 1993. pap. 80.00 (*0-900767-81-2*, Pub. by Univs Fed Animal Welfare) St Mut.

— The Welfare & Management of Bears in Zoological Gardens. UFAW Staff, ed. 1994. pap. 26.00 (*0-900767-88-X*, Pub. by Univs Fed Animal Welfare) St Mut.

*__Ames, Adele Z. & Brown, Blake Adele.__ A Flower for My Papa. (Illus.). 32p. (J). (gr. 1-6). 1999. pap. 7.50 (*0-9677692-0-5*) Butterfly Pr ME.

Ames, Agnes. Ames Ancestry-Europe to Maine. enl. ed. LC 79-91192. 210p. 1982. reprint ed. pap. 20.00 (*0-941216-05-5*) Cay-Bel.

Ames, Andrea L., et al. VRML 2.0 Sourcebook. 2nd ed. LC 96-42409. 688p. 1996. pap. text 64.99 incl. cd-rom (*0-471-16507-7*) Wiley.

Ames, Andrew. Marriage, after Sex. March, Jared A., ed. LC 95-80305. 96p. (Orig.). 1995. pap. 7.95 (*0-931673-03-8*) J March Pub Grp.

Ames, Anthony. Five Houses. (Illus.). 136p. 1988. 34.95 (*0-910413-41-X*); pap. 24.95 (*0-910413-29-0*) Princeton Arch.

Ames, Azel. The Mayflower & Her Log: July 15, 1620 - May 6, 1621. LC 99-203408. (Illus.). 230p. 1999. reprint ed. pap. 36.00 (*0-7884-1070-9*, A516) Heritage Bk.

Ames, B. Charles. Market Driven Management: Prescriptions for Success in a Turbulent World. 2nd ed. LC 96-9326. 208p. 1996. text 29.95 (*0-7863-0540-1*, Irwn Prfssnl) McGraw-Hill Prof.

Ames, B. Charles & Hlavacek, James D. Managerial Marketing Industrial. 1983. 28.95 (*0-685-07561-3*) Random.

Ames, Barry. The Deadlock of Democracy in Brazil. (Illus.). 392p. (C). text 59.50 (*0-472-11160-4*, 11160) U of Mich Pr.

Ames, Blanche A. Adelbert Ames, 1835-1933: Broken Oaths & Reconstruction in Mississippi. (Illus.). 1964. 25.00 (*0-87266-000-1*) Argosy.

Ames, Bob. Vintage Miniature Racing Cars. deluxe limited ed. (Illus.). 128p. 1992. 150.00 (*1-55868-121-3*) Gr Arts Ctr Pub.

Ames, Bobbie H., ed. see Anchell, Melvin.

Ames, Bruce, et al, eds. Ethylene Dichloride: A Potential Health Risk? LC 80-7677. (Banbury Reports: Vol. 5). (Illus.). 350p. 1980. 52.00 (*0-87969-204-9*) Cold Spring Harbor.

Ames, C. Alan. Messages to Carver Alan Ames. 237p. 1997. pap. 10.00 (*1-890137-36-7*) One Hund-One Fnd.

— Through the Eyes of Jesus, Vol. 1. 153p. 1996. pap. 8.00 (*1-890137-00-6*) One Hund-One Fnd.

*__Ames, C. Alan.__ Our Father Speaks. 1999. pap. 11.95 (*1-890137-40-5*) One Hund-One Fnd.

Ames, C. Alan. Through the Eyes of Jesus, Vol. 2. 157p. 1997. pap. text 8.00 (*1-890137-03-0*) One Hund-One Fnd.

— Through the Eyes of Jesus, Vol. 3. 168p. 1998. pap. 8.00 (*1-890137-07-3*) One Hund-One Fnd.

— Through the Eyes of Jesus: A Trilogy. 1999. 25.95 (*1-890137-09-X*) One Hund-One Fnd.

— The Way of Hope. 123p. pap. text 8.00 (*1-890137-06-5*) One Hund-One Fnd.

Ames, Carole & Ames, Russell E. Research of Motivation in Education Vol. 2: The Classroom Milieu. 1985. text 100.00 (*0-12-056702-4*) Acad Pr.

Ames, Carole, jt. auth. see Ames, Russell E.

*__Ames, Carver Alan.__ Heaven Speaks. 1999. pap. 10.00 (*1-890137-37-5*) One Hund-One Fnd.

Ames, Charles & Hlavacek, James D. Market Driven Management (Charles Ames Company Special Edition) 2nd ed. 1996. text 29.95 (*0-7863-1227-0*, Irwn McGrw-H) McGrw-H Hghr Educ.

Ames, Charlotte A. & Cawley, William K. Catholic Newspapers in Microform: A Directory of Works at Notre Dame: Detailed Holdings Version. 2nd rev. ed. LC 97-1353. 151p. 1997. spiral bd. 17.50 (*0-9656120-0-7*) C & M Cushwa.

— Catholic Newspapers in Microform: A Directory of Works at Notre Dame: Summary Holdings. 2nd rev. ed. LC 97-1362. 107p. 1997. spiral bd. 12.50 (*0-9656120-1-5*) C & M Cushwa.

Ames, Christopher. Movies about the Movies: Hollywood Reflected. LC 96-52946. (Illus.). 256p. 1997. 32.50 (*0-8131-2018-7*) U Pr of Ky.

— Movies about the Movies: Hollywood Reflected. (Illus.). 264p. (C). 1998. pap. 17.00 (*0-8131-0938-8*) U Pr of Ky.

Ames, Clifford R., tr. see Motoyama, Hiroshi.

Ames, Constance L. Gilman. The Story of the Gilmans & a Gilman Genealogy of the Descendants of Edward Gilman of Hingham, England, 1550-1950. (Illus.). 190p. 1998. reprint ed. pap. 27.00 (*0-8328-8746-3*); reprint ed. lib. bdg. 37.00 (*0-8328-8745-5*) Higginson Bk Co.

Ames, Constance L. & Gilman, Wayne C. The Gilmans of Hingham, England: A Contribution to the History of Lunenburg County & Southside Virginia, 2 vols., Set. (Illus.). 200p. (Orig.). 1996. pap. 34.00 (*0-7884-0410-5*, A518) Heritage Bk.

Ames, Daniel T. Ames on Forgery: Its Detection & Illustration with Numerous Causes Celebres. (Illus.). 293p. 1992. reprint ed. 35.00 (*0-8377-0208-9*, Rothman) W S Hein.

Ames, Dave. True Love & the Woolly Bugger. LC 96-20216. 200p. 1996. 24.95 (*0-9626663-4-3*) Greycliff Pub.

Ames, David, ed. International Journal of Geriatric Psychiatry: A Journal of the Psychiatry of Late Life & Allied Sciences. 150p. 1997. pap. 98.95 (*0-471-97521-4*) Wiley.

Ames, David & Chiu, Edmond, eds. Neuroimaging & the Psychiatry of Late Life. LC 96-52958. (Illus.). 252p. (C). 1998. text 95.00 (*0-521-49505-9*) Cambridge U Pr.

Ames, David, jt. ed. see Chiu, Edmond.

Ames, David J., et al. Quality Handbook for Small Business. Stoiaken, Larry N., ed. (Illus.). 1994. write for info. (*0-9643779-0-X*) Small Business.

— Quality Handbook for Small Business. 2nd rev. ed Stoiaken, Larry N., ed. (Illus.). 1996. pap. 29.95 (*0-9652338-0-4*) Small Business.

Ames, E. W., jt. auth. see Thayer, M. N.

Ames, Earline & Richardson, Roy. When Grandma Learned to Fly: A Flight Instructor's Nightmare. (Illus.). 195p. 1998. pap. 12.95 (*0-9663955-0-6*) Leap Frog CA.

Ames, Edward. A Look in the Mirror: A Handbook for Widowers. Johnson, Joy, ed. (Illus.). 31p. (Orig.) 1995. pap. 4.95 (*1-56123-083-9*) Centering Corp.

Ames, Edwina G. & Ames, Stanley R. Gray, Powers & Their Interrelated Families, Descendants of Col. Thomas Holden Wade: Including Arledge, Bailes, Virginia Butts, Virginia Clements, Dupree, Hendricks, Legg, Martin, Massenburg, McWilliams, Sims, Wade of Limestone County, Alabama. LC 92-71548. (Illus.). 416p. (C). 1992. 40.00 (*0-9620195-2-6*) S R Ames.

Ames, Elizabeth S. The Deaconess of the Everglades (Illus.). 80p. (Orig.). 1995. 35.00 (*0-9647244-0-5*) Cortland NY.

— Morning Dew. large type ed. (Illus.). 24p. (Orig.). (J). (gr. 3-5). 1997. pap. write for info. (*0-9647244-3-X*, 46141) Cortland NY.

Ames, Evelyn E. Dust on a Precipice. LC 80-26142. 1981. 15.00 (*0-87233-055-9*); pap. 8.95 (*0-87233-067-2*) Bauhan.

Ames, Evelyn E., et al. Designing School Health Curruculam, Planning for Good Health. 2nd ed. 256p. (C). 1994. text 32.00 (*0-697-22363-9*) Brown & Benchmark.

Ames, F. The Kashmir Shawl & Its Indo-French Influence. rev. ed. (Illus.). 348p. 1988. 89.50 (*1-85149-079-5*) Antique Collect.

Ames, Fisher. Works of Fisher Ames, 2 vol. set. Ames, Seth & Allen, William, eds. LC 83-13568. (C). 1984. 30.00 (*0-86597-013-0*) Liberty Fund.

— Works of Fisher Ames, 2 vol. set, Set. Ames, Seth & Allen, William, eds. LC 83-13568. (C). 1984. pap. 15.00 (*0-86597-016-5*) Liberty Fund.

*__Ames, Fran.__ Big Book of Horses: The Illustrated Guide to More Than 100 of the World's Best Breeds. 176p. 1999. 19.98 (*0-7624-0596-1*) Running Pr.

Ames, Francis H. Fishing the Oregon Country. rev. ed. Diness, Madelynne, ed. LC 87-83635. (Illus.). 230p. 1988. reprint ed. pap. 10.95 (*0-916473-02-3*) Flying Pencil.

Ames, Frank. The Kashmir Shawl & Its Indo-French Influence. (Illus.). 348p. 1997. 89.50 (*1-85149-265-6*) Antique Collect.

Ames, G., et al. Post-Harvest Fish Losses in the Tropics. 1991. pap. 25.00 (*0-85954-291-2*, Pub. by Nat Res Inst) St Mut.

Ames, G. M., jt. auth. see Bennett, L. A.

Ames, Gary A., jt. auth. see Bradford, C. Steven.

Ames, Gerald & Wyler, Rose. Magic Secrets. (I Can Read Bks.). (Illus.). 64p. (J). (gr. 2-4). 1978. reprint ed. pap. 3.50 (*0-06-444007-9*, HarpTrophy) HarpC Child Bks.

Ames, Gerald, jt. auth. see Wyler, Rose.

Ames, Glenn J. Colbert, Mercantilism, & the French Quest for Asian Trade. LC 95-45429. 259p. 1996. lib. bdg. 36.00 (*0-87580-207-9*) N Ill U Pr.

— Renascent Empire? Pedro II & the Quest for Stability in Portuguese Monsoon Asia. 264p. 1999. pap. 42.50 (*90-5356-382-2*, Pub. by Amsterdam U Pr) U of Mich Pr.

Ames, Helen Wattley, see Wattley-Ames, Helen.

Ames, Herbert B. The City Below the Hill: A Sociological Study of a Portion of the City of Montreal, Canada. LC 78-163831. (Social History of Canada Ser.). (Illus.). 134p. reprint ed. pap. 41.60 (*0-8357-6373-0*, 203572700096) Bks Demand.

Ames, Herman, et al, eds. The X, Y, Z Letters. (BCL History Ser.). 1899. 19.00 (*0-403-00035-1*) Scholarly.

Ames, Herman V. John C. Calhoun & the Secession Movement of 1850. LC 71-169749. (Select Bibliographies Reprint Ser.). 1977. reprint ed. 15.95 (*0-8369-5892-6*) Ayer.

Ames, Herman V., et al. The X, Y, Z, Letters. (History - United States Ser.). 36p. 1992. reprint ed. lib. bdg. 59.00 (*0-7812-6140-6*) Rprt Serv.

Ames, Irene W. Callahan Incorporates. 169p. 1992. pap. 10.00 (*1-883166-00-4*) Frst Edition.

Ames, J. M., jt. auth. see Meadows, F. L.

Ames, James B. Lectures on Legal History. Helmholz, R. H. & Reams, Bernard D., Jr., eds. LC 86-62934. (Historical Writings in Law & Jurisprudence Ser.: No. 3). viii, 553p. 1986. reprint ed. lib. bdg. 47.50 (*0-89941-517-2*, 304530) W S Hein.

— Lectures on Legal History & Miscellaneous Legal Essays. 1976. lib. bdg. 59.95 (*0-8490-2137-5*) Gordon Pr.

Ames, Janet & Lettner, Margot. Ontario Business Corporations Act. annot. ed. 328p. 1990. text 67.00 (*0-409-80911-X*, MICHIE) LEXIS Pub.

Ames, Jennifer, jt. auth. see Medved, Robert.

Ames, Jerry & Siegelman, Jim. The Book of Tap. (Illus.). 224p. 1977. pap. 6.95 (*0-679-50632-2*) McKay.

Ames, Jessie D. Changing Character of Lynching: Review of Lynching 1931-1941, with a Discussion of Recent Developments in This Field. LC 78-158249. reprint ed. 29.50 (*0-404-00134-3*) AMS Pr.

Ames, Jim. Color Theory Made Easy: A New Approach to Color Theory & How to Apply It to Mixing Paints. (Illus.). 128p. 1996. pap. text 19.95 (*0-8230-0754-5*) Watsn-Guptill.

Ames, John, ed. Speaking of Florida. (Illus.). 224p. 1991. 24.95 (*0-8130-1048-9*); pap. 17.95 (*0-8130-1090-X*) U Press Fla.

Ames, Jonathan. The Extra Man. 384p. 1999. per. 12.95 (*0-671-01558-3*, WSP) PB.

— The Extra Man. LC 98-15784. 336p. 1998. 23.00 (*0-684-84504-0*) Scribner.

— I Pass Like Night. 176p. 1999. per. 12.00 (*0-671-03426-X*, WSP) PB.

— I Pass Like Night. LC 89-40502. (Vintage Contemporaries Ser.). 176p. 1990. pap. 8.95 (*0-679-72857-0*) Vin Bks.

*__Ames, Jonathan.__ What's Not to Love? The Adventures of a Mildly Perverted Young Writer. LC 99-55758. (Illus.). 288p. 2000. 23.00 (*0-609-60514-3*, HUM003000, Crown) Crown Pub Group.

Ames, Joseph. Typographical Antiquities or the History of Printing in England, Scotland & Ireland, 4 vols. 2337p. 1969. reprint ed. lib. bdg. 785.00 (*0-685-43586-5*, 05102047) G Olms Pubs.

Ames, Joseph B. The Bladed Barrier. Reginald, R. & Melville, Douglas, eds. LC 77-84193. (Lost Race & Adult Fantasy Ser.). 1978. reprint ed. lib. bdg. 35.95 (*0-405-10951-2*) Ayer.

Ames, Joseph S. Cantey: Six Generations of the Cantey Family of South Carolina. 56p. 1997. reprint ed. pap. 11.00 (*0-8328-7837-5*); reprint ed. lib. bdg. 21.00 (*0-8328-7836-7*) Higginson Bk Co.

*__Ames, Joye.__ Only You. LC 99-90715. 192p. 1999. 18.95 (*0-8034-9372-X*, Avalon Bks) Bouregy.

Ames, Joye. A Time for Love. LC 99-90143. 192p. 1997. lib. bdg. 18.95 (*0-8034-9353-3*, Avalon Bks) Bouregy.

Ames, Julius R., jt. auth. see Branagan, Thomas.

Ames, Karen A. & Straughan, Brian. Non-Standard & Improperly Posed Problems. LC 97-21742. (Mathematics in Science & Engineering Ser.). (Illus.). 200p. 1997. text 99.00 (*0-12-056745-8*) Morgan Kaufmann.

Ames, Karyn R. & Brenner, Alan, eds. Frontiers of Supercomputing Two: A National Reassessment. LC 93-29197. (Los Alamos Series in Basic & Applied Sciences: Vol. 13). 1994. 75.00 (*0-520-08401-2*, Pub. by U CA Pr) Cal Prin Full Svc.

Ames, Kathy, jt. auth. see Marsden, Donald.

*__Ames, Kenneth & Maschner, Herbert D.__ Peoples of the Northwest Coast: Their Archaeology & Prehistory. LC 98-60253. (Illus.). 288p. 2000. reprint ed. pap. 24.95 (*0-500-28110-6*, Pub. by Thames Hudson) Norton.

Ames, Kenneth J. The Religious Language of Thomas Traherne's Centuries. (Religion & Literature Ser.). 1979. lib. bdg. 250.00 (*0-87700-260-6*) Revisionist Pr.

Ames, Kenneth L. Death in the Dining Room & Other Tales of Victorian Culture. (American Civilization Ser.). (Illus.). 280p. (C). 1992. 49.95 (*0-87722-891-4*) Temple U Pr.

— Death in the Dining Room & Other Tales of Victorian Culture. 280p. (C). 1993. pap. text 24.95 (*1-56639-333-7*) Temple U Pr.

Ames, Kenneth L., et al, eds. Ideas & Images: Developing Interpretive History Exhibits. LC 97-542. (American Association for State & Local History Book Ser.). 346p. 1992. pap. 24.95 (*0-7619-8932-3*) AltaMira Pr.

Ames, Kenneth L., jt. ed. see Martinez, Katharine A.

Ames, Kenneth M. & Maschner, Herbert D. Peoples of the Northwest Coast: Their Archaeology & Prehistory. LC 98-60253. (Illus.). 272p. 1999. 45.00 (*0-500-05091-0*, Pub. by Thames Hudson) Norton.

Ames, Laurel. Besieged. LC 96-525. 296p. 1995. per. 4.50 (*0-373-28889-1*, 1-28889-3) Harlequin Bks.

— Castaway. (Historical Ser.). 1993. per. 3.99 (*0-373-28797-6*, 1-28797-8) Harlequin Bks.

— Homeplace. 1994. per. 3.99 (*0-373-28826-3*, 1-28826-5) Harlequin Bks.

— Infamous. (Historical Ser.). 1998. per. 4.99 (*0-373-29018-7*, 1-29018-8) Harlequin Bks.

— Nancy Whiskey. 1997. per. 4.99 (*0-373-28978-2*, 1-28978-4) Harlequin Bks.

— Playing to Win. LC 96-498. (Historical Ser.). 296p. 1995. per. 4.50 (*0-373-28880-8*, 1-28880-2) Harlequin Bks.

— Tempted. (Historical Ser.). 1996. per. 4.99 (*0-373-28938-3*, 1-28938-8) Harlequin Bks.

*__Ames, Lee.__ Draw 50 Famous Cartoons. (Illus.). (gr. 4-7). 1999. pap. text 16.80 (*0-8085-3760-1*) Econo-Clad Bks.

— Draw 50 Vehicles. 1990. pap. write for info. (*0-385-44514-8*) Doubleday.

Ames, Lee & Estrada, Ric. Draw 50 Aliens: UFOS, Galaxy Ghouls, Milky Way Marauders, & Other Extraterrestrial Creatures. (Illus.). 64p. (J). 1998. pap. 8.95 (*0-385-49145-X*, Main St Bks) Doubleday.

Ames, Lee J. Draw 50 Airplanes, Aircraft, & Spacecraft. (Draw 50 Ser.). (J). 1977. 14.15 (*0-606-03239-8*, Pub. by Turtleback) Demco.

Ames, Lee J. Draw Fifty Airplanes, Aircraft & Spacecraft. LC 76-51554. (Illus.). 64p. 1987. pap. 8.95 (*0-385-23629-8*) Doubleday.

— Draw 50 Animals. LC 73-13083. (Draw 50 Ser.). (Illus.). 64p. (J). (gr. 4-7). 1985. pap. 8.95 (*0-385-19519-2*) Doubleday.

— Draw Fifty Athletes. (Illus.). 64p. 1989. pap. 8.95 (*0-385-24638-2*) Doubleday.

— Draw 50 Athletes. (Draw 50 Ser.). (J). 1985. 14.15 (*0-606-04207-5*, Pub. by Turtleback) Demco.

— Draw Fifty Beasties: And Yugglies & Turnover Uglies & Things That Go Bump in the Night. 64p. 1988. pap. 8.95 (*0-385-26767-3*) Doubleday.

A

Ames, Lee J. Draw 50 Beasties & Yugglies & Turnover Uglies & Things That Go Bump in the Night. (Draw 50 Ser.). (J). 1988. 14.15 (*0-606-03243-6*, Pub. by Turtleback) Demco.

Ames, Lee J. Draw Fifty Boats, Ships, Trucks & Trains. LC 75-19011. (Illus.). 64p. 1976. pap. 8.95 (*0-385-23630-1*) Doubleday.

— Draw 50 Boats, Ships, Trucks & Trains. (Draw 50 Ser.). (J). 1976. 14.15 (*0-606-00745-8*, Pub. by Turtleback) Demco.

— Draw Fifty Buildings & Other Structures. 64p. 1991. pap. 8.95 (*0-385-41777-2*) Doubleday.

— Draw Fifty Cars, Trucks & Motorcycles. (Illus.). 64p. 1986. pap. 8.95 (*0-385-24639-0*) Doubleday.

— Draw 50 Cars, Trucks, & Motorcycles. (Draw 50 Ser.). (J). 1986. 14.15 (*0-606-04208-3*, Pub. by Turtleback) Demco.

— Draw Fifty Cats. (Illus.). 64p. 1986. pap. 8.95 (*0-385-24640-4*) Doubleday.

— Draw 50 Cats. (Draw 50 Ser.). (J). 1986. 14.15 (*0-606-04209-1*, Pub. by Turtleback) Demco.

— Draw Fifty Creepy Crawlies: The Step-By-Step Way to Draw Bugs, Slugs, Spiders, Scorpions. 64p. (J). 1992. pap. 8.95 (*0-385-42449-3*) Doubleday.

Ames, Lee J. Draw 50 Dinosaurs & Other Prehistoric Animals. (Draw 50 Ser.). (J). 1985. 13.90 (*0-606-03516-8*, Pub. by Turtleback) Demco.

Ames, Lee J. Draw Fifty Dinosaurs & Other Prehistoric Animals. LC 76-7285. (Illus.). 64p. 1985. pap. 8.95 (*0-385-19520-6*) Doubleday.

— Draw Fifty Dogs. LC 85-16197. (Illus.). 64p. 1981. pap. 8.95 (*0-385-23431-7*) Doubleday.

— Draw Fifty Famous Cartoons. LC 78-1176. (Illus.). 64p. 1985. pap. 8.95 (*0-385-19521-4*) Doubleday.

— Draw 50 Famous Cartoons. (Draw 50 Ser.). (J). 1979. 14.15 (*0-606-04211-3*, Pub. by Turtleback) Demco.

— Draw Fifty Famous Faces. LC 77-15878. (Illus.). 64p. 1990. pap. 8.95 (*0-385-23432-5*) Doubleday.

— Draw 50 Famous Faces. (Draw 50 Ser.). (J). 1978. 14.15 (*0-606-04212-1*, Pub. by Turtleback) Demco.

— Draw Fifty Holiday Decorations. (Illus.). 64p. 1987. pap. 8.95 (*0-385-26770-3*) Doubleday.

— Draw Fifty Horses. LC 81-43646. (Illus.). 64p. 1984. pap. 8.95 (*0-385-17642-2*) Doubleday.

— Draw 50 Horses. (Draw 50 Ser.). (J). 1984. 14.15 (*0-606-04213-X*, Pub. by Turtleback) Demco.

— Draw 50 Monsters, Creeps, Superheroes, Demons, Dragons, Nerds, Dirts, Ghouls, Giants, Vampires. (Draw 50 Ser.). (J). 1983. 14.15 (*0-606-04214-8*, Pub. by Turtleback) Demco.

— Draw Fifty Monsters, Creeps, Superheroes, Demons, Dragons, Nerds, Dirts, Ghoulds, Giants, Vampires, Zombies, & Other Curiosa. LC 80-3006. (Illus.). 64p. 1986. pap. 8.95 (*0-385-17639-2*) Doubleday.

— Draw Fifty People: The Step-by-Step Way to Draw Cavemen, Queens, Aztecs, Knights, Minutemen... 64p. 1994. pap. 8.95 (*0-385-41194-4*) Doubleday.

— Draw 50 People from the Bible. LC 95-24361. (Illus.). 64p. 1995. pap. 8.95 (*0-385-47162-9*, Main St Bks) Doubleday.

— Draw Fifty Sharks, Whales & Other Sea Creatures. 64p. 1989. pap. 8.95 (*0-385-26768-1*) Doubleday.

*__Ames, Lee J.__ Draw 50 Toon Animals. 64p. 2000. pap. 8.95 (*0-7679-0544-X*) Broadway BDD.

— Draw 50 'Toon Animals: The Step-by-Step Way to Draw Dogs, Cats, Birds, Fish & Many, Many More. (Illus.). 64p. 2000. 13.95 (*0-385-49142-5*) Broadway BDD.

Ames, Lee J. Draw Fifty Trees, Flowers & Other Plants. (Illus.). 64p. 1994. pap. 8.95 (*0-385-47150-5*) Doubleday.

— Draw Fifty Vehicles. LC 77-94862. (Illus.). 64p. 1978. pap. 8.95 (*0-385-14154-8*) Doubleday.

— Draw 50 Vehicles: Selections from Draw 50 Boats, Ships, Trucks, & Trains, & Draw 50 Airplanes. (Draw 50 Ser.). (J). 1978. 13.90 (*0-606-04215-6*, Pub. by Turtleback) Demco.

— Draw 50 Buildings & Other Structures. (Draw 50 Ser.). 1980. 13.20 (*0-606-04910-X*, Pub. by Turtleback) Demco.

— Drawing with Lee J. Ames. 272p. 1990. pap. 21.00 (*0-385-23701-4*) Doubleday.

Ames, Lee J. & Budd, Warren. Draw Fifty Endangered Animals. (Illus.). 64p. 1993. pap. 8.95 (*0-385-46985-3*) Doubleday.

Ames, Lee J. & D'Adamo, Tony. Draw 50 Birds: The Step-By-Step Way to Draw Chickadees, Peacocks, Toucans, Mallards, & Many More of Our Feathered Friends. LC 96-27621. (Illus.). 64p. (J). 1996. pap. 8.95 (*0-385-47163-7*) Doubleday.

Ames-Lewis, Francis. The Draftsman Raphael. LC 86-1593. 174p. reprint ed. pap. 54.00 (*0-7837-4540-0*, 208028900004) Bks Demand.

*__Ames-Lewis, Francis.__ Drawing in Early Renaissance Italy. 196p. 1999. 27.50 (*0-300-07981-8*) Yale U Pr.

— Intellectual Life of the Early Renaissance Artist. LC 99-86289. (Illus.). 304p. 2000. 40.00 (*0-300-08304-1*) Yale U Pr.

Ames-Lewis, Francis. Tuscan Marble Carving, 1250-1350: Sculpture & Civic Pride. LC 96-40247. 270p. 1997. text 96.95 (*1-85928-376-4*, NB619.T9A47, Pub. by Scolar Pr) Ashgate Pub Co.

Ames-Lewis, Francis, ed. Sir Thomas Gresham & Gresham College: Studies in the Intellectual History of London in the 16th - 17th Centuries. LC 98-36781. 230p. 1999. text 65.95 (*1-84014-641-9*, Pub. by Ashgate Pub) Ashgate Pub Co.

Ames-Lewis, Francis & Rogers, Mary, eds. Concepts of Beauty in Renaissance Art. LC 97-17021. (Illus.). 160p. 1997. text 86.95 (*1-85928-425-6*, Pub. by Ashgate Pub) Ashgate Pub Co.

*__Ames-Lewis, Francis & Rogers, Mary, eds.__ Concepts of Beauty in Renaissance Art. 260p. 1999. 28.95 (*0-7546-0061-0*) Ashgate Pub Co.

Ames, Lois, ed. see Sexton, Anne.

Ames, Louise B. Arnold Gessell: Themes of His Work. (Illus.). 288p. 1989. 45.95 (*0-89885-421-0*, Kluwer Acad Hman Sci) Kluwer Academic.

— I'm Not Really Five. 40p. (Orig.). 1992. pap. text 6.00 (*0-935493-82-4*) Modern Learn Pr.

— What Am I Doing in This Grade? A Book for Parents about School Readiness. (Illus.). 31p. (Orig.). 1985. pap. 4.50 (*0-935493-00-X*, 156) Modern Learn Pr.

Ames, Louise B. & Metraux, Ruth W. Child Rorschach Responses: Developmental Trends from Two to Ten Years. rev. ed. LC 94-44161. (Illus.). 150p. 1995. pap. 60.00 (*1-56821-454-5*) Aronson.

Ames, Louise B., et al. Adolescent Rorschach Responses: Developmental Trends from 10 to 16 Years. 2nd rev. ed. LC 94-49579. (Master Works). (Illus.). 340p. 1995. pap. 60.00 (*1-56821-466-9*) Aronson.

— Rorschach Responses in Old Age. rev. ed. 242p. 1995. pap. 60.00 (*1-56821-490-1*) Aronson.

— Your Eight Year Old. 160p. 1990. pap. 10.95 (*0-440-50681-6*) Dell.

— Your Five Year Old. 144p. 1981. pap. 10.95 (*0-440-50673-5*) Dell.

— Your Four Year Old. 160p. 1989. pap. 11.95 (*0-440-50675-1*) Dell.

— Your Nine-Year-Old. 176p. 1991. pap. 11.95 (*0-440-50676-X*) Dell.

— Your One-Year-Old. 192p. 1983. pap. 10.95 (*0-440-50672-7*) Dell.

— Your Seven Year Old. 176p. 1987. pap. 10.95 (*0-440-50650-6*) Dell.

— Your Six Year Old. (Illus.). 144p. 1981. pap. 10.95 (*0-440-50674-3*) Dell.

— Your Three Year Old. 176p. 1980. pap. 11.95 (*0-440-50649-2*) Dell.

— Your Two Year Old. 160p. 1980. pap. 11.95 (*0-440-50638-7*) Dell.

Ames, Lynda J. & Ellsworth, Jeanne. Women Reformed, Women Empowered: Poor Mothers & the Endangered Promise of Head Start. LC 96-20537. (Women in the Political Economy Ser.). 224p. (C). 1996. pap. 22.95 (*1-56639-493-7*); lib. bdg. 69.95 (*1-56639-492-9*) Temple U Pr.

Ames, Lynda J., jt. ed. see Ellsworth, Jeanne.

*__Ames, Lynne.__ Easy Answers to Life's Hard Questions. (Charming Petites Ser.). (Illus.). 80p. 1999. pap. 4.95 (*0-88088-392-8*) Peter Pauper.

Ames, Margaret, ed. see Williams, Dorothy.

*__Ames, Mark & Taibbi, Matt.__ The Exile: Sex, Drugs & Libel in the New Russia. LC 99-25071. (Illus.). 256p. 1999. pap. 16.00 (*0-8021-3652-4*, Grove) Grove-Atltic.

Ames, Mary. From a New England Woman's Diary in Dixie in 1865. LC 70-78760. 125p. 1969. reprint ed. lib. bdg. 35.00 (*0-8371-1386-5*, AMD&) Greenwood.

— Memories of the Pasque & Prairie. (Illus.). 79p. (YA). (gr. 9-12). 1987. 13.95 (*0-9619407-0-0*) Country Messenger Inc.

Ames, Matthew M., jt. ed. see Grochow, Louise B.

Ames, Mel D. Amazon: The Adventures of Detective-Lieutenant Cathy Carruthers. 416p. 1999. pap. 20.00 (*0-88962-666-9*) Mosaic.

— The Ogopogo Affair. 96p. 1993. pap. 12.95 (*0-88962-538-7*) Mosaic.

— Tales of Terror & Titillation: A Compilation of Short Stories from the Macabre to the Erotic. 224p. 1995. pap. 15.95 (*0-88962-590-5*) Mosaic.

Ames, Meriam, et al, eds. Rancho Santa Fe: A California Village. (Illus.). 150p. (C). 1993. 45.00 (*0-938711-20-2*) Tecolote Pubns.

Ames, Michael D. Pathways to Success. (GB - Basic Business Ser.). 1994. mass mkt., wbk. ed. 19.95 (*0-538-63727-7*) S-W Pub.

— Pathways to Success: Today's Business Leaders Tell How to Excel in Work, Career, & Leadership Roles. LC 94-1870. (Illus.). 320p. (Orig.). 1994. pap. 16.95 (*1-881052-57-5*) Berrett-Koehler.

Ames, Michael D. & Wellsfry, Norval L. Small Business Management. (Illus.). 492p. (C). 1983. text 60.75 (*0-314-69631-8*) West Pub.

Ames, Michael M. Cannibal Tours & Glass Boxes: The Anthropology of Museums. 238p. 1992. pap. 22.95 (*0-7748-0483-1*) U of Wash Pr.

Ames, Michael M., jt. ed. see Halpin, Marjorie M.

Ames, Michaela, tr. see Mendoza, Plinio A., et al.

Ames, Mildred. Conjuring Summer In. LC 85-45821. 224p. (YA). (gr. 7 up). 1986. 12.95 (*0-06-020053-7*) HarpC Child Bks.

— Grandpa Jake & the Grand Christmas. LC 90-8527. 112p. (J). (gr. 5-7). 1990. 15.00 (*0-684-19241-1*) Scribner.

— Who Will Speak for the Lamb? LC 88-21208. 224p. (YA). (gr. 7 up). 1989. 13.95 (*0-06-020111-8*) HarpC Child Bks.

Ames, Nancy L. & Miller, Edward. Changing Middle Schools: How to Make Schools Work for Young Adolescents. (Education Ser.). 261p. 1994. text 29.95 (*0-7879-0006-0*) Jossey-Bass.

Ames, Oakes. Orchidaceae: Studies in the Family, Set, Vols. 1-7. (Illus.). 1547p. (C). 1988. 500.00 (*0-7855-3294-3*) St Mut.

— Orchidaceae: Studies in the Family, Vol. 1. (Illus.). 156p. (C). 1988. write for info. (*0-7855-2583-1*, Pub. by Scientific) St Mut.

— Orchidaceae: Studies in the Family, Vol. 2. (Illus.). 288p. (C). 1988. write for info. (*0-7855-2584-X*, Pub. by Scientific) St Mut.

— Orchidaceae: Studies in the Family, Vol. 3. (Illus.). 99p. (C). 1988. write for info. (*0-7855-2585-8*, Pub. by Scientific) St Mut.

— Orchidaceae: Studies in the Family, Vol. 4. (Illus.). 288p. (C). 1988. write for info. (*0-7855-2586-6*, Pub. by Scientific) St Mut.

— Orchidaceae: Studies in the Family, Vol. 5. (Illus.). 271p. (C). 1988. write for info. (*0-7855-2587-4*, Pub. by Scientific) St Mut.

— Orchidaceae: Studies in the Family, Vol. 6. (Illus.). 27p. (C). 1988. write for info. (*0-7855-2588-2*, Pub. by Scientific) St Mut.

— Orchidaceae: Studies in the Family, Vol. 7. (Illus.). 174p. (C). 1988. write for info. (*0-7855-2589-0*, Pub. by Scientific) St Mut.

— Orchids of Guatemala, 2 vols., Set. 13793p. (C). 1985. 150.00 (*0-7855-3292-7*, Pub. by Scientific) St Mut.

— Schedulae Orchidiacae, 10 pts. 594p. (C). 1922. 120.00 (*0-7855-3293-5*, Pub. by Scientific) St Mut.

Ames, Oakes & Correl, Donovan S. Orchids of Guatemala & Belize. (Nature Ser.). 800p. 1985. reprint ed. pap. 19.95 (*0-486-24834-8*) Dover.

Ames, Percy. Milton Memorial Lectures, 1909. LC 65-15895. (Studies in Milton: No. 22). 1969. reprint ed. lib. bdg. 75.00 (*0-8383-0501-6*) M S G Haskell Hse.

Ames, Robert L. Mascot Catalogs. LC 98-92429. 133 p. 1998. pap. write for info. (*0-9661017-0-7*, Pub. by R Ames) Gr Arts Ctr Pub.

*__Ames, Roger, tr.__ The Analects of Confucius: A Philosophical Translation. 1999. pap. 14.00 (*0-345-43407-2*, Ballantine) Ballantine Pub Grp.

Ames, Roger & Rosemont, Henry, trs. The Analects of Confucius: A Philosophical Translation. LC 98-27104. (Classics of Ancient China Ser.). 327p. 1998. 27.00 (*0-345-40154-9*) Ballantine Pub Grp.

Ames, Roger T. Aesthetic Turn: Reading Eliot Deutsch on Comparative Philosophy. LC 99-42789. 288p. 1999. 42.95 (*0-8126-9405-8*) Open Court.

— The Art of Rulership: A Study of Ancient Chinese Political Thought. LC 93-45477. 277p. (C). 1994. text 49.50 (*0-7914-2061-2*); pap. text 18.95 (*0-7914-2062-0*) State U NY Pr.

Ames, Roger T., ed. Wandering at Ease in the "Zhuangzi" LC 97-43323. (Series in Chinese Philosophy & Culture). 288p. (C). 1998. text 73.50 (*0-7914-3921-6*); pap. text 24.95 (*0-7914-3922-4*) State U NY Pr.

Ames, Roger T., et al, eds. Self As Image in Asian Theory & Practice. LC 95-34253. 465p. (C). 1998. pap. text 24.95 (*0-7914-2726-9*) State U NY Pr.

— Self As Image in Asian Theory & Practice. LC 95-34253. 465p. (C). 1998. text 74.50 (*0-7914-2725-0*) State U NY Pr.

— Self As Person in Asian Theory & Practice. LC 93-9297. 392p. (C). 1994. pap. text 21.95 (*0-7914-1724-7*) State U NY Pr.

— Self As Person in Asian Theory & Practice. LC 93-9297. 392p. 1994. text 63.50 (*0-7914-1723-9*) State U NY Pr.

Ames, Roger T., tr. Sun-Tzu: The Art of War: New Translation Incorporating the Recently Discovered Yin-Ch Ueh-Shan Texts. LC 92-52662. (Illus.). 400p. 1993. 25.00 (*0-345-36239-X*) Ballantine Pub Grp.

Ames, Roger T. & Dissanayake, Wimal, eds. Self & Deception: A Cross-Cultural Philosophical Enquiry. LC 96-1329. 373p. (C). 1996. text 74.50 (*0-7914-3031-6*); pap. text 24.95 (*0-7914-3032-4*) State U NY Pr.

Ames, Roger T., jt. auth. see Hall, David L.

Ames, Roger T., jt. ed. see Callicott, J. Baird.

Ames, Roger T., jt. ed. see Hall, David L.

Ames, Roger T., jt. ed. see Marks, Joel.

Ames, Roger T., jt. tr. see Lau, D. C.

Ames, Russell E. & Ames, Carole. Research on Motivation in Education: Student Motivation, Vol. 1. LC 83-12315. 1984. text 100.00 (*0-12-056701-6*) Acad Pr.

Ames, Russell E., jt. auth. see Ames, Carole.

Ames, Samuel, jt. auth. see Angell, Joseph K.

Ames, Scribner. Marsden Hartley in Maine. LC 73-153218. 1972. 8.95 (*0-89101-025-4*) U Maine Pr.

Ames, Seth, ed. see Ames, Fisher.

Ames, Sorrell. Listening In. 256p. 1998. mass mkt. 5.99 (*0-451-19233-8*, Onyx) NAL.

Ames, Stanley R. How to Write & Publish Your Family History Using WordPerfect: DOS Versions 5.1 & 6.0. LC 94-76203. 160p. (Orig.). 1994. pap. 19.95 (*1-55787-118-3*, SR01001) Hrt of the Lakes.

— How to Write & Publish Your Family History Using WordPerfect: IBM Versions 4.1 & 4.2. LC 88-16234. (Illus.). 160p. 1988. pap. 17.95 (*0-9620195-1-8*) S R Ames.

— John Fruits of Kentucky, Ohio, & Indiana, His Ancestors & Descendants: With Family Lineages for, Allen, Ammerman, Ames, Beaty, Fetty, Gray, Gordon, Hurless, Keller, Morris, Powers, Scoles, Templin, Wade, Winter. LC 87-71968. (Illus.). 317p. (C). 1987. 35.00 (*0-9620195-0-X*) S R Ames.

Ames, Stanley R., contrib. by. How to Write & Publish Your Family History Using WordPerfect: DOS Version 5.1 & 6.0. LC 94-76203. (Illus.). 160p. 1994. pap. 19.95 (*0-9620195-4-2*) S R Ames.

Ames, Stanley R., jt. auth. see Ames, Edwina G.

Ames, Steven E. Elements of Newspaper Design. LC 88-31892. 341p. 1989. pap. 24.95 (*0-275-92464-5*, B2464, Praeger Pubs) Greenwood.

— Elements of Newspaper Design. LC 88-31892. 341p. 1989. 85.00 (*0-275-92330-4*, C2330, Praeger Pubs) Greenwood.

Ames, Stuart D., jt. auth. see Cohn, Stuart R.

Ames, Sueann. Essentials of Adult Health Nursing. LC 87-27529. 1988. 61.25 (*0-201-12667-2*) Addison-Wesley.

*__Ames, Thomas, Jr.__ Hatch Guide to New England Streams. (Illus.). 260p. 2000. pap. 24.95 (*1-57188-210-3*) F Amato Pubns.

Ames, Toni, jt. auth. see Schaub, James L.

Ames, Van Meter. Introduction to Beauty. LC 68-14895. (Essay Index Reprint Ser.). 1977. 21.95 (*0-8369-0152-5*) Ayer.

— Zen & American Thought. LC 77-18523. 293p. 1978. reprint ed. lib. bdg. 35.00 (*0-313-20066-1*, AMZA, Greenwood Pr) Greenwood.

Ames, William. Conscience with the Power & Cases Thereof. LC 74-28826. (English Experience Ser.: No. 708). 1975. reprint ed. 55.00 (*90-221-0708-6*) Walter J Johnson.

— The Marrow of Theology. Eusden, John D., tr. 368p. 1997. pap. text 24.99 (*0-8010-2038-7*, Labyrinth) Baker Bks.

*__Ames, William F.__ Mathematics for Mechanical Engineers. 221p. 2000. 49.95 (*0-8493-0056-8*) CRC Pr.

Ames, William F. Numerical Methods for Partial Differential Equations. 3rd ed. (Computer Science & Scientific Computing Ser.). (Illus.). 451p. 1992. text 71.00 (*0-12-056761-X*) Acad Pr.

Ames, Wilmot S. Eames: Robert Eames (Ames), 1640-1693, of Andover & Boxford MA. 400p. 1994. reprint ed. pap. 61.50 (*0-8328-4314-8*); reprint ed. lib. bdg. 71.50 (*0-8328-4313-X*) Higginson Bk Co.

— Eames - Ames Genealogy: Descendants of Robert of Woburn & Thomas of Framingham, Mass., 1634-1931. (Illus.). 251p. 1997. reprint ed. pap. 38.00 (*0-8328-8402-2*); reprint ed. lib. bdg. 48.00 (*0-8328-8401-4*) Higginson Bk Co.

Ames, Winslow, tr. see Meder, Joseph.

Ames, Winthrop. What Shall We Name the Baby? 1990. mass mkt. 5.99 (*0-671-70962-3*) S&S Trade.

Amescua. Esclavo Del Demonio, unabridged ed. (SPA.). pap. 5.95 (*84-410-0046-8*, Pub. by Bookking Intl) Distribks Inc.

Amesoli, Fernandez. Idonapshe (Let's Eat) Traditional Zuni Foods. LC 98-43574. (A: Shiwi A: Wan Museum & Heritage Center Ser.). 160p. 1999. pap. 16.95 (*0-8263-2046-5*) U of NM Pr.

*__Amestoy, Patrick, et al, eds.__ Euro-Par'99 Parallel Processing: 5th International Euro-Par Conference, Toulouse, France, August 31-September 3, 1999: Proceedings. LC 99-40195. (Lecture Notes in Computer Science Ser.: Vol. 1685). xxxii, 1503p. 1999. pap. 125.00 (*3-540-66443-2*) Spr-Verlag.

Amesz, J. Biophysical Techniques in Photosynthesis. Hoff, A. J., ed. (Advances in Photosynthesis Ser.). 426p. (C). 1996. lib. bdg. 259.00 (*0-7923-3642-9*) Kluwer Academic.

Amesz, J., et al, eds. Current Topics in Photosynthesis. 1986. text 182.50 (*90-247-3344-8*) Kluwer Academic.

Ametistov, E. V. Heat Transfer in Boiling Cryogenic Liquids. 1990. 91.00 (*0-8493-7121-X*, TJ) CRC Pr.

Ametsbichler, Elizabeth G., jt. ed. see Frederiksen, Elke P.

Amette, Jacques-Pierre. Country Landscapes. Seide, Stuart, tr. from FRE. 56p. (Orig.). 1987. pap. text 8.95 (*0-913745-23-5*) Ubu Repertory.

Ameur, Charles. Agricultural Extension: A Step Beyond the Next Step. LC 94-16437. (World Bank Technical Papers: No. 247). 44p. 1994. pap. 22.00 (*0-8213-2843-3*, 12843) World Bank.

Amev, Lloyd R. & Egginton, Don A. Management Accounting: A Conceptual Approach. LC 73-86099. (Longman Business Ser.). 696p. reprint ed. pap. 200.00 (*0-608-13119-9*, 202522400043) Bks Demand.

Amey, Daniel. Printed Wiring Boards & Other Interconnection Technologies for High Performance Systems. 1994. 55.00 (*0-07-001614-3*) McGraw.

Amey, L. J., ed. Combining Libraries: The Canadian & Australian Experience. LC 87-16678. (Dalhousie University School of Library & Information Studies). 453p. 1987. 50.00 (*0-8108-2049-8*) Scarecrow.

Amey, Lloyd R. A Conceptual Approach to Management. LC 86-91513. 239p. 1986. 59.95 (*0-275-92311-8*, C2311, Praeger Pubs) Greenwood.

— Corporate Planning: A Systems View. LC 86-8110. 287p. 1986. 69.50 (*0-275-92077-1*, C2077, Praeger Pubs) Greenwood.

Amey, Marilyn J., jt. auth. see Moore, Kathryn M.

Amey, Peter. Pax Romana. Yapp, Malcolm et al, eds. (World History Program Ser.). (Illus.). 32p. (YA). (gr. 6-11). 1980. reprint ed. pap. text 5.90 (*0-89908-002-2*) Greenhaven.

Amey, Peter, et al. Leonardo da Vinci. Yapp, Malcolm et al, eds. (World History Program Ser.). (Illus.). (J). (gr. 6-11). 1980. reprint ed. pap. text 5.90 (*0-89908-016-2*) Greenhaven.

Amey, Vera E., jt. auth. see Eaton, Margaret H.

Amezcua, Carlos. Misa de Mariachi. (SPA.). 12p. 1978. write for info. (*0-614-04899-0*) Mex Am Cult.

Amezcua Viedma, C. & Jimenez Lara, A. Evaluacion de Programas Sociales. (SPA.). 129p. 1996. pap. 18.50 (*84-7978-241-2*, Pub. by Ediciones Diaz) IBD Ltd.

Amezquita, Hector. Thought: The Greatest Power. LC 97-67730. 120p. (Orig.). 1997. pap. 10.95 (*0-87516-708-X*) DeVorss.

AMG Publishing Staff. To Love Is to Live: 1 Corinthians 13. (Exegetical Commentary Ser.). 1998. pap. 8.99 (*0-89957-463-7*) AMG Pubs.

*__AMG Staff.__ Greek New Testament with Modern Greek Parallel. 1999. pap. text 24.99 (*0-89957-130-1*) AMG Pubs.

*__AMGA Technical Committee.__ Bevel Gear Classification, Tolerances, & Measuring Methods. (ANSI/AGMA Standard Ser.: Vol. 2009-A98). 68p. 2000. pap. text 96.00 (*1-55589-731-2*) AGMA.

AMGA Technical Committee. Measuring Instrument Calibration Pt. 1: Involute Measurement. (ANSI/AGMA Standard Ser.: Vol. 2010-A94). (Illus.). 39p. 1994. pap. text 55.00 (*1-55589-630-8*) AGMA.

Amghar, Alain. Microprocessor System Development. 1991. pap. 38.00 (*0-13-582651-9*) P-H.

An Asterisk (*) at the beginning of an entry indicates that the title is appearing for the first time.

Amgwert, John. Corvette Specifications Guide, 1953-1972. (Illus.). 168p. (Orig.). 1989. pap. 19.95 (*0-685-29080-8*) Natl Corvette.

AMHCA Staff, jt. auth. see PTI-AMHCA Staff.

AMHCA Staff, jt. auth. see Ptito, Maurice.

Amherst College Staff. The College on the Hill: Celebrating the 175th Anniversary of Amherst College, 1821-1996. LC 96-9708. 1996. 29.95 (*0-943184-05-3*) Amherst Coll Pr.

Amherst H. Wilder Foundation Staff, jt. auth. see Simon, Judy S.

Amherst Town Committee, compiled by. The History of the Town of Amherst, Massachusetts. (Illus.). 903p. 1989. reprint ed. lib. bdg. 95.00 (*0-8328-0801-6*) Higginson Bk Co.

Ami, Bel. Euros: Photos of Lukas. 11th ed. 1997. 16.95 (*3-86187-111-4*) LPC InBook.

Ami, Bel. Postcardbook No. 2: With 30 Postcards. (Illus.). 1997. pap. text 7.95 (*3-86187-109-2*) B Gmunder.

***AMI Jerusalem Staff.** Hier in Israel Series I, Lessons 1-14: Bibelstudium, 2 vols. 2nd rev. ed. (GER.). 257p. 1999. pap. 20.00 (*1-888235-26-8*) AMI-Jerusalem.

AMI Press Staff. Basic Catechism of Christian Doctrine. 72p. 1996. 0.50 (*1-56036-022-4*, 37502) AMI Pr.

— Exploring Fatima. 113p. 1989. 3.95 (*1-56036-003-8*, 37635) AMI Pr.

— Five Homilies for First Saturdays. 46p. 1995. 0.75 (*0-911988-61-0*, 38297) AMI Pr.

— The Heroic Virtues of Jacinta & Francisco Marto. 1994. 1.00 (*1-56036-005-4*, 42230) AMI Pr.

AMI®owe International Company Staff. Piano & Player Piano: Buyer's Guide of 1926. 176p. 1984. reprint ed. spiral bd. 27.50 (*0-913599-42-5*, R-64) A M C Corp.

Amiard, J. C. Oceans, Rivers, & Lakes: Energy & Substance Transfers at Interfaces. LC 98-34666. (Developments in Hydrobiology Ser.). 1998. write for info. (*0-7923-5233-5*) Kluwer Academic.

Amic, Peter J. Computer Numerical Control Programming. LC 96-33099. 302p. (C). 1996. 83.00 (*0-13-326158-1*) P-H.

Amichai, Yehuda. Great Tranquillity: Questions & Answers. Abramson, Glenda & Parfitt, Tudor, trs. from HEB. LC 97-32012. Orig. Title: Great Tranquility: Questions & Answers. 86p. 1997. pap. 12.95 (*1-878818-68-6*, Pub. by Sheep Meadow) U Pr of New Eng.

***Amichai, Yehuda.** Open Closed Open: Poems. Bloch, Chana & Kronfeld, Chana, trs. from HEB. 2000. 24.00 (*0-15-100378-5*) Harcourt.

Amichai, Yehuda. Poems of Jerusalem & Love Poems. LC 92-31558. (ENG & HEB.). 277p. 1992. pap. 13.95 (*1-878818-19-8*, Pub. by Sheep Meadow) U Pr of New Eng.

— The Selected Poetry of Yehuda Amichai. expanded rev. ed. Bloch, Chana & Mitchell, Stephen, trs. from HEB. (Literature of the Middle East Ser.: Vol. 6). 192p. 1996. pap. 15.95 (*0-520-20538-3*, Pub. by U CA Pr) Cal Prin Full Svc.

— Travels: Bilingual Edition. Nevo, Ruth, tr. LC 85-27814. (ENG & HEB.). 141p. 1986. pap. 12.95 (*0-935296-63-8*, Pub. by Sheep Meadow); text 25.00 (*0-935296-62-X*, Pub. by Sheep Meadow) U Pr of New Eng.

— Yehuda Amichai: A Life of Poetry, 1948-1994. 496p. 1995. pap. 16.00 (*0-06-092666-X*) HarperTrade.

Amichai, Yehuda, et al. Quarterly Review of Literature: The 1970s, Poetry, Vol. XVI, Nos. 1-2. 1970. pap. 35.00 (*1-888545-11-9*) Quarterly Rev.

Amici Design Staff. Fat Tire: A Celebration of the Mountain Bike. LC 98-4094. (Illus.). 144p. 1999. 24.95 (*0-8118-1982-5*) Chronicle Bks.

Amici, R., et al. Cerebellar Tumors: Clinical Analysis & Physiopathologic Correlations. (Monographs in Neural Sciences: Vol. 4). 1976. pap. 55.75 (*3-8055-2358-0*) S Karger.

Amicis, E. De, see De Amicis, E.

Amick, Benjamin, III, et al, eds. Society & Health. (Illus.). 392p. 1995. text 52.50 (*0-19-508506-X*) OUP.

Amick, Daniel S., ed. Folsom Lithic Technology: Exploration in Structure & Variation. LC 99-13738. (Archaeological Ser.). (Illus.). vi, 213p. 1999. lib. bdg. 65.00 (*1-879621-27-4*) Intl Mono Prehstry.

— Folsom Lithic Technology: Explorations in Structure & Variation. LC 99-13738. (Archaeological Ser.). (Illus.). vi, 213p. 1999. pap. 35.00 (*1-879621-26-6*) Intl Mono Prehstry.

Amick, George. Linn's U. S. Stamp Yearbook, 1998, Vol. 16. (Illus.). 504p. 1999. 35.00 (*0-940403-84-6*) Linns Stamp News.

— Linn's U. S. Stamp Yearbook, 1988. 384p. 1989. 35.00 (*0-940403-15-3*); pap. 22.00 (*0-940403-11-0*) Linns Stamp News.

— Linn's U. S. Stamp Yearbook, 1989. (Illus.). 300p. 1990. reprint ed. 35.00 (*0-940403-24-2*); reprint ed. pap. 25.00 (*0-940403-23-4*) Linns Stamp News.

— Linn's U. S. Stamp Yearbook, 1994. 504p. (Orig.). 1995. 35.00 (*0-940403-65-X*) Linns Stamp News.

— Linn's U. S. Stamp Yearbook, 1994. 512p. (Orig.). 1995. pap. 22.00 (*0-940403-64-1*) Linns Stamp News.

— Linn's U. S. Stamp Yearbook, 1990. (Illus.). 300p. (Orig.). 1991. 35.00 (*0-940403-41-2*); pap. 22.00 (*0-940403-40-4*) Linns Stamp News.

— Linn's U. S. Stamp Yearbook, 1991. (Illus.). 448p. (Orig.). 1992. 35.00 (*0-940403-47-1*); pap. 22.00 (*0-940403-46-3*) Linns Stamp News.

— Linn's U. S. Stamp Yearbook, 1992. (Illus.). 448p. (Orig.). 1993. 35.00 (*0-940403-54-4*); pap. 22.00 (*0-940403-53-6*) Linns Stamp News.

— Linn's U. S. Stamp Yearbook, 1993. (Illus.). 408p. (Orig.). 1994. 35.00 (*0-940403-61-7*); pap. 22.00 (*0-940403-60-9*) Linns Stamp News.

— Linn's U. S. Stamp Yearbook, 1996. (Illus.). 456p. 1997. 35.00 (*0-940403-73-0*); pap. 22.00 (*0-940403-72-2*) Linns Stamp News.

— U. S. Stamp Yearbook, 1996. 456p. 1997. pap. 35.00 (*0-940403-68-4*) Linns Stamp News.

Amick, James A., ed. see Symposium on Materials & New Processing Technologi.

***Amick, Wanda Codper & Jharpe, Sandra Codper.** The Mystery of the Rainbow & the Showdown Between Two Angels. Hardy, Lea, ed. 104p. (J). 1999. pap. 7.95 (*0-9675187-0-9*) Rainbow Angel.

Amico, jt. auth. see Clymer.

Amico, Eleanor, ed. Reader's Guide to Women's Studies. LC 98-138939. 732p. 1998. lib. bdg. 125.00 (*1-884964-77-X*) Fitzroy Dearborn.

Amico, Joseph. Introduction to U. S. Income Tax. 1993. pap. text 108.50 (*90-6544-716-4*) Kluwer Academic.

Amico, Leonard. Bernard Palissy: In Pursuit of the Earthly Paradise. (Illus.). 240p. 1996. 75.00 (*2-08-013614-3*, Pub. by Flammarion) Abbeville Pr.

Amico, Lorraine. The Role of Information in Broadening Education & Employment Opportunities. Glass, Karen, ed. 51p. (Orig.). 1991. pap. text 15.00 (*1-55877-139-5*) Natl Governor.

— State Capacity to Use UI Wage Records: The Vocational Education Experience. Glass, Karen, ed. 71p. (Orig.). 1993. pap. text 15.00 (*1-55877-205-7*) Natl Governor.

Amico, Michael. The Quitting Point. LC 98-207120. 1998. pap. 9.99 (*1-56043-307-8*, Treasure Hse) Destiny Image.

Amico, Robert P. The Problem of the Criterion. LC 92-37597. (Studies in Epistemology & Cognitive Theory). 188p. (C). 1995. pap. 19.95 (*0-8476-8034-7*); lib. bdg. 49.50 (*0-8476-7817-2*) Rowman.

Amico, Victoria, tr. see Hutchinson, Hanna.

Amid, Mohammad J. Poverty, Agriculture & Reform in Iran. 224p. (C). (gr. 13). 1990. text 69.95 (*0-415-03561-9*, A5538) Routledge.

Amideast Publications Staff. Introduction to the Arab World. Nucho, Leslie S., ed. (Illus.). 144p. (Orig.). 1989. student ed. 49.95 incl. VHS (*0-913957-09-7*) AMIDEAST.

***Amidei, Kathie, et al.** Dealing with Death. Cannizzo, Karen, ed. (Conversations with Teens Ser.). 16p. (YA). 1999. pap. 9.95 (*0-937997-64-1*, 3822) Hi-Time Pflaum.

Amidei, Nancy. Hunger in the Eighties: A Primer. Perry, Cecilia, ed. 166p. (Orig.). (C). 1984. pap. write for info. (*0-934220-06-9*) Food Res.

Amidon, Beulah E., ed. Democracy's Challenge to Education. LC 74-128201. (Essay Index Reprint Ser.). 1977. reprint ed. 23.95 (*0-8369-2265-4*) Ayer.

Amidon, Debra M. Innovation Strategy for the Knowledge Economy: The Ken Awakening. LC 96-52396. 192p. 1997. pap. text 17.95 (*0-7506-9841-1*) Buttrwrth-Heinemann.

Amidon, Elias L. & Roberts, Elizabeth, eds. Earth Songs - Earth Prayers Package: The Music & the Book. (Illus.). 452p. 1994. pap. 29.98 (*0-934245-32-0*) Narada Prodns.

Amidon, Elias L., jt. ed. see Roberts, Elizabeth.

Amidon, G. L. & Sadee, W., eds. Membrane Transporters as Drug Targets. LC 99-37278. (Pharmaceutical Biotechnology Ser.: Vol. 12). (Illus.). 445p. (C). 1999. write for info. (*0-306-46094-7*, Plenum Trade) Perseus Pubng.

Amidon, Gordon & Lee, Ping I. Transport Processes in Pharmaceutical Systems. (Drugs & the Pharmaceutical Sciences Ser.). Date not set. write for info. (*0-8247-9374-9*) Dekker.

***Amidon, Gordon L., ed.** Transport Processes in Pharmaceutical Systems. LC 99-51470. (Drugs & the Pharmaceutical Sciences Ser.: Vol. 102). 727p. 2000. 225.00 (*0-8247-6610-5*) Dekker.

Amidon, Gordon L., jt. auth. see Lee, I-Der.

Amidon, Gordon L., jt. ed. see Taylor, Michael D.

Amidon, Horton W. Cross-Correspondence among the Loehr-Daniels Life Readings. Loehr, Franklin, ed. (Orig.). 1985. pap. 5.95 (*0-915151-11-1*) Religious Res Pr.

Amidon, Jane, jt. auth. see Kiley, Dan.

Amidon, Philip R., tr. see Rufinus.

***Amidon, Stephen.** The New City. LC 99-25619. 464p. 2000. 24.95 (*0-385-49762-8*) Doubleday.

— The New City. 2001. reprint ed. pap. 15.00 (*0-385-49763-6*, Anchor NY) Doubleday.

Amidon, Stephen. Subdivision. 160p. 1992. 18.95 (*0-88001-279-X*) HarpC.

— Thirst. LC 92-36963. 240p. 1993. text 21.00 (*0-88001-296-X*) HarpC.

Amidrazavi, Mehdi, jt. ed. see Nasr, Seyyed Hossein.

***Amidror, Isaac.** The Theory of the Moirbe Phenomenon. LC 99-42396. (Computational Imaging & Vision Ser.). 1999. 225.00 (*0-7923-5949-6*) Kluwer Academic.

Amiel, Ilene & Michael, Angie. Business Casual Made Easy: The Complete Guide to Business Casual Dress for Men & Women. LC 99-945597. (Illus.). 160p. 1999. pap. 14.95 (*0-9672878-0-4*) Bus Casual Pubs.

Amiel, Moshe. Light for an Age of Confusion, 2 vols., Set. 1996. 39.95 (*0-87306-693-6*) Feldheim.

Amiel, Moshe A. Ethics & Legality in Jewish Law. 1992. 24.95 (*0-87306-567-0*) Feldheim.

Amiel, Philippe, jt. ed. see Bonnevie, Paul.

***Amiel-Tison, Claudine & Gosselin, Julie.** Neurological Development from Birth to Six Years: Guide for Examination & Evaluation. LC 00-9626. (Illus.). 2001. pap. write for info. (*0-8018-6564-6*) Johns Hopkins.

Amiel, Yoram, jt. auth. see Cowell, Frank.

Amien, Istiqlal, et al, eds. Conservation Policies for Sustainable Hillslope Farming. (Illus.). 368p. (C). 1992. text 35.00 (*0-935734-28-7*) Soil & Water Conserv.

Amiet, Pierre, et al. Tell el Farah: Histoire, Glyptique et Ceramologie: Sous la Direction de Henri de Contenson. (Orbis Biblicus et Orientalis Ser.: Vol. 14). (FRE.). 91p. 1996. pap. text 25.25 (*3-7278-1105-6*, Pub. by Presses Univ Fribourg) Eisenbrauns.

Amighai-Maisels, Ziva. Depiction & Interpretation: The Influence of the Holocaust on the Visual Arts. (Holocaust Ser.). (Illus.). 590p. 1993. 199.95 (*0-08-040656-4*, Prgamon Press) Buttrwrth-Heinemann.

Amighi, Janet K., et al. The Meaning of Movement: Developmental & Clinical Perspectives of the Kestenberg Movement Profile. 336p. 1998. 65.00 (*90-5700-528-X*, ECU54, Harwood Acad Pubs) Gordon & Breach.

Amigo, Cantigas De, see Fowler, Barbara H., tr.

Amigo, Cantigas De, see Fowler, Barbara H. & De Amigo, Cantigas.

Amigo, Eleanor & Neuffer, Mark. Beyond the Adirondacks: The Story of St. Regis Paper Company, 35. LC 80-1798. (Contributions in Economics & Economic History Ser.: No. 35). (Illus.). 219p. 1980. 57.95 (*0-313-22735-7*, AFN/, Greenwood Pr) Greenwood.

Amigoni, David. Victorian Biography: Intellectuals & the Ordering of Discourse. LC 93-26875. 207p. 1994. text 45.00 (*0-312-10394-8*) St Martin.

Amigoni, David & Wallace, Jeff, eds. Charles Darwin, the Origin of Species: New Interdisciplinary Essays. LC 94-26485. 204p. 1995. pap. 27.95 (*0-7190-4025-6*) St Martin.

Amihud, Yakov, ed. Leveraged Management Buyouts: Causes & Consequences. 1989. 60.00 (*1-55623-208-X*, Irwn Prfssnl) McGraw-Hill Prof.

Amihud, Yakov & Miller, Geoffrey P. Bank Mergers & Acquisitions: An Introduction & an Overview. LC 97-18259. 235p. Date not set. lib. bdg. 85.00 (*0-7923-9975-7*) Kluwer Academic.

Amiji. Physical Pharmacy (book) 2001. write for info. (*0-07-135076-4*) McGraw.

— Physical Pharmacy (set 2) 2001. 59.00 (*0-07-135075-6*) McGraw.

Amilshahi, Mahshid. Dar Safar. (PER.). 384p. (Orig.). 1995. pap. 21.95 (*1-883819-06-7*) Ketab Corp.

Amin, et al. Regional Incentives & the Quality, Vol. 41/1. (Progress in Polymer Science Ser.: No. 41/1). 120p. 1994. pap. 61.00 (*0-08-042481-3*, Pergamon Pr) Elsevier.

Amin, A. Law, Reform & Revolution in Afghanistan. 176p. (C). 1991. 150.00 (*0-7855-6802-6*, Pub. by Royston Ltd) St Mut.

Amin, A., ed. Law of Intellectual Property in the Middle East. 80p. (C). 1991. 150.00 (*0-7855-6801-8*, Pub. by Royston Ltd) St Mut.

Amin, A. & Sastris, S. Law of Easements. 5th ed. (C). 1986. suppl. ed. 160.00 (*0-7855-4709-6*) St Mut.

— Law of Easements, 1984. 5th rev. ed. (C). 1986. 130.00 (*0-7855-5580-3*) St Mut.

Amin, Adnan L., ed. see International Association for Pattern Recognition Staff.

Amin Ahsan Islahi. Islamic Law: Concept & Codification. Rauf, S. A., tr. 115p. (C). 1988. pap. text 7.50 (*1-56744-309-5*) Kazi Pubns.

Amin, Amina, jt. ed. see Jain, Jasbir.

***Amin, Arun.** Black Eyed Peas or Brahman the Absolute? Conversations with the Supreme. 53p. 2000. pap. 14.95 (*1-891253-07-7*) Aurovision Bks.

— The Cosmic Beauty of Mental Silence. (Illus.). 350p. 2000. 30.00 (*1-891253-06-9*); pap. 25.00 (*1-891253-05-0*) Aurovision Bks.

Amin, Arun. Facing Life: Basics for a Seeker. (Orig.). 1994. pap. 4.95 (*1-891253-01-8*) Aurovision Bks.

Amin, Arun & Amin, Pauitra. You Asked about SRI Aurobindo: 25 Answers. 1994. pap. 4.95 (*1-891253-00-X*) Aurovision Bks.

Amin, Arun & Amin, Pavitra. Dynamic Meditation. 1995. reprint ed. pap. 4.95 (*1-891253-02-6*) Aurovision Bks.

Amin, Arun A. Om - The Magical Mystical Sound. 24p. 1997. pap. 4.95 (*1-891253-03-4*) Aurovision Bks.

— Peace - The Womb of Power. 20p. 1997. pap. 4.95 (*1-891253-04-2*) Aurovision Bks.

Amin, Ash, ed. Post-Fordism: A Reader. LC 94-10761. (Studies in Urban & Social Change). 432p. 1994. pap. 29.95 (*0-631-18857-6*) Blackwell Pubs.

Amin, Ash & Dietrich, Michael, eds. Towards a New Europe? Structural Change in the European Economy. (European Association for Evolutionary Political Economy Ser.). 256p. 1991. text 90.00 (*1-85278-415-6*) E Elgar.

Amin, Ash & Thrift, Nigel, eds. Globalization, Institutions, & Regional Development in Europe. (Illus.). 282p. (C). 1996. pap. text 29.95 (*0-19-828916-2*) OUP.

Amin, Ash & Tomaney, John, eds. Behind the Myth of European Union: Prospects for Cohesion. LC 95-5185. 352p. (C). 1995. pap. 29.99 (*0-415-13078-6*) Routledge.

— Behind the Myth of European Union: Prospects for Cohesion. LC 95-5185. 352p. (C). (gr. 13). 1995. 100.00 (*0-415-12552-9*) Routledge.

Amin bin Qasim Nathari. Islam in America, 1995: 20 Years A. E. (after Elijah) 239p. (Orig.). (C). 1995. pap. 9.95 (*1-887513-00-0*) Sabree Pubns.

Amin, Chirag. High Yield MCAT. (Illus.). 217p. 1996. pap. 14.95 (*0-683-18058-4*) Lppncott W & W.

Amin, Chirag, jt. auth. see Bhushan, Vikas.

Amin, Farooq, jt. ed. see Friedhoff, Arnold J.

Amin, Galal. Food Supply & Economic Development with Special Reference to Egypt. 132p. 1966. 39.50 (*0-7146-1201-4*, BHA-01201, Pub. by F Cass Pubs) Intl Spec Bk.

Amin, Galal A. Egypt's Economic Predicament: A Study in the Interaction of External Pressure, Political Folly, & Social Tension in Egypt, 1960-1990. LC 94-46801. (Social, Economic, & Political Studies of the Middle East: Vol. 51). 1995. 62.00 (*90-04-10188-8*) Brill Academic Pubs.

Amin, Hussein Y., jt. auth. see Gher, Leo A.

Amin, Hussein Y., jt. ed. see Gher, Leo A.

Amin, Idi & Turyahikayo-Rugyema, Benoni. Idi Amin Speaks: An Annotated Selection of His Speeches. LC 98-40361. 1998. write for info. (*0-942615-38-7*) U Wis African Stud.

Amin, Julius A. The Peace Corps in Cameroon. LC 91-29956. (Illus.). 248p. 1992. 32.00 (*0-87338-450-4*) Kent St U Pr.

***Amin, Karima, et al.** The Adventures of Brer Rabbit & Friends: From the Stories Collected LC 99-14241. (J). 1999. write for info. (*0-7894-4925-0*) DK Pub Inc.

***Amin, Martin E.** Trends in the Demand for Primary Education in Cameroon. LC 99-21903. 288p. 1999. 42.00 (*0-7618-1397-7*) U Pr of Amer.

***Amin, Mohamed.** The Beauty of Makkah & Madinah. (Illus.). 2000. 12.95 (*1-874041-53-9*, Pub. by Camerapix) Interlink Pub.

— Journey of a Lifetime: Pilgrimage to Makkah. (Illus.). 2000. 50.00 (*1-874041-83-0*) Camerapix.

— Journey of Lifetime: Pilgrimage Mecca. (Illus.). 256p. 2000. 65.00 (*0-905743-96-2*, Pub. by Stacey Intl) Intl Bk Ctr.

Amin, Mohamed. Journey Through Pakistan. 255p. 1996. 49.95 (*0-614-21692-3*, 676); 49.95 (*0-614-21695-8*, 676) Kazi Pubns.

— Roof of the World. 1992. 45.00 (*1-869828-05-4*, Pub. by Moonstone Bks) St Mut.

Amin, Mohamed & Willetts, Duncan. Journey Through Kenya. 200p. 1991. 45.00 (*1-874041-01-6*, Pub. by Camerapix) Interlink Pub.

Amin, Mohamed & Willetts, Duncan, photos by. Journey Through Seychelles. (Journey Through Ser.). (Illus.). 200p. 2000. 45.00 (*1-874041-90-3*, Pub. by Camerapix) Interlink Pub.

***Amin, Mohamed, et al.** The Last of the Maasai. (Illus.). 2000. 45.00 (*1-874041-32-6*, Pub. by Camerapix) Interlink Pub.

Amin, Mohamed, tr. see Abul Ala Maududi, S.

***Amin, Nancy.** Century of Great African American. LC 99-20451. 1999. 12.99 (*0-517-20724-9*) Random Hse Value.

***Amin, Nazeeh.** Suse Linux Installation & Configuration Handbook with CD-ROM. 784p. 2000. 39.99 (*0-7897-2355-7*) Que.

Amin, Pauitra, jt. auth. see Amin, Arun.

Amin, Pavitra, jt. auth. see Amin, Arun.

Amin, Qasim. The Liberation of Women: A Document in the History of Egyptian Feminism. Peterson, Samiha S., tr. from ARA. 128p. 1993. pap. 14.50 (*977-424-343-9*, Pub. by Am Univ Cairo Pr) Col U Pr.

— The New Woman. Peterson, Samiha S., tr. 128p. 1996. 25.00 (*977-424-366-8*, Pub. by Am Univ Cairo Pr) Col U Pr.

Amin Razavi, Mehdi & Ambuel, David, eds. Philosophy, Religion, & the Question of Intolerance. LC 96-46170. 284p. (C). 1997. text 59.50 (*0-7914-3447-8*); pap. text 19.95 (*0-7914-3448-6*) State U NY Pr.

Amin, S. H. Commercial Arbitration in Islamic & Middle East, Glasgow. (C). 1989. 170.00 (*0-946706-46-8*, Pub. by Royston Ltd) St Mut.

— Commercial Law of Iran. 1986. 110.00 (*0-946706-29-8*, Pub. by Royston Ltd) St Mut.

— The Constitutional Law of Iran: Text & Comments. (C). 1987. 195.00 (*0-7855-6870-0*, Pub. by Royston Ltd) St Mut.

— The Constitutional Law of Iran: Texts & Comments. (C). 1987. 95.00 (*0-7855-6539-6*, Pub. by Royston Ltd) St Mut.

— International & Legal Problems of the Gulf. 240p. (C). 1981. 125.00 (*0-906559-05-7*, Pub. by Royston Ltd) St Mut.

— Iran-Iraq War Legal Implications. (C). 1983. pap. 95.00 (*0-946706-09-3*, Pub. by Royston Ltd) St Mut.

— Islamic Banking & Finance. 1986. 65.00 (*0-946706-30-1*, Pub. by Royston Ltd) St Mut.

— Islamic Law & Its Implications for the Modern World. (C). 1989. 165.00 (*0-946706-49-2*, Pub. by Royston Ltd) St Mut.

— Islamic Law in the Contemporary World: Introduction, Glossary & Bibliography. 1985. pap. 30.00 (*0-946706-24-7*, Pub. by Royston Ltd) St Mut.

— Law & Justice in Contemporary Yemen: People's Democratic Republic of Yemen & Yemen Arab Republic. 1987. 25.00 (*0-946706-36-0*, Pub. by Royston Ltd) St Mut.

— Law of Fisheries in the Persian-Arabian Gulf. (C). 1983. 39.00 (*0-946706-08-5*, Pub. by Royston Ltd) St Mut.

— The Legal System of Iraq. 1987. 90.00 (*0-946706-32-8*, Pub. by Royston Ltd) St Mut.

— Marine Pollution in International & Middle Eastern Law. 1986. 60.00 (*0-946706-26-3*, Pub. by Royston Ltd) St Mut.

— Middle East Legal Systems. 308p. (C). 1985. 210.00 (*0-946706-22-0*, Pub. by Royston Ltd) St Mut.

— Remedies for Breach of Contract in Islamic & Iranian Law. 254p. (C). 1984. 195.00 (*0-946706-21-2*, Pub. by Royston Ltd) St Mut.

— Trading with Iran: Post-Revolution Law & Practice. 1987. 150.00 (*0-946706-38-7*, Pub. by Royston Ltd) St Mut.

— Wrongful Appropriation in Islamic Law. 224p. (C). 1983. 135.00 (*0-946706-01-8*, Pub. by Royston Ltd) St Mut.

Amin, S. Hassan, et al. Mealey's International Arbitration Review, 1996. 218p. 1996. pap. 95.00 (*0-9657810-1-1*) Mealey Pubns.

A

A

Amin, Salim, jt. auth. see Smith, Bob.

Amin, Samir. Accumulation on a World Scale: A Critique of the Theory of Underdevelopment, 2 vols., 2. Pearce, Brian, tr. LC 72-92028. 314p. reprint ed. pap. 97.40 (*0-8357-6003-0*, 203435400002) Bks Demand.

— Accumulation on a World Scale: A Critique of the Theory of Underdevelopment, 2 vols., Vol. 1. Pearce, Brian, tr. LC 72-92028. 365p. reprint ed. pap. 113.20 (*0-8357-6002-2*, 203435400001) Bks Demand.

— Capitalism in the Age of Globalization: The Management of Contemporary Society. LC 96-34226. 160p. (C). 1997. text 19.95 (*1-85649-468-3*, Pub. by Zed Books) St Martin.

— Class & Nation: Historically & in the Current Crisis. LC 79-3022. 302p. reprint ed. pap. 93.70 (*0-7837-3900-1*, 204374800010) Bks Demand.

— Delinking: Towards a Polycentric World. Wolfers, Michael, tr. from FRE. LC 89-28953. 320p. (C). 1990. text 19.95 (*0-86232-803-9*, Pub. by St Martin) St Martin.

— Empire of Chaos. Anderson, W. H., tr. LC 92-9954. 1992. 22.00 (*0-85345-843-X*, Pub. by Monthly Rev); pap. 12.00 (*0-85345-844-8*, Pub. by Monthly Rev) NYU Pr.

— Eurocentrism. Moore, Russell, tr. from FRE. 144p. (C). 1989. pap. 15.00 (*0-85345-786-7*, Pub. by Monthly Rev) NYU Pr.

— Global Capitalism: The Management of Contemporary Society. LC 96-34226. 160p. (C). 1997. text 55.00 (*1-85649-467-5*, Pub. by Zed Books) St Martin.

— Imperialism & Unequal Development. LC 77-76169. 271p. reprint ed. pap. 84.10 (*0-8357-6153-3*, 203435700089) Bks Demand.

— Neo-Colonialism in West Africa. McDonagh, Francis, tr. from FRE. LC 74-7784. 320p. reprint ed. pap. 99.20 (*0-8357-6232-7*, 203435200089) Bks Demand.

— Re-Reading the Postwar Period: An Intellectual Itinerary. Wolfers, Michael, tr. from FRE. 192p. 1994. 26.00 (*0-85345-893-6*, Pub. by Monthly Rev); pap. 17.00 (*0-85345-894-4*, Pub. by Monthly Rev) NYU Pr.

— Specters of Capitalism: A Critique of Current Intellectual Fashions. LC 98-9578. 1998. 40.00 (*0-85345-934-7*, Pub. by Monthly Rev); pap. 16.00 (*0-85345-933-9*, Pub. by Monthly Rev) NYU Pr.

Amin, Samir, et al, eds. Sadcc: Problems & Prospects for Disengagement & Development in South Africa. LC 88-5534. 304p. (C). 1987. pap. 19.95 (*0-86232-749-0*, Pub. by Zed Books); text 55.00 (*0-86232-748-2*, Pub. by Zed Books) St Martin.

Amin, Samir, et al. Dynamics of Global Crisis. LC 81-84739. 256p. 1982. pap. 12.00 (*0-85345-606-2*, Pub. by Monthly Rev) NYU Pr.

Amin, Samir, ed. see International African Seminar Staff.

Amin, Shahid. Event, Metaphor, Memory: Chauri Chaura, 1922-1992. LC 94-737. (Illus.). 210p. 1995. 48.00 (*0-520-08779-8*, Pub. by U CA Pr); pap. 17.95 (*0-520-08780-1*, Pub. by U CA Pr) Cal Prin Full Svc.

— Sugarcane & Sugar in Gorakpur: An Inquiry into Peasant Production for Capitalist Enterprises in Colonial India. (Illus.). 1984. 29.95 (*0-19-561545-X*) OUP.

Amin, Shahid & Chakrabarty, Dipesh, eds. Subaltern Studies: Writings on South Asian History & Society, Vol. IX. (Oxford India Paperbacks Ser.). (Illus.). 294p. 1998. reprint ed. pap. text 9.95 (*0-19-564334-8*) OUP.

Amin, Shahid & Van der Linden, Marcel, eds. Peripheral Labour: Studies in the History of Partial Proletarianization. (International Review of Social History Supplements Ser.: Vol. 4). 177p. (C). 1997. pap. text 19.95 (*0-521-58900-2*) Cambridge U Pr.

Amin, Shahid, ed. see Crooke, William.

Amin, Sonia. The World of Muslim Women in Colonial Bengal, 1876-1939. LC 96-8399. (Social, Economic & Political Studies of the Middle East: Vol. 55). 312p. 1996. 95.00 (*90-04-10642-1*) Brill Academic Pubs.

Amin, Tahir. Afghanistan Crisis: Implications & Options for Muslim World, Iran & Pakistan. 144p. (Orig.). 1982. pap. 6.00 (*0-939830-28-0*, Pub. by Inst Pol Stud) New Era Publns MI.

Amin, Vaumini. Bankers Securities. 201p. 1990. pap. 125.00 (*0-85297-351-9*, Pub. by Chartered Bank) St Mut.

— Offshore Lending & Financing: A Practical & Legal Handbook for Lenders, Borrowers, Investors & Their Professional Advisers. 192p. 1997. 210.00 (*1-85573-329-3*, Pub. by Woodhead Pubng) Am Educ Systs.

Amina, Haji. Stories of the Prophets from the Earliest Sources, Vol. 1. 256p. (Orig.). 1995. pap. 14.95 (*0-934905-35-5*) Kazi Pubns.

Amina McCloud, Frederick T. A Question of Faith for Muslim Inmates. 72p. 1999. pap. 9.95 (*1-871031-91-5*) Kazi Pubns.

Amina Shah. The Tale of the Four Dervishes of Amir Khusru. 1976. 21.00 (*0-900860-44-8*, Pub. by Octagon Pr) ISHK.

Aminah, Ibrahim Ali. The Three Muslim Festivals. large type ed. Ghazi, A., ed. LC 98-71812. (Illus.). 68p. (J). (gr. 4-7). 1998. 9.00 (*1-56316-308-X*) Iqra Intl Ed Fdtn.

***Amineh, Mehdi P.** Global Change. LC 99-38752. 2000. text 55.00 (*0-312-22863-5*) St Martin.

Amini, Gitty M. A Larger Role for Positive Sanctions in Cases of Compellence. (New Ser.: Vol. 12). 34p. 1997. pap. 15.00 (*0-86682-128-7*) Ctr Intl Relations.

***Amini, Iradj.** Napoleon & Persia: Franco-Persian Relations under the First Empire. 288p. 1999. (*0-7007-1168-6*, Pub. by Curzon Pr Ltd) Paul & Co Pubs.

Amini, Iradj. Napoleon & Persia: Franco-Persian Relations under the First Empire. (Illus.). 228p. 1999. 34.95 (*0-934211-58-2*) Mage Pubs Inc.

Amini, Majid. Oriental Rugs: Care & Repair. 1995. pap. write for info. (*0-316-03785-0*, Pub. by Little Brown) Trafalgar.

Amini, S., et al. Coupled Boundary & Finite Element Methods for the Solution of the Dynamic Fluid-Structure Interaction Problem. Brebbia, Carlos A. & Orszag, S. A., eds. LC 92-20139. (Lecture Notes in Engineering Ser.: Vol. 77). (Illus.). 115p. 1992. 45.95 (*0-387-55562-5*) Spr-Verlag.

Aminoff. Electrodiagnosis in Clinical Neurology. 4th ed. 1999. text. write for info. (*0-443-06507-1*) Harcourt.

Aminoff, Michael J. Brown-Sequard: A Visionary of Science. LC 92-24712. 224p. 1993. text 71.50 (*0-88167-956-9*) Lppncott W & W.

— Electrodiagnosis in Clinical Neurology. 3rd ed. (Illus.). 822p. 1992. text 139.00 (*0-443-08795-4*) Church.

— Electrodiagnosis in Clinical Neurology. 4th ed. Ross, Allan, ed. LC 98-52731. (Illus.). 700p. 1999. text 135.00 (*0-443-07549-2*) Church.

— Electromyography in Clinical Practice: Clinical & Electrodiagnostic Aspects of Neuromuscular Disease. 3rd ed. LC 97-25846. 1997. text 99.00 (*0-443-07681-2*) Church.

— Neurology & General Medicine. 2nd ed. 1995. text 140.00 (*0-443-08933-7*) Church.

Aminoff, Michael J., ed. Electrodiagnosis in Clinical Neurology. 2nd ed. LC 86-13624. 769p. 1986. reprint ed. pap. 200.00 (*0-7837-2414-4*, 204274600006) Bks Demand.

— Neurology & General Medicine: The Neurological Aspects of Medical Disorders. LC 88-36459. (Illus.). 840p. reprint ed. pap. 200.00 (*0-7837-8752-9*, 204949700012) Bks Demand.

Aminoff, Michael J. & Greenberg. Clinical Neurology. 3rd ed. (C). 1995. pap. text 37.95 (*0-8385-1383-2*) P-H.

Aminov, L. K. Physics Reviews Vol. 14, Pt. 1: Magnetic Resonance & Relaxation in Dielectric Crystals of Rare Earth Compounds, Vol. 14. (Soviet Scientific Reviews Ser.: Section A). 159p. 1991. text 157.00 (*3-7186-4991-8*, Harwood Acad Pubs) Gordon & Breach.

***Aminov, Yu.** Differential Geometry & Topology of Curves. 168p. 2000. text 70.00 (*90-5699-091-8*, G & B Science) Gordon & Breach.

***Aminov, Yu.** The Geometry of Submanifolds. 388p. 1999. text 135.00 (*90-5699-087-X*) Gordon & Breach.

***Aminov, Yu.** The Geometry of Vector Fields. 210p. 1999. text 72.00 (*90-5699-201-5*, Harwood Acad Pubs) Gordon & Breach.

Aminrazavi, Mehdi. Suhrawardi & the School of Illumination. LC 97-160237. (Sufi Ser.). 220p. 1996. 70.00 (*0-7007-0451-5*, Pub. by Curzon Pr Ltd); pap. 25.00 (*0-7007-0412-4*, Pub. by Curzon Pr Ltd) Paul & Co Pubs.

Aminrazavi, Mehdi, ed. see Mushtaq, Q. & Tan, A. L.

Aminrazavi, Mehdi, ed. see Nasr, Seyyed Hossein.

Aminrazavi, Mehdi, jt. ed. see Nasr, Seyyed Hossein.

Aminzade, Ronald. Ballots & Barricades: Class Formation & Republican Politics in France, 1830-1871. LC 93-18279. (Illus.). 368p. 1993. text 57.50 (*0-691-09479-9*, Pub. by Princeton U Pr) Cal Prin Full Svc.

— Class, Politics, & Early Industrial Capitalism: A Study of Mid-Nineteenth Century Toulouse, France. LC 80-28284. (SUNY Series in European Social History). (Illus.). 334p. (C). 1981. text 74.50 (*0-87395-528-5*); pap. text 24.95 (*0-87395-529-3*) State U NY Pr.

Aminzade, Ronald, jt. auth. see Pescosolido, Bernice A.

Aminzadeh, F. Pattern Recognition & Image Processing. (Handbook of Geophysical Exploration Ser.). 379p. 1986. 258.00 (*0-08-036955-3*, CRC Reprint) Franklin.

Amipa, Sherab G. Opening the Lotus: Developing Clarity & Kindness. (Basic Book - Orange Ser.). (Illus.). 176p. (Orig.). 1987. pap. 12.95 (*0-86171-049-5*) Wisdom MA.

Amipas-Silber, G. Sephardi Jews in Occupied France under the Tyrant's Heel, 1940-1944. 420p. 1995. 30.00 (*965-09-0051-9*, 82105, Pub. by R Mass Ltd) Lambda Pubs.

Amipaz-Silber, Gitta. The Role of the Jewish Underground in American Landing in Algiers, 1940-1942. 206p. 1992. 18.95 (*965-229-077-7*, Pub. by Gefen Pub Hse) Gefen Bks.

Amir, A. & Fass, A. Elements of Linear Spaces. LC 62-16311. (International Series of Monographs on Pure & Applied Mathematics: Vol. 26). 1962. 71.00 (*0-08-009656-5*, Pub. by Pergamon Repr) Franklin.

Amir, Fred. Rapid Recovery from Back & Neck Pain: A Nine Step Recovery Plan. LC 98-94189. 150p. 1999. pap. write for info. (*0-9669826-0-6*) Hlth Advisory.

Amir, Jehoshua, tr. see Schalit, Abraham.

Amir, Joram M. Piling in Rock. 112p. (C). 1986. text 123.00 (*90-6191-586-4*, Pub. by A A Balkema) Ashgate Pub Co.

Amir, Menachem. Patterns in Forcible Rape. LC 79-14022. (C). 1971. lib. bdg. 35.00 (*0-226-01734-6*) U Ch Pr.

— Patterns in Forcible Rape. LC 79-140222. 404p. reprint ed. pap. 125.30 (*0-608-08041-1*, 206900600002) Bks Demand.

Amir, Menachem, jt. ed. see Einstein, Stanley.

Amir-Moez, Ali R. Extreme Properties of Linear Transformations. LC 90-30314. 174p. 1990. 24.00 (*0-936428-12-0*) Polygonal Pub.

— Notes on Geometric Transformations. LC 97-45226. (Illus.). 127p. 1998. text 20.00 (*0-936428-16-3*) Polygonal Pub.

Amir-Moezzi, Mohammad A. The Divine Guide in Early Shi'ism: The Sources of Esotericism in Islam. Streight, David, tr. LC 93-42680. (FRE.). 279p. (C). 1994. pap. text 19.95 (*0-7914-2122-8*) State U NY Pr.

— The Divine Guide in Early Shi'ism: The Sources of Esotericism in Islam. Streight, David, tr. LC 93-42680. (FRE.). 279p. (C). 1994. text 59.50 (*0-7914-2121-X*) State U NY Pr.

Amir, Naomi, et al, eds. Pediatric Neurology: Behavior & Cognition of the Child with Brain Dysfunction. (Pediatric & Adolescent Medicine Ser.: Vol. 1). (Illus.). x, 186p. 1991. 151.50 (*3-8055-5223-8*) S Karger.

Amir, Pervaiz & Knipscheer, Hendrik C. Conducting On-Farm Animal Research: Procedures & Economic Analysis. 244p. 1989. 12.50 (*1-57360-010-5*) Winrock Intl.

Amir, Yehuda & Sharan, Shlomo. School Desegregation: Cross-Cultural Perspectives. 288p. 1984. text 69.95 (*0-89859-335-2*) L Erlbaum Assocs.

Amira, John & Cornelius, Steven. The Music of Santeria: Traditional Rhythms of the Bata Drums. 2nd rev. ed. LC 99-29426. (Performance in World Music Ser.: No. 5). (Illus.). 128p. (YA). (gr. 9-12). 1999. pap. 24.95 (*0-941677-70-2*, Pub. by White Cliffs Media) Words Distrib.

***Amirahmadi, Hooshang.** The Caspian Region at a Crossroad: Challenges of a New Frontier of Energy & Development LC 99-27683. 1999. text 55.00 (*0-312-22351-X*) St Martin.

Amirahmadi, Hooshang. Revolution & Economic Transition: The Iranian Experience. LC 90-33035. 420p. (C). 1990. text 24.50 (*0-7914-0509-5*) State U NY Pr.

— Small Island, Big Politics: The Tonbs & Uba Musa in Iranian Foreign Policy. 262p. 1996. text 49.95 (*0-312-15910-2*) St Martin.

Amirahmadi, Hooshang, ed. The United States & the Middle East: A Search for New Perspectives. LC 91-38541. 512p. (C). 1992. pap. text 24.95 (*0-7914-1226-1*) State U NY Pr.

Amirahmadi, Hooshang & El-Shakhs, Salah S., eds. Urban Development in the Muslim World. LC 92-20103. 290p. (C). 1993. text 19.95 (*0-88285-141-1*) Ctr Urban Pol Res.

Amirahmadi, Hooshang & Hooglund, Eric, eds. U. S. - Iran Relations: Areas of Tension & Mutual Interest. 127p. 1994. pap. 15.00 (*0-916808-41-6*) Mid East Inst.

***Amirahmadi, Hooshang, et al.** A Great Game No More: Oil Gas & Stability in the Caspian Sea Region: Contributions to a Friedrich-Ebert-Stiftung Seminar. Dettke, Dieter, ed. 109p. 1999. pap. write for info. (*0-9647348-5-0*) Friedrich-Ebert Found.

Amiran, Eyal. Wandering & Home: Beckett's Metaphysical Narrative. 240p. (C). 1993. 40.00 (*0-271-00860-1*) Pa St U Pr.

Amiran, Eyal & Unsworth, John, eds. Essays in Postmodern Culture. 400p. (C). 1994. text 61.00 (*0-19-508752-6*); pap. text 25.95 (*0-19-508753-4*) OUP.

Amirault, Toby. Linus Welch. 80p. (Orig.). 1991. pap. 7.95 (*0-9625432-0-9*) Ivy Pr MA.

— Things My Mother Said II. (Illus.). 48p. (Orig.). 1991. pap. 7.95 (*0-9625432-1-7*) Ivy Pr MA.

***Amireh, Amal.** Working Women: Imagining Gender & Class in Nineteenth-Century American Fiction. (Garland Studies in American Popular History & Culture). 250p. 1999. 40.00 (*0-8153-3620-9*) Garland.

***Amireh, Amal & Majaj, Lisa Suhair, eds.** Going Global: The Transnational Reception of 3rd World Women Writers. (Reference Library of the Humanities). 300p. 2000. pap. 24.95 (*0-8153-3606-3*) Garland.

***Amireh, Amal & Suhair-Majaj, Lisa.** The Politics of Reception: Globalizing Third World Women's Texts. 300p. 2000. 55.00 (*0-8153-3605-5*) Garland.

Amirfaiz, Farhad. Official Microsoft Merchant Server Toolkit. LC 97-43124. 400p. 1997. pap. text 79.99 incl. cd-rom (*1-57231-622-5*) Microsoft.

— Official Microsoft Site Server 3.0 Commerce Edition Toolkit. 2nd ed. LC 98-11187. 600p. 79.99 incl. cd-rom (*1-57231-813-9*) Microsoft.

Amirie, Abbas, ed. The Persian Gulf & Indian Ocean in International Politics. LC 77-378100. 429p. reprint ed. pap. 133.00 (*0-608-15866-6*, 203073700070) Bks Demand.

Amirie, Abbas, jt. auth. see Amirie, Susan D.

Amirie, Susan D. & Amirie, Abbas. Expository Writing A to Z: A Manual with Outlines & Exemplars. (Illus.). 102p. 1999. pap. text 16.95 (*1-883317-04-5*) Acad Pr of Am.

— Law Enforcement Report Writing I: Source Book: A Comprehensive Reference-Text. LC 93-70806. (Illus.). 368p. (Orig.). (C). 1994. pap. 41.95 (*1-883317-00-2*) Acad Pr of Am.

— Law Enforcement Report Writing II: Source Workbook: Exercises Accompanying Text. LC 93-70804. (Illus.). 420p. (Orig.). (C). 1999. pap. 46.95 (*1-883317-01-0*) Acad Pr of Am.

— Law Enforcement Report Writing I: Source Book (Reference-Text), 2 vols. 3rd rev. ed. LC 93-70806. (Illus.). 345p. 1999. pap. text 41.95 (*1-883317-05-3*) Acad Pr of Am.

— Vocabulary in Context: Law Enforcement: For Civil Service & Scholastic Entry-Level Testing. LC 96-96346. 118p. 1997. pap. text 12.95 (*1-883317-03-7*) Acad Pr of Am.

Amirouche, Farid M. Computer-Aided Design & Manufacturing. LC 92-27575. 528p. 1992. 69.80 (*0-13-472341-4*) P-H.

Amirsadeghi, Hossein, ed. Twentieth Century Iran. LC 77-9569. (Illus.). 328p. 1977. 45.00 (*0-8419-0325-5*) Holmes & Meier.

Amirshahi, Mahshid. Suri & Co. Tales of a Persian Teenage Girl. Knorzer, J. E., tr. from IRA. (Modern Middle Eastern Literature in Translation Ser.). 100p. (Orig.). 1995. pap. 9.95 (*0-292-70463-1*) U of Tex Pr.

Amirshahy, Mahshid. Dar Hazar. 3rd ed. (Orig.). 1995. reprint ed. pap. 18.95 (*1-883819-08-3*) Ketab Corp.

Amirtham, Samuel & Pobee, John S., eds. Theology by the People: Reflections on Doing Theology in Community. LC 86-211214. 153p. reprint ed. pap. 47.50 (*0-7837-6007-8*, 204581700008) Bks Demand.

***Amirthanayagam, Guy.** The Marriage of Continents: Multiculturalism in Modern Literature. LC 99-51876. 384p. 2000. 49.50 (*0-7618-1575-9*) U Pr of Amer.

Amirthanayagam, Indran. Elephants of Reckoning. 1993. 18.00 (*0-914610-73-2*); pap. 10.00 (*0-914610-72-4*) Hanging Loose.

Amirtharaj, Paul M. Proceedings of the 1997 U. S. Workshop on the Physics & Chemistry of Li-Vi Materials. LC 98-66949. ix, 819 p. 1998. write for info. (*0-87339-410-0*) Minerals Metals.

Amirtharajah, Appiah. Filtration. Date not set. 85.00 (*0-87371-330-3*) Lewis Pubs.

Amirtharajah, Appiah, et al, eds. Mixing in Coagulation & Flocculation. 440p. 1991. 125.00 (*0-89867-561-8*, 90580) Am Water Wks Assn.

Amirxan. Deutsch-Kurdisch Woerterbuch. (GER & KUR.). 611p. 1992. 150.00 (*0-7859-7243-9*, 3190063486) Fr & Eur.

— Kurdisch-Deutsch Woerterbuch. (GER & KUR.). 542p. 1992. 150.00 (*0-7859-7244-7*, 3190063494) Fr & Eur.

Amiry, Laila. Barron's How to Prepare for the AP French: Advanced Placement Examination LC 97-77572. iv, 444 p. 1998. write for info. (*0-7641-0543-4*) Barron.

— How to Prepare for the Advanced Placement Test: AP French, 2 vols. (ENG & FRE.). 450p. 1998. pap. 24.95 incl. audio (*0-7641-7159-3*) Barron.

Amis, Debby & Green, Jeanne. Prepared Childbirth - The Family Way. 6th rev. ed. 1998. 5.00 (*0-9662875-0-9*) Family Way Pubns.

Amis, E., ed. Joint Meeting on Multicomponent Polymers & Polyelectrolytes. 54p. (C). 1998. pap. text 20.00 (*0-7881-7183-6*) DIANE Pub.

Amis, E. Newhouse. Essen Urorad. 1990. 110.00 (*0-316-03735-4*) Little.

Amis, John & Rose, Michael, eds. Words about Music: A Treasury of Writings by Celebrated Figures. 440p. 1995. pap. 14.95 (*1-56924-875-3*) Marlowe & Co.

Amis, Kingsley. The Alteration. 210p. 1988. mass mkt. 3.95 (*0-88184-432-2*) Carroll & Graf.

— The Green Man. 3rd ed. 252p. 1997. reprint ed. pap. 12.00 (*0-89733-220-2*) Academy Chi Pubs.

— The King's English: A Guide to Modern Usage. LC 98-15432. 288p. 1998. text 23.95 (*0-312-18601-0*) St Martin.

***Amis, Kingsley.** The King's English: A Guide to Modern Usage. 1999. pap. 12.95 (*0-312-20657-7*) St Martin.

Amis, Kingsley. Lucky Jim. 254p. 1993. pap. 11.95 (*0-14-018630-1*, Penguin Classics) Viking Penguin.

— Lucky Jim. 256p. 1976. reprint ed. lib. bdg. 22.95 (*0-89244-069-4*, Queens House) Amereon Ltd.

— Lucky Jim. 1990. reprint ed. lib. bdg. 29.95 (*0-89968-473-4*) Buccaneer Bks.

— New Maps of Hell. LC 74-15944. (Science Fiction Ser.). 161p. 1977. reprint ed. 21.95 (*0-405-06321-0*) Ayer.

— The Russian Girl. 304p. 1993. pap. 11.99 (*0-14-014475-7*, Penguin Bks) Viking Penguin.

— The Russian Girl. 1995. pap. 11.95 (*0-14-025172-3*, Viking) Viking Penguin.

— Take a Girl Like You. large type ed. (Romance Ser.). 688p. 1993. 27.99 (*0-7089-2927-3*) Ulverscroft.

Amis, Kingsley, ed. Harold's Years: Impressions of the Harold Wilson Era. 12.95 (*0-7043-2143-2*, Pub. by Quartet) Charles River Bks.

Amis, Kingsley, ed. The New Oxford Book of Light Verse. 384p. 1987. pap. 14.95 (*0-19-282075-3*) OUP.

Amis, Kingsley & Conquest, Robert, eds. Spectrum: A Science Fiction Anthology. 20.95 (*0-8488-0105-9*) Amereon Ltd.

Amis, Lola J. Native Son Notes. (Cliffs Notes Ser.). 56p. 1971. pap. 4.95 (*0-8220-0874-2*, Cliff) IDG Bks.

Amis, Martin. Collection of Short Stories. 1999. pap. 12.00 (*0-375-70115-X*) Vin Bks.

— Dead Babies. LC 90-50616. 224p. 1991. pap. 13.00 (*0-679-73449-X*) Vin Bks.

— Einstein's Monsters. (Vintage International Ser.). 160p. 1990. pap. 12.00 (*0-679-72996-8*) Vin Bks.

***Amis, Martin.** Experience: A Memoir. (Illus.). 406p. 2000. 23.95 (*0-7868-6652-7*, Pub. by Talk Miramax Bks) Time Warner.

Amis, Martin. Heavy Water: And Other Stories. LC 98-21779. 208p. 1999. 21.00 (*0-609-60129-6*) Harmony Bks.

— Heavy Water: And Other Stories. large type ed. LC 99-21865. 278p. 1999. 28.95 (*0-7838-8621-7*) Mac Lib Ref.

— The Information. 1996. pap. 13.00 (*0-679-73573-9*) Vin Bks.

— London Fields. LC 90-50471. 480p. 1991. pap. 14.00 (*0-679-73034-6*) Vin Bks.

— Money: A Suicide Note. (Fiction Ser.). 368p. 1986. pap. 13.95 (*0-14-008891-1*, Penguin Bks) Viking Penguin.

— The Moronic Inferno: And Other Visits to America. 1991. pap. 12.95 (*0-14-012719-4*, Viking) Viking Penguin.

— My Oxford. Thwaite, Ann, ed. & intro. by. (Illus.). 214p. (Orig.). 1987. pap. 8.95 (*0-86051-381-5*, Pub. by Robson Bks) Parkwest Pubns.

— Night Train. LC 97-28163. 175p. 1998. 20.00 (*0-609-60128-8*) Harmony Bks.

— Night Train. 175p. 1999. pap. 11.00 (*0-375-70114-1*) Vintage Am.

— Night Train. large type ed. LC 98-7829. 1998. 25.95 (*1-56895-570-7*, Compass) Wheeler Pub.

— Other People: A Mystery Story. LC 93-42062. 1994. pap. 13.00 (*0-679-73589-5*) Vin Bks.

— The Rachel Papers. LC 92-50078. 1992. pap. 12.00 (*0-679-73458-9*) Vin Bks.

— Success. LC 90-50617. 224p. 1991. pap. 11.00 (*0-679-73448-1*) Vin Bks.

— Time's Arrow: Or the Nature of the Offense. LC 91-51128. 1992. pap. 7.00 (*0-679-74170-4*) Vin Bks.

An Asterisk (*) at the beginning of an entry indicates that the title is appearing for the first time.

— Time's Arrow: Or the Nature of the Offense. LC 91-5112. 1992. pap. 11.00 (*0-679-73572-0*) Vin Bks.

Amis, Martin. Visiting Mrs. Nabokov & Other Excursions. 1995. pap. 15.00 (*0-679-75793-7*) Vin Bks.

Amis, Martin, et al. On Guard: Bella Fleace Gave a Party. 22p. 3.95 (*1-86092-000-4*, Pub. by Travelman Pub) IPG Chicago.

Amis, Moses N. Historical Raleigh: With Sketches of Wake County from 1771 & Its Important Towns, Descriptive, Biographical, Educational, Induatrial, Religious. (Illus.). 289p. 1997. reprint ed. lib. bdg. 34.00 (*0-8328-6910-4*) Higginson Bk Co.

Amis, R., intro. see Mouravieff, Boris & D'Oncieu, Manek.

Amis, Robin. A Different Christianity: Early Christian Esotericism & Modern Thought. LC 94-40813. 388p. (C). 1995. text 65.50 (*0-7914-2571-1*); pap. text 21.95 (*0-7914-2572-X*) State U NY Pr.

— The Heart of Salvation: Life & Writings of St. Theophan the Recluse. Williams, Esther, tr. from RUS. 104p. (Orig.). (C). 1992. pap. text 17.95 (*1-872292-02-X*) Praxis Inst.

Amis, Robin, ed. see Capsanis, George.

Amis, Robin, ed. see Kovalevsky, Jean.

Amis, Robin, ed. see Mouravieff, Boris & D'Oncieu, Manek.

Amis, Robin, ed. see Theophan the Recluse.

Amis, Robin, ed. & tr. see Mouravieff, Boris.

Amis, Robin, tr. see Mouravieff, Boris.

Amisano, Gianni & Giannini, Carlo. Topics in Structural VAR Econometrics, Vol. XIII. 2nd enl. rev. ed. LC 96-53414. (Illus.). 181p. 1997. 69.95 (*3-540-61942-9*) Spr-Verlag.

Amish Women Committee. Amish Cooking. rev. ed. LC 81-80123. 320p. 1992. 18.99 (*0-8361-3626-8*); spiral bd. 17.99 (*0-8361-3600-4*) Herald Pr.

Amissah, Austin, jt. auth. see Cotran, Eugene.

Amit, Daniel J. Field Theory: The Renormalization Group & Critical Phenomena. 2nd ed. 412p. (C). 1984. pap. text 33.00 (*9971-966-11-5*) World Scientific Pub.

— Field Theory: The Renormalization Group & Critical Phenomena. 2nd ed. 412p. (C). 1993. text 38.00 (*9971-966-10-7*) World Scientific Pub.

— Modelling Brain Function: The World of Attractor Neural Networks. (Illus.). 528p. (C). 1989. text 64.95 (*0-521-36100-1*) Cambridge U Pr.

Amit, Daniel J., et al, eds. Neural Networks: From Biology to High Energy Physics: Proceedings of the Third Workshop, Elba International Physics Centre, Italy 26 - 30 September 1994. 280p. 1995. text 68.00 (*981-02-2482-6*, RuBnRaPh-P2953) World Scientific Pub.

Amit, Daniel J. & Verbin, Yosef. Introductory Course in Statistical Physics. LC 99-57215. 500p. 1998. 48.00 (*981-02-3192-X*) World Scientific Pub.

Amit, Daniel J., jt. ed. see Wiser, N.

Amit-Talai, Vered. Constructing Field: Ethnographic Fieldwork in Contemporary World. LC 99-24309. 1999. pap. write for info. (*0-415-19830-5*) Routledge.

***Amit-Talai, Vered, ed.** Constructing Field: Ethnographic Fieldwork in Contemporary World. LC 99-24309. (European Association of Social Anthropologists Ser.). 232p. (C). 1999. text. write for info. (*0-415-19829-1*) Routledge.

Amit-Talai, Vered & Knowles, Caroline, eds. Re-Situating Identities: The Politics of Race, Ethnicity & Culture. 320p. 1996. pap. 24.95 (*1-55111-071-7*) Broadview Pr.

Amit-Talai, Vered & Wulff, Helena, eds. Youth Cultures: A Cross Cultural Perspective. LC 94-46793. 240p. (C). 1995. pap. 25.99 (*0-415-10984-1*, C0042) Routledge.

Amit, Yairah. The Book of Judges: The Art of Editing. (Biblical Encyclopaedia Library: No. VI). 399p. 1992. pap. text 32.00 (*965-342-592-7*, Pub. by Bialik) Eisenbrauns.

Amit, Yairah. The Book of Judges: The Art of Editing. LC 98-33359. (Biblical Interpretation Ser.). xvi, 430p. 1999. 143.50 (*90-04-10827-0*) Brill Academic Pubs.

— Covert Polemics in Biblical Narrative. (Biblical Interpretation Ser.: No. 25). 240p. 2000. 87.50 (*90-04-10153-5*, NLG132) Brill Academic Pubs.

***Amit, Yairah.** History & Ideology: Introduction to Historiography in the Hebrew Bible. (Biblical Seminar Ser.: No. 60). 128p. 1999. pap. 19.95 (*1-85075-928-6*, Pub. by Sheffield Acad) CUP Services.

— Judges: Introduction & Commentary. (Mikra Leyisra'el Ser.). (HEB.). xiv, 337p. 1999. 14.00 (*965-13-1325-0*, Pub. by Magnes Pr) Eisenbrauns.

Amitabh. Urban Land Markets & Land Price Changes: A Study in the Third World Context. LC 97-74446. 328p. 1997. text 78.95 (*1-85972-450-7*, Pub. by Ashgate Pub) Ashgate Pub Co.

Amitai-Preiss, Reuven. The Mongol Empire & Its Legacy. LC 98-4197. (Islamic History & Civilization Studies & Texts). 361p. 1999. 146.50 (*90-04-11048-8*) Brill Academic Pubs.

— Mongols & Mamluks: The Mamluk-Ilkhanid War, 1260-1281. (Studies in Islamic Civilization). (Illus.). 288p. (C). 1995. text 64.95 (*0-521-46226-6*) Cambridge U Pr.

Amitan, Daniel, ed. see Kaplan, Aryeh.

Amith, Jonathan D. Amate Tradition/La Tradicion del Amate: Innovation & Dissent in Mexican Art. 168p. 1996. pap. text 29.95 (*968-6272-08-9*) Mexican Fine Arts.

Amitrano & Lowe. Laboratory Guide to Human Biology. 2nd ed. 182p. (C). 1997. spiral bd. 40.95 (*0-7872-4277-2*, 41427701) Kendall-Hunt.

Amitsur, S. A, et al, eds. Algebraists' Homage: Papers in Ring Theory & Related Topics. LC 82-18934. (Contemporary Mathematics Ser.: vol. 13). 409p. 1983. pap. 44.00 (*0-8218-5013-X*, CONM/13) Am Math.

Amjad-Ali, Charles & Pitcher, W. Alvin, eds. Liberation & Ethics: Essays in Religious Social Ethics in Honor of Gibson Winter. LC 83-73425. (Studies in Religion & Society). 233p. 1985. text 32.95 (*0-913348-22-8*) Ctr Sci Study.

Amjad, Mohammed. Iran: From Royal Dictatorship to Theocracy, 242. LC 89-11746. (Contributions in Political Science Ser.: No. 242). 187p. 1989. 57.95 (*0-313-26441-4*, AFD/, Greenwood Pr) Greenwood.

Amjad, Rashid, jt. auth. see Ahmed, Viqar.

Amjad, Z. Mineral Scale Formation & Inhibition: Proceedings of an American Chemical Society Symposium in Washington, D.C., August 21-26, 1994. (Illus.). 368p. (C). 1996. text 125.00 (*0-306-45195-6*, Kluwer Plenum) Kluwer Academic.

Amjad, Zahid, ed. Calcium Phosphates in Biological & Industrial Systems. LC 97-41618. 529p. 1997. text 198.00 (*0-7923-8046-0*, D Reidel) Kluwer Academic.

— Water-Soluble Polymers. LC 98-39451. (Illus.). 272p. (C). 1998. text 125.00 (*0-306-45931-0*, Kluwer Plenum) Kluwer Academic.

Amjadi, Azita, et al. Did External Barriers Cause the Marginalization of Sub-Saharan Africa in World Trade? LC 96-46465. (Discussion Papers: No. 348). 164p. 1996. pap. 22.00 (*0-8213-3826-9*, 13826) World Bank.

Amkreutz, Johann J. Dictionary of Numeric Control & Machine Tools. 250p. 1992. 149.00 (*0-7859-8834-3*) Fr & Eur.

— English, German & French Dictionary of Machine Tools: Woerterbuch der Numerischen Steuerungen und Werkzeugmaschinen. 2nd ed. (ENG, FRE & GER.). 772p. 1989. 175.00 (*0-8288-3839-9*, M15531) Fr & Eur.

— Office & Data Communication Dictionary: Fachwoerterbuch der Buero und Datenkommunikation. (ENG, FRE & GER.). 1985. write for info. (*0-8288-1369-8*, M8449) Fr & Eur.

Amkreutz, Johann J., jt. auth. see Carl, Wilhelm H.

Amler, Jane F. Christopher Columbus's Jewish Roots. LC 91-16694. 304p. 1992. 24.95 (*0-87668-586-6*) Aronson.

— Christopher Columbus's Jewish Roots. LC 91-16694. 304p. 1993. reprint ed. pap. 25.00 (*1-56821-021-3*) Aronson.

***Amma, T. A. Sarasvati.** Geometry in Ancient & Medieval India. 1998. reprint ed. 26.00 (*81-208-1344-8*, Pub. by Motilal Bnarsidass) S Asia.

Amman, Daniel, jt. auth. see Fischer, Andreas.

Amman, Hans M., et al, eds. Computational Economics & Econometrics. (Advanced Studies in Theoretical & Applied Econometrics). 192p. (C). 1992. lib. bdg. 140.50 (*0-7923-1287-2*) Kluwer Academic.

— Handbook of Computational Economics. LC 96-12806. (Handbooks in Economics Ser.: No. 13). 832p. 1996. 110.00 (*0-444-89857-3*) Elsevier.

Amman, J. C. A Dissertation on Speech. Baker, C., tr. 1966. 15.00 (*0-934454-29-9*) Lubrecht & Cramer.

Amman, Janet. Theme Teaching with Art Reproductions. 150p. (Orig.). 1992. pap. 14.95 (*0-935493-26-3*) Modern Learn Pr.

Amman, Jost. Two Hundred Ninety-Three Renaissance Woodcuts for Artists & Illustrators: Jost Amman's Kunstbuchlein. LC 68-14561. 96p. 1968. reprint ed. pap. 8.95 (*0-486-21987-9*) Dover.

Amman, Jost & Sachs, Hans. Book of Trades (Standebuch) Appelbaum, Stanley & Rifkin, Benjamin A., trs. from GER. LC 72-75581. (Pictorial Archive Ser.). Orig. Title: Eygentliche Beschreibung Aller Stande Auff Erden. (Illus.). 176p. 1973. reprint ed. 6.95 (*0-486-22886-X*) Dover.

Amman, Ludwig. Vorbild und Vernunft, Band 5. (GER.). xii, 287p. 1993. 49.80 (*3-487-09773-7*) G Olms Pubs.

Ammaniti, Massimo & Stern, Daniel N., eds. Psychoanalysis & Development: Representations & Narratives. LC 94-14618. (Psychoanalytic Crosscurrents Ser.). 208p. (C). 1994. text 55.00 (*0-8147-0616-9*) NYU Pr.

Ammann, Brigitta. Late-Quaternary Palynology at Lobsigensee: Regional Vegetation History & Local Lake Development. (Dissertationes Botanicae Ser.: Band 137). (Illus.). xii, 157p. 1989. pap. 77.00 (*3-443-64049-4*, Pub. by Gebruder Borntraeger) Balogh.

Ammann, D. Ion-Selective Microelectrodes. (Illus.). 385p. 1986. 196.95 (*0-387-16222-4*) Spr-Verlag.

Ammann, Erika. Erika's Folk Art. (Illus.). 1994. pap. 9.95 (*1-883675-05-7*, 105) J Shaw Studio.

— Erika's Swiss Folk Art Design, Vol. 1. (Illus.). 36p. 1998. pap. 9.95 (*1-57377-032-9*) Easl Pubns.

Ammann, Ernst, jt. auth. see Zeitler, E.

Ammann, Herman. Canterbury Tale from the Wife of Bath: After Chaucer A Comedy in One Act. (Illus.). 33p. 1970. pap. 3.25 (*0-88680-018-8*) I E Clark.

— Canterbury Tale from the Wife of Bath: Director's Script. (Illus.). 33p. 1970. pap. 7.50 (*0-88680-019-6*) I E Clark.

— The Little Troll Without a Soul: A Search for Happiness in One-Act. (Illus.). 27p. (J). (gr. 4-9). 1976. pap. 3.25 (*0-88680-117-6*) I E Clark.

Ammann, Hermann. Ghost for Rosanda: A Scary Play in One-Act. (Illus.). 47p. 1974. pap. 3.25 (*0-88680-071-4*) I E Clark.

— Ghost for Rosanda: Director's Script. (Illus.). 47p. 1974. pap. 7.50 (*0-88680-072-2*) I E Clark.

— The Little Match Girl: One-Act Dramatization. (Illus.). 36p. (J). (gr. k up). 1970. pap. 3.25 (*0-88680-111-7*) I E Clark.

— The Little Match Girl: One-Act Dramatization - Director's Script. (Illus.). 36p. (J). (gr. k up). 1970. pap. 7.50 (*0-88680-112-5*) I E Clark.

— Magic Well: A One-Act Comedy. (Illus.). 37p. (J). (gr. k up). 1972. pap. 3.25 (*0-88680-122-2*) I E Clark.

— Magic Well: Director's Script. (Illus.). 37p. (J). (gr. k up). 1972. pap. 7.50 (*0-88680-123-0*) I E Clark.

— Steadfast Tin Soldier: A One-Act Play. (Illus.). 29p. (J). (gr. 1 up). 1969. pap. 3.25 (*0-88680-186-9*) I E Clark.

— Steadfast Tin Soldier: Director's Script. (Illus.). 29p. (J). (gr. 1 up). 1968. 7.50 (*0-88680-187-7*) I E Clark.

***Ammann, Jean-Christophe.** A Room in the Museum of Modern Art in Frankfurt. (Illus.). 96p. 1999. 19.95 (*3-929078-35-X*, Pub. by G Kehayoff) te Neues.

Ammann, Jean-Christophe & Schubert, Renate, contrib. by. Ellen Auerbach: Berlin - Tel Aviv - London - New York. (Illus.). 100p. 1998. 39.95 (*3-7913-1972-8*) te Neues.

Ammann, Jean-Christophe, et al. Views from Abroad: European Perspectives on American Art, Vol. I. LC 95-16525. (Illus.). 1996. pap. write for info. (*0-87427-101-0*) Whitney Mus.

***Ammann, Klaus, et al, eds.** Methods for Risk Assessment of Transgenic Plants Vol. III: Ecological Risks & Prospects of Transgenic Plants, Where Do We Go from Here? A Dialogue Between Biotech Industry & Science. LC 99-16245. 350p. 1999. 92.00 (*3-7643-5917-X*, Pub. by Birkhauser) Spr-Verlag.

Ammann, L. A. Self Liberation. rev. ed. Tooby, Paul, tr. from SPA. (Illus.). 225p. 1999. pap. 15.95 (*1-878977-14-8*) Latitude Pr.

Ammann, Lillie. Look Beyond Tomorrow: The Carola Spencer Story. 80p. 1998. pap. 14.95 (*0-9665912-0-8*) Lillies Lovely.

***Ammann, Paul T.** Aix RS/6000 All in One Certification Exam Guide. (All-in-One Ser.). 720p. (C). 2000. 99.99 (*0-07-212331-1*) Osborne-McGraw.

Ammann, Raymond. Kanak Dance & Music: Ceremonial & Intimate Peformance of the Melanesians of New Caledonia, Historical & Actual. (Illus.). 352p. 1997. 110.00 (*0-7103-0586-9*, Pub. by Kegan Paul Intl) Col U Pr.

Ammann, Ruth. Healing & Transformation in Sandplay: Creative Processes Become Visible. LC 91-18685. (Illus.). 160p. 1991. 37.95 (*0-8126-9140-7*); pap. 13.95 (*0-8126-9141-5*) Open Court.

Ammann, W. J., et al, eds. Impact: Effects of Fast Transient Loadings: Proceedings of the First International Conference, Lausanne, August 26-27, 1987. 400p. (C). 1988. text 220.00 (*90-6191-862-6*, Pub. by A A Balkema) Ashgate Pub Co.

Ammar, Mostafa H., jt. auth. see Saadawi, Tarek N.

Ammar, R., jt. ed. see Elmaghraby, A.

Ammar, R. A., ed. Intelligent Distributed Processing '89: Proceedings of ISMM Symposium, Fort Lauderdale, Florida, U. S. A., December 13-15, 1989. 153p. 1989. 65.00 (*0-88986-138-2*, 152) Acta Pr.

***Ammarell, Eugene.** Bugis Navigation. (Monograph Series, Yale Southeast Asia Studies: Vol. 48). (Illus.). 314p. 1999. pap. 27.00 (*0-938692-70-4*); lib. bdg. 38.00 (*0-938692-69-0*) Yale U SE Asia.

Amme, Carl H. NATO Strategy & Nuclear Defense, 69. LC 87-17746. (Contributions in Military Studies Ser.: No. 69). (Illus.). 202p. 1988. 49.95 (*0-313-26037-0*, ANS/, Greenwood Pr) Greenwood.

***Ammen.** Metalcaster's Bible. LC 99-33560. 432p. 1999. pap. 34.95 (*0-07-134246-X*) McGraw.

Ammen, Amy. Dog Training: An Owner's Guide to a Happy, Healthy Pet. LC 98-12611. (Owner's Guide to a Happy, Healthy Pet Ser.). 128p. 1998. 12.95 (*0-87605-564-1*) Howell Bks.

Ammen, Amy, jt. auth. see Fraser, Jacqueline.

Ammen, C. W. Casting Aluminum. (Illus.). 252p. (Orig.). 1985. pap. 14.95 (*0-8306-1910-0*) McGraw-Hill Prof.

— Casting Brass. (Illus.). 252p. (Orig.). 1985. 18.95 (*0-8306-0810-9*, 1810H); pap. 14.95 (*0-8306-1810-4*, 1810P) McGraw-Hill Prof.

— The Complete Handbook of Sand Casting. (Illus.). 238p. 1979. pap. 15.95 (*0-07-157204-X*) McGraw.

— The Complete Handbook of Sand Casting. (Illus.). 1979. pap. 12.95 (*0-8306-1043-X*, 1043) McGraw-Hill Prof.

— The Electroplater's Handbook. (Illus.). 224p. (Orig.). 1986. pap. 15.95 (*0-8306-0310-7*) McGraw-Hill Prof.

— The Metalcaster's Bible. 434p. 1980. pap. 27.95 (*0-07-156186-2*) McGraw.

— Recovery & Refining of Precious Metals. LC 83-12355. (Illus.). 400p. 1984. mass mkt. 44.95 (*0-442-20934-7*, VNR) Wiley.

Ammen, Sue, jt. ed. see O'Connor, Kevin J.

Ammende, Ewald. Human Life in Russia. (Illus.). xii, 320p. 1984. reprint ed. 25.00 (*0-939738-54-6*) Zubal Inc.

Ammendola, Giuseppe. From Creditor to Debtor: The U. S. Pursuit of Foreign Capital -- the Case of the Repeal of the Withholding Tax. LC 93-38435. (Foreign Economic Policy of the United States Ser.). 456p. 1994. text 35.00 (*0-8153-1565-1*) Garland.

Ammentorp, William, et al. Quality Assurance for Long-Term Care Providers: Nursing Home Management in the 1990s. (Human Services Guides Ser.: Vol. 64). (Illus.). 192p. (C). 1990. pap. text 18.95 (*0-8039-4024-6*) Sage.

Ammentrop, et al. Reforming Administrator Preparation Programs. (Orig.). (C). 1992. pap. text 7.00 (*1-55996-153-8*) Univ Council Educ Admin.

Ammer, Christine. The A to Z of Foreign Musical Terms: From Adagio to Zierlich - A Dictionary for Performers & Students. (Orig.). (C). 1989. pap. text 8.50 (*0-911318-15-1*) E C Schirmer.

— The American Heritage Dictionary of Idioms. LC 97-12390. 736p. (YA). (gr. 7 up). 1997. 30.00 (*0-395-72774-X*) HM.

— Cool Cats & Top Dogs: And Other Beastly Expressions. LC 99-24727. (Illus.). 266p. 1999. pap. 14.00 (*0-395-95730-3*) HM.

***Ammer, Christine.** Fighting Words: From War, Rebellion & Other Combative Capers. 2nd ed. LC 98-33697. (Illus.). 288p. 1999. pap. 15.95 (*0-8442-0285-1*, 02851) NTC Contemp Pub Co.

— HarCol Dict Music. 3rd ed. LC 94-28689. 528p. 1995. pap. 19.00 (*0-06-461049-7*, Perennial) HarperTrade.

— The New A to Z of Women's Health: A Concise Encyclopedia. 4th ed. LC 99-16506. 2000. 19.95 (*0-8160-4002-8*) Facts on File.

Ammer, Christine. The New A-Z Book of Women's Health. 3rd rev. ed. LC 94-25289. 576p. 1995. 40.00 (*0-8160-3121-5*) Facts on File.

***Ammer, Christine.** Unsung: A History of Women in American Music. 2nd ed. LC 00-42017. 2000. pap. write for info. (*1-57467-061-1*, Amadeus Pr) Timber.

Ammer, Christine & Ammer, Dean S. Dictionary of Business & Economics: Revised & Expanded Edition. expanded rev. ed. 517p. 1986. per. 29.50 (*0-02-901480-8*) Free Pr.

Ammer, Christine, jt. auth. see Lederer, Richard.

Ammer, Dean S., jt. auth. see Ammer, Christine.

***Ammeraal, L.** C++ for Programmers. 3rd ed. LC 99-58871. 464p. 2000. pap. 54.99 (*0-471-60697-9*) Wiley.

Ammeraal, L. Computer Graphics for Java Programmers. LC 97-51766. (Worldwide Series in Computer Science). 282p. 1998. pap. 54.99 (*0-471-98142-7*) Wiley.

Ammeraal, Leendert. Algorithms & Data Structures in C++ 368p. 1996. pap. 59.99 (*0-471-96355-0*) Wiley.

— C for Programmers: A Complete Tutorial Based on the ANSI Standard. LC 90-13077. 262p. 1991. pap. 54.95 (*0-471-92851-8*) Wiley.

— C++ for Programmers. 2nd ed. 392p. 1995. pap. text 59.99 (*0-471-95486-1*) Wiley.

— Programs & Data Structures in C: Based on ANSI C & C Plus Plus. 2nd ed. 284p. 1992. pap. 64.00 (*0-471-93123-3*) Wiley.

— STL for C++ Programmers. LC 96-43517. 236p. 1997. pap. 64.99 (*0-471-97181-2*) Wiley.

— Windows Wisdom for C & C++ Programmers. LC 93-10287. (Wiley Professional Computing Ser.). (Illus.). 255p. 1993. reprint ed. pap. 79.10 (*0-608-07294-X*, 206752200009) Bks Demand.

Ammerman. The Santa Venera Figurines. (Illus.). 1168p. (C). text 150.00 (*0-472-10899-6*, 10899) U of Mich Pr.

Ammerman, Albert J. & Cavalli-Sforza, L. L. The Neolithic Transition & the Genetics of Populations in Europe. LC 84-42587. 193p. 1984. reprint ed. pap. 59.90 (*0-608-02931-9*, 206399700008) Bks Demand.

Ammerman, Clarence B., et al, eds. Bioavailability of Nutrients for Animals: Amino Acids, Minerals, Vitamins. (Illus.). 441p. 1995. text 69.00 (*0-12-056250-2*) Acad Pr.

Ammerman, David L. In the Common Cause: American Response to the Coercive Acts of 1774. LC 74-2417. 182p. reprint ed. pap. 56.50 (*0-8357-4632-1*, 203756100008) Bks Demand.

Ammerman, David L. & Morgan, Philip D., eds. Books about Early America: Two Thousand One Titles. 134p. 1989. pap. 10.00 (*0-910776-04-0*); lib. bdg. 25.00 (*0-910776-03-2*) Omohundro Inst Early Am.

Ammerman, David L., jt. ed. see Tate, Thad W.

Ammerman, Douglas J., jt. ed. see Sammataro, Robert F.

***Ammerman, J. Mark & Ammerman, Kathy.** Help During Loss. 144p. 1999. pap. 9.95 (*1-57921-220-4*, Pub. by WinePress Pub) BookWorld.

Ammerman, Jim. Supernatural Events in the Life of an Ordinary Man. 192p. (Orig.). 1996. pap. 10.00 (*1-883893-48-8*) WinePress Pub.

Ammerman, Kathleen, jt. auth. see Ammerman, Mark.

Ammerman, Kathy, jt. auth. see Ammerman, J. Mark.

***Ammerman, Mark.** Jesus Feeds the 5,000. (Little Bible Bks.). (Illus.). 24p. (J). 1999. 1.99 (*1-57748-658-7*) Barbour Pub.

— Jonah & the Big Fish. (Little Bible Bks.). (Illus.). 24p. (J). (ps-1). 2000. 1.99 (*1-57748-684-6*) Barbour Pub.

— Longshot. LC 99-80158. (Cross & the Tomahawk Ser.: Vol. 3). 318p. 2000. pap. 11.99 (*0-88965-165-5*, Pub. by Horizon Books) Chr Pubns.

Ammerman, Mark. Rain from God. LC 97-70110. (Cross & the Tomahawk Ser.: Vol. I). (Illus.). 320p. 1997. pap. 11.99 (*0-88965-134-5*, Pub. by Horizon Books) Chr Pubns.

— The Ransom. LC 97-223067. (Cross & the Tomahawk Ser.: Vol. 2). 392p. 1997. pap. 11.99 (*0-88965-135-3*, Pub. by Horizon Books) Chr Pubns.

— Roger Williams. unabridged ed. (Young Reader's Christian Library). (Illus.). 224p. (J). (gr. 3-7). 1996. pap. 1.39 (*1-55748-761-8*) Barbour Pub.

Ammerman, Mark & Ammerman, Kathleen. Help During Grief: Hope for the Hurting. 96p. (Orig.). 1996. pap. 10.00 (*1-883893-44-5*) WinePress Pub.

***Ammerman, Mark & Wheeler, Ron.** Daniel & the Lion's Den. (Little Bible Bks.). (Illus.). 24p. (J). 1999. 1.99 (*1-57748-660-9*) Barbour Pub.

***Ammerman, Max.** Root Cause Analysis Handbook: A Simplified Approach to Identifying, Correcting, & Reporting Workplace Errors. 135p. 1998. pap. text 26.00 (*0-527-76326-8*) Productivity Inc.

Ammerman, Nancy T. Baptist Battles: Social Change & Religious Conflict in the Southern Baptist Convention. LC 89-48883. 380p. (Orig.). (C). 1990. text 40.00 (*0-8135-1556-4*); pap. text 17.95 (*0-8135-1557-2*) Rutgers U Pr.

— Bible Believers: Fundamentalists in the Modern World. 248p. 1987. pap. text 16.00 (*0-8135-1231-X*) Rutgers U Pr.

— Congregation & Community. LC 96-16173. 480p. (C). 1997. text 55.00 (*0-8135-2334-6*); pap. text 24.00 (*0-8135-2335-4*) Rutgers U Pr.

— Studying Congregations: A New Handbook. LC 98-18487. 224p. 1998. pap. 20.00 (*0-687-00651-1*) Abingdon.

Ammerman, Nancy T., ed. Southern Baptists Observed: Multiple Perspectives on a Changing Denomination. LC 92-18725. 376p. (Orig.). (C). 1993. pap. 21.00 (*0-87049-770-7*); lib. bdg. 40.00 (*0-87049-769-3*) U of Tenn Pr.

A

An Asterisk (*) at the beginning of an entry indicates that the title is appearing for the first time.

A

Ammerman, Nancy T. & Roof, Wade C., eds. Work, Family & Religion in American Society. 348p. (C). 1995. pap. 22.99 (*0-415-91172-9*, C0245) Routledge.

Ammerman, R. T., ed. Classics of Analytic Philosophy. LC 90-38344. (Hackett Classics Ser.). 424p. (C). 1990. reprint ed. pap. text 16.95 (*0-87220-101-5*); reprint ed. lib. bdg. 37.95 (*0-87220-102-3*) Hackett Pub.

Ammerman, R. T. & Hersen, M. Case Studies in Family Violence. LC 90-49558. (Illus.). 422p. (C). 1991. 75.00 (*0-306-43622-1*, Plenum Trade) Perseus Pubng.

— Children at Risk: An Evaluation of Factors Contributing to Child Abuse & Neglect. LC 90-7228. (Illus.). 332p. (C). 1990. 57.50 (*0-306-43437-7*, Kluwer Plenum) Kluwer Academic.

Ammerman, R. T., jt. ed. see Hersen, M.

Ammerman, Robert T. Handbook of Behavior Therapy with Children & Adults. LC 91-3533. Vol. 171. 552p. (C). 1993. 80.00 (*0-205-14583-3*, H45834, Longwood Div) Allyn.

— Treatment of Family Violence: Sourcebook. LC 89-39492. (Personality Processes Ser.). 480p. 1990. 147.50 (*0-471-61023-2*) Wiley.

Ammerman, Robert T., et al, eds. Handbook of Prescriptive Treatments for Children & Adolescents. 2nd ed. LC 98-39961. 426p. 1999. 79.50 (*0-205-26836-6*) Allyn.

— Prevention & Societal Impact of Drug & Alcohol Abuse. 432p. 1999. 89.95 (*0-8058-3157-6*); pap. 39.95 (*0-8058-3158-4*) L Erlbaum Assocs.

***Ammerman, Robert T. & Campo, John V., eds.** Handbook of Pediatric Psychology & Psychiatry Vol. 1: Psychological & Psychiatric Issues in the Pediatric Setting. LC 97-42736. 415p. (C). 1998. 86.00 (*0-205-16560-5*) Allyn.

Ammerman, Robert T. & Campo, John V., eds. Handbook of Pediatric Psychology & Psychiatry Vol. 2: Disease, Injury, & Illness. LC 97-42736. 400p. (C). 1998. 68.00 (*0-205-27601-6*) Allyn.

Ammerman, Robert T. & Hersen, M., eds. Case Studies in Family Violence. LC 90-49558. (Illus.). 422p. (C). 1991. pap. 37.50 (*0-306-43649-3*, Plenum Trade) Perseus Pubng.

Ammerman, Robert T. & Hersen, Michel. Assessment of Family Violence: A Clinical & Legal Sourcebook. LC 91-31397. (Series on Personality Processes). 416p. 1992. 99.95 (*0-471-52415-8*) Wiley.

— Handbook of Prevention & Treatment with Children & Adolescents: Intervention in the Real World Context. LC 96-51877. 656p. 1997. 99.95 (*0-471-12163-0*) Wiley.

***Ammerman, Robert T. & Hersen, Michel, eds.** Assessment of Family Violence: A Clinical & Legal Sourcebook. 2nd ed. LC RC569.5.F3A87 1999. 436p. 1999. 59.95 (*0-471-24256-X*) Wiley.

Ammerman, Robert T. & Hersen, Michel, eds. Handbook of Child Behavior Therapy in the Psychiatric Setting. (Series on Personality Processes). 512p. 1994. 135.00 (*0-471-57844-4*) Wiley.

Ammerman, Robert T., jt. ed. see Hersen, Michel.

Ammermann, Norbert. Subjekt, Logik, Empirie: Grundlegung und Moglichkeiten Empirischer Theologie als Erforschung Subjektiver Theorien. (GER., Illus.). 327p. 1997. 57.95 (*3-631-31551-1*) P Lang Pubng.

— Zur Konstruktion von Seelsorge: Seelsorge, Erkenntnistheorie und Methodenfrage Unter Dem Aspekt der Psychologie der Personlichen Konstrukte und Auf Dem Hintergrund Konstruktivistischer Erkenntnistheorien. (Europaische Hochschulschriften Ser.: Reihe 23, Bd. 513). (GER., Illus.). 277p. 1994. 48.95 (*3-631-47367-2*) P Lang Pubng.

Ammi, Ben. God & the Law of Relativity. LC 91-72967. 154p. 1991. pap. text 12.00 (*0-9620463-2-9*) Communicators Pr.

— God, the Black Man & Truth. rev. ed. LC 82-50906. 272p. 1988. reprint ed. pap. text 9.95 (*0-9620463-0-2*) Communicators Pr.

— God, the Black Man & Truth. 2nd ed. 281p. 1990. pap. 12.00 (*0-9620463-1-0*) Communicators Pr.

Ammianus, Marcellinus. Opera Quae Supersunt, 3 vols. in 2, Set. cxxxiv, 1634p. 1975. reprint ed. 360.00 (*3-487-05654-2*) G Olms Pubs.

— Rerum Gestarum Libri Qui Supersunt, Vol. II, 1. 1963. 90.00 (*3-296-10402-X*) G Olms Pubs.

— Roman History, 3 vols. (Loeb Classical Library: No. 300, 315, 331). write for info. (*0-318-53177-1*) HUP.

— Roman History, 3 vols., Vol. 1. (Loeb Classical Library: No. 300). 632p. 1935. 19.95 (*0-674-99331-4*) HUP.

— Roman History, 3 vols., Vol. 2. (Loeb Classical Library: No. 315). 692p. 1940. 19.95 (*0-674-99348-9*) HUP.

— Roman History, 3 vols., Vol. 3, Bks. 27-31. (Loeb Classical Library: No. 300, 315, 331). 612p. 1939. 19.95 (*0-674-99365-9*) HUP.

Ammidown, Holmes. Historical Collections, Vol. 1. (Illus.). 557p. 1995. pap. 35.00 (*0-7884-0307-9*) Heritage Bk.

— Historical Collections, Vol. 2. (Illus.). 598p. 1996. pap. 41.00 (*0-7884-0437-7*, A002) Heritage Bk.

Ammidown, Margot, et al. From Wilderness to Metropolis: The History & Architecture of Dade County, 1825-1940. 2nd ed. (Illus.). 252p. (C). 1992. pap. write for info. (*0-9618373-1-4*) MDC-Hist Preserv Div.

— The Journal of Decorative & Propaganda Arts No. 23: 1997 Florida Theme Issue. (Illus.). 300p. (Orig.). 1997. pap. 19.00 (*0-9631601-8-4*) Wolfson Fnd D&P Arts.

Ammirati, Joseph F., jt. auth. see Laursen, Gary A.

Ammirati, M., jt. auth. see Samii, Madjid.

Ammirato, Piero. La Lega: The Making of a Successful Cooperative Network. 376p. 1996. text 82.95 (*1-85521-839-9*, Pub. by Dartmth Pub) Ashgate Pub Co.

Ammitzboll, Niels-Peter. Menschenbild und Erziehungskonzeption Bei William Godwin. (Philosophische Texte und Studien: Vol. 28). (GER.). 249p. 1991. 40.00 (*3-487-09509-2*) G Olms Pubs.

Ammon, Bette D. & Sherman, Gale W. Handbook for the Newbery Medal & Honor Books, 1980-1989. 276p. 1991. pap. 8.00 (*0-913853-15-1*, 32519, Alleyside) Highsmith Pr.

— Handbook for the 2000 Young Reader's Choice Award Nominees. 155p. (Orig.). (C). 1999. pap. 12.95 (*1-884922-06-6*) Beyond Basals.

— Handbook for the Young Reader's Choice Award Nominees, 1993. 1993. 11.95 (*0-9619099-8-6*) Beyond Basals.

— Handbook for the Young Reader's Choice Award Nominees, 1995. 8th ed. 140p. 1994. pap. 12.95 (*1-884922-00-7*) Beyond Basals.

— Handbook for the Young Reader's Choice Award Nominees, 1996. 9th ed. 148p. 1995. pap. 12.95 (*1-884922-01-5*) Beyond Basals.

— Handbook for the Young Reader's Choice Award Nominees, 1997. Vol. 10. 150p. (Orig.). 1996. pap. 12.95 (*1-884922-02-3*) Beyond Basals.

— Worth a Thousand Words: An Annotated Guide to Picture Books for Older Readers. LC 96-31489. 230p. 1996. lib. bdg. 28.00 (*1-56308-390-6*) Libs Unl.

Ammon, Bette D., jt. auth. see Sherman, Gale W.

Ammon, Bette R., jt. auth. see Sherman, Gale W.

***Ammon, Betty D. & Sherman, Gale W.** Handbook for the Newbery Medal & Honor Books, 1990-1999. (Illus.). 120p. (J). (gr. 4-8). 2000. 19.95 (*1-57950-046-3*, Alleyside) Highsmith Pr.

Ammon, Betty D. & Sherman, Gale W. More Rip-Roaring Reads for Reluctant Teen Readers. 161p. 1998. pap. 26.50 (*1-56308-571-2*) Teacher Ideas Pr.

Ammon, Friedrich Von, see Von Ammon, Friedrich.

***Ammon, Harry.** James Monroe: The Quest for National Identity. Speirs, Katherine E., ed. (Signature Ser.). (Illus.). 706p. 1998. reprint ed. 35.00 (*0-945707-21-5*) Amer Political.

Ammon, Harry. James Monroe: The Quest for National Identity. 706p. 1990. reprint ed. pap. text 22.50 (*0-8139-1266-0*) U Pr of Va.

Ammon, Henry. James Monroe: A Bibliography, 5. LC 90-20397. (Bibliographies of the Presidents of the United States Ser.: No. 5). 156p. 1990. lib. bdg. 65.00 (*0-313-28163-7*, APO5, Greenwood Pr) Greenwood.

Ammon, Karl W. Historical Reports on Arab Horse Breeding & the Arabian Horse. Collected Reports from Travellers to Arabia. Staeubli, H., tr. (Illus.). 325p. 1993. lib. bdg. 55.00 (*3-487-08261-6*) G Olms Pubs.

— Nachrichten Von der Pferdezucht der Araber und Den Arabischen Pferden. (Documenta Hippologica Ser.). (Illus.). xvi, 408p. 1983. reprint ed. 55.00 (*3-487-08004-4*) G Olms Pubs.

— News of the Arab's Horse-Breeding & of the Arabian Horses. Staubli, Helen, tr. 400p. 1992. reprint ed. write for info. (*0-318-71574-0*) G Olms Pubs.

Ammon, R. L., ed. see Minerals, Metals & Materials Society Staff.

Ammon, Richard. An Amish Christmas. LC 95-33383. (Illus.). 40p. (J). (gr. k-5). 1996. 17.00 (*0-689-80377-X*) Atheneum Yung Read.

— An Amish Year. LC 98-52806. 40p. (J). (gr. k-4). 2000. 16.95 (*0-689-82622-2*) S&S Trade.

Ammon, Richard & Farnsworth, Bill. The Conestoga Wagon. LC 99-19726. (Illus.). 32p. (J). (gr. 1-5). 2000. 16.95 (*0-8234-1475-2*) Holiday.

Ammon, Richard & Patrick, Pamela. An Amish Wedding. LC 97-9740. (Illus.). 32p. (J). (gr. k-5). 1998. 17.00 (*0-689-81677-4*) Atheneum Yung Read.

***Ammon, Richard & Patrick, Pamela.** Amish Horses. LC 99-89452. (J). 2001. write for info. (*0-689-82623-0*) Atheneum Yung Read.

Ammon, Richard, jt. ed. see Tunnell, Michael O.

Ammon, Ulrich. Die Deutsche Sprach in Deutschland, Oesterreich und der Schweiz: Das Problem der Nationalen Varietaeten. (GER.). xvi, 575p. (C). 1995. lib. bdg. 98.50 (*3-11-014753-X*) De Gruyter.

— Die Internationale Stellung der Deutschen Sprache. (GER.). xx, 633p. (C). 1991. lib. bdg. 98.50 (*3-11-013179-X*, 167-91) De Gruyter.

Ammon, Ulrich, ed. Dialect & Standard in Highly Industrialized Societies. (International Journal of the Sociology of Language Ser.: No. 21). 1979. text 60.00 (*90-279-7858-1*) Mouton.

— Status & Function of Languages & Language Varieties. (Foundations of Communication & Cognition Ser.). x, 665p. (C). 1989. lib. bdg. 223.10 (*3-11-011299-X*) De Gruyter.

Ammon, Ulrich & Hellinger, Marlis, eds. Status Change of Languages. (Foundations of Communication & Cognition Ser.). (Illus.). ix, 547p. (C). 1991. lib. bdg. 190.80 (*3-11-012668-0*, 256-91) De Gruyter.

Ammon-Wexler, Jill. A Moment of Truth: A Novel. LC 97-91696. 280p. (Orig.). 1997. pap. 15.00 (*0-9657459-0-2*) Clear Vision.

Ammon, William. Walking Our Loved One Home: Love Never Fails. 144p. 1997. pap. write for info. (*1-57502-658-9*, PO1866) Morris Pubng.

Ammon, William H. Walking Our Loved One Home 2. 200p. 1997. reprint ed. pap. write for info. (*1-57502-563-9*, PO1628) Morris Pubng.

Ammondson, Pamela. Clarity Quest: How to Take a Sabbatical Without Taking More Than a Week Off. LC 99-17990. 240p. 1999. pap. 13.00 (*0-684-86320-0*) S&S Trade.

Ammonia Plant Safety Committee & Schulstok, G., eds. Ammonia Plant Safety, Vol. 37. 352p. 1997. pap. 175.00 (*0-8169-0738-2*, T-103) Am Inst Chem Eng.

Ammonius. On Aristotle's "Categories" Cohen, S. Marc & Matthews, Gareth B., trs. LC 91-55258. (Ancient Commentators on Aristotle Ser.). 176p. 1992. text 52.50 (*0-8014-2688-X*) Cornell U Pr.

— On Aristotle's "On Interpretation 9" Blank, David, tr. from GEC. LC 98-16299. (Ancient Commentators on Aristotle Ser.). 1996. text 49.95 (*0-8014-3335-5*) Cornell U Pr.

Ammonius, Hermiae. On Aristotle's "On Interpretation 1-8" Blank, David, tr. (Ancient Commentators on Aristotle Ser.). 1995. text 47.50 (*0-8014-3223-5*) Cornell U Pr.

Ammons, A. R. Brink Road. LC 95-42535. 256p. (Orig.). (C). 1997. pap. 12.00 (*0-393-31597-5*) Norton.

— Brink Road: Poems. 208p. 1996. 23.00 (*0-393-03958-7*) Norton.

— Garbage: A Poem. LC 92-42490. 1993. 17.95 (*0-393-03542-5*) Norton.

— Garbage: A Poem. 128p. 1994. pap. 10.00 (*0-393-31203-8*) Norton.

— Glare. LC 96-48506. 300p. 1998. pap. 15.00 (*0-393-31779-X*) Norton.

— Glare: Poetry. LC 96-48506. (Illus.). 224p. 1997. 25.00 (*0-393-04096-8*) Norton.

— The Really Short Poems of A. R. Ammons. 1991. 17.95 (*0-393-02870-4*) Norton.

— The Really Short Poems of A. R. Ammons. 176p. 1992. pap. 9.95 (*0-393-30850-2*) Norton.

— Selected Poems. 1987. pap. 10.95 (*0-393-30396-9*) Norton.

— Set in Motion: Essays, Interviews, & Dialogues. Burr, Zofia, ed. (Poets on Poetry Ser.). 136p. (Orig.). 1996. pap. 13.95 (*0-472-06603-X*, 06603); text 39.50 (*0-472-09603-6*, 09603) U of Mich Pr.

— Sphere: The Form of a Motion. 80p. 1995. pap. 8.95 (*0-393-31310-7*) Norton.

— Sumerian Vistas: Poems. 1987. pap. 7.95 (*0-393-30425-6*) Norton.

— Tape for the Turn of the Year. 96p. 1993. 21.00 (*0-393-03553-0*) Norton.

— Tape for the Turn of the Year. 216p. 1994. pap. 11.00 (*0-393-31204-6*) Norton.

— Worldly Hopes: Poems. 51p. 1982. pap. 5.95 (*0-393-00081-8*) Norton.

Ammons, David N. Administrative Analysis for Local Government: Practical Application of Selected Techniques. 176p. 1991. pap. 21.95 (*0-89854-145-X*) U of GA Inst Govt.

— Municipal Benchmarks: Assessing Local Performance & Establishing Community Standards. LC 96-4478. (Illus.). 256p. 1996. 39.95 (*0-8039-7253-9*) Sage.

— Municipal Productivity: A Comparison of Fourteen High-Quality Service Cities. LC 83-17821. 294p. 1984. 55.00 (*0-275-91118-7*, C1118, Praeger Pubs) Greenwood.

Ammons, David N., ed. Accountability for Performance: Measurement & Monitoring in Local Government. LC 95-40999. (Practical Management Ser.). 210p. 1995. pap. 23.95 (*0-87326-105-4*) Intl City-Cnty Mgt.

Ammons, David N. & Newell, Charldean. City Executives: Leadership Roles, Work Characteristics, & Time Management. LC 88-15380. (SUNY Series in Leadership Studies). 224p. (C). 1989. text 24.50 (*0-88706-957-6*) State U NY Pr.

Ammons, David N., et al. The Option of Prison Privatization: A Guide for Community Deliberations. LC 92-23148. 60p. 1993. pap. 11.95 (*0-89854-159-X*) U of GA Inst Govt.

— Selecting Prison Sites: State Processes, Site-Selection Criteria, & Local Initiatives. LC 92-23147. 96p. 1992. pap. 14.95 (*0-89854-158-1*, HV8815.A44) U of GA Inst Govt.

Ammons, Elizabeth. American Local Color Writing, 1880-1920. Rohy, Valerie, ed. LC 97-18115. (Penguin Classics Ser.). 1999. pap. write for info. (*0-14-018999-8*) Viking Penguin.

— Conflicting Stories: American Women Writers at the Turn into the Twentieth Century. 248p. 1992. reprint ed. pap. text 22.00 (*0-19-508038-6*) OUP.

Ammons, Elizabeth, compiled by. Short Fiction by Black Women, 1900-1920. (Schomburg Library of Nineteenth-Century Black Women Writers). 640p. 1991. text 49.95 (*0-19-506195-0*) OUP.

***Ammons, Elizabeth, ed.** Approaches to Teaching Stowe's Uncle Tom's Cabin. LC 99-89158. (Approaches to Teaching World Literature Ser.: Vol. 66). 256p. 2000. 37.50 (*0-87352-755-0*) Modern Lang.

***Ammons, Elizabeth & Belasco, Susan.** Approaches to Teaching Stowe's Uncle Tom's Cabin. LC 99-89158. (Approaches to Teaching World Literature Ser.). 2000. pap. write for info. (*0-87352-756-9*) Modern Lang.

Ammons, Elizabeth & Rohy, Valerie, eds. American Local Color Writing, 1880-1920. LC 97-18115. (Classics Ser.). xxx, 448p. 1998. pap. 13.95 (*0-14-043688-X*) Viking Penguin.

Ammons, Elizabeth & White-Parks, Annette, eds. Tricksterism in Turn-of-the-Century American Literature: A Multicultural Perspective. LC 94-20520. 217p. 1994. text 35.00 (*0-87451-680-3*) U Pr of New Eng.

Ammons, Elizabeth, ed. see Cooke, Rose T.

Ammons, Elizabeth, ed. see Stowe, Harriet Beecher.

Ammons, Elizabeth, ed. see Wharton, Edith.

Ammons Garza, Amy, ed. see Wagoner, Elisa G.

Ammons, Hiram F. Great Blacks in Wax Activity Book. (Illus.). 168p. 1995. pap. 17.50 (*0-9662436-2-5*) Dajo Pub.

Ammons, James & Ammons, Jeannine. The King & the Kingdom. 280p. 1994. 14.95 (*1-880047-26-8*) Creative Des.

Ammons, Jeannine, jt. auth. see Ammons, James.

Ammons, Kevin. Good Girl, Bad Girl: An Insider's Biography of Whitney Houston. (Illus.). 242p. 1997. mass mkt. 6.99 (*0-8065-8012-7*, Citadel Pr) Carol Pub Group.

Ammons, Kevin & Bacon, Nancy. Good Girl, Bad Girl: An Insider's Biography of Whitney Houston. (Illus.). 256p. 1996. 19.95 (*1-55972-379-3*, Birch Ln Pr) Carol Pub Group.

Ammons, Mark. American Popular Music. (Illus.). 80p. (YA). (gr. 5-8). 1996. pap. text 9.95 (*1-58037-049-7*, Pub. by M Twain Media) Carson-Dellos.

— Great Artists & Musicians. (Illus.). 80p. (YA). (gr. 5). 1996. pap. text 9.95 (*1-58037-011-X*, Pub. by M Twain Media) Carson-Dellos.

— Music: A. D. 450 to A. D. 1995. (Illus.). 80p. (YA). (gr. 5). 1995. pap. text 9.95 (*1-58037-053-5*, Pub. by M Twain Media) Carson-Dellos.

Ammons, Nelle P., jt. auth. see Core, Earl L.

Ammons, Pamela, et al. Skiing for Women. (Illus.). 1979. 16.95 (*0-88280-052-3*); pap. 16.95 (*0-88280-053-1*) ETC Pubns.

Ammoun, Denise. Crafts of Egypt. 140p. 1996. pap. 16.95 (*0-614-21572-2*, 176) Kazi Pubns.

***Amnasan, Mike.** Beyond the Safety of Dreams. 64p. 2000. pap. 9.00 (*1-928650-04-X*, Pub. by Krupskaya) SPD-Small Pr Dist.

Amnesty International. Iran: Amnesty International Briefing. LC 88-151094. 12 p. 1987. write for info. (*0-86210-119-0*) AI Pubns Intl.

Amnesty International, Dutch Section Staff. Disappearances & Political Killings: A Manual for Action. (Human Rights Crisis of the 1990s Ser.). 300p. (Orig.). 1994. pap. 16.95 (*0-939994-91-7*) Amnesty Intl USA.

Amnesty International, Human Rights for Children C. Human Rights for Children. LC 92-35575. (Illus.). 80p. (Orig.). 1992. teacher ed., spiral bd. 14.95 (*0-89793-120-3*) Hunter Hse.

Amnesty International Staff. Afghanistan: Torture of Political Prisoners. 51p. (Orig.). 1986. pap. 5.00 (*0-939994-24-0*, Pub. by Amnesty Intl Pubns) Science Pubs.

— The Americas: Human Rights Violations Against Indigenous People. (ENG & SPA.). 8.00 (*0-939994-80-1*) Amnesty Intl USA.

— The Amnesty International Handbook. LC 91-12255. (Illus.). 160p. (Orig.). 1991. pap. 9.95 (*0-89793-081-9*) Hunter Hse.

— Amnesty International Report, 1991. 360p. (Orig.). 1991. pap. 12.00 (*0-939994-61-5*) Amnesty Intl USA.

***Amnesty International Staff.** Amnesty International Report 1999. 1999. 20.00 (*1-887204-17-2*) Amnesty Intl USA.

Amnesty International Staff. Argentina: The Military Junta & Human Rights. 99p. (Orig.). 1987. pap. 5.00 (*0-939994-34-8*, Pub. by Amnesty Intl Pubns) Science Pubs.

— Brazil: Authorized violence in rural areas. LC 91-222472. 79 p. :p. 1988. write for info. (*0-86210-151-4*) AI Pubns Intl.

— Breaking the Silence: Human Rights Violations Based on Sexual Orientation. 53p. (Orig.) (C). 1994. pap. 6.00 (*0-939994-86-0*) Amnesty Intl USA.

— Bulgaria: Imprisonment of Ethnic Turks. 40p. (Orig.). 1986. pap. 5.00 (*0-86210-097-6*, Pub. by Amnesty Intl Pubns) Science Pubs.

— Childhood Stolen: Grave Human Rights Violations Against Children. (Illus.). 65p. (Orig.). 1995. pap. 8.00 (*1-873328-15-X*, Pub. by Amnesty Intl Pubns) Science Pubs.

— China: No One Is Safe: Political Repression & Abuse of Power in the 1990s. 121p. 1996. pap. 8.00 (*1-887204-05-9*) Amnesty Intl USA.

— The Death Penalty. (Illus.). 209p. (Orig.). 1979. pap. 5.00 (*0-900058-88-9*, Pub. by Amnesty Intl Pubns) Science Pubs.

— German Democratic Republic: Sweeping Laws - Secret Justice. 1989. pap. 6.00 (*0-939994-41-0*) Amnesty Intl USA.

— Getting Away with Murder: Political Killings & Disappearances in the 1990s. (Illus.). 126p. (Orig.). 1993. pap. 8.00 (*0-939994-82-8*) Amnesty Intl USA.

— Guatemala: The Human Rights Record. 234p. (Orig.). 1987. pap. 6.00 (*0-86210-118-2*, Pub. by Amnesty Intl Pubns) Science Pubs.

— Honduras: Human Rights Violations. 54p. 1988. pap. 5.00 (*0-86210-137-9*, Pub. by Amnesty Intl Pubns) Science Pubs.

— Human Rights & U. S. Security Assistance: An AIUSA Report on Human Rights Violations in Countries Receiving U. S. Security Assistance. 4th ed. 70p. 1996. pap. 10.00 (*1-887204-07-5*) Amnesty Intl USA.

— Indonesia - East Timor: Violations of Human Rights. 92p. (Orig.). 1985. pap. 3.50 (*0-939994-12-7*, Pub. by Amnesty Intl Pubns) Science Pubs.

— Iran: Violations of Human Rights. 99p. (Orig.). 1987. pap. 6.00 (*0-939994-29-1*) Amnesty Intl USA.

— It's about Time! Human Rights Are Women's Right. 152p. 1995. pap. 8.95 (*0-939994-98-4*) Amnesty Intl USA.

— Jamaica: The Death Penalty. 85p. (Orig.). 1989. pap. 6.00 (*0-939994-43-7*) Amnesty Intl USA.

— Kampuchea (Cambodia) Political Imprisonment & Torture. 84p. (Orig.). 1987. pap. 5.00 (*0-939994-31-3*, Pub. by Amnesty Intl Pubns) Science Pubs.

— Kenya: The Quest for Justice. LC 98-169157. (Briefing Ser.). 1997. write for info. (*0-86210-270-7*) AI Pubns Intl.

— The Machinery of Death: A Shocking Indictment of Capital Punishment in the United States. 216p. (Orig.). (C). 1995. pap. 17.95 (*0-939994-94-1*) Amnesty Intl USA.

— Mexico: Human Rights in Rural Areas. 136p. (Orig.). 1986. pap. 5.00 (*0-939994-19-4*, Pub. by Amnesty Intl Pubns) Science Pubs.

An Asterisk (*) at the beginning of an entry indicates that the title is appearing for the first time.

— Nicaragua: The Human Rights Record, 1986-1986. (SPA.). 67p. (Orig.). 1989. pap. 6.00 (*0-939994-50-X*, Pub. by Amnesty Intl Pubns) Science Pubs.
— The People's Republic of China: Torture & Ill-Treatment of Prisoners. 46p. (Orig.). 1987. pap. 5.00 (*0-939994-32-1*, Pub. by Amnesty Intl Pubns) Science Pubs.
— Peru: "Disappearances," Torture & Summary Executions by Government Forces after Prison Revolts of June 1986. 70p. 1987. pap. 5.00 (*0-86210-116-6*, Pub. by Amnesty Intl Pubns) Science Pubs.
— Philippines: Unlawful Killings by Military & Paramilitary Squads. (SPA.). 66p. (Orig.). 1988. pap. 6.00 (*0-939994-36-4*, Pub. by Amnesty Intl Pubns) Science Pubs.
— Sudan: What Future for Human Rights? LC 95-226499. (Briefing Ser.). 1995. pap. write for info. (*0-86210-239-1*) AI Pubns Intl.
— Torture in the '80s. (Illus.). 263p. 1984. pap. 5.95 (*0-86210-066-6*) Amnesty Intl USA.
— U. S. A. Rights for All. 1998. 12.95 (*1-887204-15-6*) Amnesty Intl USA.
— United States of America: Death Penalty Briefing. (Illus.). 245p. (Orig.). 1987. pap. 4.00 (*0-939994-26-7*, Pub. by Amnesty Intl Pubns) Science Pubs.
— Voices for Freedom. (Illus.). 208p. (Orig.). 1986. pap. 15.00 (*0-939994-20-8*, Pub. by Amnesty Intl Pubns) Science Pubs.
— Yugoslavia: Prisoners of Conscience. (SPA.). 95p. (Orig.). 1985. pap. 5.00 (*0-86210-084-4*, Pub. by Amnesty Intl Pubns) Science Pubs.

Amnesty International Staff, compiled by. Torture by Governments. 75p. 1984. 3.95 (*0-685-23311-1*) Amnesty Intl USA.

Amnesty International U. S. A. Staff. Amnesty International Report 1997. 1997. 20.00 (*1-887204-11-3*) Amnesty Intl USA.

Amnesty International USA Staff. Amnesty International Report 1997. 372p. 1997. 20.00 (*1-887204-10-5*) Amnesty Intl USA.

Amnesty International U.S.A. Staff. Amnesty International Report 1998. 1998. 20.00 (*1-887204-13-X*) Amnesty Intl USA.

Amneus, Daniel. The Case for Father Custody. 460p. Date not set. 25.00 (*0-9610864-6-7*) Primrose Pr.
— Garbage Generation. 298p. (C). 1990. 19.95 (*0-9610864-4-0*) Primrose Pr.
— Garbage Generation. 300p. 1990. pap. 12.95 (*0-9610864-5-9*) Primrose Pr.
— Garbage Generation. 300p. (C). 1990. reprint ed. pap. 12.95 (*0-9610634-5-9*) Primrose Pr.
— The Mystery of Macbeth. 1983. 10.00 (*0-9610864-0-8*); pap. 7.00 (*0-9610864-1-6*) Primrose Pr.
— The Three Othellos. 1986. 15.00 (*0-9610864-2-4*); pap. 10.00 (*0-9610864-3-2*) Primrose Pr.

Amneus, Nils. Does Chance or Justice Rule Our Lives? 97p. 1996. pap. 6.50 (*0-913004-08-1*) Point Loma Pub.

Amneus, Nils A. Life's Riddle. LC 98-10510. 264p. 1998. reprint ed. pap. 11.95 (*1-55700-130-8*) Theos U Pr.

Amo, Gary. Come Darkness. 352p. 1993. mass mkt. 4.50 (*1-55817-767-1*, Pinncle Kensgtn) Kensgtn Pub Corp.
— Come Nightfall. 1990. mass mkt. 3.95 (*1-55817-340-4*, Pinncle Kensgtn) Kensgtn Pub Corp.
— Creeping Shadows. 352p. 1992. mass mkt. 4.50 (*1-55817-633-0*, Pinncle Kensgtn) Kensgtn Pub Corp.
— Silent Night. 1991. mass mkt. 4.50 (*1-55817-510-5*, Pinncle Kensgtn) Kensgtn Pub Corp.

Amo, Stephen F. & Hoff, Raymond J. Silvics of Whitebark Pine (Pinus Albicaulis) (Illus.). 16p. 1997. reprint ed. pap. 2.60 (*0-89904-911-7*, Ecosytems Resrch) Crumb Elbow Pub.

***Amo, William C.** Microsoft SQL Server 7 OLAP Developer's Guide. 384p. 2000. pap. 39.99 (*0-7645-4643-0*) IDG Bks.

Amo, William C. Transact SQL. LC 98-72472. 528p. 1998. pap. 39.99 incl. cd-rom (*0-7645-8048-5*) IDG Bks.

Amoaku, W. M., jt. auth. see Galloway, N. R.

***Amochaev, Tania, ed.** Healdsburg Haiku. 36p. 2000. pap. write for info. (*0-9701333-0-8*) Running Wolf Pr.

Amoco Pathfinder Staff. How to Cope. 1992. pap. 2.25 (*0-671-84028-2*) S&S Trade.
— Mileage Chart. 1992. pap. 2.25 (*0-671-84029-0*) Macmillan USA.
— National Parks. 1992. pap. 2.25 (*0-671-84030-4*) S&S Trade.
— Seat Belt Laws. 1992. pap. 2.25 (*0-671-84031-2*) S&S Trade.
— Speed Laws & Motorcycle Laws. 1992. pap. 2.25 (*0-671-84032-0*) S&S Trade.
— Tourist & Camping Information. 1992. pap. 2.25 (*0-671-84033-9*) S&S Trade.
— Travel Games. 1992. pap. 2.25 (*0-671-84035-5*) Macmillan USA.

Amoda, Moyibi, ed. Festac Colloquium. 270p. 1978. 35.00 (*0-89388-218-6*); pap. 20.00 (*0-89388-219-4*) Okpaku Communications.

Amodei, Michael. Decide to Forgive. Sawyer, Kieran, ed. (Developing Faith Ser.). (Illus.). 128p. 1999. pap. text, teacher ed. 16.95 (*0-87793-559-9*) Ave Maria.
— Developing Faith: Mentor Handbook. Sawyer, Kieran, ed. (Developing Faith Ser.). (Illus.). 32p. 1996. pap. text 1.95 (*0-87793-578-5*) Ave Maria.
— Jump Start: 180 Lessons, Icebreakers, Projects & Weekend Activities for Junior High. LC 99-164735. 208p. (J). (gr. 6-8). 1998. pap. 16.95 (*0-87793-662-5*) Ave Maria.

***Amodei, Michael.** Questions of Faith: A Workbook Companion to the Catechism of the Catholic Church. 96p. (YA). 2000. pap. 6.95 (*0-87793-689-7*) Ave Maria.

Amodei, Michael, jt. auth. see Sawyer, Kieran.

Amodeo, Corine A., ed. see Panis, Patrice.

***Amodeo, John.** The Authentic Heart: An Eight-Fold Path to Midlife Love. 272p. 2001. pap. 14.95 (*0-471-38757-6*) Wiley.

Amodeo, John. Love & Betrayal: Broken Trust in Intimate Relationships. 304p. (Orig.). 1994. pap. 11.00 (*0-345-37856-3*) Ballantine Pub Grp.

Amodeo, Maryann. Social Work Approaches to Alcohol & Other Drug Problems: Case Studies & Teaching Tools. LC 96-52842. (Orig.). 1997. pap. text 13.00 (*0-87293-053-X*) Coun Soc Wk Ed.

Amodio, Mark, jt. ed. see Niles, John D.

Amodio, Mark C., ed. Oral Poetics in Middle English Poetry. LC 94-9803. (Albert Bates Lord Studies in Oral Tradition: Vol. 13). 304p. 1994. text 15.00 (*0-8153-0830-2*, H1595) Garland.

Amodio, P., jt. auth. see Steven, Andrew.

***Amoia, Alba.** No Mothers We! Italian Women & Their Revolt Against Maternity. 200p. 2000. 52.00 (*0-7618-1717-4*); pap. 29.50 (*0-7618-1718-2*) U Pr of Amer.

Amoia, Alba. Twentieth-Century Italian Women Writers. LC 95-22079. 208p. 1996. 39.95 (*0-8093-2026-6*); pap. 15.95 (*0-8093-2027-4*) S Ill U Pr.

Amoia, Alba, et al, trs. from FRE. An Anthology of Modern Belgian Theatre: Maurice Maeterlinck, Fernand Crommelynck, Michel de Ghelderode. LC 81-80286. viii, 280p. (C). 1982. 46.50 (*0-87875-215-3*) Whitston Pub.

Amoia, Alba della Fazia. Women on the Italian Literary Scene: A Panorama. LC 91-67977. xvi, 151p. 1992. 40.00 (*0-87875-428-8*) Whitston Pub.

Amoia, Alba della Fazia & Mann, Thomas. Thomas Mann's Fiorenza. (American University Studies: Theatre Arts: Ser. XXVI, Vol. 3). XIII, 197p. (C). 1990. text 30.00 (*0-8204-1091-8*) P Lang Pubng.

Amole, Gene. Amole Again. pap. text 7.95 (*0-914807-03-X*) Denver Pub Co.

Amole, Gene. Amole One More Time. LC 98-3203. 256p. 1998. pap. 12.50 (*1-55566-217-X*) Johnson Bks.

Amon. Summering in Colorado: An 1874 Guide. (Illus.). 1993. reprint ed. pap. 12.50 (*0-910746-36-2*, SUM01) Hope Farm.

***Amon, B. E.** A Kingdom of Many. 28p. 2000. 5.50 (*0-9675290-0-X*) GrapeWyrm Pr.

Amon, C., et al, eds. Proceedings of the 32nd National Heat Transfer Conference, Baltimore, Maryland, August 8-12, 1997, Vol. 5. (HTD Ser.: Vol. 343). 148p. 1997. 70.00 (*0-7918-1810-1*, H01091) ASME Pr.

Amon, C. H., et al, eds. Cooling & Thermal Design of Electronic Systems Vol. 319-15: Proceedings of the ASME International Mechanical Engineering Congress & Exposition, 1995, San Francisco, CA. LC 95-81257. (1995 ASME International Mechanical Engineering Congress & Exposition Ser.: HTD-Vol. 319/EEP-Vol. 15). 240p. 1995. 88.00 (*0-7918-1753-9*, H01034) ASME.

Amon, C. H., jt. ed. see Kandlikar, S. G.

Amon, Evelyne & Muyskens, Judity A. Vis-a-Vis: Beginning French. (C). 1996. pap., wbk. ed., lab manual ed. 34.38 (*0-07-001702-6*) McGraw.

Amon, Evelyne, et al. Vis-a-Vis: Beginning French. LC 95-45823. 1995. student ed. write for info. (*0-07-001700-X*) McGraw.

***Amon, Evelyne, et al.** Vis-a-Vis: Beginning French. 2nd ed. (FRE.). 576p. (C). 2000. pap., student ed. 68.13 incl. audio (*0-07-234223-4*); pap., student ed. 68.13 (*0-07-234226-9*) McGrw-H Hghr Educ.
— Vis-a-Vis: Beginning French. 2nd ed. (ENG & FRE.). 392p. (C). 2000. pap., wbk. ed., lab manual ed. 34.69 (*0-07-231042-1*) McGrw-H Hghr Educ.

Amon, Rene, jt. auth. see Fanella, David A.

Amon, Von. Broken Dolls. LC 81-14943. 1986. 22.95 (*0-87949-183-3*) Ashley Bks.

Amond, Janet D. Exercises for Airplanes. (Illus.). 64p. (Orig.). 1996. pap. 8.95 (*1-885064-03-9*) Excalibur Pub.

Amonette, Ruth L. Among Equals: A Memoir. LC 98-89652. 200p. 1999. 23.50 (*0-88739-219-9*) Creat Arts Bk.
— Among Equals: The Rise of IBM's First Woman Corporate Vice President. LC 98-89652. 212p. 1999. pap. 14.50 (*0-88739-218-0*) Creat Arts Bk.

Amoore, Mary, ed. see Osho.

Amoore, Susannah. Motley. LC 97-61324. (Illus.). 32p. (J). (ps-4). 1998. 14.99 (*0-670-87730-1*) Viking Penguin.

Amopoulous, Paris. Sociopolitics: Political Development in Postmodern Societies. (Essay Ser.: No. 18). 250p. 1995. pap. 15.00 (*0-920717-99-3*) Guernica Editions.

Amor, jt. auth. see Mizushima.

***Amor, Daniel.** The E-business (R)evolution: Living & Working in an Interconnected World. LC 99-44842. (Illus.). 670p. 1999. pap. text 39.99 (*0-13-085123-X*, Prentice Hall) P-H.

Amor, Monica, et al. Amnesia. (Illus.). 102p. 1998. pap. 25.00 (*1-889195-25-1*) Smart Art Pr.

Amor, Paul F. The People's Republic. 224p. 1990. 18.95 (*0-8027-1072-7*) Walker & Co.

Amorah Quan Yin. The Pleidian Tantric Workbook: Awakening Your Divine BA, Vol. II. LC 97-28684. (Illus.). 320p. (Orig.). 1997. pap. 16.00 (*1-879181-45-2*) Bear & Co.

Amorai-Stark, Shua. Wolfe Family Collection of Near Eastern Prehistoric Stamp Seals. (Orbis Biblicus et Orientalis Ser.: Vol. 16). 205p. 1997. text 52.50 (*3-7278-1136-6*, Pub. by Ed Univ Fri) Eisenbrauns.

AMORC Staff, ed. see Poole, Cecil A.

Amore, Adelaide P., intro. Aphra Behn: Oroonoko or, the Royal Slave a Critical Edition. (Illus.). 130p. (Orig.). 1987. lib. bdg. 43.50 (*0-8191-6529-8*) U Pr of Amer.

Amore, Dom. Return to the Final Four: How the UConn Women Carved Their Own Identity. Leary, Mark, ed. 144p. (Orig.). (YA). 1996. pap. text 14.95 (*0-9646638-2-1*) Hartford Courant.

Amore, JoAnn, ed. see U. S. Department of Labor Staff.

Amore, Roy C. & Shinn, Larry D. Lustful Maidens & Ascetic Kings: Buddhist & Hindu Stories of Life. (Illus.). 210p. 1981. pap. text 10.95 (*0-19-502839-2*) OUP.

Amores, Hideliza. Manual de Ministerios con Familias: Family Ministries Manual. (SPA.). 52p. 1996. pap. 7.95 (*0-88177-188-0*, DR188) Discipleship Res.

Amoretty, S. J., tr. see Kapchinskiy, I. M.

Amoretty, S. J., tr. see Nikitin, Yu P., et al.

Amoretty, Stephen J., tr. see Shpil'rain, E. E., et al.

Amoriell, Amelia & Lindbeck, Susan. Chesapeake Colors: Natural Life, History, Recipes & Local Color. LC 82-60329. (Illus.). 48p. (J). 1982. pap. 3.95 (*0-87033-298-8*, Tidewtr Pubs) Cornell Maritime.

Amoros, Andres. Bibliografia de Francisco Ayala. (SPA.). 95p. 1973. reprint ed. 3.00 (*0-87535-142-5*) Hispanic Soc.

Amoros, Andres, ed. see Alonso de Santos, Jose L.

Amoros, Jaume, et al. Fundamental Groups of Compact Kahler Manifolds. LC 96-4669. (Mathematical Surveys & Monographs Ser.: Vol. 44). 140p. 1996. pap. 39.00 (*0-8218-0498-7*, SURV/44) Am Math.

Amoros Rica, Narciso, jt. auth. see Merlin-Walch, Olivier.

Amorosa, Judith K., et al. Exercises in Diagnostic Radiology: Chest, Abdomen, Bone & Clinical Skills: A Problem-Based Text. 3rd ed. (Illus.). 380p. 1992. pap. text 38.95 (*0-7216-3129-0*, W B Saunders Co) Harcrt Hlth Sci Grp.

Amorosi, Ray. Flim Flam. LC 79-93197. (Illus.). 64p. 1980. 10.00 (*0-89924-030-5*); pap. 7.00 (*0-89924-029-1*) Lynx Hse.
— A Generous Wall. LC 76-27961. 61p. 1976. pap. 7.00 (*0-89924-008-9*) Lynx Hse.

Amorosia, D. Interplanetary Jammin' 56p. 1992. pap. 19.95 (*0-7935-2893-3*) H Leonard.
— Sounds a Little Fishy to Me. 56p. 1992. pap., teacher ed. 19.95 (*0-7935-2891-7*) H Leonard.
— Tales of Temples & Tombs: A Kids-Eye View of Ancient Egypt. 64p. 1993. pap., teacher ed. 19.95 (*0-7935-3605-7*) H Leonard.

Amorosino, Chris, ed. see McNamara, Regina.

Amoroso, Donald, jt. ed. see Khosrowpour, Mehdi.

Amoroso, E. C., ed. see Easter School in Agricultural Science (14th 1967,.

Amoroso, Edward. Fundamentals of Computer Security Technology. 432p. (C). 1994. pap. 46.60 (*0-13-108929-3*) P-H.

***Amoroso, Edward.** Fundamentals of Computer Security Technology. (Illus.). 404p. 1999. reprint ed. pap. text 20.00 (*0-7881-6531-3*) DIANE Pub.
— Intrusion Detection: An Introduction to Internet Surveillance, Correlation, Trace Back, Traps, & Response. LC 98-233169. (Illus.). 15p. (C). 1999. pap. 49.95 (*0-9666700-7-8*) IntrusionNet Bks.

***Amoroso, Richard L., et al, eds.** Science & the Primacy of Consciousness: Intimation of a 21st Century Revolution. LC 00-100695. (Readings in Consciousness Studies: Vol. 1). (Illus.). xiii, 360p. (C). 2000. pap. 37.95 (*0-9678687-1-8*) Noetic Pr CA.

***Amorth, Gabriel.** The Gospel of Mary: A Month with the Mother of God. Lane, Edmund C., tr. from ITA. LC 99-30144. x, 124p. 2000. pap. 8.95 (*0-8189-0871-8*) Alba.

***Amorth, Gabriele.** An Exorcist Tells His Story. LC 98-74066. 210p. 1999. write for info. (*0-89870-710-2*) Ignatius Pr.
— Habla un Exorcista. 1999. 21.95 (*84-08-02355-1*) Planeta Edit.

***Amory, A.** Male Order. 1998. mass mkt. 6.95 (*0-7472-5838-4*, Pub. by Headline Bk Pub) Trafalgar.

Amory, Anne R., jt. auth. see Hammond, Mason.

Amory, Cleveland. The Best Cat Ever. 2000. 7.99 (*0-517-20863-6*) Random.
— The Cat & the Curmudgeon. 2000. 8.99 (*0-517-20861-X*) Random.
— The Cat Who Came for Christmas. LC 96-202117. (Illus.). 224p. 1995. pap. 9.95 (*0-14-025273-8*, Penguin Bks) Viking Penguin.
— Cleveland Amory's Compleat Cat. 832p. 1995. 14.98 (*1-884822-58-4*) Blck Dog & Leventhal.
— Last Resorts. 1973. write for info. (*0-8371-6644-6*) Greenwood.
— The Proper Bostonians. 384p. 1984. reprint ed. pap. 9.95 (*0-940160-25-0*) Parnassus Imprints.
— The Ranch of Dreams: The Heartwarming Story of America's Most Unusual Animal Sanctuary. 320p. 1998. pap. 11.95 (*0-14-026975-4*) Viking Penguin.
— Ranch of Dreams: The Heartwarming Story of America's Most Unusual Animal Sanctuary. large type ed. LC 98-5279. (Americana Series). 1998. 25.95 (*0-7862-1421-X*) Thorndike Pr.

Amory, Cleveland, jt. auth. see Fox, Michael W.

Amory, Dita, et al. Nature Observed, Nature Interpreted: Nineteenth-Century American Landscape Drawings & Watercolors from the National Academy of Design & Cooper-Hewitt, National Design Museum, Smithsonian Institution. LC 95-5941. 1995. pap. 35.00 (*1-887149-00-7*) Nat Acad of Des.

Amory, Hugh. Bute Broadsides in the Houghton Library Harvard University, Guide & Index to the Microfilm Collection. LC 81-11939. 98p. 1981. 90.00 (*0-89235-025-3*) Primary Srce Media.
— Under the Exchange: The Unprofitable Business of Michael Perry, a Seventeenth-Century Boston Bookseller. 29p. (Orig.). 1993. pap. 9.00 (*0-944026-45-1*) Am Antiquarian.

***Amory, Hugh & Hall, David D., eds.** A History of the Book in America: The Colonial Book in the Atlantic World. LC 99-12595. (Illus.). 688p. (C). 1999. 125.00 (*0-521-48256-9*) Cambridge U Pr.

Amory, Hugh, jt. ed. see Bond, William H.

Amory, Hugh, ed. see Fielding, Henry.

***Amory, Mark.** Lord Berners: The Last Eccentric. (Illus.). 272p. 2000. pap. 22.95 (*0-7126-6578-1*, Pub. by Pimlico) Trafalgar.

Amory, Martha B. Domestic & Artistic Life of John Singleton Copley, R.A. LC 70-119925. (Select Bibliographies Reprint Ser.). 1977. 30.95 (*0-8369-5368-1*) Ayer.

Amory, Patrick. People & Identity in Ostrogothic Italy, 489-554. (Cambridge Studies in Medieval Life & Thought: No. 33). 547p. 1997. text 95.00 (*0-521-57151-0*) Cambridge U Pr.

Amory, Thomas C. Boston Police Debates: Selected Arguments. 1971. pap. 15.95 (*0-405-03363-X*) Ayer.

Amos. Bachelorette Blues. 186p. 1999. mass mkt. 3.50 (*0-373-52086-7*, Harlequin) Harlequin Bks.
— Electronics Dictionary Spanish-English/English-Spanish. 3rd ed. (ENG & SPA.). 456p. 1995. 95.00 (*0-7859-9774-1*) Fr & Eur.
— Handbook for Primary Care Options. 1999. text. write for info. (*0-7216-5921-7*, W B Saunders Co) Harcrt Hlth Sci Grp.

Amos & Prescher. Amazon Rally Long Original J. 1996. pap. text 7.00 (*0-582-08137-8*, Pub. by Addison-Wesley) Longman.

Amos, A. K., jt. ed. see Atluri, S. N.

Amos, Alcione M., ed. see Porter, Kenneth W.

Amos, Alden. Spinning Wheel Primer. 2nd rev. ed. (Illus.). 60p. 1990. reprint ed. pap. 6.00 (*0-934026-55-6*) Interweave.

***Amos, Andrew.** The Great Oyer of Poisoning: The Trial of the Earl of Somerset for the Poisoning of Sir Thomas Overbury in the Tower of London ... LC 99-73250. (Illus.). 551p. 1999. 138.00 (*1-56169-533-5*) Gaunt.

Amos, Ashley C. Linguistic Means of Determining the Dates of Old English Literary Texts. LC 79-89570. (Medieval Academy Bks: No. 90). 1980. 32.00 (*0-910956-70-7*) Medieval Acad.

Amos, Beth. Cold White Fury. 368p. 1996. mass mkt. 5.99 (*0-06-101005-7*, Harp PBks) HarpC.
— Eyes of Night. 400p. 1997. mass mkt. 6.50 (*0-06-101006-5*, Harp PBks) HarpC.
— Second Sight. 464p. 1998. mass mkt. 6.50 (*0-06-101288-2*, Harp PBks) HarpC.

***Amos, Beverly.** Calligraphy: A Handbook for Beginners. 96p. 2000. per. 13.00 (*0-684-87200-5*) S&S Trade.

Amos, Bonnie & Gehlbach, Frederick R., eds. Edwards Plateau Vegetation: Plant Ecological Studies in Central Texas. LC 88-16655. (Illus.). 154p. (Orig.). 1988. pap. 21.50 (*0-918954-50-9*) Baylor Univ Pr.

Amos, Chuck & Amos, Sheila. Clown Ministry Organizer. Lent, Penny, ed. LC 94-79468. (Illus.). 210p. 1994. ring bd. 15.99 (*1-885371-06-3*) Kldoscope Pr.
— Clowning for Beginners. Lent, Penny, ed. LC 94-79467. (Illus.). 100p. (Orig.). (J). (gr. k up). pap., per. 6.95 (*1-885371-07-1*) Kldoscope Pr.

***Amos Copelan, Ashley.** Thank You God. (Illus.). 32p. (J). (ps-3). 1999. pap. 9.95 (*1-56167-532-6*, SSE) Am Literary Pr.

Amos, Dan, ed. & photos by see Bradley, Nancy.

Amos, Eileen, tr. see Vestly, Anne-Catherine.

Amos, F. J. C., et al. Contemporary Perspectives of Urbanization. (Progress in Planning Ser.: Vol. 46/3). 70p. 1997. pap. text 102.50 (*0-08-043084-8*, Pergamon Pr) Elsevier.

Amos, Flora R. Early Theories of Translation. LC 98-20289. xiv, 178p. 1998. reprint ed. 50.00 (*0-9631902-0-2*) Canonymous.

Amos, Gary & Gardiner, Richard. Never Before in History: America's Inspired Birth. LC 98-72936. (Pandas Publications: A Series about Central Questions). (Illus.). 213p. (YA). (gr. 8-10). 1998. text 27.50 (*0-914513-51-6*) Haughton.

Amos, Gary T. Attainted: The Political Branding of Oliver North. 246p. (Orig.). 1994. pap., per. 6.95 (*0-9643427-0-7*) G T Amos.

Amos, Gary T., ed. Defending the Declaration: How the Bible & Christianity Influenced the Writing of the Declaration of Independence. 240p. 1994. reprint ed. pap. 11.95 (*1-884726-05-8*) Providence Found.

Amos, Geoff. The Flower Garden. 96p. 1988. 45.00 (*1-85283-228-2*, Pub. by Boxtree) St Mut.

Amos, H. D. & Lang, A. G. These Were the Greeks. LC 81-71846. (Illus.). 224p. (C). 1991. pap. 19.95 (*0-8023-1275-6*) Dufour.

Amos, Harriet E. Cotton City: Urban Development in Antebellum Mobile. LC 84-189. (Illus.). 336p. 1985. text 34.95 (*0-8173-0218-2*) U of Ala Pr.

Amos, Hazel C. Amos: Our Ancestry (Amos, Beverly, Goodale, Graham, Keeney, Miller, Walton) (Illus.). 202p. 1994. reprint ed. pap. 32.00 (*0-8328-4167-6*); reprint ed. lib. bdg. 42.00 (*0-8328-4166-8*) Higginson Bk Co.

Amos, James. The Memorial. 288p. 1990. pap. 3.95 (*0-380-71195-8*, Avon Bks) Morrow Avon.

Amos, James H. Focus or Failure: America At the Crossroads Where Are You? 2nd ed. 145p. (C). 1998. 21.95 (*0-937539-31-7*) Executive Bks.

Amos, Janell S. Entertaining Children: Theme Parties, Activities, Games & Fun Ideas for Groups. LC 92-50300. (Illus.). 144p. 1992. pap. 25.00 (*0-89950-738-7*) McFarland & Co.
— Fundraising Ideas: Over 225 Money Making Events for Community Groups, with a Resource Directory. LC 95-16638. (Illus.). 160p. 1995. pap. 33.00 (*0-7864-0072-2*) McFarland & Co.

A

A

Amos, Janet & Dones, John. The Successful Student Guide to Career College. 400p. (C). 1994. text 18.30 (0-256-12571-6, Irwn McGrw-H) McGrw-H Hghr Educ.

Amos, Janet & Downes, John. The Successful Student Guide to Community College. 400p. (C). 1994. text 18.30 (0-256-12572-4, Irwn McGrw-H) McGrw-H Hghr Educ.

— The Successful Student's Guide to College. LC 94-179672. 400p. (C). 1994. text 18.30 (0-256-12573-2, Irwn McGrw-H) McGrw-H Hghr Educ.

Amos, Janet & Henry, Barbara. Strategies: College, Career, Life, West Virginia State College Edition. 4th ed. 304p. (C). 1995. text 41.95 (0-256-12587-2, Irwn McGrw-H) McGrw-H Hghr Educ.

Amos, Janet, et al. CPS the Successful Student's Guide to Career Colleges, Peak Performance, & Human Relations: Selected Material for Interpersonal Skills. 200p. (C). 1995. text 11.90 (0-256-21751-3, Irwn McGrw-H) McGrw-H Hghr Educ.

***Amos, Janine.** Animals. (Picture Reference Ser.). (Illus.). (J). (gr. 2-6). 2000. 13.95 (1-58728-650-5) Two Can Pub.

Amos, Janine. Animals. LC 97-13065. (Picture Reference Ser.). (Illus.). 48p. (J). (gr. 2-6). 1997. write for info. (0-7166-9902-8) World Bk.

— Animals in Danger. 32p. (J). (gr. 1-4). 1993. pap. 4.95 (0-8114-4913-0) Raintree Steck-V.

— Animals of the Rainforest. (Animal Stars Ser.). (Illus.). 24p. (J). 1996. pap. 1.29 (1-884628-47-8, Flyng Frog) Allied Pub MD.

— Feeding the World. (J). (ps-3). 1993. pap. 4.95 (0-8114-4918-1) Raintree Steck-V.

— Pollution. 32p. (J). (gr. 1-4). 1993. pap. 4.95 (0-8114-4917-3) Raintree Steck-V.

— Waste & Recycling. (What About...? Ser.). 1996. pap. 4.95 (0-8114-4914-9) Raintree Steck-V.

***Amos, Janine & Solway, Andrew.** Animals & Nature. (First Encyclopedia Ser.). (Illus.). 96p. (J). (ps-3). 2000. pap. 7.95 (0-590-47523-1) Scholastic Inc.

Amos, Jeffrey. Transformation to Agility: Manufacturing in the Market Place of Unanticipated Change. LC 98-46666. (Transnational Business & Corporate Culture Ser.). 320p. 1998. 69.00 (0-8153-3347-1) Garland.

Amos, Jessie, ed. see O'Connor, Michol.

Amos, John F. Diagnosis & Management in Vision Care. (Illus.). 729p. 1987. pap. text 70.00 (0-7506-9669-9) Buttrwrth-Heinemann.

Amos, John J., jt. auth. see Minoli, Daniel.

Amos, John M., jt. auth. see Magad, Eugene L.

Amos, Joye. If Not For You. LC 98-97000. 192p. 1999. lib. bdg. 18.95 (0-8034-9343-6, Avalon Bks) Bouregy.

***Amos, Julie-Ann.** Job Hunt on the Net. (Illus.). 64p. 2000. pap. 9.95 (1-85703-637-9, Pub. by How To Bks) Midpt Trade.

— Making Meetings Work. 64p. 2000. pap. 9.95 (1-85703-622-0, Pub. by How To Bks) Midpt Trade.

— Making the Most of Your Time. (Essentials Ser.). 64p. 2000. pap. 9.95 (1-85703-519-4, Pub. by How To Bks) Midpt Trade.

— Moving into Management: Prepare Yourself to Be an Effective & Efficient Manager. 2nd ed. (Business & Management Ser.). (Illus.). 160p. 2000. pap. 19.95 (1-85703-552-6, Pub. by How To Bks) Trans-Atl Phila.

— Self-Management & Personal Effectiveness: How to Achieve Your Personal Goals in Life & at Work. 2nd ed. 128p. 2000. pap. 14.95 (1-85703-530-5, Pub. by How To Bks) Midpt Trade.

Amos, Linda A. & Amos, W. Bradshaw. Molecules of the Cytoskeleton. LC 91-16542. (Molecular Cell Biology Ser.). 247p. 1991. pap. text 27.95 (0-89862-527-0); lib. bdg. 52.50 (0-89862-404-5) Guilford Pubns.

Amos, M., jt. auth. see Fletcher, W. J.

***Amos, Martyn.** Theoretical & Experimental DNA Computation. 200p. 1999. 39.95 (3-540-65773-8) Spr-Verlag.

Amos, Michael P. Macroeconomics Policy Analysis: Open Economies with Quantity Constraints. 88p. 1989. text 47.95 (0-521-34387-9) Cambridge U Pr.

Amos, N. Lust at Large. mass mkt. 6.95 (0-7472-4329-8, Pub. by Headline Bk Pub) Trafalgar.

Amos, Robyn. Arabesque: True Blue. 1999. pap. 4.99 (1-58314-001-8) BET Bks.

***Amos, Robyn.** Hero at Large. (Intimate Moments Ser.: Bk. 1040). 2000. mass mkt. 4.50 (0-373-27110-7, 1-27110-5) Silhouette.

Amos, Robyn. Into the Night. 256p. 1998. pap. 4.99 (0-7860-0559-9) Kensgtn Pub Corp.

— Private Lies. 288p. 1998. pap. 4.99 (0-7860-0496-7, Pinncle Kensgtn) Kensgtn Pub Corp.

— Promise Me. 256p. 1997. mass mkt. 4.99 (0-7860-0444-4, Pinncle Kensgtn) Kensgtn Pub Corp.

Amos, Robyn, et al. I Do! 320p. 1998. mass mkt. 4.99 (0-7860-0486-X, Pinncle Kensgtn) Kensgtn Pub Corp.

Amos, Roger. Complete Book of Model Railway Electronics. LC 97-76833. (Illus.). 256p. 1998. 34.95 (1-85260-591-X) Haynes Manuals.

Amos, Roger, jt. auth. see Amos, S. W.

Amos, Ronald. Shenandoah Autumn. 42p. (Orig.). 1994. pap. 4.00 (1-57514-123-X, 1167) Encore Perform Pub.

Amos, S. Karin. Alexis de Tocqueville & the American National Identity: The Reception of De la Democratie En Amerique in the United States in the Nineteenth Century. LC 94-43413. (Komparatistische Bibliothek: Bd. 5). 313p. 1994. pap. 52.95 (3-631-47395-8) P Lang Pubng.

Amos, S. W. Spanish-English Dictionary of Electronics. (ENG & SPA.). 456p. 1988. 95.00 (0-8288-4020-2, S30010) Fr & Eur.

— Spanish-English Dictionary of Electronics with an English-Spanish Vocabulary. 2nd ed. (ENG & SPA., Illus.). 456p. 1988. 56.75 (84-283-1605-8, Pub. by Paraninfo) IBD Ltd.

Amos, S. W. & Amos, Roger. Dictionary of Electronics. 3rd ed. (Illus.). 384p. 1996. text 34.95 (0-7506-2405-1) Buttrwrth-Heinemann.

— Scroggie's Foundations of Wireless & Electronics. 11th ed. LC 97-225107. (Illus.). 300p. 1997. pap. text 39.95 (0-7506-3430-8, Newnes) Buttrwrth-Heinemann.

Amos, S. W., jt. auth. see James, Mike.

Amos, Sharon R. Alabaster & Leopard Jasper. 24p. 1994. write for info. (0-914620-05-3) Alpha Pr.

***Amos, Sharon R.** Garden Wisdom. 2000. 24.95 (1-57145-665-1, Laurel Glen Pub) Advantage Pubs.

Amos, Sharon R. Istanbul. (Great Cities Ser.). (Illus.). 96p. 1999. 20.00 (1-85995-588-6) Parkstone Pr.

Amos, Sheila, jt. auth. see Amos, Chuck.

Amos, Sheldon. Fifty Years of the English Constitution, 1830-1880. xxxii, 495p. 1987. reprint ed. 48.50 (0-8377-1904-6, Rothman) W S Hein.

— The History & Principles of the Civil Law of Rome: An Aid to the Study of Scientific & Comparative Jurisprudence. LC 89-45851. 496p. 1989. reprint ed. 125.00 (0-912004-73-8, 18172) Gaunt.

— History & Principles of the Civil Law of Rome: An Aid to the Study of Scientific & Comparative Jurisprudence. (Illus.). xv, 475p. 1987. reprint ed. 47.50 (0-8377-1903-8, Rothman) W S Hein.

— Lectures on International Law: Delivered in the Middle Temple Hall to the Students of the Inns of Court. xii, 136p. 1983. reprint ed. 30.00 (0-8377-0215-1, Rothman) W S Hein.

— Political & Legal Remedies for War. 254p. 1982. reprint ed. 35.00 (0-8377-0213-5, Rothman) W S Hein.

— Science of Law. (International Scientific Ser.: Vol. 1). xx, 417p. 1982. reprint ed. 45.00 (0-8377-0209-7, Rothman) W S Hein.

— Systematic View of the Science of Jurisprudence. 545p. 1982. reprint ed. 48.50 (0-8377-0210-0, Rothman) W S Hein.

Amos, Stephanie. Questions of the Heart. 1998. pap. 8.95 (0-533-12767-X) Vantage.

Amos, Stephen H. The Audubon Society Pocket Guide to Familiar Seashore Creatures. (Audubon Society Pocket Guides Ser.). (Orig.). 1990. pap. 5.95 (0-685-46222-6) Knopf.

— Familiar Marine Mammals North America. (National Audubon Society Pocket Guides Ser.). 1990. pap. 9.00 (0-679-72983-6) Knopf.

— Familiar Seashore Creatures: North America. LC 90-52501. (Illus.). (Orig.). 1990. pap. 5.95 (0-679-72982-8) Knopf.

Amos, Stephen H., jt. auth. see Amos, William H.

Amos, Steve, contrib. by. Force 4-150 hp Outboards Includes L-Drives, 1984-1996. LC 96-79904. (Illus.). (Orig.). 1997. pap. 36.95 (0-89287-689-1, B751-3) Intertec Pub.

Amos, Thomas, ed. Descriptive Inventories of Manuscripts Microfilmed for the Hill Monastic Manuscript Library, No. 1: Biblioteca Nacional de Lisboa, Fundo Alcobaca, Pt. 2. 1989. 50.00 (0-940250-19-5) Hill Monastic.

Amos, Thomas, jt. ed. see Black, Jonathan.

Amos, Thomas L., ed. Descriptive Inventories of Manuscripts Microfilmed for the Hill Monastic Manuscript Library, Portuguese Libraries, Vol. 1: Biblioteca Nacional de Lisboa, Fundo Alcobaca, Pt. 1. (Orig.). 1988. 50.00 (0-940250-18-7) Hill Monastic.

Amos, Thomas L., et al, eds. De Ore Domini: Preacher & Word in the Middle Ages. (Studies in Medieval Culture: Vol. 27). 1989. pap. 15.95 (0-918720-27-3); boxed set 32.95 (0-918720-28-1) Medieval Inst.

***Amos, Tori.** To Venus & Back. 1999. pap. 29.95 (0-8256-1763-4, Amsco Music) Music Sales.

Amos, Tori. Tori Amos: Little Earthquakes. (Illus.). 132p. 1992. pap. 24.95 (0-8256-1345-0, AM90041) Music Sales.

— Tori Amos: MTV Unplugged. pap. 22.95 (0-8256-1565-8) Omnibus NY.

— Tori Amos: The Bee Sides. 1996. pap. 21.95 (0-8256-1494-5, AM 931315) Music Sales.

— Tori Amos: Under the Pink. 124p. 1996. pap. 27.95 (0-8256-1405-8, AM 92048) Music Sales.

— Tori Amos Boys for Pele. 1996. pap. text 24.95 (0-8256-1544-5, AM937750) Omnibus NY.

Amos Tuck School of Business Administration-Dartmouth College Staff, et al. The Complete MBA Companion in Global Business: Your Passport to a World of Global Business. (Illus.). 356p. 1998. pap. 39.95 (0-273-63706-1) F T P H.

Amos, W. Bradshaw, jt. auth. see Amos, Linda A.

Amos, W. J. Borderline. 224p. (Orig.). 1988. mass mkt. 2.95 (0-87067-351-3) Holloway.

— M. I. A. Saigon. 224p. 1986. mass mkt. 2.50 (0-87067-274-6, BH274) Holloway.

Amos, Wally. Man with No Name: Turn Lemons into Lemonade. 142p. (Orig.). 1994. 16.95 incl. audio (1-879323-37-0) Sound Horizons AV.

Amos, Wally & Glauberman, Stuart. Watermelon Magic: Seeds of Wisdom, Slices of Life. LC 96-16177. (Illus.). 136p. 1996. 14.95 (1-885223-47-1) Beyond Words Pub.

Amos, William. Assateague Island. LC 79-607136. (Official National Park Handbook Ser.: No. 106). 1979. pap. 9.00 (0-912627-03-4) Natl Park Serv.

Amos, William E., Jr. Cuando el Sida Llega a la Iglesia: When AIDS Comes to the Church. Martinez, Jose L., tr. from ENG. (SPA.). 128p. (Orig.). 1989. pap. text 6.99 (0-311-42080-X) Casa Bautista.

Amos, William E. The Originals: Who's Really Who in Fiction. 1986. 19.95 (0-316-03741-9) Little.

Amos, William E., Jr. When AIDS Comes to the Church. LC 87-30875. 132p. 1988. pap. 14.95 (0-664-25009-2) Westminster John Knox.

Amos, William E. & Orem, Reginald C. Managing Student Behavior. LC 67-26008. 167p. reprint ed. pap. 51.80 (0-608-13998-X, 205553800028) Bks Demand.

Amos, William E. & Williams, David E. Community Counseling. LC 71-154110. 244p. 1972. 10.00 (0-87527-092-1) Green.

Amos, William E., ed. see Stevens, George L.

Amos, William H. Assateague Island, National Seashore: Maryland & Virginia. LC 79-607136. (National Park Service Handbook Ser.: No. 106). (Illus.). 175p. 1980. pap. 7.50 (0-16-003440-X, S/N 024-005-00776-8) USGPO.

Amos, William H. Life in Ponds & Streams. Crump, Donald J., ed. LC 81-47745. (Books for Young Explorers: Set 8). 32p. (J). (ps-3). 1981. lib. bdg. 16.95 (0-87044-404-2) Natl Geog.

— Time to Remember: A Biography of St. Andrew's School from the 1950s to the 1980s. LC 96-72586. (Illus.). 400p. 1997. 45.00 (0-9656434-0-9) Saint Andrews Schl.

Amos, William H. & Amos, Stephen H. Atlantic & Gulf Coasts. LC 84-48676. (Audubon Society Nature Guides Ser.). (Illus.). 670p. 1985. pap. 19.95 (0-394-73109-3) Knopf.

Amosova, S. V., jt. auth. see Trofimov, B. A.

***Amoss, Barthe.** Three Little Cajun Pigs. (Illus.). (J). 1999. pap. text 13.95 (0-922589-67-4) More Than a Card.

Amoss, Berthe. The Cajun Gingerbread Boy. LC 94-78160. (Illus.). 20p. (J). (ps-2). 1995. 12.95 (0-7868-0114-X, Pub. by Hyprn Child) Time Warner.

***Amoss, Berthe.** The Cajun Gingerbread Boy. 1999. 13.95 (0-922589-66-6) More Than a Card.

Amoss, Berthe. Car Seat Games. (Illus.). 10p. (J). (ps-7). 1989. pap. 2.95 (0-922589-14-3) More Than a Card.

— Cinderella. (Illus.). 10p. (J). (ps-7). 1989. pap. 2.95 (0-922589-04-6) More Than a Card.

— David & Goliath. (Illus.). 10p. (J). (ps-7). 1989. pap. 2.95 (0-922589-12-7) More Than a Card.

— Hansel & Gretel. (Illus.). 10p. (J). (ps-7). 1989. pap. 2.95 (0-922589-05-4) More Than a Card.

— Jack & the Beanstalk. (Illus.). 10p. (J). (ps-7). 1989. pap. 2.95 (0-922589-00-3) More Than a Card.

— Jonah. (Illus.). 10p. (J). (ps-7). 1989. pap. 2.95 (0-922589-09-7) More Than a Card.

— Little Red Riding Hood. (Illus.). 10p. (J). (ps-7). 1989. pap. 2.95 (0-922589-11-9) More Than a Card.

— Lost Magic. LC 93-10082. 192p. (J). (gr. 5-9). 1993. 14.95 (1-56282-573-9, Pub. by Hyprn Child) Little.

— Lullaby & Good Night. (Illus.). 10p. (J). (ps-7). 1989. pap. 2.95 (0-922589-13-5) More Than a Card.

— The Mockingbird Song. LC 87-45272. 128p. (J). (gr. 4-7). 1988. 12.95 (0-06-020061-8) HarpC Child Bks.

— Mother Goose Rhymes. (Illus.). 10p. (J). (ps-7). 1989. pap. 2.95 (0-922589-02-X) More Than a Card.

— Noah. (Illus.). 10p. (J). (ps-7). 1989. pap. 2.95 (0-922589-10-0) More Than a Card.

— Rumpelstiltskin. (Illus.). 10p. (J). (ps-7). 1989. pap. 2.95 (0-922589-03-8) More Than a Card.

— Snow White & the Seven Dwarfs. (Illus.). 10p. (J). (ps-7). 1989. pap. 2.95 (0-922589-01-1) More Than a Card.

Amoss, Berthe & Suben, Eric. Writing & Illustrating Children's Books for Publication: Two Perspectives. LC 95-17164. (Illus.). 128p. 1995. 24.95 (0-89879-722-5, Wrtrs Digest Bks) F & W Pubns Inc.

Amoss, Berthe, jt. auth. see Suben, Eric.

Amoss, Lindsay S. Enemy Ancestor. LC 92-43539. 1993. pap. 14.95 (0-7734-2800-3, Mellen Poetry Pr) E Mellen.

— Hiroshima. LC 97-30524. 88p. 1997. pap. 14.95 (0-7734-2809-7, Mellen Poetry Pr) E Mellen.

— Violin & Flamethrower: Poems. LC 95-20574. 68p. 1996. pap. 14.95 (0-7734-2759-7, Mellen Poetry Pr) E Mellen.

Amoss, Pamela T. & Harrell, Stevan, eds. Other Ways of Growing Old: Anthropological Perspectives. LC 79-66056. xxiv, 270p. 1981. 42.50 (0-8047-1072-4); pap. 15.95 (0-8047-1153-4) Stanford U Pr.

Amoss, Pamela T., jt. ed. see Seaburg, William R.

Amott, Teresa. Caught in the Crisis: Women & the U. S. Economy Today. LC 93-7326. (Cornerstone Bks.). (Illus.). 160p. 1993. pap. text 13.00 (0-85345-846-4, Pub. by Monthly Rev) NYU Pr.

— Caught in the Crisis: Women & the U. S. Economy Today. 2nd rev. ed. 1999. pap. 15.00 (1-58367-020-3, Pub. by Monthly Rev) NYU Pr.

Amott, Teresa & Mattaei, Julia A. Race, Gender & Work: A Multicultural Economic History of Women in the United States. rev. ed. 444p. 1996. pap. 21.00 (0-89608-537-6) South End Pr.

Amott, Teresa & Mattaei, Julie A. Race, Gender, & Work: A Multi-Cultural Economic History of Women in the United States. 420p. (Orig.). 1991. write for info. (0-921689-91-8); pap. write for info. (0-921689-90-X) Black Rose.

— Race, Gender, & Work: A Multicultural Economic History of Women in the United States. rev. ed. LC 96-10382. 444p. 1996. 40.00 (0-89608-538-4) South End Pr.

Amouroux, Jacques & Fauchais, Pierre. Progress in Plasma Processing of Materials 1999: Proceedings of the Fourth International Thermal Plasma Processes Conference, St. Petersburg, Russia, July 13-16, 1998. LC 98-55121. 1999. write for info. (1-56700-126-2) Begell Hse.

Amouroux, M. & El Jai, A., eds. Control of Distributed Parameter Systems, 1989: Selected Papers from the Fifth IFAC Symposium, Perpignan, France, 26-29 June 1989. LC 89-72118. (IFAC Proceedings Ser.: IFACI9003). 532p. 1990. 218.00 (0-08-037036-5, Pergamon Pr) Elsevier.

Amowitz, Georgette W. And after the Journey. 1990. spiral bd. 20.00 (1-878084-03-8) Danscores.

— A Day for Dancing to Music by Lloyd Pfautsch. (Illus.). (Orig.). 1990. spiral bd. 35.00 (1-878084-00-3) Danscores.

— Scherzofrenia. 1990. spiral bd. 15.00 (1-878084-04-6) Danscores.

— Themes & Variations from the Foot-Hook Rag. (Illus.). (Orig.). 1990. spiral bd. 15.00 (1-878084-02-X) Danscores.

Amp, E. S., et al, eds. New Survey Methods in Transport: 2nd International Conference, Australia, 1983. 387p. 1985. lib. bdg. 99.50 (90-6764-051-4, Pub. by VSP) Coronet Bks.

Ampalavanar, Rajeswary. The Indian Minority & Political Change in Malaya: 1945-1957. (East Asian Historical Monographs). (Illus.). 1981. 39.95 (0-19-580473-2) OUP.

Ampco Metal Division Staff. The Establishment of Foundry Procedures & Evaluation of Mechanical & Chemical Criteria (of INCRAMET 800) As Pertinent to Industries Other than Glass Making. 86p. 1965. 12.90 (0-317-34522-2, 52) Intl Copper.

— Properties of Incramute I Castings. 85p. 1974. 12.75 (0-317-34541-9, 209) Intl Copper.

Amper, Thomas. Booker T. Washington. LC 97-27454. (Carolrhoda On My Own Bks.). (Illus.). 48p. (J). (gr. 1-3). 1998. 18.60 (1-57505-094-3, Carolrhoda) Lerner Pub.

***Ampersand, Violet.** Poetry, Prose & Other Voyages to the Edge. LC 99-90883. 1999. 25.00 (0-7388-0554-8); pap. 18.00 (0-7388-0555-6) Xlibris Corp.

Amphlett, C. & Dunworth, J. Treatment & Disposal of Radioactive Wastes. Vol. 2. 1961. write for info. (0-318-69653-3, Pub. by Pergamon Repr) Franklin.

Amphlett, Hilda. Who Was Shakespeare? LC 72-126768. reprint ed. 32.50 (0-404-00325-7) AMS Pr.

Amphoux, Christian-Bernard, jt. auth. see Vaganay, Leon.

Amphoux, Nancy, tr. see Deshimaru, Taisen.

Ampiah, Kweku. Dynamics of Japan's Relations with Africa: South Africa Tanzania & Nigeria. LC 98-108263. (Nissan Institute/Routledge Japanese Studies Ser.). 256p. (C). 1997. 90.00 (0-415-14483-3) Routledge.

Ampim, Manu. Critical Issues in the Current Africentric Movement, 2 vols., Set. (Illus.). (Orig.). 1992. pap. 7.00 (0-9636447-1-8) Advan The Res.

— A Guide to Egyptian Collections in the Western World, 2 vols. (Illus.). 1994. pap. write for info. (0-9636447-3-4) Advan The Res.

— Major Egyptian Forgeries: The Fabrication of Ra-Hotep - Nofret & Nefertiti. (Illus.). 1995. pap. write for info. (0-9636447-6-9) Advan The Res.

— Martin Luther King, Jr: The Evolution of a Revolutionary. (Illus.). 1994. pap. write for info. (0-9636447-4-2) Advan The Res.

— The Origin & Use of the Word Africa. (Illus.). 1995. pap. write for info. (0-9636447-5-0) Advan The Res.

— Towards Black Community Development: Moving Beyond the Limitations of the Lecture Model. (Critical Issues in the Current Africentric Movement Ser.: Vol. II). (Illus.). 228p. (Orig.). 1993. pap. 11.95 (0-9636447-0-X) Advan The Res.

— Twelve Aspects of a Complete System of Spiritual Health & Nutrition: The Example of Ancient Egypt. (Illus.). 1994. pap. write for info. (0-9636447-2-6) Advan The Res.

Amplatz, Kurt. Atlas of Endourology. 1991. write for info. (0-8151-0137-6) Mosby Inc.

Amplatz, Kurt, et al. Radiology of Congenital Heart Disease. LC 92-49972. 1992. write for info. (0-8016-0329-3) Mosby Inc.

Ampleforth Abbey Press Staff. St. Benedict's Prayer Book. 1994. 12.95 (0-85244-258-0, Pub. by Gra1cewing) Morehouse Pub.

AMPO, Japan Asia Quarterly Review Staff, ed. Voices from the Japanese Women's Movement. LC 95-43512. (Japan in the Modern World Ser.). 232p. (C). (gr. 13). 1996. text 68.95 (1-56324-725-9); pap. text 26.95 (1-56324-726-7, East Gate Bk) M E Sharpe.

Ampola, Mary G. Metabolic Diseases in Pediatric Practice. 1982. text 39.00 (0-316-03796-6, Little Brwn Med Div) Lppncott W & W.

Amprimoz, Alexandre. Hard Confessions. 1997. pap. 7.95 (0-88801-105-9, Pub. by Turnstone Pr) Genl Dist Srvs.

Amprimoz, Alexandre L. A l'Ombre de Rimbaud. (Stanford French & Italian Studies: Vol. 43). (FRE.). 86p. (Orig.). 1986. pap. 56.50 (0-915838-58-3) Anma Libri.

— Germain Nouveau dit Humilis: Etude Biographique. LC 83-13201. (North Carolina Studies in the Romance Languages & Literatures: No. 220). (FRE.). 200p. reprint ed. pap. 62.00 (0-608-20062-X, 207133400011) Bks Demand.

— L' Inspiration Religieuse des Symbolistes: Le Cas de La Doctrine de l'amour de Germani Nouveau. LC 88-70958. (Stanford French & Italian Studies: Vol. 60). (FRE.). 128p. 1989. pap. 56.50 (0-915838-76-1) Anma Libri.

— La Poesie Erotique de Germain Nouveau: Une Lecture des Valentines. (Stanford French & Italian Studies: Vol. 28). 76p. 1983. pap. 56.50 (0-915838-09-5) Anma Libri.

***Ampudia, Ricardo.** La Iglesia de Roma: Estructura y Presencia en Mexico. 395p. 1999. pap. 12.99 (968-16-5685-7) Fondo CA.

Amr, Asad T., et al. Energy Systems in the United States. LC 81-5414. (Energy, Power, & the Environment Ser.: No. 12). (Illus.). 510p. reprint ed. pap. 158.10 (0-7837-0953-6, 204125800019) Bks Demand.

AMR Staff. Advanced French, Set. (AMR Language Ser.). 46.95 incl. audio (1-55536-287-7) Oasis Audio.

— Advanced French - Module Four, Set. (AMR Language Ser.). 46.95 incl. audio (1-55536-288-5) Oasis Audio.

— Advanced German, Set. (AMR Language Ser.: Vol. 3). 46.95 incl. audio (1-55536-314-8) Oasis Audio.

An Asterisk (*) at the beginning of an entry indicates that the title is appearing for the first time.

— Advanced Spanish - Module Four, Set. (AMR Language Ser.). 46.95 incl. audio (*1-55536-261-3*) Oasis Audio.
— Instant Conversational French - Advanced, Set. (AMR Language Ser.). (FRE.). 1999. pap. 46.95 incl. audio (*1-886463-60-3*) Oasis Audio.
— Instant Conversational French - Advanced Plus, Set. (AMR Language Ser.). (FRE.). 1999. pap. 46.95 incl. audio (*1-886463-61-1*) Oasis Audio.
— Instant Conversational French - Basic, Set. (AMR Language Ser.). (FRE.). 1998. pap. 46.95 incl. audio (*1-886463-28-X*) Oasis Audio.
— Instant Conversational French - Intermediate, Set. (AMR Language Ser.). (FRE.). 1999. pap. 46.95 incl. audio (*1-886463-34-4*) Oasis Audio.
— Instant Conversational French Vocabulary, Set. (AMR Language Ser.). (FRE.). 1999. pap. 46.95 incl. audio (*1-886463-65-4*) Oasis Audio.
— Instant Conversational German - Advanced Plus, Set. (AMR Language Ser.). (GER.). 1999. pap. 46.95 incl. audio (*1-886463-63-8*) Oasis Audio.
— Instant Conversational German - Basic, Set. (AMR Language Ser.). (GER.). 1998. 46.95 incl. audio (*1-886463-29-8*) Oasis Audio.
— Instant Conversational German - Intermediate, Set. (AMR Language Ser.). (GER.). 1998. 46.95 incl. audio (*1-886463-35-2*) Oasis Audio.
— Instant Conversational Italian - Basic, Set. (AMR Language Ser.). (ITA.). 1998. 46.95 incl. audio (*1-886463-30-1*) Oasis Audio.
— Instant Conversational Italian - Intermediate, Set. (AMR Language Ser.). (ITA.). 1998. 46.95 incl. audio (*1-886463-36-0*) Oasis Audio.
— Instant Conversational Japanese - Basic, Set. (AMR Language Ser.). (JPN.). 1998. 46.95 incl. audio (*1-886463-31-X*) Oasis Audio.
— Instant Conversational Mandarin Chinese - Basic, Set. (AMR Language Ser.). (CHI.). 1998. audio 46.95 (*1-886463-32-8*) Oasis Audio.
— Instant Conversational Spanish - Basic, Set. (AMR Language Ser.). (SPA.). 1998. vinyl bd. 46.95 incl. audio (*1-886463-27-1*) Oasis Audio.
— Instant Conversational Spanish - Intermediate, Set. (AMR Language Ser.). (SPA.). 1998. 46.95 incl. audio (*1-886463-33-6*) Oasis Audio.
— Instant Converstional Advanced English Vocabulary, Set. (AMR Language Ser.). 46.95 incl. audio Oasis Audio.

***Amra, Claude & Angus Macleod, H., eds.** Advances in Optical Interference Coatings. (Europto Ser.). 574p. 1999. pap. text 128.00 (*0-8194-3212-1*) SPIE.

Amram & Kulatilaka. Real Options: Managing Strategic Investments in an Uncertain World. LC 98-22392. 256p. 1998. 35.00 (*0-87584-845-1*, HBS Pr) Harvard Busn.

Amram, David. The Makers of Hebrew Books in Italy. 418p. (C). 1988. 150.00 (*0-900470-46-1*, Pub. by New5 Holland) St Mut.

Amram, David W. Leading Cases in the Bible. ix, 220p. 1985. reprint ed. 48.50 (*0-8377-0218-6*, Rothman) W S Hein.
— The Makers of Hebrew Books in Italy. 350p. 1983. 45.00 (*0-87556-013-X*) Saifer.
— Vibrations: The Adventures & Musical Times of David Amram. LC 79-24422. (Illus.). 469p. 1980. reprint ed. lib. bdg. 75.00 (*0-313-22230-4*, AMVI, Greenwood Pr) Greenwood.

Amram, Fred. African-American Inventors. (Scientists & Inventors Ser.). (Illus.). 48p. (J). (gr. 3-7). 1996. lib. bdg. 19.00 (*0-516-20106-9*) Childrens.

Amram, Fred, jt. auth. see Showell, Ellen H.

Amranand, Pimsai, et al. Gardening in Bangkok. LC 97-942777. 240 p. 1996. write for info. (*974-8298-33-7*) AgBe Pub.

Amranand, Ping, jt. auth. see Tamulevich, Susan.

Amrein, Matthias, jt. auth. see Marti, Othmar.

Amrein, Werner D., et al. Hardy Type Inequalities for Abstract Differential Operators. LC 87-25476. (Memoirs Ser.: Vol. 70/375). 119p. 1987. pap. 21.00 (*0-8218-2438-4*, MEMO/70/375) Am Math.

Amrein, Werner O., et al. Co-Groups, Commutator Methods & Spectral Theory of N-Body Hamiltonians. (Progress in Mathematics Ser.: Vol. 135). 480p. 1996. 98.00 (*3-7643-5365-1*) Birkhauser.
— Commutator Methods & Spectral Theory of N-Body Hamiltonians. (Progress in Mathematics Ser.: Vol. 135). 460p. 1996. 98.00 (*0-8176-5365-1*) Birkhauser.

Amrhein, Carl G., jt. auth. see Griffith, Daniel A.

Amrhein, Christopher J. & Hussey, Daniel P., Jr. Multiple-Lines Insurance Production Segment A: Commercial Liability Insurance. LC 96-79434. 262p. (C). 1999. pap. text 41.00 (*0-89462-103-3*, 8201) IIA.

Amrhein, Christopher J. & Insurance Institute of America. Agency Operations & Sales Management. LC 97-77783. (Illus.). 1997. write for info. (*0-89462-122-X*); write for info. (*0-89462-123-8*); write for info. (*0-89462-124-6*) IIA.

Amrhein, James E. Informational Guide to Grouting Masonry. 52p. 1990. pap. 5.00 (*0-940116-17-0*) Masonry Inst Am.
— Masonry Codes & Specifications Handbook, 1994. LC 94-78167. 441p. 1994. 10.00 (*0-940116-28-6*) Masonry Inst Am.
— Masonry Veneer. 2nd rev. ed. (Illus.). 109p. (Orig.). 1994. pap. text 20.00 (*0-940116-23-5*) Masonry Inst Am.
— Reinforced Grouted Brick Masonry. 13th ed. 130p. 1991. pap. 15.00 (*0-940116-19-7*) Masonry Inst Am.
— Reinforcing Steel in Masonry. 75p. (Orig.). 1991. pap. text 10.00 (*0-940116-18-9*) Masonry Inst Am.
— Residential Masonry Fireplace & Chimney Handbook. (Illus.). 235p. (Orig.). 1995. pap. 19.50 (*0-940116-29-4*) Masonry Inst Am.

Amrhein, James E. & Chrysler, John. Reinforced Concrete Masonry Construction Inspector's Handbook. 3rd ed. (Illus.). 462p. (Orig.). 1995. pap. text 29.50 (*0-940116-24-3*) Masonry Inst Am.

Amrhein, James E. & Lee, D. E. Tall Slender Walls, Estimating Curves for Area of Steel for Reinforced Masonry. 2nd ed. LC 94-77734. 110p. 1994. pap. text 15.00 (*0-940116-26-X*) Masonry Inst Am.

Amrhein, James E. & Merrigan, Michael W. Marble & Stone Slab Veneer. (Illus.). 138p. (Orig.). 1989. pap. text 20.00 (*0-940116-08-1*) Masonry Inst Am.

AmRhein, Richard, ed. Continuity & Transformation: The Promise of Confluence: Proceedings of the Seventh National Conference of ACRL. 500p. (Orig.). (C). 1995. pap. 50.00 (*0-8389-7786-3*) Assn Coll & Res Libs.

Amrine, Frederick. Goethe in the History of Science. (Studies in Modern German Literature: Vol. 29). XII, 465p. (C). 1996. 64.95 (*0-8204-1076-4*) P Lang Pubng.
— Goethe in the History of Science. (Studies in Modern German Literature: Vol. 30). VII, 464p. (C). 1996. 64.95 (*0-8204-1077-2*) P Lang Pubng.

Amrine, Frederick, et al, eds. Goethe & the Sciences: A Reappraisal. 464p. 1986. lib. bdg. 175.00 (*90-277-2265-X*, D Reidel) Kluwer Academic.

Amrine, Frederick, tr. see Steiner, Rudolf.

Amrine, Harold T., et al. Manufacturing Organization & Management. 6th ed. LC 92-12867. (International Industrial & Systems Engineering Ser.). 608p. 1992. 91.00 (*0-13-554858-6*) P-H.

Amristaswarupananda, Swami & Prasada, Ajit, eds. Purushartha-Siddhyupaya (Jaina-Pravachana-Rahasya-Kosha) LC 73-3838. (Sacred Books of the Jainas: No. 4). reprint ed. 34.50 (*0-404-57704-0*) AMS Pr.

Amritaswarupananda, Swami. Ammachi: A Biography of Mata Amritanandamayi. 2nd ed. (ENG, FRE & ITA.). 348p. 1994. 13.00 (*1-879410-60-5*) M A Ctr.
— Awaken Children, Vol. 7. 260p. 1995. 13.00 (*1-879410-63-X*) M A Ctr.
— Awaken Children: Dialogues with the Holy Mother, Vol. 1. (Illus.). 377p. (Orig.). 1989. 13.00 (*1-879410-52-4*) M A Ctr.
— Awaken Children: Dialogues with the Holy Mother, Vol. 2. (Illus.). 327p. (Orig.). 1990. 13.00 (*1-879410-53-2*) M A Ctr.
— Awaken Children: Dialogues with the Holy Mother, Vol. 3. (Illus.). 325p. (Orig.). 1991. 13.00 (*1-879410-54-0*) M A Ctr.
— Awaken Children: Dialogues with the Holy Mother, Vol. 4. (Illus.). 318p. (Orig.). 1992. 12.00 (*1-879410-55-9*) M A Ctr.
— Awaken Children: Dialogues with the Holy Mother, Vol. 5. (Illus.). 259p. (Orig.). 1993. 12.00 (*1-879410-58-3*) M A Ctr.
— Awaken Children: Dialogues with the Holy Mother, Vol. 6. (Illus.). 260p. (Orig.). 1994. 13.00 (*1-879410-64-8*) M A Ctr.
— Awaken Children Vol. 8: Dialogues with the Holy Mother. 216p. 1996. 13.00 (*1-879410-66-4*) M A Ctr.
— Awaken Children Vol. 9: Dialogues with the Holy Mother. LC 98-221763. 221p. 1998. 13.00 (*1-879410-71-0*) M A Ctr.
— For My Children: Selected Teachings of Divine Mother Ammachi. Chaitanya, Ramakrishna, ed. (Illus.). 191p. (Orig.). 1994. 6.00 (*1-879410-61-3*) M A Ctr.
— Immortal Light: Divine Mother Ammachi's Advice to Householder. Namoodiri, Neelakantan, ed. (Illus.). 104p. (Orig.). 1994. 4.00 (*1-879410-62-1*) M A Ctr.

Amro, Abn, jt. auth. see Euromoney Books Staff.

AMRO Bank Staff & Ernst & Whinney Staff. Europe! From White Paper to Blueprint Nineteen Ninety-Two: Strategy Guide for Medium-sized & Large Companies, Checklist Guide. 45p. 1990. write for info. (*0-318-67995-7*) Kluwer Law Intl.
— Europe! From White Paper to Blueprint Nineteen Ninety-Two: Strategy Guide for Medium-sized & Large Companies, Set. 1990. bds. 122.00 (*90-6544-487-4*) Kluwer Law Intl.
— Europe! From White Paper to Blueprint Nineteen Ninety-Two: Strategy Guide for Medium-sized & Large Companies, Strategy Guide. 125p. 1990. write for info. (*0-318-67994-9*) Kluwer Law Intl.

Amrouche, Fadhma. My Life Story: The Autobiography of a Berber Woman. Blair, Dorothy, tr. 197p. (C). 1989. text 35.00 (*0-8135-1425-8*); pap. text 17.00 (*0-8135-1426-6*) Rutgers U Pr.

Amroundi, Dominique, jt. auth. see Renyl, Pierre.

Amrouni, Dominique, jt. auth. see Renyi, Pierre.

Amrud, Johan. Ornamental Woodcarving in the Norwegian Tradition. 105p. (C). 1995. 35.00 (*82-00-41978-9*, Pub. by Scand Univ Pr) IBD Ltd.

***AMS-IMS-SIAM Joint Summer Research Conference on Geometric Group Theory and Computer Science.** Groups, Languages, & Geometry: 1998 AMS-IMS-SIAM Joint Summer Research Conference on Geometric Group Theory & Computer Science, July 5-9, 1998, Mount Holyoke College. Gilman, Robert H., ed. LC 99-49968. (CONM Ser.: Vol. 250). 142p. 1999. 35.00 (*0-8218-1053-7*) Am Math.

***AMS-IMS-SIAM Joint Summer Research Conference Staff.** Algebraic K-Theory: Ams-Ims-Siam Joint Summer Research Conference on Algebraic K-Theory, July 13-24, 1997, University of Washington, Seattle. Raskind, Wayne & Weibel, Charles A., eds. LC 99-37722. (Proceedings of Symposia in Pure Mathematics Ser.: Vol. 67). 315p. 1999. 79.00 (*0-8218-0927-X*) Am Math.
— Applications of Curves over Finite Fields: 1997 AMS-IMS-SIAM Joint Summer Research Conference, July 27-31, 1997, University of Washington, Seattle. Fried, Michael D., ed. LC 99-43767. (Contemporary Mathematics Ser.: Vol. 245). 226p. 1999. pap. 39.00 (*0-8218-0925-3*) Am Math.

AMS-IMS-SIAM Joint Summer Research Conference Staff. Complex Differential Geometry & Nonlinear Differential Equations: Proceedings of the AMS-IMS-SIAM Joint Summer Research Conference, Held August 12-18, 1984, with Support from the National Science Foundation. Yum-Tong Siu, ed. LC 85-28656. (Contemporary Mathematics Ser.: Vol. 49). (Illus.). 198p. reprint ed. pap. 61.40 (*0-608-09611-3*, 205276900007) Bks Demand.

AMS Planning & Research Corp. Staff. American Participation in Theatre. LC 96-7842. (National Endowment for the Arts Research Division Report Ser.: No. 35). 50p. 1996. pap. 10.95 (*0-929765-46-X*) Seven Locks Pr.

AMS Planning & Research Corp. Staff, compiled by. A Practical Guide to Arts Participation Research. LC 95-12004. (Research Division Reports: No. 30). 1995. write for info. (*0-614-32291-X*) Natl Endow Arts.

***AMS Special Session on Homotopy Theory Staff, et al.** Homotopy Invariant Algebraic Structures: A Conference in Honor of Mike Boardman: AMS Special Session on Homotopy Theory, January 1998, Baltimore, MD. LC 99-34575. (Contemporary Mathematics Ser.). 1999. write for info. (*0-8218-1057-X*) Am Math.

AMS Special Session on Invariant Theory Staff. Invariant Theory: Proceedings of an AMS Special Session on Invariant Theory, October 31-November 1, 1986, Denton, TX. Fossum, R. et al, eds. LC 89-311. (Contemporary Mathematics Ser.: Vol. 88). (Illus.). 608p. 1989. reprint ed. pap. 188.50 (*0-608-07913-8*, 205267000012) Bks Demand.

***AMS Special Session on Probability on Algebraic Structures Staff, et al.** Probability on Algebraic Structures: AMS Special Session on Probability on Algebraic Structures, March 12-13, 1999, Gainesville, Florida. LC 00-34992. (Contemporary Mathematics Ser.: Vol. 261). 238p. 2000. 59.00 (*0-8218-2027-3*) Am Math.

AMS Special Session on Stochastic Inequalities & their Applications Staff, et al. Advances in Stochastic Inequalities: AMS Special Session on Stochastic Inequalities & Their Applications, October 17-19, 1997, Georgia Institute of Technology. LC 99-22875. (Contemporary Mathematics Ser.). ix, 212p. 1999. write for info. (*0-8218-1086-3*) Am Math.

***AMS Special Session on the Functional & Harmonic Analysis of Wavelets Staff, et al.** The Functional & Harmonic Analysis of Wavelets & Frames: AMS Special Session on the Functional & Harmonic Analysis of Wavelets, January 13-14, 1999, San Antonio, Texas. Baggett, Lawrence Wasson & Larson, David Royal, eds. LC 99-52140. (Contemporary Mathematics Ser.: Vol. 247). 306p. 2000. 75.00 (*0-8218-1957-7*) Am Math.

Amsalem, Michel A. Technology Choice in Developing Countries: The Textile & Pulp & Paper Industries. (Illus.). 224p. 1983. 32.50 (*0-262-01072-0*) MIT Pr.

Amsbury, George S. Proof It! A Competency-Based Approach to Proofreading & Editing Skills. LC 93-18927. (C). 1994. mass mkt. 15.00 (*0-538-70944-8*) S-W Pub.

***Amsco Music Staff.** Best Balalaika Method. 1999. pap. text 9.95 (*0-8256-5366-5*, Amsco Music) Music Sales.
— Chopin: His Greatest Piano Solos. 1999. 11.95 (*0-8256-5140-9*, Amsco Music) Music Sales.

AMSCO Publications Staff. Emerson, Lake & Palmer Greatest Hits. 1996. pap. 14.95 (*0-8256-1536-4*, AM 934494) Music Sales.

Amsco Publications Staff. The Library of Easy Piano Classics, Vol. 2. 1996. pap. 19.95 (*0-8256-1566-6*, AM940270) Music Sales.

AMSCO Staff. Contemporary Blues Guitar. 1996. pap. 24.95 (*0-8256-1532-1*) Music Sales.
— Jazz Classics: 22 Timeless Jazz Classics. 1996. pap. 14.95 (*0-8256-1529-1*, AM934373) Music Sales.

Amsden, Alice H. Asia's Next Giant: South Korea & Late Industrialization. 400p. 1992. reprint ed. pap. text 16.95 (*0-19-507603-6*) OUP.
— International Firms & Labour in Kenya, 1945-1970. 186p. 1971. 45.00 (*0-7146-2581-7*, Pub. by F Cass Pubs) Intl Spec Bk.

***Amsden, Alice H.** The Rise of 'the Rest' Challenges to the West from Late-Industrializing Economies. (Illus.) 432p. 2000. 35.00 (*0-19-513969-0*) OUP.

Amsden, Alice H., et al. The Market Meets Its Match: Restructuring the Economies of Eastern Europe. LC 94-18600. 232p. 1994. text 43.50 (*0-674-54983-X*, AMSMAR) HUP.
— The Market Meets Its Match: Restructuring the Economies of Eastern Europe. (Illus.). 264p. 1998. pap. 18.95 (*0-674-54984-8*) HUP.

***Amsden, Charles A.** America's Earliest Man. (LC History-America-E). 1999. reprint ed. lib. bdg. 89.00 (*0-7812-4302-5*) Rprt Serv.

Amsden, Charles A. Navaho Weaving: Its Technic & History. (Illus.). 416p. 1991. pap. 12.95 (*0-486-26337-4*) Dover.
— Navaho Weaving: Its Technic & History. (Beautiful Rio Grande Classics Ser.). (Illus.). 460p. 1990. reprint ed. pap. 17.50 (*0-87380-172-5*) Popular E Commerce.
— Prehistoric Southwesterners from Basketmaker to Pueblo. xiv, 163p. 1976. reprint ed. pap. 5.00 (*0-916561-57-7*) Southwest Mus.

Amsden, Charles A. & Kidder, Alfred V. Prehistoric Southwesterners from Basketmaker to Pueblo. LC 76-43642. reprint ed. 39.50 (*0-404-15477-8*) AMS Pr.

Amsden, D., et al. SPC Simplified Workbook: Practical Steps to Quality. 2nd rev. ed. 420p. 1998. pap. text, wbk. ed. 26.95 (*0-527-76341-1*, 763411) Productivity Inc.

Amsden, Davida M., et al. SPC Simplified for Services: Practical Tools for Continuous Quality Improvement. 317p. 1991. pap. text 25.00 (*0-527-91639-0*, 916390) Productivity Inc.

Amsden, Don B., ed. see Limprecht, Jane E.

Amsden, Kay, ed. see Fuller, Mary L.

Amsden, Monroe. Archaeological Reconnaissance in Sonora. LC 76-43642. (Southwest Museum Papers: No. 1). reprint ed. write for info. (*0-404-15476-X*) AMS Pr.
— Archaeological Reconnaissance in Sonora. (Illus.). 51p. 1970. reprint ed. pap. 5.00 (*0-318-18302-1*) Southwest Mus.
— Archeological Reconnaisance in Sonora. (Illus.). 51p. 1970. reprint ed. pap. 5.00 (*0-916561-08-9*) Southwest Mus.

Amsden, Robert T., et al. SPC Simplified: Practical Steps to Quality. (Illus.). 300p. 1986. pap. text 21.00 (*0-527-91617-X*, 91617X) Productivity Inc.
— SPC Simplified: Practical Steps to Quality. 2nd rev. ed. LC 97-47363. (Illus.). 304p. 1998. 24.95 (*0-527-76340-3*) Productivity Inc.
— SPC Simplified Workbook: Practical Steps to Quality. 368p. 1990. spiral bd. 21.00 (*0-527-91638-2*, 916382) Productivity Inc.

Amsden, Robert T., jt. auth. see Cleary, Michael J.

Amse-De Jong, Tine H. The Meaning of the Finite Verb Forms in the Old Church Slavonic Codex Suprasliensis: A Synchronic Study. (Slavistic Printings & Reprintings Ser.: No. 319). 228p. (Orig.). 1974. pap. text 103.10 (*90-279-3012-0*) Mouton.

Amsel, Abram. Behaviorism, Neobehaviorism & Cognitivism in Learning Theory: Historical & Contemporary Perspectives. 116p. 1988. 24.95 (*0-8058-0332-7*) L Erlbaum Assocs.
— Frustration Theory: An Analysis of Dispositional Learning & Memory. (Problems in the Behavioral Sciences Ser.: No. 11). (Illus.). 294p. (C). 1992. text 69.95 (*0-521-24784-5*) Cambridge U Pr.

Amsel, Abram & Rashotte, Michael E. Mechanisms of Adaptive Behavior: Clark L. Hull's Theoretical Papers with Commentary. LC 84-7608. 560p. 1984. text 104.00 (*0-231-05792-X*) Col U Pr.

Amsel, Allan. Sloan's Green Guide to Antiquing in the Midwest: The Enthusiast's Guidebook to Antique Shops in the Midwest. (Illus.). 288p. 1998. pap. 15.95 (*0-7627-0383-0*) Globe Pequot.

Amsel, Eric & Renninger, K. Ann, eds. Change & Development: Issues of Theory, Method, & Application. LC 96-38151. (Jean Piaget Symposia Ser.). 336p. 1997. pap. 69.95 (*0-8058-1825-1*) L Erlbaum Assocs.

Amsel, Freda. Personally Yours. 28p. (Orig.). 1989. pap. text. write for info. (*0-9602026-1-7*) Amsel Enterps.

Amsel, Nachum. The Jewish Encyclopedia of Moral & Ethical Issues. LC 94-2484. 520p. 1994. 50.00 (*1-56821-174-0*) Aronson.
— The Jewish Encyclopedia of Moral & Ethical Issues. LC 94-2484. 520p. 1997. pap. 40.00 (*1-56821-761-7*) Aronson.

Amsel, Sheri. The Adirondack Alphabet Book: An Alphabetical Tour of the Adirondack Mountains. (Illus.). 32p. (J). 1994. pap. 7.50 (*0-925168-33-5*) North Country.
— Adirondack Counting: A Counting Adventure to the 46 Highest Peaks of the Adirondacks. (Illus.). 32p. (J). (ps-k). 1998. pap. 7.50 (*0-925168-63-7*) North Country.
— The Adirondack Nature Guide: Birds, Trees, Plants, Insects, Mammals, Reptiles & Amphibians of the North Country. (Illus.). 120p. (Orig.). 1997. pap. 14.95 (*0-9632476-3-8*) Pinto Pr.
— Vermont Nature Guide: A Field Guide to Birds, Mammals, Trees, Insects, Wildflowers, Amphibians, Reptiles & Where to Find Them. LC 98-65510. (Illus.). 120p. (YA). (gr. 9-12). 1998. pap. 14.95 (*0-9632476-7-0*) Pinto Pr.

Amselek, Paul & MacAormick, Neil, eds. Controversies about Law's Ontology. 224p. 1991. pap. text 65.00 (*0-7486-0280-1*, Pub. by Edinburgh U Pr) Col U Pr.

Amselle, Jean-Loup. Mestizo Logics: Anthropology of Identity in Africa & Elsewhere. Royal, Claudia, tr. from FRE. LC 97-26993. (Mestizo Spaces Ser.). 240p. 1997. 45.00 (*0-8047-2429-6*); pap. 15.95 (*0-8047-2431-8*) Stanford U Pr.

Amshay, Thomas & Clement, Christina. Turning Horse Power into Marketing Power: How to Use the Racing Industry As a Marketing Tool. Gottlieb, Anne, ed. LC 93-83684. 215p. (Orig.). 1993. pap. 50.00 (*0-939401-15-0*) RFTS Prod.

Amsler, C., ed. SuperLEAR Workshop Proceedings. (Institute of Physics Conference Ser.: No. 124). (Illus.). 460p. 1992. 183.00 (*0-85498-414-3*) IOP Pub.

Amsler, C., et al. Physics at LEAR with Low Energy Antiprotons, Vol. 14. xviii, 828p. 1988. text 312.00 (*3-7186-4814-8*) Gordon & Breach.

Amsler, Kevin. Final Resting Place: The Life & Death of Famous St. Louisans. Dunn, Zellie, ed. (Illus.). 257p. (Orig.). 1997. pap. 15.95 (*0-9631448-8-X*) VA Pub Corp.

Amsler, Kurt. The Caribbean Dive Guide: A Guide to the Best Sites. LC 96-52843. (Dive Guide Ser.). (Illus.). 168p. 1998. pap. 24.95 (*0-7892-0307-3*) Abbeville Pr.

***Amsler, Kurt, photos by.** The French Polynesia Dive Guide. (Illus.). 2000. pap. 24.95 (*0-7892-0660-9*) Abbeville Pr.

Amsler, Mark. Etymology & Grammatical Discourse in Late Antiquity & the Early Middle Ages. LC 88-7616. (Studies in the History of the Language Sciences: Vol. 44). xi, 280p. (C). 1989. 76.00 (*90-272-4527-4*) J Benjamins Pubng Co.

Amsler, Mark, ed. Creativity & the Imagination: Case Studies from the Classical Age to the Twentieth Century. LC 85-41031. (Studies in Science & Culture: Vol. 3). 224p. 1987. 35.00 (*0-87413-296-7*) U Delaware Pr.
— The Language of Creativity: Models, Problem-Solving, Discourse. LC 85-40360. (Studies in Science & Culture: Vol. 2). 208p. 1986. 32.50 (*0-87413-280-0*) U Delaware Pr.

Amson, J. C., tr. see Dautray, R. & Lions, J. L.

A

A

Amsoneit, Wolfgang. Contemporary European Architects. (SPA.). 1996. pap. 24.99 (*3-8228-0754-0*) Taschen Amer.

— Contemporary European Architects, Vol. 1. 1994. pap. 24.99 (*3-8228-9753-1*) Taschen Amer.

Amspaugh-Corson, Linda B., jt. auth. see Stoodt-Hill, Barbara D.

Amspaugh, Linda B., jt. auth. see Stoodt, Barbara D.

AMSS Staff. Some Aspects of the Economics of Zakah. 229p. 1979. 3.50 (*0-89259-019-X*) Am Trust Pubns.

Amstead, B. H., et al. Manufacturing Processes. 8th ed. LC 86-19094. 736p. 1987. text 92.95 (*0-471-84236-2*) Wiley.

Amstel, M. J. Ploos Van, see Farmer, David & Ploos van Amstel, M. J.

***Amstel, Marsha.** Sybil Ludington's Midnight Ride. (On My Own History Ser.). (Illus.). 56p. (J). (gr. 1-3). 2000. pap. 5.95 (*1-57505-456-6*, Carolrhoda) Lerner Pub.

Amstel, Marsha. Sybil Ludington's Midnight Ride. LC 98-44155. (On My Own History Ser.). (Illus.). 56p. (J). (gr. 1-3). 2000. 21.27 (*1-57505-211-3*, Carolrhoda) Lerner Pub.

Amster, Barbara J., ed. see Silver, Judith A.

Amster, Randall, jt. auth. see Lauderdale, Pat.

Amster, Warren. Neighbors of the Earth. (Illus.). 87p. (Orig.). 1984. pap. 5.95 (*0-86700-012-0*) P Walsh Pr.

Amsterdam, Dick, jt. auth. see Parsons, Nancy.

Amsterdam, Anthony G. Trial Manual Five for the Defense of Criminal Cases: Proceedings Between Arraignment & Trial, Vol. II. 5th ed. 343p. 1989. text 19.67 (*0-8318-0613-3*, B613) Am Law Inst.

— Trial Manual Five for the Defense of Criminal Cases Vol. I: Proceedings Through Arraignment. 5th ed. 403p. 1988. text 19.66 (*0-8318-0582-X*, B582) Am Law Inst.

— Trial Manual Five for the Defense of Criminal Cases Vol. II: Trial & Posttrial Proceedings. 5th ed. LC 88-71176. 356p. 1989. text 19.66 (*0-8318-0614-1*, B614) Am Law Inst.

***Amsterdam, Anthony G. & Bruner, Jerome S.** Minding the Law. LC 00-25428. 448p. 2000. 35.00 (*0-674-00289-X*) HUP.

Amsterdam, D., jt. auth. see Van Oss, Carel J.

Amsterdam, Daniel, ed. see Van Oss, Carel J., et al.

Amsterdam, Ezra A., ed. Cardiovascular Drug Therapy - Current Concepts: Journal: Cardiology, Vol. 72, Nos. 5 & 6. (Illus.). 164p. 1985. pap. 62.75 (*3-8055-4081-7*) S Karger.

Amsterdam, Ezra A. & Holmes, Ann M. Take Care of Your Heart: The Complete Book of Heart Facts. LC 82-12068. 355p. reprint ed. pap. 110.10 (*0-7837-1364-9*, 204151200021) Bks Demand.

Amsterdam, Jay D. Pharmacotherapy of Depression: Application for the Outpatient Practitioner. (Illus.). 496p. 1990. text 145.00 (*0-8247-8209-7*) Dekker.

Amsterdam, Jay D., ed. Refractory Depression. LC 90-9158. (Advances in Neuropsychiatry & Psychopharmacology Ser.: No. 2). (Illus.). 263p. 1991. reprint ed. pap. 81.60 (*0-608-05832-7*, 205979700007) Bks Demand.

Amsterdamska, Olga. Schools of Thought. (C). 1987. lib. bdg. 155.50 (*90-277-2391-5*) Kluwer Academic.

Amsterdamska, Olga, tr. see Amsterdamski, Stefan.

Amsterdamski, Stefan. Between Experience & Metaphysics: Philosophical Problems of the Evolution of Science. Michalowski, P., tr. from POL. LC 75-2184. (Boston Studies in the Philosophy of Science: No. 35). 211p. 1975. pap. text 62.50 (*90-277-0580-1*, D Reidel); lib. bdg. 78.00 (*90-277-0568-2*, D Reidel) Kluwer Academic.

— Between History & Method: Disputes about the Rationality of Science (Miedzy Historia a Metoda) Amsterdamska, Olga & Moore, Gene M., trs. from POL. LC 92-18172. 240p. (C). 1992. lib. bdg. 127.50 (*0-7923-1941-9*, Pub. by Kluwer Academic) Kluwer Academic.

Amstock, Joseph S. Construction Sealants & Adhesives Handbook. 656p. 1998. 75.00 (*0-07-001616-X*) McGraw.

— Handbook of Glass in Construction. LC 97-1273. (Illus.). 584p. 1997. 79.95 (*0-07-001619-4*) McGraw.

Amstutz. General Physics Pearls of Wisdom. (Pearls of Wisdom Ser.). 1999. pap. 18.00 (*1-890369-23-3*) Boston Medical.

— International Conflict. 1995. teacher ed. 12.18 (*0-697-23213-1*) McGraw.

Amstutz, Beverly. Benjamin & the Bible Donkeys. (Illus.). 36p. (J). (gr. k-7). 1981. pap. 3.50 (*0-937836-03-6*) Precious Res.

— The Fly Has Lots of Eyes. (Illus.). 34p. (J). (gr. k-9). 1981. pap. 3.50 (*0-937836-04-4*) Precious Res.

— I Love My Foster Grandparents. (Illus.). 24p. (J). (gr. k-7). 1981. pap. 3.50 (*0-937836-06-0*) Precious Res.

— Moccasins & Sneakers. (Illus.). 24p. (J). (gr. k-7). 1980. pap. 3.50 (*0-937836-02-8*) Precious Res.

***Amstutz, Beverly.** Mushi & the King of Kings: A Christmas Play for Children. (Illus.). 20p. 1999. pap. 5.50 (*0-937836-11-7*) Precious Res.

Amstutz, Beverly. Sharing Is Fun. (Illus.). 24p. (J). (gr. k-7). 1979. pap. 3.50 (*0-937836-00-1*) Precious Res.

— Sprouts: A Diary for the Foster Child. (Illus.). 38p. (Orig.). (J). (gr. k-7). 1982. pap. 3.50 (*0-937836-07-9*) Precious Res.

— That Boy, That Girl. LC 80-80372. (Illus.). 24p. (J). (gr. k-7). 1979. pap. 3.50 (*0-937836-01-X*) Precious Res.

***Amstutz, Beverly.** Tiny Wings: A Christmas Play for Children. (Illus.). (YA). (gr. k-12). 2000. pap. 5.50 (*0-937836-12-5*) Precious Res.

Amstutz, Beverly. Too Big for the Bag. (Illus.). (J). (gr. k-7). 1981. pap. 3.50 (*0-937836-05-2*) Precious Res.

— Too Big for the Bag: A Christmas Play for Children. rev. ed. (Illus.). 25p. (J). (ps-8). 1996. pap. 5.50 (*0-937836-10-9*) Precious Res.

— Touch Me Not! (Illus.). 20p. (J). (ps-7). 1983. pap. 3.50 (*0-937836-09-5*) Precious Res.

— You Are Number One! (Illus.). 30p. (J). (gr. k-9). 1986. pap. 3.50 (*0-937836-08-7*) Precious Res.

Amstutz, Donna D., jt. auth. see Whitson, Donna L.

Amstutz, Ellen, et al, eds. ACES Manual: A Guide to Government Benefit Programs for Individuals & Families in New York City. 2nd rev. ed. 550p. 1999. ring bd. 60.00 (*0-88156-166-5*, 212-614-5314) Comm Serv Soc NY.

Amstutz, G. C., et al, eds. Stratabound Ore Deposits in the Andes. (Special Publications of the Society for General Microbiology: Vol. 8). (Illus.). 800p. 1990. 238.95 (*0-387-52181-X*) Spr-Verlag.

Amstutz, G. Christian, jt. auth. see El Aref, Mortada M.

Amstutz, Galen. Interpreting Amida: History & Orientalism in the Study of Pure Land Buddhism. LC 96-24300. (SUNY Series in Buddhist Studies). 248p. (C). 1997. text 65.50 (*0-7914-3309-9*); pap. text 21.95 (*0-7914-3310-2*) State U NY Pr.

Amstutz, Harlan C. Hip Arthroplasty. (Illus.). 1001p. 1991. text 250.00 (*0-443-08505-6*) Church.

Amstutz, Harlan C. & Brighton, Carl T. Metal on Metal Hip Prostheses: Past Performance & Future Directions. 314p. 1996. text 72.00 (*0-397-51830-7*) Lppncott W & W.

Amstutz, Harold E. Church Planter's Manual: How to Plant Churches. (Illus.). 95p. (Orig.). 1985. pap. text 4.95 (*1-888796-03-0*) ABWE Pubng.

— Prepared to Endure: Nine Essentials for Missionary Success. 150p. (Orig.). 1987. pap. text 8.95 (*1-888796-05-7*) ABWE Pubng.

— Valued Heritage & Veritable Harvest, 2 vols., Set. (Illus.). 217p. (Orig.). 1995. pap. text 8.95 (*1-888796-09-X*) ABWE Pubng.

Amstutz, Harold E., jt. auth. see Commons, Harold.

Amstutz, Irina, ed. see Black-Downes, Jim.

Amstutz, Irina, ed. see DeFilippo, M. Kathleen.

Amstutz, J. Bruce. Afghanistan: The First Five Years of Soviet Occupation. (Illus.). 545p. (Orig.). (C). 1994. pap. text 50.00 (*0-7881-1111-6*) DIANE Pub.

Amstutz, J. Bruce, ed. Afghanistan First Five Years of Soviet Occupation, 3 vols. (Illus.). 574p. 1986. pap. text 55.00 (*1-57979-145-X*) DIANE Pub.

Amstutz, Linda S. Dozens of Uses for a Dead Dick. (Illus.). 112p. (Orig.). 1994. pap. 6.95 (*0-9640362-1-5*) Off Color Pr.

— More Dead Dicks. (Illus.). 112p. (Orig.). 1996. pap. 6.95 (*1-887652-26-4*) Off Color Pr.

— You Might Be a Talk Show Addict If . . . 112p. 1995. pap. 6.95 (*0-9640362-8-2*) Off Color Pr.

Amstutz, Mark R. Christian Ethics & U. S. Foreign Policy. 192p. (Orig.). 1987. pap. 12.95 (*0-310-30031-2*, 18407P) Zondervan.

— International Conflict & Cooperation: An Introduction to World Politics. LC 94-71380. 512p. (C). 1994. text. write for info. (*0-697-21960-7*) Brown & Benchmark.

— International Conflict & Cooperation: An Introduction to World Politics. 2nd ed. LC 98-20212. 560p. 1998. pap. 45.00 (*0-697-37014-3*) McGraw.

***Amstutz, Mark R.** International Ethics: Concepts, Theories, & Cases in Global Politics. LC 98-43537. 224p. 1999. 59.00 (*0-8476-9152-7*) Rowman.

Amstutz, Mark R. International Ethics: Concepts, Theories, & Cases in Global Politics. LC 98-43537. 224p. 1999. pap. 18.95 (*0-8476-9153-5*) Rowman.

Amstutz, Walter, ed. Japanese Emblems & Designs. LC 94-10952. 160p. 1994. 9.95 (*0-486-28184-1*) Dover.

Amt, Emilie, ed. Women's Lives in Medieval Europe: A Sourcebook. LC 92-12815. 256p. (C). (gr. 13). 1992. pap. 20.99 (*0-415-90628-8*, A7413) Routledge.

Amt, Emilie M. The Accession of Henry II in England: Royal Government Restored, 1149-1159. LC 93-27942. (Illus.). 240p. 1993. 75.00 (*0-85115-348-8*, Boydell Pr) Boydell & Brewer.

AMT Magazine Staff. Best of AMT Magazine Vol. 1: Professional, Legal, & FAA Issues. (Illus.). 250p. 1996. reprint ed. pap. 19.95 (*1-56027-271-6*, ASA-BAMT-G) ASA Inc.

— Best of AMT Magazine Vol. 2: Airframe Technology/Accessory Technology. 250p. 1996. pap. 19.95 (*1-56027-270-8*, ASA-BAMT-A) ASA Inc.

— Best of AMT Magazine Vol. 3: Recip Technology & Turbine Technology. (Illus.). 250p. 1996. pap. 19.95 (*1-56027-269-4*, ASA-BAMT-P) ASA Inc.

Amtenbrink, Fabian. The Democratic Accountability of Central Banks: A Comparative Study. 288p. 1999. 80.00 (*1-84113-042-7*, Pub. by Hart Pub) Intl Spec Bk.

Amthor, J. S. Respiration & Crop Productivity. (Illus.). 220p. 1989. 89.95 (*0-387-96938-1*) Spr-Verlag.

Amthor, Terry K. Artifacts & Lost Technology. (Shadow World Sourcebooks Ser.). 132p. 1999. pap. 20.00 (*1-883716-15-2*) Eidolon Studio.

— Citybook I: Haalkitaine. (Shadow World Citybooks Ser.). 130p. 1997. pap. 20.00 (*1-883716-13-6*) Eidolon Studio.

— Emer IV: The Southwest. (Shadow World Sourcebks.). (Illus.). 132p. 2000. pap. 20.00 (*1-883716-18-7*, 6140, Eidolon) Eidolon Studio.

— Emer I: Haestra & the History of the Emerian Empire. (Shadow World Sourcebooks Ser.). 132p. 1997. pap. 20.00 (*1-883716-12-8*) Eidolon Studio.

— Emer II: The Northeast. (Shadow World Sourcebooks Ser.). 132p. 1999. pap. 20.00 (*1-883716-14-4*) Eidolon Studio.

— Emer III: The Southeast. (Shadow World Sourcebks.). (Illus.). 132p. 1999. pap. 20.00 (*1-883716-17-9*, 6130, Eidolon) Eidolon Studio.

— Shadow World Atlas: Encyclopedia Kulthea. 3rd rev. ed. (Shadow World Sourcebooks Ser.). (Illus.). 200p. 1999. pap. 30.00 (*1-883716-21-7*, 6003, Eidolon) Eidolon Studio.

— Shadow World GM Screen. (Shadow World Sourcebks.). (Illus.). 32p. 1998. pap. 12.00 (*1-883716-22-5*, 6004, Eidolon) Eidolon Studio.

Amtmann, Hans H. The Vanishing Paperclips America's Aerospace Secret. Hitchcock, thomas H., ed. LC 86-62375. (Illus.). 128p. 1988. 29.95 (*0-914144-35-9*) Monogram Aviation.

Amtoft, Torben. Type & Effect Systems: Behaviors for Concurrency. 1999. 48.00 (*1-86094-154-0*) World Scientific Pub.

***Amtrup, J. W.** Incremental Speech Translation. LC 99-56375. (Lecture Notes in Computer Science Ser.: Vol. 1735). xv, 200p. 1999. pap. 45.00 (*3-540-66753-9*) Spr-Verlag.

Amundsen, Christian D. Illumination. 120p. 1999. pap. 12.95 (*1-887472-53-3*) Sunstar Pubng.

— Insights from the Secrets Teachings of Jesus: The Gospel of Thomas. 336p. 1999. pap. text 18.95 (*1-887472-57-6*) Sunstar Pubng.

Amundsen, Darrel W. Medicine, Society, & Faith in the Ancient & Medieval Worlds. LC 95-11759. 368p. 1995. text 42.50 (*0-8018-5109-2*) Johns Hopkins.

Amundsen, Darrel W., jt. auth. see Larson, Edward J.

Amundsen, Darrel W., jt. ed. see Numbers, Ronald L.

Amundsen, Hyrum. How to Terminate Income Taxes, Welfare, Government Debt & Prosper. 84p. 1998. pap. 12.00 (*1-57502-890-5*, PO2449) Morris Pubng.

***Amundsen, Janet.** Fly, the Poet. (Premiere Ser.). vii, 117p. 2000. pap. 16.95 (*0-9678610-0-4*) MindFire Pr.

Amundsen, Michael. Using Visual InterDev. 1998. pap. text 29.99 (*0-7897-1640-2*) Que.

Amundsen, Michael & Smith, Curtis. Teach Yourself Database Programming with Visual Basic 5 in 21 Days. 2nd ed. LC 96-71197. 1080p. 1997. 45.00 (*0-672-31018-X*) Sams.

Amundsen, Michael & Warren, Susan. Practical Visual InterDev 6. 750p. 1999. pap. 29.99 (*0-7897-2143-0*) Que.

***Amundsen, Mike.** Teach Yourself Database Programming with Visual InterDev in 21 Days. (Teach Yourself . . . in 21 Days Ser.). 700p. 1999. pap. 34.99 (*0-672-31563-7*) Sams.

Amundsen, Mike. Teach Yourself Visual Sourcesafe in 21 Days. 1997. 29.99 (*1-57521-332-X*) Sams.

Amundsen, Roald E. The North West Passage: Being the Record of a Voyage of Exploration of the Ship Gjoa 1903-1907, 2 vols., Set. LC 74-5824. reprint ed. 87.50 (*0-404-11625-6*) AMS Pr.

Amundson, Kristen. Brush up Your Study Skills: Tips for Students & Parents. 28p. 1995. pap. 3.50 (*0-87652-214-2*, 021-00521) Am Assn Sch Admin.

— High-Skill, High-Wage Jobs. Ries, Eric, ed. 135p. (Orig.). 1998. pap. text 19.95 (*0-89514-000-4*) ACTE.

Amundson, Kristen. Telling the Truth about America's Public Schools. 20p. (Orig.). 1996. pap. 5.00 (*0-87652-224-X*, 021-0580) Am Assn Sch Admin.

Amundson, Kristen J. Destination: Kyrgyzstan (study Guide) 80p. 1996. pap. 11.00 (*0-16-063409-1*) USGPO.

Amundson, Kristen J. Learning by Doing: How School Districts Are Preparing Students for the New American Workplace. (NSBA Best Practices Ser.). 82p. (Orig.). 1994. pap. 15.00 (*0-88364-189-5*, 04-113) Natl Sch Boards.

— Link-Up - A Resource Directory: Interagency Collaborations to Help Children Achieve. (NSBA Best Practices Ser.). (Orig.). 1991. pap. 15.00 (*0-88364-150-X*, 04-109) Natl Sch Boards.

— Restructuring Reform & Reality: What School Districts Are Really Doing. (NSBA Best Practices Ser.). 79p. 1993. pap. 15.00 (*0-88364-175-5*, 04-112) Natl Sch Boards.

Amundson, Kristen J., et al. Becoming a Better Board Member: A Guide to Effective School Board Service. 2nd rev. ed. (Illus.). 325p. (Orig.). 1996. pap. 35.00 (*0-88364-115-1*, 01-103) Natl Sch Boards.

***Amundson, Mavis.** The Lady of the Lake. (Illus.). 40p. 2000. pap. 5.95 (*0-9610910-6-1*) Western Gull Pub.

Amundson, Mavis, ed. Sturdy Folk: Personal Accounts of Life & Work on the Olympic Peninsula. 130p. (Orig.). 1995. pap. 9.95 (*0-9610910-2-9*) Western Gull Pub.

Amundson, Patricia A., ed. see Carpenter, Diana Lynn.

Amundson, Ronald, et al, eds. Factors of Soil Formation: A Fiftieth Anniversary Retrospective: Proceedings of a Symposium. LC 93-41400. (Special Publications: No. 33). 160p. 1994. pap. 15.00 (*0-89118-804-5*) Soil Sci Soc Am.

Amurskii, G. I., et al. Remote Sensing Methods in Studying Tectonic Fractures in Oil- & Gas-Bearing Formations. Rao, N. Venkat, tr. from RUS. (Russian Translation Ser.: No. 86). (Illus.). 164p. (C). 1991. text 78.00 (*90-6191-989-4*, Pub. by A A Balkema) Ashgate Pub Co.

Amusia, M. Y. Atomic Photoeffect. LC 90-6700. (Physics of Atoms & Molecules Ser.). (Illus.). 328p. (C). 1990. text 110.00 (*0-306-43548-9*, Kluwer Plenum) Kluwer Academic.

Amusia, M. Ya & Chernysheva, L. V. Computation of Atomic Structure & Processes. Pougovikin, A. P., tr. from RUS. LC 97-9082. (Illus.). 260p. 1997. 170.00 (*0-7503-0229-1*) IOP Pub.

Amussen, Susan D. An Ordered Society: Gender & Class in Early Modern England. LC 93-38125. 1994. pap. 19.50 (*0-231-09979-7*) Col U Pr.

Amussen, Susan D. & Kishlansky, Mark A., eds. Political Culture & Cultural Politics in Early Modern England: Essays Presented to David Underdown. LC 95-3505. 1995. text 69.95 (*0-7190-4695-5*, Pub. by Manchester Univ Pr) St Martin.

Amussen, Susan D. & Seeff, Adele F., eds. Attending to Early Modern Women. LC 97-47037. (Illus.). 344p. 1999. 55.00 (*0-87413-650-4*) U Delaware Pr.

Amuzegar. Managing the Oil Wealth: OPEC's Windfalls & Pitfalls. 256p. 2000. text 65.00 (*1-86064-292-6*, Pub. by I B T) St Martin.

Amuzegar, Hooshang, tr. see Behrangi, Samad.

Amuzegar, Jahangir. Dynamics of the Iranian Revolution: The Pahlavis' Triumph & Tragedy. LC 90-44904. 367p. (C). 1991. pap. text 24.95 (*0-7914-0732-2*) State U NY Pr.

— Dynamics of the Iranian Revolution: The Pahlavis' Triumph & Tragedy. LC 90-44904. 367p. (C). 1991. text 74.50 (*0-7914-0731-4*) State U NY Pr.

— Iran: An Economic Profile. LC 77-5286. 1977. 6.00 (*0-916808-14-9*) Mid East Inst.

— Iran's Economy under the Islamic Republic. 288p. (C). 1994. text 65.00 (*1-85043-603-7*, Pub. by I B T) St Martin.

— Oil Exporters' Economic Development in an Interdependent World. (Occasional Paper Ser.: No. 18). 99p. 1983. pap. 5.00 (*1-55775-078-5*) Intl Monetary.

Amuzegar, Jahangir & Fekrat, M. Ali. Iran: Economic Development under Dualistic Conditions. LC 79-153044. (Publications of the Center for Middle Eastern Studies: No. 7). 190p. reprint ed. pap. 58.90 (*0-8357-8926-8*, 205678900085) Bks Demand.

***Amy, Douglas J.** Behind the Ballot Box: A Citizen's Guide to Voting Systems. 2000. write for info. (*0-275-96585-6*); pap. write for info. (*0-275-96586-4*) Greenwood.

Amy, Douglas J. Proportional Representation: The Case for a Better Election System. LC 97-68972. (Illus.). 50p. (Orig.). 1997. pap. 2.95 (*0-9659456-3-4*) Crescent St Pr.

— Real Choices - New Voices: The Case for Proportional Representation Elections in the United States. LC 92-46631. (C). 1993. 46.00 (*0-231-08154-5*) Col U Pr.

— Real Choices - New Voices: The Case for Proportional Representation Elections in the United States. 278p. 1995. pap. 18.50 (*0-231-08155-3*) Col U Pr.

Amy, Ernest F. Text of Chaucer's Legend of Good Women. LC 65-21088. (Studies in Chaucer: No. 6). 1969. reprint ed. lib. bdg. 75.00 (*0-8383-0502-4*) M S G Haskell Hse.

***Amy, Gary L. & AWWA Research Foundation Staff.** Arsenic Treatability Options & Evaluation of Residuals Management Issues LC 99-35885. 1999. write for info. (*1-58321-003-2*) Am Water Wks Assn.

Amy, Gary L. & Knocke, William R., eds. Register of Environmental Engineering Graduate Programs. 5th ed. LC 84-70854. 626p. 1984. pap. 30.00 (*0-917567-00-5*) Assn Environ Eng.

Amy, Gary L. & Siddiqui, Mohamed S. Strategies to Control Bromate & Bromide. LC 97-44149. 1998. write for info. (*0-89867-948-6*) American Waterways Shipyard Conference.

Amy, Gary L., et al. Formation & Control of Brominated Ozone By-Products. LC 97-173945. (Illus.). 72p. 1997. pap. 112.00 (*0-89867-892-7*, 90714) Am Water Wks Assn.

Amy, Gary L., jt. ed. see Minear, Roger A.

Amy, Lawrence T. Automation Systems for Control & Data Acquisition. (Resources for Measurement & Control Ser.). Orig. Title: Computer Automation: A Practical Approach for Instrument Control & Data Acquisition. 245p. 1992. 76.00 (*1-55617-390-3*) ISA.

Amy, Fenny S. & Haldeman, Dana L. Microbiology of the Terrestrial Deep Subsurface. LC 96-82013. 368p. 1997. boxed set 129.95 (*0-8493-8362-5*) CRC Pr.

Amyes, Tim. Audio Post-Production in Video & Film. 2nd ed. LC 99-207308. 224p. 2000. pap. text 37.95 (*0-240-51542-0*, Focal) Buttrwrth-Heinemann.

— The Technique of Audio Post-Production in Video & Film. (Illus.). 208p. 1990. pap. text 34.95 (*0-240-51363-0*, Focal) Buttrwrth-Heinemann.

Amyett, Paddy. Real Estate Marketing & Sales. 388p. (C). 2001. 33.33 (*0-13-442229-5*, Macmillan Coll) P-H.

Amylase Research Society of Japan Staff. Enzyme Chemistry & Molecular Biology of Amylases & Related Enzymes. 224p. 1994. lib. bdg. 149.00 (*0-8493-2904-3*, 2904) CRC Pr.

Amylase Research Society of Japan Staff, ed. Handbook of Amylases & Related Enzymes: Their Sources, Isolation Methods, Properties & Applications. (Illus.). 288p. 1988. 127.50 (*0-08-036141-2*, Pergamon Pr) Elsevier.

Amyot, J. R. Hovercraft Technology, Economics & Applications. 770p. 1990. 311.75 (*0-444-88152-2*) Elsevier.

Amyot, Joseph R., jt. auth. see Dukkipati, Rao V.

Amyuni, Mona T. Tayeb Salih's "Season of Migration to the North" A Casebook. 174p. (Orig.). 1986. pap. text 18.00 (*0-8156-6075-8*, Pub. by Am U Beirut) Syracuse U Pr.

Amyx, D. A. Corinthian Vase-Painting of the Archaic Period, 3 Vol., Vol. Set. (California Studies in the History of Art: No. XXV). 1989. 350.00 (*0-520-03166-0*, Pub. by U CA Pr) Cal Prin Full Svc.

Amyx, D. A. & Lawrence, Patricia. Archaic Corinthian Pottery & the Anaploga Well. LC 75-4551. (Corinth Ser.: Vol. 7, Pt. 2). (Illus.). xvi, 177p. 1976. 40.00 (*0-87661-072-6*) Am Sch Athens.

— Studies in Archaic Corinthian Vase Painting. LC 96-43204. (Hesperia Supplement Ser.: No. 28). xi, 161p. 1996. pap. 65.00 (*0-87661-528-0*) Am Sch Athens.

Amyx, James W., et al. Petroleum Reservoir Engineering Physical Properties. (C). 1960. 116.25 (*0-07-001600-3*) McGraw.

Amzallag, Claude, ed. Automation in Fatigue & Fracture: Testing & Analysis, STP 1231. LC 94-36845. (Special Technical Publication Ser.: Vol. 1231). (Illus.). 670p. 1994. text 119.00 (*0-8031-1985-2*, STP1231) ASTM.

Amzallag, Claude, et al, eds. Low-Cycle Fatigue & Life Prediction- STP 770. 646p. 1982. 60.00 (*0-8031-0713-7*, STP770) ASTM.

An Asterisk (*) at the beginning of an entry indicates that the title is appearing for the first time.

An, Byong-Ro. Die Religiositat der Koreaner in Deutschland. (Jahrbuch fur Religionskultur Ser.: Bd. 8). (GER., Illus.). 203p. 1997. 42.95 (*3-631-30660-1*) P Lang Pubng.

An, Chae, et al. Model-Based Control of a Robot Manipulator. (Artificial Intelligence Ser.). 248p. 1988. 42.50 (*0-262-01102-6*) MIT Pr.

An-che, Li. History of Tibetan Religion: A Study in the Field. LC 95-203861. 267p. 1994. pap. 18.95 (*7-80005-225-7*, Pub. by New World Pr) China Bks.

***An Chen.** Restructing Political Power in China: Alliances & Opposition, 1978-1998. LC 99-11103. 300p. 1999. 59.95 (*1-55587-842-3*) L Rienner.

An, Howard. Synopsis of Orthopedics. (Illus.). 480p. 1991. text 66.00 (*0-86577-383-1*) Thieme Med Pubs.

An, Howard S. Principles & Techniques of Spine Surgery. LC 97-5525. (Illus.). 1452p. 1997. 150.00 (*0-683-30260-4*) Lppncott W & W.

— Surgery of the Cervical Spine. (Illus.). 350p. 1994. 150.00 (*0-683-00128-0*) Lppncott W & W.

— Synopsis of Spine Surgery. LC 97-747. 400p. 1997. pap. 44.95 (*0-683-18097-5*) Lppncott W & W.

An, Howard S. & Cotter, Jerome M. Spinal Instrumentation. (Illus.). 496p. 1992. 165.00 (*0-683-00127-2*) Lppncott W & W.

An, Howard S., jt. auth. see Balderston, Richard A.

An, Jiang. Chinese Word Book. LC 89-82132. (Rainbow Book Ser.). (CHI & ENG.). 106p. 1990. pap. 19.95 incl. audio (*1-880188-58-9*) Bess Pr.

— Chinese Word Book. LC 89-82132. (Rainbow Bk.). (CHI., Illus.). 106p. 1995. 11.95 (*1-57306-007-0*) Bess Pr.

An, Jung-Hee. Effects of the Text Structure-Based Reading Strategy on the Comprehension of EFL Classroom Text: An Empirical Investigation of the Effectiveness of Schemata-Based Reading Instruction for the Students of English as a Foreign Language. LC 92-25682. (European University Studies Anglo-Saxon Languages & Literature: Ser. 14, Vol. 253). VI, 228p. 1992. 45.00 (*3-631-45042-7*) P Lang Pubng.

An, K. N., et al, eds. Biomechanics of the Wrist Joint. (Illus.). 192p. 1991. 80.95 (*0-387-97674-4*) Spr-Verlag.

An Lim, Jaime L. Literature & Politics: The Colonial Experience in Nine Philippine Novels. 182p. (Orig.). 1993. pap. 16.50 (*971-10-0478-X*, Pub. by New Day Pub) Cellar.

— Trios. LC 98-947567. vii, 69p. 1998. write for info. (*971-542-151-2*) U of Philippines Pr.

An, Margaret, jt. auth. see Corrigan, Mike.

An-Min Li, et al. Global Affine Differential Geometry of Hypersurfaces. LC 93-20766. (Expositions in Mathematics Ser.: No. 11). xiv, 328p. (C). 1993. lib. bdg. 104.95 (*3-11-012769-5*) De Gruyter.

An, Myoung, jt. auth. see Tolimieri, Richard.

An-Na'Im, Abdullahi A. Human Rights in Cross-Cultural Perspectives: A Quest for Concensus. 1995. pap. 17.95 (*0-8122-1568-0*) U of Pa Pr.

An-Na'Im, Abdullahi A., ed. Proselytization & Communal Self-Determination in Africa. rev. ed. LC 99-37929. (Religion & Human Rights Ser.). 400p. 1999. pap. 25.00 (*1-57075-261-3*) Orbis Bks.

An-Na'im, Abdullahi A. & Deng, Francis M, eds. Human Rights in Africa: Cross-Cultural Perspectives. 399p. 1990. 39.95 (*0-8157-1796-2*); pap. 18.95 (*0-8157-1795-4*) Brookings.

An-Naqshbandi, Shaykh M. Divine Kingdom. 112p. (Orig.). 1995. pap. 9.95 (*0-934905-28-2*) Kazi Pubns.

— Divine Sources. (Mercy Oceans Ser.). 104p. (Orig.). 1995. pap. 9.95 (*0-934905-43-6*) Kazi Pubns.

An-Naqshbandi, Shaykh M., et al. Mystical Secrets of the Last Days. LC 96-161285. 144p. 1995. pap. 12.50 (*0-934905-27-4*) Kazi Pubns.

An-Nawawi, Shaykh M. Forty Hadith of an-Nawawi. 127p. (Orig.). 1982. pap. 7.50 (*0-933511-22-1*) Kazi Pubns.

— Forty Hadith Qudsi. Ibrahim, E. & Davies, Denys J., trs. 151p. (Orig.). 1986. pap. 8.50 (*0-933511-21-3*) Kazi Pubns.

An, Ok-Sun. Compassion & Benevolence: A Comparative Study of Early Guddhist & Classical Confucian Ethics, Vol. 31. LC 97-5219. (Asian Thought & Culture Ser.). X, 180p. (C). 1998. text 42.95 (*0-8204-3801-4*) P Lang Pubng.

An, Sung-Po. Die Vor-AG. XVII, 209p. 1997. 44.95 (*3-631-32396-4*) P Lang Pubng.

An, Tai-Sung. North Korea: A Political Handbook. LC 83-16307. (Illus.). 294p. (C). 1983. lib. bdg. 45.00 (*0-8420-2205-8*) Scholarly Res Inc.

***An, Yuehuei H. & Draughn, Robert A.** Mechanical Testing of Bone & the Bone-Implant Interface LC 99-36531. 1999. write for info. (*0-8493-0266-8*) CRC Pr.

An, Yuehuei H. & Friedman, Richard J. Animal Models in Orthopedic Research. LC 98-39579. 624p. 1998. boxed set 139.95 (*0-8493-2115-8*) CRC Pr.

***An, Yuehuei H. & Friedman, Richard J., eds.** Handbook of Bacterial Adhesion: Principles, Methods & Applications. 672p. 2000. 135.00 (*0-89603-794-0*) Humana.

Ana, Julio De Santa, see De Santa Ana, Julio, ed.

Anaand, N., jt. auth. see Harman, G.

***Anabtawi, Jehanne, ed.** Ourselves & Others: Perspectives on Morality from East & West. 512p. 2000. pap. text 43.95 (*1-889119-51-2*) Seven Bridges.

Anabtawi, Sami N. Palestinian Higher Education in the West Bank & the Gaza Strip: A Critical Assessment. 250p. 1987. text 45.00 (*0-7103-0119-7*) Routledge.

Anacker, C. Alan. Guide to Achievement & Success Philosophy Books. (Orig.). 1990. pap. 8.95 (*0-685-45542-4*) Ref Guide Bks.

Anacker, Christopher A. Exhaustive Outline of the Entire Bible. LC 81-90358. (Orig.). 1981. pap. 8.95 (*0-9607942-0-4*) Ref Guide Bks.

Anacker, Stefan. The Seven Works of Vasubandhu: The Buddhist Psychological Doctor. (Religion of Asia Ser.: No. 4). 491p. 1986. reprint ed. 24.00 (*81-208-0203-9*, Pub. by Motilal Bnarsidass) S Asia.

Anadon, Jose, jt. auth. see Durand, Jose.

Anadon, Jose, ed. see Durand, Jose.

Anadon, P., et al. Lacustrine Facies Analysis. (International Association of Sedimentologists Special Publication Ser.: No. 13). (Illus.). 328p. 1991. 95.00 (*0-632-03149-2*) Blackwell Sci.

Anaejionu, Paul, et al, eds. Space & Society - Challenges & Choices, April 14-16, 1982, University of Texas at Austin. (Science & Technology Ser.: Vol. 59). (Illus.). 442p. 1984. 55.00 (*0-87703-204-1*, Am Astronaut Soc); pap. 35.00 (*0-87703-205-X*, Am Astronaut Soc) Univelt Inc.

Anagnastopoulas, P. Flow-Induced Vibration: Theory & Practice. (Advances in Fluid Mechanics Ser.). 250p. 2000. 119.00 (*1-85312-644-6*, No. 6446) Computational Mech MA.

Anagnastopoulos, P., jt. ed. see Brebbia, Carlos A.

Anagnoson, J. Theodore. StataQuest 4 Text Companion Windows Version. 2nd ed. (Statistics Software). 1995. pap. 11.95 (*0-534-26547-2*) Wadsworth Pub.

— Stataquest 4 Text Companion Dos Version. 2nd ed. (Statistics Software). 1996. pap. 16.95 (*0-534-26548-0*) Wadsworth Pub.

— StatQuest Text Companion: DOS. (Statistical Software Ser.). 1994. pap. 7.50 incl. 3.5 hd (*0-534-23680-4*) Wadsworth Pub.

Anagnoson, J. Theodore & DeLeon, Richard E. StataQuest. 253p. 1994. pap. 18.75 incl. 3.5 hd (*0-534-23677-4*) Wadsworth Pub.

— Stataquest Text Companion For Windows 95. (Statistics Software). (C). 1997. pap. 11.95 (*0-534-52138-X*) Wadsworth Pub.

— StataQuest 4. (Statistics Software Ser.). (C). 1997. pap. 36.95 (*0-534-52137-1*) Wadsworth Pub.

— StataQuest 4. 2nd ed. (C). 1996. pap. text, mass mkt. 36.95 incl. 3.5 hd (*0-534-26545-6*); pap. text, mass mkt. 37.95 incl. disk (*0-534-26546-4*) Wadsworth Pub.

Anagnost, Ann S. National Past-Times: Narrative, Representation, & Power In Modern China. LC 96-6609. (Body, Commodity, Text Ser.). (Illus.). 272p. 1997. pap. text 16.95 (*0-8223-1969-1*); lib. bdg. 49.95 (*0-8223-1961-6*) Duke.

Anagnostakis, Manolis. The Target: Selected Poems. Friar, Kimon, tr. LC 80-81164. (ENG & GRE.). 135p. (Orig.). 1980. pap. text 9.00 (*0-918618-16-9*) Pella Pub.

Anagnostatos, G. S., ed. Atomic & Nuclear Clusters: Proceedings of the 2nd International Conference Held at Santorini, Greece, June 28-July 2, 1993. LC 95-12998. 320p. 1995. 129.95 (*3-540-59160-5*) Spr-Verlag.

Anagnostidis, K., et al, eds. Cyanophyta (Cyanobacteria). Morphology, Taxonomy, Ecology: Proceedings of the Symposium of the International Ass'n for Cyanophyte Research, 10th, Greece, 1986. (Algological Studies: No. 50-53). (Illus.). 584p. 1988. pap. text 215.00 (*0-945345-11-9*) Lubrecht & Cramer.

Anagnoston, Taki N. Surviving the AIDS Plague. Hewitt, Carla, ed. (Illus.). 340p. (Orig.). (C). 1991. pap. text 14.95 (*0-922356-44-0*) Amer West Pubs.

Anagnostoplulos, Paul C. Writing Real Programs in DCL. 1998. pap. 44.95 (*1-55558-191-9*) DEC.

Anagnostopoulos, Athan. Geotechnical Engineering of Hard Soils, Vol. 1. ed. 1993. 104.00 (*90-5410-345-0*) Ashgate Pub Co.

— Geotechnical Engineering of Hard Soils, Vol. 3. ed. 1993. 104.00 (*90-5410-347-7*) Ashgate Pub Co.

— Geotechnical Engineering of Hard Soils, Vol.2. ed. 1993. 104.00 (*90-5410-346-9*) Ashgate Pub Co.

Anagnostopoulos, Athan, ed. Geotechnical Engineering of Hard Soils Soft Rocks, 3 vols. 1994. 252.00 (*90-5410-344-2*, Pub. by A A Balkema) Ashgate Pub Co.

Anagnostopoulos, Georgios. Aristotle on the Goals & Exactness of Ethics. 474p. 1994. 65.00 (*0-520-08125-0*, Pub. by U CA Pr) Cal Prin Full Svc.

Anagnostopoulos, P. & Brebbia, C. A., eds. Water Pollution V: Modelling, Measuring & Prediction, Vol. 1. (Progress in Water Resources Ser.: Vol. 1). 608p. 1999. 299.00 (*1-85312-685-3*, 6853) Computational Mech MA.

Anagnostopoulos, Paul G. VAX-VMS: Writing Real Programs in DCL. (VAX Users Ser.). 409p. (Orig.). 1989. pap. text 42.95 (*1-55558-023-8*, EY C168E-DP, Digital DEC) Buttrwrth-Heinemann.

Anagnostopoulos, S. A., jt. ed. see Beskos, D. E.

Anagnostopoulou, Elena, et al, eds. Materials on Left Dislocation. LC 97-4489. (Linguistik Aktuell/Linguistics Today Ser.: Vol. 14). viii, 349p. 1997. lib. bdg. 86.00 (*1-55619-233-9*) J Benjamins Pubng Co.

Anagos, Gus, jt. auth. see Mitroff, Ian I.

Anahid. Save More So You Can Spend More: Hundreds of Tips to Save Thousands of Dollars. 168p. (Orig.). 1996. pap. 14.95 (*0-918751-47-0*) Delta Pr.

Anahory, Sam. Data Warehousing in the Real World. LC 97-20862. 368p. (C). 1997. 54.95 (*0-201-17519-3*) Addison-Wesley.

Anai-Otong, Deborah. Psychiatric Nursing: Biological & Behavioral Concepts. LC 94-25346. (Illus.). 1008p. 1995. text 51.00 (*0-7216-3778-7*, W B Saunders Co) Harcrt Hlth Sci Grp.

Anakiev, Aleksander & Anaklev, Maya. Lotto Winning Systems: How to Play the Lottery Smartly & Win. 128p. (Orig.). 1987. pap. 12.95 (*0-318-23367-3*) LWS Pub.

Anaklev, Maya, jt. auth. see Anakiev, Aleksander.

Anakwa, W. K., ed. Computer Applications in Industry & Engineering (CAINE-94), 7th International Conference, December 15-17, 1994, San Diego, California, U.S.A: CAINE-94, Dec. 15-17, 1994, San Diego, CA. (Conference Proceedings Ser.). 190p. (C). 1994. write for info. (*1-880843-10-2*) Int Soc Comp App.

Analoak, Gertrude, tr. see Ellanna, Frank.

Analog & Isaac Asimov's Science Fiction Magazine E. Writing Science Fiction & Fantasy. LC 92-41283 viii, 264p. 1993. pap. 9.95 (*0-312-08926-0*) St Martin

Analog Device Staff. Analog Signal Processing Handbook. 750p. (C). 1900. 40.00 (*0-13-033374-3*, Macmillan Coll) P-H.

Analog Devices Engineering Staff. Amplifier Applications Guide. (Analog Devices Technical Reference Bks.). (Illus.). 648p. 1992. pap. 20.00 (*0-916550-10-9*) Analog Devices.

— Mixed-Signal Design Seminar. Kester, Walt, ed. (Analog Devices Technical Reference Bks.). (Illus.). 392p (Orig.). 1991. pap. text 22.00 (*0-916550-08-7*) Analog Devices.

Analog Devices, Inc. Staff Computer Products Div. ADSP-21000 Family Application Handbook Vol. 1. (Analog Devices Technical Reference Bks.). (Illus.). 358p. (Orig.). 1994. pap. 22.00 (*0-916550-14-1*) Analog Devices.

Analog Magazine Staff. Analog: The Best of Science Fiction. 1994. 11.98 (*0-88365-637-X*) Galahad Bks.

Analoui, Farhad. Senior Managers & Their Effectiveness. 176p. 1997. text 59.95 (*1-85972-041-2*, Pub. by Avebry) Ashgate Pub Co.

Analoui, Farhad, ed. Effective Human Resource Development: A Challenge for Developing Countries. LC HF5549.E423 1997. 230p. 1998. text 65.95 (*1-84014-854-3*, Pub. by Ashgate Pub) Ashgate Pub Co.

— Human Resource Management Issues in Developing Countries. LC 98-72802. 206p. 1998. text 59.95 (*1-84014-143-3*, Pub. by Ashgate Pub) Ashgate Pub Co.

— The Realities of Managing Development Projects. 306p. 1994. 77.95 (*1-85628-514-6*, Pub. by Avebry) Ashgate Pub Co.

Analysis Group Staff, jt. auth. see Greenberg-Lake Staff.

Analytical Chemistry, Washington Staff. Milestones in Analytical Chemistry. LC 93-51082. 1994. 74.95 (*0-8412-2855-8*) Am Chemical.

Analytical Sciences Corp-Technical Staff. Applied Optimal Estimation. Gelb, Arthur, ed. LC 74-1604. (Illus.). 382p. 1974. pap. text 30.00 (*0-262-57048-3*) MIT Pr.

***Analytis, G.** Developmental Assessment of RELAP5/MOD3.1 with Separate- Effect & Integral Test Experiments: Model Changes & Options. 45p. 1998. pap. 4.00 (*0-16-063228-5*) USGPO.

— Implementation & Assessment of Improved Modes & Options in TRAC-BF1. 46p. 1998. pap. 4.00 (*0-16-063227-7*) USGPO.

Anami. Meditation Magic: A Course in Freedom & Dreaming. LC 96-910553. (Illus.). 240p. (Orig.) pap. 15.00 (*0-9635756-0-0*) Beyond Bks.

Anamika, Roy. Amareavatei Steupa. LC 94-905316. 1994. write for info. (*81-7320-016-5*) S Asia.

Ananasso, F. & Vatalaro, F. K., eds. Mobile & Personal Satellite Communications: Proceedings of the 1st European Workshop on Mobile-Personal Satcoms (EMPS 94) LC 95-2516. 348p. 1996. 59.00 (*3-540-19933-0*) Spr-Verlag.

Ananasso, F., jt. auth. see Vatalaro, F. K.

Anand. Anand Law of the Sea. 1981. lib. bdg. 121.50 (*90-247-2366-3*, Pub. by M Nijhoff) Kluwer Academic.

Anand & Sherrif, K. M. Desert Shadows. LC 98-908480. 270 p. 1998. 19.50 (*0-14-027824-9*) Viking Penguin.

Anand, A. & Sastri, S. Law of Torts. (C). 1990. 175.00 (*0-89771-256-0*) St Mut.

Anand, A., jt. auth. see Seithi, S.

Anand, Anita, jt. ed. see Foster, John W.

Anand, Ashok K. Buddhism in India. (C). 1996. 19.00 (*81-212-0506-9*, Pub. by Gian Publng Hse) S Asia.

Anand, C. I. A Critical Survey & Indepth Commentary on Constitutional Law & History of Government of India. (C). 1990. 238.00 (*0-89771-211-0*) St Mut.

Anand, C. L. Equality, Justice & Reverse Discrimination in India. 472p. 1987. 54.00 (*0-8364-2019-5*, Pub. by Mittal Pubs Dist) S Asia.

Anand, C. L., et al. The Teacher & Education in Emerging Indian Society. 358p. 1983. 16.95 (*0-318-36832-3*) Asia Bk Corp.

Anand, Christpoh. Harmonic Morphisms Harmonic, 001. LC 99-41247. 328p. 1999. per. 59.95 (*1-58488-032-5*) CRC Pr.

Anand, D. Krishna: The Living God of Braj. (C). 1992. 98.00 (*81-7017-280-2*, Pub. by Abhinav) S Asia.

Anand, D. K. Introduction to Control Systems. LC 72-12834. (C). 1984. text 105.00 (*0-08-030002-2*, Pergamon Pr); pap. text 40.00 (*0-08-030001-4*, Pergamon Pr) Elsevier.

Anand, D. K. & Zmood, R. B. Introduction to Control Systems. 3rd ed. LC 94-44621. (Illus.). 796p. 1995. pap. text 49.95 (*0-7506-2298-9*, Prgamon Press) Buttrwrth-Heinemann.

Anand, Davinder K. & Cunniff, Patrick F. Engineering Mechanics: Dynamics. 450p. (C). 1984. teacher ed. write for info. (*0-318-57284-2*, H82761) P-H.

— Engineering Mechanics: Statics. 450p. (C). 1984. teacher ed. write for info. (*0-318-57283-4*, H82779) P-H.

— Engineering Mechanics: Statics & Dynamics. 900p. 1984. teacher ed. write for info. (*0-318-57282-6*) P-H.

Anand, I. N. Modern English Hindi Dictionary. (C) 1996. reprint ed. 20.00 (*0-685-50024-1*, Pub. by M Manoharial) S Asia.

Anand, I. N., ed. The Modern English-Hindi Dictionary. 1136p. 1991. 57.50 (*81-215-0461-9*, Pub. by M Manoharial) Coronet Bks.

Anand, Inder S., et al, eds. Pathophysiology & Pharmacology of Heart Disease: Proceedings of the Symposium Held at Chandigarh, India, Feb. 1988. (Developments in Cardiovascular Medicine Ser.). (C). 1989. text 131.50 (*0-7923-0367-9*) Kluwer Academic.

Anand, K. J. S. & McGrath, Patrick J., eds. Pain in Neonates. LC 92-48284. (Pain Research & Clinical Management Ser.: Vol. 5). 356p. 1993. 239.50 (*0-444-81226-1*) Elsevier.

— Pain in Neonates. (Pain Research & Clinical Management Ser.: Vol. 5). 356p. 1995. pap. 92.00 (*0-444-82238-0*) Elsevier.

***Anand, K. J. S., et al.** Pain in Neonates. 2nd rev. enl. ed. LC 99-53891. (Pain Research & Clinical Management Ser.). 1999. write for info. (*0-444-50349-8*) Elsevier.

Anand, Kewal K. Indian Philosophy: The Concept of Karma. 396p. 1982. 24.95 (*0-940500-91-4*, Pub. by Bharat Vidya) Asia Bk Corp.

Anand Kumar, T. C., ed. see International Primatological Society Staff.

Anand Kumar, T. C., ed. see International Symposium on Neuroendocrine Regulation Staff.

Anand, Margo. The Art of Sexual Ecstasy: The Path of Sacred Sexuality for Western Lovers. LC 89-35137. (Illus.). 464p. 1990. pap. 19.95 (*0-87477-581-7*, Tarcher Putnam) Putnam Pub Group.

— The Art of Sexual Magic: Cultivating Sexual Energy to Transform Your Life. (Illus.). 384p. 1996. pap. 19.95 (*0-87477-840-9*, Tarcher Putnam) Putnam Pub Group.

Anand, Margot. The Art of Everyday Ecstasy: The Seven Tantric Keys for Bringing Passion, Spirit & Joy into Every Part of Your Life. LC 98-4872. 320p. 1998. 25.00 (*0-7679-0164-9*) Broadway BDD.

— The Art of Everyday Ecstasy: The Seven Tantric Keys for Bringing Passion, Spirit & Joy into Every Part of Your Life. 320p. 1999. reprint ed. pap. 13.00 (*0-7679-0199-1*) Broadway BDD.

***Anand, Margot.** Sexual Ecstasy: The Art of Orgasm. LC 00-23422. 2000. pap. 11.00 (*1-58542-028-X*, Tarcher Putnam) Putnam Pub Group.

Anand, Mulk-Raj. Anthology of Dalit Literature. Zelliot, Eleanor, ed. (C). 1992. 14.00 (*81-212-0419-4*, Pub. by Gian Publng Hse) S Asia.

— Conversations in Bloomsbury. LC 96-900239. 192p. 1995. pap. text 11.95 (*0-19-563678-3*) OUP.

— Madhubani Painting. (Illus.). 60p. 1982. 37.95 (*0-318-36343-7*) Asia Bk Corp.

— Pilpali Sahab: The Story of a Big Ego in a Small Body. (C). 1990. text 14.00 (*1-85529-059-6*, Pub. by Arnold Pubs) S Asia.

— Poet-Painter: Paintings by Rabindranath Tagore. (Illus.). 86p. 1992. 18.00 (*1-85127-039-6*, Pub. by Tricolour Bks) Asia Pub Hse.

— Sati. (C). 1989. 21.50 (*81-7018-535-1*, Pub. by Renaiss Publng Hse) S Asia.

— Sword & the Sickle. (C). 1984. 11.00 (*0-8364-2793-9*, Pub. by Arnold Pubs) S Asia.

— Untouchable. (C). 1970. reprint ed. pap. text 6.00 (*0-8364-2848-X*, Pub. by Arnold Pubs) S Asia.

Anand, Mulk Raj, see Raj Anand, Mulk.

***Anand, N.** Indian Freshwater Microalgae. (Illus.). 94p. (C). 1998. 12.50 (*81-211-0156-5*, Pub. by Bishen Singh) Lubrecht & Cramer.

Anand, N., ed. Approaches to Desgin & Synthesis of Antiparasitic Drugs, Vol. 25. LC 97-16035. (Pharmacochemistry Library: 25). 524p. 1997. 244.00 (*0-444-89476-4*) Elsevier.

Anand, N. K. Handbook of Blue-Green Algae (of Rice Fields of South India) (Illus.). 79p. 1990. text 20.00 (*81-211-0024-0*, Pub. by Mahendra Pal Singh) Lubrecht & Cramer.

Anand, N. K., et al, eds. Heat Transfer in Turbulent Flows - 1995 Vol. 1: Proceedings of the ASME International Mechanical Engineering Congress & Exposition, 1995, San Francisco, CA. LC 95-81254. (1995 International Mechanical Engineering Congress & Exposition Ser.: HTD-Vol. 318). 176p. 1995. 74.00 (*0-7918-1752-0*, H01033) ASME.

Anand, Nirmal, jt. auth. see Anand, Raj K.

Anand, Nitya, et al. Art in Organic Synthesis. 2nd ed. LC 87-14762. 448p. 1988. 110.00 (*0-471-88738-2*) Wiley.

Anand, R. P. Cultural Factors in International Relations. 1981. 20.00 (*0-8364-0727-X*, Pub. by Abhinav) S Asia.

— Origin & Development of the Law of the Sea. 1982. lib. bdg. 114.00 (*90-247-2617-4*) Kluwer Academic.

Anand, R. P., et al. Law, Science, & Environment. 1987. 44.00 (*81-7095-003-1*) S Asia.

Anand, Raj K & Anand, Nirmal. Diet for Healthy Living. 65p. (Orig.). 1985. pap. 3.95 (*0-318-04445-5*) Raj Anand.

Anand, Rakesh, ed. Techniques for the Analysis of Complex Genomes. (Illus.). 256p. 1992. 58.00 (*0-12-057620-1*) Acad Pr.

Anand, Rohini. Cultural Competence in Health Care: A Guide for Trainers. xvi, 279p. 1997. 149.95 (*1-885077-60-2*) NMCI Pubns.

— Teaching Skills & Cultural Competency: A Guide for Trainers. 3rd rev. ed. xvi, 255p. 1999. 149.95 (*1-885077-50-5*) NMCI Pubns.

***Anand, Rohini & Shipler, Laura K.** Multicultural Case Studies: Tools for Training. ix, 131p. 1998. 24.95 (*1-885077-70-X*) NMCI Pubns.

***Anand, S.** Medical Textiles ' 99. 208p. 2000. text 170.00 (*1-85573-494-X*, Pub. by Woodhead Pubng) Am Educ Systs.

Anand, S., ed. Medical Textiles 96. 208p. 1996. boxed set 164.95 (*1-85573-317-X*) Technomic.

Anand, S., jt. ed. see Horrocks, A. R.

***Anand, Sarabjot.** Foundations of Data Mining. (C). 2000. pap. text. write for info. (*0-201-39830-3*) Addison-Wesley.

Anand, Sarabot S. & Buchner, Alex G. Decision Support Using Data Mining. (Managment Briefings - Information Technology Ser.). (Illus.). 184p. 1998. pap. 92.50 (*0-273-63269-8*, Pub. by Pitman Pbg) Trans-Atl Phila.

A

An Asterisk (*) at the beginning of an entry indicates that the title is appearing for the first time.

A

Anand, Satish & Kumar, Raj. Dictionary of Biochemistry. 1990. 33.50 (81-7041-272-2, Pub. by Anmol) S Asia.
— Dictionary of Drugs. 1990. 23.00 (81-7041-240-4, Pub. by Anmol) S Asia.
— Dictionary of Physical Chemistry. 1990. 23.50 (81-7041-238-2, Pub. by Anmol) S Asia.

Anand, Satish, jt. auth. see Kumar, Raj.

Anand, Subhadra. National Integration of Sindhis. LC 95-911165. (C). 1996. 27.00 (0-7069-9970-3, Pub. by Vikas) S Asia.

Anand, Subhash. Way of Love: Bhagavata Doctrine of Bhaki. LC 95-911617. 248p. (C). 1996. 33.50 (81-215-0665-4, Pub. by M Manoharial) Coronet Bks.

Anand, Subhash, ed. Advances in Analysis of Structural Masonry. 164p. 1986. 5.00 (0-87262-553-2) Am Soc Civil Eng.
— New Analysis Techniques for Structural Masonry: Proceedings of a Session Held in Conjunction with Structures Congress '85. 130p. 1985. 5.00 (0-87262-481-1) Am Soc Civil Eng.

***Anand, Sudhir.** The Essence of the Hindu Religion: With an Introduction to the Vedas & Yoga. 2000. pap. 12.50 (0-9700929-4-6) ASK.

Anand, Uma, intro. Gods of the Byways: Wayside Shrines from Rajasthan India. (Illus.). 1982. pap. 30.00 (0-905836-28-6, Pub. by Museum Modern Art) St Mut.

Anand, V. K. Conflict in Nagaland. 1981. 18.50 (0-8364-0683-4, Pub. by Chanakya) S Asia.

Anand, Vera. Introduction to Engineering Computer Graphics. (C). 1999. pap. text. write for info. (0-201-87438-5) Addison-Wesley.

Anand, Vera B. Computer Graphics & Geometric Modeling for Engineers. LC 92-36055. 432p. 1993. text 81.95 (0-471-51417-9) Wiley.
— Computer Graphics & Geometric Modeling for Engineers. 4p. 1993. pap. text 135.95 (0-471-59844-5) Wiley.
— Computer Graphics & Geometric Modeling for Engineers. 432p. 1996. pap. 61.95 (0-471-15731-7) Wiley.

Anand, Vijay K. & Panje, William R., eds. Practical Endoscopic Sinus Surgery. LC 92-49884. (Illus.). 186p. 1992. text 129.00 (0-07-105419-7) McGraw-Hill HPD.

***Anand, Vishy.** My Best Games of Chess. 1998. pap. write for info. (1-901983-00-5, Pub. by Gambit) BHB Intl.

Anand, Yogindra N., ed. Seismic Experience Data-Nuclear & Other Plants: Proceedings of a Session Sponsored by the Structural Division. 85p. 1985. 5.00 (0-87262-501-X) Am Soc Civil Eng.
— Structural Design, Cementitious Products, & Case Histories: Proceedings of Three Sessions Sponsored by the Structural Division & the Michigan Section of ASCE. 129p. 1985. 18.00 (0-87262-502-8) Am Soc Civil Eng.

Ananda. Comparative Study of Religion: A Sufi & a Sanatani (Ramakrishna) 1993. 22.00 (81-202-0373-9, Pub. by Ajanta) S Asia.
— Myth, Symbol & Language: A Modern Perspective with Reference to India & Her Religions, Including Mythologem & Mythologene. LC 98-906958. xi, 404 p. 1998. 58.00 (81-7305-117-8, Pub. by Aryan Bks Intl) S Asia.

Ananda, A. L., et al, eds. Networks, '98: IEEE SICON'98: Proceedings of the 6th IEEE Singapore International Conference. 492p. 1998. pap. 96.00 (981-02-3584-4) World Scientific Pub.

Ananda, Joshua. Merlyn: A Guide to Soulmerging. 410p. 1995. pap. 12.95 (0-9640538-0-2) Morphos.

Ananda-Maitreya. The Religion of Burma & Other Papers. LC 77-87482. reprint ed. 45.00 (0-404-16790-X) AMS Pr.

Ananda, Shanti. Conversations with My Dark Side. LC 97-65811. 192p. (Orig.). 1997. pap. 14.95 (1-56184-127-7) New Falcon Pubns.

Ananda Yogi, Gururaj. From Darkness to Light: A Selection of Talks by Gururaj Ananda Yogi. rev. ed. Anderson, Vidya & Morosani, Roopa, eds. 224p. 1993. reprint ed. pap. write for info. (1-883797-00-4) Am Meditation.

Anandakrishnan, Satya M., jt. auth. see Regan, Frank J.

Anandamurti, Shrii S. A Guide to Human Conduct. LC 80-70792. 55p. 1981. pap. 4.95 (0-88476-010-3) Ananda Marga.

Anandamurti, Shrii Shrii. Namami Krsnasundaram - Salutations to Lord Krsna. 252p. 1981. pap. 6.95 (0-686-95432-7) Ananda Marga.

Anandan, Jeeva S. Quantum Coherence Conference: Proceedings of the Conference on Fundamental Aspects of Quantum Theory. 404p. (C). 1991. pap. 38.00 (981-02-0257-1); text 118.00 (981-02-0256-3) World Scientific Pub.

Anandan, Jeeva S. & Safko, John L. Quantum Coherence & Reality - In Celebration of the 60th Birthday of Yakir Aharonov. 384p. 1995. text 99.00 (981-02-2117-7) World Scientific Pub.

Anandanagar. Caryacarya, 3 vols. pap. write for info. (0-686-95445-9) Ananda Marga.
— Caryacarya, 3 vols., Vol. 1. 37p. pap. 3.95 (0-88476-018-9) Ananda Marga.
— Caryacarya, 3 vols., Vol. 2. 49p. pap. 3.95 (0-88476-019-7) Ananda Marga.
— Caryacarya, 3 vols., Vol. 3. pap. 3.95 (0-88476-020-0) Ananda Marga.

Anandarajah, Kala. The Bills of Sale in Singapore & Malaysia. xxiv, 167p. 1995. pap. write for info. (0-409-99792-7, MICHIE) LEXIS Pub.

Anandaram, S. Assassination of a Prime Minister As It Happened. LC 94-900646. (C). 1995. 22.00 (81-7094-096-6, Pub. by Vision) S Asia.

Anan'ev, Y. A. Laser Resonators & the Beam Divergence Problem. (Optics & Optoelectronics Ser.). (Illus.). 460p. 1992. 208.00 (0-7503-0146-5) IOP Pub.

Anang, Frederick, jt. ed. see Seidman, Ann.

Anani, Al-Hasan. Freedom & Responsibility in Quranic Perspective. 218p. 1996. pap. 12.95 (0-614-21054-2, 318) Kazi Pubns.

Anania, Michael. Constructions - Variations. 36p. 1985. 3.00 (0-933180-71-3) Spoon Riv Poetry.
— In Natural Light. LC 98-33656. 96p. 1999. pap. 14.95 (1-55921-270-5) Moyer Bell.
— In Plain Sight: Obsessions, Morals, & Domestic Laughter. 224p. 1993. pap. 9.95 (1-55921-047-8) Moyer Bell.
— Red Menace. 158p. 1985. pap. 13.95 (0-938410-19-9, Thunders Mouth) Avalon NY.
— Riversongs. fac. ed. LC 78-12900. 95p. 1978. pap. 30.00 (0-7837-7606-3, 204735900007) Bks Demand.
— Riversongs. Poems. LC 78-12900. 87p. 1978. 14.95 (0-252-00717-4) U of Ill Pr.
— Selected Poems. LC 93-46134. 224p. 1994. pap. 14.95 (1-55921-113-X) Moyer Bell.

Ananicz, Frank. The Red Overcoat & Other Stories. 24p. 1983. pap. 3.50 (0-933292-12-0) Arts End.

Anant, Suchitra, et al, eds. Women at Work in India: A Bibliography. 240p. (C). 1987. text 22.50 (0-8039-9512-1) Sage.

Ananta Toer, Pramoedya. Tales from Djakarta. (Studies on Southeast Asia: Vol. 27). 1999. pap. 15.00 (0-87727-726-5) Cornell SE Asia.

Anantananda, Swami. What's on My Mind? Becoming Inspired with New Perception. LC 96-9267. 176p. (Orig.). 1996. pap. 11.95 (0-911307-47-8) SYDA Found.

Ananth, R., ed. Ronald Rosensweig Alpha Chi Sigma Award Winner: A Special Issue of the Journal Chemical Engineering Communications. 342p. 1988. pap. text 711.00 (2-88124-281-2) Gordon & Breach.

Ananth, Sashikala. The Penguin Guide to Vastu: The Classical Indian Science of Architecture & Design. LC 98-917782. 195 p. 1998. 24.00 (0-670-88288-7, Viking) Viking Penguin.

Ananthakrishna, G., et al, eds. Non Linear Phenomena in Materials Science III: Instabilities & Patterning. (Solid State Phenomena Ser.: Vols. 42-43). (Illus.). 352p. (C). 1995. text 183.00 (3-908450-09-8, Pub. by Scitec Pubns) Enfield Pubs NH.

Ananthakrishnan, Indira, tr. see Lakshmi.

Ananthakrishnan, T. N. Bioresources Ecology. 172p. (C). 1982. text 91.00 (90-6191-402-7, Pub. by A A Balkema) Ashgate Pub Co.
— Chemical Ecology of Thrips-Host Plant Interactions. 132p. (C). 1993. text 56.00 (1-881570-23-1) Science Pubs.
— Dimensions of Insect-Plant Interactions. (C). 1992. text 30.00 (81-204-0668-0, Pub. by Oxford IBH) S Asia.
— Forest Litter Insect Communities: Biology & Chemical Ecology. (Illus.). 165p. 1996. lib. bdg. 66.00 (1-886106-58-4) Science Pubs.

Ananthakrishnan, T. N., contrib. by. Technology in Biological Control. (Illus.). 130p. 1998. 55.00 (1-57808-021-5) Science Pubs.

Ananthakrishnan, T. N., ed. Biological Control of Social Forest & Plantation Crops Insects. 270p. 1995. text 72.00 (1-886106-13-4) Science Pubs.
— Biotechnological Perspectives in Chemical Ecology of Insects. 305p. (C). 1996. text 79.00 (1-886106-73-8) Science Pubs.
— Functional Dynamics of Phytophagous Insects. (Illus.). 312p. 1994. text 79.00 (1-886106-01-0) Science Pubs.

Ananthakrishnan, T. N. & Gopichandran, R. Chemical Ecology in Thrips-Host Plant Interactions. (C). 1993. 24.00 (81-204-0792-X, Pub. by Oxford IBH) S Asia.

Ananthakrishnan, T. N. & Muraleedharan, N. Studies on the Gynaikothrips-Liophleaothrips-Liothrips Complex from India. (Oriental Insects Monographs: No. 4). 1974. pap. 30.00 (1-877711-14-4) Assoc Pubs FL.

Ananthakrishnan, T. N. & Raman, A. Chemical Ecology of Phytophagous Insects. 338p. (C). 1993. text 78.00 (1-881570-33-9) Science Pubs.
— Thrips & Gall Dynamics. (C). 1989. 31.00 (81-204-0412-2, Pub. by Oxford IBH) S Asia.

Ananthakrishnan, T. N. & Sen, A., eds. Biocommunication in Insects. (Illus.). 104p. 1998. 49.00 (1-57808-031-2) Science Pubs.

Ananthakrishnan, T. N., jt. auth. see Murthy, V. A.

Ananthanpillai, Raj. Managing Global Information Network. LC 97-22889. (Illus.). 213p. 1997. pap. 55.00 (0-07-001601-1) McGraw.
— Managing Messaging Networks. LC 94-17551. 1994. 10.00 (0-89006-703-1) Artech Hse.

Ananthapadmanabhan, K. P., ed. see Goddard, E. D.

Anantharamaiah, G. M., jt. auth. see Basava, C.

Anantharaman, T. R. Ancient Yoga & Modern Science. LC 97-900752. (C). 1996. text 20.00 (81-215-0752-9, Pub. by M Manoharial) Coronet Bks.
— Iron Pillar at Delhi. LC 95-910466. (C). 1995. 20.00 (81-7476-057-1, Pub. by UBS Pubs Dist) S Asia.

Anantharaman, T. R., ed. Metallic Glasses: Production, Properties & Applications. 312p. (C). 1984. text 100.00 (0-87849-525-8, Pub. by Trans T Pub) Enfield Pubs NH.

Anantharaman, T. R. & Krishnan, R., eds. Advanced Techniques for Microstructural Characterization. 400p. 1988. text 121.00 (0-87849-563-0, Pub. by Trans T Pub) Enfield Pubs NH.

Anantharaman, T. R. & Suryanarayana, C. Rapidly Solidified Metals: A Technological Overview. 272p. (C). 1987. text 116.00 (0-87849-557-6, Pub. by Trans T Pub) Enfield Pubs NH.

Anantharaman, V. & Tan, P. P. Manual of Medicinal Poisoning. 280p. 1995. text 61.00 (981-02-1093-0) World Scientific Pub.

Anapaugh, et al. Developing Health Promotion Programs. LC 99-34740. 320p. (C). (gr. 13). 1999. text 29.95 (0-8151-4374-5, 30778) Mosby Inc.

Anapol, Deborah. Love Without Limits: Responsible Nonmonogamy & the Quest for Sustainable Intimate Relationships. LC 91-77439. 192p. (Orig.). 1992. pap. 16.00 (1-880789-06-X) IntiNet Res Ctr.

Anapol, Deborah M. Polyamory: The New Love Without Limits. 2nd rev. ed. LC 91-77439. 182p. 1997. pap. 16.00 (1-880789-08-6) IntiNet Res Ctr.

Anapol, Sylvie, jt. auth. see Gitter, Michael.

Anapolitanos, Dionysios. Leibniz: Representation, Continuity, & the Spatio-Temporal. LC 98-47229. (Science & Philosophy Ser.). 1p. 1998. 96.00 (0-7923-5476-1) Kluwer Academic.

Anapolitanos, Dionysios, et al, eds. Philosophy & the Many Faces of Science. (CPS Publications in Philosophy of Science). 272p. (C). 1998. pap. text 23.95 (0-8476-8175-0); lib. bdg. 62.50 (0-8476-8174-2) Rowman.

Anarchism, Bob. Anarchism: There's Nothing More Revolutionary Than Marxism-Lenisim, Mao Tsetung Thoughts. 32p. 1982. 2.25 (0-89851-060-0) RCP Pubns.

Anas, Alex. Modeling in Urban & Regional Economics. Lesourne, Jacques & Sonnenschein, Hugo, eds. (Fundamentals of Pure & Applied Economics Ser.: Vol. 26). viii, 134p. 1987. pap. text 62.00 (3-7186-0467-1) Gordon & Breach.

Anas, Imam Malik Ibn. Al-Muwatta of Imam Malik Ibn Anas: The First Formulation of Islamic Law. Bewley, Aisha A., tr. 500p. 1989. 65.00 (0-7103-0361-0, A3920) Routledge.

Anasal, Arshes, tr. see Samton, Sheila W.

***Anastaplo, George.** Abraham Lincoln: A Constitutional Biography. 400p. 1999. write for info. (0-8476-9432-1) Rowman.
— Abraham Lincoln: A Constitutional Biography. LC 99-14721. 368p. 1999. 35.00 (0-8476-9431-3, Pub. by Rowman) Natl Bk Netwk.

Anastaplo, George. The Amendments to the Constitution: A Commentary. 432p. 1995. text 48.50 (0-8018-4959-4) Johns Hopkins.
— The American Moralist: On Law, Ethics, & Government. LC 91-35715. 647p. (C). 1992. text 110.00 (0-8214-1001-6) Ohio U Pr.
— The American Moralist: On Law, Ethics, & Government. LC 91-35715. 647p. (C). 1994. pap. text 35.00 (0-8214-1079-2) Ohio U Pr.
— Campus Hate - Speech Codes & Twentieth Century Atrocities. LC 95-49261. (Symposium Ser.: Vol. 44). 128p. 1996. 59.95 (0-7734-8847-2) E Mellen.
— The Constitutionalist: Notes on the First Amendment. LC 72-165793. 840p. reprint ed. pap. 200.00 (0-608-16262-0, 202623300049) Bks Demand.
— Human Being & Citizen: Essays on Virtue, Freedom & the Common Good. LC 75-21909. 1975. reprint ed. 22.95 (0-8040-0677-6) Swallow.
— Liberty, Equality & Modern Constitutionalism Vol. I: From Socrates & Pericles to Thomas Jefferson. (Focus Philosophical Library). 260p. 1999. pap. text 19.95 (0-941051-62-5) Focus Pub-R Pullins.
— Liberty, Equality & Modern Constitutionalism Vol. II: From George III to Hitler & Stalin. (Focus Philosophical Library). 260p. 1999. pap. text 19.95 (0-941051-66-8) Focus Pub-R Pullins.
— The Thinker As Artist: From Homer to Plato & Aristotle. LC 97-2389. 421p. 1997. text 49.95 (0-8214-1176-4); pap. text 24.95 (0-8214-1184-5) Ohio U Pr.

Anastas. Corporations & Partnerships in Hellas. 1993. pap. text 52.50 (90-6544-739-3) Kluwer Academic.

Anastas, Benjamin. An Underachiever's Diary. 160p. 1999. pap. 10.00 (0-380-73218-1, Avon Bks) Morrow Avon.
— An Underachiever's Diary: A Novella. LC 97-36276. 160p. 1998. 15.95 (0-385-31998-3) Delacorte.

Anastas, Jean W. & MacDonald, Marian L. Research Design for Social Work & the Human Services. LC 93-44863. 596p. 1994. 40.95 (0-669-20937-6) Jossey-Bass.

Anastas, Jeane, jt. auth. see Appleby, George.

***Anastas, Jeane W.** Research Design for Social Work & the Human Services. rev. ed. LC 99-38959. 599p. 1999. 50.00 (0-231-11890-2) Col U Pr.

***Anastas, Margaret.** Peephole Riddles. (Illus.). (J). (ps-3). 2000. 7.99 (0-8431-7595-8, Price Stern) Peng Put Young Read.

Anastas, Paul & Warner, John. Green Chemistry: Theory & Practice. LC 98-36292. (Illus.). 152p. 1998. text 85.00 (0-19-850234-6) OUP.

***Anastas, Paul & Warner, John.** Green Chemistry: Theory & Practice. (Illus.). 152p. 2000. pap. text 25.00 (0-19-850698-8) OUP.

Anastas, Paul & Williamson, Tracy C., eds. Green Chemistry: Frontiers in Benign Chemical Syntheses & Processes. LC 98-6295. (Illus.). 384p. 1998. text 115.00 (0-19-850170-6) OUP.

***Anastas, Paul, et al.** Green Engineering & Processing. (ACS Symposium Ser.). (Illus.). 464p. 2000. text 130.00 (0-8412-3677-1, Pub. by Am Chemical) OUP.

Anastas, Paul T. Green Chemistry: Designing Chemistry for the Environment. Williamson, Tracy C., ed. LC 96-162. (ACS Symmposium Ser.: No. 626). (Illus.). 238p. 1996. text 95.00 (0-8412-3399-3, Pub. by Am Chemical) OUP.

***Anastas, Paul T., et al, eds.** Green Chemical Syntheses & Processes. (ACS Symposium Ser.: No. 767). (Illus.). 464p. 2000. text 130.00 (0-8412-3678-X, Pub. by Am Chemical) OUP.

Anastas, Paul T. & Farris, Carol A., eds. Benign by Design: Alternative Synthetic Design for Pollution Prevention. LC 94-38830. (ACS Symposium Ser.: No. 577). (Illus.). 208p. 1994. text 65.00 (0-8412-3053-6, Pub. by Am Chemical) OUP.

Anastas, Paul T., jt. auth. see Tundo, Pietro.

Anastas, Peter, ed. see Olson, Charles.

Anastasi. Psychological Testing. 7th ed. (C). 1997. pap. text, student ed. 26.20 (0-13-257321-0) P-H.

Anastasi, Anne. Contributions to Differential Psychology. LC 82-9845. 258p. 1982. 49.95 (0-275-90754-6, C0754, Praeger Pubs) Greenwood.
— Individual Difference. LC 65-25851. (Perspectives in Psychology Ser.). 315p. reprint ed. pap. 97.70 (0-608-30621-5, 205129300093) Bks Demand.
— Psychological Testing. 7th ed. LC 96-41155. 721p. (C). 1996. 89.00 (0-02-303085-2, Macmillan Coll) P-H.

Anastasi, Audrey F. Audrey Frank Anastasi. 24p. (Orig.). 1995. pap. write for info. (0-9650442-0-3) Luna Publns.

Anastasi, Billie, ed. see Vogel, Donald S.

Anastasi, Peter A., ed. Fifty Birds of Town & City. (Illus.). 50p. 1998. reprint ed. text 25.00 (0-7881-4556-8) DIANE Pub.

Anastasi, Tom. The Fight-Free Marriage: The Conflict Without Casualty Strategy to a Satisfying Marriage. LC 94-49081. 1995. pap. 12.99 (0-7852-7937-7) Nelson.

Anastasia, Dina. Bear Who Couldn't Do Anything. (Teddy Bear Tales Ser.: No. S897-4). (J). (ps-2). 1989. pap. text, boxed set 3.95 (0-7214-5227-2, Ladybrd) Penguin Putnam.

Anastasia, George. Goodfella Tapes: The True Story of How the FBI Recorded a Mob War & Brought down a Mafia Don. LC 97-94928. 264p. 1998. mass mkt. 5.99 (0-380-79637-6, Avon Bks) Morrow Avon.
— Mobfather. 320p. 1994. mass mkt. 4.99 (0-7860-0043-0, Pinnacle Kensgtn) Kensgtn Pub Corp.

***Anastasia, George.** The Summer Wind: Thomas Capano & the Murder of Anne Marie Fahey. (Illus.). 256p. 1999. 24.00 (0-06-039314-9, ReganBks) HarperTrade.
— Summer Wind: Thomas Capano & the Murder of Anne Marie Fahey. 400p. 2000. mass mkt. 6.99 (0-06-103100-3, Avon Bks) Morrow Avon.

Anastasia, Patti, jt. auth. see Zubak, Cheryl Lockett.

Anastasia, Phil. Broken Wing, Broken Promise: A Season Inside the Philadelphia Eagles. LC 93-5211. (Illus.). 216p. 1993. 18.00 (0-940159-20-1) Camino Bks.

Anastasiadis, P., jt. ed. see Heine, Hartmut.

***Anastasiadis, S. H., et al, eds.** Interfaces, Adhesion & Processing in Polymer Systems: Materials Research Society Symposium Proceedings, Vol. 629. 2000. text 77.00 (1-55899-537-4) Materials Res.

Anastasio, Dina. The Case of the Glacier Park Swallow. LC 94-65091. (Juliet Stone Mystery Ser.: No. 2). (Illus.). 80p. (Orig.). (J). (gr. 4 up). 1994. pap. 6.95 (1-879373-85-8) Roberts Rinehart.
— The Case of the Grand Canyon Eagle. LC 94-65090. (Juliet Stone Mystery Ser.: No. 1). (Illus.). 80p. (Orig.). (J). (gr. 6 up). 1994. pap. 6.95 (1-879373-84-X) Roberts Rinehart.

***Anastasio, Dina.** Crazy Crosswords. (Travel Games to Go Ser.). (Illus.). 48p. (J). (gr. 2-6). 1998. pap. 3.50 (0-8431-7835-3, Price Stern) Peng Put Young Read.

Anastasio, Dina. Dolly Dolphin & the Strange New Something. (Shamu & His Crew Adventure Ser.). (Illus.). 32p. (J). (gr. k-3). 1994. 5.95 (1-884506-07-0) Third Story.
— Enemy: A Novel. (Space, Above & Beyond). 1996. 9.15 (0-606-10936-6, Pub. by Turtleback) Demco.
— Fly Trap. LC 96-16294. (Eek! Stories to Make You Shriek Ser.). (Illus.). 48p. (J). (gr. 1-3). 1997. pap. 3.95 (0-448-41557-7, G & D); lib. bdg. 13.99 (0-448-41582-8, G & D) Peng Put Young Read.
— Fly Trap. (Eek! Stories to Make You Shriek Ser.). (YA). 1997. 9.15 (0-606-11338-X, Pub. by Turtleback) Demco.
— It's about Time. (Illus.). 24p. (J). (gr. 1-3). 1993. 9.95 (0-448-40551-2, G & D) Peng Put Young Read.
— Joy to the World! (All Aboard Bks.). (Illus.). 32p. (J). (ps-3). 1992. pap. 2.95 (0-448-40479-6, G & D) Peng Put Young Read.
— Let's Start Learning Phonetics. (J). 1992. pap. 1.95 (0-590-45272-X) Scholastic Inc.
— Pass the Peas, Please: A Book of Manners. LC 99-19163. 32p. (J). 1999. pap. 7.95 (0-7373-0193-7, 01937W) NTC Contemp Pub Co.

***Anastasio, Dina.** Pinky Ball Book & the Pinky Ball. (Illus.). 176p. (J). (ps-3). 2000. pap. 9.95 (0-7611-1977-9) Workman Pub.

Anastasio, Dina. Pirates. LC 96-17597. (All Aboard Bks.). (Illus.). 32p. (J). (ps-3). 1997. pap. 2.95 (0-448-41494-5, G & D) Peng Put Young Read.

Anastasio, Dina. Pirates. LC 96-17597. (Grosset & Dunlap All Aboard Bks.). 1997. 8.15 (0-606-11752-0, Pub. by Turtleback) Demco.

Anastasio, Dina. The Teddy Bear Who Couldn't Do Anything. (S Eight Hundred Ninety-Seven Ser.). (Illus.). 24p. (J). 1993. text 2.95 (0-7214-3511-4, Ladybrd) Penguin Putnam.
— Wild, Wild West. (Illus.). 169p. (gr. 3-7). 1999. pap. 4.99 (0-439-08653-1) Scholastic Inc.
— A Year of Celebrations: Hundreds of Ideas & Activities for Family Fun. (Illus.). 164p. (Orig.). 1997. pap. write for info. (0-614-29765-6); pap. 17.95 (1-884013-00-7) CTV Workshop.

Anastasio, Janet. The Wedding Shower Book. 2nd ed. LC 94-3728. 132p. 1995. pap. 7.95 (1-55850-407-9) Adams Media.

***Anastasio, Janet & Bevilacqua, Michelle.** The Everything Wedding Checklist: The Gown, the Guests, the Groom & Everything Else You Shouldn't Forget. 2nd ed. (Everything Wedding Ser.). (Illus.). 208p. 2000. pap. 8.95 (1-58062-456-1) Adams Media.

Anastasio, Janet & Bevilacqua, Michelle. The Everything Wedding Checklist: The Gown, the Guests, the Groom & Other Things You Shouldn't Forget. (Illus.). 168p. 1993. pap. 7.00 (1-55850-278-5) Adams Media.

***Anastasio, Janet & Bevilacqua, Michelle.** The Everything Wedding Vows Book: Anything & Everything You Could Possibly Say at the Altar--And Them Some. (Everything Wedding Ser.). (Illus.). 208p. 2000. pap. 8.95 (1-58062-455-3) Adams Media.

An Asterisk (*) at the beginning of an entry indicates that the title is appearing for the first time.

Anastasio, Janet & Bevilacqua, Michelle. Everything Wedding Vows Book: Anything & Everything You Could Possibly Say at the Altar & Then Some! LC 94-231811. 143p. 1994. pap. 7.95 (*1-55850-364-1*) Adams Media.

Anastasio, Janet & Gouck, Peter. Our Wedding Memories. 1992. 18.50 (*1-55850-120-7*) Adams Media.

***Anastasio, Janet, et al.** The Everything Wedding Book: Everything You Need to Know to Survive Your Wedding & Actually Even Enjoy It! 2nd rev. expanded ed. (The Everything Ser.). (Illus.). 320p. 2000. pap. 12.95 (*1-58062-190-2*) Adams Media.

Anastasio, Philip, ed. see Society of Photographic Scientists & Engineers Sta.

Anastasio, Vittorio. Woerterbuch der Wasserchemie: German-English-French. (ENG, FRE & GER.). 362p. 1991. lib. bdg. 175.00 (*0-8288-3840-2*, F124330) Fr & Eur.

Anastasiou, C. J. Ascomycetes & Fungi Imperfecti from the Salton Sea. 1963. pap. 15.00 (*3-7682-0210-0*) Lubrecht & Cramer.

Anastasovski, Petar K. Theory of Magnetic & Electric Susceptibilities for Optical Frequencies. 301p. (C). 1991. text 165.00 (*0-941743-83-7*) Nova Sci Pubs.

Anastasovski, Petar K. & Benson, Trevor M. Quantum Mass Theory Compatible with Quantum Field Theory. (Illus.). 212p. (C). 1994. lib. bdg. 125.00 (*1-56072-157-X*) Nova Sci Pubs.

Anastassakis, E., jt. auth. see Joannopoulos, John D.

Anastassiadou, Meropi. Salonique, 1830-1912: Une Ville Ottomane a l'Age des Reformes. (Ottoman Empire & Its Heritage Ser.: Vol. 11). (FRE., Illus.). xii, 466p. 1997. 160.00 (*90-04-10798-3*) Brill Academic Pubs.

Anastassiadou, Vicky, tr. see Farris, Katherine, ed.

Anastassiou, G. & Rachev, S. T. Approximation, Probability, & Related Fields. (Illus.). 468p. (C). 1994. 125.00 (*0-306-44724-X*, Plenum Trade) Perseus Pubng.

***Anastassiou, George A.** Handbook on Analytic-Computational Methods in Applied Mathematics. LC 00-36089. 2000. write for info. (*1-58488-135-6*, Chap & Hall CRC) CRC Pr.

— Quantitative Approximations. LC 00-34615. 2000. write for info. (*1-58488-221-2*, Chap & Hall CRC) CRC Pr.

Anastassiou, George A., ed. Approximation Theory. (Lecture Notes in Pure & Applied Mathematics Ser.: Vol. 138). (Illus.). 560p. 1992. pap. text 210.00 (*0-8247-8708-0*) Dekker.

***Anastassiou, George A. & Gal, Sorin G.** Approximation Theory: Moduli of Continuity & Global Smoothness Preservation. LC 99-57004. 552p. 2000. 89.95 (*0-8176-4151-3*, Pub. by Birkhauser) Spr-Verlag.

— Approximation Theory: Moduli of Continuity & Global Smoothness Preservation. LC 99-57004. 2000. write for info. (*3-7643-4151-3*) Birkhauser.

Anastassopoulos, A., jt. ed. see Hemelrijck, D.Van.

Anastassopoulou, Jane, jt. ed. see Theophanides, Theophile.

Anastazievsky, Walter A., et al, compiled by. Svoboda: A Select Index, 4 vols., Set. LC 89-82654. (Orig.). 1994. pap. 85.00 (*0-685-67718-4*) Immig His Res.

— Svoboda: A Select Index, 4 vols., Vol. 1: 1893-1899. LC 89-82654. xix, 406p. (Orig.). 1990. pap. 25.00 (*0-932833-10-1*) Immig His Res.

— Svoboda: A Select Index, 4 vols., Vol. 2: 1900-1907. LC 89-82654. xlvi, 410p. (Orig.). 1991. pap. 25.00 (*0-932833-11-X*) Immig His Res.

— Svoboda: A Select Index, 4 vols., Vol. 3: January 1908-July 1914. LC 89-82654. xlv, 407p. (Orig.). 1993. pap. 25.00 (*0-932833-17-9*) Immig His Res.

Anastazievsky, Walter A., ed. Svoboda - A Select Index Vol. 4: August 1914 to December 1918. LC 89-82654. xlv, 394p. (Orig.). (C). 1994. pap. text 25.00 (*0-932833-14-4*) Immig His Res.

***Anastopoulos, Dimitris.** Psychoanalytic Psychotherapy of the Severely Disturbed Adolescent. 216p. 1999. pap. 31.50 (*1-85575-214-X*, Pub. by H Karnac Bks Ltd) Other Pr LLC.

Anastos, Elizabeth, ed. see Ecklund, Lois E.

Anastos, G., tr. see Pomerantzev, B. I.

Anathakrishnan, T. N. Dynamics of Insect-Plant Interaction. (C). 1988. 30.00 (*81-204-0376-2*, Pub. by Oxford IBH) S Asia.

Anatol, Frank, jt. auth. see Noori, Hamid.

Anatole, France. On Life Letters, vols. 4, Set. Date not set. 86.95 (*0-8369-4977-3*) Ayer.

Anatoli, A. Babi Yar: A Document in the Form of a Novel. Floyd, David, tr. from RUS. LC 78-74649. 1979. reprint ed. lib. bdg. 30.00 (*0-8376-0432-X*) Bentley Pubs.

Anatolii, Kuznetsov. Babii Iar: Roman-Dokument. LC 85-62294. (RUS., Illus.). 488p. 1986. reprint ed. 18.00 (*0-911971-16-5*) Effect Pub.

Anatolios, Khaled. Athanasius: The Structure of His Thought. LC 98-4029. 1998. 75.00 (*0-415-18637-4*) Routledge.

Anatolius of Mohilew & Mstislaw. Greek Orthodox Faith: Scriptural Presentation. Bjerring, Nicholas, tr. from RUS. 1974. reprint ed. pap. 1.00 (*0-89981-028-4*) Eastern Orthodox.

Anatoly, Elder. A Collection of Letters to Nuns. Luke, Igumen, ed. Holy Nativity Convent Staff, tr. from RUS.Tr. of Pisma Startsa Anatolia Monakhiniam. (Illus.). 308p. (Orig.). 1993. pap. 15.00 (*0-88465-053-7*) Holy Trinity.

Anatoly, Naiman. Oblaka V Kontse Veka. LC 93-11885. (RUS.). 100p. (Orig.). 1993. pap. 9.00 (*1-55779-069-8*) Hermitage Pubs.

***Anatomical Chart Company Staff.** Diseases & Disorders Bk. II: The World's Best Anatomical Charts Collection. (Illus.). 35p. 2000. pap. 15.95 (*1-889241-08-3*, DIS-35) Anatomical Chart.

— Piecing Together Hypertension. (Illus.). 9p. 2000. 24.95 (*1-889241-05-9*, 9767FC) Anatomical Chart.

— Piecing Together the Digestive System. (Illus.). 9p. 2000. pap. 24.95 (*1-889241-02-4*, 9859FC) Anatomical Chart.

— Piecing Together the Heart. (Illus.). 9p. 2000. pap. 24.95 (*1-889241-01-6*, 8023FC) Anatomical Chart.

— Piecing Together the Respiratory System. (Illus.). 9p. 2000. pap. 24.95 (*1-889241-03-2*, 9766FC) Anatomical Chart.

— Piecing Together the Skeletal System. (Illus.). 20p. 2000. pap. 34.95 (*1-889241-04-0*, 8943FC) Anatomical Chart.

— Systems & Structures Bk. I: The World's Best Anatomical Charts Collection. 35p. 2000. pap. 15.95 (*1-889241-07-5*, SYS-35) Anatomical Chart.

Anatomical Chart Company Staff. Trigger Points: Understanding Myofascial Pain & Discomfort. (Illus.). 1994. pap. 29.95 (*0-9603730-6-3*) Anatomical Chart.

— The World's Best Anatomical Charts. 2nd ed. (Illus.). 72p. 1993. pap. 15.95 (*0-9603730-5-5*) Anatomical Chart.

Anatta, Ivan. Flowers. LC 92-35065. (Nature Books Ser.). (Illus.). 32p. (J). (gr. 2-6). 1994. lib. bdg. 22.79 (*1-56766-005-3*) Childs World.

Anatta, Ivan M. Trees. LC 92-32286. (Nature Books Ser.). (Illus.). 32p. (J). (gr. 2-6). 1994. lib. bdg. 22.79 (*1-56766-002-9*) Childs World.

Anawalt, H. Clarke. Ideas in the Workplace: Planning for Protection. LC 86-72658. (Illus.). 170p. 1988. lib. bdg. 29.95 (*0-89089-315-2*) Carolina Acad Pr.

Anawalt, H. Clarke, et al. IP Strategy: Complete Intellectual Property Planning, Access, & Protection. LC 97-173872. (The Clark Boardman Callaghan Intellectual Property Library). xxxi, 685 p. 1997. write for info. (*0-8366-1107-1*) West Group.

Anawalt, Howard & Enayati, Elizabeth. I. P. Strategy: Complete Intellectual Property Planning, Access & Protection. LC 96-186415. (Intellectual Property Library). 1996. pap. write for info. (*0-87632-415-4*) West Group.

***Anawalt, Loretta Bonnier.** Dream Prints: Poems. LC 99-25539. 175p. 1999. 60.00 (*0-910055-51-3*) East Wash Univ.

Anawalt, Patricia R. Indian Clothing Before Cortes: Mesoamerican Costumes from the Codices. LC 80-5942. (Civilization of the American Indian Ser.: Vol. 156). (Illus.). 256p. 1990. 65.00 (*0-8061-1650-1*); pap. 39.95 (*0-8061-2288-9*) U of Okla Pr.

Anawalt, Patricia R., jt. auth. see Berdan, Frances F.

***Anawalt, Paula Bonnier.** The Crystal Palace: A Tale from the Gold Country. LC 98-93933. 44p. (J). (gr. k-4). 1999. 16.95 (*0-9668414-0-9*) Abongold.

Anawalt, Sasha. The Joffrey Ballet: Robert Joffrey & the Making of an American Dance Company. LC 97-23161. 480p. 1997. pap. 18.95 (*0-226-01755-9*) U Ch Pr.

***Anawalt, Sasha.** The Joffrey Ballet: Robert Joffrey & the Making of an American Dance Company. (Illus.). 464p. 2000. reprint ed. 35.00 (*0-7881-9335-X*) DIANE Pub.

Anaximenes. Ars Rhetorica Quae Vulgo Fertur Aristotelis Ad Alexandrum. (Illus.). xii, 275p. 1981. reprint ed. 55.00 (*3-487-07052-9*) G Olms Pubs.

Anaya, A. Paco. I Buried Billy. Earle, James H., ed. LC 91-29656. 160p. 1991. 21.95 (*0-932702-92-9*) Creative Texas.

***Anaya, Alison, ed.** 2000-2001 Accredited Institutions of Post-Secondary. (Ace Higher Education Ser.). 736p. 2001. pap. text 59.95 (*1-57356-283-1*) Oryx Pr.

***Anaya, James.** Indigenous Peoples in International Law. 288p. 2000. pap. 19.95 (*0-19-514045-1*) OUP.

***Anaya, Jose A.** Labor Market Flexibility in 13 Latin American Countries & the United States. LC 99-15436. (Latin American & Caribbean Studies). 48p. 1999. pap. 22.00 (*0-8213-4489-7*, 14489) World Bank.

Anaya, Rudolfo A. The Adventures of Juan Chicaspatas. LC 84-72301. 48p. (C). 1985. pap. 5.00 (*0-934770-45-X*) Arte Publico.

Anaya, Rudolfo A. Albuquerque. 1992. 11.09 (*0-606-06168-1*, Pub. by Turtleback) Demco.

Anaya, Rudolfo A. Albuquerque. 304p. 1994. mass mkt. 6.99 (*0-446-36544-0*, Pub. by Warner Bks) Little.

***Anaya, Rudolfo A.** Albuquerque. 2000. reprint ed. pap. 13.95 (*0-446-67615-2*) Warner Bks.

Anaya, Rudolfo A. The Anaya Reader. 592p. (Orig.). 1995. mass mkt. 12.99 (*0-446-67077-4*, Pub. by Warner Bks) Little.

Anaya, Rudolfo A. Bendiceme, Ultima. 1992. 11.09 (*0-606-06225-4*, Pub. by Turtleback) Demco.

Anaya, Rudolfo A. Bendiceme, Ultima: Bless Me, Ultima. Smithers, Alicia, tr. (SPA.). 320p. 1994. mass mkt. 6.50 (*0-446-60177-2*, Pub. by Warner Bks) Little.

— Bless Me, Ultima. (Writers' Voices Ser.). (J). 1988. 8.70 (*0-606-04174-5*, Pub. by Turtleback) Demco.

Anaya, Rudolfo A. Bless Me, Ultima. LC 93-30477. 1994. 11.09 (*0-606-06238-6*, Pub. by Turtleback) Demco.

Anaya, Rudolfo A. Bless Me, Ultima. (Illus.). 272p. 1994. mass mkt. 6.99 (*0-446-60025-3*, Pub. by Warner Bks) Little.

— Bless Me, Ultima. 304p. 1999. reprint ed. mass mkt. 12.00 (*0-446-67536-9*, Pub. by Warner Bks) Little.

— Conversations with Rudolfo Anaya. Dick, Bruce & Sirias, Silvio, eds. LC 98-24028. (Literary Conversation Ser.). 256p. 1998. pap. 17.00 (*1-57806-078-8*); text 45.00 (*1-57806-077-X*) U Pr of Miss.

***Anaya, Rudolfo A.** An Elegy on the Death of Cesar Chavez: A Poem. LC 00-24832. (Illus.). 40p. (J). (gr. 4-7). 2000. 15.95 (*0-938317-51-2*) Cinco Puntos.

Anaya, Rudolfo A. Farolitos for Abuelo. LC 97-46710. (Illus.). 32p. (J). (gr. k-4). 1999. lib. bdg. 16.49 (*0-7868-2186-8*, Pub. by Hyprn Child) Little.

***Anaya, Rudolfo A.** Farolitos for Abuelo. LC 97-46710. (Illus.). 32p. (J). (gr. k-4). 1999. 15.99 (*0-7868-0237-5*, Pub. by Hyprn Child) Time Warner.

Anaya, Rudolfo A. Farolitos Limited. (J). 1997. 15.45 (*0-7868-0393-2*, Pub. by Hyperion) Time Warner.

— The Farolitos of Christmas. LC 94-48073. (Illus.). 32p. (J). (gr. k-4). 1995. lib. bdg. 14.89 (*0-7868-2047-0*, Pub. by Hyprn Child) Little.

— The Farolitos of Christmas. limited ed. LC 94-48073. (Illus.). 32p. (J). (gr. k-4). 1995. 16.95 (*0-7868-0060-7*, Pub. by Hyprn Child) Time Warner.

— First Tortilla. 32p. (J). Date not set. lib. bdg. write for info. (*0-7868-2187-6*) Hyperion.

Anaya, Rudolfo A. First Tortilla. 32p. (J). Date not set. write for info. (*0-7868-0238-3*) Hyperion.

Anaya, Rudolfo A. Heart of Aztlan: A Novel. LC 87-35689. 209p. 1988. reprint ed. pap. 13.95 (*0-8263-1054-7*) U of NM Pr.

— Jaolamanta: A Message from the Desert. 208p. 1997. mass mkt. 12.99 (*0-446-67273-4*, Pub. by Warner Bks) Little.

— Maya's Children: The Story of La Llorona. LC 95-41973. (Illus.). 32p. (J). (gr. k-4). 1997. 14.95 (*0-7868-0152-2*, Pub. by Hyprn Child); lib. bdg. 14.89 (*0-7868-2124-8*, Pub. by Hyprn Child) Little.

***Anaya, Rudolfo A.** My Land Sings. (J). 2000. pap. write for info. (*0-380-72902-4*) Morrow Avon.

Anaya, Rudolfo A. My Land Sings: Stories from the Rio Grande. LC 99-19040. (Illus.). 144p. (J). (gr. 5-9). 1999. 17.00 (*0-688-15078-0*, Wm Morrow) Morrow Avon.

— Rio Grande Fall. 352p. 1997. mass mkt. 6.99 (*0-446-60486-0*, Pub. by Warner Bks) Little.

***Anaya, Rudolfo A.** Roadrunner's Dance. LC 99-89871. (Illus.). 32p. (J). (gr. k-4). 2000. 15.99 (*0-7868-0254-5*, Pub. by Disney Pr); lib. bdg. 16.49 (*0-7868-2209-0*, Pub. by Disney Pr) Time Warner.

Anaya, Rudolfo A. Shaman Winter. LC 97-51226. 368p. 1999. 24.00 (*0-446-52374-7*, Pub. by Warner Bks) Little.

***Anaya, Rudolfo A.** Shaman Winter. 432p. 2000. mass mkt. 7.50 (*0-446-60801-7*) Warner Bks.

Anaya, Rudolfo A. Tortuga: A Novel. LC 87-35665. 202p. 1988. reprint ed. pap. 13.95 (*0-8263-1074-5*) U of NM Pr.

— Zia Summer. 368p. (YA). 1996. mass mkt. 6.99 (*0-446-60316-3*, Pub. by Warner Bks) Little.

Anaya, Rudolfo A., ed. Blue Mesa Review, Vol. 3, No. 6. 282p. 1984. pap. 10.00 (*1-885290-05-5*) Blue Mesa Rev.

— Tierra: Contemporary Short Fiction of New Mexico. LC 89-91054. 258p. (Orig.). 1989. pap. 12.95 (*0-938317-09-1*) Cinco Puntos.

Anaya, Rudolfo A., tr. from SPA. Cuentos: Tales from the Hispanic Southwest. (Illus.). 174p. 1981. pap. 11.95 (*0-89013-111-2*) Museum NM Pr.

Anaya, Rudolfo A., tr. Cuentos: Tales from the Hispanic Southwest: Based on Stories Originally Collected by Juan B. Rae. LC 80-18790. 1980. 17.05 (*0-606-04383-7*, Pub. by Turtleback) Demco.

Anaya, Rudolfo A. & Lomeli, Francisco A. Aztlan: Essays on the Chicano Homeland. LC 89-83942. 248p. 1991. reprint ed. pap. 16.95 (*0-8263-1261-6*) U of NM Pr.

Anaya, Rudolfo A. & Marquez, Antonio, eds. Cuentos Chicanos: A Short Story Anthology. LC 84-13066. 186p. 1984. reprint ed. pap. 14.95 (*0-8263-0772-8*) U of NM Pr.

Anaya, Rudolfo A., jt. auth. see Baeza, Aberlarda.

Anaya, Rudolfo A., jt. auth. see Center for Learning Network Staff.

Anaya, Rudolfo A., jt. auth. see Linde, Barbara M.

Anaya, Rudolfo A., jt. auth. see Martinez, Ruben O.

Anaya, S. James. Indigenous Peoples in International Law. 288p. 1996. text 52.00 (*0-19-508620-1*) OUP.

Anaya Staff. Diccionario Basico Anaya de la Lengua. (SPA.). 736p. 1991. 24.95 (*0-7859-5734-0*, 8420721956) Fr & Eur.

— Diccionario de la Lengua Espanola. (SPA.). 1080p. 1991. 59.95 (*0-7859-5736-7*, 8420741485) Fr & Eur.

— Diccionario de Linguistica. (SPA.). 328p. 1986. 55.00 (*0-7859-6230-1*, 8475253660) Fr & Eur.

— Diccionario Multilingue CD-ROM. (SPA.). 36p. 1988. 1895.00 incl. cd-rom (*0-7859-5735-9*, 8420729876) Fr & Eur.

— Small Anaya Spanish Dictionary: Pequeno Diccionario Anaya de la Lengua. (SPA.). 644p. 1984. pap. 14.95 (*0-8288-2024-4*, S60163) Fr & Eur.

Anbar, Ada. How to Choose a Nursery School: A Parents' Guide to Preschool Education. 2nd ed. LC 99-23134. (Illus.). 176p. 1999. 27.95 (*0-87015-267-X*); pap. 12.95 (*0-87015-268-8*) Pacific Bks.

Anbar, Michael. Clinical Biophysics. Gardner, Alvin F., ed. (Allied Health Professions Monograph). (Illus.) 772p. 1985. 75.00 (*0-87527-316-5*) Green.

— Quantitative & Dynamic Thermal Imaging in Medical Diagnosis. 288p. 1994. lib. bdg. 110.00 (*0-8493-4409-3*) CRC Pr.

Anbar, Michael, jt. ed. see Reiser, Stanley J.

***Anbar, Moshe.** Joshua & the Covenant at Schechem: (JOS. 24:1-28) (Biblical Encyclopaedia Library: Vol. XVII). 202p. 1999. pap. text 29.00 (*965-342-705-9*, Pub. by Bialik) Eisenbrauns.

Anbar, Moshe. Josue et l'Alliance de Sichem: Josue 24: 1-28. (Beitrage zur Biblischen Exegese und Theologie Ser.: Bd. 25). (FRE.). 163p. 1992. 31.80 (*3-631-45018-4*) P Lang Pubng.

— Les Tribus Amurrites de Mari. (Orbis Biblicus et Orientalis Ser.: Vol. 108). (FRE.). 248p. 1991. text 51.25 (*3-7278-0750-4*, Pub. by Presses Univ Fribourg) Eisenbrauns.

Anbarlian, Harry. An Introduction to Multiplan: Spreadsheeting on the Hewlett Packard 75C. 1984. pap. 22.95 (*0-07-079407-3*) McGraw.

— An Introduction to Multiplan-86 Spreadsheeting on the DEC Rainbow 100: DEC Version. (Personal Programming Ser.). 416p. 1984. 1.00 (*0-07-001735-2*) McGraw.

— An Introduction to Multiplan-86 Spreadsheeting on the DEC Rainbow 100: McGraw-Hill Version. (Personal Programming Ser.). 416p. 1984. 1.00 (*0-07-001709-3*) McGraw.

— An Introduction to SuperCalc Spreadsheeting on the Osborne. disk 49.95 (*0-07-001701-8*, BYTE Bks) McGraw.

— Introduction to VisiCalc Spreadsheeting for the TRS-80 Model II & 16. (Personal Programming Ser.). 1983. write for info. (*0-07-001596-1*) McGraw.

— Spreadsheeting on the TRS-80 Color Computer. (Personal Computing Ser.). 320p. 1983. write for info. (*0-07-001595-3*, BYTE Bks) McGraw.

Anbian, Robert. Antinostalgia. (Oro Madre Ser.: Vol. 5, Nos. 1-4, 1992). (Illus.). 80p. (Orig.). 1992. pap. 12.00 (*0-910697-08-6*) Ruddy Duck Pr.

— Bohemian Airs & Other Kefs. LC 81-90581. (Literature Ser.: No. 1). (Illus.). 74p. (Orig.). 1982. pap. 6.00 (*0-941842-00-2*) Night Horn Books.

— We. (Illus.). 1999. pap. 12.00 (*0-941842-04-5*) Night Horn Books.

Anbinder, Tyler G. Nativism & Slavery: The Know-Nothing Party in the Northern United States. (Illus.). 352p. 1992. text 75.00 (*0-19-507233-2*) OUP.

— Nativism & Slavery: The Northern Know Nothings & the Politics of the 1850s. (Illus.). 352p. 1994. pap. text 19.95 (*0-19-508922-7*) OUP.

Anbury, Thomas. Travels Through the Interior Parts of America in a Series of Letters by an Officer, 2 vols., Set. LC 75-76553. (Eyewitness Accounts of the American Revolution Ser.). (Illus.). 1969. reprint ed. 45.95 (*0-405-01140-7*) Ayer.

— Travels Through the Interior Parts of America in a Series of Letters by an Officer, 2 vols., Vol. 1. LC 75-76553. (Eyewitness Accounts of the American Revolution Ser.). (Illus.). 1969. reprint ed. 22.95 (*0-405-01141-5*) Ayer.

— Travels Through the Interior Parts of America in a Series of Letters by an Officer, 2 vols., Vol. 2. LC 75-76553. (Eyewitness Accounts of the American Revolution Ser.). (Illus.). 1969. reprint ed. 22.95 (*0-405-01142-3*) Ayer.

Ancas, Mike. The Honda & Acura Performance Handbook. LC 99-19842. (Performance Handbooks Ser.). (Illus.). 160p. 1999. pap. 19.95 (*0-7603-0669-9*, 128074AP, Pub. by MBI Pubg) Motorbooks Intl.

***Ancas, Mike.** Mazda RX-7 Performance Handbook. (Illus.). 160p. 2000. pap. 21.95 (*0-7603-0802-0*, 129797AP, Pub. by MBI Pubg) Motorbooks Intl.

Ancel, Marc. Social Defense: The Future of Penal Reform. 3rd ed. Wise, Edward M., ed. Sellin, Thorsten, tr. from FRE. LC 86-15458. (Comparative Criminal Law Project Publications Ser.: Vol. 16). xxi, 314p. 1981. reprint ed. 47.50 (*0-8377-0219-4*, Rothman) W S Hein.

Ancel, Martin. Mira Conquistador. 1974. 19.95 (*0-685-52987-8*); pap. 15.95 (*0-930400-00-3*) Pleasure Trove.

— Oriental Pleasure Troves. 7th ed. LC 85-61264. (Illus.). 246p. 1985. pap. 19.95 (*0-685-04064-X*); per. 29.95 (*0-685-57741-4*) Pleasure Trove.

Ancelet, Barry J. Cajun & Creole Music Makers: Musiciens Cadiens et Creoles. 2nd rev. ed. LC 99-31746. Orig. Title: The Makers of Cajun Music. (Illus.). 176p. 1999. pap. 35.00 (*1-57806-170-9*) U Pr of Miss.

Ancelet, Barry J., et al, eds. Louisiana: A Land Apart. LC 84-72896. (Illus.). 144p. 1985. 35.00 (*0-917541-01-4*) Galerie Pr.

Ancelet, Barry J., et al. Cajun Country. Montell, Lynwood, ed. LC 90-28931. (Folklife in the South Ser.). 1991. pap. 17.00 (*0-87805-467-7*) U Pr of Miss.

Ancelet, Barry Jean. Cajun Music: Its Origins & Development. (Louisiana Life Ser.). 58p. (Orig.). 1989. pap. 5.00 (*0-940984-48-2*) Univ LA Lafayette.

— Capitaine, Voyage Ton Flag: The Traditional Cajun Country Mardi Gras. (Louisiana Life Ser.: No. 1). 38p. 1989. pap. 5.00 (*0-940984-46-6*) Univ LA Lafayette.

Ancelet, Barry Jean, anno. Cajun & Creole Folktales: The French Oral Tradition of South Louisiana. LC 93-31848. (World Folktale Library: Vol. 1). (Illus.). 296p. 1994. text 20.00 (*0-8153-1498-1*, H1792) Garland.

Ancelet, Barry Jean, ed. Cajun & Creole Folktales: The French Oral Tradition of South Louisiana. LC 93-46885. 296p. 1994. reprint ed. pap. 19.95 (*0-87805-709-9*) U Pr of Miss.

Ancelet, Barry Jean, tr. see Gould, Philip.

***Ancell, Carolyn D.** Can the Saints Come Out To Play: A Saint For Everyday June Saints. Meehan, Rosario, tr. from SPA. (Can the Saints Come Out To Play: 10). 74p. (J). (gr. k-5). 2000. 12.95 (*1-893757-17-X*, 17-x) E T Nedder.

— Can the Saints Come Out to Play: A Saint Story for Every Day - April Saints. Meehan, Rosario, tr. from ENG. 74p. (J). (gr. k-5). 2000. 12.95 (*1-893757-15-3*) E T Nedder.

— Can the Saints Come Out to Play: A Saint Story for Every Day - March Saints. Meehan, Rosario, tr. from ENG. 74p. (J). (gr. k-5). 2000. 12.95 (*1-893757-14-5*) E T Nedder.

— Can the Saints Come Out To Play: A Saint Story For Everyday - May Saints. abr. ed. Meehan, Rosario, tr. from SPA. (Can the Saints Come Out To Play: 9). 74p. (J). (gr. k-5). 2000. 12.95 (*1-893757-16-1*, 16-1) E T Nedder.

— Can the Saints Come Out to Play: A Saint Story for Everyday, February Saints, 12 vols. Meehan, Rosario, tr. 74p. (J). (gr. k-5). 2000. 12.95 (*1-893757-13-7*, 13-7) E T Nedder.

— Can the Saints Come Out to Play: July Saints. Meehan, Rosario, tr. (Saint for Every Day Ser.: Vol. 11). 74p. (J). (gr. k-5). 2000. 12.95 (*1-893757-18-8*, 18-8) E T Nedder.

— Can the Saints Come Out to Play! - A Saint Story for

A

Every Day Vol. 5: January Saints. Meehan, Rosario, tr.Tr. of Pueden Salir a Jugar los Santos. (Illus.). 74p. (J). (gr. 1-8). 2000. 12.95 (*1-893757-11-0*, 11-0) E T Nedder.

— Can the Saints Come Out to Play - August. Meehan, Rosario, tr. (Saint for Everyday Ser.: No. 12). 74p. (J). (gr. k-5). 2000. 12.95 (*1-893757-19-6*, 19-6) E T Nedder.

— Can the Saints Come Out to Play (Pueden Salin a Jugar los Santos) Vol. 3: November Saints. Meehan, Rosario, tr. 74p. (gr. 1-6). 1999. 12.95 (*1-893757-05-6*, 06) E T Nedder.

— Can the Saints Some Out to Play (Pueden Salis a Juans los Santos) Vol. 2: October Saints. Meehan, Rosario, tr. 74p. (gr. 1-6). 1999. 12.95 (*1-893757-04-8*, 05) E T Nedder.

Ancell, R. Manning. 4 Star Leadership for Leaders. Jones, Charles E., ed. LC 98-84948. 204p. 1997. pap. 12.95 (*0-937539-24-4*) Executive Bks.

Ancell, R. Manning & Miller, Christine M. Biographical Dictionary of World War II Generals & Flag Officers: The U. S. Armed Forces. LC 95-50450. 720p. 1996. lib. bdg. 110.00 (*0-313-29546-8*, Greenwood Pr) Greenwood.

Anchel, Marjorie, ed. see New York State Humane Association Staff.

Anchell, Melvin. Sex & Insanity. LC 83-81798. 169p. 1983. pap. 12.95 (*0-89420-238-3*, 110020, Halcyon) Natl Book.

— What's Wrong with Sex Education? Preteen & Teenage Sexual Development & Environmental Influences. Ames, Bobbie H., ed. (Illus.). 108p. (Orig.). 1993. pap. 7.00 (*0-9626257-4-4*) CBCCU Amer.

Anchell, Steve. The Darkroom Cookbook. (Illus.). 240p. 1994. pap. 26.95 (*0-240-80196-2*, Focal) Buttrwrth-Heinemann.

***Anchell, Steve.** Darkroom Cookbook. 2nd ed. (Illus.). 240p. 2000. pap. 27.95 (*0-240-80423-6*, Focal) Buttrwrth-Heinemann.

Anchell, Steve. The Variable Contrast Printing Manual. LC 96-46892. (Illus.). 176p. 1997. pap. 27.95 (*0-240-80259-4*, Focal) Buttrwrth-Heinemann.

Anchell, Steve & Troop, Bill. The Film Developing Cookbook. LC 98-41649. 176p. 1998. pap. text 26.95 (*0-240-80277-2*, Focal) Buttrwrth-Heinemann.

Ancheta, Angelo N. Race, Rights & the Asian American Experience. LC 97-24855. xv, 209p. 1998. 47.00 (*0-8135-2463-6*); pap. 18.00 (*0-8135-2464-4*) Rutgers U Pr.

Ancheta, Jocelyn, ed. see Metro Deaf Senior Citizens, Inc. Staff.

Ancheta, Shirley, et al, eds. Without Names: Bay Area Pilipino American Writers. 64p. 1997. pap. 8.95 (*0-9609630-2-2*) Kearny St Wkshop.

Anchlia, Than M. New Dictionary System. 1987. write for info. (*0-9621487-0-9*) T M Anchlia.

Anchondo, Mary. How We Came to the Fifth World: Como Vinimos Al Quinto Mundo. Olivarez, Anna, ed. (Creation Story from Ancient Mexico). (ENG & SPA.). (J). (gr. 2-7). 1987. 22.95 incl. audio (*0-89239-038-7*) Childrens Book Pr.

Anchondo, Mary, jt. auth. see Rohmer, Harriet.

Anchor, K. N., ed. The Handbook of Medical Psychotherapy: Cost-Effective Strategies in Mental Health. LC 90-5007. (Illus.). 429p. 1991. 64.00 (*0-920887-67-8*) Hogrefe & Huber Pubs.

Anchor, R. D., et al. Design of Structures Against Fire. (C). 1986. 300.00 (*0-7855-4185-3*, Pub. by Witherby & Co) St Mut.

Anchor, Robert. The Enlightenment Tradition. LC 78-62855. 1979. pap. 16.95 (*0-520-03784-7*, Pub. by U CA Pr) Cal Prin Full Svc.

Anchor, Robert, tr. see Lukacs, Georg.

Anchorage Chapter National Assoc. of Catering Exec. Aurora N. A. C. E. Cookbook 1994-1995. (Illus.). 200p. 1994. 15.00 (*1-884234-01-1*) Penmanship Plus.

Anchorage Museum of History & Art Staff, jt. auth. see Cook Inlet Historical Society Staff.

Anchorage Woman's Club Staff, compiled by. Alaska's Cooking. 2. (ENG.). 263p. 1988. pap. text 16.00 (*1-57833-081-5*) Todd Commns.

Anchordoguy, Marie. Computers, Inc. Japan's Challenge to IBM. (East Asian Monographs: No. 144). 300p. 1989. 35.00 (*0-674-15630-7*) HUP.

Anchors, Michael. Safer Than Phen-Fen. LC 97-15285. 240p. 1997. boxed set 20.00 (*0-7615-1149-0*) Prima Pub.

Anchors, Scott, jt. auth. see Winston, Roger B., Jr.

Anchors, William E., Jr. Ruskin & Jewel Caves: A Brief History. 94p. 1989. pap. 4.95 (*1-880417-01-4*) Star Tech.

Anchors, William E., Jr., ed. The Lost in Space Scrapbook. 150p. 1991. pap. 19.95 (*1-880417-04-9*) Star Tech.

Anchors, William E., Jr. & Stork, Gary. The Alpha Control Reference Manual. 102p. 1986. pap. 11.95 (*1-880417-00-6*) Star Tech.

— The Jupiter Two Log Book: Lost in Space. 100p. 1992. pap. 19.95 (*1-880417-07-3*) Star Tech.

Anchors, William E., Jr., jt. auth. see Mitchell, Flint.

Ancikov, A. M., et al. Seventeen Papers on Topology & Differential Geometry. LC 51-5559. (Translations Ser.: Series 2, Vol. 92). 284p. 1970. 49.00 (*0-8218-1792-2*, TRANS2/92) Am Math.

***Ancill, R. J., et al.** Therapeutics in Geriatric Neuropsychiatry. LC 97-29971. 170p. 1998. 93.50 (*0-471-97947-3*) Wiley.

Ancilli, Ermano. Diccionario de Linguistica. (SPA.). 732p. 1982. 105.00 (*0-7859-5822-3*, 8425412641) Fr & Eur.

— Diccionario Espiritualidad, Vol. 1. (SPA.). 728p. 1983. 105.00 (*0-7859-5823-1*, 8425413370) Fr & Eur.

— Diccionario Espiritualidad, Vol. 3. (SPA.). 652p. 1983. 105.00 (*0-7859-5824-X*, 8425413656) Fr & Eur.

— Dicionario Espiritualidad, 3 vols. 2nd ed. (SPA.). 524p. 1987. 295.00 (*0-7859-3442-1*) Fr & Eur.

***Ancinec, G. Dennis, ed.** Experiences on General Biology 5th ed. 288p. 1999. pap. text, lab manual ed. 30.00 (*0-536-02410-3*) S&S Trade.

Ancinec, G. Dennis, ed. Natural History Southern: First Edition (Hardcover Book) (C). 1997. text 72.00 (*0-321-01236-4*) Addison-Wesley.

***Ancitipova, Anastasiya.** Favorite Grimm's Tales. (Illus.). (J). 2000. 25.00 (*0-86315-318-6*) Floris Bks.

Ancker, C. J., Jr. & Gafarian, A. V. Modern Combat Models: A Critique of Their Foundations. (Topics in Operations Research Ser.). x, 196p. 1992. pap. 17.00 (*1-877640-11-5*) INFORMS.

Anckner, Joy, jt. auth. see Hiney, Mary Jo.

Ancoli-Israel, Sonia. All I Want Is a Good Night's Sleep. LC 96-201. (Illus.). 144p. (C). (gr. 13). 1996. pap. text 9.95 (*0-8151-4843-7*, 26864) Mosby Inc.

Ancona & Kochan. Ancona Modules. (Swc-Management Ser.). Date not set. 40.00 (*0-538-95341-1*) Sth-Wstrn College.

Ancona, et al. Culture Module 10: Managing for the Future. (GI - Organizational Behavior Ser.). 1995. mass mkt. 6.25 (*0-538-85890-7*) S-W Pub.

— Managing for the Future. 1995. 6.50 (*0-538-85895-8*); 6.50 (*0-538-85896-6*) Thomson Learn.

— Managing Organizational Change, Module 11. (GI - Organizational Behavior Ser.). 1995. text 7.95 (*0-538-85891-5*) S-W Pub.

Ancona, A., et al. Ecole d'Ete de Probabilites de Saint-Flour XVIII - 1988. (Lecture Notes in Mathematics Ser.: Vol. 1427). vii, 330p. 1991. 58.95 (*0-387-53508-X*) Spr-Verlag.

Ancona, C., jt. auth. see Drabowitch, S.

Ancona, Deborah & Kochan. Managing for the Future: Organizational. 2nd ed. (GC - Principles of Management Ser.). 1998. 74.95 (*0-538-87546-1*) S-W Pub.

Ancona, Deborah, et al. Making Teams Work Module 3: Managing for the Future. (GI - Organizational Behavior Ser.). 1995. pap. 7.95 (*0-538-85875-3*) S-W Pub.

— Managing Diversity & Change, Module 12. (GI - Organizational Behavior Ser.). 1995. text 7.95 (*0-538-85892-3*) S-W Pub.

— Managing for the Future. (GI - Organizational Behavior Ser.). 1996. ring bd. 57.95 (*0-538-86158-4*) S-W Pub.

— Managing for the Future, Module 4. (GI - Organizational Behavior Ser.). 1995. mass mkt. 6.25 (*0-538-85876-1*) S-W Pub.

— Managing for the Future: Organizational Behavior. (GI - Organizational Behavior Ser.). (C). 1996. mass mkt. 69.95 (*0-538-84890-1*) S-W Pub.

— Negotiation - Dispute Resolution: Module 13, Module 13. (GI - Organizational Behavior Ser.). 1995. text 7.95 (*0-538-85893-1*) S-W Pub.

— The New Organization - Managing: Module 1. (GI - Organizational Behavior Ser.). 1995. mass mkt. 7.95 (*0-538-85877-X*) S-W Pub.

— New Organizational Forms Module 8: Managing for the Future. (GI - Organizational Behavior Ser.). 1995. mass mkt. 6.25 (*0-538-85882-6*) S-W Pub.

— Organizational Project & Diagnosis, Module 2. (GI - Organizational Behavior Ser.). 1995. mass mkt. 7.95 (*0-538-85878-8*) S-W Pub.

— Stakeholders/Allies/Adversaries: Module 9, Module 9. (GI - Organizational Behavior Ser.). (Illus.). 1995. mass mkt. 7.95 (*0-538-85889-3*) S-W Pub.

— Team Processes Module 5: Managing for the Future. (GI - Organizational Behavior Ser.). 1995. mass mkt. 6.95 (*0-538-85879-6*) S-W Pub.

— Teams in Organizations Module 6: Managing for the Future. (GI - Organizational Behavior Ser.). 1995. mass mkt. 7.95 (*0-538-85880-X*) S-W Pub.

— Workforce Management Module 7: Managing for the Future. (GI - Organizational Behavior Ser.). 1995. mass mkt. 6.25 (*0-538-85881-8*) S-W Pub.

Ancona, Francesco A. Crisis in America: Father Absence. LC 98-7503. 132p. 1998. 34.00 (*1-56072-569-9*) Nova Sci Pubs.

— Myth: Matter of Mind? LC 94-4718. 186p. (Orig.). pap. 27.50 (*0-8191-9494-8*); lib. bdg. 46.00 (*0-8191-9493-X*) U Pr of Amer.

Ancona, George. The American Family Farm: A Photo Essay. LC 88-30068. (Illus.). 96p. (J). (gr. 3-7). 1989. 18.95 (*0-15-203025-5*) Harcourt.

Ancona, George. The American Family Farm: A Photo Essay. 1997. 14.20 (*0-606-11038-0*, Pub. by Turtleback) Demco.

Ancona, George. The American Family Farm: A Photo Essay. large type ed. (J). 1993. 25.00 (*0-614-09815-7*, L-34126-00) Am Printing Hse.

— Aquarium Book. 1991. 12.15 (*0-606-07205-5*, Pub. by Turtleback) Demco.

— Bananas. (J). (gr. 4-7). 1990. pap. 5.95 (*0-395-54787-3*, Clarion Bks) HM.

— Bananas: From Manolo to Margie. (J). 1982. 11.15 (*0-606-04612-7*, Pub. by Turtleback) Demco.

— Barrio: Jose's Neighborhood. LC 97-29667. (Illus.). 48p. (J). (gr. 2-7). 1998. 18.00 (*0-15-201049-1*); pap. 9.00 (*0-15-201808-5*) Harcourt.

***Ancona, George.** Barrio: Jose's Neighborhood. LC 97-29667. (Illus.). 48p. (J). (gr. 2-7). 1998. pap. 9.00 (*0-15-201048-3*) Harcourt.

— Carnaval. LC 98-47297. 48p. (J). (gr. 2-5). 1999. 18.00 (*0-15-201793-3*, Harcourt Child Bks); pap. 9.00 (*0-15-201792-5*, Harcourt Child Bks) Harcourt.

Ancona, George. Charro. 1999. 27.12 (*0-8172-3773-9*) Raintree Steck-V.

— Charro: The Mexican Cowboy. LC 98-13396. (Illus.). 48p. (J). 1999. 18.00 (*0-15-201047-5*); pap. 9.00 (*0-15-201046-7*); pap. 9.00 (*0-15-202026-8*) Harcourt.

Ancona, George. Come & Eat! (Illus.). (J). 1924. 15.95 (*0-688-16235-5*, Wm Morrow); lib. bdg. 15.89 (*0-688-16236-3*, Wm Morrow) Morrow Avon.

— Cuban Family Book. 2000. write for info. (*0-688-16655-5*); lib. bdg. write for info. (*0-688-16656-3*) Lothrop.

— Cuban Kids. LC 00-29522. (Illus.). (J). 2000. write for info. (*0-7614-5077-7*) Marshall Cavendish.

Ancona, George. Fiesta Fireworks. LC 97-21608. (Illus.). 32p. (J). 1998. 16.00 (*0-688-14817-4*); lib. bdg. 15.93 (*0-688-14818-2*) Lothrop.

— Fiesta U. S. A. LC 94-34828. (Illus.). 48p. 1995. 16.99 (*0-525-67498-5*, Dutton Child) Peng Put Young Read.

— Freighters. (J). (gr. 5 up). 1985. lib. bdg. 12.89 (*0-690-04359-7*) HarpC Child Bks.

— The Golden Lion Tamarin Comes Home. LC 93-23705. (Illus.). 40p. (J). 1994. mass mkt. write for info. (*0-02-700905-X*, Mac Bks Young Read) S&S Childrens.

— Handtalk Zoo. LC 88-36861. 1996. 10.19 (*0-606-09374-5*, Pub. by Turtleback) Demco.

— Helping Out. (J). (ps-3). 1991. pap. 191.36 (*0-395-55774-7*, Clarion Bks) HM.

— Helping Out. (J). 1985. 11.15 (*0-606-04694-1*, Pub. by Turtleback) Demco.

— Let's Dance. LC 97-29436. (J). 1998. 15.99 (*0-525-67536-1*, Dutton Child) Peng Put Young Read.

***Ancona, George.** Let's Dance! LC 97-52022. (Illus.). 40p. (J). (ps-3). 1998. 16.00 (*0-688-16211-8*, Wm Morrow); 15.89 (*0-688-16212-6*, Wm Morrow) Morrow Avon.

Ancona, George. Man & Mustang. LC 91-29513. (Illus.). 48p. (J). (gr. 3-7). 1992. lib. bdg. 15.95 (*0-02-700802-9*, Mac Bks Young Read) S&S Childrens.

— Mayeros: A Yucatec Maya Family. LC 96-2309. (Illus.). 40p. (J). (gr. 1 up). 1997. 16.00 (*0-688-13465-3*); lib. bdg. 15.93 (*0-688-13466-1*) Lothrop.

— Pablo Remembers: The Fiesta of the Day of the Dead. LC 92-22819. (Illus.). (J). (gr. 4 up). 1993. 16.00 (*0-688-11249-8*); lib. bdg. 15.93 (*0-688-11250-1*) Lothrop.

— The Pinata Maker. LC 93-2389.Tr. of El Pinatero. (Illus.). 40p. (J). 1994. pap. 9.00 (*0-15-200060-7*, Harcourt Child Bks) Harcourt.

— Pinata Maker: El Pinatero. 1995. 15.20 (*0-606-06668-3*, Pub. by Turtleback) Demco.

— The Pinatamaker - El Pinatero. LC 93-2389. (Illus.). 40p. (YA). (gr. 7 up). 1994. 17.00 (*0-15-261875-9*) Harcourt.

— Powwow. LC 92-15912. (Illus.). 48p. (C). (gr. 1-7). 1993. pap. 9.00 (*0-15-263269-7*) Harcourt.

— Team Work. LC 82-45579. (Illus.). 48p. (J). (gr. 3-6). 1983. 12.95 (*0-690-04247-7*); lib. bdg. 11.89 (*0-690-04248-5*) HarpC Child Bks.

Ancona, George, photos by. Cowboys: Roundup on an American Ranch. LC 95-8866. (Illus.). 48p. (J). (gr. 2 up). 1996. 16.95 (*0-590-48424-9*) Scholastic Inc.

— Powwow. LC 92-15912. (Illus.). 48p. (J). (gr. 1-7). 1993. 17.00 (*0-15-263268-9*) Harcourt.

Ancona, George & Beth, Mary. Handtalk Zoo. (Illus.). 32p. (J). (gr. k-12). 1996. mass mkt. 4.99 (*0-689-80392-3*) Aladdin.

Ancona, George & Miller, Mary B. Handtalk School. LC 90-24030. (Illus.). 32p. (J). (gr. k-6). 1991. text 14.95 (*0-02-700912-2*, Mac Bks Young Read) S&S Childrens.

— Handtalk Zoo. LC 88-36861. (Handtalk Ser.). (Illus.). 32p. (J). (ps up). 1989. text 14.95 (*0-02-700801-0*, Mac Bks Young Read) S&S Childrens.

Ancona, Joe, ed. see Moore, John.

Ancona, Leonardo. Thematic Encyclopedia of Psychology: Enciclopedia Tematica de Psicologia, 2 vols. 1892p. 1985. 150.00 (*0-8288-2213-1*, S35828) Fr & Eur.

Ancona, Paula. SuccessAbilities! 1,003 Practical Ways to Keep up, Stand Out, & Move Ahead at Work. LC 97-36833. (Illus.). 271p. (Orig.). 1997. pap. 14.95 (*1-56370-444-7*) Park Ave.

Ancona, Ronnie. Time & the Erotic in Horace's Odes. LC 93-46913. 208p. 1994. text 42.95 (*0-8223-1476-2*) Duke.

Ancona, Ronnie, ed. Horace: Selected Odes & Satire 1.9. 1999. pap., teacher ed. 20.00 (*0-86516-430-4*) Bolchazy-Carducci.

Ancona, Ronnie, ed. see Horace.

Ancona, V. & Silva, A. Complex Analysis & Geometry. (University Series in Mathematics). (Illus.). 426p. (C). 1993. 95.00 (*0-306-44179-9*, Plenum Trade) Perseus Pubng.

Ancona, Vincenzo. Malidittu la Lingua: Damned Language. Cipolla, Gaetano, tr. 212p. 1991. pap. 16.00 incl. audio (*0-921252-14-5*) LEGAS.

Ancona, Vincenzo, et al, eds. Complex Analysis & Geometry. (Lecture Notes in Pure & Applied Mathematics Ser.: Vol. 173). (Illus.). 576p. 1995. pap. text 190.00 (*0-8247-9672-1*) Dekker.

***Anconca, Deborah.** Managing for the Future. 3rd ed. (SWC-General Business Ser.). 2001. pap. 50.00 (*0-324-05575-7*) Sth-Wstrn College.

Ancot, J. P. Micro-Qualiflex. (C). 1988. lib. bdg. 814.50 (*90-247-3615-5*) Kluwer Academic.

Ancowitz, Arthur. The Stroke Book: One on One Advice about Stroke Prevention, Management & Rehabilitation. large type ed. LC 93-40726. 1994. 24.95 (*0-7862-0115-0*) Thorndike Pr.

— The Stroke Book: One on One Advice about Stroke Prevention, Management & Rehabilitation. large type ed. LC 93-40726. 1994. pap. 17.95 (*0-7862-0116-9*) Thorndike Pr.

Ancrum, Nancy, ed. see Miami Herald Staff.

Ancrum, Ron, jt. auth. see Swann, Claire.

Ancsel, Eva. Dilemmas of Freedom. 104p. 1978. 50.00 (*0-7855-1216-0*, Pub. by Collets) St Mut.

— The Dilemmas of Freedom. 104p. (C). 1978. pap. 30.00 (*963-05-1694-2*, Pub. by Akade Kiado) St Mut.

— Ethos, Knowing, History. LC 97-126095. 157p. 1996. pap. 70.00 (*963-05-6936-1*, Pub. by Akade Kiado) St Mut.

— The Silence of History. 110p. (C). 1991. pap. 40.00 (*963-05-4907-7*, Pub. by Akade Kiado) St Mut.

And, Miekal. SASE, a Mail Installation. (Samsara Congeries Ser.: Bk. 8). 35p. 1990. pap. 5.00 (*0-945112-11-4*) Generator Pr.

And, Miekal & Was, Elizabeth. Fluxonyms. 30p. (Orig.). 1989. pap. 3.00 (*0-926935-09-7*) Runaway Spoon.

And, Miekal, ed. see Storch, Rotar.

***Anda, Michael O.** International Relations in Contemporary Africa. LC 99-55517. 312p. 2000. 44.50 (*0-7618-1585-6*) U Pr of Amer.

Anda, Michael O. Yoruba, 14 vols. Bond, George & Wyk, Gary V., eds. LC 95-15070. (Heritage Library of African Peoples). (Illus.). 64p. (YA). (gr. 7-12). 1996. lib. bdg. 16.95 (*0-8239-1988-9*) Rosen Group.

Anda, Miriam Curet De, see Curet De Anda, Miriam.

***Andacht, Sandra.** Collector's Value Guide to Japanese Woodblock Prints. LC 00-104097. (Illus.). 272p. 2000. pap. 26.95 (*1-58221-005-5*) Krause Pubns.

Andacht, Sandra. Collector's Value Guide to Oriental Decorative Arts, 2 vols., Vol. 1. (Illus.). 240p. 1997. pap. 24.95 (*0-930625-80-3*, AT5803, Antique Trader) Krause Pubns.

— Oriental Antiques & Art: An Identification & Value Guide. LC 87-50296. (Illus.). 428p. (Orig.). 1987. pap. 21.95 (*0-87069-485-5*, Wllce-Homestd) Krause Pubns.

— The Orientalia Journal Annual of Articles, Vol. 1. (Illus.). 144p. (Orig.). 1981. pap. 9.95 (*0-9607616-0-8*) S Andacht.

Andahazi, Federico. The Anatomist. 224p. 1999. pap. 12.95 (*0-385-49133-6*) Doubleday.

— The Anatomist: A Novel. LC 98-10125. 224p. 1998. 22.95 (*0-385-49132-8*) Doubleday.

— Anatomist: A Novel. Manguel, Alberto, tr. 256p. 1998. pap. 22.95 (*950-742-787-2*) Doubleday.

— El Anatomista. 1998. mass mkt. 12.00 (*0-385-49210-3*) Doubleday.

Andahazi, Federico. El Anatomista. (SPA.). 1997. 21.95 (*84-08-02083-8*) Planeta Edit.

— The Merciful Women. 2000. write for info. (*0-8021-1674-4*, Pub. by Grove-Atltic) Publishers Group.

Andahazi, Federico. Las Piadosas.Tr. of Pious. 219p. 1999. pap. 12.95 (*0-553-06099-6*) Bantam.

Andaiye, ed. see Lamming, George.

Andalis, Kristin E. My Impossible Dreams. LC 97-91319. (Orig.). 1999. pap. 8.95 (*0-533-12640-1*) Vantage.

Andall. Politics of Gender & Domestic Service. 61.95 (*0-7546-1088-8*) Ashgate Pub Co.

Andamo, Evelyn M., ed. Guide to Program Evaluation for Physical Therapy & Occupational Therapy Services. LC 84-8962. 151p. (C). 1984. text 4.95 (*0-86656-261-3*) Haworth Pr.

Anday, Melih Cevdet. Rain One Step Away. Halman, Talat S. & Swann, Brian, trs. LC 80-68880. 1980. 7.50 (*0-910350-00-0*) Charioteer.

Andaya, Barabara W. History of Malaysia. pap. 23.75 (*0-333-27673-6*, Pub. by Macmillan) St Martin.

Andaya, Barbara W. Perak, the Abode of Grace: A Study of an Eighteen-Century Malay State. (East Asian Historical Monographs). 1979. 34.00 (*0-19-580385-X*) OUP.

— To Live As Brothers: Southeast Sumatra in the Seventeenth & Eighteenth Centuries. LC 93-1347. 336p. (C). 1993. text 38.00 (*0-8248-1489-4*) UH Pr.

***Andaya, Barbara Watson, ed.** Other Pasts: Women, Gender & History in Early Modern Southeast Asia. (Southeast Asia Papers). 384p. 2000. pap. text 30.00 (*1-930734-00-X*) Ctr for SE.

Andaya, Leonard Y. The World of Maluku: Eastern Indonesia in the Early Modern Period. LC 93-18245. 304p. (C). 1993. text 38.00 (*0-8248-1490-8*) UH Pr.

Andazola, Julianne. Hoarse. (Illus.). 1996. 20.00 (*0-9652709-0-4*) Hoarse.

Ande, Nicholas & Ismailov, Famil. Azerbaijani-English, English-Azerbaijani Dictionary & Phrasebook. (AZE & ENG.). 150p. 1998. pap. 11.95 (*0-7818-0684-4*) Hippocrene Bks.

Ande, Nicholas, et al. Somali-English, English-Somali Dictionary & Phrasebook. (ENG & SOM.). 180p. 1998. pap. 13.95 (*0-7818-0621-6*) Hippocrene Bks.

Ande, Nicholas, jt. ed. see Shackle, Christopher.

Andebsihane, Berhanc, jt. auth. see Gambatta, Vern.

Andel, G. K. Christian Concept of History in the Chronicle of Sulpicius Severus. iv, 195p. (Orig.). 1976. pap. text 54.00 (*0-317-57956-8*, Pub. by AM Hakkert) Coronet Bks.

Andel, J., et al, eds. Disturbance in Grasslands: Causes, Effects & Processes. (Geobotany Ser.). (C). 1987. text 294.00 (*90-6193-640-3*) Kluwer Academic.

Andel, Tjeerd H., et al. Cenozoic History & Paleoceanography of the Central Equatorial Pacific Ocean: A Regional Synthesis Deep Sea Drilling Project Data. LC 75-20815. (Geological Society of America, Memoir Ser.: No. 143). 231p. reprint ed. pap. 71.70 (*0-608-13944-0*, 202373200033) Bks Demand.

Andel, Tjeerd H. Van, see Van Andel, Tjeerd H.

Andelin, Aubrey P. Man of Steel & Velvet. 301p. 1994. mass mkt. 5.99 (*0-911094-23-7*) Pacific Santa Barbara.

Andelin, Darline. Easy String Art for All Seasons. 70p. (J). (gr. 1-6). pap. 7.95 (*1-56861-047-5*) Swift Lrn Res.

Andelin, Helen. All about Raising Children. 410p. 1981. 18.00 (*0-911094-07-5*) Pacific Santa Barbara.

— Fascinating Womanhood. rev. ed. 416p. 1992. mass mkt. 6.99 (*0-553-29220-X*) Bantam.

— La Mujer Encantadora: Fascinating Womanhood. (SPA.). 234p. 1979. pap. 10.00 (*0-911094-08-3*) Pacific Santa Barbara.

— The Secrets of Winning Men. Orig. Title: The Fascinating Girl. 262p. 1994. pap. 12.00 (*0-911094-19-9*) Pacific Santa Barbara.

Andelman, Bob. Why Men Watch Football: A Report from the Couch. Angers, Trent, ed. (Illus.). 176p. 1993. 14.95 (*0-925417-14-9*) Acadian Hse Pub.

Andelman, Bob, jt. auth. see Gackle, Merlin.

Andelman, Bob, jt. auth. see Groppel, Jack L.

Andelman, Julian B. & Underhill, Dwight W., eds. Health Effects from Hazardous Waste Sites. LC 86-27290. (Illus.). 308p. 1987. lib. bdg. 97.50 (*0-87371-046-0*, L046) Lewis Pubs.

Andelora. Horizons: Cmpt Acr the Curr-MS Works 3 Mac. (DA - Computer Education Ser.). 1995. text 28.95 (*0-538-62572-4*) S-W Pub.

— Horizons: Cmpt Acr the Curr-MS Works 3 Mac. (DA - Computer Education Ser.). 1995. text 30.95 (*0-538-62563-5*) S-W Pub.

— Horizons: Cmpt Acr the Curr-MS Works 3 Mac. (DA - Computer Education Ser.). 1995. text 30.95 (*0-538-63307-7*) S-W Pub.

— Horizons: MS Works 2.0 MAC. (DA - Computer Education Ser.). (J). (gr. k-8). 1995. spiral bd. 36.95 (*0-538-62560-0*) S-W Pub.

— Horizons: Clarisworks 3 for Windows. (DA - K-8 Computer Education Ser.). (YA). 1996. text 30.95 (*0-538-65171-7*) S-W Pub.

— Horizons, Teacher's Print Mat: WP Works 2.1 for Windows. (DA - Computer Education Ser.). 1996. pap. 14.95 (*0-538-64181-9*) S-W Pub.

— Horizons Tutorial. (DA - Computer Education Ser.). 1995. text, suppl. ed. 28.95 incl. 3.5 hd, 5.25 hd, 5.25 ld (*0-538-62558-9*); text, suppl. ed. 30.95 (*0-538-62566-X*) S-W Pub.

— Horizons Tutorial. (DA - Computer Education Ser.). 1995. text, suppl. ed. 25.95 incl. 3.5 hd, 3.5 ld (*0-538-62575-9*) S-W Pub.

— Horizons Tutorial. (DA - Computer Education Ser.). (J). (gr. k-8). 1995. text 22.95 (*0-538-62586-4*) S-W Pub.

— Tutorial Horizons: Microsoft Works 4.0 Mac. (DA - Computer Education Ser.). (J). (gr. k-8). 1996. pap. 30.95 (*0-538-64585-7*) S-W Pub.

Andelora, Rob. Horizons: Cmpt Acr the Curr-MS Works 3 Mac. (DA - Computer Education Ser.). 1995. text 28.95 (*0-538-63302-6*) S-W Pub.

Andelora, Sharon. ClarisWorks 5.0, Macintosh Tutorial. LC 98-3907. (Horizons, Computing Across the Curriculum Ser.). (YA). 1998. spiral bd. 24.95 (*0-02-804225-5*) Glencoe.

Andelson, Robert V., ed. Commons Without Tragedy. 210p. (C). 1991. 54.00 (*0-389-20958-9*) B&N Imports.

Andelson, Robert V. & Dawsey, James. From Wasteland to Promised Land. 146p. 1994. pap. 30.00 (*0-85683-133-6*, Pub. by Srch Pr) St Mut.

Andemicael, Berhanykun. The OAU & the U. N. Relations Between the Organization of African Unity & the United Nations. LC 74-84658. 350p. 1976. 49.50 (*0-8419-0186-4*, Africana) Holmes & Meier.

Andemichael, B. Regionalism & the United Nations. 623p. 1979. lib. bdg. 104.50 (*90-286-0109-0*) Kluwer Academic.

Andenaes, Johannes. General Part of the Criminal Law of Norway. Ogle, Thomas P., tr. (N. Y. U. Criminal Law Education & Research Center Publications: Vol. 3). xxiii, 346p. Date not set. 35.00 (*0-8377-0202-X*, Rothman) W S Hein.

Andenaes, Olav & Naess, Tor, eds. Floating Production Platforms in Combination with Fixed Lightweight Wellhead Structures. (C). 1989. 95.00 (*0-89771-743-0*, Pub. by Lorne & MacLean Marine) St Mut.

Andenaes, Olav & Ness, Tor. Floating Production in Combination & Fixed Lightweight Wellhead Structures. 1989. 150.00 (*90-6314-860-7*, Pub. by Lorne & MacLean Marine) St Mut.

Andenas, Mads, et al, eds. European Economic & Monetary Union Vol. EEFS 1: The Institutional Framework. LC 98-116825. (International Banking & Finance Law Ser.). 592p. 1997. 233.00 (*90-411-0687-1*) Kluwer Academic.

Andenas, Mads, jt. auth. see Norton, Joseph J.

Andenas, Mads, jt. ed. see Jacobs, Francis.

Andenas, Mads, jt. ed. see Rider, Barry A. K.

Andenoro, Amy L., ed. see Andenoro, Nanetta.

Andenoro, Nanetta. The Long Journey. Andenoro, Amy L., ed. (Orig.). 1997. mass mkt. 5.95 (*0-9658602-0-5*) Three G.

Andeo, Hikotareo. Peking. LC 77-400603. (This Beautiful World Bks.). 150 p. 1968. write for info. (*0-7063-1088-8*, Pub. by WrLock) Sterling.

Andeo, Nisuke & Kokusaiheo Gakkai (Japan) Staff. Japan & International Law: Past, Present & Future: International Symposium to Mark the Centennial of the Japanese Association of International Law. LC 99-22826. (International Law in Japanese Perspective Ser.). 1999. 135.00 (*90-411-1194-8*) Kluwer Law Intl.

Ander, Gregg D. Daylighting Performance & Design. (Architecture Ser.). 241p. 1995. 80.00 (*0-471-28661-3*, VNR) Wiley.

Ander, Gregg D. Daylighting Performance & Design. LC 94-45674. (Illus.). 240p. 1995. text 62.95 (*0-442-01921-1*, VNR) Wiley.

Ander, O. Fritiof. The Cultural Heritage of the Swedish Immigrant. Scott, Franklyn D., ed. LC 78-15203. (Scandinavians in America Ser.). 1979. reprint ed. lib. bdg. 18.95 (*0-405-11629-2*) Ayer.

— T. N. Hasselquist. Scott, Franklyn D., ed. LC 78-15208. (Scandinavians in America Ser.). 1979. reprint ed. lib. bdg. 23.95 (*0-405-11630-6*) Ayer.

Ander, O. Fritiof, ed. The John Hauberg Historical Essays. LC 54-14973. (Augustana College Library Publications: No. 26). 70p. 1954. 13.00 (*0-910182-21-3*) Augustana Coll.

— Lincoln Images: Augustana College Centennial Essays. LC 60-12543. (Augustana College Library Publications: No. 29). (Illus.). 161p. 1960. 13.00 (*0-910182-29-9*) Augustana Coll.

Ander, O. Fritiof & Nordstrom, Oscar L. The American Origin of the Augustana Synod & Contemporary Lutheran Periodicals, 1851-1860. LC 43-9754. (Augustana Historical Society Publications: Vol. 9). 192p. 1942. pap. 3.00 (*0-910184-09-7*) Augustana.

Andera, Frank, jt. auth. see Condon, Gregg.

Andera, Margaret, et al. Warrington Colescott. LC 96-77357. (Illus.). 32p. (Orig.). 1996. pap. 10.95 (*0-944110-48-7*) Milwauk Art Mus.

Andereck, C. D. & Hayot, F. Ordered & Turbulent Patterns in Taylor-Couette Flow. LC 92-18440. (NATO ASI Ser.: Vol. 297). (Illus.). 370p. (C). 1992. text 125.00 (*0-306-44238-8*, Kluwer Plenum) Kluwer Academic.

Andereck, Gene. Trial at Grand Marais. LC 97-68211. 280p. 1997. 15.00 (*1-890826-01-4*) Rock Creek Pr.

Andereck, Mary E. Ethnic Awareness & the School: An Ethnographic Study. (Series on Race & Ethnic Relations: Vol. 5). (Illus.). 172p. 1992. 52.00 (*0-8039-3886-1*); pap. 24.00 (*0-8039-3887-X*) Sage.

— Ethnic Awareness & the School: An Ethnographic Study. LC 91-44223. (Sage Series on Race & Ethnic Relations: No. 5). 155p. 1992. reprint ed. pap. 48.10 (*0-608-04296-X*, 206507500012) Bks Demand.

Anderegg, M. L., jt. auth. see Vergason, Glenn A.

***Anderegg, Michael.** Orson Welles, Shakespeare, & Popular Culture. LC 98-24770. (Film & Culture Ser.). (Illus.). 216p. 1998. lib. bdg. 42.50 (*0-231-11228-9*) Col U Pr.

— Orson Welles, Shakespeare, & Popular Culture. LC 98-24770. (Film & Culture Ser.). (Illus.). xiv, 213 p. 1999. pap. 16.50 (*0-231-11229-7*) Col U Pr.

Anderegg, Michael, ed. Inventing Vietnam: The War in Film & Television. (Culture & the Moving Image Ser.). (Illus.). (C). 1991. 69.95 (*0-87722-861-2*); pap. 22.95 (*0-87722-862-0*) Temple U Pr.

Anderer, Paul. Other Worlds: Arishima Takeo & the Bounds of Modern Japanese Fiction. LC 84-12171. 224p. 1984. text 46.00 (*0-231-05884-5*) Col U Pr.

Anderes, Fred & Agranoff, Ann. Ice Palaces. LC 83-6061. (Illus.). 132p. 1983. pap. 35.00 (*0-89659-393-2*) Abbeville Pr.

***Anderes, Marilyn.** The Great Encourager: A Study of John XIV. 86p. 1998. reprint ed. pap. 5.95 (*1-885224-22-2*) Bristol Hse.

Anderes, Marilyn. A Workshop on Self-Giving. 144p. (Orig.). 1989. pap. 6.99 (*0-310-52251-X*) Zondervan.

Anderes, Marilyn N. From the Heart of the Word: Building Biblical Lives. 96p. 1997. pap. 11.95 (*1-885224-15-X*) Bristol Hse.

Anderes, Thomas. Outcome Based Budgeting: Connecting Budget Development, Allocation & Outcomes. 1995. 10.00 (*0-614-13553-2*) SHEEO.

Anderhalden, A., ed. see Roelli, H. J.

Anderheggen, George C. Willie the Weenie Whiner. (Illus.). 20p. (Orig.). (J). (gr. 5 up). 1983. 3.95 (*0-910717-01-X*) Bookling Pubs.

— A Wish for Your Christmas. (Illus.). 13p. (Orig.). 1982. write for info. (*0-318-56854-3*) Bookling Pubs.

Anderheggew, George C. The Harmonic Mind. (Orig.). 1989. 19.95 (*0-910717-02-8*) Bookling Pubs.

Anderholm, K. D. Understanding New Testament Judgments. unabridged ed. 100p. (Orig.). Date not set. pap. text 6.99 (*0-9655407-1-5*) True Light Pubns.

Anderholm, Kerry D. Beware of Men: Exposing the Spirit of the Modern-Day Pharisee. unabridged ed. 192p. (Orig.). 1997. pap. 9.99 (*0-9655407-0-7*) True Light Pubns.

— You Need . . . Dispensational Understanding. unabridged ed. Jensen, Jerry, ed. (Illus.). 100p. (Orig.). 1995. pap. 5.99 (*0-9655407-9-0*) True Light Pubns.

Anderhub, Beth. General Sonography: A Clinical Guide. (Illus.). 416p. (C). (gr. 13). 1994. text 53.00 (*0-8016-7421-2*, 00031) Mosby Inc.

— General Sonography: A Clinical Guide. 224p. 1995. pap. text, teacher ed. write for info. (*0-8151-0099-X*) Mosby Inc.

Anderhub, Beth & Anderhub, O'Brien. Ultrasonic Physics & Instrumentation. (Illus.). 304p. 1988. pap. text. write for info. (*0-316-03918-7*, Little Brwn Med Div) Lppncott W & W.

Anderhub, O'Brien, jt. auth. see Anderhub, Beth.

Anderhub, Rita, jt. auth. see Polek, David.

Anderko, Andrzej, jt. auth. see Malanowski, Stanislaw.

Anderko, Andrzej, ed. see Malanowski, Stanislaw.

Anderko, Kurt, jt. ed. see Hansen, Max.

Anderla, Georges & Dunning, Anthony. Computer Strategies, 1990-1999: Technologies - Costs - Markets. LC 87-8173. 321p. reprint ed. pap. 99.60 (*0-7837-3212-0*, 204323000007) Bks Demand.

Anderla, Georges, et al. Chaotics: An Agenda for Business & Society in the 21st Century. LC 96-37727. (Praeger Studies on the 21st Century). 240p. 1997. 69.50 (*0-275-95691-1*, Praeger Pubs); pap. 23.95 (*0-275-95882-5*, Praeger Pubs) Greenwood.

Anderlini-D'Onofrio, Serena. The Weak Subject: On Modernity, Eros, & Women's Playwriting. LC 97-13826. 352p. 1998. 48.50 (*0-8386-3730-2*) Fairleigh Dickinson.

Anderlini, Fausto, jt. ed. see Leonardi, Robert.

Anderlini, Sanam Naraghi, jt. auth. see Rupesinghe, Kumar.

Anderloni, L., jt. ed. see Ruozi, R.

Andermahr, Sonya, et al. A Concise Glossary of Feminist Theory. LC 97-13574. (An Arnold Publication). 296p. 1997. pap. text 19.95 (*0-340-59663-5*) OUP.

— A Glossary of Feminist Theory. LC 97-3800. (An Arnold Publication). 356p. 1997. text 65.00 (*0-340-59662-7*) OUP.

Andermahr, Sonya, jt. auth. see Griffin, Gabriele.

Anderman, Barbara, ed. see Wilmerding, John, et al.

Anderman, Eric M., jt. ed. see Anderman, Lynley H.

Anderman, Gunilla, ed. New Swedish Plays. Foster, Duncan et al, trs. 212p. 1993. pap. 25.00 (*1-870041-19-4*, Pub. by Forest Bks) Dufour.

Anderman, Gunilla & Rogers, Margaret, eds. Words, Words, Words: The Translator & the Language Learner. LC 95-43551. (Topics in Translation Ser.: Vol. 7). 120p. 1996. 69.00 (*1-85359-332-X*, Pub. by Multilingual Matters); pap. 26.95 (*1-85359-331-1*, Pub. by Multilingual Matters) Taylor & Francis.

***Anderman, Gunilla M., et al.** Word, Text & Translation: Liber Amicorum for Peter Newmark. LC 99-43741. 1999. pap. write for info. (*1-85359-460-1*, Pub. by Multilingual Matters) Taylor & Francis.

Anderman, Janusz. The Edge of the World. Taylor, Nina, tr. LC 88-61402. (Readers International Ser.). (POL., Illus.). 150p. (Orig.). 1988. 14.95 (*0-930523-49-0*); pap. 7.95 (*0-930523-50-4*) Readers Intl.

— Poland under Black Light. Short, Andrew & Taylor, Nina, trs. from POL. (Readers International Ser.). 131p. (Orig.). 1988. 12.50 (*0-930523-13-X*); pap. 6.95 (*0-930523-14-8*) Readers Intl.

***Anderman, Lynley H. & Anderman, Eric M., eds.** The Role of Social Context in Educational Psychology: Substantive & Methodological Issues. A Special Issue of Educational Psychologist. 87p. 2000. pap. write for info. (*0-8058-9754-2*) L Erlbaum Assocs.

Anderman, Paul. Word Carvings: Valley Notes. (Illus.). 122p. 1999. pap. 10.00 (*0-9644370-8-2*) Dryden Publ.

Anderman, Steven D. EC Competition Law & Intellectual Property Rights: The Regulation of Innovation. LC 98-3003. 348p. 1998. text 98.00 (*0-19-825977-8*) OUP.

Anderman, Steven D., et al, eds. Law & the Weaker Party. 1992. write for info. (*0-406-99845-0*, LWPAASET, MICHIE) LEXIS Pub.

Anderman, Steven D., et al. Law & the Weaker Party, 5 vols., Set. boxed set 220.00 (*0-614-05550-4*, UK, MICHIE) LEXIS Pub.

Andermann, Frederick. Occipital Seizures & Epilepsies in Children. 256p. 68.00 (*0-86196-385-7*, Pub. by J Libbey Med) Bks Intl VA.

Andermann, Frederick, ed. Alternating Hemiplegia of Childhood. (International Review of Child Neurology Ser.). 240p. 1994. text 89.00 (*0-7817-0163-5*) Lppncott W & W.

Andermann, Frederick, et al, eds. Magnetic Resonance Scanning & Epilepsy. (NATO ASI Ser.: Vol. 264). (Illus.). 334p. (C). 1994. text 105.00 (*0-306-44735-5*, Kluwer Plenum) Kluwer Academic.

Anders, et al. Exploring Unity of Organisms. 3rd ed. 266p. (C). 1998. spiral bd. 20.95 (*0-7872-4681-6*) Kendall-Hunt.

Anders, Andre. A Formulary for Plasma Physics. 276p. 1990. 55.00 (*3-05-501263-1*, Pub. by Akademie Verlag) Wiley.

***Anders, Andre.** Handbook of Plasma Immersion Ion Implantation & Deposition. 704p. 2000. text 175.00 (*0-471-24698-0*) Wiley.

***Anders, C. J.** A Capeside Christmas. (Dawson's Creek Ser.: No. 12). (Illus.). 176p. (YA). (gr. 8 up). 2000. mass mkt. 5.99 (*0-671-77541-3*, Pocket Pulse) PB.

Anders, C. J. Don't Scream. (Dawson's Creek Ser.: No. 8). 192p. (YA). (gr. 7-12). 1999. mass mkt. 4.99 (*0-671-03529-0*) S&S Trade.

— Double Exposure. (Dawson's Creek Ser.: No.5). (YA). (gr. 8 up). 1999. per. 4.99 (*0-671-03526-6*) PB.

***Anders, C. J.** Playing for Keeps. (Dawson's Creek Ser.: No. 10). 192p. (YA). (gr. 8 up). 2000. mass mkt. 5.99 (*0-671-77536-7*, Pocket Pulse) PB.

— Running on Empty. (Dawson's Creek Ser.: No. 11). (Illus.). 176p. (YA). (gr. 8 up). 2000. mass mkt. 5.99 (*0-671-77540-5*) PB.

Anders, C. J. Shifting into Overdrive, Vol. 3. (Dawson's Creek Ser.: No. 3). (YA). (gr. 8 up). 1998. per. 4.99 (*0-671-02476-0*) PB.

— Too Hot to Handle. (Dawson's Creek Ser.: No. 7). (YA). (gr. 8 up). 1999. per. 4.99 (*0-671-03528-2*) S&S Trade.

***Anders, C. J.** Tough Enough. (Dawson's Creek Ser.: No. 9). 176p. (YA). (gr. 8 up). 2000. per. 5.99 (*0-671-77533-2*, Pocket Pulse) PB.

Anders, C. J. Trouble in Paradise. (Dawson's Creek Ser.: No. 6). 192p. (YA). (gr. 7-12). 1999. per. 4.99 (*0-671-03527-4*) PB.

Anders, Curt. Disaster in Damp Sand: The Red River Expedition. 1998. 22.95 (*1-57860-015-4*); pap. 14.95 (*1-57860-016-2*) Guild Pr IN.

— Hearts in Conflict: A One-Volume History of the Civil War. LC 92-39497. 1993. 29.95 (*1-55972-184-7*, Birch Ln Pr) Carol Pub Group.

— Henry Halleck's War: A Fresh Look at Lincoln's Controversial General-in-Chief. 1999. pap. 35.95 (*1-57860-071-5*) Guild Pr IN.

Anders, Donna. Another Life, Vol. 1. 1984. mass mkt. 1.50 (*0-671-00910-9*) PB.

***Anders, Donna.** Dead Silence. 352p. 2000. 6.99 (*0-671-03881-8*, Pocket Star Bks) PB.

Anders, Donna. The Flower Man. 320p. 1995. per. 5.99 (*0-671-88043-8*) PB.

— Mari. (Historical Ser.: No. 73). 1991. per. 3.95 (*0-373-28673-2*) Harlequin Bks.

— Paradise Moon. (Historical Ser.: No. 713). 1992. mass mkt. 3.99 (*0-373-28713-5*, 1-28713-5) Harlequin Bks.

***Anders, Donna J.** The Road Back from Hell. LC 99-93819. 2000. pap. 9.95 (*0-533-13152-9*) Vantage.

Anders, Elizabeth. Field Hockey: Steps to Success. LC 98-27574. (Illus.). 200p. 1999. pap. 16.95 (*0-88011-673-0*, PAND0673) Human Kinetics.

— My Doll Is Missing! LC 96-76135. (Puzzle Place Ser.). (Illus.). 32p. (Orig.). (J). (ps-1). 1996. pap. 4.95 (*0-448-41313-2*, G & D) Peng Put Young Read.

— Sizzle Cleans Up. (Puzzle Place Ser.). (Illus.). 32p. (Orig.). (J). (ps-1). 1997. pap. 5.95 (*0-448-41300-0*, G & D) Peng Put Young Read.

Anders, F., intro. Codex Tro-Cortesianus. fac. ed. (Codices Selecti C Ser.: Vol. VIII). (Illus.). 54p. 1967. lthr. 459.00 (*3-201-00759-5*, Pub. by Akademische Druck-und) Balogh.

— Codex Vaticanus 3773. fac. ed. (Codices Selecti C Ser.: Vol. XXXVI). (Illus.). 48p. 1972. lthr. 321.00 (*3-201-00780-3*, Pub. by Akademische Druck-und) Balogh.

Anders, F., intro. Codex Magliabechiano CL. XIII.3 (B. R. 232) Anon. Vida de los Yndios. fac. ed. (Codices Selecti C Ser.: Vol. XXIII). 78p. 1970. lthr. 320.00 (*3-201-00763-3*, Pub. by Akademische Druck-und) Balogh.

Anders, F., pref. Codex Zouche-Nuttall. fac. ed. (Codices Selecti C Ser.: Vol. LXXXIV). (ENG & GER., Illus.). 60p. 1987. lthr. 779.00 (*3-201-01350-1*, Pub. by Akademische Druck-und) Balogh.

Anders, F. & Deckert, H., contrib. by. Codex Dresdensis. fac. ed. (Codices Selecti C Ser.: Vol. LIV). (Illus.). 78p. 1975. lthr. 309.00 (*3-201-00960-1*, Pub. by Akademische Druck-und) Balogh.

Anders, Ferdinand. Codice Vaticano B (Codex Vaticanus B), 2 vols. deluxe ed. (SPA.). 1993. pap. text 129.99 (*968-16-4155-8*, Pub. by Fondo) Continental Bk.

Anders, Ferdinand, et al, comments. Codice Borbonico: Codex Borbonicus, 2 vols., Set. 251p. 1996. text 179.99 (*0-8061-9939-3*, 9939) U of Okla Pr.

— Codice Borgia: Codex Borgia, 2 vols., Set. 394p. 1996. text 155.99 (*0-8061-9940-7*, 9940) U of Okla Pr.

— Codice Zouche-Nuttall: Codex Zouche-Nuttall, 2 vols., Set. 256p. 1996. text 155.99 (*0-8061-9941-5*, 9941) U of Okla Pr.

Anders, Ferdinand & Jansen, Maarteen. Codice Borgia (Codex Borgia), 2 vols. deluxe ed. (SPA.). 1993. pap. text 169.99 (*968-16-4154-X*, Pub. by Fondo) Continental Bk.

Anders, Ferdinand & Jansen, Maarten. Codice Borbonico (Codex Borbonicus), 2 vols. deluxe ed. (SPA.). 1993. pap. text 179.99 (*968-16-3630-9*, Pub. by Fondo) Continental Bk.

— Codice Cospi (Codex Cospi), 2 vols. deluxe ed. (SPA.). 20p. 1994. text 155.99 (*968-16-4481-6*, Pub. by Fondo) Continental Bk.

— Codice Egerton y Becker II (Codex Egerton & Becker II), 2 vols. deluxe ed. (SPA.). 16p. 1994. text 179.99 (*968-16-4482-4*, Pub. by Fondo) Continental Bk.

— Codice Vindobonensis (Codex Vindobonensis), 2 vols. deluxe ed. (SPA.). 1993. pap. text 169.99 (*968-16-3710-0*, Pub. by Fondo) Continental Bk.

— Codice Zouche-Nuttall (Codex Zouche-Nuttall), 2 vols. deluxe ed. (SPA.). 1993. pap. text 169.99 (*968-16-3711-9*, Pub. by Fondo) Continental Bk.

Anders, Ferdinand, et al. Codice Laud (Codex Laud), 2 vols. deluxe ed. (SPA.). 24p. 1994. text 159.99 (*968-16-4479-4*, Pub. by Fondo) Continental Bk.

Anders, George. Health Against Wealth. 304p. 1998. pap. 15.00 (*0-395-82282-3*) HM.

— Health Against Wealth: HMOs & the Breakdown of Medical Trust. large type ed. LC 96-49737. 523p. 1997. 26.95 (*0-7838-8054-5*, G K Hall Lrg Type) Mac Lib Ref.

Anders, George J. Probability Concepts in Electric Power Systems. LC 89-8932. 682p. 1990. 198.50 (*0-471-50229-4*) Wiley.

— Rating of Electric Power Cables: Ampacity Computations for Transmission, Distribution & Industrial Applications. LC 96-43345. (Press Power Engineering Ser.). 464p. 1997. 129.95 (*0-7803-1177-9*, PC5647) Inst Electrical.

— Rating of Electric Power Cables: Ampacity Computations for Transmission, Distribution, & Industrial Applications. (Illus.). 424p. 1997. 99.95 (*0-07-001791-3*) McGraw-Hill Prof.

Anders, Gerhard, ed. see Gramm, W. Phillip.

Anders, Greg, et al. Microcomputing Accounting: Tutorial & Applications with Peachtree for DOS. 1994. teacher ed. 79.76 incl. disk (*0-02-801067-1*) Glencoe.

— Spreadsheet Accounting: Tutorial & Applications Using Lotus 1-2-3. 1995. teacher ed. 30.70 incl. disk (*0-02-800730-1*) Glencoe.

Anders, Gregory E. Spreadsheet Applications for Accounting. LC 95-115637. 1994. pap. 27.00 (*0-02-800729-8*) Glencoe.

***Anders, Gregory E., et al.** Microcomputer Accounting: Tutorial & Applications for Peachtree Accounting, Release 7.0. 3rd ed. LC 99-40025. 1999. write for info. (*0-02-804754-0*) Glencoe.

— Microcomputer Accounting: Tutorial & Applications for Peachtree Accounting, Release 7.0. 3rd ed. LC 99-40025. 1999. write for info. (*0-02-804752-4*); write for info. (*0-02-804753-2*) Glencoe.

Anders, Gregory E., et al. Microcomputer Accounting: Tutorial & Applications with ACCPAC Simply Accounting. LC 94-8323. 1994. 98.00 (*0-02-801068-X*) Glencoe.

— Microcomputer Accounting: Tutorial & Applications with Peachtree for Windows. LC 95-35134. 1995. 72.44 (*0-02-802250-5*) Glencoe.

Anders, Gregory E., et al. Microcomputing Accounting: Tutorial & Applications with Peachtree for Windows. 1996. teacher ed. 75.52 incl. disk (*0-02-802251-3*) Glencoe.

Anders, Heidi. Never Say Die: Englische Idiome um Den Tod und das Sterben. (Europaische Hochschulschriften Ser.: No.14, Vol. 298). (GER.). 324p. 1995. 57.95 (*3-631-49351-7*) P Lang Pubng.

Anders, Henry R. Shakespeare's Books. LC 76-158251. reprint ed. 34.50 (*0-404-00355-9*) AMS Pr.

Anders, Isabel. A Book of Blessings for Working Mothers. LC 94-76024. (Illus.). 48p. 1994. pap. 4.95 (*0-89243-675-1*) Liguori Pubns.

***Anders, Isabel.** Easter ABC's. 32p. 2000. teacher ed. 7.99 (*1-570-07020-1*, 56-2040) Concordia.

— Real Night Before Christmas. 32p. (J). (gr. k-2). 1999. 7.99 (*0-570-05480-X*) Concordia.

Anders, Isabel. Sand & Shell, Carousels & Silver Bells: A Child's Seasons of Prayer. LC 97-131086. (Illus.). 32p. 1997. 6.99 (*0-570-04881-8*, 56-1830) Concordia.

— Simple Blessings for Sacred Moments Series 1: A Compilation by Isabel Anders. LC 97-17287. 256p. 1998. pap. 11.00 (*0-7648-0221-6*, Liguori Triumph) Liguori Pubns.

— Soul Moments: Times when Heaven Touches Earth. 144p. 1999. pap. 13.95 (*0-88347-430-1*, Pub. by T More) BookWorld.

Anders, Isabel, ed. see Bomar, Wayne.

Anders, Isabel, ed. see Shemin, Robert.

Anders, J. The Postischemic Myocardium: Energetic State & Its Relation to Contractile Failure. No. 7. 96p. (Orig.). 1988. pap. 29.50 (*90-6186-291-4*, Pub. by Leuven Univ) Coronet Bks.

Anders, James E., Sr. Cleaning & Flushing Hydraulics Systems. (Illus.). 100p. (Orig.). 1994. 30.00 (*0-9636737-1-8*) Hydraulics.

— Industrial Hydraulics Troubleshooting. (Illus.). 192p. 1989. reprint ed. text 30.00 (*0-07-001592-9*) Hydraulics.

— Solenoid-Actuated Directional Control Valves for Hydraulic Service. (Illus.). 144p. 1997. spiral bd. 40.00 (*0-9636737-3-4*) Hydraulics.

— User-Friendly Hydraulics Specifications. 292p. 1993. 30.00 (*0-9636737-0-X*) Hydraulics.

— What You Should Know about Hydraulic Cylinders. 1995. spiral bd. 30.00 (*0-9636737-2-6*) Hydraulics.

Anders, Jaroslaw, tr. see Herbert, Zbigniew.

Anders, Jaroslaw, tr. see Krall, Hanna.

Anders, Jeanne. Language of the Heart. No. 24. (Serenade Serenata Ser.). 1985. pap. 1.49 (*0-310-46922-8*, 15551P) Zondervan.

Anders, Jeffrey L. & Jefferson, James W. Trichotillomania: A Guide. vii, 45p. 1994. pap. 4.50 (*1-890802-10-7*) Madison Inst of Med.

***Anders, Jeffrey L. & Jefferson, James W.** Trichotillomania: A Guide. rev. ed. 49p. 1998. pap. 4.95 (*1-890802-14-X*) Madison Inst of Med.

Anders, Jim. Networking Starter Kit for Macintosh. (Illus.). 500p. (Orig.). 1995. pap. text 40.00 (*1-56830-131-6*) Hayden.

Anders, Joe, et al. A Look at Life: Exploring the Unity of Organisms. 3rd ed. 256p. (C). 1996. pap. text 20.95 (*0-7872-2361-1*) Kendall-Hunt.

Anders, John P. Willa Cather's Sexual Aesthetics & the Male Homosexual Literary Tradition. LC 99-10701. 1999. text 40.00 (*0-8032-1053-1*) U of Nebr Pr.

Anders, Joyce J. Anders of Two Rivers: A California Family Homesteads in Alaska. L'Ecuyer, Rosalie E., ed. LC 97-195483. (Illus.). 121p. 1997. pap. 9.95 (*0-9655844-0-2*) Jenny M Pubs.

Anders, Judy & Anders, Richard. Anders CD-ROM Guide 1997 Edition. 256p. (Orig.). 1996. pap. 10.95 (*1-888056-02-9*) Andiron Press.

Anders, Karen. Jennifer's Outlaw. 1997. per. 3.99 (*0-373-07780-7*, 1-07780-9) Silhouette.

Anders, Karl. Murder to Order. (Illus.). 1967. 6.95 (*0-8159-6207-X*) Devin.

Anders, Karl H., jt. ed. see Vinters, Harry V.

Anders, Leslie. Confederate Roll of Honor: Missouri. (Illus.). 180p. 1989. lib. bdg. 29.00 (*0-9624743-0-4*) WCMGS&L.

— Gentle Knoght: The Life & Times of Major General Edwin Forrest Harding. LC 84-27839. 394p. reprint ed. pap. 122.20 (*0-7837-1981-7*, 204225500002) Bks Demand.

— The Twenty-First Missouri: From Home Guard to Union Regiment, 11. LC 75-64. (Contributions in Military History Ser.: No. 11). (Illus.). 298p. 1975. 59.95 (*0-8371-7962-9*, AVI/, Greenwood Pr) Greenwood.

Anders, Lizzie & Hayes, Katie. Hijack: Our Story of Survival. large type ed. (Illus.). 288p. 31.99 (*0-7089-4056-0*) Ulverscroft.

Anders, Louis H., et al. Alabama Limited Liability Company Forms & Practice Manual, 2 vols. LC 96-23181. 736p. 1996. ring bd. 239.90 (*1-57400-012-8*) Data Trace Pubng.

Anders, M. 30 Days to Understanding the Bible. rev. ed. LC 95-113338. 12.99 (*0-8499-3575-X*) Word Pub.

Anders, M. W., et al, eds. Advances in Pharmacology: Intracellular Signal Transduction, Vol. 36. (Illus.). 310p. 1996. text 69.00 (*0-12-032937-9*); pap. text 39.00 (*0-12-513805-9*) Acad Pr.

Anders, Max. God. (What You Need to Know Ser.). 1998. pap. 8.99 (*0-7852-1344-9*) Nelson.

Anders, Max. Guerra Espiritual en 12 Lecciones (Spiritual Warfare in 12 Lessons) (What You Need to Know about ... in 12 Lessons Ser.). (ENG & SPA.). 192p. 8.99 (*0-89922-524-1*) Caribe Betania.

Anders, Max. Jesus. (What You Need to Know Ser.). 1998. pap. text 8.99 (*0-7852-1346-5*) Nelson.

— The New Christian's Handbook. LC 99-11283. 320p. 1999. pap. 10.99 (*0-7852-0707-4*) Nelson.

Anders, Max. Profecia Biblica en 12 Lecciones (Bible Prophecy in 12 Lessons) (What You Need to Know about ... in 12 Lessons Ser.). (ENG & SPA.). 192p. 8.99 (*0-89922-467-9*) Caribe Betania.

Anders, Max. 30 Dias para Entender la Biblia. (SPA.). 272p. 1996. 12.99 (*0-89922-503-9*, C008-5039) Caribe Betania.

— 30 Dias Para Entender Lo Que Creen los Cristianos. (SPA.). 304p. 1996. 12.99 (*0-89922-505-5*, C008-5055) Caribe Betania.

***Anders, Max & Walls, David.** 1 & 2 Peter, 1,2 & 3 John & Jude. (Holman New Testament Commentary Ser.: Vol. 11). 400p. 1999. 16.99 (*0-8054-0210-1*) Broadman.

Anders, Max E. Bible. (What You Need to Know Ser.). 1998. pap. 8.99 (*0-7852-1345-7*) Nelson.

— Bible Prophecy: Revealing the Final Victory. LC 96-52882. (What You Need to Know Ser.: Vol. 7). 192p. 1997. pap. 8.99 (*0-8407-1938-8*) Nelson.

— The Church: Finding Your Place in the Body of Christ. LC 96-5898. (What You Need to Know Ser.). 192p. 1997. pap. 8.99 (*0-7852-1153-5*) Nelson.

— Defending Your Faith: In 12 Lessons. LC 97-46644. (What You Need to Know About Ser.). 192p. 1998. pap. 8.99 (*0-7852-1192-6*) Nelson.

— The Holy Spirit: In 12 Lessons. (What You Need to Know Ser.). 1998. pap. 8.99 (*0-7852-1347-3*) Nelson.

— Jesus: Knowing Our Savior. LC 94-45930. (We Believe! Ser.). 1995. pap. 8.99 (*0-8407-8486-4*) Nelson.

— Salvation: In 12 Lessons. LC 97-48678. (What You Need to Know Ser.). 192p. 1998. pap. 8.99 (*0-7852-1191-8*) Nelson.

— Spiritual Growth. LC 97-8578. (What You Need to Know Ser.). 1997. pap. 8.99 (*0-8407-1936-1*) Nelson.

— Spiritual Warfare. LC 96-12964. (We Believe! Ser.). 192p. 1996. pap. 8.99 (*0-7852-1149-7*) Nelson.

— 30 Days to Understanding the Christian Life in 15 Minutes a Day. LC 98-14124. 1998. pap. 12.99 (*0-7852-0998-0*) Nelson.

— 30 Days to Understanding What Christians Believe in 15 Minutes a Day. LC 98-14123. 1998. pap. 12.99 (*0-7852-0999-9*) Nelson.

— Twenty-One Unbreakable Laws of Life. 240p. 1996. 16.99 (*0-7852-7611-4*) Nelson.

Anders, N. L., et al. An Evaluation of Potential Export Markers for Selected U. S. Fish Products. 1992. 3.00 (*0-685-10181-9*) MD Sea Grant Col.

Anders, Nedda C. Applique Old & New, Including Patchwork & Embroidery. LC 75-19756. (Illus.). 128p. 1976. reprint ed. pap. 4.95 (*0-486-23246-8*) Dover.

Anders, Patricia. Literacy Instruction Content Area. LC 95-79772. (C). 1995. pap. text 34.00 (*0-15-500820-X*, Pub. by Harcourt Coll Pubs) Harcourt.

Anders, Peter. Envisioning Cyberspace: Designing 3-D Electronic Spaces. LC 98-26053. (Illus.). 228p. 1998. pap. 49.95 (*0-07-001632-1*) McGraw.

Anders, Richard. The Anders CD-ROM Survey. Shipley, Chris, ed. & pref. by. 250p. (Orig.). 1995. pap. 9.95 (*1-888056-00-2*) Andiron Press.

***Anders, Richard.** From One Who Has Not Stepped Forth. 32p. 2000. pap. 5.00 (*0-9675144-2-8*, Black Sq) Neko Buildings.

Anders, Richard, jt. auth. see Anders, Judy.

Anders, Robert L. Biograffiti. 1997. write for info. (*1-57074-361-4*) Greyden Pr.

Anders, Roger M., ed. Forging the Atomic Shield: Excerpts from the Office Diary of Gordon E. Dean. LC 86-11385. xxxii, 309p. 1987. 42.50 (*0-8078-1714-7*) U of NC Pr.

Anders, Roger M., ed. see Dean, Gordon E.

Anders, Roger M., jt. intro. see Holl, Jack M.

Anders, Shirley B. The Bus Home: Poems. LC 85-24644. (Breakthrough Ser.: No. 49). 64p. 1986. pap. 12.95 (*0-8262-0603-4*) U of Mo Pr.

Anders, Thomas F., jt. auth. see Morrison, James.

Anders, Tim, ed. see Hope.

Anders, Timothy. The Evolution of Evil: An Inquiry into the Ultimate Origins of Human Suffering. 396p. 1994. 54.95 (*0-8126-9174-1*); pap. 22.95 (*0-8126-9175-X*) Open Court.

Anders, Vicki. Automated Information Retrieval in Libraries: A Management Handbook. LC 91-44401. (Library Management Collection). 264p. 1992. lib. bdg. 65.00 (*0-313-27361-8*, AAO/, Greenwood Pr) Greenwood.

Andersch, Alfred. Efraim's Book. Manheim, Ralph, tr. from GER. LC 93-38230. (New Directions Classics Ser.). 304p. 1994. reprint ed. pap. 11.95 (*0-8112-1262-9*, NDP779, Pub. by New Directions) Norton.

— The Father of a Murderer. Vennewitz, Leila, tr. from GER. LC 93-50806. 128p. 1994. 17.95 (*0-8112-1261-0*, Pub. by New Directions) Norton.

— Winterspelt: A Novel about the Last Days of World War II. 480p. 1980. 30.00 (*0-7206-0550-4*) Dufour.

Andersdatter, Karla. Anazazi Woman. 20p. 1985. 8.00 (*0-935430-07-5*) In Between.

— The Broken String. (Illus.). 135p. 1994. per. 14.95 (*0-911051-63-5*, Pub. by Plain View) In Between.

— The Doorway. 275p. 1990. 17.95 (*0-911051-50-3*, Pub. by Plain View) In Between.

— Follow the Blue Butterfly. (Illus.). 230p. (J). (gr. 4-8). 1980. per. 7.00 (*0-935430-00-8*) In Between.

— The Girl Who Struggled with Death. 102p. 1985. per. 12.95 (*0-911051-14-7*, Pub. by Plain View) In Between.

— I Don't Know Whether to Laugh or Cry Cause I Lost the Map to Where I Was Going. (Illus.). 39p. 1978. per. 7.00 (*0-935430-06-7*) In Between.

— Marissa the Tooth Fairy. 100p. (J). 1979. per. 5.95 (*0-935430-03-2*) In Between.

— Naked in the Garden. LC 88-60408. 210p. 1988. per. 12.95 (*0-911051-46-5*, Pub. by Plain View) In Between.

— The Princess Who Was Afraid of the Dark. 1988. 8.00 (*0-935430-09-1*) In Between.

— To a Chinese Girl, Singing. 36p. 1984. 8.00 (*0-935430-08-3*) In Between.

***Andersdatter, Karla.** White Moon Woman: Or the Education of Imogene Love. large type ed. 100p. 1999. per. 15.95 (*0-935430-11-3*) In Between.

Andersdatter, Karla. Wild Onions. 295p. 1997. 24.95 (*0-911051-89-9*, Pub. by Plain View) In Between.

Andersdatter, Karla & Brookes, C. E. The Woman Who Was Wild & Other Tales. LC 94-28084. 161p. 1995. pap. 16.95 (*0-933029-76-4*, Pub. by Chiron Pubns) In Between.

Andersen. Basic Algebra Review. 1998. pap. 8.25 (*0-07-154062-8*) McGraw.

— China Business Guide. Date not set. pap. text. write for info. (*0-582-99802-6*, Pub. by Addison-Wesley) Longman.

***Andersen.** Consumer Culture & TV Programming. 2000. pap. 28.00 (*0-8133-6633-X*, Pub. by Westview) HarpC.

— The Day JFK, Jr. Died. 352p. 2000. 26.00 (*0-688-17204-0*, Wm Morrow) Morrow Avon.

Andersen. Law of Estates, Trusts, & Gifts. 1996. text 50.36 (*0-256-22170-7*) McGraw.

— The Little Mermaid & Other Stories. (Illus.). 96p. (J). 1997. pap. 5.95 incl. audio (*0-486-29616-4*, 29616-4) Dover.

Andersen. M. P. B. Cerillera. (SPA., Illus.). (J). (ps-k). 1997. pap. 2.49 (*968-13-2434-X*) Edit Diana.

Andersen. Nursing Student to Nursing Leader: The Critical Path to Leadership Development. LC 98-2907. 384p. 1998. text 29.95 (*0-7668-0255-8*) Delmar.

***Andersen.** On Kuhn. 2000. pap. 8.25 (*0-534-58356-3*) Wadsworth Pub.

Andersen. Precalculus. (C). 2000. text. write for info. (*0-03-024964-3*); pap. text 29.50 (*0-03-022228-1*) Harcourt Coll Pubs.

***Andersen.** Project For Precalculus. (C). 1999. pap. text, teacher ed. 33.50 (*0-03-028261-6*, Pub. by Harcourt Coll Pubs) Harcourt.

— Projects For Precalculus. (C). 1999. pap. text, student ed. 17.00 (*0-03-027061-8*) Harcourt Coll Pubs.

Andersen. Sociology. (Sociology - Intro Level Ser.). 1999. pap., student ed. 16.00 (*0-534-56671-5*) Wadsworth Pub.

Andersen, ed. Sociology: Understanding a Diverse Society. (C). 1998. pap. text, student ed. write for info. (*0-321-01036-1*) Addison-Wesley.

— Sociology: Understanding a Diverse Sociology. (C). 1998. write for info. (*0-321-40017-8*) Addison-Wesley.

— Sociology Understanding. (C). 1998. text. write for info. (*0-321-01035-3*) Addison-Wesley Educ.

Andersen & Clancy. Cost Accounting. 2nd ed. LC 96-71824. 1997. 77.95 (*0-87393-328-1*) Dame Pubns.

Andersen & Rogers. Antitrust Law: Policy & Practice. 1987. suppl. ed. write for info. (*0-318-67317-7*) Bender.

***Andersen & Taylor.** The Essentials of Sociology. 2000. pap. 5.00 (*0-534-56699-5*) Wadsworth Pub.

— Sociology: A Reader. (Sociology-Introduction Level Ser.). 2000. pap. 19.00 (*0-534-56666-9*) Wadsworth Pub.

— Sociology: The Essentials. 2000. pap. 15.25 (*0-534-56698-7*) Wadsworth Pub.

— Sociology Practice Tests: Understanding a Diverse Society. (Sociology - Intro Level). 1999. pap. text 5.25 (*0-534-56687-1*) Thomson Learn.

— Telecourse Guide for Sociology: Understanding a Diverse Society. (Sociology Ser). 1999. pap. text 24.50 (*0-534-56688-X*) Thomson Learn.

Andersen, et al. Child Growth & Nutrition in Developing Countries. 1997. pap. 116.00 (*0-7855-7374-7*, Pub. by Ratna Pustak Bhandar) St Mut.

***Andersen, et al.** Gunther Keusen: Holunder. Ein Dialog. (Illus.). 192p. 2000. 65.00 (*3-932189-04-3*, Pub. by Salon-Verlag) Nazraeli Press.

Andersen, A. Managing the Future: Benchmarking Compensation Trends in Commercial Real Estate, 1994 Edition. (Illus.). (Orig.). 1994. pap. text 595.00 (*0-943130-09-3*) Build Own & Man.

Andersen, Alfred F. Challenging Newt Gingrich Chapter by Chapter: An In-Depth Analysis of America's Options at its Economic, Political, & Military Crossroads. LC 95-51201. 264p. 1996. 19.95 (*0-931803-05-5*) T Paine Inst.

— Liberating the Early American Dream: A Way to Transcend the Capitalist-Communist Dilemma Nonviolently. LC 85-51336. (Illus.). xiii, 273p. (Orig.). 1985. 12.00 (*0-931803-02-0*); pap. 10.00 (*0-931803-01-2*) T Paine Inst.

Andersen, Ann F., jt. auth. see Wold, Lucy F.

Andersen, Ann H., ed. see Jacobsen.

Andersen, Arden A. Science & Agriculture. LC 92-71951. 370p. 1992. pap. 25.00 (*0-911311-35-1*) Acres USA.

Andersen, Arden B. The Anatomy of Life & Energy in Agriculture. LC 89-83872. 115p. 1989. pap. 13.00 (*0-911311-19-X*) Acres USA.

— Applied Body Electronics: A Preview into the Field of Electrobiology. (Illus.). 100p. 1987. teacher ed. 30.00 (*0-9620023-0-5*) Andersen Pubns.

Andersen, Arlow W. The Immigrant Takes His Stand: The Norwegian-American Press & Public Affairs, 1847-1872. LC 53-11606. 184p. reprint ed. pap. 57.10 (*0-8357-3436-6*, 203969300013) Bks Demand.

Andersen, Arnold, et al. Making Weight: Healing Men's Conflicts with Food, Weight & Shape. LC 00-8779. 256p. 1999. pap. 14.95 (*0-936077-35-2*, Pub. by Gurze Bks) Publishers Group.

Andersen, Arnold E. Practical Comprehensive Treatment of Anorexia Nervosa & Bulimia. LC 84-47958. (Johns Hopkins Series in Contemporary Medicine & Public Health). 224p. 1985. reprint ed. pap. 69.50 (*0-608-03639-0*, 206446500009) Bks Demand.

Andersen, Arnold E., ed. Males with Eating Disorders. LC 89-23909. (Eating Disorders Monographs: No. 4). (Illus.). 274p. 1990. text 39.95 (*0-87630-556-7*) Brunner-Mazel.

Andersen, Arnold E., jt. ed. see Mehler, Philip S.

Andersen, Arthur. The Arthur Andersen North American Business Sourcebook: The Most Comprehensive, Authoritative Reference Guide Ever Assembled on NAFTA & the North American Market. LC 95-14127. (Illus.). 600p. 1993. lib. bdg. 195.00 (*1-880141-51-5*) Triumph Bks.

— Control Self-Assessment: Experience, Current Thinking, & Best Practices. Campbell, Lee A., ed. LC 97-178491. 250p. 1996. pap. 65.00 (*0-89413-370-5*, A316) Inst Inter Aud.

— International GAAP Analysis, 2 vols. 1998. ring bd. write for info. (*1-895333-42-3*) STP.

— The Law & Practice of Corporate Receiverships in Malaysia & Singapore. LC 98-474083. 641p. 1997. write for info. (*0-409-99706-4*, MICHIE) LEXIS Pub.

— Managing Business Risks in the Information Age. LC 99-194068. 1998. 595.00 (*0-85058-943-6*) Economist Intell.

— Sales Tax: A Practical Guide to Simplification. 258p. 1993. pap. 71.00 (*0-409-30764-5*, Austral, MICHIE) LEXIS Pub.

— Small Store Survival: Success Strategies for Retailers. LC 96-24438. (Illus.). 400p. 1996. 35.00 (*0-471-16468-2*) Wiley.

— Software & Services State Tax Report. LC 95-95130. 303p. (Orig.). 1995. pap. text 195.00 (*0-942319-49-4*) A Andersen.

— Tolley's Personal Tax & Investment Planning, 1993-94. 220p. 1993. 90.00 (*0-85459-786-7*, Pub. by Tolley Pubng) St Mut.

Andersen, Arthur, et al. Arthur Andersen European Community Sourcebook: The Most Authoritative, Comprehensive Reference Guide Ever Assembled on the European Market. 500p. 1991. lib. bdg. 150.00 (*0-9624436-4-6*) Triumph Bks.

***Andersen, Arthur, et al.** Best Practices: Building Your Business with Customer Focused Solutions. LC 97-45739. 240p. 2000. per. 13.00 (*0-684-84804-X*) S&S Trade.

Andersen, Arthur, jt. auth. see Hall, William D.

Andersen, Arthur, jt. auth. see Wing, Michael.

Andersen, Arthur, & Co. Staff. Guide to Companies Act 1981. 294p. 1982. pap. text 27.50 (*0-86010-345-5*) G & T Inc.

Andersen, Arthur, & Co. Staff. Guide to Companies Act 1980. 202p. 1980. pap. text 27.50 (*0-86010-256-4*) G & T Inc.

Andersen, Arthur & Co. Staff. Tax Shelters: The Basics. LC 82-74373. (Illus.). iii, 147p. 1985. 15.95 (*0-318-11685-5*) A Andersen.

Andersen, Arthur, & Co. Staff. Trends in Information Technology: A Handbook for Senior Management Who Must Understand Information Technology in a Competitive Context. (JPN.). 128p. (Orig.). (C). 1988. pap. text. write for info. (*0-942319-02-8*) A Andersen.

Andersen, Arthur & Co. Staff. Trends in Information Technology: A Handbook for Senior Management Who Must Understand Information Technology in a Competitive Context. 3rd ed. (Illus.). 88p. (Orig.). (C). 1987. pap. 9.95 (*0-942319-00-1*) A Andersen.

Andersen, Arthur W. Bee Prepared. (Illus.). 144p. 1975. 9.95 (*0-935596-36-4*) LM Pubns.

***Andersen, Ashley C.** First Book of Flight: A Child's History of Aviation & Flight Log. (Illus.). 48p. (J). (gr. 1-5). 2000. pap. 7.95 (*1-882663-48-9*) Plymouth VT.

Andersen, Ashley C., ed. Crew Flight Log. 224p. 1999. spiral bd. 5.95 (*1-882663-46-2*) Plymouth VT.

Andersen, B. L., ed. Women with Cancer. (Contributions to Psychology & Medicine Ser.). (Illus.). 330p. 1986. 135.00 (*0-387-96360-X*) Spr-Verlag.

Andersen, Barry W. & Craven, Robert M. All Possible Worlds: Photographs by Douglas D. Prince. (Illus.). 104p. 1999. pap. 25.00 (*0-9672678-1-1*, Pub. by Northern Kentucky) Photo-Eye.

— All Possible Worlds: Photographs by Douglas D. Prince. limited ed. (Illus.). 104p. 1999. 35.00 (*0-9672678-0-3*, Pub. by Northern Kentucky) Photo-Eye.

Andersen, Benny. The Pillows. LC 83-7166. 184p. 1983. pap. 8.95 (*0-915306-37-9*) Curbstone.

— Selected Poems. LC 74-27873. 1997. pap. text 10.95 (*1-880684-53-5*) Curbstone.

— Selected Poems. LC 74-27873. (Lockert Library of Poetry in Translation). 96p. 1975. reprint ed. pap. 30.00 (*0-608-04632-9*, 206531900003) Bks Demand.

— Selected Stories. LC 82-23459. 96p. 1983. pap. 8.95 (*0-915306-25-5*) Curbstone.

Andersen, Bjorn. Business Process Improvement Toolbox. LC 98-14191. 233p. 1998. 38.50 (*0-87389-438-3*, H1010) ASQ Qual Pr.

— Kama Sutra of Gay Sex. 1996. pap. text 30.00 (*0-9524647-0-5*, Pub. by Prowler Pr) LPC InBook.

Andersen, Bjorn, jt. auth. see Rolstadjas, A.

Andersen, Bjorn F., jt. ed. see Scholl, Marija S.

Andersen, Bjorn G. & Borns, Harold W. The Ice Age World: An Introduction to Quaternary History & Research. (Illus.). 208p. 1994. 37.00 (*82-00-21810-4*) Scandnvan Univ Pr.

Andersen, Bjorn G. & Borns, Harold W., Jr. The Ice Age World: An Introduction to Quaternary History on Research. 2nd rev. ed. (Illus.). 208p. (C). 1997. pap. text 37.00 (*82-00-37683-4*) Scandnvan Univ Pr.

Andersen, Bob. Illinois Professional Fishing Guides. 96p. 1993. pap. write for info. (*1-883347-02-5*) Fish Guides.

— Wisconsin's Northwoods Fishing Guides. 160p. 1993. pap. write for info. (*1-883347-00-9*) Fish Guides.

— Wisconsin's Professional Fishing Guides: South-Central Edition. 120p. 1993. pap. write for info. (*1-883347-01-7*) Fish Guides.

Andersen, Borge B., jt. photos by see Dimond, Craig W.

***Andersen, C. B.** The Book of Mormon Sleuth. LC 00-25616. 2000. pap. write for info. (*1-57345-664-0*) Deseret Bk.

Andersen, Carl. How to Play Music by Numbers. (Self Improvement Ser.). 96p. (Orig.). 1985. pap. text 7.95 (*0-8494-1701-5*, 85-11) Hansen Ed Mus.

Andersen, Carl C., et al. Critical Thinking Approach to Intermediate Algebra. (Reivew Sequence in Mathematics of MTE Ser.). (Illus.). x, 286p. 1989. text 28.00 (*1-888679-04-2*, 5400) MTE.

Andersen, Charles J. Fact Book on Higher Education: 1997 Edition. (Series on Higher Education). (Illus.). 276p. 1997. boxed set 49.95 (*0-89774-820-4*) Oryx Pr.

Andersen, Charles J., et al, compiled by. Fact Book on Higher Education, 1989-1990: Division of Policy Analysis & Research, ACE. (Ace-Macmillan Series on Higher Education). 224p. 1989. 41.95 (*0-02-897511-1*) Macmillan.

Andersen, Charlotte W. Faces & Places: Images in Applique. (Illus.). 128p. 1995. pap. 24.95 (*1-57120-000-2*, 10122) C & T Pub.

— Focus on Features: Life-Like Portrayals in Applique. LC 98-3694. (Illus.). 96p. 1998. pap. 23.95 (*1-57120-053-3*, 10177) C & T Pub.

Andersen, Christopher. The Day Diana Died. 400p. 1999. mass mkt. 6.99 (*0-440-23533-2*) Dell.

— The Day Diana Died. 339p. 1999. pap. 30.00 (*0-7838-0422-9*, G K Hall & Co) Mac Lib Ref.

— The Day Diana Died. LC 98-29767. (Illus.). 320p. 1998. 27.00 (*0-688-16082-4*, Wm Morrow) Morrow Avon.

— The Day Diana Died. large type ed. LC 98-44166. 1999. 30.00 (*0-7838-0421-0*, G K Hall Lrg Type) Mac Lib Ref.

***Andersen, Christopher.** The Day John Died. (Illus.). 384p. 2000. 26.00 (*0-688-17203-2*, Wm Morrow) Morrow Avon.

Andersen, Christopher. Michael Jackson. 1999. pap. write for info. (*0-451-18262-6*, Sig) NAL.

— Michael Jackson. 1995. pap. 6.99 (*0-671-89240-1*) PB.

— Michael Jackson Unauthorized. (Illus.). 352p. 1994. 23.00 (*0-671-89239-8*) S&S Trade.

Andersen, Christopher, jt. auth. see Clark, Donald.

Andersen, Christopher P. An Affair to Remember. 624p. 1998. mass mkt. 7.99 (*0-380-73158-4*, Avon Bks) Morrow Avon.

— An Affair to Remember: The Remarkable Love Story of Katharine Hepburn & Spencer Tracy. large type ed. LC 97-15741. (Core Ser.). 518p. 1997. lib. bdg. 27.95 (*0-7838-8238-6*, G K Hall Lrg Type) Mac Lib Ref.

— Bill & Hillary: The Marriage. LC 99-29993. (Illus.). 352p. 1999. 27.50 (*0-688-16755-1*, Wm Morrow) Morrow Avon.

— Jack & Jackie: Portrait of an American Marriage. large type ed. LC 96-34826. 1997. pap. 23.95 (*0-7862-0886-4*) Thorndike Pr.

— Jackie after Jack: Portrait of the Lady. LC 98-17240. 1998. 28.95 (*0-7862-1501-1*) Thorndike Pr.

— Jackie after Jack: Portrait of the Lady. 260p. 1999. mass mkt. 7.50 (*0-446-60743-6*, Pub. by Warner Bks) Little.

— Jackie After Jack: Portrait of the Lady. LC 97-49673. (Illus.). 336p. 1998. 25.00 (*0-688-15312-7*, Wm Morrow) Morrow Avon.

***Andersen, Christopher P.** Jackie after Jack: Portrait of the Lady. large type ed. LC 98-17240. 619p. 1999. pap. 20.00 (*0-7862-1502-X*) Thorndike Pr.

Andersen Consulting Logistics Strategy Group Staff, compiled by. The Mass Merchant Distribution Channel: Challenges & Opportunities. (Illus.). 31p. 1994. pap. 25.00 (*1-892663-07-4*) WERC.

Andersen Consulting Staff. Warehouse Systems & the Supply Chain: A Survey of Success Factors. Coleman, Rita M., ed. (Illus.). 56p. 1998. pap. 30.00 (*1-892663-15-5*) WERC.

Andersen Consulting Staff, contrib. by. Financial Services in a Virtual World. LC 98-180278. 1998. 495.00 (*0-85058-941-X*) Economist Intell.

Andersen, D. P., jt. ed. see Hennessen, W.

Andersen, Daniel. Be Likeminded - One to Another. 24p. (Orig.). 1992. pap. 2.50 (*1-880573-04-0*) Bible Search Pubns.

Andersen, David, et al. Introduction to Computer Simulation: The System Dynamics Approach. (Illus.). 1983. text 21.56 (*0-201-06414-6*) Addison-Wesley.

Andersen, David, jt. auth. see Klare, Michael T.

Andersen, David W. & Rymer, Michael J., eds. Tectonics & Sedimentation along Faults of the San Andreas System. (Illus.). 120p. (Orig.). 1983. pap. 6.00 (*1-878861-42-5*) Pac Section SEPM.

Andersen, Dines. Pali Reader & Pali Glossary, 2 vols. 1996. 54.00 (*81-206-1197-7*, Pub. by Asian Educ Servs) S Asia.

— A Pali Reader with Notes & Glossary. 1988. reprint ed. lib. bdg. 49.00 (*0-7812-0120-9*) Rprt Serv.

— A Pali Reader with Notes & Glossary. 1976. reprint ed. 49.00 (*0-403-05978-X*, Regency) Scholarly.

Andersen, Dines & Smith, Helmer, eds. The Sutta-Nipata. LC 78-70124. reprint ed. 34.00 (*0-404-17383-7*) AMS Pr.

Andersen, Dorothy N., et al. Downwardly Mobile for Conscience Sake: Ten Autobiographical Sketches: Each a Personal Search for Justice, Peace, & Eco-sanity. rev. ed. (Illus.). 206p. (Orig.). 1995. per. 10.00 (*0-931803-04-7*) T Paine Inst.

Andersen, E. B. The Statistical Analysis of Categorical Data. (Illus.). ix, 523p. 1990. pap. 104.70 (*0-387-52139-9*) Spr-Verlag.

— The Statistical Analysis of Categorical Data. 2nd enl. rev. ed. (Illus.). xi, 532p. 1991. 108.00 (*0-387-54463-1*) Spr-Verlag.

Andersen, E. B., et al. Statistics for Economics, Business Administration & the Social Sciences. (Illus.). 455p. 1987. 50.95 (*0-387-17720-5*) Spr-Verlag.

Andersen, Edwin, jt. auth. see Lund, Charles.

Andersen, Edwin D., jt. auth. see Lund, Charles.

Andersen, Elaine S. Speaking with Style: The Socio-Linguistic Skills of Children. 176p. 1989. 45.00 (*0-415-02256-8*) Routledge.

***Andersen, Elmer L.** A Man's Reach. LC 00-8891. 2000. pap. write for info. (*0-8166-3739-3*) U of Minn Pr.

***Andersen, Erik Andre.** An Ethnic Perspective on Economic Reform: The Case of Estonia. LC 98-74692. 560p. 1999. text 96.95 (*1-84014-418-1*, Pub. by Ashgate Pub) Ashgate Pub Co.

Andersen, Erling B. Introduction to the Statistical Analysis of Categorical Data Analysis. LC 97-6584. 265p. 1997. 44.95 (*3-540-62399-X*) Spr-Verlag.

— The Statistical Analysis of Categorical Data. 2nd ed. LC 94-3807. 1997. text 125.00 (*0-387-57696-7*) Spr-Verlag.

Andersen, Erling S. Goal Directed Project Management: Effective Techniques & Strategies. 2nd ed. 1998. pap. text 24.95 (*0-7494-2615-2*) Kogan Page Ltd.

Andersen, Esben S. Evolutionary Economics: Post-Schumpeterian Contributions. 250p. 1996. pap. 24.95 (*1-85567-383-5*) Bks Intl VA.

— Evolutionary Economics: Post-Schumpeterian Contributions. LC 93-39415. 1994. 49.00 (*1-85567-042-9*) St Martin.

Andersen, Eugene C. Tales from the Edge of the Ozarks. LC 98-90415. 1998. pap. 10.95 (*0-533-12798-X*) Vantage.

Andersen, F. J. & Forbes, A. Dean. A Key-Word-in-Context Concordance of the Pentateuch. (Computer Bible Ser.: Vol. 35-A). 1995. pap. 269.85 (*0-935106-32-4*) E Mellen.

Andersen, Flemming G. Shiloh. The Remains from the Hellenistic to the Mamluk Periods: The Dansih Excavations at Tall Sailun, Palestine in 1926, 1929, 1932, & 1963. (Publications of the National Museum, Archaeological-Historical Ser.: No. 23). (Illus.). 126p. (C). 1985. pap. 37.00 (*87-480-0567-3*, Pub. by Aarhus Univ Pr) David Brown.

Andersen, Flemming G., et al, eds. Medieval Iconography & Narrative. 215p. (Orig.). 1980. pap. 26.00 (*87-7492-307-2*, Pub. by Odense Universitets Forlag) Coronet Bks.

Andersen, Flemming G., jt. ed. see Pedersen, Rita.

***Andersen, Francis I.** Habakkuk: A New Translation with Introduction & Commentary. LC 00-31673. (Anchor Bible Ser.). 2001. write for info. (*0-385-08396-3*) Doubleday.

Andersen, Francis I. The Hebrew Verbless Clause in the Pentateuch. LC 78-97574. (Journal of Biblical Literature. Monograph: No. 14). 128p. reprint ed. pap. 39.70 (*0-7837-5399-3*, 204516300005) Bks Demand.

— Job. Wiseman, Donald J., ed. LC 76-12298. (Tyndale Old Testament Commentary Ser.). 294p. 1976. pap. 12.99 (*0-87784-263-9*, 263) InterVarsity.

Andersen, Francis I. & Forbes, A. Dean. Eight Minor Prophets: A Linguistic Concordance. (Computer Bible Ser.: Vol. 10). 1976. pap. 99.95 (*0-935106-11-1*) E Mellen.

— A Key-Word-in-Context Concordance of Psalms, Job & Proverbs. (Computer Bible Ser.: Vol. XXXIV). 816p. 1992. 149.95 (*0-935106-31-6*) E Mellen.

— A Linguistic Concordance of Ruth & Jonah: Hebrew Vocabulary & Idiom. (Computer Bible Ser.: Vol. 9). 1976. pap. 89.95 (*0-935106-12-X*) E Mellen.

Andersen, Francis I. & Freedman, David Noel. Micah: A New Translation with Introduction & Commentary. LC 99-22814. (Anchor Bible Ser.). 720p. 2000. 42.50 (*0-385-08402-1*) Doubleday.

***Andersen, Frank.** Making the Eucharist Matter. LC 99-37728. 144p. 1999. pap. 12.95 (*0-87793-695-1*) Ave Maria.

Andersen, Frank E. & Weinstock, John, eds. The Nordic Mind: Current Trends in Scandinavian Literary Criticism. LC 86-22476. 400p. (Orig.). (C). 1987. pap. text 36.00 (*0-8191-5692-2*) U Pr of Amer.

Andersen, Gerda M. Say It in Danish. 165p. (Orig.). 1958. pap. 3.95 (*0-486-20818-4*) Dover.

***Andersen, Gisle & Fretheim, Thorstein.** Pragmatic Markers & Propositional Attitude. LC 00-28921. (Pragmatics & Beyond Ser.). vi, 279p. 2000. 69.00 (*1-55619-797-7*) J Benjamins Pubng Co.

Andersen, H. A. & Hohl, E. Studies in Cassius Dio & Herodian. LC 75-7342. (Roman History Ser.). (GER., Illus.). 1975. reprint ed. 19.95 (*0-405-07063-2*) Ayer.

Andersen, H. Hellmuth, jt. auth. see Hojlund, Flemming.

Andersen, H. Verlan. The Book of Mormon & the Constitution. Andersen, Hans V., Jr., ed. LC 95-70298. 264p. (Orig.). 1995. pap. text 12.95 (*0-9644552-1-8*) SunRise Pbl.

— The Great & Abominable Church of the Devil. LC 94-74044. 234p. 1994. pap. text 11.95 (*0-9644552-0-X*) SunRise Pbl.

— Many Are Called but Few Are Chosen. Andersen, Hans V., Jr., ed. 110p. 1997. pap. 8.95 (*1-57636-043-1*) SunRise Pbl.

— The Moral Basis of a Free Society. Andersen, Hans V., Jr., ed. LC 96-70759. 204p. 1996. pap. 12.95 (*1-57636-027-X*) SunRise Pbl.

Andersen, Hans Christian. Andersen's Fairy Tales. (Children's Classics Ser.). (Illus.). (J). 1992. write for info. (*0-89434-122-7*) Ferguson.

— Andersen's Fairy Tales. 1987. mass mkt. 4.95 (*0-451-52107-2*, Sig Classics) NAL.

— Andersen's Fairy Tales. 1999. 5.99 (*0-517-20573-4*) Random Hse Value.

— Andersen's Fairy Tales. LC 58-6191. (Illustrated Junior Library). (Illus.). 352p. (J). (gr. 3-9). 1945. reprint ed. 15.99 (*0-448-06005-1*, G & D) Peng Put Young Read.

— Ariel & the Mysterious World Above. unabridged ed. (Disney Read-Alongs Ser.). (J). 7.99 incl. audio (*0-7634-0288-5*) Walt Disney.

Andersen, Hans Christian. Ariel & the Secret Grotto. (Disney Read-Alongs Ser.). (J). 7.99 incl. audio (*0-7634-0287-7*) W Disney Records.

Andersen, Hans Christian. Brothers, Very Far Away & Other Poems. 44p. 1991. pap. 4.95 (*1-880755-03-3*) Mermaid Pr.

— The Classic Treasury Hans Christian Anderson Fairy Tales. (Children's Storybook Classics Ser.). (Illus.). 56p. (J). 1997. 6.98 (*0-7624-0185-0*, Courage) Running Pr.

— Complete Fairy Stories. (Complete Classics Library). 1152p. 1998. pap. 11.95 (*1-85326-899-2*, 8992WW, Pub. by Wrdsworth Edits) NTC Contemp Pub Co.

— The Complete Hans Christian Andersen Fairy Tales. Owens, Lily, ed. (Illus.). 816p. 1993. 12.99 (*0-517-09291-3*) Random Hse Value.

— Contes Choisis. (FRE.). 352p. 1987. pap. 13.95 (*0-7859-2074-9*, 2070378853) Fr & Eur.

— Disney's the Little Mermaid. (Look & Find Ser.). (Illus.). 24p. (J). (gr. k-6). 1995. lib. bdg. 14.95 (*1-56674-095-9*, HTS Bks) Forest Hse.

— Emperor & the Nightingale. LC 78-18065.Tr. of Nattergalen. (Illus.). 32p. (J). (gr. k-4). 1997. pap 3.95 (*0-89375-112-X*) Troll Communs.

— Emperor & the Nightingale.Tr. of Nattergalen. (J). 1979. 9.15 (*0-606-02786-6*, Pub. by Turtleback) Demco.

— The Emperor & the Nightingale. LC 88-11541.Tr. of Nattergalen. (Illus.). (J). (gr. 1-4). 1995. pap. 10.95 incl. audio (*0-689-80363-X*, Rabbit Ears) Litle Simon.

— The Emperor's New Clothes. (Children's Classics Ser.).Tr. of Kejserens Nye Klaeder. (Illus.). 32p. (J). 1991 6.95 (*0-8362-4928-3*) Andrews & McMeel.

— The Emperor's New Clothes. LC 98-70451.Tr. of Kejserens Nye Klaeder. (Illus.). 32p. (J). (gr. 2-4). 1998. 15.95 (*1-56397-699-4*) Boyds Mills Pr.

— The Emperor's New Clothes. Lewis, Naomi, tr. LC 96-45004.Tr. of Kejserens Nye Klaeder. (Illus.). 32p. (J). (gr. 1-4). 1997. 15.99 (*0-7636-0119-5*) Candlewick Pr.

Andersen, Hans Christian. The Emperor's New Clothes, 001. LC 83-19610.Tr. of Kejserens Nye Klaeder. (Illus.). 48p. (J). (gr. k-3). 1979. pap. 6.95 (*0-395-28594-1*) HM.

Andersen, Hans Christian. The Emperor's New Clothes. LC 86-2509.Tr. of Kejserens Nye Klaeder. (Illus.). 32p. (J). (gr. k-3). 1986. 16.95 (*1-55858-036-0*, Pub. by North-South Bks NYC) Chronicle Bks.

— The Emperor's New Clothes. LC 86-2509.Tr. of Kejserens Nye Klaeder. (Illus.). 32p. (J). (gr. k-3). 1997. pap. 7.95 (*1-55858-689-X*, Pub. by North-South Bks NYC) Chronicle Bks.

***Andersen, Hans Christian.** The Emperor's New Clothes. LC 00-36169.Tr. of Kejserens Nye Klaeder. (Illus.). 32p. 2000. 15.95 (*0-7358-1340-X*) North-South Bks NYC.

Andersen, Hans Christian. The Emperor's New Clothes. LC 97-62026. (We Both Read Ser.).Tr. of Kejserens Nye Klaeder. (Illus.). 48p. (J). (gr. k-2). 1998. 7.99 (*1-891327-03-8*) Treas Bay Inc.

— The Emperor's New Clothes.Tr. of Kejserens Nye Klaeder. (J). 1949. 12.15 (*0-606-00437-8*, Pub. by Turtleback) Demco.

***Andersen, Hans Christian.** Emperor's New Clothes. Lewis, Naomi, tr.Tr. of Kejserens nye klaeder. (Illus.). 32p. (J). (gr. 1-4). 2000. pap. 5.99 (*0-7636-1281-2*) Candlewick Pr.

Andersen, Hans Christian. Emperor's New Clothes. LC 78-18063.Tr. of Kejserens nye klaeder. (Illus.). 32p. (J). (gr. k-4). 1979. lib. bdg. 15.85 (*0-89375-132-4*) Troll Communs.

— Emperor's New Clothes. LC 78-18063.Tr. of Kejserens nye klaeder. (Illus.). 32p. (J). (gr. k-4). 1997. pap. 3.95 (*0-89375-110-3*) Troll Communs.

— The Emperor's New Clothes. abr. adapted ed. Metaxas, Eric, tr. & adapted by by. LC 90-25376. (Storybook Classics Ser.).Tr. of Kejserens Nye Klaeder. (Illus.). 32p. (J). (ps up). 1991. 19.95 incl. audio (*0-88708-161-4*, Rabbit Ears) Litle Simon.

— The Emperor's New Clothes: An All-Star Retelling of the Classic Fairy Tale. Starbright Foundation Staff, ed. LC 97-32021. (Illus.). 96p. (J). (ps-3). 1998. 27.95 (*0-15-100109-X*) Harcourt Coll Pubs.

***Andersen, Hans Christian.** Fairy Tale of My Life. 2000. reprint ed. pap. 22.95 (*0-8154-1105-7*, Pub. by Cooper Sq) Natl Bk Netwk.

Andersen, Hans Christian. Fairy Tales. Spink, Reginald, tr. from DAN. LC 92-53178. (Illus.). 416p. (J). 1992. 14.95 (*0-679-41791-5*, Evrymans Lib Childs) Knopf.

— Fairy Tales from Hans Christian Andersen. Higton, Bernard, ed. (Classic Illustrated Treasury Ser.). (Illus.). 128p. (J). 1992. 17.95 (*0-8118-0230-2*) Chronicle Bks.

— Favorite Tales of Hans Christian Andersen. 96p. (J). (gr. 2 up). 1988. 9.95 (*1-56288-253-8*) Checkerboard.

— The Fir Tree. LC 73-121800.Tr. of Grantraeet. (Illus.). 48p. (J). (gr. 3-6). 1970. 13.95 (*0-06-020077-4*, HarpC Child Bks.

— The Fir Tree. LC 89-43730.Tr. of Grantraeet. (Illus.). 32p. (J). (gr. k-3). 1990. 14.95 (*1-55858-093-X*, Pub. by North-South Bks NYC) Chronicle Bks.

***Andersen, Hans Christian.** Les Habits Neufs De L'empereur. 1999. pap. 11.95 (*2-09-202111-7*) Distribks Inc.

Andersen, Hans Christian. Hans Andersen's Fairy Tales. Kingsland, L. W., tr. LC 97-182259. (Oxford Illustrated Classics Ser.). (Illus.). 268p. (J). (gr. 4 up). 1997. pap. 14.95 (*0-19-274173-X*) OUP.

— Hans Andersen's Fairy Tales: A Selection. Kingsland, L. W., tr. (Oxford World's Classics Ser.). (Illus.). 374p. 1998. pap. 6.95 (*0-19-283507-6*) OUP.

— Hans Christian Andersen. (Illus.). 32p. 1982. pap. 8.95 (*0-88188-202-X*, 00446431) H Leonard.

— Hans Christian Andersen: The Complete Fairy Tales & Stories. Haugaard, Erik C., tr. from DAN. LC 73-83883. (Anchor Folktale Library). 1120p. 1983. pap. 19.95 (*0-385-18951-6*, Anchor NY) Doubleday.

— Hans Christian Andersen Fairy Tales. Bell, Anthea, tr. from DAN. LC 91-13132. Orig. Title: Hans Christian Andersen Marchen. (Illus.). 68p. (J). (ps up). 1992. 19.95 (*0-88708-182-7*, Picture Book Studio) S&S Childrens.

— Hans Christian Andersen's the Snow Queen. 1996. 13.19 (*0-606-10933-1*, Pub. by Turtleback) Demco.

— Hans Christian Anderson's Fairy Tales. Lewis, Naomi, ed. (Illus.). 208p. (YA). (gr. 5 up). 1996. pap. 4.99 (*0-14-036737-3*, PuffinBks) Peng Put Young Read.

— Hans Clodhopper. LC 74-23674. (J). (gr. k-3). 1975. 10.78 (*0-397-31614-3*) HarpC Child Bks.

***Andersen, Hans Christian.** The Improvisatore. LC 99-80206. (Library of Classical Historical Fiction). 275p. 1999. pap. 14.95 (*0-594-00744-5*) Eighth Hundrd.

Andersen, Hans Christian. Listen & Read the Ugly Duckling & Other Fairy Tales. (Illus.). 96p. (Orig.). (J). 1996. pap. text 5.95 incl. audio (*0-486-29100-6*) Dover.

— The Little Match Girl. (Illus.). 32p. (J). (ps-3). 1992. 6.95 (*0-8362-4931-3*) Andrews & McMeel.

— The Little Match Girl. LC 94-79160. (Illus.). 32p. (J). (gr. k-4). 1995. 14.95 (*1-56397-470-3*) Boyds Mills Pr.

— The Little Match Girl. (Scheherezade Children's Stories Ser.). (Illus.). 16p. (J). 1997. 4.95 (*1-873938-89-6*, Pub. by Garnet-Ithaca) LPC InBook.

— The Little Match Girl. LC 68-28050. (Illus.). (J). (gr. k-3). 1975. pap. 1.95 (*0-685-02294-3*) HM.

Andersen, Hans Christian. The Little Match Girl. LC 85-30082. 1996. 11.15 (*0-606-10253-1*, Pub. by Turtleback) Demco.

Andersen, Hans Christian. The Little Match Girl.Tr. of Lille pige med svovlstikkerne. (Illus.). 32p. (J). (ps-3). 1987. 15.95 (*0-399-21336-8*, G P Putnam) Peng Put Young Read.

— The Little Match Girl: A Musical. 20p. (Orig.). (J). (gr. 1-8). 1992. pap. 3.50 (*1-57514-221-X*, 0047) Encore Perform Pub.

— The Little Mermaid. (Illus.). 32p. (J). (ps-3). 1992. 6.95 (*0-8362-4918-6*) Andrews & McMeel.

— The Little Mermaid. (J). 1980. pap. 2.95 (*0-88388-039-3*) Bellerophon Bks.

— The Little Mermaid. (Hans Christian Andersen's Tales Ser.). 36p. (J). 24.95 (*0-915035-39-1*) Dawn Sign.

— The Little Mermaid. 1994. 3.95 (*0-87129-435-4*, L79) Dramatic Pub.

— The Little Mermaid. LC 92-29807. (Illus.). (J). 1995. 16.95 (*0-8050-1010-6*, Bks Young Read) H Holt & Co.

— The Little Mermaid. LC 89-31602. (Illus.). 42p. (J). (gr. k-3). 1989. 15.95 (*0-15-246320-8*) Harcourt.

— The Little Mermaid. (J). 1997. pap. 6.00 (*0-15-201561-2*, Harcourt Child Bks) Harcourt.

Andersen, Hans Christian. The Little Mermaid. LC 97-8819. (Illus.). 64p. (J). (gr. 4-7). 1997. 11.45 (*0-7868-0383-5*, Pub. by Hyperion) Little.

Andersen, Hans Christian. The Little Mermaid. LC 97-8819. (Illus.). 64p. (J). 1997. lib. bdg. 11.89 (*0-7868-2331-3*, Pub. by Hyprn Child) Little.

— The Little Mermaid. (Fun-to-Read Fairy Tales Ser.). (Illus.). 24p. (J). 1992. pap. 2.50 (*1-56144-093-0*) Modern Pub NYC.

— The Little Mermaid. (Classics Ser.). (Illus.). 96p. (J). 1994. 7.98 (*1-57082-042-2*, Pub. by Mouse Works) Little.

— The Little Mermaid. (J). 1997. 7.98 (*1-57082-727-3*, Pub. by Mouse Works) Time Warner.

— The Little Mermaid. (Disney's Look & Find Ser.). (Illus.). 24p. (J). 1993. write for info. (*0-7853-0106-2*); 12.98 (*0-7853-0133-X*) Pubns Intl Ltd.

— The Little Mermaid. LC 91-6632. (Step into Reading Ser.: A Step 3 Book). (Illus.). 48p. (J). (gr. 2-3). 1991. pap. 3.99 (*0-679-82241-0*, Pub. by Random Bks Yng Read) Random.

— The Little Mermaid. (Disney Read-Alongs Ser.). (J). 7.99 incl. audio (*0-7634-0286-9*) Walt Disney.

— The Little Mermaid. Michel, Petra, tr. LC 96-21504. (Illus.). 32p. (J). 1996. 18.95 (*1-885394-17-9*) Bluestar Communs.

— The Little Mermaid. LC 97-4979. Orig. Title: Lille havfrue. (Illus.). (J). 1997. 18.00 (*0-679-88757-1*, Pub. by Random Bks Yng Read) Random.

***Andersen, Hans Christian.** Little Mermaid. (Illus.). (J). 2000. 12.44 (*0-606-18420-1*) Turtleback.

Andersen, Hans Christian. The Little Mermaid: An under the Sea Christmas: A Holiday Songbook. LC 93-70939. (Little Mermaid Novels Ser.). (Illus.). 48p. (J). 1993. pap. 9.95 (*1-56282-504-6*, Pub. by Disney Pr) Time Warner.

Andersen, Hans Christian. The Little Mermaid: My Coloring Book.Tr. of Lille havfrue. (J). pap. text 1.09 (*0-307-08630-5*, 08630) Gldn Bks Pub Co.

Andersen, Hans Christian. The Little Mermaid & Other Fairy Tales. Philip, Neil, tr. LC 98-60069. 144p. (J). 1998. text 21.99 (*0-670-87840-5*) Viking Penguin.

— The Little Mermaid & Other Fairy Tales. LC 93-14418. (Children's Thrift Classics Ser.). (Illus.). 96p. (J). 1993. reprint ed. pap. 1.00 (*0-486-27816-6*) Dover.

— The Little Mermaid & Other Hans Christian Andersen Stories. 1999. 6.99 (*0-517-20733-8*) Random Hse Value.

— The Little Mermaid & Other Tales. (Library of Folklore). (Illus.). 508p. (J). (gr. 3-4). 1998. 19.95 (*0-7818-0720-4*) Hippocrene Bks.

Andersen, Hans Christian. Little Mermaid Coloring Book. (J). 1992. pap. 2.95 (*0-486-27130-7*) Dover.

Andersen, Hans Christian. The Little Mermaid Hunts for Treasure. LC 91-73811. (Surprise Lift-the-Flap Bk.). (Illus.). 18p. (J). (ps-1). 1992. 8.95 (*1-56282-146-6*, Pub. by Disney Pr) Time Warner.

— The Little Mermaid Treasury Exclusive for AMS. 176p. (J). (ps-2). 1997. pap. 17.95 (*0-7868-3182-0*, Pub. by Disney Pr) Time Warner.

— Mary Engelbreit's the Snow Queen. LC 93-11436.Tr. of Snedronningen. (Illus.). 48p. (J). (gr. k up). 1993. 16.95 (*1-56305-438-8*, 3438) Workman Pub.

— Michael Hague's Favourite Hans Christian Andersen Fairy Tales. LC 81-47455. (Illus.). 168p. (J). (ps-2). 1995. 19.95 (*0-8050-0659-1*, Bks Young Read) H Holt & Co.

A

An Asterisk (*) at the beginning of an entry indicates that the title is appearing for the first time.

A

— The Nightingale.Tr. of Nattergalen. (Illus.). 32p. (J). (ps-3). 1992. 6.95 (*0-8362-4927-5*) Andrews & McMeel.

— The Nightingale. LC 85-2765.Tr. of Nattergalen. (Illus.). 32p. (J). (ps-3). 1988. pap. 3.95 (*0-15-257428-X*, Voyager Bks) Harcourt.

— The Nightingale. Le Gallienne, Eva, tr. LC 64-18574.Tr. of Nattergalen. (Illus.). 48p. (J). (gr. 3 up). 1965. 13.95 (*0-06-023780-5*) HarpC Child Bks.

***Andersen, Hans Christian.** The Nightingale. Bell, Anthea, tr. from DAN. LC 98-45563.Tr. of Nattergalen. (Illus.). 32p. (J). (gr. k-3). 1999. pap. 6.95 (*0-7358-1120-2*, Pub. by North-South Bks NYC) Chronicle Bks.

— The Nightingale. Bell, Anthea, tr. from DAN. LC 98-45563.Tr. of Nattergalen. (Illus.). 32p. (J). (gr. k-3). 1999. 15.95 (*0-7358-1118-0*, Pub. by North-South Bks NYC) Chronicle Bks.

Andersen, Hans Christian. Oeuvres, Vol. 1. (FRE.). 1648p. 1992. 185.00 (*0-7859-6512-2*) Fr & Eur.

— El Patito Feo. (Spanish Well Loved Tales Ser.: No. 700-1). (SPA.). (J). (gr. 1). 1990. boxed set 3.50 (*0-7214-1407-9*, Ladybrd) Penguin Putnam.

— El Patito Feo. (SPA.). (J). 1997. pap. 3.95 (*0-8167-3066-0*) Troll Communs.

***Andersen, Hans Christian.** Patito Feo.Tr. of Grimme Aelling. (SPA.). 1999. pap. 7.95 (*88-8148-251-7*) Europ Lang Inst.

Andersen, Hans Christian. El Patito Feo (The Ugly Duckling) (SPA., Illus.). 32p. (J). (ps-3). 1999. 8.95 (*0-7641-5150-9*) Barron.

— A Poet's Bazaar: A Journey to Greece, Turkey & up the Danube. Thornton, Grace, tr. from DAN. LC 87-30993.Tr. of Digters bazar. (Illus.). 208p. 1990. pap. 15.95 (*0-935576-34-7*) Kesend Pub Ltd.

— The Princess & the Pea. LC 81-13395.Tr. of Prindsessen Paa Aerten. (Illus.). 32p. (J). (gr. k-3). 1982. lib. bdg. 15.95 (*0-8234-0442-0*) Holiday.

— The Princess & the Pea. LC 81-13395.Tr. of Prindsessen Paa Aerten. (Illus.). 32p. (J). (gr. k-3). 1989. pap. 6.95 (*0-8234-0753-5*) Holiday.

— The Princess & the Pea. (Ladybird Stories Ser.).Tr. of Prindsessen Paa Aerten. (ARA., Illus.). 52p. (J). (gr. 4-6). 1989. 4.95 (*0-86685-218-2*, LDL163); audio 12.95 (*0-86685-633-1*) Intl Bk Ctr.

— The Princess & the Pea. LC 85-7199.Tr. of Prindsessen Paa Aerten. (Illus.). 32p. (J). (gr. k-3). 1985. 15.95 (*1-55858-034-4*, Pub. by North-South Bks NYC) Chronicle Bks.

— The Princess & the Pea. LC 85-7199.Tr. of Prindsessen Paa Aerten. (Illus.). 32p. (J). (gr. k-3). 1995. pap. 6.95 (*1-55858-381-5*, Pub. by North-South Bks NYC) Chronicle Bks.

— The Princess & the Pea. (Fairy Tale Fun Ser.).Tr. of Prindsessen Paa Aerten. (J). 3.95 (*0-7214-5433-X*, Ladybrd) Penguin Putnam.

— The Princess & the Pea. (Story Activity Bks.: No. S909-5).Tr. of Prindsessen Paa Aerten. (J). 1991. pap. 1.95 (*0-7214-5282-5*, Ladybrd) Penguin Putnam.

Andersen, Hans Christian. The Princess & the Pea.Tr. of Prindsessen Paa Aerten. 1995. 12.15 (*0-606-08849-0*, Pub. by Turtleback) Demco.

Andersen, Hans Christian. The Princess & the Pea. (Fairy Tale Pop-ups Ser.). (Illus.). 16p. (J). 1994. 3.95 (*0-7214-9421-8*, Ladybrd) Penguin Putnam.

— The Princess & the Pea: A Fairy Tale. LC 98-35941. (Little Pebbles Ser.). (Illus.). 32p. (J). (ps-1). 1999. 6.95 (*0-7892-0515-7*, Abbeville Kids) Abbeville Pr.

***Andersen, Hans Christian.** La Princesse Aux Petit Pois. 1999. pap. 11.95 (*2-09-202112-5*) Distribks Inc.

Andersen, Hans Christian. The Red Shoes. LC 96-29257. (Illus.). 40p. (J). (gr. 1-5). 1997. 15.95 (*1-879085-56-9*, Whispering Coyote) Charlesbridge Pub.

— Rossignol de l'Empereur de Chine. (Folio - Cadet Rouge Ser.: No. 179). (FRE., Illus.). 56p. (J). (gr. 3-7). 1990. pap. 8.95 (*2-07-031179-1*) Schoenhof.

— La Sirenita - The Little Mermaid. (J). (ps-3). 1998. pap. 2.95 (*0-486-28001-2*) Dover.

— The Snow Queen.Tr. of Snedronningen. 29p. (J). (gr. 3-8). 1990. pap. 3.00 (*1-57514-230-9*, 1099) Encore Perform Pub.

— The Snow Queen. Le Gallienne, Eva, tr. from DAN. LC 83-47711.Tr. of Snedronningen. (Illus.). 128p. (J). (gr. 2-5). 1985. 14.95 (*0-06-023694-9*) HarpC Child Bks.

— The Snow Queen. LC 87-1518.Tr. of Snedronningen. (Illus.). 32p. (J). (gr. k-3). 1997. pap. 7.95 (*1-55858-779-9*, Pub. by North-South Bks NYC) Chronicle Bks.

***Andersen, Hans Christian.** The Snow Queen.Tr. of Snedronningen. 104p. 1998. pap. 12.95 (*1-84002-025-3*, Pub. by Oberon Bks Ltd) Theatre Comm.

Andersen, Hans Christian. The Snow Queen. Lewis, Naomi, tr. LC 92-54412.Tr. of Snedronningen. (Illus.). 48p. (J). (gr. 2-6). 1996. reprint ed. pap. 6.99 (*1-56402-979-4*) Candlewick Pr.

— The Snow Queen: A New Adapted Version by Naomi Lewis. LC 68-17218. (Illus.). 32p. (J). (ps-5). 16.95 (*0-87592-048-9*) Scroll Pr.

Andersen, Hans Christian. Starship. 1991. mass mkt. 3.95 (*0-8125-1365-7*) Tor Bks.

Andersen, Hans Christian. The Steadfast Tin Soldier. (Children's Classics Ser.).Tr. of Standhaftige Tinsoldat. (Illus.). 32p. (J). 1991. 6.95 (*0-8362-4929-1*) Andrews & McMeel.

***Andersen, Hans Christian.** The Steadfast Tin Soldier. LC 99-29919.Tr. of Standhaftige Tinsoldat. (Illus.). 32p. (YA). 2000. lib. bdg. 13.95 (*1-56846-132-1*, Creat Educ) Creative Co.

Andersen, Hans Christian. The Steadfast Tin Soldier. LC 91-71342. (From the Disney Archives Ser.).Tr. of Standhaftige Tinsoldat. (Illus.). 32p. (J). (gr. 1-4). 1991. 13.95 (*1-56282-016-8*, Pub. by Disney Pr); lib. bdg. 13.89 (*1-56282-073-7*, Pub. by Disney Pr) Little.

— The Steadfast Tin Soldier. LC 92-52690. (Michael di Capua Bks.).Tr. of Standhaftige Tinsoldat. (Illus.). 32p. (J). (ps-3). 1992. 14.95 (*0-06-205000-1*) HarpC Child Bks.

— The Steadfast Tin Soldier. LC 92-52690. (Michael di Capua Bks.).Tr. of Standhaftige Tinsoldat. (Illus.). 32p. (J). 1997. reprint ed. pap. 6.95 (*0-06-205900-9*, HarpTrophy) HarpC Child Bks.

— Stories from Hans Christian Andersen. LC 92-45627. (Illus.). 96p. (J). (gr. 2-5). 1993. 18.95 (*0-531-05463-2*) Orchard Bks Watts.

— The Story of the Ugly Duckling. LC 94-1298. Orig. Title: Grimme aelling. (Illus.). 32p. (J). (gr. 1 up). 1994. pap. 1.00 (*0-486-28300-3*) Dover.

— The Swan's Stories. Alderson, Brian, tr. & selected by by. LC 96-47197. (Illus.). 144p. (J). (gr. 3-7). 1997. 22.99 (*1-56402-894-1*) Candlewick Pr.

— The Swineherd.Tr. of Svinedrengen. 15.95 (*0-86315-129-9*, 1297, Pub. by Floris Bks) Anthroposophic.

— The Swineherd. Bell, Anthea, tr. LC 94-32153.Tr. of Svinedrengen. (Illus.). 32p. (J). (gr. k-3). 1995. 14.95 (*1-55858-428-5*, Pub. by North-South Bks NYC) Chronicle Bks.

Andersen, Hans Christian. The Swineherd.Tr. of Svinedrengen. 1995. 11.15 (*0-606-08885-7*, Pub. by Turtleback) Demco.

— Swineherd. (North-South Picture Book Ser.). (Illus.). 1987. 13.95 (*0-8050-0232-4*) H Holt & Co.

Andersen, Hans Christian. Tales Stories H. C. Andersen. LC 80-50867. (Illus.). 316p. 1980. pap. 14.95 (*0-295-95936-3*) U of Wash Pr.

— Thumbelina. LC 79-50146. (Children's Classics Ser.).Tr. of Tommelise. (Illus.). 32p. (J). (ps-3). 1992. 6.95 (*0-8362-4926-7*) Andrews & McMeel.

— Thumbelina. (Pocket Play Bks.).Tr. of Tommelise. (Illus.). 24p. (J). (ps-2). 1996. 9.95 (*0-8362-0956-7*) Andrews & McMeel.

— Thumbelina. Haugaard, Erik C., tr. LC 95-53284.Tr. of Tommelise. (Illus.). 32p. (J). (ps-3). 1997. 16.95 (*0-385-32251-8*, DD Bks Yng Read) BDD Bks Young Read.

— Thumbelina. Roberts, Tom, ed. LC 89-8484.Tr. of Tommelise. (Illus.). 32p. (J). (ps up). 1991. 14.95 (*0-88708-113-4*, Rabbit Ears) Litle Simon.

— Thumbelina. (Fun-to-Read Fairy Tales Series III).Tr. of Tommelise. (Illus.). 24p. (J). (gr. k-3). 1993. pap. 2.50 (*1-56144-298-4*, Honey Bear Bks) Modern Pub NYC.

— Thumbelina. LC 79-50146.Tr. of Tommelise. 32p. (J). 1992. pap. 2.99 (*0-8125-2318-0*, Pub. by Tor Bks) St Martin.

— Thumbelina. LC 78-18080.Tr. of Tommelise. (Illus.). 32p. (J). (gr. k-4). 1979. lib. bdg. 15.85 (*0-89375-141-3*) Troll Communs.

— Thumbelina. LC 78-18080.Tr. of Tommelise. (Illus.). 32p. (J). (gr. k-4). 1997. pap. 3.95 (*0-89375-119-7*) Troll Communs.

— Thumbelina. LC 79-50146.Tr. of Tommelise. (J). 1994. pap. 6.99 (*0-14-054714-2*) Viking Penguin.

— Thumbelina.Tr. of Tommelise. 1994. 7.98 (*1-57042-086-6*) Warner Bks.

— Thumbelina. (Pudgy Pal Board Bks.). Orig. Title: Tommelise. (Illus.). 18p. (J). (ps). 1995. bds. 3.95 (*0-448-40855-4*, G & D) Peng Put Young Read.

— Thumbelina. LC 79-50146.Tr. of Tommelise. (Illus.). 40p. (J). (gr. 2 up). 1992. reprint ed. 9.95 incl. audio (*0-88708-256-4*, Rabbit Ears) Litle Simon.

— Thumbelina: Story Pak. (Graphic Learning Literature Program Series: Folk Tales). (ENG & SPA., Illus.). (J). 1992. 45.00 (*0-87746-235-6*) Graphic Learning.

***Andersen, Hans Christian.** Thumbeline.Tr. of Tommelise. (Illus.). 32p. (J). (gr. k-3). 2000. 15.95 (*0-7358-1213-6*, Pub. by North-South Bks NYC); pap. 6.95 (*0-7358-1210-1*, Pub. by North-South Bks NYC) Chronicle Bks.

Andersen, Hans Christian. Thumbeline. Bell, Anthea, tr. from DAN. LC 85-12062.Tr. of Tommelise. (Illus.). 28p. (J). (gr. 1 up). 1991. 16.00 (*0-88708-006-5*, Picture Book Studio) S&S Childrens.

— The Tinder Box. LC 89-48014. Orig. Title: Fyrtojet. (Illus.) (J). 1991. pap. 14.95 (*0-671-70546-6*) S&S Bks Yung.

— The Tinderbox. LC 88-9206. Orig. Title: Fyrtojet. (Illus.). 32p. (J). (gr. 1 up). 1988. mass mkt. 14.95 (*0-689-50458-6*) McElderry Bks.

— The Top & the Ball. LC 92-83.Tr. of Toppen og bolden. (Illus.). 32p. (J). (gr. k-3). 1992. 14.95 (*0-8249-8547-8*, Ideals Child); lib. bdg. 15.00 (*0-8249-8583-4*, Ideals Child) Hambleton-Hill.

— Travels. Little, Anastazia, tr. (Green Integer Ser.: No. 10). 385p. 1999. pap. 10.95 (*1-55713-344-1*, Pub. by Green Integer) SPD-Small Pr Dist.

— A Treasury of Stories from Hans Christian Andersen. LC 95-36161. (Treasury of Stories Ser.). (Illus.). 160p. (J). (ps-4). 1996. pap. 5.95 (*1-85697-676-9*) LKC.

— The Ugly Duckling. LC 78-18059. (Illus.). 32p. (J). (ps-3). 1992. 6.95 (*0-8362-4911-9*) Andrews & McMeel.

— The Ugly Duckling. (Fun-to-Read Fairy Tales Series III). (Illus.). 24p. (J). (gr. k-3). 1993. pap. 2.50 (*1-56144-299-2*, Honey Bear Bks) Modern Pub NYC.

***Andersen, Hans Christian.** The Ugly Duckling. LC 98-23604. 48p. (J). 1999. 15.95 (*0-688-15932-X*, Wm Morrow) Morrow Avon.

— The Ugly Duckling. LC 00-35125. (Illus.). 32p. (gr. k-3). 2000. 15.95 (*0-7358-1388-4*) North-South Bks NYC.

Andersen, Hans Christian. The Ugly Duckling. (Fairy Tale Fun Ser.). (J). 3.95 (*0-7214-5432-1*, Ladybrd) Penguin Putnam.

— The Ugly Duckling. (Square Format Fairy Tales Ser.: No. S874-5). (Illus.). 28p. (J). (ps up). 1987. boxed set 3.95 (*0-7214-5032-6*, Ladybrd) Penguin Putnam.

Andersen, Hans Christian. The Ugly Duckling. (Favorite Fairy Tales Ser.). (Illus.). 24p. (J). 1993. 4.98 (*1-56173-912-X*) Pubns Intl Ltd.

Andersen, Hans Christian. The Ugly Duckling. (Illus.). 48p. (J). (ps-2). 1988. pap. 4.99 (*0-590-43794-1*) Scholastic Inc.

— The Ugly Duckling. LC 75-145207. (Illus.). 32p. (J). (ps-3). 16.95 (*0-87592-055-1*) Scroll Pr.

— The Ugly Duckling. (Froggy's Country Storybook Ser.: Vol. 3). (Illus.). 16p. (J). (gr. k-3). 1998. pap. 12.98 incl. audio (*1-890818-28-3*) Virginia Recs.

— Ugly Duckling. (Story Activity Bks.: No. S909-3).Tr. of Grimme aelling. (J). 1991. pap. 1.95 (*0-7214-5280-9*, Ladybrd) Penguin Putnam.

— Ugly Duckling.Tr. of Grimme aelling. (J). 1989. pap. 1.25 (*0-8167-1347-2*) Troll Communs.

— Ugly Duckling. LC 78-18059.Tr. of Grimme aelling. (Illus.). 32p. (J). (gr. k-2). 1997. pap. 3.95 (*0-89375-106-5*) Troll Communs.

— The Ugly Duckling. (Happytime Storybks.). (Illus.). 24p. (J). (ps-1). 1991. pap. 1.25 (*0-7214-5304-X*, S9016-5, Ladybrd) Penguin Putnam.

— Ugly Duckling. (Once Upon a Time Ser.). (Illus.). 24p. (J). (ps-1). 1996. 3.98 (*1-85854-416-5*) Brimax Bks.

— The Ugly Duckling: Based on the Tale by Hans Christian Andersen. (Illus.). 30p. (J). (ps up). 1995. pap. 3.25 (*0-88680-408-6*, 408-6) I E Clark.

— The Ugly Duckling & Other Fairy Tales. (Illus.). 96p. (Orig.). (J). 1992. pap. 1.00 (*0-486-27081-5*) Dover.

— Le Vilain Petit Canard. adapted ed. LC 96-940390. (Best-Sellers Ser.).Tr. of The Ugly Duckling. (FRE., Illus.). (J). (ps-2). 2000. pap., boxed set 9.95 incl. audio (*2-921997-05-3*) Coffragants.

— A Visit to Germany, Italy & Malta, 1840-1841: A Poet's Bazaar. Thornton, Grace, tr. from DAN. & intro. by.Tr. of Digters bazar. (Illus.). 182p. 1986. 30.00 (*0-7206-0636-5*, Pub. by P Owen Ltd) Dufour.

Andersen, Hans Christian. The Wicked Prince. LC 94-45650. (Illus.). (J). 1995. 26.00 (*1-56846-107-0*, Creat Educ) Creative Co.

Andersen, Hans Christian. The Wild Swans. LC 80-27685.Tr. of Villijoutsenet. (Illus.). 32p. (J). (gr. k-4). 1981. lib. bdg. 15.85 (*0-89375-480-3*) Troll Communs.

Andersen, Hans Christian, ed. New Danish Plays. LC 96-226095. 264p. 1996. pap. 22.95 (*1-870041-32-1*, Pub. by Norvik Pr) Dufour.

***Andersen, Hans Christian & Isadora, Rachel.** The Little Mermaid. (Picture Puffin Ser.). (Illus.). 32p. (J). (ps-3). 2000. pap. 6.99 (*0-698-11829-4*, PuffinBks) Peng Put Young Read.

Andersen, Hans Christian & Weghorst, Suzanne J. The Little Mermaid Novels, 4 bks., Set. (Little Mermaid Novels Ser.). (Illus.). (J). (gr. 1-4). 1993. pap., boxed set 11.80 (*1-56282-562-3*, Pub. by Disney Pr) Little.

***Andersen, Hans Christian, et al.** The Emperor's New Clothes. LC 00-36169.Tr. of Kejserens Nye Klaeder. (Illus.). 32p. (J). 2000. pap. 15.88 (*0-7358-1341-8*) North-South Bks NYC.

Andersen, Hans Christian, et al. The Emperor's New Clothes - Musical. 1969. 5.95 (*0-87129-499-0*, E02) Dramatic Pub.

Andersen, Hans Christian, jt. auth. see Erwin, Gail.

Andersen, Hans Christian, jt. auth. see Jeffers, Susan.

Andersen, Hans Christian, jt. auth. see Setterington, Ken.

Andersen, Hans Christian, jt. auth. see Watts, Bernadette.

Andersen, Hans V., Jr. Teachings of H. Verlan Andersen. LC 95-70913. 450p. 1996. text 29.95 (*0-9644552-2-6*) SunRise Pbl.

Andersen, Hans V., Jr., ed. see Andersen, H. Verlan.

***Andersen, Heine & Kaspersen, Lars Bo, eds.** Classical & Modern Social Theory. LC 99-58779.Tr. of Klassisk og Moderne Sanfundsteori. (Illus.). 528p. 2000. text 72.95 (*0-631-21287-6*); pap. text 39.95 (*0-631-21288-4*) Blackwell Pubs.

Andersen, Henning. Reconstructing Prehistorical Dialects: Initial Vowels in Slavic & Baltic. LC 96-12946. (Trends in Linguistics Ser.: Vol. 91). x, 238p. (C). 1996. lib. bdg. 141.45 (*3-11-014705-X*) Mouton.

Andersen, Henning, ed. Historical Linguistics 1993: Selected Papers from the 11th International Conference on Historical Linguistics, Los Angeles, 16-20 August 1993. (Current Issues in Linguistic Theory Ser.: No. 124). x, 460p. 1995. lib. bdg. 110.00 (*1-55619-578-8*) J Benjamins Pubng Co.

— Sandhi Phenomena in the Languages of Europe. (Trends in Linguistics, Studies & Monographs: No. 33). (Illus.). xii, 616p. 1986. lib. bdg. 215.40 (*0-89925-070-X*) Mouton.

Andersen, Henning & Koerner, Konrad, eds. Historical Linguistics, 1987: Papers from the 8th International Conference on Historical Linguistics, Lille, August 30-September 4, 1987. LC 89-26711. (Current Issues in Linguistic Theory Ser.: Vol. 66). xii, 577p. 1990. 100.00 (*90-272-3563-5*) J Benjamins Pubng Co.

Andersen, Henning, et al. Proceedings of the 7th UCLA Indo-European Conference, Los Angeles, 1995. Della Volpe, Angela, ed. LC 99-165919. (Journal of Indo-European Studies Monograph Ser.: No. 27). 248p. (C). 1998. pap. text 46.00 (*0-941694-64-X*) Inst Study Man.

Andersen, Honey. Which Comes First? LC 93-18113. (Illus.). (J). 1994. write for info. (*0-383-03726-3*) SRA McGraw.

Andersen, Honey & Reinholdt, Bill. Pop's Truck. LC 93-18050. (Illus.). (J). 1994. write for info. (*0-383-03709-3*) SRA McGraw.

Andersen, Ian. Burning the Tables in Las Vegas. (Illus.). 305p. 1999. 27.95 (*0-929712-83-8*) Huntington Pr.

***Andersen, Ib.** On the Art of Doing Field Studies: An Experience-Based Research Methodology. LC 98-106335. 1999. 48.00 (*87-16-13269-6*) Mksgaard.

Andersen, J. Eighteen Studies for Flute Opus 41. 20p. 1986. pap. 4.95 (*0-7935-5203-6*, 50260300) H Leonard.

— Twenty Four Etudes: Opus 15 Flute. 72p. 1986. pap. 9.95 (*0-7935-5266-4*, 50335090) H Leonard.

— Twenty-Four Studies in All Major & Minor Keys: For the Flute Opus 21. 28p. 1986. pap. 5.95 (*0-7935-5417-9*, 50260890) H Leonard.

Andersen, J. E., ed. see Metallurgical Society of AIME Staff.

Andersen, Jeffrey W. Harry L. Hoffman: A World of Color. (Illus.). 89p. (Orig.). 1988. 19.00 (*1-880897-07-5*); pap. 14.00 (*1-880897-06-7*) Lyme Hist.

Andersen, Jeffrey W. & Ferguson, Charles B. The Harmony of Nature: The Art of Frank Vincent DuMond. (Illus.). 32p. (Orig.). 1990. pap. 10.00 (*1-880897-12-1*) Lyme Hist.

***Andersen, Jens.** Memoirs of an Idaho Elk Hunter. 1998. pap. 19.95 (*0-912299-78-9*) Stoneydale Pr Pub.

Andersen, Jim. Courageous Teaching: Creating a Caring Community in the Classroom. (Illus.). 104p. 1995. pap. 24.95 (*0-8039-6239-8*) Corwin Pr.

***Andersen, Jodi.** The Latchkey Dog: How the Way You Live Shapes the Behavior of the Dog You Love. 2000. 22.00 (*0-06-270240-8*, HarpRes) HarpInfo.

Andersen, Johannes C. Maori Life in Ao-tea. LC 75-35221. reprint ed. 74.50 (*0-404-14400-4*) AMS Pr.

— Maori Music, with Its Polynesian Background. LC 75-35222. reprint ed. 87.50 (*0-404-14401-2*) AMS Pr.

— Maori String Figures. LC 75-35223. reprint ed. 41.50 (*0-404-14402-0*) AMS Pr.

— The Maori Tohunga & His Spirit World. LC 75-35224. reprint ed. 37.50 (*0-404-14403-9*) AMS Pr.

— Myths & Legends of the Polynesians. (Illus.). 592p. 1995. pap. text 12.95 (*0-486-28582-0*) Dover.

— Myths & Legends of the Polynesians. LC 75-35170. (Illus.). reprint ed. 52.50 (*0-404-14200-1*) AMS Pr.

Andersen, John M., jt. auth. see Eaton, David J.

Andersen, Jon, jt. auth. see Williamson, Martha.

Andersen, Jorgen E. Geometry & Physics: Proceedings of the Conference at Aarhus University, Aarhus, Denmark. LC 96-41101. (Lecture Notes in Pure & Applied Mathematics Ser.: Vol. 10). (Illus.). 768p. 1996. pap. text 199.00 (*0-8247-9791-4*) Dekker.

Andersen, Jorgen G., jt. auth. see Borre, Ole.

Andersen, K. Brook Taylor's Role in the History of Linear Perspective. Toomer, G. J., ed. (Sources in the History of Mathematics & Physical Sciences Ser.: Vol. 10). (Illus.). 272p. 1991. 79.95 (*0-387-97486-5*) Spr-Verlag.

Andersen, K., et al. Medicine & Public Health in the Arctic & Antarctic: Selected Papers from a Conference. (Public Health Papers: No. 18). 169p. 1963. pap. text 6.00 (*92-4-130018-3*, 1110018) World Health.

Andersen, K. E. & Maibach, Howard I., eds. Contact Allergy Predictive Test in Guinea Pigs. (Current Problems in Dermatology Ser.: Vol. 14). (Illus.). viii, 300p. 1985. 141.00 (*3-8055-4053-1*) S Karger.

Andersen, K. Lange, et al. Fundamentals of Exercise Testing. 116p. 1970. pap. text 21.60 (*92-4-156001-0*, 1150046) World Health.

Andersen, Kenneth E. Persuasion: Theory & Practice. 2nd ed. (Illus.). 431p. 1983. pap. text 24.95 (*0-89641-117-6*) American Pr.

Andersen, Kenneth L. & Szany, Patrick A. Guidelines for the Buying & Selling of Used Corrugated Machinery: A Project of the Engineering Committee of the Corrugated Division. LC 92-24514. 1992. pap. 28.00 (*0-89852-303-6*, 0101R210) TAPPI.

Andersen, Kenneth W. Bats of San Salvador Island, Bahamas. (Occasional Papers - 1990: No. 1). (Illus.). 4p. (Orig.). (C). 1990. pap. text 2.00 (*0-935909-33-8*) Bahamian.

Andersen, Kenneth W. & Jones, J. Knox, Jr. Mammals of Northwestern South Dakota. (Museum Ser.: Vol. 19, No. 5). 33p. 1971. pap. 1.75 (*0-317-04914-3*) U KS Nat Hist Mus.

Andersen, Kim & Pemberton, Scott, eds. Indispensable You. LC 96-86313. (Illus.). 213p. 1996. pap. 21.95 incl. audio (*0-85013-289-4*) Dartnell Corp.

Andersen, Kim V., ed. EDI & Data Networking in the Public Sector. LC 97-40752. 352p. 1998. lib. bdg. 138.50 (*0-7923-8021-5*) Kluwer Academic.

Andersen, Kristi. After Suffrage: Women in Partisan & Electoral Politics Before the New Deal. LC 95-43395. (American Politics & Political Economy Ser.). (Illus.). 208p. (C). 1996. pap. text 14.00 (*0-226-01957-8*); lib. bdg. 38.00 (*0-226-01955-1*) U Ch Pr.

— The Creation of a Democratic Majority, 1928-1936. LC 78-11660. (Illus.). 175p. reprint ed. pap. 54.30 (*0-608-09260-6*, 205406200002) Bks Demand.

— Creation of a Democratic Majority, 1928-1936. LC 78-11660. (Illus.). 175p. 1979. 16.95 (*0-226-01884-9*) U Ch Pr.

***Andersen, Kurt.** Turn of the Century. 672p. 2000. pap. 14.95 (*0-385-33504-0*, Delta Trade) Dell.

Andersen, Kurt. Turn of the Century: A Novel. LC 99-18954. 659p. 1999. 24.95 (*0-375-50008-1*) Random.

Andersen, Lauri. Heikki Heikkinen: And Other Stories of Upper Peninsula Finns. 144p. 1995. pap. 12.95 (*0-87839-097-9*) North Star.

Andersen, Laurie H. Ndito Runs. LC 94-44649. (Illus.). 32p. (J). (ps-2). 1995. 15.95 (*0-8050-3265-7*) H Holt & Co.

Andersen, Lee. The Casual You: Knitting Designs for the Family. (Unique Ser.). (Illus.). 112p. 1991. text 23.95 (*0-9629520-0-1*) Eagle-Anderson.

***Andersen, Linda.** Love Adds the Chocolate. (Illus.). 32p. 2000. 10.95 (*1-57856-325-9*) Waterbrook Pr.

***Andersen, Lorraine, et al.** Islanders Speak: Profiles & Personalities. (Illus.). 100p. 2000. pap. 6.95 (*1-890352-11-X*) Jackson Harbor.

An Asterisk (*) at the beginning of an entry indicates that the title is appearing for the first time.

Andersen, Lydia. Titan U. LC 89-80152. 135p. (C). 1989. pap. 8.50 (*0-9622399-1-7*); lib. bdg. 11.95 (*0-9622399-2-5*); lib. bdg. 9.00 (*0-9622399-0-9*) Inniea Pub Co.

Andersen, M. L. M. Nucleic Acid Hybridization. 1998. pap. 34.95 (*0-387-91556-7*) Spr-Verlag.

Andersen, M. Paul. Guide to Pari-Mutual Wagering in North America. 106p. 1995. pap. 9.95 (*1-888405-00-7*) Mutuel Pr.

***Andersen, Marcellus B.** How to Reinvent Yourself: Inspiring Strategies for Personal Renewal. 296p. 1999. pap. 16.00 (*0-9684682-0-9*) BrookePress.

***Andersen, Margaret.** Thinking about Women. 5th ed. LC 99-26314. 434p. 1999. pap. text 44.00 (*0-205-30226-2*) Allyn.

Andersen, Margaret, et al. Sociology: CUNY Panel: Rethinking the Disciplines, Vol. 8G. (Women in the Curriculum Ser.). 65p. 1997. pap. 10.00 (*1-885303-15-7*) Towson St Univ.

***Andersen, Margaret L.** Race, Class & Gender: An Anthology. 4th ed. 2000. 28.50 (*0-534-56889-0*) Brooks-Cole.

Andersen, Margaret L. & Collins, Patricia H. Race, Class, & Gender: An Anthology. 518p. (C). 1991. pap. 24.95 (*0-534-13566-8*) Wadsworth Pub.

— Race, Class, & Gender: An Anthology. 2nd ed. LC 94-19800. 640p. 1994. mass mkt. 25.50 (*0-534-24768-7*) Wadsworth Pub.

Andersen, Margaret L. & Collins, Patricia H. Race, Class & Gender: An Anthology. 3rd ed. LC 97-29045. (Sociology Ser.). (C). 1997. pap. 41.95 (*0-534-52879-1*) Wadsworth Pub.

***Andersen, Margaret L. & Collins, Patricia Hill.** Race, Class & Gender: An Anthology. 4th ed. LC 00-29018. 2000. pap. write for info. (*0-534-56890-4*) Wadsworth Pub.

***Andersen, Margaret L. & Taylor, Howard F.** Sociology: Understanding a Diverse Society. LC 99-33633. 1999. 50.00 (*0-534-56664-2*) Wadsworth Pub.

— Sociology: Understanding a Diverse Society. LC 99-33633. 660p. 2000. 67.95 (*0-534-56685-5*) Wadsworth Pub.

Andersen, Margaret L., jt. auth. see Scarpitti, Frank R.

Andersen, Margret, ed. Mother Was Not a Person. 274p. 1972. 36.99 (*0-919618-12-X*, Pub. by Black Rose); pap. 7.99 (*0-919618-00-6*, Pub. by Black Rose) Consort Bk Sales.

Andersen, Maria. Howlin' Marie. Elgaard, Elin, tr. 140p. (YA). (gr. 9-12). 1985. 7.95 (*0-920806-71-6*, Pub. by Penumbra Pr) U of Toronto Pr.

***Andersen, Mark & Jenkins, Mark.** The Dance of Days: A History of the DC Punk Scene. 200p. 2000. pap. 16.00 (*1-887128-49-2*) Soft Skull Pr.

***Andersen, Mark B.** Doing Sport Psychology. (Illus.). 312p. 2000. pap. write for info. (*0-7360-0086-0*) Human Kinetics.

Andersen, Mary K., jt. auth. see Read, Hadley.

Andersen, Mikael S. Governance by Green Taxes: Making Pollution Prevention Pay. LC 93-44232. (Issues in Environmental Politics Ser.). 247p. 1994. text 29.95 (*0-7190-4232-1*, Pub. by Manchester Univ Pr) St Martin.

***Andersen, Mikael Skou & Liefferink, Duncan, eds.** European Environmental Policy: The Pioneers. 340p. 2000. pap. 24.95 (*0-7190-5717-5*, Pub. by Manchester Univ Pr) St Martin.

***Andersen, Mikael Skou & Sprenger, Rolf-Ulrich.** Market Based Instruments for Environmental Management. LC 99-49220. (International Studies in Environmental Policy Making Ser.). 288p. 2000. text 100.00 (*1-84064-039-1*) E Elgar.

Andersen, Niels H. The Sarup Enclosures. LC 97-226340. (Jutland Archaeological Society Publications: Vol. XXXIII, 1). (Illus.). 404p. (C). 1997. 46.50 (*87-7288-588-2*, Pub. by Aarhus Univ Pr) David Brown.

Andersen, O. K., et al. Methods of Electronic Structure Calculations. 396p. 1995. text 116.00 (*981-02-1485-5*) World Scientific Pub.

Andersen, Oivind & Dickie, Matthew, eds. Homer's World: Fiction, Tradition, Reality. (Papers from the Norwegian Institute at Athens: No. 3). (Illus.). 173p. (Orig.). 1995. pap. 34.50 (*82-991411-9-2*, Pub. by P Astroms) Coronet Bks.

Andersen, Oivind & Whittaker, Helene, eds. The Norwegian Institute at Athens: The First Five Lectures. (Papers from the Norwegian Institute at Athens). (Illus.). 86p. 1991. pap. 22.50 (*960-85145-0-9*, Pub. by P Astroms) Coronet Bks.

Andersen, P. B., et al, eds. The Computer As Medium. (Learning in Doing: Social, Cognitive & Computational Perspectives Ser.). (Illus.). 505p. (C). 1994. text 59.95 (*0-521-41995-6*) Cambridge U Pr.

Andersen, P. K. & Bjedov, G. Essential C: An Introduction for Scientists & Engineers. LC 94-67128. (Illus.). 408p. (C). 1994. pap. text 47.95 (*0-03-004158-9*) OUP.

Andersen, P. K., et al. Essential C: An Introduction for Scientists & Engineers. 224p. (C). 1995. pap. text, student ed. write for info. (*0-03-010548-X*) OUP.

Andersen, Paul. Aspen: Body, Mind & Spirit: In Celebration of the Aspen Idea. Ohlrich, Warren H., ed. LC 98-94036. (Illus.). 128p. 1999. 39.95 (*1-882426-11-8*) W H O Pr.

— Statically Indeterminate Structures: Their Analysis & Design. LC 52-11520. (Illus.). 326p. reprint ed. pap. 101.10 (*0-608-11488-X*, 201256800082) Bks Demand.

— Substructure Analysis & Design. 2nd ed. LC 56-6804. 348p. reprint ed. pap. 107.90 (*0-608-30452-2*, 201244600081) Bks Demand.

Andersen, Paul & Johnson, Ken. Elk Mountains Odyssey: The West Elk Loop Scenic & Historic Byway Guide LC 98-91476. 128p. 1998. write for info. (*0-9664445-0-7*) Redstone Pr.

Andersen, Paul & Nordby, Gene M. Introduction to Structural Mechanics. LC 60-13150. 352p. reprint ed. pap. 109.20 (*0-608-11486-3*, 201244500081) Bks Demand.

Andersen, Paul K. Just Enough UNIX. 272p. (C). 1992. text 23.20 (*0-697-13172-6*, WCB McGr Hill) McGrw-H Hghr Educ.

— Just Enough UNIX. 2nd ed. LC 97-103247. 416p. (C). 1996. text 19.96 (*0-256-21276-7*, Irwn McGrw-H) McGrw-H Hghr Educ.

— Just Enough UNIX. 3rd ed. LC 99-462552. 456p. 1999. pap. 43.75 (*0-07-230297-6*) McGraw.

Andersen, Paul Kent. Word Order Typology & Comparative Constructions. (Current Issues in Linguistic Theory Ser.: Vol. 25). xvii, 245p. 1983. 59.00 (*90-272-3517-1*) J Benjamins Pubng Co.

Andersen, Peter A. Nonverbal Communication: Forms & Functions. LC 98-36051. 416p. 1998. pap. text 41.95 (*1-55934-726-0*) Mayfield Pub.

Andersen, Peter A. & Guerrero, Laura K., eds. Handbook of Communication & Emotion: Research, Theory, Applications, & Contexts. LC 97-23315. (Illus.). 590p. 1997. text 120.00 (*0-12-057770-4*) Morgan Kaufmann.

Andersen, Peter B. The Theory of Computer Semiotics: Semiotic Approaches to Construction & Assessemnt of Computer Systems. (Series in Human-Computer Interaction). (Illus.). 424p. (C). 1991. text 74.95 (*0-521-39336-1*) Cambridge U Pr.

— The Theory of Computer Semiotics: Semiotic Approaches to Construction & Assessment of Computer Systems. LC 97-181297. (Cambridge Series in Human-Computer Interaction: No. 3). 416p. 1997. pap. text 29.95 (*0-521-44868-9*) Cambridge U Pr.

***Andersen, Peter Bogh, et al, eds.** Downward Causation: Minds, Bodies & Matter. 352p. 2000. 34.95 (*87-7288-814-8*, Pub. by Aarhus Univ Pr) David Brown.

Andersen, Poul, jt. auth. see Breslin, John P.

Andersen, R., et al. Advanced Information Systems Engineering: Proceedings of the Third Nordic Conference CAiSE '91, Trondheim, Norway, May 13-15, 1991. Goos, G. & Hartmanis, J., eds. (Lecture Notes in Computer Science Ser.: Vol. 498). vi, 579p. 1991. 58.95 (*0-387-54059-8*) Spr-Verlag.

Andersen, R. C. The Privateer. Kaiser, Kathy, ed. LC 98-96572. 192p. 1999. 19.95 (*0-9666946-0-0*) Spring Pubg.

Andersen, Raoul, ed. North Atlantic Maritime Cultures. (World Anthropology Ser.). (Illus.). xviii, 365p. 1979. 63.10 (*90-279-7830-1*) Mouton.

***Andersen, Reidar, et al, eds.** The European Roe Deer: The Biology of Success. 376p. (C). 1998. 47.00 (*82-00-37682-6*, Pub. by Scand Univ Pr) IBD Ltd.

Andersen, Richard. Arranging Deck Chairs on the Titanic: Crises in Education. 250p. (Orig.). 1987. pap. 8.95 (*0-915597-62-4*) Amana Bks.

— The Red Aristocrats: Michael & Catherine Karolyi. 250p. 1991. pap. 12.50 (*0-915597-85-3*) Amana Bks.

— Straight Cut Ditch. Hammond, Debbie, ed. LC 79-7034. 1979. 22.95 (*0-87949-139-6*) Ashley Bks.

Andersen, Richard & Hinis, Helene. Write It Right! A Guide for Clear & Correct Writing. (Self-Study Sourcebook Ser.). ix, 158p. 1993. pap. 15.95 (*1-878542-30-3*, 13-0001) SkillPath Pubns.

Andersen, Richard, et al. Infections in Children. 2nd ed. 286p. 1993. 42.00 (*0-8342-0387-1*, 20387) Aspen Pub.

Andersen, Richard A., jt. ed. see Kosslyn, Stephen M.

Andersen, Richard E. Foreign Tax Credits. 410p. 1996. 185.00 (*0-7913-2545-8*) Warren Gorham & Lamont.

Andersen, Richard E., ed. Foreign Investment in the United States, Vol. 1. 2000. ring bd. 225.00 (*0-379-00841-6*, 0393010) Oceana.

Andersen, Robert. Second Choice: Growing up Adopted. LC 92-90502. (Illus.). 176p. (Orig.). (C). 1993. pap. 10.00 (*0-9632648-4-2*) Badger Hill.

***Andersen, Robert & Tucker, Rhonda.** A Bridge Less Traveled: Twice Visited. 320p. 2000. pap. 15.00 (*0-9632648-8-5*) Badger Hill.

Andersen, Robin K. Consumer Culture & TV Programming. Schiller, Herbert I., ed. (Critical Studies in Communication & in the Cultural Industries). (Illus.). 320p. (C). 1995. pap. 32.00 (*0-8133-1542-5*, Pub. by Westview) HarpC.

***Andersen, Robin K.** Critical Studies in Media Commercialism. 350p. 2000. pap. 24.95 (*0-19-874277-0*) OUP.

Andersen, Roger W. Fundamentals of Trusts & Estates 1996. annuals text 55.00 (*0-8205-2662-2*) Bender.

— Understanding Trusts & Estates. 2nd ed. LC 99-28255. (Legal Text Ser.). 1999. 30.00 (*0-8205-4059-5*) Bender.

Andersen, Ron. The Lebensohl Convention Complete in Contract Bridge. 105p. (Orig.). 1987. pap. 6.95 (*0-87643-048-5*) Barclay Bridge.

Andersen, Ron & Zenkel, Sabine. Preempts from A to Z. 300p. 1993. pap. text 14.95 (*0-9637533-0-4*) Magnus Bks.

— Preempts from A to Z. 2nd rev. ed. Francis, Henry, ed. 328p. 1996. pap. 15.95 (*0-9637533-3-9*) Magnus Bks.

Andersen, Ron, jt. auth. see Wei, C. C.

Andersen, Ron, jt. auth. see Wei, Kathie.

Andersen, Ronald M., et al, eds. Changing the U. S. Health Care System: Key Issues in Health Services, Policy, & Management. LC 96-22517. (Health Ser.). 464p. 1996. 43.95 (*0-7879-0224-1*) Jossey-Bass.

Andersen, Ronald M., et al. Total Survey Error. LC 79-88104. (Jossey-Bass Social & Behavioral Science Ser.). 236p. reprint ed. pap. 104.20 (*0-8357-4963-0*, 203789600009) Bks Demand.

Andersen, Ross J. Specifications & Tolerances for Reference Standards & Field Standard Weights & Measures: 5. Specifications & Tolerances for Field Standard Stopwatches. 16p. 1998. pap. 1.75 (*0-16-054741-5*) USGPO.

***Andersen, Roy, et al.** Politics & Change in the Middle East: Sources of Conflict & Accommodation. 6th ed. LC 00-29804. 2000. write for info. (*0-13-026009-6*) P-H.

Andersen, Roy R. & Seibert, Robert F. Politics & Change in the Middle East: Sources of Conflict & Accommodation. 5th ed. LC 97-2062. 396p. 1997. pap. text 49.00 (*0-13-621822-9*) P-H.

***Andersen, Scott.** Homosexuality - Symptoms & Free Agency. 1999. pap. 11.95 (*1-55517-410-8*) CFI Dist.

Andersen, Sigrid, jt. auth. see Clute, Robin.

Andersen, Stig. The Siphonini: (Diptera: Tachinidae) of Europe. LC 97-124330. (Fauna Entomologica Scandinavica Ser.: Vol. 33). (Illus.). 148p. 1996. text 71.50 (*90-04-10731-2*, NLG145) Brill Academic Pubs.

Andersen, Sue & Pryor, Burt. Speech Fundamentals: A Contemporary Approach. 2nd ed. 216p. (C). 1992. pap. text 38.20 (*0-536-58230-0*) Pearson Custom.

***Andersen, Susan.** Baby, Don't Go. LC 99-96449. 384p. 2000. mass mkt. 6.50 (*0-380-80712-2*, Avon Bks) Morrow Avon.

Andersen, Susan. Baby, I'm Yours. LC 97-94412. 384p. 1998. mass mkt. 5.99 (*0-380-79511-6*, Avon Bks) Morrow Avon.

— Be My Baby. LC 98-93542. 384p. 1999. mass mkt. 5.99 (*0-380-79512-4*, Avon Bks) Morrow Avon.

— Exposure. 1996. mass mkt. 4.99 (*0-8217-5289-8*, Zebra Kensgtn) Kensgtn Pub Corp.

***Andersen, Susan.** Exposure. 1999. mass mkt. 5.99 (*0-8217-6403-9*) Kensgtn Pub Corp.

Andersen, Susan. Obsessed. 320p. 1993. mass mkt. 4.50 (*0-8217-4330-9*, Zebra Kensgtn) Kensgtn Pub Corp.

— Present Danger. 288p. 1993. mass mkt. 4.50 (*0-8217-4067-9*, Zebra Kensgtn) Kensgtn Pub Corp.

Andersen, Svein S. The Struggle over North Sea Oil & Gas: Government Strategies in Denmark, Britain, & Norway. 204p. (C). 1993. 12.00 (*82-00-21815-5*, 14493) Scandnvan Univ Pr.

Andersen, Svein S., jt. auth. see Burns, Tom.

Andersen, Svend. Ideal und Singularitat: Uber die Funktion des Gottesbegriffes in Kants theoretischer Philosophie. 278p. 1983. 68.50 (*3-11-009649-8*) De Gruyter.

Andersen, Svend, ed. Traditional Theism & Its Modern Alternatives. LC 95-157561. (Acta Jutlandica Ser.: Vol. 70:1). 240p. (Orig.). (C). 1994. pap. 27.00 (*87-7288-482-7*, Pub. by Aarhus Univ Pr) David Brown.

Andersen, Svend & Peacocke, Arthur, eds. Evolution & Creation: A European Perspective. (Illus.). 215p. (Orig.). (C). 1987. pap. 25.00 (*87-7288-114-3*, Pub. by Aarhus Univ Pr) David Brown.

Andersen, T. Pelagic Nutrient Cycles: Herbivores As Sources & Sinks. LC 96-49478. (Ecological Studies: Vol. 129). (Illus.). 192p. 1997. 79.95 (*3-540-61881-3*) Spr-Verlag.

Andersen, T., et al, eds. The Physics of Electronic & Atomic Collisions: XVIII International Conference. (AIP Conference Proceedings Ser.: No. 295). 1300p. 1993. text 834.00 (*1-56396-290-X*) Am Inst Physics.

Andersen, Thayne I. Alaska Hooch: The History of Alcohol in Early Alaska. (Illus.). 300p. (Orig.). 1988. pap. 14.95 (*0-685-24051-7*) Temp Counsel Serv.

— Alaska Hooch: The History of Alcohol in Early Alaska. LC 88-71043. (Illus.). 272p. (Orig.). (C). 1988. pap. text 14.95 (*0-317-93044-3*) Temp Counsel Serv.

Andersen, Theodore A. A Century of Banking in Wisconsin. Bruchey, Stuart, ed. LC 80-1130. (Rise of Commercial Banking Ser.). 1981. reprint ed. lib. bdg. 23.95 (*0-405-13630-7*) Ayer.

Andersen, Tim. Jet Plane. 64p. (Orig.). 1987. pap. 5.00 (*0-944195-00-8*) A&B Pr Chi.

Andersen, Toirben J. Currency & Interest Rate Hedging: A User's Guide to Options, Futures, Swaps, & Forward Contracts. 2nd ed. (C). 1993. text 49.95 (*0-13-226101-4*) NY Inst Finance.

Andersen, Tom, ed. The Reflecting Team: Dialogues & Dialogues about the Dialogues. 192p. 1991. 22.95 (*0-393-70120-4*) Norton.

***Andersen, Tony.** Small Town Minnesota: A-Z. 120p. 2000. pap. 24.95 (*1-890434-25-6*) Afton Hist Soc.

Andersen, Torben J. Euromarket Instruments: A Guide to the World's Largest Debt Market. 1990. 34.95 (*0-13-298845-3*) NY Inst Finance.

Andersen, Torben M. Price Rigidity: Causes & Macroeconomic Implications. (Illus.). 194p. 1995. text 38.00 (*0-19-828760-7*) OUP.

Andersen, Torben M., et al, eds. The Future of the Welfare State. 208p. (Orig.). 1996. pap. text 30.95 (*0-631-19576-9*) Blackwell Pubs.

Andersen, Torben M. & Moene, Karl O., eds. Public Policy & Economic Theory. LC 98-29798. 275p. 1998. pap. 32.95 (*0-631-20943-3*) Blackwell Pubs.

Andersen, U. S. Greatest Power in the Universe. 270p. 1978. pap. 10.00 (*0-87980-339-8*) Wilshire.

— Secret Power of the Pyramids. 266p. 1977. pap. 7.00 (*0-87980-343-6*) Wilshire.

Andersen, Uell S. Magic in Your Mind. 1976. pap. 15.00 (*0-87980-089-5*) Wilshire.

— Secret of Secrets. 318p. 1976. pap. 10.00 (*0-87980-134-4*) Wilshire.

— Success Cybernetics. 1975. pap. 10.00 (*0-87980-155-7*) Wilshire.

— Three Magic Words. 323p. 1977. pap. 15.00 (*0-87980-165-4*) Wilshire.

Andersen, Velma R. & Thompson, Sheryl K. Test of Written English (TWE) 1979. student ed. 36.00 (*0-685-44977-7*); pap., teacher ed. 19.00 (*0-87879-234-1*); teacher ed. 18.00 (*0-685-31200-3*) Acad Therapy.

Andersen, Verlan. Many Are Called but Few Are Chosen. 96p. 1967. pap. 3.95 (*0-89036-002-2*) Liahona Pub Trust.

Andersen, Virginia. Access 2000: The Complete Reference. (Complete Reference Ser.). (Illus.). 1319p. 1999. pap. 39.99 (*0-07-882512-1*) Osborne-McGraw.

— Maximizing Access '97. 1998. pap. 39.99 (*0-07-882473-7*) Intl Marine.

***Andersen, Virginia.** Troubleshooting Microsoft Access Databases. 352p. 2000. pap. 19.99 (*0-7356-1160-2*) Microsoft Pr.

Andersen, Virginia, jt. auth. see Norton, Peter.

Andersen, Walter K. Indian Elections of 1989. (C). 1996. pap. text 27.95 (*0-8133-8123-1*) Westview.

Andersen, Wayne, tr. see Spring, Gardiner.

Andersen, William D. Genealogists in the United States & Canada 1984. 65p. (Orig.). 1984. pap. 10.00 (*0-930373-01-4*) W D Andersen.

Andersen, William E., jt. ed. see Young, Vigor.

Andersen, William R. & Rogers, C. Paul. Antitrust Law: Policy & Practice. 2nd ed. 1985. teacher ed. write for info. (*0-8205-0317-7*) Bender.

***Andersen, William R. & Rogers, C. Paul.** Antitrust Law: Policy & Practice. 3rd ed. LC 99-27249. (Casebook Ser.). 1999. 56.00 (*0-8205-4129-X*) Bender.

Andersland, Orlando B. & Sayles, Francis H, eds. Research on Transportation Facilities in Cold Regions. LC 86-25920. 112p. 1986. pap. 5.00 (*0-87262-568-0*) Am Soc Civil Eng.

Andersland, Orlando B., jt. auth. see Al-Khafaji, Amir W.

Andersland, Orlando B., jt. auth. see Khafaji, Amir W.

Anderson. Airplane Performance & Design. LC 98-48481. 1998. pap. (*0-07-001971-1*) McGrw-H Hghr Educ.

— American Revolution: A Narrative History. 1998. 144.80 (*0-07-001916-9*) McGraw.

— Anderson Public Policymaking. 4th ed. 1999. pap. text 34.77 (*0-395-96104-1*) HM.

Anderson. Anderson Strategic Marketing & Management: Cases. Date not set. pap. text 35.97 (*0-395-87053-4*) HM.

— Anderson Strategic Marketing & Management: Theory. Date not set. text 51.87 (*0-395-87050-X*) HM.

Anderson. Asking Questions. 228p. (C). 1998. pap. text 32.75 (*0-536-01550-3*) Pearson Custom.

— The Book of the Bible, Vol. 1. 1989. 110.00 (*0-684-19098-2*) Simon & Schuster.

— The Book of the Bible, Vol. 2. 1990. 110.00 (*0-684-19099-0*) Simon & Schuster.

Anderson. Built Surface, Vol.1. 87.95 (*0-7546-0022-X*) Ashgate Pub Co.

— Built Surface, Vol.2. 87.95 (*0-7546-0023-8*) Ashgate Pub Co.

Anderson. Caminando en la Luz - Walking Through the Darkness. (SPA.). 1994. write for info. (*0-614-24351-3*) Editorial Unilit.

— Care of the Critically ill Surgical Patient. (Illus.). 224p. 1999. pap. text 45.00 (*0-340-70092-0*, Pub. by E A) OUP.

— Cognitive Psychology. 4th ed. 1995. pap. text 24.00 (*0-7167-2684-X*) W H Freeman.

— Cognitive Psychology. 5th ed. 1999. pap. text 65.95 (*0-7167-3678-0*) St Martin.

— Compact Classics: Your Personal Portable Library, Vol. I. (Illus.). 624p. 1991. pap. 19.95 (*1-880184-01-X*) Compact Classics.

— Controlling Electrohydraulic Systems. (Fluid Power & Control Ser.: Vol. 7). (Illus.). 352p. 1988. text 175.00 (*0-8247-7825-1*) Dekker.

— Costume Design. 2nd ed. LC 98-86089. (C). 1998. pap. 58.00 (*0-15-508379-1*, Pub. by Harcourt Coll Pubs) Harcourt.

***Anderson.** Cpsq Essentials of Person Sel. 1998. pap. text 34.25 (*0-07-230700-5*) McGraw.

Anderson. Dental Assistant. (Dental Assisting Procedures Ser.). 1987. pap., teacher ed. 10.00 (*0-8273-2753-6*) Delmar.

— Dental Assisting Essentials. 7th ed. (Dental Assisting Procedures Ser.). (C). 2000. pap. 40.00 (*0-7668-1113-1*) Delmar.

— Discrete Mathematics. (C). 2000. write for info. (*0-13-793787-3*, Macmillan Coll) P-H.

— Education at West Texas A & M. 1996. pap. text. write for info. (*0-205-26629-0*) Allyn.

— The Effective Teacher. (C). 1994. pap. text 25.00 (*0-07-002038-8*) McGraw.

— Element of Literature. 1989. text 60.25 (*0-15-717500-6*) Holt R&W.

— Elements of Literature. 1989. text 65.25 (*0-15-717520-0*, Pub. by Harcourt Coll Pubs) Harcourt.

— Elements of Literature. (J). (gr. 8-9). 1989. text 60.25 (*0-15-717510-3*) Holt R&W.

— Elements of Literature. (YA). (gr. 9-10). 1989. text 65.25 (*0-15-717530-8*) Holt R&W.

— Elements of Literature. (YA). (gr. 10-11). 1989. text 66.50 (*0-15-717540-5*) Holt R&W.

Anderson. Encyclopedia of Hydrological Problems. text. write for info. (*0-471-49103-9*) Wiley.

Anderson. Environmental Protection: Law & Policy. 2nd ed. 960p. 1990. 53.00 (*0-316-03960-8*) Aspen Pub.

***Anderson.** Estadistica Para Administracion Y Economia. 7th ed. (SWC-Business Statistics Ser.). 1999. pap. 87.95 (*968-7529-41-5*) Sth-Wstrn College.

Anderson. European Film Production Guide. LC 95-83011. 480p. (C). 1996. 140.00 (*0-415-13665-2*) Routledge.

— Fairy Tales. (J). 1998. pap. 3.95 (*1-85326-100-9*, 1009WW, Pub. by Wrdsworth Edits) NTC Contemp Pub Co.

— Fast Cycle Organizational Development. LC 99-28180. (SWC-Management Ser.). 200p. 1999. pap. 29.95 (*0-324-01328-0*) Thomson Learn.

— Federico Garcia Lorca. (Modern Dramatists Ser.). (Orig.). 1990. pap. 11.95 (*0-333-31888-9*) St Martin.

— Finite Mathematics. 156p. (C). 1998. pap. text 14.00 (*0-536-01188-5*) S&S Trade.
— Forensic Sciences in Clinical Medicine: A Case Study Approach. (Illus.). 304p. 1998. text 185.00 (*0-397-58777-5*) Lppncott W & W.
— Freestyle. (C). 1991. pap. text, teacher ed. 2.76 (*0-395-57733-0*) HM.
— Fundamentals of Aerodynamics. 2nd ed. 1991. 34.68 (*0-07-001680-1*) McGraw.
Anderson. Fundamentals of Sports Injury Management. wbk. ed. 49.95 (*0-683-30345-7*) Lppncott W & W.
Anderson. Gynecological Imaging. (C). 1998. text 195.00 (*0-443-05239-5*) Church.
— Les Habits Neufs de l'Empereur, la Petite Sirene. (FRE.). 1996. pap. 7.95 (*2-87714-328-7*, Pub. by Bookking Intl) Distribks Inc.
— Herpetology of Arabia. LC 84-51123. 1984. write for info. (*0-916984-15-X*) SSAR.
— High Availability Servers: UNIX & NT. 2001. pap. write for info. (*0-13-096180-9*) P-H.
— How to Do What You Love for a Living. 336p. 1999. 7.98 (*1-56731-317-5*, MJF Bks) Fine Comms.
— IBM Test Bank Cognitive Psychology. 4th ed. 48.00 (*0-7167-2685-8*) W H Freeman.
— Instrumentation for Process Measurement & Control. 3rd ed. 512p. 1997. boxed set 54.95 (*0-8493-9871-1*) CRC Pr.
***Anderson.** Insulting the Public. LC 98-45964. 240p. (C). 1999. pap. text 26.95 (*0-582-31740-1*) Longman.
— Integrating Music in the Elementary Classroom. 5th ed. (Music Ser.). 2000. 46.75 (*0-534-51751-X*) Wadsworth Pub.
Anderson. International Politics Central Asia. LC 97-5365. 1997. pap. 24.95 (*0-7190-4373-5*, Pub. by Manchester Univ Pr) St Martin.
— Introduction to Flight. 3rd ed. 1989. student ed. 31.25 (*0-07-001642-9*) McGraw.
— Introduction to Management Science. 7th ed. 1994. text 75.80 (*0-314-03483-8*) Thomson Learn.
— Introduction to Management Science, Quantitative Approach to Decision Making. 7th ed. (SWC-Management). 1993. pap. text, student ed. 23.25 (*0-314-03368-8*) West Pub.
— Irwin's Introduction to Law. 1997. text 39.16 (*0-256-19485-8*, Irwn McGrw-H) McGrw-H Hghr Educ.
— Journeying in His Light. 1993. pap. 9.00 (*0-697-02243-9*, WCB McGr Hill) McGrw-H Hghr Educ.
— Journeys in Listening 3. (C). 1999. pap. text, teacher ed. 13.93 (*0-13-242124-0*) P-H.
— Journeys Listening Speak, Vol. 3. 1998. pap. 27.73 (*0-13-233362-7*) P-H.
— Keys to Successful College Writing. LC 98-30750. 500p. (C). 1998. pap. text 47.00 (*0-321-01576-2*) Addson-Wesley Educ.
— The Kingdom of Saudi Arabia. 9th ed. (Illus.). 256p. 1986. 60.00 (*0-86685-518-1*, Pub. by Stacey Intl) Intl Bk Ctr.
— Libertando A Su Iglesia - Setting Your Church Free. pap. write for info. (*0-7899-0379-2*) Editorial Unilit.
— Life Insurance Set, Set. 1992. 145.00 (*0-316-03971-3*) Aspen Pub.
Anderson. Little Woman. 32p. (J). Date not set. pap. 5.95 (*0-06-443574-1*) HarpC Child Bks.
Anderson. The Living World of the Old Testament. 1988. pap. text. write for info. (*0-582-02561-3*, Pub. by Addison-Wesley) Longman.
— Mac Cognitive Psychology. 4th ed. (C). 48.00 (*0-7167-2686-6*) W H Freeman.
— Magic, Science, & Health. (C). 1995. pap. text 50.00 (*0-15-500828-5*, Pub. by Harcourt Coll Pubs); pap. text, teacher ed. 26.75 (*0-15-503183-X*) Harcourt Coll Pubs.
— Management: Skills, Functions & Organization Performance. 2nd ed. 1988. student ed. 18.00 (*0-205-11435-0*, H1435-0) Allyn.
— Management Science. 7th ed. Date not set. text, teacher ed. write for info. (*0-314-02504-9*); pap. text. write for info. (*0-314-03052-2*); pap. text, student ed. 23.25 (*0-314-03306-8*) West Pub.
— Management Scientist Version 3.0: Software Pkg. 3rd ed. (SWC-Management). 1993. 3.5 hd 38.25 (*0-314-03458-7*) West Pub.
Anderson. Managerial Accounting, 001. (C). 1989. mass mkt., teacher ed. 7.56 (*0-395-32469-6*) HM.
— Managerial Accounting, 001. (C). 1989. pap., student ed. 25.16 (*0-395-32466-1*); pap., wbk. ed. 31.96 (*0-395-32467-X*); mass mkt., teacher ed. 7.56 (*0-395-32468-8*) HM.
Anderson. Managerial Accounting. 8th ed. (SWC-Accounting Ser.). 1992. 41.00 (*0-538-81328-8*) S-W Pub.
— Managerial Accounting. 8th ed. (Swc-Accounting Ser.). 1992. teacher ed. 31.25 (*0-538-81331-8*) S-W Pub.
— Managing Our Wildlife Resources. 3rd ed. LC 98-5859. 560p. (C). 1998. 105.00 (*0-13-901232-X*) P-H.
***Anderson.** Marmaduke: Everlovin' 1999. mass mkt. 3.50 (*0-8125-1743-1*) Tor Bks.
— Marmaduke: Laps it. 1989. mass mkt. 2.95 (*0-8125-0309-0*) Tor Bks.
Anderson. Melting & Casting Aluminum. 1987. reprint ed. pap. 9.95 (*0-917914-59-7*) Lindsay Pubns.
Anderson. Metal Minds. 1986. mass mkt. 2.95 (*0-8125-3070-5*) Tor Bks.
— Millennium. 336p. 2000. text 15.95 (*0-312-87394-8*) Forge NYC.
— My First Joke Book. (J). 2000. pap. 5.95 (*0-552-54278-4*, Pub. by Transworld Publishers Ltd) Trafalgar.
Anderson. Mystery of Blue Mines. 1992. pap. text. write for info. (*0-582-05478-8*, Pub. by Addison-Wesley) Longman.
— 95 Supplemental Life Insurance. 1995. suppl. ed. 80.00 (*0-316-03975-6*) Aspen Pub.
— Nursing, Communication & Education in an Information Age. (Nursing Education Ser.). 1990. pap., teacher ed. 12.75 (*0-8273-3434-6*) Delmar.
***Anderson.** On Kierkegaard. (Philosophy Ser.). 1999. pap. text 13.95 (*0-534-57601-X*) Brooks-Cole.
— On Mill. 1999. pap. text 13.95 (*0-534-57600-1*) Brooks-Cole.
— Operation Chaos. 1999. mass mkt. 5.99 (*0-8125-7927-5*) Tor Bks.
Anderson. Paediatric Gastroenterology, No. 2. 2nd ed. (gr. 13). 1989. 145.00 (*0-86793-176-0*) Mosby Inc.
— Pasos Hacia la Libertad en Cristo.Tr. of Steps to Freedom in Christ. (SPA.). 1995. write for info. (*0-614-27104-5*) Editorial Unilit.
— Pasos Hacia la Libertad en Cristo - Steps to Freedom in Christ. (SPA.). 1995. write for info. (*0-614-24390-4*) Editorial Unilit.
— Pediatric Cardiology. 2nd ed. 2000. text 375.00 (*0-443-07990-0*, W B Saunders Co) Harcrt Hlth Sci Grp.
— Peyote 2nd: The Divine Cactus. 2nd ed. LC 95-50224. (Illus.). 272p. 1996. 50.00 (*0-8165-1653-7*) U of Ariz Pr.
— POP 11 Comes of Age. 1990. boxed set. write for info. (*0-318-68277-X*) P-H.
— Power System Protection. (Illus.). 1236p. 1998. 124.95 (*0-07-134323-7*) McGraw.
— Principles of Reading. (Teaching Methods Ser.). 1999. pap. 22.95 (*0-8384-6685-0*) Wadsworth Pub.
— Proceedings of the Conference on Simulation in Health Care & Social Services. 120p. 1992. pap. 48.00 (*1-56555-010-2*, MC92-4) Soc Computer Sim.
— Professional Sales Management. 2nd ed. 1992. teacher ed. 50.00 (*0-07-001688-7*) McGraw.
Anderson. Quantum Mechanics. (C). 1912. text 65.00 (*0-03-005647-0*) Harcourt Coll Pubs.
Anderson. Questions of Communication. LC 97-65198. 348p. 1997. pap. text 51.95 (*0-312-17086-6*) St Martin.
— Real Contexts. (College ESL Ser.). 200p. (J). 1996. pap. 20.95 (*0-8384-4706-6*) Heinle & Heinle.
— Retailing. Date not set. pap. text, teacher ed. write for info. (*0-314-01310-5*) West Pub.
Anderson. River Boy. 32p. (J). Date not set. pap. 5.95 (*0-06-443573-3*) HarpC Child Bks.
Anderson. River Boy. 32p. (J). 2001. 15.95 (*0-06-028400-5*); lib. bdg. 15.89 (*0-06-028401-3*) HarpC Child Bks.
— Rompiendo las Cadenas - Bondage Breaker: Ed. Jovenes - The Youth Edition. (SPA.). 1995. write for info. (*0-614-24403-X*) Editorial Unilit.
***Anderson.** Rose Wilder Lane Biography. 256p. (J). (gr. 3-7). 2001. lib. bdg. 14.89 (*0-06-026433-0*) HarpC Child Bks.
— SAAB Aircraft Since 1937. rev. ed. 192p. 2000. 49.95 (*0-85177-886-0*, Pub. by Conway) Motorbooks Intl.
Anderson. Sensory Motor Issues in Autism. 64p. (C). 1999. pap. text 35.00 (*0-12-785073-2*) Acad Pr.
— The Sociology Game. 1985. pap. text. write for info. (*0-582-29641-2*, Pub. by Addison-Wesley) Longman.
— Solution Manual to Accompany Horowitz. (C). 1990. 16.80 (*0-7167-8234-0*, Computer Sci Pr) W H Freeman.
— Statistical Business Economics 5. Date not set. pap. text, student ed. write for info. (*0-314-01708-9*) West Pub.
— Statistical Models Based on Counting Processes. 1995. 39.95 (*0-387-94519-9*) Spr-Verlag.
— Statistics Business Economics. 6th ed. 1995. pap., student ed. 19.50 (*0-314-08588-2*); pap., wbk. ed. 22.25 (*0-314-08459-2*) West Pub.
— The Status of Alternative Methods in Toxicology. 1996. 95.00 (*0-85404-404-3*) CRC Pr.
— Supplement Environmental '88. 1988. pap. 10.95 (*0-316-03944-6*) Aspen Pub.
— Systemic Path: Female Reproduction, Vol. 6. 4th ed. (C). 2001. text. write for info. (*0-443-05595-5*, W B Saunders Co) Harcrt Hlth Sci Grp.
— Technical Communication. 4th ed. LC 98-28047. (C). 1998. pap. text 63.50 (*0-15-508309-0*, Pub. by Harcourt Coll Pubs) Harcourt.
— Technical Writing. 3rd ed. (C). 1995. pap. text, teacher ed. 33.75 (*0-15-502325-X*) Harcourt Coll Pubs.
— Technical writing guide for nonnative speakers of English. 3rd ed. LC 95-191831. (C). 1994. pap. text, lab manual ed. 12.50 (*0-15-502326-8*) Harcourt Coll Pubs.
— Technical Writing 1995. 3rd ed. (C). 1994. otabind 70.00 (*0-15-502913-4*) Harcourt.
— Thermo Using Mathcad. (Miscellaneous/Catalogs Ser.). 1998. text 20.95 (*0-534-95105-8*) Wadsworth Pub.
— Video Editing & Post Production. LC 97-194194. 218p. 1997. pap. 37.95 (*0-240-80302-7*) Buttrwrth-Heinemann.
— Wkbk Stats For Bus & Econ 5e. 5th ed. (SWC-Business Statistics). 1992. mass mkt., wbk. ed. 16.75 (*0-314-01711-9*) West Pub.
— The World of Computing. (C). 1988. pap., student ed. 22.36 (*0-395-43556-0*) HM.
— Writing the News. 1987. teacher ed. 26.25 (*0-07-553932-2*) McGraw.
— The Wrong Man. 1992. pap. text. write for info. (*0-582-06071-0*, Drumbeat) Longman.
Anderson, ed. Literature & the Environment. LC 98-29887. 510p. (C). 1998. pap. 44.00 (*0-321-01149-X*) Addson-Wesley Educ.
— Ovidii, Nasonis: Metamorphoses. 1996. pap. 29.95 (*3-8154-1565-9*, T1565, Pub. by B G Teubner) U of Mich Pr.
***Anderson, ed.** The Sixties. LC 98-24046. 256p. (C). 1998. pap. 24.60 (*0-321-01128-7*) Addson-Wesley Educ.
Anderson & Arenau. Fundamentals in Education Research. 2nd ed. 1998. text 25.95 (*0-7507-0857-3*) Taylor & Francis.
***Anderson & Beveridge.** Threshold Competitor: Team & Solo. 2nd ed. 109p. (C). 1998. pap. text 52.00 (*0-13-020237-1*) P-H.
Anderson & Blakers, Anderson. Youth Transit & Social Research. (Australian National University Press Ser.). 1983. pap. text 19.50 (*0-08-032988-8*, Pergamon Pr) Elsevier.
Anderson & Coates. Explanations & Ideologies. (C). 1996. pap. text. write for info. (*0-582-09200-0*, Pub. by Addison-Wesley) Longman.
Anderson & Connin, D. M. Experimental Toxicology. 1990. 55.00 (*0-85186-682-4*) CRC Pr.
Anderson & Forbes. A Linguistic Concordance of Jeremiah: Hebrew Vocabulary & Idiom, Vol. 14. 1977. 129.95 (*0-935106-06-5*) E Mellen.
Anderson & Fox. Business Law & Regulatory Environment: Principles & Cases. 12th ed. (LA - Business Law Ser.). (C). 1994. mass mkt., student ed. 20.50 (*0-538-84229-6*) S-W Pub.
— Business Law & the Legal Environment Comprehension. 16th ed. (LA - Business Law Ser.). (C). 1995. pap. 79.95 (*0-538-84526-0*) S-W Pub.
— Business Law & the Regulatory Environment. 14th ed. (SWC -Business Law Ser.). 2000. pap. 109.95 (*0-324-01500-3*) Sth-Wstrn College.
— Business Law Principle Cases. 11th ed. (SWC-Business Law Ser.). 1991. mass mkt., student ed. 4.75 (*0-538-81274-5*) S-W Pub.
— Business Law Principle Cases. 11th ed. (LA - Business Law Ser.). (C). 1991. mass mkt., student ed. 22.50 (*0-538-81271-0*) S-W Pub.
— Business Law Principle Cases. 11th ed. (SWC-Business Law Ser.). 1992. teacher ed. 91.00 (*0-538-81276-1*) S-W Pub.
Anderson & Gillison. Vegetable Classification in Australia. (Australian National University Press Ser.). 1981. text 37.00 (*0-08-032945-4*, Pergamon Pr) Elsevier.
Anderson & Katzper, eds. Simulation in Health Sciences, 1994. 151p. 1994. pap. 60.00 (*1-56555-068-4*, MC-94-3) Soc Computer Sim.
Anderson & Katzper, Meyer. Simulation in Health Sciences & Services: 1993 Conference. 116p. 1993. pap. 48.00 (*1-56555-021-8*, MC93-2) Soc Computer Sim.
Anderson & Scott. Threshold Competitor: Solo. 2nd ed. 103p. (C). 1998. pap. text 37.80 (*0-13-020235-5*) P-H.
Anderson & Sweeney. Introduction to Statistics: Concepts & Applications. 3rd ed. 1994. pap. 17.00 (*0-314-03309-2*) West Pub.
***Anderson & Sweeney, Pete.** Metodos Cuantitativos para la Administracion. 7th ed. 1999. pap. 79.95 (*968-7529-56-3*) Thomson Learn.
***Anderson & Zuehlk.** Christ-Centered Therapy: The Practical Integration of Theology & Psychology. 2000. 24.99 (*0-310-23113-2*) Zondervan.
Anderson, et al. Clinical Decisions in Glaucoma. (Illus.). 216p. (C). (gr. 13). 1993. text 93.00 (*0-8016-6799-2*, 06799) Mosby Inc.
— Essentials of Statistics for Business & Economics. 1996. text 20.75 (*0-314-20473-3*) West Pub.
— Introduction to Management Science. 8th ed. 1996. 20.75 (*0-314-20800-3*) West Pub.
— LOEX of the West: Collaboration & Instructional Design in a Virtual Environment. LC 99-12397. (Foundations in Library & Information Science: Vol. 43). 1999. 78.50 (*0-7623-0549-5*) Jai Pr.
— Management Scientist Version 4.0 for Windows. 8th ed. 1996. 34.75 (*0-314-21646-4*) West Pub.
— Professional Sales Management. 1998. 69.95 (*0-87393-751-1*) Dame Pubns.
Anderson, jt. auth. see Compact Classics Staff.
Anderson, jt. auth. see Cross.
Anderson, jt. auth. see Damjanov, Ivan.
Anderson, jt. auth. see Davis.
Anderson, jt. auth. see Gardner.
Anderson, jt. auth. see Gold.
Anderson, jt. auth. see Nahikian-Nelms, Marcia.
Anderson, jt. auth. see Stewart.
Anderson, ed. see Sauer, John R.
Anderson, Brian C., ed. see Novak, Michael.
***Anderson, Pati.** Consider the Lilies. LC 00-90242. 2000. pap. 7.95 (*0-533-13489-7*) Vantage.
***Anderson, Reb.** Being Upright: Zen Meditation & the Bodhisatva Precepts. 288p. 2001. 24.95 (*0-9627138-9-9*, Pub. by Rodmell Pr) SCB Distributors.
Anderson, Reb. Warm Smiles from Cold Mountains: Dharma Talks on Zen Meditation. 173p. 1999. pap. 12.95 (*0-9627138-7-2*) Rodmell Pr.
Anderson, Richard P. & Nibley, Reid. Simple Steps to Playing the Piano. 244p. (C). 1999. pap. 29.95 (*1-57766-052-8*) Waveland Pr.
***Anderson & Miller Staff.** Caminando Con Libertad. (SPA.). 2000. pap. 8.99 (*0-7899-0685-6*) Spanish Hse Distributors.
Anderson, A. Diccionario Espiritualidad, Vol. 3. 3rd ed. (ENG & GER.). 277p. 1989. lib. bdg. 95.00 (*0-8288-3878-X*, F107850) Fr & Eur.
— Interpreting Data. 240p. (gr. 13). 1989. per. 36.95 (*0-412-29570-9*, Chap & Hall CRC) CRC Pr.
— Interpreting Data. 200p. 1989. text 52.50 (*0-412-29560-1*) Chapman & Hall.
Anderson, A., ed. see Royal Academy of Letters, History, & Antiquities S.
Anderson, A. A. Experiences & Impressions: The Autobiography of Colonel A. A. Anderson. LC 72-124223. (Select Bibliographies Reprint Ser.). 1977. 23.95 (*0-8369-5411-4*) Ayer.
Anderson, A. C. Phonon Scattering in Condensed Matter. Wolfe, J. P., ed. (Solid-State Sciences Ser.: Vol. 68). (Illus.). 430p. 1986. 73.95 (*0-387-17057-X*) Spr-Verlag.
Anderson, A. E., et al, eds. Knowledge & Industrial Organization. (Illus.). 320p. 1989. 93.95 (*0-387-51529-1*) Spr-Verlag.
Anderson, A. J. The Artistic Side of Photography in Theory & Practice. LC 72-9179. (Literature of Photography Ser.). 1978. reprint ed. 28.95 (*0-405-04890-4*) Ayer.
— Dr. Sparkplug: "A Car Owners Bible" LC 87-91237. (Illus.). 260p. 1987. pap. 14.95 (*0-930942-14-0*) Sutherland IA.
— E. B. White: A Bibliography. LC 78-2783. (Author Bibliographies Ser.: No. 37). 205p. 1978. 24.00 (*0-8108-1121-9*) Scarecrow.
Anderson, A. Janell, jt. auth. see Raza, M. Ali.
Anderson, Abbe, jt. auth. see Rush, John.
Anderson, Abraham, tr. from FRE. The Treatise of the Three Impostors & the Problem of Enlightenment. LC 97-7424. 192p. 1997. 55.50 (*0-8476-8430-X*); pap. 23.95 (*0-8476-8431-8*) Rowman.
Anderson, Adam. An Historical & Chronological Account of the Origin of Commerce, 4 vols., Set. LC 67-20805. (Reprints of Economic Classics Ser.). 1967. reprint ed. 295.00 (*0-678-00259-2*) Kelley.
Anderson, Adele, jt. auth. see Reeves-Ellington, Richard H.
Anderson, Adreinne R., ed. see Anderson, Dona S.
Anderson, Adrian. Living a Spiritual Year: Seasonal Festivals in Northern & Southern Hemispheres: an Esoteric Study. LC 92-34742. (Illus.). 336p. (Orig.). 1993. pap. 19.95 (*0-88010-365-5*) Anthroposophic.
Anderson, Adrian, jt. auth. see Richardson, Rupert N.
Anderson, Adrienne E. Fun & Games for Family Gatherings. LC 95-41090. (Illus.). 134p. (Orig.). 1996. pap. 12.95 (*0-9610470-5-4*) Reunion Research.
***Anderson, Adrienne E. & Anderson, Dona S.** Let's Face It: Bg Beading Hearts Designs Inc. (Beading Heart Designs). (Illus.). 34p. (C). 2000. pap. text 22.00 (*1-892980-01-0*) Buckaroo Pr.
Anderson, Adrienne W. Firefighter: Read Me a Book! LC 92-41484. (Illus.). 300p. 1993. 37.00 (*0-8108-2651-8*) Scarecrow.
Anderson, Agnes G. Approaching the Magic Hour: Memories of Walter Anderson. Black, Patti C., ed. LC 85-5407. (Illus.). 178p. 1995. pap. 15.95 (*0-87805-803-6*) U Pr of Miss.

Anderson, Aimee D. & Anderson, Albert E.Broken Yet Triumphant: True Romance & Murder Mystery. Aimee D. Anderson. 221p. 1985. 14.95 (*0-9650875-1-4*); pap. 9.95 (*0-9650875-2-2*) A & A Anderson.
BROKEN, YET TRIUMPHANT - True romance & murder mystery - Aimee Anderson, a pastor's wife, reveals the discovery of two brutal murders, challenge of pastoral life, drama of a parsonage fire, & private episodes that touch the heartstrings. There is also revealed the indomitable spirit overcoming all obstacles. "I remember walking into their house that night in a daze & viewing the dead bodies of our dear friends. The man of the house was lying curled up in a heap in his own blood on the kitchen floor. His wife was sprawled face down on her blood-spattered bed." (Quotes from the book). (A sequel is presently in progress. Together with her husband, Albert, she has authored the book WHITED SEPULCHRES). *Publisher Paid Annotation.*

— Whited Sepulchres: An Expose of Corruption in Church Hierarchies. Aimee D. Anderson & Albert E. Anderson. (Illus.). 352p. (Orig.). 1996. pap. 15.95 (*0-9650875-0-6*) A & A Anderson.
WHITED SEPULCHRES--AN EXPOSE--Illegal & deceitful activities involving the Northwest District Council of the Assemblies of God, Executive Presbytery & the General Council of the Assemblies were whitewashed, ignored & set aside; subsequently allowing the accused to determine the fate of the accuser. Currently, it is a Grand Jury case. The unscrupulous, unethical & unprofessional manner in which both the Northwest District & General Council Executive Presbytery of the Assemblies of God handled the complaints & complaintants is appalling. "Albert & Aimee Anderson have done a great service in writing this book...This book is more than an expose of one scandal, in one denominatin, in part of the country. It is an autopsy on the politically correct, powerful & politically motivated church of today...these pastors have done first-class investigation & fine reporting. Their facts are so well verifed & the documentation so overwhelming...WHITED SEPULCHRES...turns a spotlight on the crisis of integrity in the church today." This true account uses real names of people & places.--Quotes from the Foreword by Larry Thomas (Publisher, THE INKHORN). (A sequel is presently in process). Aimee also authored BROKEN, YET TRIUMPHANT. *Publisher Paid Annotation.*

Anderson, Al. Game Fish Tag & Release. Barrett, Linda, ed. (Illus.). 200p. (Orig.). 1995. pap. write for info. (*0-923155-22-8*) Fisherman Lib.

An Asterisk (*) at the beginning of an entry indicates that the title is appearing for the first time.

— Meeting God in the Breakdown Lane: Stories from the Journey. 192p. 1995. 20.00 (0-9649789-1-1) Mtntop Graphics.
— To Catch a Tuna. (Illus.). 160p. (Orig.). 1990. pap. 9.95 (0-929775-03-1) MT Pubns.
Anderson, Alan D. The Origin & Resolution of an Urban Crisis: Baltimore, 1890. LC 77-4553. (Johns Hopkins Studies in Urban Affairs). 155p. reprint ed. pap. 48.10 (0-608-14630-7, 202582300046) Bks Demand.
Anderson, Alan D., ed. & tr. see Adomnan.
Anderson, Alan H. Effective Business Policy: Instructor's Manual. 80p. (Orig.). (C). pap. 33.95 (0-631-19854-7) Blackwell Pubs.
— Effective Marketing: Instructor's Manual. (Effective Management Ser.). 100p. (Orig.). (C). pap. 36.95 (0-631-19853-9) Blackwell Pubs.
— Effective Personnel Management: A Skills & Activity-Based Approach. (Effective Management Ser.). 256p. 1994. pap. 40.95 (0-631-19116-X) Blackwell Pubs.
— Effective Personnel Management: Instructor's Manual. (Effective Management Ser.). 100p. (Orig.). (C). pap. 38.95 (0-631-19799-0) Blackwell Pubs.
— Effective Self-Development. (C). 1996. pap. text 40.95 (0-631-20015-0) Blackwell Pubs.
Anderson, Alan H. & Barker, Dennis. Effective Business Policy: A Skills & Activity-Based Approach. (Effective Management Ser.). 256p. 1994. pap. 40.95 (0-631-19125-9) Blackwell Pubs.
— Effective Enterprise & Change Management. (Effective Management Ser.). (Illus.). 350p. 1995. pap. 44.95 (0-631-19124-0) Blackwell Pubs.
Anderson, Alan H. & Kleiner, David. Effective Marketing Communications: A Skills & Activity-Based Approach. (Effective Management Ser.). 256p. (Orig.). (C). 1995. pap. 40.95 (0-631-19126-7) Blackwell Pubs.
Anderson, Alan H. & Nix, Eileen. Effective Labour Relations: A Skills & Activity-Based Approach. (Effective Management Ser.). 256p. 1994. pap. 40.95 (0-631-19122-4) Blackwell Pubs.
Anderson, Alan H. & Woodcock, Peter. Effective Entrepreneurship: A Skills & Activity-Based Approach. (Effective Management Ser.). (Illus.). 250p. (Orig.). (C). 1996. pap. 40.95 (0-631-19117-8) Blackwell Pubs.
Anderson, Alan R., et al, eds. The Logical Enterprise. LC 74-20084. 271p. reprint ed. pap. 84.10 (0-8357-8735-4, 203366000087) Bks Demand.
Anderson, Alan R. & Belnap, Nuel D., Jr. Entailment: The Logic of Relevance & Necessity. LC 72-14016. 575p. reprint ed. pap. 178.30 (0-608-08021-7, 206798600001) Bks Demand.
— Entailment: The Logic of Relevance & Necessity, Vol. 1. LC 72-14016. 567p. 1975. text 99.50 (0-691-07192-6, Pub. by Princeton U Pr) Cal Prin Full Svc.
Anderson, Alan R., et al. Entailment Vol. II: The Logic of Relevance & Necessity. (Illus.). 784p. (C). 1990. text 99.50 (0-691-07339-2, Pub. by Princeton U Pr) Cal Prin Full Svc.
***Anderson, Alasdair & MacLeod, Isabail, eds.** Early Word Skills: Exercises. (J). (gr. 1-2). 1999. pap. 29.00 (0-7217-0674-6, Pub. by Schofield) St Mut.
— Early Words Dictionary. (J). (gr. 1-2). 1999. pap. 29.00 (0-7217-0672-X, Pub. by Schofield) St Mut.
— A Keyword Dictionary. (J). (gr. 2-3). 1999. pap. 39.00 (0-7217-0677-0, Pub. by Schofield) St Mut.
— A Keyword Dictionary: Exercises. (J). (gr. 2-3). 1999. pap. 39.00 (0-7217-0678-9, Pub. by Schofield) St Mut.
Anderson, Albert. Ethics for Fundraisers. LC 95-4612. (Philanthropic Studies). 168p. Date not set. pap. 12.95 (0-253-21052-6) Ind U Pr.
Anderson, Albert E., jt. auth. see Anderson, Aimee D.
***Anderson, Alex.** Fabric Shopping with Alex Anderson: Seven Projects to Help You Make Successful Choices, Build Your Confidence, Add to Your Fabric Stash. Aneloski, Liz & Lytle, Joyce, eds. LC 99-50433. (Quilting Basics Ser.). (Illus.). 48p. 2000. pap. 14.95 (1-57120-089-4, 10206, Pub. by C & T Pub) Watsn-Guptill.
Anderson, Alex. Hand Quilting with Alex Anderson: Six Projects for Hand Quilters. LC 97-31930. (Illus.). 40p. 1999. 12.95 (1-57120-039-8) C & T Pub.
— Quilts for Fabric Lovers. Nadel, Harold & Lytle, Joyce E., eds. LC 94-15499. (Illus.). 64p. 1994. pap. 19.95 (0-914881-87-6, 10102) C & T Pub.
— Rotary Cutting with Alex Anderson: Tips, Techniques, Projects. Aneloski, Liz & Lanzarotti, Sally, eds. LC 98-46591. (Illus.). 48p. 1999. pap. text 14.95 (1-57120-066-5, 10187) C & T Pub.
— Simply Stars: Quilts That Sparkle. Jonsson, Lee, ed. LC 96-15854. (Illus.). 96p. (Orig.). 1996. pap. 21.95 (1-57120-019-3, 10143) C & T Pub.
***Anderson, Alex.** Stars Galore Gift Wrap. 1999. 12.95 (1-57120-083-5) C & T Pub.
Anderson, Alex. Start Quilting with Alex Anderson: Six Projects for First-Time Quilters. Aneloski, Elizabeth & Roberts, Diana, eds. LC 97-179003. (Illus.). 40p. (Orig.). 1997. pap. 12.95 (1-57120-029-0, 10154) C & T Pub.
Anderson, Alexander W. How We Got Our Flowers. (Illus.). 1990. 15.00 (0-8446-1533-1) Peter Smith.
Anderson, Alice. Human Nature: Poems. LC 94-34303. (C). 1994. pap. 12.95 (0-8147-0633-9); text 25.00 (0-8147-0632-0) NYU Pr.
Anderson, Alice H. Extraordinary Ordinary Women: Making a Difference. LC 97-76405. (Illus.). 256p. 1998. pap. 17.95 (1-889409-20-0) Ladybug Pr CA.
Anderson, Aline F. Anderson's Indiana Probate Forms. 2nd ed. LC 96-75621. (Indiana Practitioners' Ser.). 1500p. 1996. text. write for info. (0-7620-0045-7) West Group.
— Anderson's Indiana Wills, Trusts, & Estate Planning. LC 96-75620. (Indiana Practitioners' Ser.). 1000p. 1996. text. write for info. (0-7620-0046-5) West Group.
Anderson, Alison. Hidden Latitudes. 1997. per. 12.00 (0-671-00888-9, WSP) PB.
— Hidden Latitudes: A Novel. large type ed. LC 96-23994. 1996. pap. 20.95 (0-7838-1902-1, G K Hall Lrg Type) Mac Lib Ref.
— Media, Culture, & the Environment. LC 96-39287. (Communications, Media, & Culture Ser.). (Illus.). 236p. (C). 1997. text 50.00 (0-8135-2394-X); pap. text 17.95 (0-8135-2395-8) Rutgers U Pr.
— Media, Culture & the Environment, 1. 1997. 65.00 (1-85728-383-X); pap. text 23.95 (1-85728-384-8) Taylor & Francis.
Anderson, Alison, tr. see Dalai Lama XIV.
Anderson, Alison, tr. see De Kersauson, Olivier.
Anderson, Alison, tr. see Le Clezio, J. M.
***Anderson, Alison D.** On the Verge of War: International Relations & the Jhulich-Kleve Succession Crises, 1609-1614. LC 99-25332. (Studies In Central European Histories). 1999. write for info. (0-391-04092-8) Humanities.
Anderson, Alison D., ed. from GER. Admiral Steven van der Haghen's Voyage to the East Indies, 1603-1606. (Illus.). 128p. (C). 1997. text 15.00 (0-9601798-6-0) Assocs James Bell.
***Anderson, Allan H. & Hollenweger, Walter J., eds.** Pentecostals after a Century: Global Perspectives on a Movement in Transition. (Journal of Pentecostal Theology Supplement Ser.: No. 15). 232p. 1999. pap. 21.95 (1-84127-006-7, Pub. by Sheffield Acad) CUP Services.
Anderson, Allen J. & Anderson, Linda. Angel Animals: Exploring Our Spiritual Connection with Animals. LC 99-13700. 256p. 1999. pap. 12.95 (0-452-28072-9, Plume) Dutton Plume.
Anderson-Allen, Moira. Belgian Tervuren. (KW Ser.). (Illus.). 192p. 1992. 9.95 (0-86622-571-4, KW-201) TFH Pubns.
— Belgian Tervurens. (Illus.). 192p. Date not set. pap. 9.95 (0-7938-2302-1, KW-201S) TFH Pubns.
— Writing.com: Creative Internet Strategies to Advance Your Writing Career. 256p. 1999. pap. text 16.95 (1-58115-029-6) Allworth Pr.
Anderson, Alun M. Science & Technology in Japan. (Guides to World Science & Technology Ser.). 421p. 1984. 88.00 (0-582-90015-8, 076403-99584) Longman.
— Science & Technology in Japan. 2nd ed. 350p. 1991. text 149.00 (0-582-03684-4) Longman.
Anderson, Amanda. Tainted Souls & Painted Faces: The Rhetoric of Fallenness in Victorian Culture. LC 93-17254. (Reading Women Writing Ser.). 256p. 1993. text 42.50 (0-8014-2781-9); pap. text 16.95 (0-8014-8148-1) Cornell U Pr.
Anderson, Anders H. A Bibliography of Arizona Ornithology. LC 76-163008. 253p. 1972. pap. 78.50 (0-608-05651-0, 206610500006) Bks Demand.
Anderson, Anders H. & Anderson, Anne. The Cactus Wren. LC 72-77133. (Illus.). 240p. reprint ed. pap. 74.40 (0-8357-7957-2, 202964700062) Bks Demand.
Anderson, Andrew, jt. auth. see Rugman, Alan A.
Anderson, Andrew J. Seaside Park. LC 98-87318. (Images of America Ser.). (Illus.). 1998. pap. 18.99 (0-7524-1388-0) Arcadia Publng.
Anderson, Andrew R. Alexander's Gate, Gog & Magog & the Inclosed Nations. (Medieval Academy Bks.: No. 12). 1932. 20.00 (0-910956-07-3) Medieval Acad.
Anderson, Andy. Hungary Nineteen Fifty-Six. 1976. reprint ed. pap. 3.00 (0-934868-01-8) Black & Red.
Anderson, Angela. Crime & Punishment: A Study Across Time. (Illus.). 192p. (YA). (gr. 9-11). 1998. pap. 32.50 (0-7487-3057-5, Pub. by S Thornes Pubs) Trans-Atl Phila.
— Crime & Punishment: Teacher's Guide. 64p. 1998. pap., teacher ed. 27.50 (0-7487-3058-3, Pub. by S Thornes Pubs) Trans-Atl Phila.
Anderson, Angela, jt. auth. see Eickberg, A. I.
Anderson, Anita L. Hidden Places, Secret Words: An Anthology of Fantasy Poetry. LC 80-81307. 62 p. 1980. write for info. (0-89002-158-9) Am Hist Pr.
***Anderson, Ann.** Snake Oil, Hustlers & Hambones: The American Medicine Show of the Nineteenth Century. (Illus.). 200p. 2000. 38.00 (0-7864-0800-6) McFarland & Co.
Anderson, Ann K. Knightly Dreams. 1996. pap. 3.50 (1-57514-284-8, 0001) Encore Perform Pub.
— Seduced by Success: No Longer Addicted to Pills, Performance, & Praise. LC 98-27232. 192p. 1998. 16.99 (0-7852-7076-0) Nelson.
— This Is a Story about God: The True Account of Two Men, an Impossible Surgery & the God of the Universe. LC 97-47014. 96p. 1998. 14.99 (0-8341-1731-2) Beacon Hill.
***Anderson, Anne.** Cube Teapot: The Story of the Patent Teapot. Atterbury, Paul, ed. (Illus.). 84p. 2000. pap. 24.95 (0-903685-76-0) R Dennis.
Anderson, Anne. Heads of the Masters. LC 98-2953. (Illus.). 64p. 1998. 6.95 (1-57601-054-6) Anderson.
Anderson, Anne & Lynch, Tony. Listening. Candlin, C. N. & Widdowson, H. G., eds. (Illus.). 160p. 1988. pap. text 14.95 (0-19-437135-2) OUP.
Anderson, Anne, jt. auth. see Anderson, Anders H.
Anderson, Anne S. & Pitre, Marianne R. Land Claims of Hancock County, Mississippi, Filed April 2nd 1894. 50p. 1985. lib. bdg. 15.00 (0-318-04436-6) L W Anderson Genealogical.
Anderson, Annelise G. Political Money: The New Prohibition. LC 97-42649. (Essays in Public Policy Ser.: No. 83). 1997. pap. 5.00 (0-8179-5882-7) Hoover Inst Pr.
— The Ruble Problem: A Competitive Solution. LC 92-17681. (Essays in Public Policy Ser.: No. 31). 20p. 1992. pap. text 5.00 (0-8179-5362-0) Hoover Inst Pr.
***Anderson, Annelise Graener.** Political Money: Deregulating American Politics, Selected Writings on Campaign Finance Reform. LC 00-21268. 2000. write for info. (0-8179-9672-9) Hoover Inst Pr.
Anderson, Anthony, ed. The Raman Effect, Vol. 1. LC 77-134788. 416p. reprint ed. pap. 129.00 (0-608-30860-9, 205506700001) Bks Demand.
— The Raman Effect Vol. 2: Applications. LC 77-134788. (Illus.). 642p. reprint ed. pap. 199.10 (0-7837-0922-6, 204122700002) Bks Demand.
Anderson, Anthony B., ed. Alternatives to Deforestation: Steps Toward Sustainable Use of the Amazon Rain Forest. 296p. 1992. pap. text 27.00 (0-231-06893-X) Col U Pr.
Anderson, Anthony B., et al. The Subsidy from Nature. (Illus.). 256p. 1991. text 44.00 (0-231-07222-8) Col U Pr.
***Anderson, Anthony C.** The Radiology Technologist's Handbook to Surgical Procedures. 152p. 1999. boxed set 59.95 (0-8493-1506-9) CRC Pr.
Anderson, Arlow W. Rough Road to Glory. LC 88-62780. 271p. 1990. 44.50 (0-944190-02-2) Balch IES Pr.
Anderson, Arne. A Progressive Answer to the Fiscal Deficit. 38p. 1989. 10.00 (0-944826-09-1) Economic Policy Inst.
Anderson, Arnold A. Second Samuel. (Biblical Commentary Ser.: Vol. 11). 29.99 (0-8499-0210-X) Word Pub.
Anderson, Arnold P. Wisconsin Insurance Law. 4th rev. ed. LC 98-92622. 900p. 1998. 245.00 (0-9663376-0-3) A P A Pub.
Anderson, Art. Casinos & Their Ashtrays: A Collector's Guide with Values & Casino Histories. (Illus.). 208p. 1994. pap. 19.95 (0-9640238-0-6) A Anderson.
***Anderson, Arthur.** Dark Mormon Beginnings. 400p. 2000. 18.95 (1-57532-292-7, Pub. by Press-Tige Pub) An Wholesale.
Anderson, Arthur. 50 Top Outpatient Procedures: Benchmarks, Standards & Trends, 1997. 1997. pap. 245.00 (1-57372-089-5) HCIA.
— The Guide to the Nursing Home Industry, 1997. 1997. pap. 249.00 (1-57372-098-4) HCIA.
— Professional Dictionary: Accounting/Tax/Banking/EPD. 4th ed. 232p. 1996. 95.00 (0-7859-9463-7) Fr & Eur.
Anderson, Arthur, jt. ed. see Kvint, Vladimir L.
Anderson, Arthur E., jt. auth. see Heinze, William J., Jr.
Anderson, Arthur J. Grammatical Examples, Exercises & Review: For Use with Rules of the Aztec Language. LC PM4063.A620. 148p. reprint ed. pap. 45.90 (0-8357-6851-1, 203554600095) Bks Demand.
— Problems in Intellectual Freedom & Censorship. LC 74-4107. (Bowker Series in Problem-Centered Approaches to Librianship). 219p. reprint ed. pap. 57.90 (0-608-11872-9, 202305400031) Bks Demand.
— Rules of the Aztec Language: Classical Nahuatl Grammar. LC 72-88553. 124p. reprint ed. pap. 38.50 (0-8357-6850-3, 203554500095) Bks Demand.
Anderson, Arthur J. & Dahlstrom, William S. Texas Zoning & Land Use Forms. LC 92-40671. 400p. 1992. spiral bd. 115.00 (1-56257-953-3, MICHIE) LEXIS Pub.
Anderson, Arthur J. & Schroeder, Susan, eds. Codex Chimalpahin Vol. 1: Society & Politics in Mexico, Tenochtitlan, Tlatelolco, Texcoco, Culhuacan, & Other Nahua Altepetl in Central Mexico. LC 96-39926. (Civilization of the American Indian Ser.: Vol. 225). (Illus.). 256p. 1997. 45.00 (0-8061-2921-2) U of Okla Pr.
— Codex Chimalpahin: Society & Politics in Mexico Tenochtitlan, Tlatelolco, Texcoco, Culhuacan, & Other Nahua Altepetl in Central America, Vol. 2. LC 96-39926. (Civilization of the American Indian Ser.: Vol. 226). (Illus.). 1997. 48.50 (0-8061-2950-6) U of Okla Pr.
Anderson, Arthur J., tr. see De Sahagun, Bernardino.
Anderson, Arthur J., tr. see Leon-Portilla, Miguel, ed.
Anderson, Arthur J., tr. see Sahagun, Bernardino de.
Anderson, Arthur W. Pension Mathematics for Actuaries. 2nd ed. LC 85-11231. 217p. (C). 1992. text 70.00 (0-936031-10-7) Actex Pubns.
Anderson, Arvid C. Masters of Music. LC 70-117320. (Biography Index Reprint Ser.). 1977. 19.95 (0-8369-8012-3) Ayer.
Anderson Associates Staff, jt. auth. see Anderson, Carolyn.
Anderson, Atholl. Prodigious Birds: Moas & Moa-Hunting in New Zealand. (Illus.). 256p. (C). 1990. text 95.00 (0-521-35209-6) Cambridge U Pr.
***Anderson, Atholl.** The Welcome of Strangers: An Ethno-History of the Southern Maori, 1650-1850. (Illus.). 249p. 1998. pap. 29.95 (1-877133-41-8, Pub. by Univ Otago Pr) Intl Spec Bk.
Anderson, Audrey, ed. Needlecrafters' Travel Companion: 1999-2001. 2nd ed. (Illus.). 192p. 1999. pap. 10.95 (0-9635290-8-0) Chalet CO.
— Quilters' Travel Companion, 1998-2000. 5th ed. (Illus.). 384p. 1998. pap. 12.95 (0-9635290-7-2) Chalet CO.
***Anderson, Audrey, ed.** Quilters' Travel Companion, 2000-2002. 6th ed. (Illus.). 2000. pap. 12.95 (0-9635290-9-9) Chalet CO.
Anderson, August K. Blonde, Like Me...Dispelling the Myths of Beauty's Advantages: A View from a Former Fashion Model Turned Attorney. Anderson, Nola, ed. 210p. 1995. pap. 14.95 (1-885351-02-X) Cheval Intl.
— Body Building for Your Horse: Horses - Create the Ultimate Physique on Any Horse. Anderson, Nola, ed. (Illus.). 150p. 1995. mass mkt. 24.95 (1-885351-04-6) Cheval Intl.
— The Equestrian Green Book: An Objective Guide to Valuing Horses. Kelsey, Avonelle & Kelsey, Nola, eds. 50p. (Orig.). 1995. pap. 9.95 (1-885351-09-7) Cheval Intl.
***Anderson, August K.** Equestrian Websites, the Complete Guide. 200p. 1999. pap. 15.95 (1-885351-33-X) Cheval Intl.
Anderson, August K. Horse Forms: Legal Forms for All Horse Owners. 4th ed. 80p. 1984. pap. 14.95 (1-885351-01-1, C18401) Cheval Intl.
— Transcending unto Heaven. (Illus.). 200p. (Orig.). 1994. pap. 9.95 (0-9640610-4-X) Cheval Intl.
— You Can't Handle the Truth! 150p. 1999. mass mkt. 19.95 (1-885351-28-3) Cheval Intl.
Anderson, August K., see Rasputin, pseud.
Anderson, Austin G. Marketing Your Practice: A Practical Guide to Client Development. LC 86-82074. (Illus.). 204p. 1986. pap. 54.95 (0-89707-258-8, 511-0215) Amer Bar Assn.
— Marketing Your Practice: A Practical Guide to Client Development. LC 86-82074. (ABA Law Practice Management Section Ser.). 204p. 1986. pap. 60.00 (0-685-22731-6, 87-017) U MI Law CLE.
Anderson, Avdis H., jt. auth. see Thogmartin, Gwen H.
Anderson, B. Infectious Diseases. (Illus.). 766p. 1992. pap. text 79.50 (0-19-854040-X) OUP.
Anderson, B., et al, eds. Molecular Genetics of Photosynthesis. (Frontiers in Molecular Biology Ser.: No. 14). (Illus.). 268p. 1996. text 110.00 (0-19-963448-3); pap. text 55.00 (0-19-963447-5) OUP.
Anderson, B. C. & Imanishi, Y., eds. Progress in Pacific Polymer Science: Proceedings of the First Pacific Polymer Conference Maui, Hawaii, U. S. A., 12-15 December 1989. xi, 431p. 1991. 122.95 (0-387-52222-0) Spr-Verlag.
Anderson, B. D. & Ljung, Lennart, eds. Adaptive Control. 232p. 1984. pap. 44.00 (0-08-031660-3, Pergamon Pr) Elsevier.
Anderson, B. H., jt. auth. see Amberson, Max L.
Anderson, B. L. Containment Analysis for Type B Packages Used to Transport Various Contents. 64p. 1996. pap. 9.00 (0-16-062785-0) USGPO.
***Anderson, B. Ray & Johnson, F. McKay.** Trusts You Can Trust: All the Legal Ways to Transfer Your Wealth & Disinherit The IRS : Including Useful Strategies from the Taxpayer Relief Act of 1997. LC 98-92839. xx, 364 p. 1998. write for info. (0-9663866-0-4) B R Anderson.
Anderson, B. Robert. Professional Selling. 2nd ed. (Illus.). 400p. 1981. text 19.95 (0-13-725960-3) P-H.
Anderson, Babette & Kornberg, Patti. Off the Menu: Central Florida's Top Restaurants Recipes. LC 97-94402. (Illus.). 1997. pap. 15.95 (0-9660679-0-8) Il Diners.
Anderson, Barbara. First Fieldwork: The Misadventures of an Anthropologist. 150p. (C). 1990. pap. text 10.95 (0-88133-491-X) Waveland Pr.
— The House Guest. 312p. 1997. 24.95 (0-224-04380-3, Pub. by Jonathan Cape) Trafalgar.
— Junk City: Poems. (National Poetry Ser.: 1986). 72p. 1987. pap. 8.95 (0-89255-120-8) Persea Bks.
— 1-800-911. LC 96-48231. (Illus.). 104p. (Orig.). 1996. 25.00 (0-933313-30-6); pap. 14.95 (0-933313-31-4) SUN Gemini Pr.
— 1-800-911. deluxe ed. (Illus.). 104p. (Orig.). 1996. 35.00 (0-933313-29-2) SUN Gemini Pr.
Anderson, Barbara, ed. see Hill, Harry & Stainken, Fred.
Anderson, Barbara G. & Shapiro, Pamela J. Basic Maternal - Newborn Nursing. 6th ed. LC 93-28313. 416p. (C). 1994. mass mkt. 46.95 (0-8273-5747-8) Delmar.
— Basic Maternal Newborn Nursing: Instructor's Guide. 6th ed. 27p. 1994. teacher ed. 12.95 (0-8273-5748-6) Delmar.
Anderson, Barbara G., jt. auth. see Anderson, Robert T.
Anderson, Barbara G., jt. auth. see Clark, Margaret.
***Anderson, Barbara Gallatin.** Around the World in 30 Years: Life As a Cultural Anthropologist. 181p. (C). 1999. pap. 11.95 (1-57766-057-9) Waveland Pr.
Anderson, Barbara J., et al. Practical Psychology for Diabetes Clinicians: How to Deal with the Key Behavioral Issues Faced by Patients & Health Care Teams. LC 96-15937. (Practical Approaches in Diabetes Care Ser.). (Orig.). 1996. pap. 24.95 (0-945448-73-2, PPPDC) Am Diabetes.
Anderson, Barbara N. Llama Babies: Up, Dry, & Nursing. LC 96-86675. (Illus.). 192p. 1996. pap. 14.95 (0-9654791-0-2) A Plus Llamas.
Anderson, Barbara S. The Counselor & the Law. 4th ed. 150p. (Orig.). 1996. pap. text 24.95 (1-55620-152-4, 72623) Am Coun Assn.
Anderson, Barbara V. The Art & Science of Computer Assisted Ordering: Methods for Management. LC 95-41390. 248p. 1996. 65.00 (1-56720-049-4, Quorum Bks) Greenwood.
Anderson, Barrie. Naroh's Task. 142p. 1986. 19.95 (0-7212-0727-8, Pub. by Regency Pr GBR) St Mut.
Anderson, Barry, jt. auth. see Anderson, Hilda.
Anderson, Barry F., et al. Concepts in Judgement & Decision Research: Definitions, Sources, Interrelations, Comments. LC 81-7345. 310p. 1981. 69.50 (0-275-90577-2, C0577, Praeger Pubs) Greenwood.
Anderson, Barry M. The Death Penalty & Public Opinion: The Example of the State of Iowa. (Illus.). 296p. 1998. 74.95 (1-57292-035-1) Austin & Winfield.
***Anderson, Barry M.** The Death Penalty & Public Opinion: The Example of the State of Iowa. (Illus.). 296p. 1998. pap. 54.95 (1-57292-034-3) Austin & Winfield.
Anderson, Basil. Spectroscope & Gemmology. 1997. 60.00 (0-7198-0261-X, Pub. by NAG Press) Antique Collect.
Anderson, Basil & Jobbins, Alan. Gem Testing. 10th rev. ed. 390p. 1990. 34.95 (0-408-02320-1) Buttrwrth-Heinemann.
Anderson, Basil W., et al. The Spectroscope & Gemmology. Mitchell, R. Keith, ed. LC 98-12283. (Illus.). 288p. 1998. 60.00 (0-943763-18-5) GemStone Pr.

A

An Asterisk (*) at the beginning of an entry indicates that the title is appearing for the first time.

A

***Anderson, Bendix.** Quetzal & the Cool School. (Dragon Tales Ser.). (Illus.). 24p. (J). (ps-k). 2000. pap. 3.25 (*0-375-80634-2*, Pub. by Random Bks Yng Read) Random.

Anderson, Benedict. Imagined Communities: Reflections on the Origin & Spread of Nationalism. rev. ed. 192p. (C). (gr. 13). 1991. pap. 19.00 (*0-86091-546-8*, A5361, Pub. by Verso) Norton.

— Spectre of Comparison: Politics, Culture & the Nation. LC 98-35495. 368p. 1998. pap. 20.00 (*1-85984-184-8*, Pub. by Verso) Norton.

— Spectre of Comparisons: Politics, Culture & the Nation. LC 98-35495. 368p. (C). 1998. 60.00 (*1-85984-813-3*, Pub. by Verso) Norton.

Anderson, Benedict & Kahin, Audrey R., eds. Interpreting Indonesian Politics Vol. 62: Thirteen Contributions to the Debate, 1964-1981. (Modern Indonesia Project Ser.). 172p. 1982. reprint ed. pap. 9.00 (*0-87763-028-3*) Cornell Mod Indo.

Anderson, Benedict R. Language & Power: Exploring Indonesian Political Culture. Laitin, David, ed. LC 90-55126. (Wilder House Series in Politics, History, & Culture). (Illus.). 352p. 1990. 49.95 (*0-8014-2354-6*); pap. text 18.95 (*0-8014-9758-2*) Cornell U Pr.

— Mythology & the Tolerance of the Javanese. 2nd rev. ed. LC 97-208972. (Modern Indonesia Project Ser.: Vol. 37). (Illus.). 104p. (C). 1997. pap. 12.00 (*0-87763-041-0*) Cornell SE Asia.

— Some Aspects of Indonesian Politics under the Japanese Occupation, 1944-1945. LC 61-66733. (Cornell University, Modern Indonesian Project, Interim Report Ser.). 136p. reprint ed. pap. 42.20 (*0-608-11725-0*, 201081000069) Bks Demand.

Anderson, Benedict R., ed. Indonesia Journal. (Orig.). (C). 1997. pap. 12.50 (*0-87727-863-6*, INDO-63) Cornell SE Asia.

Anderson, Benedict R. & McVey, Ruth T. A Preliminary Analysis of the October 1, 1965, Coup in Indonesia. LC 71-30341. (Cornell University, Modern Indonesia Project, Monograph Ser.: No. 52). 174p. reprint ed. pap. 54.00 (*0-8357-3667-9*, 203639300003) Bks Demand.

— A Preliminary Analysis of the October 1, 1965, Coup in Indonesia (Prepared in Jan. 1966), No. 52. 4th ed. (Modern Indonesia Project Ser.). (C). 1991. reprint ed. pap. 10.75 (*0-87763-008-9*) Cornell Mod Indo.

Anderson, Benedict R. & Mendiones, Ruchira C., eds. In the Mirror: Literature & Politics in Siam in the American Era. 2nd ed. 303p. 1991. pap. 12.00 (*974-210-380-1*) Cornell SE Asia.

Anderson, Benjamin. Narrative of a Journey to Musardu: The Capitol of the Mandingoes. 172p. 1971. 45.00 (*0-7146-1785-7*, BHA-01785, Pub. by F Cass Pubs) Intl Spec Bk.

Anderson, Benjamin M. Economics & the Public Welfare: Financial & Economic History of the United States, 1914-1946. LC 79-20911. 1980. reprint ed. 20.00 (*0-913966-68-1*); reprint ed. pap. 8.00 (*0-913966-69-X*) Liberty Fund.

Anderson, Benjamin M., Jr. Social Value: A Study in Economic Theory Critical & Constructive. LC 65-26357. (Reprints of Economic Classics Ser.). xviii, 204p. 1966. reprint ed. 35.00 (*0-678-00177-4*) Kelley.

Anderson, Bentley J. Annual Reporting under the Federal Securities Laws. 2nd ed. (Corporate Practice Ser.: No. 33). 1999. 95.00 (*1-55871-395-6*) BNA.

Anderson, Bentley J., jt. auth. see Gutterman, Alan S.

Anderson, Bern. By Sea & by River: A Naval History of the Civil War. (Quality Paperbacks Ser.). (Illus.). 344p. 1989. pap. 13.95 (*0-306-80367-4*) Da Capo.

Anderson, Bernard E. The Opportunities Industrialization Centers: A Decade of Community - Based Manpower Services. LC 76-48860. (Manpower & Human Resources Studies: No. 6). 170p. reprint ed. pap. 52.70 (*0-8357-3159-6*, 203942200012) Bks Demand.

Anderson, Bernard E. & Sawhill, Isabel V., eds. Youth Employment & Public Policy. LC 79-27022. 1980. 11.95 (*0-13-982413-8*) Am Assembly.

Anderson, Bernard E., jt. auth. see America, Richard F.

Anderson, Bernhard W. The Books of the Bible, 2 vols., Set. 888p. 1989. text 179.00 (*0-684-18487-7*, Scribners Ref) Mac Lib Ref.

— Contours of Old Testament Theology. LC 99-10518. ix, 358p. 1999. 27.00 (*0-8006-3074-2*, Fortress Pr) Augsburg Fortress.

***Anderson, Bernhard W.** Creation Theology as a Basis for Global Witness. (Mission Evangelism Ser.: Vol. 3). 36p. 1999. pap. 3.00 (*1-890569-12-7*, 2745) Gnl Brd Glbl Minis.

Anderson, Bernhard W. From Creation to New Creation: Old Testament Perspectives. (Overtures to Biblical Theology Ser.). 272p. 1994. pap. 22.00 (*0-8006-2847-0*, 1-2847, Fortress Pr) Augsburg Fortress.

— Out of the Depths: The Psalms Speak for Us Today. expanded rev. ed. LC 83-19801. 254p. (C). 1983. pap. 19.95 (*0-664-24504-8*) Westminster John Knox.

***Anderson, Bernhard W.** Out of the Depths: The Psalms Speak for Us Today. 3rd rev. expanded ed. (Illus.). 264p. 2000. pap. 24.95 (*0-664-25832-8*, Pub. by Westminster John Knox) Presbyterian Pub.

Anderson, Bernhard W. Understanding the Old Testament. 4th ed. (Illus.). 672p. 1986. text 69.00 (*0-13-935925-7*) P-H.

— Understanding the Old Testament. 4th abr. ed. LC 96-31386. 635p. (C). 1997. pap. 48.00 (*0-13-948399-3*) P-H.

— The Unfolding Drama of the Bible: Eight Studies Introducing the Bible as a Whole. 3rd ed. LC 87-45884. 96p. 1988. pap. 12.00 (*0-8006-2098-4*, 1-2098, Fortress Pr) Augsburg Fortress.

Anderson, Bernhard W., jt. auth. see Noth, Martin.

***Anderson, Bernice.** Rutland. (Images of America Ser.). (Illus.). 128p. 2000. pap. 18.99 (*0-7385-0173-5*) Arcadia Publng.

Anderson, Bernice, jt. auth. see Clewell, Beatriz C.

Anderson, Bernice E., jt. auth. see Lesnik, Milton.

Anderson, Bernice May. Rutland. (Images of America Ser.). 1999. pap. 18.99 (*0-7524-0449-0*) Arcadia Publng.

Anderson, Bert M. Write True to Yourself So You Sell: 19 Lessons in Folios. ring bd. 95.00 (*0-917628-02-0*) Coraco.

***Anderson, Beth.** In Residence. 32p. 1999. pap. write for info. (*0-9674857-0-3*) Pressed Wafer Pr.

Anderson, Beth. Pollution Prevention Directory. 103p. (C). 1996. pap. text 35.00 (*0-7881-2913-9*) DIANE Pub.

— Wild Rice for All Season Cook Book. 179p. 1984. 9.95 (*0-9610030-0-6*) B Anderson Assocs.

Anderson, Beth, ed. Directory of Curriculum Materials Center. 4th ed. 175p. (C). 1996. pap. 26.50 (*0-8389-7862-2*) Assn Coll & Res Libs.

Anderson, Beth, jt. auth. see Baker, Lois.

Anderson, Beth, jt. auth. see Dutton, Bob.

Anderson, Beth, ed. see Reynolds, Larry A. & La Belle, Tim.

Anderson, Beth H. & Suggs, Kimberly. Review Book for MRA & MRT Certification Exams. (Health Services Administration Ser.). (Illus.). 200p. (C). 1996. mass mkt. 35.95 (*0-8273-6897-6*) Delmar.

***Anderson, Beth Ranes.** Joe's New Glasses. 4p. 1999. pap. 2.50 (*0-7390-0385-2*, 18526) Alfred Pub.

Anderson, Betsy. Fly on, My Sweet Angel. 168p. 1998. pap. 12.00 (*1-885937-07-5*, 1-885937) Casco Commns.

Anderson, Bette. We Just Got On with It. LC 95-138326. 176p. 1990. 54.00 (*0-948251-58-1*, Pub. by Picton) St Mut.

Anderson, Bettina G., jt. auth. see Anderson, Wesley.

Anderson, Beverly M. & Hamilton, Donna M. The New High Altitude Cookbook. LC 80-5287. (Illus.). 320p. 1980. 17.95 (*0-685-04236-7*) Random.

Anderson, Bijorn & Hedberg, Neils B. The Impact of Systems Change in Organizations, No. 2. (Information Systems Ser.). 356p. 1980. text 196.50 (*90-286-0549-5*) Kluwer Academic.

Anderson, Bill. Fishing the Rivers of the Mid-Atlantic. LC 90-53072. (Illus.). 185p. 1991. pap. 14.95 (*0-87033-413-1*, Tidewtr Pubs) Cornell Maritime.

— I Hope You're Living As High on the Hog As the Pig You Turned Out To Be. LC 94-45221. 1995. pap. 10.00 (*0-684-80174-4*, Fireside) S&S Trade Pap.

***Anderson, Bill.** Java 2 Platform Sun Certified Programmer: Exam 310-025. 600p. 2000. pap. text 44.99 incl. cd-rom, audio compact disk (*0-13-014265-4*) P-H.

Anderson, Bill & Cunliffe, Tom. Boat Handling under Sail & Power. (Illus.). 96p. 1998. pap. 16.95 (*1-898660-15-8*, 128326AE) Motorbooks Intl.

Anderson, Bill, jt. auth. see Anderson, Kate.

Anderson, Bill, ed. see McDaniel, Kristyne.

Anderson, Blaine. Destiny's Kiss. 1989. mass mkt. 3.95 (*0-445-20881-3*, Pub. by Warner Bks) Little.

— Heartspell. 352p. (Orig.). 1992. mass mkt. 4.99 (*0-446-36199-2*, Pub. by Warner Bks) Little.

Anderson, Bo, ed. Essays on Social Action & Social Structure. (Studia Sociologica Upsaliensia: No. 29). 181p. 1988. pap. 47.50 (*91-554-2252-7*, Pub. by Uppsala Univ Acta Univ Upsaliensis) Coronet Bks.

Anderson, Bo, jt. auth. see Davis, Nanette J.

Anderson, Bo, jt. auth. see Willer, David.

Anderson, Bob. Obo. LC 98-73916. (Illus.). 48p. (J). (gr. 2-6). 1999. bds. 16.00 (*1-57174-124-0*) Hampton Roads Pub Co.

— Stretch Yourself for Health & Fitness. (C). 1993. 8.00 (*81-85674-96-5*, Pub. by UBS Pubs Dist) S Asia.

— Stretching. LC 97-5567. 192p. 1980. pap. 13.95 (*0-936070-01-3*) Shelter Pubns.

***Anderson, Bob.** Stretching. 20th rev. ed. Kahn, Lloyd, ed. LC 00-36525. (Illus.). 224p. 2000. pap. 14.95 (*0-936070-22-6*, Pub. by Shelter Pubns) Publishers Group.

Anderson, Bob, ed. Sport-Source. LC 75-16003. (Illus.). 430p. (Orig.). 1975. 18.95 (*0-89037-061-3*) Anderson World.

Anderson, Bob & Anderson, Jean. Stretching at Your Computer or Desk. Kahn, Lloyd, ed. LC 96-34996. (Illus.). 128p. (Orig.). 1997. pap. 9.95 (*0-679-77084-4*) Random.

— Stretching at Your Computer or Desk. Kahn, Lloyd, ed. LC 96-34996. (Illus.). 128p. (Orig.). 1997. pap. 9.95 (*0-936070-19-6*) Shelter Pubns.

Anderson, Bob & Bornell, Donald G. Stretch & Strengthen for Rehabilitation & Development. (Illus.). 91p. 1984. spiral bd. 7.95 (*0-9601066-2-6*) Stretching Inc.

Anderson, Bob & Carlson, Sally. Stretching for Working America. (Illus.). 72p. (Orig.). 1988. spiral bd. 7.95 (*0-9601066-4-2*) Stretching Inc.

Anderson, Bob, et al. Getting in Shape: Workout Programs for Men & Women. Kahn, Lloyd & Kenter, Stuart, eds. LC 94-21737. 220p. 1995. pap. 15.00 (*0-936070-16-1*) Shelter Pubns.

Anderson, Bonnie S. Joyous Greetings: The First International Women's Movement, 1830-1860. 256p. 1999. 25.00 (*0-06-017072-7*) HarperTrade.

***Anderson, Bonnie S.** Joyous Greetings: The First International Women's Movement, 1830-1860. LC 99-14778. (Illus.). 314p. 2000. 30.00 (*0-19-512623-8*) OUP.

***Anderson, Bonnie S. & Zinsser, Judith.** A History of Their Own: Women in Europe from Prehistory to the Present, Vol. 1. rev. ed. LC 98-46743. (Illus.). 624p. 1999. pap. 24.50 (*0-19-512838-9*) OUP.

Anderson, Bonnie S. & Zinsser, Judith P. A History of Their Own: Women in Europe from Prehistory to the Present, Vol. 2. rev. ed. LC 98-46743. (The Practical Approach in Chemistry Ser.). (Illus.). 624p. 1999. pap. 24.50 (*0-19-512839-7*) OUP.

Anderson, Brad. Marmaduke: I Am Lovable. (Illus.). 128p. 1991. pap. 3.50 (*0-8125-1293-6*, Pub. by Tor Bks) St Martin.

— Marmaduke: It's a Dog's Life. (Illus.). 128p. 1989. pap. 2.95 (*0-8125-7355-2*, Pub. by Tor Bks) St Martin.

— Marmaduke: Large & Loveable. (Illus.). 128p. (Orig.). 1990. pap. 2.95 (*0-8125-1281-2*, Pub. by Tor Bks) St Martin.

— Marmaduke: Up & at 'Em. (Illus.). 128p. 1990. pap. 2.95 (*0-8125-0597-2*, Pub. by Tor Bks) St Martin.

— Marmaduke Laps it Up. (Illus.). 128p. 1989. pap. 2.95 (*0-8125-7335-8*, Pub. by Tor Bks) St Martin.

— Wake up! On the Road with a Zen Master. 1996. 29.95 incl. VHS (*0-942795-07-5*) Primary Point Pr.

Anderson, Brett, ed. Home Theater Magazine Presents Theo Kalomirakis' "Private Theaters" (Illus.). 170p. 1996. write for info. (*0-9653179-0-0*) Curtco Freedom.

Anderson, Brian & Anderson, Eileen. Algarve & Southern Portugal. (Passport's Regional Guides of Portugal Ser.). (Illus.). 192p. (Orig.). 1996. pap. 17.95 (*0-8442-4545-3*, 45453, Passprt Bks) NTC Contemp Pub Co.

— Writing about Travel: How to Research, Write & Sell Travel Guides & Articles. 144p. 2000. pap. 14.95 (*1-85703-259-4*, Pub. by How To Bks) Midpt Trade.

Anderson, Brian, jt. ed. see Cross, Derek.

Anderson, Brian C. Raymond Aron: The Recovery of the Political. LC 97-24239. (Twentieth Century Political Thinkers Ser.). 224p. 1998. 58.00 (*0-8476-8757-0*); pap. 19.95 (*0-8476-8758-9*) Rowman.

Anderson, Brian C., ed. The Pope in America. (Illus.). 164p. (Orig.). 1996. pap. 13.95 (*1-883357-24-1*, Crisis Bks) Dumb Ox Bks.

Anderson, Brian C., ed. see Novak, Michael.

Anderson, Brian L., et al. A Guide for Wisconsin Nonprofit Organizations. 700p. 1990. ring bd. 95.00 (*0-945574-32-0*) State Bar WI.

Anderson, Bridget. Arabesque: Lost to Love. pap. 4.99 (*1-58314-010-7*) BET Bks.

***Anderson, Bridget.** Doing the Dirty Work? The Global Politics of Domestic Labor. LC 99-87818. 2000. pap. 25.00 (*1-85649-761-5*) Zed Books.

— Rendezvous, Vol. 1. 1999. mass mkt. 5.99 (*1-58314-061-1*) BET Bks.

Anderson, Bridget. Rendezvous. 256p. 1998. mass mkt. 4.99 (*0-7860-0485-1*, Pinncle Kensgtn) Kensgtn Pub Corp.

— Soul Mates. 288p. 1997. mass mkt. 4.99 (*0-7860-0386-3*, Pinncle Kensgtn) Kensgtn Pub Corp.

***Anderson, Bridget Jane.** Doing The Dirty Work? The Global Politics of Domestic Labour. LC 99-87818. 2000. text 65.00 (*1-85649-760-7*, Pub. by Zed Books) St Martin.

Anderson, Bruce. Discovery in Legal Decision Making. LC 97-216221. (Law & Philosophy Library: No. 24). 180p. (C). 1996. lib. bdg. 110.50 (*0-7923-3981-9*) Kluwer Academic.

— Porsche 911 Performance Handbook. 2nd ed. LC 96-43706. (Performance Handbook Ser.). (Illus.). 272p. 1996. pap. 21.95 (*0-7603-0033-X*) MBI Pubg.

Anderson, Bruce & Riordan, Michael. The New Solar Home Book. 2nd ed. LC 86-23214. (Illus.). 204p. (Orig.). 1996. pap. 20.00 (*0-931790-70-0*) Brick Hse Pub.

Anderson, Bruce & Wells, Malcolm. Passive Solar Energy: The Homeowner's Guide to Natural Heating & Cooling. 2nd ed. (Illus.). 197p. (Orig.). 1993. pap. 24.95 (*0-931790-95-6*) Brick Hse Pub.

— Passive Solar Energy: The Homeowner's Guide to Natural Heating & Cooling. 2nd ed. (Illus.). 168p. (Orig.). 1996. pap. 24.95 (*0-931790-22-0*) Brick Hse Pub.

Anderson, Bruce, et al. Watchmen on the Walls: Pastors Equipping Christians for Their Civil Duties. 70p. 1995. pap. 5.95 (*1-887456-02-3*) Providence Found.

Anderson, Bruce, jt. auth. see Factor, TR.

Anderson, Bruce C. Office Orthopedics for Primary Care: Diagnosis & Treatment. LC 94-25753. (Illus.). 208p. (C). 1994. pap. text 42.00 (*0-7216-4576-3*, W B Saunders Co) Harcrt Hlth Sci Grp.

— Office Orthopedics for Primary Care: Diagnosis & Treatment. 2nd ed. Kersey, Ray, ed. LC 98-36303. (Illus.). 285p. (C). 1998. pap. text 42.00 (*0-7216-7089-X*, W B Saunders Co) Harcrt Hlth Sci Grp.

Anderson, Bruce H., jt. auth. see Stevenson, Henry M.

Anderson, Bruce N., ed. The Fuel Savers: A Kit of Solar Ideas for Your Home, Apartment, or Business. (Illus.). 83p. 1991. pap. 4.95 (*0-9629069-0-5*, Pub. by Morn Sun Pr) Chelsea Green Pub.

Anderson, Bryon D., jt. auth. see Spielberg, Nathan.

Anderson, Bryond D., jt. auth. see Spielberg, Nathan.

Anderson, Buist M. Life Insurance. 1991. 145.00 (*0-316-03961-6*) Aspen Pub.

Anderson, Burt, et al, eds. Rickettsial Infection & Immunity. LC 97-22825. (Infectious Agents & Pathogenesis Ser.). (Illus.). 264p. (C). 1997. text 79.50 (*0-306-45528-5*, Kluwer Plenum) Kluwer Academic.

Anderson, Burton. Italian Table-Treasures. LC 93-14272. 318p. 1994. 20.00 (*0-688-11557-8*, Wm Morrow) Morrow Avon.

***Anderson, Burton.** Wines of Italy. (Illus.). 304p. 2000. 14.95 (*1-84000-251-4*, Pub. by Mitchell Beazley) Antique Collect.

Anderson, Burton & Pigott, Stuart. The Wine Atlas of Italy: And Traveller's Guide to the Vineyards. 1997. 45.00 (*0-85533-793-1*, Pub. by Mitchell Beazley) Antique Collect.

Anderson, Burton, jt. auth. see Sutcliffe, Serena.

Anderson, Burton F. We Claim the Title: Korean War Marines. 2nd rev. ed. LC 99-76950. (Illus.). 400p. 2000. pap. 19.95 (*0-9643110-1-1*) Tracy Pubng.

Anderson, Byron, ed. Library Services for Career Planning, Job Searching & Employment Opportunities. LC 92-11277. (Reference Librarian Ser.: No. 36). (Illus.). 183p. 1992. 39.95 (*1-56024-303-1*) Haworth Pr.

— Library Services for Career Planning, Job Searching & Employment Opportunities. LC 92-11277. (Reference Librarian Ser.: No. 36). 183p. 1996. reprint ed. pap. 19.95 (*0-7890-0054-7*) Haworth Pr.

— Worship Matters: A United Methodist Guide to Ways to Worship, Vol. I. LC 98-96831. 176p. 1999. pap. 24.95 (*0-88177-279-8*, DR279) Discipleship Res.

Anderson, C. Invitations. mass mkt. 6.95 (*0-7472-5212-2*, Pub. by Headline Bk Pub) Trafalgar.

— Liaison: Flood Tide. 1998. mass mkt. 6.95 (*0-7472-5826-0*, Pub. by Headline Bk Pub) Trafalgar.

— Liaison Private Education. 1997. mass mkt. 6.95 (*0-7472-5518-0*, Pub. by Headline Bk Pub) Trafalgar.

— Liaison Private Performance. 1997. mass mkt. 6.95 (*0-7472-5674-8*, Pub. by Headline Bk Pub) Trafalgar.

Anderson, C. A Monograph of the Mexican & Central American Species of Trixis (Compositae) (Memoirs Ser.: Vol. 22 (3)). (Illus.). 68p. 1972. pap. 8.00 (*0-89327-076-8*) NY Botanical.

Anderson, C. Private Affair. mass mkt. 6.95 (*0-7472-5211-4*, Pub. by Headline Bk Pub) Trafalgar.

Anderson, C. & Greengard, C. Vortex Dynamics & Vortex Methods. LC 91-29692. (Lectures in Applied Mathematics: Vol. 28). 751p. 1991. pap. 149.00 (*0-8218-1135-5*, LAM/28) Am Math.

Anderson, C. & Senne, J., eds. Walkway Surfaces: Measurement of Slip Resistance - STP 649. 117p. 1982. pap. 15.00 (*0-8031-0596-7*, STP649) ASTM.

Anderson, C., jt. auth. see Morrison, D.

Anderson, C. Alan. God in a Nutshell. (Illus.). 28p. (Orig.). 1981. pap. 5.00 (*0-9607532-0-6*) Squantum Pr.

— Healing Hypotheses: Horatio W. Dresser & the Philosophy of New Thought. LC 92-34575. (Cults & Nonconventional Religious Groups Ser.). 504p. 1993. text 50.00 (*0-8153-0778-0*) Garland.

Anderson, C. Alan & Whitehouse, Deborah G. New Thought: A Practical American Spirituality. LC 94-47380. 160p. 1995. 19.95 (*0-8245-1480-7*) Crossroad NY.

Anderson, C. Anthony & Owens, Joseph. Propositional Attitudes: The Role of Content in Logic, Language, & Mind. LC 90-34223. (CSLI Lecture Notes Ser.: No. 20). 342p. (C). 1990. 49.95 (*0-937073-51-2*); pap. 17.95 (*0-937073-50-4*) CSLI.

Anderson, C. B. & Boardman, Mark R. Sedimentary Gradients in a High Energy Carbonate Lagoon, Snow Bay, San Salvador, Bahamas. (Occasional Papers: No. 1). 25p. 1987. pap. text 4.00 (*0-935909-25-7*) Bahamian.

***Anderson, C. D.** Exploring Texas Skies with Children: Night Skies, Day Skies & All about the Weather. (Illus.). (J). 2000. pap. text 18.95 (*1-55622-726-4*) Wordware Pub.

Anderson, C. Dean. Buried Screams. 1992. mass mkt. 4.50 (*0-8217-3723-6*, Zebra Kensgtn) Kensgtn Pub Corp.

— I Am Frankenstein. 352p. 1996. mass mkt. 5.99 (*0-8217-5422-X*, Zebra Kensgtn) Kensgtn Pub Corp.

Anderson, C. Dixon & Meredith, R. Alan. Hablame. 661p. (C). 1988. 14.00 (*0-15-530624-3*) Harcourt Coll Pubs.

Anderson, C. E. A Stock Market Strategy. 280p. (Orig.). 1993. pap. 17.95 (*0-9618383-3-7*) GN Inc.

Anderson, C. E., ed. Hypervelocity Impact: Proceedings of the Symposium, San Antonio, TX, USA, 21-24 October 1986. (Impact Engineering Ser.). 760p. 1987. 127.50 (*0-08-035899-3*, Pergamon Pr) Elsevier.

Anderson, C. K., et al, eds. Germ Cell Tumours. 450p. 1981. 53.00 (*0-85066-223-0*) Taylor & Francis.

Anderson, C. LeRoy. Joseph Morris & the Sage of the Morrisites. LC 88-1292. (Illus.). 287p. reprint ed. pap. 89.00 (*0-7837-7065-0*, 204687700054) Bks Demand.

Anderson, C. Leroy, et al, eds. No Longer Silent: World-Wide Memories of the Children of World War II. LC 95-70124. (Illus.). 370p. (Orig.). 1995. pap. 22.95 (*1-57510-003-7*) Pictorial Hist.

Anderson, C. R. & Greengard, C., eds. Vortex Methods. rev. ed. (Lecture Notes in Mathematics Ser.: Vol. 1360). (Illus.). 141p. 1988. 36.10 (*0-387-50526-1*) Spr-Verlag.

Anderson, C. R., ed. see Lanier, Sidney.

Anderson, C. W. Billy & Blaze. (Billy & Blaze Ser.). 1992. 10.19 (*0-606-01586-8*, Pub. by Turtleback) Demco.

— Billy & Blaze. (Illus.). 56p. (J). 1992. reprint ed. lib. bdg. 21.95 (*0-89966-947-6*) Buccaneer Bks.

— Billy & Blaze: A Boy & His Pony. 2nd ed. LC 91-29882. (Illus.). 56p. (J). (gr. k-3). 1992. reprint ed. mass mkt. 4.99 (*0-689-71608-7*) Aladdin.

***Anderson, C. W.** Blaze & the Forest Fire. (J). (gr. 1-4). 1999. 19.25 (*0-8446-7000-6*) Peter Smith.

Anderson, C. W. Blaze & the Forest Fire. (Billy & Blaze Ser.). 1992. 10.19 (*0-606-01589-2*, Pub. by Turtleback) Demco.

— Blaze & the Forest Fire. 1999. reprint ed. 21.95 (*1-56849-718-0*) Buccaneer Bks.

— Blaze & the Forest Fire: Billy & Blaze Spread the Alarm. 2nd ed. LC 91-26586. (Illus.). 56p. (J). (gr. k-3). 1992. reprint ed. mass mkt. 4.99 (*0-689-71605-2*) Aladdin.

— Blaze & the Gary Spotted Pony. 1999. reprint ed. 21.95 (*1-56849-717-2*) Buccaneer Bks.

— Blaze & the Gray Spotted Pony. LC 97-197169. (Illus.). 32p. (J). (gr. k-3). 1997. per. 4.99 (*0-689-81741-X*) S&S Childrens.

— Blaze & the Gray Spotted Pony. (J). 1997. 10.19 (*0-606-13207-4*, Pub. by Turtleback) Demco.

***Anderson, C. W.** Blaze & the Lost Quarry. (gr. 1-4). 1999. 19.00 (*0-8446-7001-4*) Peter Smith.

An Asterisk (*) at the beginning of an entry indicates that the title is appearing for the first time.

— Blaze & the Lost Quarry. (Billy & Blaze Ser.). (J). 1994. 10.19 (*0-606-05758-7*, Pub. by Turtleback) Demco.

Anderson, C. W. Blaze & the Lost Quarry: Billy & Blaze Find the Way. LC 93-10721. (Illus.). 48p. (J). (gr. k-3). 1994. reprint ed. mass mkt. 4.99 (*0-689-71775-X*) Aladdin.

***Anderson, C. W.** Blaze & the Mountain Lion. (gr. 1-4). 1999. 19.00 (*0-8446-6999-7*) Peter Smith.

Anderson, C. W. Blaze & the Mountain Lion. (J). 1993. 10.19 (*0-606-02524-3*, Pub. by Turtleback) Demco.

— Blaze & the Mountain Lion: Billy & Blaze to the Rescue. LC 92-27148. (Illus.). 48p. (J). (gr. k-3). 1993. reprint ed. mass mkt. 4.99 (*0-689-71711-3*) Aladdin.

— Blaze & Thunderbolt. (J). 1993. 10.19 (*0-606-02526-X*, Pub. by Turtleback) Demco.

— Blaze & Thunderbolt: Billy & Blaze Head West. LC 92-27153. (Illus.). 48p. (J). (gr. k-3). 1993. reprint ed. mass mkt. 4.99 (*0-689-71712-1*) Aladdin.

***Anderson, C. W.** Blaze Finds the Trail. LC 99-52655. (Illus.). 48p. (J). (ps-3). 2000. pap. 4.99 (*0-689-83520-5*) Aladdin.

— Blaze Finds the Trail. (Illus.). (J). 2000. 10.44 (*0-606-17915-1*) Turtleback.

— Blaze Shows the Way. (Billy & Blaze Ser.). (J). 1994. 10.19 (*0-606-05759-5*, Pub. by Turtleback) Demco.

Anderson, C. W. Blaze Shows the Way: Billy & Blaze Help a Friend. LC 93-1454. (Illus.). 48p. (J). (gr. k-3). 1994. reprint ed. mass mkt. 4.99 (*0-689-71776-8*) Aladdin.

Anderson, Camilla M. Camilla, Montana Prairie Pioneer. LC 96-83562. 1996. write for info. (*1-888875-01-1*) P Diamond.

Anderson, Camille J. & Price, Don L. The Business of Gift Baskets: How to Make a Profit Working from Home. Porter, Carolyn, ed. LC 91-91375. (Illus.). 202p. (Orig.). 1993. pap. 24.95 (*0-9630396-2-8*) Those Bloomin Baskets.

***Anderson, Candace E.** Genealogical Abstracts of Orphans Court Records: 10,000 Early Residents of the County, Vol. 2. LC 98-71576. 1998. 45.00 (*1-55856-319-9*, 238) Closson Pr.

— Genealogical Abstracts of Orphans Court Records, Northampton County, Pennsylvania: 1752-1795. LC 98-71576. 1998. per. 35.00 (*1-55856-280-X*, 237) Closson Pr.

Anderson, Carl, compiled by. All I Want for Christmas Is . . . Letters from Santa's Mailbag. LC 98-29010. 200p. 1998. pap. 10.95 (*1-55874-636-6*) Health Comm.

Anderson, Carl & Fox, John. Hold-Em for Winners: Gamesmam Hold-Em. 1982. 14.95 (*0-940416-03-4*) Bacchus Pr.

Anderson, Carl C., et al. Critical Thinking Approach to Intermediate Algebra. 2nd rev. ed. (Reivew Sequence in Mathematics of MTE Ser.). (Illus.). xii, 310p. 1994. text 30.00 (*1-888679-05-0*, 6400) MTE.

Anderson, Carl L., ed. see Roos, Rosalie.

Anderson, Carl R. Management: Skills, Functions & Organization Performance. 2nd ed. 1988. teacher ed. write for info. (*0-205-11437-7*, H1437-6); write for info. (*0-205-11438-5*, H1438-4); trans. write for info. (*0-205-11439-3*, H1439-2) Allyn.

***Anderson, Carla.** Civil War. (J). 1999. pap. 10.99 (*0-8431-7462-5*, Price Stern) Peng Put Young Read.

— Civil War 2001 Desk Calendar. 640p. 2000. pap. 10.99 (*0-8431-7574-5*) Peng Put Young Read.

— World War II 2001 Desk Calendar. 640p. 2000. pap. 10.99 (*0-8431-7575-3*) Peng Put Young Read.

— Your Day Could Be Worse 2001 Desk Calendar. 640p. 2000. pap. 10.99 (*0-8431-7577-X*) Peng Put Young Read.

Anderson, Carlotta. All-American Anarchist: Joseph A. Labadie & the Labor Movement. LC 97-42353. (Great Lakes Books Publication). (Illus.). 328p. 1998. 34.95 (*0-8143-2707-9*) Wayne St U Pr.

Anderson, Carol. Knowing Jesus in Your Life. LC 95-3419. 96p. 1995. pap. 9.95 (*0-8192-1643-7*) Morehouse Pub.

— Pain & Its Ending: The Four Noble Truths in the Theravada Buddhist Canon. (Critical Studies in Buddhism: Vol. 10). 288p. 1999. text 55.00 (*0-7007-1065-5*, Pub. by Curzon Pr Ltd) UH Pr.

Anderson, Carol, ed. see Thomas, Sandy.

Anderson, Carol, jt. ed. see Walsh, Froma.

Anderson, Carol B. North Carolina Trial Practice. LC 95-82262. 845p. 1996. 95.00 (*1-55834-312-1*, 65160-10, MICHIE) LEXIS Pub.

— North Carolina Trial Practice, 1998 Cumulative Supplement. 100p. 1998. pap. write for info. (*0-327-00616-1*, 6516111) LEXIS Pub.

Anderson, Carol G. Get Fired up Without Burning Out. 178p. 1997. pap. 14.95 (*0-9660276-0-4*) Rock Hill Pubng.

Anderson, Carol L. Do You Know What You Are Doing, Lord? A Jungle Journey in Search of God. LC 98-21482. 192p. (C). (gr. 13). 1998. pap. 8.99 (*0-8007-9261-0*) Chosen Bks.

Anderson, Carol L. & Hauptman, Robert. Technology & Information Services: Challenges for the 1990s. LC 92-40228. (Information Management, Policies & Services Ser.). 242p. 1993. pap. 39.50 (*1-56750-021-8*); text 73.25 (*1-56750-020-X*) Ablx Pub.

Anderson, Carol L. & Wright, William E. The Ready Mapbook of Kauai, Vol. 1. unabridged ed. (Illus.). 68p. 1998. pap. 9.95 (*0-9654158-0-5*, K98) Odyssey Pub LLC.

Anderson, Carol L., jt. auth. see Fraley, Ruth A.

Anderson, Carol M. & Stewart, Susan. Mastering Resistance: A Practical Guide to Family Therapy. LC 82-21033. (Family Therapy Ser.). 259p. 1983. lib. bdg. 32.50 (*0-89862-044-9*) Guilford Pubns.

Anderson, Carol M., et al. Flying Solo: Single Women in Midlife. 320p. 1995. pap. 13.95 (*0-393-31347-6*, Norton Paperbks) Norton.

— Schizophrenia & the Family: A Practitioner's Guide to Psychoeducation & Management. LC 85-17218. 365p. 1986. lib. bdg. 41.95 (*0-89862-065-1*) Guilford Pubns.

Anderson, Carol S., jt. auth. see Anderson, Roger.

Anderson, Carol Shively, jt. auth. see Anderson, Roger.

Anderson, Caroline. Anyone Can Dream. large type ed. 288p. 1995. 23.99 (*0-263-14624-3*, Pub. by Mills & Boon) Ulverscroft.

***Anderson, Caroline.** Captive Heart. large type ed. 1999. 25.99 (*0-263-15818-7*) Mills & Boon.

Anderson, Caroline. Definitely Maybe. (Promo Ser.). 1999. per. 3.75 (*0-373-83382-2*, 1-83382-1) Harlequin Bks.

— A Familiar Stranger. large type ed. 288p. 1996. 23.99 (*0-263-14640-5*, Pub. by Mills & Boon) Ulverscroft.

— A Funny Thing Happened... (Romance Ser.: Vol. 427). 1999. mass mkt. 3.50 (*0-373-17427-6*, 1-17427-5, Harlequin) Harlequin Bks.

— The Ideal Choice. large type ed. (Mills & Boon Large Print Ser.). 288p. 1997. 23.99 (*0-263-15003-8*) Ulverscroft.

— If You Need Me... large type ed. (Mills & Boon Large Print Ser.). 288p. 1997. 23.99 (*0-263-15097-6*, Pub. by Mills & Boon) Ulverscroft.

— Just Another Miracle! 1999. mass mkt. 3.50 (*0-373-17408-X*, 1-17408-5, Mira Bks) Harlequin Bks.

***Anderson, Caroline.** Just Say Yes! (Romance Ser.: Vol. 3605). 186p. 2000. per. 3.50 (*0-373-03605-1*) Harlequin Bks.

— Just Say Yes! large type ed. Vol. 451. 2000. mass mkt. 3.50 (*0-373-15851-3*) Harlequin Bks.

— Kids Included. large type ed. 288p. 2000. 25.99 (*0-263-16281-8*, Pub. by Mills & Boon) Ulverscroft.

Anderson, Caroline. A Man of Honour. large type ed. 1995. 11.50 (*0-7505-0819-1*, Pub. by Mgna Lrg Print) Ulverscroft.

— Not Husband Material! large type ed. (Mills & Boon Large Print Ser.). 288p. 1998. 24.99 (*0-263-15328-2*, Pub. by Mills & Boon) Ulverscroft.

— Nothing Left to Give. large type ed. 288p. 1995. 23.99 (*0-263-14175-6*, Pub. by Mills & Boon) Ulverscroft.

— Once More, with Feeling. large type ed. 288p. 1995. 23.99 (*0-263-14329-5*, Pub. by Mills & Boon) Ulverscroft.

***Anderson, Caroline.** Une Partie de Campagne. (FRE.). 2000. mass mkt. 3.99 (*0-373-34811-8*) Harlequin Bks.

Anderson, Caroline. Un Piege de Tendresse. (Azur Ser.: No. 745). (FRE.). 1999. mass mkt. 3.50 (*0-373-34745-6*, 1-34745-9) Harlequin Bks.

***Anderson, Caroline.** Practically Perfect. 288p. 2000. 26.99 (*0-263-16330-X*, Pub. by Mills & Boon) Ulverscroft.

Anderson, Caroline. Practice Makes Perfect. large type ed. (Dales Large Print Ser.). 265p. 1998. pap. 19.99 (*1-85389-805-8*, Dales) Ulverscroft.

— The Real Fantasy. large type ed. (Mills & Boon Large Print Ser.). 288p. 1997. 23.99 (*0-263-14997-8*) Ulverscroft.

***Anderson, Caroline.** Sarah's Gift. large type ed. 288p. 1999. 25.99 (*0-263-15904-3*, Pub. by Mills & Boon) Ulverscroft.

Anderson, Caroline. Second Thoughts. large type ed. 1995. 11.50 (*0-7505-0816-7*, Pub. by Mgna Lrg Print) Ulverscroft.

— Taken for Granted. large type ed. 288p. 1995. 23.99 (*0-263-14513-1*, Pub. by Mills & Boon) Ulverscroft.

— Tender Touch. large type ed. (Mills & Boon Large Print Ser.). 288p. 1996. 23.99 (*0-263-14770-3*, Pub. by Mills & Boon) Ulverscroft.

***Anderson, Caroline.** An Unexpected Bonus. large type ed. 288p. 1999. 25.99 (*0-263-16111-0*, Pub. by Mills & Boon) Ulverscroft.

Anderson, Carolyn. The Anderson Guide to Enjoying Greenwich: An Insider's Favorite Places. LC 97-80547. 128p. 1997. pap. 12.95 (*0-9661072-0-9*, Ickus Guides) Avocet Pr.

***Anderson, Carolyn.** Brain Stretchers Bk 4: Advanced. 70p. (Orig.). (YA). (gr. 6 up). 1998. pap. 10.95 (*0-89455-674-6*) Crit Think Bks.

Anderson, Carolyn. Cry Revenge! The Novel. 250p. 1994. pap. write for info. (*1-883778-03-4*) Starlite Prods.

— How to Protect Your Child from Becoming a Missing Person. unabridged ed. 46p. (J). (ps-7). 1992. pap., wbk. ed. 5.00 incl. audio (*1-883778-00-X*) Starlite Prods.

— How to Protect Your Child from Becoming a Missing Person: The Manual. 2nd rev. ed. (Illus.). 41p. 1995. pap. 12.00 (*1-883778-04-2*) Starlite Prods.

— The 1999 Anderson Guide to Enjoying Greenwich, CT. LC 98-88785. (Illus.). 200p. 1998. pap. 12.95 (*0-9661072-3-3*) Avocet Pr.

— The Rings of Empowerment: A Guide to Discovering & Fulfilling Your Life Purpose As Part of a Co-Creative Team. (Illus.). 168p. (Orig.). 1993. pap. text 20.00 (*1-883208-00-9*) Global Family.

***Anderson, Carolyn & Anderson Associates Staff.** The Anderson Guide to Enjoying Greenwich, CT: An Insider's Favorite Places. 4th ed. LC 00-8450. (Illus.). 2000. write for info. (*0-9677346-0-6*) Avocet Pr.

Anderson, Carolyn & Benson, Thomas W. Documentary Dilemmas: Frederick Wiseman's "Titicut Follies" LC 88-29834. 176p. (Orig.). (C). 1991. pap. 16.95 (*0-8093-1518-1*) S Ill U Pr.

Anderson, Carolyn & Haller, Jackie. Brain Stretchers Bk 1. 76p. (Orig.). (YA). (gr. 5-9). 1975. pap. 10.95 (*0-89455-644-4*) Crit Think Bks.

— Brain Stretchers Bk 2. 70p. (Orig.). (YA). (gr. 5-9). 1977. pap. 10.95 (*0-89455-645-2*) Crit Think Bks.

Anderson, Carolyn & Haller, Jackie. Brain Stretchers-Book I. 1975. pap. 10.95 (*0-910974-87-X*) Crit Think Bks.

Anderson, Carolyn S., jt. auth. see Witmer, Judith T.

Anderson, Carolyn T. A Unique Experience. 173p. (Orig.). 1987. pap. 6.00 (*0-935132-08-2*) C H Fairfax.

Anderson, Carrie & Wendelken, David. The Oracle Designer - 200 Handbook. 624p. (C). 1996. pap. 41.95 (*0-201-63445-7*) Addison-Wesley.

Anderson, Cary. Alaska's Magnificent Eagles. (Alaska Geographic Ser.: Vol. 24, No. 4). (Illus.). 1997. pap. 19.95 (*1-56661-039-7*) Alaska Geog Soc.

— The Valley of the Eagles. (Illus.). 24p. 1995. pap. 5.95 (*0-9607358-9-5*) Fathom Pub.

Anderson, Catherine. Annie's Song. 416p. (Orig.). 1996. mass mkt. 6.50 (*0-380-77961-7*, Avon Bks) Morrow Avon.

— Baby Love. LC 99-94805. 432p. 1999. mass mkt. 5.50 (*0-380-79937-5*, Avon Bks) Morrow Avon.

— Basic Watercolor Answer Book. LC 98-38525. (Illus.). 128p. 1999. pap. 24.99 (*0-89134-877-8*, North Light Bks) F & W Pubns Inc.

***Anderson, Catherine.** Bits & Pieces II. 1998. pap. 18.15 (*1-57232-617-4*) Seymour Pubns.

Anderson, Catherine. Cherish. LC 98-92774. 391p. 1998. mass mkt. 6.50 (*0-380-79936-7*, Avon Bks) Morrow Avon.

— Forever After. 448p. 1998. mass mkt. 5.99 (*0-380-79104-8*, Avon Bks) Morrow Avon.

***Anderson, Catherine.** Forever After. large type ed. LC 99-48260. 1999. 22.95 (*1-56895-781-5*, Wheeler) Wheeler Pub.

— Frogs, Fleas & Painted Cube. (Illus.). 1997. pap. 18.15 (*1-57232-185-7*) Seymour Pubns.

— How Likely Is It? 1998. pap. 18.15 (*1-57232-627-1*) Seymour Pubns.

Anderson, Catherine. In the Mother Tongue. LC 83-82377. 64p. 1983. 6.95 (*0-914086-47-2*); pap. 3.95 (*0-914086-46-4*) Alice James Bks.

— Keegan's Lady. 1996. mass mkt. 5.99 (*0-380-77962-5*, Avon Bks) Morrow Avon.

***Anderson, Catherine.** Prime Time. 1998. pap. 18.15 (*1-57232-621-2*) Seymour Pubns.

— Seventh Heaven. 384p. 2000. mass mkt. 6.99 (*0-380-79938-3*, Avon Bks) Morrow Avon.

Anderson, Catherine. Simply Love. LC 96-97081. 400p. 1997. mass mkt. 5.99 (*0-380-79102-1*, Avon Bks) Morrow Avon.

— Simply Love. LC 99-11185. 1999. 23.95 (*1-56895-541-X*) Wheeler Pub.

***Anderson, Catherine.** The Work of Hands. LC 00-101746. 88p. 2000. pap. 11.95 (*0-9660459-3-9*, Pub. by Perugia Pr) SPD-Small Pr Dist.

Anderson, Catherine & Hayes, Jeri, eds. Chemicals: Choosing Wisely. (Environmental ACTION Ser.). (Illus.). 153p. (Orig.). 1997. pap. text, teacher ed. 13.95 (*0-201-49534-1*, 36864) Seymour Pubns.

Anderson, Catherine, jt. auth. see Loughlin, Caroline.

Anderson, Catherine, ed. see Akers, Joan, et al.

Anderson, Catherine, ed. see Battista, Michael T. & Berle-Carman, Mary.

Anderson, Catherine, ed. see Battista, Michael T. & Clements, Douglas H.

Anderson, Catherine, ed. see Berle-Carman, Mary, et al.

Anderson, Catherine, ed. see Blank, Carla & Roberts, Jody.

Anderson, Catherine, ed. see Bryan, Virginia, et al.

Anderson, Catherine, ed. see Clements, Douglas H., et al.

Anderson, Catherine, ed. see Clements, Doug, et al.

Anderson, Catherine, ed. see Economopoulos, Karen & Murray, Megan.

Anderson, Catherine, ed. see Economopoulos, Karen & Russell, Susan J.

Anderson, Catherine, ed. see Economopoulos, Karen, et al.

Anderson, Catherine, ed. see Eston, Rebeka & Economopoulos, Karen.

Anderson, Catherine, ed. see Fey, James T., et al.

Anderson, Catherine, ed. see Glatzer, David J. & Glatzer, Joyce.

Anderson, Catherine, ed. see Goodrow, Anne, et al.

Anderson, Catherine, ed. see Ham, Jan.

Anderson, Catherine, ed. see Kilman, Marlene, et al.

Anderson, Catherine, ed. see Kliman, Marlene & Russell, Susan J.

Anderson, Catherine, ed. see Kliman, Marlene, et al.

Anderson, Catherine, ed. see Lapan, Glenda, et al.

Anderson, Catherine, ed. see Lappan, Glenda, et al.

Anderson, Catherine, ed. see Miller, Elizabeth D.

Anderson, Catherine, ed. see Miller, Lucy.

Anderson, Catherine, ed. see Murray, Megan, et al.

Anderson, Catherine, ed. see Reys, Barbara J., et al.

Anderson, Catherine, ed. see Rockwell, Robert E., et al.

Anderson, Catherine, ed. see Rubin, Andee & Mokros, Jan.

Anderson, Catherine, ed. see Rubin, Andee, et al.

Anderson, Catherine, ed. see Russell, Susan J. & Rubin, Andee.

Anderson, Catherine, ed. see Russell, Susan J., et al.

Anderson, Catherine, ed. see Singer, Margie, et al.

Anderson, Catherine, ed. see Theo Carus Harter, Kaboblin.

Anderson, Catherine, ed. see Tierney, Cornelia.

Anderson, Catherine, ed. see Tierney, Cornelia, et al.

Anderson, Catherine, ed. see Underwood, Larry, et al.

Anderson, Catherine, ed. see Virginia Space Grant Consortium Staff.

Anderson, Catherine, ed. see Winnett, David A., et al.

Anderson, Catherine, ed. see Wright, Tracey & Makros, Jan.

Anderson, Catherine, ed. see Wright, Tracey, et al.

Anderson, Catherine C. Jacqueline Kennedy Onassis: Woman of Courage. LC 94-37241. (Achievers Ser.). (J). 1995. lib. bdg. 19.93 (*0-8225-2885-1*) Lerner Pub.

Anderson, Catherine E., ed. see Smithsonian Institute, National Museum of American.

Anderson, Cathy, ed. San Diego Film & Video Resource Guide, 1995. 306p. 1995. 15.00 (*0-9646317-0-9*) San Diego Film Comm.

Anderson, Cathy, ed. see Burrill, Gail F. & Hopfensperger, Patrick.

Anderson, Cathy, ed. see Burrill, Gail & Hopfensperger, Patrick.

Anderson, Cathy, ed. see Charles, R., et al.

Anderson, Cathy, ed. see Cook, Nancy & Johnson, Christine V.

Anderson, Cathy, ed. see EZ: Environment & Education Staff.

Anderson, Cathy, ed. see E2: Environment & Education Staff.

Anderson, Cathy, ed. see Wright, Russell.

Anderson, Charlene. Berkeley's Best Buddhist Bookstore. LC 99-61369. 300p. 2000. pap. 14.95 (*0-88739-263-6*) Creat Arts Bk.

— The Greatest Puppet Show on Earth. 40p. 1998. pap. 3.25 (*0-8341-1684-7*) Nazarene.

Anderson, Charles. Charleston: A Golden Memory. (Illus.). 116p. (Orig.). 1992. pap. 9.95 (*0-941711-18-8*) Wyrick & Co.

— Papua: The United States Army Campaigns of World War 2. 22p. 1992. pap. 1.00 (*0-16-035883-3*) USGPO.

Anderson, Charles & Blakemore, Derek. Modern Food Service. 240p. 1991. pap. 34.95 (*0-7506-0057-8*) Buttrwrth-Heinemann.

Anderson, Charles & Wilkie, Patricia, eds. Reflective Helping in HIV & AIDs. 256p. 1991. 123.00 (*0-335-15632-0*); pap. 41.95 (*0-335-15631-2*) OpUniv Pr.

Anderson, Charles, ed. & intro. see James, Henry.

***Anderson, Charles A.** Shall We Gather at the River. LC 98-90376. 1999. 22.95 (*0-533-12776-9*) Vantage.

Anderson, Charles G. In Search of the Buffalo: The Story of J. Wright Mooar. (Illus.). 145p. (Orig.). 1996. pap. 13.95 (*1-877704-24-5*) Pioneer Pr.

Anderson, Charles M. Isle of View: A History of South Manitou Island. (Illus.). 111p. (Orig.). (C). 1979. pap. 7.50 (*1-878526-07-3*) Pineapple MI.

— Memos of Betsie Bay: A History of Frankfort. (Illus.). 128p. (Orig.). (C). 1988. pap. 8.50 (*1-878526-08-1*) Pineapple MI.

— Richard Selzer & the Rhetoric of Surgery. LC 88-26454. 160p. (C). 1989. 21.95 (*0-8093-1502-5*) S Ill U Pr.

***Anderson, Charles M. & MacCurely, Marian M., eds.** Writing & Healing: Toward an Informed Practice. LC 99-48921. (Illus.). 493p. 2000. pap., teacher ed. 29.95 (*0-8141-5860-9*, 58609) NCTE.

Anderson, Charles M., et al. Clinical Magnetic Resonance Angiography. LC 93-10272. 528p. 1993. text 160.00 (*0-7817-0094-9*) Lppncott W & W.

Anderson, Charles R. Algeria-French Morocco: The United States Army Campaigns of World War 2. 32p. 1993. pap. 1.25 (*0-16-038105-3*) USGPO.

— East Indies: The United States Army Campaigns of World War 2. 23p. 1995. pap. 1.75 (*0-16-042087-3*) USGPO.

— Emily Dickinson's Poetry: Stairway of Surprise. LC 82-15844. (Illus.). 334p. 1982. reprint ed. lib. bdg. 52.50 (*0-313-23733-6*, ANED, Greenwood Pr) Greenwood.

— The Grunts. 256p. 1987. mass mkt. 5.99 (*0-425-10403-6*) Berkley Pub.

Anderson, Charles R. Guadalcanal: United States Army Campaigns of World War 2. 28p. 1993. pap. 1.00 (*0-16-061301-9*) USGPO.

Anderson, Charles R. Person, Place & Thing in Henry James's Novels. LC 77-75619. 318p. reprint ed. pap. 98.60 (*0-608-17316-9*, 205223400068) Bks Demand.

Anderson, Charles R. Tunisia: The United States Army Campaigns of World War II. 30p. 1993. pap. 1.25 (*0-16-038106-1*) USGPO.

Anderson, Charles R. Western Pacific: The United States Army Campaigns of World War 2. 36p. 1994. pap. 2.00 (*0-16-045116-7*) USGPO.

Anderson, Charles R., ed. Centennial Edition of the Works of Sidney Lanier, 10 vols., Set. Incl. English Novel & Essays on Literature. Gohdes, Clarence & Malone, Kemp, eds. 411p. 1945. 55.00 (*0-8018-0032-3*); Florida & Miscellaneous Prose. Graham, Philip, ed. 437p. 1945. 55.00 (*0-8018-0034-X*); Letters. Starke, Aubrey H., ed. 450p. 1945. 55.00 (*0-8018-0036-6*); Letters. Starke, Aubrey H., ed. 575p. 1945. 55.00 (*0-8018-0037-4*); Poems & Poem Outlines. 396p. 1945. 55.00 (*0-8018-0029-3*); Science of English Verse & Essays on Music. Baum, Paull F., ed. 389p. 1945. 55.00 (*0-8018-0030-7*); Shakespeare & His Forerunners. Malone, Kemp, ed. 443p. 1945. 55.00 (*0-8018-0031-5*); Tiger Lilies & Southern Prose. Greever, Garland & Abernethy, Cecil, eds. 407p. 1945. 55.00 (*0-8018-0033-1*); Vol. 7. Letters. Starke, Aubrey H., ed. 401p. 1945. 55.00 (*0-8018-0035-8*); 4241p. 1945. 450.00 (*0-8018-0028-5*) Johns Hopkins.

— Journal of a Cruise to the Pacific Ocean, 1842-1844, in the Frigate United States with Notes on Herman Melville. LC 70-158282. reprint ed. 29.50 (*0-404-00356-7*) AMS Pr.

Anderson, Charles S. Augsburg Historical Atlas of Christianity in the Middle Ages & Reformation. LC 67-11723. 64p. 1973. pap. 18.99 (*0-8066-1317-3*, 10-0521, Augsburg) Augsburg Fortress.

— CSA Archive Book. (Illus.). 500p. 1995. 50.00 (*0-9622431-1-6*) C S Anderson.

Anderson, Charles W. Political Economy of Modern Spain: Policy-Making in an Authoritarian System. LC 72-106036. 296p. reprint ed. pap. 91.80 (*0-7837-7019-7*, 204683500004) Bks Demand.

— Pragmatic Liberalism. LC 90-30177. 234p. 1990. 33.00 (*0-226-01801-6*) U Ch Pr.

A

A

— Pragmatic Liberalism. 234p. 1994. pap. text 14.95 (*0-226-01802-4*) U Ch Pr.

— Prescribing the Life of the Mind: An Essay on the Purpose of the University, the Aims of Liberal Education, the Competence of Citizens, & the Cultivation of Practical Reason. LC 92-45196. 192p. (C). 1993. 22.95 (*0-299-13830-5*) U of Wis Pr.

— Prescribing the Life of the Mind: An Essay on the Purpose of the University, the Aims of Liberal Education, the Competence of Citizens, & the Cultivation of Practical Reason. LC 92-45196. 190p. (C). 1996. pap. 12.95 (*0-299-13834-8*) U of Wis Pr.

— Value Judgment & Income Distribution. Solo, Robert A., ed. LC 81-10553. 410p. 1981. 69.50 (*0-275-90722-8*, C0722, Praeger Pubs) Greenwood.

Anderson, Charles W., jt. auth. see Glade, William P.

Anderson, Charlotte. Images of Japan: Matsuri: World of Japanese Festivals. (Postcard Book Ser.). (Illus.). 22p. 1997. pap. 11.95 (*4-07-976280-1*, Pub. by Shufunotomo) Weatherhill.

Anderson, Charlotte, jt. auth. see Vilhar, Gorazd.

Anderson, Charlotte C., et al. Global Understandings: A Framework for Teaching & Learning. LC 94-38856. 1994. pap. 17.95 (*0-87120-240-9*) ASCD.

Anderson, Cherrie & Sinclair Wood, Kathleen. Cleveland Park: A Guide to Architectural Styles & Building Types. LC 98-144215. (Illus.). 27p. 1997. pap. 12.00 (*0-9662090-0-1*) Cleve Pk Hist.

Anderson, Cheryl P. Shaker Hymnal: A Facsimile Edition of the Hymnal of the Canterbury Shakers. 288p. 1996. pap. 15.95 (*0-87951-640-2*, Pub. by Overlook Pr) Penguin Putnam.

Anderson, Cheryl P., intro. Shaker Hymnal: A Facsimile Edition of the Hymnal of the Canterbury Shakers. 288p. 1990. 21.95 (*0-87951-402-7*, Pub. by Overlook Pr) Penguin Putnam.

Anderson, Chester. Fox & Hare. LC 80-66869. (Illus.). 192p. 1980. 20.00 (*0-9601428-0-0*); pap. 9.95 (*0-9601428-9-4*) Entwhistle Bks.

Anderson, Chester G. James Joyce. LC 85-51358. (Literary Lives Ser.). (Illus.). 144p. 1998. reprint ed. pap. 12.95 (*0-500-26018-4*, Pub. by Thames Hudson) Norton.

Anderson, Chester G., ed. Growing up in Minnesota: Ten Writers Remember Their Childhoods. LC 75-40546. 256p. 1976. pap. 16.95 (*0-8166-0921-7*) U of Minn Pr.

Anderson, Chester G., ed. see Joyce, James.

Anderson, Chris. Edge Effects: Notes from an Oregon Forest. LC 93-20638. (American Land & Life Ser.). (Illus.). 207p. 1993. pap. 11.95 (*0-87745-438-8*) U of Iowa Pr.

— Free - Style. (C). 1991. pap. text 18.36 (*0-395-57732-2*) HM.

— Style As Argument: Contemporary American Nonfiction. LC 86-21970. 202p. 1987. pap. 14.95 (*0-8093-1373-1*); text 16.95 (*0-8093-1314-6*) S Ill U Pr.

Anderson, Chris, ed. Literary Nonfiction: Theory, Criticism, Pedagogy. LC 88-18726. 256p. (C). 1989. text 31.95 (*0-8093-1405-3*) S Ill U Pr.

***Anderson, Chris & McGehee, Sharon.** Bodies of Evidence. 2000. mass mkt. 6.50 (*0-312-92806-8*) St Martin.

Anderson, Chris & Runciman, Lex. Asking Questions: A Rhetoric for the Intellectual Life. LC 99-42044. 272p. (C). 2000. pap. text 29.00 (*0-205-27828-0*, Macmillan Coll) P-H.

***Anderson, Chris & Runciman, Lex.** A Forest of Voices: Conversations in Ecology. 2nd ed. LC 99-39787. xii, 625p. 2000. pap. text 34.95 (*0-7674-1147-1*, 1147-1) Mayfield Pub.

Anderson, Chris, et al. Raging Bull II. 288p. 16.95 (*0-8184-0407-8*) Carol Pub Group.

Anderson, Christa. Mastering Local Area Networks. (Mastering Ser.). 784p. 1999. pap. 39.99 (*0-7821-2258-2*) Sybex.

***Anderson, Christa.** Windows 2000 Terminal Services & Citrix MetaFrame 24seven. (24x7 Ser.). (Illus.). 576p. 2000. pap. 34.99 (*0-7821-2594-8*) Sybex.

Anderson, Christeen L. & Keyston, David L., compiled by. Mother in Israel. (Illus.). 120p. 1998. pap. 14.95 (*0-9645803-6-5*, PB-M1) Healing Unltd.

Anderson, Christian S. & Musselman, Eric P. Musselman's Guide to Minor League Basketball, Vol. I, No. 1. rev. ed. 250p. (Orig.). 1995. pap. text 45.00 (*0-9636968-0-7*) Goose Prods.

Anderson, Christiane. Monograph of Stigmaphyllon (Malpighiaceae) Daniel, Thomas F., ed. (Systematic Botany Monographs: Vol. 51). (Illus.). 313p. 1997. 40.00 (*0-912861-51-7*) Am Soc Plant.

Anderson, Christiane, ed. see Affolter, James M.

Anderson, Christiane, ed. see Argus, George W.

Anderson, Christiane, ed. see Beaman, John H.

Anderson, Christiane, ed. see Beyra M., Angela & Lavin, Matt.

Anderson, Christiane, ed. see Chase, Mark W.

Anderson, Christiane, ed. see Chen, Chia-jui, et al.

Anderson, Christiane, ed. see Christensen, Knud I.

Anderson, Christiane, ed. see Chuang, Tsan I. & Heckard, Lawrence R.

Anderson, Christiane, ed. see Clark, Lynn G.

Anderson, Christiane, ed. see Daniel, Thomas F.

Anderson, Christiane, ed. see Darwin, Steven P.

Anderson, Christiane, ed. see Dietrich, Werner & Wagner, Warren L.

Anderson, Christiane, ed. see Dietrich, Werner, et al.

Anderson, Christiane, ed. see Elisens, Wayne J.

Anderson, Christiane, ed. see Esslinger, Theodore L.

Anderson, Christiane, ed. see Evans, Randall J.

Anderson, Christiane, ed. see Fryxell, G. A., et al.

Anderson, Christiane, ed. see Fryxell, Paul A.

Anderson, Christiane, ed. see Graham, Shirley A.

Anderson, Christiane, ed. see Hensold, Nancy.

Anderson, Christiane, ed. see Hughes, Colin.

Anderson, Christiane, ed. see Jansen, Robert K.

Anderson, Christiane, ed. see Johnson, David M.

Anderson, Christiane, ed. see Kuijt, Job.

Anderson, Christiane, ed. see Lammers, Thomas G.

Anderson, Christiane, ed. see Lavin, Matt.

Anderson, Christiane, ed. see Lavin, Matt & Sousa, Mario.

Anderson, Christiane, ed. see Luckow, Melissa.

Anderson, Christiane, ed. see MacDougal, John M.

Anderson, Christiane, ed. see Murray, Nancy A.

Anderson, Christiane, ed. see Panero, Jose L.

Anderson, Christiane, ed. see Peterson, Paul M. & Annable, Carol R.

Anderson, Christiane, ed. see Prather, L. Alan.

Anderson, Christiane, ed. see Sanders, Roger W.

Anderson, Christiane, ed. see Saunders, Richard M.

Anderson, Christiane, ed. see Schlessman, Mark A.

Anderson, Christiane, ed. see Skean, James D., Jr.

Anderson, Christiane, ed. see Smith, James F.

Anderson, Christiane, ed. see Spooner, David M.

Anderson, Christiane, ed. see Standley, Lisa A.

Anderson, Christiane, ed. see Strother, John L.

Anderson, Christiane, ed. see Taylor, Charlotte M.

Anderson, Christiane, ed. see Thompson, David M.

Anderson, Christiane, ed. see Tucker, Gordon C.

Anderson, Christiane, ed. see Wells, Elizabeth F. & Elvander, Patrick E.

Anderson, Christiane, ed. see Whalen, M. A.

Anderson, Christiane, ed. see Wiersema, John H.

***Anderson, Christina.** Tutti Nudi: Reflections on the Re-Emergence of the Nude During the Italian Renaissance. LC 99-76784. (Illus.). 80p. 2000. pap. 15.00 (*1-877675-34-2*) Midmarch Arts.

Anderson, Christina. Working While They Nap: An Inspirational Guide for Parents Who Want to Work from Home. (Illus.). 48p. 1997. pap. 6.95 (*1-885273-07-X*) First Century.

***Anderson, Christine.** The Poinsettia Tradition. LC 99-94939. 1999. 9.95 (*0-9656224-7-9*) Wtrs Edge.

Anderson, Christine. Poinsettias: Myth & Legend - History & Botanical Fact. LC 96-60667. (Illus.). 64p. 1997. 21.95 (*0-9656224-9-5*) Wtrs Edge.

Anderson, Christine & Dorfman, Merlin. Aerospace Software Engineering. (Progress in Astronautics & Aeronautics Ser.: Vol. 136). (Illus.). 630p. 1991. 79.95 (*1-56347-005-5*, V-136) AIAA.

Anderson, Christine M., et al. Christmas Time & Juletid: Traditions from the United States & Norway with Songs, Food, Decorations & Stories for the Season. LC 97-92750. (Illus.). ix, 256p. 1997. spiral bd., wbk. ed. 29.95 (*0-9661699-0-5*) Leikarringen.

Anderson, Christopher. Blaming the Government: Citizens & the Economy in Five European Democracies. LC 95-18912. (Comparative Politics Ser.). (Illus.). 248p. (gr. 13). 1995. text 70.95 (*1-56324-447-0*); pap. text 34.95 (*1-56324-448-9*) M E Sharpe.

— Hollywood TV: The Studio Systems in the Fifties. LC 93-37276. (Film Studies). (Illus.). 352p. (C). 1994. pap. 19.95 (*0-292-70457-7*); text 45.00 (*0-292-73059-4*) U of Tex Pr.

— Jack & Jackie: Portrait of an American Marriage. 1997. mass mkt. 6.99 (*0-380-73031-6*, Avon Bks) Morrow Avon.

— Michel Tournier's Children: Myth, Intertext, Initiation. Vol. 180. LC 91-43009. (American University Studies: No. II). XV, 145p. (C). 1998. text 34.95 (*0-8204-1654-1*) P Lang Pubng.

***Anderson, Christopher.** Prayer Book for Catholic Families. 186p. 1999. pap. 9.95 (*0-8294-1528-9*) Loyola Pr.

Anderson, Christopher. Prayer Primer for Catholic Families. 1998. pap. 3.15 (*0-8294-1015-5*) Loyola Pr.

— Primitives, Patriarchy, & the Picaresque in Vicente Blasco Ibanez's "Canas y Barro" xi, 186p. 1995. 65.00 (*1-882528-16-6*) Scripta.

Anderson, Christopher, et al, eds. The Domestic Politics of German Unification. LC 93-10015. 254p. 1993. lib. bdg. 18.50 (*1-55587-409-6*) L Rienner.

— A Prayer Book for Catholic Families. LC 97-49896. (Illus.). 218p. 1998. 14.95 (*0-8294-1076-7*) Loyola Pr.

Anderson, Christopher A. The Discovery of Life. LC 93-74324. (Illus.). 154p. (Orig.). 1994. pap. text 12.00 (*0-931353-35-1*) Andersons Pubns.

***Anderson, Christopher A.** Healing in the Light & the Art & Practice of Creativity. 135p. 1998. pap. 10.50 (*0-931353-43-2*) Andersons Pubns.

Anderson, Christopher A. Illumination. LC 89-83312. (Illus.). 208p. 1990. 17.00 (*0-931353-19-X*) Andersons Pubns.

— The Man & Woman Manifesto: Let the Revolution Begin. LC 93-74322. (Illus.). 167p. (Orig.). 1994. pap. 12.50 (*0-931353-33-5*) Andersons Pubns.

— The Man & Woman Relationship: A New Center for the Universe. LC 85-71216. (Illus.). 235p. 1985. 18.00 (*0-931353-00-9*) Andersons Pubns.

— Man, Woman, & God. LC 93-74323. (Illus.). 514p. (Orig.). 1994. pap. 18.00 (*0-931353-34-3*) Andersons Pubns.

— Meditations for Deepening Love. LC 93-74325. (Illus.). 206p. 1994. 15.50 (*0-931353-36-X*) Andersons Pubns.

— Psychotherapy As If Life Really Mattered. LC 95-76211. (Illus.). 147p. (Orig.). 1995. pap. 12.00 (*0-931353-39-4*) Andersons Pubns.

— Selected Writings. LC 88-71661. (Illus.). 287p. (Orig.). 1988. pap. text 14.00 (*0-931353-15-7*) Andersons Pubns.

— Selected Writings, Vol. 2. LC 88-71661. (Illus.). 391p. (Orig.). 1991. pap. text 15.50 (*0-931353-26-2*) Andersons Pubns.

— To Cassandra - Early Years. rev. ed. LC 93-74326. 157p. 1994. pap. 12.50 (*0-931353-37-8*) Andersons Pubns.

— The Truth Revealed: My Answer to the World. LC 96-95070. 124p. (Orig.). 1996. pap. 10.50 (*0-931353-42-4*) Andersons Pubns.

— The Universal Religion: The Final Destiny of Mankind. LC 93-74928. (Illus.). 135p. (Orig.). 1994. pap. 12.00 (*0-931353-38-6*) Andersons Pubns.

Anderson, Christopher J. Fall of Fortress Europe: From the Battle of the Bulge to the Crossing of the Rhine. LC 99-35085. (G. I. Ser.: Vol. 18). (Illus.). 72p. 1999. pap. text 13.95 (*1-85367-379-X*, Pub. by Greenhill Bks) Stackpole.

— Grunts: U.S. Infantry in Vietnam. LC 99-20165. (G.I. Ser.). (Illus.). 84p. 1999. 19.95 (*0-7910-5377-6*) Chelsea Hse.

— Hell on Wheels: The Men of the U. S. Armored Forces, 1918 to the Present. LC 99-32807. (G. I. Ser.: Vol. 17). (Illus.). 72p. 1999. pap. text 13.95 (*1-85367-378-1*, Pub. by Stackpole) Stackpole.

***Anderson, Christopher J.** The Marines II World War II: From Pearl Harbor to Tokyo Bay. LC 00-30809. (G. I. Ser.). (Illus.). 2000. write for info. (*1-85367-426-5*, Pub. by Greenhill Bks) Stackpole.

Anderson, Christopher J. Patton's Third Army. LC 99-20139. (G.I. Ser.). 1999. 19.95 (*0-7910-5374-1*) Chelsea Hse.

— Patton's Third Army. LC 98-130315. (G. I.: Vol. 10). (Illus.). 80p. 1997. pap. 12.95 (*1-85367-290-4*, Pub. by Greenhill Bks) Stackpole.

***Anderson, Christopher J.** Screaming Eagles: The 101st Airborne Division from D-Day to Desert Storm. LC 00-38080. (G. I. Ser.). 2000. pap. write for info. (*1-85367-425-7*) Stackpole.

Anderson, Christopher J. The U. S. Army Today: From the End of the Cold War to the Present Day. LC 99-13176. (G.I. Ser.). (Illus.). 84p. 1999. 19.95 (*0-7910-5372-5*) Chelsea Hse.

— The U. S. Army Today: From the End of the Cold War to the Present Day. LC 96-39716. (GI: The Illustrated History of the American Soldier, His Uniform, & His Equipment Ser.). 80p. 1997. 13.95 (*1-85367-269-6*) Stackpole.

Anderson, Christopher J. & Zelle, Carsten, eds. Stability & Change in German Elections: How Electronics Merge, Converge or Collide. LC 98-15651. 376p. 1998. 69.50 (*0-275-96254-7*, Praeger Pubs) Greenwood.

Anderson, Christopher J., et al. Grunts: U.S. Infantry in Vietnam. LC 98-18239. (G. I. Ser.). (Illus.). 72p. 1998. 12.95 (*1-85367-326-9*) Stackpole.

Anderson, Cindi, ed. see McClellan, Bill.

Anderson, Claire M., jt. auth. see Jenkins, Joseph.

***Anderson, Clarence.** Convicts in the Indian Ocean: Transportation from the South Asia. LC 99-44579. 2000. text 65.00 (*0-312-22789-2*) St Martin.

Anderson, Clarence E. & Hamelin, Joseph P. To Fly & Fight: Memoirs of a Triple Ace. LC 99-24801. (Illus.). 340p. 1999. reprint ed. 29.95 (*0-935553-34-7*) Pacifica Military.

Anderson, Clarita S. Weaving a Legacy: The Don & Jean Stuck Coverlet Collection. LC 94-47602. (Illus.). 234p. 1995. 49.50 (*0-8109-3984-3*, Pub. by Abrams) Time Warner.

— Weaving a Legacy: The Don & Jean Stuck Coverlet Collection. LC 94-47602. 1995. 42.95 (*0-918881-33-1*) Columbus Mus Art.

Anderson, Claud. Black Labor, White Wealth: The Search for Power & Economic Justice. 2nd rev. ed. Sargent, Edward D. & Scott, Reginald B., Jr., eds. (Illus.). 250p. 1994. text 23.95 (*0-9661702-1-0*) PowerNomics Corp.

— Dirty Little Secrets about Black History, Heroes & Other Troublemakers. Anderson, Joann & Jekins, Florence, eds. (Illus.). 270p. 1997. pap. 14.95 (*0-9661702-0-2*) PowerNomics Corp.

Anderson, Clay. Portrait of the Ozarks. 1995. pap. text 12.95 (*1-55868-205-8*) Gr Arts Ctr Pub.

***Anderson, Clayton.** Arizona & Grand Canyon. (Illus.). 2001. pap. 17.95 (*2-89464-392-6*) Ulysses Travel.

— Phoenix. (Illus.). 2000. pap. 12.95 (*2-89464-386-1*) Ulysses Travel.

Anderson, Cleasther H. Victory in Spite of the Circumstances. 155p. 1998. pap. write for info. (*1-57502-849-2*, PO2324) Morris Pubng.

Anderson, Clifford. The Stages of Life: A Groundbreaking Look at How We Mature. LC 94-43724. 240p. 1995. 23.00 (*0-87113-481-0*, Atlntc Mnthly) Grove-Atltic.

Anderson, Clinton L. & Kime, Steve F. Adult Higher Education & the Military: Blending Traditional & Nontraditional Education. 70p. (Orig.). 1990. pap. text 14.00 (*0-88044-126-7*) AASCU Press.

Anderson, Clinton W. & Adley, Amanda R., eds. Gay & Lesbian Issues: Abstracts of the Psychological & Behavioral Literature, 1985-1996. LC 97-12944. (Bibliographies in Psychology Ser.: Vol. 17). 227p. 1997. pap. text 27.50 (*1-55798-445-X*) Am Psychol.

Anderson, Colin. Manual for the Examination of Bone. 128p. 1982. 78.00 (*0-8493-0725-2*, RC930, CRC Reprint) Franklin.

Anderson, Colleen. The New West Virginia One-Day Trip Book: More Than 200 Affordable Adventures in the Mountain State. LC 98-22753. 1998. pap. 12.95 (*1-889324-13-2*, EPM) Howell Pr VA.

Anderson, Connie. Save Our Earth: A Musical Story. Anderson, Lindsay, tr. (SPA., Illus.). 28p. (Orig.). (J). (ps-5). 1997. write for info. incl. audio (*0-614-30093-2*) Iguana Prodns.

Anderson, Connie, ed. see Azzam, Fouad.

Anderson, Connie K. From Grandma's Piano Bench: Fifty Years of Children's Music. unabridged ed. 36p. (J). (ps-2). 1995. 11.95 incl. audio (*0-9649986-0-2*) Iguana Prodns.

Anderson, Constance, jt. auth. see Molinski, Michael.

Anderson Consulting Staff. Foundations of Business Systems: Test Bank. 2nd ed. 160p. (C). 1992. pap. text 43.50 (*0-03-092697-1*) Dryden Pr.

Anderson, Cordelia, contrib. by. It's Not Okay to Bully. (Illus.). 16p. (J). (gr. k-5). 1994. pap. 1.75 (*1-56838-033-X*) Hazelden.

Anderson County Chamber of Commerce Staff. History & Families of Anderson County, Kentucky. LC 90-71717. (Illus.). 169p. 1990. 49.95 (*1-56311-007-5*) Turner Pub KY.

Anderson, Courbet. Senior Housing Options. large type ed. Gray, Cecilia, ed. 171p. 1996. 30.00 (*0-9659829-0-4*) ABC Sr Housing.

Anderson, Courtney. To the Golden Shore: The Life of Adoniram Judson. 544p. (Orig.). 1987. pap. 17.00 (*0-8170-1121-8*) Judson.

Anderson, Craig & Rampp, Lary C. Vocational Education in the 1990's II: A Sourcebook for Strategies, Methods, & Materials. 294p. (Orig.). 1993. pap. text 19.50 (*0-911168-87-7*) Prakken.

Anderson, Craig, et al. Digital Projects for Musicians. LC 94-218940. 368p. pap. 24.95 (*0-8256-1384-1*, AM91244) Omnibus NY.

Anderson, Craig V. Talking with Your Child about the Bible. LC 92-26093. (Growing Together Ser.). 32p. 1992. pap. 2.25 (*0-8298-0943-0*) Pilgrim OH.

Anderson, Curt. Bent Antenna. 1992. pap. 5.00 (*0-938979-42-6*) EG Bksellers.

Anderson, Curtiss, jt. auth. see Hall, Joyce C.

Anderson, Cynthia. Hawaii Tropical Botanical Gardens: A Garden in a Valley on the Ocean Floor. (Illus.). 96p. (Orig.). 1994. pap. 14.95 (*0-9639711-0-7*) Hawaii Trop Bot.

Anderson, Cynthia & Bislo, Robin. Heaven & Earth in Geologic Time/Sea Madonna. (Illus.). 28p. (Orig.). 1994. pap. 5.00 (*0-9638843-3-6*) Mille Grazie.

Anderson, Cynthia Peabody, see Peabody Anderson, Cynthia.

Anderson, D., ed. Exotic Species in Australia: Their Establishment & Success. 186p. (C). 1977. text 115.00 (*0-909436-03-7*, Pub. by Surrey Beatty & Sons) St Mut.

***Anderson, D., ed.** Human Monitoring after Enviromental & Occupational Exposure to Chemical & Physical Agents. (NATO Science Ser.: Vol. 313). 350p. 2000. 114.00 (*90-5199-495-8*) IOS Press.

Anderson, D., et al, eds. Calorimetry in High Energy Physics: International Conference. 600p. (C). 1991. text 151.00 (*981-02-0562-7*) World Scientific Pub.

Anderson, D. & Conning, D. M., eds. Experimental Toxicology: The Basic Issues. 2nd ed. 566p. 1994. pap. 59.95 (*0-85186-461-9*) Royl Soc Can.

Anderson, D., jt. auth. see Johnson, R. P.

Anderson, D. A. Finally Free. 52p. 1991. pap. text 4.50 (*1-878886-12-6*) Maryheart Crusaders.

Anderson, D. A. & Burnham, K. P. Model Selection & Inference: A Practical Information Theoretic Approach. LC 98-13046. (Illus.). 320p. 1998. 69.95 (*0-387-98504-2*) Spr-Verlag.

Anderson, D. C., jt. auth. see Vinson, Gavin P.

Anderson, D. F. The Elder & the Sacraments. 1993. pap. 30.00 (*0-7152-0676-1*) St Mut.

Anderson, D. H. Compartmental Modeling & Tracer Kinetics. (Lecture Notes in Biomathematics Ser.: Vol. 50). 302p. 1983. pap. 35.70 (*0-387-12303-2*) Spr-Verlag.

Anderson, D. L., ed. see North Atlantic Treaty Organization Staff.

Anderson, D. L., jt. ed. see Willebrand, Jurgen.

Anderson, D. M., et al, eds. Physiological Ecology of Harmful Algal Blooms. LC 98-5063. (NATO ASI Ser.: Series G, Vol. 41). (Illus.). xix, 662p. 1998. 275.00 (*3-540-64117-3*) Spr-Verlag.

Anderson, D. M., ed. see Anderson, Maxwell.

Anderson, D. R., jt. ed. see Garber, W. F.

Anderson, D. T. Atlas of Invertebrate Anatomy. (Illus.). 1996. pap. 34.95 (*0-86840-207-9*, Pub. by New South Wales Univ Pr) Intl Spec Bk.

Anderson, D. V. Illusions of Power: A History of the Washington Public Power Supply System. LC 84-18329. 159p. 1985. 55.00 (*0-275-90053-3*, C0053, Praeger Pubs) Greenwood.

Anderson, D. W., jt. ed. see Seyed-Yagoobi, J.

Anderson, Dale. Battles That Changed the Modern World. LC 93-17028. (Twenty Events Ser.). (Illus.). 48p. (J). (gr. 5-7). 1993. lib. bdg. 24.26 (*0-8114-4928-9*) Raintree Steck-V.

— Explorers Who Found New Worlds. LC 93-19016. (Twenty Events Ser.). (Illus.). 48p. (J). (gr. 5-6). 1993. lib. bdg. 24.26 (*0-8114-4931-9*) Raintree Steck-V.

— Muscle Pain Relief in Ninety Seconds: The Fold & Hold Method. (Illus.). 192p. 1995. 10.95 (*1-56561-058-X*) Wiley.

***Anderson, Dale.** Westward Expansion. (Making of America Ser.). (Illus.). 2000. 28.54 (*0-8172-5705-5*) Raintree Steck-V.

Anderson, Dale, ed. Folktales of the High Plains. 290p. (C). 1992. pap. text 39.80 (*0-536-58243-2*) Pearson Custom.

Anderson, Dale A. Computational Fluid Mechanics & Heat Transfer. 599p. 1984. 66.95 (*0-89116-471-5*) Hemisp Pub.

Anderson, Dale G., jt. ed. see Felton, John R.

Anderson, Dale L. The Log House in America: And the History & Preservation of the Lewis Anderson Homestead. 2nd rev. ed. (Illus.). 60p. 1999. 19.95 (*1-887188-06-1*); pap. 15.00 (*1-887188-05-3*) Silesia Cos.

— Muscle Pain Relief in 90 Seconds: The Fold & Hold Method. 160p. 1994. pap. 11.95 (*0-471-34689-6*) Wiley.

— The Orchestra Conductor's Secret to Health & Long Life:

An Asterisk (*) at the beginning of an entry indicates that the title is appearing for the first time.

An Asterisk (*) at the beginning of an entry indicates that the title is appearing for the first time.

A

Anderson, David W. More Than Merkle: A History of the Best & Most Exciting Baseball Season in Human History. LC 99-35024. (Illus.). 304p. 2000. 29.95 (0-8032-1056-6) U of Nebr Pr.

***Anderson, Dawn.** Creepy, Crafty Halloween. (Illus.). 96p. 2000. pap. 19.95 (1-56477-306-X, B445, Pub. by Martingale & Co) F & W Pubns Inc.

Anderson, Dawn H. & Cornwall, Marie, eds. Women Steadfast in Christ: Talks Selected from the 1991 BYU Women's Conference. LC 91-47724. 312p. 1992. 13.95 (0-87579-597-8) Deseret Bk.

Anderson, Dawn H. & Green, Susette F., eds. Women in the Covenant of Grace: Talks Selected from the 1993 Women's Conference. LC 93-42368. vii, 280p. 1994. 14.95 (0-87579-829-2) Deseret Bk.

Anderson, Dawn H., et al. Clothed with Charity: Talks from the 1996 Women's Conference. LC 96-53165. 1997. 15.95 (1-57345-240-8) Deseret Bk.

— Every Good Thing: Talks from the 1997 BYU Women's Conference. LC 98-10030. 1998. write for info. (1-57345-367-6) Deseret Bk.

Anderson, Dawn H., jt. ed. see Green, Susette F.

Anderson, Dean. Mortal Combat Jr. Novel Vol. 1: Reptile's World. (Mortal Kombat Ser.). 1996. mass mkt. 4.50 (1-57297-131-2) Blvd Books.

Anderson, Dean, jt. ed. see Grubb, Michael.

Anderson, Dean B., compiled by. A History of the IEEE Lasers & Electro-Optics Society. LC 93-10427. 1993. write for info. (0-7803-9967-6) Inst Electrical.

Anderson, Dean H., ed. Changing Physician Behavior Through Practice Guidelines: The Zitter Group's 1996 Implementing Practice Guidelines Seminar Proceedings. 131p. (Orig.). 1996. pap. text 247.00 (0-9645360-3-X) Cor Hlthcare.

Anderson, Debbie. I Can ABC. LC 96-159136. (Illus.). 36p. (J). (ps-1). 1996. 10.99 (0-7814-0281-6) Chariot Victor.

Anderson, Debbie. Imitators of God: The Art of Improv. (Illus.). 92p. (C). 1997. pap. 7.00 (1-886232-34-2) Majesty Pubns.

Anderson, Debbie, adapted by. Aspects of Praise & Worship. (Illus.). 64p. (C). 1995. pap. 9.50 (1-886232-16-4) Majesty Pubns.

— Teaching Flag Techniques. (Illus.). 42p. (C). 1992. pap. 6.50 (1-886232-29-6) Majesty Pubns.

Anderson, Debby. Are Tigers Ticklish? LC 96-101543. (Illus.). 36p. (J). 1995. bds. 6.99 (0-88070-853-0, Gold n Honey) Zondervan.

— Do Bugs Have Noses? LC 99-23958. 1999. 15.99 (0-7814-3060-7) Chariot Victor.

— Everyday Prayer & Praise. 1999. 10.99 (0-7814-3069-0) Chariot Victor.

— God Is with Me. LC 83-51627. (Happy Day Bks.). (Illus.). 24p. (J). (ps). 1995. pap. 1.99 (0-7847-0349-3, 04229) Standard Pub.

— God Loves Even Me. Beegle, Shirley, ed. LC 84-52169. (Happy Day Bks.). (Illus.). 24p. (J). 1994. reprint ed. pap. 1.99 (0-7847-0254-3, 04204) Standard Pub.

— Here & There, Everywhere! LC 87-72709. (Cuddle & Sing Bks.). (Illus.). 18p. (J). (ps). 1988. bds. 4.29 (1-55513-643-5, Chariot Bks) Chariot Victor.

— Jesus is with Me. 1998. 4.99 (0-7814-3076-3) Chariot Victor.

— Jesus Loves Me. LC 87-72711. (Cuddle & Sing Bks.). (Illus.). 18p. (J). (ps). 1988. bds. 4.49 (1-55513-647-8) Chariot Victor.

— Jesus Loves Me. 1998. 4.99 (0-7814-3075-5) Chariot Victor.

— Jesus Loves the Little Children. LC 92-74367. (Cuddle & Sing Bks.). 18p. (J). (ps). 1993. bds. 4.49 (0-7814-0687-0, Chariot Bks) Chariot Victor.

— Jesus Loves the Little Children. 1998. 4.99 (0-7814-3074-7) Chariot Victor.

— Let's Talk about Children Around the World. Norton, LoraBeth, ed. LC 94-9161. (Illus.). 32p. (J). (ps-2). 1994. 9.99 (0-7814-0178-X, Chariot Bks) Chariot Victor.

— Let's Talk about Heaven. Smith, Julie, ed. LC 91-312. 32p. (J). (gr. 1-2). 1991. 9.99 (1-55513-531-5) Chariot Victor.

— Let's Talk about Heaven. 32p. (J). (ps-2). 1998. 12.99 (0-7814-3077-1) Chariot Victor.

— My Friend Noah. LC 87-72710. (Cuddle & Sing Bks.). (Illus.). 18p. (J). (ps). 1988. bds. 4.29 (1-55513-665-6, Chariot Bks) Chariot Victor.

Anderson, Debby & Norton, L. B. My First Prayers: A Book about Talking to Jesus. (Illus.). 320p. (J). (ps). 1995. 10.99 (0-7814-0210-7, Chariot Bks) Chariot Victor.

Anderson, Debby, jt. auth. see Pingree, Chellie.

Anderson, Deborah, jt. auth. see Evans, Mary J.

Anderson, Deborah L., et al, eds. Navigating the Networks. 255p. 1994. pap. 29.95 (0-938734-85-7) Info Today Inc.

Anderson, Deborah Y. Marvin Gaye the Untold Chapter: Based on the Upcoming Feature Film "The Untold Chapter" LC 97-66302. x, 130p. (Orig.). 1997. pap. 16.95 (0-9657332-0-3) DeVonne Prod.

Anderson, Deborah Y. & Hayes, Christopher L. Gender, Identity & Self-Esteem: A New Look at Adult Development. LC 96-18388. 360p. 1996. 39.95 (0-8261-9410-9) Springer Pub.

Anderson, Debra, compiled by. Voyageur: Northeast Wisconsin's Historical Review Index to Volumes 1-10: Spring 1984 - Winter/Spring 1994. LC 95-77399. (Illus.). 102p. (Orig.). 1996. pap. 10.00 (0-9641499-2-3) Brown County Hist.

Anderson, Debra & Bell, Peter. Porcelain Doll Making. rev. ed. (Illus.). 44p. 1997. pap. 13.95 (0-916809-93-5) Scott Pubns MI.

Anderson, Debra J., et al. Hope, Intolerance & Greed: A Reality Check for Teachers. LC 94-32924. 176p. 1995. 55.00 (0-275-94821-8, Praeger Pubs) Greenwood.

— Teacher Supervision That Works: A Guide for University Supervisors. LC 91-39696. 184p. 1992. 49.95 (0-275-94264-3, C4264, Praeger Pubs) Greenwood.

Anderson, Debra L. Decolonizing the Text: Glissanntian Readings in Caribbean & African American Literatures. LC 94-11769. (Francophone Cultures & Literatures Ser.: Vol. 1). 128p. (C). 1995. text 46.95 (0-8204-2521-4) P Lang Pubng.

Anderson, Debra N., et al. The Occupational Therapy Examination Review Guide. LC 95-46117. (Illus.). 212p. (C). 1996. pap. text 28.95 (0-8036-0029-1) Davis Co.

Anderson, Dee. Amazingly Easy Puppet Plays: 42 New Scripts for One-Person Puppetry. LC 96-32752. 248p. 1996. 27.00 (0-8389-0697-4) ALA.

Anderson, Deland S. Hegel's Speculative Good Friday: The Death of God in Philosophical Perspective, Vol. 4. LC 95-22988. (AAR Reflection & Theory in the Study of Religion Ser.). 240p. 1996. pap. 29.95 (0-7885-0124-0, 01 10 04) OUP.

***Anderson, Denise, et al.** Creative Jolt. (Illus.). 144p. 2000. pap. 24.99 (1-58180-011-8, North Lght Bks) F & W Pubns Inc.

— Creative Jolt Inspirations. (Illus.). 144p. 2000. pap. 24.99 (1-58180-012-6, North Lght Bks) F & W Pubns Inc.

Anderson, Denise, ed. see Willis, Jan.

Anderson, Dennis. An Hour Before Dawn: Stories of the Outdoors. 240p. (Orig.). 1993. pap. 1.99 (0-89658-180-2) Voyageur Pr.

Anderson, Dennis & Ahmed, Kulsum. The Case for Solar Energy Investments. LC 95-1466. (World Bank Technical Papers: No. 279). 30p. 1995. pap. 22.00 (0-8213-3196-5, 13196) World Bank.

Anderson, Dennis, jt. auth. see Turvey, Ralph.

Anderson, Dennis R. 300 Years of American Art in the Chrysler Museum. LC 75-42583. (Illus.). 270p. 1976. pap. 10.00 (0-940744-11-2) Chrysler Museum.

Anderson, Diana & Conning, D. M., eds. Experimental Toxicology: The Basic Issues. 2nd ed. 566p. 1994. 168.00 (0-85186-451-1, R6451) CRC Pr.

Anderson, Diane & Anderson, Glenn. Relationship Renewal: Step up to Intimacy. 179p. 1992. student ed. 15.00 (0-9647544-0-1) Wolf Song.

Anderson, Diane M. PAF Help Guide. 89p. pap. 14.95 (1-877677-86-8) Herit Quest.

Anderson, Diann L., jt. auth. see Cosgriff, James H., Jr.

Anderson, Dick. Diving & Dredging for Gold. (Illus.). 147p. (C). 1994. 12.95 (0-941332-31-4, D482) Best Pub Co.

***Anderson, Dillon.** I & Claudie. LC 99-55783. 256p. 2000. 15.95 (0-89672-429-8) Tex Tech Univ Pr.

Anderson, Dines. A Pali Reader. 130p. 1985. reprint ed. 39.00 (0-932051-66-9) Rprt Serv.

Anderson, Don. AMD K5 Processor System Architecture. 1996. pap. 29.95 (0-201-48409-9) Addison-Wesley.

— PCMCIA System Architecture. 2nd ed. (PC System Architecture Ser.). 464p. (Orig.). (C). 1995. pap. text 34.95 (0-201-40991-7) Addison-Wesley.

— Theory of the Earth. (Illus.). 384p. (C). 1989. reprint ed. pap. text 49.95 (0-86542-123-4) Blackwell Sci.

— Universal Serial Business System Architecture. LC 96-52321. 352p. (C). 1997. pap. text 29.95 (0-201-46137-4) Addison-Wesley.

Anderson, Don & Shanley, Tom. CardBus System Architecture. (PC System Architecture Ser.). 432p. (C). 1995. pap. text 29.95 (0-201-40997-6) Addison-Wesley.

Anderson, Don, et al. Pentium Processor System Architecture. 2nd ed. LC 95-1804. (PC System Architecture Ser.). 464p. (C). 1995. pap. text 34.95 (0-201-40992-5) Addison-Wesley.

Anderson, Don, jt. auth. see Shanley, Tom.

Anderson, Dona S. Beading Heart Designs Amulet Purses. Anderson, Adreinne R., ed. (Illus.). 20p. 1998. pap. text 14.95 (1-892980-00-2) Buckaroo Pr.

Anderson, Dona S., jt. auth. see Anderson, Adrienne E.

Anderson, Donald. Rocky Mountain Traveler: A Visitor's Guide to the U. S. Air Force Academy. LC 94-219686. (American Traveler Ser.: Vol. 33). 1994. pap. 4.95 (1-55838-154-6) R H Pub.

Anderson, Donald, ed. Aftermath: An Anthology of Post-Vietnam Fiction. LC 94-33932. 304p. 1995. 25.00 (0-8050-3655-5); pap. 12.95 (0-8050-3656-3) H Holt & Co.

Anderson, Donald & Swanson, Carl D. Legal Issues in Licensure. LC 93-33196. (ACA Legal Ser.: Vol. 11). 67p. 1994. pap. text 18.95 (1-55620-129-X, 72311) Am Coun Assn.

Anderson, Donald, jt. auth. see Holland, Stuart.

Anderson, Donald D. The Status of Deer in Kansas. (Miscellaneous Publications: No. 39). 36p. 1964. pap. 2.00 (0-317-04916-X) U KS Nat Hist Mus.

Anderson, Donald K. Los Distintivos Biblicos de los Bautistas. Meyer, Richard, ed. (Adult Sunday School Ser.). (SPA.). 95p. 1992. 4.40 (1-879892-35-9) Editorial Bautista.

Anderson, Donald K., Jr., ed. Concord in Discord: The Plays of John Ford, 1586-1986. LC 85-48063. (Studies in the Renaissance: No. 17). 1986. 39.50 (0-404-62287-9) AMS Pr.

Anderson, Donald K., Jr., ed. see Ford, John.

Anderson, Donald M. Calligraphy: The Art of Written Forms. unabridged ed. LC 92-12563. Orig. Title: The Art of Written Forms. (Illus.). 367p. 1992. reprint ed. pap. text 19.95 (0-486-27212-5) Dover.

Anderson, Donald Thomas. Invertebrate Zoology. LC 99-200463. (Illus.). 480p. 1999. pap. text 55.00 (0-19-553941-9) OUP.

Anderson, Donna. Donna Anderson: Whose Kingdom Are You Living In? 48p. 1999. pap. 5.99 (1-57921-163-1, Pub. by WinePress Pub) BookWorld.

Anderson, Donna K. Charles T. Griffes: A Life in Music. LC 92-21844. (Studies of American Musicians). (Illus.). 272p. 1993. text 49.00 (1-56098-191-1) Smithsonian.

— The Works of Charles T. Griffes: A Descriptive Catalogue. LC 83-4983. (Studies in Musicology: No. 68). (Illus.). 588p. reprint ed. pap. 182.30 (0-8357-1419-5, 207033500085) Bks Demand.

Anderson, Donny, jt. auth. see Cohn, Linkie S.

Anderson, Doris. Unfinished Revolution. 312p. 1992. pap. 15.00 (0-385-25377-X) Doubleday.

***Anderson, Dorothy.** Biblical Narrative Poetry. 2000. pap. write for info. (1-58235-440-5) Watermrk Pr.

Anderson, Dorothy. A Guide to Information Sources for the Preparation, Editing & Production of Documents. 128p. 1989. text 59.95 (0-566-05743-3, Pub. by Gower) Ashgate Pub Co.

Anderson, Dorothy & Anderson, Robert. Recipes from the Bottom of the Sea. Lampert, Eva & Lampert, Erv, eds. (Illus.). 168p. (Orig.). 1993. pap. 12.95 (0-932855-32-6) Winner Enter.

Anderson, Dorothy, jt. auth. see Anderson, Stanley F.

Anderson, Dorothy, ed. see Hovis, Joyce.

Anderson, Dorothy D. Arizona Legends & Lore. LC 91-10594. (Illus.). 176p. (Orig.). 1991. pap. 6.95 (0-914846-55-8) Golden West Pub.

Anderson, Dorothy P. Leader's Guide for Jay E. Adams's Christian Living in the Home: A Teaching Manual for Use in Adult Study Groups. (Orig.). 1977. pap. 3.95 (0-934688-05-2) Great Comm Pubns.

Anderson, Dorothy Porter. Different Breed. LC 99-70439. 160p. 1999. pap. 12.95 (1-57197-175-0) Pentland Pr.

Anderson, Doug. Bamboo Bridge. (Amherst Writers & Artists Chapbook Ser.: No. 7). 34p. (Orig.). 1991. pap. 12.00 (0-941895-07-6) Amherst Wri Art.

***Anderson, Doug.** Blues for Unemployed Secret Police. 90p. 2000. pap. 12.95 (1-880684-70-5) Curbstone.

Anderson, Doug. The Moon Reflected Fire. LC 94-26156. 80p. 1994. pap. 9.95 (1-882295-03-X) Alice James Bks.

— Tricky, Sneaky Puzzle Pictures. LC 97-173701. (Illus.). 128p. 1997. reprint ed. pap. 5.95 (0-8069-9608-0) Sterling.

Anderson, Doug, jt. auth. see Tribble, Mike.

Anderson, Douglas. Gold in Trib 1: A Story of Flying, Hiking & Gold Prospecting in Alaska Wilderness. LC 96-71689. 192p. 1997. pap. 12.95 (1-888125-11-X) Publ Consult.

— A House Undivided: Domesticity & Community in American Literature. (Cambridge Studies in American Literature & Culture: No. 38). 246p. (C). 1990. text 69.95 (0-521-38287-4) Cambridge U Pr.

— Jazz & Show Choir Handbook, Vol. II. 2nd ed. 1993. pap. 29.95 (0-937276-14-6, HMB188) Hinshaw Mus.

— The Planet of Waters. 135p. (Orig.). 1983. pap. 7.95 (0-912549-00-9) Bread & Butter.

— Profane & Sacred Dances. 71p. 1989. pap. 7.95 (0-912549-16-5) Bread & Butter.

— The Radical Enlightenments of Benjamin Franklin. LC 96-33236. (New Studies in American Intellectual & Cultural History). (Illus.). 288p. 1997. text 39.95 (0-8018-5445-8) Johns Hopkins.

— Yes. 111p. 1979. pap. 6.95 (0-912549-08-4) Bread & Butter.

Anderson, Douglas, jt. auth. see Itule, Bruce D.

Anderson, Douglas A. New Approaches to Family Pastoral Care. LC 79-8898. (Creative Pastoral Care & Counseling Ser.). 96p. (Orig.). reprint ed. pap. 30.00 (0-608-15327-3, 202961400061) Bks Demand.

Anderson, Douglas A., jt. auth. see Itule, Bruce D.

Anderson, Douglas D. Lang Rongrien Rockshelter: A Pleistocene, Early Holocene Archaeological Site from Krabi, Southwestern Thailand. LC 90-11175. (University Museum Monographs: No. 71). (Illus.). x, 86p. 1990. text 25.00 (0-924171-02-2) U Museum Pubns.

— Regulatory Politics & Electric Utilities. LC 80-26943. 206p. 1981. 49.95 (0-86569-058-8, Auburn Hse) Greenwood.

Anderson, Douglas F., jt. auth. see Ernst, Eldon G.

Anderson, Douglas R. Automated Static Perimetry. 2nd ed. LC 98-29287. (Illus.). 377p. 1998. text 84.95 (0-8151-4384-2, 31269) Mosby Inc.

— Strands of System: The Philosophy of Charles Peirce. LC 94-3571. (Series in the History of Philosophy). 218p. (C). 1995. 39.95 (1-55753-058-0); pap. 17.95 (1-55753-059-9) Purdue U Pr.

Anderson, Douglas R. & Munkholm, Hans J. Boundedly Controlled Topology: Foundations of Algebraic Topology & Simple Homotopy Theory. LC 88-16054. (Lecture Notes in Mathematics Ser.). xii, 309p. 1988. write for info. (0-387-19397-9) Spr-Verlag.

Anderson, Douglas R., jt. ed. see Hart, Richard E.

Anderson, Douglas T. The Hard Disk Technical Guide. rev. ed. (Illus.). 1992. pap. 59.95 (1-880252-13-9) Micro Hse.

— Micro House Encyclopedia of Hard Drives, Rev. A-3, Vol. 2: Drive Settings. (Illus.). 1992. write for info. (1-880252-07-4) Micro Hse.

— Micro House Encyclopedia of Hard Drives, Rev. A-3, Vol. 3: Controller Cards. (Illus.). 1992. write for info. (1-880252-08-2) Micro Hse.

— Micro House Encyclopedia of Hard Drives, Rev. B, 3 vols., Set, Vols. 1-3. (Illus.). 1992. write for info. (1-880252-12-0) Micro Hse.

— Micro House Encyclopedia of Hard Drives, Rev. B, 3 vols., Vol. 1: Setup Guide. (Illus.). 1992. write for info. (1-880252-09-0) Micro Hse.

— Micro House Encyclopedia of Hard Drives, Rev. B, 3 vols., Vol. 2: Drive Settings. (Illus.). 1992. write for info. (1-880252-10-4) Micro Hse.

— Micro House Encyclopedia of Hard Drives, Rev. B, 3 vols., Vol. 3: Controller Cards. (Illus.). 1992. write for info. (1-880252-11-2) Micro Hse.

Anderson, Douglas T. & Bethany, Michael, eds. The Network Interface Technical Guide. (Illus.). (Orig.). 1992. pap. 89.95 (1-880252-21-X) Micro Hse.

Anderson, Douglas T. & Newkirk, Robert, Jr., eds. The Network Interface Technical Guide, Vol. S-B. rev. ed. (Illus.). (Orig.). 1993. write for info. (1-880252-26-0) Micro Hse.

Anderson, Douglas T. & Stein, Todd P., eds. The Encyclopedia of Main Boards, 8 vols., 1. 1992. write for info. (1-880252-14-7) Micro Hse.

— The Encyclopedia of Main Boards, 8 vols., 2. 1992. write for info. (1-880252-15-5) Micro Hse.

— The Encyclopedia of Main Boards, 8 vols., 3. 1992. write for info. (1-880252-16-3) Micro Hse.

— The Encyclopedia of Main Boards, 8 vols., 4. 1992. write for info. (1-880252-17-1) Micro Hse.

— The Encyclopedia of Main Boards, 8 vols., 5. 1992. write for info. (1-880252-22-8) Micro Hse.

— The Encyclopedia of Main Boards, 8 vols., Set. 1992. pap. 399.00 (1-880252-20-1) Micro Hse.

— The Encyclopedia of Main Boards, Vol. X, Index. 1992. write for info. (1-880252-18-X); write for info. (1-880252-23-6) Micro Hse.

— The Encyclopedia of Main Boards, Vol. R, Reference. 1992. write for info. (1-880252-19-8) Micro Hse.

Anderson, Douglas T. & Tribble, Mike. Hard Disk Technical Guide. 11th ed. Dawson, Patrick, ed. (Illus.). 512p. (Orig.). 1995. pap. 49.95 incl. disk (1-880252-28-7) Micro Hse.

Anderson, Duane. All That Glitters: The Emergence of Native American Micaceous Art Pottery in Northern New Mexico. LC 99-19916. (Illus.). 216p. 1999. pap. 27.50 (0-933452-58-6) Schol Am Res.

***Anderson, Duane.** All That Glitters: The Emergence of Native American Micaceous Art Pottery in Northern New Mexico. LC 99-19916. (Illus.). 216p. 1999. 55.00 (0-933452-53-5) Schol Am Res.

Anderson, Duane. Legacy: Southwest Indian Art at the School of American Research. LC 98-36554. 224p. 1998. pap. 49.95 (0-933452-57-8) Schol Am Res.

— Legacy: Southwest Indian Art at the School of American Research. LC 98-36554. 3p. 1998. 100.00 (0-933452-54-3) Schol Am Res.

***Anderson, Duncan.** The Fall of the Reich: D-Day to the Fall of Berlin. (Illus.). 256p. 2000. 29.95 (0-7603-0922-1, 130443AP, Pub. by MBI Pubg) Motorbooks Intl.

Anderson, Duncan, ed. see Syngress Media, Inc. Staff.

Anderson, Duwayne & Bell, Florian. Optical Time-Domain Reflectometry. (Illus.). 395p. 1997. 59.95 (0-927489-01-5, 001-1134-00) Tektronix.

Anderson, Dwight. Foundations of Financial Management. 6th ed. (C). 1991. student ed. 22.50 (0-256-08357-6, Irwn McGrw-H) McGrw-H Hghr Educ.

***Anderson, E., et al.** LAPACK Users' Guide. 3rd rev. ed. LC 99-48954. (Software, Environments & Tools Ser.: No. 9). xxii, 407p. 2000. pap. 39.00 (0-89871-447-8, SE0009) Soc Indus-Appl Math.

Anderson, E. Byron. Belief & Belonging: Living & Celebrating the Faith: A Teaching Companion. 24p. (Orig.). 1993. pap. 2.95 (0-8146-2214-3) Liturgical Pr.

— Belief & Belonging - Living & Celebrating the Faith: A Teaching Companion, Tchr's. preview pack. (Orig.). 1993. pap., teacher ed. 11.95 (0-8146-0013-1) Liturgical Pr.

***Anderson, E. Byron, ed.** Worship Matters Vol. II: A United Methodist Guide to Worship Work. LC 98-96831. 184p. 1999. pap. 24.95 (0-88177-280-1, Pub. by Discipleship Res) P B D Inc.

Anderson, E. Byron & Morrill, Bruce. Liturgy & the Moral Self: Humanity at Full Stretch Before God. LC 97-52051. xii, 231 p. 1998. pap. 27.95 (0-8146-6168-8) Liturgical Pr.

Anderson, E. F., et al. Threatened Cacti of Mexico. (Succulent Plant Research Ser.: Vol. 2). 135p. 1994. 66.00 (0-947643-70-2, Pub. by Royal Botnic Grdns); pap. 36.00 (0-947643-69-9, Pub. by Royal Botnic Grdns) Balogh.

Anderson, E. J. & Philpott, A. B., eds. Infinite Programming. (Lecture Notes in Economics & Mathematical Systems Ser.: Vol. 259). 244p. 1985. 38.50 (0-387-15996-7) Spr-Verlag.

Anderson, E. N. Bird of Paradox: Unpublished Writings of Wilson Duff. LC 97-166151. (Illus.). 316p. 1996. pap. 24.95 (0-88839-360-1) Hancock House.

— The Floating World of Castle Peak Bay. (American Anthropological Association-Anthropological Studies: No. 4). 279p. reprint ed. pap. 79.60 (0-317-10012-2, 2000776) Bks Demand.

— The Food of China. LC 87-29466. (C). 1990. pap. 20.00 (0-300-04739-8) Yale U Pr.

Anderson, Earl R. Cynewulf: Structure, Style, & Theme in His Poetry. LC 81-65464. 248p. 1983. 39.50 (0-8386-3091-X) Fairleigh Dickinson.

— A Grammar of Iconism. LC 98-14041. (Illus.). 400p. 1998. 55.00 (0-8386-3764-7) Fairleigh Dickinson.

Anderson, Ed. Affected: A Vagabonds Journey Through Life. Pasqua, Sandra, ed. LC 96-71728. (Illus.). 136p. (Orig.). 1997. pap. 13.95 (1-886580-17-0) Pinnacle-Syatt.

— Climbing Jacob's Ladder to Wealth & Success: The Making of a Millionaire. LC 98-13168. (Illus.). 208p. 1998. pap. 14.95 (1-880090-63-5) Galde Pr.

***Anderson, Ed.** Passion for the Game: Keeping Faith in Every Inning of Life. 2000. 19.99 (1-56292-848-1) Honor Bks OK.

— Racer's Edge. 2000. 19.99 (1-56292-847-3) Honor Bks OK.

Anderson, Edgar. The Considered Landscape. 52p. 1985. 7.00 (0-934834-60-1) White Pine.

— Plants, Man & Life. LC 52-5870. (Illus.). 265p. reprint ed. pap. 82.20 (0-608-18284-2, 203153100075) Bks Demand.

— Plants, Man & Life. (Illus.). 272p. 1997. reprint ed. 16.95 (0-915279-44-4, PLANTSMAN) Miss Botan.

An Asterisk (*) at the beginning of an entry indicates that the title is appearing for the first time.

Anderson, Edith. Love in Exile: An American Writer's Memoir of Life in Divided Berlin. LC 99-13795. (Illus.). 408p. 1999. 29.50 (*1-883642-67-1*) Steerforth Pr.

Anderson, Edward. Hungry Men. LC 93-13386. 1993. 14.95 (*0-8061-2556-X*) U of Okla Pr.

— Thieves Like Us. (Film Ink Ser.). 1999. pap. 12.00 (*1-85375-311-4*, Pub. by Prion) Trafalgar.

Anderson, Edward, ed. see Anderson Publishing Company Staff.

Anderson, Edward C., et al. The Noel Levitz Student Athlete Retention Program. (C). 1995. write for info. (*1-887842-00-4*) USA Grp N-Levitz.

— The Noel Levitz Student Athlete Retention Program: Leader's Guide. 282p. (C). 1995. teacher ed., ring bd. write for info. (*1-887842-02-0*) USA Grp N-Levitz.

— The Noel Levitz Student Athlete Retention Program: Work-Text: Planning for Success in Athletics, Academics, & Careers. (C). 1995. pap., wbk. ed. write for info. (*1-887842-01-2*) USA Grp N-Levitz.

Anderson, Edward D. Poems in Black & White with Shades of Color, No. 1000. (Illus.). 52p. (Orig.). 1996. pap. 6.95 (*0-9655341-0-3*) Small Caps.

Anderson, Edward E. Fundamentals of Solar Thermal Energy Conversion. LC 81-22852. 576p. 1983. text 46.36 (*0-201-00008-3*) Addison-Wesley.

Anderson, Edward F. Peyote: The Divine Cactus. 2nd rev. ed. LC 95-50224. (Illus.). 272p. 1996. pap. 19.95 (*0-8165-1654-5*) U of Ariz Pr.

— Plants & People of the Golden Triangle: Ethnobotany of the Hill Tribes of Northern Thailand. LC 92-25857. (Illus.). 272p. 1993. 69.95 (*0-931146-25-9*, Dioscorides) Timber.

Anderson, Edward J. & Nash, Peter. Linear Programming in Infinite-Dimensional Spaces: Theory & Applications. fac. ed. LC 86-32579. (Wiley-Interscience Series in Discrete Mathematics & Optimization). (Illus.). 184p. 1987. reprint ed. pap. 57.10 (*0-608-00992-X*, 206184900012) Bks Demand.

***Anderson, Edward R.** They Musta Had Wings: A True Story of Courage & Triumph. 128p. 1999. pap. 10.95 (*1-929978-01-4*) Diamond Life Pr.

Anderson, Edwin. Loving Words Every Child Needs to Hear, 1. 96p. 1999. 9.99 (*0-8499-5404-5*) Word Pub.

Anderson, Edwin & Peterson, John. Loving Words Every Woman Wants to Hear. (Illus.). 96p. 1999. 9.99 (*0-8499-5402-9*) Word Pub.

Anderson, Edwin C. The Promise That Was America. LC 97-32193. 1998. write for info. (*0-9660522-2-6*) Jems Mont Pr.

Anderson, Edwin C., Jr. & Kasten, Sandy. California Decedent Estate Practice 1, 2, 2 vols. Tom, Janette, ed. LC 86-70193. 475p. 1996. ring bd. 67.00 (*0-7626-0000-4*, ES-35668) Cont Ed Bar-CA.

Anderson, Edwin C., Jr., jt. auth. see Richardson, Joan.

Anderson, Edwin P. Air Conditioning. 2nd ed. Miller, Rex, ed. (Illus.). 1984. write for info. (*0-318-58077-2*) Macmillan.

— Air Conditioning: Home & Commercial. 4th ed. 528p. 1990. 24.00 (*0-02-584885-2*) Macmillan.

— Refrigeration: Home & Commercial. 2nd ed. Miller, Rex, ed. (Illus.). 1984. 19.95 (*0-685-08249-0*) Macmillan.

— Refrigeration: Home & Commercial. 4th ed. 768p. 1990. 36.00 (*0-02-584875-5*, Aude IN) IDG Bks.

Anderson, Eileen, jt. auth. see Anderson, Brian.

Anderson, Eileen L. Mastering Change Using Principles of Synergy: How to Solve Problems Together & Build Joyous, Lasting Relationships! rev. ed. 320p. (Orig.). (C). 1994. pap. 28.95 (*0-9638150-9-1*) Tahirih Inst.

Anderson, Einar. History & Beliefs of Mormonism. LC 81-13671. Orig. Title: Inside Story of Mormonism. 168p. (C). 1981. pap. 10.99 (*0-8254-2122-5*) Kregel.

Anderson, Elaine. Giraffe's Tale. 32p. (J). (ps-3). 1995. 8.99 (*1-873796-46-3*) Review & Herald.

— A Mouse's Tale. 32p. (J). (gr. k-4). 1991. 8.99 (*0-904748-63-4*) Review & Herald.

— Owl's Tale. 32p. (J). (ps-3). 1994. 8.99 (*0-904748-69-3*) Review & Herald.

— Rabbit's Tale. 32p. (J). (ps-3). 1993. 8.99 (*1-873796-15-3*) Review & Herald.

***Anderson, Elaine.** Wings of Faith Leaders Guide. 52p. 2000. pap., teacher ed. 10.00 (*0-9673200-1-1*) Wings of Faith.

— Wings of Faith Workbook. 102p. 1999. pap., wbk. ed. 25.00 (*0-9673200-0-3*) Wings of Faith.

Anderson, Elaine. With God's Help Flowers Bloom. 1978. pap. 6.95 (*0-89137-411-6*); student ed. 3.85 (*0-89137-412-4*) Quality Pubns.

Anderson, Elaine, jt. auth. see Kurten, Bjorn.

Anderson, Elaine, jt. ed. see Skinner, Denise.

Anderson, Elaine A. & Hula, Richard, eds. Family Policy. (Orig.). 1989. pap. 15.00 (*0-944285-08-2*) Pol Studies.

Anderson, Elaine A. & Hula, Richard C., eds. The Reconstruction of Family Policy, 15. LC 91-46. (Contributions in Family Studies: No. 15). 296p. 1991. 65.00 (*0-313-27899-7*, HRK, Greenwood Pr) Greenwood.

Anderson, Elaine B. A Contemporary Princess: The Journey Back from Anorexia. LC 87-90743. (Illus.). 135p. (Orig.). 1987. pap. 9.98 (*0-318-23783-0*) Monthly Planet Pr.

Anderson, Elaine V., jt. auth. see Tompkins, Phillip K.

Anderson, Elbridge. Through the Awakening Eye: Poems. (Illus.). 1976. pap. 4.00 (*0-915242-08-7*) Pygmalion Pr.

***Anderson, Eleanor.** Miracle at Sea: The Sinking of the Zamzam & Our Family's Astrounding Rescue. (Illus.). 148p. 2000. pap. 16.00 (*0-9663966-3-4*) Quiet Waters.

Anderson, Eleanor. Reading the Changes. (Rethinking Reading Ser.). 128p. 1992. 110.00 (*0-335-15643-6*); pap. 32.95 (*0-335-15642-8*) OpUniv Pr.

***Anderson, Elijah.** Code of the Street: Decency, Violence, & the Moral Life of the Inner City. LC 98-36800. 224p. 1999. 25.95 (*0-393-04023-2*) Norton.

— Code of the Street: Decency, Violence & the Moral Life of the Inner City. 352p. 2000. pap. 14.95 (*0-393-32078-2*) Norton.

Anderson, Elijah. A Place on the Corner: Identity & Rank among Black Streetcorner Men. LC 78-1879. (Studies of Urban Society). 1978. lib. bdg. 20.00 (*0-226-01953-5*) U Ch Pr.

— A Place on the Corner: Identity & Rank among Black Streetcorner Men. LC 78-1879. (Studies of Urban Society). 248p. 1981. pap. text 10.95 (*0-226-01954-3*) U Ch Pr.

— Streetwise: Race, Class, & Change in An Urban Community. LC 90-34048. (Illus.). 288p. 1990. 23.95 (*0-226-01815-6*) U Ch Pr.

— Streetwise: Race, Class, & Change in an Urban Community. LC 90-18646. 288p. 1992. pap. 13.00 (*0-226-01816-4*) U Ch Pr.

Anderson, Elisabeth, et al. Cabin Comments: A Journal of Life in Jackson Hole. LC 80-53090. (Illus.). 286p. (gr. 7-12). 1980. 14.75 (*0-933160-08-9*); pap. 7.75 (*0-933160-09-7*) Teton Bkshop.

***Anderson, Elizabeth.** My Bondage & My Freedom. (Illus.). 244p. 1999. pap. 14.95 (*1-881524-57-4*, Pub. by Milligan Bks) Baker & Taylor.

Anderson, Elizabeth. Value in Ethics & Economics. 1993. text 43.50 (*0-674-93189-0*) HUP.

— Value in Ethics & Economics. LC 93-365. 261p. 1993. 35.00 (*0-674-09732-7*) HUP.

— Value in Ethics & Economics. 264p. 1995. pap. text 19.50 (*0-674-93190-4*) HUP.

Anderson, Elizabeth, ed. How to Potty Train Your Parrot in 14 Days: Communicate with, Understand & Train Your Parrot. rev. ed. (Illus.). 112p. 1997. mass mkt. 15.99 (*0-9657330-0-9*) L Andreoli.

Anderson, Elizabeth & Emmons, Pauline. Unlocking the Mysteries of Sensory Dysfunction. 91p. (Orig.). 1996. pap. 19.95 (*1-885477-25-2*) Fut Horizons.

Anderson, Elizabeth, ed. see Anderson, Emily.

Anderson, Elizabeth, ed. see Robbins, Roland.

Anderson, Elizabeth A. Colour All My Wings: A Poetry Journal. LC 98-221669. 140p. 1998. pap. text 8.95 (*1-896867-05-7*) Moulin Publ.

Anderson, Elizabeth B. Annapolis: A Walk Through History. LC 83-40548. (Illus.). 152p. 1984. pap. 9.95 (*0-87033-311-9*, Tidewtr Pubs) Cornell Maritime.

Anderson, Elizabeth L., ed. Newspaper Libraries in the U. S. & Canada: An SLA Directory. LC 80-25188. 331p. reprint ed. pap. 102.70 (*0-7837-6301-8*, 204601600010) Bks Demand.

Anderson, Elizabeth T. & McFarlane, Judith. Community As Partner: Theory & Practice in Nursing. 2nd ed. LC 95-14909. 496p. 1995. pap. text 29.95 (*0-397-55088-X*) Lppncott W & W.

Anderson, Elizabeth T. & McFarlane, Judith M. Community As Partner: Theory & Practice in Nursing. 3rd ed. 484p. pap. text. write for info. (*0-7817-2125-3*) Lppncott W & W.

Anderson, Elizabeth Y. Faith in the Furnace. LC 84-72818. (Illus.). 1985. 10.00 (*0-9614002-0-X*) E Y Anderson.

Anderson, Ella J. The Teacher's Friend. 1970. pap. 3.10 (*0-87813-905-2*) Christian Light.

Anderson, Ellen K. Pregnancy Workbook. (Illus.). 96p. (Orig.). 1983. pap. 8.95 (*0-939374-01-3*) Homefront Graphics.

***Anderson, Ellen M. & Williamsen, Amy R., eds.** Ingeniosa Invencion: Essays on Golden Age Spanish Literature for Geoffrey L. Stagg in Honor of His Eighty-Fifth Birthday. (Homenajes Ser.: Vol. 14). 285p. 1999. 23.00 (*0-936388-83-8*) Juan de la Cuesta.

***Anderson, Ellen Moore.** As Long as the Moon Shall Rise. (Illus.). 80p. 2000. 16.95 (*0-930100-94-8*, Pub. by Holy Cow) Consort Bk Sales.

Anderson, Elliott, jt. ed. see Hayman, David.

Anderson Embree, Jean. A Practical English Grammar: A Sentence-to-Paragraph Approach. LC 95-10619. (Illus.). 336p. 1996. pap. text 38.95 (*1-55934-348-6*, 1348) Mayfield Pub.

Anderson, Emily. All-American Comfort Food: Recipes for the Great-Tasting Food Everyone Loves. Anderson, Elizabeth, ed. LC 96-49095. 304p. (Orig.). 1997. pap. 17.95 (*1-888952-32-6*) Cumberland Hse.

— The Letters of Mozart & His Family. 2nd rev. ed. (Illus.). 1986. 75.00 (*0-393-02248-X*) Norton.

Anderson, Enoch & Bellas, Henry H. Personal Recollections of Captain Enoch Anderson, an Officer of the Delaware Regiments in the Revolutionary War. LC 76-140851. (Eyewitness Accounts of the American Revolution Ser.). 1971. reprint ed. 14.95 (*0-405-01221-7*) Ayer.

Anderson, Enrique I. Spanish-American Literature: A History, Vol. 2. 2nd ed. LC 70-75087. (Waynebook Ser.: Vol. 29). 370p. reprint ed. pap. 114.70 (*0-608-10502-3*, 203203300078) Bks Demand.

Anderson, Eric. Structuring IDBs: A Guide to Conventional & Innovative IDB Financing. Murphy, Jenny & Kailo, Andrea, eds. 24p. (Orig.). 1985. pap. 16.00 (*0-317-04903-8*) Natl Coun Econ Dev.

***Anderson, Eric.** Trailblazing: The True Story of America's First Openly Gay Track Coach. LC 99-88235. 210p. 2000. pap. 13.95 (*1-55583-524-4*, Pub. by Alyson Pubns) Consort Bk Sales.

Anderson, Eric. Training Games: Coaching Runners Creatively. 2nd ed. LC 97-150950. (Illus.). 152p. (Orig.). 1996. pap. 15.00 (*0-911521-47-X*) Tafnews.

***Anderson, Eric & Moss, Alfred A., Jr.** Dangerous Donations: Northern Philanthropy & Southern Black Education, 1902-1930. LC 99-28263. (Illus.). 264p. 1999. 34.95 (*0-8262-1226-3*) U of Mo Pr.

Anderson, Eric & Moss, Alfred A., Jr., eds. The Facts of Reconstruction: Essays in Honor of John Hope Franklin. LC 90-47141. 264p. 1991. text 37.50 (*0-8071-1666-1*) La State U Pr.

— The Facts of Reconstruction: Essays in Honor of John Hope Franklin. LC 90-47141. 264p. 1991. pap. text 18.95 (*0-8071-1691-2*) La State U Pr.

Anderson, Eric G. American Indian Literature & the Southwest. LC 98-24862. (Illus.). 228p. 1999. pap. 17.95 (*0-292-70488-7*) U of Tex Pr.

Anderson, Eric S. Medical Consultations - Practice, Methods, Preferences, Importance & Necessity: Index of New Information with Authors & Subjects. 180p. 1993. 47.50 (*1-55914-910-8*); pap. 44.50 (*1-55914-911-6*) ABBE Pubs Assn.

Anderson, Erik, et al, eds. Performance of HUD Assisted Properties During the January 17, 1994 Northridge Earthquake. (Illus.). 47p. 1998. pap. text 30.00 (*0-7881-4161-9*) DIANE Pub.

Anderson, Erin, ed. Campus Use of the Teaching Portfolio: Twenty-Five Profiles. 120p. 1993. pap. 15.00 (*1-56377-027-X*, TI9301) Am Assn Higher Ed.

Anderson, Erland, tr. see Aggestam, Rolf.

Anderson, Ernest C. & Sullivan, Elizabeth M., eds. Impact of Energy Production on Human Health: An Evaluation of Means for Assessment: Proceedings. LC 76-22540. (ERDA Symposium Ser.). 154p. 1976. pap. 11.75 (*0-87079-032-3*, CONF-751022); fiche 9.00 (*0-87079-245-8*, CONF-751022) DOE.

Anderson, Ernest L. & Morgan, James P. The Systems Purchasing Breakthrough. (Illus.). 216p. 1999. pap. write for info. (*0-9644791-0-9*, Purchasing Mag) Cahners Business.

Anderson, Eskil. Asbestos & Jade in the Kobuk River Region of Alaska. (Shorey Prospecting Ser.). 26p. reprint ed. pap. 10.00 (*0-8466-0037-4*, S37) Shoreys Bkstore.

Anderson, Esther, et al. Bible Crafts. LC 97-221776. (Illus.). 48p. (J). 1997. write for info. (*0-7853-2328-7*) Pubns Intl Ltd.

Anderson, Eugene. The Chumash Indians of Southern California. 1973. pap. 2.00 (*0-939046-13-X*) Malki Mus Pr.

Anderson, Eugene, et al. Self Esteem for Tots to Teens. LC 90-92130. 1991. pap. 8.95 (*1-879276-00-3*) Parent Tching Pubns.

Anderson, Eugene N. Ecologies of the Heart: Emotion, Belief & the Environment. 272p. 1996. 30.00 (*0-19-509010-1*) OUP.

Anderson, Eugene N., ed. see Kehr, Eckart.

Anderson, Evan. Middle East. LC 99-49755. 400p. (C). 1998. 99.99 (*0-415-07667-6*); pap. 29.99 (*0-415-07668-4*) Routledge.

Anderson, Evelyn M., jt. ed. see Carney, Andrew L.

Anderson, Evert. Verb Complementation in Written English. 292p. (Orig.). 1985. pap. text 35.00 (*0-614-03099-4*) Coronet Bks.

Anderson, Ewan, ed. In Loco Parentis: Training Issues in Boarding & Residential Environments. 224p. 1994. pap. 32.00 (*1-85346-328-0*, Pub. by David Fulton) Taylor & Francis.

Anderson, Ewan W. Strategic Minerals: The Geopolitical Problems for the United States. LC 88-12028. 172p. 1988. 57.95 (*0-275-93062-9*, C3062, Praeger Pubs) Greenwood.

— The Structure & Dynamics of U. S. Government Policymaking: The Case of Strategic Minerals. LC 88-11757. 239p. 1988. 59.95 (*0-275-93061-0*, C3061, Praeger Pubs) Greenwood.

Anderson, Ewan W. & Anderson, Liam D. Strategic Minerals: Resource Geopolitics & Global Geo-Economics. LC 97-34183. 180p. 1997. 100.00 (*0-471-97402-1*) Wiley.

Anderson, Ewan W. & Davison, Alan J., eds. Applying the Children Act in Boarding & Residential Environments, 1989. 208p. 1993. pap. 36.00 (*1-85346-257-8*, Pub. by David Fulton) Taylor & Francis.

Anderson, Ewan W. & Dupree, Nancy H. The Cultural Basis of Afghan Nationalism. 256p. 1990. text 49.00 (*0-86187-869-8*) St Martin.

Anderson, Ewan W., et al. Economic Power in a Changing International System. LC 99-22983. 1999. 26.95 (*1-85567-633-8*) CRC Pr.

Anderson, F. J., jt. ed. see Freier, G. D.

Anderson, Farris. Alfonso Sastre. LC 78-125251. (Twayne's World Authors Ser.). 1971. lib. bdg. 20.95 (*0-8057-2802-3*) Irvington.

— One Man - Unconquered. (Illus.). 175p. 1998. pap. 19.95 (*0-9663207-1-9*) F Anderson.

Anderson, Florence M. Religious Cults Associated with the Amazons. LC 73-158253. reprint ed. 37.50 (*0-404-00749-X*) AMS Pr.

Anderson, Fran, ed. see Maass, Eliezer.

Anderson, Frances E. Art-Centered Education & Therapy for Children with Disabilities. LC 93-33203. (Illus.). 284p. 1994. pap. 35.95 (*0-398-06006-1*) C C Thomas.

— Art-Centered Education & Therapy for Children with Disabilities. LC 93-33203. (Illus.). 284p. (C). 1994. text 49.95 (*0-398-05896-2*) C C Thomas.

— Art for All the Children: Approaches to Art Therapy for Children with Disabilities. 2nd ed. (Illus.). 398p. 1992. pap. 48.95 (*0-398-06007-X*) C C Thomas.

— Art for All the Children: Approaches to Art Therapy for Children with Disabilities. 2nd ed. (Illus.). 398p. (C). 1992. text 69.95 (*0-398-05797-4*) C C Thomas.

Anderson, Frances J. Classroom Newspaper Activities: A Resource for Teachers, Grades K-8. (Illus.). 276p. 1985. pap., spiral bd. 37.95 (*0-398-05145-3*) C C Thomas.

Anderson, Frances S., jt. ed. see Aron, Lewis.

Anderson, Francis D. Commentary about the Book of Revelation. 170p. 1996. pap. text 17.50 (*0-9655450-0-3*) F & R Enterprises.

Anderson, Francis I. Hosea. LC 73-9008. (Anchor Bible Ser.: Vol. 24). 720p. 1980. 44.95 (*0-385-00768-X*) Doubleday.

Anderson, Frank. Cultivated Flowers. (Illus.). 1996. pap. 4.95 (*0-89659-182-4*) Abbeville Pr.

— Orchids. (Illus.). 1996. pap. 4.95 (*0-89659-122-0*) Abbeville Pr.

— Southwest Seminar on Energy & Economic Development. 117p. 1989. pap. 5.00 (*0-936440-79-1*) U TX SUPA.

Anderson, Frank, ed. see Allen, Virginia.

Anderson, Frank J., ed. The Illustrated Bartsch Vol. 90: Herbals Through 1500. (Illus.). 1985. 149.00 (*0-89835-059-X*) Abaris Bks.

— The Illustrated Bartsch Vol. 90, Commentary: Herbals Through 1500. 1985. lib. bdg. 149.00 (*0-89835-189-8*) Abaris Bks.

***Anderson, Frank W.** Bill Miner: Stagecoach & Train Robber. 4th ed. (Illus.). 64p. 2000. reprint ed. pap. 7.95 (*1-894384-04-0*, Pub. by Heritage Hse) Midpt Trade.

Anderson, Frank W. Border Bank Bandits: Living History of the West. 88p. 1990. pap. 7.95 (*0-88839-255-9*) Hancock House.

— The Rum Runners. Spalding, Jane, ed. 64p. 1991. pap. 5.95 (*0-919433-22-7*) Lone Pine.

Anderson, Frank W. & Fuller, Kent R. Rings & Categories of Modules. 2nd ed. Ewing, J. H. et al, eds. LC 92-10019. (Graduate Texts in Mathematics Ser.: Vol. 13). 392p. 1992. 59.95 (*0-387-97845-3*) Spr-Verlag.

Anderson, Franklin K., jt. auth. see Treshow, Michael.

Anderson, Franz. Introductory Oceanography. 3rd ed. 326p. (C). 1998. pap. text 39.95 (*0-7872-5458-4*, 41545801); spiral bd., lab manual ed. 35.95 (*0-7872-5459-2*) Kendall-Hunt.

— Lobstah: A Board Game. 3rd ed. 60p. (C). 1998. 35.95 (*0-7872-5460-6*) Kendall-Hunt.

Anderson, Fred. Celebrating Your Church's Anniversary. Deweese, Charles W., ed. (Resource Kit for Your Church's History Ser.). 8p. 1984. pap. 0.60 (*0-939804-23-9*) Hist Comm S Baptist.

***Anderson, Fred.** Crucible of War: The Seven Years' War & the Fate of Empire in British North America, 1754-1766. LC 99-18512. (Illus.). 960p. 2000. 40.00 (*0-375-40642-5*) Knopf.

Anderson, Fred. A People's Army: Massachusetts Soldiers & Society in the Seven Years' War. 292p. (C). 1996. pap. text 16.95 (*0-8078-4576-0*) U of NC Pr.

— A People's Army: Massachusetts Soldiers & Society in the Seven Years' War. LC 84-2344. (Illus.). 292p. 1984. reprint ed. pap. 90.60 (*0-7837-9890-3*, 206061600006) Bks Demand.

— The Traditional Way: The Mystic & Heritage of Archery. (Illus.). 269p. 1997. per. 19.95 (*0-9651617-0-6*) Tox Press.

Anderson, Frederick, ed. Mark Twain. (Critical Heritage Ser.). 364p. (C). 1997. 140.00 (*0-415-15932-6*) Routledge.

Anderson, Frederick, ed. see Hempl, George.

Anderson, Frederick, ed. see Twain, Mark, pseud.

Anderson, Frederick R. & Daniels, Robert H. NEPA in the Courts: A Legal Analysis of the National Environmental Policy Act. 324p. 1973. pap. 23.95 (*0-8018-1559-2*) Resources Future.

Anderson, Frederick R., et al. Environmental Improvement Through Economic Incentives. LC 76-47400. 195p. 1977. 19.95 (*0-8018-2000-6*) Resources Future.

— Environmental Improvement Through Economic Incentives. LC 76-47400. 195p. 1978. pap. 12.95 (*0-8018-2100-2*) Resources Future.

— Environmental Protection: Law & Policy. LC 83-82691. 1127p. (C). 1984. 37.00 (*0-316-03950-0*) Aspen Pub.

— Environmental Protection: Law & Policy. 2nd ed. 960p. 1990. teacher ed. write for info. (*0-316-03962-4*, 39624) Aspen Law.

— Environmental Protection: Selected Statutes with New Cases: 1991 Edition. 704p. 1991. pap. text 27.95 (*0-316-03943-8*, 39438) Aspen Law.

***Anderson, Freedolph.** Build Bone Health: Prevent & Treat Osteoporosis. LC 99-61964. 1999. pap. 7.95 (*1-890694-22-3*) IMPAKT Communs.

Anderson, Fulton H. Francis Bacon: His Career & His Thought. LC 77-18070. (Aresnberg Lectures: 2nd Ser. 1957). 367p. 1978. reprint ed. lib. bdg. 85.00 (*0-313-20108-0*, ANFB, Greenwood Pr) Greenwood.

Anderson, Fulton H., ed. The New Organon: Bacon. 336p. (C). 1960. pap. text 14.00 (*0-02-303380-0*, Macmillan Coll) P-H.

Anderson, G. Channel Tunnel Story. (Illus.). 240p. 1994. pap. 35.00 (*0-419-19620-X*, E & FN Spon) Routledge.

— Fundamentals in Educational Research. 2nd ed. LC 98-166855. 266p. 1998. text 79.95 (*0-7507-0858-1*) Taylor & Francis.

Anderson, G., jt. auth. see Bryant, Barbara.

Anderson, G. A. Surgery with Coefficients. (Lecture Notes in Mathematics Ser.: Vol. 591). 1977. 13.00 (*3-540-08250-6*) Spr-Verlag.

Anderson, G. H. African Safaris. (Illus.). 173p. 1997. 35.00 (*1-57157-074-8*) Safari Pr.

***Anderson, G. Harvey.** Nutritional Implications of Macronutrient Substitutes. 1999. pap. text 24.95 (*0-8018-6212-4*) Johns Hopkins.

Anderson, G. Harvey, et al, eds. Nutritional Implications of Macronutrient Substitutes, Vol. 819. LC 97-19405. 1997. 95.00 (*1-57331-084-0*) NY Acad Sci.

Anderson, G. Harvey, et al. Nutritional Implications of Macronutrient Substitutes. LC 97-19405. (Annals of the New York Academy of Sciences Ser.: Vol. 819). 1997. pap. 95.00 (*1-57331-085-9*) NY Acad Sci.

Anderson, G. L., ed. Masterpieces of the Orient. expanded ed. (C). 1976. pap. text 46.00 (*0-393-09196-1*) Norton.

Anderson, G. L., jt. ed. see Tzou, H. S.

A

An Asterisk (*) at the beginning of an entry indicates that the title is appearing for the first time.

Anderson, G. M. Thermodynamics of Natural Systems. LC 95-23040. 400p. (C). 1995. pap. 37.95 (*0-471-10943-6*) Wiley.

Anderson, G. Norman. Sudan in Crisis: The Failure of Democracy. LC 98-54870. 1999. 49.95 (*0-8130-1671-1*) U Press Fla.

Anderson, G. W. The History & Religion of Israel. (New Clarendon Bible Ser.). (Illus.). 222p. 1975. pap. 18.95 (*0-19-836915-8*) OUP.

— Tradition & Interpretation. 1979. 59.00 (*0-19-826315-5*) OUP.

***Anderson, Gabriella.** Destiny Coin: A Matter of Convenience. (Ballad Romances Ser.). 2000. mass mkt. 5.50 (*0-8217-6682-1*, Zebra Kensgtn) Kensgtn Pub Corp.

Anderson, Gail. Learning & Using C++ LC 97-27828. 800p. (C). 1997. pap. text 49.95 (*0-13-532748-2*) P-H.

Anderson, Gail, ed. Museum Mission Statements: Building a Distinct Identity. (Professional Practice Ser.). 137p. 1998. pap. 25.00 (*0-931201-41-1*) Am Assn Mus.

Anderson, Gail & Anderson, Paul. The UNIX C Shell Field Guide. (Illus.). 374p. (C). 1986. pap. text 44.95 (*0-13-937468-X*) P-H.

Anderson, Gail & Hill, Marcia, eds. Children's Rights, Therapists' Responsibilities: Feminist Commentaries. LC 97-5226. 141p. 1997. 34.95 (*0-7890-0326-0*); pap. 19.95 (*1-56023-100-9*, Harrington Park) Haworth Pr.

Anderson, Gail S., jt. auth. see Anderson, Hal W.

***Anderson, Gale.** Cultural Geography: Australian Publication. 2nd ed. 1999. pap. text. write for info. (*0-582-81086-8*) Addison-Wesley.

Anderson Galleries, New York Staff. Forum Exhibition of Modern American Painters. LC 68-9240. (Contemporary Art Ser.). (Illus.). 1968. reprint ed. 7.00 (*0-405-00722-1*) Ayer.

Anderson, Garrett. Brennan's Book. 1976. 25.00 (*0-8464-0207-6*) Beekman Pubs.

Anderson, Gary, ed. Courage to Care: Responding to the Crisis of Children with AIDS. 1990. pap. 15.95 (*0-87868-401-8*) Child Welfare.

Anderson, Gary, et al, eds. Children & HIV/AIDS. LC 98-29901. 271p. 1999. pap. 22.95 (*0-7658-0488-3*) Transaction Pubs.

Anderson, Gary, jt. auth. see Heinerman, John.

Anderson, Gary, jt. compiled by see Goldstone, Richard H.

Anderson, Gary A. Floral Design & Marketing. 2nd ed. King, Muriel N., ed. (Illus.). 510p. 1995. 49.95 (*1-56502-009-X*, 9516M) Ohio Agri Educ.

— A Time to Mourn, a Time to Dance: The Expression of Grief & Joy in Israelite Religion. 152p. 1991. 32.50 (*0-271-00729-X*) Pa St U Pr.

Anderson, Gary A. & Olyan, Saul M., eds. Priesthood & Cult in Ancient Israel. (Journal for the Study of the Old Testament Supplement Ser.: No. 125). 217p. (C). 1991. 60.00 (*1-85075-322-9*, Pub. by Sheffield Acad) CUP Services.

Anderson, Gary C. Kinsmen of Another Kind: Dakota-White Relations in the Upper Mississippi Valley, 1650-1862. LC 83-23411. 399p. 1984. reprint ed. pap. 123.70 (*0-608-02778-2*, 206384500007) Bks Demand.

— Kinsmen of Another Kind: Dakota-White Relations in the Upper Mississippi Valley, 1650-1862. LC 97-3712. (Borealis Bks.). (Illus.). xxxii, 383p. 1997. reprint ed. pap. 15.95 (*0-87351-353-3*) Minn Hist.

— Little Crow, Spokesman for the Sioux. LC 86-795. (Illus.). 259p. (Orig.). 1986. pap. 11.95 (*0-87351-196-4*) Minn Hist.

Anderson, Gary C., ed. see Woolworth, Alan R.

Anderson, Gary Clayton. Indian Southwest, 1580-1830: Ethnogenesis & Reinvention. LC 98-45331. 1999. 39.95 (*0-8061-3111-X*) U of Okla Pr.

— Sitting Bull & the Paradox of Lakota Nationhood. (Library of American Biography Ser.). 192p. (C). 1997. pap. 20.20 (*0-06-501033-7*) Addson-Wesley Educ.

Anderson, Gary D., ed. see Abbott, Dan.

***Anderson, Gary G.** Austin-Healey 100, 100-6, 3000 Restoration Guide. (Authentic Restoration Guides Ser.). (Illus.). 192p. 2000. pap. write for info. (*0-7603-0673-7*, 129991AP, Pub. by MBI Pubg) Motorbooks Intl.

Anderson, Gary H. Video Editing & Post-Production: A Professional Guide. 4th ed. LC 98-18276. 244p. 1998. pap. 34.95 (*0-240-80337-X*, Focal) Buttrwrth-Heinemann.

Anderson, Gary L. Solving Alcohol Drug Problems in Your School: Why Student Assistance Programs Work. 32p. 1988. pap. 3.25 (*0-935908-44-7*, 3177, HazeldenJohnson Inst) Hazelden.

— Enabling in the School Setting. 40p. 1988. pap. 3.25 (*0-935908-43-9*, 3175, HazeldenJohnson Inst) Hazelden.

— Intervening with Parents. (Illus.). 128p. (Orig.). (C). 1993. pap. 24.95 (*0-9618023-4-0*) Community Rec Pr.

— When Chemicals Come to School: The Core Team Model of Student Assistance Programs. 3rd rev. ed. (Illus.). 452p. (Orig.). 1993. pap. 34.95 (*0-9618023-5-9*) Community Rec Pr.

Anderson, Gary L. & Montero-Sieburth, Martha, eds. Educational Qualitative Research in Latin America: The Struggle for a New Paradigm. LC 97-22805. (Studies In Education & Culture: Vol. 11). 268p. 1997. pap. text 72.00 (*0-8153-1353-5*, H1751) Garland.

Anderson, Gary L., et al. Studying Your Own School: An Educator's Guide to Qualitative Practitioner Research. LC 94-30532. (Illus.). 232p. 1994. 61.95 (*0-8039-6113-8*); pap. 27.95 (*0-8039-6114-6*) Corwin Pr.

Anderson, Gary L., jt. ed. see Blase, Joseph R.

Anderson, Gary R., ed. Courage to Care: Responding to the Crisis of Children with AIDS. 1990. 24.95 (*0-87868-384-4*, 3844) Child Welfare.

Anderson, Gary R., et al, eds. The Challenge of Permanency Planning in a Multicultural Society. LC 97-1461. 215p. 1997. pap. 19.95 (*0-7890-0302-3*) Haworth Pr.

— The Challenge of Permanency Planning in a Multicultural Society. LC 97-1461. 215p. 1997. 49.95 (*0-7890-0034-2*) Haworth Pr.

***Anderson, Gavin W., ed.** Rights & Democracy: Essays in UK-Canadian Constitutionalism. (Law in Its Social Setting Ser.). 276p. 1999. 36.00 (*1-85431-705-9*, Pub. by Blackstone Pr) Gaunt.

Anderson, Gene. Coyote Space. (Kestrel Ser.: No. 6). 28p. 1983. pap. 3.00 (*0-914974-38-6*) Holmgangers.

Anderson, Gene C., jt. ed. see Raff, Beverly S.

Anderson, Genevieve, jt. ed. see Miller, John.

Anderson, Geoff, et al. Learning Contracts. 192p. 1996. pap. 29.95 (*0-7494-1847-8*, Kogan Pg Educ) Stylus Pub VA.

***Anderson, George.** American Hard-Boiled Crime Writers. LC 00-28761. (Dictionary of Literary Biography Ser.). 400p. 2000. text 204.75 (*0-7876-3133-7*) Gale.

***Anderson, George & Barone, Andrew.** Lessons from the Light: Extraordinary Messages of Comfort & Hope from the Other Side. 336p. 2000. pap. text 12.95 (*0-425-17416-6*) Berkley Pub.

Anderson, George & Barone, Andrew. Lessons from the Light: Extraordinary Messages of Love & Comfort from the Other Side. LC 98-56039. 320p. 1999. 23.95 (*0-399-14510-9*, G P Putnam) Peng Put Young Read.

Anderson, George, jt. auth. see Berson, Alex.

Anderson, George A. Winning: A Race Driver's Handbook. (Illus.). 192p. 1993. pap. 19.95 (*0-87938-776-9*) MBI Pubg.

Anderson, George B. Landmarks of Rensselaer County, New York, (with Biographies & Genealogies) (Illus.). 1195p. 1992. reprint ed. lib. bdg. 109.00 (*0-8328-2446-1*) Higginson Bk Co.

— One Hundred Booming Years. Row, H. J. & Stupek, D., eds. LC 80-65338. (Illus.). 305p. 1980. 55.00 (*0-9604136-0-X*) Bucyrus-Erie Co.

Anderson, George B., jt. auth. see Saratogian Staff.

***Anderson, George C.** What Christians Believe. (Illus.). 64p. 1999. pap. text 10.95 (*1-57895-035-X*) Curriculm Presbytrn KY.

Anderson, George E., jt. auth. see Hickey, Patrick M.

Anderson, George K. Breadloaf School of English: The First Fifty Years. 1969. pap. 3.50 (*0-910408-15-7*) Coll Store.

Anderson, George K., tr. The Saga of the Volsungs. LC 80-65685. 272p. 1982. 38.50 (*0-87413-172-3*) U Delaware Pr.

Anderson, George K. & Buckler, William E. Literature England Single Vol Edition. 3rd ed. 1263p. (C). 1999. 95.00 (*0-673-15155-7*) Addison-Wesley Educ.

Anderson, George L. Essays in Kansas History: In Memorium. Williams, Burton J., ed. 1977. 10.00 (*0-87291-086-5*) Coronado Pr.

— Essays on the History of Banking. 217p. 1972. 10.00 (*0-87291-037-7*) Coronado Pr.

Anderson, George W. Client/Server Databases with SYBASE: A High Performance & Fine Tuning Guide. (Illus.). 580p. 1996. 55.00 (*0-07-001697-6*) McGraw.

— Using Datablades. (McGraw Hill Series on Data Warehousing). (Illus.). 312p. 1997. pap. text 39.95 (*0-07-001737-9*) McGraw.

Anderson, George W., Jr., tr. from NOR. Early Records of the LeSueur River Church of Waseca & Steele Counties, Minnesota. LC 93-26426. (Illus.). 54p. 1993. pap. 7.50 (*0-915709-09-0*) Pk Geneal Bk.

Anderson, Georgene, jt. auth. see Anderson, Raymond.

Anderson, Gerald. The Uffda Trial. 202p. 1995. pap. 9.95 (*0-9613437-3-7*, Martin Hse Pubns) Redbird Prods.

Anderson, Gerald & Frost, Robert. All for Strings: Conductor, Bk. 3: Cello. 1990. 4.95 (*0-8497-3306-5*, 80CO) Kjos.

— All for Strings: Conductor, Bk. 3: Piano Accompaniment. 1990. 4.95 (*0-8497-3308-1*, 80PA) Kjos.

— All for Strings: Conductor, Bk. 3: String Bass. 1990. 4.95 (*0-8497-3307-3*, 80SB) Kjos.

— All for Strings: Conductor, Bk. 3: Viola. 1990. 4.95 (*0-8497-3305-7*, 80VA) Kjos.

— All for Strings: Conductor, Bk. 3: Violin. 1990. 4.95 (*0-8497-3304-9*, 80VN) Kjos.

— All for Strings: Conductor Score, Bk. 1: Cello. 1985. 4.95 (*0-8497-3224-7*, 78CO) Kjos.

— All for Strings: Conductor Score, Bk. 1: Piano Accompaniment. 1985. 4.95 (*0-8497-3227-1*, 78PA) Kjos.

— All for Strings: Conductor Score, Bk. 1: Score. 1985. 14.95 (*0-8497-3226-3*, 78F) Kjos.

— All for Strings: Conductor Score, Bk. 1: String Bass. 1985. 4.95 (*0-8497-3225-5*, 78SB) Kjos.

— All for Strings: Conductor Score, Bk. 1: Viola. 1985. 4.95 (*0-8497-3223-9*, 78VA) Kjos.

— All for Strings: Conductor Score, Bk. 1: Violin. 1985. 4.95 (*0-8497-3222-0*, 78VN) Kjos.

— All for Strings: Conductor Score, Bk. 3: Score. 180p. 1991. 14.95 (*0-8497-3309-X*, 80F) Kjos.

— All for Strings Bk. 2: Conductor Score. 208p. 1987. 14.95 (*0-8497-3240-9*, 79F) Kjos.

— All for Strings Bk. 2: Conductor Score, Piano Accompaniment. 180p. 1988. 4.95 (*0-8497-3239-5*, 79PA) Kjos.

— All for Strings Conductor Score Bk. 2: Cello. 180p. 1986. 4.95 (*0-8497-3237-9*, 79CO) Kjos.

— All for Strings Conductor Score Bk. 2: String Bass. 180p. 1987. 4.95 (*0-8497-3238-7*, 79SB) Kjos.

— All for Strings Conductor Score Bk. 2: Viola. 180p. 1987. 4.95 (*0-8497-3236-0*, 79VA) Kjos.

— All for Strings Conductor Score Bk. 2: Violin. 180p. 1986. 4.95 (*0-8497-3235-2*, 79VN) Kjos.

— All for Strings Theory No. 1: Cello. 32p. 1988. wbk. ed. 3.45 (*0-8497-3248-4*, 84CO) Kjos.

— All for Strings Theory No. 1: Conductor Answer Key. 32p. 1989. wbk. ed. 3.45 (*0-8497-3265-4*, 84F) Kjos.

— All for Strings Theory No. 1: String Bass. 32p. 1987. wbk. ed. 3.45 (*0-8497-3249-2*, 84SB) Kjos.

— All for Strings Theory No. 1: Viola. 32p. 1987. wbk. ed. 3.45 (*0-8497-3247-6*, 84VA) Kjos.

— All for Strings Theory No. 1: Violin. 32p. 1987. wbk. ed. 3.45 (*0-8497-3246-8*, 84VN) Kjos.

— All for Strings Theory No. 2: Cello. 32p. 1988. wbk. ed. 3.45 (*0-8497-3252-2*, 85CO) Kjos.

— All for Strings Theory No. 2: Conductor Answer Key. 32p. 1988. wbk. ed. 3.45 (*0-8497-3266-2*, 85F) Kjos.

— All for Strings Theory No. 2: String Bass. 32p. 1988. wbk. ed. 3.45 (*0-8497-3253-0*, 85SB) Kjos.

— All for Strings Theory No. 2: Violin. 32p. 1988. wbk. ed. 3.45 (*0-8497-3250-6*, 85VN) Kjos.

Anderson, Gerald H. Asian Voices in Christian Theology. LC 75-13795. 333p. reprint ed. pap. 103.30 (*0-8357-5790-0*, 202511500042) Bks Demand.

Anderson, Gerald H., ed. Biographical Dictionary of Christian Missions. LC 99-28087. 873p. 1999. pap. 50.00 (*0-8028-4680-7*) Eerdmans.

Anderson, Gerald H., et al, eds. Mission Legacies: Biographical Studies of Leaders of the Modern Missionary Movements. LC 94-16771. (American Society of Missiology Ser.: Vol. 19). 640p. 1994. 38.00 (*0-88344-964-1*) Orbis Bks.

Anderson, Gerald H. & Stransky, Thomas F., eds. Christ's Lordship & Religious Pluralism. LC 80-25406. 224p. (Orig.). reprint ed. pap. 69.50 (*0-7837-5513-9*, 204528300005) Bks Demand.

Anderson, Gerald L., jt. auth. see Hadden, David M.

Anderson, Gerald R. Sons of Disobedience, 2 vols. 340p. 1998. pap. 19.95 (*0-9662015-0-7*) Marvin Bks.

Anderson, Gerard F. Providing Hospital Services: The Changing Financial Environment. LC 89-1855. (Johns Hopkins Studies in Health Care Finance & Administration: No. 2). (Illus.). 246p. 1989. reprint ed. pap. 76.30 (*0-608-05922-6*, 206625800008) Bks Demand.

Anderson, Geri. Any Body Can Hiking Guide: Routt County Trails, My 15 Favorite Day Hikes Near Steamboat Springs, Colorado. (Illus.). 46p. (Orig.). 1994. pap. 5.00 (*1-883546-03-6*) Trail Finders.

— Come Walk in Their Footsteps: The Flat Tops Trail Scenic Byway. 58p. 1993. pap. 7.95 (*1-883546-00-1*) Trail Finders.

— Cross-Country Ski Trails Near Steamboat Springs. (Illus.). 75p. 1993. pap. 7.95 (*1-883546-02-8*) Trail Finders.

Anderson, Geroge, jt. auth. see Berson, Alex.

Anderson, Gillian B. Music in New York During the American Revolution: An Inventory of Musical References in Rivington's New York Gazette. (Music Library Association Index & Bibliography Ser.: No. 24). 135p. 1987. pap. 15.00 (*0-914954-33-4*) Scarecrow.

Anderson, Gillian B., ed. Freedom's Voice in Poetry & Song. LC 77-78353. 888p. 1977. 85.00 (*0-8420-2124-8*) Scholarly Res Inc.

Anderson, Girard F., jt. auth. see Leer, Steven F.

Anderson, Glen D., et al. Conformal Invariants, Inequalities & Quasiconformal Maps. LC 97-13356. (Canadian Mathematical Society Ser.). 505p. 1997. 109.95 (*0-471-59486-5*) Wiley.

Anderson, Glenn, jt. auth. see Anderson, Diane.

Anderson, Glenn L. The Doomsday Factor. LC 87-82113. 160p. 1987. 11.98 (*0-88290-319-5*) Horizon Utah.

Anderson, Glenn P., ed. Covenant Roots: Sources & Affirmations. Jansson, Fred O. et al, trs. from SWE. 238p. (Orig.). 1980. pap. 7.95 (*0-910452-46-6*) Covenant.

***Anderson-Gold, Sharon.** Unnecessary Evil: History & Moral Progress in the Philosophy of Immanuel Kant. (C). 2000. pap. text 16.95 (*0-7914-4820-7*) State U NY Pr.

— Unnecessary Evil: History & Moral Progress in the Philosophy of Immanuel Kant. (C). 2001. text 49.50 (*0-7914-4819-3*) State U NY Pr.

Anderson, Gordon. Butterworths Employment Law Guide: New Zealand Edition. 863p. 1993. pap. 90.00 (*0-409-47051-1*, NZ, MICHIE) LEXIS Pub.

Anderson, Gordon, jt. auth. see Benedict, Bert.

Anderson, Gordon A. Latin Compositions in the Sixth Fasciale of the Notre-Dame Manuscript Wolfenbuttel 1099, Pt. 1. (Wissenschaftliche Abhandlungen-Musicological Studies: Vol. 24). 1981. lib. bdg. 67.00 (*0-931902-02-9*) Inst Mediaeval Mus.

— Latin Compositions in the Sixth Fasciale of the Notre-Dame Manuscript Wolfenbuttel 1099, Pt. 2. (Wissenschaftliche Abhandlungen-Musicological Studies: Vol. 24). 1981. lib. bdg. 67.00 (*0-931902-03-7*) Inst Mediaeval Mus.

Anderson, Gordon A., ed. Notre-Dame & Related Conductus. (Gesamtausgaben - Collected Works: Vol. X). 140p. lib. bdg. 94.00 (*0-937902-27-6*) Inst Mediaeval Mus.

— Notre-Dame & Related Conductus, Pt. 1. (Gesamtausgaben - Collected Works: Vol. X). 140p. 1981. lib. bdg. 85.00 (*0-931902-20-7*) Inst Mediaeval Mus.

— Notre-Dame & Related Conductus, Pt. 3. (Gesamtausgaben - Collected Works: Vol. X). 140p. 1981. lib. bdg. 94.00 (*0-912024-17-8*) Inst Mediaeval Mus.

— Notre-Dame & Related Conductus, Pt. 4. (Gesamtausgaben - Collected Works: Vol. X). 140p. lib. bdg. 94.00 (*0-937902-22-5*) Inst Mediaeval Mus.

— Notre-Dame & Related Conductus, Pt. 5. (Gesamtausgaben - Collected Works: Vol. X). 140p. 1981. lib. bdg. 60.00 (*0-931902-11-8*) Inst Mediaeval Mus.

— Notre-Dame & Related Conductus, Pt. 6. (Gesamtausgaben - Collected Works: Vol. X). 140p. 1981. lib. bdg. 94.00 (*0-912024-18-6*) Inst Mediaeval Mus.

Anderson, Gordon A. & Dittmer, Luther, eds. Canberra, Nan Kivell Collecton. (Veroffentlichungen Mittelalterlicher Musikhandschriften - Publications of Mediaeval Musical Manuscripts Ser.: Vol. 13). (ENG & GER.). 1981. lib. bdg. 47.00 (*0-912024-13-5*) Inst Mediaeval Mus.

Anderson, Gordon A., ed. see Tischler, Hans.

Anderson, Gordon L., ed. The Family in Global Transition. LC 97-2955. 540p. 1997. 29.95 (*1-885118-05-8*); pap. 19.95 (*1-885118-06-6*) Prof World Peace.

— Worldwide State of the Family: Reports & Observations Prepared for the 6th International Congress of Professors World Peace Academy. LC 96-18496. 222p. (Orig.). 1995. pap. 19.95 (*1-885118-00-7*) Prof World Peace.

Anderson, Gordon L. & Kaplan, Morton A., intros. Morality & Religion in Liberal Democratic Societies. LC 91-11309. 368p. (C). 1992. 24.95 (*0-943852-96-X*); pap. text 14.95 (*0-943852-97-8*) Prof World Peace.

Anderson, Gordon S. A Whole Language Approach to Reading. LC 84-13229. (Illus.). 642p. (Orig.). 1984. pap. text 43.50 (*0-8191-4197-6*) U Pr of Amer.

Anderson, Gordon T., ed. see Mitchell, Alice, et al.

Anderson-Gough, Fiona, et al, eds. Making up Accountants: The Organizational & Professional Socialization of Trainee Charted Accountants. (Institute of Charted Accountants Ser.). 147p. 1998. text 55.95 (*1-84014-539-0*, Pub. by Ashgate Pub) Ashgate Pub Co.

Anderson, Graham. Ancient Fiction: The Novel in the Graeco-Roman World. LC 84-12319. 256p. (C). 1984. 57.50 (*0-389-20516-8*, N8078) B&N Imports.

***Anderson, Graham.** Fairytale in the Ancient World. LC 00-29109. 2000. pap. write for info. (*0-415-23703-3*) Routledge.

Anderson, Graham. Philostratus: Biography & Belles-Lettres in the Third Century A. D. LC 85-28013. 352p. 1987. 57.00 (*0-7099-0575-0*, Pub. by C Helm) Routldge.

— Sage, Saint, & Sophist: Holy Men & Their Associates in the Early Roman Empire. LC 93-27965. 304p. (C). (gr. 13). 1994. 80.00 (*0-415-02372-6*) Routledge.

Anderson, Graham, tr. see Beaumarchais, Pierre De.

Anderson, Graham, tr. see Feydeau, Georges.

Anderson, Grant J. Genealogy in Part, of the Anderson-Owen-Beall Families. 159p. 1988. reprint ed. pap. 24.00 (*0-8328-0119-4*); reprint ed. lib. bdg. 32.00 (*0-8328-0118-6*) Higginson Bk Co.

Anderson, Greg. All a Parent Needs to Know about Homework. (Illus.). 8p. (Orig.). 1996. pap. 2.50 (*1-884241-75-1*, AN1022) Energeia Pub.

— Cancer: 50 Essential Things to Do Revised & Updated. LC 98-53091. 208p. 1999. pap. 11.95 (*0-452-28074-5*) NAL.

— Communicating with Your 11-15 Year Old. (Illus.). 8p. (Orig.). 1996. pap. 2.50 (*1-884241-81-6*, AN1028) Energeia Pub.

— Discipline at Schools: Does It Exist? (Illus.). 8p. (Orig.). 1996. pap. 2.50 (*1-884241-80-8*, AN1027) Energeia Pub.

— Does Your Child Need Special Education? (Illus.). 8p. (Orig.). 1996. pap. 2.50 (*1-884241-76-X*, AN1023) Energeia Pub.

— How to Deal with Bullying at School. (Illus.). 8p. (Orig.). (J). 1996. pap. 2.50 (*1-884241-77-8*, AN1024) Energeia Pub.

— How to Help Your Child Cope with Peer Pressure. (Illus.). 8p. (Orig.). 1996. pap. 2.50 (*1-884241-78-6*, AN1025) Energeia Pub.

***Anderson, Greg.** Journeys with the Cancer Conqueror: Mobilizing Mind & Spirit. LC 99-22165. 240p. 1999. 14.95 (*0-7407-0020-0*) Andrews & McMeel.

— Laria. 2000. 23.95 (*1-891400-50-9*) Champion Pr.

Anderson, Greg. Living Life on Purpose: A Guide to Creating a Life of Success & Significance. LC 96-32302. 1999. pap. 12.00 (*0-06-060232-5*) HarpC.

— Separation/Divorce & Your Child at School. (Illus.). 8p. (Orig.). 1996. pap. 2.50 (*1-884241-73-5*, AN1020) Energeia Pub.

— Setting Rules for Your 11-15 Year Old. (Illus.). 8p. (Orig.). 1996. pap. 2.50 (*1-884241-82-4*, AN1029) Energeia Pub.

— Tatiana, Bk. 1. LC 97-76840. 336p. 1998. 22.95 (*1-891400-40-1*) Champion Pr.

— 22 Non-Negotiable Laws of Wellness: Feel, Think, & Live Better Than You Ever Thought Possible. 1996. pap. 12.00 (*0-614-97841-6*) Harper SF.

— The 22 Non-Negotiable Laws of Wellness: Take Your Health into Your Own Hands to Feel, Think & Live Better Than You Ever Thought Possible. LC 94-42770. 256p. 1996. pap. 14.00 (*0-06-251238-2*, Pub. by Harper SF) HarpC.

— Understanding the Parent-Teacher Conference. (Illus.). 8p. (Orig.). 1996. pap. 2.50 (*1-884241-79-4*, AN1026) Energeia Pub.

— What Makes a Good Teacher? (Illus.). 8p. (Orig.). 1996. pap. 2.50 (*1-884241-74-3*, AN1021) Energeia Pub.

Anderson, Greg, jt. auth. see Singh, T. D.

Anderson, Greg M. & Crerar, David A. Thermodynamics in Geochemistry. (Illus.). 608p. 1993. text 95.00 (*0-19-506464-X*) OUP.

Anderson, Gregory L. Victorian Clerks. (Illus.). 145p. 1976. lib. bdg. 29.50 (*0-678-06794-5*) Kelley.

Anderson, Greta, ed. see Lagerlof, Selma.

An Asterisk (*) at the beginning of an entry indicates that the title is appearing for the first time.

Anderson, Gunnar, ed. Clarian de Landanis. (Ediciones Criticas Ser.: Vol. 7). 529p. (Orig.). 1995. pap. 26.00 (*0-936388-73-0*) Juan de la Cuesta.

Anderson, Gunnar, et al, eds. La Coronica de Adramon, 2 pts., set, Pt. I. (SPA.). 300p. 1992. pap. 23.00 (*0-936388-59-5*) Juan de la Cuesta.

— La Coronica de Adramon, 2 pts., set, Pt. II. (SPA.). 1992. pap. 23.00 (*0-936388-60-9*) Juan de la Cuesta.

Anderson, Gunnar, jt. ed. see Radnitzky, Gerard.

Anderson-Gutherie, Carol. Native American Housing: Information on HUD's Funding of Indian Housing Programs. (Illus.). 63p. (C). 1999. pap. text 20.00 (*0-7881-7755-9*) DIANE Pub.

Anderson, H. Secrets of Cruising British Columbia Coast. (Illus.). 240p. 1996. pap. 16.95 (*0-945989-25-3*) Anderson WA.

Anderson, H., ed. Gospel of Mark. (New Century Bible Ser.). 384p. 1976. 9.50 (*0-551-00579-3*) Attic Pr.

Anderson, H., jt. auth. see McGuire, William T.

Anderson, H. Allen. The Chief: Ernest Thompson Seton & the Changing West. LC 85-40751. (Illus.). 378p. 1986. 44.95 (*0-89096-239-1*) Tex A&M Univ Pr.

Anderson, H. D., jt. ed. see Craig, B. D.

Anderson, H. H. Centrifugal Pumps. 4th ed. LC 95-119248. 480p. Date not set. 184.00 (*1-85617-231-7*, R104) Elsevier.

Anderson, H. M., et al, eds. Plant Roots: From Cells to Systems. LC 97-29302. (Developments in Plant & Soil Sciences Ser.: No. 73). 160p. 1997. text 120.50 (*0-7923-4369-7*) Kluwer Academic.

Anderson, H. Michael, jt. auth. see Wilkinson, Charles F.

Anderson, H. R., Jr., jt. ed. see Mittal, K. L.

Anderson, H. T. The Diamonds Are Dancing: A History of Conesus Lake. 57p. 1993. 25.00 (*1-884849-06-7*) R&R Bks.

Anderson, H. U., et al, eds. Ceramic Membranes: 1st International Symposium. LC 95-61597. (Proceedings Ser.: Vol. 95-24). (Illus.). 336p. 1997. 71.00 (*1-56677-119-6*) Electrochem Soc.

— Ceramic Sensors III. LC 97-197076. (Proceedings Ser.: Vol. 96-27). (Illus.). 230p. 1997. 43.00 (*1-56677-127-7*) Electrochem Soc.

Anderson, H. William, jt. auth. see Fisk, Marion J.

Anderson, Hal W. & Anderson, Gail S. Mom & Dad Are Divorced, but I'm Not: Parenting after Divorce. LC 80-27602. 284p. 1981. text 28.95 (*0-88229-522-5*) Burnham Inc.

Anderson, Hans & Forbes, A. Dean. A Key-Word-in-Context to the Pentateuch, Vol. 35, Pt. B. pap. 269.95 (*0-7734-4096-8*) E Mellen.

Anderson, Harlene. Conversation, Language & Possibilities: A Postmodern Approach to Therapy. LC 96-17802. 224p. 1997. 42.00 (*0-465-03805-0*, Pub. by Basic) HarpC.

Anderson, Harlyn E., Jr. Tales of Happy Harley, Vol. I. (Illus.). 32p. 1999. pap. 18.95 (*1-57532-140-8*) Press-Tige Pub.

Anderson, Harold C. Missionary Notebook. 75p. 1998. pap. text 6.59 (*1-57636-056-3*) SunRise Pbl.

Anderson, Harriet. Utopian Feminism: Women's Movements in Fin-de-Siecle Vienna. LC 92-5739. (Illus.). 368p. (C). 1993. 42.50 (*0-300-05736-9*) Yale U Pr.

Anderson, Harriet, tr. see Ecker, Gisela, ed.

Anderson, Harry. Games You Can't Lose: A Guide for Suckers. 1991. pap. 10.00 (*0-671-74552-2*) PB.

Anderson, Harry, jt. auth. see Eiserman, Monte.

Anderson, Harry H., ed. The German-American Pioneers in Wisconsin & Michigan: The Frank-Kerler Letters, 1849-1864. LC 70-134341. (Illus.). 600p. 1989. 19.00 (*0-938076-00-0*) Milwaukee Cty Hist Soc.

Anderson, Harry H. & Olson, Frederick I. Milwaukee: At the Gathering of the Waters. LC 81-65676. (Illus.). 224p. 1981. 32.95 (*0-938076-06-X*) Milwaukee Cty Hist Soc.

Anderson, Heidi M., jt. auth. see Anderson, John M.

Anderson, Henry, jt. auth. see Hill, Anthony.

Anderson, Henry, ed. see Hill, Anthony.

Anderson, Henry H. Centennial History of the United States Sailing Association. 1998. 39.95 (*1-882502-51-5*) US Sail Assn.

Anderson, Henry P. The Bracero Program in California: With Particular Reference to Health Status, Attitudes, & Practices. Cortes, Carlos E., ed. LC 76-1225. (Chicano Heritage Ser.). (Illus.). 1977. 28.95 (*0-405-09482-5*) Ayer.

Anderson, Henry R. The Windham Company: A Managerial Practice Set, 6 vols. 6th ed. (C). 1990. pap. text, teacher ed. 11.96 (*0-395-52978-6*) HM.

Anderson, Henry R., et al. Accounting Course Manual, 6 vols. (C). 1995. text 13.96 (*0-395-75950-1*) HM.

Anderson, Henry R., et al. Managerial Accounting. LC 88-8138. 1989. teacher ed. 7.56 (*0-318-36876-5*); teacher ed., student ed. 7.56 incl. trans. (*0-318-36875-7*) HM.

Anderson, Henry R., et al. Managerial Accounting, 001. LC 88-8138. (C). 1989. text 93.16 (*0-395-32458-0*) HM.

Anderson, Herbert. Living Alone. large type ed. LC 98-6247. 1998. 23.95 (*0-7862-1449-X*) Thorndike Pr.

Anderson, Herbert, et al, eds. Promising Again. (Family Living in Pastoral Perspective Ser.). 144p. 1995. pap. 14.00 (*0-664-25124-2*) Westminster John Knox.

Anderson, Herbert & Fite, Robert C. Becoming Married. LC 93-4537. (Family Living in Pastoral Perspective Ser.). 160p. 1993. pap. 14.00 (*0-664-25126-9*) Westminster John Knox.

Anderson, Herbert & Foley, Edward. Mighty Stories, Dangerous Rituals: Weaving Together the Human & the Divine. LC 97-21075. 1997. 21.95 (*0-7879-0880-0*) Jossey-Bass.

Anderson, Herbert & Gardner, Freda. Living Alone. LC 96-36563. (Family Living in Pastoral Perspective Ser.). 152p. 1997. pap. 14.00 (*0-664-25123-4*) Westminster John Knox.

Anderson, Herbert & Johnson, Susan B. Regarding Children: A New Respect for Childhood & Families. (Family Living in Pastoral Perspective Ser.). 144p. 1994. pap. 14.00 (*0-664-25125-0*) Westminster John Knox.

Anderson, Herbert & Mitchell, Kenneth R. Leaving Home. LC 92-33115. (Family Living in Pastoral Perspective Ser.). 1993. pap. 14.00 (*0-664-25127-7*) Westminster John Knox.

Anderson, Herbert, jt. auth. see Mitchell, Kenneth R.

Anderson, Herbert, ed. see Van Leeuwen, Mary S.

Anderson, Herbert L., ed. A Physicist's Desk Reference: Physics Vade Mecum. 2nd ed. 356p. 1989. 70.00 (*0-88318-629-2*); pap. 45.00 (*0-88318-610-1*) Am Inst Physics.

— Physics Vade Mecum. LC 81-69849. 340p. 1981. 25.00 (*0-88318-289-0*) Am Inst Physics.

Anderson, Hershal, et al. Decision Analysis & Information Systems. 4th rev. ed. Newton, Grant, ed. (Certified Management Accountant Review Ser.: Vol. 4). (Illus.). 386p. (C). 1995. pap. text 30.00 (*0-918937-25-6*) Malibu Pub.

— Financial Accounting & Reporting. 4th rev. ed. Newton, Grant, ed. (Certified Management Accountant Review Ser.: Vol. 2). (Illus.). 600p. (C). 1995. pap. text 30.00 (*0-918937-24-8*) Malibu Pub.

***Anderson, Hesper.** South Mountain Road: A Daughter's Journey of Discovery. LC 99-52819. (Illus.). 288p. 2000. 23.00 (*0-684-85901-7*) S&S Trade.

Anderson, Hilda & Anderson, Barry. Short Trips in the Pacific Northwest: 52 Weekend Destination to Seattle. LC 97-37225. 256p. 1998. pap. 16.00 (*0-609-80111-2*) Crown Pub Group.

Anderson, Ho C. King, Vol. 1. 80p. 1993. per. 8.95 (*1-56097-112-6*) Fantagraph Bks.

— Young Hoods in Love. 72p. 1995. pap. 9.95 (*1-56097-192-4*) Fantagraph Bks.

Anderson, Ho Che. I Want to Be Your Dog. pap. 16.95 (*1-56097-228-9*, Pub. by Fantagraph Bks) Seven Hills Bk.

Anderson, Ho Che. The No-Boys Club. 160p. (J). (gr. 4-7). 1998. pap. write for info. (*0-88899-321-8*, Pub. by Gro1undwood-Douglas); text 14.95 (*0-88899-322-6*, Pub. by Gro1undwood-Douglas) Publishers Group.

Anderson, Holly. Teaching Through Texts: Promoting Literacy Through Popular & Literary Texts in the Primary Classroom LC 99-28349. 1999. pap. write for info. (*0-415-20307-4*) Routledge.

***Anderson, Holly & Styles, Morag, eds.** Teaching Through Texts: Promoting Literacy Through Popular & Literary Texts in Primary Classroom. LC 99-28349. 176p. (C). 2000. text. write for info. (*0-415-20306-6*) Routledge.

Anderson, Honey & Reinholdt, Bill. Don't Cut down This Tree. LC 92-21446. (Voyages Ser.). (Illus.). (J). 1993. 3.75 (*0-383-03621-6*) SRA McGraw.

— Getting the Mail. LC 92-34338. (Voyages Ser.). (Illus.). (J). 1993. 3.75 (*0-383-03624-0*) SRA McGraw.

— What Are You Called? LC 92-31953. (Voyages Ser.). (Illus.). (J). 1993. 3.75 (*0-383-03604-6*) SRA McGraw.

Anderson, Howard, et al, eds. Familiar Letter in the Eighteenth Century. LC 66-17466. viii, 312p. 1968. pap. 16.95 (*0-7006-0003-5*) U Pr of KS.

Anderson, Howard, ed. see Lewis, Matthew.

Anderson, Howard, ed. see Sterne, Laurence.

Anderson, Howard J. Major Employment Law Principles Established by the EEOC, the OFCCP & the Courts. LC 80-607842. 117p. reprint ed. pap. 36.30 (*0-608-12747-7*, 202434000036) Bks Demand.

— New Techniques in Labor Dispute Resolution: A Report of the 23rd Conference of the Association of Labor Mediation Agencies. LC 76-13538. 259p. reprint ed. pap. 80.30 (*0-608-12743-4*, 202434200036) Bks Demand.

Anderson, Howard S. & Riley, Lee H. An Atlas of Surgery of the Spine. 500p. 1998. text. write for info. (*0-7817-1219-X*) Lppncott W & W.

Anderson, Hoyt. Accepting Disability. 175p. 1996. pap. write for info. (*0-937743-01-1*) Successful Living.

— Positive Attitudes for the Physically Challenged. 20p. (Orig.). 1986. pap. 3.95 (*0-937743-00-3*) Successful Living.

Anderson, Hugo. The Inside Passage to Alaska: A Short History. (Illus.). 128p. 1998. pap. 12.95 (*0-945989-21-0*) Anderson WA.

— Secrets of Cruising: North to Alaska. (Illus.). 256p. 1993. pap. 16.95 (*0-945989-23-7*) Anderson WA.

Anderson, I., et al. Physical Resource Inventory of the Communal Lands of Zimbabwe: An Overview. (Illus.). 186p. 1993. pap. 60.00 (*0-85954-340-4*, Pub. by Nat Res Inst) St Mut.

Anderson, I. F., et al. Radiology of Sports Injuries. (Illus.). 248p. 1999. 85.00 (*0-07-470497-4*) McGraw-Hill Prof.

Anderson, I. G., ed. Directory of European Associations, 2 vols. 2nd ed. LC 76-11697. (ENG, FRE & GER.). 906p. write for info. (*0-318-53674-9*) Intl Pubns Serv.

Anderson, Ian. Combinatorial Designs & Tournaments. (Oxford Lecture Series in Mathematics & Its Applications: No. 6). (Illus.). 248p. 1998. text 67.00 (*0-19-850029-7*) OUP.

***Anderson, Ian.** Sitting Bull's Boss: Above the Medicine Line with James Morrow Walsh. 192p. 2000. pap. 16.95 (*1-895811-63-5*) Heritage Hse.

Anderson, Ian & Thompson, Gerald. The Inverse Problem of the Calculus of Variations for Ordinary Differential Equations. LC 92-10610. (Memoirs Ser.: No. 475). 110p. 1992. pap. 26.00 (*0-8218-2533-X*, MEMO/99/475) Am Math.

Anderson, Ian C. Combinatorial Designs. 1990. text 79.95 (*0-470-21643-3*) P-H.

— A First Course in Combinatorial Mathematics. 2nd ed. (Oxford Applied Mathematics & Computing Science Ser.). (Illus.). 144p. 1989. pap. text 35.00 (*0-19-859673-1*) OUP.

— A First Course in Combinatorial Mathematics. 2nd ed. (Oxford Applied Mathematics & Computing Science Ser.). (Illus.). 144p. 1989. 65.00 (*0-19-859674-X*) OUP.

— The Scarlet Riders No. 6: The Flying Patrol. 240p. 1988. mass mkt. 2.50 (*0-8217-2437-1*, Zebra Kensgtn) Kensgtn Pub Corp.

Anderson, Ian C., ed. Editor & Publisher/Free Paper Publisher, Community, Specialty & Free Publications Year Book: A Media Buyers Guide. 500p. (Orig.). 1996. pap. text. write for info. (*0-9646364-5-X*) ASM Communs.

Anderson III, Walter E. The Blood: In the Name of Jesus. 110p. (Orig.). 1999. pap. 9.95 (*0-9647596-7-5*, Pub. by Mlk & Hny Pub) Herveys Bklink.

***Anderson, Ilana.** Sad Strangeness. 88p. 1999. pap. write for info. (*0-7541-0774-4*, Pub. by Minerva Pr) Unity Dist.

Anderson-Imbert, Enrique. Woven on the Loom of Time: Stories by Enrique Anderson-Imbert. Vail, Carleton, tr. from SPA. (Texas Pan American Ser.). 200p. (Orig.). 1990. text 32.50 (*0-292-79054-6*) U of Tex Pr.

Anderson-Imbert, Florit. LITERAT HISPANOAMER REV VOL 1, 2 vols., I. (SPA.). (C). 1970. pap. text 58.50 (*0-03-083454-6*) Harcourt Coll Pubs.

— LITERAT HISPANOAMER REV VOL 2, 2 vols., II. (SPA.). (C). 1970. pap. text 58.50 (*0-03-083455-4*) Harcourt Coll Pubs.

Anderson, Iris I. Destiny. LC 94-90829. 1998. pap. 10.95 (*0-533-11385-7*) Vantage.

Anderson, Irvine H. Aramco, the United States, & Saudi Arabia: A Study of the Dynamics of Foreign Oil Policy, 1933-1950. LC 80-8535. 276p. reprint ed. pap. 85.60 (*0-7837-0045-8*, 204029200016) Bks Demand.

— History in a Teilhardian Context: The Thought of Teilhard de Chardin As a Guide to Social Science. (Teilhard Studies: No. 17). 1987. pap. 3.50 (*0-89012-046-5*) Am Teilhard.

— The Standard-Vacuum Oil Company & United States East Asian Policy, 1933-1941. LC 74-25611. 273p. reprint ed. pap. 84.70 (*0-608-17849-7*, 203263200080) Bks Demand.

Anderson, Isaac, tr. see Christiansen, Sigurd.

Anderson, Isabel. Building to Last: Stories for Families to Read Together in Their Daily Prayer Time. LC 94-14010. (Illus.). 1994. write for info. (*1-878997-53-X*) St Tikhons Pr.

Anderson, J. Butterworths' Student Companions - Evidence. 2nd ed. 96p. 1996. pap. write for info. (*0-409-31325-5*, MICHIE) LEXIS Pub.

— Communications Research: Issues & Methods. (Mass Communications Ser.). 416p. (C). 1987. text 63.74 (*0-07-001651-8*) McGraw.

— Foundations of Computer Technology. 1994. pap. 42.50 (*0-412-59810-8*, Chap & Hall NY) Chapman & Hall.

Anderson, J., ed. Tacitus: Germania. 296p. 1996. pap. text 35.95 (*1-85399-503-7*, Pub. by Brist Class Pr) Focus Pub-R Pullins.

Anderson, J., et al. Manual on the Diagnosis of Rinderpest: Animal Health Manual. 2nd ed. (Animal Health Ser.: No. 1). (Illus.). 143p. 1997. pap. 28.00 (*92-5-103814-7*, F38147, Pub. by FAO) Bernan Associates.

Anderson, J., jt. auth. see Akemann, C.

Anderson, J. A. Real Analysis. x, 346p. 1969. text 497.00 (*0-677-61460-8*) Gordon & Breach.

— What Neural Networks Can Do. 144p. 1988. lab manual ed. write for info. (*1-56321-003-7*); lab manual ed. 295.00 incl. VHS (*1-56321-000-2*); VHS 235.00 (*1-56321-004-5*); VHS 15.00 (*1-56321-002-9*) L Erlbaum Assocs.

Anderson, J. A., jt. ed. see Hinton, Geoffrey E.

Anderson, J. B., ed. Alaska: Anchorage & South Central. 32p. (Orig.). 1995. pap. 4.99 (*1-886462-08-9*) J & H Sales.

Anderson, J. B. & Ashley, Gail M., eds. The Glacial Marine Sedimentation: Paleoclimatic Significance. (Special Papers: No. 261). (Illus.). 240p. 1991. pap. 28.50 (*0-8137-2261-6*) Geol Soc.

Anderson, J. B. & Molnia, Bruce F., eds. Glacial-Marine Sedimentation. (Short Course Ser.: Vol. 9). 127p. 1989. 22.00 (*0-87590-706-7*) Am Geophysical.

Anderson, J. B., et al. Digital Phase Modulation. (Applications of Communications Theory Ser.). (Illus.). 516p. (C). 1986. 120.00 (*0-306-42195-X*, Plenum Trade) Perseus Pubng.

Anderson, J. D., jt. ed. see Wendt, J. F.

Anderson, J. G. & Jay, S. J., eds. Use & Impact of Computers in Clinical Medicine. (Computers & Medicine Ser.). (Illus.). 375p. 1986. 58.00 (*0-387-96362-6*) Spr-Verlag.

Anderson, J. I. I Can Read About Dogs & Puppies. LC 72-96953. (Illus.). (J). (gr. 2-4). 1997. pap. 2.95 (*0-89375-053-0*) Troll Communs.

— I Can Read About Paul Bunyan. LC 76-54494. (Illus.). (J). (gr. 2-5). 1977. pap. 2.95 (*0-89375-041-7*) Troll Communs.

— I Can Read About Pecos Bill. LC 76-54575. (Illus.). (J). (gr. 2-5). 1977. pap. 2.95 (*0-89375-042-5*) Troll Communs.

— I Can Read about Whales & Dolphins. LC 95-5949. (I Can Read about Ser.). (Illus.). 48p. (J). (gr. k-3). 1996. pap. 4.95 (*0-8167-3645-6*) Troll Communs.

— I Can Read About Whales & Dolphins. LC 72-96955. (Illus.). (J). (gr. 2-4). 1973. pap. 2.95 (*0-89375-052-2*) Troll Communs.

Anderson, J. J. Newcastle upon Tyne. (Records of Early English Drama Ser.). (Illus.). 264p. 1982. text 60.00 (*0-8020-5610-5*) U of Toronto Pr.

Anderson, J. J., ed. Sir Gawain & the Green Knight, Pearl, Cleanness & Patience. rev. ed. (Everyman Paperback Classics Ser.). 288p. (C). 1996. pap. 6.95 (*0-460-87510-8*, Everyman's Classic Lib) Tuttle Pubng.

Anderson, J. J., jt. ed. see McCully, C. B.

Anderson, J. K. Ancient Faces. 1987. pap. 5.95 (*0-88388-080-6*) Bellerophon Bks.

— Birds of California. (J). (gr. 1-9). 1992. pap. 4.95 (*0-88388-101-2*) Bellerophon Bks.

— Castles. (J). (gr. 1-9). 1992. pap. 4.95 (*0-88388-088-1*) Bellerophon Bks.

— Castles of Scotland. (J). (gr. 1-9). 1992. pap. 4.95 (*0-88388-111-X*) Bellerophon Bks.

— Genetic Engineering: The Ethical Issues. 128p. (Orig.). 1982. pap. 4.95 (*0-310-45051-9*, 12707P) Zondervan.

— Gorgons. (J). (gr. 1-9). 1992. pap. 3.95 (*0-88388-109-8*) Bellerophon Bks.

— Unicorns-Coloring Book. (J). 1985. pap. 4.95 (*0-88388-086-5*) Bellerophon Bks.

Anderson, J. K., ed. see Smith, Henry R.

Anderson, J. Kerby. Moral Dilemmas: Biblical Perspectives on Contemporary Ethical Issues. Swindoll, Charles R., ed. LC 98-15087. (Swindoll Christian Leadership Library). 262p. 1998. 24.99 (*0-8499-1446-9*) Word Pub.

— Moral Dilemmas Supersaver ed. Biblical Perspectives on Contemporary Ethical Issues. Swindoll, Charles R., ed. (Swindoll Leadership Library). 1998. 19.97 (*0-8499-1565-1*) Word Pub.

Anderson, J. L. Explaining Long-Term Economic Change. (New Studies in Economic & Social History: No. 10). 91p. (C). 1995. text 34.95 (*0-521-55269-9*); pap. text 10.95 (*0-521-55784-4*) Cambridge U Pr.

Anderson, J. L., ed. Critical Care Cardiology. (Progress in Critical Care Medicine Ser.: Vol. 3). (Illus.). vii, 260p. 1988. 113.25 (*3-8055-4734-X*) S Karger.

— The Nature & Origin of Cordilleran Magmatism. (Memoir Ser.: No. 174). (Illus.). 440p. 1990. 40.00 (*0-8137-1174-6*) Geol Soc.

Anderson, J. M. The Biostratigraphy of the Permian & Triassic Pt. 3: A Review of Gondwana Permian Palynology with Particular Reference to the Northern Karoo Basin, South Africa. (Memoirs of the Botanical Survey of South Africa Ser.: No. 41). (Illus.). 200p. 1977. 16.00 (*0-621-03834-2*, Pub. by Natl Botanical Inst) Balogh.

Anderson, J. M., et al, eds. Advances in Drug Delivery Systems 6: Proceedings of the Sixth International Symposium on Recent Advances in Drug Delivery Systems, Salt Lake City, UT, U. S. A., 21-24 February 1993. 350p. 1994. text 227.25 (*0-444-82027-2*) Elsevier.

Anderson, J. M. & Ingram, J. S., eds. Tropical Soil Biology & Fertility: A Handbook of Methods. 2nd ed. 240p. (Orig.). 1993. pap. text 50.00 (*0-85198-821-0*) OUP.

Anderson, J. M. & Mikhail, Edward M. Surveying, Theory & Practice. 7th ed. LC 97-28584. 1200p. 1997. 99.38 (*0-07-015914-9*) McGraw.

Anderson, J. M., jt. auth. see Gest, T. R.

Anderson, J. M., tr. see Heidegger, Martin.

Anderson, J. N., ed. The World's Religions. rev. ed. LC 75-26654. 1954. pap. 16.00 (*0-8028-1636-3*) Eerdmans.

Anderson, J. N. & Queneau, P. E., eds. Pyrometallurgical Processes in Nonferrous Metallurgy. LC 67-26570. (Metallurgical Society Conference Ser.: Vol. 39). 529p. reprint ed. pap. 164.00 (*0-608-11342-5*, 200152800079) Bks Demand.

Anderson, J. R. Death in a High Latitude. large type ed. 432p. 1983. 27.99 (*0-7089-0940-X*) Ulverscroft.

— A Geography of Agriculture in the United States: Southeast. (Geography of World Agriculture Ser.: No. 2). 136p. 1973. 25.00 (*0-7855-2776-1*, Pub. by Akade Kiado) St Mut.

— A Sprig of Sea Lavender. large type ed. 324p. 1979. 27.99 (*0-7089-0364-9*) Ulverscroft.

Anderson, J. R., ed. Agricultural Technology: Policy Issues for the International Community. (Illus.). 672p. 1994. text 130.00 (*0-85198-880-6*) OUP.

Anderson, J. R. & Boudart, M., eds. Catalysis: Science & Technology, 11 vols. Incl. Vol. 5. Catalysis: Science & Technology. (Illus.). 280p. 1984. 126.95 (*0-387-12665-1*); Vol. 6. Catalysis: Science & Technology. (Illus.). 320p. 1984. 135.95 (*0-387-12815-8*); Vol. 1. (Illus.). 320p. 1981. 126.95 (*0-387-10353-8*); Vol. 2. (Illus.). 280p. 1982. 116.95 (*0-387-10593-X*); Vol. 4. (Illus.). 280p. 1983. 126.95 (*0-387-11855-1*); Vol. 7. (Illus.). 230p. 1985. 125.95 (*0-387-15035-8*); Vol. 8. (Illus.). 280p. 1987. 108.95 (*0-387-15034-X*); Vol. 9. Burwell, R. L., et al, contrib. by. (Illus.). 192p. 1991. 103.95 (*0-387-52972-1*); Vol. 10. 164p. 1996. 125.00 (*3-540-60109-0*); Vol. 11. 201p. 1996. 129.00 (*3-540-60380-8*); Vol. 3. (Illus.). 290p. 1983. 126.95 (*0-387-11634-6*); 999.00 (*3-540-11634-6*) Spr-Verlag.

Anderson, J. S. Electronics Servicing. LC 98-163257. 288p. 1998. pap. text 32.95 (*0-7506-3554-1*) Buttrwrth-Heinemann.

Anderson, J. Stuart. Lawyers & the Making of English Land Law, 1832-1940. (Illus.). 376p. 1992. text 79.00 (*0-19-825670-1*) OUP.

Anderson, Jack. The American Dance Festival. LC 86-23942. (Illus.). x, 324p. 1987. text 37.95 (*0-8223-0683-2*) Duke.

— Art Without Boundaries: The World of Modern Dance. LC 96-52226. (Illus.). 384p. 1997. 34.95 (*0-87745-583-X*) U of Iowa Pr.

— Art Without Boundaries: The World of Modern Dance. LC 96-52226. (Illus.). 384p. 1999. reprint ed. pap. 19.95 (*0-87745-677-1*) U of Iowa Pr.

— Ballet & Modern Dance: A Concise History. 2nd ed. (Illus.). 288p. 1992. pap. 17.95 (*0-87127-172-9*, Dance Horizons) Princeton Bk Co.

A

— Choreography Observed. LC 87-6021. (Illus.). 304p. 1987. text 35.00 (*0-87745-172-9*) U of Iowa Pr.

— Choreography Observed. LC 87-6021. (Illus.). 304p. 1997. reprint ed. pap. 12.95 (*0-87745-593-7*) U of Iowa Pr.

— The Clouds of That Country. 1982. pap. 7.00 (*0-914610-29-5*) Hanging Loose.

— Control. 1988. 19.95 (*0-8217-2428-2*, Zebra Kensgtn) Kensgtn Pub Corp.

— Control. 1990. mass mkt. 4.95 (*1-55817-312-9*, Pinncle Kensgtn) Kensgtn Pub Corp.

— Field Trips on the Rapid Transit. 1990. 15.00 (*0-914610-69-4*); pap. 9.00 (*0-914610-68-6*) Hanging Loose.

— The Japan Conspiracy. large type ed. LC 93-39748. 510p. 1994. lib. bdg. 17.95 (*0-7862-0110-X*) Thorndike Pr.

— Millennium. 416p. 1995. mass mkt. 5.99 (*0-8125-2258-3*, Pub. by Tor Bks) St Martin.

— The One & Only: The Ballet Russe de Monte Carlo. (Illus.). 333p. 1981. 29.95 (*0-903102-65-X*, Pub. by Dance Bks) Princeton Bk Co.

— Peace, War & Politics: An Eyewitness Account. LC 99-26647. 1999. 27.95 (*0-312-85602-4*, Pub. by Forge NYC) St Martin.

— Stormin' Norman: An American Hero. 1991. mass mkt. 4.50 (*0-8217-3562-4*, Zebra Kensgtn) Kensgtn Pub Corp.

— Traffic: New & Selected Prose Poems. LC 98-66584. (Marie Alexander Poetry Ser.: Vol. 1). 96p. 1998. pap. 12.95 (*0-89823-191-4*) New Rivers Pr.

— The Washington Money Go-Round, Vol. 1. 288p. (C). 1997. 28.95 (*0-9637899-3-7*) Elliott & James Pubs.

— Zero Time. 512p. 1993. mass mkt. 4.99 (*0-8217-4087-3*, Zebra Kensgtn) Kensgtn Pub Corp.

***Anderson, Jack & Gibson, Daryl.** Peace War & Politics. 432p. 2000. pap. 14.95 (*0-312-87497-9*) St Martin.

Anderson, Jack & Schatz, Thomas. The Best President Money Can Buy. (Illus.). 300p. 1997. 26.95 (*0-9637899-9-6*) Elliott & James Pubs.

Anderson, Jack M. Warrior by Choice & Warrior by Chance. LC 96-61939. 448p. 1997. 24.95 (*1-883893-97-6*, Pub. by WinePress Pub) BookWorld.

Anderson, Jacqueline M. How to Find & Manage H. U. D. & Rental Property: Property Management Advice for Landlords. Black, Marge, ed. (Illus.). 1989. text 9.95 (*0-685-24085-1*) J M Anderson.

***Anderson, James.** The Affair of the Bloodstained Egg Cosy. (Missing Mysteries Ser.: Vol. 6). 227p. 1999. pap. text 11.95 (*1-890208-09-4*) Poisoned Pen.

— Arctic Bush Pilot: From Navy Combat to Flying Alaska's Northern Wilderness. (Illus.). 2000. pap. 16.95 (*0-945397-83-6*) Epicenter Pr.

— Dis-Agreeing Ireland. 192p. 1999. pap. 19.95 (*0-7453-1275-6*, Pub. by Pluto GBR) Stylus Pub VA.

Anderson, James. Illustrated Bradbury. (Illus.). 56p. 1989. pap. 5.95 (*0-910619-06-9*) Niekas Pubns.

— Observations on the Means of Exciting a Spirit of National Industry. LC 68-25541. (Reprints of Economic Classics Ser.). xii, 526p. 1968. reprint ed. 67.50 (*0-678-00391-2*) Kelley.

— Public Policymaking, 2 vols. 2nd ed. LC 93-78691. (C). 1993. pap. text 41.56 (*0-395-67529-4*) HM.

— Public Policymaking: An Introduction, 3 vols. 3rd ed. 352p. (C). 1996. pap. text 42.76 (*0-395-75396-1*) HM.

— Roman Brickstamps: The Thomas Ashby Collection in the American Academy at Rome. (British School at Rome Archaeological Monographs). (Illus.). 141p. 1991. pap. 81.00 (*0-904152-18-9*, Pub. by British Schl Rome) David Brown.

— They Finished Their Course. 1996. pap. 14.99 (*0-946351-22-8*, Pub. by John Ritchie) Loizeaux.

Anderson, James, ed. Economic Regulatory Policy. (C). 1975. pap. 15.00 (*0-918592-12-7*) Pol Studies.

Anderson, James, et al, eds. A Global World? Re-Ordering Political Space. (Shape of the World Ser.). (Illus.). 296p. (C). 1996. pap. text 24.95 (*0-19-874193-6*) OUP.

— A Global World? Re-Ordering Political Space. (Shape of the World Ser.: Vol. 5). (Illus.). 296p. (C). 1996. text 59.95 (*0-19-874192-8*) OUP.

Anderson, James & Goodman, James. Dis-Agreeing Ireland. LC 98-34974. (Contemporary Irish Studies). 192p. 1999. 59.95 (*0-7453-1280-2*, Pub. by Pluto GBR) Stylus Pub VA.

Anderson, James & Narus, James. Business Market Management: Understanding, Creating & Delivering Value. LC 98-42009. 430p. 1998. 79.00 (*0-13-522657-0*) P-H.

Anderson, James, et al. Redundant Spaces in Cities & Regions? Studies in Industrial Decline & Social Change. LC 83-70171. (Special Publications/Institute of British Geographers). x, 354p. 1983. write for info. (*0-12-058480-8*) Acad Pr.

Anderson, James, jt. auth. see Gaarder, Jostein.

Anderson, James, jt. auth. see Shingleton, John D.

Anderson, James, jt. ed. see Cochrane, Allan.

Anderson, James, jt. ed. see Parker, Donn B.

Anderson, James, tr. see Steen, Thorvald.

Anderson, James, tr. see Va, Leong.

***Anderson, James A.** The Black Enterprise Guide to Investing. 336p. 2000. pap. 19.95 (*0-471-38184-5*, Wiley Heyden) Wiley.

Anderson, James A. Communication Theory: Epistemological Foundations. LC 96-12352. (Communication Ser.). 259p. 1996. lib. bdg. 35.00 (*1-57230-083-3*) Guilford Pubns.

— A Comparative Analysis of Selected Income Measurement Theories in Financial Accounting, Vol. 12. (Studies in Accounting Research). 120p. 1976. 12.00 (*0-86539-024-X*) Am Accounting.

— Encina & Virgil. LC 74-75722. (Romance Monographs: No. 8). 1974. 15.00 (*84-399-2158-6*) Romance.

— An Introduction to Neural Networks. 1995. pap. text 34.50 (*0-262-51081-2*) MIT Pr.

— An Introduction to Neural Networks. (Illus.). 771p. 1995. 66.00 (*0-262-01144-1*, Bradford Bks) MIT Pr.

Anderson, James A., ed. Communication Yearbook. (Communication Yearbook Ser.: Vol. 12). 640p. (C). 1989. text 60.00 (*0-8039-3348-7*) Sage.

— Communication Yearbook, Vol. 11. 640p. 1988. text 45.00 (*0-8039-3138-7*) Sage.

— Communication Yearbook, Vol. 13. 640p. (C). 1990. text 85.00 (*0-8039-3349-5*) Sage.

— Communication Yearbook, Vol. 13-1990. LC 76-45943. 589p. 1990. reprint ed. pap. 182.60 (*0-608-02999-8*, 206344900013) Bks Demand.

— Communication Yearbook, Vol. 14. (Illus.). 640p. (C). 1990. text 69.95 (*0-8039-3543-9*) Sage.

— Communication Yearbook, Vol. 14, 1991. fac. ed. LC 76-45943. (Illus.). 599p. 1991. reprint ed. pap. 185.70 (*0-608-01021-9*, 206187900014) Bks Demand.

Anderson, James A. & Bell, James M. Number Theory with Applications. LC 96-25134. 566p. 1996. 89.33 (*0-13-190190-7*) P-H.

Anderson, James A. & Meyer, Timothy P. Mediated Communication: A Social Action Perspective. (Current Communication An Advanced Text Ser.: Vol. 1). 320p. (C). 1988. text 45.00 (*0-8039-3050-X*) Sage.

— Mediated Communication: A Social Action Perspective. LC 88-23903. (Current Communication Ser.: Vol. 1). 368p. 1988. reprint ed. pap. 114.10 (*0-608-02770-7*, 206383600007) Bks Demand.

Anderson, James A. & Rosenfeld, Edward, eds. Neurocomputing: Foundations of Research. 600p. 1988. 85.00 (*0-262-01097-6*, Bradford Bks) MIT Pr.

— Neurocomputing: Foundations of Research. 752p. 1989. reprint ed. pap. text 39.95 (*0-262-51048-0*) MIT Pr.

— Talking Nets: An Oral History of Neural Networks. LC 97-23868. (Illus.). 422p. 1998. 39.95 (*0-262-01167-0*, Bradford Bks) MIT Pr.

***Anderson, James A. & Rosenfeld, Edward, eds.** Talking Nets: An Oral History of Neural Networks. LC 97-23868. (Illus.). 448p. 2000. reprint ed. pap. 22.95 (*0-262-51111-8*) MIT Pr.

Anderson, James A., et al. Neurocomputing 2: Directions for Research. (Illus.). 750p. 1993. pap. text 42.50 (*0-262-51075-8*, Bradford Bks) MIT Pr.

Anderson, James A., jt. ed. see Hinton, Geoffrey E.

Anderson, James B. Speaking to Groups: Eyeball to Eyeball. (Illus.). 368p. (Orig.). 1989. 29.95 (*0-922749-05-1*); pap. 19.95 (*0-922749-06-X*) Wyndmoor Pr.

Anderson, James C., Jr. Roman Architecture & Society. LC 96-48315. (Ancient Society & History Ser.). (Illus.). 474p. 1997. text 39.95 (*0-8018-5546-2*) Johns Hopkins.

Anderson, James C., jt. auth. see Naeim, Farzad.

Anderson, James D. The Education of Blacks in the South, 1860- 1935. LC 87-35196. (Illus.). xv, 366p. (C). 1988. pap. 17.95 (*0-8078-4221-4*) U of NC Pr.

— A Woodsman Remembers: The Life & Times of James D. Anderson. (Illus.). 158p. (Orig.). 1996. pap. 9.95 (*0-9655356-0-6*, 1) J D Anderson.

Anderson, James D. & Jones, Ezra E. The Management of Ministry: Building Leadership in a Changing World. LC 93-73930. 224p. (Orig.). 1993. pap. 12.95 (*0-88177-131-7*, DR131) Discipleship Res.

Anderson, James D., jt. auth. see Catala, Rafael.

Anderson, James D., jt. ed. see Catala, Rafael.

Anderson, James E. Economic Regulatory Policies. 242p. 1985. reprint ed. pap. 17.50 (*0-8191-5154-8*) U Pr of Amer.

— The Relative Inefficiency of Quotas. 240p. 1988. 27.50 (*0-262-01103-4*) MIT Pr.

— Two Literary Riddles in the Exeter Book: Riddle 1 & the Easter Riddle. LC 85-40471. (Illus.). 288p. 1986. 37.95 (*0-8061-1947-0*) U of Okla Pr.

Anderson, James E. & Hazleton, Jared E. Managing Macroeconomic Policy: The Johnson Presidency. LC 85-15064. (Administrative History of the Johnson Presidency Ser.). 301p. 1986. text 30.00 (*0-292-75084-6*) U of Tex Pr.

— Managing Macroeconomic Policy: The Johnson Presidency. LC 85-15064. (Administrative History of the Johnson Presidency Ser.). 301p. reprint ed. pap. 93.40 (*0-608-20095-6*, 207136700011) Bks Demand.

Anderson, James E., ed. see Hammond, Paul Y.

Anderson, James E., ed. see Herring, George C.

Anderson, James E., ed. see Welborn, David M.

Anderson, James F., et al. Boot Camps: An Intermediate Sanction. LC 98-38405. 180p. 1998. 49.00 (*0-7618-1256-3*); pap. 24.50 (*0-7618-1257-1*) U Pr of Amer.

***Anderson, James F., et al.** Boot Camps: An Intermediate Sanction - A Student's Guide. 120p. (C). 1999. pap. 23.50 (*0-7618-1495-7*) U Pr of Amer.

Anderson, James F., tr. see Aquinas, Thomas, Saint.

Anderson, James G., et al, eds. Evaluating Health Care Information Systems: Methods & Applications. (Illus.). 320p. (C). 1993. text 58.00 (*0-8039-4935-9*); pap. text 27.95 (*0-8039-4936-7*) Sage.

Anderson, James G. & Katzper, Meyer, eds. Health Sciences, Physiological & Pharmacological Simulation Studies. 217p. (Orig.). 1995. pap. 80.00 (*1-56555-042-0*, HSS-95) Soc Computer Sim.

***Anderson, James G. & Katzper, Meyer, eds.** Health Sciences Simulation. 216p. 1999. pap. 80.00 (*1-56555-160-5*) Soc Computer Sim.

— Medical Sciences 1998. 201p. 1998. 40.00 (*1-56555-138-9*) Soc Computer Sim.

Anderson, James G. & Katzper, Meyer, eds. Simulation in the Medical Sciences. 226p. 1996. pap. 80.00 (*1-56555-091-9*, HSS-96) Soc Computer Sim.

***Anderson, James G. & Katzper, Meyer, eds.** Simulation in the Medical Sciences Held in Phoenix, Arizona - January, 1997. 199p. 1998. pap. 80.00 (*1-56555-105-2*, HSS-97) Soc Computer Sim.

***Anderson, James H.** America at Risk. 2000. pap. 6.95 (*0-89195-249-7*) Heritage Found.

***Anderson, James L., et al, eds.** Year in Review - U. S. Seafood Trade Report: U. S. Exports, Vol. II. 5th ed. 185p. 2000. 50.00 (*0-9673524-5-2*) J L Anderson Assoc.

— Year in Review - U. S. Seafood Trade Report: U. S. Imports, Vol. I. 5th ed. 245p. 2000. 50.00 (*0-9673524-4-4*) J L Anderson Assoc.

Anderson, James L. & Gardiner, Barbara S., eds. 1995 Year in Review - U. S. Seafood Trade Report. (Illus.). xii, 390p. 1996. pap. 19.95 (*0-9673524-0-1*) J L Anderson Assoc.

— 1997 Year in Review - U. S. Seafood Trade Report. 3rd ed. (Illus.). iv, 420p. 1998. pap. 39.95 (*0-9673524-2-8*) J L Anderson Assoc.

— 1996 Year in Review - U. S. Seafood Trade Report. 2nd ed. (Illus.). v, 400p. 1997. pap. 29.95 (*0-9673524-1-X*) J L Anderson Assoc.

— Year in Review - U. S. Seafood Trade Report. 4th ed. (Illus.). vii, 94p. 1999. pap. 69.95 incl. cd-rom (*0-9673524-3-6*) J L Anderson Assoc.

Anderson, James L., jt. auth. see Kennett, Lee B.

Anderson, James M. & Creore, JoAnn. Readings in Romance Linguistics. (Illus.). 472p. (Orig.). 1972. pap. text 50.00 (*90-279-2303-5*) Mouton.

Anderson, James M. & Kim, Sung W., eds. Recent Advances in Drug Delivery Systems. LC 84-3387. 404p. 1984. 95.00 (*0-306-41627-1*, Plenum Trade) Perseus Pubng.

Anderson, James N. Islamic Law in the Modern World. LC 75-31816. 106p. 1975. reprint ed. lib. bdg. 35.00 (*0-8371-8451-7*, ANIL, Greenwood Pr) Greenwood.

Anderson, James N., et al. Critical Issues in Philippine Research: A Selected & Annotated Literature Review on the Women's Movement, Conflict in Luzon's Cordillera, Muslim Autonomy, & Recent Political Resistence. LC 96-9139. (Occasional Papers). 1996. pap. text 25.00 (*0-944613-27-6*) UC Berkeley Ctrs SE Asia.

Anderson, James R. & Walker, Steven. Diccionario de Terminologia Forestal. 2nd ed.Tr. of Dictionary of Forest Terminology. (SPA.). 92p. reprint ed. pap. text. write for info. (*0-9619526-0-1*) J R Anderson.

***Anderson, James V.** Not Unlike a Madman in Cheap Sandals. 110p. 1999. pap. 11.95 (*0-9675981-4-1*) J V Anderson.

Anderson, James W. Be Heart Smart: The HCF Way to a Healthy Heart. (Illus.). 120p. (Orig.). 1989. pap. 5.95 (*0-922859-00-0*) HCF NRF.

— Diabetes. 224p. 1987. mass mkt. 5.99 (*0-446-34399-4*, Pub. by Warner Bks) Little.

***Anderson, James W.** Hyperbolic Geometry. LC 99-37719. (Undergraduate Mathematics Ser.). (Illus.). 255p. 1999. pap. 35.00 (*1-85233-156-9*, Pub. by Spr-Verlag) Spr-Verlag.

Anderson, James W. & Breecher, Maury M. Dr. Anderson's Antioxidant Antiaging Health Program. 288p. 1996. 21.00 (*0-7867-0304-0*) Carroll & Graf.

— Live Longer Better: Dr. Anderson's Complete Antiaging Health Program. LC 97-31746. 288p. 1997. pap. 12.95 (*0-7867-0472-1*) Carroll & Graf.

Anderson, James W. & Gustafson, Nancy J. Dr. Anderson's High-Fiber Fitness Plan. LC 93-45451. 264p. 1994. 19.95 (*0-8131-1867-0*) U Pr of Ky.

Anderson, Jane. Deception's Bride. 288p. 1998. pap. 5.99 (*0-7860-0509-2*, Pinncle Kensgtn) Kensgtn Pub Corp.

— Guide to State Medicaid Managed Care Laws & Rules: 1996-97 Edition. 2nd ed. Towler, Ashli, ed. 85p. 1996. pap. 134.00 (*1-56925-053-7*, SMM2) Capitol Publns.

***Anderson, Jane.** Mountain Moonlight. 1999. mass mkt. 3.99 (*0-8217-6440-3*) Kensgtn Pub Corp.

Anderson, Jane. State-By-State Laws & Regulations on Workers' Compensation Managed Care: 1997 Edition. 3rd ed. Towler, Ashli, ed. 150p. 1996. pap. 79.00 (*1-56925-059-6*, SBS3) Capitol Publns.

Anderson, Jane, et al. A Hard Night's Run. (Follet Adult Basic Reading Comprehension Program Ser.). 64p. 1988. pap. text 4.00 (*0-8428-2251-8*) Cambridge Bk.

— Hello, World & Other Stories. (Follet Adult Basic Reading Comprehension Program Ser.). 64p. 1988. pap. text 4.00 (*0-8428-2250-X*) Cambridge Bk.

— Instructional Guide to the Follet Adult Basic Reading Comprehension Program: Instructional Guide for All Books. (Follet Adult Basic Reading Comprehension Program Ser.). 112p. 1988. pap. text. write for info. (*0-8428-2258-5*) Cambridge Bk.

— A Notebook for the Rest of Your Life. (Illus.). 95p. 1995. ring bd. 20.00 (*0-9634836-2-5*) Sheep Shoppe.

Anderson, Jane C. A History of Channing-Murray Foundation & Its Red Herring: A Liberal Ministry to the Campus of the University of Illinois. (Illus.). 68p. 1992. reprint ed. 5.00 (*0-932884-25-3*) Red Herring.

Anderson, Jane L., jt. auth. see Lintz, Christopher R.

***Anderson, Janet.** Going Through the Gate. 144p. (YA). (gr. 3-7). 2000. pap. 4.99 (*0-14-130698-X*, PuffinBks) Peng Put Young Read.

— Going Through the Gate. (Illus.). (J). 2000. 10.34 (*0-606-18407-4*) Turtleback.

Anderson, Janet. The Storms of Life. 112p. write for info. (*0-8187-0139-0*) Harlo Press.

Anderson, Janet A. Pedro De Mena, Seventeenth-Century Spanish Sculptor. LC 98-2589. (Studies in Art & Religious Interpretation: Vol. 22). (Illus.). 316p. 1998. text 99.95 (*0-7734-8481-7*) E Mellen.

— A Taste of Kentucky. LC 86-9197. (Illus.). 112p. 1986. 15.00 (*0-8131-1580-9*) U Pr of Ky.

— Women in the Fine Arts: A Bibliography & Illustration Guide. LC 90-53608. 368p. 1991. lib. bdg. 65.00 (*0-89950-541-4*) McFarland & Co.

Anderson, Janet S. The Monkey Tree. LC 98-24315. (Illus.). 176p. (J). (gr. 7-9). 1998. 15.99 (*0-525-46032-2*, Dutton Child) Peng Put Young Read.

— Sunflower Sal. LC 96-53906. (Illus.). 32p. (J). (gr. 1-4). 1997. lib. bdg. 15.95 (*0-8075-7662-X*) A Whitman.

— Sunflower Sal. (Illus.). 32p. (J). (gr. 1-4). 1999. pap. 6.95 (*0-8075-7663-8*) A Whitman.

Anderson, Janette J. Bankruptcy for Paralegal. 400p. (C). 1996. 68.00 (*0-13-360058-0*) P-H.

Anderson, Jani. Bringing down the Moon: Fifteen Tales of Fantasy & Terror. LC 85-10904. (Illus.). 272p. (Orig.). 1985. 15.95 (*0-917053-03-6*); pap. 7.95 (*0-917053-02-8*) Space And.

Anderson, Janice. A Celebration of Ireland. (Illus.). 80p. 10.99 (*1-57215-219-2*, JG2192) World Pubns.

***Anderson, Janice.** Children in Art. (Illus.). 128p. 1998. 16.98 (*1-880908-95-6*) Todtri Prods.

— Illuminated Manuscripts. 1999. 16.95 (*1-57717-155-1*) Todtri Prods.

Anderson, Janice & Swinglehurst, Edmund. Train & Transport: A Collector's Guide. (Illus.). 96p. 1998. text 20.00 (*0-7881-5268-8*) DIANE Pub.

Anderson, Janice C. & Moore, Stephen D., eds. Mark & Method: New Approaches in Biblical Studies. LC 92-17158. 192p. 1992. pap. 18.00 (*0-8006-2655-9*, 1-2655) Augsburg Fortress.

Anderson, Janice Capel. Matthew's Narrative Web: Over, & Over, & Over Again. (JSNT Supplement Ser.: No. 91). 262p. 1994. 75.00 (*1-85075-450-0*, Pub. by Sheffield Acad) CUP Services.

Anderson, Janice R. Atlas of Skeletal Muscle Pathology. LC 85-2956. 1985. text 309.00 (*0-85200-325-0*) Kluwer Academic.

Anderson, Janice R., jt. auth. see Bragg, Steven M.

Anderson, Janice W., et al. Communication Skills for Surviving Conflicts at Work. 200p. 1996. 45.00 (*1-57273-056-0*); pap. 22.95 (*1-57273-057-9*) Hampton Pr NJ.

Anderson, Jay, ed. A Living History Reader Vol. 1: Museums. LC 91-14576. (American Association for State & Local History Book Ser.). (Illus.). 240p. 1991. reprint ed. pap. 25.95 (*0-942063-13-9*) AltaMira Pr.

Anderson, Jaynie. Giorgione: The Painter of Poetic Brevity. LC 97-33012. (Illus.). 392p. 1997. 95.00 (*2-08-013644-5*, Pub. by Flammarion) Abbeville Pr.

Anderson, Jaynie, ed. see Wind, Edgar.

Anderson, Jean. The American Century Cookbook: 100 Years of Culinary Invention. LC 97-3600. 608p. 1997. 35.00 (*0-517-70576-1*) Random.

— Dinners in a Dish or a Dash: Delicious One-Pot Meals You Can Prepare with Ease. LC 99-49514. 384p. 2000. 25.00 (*0-688-14572-8*, Wm Morrow) Morrow Avon.

***Anderson, Jean.** Eric Benhamou Focus on Education. 18p. 2000. pap. 9.95 (*0-9678605-5-5*) InfoHi.

Anderson, Jean. The Food of Portugal. 1994. pap. 16.00 (*0-688-13415-7*, Hearst) Hearst Commns.

Anderson, Jean. Handling Hostile People. (Lifestyle Ser.). 31p. 1988. pap. 0.99 (*0-8163-0779-2*) Pacific Pr Pub Assn.

Anderson, Jean. In Extremis & Other Alaskan Stories. LC 89-3507. 120p. 1989. 14.95 (*0-917635-06-X*); pap. 9.95 (*0-917635-07-8*) Plover Pr.

***Anderson, Jean.** The Secret Surfwoman. (Illus.). 44p. 2000. pap. 14.95 (*0-9678605-0-4*) InfoHi.

— 10 Steps to Becoming a Technical Writer. 39p. 2000. pap. 19.95 (*0-9678605-3-9*) InfoHi.

Anderson, Jean. 1,001 Secrets of Great Cooks. LC 95-3. 272p. (Orig.). 1995. pap. 12.00 (*0-399-52153-4*, Perigee Bks) Berkley Pub.

— Wigmaking Step by Step Pt. 1: Weft Work. 138p. 1992. 150.00 (*0-9519080-0-6*, Pub. by JA Pubns) St Mut.

— Wigmaking Step by Step Pt. 2: Foundation Work. 250p. 1992. 175.00 (*0-9519080-1-4*, Pub. by JA Pubns) St Mut.

Anderson, Jean & Deskins, Barbara. The Nutrition Bible: A Comprehensive, No-Nonsense Guide to Foods, Nutrients, Additives, Preservatives, Pollutants, & Everything Else We Eat & Drink. LC 94-38080. 544p. 1996. 30.00 (*0-688-11619-1*, Wm Morrow) Morrow Avon.

— The Nutrition Bible: A Comprehensive, No-Nonsense Guide to Foods, Nutrients, Additives, Preservatives, Pollutants & Everything Else We Eat & Drink. (Illus.). 480p. 1997. reprint ed. pap. 17.00 (*0-688-15559-6*, Quil) HarperTrade.

Anderson, Jean & Hanna, Elaine. The New Doubleday Cookbook. LC 85-16844. (Illus.). 992p. 1990. 35.00 (*0-385-19577-X*) Doubleday.

Anderson, Jean & Lininger, Linda. Birdman of Altamount. 47p. Date not set. pap. 9.95 (*0-9678605-4-7*) InfoHi.

— Calistoga Candlestick Caper. 124p. (YA). (gr. 4 up). 2000. pap. 14.95 (*0-9678605-9-8*) InfoHi.

— 10 Steps to Protecting Your Man from Monica Wannabees. 21p. 2000. pap. 11.00 (*0-9678605-6-3*) InfoHi.

Anderson, Jean, et al. The New German Cookbook: More Than 230 Contemporary & Traditional Recipes. LC 92-56211. (Illus.). 416p. 1993. 27.50 (*0-06-016202-3*) HarperTrade.

Anderson, Jean, jt. auth. see Anderson, Bob.

Anderson, Jean, jt. auth. see Kasten, Lloyd A.

Anderson, Jean, jt. auth. see Kimball, Yeffe.

Anderson, Jean, jt. auth. see Moulton, Sara.

Anderson, Jean, ed. see Bullock, Harold B.

Anderson, Jean, jt. ed. see Kasten, Lloyd A.

Anderson, Jean B. Durham County: A History of Durham County, North Carolina. LC 90-3509. (Illus.). 628p. (C). 1990. text 34.95 (*0-8223-1056-2*) Duke.

— The Kirklands of Ayr Mount. LC 90-12409. (Illus.). xii, 265p. 1991. 29.95 (*0-8078-1930-1*) U of NC Pr.

— The Kirklands of Ayr Mount. LC 90-12409. (Illus.). 289p. 1991. reprint ed. pap. 89.60 (*0-7837-9894-6*, 206062000006) Bks Demand.

— Piedmont Plantation: The Bennehan-Cameron Family & Lands in North Carolina. LC 85-81002. (Illus.). xix, 227p. 1985. 24.95 (*0-9615577-1-0*) HPS Durham.

Anderson, Jeff. The Graphic Bible. Maddox, Mike, ed. (Illus.). 256p. 1998. 29.99 (*0-8054-1813-X*) Broadman.

***Anderson, Jeff & Maddox, Mike.** Biblia Grafica. (SPA., Illus.). 1999. 29.99 (*0-7899-0627-9*) Spanish Hse Distributors.

Anderson, Jeffrey. German Unification & the Union of Europe: The Domestic Politics of Integration Policy. LC 98-41171. (Illus.). 280p. (C). 1999. text 54.95 (*0-521-64355-4*); pap. text 19.95 (*0-521-64390-2*) Cambridge U Pr.

Anderson, Jeffrey, ed. Modern Management of Acute Myocardial Infarction in the Community Hospital. 560p. 1991. text 125.00 (*0-8247-8432-4*) Dekker.

Anderson, Jeffrey, et al. Inklings. 80p. 1995. pap. 12.50 (*0-9644863-0-X*) E Johnstone.

Anderson, Jeffrey C. The New York Cruciform Lectionary. (Illus.). 192p. 1992. 47.50 (*0-271-00743-5*) Pa St U Pr.

Anderson, Jeffrey J. The Territorial Imperative: Pluralism, Corporatism & Economic Crisis. (Illus.). 268p. (C). 1992. text 69.95 (*0-521-41378-8*) Cambridge U Pr.

Anderson, Jeffrey J., ed. Regional Integration & Democracy: Expanding on the European Experience. LC 98-36858. (Marks/Governance in Europe Ser.). 344p. 1999. pap. 24.95 (*0-8476-9025-3*) Rowman.

***Anderson, Jeffrey J., ed.** Regional Integration & Democracy: Expanding on the European Experience. LC 98-36858. (Marks/Governance in Europe Ser.). 344p. 1999. 67.00 (*0-8476-9024-5*) Rowman.

Anderson, Jeffrey W., jt. auth. see Cummings, Hildegard.

Anderson, Jenna, ed. see Doherty, Kieran.

Anderson, Jenna, ed. see McLean, Jacqueline.

Anderson, Jenna, ed. see Wills, Susan & Wills, Steven R.

Anderson, Jennifer. The Limits of Sino-Russian Strategic Partnership. LC U162.A3 no. 315. (Adelphi Papers: No. 315). (Illus.). 96p. 1998. pap. text 28.95 (*0-19-829427-1*) OUP.

Anderson, Jerry D. Success Strategies for Investment Real Estate: The Professionals Guide to Better Service & Increased Commissions. 2nd ed. Berlin, Helene, ed. LC 82-61402. (Illus.). 322p. (Orig.). (C). 1985. pap. text 17.95 (*0-913652-33-4*, BK 153) Realtors Natl.

***Anderson, Jerry L.** Jerry Anderson's Joy of Fitness for Women: The Best & Easiest Way to Gain a Healthy Body & Peace of Mind. LC 99-98089. (Illus.). 184p. 2000. pap. 24.95 (*0-9677093-0-X*) Apex Fitness.

Anderson, Jerry L., ed. Water Resources Planning & Management & Urban Water Resources. LC 91-12629. 1064p. 1991. pap. text 12.00 (*0-87262-805-1*) Am Soc Civil Eng.

Anderson, Jerry L. & Hirsch, Dennis D. Environmental Law Practice: Problems & Exercises for Skills Development. LC 98-43983. 296p. 1999. pap. 25.00 (*0-89089-657-7*) Carolina Acad Pr.

Anderson, Jerry W., Jr. Corporate Social Responsibility: Guidelines for Top Management. LC 88-23952. 294p. 1989. 62.95 (*0-89930-272-6*, ACS/, Quorum Bks) Greenwood.

Anderson, Jerry W., Jr. & Camealy, John B. Corporate Operational Analysis: A Procedure for Evaluating Key Factors in Internal Operations, Acquisitions, & Takeovers. LC 90-47592. 362p. 1991. 79.50 (*0-89930-535-0*, ACB/, Quorum Bks) Greenwood.

Anderson, Jervis. A. Philip Randolph: A Biographical Portrait. LC 73-12847. 1986. pap. 17.95 (*0-520-05505-5*, Pub. by U CA Pr) Cal Prin Full Svc.

Anderson, Jervis. Bayard Rustin: Troubles I've Seen: A Biography. LC 97-33075. 432p. 1997. pap. 17.95 (*0-520-21418-8*, Pub. by U CA Pr) Cal Prin Full Svc.

Anderson, Jill. Bright Beginnings Storybook: Building Self-Esteem Skills with Pumsy. (Illus.). 200p. 1990. teacher ed. 80.00 (*0-9608284-6-X*) Timberline Pr.

— Bright Beginnings Storybook: Building Self-Esteem Skills with Pumsy. (Illus.). 42p. (J). (gr. k-4). 1990. pap. text 3.95 (*0-9608284-7-8*) Timberline Pr.

— The Land of No. Blackwelder, Kathy, ed. LC 87-51628. (Illus.). 40p. (J). (gr. 1-4). 1990. lib. bdg. 14.95 (*0-9608284-5-1*) Timberline Pr.

— Pumsy in Pursuit of Excellence: Self-Esteem for the Elementary School Child. (Illus.). 270p. 1990. teacher ed. 80.00 (*0-9608284-3-5*) Timberline Pr.

— Pumsy Storybook. (Illus.). 40p. (Orig.). (J). (gr. 2-5). 1990. pap. text 4.95 (*0-9608284-2-7*) Timberline Pr.

— Thinking, Changing, Rearranging. 1985. reprint ed. student ed. 8.00 (*0-9608284-0-0*); reprint ed. pap. text, teacher ed. 17.00 (*0-7648-0149-3*) Timberline Pr.

— Thinking, Changing, Rearranging: Improving Self Esteem in Young People. LC 88-2289. (Illus.). 80p. (J). (gr. 2). 1990. reprint ed. pap., student ed. 7.50 (*0-943920-30-2*) Metamorphous Pr.

Anderson, Jill & Weinman, Susan. Skill Builders: Course Code 392-1. Schroeder, Bonnie & Doheny, Catherine, eds. (Illus.). 86p. 1989. reprint ed. pap. text 5.95 (*0-917531-87-6*) CES Compu-Tech.

— Skill Builders: Course Code 392-2. Schroeder, Bonnie & Doheny, Catherine, eds. (Illus.). 90p. (J). (gr. 4). 1989. reprint ed. pap. text 5.95 (*0-917531-88-4*) CES Compu-Tech.

Anderson, Jill, et al. Skill Builders: Lab Pack 1. Schroeder, Bonnie & Doheny, Cathy, eds. (Illus.). 100p. teacher ed. 19.95 (*1-56177-070-1*, T392-1); teacher ed., student ed. 229.95 incl. disk (*1-56177-068-X*, L392-1); disk 15.95 (*1-56177-066-3*, D392-1) CES Compu-Tech.

— Skill Builders: Lab Pack 2. Schroeder, Bonnie & Doheny, Cathy, eds. (Illus.). 100p. teacher ed. 19.95 (*1-56177-071-X*, TE392-2); teacher ed., student ed. 229.95 incl. disk (*0-685-45804-0*, L392-2); disk 15.95 (*1-56177-067-1*, D392-2) CES Compu-Tech.

Anderson, Jim. Live Free Forever, Guaranteed (by New Law) & Save up to 25on Home Purchase: All Because of Jim Anderson's New Home Buyer Law. 1996. pap. 20.00 incl. VHS (*0-932574-11-4*) Brun Pr.

— Live Free Forever, Guaranteed (by New Law) & Save up to 25on Home Purchase: All Because of Jim Anderson's New Home Buyer Law. 12th enl. rev. ed. LC 78-113752. (Illus.). 650p. 1991. reprint ed. 40.00 (*0-932574-10-6*) Brun Pr.

— Runabout Renovation: How to Find & Fix up an Old Fiberglass Speedboat. (Illus.). 160p. 1992. pap. 16.95 (*0-87742-295-8*) Intl Marine.

— Runabout Renovation: How to Find & Fix up an Old Fiberglass Speedboat. 160p. 1992. pap. 16.95 (*0-07-158008-5*) McGraw.

Anderson, Jim & Anderson, Lisa. Philly's Best Bars. LC 90-84771. (Illus.). (Orig.). 1990. pap. 8.95 (*0-9628362-0-6*) Black Tooth Pr.

— Philly's Best Bars. 2nd ed. LC 90-84771. (Illus.). (Orig.). 1991. pap. 8.95 (*0-9628362-1-4*) Black Tooth Pr.

Anderson, Jim A. Fifty Strategies for Quality Teaching: A Handbook for the Application of Control Theory in Classroom Settings. (Illus.). 74p. (Orig.). 1995. pap. 14.95 (*0-9654291-0-5*) Jackpine Pubng.

Anderson, J'Lynn, jt. auth. see Miller, Donna.

Anderson, Joan. After Residency: The Young Physician's Guide to the Universe. 1998. pap. 19.95 (*1-890114-01-4*) Physicians Pr.

— The American Family Farm. LC 88-30068. (Illus.). 96p. (J). 1997. pap. 9.00 (*0-15-201481-0*) Harcourt.

— Batboy: An Inside Look at Spring Training. LC 95-11793. (Illus.). 48p. (J). (gr. 3-7). 1996. 16.99 (*0-525-67511-6*, Dutton Child) Peng Put Young Read.

— The First Thanksgiving Feast. LC 84-58040. (Illus.). 48p. (J). (ps-3). 1989. pap. 6.95 (*0-395-51886-5*, Clarion Bks) HM.

— The First Thanksgiving Feast. 1989. 10.90 (*0-606-01089-0*, Pub. by Turtleback) Demco.

— Getting Unplugged: Take Control of Your Family's Television, Video Game, & Computer Habits. LC 98-14645. 164p. 1998. pap. 12.95 (*0-471-17889-6*) Wiley.

***Anderson, Joan.** Rookie: A First Year in the WNBA. LC 00-20516. (Illus.). 40p. (J). (gr. 4-8). 2000. 16.99 (*0-525-46412-3*, Dutton Child) Peng Put Young Read.

— Rookie: A First Year with the WNBA. (Illus.). (J). (ps-3). 2000. pap. 7.99 (*0-14-056740-2*, PuffinBks) Peng Put Young Read.

Anderson, Joan. 1787. LC 86-29403. (Illus.). 176p. (J). (gr. 3-7). 1987. 14.95 (*0-15-200582-X*, Gulliver Bks) Harcourt.

— The Single Mother's Book: A Practical Guide to Managing Your Children, Career, Home, Finances & Everything Else. 320p. 1990. pap. 13.95 (*0-934601-84-4*) Peachtree Pubs.

— Spanish Pioneers of the Southwest. 1989. pap. 16.99 (*0-525-67546-9*) NAL.

— Wearable Art: Cut-to-Fit. (Illus.). 64p. 1997. pap. text 11.95 (*0-614-31265-5*) Sew-Fit.

Anderson, Joan. Williamsburg Household. 1988. 11.15 (*0-606-04848-0*, Pub. by Turtleback) Demco.

Anderson, Joan. A Year by the Sea: Thoughts of an Unfinished Woman. LC 98-37082. (Illus.). 208p. 1999. 22.95 (*0-385-49139-5*) Doubleday.

***Anderson, Joan.** A Year by the Sea: Thoughts of an Unfinished Woman. LC 99-53128. 2000. 30.00 (*0-7838-8821-X*, G K Hall Lrg Type) Mac Lib Ref.

— Year by the Sea: Thoughts of an Unfinished Woman. 196p. 2000. pap. 12.95 (*0-7679-0593-8*) Broadway BDD.

Anderson, Joan, jt. auth. see Oblander, Ruth.

Anderson, Joan B. Economic Policy Alternatives for the Latin American Crisis. 144p. 1990. 75.00 (*0-8448-1677-9*, Crane Russak) Taylor & Francis.

Anderson, Joan B., jt. ed. see Randall, Laura.

Anderson, Joan M., jt. ed. see Kinsey, Bruce.

Anderson, Joan W. Abortion: The Prolife Point of View. 72p. (YA). (gr. 7-12). 1992. pap. 6.95 (*1-57515-020-4*) PPI Pubng.

— Un Angel Que Vele Por Mi. (SPA.). 176p. 1996. pap. 12.00 (*0-345-40255-3*) Ballantine Pub Grp.

— An Angel to Watch over Me: True Stories of Children's Encounters with Angels. 160p. 1996. pap. 12.00 (*0-345-39773-8*) Ballantine Pub Grp.

— Angels We Have Heard on High: A Book of Seasonal Blessings. LC 97-20969. 128p. 1997. 12.95 (*0-345-41203-6*) Ballantine Pub Grp.

— Making Your Marriage Last. 32p. 1998. pap. 1.95 (*0-7648-0147-3*) Liguori Pubns.

— Pioneer Children of Appalachia. LC 86-2624. 48p. (J). (gr. 4-7). 1990. pap. 7.95 (*0-395-54792-X*, Clarion Bks) HM.

— Power of Miracles: Stories of God in the Everyday. rev. ed. LC 98-13966. 1998. 23.00 (*0-345-39732-0*) Ballantine Pub Grp.

— Where Angels Walk: True Stories of Heavenly Visitors. 224p. 1992. 16.95 (*0-9631981-0-6*) Barton & Brett.

— Where Angels Walk: True Stories of Heavenly Visitors. large type ed. LC 93-10047. 254p. 1993. lib. bdg. 22.95 (*0-8161-5818-5*, G K Hall Lrg Type) Mac Lib Ref.

— Where Angels Walk: True Stories of Heavenly Vistors. LC 92-97538. 224p. 1993. pap. 12.00 (*0-345-38338-9*, Ballantine Epiphany) Ballantine Pub Grp.

— Where Miracles Happen. 272p. 1995. pap. 12.00 (*0-345-39305-8*) Ballantine Pub Grp.

— Where Miracles Happen: True Stories of Heavenly Encounters. large type ed. LC 94-41966. 329p. 1995. lib. bdg. 21.95 (*0-7838-1202-7*, G K Hall Lrg Type) Mac Lib Ref.

— Where Wonders Prevail: True Accounts That Bear Witness to the Existence of Heaven. 288p. 1997. pap. 12.00 (*0-345-40910-8*) Ballantine Pub Grp.

— Where Wonders Prevail: True Accounts That Bear Witness to the Existence of Heaven. large type ed. LC 97-22183. (Inspirational Ser.). 303p. 1997. lib. bdg. 23.95 (*0-7838-8263-7*, G K Hall Lrg Type) Mac Lib Ref.

— A Williamsburg Household. LC 87-33803. 48p. (J). (gr. 4-7). 1990. pap. 7.95 (*0-395-54791-1*, Clarion Bks) HM.

Anderson, Joan Wester. Angels We Have Heard on High: A Book of Seasonal Blessings. 1999. mass mkt. 5.99 (*0-345-43608-3*) Ballantine Pub Grp.

Anderson, Joann, ed. see Anderson, Claud.

Anderson, Joanne, jt. auth. see Anderson, Neil T.

Anderson, Joanne M. Small-Town Restaurants in Virginia. LC 98-15963. (Illus.). 1998. pap. 16.95 (*0-89587-211-0*) Blair.

Anderson, Joanne S., ed. Guide for Written Collection Policy Statements. 2nd ed. LC 95-53047. (ALCTS Collection Management & Development Guides Ser.: 7). 40p. 1996. pap. 15.00 (*0-8389-3455-2*, 3455-2-2045) ALA.

Anderson, Jock R. & Hazell, Peter B., eds. Variability in Grain Yields: Implications for Agricultural Research & Policy in Developing Countries. LC 88-32079. 384p. 1989. text 45.00 (*0-8018-3793-6*) Johns Hopkins.

Anderson, Jock R. & Thampapillai, Jesuthason. Soil Conservation in Developing Countries: Project & Policy Intervention. (Policy & Research Ser.: No. 8). 52p. 1990. pap. 22.00 (*0-8213-1448-3*, 11448) World Bank.

Anderson, Jock R., et al. Agricultural Decision Analysis. LC 76-46456. 354p. reprint ed. pap. 109.80 (*0-8357-5267-4*, 202972000064) Bks Demand.

Anderson, Jock R., jt. auth. see Purcell, Dennis L.

Anderson, Joel. David & the Trash-Talkin Giant. LC 98-46163. (Illus.). 32p. (J). (ps-3). 1999. 12.99 (*0-8499-5918-7*) Tommy Nelson.

***Anderson, Joel.** God Knows Me! From Psalm 139. LC 98-89073. 24p. 1999. 9.95 (*0-307-25177-2*) Gldn Bks Pub Co.

— Lord is My Shepherd! From Psalm 23. LC 98-89074. 24p. 1999. 9.95 (*0-307-25176-4*) Gldn Bks Pub Co.

Anderson, Joel & Goolsby, Abe. Jonah's Trash...God's Treasure: Mr. Grungy's Junkyard Bible Stories. LC 97-32655. (Illus.). 32p. (J). (ps-3). 1998. 12.99 (*0-8499-5825-3*) Tommy Nelson.

Anderson, Joel, tr. see Honneth, Axel.

Anderson, Johana G. Sewing for Twentieth Century Dolls. Vol. 1. (Illus.). 264p. 1996. reprint ed. 24.95 (*0-87588-467-9*, 5200) Hobby Hse.

Anderson, John. Civil War Infantry, the 57th Regiment of Massachusetts Volunteers in the War of the Rebellion, Army of the Potomac. (Illus.). 512p. 1995. reprint ed. lib. bdg. 56.00 (*0-8328-4630-9*) Higginson Bk Co.

— English Intercourse with Siam in the Seventeenth Century. 1976. reprint ed. 69.00 (*0-403-05983-6*, Regency) Scholarly.

— An Essay Concerning Aspect: Some Considerations of a General Character Arising from the Abbe Darrigol's Analysis of the Basque Verb. (Janua Linguarum, Series Minor: No. 167). 1973. pap. text 41.55 (*90-279-2408-2*) Mouton.

— How to Buy Government Surplus. 112p. 1987. 25.00 (*0-934748-24-1*) Broughton Hall.

***Anderson, John.** Kyrgyzstan: Central Asia's Island of Democracy? (Postcommunist States & Nations Ser.). 107p. 1999. pap. text 19.95 (*90-5702-390-3*, Harwood Acad Pubs) Gordon & Breach.

— Kyrgyzstan: Central Asia's Island of Democracy. 107p. 1999. text 33.00 (*90-5702-389-X*, Harwood Acad Pubs) Gordon & Breach.

Anderson, John. Religion, State, & Politics in the Soviet Union & the Successor States, 1953-1993. LC 93-44304. 248p. (C). 1994. pap. text 20.95 (*0-521-46784-5*) Cambridge U Pr.

— Reptilia & Batrachia. (Zoology of Egypt Ser.: No. 1). (Illus.). 1965. reprint ed. 250.00 (*3-7682-0240-2*) Lubrecht & Cramer.

— The Story of the Life of John Anderson, the Fugitive Slave. Twelvetrees, Harper, ed. LC 72-164378. (Black Heritage Library Collection). 1977. reprint ed. 26.95 (*0-8369-8837-X*) Ayer.

***Anderson, John.** Sundancing: Hanging Out & Listening in at America's Most Important Film Festival, Vol. 1. LC 99-39934. (Illus.). 288p. 2000. pap. 12.50 (*0-380-80480-8*, Avon Bks) Morrow Avon.

Anderson, John, ed. Surface Infrastructure: Costs, Financing & Schedules for Large-Dollar Transportation Projects. (Illus.). 87p. (C). 1998. pap. text 20.00 (*0-7881-7322-7*) DIANE Pub.

***Anderson, John & Aberman, Rick.** Coaching Coaches: How to Cope with the Realities of Modern Sports: A Guide for Coaches from Youth Leagues to College. LC 98-50806. 192p. 1999. pap. 15.95 (*1-57749-067-3*, Pub. by Fairview Press) Natl Bk Netwk.

Anderson, John & Bratos-Anderson, Magda. Noise: Its Measurement, Analysis, Rating & Control. 494p. 1993. 96.95 (*0-291-39794-8*, Pub. by Avebury Technical) Ashgate Pub Co.

Anderson, John & Cassady, Marsh. The Newhall Incident: America's Worst Uniformed Cop Massacre. (Illus.). 212p. 1999. 24.95 (*1-884956-09-2*) Quill Driver.

Anderson, John & Varuzza, Jose. International Dominos. (Illus.). 64p. (Orig.). 1989. pap. 14.95 (*0-9624571-0-8*) Avid Pr.

Anderson, John, jt. auth. see De Blassie, Richard R.

Anderson, John, jt. auth. see Rose, Peter.

Anderson, John, tr. see Elsass, Peter.

Anderson, John A. How to Steal Food from the Supermarket. LC 92-74896. 67p. (Orig.). 1992. pap. 10.00 (*1-55950-091-3*, 40079) Loompanics.

Anderson, John A. & Groten, Frank J., Jr. Latin: A Course for Schools & Colleges. rev. ed. LC 71-102077. (Illus.). 357p. (YA). (gr. 7-12). 1988. reprint ed. 20.00 (*0-942573-00-5*) Hill School.

Anderson, John A., jt. ed. see Lieberman, Phil.

Anderson, John B. Antarctic Marine Geology. LC 98-37219. (Illus.). 496p. (C). 1999. 115.00 (*0-521-59317-4*) Cambridge U Pr.

— Digital Transmission Engineering. LC 98-3517. 400p. 1998. 89.95 (*0-7803-3457-4*, PC5714-QOE) Inst Electrical.

— Digital Transmission Engineering. 369p. (C). 1998. 105.00 (*0-13-082961-7*) P-H.

— A Proper Institution: Guaranteeing Televised Presidential Debates - A Twentieth Century Fund Paper. 61p. 1988. 18.95 (*0-87078-253-3*); pap. 8.95 (*0-87078-252-5*) Century Foundation.

Anderson, John B. & Mohan, Seshadri. Source & Channel Coding: An Algorithmic Approach. 448p. (C). 1991. text 93.00 (*0-7923-9210-8*) Kluwer Academic.

Anderson, John C. Chapter Eleven Reorganizations. 778p. 1983. text 105.00 (*0-07-001691-7*) Shepards.

— Cosmic Omelet. LC 79-89328. 1980. 5.95 (*0-87212-102-X*) Libra.

— Mackinaws down the Missouri: John C. Anderson's Journal of a Trip from Saint Louis, Mo., to Virginia City, Montana & Return, 1866. Barrett, Glen, ed. LC 73-79903. (Illus.). 111p. reprint ed. pap. 34.50 (*0-8357-6197-5*, 203460500090) Bks Demand.

— Why Lawyers Derail Justice: Probing the Roots of Legal Injustices. LC 98-16936. 1998. 40.00 (*0-271-01842-9*); 18.95 (*0-271-01843-7*) Pa St U Pr.

Anderson, John C., et al, eds. Material Requirements Planning: A Study of Implementation & Practice. LC 81-68514. 57p. 1981. pap. 10.00 (*0-935406-03-4*) Am Prod & Inventory.

Anderson, John D., Jr. Computational Fluid Dynamics: The Basics with Applications. LC 94-21237. (Series in Mathematical Engineering). 574p. (C). 1995. 75.94 (*0-07-001685-2*) McGraw.

Anderson, John D. Fundamentals of Aerodynamics. 2nd ed. 800p. (C). 1991. 96.88 (*0-07-001679-8*) McGraw.

Anderson, John D., Jr. A History of Aerodynamics: And Its Impact on Flying Machines. (Cambridge Aerospace Ser.: No. 8). (Illus.). 490p. (C). 1997. text 95.00 (*0-521-45435-2*) Cambridge U Pr.

— A History of Aerodynamics: And Its Impact on Flying Machines. (Aerospace Ser.: No. 8). (Illus.). 478p. (C). 1999. pap. text 39.95 (*0-521-66955-3*) Cambridge U Pr.

— Hypersonic & High Temperature Gas Dynamics. (Aeronautical & Aerospace Engineering Ser.). 704p. (C). 1988. text 82.50 (*0-07-001671-2*) McGraw.

— Introduction to Flight. 3rd ed. (Aeronautical & Aerospace Engineering Ser.). 616p. (C). 1988. 96.88 (*0-07-001641-0*) McGraw.

Anderson, John D. Introduction to Flight. 4th ed. LC 99-32638. 784p. 1999. 97.50 (*0-07-109282-X*) McGraw.

Anderson, John D., Jr. Modern Compressible Flow: With Historical Perspective. 2nd ed. (Aeronautical & Aerospace Engineering Ser.). 650p. (C). 1989. 98.13 (*0-07-001673-9*) McGraw.

— Modern Compressible Flow: With Historical Perspective. 2nd ed. (Aeronautical & Aerospace Engineering Ser.). 672p. (C). 1990. pap. text, teacher ed. 27.50 (*0-07-001674-7*) McGraw.

Anderson, John D. The Rich Register: A Directory of America's Wealthiest People, 1996. 240p. 1998. 395.00 (*0-9633933-0-8*) Rich Register.

Anderson, John D. & Edwards, Ann T. Out for Life. LC 96-784. (Illus.). iv, 182p. (Orig.). 1996. pap. 14.00 (*0-86663-208-5*) Ide Hse.

Anderson, John E. Fiscal Equalization for State & Local Government Finance. LC 94-2985. 224p. 1994. 49.95 (*0-275-94654-1*, Praeger Pubs) Greenwood.

***Anderson, John E. & Wassmer, Robert W.** Bidding for Business: The Efficacy of Local Economic Development Incentives in a Metropolitan Area. LC 00-22199. 220p. (C). 2000. 35.00 (*0-88099-202-6*) W E Upjohn.

— Bidding for Business: The Efficacy of Local Economic Development Incentives in a Metropolitan Area. LC 00-22199. 220p. 2000. pap. 17.00 (*0-88099-201-8*) W E Upjohn.

Anderson, John E., jt. ed. see Darby, Michael R.

Anderson, John F., et al. Questionnaires: Design & Use. 2nd ed. LC 86-1783. 344p. 1986. 34.50 (*0-8108-1884-1*) Scarecrow.

Anderson, John G. Hidden Montana. 2nd rev. ed. (Hidden Travel Ser.). (Illus.). 304p. 1999. pap. 14.95 (*1-56975-176-5*) Ulysses Pr.

— Technical Shop Mathematics. 2nd ed. LC 82-11847. (Illus.). 500p. (C). 1983. 25.95 (*0-8311-1145-3*) Indus Pr.

***Anderson, John G.** Technical Shop Mathematics. 3rd ed. 1999. text 29.95 (*0-8311-3086-5*) Indus Pr.

Anderson, John G. & Rose, Peter. The Insiders' Guide to Boise & Sun Valley. (Insiders' Guide Travel Ser.). 1998. pap. 15.95 (*1-57380-057-0*, The Insiders Guide) Falcon Pub Inc.

Anderson, John G., jt. auth. see Drury, William Holland.

***Anderson, John H.** Kareers: A "Useful" Guide to 111 Really Odd Jobs. (Illus.). 250p. 1999. pap. 14.95 (*1-55152-070-2*, Pub. by Arsenal Pulp) LPC InBook.

Anderson, John H. National Airspace System: FAA Has Implemented Some Free Flight Initiatives, but Challenges Remain. (Illus.). 76p. 1999. text 20.00 (*0-7881-7914-4*) DIANE Pub.

— Thru One Orphan's Eyes: The Girard Story. unabridged ed. LC 96-96316. (Illus.). 400p. 1996. 25.00 (*0-9654295-0-4*) Pocono.

A

An Asterisk (*) at the beginning of an entry indicates that the title is appearing for the first time

A

Anderson, John H., et al. Aviation Safety: Weaknesses in Inspection & Enforcement Limit FAA in Identifying & Responding to Risks. (Illus.). 124p. 1998. pap. text 30.00 (*0-7881-7317-0*) DIANE Pub.

Anderson, John H., jt. auth. see Beitz, Alvin J.

Anderson, John J. Dietary Excesses & Health Disease Implications. (Illus.). 1984. pap. 18.95 (*0-938938-13-4*) Health Sci Comm.

Anderson, John J. The Markagunt Megabreccia: Large Miocene Gravity Slides Mantling the Northern Markagunt Plateau, Southwestern Utah. (Miscellaneous Publication Ser.: Vol. 93-2). (Illus.). 37p. 1993. pap. 5.00 (*1-55791-321-8*, MP-93-2) Utah Geological Survey.

Anderson, John J. & Garner, Sanford C., eds. Calcium & Phosphorus in Health & Disease. (Modern Nutrition Ser.). 416p. 1995. boxed set 179.95 (*0-8493-7845-1*, 7845) CRC Pr.

Anderson, John J., et al. Cenozoic Geology of Southwestern High Plateaus of Utah. LC 75-10395. (Geological Society of America, Special Paper: No. 160). 134p. reprint ed. pap. 41.60 (*0-608-13552-6*, 202545700044) Bks Demand.

Anderson, John J., jt. auth. see Kurlich, Richard A., III.

Anderson, John K. Alexander the Great. (Illus.). 1981. pap. 4.95 (*0-88388-085-7*) Bellerophon Bks.

— Amazons. (Illus.). 48p. (J). (gr. 4-8). 1997. pap. 4.95 (*0-88388-201-9*) Bellerophon Bks.

— Horses & Riding. (Illus.). 48p. (J). (gr. 4-7). 1979. pap. 4.95 (*0-88388-066-0*) Bellerophon Bks.

— Tales of Great Dragons. (Illus.). 64p. 1980. pap. 4.95 (*0-88388-075-X*) Bellerophon Bks.

Anderson, John L. An Exegetical Summary of 1, 2, & 3 John. 272p. 1992. pap. 14.70 (*0-88312-827-6*) S I L Intl.

Anderson, John L. Night of the Silent Drums. (Illus.). 449p. 1992. reprint ed. 29.95 (*0-926330-05-5*); reprint ed. pap. 19.95 (*0-926330-06-3*) Mapes Monde.

— Off the Bridal Path. 1992. pap. 17.95 (*0-9616967-2-9*) Nordbook.

— Scandinavian Humor & Other Myths. 218p. 1987. pap. 9.95 (*0-9616967-0-2*) Nordbook.

Anderson, John M. The Kincade Chronicles. LC 86-80062. 303p. 1986. 17.50 (*0-937884-12-X*, Bennington Bks) Hystry Mystry.

— Linguistic Representation: Structural Analogy & Stratification. LC 92-26797. (Trends in Linguistics, Studies & Monographs: Vol. 67). x, 254p. (C). 1992. lib. bdg. 113.85 (*3-11-013531-0*) Mouton.

— A Notional Theory of Syntactic Categories. LC 96-21789. (Cambridge Studies in Linguistics: No. 82). 365p. 1997. text 69.95 (*0-521-58023-4*) Cambridge U Pr.

— West Highland Cattle! The Grand Olde Breed. (Illus.). 96p. 1985. 14.00 (*0-9615813-0-1*) J Mac Anderson.

***Anderson, John M.** Wildlife Sanctuaries & the Audubon Society: Places to Hide & Seek. LC 99-44164. (Illus.). 286p. 2000. 45.00 (*0-292-70498-4*); pap. 22.95 (*0-292-70499-2*) U of Tex Pr.

Anderson, John M. & Anderson, Heidi M. Palaeoflora of Southern Africa: Prodromus of South African Megafloras, Devonia to Lower Cretaceous. 424p. 1985. text 214.00 (*90-6191-575-9*, Pub. by A A Balkema) Ashgate Pub Co.

— Palaeoflora of Southern Africa - Molteno Formation (Triassic) Fruits & Seeds; Spores & Pollen Grains, Vol. 4, Pts. 5 & 6. (C). Date not set. text 150.00 (*90-6191-286-5*, Pub. by A A Balkema) Ashgate Pub Co.

— Palaeoflora of Southern Africa - Molteno Formation (Triassic) Gymnosperms, Vol. 2, Pt. 3. (C). 1988. text 150.00 (*90-6191-284-9*, Pub. by A A Balkema) Ashgate Pub Co.

— Palaeoflora of Southern Africa - Molteno Formation (Triassic) Introduction; Dicroidium, Vol. 1 Pts. 1 & 2. (Illus.). 240p. 1983. text 150.00 (*90-6191-283-0*, Pub. by A A Balkema) Ashgate Pub Co.

— Palaeoflora of Southern Africa - Molteno Formation (Triassic) Localities & Communities; General Synthesis, Vol. 6 Pts. 9 & 10. (C). Date not set. text 150.00 (*90-6191-288-1*, Pub. by A A Balkema) Ashgate Pub Co.

— Palaeoflora of Southern Africa - Molteno Formation (Triassic) Non-Gymnosperms, Vol. 3, Pt. 4. (C). 1991. text 150.00 (*90-6191-285-7*, Pub. by A A Balkema) Ashgate Pub Co.

— Palaeoflora of Southern Africa - Molteno Formation (Triassic) Wood; Fauna, Vol. 5 Pts. 7 & 8. (C). 1993. text 150.00 (*90-6191-287-3*, Pub. by A A Balkema) Ashgate Pub Co.

Anderson, John O. The Cry of Compassion: A Prophetic Call to Defend Biblical Values & Make a Difference in Our World. 238p. (Orig.). 1994. pap. 7.99 (*0-88270-681-0*) Bridge-Logos.

Anderson, John O. & Brendel, Doug. Cry of the Innocents: Abortion & the Race Towards Judgement. LC 85-70539. 187p. 1985. mass mkt. 4.99 (*0-88270-586-5*) Bridge-Logos.

Anderson, John P. & Cassady, Marsh. The Newhall Incident: America's Worst Uniformed Cop Massacre. LC 98-40994. (Illus.). 1998. pap. 14.95 (*1-884956-01-7*) Quill Driver.

Anderson, John Q. Texas Folk Medicine: 1,333 Cures, Remedies, Preventives & Health Practices. (Illus.). 91p. 1970. reprint ed. 16.95 (*1-57441-056-3*) UNTX Pr.

— With the Bark On: Popular Humor of the Old South. LC 67-13998. (Illus.). 349p. reprint ed. pap. 108.20 (*0-8357-3200-2*, 203947100012) Bks Demand.

Anderson, John Q., ed. Brokenburn: The Journal of Kate Stone, 1861-1868. 1995. pap. text 17.95 (*0-8071-2017-0*) La State U Pr.

— Texas Folk Medicine, Vol. 5. (Texas Folklore Society Paisano Books Ser.). 1970. 15.00 (*0-88426-013-5*) Encino Pr.

Anderson, John R. The Architecture of Cognition. 352p. 1995. pap. text 39.95 (*0-8058-2233-X*) L Erlbaum Assocs.

— Cognitive Psychology & Its Implications. 3rd ed. LC 89-28409. (Illus.). 400p. (C). 1990. text 36.80 (*0-7167-2085-X*) W H Freeman.

— Cognitive Psychology & Its Implications. 3rd ed. LC 89-28409. (Illus.). 400p. (C). 1991. teacher ed. 24.00 (*0-7167-2251-8*) W H Freeman.

— Cognitive Psychology & Its Implications. 4th ed. LC 94-39006. 544p. (C). 1995. pap. text 64.95 (*0-7167-2385-9*) W H Freeman.

— Language, Memory, & Thought. LC 76-21791. 546p. (C). 1976. text 99.95 (*0-89859-107-4*) L Erlbaum Assocs.

— Learning & Memory: An Integrated Approach. LC 94-14189. 504p. 1994. text 80.95 (*0-471-58685-4*) Wiley.

***Anderson, John R.** Learning & Memory: An Integrated Approach. 2nd ed. LC 99-32553. 512p. 1999. text 77.95 (*0-471-24925-4*) Wiley.

Anderson, John R. Rules of the Mind. 336p. 1993. pap. 32.50 (*0-8058-1200-8*); text 69.95 (*0-8058-1199-0*) L Erlbaum Assocs.

Anderson, John R., ed. The Adaptive Character of Thought. (Studies in Cognition). 304p. (C). 1990. text 69.95 (*0-8058-0419-6*) L Erlbaum Assocs.

— Cognitive Skills & Their Acquisition. (Carnegie-Mellon Symposia on Cognition Ser.). 384p. 1981. text 79.95 (*0-89859-093-0*) L Erlbaum Assocs.

Anderson, John R., et al, eds. AIDS: Abstracts of the Psychological & Behavioral Literature, 1983-1991. 3rd ed. LC 91-22115. (Bibliographies in Psychology Ser.: No. 1). 301p. 1991. pap. 19.95 (*1-55798-148-5*) Am Psychol.

Anderson, John R. & Bower, Gordon H. Human Associative Memory. LC 79-28349. 538p. 1980. 89.95 (*0-89859-108-2*); pap. 29.95 (*0-89859-020-5*) L Erlbaum Assocs.

Anderson, John R. & Kemp, Cassandra E., eds. AIDS Vol. 2, 1991-1995: Abstracts of the Psychological & Behavioral Literature, Vol. 2. 463p. 1996. pap. 19.95 (*1-55798-377-1*) Am Psychol.

Anderson, John R. & Lebiere, Christian J. The Atomic Components of Thought. 400p. 1998. write for info. (*0-8058-2816-8*); pap. write for info. (*0-8058-2817-6*) L Erlbaum Assocs.

Anderson, John R., jt. auth. see Rubenson, David.

Anderson, John R., jt. auth. see Singley, Mark K.

Anderson, John S. Witch What & the Wye of Time. (Illus.). 40p. (J). (gr. 1-4). 1992. 12.95 (*0-929141-15-6*) Napoleon Publ.

Anderson, John T., jt. auth. see Stewart.

Anderson, John W. The Tale of the Great Fruit Tree. (Illus.). 40p. (YA). 1992. 15.00 (*0-9633296-0-X*) Koinonia TX.

Anderson, John W., jt. auth. see Burban, Lisa L.

Anderson, Jolivette. Past Lives, Still Living: Traveling the Pathways to Freedom. xv, 41p. 1999. pap. 7.95 (*1-893926-00-1*) Sisterlove Prodns.

Anderson, Jon. The Milky Way. LC 82-11491. (American Poetry Ser.: No. 25). 175p. 1985. pap. 8.50 (*0-88001-007-X*) HarpC.

— Since 1794 the History of the Onondaga County Sheriff Department. 110p. 1994. pap. 10.00 (*0-9648622-4-7*) Pine Grve Pr.

Anderson, Jon G. Idaho. (Compass American Guides Ser.). (Illus.). 288p. 1996. pap. 18.95 (*1-878867-78-4*, Compass Amrcn) Fodors Travel.

***Anderson, Jon Lee.** Che Guevara: A Revolutionary Life. 832p. 1998. reprint ed. pap. 18.50 (*0-8021-3558-7*, Grove) Grove-Atltic.

Anderson, Jon M., ed. see Denny, Walter B. & Walker, Daniel.

Anderson, Jon P., ed. 1998 Random Lengths Buyers' & Sellers' Guide: A Directory of the Forest Products Industry. 1044p. 1998. 185.00 (*1-884311-03-2*) Random Lgths Pubns.

— 1999 Random Lengths Buyers' & Sellers' Guide: A Directory of the Forest Products Industry. 1102p. 1999. 195.00 (*1-884311-06-7*) Random Lgths Pubns.

***Anderson, Jon P., ed.** 2000 Random Lengths Buyers' & Sellers' Guide: A Directory of the Forest Products Industry. 1096p. 2000. 219.95 (*1-884311-08-3*) Random Lgths Pubns.

Anderson, Jon W. & Friend, William B., eds. The Culture of Bible Belt Catholics. LC 95-8222. 320p. (Orig.). 1995. pap. 14.95 (*0-8091-3574-4*) Paulist Pr.

Anderson, Jon W., jt. auth. see Eickelman, Dale F.

Anderson, Joseph. The Orkneyinga Saga. 368p. (C). 1989. 44.00 (*0-901824-25-9*, Pub. by Mercat Pr Bks) St Mut.

— Prayerbook Hebrew Answer Book & Teacher's Guide. Simon, Ethelyn & Kelman, Victoria, eds. 110p. (Orig.). (C). 1994. pap. text 8.95 (*0-939144-19-0*) EKS Pub Co.

— Social Work with Groups: A Process Model. LC 96-15770. 352p. (C). 1996. 72.00 (*0-8013-1837-8*) Longman.

Anderson, Joseph, ed. The Town & City of Waterbury, CT, from the Aboriginal Period, 3 vols. (Illus.). 1380p. 1994. reprint ed. lib. bdg. 140.00 (*0-8328-3903-5*) Higginson Bk Co.

— Town & City of Waterbury, CT, from the Aboriginal Period to the Year 1895. (Illus.). 2264p. 1997. reprint ed. lib. bdg. 232.50 (*0-8328-5692-4*) Higginson Bk Co.

***Anderson, Joseph, et al.** Prayerbook Hebrew the Easy Way. 3rd ed. 312p. 2000. pap. 18.95 (*0-939144-32-8*) EKS Pub Co.

Anderson, Joseph, jt. auth. see Simon, Ethelyn.

Anderson, Joseph C. Maine Families in 1790 No. 31, Vol. 6: Maine Genealogical Society Special Publication. LC 88-62540. 608p. 1998. 45.00 (*0-89725-361-2*, 1895) Picton Pr.

Anderson, Joseph C., II. York County, Maine Will Abstracts, 1801-1858. LC 97-69582. 1376p. 1997. 99.50 (*0-89725-326-4*, 1845) Picton Pr.

Anderson, Joseph C., II, ed. Maine Families in 1790, Vol. 5. 402p. 1996. 35.00 (*0-89725-255-1*, 1726) Picton Pr.

Anderson, Joseph C. & Thurston, Lois, eds. Maine Families in 1790, Vol. 4. LC 88-62540. 416p. 1994. 35.00 (*0-89725-126-1*, 1439) Picton Pr.

Anderson, Joseph C., II, jt. ed. see Frost, John E.

Anderson, Joseph C., jt. ed. see Gray, Ruth.

***Anderson, Joseph Crook, II, ed.** Berwick, ME: The First & Second Churches Of. 352p. 1999. 34.50 (*0-89725-125-3*) Picton Pr.

Anderson, Joseph Crook, II & Thurston, Lois Ware. Kittery, Maine Vital Records of Prior to 1892: MGS Special Pub. No. 8. LC 91-62157. (Illus.). 740p. 1991. 54.50 (*0-929539-73-7*, 1173) Picton Pr.

Anderson, Joseph D. The Reality of Illusion: An Ecological Approach to Cognitive Film Theory. LC 94-48221. 232p. (C). 1995. 29.95 (*0-8093-2000-2*) S Ill U Pr.

— Reality of Illusion: An Ecological Approach to Cognitive Film Theory. 1998. pap. text 18.95 (*0-8093-2196-3*) S Ill U Pr.

Anderson, Joseph L. & Richie, Donald. The Japanese Film: Art & Industry. LC 81-47985. (Illus.). 500p. 1982. reprint ed. pap. text 26.95 (*0-691-00792-6*, Pub. by Princeton U Pr) Cal Prin Full Svc.

Anderson, Joy & Burlison, Steve, eds. Peoria-Pekin MSA. (Illus.). 32p. (C). 1994. pap. text 7.95 (*0-9634793-8-5*) Peoria Jrnl.

Anderson, Judith. Best Recipes of the Great Food Companies. (Illus.). 528p. 1997. 11.99 (*0-88365-996-4*) Galahad Bks.

Anderson, Judith & Bloom, Claire. Bk of Judith & Ruth. unabridged ed. 1977. audio 14.00 (*0-694-50041-0*, SWC 1052, Caedmon) HarperAudio.

***Anderson, Judith D.** Taming of the Shrew. (Streamline Shakespeare Ser.). 2000. pap. 7.00 (*1-57128-155-X*) Acad Therapy.

Anderson, Judith D., jt. ed. see Anderson, Peggy L.

Anderson, Judith H. Biographical Truth: The Representation of Historical Persons in Tudor-Stuart Writing. LC 83-14520. (Illus.). 244p. 1984. 40.00 (*0-300-03085-1*) Yale U Pr.

— Words That Matter: Linguistic Perception in Renaissance English. LC 96-3159. 1996. write for info. (*0-8047-2631-0*) Stanford U Pr.

Anderson, Judith H., et al, eds. Spenser's Life & the Subject of Biography. LC 96-19287. (Massachusetts Studies in Early Modern Culture). 232p. (C). 1996. 37.50 (*1-55849-050-7*) U of Mass Pr.

Anderson, Judith H., ed. see Langland, William.

Anderson, Judith I., jt. ed. see Sweet, Anne P.

Anderson, Judy. Fragments from the Stacked Deck. (Illus.). 1995. boxed set 22.00 (*0-932526-52-7*) Nexus Pr.

— Plagiarism, Copyright Violation & Other Thefts of Intellectual Property: An Annotated Bibliography with a Lenghty Introduction. LC 97-44084. 212p. 1998. pap. 42.50 (*0-7864-0463-9*) McFarland & Co.

Anderson, Judy. Teeing off to the Green: Using Golf As a Business Tool. LC 95-230860. 224p. (Orig.). 1995. pap., per. 14.95 (*0-7872-1105-2*) Kendall-Hunt.

Anderson, Judy. Teeing off to the Green: Using Golf as a Business Tool. 1997. pap. text 14.95 (*1-885640-33-1*) Intl Netwrk.

Anderson, Judy, jt. auth. see Gossen, Diane.

Anderson, Judy C. & Rogers, George E. For the Love of Postcards. LC 98-93097. (Illus.). iv, 124p. 1998. pap. 14.95 (*0-9665417-0-7*) Epitaph Pr.

Anderson, Judy L., ed. Catch Me a Poem. (Illus.). 160p. (Orig.). 1995. pap. 9.95 (*0-9650317-0-5*) M T Haack.

Anderson, Juel E. Trading, Sex & Dying. 283p. 1998. pap. 39.95 (*1-883272-24-6*) Traders Lib.

Anderson, Julia. Labeled for Life. LC 98-67375. 240p. 1998. text 26.95 (*0-7872-5129-1*, 41512901) Kendall-Hunt.

Anderson, Julia, ed. see Pakizer, Debi & Sears, Mary A.

Anderson, Julie & Prosser, Kevin, contrib. by. Mellows: Taxation for Executors & Trustees. 1991. ring bd. write for info. (*0-406-99833-7*, MWTESSET, MICHIE) LEXIS Pub.

***Anderson, Julie K.** Human Resources Best Practices During A Merger 2p. 1998. (*0-88886-506-6*) Queßens U Indus Relat.

***Anderson, Julie Wofford.** The Answers--To Questions That Teachers Most Frequently Ask. LC 00-9505. 2000. pap. write for info. (*0-7619-7659-0*) Corwin Pr.

Anderson, June. Honoring the Ancestors: The Woodcarvings of Claude Lockhart Clark. LC 98-103658. (Illus.). 48p. 1997. pap. 15.00 (*0-940228-42-4*) Calif Acad Sci.

— Return to Tradition: The Revitalization of Turkish Village Carpets. LC 98-148479. (Illus.). 88p. 1998. pap. 24.95 (*0-295-97689-6*) U of Wash Pr.

***Anderson, June & Kirwan, Larry.** Rafferty Rescues the Moon (Musical) 56p. 1999. pap. 5.95 (*0-87129-936-4*, R04) Dramatic Pub.

Anderson, Justo C. Historia de los Bautistas: Baptist History, Tomo II. (Sus Comienzos y Desarrollo en Europa y Norteamerica - Beginnings & Development in Europe & North America Ser.). (SPA.). 400p. (Orig.). 1991. pap. 15.99 (*0-311-15037-3*) Casa Bautista.

— Historia de los Bautistas: Baptist History, Tomo III. (SPA.). 640p. (Orig.). 1991. pap. 23.99 (*0-311-15038-1*) Casa Bautista.

Anderson, Justo C. Historia de los Bautistas - Sus Bases y Principios Tomo I: Baptist History. 1978. reprint ed. pap. 11.25 (*0-311-15036-5*) Casa Bautista.

— Manual de Homiletica Para Laicos.Tr. of Homiletic for Laymen. (SPA., Illus.). 128p. (C). 1987. reprint ed. 6.50 (*0-311-42073-7*) Casa Bautista.

Anderson, K. Young People & Alcohol, Drugs & Tobacco. (WHO Regional Publications, European Ser.: No. 66). 87p. 1995. pap. text 20.00 (*92-890-1330-3*) World Health.

Anderson, K. & Hall, D. W. Elementary Real Analysis. 1972. write for info. (*0-07-001620-8*) McGraw.

Anderson, K. & Mafera, G. EDV Fachworterbuch Rechnungslegung Steuern: German-English, English-German. 2nd ed. 485p. 1980. 95.00 (*0-7859-6513-0*, M1286) Fr & Eur.

Anderson, K. M., et al, eds. Recent Advances in the Biochemistry & Biology of Cancer. (Journal: Clinical Physiology & Biochemistry: Vol. 5, No. 3-4). (Illus.). 132p. 1987. pap. 75.75 (*3-8055-4643-2*) S Karger.

***Anderson, Kai.** Hedley Bull on International Politics. LC 99-46716. 2000. text 65.00 (*0-312-22859-7*) St Martin.

Anderson, Kare. Resolving Conflict Sooner. LC 98-56511. 1999. pap. 10.95 (*0-89594-976-8*) Crossing Pr.

Anderson, Karen. Cats Have No Masters . . . Just Friends: An Investigation into the Feline Mind. LC 98-2793. (Illus.). 111p. 1998. 24.50 (*1-57223-135-1*, 1351) Willow Creek Pr.

— Changing Woman: A History of Racial Ethnic Women in Modern America. 304p. 1997. reprint ed. pap. 19.95 (*0-19-511788-3*) OUP.

— Disney's Big Bad Book of Puzzlers: Deviously Difficult Games & Brainteasers Featuring Favorite Disney Villains. LC 94-74820. (Illus.). 176p. (J). (gr. 2-7). 1996. pap. 9.95 (*0-7868-4032-3*, Pub. by Disney Pr) Time Warner.

— Disney's Puzzlers Book. 350p. (J). (gr. 2-7). 1997. pap. 4.95 (*0-7868-4205-9*, Pub. by Disney Pr) Time Warner.

— Games Magazine Junior Kids' Big Book of Games. LC 89-40727. (Illus.). 176p. (J). (gr. 1-7). 1999. pap. 8.95 (*0-89480-657-2*, 1657) Workman Pub.

— Games Magazine Presents Riddlers: Puzzles to Tickle Your Mind. 1994. pap. 12.00 (*0-8129-2385-5*, Times Bks) Crown Pub Group.

***Anderson, Karen.** Glad to Be Human: Meditations. LC 00-21174. 2000. pap. write for info. (*1-55896-404-5*, Skinner Hse Bks) Unitarian Univ.

Anderson, Karen. Just Cats. LC 98-30021. (Just Ser.). (Illus.). 144p. 1998. 29.50 (*1-57223-187-4*) Willow Creek Pr.

— Just Cats: Half-Pint Edition. LC 98-52369. (Half-Pint Ser.). (Illus.). 96p. 1999. 12.95 (*1-57223-220-X*, 220X) Willow Creek Pr.

— Proof Positive: How to Find Errors Before They Embarrass You. Scanlon, Kelly, ed. LC 96-67393. (Self-Study Sourcebook Ser.). (Illus.). 193p. 1996. pap. 15.95 (*1-57294-043-3*, 13-0016) SkillPath Pubns.

— Teaching Gender in U. S. History. Painter, Nell I. & Rios-Bustamante, Antonio, eds. LC 97-73597. (Teaching Diversity Ser.). 56p. 1997. pap. 8.00 (*0-87229-078-6*) Am Hist Assn.

— Y2K for Women: How to Protect Your Home & Family in the Coming Crises. 1999. pap. 12.99 (*0-7852-6853-7*) Nelson.

Anderson, Karen. Y2K for Women: How to Protect Your Home & Family in the Coming Crises. xiii, 224p. 1999. pap. 19.95 (*0-9654974-1-0*) Sterling Pr Int.

Anderson, Karen & Irwin, Dayle. Decatur Entertainment: A Pictorial History. (Illinois Pictorial History Ser.). (Illus.). 1997. write for info. (*0-943963-55-9*) G Bradley.

Anderson, Karen, jt. auth. see Anderson, Poul.

Anderson, Karen, jt. ed. see Fitness Magazine Editors.

Anderson, Karen, ed. see Powers, Marie.

Anderson, Karen, ed. see Siler, George & Siler, Betty.

Anderson, Karen C. & Cumbaa, Stephen. The Bones & Skeleton Gamebook. LC 93-14455. (Illus.). 96p. (Orig.). (J). (gr. 1-5). 1993. pap. 7.95 (*1-56305-497-3*, 3497) Workman Pub.

Anderson, Karen C., jt. auth. see Cumbaa, Stephen.

***Anderson, Karen E., et al.** California Trust Administration: February 2000 Update. rev. ed. Gerber, Mary, ed. LC 86-70263. 1157p. 2000. 56.00i (*0-7626-0391-7*, ES-31708) Cont Ed Bar-CA.

Anderson, Karen E., ed. see Fink, Diane D.

Anderson, Karen H., et al. Missing Person: A Radio Play. (Intermediate Listening Ser.: No. 1). (Illus.). 92p. (Orig.). 1983. pap. text 29.40 (*0-582-79789-6*, 75043) Longman.

— Missing Person Package. (Intermediate Listening Ser.: No. 1). (Illus.). 92p. 1989. pap. text 40.50 incl. audio (*0-582-79814-0*, 75064) Addison-Wesley.

Anderson, Karen L. Chain Her by One Foot: The Subjugation of Native Women in Seventeenth-Century New France. LC 93-19097. 252p. (C). 1993. pap. 19.99 (*0-415-90827-2*, B2291) Routledge.

Anderson, Karen L. Games Magazine Presents Kids' Giant Book of Games. (J). (gr. 4-7). 1993. pap. 13.00 (*0-8129-2199-2*, Times Bks) Crown Pub Group.

— Wartime Women: Sex Roles, Family Relations, & the Status of Women During World War II, 20. LC 80-1703. (Contributions in Women's Studies: No. 20). 198p. 1981. 55.00 (*0-313-20884-0*, AWW/, Greenwood Pr) Greenwood.

Anderson, Karl. The Astrology of the Old Testament. 502p. 1996. spiral bd. 32.50 (*0-7873-0033-0*) Hlth Research.

— The Astrology of the Old Testament or the Lost Word Regained (1892) 502p. 1996. reprint ed. pap. 32.00 (*1-56459-930-2*) Kessinger Pub.

Anderson, Karl, jt. auth. see Iuppa, Nicholas V.

Anderson, Karl H., jt. auth. see Collins, Beryl R.

Anderson, Karl R. Joseph Smith's Kirtland. LC 89-30535. x, 286p. 1996. pap. 13.95 (*1-57345-205-X*) Deseret Bk.

Anderson, Kat, jt. compiled by see Blackburn, Thomas C.

Anderson, Kate & Anderson, Bill. There's a Pig in the Closet! (Illus.). 32p. (J). (ps-3). 1997. 16.00 (*0-9642979-3-0*) New Energy Pr.

***Anderson, Katharine.** Wildlife Gardens. LC 99-484106. (Illus.). 1998. write for info. (*0-914697-99-4*) N Amer Outdoor Grp.

An Asterisk (*) at the beginning of an entry indicates that the title is appearing for the first time.

Anderson, Katherine E. Creativity Lives for Creative Thinkers: Journal & Calendar Set. (Illus.). (Orig.). 1996. pap., spiral bd. 21.95 (*1-57876-196-4*) Triple U Enterprises.
— Creativity Lives for Parents: Journal & Calendar Set. (Illus.). (Orig.). 1996. pap., spiral bd. 21.95 (*1-57876-195-6*) Triple U Enterprises.
— Creativity Lives for Teachers: Journal & Calendar Set. (Illus.). (Orig.). 1996. pap., spiral bd. 21.95 (*1-57876-194-8*) Triple U Enterprises.
— Creativity Lives for the Courageous: Journal & Calendar Set. 1996. pap., spiral bd. 21.95 (*1-57876-199-9*) Triple U Enterprises.
— Creativity Lives for Those Who Dream Inpossible Things: Journal & Calendar Set. (Illus.). (Orig.). 1996. pap., spiral bd. 21.95 (*1-57876-197-2*) Triple U Enterprises.
— Creativity Lives in Creative Definance: Journal & Calendar Set. (Illus.). (Orig.). 1996. pap., spiral bd. 21.95 (*1-57876-198-0*) Triple U Enterprises.
— Creativity Lives Journal for Creative Thinkers. (Illus.). 150p. (Orig.). 1994. pap., spiral bd. 15.95 (*1-57876-102-6*) Triple U Enterprises.
— Creativity Lives Journal for Parents. (Illus.). 150p. (Orig.). 1994. pap., spiral bd. 15.95 (*1-57876-101-8*) Triple U Enterprises.
— Creativity Lives Journal for Teachers. (Illus.). 150p. (Orig.). 1994. pap., spiral bd. 15.95 (*1-57876-100-X*) Triple U Enterprises.
— Creativity Lives Journal for the Courageous. 150p. (Orig.). 1994. pap., spiral bd. 15.95 (*1-57876-105-0*) Triple U Enterprises.
— Creativity Lives Journal for Those Who Dream Impossible Things. 150p. (Orig.). 1994. pap., spiral bd. 15.95 (*1-57876-103-4*) Triple U Enterprises.
— Creativity Lives Journal of Creative Defiance. 150p. (Orig.). 1994. pap., spiral bd. 15.95 (*1-57876-104-2*) Triple U Enterprises.
— Current Science & Medicine: In Light of a Yeast Causal Hypothesis. 30p. (Orig.). 1996. pap. 4.95 (*1-57876-903-5*) Triple U Enterprises.
— Disease Etiologies of the Unsolved Mystery Diseases. 135p. (Orig.). 1996. pap., spiral bd. 15.95 (*1-57876-902-7*) Triple U Enterprises.
— Education Lives for Home School Teachers: Journal & Calendar Set. (Illus.). (Orig.). 1996. pap., spiral bd. 21.95 (*1-57876-796-2*) Triple U Enterprises.
— Education Lives for Mentors: Journal & Calendar Set. (Illus.). (Orig.). 1996. pap., spiral bd. 21.95 (*1-57876-798-9*) Triple U Enterprises.
— Education Lives for Parents & Grandparents: Journal & Calendar Set. (Illus.). (Orig.). 1996. pap., spiral bd. 21.95 (*1-57876-797-0*) Triple U Enterprises.
— Education Lives for Students: Journal & Calendar Set. (Illus.). (Orig.). 1996. pap., spiral bd. 21.95 (*1-57876-794-6*) Triple U Enterprises.
— Education Lives for Teachers: Journal & Calendar Set. 1996. pap. 21.95 (*1-57876-795-4*) Triple U Enterprises.
— Education Lives for the Culturally Elite: Journal & Calendar Set. (Illus.). (Orig.). 1996. pap., spiral bd. 21.95 (*1-57876-799-7*) Triple U Enterprises.
— Education Lives Journal for Home School Teachers. (Illus.). 150p. (Orig.). 1994. pap., spiral bd. 15.95 (*1-57876-702-4*) Triple U Enterprises.
— Education Lives Journal for Mentors. (Illus.). 150p. (Orig.). 1994. pap. 15.95 (*1-57876-704-0*) Triple U Enterprises.
— Education Lives Journal for Parents & Grandparents. (Illus.). 150p. (Orig.). 1994. pap., spiral bd. 15.95 (*1-57876-703-2*) Triple U Enterprises.
— Education Lives Journal for Students. (Illus.). 150p. (Orig.). 1994. pap., spiral bd. 15.95 (*1-57876-700-8*) Triple U Enterprises.
— Education Lives Journal for Teachers. (Illus.). 150p. (Orig.). 1994. pap., spiral bd. 15.95 (*1-57876-701-6*) Triple U Enterprises.
— Education Lives Journal for the Culturally Elite. (Illus.). 150p. (Orig.). 1994. pap., spiral bd. 15.95 (*1-57876-705-9*) Triple U Enterprises.
— Future Shock: The Future of the Insurance Industry & the Curing of the Unsolved Mystery Diseases. (Illus.). 100p. (Orig.). 1997. pap., spiral bd. 15.95 (*1-57876-998-1*) Triple U Enterprises.
— God Lives for Knowledge Hunters: Journal & Calendar Set. (Illus.). (Orig.). 1996. pap., spiral bd. 21.95 (*1-57876-599-4*) Triple U Enterprises.
— God Lives for Promise Keepers: Journal & Calendar Set. (Illus.). (Orig.). 1996. pap., spiral bd. 21.95 (*1-57876-598-6*) Triple U Enterprises.
— God Lives for the Struggling Heart: Journal & Calendar Set. (Illus.). (Orig.). 1996. pap., spiral bd. 21.95 (*1-57876-594-3*) Triple U Enterprises.
— God Lives for Those Who Suffer: Journal & Calendar Set. (Illus.). (Orig.). 1996. pap., spiral bd. 21.95 (*1-57876-595-1*) Triple U Enterprises.
— God Lives for Truth Seekers: Journal & Calendar Set. (Illus.). (Orig.). 1996. pap., spiral bd. 21.95 (*1-57876-597-8*) Triple U Enterprises.
— God Lives Journal for Knowledge Hunters. (Illus.). 150p. (Orig.). 1994. pap., spiral bd. 15.95 (*1-57876-505-6*) Triple U Enterprises.
— God Lives Journal for Prayer Warriors. (Illus.). 150p. (Orig.). 1996. pap., spiral bd. 15.95 (*1-57876-502-1*) Triple U Enterprises.
— God Lives Journal for Promise Keepers. (Illus.). 150p. (Orig.). 1994. pap., spiral bd. 15.95 (*1-57876-504-8*) Triple U Enterprises.
— God Lives Journal for the Struggling Heart. (Illus.). 150p. (Orig.). 1996. pap., spiral bd. 15.95 (*1-57876-500-5*) Triple U Enterprises.
— God Lives Journal for Those Who Suffer. (Illus.). 150p. (Orig.). 1996. pap., spiral bd. 15.95 (*1-57876-501-3*) Triple U Enterprises.
— God Lives Journal for Truth Seekers. (Illus.). 150p. (Orig.). 1994. pap., spiral bd. 15.95 (*1-57876-503-X*) Triple U Enterprises.
— The Idea Workshop: Strategies for the Creative Thinker - Original Edition. large type ed. (Illus.). 200p. (Orig.). 1996. pap., spiral bd. 15.95 (*1-57876-000-3*) Triple U Enterprises.
— The Idea Workshop Reproducible Handouts: Games from the Original Edition, Vol. 1. large type ed. (Illus.). 100p. (Orig.). 1996. pap., spiral bd. 12.95 (*1-57876-003-8*) Triple U Enterprises.
— Love Lives for Believers Journal. 150p. 1998. pap., spiral bd. 15.95 (*1-57876-400-9*, Love Lives) Triple U Enterprises.
— Love Lives for Believers Journal & Calendar Set. 1998. pap., spiral bd. 21.95 (*1-57876-494-7*, Love Lives) Triple U Enterprises.
— Love Lives for Families. 150p. 1998. pap., spiral bd. 15.95 (*1-57876-402-5*, Love Lives) Triple U Enterprises.
— Love Lives for Families Journal & Calendar Set. 1998. pap., spiral bd. 21.95 (*1-57876-496-3*, Love Lives) Triple U Enterprises.
— Love Lives for Friends Journal. 150p. 1998. pap., spiral bd. 15.95 (*1-57876-403-3*, Love Lives) Triple U Enterprises.
— Love Lives for Friends Journal & Calendar Set. 1998. pap., spiral bd. 21.95 (*1-57876-497-1*, Love Lives) Triple U Enterprises.
— Love Lives for the Faithful Journal. 150p. 1998. pap., spiral bd. 15.95 (*1-57876-401-7*, Love Lives) Triple U Enterprises.
— Love Lives for the Faithful Journal & Calendar Set. 1998. pap., spiral bd. 21.95 (*1-57876-495-5*, Love Lives) Triple U Enterprises.
— Love Lives for Those Who Wait Journal. 150p. 1998. pap., spiral bd. 15.95 (*1-57876-404-1*, Love Lives) Triple U Enterprises.
— Love Lives for Those Who Wait Journal & Calendar Set. 1998. pap., spiral bd. 21.95 (*1-57876-498-X*, Love Lives) Triple U Enterprises.
— Love Lives for True Lovers Journal & Calendar Set. 1998. pap., spiral bd. 21.95 (*1-57876-499-8*, Love Lives) Triple U Enterprises.
— Loves Lives for True Lovers Journal. 150p. 1998. pap., spiral bd. 15.95 (*1-57876-405-X*, Love Lives) Triple U Enterprises.
— Morality Lives for Knowledge Hunters: Journal & Calendar Set. (Illus.). (Orig.). 1996. pap., spiral bd. 21.95 (*1-57876-696-6*) Triple U Enterprises.
— Morality Lives for Promise Keepers: Journal & Calendar Set. (Illus.). (Orig.). 1996. pap., spiral bd. 21.95 (*1-57876-695-8*) Triple U Enterprises.
— Morality Lives for the Integrity Seekers: Journal & Calendar Set. (Illus.). (Orig.). 1996. pap., spiral bd. 21.95 (*1-57876-697-4*) Triple U Enterprises.
— Morality Lives for the Rich & Famous: Journal & Calendar Set. (Illus.). (Orig.). 1996. pap., spiral bd. 21.95 (*1-57876-699-0*) Triple U Enterprises.
— Morality Lives for the Young & Restless: Journal & Calendar Set. (Illus.). (Orig.). 1996. pap., spiral bd. 21.95 (*1-57876-698-2*) Triple U Enterprises.
— Morality Lives for Truth Seekers: Journal & Calendar Set. (Illus.). (Orig.). 1996. pap., spiral bd. 21.95 (*1-57876-694-X*) Triple U Enterprises.
— Morality Lives Journal for Integrity Seekers. (Illus.). 150p. (Orig.). 1994. pap. 15.95 (*1-57876-603-6*) Triple U Enterprises.
— Morality Lives Journal for Knowledge Hunters. (Illus.). 150p. (Orig.). 1994. pap., spiral bd. 15.95 (*1-57876-602-8*) Triple U Enterprises.
— Morality Lives Journal for Promise Keepers. (Illus.). 150p. (Orig.). 1994. pap. 15.95 (*1-57876-601-X*) Triple U Enterprises.
— Morality Lives Journal for the Rich & Famous. (Illus.). 150p. (Orig.). 1994. pap., spiral bd. 15.95 (*1-57876-605-2*) Triple U Enterprises.
— Morality Lives Journal for the Young & Restless. (Illus.). 150p. (Orig.). 1994. pap., spiral bd. 15.95 (*1-57876-604-4*) Triple U Enterprises.
— Morality Lives Journal for Truth Seekers. (Illus.). 150p. (Orig.). 1994. pap., spiral bd. 15.95 (*1-57876-600-1*) Triple U Enterprises.
— Nine Pathological Mechanisms. 30p. (Orig.). 1996. pap., spiral bd. 4.95 (*1-57876-901-9*) Triple U Enterprises.
— Science Lives for Geniuses: Journal & Calendar Set. (Illus.). (Orig.). 1996. pap., spiral bd. 21.95 (*1-57876-897-7*) Triple U Enterprises.
— Science Lives for Health Care Workers: Journal & Calendar Set. (Illus.). (Orig.). 1996. pap., spiral bd. 21.95 (*1-57876-899-3*) Triple U Enterprises.
— Science Lives for Intellectuals: Journal & Calendar Set. (Illus.). (Orig.). 1996. pap., spiral bd. 21.95 (*1-57876-896-9*) Triple U Enterprises.
— Science Lives for Researchers: Journal & Calendar Set. (Illus.). (Orig.). 1996. pap., spiral bd. 21.95 (*1-57876-898-5*) Triple U Enterprises.
— Science Lives for Students: Journal & Calendar Set. (Illus.). (Orig.). 1996. pap., spiral bd. 21.95 (*1-57876-894-2*) Triple U Enterprises.
— Science Lives for Teachers: Journal & Calendar Set. (Illus.). (Orig.). 1996. pap., spiral bd. 21.95 (*1-57876-895-0*) Triple U Enterprises.
— Science Lives Journal for Health Care Workers. (Illus.). 150p. (Orig.). 1994. pap., spiral bd. 15.95 (*1-57876-805-5*) Triple U Enterprises.
— Science Lives Journal for Intellectuals. (Illus.). 150p. (Orig.). 1994. pap., spiral bd. 15.95 (*1-57876-802-0*) Triple U Enterprises.
— Science Lives Journal for Researchers. (Illus.). 150p. (Orig.). 1994. pap., spiral bd. 15.95 (*1-57876-804-7*) Triple U Enterprises.
— Science Lives Journal for Students. (Illus.). 150p. (Orig.). 1994. pap., spiral bd. 15.95 (*1-57876-800-4*) Triple U Enterprises.
— Science Lives Journal for Teachers. (Illus.). 150p. (Orig.). 1994. pap., spiral bd. 15.95 (*1-57876-801-2*) Triple U Enterprises.
— Secondary Infections & ISR Testing. 150p. 1998. pap., spiral bd. 19.95 (*1-57876-930-2*, Love Lives) Triple U Enterprises.
— So in the Meantime, 3 vols. Incl. How Do I Help? Caregiver's Guide. large type ed. (Illus.). 100p. (Orig.). 1997. pap., spiral bd. 12.95 (*1-57876-927-2*); What Do I Do? Patient's Guide. large type ed. (Illus.). 100p. (Orig.). 1997. pap., spiral bd. 12.95 (*1-57876-925-6*); What Do I Tell Them? Doctor's Guide. (Illus.). 100p. (Orig.). 1997. pap., spiral bd. 12.95 (*1-57876-928-0*); 32.95 (*1-57876-929-9*) Triple U Enterprises.
— So In the Meantime, What Do I Do? Patient Guide. large type ed. (Illus.). 150p. (Orig.). 1997. pap., spiral bd. 15.95 (*1-57876-926-4*) Triple U Enterprises.
— Testing Yeast & Bacteria Reproducible Forms. (Illus.). 60p. (Orig.). 1996. pap., spiral bd. 9.95 (*1-57876-904-3*) Triple U Enterprises.
— Unsolved Mystery Diseases. large type ed. (Illus.) 240p. (Orig.). 1996. pap., spiral bd. 24.95 (*1-57876-900-0*) Triple U Enterprises.
— Your Mission Should You Choose to Accept It. large type ed. (Illus.). 120p. (Orig.). 1997. pap., spiral bd. 9.95 (*1-57876-999-X*) Triple U Enterprises.

Anderson, Katherine H. Introduction to Medical Sciences for Clinical Practice: A Self-Instructional-Tutorial Curriculum. LC 76-43143. (Illus.). 454p. reprint ed. pap. 140.80 (*0-8357-7670-0*, 205699800001) Bks Demand.

Anderson, Katherine S. & Turco, Peggy. Walks & Rambles in Westchester & Fairfield Counties: A Nature Lover's Guide to 36 Parks & Sanctuaries. 2nd rev. ed. LC 93-29152. (Walks & Rambles Ser.). 176p. 1993. pap. 14.00 (*0-88150-277-4*, Pub. by Countryman) Norton.

Anderson, Kathie J., jt. auth. see Clouse, Michael S.

Anderson, Kathie R. Dakota: The Literary Heritage of the Northern Prairie State. (North Dakota Centennial Heritage Ser.). (Illus.). 186p. 1990. 18.95 (*0-9608700-4-0*) U NDak Pres.

Anderson, Kathl Holly, jt. ed. see Wells, Danny.

Anderson, Kathleen & Miller, Pamela C. Lessons for the Right Brain: Complete Kit, 5 bks. 64p. 1984. pap. text 44.00 (*0-88120-212-6*, 2700) PRO-ED.
— Lessons for the Right Brain: Memory Workbook. 64p. 1984. pap. text 44.00 (*0-88120-213-4*, 2701) PRO-ED.
— Lessons for the Right Brain: Reading & Writing Workbook. 64p. 1984. pap. text 44.00 (*0-88120-214-2*, 2702) PRO-ED.
— Lessons for the Right Brain: Self Perception-Organizing Functional Information Workbook. 64p. 1984. pap. text 44.00 (*0-88120-217-7*, 2705) PRO-ED.
— Lessons for the Right Brain: Thought Organization Workbook. 64p. 1984. pap. text 44.00 (*0-88120-216-9*, 2704) PRO-ED.
— Lessons for the Right Brain: Visual Perception & Attention Workbook. 64p. 1984. pap. text 44.00 (*0-88120-215-0*, 2703) PRO-ED.

***Anderson, Kathryn.** Listen, Love & Advocate: A Parent's Story of Living with Attention Deficit Disorder. LC 00-34126. 2000. write for info. (*0-936389-80-X*) Tudor Pubs.

Anderson, Kathryn. Nursing Your Adopted Baby. (Illus.). 32p. 1986. pap. 2.50 (*0-912500-15-8*) La Leche.

Anderson, Kathryn R., ed. see Staccia, Donald A.

Anderson, Kathy. Sweet & Sassy: Counted Cross Stitch Designs for Children & Beginners. 32p. (Orig.). 1983. pap. 5.98 (*0-88290-216-4*) Horizon Utah.

Anderson, Kathy & Anderson, Thor. Wedding Planning Made Easy: Timelines, Tips, & Techniques. 120p. 1997. pap. 14.95 (*0-9659400-0-4*) Thor & Kathy.

Anderson, Kathy P. Illinois. (Illus.). 72p. (J). 1995. pap. 5.95 (*0-8225-9706-3*) Lerner Pub.
— Illinois: Hello U. S. A. (Illus.). 72p. (J). (gr. 3-6). 1993. lib. bdg. 19.93 (*0-8225-2723-5*, Lerner Publctns) Lerner Pub.

Anderson, Kathy S. Stories of the Journey in the Circle of Life. 1992. pap. 9.95 (*0-87839-075-8*) North Star.

Anderson, Kay. The Magic of Ribbons. (Illus.). 158p. (Orig.). 1998. pap. 29.50 (*1-85486-186-7*) Nexus Special Interests.

Anderson, Kay J. Vancouver's Chinatown: Racial Discourse in Canada, 1875-1980. (McGill-Queen's Studies in Ethnic History). (Illus.). 336p. 1991. text 65.00 (*0-7735-0844-9*, Pub. by McG-Queens Univ Pr) CUP Services.
— Vancouver's Chinatown: Racial Discourse in Canada, 1875-1980. 336p. 1995. pap. 24.95 (*0-7735-1329-9*, Pub. by McG-Queens Univ Pr) CUP Services.

Anderson, Kay W. Don't Forget Me, Mommy! (Orig.). 1982. 6.95 (*0-318-70109-X*) Marin Pub.
— Don't Forget Me, Mommy! LC 81-85048. (Illus.). 118p. (Orig.). 1982. pap. 6.95 (*0-685-05552-3*) Marin Pub.

Anderson, Kaye. Cold Feet: Beginning Waltz & Two-Step Basics, II. (Fancy Dancing Ser.). (Illus.). 164p. (Orig.). 1994. pap. 18.95 (*0-9625895-7-8*) Dance Action.
— Fancy Dancing Series, Set. (Illus.). 1992. pap. write for info. (*0-9625895-5-1*) Dance Action.
— Fancy Figures: Phase III Latins (Cha Cha, Rumba, Mambo, Jive) with Advanced Variations. (Fancy Dancing Ser.). (Illus.). 165p. (Orig.). 1992. pap. 18.95 (*0-9625895-6-X*) Dance Action.
— Fancy Figures: Phase III Moderns (Foxtrot, Quickstep, Argentine Tango) with Advanced Variations. LC 92-81582. (Fancy Dancing Ser.). (Illus.). 150p. (Orig.). 1992. pap. 18.95 (*0-9625895-4-3*) Dance Action.
— Fancy Figures, Phases 1-3: Easy Level Waltz. (Fancy Dancing Ser.). (Illus.). 142p. 1992. pap. 18.95 (*0-9625895-2-7*) Dance Action.
— Fancy Figures, Phases 1-3: Two-Step. (Fancy Dancing Ser.). (Illus.). 169p. (Orig.). 1992. pap. 18.95 (*0-9625895-1-9*) Dance Action.
— Fancy Footwork: The Art of Round Dancing - Conventions, Positions, & Terminology. 2nd ed. (Fancy Dancing Ser.). (Illus.). 154p. (Orig.). 1992. pap. 15.95 (*0-9625895-3-5*) Dance Action.

Anderson, Keith. Friendships That Run Deep: 7 Ways to Build Lasting Relationships. LC 97-12918. 132p. 1997. pap. 8.99 (*0-8308-1966-5*, 1966) InterVarsity.
— Is This the One? 9 Tests for Marriage. (IVP Booklets Ser.). 32p. (Orig.). (C). 1996. pap. 0.99 (*0-87784-099-7*, 099) InterVarsity.
— Jensen & Jensen-Healey. LC 99-185229. (Photographic History of Transport Ser.). (Illus.). 160p. 1998. pap. 29.95 (*0-7509-1766-0*, Pub. by Sutton Pub Ltd) Intl Pubs Mktg.
— On Your Own Again: The Down-to-Earth Guide to Getting Through a Divorce Or Separation & Getting on with Your LIfe. 1998. pap. 12.95 (*0-7710-0750-7*) McCland & Stewart.

Anderson, Keith M. Highway Salvage on Arizona State Highway 98: Kayenta Anasazi Sites Between Kaibito & the Klethla Valley. (Archaeological Ser.: No. 140). (Illus.). 70p. 1980. pap. 5.95 (*1-889747-11-4*) Ariz St Mus.

Anderson, Keith R. Does God Believe in You? Developing Spiritual Self-Confidence. LC 96-42258. 180p. (Orig.). 1997. pap. 10.99 (*0-8308-1999-1*, 1999, Saltshaker Bk) InterVarsity.
— What They Don't Always Teach You at a Christian College. 192p. (Orig.). 1995. pap. 9.99 (*0-8308-1611-9*, 1611) InterVarsity.

Anderson, Keith R. & Reese, Randy. Spiritual Mentoring: A Guide for Seeking & Giving Direction. LC 99-21817. 180p. 1999. pap. 11.99 (*0-8308-2210-0*, 2210) InterVarsity.

Anderson, Kelly. Rebels on the Rise: An Athletic History. Missouri Editing Group Staff, ed. (Illus.). 1992. write for info. (*1-56166-020-5*) Walsworth Pub.

Anderson, Kelly, ed. see Broeg, Bob.

Anderson, Kelly, ed. see Hendel, John & Carr, Jim.

Anderson, Kelly, ed. see McKenzie, Mike.

Anderson, Kelly C. Police Brutality. LC 94-9707. (Overview Ser.). (Illus.). (YA). (gr. 5-8). 1995. 22.45 (*1-56006-164-2*) Lucent Bks.

Anderson, Kelly P., ed. Cardiac Electrophysiology Review. 1997. write for info. (*0-614-30263-3*) Kluwer Academic.

***Anderson, Ken.** Bible-Based Prayer Power: Using Relevant Scripture to Pray with Confidence for All Your Needs. 348p. 2000. pap. 14.99 (*0-7852-6869-3*) Nelson.

Anderson, Ken. Bold As a Lamb: Pastor Samuel Lamb & the Underground Church of China. 192p. 1991. pap. 10.99 (*0-310-53221-3*) Zondervan.
— The Coincidence File. 1999. pap. 14.95 (*0-7137-2749-7*) Blandford Pr.
— Coincidences: Chance or Fate? LC 95-179208. 320 sp. 1995. pap. 14.95 (*0-7137-2523-0*, Pub. by Blandford Pr) Sterling.
— Crime in Texas: Your Complete Guide to the Criminal Justice System. LC 96-41661. 204p. 1997. 25.00 (*0-292-70477-1*); pap. 12.95 (*0-292-70478-X*) U of Tex Pr.

***Anderson, Ken.** Donde Hallarlo en la Biblia. (What You Need to Know about ... in 12 Lessons Ser.).Tr. of Where to Find It in the Bible. 592p. 1998. 19.99 (*0-89922-388-5*) Caribe Betania.
— Extreme A - Z: Find It in the Bible. LC 00-41580. 2000. write for info. (*0-7852-4580-4*) Tommy Nelson.

Anderson, Ken. Himalayan Heartbeat. (Illus.). 262p. (Orig.). 1992. pap. 8.25 (*0-87508-004-9*) Chr Lit.
— Hitler & the Occult. LC 95-3701. (Illus.). 244p. 1995. 26.95 (*0-87975-973-9*) Prometheus Bks.
— The Intense Lover: Suite of Poems. 96p. (Orig.). 1995. pap. 9.00 (*1-877978-80-9*, STARbks Pr) FL Lit Foundation.

***Anderson, Ken.** Nolan Ryan: Fastball to Cooperstown. LC 99-42362. 1999. pap. 5.95 (*1-57168-349-6*, Eakin Pr) Sunbelt Media.
— Nolan Ryan: Fastball to Cooperstown. LC 99-42362. 1999. 16.95 (*1-57168-350-X*, Eakin Pr) Sunbelt Media.

Anderson, Ken. Texas Crime Victims Handbook. 152p. (Orig.). 1998. pap. 27.50 (*0-9644421-1-6*) Georgetwn Pr.
— Using ACT! 4. LC 98-84199. 456p. 1998. pap. text 29.99 (*0-7897-1637-2*) Que.
— Where to Find It in the Bible: The Ultimate A to Z Resource. LC 95-50965. (Illus.). 608p. 1996. pap. 19.99 (*0-7852-1157-8*) Nelson.

***Anderson, Ken.** You Can't Do That, Dan Moody! The Klan Fighting Governor of Texas. LC 98-139361. (Illus.). 176p. (YA). (gr. 6 up). 1998. 15.95 (*1-57168-181-7*, Eakin Pr) Sunbelt Media.
— You Can't Do That, Dan Moody! The Klan Fighting Governor of Texas. LC 99-47815. (Illus.). 1999. pap. write for info. (*1-57168-358-5*, Eakin Pr) Sunbelt Media.

***Anderson, Ken & Bradley, John.** Texas Sentencing. 3rd ed. LC 98-65274. (Illus.). 576p. 1998. write for info. (*1-55834-886-7*) LEXIS Pub.

Anderson, Ken & Carlson, Merry. Games for All Occasions. 128p. 1988. reprint ed. mass mkt. 5.99 (*0-310-20151-9*, 9052P) Zondervan.

Anderson, Ken, jt. auth. see Tam, Stanley.

Anderson, Ken, Sr., ed. see Sims, Rose G.

A

An Asterisk (*) at the beginning of an entry indicates that the title is appearing for the first time.

Anderson, Ken B. & Crelling, John C., eds. Amber, Resinite & Fossil Resins. LC 95-44645. (ACS Sympsoium Ser.: No. 617). (Illus.). 295p. 1996. text 89.00 (*0-8412-3336-5*, Pub. by Am Chemical) OUP.

Anderson, Kenneth. Mosby's Trade Dictionary. 5th ed. LC 97-33687. (Illus.). 2128p. (C). (gr. 13). 1997. text 28.95 (*0-8151-4631-0*, 29951) Mosby Inc.

— Nine Man-Eaters & One Rogue. 264p. 1997. 21.95 (*1-887269-11-8*) J Culler & Sons.

— Tiger Walks. 1997. pap. text 16.95 (*1-887269-29-0*) J Culler & Sons.

— The Tiger Walks. 430p. 1997. 23.95 (*1-887269-07-X*) J Culler & Sons.

Anderson, Kenneth & Harmo, Lois. The Prentice-Hall Dictionary of Nutrition & Health. LC 84-11590. 257p. 1985. 21.95 (*0-13-695610-6*); pap. 9.95 (*0-13-695602-5*) P-H.

Anderson, Kenneth, et al. Mosby's Medical, Nursing & Allied Health Dictionary. 5th ed. LC 97-33687. (Illus.). 2112p. (C). (gr. 13). 1997. text 32.95 (*0-8151-4800-3*, 29948) Mosby Inc.

— Mosby's Medical, Nursing & Allied Health Dictionary. 5th ed. LC 97-33687. 1998. write for info. (*1-55664-566-X*) Mosby Inc.

Anderson, Kenneth A., jt. auth. see Tver, David F.

Anderson, Kenneth C. & Ness, Paul M. Scientific Basis of Transfusion Medicine. 2nd ed. Strauss, Marc, ed. LC 99-37690. (Illus.). 658p. 1999. text. write for info. (*0-7216-7684-7*, W B Saunders Co) Harcrt Hlth Sci Grp.

***Anderson, Kenneth E.** Prentice Hall's Federal Taxation 1999. 1999. 87.50 (*0-13-022582-7*) P-H.

***Anderson, Kenneth E., et al.** Prentice Hall's Federal Taxation 2001: Corporations, Partnerships, Estates, & Trusts. 1040p. 2000. 89.33 (*0-13-026047-9*, Prentice Hall) P-H.

Anderson, Kenneth E., jt. auth. see Berger, Bill D.

Anderson, Kenneth L. Someone Bought the House on the Island: A Novel. LC 98-61108. 320p. 1998. pap. 12.95 (*1-891855-04-2*, STARbks Pr) FL Lit Foundation.

Anderson, Kenneth N. & Anderson, Lois E. The International Dictionary of Food & Nutrition. LC 92-38971. 336p. 1993. 34.95 (*0-471-55957-1*) Wiley.

— International Menu Speller. LC 93-7261. 208p. 1993. pap. 27.95 (*0-471-58435-5*) Wiley.

— Mosby's Pocket Dictionary of Medicine, Nursing & Allied Health, Vol. 3. 3rd ed. LC 98-3311. 1312p. (C). (gr. 13). 1998. text 25.95 (*0-8151-3166-6*, 28931) Mosby Inc.

Anderson, Kenneth N. & Mosby, C. V. Mosby's Medical, Nursing & Allied Health Dictionary. 4th ed. (Illus.). 2208p. (C). (gr. 13). 1993. text 32.95 (*0-8016-7225-2*, 07225) Mosby Inc.

Anderson, Kennie. Enlightenment. 100p. 1999. pap. 8.00 (*0-7392-0090-9*, PO2962) Morris Pubng.

— The Real You. 96p. (Orig.). 1997. pap. 5.00 (*1-57502-401-2*, P01245) Morris Pubng.

Anderson, Kent. Liquor, Guns & Ammo: The Collected Short Fiction & Non-Fiction of Kent Anderson. 296p. 1998. 30.00 (*0-939767-29-5*) D McMillan.

— Night Dogs. 544p. 1999. reprint ed. mass mkt. 6.50 (*0-553-57877-4*) Bantam.

— Sympathy for the Devil. 352p. 1999. pap. 12.95 (*0-553-38057-5*) Bantam.

***Anderson, Kent.** Sympathy for the Devil. 2000. mass mkt. 6.50 (*0-553-58087-6*) Bantam.

Anderson, Kent. Sympathy for the Devil. 1989. mass mkt. 4.95 (*0-446-35222-5*) Warner Bks.

Anderson, Kent, ed. Television Fraud: The History & Implications of the Quiz Show Scandals, 39. LC 77-94755. (Contributions in American Studies: No. 39). 226p. 1979. 29.95 (*0-313-20321-0*, ATF/, Greenwood Pr) Greenwood.

Anderson, Kera. Branson's Cookin' Celebrity Cookbook. 4th rev. ed. Orig. Title: Branson's Country Music Cookbook. (Illus.). 144p. (Orig.). 1996. pap. 12.95 (*0-9636666-0-6*) Anderson MO.

Anderson, Kera, ed. Branson's Cookin' Celebrity Cookbook. 4th rev. ed. Orig. Title: Branson's Country Music Cookbook. (Illus.). 144p. (Orig.). 1996. pap. 12.95 (*0-9636666-9-X*) Anderson MO.

***Anderson, Kerby.** Creation, Ecolution & Modern Science. (Issues in Focus Ser.). 160p. 2000. pap. 10.99 (*0-8254-2033-4*) Kregel.

— Kids, Classrooms & Contemporary Education. LC 00-35726. (Issues in Focus Ser.). 160p. 2000. pap. 10.99 (*0-8254-2034-2*) Kregel.

***Anderson, Kerby, ed.** Entertainment, the Internet & Contemporary Culture. LC 99-43118. (Issues in Focus Ser.). 160p. 1999. pap. 10.99 (*0-8254-2032-6*) Kregel.

— Marriage, Family & Sexuality. LC 99-33450. (Issues in Focus Ser.). 160p. 1999. pap. 10.99 (*0-8254-2031-8*) Kregel.

Anderson, Kevin. Lenin, Hegel, & Western Marxism: A Critical Study. LC 94-45414. 344p. 1995. text 49.95 (*0-252-02167-3*) U of Ill Pr.

— Lenin, Hegel, & Western Marxism: A Critical Study. 344p. (C). 1995. pap. text 17.95 (*0-252-06503-4*) U of Ill Pr.

Anderson, Kevin, ed. Tales of the Bounty Hunters. 368p. (YA). 1996. mass mkt. 5.99 (*0-553-56816-7*) Bantam.

Anderson, Kevin & Beason, Doug. Ill Wind. 1996. pap. 5.99 (*0-614-98098-4*) Tor Bks.

Anderson, Kevin & Kaufman, Mitchell. Poltergeist: The Legacy. 224p. Date not set. pap. 12.95 (*1-58185-702-0*) Quadrillion Media.

***Anderson, Kevin & Moesta, Rebecca.** Titan A. E. Akima's Story. 240p. 2000. mass mkt. 5.99 (*0-441-00738-4*) Ace Bks.

— Titan A. E. Cale's Story. 240p. 2000. mass mkt. 5.99 (*0-441-00737-6*) Ace Bks.

***Anderson, Kevin, et al.** Erich Fromm & Critical Criminology: Beyond the Punitive Society. LC 99-6327. 2000. 15.95 (*0-252-06830-0*) U of Ill Pr.

Anderson, Kevin, jt. auth. see Severson, Susan J.

Anderson, Kevin, ed. & tr. see Marx, Karl.

Anderson, Kevin G. Antibodies, No. 5. Vol. 5. 288p. 1998. mass mkt. 6.50 (*0-06-105624-3*, HarperPrism) HarpC.

— X-Files No. 4: Skin. 336p. 2000. mass mkt. 6.50 (*0-06-105644-8*, HarperPrism) HarpC.

Anderson, Kevin J. Champions of the Force. (Star Wars: No. 3). (YA). (gr. 5 up). 1994. 11.09 (*0-606-08204-2*, Pub. by Turtleback) Demco.

— Champions of the Force, No. 3. LC 00-1713. (Star Wars: No. 3). 368p. (YA). (gr. 5 up). 1994. mass mkt. 5.99 (*0-553-29802-X*) Bantam.

— Climbing Olympus. 304p. 1994. mass mkt. 5.50 (*0-446-60158-6*, Aspect) Warner Bks.

— Dark Apprentice. (Star Wars: No. 2). (YA). (gr. 5 up). 1994. 11.09 (*0-606-08203-4*, Pub. by Turtleback) Demco.

— Dark Apprentice, No. 2. LC 00-1429. (Star Wars: No. 2). 368p. (YA). (gr. 5 up). 1994. mass mkt. 5.99 (*0-553-29799-6*) Bantam.

— Darkest Knight. (Star Wars: No. 5). (J). (gr. 7-12). 1996. mass mkt. 5.99 (*0-425-16950-2*) Berkley Pub.

— Darksaber. (Star Wars Ser.). 1995. 22.95 (*0-614-15489-8*) Bantam.

— Darksaber. (Star Wars Ser.). 430p. (YA). 1996. mass mkt. 5.99 (*0-553-57611-9*, Spectra) Bantam.

— Darksaber. (Star Wars Ser.). 464p. (YA). 1996. pap. 10.95 (*0-553-84011-8*) Bantam.

— Delusions of Grandeur. (Star Wars: No. 9). (J). 1997. mass mkt. 5.99 (*0-425-17061-6*) Berkley Pub.

— Diversity Alliance. (Star Wars: No. 8). (J). (gr. 3-5). 1997. mass mkt. 5.99 (*0-425-16905-7*) Berkley Pub.

***Anderson, Kevin J.** The Emperor's Plague. (Star Wars: No. 11). (J). (gr. 3-5). 1999. mass mkt. 5.99 (*0-425-17314-3*) Berkley Pub.

Anderson, Kevin J. Fall of the Sith Empire. (Star Wars). (Illus.). (YA). (gr. 5 up). 1998. pap. text 15.95 Dark Horse Comics.

— Ground Zero. (X-Files Ser.). 304p. 1996. mass mkt. 6.50 (*0-06-105677-4*, HarperPrism) HarpC.

Anderson, Kevin J. Ground Zero: TV Guide Edition. 304p. 1995. mass mkt. 5.99 (*0-06-105847-5*) HarpC.

— Heirs of the Force. (Star Wars: Vol. 1). (J). 1995. mass mkt. 5.99 (*0-425-16949-9*) Berkley Pub.

Anderson, Kevin J. Ill Wind. 1996. mass mkt. 6.99 (*0-8125-5018-8*, Pub. by Tor Bks) St Martin.

***Anderson, Kevin J.** Jedi Bounty. (Star Wars: No. 10). (J). (gr. 3-5). 1999. mass mkt. 5.99 (*0-425-17313-5*) Berkley Pub.

Anderson, Kevin J. Jedi Search. (Star Wars: No. 1). (YA). (gr. 5 up). 1994. 11.09 (*0-606-08202-6*, Pub. by Turtleback) Demco.

— Jedi Search, No. 1. LC 00-1423. (Star Wars: No. 1). 384p. (YA). (gr. 5 up). 1994. mass mkt. 5.99 (*0-553-29798-8*) Bantam.

— Jedi Trilogy Boxed Set: Jedi Search; Dark Apprentice; Champions of the Force, 3 vols., Set. (Star Wars). (YA). (gr. 5). 1998. mass mkt., boxed set 17.95 Bantam.

— Jedi under Siege. (Star Wars: No. 6). (J). (gr. 8-12). 1996. mass mkt. 5.99 (*0-425-16633-3*) Berkley Pub.

— Lethal Exposure. 1998. mass mkt. 5.99 (*0-441-00536-5*) Ace Bks.

— Lightsabers. (Star Wars: No. 4). (Orig.). (J). (gr. 3-5). 1996. mass mkt. 5.99 (*0-425-16951-0*) Berkley Pub.

— The Lost Ones. (Star Wars: No. 3). (Orig.). (J). (gr. 4-7). 1998. mass mkt. 5.99 (*0-425-16999-5*) Berkley Pub.

Anderson, Kevin J. The Outer Limits: Armageddon Dreams. 224p. Date not set. pap. 12.95 (*1-58185-700-4*) Quadrillion Media.

Anderson, Kevin J. Resurrection Inc. Tenth Anniversary - Lettered 1-52. 10th num. ed. (Illus.). 300p. 1999. boxed set 350.00 (*1-892950-05-7*) Overlook Connect.

— Resurrection Inc. Tenth Anniversary - Limited. 10th limited ed. (Illus.). 300p. 1999. 45.00 (*1-892950-07-3*) Overlook Connect.

— Resurrection Inc. Tenth Anniversary - Sterling 1-100. 10th ed. (Illus.). 300p. 1999. 85.00 (*1-892950-06-5*) Overlook Connect.

— Ruins. Vol. 4. 272p. 1997. mass mkt. 6.50 (*0-06-105736-3*, HarperPrism) HarpC.

— Shadow Academy. (Star Wars: No. 2). 225p. (Orig.). (J). (gr. 7-12). 1995. mass mkt. 5.99 (*0-425-17153-1*) Berkley Pub.

— Shards of Alderaan. (Star Wars: No. 7). (J). (gr. 8-12). 1997. mass mkt. 5.99 (*0-425-16952-9*) Berkley Pub.

— Star Wars: The Mos Eisley Cantina Pop-Up Book. LC 94-73767. (Illus.). 16p. (J). (gr. 2 up). 1995. 19.45 (*0-316-53511-7*) Little.

— Tales from Jabba's Palace. (Star Wars Ser.). 1996. 11.09 (*0-606-09892-5*, Pub. by Turtleback) Demco.

— Tales from the Mos Eisley Cantina. (Star Wars Ser.). 1995. 11.09 (*0-606-08200-X*, Pub. by Turtleback) Demco.

— Viento de Sangre. (Expediente X/X Files Ser.). 1998. pap. text 6.50 (*84-01-47372-1*) Lectorum Pubns.

Anderson, Kevin J. The X-Files: Antibodies, Set. abr. ed. 1997. audio 18.00 (*0-694-51762-3*, CPN2618) HarperAudio.

— The X-Files: Ground Zero. unabridged ed. 1995. audio 18.00 (*0-694-51620-1*, CPN 2530, Pub. by HarperAudio) Lndmrk Audiobks.

— X-Files: Ruin: Pileggi,&Mitch, Set. abr. ed. 1996. audio 18.00 (*0-694-51688-0*, CPN 2567) HarperAudio.

Anderson, Kevin J. The X-Files: Ruins. 1997. mass mkt. 5.99 (*0-614-20511-5*, Harp PBks) HarpC.

Anderson, Kevin J., ed. Chemical Protective Clothing Vol. 2: Product & Performance Information. 435p. 1990. 75.00 (*0-932627-44-7*) Am Indus Hygiene.

— Tales from Jabba's Palace. (Star Wars Ser.). 464p. (YA). 1995. mass mkt. 5.99 (*0-553-56815-9*, Spectra) Bantam.

— Tales from the Mos Eisley Cantina. (Star Wars Ser.). 416p. (YA). 1995. mass mkt. 5.99 (*0-553-56468-4*) Bantam.

Anderson, Kevin J. & Beason, Doug. Fallout. 320p. 1997. mass mkt. 5.99 (*0-441-00425-3*); mass mkt. 5.99 (*0-614-27691-8*) Ace Bks.

— Ignition. LC 96-29343. 304p. 1997. 23.95 (*0-312-86270-9*, Pub. by Forge NYC) St Martin.

— Ignition. LC 96-29343. 1998. mass mkt. 6.99 (*0-8125-4548-6*, Pub. by Tor Bks) St Martin.

— Virtual Destruction. 336p. (Orig.). 1996. mass mkt. 5.99 (*0-441-00308-7*) Ace Bks.

Anderson, Kevin J. & Betancourt, John G. Born of Elven Blood. (Illus.). (YA). (gr. 7 up). 1995. 15.00 (*0-689-31815-4*) Atheneum Yung Read.

Anderson, Kevin J. & Moesta, Rebecca. Crisis at Crystal Reef. (Star Wars: No. 14). 215p. (J). (gr. 3-5). 1998. mass mkt. 5.99 (*0-425-16519-1*, JAM) Berkley Pub.

— Darkest Knight. (Star Wars: No. 5). (J). (gr. 3-5). 1996. mass mkt. 5.99 (*1-57297-129-0*) Blvd Books.

— Delusions of Grandeur. (Star Wars: No. 9). 229p. (J). (gr. 3-5). 1997. mass mkt. 5.99 (*1-57297-272-6*) Blvd Books.

— Diversity Alliance. (Star Wars: No. 8). 232p. (J). (gr. 3-5). 1997. mass mkt. 5.99 (*1-57297-234-3*) Blvd Books.

— The Emperor's Plague. (Star Wars: No. 11). 208p. (J). (gr. 3-5). 1998. mass mkt. 5.99 (*1-57297-331-5*) Blvd Books.

— Heirs of the Force. (Star Wars: No. 1). 240p. (J). (gr. 3-5). 1995. mass mkt. 4.99 (*1-57297-000-6*); mass mkt. 4.99 (*1-57297-066-9*) Blvd Books.

— Jabba's Palace Pop-Up Book. LC 95-78657. (Illus.). 14p. (J). 1996. 19.45 (*0-316-53513-3*) Little.

— Jedi Bounty. (Star Wars: No. 10). 231p. (J). (gr. 3-5). 1997. mass mkt. 5.99 (*1-57297-297-1*) Blvd Books.

— Jedi under Siege. (Star Wars: No. 6). 230p. (J). (gr. 3-5). 1996. mass mkt. 5.99 (*1-57297-163-0*) Blvd Books.

— Lightsabers. (Star Wars: No. 4). 240p. (Orig.). (J). (gr. 3-5). 1996. mass mkt. 5.99 (*1-57297-091-X*) Blvd Books.

— The Lost Ones. (Star Wars: No. 3). 232p. (Orig.). (J). (gr. 3-5). 1995. mass mkt. 4.99 (*1-57297-052-9*) Blvd Books.

— Return to Ord Mantell. (Star Wars: No. 12). 230p. (J). (gr. 7-12). 1998. mass mkt. 5.99 (*0-425-16362-8*, JAM) Berkley Pub.

— Shadow Academy. (Star Wars: No. 2). 224p. (Orig.). (J). (gr. 3-5). 1995. mass mkt. 4.99 (*1-57297-025-1*) Blvd Books.

— Shards of Alderaan. (Star Wars: No. 7). (J). (gr. 3-5). 1997. mass mkt. 5.99 (*1-57297-207-6*) Blvd Books.

— Trouble on Cloud City. (Star Wars: No. 13). 210p. (J). (gr. 8-12). 1998. mass mkt. 5.99 (*0-425-16416-0*) Berkley Pub.

Anderson, Kevin J. & Rusch, Kristine K. Afterimage Aftershock. 456p. 1998. pap. 18.00 (*0-9658345-7-3*) Meisha Merlin.

Anderson, Kevin J. & Veitch, Tom. Dark Lords of the Sith. unabridged ed. (Star Wars). (Illus.). 160p. (YA). (gr. 5 up). 1996. pap. 17.95 (*1-56971-095-3*) Dark Horse Comics.

— Tales of the Jedi. abr. ed. (Star Wars). 1997. pap. 16.95 incl. audio Penguin Putnam.

— Tales of the Jedi. 2nd ed. (Star Wars). (Illus.). 136p. (YA). (gr. 5 up). 1994. pap. 14.95 Dark Horse Comics.

***Anderson, Kevin J. & Wallace, Daniel.** Star Wars: The Essential Chronology. (Star Wars Ser.). 224p. 2000. pap. 18.95 (*0-345-43439-0*, Del Rey) Ballantine Pub Grp.

Anderson, Kevin J., et al. Dark Lords of the Sith. (Star Wars). (Illus.). 160p. (YA). (gr. 5 up). 1996. pap. 17.95 (*1-56971-173-9*) Dark Horse Comics.

— Golden Age of Sith. (Star Wars). (Illus.). 144p. (YA). (gr. 5 up). 1997. pap. text 16.95 (*1-56971-229-8*) Dark Horse Comics.

***Anderson, Kevin J., et al.** Science Fiction Theater. Forbes, Brian, ed. 224p. 1999. pap. 19.95 (*1-58185-701-2*) Quadrillion Media.

Anderson, Kevin J., jt. auth. see Herbert, Brian.

Anderson, Kevin J., jt. auth. see Hubbard, L. Ron.

Anderson, Kevin J., jt. ed. see Johnson, James S.

***Anderson, Kim.** Analytical Techniques for Inorganic Contaminants. 200p. 1999. pap. 99.00 (*0-935584-65-X*, 2085) AOAC Intl.

— The Art of Kim Anderson. LC 98-18890. (Illus.). 192p. 1999. 30.00 (*0-7611-1062-3*) Workman Pub.

— Babies Are a Special Gift: Kim Anderson Collection. (Illus.). 2000. 8.99 (*0-7667-6651-9*) Gibson.

— For My Friend: Kim Anderson Collection. (Illus.). 2000. 8.99 (*0-7667-6649-7*) Gibson.

Anderson, Kim. Life Favors. 1997. 6.99 (*0-676-54053-8*) Random.

— Listen to Your Angel. 1998. 10.00 (*0-7852-1731-2*) Gibson.

***Anderson, Kim.** Listen to Your Angel: Kim Anderson Collection. (Illus.). 2000. 8.99 (*0-7667-6653-5*) Gibson.

— Our Lives Were Meant to Be Shared: Kim Anderson Collection. (Illus.). 2000. 8.99 (*0-7667-6654-3*) Gibson.

Anderson, Kim. Para Mi Mejor Amiga. 1997. 7.95 (*987-9201-04-3*) Great Quotations.

— Thank You for Being You. 1995. 7.95 (*0-8378-9858-7*) Gibson.

***Anderson, Kim.** Thank You for Being You: Kim Anderson Collection. (Illus.). 2000. 8.99 (*0-7667-6652-7*) Gibson.

Anderson, Kim. To My Sister. 1997. 6.95 (*0-7667-0953-1*) Gibson.

***Anderson, Kim.** To My Sister: Kim Anderson Collection. (Illus.). 2000. 8.99 (*0-7667-6650-0*) Gibson.

— Wonder of Boys: Kim Anderson Collection. (Illus.). 2000. 6.95 (*0-7667-6157-6*) Gibson.

— Wonder of Fathers: Kim Anderson Collection. (Illus.). 2000. 6.99 (*0-7667-6755-8*) Gibson.

— Wonder of Friends: Kim Anderson Collection. (Illus.). 2000. 6.95 (*0-7667-6159-2*) Gibson.

— Wonder of Girls: Kim Anderson Collection. (Illus.). 2000. 6.95 (*0-7667-6158-4*) Gibson.

— Wonder of Grandfathers: Kim Anderson Collection. (Illus.). 2000. 6.99 (*0-7667-6756-6*) Gibson.

— Wonder of Mothers: Kim Anderson Collection. (Illus.). 2000. 6.99 (*0-7667-6754-X*) Gibson.

— Wonder of Sisters: Kim Anderson Collection. (Illus.). 2000. 6.95 (*0-7667-6160-6*) Gibson.

— Wonder of Teachers: Kim Anderson Collection. (Illus.). 2000. 6.99 (*0-7667-6757-4*) Gibson.

Anderson, Kim & Murphy, Troy. Programming with Purpose: Developing a Process for Programming. LC 97-34170. (Student Impact Ser.). (Illus.). 176p. (Orig.). 1997. pap. 14.99 (*0-310-20129-2*) Zondervan.

Anderson, Kim, jt. auth. see Boshers, Bo.

Anderson, Kingdon P. Undercover Operations. 1990. pap. 5.95 (*0-8065-1166-4*, Citadel Pr) Carol Pub Group.

— Undercover Operations: A Manual for the Private Investigator. 88p. 1988. pap. 12.00 (*0-87364-486-7*) Paladin Pr.

Anderson, Kirk, tr. see Brovelli, Tito A.

Anderson, Kirk, tr. see Brovelli, Tito Alberto.

Anderson, Kirk A. Fighting Fire with Napalm: A Roadmap Through the Mailorder Minefield. (Illus.). 90p. 1998. pap. text 19.95 (*0-9671526-0-7*) K A Anderson.

***Anderson, Kirsteen.** Paul Valery & the Voice of Desire. (Legenda Ser.). 200p. (C). 2000. pap. 49.50 (*1-900755-40-8*, Pub. by E H R C) David Brown.

Anderson, Kirsteen, ed. see Boylston, Eula & O'Day, Carol.

Anderson, Kirsteen, ed. see Lewis, Jan.

Anderson, Kirsteen, ed. see Marsh, Nory.

Anderson, Kirsteen, ed. see Middleton, Grace F. & Pannbacker, Mary.

Anderson, Kirsteen, ed. see Walton, Patty & Wallace, Mary.

Anderson, Kitty K. & Berry, Nancy M., eds. A Dash of Down East. LC 86-80636. (Illus.). 340p. 1986. 13.95 (*0-9616940-0-9*) Jr Guild Rocky Mt NC.

Anderson, Kris. Julie Chan is Missing, 3. (Longman Originals Ser.). 1996. pap. text 5.51 (*0-582-08141-6*) Addison-Wesley.

Anderson, Kristen. Creative Writing. 324p. (C). 1984. pap. text 15.75 (*0-911337-00-8*) Intell Pr CA.

Anderson, Kristen & Ross, Imogen. Contemporary Australian Performance Design. (Illus.). 246p. 1998. text 85.00 (*90-5703-441-7*) Gordon & Breach.

Anderson, Kristin. 500 Years of Graphic Art Techniques. 2nd rev. ed. Caiaccia, Laura, ed. (Illus.). 78p. 1996. pap. 20.00 (*0-9664282-0-X*, B-GAT-500) FACTS.

— Great Customer Service on the Telephone. LC 92-22159. 96p. 1992. pap. 10.95 (*0-8144-7795-X*) AMACOM.

Anderson, Kristin & Zemke, Ron. Coaching Knock Your Socks off Service. (Illus.). 148p. 1999. pap. 25.95 (*0-8144-7935-9*) AMACOM.

— Delivering Knock Your Socks off Service. 130p. 1991. pap. 16.95 (*0-8144-7777-1*, 040533) AMACOM.

— Delivering Knock Your Socks off Service. 2nd rev. ed. LC 97-37663. (Illus.). 149p. 1999. pap. 25.95 (*0-8144-7970-7*) AMACOM.

— Knock Your Socks off Answers: Solving Customer Nightmares & Soothing Nightmare Customers. LC 95-30884. (Illus.). 143p. 1999. pap. 22.95 (*0-8144-7884-0*) AMACOM.

Anderson, Kristin, jt. auth. see Zemke, Ron.

Anderson, Kym, ed. New Silk Roads: East Asia & World Textile Markets. (Trade & Development Ser.). (Illus.). 271p. (C). 1992. text 59.95 (*0-521-39278-0*) Cambridge U Pr.

Anderson, Kym & Tyers, Rodney. Global Effects of Liberalizing Trade in Farm Products. 116p. (C). 1992. text 49.50 (*0-472-10320-2*, 10320) U of Mich Pr.

Anderson, Kym, jt. auth. see Tyers, Rodney.

Anderson, L., et al, eds. The Origins of Arab Nationalism. 1991. text 57.50 (*0-231-07434-4*) Col U Pr.

Anderson, L., et al. Performance Guide for Understanding Business & Personal Law. 8th ed. 160p. 1987. pap. text 7.96 (*0-07-008434-3*) McGraw.

Anderson, L. H., et al. Occult Science or Hidden Forces. 271p. 1955. 9.95 (*0-932785-35-2*) Philos Pub.

— Occult Science or Hidden Forces. deluxe ed. 271p. 1955. lthr. 20.00 (*0-932785-97-2*) Philos Pub.

Anderson, L. I., ed. see Tesla, Nikola.

Anderson, L. J. & Young, N. S., eds. Human Parvovirus B19. Neal, S., tr. LC 96-50380. (Monographs in Virology: Vol. 20, 1996). (Illus.). viii, 154p. 1997. 139.25 (*3-8055-6353-1*) S Karger.

Anderson, L. O. & Zornig, Harold F. Build Your Own Low Cost Home. 204p. 1972. pap. 15.95 (*0-486-21525-3*) Dover.

Anderson, L. S. Caught in the Loop: How Eastern Money Won the West . . . Or Did It? 224p. (Orig.). 1992. pap. 12.95 (*0-9633672-1-8*) Hot Iron Pr.

Anderson, L. W., ed. Polarized Ion Sources & Polarized Gas Targets. (AIP Conference Proceedings Ser.: No. 293). 320p. 1994. text 288.00 (*1-56396-220-9*) Am Inst Physics.

Anderson, Laird B., ed. Pulitzer Prize-Winning Editorials: America's Best Editorial Writing, 1917-1993. 2nd ed. LC 93-45742. 292p. (C). 1994. pap. text 24.95 (*0-8138-1491-X*) Iowa St U Pr.

Anderson, Lance. Fort Sumter: The Illustrated Story. (Illus.). 24p. (J). (gr. 2 up). 1993. pap. 3.95 (*0-9640446-0-9*) Typesetters.

Anderson, Lane K. Accounting for Government Contracts: Cost Accounting Standards. 1981. ring bd. 220.00 incl. cd-rom (*0-8205-1024-6*) Bender.

— Accounting for Government Contracts: Federal Acquisition Regulation. 1985. ring bd. 220.00 incl. cd-rom (*0-8205-1183-8*) Bender.

Anderson, Lane K. & Sollenberger, Harold M. Managerial Accounting. 8th ed. (C). 1992. mass mkt. 55.75 (*0-538-81326-1*, AQ96HA) S-W Pub.

Anderson, Lara. An Echo from a Cliff. (Illus.). 28p. 1997. pap. write for info. (*0-9659450-0-6*) L Anderson.

Anderson, Larry. Working for Success. LC 88-70593. 245p. (Orig.). 1990. pap. 9.95 (*0-9620270-0-6*) Anderson OH.

Anderson, Larry E., ed. see Zimmerman, John J.

Anderson, Larry L. Soldier's Guide to a College Degree. LC 97-42004. 176p. 1998. pap. 12.95 (*0-8117-2929-X*) Stackpole.

Anderson, Larry L. & Tillman, David A. Synthetic Fuels from Coal: Overview & Assessment. LC 79-17786. (Wiley-Interscience Publications). 172p. reprint ed. pap. 53.40 (*0-608-12355-2*, 202518400042) Bks Demand.

***Anderson, Lars.** Nascar Stars & Cars. Holder, Sherie, ed. (Illus.). 32p. (J). (gr. 2-8). 1999. pap. 3.99 (*1-886749-78-7*) SI For Kids.

Anderson, Lars. Pickup Artists: Street Basketball in America. LC 98-17460. 240p. 1998. 25.00 (*1-85984-235-6*, Pub. by Verso) Norton.

***Anderson, Lars.** Pickup Artists: Street Basketball in America. 1999. pap. text 15.00 (*1-85984-243-7*, Pub. by Verso) Norton.

Anderson, Larz. Guidelines for Preparing Urban Plans. LC 94-77951. (Illus.). 231p. (C). 1995. lib. bdg. 49.95 (*1-884829-07-4*, Planners Press) Am Plan Assn.

Anderson, Launi K. Clarissa's Crossing. LC 95-16734. (Latter-Day Daughters Ser.: Vol. 2). 80p. (J). (gr. 2 up). 1995. pap. 4.95 (*1-56236-500-2*, Pub. by Aspen Bks) Origin Bk Sales.

— Clarissa's Heart. LC 98-33731. (Latter-Day Daughters Ser.). 1998. 5.95 (*1-57345-416-8*) Deseret Bk.

— Ellie's Gold. LC 95-40536. (Latter-Day Daughters Ser.). (J). 1995. pap. 4.95 (*1-56236-505-3*, Pub. by Aspen Bks) Origin Bk Sales.

— Gracie's Angel. Utley, Jennifer, ed. LC 96-12976. (Latter-Day Daughters Ser.). (Illus.). 80p. (J). (gr. 3-9). 1996. pap. 4.95 (*1-56236-508-8*, Pub. by Aspen Bks) Origin Bk Sales.

— Hannah's Treasure. LC 96-20044. (The Latter-Day Daughters Ser.). (J). 1996. pap. 4.95 (*1-57345-297-1*, Cinnamon Tree) Deseret Bk.

— Janey's Own. LC 97-37259. (The Latter-Day Daughters Ser.). (J). 1997. pap. 4.95 (*1-57345-319-6*, Cinnamon Tree) Deseret Bk.

— Maren's Hope. LC 95-33437. (Latter-Day Daughters Ser.). (Illus.). 80p. (J). 1995. pap. 4.95 (*1-56236-503-7*, Pub. by Aspen Bks) Origin Bk Sales.

— Sadie's Trade. LC 98-33733. (Latter-Day Daughters Ser.). (J). 1998. write for info. (*1-57345-415-X*) Deseret Bk.

— Violet's Garden. LC 96-3443. (Latter-Day Daughters Ser.). (Illus.). 80p. (J). (gr. 3-9). 1996. pap. 4.95 (*1-56236-506-1*, Pub. by Aspen Bks) Origin Bk Sales.

Anderson, Laura & Malaski, Christine. Occupational Therapy As a Career: An Introduction to the Field & a Structured Method for Observation. LC 98-28653. (Illus.). 156p. (C). 1998. pap. text 18.95 (*0-8036-0387-8*) Davis Co.

Anderson, Laura K. Handbook For Proofreading. (Illus.). 256p. 1994. pap. 12.95 (*0-8442-3266-1*, 32661, Natl Textbk Co) NTC Contemp Pub Co.

— Handbook for Proofreading. (Illus.). 256p. 1993. 24.95 (*0-8442-3265-3*, NTC Business Bks) NTC Contemp Pub Co.

Anderson, Laurel, tr. see Bender, Ida.

Anderson, Laurens & Unger, Frank M., eds. Bacterial Lipopolysaccharides: Structure, Synthesis, & Biological Activities. LC 83-15828. (ACS Symposium Ser.: No. 231). 330p. 1983. lib. bdg. 49.95 (*0-8412-0800-X*) Am Chemical.

— Bacterial Lipopolysaccharides: Structure, Synthesis, & Biological Activities. LC 83-15828. (ACS Symposium Ser.: Vol. 231). 335p. 1983. reprint ed. pap. 103.90 (*0-608-03080-5*, 206353300007) Bks Demand.

Anderson, Lauri. Children of the Kalevala: Contemporary American Finns Relive the Timeless Tales of the Kalevala. LC 97-16932. 128p. 1997. pap. 12.95 (*0-87839-119-3*) North Star.

Anderson, Laurie. Bones Appetit' Gourmet Dog Biscuit Recipes & More. rev. ed. (Illus.). vii, 53p. (Orig.). 1995. spiral bd. 6.95 (*0-9653142-0-0*) Lucky Dog.

— Dal Vivo. 1999. pap. 40.00 (*88-87029-10-5*) Fondazione Prada.

— Dal Vivo. (Illus.). 327p. 1999. pap. 40.00 (*88-87029-08-3*, 910861, Pub. by Fondazione Prada) Dist Art Pubs.

— Words in Reverse. 16p. (Orig.). 1979. pap. 3.00 (*0-917061-02-0*) Top Stories.

Anderson, Laurie, et al. Blasted Allegories: An Anthology of Artists' Writings. Wallis, Brian, ed. (Illus.). 429p. 1987. 21.95 (*0-262-23128-X*) New Mus Contemp Art.

— Parkett, No. 49. 240p. 1997. pap. 29.00 (*3-907509-99-4*, 710553, Pub. by Parkett Verlag AG) Dist Art Pubs.

— Parkett Nos. 50/51: Special Double Issue. (Illus.). 350p. 1998. pap. 48.00 (*3-907582-00-4*, 720991, Pub. by Parkett Verlag AG) Dist Art Pubs.

Anderson, Laurie, jt. auth. see Goldberg, RoseLee.

***Anderson, Laurie H.** Saudi Arabia. LC 99-16276. 2000. lib. bdg. 22.60 (*1-57505-122-2*, Carolrhoda) Lerner Pub.

Anderson, Laurie Halse, see Halse Anderson, Laurie.

***Anderson, Laurie Halse.** Homeless: Sunita. LC 00-24206. (Wild at Heart Ser.: Bk. 2). (Illus.). 128p. (J). (gr. 5-9). 2000. pap. write for info. (*1-58485-045-0*) Pleasant Co.

— Saudi Arabia. (Ticket to Ser.). (Illus.). 48p. (J). (ps-3). 2000. 22.60 (*1-57505-147-8*, Carolrhoda) Lerner Pub.

Anderson, Laurie Halse. Speak. LC 98-31933. 208p. (YA). (gr. 7-12). 1999. 16.00 (*0-374-37152-0*) FS&G.

***Anderson, Laurie Halse.** Speak. large type ed. (Thorndike Young Adult Ser.). (YA). 2000. 20.95 (*0-7862-2525-4*) Thorndike Pr.

— Trickster: David. (Wild at Heart Ser.: Bk. 3). (Illus.). 128p. (YA). (gr. 5-9). 2000. pap. 4.95 (*1-58485-047-7*) Pleasant Co.

Anderson, Lavina F., ed. In Love with Eloquence. 372p. (Orig.). 1989. pap. text 14.95 (*0-922804-0-2*) S S Smith.

Anderson, Lavina F., jt. ed. see Beecher, Maureen U.

Anderson, Lavina F., jt. ed. see England, Eugene.

Anderson, Lawrence, jt. auth. see Rochfort, Luke.

Anderson, Lawrence, ed. see Symposuim on Laser & Electron Beam Processing of E.

Anderson, Leale G. Freedom from AIDS: Messmate to Helpmeet. Anderson, Mary E., ed. 236p. (Orig.). 1993. pap. 15.00 (*0-9636771-0-1*) White Dove Ent.

Anderson, Leann, jt. auth. see Lesonsky, Rieva.

Anderson, Lee. Internal Medicine & the Structures of Modern Medical Science: The University of Iowa, 1870-1990. LC 95-26592. (Illus.). 296p. (C). 1996. text 54.95 (*0-8138-2332-3*) Iowa St U Pr.

— Iowa Pharmacy, 1880-1905: An Experiment in Professionalism. LC 89-5036. (Illus.). 190p. 1989. text 27.95 (*0-87745-249-0*) U of Iowa Pr.

Anderson, Lee & Penningroth, Kathy. Complete in All Its Parts: Nursing Education at the University of Iowa, 1898-1998. LC 98-13929. (Illus.). 320p. 1998. text 42.50 (*0-472-10966-9*, 10966) U of Mich Pr.

Anderson, Lee G. The Economics of Fisheries Management. enl. rev. ed. LC 85-24061. 1986. text 50.00 (*0-8018-3253-5*) Johns Hopkins.

Anderson Lee, Pamela. Pamdemonium. (Illus.). 1997. 23.00 (*0-446-52269-4*) Warner Bks.

Anderson, Leif. Dancing Through Airth. (Illus.). 50p. 1986. pap. 15.00 (*0-9616720-0-5*) Airth Pubns.

Anderson, Leigh. Two-Dimensional Electrophoresis: Operation of the ISO-DALTR System. (Illus.). 174p. (C). 1988. teacher ed. 35.00 (*0-945532-00-8*) Large Scale Biol.

Anderson, Leigh & Hennes, David A. Principles of Microeconomics. 1995. pap. text, student ed. 26.00 (*0-13-157703-4*) P-H.

Anderson, Leith. A Church for the Twenty-First Century. 256p. (Orig.). 1992. text 15.99 (*1-55661-231-1*) Bethany Hse.

— Cuando Dios Dice Que No.Tr. of When God Says No. (SPA.). 1997. 9.99 (*0-88113-461-9*, B052-4619) Caribe Betania.

— Dying for Change. 28p. 1998. pap. 10.99 (*1-55661-665-1*) Bethany Hse.

— Leadership That Works. LC 99-6592. 224p. 1999. 16.99 (*1-55661-994-4*) Bethany Hse.

— Praying...God You Can Trust. 28p. 1998. pap. 9.99 (*0-7642-2119-1*, 212119) Bethany Hse.

— Winning the Values War in a Changing Culture: Thirteen Distinct Values That Mark a Follower. LC 94-38361. 28p. 1994. text 14.99 (*1-55661-340-7*) Bethany Hse.

Anderson, Leland I., jt. auth. see Ratzlaff, John T.

Anderson, Leland I., ed. see Tesla, Nikola.

Anderson, Lena. Stina. (Illus.). 40p. (J). (ps-3). 1989. 13.88 (*0-688-08881-3*, Grenwillow Bks) HarpC Child Bks.

— Tea for Ten. Dyssegaard, Elisabeth Kallick, tr. (Illus.). 28p. (J). (ps-k). 2000. 14.00 (*91-29-64557-3*) R&S Bks SW.

Anderson, Lena. Tick Tock. LC 97-12075. (J). 1998. write for info. (*0-385-32554-1*, DD Bks Yng Read) BDD Bks Young Read.

— Tick Tock. LC 97-69293. 28p. (J). 1998. pap. text 13.00 (*91-29-64074-1*) FS&G.

Anderson, Leon. Japanese Rage: Japanese Business & Its Assault on the West. LC 90-25372. 250p. 1992. 22.00 (*0-941423-59-X*) FWEW.

***Anderson, Leon.** Japanese Rage: Japanese Business & Its Assault on the West. 211p. 1999. reprint ed. text. write for info. (*0-7881-6392-2*) DIANE Pub.

Anderson, Leon, jt. auth. see Snow, David A.

Anderson, Leona M. Vasantotsava: The Spring Festivals of India. (Illus.), xi, 254p. 1993. 20.00 (*81-246-0011-2*, Pub. by D K Printwrld) Nataraj Bks.

Anderson, Leone C. Sean's War. LC 97-68725. (Illus.). 192p. (J). (gr. 3-9). 1998. 16.95 (*0-9638819-4-9*); pap. 10.95 (*0-9638819-5-7*) ShadowPlay Pr.

Anderson, Les, jt. auth. see Harrington, H. James.

Anderson, Lesley C., ed. see McGowan, James A.

Anderson, Leslie. Industrial Information Systems. 1980. 100.00 (*0-86176-034-4*) St Mut.

Anderson, Leslie E. The Political Ecology of the Modern Peasant: Calculation & Community. LC 93-5388. 1994. text 49.95 (*0-8018-4708-7*) Johns Hopkins.

Anderson, Lester W. & Lee, Shelley A. You Are the Product: Powerful Self-Marketing for Practicing Professionals. 215p. 1996. reprint ed. 29.95 (*0-9634809-4-4*) Financial Mktg.

Anderson, Lewis. So What. LC 89-80861. 280p. (Orig.). 1989. pap. 9.95 (*0-9623580-4-5*) Avalanche Pr.

Anderson, Lewis E., jt. auth. see Crum, Howard A.

Anderson, Lewis F., compiled by. Pestalozzi. LC 75-130984. 1975. reprint ed. 14.00 (*0-404-00357-5*) AMS Pr.

Anderson, Lewis F., ed. see Pestalozzi, Johann H.

Anderson, Liam D., jt. auth. see Anderson, Ewan W.

Anderson, Libby. A New Horse for Marny. (Illus.). 1994. pap. 9.95 (*0-939481-41-3*) Half Halt Pr.

Anderson, Lieselotte, ed. see Kant, Immanuel.

***Anderson, Linda.** Autobiography. 2000. 50.00 (*0-415-18634-X*) Routledge.

— Autobiography. 2000. pap. 14.99 (*0-415-18635-8*) Routledge.

— Home Before Dark. 2000. mass mkt. 6.50 (*0-671-02769-7*) PB.

Anderson, Linda. A Kind of Wild Justice: Revenge in Shakespeare's Comedies. LC 86-40586. 192p. 1987. 36.50 (*0-87413-319-X*) U Delaware Pr.

***Anderson, Linda.** Love Adds the Chocolate. (Illus.). 32p. 2000. 10.95 (*1-57856-377-1*) Waterbrook Pr.

Anderson, Linda. Saint Babe. 1999. pap. 5.99 (*0-451-19077-7*) NAL.

— The Secrets of Sadie Maynard. 452p. 1999. mass mkt. 6.50 (*0-671-02768-9*, Pocket Star Bks) PB.

***Anderson, Linda.** When Night Falls. 448p. 2000. 6.99 (*0-7434-1147-1*) PB.

Anderson, Linda, ed. Plotting Change: Contemporary Women's Fiction. (Stratford-upon-Avon Ser.). 160p. 1990. pap. 13.95 (*0-7131-6603-7*, A4124, Pub. by E A) Routldge.

Anderson, Linda. On Top of Old Smoky: A Collection of Songs & Stories from Appalachia. LC 92-14437. 40p. (J). 1992. 13.95 (*0-8249-8569-9*, Ideals Child) Hambleton-Hill.

Anderson, Linda, et al. A Handbook of Social Welfare Policy & Programs. LC 99-39532. 303p. (C). 1999. pap. text 35.00 (*0-205-28264-4*, Macmillan Coll) P-H.

Anderson, Linda, jt. auth. see Anderson, Allen J.

Anderson, Linda, jt. auth. see Collins, Marcia R.

Anderson, Linda, jt. ed. see Blumenfeld, Phyllis C.

Anderson, Linda, jt. ed. see Broughton, Trev L.

Anderson, Linda, ed. see James, Alice.

Anderson, Linda A., ed. see Whitlock, Ruth.

Anderson, Linda C. 35 Golden Keys about Who You Are & Why You're Here. LC 96-46477. 472p. (Orig.). 1997. pap. 14.00 (*1-57043-118-3*) Eckankar.

Anderson, Lindsay, tr. see Anderson, Connie.

Anderson, Lisa. Proud to Be Me, Peewee Platypus. (Illus.). 40p. (Orig.). (J). (ps-4). 1990. pap. 12.95 (*0-9628323-0-8*) Ridge Enter.

— The State & Social Transformation in Tunisia & Libya, 1830-1980. LC 85-43266. (Princeton Studies on the Near East). 350p. reprint ed. pap. 108.50 (*0-608-06404-1*, 206676500008) Bks Demand.

***Anderson, Lisa.** Transitions to Democracy. LC 99-19925. 336p. 1999. 45.00 (*0-231-11590-3*); pap. 17.50 (*0-231-11591-1*) Col U Pr.

Anderson, Lisa, jt. auth. see Anderson, Jim.

Anderson, Lisa, tr. see Norbu, Thinley.

Anderson, Lisa M. Mammies No More: The Changing Image of Black Women on Stage & Screen. LC 97-9782. (Illus.). 160p. 1997. 22.95 (*0-8476-8419-9*) Rowman.

Anderson, Lisa M., jt. auth. see Stevens, Susan K.

Anderson, Lloyd B. The Writing System of La Mojarra & Associated Monuments, 2 vols., Set. 212p. 1995. 29.00 (*1-879910-00-4*) Ecological Linguistics.

***Anderson, Lloyd C.** Voices from a Southern Prison. LC 00-20949. 2000. 29.95 (*0-8203-2235-0*) U of Ga Pr.

Anderson, Lois, et al. Understanding Business & Personal Law. 8th ed. 1987. pap. text 48.16 (*0-07-008438-6*) Gregg-McGraw.

Anderson, Lois E., jt. auth. see Anderson, Kenneth N.

Anderson, Loni. My Life in High Heels. 1997. mass mkt. 6.99 (*0-380-72854-0*, Avon Bks) Morrow Avon.

Anderson, Loni & Warren, Larkin. Life in High Heels. (Illus.). 306p. 1998. text 23.00 (*0-7881-5944-5*) DIANE Pub.

— My Life in High Heels. 1997. mass mkt. 6.99 (*0-614-27698-5*, Avon Bks) Morrow Avon.

Anderson, Loraine. Sisters of the Earth: Women's Prose & Poetry about Nature. LC 90-55686. 446p. 1991. pap. 14.00 (*0-679-73382-5*) Vin Bks.

Anderson, Loren R., ed. Geotechnical Practice in Dam Rehabilitation: Proceedings of the Specialty Conference. LC 93-18961. 1064p. 1993. 67.00 (*0-87262-911-2*) Am Soc Civil Eng.

Anderson, Loren W. & Walberg, Herbert J., eds. Timepiece: Extending & Enhancing Learning Time. 56p. (Orig.). (C). 1993. pap. text 9.00 (*0-88210-280-X*) Natl Assn Principals.

Anderson, Lori. Cultivating Excess. LC 92-3104. 128p. 1992. pap. 9.95 (*0-933377-18-5*, Pub. by Eighth Mount Pr); lib. bdg. 21.95 (*0-933377-19-3*, Pub. by Eighth Mount Pr) Consort Bk Sales.

— Walking the Dead. (Illus.). 24p. (Orig.). (C). 1991. pap. 4.95 (*0-9623693-2-2*) Heaven Bone Pr.

Anderson, Lori, jt. ed. see Alatalo, Frances.

Anderson, Lorin. Charles Bonnet & the Order of the Known. 176p. 1982. lib. bdg. 121.50 (*90-277-1389-8*, D Reidel) Kluwer Academic.

Anderson, Lorin W., ed. International Encyclopedia of Teaching & Teacher Education. 2nd ed. LC 95-45385. 652p. 1996. write for info. (*0-08-042304-3*, Pergamon Pr) Elsevier.

Anderson, Lorin W. & Burns, Robert A. Research in Classrooms: The Study of Teachers, Teaching, & Instruction. LC 89-16156. (Illus.). 385p. reprint ed. pap. 119.40 (*0-608-06257-X*, 206658600008) Bks Demand.

Anderson, Lorin W. & Burns, Robert B. Research in Classrooms: The Study of Teachers, Teaching & Instruction. (Illus.). 386p. (C). 1989. pap. text 39.95 (*0-08-034059-8*, Prgamon Press) Buttrwrth-Heinemann.

Anderson, Lorin W. & Carroll, John B., eds. Perspectives on School Learning: Selected Writings of John B. Carroll. 440p. (C). 1985. text 99.95 (*0-89859-343-X*) L Erlbaum Assocs.

Anderson, Lorin W., et al. The IEA Classroom Environment Study. (International Studies in Educational Achievement: Vol. 4). 350p. 1989. 83.00 (*0-08-037268-6*, Pergamon Pr) Elsevier.

Anderson, Lorin W., jt. auth. see Pellicer, Leonard O.

Anderson, Lorin W., ed. see Sosniak, Lauren A.

Anderson, Lorraine, et al. Literature & the Environment: A Reader on Nature & Culture. 18.00 (*0-321-02741-8*) Addson-Wesley Educ.

Anderson, Louis E., jt. auth. see Baker, Paul J.

Anderson, Louise. I-Got-Funner-Things-To-Do-Than-Cookin' Cookbook. (Illus.). 208p. (Orig.). 1992. spiral bd. 11.95 (*1-878488-69-4*) Hearts N Tummies.

Anderson, Louise V. B., jt. ed. see Bushby, Katherine M. D.

Anderson, Lowell, et al. California Real Estate Practice. 3rd ed. LC 97-211727. (Illus.). vii, 476p. 1997. write for info. (*0-7931-2552-9*) Dearborn.

***Anderson, Lowell, et al.** California Real Estate Practice. 4th ed. LC 99-87481. 2000. pap. 39.95 (*0-7931-3511-7*) Dearborn.

Anderson, Lowell A. California Real Estate Practice: 1997 Update. 3rd ed. 1997. pap. text 39.95 (*0-7931-2522-7*, 1523-013A) Dearborn.

***Anderson, Luke.** Genetic Engineering, Food & Our Environment. 160p. 2000. pap. 7.95 (*1-890132-55-1*) Chelsea Green Pub.

— Genetic Engineering, Food & Our Environment, Vol. 1. 80p. 1999. pap. 3.95 (*1-870098-78-1*) Green Bks.

Anderson, Luleen S. Sunday Came Early This Week. 140p. 1982. pap. 11.95 (*0-87073-575-6*) Schenkman Bks Inc.

Anderson, Lyn. Golden Retrievers: An Owners Companion. (Illus.). 240p. 1992. 39.95 (*1-85223-609-4*, Pub. by Crolwood) Trafalgar.

Anderson, Lynn. The Feasibility of Health Maintenance Organizations in Texas. (Policy Research Project Report Ser.: No. 11). 110p. 1975. pap. 3.00 (*0-89940-607-6*) LBJ Sch Pub Aff.

***Anderson, Lynn.** If I Really Believe, Why Do I Have These Doubts? rev. ed. xii, 202p. (Orig.). 2000. pap. 12.99 (*1-58229-117-9*) Howard Pub LA.

Anderson, Lynn. The Shepherd's Song: Finding the Heart to Go On. LC 96-14377. 230p. 1996. 14.99 (*1-878990-62-4*) Howard Pub LA.

— Si Realmente Creo, Por Que Tengo Estas Dudas?Tr. of If I Really Believe, Why Do I Have Doubts?. (SPA.). 208p. 9.99 (*0-88113-327-2*, B052-3272) Caribe Betania.

— A Study of the Feasibility of No-Fault Automobile Insurance for Texas. (Policy Research Project Report Ser.: No. 10). 85p. 1975. pap. 3.00 (*0-89940-606-8*) LBJ Sch Pub Aff.

— They Smell Like Sheep: Spiritual Leadership for the Twenty-First Century. LC 97-3349. 250p. 1997. 15.99 (*1-878990-73-X*) Howard Pub LA.

Anderson, Lynn M. Easy to Read Book of Mormon. Burch, Allen W., ed. 448p. 1995. 16.95 (*0-9644957-0-8*) Estes Bk.

Anderson, M. The Unsinkable Molly Malone. LC 91-10967. 208p. (YA). (gr. 7 up). 1991. 16.95 (*0-15-213801-3*, Harcourt Child Bks) Harcourt.

Anderson, M. & Arnoldi, Mary Jo. Art in Achebe's "Things Fall Apart" & "Arrow of God" 1978. 2.00 (*0-941934-25-X*) Indiana Africa.

Anderson, M. A. Tracey: A Mother's Journal of Teenage Addiction. 115p. 1988. 15.95 (*0-930773-07-1*); pap. 7.95 (*0-930773-08-X*) Black Heron Pr.

Anderson, M. B., tr. see Hugo, Victor.

Anderson, M. Brownwell & Bryan, George T., eds. Advances in Educating Medical Students: A Special Issue of Teaching & Learning in Medicine. 88p. 1994. pap. 20.00 (*0-8058-9959-6*) L Erlbaum Assocs.

Anderson, M. D. History & Imagery in British Churches. (Illus.). 320p. 1996. pap. 35.00 (*0-7195-5414-4*, Pub. by John Murray) Trafalgar.

— History by the Highway. 1967. 69.50 (*0-614-00169-2*); 69.50 (*0-614-00274-5*) Elliots Bks.

Anderson, M. Frank, ed. Physics Exam III File: Electricity & Magnetism. LC 85-25306. (Exam File Ser.). 346p. 1986. pap. 19.50 (*0-910554-56-0*) Engineering.

Anderson, M. G. & Brooks, Sue M. Advances Hillslope Processes V. LC 96-32934. (British Geomorphological Research Group Symposia Ser.). 1999. text 385.00 (*0-471-96774-2*) Wiley.

— Advances in Hillslope Processes. LC 96-32934. (British Geomorphological Research Group Symposia Ser.). 1996. write for info. (*0-471-96775-0*); write for info. (*0-471-96776-9*) Wiley.

Anderson, M. G. & Burt, T. P., eds. Process Studies in Hillslope Hydrology. LC 90-12111. 550p. 1990. 360.00 (*0-471-92714-7*) Wiley.

Anderson, M. G. & Richards, K. S., eds. Slope Stability: Geotechnical Engineering & Geomorphology. LC 86-4063. (Illus.). 656p. 1987. reprint ed. pap. 200.00 (*0-608-03996-9*, 206473300011) Bks Demand.

Anderson, M. R. & Semar, H. W. The VH-2000 Hobber. (AGMA Technical Paper: Vol. P129.17). (Illus.). 18p. 1966. pap. text 30.00 (*1-55589-162-4*) AGMA.

Anderson, M. S. Europe 18TH Century. 3rd ed. Hay, Denys, ed. (General History of Europe Ser.). 552p. (C). 1987. pap. text 33.95 (*0-582-49389-7*, 73599) Longman.

— Peter the Great. 2nd ed. LC 94-44378. (Profiles in Power Ser.). 240p. (C). 1995. text 57.75 (*0-582-08412-1*, Pub. by Addison-Wesley) Longman.

— Peter the Great. 2nd ed. LC 94-44378. (Profiles in Power Ser.). 240p. (C). 1996. pap. text 22.50 (*0-582-08411-3*, Pub. by Addison-Wesley) Longman.

— War & Society in Europe of the Old Regime, 1618-1789. 240p. 1998. pap. 19.95 (*0-7735-1759-6*, Pub. by McG-Queens Univ Pr) CUP Services.

— War & Society in Europe of the Old Regime, 1618-1789. 1998. pap. text 17.95 (*0-7509-1603-6*, Pub. by Sutton Pub Ltd) Intl Pubs Mktg.

— War Austrian Succession. LC 94-15591. (Modern Wars in Perspective Ser.). 264p. (C). 1995. text 59.75 (*0-582-05951-8*, 76987, Pub. by Addison-Wesley); pap. text 26.25 (*0-582-05950-X*, 76986, Pub. by Addison-Wesley) Longman.

***Anderson, M. T.** Burger Wuss. LC 99-14257. (Illus.). 192p. (YA). (gr. 8-10). 1999. 16.99 (*0-7636-0680-4*) Candlewick Pr.

Anderson, M. T. Thirsty. LC 96-30744. (YA). (gr. 9-12). 1997. 17.99 (*0-7636-0048-2*) Candlewick Pr.

— Thirsty. LC 96-30744. 256p. (J). (gr. 9-12). 1998. pap. text 4.99 (*0-7636-0699-5*) Candlewick Pr.

Anderson, Mac. Companies Don't Succeed . . . People Do! The Art of Recognition. (Power of One Ser.). 48p. 1998. pap. 5.95 (*1-880461-47-1*) Successories Inc.

Anderson, Mac, ed. Aged to Perfection. (Illus.). 78p. (Orig.). 1989. pap., spiral bd. 7.95 (*0-931089-27-1*) Great Quotations.

— An Apple a Day: Motivational Food for Thought. 78p. (Orig.). 1991. pap., spiral bd. 7.95 (*1-56245-019-0*) Great Quotations.

— A Friend Is a Present You Give Yourself: Quotations on Friendship & Love. (Illus.). 78p. (Orig.). 1990. pap. 7.95 (*1-56245-004-2*) Great Quotations.

— Golf Humor. (Illus.). 78p. (Orig.). 1990. pap. 7.95 (*0-931089-76-X*) Great Quotations.

— How to Handle Stress. (Illus.). 78p. (Orig.). 1988. pap. 7.95 (*0-931089-45-X*) Great Quotations.

— The Joy of Family. 78p. (Orig.). 1991. pap. 7.95 (*1-56245-015-8*) Great Quotations.

— Mothers & Babies. 78p. (Orig.). 1988. pap. 7.95 (*1-56245-012-3*) Great Quotations.

— Real Friends. (Illus.). 78p. (Orig.). 1989. pap. 7.95 (*0-931089-26-3*) Great Quotations.

— A Smile Increases Your Face Value. (Illus.). 78p. (Orig.). 1991. pap. 7.95 (*1-56245-011-5*) Great Quotations.

— Teacher's Inspirations. 78p. (Orig.). 1990. pap. 7.95 (*0-931089-95-6*) Great Quotations.

— Thoughts from the Heart. 78p. (Orig.). 1991. pap. 7.95 (*1-56245-016-6*) Great Quotations.

— To the Graduate - Keys to Success. 78p. (Orig.). 1985. pap. 7.95 (*0-931089-15-8*) Great Quotations.

— What to Tell Your Children. 78p. (Orig.). 1991. pap. 7.95 (*1-56245-014-X*) Great Quotations.

— The Wonders & Joys of Christmas. 78p. (Orig.). 1990. pap. 7.95 (*1-56245-002-6*) Great Quotations.

Anderson, Mac & Ryan, Michael. Great Men, Great Leaders: Wisdom & Inspiration from Prominent Leaders, Past & Present. Caton, Patrick, ed. (Illus.). 78p. (Orig.). 1997. pap., spiral bd. 7.95 (*1-56245-248-7*) Great Quotations.

Anderson, Mac, ed. see Golf Magazine Editors.

Anderson, Mac, ed. see Ireland, Karen.

Anderson, Mac, ed. see Lucas, Elizabeth.

***Anderson, Madelyn K.** North American Indian Games LC 99-30240. (Library Ser.). 2000. 24.00 (*0-531-20403-0*) Watts.

— North American Indian Games. (Indians of the Americas Library). (Illus.). (YA). 2000. pap. 8.95 (*0-531-16474-8*) Watts.

— The Omaha. LC 99-29816. (Watts Library). 2000. 24.00 (*0-531-20404-9*) Watts.

— Omaha. (Indians of the Americas Library). (Illus.). (YA). 2000. pap. 8.95 (*0-531-16481-0*) Watts.

Anderson, Madelyn K. Robert E. Peary & the Fight for the North Pole. (Illus.). 160p. (YA). (gr. 9-12). 1992. lib. bdg. 23.60 (*0-531-13004-5*) Watts.

***Anderson, Maggie.** Windfall: New & Selected Poems. 112p. 2000. pap. 12.95 (*0-8229-5719-1*) U of Pittsburgh Pr.

Anderson, Maggie, et al, eds. A Gathering of Poets. LC 92-3198. 320p. (Orig.). 1992. pap. 18.00 (*0-87338-468-7*) Kent St U Pr.

Anderson, Maggie & Hassler, David, eds. Learning by Heart: Contemporary American Poetry about School. LC 98-47405. 246p. 1999. pap. 14.95 (*0-87745-663-1*); text 29.95 (*0-87745-662-3*) U of Iowa Pr.

Anderson, Maggie, ed. see McNeill, Louise.

Anderson, Maggie O. Murder by Prophecy. 280p. 1998. pap. 13.00 (*0-9639147-4-X*) ReGeJe Press.

Anderson, Malcolm. Frontiers: Territory & State Formation in the Modern World. LC 97-29548. (Illus.). 255p. (C). 1996. text 60.95 (*0-7456-1652-6*, Pub. by Polity Pr) Blackwell Pubs.

— Frontiers: Territory & State Formation in the Modern World. LC 97-29548. (Illus.). 255p. (C). 1997. pap. text 23.95 (*0-7456-2008-6*, Pub. by Polity Pr) Blackwell Pubs.

— Policing the World: Interpol & the Politics of International Police Co-Operation. (Illus.). 222p. 1989. text 49.95 (*0-19-827597-8*) OUP.

***Anderson, Malcolm.** States & Nationalism in Europe since 1945. LC 00-25486. (Making of the Contemporary World Ser.). 2000. pap. write for info. (*0-415-19558-6*) Routledge.

Anderson, Malcolm, ed. Frontier Regions in Western Europe. 144p. 1983. text 35.00 (*0-7146-3217-1*, BHA-03217, Pub. by F Cass Pubs) Intl Spec Bk.

Anderson, Malcolm & Bort, Eberhard, eds. The Irish Border: History, Politics, Culture. LC 98-100752. 288p. 1998. pap. 21.95 (*0-85323-951-7*, Pub. by Liverpool Univ Pr) Intl Spec Bk.

Anderson, Malcolm & Den Boer, Monica. Policing Across National Boundaries. LC 93-42935. 256p. 1994. text 55.00 (*1-85567-195-6*) St Martin.

— Policing the European Union. (Clarendon Studies in Criminology). 346p. 1996. text 85.00 (*0-19-825965-4*) OUP.

Anderson, Malcolm, jt. auth. see Pick, John.

Anderson, Malcolm G., et al, eds. Floodplain Processes. LC 96-12987. 1996. text 195.00 (*0-471-96679-7*) Wiley.

***Anderson, Marbury E.** The Lord's Prayer in My Life: The Basic Lessons of Prayer. 96p. 2000. pap. 9.95 (*1-886513-23-6*) Kirk Hse Pubs.

Anderson, Marc & Quillen, Maureen, eds. Rockhurst Review, 1989: A Fine Arts Journal, Vol. II. 80p. 1989. pap. 5.00 (*1-886761-01-9*) Rockhurst Col.

Anderson, Marcella F. Hospitalized Children & Books: A Guide for Librarians, Families, & Caregivers. 2nd ed. LC 91-41698. (Illus.). 154p. 1992. reprint ed. 25.00 (*0-8108-2519-8*) Scarecrow.

Anderson, Marcia & Hall, Susan. Sports Injury Management. 2nd ed. 640p. 54.95 (*0-683-30602-2*) Lppncott W & W.

Anderson, Marcia K. & Hall, Susan J. Sports Injury Management. LC 94-12487. 1995. 45.95 (*0-683-01752-7*) Lppncott W & W.

— Sports Injury Management. LC 94-22447. (Illus.). 844p. 1995. 45.95 (*0-683-00175-2*) Lppncott W & W.

Anderson, Marcia K. & Martin, Malissa. Field Manual in Athletic Training. LC 98-15945. (Illus.). 300p. 1998. 29.95 (*0-683-30235-3*) Lppncott W & W.

Anderson, Marcia K., et al. Fundamentals of Sports Injury Management. LC 96-46312. (Illus.). 689p. 1997. 39.95 (*0-683-30001-6*) Lppncott W & W.

Anderson, Marcie, jt. auth. see Kovash, Arlene.

Anderson, Margaret. European Economic Interest Groupings. 150p. 1990. pap. 175.00 (*0-406-04567-4*, U.K., MICHIE) LEXIS Pub.

— Forbidden Fires. Hills, Mathilda, ed. & intro. by. (Illus.). 176p. 1996. text 21.95 (*1-56280-123-6*) Naiad Pr.

— My Thirty Years' War, an Autobiography. LC 76-136511. (Illus.). 320p. 1971. reprint ed. lib. bdg. 69.50 (*0-8371-5429-4*, ANTY, Greenwood Pr) Greenwood.

— Structured Programming Using Turbo Pascal: A Brief Introduction. 2nd ed. 200p. (C). 1990. pap. text 16.50 (*0-15-584081-9*) Dryden Pr.

— Structured Programming Using Turbo Pascal: A Brief Introduction. 2nd ed. LC 89-81791. 1990. pap. text 20.00 (*0-15-504365-X*, Pub. by Harcourt Coll Pubs) Harcourt.

***Anderson, Margaret & Halpin, Marjorie, eds.** Potlatch at Gitsegukla: William Beynon's 1945 Field Notebooks. (Illus.). 256p. 2000. text 75.00 (*0-7748-0743-1*) UBC Pr.

Anderson, Margaret, et al. Ancient Forests. (Illus.). 40p. (Orig.). (J). (gr. 3-8). 1995. pap. 5.95 (*0-941042-14-6*) Dog Eared Pubns.

— Test Book to Accompany Living with Computers Version 5.0. 5th ed. 903p. (C). 1995. pap. text, teacher ed. 43.50 (*0-03-015357-3*) Dryden Pr.

Anderson, Margaret, jt. auth. see Pound, Ezra.

Anderson, Margaret, ed. see Jansky, Robert C.

Anderson, Margaret, ed. see Pelletier, Robert.

Anderson, Margaret J. Bizarre Insects. LC 94-23725. (Weird & Wacky Science Ser.). (Illus.). 48p. (J). (gr. 4-10). 1996. lib. bdg. 18.95 (*0-89490-613-5*) Enslow Pubs.

— Carl Linnaeus: Father of Classification. LC 96-48900. (Great Minds of Science Ser.). 128p. (J). (gr. 4-10). 1997. lib. bdg. 20.95 (*0-89490-786-7*) Enslow Pubs.

— Charles Darwin: Naturalist. LC 93-29839. (Great Minds of Science Ser.). (Illus.). 128p. (J). (gr. 4-10). 1994. lib. bdg. 20.95 (*0-89490-476-0*) Enslow Pubs.

— Children of Summer. LC 96-16937. (Illus.). 112p. (J). (gr. 3 up). 1997. 14.00 (*0-374-31243-5*) FS&G.

— Isaac Newton: The Greatest Scientist of All Time. LC 96-4958. (Great Minds of Science Ser.). (Illus.). 128p. (J). (gr. 4-10). 1996. lib. bdg. 20.95 (*0-89490-681-X*) Enslow Pubs.

Anderson, Margaret J. & Stephenson, Karen F. Scientists of the Ancient World. LC 98-3912. (Collective Biographies Ser.). 104p. (YA). (gr. 6 up). 1999. lib. bdg. 20.95 (*0-7660-1111-9*) Enslow Pubs.

Anderson, Margaret U., et al. Archaeological Investigations of the Weber I (20SA581) & Weber II (20SA582) Sites, Frankenmuth Township, Saginaw County, Michigan. Lovis, William A., ed. (Illus.). 388p. (C). 1989. pap. text. write for info. (*0-9623670-0-1*) MI Dept Trans.

Anderson, Margo & Feinberg, Stephen. Who Counts? The Politics of Census Taking in Contemporary America. LC 99-25035. (Illus.). 256p. 1999. 34.95 (*0-87154-256-0*) Russell Sage.

Anderson, Margo J. The American Census: A Social History. LC 87-29828. (C). 1990. pap. 18.00 (*0-300-04709-6*) Yale U Pr.

***Anderson, Margo J.** Encyclopedia of the U. S. Census. 2000. 125.00 (*1-56802-428-2*) CQ Pr.

Anderson, Margo J., jt. ed. see Greenwald, Maurine W.

Anderson, Margot & Magleby, Richard, eds. Agricultural Resources & Environmental Indicators, 1996-97. (Illus.). 347p. (C). 1998. pap. text 45.00 (*0-7881-4903-2*) DIANE Pub.

Anderson, Maria K. & Hall, Susan J. Sports Injury Management. 1994. 43.95 (*0-8121-1754-9*) Lppncott W & W.

Anderson, Marian. Cairo Guidebook: A 1920s Guide for Call of Cthulhu. Willis, Lynn, ed. (Call of Cthulhu Roleplaying Game Ser.). (Illus.). 96p. (Orig.). (YA). 1995. pap. 16.95 (*1-56882-025-9*, 2351) Chaosium.

— My Lord, What a Morning: An Autobiography. 312p. reprint ed. lib. bdg. 59.00 (*0-685-14834-3*) Rprt Serv.

***Anderson, Marilyn.** Artes y Artesanias Mayas de Guatemala. (SPA & MYN.). 2000. 11.95 (*1-886502-30-7*) Yax Te Found.

— Maya Arts & Crafts of Guatemala: Artes y Artesanias de Guatemala. (SPA.). 64p. 2000. pap. 9.95 (*1-886502-36-6*) Yax Te Found.

Anderson, Marilyn, jt. auth. see Martens, Mert.

***Anderson, Marilyn D.** Chris Farley. LC 00-27711. (They Died Too Young Ser.). (Illus.). 2000. 16.95 (*0-7910-5860-3*) Chelsea Hse.

Anderson, Marina. The Crayon Design Workbook. (Illus.). 40p. (Orig.). 1985. pap. 6.00 (*0-932946-23-2*) Burdett CA.

Anderson, Marjorie O., tr. see Adomnan.

Anderson, Mark. The Adirondack Kobold. LC 96-71114. (Illus.). 39p. (J). (gr. k-5). 1996. spiral bd. 6.95 (*1-886623-01-5*) Canal Side Pubs.

— The Broken Boat. LC 78-14534. 75p. 1978. 3.50 (*0-87886-104-1*, Greenfld Rev Pr) Greenfld Rev Lit.

— Kafka's Clothes: Ornament & Aestheticism in the Habsburg Fin de Siecle. (Illus.). 244p. 1992. text 55.00 (*0-19-815162-4*) OUP.

— Serious Joy. LC 90-34156. 64p. (Orig.). 1990. pap. 10.00 (*0-914061-14-3*) Orchises Pr.

***Anderson, Mark & Anderson, Peter.** Anderson Anderson: Architecture & Construction. (Illus.). 192p. 2001. pap. 35.00 (*1-56898-243-7*) Princeton Arch.

Anderson, Mark, jt. auth. see Jensen, Bernard.

Anderson, Mark, ed. see Ashe, Karen.

Anderson, Mark, ed. see Bartsch, Renate.

Anderson, Mark, ed. see Brown, Marcia H.

Anderson, Mark, ed. see Bulanda, Susan.

Anderson, Mark, ed. see Christain, Kathy.

Anderson, Mark, ed. see Coe, Susan.

Anderson, Mark, ed. see Furstinger, Nancy.

Anderson, Mark, ed. see Hoffman, Martha.

Anderson, Mark, ed. see Link, Valerie & Skerritt, Linda.

Anderson, Mark, ed. see Rafe, Stephen C. & Rafe, Kathleen B.

Anderson, Mark, ed. see Turner, Deborah & Mohler, Diana.

Anderson, Mark, tr. see Bachmann, Ingeborg.

Anderson, Mark A., jt. ed. see Mular, Andrew L.

Anderson, Mark Cronlund. Pancho Villa's Revolution by Headlines. LC 99-14135. (Illus.). 320p. 1999. 34.95 (*0-8061-3172-1*) U of Okla Pr.

Anderson, Mark H. Risk Assessment of Ventricular Tachyarrhythmias, No. 3. LC 94-23609. (Clinical Approaches to Tachyarrhythmias Ser.: Vol. 3). (Illus.). 80p. 1995. 16.00 (*0-87993-612-6*) Futura Pub.

Anderson, Mark J. A Sourcebook of Nineteenth-Century American Sacred Music for Brass Instruments, 59. LC 97-8763. (Music Reference Collection: Vol. 59). 144p. 1997. lib. bdg. 65.00 (*0-313-30380-0*, Greenwood Pr) Greenwood.

***Anderson, Mark J. & Whitcomb, Patrick J.** Doe Simplified: Practical Tools for Effective Experimentation. LC 99-86646. 2000. 39.95 (*1-56327-225-3*) Productivity Inc.

Anderson, Mark M. Kafka's Clothes: Ornament & Aestheticism in the Habsburg Fin de Siecle. (Illus.). 244p. 1995. pap. text 22.00 (*0-19-815907-2*) OUP.

Anderson, Mark M., ed. Hitler's Exiles: Personal Stories of the Flight from Nazi Germany to America. LC 98-91189. 384p. 1998. 30.00 (*1-56584-394-0*, Pub. by New Press NY) Norton.

***Anderson, Mark M., ed.** Hitler's Exiles: Personal Stories of the Flight from Nazi Germany to America. 2000. pap. 16.95 (*1-56584-591-9*, Pub. by New Press NY) Norton.

Anderson, Mark S. Technology: The Law of Exploitation & Transfer. 1995. boxed set. write for info. (*0-406-01304-7*, UK, MICHIE) LEXIS Pub.

Anderson, Mark V., jt. auth. see Bedward, Marvin V.

Anderson, Marlow & Feil, Todd, eds. Lattice-Ordered Groups: An Introduction. (C). 1988. text 106.00 (*90-277-2643-4*) Kluwer Academic.

Anderson, Marston. The Limits of Realism: Chinese Fiction in the Revolutionary Period. 1989. 50.00 (*0-520-06436-4*, Pub. by U CA Pr) Cal Prin Full Svc.

Anderson, Martha, jt. auth. see Biedermann, Gertrude.

Anderson, Martha G. & Kreamer, Christine M. Wild Spirits: Strong Medicine: African Art & the Wilderness. Schildkrout, Enid, ed. LC 89-7124. (Illus.). 96p. 1989. pap. text 25.00 (*0-945802-03-X*) Museum African.

Anderson, Martha S. Good Love Gone Bad: And Other Rhymes. (Illus.). 102p. (Orig.). 1996. pap. 10.00 (*0-934852-64-2*) Lorien Hse.

Anderson, Martin. The Adult Class Manual. 93p. 1992. reprint ed. pap. text 3.95 (*1-58572-008-9*) Ambasdor Pubns.

— The Ash Circle. Sherman, Alana & De Gennard, Lorraine, eds. 48p. (Orig.). 1989. pap. text 4.95 (*0-939689-06-5*) Alms Hse Pr.

— Heard Lanes. Sherman, Alana & De Gennaro, Lorraine, eds. (Chapbooks Second Ser.). 24p. (Orig.). 1989. pap. 4.95 (*0-939689-07-3*) Alms Hse Pr.

— Impostors in the Temple. (Publication Ser.: No. 436). 270p. 1996. pap. 18.95 (*0-8179-9442-4*) Hoover Inst Pr.

— Impostors in the Temple: The Decline of the American University. 448p. 1992. 22.00 (*0-671-70915-1*) S&S Trade.

— Revolution. (Illus.). 400p. 1988. 19.95 (*0-15-177087-5*) Harcourt.

— Revolution: The Reagan Legacy. (Publication Ser.: No. 399). 486p. (C). 1990. reprint ed. pap. text 18.95 (*0-8179-8992-7*) Hoover Inst Pr.

— The Ten Causes of the Reagan Boom, 1982-1997. LC 97-45718. (Essays in Public Policy Ser.: No. 84). 1997. pap. 5.00 (*0-8179-5892-4*) Hoover Inst Pr.

— Welfare: The Political Economy of Welfare Reform in the United States. (Publication Ser.: No. 181). 1978. 6.78 (*0-8179-6811-3*) Hoover Inst Pr.

Anderson, Martin, ed. The Military Draft: Selected Readings on Conscription. LC 81-84641. (Publication Ser.: No. 258). 668p. 1982. 7.98 (*0-8179-7581-0*) Hoover Inst Pr.

— Registration & the Draft. (Publication Ser.: No. 242). 415p. (C). 1982. 7.98 (*0-8179-7421-0*) Hoover Inst Pr.

Anderson, Marvel, ed. see Carpenter, Patricia.

Anderson, Marvin W. Evangelical Foundations: Religion in England, 1378-1683. (American University Studies: Theology & Religion: Ser. VII, Vol. 33). XIV, 488p. (C). 1987. text 65.90 (*0-8204-0486-1*) P Lang Pubng.

— Peter Martyr, a Reformer in Exile, 1542-1562: A Chronology of Biblical Writings in England & Europe. 607p. 1975. 125.00 (*90-6004-343-X*, Pub. by B De Graaf) Coronet Bks.

Anderson, Mary. Color Therapy: The Application of Color for Healing, Diagnosis, & Well-Being. 112p. 1991. pap. 9.00 (*1-85538-010-2*, Pub. by Aqrn Pr) Harper SF.

— Suzy's Secret Snoop Society. (J). (gr. 3-7). 1991. pap. 2.95 (*0-380-75917-9*, Avon Bks) Morrow Avon.

— Tune in Tomorrow. 192p. (J). (gr. 7 up). 1985. pap. 2.50 (*0-380-69870-6*, Avon Bks) Morrow Avon.

— Woman at Work. LC 73-13451. (Illus.). 266p. 1973. reprint ed. lib. bdg. 59.50 (*0-8371-7133-4*, ANWW, Greenwood Pr) Greenwood.

Anderson, Mary, et al, eds. Doing Feminism: Teaching & Research in the Academy. LC 97-15338. (Illus.). 250p. (Orig.). 1997. pap. 24.95 (*0-87013-472-8*) Mich St U Pr.

Anderson, Mary, jt. auth. see Ashby, Eric.

Anderson, Mary Alice, jt. ed. see Allen, Christine.

Anderson, Mary Ann. Ain't Nothing Sweeter Than a Magnolia Moon. 128p. 1995. pap. 12.95 (*0-86554-489-1*, MUP/P129) Mercer Univ Pr.

— Portrait of a Soap Star, the Emily McLaughlin Story. (Illus.). 155p. (Orig.). 1994. pap. text 14.95 (*0-9643167-8-1*) Orchard Books.

— To Be a Nurse: Personal-Vocational Relations for the LPN/LVN. LC 99-58026. (Illus.). 384p. 2000. pap. text 23.95 (*0-8036-0573-0*) Davis Co.

Anderson, Mary Ann, et al, eds. The Long-Term Care Nursing Assistant Training Manual. 2nd ed. LC 95-46849. (Illus.). 352p. (Orig.). 1996. pap. 29.95 (*1-878812-28-9*) Hlth Prof Pr.

***Anderson, Mary Ann & Braun, Judith V.** Caring for the Elderly Client. 2nd ed. LC 98-51166. 400p. 1999. 24.95 (*0-8036-0462-9*) Davis Co.

Anderson, Mary Ann, et al. Nursing Leadership, Management, & Professional Practice for the LPN/LVN. LC 96-52836. (Illus.). 252p. (C). 1997. pap. text 22.95 (*0-8036-0209-X*) Davis Co.

***Anderson, Mary B.** Do No Harm: How Aid Can Support Peace - or War. LC 98-44669. 161p. 1999. pap. 16.95 (*1-55587-834-2*) L Rienner.

— Do No Harm: How Aid Can Support Peace - Or War. LC 98-44669. 161p. 1999. lib. bdg. 35.00 (*1-55587-833-4*) L Rienner.

Anderson, Mary B. Focusing on Women: UNIFEM's Experience in Mainstreaming. 28p. (Orig.). 1993. pap. 7.95 (*0-912917-42-3*) UNIFEM.

Anderson, Mary B. & Woodrow, Peter J. Rising from the Ashes: Development Strategies in Times of Disaster. LC 97-45940. 340p. 1998. pap. 22.50 (*1-55587-800-8*) L Rienner.

Anderson, Mary C., ed. Two Scholarly Friends: Yates Snowden-John Bennett Correspondence, 1902-1932. LC 93-14054. 421p. 1993. text 29.95 (*0-87249-961-8*) U of SC Pr.

Anderson, Mary E. Link Across America: A Story of the Historic Lincoln Highway. LC 97-65052. (Illus.). 52p. (J). (gr. 1-8). 1997. 14.95 (*1-877810-97-5*, LINK) Rayve Prodns.

Anderson, Mary E., ed. see Anderson, Leale G.

***Anderson, Mary Elizabeth.** Taking Cerebral Palsy to School. Gosselin, Kim, ed. (Special Kids in School Ser.: Vol. 6). (Illus.). 32p. (J). (gr. k-5). 2000. pap. 11.95 (*1-891383-08-6*, Pub. by JayJo Bks) Unique Bks Inc.

Anderson, Mary J. & Venable, Ginger. Graduation - Celebrate with Style! A Graduation Party Planning Guide. (Illus.). 40p. 1999. 9.95 (*0-9671253-0-8*) Lanewood Mktg.

***Anderson, Mary J. & Venable, Ginger.** Graduation - Celebrate with Style! A Graduation Party Planning Guide. rev. ed. (Illus.). 96p. 2000. pap. 9.95 (*0-9671253-1-6*) Lanewood Mktg.

Anderson, Mary M. Hidden Power: The Palace Eunuchs of Imperial China. LC 80-70053. 318p. (C). 1990. 34.95 (*0-87975-574-1*) Prometheus Bks.

Anderson, Mary P. & Woessner, William W. Applied Groundwater Modeling: Simulation of Flow & Advective Transport. 381p. 1991. text 94.00 (*0-12-059485-4*) Acad Pr.

Anderson, Mary P., jt. auth. see Wang, Herbert F.

Anderson, Mary P., jt. ed. see Chen, S. P.

Anderson, Mary P., ed. see Minerals, Metals & Materials Society Staff.

Anderson, Mary S. Whatever Happened to the Hippies? LC 90-91784. (Illus.). 192p. (Orig.). 1990. pap. 10.95 (*0-936810-19-X*) M & M.

Anderson, Marylynn. Christmas List Organizer. 160p. 1991. pap. 12.95 (*0-9630945-0-5*) M L Pr.

Anderson, Mathew. La Europa del Siglo XVIII (1738-1789) (Breviarios Ser.). (SPA.). pap. 8.99 (*968-16-0430-X*, Pub. by Fondo) Continental Bk.

Anderson, Matthew S. The Ascendancy of Europe, 1815-1914. 2nd ed. (Illus.). 411p. (C). 1989. pap. 49.00 (*0-582-49386-2*, 73597) Longman.

Anderson, Matthew S. The Origins of the Modern European State System, 1494-1618. LC 97-31324. (C). 1998. text 68.44 (*0-582-22945-6*, Pub. by Addison-Wesley) Longman.

Anderson, Maxwell. Anne of the Thousand Days. 1950. pap. 5.25 (*0-8222-0049-X*) Dramatists Play.

— Barefoot in Athens: Manuscript Edition. 1952. pap. 13.00 (*0-8222-0094-5*) Dramatists Play.

— Dramatist in America: Letters of Maxwell Anderson, 1912-1958. Avery, Laurence G., ed. LC 77-4491. 451p. reprint ed. pap. 139.90 (*0-7837-5235-0*, 204496900005) Bks Demand.

— Four Verse Plays. Incl. Elizabeth the Queen. LC 59-1731. 1959. High Tor. LC 59-1731. 1959. Mary of Scotland. LC 59-1731. 1959. Winterset. LC 59-1731. 1959. LC 59-1731. 560p. (Orig.). 1959. Set pap. 9.95 (*0-15-633329-5*, Harvest Bks) Harcourt.

— The Golden Six. 1959. pap. 5.25 (*0-8222-0457-6*) Dramatists Play.

— Joan of Lorraine. 1947. pap. 5.25 (*0-8222-0593-9*) Dramatists Play.

An Asterisk (*) at the beginning of an entry indicates that the title is appearing for the first time.

A

***Anderson, Niki.** What I Learned from God While Gardening. 2000. pap. text 8.99 (*1-57748-853-9*) Barbour Pub.

Anderson, Niki. What My Cat Has Taught Me about Life: Meditations for Cat Lovers. LC 99-214314. 208p. 1997. 17.99 (*1-56292-366-8*, HB-366) Honor Bks OK.

Anderson, Nils. Chemicals, Metals & Men: The Coke & Coal By-Product Industry in the United States. 1995. 19.95 (*0-533-10998-1*) Vantage.

***Anderson, Nils.** Polarization, Alignment & Orientation in Atomic Collisions. (Illus.). 2000. write for info. (*0-387-98989-7*) Spr-Verlag.

***Anderson, Nina.** ADD: El Metodo Natural: Una Ayuda Para Ninos Con Trastorno Deficitario de la Atencion E Hipe. 56p. 1999. pap. 6.95 (*1-884820-49-2*) SAFE GOODS.

Anderson, Nina. The Backseat Flyer. LC 98-90505. (Illus.). 80p. 1998. pap. 9.95 (*1-884820-35-2*) ATN Grp Pub.

— Eliminating Pilot Error: The Final Step in Flight Training. large type ed. 64p. 1999. pap. 7.95 (*1-884820-44-1*) ATN Grp Pub.

Anderson, Nina & Peiper, Howard. A. D. D. the Natural Approach: Help for Attention Deficit Disorder & Hyperactivity. 40p. 1996. pap. 4.95 (*1-884820-19-0*) SAFE GOODS.

— The All Natural, High-Performance Diet: Improving Your Physical, Mental & Sexual Performance. LC 99-71261. 64p. 1999. pap. 7.95 (*1-884820-46-8*) SAFE GOODS.

— Are You Poisoning Your Pets? A Guidebook to How Our Lifestyles Affect the Health of Our Pets. LC 98-4712. 192p. 1998. pap. 9.95 (*0-89529-829-5*, Avery) Penguin Putnam.

***Anderson, Nina & Peiper, Howard.** Super Nutrition for Dogs n' Cats: Preventive Medicine for Pets. rev. ed. LC 00-132683. (Illus.). 104p. 2000. pap. 9.95 (*1-884820-59-X*) SAFE GOODS.

***Anderson, Nina, et al.** Nutritional Leverage for Great Golf. Orenstein, Neil, ed. LC 99-72917. 152p. (Orig.). 1999. pap. 9.95 (*1-884820-53-0*) ATN Grp Pub.

Anderson, Nina, et al. The Secrets of Staying Young: Over 50 Looking 30. large type rev. ed. LC 98-61785. (Illus.). 176p. 1999. pap. 9.95 (*1-884820-43-3*) SAFE GOODS.

— Super Nutrition for Animals. LC 96-70946. (Illus.). 192p. (Orig.). 1997. pap. 12.95 (*1-884820-16-6*) SAFE GOODS.

Anderson, Nina, jt. auth. see Carden, Gary.

Anderson, Nina, jt. auth. see Peiper, Howard.

Anderson, Nina, ed. see Bell, Rachel & Peiper, Howard.

Anderson, Nola, ed. see Anderson, August K.

Anderson, Noma B., jt. auth. see Payne, K. T.

Anderson, Noma B., jt. auth. see Screen, Robert M.

Anderson, Norma, ed. see Taylor, Eldon.

Anderson, Norma R. An Elfindale Story. LC 81-5977. (Illus.). 36p. (Orig.). (J). (gr. 1-6). 1981. pap. 5.95 (*0-913504-64-5*) Lowell Pr.

Anderson, Norman. Christianity & World Religions. rev. ed. LC 84-115291. 216p. (Orig.). 1984. pap. 14.99 (*0-87784-981-1*, 981) InterVarsity.

— Ferris Wheels: An Illustrated History. (Illus.). 280p. (C). 1992. 59.95 (*0-87972-531-1*); pap. 29.95 (*0-87972-532-X*) Bowling Green Univ Popular Press.

— Islamic Law in Africa. 396p. 1970. 49.50 (*0-7146-1905-1*, BHA-01905, Pub. by F Cass Pubs) Intl Spec Bk.

— Las Religiones del Mundo.Tr. of World's Religions. (SPA.). 1993. pap. 11.99 (*0-311-05767-5*) Casa Bautista.

Anderson, Norman, ed. Contributions to Information Integration Theory, Set, Vols. 1-3. 1991. text 85.00 (*0-8058-0855-8*) L Erlbaum Assocs.

— Contributions to Information Integration Theory Vol. 1: Cognition. 424p. 1991. text 39.95 (*0-8058-0836-1*) L Erlbaum Assocs.

— Contributions to Information Integration Theory Vol. 2: Social. 304p. 1991. text 34.50 (*0-8058-0837-X*) L Erlbaum Assocs.

— Contributions to Information Integration Theory Vol. 3: Developmental. 264p. 1991. text 32.50 (*0-8058-0838-8*) L Erlbaum Assocs.

Anderson, Norman & Weiss, Margene, eds. Interspace & the Inward Sphere: Essays on Romantic & Victorian Self. LC 78-58247. 1978. pap. 5.00 (*0-934312-01-X*) WIU Essays Lit.

Anderson, Norman D. & Fowler, B. T. Raleigh, North Carolina: North Carolina's Capital City on Postcards. LC 97-112774. (Images of America Ser.). (Illus.). 128p. 1996. pap. 16.99 (*0-7524-0495-4*) Arcadia Publng.

Anderson, Norman H. A Functional Theory of Cognition. 512p. 1996. 69.95 (*0-8058-2244-5*) L Erlbaum Assocs.

Anderson, O., et al, eds. Mesozoic Geology & Paleontology of the Four Corners Area. (Guidebook Ser.: No. 48). (Illus.). 288p. 1997. pap. 60.00 (*1-58546-083-4*) NMex Geol Soc.

Anderson, O. J., et al, eds. Southwestern Colorado Plateau. (Guidebook Ser.: No. 40). (Illus.). 345p. 1989. 50.00 (*1-58546-075-3*) NMex Geol Soc.

Anderson, O. Roger. Comparative Protozoology. (Illus.). 440p. 1987. 107.95 (*0-387-18082-6*) Spr-Verlag.

— Radiolaria. (Illus.). 350p. 1983. 205.00 (*0-387-90832-3*) Spr-Verlag.

— Teaching Modern Ideas of Biology. LC 73-185961. (Studies in Science Education). 251p. reprint ed. pap. 77.90 (*0-608-14900-4*, 202598700048) Bks Demand.

Anderson, O. Roger & Druger, Marvin, eds. Explore the World Using Protozoa. (Illus.). 240p. (Orig.). 1997. pap. text 29.95 (*0-87355-159-1*, PB137X) Natl Sci Tchrs.

Anderson, O. Roger, jt. ed. see Lee, John J.

Anderson, Odin W. Health Care: Can There Be Equity? the United States, Sweden, & England. LC 72-7449. 295p. reprint ed. 91.50 (*0-8357-9902-6*, 201952400012) Bks Demand.

— The Uneasy Equilibrium: Private & Public Financing of Health Services in the United States, 1875-1965. 1968. pap. 9.95 (*0-8084-0305-2*) NCUP.

Anderson, Odin W., jt. auth. see Anderson, Ronald.

Anderson, Odin W., jt. auth. see Sinai, Nathan.

Anderson, Odin W., ed. & tr. see Sundt, Eilert.

Anderson, Olive. A Liberal State at War: English Politics & Economics During the Crimean War. (Modern Revivals in History Ser.). 320p. (C). 1994. text 63.95 (*0-7512-0279-7*, Pub. by Gregg Revivals) Ashgate Pub Co.

Anderson, Olive M. Utopia in Upper Michigan. LC 81-84595. (Illus.). 68p. 1982. pap. 5.95 (*0-918616-10-7*) Northern Mich.

Anderson, Olof W. The Treasure Vault of Atlantis. Reginald, R. & Melville, Douglas, eds. LC 77-84194. (Lost Race & Adult Fantasy Ser.). 1978. reprint ed. lib. bdg. 29.95 (*0-405-10952-0*) Ayer.

Anderson, Orson. Equations of State for Solids in Geophysics & Ceramic Science. (Monographs on Geology & Geophysics: No. 31). (Illus.). 432p. 1995. text 90.00 (*0-19-505606-X*) OUP.

***Anderson, Osborne P.** A Voice from Harper's Ferry 1859. LC 99-54102. 2000. write for info. (*0-89567-136-0*) World View Forum.

Anderson, Osborne P. A Voice from Harper's Ferry. LC 72-8569. (Black Heritage Library Collection). 1977. reprint ed. 19.95 (*0-8369-9182-6*) Ayer.

Anderson, Oscar E., Jr., jt. auth. see Hewlett, Richard G.

Anderson, Owanah. 400 Years: Anglican/Episcopal Mission among American Indians. (Illus.). 416p. (Orig.). 1997. pap. 12.95 (*0-88028-182-0*, 1421) Forward Movement.

Anderson, Owen. Lactate Lift-Off: How to Use Lactate Training to Maximize Your Fitness. unabridged ed. LC 98-96158. 180p. 1998. pap. 21.95 (*0-9663726-0-3*) SSS MI.

Anderson, Owen & Romanov, Jane F., eds. Texas Oil & Gas Law Journal. 20p. 1986. ring bd. 125.00 (*0-409-25264-6*, MICHIE) LEXIS Pub.

Anderson, Owen L., et al. Oil & Gas, Cases & Materials On. 3rd ed. LC 98-16545. 1000p. 1998. 65.00 (*0-314-22640-0*) West Pub.

Anderson, P. Go for Growth. 5.99 (*0-614-11438-1*, Pub. by Christian Focus); 5.99 (*1-871676-70-3*, Pub. by Christian Focus) Spring Arbor Dist.

Anderson, P. & Lehto, J. Evaluation & Monitoring of Action on Alcohol. LC 96-145876. (WHO Regional Publications, European Ser.). 92p. 1995. pap. text 14.00 (*92-890-1323-0*) World Health.

Anderson, P. A., ed. Evolution of the First Nervous Systems. LC 90-34441. (NATO ASI Ser.: Vol. 188). (Illus.). 446p. (C). 1990. text 156.00 (*0-306-43529-2*, Kluwer Plenum) Kluwer Academic.

Anderson, P. A., jt. ed. see Corell, R. W.

Anderson, P. D. In Its Own Image: The Cinematic Vision of Hollywood. LC 77-22903. (Dissertations on Film Ser.). 1978. lib. bdg. 26.95 (*0-405-10749-8*) Ayer.

Anderson, P. K., et al. Essential C. (C). 1993. student ed. 30.00 (*1-881592-11-1*) Hayden-McNeil.

— Statistical Models Based on Counting Processes. (Statistics Ser.). 767p. 1995. 39.95 (*3-540-94519-9*) Spr-Verlag.

Anderson, P. K., jt. auth. see Lhotka, John F.

Anderson, P. M., et al, eds. Subsynchronous Resonance in Power Systems. LC 89-28366. (Illus.). 282p. 1990. text 69.95 (*0-87942-258-0*, PC02477) Inst Electrical.

Anderson, P. W. Basic Notion of Condensed Matter Physics. 2nd ed. LC 97-39043. 1997. pap. 39.00 (*0-201-32830-5*) Addison-Wesley.

— Basic Notions of Condensed Matter Physics, No. 55. (Frontiers in Physics Ser.). 1984. text 51.75 (*0-8053-0220-4*) Addison-Wesley.

— Basic Notions of Condensed Matter Physics, No. 55. (Frontiers in Physics Ser.). (C). 1984. pap. 44.95 (*0-8053-0219-0*) Addison-Wesley.

— Concepts in Solids: Lectures on the Theory of Solids. 188p. 1997. pap. text 24.00 (*981-02-3195-4*) World Scientific Pub.

— The Theory of Superconductivity in the High-TC Cuprate Superconductors. LC 96-43338. (Princeton Series in Physics). 352p. 1997. text 49.50 (*0-691-04365-5*, Pub. by Princeton U Pr) Cal Prin Full Svc.

Anderson, P. W., et al. The Economy As an Evolving Complex System. (Santa Fe Institute Ser.). (Illus.). 336p. (C). 1988. pap. 45.00 (*0-201-15685-7*) Addison-Wesley.

Anderson, Paige. Hobnob Inn: Inquiring Minds Want to Know. (Illus.). 152p. 1999. pap. 12.95 (*0-9660676-2-2*) Plan Nine Publ.

***Anderson, Pam.** How to Cook Without a Book: Recipes & Techniques Every Cook Should Know by Heart. LC 99-43776. (Illus.). 304p. 2000. 25.00 (*0-7679-0279-3*) Broadway BDD.

Anderson, Pam. The Perfect Recipe: Getting It Right Every Time: Making Our Favorite Dishes the Absolute Best They Can Be. LC 98-17821. (Illus.). 372p. 1998. 27.00 (*0-395-89403-4*) HM.

Anderson, Pamela S. The Complete Student's Handbook. LC 97-10145. (Illus.). 256p. (C). 1997. pap. text 26.95 (*0-631-19383-9*) Blackwell Pubs.

— A Feminist Philosophy of Religion: The Rationality & Myths of Religious Belief. 256p. (C). 1997. text 62.95 (*0-631-19382-0*) Blackwell Pubs.

Anderson-Parente, Janet K., jt. auth. see Parente, Rick.

Anderson, Pat R. My Own Cruising Journal. LC 92-97098. 80p. 1997. spiral bd. 19.95 (*0-9634391-0-3*) P Russel Anderson.

Anderson, Patricia. Affairs in Order: A Complete Resource Guide to Wills & Other Financial-Legal Plans - Terminal Care & Counseling; Bioethics; Funeral & Disposition Options; Notification & Documents; Executor-Survivor Aid; Bereavement Help & More. 256p. 1991. text 21.95 (*0-02-501991-0*) Macmillan.

— Contemporary Jewellery in Australia & New Zealand. LC 99-158614. (Illus.). 168p. 1998. text 80.00 (*90-5703-371-2*) Gordon & Breach.

— The Printed Image & the Transformation of Popular Culture, 1790-1860. (Illus.). 224p. 1994. pap. 18.95 (*0-19-818276-7*) OUP.

Anderson, Patricia & Rose, Jonathan. British Literary Publishing Houses, 1820-1880 LC 91-13358. (Dictionary of Literary Biography Ser.). 412p. 1991. text 155.00 (*0-8103-4586-2*) Gale.

Anderson, Patricia, jt. auth. see Rose, Jonathan.

Anderson, Patricia A., intro. North Country Landscape. (Illus.). 23p. 1986. pap. 7.00 (*0-685-18656-3*) SUNYP R Gibson.

Anderson, Patricia C., ed. Prehistory of Agriculture: New Experimental & Ethnographic Approaches. LC 98-31101. (Monograph Ser.: No. 40). (Illus.). 1999. pap. text 50.00 (*0-917956-93-1*) UCLA Arch.

Anderson, Patricia J. Breast Cancer: A Patient Guide. LC 92-81894. (Illus.). 191p. 1992. pap. 14.95 (*1-881915-00-X*) Creat Hlth Srvs.

Anderson, Patricia M. The Architecture of Bowdoin College. LC 87-71827. (Illus.). 225p. (Orig.). 1988. pap. 15.95 (*0-685-22205-5*) Bowdoin Coll.

Anderson, Patricia M., et al. Portland. rev. ed. Summers, Lydia B., ed. (Illus.). 229p. 1986. pap. 19.95 (*0-685-17690-8*) Greater Portland.

Anderson, Patricia S. Happy Hearts in the Kitchen. Anderson, Robert E., ed. (Illus.). 350p. (Orig.). 1989. pap. text 14.95 (*0-9623124-0-1*) DOBEES Found.

Anderson, Patrick. Electing Jimmy Carter: Campaign of 1976. LC 94-28320. (Illus.). 192p. 1994. 24.95 (*0-8071-1916-4*) La State U Pr.

— The Pleasure Business. 291p. 1989. 17.95 (*0-15-172047-9*) Harcourt.

***Anderson, Patrick & Henderson, Michael.** Right on the Money: ActiveStore - Your Guide to E-Commerce. 83p. 1999. ring bd. 97.00 (*1-930336-08-X*) Adnet Intl.

Anderson, Patrick R. Introduction to Criminal Justice. 6th ed. LC 97-18086. 544p. (C). 1997. pap. 40.63 (*0-07-006166-1*) McGraw.

Anderson, Patrick R. & Newman, Donald J. Introduction to Criminal Justice. 5th ed. LC 92-19224. (C). 1993. pap. text 46.50 (*0-07-001958-4*) McGraw.

Anderson, Patrick R. & Winfree, L. Thomas, Jr., eds. Expert Witnesses: Criminologists in the Courtroom. LC 86-14519. (SUNY Series in Critical Issues in Criminal Justice). 237p. (C). 1987. text 89.50 (*0-88706-448-5*); pap. text 29.95 (*0-88706-449-3*) State U NY Pr.

Anderson, Paul. A Call from the 21st Century: The Technology of Customer Contact. LC 96-71809. 225p. (Orig.). 1997. pap. 22.95 (*0-9653359-0-9*) Doyle Pub.

— Safety First: The Making of New Labour. 456p. 1997. pap. text 14.95 (*1-86207-070-9*) Granta.

Anderson, Paul & Bontrager, Lisa. Brass Ensemble. 1987. 14.00 (*0-318-37568-0*) Instrumental.

Anderson, Paul & Rosenberg, Art. The Digital Caller Center: Gateway to Technical Intimacy. LC 99-72185. 170p. 1999. pap. 22.95 (*0-9653359-1-7*) Doyle Pub.

***Anderson, Paul & Rosenberg, Art.** The Executive's Guide to Customer Relationship Management: Retention - Loyalty - Profit. 2nd ed. 204p. 2000. pap. 22.95 (*0-9653359-4-1*) Doyle Pub.

Anderson, Paul, jt. auth. see Anderson, Gail.

Anderson, Paul A., et al. Program & Abstract Book. 180p. (C). 1990. pap. 22.00 (*0-9627560-0-8*) U of MD Physical Therapy.

Anderson, Paul D. Basic Human Anatomy & Physiology: Clinical Implications for the Health Professionals. LC 83-23511. (C). 1984. pap., teacher ed. 10.00 (*0-534-03090-4*); pap. text 35.00 (*0-534-03089-0*) Jones & Bartlett.

— The Devil Made Me Do It Again: Thirty-Three Tales of Terror. 128p. 1998. pap. 14.95 (*0-937491-07-1*) TwoAM Pubns.

— Human Anatomy & Physiology Coloring Workbook & Study Guide. 304p. 1990. pap., student ed., wbk. ed. 28.75 (*0-86720-145-2*) Jones & Bartlett.

Anderson, Paul D. & Spitzer. Human Anatomy & Physiology Coloring Workbook. 2nd ed. (Health Science Ser.). 304p. 1997. pap. 29.50 (*0-7637-0499-7*) Jones & Bartlett.

Anderson, Paul F., et al, eds. Utah's Aerospace Heritage: The Aircraft & Artifacts of Hill Aerospace Museum. LC 96-80367. (Illus.). 144p. (Orig.). 1996. pap. 11.95 (*0-9656079-0-9*, UAH-1) Persistence of Vision.

Anderson, Paul G. Brass Solo & Study Guide. 14.00 (*0-686-15889-X*) Instrumental.

Anderson, Paul L. The Fine Art of Photography. LC 72-9180. (Literature of Photography Ser.). 1979. reprint ed. 34.95 (*0-405-04891-2*) Ayer.

— For Freedom & for Gaul. LC 57-9449. (Illus.). (YA). (gr. 7-11). 1931. pap. 18.00 (*0-8196-0102-0*) Biblo.

— Pugnax the Gladiator. LC 61-1111. (Illus.). (J). (gr. 7-11). 1939. pap. 18.00 (*0-8196-0104-7*) Biblo.

— Slave of Catiline. LC 57-9446. 255p. (J). (gr. 7-11). 1930. pap. 20.00 (*0-8196-0101-2*) Biblo.

— Swords in the North. LC 57-9448. 270p. (J). (gr. 7-11). 1935. 21.00 (*0-8196-0103-9*) Biblo.

— With the Eagles. LC 57-9447. (Illus.). (J). (gr. 7-11). 1929. pap. 21.00 (*0-8196-0100-4*) Biblo.

Anderson, Paul M. Analysis of Faulted Power Systems. LC 95-15246. (Power Systems Engineering Ser.). 536p. 1995. reprint ed. 69.95 (*0-7803-1145-0*, PC5616) Inst Electrical.

***Anderson, Paul M.** Power System Protection. LC 98-28659. (Power Engineering Ser.). 1998. 124.95 (*0-7803-3427-2*) IEEE Standards.

Anderson, Paul M., ed. Professors Who Believe: The Spiritual Journeys of Christian Faculty. LC 98-27832. 252p. 1998. pap. 14.99 (*0-8308-1599-6*, 1599) InterVarsity.

Anderson, Paul M. & Fouad, Aziz A. Power System Control & Stability. rev. ed. LC 93-10958. 480p. 1993. 69.95 (*0-7803-1029-2*, PC0379-8) Inst Electrical.

Anderson, Paul N. The Christology of the Fourth Gospel. LC 97-7838. 352p. (Orig.). 1997. pap. 25.00 (*1-56338-199-0*) TPI PA.

Anderson, Paul N. & Macy, Howard R., eds. Truth's Bright Embrace: Essays & Poems in Honor of Arthur O. Roberts. 375p. 1996. 25.00 (*0-9653474-0-0*); pap. 20.00 (*0-9653474-1-9*) G Fox Univ.

Anderson, Paul S. The MDT Innovation: Machine Scoring of Fill-in-the-Blank Tests. (Illus.). 198p. 1987. pap. text 9.95 (*0-940387-01-8*); pap. text 14.95 (*0-317-60239-X*) Multi Digit Tech.

— Storytelling with the Flannel Board, 3 Bks., Bk. 1. LC 21-650. (Illus.). 270p. (J). (ps). 1963. 15.95 (*0-513-00105-0*) Denison.

— Storytelling with the Flannel Board, 3 bks., Bk. 2. LC 21-650. (Illus.). 260p. (J). (ps). 1970. 15.95 (*0-513-00137-9*) Denison.

Anderson, Paul S. & Lapp, Diane K. Language Skills in Elementary Education. 4th ed. 496p. (C). 1987. text 53.25 (*0-02-303170-0*, Macmillan Coll) P-H.

Anderson, Paul T. Boogie Nights. 144p. 1998. pap. 13.95 (*0-571-19539-3*) Faber & Faber.

***Anderson, Paul Thomas.** Magnolia: The Shooting Script. LC 99-59360. 224p. 2000. 32.95 (*1-55704-409-0*, Pub. by Newmarket); pap. text 22.95 (*1-55704-406-6*, Pub. by Newmarket) Norton.

Anderson, Paul V. Technical Writing: A Reader-Centered Approach. 3rd ed. LC 93-81248. (Illus.). 800p. (C). 1994. pap. text 63.50 (*0-15-501185-5*) Harcourt Coll Pubs.

Anderson, Paul V., et al, eds. New Essays in Technical & Scientific Communications: Theory, Research, & Practice. (Baywood Technical Communication Ser.: Vol. 2). 254p. (C). 1983. pap. text 33.95 (*0-89503-036-5*) Baywood Pub.

Anderson, Pauline C. & Burkard, Martha R. The Dental Assistant. 6th ed. LC 93-40765. 784p. (C). 1994. pap. 56.95 (*0-8273-5281-6*) Delmar.

— The Dental Assistant. 6th ed. 69p. 1994. pap., teacher ed. 18.95 (*0-8273-5282-4*) Delmar.

Anderson, Pauline C. & Clifford, Susan B. Dental Radiology. rev. ed. LC 79-56352. (Dental Assisting Ser.). (Illus.). 152p. (C). 1982. teacher ed. 13.00 (*0-8273-1872-3*) Delmar.

— Dental Radiology. 2nd rev. ed. LC 79-56352. (Dental Assisting Ser.). (Illus.). 152p. (C). 1981. mass mkt. 42.95 (*0-8273-1871-5*) Delmar.

Anderson, Pauline R., ed. see Kehr, Eckart.

***Anderson, Peggy.** Improving with Age: The Best Is yet to Come. 1999. 7.95 (*1-56245-366-1*) Great Quotations.

Anderson, Peggy. Nurse. 1990. mass mkt. 6.99 (*0-425-12286-7*, Berkley-Pacer) Berkley Pub.

— Wisconsin Cranberry Growers' Favorite Recipes. 2nd rev. ed. 138p. 1991. pap. 12.00 (*0-9656821-0-2*) Peggy Anderson.

Anderson, Peggy, compiled by. Great Quotes from Great Leaders. rev. ed. LC 96-51684. (Successories Ser.). (Illus.). 128p. 1997. pap. 7.99 (*1-56414-286-8*) Career Pr Inc.

— Great Quotes from Great Women. rev. ed. LC 96-51678. (Successories Ser.). (Illus.). 128p. 1997. pap. 7.99 (*1-56414-288-4*) Career Pr Inc.

Anderson, Peggy K. First Day Blues. LC 91-67808. (Decision Is Yours Ser.). (Illus.). 64p. (Orig.). (J). (gr. 3-6). 1992. pap. 5.95 (*0-943990-72-6*); lib. bdg. 16.95 (*0-943990-73-4*) Parenting Pr.

Anderson, Peggy K., jt. auth. see Szablya, Helen M.

Anderson, Peggy King. Safe at Home! (J). 1995. 9.05 (*0-606-08126-7*) Turtleback.

Anderson, Peggy L. Case Studies for Inclusive Schools. LC 96-3414. 260p. 1997. spiral bd. 24.00 (*0-89079-703-X*, 7473) PRO-ED.

— Denver Handwriting Analysis. 80p. (J). (gr. 3-8). 1983. pap. 45.00 (*0-87879-334-8*); lp 12.00 (*0-87879-335-6*) Acad Therapy.

— Denver Handwriting Analysis, Remedial checklists. 80p. (J). (gr. 3-8). 1983. 10.00 (*0-685-06661-4*) Acad Therapy.

***Anderson, Peggy L.** Hamlet. (Streamline Shakespeare Ser.). 2000. pap. 7.00 (*1-57128-154-1*) Acad Therapy.

Anderson, Peggy L. & Anderson, Judith D., eds. The Merchant of Venice. (Streamline Shakespeare Ser.). 72p. (J). (gr. 4-12). 1999. pap. 7.00 (*1-57128-123-1*, 8123-1) High Noon Bks.

— Romeo & Juliet. (Streamline Shakespeare Ser.). 108p. (J). (gr. 4-12). 1999. pap. 7.00 (*1-57128-124-X*, 8124-X) High Noon Bks.

Anderson, Peggy P. Out to Lunch. LC 97-30836. 32p. (J). (ps-1). 1998. 14.00 (*0-395-89826-9*) HM.

— Time for Bed, the Babysitter Said. LC 86-27388. 32p. (J). (ps). 1987. 15.00 (*0-395-41851-8*) HM.

— Time for Bed, the Babysitter Said. (Illus.). 32p. (J). (ps-k). 1995. pap. 4.95 (*0-395-74511-X*, Sandpiper) HM.

— To the Tub. LC 95-53267. (Illus.). 32p. (J). (ps-2). 1996. 13.95 (*0-395-77614-7*) HM.

Anderson Penno, Ellen E., jt. auth. see Gimbel, Howard.

Anderson Penno, Ellen E., jt. auth. see Gimbel, Howard V.

Anderson, Penny, jt. auth. see Gilbert, Oliver L.

Anderson, Per M., jt. intro. see Schweiker, William.

An Asterisk (*) at the beginning of an entry indicates that the title is appearing for the first time.

Anderson, Perry. English Questions. LC 92-9259. 416p. (C). 1992. pap. 22.00 (*0-86091-591-3*, Pub. by Verso) Norton.
— In the Tracks of Historical Materialism. LC 84-110. (Wellek Library Lectures). 120p. 1984. 18.00 (*0-226-01788-5*) U Ch Pr.
— Lineages of the Absolutist State. 576p. (C). 1985. pap. 25.00 (*0-86091-710-X*, Pub. by Verso) Norton.
— The Origins of Postmodernity. LC 99-237049. 160p. 1998. 65.00 (*1-85984-864-8*, Pub. by Verso); pap. 18.00 (*1-85984-222-4*, Pub. by Verso) Norton.
— Passages from Antiquity to Feudalism. (C). 1996. pap. 19.00 (*1-85984-107-4*, Pub. by Verso) Norton.
— A Zone of Engagement. 400p. (C). 1992. pap. 22.00 (*0-86091-595-6*, Pub. by Verso) Norton.
Anderson, Perry & Camiller, Patrick, eds. Mapping the West European Left. (Mapping Ser.). 288p. (C). 1994. pap. 19.00 (*0-86091-927-7*, A2706, Pub. by Verso) Norton.
Anderson, Pete, jt. auth. see Watkinson, Mike.
Anderson, Peter. Aldo Leopold: American Ecologist. LC 95-2596. (First Bks.). 64p. (J). (gr. 4-6). 1995. lib. bdg. 22.00 (*0-531-20203-8*) Watts.
— Aldo Leopold: American Ecologist. (First Bks.). (Illus.). 64p. (J). (gr. 4-6). 1996. reprint ed. pap. 6.95 (*0-531-15759-8*) Watts.
— Before the Blueprint: Science Center Buildings. (Illus.). 96p. 1991. spiral bd. 22.00 (*0-944040-27-6*) AST Ctrs.
— Gifford Pinchot: American Forester. LC 95-2041. (First Bks.). 64p. (J). (gr. 4-6). 1995. lib. bdg. 22.00 (*0-531-20205-4*) Watts.
— Gifford Pinchot: American Forester. (First Bks.). (Illus.). 64p. (J). (gr. 4-6). 1996. reprint ed. pap. 6.95 (*0-531-15760-1*) Watts.
— Global Politics of Power, Justice & Death. 320p. (C). 1996. 90.00 (*0-415-10945-0*); pap. 24.99 (*0-415-10946-9*) Routledge.
— A Grand Canyon Journey: Tracing Time in Stone. LC 96-36144. (First Book Ser.). (J). (gr. 4-6). 1997. lib. bdg. 22.00 (*0-531-20259-3*) Watts.
— A Grand Canyon Journey: Tracing Time in Stone. (First Books). (Illus.). 64p. (J). (gr. 4-6). 1997. pap. text 6.95 (*0-531-15839-X*) Watts.
— Henry David Thoreau: American Naturalist. LC 95-3225. (First Bks.). 64p. (J). (gr. 4-6). 1995. lib. bdg. 22.00 (*0-531-20206-2*) Watts.
— Henry David Thoreau: American Naturalist. (First Bks.). (Illus.). 64p. (J). (gr. 4-6). 1996. reprint ed. pap. 6.95 (*0-531-15761-X*) Watts.
— John James Audubon: Wildlife Artist. LC 95-2597. (First Bks.). 64p. (J). (gr. 4-6). 1995. lib. bdg. 22.00 (*0-531-20202-X*) Watts.
— John James Audubon: Wildlife Artist. (First Bks.). (Illus.). 64p. (J). (gr. 4-6). 1996. reprint ed. pap. 6.95 (*0-531-15762-8*) Watts.
— John Muir: Wilderness Prophet. LC 95-2598. (First Bks.). 64p. (J). (gr. 4-6). 1995. lib. bdg. 22.00 (*0-531-20204-6*) Watts.
— John Muir: Wilderness Prophet. (First Bks.). (Illus.). 64p. (J). (gr. 4-6). 1996. reprint ed. pap. 6.95 (*0-531-15781-4*) Watts.
— Looking for the Lilac Line & Other Stories from off the Road. 272p. 1991. 26.95 (*1-879601-03-6*); pap. 16.95 (*1-879601-02-8*) Semaphore Bks.
— The Pony Express. (Cornerstones to Freedom Ser.). (Illus.). 32p. (J). (gr. 4-6). 1996. lib. bdg. 19.50 (*0-516-20002-X*) Childrens.
— Pony Express. (Cornerstones to Freedom Ser.). (Illus.). 32p. (J). (gr. 3-7). 1998. pap. text 5.95 (*0-516-26286-6*) Childrens.
— Satan's Snare. 1988. pap. 3.99 (*0-85234-245-4*, Pub. by Evangelical Pr) P & R Pubng.
— The Transcontinental Railroad. LC 95-33593. (Cornerstones to Freedom Ser.). (Illus.). 32p. (J). (gr. 1-4). 1996. lib. bdg. 19.50 (*0-516-06635-8*) Childrens.
— The Transcontinental Railroad. LC 95-33593. (Cornerstones to Freedom Ser.). (Illus.). 32p. (J). (gr. 4-7). 1996. pap. 5.95 (*0-516-26035-9*) Childrens.
Anderson, Peter & Roe, Bonnie C. Museum Impact & Evaluation Study: Roles of Affect in the Museum, Visit & Ways of Assessing Them, 3 vols., Set. 500p. 1993. 97.50 (*0-9638657-0-6*) Mus of Sci.
— Museum Impact & Evaluation Study: Roles of Affect in the Museum, Visit & Ways of Assessing Them, 3 vols., Vol. 1. 500p. 1993. 12.50 (*0-9638657-1-4*) Mus of Sci.
— Museum Impact & Evaluation Study: Roles of Affect in the Museum, Visit & Ways of Assessing Them, 3 vols., Vol. 2. 500p. 1993. 35.00 (*0-9638657-2-2*) Mus of Sci.
— Museum Impact & Evaluation Study: Roles of Affect in the Museum, Visit & Ways of Assessing Them, 3 vols., Vol. 3. 500p. 1993. 50.00 (*0-9638657-3-0*) Mus of Sci.
Anderson, Peter, et al. Alcohol Problems. (Practical Guides for General Practice Ser.: No. 5). (Illus.). 96p. 1989. pap. text 15.95 (*0-19-261752-4*) OUP.
— Does Anyone Still Remember When Sex Was Fun? 256p. (C). 1996. pap. text, per. 15.95 (*0-7872-2723-4*) Kendall-Hunt.
Anderson, Peter, jt. auth. see Anderson, Mark.
Anderson, Peter, ed. see Arches National Park Intrepretive Staff.
Anderson, Peter B. & Struckman-Johnson, Cynthia. Sexually Aggressive Women: Current Perspectives & Controversies. LC 98-2635. 244p. 1998. 31.00 (*1-57230-165-1*) Guilford Pubns.
Anderson, Peter D. Black Patie: Patrick Stewart, Earl of Orkney, Lord of Shetland. 250p. (C). 1997. text 44.00 (*0-85976-355-2*, Pub. by J Donald) St Mut.
Anderson, Peter H. Use of a PC Printer Port for Control & Data Acquisition. LC 96-96562. (Illus.). 150p. (Orig.). (C). 1996. pap. 15.00 (*0-9653357-0-4*) P H Anderson.
Anderson, Peter J. A Consumer's Guide to Home Buying & Mortgage Financing. LC 91-70986. (Illus.). 128p. 1991. pap. 16.95 (*0-9628794-0-1*) Anderson Saginaw.
Anderson, Phil, et al. Mortality of Indigenous Australians. LC 98-119419. (Occasional Papers.). v, 76 p. 1996. write for info. (*0-642-23190-7*) Aust Inst Criminology.
***Anderson, Philip, et al.** Threshold Competitor: A Management Simulation, Team Version 2.1. 2nd ed. LC 99-25826. 112p. (C). 1999. pap. text 37.80 (*0-13-022841-9*) P-H.
Anderson, Philip C. & Malaker, Kristin S. Managing Skin Diseases. LC 98-25827. 368p. 1998. pap. 39.95 (*0-683-30598-0*) Lppncott W & W.
Anderson, Philip C., jt. auth. see Tushman, Michael L.
***Anderson, Philip H., et al.** Threshold Entrepreneur: A New Business Venture Simulation, Solo Version. LC 99-44998. 2000. 29.33 (*0-13-021921-5*) P-H.
— Threshold Entrepreneur: A New Business Venture Simulation, Team Version. LC 99-44996. 2000. 29.33 (*0-13-020633-4*) P-H.
Anderson, Philip J. One Body . . . Many Members. 35p. 1983. pap. 2.95 (*0-910452-53-9*) Covenant.
Anderson, Philip J., et al, eds. Scandinavian Immigrants & Education in North America. LC 95-68623. (Illus.). 224p. 1995. 19.95 (*0-914819-01-1*) Swedish-Am.
Anderson, Philip J. & Blanck, Dag, eds. Swedish-American Life in Chicago: Cultural & Urban Aspects of an Immigrant People, 1850-1930. (Studia Multiethnica Upsaliensia: No. 9). 394p. 1992. pap. 65.00 (*91-554-2734-0*) Coronet Bks.
Anderson, Philip Longfellow. The Gospel According to Disney: Christian Values in the Early Animated Classics. LC 98-97013. 264p. 1999. pap. 15.00 (*0-9669564-0-0*) Longfellow Pubng.
Anderson, Philip M., ed. Reading & Writing Non-Fiction. (Illus.). 109p. (C). 1994. pap. text 10.00 (*0-930348-19-2*) NY St Eng Coun.
Anderson, Philip M., intro. English Language Arts & the At-Risk Student. (Monographs). xii, 127p. (Orig.). 1993. pap. text 10.00 (*0-930348-18-4*) NY St Eng Coun.
Anderson, Philip M. & Rubano, Gregory L. Enhancing Aesthetic Reading & Response. 91p. 1991. pap. 9.95 (*0-8141-1561-6*) NCTE.
Anderson, Philip N. Computers & the Radio Amateur. (Illus.). 224p. 1982. pap. text 34.00 (*0-13-166306-2*) P-H.
— Pager Handbook for the Radio Amateur. 124p. 1996. pap. 14.95 (*1-887736-08-5*) Xtal Set Soc.
Anderson, Philip O. & Knoben, James E. Handbook of Clinical Drug Data 97-98. 8th ed. (C). 1996. pap. text 47.95 (*0-8385-3561-5*, Medical Exam) Appleton & Lange.
Anderson, Philip W. A Career in Theoretical Physics. LC 94-13919. (Series in Twentieth Century Physics). 696p. 1994. text 99.00 (*981-02-1717-X*); pap. text 48.00 (*981-02-1718-8*) World Scientific Pub.
— The Crystal Set Handbook & Xtal Set Society Newsletter, Vol. III. 1994. pap. 10.95 (*1-887736-03-4*) Xtal Set Soc.
— Crystal Set Projects. LC 97-186686. 135p. 1996. pap. 10.95 (*1-887736-06-9*) Xtal Set Soc.
— The Xtal Set Society Newsletter, Vol. 1. 36p. 1992. pap. 9.95 (*1-887736-01-8*) Xtal Set Soc.
— The Xtal Set Society Newsletter, Vol. 2. 36p. 1993. pap. 9.95 (*1-887736-02-6*) Xtal Set Soc.
— The Xtal Set Society Newsletter, Vol. 4. 85p. 1994. pap. 9.95 (*1-887736-04-2*) Xtal Set Soc.
— The Xtal Set Society Newsletter, Vol. 5. 85p. 1995. pap. 9.95 (*1-887736-07-7*) Xtal Set Soc.
Anderson, Philip W., jt. auth. see Genetsky, Barry.
Anderson, Philip W., jt. auth. see Yoshimura, Naboru.
Anderson, Philip W., ed. see Rivasseau, Vincent.
***Anderson, Phillip.** Your Destiny. LC 00-9297. 2000. write for info. (*0-9673076-0-0*) P C R Pubng.
Anderson, Phoebe M. Teaching Preschoolers in the Christian Community. rev. ed. LC 94-6910. (Illus.). 288p. 1994. pap. 19.95 (*0-8298-0922-8*) Pilgrim OH.
Anderson, Phyllis & Statz, Harriet T. Prayers Without Words. (Illus.). 40p. 1993. pap. 12.00 (*0-9636957-0-3*) Bethel Luth.
Anderson, Poul. Alight in the Void. 1993. reprint ed. mass mkt. 4.50 (*0-8125-3436-0*, Pub. by Tor Bks) St Martin.
— All One Universe. 1997. pap. 9.99 (*0-8125-3909-5*, Pub. by Tor Bks); mass mkt. 9.99 (*0-614-27800-7*) Tor Bks.
— The Armies of Elfland. 1992. mass mkt. 3.99 (*0-8125-1919-1*, Pub. by Tor Bks) St Martin.
— The Boat of a Million Years. 544p. 1993. mass mkt. 5.99 (*0-8125-3135-3*, Pub. by Tor Bks) St Martin.
— Brain Wave. 1993. reprint ed. lib. bdg. 18.95 (*0-89968-327-4*, Lghtyr Pr) Buccaneer Bks.
— Cold Victory. (Orig.). 1985. pap. 2.95 (*0-8125-3057-8*, Pub. by Tor Bks) St Martin.
— Conflict. 288p. (Orig.). 1985. pap. 2.95 (*0-8125-3088-8*, Pub. by Tor Bks) St Martin.
— The Day of Their Return. 224p. 1994. mass mkt. 4.99 (*0-8125-2309-1*, Pub. by Tor Bks) St Martin.
— The Devil's Game. 1985. per. 4.99 (*0-671-55995-8*) Baen Bks.
— Explorations. 1991. mass mkt. 3.99 (*0-8125-1536-6*) Tor Bks.
— Firetime. 288p. 1988. mass mkt. 5.99 (*0-671-65415-2*) Baen Bks.
— Flandry. 400p. 1993. per. 4.99 (*0-671-72149-6*) Baen Bks.
— The Fleet of Stars. LC 96-32450. 352p. 1997. 24.95 (*0-312-86036-6*, Pub. by Tor Bks) St Martin.
— The Fleet of Stars. 1998. pap. 6.99 (*0-8125-4598-2*, Pub. by Tor Bks) St Martin.
— The Game of Empire. 1994. reprint ed. lib. bdg. 20.00 (*0-7278-4684-1*) Severn Hse.
***Anderson, Poul.** Genesis. LC 99-58829. 256p. 2000. 23.95 (*0-312-86707-7*, Pub. by Tor Bks) St Martin.
— Genesis. 2001. mass mkt. 6.99 (*0-8125-8028-1*) Tor Bks.
Anderson, Poul. The Guardians of Time. 256p. 1988. pap. 3.50 (*0-8125-3091-8*, Pub. by Tor Bks) St Martin.
— Harvest of Stars. 544p. 1992. pap. 91.64 (*0-8125-2546-4*) Tor Bks.
— Harvest of Stars. 544p. 1994. mass mkt. 5.99 (*0-8125-1946-9*, Pub. by Tor Bks) St Martin.
— Harvest the Fire. 192p. 1995. 19.95 (*0-312-85943-0*) Tor Bks.
— Harvest the Fire, Vol. 1. 1997. mass mkt. 5.99 (*0-8125-5375-6*, Pub. by Tor Bks) St Martin.
— Inconstant Star: Man-Kzin Wars. 320p. 1991. per. 4.95 (*0-671-72031-7*) Baen Bks.
— Kinship with the Stars. (Orig.). 1991. mass mkt. 3.99 (*0-8125-1814-4*, Pub. by Tor Bks) St Martin.
— A Knight of Ghosts & Shadows. 256p. 1993. mass mkt. 4.99 (*0-8125-2225-7*, Pub. by Tor Bks) St Martin.
— The Long Night. 1999. pap. 3.50 (*0-8125-1396-7*, Pub. by Tor Bks) St Martin.
— Maurai & Kith. 240p. 1992. mass mkt. 3.99 (*0-8125-1397-5*, Pub. by Tor Bks) St Martin.
— New America. 288p. 1985. pap. 2.95 (*0-8125-3054-3*, Pub. by Tor Bks) St Martin.
— The Night Face & Other Stories. LC 77-28644. 221p. 1978. 25.00 (*0-89366-148-1*) Ultramarine Pub.
***Anderson, Poul.** Operation Chaos. 256p. 1999. pap. 12.95 (*0-312-87242-9*, Pub. by Tor Bks) St Martin.
Anderson, Poul. Operation Chaos. 288p. 1995. reprint ed. 20.00 (*0-7278-4763-5*) Severn Hse.
— Operation Luna. LC 99-24483. 320p. 1999. 22.95 (*0-312-86706-9*, Pub. by Tor Bks) St Martin.
***Anderson, Poul.** Operation Luna. 416p. 2000. mass mkt. 6.99 (*0-8125-8027-3*) Tor Bks.
Anderson, Poul. Orion Shall Rise. 1991. reprint ed. per. 4.99 (*0-671-72090-2*) Baen Bks.
— The Rebel Worlds. (Science Fiction Ser.). 1979. lib. bdg. 12.50 (*0-8398-2525-0*, G K Hall & Co) Mac Lib Ref.
— The Rebel Worlds. 1969. mass mkt. 2.95 (*0-451-15145-3*, Sig) NAL.
— The Shield of Time. 1991. mass mkt. 4.99 (*0-8125-1000-3*, Pub. by Tor Bks) St Martin.
— The Sign of the Raven. (Last Viking Ser.: No. 3). (Orig.). 1981. mass mkt. 2.50 (*0-8217-0625-X*, Zebra Kensgtn) Kensgtn Pub Corp.
— Starfarers. LC 98-21766. 384p. 1998. text 25.95 (*0-312-86037-4*) St Martin.
***Anderson, Poul.** Starfarers. 512p. 1999. mass mkt. 6.99 (*0-8125-4599-0*, Pub. by Tor Bks) St Martin.
Anderson, Poul. The Stars Are Also Fire. 544p. 1995. 5.99 (*0-8125-3022-5*, Pub. by Tor Bks) St Martin.
— Tales of the Flying Mountains. 288p. (Orig.). 1984. pap. 2.95 (*0-8125-3073-X*, Pub. by Tor Bks) St Martin.
— There Will Be Time. 1976. mass mkt. 2.95 (*0-451-15412-6*, AE1752, Sig) NAL.
— There Will Be Time. 1993. mass mkt. 4.99 (*0-8125-2308-3*, Pub. by Tor Bks) St Martin.
— Three Hearts & Three Lions. 256p. 1993. mass mkt. 4.99 (*0-671-72186-0*) Baen Bks.
— Three Hearts & Three Lions. 1993. reprint ed. lib. bdg. 18.95 (*0-89968-389-4*, Lghtyr Pr) Buccaneer Bks.
— The Time Patrol. 464p. 1994. pap. 14.95 (*0-312-85635-9*) Tor Bks.
***Anderson, Poul.** Virgin Planet. 384p. 2000. mass mkt. 5.99 (*0-671-31944-2*) Baen Bks.
Anderson, Poul. War of the Gods. LC 97-19383. 304p. 1997. text 22.95 (*0-312-86315-2*) St Martin.
— War of the Gods. 1999. mass mkt. 5.99 (*0-8125-3925-7*, Pub. by Tor Bks) St Martin.
— War of the Gods. large type ed. LC 98-21827. 1998. 23.95 (*0-7838-0300-1*, G K Hall & Co) Mac Lib Ref.
— The Winter of the World. 256p. 1995. mass mkt. 4.99 (*0-8125-2311-3*, Pub. by Tor Bks) St Martin.
Anderson, Poul, ed. Time Wars. 384p. (Orig.). 1990. pap. 3.95 (*0-8125-1311-8*) Tor Bks.
Anderson, Poul & Anderson, Karen. The King of Ys. 1376p. 1996. pap. 15.00 (*0-671-87729-1*) Baen Bks.
***Anderson, Poul & Dickson, Gordon R.** Hokas Pokas! 288p. 2000. mass mkt. 6.99 (*0-671-57858-8*) Baen Bks.
Anderson, Poul & Dickson, Gordon Rupert. Earthman's Burden. 192p. 1979. pap. 2.95 (*0-380-47993-1*, Avon Bks) Morrow Avon.
Anderson, Poul & Popkes, Steve. Longest Voyage & Slow Lightning. (Double Ser.: No. 30). 1991. pap. 3.95 (*0-8125-1170-0*, Pub. by Tor Bks) St Martin.
Anderson, Poul, et al. Space Wars. Greenberg, Martin H. & Waugh, Charles G., eds. 384p. 1988. pap. 3.95 (*0-8125-3046-2*) Tor Bks.
Anderson, Poul, jt. auth. see Dickson, Gordon Rupert.
***Anderson Publishing Co. Staff.** Federal Rules of Civil Procedure: 1999-2000 Edition. 160p. (C). 1999. pap. 5.95 (*1-58360-761-7*) Anderson Pub Co.
— Federal Rules of Evidence Handbook. 185p. (C). 1999. pap. 5.95 (*1-58360-760-9*) Anderson Pub Co.
— Indiana Arrest, Search & Seizure. 1999. pap. 29.00 (*1-58360-134-1*) Anderson Pub Co.
— Indiana Interrogations, Confessions & Identifications. 300p. 1999. pap. 24.00 (*1-58360-184-8*) Anderson Pub Co.
— Kentucky Criminal Code: Handbook for Law Enforcement Officers. rev. ed. 270p. 1999. pap. 14.95 (*1-58360-135-X*) Anderson Pub Co.
— Michigan Criminal Code 2000: Handbook for Law Enforcement Officers. rev. ed. 576p. 1999. pap. 14.95 (*1-58360-100-7*) Anderson Pub Co.
— New Jersey Criminal Code: Handbook for Law Enforcement Officers. 360p. 1999. pap. 14.95 (*1-58360-036-1*) Anderson Pub Co.
— North Carolina Criminal Code: Handbook for Law Enforcement Officers. rev. ed. 642p. 1999. pap. 14.95 (*0-87084-479-2*) Anderson Pub Co.
— Ohio Bankruptcy Handbook. rev. ed. 1999. pap. 59.00 (*1-58360-085-X*) Anderson Pub Co.
Anderson Publishing Company Staff. Anderson's Manual for Notaries Public. annuals 7th ed. 666p. 1997. pap. 25.00 (*0-87084-041-X*) Anderson Pub Co.
***Anderson Publishing Company Staff.** Anderson's Manual for Notaries Public. 8th ed. 753p. 1999. pap. 25.00 (*1-58360-110-4*) Anderson Pub Co.
Anderson Publishing Company Staff. Mickey Gilley's Favorite Recipes. Anderson, Edward, ed. (Illus.). 106p. 1992. 7.95 (*0-9636666-1-4*) Anderson MO.
***Anderson Publishing Company Staff.** Northwest Boat Travel. Cole, Gwen & Cole, Phil, eds. 2000. pap. 19.95 (*0-945989-12-1*) Anderson WA.
Anderson Publishing Company Staff. Northwest Boat Travel, Vol. 22. Cole, Gwen & Cole, Phil, eds. 344p. 1999. pap. 19.95 (*0-945989-09-1*) Anderson WA.
Anderson Publishing Company Staff. Ohio Criminal Code Handbook. 17th ed. pap. 12.95 (*1-58360-153-8*) Anderson Pub Co.
— Ohio Tort Reform Guide. pap. 35.50 (*1-58360-269-0*) Anderson Pub Co.
Anderson Publishing Company Staff. Page's Ohio Revised Code Annotated, 36 vols., annot. ed. 1997. 1100.00 (*0-87084-950-6*) Anderson Pub Co.
***Anderson Publishing Company Staff.** Rules Governing the Courts of Ohio. 1498p. 2000. pap. 41.50 (*1-58360-127-9*) Anderson Pub Co.
Anderson, Quentin. Making Americans: An Essay on Individualism & Money. LC 92-8693. 1992. 21.95 (*0-15-155941-4*) Harcourt.
Anderson, R. Blackthorn Whitehorn. 1997. mass mkt. 11.95 (*0-340-68127-6*, Pub. by Hodder & Stought Ltd) Trafalgar.
Anderson, R. Sea Gypsy. 1980. pap. 1.50 (*0-373-58052-5*) Harlequin Bks.
— A Step by Step Book about Snakes. (Step-by-Step Ser.). (Illus.). 64p. 1987. pap. 5.95 (*0-86622-460-2*, SK-017) TFH Pubns.
Anderson, R., ed. Information Hiding: First International Workshop, Cambridge, U. K., May 30-June 1, 1996: Proceedings. LC 96-48644. (Lecture Notes in Computer Science Ser.: Vol. 1174). 357p. 1996. text 62.00 (*3-540-61996-8*) Spr-Verlag.
Anderson, R., et al, eds. Specimen Preparation for Transmission Electron Microscopy of Materials III. (Symposium Proceedings Ser.: Vol. 254). 287p. 1992. text 62.00 (*1-55899-148-4*) Materials Res.
Anderson, R., jt. auth. see Dewar, J. D.
Anderson, R., jt. auth. see Sharrock, W. W.
Anderson, R. B., tr. see Brandes, George M.
***Anderson, R. C.** Nematode Parasites of Vertebrates: Their Development & Transmission. 2nd ed. LC 99-42444. 750p. 2000. 185.00 (*0-85199-421-0*) OUP.
Anderson, R. C. The Rigging of Ships in the Days of the Spritsail Topmast, 1600-1720. LC 93-43440. (Illus.). 320p. 1994. reprint ed. pap. 9.95 (*0-486-27960-X*) Dover.
Anderson, R. C., et al, eds. Learning to Read in American Schools: Basic Readers & Content Texts. LC 83-20701. 320p. (C). 1984. text 59.95 (*0-89859-219-4*) L Erlbaum Assocs.
Anderson, R. C. & May, Raoul M., eds. Population Biology of Infectious Diseases: Berlin, 1982. (Dahlem Workshop Reports: Vol. 25). (Illus.). 320p. 1982. 35.00 (*0-387-11650-8*) Spr-Verlag.
Anderson, R. C., jt. auth. see Anderson, Romola.
Anderson, R. D. France Eighteen-Seventy to Nineteen-Fourteen: Politics & Society. 224p. 1984. pap. 9.95 (*0-7102-0175-3*, Routledge Thoemms) Routledge.
— The Student Community at Aberdeen, 1860-1939. (Quincentennial Studies in the History of the University of Aberdeen). 146p. 1988. pap. 17.00 (*0-08-036588-4*, Pub. by Aberdeen U Pr) Macmillan.
— Universities & Elites in Britain Since 1800. LC 96-125519. (New Studies in Economic & Social History: No. 16). 92p. (C). 1995. text 34.95 (*0-521-55275-3*) Cambridge U Pr.
— Universities & Elites in Britain Since 1800. LC 96-125519. (New Studies in Economic & Social History: No. 16). 90p. (C). 1996. pap. text 10.95 (*0-521-55778-X*) Cambridge U Pr.
Anderson, R. G., et al. Handlist of Scientific Instrument Maker's Trade Catalogues. 107p. 29.95 (*0-948636-46-7*, Pub. by Natl Mus Scotland) A Schwartz & Co.
— Making Instruments Count: Essays on Historical Scientific Instruments Presented to Gerard L'Estrange Turner. 512p. 1993. 111.95 (*0-86078-394-4*, Pub. by Variorum) Ashgate Pub Co.
Anderson, R. J. & Hughes, J. A., eds. Classic Disputes in Sociology. 256p. (C). 1987. pap. 24.95 (*0-415-07902-0*) Routledge.
Anderson, R. J. & Sharrock, W. W., eds. Applied Sociological Perspectives. (Illus.). 192p. 1984. pap. text 15.95 (*0-04-301168-3*) Routledge.
Anderson, R. J., et al. The Sociology Game: An Introduction to Sociological Reasoning. LC 84-19442. 175p. reprint ed. pap. 54.30 (*0-7837-1601-X*, 204189300024) Bks Demand.
Anderson, R. Joseph, jt. auth. see Bourque, Monique.
Anderson, R. Joseph, jt. ed. see Bourque, Monique.
Anderson, R. L. Elizabethan Psychology & Shakespeare. LC 65-15887. 1964. reprint ed. lib. bdg. 75.00 (*0-8383-0503-2*) M S G Haskell Hse.
Anderson, R. L. Handbook of Lie Group Differential Equations Vol. 3: New Trends in Theoretical Developments & Computational Methods. Ibragimov, Nail H., ed. 560p. 1995. pap. 144.95 incl. disk (*0-8493-9419-8*, 9419) CRC Pr.

A

An Asterisk (*) at the beginning of an entry indicates that the title is appearing for the first time.

Anderson, R. L. & Ibragimov, N. H. Lie-Backlund Transformations in Applications. LC 78-78207. (Studies in Applied Mathematics: No. 1). x, 124p. 1979. text 32.50 (0-89871-151-7) Soc Indus-Appl Math.

Anderson, R. M. & Walck, S. D., eds. Specimen Preparation for Transmission Electron Microscopy of Materials IV: Materials Research Society Symposium Proceedings, Vol. 480. LC 97-33239. 295p. 1997. text 62.00 (1-55899-384-3) Materials Res.

Anderson, R. O., jt. ed. see Taswell, Ruth.

Anderson, R. R., et al. Healthways: Newfoundland Elders: Their Lifestyles & Values. 180p. 1998. pap. 9.95 (1-895387-97-3) Creative Bk Pub.

***Anderson, R. Rox, et al, eds.** Lasers in Surgery. 520p. 1999. pap. text 120.00 (0-8194-3060-9) SPIE.

Anderson, R. Rox, et al, eds. Lasers in Surgery: Advanced Characterization, Therapeutics & Systems VIII. LC 99-192207. (Proceedings of SPIE Ser.: Vol. 3245). 474p. 1998. 116.00 (0-8194-2684-9) SPIE.

— Lasers in Surgery Vol. 2970: Advanced Characterization, Therapeutics & Systems VII. 632p. 1997. 132.00 (0-8194-2381-5) SPIE.

Anderson, R. S., ed. Nutrition & Behavior in Dogs & Cats: Proceedings of the First Nordic Symposium on Small Animal Veterinary Medicine, Oslo, Norway, September 15-18, 1982. LC 83-17281. 246p. 1984. 113.00 (0-08-029778-1, Pub. by Pergamon Repr) Franklin.

Anderson, R. S., et al, eds. Application & Numerical Solution of Intergral Equations. (Mechanics Analysis Ser.: No. 6). 265p. 1980. text 88.00 (90-286-0450-2) Kluwer Academic.

Anderson, R. T. Study Guide Some Fundamental Spiritual Verities: A Study Guide to the Revelation of Baha'u'llah. 42p. 1988. pap., student ed. 4.95 (0-85398-282-1) G Ronald Pub.

Anderson, R. Y. & Harshbarger, J. W., eds. Black Mesa Basin: Northeastern Arizona. (Guidebook Ser.: No. 9). (Illus.). 205p. 1958. reprint ed. pap. 11.00 (1-58546-039-7) NMex Geol Soc.

Anderson, Rachel. Black Water. 88p. (J). (gr. 5-8). 1995. 14.95 (0-8050-3847-7) H Holt & Co.

— Black Water. 1996. 10.05 (0-606-11141-7, Pub. by Turtleback) Demco.

— The Bus People. LC 92-1506. 112p. (YA). (gr. 5 up). 1995. 13.95 (0-8050-2297-X, Bks Young Read); pap. 5.95 (0-8050-4250-4) H Holt & Co.

— Bus People. 1995. 11.05 (0-606-08708-7, Pub. by Turtleback) Demco.

— Kin 262: Human Anatomy. 100p. (C). 1997. spiral bd. 21.95 (0-7872-3882-1) Kendall-Hunt.

— Paper Faces. 88p. (J). (gr. 4-7). 1995. 14.95 (0-8050-2527-8, Bks Young Read) H Holt & Co.

Anderson, Rachel & Bradby, David. Reynard the Fox. (Oxford Myths & Legends Ser.). (Illus.). 80p. (YA). (gr. 5-12). 1987. 20.00 (0-19-274129-2) OUP.

Anderson, Rachell N. Hindsight & Blindspots: Poems about Relationships. Cape, Diane, ed. (Illus.). 100p. (Orig.). 1997. pap. 10.95 (0-614-16471-0) Marriage & Fam LEC.

— Responsible Children in Today's World: A Guide for Parents, 2nd ed. 1992. pap. text 7.95 (0-9634548-6-2) Marriage & Fam LEC.

Anderson, Ralph E., et al. Human Behavior in the Social Environment: A Social Systems Approach. 5th ed. LC 98-45357. (Modern Applications of Social Work Ser.). (Illus.). 330p. 1999. pap. text 25.95 (0-202-36116-0); lib. bdg. 49.95 (0-202-36115-2) Aldine de Gruyter.

Anderson, Ralph K. South Carolina Civil Trial Techniques Handbook. LC 97-205705. 1997. write for info. (0-943856-88-4) SC Bar CLE.

Anderson, Raoul & Thornhill, Archibald. Voyage to the Grand Banks: The Saga of Captain Arch Thornhill. 376p. 1998. pap. 15.95 (1-895387-25-6) Creative Bk Pub.

Anderson, Rasmos B., tr. see Bjornson, Bjornstjerne.

Anderson, Ray. Father Knows Best. (Inter Acta Ser.). (Illus.). 6p. (C). 1994. teacher ed., ring bd. 1.25 (1-885702-05-1, 741-014t, Inter Acta); student ed., ring bd. 3.25 (1-885702-04-3, 741-014s, Inter Acta) WSN Pr.

— Mid-Course Correction: Toward a Sustainable Enterprise: The Interface Model. 1999. pap. 17.95 (0-9645953-5-4, Pub. by Peregrinzilla) Chelsea Green Pub.

Anderson, Ray, et al. Face It: A Spiritual Journey of Leadership. (Illus.). 150p. (C). 1996. pap. text 14.95 (0-9645953-1-1) Peregrinzilla.

Anderson, Ray H. The Usefulness of Corporate Annual Reports to Shareholders in Australia, New Zealand & the United States. Epstein, Marc J., ed. LC 96-48394. (Studies in Managerial & Financial Accounting: Vol. 4). 240p. 1996. 78.50 (0-7623-0162-7) Jai Pr.

Anderson, Ray S. Christians Who Counsel: The Vocation of Wholistic Therapy. 256p. 1990. pap. 17.99 (0-310-52231-5) Zondervan.

— Christians Who Counsel: The Vocation of Wholistic Therapy. 256p. 1990. reprint ed. pap. 18.00 (0-9602638-6-1) Fuller Seminary.

— Living the Spiritually Balanced Life. LC 98-8101. 192p. 1998. pap. 12.99 (0-8010-5803-1) Baker Bks.

— Minding God's Business. LC 86-6367. 164p. (Orig.). reprint ed. pap. 50.90 (0-8357-4351-9, 203717800007) Bks Demand.

— Minding God's Business. 156p. (Orig.). 1992. reprint ed. pap. 18.00 (0-9602638-7-X) Fuller Seminary.

— Ministry on the Fireline. Hsiao, Sharman, tr. (Theology Ser.). 265p. 1996. pap. 12.95 (1-885216-04-1) Evan Formosan.

— Ministry on the Fireline: A Practical Theology for an Empowered Church. 235p. (Orig.). 1998. reprint ed. pap. 18.00 (0-9602638-8-8) Fuller Seminary.

— On Being Human: Essays in Theological Anthropology. 234p. (Orig.). (C). 1991. reprint ed. pap. 20.00 (0-9602638-4-5) Fuller Seminary.

— The Soul of Ministry. LC 97-11496. 1997. pap. 14.00 (0-664-25744-5) Westminster John Knox.

— Soulprints: Personal Reflections on Faith, Hope & Love. 195p. 1996. pap. 18.00 (1-881266-00-1) Fuller Seminary.

— Theological Foundations for Ministry. 1996. pap. 33.95 (0-567-22355-8, Pub. by T & T Clark) Bks Intl VA.

— Theology, Death & Dying. 170p. 1994. reprint ed. pap. 16.00 (1-881266-01-X) Fuller Seminary.

— Unspoken Wisdom: Truths My Father Taught Me. LC 94-44754. 128p. 1995. pap. 10.99 (0-8066-2811-1, 9-2811, Augsburg) Augsburg Fortress.

Anderson, Ray S. & Guensey, Dennis B. On Being Family: A Social Theology of the Family. 168p. 1992. reprint ed. pap. 20.00 (0-9602638-9-6) Fuller Seminary.

Anderson, Raymond & Anderson, Georgene. The Jesse Tree: Stories & Symbols of Advent. 64p. (J). 1990. pap. 5.99 (0-8066-2524-4, 10-25244) Augsburg Fortress.

Anderson, Raymond L., jt. auth. see Maass, Arthur.

Anderson, Raymond R., jt. ed. see Koeberl, Christian.

***Anderson, Rebecca.** Glass-Slipper.com. 2000. pap. 8.50 (1-893896-16-1) Ima Jinn.

Anderson, Rebecca. Promoting Employee Health: A Guide for Worksite Wellness. 73p. 1986. 20.00 (0-939874-74-1) ASSE.

Anderson, Rebecca C. Promoting Employee Health: A Guide for Worksite Wellness. 2nd rev. ed. LC 99-12633. (Illus.). 98p. 1999. pap. 16.95 (1-885581-25-4, 4374) ASSE.

Anderson, Rebecca R. & Buehler, Bruce A. Sotos Syndrome: A Handbook for Families. (Illus.). 55p. (Orig.). 1992. spiral bd. 11.00 (1-889843-01-6) Munroe-Meyer Inst.

***Anderson-Redick, Stacey.** Windows System Policy Editor. Denn, Robert, ed. (Illus.). 350p. 2000. pap. 29.95 (1-56592-649-8) OReilly & Assocs.

Anderson-Reece, Erik. My Muse Was Supposed to Meet Me Here. 72p. 1992. pap. 10.00 (0-917453-25-5) Bamberger.

Anderson Retail. Activity Man. Date not set. pap. text 19.00 (0-314-01247-8) West Pub.

Anderson, Rica, jt. ed. see Nandi, Jean.

Anderson, Richard. Abortion Pro & Con: (Debater's Manual) 1977. pap. 3.00 (0-686-31357-7) Right to Life.

— Cleanse & Purify Thyself, Book 2. 5th rev. ed. Getreu, G. Renee, ed. (Illus.). 450p. 1998. pap. 19.95 (0-9664973-0-9) Christobe Publishing.

— Market Timing Models: Constructing, Implementing & Optimizing a Market Timing Based Investment Strategy. LC 96-20989. 240p. 1996. 50.00 (0-7863-1099-5, Irwn Prfssnl) McGraw-Hill Prof.

— Sample Pretreatment & Seperati. LC 87-10655. (Analytical Chemistry by Open Learning Ser.). 668p. 1987. pap. 190.00 (0-471-91361-8) Wiley.

***Anderson, Richard, et al.** Beginning Components for ASP. (Professional Ser.). 800p. 1999. pap. 39.99 (1-86100-288-2) Wrox Pr Inc.

— Professional Active Server Pages 3.0. 1200p. 1999. pap. 59.99 (1-86100-261-0) Wrox Pr Inc.

Anderson, Richard, jt. auth. see Greenberg, Michael R.

Anderson, Richard, jt. auth. see Seymour, James D.

Anderson, Richard, jt. ed. see Meyerson, Joel W.

Anderson, Richard C. Diary & Journal of Richard Clough Anderson, Jr., 1814-1826. Parks, E. Taylor & Tischendorf, Alfred P., eds. LC 64-19178. 374p. reprint ed. pap. 116.00 (0-608-15270-6, 205220800060) Bks Demand.

— Peace Was in Their Hearts: Conscientious Objectors in World War II. 318p. 1996. pap. 17.99 (0-8361-9053-X) Herald Pr.

Anderson, Richard C., ed. Tacoma. (Illus.). 120p. 1988. 39.95 (0-685-22942-4) Baker Anderson.

Anderson, Richard C. & Commission on Reading Staff. Becoming a Nation of Readers. 147p. 1985. 10.95 (0-318-21645-0) NCTE.

Anderson, Richard C., Jr., jt. auth. see Johnson, Curt.

Anderson, Richard C., jt. ed. see Schroeder, David A.

Anderson, Richard D., Jr. Public Politics in an Authoritarian State: Making Foreign Policy During the Brezhnev Years. LC 93-15240. 288p. 1993. text 45.00 (0-8014-2900-5) Cornell U Pr.

Anderson, Richard E. Strategic Policy Changes at Private Colleges. LC 77-13257. 112p. reprint ed. 34.80 (0-608-16117-9, 201317200086) Bks Demand.

Anderson, Richard E. & Leslie, Larry L. ASHE Reader on Finance in Higher Education. (C). 1989. pap. text 50.00 (0-536-05556-4) Pearson Custom.

Anderson, Richard E. & Meyerson, Joel W. Financing Higher Education in a Global Economy. (ACE-Oryx Series on Higher Education). (Illus.). 160p. 1990. 27.95 (0-02-900965-0) Free Pr.

— Financing Higher Education in a Global Economy: Sponsored by the National Center for Postsecondary Governance & Finance. LC 89-35925. (American Council on Education/Macmillan Series on Higher Education). 160p. reprint ed. pap. 49.60 (0-608-20853-1, 207195200003) Bks Demand.

Anderson, Richard E. & Meyerson, Joel W., eds. Financial Planning under Economic Uncertainty. LC 85-644752. (New Directions for Higher Education Ser.: No. HE 69). 1990. 22.00 (1-55542-826-6) Jossey-Bass.

Anderson, Richard F., jt. auth. see Gordon, Steven I.

Anderson, Richard J., et al. Alternative Energy Sources for the United States. 19p. (C). 1975. pap. 19.95 (0-87855-743-1) Transaction Pubs.

***Anderson, Richard L.** American Muse: Anthropological Excursions into Art & Aesthetics. LC 99-35355. 235p. 1999. pap. text 26.60 (0-13-084313-X) P-H.

Anderson, Richard L. Art in Small-Scale Societies. 2nd ed. 288p. (C). 1988. pap. text 39.20 (0-13-047762-1) P-H.

— Calliope's Sisters. LC 89-8389. 320p. 1989. pap. text 37.80 (0-13-155425-5) P-H.

— LeConte History & Genealogy, with Particular Reference to Guillaume LeConte of New Rochelle & New York, & His Descendants. 1350p. 1992. reprint ed. pap. 159.00 (0-8328-2433-X); reprint ed. lib. bdg. 169.00 (0-685-59664-8) Higginson Bk Co.

— Understanding Paul. LC 83-72103. xv, 448p. 1990. reprint ed. pap. 8.95 (0-87579-477-7) Deseret Bk.

Anderson, Richard L. & Field, Karen L. Art in Small Scale Societies: Contemporary Readings. 3rd ed. LC 92-14754. 452p. 1992. pap. text 29.00 (0-13-045451-6) P-H.

***Anderson, Richard L., et al.** The Disciple as Scholar: Essays on Scripture & the Ancient World in Honor of Richard Lloyd Anderson. LC 99-88955. 2000. write for info. (0-934893-49-7) Res Press UT.

— The Disciple as Witness: Essays on Latter-Day Saint History & Doctrine in Honor of Richard Lloyd Anderson. LC 99-86523. 2000. write for info. (0-934893-45-4, F A R M S) Brigham.

Anderson, Richard L., jt. auth. see Jordan, David R.

Anderson, Richard O., ed. Strategies & Tactics for Management of Fertilized Hatchery Ponds. LC 93-44926. (Journal of Applied Aquaculture). (Illus.). 290p. 1994. lib. bdg. 49.95 (1-56022-048-1) Haworth Pr.

— Strategies & Tactics for Management of Fertilized Hatchery Ponds. LC 93-44926. (Journal of Applied Aquaculture). (Illus.). 290p. 1994. pap. text 24.95 (1-56022-049-X) Haworth Pr.

Anderson, Rickie W. How to Repair & Install Your Home & Business Phones. Fields, Harriet, ed. Rifkind, Marion, tr. from ENG. (SPA., Illus.). 18p. (Orig.). 1984. pap. 3.00 (0-940783-00-2, 143-580) Telco Systs Pub.

Anderson, Rita & Neumann, Linda C. Partners in Play: Homemade Toys for Toddlers. (Illus.). 184p. 1991. pap. 12.95 (1-880202-01-8) Partners Pr.

Anderson, Rob. Business Law & the Regulatory Environment Comprehension, 1. 16th ed. (LA - Business Law Ser.). (C). 1995. pap., student ed. 25.95 (0-538-84527-9) S-W Pub.

— Generic Computer Applications for Reinforce. (DF - Computer Applications Ser.). 1997. mass mkt. 32.95 (0-538-71737-8) S-W Pub.

— Interpersonal Communication & Education: Students as Real People. 134p. 1979. pap. text 8.95 (0-8104-5764-4) Transaction Pubs.

— Lotus 1-2-3 5.0 for Windows: Applications for Reinforcement. (Computer Applications Ser.). 1996. mass mkt. 31.95 (0-538-71450-6) S-W Pub.

— Managerial Accounting. 8th ed. (AB - Accounting Principles Ser.). (C). 1992. mass mkt., student ed. 22.50 (0-538-81327-X) S-W Pub.

— Using Lotus 1-2-3 Applications for Reinforcement. (DF - Computer Applications Ser.). 1995. 60.95 (0-538-63353-0); mass mkt. 27.95 (0-538-62909-6) S-W Pub.

— WordPerfect 6.0 Applications for Reinforcement. (DF - Computer Applications Ser.). 1995. mass mkt. 27.95 (0-538-63444-8) S-W Pub.

Anderson, Rob & Cissna, Kenneth N. The Martin Buber-Carl Rogers Dialogue: A New Transcript with Commentary. LC 96-44106. (SUNY Series in Speech Communication). 138p. (C). 1997. text 29.50 (0-7914-3437-0); pap. text 9.95 (0-7914-3438-9) State U NY Pr.

Anderson, Rob & Fox. Business Law & the Legal Environment. 15th ed. (LA - Business Law Ser.). (C). 1992. mass mkt., student ed. 23.25 (0-538-81986-3) S-W Pub.

— Business Law & the Legal Environment. 15th ed. (LA - Business Law Ser.). (C). 1992. mass mkt. 51.25 (0-538-81999-5) S-W Pub.

— Business Law & the Legal Environment - Standard Volume. 16th ed. (LA - Business Law Ser.). 1995. pap., student ed. 27.95 (0-538-86200-9) S-W Pub.

— Business Law & the Regulatory Environment. 13th ed. LC 97-12703. (LA - Business Law Ser.). (C). 1997. 107.95 (0-538-86899-6) S-W Pub.

***Anderson, Rob & Killenberg, George M., eds.** Interviewing: Speaking, Listening & Learning for Professional Life. LC 98-44466. xv, 432p. 1999. pap. text 34.95 (1-55934-956-5, 956-5) Mayfield Pub.

Anderson, Rob & Sweeney. Essentials of Management Science. LC 98-13629. (MI - Management Science Ser.). 1998. mass mkt. 49.95 (0-538-87609-3) S-W Pub.

— Introduction to Management Science Quantitation. 8th ed. (GC - Principles of Management Ser.). (C). 1996. mass mkt., student ed. 24.00 (0-314-20798-8) S-W Pub.

— Quantitative Methods for Business. 7th ed. LC 97-16589. (QM - Quantitative Methods Ser.). 1997. mass mkt. 85.95 (0-538-87601-8); mass mkt. 18.95 (0-538-87605-0); mass mkt., student ed. 18.95 (0-538-87602-6) S-W Pub.

— Statistics for Business & Economics. (ME - Statistics Ser.). 1998. pap., student ed. 18.95 (0-538-87594-1) S-W Pub.

— Statistics for Business & Economics. 7th ed. (ME - Statistics Ser.). 1998. pap., student ed. 18.95 (0-538-87597-6) S-W Pub.

— Statistics for Business & Economics. 7th ed. 1998. pap. 87.95 (0-538-87593-3) S-W Pub.

Anderson, Rob, et al. The Conversation of Journalism: Communication, Community, & News. LC 93-40573. 232p. 1994. 55.00 (0-275-94448-4, Praeger Pubs) Greenwood.

— The Reach of Dialogue: Confirmation, Voice & Community. Dervin, Brenda, ed. LC 94-29161. (Communication Series: Communication Alternatives). 336p. (C). 1994. text 69.50 (1-881303-00-4); pap. text 27.50 (1-881303-01-2) Hampton Pr NJ.

Anderson, Rob, jt. auth. see Jian.

Anderson, Rob, jt. auth. see Killenberg, George M.

Anderson, Rob M. & Dardenne, Robert. The Conversation of Journalism: Communication, Community & News. LC 93-40573. 232p. 1996. pap. 20.95 (0-275-95674-1, Praeger Pubs) Greenwood.

Anderson, Robert. The Aftermath of Stroke: The Experience of Patients & Their Families. 272p. (C). 1992. text 80.00 (0-521-40196-8) Cambridge U Pr.

Anderson, Robert. Artillery Officer in the Mexican War, 1846-1847: Letters of Robert Anderson. LC 74-148870. (Select Bibliographies Reprint Ser.). 1977. reprint ed. 26.95 (0-8369-5642-7) Ayer.

— Beartooth Country: Montana's Absaroka & Beartooth Mountains. rev. ed. LC 94-30004. (Montana Geographic Ser.: No. 7). (Illus.). 112p. 1994. pap. 17.95 (1-56037-065-3) Am Wrld Geog.

Anderson, Robert. Canoeing Florida, Vol. 1: The Panhandle. (Illus.). 72p. (Orig.). 1990. pap. 4.95 (0-932855-36-9) Winner Enter.

— Canoeing Florida, Vol. 2: Northern Peninsula. (Illus.). 72p. (Orig.). 1990. pap. 4.95 (0-932855-37-7) Winner Enter.

— Canoeing Florida, Vol. 3: Southern Peninsula. (Illus.). 64p. (Orig.). 1990. pap. 4.95 (0-932855-38-5) Winner Enter.

Anderson, Robert. The Coming Prince. LC 63-11464. (Sir Robert Anderson Library). 384p. 1975. pap. 13.99 (0-8254-2115-2, Kregel Class) Kregel.

— Daniel in the Critics' Den: A Defense of the Historicity of the Book of Daniel. 3rd ed. LC 90-4683. 200p. 1990. reprint ed. pap. 10.99 (0-8254-2133-0, Kregel Class) Kregel.

— Education & Opportunity in Victorian Scotland: Schools & Universities. (Edinburgh Education & Society Ser.). 384p. 1989. pap. 35.00 (0-85224-617-X, Pub. by Edinburgh U Pr) Col U Pr.

— Elements of Literature. (YA). (gr. 11-12). 1989. text 66.50 (0-15-717550-2) Holt R&W.

— Florida Snakes. Allyn, Joyce, ed. (Illus.). 136p. (Orig.). 1989. pap. 10.95 (0-8200-0305-0) Great Outdoors.

Anderson, Robert. Forests: Identifying Propaganda Techniques. LC 92-28185. (Opposing Viewpoints Juniors Ser.). (Illus.). 36p. (J). (gr. 4-7). 1992. lib. bdg. 16.20 (0-89908-099-5) Greenhaven.

Anderson, Robert. Forgotten Truths. LC 80-17526. (Sir Robert Anderson Library). 168p. 1980. reprint ed. pap. 9.99 (0-8254-2130-6, Kregel Class) Kregel.

— Gamefish Cookbook: Fresh - Saltwater. Lampert, Eva & Lampert, Erv, eds. (Illus.). 320p. (Orig.). 1992. pap. 16.95 (0-932855-33-4) Winner Enter.

— Garbage: Understanding Words in Context. LC 91-22100. (Opposing Viewpoints Juniors Ser.). (Illus.). 36p. (J). (gr. 4-7). 1991. lib. bdg. 16.20 (0-89908-609-8) Greenhaven.

— The Gospel & Its Ministry. LC 78-9539. (Sir Robert Anderson Library). 224p. 1978. reprint ed. pap. 10.99 (0-8254-2126-8, Kregel Class) Kregel.

— Guide to Florida Alligator & Crocodile. (Illus.). 60p. (Orig.). 1985. pap. 4.95 (0-932855-01-6) Winner Enter.

— Guide to Florida Backyard Birds. (Illus.). 60p. (Orig.). 1986. pap. 4.95 (0-932855-02-4) Winner Enter.

— Guide to Florida Birds of Prey. (Illus.). 60p. (Orig.). 1989. pap. 4.95 (0-932855-16-4) Winner Enter.

— Guide to Florida Camping. (Illus.). 72p. (Orig.). 1988. pap. 4.95 (0-932855-21-0) Winner Enter.

— Guide to Florida Corals, Anemones & Sponges. (Illus.). 60p. (Orig.). 1988. pap. 4.95 (0-932855-24-5) Winner Enter.

— Guide to Florida Dangerous Creatures. (Illus.). 72p. (Orig.). 1987. pap. 4.95 (0-932855-13-X) Winner Enter.

— Guide to Florida Fishing Tips. (Illus.). 72p. (Orig.). 1989. pap. 4.95 (0-932855-35-0) Winner Enter.

— Guide to Florida Freshwater Fish & Fishing. (Illus.). 72p. (Orig.). 1984. reprint ed. pap. 4.95 (0-932855-05-9) Winner Enter.

— Guide to Florida Hunting. (Illus.). 72p. (Orig.). 1987. pap. 4.95 (0-932855-14-8) Winner Enter.

— Guide to Florida Insects. (Illus.). 60p. (Orig.). 1988. pap. 4.95 (0-932855-18-0) Winner Enter.

— Guide to Florida Lizards & Amphibians. (Illus.). 60p. (Orig.). 1988. pap. 4.95 (0-932855-17-2) Winner Enter.

— Guide to Florida Mammals. (Illus.). 60p. (Orig.). 1985. pap. 4.95 (0-932855-07-5) Winner Enter.

— Guide to Florida Non-Poisonous Snakes. (Illus.). 60p. (Orig.). 1985. pap. 4.95 (0-932855-00-8) Winner Enter.

— Guide to Florida Pier & Bridge Fishing. (Illus.). 72p. (Orig.). 1988. pap. 4.95 (0-932855-19-9) Winner Enter.

— Guide to Florida Poisonous Snakes. (Illus.). 60p. (Orig.). 1984. reprint ed. pap. 4.95 (0-932855-04-0) Winner Enter.

— Guide to Florida Prehistoric Animals. (Illus.). 72p. (Orig.). 1988. pap. 4.95 (0-932855-15-6) Winner Enter.

— Guide to Florida Rocks, Minerals & Fossils. (Illus.). 72p. (Orig.). 1988. pap. 4.95 (0-932855-23-7) Winner Enter.

— Guide to Florida Saltwater Fishing. (Illus.). 60p. (Orig.). 1984. pap. 4.95 (0-932855-11-3) Winner Enter.

— Guide to Florida Sea & Shore Birds. (Illus.). 60p. (Orig.). 1985. pap. 4.95 (0-932855-09-1) Winner Enter.

— Guide to Florida Seashells. (Illus.). 60p. (Orig.). 1985. pap. 4.95 (0-932855-10-5) Winner Enter.

— Guide to Florida Seashore Life. (Illus.). 60p. (Orig.). 1985. pap. 4.95 (0-932855-03-2) Winner Enter.

— Guide to Florida Sharks & Shark Fishing: Rays Included. (Illus.). 76p. (Orig.). 1983. pap. 4.95 (0-932855-12-1) Winner Enter.

— Guide to Florida Trees. (Illus.). 72p. (Orig.). 1988. pap. 4.95 (0-932855-20-2) Winner Enter.

— Guide to Florida Turtles. (Illus.). 60p. (Orig.). 1984. pap. 4.95 (0-932855-06-7) Winner Enter.

— Guide to Florida Vanishing Wildlife. (Illus.). 72p. (Orig.). 1988. pap. 4.95 (0-932855-22-9) Winner Enter.

— Guide to Florida Wading Birds. (Illus.). 60p. (Orig.). 1985. pap. 4.95 (0-932855-08-3) Winner Enter.

— Guide to Florida Whales & Their Relatives. (Illus.). 76p. (Orig.). 1989. pap. 4.95 (*0-932855-34-2*) Winner Enter.
— Guide to Florida Wildflowers. (Illus.). 60p. (Orig.). 1989. pap. 4.95 (*0-932855-30-X*) Winner Enter.
Anderson, Robert. Hiking & Backpacking Florida: Northern Peninsula. (Illus.). 72p. (Orig.). 1991. pap. 4.95 (*0-932855-40-7*) Winner Enter.
— Hiking & Backpacking Florida: Southern Peninsula. (Illus.). 72p. (Orig.). 1991. pap. 4.95 (*0-932855-41-5*) Winner Enter.
— Hiking & Backpacking Florida: The Panhandle. (Illus.). 72p. (Orig.). 1991. pap. 4.95 (*0-932855-39-3*) Winner Enter.
Anderson, Robert. I Never Sang for My Father. 1968. pap. 5.25 (*0-8222-0548-3*) Dramatists Play.
***Anderson, Robert.** Ice Age: Stories. LC 00-29901. 200p. 2000. 24.95 (*0-8203-2243-1*) U of Ga Pr.
Anderson, Robert. Legal Boundaries of California Nursing Practice. 5th ed. 300p. 1997. pap. 20.00 (*0-942028-50-3*) Andrsn Cont Educ.
— The Life of Samuel Johnson with Critical Observations on His Work. 3rd ed. 678p. 1973. reprint ed. lib. bdg. 150.00 (*3-487-04534-6*) G Olms Pubs.
***Anderson, Robert, 3rd.** Life's Journey for One Man. 32p. 1999. pap. 8.00 (*0-8059-4829-5*) Dorrance.
Anderson, Robert. Pollution: Examining Cause & Effect Relationships. LC 92-25958. (Opposing Viewpoints Juniors Ser.). (Illus.). 36p. (J). (gr. 4-7). 1992. lib. bdg. 16.20 (*0-89908-574-1*) Greenhaven.
Anderson, Robert. El Principe Que Ha de Venir.Tr. of Coming Prince. (SPA.). 288p. 1980. pap. 8.99 (*0-8254-1021-5*, Edit Portavoz) Kregel.
Anderson, Robert. Redemption Truths. LC 80-16161. (Sir Robert Anderson Library). Orig. Title: For Us Men. 192p. 1980. reprint ed. pap. 9.99 (*0-8254-2131-4*, Kregel Class) Kregel.
— Saltwater Fishing. (Illus.). 120p. (Orig.). 1989. pap. 5.95 (*0-8200-0128-7*) Great Outdoors.
— The Silence of God. LC 78-9528. (Sir Robert Anderson Library). 232p. 1978. reprint ed. pap. 10.99 (*0-8254-2128-4*, Kregel Class) Kregel.
— Solitaire/Double Solitaire. 1971. pap. 5.25 (*0-8222-1050-9*) Dramatists Play.
— Spanish American Modernism: A Selected Bibliography. LC 73-82616. 191p. reprint ed. pap. 59.30 (*0-608-12777-9*, 202431500037) Bks Demand.
— Story of Extinct Civilizations of the West. 1972. 59.95 (*0-8490-1133-7*) Gordon Pr.
Anderson, Robert. Types in Hebrews. LC 78-9545. (Sir Robert Anderson Library). 192p. 1978. reprint ed. pap. 9.99 (*0-8254-2129-2*, Kregel Class) Kregel.
Anderson, Robert. You Know I Can't Hear You When the Water's Running: Four Plays. 1968. pap. 5.25 (*0-8222-1288-9*) Dramatists Play.
Anderson, Robert, et al, eds. Innovation Systems in a Global Context: The North American Experience. 303p. 1998. 60.00 (*0-7735-1780-4*) McG-Queens Univ Pr.
— Security in Cyberspace: Challenges for Society: Proceedings of an International Conference. LC 97-173197. 72p. (Orig.). 1996. pap. 9.00 (*0-8330-2470-1*, CF-128-RC) Rand Corp.
Anderson, Robert & Fawzy, Ibrahim, eds. Egypt Revealed: Scenes from Description de l'Egypte. (Illus.). 200p. 1988. 50.00 (*977-424-172-X*, Pub. by Am Univ Cairo Pr) Col U Pr.
Anderson, Robert & Pavan, Barbara N. Nongradedness: Helping It to Happen. LC 92-62813. 250p. 1999. pap. text 24.95 (*0-87762-980-3*) Scarecrow.
***Anderson, Robert, et al.** Securing the U. S. Defense Information Infrastructure: A Proposed Approach. LC 99-19989. 163p. 1999. pap. text 20.00 (*0-8330-2713-1*, MR-993-OSD/DARP) Rand Corp.
Anderson, Robert, jt. auth. see Anderson, Dorothy.
Anderson, Robert, jt. auth. see Goodlad, John I.
Anderson, Robert, jt. auth. see Mills, Hugh L., Jr.
Anderson, Robert, jt. auth. see Snyder, Karolyn J.
Anderson, Robert, jt. ed. see Cohn, Theodore.
Anderson, Robert, ed. & tr. see Aquinas, Thomas, Saint.
Anderson, Robert A. Service for the Dead. 288p. 1987. pap. 3.95 (*0-380-89980-9*, Avon Bks) Morrow Avon.
— Wellness Medicine. LC 87-70316. (Illus.). 520p. 1987. lib. bdg. 34.95 (*0-942767-00-4*) Amer Health Pr.
***Anderson, Robert A., et al.** Studies in Frank Waters vol. 20: Explication. 87p. 1998. pap. 10.00 (*1-878277-15-4*) Frank Waters Soc.
Anderson, Robert C. The Great Migration Begins: Immigrants to New England, 1620-1633, Vols. 3. (State & Regional Guides Ser.). 1996. 125.00 (*0-88082-042-X*) New Eng Hist.
Anderson, Robert C. The Great Migration Newsletter Vols. 1-5: 1990-1994. 174p. 1998. 19.50 (*0-88082-083-7*) New Eng Hist.
— The Interorganizational Community. LC 93-1353. 272p. 1993. pap. 89.95 (*0-7734-9300-X*) E Mellen.
***Anderson, Robert C.** The Interorganizational Community. 2nd ed. LC 00-32457. 240p. 2000. reprint ed. 89.95 (*0-7734-7757-8*) E Mellen.
Anderson, Robert C. Living Memories. Drieci, Paula, ed. 300p. 1999. pap. 19.95 (*1-57635-053-3*) WeWrite.
— A Look Back: The Birth of the Americans with Disabilities Act. LC 96-19551. (Journal of Religion in Disability & Rehabilitation Ser.: Vol. 2, No. 4). 90p. 1996. 39.95 (*0-7890-0007-5*, Haworth Pastrl) Haworth Pr.
— Medical Terminology. 52p. (C). 1992. 13.95 incl. audio (*0-9634298-3-3*) Cricket Sci.
— Scientific Processes: Origin of Knowledge. (Illus.). 102p. (C). 1994. 18.95 (*0-9634298-9-2*) Cricket Sci.
Anderson, Robert D. Education & the Scottish People, 1750-1918. (Illus.). 348p. 1995. text 65.00 (*0-19-820515-5*) OUP.
Anderson, Robert D. Inside the Mind of Joseph Smith: Psychobiography & the Book of Mormon. LC 98-46501. (Illus.). 308p. 1999. pap. 19.95 (*1-56085-125-2*) Signature Bks.
Anderson, Robert E. The Merchant Marine & World Frontiers. LC 78-5585. (Illus.). xvii, 205p. 1978. reprint ed. lib. bdg. 22.50 (*0-313-20437-3*, ANMM, Greenwood Pr) Greenwood.
***Anderson, Robert E.** The Story of Extinct Civilizations of the West. (LC History-America-E). 195p. 1999. reprint ed. lib. bdg. write for info. (*0-7812-4232-0*) Rprt Serv.
Anderson, Robert E., ed. Biochemistry of the Eye. (Illus.). 267p. 1983. 27.50 (*0-317-94078-3*) Am Acad Ophthal.
Anderson, Robert E., et al, eds. Degenerative Diseases of the Retina: Proceedings of the Sixth International Symposium Held in Jerusalem, Israel, November 4-9, 1994. (Illus.). 428p. 1995. 120.00 (*0-306-45137-9*, Kluwer Plenum) Kluwer Academic.
Anderson, Robert E., et al. Retinal Degenerations. (Illus.). 544p. 1991. lib. bdg. 116.00 (*0-8493-0178-5*, RE551, CRC Reprint) Franklin.
Anderson, Robert E., ed. see Anderson, Patricia S.
Anderson, Robert F. Hume's First Principles. LC 65-18415. 204p. 1966. reprint ed. pap. 63.30 (*0-608-02680-8*, 206333300004) Bks Demand.
Anderson, Robert G., et al. Property Loss Adjusting, 2 vols. 2nd ed. Markham, James J., ed. LC 95-77155. (C). 1995. pap. 41.00 (*0-89462-091-6*, 3502/3503) IIA.
Anderson, Robert G., jt. auth. see Anderson, Sandy S.
Anderson, Robert H. Echo-Morphologic Correlates: The Normal Heart. 32p. 1998. 140.00 (*1-86094-110-9*, Pub. by Imperial College) World Scientific Pub.
Anderson, Robert H. & Becker, Anton E. Controversies in the Description of Congenitally Malformed Hearts. 260p. 1997. text 78.00 (*1-86094-067-6*) World Scientific Pub.
Anderson, Robert H. & Hearn, Anthony C. An Exploration of Cyberspace Security R&D Investment Strategies for DARPA: The Day After-- In Cyberspace II. LC 96-41146. 1996. pap. text 13.00 (*0-8330-2452-3*) Rand Corp.
Anderson, Robert H., et al. Connecticut Real Property Law. Burke, Richard E., ed. 543p. 1984. text 95.00 (*1-878698-00-1*) Atlantic Law.
— Universal Access to E-Mail: Feasibility & Societal Implications. LC 95-53853. 295p. (Orig.). 1995. pap. 20.00 (*0-8330-2331-4*, MR-650-RC) Rand Corp.
Anderson, Robert L. The Diggs-Caminetti Case, 1913-1917: For Any Other Immoral Purpose, Set. LC 90-6004. (Studies in Twentieth Century American History: Vol. 1). 468p. 1990. lib. bdg. 109.95 (*0-88946-320-4*) E Mellen.
— Practical Statistics for Analytical Chemists. (Illus.). 352p. 1987. text 52.95 (*0-442-20973-8*, Chap & Hall CRC) CRC Pr.
Anderson, Robert M. American Law of Zoning, 5 vols. 3rd ed. LC 86-80879. (Real Property - Zoning Ser.). 1986. suppl. ed. 550.00 (*0-685-59795-4*) West Group.
— Great Rams & Great Ram Hunters. 264p. 1994. 65.00 (*0-9632969-3-0*) Collect Covey.
— Law of Zoning in New Jersey, 2 vols. LC 89-84975. 1612p. 1993. suppl. ed. 65.00 (*0-317-03774-9*) West Group.
— Law of Zoning in New Jersey, 2 vols., Set. LC 89-84975. 1612p. 1989. 200.00 (*0-317-02791-3*) West Group.
— Law of Zoning in Pennsylvania, 2 vols. LC 82-82349. 1993. suppl. ed. 71.50 (*0-317-03158-9*) West Group.
— Law of Zoning in Pennsylvania, 2 vols., Set. LC 82-82349. 1982. 220.00 (*0-317-00349-6*) West Group.
— New York Zoning Law & Practice, 2 vols. 3rd ed. LC 84-81189. 1984. 220.00 (*0-318-03855-2*) West Group.
— New York Zoning Law & Practice, 2 vols. 3rd ed. LC 84-81189. 1993. suppl. ed. 60.00 (*0-317-03252-6*) West Group.
Anderson, Robert M., Jr. Practitioner's Guide to Clinical Neuropsychology. LC 94-2057. (Critical Issues in Neuropsychology Ser.). 406p. (C). 1994. spiral bd. 49.50 (*0-306-44616-2*, Kluwer Plenum) Kluwer Academic.
Anderson, Robert M. Summit: Climbing the Seven Summits. 160p. 1995. 65.00 (*0-614-11915-4*) C Potter.
— To Everest Via Antarctica: Climbing Solo on the Highest Peak on Each of the World's Seven Continents. (Illus.). 224p. 1996. 29.95 (*0-8117-1598-1*) Stackpole.
***Anderson, Robert M.** To Everest Via Antarctica: Climbing Solo on the Highest Peak on Each of the World's Seven Continents. (Illus.). 219p. 1999. reprint ed. text 25.00 (*0-7881-6671-9*) DIANE Pub.
Anderson, Robert M. Vision of the Disinherited: The Making of American Pentecostalism. LC 92-30434. 334p. 1992. reprint ed. pap. 14.95 (*1-56563-000-9*) Hendrickson MA.
Anderson, Robert M., Jr., et al, eds. Avoiding Ethical Misconduct in Psychology Specialty Areas. LC 97-23109. 340p. 1998. text 69.95 (*0-398-06797-X*); pap. text 52.95 (*0-398-06798-8*) C C Thomas.
***Anderson, Robert M. & Funnell, Martha Mitchell.** Putting Empowerment into Practice: Stories & Strategies for Diabetes Educators. LC 00-28898. 2000. pap. write for info. (*1-58040-010-8*) Am Diabetes.
Anderson, Robert M., jt. auth. see Anderson, David J.
Anderson, Robert M., Jr., jt. auth. see Tsushima, William T.
***Anderson, Robert N.** Method for Constructing Complete Annual United States Life Tables. 32p. 2000. pap. 3.00 (*0-16-050256-X*) USGPO.
— Report of the Second Workshop on Age-Adjustment. 43p. 1999. pap. 6.00 (*0-16-049852-X*) USGPO.
— United States Decennial Life Tables for 1989- 91, United States Life Tables Eliminating Certain Causes of Death, 1, 4. 190p. 1999. per. 18.00 (*0-16-050156-3*) USGPO.
***Anderson, Robert N. & National Center for Health Statistics Staff.** Method for Constructing Complete Annual United States Life Tables. LC 99-58350. (Vital & Health Statistics Ser.). 1999. pap. write for info. (*0-8406-0560-9*) Natl Ctr Health Stats.
Anderson, Robert N., et al. Report of Final Mortality Statistics (1995) (Illus.). 80p. (C). 1999. pap. text 20.00 (*0-7881-7820-2*) DIANE Pub.
Anderson, Robert O. Fundamentals of the Petroleum Industry. LC 84-40271. (Illus.). 400p. 1984. 39.95 (*0-8061-1909-8*); pap. 26.95 (*0-8061-1916-0*) U of Okla Pr.
Anderson, Robert R., et al, contrib. by. Fruhneuhochdeutsches Worterbuch. 512p. 1997. 99.00 (*3-11-015464-1*); 96.00 (*3-11-015465-X*); 96.00 (*3-11-015608-3*) De Gruyter.
— Fruhneuhochdeutsches Worterbuch. 512p. 1998. 96.00 (*3-11-015609-1*) De Gruyter.
Anderson, Robert S., et al. Rice Science & Development Politics: Research Strategies & IRRI's Technologies Confront Asian Diversity (1950-1980) (Illus.). 415p. 1991. 72.00 (*0-19-828341-5*, 5009) OUP.
Anderson, Robert S., ed. see Bayne-Jones, Stanhope.
Anderson, Robert T. Denmark: Success of a Developing Nation. (Illus.). 186p. (C). 1975. 39.95 (*0-87073-738-4*); pap. text 24.95 (*0-87073-739-2*) Transaction Pubs.
Anderson, Robert T. & Anderson, Barbara G. The Vanishing Village: Danish Maritime Community. LC 77-87704. (American Ethnological Society Monographs: No. 39). reprint ed. 39.50 (*0-404-16498-6*) AMS Pr.
Anderson, Robert V. Franchising As It Relates to Location & Valuation Considerations. LC 88-50359. 137p. 1988. text 19.50 (*0-935988-30-0*, 323) Todd Pub.
— An Introduction to Linear Algebra. 400p. (C). 1986. text 76.50 (*0-03-921835-X*) SCP.
— Simplifying the Complicated in Real Estate & Appraising. LC 84-70613. (Illus.). 95p. 1984. 14.95 (*0-910436-27-4*) Conway Data.
Anderson, Robert W. A Discarded Rose Petal: A Powerful Drama. LC 96-48574. 55p. (Orig.). 1997. pap. 6.00 (*0-88734-241-8*) Players Pr.
Anderson, Robin. Between Two Wars: The Story of Pope Pius XI. 154p. 1978. 3.95 (*0-8199-0687-5*, Frncscn Herld) Franciscan Pr.
— St. Pius V - A Brief Account of His Life, Times, Virtues & Miracles. LC 78-55637. 1992. reprint ed. pap. 5.00 (*0-89555-068-7*) TAN Bks Pubs.
Anderson, Robin, ed. Clinical Lectures on Klein & Bion. (New Library of Psychoanalysis Ser.: No. 14). 155p. (C). 1991. pap. 25.99 (*0-415-06993-9*, A6481) Routledge.
Anderson, Robin & Darlington, Anna. Facing it Out. LC 98-35023. (Tavistock Clinic Ser.). 1999. 80.00 (*0-415-92262-3*); pap. 25.00 (*0-415-92263-1*) Routledge.
***Anderson, Robin L.** Colonization As Exploitation in The Amazon Rain Forest: 1758-1911. LC 99-36929. 1999. 49.95 (*0-8130-1719-X*) U Press Fla.
Anderson, Rodger I., jt. auth. see White, Rhea A.
Anderson, Rodney D. Outcasts in Their Own Land: Mexican Industrial Workers, 1906-1911. LC 74-28896. (Origins of Modern Mexico Ser.). (Illus.). 407p. 1976. 35.00 (*0-87580-054-8*) N Ill U Pr.
Anderson, Roger & Anderson, Carol S. Yellowstone: The Story Behind the Scenery. 2nd rev. ed. LC 98-65027. (Illus.). 48p. 1998. pap. 7.95 (*0-88714-140-4*) KC Pubns.
***Anderson, Roger & Anderson, Carol Shively.** A Ranger's Guide to Yellowstone Day Hikes. (Illus.). 152p. 2000. pap. 11.95 (*1-56037-157-9*, Montana Magazine) Am Wrld Geog.
Anderson, Roger, ed. see Stocking, Jerry.
Anderson, Roger B. Dostoevsky: Myths of Duality. LC 86-15650. (University of Florida Humanities Monographs: No. 58). 160p. (Orig.). 1986. pap. 22.95 (*0-8130-0803-4*) U Press Fla.
Anderson, Roger B. & Debreczeny, Paul, eds. Russian Narrative & Visual Art: Varieties of Seeing. LC 93-34786. (Illus.). 216p. (C). 1994. 49.95 (*0-8130-1255-4*) U Press Fla.
Anderson, Roger B., jt. ed. see Nelson, Daniel N.
Anderson, Roger C., et al, eds. Savannas, Barrens, & Rock Outcrop Plant Communities of North America. LC 98-25688. (Illus.). 497p. (C). 1999. text 110.00 (*0-521-57322-X*) Cambridge U Pr.
Anderson, Roger N. Marine Geology: A Planet Earth Perspective. rev. ed. 336p. 1989. pap. 87.95 (*0-471-50407-6*) Wiley.
Anderson, Rolf R. Atlas of the American Economy: An Illustrated Guide to Industries & Trends. LC 94-23105. (Illus.). 176p. (YA). (gr. 11). 1995. pap. text 17.3? (*1-56802-052-X*) Congr Quarterly.
Anderson, Rolph E., et al. Professional Sales Management. 2nd ed. 1992. pap. text. write for info. incl. disk (*0-07-836702-6*); boxed set, suppl. ed. write for info. (*0-07-001687-9*) McGraw.
— Professional Sales Management. 2nd ed. (C). 1992. text 66.25 (*0-07-001686-0*) McGraw.
Anderson, Romola & Anderson, R. C. The Sailing Ship: Six Thousand Years of History. LC 79-177507. 1972. 24.95 (*0-405-08205-3*) Ayer.
Anderson, Ron. Boiler Efficiency Manual. (Illus.). 1p. (C). 1997. text 29.67 (*0-13-079724-3*) P-H.
Anderson, Ron, jt. auth. see Wei, C. C.
Anderson, Ronald. Couch on Insurance, 33 vols., Set. 2nd ed. LC 59-1915. 1984. 2900.00 (*0-685-59868-3*) West Group.
Anderson, Ronald & Anderson, Odin W. A Decade of Health Services: Social Survey Trends in Use & Expenditure. LC 67-30125. (University of Chicago, Graduate School of Business, Studies in Business & Society). 264p. reprint ed. pap. 81.90 (*0-608-12637-3*, 202408100035) Bks Demand.
Anderson, Ronald & Kegels, Chantal. Transition Banking: A Comparison of Financial Reforms in the Czech Republic, Hungary, & Poland. (Illus.). 316p. 1998. text 75.00 (*0-19-829013-6*) OUP.
Anderson, Ronald & Koval, Anne. James McNeill Whistler: Beyond the Myth. (Illus.). 544p. 1995. 30.00 (*0-7867-0187-0*) Carroll & Graf.
Anderson, Ronald A. Bus Law & Leg Envirnment Stndr. 17th ed. LC 98-6847. (SWC-Business Law Ser.). 1998. pap. 104.95 (*0-538-88245-X*) Thomson Learn.
— Hotelman's Basic Law. 18.50 (*0-914770-00-4*) Littoral Develop.
— Insurers' Tort Law. 14.30 (*0-914770-01-2*) Littoral Develop.
— Running a Professional Corporation. 7.50 (*0-914770-02-0*) Littoral Develop.
— Uniform Commercial Code, 11 vols. 1992. boxed set 1000.00 (*0-685-63104-4*) West Group.
Anderson, Ronald A., et al. Business Law: Comprehensive. 14th ed. (C). 1989. mass mkt. 62.25 (*0-538-80222-7*, LA68NA) S-W Pub.
— Business Law & the Legal Environment. 15th ed. LC 92-29951. (C). 1992. 70.50 (*0-538-81985-5*) S-W Pub.
— Business Law & the Legal Environment. 17th ed. LC 98-6847. 1998. pap. 109.95 (*0-538-88244-1*) S-W Pub.
Anderson, Ronald D. Study of Curriculum Reform. 114p. 1996. pap. 10.00 (*0-16-048865-6*) USGPO.
Anderson, Ronald D., et al. Issues of Curriculum Reform in Science, Mathematics & Higher Order Thinking Across the Disciplines. 145p. (Orig.). (C). 1994. pap. text 30.00 (*0-7881-1526-X*) DIANE Pub.
Anderson, Ronald E., et al. Cross National Policies & Practices on Computers on Education. Plomp, Tjeerd, ed. LC 96-33526. (Technology-Based Education Series TBES: Vol. 001). 480p. (C). 1996. lib. bdg. 157.50 (*0-7923-4217-8*) Kluwer Academic.
Anderson, Ronald E., jt. auth. see Brent, Edward E., Jr.
Anderson, Ronald J., et al, eds. Enhancing Diversity: Educators with Disabilities. LC 98-38159. (Illus.). 336p. 1998. 60.00 (*1-56368-071-8*) Gallaudet Univ Pr.
— Enhancing Diversity: Educators with Disabilities in the Educational Enterprise. (C). 1998. text 60.00 (*1-56368-065-3*) Gallaudet Univ Pr.
Anderson, Ronald O., jt. auth. see Tennyson, Robert D.
Anderson, Ronald T. On the Divide. (Illus.). 96p. (Orig.). 1986. pap. 5.95 (*0-9616710-0-9*) Buck Mntn Pr.
Anderson, Ronald T., jt. auth. see Lakner, Armand A.
Anderson, Ronald W., et al. Banking Sector Development in Central & Eastern Europe No. 1: Forum Report of the Economic Policy Initiative. Ambrus-Lakatos, Lorand & Schaffer, Mark E., eds. 109p. 1996. pap. 14.95 (*1-898128-24-3*, Pub. by Ctr Econ Policy Res) Brookings.
Anderson, Rosalind C., jt. auth. see Gad, Shayne C.
Anderson, Rosemarie. Celtic Oracles. 2000. pap. 12.95 (*0-609-80275-5*) Harmony Bks.
— Celtic Oracles: A New System for Spiritual Growth & Divination. LC 97-30944. 240p. 1998. 18.95 (*0-609-60082-6*) Crown Pub Group.
Anderson, Rosemarie & Braud, William. Transpersonal Research Methods in the Social Sciences: Honoring Human Experience. LC 98-8870. 1998. 53.00 (*0-7619-1012-3*); pap. 24.95 (*0-7619-1013-1*) Sage Pubng.
***Anderson, Rosemary C.** Haiku. unabridged ed. ii, 32p. 1998. 50.00 (*1-929706-09-X*) Anderson Pubng.
Anderson, Rosemary C., ed. Christmas Poems. unabridged ed. iv, 15p. 1997. pap. write for info. (*1-929706-04-9*) Anderson Pubng.
— Ink Blot Poems. unabridged ed. (Illus.). ii, 14p. 1994. pap. write for info. (*1-929706-01-4*) Anderson Pubng.
— Patience: A Book of Quotations. unabridged ed. iv, 16p. 1990. write for info. (*1-929706-00-6*) Anderson Pubng.
***Anderson, Ross.** Forgotten Truths: What a Man Really Wants in a Woman. 1999. 18.95 (*0-9671488-1-2*) Renaissance Ctr.
— Games Women Play: The Authoritative Handbook on Bringing a Good Man to His Knees & Keeping Him There, Wanting More. 65p. 1998. 18.95 (*0-9671488-0-4*) Renaissance Ctr.
Anderson, Ross, ed. Fast Software Encryption: Cambridge Security Workshop, Cambridge, UK, December 9-11, 1993, Proceedings. LC 94-20769. (Lecture Notes in Computer Science Ser.: Vol. 809). 1994. 39.95 (*0-387-58108-1*) Spr-Verlag.
Anderson, Ross & Perry, Barbara. The Diversions of Keramos: American Clay Sculpture, 1925-1950. Grover-Rogoff, Annis, ed. LC 83-82416. (Illus.). 118p. (Orig.). 1983. pap. text 12.00 (*0-914407-00-7*) Everson Mus.
Anderson, Ross, et al. The Global Trust Register: 1999 Edition. LC 98-88653. (Illus.). 150p. 1999. pap. text 24.95 (*0-262-51105-3*) MIT Pr.
Anderson, Ross, ed. see Isaac Newton Institute for Mathematical Sciences S, et al.
Anderson, Roy. Excel 5.0 for Windows: Applications for Reinforcement. (Computer Applications Ser.). 1996. mass mkt. 31.95 (*0-538-71447-6*) S-W Pub.
***Anderson, Roy.** First Steps: A Physical Basis of Concentration. 1999. pap. 14.95 (*1-899836-34-9*, Pub. by Crown Hse) LPC Group.
Anderson, Roy. Management, Information Systems & Computers: An Introduction. 285p. (C). 1987. 40.00 (*0-333-39852-1*); pap. text 30.00 (*0-333-39853-X*) Scholium Intl.
Anderson, Roy & Fox. Business Law & the Legal Environment - Standard Volume. 16th ed. (LA - Business Law Ser.). (C). 1995. pap. 75.95 (*0-538-84542-2*) S-W Pub.
Anderson, Roy C., jt. ed. see Davis, John W.

A

Anderson, Roy N. The Disabled Man & His Vocational Adjustment: A Study of the Types of Jobs Held by 4,404 Orthopedic Cases in Relation to the Specific Disability. Phillips, William R. & Rosenberg, Janet, eds. LC 79-6893. (Physically Handicapped in Society Ser.). 1980. reprint ed. lib. bdg. 17.95 (0-405-13104-6) Ayer.

Anderson, Roy R. Damages under the UCC, 2 vols. 1992. 230.00 (0-685-28162-0) West Group.

— Damages under the UCC, 2 vols. annuals 1992. suppl. ed. write for info. (0-318-65582-9) West Group.

Anderson, Russell F. Lectionary Preaching Workbook. LC 96-12704. (Series V). 1996. pap., wbk. ed. 34.50 (0-7880-0821-8) CSS OH.

— Lectionary Preaching Workbook. LC 96-30030. (Series V, Cycle C: Vol. 3). 362p. 1997. pap. 34.50 (0-7880-1041-7) CSS OH.

***Anderson, Russell F.** Lectionary Preaching Workbook. 1998. cd-rom 34.50 (0-7880-0521-9); mac hd 34.50 (0-7880-0523-5) CSS OH.

Anderson, Russell F. Lectionary Preaching Workbook, Series V, Cycle A. LC 95-13959. 1995. pap., wbk. ed. 34.50 (0-7880-0520-0) CSS OH.

Anderson, Ruth. Gallegan Provinces of Spain: Pontevedra & la Coruna. (Illus.). 1939. 15.00 (0-87535-047-X) Hispanic Soc.

— Life in the Slow Lane. 36p. (Orig.). 1996. pap. 8.43 (0-9648461-2-8) Ebert Desgn.

Anderson, Ruth M. Hispanic Costume Fourteen Eighty to Fifteen Thirty. LC 78-66860. (Hispanic Notes & Monographs: Peninsular). (Illus.). 1979. 29.00 (0-87535-126-3) Hispanic Soc.

— Spanish Costume: Extremadura. (Illus.). 1951. 15.00 (0-87535-067-4) Hispanic Soc.

Anderson, Ruth Yaeger. It's Kitzel- -it's Me! A Memoir, 1918-1932. LC 98-52057. 1998. write for info. (1-880397-29-3) Patrice Pr.

***Anderson, Ruthann P.** Duck "Tails" from Quacker Inn. deluxe ed. LC 00-132301. (Illus.). x, 182p. 2000. pap. 15.00 (0-9701122-0-3, Gateway GA) R P Anderson.

Anderson, Ryan, jt. ed. see Jackson, Scott.

Anderson, S. Mussels at Midnight. Date not set. pap. 6.99 (0-906731-93-3, Pub. by Christian Focus) Spring Arbor Dist.

Anderson, S., jt. ed. see Agnoletti, M.

***Anderson, S. Chris & Thode, Ernest.** A Genealogist's Guide to Discovering Your Germanic Ancestors. LC 00-29753. (Genealogist's Guide to Discovering Your Ancestors Ser.). (Illus.). 192p. 1999. pap. 18.99 (1-55870-520-1, 70446, Betrwy Bks) F & W Pubns Inc.

Anderson, S. E. The Black Holocaust for Beginners. (Illus.). 192p. 1995. pap. 11.00 (0-86316-178-2) Writers & Readers.

Anderson, S. E. & Medina, Tony, eds. In Defense of Mumia. (Illus.). 400p. 1996. pap. 14.00 (0-86316-099-9) Writers & Readers.

Anderson, S. W., jt. auth. see Anderson, W. L.

Anderson, Samantha, ed. see Sankara, Thomas.

Anderson, Sandra. Angels Can Fall. 176p. 1998. pap. 9.99 (1-57921-111-9, Pub. by WinePress Pub) BookWorld.

— Computer Literacy for Health Care Professionals. (C). 1992. mass mkt. 44.95 (0-8273-4171-7) Delmar.

— Computer Literacy for Health Care Professions Instructors Guide. 1992. pap., teacher ed. 13.00 (0-8273-4172-5) Delmar.

***Anderson, Sandra & Sovik, Rolf.** Yoga: Mastering the Basics. LC 99-53823. (Illus.). 2000. pap. write for info. (0-89389-155-X) Himalayan Inst.

Anderson, Sandra M. Let's Get Ready for Christmas: Advent Activities for Preschool Children. (Illus.). 32p. 1993. pap. 7.99 (0-8066-2662-3, 10-26623) Augsburg Fortress.

Anderson, Sandy. Jeanne Was Once a Player of Pianos. 36p. 1998. pap. 15.00 (0-931659-45-0) Limberlost Pr.

— Jeanne Was Once a Player of Pianos. aut. limited ed. 36p. 1998. 50.00 (0-931659-46-9) Limberlost Pr.

***Anderson, Sandy.** Women in Career & Life Transitions: Mastering Change in the New Millennium. Jarrett, Kitty, ed. LC 99-47165. 248p. 1999. pap. 16.95 (1-56370-670-9, J6709) Park Ave.

Anderson, Sandy. Work-at-Home Balancing Act: The Professional Resource Guide for Managing Yourself, Your Work. LC 98-20230. 272p. 1998. pap. 12.00 (0-380-79801-8, Avon Bks) Morrow Avon.

Anderson, Sandy S. & Anderson, Robert G. Willpower: How to Gain It & Maintain It--A Simple Building Block Approach. LC 87-70328. (Illus.). 96p. (Orig.). 1987. pap. 7.95 (0-9617964-0-5, 964A) Calif Dream Pubns.

Anderson-Sankofa, David A. The Origin of Life on Earth: An African Creation Myth. (Illus.). 32p. (YA). 1991. lib. bdg. 18.95 (0-9629978-5-4) Sights Prods.

— The Origin of Life on Earth: An African Creation Myth. (Illus.). 32p. (YA). 1996. pap. 9.95 (1-886366-09-8) Sights Prods.

— The Rebellion of Humans. (Illus.). 32p. (J). 1994. 18.95 (0-9629978-6-2) Sights Prods.

Anderson-Sannes, Barbara. Alma on the Mississippi, 1848-1932. Doyle, Michael et al, eds. LC 80-68241. (Illus.). 198p. (Orig.). 1980. pap. 11.95 (0-9604684-0-4) Alma Hist Soc.

Anderson, Sara. Colors. rev. ed. (Illus.). 7p. (J). (ps-3). 1997. pap. 9.00 (1-56021-275-6) W J Fantasy.

— Numbers. rev. ed. (Illus.). 10p. (J). (ps-1). 1997. pap. 9.00 (1-56021-274-8) W J Fantasy.

— Some of My Best Friends Are Polka Dot Pigs. (Illus.). 30p. (J). (ps-3). 1997. 13.00 (1-56021-270-5) W J Fantasy.

Anderson, Sara, ed. Armor Quest: The Search for the Armor of God. 150p. 1994. student ed., ring bd. 79.95 (0-917851-96-X) Bristol Hse.

Anderson, Sara L. & Cooper, Charles, eds. We Believe: Junior High Basic Belief Studies. (Illus.). 1996. pap., teacher ed. 7.95 (1-885224-05-2); pap., student ed. 6.95 (1-885224-06-0) Bristol Hse.

— We Believe - Discovery. rev. ed. (Illus.). 64p. (YA). 1988. pap., student ed. 6.95 (1-885224-09-5) Bristol Hse.

***Anderson, Sara L. & Lanning, Cynthia, eds.** Solid Rock Construction Company. 163p. 1999. teacher ed. 89.95 (1-885224-23-0) Bristol Hse.

Anderson, Sara Long., jt. auth. see Grodner, Michelle.

Anderson, Sarah. Anderson's Travel Companion: A Guide to the Best Fiction & Non-Fiction. 584p. 1996. 69.95 (1-85928-013-7, Pub. by Scolar Pr) Ashgate Pub Co.

— Heaven's Face Thinly Veiled. LC 97-42873. 1998. pap. 16.95 (1-57062-363-5, Pub. by Shambhala Pubns) Random.

***Anderson, Sarah, et al.** The Field Guide to the Global Economy. LC 99-15595. 2000. pap. 16.95 (1-56584-421-1, Pub. by New Press NY) Norton.

Anderson, Sarah A., et al, eds. North Park Faculty Publications & Creative Works. 101p. (Orig.). 1992. pap. text 10.00 (0-9643677-2-6) North Pk Coll.

***Anderson, Sarah M. & Swenson, Karen, eds.** Cold Counsel: The Women of Old Norse Literature & Myth. 300p. 1999. 55.00 (0-8153-1966-5) Garland.

Anderson, Sarah T. Lewises, Meriwethers & Their Kin. LC 84-80082. (Illus.). 652p. 1995. reprint ed. 40.00 (0-8063-1072-3) Genealog Pub.

Anderson, Scarvia B. & Ball, Samuel. The Profession & Practice of Program Evaluation. LC 78-1154. (Jossey-Bass Series in Social & Behavioral Science & in Higher Education). (Illus.). 272p. reprint ed. pap. 84.40 (0-8357-4798-0, 203773500009) Bks Demand.

Anderson, Scarvia B. & Helmick, John S., eds. On Educational Testing. LC 83-48155. (Jossey-Bass Social & Behavioral Science Ser.). 311p. reprint ed. pap. 96.50 (0-7837-0161-6, 204045800017) Bks Demand.

Anderson, Scarvia B., et al. Encyclopedia of Educational Evaluation. LC 74-6736. 541p. reprint ed. pap. 167.80 (0-8357-4929-0, 203785900009) Bks Demand.

Anderson, Scott. Connect.Web Password. (C). pap. text. write for info. (0-393-10316-1) Norton.

Anderson, Scott. Desktop Publishing: Dollars & Sense. 208p. 1992. pap. 14.95 (0-936085-51-7) Blue Heron OR.

— Distant Fires. LC 90-61838. (Illus.). 176p. 1990. pap. 14.95 (0-938586-33-5) Pfeifer-Hamilton.

— Distant Fires. 1990. 18.05 (0-606-12591-4, Pub. by Turtleback) Demco.

— The Man Who Tried to Save the World: The Dangerous Life & Mysterious Disappearance of Fred Cuny. LC 98-43936. 384p. 1999. 24.95 (0-385-48665-0) Doubleday.

***Anderson, Scott.** The Man Who Tried to Save the World: The Dangerous Life & Mysterious Disappearance of Fred Cuny. 400p. 2000. pap. 14.00 (0-385-48666-9, Anchor NY) Doubleday.

— Triage. 240p. 1999. per. 12.00 (0-684-85653-0) S&S Trade Pap.

Anderson, Scott. Triage: A Novel. LC 98-12821. 235p. 1998. 23.00 (0-684-84695-0) Scribner.

***Anderson, Scott.** Triage: A Novel. large type ed. 408p. 1999. 31.99 (0-7089-4117-6) Ulverscroft.

Anderson, Scott. Unknown Rider. rev. ed. 205p. 1995. pap. 12.50 (0-9644521-0-3) DENNOCH.

Anderson, Scott & Dierkins, Tony. The Mosquito Book. LC 98-92515. (Illus.). 128p. 1998. pap. 6.95 (0-9644521-1-1) DENNOCH.

Anderson, Scott A., jt. ed. see Haneberg, William C.

Anderson, Scott E. Walks in Nature's Empire: Exploring the Nature Conservancy's Preserves in New York State. LC 95-40. (Illus.). 224p. (Orig.). 1995. pap. 15.00 (0-88150-313-4, Pub. by Countryman) Norton.

Anderson, Scoubar. A Puzzling Day in the Land of the Pharaohs. LC 95-41016. (Candlewick Gamebook Ser.). (Illus.). 32p. (J). (gr. 2-5). 1997. reprint ed. pap. write for info. (0-7636-0139-X) Candlewick Pr.

Anderson, Scoular. Images of Dunoon & the Cowal Peninsula LC 98-188453. 125 p. 1998. write for info. (1-874640-98-X) Argyll Pubng.

— MacPelican's American Adventure. LC 97-37127. (Gamebook Ser.). (Illus.). 32p. (J). (gr. 1-3). 1998. 12.99 (0-7636-0443-7) Candlewick Pr.

— A Puzzling Day at Castle MacPelican: A Search & Solve Gamebook. LC 94-14835. (Candlewick Gamebks.). (Illus.). 32p. (J). (gr. 1-5). 1996. reprint ed. pap. 7.99 (1-56402-852-6) Candlewick Pr.

— A Puzzling Day in the Land of the Pharaohs. LC 95-43949. (Illus.). 32p. (J). (gr. 4-7). 1996. 14.99 (1-56402-877-1) Candlewick Pr.

— A Puzzling Day in the Land of the Pharaohs Level 2: A Search-&-Solve Gamebook. LC 95-43949. (J). (gr. 2-5). 1997. pap. text 7.99 (0-7636-0138-1) Candlewick Pr.

Anderson, Scoular. 1314 & All That. 1999. pap. 7.95 (0-86241-776-7) Interlink Pub.

Anderson, Sean & Sloan, Stephen. Historical Dictionary of Terrorism. LC 94-17408. (Religions, Philosophies, & Movements Ser.: No. 4). 496p. 1995. 62.00 (0-8108-2914-2) Scarecrow.

Anderson, Sean, jt. auth. see Ashley, Stephen.

Anderson, Sean E. & Howard, Gregory J., eds. Interrogating Popular Culture: Deviance, Justice & Social Order. LC 97-43926. (Illus.). 160p. (C). 1997. pap. text 19.90 (0-911577-42-4, POP7424, Criminal Justice) Willow Tree NY.

Anderson, Selby. Center Counter Defense: The Portuguese Variation. 96p. 1997. pap. 11.95 (1-886846-10-3) Pickard & Son.

Anderson, Seth C. Closed-End Investment Companies: Issues & Answers. 160p. (C). 1992. lib. bdg. 94.00 (0-7923-9229-9) Kluwer Academic.

Anderson, Seth C., et al. Initial Public Offerings: Findings & Theories. (Innovations in Financial Markets & Institutions Ser.). 160p. (C). 1995. lib. bdg. 91.00 (0-7923-9633-2) Kluwer Academic.

Anderson, Shane M. The Complete Lincoln Cent Encyclopedia. LC 96-76701. 144p. 1996. pap. 14.95 (0-87341-445-4) Krause Pubns.

***Anderson, Sharon.** Reminders for the Journey: Reflections for Mothers. (Illus.). 160p. 2000. 15.99 (0-9642838-1-6) Bridges of Hope.

Anderson, Sharon A. And the Two Became One Plus: An Upfront Look at Today's Blended Family. LC 94-96253. 175p. 1994. pap. text 11.95 (0-9642838-0-8) Bridges of Hope.

Anderson, Sharon A., et al. Statistical Methods for Comparative Studies: Techniques for Bias Reduction. LC 79-27220. (Probability & Mathematical Statistics: Applied Probability & Statistics Section Ser.). 289p. 1980. 159.95 (0-471-04838-0) Wiley.

Anderson, Shauna C. & Cockayne, Susan. Clinical Chemistry: Concepts & Applications. (Illus.). 768p. 1992. text 65.00 (0-7216-3372-2, W B Saunders Co) Harcrt Hlth Sci Grp.

Anderson, Shauna C., et al. Clinical Simulations in Laboratory Medicine. LC 65-9095. (Illus.). 224p. 1986. text 28.50 (0-397-50746-1, Lippnctt) Lppncott W & W.

Anderson, Shawn. Countdown to College: Preparing Your Student for Success in the Collegiate Universe. LC 97-1671. 192p. (Orig.). 1997. pap. 14.95 (0-933025-55-6) Blue Bird Pub.

Anderson, Sheila. The Grey Seal. (Natural History Ser.: No. 26). (Illus.). 24p. 1989. pap. 5.25 (0-85263-947-3, Pub. by Shire Pubns) Parkwest Pubns.

Anderson, Sheldon R. A Dollar to Poland Is a Dollar to Russia: U. S. Economic Policy Toward Poland, 1945-1952. 9303rd ed. LC 92-40971. (Foreign Economic Policy of the United States Ser.). 272p. 1993. text 20.00 (0-8153-1108-7) Garland.

Anderson, Shelley. Out in the World: International Lesbian Organizing. LC 91-22999. 56p. 1991. pap. 4.95 (1-56341-005-2) Firebrand Bks.

Anderson, Shelley, et al, eds. Side Show: 1991 Short Story Annual. 276p. 1991. 12.50 (0-9630563-0-1) Somersault.

— Side Show: 1994 Annual Anthology of Contemporary Fiction. 257p. 1994. 12.00 (0-9630563-2-8) Somersault.

— Side Show: 1995 Annual Anthology of Contemporary Fiction. 308p. 1995. 12.50 (0-9630563-3-6) Somersault.

— Side Show: 1996 Annual Anthology of Contemporary Fiction. 320p. (Orig.). 1996. pap. 13.00 (0-9630563-4-4) Somersault.

— Side Show Vol. 7: Tales for the Imagination. 368p. pap. 15.00 (0-9630563-7-9) Somersault.

— Side Show, 1992-93: An Annual of Contemporary Fiction. (Annual Ser.). 448p. (Orig.). 1992. 15.00 (0-9630563-1-X) Somersault.

Anderson, Shelli, jt. auth. see Leung, Tao.

Anderson, Sheridan. Baron Von Mabel's Backpacking. (Illus.). 96p. 1993. pap. 4.95 (0-89732-123-5) Menasha Ridge.

— Curtis Creek Manifesto. (Illus.). 48p. (Orig.). 1978. pap. 7.95 (0-936608-06-4) F Amato Pubns.

Anderson, Sherry R. & Hopkins, Patricia. The Feminine Face of God: The Unfolding of the Sacred in Women. 272p. 1991. pap. 14.95 (0-553-35266-0) Bantam.

Anderson, Sherry Ruth, jt. auth. see Ray, Paul H.

Anderson, Sherwood. American Short Stories. 1999. pap. text 18.95 (3-423-09365-X) Bibliogr Inst Brockhaus.

— The Buck Fever Papers. Taylor, Welford D., ed. LC 73-151252. (Illus.). 286p. reprint ed. pap. 88.70 (0-8357-7453-8, 203311600083) Bks Demand.

— Certain Things Last: The Selected Stories of Sherwood Anderson. Modlin, Charles E., ed. & intro. by. LC 94-45830. 360p. 1992. 24.95 (0-941423-85-9) FWEW.

***Anderson, Sherwood.** Come Together. 1999. pap. text 14.95 (3-423-09339-0) Bibliogr Inst Brockhaus.

Anderson, Sherwood. Dark Laughter. 24.95 (0-88411-277-2) Amereon Ltd.

— Dark Laughter. (Collected Works of Sherwood Anderson). 319p. 1998. reprint ed. lib. bdg. 98.00 (1-58201-500-7) Classic Bks.

— Death in the Woods: And Other Stories. (Shoreline Bks.). 298p. 1986. pap. 7.95 (0-87140-140-1) Norton.

— Death in the Woods & Other Stories. Date not set. lib. bdg. 23.95 (0-8488-1952-7) Amereon Ltd.

— Egg: And Other Stories. LC 98-130404. (Penguin Twentieth-Century Classics Ser.). 400p. 1998. pap. 11.95 (0-14-118079-X, Penguin Bks) Viking Penguin.

***Anderson, Sherwood.** The Egg & Other Stories. LC 00-22699. (Thrift Editions Ser.). 2000. write for info. (0-486-41411-6) Dover.

Anderson, Sherwood. Hometown. 1975. reprint ed. 20.00 (0-911858-11-3) Appel.

***Anderson, Sherwood.** Horses & Men. (Collected Works of Sherwood Anderson). 347p. 1998. reprint ed. lib. bdg. 98.00 (1-58201-501-5) Classic Bks.

Anderson, Sherwood. I'm a Fool. 34p. 1942. pap. 3.50 (0-87129-676-4, I15) Dramatic Pub.

— Letters to Bab: Sherwood Anderson to Marietta D. Finley, 1916-33. Sutton, William A., ed. LC 83-18258. 376p. 1985. text 29.95 (0-252-00979-7) U of Ill Pr.

— Many Marriages. (Collected Works of Sherwood Anderson). 290p. 1998. reprint ed. lib. bdg. 88.00 (1-58201-502-3) Classic Bks.

— Marching Men. (Collected Works of Sherwood Anderson). 314p. 1998. reprint ed. lib. bdg. 98.00 (1-58201-503-1) Classic Bks.

— Marching Men. 1993. reprint ed. lib. bdg. 89.00 (0-7812-5421-3) Rprt Serv.

— Mid-American Chants (Poems in Prose) (Collected Works of Sherwood Anderson). 82p. 1998. reprint ed. lib. bdg. 88.00 (1-58201-504-X) Classic Bks.

— Midwest Childhood. 1993. reprint ed. lib. bdg. 89.00 (0-7812-5337-3) Rprt Serv.

— The Modern Writer: Includes Homage to Sherwood Anderson. 212p. 15.00 (0-614-09416-X) Appel.

— No Swank. LC 70-105302. (Illus.). 130p. 1970. reprint ed. 12.50 (0-911858-06-7) Appel.

— Perhaps Women (1931) LC 76-105301. 144p. 1970. reprint ed. 12.50 (0-911858-05-9) Appel.

— Poor White. (Collected Works of Sherwood Anderson). 371p. 1998. reprint ed. lib. bdg. 98.00 (1-58201-505-8) Classic Bks.

— Poor White. LC 92-44725. (New Directions Classics Ser.). 384p. 1993. reprint ed. pap. 12.95 (0-8112-1242-4, NDP763, Pub. by New Directions) Norton.

— Puzzled America. (History - United States Ser.). 287p. 1993. reprint ed. lib. bdg. 79.00 (0-7812-4916-3) Rprt Serv.

— Puzzled America (1935) 287p. 1970. reprint ed. 15.00 (0-911858-07-5) Appel.

— Selected Letters. Modlin, Charles E., ed. LC 83-6530. 279p. 1984. reprint ed. pap. 86.50 (0-608-01432-X, 206219400002) Bks Demand.

— Sherwood Anderson: Early Writings. White, Ray L., ed. LC 88-13931. 195p. reprint ed. pap. 60.50 (0-608-07365-2, 206759300009) Bks Demand.

— Sherwood Anderson: Selected Letters. Modlin, Charles E., ed. LC 83-6530. (Illus.). 280p. 1983. text 34.00 (0-87049-404-X) U of Tenn Pr.

— Sherwood Anderson's Winesburg, Ohio: With Variant Readings & Annotations. White, Ray L., ed. LC 97-711. (Illus.). 230p. 1997. reprint ed. text 44.95 (0-8214-1180-2) Ohio U Pr.

— Southern Odyssey: Selected Writings by Sherwood Anderson. Taylor, Welford D. & Modlin, Charles E., eds. LC 96-30789. 1997. 29.95 (0-8203-1899-X) U of Ga Pr.

— The Story Teller's Story. (Collected Works of Sherwood Anderson). 442p. 1998. reprint ed. lib. bdg. 108.00 (1-58201-506-6) Classic Bks.

— A Story Teller's Tale. 29.95 (0-88411-278-0) Amereon Ltd.

— The Teller's Tales: Short Stories. LC 83-80751. (Signature Ser.). 229p. (Orig.). (C). 1983. pap. text 5.95 (0-912756-08-X) Union Coll.

— The Triumph of the Egg. (Collected Works of Sherwood Anderson). 269p. 1998. reprint ed. lib. bdg. 88.00 (1-58201-507-4) Classic Bks.

— Whinesburg, Ohio: One of Modern Library's 100 Best Novels. LC 98-31438. 1999. pap. 8.95 (0-375-75313-3) Modern Lib NY.

— Windy McPherson's Son. LC 93-11209. (Prairie State Bks.). 392p. 1993. 14.95 (0-252-06357-0) U of Ill Pr.

— Windy McPherson's Son. (Collected Works of Sherwood Anderson). 347p. 1998. reprint ed. lib. bdg. 98.00 (1-58201-508-2) Classic Bks.

— Winesburg, Ohio. 1988. 22.95 (0-8488-0417-1) Amereon Ltd.

— Winesburg, Ohio. 256p. 1995. mass mkt. 5.95 (0-553-21439-X) Bantam.

— Winesburg, Ohio. LC 94-23229. 252p. 1995. 14.95 (0-679-60146-5) Modern Lib NY.

— Winesburg, Ohio. 272p. 1993. mass mkt. 5.95 (0-451-52569-8, Sig Classics) NAL.

— Winesburg, Ohio. Love, Glen A., ed. (Oxford World's Classics Ser.). 240p. 1999. pap. 7.95 (0-19-283977-2) OUP.

Anderson, Sherwood. Winesburg, Ohio. (Penguin Twentieth-Century Classics). 1976. 12.05 (0-606-01787-9, Pub. by Turtleback) Demco.

Anderson, Sherwood. Winesburg, Ohio. 256p. 1988. pap. 3.95 (0-14-043304-X, Penguin Bks) Viking Penguin.

— Winesburg, Ohio. 256p. 1992. pap. 8.95 (0-14-018655-7, Penguin Classics) Viking Penguin.

Anderson, Sherwood. Winesburg Ohio. 102p. 1960. pap. 5.50 (0-87129-804-X, W36) Dramatic Pub.

— Winesburg, Ohio. large type ed. LC 99-26432. 1999. pap. 26.95 (0-7838-8625-X) Mac Lib Ref.

Anderson, Sherwood. Winesburg, Ohio. large type ed. 370p. 1999. 27.95 (1-56000-498-3) Transaction Pubs.

— Winesburg, Ohio. large type ed. (Large Print Ser.). 330p. 1993. reprint ed. lib. bdg. 24.00 (0-939495-45-7) North Bks.

— Winesburg, Ohio. (Collected Works of Sherwood Anderson). 303p. 1998. reprint ed. lib. bdg. 98.00 (1-58201-509-0) Classic Bks.

***Anderson, Sherwood.** Winesburg, Ohio. 210p. 1998. reprint ed. lib. bdg. 24.00 (1-58287-081-0) North Bks.

Anderson, Sherwood. Winesburg, Ohio. 1993. reprint ed. lib. bdg. 89.00 (0-7812-5336-5) Rprt Serv.

— Winesburg, Ohio. unabridged ed. 160p. 1995. pap. 2.00 (0-486-28269-4) Dover.

***Anderson, Sherwood.** Winesburg, Ohio, Set. unabridged ed. 1998. 29.95 incl. audio (1-55685-596-6) Audio Bk Con.

Anderson, Sherwood. Winesburg, Ohio: Text & Criticism. Feres, John H., ed. LC 95-52436. 512p. 1996. pap. 14.95 (0-14-024779-3, Penguin Bks) Viking Penguin.

— The Writer at His Craft. Salzman, Jack et al, eds. 1978. 22.50 (0-911858-37-7) Appel.

Anderson, Sherwood, jt. auth. see Center for Learning Network Staff.

Anderson, Sheryl J. The Twelve Plays of Christmas. LC 98-53386. 1999. pap. 12.00 (0-8170-1312-1) Judson.

Anderson, Sheryl J., jt. auth. see Wolfe, William D.

Anderson, Shirle. A Gift for Eternity, 5 vols., Set, Vol. 1. 80p. 1997. 12.95 (0-9661657-0-5) Mead.

Anderson, Shirley A. & Smith. Delmar's Handbook for HIM Careers. LC 97-13364. (Allied Health Ser.). 336p. (C). 1997. mass mkt. 36.95 (0-8273-8083-6) Delmar.

An Asterisk (*) at the beginning of an entry indicates that the title is appearing for the first time.

Anderson-Siebert, Barbara. STS: Sustainable Living Module 1. 80p. 1997. per. 12.95 (*0-7872-4602-6*, 41460201) Kendall-Hunt.
***Anderson, Simon.** Arranged Marriage: Wallace Berman & Robert Watts. (Illus.). 39p. 1999. 45.00 (*0-9670774-0-0*) R Horowitz LLC.
Anderson, Simon, et al. Cautionary Tales: Young People, Crime & Policing in Edinburgh. LC 94-18854. 192p. 1994. 61.95 (*1-85628-851-X*, Pub. by Avebry) Ashgate Pub Co.
— In the Spirit of Fluxus' (Illus.). 192p. 1993. 55.00 (*0-935640-40-1*); pap. 35.00 (*0-935640-41-X*) Walker Art Ctr.
Anderson, Simon P. & De Palma, Andre. Discrete Choice Theory of Product Differentiation. (Illus.). 398p. 1992. 55.00 (*0-262-01128-X*) MIT Pr.
Anderson, Sonia P. An English Consul in Turkey: Paul Rycaut at Smyrna, 1667-1678. (Illus.). 336p. 1989. text 85.00 (*0-19-820132-X*) OUP.
Anderson, Sonia P. & Owen, G. Dynfallt, eds. Manuscripts of the Marquess of Downshire, Papers of William Trumbull the Elder, September 1616 - December 1618. (Reports & Calendars, Series 75: Vol. 6). 1995. 245.00 (*0-11-440230-2*, HM402302, Pub. by Statnry Office) Bernan Associates.
Anderson, Sparky & Ewald, Dan. They Call Me Sparky. LC 98-13339. (Illus.). 256p. 1998. 24.95 (*1-886947-23-6*) Sleepng Bear.
Anderson-Spivy, Alexandra. Keith Haring: Works on Paper, 1989. (Illus.). 38p. 1995. pap. 20.00 (*0-9646171-0-2*) Dist Art Pubs.
— Robert Kushner: Gardens of Earthly Delight. LC 97-2590. (Illus.). 174p. 1997. 50.00 (*1-55595-121-X*) Hudson Hills.
Anderson-Spivy, Alexandra, contrib. by. Elizabeth Osborne. (Illus.). 28p. 1992. pap. 20.00 (*1-879173-10-7*) Locks Gallery.
Anderson, Stanford. Peter Behrens & a New Architecture for the Twentieth Century. LC 99-49154. (Illus.). 393p. 2000. 59.95 (*0-262-01176-X*) MIT Pr.
Anderson, Stanford, ed. On Streets. (Illus.). 424p. 1986. pap. text 27.50 (*0-262-51039-1*) MIT Pr.
Anderson, Stanford, et al. The Architecture of Politics: 1910-1940. Kendall, Samuel C., ed. (Illus.). 78p. (Orig.). (C). Date not set. pap. 10.00 (*0-614-08064-9*) Wolfsonian Fnd.
Anderson, Stanford, tr. & intro. see Muthesius, Hermann.
***Anderson, Stanice.** 12-Step Programs: A Resource Guide for Helping Professionals. 160p. 1999. 24.95 (*1-55691-163-7*) Learning Pubns.
Anderson, Stanley, et al. Advanced Electrocardiography. (Biophysical Measurement Ser.). (Illus.). 120p. (Orig.). (C). 1992. 28.00 (*0-9627449-4-8*) SpaceLabs.
Anderson, Stanley F. & Anderson, Dorothy. Winemaking. (Illus.). 302p. 1989. pap. 21.00 (*0-15-697095-3*) Harcourt.
Anderson, Stanley F. & Healey, Ken. The New Art of Making Beer. 2nd ed. LC 97-46752. 192p. 1998. pap. 11.95 (*0-452-26939-3*, Plume) Dutton Plume.
Anderson, Stanley F. & Hull, Raymond. The Art of Making Wine. 1991. pap. 9.95 (*0-452-26744-7*, Plume) Dutton Plume.
Anderson, Stanley H. & Squires, John R. The Prairie Falcon. LC 96-41375. (Corrie Herring Hooks Ser.). (Illus.). 168p. 1997. 29.95 (*0-292-70473-9*); pap. 16.95 (*0-292-70474-7*) U of Tex Pr.
Anderson, Stanley V., ed. Ombudsman for American Government? LC 68-14460. 1968. 4.95 (*0-317-02958-4*, 63420) Am Assembly.
Anderson, Stephanie S. Original Sins: And Other Poems from Afterlife. (Orig.). (C). 1995. pap. 6.00 (*0-9645709-0-4*) Selene River Pr.
Anderson, Stephen. So, You Wanna Be a Rockstar? How to Create Music, Get Gigs & maybe even make it BIG! LC 98-52673. (Illus.). 144p. (J). (gr. 5-11). 1999. pap. 8.95 (*1-885223-99-4*) Beyond Words Pub.
Anderson, Stephen, ed. see Calais-Germain, Blandine & Lamotte, Andree.
Anderson, Stephen, jt. ed. see Miyagawa, Shigeru.
Anderson, Stephen A. & Bagarozzi, Dennis A. Family Myths: Psychotherapy Implications. LC 88-30091. (Journal of Psychotherapy & the Family: Vol. 4, Nos. 3-4). (Illus.). 213p. 1989. text 49.95 (*0-86656-775-5*) Haworth Pr.
***Anderson, Stephen A. & Couch, Greg.** I Know the Moon. LC 99-36027. (J). 2001. 15.99 (*0-399-23425-X*) Peng Put Young Read.
Anderson, Stephen A. & Sabatelli, Ronald M. Family Interaction: A Multigenerational Developmental Perspective. 2nd ed. LC 98-16482. 372p. (gr. 2). 1998. pap. text 46.00 (*0-205-27759-4*) Allyn.
Anderson, Stephen B. We Are Not Alone Fountain House & the Development of Clubhouse Culture. Haas, Peter, ed. LC 98-93642. viii, 217p. 1998. pap. 14.95 (*0-9667686-0-4*) Fountain Hse.
Anderson, Stephen J. Corporate Tax Practice Manual. Kaiser, Laura B., ed. 1990. ring bd. 99.00 (*1-878375-19-9*) Panel Pubs.
— Welfare Policy & Politics in Japan: Beyond the Developmental State. 194p. 1994. 46.95 (*1-56924-953-9*) Marlowe & Co.
Anderson, Stephen J., ed. The Closely Held Corporation: Planning & Operation. 1988. 150.00 (*0-916592-47-2*) Panel Pubs.
Anderson, Stephen R. A-Morphous Morphology. (Cambridge Studies in Linguistics: No. 62). (Illus.). 448p. (C). 1992. pap. text 32.95 (*0-521-37866-4*) Cambridge U Pr.
— Phonology in the Twentieth Century: Theories of Rules & Theories of Representations. LC 85-2773. 384p. 1985. pap. text 23.50 (*0-226-01916-0*) U Ch Pr.
Anderson, Stephen R., et al, eds. Syntax & Semantics, Vol. 24: Modern Icelandic Syntax. 443p. 1990. pap. text 75.00 (*0-12-606105-X*) Acad Pr.
Anderson, Stephen R. & Hendrick, Randall, eds. Syntax & Semantics, Vol. 23: The Syntax of the Modern Celtic Languages. 262p. 1990. text 110.00 (*0-12-613523-1*); pap. text 59.95 (*0-12-606104-1*) Acad Pr.
Anderson, Stephen R. & Rothstein, Susan, eds. Syntax & Semantics, Vol. 25: Perspectives on Phrase Structure: Heads & Licensing. 264p. 1991. pap. text 55.00 (*0-12-606106-8*) Acad Pr.
Anderson, Steve. The Enoch Sroll & the Final Battle. 275p. (YA). (gr. 7-12). 1997. pap. 14.99 (*0-9662029-0-2*) S Anderson Prods.
Anderson, Steven. The Great American Bathroom Book Vol. 2: The Second Sitting. 1993. pap. 19.95 (*1-880184-10-9*) Compact Classics.
***Anderson, Steven C.** The Lizards of Iran. LC 99-70849. 1999. write for info. (*0-916984-49-4*) SSAR.
Anderson, Steven C., et al. The Reluctant Dragon. 59p. 1990. pap. 5.50 (*0-87129-066-9*, R50) Dramatic Pub.
***Anderson, Steven J., et al.** Care of the Young Athlete. LC 99-86578. 2000. write for info. (*0-89203-214-6*) Amer Acad Ortho Surg.
Anderson, Stevens, ed. see Lancaster, Derek.
Anderson, Stevens, ed. see Merrell, Ken.
Anderson, Stevens, ed. see Peek, Fran.
Anderson, Stevens W., ed. Compact Classics Vol. II: Your Personal Portable Library. 626p. (Orig.). 1993. 39.95 (*1-880184-14-1*); pap. 19.95 (*1-880184-11-7*); ring bd. 39.95 (*1-880184-12-5*) Compact Classics.
— Compact Classics Vol. II: Your Personal Portable Library, 3 vols., Set. 1799p. (Orig.). 1994. pap., boxed set 56.95 (*1-880184-30-3*) Compact Classics.
— The Great American Bathroom Book: Your Personal Portable Library, 3 vols., Set. 1799p. (Orig.). 1994. pap. 56.95 (*1-880184-29-X*) Compact Classics.
Anderson, Stevens W. & England, Lan C., eds. The Great American Bathroom Book Vol. 1: Single-Sitting Summaries of All Time Great Books. 606p. 1998. pap. 19.95 (*1-880184-04-4*) Compact Classics.
Anderson, Stevens W., ed. see Peek, Francis.
Anderson-Stojanovic, Virginia R. Stobi: Results of the Joint American-Yugoslav Archaeological Investigations, 1970-1981. (Hellenistic & Roman Pottery Ser.: Vol. I). (Illus.). 400p. 1992. text 210.00 (*0-691-03605-5*, Pub. by Princeton U Pr) Cal Prin Full Svc.
Anderson, Stuart. Here's the Beef! LC 96-79664. (Illus.). 308p. 1996. 23.95 (*1-883697-94-8*) Hara Pub.
— Microprocessor Technology. LC 94-22233. (Illus.). 240p. 1995. pap. text 34.95 (*0-7506-1839-6*) Buttrwrth-Heinemann.
— Race & Rapprochement. LC 79-24185. 240p. 1981. 33.50 (*0-8386-3001-4*) Fairleigh Dickinson.
Anderson, Stuart, et al. An Atlas of South-Central Los Angeles. 34p. 1992. pap. text 195.00 (*1-883638-13-5*) Rose Inst.
Anderson, Stuart D., ed. see American Society of Civil Engineers Staff.
***Anderson, Sue, ed.** Current & Recent Research in Osteoarchaeology Vol. 2: Proceedings of the Fourth, Fifth & Sixth Meetings of the Osteoarchaeological Research Group. (Illus.). 68p. (C). 2000. pap. 17.95 (*1-900188-97-X*, Pub. by Oxbow Bks) David Brown.
Anderson, Sue & Boyle, Katherine, eds. Ritual Treatment of Human & Animal Remains. (Illus.). 72p. 1996. pap. 14.95 (*1-900188-20-1*, Pub. by Oxbow Bks) David Brown.
Anderson, Sue A., ed. see Anderson, Tracey A.
***Anderson, Susan.** Black Swan: The Twelve Lessons of Abandonment Recovery. LC 99-93501. (Illus.). 112p. 2000. pap. 16.99 (*0-9673755-1-7*, Pub. by Rock Found) Partners Pubs Grp.
Anderson, Susan. Divine Intervention: An Unexpected Journey from Chaos to Clarity. LC 98-37211. 224p. 1999. pap. 13.95 (*1-58270-000-1*) Beyond Words Pub.
— Flowers for Mommy. LC 95-10046. (Illus.). (J). (ps-3). 1995. 16.95 (*0-86543-452-2*) Africa World.
— Flowers for Mommy. 1995. pap. 8.95 (*0-86543-453-0*) Africa World.
— From Native Soil: A Selection of American Regionalist Prints. (Illus.). 16p. 1987. 3.00 (*0-915478-53-6*) Montgomery Gallery.
— Grass & Grimmelshausen: Gunter Grass's "Das Treffen in Telgte" & Rezeptionstheorie. LC 86-72132. (GERM Ser.: Vol. 28). (Illus.). x, 108p. 1986. 35.00 (*0-938100-48-3*) Camden Hse.
— Indonesian Flavors. LC 95-18916. (Illus.). 200p. (Orig.). (C). 1995. pap. 16.95 (*1-883319-28-5*) Frog Ltd CA.
***Anderson, Susan.** Journey from Abandonment to Healing: Surviving Through - & Recovering From - the Five Stages that Accompany the Loss of Love. 368p. 2000. pap. 13.95 (*0-425-17228-7*) Berkley Pub.
— Lab Guide for Human Anatomy, Vol. 201. 220p. (C). 2000. spiral bd. 35.95 (*0-7872-7244-2*) Kendall-Hunt.
Anderson, Susan. Living in Wyoming Settling for More: Pioneer Trails Edition. 2nd rev. ed. LC 97-69636. (Illus.). 172p. 1997. 39.95 (*0-9660022-0-2*) Rockridge Pr.
— On Thin Ice. 320p. 1995. mass mkt. 4.99 (*0-8217-5046-1*, Zebra Kensgtn) Kensgtn Pub Corp.
Anderson, Susan & Pryor, Burt. Speech Fundamentals: Contemporary Approach. 140p. (C). 1993. pap. 16.20 (*0-536-58335-8*) Pearson Custom.
Anderson, Susan E., jt. ed. see Greydanus, Herbert W.
Anderson, Susan F., ed. see Franken, Wallace L.
Anderson, Susan M. Body to Earth: Three Artists from Brazil (Cildo Meireles, Mario Cravo Neto, Tunga) LC 92-73010. (Illus.). 40p. (Orig.). (C). 1993. pap. 15.00 (*0-945192-10-X*) USC Fisher Gallery.
Anderson, Susan M., ed. Selected Annotated Bibliography of the Physician Assistant Profession. 2nd ed. 119p. 1980. pap. 20.00 (*0-318-13477-2*) Assn Phys Asst Prog.
— Selected Annotated Bibliography of the Physician Assistant Profession. 3rd ed. 155p. 1984. pap. 15.00 (*0-318-50054-X*) Assn Phys Asst Prog.
Anderson, Susan M., et al. The Column Show: Metaphor & Motif. 28p. 1986. pap. 5.00 (*0-9602974-4-8*) USC Fisher Gallery.
Anderson, Susan N. At the End of Your Rope, There's Hope: Parenting Teens in Crisis. LC 97-36163. xii, 146p. 1997. 14.95 (*1-57345-249-1*) Deseret Bk.
Anderson, Susan S., et al, eds. Water Management: Proceedings of the USCID 1987 Regional Meetings. 592p. (Orig.). 1988. pap. 40.00 (*0-9618257-1-5*) US Comm Irrigation.
Anderson, Susan S. & Summers, Joseph B., eds. Toxic Substances in Agricultural Water Supply & Drainage - Searching for Solutions: Proceedings of the USCID 1987 National Meeting. 176p. (Orig.). 1988. pap. 36.00 (*0-9618257-2-3*) US Comm Irrigation.
Anderson, Susan S., jt. ed. see Deason, Wayne O.
Anderson, Susan S., jt. ed. see Schaack, Jerry.
Anderson, Susan S., jt. ed. see Summers, Joseph B.
Anderson, Suzan K. Mirror of Sumari. (Illus.). 32p. (J). (ps-6). 1985. 13.95 (*0-942494-93-8*, #129) Coleman Pub.
Anderson, Svein S. & Eliassen, Kjell A., eds. The European Union: How Democratic Is It? LC 96-123116. 1995. pap. 26.95 (*0-7619-5113-X*) Sage.
— The European Union: How Democratic Is It? LC 96-123116. 295p. (C). 1995. 75.00 (*0-7619-5112-1*) Sage.
— Making Policy in Europe. 1993. text 62.00 (*0-8039-8969-5*); pap. text 22.95 (*0-8039-8970-9*) Sage.
Anderson, Sven A. Viking Enterprise. LC 77-158254. (Columbia University. Studies in the Social Sciences: No. 424). reprint ed. 22.50 (*0-404-51424-3*) AMS Pr.
Anderson, Sydney. Autumn Reason: A Collection of Letters in Essay Form. unabridged ed. Kuypers, Janet, ed. 88p. 1996. pap. 7.00 (*1-891470-08-6*) Scars Pubns.
— The Baculum in Microtine Rodents. (Museum Ser.: Vol. 12, No. 3). 36p. 1960. pap. 2.00 (*0-317-04935-6*) U KS Nat Hist Mus.
— Mammals of Mesa Verde National Park, Colorado. (Museum Ser.: Vol. 14, No. 3). 39p. 1961. pap. 2.25 (*0-317-04937-2*) U KS Nat Hist Mus.
— Mammals of the Grand Mesa, Colorado. (Museum Ser.: Vol. 9, No. 16). 10p. 1959. pap. 1.00 (*0-317-04923-2*) U KS Nat Hist Mus.
— Neotropical Bats from Western Mexico. (Museum Ser.: Vol. 14, No. 1). 8p. 1960. pap. 1.00 (*0-317-04936-4*) U KS Nat Hist Mus.
Anderson, Sydney, ed. Simon & Schuster's Guide to Mammals. (Illus.). 512p. 1984. pap. 15.00 (*0-671-42805-5*) S&S Trade.
Anderson, T. Introducing Jazz Improvisation B Flat: Maiden Voyage. 40p. 1997. pap. 14.95 (*0-7935-6587-1*) H Leonard.
— Introducing Jazz Improvisation Bass Clef: Maiden Voyage. 40p. 1997. pap. 14.95 (*0-7935-6588-X*) H Leonard.
— Introducing Jazz Improvisation E Flat: Maiden Voyage. 40p. 1997. pap. 14.95 (*0-7935-6586-3*) H Leonard.
— Introducing Jazz Improvisation Treble Clef: Maiden Voyage. 40p. 1997. pap. 14.95 (*0-7935-6589-8*) H Leonard.
Anderson, T., jt. auth. see Lee, P. A.
Anderson, T. J., jt. auth. see Page, D. L.
Anderson, T. L. Fracture Mechanics. 2nd ed. 78p. 1995. lib. bdg., lab manual ed. 0.50 (*0-8493-9482-1*) CRC Pr.
— Fracture Mechanics: Fundamentals & Applications. 2nd ed. LC 94-42871. 704p. (C). 1994. boxed set 83.95 (*0-8493-4260-0*, 4260) CRC Pr.
Anderson, T. W. An Introduction to Multivariate Statistical Analysis. 2nd ed. LC 84-7334. (Probability & Mathematical Statistics Ser.). 704p. 1984. 135.00 (*0-471-88987-3*) Wiley.
— The Statistical Analysis of Time Series. 720p. 1994. pap. 64.95 (*0-471-04745-7*) Wiley.
Anderson, T. W., et al, eds. Multivariate Analysis & Its Applications. LC 94-79714. (Lecture Notes-Monographs: Vol. 24). (Illus.). 472p. 1994. pap. 45.00 (*0-940600-35-8*) Inst Math.
Anderson, T. W. & Finn, Jeremy D. The New Statistical Analysis of Data. LC 95-44885. 712p. (C). 1996. text 59.95 (*0-387-94619-5*) Spr-Verlag.
Anderson, T. W., ed. see American Water Resources Association Staff.
Anderson, T. W., jt. ed. see Fang, Kai-Tai.
Anderson, Talmadge. Introduction to African American Studies. 304p. (C). 1995. per. 33.95 (*0-8403-9349-0*) Kendall-Hunt.
Anderson, Talmadge, ed. Black Studies: Theory, Method, & Cultural Perspectives. LC 90-42949. 227p. (Orig.) (C). 1990. pap. 15.00 (*0-87422-074-2*) Wash St U Pr.
Anderson, Tammy L., ed. California Redwoods Color Book. 26p. (J). (ps-8). 1988. pap. 1.95 (*0-915687-03-8*) FVN Corp.
Anderson, Ted L. Fracture Mechanics: Fundamentals & Applications. 800p. 1991. lib. bdg. 79.00 (*0-8493-4277-5*, TA409) CRC Pr.
Anderson, Ted R. Population Studies of European Sparrows in North America. (Occasional Papers: No. 70). 58p. 1978. pap. 1.00 (*0-317-04581-4*) U KS Nat Hist Mus.
Anderson, Terence A. Analysis of Evidence: How to Do Things with Facts Based on Wigmore's Science of Judicial. LC 98-39087. 496p. 1998. pap. text 29.95 (*0-8101-1676-6*) Northwestern U Pr.
Anderson, Terence J. & Twining, William. Analysis of Evidence: How to Do Things with Facts Based on Wigmore's Science of Judicial Proof. 1991. teacher ed. write for info. (*0-316-03964-0*, 39640) Aspen Law.
— Analysis of Evidence: How to Do Things with Facts Based on Wigmore's Science of Judicial Proof. 496p. 1991. pap. 34.00 (*0-316-03963-2*, 39632) Aspen Law.
***Anderson, Teresa, et al.** Rural Energy Services: A Handbook for Sustainable Energy Development. 234p. 1999. pap. 22.50 (*1-85339-462-9*) Intermed Tech.
***Anderson, Teresa L.** U. S. Postal Service: Postal & Telecommunications Sector Representation in International Organizations. (Illus.). 54p. 1999. pap. text 20.00 (*0-7881-8283-8*) DIANE Pub.
Anderson, Teresa L., et al. U. S. Postal Service: Little Progress Made in Addressing Persistent Labor Management Problems. Motley, Michael E., ed. (Illus.). 108p. (C). 1999. pap. text 20.00 (*0-7881-7425-8*) DIANE Pub.
Anderson, Terry. Den of Lions. 432p. 1994. mass mkt. 5.99 (*0-345-39054-7*) Ballantine Pub Grp.
— Transforming Leadership: Equipping Yourself & Others to Build the Leadership Organization. 2nd ed. LC 97-37206. (Illus.). 368p. 1998. boxed set 44.95 (*1-57444-109-4*) St Lucie Pr.
Anderson, Terry, jt. auth. see Gardner, Thomas J.
Anderson, Terry, jt. auth. see McTear, Michael.
***Anderson, Terry A.** Knowing God Personally: An Exchange of Love. 128p. 2000. pap. 5.95 (*0-9678900-0-4*) New Life Pubng.
Anderson, Terry D., et al. Every Officer Is a Leader: Transforming Leadership in Police, Justice & Public Safety. 2nd ed. LC 99-42156. 472p. 1999. boxed set 39.95 (*1-57444-118-3*, SL1183) St Lucie Pr.
Anderson, Terry H. The Movement & the Sixties. (Illus.). 544p. (C). 1996. pap. text 17.95 (*0-19-510457-9*) OUP.
— The United States, Great Britain, & the Cold War, 1944-1947. LC 80-25838. 270p. reprint ed. pap. 83.70 (*0-7837-4206-1*, AU0043600012) Bks Demand.
Anderson, Terry H., jt. auth. see Bond, Charles R., Jr.
Anderson, Terry L. The Economic Growth of Seventeenth-Century New England: A Measurement of Regional Income. LC 75-2574. (Dissertations in American Economic History Ser.). (Illus.). 1979. 24.95 (*0-405-07255-4*) Ayer.
— Water Markets: Priming the Invisible Pump. LC 97-14369. 184p. 1997. 19.95 (*1-882577-43-4*); pap. text 10.95 (*1-882577-44-2*) Cato Inst.
Anderson, Terry L., ed. Breaking the Environmental Policy Gridlock. LC 96-41981. (Publication Ser.: No. 439). 182p. (Orig.). 1997. pap. 17.95 (*0-8179-9472-6*) Hoover Inst Pr.
— Multiple Conflicts over Multiple Uses. 130p. (Orig.). (C). 1994. pap. text 14.95 (*0-8191-9748-3*, Pub. by Pol Eco Res) U Pr of Amer.
— NAFTA & the Environment. LC 93-1031. 1993. pap. write for info. (*0-936488-73-5*) PRIPP.
— Property Rights & Indian Economies. 320p. (C). 1992. text 48.50 (*0-8476-7708-7*) Rowman.
Anderson, Terry L. & Hill, Peter J., eds. Environmental Federalism. LC 97-19208. (Political Economy Forum Ser.). 225p. 1997. 66.50 (*0-8476-8570-5*); pap. 25.95 (*0-8476-8571-3*) Rowman.
— The Political Economy of the American West. 194p. (C). 1994. lib. bdg. 47.00 (*0-8476-7911-X*) Rowman.
— The Privatization Process: A Worldwide Perspective. (Political Economy Forum Ser.). 284p. (C). 1996. pap. text 25.95 (*0-8476-8187-4*); lib. bdg. 66.00 (*0-8476-8186-6*) Rowman.
— Water Marketing: The Next Generation. LC 96-31065. (Political Economy Forum Ser.: No. 37). 216p. 1996. 60.50 (*0-8476-8397-4*); pap. 24.95 (*0-8476-8398-2*) Rowman.
— Wildlife in the Marketplace. 208p. (C). 1995. pap. text 22.95 (*0-8476-8025-8*); lib. bdg. 57.50 (*0-8476-8024-X*) Rowman.
Anderson, Terry L. & Leal, Donald R. Enviro-Capitalists: Doing Good While Doing Well. LC 96-40115. (Political Economy Forum Ser.: No. 37). 200p. 1997. 55.50 (*0-8476-8381-8*); pap. 17.95 (*0-8476-8382-6*) Rowman.
— Free Market Environmentalism. LC 90-48035. 225p. (C). 1991. pap. 55.00 (*0-936488-33-6*) PRIPP.
Anderson, Terry L. & Simmons, Randy. The Political Economy of Customs & Culture: Informal Solutions to the Common Problem. (Political Economy Forum Ser.). 260p. (C). 1993. text 54.00 (*0-8476-7786-9*) Rowman.
***Anderson, Terry L. & Yandle, Bruce, eds.** Agriculture & the Environment: Searching for Greener Pastures. 2000. 17.95 (*0-8179-9912-4*) Hoover Inst Pr.
***Anderson, Terry Lee & Miller, Henry I.** The Greening of U. S. Foreign Policy. LC 00-29588. 2000. write for info. (*0-8179-9862-4*) Hoover Inst Pr.
Anderson, Terry M., jt. auth. see Gardner, Thomas J.
Anderson, Thayle & Forrester, Kent. Point Counterpoint: 8 Cases for Composition. 2nd ed. LC 92-73716. 512p. (C). 1993. pap. text 37.00 (*0-15-500169-8*) Harcourt Coll Pubs.
— Reading, Then Writing: From Source to Essay. 448p. (C). 1991. pap. 34.69 (*0-07-001957-6*) McGraw.
Anderson, Thelma. The Golden Lao. 152p. (J). 1997. pap. 7.95 (*1-57502-589-2*, PO1684) Morris Pubng.
— Gumbo Lillies. LC 98-93952. 328p. 1998. pap. write for info. (*0-7392-0018-6*, PO2763) Morris Pubng.
Anderson, Theodore M. & Barney, Stephen, eds. Contradictions: From Beowulf to Chaucer. 346p. 1995. 86.95 (*1-85928-173-7*, Pub. by Scolar Pr) Ashgate Pub Co.

A

A

Anderson, Theresa R. Nannies Grannies & Babysitters: Everything You Need to Know Before Hiring Child Care Providers in Your Home. 106p. 1997. pap. 19.95 (*0-9657440-1-9*); ring bd., wbk. ed. 49.95 (*0-9657440-0-0*) Lord & Anderson.

Anderson, Thomas. Java for Business: Using Java to Win Customers, Cut Costs, & Drive Growth. LC 97-14574. (Business Technology Ser.). 288p. (Orig.). 1997. text 24.95 (*0-442-02517-3*, VNR) Wiley.

Anderson, Thomas. Java for Business: Using Java to Win Customers, Cut Costs, & Drive Growth. 368p. (Orig.). 1997. pap. 27.95 (*0-471-28829-2*, VNR) Wiley.

Anderson, Thomas. Matanza. 2nd ed. LC 92-24610. 220p. (C). 1992. pap. 12.95 (*1-880684-04-7*) Curbstone.

— Outback Outfitters, Incorporated Family Camping Guide. (Illus.). 126p. 1998. per. 10.00 (*0-9663759-0-4*) Outback.

— Paradise Mountain. 93p. (Orig.). (J). (gr. 4-6). 1995. pap. 9.99 (*0-88092-162-5*) Royal Fireworks.

— Way of the Topi. (Orig.). (J). (gr. 6-9). 1996. pap. 9.99 (*0-88092-125-0*) Royal Fireworks.

Anderson, Thomas C. Sartre's Two Ethics: From Authenticity to Integral Humanity. LC 93-23370. 230p. 1993. 36.95 (*0-8126-9232-2*); pap. 19.95 (*0-8126-9233-0*) Open Court.

Anderson, Thomas D. Geopolitics of the Caribbean: Ministates in a Wider World. LC 83-21200. (Politics in Latin America, A Hoover Institution Ser.). 175p. 1984. 52.95 (*0-275-91119-5*, C1119, Praeger Pubs) Greenwood.

Anderson, Thomas E. The Poison Ivy, Oak & Sumac Book: A Short Natural History & Cautionary Account. LC 95-75276. (Illus.). 152p. (Orig.). 1995. pap. 14.95 (*0-9639371-8-9*) Acton Circle.

Anderson, Thomas H., et al. Foundational Studies in Teacher Education: A Reexamination. 176p. (C). 1990. reprint ed. pap. text 17.95 (*0-8077-3059-9*) Tchrs Coll.

Anderson, Thomas J., jt. auth. see Page, David L.

Anderson, Thomas P. Politics in Central America: Guatemala, El Salvador, Honduras, & Nicaragua. rev. ed. LC 87-29944. 264p. 1988. 59.95 (*0-275-92805-5*, C2805, Praeger Pubs); pap. 17.95 (*0-275-92883-7*, B2883, Praeger Pubs) Greenwood.

— The War of the Dispossessed: Honduras & El Salvador, 1969. LC 80-24080. (Illus.). xiv, 203p. 1981. text 40.00 (*0-8032-1009-4*) U of Nebr Pr.

Anderson, Thomas P. & Springer, Robert W., eds. Advances in Plasma Dynamics: Proceedings of the 6th Biennial Gas Dynamics Symposium: August 25-27, 1965. LC 58-5928. 341p. reprint ed. pap. 105.80 (*0-8357-5177-5*, 201531000094) Bks Demand.

Anderson, Thomas P., jt. ed. see Cambel, Ali B.

Anderson, Thor, jt. auth. see Anderson, Kathy.

Anderson, Thornton. Creating the Constitution: The Convention of 1787 & the First Congress. LC 92-31502. 240p. 1993. 35.00 (*0-271-00913-6*); pap. 17.95 (*0-271-00920-9*) Pa St U Pr.

Anderson, Tim. The Liberation of Class: P. R. Sarkar's Theory of Class & History. 72p. (Orig.). (C). 1984. pap. 3.50 (*0-9591792-2-4*) Proutist Universal.

Anderson, Tim, ed. see Prabhat Rainjan Sarkar.

Anderson, Timothy J., jt. ed. see Holloway, Paul H.

Anderson, Timothy R., jt. ed. see Gilkey, Robert.

Anderson, Todd A. & Coats, Joel R., eds. Biomediation Through Rhizosphere Technology. LC 94-5331. (ACS Symposium Ser.: No. 563). (Illus.). 216p. 1994. text 65.00 (*0-8412-2942-2*, Pub. by Am Chemical) OUP.

Anderson, Tom. Black Bear: Seasons in the Wild. LC 91-41365. (Illus.). 120p. 1992. pap. 19.95 (*0-89658-203-5*) Voyageur Pr.

— Challenge: A Man's Adventures & Love During an Exhaustive Odyssey. LC 98-75336. 370p. 1998. pap. 14.95 (*1-890622-53-2*) Leathers Pub.

— Hunting Unlimited: Shooting Birds with a Camera. (Illus.). 128p. (C). 1999. pap. 28.00 (*0-536-01832-4*) Pearson Custom.

***Anderson, Tom.** Real Lives: Art Teachers & the Cultures of Schools. 160p. 2000. pap. text 22.00 (*0-325-00296-7*, Pub. by Boynton Cook Pubs) Heinemann.

Anderson, Tom, jt. auth. see Redmill, Felix.

Anderson, Tom, jt. auth. see Wilson, Linda.

Anderson, Tom, jt. ed. see Redmill, Felix.

Anderson, Tracey, jt. auth. see Swinney, Bridget.

Anderson, Tracey A. Professor Anderson's Tax Guide, 1989: Step by Step Approach for Tax Return Preparation Forms 1040, 1040A & 1040EZ. (Orig.). (C). 1989. pap. 8.00 (*0-685-29801-9*) Samco Educ Series.

— Professor Anderson's Tax Guide, 1990: Step-By-Step Approach for Tax Return Preparation, 1989 Forms 1040, 1040A, & 1040EZ. Anderson, Sue A., ed. 100p. (Orig.). 1990. pap. text 9.95 (*0-9624939-0-2*) Samco Educ Series.

***Anderson, Tracey A.** 300 Activities to Do with Children. Anderson, Sue A., ed. (Illus.). 104p. 2000. pap. 8.50 (*0-9624939-1-0*) Samco Educ Series.

Anderson, Tracy, jt. auth. see Swinney, Bridget.

Anderson, Troyer S. The Command of the Howe Brothers During the American Revolution. (History - United States Ser.). 368p. 1993. reprint ed. lib. bdg. 89.00 (*0-7812-4876-0*) Rprt Serv.

— The Command of the Howe Brothers During the American Revolution. LC 77-144861. 1971. reprint ed. 25.00 (*0-403-00816-6*) Scholarly.

Anderson, U. S. Three Magic Words. 10.00 (*0-685-70722-9*) Wehman.

***Anderson, Uffe, et al.** Strategic Budgeting: An Electronic-Based Program for Strategic Budgeting & Perform Assessment. 200p. 2000. 44.00 (*87-16-13464-8*, Pub. by Copenhagen Busn Schl) Bks Intl VA.

Anderson, Ursula. Immunology of the Soul: The Paradigm for the Future. 231p. 1998. pap. 19.95 (*0-9655435-4-4*) She-Bear Pubs.

Anderson, Ursula M. Connections. (Illus.). 1998. pap. 17.00 (*0-9655435-2-8*) She-Bear Pubs.

***Anderson, Ursula M.** Immunology of the Soul: The Paradigm for the Future. LC 00-103409. 250p. 2000. pap. 19.95 (*1-929902-02-6*) InSync Commn.

Anderson, Ursula M. The Psalms of Children: Their Songs & Laments: Understanding & Healing the Scars on the Souls of Children. LC 97-219682. (Illus.). v, 231p. (YA). 1997. 25.00 (*0-9655435-1-X*); pap. 15.95 (*0-9655435-0-1*) She-Bear Pubs.

Anderson, V. Elving, jt. auth. see Reichenbach, Bruce R.

***Anderson, V. S.** King of the Roses. 348p. 1999. pap. 19.95 (*1-58444-017-1*, Looking Glass Pr) DiscUs Bks.

Anderson, V. V. Psychiatry in Industry. Stein, Leon, ed. LC 77-70477. 1977. reprint ed. lib. bdg. 35.95 (*0-405-10151-1*) Ayer.

Anderson, Valborg, ed. & tr. see Strindberg, August.

Anderson, Valerie & Bereiter, Carl. Thinking Games, 2 bks. Incl. Vol. 1. Thinking Games. 80p. (J). (gr. k-3). 10.99 (*0-8224-6941-3*, FE6941); Vol. 2. Thinking Games. 96p. (J). (gr. 4-7). 10.99 (*0-8224-6942-1*, FE6942); 1980. pap. write for info. (*0-318-55299-X*) Fearon Teacher Aids.

Anderson, Valetta & Denobriga, Kathie, eds. Alternate Roots: Plays from the Southern Theatre. LC 93-20879. 340p. (C). 1994. pap. 17.95 (*0-435-08632-4*, 08632) Heinemann.

Anderson, Vera, photos by. A Woman Like You: The Face of Domestic Violence. LC 90-20603. (New Leaf Ser.). (Illus.). 96p. (Orig.). 1997. pap. 16.00 (*1-878067-07-9*) Seal Pr WA.

Anderson, Verily. The De Veres of Castle Hedingham. 272p. 1990. 60.00 (*0-86138-062-2*, Pub. by T Dalton) St Mut.

Anderson, Verily, ed. The Northrepps Grandchildren. 272p. (C). 1989. 25.00 (*0-904623-97-1*, Pub. by T Dalton) St Mut.

Anderson, Vernon E. & Gruhn, William T. Principles & Practices of Secondary Education. 2nd ed. LC 62-11648. 523p. reprint ed. pap. 162.20 (*0-8357-9958-1*, 201246300081) Bks Demand.

Anderson, Vernon F. Sudden Glory. (Caribbean Writers Ser.). 274p. (Orig.). (C). 1987. pap. 9.95 (*0-435-98808-5*, 98808) Heinemann.

Anderson, Vicki. Cultures Outside the United States in Fiction: A Guide to 2,875 Books for Librarians & Teachers, K-9. LC 94-6272. 424p. 1994. lib. bdg. 42.50 (*0-89950-905-3*) McFarland & Co.

— Fiction Index for Readers Ten to Sixteen: Subject Access to Over 8200 Books (1960-1990) LC 91-50954. 488p. (YA). (gr. 7-12). 1992. lib. bdg. 45.00 (*0-89950-703-4*) McFarland & Co.

— Fiction Sequels for Readers 10 to 16: An Annotated Bibliography of Books in Succession. 2nd ed. LC 98-5236. 182p. 1998. pap. 35.00 (*0-7864-0185-0*) McFarland & Co.

— Immigrants in the United States in Fiction: A Guide to 705 Books for Librarians & Teachers, K-9. LC 94-1231. 143p. 1994. lib. bdg. 29.50 (*0-89950-906-1*) McFarland & Co.

— Native Americans in Fiction: A Guide to 765 Books for Librarians & Teachers, K-9. LC 94-6271. 180p. 1994. lib. bdg. 31.50 (*0-89950-907-X*) McFarland & Co.

— Sequels in Children's Literature: An Annotated Bibliography of Books in Succession or with Shared Themes & Characters, K-6. LC 97-51207. 320p. 1998. pap. 39.95 (*0-7864-0285-7*) McFarland & Co.

Anderson, Vicki J. History Reborn. 405p. 1994. pap. 17.95 (*0-9642524-1-4*) Zichron Histrcl.

— The "Other Eminent Men of Wilford Woodruff" 413p. 1994. 17.95 (*0-9642524-0-6*) Zichron Histrcl.

Anderson, Victor. Beyond Ontological Blackness: An Essay on African American Religious & Cultural Criticism. 180p. 1999. pap. 18.95 (*0-8264-1152-5*) Continuum.

— Pragmatic Theology: Negotiating the Intersections of an American Philosophy of Religion & Public Theology. LC 97-12086. (SUNY Series, Religion & American Public Life). 224p. (C). 1998. pap. text 19.95 (*0-7914-3638-1*) State U NY Pr.

— Pragmatic Theology: Negotiating the Intersections of an American Philosophy of Religion & Public Theology. LC 97-12086. (SUNY Series, Religion & American Public Life). 224p. (C). 1998. text 59.50 (*0-7914-3637-3*) State U NY Pr.

Anderson, Victor D. Bibliografia Municipal Geografica Puertorriquena. LC 78-18780. 1980. pap. 5.00 (*0-8477-2007-1*) U of PR Pr.

Anderson, Victor E., et al, eds. Genetic Basis of the Epilepsies. fac. ed. LC 80-6278. (Illus.). 396p. pap. 122.80 (*0-7837-7208-4*, 204709100005) Bks Demand.

Anderson, Vidya, ed. see Ananda Yogi, Gururaj.

Anderson, Vincent P., compiled by. Robert Browning as a Religious Poet: An Annotated Bibliography of the Criticism. LC 82-50407. x, 325p. 1983. 48.50 (*0-87875-221-8*) Whitston Pub.

Anderson, Violet, jt. auth. see Mandarino, Joseph A.

Anderson, Virgil A. Training the Speaking Voice. 3rd ed. (Illus.). 494p. (C). 1977. text 49.95 (*0-19-502150-9*) OUP.

Anderson, Virgil L. & McLean, Robert A. Design of Experiments: A Realistic Approach. (Statistics: Textbooks & Monographs: Vol. 5). (Illus.). 440p. 1974. text 59.75 (*0-8247-6131-6*) Dekker.

Anderson, Virgil L., jt. auth. see Lorenzen, Thomas J.

Anderson, Virgil L., jt. auth. see McLean, Robert A.

Anderson, Virginia & Johnson, Lauren. Systems Thinking Basics: From Concepts to Causal Loops. LC 96-39762. 144p. 1997. pap. 34.95 (*1-883823-12-9*) Pegasus Comm.

Anderson, Virginia, jt. auth. see Kim, Daniel H.

Anderson, Virginia D. New England's Generation: The Great Migration & the Formation of Society & Culture in the Seventeenth Century. 244p. (C). 1992. pap. text 15.95 (*0-521-44764-X*) Cambridge U Pr.

Anderson, Virginia Johnson, see Walvoord, Barbara & Johnson Anderson, Virginia.

Anderson, Vivian, tr. see Piaget, Jean, et al.

Anderson, W. B., tr. Poems & Letters, 2 vols., 1. (Loeb Classical Library: Nos. 296, 420). 560p. 1936. 18.95 (*0-674-99327-6*) HUP.

— Poems & Letters, 2 vols., 2. (Loeb Classical Library: Nos. 296, 420). 668p. 1965. 18.95 (*0-674-99462-0*) HUP.

Anderson, W. C. Stabilization/Solidification. (Innovative Site Remediation Technology Ser.: Vol. 4). 146p. 1995. 75.95 (*3-540-59064-1*) Spr-Verlag.

— Thermal Desorption. (Innovative Site Remediation Technology Ser.: Vol. 6). 130p. 1995. 59.95 (*3-540-59066-8*) Spr-Verlag.

— Thermal Destruction. (Innovative Site Remediation Technology Ser.: Vol. 7). 110p. 1995. 75.95 (*3-540-59067-6*) Spr-Verlag.

Anderson, W. C., ed. Chemical Treatment. (Innovative Site Remediation Technology Ser.: Vol. 2). 187p. 1995. 75.95 (*3-540-58911-2*) Spr-Verlag.

— Innovative Site Remediation Technology Vol. 1: Bioremediation. 288p. 1996. 69.00 (*3-540-59218-0*) Spr-Verlag.

— Soil Washing - Soil Flushing. (Innovative Site Remediation Technology Ser.: Vol. 3). 174p. 1995. 75.95 (*3-540-59062-5*) Spr-Verlag.

Anderson, W. E., ed. The Journal of Sir Walter Scott. 1999. pap. 19.95 (*0-86241-828-3*) Interlink Pub.

Anderson, W. H., tr. see Amin, Samir.

Anderson, W. J. Continuous Time Markov Chains: An Applications-Oriented Approach. Gani, J. & Heyde, C. C., eds. (Series in Statistics-Subseries: Probability & Its Applications). (Illus.). 368p. 1992. 92.95 (*0-387-97369-9*) Spr-Verlag.

Anderson, W. J., ed. see International Conference on Bearing Design Staff.

Anderson, W. J., jt. ed. see Marwaha, J.

Anderson, W. K. James Connolly & the Irish Left. (Illus.). 160p. 1994. pap. 22.50 (*0-7165-2645-X*, Pub. by Irish Acad Pr) Intl Spec Bk.

Anderson, W. L. & Anderson, S. W. The Debonair Bachelor: A Guide to Love & Laughter. LC 81-82186. (Illus.). 128p. 1983. 19.95 (*0-940452-00-6*) Marduk Manumit.

— Outfitting Your Van for Camping. (Illus.). 300p. 1988. 9.95 (*0-940452-01-4*) Marduk Manumit.

Anderson, W. N. James Connolly & the Irish Left. 200p. 1996. 15.00 (*0-7165-2615-8*, Pub. by Irish Acad Pr) Intl Spec Bk.

Anderson, W. P. Anderson - Overton Genealogy: A Continuation of Anderson Family Records (1936) & Early Descendants of William Overton & Elizabeth Waters of VA (1938) (Illus.). 376p. 1991. reprint ed. pap. 59.50 (*0-8328-1774-0*); reprint ed. lib. bdg. 69.59 (*0-8328-1773-2*) Higginson Bk Co.

— Anderson Family Records. (Illus.). 174p. 1997. reprint ed. pap. 25.00 (*0-8328-7263-6*); reprint ed. lib. bdg. 35.00 (*0-8328-7262-8*) Higginson Bk Co.

Anderson, W. R. Norse America: Tenth Century Onward. LC 97-207482. (Illus.). 220p. 1996. 25.00 (*0-9607070-2-6*) Valhalla Pr.

Anderson, Wallace E., ed. see Edwards, Jonathan.

Anderson, Wallace E., jt. ed. see Edwards, Jonathan.

Anderson, Wallace L. Edwin Arlington Robinson: A Critical Introduction. LC PS3535.O25.A. 191p. reprint ed. pap. 59.30 (*0-7837-1668-0*, 205720000024) Bks Demand.

Anderson, Walt. Me, Candido! 1958. pap. 5.25 (*0-8222-0743-5*) Dramatists Play.

— The Sutter Buttes: A Naturalist's View. LC 82-90753. (Illus.). 326p. (Orig.). (C). 1983. pap. 16.00 (*0-9610722-1-0*) Nat Select.

Anderson, Walter. An Alphabet. LC 84-7291. (Illus.). 64p. 1992. pap. 10.95 (*0-87805-573-8*) U Pr of Miss.

— Birds. limited ed. LC 90-12883. (Illus.). 1990. 150.00 (*0-87805-460-X*) U Pr of Miss.

— The Confidence Course: Seven Steps to Self-Fulfillment. 256p. 1998. pap. 13.00 (*0-06-109453-6*, Perennial) HarperTrade.

Anderson, Walter. The Confidence Course: Seven Steps to Self-Fulfillment. abr. ed. 1997. audio 18.00 (*0-694-51782-8*, CPN 2624) HarperAudio.

— The Confidence Course: Seven Steps to Self-Fulfillment. 237p. 1999. reprint ed. text 22.00 (*0-7881-6316-7*) DIANE Pub.

Anderson, Walter. Robinson, the Pleasant History of an Unusual Cat. LC 82-10868. 1996. pap. 16.95 (*0-87805-948-2*) U Pr of Miss.

— The Walter Anderson Birthday Book. Black, Patti C., ed. & intro. by. (Illus.). 125p. 1986. text 15.00 (*0-938896-47-4*) Mississippi Archives.

Anderson, Walter. The Magic Carpet & Other Tales. LC 87-10434. 186p. (J). (ps up). 1997. reprint ed. 50.00 (*0-87805-327-1*) U Pr of Miss.

— A Symphony of Animals. LC 96-14276. 144p. 1996. 50.00 (*0-87805-909-1*) U Pr of Miss.

Anderson, Walter E., III. At Random. 110p. (Orig.). 1999. pap. 9.95 (*0-9647596-5-9*, Pub. by Mlk & Hny Pub) Herveys Bklink.

— Frat Boyz. 110p. 1999. pap. 9.95 (*0-9647596-9-1*, Pub. by Mlk & Hny Pub) Herveys Bklink.

Anderson, Walter T. Evolution Isn't What It Used to Be: The Augmented Animal & the Whole Wired World. 223p. 1997. pap. text 14.95 (*0-7167-3134-7*) W H Freeman.

— The Future of the Self: Inventing the Post-Modern Person. LC 97-19571. 304p. 1997. 24.95 (*0-87477-881-6*, Tarcher Putnam) Putnam Pub Group.

— Reality Isn't What It Used to Be: Theatrical Politics, Ready-to-Wear Religion, Global Myths, Primitive Chic, & Other Wonders of the Post Modern World. LC 89-45950. 304p. 1992. reprint ed. pap. 15.00 (*0-06-250017-1*, Pub. by Harper SF) HarpC.

— To Govern Evolution: Further Adventures of the Political Animal. LC 86-19477. 392p. 1987. 22.95 (*0-15-190483-9*) Harcourt.

Anderson, Warren D. The Classical Tradition. 320p. 1988. reprint ed. pap. text 14.95 (*0-472-06177-1*, 06177, Ann Arbor Bks) U of Mich Pr.

— Ethos & Education in Greek Music: The Evidence of Poetry & Philosophy. LC 66-21328. 316p. reprint ed. pap. 98.00 (*0-7837-4097-2*, 205792000011) Bks Demand.

— Music & Musicians in Ancient Greece. (Illus.). 264p. 1995. text 45.00 (*0-8014-3083-6*) Cornell U Pr.

— Music & Musicians in Ancient Greece. (Illus.). 264p. 1996. pap. text 15.95 (*0-8014-8432-4*) Cornell U Pr.

Anderson, Warrigal. Warrigal's Way. LC 96-216894. 1996. 16.95 (*0-7022-2909-1*, Pub. by Univ Queensland Pr) Intl Spec Bk.

Anderson, Wayne. Wayne Anderson's Horrorble Book. LC 96-206028. (Illus.). 24p. (J). (ps-3). 1996. 14.95 (*0-7894-1119-9*) DK Pub Inc.

Anderson, Wayne. The Flight of Dragons. LC 97-24206. 128p. 1998. pap. 24.95 (*0-87951-839-1*, Pub. by Overlook Pr) Penguin Putnam.

Anderson, Wayne, et al. Stress Management for Law Enforcement Officers. LC 94-36883. 384p. (C). 1994. pap. text 29.40 (*0-13-146945-2*) Prntice Hall Bks.

Anderson, Wayne, jt. ed. see Bray, Michael A.

Anderson, Wayne E. You Have a Right to Be Free. 40p. 1986. pap. 1.95 (*0-913748-08-0*) Orovan Bks.

Anderson, Wayne F., et al, eds. Managing Human Services. LC 77-2464. (Municipal Management Ser.). (Illus.). 591p. 1977. text 30.00 (*0-87326-017-1*) Intl City-Cnty Mgt.

Anderson, Wayne I. Iowa's Geological Past: Three Billion Years of Change. LC 98-38373. (Illus.). 484p. 1998. text 49.95 (*0-87745-639-9*); pap. text 24.95 (*0-87745-640-2*) U of Iowa Pr.

Anderson, Wayne K., ed. Advances in Antineoplastic Agent Design, Vol. 1. Date not set. 109.50 (*1-55938-154-X*) Jai Pr.

Anderson, Wayne R. The Custody Hoax: Why Men Don't Win Custody & Shouldn't Pay Support. unabridged ed. LC 91-91373. (Illus.). iii, 271p. 1992. pap. 12.95 (*0-9672463-0-X*) Vindicator Bks.

Anderson, Wayne R., jt. auth. see Payne, Michael N.

Anderson, Wendy. Wild Things in the Yard. 64p. (Orig.). 1986. 9.95 (*0-939395-00-2*); pap. 5.95 (*0-939395-01-0*) Thorntree Pr.

Anderson, Wendy H. The Art of Grantwriting. (Illus.). v, 112p. 1998. pap. 16.95 (*0-9664879-2-3*) WORDS Pubns.

Anderson, Wes & Wilson, Owen. Rushmore. (Illus.). 144p. 1999. pap. 14.00 (*0-571-20012-5*) Faber & Faber.

Anderson, Wesley & Anderson, Bettina G. Atlas of Canine Anatomy. (Illus.). 1230p. 1994. 85.00 (*0-8121-1535-X*) Lppncott W & W.

— Atlas of Canine Anatomy. (Illus.). 1200p. 1994. sl. 995.00 (*0-8121-1690-9*) Lppncott W & W.

Anderson, Wilbert L. The Country Town: A Study of Rural Evolution. LC 73-11914. (Metropolitan America Ser.). 318p. 1979. reprint ed. 21.95 (*0-405-05382-7*) Ayer.

Anderson, Wilda C. Diderot's Dream. LC 89-43478. (Illus.). 269p. 1990. reprint ed. pap. 83.40 (*0-608-06707-5*, 206690400009) Bks Demand.

Anderson, Will. The Great State of Maine Beer Book: A Lively & Engaging Look at Maine's Brewing Past & Present. LC 96-83097. (Illus.). 184p. (Orig.). 1996. pap. 22.95 (*0-9601056-8-9*) Anderson & Sons.

— Mid-Atlantic Roadside Delights: Roadside Architecture of Yesterday & Today in New Jersey, New York, & Pennsylvania. LC 90-85283. (Illus.). 164p. (Orig.). 1991. pap. 19.95 (*0-9601056-4-6*) Anderson & Sons.

— More Good Old Maine: 101 Past & Present Pop Delights. LC 95-75481. (Illus.). 140p. (Orig.). 1995. pap. 17.95 (*0-9601056-7-0*) Anderson & Sons.

— Where Have You Gone, Starlight Cafe? America's Golden Era Roadside Restaurants. LC 97-95027. (Illus.). 144p. 1998. pap. 24.95 (*0-9601056-9-7*) Anderson & Sons.

— You Auto See Maine: When Old Cars Were Young & for Sale in Maine. LC 99-72411. (Illus.). 168p. 1999. pap. 18.95 (*1-893804-00-3*) Anderson & Sons.

Anderson, William. Almanzo Picture Book Biography. 40p. (ps-3). pap. 5.95 (*0-06-443684-5*) HarpC.

— Almanzo Picture Book Biography. 40p. (J). (ps-3). Date not set. 15.95 (*0-06-028975-9*); lib. bdg. 15.89 (*0-06-028976-7*) HarpC Child Bks.

Anderson, William. Dante the Maker. (Illus.). 1981. 39.50 (*0-7100-0322-6*, Routledge Thoemms) Routledge.

— The Face of Glory: Creativity, Consciousness, & Civilization. LC 96-61114. (Illus.). 384p. 1996. pap. 24.95 (*0-87451-804-0*) U Pr of New Eng.

***Anderson, William.** Genealogy & Surnames: With Some Heraldic & Biographical Notices. (Illus.). 182p. 1999. 18.00 (*0-7884-1277-9*) Heritage Bk.

Anderson, William. God's Arm: A Novel about Jesus the Man, Vol. 1. 289p. 1998. 12.00 (*0-9665914-0-2*) Morn Star.

— Green Man: The Archetype of Our Oneness with the Earth. LC 90-55342. (Illus.). 176p. (Orig.). 1990. pap. 19.00 (*0-06-250075-9*, Pub. by Harper SF) HarpC.

Anderson, William. Les Kelly, Vol. 1. (Illus.). (J). (gr. 3-7). 9.95 (*0-06-440851-5*) HarpC Child Bks.

— Les Kelly, Vol. 2. (Illus.). (J). (gr. 3-7). 9.95 (*0-06-440850-7*) HarpC Child Bks.

— Laura Chapter Book Biography. 80p. 13.95 (*0-06-028973-2*) HarpC.

An Asterisk (*) at the beginning of an entry indicates that the title is appearing for the first time.

— Laura Chapter Book Biography. (Illus.). 80p. (gr. 2-5). mass mkt. 3.95 (*0-06-442133-3*) HarpC.

— Laura Chapter Book Biography. (Illus.). 80p. (J). (gr. 2-5). 13.89 (*0-06-028974-0*) HarpC Child Bks.

Anderson, William. Laura Ingalls Wilder: A Biography. LC 91-33805. (Illus.). 240p. (J). (gr. 4-6). 1992. 16.95 (*0-06-020113-4*) HarpC Child Bks.

Anderson, William. Laura Ingalls Wilder: A Biography. LC 91-33805. 256p. (J). (gr. 3-7). 1995. pap. 6.95 (*0-06-446103-3*, HarpTrophy) HarpC Child Bks.

— Laura Ingalls Wilder: A Biography. (J). 1995. 11.05 (*0-606-12977-4*, Pub. by Turtleback) Demco.

Anderson, William. Laura Ingalls Wilder Country Ri. LC 89-46512. (Illus.). 120p. 1996. reprint ed. pap. 22.50 (*0-06-097346-3*, Perennial) HarperTrade.

— Laura Ingalls Wilder's: The Iowa Story. (Illus.). 50p. 1989. pap. 4.95 (*0-9610088-9-X*) Anderson Publns.

— Laura's Album: A Remembrance Scrapbook of Laura Ingalls Wilder. LC 97-49332. (Illus.). 80p. (J). (gr. 3-7). 1998. 21.95 (*0-06-027842-0*) HarpC.

Anderson, William. The Little House Guidebook. (Illus.). 96p. (J). (gr. 3 up). 1996. pap. 9.95 (*0-06-446177-7*, HarpTrophy) HarpC Child Bks.

Anderson, William. The Little House Guidebook. 1996. 14.15 (*0-606-12984-7*, Pub. by Turtleback) Demco.

— Little Woman. 32p. (J). (gr. 2-5). 2001. 15.95 (*0-06-028402-1*) HarpC Child Bks.

***Anderson, William.** Little Woman. 32p. (J). (gr. 2-5). 2001. lib. bdg. 15.89 (*0-06-028403-X*) HarpC Child Bks.

Anderson, William. Michigan's Marguerite de Angeli. (Illus.). 70p. 1987. pap. 10.00 (*0-9610088-6-5*) Anderson Publns.

— The Nation & the States, Rivals or Partners? LC 73-16640. 263p. 1974. reprint ed. lib. bdg. 69.50 (*0-8371-7210-1*, ANNS, Greenwood Pr) Greenwood.

— Pioneer Girl: The Story of Laura Ingalls Wilder. LC 96-31203. (Illus.). 32p. (J). (gr. 2 up). 1998. 15.95 (*0-06-027243-0*); lib. bdg. 15.89 (*0-06-027244-9*) HarpC.

***Anderson, William.** Pioneer Girl: The Story of Laura Ingalls Wilder. (Illus.). 32p. (YA). (gr. 2 up). 2000. pap. 5.95 (*0-06-446234-X*) HarpC Child Bks.

Anderson, William. Powers Northeast Golf Guide, 1993. 250p. 1992. pap. 14.95 (*0-9631658-1-X*) Briarcliff NY.

— The Scottish Nation, Vol. D-F. (Illus.). 280p. (Orig.). 1995. reprint ed. pap. 34.50 (*0-7884-0310-9*) Heritage Bk.

— The Scottish Nation, Vol. M. 286p. (Orig.). 1995. pap. 35.50 (*0-7884-0362-1*, A00M) Heritage Bk.

— The Scottish Nation, Vol. G-L. (Illus.). 439p. (Orig.). 1995. pap. 51.00 (*0-7884-0361-3*, A00G) Heritage Bk.

— The Scottish Nation: Or the Surnames, Families, Literature, Honours, & Biographical History of the People of Scotland, Vol. B. (Illus.). 345p. 1995. pap. text 41.50 (*0-7884-0246-3*) Heritage Bk.

— The Scottish Nation Vol. A: Or the Surnames, Families, Literature, Honours, & Biographical History of the People of Scotland. (Illus.). 172p. 1995. pap. text 24.00 (*0-7884-0245-5*) Heritage Bk.

— The Scottish Nation Vol. T-Z: Or the Surnames, Families, Literature, Honours, & Biographical History of the People of Scotland. (Illus.). 193p. 1996. reprint ed. pap. 28.00 (*0-7884-0381-8*, A00T) Heritage Bk.

— The Scottish Nation or the Surnames, Families, or Literature, Honours & Biographical History of the People of Scotland, Vol. N-5. (Illus.). 320p. 1996. pap. 41.00 (*0-7884-0380-X*, A00N) Heritage Bk.

— Surnames of Scotland: Genealogy & Surnames with Some Heraldic & Biographical Notes. 1991. reprint ed. pap. 15.00 (*0-89979-054-2*) British Am Bks.

— They Died to Make Men Free: The 19th Michigan Infantry. rev. ed. (Illus.). 397p. 1994. 30.00 (*0-89029-322-8*) Morningside Bkshop.

— The Walnut Grove Story of Laura Ingalls Wilder. (Illus.). 50p. 1987. pap. 4.95 (*0-9610088-7-3*) Anderson Publns.

— The World of Louisa May Alcott. LC 95-24373. (Illus.). 120p. 1995. pap. 22.50 (*0-06-095156-7*, Perennial) HarperTrade.

— The World of the Trapp Family: The Life Story of the Legendary Family Who Inspired the Sound of Music. LC 98-156063. (Illus.). 168p. 1998. pap. 24.95 (*1-890757-00-4*) Anderson Publns.

Anderson, William, ed. The Scottish Nation, Vol. C. (Illus.). 241p. (Orig.). 1995. reprint ed. pap. 30.00 (*0-7884-0309-5*) Heritage Bk.

Anderson, William & Gattis, L. S. Basic Houseplants. (Illus.). 20p. (Orig.). 1987. pap., teacher ed. 9.95 (*0-936241-21-7*) Cheetah Pub.

Anderson, William, et al. Sounds of the World: Music of East Asia (Teacher's Guide) (Sounds of the World Ser.). (Illus.). 5p. 1989. pap., teacher ed. write for info. incl. audio (*0-940796-69-4*, 3036) MENC.

Anderson, William, jt. auth. see Wilder, Laura Ingalls.

Anderson, William, ed. see American Academy of Environmental Engineers Staff.

Anderson, William, ed. see McFarland, Michael J., et al.

Anderson, William, ed. see Wilder, Laura Ingalls.

Anderson, William A. The Book of Revelation. LC 98-67726. (Christian Scripture Study Ser.). 64p. 1999. pap. text 3.95 (*0-7648-0246-1*) Liguori Pubns.

***Anderson, William A.** The Gospel of John. LC 98-75392. (Christian Scripture Study Ser.). 80p. 1999. pap. 4.95 (*0-7648-0239-9*) Liguori Pubns.

— The Gospel of Mark. LC 98-75391. (Christian Scripture Study Ser.). 96p. 1999. pap. 5.95 (*0-7648-0237-2*) Liguori Pubns.

— The Gospel of Matthew. LC 98-67723. (Christian Scripture Study Ser.). 64p. 1999. pap. 3.95 (*0-7648-0236-4*) Liguori Pubns.

Anderson, William A. In His Light: A Path into Catholic Belief. 2nd ed. LC 95-161885. 1995. pap. text 10.95 (*0-697-17853-6*, WCB McGr Hill) McGrw-H Hghr Educ.

— Rite of Christian Initiation of Adults A Total Parish Process. 1998. pap. text 24.00 (*0-697-02808-9*) Brown & Benchmark.

***Anderson, William A.** Romans & Galatians. LC 98-67725. (Christian Scripture Study Ser.). 64p. 1999. pap. 3.95 (*0-7648-0242-9*) Liguori Pubns.

— Understanding the Christian Scripture's. LC 98-67724. (Christian Scripture Study Ser.). 64p. 1999. pap. 3.95 (*0-7648-0235-6*) Liguori Pubns.

Anderson, William C. A Dictionary of Law, Consisting of Judicial Definitions & Explanations of Words, Phrases, & Maxims, & an Exposition of the Principles of Law, 1889. LC 96-35844. viii, 1140p. 1996. reprint ed. lib. bdg. 125.00 (*1-886363-23-4*) Lawbk Exchange.

— How to Prepare for the Examinations for the Environmental Specialty Certification. LC TD157.A65 1995. (Illus.). 72p. 1995. pap. 35.00 (*1-883767-10-5*, 95-15274) Am Acad Environ.

— How to Survive Hospital Care: Why They Keep Bedpans in the Freezer. Terra, Jean, ed. LC 95-80408. (Illus.). 108p. 1996. per. 6.95 (*1-887747-00-1*, 297-231-X) Legendary Pub.

— Lady Bluebeard: The True Story of Love & Marriage, Death & Flypaper. (Illus.). 208p. 1994. 24.95 (*0-9623868-7-1*) F Pruett.

— Please Don't Tailgate the Real Estate. 224p. 1997. 16.95 (*0-934798-51-6*) TL Enterprises.

Anderson, William C., ed. Environmental Engineering Education: The Relationship to Engineering Practice. LC 97-1186. (Illus.). 160p. (Orig.). (C). 1997. pap. 10.95 (*1-883767-16-4*) Am Acad Environ.

— Innovative Site Remediation Technology, 8 vols., Set. LC 93-20786. (Illus.). 1995. 295.00 (*1-883767-00-8*) Am Acad Environ.

— Innovative Site Remediation Technology Vol. 6: Thermal Desorption. LC 93-20786. (Illus.). 120p. 1993. 79.95 (*1-883767-06-7*) Am Acad Environ.

— Natural Disaster Experiences: Preparing Environmental Facilities for the Worst. LC 95-15285. (Illus.). 88p. 1995. pap. 5.95 (*1-883767-09-1*) Am Acad Environ.

Anderson, William C., ed. see Colombo, Peter, et al.

Anderson, William C., ed. see Donnelly, James R., et al.

Anderson, William C., ed. see Hickman, H. Lanier.

Anderson, William C., ed. see Hickman, H. Lanier, Jr.

Anderson, William C., ed. see Holbrook, Timothy B., et al.

Anderson, William C., ed. see Holm, Francis W., et al.

Anderson, William C., ed. see Johnson, Paul, et al.

Anderson, William C., ed. see King, W. Christopher.

Anderson, William C., ed. see Kumar, Ashok & Vashisth, Sumant.

Anderson, William C., ed. see Loehr, Raymond, et al.

Anderson, William C., ed. see Magee, Richard S., et al.

Anderson, William C., ed. see Mann, Michael J., et al.

Anderson, William C., ed. see Rich, Linvil G.

Anderson, William C., ed. see Troxler, William, et al.

Anderson, William C., ed. see Weitzman, Leo, et al.

Anderson, William D., jt. auth. see Pietsch, Theodore W.

Anderson, William D., jt. auth. see Sanders, Albert E.

Anderson, William E., ed. Research for Electric Energy Systems. (Illus.). 97p. (Orig.). (C). 1992. pap. text 30.00 (*1-56806-003-3*) DIANE Pub.

Anderson, William F. Client/Server JavaScript for Netscape 3.0. LC 98-25175. 784p. (C). 1998. pap. text 49.99 (*0-13-719279-7*) P-H.

Anderson, William G. The Price of Liberty: The Public Debt of the American Revolution. LC 82-17420. (Illus.). 192p. reprint ed. pap. 59.60 (*0-7837-1769-5*, 204196600001) Bks Demand.

Anderson, William H. Qoheleth & Its Pessimistic Theology: Hermeneutical Struggles in Wisdom Literature. LC 97-12632. (Mellen Biblical Press Ser.: No. 54). 294p. 1997. text 89.95 (*0-7734-2429-6*) E Mellen.

Anderson, William H., jt. auth. see Stowers, Walter H.

Anderson, William J. The Architecture of Ancient Greece. LC 75-41010. reprint ed. 49.50 (*0-404-14725-9*) AMS Pr.

Anderson, William J., et al. The Architecture of Ancient Rome. LC 71-37326. (Select Bibliographies Reprint Ser.). 1977. reprint ed. 26.95 (*0-8369-6675-9*) Ayer.

Anderson, William K. James Connolly & the Irish Left. (Illus.). 160p. 1994. 24.95 (*0-7165-2522-4*, Pub. by Irish Acad Pr) Intl Spec Bk.

Anderson, William K., ed. Protestantism. LC 69-18918. (Essay Index Reprint Ser.). 1977. 20.95 (*0-8369-1018-4*) Ayer.

Anderson, William L., ed. Cherokee Removal: Before & After. LC 90-36731. (Brown Thrasher Bks.). (Illus.). 176p. 1992. pap. 15.95 (*0-8203-1482-X*) U of Ga Pr.

Anderson, William L. & Lewis, James A. A Guide to Cherokee Documents in Foreign Archives. LC 83-4636. (Native American Bibliography Ser.: No. 4). 770p. 1983. 42.00 (*0-8108-1630-X*) Scarecrow.

Anderson, William M. The Detroit Tigers: A Pictorial Celebration of the Greatest Moments in Tigers' History. rev. ed. LC 98-24774. 1999. 34.95 (*0-8143-2826-1*) Wayne St U Pr.

***Anderson, William M.** Immunology. (Integrated Medical Sciences Ser.). 1998. pap. text 22.95 (*1-889325-34-1*) Fence Crk Pubng.

Anderson, William M. The Rocky Mountain Journals of William Marshall Anderson: The West in 1834. Morgan, Dale L. & Harris, Eleanor T., eds. LC 66-25064. (Huntington Library Publications). 438p. reprint ed. pap. 135.80 (*0-608-13999-8*, 205553900028) Bks Demand.

— Teaching Music with a Multicultural Approach. LC 91-193013. (Illus.). 102p. (Orig.). reprint ed. pap. 31.70 (*0-608-20263-0*, 207152200012) Bks Demand.

Anderson, William M. & Campbell, Patricia S. Multicultural Perspectives in Music Education. 2nd ed. (Illus.). 436p. 1996. pap. 48.00 (*1-56545-097-3*, 1509) MENC.

Anderson, William M. & Lawrence, Joy E. Integrating Music into the Classroom. 356p. (C). 1985. pap. write for info. (*0-534-03933-2*) Wadsworth Pub.

— Integrating Music into the Classroom. 2nd ed. 430p. (C). 1991. pap. 34.95 (*0-534-14520-5*) Wadsworth Pub.

— Integrating Music into the Elementary Classroom. 3rd ed. LC 94-29737. (Illus.). 516p. 1994. pap. 48.50 (*0-534-23736-3*) Wadsworth Pub.

— Integrating Music into the Elementary Classroom. 4th ed. LC 97-29330. (Music Ser.). (C). 1997. 76.95 (*0-534-52596-2*) Wadsworth Pub.

Anderson, William M. & Moore, Marvelene C., eds. Making Connections: Multicultural Music & the National Standards. 128p. 1998. 30.00 incl. audio compact disk (*1-56545-108-2*) MENC.

— Making Connections: Multicultural Music & the National Standards. 144p. 1998. pap. 20.00 incl. audio compact disk (*1-56545-106-6*, 1510) MENC.

Anderson, William R. Introduction to the Music of Brahms: Music Book Index. 78p. 1993. reprint ed. lib. bdg. 59.00 (*0-7812-9588-2*) Rprt Serv.

Anderson, William R. B. & Taylor, Jesse F. Chronic Pain: Taking Command of Our Healing: Understanding the Emotional Trauma Underlying Chronic Pain. (Illus.). 130p. (Orig.). 1995. pap. 10.95 (*0-9642979-0-6*) New Energy Pr.

Anderson, William S. The Art of the Aeneid. Betts, John H., ed. (Illus.). 121p. (C). 1989. reprint ed. pap. 12.00 (*0-86516-237-9*) Bolchazy-Carducci.

— Barbarian Play: Plautus' Roman Comedy. (Robson Classical Lectures). 194p. 1996. pap. text 19.95 (*0-8020-7941-5*) U of Toronto Pr.

— Barbarian Play: Plautus' Roman Comedy. LC 93-93219. (Robson Classical Lectures: Vol. 1). 194p. 1996. text 50.00 (*0-8020-2815-2*) U of Toronto Pr.

Anderson, William S., ed. Ballentine's Law Dictionary. 25.00 (*0-327-12700-7*) LEXIS Pub.

Anderson, William S., ed. Ovid's Metamorphoses, Bks. 6-10. LC 74-160488. (American Philological Association Ser.: Vol. 2). 540p. 1972. pap. 19.95 (*0-8061-1456-8*) U of Okla Pr.

Anderson, William S., ed. Why Horace? A Collection of Interpretations. LC 98-45905. 1999. pap. 30.00 (*0-86516-417-7*) Bolchazy-Carducci.

***Anderson, William S., ed.** Why Horace? A Collection of Interpretations. LC 98-45905. 1999. 60.00 (*0-86516-434-7*) Bolchazy-Carducci.

Anderson, William S., ed. Ovid's Metamorphoses, Bks. 1-5. LC 96-11064. 584p. 1997. text 49.95 (*0-8061-2845-3*) U of Okla Pr.

— Ovid's Metamorphoses: Books 1-5, Bks. 1-5. LC 96-11064. (Illus.). 584p. 1998. pap. 21.95 (*0-8061-2894-1*) U of Okla Pr.

Anderson, William S. & Frederick, Mary P. Selections from Ovid's Metamorphoses. 1987. pap. text 10.47 (*0-582-36748-4*, 72524) Longman.

Anderson, William T. Laura Wilder of Mansfield: Laura Ingalls Wilder Biography. (Laura Ingalls Wilder Family Ser.). (Illus.). 36p. 1982. pap. 3.95 (*0-9610088-1-4*) Anderson Publns.

— Laura's Rose: The Story of Rose Wilder Lane. (Laura Ingalls Wilder Family Ser.). (Illus.). 48p. (Orig.). 1984. pap. text 3.95 (*0-9610088-3-0*) Anderson Publns.

— The Masonic Token: A Gift Book. 300p. 1997. reprint ed. pap. 19.95 (*0-7661-0044-8*) Kessinger Pub.

— The Story of the Ingalls. (Laura Ingalls Wilder Family Ser.). (Illus.). 40p. (Orig.). 1993. pap. text 3.95 (*0-9610088-0-6*) Anderson Publns.

— The Story of the Wilders. (Laura Ingalls Wilder Family Ser.). (Illus.). 32p. 1983. pap. 3.95 (*0-9610088-2-2*) Anderson Publns.

— A Wilder in the West: Eliza Jane's Story of a Lady Homesteader. (Laura Ingalls Wilder Family Ser.). (Illus.). 44p. 1985. pap. 3.95 (*0-9610088-4-9*) Anderson Publns.

Anderson, William T., jt. auth. see Hargrave, Terry D.

Anderson, William T., ed. see Wilder, Laura Ingalls & Lane, Rose W.

Anderson, Winifred, et al. Guiandose por la Intrincada Senda de la Educacion Especial (Negotiating the Special Education Maze) Una Guia para Padres y Maestros (A Guide for Parents & Teachers) 3rd ed. Brawn, Nellie L., tr. (SPA.). 312p. (C). 1999. pap. 16.95 (*1-890627-07-0*) Woodbine House.

— Negotiating the Special Education Maze: A Guide for Parents & Teachers. 3rd ed. LC 96-37779. 264p. (Orig.). 1997. pap. 16.95 (*0-933149-72-7*) Woodbine House.

Anderson, Winn. A Rather Special Place. 173p. 1993. pap. 19.95 (*0-8464-4655-3*) Beekman Pubs.

Anderson, Winston. The Law of Caribbean Marine Pollution, Vol. IELP. LC 97-2541. 1997. 210.00 (*90-411-0662-6*) Kluwer Law Intl.

***Anderson, Wood Powell.** Perennial Weeds: Characteristics & Identification of Selected Herbaceous Species. LC 99-35933. (Illus.). 244p. 1999. 64.95 (*0-8138-2520-2*) Iowa St U Pr.

Anderson, Wood Powell. Weed Science: Principles. 2nd ed. (Illus.). 655p. (C). 1983. text 67.00 (*0-314-69632-6*) West Pub.

— Weed Science: Principles & Applications. 3rd ed. LC 95-30901. 410p. (C). 1995. 103.95 (*0-314-04627-5*) West Pub.

Anderson, Wynema. Using WordPerfect 5.0-5.1: Applications. (DF - Computer Applications Ser.). 1992. mass mkt. 27.95 (*0-538-61755-1*) S-W Pub.

Anderson, Wynema & Golightly, Stacey. Business Computer Applications for Reinforcement. LC 96-37656. 1997. write for info. (*0-538-71739-4*) S-W Pub.

— WordPerfect for Windows: Easy Reference Guide. LC 93-4307. 1994. mass mkt. 7.95 (*0-538-62675-5*) S-W Pub.

— WordPerfect 6.0 DOS Applications for Reinforcement. large type ed. 1995. 96.50 (*0-614-09617-0*, L-83778-00) Am Printing Hse.

Anderson-Yates, Marcia, jt. auth. see Henry, Janice S.

Anderson, Zane, jt. auth. see Coyle, Neva.

Andersonn, Barbara, jt. auth. see Andersonn, Christopher.

Andersonn, Christian, jt. auth. see Hemmert, Martin.

***Andersonn, Christopher & Andersonn, Barbara.** Will You Still Love Me If I Don't Win: A Guide for Parents of Young Athletes. LC 99-56883. 2000. pap. 12.95 (*0-87833-172-7*) Taylor Pub.

Andersonn, Lennart, jt. ed. see Harling, G.

Anderssen, Claes-Axel, et al. Road Maintenance & Regravelling Using Labour-Based Methods (ROMAR) Workbook. (Orig.). 1996. pap. 19.50 (*1-85339-349-5*, Pub. by Intermed Tech) Stylus Pub VA.

— Road Maintenance & Regravelling Using Labour-Bated Methods (ROMAR) Handbook. (Orig.). 1996. pap. 25.00 (*1-85339-348-7*, Pub. by Intermed Tech) Stylus Pub VA.

Anderssen, Lia. The Angel of Lust. 1998. pap. 9.95 (*1-897809-48-4*) Silver Moon.

— Bush Slave. 1998. pap. text 8.95 (*1-897809-37-9*) Silver Moon.

Andersson, et al. Bioceramics, 3 vols. 1996. pap. 469.00 (*0-08-042687-5*, Pergamon Pr) Elsevier.

Andersson, Ake E., et al, eds. Economics of Space & Time: Scientific Papers of Tsnu Puu. LC 97-29383. (Illus.). xviii, 266p. 1997. 89.95 (*3-540-63315-4*) Spr-Verlag.

***Andersson, Ake E. & Andersson, David E.** Gateways to the Global Economy. LC 00-37619. 416p. (C). 2000. text 110.00 (*1-84064-389-7*) E Elgar.

Andersson, Ake E. & Sahlin, Nils-Eric. The Complexity of Creativity. LC 96-50128. (Synthese Library Ser.). 1996. lib. bdg. 77.00 (*0-7923-4346-8*) Kluwer Academic.

Andersson, Ake E., et al. Government for the Future: Unification, Fragmentation & Regionalism, Vol. 238. LC 97-12804. (Contributions to Economic Analysis Ser.: 238). 334p. 1997. 129.50 (*0-444-82767-6*) Elsevier.

Andersson, Anders. Runes. LC 98-208104. (Illus.). 72p. 1998. 9.95 (*1-85368-948-3*, Pub. by New5 Holland) Sterling.

Andersson, Billie V. Simple & Classic: Greek Elegance for the Everyday Cook. (Illus.). 88p. (Orig.). 1991. pap. 10.00 (*0-9615556-0-2*) Andesign.

Andersson, Bo. The Lund Model. LC 97-32156. (Cambridge Monographs on Particle Physics, Nuclear Physics & Cosmology: No. 4). (Illus.). 484p. (C). 1998. text 130.00 (*0-521-42094-6*) Cambridge U Pr.

Andersson, Bo & Schade, Richard E., eds. Cultura Baltica: Literary Culture Around the Baltic 1600-1700. LC 97-176967. (Studia Germanistica Upsaliensia: No. 35). 147p. (Orig.). 1996. pap. 39.50 (*91-554-3806-7*, Pub. by Uppsala Univ Acta Univ Uppsaliensis) Coronet Bks.

Andersson, C. A., et al. Business Management: Handbook & Workbook. (Improve Your Construction Business Ser.: Vol. 3). 128p. 1996. pap. 24.75 (*92-2-109314-X*) Intl Labour Office.

— Business Management Handbook. LC 97-123558. (Improve Your Construction Business Ser.: No. 3). 1996. 13.50 (*92-2-108755-7*) Intl Labour Office.

— Pricing & Bidding Handbook. LC 94-223507. (Improve Your Construction Business Ser.: No. 1). 1996. 13.50 (*92-2-108738-7*) Intl Labour Office.

— Site Management Handbook. (Improve Your Construction Ser.: No. 2). 1996. 13.50 (*92-2-108753-0*) Intl Labour Office.

Andersson, C. Dean. I Am Dracula. 352p. 1998. mass mkt. 4.99 (*0-8217-6025-4*, Zebra Kensgtn) Kensgtn Pub Corp.

— Mortal Kombat: Shango's Thunder. 1996. mass mkt. 4.50 (*1-57297-149-5*) Blvd Books.

***Andersson, C. Dean.** Warrior Beast. (Bloodsong Saga Ser.: Vol. 3). 250p. 2000. pap. 14.95 (*1-930709-01-3*) HAWK Pubng Grp.

— Warrior Rebel. (Bloodsong Saga Ser.: Vol. 2). 263p. 2000. pap. 14.95 (*1-930709-00-5*) HAWK Pubng Grp.

— Warrior Witch. (Bloodsong Saga Ser.: Vol. 1). 218p. 2000. pap. 14.95 (*0-9673131-9-8*) HAWK Pubng Grp.

Andersson, Christian. Peasant or Proletarian? Wage Labour & Peasant Economy during Industrialization (The Algerian Experience) (Illus.). 236p. 1985. pap. text 51.00 (*91-22-00771-7*) Coronet Bks.

Andersson, Christina. The Children of Maria: Adolescent Substance Abusers, Their Families & Schooling. (Uppsala Studies in Education: No. 46). 136p. (Orig.). 1993. pap. 41.50 (*91-554-3086-4*, Pub. by Uppsala Universitet) Coronet Bks.

Andersson, Claes. On the Use of Two-Phase Sampling in Estimation of Parameters in Domains Where Data Contain Misclassification & Measurement Errors. LC 95-109317. (Studia Statistica Upsaliensia: No. 3). 120p. (Orig.). 1994. pap. 34.50 (*91-554-3305-7*) Coronet Bks.

— Poems in Our Absence. Bruce, Lennart & Bruce, Sonja, trs. from FIN. LC 94-1387. 128p. (Orig.). 1994. pap. 12.95 (*0-9638398-5-3*) Bonne Chance.

— What Became Words. Barkan, Stanley H., ed. Lesser, Rika, tr. (Review Chapbook Ser.: No. 22: Swedish Poetry 2). (ENG & SWE.). 32p. 1991. 15.00 (*0-89304-890-9*); pap. 5.00 (*0-89304-891-7*) Cross-Cultrl NY.

A

A

— What Became Words: A Bilingual Edition. Lesser, Rika, tr. from FIN. (Classics Ser.: No. 135). (ENG & SWE.). 120p. (Orig.). 1997. pap. 11.95 (*1-55713-302-6*) Sun & Moon CA.

— What Became Words: Mini Book. Barkan, Stanley H., ed. Lesser, Rika, tr. (Review Chapbook Ser.: No. 22: Swedish Poetry 2). (ENG & SWE.). 32p. 1991. 15.00 (*0-89304-892-5*); pap. 5.00 (*0-89304-893-3*) Cross-Cultrl NY.

***Andersson, David E. & Poon, Jessie P. H.** Asia Pacific Transitions. LC 00-31112. 2000. write for info. (*0-312-23652-2*) St Martin.

Andersson, David E., jt. auth. see Andersson, Ake E.

Andersson, Dee Dee. The Mastiff: The Aristocratic Guardian. Luther, Luana, ed. LC 98-70320. (Pure-Bred Ser.). (Illus.). 312p. 1999. 28.50 (*0-944875-51-3*, Pub. by Doral Pub) Natl Bk Netwk.

Andersson, Fredrik. The International Diffusion of New Chemical Entities: A Cross-National Study of the Determinants of Differences in Drug Lag. (Linkoping Studies in Arts & Sciences: No. 51). (Illus.). 272p. (Orig.). 1990. pap. 78.00 (*91-7870-578-9*) Coronet Bks.

Andersson, G., ed. Rationality in Science & Politics. (Boston Studies in the Philosophy of Science Ser.: No. 79). 320p. 1985. pap. text 79.50 (*90-277-1953-5*) Kluwer Academic.

Andersson, G., jt. auth. see Kapadia, R.

Andersson, Gunnar B. Criticism & the History of Science: Kuhn's, Lakato's, & Feyrabend's Criticisms of Critical Rationalism. LC 94-26308. (Philosophy of History & Culture Ser.: Vol. 13).Tr. of Kritik und Wissenschaftgeschichte. 1994. 81.00 (*90-04-10050-4*) Brill Academic Pubs.

Andersson, Gunnar B., ed. Rationality in Science & Politics. (Boston Studies in the Philosophy of Science: 79). 312p. 1984. lib. bdg. 139.50 (*90-277-1575-0*) Kluwer Academic.

Andersson, Gunnar B. & McNeill, T. W. Lumbar Spine Syndromes. (Illus.). 250p. 1989. 118.00 (*0-387-82070-1*) Spr-Verlag.

Andersson, Gunnar B. J., et al. Occupational Orthopaedics. Nordin, Margareta, ed. (Illus.). 688p. (C). (gr. 13). 1996. text 125.00 (*0-8016-7984-2*, 07984) Mosby Inc.

Andersson, Hans. Strindberg's Master Olof & Shakespeare. (Essays & Studies on English Language & Literature: Vol. 11). 1974. reprint ed. 25.00 (*0-8115-0209-0*) Periodicals Srv.

Andersson, Hans, et al, eds. Visions of the Past: Trends & Traditions in Swedish Medieval Archaeology. (Lund Studies in Medieval Archaeology: No. 19). (Illus.). 808p. 1997. pap. 77.50 (*91-7209-082-0*, Pub. by Almqvist Wiksell) Coronet Bks.

Andersson, Hans & Wienberg, Jes, eds. The Study of Medieval Archaeology: European Symposium, June 1990. (Lund Studies in Medieval Archaeology: No. 13). (Illus.). 387p. (Orig.). 1993. pap. 70.00 (*91-22-01557-4*) Coronet Bks.

Andersson, Hilary. Mozambique: A War Against the People. LC 92-8426. 1992. text 49.95 (*0-312-08406-4*) St Martin.

***Andersson, Hjakan & Britton, Tom.** Stochastic Epidemic Models & Their Statistical Analysis. LC 00-41911. (Lecture Notes in Statistics). 2000. pap. write for info. (*0-387-95050-8*) Spr-Verlag.

Andersson, Ingvar. A History of Sweden. Hannay, Carolyn, tr. from SWE. LC 75-8717. (Illus.). 461p. 1975. reprint ed. lib. bdg. 35.00 (*0-8371-8044-9*, ANHS, Greenwood Pr) Greenwood.

Andersson, Johan G. Children of the Yellow Earth: Studies in Prehistoric China. 1976. lib. bdg. 59.95 (*0-8490-1602-9*) Gordon Pr.

Andersson, L. Flora of Ecuador No. 221: Musaceae. (Opera Botanica Series B). 86p. 1985. pap. 25.00 (*91-86344-30-7*, Pub. by Coun Nordic Pubs) Balogh.

— A Provisional Checklist of Neotropical Rubiaceae. (Scripta Botanica Belgica Ser.: Vol. 1). 199p. 1992. 64.00 (*90-72619-06-4*, Pub. by Natl Botanic Grdn Belgium) Balogh.

Andersson, L. & Dempster, L. T. Flora of Ecuador Nos. 162, 162(22), & 162(23) Rubiaceae-Introduction, Rubiaceae-Anthospermeae, Rubiaceae-Rubieae. (Opera Botanica Series B). 36p. 1993. pap. 28.00 (*87-88702-66-9*, Pub. by Coun Nordic Pubs) Balogh.

Andersson, L. & Taylor, C. M. Flora of Ecuador No. 162(1-4) Rubiaceae - Cinchoneae - Coptosapelteae. (Opera Botanica Series B). 112p. 1994. pap. 62.00 (*87-88702-72-3*, Pub. by Coun Nordic Pubs) Balogh.

Andersson, L., jt. auth. see Liden, M.

Andersson, Lennart. A Revision of the Genus Cinchona (Rubiaceae-Cinchoneae) LC 97-24318. (Memoirs of the New York Botanical Garden Ser.: Vols. 80 & 81). 1997. 24.00 (*0-89327-416-X*) NY Botanical.

— Soviet Aircraft & Aviation, 1917-1941. (Illus.). 352p. 1995. 59.95 (*1-55750-770-8*) Naval Inst Pr.

***Andersson, Magnus.** Change & Continuity in Poland's Environmental Policy. LC 99-50122. (Environment & Policy Ser.). 1999. write for info. (*0-7923-6051-6*) Kluwer Academic.

Andersson, Malte. Sexual Selection. LC 93-33276. (Monographs in Behavior & Ecology). 624p. 1994. pap. text 27.95 (*0-691-00057-3*, Pub. by Princeton U Pr) Cal Prin Full Svc.

Andersson, Mari, ed. see Daugherty, Jackson.

Andersson, Mats. Topics in Complex Analysis. LC 96-11793. (Universitext Ser.). 157p. 1996. pap. 32.50 (*0-387-94754-X*) Spr-Verlag.

Andersson, Max. Pixy. 72p. 1993. pap. 11.95 (*1-56097-131-2*) Fantagraph Bks.

Andersson, S., et al, eds. Chronic Non-Cancer Pain: Assessment & Practical Management. 1987. pap. text 55.50 (*0-7462-0047-1*) Kluwer Academic.

Andersson, S. I. Non-Abelian Cohomology Theory & Applications to the Yang-Mills & Backlund Problems. 280p. 1998. text 54.00 (*9971-5-0013-2*) World Scientific Pub.

Andersson, S. I. & Doebner, H. D., eds. Non-Linear Partial Differential Operators & Quantization Procedures. (Lecture Notes in Mathematics Ser.: Vol. 1037). 334p. 1983. 42.95 (*0-387-12710-0*) Spr-Verlag.

Andersson, S. I. & Lapidus, Michel L. Progress in Inverse Spectral Geometry. LC 97-35734. (Trends in Mathematics Ser.). (ENG & FRE.). 1997. write for info. (*3-7643-5755-X*) Birkhauser.

Andersson-Skog, Lena & Krantz, Olle, eds. Institutions in the Transport & Communications Industries: State & Private Actors in the Making of Institutional Patterns, 1850-1990. LC 98-27714. (Illus.). 359p. 1999. 40.00 (*0-88135-201-2*, Sci Hist) Watson Pub Intl.

Andersson, Staffan, jt. auth. see Cunningham-Andersson, Una.

Andersson, Stefan. In Quest of Certainty: Bertrand Russell's Search for Certainty in Religion & Mathematics. (Studia Philosophiae Religiosis: No. 18). 192p. (Orig.). 1994. pap. 45.50 (*91-22-01607-4*) Coronet Bks.

Andersson, Stellan, ed. see Myrdal, Gunnar.

***Andersson, Sten.** Biomathematics: Structure & Dynamics in Molecular Biology. LC 99-48245. 1999. write for info. (*0-444-50273-4*) Elsevier.

Andersson, Sten, jt. auth. see Hyde, Bruce.

Andersson, Sten, jt. auth. see Jacob, Michael.

Andersson, Stig I., ed. Analysis of Dynamical & Cognitive Systems: Proceedings of Advanced Course, Stockholm, Sweden, August 1993. LC 94-46541. (Lecture Notes in Computer Science Ser.: Vol. 888). 1995. write for info. (*0-387-58843-4*) Spr-Verlag.

Andersson, Stig I., et al, eds. Dynamical Systems: Theory & Applications. LC 93-17904. 300p. 1993. text 109.00 (*981-02-1468-5*) World Scientific Pub.

— Theory & Control of Dynamical Systems: Applications to Systems in Biology, Huddinge, Stockholm, 4-10 August, 1991. LC 92-10268. 340p. 1992. text 93.00 (*981-02-0895-2*) World Scientific Pub.

Andersson, Theodore M. A Preface to the 'Nibelungenlied' LC 86-28064. viii, 307p. 1987. 45.00 (*0-8047-1362-6*) Stanford U Pr.

***Andersson, Theodore M. & Gade, Kari E.** Morkinskinna: The Earliest Icelandic Chronicle of the Norwegian Kings. LC 99-43299. (Islandica Ser.). 2000. 75.00 (*0-8014-3694-X*) Cornell U Pr.

Andersson, Theodore M. & Miller, William I. Law & Literature in Medieval Iceland: 'Ljosvetninga Saga' & 'Valla-Ljots Saga' LC 88-38439. 352p. 1989. 45.00 (*0-8047-1532-7*) Stanford U Pr.

Andersson, Thomas. Foreign Direct Investment in Competing Host Countries: A Study of Taxation & Nationalization. 208p. (Orig.). 1989. pap. 98.00 (*91-7258-278-2*) Coronet Bks.

— Managing Trade Relations in the New World Economy. LC 93-9831. 192p. (C). (gr. 13). 1993. 85.00 (*0-415-09568-9*) Routledge.

Andersson, Thomas, ed. Japan: A European Perspective. LC 92-38068. 176p. 1993. text 69.95 (*0-312-09146-X*) St Martin.

Andersson, Thomas, et al. Multinational Restructuring, Internationalization & Small Economies: The Case of Sweden. LC 95-12518. 208p. (C). (gr. 13). 1995. 85.00 (*0-415-12286-4*) Routledge.

***Andersson, Ulf L.** Humanware - Practical Usability Engineering. (Illus.). 242p. 1999. spiral bd. 19.50 (*1-55212-280-8*, 99-0031, Pub. by Tra3fford) Trafford Pub.

Anderst, Lee, compiled by. Weaver's & PWC Index, 1981-1995. 45p. (Orig.). 1996. pap. 9.95 (*0-9646391-1-4*) XRX Inc.

Anderton, Basil. Fragrance among Old Volumes: Essays & Idylls of a Book Lover. LC 67-30171. (Essay Index Reprint Ser.). 1977. 19.95 (*0-8369-0153-3*) Ayer.

— Sketches from a Library Window. LC 68-16903. (Essay Index Reprint Ser.). 1977. 18.95 (*0-8369-0154-1*) Ayer.

Anderton, Bill. Guide to Ancient Britain. 224p. 1995. pap. 12.95 (*0-572-01620-4*, Pub. by Foulsham UK) Assoc Pubs Grp.

— Life Cycles: The Astrology of Inner Space & Its Application to the Rhythms of Life. LC 90-49411. (Illus.). 160p. 1999. reprint ed. pap. 9.95 (*0-87542-021-4*) Llewellyn Pubns.

— Meditation for Every Day. 1999. pap. 6.95 (*0-7499-1871-3*, Pub. by Piatkus Bks) London Brdge.

— Meditation for Everyday. LC 97-109285. 250p. (Orig.). 1996. pap. text 14.95 (*0-7499-1485-8*, Pub. by Piatkus Bks) London Brdge.

Anderton, Charles H., jt. ed. see Isard, Walter.

Anderton, Craig. Do-it-Yourself Projects for Guitarists: 35 Useful, Inexpensive Electronic Projects to Help Unlock Your Instrument's Potential. (Illus.). 170p. 1995. pap. 19.95 (*0-87930-359-X*) Miller Freeman.

— The Electronic Musician's Dictionary. LC 88-176371. (Illus.). 120p. 1988. pap. 9.95 (*0-8256-1125-3*, AM67166) Music Sales.

— Electronic Projects for Musicians. rev. ed. (Illus.). 140p. cd-rom 21.95 (*0-8256-9502-3*, AM32707) Music Sales.

— Home Recording for Musicians. 2nd rev. ed. LC 97-122588. (Illus.). 256p. 1996. pap. 24.95 (*0-8256-1500-3*, AM931370) Omnibus NY.

— MIDI for Musicians. 105p. 1986. pap. 17.95 (*0-8256-1050-8*) Omnibus NY.

— Multieffects for Musicians. LC 95-140669. (Illus.). 144p. (Orig.). (C). 1995. pap. 19.95 (*0-8256-1447-3*, AM 91245, Amsco Music) Music Sales.

— Power Sequencing with Master Tracks Pro-Pro 4. (Illus.). 112p. 1990. pap. 19.95 (*0-8256-2585-8*, AM76613) Music Sales.

Anderton, Craig, jt. ed. see Keatinge, Carolyn.

Anderton, Douglas L., et al. The Population of the United States. 3rd ed. LC 96-48990. (Illus.). 736p. 1997. 150.00 (*0-684-82774-3*) Free Pr.

***Anderton, Frances.** You Are Here: The Jerde Partnership International. 240p. 1999. pap. 75.00 (*0-7148-3830-6*) Phaidon Pr.

Anderton, Frances & Chase, John. Las Vegas. LC 98-127802. (Architecture in Context Ser.). (ENG, FRE & GER., Illus.). 80p. 1997. pap. 9.95 (*3-89508-288-0*, 810091) Konemann.

— Las Vegas. (Architecture Guides Ser.). (Illus.). 320p. 1998. pap. 5.95 (*3-89508-639-8*, 520204) Konemann.

Anderton, Johana G. Sewing for 20th Century Dolls, Vol. 2. Vol. 2. (Illus.). 264p. 1998. 24.95 (*0-87588-514-4*, H5457) Hobby Hse.

Anderton, Mark. Encyclopedia of Petroliana: Identifications & Price Guide. LC 98-87377. (Illus.). 256p. 1999. pap. 29.95 (*0-87341-694-5*, PETI) Krause Pubns.

Anderton, Mary. A Great Way to Get Wealth: How to Start & Build a Network Marketing Business from Your Home. LC 93-72227. (Illus.). 300p. 1993. pap. 19.95 (*1-56883-011-4*) Colonial Pr AL.

Anderton, Richard L., et al. Design of Wastewater & Stormwater Pumping Stations. LC 93-6136. (Manual of Practice Ser.: Vol. FD-4). 1993. 70.00 (*1-881369-36-6*) Water Environ.

Anderton, Stephen. Garden Answers: Perennial Problems Solved. LC 98-70044. 270p. 1999. pap. 14.95 (*1-86105-117-4*, Pub. by Robson Bks) Parkwest Pubns.

***Anderton, Stephen.** Rejuvenating a Garden. LC 99-33053. (Illus.). 160p. 2000. 25.00 (*1-57959-057-8*, SOMA) BB&T Inc.

Andes, Karen. The Complete Book of Fitness: Mind, Body, Spirit. Fitness Magazine Staff, ed. LC 98-25292. 496p. 1998. pap. 24.95 (*0-609-80155-4*, Crown) Crown Pub Group.

— A Woman's Book of Balance: Finding the Spiritual, Physical, Emotional Center. LC 99-45745. 224p. 1999. pap. 15.95 (*0-399-52567-X*, Perigee Bks) Berkley Pub.

— A Woman's Book of Power. LC 97-23333. 256p. 1998. pap. 14.00 (*0-399-52372-3*, Perigee Bks) Berkley Pub.

— A Woman's Book of Strength. LC 94-29498. 288p. (Orig.). 1995. pap. 14.00 (*0-399-51899-1*, Perigee Bks) Berkley Pub.

Andes, Karrie K., jt. auth. see Norman, Sandra J.

Andia, Ysabel De, see De Andia, Ysabel.

Andic, Martin, ed. see Finch, Henry L.

Andic, Suphan & Cao Garcia, Ramon I. La Reforma Contributiva en Puerto Rico, 1994: Estudio Tecnico. 588p. 1996. 60.00 (*0-8477-0276-6*) U of PR Pr.

***Andidora, Ronald W.** Iron Admirals: Naval Leadership in the Twentieth Century, 194. LC 99-49147. (Contributions in Military Studies Ser.). 208p. 2000. write for info. (*0-313-31266-4*, Greenwood Pr) Greenwood.

Andima, Susan, ed. General Topology & Applications. (Lecture Notes in Pure & Applied Mathematics Ser.: Vol. 134). (Illus.). 440p. 1991. pap. text 195.00 (*0-8247-8552-5*) Dekker.

— Papers on General Topology & Applications: Eleventh Summer Conference at the University of Southern Maine. LC 96-51642. (Annals of the New York Academy of Sciences Ser.). 492p. 1997. pap. 110.00 (*1-57331-091-3*) NY Acad Sci.

Andima, Susan, et al, eds. Papers on General Topology & Applications: Eleventh Summer Conference at University of Southern Maine, Vol. 806. LC 96-51642. 492p. 1997. 110.00 (*1-57331-090-5*) NY Acad Sci.

— Papers on General Topology & Applications: Seventh Conference at the University of Wisconsin. LC 93-48367. (Annals Ser.: Vol. 704). 367p. 1993. pap. 160.00 (*0-89766-720-4*) NY Acad Sci.

Anding, Robert, et al. Clinical Diagnosis & Management of Eating Disorders. Hall, Richard C., ed. LC 89-64482. 334p. 1990. text 50.00 (*0-9625272-0-3*) Ryandic Pub.

Andino, Alberto. Frutos De Mi Trasplante. LC 79-52356. (Coleccion Caniqui). (SPA.). 102p. 1980. pap. 5.95 (*0-89729-230-8*) Ediciones.

— Pero el Diablo Metio el Rabo: Profana y Atortoradora Novelita Velivola en 22 Trances y 1 Introito. LC 85-70433. (Coleccion Caniqui). (SPA.). 97p. (Orig.). 1985. pap. 8.95 (*0-89729-370-3*) Ediciones.

Andino, Sandra, ed. Indigenous Land Rights Reader: Five Hundred Years of Resistance. 97p. (Orig.). 1992. pap. 7.00 (*0-910082-18-9*) Am Fr Serv Comm.

Andioc, Rene, ed. see Fernandez de Moratin, Leandro.

Andis, Kitrell. Bookstore. 150p. 1996. pap. 10.00 (*1-885710-19-4*) Geekspeak Unique.

— Hearts Make Fists: Nineteen Poems. 36p. 1994. pap. 5.00 (*1-885710-08-9*) Geekspeak Unique.

Andis, Kitrell, et al. PlopLop No. 3: An "Antholozine" of Poetry, Prose & Artwork. 32p. 1993. pap. 5.00 (*1-885710-02-X*) Geekspeak Unique.

— PlopLop No. 4: An "Antholozine" of Poetry, Prose & Artwork. 48p. 1993. pap. 6.00 (*1-885710-03-8*) Geekspeak Unique.

— PlopLop No. 5: An "Antholozine" of Poetry, Prose & Artwork. Clark, John, ed. & illus. by. Quinet, Bart, illus. 50p. 1994. pap. 5.00 (*1-885710-05-4*) Geekspeak Unique.

— PlopLop No. 6: An "Antholozine" of Poetry, Prose & Artwork. 50p. 1995. pap. 5.00 (*1-885710-11-9*) Geekspeak Unique.

— PlopLop No. 7: An "Antholozine" of Poetry, Prose & Artwork. Clark, John, ed. (Illus.). 50p. 1995. pap. 5.00 (*1-885710-14-3*) Geekspeak Unique.

— Ploplop No. 10: An "Antholozine" of Poetry, Prose, & Artwork. Clark, John, ed. & illus. by. 50p. 1998. pap. 5.00 (*1-885710-23-2*) Geekspeak Unique.

Andis, Kitrell, ed. see Dawson, Fielding, et al.

Andis, Mary F., et al. CBEST with Software. 272p. 1998. pap. 29.95 incl. disk (*0-87891-122-7*) Res & Educ.

Andison, Mabelle L., tr. see Bergson, Henri.

***Andite Corporation Staff.** El Libro de Urantia. 5th ed. (SPA.). lxvi, 2097p. 1999. reprint ed. 24.95 (*1-883395-03-8*) Andite IL.

Andite Corporation Staff, ed. El Libro de Urantia. 1998. pap. 24.95 (*1-883395-01-1*) Andite IL.

***Andite Corporation Staff, ed.** El Libro de Urantia. 6th ed. (SPA.). lxvi, 2097p. 1999. reprint ed. pap. 19.95 (*1-883395-02-X*) Andite IL.

Andlaw, R. J. & Rock, W. P. A Manual of Paediatric Dentistry. 4th ed. LC 96-39210. (C). 1998. pap. text 49.50 (*0-443-05372-3*) Church.

Andleigh, Prabhat K. UNIX System Architecture. 320p. (C). 1989. 44.99 (*0-13-949843-5*) P-H.

— UNIX System Architecture, System V, Version IV. 2nd ed. 270p. (C). 2002. pap. 35.00 (*0-13-948423-X*) P-H.

Andleigh, Prabhat K. & Gretzinger, Michael A. Distributed Object Oriented Data-Systems Design. 448p. (C). 1992. text 48.00 (*0-13-174913-7*) P-H.

Andleman, Bob, jt. auth. see Dunlap, Albert J.

Andler, Daniel. Facets of Rationality. LC 94-45238. 394p. 1995. 29.95 (*0-8039-9225-4*) Sage.

Andler, Daniel, et al, eds. Facets of Rationality. LC 94-45238. 1995. text 29.95 (*81-7036-453-1*) Sage.

Andler, Edward C. The Complete Reference Checking Handbook: Smart, Fast, Legal Ways to Check Out Job Applicants. LC 97-32352. 240p. 1998. 29.95 (*0-8144-0405-7*) AMACOM.

— Winning the Hiring Game: Smart Interviewing & Effective Reference Checking are Vital to Survival in the 90's. LC 91-66848. 174p. (Orig.). 1992. pap. 15.95 (*0-9623414-2-8*) Smith Collins.

Andler, Sten F., ed. see International Workshop on Active and Real-Time Database Systems.

Andleton, Bobbie & Decoteau, Al E. Encyclopedia of Cockatiels. (Illus.). 400p. Date not set. 50.00 (*0-88839-414-4*) Hancock House.

Ando, Albert, et al, eds. Monetary Policy in Our Times. (Illus.). 356p. 1985. 42.00 (*0-262-01082-8*) MIT Pr.

— Saving & the Accumulation of Wealth: Essays on Italian Household & Government Saving Behavior. LC 93-34758. 424p. (C). 1994. text 54.95 (*0-521-45208-2*) Cambridge U Pr.

Ando, Albert, et al. The Structure & Reform of the U. S. Tax System. 184p. 1985. 25.00 (*0-262-01086-0*) MIT Pr.

Ando, Arnell. Transformational Tarot. 96p. 1995. pap. 24.95 (*0-9649386-3-4*) Ink Well.

Ando, Cheryl, tr. see Suwa, Shigeo & Suwa, Shizuko.

***Ando, Clifford.** Imperial Ideology & Provincial Loyalty in the Roman Empire. LC 99-41499. (Classics & Contemporary Thought : Vol. 6). (Illus.). 422p. 2000. 60.00 (*0-520-22067-6*, Pub. by U CA Pr) Cal Prin Full Svc.

Ando, D. J. & Pellatt, M. G. Fine Chemicals/Electronics Industry, II, No. 88. 1991. 143.00 (*0-85186-887-8*) CRC Pr.

Ando, D. J., jt. auth. see Stuart, Barbara.

Ando, David J., ed. see Thomas, Michael J.

Ando, Hirofumi, jt. auth. see Ness, Gayl D.

Ando, Hisao. Paleobiological Study of the Late Triassic Bivalve Honotis from Japan. (Illus.). 148p. 1987. 44.50 (*0-86008-416-7*, Pub. by U of Tokyo) Col U Pr.

Ando, I. & Asakura, Tetsuo. Solid State NMR of Polymers. LC 97-53184. (Studies in Physical & Theoretical Chemistry: 84). 1000p. 1998. write for info. (*0-444-82924-5*) Elsevier.

Ando, Isal & Webb, Graham A. Theory of NMR Parameters. 1984. text 125.00 (*0-12-056820-9*) Acad Pr.

Ando, M. Modern Imaging of the Alimentary Tube. Margulis, Alexander R., ed. LC 97-13066. (Medical Radiology Ser.). (Illus.). 350p. 1997. 159.00 (*3-540-61441-9*) Spr-Verlag.

Ando, M., et al, eds. Medical Applications of Synchrotron Radiation. (Illus.). xii, 200p. 1998. 99.00 (*4-431-70229-6*) Spr-Verlag.

Ando, Mitsuko. A Two-Head Bird: One Life. Yokogawa, Ken'ichi, tr. from JPN. Orig. Title: Gumyo No Tori. 171p. (Orig.). 1996. pap. 14.95 (*0-9651914-0-0*) Daishinkai Pr.

Ando, Nicholas. Igbo-English, English-Igbo Dictionary & Phrasebook. 190p. 1998. pap. 11.95 (*0-7818-0661-5*) Hippocrene Bks.

Ando, Nisuke. Surrender, Occupation, & Private Property in International Law: An Evaluation of U. S. Practice in Japan. (Oxford Monographs in International Law). (Illus.). 224p. 1991. text 72.00 (*0-19-825411-3*) OUP.

Ando, Sadao, ed. A Descriptive Syntax of Christopher Marlowe's Language. 721p. 1976. 115.00 (*0-86008-162-1*, Pub. by U of Tokyo) Col U Pr.

Ando, T. Metaphysics: A Critical Survey of Its Meaning. 2nd enl. ed. 158p. 1974. pap. text 57.00 (*90-247-0007-8*, Pub. by M Nijhoff) Kluwer Academic.

Ando, T. & Fukuyama, H., eds. Anderson Localization. (Proceedings in Physics Ser.: Vol. 28). (Illus.). 376p. 1988. 84.95 (*0-387-19122-4*) Spr-Verlag.

Ando, T. & Gohberg, I., eds. Operator Theory & Complex Analysis. LC 92-36581. (Operator Theory, Advances & Applications Ser.: Vol. 59). x, 460p. 1992. 117.50 (*0-8176-2824-X*) Birkhauser.

Ando, T., jt. auth. see Fukuyama, H.

Ando, Tadao, et al, eds. Plant Nutrition for Sustainable Food Production & Environment. LC 98-122134. 982p. 1998. text 468.00 (*0-7923-4796-X*) Kluwer Academic.

Ando, Tsuneya, et al, eds. Mesoscopic Physics & Electronics. LC 97-43404. (Nanoscience & Technology Ser.). (Illus.). xii, 270p. 1997. 69.95 (*3-540-63587-4*) Spr-Verlag.

An Asterisk (*) at the beginning of an entry indicates that the title is appearing for the first time.

Ando, W. Photoxidation of Organosulfur Compounds, Vol. 1. (Sulfur Reports). 80p. 1981. pap. text 87.00 (*3-7186-0073-0*) Gordon & Breach.

Ando, Y. Concert Hall Acoustics. (Electrophysics Ser.: Vol. 17). (Illus.). 170p. 1985. 79.00 (*0-387-13505-7*) Spr-Verlag.

Ando, Yoichi. Architectural Acoustics: Blending Sound Sources, Sound Fields, & Listeners. Beyer, R., ed. LC 97-33261. (Modern Acoustics & Signal Processing Ser.). 224p. 1998. 49.95 (*0-387-98333-3*) Spr-Verlag.

Ando, Yoichi & Noson, Dennis, eds. Music & Concert Hall Acoustics: Conference Proceedings from MCHA, 1995. (Illus.). 448p. 1996. text 95.00 (*0-12-059555-9*) Acad Pr.

Ando, Yukie. A Comparison of Keats's Hyperion & the Fall of Hyperion. LC 95-16580. (European University Studies, Ser. 14, Anglo-Saxon Language & Literature: Vol. 282). (Illus.). 197p. 1995. pap. 42.95 (*3-631-47901-8*) P Lang Pubng.

Andocides, jt. auth. see Antiphon.

Andoh, Anthony K. The Science & Romance of Selected Herbs Used in Medicine & Religious Ceremony. LC 86-617535. (Illus.). 324p. 1986. 27.95 (*0-916299-01-5*) North Scale Co.

— The Science & Romance of Selected Herbs Used in Medicine & Religious Ceremony. (Illus.). 324p. 1991. pap. 19.95 (*0-916299-24-4*) North Scale Co.

Andoh, Anthony K. & Sichen, Kali. Astrological Symbols & African Gods. (Illus.). 1995. pap. 14.95 (*0-916299-05-8*) North Scale Co.

Andoh, Anthony K., ed. see Eleburuibon, Ifayemi.

Andoh, Anthony K., ed. & intro. see Enti, Albert A.

Andoh, Benjamin & Marsh, Stephen. Civil Remedies. LC 96-41977. (Illus.). 448p. 1997. 91.95 (*1-85521-788-0*, Pub. by Dartmth Pub); pap. 38.95 (*1-85521-792-9*, Pub. by Dartmth Pub) Ashgate Pub Co.

Andoh, Toshiwo, et al, eds. Molecular Biology of DNA Topoisomerases & Its Application to Chemotherapy: Proceedings of the International Symposium on DNA Topoisomerases in Chemotherapy, Nagoya, Japan, November 18-20, 1991. 400p. 1992. lib. bdg. 239.00 (*0-8493-4970-2*, QP616) CRC Pr.

Andokides. On the Mysteries. 236p. 1989. pap. text 40.00 (*0-19-814692-2*) OUP.

Andolenko, S. Badges of Imperial Russia, Including Military, Civil & Religious. Werlich, Robert, tr. (Illus.). 1983. lib. bdg. 50.00 (*0-911200-02-9*) Quaker.

Andolfi, Maurizio. Family Therapy: An Interactional Approach. LC 78-27741. 186p. 1979. 37.50 (*0-306-40200-9*, Plenum Trade) Perseus Pubng.

Andolfi, Maurizio & Haber, Russell, eds. Please Help Me with This Family: Using Consultants As Resources in Family Therapy. LC 94-25864. 294p. 1995. text 35.95 (*0-87630-748-9*) Brunner-Mazel.

Andolfi, Maurizio & Zwerling, Israel, eds. Dimensions of Family Therapy. LC 79-25485. 296p. reprint ed. pap. 91.80 (*0-7837-0692-8*, 204102500019) Bks Demand.

Andolfi, Maurizio, et al. The Myth of Atlas: Families & the Therapeutic Story. LC 89-32190. 256p. 1989. text 35.95 (*0-87630-549-4*) Brunner-Mazel.

***Andolina, Valerie F.** Critical Thinking for Working Students. (C). 2001. pap. 30.00 (*0-7668-2253-2*) Delmar.

— Successful Study Skills. (C). 2002. text 22.50 (*0-7668-2255-9*) Delmar.

Andolina, Valerie F., et al. Mammographic Imaging: A Practical Guide. 2nd ed. 416p. text 56.00 (*0-7817-1696-9*) Lppncott W & W.

Andolsek, Kathryn M. Obstetric Care: Standards of Prenatal, Intrapartum, & Postpartum Management. LC 89-8359. (Illus.). 293p. 1989. pap. text 46.50 (*0-8121-1250-4*) Lppncott W & W.

Andolsen, Barbara H. Daughters of Jefferson, Daughters of Bootblacks: Racism & American Feminism. LC 86-86. xiv, 130p. (Orig.). 1986. pap. text 13.95 (*0-86554-205-8*, P023) Mercer Univ Pr.

— Good Work at the Video Display Terminal: A Feminist Ethical Analysis of Changes in Clerical Work. LC 89-4884. 224p. 1989. text 32.00 (*0-87049-618-2*) U of Tenn Pr.

— The New Job Contract: Economic Justice in an Age of Insecurity. LC 98-35073. 164p. 1998. pap. 15.95 (*0-8298-1272-5*) Pilgrim OH.

Andolsen, Barbara H., et al, eds. Women's Consciousness, Women's Conscience: A Reader in Feminist Ethics. LC 85-50124. 340p. 1985. 24.95 (*0-86683-958-5*, AY8540) Harper SF.

Andolshek, Margaret D. & Hobbs, Horton H. The Entocytherid Ostracod Fauna of Southeastern Georgia. LC 85-14437. (Smithsonian Contributions to Zoology Ser.: No. 424). 47p. reprint ed. pap. 30.00 (*0-608-16198-5*, 202713600054) Bks Demand.

Andomus & Powell. Flight into the Source: The Andomus Material I. LC 90-80751. 192p. (Orig.). 1990. pap. 8.95 (*0-9625738-0-9*) Gala Pub.

— Stations in Life: The Andomus Material Three. Krueger, ed. 224p. (Orig.). 1992. pap. 12.95 (*0-9625738-2-5*) Gala Pub.

Andon, Mark. Super Calcium Miracle: The Calcium Citrate Malate Breakthrough. LC 98-25969. 208p. 1998. per. 15.00 (*0-7615-1456-2*) Prima Pub.

Andonian, Aramais, tr. see Lewis, Clarissa.

Andonian, Cathleen C., ed. The Critical Response to Samuel Beckett, 30. LC 97-44888. (Critical Responses in Arts & Letters Ser.: Vol. 30). 440p. 1998. lib. bdg. 79.50 (*0-313-28910-7*, Greenwood Pr) Greenwood.

Andonian, Hagop. Beginner's Armenian. (Hippocrene Beginner's Language Ser.). (ARM & ENG.). 216p. 1999. pap. 14.95 (*0-7818-0723-9*) Hippocrene Bks.

Andonov, Nicole. Portraits Exposed. LC 95-90214. 80p. 1995. pap. 6.95 (*0-9646048-0-9*) Westonian.

Andonovic, Ivan & Uttamchandani, Deepak, eds. Principles of Modern Optical Systems, Vol. 1. fac. ed. LC 89-304. (Artech House Telecommunications Library). (Illus.). 624p. 1989. reprint ed. pap. 193.50 (*0-608-00943-1*, 206173500011) Bks Demand.

Andor, L. Southern African Political History: A Chronology of Key Political Events from Independence to Mid-1997. LC 98-44996. 936p. 1999. lib. bdg. 145.00 (*0-313-30247-2*) Greenwood.

***Andor, Laszlo.** Hungary on the Road to the European Union: Transition in Blue. LC 99-43101. 216p. 2000. 65.00 (*0-275-96394-2*, Praeger Pubs) Greenwood.

Andor, Lotte, jt. auth. see Leyens, Erich.

***Andorka, Catherine.** Once upon a Secret. 216p. 1999. pap. 7.99 (*1-893108-17-1*) Neighbrhd Pr Pubng.

Andorka, Rudolf, et al, eds. A Society Transformed: Hungary in Time-Space Perspective. LC 99-26032. 206p. (C). 1999. pap. 27.95 (*963-9116-49-1*) Ctrl Europ Univ.

Andors, Phyllis. The Unfinished Liberation of Chinese Women, 1949-1980. LC 81-48323. 224p. reprint ed. pap. 69.50 (*0-8357-3963-5*, 205705900004) Bks Demand.

Andors, Stephen, ed. Workers & Workplaces in Revolutionary China. LC 76-53710. (China Book Project Ser.). 439p. reprint ed. pap. 136.10 (*0-608-18119-6*, 203277100081) Bks Demand.

Andouard, Loeiz. Geriadur Iwerzhoneg-Brezhoneg: Dictionnaire Irlandais-Breton. (BRE.). 212p. 1987. pap. 32.95 (*0-7859-8162-4*, 2868630251) Fr & Eur.

Andover, James J., ed. see Berman, Ben.

Andow, David A., ed. Ecological Interactions & Biological Control. LC 97-6907. 352p. (C). 1997. text 79.00 (*0-8133-8758-2*, Pub. by Westview) HarpC.

Andra, Wilfried. Magnetism in Medicine. 512p. 1998. 205.00 (*3-527-40221-7*, Wiley-VCH) Wiley.

Andracki, Stanislaw. Immigration of Orientals into Canada with Special Reference to Chinese. Daniels, Roger, ed. LC 78-54806. (Asian Experience in North America Ser.). (Illus.). 1979. lib. bdg. 23.95 (*0-405-11262-9*) Ayer.

Andradas, Carlos & Ruiz, Jesus M. Algebraic & Analytic Geometry of Fans. LC 95-1556. (Memoirs Ser.: No. 553). 117p. 1995. pap. text 35.00 (*0-8218-2612-3*, MEMO/115/553) Am Math.

Andradas, Carlos, et al. Constructible Sets in Real Geometry. LC 95-51853. (Series of Modern Surveys in Mathematics: Vol. 33). (Illus.). 289p. 1996. 119.00 (*3-540-60451-0*) Spr-Verlag.

Andrade. Science Without Walls. 512p. (C). 1998. pap. text 30.00 (*0-536-00673-3*, Pub. by P-H) S&S Trade.

Andrade, Albert, jt. auth. see Tishman, Shari.

***Andrade, Allan.** Leopoldville Troopship Disaster in Memoriam. unabridged ed. LC 99-75433. (Illus.). VIII, 72p. 1999. pap. 19.95 (*0-9675950-0-2*) A Andrade.

Andrade, Allan. S. S. Leopoldville Disaster. LC 97-22938. (Illus.). 288p. 1997. pap. 21.95 (*1-890309-54-0*) Tern Bk Co.

Andrade, Ana, et al. Las Piedras. (SPA.). 24p. 1995. pap. text 5.00 (*0-435-08856-4*, 08856) Heinemann.

Andrade, Angela. Investigacion Arqueologica de los Antrosoles de Araracuara. (SPA., Illus.). 104p. 1986. pap. 8.50 (*1-877812-26-9*, BR024) UPLAAP.

Andrade, Barbara. Gott Mitten unter Uns. 486p. 1998. 67.95 (*3-631-32437-5*) P Lang Pubng.

Andrade, Camilo De, see Hardin, Jerry W. & De Andrade, Camilo.

Andrade, Carla-Krystin. Stay in Control: How to Cope & Still Get the Job You Really Want. 212p. 1994. pap. text 14.95 (*1-880030-27-6*) DBM Pub.

Andrade, Carla-Krystin & Clifford, Paul. Outcome Oriented Therapeutic Massage. 400p. pap. text 34.95 (*0-7817-1743-4*) Lppncott W & W.

***Andrade, Chittaranjan.** Psychiatry: Current Trends & Practices. 328p. 2000. text 29.95 (*0-19-564985-0*) OUP.

Andrade, Cynthia C., et al. Marketing Guide for Money Market Mutual Funds. 82p. 1996. write for info. (*0-913755-35-4*) IBC Financial.

Andrade, Dale. Luzon: The United States Army Campaigns of World War 2. 31p. 1996. pap. 1.75 (*0-16-045115-9*) USGPO.

Andrade, Dale, jt. auth. see Conboy, Kenneth J.

Andrade, Edward N. Sir Isaac Newton. LC 79-15162. 140p. 1979. reprint ed. lib. bdg. 62.50 (*0-313-22022-0*, ANNE, Greenwood Pr) Greenwood.

Andrade, Ernest, Jr. Unconquerable Rebel: Robert W. Wilcox & Hawaiian Politics, 1880-1903. (Illus.). 376p. 1996. text 39.95 (*0-87081-417-6*) Univ Pr Colo.

Andrade, Fernando A. El Desarrollo de la Tecnologia. (Ciencia Para Todos Ser.). (SPA.). pap. 6.99 (*968-16-2538-2*, Pub. by Fondo) Continental Bk.

Andrade, Gene. Star Wisdom. Maceri, Eileen, ed. (Illus.). 153p. (Orig.). 1997. pap. 15.00 (*1-885757-10-7*) Pleiades Proj.

Andrade, Joseph D., ed. Hydrogels for Medical & Related Applications. LC 76-28170. (ACS Symposium Ser.: No. 31). 1976. 32.95 (*0-8412-0338-5*) Am Chemical.

— Hydrogels for Medical & Related Applications: A Symposium Sponsored by the Division of Polymer Chemistry, Inc. at the 170th Meeting of the American Chemical Society, Chicago, Ill., August 27-28, 1975. LC 76-28170. (ACS Symposium Ser.: No. 31). (Illus.). 373p. reprint ed. pap. 115.70 (*0-7837-1963-9*, 205244100001) Bks Demand.

— Medical & Biological Engineering in the Future of Health Care. LC 94-8413. (Illus.). 176p. (Orig.). (C). 1994. pap. 24.95 (*0-87480-454-X*) U of Utah Pr.

— Polymer Surface Dynamics. LC 87-35942. (Illus.). 190p. (C). 1988. text 102.00 (*0-306-42788-5*, Kluwer Plenum) Kluwer Academic.

— Surface & Interfacial Aspects of Biomedical Polymers Vol. 1: Surface Chemistry & Physics. (Illus.). 486p. (C). 1985. text 156.00 (*0-306-41741-3*, Kluwer Plenum) Kluwer Academic.

— Surface & Interfacial Aspects of Biomedical Polymers Vol. 2: Protein Adsorption. LC 84-26601. (Illus.). 338p. reprint ed. pap. 104.80 (*0-608-09369-6*, 205411400002) Bks Demand.

Andrade, Juan, et al. The Tuxedo System: A Guide to Constructing Distributed Business Applications. 496p. (C). 1996. 49.95 (*0-201-63493-7*) Addison-Wesley.

Andrade, Lucia M. De, see De Andrade, Lucia M., ed.

Andrade, M. J., ed. Folk-Lore from the Dominican Republic. LC 33-10559. (American Folklore Society Memoirs Ser.: Vol. 23). 1972. reprint ed. 45.00 (*0-527-01075-8*) Periodicals Srv.

Andrade, Magdalena, jt. auth. see Terrell, Tracy D.

Andrade, Manuel J. Quileute. pap. 15.00 (*0-685-71707-0*) J J Augustin.

— Quileute Texts. fac. ed. (Columbia University Contributions to Anthropology Ser.: Vol. 12). 223p. (C). 1931. reprint ed. pap. text 23.75 (*1-55567-683-9*) Coyote Press.

— Quileute Texts. LC 75-82358. (Columbia Univ. Contributions to Anthropology Ser.: Vol. 12). reprint ed. 27.50 (*0-404-50562-7*) AMS Pr.

Andrade, Marcel. El Cid. 48p. 1992. pap. 6.75 (*0-8442-7119-5*) NTC Contemp Pub Co.

Andrade, Marcel, adapted by. El Diario de Cristobal Colon. LC 97-69173.Tr. of Diary of Christopher Columbus. (SPA., Illus.). 160p. 1997. pap. 17.19 (*0-8442-7249-3*, 72493) NTC Contemp Pub Co.

Andrade, Marcel C. Adventuras del Ingenioso Hidalgo Don Quijote de la Mancha: An Adaptation for Intermediate & Advanced Students. abr. ed. LC 94-143809. (SPA & ENG., Illus.). 192p. 1993. pap. 15.31 (*0-8442-7361-9*, 73619, Natl Textbk Co) NTC Contemp Pub Co.

Andrade, Marcel C. El Burlador de Sevilla. 96p. 1990. pap. 8.40 (*0-8442-7356-2*) NTC Contemp Pub Co.

— La Celestina. (SPA.). 56p. 1987. pap. 7.95 (*0-8442-7121-7*) NTC Contemp Pub Co.

— El Conde Lucanor. (SPA.). 64p. 1988. pap. 8.40 (*0-8442-7363-5*) NTC Contemp Pub Co.

Andrade, Mary & Fisher, Shirley I. Cinco de Mayo en San Jose. (SPA., Illus.). 115p. (Orig.). 1987. pap. 15.00 (*0-942607-00-7*) Hispanic Anglo Pubns.

Andrade, Mary J. Through the Eyes of the Soul, Day of the Dead in Mexico Vol. 1: Michoacan.Tr. of A Traves de los Ojos del Alma, Dia de Muertos en Mexico. (Illus.). 82p. 1998. pap. 26.90 (*0-9665876-0-X*) La Oferta Pubg.

— Through the Eyes of the Soul, Day of the Dead in Mexico Vol. II: Oaxaca.Tr. of A Traves de los Ojos Del Alma, Dia de Muertos en Mexico-Oaxaca. (Illus.). iv, 84p. 1999. 26.90 (*0-9665876-1-8*) La Oferta Pubg.

***Andrade, Mary J.** Through the Eyes of the Soul, Day of the Dead in Mexico Vol. 3: Mexico City, Mixquic & Morelos, 5. (Through the Eyes of the Soul, Day of the Dead in Mexico: 3).Tr. of Traves de los Ojos Den Alma, Dia de Muertos en Mexico. (Illus.). iv, 100p. (YA). 2000. pap. 26.90 (*0-9665876-2-6*) La Oferta Pubg.

Andrade, Sally J., et al. Metodos Cualitativos para La Evaluacion de Programas: Un Manual par Programas de Salud, Planificacion Familiar Y Servicios Sociales. (SPA., Illus.). 146p. (Orig.). 1987. pap. text 3.00 (*0-317-59568-7*) Pathfinder Fund.

Andrade, T. Soy, see Soy Andrade, T.

Andrade, Victor. My Missions for Revolutionary Bolivia, 1944-1962. LC 76-6656. (Pitt Latin American Ser.). 217p. reprint ed. 67.30 (*0-8357-9758-9*, 201786300009) Bks Demand.

Andrade-Watkins, Claire, jt. auth. see Cham, Mbye.

Andrae, Christian. Ferdinand Christian Baur als Prediger: Exemplarische Interpretationen zu Seinem Handschriftlichen Predigtnachlass. (Arbeiten zur Kirchengeschichte Ser.: Band 61). (GER.). x, 554p. (C). 1993. lib. bdg. 152.35 (*3-11-013920-0*) De Gruyter.

Andrae, Gunilla. Industry in Ghana: Production Form & Spatial Structure. 181p. 1981. write for info. (*91-7106-189-4*, Pub. by Nordic Africa) Transaction Pubs.

Andrae, Gunilla & Beckman, Bjorn. Industry Goes Farming: The Nigerian Raw Material Crisis & the Case of Textiles & Cotton. (Research Report Ser.: No. 80). 68p. 1987. 10.95 (*91-7106-273-4*, Pub. by Nordic Africa) Transaction Pubs.

— Union Power in the Nigerian Textile Industry: Labour Regime & Adjustment. LC 98-33329. 317p. 1999. write for info. (*0-7658-0601-0*) Transaction Pubs.

Andrae, Johann V. The Chemical Wedding of Christian Rosenkreutz. Holmes, J. D., ed. Foxcroft, E., tr. from DUT. 1991. reprint ed. pap. 9.95 (*1-55818-145-8*) Holmes Pub.

Andrae, Tor. Mohammed: The Man & His Faith. Menzel, Theophil, tr. LC 79-160954. (Select Bibliographies Reprint Ser.). 1977. reprint ed. 25.95 (*0-8369-5821-7*) Ayer.

— Mohammed, Sein Leben und Sein Glaube. 160p. 1977. reprint ed. 32.00 (*3-487-06302-6*) G Olms Pubs.

Andrain, Charles F. Comparative Political Systems: Policy Performance & Social Change. LC 93-35886. (Comparative Politics Ser.). 256p. (C). (gr. 13). 1994. text 77.95 (*1-56324-280-X*); pap. text 32.95 (*1-56324-281-8*) M E Sharpe.

— Political Change in the Third World. 1988. 44.95 (*0-04-497029-3*); pap. 17.95 (*0-04-497030-7*) Routledge.

— Public Health Policies & Social Inequality. LC 97-48835. 292p. 1998. text 50.00 (*0-8147-0676-2*) NYU Pr.

Andrain, Charles F. & Apter, David E. Political Protest & Social Change: Analyzing Politics. LC 94-30981. 387p. (C). 1995. text 50.00 (*0-8147-0630-4*) NYU Pr.

— Political Protest & Social Change: Analyzing Politics. 387p. (C). 1995. pap. text 20.00 (*0-8147-0634-7*) NYU Pr.

Andraisk, F., jt. auth. see Blanchard, Edward.

Andrande, Mario De, see De Andrande, Mario.

Andranovich, Gregory D. & Riposa, Gerry. Doing Urban Research. (Applied Social Research Methods Ser.: Vol. 33). (Illus.). 160p. (C). 1993. text 42.00 (*0-8039-3988-4*) Sage.

Andras, Adam. The Behavior & Simplicity of Finite Moore Automata. LC 97-184179. 200p. 1996. pap. 110.00 (*963-05-7319-9*, Pub. by Akade Kiado) St Mut.

Andras, L. T. How to Say It in Hungarian: Hungarian Phrasebook. 8th ed. (ENG & HUN.). 238p. 1987. pap. 12.95 (*0-7859-7455-5*, 9631804763) Fr & Eur.

Andras, Tor. In the Garden of Myrtles: Studies in Early Islamic Mysticism. 160p. 1996. pap. 16.95 (*0-614-21289-8*, 495) Kazi Pubns.

***Andras, Tor.** Mohammed, the Man & His Faith. LC 99-57349. (Illus.). 2000. pap. 6.95 (*0-486-41136-2*) Dover.

Andrasfai, Bela. Graph Theory: Flows, Matrices. 290p. 1991. 105.00 (*963-05-5585-9*, Pub. by Akade Kiado) St Mut.

— Graph Theory - Flows, Matrices. (Illus.). 284p. 1991. 130.00 (*0-85274-222-3*) IOP Pub.

Andrasick, Kathleen D. Opening Texts: Using Writing to Teach Literature. LC 90-30045. 208p. (Orig.). (C). (gr. 9). 1990. pap. text 21.50 (*0-435-08522-0*, 08522) Heinemann.

Andrasik, Frank, jt. ed. see Matson, Johnny L.

Andraski, Katherine. When the Plow Cuts. 64p. (Orig.). 1988. pap. 5.95 (*0-939395-11-8*) Thorntree Pr.

Andrassy, Gyula. Bismarck, Andrassy, & Their Successors. 1977. 20.95 (*0-8369-7101-9*, 7935) Ayer.

Andrassy, Richard J. Pediatric Surgical Oncology. Lampert, Richard, ed. LC 96-53983. (Illus.). 400p. 1998. text 165.00 (*0-7216-6378-8*, W B Saunders Co) Harcrt Hlth Sci Grp.

Andrassy, Richard J., jt. auth. see Ford, Edward G.

***Andrawis, Wadie M.** He Fell in the Crowd - Fool in Eternity. LC 99-91838. 96p. 2000. pap. 14.95 (*1-56167-597-0*) Am Literary Pr.

Andre, Alain. Fictions. Lire, Ecrire et en Parler. (Hatier Ser.). (FRE.). 153p. 1988. pap. 17.95 (*2-218-00979-X*) Schoenhof.

Andre, Alain, jt. auth. see Nony, Daniele.

Andre, Anthony D. & Hancock, P. A., eds. Pilot Workload Vol. 5, No. 1, 1995: Contemporary Issues: A Special Issue of "The International Journal of Aviation Psychology", Vol. 5, No. 1. 136p. 1995. pap. 20.00 (*0-8058-9953-7*) L Erlbaum Assocs.

Andre, Bernard, et al. French Made Easy - Beginners. LC 95-75593. 320p. 1995. 19.95 incl. audio (*0-8120-8352-0*) Barron.

Andre, Bruce, jt. auth. see Allen, Dodie.

Andre, Carl. Quincy Book. (Illus.). 1973. pap. write for info. (*1-879886-21-9*) Addison Gallery.

***Andre, Dom Emmanuel Marie.** Treatise on the Ecclesiastical Ministry.Tr. of Traite du Ministere Ecclesiastique. 40p. 2000. pap. 5.45 (*0-9639032-7-6*, Pub. by Sarto Hse) Spring Arbor Dist.

Andre-Driussi, Michael. Lexicon Urthus: A Dictionary for the Urth Cycle. LC 95-120345. (Illus.). 304p. 1994. 39.95 (*0-9642795-9-2*) Sirius Fiction.

Andre, Edouard F. Bromeliaceae Andre Anae. deluxe ed. Rothenberg, Michael, ed. Love, Doris, tr. from FRE. (Illus.). 211p. 1983. reprint ed. 150.00 (*1-878471-03-1*) Big Bridge Pr.

Andre, G. Gideon-Samson: And Other Judges of Israel. 52p. (Orig.). 1993. pap. 3.95 (*0-88172-132-8*) Believers Bkshelf.

— Jeremiah, the Prophet. (Let's Discuss It Ser.). pap. 3.95 (*0-88172-135-2*) Believers Bkshelf.

— Moses: The Man of God. 78p. (Orig.). 1988. pap. 2.50 (*0-88172-134-4*) Believers Bkshelf.

— Moses, the Man of God - Gideon, Samson (Combination) pap. 2.75 (*0-88172-133-6*) Believers Bkshelf.

Andre, Gunnel. Determining the Destiny: P. Q. D. in the Old Testament. (Coniectanea Biblica. Old Testament Ser.: No. 16). 264p. (Orig.). 1980. pap. text 49.00 (*91-40-04759-8*) Coronet Bks.

Andre, Hans-Jurgen. Empirical Poverty Research in a Comparative Perspective. LC 97-76950. 434p. 1998. text 84.95 (*1-85972-688-7*, Pub. by Ashgate Pub) Ashgate Pub Co.

Andre, J., et al, eds. Quantum Theory of Polymers. (NATO Advanced Study Institute Ser.). 1978. text 141.50 (*90-277-0870-3*) Kluwer Academic.

— Structured Documents. (Cambridge Series on Electronic Publishing). (Illus.). 232p. (C). 1989. text 80.00 (*0-521-36554-6*) Cambridge U Pr.

Andre, J., jt. ed. see Morris, R. A.

Andre, J. C., jt. ed. see Schmugge, T. J.

Andre, J. J., jt. auth. see Simon, J.

Andre, J. M., et al, eds. Quantum Chemistry Aided Design of Organic Polymers for Molecular Electronics: An Introduction to the Quantum Chemistry of Polymers & Its Applications. 392p. (C). 1991. text 74.00 (*981-02-0004-8*) World Scientific Pub.

— Recent Advances in the Quantum Theory of Polymers: Proceedings. (Lecture Notes in Physics Ser.: Vol. 113). 306p. 1980. pap. 26.00 (*3-540-09731-7*) Spr-Verlag.

Andre, Jacques, ed. see International Conference on Raster Imaging & Digital Typography Staff.

Andre, Jean, ed. The Sperm Cell. 1982. text 234.00 (*90-247-2784-7*) Kluwer Academic.

Andre, Jean, jt. auth. see Bofill, Ricardo.

Andre, Jean-Marie, jt. ed. see Ladik, Janos J.

Andre, Johann. Der Topfer: Hanau, 1773. Bauman, Thomas, ed. (German Opera Ser., 1770-1800). 375p. 1986. lib. bdg. 15.00 (*0-8240-8858-1*) Garland.

Andre, John. Major Andre's Journal: Eyewitness Accounts of the American Revolution. LC 67-29031. 128p. reprint ed. pap. 18.95 (*0-405-01103-2*) Ayer.

Andre, Joli. Business Etiquette Mastery. Dashefsky, Helene, ed. (Illus.). 64p. 1997. pap. 12.95 (*0-9635392-2-1*) Sci-Tech Commun.

Andre, Jouette. Dictionnaire d'Orthographe et d'Expression Ecrite. (FRE.). 775p. 1994. 95.00 (*0-7859-9186-7*) Fr & Eur.

Andre, Judith. Rethinking College Athletics. 1992. pap. 22.95 (*1-56639-002-8*) Temple U Pr.

Andre, Judith & James, David N., eds. Rethinking College Athletics. 208p. 1991. 49.95 (*0-87722-716-0*) Temple U Pr.

Andre, Lee & Lipe, David. Decorative Painting for the Home: Creating Exciting Effects with Water-Based Paints. (Illus.). 144p. 1995. pap. 14.95 (*0-8069-0805-X*) Lark Books.

Andre-Levy, Michel, jt. auth. see De Clermont-Tonnerre, Alban.

Andre, Lyn. Good Morning World. LC 74-31663. (Illus.). 1975. 10.95 (*0-930422-06-6*) Dennis-Landman.

Andre, Marion. Verdict of Fate. 160p. 1995. pap. 10.95 (*0-88962-375-9*) Mosaic.

Andre, Michael. It As It. (Money for Food Press Ser.). (Illus.). 1992. pap. 3.00 (*0-934450-24-2*) Unmuzzled Ox.

— Jabbing the Oss Hole is High Comedy. 12p. 1981. pap. 4.95 (*0-934450-14-5*) Unmuzzled Ox.

— Letters Home. 24p. 1979. pap. 1.50 (*0-916696-14-6*) Cross Country.

Andre, Michael, ed. Unmuzzled Ox Anthology, No. 7. (Illus.). 78p. 1974. pap. 10.95 (*0-934450-13-7*) Unmuzzled Ox.

Andre, Michael & Wright, James, eds. Unmuzzled Ox Anthology, No. 13. 1980. pap. 19.95 (*0-934450-06-4*) Unmuzzled Ox.

Andre, Michael, et al. Canada: A to Don't. (Poets' Guide to Canada Ser.: No. XIV). (Illus.). 1996. pap. 8.95 (*0-934450-52-8*) Unmuzzled Ox.

Andre, Michael, ed. see Barnes, Djuna, et al.

Andre, Michael, ed. see Cage, John M. & Ginsberg, Allen.

Andre, Michael, ed. see Corso, Gregory.

Andre, Michael, ed. see Ginsberg, Allen & Creeley, Robert.

Andre, Michael, ed. see Goldoni, Carlo.

Andre, Michael, ed. see Pound, Ezra.

Andre, Michael, ed. see Seidman, Hugh.

Andre, Michael, ed. see Stafford, William, et al.

Andre, Michel L., ed. Solid State Lasers for Application to Inertial Confinement Fusion: Second Annual International Conference, Vol. 3047. LC 98-161686. 1140p. 1997. 158.00 (*0-8194-2460-9*) SPIE.

Andre, Rae. Homemakers: The Forgotten Workers. LC 80-21258. xii, 300p. (C). 1983. pap. 10.95 (*0-226-01994-2*) U Ch Pr.

— Homemakers, the Forgotten Workers. LC 80-21258. 311p. reprint ed. pap. 96.50 (*0-608-08042-X*, 206900700002) Bks Demand.

Andre, Rae & Forst, Peter J., eds. Researchers Hooked on Teaching: Noted Scholars Discuss the Synergies of Teaching & Research. (Foundations for Organizational Science Ser.). 332p. 1996. 45.00 (*0-7619-0622-3*); pap. 21.95 (*0-7619-0623-1*) Sage.

Andre, Richard, et al. Bullets & Steel: The Fight for the Great Kanawha Valley, 1861-1865. LC 95-72166. (Illus.). 200p. 1995. pap. 14.95 (*1-57510-006-1*) Pictorial Hist.

Andre, Richard, jt. auth. see Cohen, Stan B.

Andre, Robert. L' Enfant Miroir. (FRE.). 416p. 1979. pap. 12.95 (*0-7859-1902-3*, 2070371417) Fr & Eur.

***Andre, Serge.** What Does a Woman Want? LC 98-50494. (Lacanian Clinical Field Ser.). (Illus.). 360p. 1999. pap. 19.95 (*1-892746-28-X*, 4628X) Other Pr LLC.

Andre, Thomas J., Jr. Louisiana Wrongful Death & Survival Actions. 2nd ed. 500p. 1992. ring bd. 120.00 (*1-56257-954-1*, MICHIE) LEXIS Pub.

— Louisiana Wrongful Death & Survival Actions. 2nd ed. 1993. ring bd., suppl. ed. 60.00 (*0-685-74597-X*, MICHIE) LEXIS Pub.

***Andre, Ty.** On My Brother's Shoulders. LC 97-205475. 1998. 16.95 (*1-86254-378-X*) Wakefield Pr.

Andre, Wayne & Balsiger, David. Face in the Mirror. LC 93-72057. 360p. (Orig.). 1993. pap. 11.99 (*0-88270-678-0*) Bridge-Logos.

Andrea. The Human Record, Vol. 7. 3rd ed. LC 97-72433. 1997. pap. 27.87 (*0-395-87088-7*) HM.

Andrea, Alfred J. The Capture of Constantinople: The "Hystoria Constantinopolitana" of Gunther of Pairis. (Middles Ages Ser.). 192p. 1997. pap. text 16.50 (*0-8122-1586-9*) U of Pa Pr.

— The Human Record, 2 vols. (C). 1993. pap., teacher ed. 3.96 (*0-395-66874-3*) HM.

— The Human Record, 2 vols. 2nd ed. LC 93-78666. (C). 1993. pap. text 31.96 (*0-395-66872-7*) HM.

— The Human Record, 2 vols. 2nd ed. (C). 1995. pap. text 35.96 (*0-395-77390-3*) HM.

— The Human Record, 2 vols., Vol. 2. 2nd ed. (C). 1995. pap. text 32.36 (*0-395-77391-1*) HM.

— The Human Record, 2 vols., Vol. 3. 2nd ed. (C). 1995. pap. text 32.36 (*0-395-77392-X*) HM.

— The Human Record Vol. 2, 2 vols. 2nd ed. LC 93-78666. (C). 1993. pap. text 31.96 (*0-395-66873-5*) HM.

— The Medieval Record. 416p. (C). 1997. pap. text 25.16 (*0-395-71862-7*) HM.

Andrea, Alfred J. & Overfield, James H. The Human Record: Sources of Global History. (C). 1990. teacher ed. write for info. (*0-318-66706-1*) HM.

Andrea, Alfred J., ed. & tr. see Gunther, Von Pairis.

Andrea, I., jt. auth. see Perine, Robert.

Andrea, Mario & Dias, Oscar. Atlas of Rigid & Contact Endoscopy in Microlaryngeal Surgery: Technique & Atlas of Clinical Cases. LC 95-14124. (Illus.). 128p. 1995. text 105.00 (*0-7817-0328-X*) Lppncott W & W.

Andrea, Raymond. The Mystic Path. LC 87-63342. 163p. (Orig.). 1990. pap. 11.95 (*0-912057-56-4*, 502080) GLELJ AMORC.

— Technique of the Disciple. LC 36-35. 120p. 1935. pap. 12.95 (*0-912057-12-2*, 501870) GLELJ AMORC.

— The Technique of the Master. LC 35-11449. 174p. 1932. pap. 12.95 (*0-912057-10-6*, 501680) GLELJ AMORC.

Andrea, Raymund. Mystic Way. 142p. 1998. reprint ed. pap. 16.95 (*0-7661-0467-2*) Kessinger Pub.

— The Way of the Heart. rev. ed. LC 96-68945. 120p. 1996. pap. 9.95 (*0-912057-93-9*, 510494) GLELJ AMORC.

Andreacchi, Grace. Give My Heart Ease. LC 88-92640. 224p. 1989. 22.00 (*0-932966-90-X*) Permanent Pr.

Andreach, Robert J. Creating the Self in the Contemporary American Theatre. LC 97-36106. 1998. 39.95 (*0-8093-2178-5*) S Ill U Pr.

Andreadakis & Christoulas. Pretreatment of Industrial Wastewaters. (Water Science & Technology Ser.: No. 29). 354p. 1994. pap. 210.50 (*0-08-042542-9*, Pergamon Pr) Elsevier.

Andreadakis, A., ed. Pretreatment of Industrial Wastewaters II: Selected Proceedings of the 2nd IAWQ International Conference on Pretreatment of Industrial Wastewaters, Held in Athens, Greece, 16-18 October, 1996. 402p. 1997. pap. 255.00 (*0-08-043371-5*, Pergamon Pr) Elsevier.

Andreadakis, A. D., jt. ed. see Nicolaou, M. L.

Andreadakis, Katya B., jt. auth. see Berger, John.

Andreade, B., et al. Bildkatalog der Skulpteren des Vatikanischen Museums: Band I: Museo Chiaramonti, 3 pts. Liverani, P. & Mathea-Foertsch, M., eds. (GER.). 1106p. (C). 1994. lib. bdg. 646.15 (*3-11-013899-9*) De Gruyter.

Andreades, Andreas M. Geschichte der Griechischen Staatswirtschaft. xvii, 459p. 1965. reprint ed. 95.00 (*0-318-70852-3*) G Olms Pubs.

Andreades, Andreas M. & Finley, Moses, eds. A History of Greek Public Finance, Vol. I. enl. rev. ed. Brown, Carroll N., tr. LC 79-4959. (Ancient Economic History Ser.). 1979. reprint ed. lib. bdg. 40.95 (*0-405-12347-7*) Ayer.

Andreadis, Athena. To Seek Out New Life: The Biology of Star Trek. 1999. pap. 14.00 (*0-609-80421-9*, Three Riv Pr) Three Rivers Pr.

Andreadou, Ioanna. Software Fur Den Fremdsprachenunterricht. (Sprache und Computer Ser.: Bd. 6). (GER.). viii, 211p. 1987. write for info. (*3-487-07826-0*) G Olms Pubs.

Andreae, Bernard. The Art of Rome LC 79-313023. (ENG.). 655p. 1978. write for info. (*0-333-25689-1*) Macmillan.

— Farming, Development & Space: A World Agricultural Geography. (Illus.). 345p. 1981. 63.10 (*3-11-007632-2*) De Gruyter.

Andreae, Bernard, ed. Bildkatalog der Skulpturen des Vatikanischen Museums Vol. 2: Der Cortile Ottagono Im Belvedere. (GER., Illus.). 530p. (C). 1997. lib. bdg. 240.00 (*3-11-014629-0*) De Gruyter.

Andreae, Christine. Grizzly: A Mystery. (Worldwide Library Mysteries). 1996. per. 4.99 (*0-373-26202-7*, 1-26202-1, Wrldwide Lib) Harlequin Bks.

— A Small Target. (WWL Mystery Ser.). 1998. per. 4.99 (*0-373-26264-7*, 1-26264-1, Wrldwide Lib) Harlequin Bks.

— A Small Target, Vol. 1. LC 96-20047. 272p. 1996. 21.95 (*0-312-14543-8*, Thomas Dunne) St Martin.

***Andreae, Christine.** Smoke Eaters. LC 99-54818. 384p. 2000. text 24.95 (*0-312-25206-4*, Thomas Dunne) St Martin.

Andreae, Christine. Trail of Murder. LC 95-22349. (Mystery Ser.). 253p. 1995. per. 3.99 (*0-373-26183-7*, 1-26183-3, Wrldwide Lib) Harlequin Bks.

***Andreae, Christine.** When Evening Comes: The Education of a Hospice Volunteer. LC 00-40249. 256p. 2000. 23.95 (*0-312-26871-8*, Thomas Dunne) St Martin.

Andreae, Christopher. Lines of Country: An Atlas of Railway & Waterway History in Canada. (Illus.). 240p. 1996. 68.00 (*0-614-17726-X*, Pub. by Boston Mills) Genl Dist Srvs.

— Lines of Country: An Atlas of Railway & Waterway History in Canada. (Illus.). 240p. 1997. 68.00 (*1-55046-133-8*, Pub. by Boston Mills) Genl Dist Srvs.

Andreae, Christopher, contrib. by. Mary Newcomb. (Illus.). 200p. 1996. 80.00 (*0-85331-695-3*, Pub. by Lund Humphries) Antique Collect.

Andreae, Giles. Commotion in the Ocean. LC 98-15772. (Illus.). 32p. (J). (gr. k-5). 1998. 14.95 (*1-888444-39-8*) Little Tiger.

— The Lion Who Wanted to Love. LC 97-24542. (Illus.). 32p. (J). (ps-2). 1998. 14.95 (*1-888444-25-8*, 21023) Little Tiger.

***Andreae, Giles.** Love Is a Handful of Honey. LC 99-12767. (Illus.). 32p. (J). (ps-2). 1999. 14.95 (*1-888444-58-4*) Little Tiger.

***Andreae, Giles & Wojtowycz, David.** Christopher Crocodile's Jungly Jingles. (Illus.). (J). (ps-1). 2000. bds. 6.95 (*1-888444-67-3*) Little Tiger.

— Cock-a-Doodle-Doo! Barnyard Hullabaloo. (Illus.). 32p. (J). (ps-2). 2000. pap. 14.95 (*1-888444-75-4*) Little Tiger.

— Larry Lion's Rumbly Rhymes. (Illus.). (J). (ps-1). 2000. bds. 6.95 (*1-888444-68-1*) Little Tiger.

— Olive Octopus's Deep Sea Ditties. (Illus.). (J). (ps-1). 2000. bds. 6.95 (*1-888444-69-X*) Little Tiger.

Andreae, Giles & Wojtowycz, David. Rumble in the Jungle. LC 96-34423. (Illus.). 32p. (J). (ps-2). 1997. 14.95 (*1-888444-08-8*, 21009) Little Tiger.

***Andreae, Giles & Wojtowycz, David.** Sidney Shark's Seaside Shanties. (Illus.). (J). (ps-1). 2000. bds. 6.95 (*1-888444-70-3*) Little Tiger.

Andreae, J. P. Important Chapter from the History of Legal Interpretation. 159p. 1983. reprint ed. 39.50 (*0-89941-274-2*, 303100) W S Hein.

Andreae, John H. Associative Learning for a Robot Intelligence. LC 98-26352. 1998. 48.00 (*1-86094-132-X*, Pub. by Imperial College) World Scientific Pub.

Andreae, Meinrat D. & Schimel, David S., eds. Exchange of Trace Gases between Terrestrial Ecosystems & the Atmosphere. LC 89-22459. (Dahlem Workshop Reports - Life Sciences). 364p. 1990. 350.00 (*0-471-92551-9*) Wiley.

Andreani. Current Views of Insulin Receptors. 625p. 1982. 105.00 (*0-12-058620-7*) Acad Pr.

Andreani, Domenico, et al, eds. Diabetic Complications: Early Diagnosis & Treatment. LC 87-18967. (Wiley-Medical Publication). (Illus.). 330p. reprint ed. pap. 102.30 (*0-8357-8629-3*, 203505300092) Bks Demand.

Andreano, Michael. Families. LC 97-93669. 226p. (Orig.). 1997. pap. 12.00 (*1-57502-504-3*, P01500) Morris Pubng.

— For You, Mom. 232p. 1999. pap. 14.95 (*0-7414-0061-8*) Buy Books.

— I Want Mine. 230p. 1999. pap. 14.95 (*0-7414-0063-4*) Buy Books.

***Andreano, Michael.** Incendiary Mary... & Beyond: A Search for the Remains of a World War II Flier. 192p. 1999. pap. write for info. (*0-7392-0427-0*, PO3701) Morris Pubng.

Andreas. Rork No 1: Fragments. Bell & Lofficier, Jean-Marc, trs. from FRE. 54p. 1991. pap. 2.99 (*1-56163-016-0*) NBM.

Andreas. Rork No. 2: Passages. Lofficier, Jean-Marc, tr. 1991. pap. 2.99 (*1-56163-028-4*) NBM.

Andreas. Rork Vol. 3: The Graveyard of Cathedrals & Starlight. 96p. 1996. pap. 2.99 (*1-56163-150-7*) NBM.

Andreas, A. T. History of Chicago, from the Earliest Period to the Present Time, 3 vols. (Illus.). 1997. reprint ed. lib. bdg. 199.00 (*0-8328-5724-6*) Higginson Bk Co.

— History of Cook County, Illinois: From the Earliest Period to the Present Time (1884) with Biographical Sketches. (Illus.). 888p. 1997. reprint ed. lib. bdg. 89.50 (*0-8328-5728-9*) Higginson Bk Co.

Andreas, Alfred T. History of Chicago: From the Earliest Period to the Present Time, 3 vols., Set. LC 75-80. (Mid-American Frontier Ser.). (Illus.). 1975. reprint ed. 286.95 (*0-405-06846-8*) Ayer.

— History of Chicago: From the Earliest Period to the Present Time, 3 vols., Vol. 1. LC 75-80. (Mid-American Frontier Ser.). (Illus.). 1975. reprint ed. 84.95 (*0-405-06847-6*) Ayer.

— History of Chicago: From the Earliest Period to the Present Time, 3 vols., Vol. 2. LC 75-80. (Mid-American Frontier Ser.). (Illus.). 1975. reprint ed. 94.95 (*0-405-06848-4*) Ayer.

— History of Chicago: From the Earliest Period to the Present Time, 3 vols., Vol. 3. LC 75-80. (Mid-American Frontier Ser.). (Illus.). 1975. reprint ed. 111.95 (*0-405-06849-2*) Ayer.

Andreas, Barbara K. Vascular Flora of the Glaciated Allegheny Plateau Region of Ohio. LC 87-72905. (Bulletin New Ser.: Vol. 8, No. 1). (Illus.). 191p. 1989. pap. text 15.00 (*0-86727-104-3*) Ohio Bio Survey.

Andreas, Barbara K., et al. Ohio Endangered & Threatened Vascular Plants: Abstract of State-Listed Taxa. Burns, James F. & McCance, Robert M., Jr., eds. LC 84-620010. xii, 635p. (Orig.). 1984. pap. 10.00 (*0-931079-00-4*) Ohio Nat Res.

Andreas, Barbara K., jt. auth. see Snider, Jerry A.

Andreas, Brian. Going Somewhere Soon Vol. 3: Collected Stories & Drawings. (Illus.). 80p. 1995. pap. 20.00 (*0-9642660-2-4*) StoryPeople.

— Mostly True: Collected Stories & Drawings. 80p. 1993. pap. 20.00 (*0-9642660-0-8*) StoryPeople.

— Still Mostly True: Collected Stories & Drawings. 80p. 1994. pap. 20.00 (*0-9642660-1-6*) StoryPeople.

— Story People: Collected Stories & Drawings. (Illus.). 160p. 1997. pap. 12.95 (*0-9642660-4-0*) StoryPeople.

— Strange Dreams Vol. 4: Collected Stories & Drawings. (Illus.). 80p. 1996. pap. 20.00 (*0-9642660-3-2*) StoryPeople.

Andreas, Burton G. Experimental Psychology. 2nd ed. LC 78-171910. (Series in Psychology). (Illus.). 620p. reprint ed. pap. 192.20 (*0-608-30665-7*, 205548800022) Bks Demand.

Andreas, Carol. Nothing Is As It Should Be: A North American Woman in Chile. LC 76-7836. (Illus.). 140p. 1976. pap. text 16.95 (*0-87073-779-1*) Schenkman Bks Inc.

Andreas, Connirae. Change Your Mind & Keep the Change: Advanced Submodalities Intervention. 215p. 1987. pap. 13.50 (*0-911226-29-X*) Real People.

— Change Your Mind & Keep the Change: Neuro-Linguistic Programming. 215p. 1987. 19.00 (*0-911226-28-1*) Real People.

Andreas, Connirae, jt. auth. see Andreas, Steve.

***Andreas, Demetriou & Kazi, Smargada.** Unity & Modularity in the Mind & the Self: Studies on the Relationships Between Self-Awareness, Personality & Intellectual Development from Childhood to Adolescence. LC 00-38960. 2000. write for info. (*0-415-23399-2*) Routledge.

Andreas, E. L., ed. Selected Papers on Turbulence in a Refractive Medium. 720p. 1990. pap. 35.00 (*0-8194-0545-0*, VOL. MS25) SPIE.

Andreas, John C., ed. Energy-Efficient Electric Motors: Selection & Application. 2nd ed. (Electrical Engineering & Electronics Ser.: Vol. 78). (Illus.). 280p. 1992. text 85.00 (*0-8247-8596-7*) Dekker.

Andreas, Osborn. Henry James & the Expanding Horizon. LC 72-90463. 179p. 1970. reprint ed. lib. bdg. 45.00 (*0-8371-2133-7*, ANJH, Greenwood Pr) Greenwood.

***Andreas, Peter.** Border Games: Policing the U. S.-Mexico Divide. LC 00-24022. 2000. 26.00 (*0-8014-3796-2*) Cornell U Pr.

— The Illicit Global Economy & State Power. Friman, H. Richard, ed. 208p. 1998. pap. 22.95 (*0-8476-9304-X*) Rowman.

***Andreas, Peter.** The Illicit Global Economy & State Power. Friman, H. Richard, ed. 208p. 1998. 65.00 (*0-8476-9303-1*) Rowman.

Andreas-Salome, Lou. Fenitschka & Deviations: Two Novellas. Krahn, Dorothee E., tr. from GER. & intro. by. 94p. (C). 1990. lib. bdg. 31.00 (*0-8191-7649-4*) U Pr of Amer.

— Frederic Nietzsche: Science Humaines et Philosophie. 310p. 1971. pap. text 44.00 (*0-677-50405-5*) Gordon & Breach.

— Looking Back: Memoirs. (Illus.). 226p. 1995. pap. 12.95 (*1-56924-848-6*) Marlowe & Co.

— Rilke. Von der Lippe, A., ed. (Austrian-German Culture Ser.). 120p. 1995. 25.00 (*0-933806-30-2*) Black Swan CT.

Andreas-Salome, Lou, jt. auth. see Freud, Sigmund.

Andreas, Steve. Nlp: The New Technology. 1996. pap. 14.00 (*0-688-14619-8*, Quil) HarperTrade.

— Virginia Satir: The Patterns of Her Magic. LC 90-63678. 1991. pap. 14.95 (*0-8314-0076-5*) Sci & Behavior.

Andreas, Steve, ed. Is There Life Before Death? I Was an Imaginary Playmate in My Past Lives - Anthology. 1995. 19.95 (*0-911226-34-6*) Real People.

Andreas, Steve & Andreas, Connirae. Heart of the Mind: Engaging Your Inner Power to Change with Neuro-Linguistic Programming. 288p. 1989. 14.00 (*0-911226-30-3*); pap. 10.50 (*0-911226-31-1*) Real People.

Andreas, Tamara, jt. auth. see Connirae, Andreas.

***Andreasen, Alan, et al, eds.** Marketing & Public Policy Proceedings, Vol. 8. 117p. 1998. pap. 45.00 (*0-87757-272-0*) Am Mktg.

Andreasen, Alan A. Marketing Social Change: Changing Behavior to Promote Health, Social Development, & the Environment. (Nonprofit Sector, Public Administration & Health Ser.). 367p. 1995. text 30.95 (*0-7879-0137-7*) Jossey-Bass.

Andreasen, Alan R. Expanding the Audience for the Performing Arts. LC 90-23150. (Research Division Report, National Endowment for the Arts Ser.: No. 24). 64p. 1991. pap. 10.95 (*0-929765-01-X*, 2900) Seven Locks Pr.

Andreasen, Alan R. & Gardner, David M., eds. Diffusing Marketing Theory & Research: The Contributions of Bauer, Green, Kotler, & Levitt. LC 78-10544. (American Marketing Association, Proceedings Ser.). 154p. reprint ed. pap. 47.80 (*0-8357-6873-2*, 203557100095) Bks Demand.

Andreasen, Alan R. & Kotler, Philip. Strategic Marketing for Nonprofit Organizations. 5th rev. ed. LC 95-40725. Orig. Title: Strategic Marketing for Nonprofit Organizations. 528p. 1995. 90.33 (*0-13-232547-0*) P-H.

Andreasen, Alan R. & Sturdivant, Frederick D., eds. Minorities & Marketing: Research Challenges. LC 77-6819. 150p. reprint ed. pap. 46.50 (*0-608-13067-2*, 201462600093) Bks Demand.

***Andreasen, Dan.** Just Like Me. 32p. (J). (ps-3). 2000. 14.95 (*0-06-027811-0*) HarpC Child Bks.

Andreasen, Dan, et al. Rose Red & the Bear Prince. LC 98-47525. (Illus.). 40p. (J). (ps-4). 2000. 16.95 (*0-06-027966-4*) HarpC.

Andreasen, Dan, jt. auth. see Kay, Verla.

Andreasen, Don. Felicity's Stationery Set. (J). (gr. 3-7). 1996. pap. 9.95 (*1-56247-486-3*) Pleasant Co.

Andreasen, Esben. Popular Buddhism in Japan: Shin Buddhist Religion & Culture. LC 97-33209. 248p. 1997. text 39.00 (*0-8248-2027-4*, Latitude Twenty); pap. text 22.95 (*0-8248-2028-2*, Latitude Twenty) UH Pr.

Andreasen, J. H., jt. auth. see Karihaloo, Bhushan L.

Andreasen, Jens O. Atlas of Replantation & Transplantation of Teeth. (Illus.). 304p. 1992. text 142.00 (*0-7216-6711-2*, W B Saunders Co) Harcrt Hlth Sci Grp.

***Andreasen, Jens O., et al.** Textbook & Color Atlas of Tooth Impactions. (C). 1998. text. write for info. (*0-323-00146-7*) Mosby Inc.

Andreasen, Lars Erik. Europe's Next Step. 1995. 45.00 (*0-7146-4630-X*, Pub. by F Cass Pubs) Intl Spec Bk.

— Europe's Next Step. 1995. pap. 22.00 (*0-7146-4151-0*, Pub. by F Cass Pubs) Intl Spec Bk.

Andreasen, M. L. Letters to the Churches. LC 96-60002. 96p. 1996. reprint ed. per. 7.95 (*1-57258-074-7*) Teach Servs.

— The Sabbath - Which Day & Why? fac. ed. LC 95-61755. 256p. 1996. reprint ed. per. 9.95 (*1-57258-053-4*) Teach Servs.

Andreasen, M. Myrup. Flexible Assembly Systems. 250p. 1988. 119.00 (*0-387-50246-7*) Spr-Verlag.

— Integrated Product Development. (Illus.). 200p. 1987. 157.95 (*0-387-16679-3*) Spr-Verlag.

Andreasen, M. Myrup, et al. Design for Assembly. 189p. 1983. 45.00 (*0-387-12544-2*) Spr-Verlag.

— Design for Assembly. (Illus.). 220p. 1988. 103.95 (*0-387-18929-7*) Spr-Verlag.

Andreasen, Nancy C. The Broken Brain. LC 83-48782. (Illus.). 288p. 1985. pap. 15.00 (*0-06-091272-3*, PL 1272, Perennial) HarperTrade.

An Asterisk (*) at the beginning of an entry indicates that the title is appearing for the first time.

— Can Schizophrenia Be Localized in the Brain? LC 85-26875. (Progress in Psychiatry Ser.). 97p. reprint ed. pap. 30.10 (*0-608-06670-2*, 206686700009) Bks Demand.

Andreasen, Nancy C., ed. Brain Imaging: Applications in Psychiatry. LC 88-16775. 384p. 1989. 29.95 (*0-88048-229-X*, 8229) Am Psychiatric.

— Schizophrenia: From Mind to Molecule. LC 93-9585. (American Psychopathological Association Ser.). 278p. 1994. text 36.00 (*0-88048-950-2*, 8950) Am Psychiatric.

Andreasen, Nancy C. & Black, Donald W. Introductory Textbook of Psychiatry. 2nd ed. LC 94-44481. 768p. 1995. pap. text 49.95 (*0-88048-705-4*, 8705) Am Psychiatric.

Andreasen, Nancy C., et al. Eminent Creativity, Everyday Creativity, & Health. Runco, Mark A. & Richards, Ruth, eds. LC 96-5371. (Creativity Research Monographs). (Illus.). 275p. 1998. pap. 49.50 (*1-56750-175-3*); text 82.50 (*1-56750-174-5*) Ablx Pub.

Andreasen, Tayo, et al, eds. Moving On: New Perspectives on the Women's Movement. (Acta Jutlandica Ser.: Vol. 67:1). (Illus.). 224p. (Orig.). (C). 1991. pap. 32.00 (*87-7288-368-5*, Pub. by Aarhus Univ Pr) David Brown.

Andreasen, Troeis, et al, eds. Flexible Query Answering Systems. LC 97-29083. 304p. 1997. text 137.50 (*0-7923-8001-0*) Kluwer Academic.

Andreasen, Troels, et al. Flexible Query Answering Systems: Third Internaitonal Conference, FQAS '98, Roskilde, Denmark, May 13-15, 1998: Proceedings. LC 98-41916. (Lecture Notes in Artificial Intelligence: Vol. 149). 1998. pap. 67.00 (*3-540-65082-2*) Spr-Verlag.

Andreassen, Norman. Donleavey's Maelstrom. (Illus.). 302p. (Orig.). 1997. pap. 14.00 (*0-9659158-1-6*) Global Outlook.

Andreassen, Steen, et al, eds. Artificial Intelligence in Medicine: Proceedings of the 4th Conference on Artificial Intelligence in Medicine Europe, Munich, Germany, October 3-6, 1993, Vol. 10. LC 93-61133. (Studies in Health Technology & Informatics). 508p. 1993. 116.00 (*90-5199-141-X*, Pub. by IOS Pr) IOS Press.

Andreassi, John L. Psychophysiology: Human Behavior & Physiological Response. 2nd ed. 488p. 1989. pap. 34.50 (*0-8058-0180-4*) L Erlbaum Assocs.

— Psychophysiology: Human Behavior & Physiological Response. 3rd ed. 400p. 1995. pap. 55.00 (*0-8058-1104-4*); text 99.95 (*0-8058-1103-6*) L Erlbaum Assocs.

Andreassi, John L. Psychophysiology: Human Behavior & Physiological Response. 4th ed. LC 99-41207. 450p. 2000. pap. text. write for info. (*0-8058-2833-8*) L Erlbaum Assocs.

***Andreassi, John L.** Psychophysiology: Human Behavior & Physiological Response. 4th ed. LC 99-41207. 450p. 2000. write for info. (*0-8058-2832-X*) L Erlbaum Assocs.

Andreassi, K. Robert. Gargantua. 224p. 1998. mass mkt. 5.99 (*0-8125-7098-7*, Pub. by Tor Bks) St Martin.

Andreatta, Marco & Peternell, Thomas, eds. Higher Dimensional Complex Varieties: Proceedings of the International Conference Held in Trento, Italy, June 15-24, 1994. LC 96-7246. 1996. 152.95 (*3-11-014503-0*) De Gruyter.

Andreatta, Pat. Applique Can Be Easy. (Illus.). 19p. 1988. student ed. 14.95 (*0-9616848-2-8*) Heirloom Stitches.

— Heirloom Applique. (Illus.). 33p. 1985. student ed. 14.95 (*0-9616848-0-1*) Heirloom Stitches.

— Heirlooms for Tomorrow. 30p. 1988. student ed. 14.95 (*0-9616848-3-6*) Heirloom Stitches.

— Tomorrow's Treasures. (Illus.). 28p. 1987. student ed. 14.95 (*0-9616848-1-X*) Heirloom Stitches.

— Treasures from the Garden. 34p. 1990. student ed. 14.95 (*0-9616848-4-4*) Heirloom Stitches.

***Andreau, Jean.** Banking & Business in the Roman World. LC 98-48325. (Key Themes in Ancient History Ser.). 211p. 1999. 59.95 (*0-521-38031-6*); pap. 22.95 (*0-521-38932-1*) Cambridge U Pr.

Andreau, Paul, pref. Paul Andreau: The Discovery of Universal Space. (I Talenti Ser.). (FRE, ITA & KOR., Illus.). 144p. 1997. pap. write for info. (*88-7838-036-9*) Rockport Pubs.

Andrecht, Summer, ed. see Andrecht, Venus.

Andrecht, Summer, ed. see Andrecht, Venus C.

Andrecht, Summer, ed. see McWhorter, Margaret L.

Andrecht, Summer, ed. see Meyers, Ron.

Andrecht, Summer, ed. see Moore, Lisa.

Andrecht, Venus. When the Roses Start Stinking, It's Time to Throw Them Out. Andrecht, Summer, ed. LC 96-72083. 200p. 1997. write for info. (*0-941903-22-2*) Ransom Hill.

Andrecht, Venus C. Bad Blues: The Ups & Downs of Multilevel & How to Cope. Andrecht, Summer & Elliott, Cindy, eds. 128p. (Orig.). 1995. pap. 13.95 (*0-941903-16-8*) Ransom Hill.

— The Herb Lady's Notebook, an Outrageous Herbal. LC 83-63072. (Illus.). 300p. 1984. reprint ed. pap. 16.95 (*0-9604342-4-0*) Ransom Hill.

— La Magia del Multinivel: Como Cualquier Persona Puede Lograr un Negocio Colosal de Ventas de Multinivel a Par de Cero. (SPA.). 290p. (Orig.). 1994. pap. 18.95 (*0-941903-08-7*) Ransom Hill.

— MLM Magic Multilevel Marketing: How an Ordinary Person Can Build an Extra-Ordinary Networking Business from Scratch. 2nd ed. Andrecht, Summer, ed. LC 91-61552. (Illus.). 274p. (C). 1993. pap. 16.95 (*0-941903-07-9*, 3000) Ransom Hill.

— MLM Magic Workbook: Companion Workbook to the Award Winning Book MLM Magic-How an Ordinary Person Can Build an Extra Ordinary Networking Business from Scratch. Andrecht, Summer, ed. 112p. (Orig.). 1994. pap. 18.95 (*0-941903-11-7*) Ransom Hill.

— Prospecting: Prospects: How to Find 'Em, Sign 'Em & What To Do with 'Em in Multilevel. Andrecht, Summer, ed. 120p. (Orig.). 1995. pap. 12.95 (*0-941903-13-3*) Ransom Hill.

— Simple, Cheap & Easy: How to Build a Cell Tech Business off Your Kitchen Table. Andrecht, Summer, ed. (Illus.). 112p. (Orig.). 1996. mass mkt. write for info. (*0-941903-17-6*) Ransom Hill.

Andree, Herb, et al. Santa Barbara Architecture. 3rd ed. Easton, Bob & McCall, Wayne, eds. LC 95-42956. (Illus.). 316p. 1995. 89.95 (*0-88496-400-0*) Capra Pr.

Andree, Josephine P., ed. Chips from the Mathematical Log. 1966. pap. 2.00 (*0-686-00750-6*) Mu Alpha Theta.

— Lines from the O. U. Mathematics Letter. Incl. Vol. 1, Number Extensions. 1.00 Vol. 2, Theory of GAmes. 0.75 Vol. 3, Geometric Extensions. 1985. 1.25 write for info. (*0-318-59521-4*) Mu Alpha Theta.

— More Chips from the Mathematical Log. 1978. pap. 1.25 (*0-686-00324-1*) Mu Alpha Theta.

Andree, Josephine P. & Andree, Richard. Cryptarithms. 1978. teacher ed. 2.00 (*0-686-28564-6*); pap. 2.95 (*0-686-23790-0*) Mu Alpha Theta.

Andree, Marie. The Bulldog: An Owner's Guide to a Happy Healthy Pet. LC 97-35869. (Illus.). 158p. 1997. 12.95 (*0-87605-432-7*) Howell Bks.

Andree, Richard, jt. auth. see Andree, Josephine P.

Andree, Robert G. Collective Negotiations: A Guide to School Board-Teacher Relations. LC 74-121401. 1970. 52.50 (*0-89197-704-X*) Irvington.

Andreeff, Michael & Pinkel, Daniel, eds. Introduction to Fluorescent In-Situ Hybridization: Principles & Clinical Applications. LC 98-37311. 455p. 1999. 225.00 (*0-471-01345-5*) Wiley.

Andreen, B. H., et al. Instrumental Methods of Analysis for Odorant Compounds in Natural Gas, No. 7. vi, 32p. 1963. pap. 25.00 (*1-58222-027-1*) Inst Gas Tech.

Andreen, Gustav. Studies in the Idyl in German Literature. LC 06-19423. (Augustana College Library Publications: No. 3). 96p. 1984. reprint ed. pap. 1.00 (*0-910182-01-9*) Augustana Coll.

***Andreescu, T. & Gelca, R.** Mathematical Olympiad Challenges. (Illus.). 240p. (C). 2000. text 59.95 (*0-8176-4190-4*, Pub. by Birkhauser) Spr-Verlag.

— Mathematical Olympiad Challenges. LC 99-86229. (Illus.). 280p. 2000. 24.95 (*0-8176-4155-6*, Pub. by Birkhauser) Spr-Verlag.

***Andreescu, Titu & Gelca, Riazvan.** Mathematical Olympiad Challenges. LC 99-86229. 2000. write for info. (*3-7643-4155-6*) Birkhauser.

Andreesen, R., ed. The Macrophage, 1990, Pt. 1. (Journal: Vol. 59, No. 3, 1991). (Illus.). 92p. 1991. pap. 51.50 (*3-8055-5407-9*) S Karger.

— The Macrophage, 1990, Pt. 2. (Journal: Pathobiology: Vol. 59, No. 4, 1991). (Illus.). 100p. 1991. pap. 51.50 (*3-8055-5408-7*) S Karger.

— The Macrophage, 1992: Abstracts, European Conference on Basic & Clinical Aspects of Macrophage Biology, Regensburg, FRG, September 1992. (Journal: Pathobiology: Vol. 60, Suppl. 1, 1992). (Illus.). x, 42p. 1992. pap. 24.50 (*3-8055-5689-6*) S Karger.

Andreetti, Keith. Teaching History Primary Evidence. 128p. 1993. pap. 22.00 (*1-85346-183-0*, Pub. by David Fulton) Taylor & Francis.

Andreev. Short Stories. unabridged ed. (World Classic Literature Ser.). (RUS.). pap. 8.95 (*2-87714-276-0*, Pub. by Bookking Intl) Distribks Inc.

Andreev, A. E., et al. Twelve Papers on Function Theory, Probability, & Differential Equations. (Translations Ser.: Series 2, Vol. 8). 356p. 1957. 59.00 (*0-8218-1708-6*, TRANS2/8) Am Math.

Andreev, A. V., et al. Cooperative Effects in Optics: Superradiance & Phase Transitions. (Malvern Physics Ser.). (Illus.). 470p. 1993. 210.00 (*0-7503-0219-4*) IOP Pub.

***Andreev, Alexander A., et al.** An Introduction to Hot Laser Plasma Physics, Vol. 233. LC 00-27320. (Horizons in World Physics Ser.). 163p. 2000. lib. bdg. 89.00 (*1-56072-803-5*) Nova Sci Pubs.

***Andreev, Anatoli V., et al, eds.** Quantum Optics. 452p. 1999. pap. text 92.00 (*0-8194-3210-5*) SPIE.

Andreev, B. M., et al. Interaction of Hydrogen Isotopes with Transition-Metals & Intermetallic Compounds. 112p. 1996. 99.00 (*3-540-58369-6*) Spr-Verlag.

Andreev, Boris V. Sleep Therapy in Neuroses. Haigh, Basil, tr. LC 60-13947. (International Behavioral Science Ser.). 121p. reprint ed. pap. 37.60 (*0-608-10827-8*, 202065900018) Bks Demand.

Andreev, Daniel, jt. auth. see Powell, Robert.

Andreev, Daniil, et al. The Rose of the World. (Esalen-Lindisfarne Library of Russian Philosophy). (Illus.). 416p. (Orig.). 1997. pap. 24.95 (*0-940262-83-5*, 2040, Lindisfarne) Anthroposophic.

Andreev, George E. Brittle Failure of Rock Materials: Test Results & Constitutive Models. LC 99-226657. (Illus.). 380p. (C). 1995. text 149.00 (*90-5410-602-6*, Pub. by A A Balkema) Ashgate Pub Co.

Andreev, Grigorii L., compiled by. A Catalog of Russian Christian Serials, 1801-1917, Vol. 1. 1998. lib. bdg. 250.00 (*0-88354-132-7*) N Ross.

Andreev-Khomiakov, Gennady. Bitter Waters: Life & Work in Stalin's Russua. 224p. (C). 1998. pap. 17.00 (*0-8133-2374-6*, Pub. by Westview) HarpC.

Andreev, Leonid N. He Who Gets Slapped: A Play in Four Acts. Zilboorg, Gregory, tr. LC 74-14348. (Illus.). 193p. 1975. reprint ed. lib. bdg. 35.00 (*0-8371-7796-0*, ANHW, Greenwood Pr) Greenwood.

— Little Angel, & Other Stories. LC 78-167439. (Short Story Index Reprint Ser.). 1977. reprint ed. 32.95 (*0-8369-3965-4*) Ayer.

— When the King Loses His Head, & Other Stories. Wolfe, Archibald J., tr. LC 74-116927. (Short Story Index Reprint Ser.). 1977. 21.95 (*0-8369-3429-6*) Ayer.

Andreev, N. N., jt. auth. see Kapustina, O. A.

Andreev, Nikolai, jt. ed. see Balkanski, Minko.

Andreev, Nikolai P. Ukazatel' Skazochnykh Siuzhetov Po Sisteme Aarne. (RUS.). 118p. (C). 1993. reprint ed. pap. 12.00 (*0-933884-90-7*) Berkeley Slavic.

Andreev, S. V. Hematology Reviews Vol. 3, Pt. 1: Biochemical Mechanisms of the System Regulating the Aggregate State of Blood, Vol. 3. (Soviet Medical Reviews Ser.: Section C). iv, 126p. 1990. pap. text 142.00 (*3-7186-4963-2*, Harwood Acad Pubs) Gordon & Breach.

Andreev, S. V., et al. Hematology Reviews: Cellular Mechanisms of the System Regulating the Aggregate State of Blood, Vol. 3. (Soviet Medical Reviews Ser.: Vol. 3, Pt. 3). 76p. 1990. pap. text 82.00 (*3-7186-4961-6*) Gordon & Breach.

Andreev, Tania. Food in Russia. LC 88-32179. (International Food Library: Set I). (Illus.). 32p. (J). (gr. 3-6). 1989. lib. bdg. 21.27 (*0-86625-343-2*) Rourke Pubns.

Andreev, V. C. Skin Manifestations in Visceral Cancer. (Current Problems in Dermatology Ser.: Vol. 8). (Illus.). 1978. pap. 86.25 (*3-8055-2878-7*) S Karger.

Andreev, V. K. Applications of Group-Theoretical Methods in Hydrodynamics. LC 98-29283. (Mathematics & Its Applications Ser.). 1998. write for info. (*0-7923-5215-7*) Kluwer Academic.

Andreev, V. M., et al. Photovoltaic Conversion of Concentrated Sunlight. LC 97-3769. 308p. 1997. 159.95 (*0-471-96765-3*) Wiley.

Andreeva, Vasina N. Dictionary of Russian Folk Dialects, Vol. 23. (ENG & RUS.). 376p. (C). 1987. 90.00 (*0-7855-6434-9*, Pub. by Collets) St Mut.

Andreeva, Yekaterina. Sots Art: Soviet Artists of the 1970s & 1980s. (Illus.). 120p. 1995. text 39.95 (*976-8097-85-X*) Gordon & Breach.

Andrefsky, William, Jr. Lithics: Macroscopic Approaches to Analysis. LC 97-35227. (Cambridge Manuals in Archaeology). (Illus.). 286p. (C). 1998. text 69.95 (*0-521-57084-0*); pap. text 27.95 (*0-521-57815-9*) Cambridge U Pr.

Andregg, Caron. Dangerous Curves. 40p. (Orig.). 1995. pap. 4.50 (*1-886895-01-5*) Poetry Harbor.

— Pavlov's Mistress. 30p. (Orig.). 1996. pap. 5.00 (*1-886895-02-3*) Poetry Harbor.

***Andregg, Caron & Wynne, Robert, eds.** Cider Press Review, Vol. 1. 144p. 2000. pap. 12.00 (*0-9661399-2-5*) Cider Pr CA.

Andreggen, Anton. France's Involvement with Subsaharan Africa. LC 93-5446. 216p. 1994. 59.95 (*0-275-94756-4*, Praeger Pubs) Greenwood.

Andreha, Johann V. Christianopolis. LC 99-26400. (Archives Internationales d'Histoire des Idbees Ser.). 1999. write for info. (*0-7923-5745-0*) Kluwer Academic.

Andrei, Eva Y., ed. Two-Dimensional Electron Systems: On Helium & Other Cryogenic Substrates. LC 97-33975. (Physics & Chemistry of Materials with Low-Dimensional Structures Ser.: No. 19). 404p. 1997. text 217.50 (*0-7923-4738-2*) Kluwer Academic.

***Andrei, Josee.** Pageant of a Woman. (Illus.). 146p. 2000. pap. 30.00 (*1-892453-05-3*) AMP Pr.

Andrei, Moscovit. Did Castro Kill Kennedy? Leyva, Adolfo & Lozano, Robert, eds. Vladimir, Klimenko, tr. from RUS. LC 96-84073.Tr. of Kto Ubil Presidenta Kennedy?. (Illus.). 392p. 1998. pap. 15.00 (*1-884619-08-8*, Pub. by Endowment CAS) Hermitage Pubs.

Andrei of Novo-Diveyevo. The One Thing Needful. (Illus.). 160p. 1992. 15.00 (*0-912927-29-1*, X029) St John Kronstadt.

***Andreini, Laura.** Cafes & Restaurants. (Illus.). 400p. 2000. pap. 22.50 (*3-8238-5478-X*) te Neues.

Andreis, Flavio. Colloquial Italian. (Colloquials Ser.). 244p. 1983. pap. 14.95 (*0-685-04385-1*) Routledge.

— Colloquial Italian. 1986. 13.95 (*0-7100-0876-7*, Routledge Thoemms) Routledge.

— Colloquial Italian. (Colloquials Ser.). 256p. 1989. pap. 14.95 (*0-415-03946-0*, 08767) Routledge.

Andrejev, Vladislav, contrib. by. Illuminated Gospel of St. Matthew: Iconographic Calligraphy & Illuminations in the Byzantine - Slavic Tradition. LC 93-83264. (Illus.). 112p. 1993. 39.95 (*1-879038-08-0*) Oakwood Pubns.

Andrejko, Dennis A. & Hayes, John, eds. Solar, 1987: Twelfth National Passive Solar Conference Proceedings, July 11-16, 1987. 12th ed. (Illus.). 574p. 50.00 (*0-89553-203-4*) Am Solar Energy.

Andrejko, Dennis A., jt. ed. see Hayes, John.

Andrejtscheff, W., et al, eds. Nuclei, Neutrons & Energy: Proceedings of the VIII International School. 492p. 1988. text 117.00 (*9971-5-0692-0*) World Scientific Pub.

Andrejtscheff, W. & Elenkov, D., eds. Nuclear Physics, Neutron Physics & Nuclear Energy: Proceedings of the 9th International School. 492p. (C). 1990. text 151.00 (*981-02-0253-9*) World Scientific Pub.

Andrejtschitsch, Jan, et al. Action Skateboarding. LC 91-40328. (Illus.). 128p. (YA). (gr. 10-12). 1992. 16.95 (*0-8069-8500-3*) Sterling.

— Action Skateboarding. (Illus.). 128p. (YA). (gr. 10-12). 1993. pap. 10.95 (*0-8069-8501-1*) Sterling.

Andreka, H., et al. Decision Problems for Equational Theories of Relation Algebras. LC 96-37450. (Memoirs of the American Mathematical Society Ser.: Vol. 126/604). 126p. 1997. pap. 39.00 (*0-8218-0595-9*, MEMO/126/604) Am Math.

Andrel, Vika. How to Adopt Your Stepchildren. rev. ed. McEachern, Trudy, ed. 86p. 1997. 25.00 (*0-9657618-0-0*) V Andrel.

Andren, A. Between Artifacts & Texts: Historical Archaeology in Global Perspective. LC 97-40651. (Contributions to Global Historical Archaeology Ser.). (Illus.). 228p. (C). 1998. 39.50 (*0-306-45556-0*, Plenum Trade) Perseus Pubng.

Andren, Arvid. Capri: From the Stone Age to the Tourist Age. (Studies in Mediterranean Archaeology & Literature: No. 13). (Illus.). 250p. (Orig.). 1980. pap. 42.50 (*91-85058-98-X*, Pub. by P Astroms) Coronet Bks.

— Deeds & Misdeeds in Classical Art & Antiquities. (Studies in Mediterranean Archaeology & Literature: Pocket-Book 36). (Illus.). 176p. (Orig.). (C). 1986. pap. 43.50 (*91-86098-31-4*, Pub. by P Astroms) Coronet Bks.

Andren, Arvid, contrib. by. Tuscanica: An Etruscan Picture-Book. (Studies in Mediterranean Archaeology & Literature: Pocket-Book 133). (Illus.). 62p. (Orig.). 1995. pap. 47.50 (*91-7081-100-8*, Pub. by P Astroms) Coronet Bks.

Andren, John, Jr., et al. IBM PC to Apple II BASIC Program Translation. 100p. 1984. 15.00 (*0-685-08622-4*) Med Software.

Andren, Nils & Birnbaum, Karl E. Belgrade & Beyond: The CSCE Process in Perspective. (East West Perspectives Ser.: No. 5). 1980. lib. bdg. 64.50 (*90-286-0250-X*) Kluwer Academic.

Andren, O., ed. see Lindberg, T., et al.

Andren-Sandberg, A., jt. ed. see Ihse, I.

Andrenyak, Gail M. An Epidemiological Study of Demographic Factors Associated with Infant Mortality in Bridgeport, Connecticut, 1981-1984. (Studies in Historical Demography). 150p. 1990. reprint ed. text 10.00 (*0-8240-4959-4*) Garland.

Andreo, Augusto V. Diccionario De Grafologia y Terminos Psicologicos Afines. 4th ed. (SPA.). 532p. 1991. pap. 49.95 (*0-7859-6454-1*) Fr & Eur.

Andreola, Karen. Beautiful Girlhood. 1993. pap. text 8.99 (*1-883934-02-8*) Grt Expect Bk.

— A Charlotte Mason Companion: Personal Reflections on the Gentle Art of Learning. (Illus.). 384p. 1998. pap. 18.99 (*1-889209-02-3*) C Mason Res.

— Simply Grammar: An Illustrated Primer. 1993. pap. text 24.95 (*1-889209-01-5*) C Mason Res.

Andreoli, Anthony L. & Shuman, D. Robert. Guide to Unclaimed Property & Escheat Laws. 3rd ed. LC 85-220478. 1988. ring bd. 249.50 (*0-943882-02-8*) Commonwlth Pub.

Andreoli, Anthony L. & Spotswood, J. Brooke. Guide to Unclaimed Property & Escheat Laws, 3 vols., Set. 2nd ed. LC 93-39071. 3312p. 1993. 415.00 (*0-13-121914-6*) Aspen Law.

Andreoli-Devillers, Jean P. Futurism & the Arts: A Bibliography, 1959-73. LC 74-79005. 220p. reprint ed. pap. 68.20 (*0-608-17112-3*, 202644500049) Bks Demand.

Andreoli, J. M., et al, eds. Coordination Programming: Mechanisms, Models & Semantics. LC 97-112405. 396p. 1996. 76.00 (*1-86094-023-4*) World Scientific Pub.

Andreoli, Kathleen G., et al, eds. Health Care for the Elderly: Regional Responses for National Policy Issues. LC 86-14869. (Home Health Care Services Quarterly Ser.: Vol. 7, Nos. 3 & 4). 363p. 1987. text 11.95 (*0-86656-607-4*) Haworth Pr.

Andreoli, T. E., et al. Clinical Disorders of Membrane Transport Processes: Physiology of Membrane Disorders, Chapters 42-56 2nd ed. LC 87-20247. (Illus.). 296p. (C). 1987. reprint ed. pap. text 55.00 (*0-306-42699-4*, Kluwer Plenum) Kluwer Academic.

— Membrane Physiology: Physiology of Membrane Disorders, Chapters 1-23 2nd ed. (Illus.). 384p. (C). 1987. reprint ed. text 59.50 (*0-306-42697-8*, Kluwer Plenum) Kluwer Academic.

— Membrane Transport Processes in Organized Systems: Physiology of Membrane Disorders, Chapters 24-41. 2nd ed. LC 87-18655. (Illus.). 408p. (C). 1987. reprint ed. text 59.50 (*0-306-42698-6*, Kluwer Plenum) Kluwer Academic.

Andreoli, Thomas E., et al, eds. Physiology of Membrane Disorders. 2nd ed. LC 85-19367. (Illus.). 1094p. 1986. 234.00 (*0-306-41774-X*, Kluwer Plenum) Kluwer Academic.

Andreoli, Thomas E., et al. Cecil Essentials of Medicine. 4th ed. Bralow, Lisette, ed. LC 96-18701. (Illus.). 780p. 1997. pap. text 45.00 (*0-7216-6697-3*, W B Saunders Co) Harcrt Hlth Sci Grp.

***Andreoli, Thomas E., et al.** Cecil Essentials of Medicine. 5th ed. LC 99-89413. (Illus.). 860p. Date not set. pap. text. write for info. (*0-7216-8179-4*, W B Saunders Co) Harcrt Hlth Sci Grp.

Andreone, Carl F. & Yokell, Stanley. Tubular Heat Exchanger Operation & Repair. LC 97-26077. (Illus.). 512p. 1997. 110.00 (*0-07-001778-6*) McGraw.

Andreone, D., et al. Advances in High Temperature Superconductivity. 364p. 1993. text 121.00 (*981-02-1297-6*) World Scientific Pub.

Andreoni, Coleen P., jt. auth. see Tipsord-Klinkhammer, Beverley.

Andreoni, Colleen. Quick Reference for Pediatric Emergency Nursing. LC 99-35201. (Illus.). 445p. 2000. pap. text. write for info. (*0-7216-8327-4*, W B Saunders Co) Harcrt Hlth Sci Grp.

***Andreoni, Wanda.** The Physics of Fullerene-Based & Fullerene-Related Materials. 464p. 2000. 199.00 (*0-7923-6234-9*) Kluwer Academic.

Andreoni, Wanda, ed. The Chemical Physics of Fullerenes 10 (& 5) Years Later: Proceedings of the NATO Advanced Research Workshop, Varenna, Italy, June 12-16, 1995. (NATO Advanced Science Institutes Ser.: Pt. E). 512p. (C). 1996. text 261.50 (*0-7923-4000-0*) Kluwer Academic.

Andreopoulos, George J., ed. Genocide: Conceptual & Historical Dimensions. LC 93-44384. (Pennsylvania Studies in Human Rights). (Illus.). 280p. (C). 1994. text 36.50 (*0-8122-3249-6*) U of Pa Pr.

— Genocide: Conceptual & Historical Dimensions. (Illus.). 280p. 1997. pap. text 15.95 (*0-8122-1616-4*) U of Pa Pr.

An Asterisk (*) at the beginning of an entry indicates that the title is appearing for the first time.

Andreopoulos, George J. & Claude, Richard P. Human Rights Education for the Twenty-First Century. LC 96-40949. (Pennsylvania Studies in Human Rights). 656p. 1997. text 49.95 (*0-8122-3388-3*) U of Pa Pr.

Andreopoulos, George J. & Selesky, Harold E., eds. The Aftermath of Defeat: Societies, Armed Forces, & the Challenge of Recovery. LC 94-3989. 195p. 1994. 27.50 (*0-300-05853-5*) Yale U Pr.

Andreopoulos, Spyros & Hogness, John R., eds. Health Care for an Aging Society. LC 88-25643. 265p. reprint ed. pap. 82.20 (*0-7837-6808-7*, 204664000003) Bks Demand.

Andreopouos, George J. & Claude, Richard P., eds. Human Rights Education for the Twenty-First Century. LC 96-40949. (Pennsylvania Studies in Human Rights). 656p. 1997. pap. text 26.95 (*0-8122-1607-5*) U of Pa Pr.

Andreose, Mario, ed. The Pirelli Calendar. Ellis, Andrew, tr. LC 97-65574. (Illus.). 396p. 1997. 70.00 (*0-8478-2032-7*, Pub. by Rizzoli Intl) St Martin.

Andreosso-O'Callaghan, Bernadette, jt. auth. see Jacobson, David.

Andreotti, Aldo. Complexes of Partial Differential Operators. LC 75-8440. (Yale Mathematical Monographs: No. 6). 59p. reprint ed. pap. 30.00 (*0-8357-9106-8*, 201679300005) Bks Demand.

Andreotti, F., et al. Physiology & Pharmacology of Biological Rhythms. LC 96-2935. (Handbook of Experimental Pharmacology Ser.). (Illus.). 600p. 1997. 445.00 (*3-540-61525-3*) Spr-Verlag.

Andreotti, Guilio. The U. S. A. up Close: From the Atlantic Pact to Bush. Farrell, Peter, tr. from ITA. 240p. (C). 1993. pap. text 18.50 (*0-8147-0627-4*) NYU Pr.

Andreotti, Libero. Theory of the Derive & Other Situationist Writings on the City. 1998. pap. 22.00 (*84-89698-21-X*, Pub. by Actar) Dist Art Pubs.

Andreotti, Margherita. The Early Sculpture of Jean Arp. Foster, Stephen, ed. LC 89-4746. (Studies in the Fine Arts: The Avant-Garde: No. 65). 366p. reprint ed. 113.50 (*0-8357-1939-1*, 207068800004) Bks Demand.

Andreotti, Margherita, ed. see Ades, Dawn.

Andreou, Andreas, jt. auth. see Sanchez-Sinencio, Edgar.

Andreou, Andreas, jt. ed. see Sanchez-Sinencio, Edgar.

Andreozzi, John, compiled by. Guide to the Records of the Order Sons of Italy in America. (Illus.). vii, 196p. 1989. pap. 12.50 (*0-932833-07-1*, G-5) Immig His Res.

Andreozzi, Lucille L. Child-Centerd Family Therapy. LC 95-52822. (Wiley Series in Couples & Family Dynamics & Treatment). 374p. 1996. 64.50 (*0-471-14858-X*) Wiley.

Andres. Hands-On Illustrator 7 for Mac & Windows. 1997. 34.95 incl. audio compact disk (*0-8052-8571-7*, M&T Bks) IDG Bks.

Andres, ed. Children's Literature Review: Excerpts from Reviews, Criticism, & Commentary on Books for Children & Young People, Vol. 44. 300p. 1997. text 140.00 (*0-7876-1138-7*, 00156242) Gale.

Andres & Telgen, eds. Children's Literature Review: Excerpts from Reviews, Criticism, & Commentary on Books for Children & Young People, Vol. 43. 300p. 1997. text 140.00 (*0-8103-9986-5*, 00007661) Gale.

Andres, Alice, jt. auth. see Leslie-Spinks, Tim.

Andres, Barry C. Human Desires & Life Expectations Including Views of the Future: Index of New Information with Authors & Subjects. 180p. 1993. 47.50 (*1-55914-918-3*); pap. 44.50 (*1-55914-919-1*) ABBE Pubs Assn.

Andres, Brad A., jt. auth. see Earnst, Susan L.

Andres, Cameron K., jt. auth. see Smith, Ronald C.

Andres, Clay. Hands on Photoshop 4.0 for Macintosh & Windows: With CD-ROM. LC 97-862. 552p. 1997. pap. text 34.95 (*1-55828-538-5*, MIS Pr) IDG Bks.

Andres, Clay. Integrated Design Solutions with QuarkXPress, Adobe PhotoShop & Adobe Illustrator. 1994. pap. 29.95 (*1-56830-114-6*) Hayden.

***Andres, Clay.** Web Architecture Studio Secrets. LC 99-28480. 256p. 1999. pap. 49.99 (*0-7645-3246-4*) IDG Bks.

Andres, Constantine, tr. see Cavadas, Athenagoras.

Andres, David. Chest Pain - Is It Your Heart? Shemtov, Rhonda L. & Andres, Janet, eds. LC 87-70554. (Illus.). 140p. (Orig.). 1987. pap. 9.95 (*0-9618345-0-1*) Colco Pub.

Andres, Dayna & Cooke, Kelly. CUES PolicyMaker: Essentials for Developing Board Policy. 76p. (Orig.). 1995. pap. 59.00 (*1-889394-24-6*) Credit Union Execs.

Andres, Domingo, jt. auth. see Juan, Jose.

Andres-Gallego, Jose. Esquilache y el Pan (1766) El Pueblo y el Poder en el Antiguo Regimen Hispano. (Iberian Studies: No. 4). (SPA.). 222p. (Orig.). 1996. pap. text 39.95 (*1-889431-04-4*) Univ Pr South.

— Los Hispanos y la Justicia Hacia 1766: El Pueblo y el Poder en el Antiguo Regimen Hispano. (Iberian Studies: No. 5). (SPA.). 227p. 1996. pap. text 39.95 (*1-889431-05-2*) Univ Pr South.

Andres, Giuseppe A., jt. ed. see McCluskey, Robert T.

Andres, Glenn, et al. The Art of Florence, Vol. 2. (Illus.). 1312p. 1999. 135.00 (*0-89660-111-0*, Artabras) Abbeville Pr.

— The Art of Florence, 2 vols., Set. LC 83-6394. (Illus.). 1348p. 1989. 425.00 (*0-89659-402-5*) Abbeville Pr.

Andres, Glenn M. Hardy Holzman Pfeiffer Associates. 224p. 60.00 (*0-8478-2208-7*, Pub. by Rizzoli Intl) St Martin.

Andres, Glenn M. Hardy Holzman Pfeiffer Associates: Concepts & Buildings. Graff, Nancy P., ed. LC 92-21528. (Illus.). 76p. (C). 1993. spiral bd. 22.95 (*0-9625262-4-X*) Middlebury Coll Mus.

Andres, Hermano. El Contrabandista de Dios.Tr. of God's Smuggler. (SPA.). 282p. 1989. pap. 4.50 (*0-945792-89-1*, 498522) Editorial Unilit.

Andres, Janet, ed. see Andres, David.

Andres, Javier, et al. Spanish Unemployment: Is There a Solution? LC 96-145728. 146p. (C). 1995. pap. 21.95 (*1-898128-18-9*, Pub. by Ctr Econ Policy Res) Brookings.

Andres, Jean U., ed. see Corippus.

***Andres, Katharina.** Antike Physiognomie in Renaissanceportrats. (Europaische Hochschulschriften, Reihe 28). (Illus.). 304p. 1999. 56.95 (*3-631-34184-9*) P Lang Pubng.

Andres, Katherine. Fish Story. LC 92-14677. (Illus.). (J). 1993. pap. 15.00 (*0-671-79270-9*) S&S Trade.

Andres, Lenora, jt. auth. see Van Nes, Patricia.

Andres, Linda R., ed. Children's Literature Review: Excerpts from Reviews, Criticism, & Commentary on Books for Children & Young People, Vol. 45. 300p. 1997. text 140.00 (*0-7876-1139-5*, 00156243) Gale.

Andres, Lorie. Volcanoes . . . And Other Earth. (Illus.). 48p. (J). (gr. 1-3). 1999. mass mkt. 4.99 (*0-7681-0089-5*, McClanahan Book) Learn Horizon.

Andres, M. F. Spanish Dictionary of Synonyms, Equivalences & Related Ideas: Diccionario Espanol de Sinonimos, Equivalencias e Ideas Afines. 9th ed. (SPA.). 443p. 1982. 19.95 (*0-8288-2014-7*, S12233) Fr & Eur.

Andres Martin, Melquiades, et al. Historia de Espana Vol. 1, No. 26: El Siglo del Quijote (1580-1680): Religion, Filosofia, Ciencia. 913p. 1992. 189.50 (*84-239-4990-7*) Elliots Bks.

Andres Ordax, S. Extremadura y America. (Gran Enciclopedia de Espana y America Ser.). (SPA., Illus.). 1989. 200.00 (*84-87053-13-0*) Elliots Bks.

Andres, Patricia. Secrets of Sewing with Plaid. 80p. (Orig.). 1985. pap. text 6.00 (*0-9618825-0-6*) Value Pubns.

Andres, Rachel & Lane, James R., eds. Cults & Consequences: The Definitive Handbook. 288p. (Orig.). (C). 1988. pap. 14.95 (*0-9621478-7-7*) JFC GLA.

Andres, Ralph W. How to Build a 4" Case Traction Engine & Water Wagon. (Illus.). 95p. (Orig.). 1997. spiral bd. 39.95 (*0-9627766-3-7*) Apple Blossom.

Andres, Stefan. El Greco Paints the Grand Inquisitor. Willson, Jeanne, tr. (Illus.). 78p. 1989. 11.95 (*0-911173-01-3*); pap. 15.95 (*0-911173-02-1*) Dimension Pr.

Andres, Stella & Steiger, Brad. Stella: One Woman's Victory over Cancer. 160p. 1986. 14.95 (*0-86700-015-5*, Synergy Bks) P Walsh Pr.

Andres, Tomas D. Human Resource Management in the Philippines Setting. 336p. (Orig.). (C). 1991. pap. 15.00 (*971-10-0348-1*, Pub. by New Day Pub) Cellar.

— Management by Filipino Values: A Sequel to Understanding Filipino Values. vi, 276p. (Orig.). 1985. pap. 15.75 (*971-10-0209-4*, Pub. by New Day Pub) Cellar.

— Positive Filipino Values. xi, 196p. (Orig.). (C). 1990. pap. 17.50 (*971-10-0408-9*, Pub. by New Day Pub) Cellar.

— Understanding Filipino Values: A Management Approach. 180p. (C). 1981. 15.00 (*971-10-0117-9*, Pub. by New Day Pub) Cellar.

Andres, Tomas D. & Ilada-Andres, Pilar B. Understanding the Filipino. xii, 184p. (Orig.). 1987. pap. 17.50 (*971-10-0337-6*, Pub. by New Day Pub) Cellar.

Andres, William, et al. When Eastern Michigan Rode the Rails, Vol. III. LC 84-19180. (Special Ser.: No. 109). 224p. 1988. 39.95 (*0-916374-80-7*) Pentrex Media.

Andresco, Victor, tr. see Turguieniev, Ivan S.

Andrescu, D. Dictionary of Aeronautics: Dictionar de Astronautica. (RUM.). 1983. write for info. (*0-8288-1172-5*, M15850) Fr & Eur.

Andresen, Andreas. Handbuch Fur Kupferstichsammler, 2 vols., Set. 1982. reprint ed. 320.00 (*3-487-07171-1*) G Olms Pubs.

Andresen, Andreas & Weigel, Rudolph. Der Deutsche Peintre-Graveur, 5 vols., Set. 1971. reprint ed. 305.00 (*3-487-04004-2*) G Olms Pubs.

Andresen, Bernd. Ernst von Dryander: Eine Biographische Studie. (Arbeiten zur Kirchengeschichte: No. 63). (GER.). ix, 435p. (C). 1995. lib. bdg. 152.30 (*3-11-014814-5*) De Gruyter.

Andresen, Bjhorn F., et al. Infrared Technology & Applications XXII: 8-12 April, 1996, Orlando, Florida. LC 95-73014. xiv, 764p. 1996. pap. write for info. (*0-8194-2125-1*) SPIE.

Andresen, Bjorn F. & Scholl, Marija S., eds. Infrared Technology & Applications XXIII. LC 98-122071. 120p. 1997. pap. 158.00 (*0-8194-2476-5*) SPIE.

— Infrared Technology & Applications XXIV, Vol. 3436. LC 99-208069. 1998. 158.00 (*0-8194-2891-4*) SPIE.

***Andresen, Bjorn F. & Scholl, Marija Strojnik, eds.** Infrared Technology & Applications XXV. 958p. 1999. pap. text 153.00 (*0-8194-3172-9*) SPIE.

Andresen, Bjorn F., jt. ed. see Scholl, Marija Strojnik.

Andresen, Bjorn F., jt. ed. see Scholl, Marija S.

Andresen, Carl & Denzler, Georg. DTV Dictionary of Church History: DTV Woerterbuch der Kirchengeschichte. (GER.). 1984. 39.95 (*0-8288-2305-7*, M15221) Fr & Eur.

Andresen, Dan, jt. illus. see Tripp, Valerie.

Andresen, Elena, et al, eds. Assessing the Health Status of Older Adults. LC 97-20430. 304p. 1997. 38.95 (*0-8261-9780-9*) Springer Pub.

Andresen, Gayle. Caring for People with Alzheimer's Disease: A Training Manual for Direct Care Providers. LC 94-31057. 208p. 1995. pap. 26.95 (*1-878812-22-X*) Hlth Prof Pr.

Andresen, Georg, jt. ed. see Nipperdey, Karl.

Andresen, Gregory G., jt. auth. see Blackman, Irving L.

Andresen, Jens, et al, eds. Computing the Past: Computer Applications & Quantitative Methods in Archaeology. (CAA 92 Ser.). (Illus.). 464p. (C). 1993. text 42.00 (*87-7288-112-7*, Pub. by Aarhus Univ Pr) David Brown.

Andresen, Julie T. The Blue Hour. (Twice upon a Time Ser.). (Illus.). 400p. 1998. 23.50 (*0-9654499-1-2*) Windows on Hist.

— Linguistics in America, 1769-1924: A Critical History. (History of Linguistic Thought Ser.). 320p. (C). 1996. pap. 25.99 (*0-415-13259-2*) Routledge.

— Swept Away. 355p. 1997. reprint ed. pap. 12.50 (*0-9654499-0-4*) Windows on Hist.

Andresen, Karl. Lexikon der Alten Welt. (GER.). 1965. 495.00 (*0-8288-6749-6*, M7281) Fr & Eur.

***Andresen, Lee.** Music of the Vietnam War. (Illus.). 192p. 2000. pap. 14.95 (*1-886028-05-2*, Pub. by Savage Pr) Bookmen Inc.

Andresen, Roberta C. My Daddy Died: When Someone You Love Dies, & You Need to Tell a Child. (Illus.). 50p. (J). (ps-5). 1994. lib. bdg. 6.95 (*0-9641718-0-5*) Andresen Ent.

Andresen, Roy, et al. Night Wrighters' Chapbook. 103p. 1999. mass mkt. 8.00 (*0-9657568-4-X*) J B Strout.

***Andresen, Sabine & Schon, Barbel.** Lehrerbildung fur Morgen: Wissenschaftlicher Nachwuchs Stellt Sich Vor. (Erziehungskonzeptionen und Praxis. Bd. 40 Ser.). 170p. 1999. 31.95 (*3-631-35672-2*) P Lang Pubng.

***Andresen, Steinar.** Science in International Environmental Regimes: Between Integrity & Involvement. LC 99-42961. (Issues in Environmental Politics Ser.). 2000. 69.95 (*0-7190-5806-6*) Manchester Univ Pr.

Andresen, William, et al. Laboratory Inquiries into Concepts of Biology. 7th ed. 110p. (C). 1996. spiral bd. 24.95 (*0-7872-2294-1*) Kendall-Hunt.

Andreski, Stanislav. Max Weber's Insights & Errors. (International Library of Sociology Ser.). 164p. 1985. 27.50 (*0-7102-0051-X*, Routledge Thoemms) Routledge.

Andreski, Stanislav, ed. Wars, Revolutions, Dictatorships. 240p. 1992. text 45.00 (*0-7146-3452-2*, Pub. by F Cass Pubs) Intl Spec Bk.

Andreson, Steve. The Orienteering Book. LC 77-73875. (Illus.). 100p. 1977. reprint ed. pap. 3.95 (*0-89037-118-0*) Anderson World.

Andress. French Society in Revolution, 1789-1799. 277p. 1999. pap. 24.95 (*0-7190-5191-6*); text 69.95 (*0-7190-5190-8*) St Martin.

Andress, Alice A. Saunders Manual of Medical Office Management. Biblis, Margaret, ed. LC 95-4642. (Illus.). 352p. 1996. text 42.00 (*0-7216-4820-7*, W B Saunders Co) Harcrt Hlth Sci Grp.

Andress, Barbara. Music for Young Children. LC 96-79966. 208p. (C). 1997. pap. text 42.00 (*0-15-503071-X*, Pub. by Harcourt Coll Pubs) Harcourt.

Andress, Barbara L., ed. Promising Practices: Prekindergarten Music Education. (Illus.). 120p. (Orig.). (C). 1989. pap. text 21.00 (*0-940796-64-3*, 1498) MENC.

Andress, Barbara L. & Walker, Linda M. Readings in Early Childhood Music Education. 112p. 1992. pap., teacher ed. 21.50 (*1-56545-015-9*, 1043) MENC.

Andress, Faye, ed. see London, Bonnie.

***Andress, Reinhard.** Protokolliteratur in der DDR: Der Dokumentierte Alltag. (DDR-Studien/East German Studies: No. 14). (GER.). 232p. 2000. text 50.95 (*0-8204-4492-8*) P Lang Pubng.

Andress, Stanford E. & Deasy, Irene M. The Civil War: The Sound of Thunder. unabridged ed. (Illus.). 273p. (Orig.). 1996. pap. 15.95 (*0-9656257-1-0*, I E A F) S E Andress.

— In That Very Day. LC 95-96087. (Illus.). 382p. (Orig.). 1995. pap. 15.95 (*0-9656257-0-2*, I E A F) S E Andress.

— Money Is Power: Harness It! unabridged ed. (Orig.). 1997. pap. 15.95 (*0-9656257-3-7*) S E Andress.

Andress, Stanford E., jt. auth. see Deasy, Irene M.

Andress, William & Gohde, Winnie. Grandma Whitney: Queen of the Mountain. LC 95-70521. 112p. 1996. per. 8.95 (*1-57258-051-8*) Teach Servs.

Andressen, B. Michael. Spectacles: Utility Article & Cult Object. (ENG & GER., Illus.). 160p. 1998. 75.00 (*3-925369-49-X*, Pub. by Arnoldsche Art Pubs) Antique Collect.

Andressen, S. & Ostreng, Willy, eds. International Resource Management. 288p. 1992. 57.95 (*1-85293-097-7*, Pub. by P P Pubs) CRC Pr.

Andressohn, John C. Ancestry & Life of Godfrey of Bouillon. LC 70-38379. (Biography Index Reprints - Social Science Ser.: No. 5). 1977. reprint ed. 17.95 (*0-8369-8114-6*) Ayer.

Andretta, G., et al, eds. Stochastics in Combinatorial Optimization. 272p. (C). 1988. text 89.00 (*9971-5-0456-1*) World Scientific Pub.

Andretta, Helen. Chaucer's "Troilus & Criseyde" A Poet's Response to Ockhamism. LC 96-21407. (Studies in the Humanities: No. 29). VII, 201p. (C). 1997. text 44.95 (*0-8204-3361-6*) P Lang Pubng.

Andretta, Richard A. Shakespeare's Romances. 152p. (C). 1981. text 15.00 (*0-7069-1420-1*, Pub. by Vikas) S Asia.

— Tom Stoppard: An Analytical Study of His Plays. (C). 1991. 40.00 (*0-7069-5827-6*) Advent Bks Div.

***Andretti, Daniel.** Joy. (Illus.). 116p. 1999. pap. 8.99 (*0-9674809-0-6*) D Andretti.

Andretti, Michael, et al. Michael Andretti at Indianapolis. LC 91-38815. (Illus.). 64p. (J). (gr. 3-7). 1993. pap. 5.95 (*0-671-79674-7*) S&S Bks Yung.

Andreu, Alicia G. Modelos Dialogicos en la Narrativa de Benito Perez Galdos. LC 89-31929. (Purdue University Monographs in Romance Languages: Vol. 27). (SPA.). xvi, 126p. 1989. 38.00 (*1-55619-057-3*); pap. 19.95 (*1-55619-058-1*) J Benjamins Pubng Co.

Andreu, Athena S. Mirror of Life: Exercise Equipment for Your Spirit. Date not set. pap., wbk. ed. 19.95 (*1-892645-00-9*, MOL) Phx Rising.

Andreu, Fatima, tr. see Braz, Julio E.

Andreu, Fatima, tr. see Garcia, Edson G.

Andreu, Guillemette. Egypt in the Age of Pyramids. Lorton, David, tr. from FRE. LC 96-48461. (Illus.). 192p. 1996. text 39.95 (*0-8014-3222-7*); pap. text 13.95 (*0-8014-8313-1*) Cornell U Pr.

Andreu-Iglesias, Cesar, ed. Memorias de Bernardo Vega. LC 80-83696. (Coleccion Norte). 278p. 1977. reprint ed. pap. 8.75 (*0-940238-26-8*) Ediciones Huracan.

Andreucci, L. & Schenone, A. Topics on Biomedical Physics: Proceedings of the 6th National Congress of the Italian Association of Medical Physicians. 700p. 1992. text 121.00 (*981-02-1037-X*) World Scientific Pub.

Andreucci, Vittorio E. The Kidney in Pregnancy. LC 85-11437. (Topics in Renal Medicine Ser.). 1985. text 160.50 (*0-89838-741-8*) Kluwer Academic.

Andreucci, Vittorio E., ed. Acute Renal Failure. 1984. text 266.00 (*0-89838-627-6*) Kluwer Academic.

— New Frontiers in Renal Stone Disease: International ASTIF Meeting, Fiuggi, July 1998. (Nephron Ser.: Vol. 81, Supplement 1 (1999)). (Illus.). iv, 104p. 1998. pap. 34.00 (*3-8055-6818-5*) S Karger.

— Vascular & Peritoneal Access for Dialysis. (Topics in Renal Medicine Ser.). (C). 1989. text 246.50 (*0-7923-0119-6*) Kluwer Academic.

Andreucci, Vittorio E., et al, eds. International Yearbook of Nephrology, 1989. (C). 1988. text 190.00 (*0-7923-0015-7*) Kluwer Academic.

— International Yearbook of Nephrology, 1990. 1989. text 163.50 (*0-7923-0562-0*) Kluwer Academic.

Andreucci, Vittorio E. & Canton, Antonio D., eds. New Therapeutic Strategies in Nephrology: Proceedings of the 3rd International Meeting on Current Therapy in Nephrology. (Developments in Nephrology Ser.). 576p. 1991. text 197.00 (*0-7923-1199-X*) Kluwer Academic.

Andreucci, Vittorio E. & Dal Canton, Antonio, eds. Nephrology: Diuretics: Basic, Pharmacological, & Clinical Aspects. (Developments in Nephrology Ser.). 640p. (C). 1987. text 208.00 (*0-89838-885-6*) Kluwer Academic.

Andreucci, Vittorio E. & Fine, Leon G., eds. International Yearbook of Nephrology Dialysis Transplantation, 1994. (Illus.). 196p. 1994. 90.00 (*0-19-262491-1*) OUP.

— International Yearbook of Nephrology Dialysis Transplantation, 1995. (Illus.). 180p. 1995. 115.00 (*0-19-262649-3*) OUP.

— International Yearbook of Nephrology Dialysis Transplantation, 1996. (Illus.). 204p. 1996. 120.00 (*0-19-262771-6*) OUP.

— International Yearbook of Nephrology, 1991. (International Yearbooks of Nephrology Ser.). (C). 1990. text 191.00 (*0-7923-1002-0*) Kluwer Academic.

— International Yearbook of Nephrology, 1992. (Illus.). xi, 360p. 1992. 122.00 (*0-387-19697-8*) Spr-Verlag.

— International Yearbook of Nephrology, 1993. (Illus.). 376p. 1993. 247.00 (*0-387-19729-X*) Spr-Verlag.

Andreus, Alejanoro, jt. auth. see Ponce de Leon, Carolina.

***Andrew.** Sword & The Shield: The Mitrokhin Archive & the Secret History of the KGB. 700p. 2000. pap. 18.00 (*0-465-00312-5*, Pub. by Basic) HarpC.

Andrew, jt. auth. see Huebner, Kenneth H.

Andrew, A. M. Computational Techniques in Operations Research. (Cybernetics & Systems Ser., Abacus Bks.). x, 202p. 1985. text 142.00 (*0-85626-425-3*) Gordon & Breach.

— Self-Organizing Systems. x, 244p. 1989. pap. text 162.00 (*2-88124-686-9*) Gordon & Breach.

Andrew, A. Piatt & Kent, Frederick I. Banking Problems. Bruchey, Stuart, ed. LC 80-1178. (Rise of Commercial Banking Ser.). 1981. reprint ed. lib. bdg. 20.95 (*0-405-13631-5*) Ayer.

Andrew, Aletha. An Annotated Bibliography & Study of the Contemporary Criticism of Tennyson's Idylls of the King, 1859-1886. LC 93-469. (American University Studies: English Language & Literature: Ser. IV, Vol. 163). IX, 244p. (C). 1993. text 43.95 (*0-8204-2084-0*) P Lang Pubng.

Andrew, Alfred D. & Cain, G. F. Calculus Projects Using Mathematica. LC 95-81741. (C). 1996. pap. 31.88 (*0-07-001790-5*) McGraw.

Andrew, Alfred D., et al. Calculus Projects Using Mathematica. rev. ed. (C). 1993. pap. text 16.74 (*0-07-001867-7*) McGraw.

Andrew, Alice & Oscar, Ina. Tulukaruk Tunutellek-Ilu. large type ed. (ESK., Illus.). 8p. (J). (gr. k-3). 1998. pap. text 6.00 (*1-58084-017-5*) Lower Kuskokwim.

Andrew, Alice, et al. Castun Neqliyarer. large type ed.Tr. of How to Prepare Fish. (ESK., Illus.). 8p. (J). (gr. k-3). 1999. pap. text 6.00 (*1-58084-115-5*) Lower Kuskokwim.

— Cin'at (Roe) large type ed. (ESK., Illus.). 8p. (J). (gr. k-3). 1999. pap. text 6.00 (*1-58084-153-8*) Lower Kuskokwim.

***Andrew, Alice, et al.** Hannairniaqtaa Iqaluum. large type ed.Tr. of How to Prepare Fish. (ESK., Illus.). 8p. (J). (gr. k-3). 1999. pap. text 6.00 (*1-58084-131-7*) Lower Kuskokwim.

Andrew, Alice, et al. How to Prepare Fish. large type ed. (Illus.). 8p. (J). (gr. k-3). 1999. pap. text 6.00 (*1-58084-052-3*) Lower Kuskokwim.

***Andrew, Alice, et al.** Iqaluum Sannaiyautaa. large type ed.Tr. of How to Prepare Fish. (ESK., Illus.). 8p. (J). (gr. k-3). 1999. pap. text 6.00 (*1-58084-124-4*) Lower Kuskokwim.

Andrew, Alice, et al. Meluk (Roe) large type ed. (ESK., Illus.). 8p. (J). (gr. k-3). 1999. pap. text 6.00 (*1-58084-104-X*) Lower Kuskokwim.

— Neqliuryaraq. large type ed.Tr. of How to Prepare Fish. (ESK., Illus.). 8p. (J). (gr. k-3). 1999. pap. text 6.00 (*1-58084-053-1*) Lower Kuskokwim.

— Qanuq Itqanaiyarnagpat Qalut. large type ed.Tr. of How to Prepare Fishs. (ESK., Illus.). 8p. (J). (gr. k-3). 1999. pap. text 6.00 (*1-58084-139-2*) Lower Kuskokwim.

An Asterisk (*) at the beginning of an entry indicates that the title is appearing for the first time.

— Roe. large type ed. (Illus.). 8p. (J). (gr. k-3). 1999. pap. text 6.00 (*1-58084-103-1*) Lower Kuskokwim.

Andrew, Anita M., jt. auth. see Rapp, John A.

Andrew, Arthur E. Unbonded Tendons in Post-Tensioned Construction. 48p. 1987. 30.00 (*0-7277-0379-X*, Pub. by T Telford) RCH.

Andrew, Bryan H., ed. Interstellar Molecules. (International Astronomical Union Symposia Ser.: No. 87). 500p. 1980. lib. bdg. 171.00 (*90-277-1160-7*) Kluwer Academic.

Andrew, C. E., et al, eds. More Light for the Day. 370p. 1991. spiral bd. 6.50 (*0-9624991-1-0*) NWestern Prods.

Andrew, Caroline. The Wild 'Uns. 1985. 15.00 (*0-7855-2135-6*, Pub. by Pentland Pr) St Mut.

Andrew, Caroline, et al, eds. Women & the Canadian State. LC 98-122171.Tr. of Femmes et l'Etat Canadien. 392p. 1996. pap. 24.95 (*0-7735-1513-5*, Pub. by McG-Queens Univ Pr) CUP Services.

Andrew, Caroline & Rodgers, Sanda, eds. Women & the Canadian State/Les Femmes et l'Itat Canadien. LC 98-122171. 392p. 1996. 65.00 (*0-7735-1423-6*, Pub. by McG-Queens Univ Pr) CUP Services.

Andrew Center Staff Members. Evangelism: Good News or Bad News? Clapp, Steve, ed. 60p. 1996. pap. 8.00 (*0-9637206-7-8*) LifeQuest IN.

Andrew, Christopher. For the President's Eyes Only: Secret Intelligence & the American Presidency from Washington to Bush. (Illus.). 660p. 30.00 (*0-614-32218-9*) HarperTrade.

— For the President's Eyes Only: Secret Intelligence & the American Presidency from Washington to Bush. (Illus.). 688p. 1996. pap. 18.00 (*0-06-092178-1*, Perennial) HarperTrade.

***Andrew, Christopher & Curry, John Court.** The Security Service, 1908-1945: The Official History. 448p. 1999. 74.95 (*1-873162-79-0*, Pub. by PRO Pubns) Midpt Trade.

Andrew, Christopher & Gordievsky, Oleg. Comrade Kryuchkov's Instructions: Top Secret Files on KGB Foreign Operations, 1975-1985. (Illus.). 264p. (C). 1993. pap. 15.95 (*0-8047-2228-5*) Stanford U Pr.

— KGB: The Inside Story of Its Foreign Operations from Lenin to Gorbachev. pap. 16.00 (*0-685-51783-7*, Perennial) HarperTrade.

Andrew, Christopher & Gordievsky, Oleg, eds. More Instructions from the Centre: Top Secret Files on KGB Global Operations, 1975-1985. 130p. 1992. text 35.00 (*0-7146-3475-1*, Pub. by F Cass Pubs) Intl Spec Bk.

***Andrew, Christopher & Mitrokhin, Vasili.** The Sword & the Shield: The Mitrokhin Archive & the Secret History of the KGB. 736p. 1999. text 32.50 (*0-465-00310-9*, Pub. by Basic) HarpC.

Andrew, Christopher & Noakes, Jeremy, eds. Intelligence & International Relations, 1900-1945. 322p. 1987. pap. text 25.95 (*0-85989-243-3*, Pub. by Univ Exeter Pr) Northwestern U Pr.

Andrew, Christopher, jt. auth. see Jeffreys-Jones, Rhodri.

Andrew Cohen Students. Letters of Love. Cohen, Andrew, ed. LC 92-60070. 155p. (Orig.). 1992. pap. 10.95 (*0-9622678-5-6*) Moksha Pr.

Andrew, D. W. Dangerous Currency. unabridged ed. LC 98-93109. 200p. 1998. pap. 6.95 (*0-9664893-0-6*, 660658) Dair Pubg.

***Andrew, David & Rhind, Susan.** Watching Wildlife East Africa. (Watching Wildlife Ser.). (Illus.). 336p. 2000. pap. 19.95 (*1-86450-033-6*) Lonely Planet.

Andrew, David, jt. auth. see Finlay, Hugh.

Andrew, David S. Louis Sullivan & the Polemics of Modern Architecture: The Present Against the Past. LC 83-18164. (Illus.). 216p. 1985. text 24.95 (*0-252-01044-2*) U of Ill Pr.

Andrew, Dolores M. American Sampler Designs. (International Design Library). (Illus.). 48p. (Orig.). 1996. pap. 6.95 (*0-88045-133-5*) Stemmer Hse.

— Italian Renaissance Textile Designs. (International Design Library). (Illus.). 48p. 1986. pap. 5.95 (*0-88045-081-9*) Stemmer Hse.

— Medieval Tapestry Design. (International Design Library). (Illus.). 48p. 1992. pap. 5.95 (*0-88045-121-1*) Stemmer Hse.

Andrew, Dudley. Concepts in Film Theory. LC 83-17365. 350p. 1984. pap. 13.95 (*0-19-503428-7*) OUP.

Andrew, Dudley. Image Theory, Image Culture & Contemporary Japan. 1995. pap. 12.95 (*0-253-30016-9*) Ind U Pr.

Andrew, Dudley. The Major Film Theories: An Introduction. (Illus.). 288p. (Orig.). 1976. pap. text 13.95 (*0-19-501991-1*) OUP.

— Mists of Regret: Culture & Sensibility in Classic French Film. LC 09-415486. 384p. 1995. text 65.00 (*0-691-05686-2*, Pub. by Princeton U Pr); pap. text 24.95 (*0-691-00883-3*, Pub. by Princeton U Pr) Cal Prin Full Svc.

***Andrew, Dudley.** Sansho Dayu (Sansho the Bailiff) 1999. pap. 10.95 (*0-85170-541-3*) British Film Inst.

Andrew, Dudley, ed. The Image in Dispute: Art & Cinema in the Age of Photography. LC 96-22106. (Illus.). 347p. 1997. 40.00 (*0-292-70475-5*); pap. 19.95 (*0-292-70476-3*) U of Tex Pr.

Andrew, Dudley & Truffaut, Francois. Andre Bazin. (Illus.). 304p. 1990. pap. text 20.50 (*0-231-07399-2*) Col U Pr.

Andrew, Dudley, ed. see Godard, Jean-Luc.

Andrew, Ed. Closing the Iron Cage: The Scientific Management of Work & Leisure. 205p. 1999. pap. 19.99 (*1-55164-128-3*, Pub. by Black Rose) Consort Bk Sales.

— Closing the Iron Cage: The Scientific Management of Work & Leisure. 205p. 1999. 48.99 (*1-55164-129-1*, Pub. by Black Rose) Consort Bk Sales.

Andrew, Edward. Shylock's Rights: A History of Lockian Doctrine. 192p. 1987. pap. 15.95 (*0-8020-6660-7*); text 35.00 (*0-8020-2611-7*) U of Toronto Pr.

Andrew, Edward G. The Genealogy of Values: The Aesthetic Economy of Nietzsche & Proust. 204p. (C). 1995. pap. text 22.95 (*0-8476-8062-2*); lib. bdg. 55.00 (*0-8476-8061-4*) Rowman.

Andrew, Geoff. The Director's Vision: A Concise Guide to the Art of 250 Great Filmmakers. (Illus.). 252p. 1999. pap. 24.95 (*1-55652-366-1*, Pub. by A Cappella Bks) IPG Chicago.

— Stranger Than Paradise: Maverick Film-Makers in Recent American Cinema. LC 98-54603. (Illus.). 374p. 1999. 40.00 (*0-87910-277-2*) Limelight Edns.

— Three Colours. LC 98-212237. (Modern Classics Ser.). (Illus.). 96p. 1998. pap. 10.95 (*0-85170-569-3*) Ind U Pr.

Andrew George Jr & Gaines. Feasts! (Illus.). 208p. 1997. pap. 29.95 (*0-385-25580-2*) Doubleday.

Andrew, Hubert. Scottish Island Hopping: A Guide for the Independent Traveller. 208p. (Orig.). 1994. pap. 12.95 (*0-7486-6164-6*, Pub. by Polygon) Subterranean Co.

Andrew, J., et al. 5: Exhibition of Works by Judith Dolnick, Bruce Dorfman, Robert Natkin, Joel Perlman & Larry Perlman. 24p. 1999. 5.00 (*0-9672926-0-3*) J Andrew.

Andrew, J., jt. ed. see Gregory, F.

Andrew, James Dudley. Film in the Aura of Art. LC 84-1788. 240p. reprint ed. pap. 74.40 (*0-7837-1424-6*, 204177900023) Bks Demand.

Andrew, Jennifer, jt. auth. see Robottom, Ian.

Andrew, Joe. Narrative & Desire in Russian Literature, 1822-1849: The Feminine & the Masculine. LC 92-33089. 1993. text 39.95 (*0-312-09123-0*) St Martin.

***Andrew, Joe.** Russian Women's Shorter Fiction: An Anthology, 1835-1860. (Illus.). 1999. pap. 18.00 (*0-87501-173-X*) Ardis Pubs.

— Why Europe? LC 99-36945. 1999. text 65.00 (*0-312-22793-0*) St Martin.

Andrew, Joe, ed. Russian Women's Shorter Fiction: An Anthology, 1935-1860. 486p. 1996. text 95.00 (*0-19-815884-X*) OUP.

***Andrew, Joe, et al.** Why Europe? Problems of Culture & Identity LC 99-36945. 1999. text 65.00 (*0-312-22794-9*) St Martin.

***Andrew, John.** The Hanging of Arthur Hodge: A Caribbean Anti-Slavery Milestone. LC 00-190698. 232p. 2000. 25.00 (*0-7388-1930-1*); pap. 18.00 (*0-7388-1931-X*) Xlibris Corp.

Andrew, John. My Heart Is Ready: Feasts & Fasts from Fifth Avenue. LC 94-41666. (Church Year Sermons Ser.). 195p. 1995. pap. 11.95 (*1-56101-107-X*) Cowley Pubns.

— The Other Side of the '60s: Young Americans for Freedom & the Rise of Conservative Politics. LC 96-48088. (Perspectives on the Sixties Ser.). 280p. (C). 1997. text 50.00 (*0-8135-2400-8*); pap. text 19.95 (*0-8135-2401-6*) Rutgers U Pr.

Andrew, John A., III. Lyndon Johnson & the Great Society. LC 97-38966. (American Ways Ser.). 224p. 1998. 24.95 (*1-56663-184-X*, Pub. by I R Dee) Natl Bk Netwk.

— Lyndon Johnson & the Great Society. LC 97-38966. (American Ways Ser.). 224p. 1999. pap. text 12.95 (*1-56663-185-8*) I R Dee.

— Rebuilding the Christian Commonwealth: New England Congregationalists & Foreign Missions, 1800-1830. LC 75-38214. 240p. 1976. 29.95 (*0-8131-1333-4*) U Pr of Ky.

Andrew, Joseph D., jt. auth. see Gallagher, Timothy J.

Andrew, Joseph D., jt. auth. see Gallagher, Timothy James.

Andrew, Keith. The Skills of Cricket: The Skills of the Game. (Illus.). 144p. 1989. pap. 19.95 (*1-85223-237-4*, Pub. by Cro1wood) Trafalgar.

Andrew, Ken, jt. auth. see Strawhorn, John.

Andrew, Larry D. & Andrew, Patricia. Math Exercises (in Division) 1980. pap. 3.00 (*0-931992-39-7*) Penns Valley.

— Math Exercises (in Multiplication) 1980. pap. 3.00 (*0-931992-38-9*) Penns Valley.

— Math Exercises (in Subtraction) 1980. pap. 3.00 (*0-931992-37-0*) Penns Valley.

Andrew, Laura. Northstar: Focus on Reading/Writing High-Intermediate Tests. 52p. (C). 1999. pap. 13.27 (*0-201-45821-7*) Addison-Wesley.

Andrew, Lee, jt. auth. see Midgley, Michael.

Andrew, M. G., jt. auth. see Adey, A. D.

***Andrew, Mac A.** An Independent Guide to Cognac: The People, the Product & the Region. Goode, Ros, ed. (Illus.). 200p. 1999. spiral bd. 20.00 (*0-9673297-0-1*) Lusina Pubg.

Andrew, Malcolm, ed. Critical Essays on Chaucer's Canterbury Tales. 256p. 1991. text 65.00 (*0-8020-5005-0*); pap. text 18.95 (*0-8020-6936-3*) U of Toronto Pr.

— Critical Essays on Chaucer's 'Canterbury Tales' 240p. 1991. 9.00 (*0-335-09601-8*); pap. 9.00 (*0-335-09600-X*) OpUniv Pr.

— Geoffrey Chaucer: Comic & Bawdy Tales. (Everyman's Poetry Ser.). 128p. 1997. pap. 3.50 (*0-460-87869-7*, Everyman's Classic Lib) Tuttle Pubng.

— Two Early Renaissance Bird Poems: The Harmony of Birds & the Parliament Birds. LC 83-48646. 120p. 1985. 24.50 (*0-918016-73-8*) Folger Bks.

Andrew, Malcolm & Waldron, Ronald, eds. The Poems of the Pearl Manuscript. 3rd ed. (Exeter Medieval English Texts & Studies Ser.). 382p. 1997. pap. 19.95 (*0-85989-514-9*, Pub. by Univ Exeter Pr) Northwestern U Pr.

Andrew, Malcom & Waldron, Ronald, eds. The Poems of the Pearl Manuscript: Pearl, Cleanness, Patience & Sir Gawain & the Green Knight. 384p. 1995. pap. text 17.95 (*0-85989-273-5*, Pub. by Univ Exeter Pr) Northwestern U Pr.

***Andrew, Maureen.** Blood Clots & Strokes: A Guide for Parents & Little Folks. LC 99-180210. 40p. 1998. pap. 6.95 (*1-55009-064-X*) DEKR.

Andrew, Maureen. Thromboembolic Complications During Infancy & Childhood. 4000p. 1999. boxed set 99.95 (*1-55009-036-4*) DEKR.

Andrew, Maureen & DeVebers, Gabrielle. Pediatric Thromboembolism & Stroke Protocols. 72p. 1997. pap. 15.95 (*1-55009-055-0*) DEKR.

Andrew, Meredith. Deadly by Nature. LC 96-105578. 240p. 1997. pap. 15.95 (*1-55128-022-1*, Pub. by Mercury Bk) LPC InBook.

Andrew, Moira. Language in Colour: Themes for Teaching Children from Five to Nine Years with Poetry as the Starting Point. 1995. pap. 15.95 (*0-947882-10-3*) Incentive Pubns.

Andrew, Moira. Legend into Language: Myths & Legends as a Springboard for Language & Artwork with Children from Five to Eleven Years. (Illus.). 72p. (J). (gr. k-4). 1998. pap. 15.95 (*0-947882-69-3*, IP 342-6) Incentive Pubns.

***Andrew, Moira.** Paint a Poem. (Kids' Stuff Ser.). (J). 1999. pap. text 15.95 (*0-947882-44-8*) Belair Pubns Ltd.

Andrew, Nancy, tr. see Murakami, Ryu.

***Andrew, Neil, ed.** Under Southern Seas: The Ecology of Australia's Rocky Reefs. 238p. 2000. 49.50 (*1-57524-141-2*) Krieger.

— Under Southern Seas: The Ecology of Australia's Rocky Reefs. (Illus.). 297p. 1999. 49.95 (*0-86840-657-0*, Pub. by New South Wales Univ Pr) Intl Spec Bk.

Andrew, Nell, tr. see Casetti, Francesco.

Andrew, Nicholas J., ed. see Dryden, John.

Andrew, Nicol, jt. auth. see Robertson, Geoffrey.

Andrew of Neuchateau. Questions on an Ethics of Divine Commands. Idziak, Janine M., ed. & tr. by. from LAT. LC 96-26435. (Texts in Medieval Culture Ser.: Vol. 3). Orig. Title: Primum Scriptum Sententiarum. 208p. (C). 1997. text 30.00 (*0-268-03977-1*) U of Notre Dame Pr.

Andrew of New Diveyevo. The Restoration of the Orthodox Way of Life. Rose, Seraphim, tr. from RUS. & intro. by. (Illus.). 16p. (Orig.). 1987. pap. 2.00 (*0-912927-19-4*, X019) St John Kronstadt.

***Andrew, Paige G. & Lasrgaard, Mary Lynette, eds.** Maps & Related Cartographic Materials: Cataloging, Classification & Bibliographic Control. LC 99-51487. (Monograph Published Simultaneously as Cataloging & Classification Quarterly Ser.: Vol. 27, Nos. 1-4). 437p. 1999. pap. text 39.95 (*0-7890-0813-0*) Haworth Pr.

— Maps & Related Cartographic Materials: Cataloging, Classification & Bibliographic Control. LC 99-51487. (Monograph Published Simultaneously as Cataloging & Classification Quarterly Ser.: Vol. 27, Nos. 1-4). 437p. (C). 1999. 69.95 (*0-7890-0778-9*) Haworth Pr.

Andrew, Patricia, jt. auth. see Andrew, Larry D.

Andrew, Peter, ed. see Vivaldi, Steven T.

Andrew, R. H. Practical Guidelines for Corrosion Protection in the Mining & Metallurgy Industry. 1997. pap. 97.00 (*1-57590-025-4*, 37547) NACE Intl.

Andrew, R. J. & Huber, Ernst. Evolution of Facial Expression: Two Accounts. Incl. Evolution of Facial Musculature & Facial Expression. LC 72-344. 1931. lib. bdg. Origin & Evolution of the Calls & Facial Expressions of the Primates. LC 72-344. 1963. lib. bdg. LC 72-344. (Body Movement Perspectives in Research Ser.). 312p. 1973. reprint ed. 25.95 (*0-405-03143-2*) Ayer.

Andrew, Ralph, jt. auth. see Sacks, Seymour.

Andrew, Rick & Equiano, Olaudah. Equiano: The Slave Who Fought to Be Free. LC 91-155527. (People's College Comics Ser.). 48p. 1988. write for info. (*0-86975-330-4*) Ravan Pr.

Andrew, Rob. A Game & a Half. (Illus.). 224p. 1995. 34.95 (*0-340-62481-7*, Pub. by Hodder & Stought Ltd) Trafalgar.

Andrew, Sheila M. The Development of Elites in Acadian New Brunswick, 1861-1881. LC 97-187602. (McGill-Queen's Studies in Ethnic History). (Illus.). 280p. 1996. 55.00 (*0-7735-1508-9*, Pub. by McG-Queens Univ Pr) CUP Services.

Andrew, Stephen, jt. auth. see Jowett, Phillip S.

Andrew, Stephen, jt. auth. see Thomas, Nigel.

***Andrew, Susan, ed.** Winning: The Design of Sport. (Illus.). 160p. 1999. pap. 35.00 (*1-85669-152-7*, Pub. by L King Pubng) Gingko Press.

Andrew, Susan, jt. ed. see Maurer, Ingo.

***Andrew, Sylvia.** Annabelle. large type ed. 1999. 25.99 (*0-263-15901-9*, Pub. by Mills & Boon) Ulverscroft.

Andrew, Sylvia. Francesca. large type ed. 350p. 1998. 24.99 (*0-263-15413-0*, Pub. by Mills & Boon) Ulverscroft.

***Andrew, Sylvia.** Rosabella. large type ed. 1999. 25.99 (*0-263-15900-0*, Pub. by Mills & Boon) Ulverscroft.

Andrew, Sylvia. Serafina. large type ed. 350p. 1995. 25.99 (*0-263-14192-6*) Ulverscroft.

***Andrew, Sylvia.** Serena. (Readers Choice Ser.). 2000. mass mkt. 4.50 (*0-373-51116-7*, 1-51116-1, Harlequin) Harlequin Bks.

Andrew, Sylvia, jt. auth. see Marshall, Paula.

Andrew, Tommy. Neqsulartukut.Tr. of We Fish. (ESK., Illus.). 8p. (J). (gr. k-3). 1998. pap. text 6.00 (*1-58084-032-9*) Lower Kuskokwim.

Andrew, W. P. India & Her Neighbours. 413p. 1986. 39.95 (*81-210-0050-5*) Asia Bk Corp.

Andrew, William G. Applied Instrumentation in the Process Industries Vol. 4: Control Systems: Theory, Troubleshooting & Design by Leslie M. Zoss. LC 72-94067. (Illus.). 191p. 1979. reprint ed. pap. 59.30 (*0-608-04534-9*, 206527700004) Bks Demand.

Andrew, William G. & Williams, H. B. Applied Instrumentation in the Process Industries: Engineering Data & Resource Material, Vol. 3. 3rd ed. LC 92-35107. (Illus.). 680p. 1993. 89.00 (*0-87201-047-3*) Gulf Pub.

— Applied Instrumentation in the Process Industries Vol. 1: A Survey. 2nd ed. LC 79-9418. 408p. 1979. 69.00 (*0-87201-382-0*) Gulf Pub.

— Applied Instrumentation in the Process Industries Vol. 2: Practical Guidelines. 2nd ed. LC 79-9418. (Illus.). 320p. 1979. reprint ed. pap. 99.20 (*0-608-07563-9*, 206527700002) Bks Demand.

Andrew, William P., jt. auth. see Schmidgall, Raymond S.

Andrewartha, Herbert G. Introduction to the Study of Animal Populations. 2nd ed. LC 73-135741. (Illus.). xiv, 2841p. 1971. lib. bdg. 12.00 (*0-226-02029-0*, P519) U Ch Pr.

Andrewartha, Herbert G. & Birch, L. C. The Ecological Web: More on the Distribution & Abundance of Animals. LC 84-70. (Illus.). xiv, 506p. (C). 1985. lib. bdg. 40.00 (*0-226-02033-9*) U Ch Pr.

— The Ecological Web: More on the Distribution & Abundance of Animals. LC 84-70. (Illus.). xiv, 520p. (C). 1986. pap. text 24.00 (*0-226-02034-7*) U Ch Pr.

— Selections from the Distribution & Abundance of Animals. LC 82-6948. (Illus.). 288p. (C). 1982. pap. text 14.95 (*0-226-02032-0*); lib. bdg. 30.00 (*0-226-02031-2*) U Ch Pr.

— Selections from the Distribution & Abundance of Animals. LC 82-6948. (Illus.). 287p. reprint ed. pap. 89.00 (*0-608-08043-8*, 206900800002) Bks Demand.

Andrewe, L., tr. see Hieronymus, Von Braunschweig.

Andrewes, C. & Burnet, M. Influenza: A Review of Current Research. (WHO Monograph Ser.: No. 20). 223p. 1954. 12.00 (*92-4-140020-X*) World Health.

Andrewes, Christopher. Natural History of Viruses. (World Naturalist Ser.). (Illus.). (C). 1967. 14.00 (*0-393-06277-5*) Norton.

Andrewes, Lancelot. Complete Works, 11 vols. Wilson, J. P. & Bliss, J., eds. LC 78-158257. (BCL Ser.: No. 1). reprint ed. 1275.00 (*0-404-52020-0*) AMS Pr.

— Lancelot Andrewes: Selected Writing. Hewison, P.E., ed. LC 96-138261. 192p. 1996. pap. 18.95 (*1-85754-118-9*, Pub. by Carcanet Pr) Paul & Co Pubs.

— Private Devotions of Lancelot Andrewes. Brightman, F. E., tr. & intro. by. 1990. 25.75 (*0-8446-1534-X*) Peter Smith.

Andrewes, S., ed. see Eltringham, R. J., et al.

Andrewes, William, ed. The Quest for Longitude. (Illus.). 450p. 1996. 75.00 (*0-9644329-0-0*) Collect Hist Sci.

***Andrews.** A+ Troubleshooting Pocket Guide. (Programming Ser.). (C). 1999. pap. text 16.95 (*0-619-01537-3*) Course Tech.

— Courseprep for A+ Certification. (Programming Ser.). (C). 2000. pap., student ed. 45.00 (*0-619-01627-2*) Course Tech.

Andrews. Dancing in My Bones. 24p. (J). (ps up). 2001. 9.95 (*0-694-01316-1*) HarpC Child Bks.

***Andrews.** Ellan Vinnin. 2000. pap. 10.95 (*0-552-13855-X*, Pub. by Transworld Publishers Ltd) Trafalgar.

Andrews. Ethics in Practice: Managing Morals. 294p. 1989. 35.00 (*0-07-103200-2*) McGraw.

***Andrews.** Free Market Racism. 1999. pap. text 18.00 (*0-8147-0680-0*) NYU Pr.

Andrews. Guide to Managing & Maintaining a PC. 2nd ed. Date not set. write for info. (*0-534-36469-1*) Wadsworth Pub.

— Intermediate Differential Equation. (C). 1991. pap. 18.00 (*0-06-500002-1*) Addson-Wesley Educ.

— Introduction to Dental Assisting. (Dental Assisting Procedures Ser.). 1995. pap. 29.95 (*0-8273-6141-6*) Delmar.

— Introduction to Dental Assisting. (Dental Assisting Procedures Ser.). 1995. pap., teacher ed. 12.00 (*0-8273-6142-4*, VNR) Wiley.

— Kids Musical Year: Preschool Director. 1993. pap. 8.95 (*1-55897-411-3*) Brentwood Music.

***Andrews.** Leaving Liverpool. 2000. pap. 6.95 (*0-552-13933-5*, Pub. by Transworld Publishers Ltd) Trafalgar.

— Liverpool Lou. (J). 2000. pap. 8.95 (*0-552-13718-9*, Pub. by Transworld Publishers Ltd) Trafalgar.

— Maggie Way. (J). 2000. pap. 8.95 (*0-552-14036-8*, Pub. by Transworld Publishers Ltd) Trafalgar.

— Manufacturing Business. 328p. 1994. 65.95 (*0-7512-0292-4*) Ashgate Pub Co.

— Mercey Blues. 2000. pap. 8.95 (*0-552-14060-0*, Pub. by Transworld Publishers Ltd) Trafalgar.

— Mist over the Mersey. (J). 2000. pap. 8.95 (*0-552-14058-9*, Pub. by Transworld Publishers Ltd) Trafalgar.

Andrews. Novell's NDS Developer's Guide. 744p. 1999. 59.99 (*0-7645-4557-4*) IDG Bks.

— Opening the Books: Essays on the Social & Cultural History of British Communism. LC 94-42972. pap. 22.95 (*0-7453-0872-4*, Pub. by Pluto GBR) Stylus Pub VA.

— Opening the Books: Essays on the Social & Cultural History of British Communism. LC 94-42972. (C). 54.95 (*0-7453-0871-6*, Pub. by Pluto GBR) Stylus Pub VA.

— Organization Communication. (C). 1996. text, suppl. ed. 49.16 (*0-395-78242-2*) HM.

— Rediscovery of America: Transatlantic Crosscurrents in an Age of Revolution. LC 97-52924. 256p. 1998. text 69.95 (*0-312-21405-7*) St Martin.

— Rehabilitation of the Older Adult. (*0-340-54825-8*) E A.

***Andrews.** Voice Treatment for Children & Adolescents. 2001. pap. 44.00 (*0-7693-0107-X*) Singular Publishing.

— White Empress. (J). 2000. pap. 10.95 (*0-552-13482-1*, Pub. by Transworld Publishers Ltd) Trafalgar.

Andrews. William Shakespeare, Vol. 1. 1986. 105.00 (*0-684-18773-6*) Mac Lib Ref.

— William Shakespeare, Vol. 2. 1986. 105.00 (*0-684-18774-4*) Mac Lib Ref.

— William Shakespeare, Vol. 3. 1986. 105.00 (*0-684-18775-2*) Mac Lib Ref.

— Women's Sexual Health. 1996. pap. text 47.00 (*0-7020-1898-8*, W B Saunders Co) Harcrt Hlth Sci Grp.

*Andrews, ed.** Business Communication. 4th ed. 632p. 1999. pap. text 44.00 (*0-536-02689-0*) P-H.

Andrews, ed. Citizenship. (C). 1991. pap. 19.50 (*0-85315-733-2*, Pub. by Lawrence & Wishart) NYU Pr.

***Andrews & Courtney.** Essentials of McTimoney Chiropractic: The Gentle Art of Whole Body Alignment. 1999. pap. 21.00 (*0-7225-3747-6*) Thorsons PA.

Andrews & Morely. Linear Algebra Projects Using Mathematica. (C). 1993. pap. text 11.74 (*0-07-001868-5*) McGraw.

Andrews & Sansone. Who Runs the Rivers? Dams & Decisions in the New West. 452p. 1983. 12.00 (*0-318-04411-0*) Stanford Enviro.

Andrews, et al. Politics & Poetic Form. (Roof Bks.). 250p. 1989. 21.95 (*0-937804-36-3*); pap. 12.95 (*0-937804-35-5*) Segue NYC.

Andrews, jt. ed. see Killion.

***Andrews, Francis B.** The Medieval Builder & His Methods. LC 98-48800. 1999. pap. text 6.95 (*0-486-40672-5*) Dover.

Andrews & McMeel. Aquarius: Little Birth Sign. (Illus.). 80p. 1994. 4.95 (*0-8362-3069-8*) Andrews & McMeel.

— Aries: Little Birth Sign. (Illus.). 80p. 1994. 4.95 (*0-8362-3070-1*) Andrews & McMeel.

— Creation. LC 98-84236. (Illus.). 80p. 1999. 4.95 (*0-8362-6807-5*) Andrews & McMeel.

— Gemini: Little Birth Sign. (Illus.). 80p. 1994. 4.95 (*0-8362-3073-6*) Andrews & McMeel.

— Leo: Little Birth Sign. (Illus.). 80p. 1994. 4.95 (*0-8362-3074-4*) Andrews & McMeel.

— Libra: Little Birth Sign. (Illus.). 80p. 1994. 4.99 (*0-8362-3075-2*) Andrews & McMeel.

***Andrews & McMeel Publishing Staff.** Believe in Yourself. 1999. pap. text 5.95 (*0-7407-0406-0*) Andrews & McMeel.

— Chicken Soup for the Soul, 4 vols. 2000. boxed set 19.95 (*0-7407-0862-7*) Andrews & McMeel.

— Chinese Astrology: A Guide to the Signs, Mini Edition. abr. ed. (Illus.). 2000. 4.95 (*0-7407-0061-8*) Andrews & McMeel.

— Classic Ornament. (Illus.). 2000. 8.95 (*0-7407-0593-8*) Andrews & McMeel.

— Collette. 2000. 8.95 (*0-7407-0623-3*) Andrews & McMeel.

— Commute. 2000. 8.95 (*0-7407-0626-8*) Andrews & McMeel.

— Complete Guide to Life after Graduation. 2000. pap. 4.95 (*0-7407-0888-0*) Andrews & McMeel.

— Doctors. 1999. pap. text 5.95 (*0-7407-0408-7*) Andrews & McMeel.

— Don't Sweat the Small Stuff: A Special Collection for the Office, Mini Edition. 2000. 5.95 (*0-7407-0669-1*) Andrews & McMeel.

— Don't Sweat the Small Stuff Treasury: A Special Collection for Friends, Mini Edition. 2000. 5.95 (*0-7407-0666-7*) Andrews & McMeel.

— Don't Sweat the Small Stuff Treasury: A Special Collection for New Parents, Mini Edition. 2000. 5.95 (*0-7407-0668-3*) Andrews & McMeel.

— Don't Sweat the Small Stuff Treasury: A Special Collection for Newlyweds, Mini Edition. 2000. 5.95 (*0-7407-0667-5*) Andrews & McMeel.

— For the Graduate, 4 vols. 2000. boxed set 19.95 (*0-7407-0864-3*) Andrews & McMeel.

— Forever Friends. 1999. pap. text 5.95 (*0-7407-0405-2*) Andrews & McMeel.

— Going for the Gold. 1999. pap. text 5.95 (*0-7407-0404-4*) Andrews & McMeel.

Andrews & McMeel Publishing Staff. Goldenrod & Dayflowers. 1999. 7.95 (*0-8362-8281-7*) Andrews & McMeel.

***Andrews & McMeel Publishing Staff.** High Fashion. (Illus.). 2000. 8.95 (*0-7407-0627-6*) Andrews & McMeel.

— Irises. (Illus.). 2000. 8.95 (*0-7407-0624-1*) Andrews & McMeel.

— Joy of Getting Older. 2000. pap. 4.95 (*0-7407-0886-4*) Andrews & McMeel.

— Lawyers. 1999. pap. text 5.95 (*0-7407-0407-9*) Andrews & McMeel.

— Lawyers: Jokes, Quotes, & Anecdotes. 1999. pap. 5.95 (*0-8362-1543-5*) Andrews & McMeel.

— Lefties: A Book for Southpaws, Mini Edition. (Illus.). 2000. 4.95 (*0-7407-0512-1*) Andrews & McMeel.

Andrews & McMeel Publishing Staff. Mysterious Kitties. 1999. 7.95 (*0-8362-8275-2*) Andrews & McMeel.

***Andrews & McMeel Publishing Staff.** Quill Pen. 2000. 8.95 (*0-7407-0622-5*) Andrews & McMeel.

Andrews & McMeel Publishing Staff. Spectrums. 1999. 7.95 (*0-8362-8288-4*) Andrews & McMeel.

— Sunflower on Purple. 1999. 7.95 (*0-8362-8280-9*) Andrews & McMeel.

***Andrews & McMeel Publishing Staff.** Teachers. 1999. pap. text 5.95 (*0-7407-0409-5*) Andrews & McMeel.

— Ultimate Guide to a Stress-Free Life. 2000. pap. 4.95 (*0-7407-0889-9*) Andrews & McMeel.

Andrews & McMeel Publishing Staff. Warm Faces. 1999. 7.95 (*0-8362-8276-0*); 7.95 (*0-8362-8279-5*) Andrews & McMeel.

***Andrews & McMeel Publishing Staff.** Women's Wisdom Mixed, 4 vols. 2000. boxed set 19.95 (*0-7407-0863-5*) Andrews & McMeel.

Andrews & McMeel Publishing Staff. Work: The Wally Way. 1999. pap. 4.95 (*0-8362-7480-6*) Andrews & McMeel.

***Andrews & McMeel Publishing Staff, ed.** Fitzgraphics Daisies Journal. (Illus.). 128p. 2000. 10.95 (*0-7407-1206-3*) Andrews & McMeel.

— Two Women Boxing Gingko Journal. (Illus.). 128p. 2000. 10.95 (*0-7407-1221-7*) Andrews & McMeel.

***Andrews & McMeel Staff.** Allure of Angels: Mini Edition. 272p. 2000. mass mkt. 5.95 (*0-7407-0535-0*) Andrews & McMeel.

Andrews & McMeel Staff. Angels. LC 98-194738. (Tiny Tomes Ser.). (Illus.). 12p. (J). 1997. 3.95 (*0-8362-3641-6*) Andrews & McMeel.

— Another Sip of Chicken Soup for the Soul. LC 98-125565. (Chicken Soup for the Soul Ser.). 80p. 1997. 4.95 (*0-8362-5088-5*) Andrews & McMeel.

— Any Way You Slice It: A Golf Pop-Up Book. LC 98-120199. (Illus.). 12p. 1997. 4.95 (*0-8362-3615-7*) Andrews & McMeel.

— Art of Reflexology: Mapping the Sole. (Little Bks.). 1998. 4.95 (*0-8362-5223-3*) Andrews & McMeel.

— Baby Love: A Treasury for New Mothers. (Illus.). 40p. 1994. 6.95 (*0-8362-4716-7*) Andrews & McMeel.

— Baseball: Diamonds Are Forever. LC 98-194443. (Tiny Tomes Ser.). (Illus.). 128p. 1997. 3.95 (*0-8362-3631-9*) Andrews & McMeel.

— Bassets: A Book of Postcards. 1997. pap. 8.95 (*0-8362-2882-0*) Andrews & McMeel.

***Andrews & McMeel Staff.** Because It's Your Birthday: Mini Edition. (Illus.). 48p. (J). 2000. 4.95 (*0-7407-0078-2*) Andrews & McMeel.

Andrews & McMeel Staff. Best Birthday Wishes. LC 98-194423. (Tiny Tomes Ser.). (Illus.). 128p. 1997. 3.95 (*0-8362-3632-7*) Andrews & McMeel.

— The Best of Friends. (Illus.). 40p. 1994. 6.95 (*0-8362-4724-8*) Andrews & McMeel.

— Birthday: Life, Liberty, & the Pursuit of Cake. LC 97-71524. (Little Bks.). (Illus.). 80p. 1997. 4.95 (*0-8362-3599-1*) Andrews & McMeel.

***Andrews & McMeel Staff.** Blue Bugs. 1999. 8.95 (*0-8362-8284-1*) Andrews & McMeel.

Andrews & McMeel Staff. The Book of Sports Quips & Quotes. LC 98-84248. (Little Bks.). (Illus.). 80p. 1999. 4.95 (*0-8362-6811-3*) Andrews & McMeel.

— Brandy. 1999. pap. text 4.95 (*0-8362-1646-6*) Andrews & McMeel.

— Bundles of Joy. (Illus.). 80p. 1998. 4.95 (*0-8362-6795-8*) Andrews & McMeel.

— Butterflies: Grace on the Wing. LC 97-71525. (Little Bks.). (Illus.). 80p. 1997. 4.95 (*0-8362-3603-3*) Andrews & McMeel.

— Cancer: Little Birth Sign. (Illus.). 80p. 1994. 4.95 (*0-8362-3084-1*) Andrews & McMeel.

— Candles. (Little Bks.). 1998. 4.95 (*0-8362-5296-9*) Andrews & McMeel.

— Capricorn: Little Birth Sign. (Illus.). 80p. 1994. 4.95 (*0-8362-3072-8*) Andrews & McMeel.

— Cat Crazy: A Pop-Up Book. LC 98-176763. (Illus.). 12p. 1997. 4.95 (*0-8362-3614-9*) Andrews & McMeel.

— Cat's Meow. (Illus.). 40p. 1994. 6.95 (*0-8362-4722-1*) Andrews & McMeel.

— Celebrating the Beauty Within: A Book For Women. LC 97-224883. (Believing in Ourselves Ser.). 48p. 1997. 6.95 (*0-8362-2654-2*) Andrews & McMeel.

— Celebration of Sisters. LC 98-194640. (Tiny Tomes Ser.). (Illus.). 128p. (J). 1997. 3.95 (*0-8362-3633-5*) Andrews & McMeel.

— Cheer Up! Words of Encouragement. (Tiny Tomes Ser.). 1998. 3.95 (*0-8362-5240-3*) Andrews & McMeel.

— The Classic Cocktails Book. (Little Bks.). (Illus.). 80p. 1998. 4.95 (*0-8362-6796-6*) Andrews & McMeel.

— Congratulations You Did It! LC 98-84235. (Illus.). 80p. 1998. 4.95 (*0-8362-6797-4*) Andrews & McMeel.

— Conjunction Junction & Interjection: What's Your Function?, 2 bks. in 1. LC 98-125531. (Illus.). 80p. 1997. 4.95 (*0-8362-5116-4*) Andrews & McMeel.

— Dear Friend: A Treasury of Friendship. (Little Bks.). 1998. 4.95 (*0-8362-3607-6*) Andrews & McMeel.

— Diana. (Little Bks.). 1998. 4.95 (*0-8362-5537-2*) Andrews & McMeel.

— Dolphins. LC 97-71545. (Little Bks.). (Illus.). 80p. 1997. 4.95 (*0-8362-3606-8*) Andrews & McMeel.

***Andrews & McMeel Staff.** Dream Discovery: Mini Edition. 272p. 2000. mass mkt. 5.95 (*0-7407-0537-7*) Andrews & McMeel.

— Dreamy Passage. 1999. 8.95 (*0-8362-8226-4*) Andrews & McMeel.

Andrews & McMeel Staff. Elvis: The Legend. (Tiny Tomes Ser.). 1998. 3.95 (*0-8362-5244-6*) Andrews & McMeel.

— Essence of Aromatherapy. (Little Bks.). 1998. 4.95 (*0-8362-5226-8*) Andrews & McMeel.

***Andrews & McMeel Staff.** Essence of Fathers: Mini Edition. 272p. 2000. mass mkt. 5.95 (*0-7407-0538-5*) Andrews & McMeel.

Andrews & McMeel Staff. Fathers. LC 98-194693. (Tiny Tomes Ser.). (Illus.). 12p. 1997. 3.95 (*0-8362-3643-2*) Andrews & McMeel.

— Finding Our Selves: Insights for Young Women. (Tiny Tomes Ser.). 1998. 3.95 (*0-8362-5238-1*) Andrews & McMeel.

***Andrews & McMeel Staff.** Fleurs de Pastel. 1999. 8.95 (*0-8362-8222-1*) Andrews & McMeel.

Andrews & McMeel Staff. For My Friend. LC 98-194719. (Tiny Tomes Ser.). (Illus.). 12p. 1997. 3.95 (*0-8362-3645-9*) Andrews & McMeel.

— For My Teacher. (Tiny Tomes Ser.). 1998. 3.95 (*0-8362-5247-0*) Andrews & McMeel.

— For the Graduate. LC 98-84949. (Little Bks.). (Illus.). 80p. 1999. 4.95 (*0-8362-6989-6*) Andrews & McMeel.

— Forever & Always. (Illus.). 80p. 1997. 4.95 (*0-8362-3740-4*) Andrews & McMeel.

— Get Real! Women Speak Out. LC 98-194461. (Tiny Tomes Ser.). (Illus.). 128p. 1997. 3.95 (*0-8362-3640-8*) Andrews & McMeel.

— Get Well: Words to Make You Feel Better. (Little Bks.). (Illus.). 80p. 1998. 4.95 (*0-8362-6798-2*) Andrews & McMeel.

— The Gift of Friendship. (Little Bks.). (Illus.). 80p. 1998. 4.95 (*0-8362-6809-1*) Andrews & McMeel.

***Andrews & McMeel Staff.** Girls! Girls! Girls! 1999. 8.95 (*0-8362-8283-3*) Andrews & McMeel.

Andrews & McMeel Staff. Golf: Life on the Course. (Illus.). 48p. 1994. 6.95 (*0-8362-4718-3*) Andrews & McMeel.

— Golfer's Companion: A Book of Wit & Wisdom. LC 98-84252. (Illus.). 80p. 1998. 4.95 (*0-8362-6810-5*) Andrews & McMeel.

— Grandmothers. LC 98-194700. (Tiny Tomes Ser.). (Illus.). 12p. (J). 1997. 3.95 (*0-8362-3646-7*) Andrews & McMeel.

— Hanson. (Little Bks.). 1998. 4.95 (*0-8362-5536-4*) Andrews & McMeel.

— Happy Birthday Book. (Illus.). 32p. 1994. 6.95 (*0-8362-4717-5*) Andrews & McMeel.

— Happy Fiftieth Birthday: A Book of Wit & Wisdom. (Illus.). 80p. 1994. 4.95 (*0-8362-3093-0*) Andrews & McMeel.

— Happy Fortieth Birthday: A Book of Wit & Wisdom. (Illus.). 80p. 1994. 4.95 (*0-8362-3095-7*) Andrews & McMeel.

— Happy Sixtieth Birthday: A Book of Wit & Wisdom. LC 98-84240. (Illus.). 80p. 1998. 4.95 (*0-8362-6791-5*) Andrews & McMeel.

— Heart to Heart: A Book of Love. (Illus.). 48p. 1994. 6.95 (*0-8362-4719-1*) Andrews & McMeel.

***Andrews & McMeel Staff.** Heaven & Earth. 1999. 8.95 (*0-8362-8282-5*) Andrews & McMeel.

Andrews & McMeel Staff. Herbal Medicine. (Little Bks.). 1998. 4.95 (*0-8362-5218-7*) Andrews & McMeel.

— I Ching: A Guide to Your Destiny. (Little Bks.). 80p. 1998. 4.95 (*0-8362-5219-5*) Andrews & McMeel.

***Andrews & McMeel Staff.** I Do: Mini Edition. 272p. 2000. mass mkt. 5.95 (*0-7407-0536-9*) Andrews & McMeel.

Andrews & McMeel Staff. I'm Just a Bill & Lolly, Lolly, Lolly, 2 bks. in 1. (Illus.). 80p. (J). 1997. 4.95 (*0-8362-5117-2*) Andrews & McMeel.

— In Praise of Moms. (Little Bks.). (Illus.). 80p. 1998. 4.95 (*0-8362-6800-8*) Andrews & McMeel.

— Jennifer Love Hewitt. abr. ed. 1999. 4.95 (*0-8362-1647-4*) Andrews & McMeel.

— Journey Ahead: A Book for Women. LC 97-224878. 48p. 1997. 6.95 (*0-8362-2655-0*) Andrews & McMeel.

— Joy of Angels. (Tiny Tomes Ser.). 1998. 3.95 (*0-8362-5237-3*) Andrews & McMeel.

— Joys of Friendship: A Book for Women. LC 97-224889. 48p. 1997. 6.95 (*0-8362-2656-9*) Andrews & McMeel.

— Kiss, Kiss. (Illus.). 80p. 1998. 4.95 (*0-8362-6801-6*) Andrews & McMeel.

— Kitten Caboodle. LC 98-194628. (Tiny Tomes Ser.). (Illus.). 128p. (J). 1997. 3.95 (*0-8362-3635-1*) Andrews & McMeel.

— Leonardo DiCaprio. LC 98-85112. (Illus.). 80p. 1998. 4.95 (*0-8362-6986-1*) Andrews & McMeel.

— Little Book of Coffee. (Tiny Tomes Ser.). 1998. 3.95 (*0-8362-5243-8*) Andrews & McMeel.

— Little Book of Love. LC 98-194454. (Tiny Tomes Ser.). (Illus.). 128p. (J). 1997. 3.95 (*0-8362-3637-8*) Andrews & McMeel.

— The Little Book of Proverbs. LC 98-84246. (Little Bks.). (Illus.). 80p. 1999. 4.95 (*0-8362-6803-2*) Andrews & McMeel.

— Little Book of Psalms. LC 98-84247. (Illus.). 80p. 1999. 4.95 (*0-8362-6804-0*) Andrews & McMeel.

— Little Book of Puppies. LC 98-194455. (Tiny Tomes Ser.). (Illus.). 128p. (J). 1997. 3.95 (*0-8362-3639-4*) Andrews & McMeel.

— Little Book of Tea. (Little Bks.). 1998. 4.95 (*0-8362-5227-6*) Andrews & McMeel.

— Little Books for Cooks Apples. (Little Books for Cooks). 1998. 4.95 (*0-8362-5228-4*) Andrews & McMeel.

— Little Books for Cooks Herbs. (Little Books for Cooks). 1998. 4.95 (*0-8362-5229-2*) Andrews & McMeel.

— Little Books for Cooks Salsas. LC 97-74527. (Little Books for Cooks). 1998. 4.95 (*0-8362-5230-6*) Andrews & McMeel.

— Little Sip of Chicken Soup for the Soul: Inspiring Stories of Self-Affirmation. LC 98-125547. (Chicken Soup for the Soul Ser.). 80p. 1997. 4.95 (*0-8362-5087-7*) Andrews & McMeel.

— A Look at the Stars. 1994. 4.95 (*0-8362-3092-2*) Andrews & McMeel.

— A Look at the Stars. (Illus.). 80p. 1994. 4.95 (*0-8362-3109-0*) Andrews & McMeel.

***Andrews & McMeel Staff.** Lure of Fishing: Mini Edition. 272p. 2000. mass mkt. 5.95 (*0-7407-0539-3*) Andrews & McMeel.

Andrews & McMeel Staff. Many Thanks: A Book of Gratitude. (Tiny Tomes Ser.). 1998. 3.95 (*0-8362-5248-9*) Andrews & McMeel.

— Martini. (Little Bks.). 1998. 4.95 (*0-8362-5220-9*) Andrews & McMeel.

— Mary Engelbreit's Queen of the Kitchen Cookbook: Cooking for Family & Friends. LC 98-22459. (Illus.). 144p. 1998. 24.95 (*0-8362-6761-3*) Andrews & McMeel.

— Massage: The Healing Power of Touch. (Little Bks.). 1998. 4.95 (*0-8362-5221-7*) Andrews & McMeel.

— Merry Christmas. LC 98-194717. (Tiny Tomes Ser.). (Illus.). 12p. (J). 1997. 3.95 (*0-8362-3642-4*) Andrews & McMeel.

Andrews & Mcmeel Staff. The Millennium. (Little Bks.). (Illus.). 80p. 1998. 4.95 (*0-8362-5222-5*) Andrews & McMeel.

Andrews & McMeel Staff. Mom: You're the Greatest! (Tiny Tomes Ser.). (J). 1998. 3.95 (*0-8362-3638-6*) Andrews & McMeel.

— Mothers & Daughters: A Lasting Bond. (Tiny Tomes Ser.). 1998. 3.95 (*0-8362-5245-4*) Andrews & McMeel.

— The Mutts: Little Big Book. (Little Bks.). (Illus.). 80p. 1998. 4.95 (*0-8362-6980-2*) Andrews & McMeel.

***Andrews & McMeel Staff.** My Thanks to You: Mini Edition. 272p. 2000. mass mkt. 5.95 (*0-7407-0545-8*) Andrews & McMeel.

Andrews & McMeel Staff. Mystery of Runes. (Little Bks.). 1998. 4.95 (*0-8362-5224-1*) Andrews & McMeel.

— 'N Sync. 1999. 4.95 (*0-8362-1648-2*) Andrews & McMeel.

— Oy Vey the - Things They Say: A Book of Jewish Wit. (Illus.). 80p. 1994. 4.95 (*0-8362-3096-5*) Andrews & McMeel.

— Parrots. LC 97-71539. (Little Bks.). (Illus.). 80p. (J). 1997. 4.95 (*0-8362-3608-4*) Andrews & McMeel.

— Piece on Earth: A Little Book Made with Special Quilting. LC 97-71548. (Little Library to Make It Special). (Illus.). 80p. 1997. 4.95 (*0-8362-3612-2*) Andrews & McMeel.

***Andrews & McMeel Staff.** Psychedelic Daisy. 1999. 8.95 (*0-8362-8274-4*) Andrews & McMeel.

Andrews & McMeel Staff. Purr-Fect Little Book of Cats. (Little Bks.). 1998. 4.95 (*0-8362-3604-1*) Andrews & McMeel.

— Scents. (Little Bks.). 1998. 4.95 (*0-8362-5297-7*) Andrews & McMeel.

— The Sermon on the Mount. LC 98-84243. (Little Bks.). (Illus.). 80p. 1999. 4.95 (*0-8362-6805-9*) Andrews & McMeel.

— Sew Yourself a Garden: A Little Book Made Special with Ribbon Embroidery. LC 97-71547. (Little Library to Make It Special). (Illus.). 80p. 1997. 4.95 (*0-8362-3613-0*) Andrews & McMeel.

— Sex: A Book of Quotations. (Tiny Tomes Ser.). 1998. 3.95 (*0-8362-5246-2*) Andrews & McMeel.

— Silver Lining: Thoughts on Finding the Bright Side. (Illus.). 80p. 1994. 4.95 (*0-8362-3094-9*) Andrews & McMeel.

— Sisters: The Unbreakable Bond. LC 98-84244. (Illus.). 80p. 1998. 4.95 (*0-8362-6806-7*) Andrews & McMeel.

— Soaps. (Little Bks.). 1998. 4.95 (*0-8362-5298-5*) Andrews & McMeel.

***Andrews & McMeel Staff.** Soul of Africa: Mini Edition. 272p. 2000. 5.95 (*0-7407-0534-2*) Andrews & McMeel.

Andrews & McMeel Staff. Speaking for Ourselves: Women's Wit & Wisdom. (Illus.). 48p. 1994. 6.95 (*0-8362-4721-3*) Andrews & McMeel.

***Andrews & McMeel Staff.** Speaking Our Minds: Sage Advice from Sassy Women. LC 98-84245. (Little Bks.). (Illus.). 80p. 1998. 4.95 (*0-8362-6812-1*) Andrews & McMeel.

— Spirit of Teaching: Mini Edition. 272p. 2000. mass mkt. 5.95 (*0-7407-0547-4*) Andrews & McMeel.

Andrews & McMeel Staff. Ten Commandments. LC 98-84249. (Illus.). 80p. 1999. 4.95 (*0-8362-6808-3*) Andrews & McMeel.

— Thank You. LC 98-194708. (Tiny Tomes Ser.). (Illus.). 12p. (J). 1997. 3.95 (*0-8362-3647-5*) Andrews & McMeel.

— Those Who Touch Our Lives. (Illus.). 80p. 1997. 4.95 (*0-8362-3741-2*) Andrews & McMeel.

— Tiger Woods. LC 98-89397. 1999. 4.95 (*0-8362-1677-6*) Andrews & McMeel.

— Timewarped: Classic Moments & Hip Quips from the Cast of the Drew Carey Show. (Little Bks.). 1998. pap. 4.95 (*0-8362-5889-4*) Andrews & McMeel.

— Tiny Treasury of African Proverbs. (Tiny Tomes Ser.). 1998. 3.95 (*0-8362-5236-5*) Andrews & McMeel.

— Tiny Treasury of Friendship. LC 98-194612. (Tiny Tomes Ser.). (Illus.). 128p. (J). 1997. 3.95 (*0-8362-3634-3*) Andrews & McMeel.

***Andrews & McMeel Staff.** To a Tee: Mini Edition. 272p. 2000. mass mkt. 5.95 (*0-7407-0541-5*) Andrews & McMeel.

Andrews & McMeel Staff. To Mother with Love. (Illus.). 48p. 1994. 6.95 (*0-8362-4720-5*) Andrews & McMeel.

— Treasury of Christmas Cheer. LC 99-165514. (Tiny Tomes Ser.). 1998. 3.95 (*0-8362-5241-1*) Andrews & McMeel.

— Tribute to Grandmothers. LC 98-84250. (Illus.). 80p. 1998. 4.95 (*0-8362-6799-0*) Andrews & McMeel.

— Voices of Africa: Its Words & People. (Little Bks.). (Illus.). 80p. 1998. 4.95 (*0-8362-6793-1*) Andrews & McMeel.

***Andrews & McMeel Staff.** Wisdom of Grandmothers: Mini Edition. 272p. 2000. mass mkt. 5.95 (*0-7407-0543-1*) Andrews & McMeel.

Andrews & McMeel Staff. Wolves: The Howl of the Wild. LC 97-71532. (Little Bks.). (Illus.). 80p. (J). 1997. 4.95 (*0-8362-3609-2*) Andrews & McMeel.

— Zapped by the Zodiac: The Cynic's Astrology Guide. (Little Bks.). 1998. 4.95 (*0-8362-3598-3*) Andrews & McMeel.

— Ziggy's Little Book of Friendship. LC 99-158846. (Little Bks.). (Illus.). 80p. 1998. 4.95 (*0-8362-6606-4*) Andrews & McMeel.

Andrews & Mcmeel Staff. Ziggy's Little Book of Heart Thoughts To Cheer You. LC 99-158951. (Illus.). 80p. 1998. 4.95 (*0-8362-6607-2*) Andrews & McMeel.

***Andrews & McMeel Staff, ed.** Keepsake for the Class of 2000: A Gift for the Graduate. (Illus.). 2000. 4.95 (*0-7407-0511-3*) Andrews & McMeel.

Andrews & McMeel Staff, ed. Millennium: My Reflections on the End of One Era & the Beginning of Another. 1998. 14.95 (*0-8362-8298-1*) Andrews & McMeel.

Andrews & McMeel Staff & Ariel. For My Daughter. LC 98-194683. (Tiny Tomes Ser.). (Illus.). 12p. 1997. 3.95 (*0-8362-3644-0*) Andrews & McMeel.

Andrews & McMeeol Publishing Staff. Alice in Blunderland. 1999. pap. 4.95 (*0-8362-7479-2*) Andrews & McMeel.

Andrews, A. Australasian Tokens & Coins. (Illus.). 1982. reprint ed. lib. bdg. 35.00 (*0-942666-10-0*) S J Durst.

An Asterisk (*) at the beginning of an entry indicates that the title is appearing for the first time.

— Genealogical & Ecclesiastical History of New Britain, Connecticut. 538p. 1988. reprint ed. lib. bdg. 55.00 (*0-8328-0007-4*, CT0007) Higginson Bk Co.

Andrews, A. A. Marshal Redleaf. large type ed. (Linford Western Library). 1991. pap. 16.99 (*0-7089-7009-5*) Ulverscroft.

***Andrews, A. H.** The Health of Dairy Cattle. (Illus.). 320p. 2000. text 92.95 (*0-632-04103-X*, Pub. by Blckwell Science) Iowa St U Pr.

Andrews, A. T. & Varley, J., eds. Biochemistry of Milk Products. (Special Publication Ser.: No. 150). 190p. 1994. 84.00 (*0-85186-702-2*, R6702) CRC Pr.

Andrews, Adele. Andrews. Ancestors & Descendants of Laban Andrews, Revolutionary Patriot, & His Wife, Pridence Stanley Andrews. (Illus.). 136p. 1997. reprint ed. pap. 21.00 (*0-8328-7285-7*); reprint ed. lib. bdg. 31.00 (*0-8328-7284-9*) Higginson Bk Co.

Andrews, Adrianne R. Language, Rhythm, & Sound: Black Popular Culture into the Twenty-First Century. Adjaye, Joseph K., ed. LC 96-45890. 324p. 1997. pap. 19.95 (*0-8229-5620-9*); text 45.00 (*0-8229-3967-3*) U of Pittsburgh Pr.

Andrews, Albert & Elder, Marc. Renoir's Atelier: L'Atelier de Renoir. rev. ed. (Illus.). 288p. 1989. 225.00 (*1-55660-033-X*) A Wofsy Fine Arts.

Andrews, Alex. Black Saxon. large type ed. (Linford Romance Library). 329p. 1996. pap. 16.99 (*0-7089-7894-0*, Linford) Ulverscroft.

— Lady of the Moon. large type ed. (Dales Large Print Ser.). 272p. 1997. pap. 18.99 (*1-85389-716-7*, Dales) Ulverscroft.

Andrews, Alexander. History of British Journalism: From the Foundation of the Newspaper Press in England to the Repeal of the Stamp Act, 2 Vols. LC 68-24958. (British History Ser.: No. 30). 1969. reprint ed. lib. bdg. 150.00 (*0-8383-0154-1*) M S G Haskell Hse.

— History of British Journalism from the Foundation of the Newspaper Press in England to the Repeal of the Stamp Act in 1855, 2 vols., Set. 1968. 59.00 (*0-403-00139-0*) Scholarly.

Andrews, Alfred. Genealogical History of John & Mary Andrews, Who Settled in Farmington, Conn., 1640 Embracing Their Descendants to 1872. (Illus.). 652p. 1988. reprint ed. pap. 82.00 (*0-8328-0121-6*); reprint ed. lib. bdg. 92.00 (*0-8328-0120-8*) Higginson Bk Co.

— Genealogy & Ecclesiastical History of New Britain, CT. 540p. (Orig.). 1995. reprint ed. pap. 34.00 (*0-7884-0270-6*) Heritage Bk.

Andrews, Alice. Hooked on Bingo. Welton, Beverly, ed. LC 87-91893. (Illus.). 144p. (Orig.). 1988. pap. 6.95 (*0-945547-00-5*) Aecila Pub Co.

Andrews, Alice C. & Fonseca, James W. The Atlas of American Society. (Illus.). 303p. (C). 1995. 50.00 (*0-8147-2626-7*) NYU Pr.

— The Atlas of American Society. 303p. (C). 1996. pap. 20.00 (*0-8147-2658-5*) NYU Pr.

Andrews, Alice C., jt. auth. see Fonseca, James W.

***Andrews, Andy.** Miracles One at a Time. 2000. pap. 12.95 (*0-9629620-8-2*) Lightning Crown Pub.

Andrews, Andy. Storms of Perfection: In Their Own Words. 168p. 1991. pap. 12.95 (*0-9629620-1-5*) Lightning Crown Pub.

— Storms of Perfection Vol. 2: Letters from the Heart. 171p. 1994. pap. 12.95 (*0-9629620-3-1*) Lightning Crown Pub.

— Storms of Perfection Vol. 3: A Pathway to Personal Achievement. 176p. 1996. pap. 12.95 (*0-9629620-5-8*) Lightning Crown Pub.

— Storms of Perfection Vol. IV: Letters from the Past. (Storms of Perfection: Vol. 4). 222p. 1997. pap. 12.95 (*0-9629620-7-4*) Lightning Crown Pub.

— Tales from Sawyerton Springs: Somewhere down the Road & across the Holler from Your Hometown. 224p. 1995. pap. 12.95 (*0-9629620-4-X*) Lightning Crown Pub.

Andrews, Angus P., jt. auth. see Grewal, Mohinder S.

Andrews, Anthony P. The First Cities. LC 94-39479. (Exploring the Ancient World Ser.). (Illus.). 176p. 1996. text 24.95 (*0-89599-043-1*) Smithsonian.

— Maya Salt Production & Trade. LC 83-9306. 173p. 1983. 25.95 (*0-8165-0813-5*) U of Ariz Pr.

Andrews, Anthony P., jt. auth. see Andrews, E. Wyllys, IV.

Andrews, Anthony T. Electrophoresis: Theory, Techniques & Biochemical & Clinical Applications. 2nd ed. (Monographs on Physical Biochemistry). (Illus.). 450p. 1986. pap. text 60.00 (*0-19-854632-7*) OUP.

Andrews, Arlene B. Victimization & Survivor Services: A Guide to Victim Assistance. LC 91-15488. (Social Work Ser.: Vol. 21). 280p. (C). 1991. text 39.95 (*0-8261-7160-5*) Springer Pub.

Andrews, Arlene Bowers & Kaufman, Natalie Hevener, eds. Implementing the U. N. Convention on the Rights of the Child: A Standard of Living Adequate for Development. LC 98-21661. 280p. 1999. 65.00 (*0-275-96265-2*, Praeger Pubs) Greenwood.

Andrews, Arthur L. & Andrews, Dorothy, eds. Beyond Ultima Thule. 252p. (Orig.). 1996. pap. text. write for info. (*0-9639999-9-0*) Jay St Pubs.

***Andrews, Audrey.** Be Good, Sweet Maid: The Trials of Dorothy Joudrie. 240p. 1999. pap. 21.95 (*0-88920-334-2*) W Laurier U Pr.

Andrews, Avery D. Andrews. A Few Family Notes, Genealogical & Otherwise. (Illus.). 48p. 1997. reprint ed. lib. bdg. 19.50 (*0-8328-7282-2*) Higginson Bk Co.

Andrews, Avery D. & Manning, Christopher D. Complex Predicates & Information Spreading in LFG. LC 98-45541. (Stanford Monographs in Linguistics). 152p. (C). 1999. text 49.00 (*1-57586-165-8*); pap. text 18.00 (*1-57586-164-X*) CSLI.

Andrews, Barbara A., jt. ed. see Asenjo, Juan A.

Andrews, Barbara J. Miniature Bull Terrier. (Illus.). 96p. 1997. 19.95 (*0-7938-0768-9*, RX118) TFH Pubns.

— A New Owner's Guide to Akitas: AKC Rank #35. (New Owner's Guide to Ser.). (Illus.). 160p. 1996. 12.95 (*0-7938-2760-4*, JG-111) TFH Pubns.

— The World of the Akita. (Illus.). 416p. 1997. 69.95 (*0-7938-2080-4*, TS-256) TFH Pubns.

Andrews, Barry & Hoertdoerfer, Patricia. In Our Hands, Grades Four - Six. Marshak, David et al, eds. (Peace & Social Justice Program Ser.). (Illus.). 106p. (Orig.). 1993. pap. text 15.00 (*1-55896-158-5*) Unitarian Univ.

Andrews, Bart. I Love Lucy Book. LC 84-6033. (Illus.). 448p. 1985. pap. 14.95 (*0-385-19033-6*) Doubleday.

Andrews, Bart & Watson, Thomas. Loving Lucy. (Illus.). 383p. 1982. pap. 14.95 (*0-312-49975-2*) St Martin.

Andrews, Becky, ed. The Mailbox, 1995-1996 Intermediate Yearbook. (Illus.). 320p. 1996. 29.95 (*1-56234-138-3*) Educ Ctr.

— The Mailbox, 1996-1997 Intermediate Yearbook. (Illus.). 320p. 1997. 29.95 (*1-56234-167-7*) Educ Ctr.

Andrews, Becky S. The Mailbox Superbook: Your Complete Resource for an Entire Year of Fourth-Grade Success! LC 97-44710. (J). (gr. 4). 1997. pap. write for info. (*1-56234-177-4*) Educ Ctr.

— The Mailbox Superbook, Grade 4: Your Complete Resource for an Entire Year of Fourth-Grade Success! LC 97-44710. 1997. pap. 29.95 (*1-56234-200-2*) Educ Ctr.

Andrews, Benny. Between the Lines. (Illus.). 111p. 1978. pap. text 10.00 (*0-918618-13-4*) Pella Pub.

Andrews, Benny. Appalachee Red. LC 87-5901. (Brown Thrasher Bks.). 298p. 1987. reprint ed. pap. 12.95 (*0-8203-0961-3*) U of Ga Pr.

Andrews, Benny, jt. illus. see Fraustino, Lisa Rowe.

Andrews, Bernice, jt. ed. see Gilbert, Paul.

Andrews, Bert, jt. auth. see Harrison, Paul C.

Andrews, Beth. The Marplot Marriage. 224p. 1999. 19.95 (*1-929085-02-8*); lib. bdg. 17.95 (*1-929085-03-6*); mass mkt. 4.95 (*1-929085-01-X*) Rgncy Pr.

— The Marplot Marriage. large type ed. 336p. 1999. lib. bdg. 23.95 (*1-929085-04-4*); per. 19.95 (*1-929085-05-2*) Rgncy Pr.

***Andrews, Beth.** One Night Enjoyed. 200p. 2000. 19.95 (*1-929085-32-X*); 17.95 (*1-929085-33-8*); mass mkt. 4.95 (*1-929085-31-1*) Rgncy Pr.

— One Night Enjoyed. large type ed. 336p. 2000. 23.95 (*1-929085-34-6*); pap. 19.95 (*1-929085-35-4*) Rgncy Pr.

Andrews, Betsy, ed. see Page, Winni R.

Andrews, Betty. No Wider Than the Heart. 1994. 5.50 (*0-87129-495-8*, N37) Dramatic Pub.

Andrews, Brian. Knife under Fire. 1993. write for info. (*1-881529-01-0*) Custom & Limited.

— Northern Balcony Gardening. 1992. pap. 5.95 (*0-919433-98-7*) Lone Pine.

Andrews, Brian T., ed. Neurosurgical Intensive Care. LC 92-49880. (Illus.). 560p. 1993. text 74.00 (*0-07-001849-9*) McGraw-Hill HPD.

Andrews, Brian T. & Hammer, Gregory B., eds. Pediatric Neurosurgical Intensive Care. (Neurosurgical Topics Ser.). (Illus.). 250p. 1997. 95.00 (*1-879284-45-6*) Am Assn Neuro.

Andrews, Bruce. Aerial 9: Bruce Andrews: Contemporary Poetics As Critical Theory, Vol. 2. Smith, Rod, ed. 300p. 1999. pap. 15.00 (*1-890311-07-3*, Pub. by Edge Bks) SPD-Small Pr Dist.

— Divestiture-A. 56p. (Orig.). 1994. pap. 7.00 (*0-9628456-3-9*) Drogue Pr.

— Ex Why Zee. LC 95-68168. (Illus.). 109p. (Orig.). 1995. pap. 10.95 (*0-937804-60-6*) Segue NYC.

— Executive Summary. 96p. (Orig.). 1990. pap. 9.00 (*0-937013-31-5*) Potes Poets.

— Getting Ready to Have Been Frightened. LC 88-90723. (Roof Bks.). 100p. (Orig.). 1988. pap. 7.00 (*0-937804-31-2*) Segue NYC.

— Give Em Enough Rope. 192p. (Orig.). 1986. pap. 10.95 (*0-940650-73-8*) Sun & Moon CA.

— I Don't Have Any Paper So Shut up (or, Social Romanticism) (New American Poetry Ser.: No. 11). 312p. 1989. pap. 13.95 (*1-55713-077-9*) Sun & Moon CA.

— Moebius. 24p. (Orig.). 1993. pap. text 6.00 (*0-945112-17-3*) Generator Pr.

— Paradise & Method: Poetry & Praxis. (Avant-Garde & Modernism Studies). 296p. 1996. text 59.95 (*0-8101-1307-4*); pap. text 19.95 (*0-8101-1308-2*) Northwestern U Pr.

— R & B. (Segue Bks.). 32p. 1983. pap. text 5.00 (*0-937804-05-3*) Segue NYC.

— Strictly Confidential. 1994. pap. 10.00 (*84-87467-22-9*, Pub. by Zasterle Pr) SPD-Small Pr Dist.

— Tizzy Boost. 1993. pap. 10.00 (*0-935724-62-1*) Figures.

— Wobbling. 93p. 1981. pap. 60.00 (*0-937804-06-1*) Segue NYC.

Andrews, Bruce & Bennett, John M. Joint Words. 1979. pap. 3.00 (*0-935350-75-6*) Luna Bisonte.

Andrews, Bruce, et al. Translations, "C" Wellman, Don et al, eds. Rothenberg, Jerome et al, trs. (Translations: Experiments in Reading Ser.). (Illus.). 104p. (Orig.). 1983. pap. 4.50 (*0-942030-06-0*) O ARS.

Andrews, Bud & Carter, W. Horace. Lures for Lunker Bass. LC 89-84506. (Illus.). 246p. (Orig.). 1989. 12.95 (*0-937866-20-2*) Atlantic Pub Co.

Andrews, Bud, jt. auth. see Carter, W. Horace.

Andrews, C. C. Minnesota & Dakotah: In Letters Descriptive of a Tour Through the North-West in the Autumn of 1856. (Illus.). 216p. 1997. reprint ed. lib. bdg. 29.00 (*0-8328-6795-0*) Higginson Bk Co.

Andrews, C. C., ed. History of St. Paul: With Illustrations & Biographical Sketches of Some of Its Prominent Men & Pioneers. (Illus.). 827p. 1997. reprint ed. lib. bdg. 85.00 (*0-8328-6814-0*) Higginson Bk Co.

Andrews, C. E. & Percival, M. O., eds. Poetry of the '90's. LC 78-116392. (Granger Index Reprint Ser.). 1977. 20.95 (*0-8369-6133-1*) Ayer.

Andrews, C. F. The True India. 251p. 1985. 34.95 (*0-318-36983-4*) Asia Bk Corp.

Andrews, C. F. & Morgan, E. B. Supermarine Aircraft since 1914. rev. ed. (Putnam Aviation Ser.). (Illus.). 416p. 1989. 31.95 (*0-87021-614-7*) Naval Inst Pr.

Andrews, C. F., ed. see Gandhi, Mahatma.

Andrews, C. M. & Davenport, Frances Gardiner. Guide to the Manuscript Materials for the History of the United States to 1783. (C1.G Ser.: Vol. 5). 55.00 (*0-527-00685-8*) Periodicals Srv.

Andrews, C. M., jt. ed. see Andrews, E. W.

Andrews, C. Y. Andrews. Genealogical Biography of Charles T. & Mary E. Clark Andrews. (Illus.). 63p. 1997. reprint ed. pap. 13.00 (*0-8328-7281-4*); reprint ed. lib. bdg. 23.00 (*0-8328-7280-6*) Higginson Bk Co.

Andrews, Carol. Amulets of Ancient Egypt. (Illus.). 128p. (Orig.). (C). 1994. pap. 19.95 (*0-292-70464-X*) U of Tex Pr.

— Ancient Egyptian Jewelry. (Illus.). 208p. 1997. pap. 24.95 (*0-8109-2677-6*, Pub. by Abrams) Time Warner.

— Egyptian Mummies. (British Museum Paperbacks Ser.). (Illus.). 72p. 1984. pap. 14.00 (*0-674-24152-5*) HUP.

Andrews, Carol, ed. The Rosetta Stone. (Illus.). 24p. 1989. 14.95 (*0-8109-1572-3*) Abrams.

Andrews, Carol, ed. see Faulkner, Raymond O.

Andrews, Carolyn. The Black Sheep. (Rebels & Rogues Ser.). 1997. per. 3.50 (*0-373-25735-X*, 1-25735-1) Harlequin Bks.

— C. J.'s Defense. (Temptation Ser.). 1994. pap. 2.99 (*0-685-71209-5*, 1-25598-3) Harlequin Bks.

***Andrews, Carolyn.** Circonstances Aggravantes. 1999. mass mkt. 3.99 (*0-373-37534-4*) Silhouette.

Andrews, Carolyn. The Last Bachelor. (Temptation Ser.: Vol. 700). 1998. per. 3.75 (*0-373-25800-3*, 1-25800-3) Harlequin Bks.

— Manhunting in Manhattan. (Temptation Ser.). 1998. per. 3.75 (*0-373-25773-2*, 1-25773-2) Harlequin Bks.

— The Marriage Curse. (Temptation Ser.). 1996. per. 3.50 (*0-373-25681-7*, 1-25681-7) Harlequin Bks.

***Andrews, Carolyn.** Mientras Dormias. Vol. 212.Tr. of While You Sleep. (SPA.). 2000. per. 3.50 (*0-373-35342-1*, 1-35342-1) Harlequin Bks.

Andrews, Carolyn. Service with a Smile. LC 95-6894. (Temptation Ser.). 216p. 1995. per. 3.25 (*0-373-25528-0*, 1-25628-8) Harlequin Bks.

— While He Was Sleeping: The Wrong Bed. (Temptation Ser.: No. 735). 1999. per. 3.75 (*0-373-25835-6*, 1-25835-9, Harlequin) Harlequin Bks.

Andrews, Carolynn M. Newsletter Principles, Pitfalls & Pizzazz! (Illus.). 42p. 1996. reprint ed. pap. text 7.00 (*0-9653191-0-5*) Designer Bytes.

Andrews, Caryn. Which Way to the Dojo? (Illus.). 60p. (Orig.). 1986. pap. text 5.95 (*0-9617494-0-7*) Laughing Stock.

Andrews, Catherine, ed. see Goldman, Julius.

Andrews, Cecile. The Circle of Simplicity: Return to the Good Life. LC 96-51531. 288p. 1997. 20.00 (*0-06-017814-0*) HarpC.

— The Circle of Simplicity: Return to the Good Life. 288p. 1998. pap. 12.00 (*0-06-092872-7*) HarpC.

Andrews, Charles. Profit Fever: The Drive to Corporatize Health Care & How to Stop It. 150p. 1995. text 29.95 (*1-56751-057-4*) Common Courage.

— Profit Fever: The Drive to Corporatize Health Care & How to Stop It. 150p. 1995. pap. text 11.95 (*1-56751-056-6*) Common Courage.

Andrews, Charles M. The Colonial Period of American History Vol. 2: The Settlements. LC 64-54917. 417p. reprint ed. pap. 129.30 (*0-8357-8695-1*, 203366100002) Bks Demand.

— Colonial Self-Government, 1652-1689. LC 04-32334. 1971. 11.00 (*0-403-00138-2*) Scholarly.

— Colonial Self-Government, 1652-1689. LC 73-98630. reprint ed. 37.50 (*0-404-00359-1*) AMS Pr.

— Colonial Self-Government, 1652-1689. (BCL1 - U. S. History Ser.). 369p. 1991. reprint ed. lib. bdg. 89.00 (*0-7812-6094-9*) Rprt Serv.

— The Fathers of New England: A Chronicle of the Puritan Commonwealth. (BCL1 - United States Local History Ser.). 210p. 1991. reprint ed. text 79.00 (*0-7812-6263-1*) Rprt Serv.

— The Old English Manor: A Study in English Economic History. LC 78-64257. (Johns Hopkins University. Studies in the Social Sciences. Thirtieth Ser. 1912: 12). reprint ed. 41.50 (*0-404-61360-8*) AMS Pr.

— The River Towns of Connecticut: A Study of Wethersfield, Hartford & Windsor. LC 78-63790. (Johns Hopkins University. Studies in the Social Sciences. Thirtieth Ser. 1912: 7-9). reprint ed. 37.50 (*0-404-61055-2*) AMS Pr.

— The River Towns of Connecticut: A Study of Wethersfield, Hartford, & Windsor. 126p. 1995. reprint ed. pap. 15.50 (*0-8328-4459-4*) Higginson Bk Co.

Andrews, Charles M., ed. Narratives of the Insurrections, 1675-1690. (Original Narratives Ser.). 414p. 1967. reprint ed. 33.00 (*0-06-480028-8*, 06316) B&N Imports.

Andrews, Charles M., jt. ed. see Andrews, Evangeline W.

Andrews, Charlotte J. & Nicholson, Susan T. Forty-Eight Precious Moments from George Bush's Perfect Little War. 96p. (Orig.). 1991. pap. 14.95 (*0-9631029-0-7*) Cove Prints.

Andrews, Chris. Aquascaping. (Illus.). 1988. pap. 3.15 (*3-923880-46-4*, 16850) Tetra Pr.

— A Fishkeeper's Guide to Fancy Goldfishes. (Illus.). 117p. 1995. 10.95 (*1-56465-162-2*, 16058) Tetra Pr.

— A Fishkeeper's Guide to Fish Breeding. (Illus.). 117p. Date not set. 10.95 (*1-56465-126-6*, 16066) Tetra Pr.

— Hobbyist Guide to Marine Fish & Invertebrates. (Aquarium Digest International - Collector's Edition Ser.). 1992. 12.95 (*3-89356-133-1*, 16582) Tetra Pr.

— Hobbyist Guide to the Natural Aquarium. (Illus.). 132p. 1991. 12.95 (*3-89356-132-3*, 16581) Tetra Pr.

— Labyrinth Fish. (Illus.). 1988. pap. 3.15 (*3-923880-87-1*, 16846) Tetra Pr.

— Marine Invertebrates. (Illus.). 1988. pap. 3.15 (*3-923880-49-9*, 16853) Tetra Pr.

Andrews, Chris & Baensch, Ulrich. Tropical Aquarium Fish: Comprehensive Edition. (Illus.). 280p. 1991. 23.95 (*3-89356-131-5*, 16002) Tetra Pr.

Andrews, Chris & Carrington, Neville. The Manual of Fish Health. (Illus.). 210p. 1995. 26.95 (*1-56465-160-6*, 16068) Tetra Pr.

Andrews, Chris, tr. see Briongos, Ana M.

Andrews, Chris, tr. see Sepulveda, Luis.

***Andrews, Christopher.** Pandora's Game. LC 99-90687. 248p. 1999. 25.00 (*0-7388-0484-3*); pap. 18.00 (*0-7388-0485-1*) Xlibris Corp.

Andrews, Christopher C. Minnesota & Dacotah: In Letters Descriptive of a Tour Through the Northwest... LC 75-81. (Mid-American Frontier Ser.). 1975. reprint ed. 19.95 (*0-405-06850-6*) Ayer.

Andrews, Christopher J. Lightning Injuries: Electrical, Medical, Legal Aspects. 208p. 1991. lib. bdg. 139.00 (*0-8493-5458-7*, RD96) CRC Pr.

Andrews, Chryl Y. State Medicaid Coverage of Family Planning Services. 59p. 1996. pap. 4.00 (*0-16-061589-5*) USGPO.

Andrews, Clarence A. Chicago in Story: A Literary History. (Illus.). 414p. 1983. lib. bdg. 19.95 (*0-934582-03-3*) Midwest Heritage.

— A Literary History of Iowa. LC 72-76304. 301p. 1972. text 34.95 (*0-87745-032-3*) U of Iowa Pr.

— Michigan in Literature. LC 91-31020. (Great Lakes Bks.). 334p. reprint ed. pap. 103.60 (*0-608-10590-2*, 207121100009) Bks Demand.

Andrews, Clarence A., ed. Growing up in Iowa. LC 87-34495. (Iowa Heritage Collection). (Illus.). 164p. 1988. reprint ed. pap. 10.95 (*0-8138-0802-2*) Iowa St U Pr.

Andrews, Clarence A., ed. see Childs, Marquis & Engel, Paul.

Andrews, Clarence A., tr. see Gravel, Fern, pseud.

Andrews, Clarence L. Wrangell & the Gold of the Cassiar. 61p. reprint ed. pap. 10.00 (*0-8466-0267-9*, S267) Shoreys Bkstore.

Andrews, Claudia E. Pharaoh, Pharaoh. LC 97-7077. (Southern Messenger Poets Ser.). 72p. 1997. pap. 15.95 (*0-8071-2159-2*) La State U Pr.

Andrews, Clinton. Regulating Regional Power Systems: Case Studies & Perspectives on Emerging Competition. 416p. 1995. pap. 59.95 (*0-7803-1139-6*, PP5369) Inst Electrical.

Andrews, Clinton J. Regulating Regional Power Systems. LC 94-21702. 416p. 1995. 79.50 (*0-89930-943-7*, Quorum Bks) Greenwood.

Andrews, Colin, jt. auth. see Delgado, Pat.

Andrews, Colman. Catalan Cuisine: Europe's Last Great Culinary Secret. LC 99-17176. (Illus.). 352p. 1999. pap. 14.95 (*1-55832-154-3*) Harvard Common Pr.

Andrews, D. A. & Bonta, James. The Psychology of Criminal Conduct. 2nd ed. LC 98-6867. 423p. (C). 1998. pap. 39.95 (*0-87084-712-0*) Anderson Pub Co.

Andrews, D. A., jt. auth. see Hoge, Robert D.

Andrews, D. C., jt. ed. see Jewell, R. J.

Andrews, D. F. & Herzberg, A. M. Data. (Series in Statistics). (Illus.). 460p. 1985. 67.95 (*0-387-96125-9*) Spr-Verlag.

***Andrews, D. F. & Stafford, J. E. H.** Symbolic Computation for Statistical Inference. (Oxford Statistical Science Ser.). (Illus.). 176p. 2000. text 80.00 (*0-19-850705-4*) OUP.

Andrews, D. J., et al. Semantics of Specification Langauges (SoSL) Proceedings of the International Workshop on Semantics of Specification Languages, Utrecht, the Netherlands, October 1993. LC 94-2518. (Workshops in Computing Ser.). 1994. 78.95 (*0-387-19854-7*) Spr-Verlag.

Andrews, D. L. Lasers in Chemistry. (Illus.). 160p. 1986. pap. 45.00 (*0-387-16161-9*) Spr-Verlag.

— Lasers in Chemistry. 2nd ed. (Illus.). 192p. 1995. 53.95 (*0-387-51777-4*) Spr-Verlag.

Andrews, D. L., ed. Applied Laser Spectroscopy: Techniques, Instrumentation & Applications. 471p. 1992. 175.00 (*0-471-18782-8*) Wiley.

Andrews, D. L., ed. Perspectives in Modern Chemical Spectroscopy. (Illus.). 352p. 1990. 59.95 (*0-387-52218-2*) Spr-Verlag.

Andrews, D. W. Cheques Sent in Settlement. (Waterlow Publications). 152p. 1991. pap. 33.90 (*0-08-040874-5*) Macmillan.

Andrews, Dana L. Blueberry. (Illus.). 40p. (Orig.). (J). (gr. 1-4). 1996. pap. 4.95 (*1-888530-00-6*) Starchild Rdrs.

— Sonnets of Heart & Soul. (Illus.). 50p. (Orig.). 1996. pap. 6.95 (*1-888530-01-4*) Starchild Rdrs.

Andrews, Darrell, jt. auth. see Andrews, Pamela R.

Andrews, Dave. Building a Better World. LC 97-49372. 280p. 1998. pap. 14.95 (*0-8245-1726-1*, Crsrd) Crossroad NY.

Andrews, Dave & King, Rusty. Nevada Silver Rounds, 1964-1989. (Illus.). 80p. 1998. pap. 14.95 (*0-932151-03-5*) Gypsyfoot Ent.

Andrews, David. Aestheticism, Nabokov & Lolita. LC 99-25605. (Studies in American Literature: Vol. 31). 172p. 1999. text 79.95 (*0-7734-7960-0*) E Mellen.

— Science, Technology & Society. 192p. (C). 1994. 97.50 (*0-7478-1293-4*, Pub. by S Thornes Pubs) Trans-Atl Phila.

A

Andrews, David, et al, contrib. by. Reading the Sea: New Essays on Sea Literature. 1999. write for info. (*0-9670328-1-4*) Fort Schuyler Pr.

Andrews, David, jt. ed. see Barnes, Anthony.

Andrews, David A., jt. ed. see Andrews, David L.

Andrews, David F., et al. Robust Estimates of Location: Survey & Advances. LC 72-39019. 383p. 1972. reprint ed. pap. 118.80 (*0-608-02871-1*, 206393500007) Bks Demand.

Andrews, David G. An Introduction to Atmospheric Physics. LC 99-20191. (Illus.). 240p. (C). 1999. pap. write for info. (*0-521-62958-6*) Cambridge U Pr.

*__Andrews, David G.__ An Introduction to Atmospheric Physics. LC 99-20191. (Illus.). 240p. (C). 1999. 74.95 (*0-521-62051-1*) Cambridge U Pr.

Andrews, David G., et al, eds. Middle Atmosphere Dynamics. (International Geophysics Ser.: No. 40). 489p. 1987. pap. text 54.00 (*0-12-058576-6*) Acad Pr.

Andrews, David L. Lasers in Chemistry. 3rd ed. LC 97-15162. 228p. 1997. text 57.95 (*3-540-61982-8*) Spr-Verlag.

Andrews, David L. & Andrews, David A., eds. Applied Laser Spectroscopy: Techniques, Instrumentation, & Applications. LC 92-38383. 472p. 1992. 125.00 (*1-56081-023-8*, Wiley-VCH) Wiley.

Andrews, David L. & Demidov, Andrey A. Resonance Energy Transfer. LC 98-38684. 488p. 1999. 245.00 (*0-471-98732-8*) Wiley.

Andrews, David L. & Demidov, Audrey A., eds. An Introduction to Laser Spectroscopy. LC 95-45655. (Illus.). 240p. (C). 1995. text 69.50 (*0-306-45203-0*, Kluwer Plenum) Kluwer Academic.

Andrews, David R. Sociocultural Perspectives on Language Change in Diaspora: Soviet Immigrants in the United States. LC 98-50929. (Impact, Studies in Language & Society: Vol. 5). xviii, 182p. 1999. 69.00 (*1-55619-854-X*) J Benjamins Pubng Co.

Andrews, David W. & Parsons, Andrew W. Tenant Default under Commercial Leases. 256p. 1996. pap. 60.00 (*1-85811-059-9*, Pub. by CLT Prof) Gaunt.

Andrews, Dean T., tr. see Sylligardakis, Titus M.

Andrews, Deborah, ed. Annual Obituary, 1989. 89th ed. 913p. 1990. 100.00 (*1-55862-056-7*) St James Pr.

— Annual Obituary, 1990. 90th ed. 875p. 1991. 100.00 (*1-55862-092-3*, 200152) St James Pr.

— Annual Obituary, 1991. 91st ed. 850p. 1992. 100.00 (*1-55862-175-X*, 200153) St James Pr.

Andrews, Deborah C. Technical Communication in the Global Community. LC 97-805. 588p. (C). 1997. pap. text 61.00 (*0-13-103060-4*) P-H.

Andrews, Dee. Learning Math with God's Sea Creatures. (Illus.). (J). 1997. pap. text 2.29 (*0-7647-0089-8*) Schaffer Pubns.

— Learning Math with Joseph. (Illus.). (J). 1997. pap. text 2.29 (*0-7647-0091-X*) Schaffer Pubns.

— Learning Math with Noah. (Illus.). (J). 1997. pap. text 2.29 (*0-7647-0090-1*) Schaffer Pubns.

Andrews, Denison. How to Beat the System. LC 86-63744. 284p. 1987. 22.00 (*0-932966-74-8*) Permanent Pr.

Andrews, Derek J. A Theory & Practice of Program Development. LC 97-19343. (Formal Approaches to Computing & Information Technology Ser.). 400p. 1997. pap. 39.95 (*3-540-76162-4*) Spr-Verlag.

Andrews, Dianne, ed. see Avery, Louisia.

Andrews, Dianne, ed. see Fuller, Louisia.

Andrews, Dominick T. What's Your Excuse? LC 98-13300. 48p. 1998. 9.95 (*1-58141-000-X*) Rivercross Pub.

Andrews, Don. Interpreting the Figure in Watercolor. 2nd ed. (Illus.). 143p. 1996. reprint ed. pap. 24.95 (*0-614-25986-X*) D Andrews.

*__Andrews, Donna.__ Murder with Peacocks. LC 98-46254. 320p. 1999. mass mkt. 5.99 (*0-312-97063-3*, St Martins Paperbacks) St Martin.

— Murder with Puffins. LC 00-25476. 288p. 2000. text 24.95 (*0-312-26221-3*, Minotaur) St Martin.

Andrews, Dorine C. Street Smarts for Business Reengineers. 320p. 1994. 18.80 (*0-13-014853-9*) P-H.

Andrews, Dorothy. God's World & Johnny. (Illus.). 102p. (J). (ps-2). 1983. pap. 5.15 (*0-7399-0000-5*, 2258) Rod & Staff.

Andrews, Dorothy, jt. ed. see Andrews, Arthur L.

Andrews, E. M. The Anzac Illusion: Anglo-Australian Relations During World War I. (Illus.). 288p. (C). 1994. text 59.95 (*0-521-41914-X*) Cambridge U Pr.

Andrews, E. W. Research & Reflections in Archaeology & History: Essays in Honor of Doris Stone. LC 85-62925. (Publications: No. 57). 217p. 1986. 35.00 (*0-939238-87-X*) Tulane MARI.

Andrews, E. W. & Andrews, C. M., eds. Journal of a Lady of Quality: Being the Narrative of a Journey from Scotland to the West Indies, North Carolina & Portugal, 1774-1776. (Illus.). 341p. 1997. reprint ed. lib. bdg. 39.50 (*0-8328-6894-9*) Higginson Bk Co.

Andrews, E. Wyllys, IV. The Archaeological Use & Distribution of Mollusca in the Maya Lowlands. (Publications: No. 34). (Illus.). 115p. 1969. 25.00 (*0-939238-38-1*) Tulane MARI.

— The Archaeology of Quelepa, El Salvador. (Publications: No. 42). (Illus.). xii, 199p. 1976. 25.00 (*0-939238-47-0*) Tulane MARI.

Andrews, E. Wyllys, IV & Andrews, Anthony P. A Preliminary Study of the Ruins of Xcaret, Quintana Roo, Mexico, with Notes on Other Archaeological Remains on the Central East Coast of the Yucatan Peninsula. (Publications: No. 40). (Illus.). xii, 117p. 1975. 25.00 (*0-939238-45-4*) Tulane MARI.

Andrews, E. Wyllys, IV & Andrews, E. Wyllys. Excavations at Dzibilchaltun, Yucatan, Mexico. (Publication Ser.: No. 48). (Illus.). xxi, 339p. 1980. 35.00 (*0-939238-53-5*) Tulane MARI.

Andrews, E. Wyllys, jt. auth. see Andrews, E. Wyllys, IV.

Andrews, Earl & Dickens, Albert, eds. Voices from the Big House. LC 72-86910. 192p. 1972. 7.00 (*0-8187-0009-2*) Harlo Press.

Andrews, Earl H. The Spirit Has Come. 1991. pap. 14.00 (*0-85234-162-8*) Pilgrim Pubns.

Andrews, Ed. Caravans of Mars. (Space: 1889 Ser.). (Illus.). 64p. (Orig.). (YA). 1989. pap. 8.00 (*1-55878-023-8*) Game Designers.

Andrews, Edgar. Free in Christ. 1996. pap. 13.99 (*0-85234-353-1*, Pub. by Evangelical Pr) P & R Pubng.

Andrews, Edgar H. Christ & the Cosmos. 1986. pap. 8.99 (*0-85234-220-9*, Pub. by Evangelical Pr) P & R Pubng.

— From Nothing to Nature. 1978. pap. 9.99 (*0-85234-120-2*, Pub. by Evangelical Pr) P & R Pubng.

Andrews, Edmund & Andrews, Irene D. A Comparative Dictionary of the Tahitian Language: Tahitian-English with an English-Tahitian Finding List. LC 75-35171. reprint ed. 37.50 (*0-404-14201-X*) AMS Pr.

Andrews, Edna. Markedness Theory: The Union of Asymmetry & Semiosis in Language. Van Schooneveld, C. H., ed. LC 89-7906. (Sound & Meaning: The Roman Jakobson Series in Linguistics & Poetics). 200p. 1989. text 49.95 (*0-8223-0959-9*) Duke.

Andrews, Edna & Tobin, Yishai, eds. Towards a Calculus of Meaning: Studies in Markedness, Distinctive Features & Deixis. LC 96-37217. (Studies in Functional & Structural Linguistics: Vol. 43). xxviii, 432p. 1996. lib. bdg. 99.00 (*1-55619-268-1*) J Benjamins Pubng Co.

Andrews, Edward. Community Industries of the Shakers. 322p. 1993. reprint ed. lib. bdg. 89.00 (*0-7812-5208-3*) Rprt Serv.

Andrews, Edward D. Gift to Be Simple. (Illus.). 170p. 1962. pap. 5.95 (*0-486-20022-1*) Dover.

— People Called Shakers. enl. ed. 1990. 23.00 (*0-8446-1535-8*) Peter Smith.

— People Called Shakers: A Search for the Perfect Society. (Illus.). 351p. 1963. pap. 8.95 (*0-486-21081-2*) Dover.

Andrews, Edward D. & Andrews, Faith. Shaker Furniture: The Craftsmanship of an American Communal Sect. (Illus.). 192p. 1961. pap. 9.95 (*0-486-20679-3*) Dover.

— Visions of the Heavenly Sphere: A Study in Shaker Religious Art. LC 79-83652. (Illus.). 155p. reprint ed. pap. 48.10 (*0-608-11218-6*, 201765000007) Bks Demand.

— Work & Worship among the Shakers. (Illus.). 224p. 1982. pap. 7.95 (*0-486-24382-6*) Dover.

Andrews, Edward Demin. Masterpieces of Shaker Furniture. LC 99-42700. 128p. 1999. pap. text 9.95 (*0-486-40724-1*) Dover.

Andrews, Edwin J., et al, eds. Spontaneous Animal Models of Human Disease, Vol. 2. LC 78-20039. (American College of Laboratory Animal Medicine Ser.). 1980. text 104.00 (*0-12-058502-2*) Acad Pr.

Andrews, Elaine. Indians of the Plains. (First Americans Ser.). (Illus.). 96p. (J). (gr. 5-9). 1992. lib. bdg. 23.95 (*0-8160-2387-5*) Facts on File.

Andrews, Elaine, et al, eds. Action Models in Adult Environmental Education. 56p. (Orig.). 1994. pap. 12.00 (*1-884008-10-0*) NAAEE.

Andrews, Elaine, et al. Home-A-System: An Environmental Risk-Assessment Guide for the Home. Eagan, David J., ed. (Illus.). 116p. 1997. pap. text 8.00 (*0-935817-30-1*, NRAES-87) NRAES.

Andrews, Eliza F. The War-Time Journal of a Georgia Girl, 1864-1865. LC 75-39489. xvii, 396 p. 1976. 34.95 (*0-87797-033-5*) Cherokee.

— The War-Time Journal of a Georgia Girl, 1864-1865. LC 97-24622. (Illus.). xvii, 403p. 1997. pap. 16.95 (*0-8032-5931-X*, Bison Books) U of Nebr Pr.

— The War-Time Journal of a Georgia Girl, 1864-1865. King, Spencer B., Jr., ed. LC 75-39489. 416p. 1981. reprint ed. pap. 14.95 (*0-87797-214-1*) Cherokee.

Andrews, Elizabeth H. Andrews-Hayward Genealogies. (Illus.). 115p. 1997. reprint ed. pap. 18.50 (*0-8328-7279-2*); reprint ed. lib. bdg. 28.50 (*0-8328-7278-4*) Higginson Bk Co.

*__Andrews, Elmer.__ The Poetry of Seamus Heaney. LC 99-41368. (Critical Guides Ser.). 2000. pap. 14.50 (*0-231-11927-5*) Col U Pr.

Andrews, Elsie M. Facing & Fulfilling the Later Years. LC 68-16318. (Orig.). 1968. pap. 4.00 (*0-87574-157-6*) Pendle Hill.

Andrews, Emily S. The Changing Profile of Pensions in America. LC 85-25296. 234p. 1985. 39.95 (*0-86643-043-1*); pap. 24.95 (*0-86643-038-5*) Empl Benefit Res Inst.

— Pension Policy & Small Employers: At What Price Coverage? 1989. 39.95 (*0-86643-050-4*) Empl Benefit Res Inst.

Andrews, Emily S. & Rashid, Mansoora. The Financing of Pension Systems in Central & Eastern Europe: An Overview of Major Trends & Their Determinants, 1990-1993. LC 96-34970. (Technical Papers: No. 339). 56p. 1996. pap. 22.00 (*0-8213-3749-1*) World Bank.

Andrews, Eric. The Writing on the Wall: The Commonwealth & the Manchurian Crisis. 304p. (C). 1987. text 44.95 (*0-04-909027-5*) Routledge.

Andrews, Ethan A. Slavery & the Domestic Slave Trade in the U. S. LC 76-138331. (Black Heritage Library Collection). 1977. 22.95 (*0-8369-8723-3*) Ayer.

— Slavery & the Domestic Slave Trade in the U. S. LC 74-92412. 1836. 12.00 (*0-403-00148-X*) Scholarly.

Andrews, Eugene, jt. auth. see Andrews, Lorraine.

Andrews, Evangeline W. & Andrews, Charles M., eds. Jonathan Dickinson's Journal. LC 61-11399. (Florida Classics Ser.). Orig. Title: God's Protecting Providence. (Illus.). 109p. 1985. reprint ed. pap. 9.95 (*0-912451-00-9*) Florida Classics.

Andrews, F. Emerson. Corporation Giving. (Richard Magat Ser.). 375p. (C). 1992. 49.95 (*1-56000-022-8*) Transaction Pubs.

— Foundation Watcher. LC 73-7398. 1973. 7.50 (*0-685-40252-5*) Franklin & Marshall.

— New Numbers. 2nd ed. LC 61-5320. 168p. 1944. reprint ed. 12.00 (*0-317-36274-7*) Dozenal.

— Philanthropic Giving. LC 56-5824. 318p. 1950. 45.00 (*0-87154-022-3*) Russell Sage.

Andrews, F. Emerson, ed. Legal Instruments of Foundations. LC 58-9443. 318p. 1958. 45.00 (*0-87154-020-7*) Russell Sage.

Andrews, F. T. Building Mechanical Systems. 2nd ed. LC 75-11895. 412p. 1977. 41.50 (*0-07-001847-2*) Krieger.

Andrews, Faith, jt. auth. see Andrews, Edward D.

Andrews, Fannie. Memory Pages of My Life. (American Autobiography Ser.). 205p. 1995. reprint ed. lib. bdg. 79.00 (*0-7812-8443-0*) Rprt Serv.

*__Andrews, Frances.__ The Early Humiliati. LC 98-48328. (Cambridge Studies in Medieval Life & Thought: No. 43). (Illus.). 368p. (C). 2000. 69.95 (*0-521-59189-9*) Cambridge U Pr.

Andrews, Frances E., et al. Leadership: Reflective Human Action. 168p. 1995. ring bd. 75.00 (*1-929083-03-3*) Kappa Omi Nu.

— Leadership for a Culturally Diverse Society. 131p. 1993. ring bd. 35.00 (*1-929083-00-9*) Kappa Omi Nu.

Andrews, Francis, ed. see Francey, Nicolette.

Andrews, Frank. The Art & Practice of Loving. 236p. 1992. pap. 13.95 (*0-87477-690-2*, Tarcher Putnam) Putnam Pub Group.

Andrews, Frank C. Equilibrium Statistical Mechanics. 2nd ed. 272p. 1975. 125.00 (*0-471-03123-2*) Wiley.

— Thermodynamics: Principles & Applications. LC 77-150607. 300p. reprint ed. 93.00 (*0-8357-9993-X*, 205527800012) Bks Demand.

Andrews, Frank D. Ayars. Robert Ayars & His Descendants. (Illus.). 98p. 1997. reprint ed. pap. 18.00 (*0-8328-7311-X*); reprint ed. lib. bdg. 28.00 (*0-8328-7310-1*) Higginson Bk Co.

— Connecticut Soldiers in the French & Indian War: Bills, Receipts & Documents. (Illus.). 41p. 1997. reprint ed. pap. 8.00 (*0-8328-5621-5*) Higginson Bk Co.

Andrews, Frank D., compiled by. Maskell. Thomas Maskell of Simsbury, Conn., His Son Thomas Maskell of Greenwich, New Jersey, & Some of Their Descendants. 38p. 1995. reprint ed. pap. 8.00 (*0-8328-4880-8*); reprint ed. lib. bdg. 18.00 (*0-8328-4879-4*) Higginson Bk Co.

Andrews, Frank M., ed. Research on the Quality of Life. 384p. 1986. text 46.50 (*0-472-00700-9*, 00700) U of Mich Pr.

Andrews, Frank M. & Withey, Stephen B. Social Indicators of Well-Being: Americans' Perception of Life Quality. LC 76-26179. (Illus.). 476p. 1976. 59.50 (*0-306-30935-1*, Plenum Trade) Perseus Pubng.

Andrews, Frank M., et al. Selecting Statistical Techniques for Social Science Data: A Guide for Sas(R) Users. LC 99-461796. 112p. (C). 1998. pap. 24.95 (*1-58025-118-8*, BR55854) SAS Publ.

Andrews, G. Q-Series: Their Development & Application in Analysis, Number Theory, Combinatorics, Physics & Computer Algebra. LC 86-14061. (CBMS Regional Conference Series in Mathematics: No. 66). 130p. 1986. pap. 18.00 (*0-8218-0716-1*, CBMS/66) Am Math.

— Recipes for Gourmet Vegetables. 1989. pap. 2.95 (*0-88266-552-9*, Storey Pub) Storey Bks.

Andrews, G. Ruskin College. pap. text 23.00 (*0-85315-899-1*) Lawrence & Wishart.

Andrews, G. Salsas. LC 97-51612. 1998. pap. 2.95 (*0-88266-729-7*, Storey Pub) Storey Bks.

Andrews, G. E., et al. The Continued Fractions Found in the Unorganized Portions of Ramanujan's Notebooks. LC 92-18059. (Memoirs Ser.: No. 477). 71p. 1992. pap. 23.00 (*0-8218-2538-0*, MEMO/99/477) Am Math.

Andrews, G. R., et al. Aging in the Western Pacific: A Four-Country Study. (Western Pacific Reports & Studies: No. 1). 165p. 1986. pap. text 25.00 (*92-9061-161-8*, 1530001) World Health.

Andrews, G. W. & Abbott, W. H. Bulletins of American Paleontology Vol. 87, No. 321: Miocene Diatoms from the Hawthorn Formation, Thomas County, Georgia. 56p. 1985. 15.00 (*0-87710-397-6*) Paleo Res.

*__Andrews, Gavin & Henderson, Scott, eds.__ Unmet Need in Psychiatry: Problems, Resources, Responses. (Illus.). 456p. (C). 2000. text 90.00 (*0-521-66229-X*) Cambridge U Pr.

Andrews, Gavin, et al. Treatment of Anxiety Disorders: Clinician's Guide & Treatment Manuals. (Illus.). 437p. (C). 1995. text 100.00 (*0-521-46521-4*); pap. text 44.95 (*0-521-46927-9*) Cambridge U Pr.

Andrews, George. Andrews Memorial: Genealogy of the Andrews of Taunton & Stoughton, Mass., Descendants of John & Hannah Andrews of Boston, Mass., 1656-1886. 86p. 1988. reprint ed. pap. 17.00 (*0-8328-0123-2*); reprint ed. lib. bdg. 27.00 (*0-8328-0122-4*) Higginson Bk Co.

Andrews, George C. Extra-Terrestrial Friends & Foes. LC 93-3037. (Illus.). 342p. (Orig.). 1993. pap. 14.95 (*0-9626534-8-9*) IllumiNet Pr.

— Extra-Terrestrials among Us. LC 92-28281. (Psi-Tech Ser.). (Illus.). 352p. (Orig.). 1999. mass mkt. 4.95 (*0-87542-001-X*) Llewellyn Pubns.

Andrews, George C., ed. Drugs & Magic. LC 97-12624. 608p. (Orig.). 1997. reprint ed. pap. 19.95 (*1-881532-12-7*) IllumiNet Pr.

Andrews, George E. Generalized Frobenius Partitions. LC 84-3059. (Memoirs Ser.: No. 49/301). 44p. 1984. pap. 15.00 (*0-8218-2302-7*, MEMO/49/301) Am Math.

— Number Theory. LC 94-5243. (Illus.). 259p. 1998. pap. text 7.95 (*0-486-68252-8*) Dover.

— Number Theory: The Theory of Partitions. LC 76-41770. (Encyclopedia of Mathematics & Its Applications Ser.: Vol. 2). (Illus.). 1976. text. write for info. (*0-201-13501-9*) Addison-Wesley.

— On the General Rogers-Ramanujan Theorem. LC 74-18067. (Memoirs Ser.: No. 1/152). 86p. 1974. pap. 17.00 (*0-8218-1852-X*, MEMO/1/152) Am Math.

— On the General Rogers-Ramanujan Theorem. LC 52-42839. (American Mathematical Society Ser.: No. 152). (Illus.). 88p. reprint ed. pap. 30.00 (*0-608-09179-0*, 205268300002) Bks Demand.

— The Theory of Partitions. (Mathematical Library). (Illus.). 269p. (C). 1998. pap. text 29.95 (*0-521-63766-X*) Cambridge U Pr.

Andrews, George E., et al, eds. The Rademacher Legacy to Mathematics: Proceedings of the Centenary Conference in Honor of Hans Rademacher, July 1992, the Pennsylvania State University. LC 94-12052. (Contemporary Mathematics Ser.: Vol. 166). 369p. 1994. pap. 60.00 (*0-8218-5173-X*, CONM/166) Am Math.

Andrews, George E., et al. Special Functions. LC 98-25757. (Encyclopedia of Mathematics & Its Applications Ser.: No. 71). 560p. (C). 1998. 69.95 (*0-521-62321-9*) Cambridge U Pr.

*__Andrews, George E., et al.__ Special Functions. (Encyclopedia of Mathematics & Its Applications Ser.). 620p. 2000. pap. write for info. (*0-521-78988-5*) Cambridge U Pr.

Andrews, George E., ed. see MacMahon, Percy A.

Andrews, George F. Comalcalco, Tabasco, Mexico: Maya Art & Architecture. 2nd ed. LC 89-92394. (Illus.). 176p. (C). 1990. pap. 40.00 (*0-911437-11-8*) Labyrinthos.

— Pyramids & Palaces, Monsters & Masks: The Golden Age of Maya Architecture, 3 vols. LC 93-77664. (Illus.). 1090p. (C). 1999. text 150.00 (*0-911437-82-7*) Labyrinthos.

— Pyramids & Palaces, Monsters & Masks Vol. II: The Golden Age of Maya Architecture. LC 93-77664. (Illus.). 332p. (C). 1997. text 65.00 (*0-911437-81-9*) Labyrinthos.

Andrews, George F., ed. see Gendrop, Paul.

Andrews, George H. & Beekman, John A. Actuarial Projections for the Old-Age, Survivors & Disability Insurance Program of Social Security in the United States of America. LC 87-1101. (Illus.). 188p. 1987. text 25.00 (*0-9623118-1-2*) Actuarial Education.

Andrews, George P. Audio Computer Tutorial Guide for Medical Terminology. (Realtime Machine Shorthand Ser.). 67p. (C). 1993. pap. text 7.00 (*0-938643-28-2*) Stenotype Educ.

— Medical Dictionary for Stenotypists. (Realtime Machine Shorthand Ser.). 526p. (C). 1994. pap. text 46.75 (*0-938643-32-0*) Stenotype Educ.

— Stenotype Text Entry. (Realtime Machine Shorthand Ser.). 15p. (C). 1993. pap. text, student ed. 8.00 incl. audio (*0-938643-61-4*) Stenotype Educ.

Andrews, George P. & Ritter, Beverly L. Global Tutorial User Manual. (Realtime Machine Shorthand Ser.). 65p. (Orig.). (C). 1995. pap. text 10.00 (*0-938643-63-0*) Stenotype Educ.

— Medical Terminology Companion Dictionary. (Realtime Machine Shorthand Ser.). 69p. (C). 1992. pap. text 8.00 (*0-938643-29-0*) Stenotype Educ.

— Stenotype Text Entry. 15p. (C). 1993. pap. text 4.00 (*0-938643-59-2*) Stenotype Educ.

— Stenotype Text Entry: FasText Edition. (Realtime Machine Shorthand Ser.). 196p. (Orig.). (C). 1992. pap. text 29.00 (*0-938643-56-8*) Stenotype Educ.

— Stenotype Text Entry: Package. (Realtime Machine Shorthand Ser.). 234p. (Orig.). (C). 1993. pap. text 33.00 incl. audio (*0-938643-62-2*) Stenotype Educ.

— Stenotype Text Entry: Rapidtext Edition. 214p. (Orig.). (C). 1993. pap. text 29.00 (*0-938643-57-6*) Stenotype Educ.

Andrews, George P. & Ritter, Beverly L. Stenotype Text Entry: RapidWrite Edition. 234p. (Orig.). (C). 1994. pap. text 29.00 (*0-938643-58-4*) Stenotype Educ.

Andrews, George P., jt. auth. see Ritter, Beverly L.

Andrews, George R. The Afro-Argentines of Buenos Aires, 1800-1900. LC 80-5105. (Illus.). 301p. reprint ed. pap. 93.40 (*0-608-09840-X*, 206922800003) Bks Demand.

— Blacks & Whites in Sao Paulo, Brazil, 1888-1988. LC 91-50320. 376p. (C). 1991. pap. 19.95 (*0-299-13104-1*) U of Wis Pr.

Andrews, George R. & Chapman, Herrick, eds. The Social Construction of Democracy, 1870-1990. 432p. (C). 1995. text 45.00 (*0-8147-1508-7*) NYU Pr.

— The Social Construction of Democracy, 1870-1990. 432p. (C). 1997. pap. text 20.00 (*0-8147-1506-0*) NYU Pr.

Andrews, Gerald D. & Subramanian, Pallatheri M., eds. Emerging Technologies in Plastics Recycling. LC 92-27130. (ACS Symposium Ser.: No. 513). (Illus.). 322p. 1992. text 85.00 (*0-8412-2499-4*, Pub. by Am Chemical) OUP.

Andrews, Ginger. An Honest Answer. LC 99-25959. 112p. 1999. pap. 12.95 (*1-885266-78-2*, Pub. by Story Line) Consort Bk Sales.

Andrews, Gini. Esther: The Star & the Sceptre. 288p. 1981. pap. 7.70 (*0-310-20181-0*, 10859P) Zondervan.

— A Violent Grace. 112p. 1986. pap. 6.95 (*0-310-20131-4*, 10862P) Zondervan.

Andrews, Glenn. Growing & Cooking with Mint. LC 95-51165. 1996. write for info. (*0-88266-040-3*) Scovill Paterson.

— Growing & Using Cilantro. LC 98-4600. 1998. pap. 2.95 (*1-58017-021-8*) Storey Bks.

*__Andrews, Glenn.__ Growing & Using Dill. LC 99-34997. 1999. pap. 3.95 (*1-58017-221-0*) Storey Bks.

Andrews, Glenn. Growing & Using Garlic. LC 98-4595. (Country Wisdom Bulletins: Vol. A-183). 1998. 2.95 (*1-58017-085-4*) Storey Bks.

— Growing & Using Hot Peppers. LC 96-53550. (Storey Publishing Bulletin Ser.: Vol. A-170). 1997. pap. 2.95 (*0-88266-711-4*) Storey Bks.

An Asterisk (*) at the beginning of an entry indicates that the title is appearing for the first time.

— Growing & Using Hot Peppers. 1997. pap. 2.95 (*0-88266-781-5*, Storey Pub) Storey Bks.

***Andrews, Glenn.** Growing & Using Tarragon. LC 99-15837. 1999. pap. 3.95 (*1-58017-236-9*) Storey Bks.

Andrews, Glenn. Making & Using Flavored Oils & Vinegars. 1989. pap. 2.95 (*0-88266-556-1*, Garden Way Pub) Storey Bks.

— Making European Breads. LC 97-13175. 1997. pap. 2.95 (*0-88266-998-2*, Storey Pub) Storey Bks.

— Making Homemade Candy. 1989. pap. 2.95 (*0-88266-568-5*, Garden Way Pub) Storey Bks.

Andrews, Glennis, et al. The Arts in the Primary School. (Library on Aesthetic Education). 224p. 1993. 89.95 (*1-85000-771-3*, Falmer Pr) Taylor & Francis.

Andrews, Gordon. Gordon Andrews: A Designer's Life. 192p. 1993. 69.95 (*0-86840-245-1*, Pub. by New South Wales Univ Pr) Intl Spec Bk.

Andrews, Gould A., et al, eds. Radioactive Pharmaceuticals: Proceedings. LC 66-60068. (AEC Symposium Ser.). 702p. 1966. pap. 25.50 (*0-87079-325-X*, CONF-651111); fiche 9.00 (*0-87079-326-8*, CONF-651111) DOE.

Andrews, Gould A., jt. ed. see Kniseley, Ralph M.

Andrews Grace, Susan, see Grace, Susan Andrews.

Andrews, Graham. You're on Air. 156p. (C). 1994. pap. 19.95 (*0-86819-404-2*, Pub. by Currency Pr) Accents Pubns.

***Andrews, Grant.** The 43rd Mistress: A Sensual Odyssey. 208p. 2000. pap. 11.95 (*1-890159-21-2*) Greenery Pr.

***Andrews, Greg R.** Foundations of Parallel & Distributed Programming. LC 99-45285. 664p. (C). 1999. pap. text 36.00 (*0-201-35752-6*) Addison-Wesley.

Andrews, Gregg. City of Dust: A Cement Company Town in the Land of Tom Sawyer. (Illus.). 376p. (C). 1996. 42.50 (*0-8262-1074-0*) U of Mo Pr.

— Insane Sisters: Or the Price Paid for Challenging a Company Town. LC 99-29913. (Illus.). 280p. 1999. 29.95 (*0-8262-1240-9*) U of Mo Pr.

Andrews, Gregory A. The Complete Guide to Premedical Success: Achieving the Doctor Dream. LC 98-204564. 317p. 1998. per. 20.00 (*0-9660525-0-1*) MedLaw Bks Inc.

Andrews, Guy. Master the Manual: A Study Guide to Accompany the Ace Aerobics Instructor Manual. Cotton, Richard T., ed. (Illus.). 98p. (Orig.). 1995. pap. text. write for info. (*0-9618161-4-7*) Am Coun Exer.

Andrews, H. The Construction Design & Management Regulations. 1996. pap. 129.00 (*1-85953-031-1*, Pub. by Tech Comm) St Mut.

— Introduction to Timber Engineering. LC 67-21926. 1967. 102.00 (*0-08-011516-0*, Pub. by Pergamon Repr) Franklin.

Andrews, H. C. Hinsdale Genealogy: Descendants of Robert Hinsdale of Dedham, Medfield, Hadley & Deerfield (Mass.) with an Account of the French Family of De Hinnidal. (Illus.). 508p. 1990. reprint ed. pap. 74.50 (*0-8328-1601-9*); reprint ed. pap. 74.50 (*0-8328-1469-5*); reprint ed. lib. bdg. 82.50 (*0-8328-1600-0*); reprint ed. lib. bdg. 82.50 (*0-8328-1468-7*) Higginson Bk Co.

Andrews, H. E. Coleoptera: Carabidae-Carabinae. (Fauna of British India Ser.: Vol. 1). (Illus.). xxvii, 433p. 30.00 (*0-88065-006-0*) Scholarly Pubns.

Andrews, H. E., ed. Coleoptera: Carabidae-Harpalinae 1. (Fauna of British India Ser.: Vol. 2). (Illus.). xvi, 340p. 1977. reprint ed. 25.00 (*0-88065-009-5*) Scholarly Pubns.

Andrews, H. F. The Hamlin Family: A Genealogy of Captain Giles Hamlin of Middletown, Connecticut, 1654-1900. (Illus.). 479p. 1989. reprint ed. pap. 72.00 (*0-8328-0636-6*); reprint ed. lib. bdg. 80.00 (*0-8328-0635-8*) Higginson Bk Co.

Andrews, H. Franklin. A History of the Andrews Family: A Genealogy of Robert Andrews & His Descendants, 1635-1890. (Illus.). 234p. 1988. reprint ed. pap. 35.00 (*0-8328-0125-9*); reprint ed. lib. bdg. 43.00 (*0-8328-0124-0*) Higginson Bk Co.

Andrews, Hans A. Evaluating for Excellence: Addressing the Need for Responsible & Effective Faculty Evaluation. 180p. (C). 1985. pap. text 17.95 (*0-913507-04-0*, Pub. by New Forums) Booksource.

— Merit in Education. 120p. (Orig.). 1987. pap. 15.95 (*0-913507-05-9*) New Forums.

— Teachers Can Be Fired! The Quest for Quality. 286p. 1995. 38.95 (*0-8126-9280-2*); pap. 18.95 (*0-8126-9281-0*) Open Court.

Andrews, Harry C. Introduction to Mathematical Techniques in Pattern Recognition. LC 82-6543. 256p. 1983. reprint ed. 32.50 (*0-89874-506-3*) Krieger.

Andrews, Heather A., jt. auth. see Roy, Carrista.

Andrews, Heather S. & Berry, P. J. Atlas of Diagnostic Ultrasound & Pathology of Fetal Malformation. (Illus.). 250p. 1997. write for info. (*0-7020-1405-2*, Pub. by W B Saunders) Saunders.

Andrews, Henrietta. The Function of Verb Prefixes in Southwestern Otomi. LC 93-60250. (Publications in Linguistics Ser.: Vol. 115). xi, 120p. 1993. pap. 10.00 (*0-88312-605-2*) S I L Intl.

Andrews, Henry B. Group Design & Leadership: Strategies for Creating Successful Common Theme Groups. LC 93-49555. 192p. (C). 1994. 58.00 (*0-205-16197-9*, Longwood Div) Allyn.

Andrews, Henry F. Company D, 16 Maine Volunteers. 40p. 1995. reprint ed. pap. 4.95 (*0-9642029-4-8*) Union Pubng.

Andrews, Henry N. The Fossil Hunters: In Search of Ancient Plants. LC 79-24101. (Illus.). 420p. 1980. text 57.50 (*0-8014-1248-X*) Cornell U Pr.

Andrews, Henry N., jt. auth. see Gensel, Patricia G.

Andrews, Herbert C. Hinsdale Genealogy: Descendants of Robert Hinsdale of Dedham, Medfield, Hadley & Deerfield (Mass.) with an Account of the French Family of De Hinnidal. Holman, Alfred L., ed. 507p. 1989. reprint ed. pap. 74.50 (*0-8328-1406-7*); reprint ed. lib. bdg. 82.50 (*0-8328-1405-9*) Higginson Bk Co.

Andrews, Hilda, ed. see Byrd, William.

Andrews, Hilda, tr. see Walicki, Andrzej.

Andrews, Hope. Do Psychics Really Know? LC 93-90623. (Illus.). 186p. 1994. pap. 9.85 (*1-882734-01-7*) Creat of Hope.

— The Father & Me. LC 77-81282. (Illus.). 84p. (Orig.). 1992. pap. 8.95 (*1-882734-00-9*) Creat of Hope.

Andrews, Ian. Pompeii. (Cambridge Introduction to World History Topic Bks.). (Illus.). 48p. (YA). (gr. 7 up). 1978. pap. 12.95 (*0-521-20973-0*) Cambridge U Pr.

Andrews, Irene D., jt. auth. see Andrews, Edmund.

Andrews, Isabelle & Clark-Andrews. Guerilla Guide to Theatre. (Illus.). 448p. 1998. pap. 24.95 (*0-304-70341-9*) Continuum.

Andrews, Israel D. Communication from the Secretary of the Treasury. LC 75-22797. (America in Two Centuries Ser.). 1976. reprint ed. 75.95 (*0-405-07668-1*) Ayer.

Andrews, J. Logic Programming: Operational Semantics & Proof Theory. (Distinguished Dissertations in Computer Science Ser.: No. 4). (Illus.). 116p. (C). 1993. text 49.95 (*0-521-43219-7*) Cambridge U Pr.

Andrews, J., et al, eds. Advances in Botanical Research Incorporating Advances in Plant Pathology Vol. 23: Pathogen Indexing Technologies. (Illus.). 256p. 1996. text 88.00 (*0-12-005923-1*) Acad Pr.

Andrews, J. & Lunati, M., eds. Viajeros Perdidos: Contemporary Spanish Short Stories. (Bristol Spanish Texts Ser.). (SPA.). 1998. pap. 18.95 (*1-85399-460-X*, Pub. by Brist Class Pr) Focus Pub-R Pullins.

Andrews, J. & Von Hahn, H. P., eds. Geriatrics for Everyday Practice. (Illus.). viii, 220p. 1981. pap. 34.00 (*3-8055-1803-X*) S Karger.

Andrews, J. & Williams, E. Woodford, eds. Iron, Anemia, & Old Age. (Gerontologia Clinica Ser.: Vol. 13, No. 1-2). 1970. reprint ed. pap. 19.25 (*3-8055-0889-1*) S Karger.

Andrews, J., et al. Heat Pipe Technology: Theory, Applications & Prospects: Proceedings of the 5th International Heat Pipe Symposium, Melbourne, Australia, 17-20 November, 1996. LC 97-27634. 464p. 1997. 209.00 (*0-08-042842-8*, Pergamon Pr) Elsevier.

Andrews, J., jt. ed. see Shennan, I.

Andrews, J. A. Criminal Evidence: Statutes & Materials. 256p. 1990. pap. 39.95 (*0-08-036900-6*) Macmillan.

— Human Rights in Criminal Procedure. 1982. lib. bdg. 197.50 (*90-247-2552-6*) Kluwer Academic.

— What Is Communism & Other Anarchist Essays. James, Bob, ed. (Illus.). 190p. (Orig.). 1984. pap. 7.95 (*0-949300-00-4*) Left Bank.

Andrews, J. A. & Hirst, M. Criminal Evidence. (Criminal Law Library). 512p. 1987. 75.00 (*0-08-039237-7*, Pergamon Pr) Elsevier.

Andrews, J. Austin. Introduction To Music Fundamentals. 6th ed. LC 92-18865. 272p. (C). 1993. pap. text 41.20 (*0-13-474958-8*) P-H.

Andrews, J. Cutler. The North Reports the Civil War. LC 55-6873. (Illus.). 848p. 1955. pap. 200.00 (*0-608-05161-6*, 201049700068) Bks Demand.

— The South Reports the Civil War. LC 84-25610. (Illus.). 632p. 1985. reprint ed. pap. 24.95 (*0-8229-5902-X*) U of Pittsburgh Pr.

Andrews, J. David. Full Moon Is Rising: "Lost Haiku" of Matsuo Basho (1644-1694) & Travel Haiku of Matsuo Basho, a New Rendering. LC 75-32845. (Illus.). 1976. 15.95 (*0-8283-1651-1*) Branden Bks.

Andrews, J. E., et al. Environmental Chemistry. 1996. pap. 29.95 (*0-632-03854-3*) Blackwell Sci.

Andrews, J. H. Comparative Ecology of Microorganisms & Macroorganisms. (Contemporary Bioscience Ser.). (Illus.). 320p. 1991. 71.95 (*0-387-97439-3*) Spr-Verlag.

— Interpreting the Irish Landscape: Explorations in Settlement History. 96p. 1998. pap. 14.95 (*1-85182-256-9*, Pub. by Four Cts Pr) Intl Spec Bk.

Andrews, J. H. & Hirano, S. S., eds. Microbial Ecology of Leaves. (Contemporary Bioscience Ser.). (Illus.). xvii, 499p. 1991. 144.00 (*0-387-97579-9*) Spr-Verlag.

Andrews, J. H. & Tommerup, Inez C., eds. Advances in Plant Pathology, Vol. 8. (Illus.). 232p. 1992. text 104.00 (*0-12-033708-8*) Acad Pr.

Andrews, J. J. The Well-Built Elephant & Other Roadside Attractions: A Tribute to American Eccentricity. LC 83-11107. (Illus.). 146p. 1983. pap. 16.95 (*0-685-07029-8*) St Martin.

Andrews, J. N. History of the Sabbath. 3rd ed. LC 98-85408. 548p. 1998. otabind 15.95 (*1-57258-107-7*) Teach Servs.

— The Three Messages of Revelation 14. LC 97-80511. 144p. 1997. reprint ed. per. 7.95 (*1-57258-125-5*) Teach Servs.

Andrews, J. Richard, ed. see Ruiz de Alarcon, Hernando.

Andrews, J. S. A Study of German Hymns in Current English Hymnals. (European University Studies: German Language & Literature: Ser. 1, Vol. 614). 398p. 1982. pap. 56.00 (*3-261-05068-3*) P Lang Pubng.

Andrews, J. T. Quaternary Environments: The Eastern Canadian Arctic, Baffin Bay & West Greenland. (Illus.). 750p. (C). 1985. text 115.00 (*0-04-551094-6*) Routledge.

Andrews, J. T., et al, eds. Late Quaternary Palaeoceanography of the North Atlantic Margins. (Geological Society Special Publication Ser.: No. 111). (Illus.). viii, 376p. 1996. 98.00 (*1-897799-61-6*, 350, Pub. by Geol Soc Pub Hse) AAPG.

Andrews, J. T., et al. Nuclear Medicine: Clinical & Technological Bases. LC 91-46493. 241p. reprint ed. pap. 74.80 (*0-608-08654-1*, 206917700003) Bks Demand.

***Andrews, J. W. & McCall, Donald D.** Place of Angels. (Illus.). 74p. 1999. pap. 14.95 (*0-9674400-0-9*) RL Fromm.

Andrews, Jack. New Edge of the Anvil: A Resource Book for the Blacksmith. rev. ed. (Illus.). 256p. (C). 1994. pap. text 24.95 (*1-879535-09-2*) Skipjack Pr.

— Samuel Yellin: Metalworker. (Illus.). 16p. 1982. 10.00 (*0-685-70734-2*) Gal Assn NY.

— Samuel Yellin, Metalworker. LC 92-90938. (Illus.) 1992. 40.00 (*1-879535-05-X*) Skipjack Pr.

Andrews, James & Wise, Kenneth. The Best Overnight Hikes in the Great Smoky Mountains. LC 96-45800. (Illus.). 104p. (Orig.). 1997. pap. 12.95 (*0-87049-972-6*) U of Tenn Pr.

Andrews, James, jt. auth. see Wise, Kenneth.

Andrews, James, ed. see Wallach, Michael.

Andrews, James C., frwd. Guia Postal de Guatemala...1873. (Guatemala Postal History Pamphlet Ser.: No. 5). (Illus.). 33p. 1985. reprint ed. pap. 4.50 (*0-913129-07-0*) La Tienda.

Andrews, James C., intro. The Poyais Bubble. (Quarterly Review Ser.: Vol. XXVIII). 2157p. 1987. reprint ed. pap. 3.25 (*0-913129-16-X*) La Tienda.

Andrews, James R. Introduction to Classical Nahuatl Workbook. LC 74-30370. 234p. reprint ed. pap., wbk. ed. 72.60 (*0-608-20096-4*, 207136800011) Bks Demand.

— On Field Evaluation & Treatment of Sport Injuries. Clancy, William G., ed. LC 96-49798. (Illus.). 288p. (C). (gr. 13). 1997. pap. text 32.95 (*0-8151-0218-6*, 24095) Mosby Inc.

Andrews, James R., ed. Injuries in Baseball. LC 97-29923. 631p. 1998. 139.00 (*0-7817-0259-3*) Lppncott W & W.

Andrews, James R. & Andrews, Mary A. Family Based Treatment in Communicative Disorders: A Systemic Approach. (C). 1990. text 25.00 (*0-9626939-0-1*) Janelle Pubns.

***Andrews, James R. & Andrews, Mary A.** Family-Based Treatment in Communicative Disorders: A Systemic Approach. 2nd rev. ed. 198p. 2000. pap. text 35.00 (*1-890265-03-9*) Janelle Pubns.

Andrews, James R. & Harrelson, Gary L. Physical Rehabilitation of the Injured Athlete. 2nd ed. Lampert, Richard, ed. LC 97-9769. (Illus.). 608p. 1997. text 75.00 (*0-7216-6549-7*, W B Saunders Co) Harcrt Hlth Sci Grp.

Andrews, James R. & Timmerman, Laura A. Diagnostic & Operative Arthroscopy. Lampert, Richard, ed. (Illus.). 496p. 1997. text 190.00 (*0-7216-5690-0*, W B Saunders Co) Harcrt Hlth Sci Grp.

Andrews, James R. & Wilk, Kevin E., eds. The Athlete's Shoulder. (Illus.). 600p. 1993. text 158.00 (*0-443-08847-0*) Church.

Andrews, Jan. Keri. 96p. (J). (gr. 5-8). 1996. pap. 6.95 (*0-88899-240-8*) Publishers Group.

***Andrews, Jan.** Out of the Everywhere: Tales for the New World. (Illus.). 80p. (J). (ps-3). 2000. 19.95 (*0-88899-402-8*) Grndwd Bks.

— Pa's Harvest. (Illus.). (J). 2000. 12.95 (*0-88899-405-2*) Grndwd Bks.

Andrews, Jan. Pumpkin Time. (Illus.). 32p. (J). (ps-3). 1991. text 12.95 (*0-88899-112-6*) Publishers Group.

— Very Last First Time. LC 85-71606. (Illus.). 32p. (J) (gr. k-4). 1986. 17.00 (*0-689-50388-1*) McElderry Bks.

— Very Last First Time: An Inuit Tale. (Illus.). 32p. (J) (gr. k-3). 1998. per. 5.99 (*0-689-81960-9*) S&S Childrens.

***Andrews, Jan.** Very Last First Time: An Inuit Tale. 1998. 11.44 (*0-606-13885-4*) Turtleback.

Andrews, Janice. Tunes for Tots. (J). (ps). 1987. teacher ed. write for info. incl. audio (*1-878079-04-2*) Arts Pubns.

Andrews, Janice D. Cultural, Ethnic, & Religious Reference Manual for Health Care Providers. 92p. 1995. ring bd. 59.95 (*0-9663552-1-0*) Jamarda NC.

Andrews, Janice H. The Janan Curriculum: A Pre-School-Kindergarten Teachers Handbook. Linse, Barbara B. & Dresser, Ginny, eds. (Illus.). 200p. (C). 1985. pap. 16.95 (*0-9607458-4-X*) Arts Pubns.

Andrews, Jay D. The Young Kennedys: The New Generation: Continuing the Legacy of America's Royal Family. LC 98-4385. 208p. 1998. pap. 12.00 (*0-380-79593-0*, Avon Bks) Morrow Avon.

Andrews, Jean. A+ A Guide to Managing & Maintaining Your PC. 2nd ed. 912p. (C). 1998. pap. 48.00 incl. cd-rom (*0-7600-5083-X*) Course Tech.

***Andrews, Jean.** A+ Exam Prep. 2nd ed. LC 99-86269. (Exam Prep Ser.). (Illus.). 1143p. 1999. pap. 59.99 (*1-57610-540-7*) Coriolis Grp.

— A+ Guide to Managing & Maintaining Your PC: Comprehensive. 3rd ed. (Illus.). 1999. pap. 67.95 (*0-619-00038-4*) Course Tech.

— A+ Guide to Managing & Maintaining Your PC: Enhanced Edition. 2nd ed. (Illus.). 1999. pap. 65.95 (*0-619-00064-3*) Course Tech.

Andrews, Jean. A+ KSO PC Repair & Maintenance Exam Prep. 10th ed. LC 98-3510. (Exam Prep Ser.). 1998 mass mkt. 59.99 (*1-57610-241-6*) Coriolis Grp.

— American Wildflower Florilegium. LC 92-22135. (Illus.). 125p. 1992. text 50.00 (*0-929398-43-2*) UNTX Pr.

— American Wildflower Florilegium. limited ed. LC 92-22135. (Illus.). 125p. 1992. 200.00 (*0-929398-45-9*) UNTX Pr.

— Field Guide to Shells of the Florida Coast. 182p. 1994. 23.95 (*0-87719-249-9*, 9249) Gulf Pub.

— Field Guide to Shells of the Florida Coast. LC 93-28090. (Gulf's Field Guide Ser.). (Illus.). 182p. 1994. pap. 16.95 (*0-87719-234-0*, 9234) Gulf Pub.

***Andrews, Jean.** Guide to Managing & Maintaining Your PC Introduction. 3rd ed. 1999. pap. text 54.95 (*0-619-00037-6*) Course Tech.

Andrews, Jean. Managing & Maintaining Your PC. (DC - Introduction to Computing Ser.). 320p. 1996. mass mkt. 27.95 (*0-7895-0654-8*) Course Tech.

— Managing & Maintaining Your PC. (Networking Ser.) (C). 1998. pap. 37.00 (*0-7600-1116-8*) Course Tech.

— Managing & Maintaining Your PC. (Networking Ser.). (C). 1998. pap., teacher ed. 18.50 (*0-7600-1117-6*) Course Tech.

— The Pepper Lady's Pocket Pepper Primer. LC 96-51216. (Illus.). 190p. 1998. pap. 17.95 (*0-292-70483-6*, ANDPPP) U of Tex Pr.

***Andrews, Jean.** The Pepper Trail: History & Recipes from Around the World. LC 99-22244. (Illus.). 264p. 1999. 50.00 (*1-57441-070-9*, Pub. by UNTX Pr) Tex A&M Univ Pr.

Andrews, Jean. Peppers: The Domesticated Capsicums. 2nd ed. (Illus.). 274p. 1995. 65.00 (*0-292-70467-4*) U of Tex Pr.

— Red Hot Peppers: A Cookbook for the Not So Faint of Heart. LC 93-25604. (Illus.). 256p. 1993. 25.00 (*0-02-502251-2*) Macmillan.

— Spanish Reactions to the Anglo-Irish Literary Revival in the Early Twentieth Century: The Stone by the Elixir. LC 91-32592. (Studies in Comparative Literature: Vol. 17). 228p. 1991. lib. bdg. 89.95 (*0-7734-9698-X*) E Mellen.

Andrews, Jean F. Hasta Luego, San Diego. LC 90-27125. (Flying Fingers Club Ser.: Vol. 3). 104p. (Orig.). (YA). (gr. 3-6). 1991. pap. 4.95 (*0-930323-83-1*, Pub. by K Green Pubns) Gallaudet Univ Pr.

— Secret in the Dorm Attic. LC 90-2972. 104p. (Orig.). (J). (gr. 3-6). 1990. pap. 4.95 (*0-930323-66-1*, Pub. by K Green Pubns) Gallaudet Univ Pr.

Andrews, Jean F., jt. auth. see Nojer, Stephen M.

Andrews, Jean F., jt. auth. see Vernon, McCay.

Andrews, Jenne. Reunion. LC 82-22928. 59p. (Orig.). 1983. pap. 7.00 (*0-89924-038-0*) Lynx Hse.

Andrews, Jill, jt. auth. see Bair, Linda.

Andrews, Jim. Quincy Blues: Stories from a River Town. LC 96-68694. (Illus.). 83p. (Orig.). 1996. pap. 10.95 (*0-9646037-5-6*) Rosehill Pr IL.

Andrews, Joan & Davis, Denise E. Add Kaleidoscope: The Many Facets of Adult Attention Deficit Disorder. LC 97-2618. 1997. 24.95 (*1-878267-03-5*) Hope Pr CA.

***Andrews, Joan M. & Davis, Denise E.** Check up from the Neck Up: Ensuring Your Mental Health in the New Millennium. 550p. 2000. pap. 19.95 (*1-878267-09-4*) Hope Pr CA.

Andrews, Joel. A Harp Full of Stars: The Journey of a Music Healer. LC 89-80782. (Illus.). 264p. (Orig.). 1989. pap. 14.95 (*0-9623165-4-7*) Golden Harp.

Andrews, John. Antique Furniture. (Illus.). 180p. 1996. 25.00 (*1-85149-241-0*) Antique Collect.

— British Antique Furniture. (Illus.). 392p. 1990. 69.50 (*1-85149-090-6*) Antique Collect.

— Classrooms for the Free Society: An Education Reform Project of the Independence Institute. 21p. 1988. pap. text 8.00 (*1-57655-113-X*) Independ Inst.

— Estimating the Fiscal Impact of School Vouchers: Modest Startup Cost Could Yield Savings by 1995. (Issue Papers: No. 18-92). 6p. 1992. pap. text 8.00 (*1-57655-080-X*) Independ Inst.

— Heavy Job Losses Forseen if Tax Hike Passes. 2p. 1992. pap. text 8.00 (*1-57655-099-0*) Independ Inst.

— How Net to Improve the Schools: Facts & Fallacies about the Amendment 6 Tax Increase. 7p. 1992. pap. text 8.00 (*1-57655-098-2*) Independ Inst.

— Paper Flying Machines. (Illus.). 36p. (Orig.). 1994. pap. 8.95 (*0-906212-93-6*, Pub. by Tarquin Pubns) Parkwest Pubns.

— Reliability & Risk Assessment. 1993. 92.07 (*0-582-09615-4*) Addison-Wesley.

— Rome & Juliet: Critical Essays. Kolin, Philip C., ed. LC 93-16203. (Shakespeare Criticism Ser.: Vol. 10). 440p. 1993. text 25.00 (*0-8240-4795-8*) Garland.

— This, Our Lofty Scene. 1999. 19.95 (*0-670-83313-4*) Viking Penguin.

— Victorian & Edwardian Furniture: Price Guide & Reasons for Values. (Illus.). 300p. 1993. 59.50 (*1-85149-118-X*) Antique Collect.

Andrews, John & Antique Collectors Club Staff. The Price Guide to Victorian, Edwardian & 1920s Furniture (1860-1930) LC 82-234219. 217p. 1980. write for info. (*0-902028-89-8*) Antique Collect.

Andrews, John, jt. auth. see Fonte, John.

Andrews, John, jt. auth. see Kopel, David.

Andrews, John, ed. see Shakespeare, William.

Andrews, John B. & Bliss, William D., eds. History of Women in Trade Unions (Report on Conditions of Women & Child Wage-Earners in the United States, 61st Congress, 2nd Session, Senate Document No. 645), Vol. X. LC 74-3925. (Women in America Ser.). 236p. 1976. reprint ed. 19.95 (*0-405-06071-8*) Ayer.

Andrews, John B., jt. auth. see Commons, John R.

Andrews, John C. The Airborne Album, 1943-45: From Normandy to Victory Parade. Phillips, Jim, ed. (Illus.). 125p. 1993. 29.95 (*0-932572-16-2*) Phillips Pubns.

Andrews, John F., ed. Dynamics & Control of the Activated Sludge Process. LC 92-53522. (Water Quality Management Library: Vol. 6). 230p. 1992. text 99.95 (*0-87762-937-4*) Technomic.

— William Shakespeare: His World, His Work, His Influence, 3 vols. LC 85-8305. 1008p. 1985. 300.00 (*0-684-17851-6*) S&S Trade.

Andrews, John F., ed. see Shakespeare, William.

Andrews, John H. The Extraterrestrials & Their Reality. (Illus.). 102p. (Orig.). 1989. pap. 10.00 (*0-9622970-1-1*) JACO Bk Pubs.

Andrews, John H. & Tommerup, Inez C., eds. Advances in Plant Pathology, Vol. II. (Illus.). 336p. 1995. text 121.00 (*0-12-033711-8*) Acad Pr.

Andrews, John K., Jr. Better Thinking Better Government: Origins & Aims of the Independence Institute. (Issue Paper #4-88 Ser.). 9p. 1998. pap. text 8.00 (*1-57655-026-5*) Independ Inst.

A

An Asterisk (*) at the beginning of an entry indicates that the title is appearing for the first time.

— Consumer Sovereignty in the Schools: Will Colorado Opt for School Choice as Minnesota Did? 15p. 1999. pap. text 8.00 (1-57655-118-0) Independ Inst.

— Election Watch, 1986: What Governor Growth' Could Do for Colorado. (Issue Papers: No. 5-86). 5p. 1986. pap. text 8.00 (1-57655-002-8) Independ Inst.

— Helping the New Russia: A Primer for Donors. 32p. 1989. pap. text 8.00 (1-57655-119-9) Independ Inst.

— No Weakness No War: Peace & Principle in America's Third Century. 120p. (Orig.). 1989. pap. 8.00 (0-317-93469-4) Independ Inst.

— Quality Checklist for Education Consumers: Thirty Tools to Improve Colorado Schools Without New Laws or New Money. (Issue Papers: No. 2-90). 9p. 1990. pap. text 8.00 (1-57655-035-4) Independ Inst.

Andrews, John K., Jr. Time for the Legislature & the Governor to Embrace Metro Cooperation. (Issue Paper #3-88 Ser.). 10p. 1988. pap. text 8.00 (1-57655-027-3) Independ Inst.

Andrews, John K., Jr. When Educating for World Affairs, First Cover Home Base. 10p. 1989. pap. text 8.00 (1-57655-125-3) Independ Inst.

— Why Not an Economic Miracle for Colorado? A Symposium of 35 Western Leaders. (Issue Papers: No. 3-86). 18p. 1986. pap. text 8.00 (1-57655-003-6) Independ Inst.

Andrews, John K., Jr., et al. Avoiding an Automatic Tax Increase in 1987. (Issue Papers: No. 14-87). 12p. 1986. pap. text 8.00 (1-57655-009-5) Independ Inst.

Andrews, John K., jt. auth. see Hendrickson, Mark.

Andrews, John M. & Schumann, G. Berry. Neurocytopathology. (Illus.). 352p. 1992. 125.00 (0-683-00227-9) Lppncott W & W.

Andrews, John N. & Marsden, Carl A., eds. Tomorrow in the Making. LC 72-546. (Essay Index Reprint Ser.). 1977. reprint ed. 30.95 (0-8369-2782-6) Ayer.

***Andrews, John R.** The Ghost Towns of Amador. LC 00-42276. (Illus.). 2000. write for info. (1-884244-20-3) Volcano Pr.

Andrews, Jonathan. The Country Diary Book of Creating a Wild Flower Garden. Huxley, Anthony, ed. (Illus.). 160p. 1996. reprint ed. 14.98 (1-56731-149-0, MJF Bks) Fine Comms.

— The History of Bethlem. LC 96-52471. (Illus.). 768p. (C). 1997. 250.00 (0-415-01773-4) Routledge.

Andrews, Joseph. The Complete Win at Hearts. rev. ed. 200p. pap. 13.95 (1-56625-147-8) Bonus Books.

Andrews, Joseph. Journey from Buenos Ayres Undertaken on Behalf of the Chilian & Peruvian Mining Assn., 1825-26, 2 vols. LC 74-128437. reprint ed. 82.50 (0-404-00410-5) AMS Pr.

***Andrews, Joseph D.** Complete Win at Spades: Basic, Intermediate & Advanced Strategies & Official Rules. (Illus.). 2000. pap. 13.95 (1-56625-145-1) Bonus Books.

Andrews, Joseph D. Win at Hearts: Revised Rules, Variations, & Strategy - How to Play & Win. 2nd rev. ed. LC 98-72846. (Illus.). 120p. 1998. pap. 12.95 (1-56625-110-9) Bonus Books.

***Andrews, Joseph D.** Win at Spades: Advanced Strategy. LC 99-12807. (Illus.). 120p. 1999. pap. 11.95 (1-56625-118-4) Bonus Books.

Andrews, Joseph D. Win at Spades: Basic & Intermediate Techniques. LC 98-48840. (Illus.). 98p. 1999. pap. 11.95 (1-56625-117-6) Bonus Books.

Andrews, Joseph L., Jr. Revolutionary Boston, Lexington & Concord: The Shots Heard Round the World! 2nd rev. ed. LC 98-175942. Orig. Title: Revolutionary Lexington & Concord. (Illus.). 144p. 1999. pap. 12.95 (0-9664112-1-8) Concrd Guide.

— Revolutionary Lexington & Concord: The Shot(s) Heard Round the World! LC 98-175942. (Illus.). 64p. 1998. pap. 9.95 (0-9664112-0-X) Concrd Guide.

Andrews, Joy, jt. auth. see Kegley, Susan E.

Andrews, Joyce. Palm Reading: For Fun, Health & Success. 96p. 1991. pap. 6.95 (0-9631450-0-2) Drew Pubs.

Andrews, Judith M., ed. A History of South Carolina's State House. LC 94-621659. 60p. 1994. pap. 8.00 (1-880067-24-2) SC Dept of Arch & Hist.

Andrews, Judith M., ed. see Begley, Paul R., et al.

Andrews, Judith M., ed. see Helsley, Alexia J.

Andrews, Judith M., ed. see Helsley, Alexia S.

Andrews, Judith M., ed. see Lesser, Charles H.

Andrews, Judith M., ed. see Lipscomb, Terry W.

Andrews, Judith M., ed. see McCawley, Patrick J.

Andrews, Judith M., ed. see McGahee, Susan H. & Edmonds, Mary W.

Andrews, Judith M., ed. see S. C. Department of Archives & History Staff.

Andrews, Judith M., ed. see Smith, Steven D.

Andrews, Judith M., ed. see South Carolina Department of Archives & History St.

Andrews, Judith M., ed. see Stauffer, Michael E.

Andrews, Judith M., ed. see Wates, Wylma A.

Andrews, Julia, et al. Fragmented Memory: The Chinese Avant-Garde in Exile. (Illus.). 37p. 1993. pap. 10.00 (1-881390-04-7) OSU Wexner Ctr.

Andrews, Julia, jt. auth. see McCreedy, Dale.

Andrews, Julia F. Painters & Politics in the People's Republic of China, 1949-1979. LC 93-38071. 480p. 1994. 65.00 (0-520-07981-7, Pub. by U CA Pr) Cal Prin Full Svc.

Andrews, Julia F. & Shen, Kuiyi. Century in Crisis: Modernity & Tradition in the Art of Twentieth-Century China. LC 99-184689. (Illus.). 336p. 1998. 85.00 (0-8109-6909-2, Pub. by Abrams) Time Warner.

***Andrews, Julia F., et al.** A Century in Crisis. LC 99-184689. 329 p. 1998. pap. write for info. (0-89207-211-3) S R Guggenheim.

Andrews, Julian. David Nash, the Sculpture Of. LC 97-145687. (Illus.). 160p. 1996. 90.00 (0-85331-692-9, Pub. by Lund Humphries) Antique Collect.

***Andrews, Julian.** The Sculpture of David Nash. LC 97-145687. (Illus.). 180p. 1999. pap. 29.95 (0-520-22044-7, Pub. by U CA Pr) Cal Prin Full Svc.

***Andrews, Julie.** Little Bo: The Story of Bonnie Boadicea. 96p. (J). 1999. 16.99 (0-7868-0598-6) Little.

— Untitled Adult Memoir Julie Andrews 2001. pap. write for info. (0-7868-8475-4) Disney Pr.

Andrews, Jullie S. & Raaf, John, eds. Horseman's Service Directory & Desk Reference, 1990. 112p. 1990. pap. 5.95 (0-930757-07-6) Esperance Enter.

Andrews, K. R. The Spanish Caribbean: Trade & Plunder, 1530-1630. LC 77-90944. 1978. 30.00 (0-300-02197-6) Yale U Pr.

***Andrews, Kate.** Cool It, Carrie. LC 99-94731. (Making Friends Ser.: No. 2). (Illus.). 128p. (J). (gr. 3-7). 1999. mass mkt. 3.99 (0-380-80931-1, Avon Bks) Morrow Avon.

— Making Friends: Face Facts, Sky, , Vol. 3. (Making Friends Ser.: No. 3). 128p. (J). (gr. 3-7). 1999. mass mkt. 3.99 (0-380-80932-X, Avon Bks) Morrow Avon.

— Making Friends: Grow Up, Amy, Vol. 4. (Making Friends Ser.: No. 4). 128p. (J). (gr. 3-7). 1999. mass mkt. 3.99 (0-380-80933-8, Avon Bks) Morrow Avon.

— Wise up, Alex. (Making Friends Ser.: No. 1). (Illus.). 128p. (J). (gr. 3-7). 1999. mass mkt. 3.99 (0-380-80930-3, Avon Bks) Morrow Avon.

Andrews, Kay, et al. Good Policy & Practice for the After-School Hours. 1995. pap. 57.50 (0-273-61628-5, Pub. by F T P-H) Trans-Atl Phila.

Andrews, Keith. The Nazarenes: A Brotherhood of German Painters in Rome. LC 86-81980. (Illus.). 148p. 1989. reprint ed. lib. bdg. 50.00 (0-87817-306-4) Hacker.

Andrews, Kenneth R. The Spanish Caribbean: Trade & Plunder, 1530-1630. LC 77-90944. 279p. reprint ed. pap. 86.50 (0-8357-8764-8, 203366200087) Bks Demand.

***Andrews, Kenneth T.** Freedom is Constant Struggle. 1999. 22.00 (0-226-02040-1) U Ch Pr.

Andrews, L. F. Pioneers of Polk County, Iowa, Vols. I & II. (Illus.). 928p. 1993. reprint ed. lib. bdg. 105.00 (0-8328-3465-3) Higginson Bk Co.

Andrews, L. McMeel. Taurus: Little Birth Sign. (Illus.). 80p. 1994. 4.95 (0-8362-3079-5) Andrews & McMeel.

— A Vow of Love. (Illus.). 96p. 1992. 15.00 (0-8362-7992-1) Andrews & McMeel.

Andrews, Larry. Language Exploration & Awareness: A Resource Book for Teachers. 224p. 1996. pap. write for info. (0-8058-2627-0) L Erlbaum Assocs.

— Language Exploration & Awareness: A Resource Book for Teachers. 2nd ed. LC 97-37791. 256p. 1997. pap. write for info. (0-8058-2367-0) L Erlbaum Assocs.

Andrews, Larry C. Special Functions of Mathematics for Engineers. LC 97-13896. 1997. 80.00 (0-8194-2616-4) SPIE.

Andrews, Larry C. & Phillips, Ronald L. Laser Beam Propagation Through Random Media. LC 97-43433. xx, 434p. 1998. 80.00 (0-8194-2787-X) SPIE.

Andrews, Larry C. & Shivamoggi, Bhimsen K. Integral Transforms for Engineers & Applied Mathematicians. LC 99-14143. 353p. 1999. 55.00 (0-8194-3232-6) SPIE.

Andrews, Larry F., et al. Cumberland Islands: A Treasure of Memories. LC 85-51860. (Illus.). 64p. 1985. pap. 10.95 (0-911977-03-1) Wrld Tampa.

Andrews, Larry L. The Cutting Edge, a Practical Guide to the Use of Highland Weapons: "The Broadsword & Targe" Purke, Terry, ed. (Illus.). 42p. 1997. pap. 10.00 (0-9663672-0-0, P&P-001-A) Past & Present.

Andrews, Laura, ed. see Amaral, Grant.

Andrews, Laurie J. & Novick, Laurie B. HIV Care: A Comprehensive Handbook for Providers. 250p. 1995. text 48.00 (0-8039-7083-8); pap. text 21.95 (0-8039-7150-8) Sage.

Andrews, Lawrence F. Straight Wire. Valleau, John & Olfe, Julie T., eds. (Illus.). 448p. (C). 1990. text 125.00 (0-9616256-0-0) L A Wells.

***Andrews, Leighton.** Wales Says Yes. 180p. 1999. pap. (1-85411-253-8, Pub. by Seren Bks) Dufour.

Andrews, Les. Model A Ford Mechanics Handbook. LC 97-9151. (Illus.). 424p. 1997. pap. 32.95 (0-9658240-0-4, MHDC 970915-1) Cottage Hill.

***Andrews, Les.** Model A Ford Troubleshooting & Diagnostics. (Illus.). 200p. 2000. pap. 26.00 (0-9658240-1-2, TDDC 031500-0) Cottage Hill.

Andrews, Lew. Story & Space in Renaissance Art: The Rebirth of Continuous Narrative. (Illus.). 206p. (C). 1998. pap. text 18.95 (0-521-64663-4) Cambridge U Pr.

***Andrews, Lewis M., Jr.** Tempest, Fire & Foe: Destroyer Escorts in World War II & the Men Who Manned Them. LC 98-66132. (Illus.). xv, 463p. 1999. pap. 29.95 (1-886391-31-9); lib. bdg. 49.95 (1-886391-30-0) Narwhal Pr.

Andrews, Lilinoe. "At I Kekahi, E Kapi Kekahi" (HAW., Illus.). 36p. (J). (gr. 1-3). 1988. pap. 8.95 incl. audio (1-890270-03-2) Aha Punana Leo.

— Hawai'iloa. (HAW., Illus.). 35p. (J). (gr. 1-3). 1994. pap. 6.95 incl. audio (1-890270-18-0) Aha Punana Leo.

— Hiki I Na 'Elala Ke Kokua Ia 'Oe. (HAW., Illus.). 37p. (J). (gr. k-2). 1999. pap. 6.95 incl. audio (1-58191-056-8) Aha Punana Leo.

— I Mea Aha Ke Kai? (HAW., Illus.). 25p. (J). (gr. k). 1999. pap. 6.95 incl. audio (1-58191-080-0) Aha Punana Leo.

— Ka 'Ekake Li'ili'i O Mekiko. (HAW., Illus.). 34p. (J). (gr. 2-3). 1999. pap. 6.95 incl. audio (1-58191-086-X) Aha Punana Leo.

— Ka Holo Ka'a Me Tutu. (HAW., Illus.). 36p. (J). (gr. k). 1992. pap. 8.95 incl. audio (1-890270-17-2) Aha Punana Leo.

— Ka Nohona Kua'aina. (HAW., Illus.). 41p. (J). (gr. 2-3). 1999. pap. 6.95 incl. audio (1-58191-053-3) Aha Punana Leo.

— Ke Kanaka Mahi'ai Pomaika'i. (HAW., Illus.). 16p. (J). (gr. k). 1999. pap. 6.95 incl. audio (1-58191-076-2) Aha Punana Leo.

— Ko Sepa Paikikala. (HAW., Illus.). 32p. (J). (gr. k). pap. 6.95 incl. audio (1-890270-21-0) Aha Punana Leo.

— 'O Kelekolio Ka Manini Li'ili'i. (HAW., Illus.). 33p. (J). (gr. k). 1999. pap. 6.95 incl. audio (1-58191-070-3) Aha Punana Leo.

Andrews, Lily. A Guide to Channeling & Channeled Material. (Illus.). 136p. (Orig.). 1990. 9.95 (0-945946-10-4) Cassandra Pr.

Andrews, Linda. Escape of the Birdwomen. Bodeen, Jim, ed. (Birdwomen Ser.: Vol. 6). (Illus.). 78p. 1998. pap. 12.00 (0-911287-25-6) Blue Begonia.

Andrews, Linda G., jt. auth. see Leggett, Linda R.

Andrews, Linda L. How to Choose a College Major. LC 97-14985. (Illus.). 160p. 1997. pap. 12.95 (0-8442-8120-4, 81204, VGM Career) NTC Contemp Pub Co.

Andrews, Linda M., et al. Data Cleaning Procedures for the 1993 Robert Wood Johnson Foundation Family Health Insurance Survey. LC 97-18144. 1997. pap. text 9.00 (0-8330-2523-6) Rand Corp.

Andrews, Lisa. Dangerous Deception. (Scarlet Ser.). 1998. mass mkt. 3.99 (1-85487-866-2, Pub. by Scarlet Bks) London Brdge.

— Too Late for Love. (Scarlet Ser.). 1998. mass mkt. 3.99 (1-85487-591-4, Pub. by Scarlet Bks) London Brdge.

Andrews, Lori. Black Power, White Blood: The Life & Times of Johnny Spain. 2nd ed. LC 99-54411. 300p. 2000. reprint ed. pap. 19.95 (1-56639-750-2) Temple U Pr.

***Andrews, Lori B.** The Clone Age. 2000. pap. 15.00 (0-8050-6446-X) St Martin.

Andrews, Lori B. The Clone Age: Adventures in the New World of Reproductive Technology. LC 98-32099. 272p. 1999. 25.00 (0-8050-6080-4) H Holt & Co.

***Andrews, Lori B. & Nelkin, Dorothy.** Body Product: The War over Body Tissue in the Biotechnology Age. LC 00-34559. 2001. 24.00 (0-609-60540-2, Crown) Crown Pub Group.

Andrews, Lori B., ed. see Institute of Medicine, Committee on Assessing Gene.

Andrews, Lori P., ed. see Center for Labor Education & Research Staff.

Andrews, Lorraine & Andrews, Eugene. Defiance, Ohio. (Illus.). 313p. 1991. 60.00 (0-88107-192-7) Curtis Media.

Andrews, Lorrin. Grammar of the Hawaiian Language. LC 75-35173. reprint ed. 41.50 (0-404-14202-8) AMS Pr.

Andrews, Lucilla. No Time for Romance: An Autobiographical Account of a Few Moments in British & Personal History LC 78-308938. 239 p. 1977. write for info. (0-245-53087-8) H Larousse Ltd.

— The Sinister Side. large type ed. (Ulverscroft Large Print Ser.). 336p. 1997. 27.99 (0-7089-3768-3) Ulverscroft.

Andrews, Lyman, et al. Red Dust One: New Writing. LC 78-127954. 180p. 1971. 4.25 (0-87376-016-6); pap. 3.00 (0-87376-017-4) Red Dust.

Andrews, Lyn. Liverpool Songbird. large type ed. (Magna Large Print Ser.). 571p. 1997. 27.50 (0-7505-1124-9) Thorndike Pr.

***Andrews, Lyn.** The Sisters O'Donnell. 2000. pap. 10.95 (0-552-13600-X, Pub. by Transworld Publishers Ltd) Trafalgar.

— Take These Broken Wings. 2000. pap. 11.00 (0-7472-5809-0, Pub. by Headline Bk Pub) Trafalgar.

Andrews, Lynn A. Teachings Around the Sacred Wheel. LC 89-45524. 160p. 1989. pap. 15.00 (0-06-250022-8, Pub. by Harper SF) HarpC.

Andrews, Lynn V. Crystal Woman. 287p. 1988. mass mkt. 13.99 (0-446-38572-7, Pub. by Warner Bks) Little.

Andrews, Lynn V. Dark Sister: A Sorcerer's Love Story. 272p. 1996. pap. 13.00 (0-06-092765-8) HarpC.

— Flight of the Seventh Moon: The Teaching of the Shields. LC 83-48414. 216p. 1985. pap. 13.00 (0-06-250028-7, Pub. by Harper SF) HarpC.

— Love & Power. LC 97-8458. 256p. 1997. 23.00 (0-06-018646-1) HarpC.

— Love & Power. 176p. 1998. pap. 13.00 (0-06-092955-3, Perennial) HarperTrade.

— The Love & Power Journal: A Workbook for the Fine Art of Living. (Illus.). 208p. 1999. text, wbk. ed. 15.95 (1-56170-605-1, 574) Hay House.

— Medicine Woman. LC 81-47546. 224p. 1983. pap. 14.00 (0-06-250026-0, CN 4062, Pub. by Harper SF) HarpC.

— The Power Deck: The Cards of Wisdom. LC 90-56474. (Illus.). 114p. (Orig.). 1991. pap., boxed set 30.00 (0-06-250078-3, Pub. by Harper SF) HarpC.

— Shakkai: Woman of the Sacred Garden. LC 91-58368. (Illus.). 320p. 1993. reprint ed. pap. 14.00 (0-06-092179-X, Perennial) HarperTrade.

— Walk in Balance: Meditations with Lynn Andrews. LC 92-56125. (Illus.). 288p. 1994. pap. 15.00 (0-06-250009-0, Pub. by Harper SF) HarpC.

— Walk in Spirit: Prayers for the Seasons of Life. (Illus.). 120p. 1996. 14.95 (0-9650958-0-0) Acacia Pubng.

— Windhorse Woman. 224p. 1990. mass mkt. 13.99 (0-446-39172-7, Pub. by Warner Bks) Little.

— Woman at the Edge of Two Worlds. LC 92-56215. 304p. 1994. pap. 14.00 (0-06-092550-7) HarpC.

— The Woman of Wyrrd: The Arousal of the Inner Fire. LC 90-56420. 272p. 1991. reprint ed. pap. 13.00 (0-06-097410-9, Perennial) HarperTrade.

Andrews, M. E. Gregg Office Job Training Program, Classroom Installation. Incl. Accounts Payable Clerk. 1972. pap. text 7.56 (0-07-001821-9); Accounts Receivable Clerk. 1972. pap. text 7.56 (0-07-001823-5); Billing Clerk. 1972. pap. text 7.56 (0-07-001839-1); Clerk Typist. 1973. pap. text 7.56 (0-07-001819-7); Credit Clerk. 1972. pap. text 7.56 (0-07-001827-8); Office Cashier. 1972. pap. text 7.56 (0-07-001831-6); Order Clerk. 1972. pap. text 7.56 (0-07-001825-1); Purchasing Clerk. 1972. pap. text 7.56 (0-07-001833-2); Stock Control Clerk. 1972. pap. text 7.56 (0-07-001829-4); Typist. 1972. pap. text 8.56 (0-07-001817-0); 1973. pap. write for info. (0-318-54186-6) McGraw.

Andrews, M. E., jt. auth. see Mulkerne, D. D.

Andrews, Maggie & Talbot, Mary M. All The World & Her Husband: Women in the 20th-Century Consumer Culture. Andrews, Margaret R., ed. LC 99-19273. 288p. 1999. 65.00 (0-304-70151-3) Continuum.

Andrews, Malachi. Color Me Right...Then Frame Me in Motion. Warnette, Ken, ed. LC 90-60395. (Illus.). 80p. (Orig.). (C). 1989. pap. text 14.95 (0-9624889-0-9) Seymour-Smith.

Andrews, Malachi & Warnette, Ken. African Origins in Sports: An Empirical Study of Why Black Athletes Achieve High Levels of Success. Martin, Reginald, ed. (Illus.). 264p. (Orig.). (C). 1998. 39.95 (0-9624889-1-7) Seymour-Smith.

Andrews, Malcolm. Landscape: And Western Art. (Oxford History of Art Ser.). (Illus.). 256p. 2000. 39.95 (0-19-210046-7) OUP.

— Landscape & Western Art. (Oxford History of Art Ser.). (Illus.). 256p. 2000. pap. 17.95 (0-19-284233-1) OUP.

— Search for the Picturesque: Landscape Aesthetics & Tourism in Britain, 1760-1800. LC 68-63668. (Illus.). xviii, 269p. 1989. 59.50 (0-8047-1402-9); pap. 24.95 (0-8047-1834-2) Stanford U Pr.

Andrews, Malcolm, ed. see Dickens, Charles.

Andrews, Marcellus. The Political Economy of Hope & Fear: Capitalism & the Black Condition in America. LC 98-58107. 1999. 29.95 (0-8147-0679-7) NYU Pr.

Andrews, Margaret M. & Boyle, Joyceen. Transcultural Concepts in Nursing. 3rd ed. LC 98-3026. 496p. 1998. pap. text 34.95 (0-7817-1038-3) Lppncott W & W.

Andrews, Margaret M. & Boyle, Joyceen S. Transcultural Concepts in Nursing Care. 2nd ed. LC 94-27740. 496p. 1994. pap. text 31.00 (0-397-55115-0) Lppncott W & W.

***Andrews, Margaret R. & Talbot, Mary M.** All the World & Her Husband: Women in the 20th-Century Consumer Culture. LC 99-19273. 288p. 1999. pap. 19.95 (0-304-70152-1) Continuum.

Andrews, Margaret R., ed. see Andrews, Maggie & Talbot, Mary M.

Andrews, Mark. C++ for Windows NT Programming. LC 94-26300. 736p. 1994. pap. 39.95 (1-55828-300-5, MIS Pr) IDG Bks.

***Andrews, Mark.** Colossus. (Illus.). 120p. (YA). 2000. pap. 9.95 (0-9700387-2-0) Crazyfish.

Andrews, Mark, jt. auth. see Bell, Ronald E.

Andrews, Mark, jt. auth. see Robison, Jim.

Andrews, Mark P., ed. Photosensitive Optical Materials & Devices, Vol. 2998. LC 97-207734. 364p. 1997. 80.00 (0-8194-2409-9) SPIE.

— Photosensitive Optical Materials & Devices II. LC 98-227281. (Proceedings of SPIE Ser.: Vol. 3282). 134p. 1998. 59.00 (0-8194-2721-7) SPIE.

Andrews, Mark P. & Najafi, S. Iraj. Sol-Gel & Polymer Photonic Devices. LC 97-23157. 1997. pap. write for info. (0-8194-2599-0) SPIE.

Andrews, Mary. Bob & the Guides. LC 77-163019. (Short Story Index Reprint Ser.). 1977. reprint ed. 23.95 (0-8369-3933-6) Ayer.

Andrews, Mary, et al. 5 Orange County Poets. Rayl, Nancy B., ed. (Illus.). 116p. 1993. pap. 15.00 (0-9632702-4-9) Lightning.

Andrews, Mary A., jt. auth. see Andrews, James R.

Andrews, Mary R. The Perfect Tribute. 56p. 1992. reprint ed. lib. bdg. 15.95 (0-89966-920-4) Buccaneer Bks.

Andrews, Maxene & Gilbert, Bill. Over Here, over There. (Illus.). 288p. 1993. 22.95 (0-8217-4117-9, Zebra Kensgtn) Kensgtn Pub Corp.

— Over Here, over There. 288p. 1994. pap. 12.95 (0-8217-4645-6, Zebra Kensgtn) Kensgtn Pub Corp.

— Over Here, over There: The Andrews Sisters & the USO Stars in World War II. large type ed. LC 93-33463. 1994. lib. bdg. 18.95 (0-7862-0094-4) Thorndike Pr.

Andrews, Mcmeel. Country Music: Hall of Fame & Museum, 1999 Edition. 1998. 10.99 (0-8362-5498-8) Andrews & McMeel.

***Andrews, Mcmeel.** Mother's Treasury: Expectations: Best Kept Secrets Every New Mother Should Know: The Little Baby Book. 2000. pap. 19.95 (0-7407-1181-4) Andrews & McMeel.

— Treasury of Cats: Smitten with Kittens, Cats: A Feline Potpourri, the Purr-Fect Little Book of Cats. (Illus.). (J). 2000. pap. 19.95 (0-7407-1180-6) Andrews & McMeel.

— Treasury of Christmas: A Very Merry Christmas, Angels, a Christmas Alphabet, the Little Book of. (Illus.). (J). 2000. pap. 19.95 (0-7407-1178-4) Andrews & McMeel.

— Treasury of Friendship: Stories of the Gift of Friendship, My Best Friend, Girlfriends Are Forever. (Illus.). (J). 2000. pap. 19.95 (0-7407-1179-2) Andrews & McMeel.

***Andrews McMeel Publishing Staff.** Backstreet Boys. (Illus.). 1999. pap. 9.95 (0-7407-0433-8) Andrews & McMeel.

— Believe in Yourself: Inspirational Thoughts for Women. 1999. pap. 5.95 (0-8362-1542-7) Andrews & McMeel.

— Britney Spears. 1999. 4.95 (0-7407-0421-4) Andrews & McMeel.

— Britney Spears. (Illus.). 1999. pap. 9.95 (0-7407-0731-0) Andrews & McMeel.

Andrews McMeel Publishing Staff. Celebrating Babies Mini Edition: A Treasury for New Mothers. 1999. 4.95 (0-8362-7831-3) Andrews & McMeel.

***Andrews McMeel Publishing Staff.** Chamique Holdsclaw. (Illus.). 2000. pap. 4.95 (0-7407-0603-9) Andrews & McMeel.

An Asterisk (*) at the beginning of an entry indicates that the title is appearing for the first time.

— Enrique Iglesias. (Illus.). 2000. pap. 4.95 (*0-7407-0606-3*) Andrews & McMeel.
— Ewan Mcgregor. 1999. 4.95 (*0-7407-0435-4*) Andrews & McMeel.
— Five. (Illus.). 80p. (gr. 4-7). 1999. 4.95 (*0-7407-0419-2*) Andrews & McMeel.
— Forever Friends. 1999. pap. 5.95 (*0-8362-1541-9*) Andrews & McMeel.
— Freddie Prinze, Jr. LC 99-63417. (Illus.). 80p. (gr. 4-7). 2000. 4.95 (*0-7407-0424-9*) Andrews & McMeel.
— Going for the Gold: Thoughts on Success & Achievement. 1999. pap. 5.95 (*0-8362-1547-8*) Andrews & McMeel.
— Jennifer Lopez. (Illus.). 2000. pap. 4.95 (*0-7407-0605-5*) Andrews & McMeel.
— Lauryn Hill. 1999. 4.95 (*0-7407-0420-6*) Andrews & McMeel.
— Lisa Leslie. (Illus.). 2000. pap. 4.95 (*0-7407-0604-7*) Andrews & McMeel.
— Mia Hamm. (Illus.). 2000. 4.95 (*0-7407-0602-0*) Andrews & McMeel.
— N'Sync. (Illus.). 1999. pap. 9.95 (*0-7407-0434-6*) Andrews & McMeel.
— Ricky Martin. 1999. 4.95 (*0-7407-0422-2*) Andrews & McMeel.
— Ricky Martin. (Illus.). 1999. pap. 9.95 (*0-7407-0732-9*) Andrews & McMeel.
— Ryan Philippe. LC 99-63408. (Illus.). 80p. (gr. 4-7). 2000. 4.95 (*0-7407-0423-0*) Andrews & McMeel.
— Teachers: Jokes, Quotes, & Anecdotes. 1999. pap. 5.95 (*0-8362-1616-4*) Andrews & McMeel.
***Andrews McMeel Publishing Staff, abr.** 98 Degrees. 1999. 4.95 (*0-7407-0418-4*) Andrews & McMeel.
Andrews, Michael. Coffin Lumber. LC 95-80485. 128p. pap. 12.00 (*0-941017-50-8*) Bombshelter Pr.
— A Lone Black Gull. 148p. 2000. pap. 14.00 (*0-941017-62-1*) Bombshelter Pr.
Andrews, Michael. The Poet from the City of the Angels: Poems & Photographs: 1969-1989. (Illus.). 234p. (Orig.). 1990. pap. 19.95 (*0-941017-16-8*) Bombshelter Pr.
— Wildspace. (Endless Quest Ser.). 192p. (Orig.). 1994. 3.95 (*1-56076-928-9*, Pub. by TSR Inc) Random.
Andrews, Michael & Widup, David. In Country. 1995. pap. 10.00 (*0-941017-28-1*) Bombshelter Pr.
Andrews, Michael C. This Action of Our Death: The Performance of Death in English Renaissance Drama. LC 88-45743. 216p. 1989. 38.50 (*0-87413-354-8*) U Delaware Pr.
Andrews, Michael F., ed. Aesthetic Form of Education. LC 58-11799. (Illus.). 115p. reprint ed. pap. 35.70 (*0-8357-5216-X*, 201947100012) Bks Demand.
Andrews, Mildred. Seattle Women: A Legacy of Community Development. LC 84-60808. 64p. 1984. pap. 4.50 (*0-9615533-0-8*) YWCA WA.
Andrews, Mildred & Riddle, Pauline. Church Organ Method. 123p. 1973. pap. 16.95 (*0-8258-0050-1*, 04904) Fischer Inc NY.
Andrews, Mildred G. The Men & the Mills: A History of the Southern Textile Industry. LC 87-29653. (Illus.). 360p. 1988. 35.00 (*0-86554-289-9*, H259) Mercer Univ Pr.
Andrews, Mildred T. Woman's Place: A Guide to Seattle & King County History. LC 93-79116. (Illus.). 344p. (Orig.). 1994. pap. 14.95 (*0-9640239-0-3*) Gemil Pr.
***Andrews, Molly.** Lines of Narrative: Psychosocial Perspectives. LC 00-42472. 2000. write for info. (*0-415-24233-9*) Routledge.
Andrews, Moya L. Manual of Voice Treatment. 2nd rev. ed. LC 98-37605. (Illus.). 700p. 1999. pap. 59.95 (*1-56593-998-0*, 1976) Thomson Learn.
— Manual of Voice Treatment: Pediatrics to Geriatrics. LC 94-40347. (Illus.). 632p. (C). 1994. pap. 59.95 (*1-56593-162-9*, 0472) Thomson Learn.
— Voice Therapy for Children. (Illus.). 336p. (C). 1991. reprint ed. pap. 39.95 (*1-879105-48-9*, 0231) Thomson Learn.
Andrews, Moya L. & Sommers, Anne C. Voice Therapy for Adolescents. (Illus.). 220p. (Orig.). (C). 1991. reprint ed. pap. 34.95 (*1-879105-21-7*, A001) Thomson Learn.
Andrews, Nancy. The Invisible Season. LC 98-90331. 128p. 1998. pap. 13.95 (*0-933573-17-0*) Wayland Pr.
Andrews, Nancy, jt. auth. see Henderson, Cary S.
Andrews, Nancy, ed. see Dubrava, Patricia.
Andrews, Nancy, ed. see Gonzalez, Ray.
Andrews, Nancy, ed. see Hutchison, Joseph.
Andrews, Nanette N. Verbal Power: Rootword Flashcards. LC 91-73379. 332p. 1992. pap. text 16.00 (*0-9630715-0-5*) Guid Acad Achieve.
Andrews, Neil. Principles of Civil Procedure. 1994. 104.00 (*0-421-48710-0*, Pub. by Sweet & Maxwll) Gaunt.
Andrews, Nigel. Jaws: Movie Guide. 208p. 1999. pap. 15.95 (*1-58234-042-0*) Bloomsbury Pubg.
— Travolta: The Life. 346p. 1998. 24.95 (*1-58234-002-1*) Bloomsbury Pubg.
— True Myths: The Life & Times of Arnold Schwarzenegger. (Illus.). 288p. 1996. 21.95 (*1-55972-364-5*, Birch Ln Pr) Carol Pub Group.
***Andrews, Nin.** The Book of Orgasms. (Imagination Ser.: Vol. 4). 64p. 1999. reprint ed. pap. 9.00 (*1-880834-48-0*) Cleveland St Univ Poetry Ctr.
Andrews, Nin. Spontaneous Breasts. 36p. 1998. pap. 6.00 (*1-888219-08-4*) Pearl Edit.
***Andrews, Obediah, Jr.** Child Care Log. unabridged ed. (Illus.). 64p. 1999. 11.95 (*0-9670858-0-2*); pap. 4.95 (*0-9670858-1-0*); lib. bdg. 4.95 (*0-9670858-2-9*); mass mkt. 2.50 (*0-9670858-3-7*) Innovatv Prods.
Andrews, Oliver. Living Materials: A Sculptor's Handbook. LC 77-71057. (Illus.). 348p. 1983. pap. 34.95 (*0-520-06452-6*, Pub. by U CA Pr) Cal Prin Full Svc.
Andrews, Ondre H., ed. see Huston, Harvey.
Andrews, Owen. A Moment of Silence: Arlington National Cemetery. LC 93-27115. (Illus.). 64p. 1995. 14.95 (*0-471-14367-7*) Wiley.
Andrews, Owen, ed. see Goetzmann, William H.
Andrews, P. & Banham, P., eds. Late Cenzoic Environments & Hominid Evolution: A Tribute to Bill Bishop. LC 99-491045. 276p. 1999. 115.00 (*1-86239-036-3*, Pub. by Geol Soc Pub Hse) AAPG.
Andrews, P. B. Facies & Genesis of a Hurricane-Washover Fan, St. Joseph Island, Central Texas Coast. (Reports of Investigations: RI 67). (Illus.). 147p. 1970. 3.00 (*0-318-03167-1*) Bur Econ Geology.
Andrews, P. J. & Stringer, C. B. Human Evolution: An Illustrated Guide. (Illus.). 50p. (C). 1990. pap. 14.95 (*0-521-38824-4*) Cambridge U Pr.
Andrews, P. L. & Widdicombe, J. G. The Pathophysiology of the Gut & Airways. 150p. 1993. 37.40 (*1-85578-022-4*, Pub. by Portland Pr Ltd) Ashgate Pub Co.
Andrews, P. R. & Morley, J. S., eds. RACI National Convention, 8th, August 1987, Vol. 13, No. 2. (Drug Design & Delivery Ser.: Vol. 3, No. 2). 108p. 1988. pap. text 218.00 (*3-7186-4836-9*) Gordon & Breach.
Andrews, Pamela R. & Andrews, Darrell. The Visionizer: A Complete Guide to Developing, Planning & Implementing Goals. 85p. 1997. 19.99 (*0-9660103-0-2*) FamQuest Pr.
Andrews, Pat. Government in Action. 230p. (Orig.). (C). 1990. pap. text 22.00 (*0-8191-7789-X*) U Pr of Amer.
Andrews, Patricia. Voices of Diversity: Perspectives on American Political Ideals & Institutions. 287p. (C). 1995. text 18.77 (*1-56134-251-3*, Dshkn McG-Hill) McGrw-H Hghr Educ.
***Andrews, Patricia.** Voices of Diversity: Twentieth-Century Perspectives on History & Government. 2nd ed. 256p. (C). 1999. pap., student ed. 22.50 (*0-07-366156-2*) McGrw-H Hghr Educ.
***Andrews, Patricia, et al.** Public Speaking: Connecting You & Your Audience. LC 98-71976. 1999. write for info. (*0-395-84603-X*) HM.
Andrews, Patricia B. Basic Public Speaking. (Illus.). 174p. (C). 1993. reprint ed. pap. text 19.50 (*0-8191-8492-6*) U Pr of Amer.
Andrews, Patricia H. & Baird. Communication for Business & the Professions. 6th ed. 1995. teacher ed. 15.31 (*0-697-20121-X*) McGraw.
Andrews, Patricia H. & Baird, John E. Communication for Business & the Professions. 6th ed. LC 94-71285. 512p. (C). 1994. text. write for info. (*0-697-20120-1*) Brown & Benchmark.
— Communication for Business & the Professions. 7th ed. LC 99-31252. 512p. 1999. pap. 47.19 (*0-697-32727-2*) McGraw.
Andrews, Patricia H. & Herschel, Richard T. Organizational Communication: Empowerment in a Technological Society. 416p. (C). 1995. text 49.16 (*0-395-72800-2*); text, teacher ed. 11.96 (*0-395-72801-0*) HM.
Andrews, Patrick. Amazon Gold. 1986. pap. 2.50 (*0-373-62013-6*) Harlequin Bks.
— Drug Runner. 1986. pap. 2.50 (*0-373-62012-8*) Harlequin Bks.
— The Ghost Dancers. 1986. pap. 2.50 (*0-373-62011-X*) Harlequin Bks.
***Andrews, Patrick.** Sky Fire. (Talon Force Ser.: Vol. 3). 336p. 2000. mass mkt. 5.99 (*0-451-19956-1*, Sig) NAL.
Andrews, Patrick E. Blood of Apache Mesa. 1988. mass mkt. 2.95 (*0-8217-2538-6*, Zebra Kensgtn) Kensgtn Pub Corp.
— Buffalo War. 256p. 1993. mass mkt. 3.50 (*0-8217-4299-X*, Zebra Kensgtn) Kensgtn Pub Corp.
— Colorado Crossfire. 1989. mass mkt. 2.95 (*0-8217-2820-2*, Zebra Kensgtn) Kensgtn Pub Corp.
— Death on the Texas Range. 224p. 1992. mass mkt. 3.50 (*0-8217-3804-6*, Zebra Kensgtn) Kensgtn Pub Corp.
— The Scalphunters. 256p. 1993. mass mkt. 3.50 (*0-8217-4101-2*, Zebra Kensgtn) Kensgtn Pub Corp.
— Texas Drawdown. 224p. 1991. mass mkt. 3.50 (*0-8217-3399-0*, Zebra Kensgtn) Kensgtn Pub Corp.
— Texican Blood Fight. 1992. mass mkt. 3.50 (*0-8217-3699-X*, Zebra Kensgtn) Kensgtn Pub Corp.
— Whiskey River. 256p. 1993. mass mkt. 3.50 (*0-8217-4409-7*, Zebra Kensgtn) Kensgtn Pub Corp.
***Andrews, Paul.** How the Web Was Won. 368p. 2000. pap. 15.95 (*0-7679-0049-9*) Broadway BDD.
Andrews, Paul. How the Web Was Won: Microsoft from Windows to the Web: The Inside Story of How Bill Gates & His Band of Internet Ideal. LC 99-14176. (Illus.). 352p. 1999. 27.50 (*0-7679-0048-0*) Broadway BDD.
Andrews, Paul, Jr. & Peterson, Marilyn B., eds. Criminal Intelligence Analysis. (Illus.). 215p. 1990. 20.00 (*0-912479-07-8*) Palmer Pr.
Andrews, Paul, jt. auth. see Manes, Stephen.
Andrews, Paul M. We're Poor Little Lambs: The Last Misson of Crew 22 & "Picadilly Lilly," 100th Bombardment Group, October 8, 1943. McDowell, Charles P., ed. LC 95-60246. (Illus.). 96p. (Orig.). 1995. pap. 12.95 (*0-915779-04-8*) Foxfall Pr.
Andrews, Peggy. Sisters Listening to Sisters: Women of the World Share Stories of Personal Empowerment. LC 96-15355. 200p. 1996. 57.95 (*0-89789-475-8*, Bergin & Garvey); pap. 18.95 (*0-89789-476-6*, Bergin & Garvey) Greenwood.
Andrews, Peter. Owls, Caves & Fossils: Predation, Preservation & Accumulation of Small Mammal Bones in Caves, with An Analysis of the Ple. LC 90-33933. (Illus.). 240p. 1990. 47.95 (*0-226-02037-1*) U Ch Pr.
— Revenge by Coincidence. Ludwig, Katherine, ed. 200p. (Orig.). 1997. pap. 7.99 (*1-885778-27-9*) Seaburn.
Andrews, Peter J. For Winners Only: The Only Cas no Gambling Guide You'll Ever Need. 288p. 1996. pap. 18.95 (*0-8065-1728-X*, Citadel Pr) Carol Pub Group.
Andrews, Peter P., et al, eds. Excavations on Black Mesa, 1980: A Descriptive Report. LC 82-72189. (Center for Archaeological Investigations Research Paper Ser.: No. 24). (Illus.). xv, 359p. 1982. pap. 17.50 (*0-88104-003-7*) Center Archaeol.
Andrews, Philip W. On Competition in Economic Theory. LC 81-6246. 141p. 1981. reprint ed. lib. bdg. 55.00 (*0-313-23053-6*, ANOC, Greenwood Pr) Greenwood.
Andrews, R., et al. B. Ioannis Duns Scoti Series, 4 vols. Incl. Vol. IV: Quaestiones Super Libros Metaphysicorum Aristotelis. 800p. 1997. text 125.00 (*1-57659-124-7*); Vol. III: Quaestiones Super Libros Metaphysicorum Aristotelis. 800p. 1997. text 125.00 (*1-57659-123-9*); Vol. II: Quaestiones Super Libros Metaphysicorum Aristotelis. 800p. 1997. text (*1-57659-122-0*); Vol. I: Quaestiones Super Libros Metaphysicorum Aristotelis. 800p. 1997. text 125.00 (*1-57659-121-2*); 437.00 (*1-57659-120-4*) Franciscan Inst.
Andrews, Ralph W. Glory Days of Logging. LC 93-87501. (Illus.). 176p. (Orig.). 1993. pap. 15.95 (*0-88740-593-2*) Schiffer.
— Redwood Classic. LC 85-61521. (Illus.). 174p. 1985. reprint ed. pap. 12.95 (*0-88740-049-3*) Schiffer.
— This Was Logging: Drama in the Northwest Timber Country. (Illus.). 157p. 1985. reprint ed. pap. 14.95 (*0-88740-035-3*) Schiffer.
— This Was Sawmilling. LC 93-87502. (Illus.). 176p. 1993. pap. 15.95 (*0-88740-594-0*) Schiffer.
— Timber: Loggers Challenge the Great Northwest Forests. (Illus.). 182p. 1985. reprint ed. pap. 12.95 (*0-88740-036-1*) Schiffer.
Andrews, Raymond. Baby Sweet's. LC 88-15344. (Brown Thrasher Bks.). (Illus.). 232p. 1988. reprint ed. pap. 12.95 (*0-8203-1069-7*) U of Ga Pr.
— Jessie & Jesus & Cousin Claire. (Illus.). 208p. 199 . 16.95 (*1-56145-032-4*) Peachtree Pubs.
— Jessie & Jesus & Cousin Claire. (Illus.). 208p. 199 . reprint ed. pap. 11.95 (*1-56145-090-1*) Peachtree Pubs.
— The Last Radio Baby: A Memoir. LC 90-41751. (Illus.). 232p. 1990. 15.95 (*1-56145-004-9*) Peachtree Pubs.
— Rosiebelle Lee Wildcat Tennessee. LC 87-21160. (Brown Thrasher Bks.). (Illus.). 290p. 1998. reprint ed. pap. 12.95 (*0-8203-0994-X*) U of Ga Pr.
Andrews, Raymond J., ed. see Lowell, Edward J.
Andrews, Rex. International Dimensions in the National Curriculum. 200p. 1994. pap. 18.00 (*0-948080-62-0*, Trentham Bks) Stylus Pub VA.
Andrews, Richard. Learning to Argue. LC 94-41443. (Education Ser.). (Illus.). 192p. 1995. 95.00 (*0-304-33279-8*); pap. 31.95 (*0-304-33281-X*) Continuum.
— Narrative & Argument. 160p. 1989. pap. 33.95 (*0-335-09219-5*) OpUniv Pr.
— Scripts & Scenarios: The Performed Comic Text in Renaissance Italy. LC 92-23446. 312p. (C). 1993. text 74.95 (*0-521-35357-2*) Cambridge U Pr.
— The Tomb of God. LC 96-77941. 513p. (gr. 8). 1996. 29.95 (*0-316-04275-7*) Little.
***Andrews, Richard & Mitchell, Sally, eds.** Learning to Argue in Higher Education. 237p. 2000. pap. text 27.00 (*0-86709-498-2*, Pub. by Boynton Cook Pubs) Heinemann.
Andrews, Richard, jt. auth. see Bruce, Chris.
Andrews, Richard, ed. see Shakespeare, William.
Andrews, Richard B. State Economic Development: Wisconsin's Planning Methods & Potentials. LC 68-9014. (Land Economics Monographs: No. 2). 116p. reprint ed. pap. 36.00 (*0-8357-6796-5*, 203547600095) Bks Demand.
Andrews, Richard M. Law, Magistracy & Crime in Old Regime Paris, 1735-1789 Vol. 1: The System of Criminal Justice. (Illus.). 630p. (C). 1994. text 80.00 (*0-521-36169-9*) Cambridge U Pr.
Andrews, Richard M., ed. Perspectives on Punishment: An Interdisciplinary Exploration. LC 92-30407. VIII, 200p. (C). 1997. text 44.95 (*0-8204-1791-2*) P Lang Pubng.
Andrews, Richard N. Managing the Environment, Managing Ourselves: A History of American Environmental Policy. LC 98-34987. 1999. 65.00 (*0-300-07358-5*) Yale U Pr.
***Andrews, Richard N.** Managing the Environment, Managing Ourselves: A History of American Environmental Policy. LC 98-34987. (Illus.). 416p. 1999. pap. 30.00 (*0-300-07795-5*) Yale U Pr.
Andrews, Robert. Cassell Dictionary of Contemporary Quotations. LC 97-124924. 576p. 1997. 29.95 (*0-304-34640-3*, Pub. by Cassell) Sterling.
— Cassell Dictionary of Contemporary Quotations. 576p. 1998. pap. 22.95 (*0-304-35032-X*, Pub. by Cassell) Sterling.
— The Columbia Dictionary of Quotations. LC 93-27305. 1,552p. 1993. 42.00 (*0-231-07194-9*) Col U Pr.
— The Concise Columbia Dictionary of Quotations. 343p. 1989. 25.50 (*0-231-06990-1*) Col U Pr.
— The Concise Columbia Dictionary of Quotations in Large Print. large type ed. LC 92-14134. (Reference Bks.). 700p. 1992. 34.95 (*0-8161-5568-2*, G K Hall Lrg Type) Mac Lib Ref.
— The Family, God's Weapon for Victory. 370p. 1996. pap. 16.95 (*1-883893-24-0*, Pub. by WinePress Pub) BookWorld.
***Andrews, Robert.** A Murder of Honor. LC 00-39015. (YA). 2001. write for info. (*0-399-14684-9*, G P Putnam) Peng Put Young Read.
Andrews, Robert. The Towers. 1996. pap. 6.50 (*0-671-86652-4*, PB Trade Paper) PB.
Andrews, Robert, ed. Famous Lines: A Columbia Desk Reference of the Most Familiar Quotations of All Time. LC 96-43879. 448p. 1996. 31.50 (*0-231-10218-6*) Col U Pr.
Andrews, Robert & Ericson, E. E. Teaching Industrial Education: Principles & Practices. 1976. pap. text 15.40 (*0-02-665790-2*) Glencoe.
Andrews, Robert & Righter, Robert W. Colorado Birds: A Reference to Their Distribution & Habitat. (Illus.). 480p. (Orig.). 1992. pap. 24.95 (*0-916278-68-9*) Denver Mus.
Andrews, Robin, ed. A Best Friend Is Forever. LC 92-271. (Illus.). 64p. 1992. 16.95 (*0-88396-357-4*) Blue Mtn Art.
— I'll Never Forget the Love That I Shared with You. LC 91-73569. (Illus.). 64p. 1991. pap. 8.95 (*0-88396-349-3*) Blue Mtn Art.
— A Sister Is a Very Special Friend. LC 91-73571. (Illus.). 64p. 1991. pap. 8.95 (*0-88396-348-5*) Blue Mtn Art.
— To a Very Special Friend on Your Birthday. LC 90-83141. (Illus.). 64p. 1990. pap. 8.95 (*0-88396-285-3*) Blue Mtn Art.
Andrews, Robin M., jt. auth. see Pough, F. H.
Andrews, Rollins D., III, et al, eds. Proceedings of the Symposium on Terrestrial & Aquatic Ecological Studies of the Northwest. 397p. (Orig.). 1977. pap. 10.00 (*0-910055-04-1*) East Wash Univ.
Andrews, Roy C. Ends of the Earth. 1988. 27.00 (*0-935632-72-7*) Wolfe Pub Co.
Andrews-Rusiecka, Hilda, tr. see Walicki, Andrzej.
Andrews, Russell. Gideon. LC 98-47422. 435p. 1999. 24.95 (*0-345-42346-1*) Ballantine Pub Grp.
***Andrews, Russell.** Gideon. 480p. 2000. mass mkt. 6.99 (*0-345-43478-1*) Ballantine Pub Grp.
Andrews, Russell J., ed. Intraoperative Neuroprotection. LC 95-21071. (Illus.). 535p. 1996. 139.00 (*0-683-00228-7*) Lppncott W & W.
Andrews, Samuel J. & Tregillis, Helen C. Sufferings of Union Soldiers in Southern Prisons: Transcript of the Andersonville Trial. LC 97-163739. xii, 86p. 1996. reprint ed. pap. 18.50 (*0-7884-0573-X*, A516) Heritage Bk.
***Andrews, Sarah.** Bone Hunter. 352p. 1999. mass mkt. 6.50 (*0-312-97317-9*) St Martin.
Andrews, Sarah. Bone Hunter. 2nd ed. LC 99-23850. 320p. 1999. text 24.95 (*0-312-20381-0*, Minotaur) St Martin.
***Andrews, Sarah.** An Eye for Gold. 336p. 2000. 24.95 (*0-312-25349-4*, Minotaur) St Martin.
Andrews, Sarah. A Fall in Denver: An Em Hansen Mystery. 1995. 20.00 (*1-883402-34-4*) S&S Trade.
— Only Flesh & Bones. LC 98-14171. 336p. 1998. text 23.95 (*0-312-18642-8*) St Martin.
— Only Flesh & Bones, Vol. 1. 1999. mass mkt. 5.99 (*0-312-96702-0*, Pub. by Tor Bks) St Martin.
— Tensleep: An Em Hansen Mystery. 288p. 1994. 20.00 (*1-883402-33-6*) S&S Trade.
Andrews, Scottie D. Dude's Mountain Vittles: Country Food, Mountain Style. (Illus.). x, 130p. 1997. pap. 12.95 (*0-9664996-1-1*) Broguin.
— Maggie Valley, North Carolina . . . Then & Now. (Illus.). xii, 108p. 1998. reprint ed. pap. 12.95 (*0-9664996-2-X*) Broguin.
— Travels in the Southern Appalachian Mountains: Jes' 'a Broquin' About. 2nd ed. Montgomery, Michael B., ed. (Illus.). xvi, 195p. 1995. reprint ed. pap. 12.95 (*0-9664996-0-3*) Broguin.
Andrews, Sekou, et al. Movement Is the Rhythm of the World: Lyrical Essays, Poetry & Prophecy from Three Black Men. 56p. 1999. 18.95 (*0-9624889-7-6*) Seymour-Smith.
Andrews, Sharon V. & Ali, Cynthia D. Teach Your Children Values: 95 Things Parents Can Do! LC 97-4571. (Illus.). 136p. (Orig.). 1997. pap. 12.95 (*1-883790-24-7*, EDINFO Pr) Grayson Bernard Pubs.
***Andrews, Sharon Vincz & Martin, Donna Marie.** Teaching Kids to Care: Exploring Values in the Public School. 169p. 1999. 109.95 (*1-56676-750-4*) Rowman.
— Teaching Kids to Care: Exploring Values in the Public School. 169p. 1999. 99.95 incl. VHS (*1-56676-702-4*) Scarecrow.
Andrews, Shirley. Atlantis: Insights from a Lost Civilization. LC 97-18360. (Illus.). 288p. (Orig.). 1997. pap. 12.95 (*1-56718-023-X*, K023-X) Llewellyn Pubns.
Andrews, Sidney. South Since the War. LC 69-18546. (American Negro: His History & Literature, Ser. No. 2). 1969. reprint ed. 32.95 (*0-405-01847-9*) Ayer.
Andrews, Siri, ed. Hewins Lectures: Nineteen Forty-Seven to Nineteen Sixty-Two. LC 63-21644. 375p. 1963. pap. 7.00 (*0-87675-164-8*) Horn Bk.
Andrews, Sona K., et al. Beyond Seeing & Hearing: Teaching Geography to Sensory Impaired Children - An Integrated Based Curriculum. (Pathways in Geography Ser.: No. 2). (Illus.). 62p. (Orig.). 1991. pap. text 7.00 (*0-9627379-4-1*) NCFGE.
Andrews-Speed, Anthony. Discover Your Leader Self: Training the Leader Inside You. LC 96-70425. 160p. (Orig.). 1997. pap. 16.95 (*0-9638880-2-1*) Osmyrrah Pub.
— Living, Loving & Laughing: A Guide to Self-Awareness. 160p. (Orig.). 1993. pap. 14.95 (*0-9638880-0-5*) Osmyrrah Pub.
— The Relationship Roller Coaster: Riding Out the Ups & Downs. LC 94-66824. 176p. (Orig.). 1994. pap. 14.95 (*0-9638880-1-3*) Osmyrrah Pub.
Andrews, Starra. The Pursuit of Acting: Working Actors Share Their Experience & Advice. LC 98-10919. 192p. 1998. 49.95 (*0-275-95692-X*, Praeger Pubs); pap. 16.95 (*0-275-96281-4*, Praeger Pubs) Greenwood.
Andrews, Stephen P. Primary Synopsis of Universology & Alwato: The New Scientific Universal Language. Stern, Madeleine B., ed. (C). 1971. 20.00 (*0-87730-007-0*) M & S Pr.

A

— The Science of Society. 1972. 250.00 (*0-8490-1003-9*) Gordon Pr.

— The Science of Society. Shively, Charles, ed. 184p. 1970. 20.00 (*0-87730-004-6*) M & S Pr.

— Sovereignty of the Individual. 1972. 250.00 (*0-8490-1094-2*) Gordon Pr.

— The Works of Stephen Pearl Andrews, 1812-1886, Set. 1987. reprint ed. lib. bdg. 500.00 (*0-685-18596-6*) Rprt Serv.

Andrews, Stephen P., et al, contrib. by. Love, Marriage & Divorce. 121p. 1985. reprint ed. 39.00 (*0-932051-63-4*) Rprt Serv.

***Andrews, Stuart M.** The British Periodical Press & the French Revolution, 1789-1999. LC 00-33321. (Illus.). 2000. write for info. (*0-312-23781-2*) St Martin.

Andrews, Stuart M. A Tenant Advocate's Guide to the South Carolina Residential Landlord & Tenant Act. 298p. 1986. 21.00 (*0-685-23182-8*, 41,235) NCLS Inc.

Andrews, Susan B. & Creed, John. Authentic Alaska: Voices of Its Native Writers. LC 97-21791. (American Indians Lives Ser.). (Illus.). xxx, 180p. 1998. pap. 15.00 (*0-8032-5933-6*) U of Nebr Pr.

Andrews, Susan B. & Creed, John, eds. Authentic Alaska: Voices of Its Native Writers. LC 97-21791. (Illus.). xxx, 180p. 1998. text 40.00 (*0-8032-1041-8*) U of Nebr Pr.

***Andrews, Susyn, et al, eds.** Taxonomy of Cultivated Plants. 500p. 1999. 54.00 (*1-900347-89-X*, Pub. by Royal Botnic Grdns) Balogh.

Andrews, Sylvia. Rattlebone Rock. LC 93-4426. 1997. 11.15 (*0-606-11783-0*, Pub. by Turtleback) Demco.

— Rattlebone Rock. LC 93-4426. (Trophy Bk.). (Illus.). 32p. (J). (ps-2). 1997. reprint ed. pap. 5.95 (*0-06-443484-2*, HarpTrophy) HarpC Child Bks.

Andrews, T. Getting It. (In the Pink Ser.). 1996. mass mkt. 11.95 (*0-340-63489-8*, Pub. by Hodder & Stought Ltd) Trafalgar.

— Lustathon. 1996. mass mkt. 11.95 (*0-340-65811-8*, Pub. by Hodder & Stought Ltd) Trafalgar.

— Sin City. mass mkt. 11.95 (*0-340-63492-8*, Pub. by Hodder & Stought Ltd) Trafalgar.

***Andrews, Tamra.** Dictionary of Nature Myths: Legends of the Earth, Sea, & Sky. LC 99-40342. 336p. 2000. 16.95 (*0-19-513677-2*) OUP.

— Nectar & Ambrosia: An Encyclopedia of Food in World Mythology. 2000. lib. bdg. 65.00 (*1-57607-036-0*) ABC-CLIO.

Andrews, Tamra, ed. Legends of the Earth, Sea & Sky: An Encyclopedia of Nature Myths. LC 98-40603. (Illus.). 336p. 1998. lib. bdg. 65.00 (*0-87436-963-0*, AD-EASKYC) ABC-CLIO.

Andrews, Tamsey K., jt. ed. see Tykot, Robert H.

Andrews, Ted. Animal-Speak: The Spiritual & Magical Powers of Creatures Great & Small. LC 93-28673. (Illus.). 400p. 1993. pap. 19.95 (*0-87542-028-1*) Llewellyn Pubns.

***Andrews, Ted.** Animal-Wise: The Spirit Language & Signs of Nature. LC 98-84420. (Illus.). 438p. 1999. pap. 19.95 (*1-888767-34-0*, Pub. by Dragonhawk Pubg) Bookpeople.

Andrews, Ted. The Animal-Wise Tarot. LC 98-85912. (Illus.). 246p. 1998. pap. 34.95 (*1-888767-35-9*) Dragonhawk Pubg.

— Basic Fly Tying in Pictures. (Illus.). 91p. 1998. pap. text 10.00 (*0-7881-5270-X*) DIANE Pub.

— Crystal Balls & Crystal Bowls: Tools for Ancient Scrying & Modern Seership. LC 94-44921. (Illus.). 256p. 1999. pap. 12.95 (*1-56718-026-4*) Llewellyn Pubns.

— Enchantment of the Faerie Realm: Communicate with Nature Spirits & Elementals. LC 92-33148. (Illus.). 240p. 1999. pap. 10.00 (*0-87542-002-8*) Llewellyn Pubns.

— The Healer's Manual: A Beginner's Guide to Energy Therapies. LC 93-34270. (Illus.). 256p. 1999. pap. 12.95 (*0-87542-007-9*) Llewellyn Pubns.

— How to Develop & Use Psychic Touch. LC 94-3524. (How to Ser.). (Illus.). 224p. 1997. mass mkt. 4.99 (*1-56718-027-2*) Llewellyn Pubns.

— How to Heal with Color. LC 92-13176. (How to Ser.). (Illus.). 224p. 1992. mass mkt. 4.99 (*0-87542-005-2*) Llewellyn Pubns.

— How to Meet & Work with Spirit Guides. LC 92-5767. (How to Ser.). (Illus.). 192p. 1992. pap. 4.99 (*0-87542-008-7*) Llewellyn Pubns.

— How to See & Read the Aura. LC 90-28285. (How to Ser.). (Illus.). 160p. (Orig.). 1991. pap. 3.95 (*0-87542-013-3*) Llewellyn Pubns.

— How to Uncover Your Past Lives. LC 91-44586. (How to Ser.). (Illus.). 240p. 1992. mass mkt. 4.99 (*0-87542-022-2*) Llewellyn Pubns.

***Andrews, Ted.** Magic of Believing. Alexander-Harding, Pagyn & Haugen, Diane, eds. LC 00-100043. 220p. 2000. 17.95 (*1-888767-43-X*, Pub. by Dragonhawk Pubg) Partners Pubs Grp.

Andrews, Ted. Magickal Dance: Your Body As an Instrument of Power. LC 92-18981. (Practical Guide to Personal Power Ser.). (Illus.). 240p. 1993. pap. 9.95 (*0-87542-004-4*) Llewellyn Pubns.

— More Simplified Magic: Pathworking & the Tree of Life. rev. ed. Alexander-Harding, Pagyn, ed. LC 96-71460. Orig. Title: Imagick - Qabalistic Pathworking for Imaginative Magicians. (Illus.). 450p. 1997. pap. 14.95 (*1-888767-28-6*) Dragonhawk Pubg.

— Music Therapy for Non-Musicians. Alexander-Harding, Pagan, ed. (Beginnings, a Dragonhawk Ser.). (Illus.). 324p. 1996. pap. 9.95 (*1-888767-31-6*) Dragonhawk Pubg.

— The Occult Christ: Angelic Mysteries: The Divine Feminine. LC 93-3724. (Illus.). 224p. 1999. pap. 12.95 (*0-87542-019-2*) Llewellyn Pubns.

***Andrews, Ted.** Psychic Power. Alexander-Harding, Pagyn & Haugen, Diane, eds. LC 00-100045. (Young Person's School of Magic & Mystery Ser.: Vol. 3). (Illus.). 220p. 2000. 17.95 (*1-888767-40-5*, Pub. by Dragonhawk Pubg) Partners Pubs Grp.

Andrews, Ted. Psychic Protection. Alexander-Harding, Pagan & Haugen, Diane, eds. LC 98-84419. (Beginnings Ser.). (Illus.). 368p. 1998. pap. 12.95 (*1-888767-30-8*) Dragonhawk Pubg.

— The Sacred Power in Your Name. LC 89-77238. (Practical Guide Ser.). (Illus.). 336p. (Orig.). 1990. pap. 12.95 (*0-87542-012-5*) Llewellyn Pubns.

— Sacred Sounds: Transformation Through Music & Word. LC 91-45962. (Practical Guide to Personal Power Ser.). (Illus.). 232p. 1999. pap. 9.95 (*0-87542-018-4*) Llewellyn Pubns.

— Simplified Magic: A Beginner's Guide to the New Age Qabala. LC 88-45192. (New Age Ser.). (Illus.). 208p. (Orig.). 1989. mass mkt. 4.99 (*0-87542-015-X*) Llewellyn Pubns.

— Ted Andrews Gift Set. (Illus.). (Orig.). 1996. pap. 13.89 (*1-56718-893-1*) Llewellyn Pubns.

— Treasures of the Unicorn: The Return to the Sacred Quest. Alexander, Pagan, ed. (Illus.). 250p. 1996. 24.95 (*1-888767-26-X*); pap. 12.95 (*1-888767-25-1*) Dragonhawk Pubg.

Andrews, Thomasin C. Update for the MRCP. LC 96-30950. 1996. pap. text 25.00 (*0-443-05589-0*) Church.

Andrews, Tim. Raku: A Review of Contemporary Work. 176p. 1994. text 60.00 (*976-8097-99-X*, Pub. by Craftsman House) Gordon & Breach.

— Raku: A Review of Contemporary Work. (Illus.). 160p. 1994. 34.95 (*0-8019-8633-8*) Krause Pubns.

***Andrews, Tina.** Sally Hemings an American Scandal: The Myths, the Madness, the Making. LC 00-104155. (Illus.). x, 246p. 2000. 24.95 (*0-9701295-4-8*) Malibu.

Andrews, Tom. The Brother's Country: Poems. (National Poetry Ser.: 1989). 76p. (Orig.). 1990. pap. 9.95 (*0-89255-151-8*) Persea Bks.

— Codeine Diary: A Memoir. LC 97-17248. 256p. 1998. 22.95 (*0-316-04244-7*) Little.

— Codeine Diary: True Confessions of a Reckless Hemophiliac. LC 99-18031. 256p. 1999. pap. 13.00 (*0-15-600657-X*) Harcourt.

— The Hemophiliac's Motorcycle. LC 93-43994. (Iowa Poetry Prize Ser.). 89p. (Orig.). 1994. pap. 11.95 (*0-87745-452-3*) U of Iowa Pr.

— Hymning the Kanawha. limited ed. 18p. (Orig.). 1989. pap. 20.00 (*0-9621666-2-6*) Haw River Bk.

— On William Stafford: The Worth of Local Things. 296p. 1995. pap. text 18.95 (*0-472-08321-X*, 08321) U of Mich Pr.

Andrews, Tom, ed. The Point Where All Things Meet: Essays on Charles Wright. LC 95-67732. 300p. (Orig.). 1995. pap. 19.95 (*0-932440-72-X*) Oberlin Coll Pr.

Andrews, V. C. All That Glitters. 352p. 1995. per. 6.99 (*0-671-87319-9*) PB.

— All That Glitters. large type ed. 1995. 25.95 (*1-56895-236-8*, Compass) Wheeler Pub.

— Angel Negro. 1998. pap. 6.95 (*84-01-49754-X*) Lectorum Pubns.

— Brooke. (J). 1998. per. 3.99 (*0-671-02032-3*) PB.

— Brooke. (Orphans Ser.). 1998. 9.09 (*0-606-13229-5*, Pub. by Turtleback) Demco.

— Brooke. large type ed. LC 98-35890. 203p. (J). 1998. 30.00 (*0-7838-0329-X*, G K Hall Lrg Type) Mac Lib Ref.

— Butterfly. (The Orphans Ser.). 1998. per. 3.99 (*0-671-02029-3*) PB.

— Butterfly. (Orphans Ser.). 1998. 9.09 (*0-606-13233-3*, Pub. by Turtleback) Demco.

***Andrews, V. C.** Butterfly. large type ed. LC 98-29032. 198 p. 1998. write for info. (*0-7540-1205-0*, G K Hall Lrg Type) Mac Lib Ref.

— Cat. (Wildflowers Ser. : No. 4). (YA). 1999. per. 3.99 (*0-671-02803-0*) PB.

— Cat. large type ed. LC 99-51865. (YA). 2000. 30.00 (*0-7838-8805-8*, G K Hall Lrg Type) Mac Lib Ref.

Andrews, V. C. Corazones Caidos, 1. 1998. pap. 6.95 (*84-01-49329-3*) Lectorum Pubns.

— Crystal. 1998. per. 3.99 (*0-671-02030-7*) PB.

— Crystal. (Orphans Ser.). 1998. 9.09 (*0-606-13295-3*, Pub. by Turtleback) Demco.

— Crystal. large type ed. LC 98-34400. 192p. 1998. pap. write for info. (*0-7540-1212-3*, G K Hall Lrg Type) Mac Lib Ref.

— Crystal. large type ed. LC 98-34400. 206p. 1998. 26.95 (*0-7838-0328-1*, G K Hall Lrg Type) Mac Lib Ref.

— Dark Angel. Marrow, Linda, ed. 1990. per. 7.50 (*0-671-72939-X*) PB.

— Dark Angel. 440p. 1986. 17.45 (*0-671-63370-8*) S&S Trade.

— Dark Angel. (J). 1986. 12.60 (*0-606-02624-X*, Pub. by Turtleback) Demco.

— Darkest Hour. 1993. 12.09 (*0-606-05225-9*, Pub. by Turtleback) Demco.

— Darkest Hour. large type ed. LC 93-31583. 471p. 1993. lib. bdg. 23.95 (*0-8161-5875-4*, G K Hall Lrg Type) Mac Lib Ref.

— Darkest Hour. large type ed. LC 93-31583. 471p. 1994. lib. bdg. 18.95 (*0-8161-5876-2*, G K Hall Lrg Type) Mac Lib Ref.

— Darkest Hour, Vol. 4. Marrow, Linda, ed. 400p. 1993. per. 6.99 (*0-671-75932-9*) PB.

— Dawn. Marrow, Linda, ed. 416p. 1990. 19.95 (*0-685-46977-8*); per. 7.99 (*0-671-67068-9*) PB.

— Dawn. 1990. 12.09 (*0-606-04649-6*, Pub. by Turtleback) Demco.

— Dawn. large type ed. (General Ser.). 472p. 1991. pap. 17.95 (*0-8161-5186-5*, G K Hall Lrg Type); lib. bdg. 20.95 (*0-8161-5184-9*, G K Hall Lrg Type) Mac Lib Ref.

***Andrews, V. C.** End of the Rainbow. 2001. 24.00 (*0-671-03984-9*, PB Hardcover) PB.

— Eye of the Storm. (Hudson Ser.: Vol. 3). 400p. 2000. 24.95 (*0-671-03982-2*); per. 7.99 (*0-671-03983-0*, Pocket Star Bks) PB.

Andrews, V. C. Fallen Hearts. Marrow, Linda, ed. LC 00-1513. 1990. mass mkt. 7.99 (*0-671-72940-3*) PB.

— Fallen Hearts. 1988. 12.09 (*0-606-03782-9*, Pub. by Turtleback) Demco.

Andrews, V. C. Flores en el Atico. Pardo, Jesus, tr. (SPA.). 469p. 1996. pap. 14.58 (*84-01-49747-7*) Lectorum Pubns.

Andrews, V. C. Flowers in the Attic. Marrow, Linda, ed. 416p. 1909. mass mkt. 7.99 (*0-671-72941-1*) PB.

— Flowers in the Attic. 1997. per. 3.99 (*0-671-01944-9*) PB.

— Flowers in the Attic. 1979. 12.60 (*0-606-00295-2*, Pub. by Turtleback) Demco.

— Flowers in the Attic, Set. Incl. If There Be Thorns. 1984. 1984. Set boxed set 15.80 (*0-671-90083-8*) PB.

— Flowers in the Attic - If There Be Thorns - Petals on the Wind - Seeds of Yesterday. (The Dollanger Saga). 1996. pap. 27.96 (*0-671-85156-X*) PB.

***Andrews, V. C.** Fulgor Oculto. (SPA.). 1998. pap. 6.95 (*84-01-49797-3*) Plaza.

Andrews, V. C. Garden of Shadows. 1990. 11.84 (*0-606-03582-6*, Pub. by Turtleback) Demco.

— Garden of Shadows, Vol. 1. Marrow, Linda, ed. 1990. per. 6.99 (*0-671-72942-X*) PB.

— Gates of Paradise. Marrow, Linda, ed. 1990. mass mkt. 7.50 (*0-671-72943-8*) PB.

— Gates of Paradise. (J). 1989. 12.60 (*0-606-04227-X*, Pub. by Turtleback) Demco.

— Heart Song. 400p. 1997. 23.00 (*0-671-53468-8*, PB Hardcover); per. 7.99 (*0-671-53472-6*, Pocket Books) PB.

— Heart Song. 1997. 12.60 (*0-606-13471-9*, Pub. by Turtleback) Demco.

— Heart Song. large type ed. LC 97-40813. 478p. 1997. 28.95 (*0-7838-8346-3*, G K Hall Lrg Type) Mac Lib Ref.

Andrews, V. C. Heaven. Marrow, Linda, ed. 1990. per. 6.99 (*0-671-72944-6*) PB.

Andrews, V. C. Heaven. 1985. 12.09 (*0-606-00660-5*, Pub. by Turtleback) Demco.

— Hidden Jewel. 384p. 1995. per. 7.99 (*0-671-87320-2*) PB.

— Hidden Jewel. large type ed. 459p. 1997. pap. 24.95 (*0-614-25128-1*, G K Hall Lrg Type) Mac Lib Ref.

— If There Be Thorns. Marrow, Linda, ed. 1990. mass mkt. 7.99 (*0-671-72945-4*) PB.

— If There Be Thorns. 1981. 12.60 (*0-606-00256-1*, Pub. by Turtleback) Demco.

— Into the Garden. 1999. per. 7.99 (*0-671-00771-8*) PB.

***Andrews, V. C.** Into the Garden. 400p. 1999. 24.00 (*0-671-00770-X*) PB.

— Into the Garden. (Illus.). (J). 1999. 13.34 (*0-606-18375-2*) Turtleback.

— Into the Garden. large type ed. LC 99-88110. (Core Ser.). 2000. 29.95 (*0-7838-8806-6*, G K Hall Lrg Type) Mac Lib Ref.

Andrews, V. C. Jade. (Wildflowers Ser.: No. 3). 192p. (YA). 1999. per. 3.99 (*0-671-02802-2*) PB.

***Andrews, V. C.** Jade. large type ed. LC 99-55681. (YA). 2000. 30.00 (*0-7838-8804-X*, G K Hall Lrg Type) Mac Lib Ref.

Andrews, V. C. Jardin Sombrio. (SPA.). 336p. 1992. pap. 4.95 (*1-56780-059-9*) La Costa Pr.

— Jardin Sombrio. 1998. pap. 6.95 (*84-01-49752-3*) Lectorum Pubns.

***Andrews, V. C.** Lightning Strikes. (Hudson Ser.: Vol. 2). 384p. 2000. 24.95 (*0-671-00768-8*, PB Hardcover); per. 7.99 (*0-671-00769-6*, Pocket Star Bks) PB.

— Lightning Strikes. (Illus.). (J). 2000. 13.34 (*0-606-18830-4*) Turtleback.

Andrews, V. C. Melody. LC 97-160353. 384p. 1996. 23.00 (*0-671-53470-X*); per. 7.99 (*0-671-53471-8*) PB.

— Melody. 1996. 12.60 (*0-606-13603-7*, Pub. by Turtleback) Demco.

— Melody. large type ed. LC 96-27669. 1996. 25.95 (*0-7838-1906-4*, G K Hall Lrg Type) Mac Lib Ref.

— Midnight Whispers. 1992. 12.09 (*0-606-02201-5*, Pub. by Turtleback) Demco.

Andrews, V. C. Midnight Whispers. large type ed. LC 93-14808. 515p. 1993. lib. bdg. 23.95 (*0-8161-5655-7*, G K Hall Lrg Type) Mac Lib Ref.

Andrews, V. C. Midnight Whispers. large type ed. LC 93-14808. (Large Print Bks.). 515p. 1993. 19.95 (*0-8161-5656-5*, G K Hall Lrg Type) Mac Lib Ref.

— Midnight Whispers, Vol. 5. Marrow, Linda, ed. 448p. 1992. mass mkt. 6.99 (*0-671-69516-9*) PB.

— Misty. (Wildflowers Ser. : No. 1). (YA). 1999. mass mkt. 3.99 (*0-671-02800-6*, Pocket Books) PB.

***Andrews, V. C.** Misty. large type ed. LC 99-46976. (G. K. Hall Core Ser.). (YA). 1999. 26.95 (*0-7838-8802-3*, G K Hall Lrg Type) Mac Lib Ref.

Andrews, V. C. Music in the Night. LC 98-169961. 1998. 24.00 (*0-671-53467-X*); per. 7.99 (*0-671-53474-2*) PB.

— Music in the Night. 1998. 12.60 (*0-606-13627-4*, Pub. by Turtleback) Demco.

— Music in the Night. large type ed. LC 98-56121. 1999. 28.95 (*0-7838-8533-4*, G K Hall Lrg Type) Mac Lib Ref.

***Andrews, V. C.** Musica en la Noche. 1999. 24.95 (*84-08-02872-3*) Planeta Edit.

Andrews, V. C. My Sweet Audrina. Marrow, Linda, ed. 1990. mass mkt. 7.99 (*0-671-72946-2*) PB.

— My Sweet Audrina. (J). 1989. 12.65 (*0-606-02956-7*, Pub. by Turtleback) Demco.

— Olivia. 400p. 1999. 24.00 (*0-671-00760-2*) S&S Trade.

— Olivia. (YA). 1999. per. 7.99 (*0-671-00761-0*) S&S Trade.

— Olivia. large type ed. LC 99-18825. 1999. 27.95 (*0-7838-8592-X*) Mac Lib Ref.

***Andrews, V. C.** Orphans. 672p. 2000. reprint ed. mass mkt. 7.99 (*0-7434-0361-4*, Pocket Books) PB.

Andrews, V. C. Pearl in the Mist. Marrow, Linda, ed. 384p. 1994. per. 7.99 (*0-671-75936-1*) PB.

— Pearl in the Mist. 1994. 12.09 (*0-606-07067-2*, Pub. by Turtleback) Demco.

— Pearl in the Mist. large type ed. 1995. 24.95 (*0-7838-1164-0*, G K Hall Lrg Type) Mac Lib Ref.

— Petalos Al Viento. 1998. pap. 6.95 (*84-01-49748-5*) Lectorum Pubns.

Andrews, V. C. Petals on the Wind. LC 80-15638. 1980. pap. write for info. (*0-671-82977-7*) Litle Simon.

Andrews, V. C. Petals on the Wind. 1984. write for info. (*0-318-57961-8*) PB.

— Petals on the Wind. Marrow, Linda, ed. LC 00-1495. 1990. per. 7.99 (*0-671-72947-0*) PB.

— Petals on the Wind. 1980. 12.09 (*0-606-00253-7*, Pub. by Turtleback) Demco.

— Rain. (Hudson Ser.: Vol. 1). 384p. 2000. 24.00 (*0-671-00764-5*, PB Hardcover); per. 7.99 (*0-671-00767-X*) PB.

— Raven. LC 98-39757. 205p. 1999. 27.95 (*0-7540-1235-2*) Mac Lib Ref.

— Raven. 1998. per. 3.99 (*0-671-02031-5*) PB.

— Raven. large type ed. LC 98-39757. 189p. 1999. 30.00 (*0-7838-0330-3*, G K Hall Lrg Type) Mac Lib Ref.

— Ruby. Marrow, Linda, ed. 448p. 1994. per. 7.99 (*0-671-75934-5*) PB.

Andrews, V. C. Ruby. 1994. 12.09 (*0-606-05989-X*, Pub. by Turtleback) Demco.

Andrews, V. C. Ruby. large type ed. 1994. 25.95 (*1-56895-074-8*) Wheeler Pub.

***Andrews, V. C.** Runaways. 368p. 1998. per. 7.99 (*0-671-00763-7*) PB.

Andrews, V. C. Runaways. 1998. 24.00 (*0-671-00762-9*) S&S Trade.

— Runaways LC 98-31643. 407p. 1999. write for info. (*0-7540-1246-8*) Chivers N Amer.

— Runaways. large type ed. LC 98-31643. Date not set. 28.95 (*0-7838-0436-9*, G K Hall Lrg Type) Mac Lib Ref.

— Secretos del Amanecer. 1998. pap. 6.95 (*84-01-49760-4*) Lectorum Pubns.

— Secrets of the Morning. Marrow, Linda, ed. 416p. 1991. per. 7.99 (*0-671-69512-6*) PB.

— Secrets of the Morning. 1991. 12.60 (*0-606-05012-4*, Pub. by Turtleback) Demco.

— Secrets of the Morning. large type ed. (General Ser.). 487p. 1992. pap. 17.95 (*0-8161-5386-8*, G K Hall Lrg Type); lib. bdg. 20.95 (*0-8161-5385-X*, G K Hall Lrg Type) Mac Lib Ref.

— Seeds of Yesterday. 416p. 1987. pap. 4.95 (*0-317-63632-4*) NAL.

— Seeds of Yesterday. 1984. write for info. (*0-318-57962-6*) PB.

— Seeds of Yesterday. 1983. 3.95 (*0-671-44328-3*) S&S Trade.

— Seeds of Yesterday. 11.84 (*0-606-03235-5*, Pub. by Turtleback) Demco.

— Seeds of Yesterday, Vol. 5. Marrow, Linda, ed. 1990. per. 7.50 (*0-671-72948-9*) PB.

— Semmillas del Ayer. 1998. pap. 6.95 (*84-01-49794-9*) Lectorum Pubns.

***Andrews, V. C.** Sintonia Inacabada. (SPA.). 1999. 27.95 (*84-08-02711-5*) Planeta Edit.

Andrews, V. C. Star. (Wildflowers Ser. : No. 2). 160p. (YA). 1999. mass mkt. 3.99 (*0-671-02801-4*, Pocket Books) PB.

***Andrews, V. C.** Star. large type ed. LC 99-47006. (G. K. Hall Core Ser.). (YA). 1999. 27.95 (*0-7838-8803-1*, G K Hall Lrg Type) Mac Lib Ref.

— Tarnished Gold. 1996. mass mkt. 6.99 (*0-671-87321-0*) PB.

Andrews, V. C. Tarnished Gold. large type ed. LC 96-17810. (Large Print Bks.). 1996. 26.95 (*1-56895-338-0*) Wheeler Pub.

Andrews, V. C. Three Complete Novels by V. C. Andrews. 1997. 14.00 (*0-671-01688-1*, PB Trade Paper) PB.

Andrews, V. C. Three Complete Novels by V. C. Andrews: Heaven, Dawn, & Ruby. 955p. 1998. text 14.00 (*0-7881-5750-7*) DIANE Pub.

— Twilight's Child. 1992. 12.09 (*0-606-00810-1*, Pub. by Turtleback) Demco.

— Twilight's Child. large type ed. LC 92-19028. (General Ser.). 555p. 1993. pap. 17.95 (*0-8161-5525-9*, G K Hall Lrg Type); lib. bdg. 20.95 (*0-8161-5524-0*, G K Hall Lrg Type) Mac Lib Ref.

— Twilight's Child, Vol. 3. Marrow, Linda, ed. 416p. 1992. per. 7.50 (*0-671-69514-2*) PB.

— Unfinished Symphony. LC 98-160780. 1997. 24.00 (*0-671-53469-6*, PB Hardcover); per. 7.50 (*0-671-53473-4*) PB.

— Unfinished Symphony. 1997. 12.60 (*0-606-13883-8*, Pub. by Turtleback) Demco.

— Unfinished Symphony. large type ed. LC 97-49396. (Core Ser.). 482p. 1998. 28.95 (*0-7838-8407-9*, G K Hall Lrg Type) Mac Lib Ref.

— Web of Dreams. Marrow, Linda, ed. 432p. 1990. per. 7.99 (*0-671-72949-7*) PB.

— Web of Dreams. (Casteel Saga Ser.). (J). 1990. 12.09 (*0-606-04418-3*, Pub. by Turtleback) Demco.

An Asterisk (*) at the beginning of an entry indicates that the title is appearing for the first time.

— Web of Dreams. large type ed. (General Ser.). 581p. 1991. pap. 17.95 (*0-8161-5039-7*, G K Hall Lrg Type); lib. bdg. 20.95 (*0-8161-5038-9*, G K Hall Lrg Type) Mac Lib Ref.

Andrews, Val. Sherlock Holmes & the Baker Street Dozen: A Collection of Thirteen Short Stories. 126p. 1997. pap. 13.95 (*0-947533-41-9*, Pub. by Breese Bks) Firebird Dist.

— Sherlock Holmes & the Brighton Pavilion Mystery. 124p. 1991. 25.00 (*0-86025-269-8*, Pub. by I Henry Pubns) Empire Pub Srvs.

— Sherlock Holmes & the Circus of Fear. 112p. 1997. pap. 13.95 (*0-947533-17-6*, Pub. by Breese Bks) Firebird Dist.

— Sherlock Holmes & the Egyptian Hall Adventure. 112p. 1997. pap. 9.95 (*0-947533-43-5*, Pub. by Breese Bks) Firebird Dist.

— Sherlock Holmes & the Eminent Thespian. 124p. 1991. 25.00 (*0-86025-268-X*, Pub. by I Henry Pubns) Empire Pub Srvs.

— Sherlock Holmes & the GreyFriars School Mystery. 109p. 1997. pap. 10.95 (*0-947533-55-9*, Pub. by Breese Bks) Firebird Dist.

Andrews, Val. Sherlock Holmes & the Greyfriars School Mystery. large type ed. 192p. pap. 18.99 (*0-7089-5442-1*) Ulverscroft.

Andrews, Val. Sherlock Holmes & the Houdini Birthright. 160p. 1997. pap. 10.95 (*0-947533-91-5*, Pub. by Breese Bks) Firebird Dist.

***Andrews, Val.** Sherlock Holmes & the Long Acre Vampire: A Sherlock Holmes Mystery. 128p. 2000. pap. 14.95 (*0-947533-29-X*, Pub. by Breese Bks) Midpt Trade.

Andrews, Val. Sherlock Holmes & the Man Who Lost Himself. 112p. 1997. pap. 10.95 (*0-947533-70-2*, Pub. by Breese Bks) Firebird Dist.

— Sherlock Holmes & the Sandringham House Mystery. 1999. pap. 14.95 (*0-947533-53-2*) Breese Bks.

— Sherlock Holmes & the Theatre of Death. 125p. 1997. pap. 13.95 (*0-947533-12-5*, Pub. by Breese Bks) Firebird Dist.

— Sherlock Holmes & the Tomb of Terror. (Sherlock Holmes... Ser.). 2000. pap. 14.95 (*0-947533-72-9*, Pub. by Breese Bks) Midpt Trade.

— Sherlock Holmes & the Yule-Tide Mystery. 112p. 1996. pap. 10.95 (*0-947533-11-7*, Pub. by Breese Bks) Firebird Dist.

***Andrews, Val.** Sherlock Holmes at the Varieties. 196p. 2000. pap. 12.95 (*0-947533-82-6*, Pub. by Breese Bks) Midpt Trade.

Andrews, Val. Sherlock Holmes on the Western Front. (Sherlock Holmes... Ser.). 2000. pap. 14.95 (*0-947533-87-7*, Pub. by Breese Bks) Midpt Trade.

***Andrews, Val.** Torment of Sherlock Holmes. 2000. pap. 12.95 (*0-947533-23-0*, Pub. by Breese Bks) Midpt Trade.

***Andrews, Vicki.** Lighter Shade of Brown. 1999. pap. text 8.95 (*1-885478-75-5*, Pub. by Genesis Press) BookWorld.

Andrews, Vicki. Midnight Peril. LC 98-208439. 247p. 1998. pap. 10.95 (*1-885478-27-5*, Pub. by Genesis Press) BookWorld.

Andrews, W. Guide to the Study of Environmental Pollution. 1972. text 12.40 (*0-13-370858-6*); pap. text 14.56 (*0-13-370833-0*) P-H.

— Guide to the Study of Freshwater Ecology. 1971. 12.40 (*0-13-370866-7*); pap. text 13.12 (*0-13-370759-8*) P-H.

Andrews, W., et al. Guide to the Study of Terrestrial Ecology. 1974. pap. text 12.40 (*0-13-370932-9*); lib. bdg. 13.12 (*0-13-370940-X*) P-H.

— Urban Studies. 1976. teacher ed. 8.44 (*0-13-939454-0*); pap. text 20.04 (*0-13-939280-7*) P-H.

Andrews, W. H. Footprints of a Regiment: A Recollection of the 1st Georgia Regulars, 1861-1865. LC 91-77195. 304p. 1992. 19.95 (*1-56352-030-3*) Longstreet.

Andrews, W. L. New York As Washington Knew It after the Revolution. 1973. 59.95 (*0-8490-0726-7*) Gordon Pr.

— The Old Booksellers of New York. 1972. 59.95 (*0-8490-0753-4*) Gordon Pr.

Andrews, W. P., ed. see Brooks, Charles T.

Andrews, W. S., et al. Magic Squares & Cubes. 419p. 1960. pap. 9.95 (*0-486-20658-0*) Dover.

Andrews, W. T. A Waif - A Prince. LC 73-37581. (Black Heritage Library Collection). 1977. reprint ed. 27.95 (*0-8369-8957-0*) Ayer.

Andrews, W. T., ed. Critics on D. H. Lawrence. LC 77-159294. (Readings in Literary Criticism Ser.: No. 9). 1979. pap. 19.95 (*0-87024-207-5*) U of Miami Pr.

Andrews, Walter G. An Introduction to Ottoman Poetry. LC 74-27615. (Studies in Middle Eastern Literatures: No. 7). 1976. pap. 20.00 (*0-88297-034-8*) Bibliotheca.

Andrews, Walter G., et al, trs. from TUR. Ottoman Lyric Poetry: An Anthology. LC 96-24262. (Illus.). 328p. 1997. 40.00 (*0-292-70471-2*); pap. 14.95 (*0-292-70472-0*) U of Tex Pr.

Andrews, Wayne. Architecture, Ambition, & Americans: A Social History of American Architecture. rev. ed. LC 78-50786. (Illus.). 1979. pap. 16.95 (*0-02-900750-X*) Free Pr.

— Architecture in Michigan. enl. rev. ed. LC 82-10886. (Illus.). 182p. 1982. pap. 21.95 (*0-8143-1719-7*) Wayne St U Pr.

— Architecture in New York: A Photographic History. LC 94-25294. (Illus.). 212p. 1995. pap. 24.95 (*0-8156-0309-6*) Syracuse U Pr.

— The Surrealist Parade. LC 89-14037. (Illus.). 192p. 1990. 22.95 (*0-8112-1126-6*, Pub. by New Directions); pap. 11.95 (*0-8112-1127-4*, NDP689, Pub. by New Directions) Norton.

— Voltaire. LC 80-29565. (Illus.). (C). 1981. 7.95 (*0-8112-0800-1*, Pub. by New Directions) Norton.

Andrews, William. Punishments in the Olden Time: Being an Historical Account of the Dunking Stool, Brand, Pillory, Stocks, Drunkard's Cloak, Whipping Post, Riding the Stang, Etc. viii, 76p. 1993. reprint ed. 24.00 (*0-8377-1909-7*, Rothman) W S Hein.

Andrews, William, ed. Lawyer in History, Literature & Humour. 276p. 1982. reprint ed. 35.00 (*0-8377-0211-9*, Rothman) W S Hein.

— Legal Core: Curiosities of Law & Lawyers. xii, 117p. 1982. reprint ed. 32.50 (*0-8377-0212-7*, Rothman) W S Hein.

Andrews, William D. Basic Federal Income Taxation. 3rd ed. LC 84-82457. (C). 1985. 40.95 (*0-316-04228-5*, Aspen Law & Bus) Aspen Pub.

— Basic Federal Income Taxation. 4th ed. 1328p. 1991. teacher ed. write for info. (*0-316-04238-2*, 42382); suppl. ed. write for info. (*0-316-04241-2*, 42412) Aspen Law.

— Basic Federal Income Taxation. 5th ed. LC 99-21254. 1008p. 1999. boxed set 60.00 (*0-7355-0021-5*) Panel Pubs.

— Basic Income Tax. 4th ed. 1328p. 1991. 56.00 (*0-316-04232-3*, Aspen Law & Bus) Aspen Pub.

— Federal Income Taxation of Corporate Transactions. 2nd ed. 1979. 45.00 (*0-316-04212-9*, Aspen Law & Bus) Aspen Pub.

— 1982 Supplement to Federal Income Taxation of Corporate Transactions. (C). 1982. pap. 12.00 (*0-316-04224-2*) Little.

Andrews, William D. & Feld, Alan L. Federal Income Taxation of Corporate Transactions. 3rd ed. 816p. 1994. teacher ed. 62.00 (*0-316-04243-9*, 42439) Aspen Law.

— Federal Income Taxation of Corporate Transactions. 3rd ed. LC 93-80969. 816p. 1994. lib. bdg. 62.00 (*0-316-04239-0*, 42390) Aspen Pub.

Andrews, William D., ed. see Institutional Staff.

Andrews, William G. The Land & People of the Soviet Union. LC 90-5746. (Portraits of the Nations Ser.). (Illus.). 320p. (J). (gr. 6 up). 1991. 17.95 (*0-06-020034-0*) HarpC Child Bks.

— The Land & People of the Soviet Union. LC 90-5746. (Portraits of the Nations Ser.). (Illus.). 320p. (YA). (gr. 6 up). 1991. lib. bdg. 17.89 (*0-06-020035-9*) HarpC Child Bks.

— Presidential Government in Gaullist France: A Study of Executive-Legislative Relations, 1958-1974. LC 82-222528. 304p. (C). 1983. text 24.50 (*0-87395-604-4*) State U NY Pr.

Andrews, William G., ed. International Handbook of Political Science. LC 81-6245. (Illus.). 464p. 1982. lib. bdg. 115.00 (*0-313-22889-2*, AIH/, Greenwood Pr) Greenwood.

Andrews, William G. & Hoffmann, Stanley, eds. The Fifth Republic at Twenty. LC 80-14528. 518p. (C). 1980. text 29.50 (*0-87395-413-0*) State U NY Pr.

Andrews, William J. Can There Be a Future? (Worth Having, That Is) (Illus.). 160p. (Orig.). 1994. pap. 8.30 (*0-9643597-0-7*) W J Andrews.

Andrews, William J. H., jt. auth. see Sobel, Dava.

Andrews, William L. Classic Fiction of the Harlem Renaissance. (Illus.). 416p. (C). 1994. pap. text 26.95 (*0-19-508196-X*) OUP.

— Critical Essays on Frederick Douglass. (Critical Essays on American Literature Ser.). 256p. (C). 1991. 49.00 (*0-8161-7301-X*, Hall Reference) Macmillan.

— The Literary Career of Charles W. Chesnutt. LC 79-25875. (Southern Literary Studies). (Illus.). 308p. reprint ed. pap. 95.50 (*0-608-09820-5*, 206998800007) Bks Demand.

— To Tell a Free Story: The First Century of Afro-American Autobiography, 1760-1865. 368p. 1986. text 29.95 (*0-252-01222-4*); pap. text 19.95 (*0-252-06033-4*) U of Ill Pr.

Andrews, William L., ed. African American Autobiography: A Collection of Critical Essays. 231p. (C). 1992. pap. text 9.80 (*0-13-019845-5*) P-H.

Andrews, William L., et al, eds. Journeys in New Worlds: Early American Women's Narratives. LC 90-50078. (Studies in American Autobiography). 232p. (Orig.). (C). 1991. pap. text 14.95 (*0-299-12584-X*) U of Wis Pr.

— The Oxford Companion to African-American Literature. LC 96-41565. 896p. 1997. 55.00 (*0-19-506510-7*) OUP.

Andrews, William L., intro. Six Women's Slave Narratives. (Schomburg Library of Nineteenth-Century Black Women Writers). (Illus.). 384p. 1989. reprint ed. pap. 14.95 (*0-19-506083-0*) OUP.

Andrews, William L. & Gates, Henry Louis, Jr., eds. The Civitas Anthology of African American Slave Narratives. LC 98-49051. 656p. 1998. text 40.00 (*1-58243-019-5*, Pub. by Counterpt DC) HarpC.

***Andrews, William L. & Gates, Henry Louis, Jr., eds.** Slave Narratives. LC 99-40360. 1035p. 2000. 40.00 (*1-883011-76-0*, Pub. by Library of America) Penguin Putnam.

Andrews, William L. & McKay, Nellie Y., eds. Toni Morrison's Beloved: A Casebook. LC 98-10126. (Casebooks in Contemporary Fiction Ser.). 240p. 1999. pap. 14.95 (*0-19-510797-7*) OUP.

Andrews, William L., ed. see Douglass, Frederick.

Andrews, William L., ed. see Douglass, Frederick, et al.

Andrews, William L., ed. see Elaw, Zilpha, et al.

Andrews, William L., jt. ed. see Gates, Henry Louis, Jr.

Andrews, William L., ed. see Washington, Booker T.

Andrews, William L., ed. & intro. see Douglass, Frederick.

Andrews, William L., ed. & intro. see Rowlandson, Mary, et al.

Andrews, William L., ed. & intro. see Washington, Booker T.

Andrews, William Loring, ed. William Loring Andrews on Bookbinding History, Vol. 13. (History of Bookbinding & Design Ser.). (Illus.). 210p. 1990. text 30.00 (*0-8240-4040-6*) Garland.

Andrews, William X., tr. see Brindle, Susan A., et al.

Andrews, Wyndham T. Critics on D. H. Lawrence. LC 72-179351. (Readings in Literary Criticism Ser.). 1971. write for info. (*0-04-801013-8*) Routledge.

Andrews, Zelle W. War in Slow Motion: The Economic & Social Impact of Militarism. 1985. 6.95 (*0-377-00155-4*) Friendship Pr.

***Andreychuk, Ed.** Burt Lancaster: A Filmography & Biography. LC 99-86393. (Illus.). 256p. 2000. 49.95 (*0-7864-0436-1*) McFarland & Co.

Andreychuk, Ed. The Golden Corral: A Roundup of Magnificent Western Films. LC 97-21512. 192p. 1997. pap. 29.95 (*0-7864-0393-4*) McFarland & Co.

Andreyeu, Leonid. The Red Laugh. 2nd ed. Willon, Mark, ed. Linden, Alexandra, tr. from RUS. (European Classics). 192p. 1999. reprint ed. pap. 8.95 (*0-946626-41-3*, Pub. by Dedalus) Hippocrene Bks.

Andreyev, Alexey V. Moyayama: Russian Haiku: A Diary. Lugowski, Marek & Hodges, Kim, eds. LC 96-203571.Tr. of My Ditch. (Illus.). 44p. 1996. pap. 3.00 (*1-888431-08-3*) ASGP.

Andreyev Carlisle, Olga, ed. see Andreyev, Leonid.

Andreyev, Catherine. Vlasov & the Russian Liberation Movement, 1941-1945. (Cambridge Russian, Soviet & Post-Soviet Studies: No. 51). (Illus.). 272p. 1987. text 64.95 (*0-521-30545-4*) Cambridge U Pr.

— Vlasov & the Russian Liberation Movement, 1941-1945. (Cambridge Russian, Soviet & Post-Soviet Studies: No. 51). 265p. (C). 1990. pap. text 24.95 (*0-521-38960-7*) Cambridge U Pr.

Andreyev, I. M. Ockerki po Istoriji Russkoi Literaturi XIX Vjeka.Tr. of Essays on the History of Russian Literature of the XIX Century. 316p. 1968. pap. text 10.00 (*0-317-30303-1*) Holy Trinity.

— Orthodox Apologetic Theology. LC 94-67834. (Illus.). 216p. 1995. pap. 10.00 (*0-938635-48-4*) St Herman Pr.

— Pravoslavno-Khristijanskaja Apologetika.Tr. of Orthodox-Christian Apologetics. 92p. 1965. pap. text 5.00 (*0-317-30249-3*) Holy Trinity.

— Pravoslavno-Khristijanskoe Nravstvennoje Bogoslovije.Tr. of Orthodox-Christian Moral Theology. 148p. 1966. pap. text 5.00 (*0-317-30264-7*) Holy Trinity.

Andreyev, Leonid. King Hunger. Kayden, Eugene M., tr. LC 73-80864. 122p. 1973. pap. 5.95 (*0-918769-11-6*) Univ South Pr.

— The Little Angel: And Other Stories. Willson, Mark, ed. (European Classics). 255p. 1997. reprint ed. pap 8.95 (*0-946626-42-1*, Pub. by Dedalus) Subterranean Co.

— The Seven That Were Hanged. Date not set. lib. bdg. 20.95 (*0-8488-1867-9*) Amereon Ltd.

— Three Plays: The Black Maskers. The Life of Man. The Sabine Woman. Meador, C. & Scott, F., trs. from RUS. LC 88-7108. xxvi, 214p. 1989. reprint ed. lib. bdg. 35.00 (*0-86527-388-X*) Fertig.

— Visions: Stories & Photographs. Andreyev Carlisle, Olga, ed. 1987. 21.95 (*0-15-193900-4*) Harcourt.

***Andreyev, Sergi.** Sufi Illuminati: The Rawshani Movement in Muslim Mysticism, Society & Politics. 288p. 2000. 85.00 (*0-7007-0668-2*, Pub. by Curzon Pr Ltd) Paul & Co Pubs.

Andreyev, Vadim. Stikhotvoreniia i Poemy. Shevelenko, Irina, ed. (Modern Russian Literature & Culture, Studies & Text: Vol. 35). (RUS.). 326p. (Orig.). 1995. pap. 20.00 (*1-57201-015-0*) Berkeley Slavic.

— Stikhotvoreniia i Poemy. Shevelenko, Irina, ed. (Modern Russian Literature & Culture, Studies & Text: Vol. 36). (RUS.). 334p. (Orig.). 1995. pap. 20.00 (*1-57201-016-9*) Berkeley Slavic.

Andreyeva-Georg, V. The Russian Verb: Prepositional & Non-Prepositional Government. 336p. 1987. text 12.95 (*0-8285-3474-8*) Firebird NY.

Andreyeva, Victoria. Treasury of Russian Love Poems, Quotations & Proverbs. 128p. 1995. 11.95 (*0-7818-0298-9*) Hippocrene Bks.

Andrian & Stores. Trees & Shrubs of Nepal & the Himalayas. 1998. pap. 134.00 (*0-7855-7502-2*, Pub. by Ratna Pustak Bhandar) St Mut.

***Andrian, Gustave W.** Modern Spanish Prose: Literary Selections from Spain & Latin America. 6th ed. 228p. (C). 1999. pap. text 30.80 (*0-13-013052-4*) P-H.

Andrian, Gustave W. Modern Spanish Prose: With a Selection of Poetry. 5th ed. 226p. 1995. pap. 37.00 (*0-13-228883-4*) P-H.

Andrianarivo, Jonah, ed. see Ratrimonimerina.

Andriano, Joseph. Our Ladies of Darkness: Feminine Daemonology in Male Gothic Fiction. 192p. (C). 1993. 35.00 (*0-271-00870-9*) Pa St U Pr.

Andriano, Joseph D. Immortal Monster: The Mythological Evolution of the Fantastic Beast in Modern Fiction & Film, 78. LC 98-28258. (Contributions to the Study of Science Fiction & Fantasy: Vol. 78). 200p. 1999. 57.95 (*0-313-30667-2*, Greenwood Pr) Greenwood.

Andriano, Sylvester, tr. see Civardi, Luigi.

Andrianov, A. N. Quadratic Forms & Hecke Operators. (Grundlehren der Mathematischen Wissenschaften Ser.: Band 286). (Illus.). 400p. 1987. 182.95 (*0-387-15294-6*) Spr-Verlag.

Andrianov, A. N., et al, eds. Algebra, Theory of Numbers & Their Applications. LC 80-28539. (STEKLO Ser.: No. 148). 283p. 1981. pap. 137.00 (*0-8218-3046-5*, STEKLO/148) Am Math.

Andrianov, A. N. & Zhuravlev, V. G. Modular Forms & Hecke Operators. LC 95-30915. (Translations of Mathematical Monographs: Vol. 145). 334p. 1995. text 95.00 (*0-8218-0277-1*, MMONO/145) Am Math.

Andrianov, A. N., et al. Thirteen Papers on Group Theory, Algebraic Geometry & Algebraic Topology. (Translations Ser.: Series 2, Vol. 66). 272p. 1968. 49.00 (*0-8218-1766-3*, TRANS2/66) Am Math.

Andrianov, I. P., et al. Physicochemical Aspects of Medicine Reviews: Affinity Chromatography in Artificial Detoxification Systems; Hemosorption in the Management of Atherosclerosis; Fertility Alpha2-Microglobulin (FAMG), Vol. 2. (Soviet Medical Reviews Ser.: Vol. 2, Pt. 1). ii, 84p. 1989. pap. text 63.00 (*3-7186-4966-7*) Gordon & Breach.

Andrianov, I. V., et al. Asymptotic Approaches in Nonlinear Dynamics. LC 98-7666. (Springer Series in Synergetics). (Illus.). xi, 310p. 1997. 79.95 (*3-540-63894-6*) Spr-Verlag.

Andrianov, S. N. English-Russian Law Dictionary. (ENG & RUS.). 510p. 1993. 95.00 (*0-7859-9084-4*) Fr & Eur.

Andrianov, S. N., et al. English - Russian Law Dictionary. (ENG & RUS.). 509p. (C). 1993. 49.95 (*0-8285-5237-1*) Firebird NY.

Andrianov, Y. N., jt. auth. see Akoev, G. N.

Andric, Ivo. The Bosnian Chronicle. Hitreck, Joseph, tr. from SER. 442p. 1993. reprint ed. pap. 10.45 (*1-55970-236-2*, Pub. by Arcade Pub Inc) Time Warner.

— The Bridge on the Drina. Edwards, Lovett F., tr. from SER. 314p. 1977. reprint ed. pap. 12.00 (*0-226-02045-2*, P746) U Ch Pr.

— The Damned Yard & Other Stories. Hawkesworth, Celia, ed. & tr. by. 198p. 1993. pap. 24.00 (*1-85610-022-7*, Pub. by Forest Bks) Dufour.

— The Days of the Consuls. Hawkesworth, Celia & Rakic, Bogdan, trs. from CRO. LC 92-72470. 416p. 1993. pap. 27.00 (*1-85610-024-3*, Pub. by Forest Bks) Dufour.

— The Development of Spiritual Life in Bosnia under the Influence of Turkish Rule. Juricic, Zelimir B. & Loud, John F., eds. & trs. by. LC 90-37059.Tr. of Die Entwicklung des geistegen Lebens in Bosnien unter der Einwirkung der turkischen Herrschaft. 151p. (C). 1990. text 34.95 (*0-8223-1063-5*) Duke.

— Devil's Yard. Johnstone, Kenneth, tr. LC 75-15692. 137p. 1975. reprint ed. lib. bdg. 55.00 (*0-8371-8218-2*, ANDY, Greenwood Pr) Greenwood.

***Andric, Stanko.** The Miracles of St. John Capistan. 2000. 49.95 (*963-9116-68-8*) Ctrl Europ Univ.

***Andricacos, P. C., et al, eds.** Electrochemical Processing in ULSI Fabrication & Semiconductor/Metal Deposition II. 400p. 2000. 74.00 (*1-56677-231-1*, PV 99-9) Electrochem Soc.

Andrich, David. Rasch Models for Measurement. (Quantitative Applications in the Social Sciences Ser.: Vol. 68). 88p. 1988. pap. 10.95 (*0-8039-2741-X*) Sage.

Andrich, Vujka. Soaring. 1993. write for info. (*0-9638160-0-4*) Happy Hands.

Andrick, Frank. Soluna. Mead, John, ed. 44p. 1998. pap. 5.00 (*1-892453-01-0*) AMP Pr.

Andrick, Frank, ed. see Mead, John.

Andriddle, Iva P. Ticklish Tales for Tellers: 99 Jokes & Riddles about Storytellers. Kallevig, Christine P., ed. (Illus.). 32p. 1997. pap. 4.99 (*0-9628769-5-X*) Storytime Ink.

Andrien, Kenneth J. The Kingdom of Quito, 1690-1830: The State & Regional Development. (Cambridge Latin American Studies: No. 80). (Illus.). 269p. (C). 1995. text 74.95 (*0-521-48125-2*) Cambridge U Pr.

Andrien, Kenneth J. & Adorno, Rolena, eds. Transatlantic Encounters: Europeans & Andeans in the Sixteenth Century. (Illus.). 353p. 1991. 60.00 (*0-520-07228-6*, Pub. by U CA Pr) Cal Prin Full Svc.

***Andries, Donald.** Investing in IRAs. (Cliffs Notes Ser.). 128p. 1999. pap. text 8.99 (*0-7645-8545-2*) IDG Bks.

Andries, E., ed. How to Face the Faces of Cardiac Pacing. (Developments in Cardiovascular Medicine Ser.). 296p. (C). 1992. text 213.50 (*0-7923-1528-6*) Kluwer Academic.

Andries, E. & Stroobandt, R., eds. Hemodynamics in Daily Practice. (DICM Ser.). (C). 1991. text 144.00 (*0-7923-0725-9*) Kluwer Academic.

Andries, Luc J. Endocardial Endothelium: Functional Morphology. LC 93-45589. (Medical Intelligence Unit Ser.). 121p. 1994. 99.00 (*1-57059-072-9*, LN9072) Landes Bioscience.

Andries, Pool, et al, contrib. by. Davide Masconi. (Illus.). 62p. 1998. pap. 19.95 (*88-8158-116-7*, 810931, Pub. by Charta) Dist Art Pubs.

Andriesh, A. M., jt. auth. see Bertolotti, Mario.

Andriessen & Koopman. The Introduction of Information & Communication Technology (ICT) in Organizations: A Special Issue of the "European Journal of Work & Organizational Psychology", Vol. 5, No. 3, 1996. 1997. pap. 39.95 (*0-86377-949-2*) L Erlbaum Assocs.

Andriessen, Jerry & Coirier, Pierre, eds. Foundations of Argumentative Text Processing. (International Series on the Research of Learning & Instruction of Writing Ser.). 250p. 1999. pap. 44.50 (*90-5356-340-7*, Pub. by Amsterdam U Pr) U of Mich Pr.

Andrieu, Jean-Marie & Lu, Wei, eds. Cell Activation & Apoptosis in HIV Infection: Implications for Pathogenesis & Therapy. LC 95-17728. (Advances in Experimental Medicine & Biology Ser.: Vol. 374). 258p. 1995. 89.50 (*0-306-45063-1*, Kluwer Plenum) Kluwer Academic.

Andrieux, Ruth E. Songs for All of God's Children. 40p. 1997. pap. 9.33 (*0-9662538-0-9*) Andrieux Hse Mus.

Andrievska & Javorska. Dictionary Francais-Ukrainien. (FRE & UKR.). 792p. 1994. 75.00 (*0-320-00986-6*) Fr & Eur.

— Dictionary Ukrainien-Francais. (FRE & UKR.). 836p. 1994. 75.00 (*0-320-00985-8*) Fr & Eur.

***Andrijich, Frances & Scourfield, Stephen.** Being Australian. (Illus.). 9p. 1998. pap. 29.95 (*1-86368-243-0*, Pub. by Fremantle Arts) Intl Spec Bk.

Andrijich, Frances, jt. auth. see Scourfield, Stephen.

A

An Asterisk (*) at the beginning of an entry indicates that the title is appearing for the first time.

A

Andrikopoulos, Bonnie, jt. ed. see Hern, Warren M.

Andriks, Susan E. Bridal Gowns: The Basics of Designing, Fitting & Sewing Your Wedding Dress. 1999. pap. 19.95 (*0-935278-51-6*) Palmer-Pletsch.

Andrillat, Y., jt. ed. see Jaschek, Carlos.

Andrilli, Stephen & Heeker, David. Linear Algebra. (C). 1993. text 77.95 (*0-534-17964-9*) PWS Pubs.

***Andrilli, Stephen F. & Hecker, David.** Elementary Linear Algebra. 2nd ed. LC 98-25761. 602p. 1999. 74.95 (*0-12-058690-8*) Acad Pr.

Andringa, Patty P. The National Symphony Orchestra Cookbook. Landfield, Lonie, ed. LC 84-82184. (Illus.). 320p. pap. 11.95 (*0-9613672-0-2*) Natl Symp Orches.

Andringa, Robert. The Executive Committee, No. 59. 16p. 1994. pap. text 12.00 (*0-925299-34-0*) Natl Ctr Nonprofit.

Andringa, Robert C. & Engstrom, Ted W. Nonprofit Board Answer Book: Practical Guidelines for Board Members & Chief Executives. LC 97-32835. 1998. 29.95 (*0-925299-80-4*) Natl Ctr Nonprofit.

Andrini, Beth. Cooperative Learning & Mathematics. (Illus.). 100p. 1992. pap. text 25.00 (*1-879097-04-4*) Kagan Cooperative.

Andriole. 1998 Year Book of Urology. 2nd ed. (Illus.). 384p. (C). (gr. 13). 1998. text 82.00 (*0-8151-2548-8*, 24061) Mosby Inc.

Andriole, Stephen J. Artificial Intelligence & National Defense: Applications to C3I & Beyond. LC 87-1150. (AIP Monograph Ser.: Vol. III). (Illus.). 186p. 1986. pap. text 8.95 (*0-916159-13-2*) AFCEA Intl Pr.

— Corporate Crisis Management. LC 84-19068. (Illus.). 250p. 1984. text 32.95 (*0-89433-216-3*) Petrocelli.

— Decision Support Systems: A Handbook to Design, Development Applications. (Illus.). 390p. 1988. text 39.95 (*0-89433-314-3*) Petrocelli.

— Handbook of Problem Solving. (Illus.). 327p. 1983. text 27.50 (*0-89433-186-8*) Petrocelli.

— Information System Design Principles for the Nineties: Getting It Right! LC 89-18522. (Illus.). 136p. (Orig.). 1990. pap. text 14.95 (*0-916159-20-5*) AFCEA Intl Pr.

— Systems Requirements & Process Reengineering: A Modeling & Prototyping Guide. LC 96-19092. (Illus.). 318p. 1996. 55.00 (*0-07-001974-6*) McGraw.

Andriole, Stephen J., ed. Advanced Technology for Command & Control Systems Engineering. LC 90-19757. 1990. 29.95 (*0-916159-22-1*) AFCEA Intl Pr.

— The Future of Information Processing Technology: A Source Book. 1986. text 32.50 (*0-89433-263-5*) Petrocelli.

— High Technology Initiatives in C3I. LC 86-3440. (AFCEA Signal Magazine C3I Ser.: Vol. V). (Illus.). 420p. 1986. 24.95 (*0-916159-09-4*) AFCEA Intl Pr.

Andriole, Stephen J. & Adelman, Leonard. Cognitive Systems Engineering for User-Computer Interface Design, Prototyping, & Evaluation. 280p. 1995. text 69.95 (*0-8058-1244-X*) L Erlbaum Assocs.

Andriole, Stephen J. & Hopple, Gerald W. Sourcebook on Artificial Intelligence. 500p. 1988. 49.95 (*0-89433-274-0*, 8263) Petrocelli.

Andriole, Stephen J. & Hopple, Gerald W., eds. Applied Artificial Intelligence: A Sourcebook. 696p. 1992. 69.95 (*0-07-157933-8*) McGraw.

— Applied Artificial Intelligence: A Sourcebook. (Illus.). 696p. 1992. 69.95 (*0-8306-8263-5*, 8263) McGraw-Hill Prof.

Andriole, Stephen J., jt. ed. see Boyes, Jon L.

Andriole, V. T., ed. Cost-Effective Use of Once-Daily Ceftriaxone in the Treatment of Moderate to Severe Infections, Vol. 37, Supplement 3, 1991: Journal: Chemotherapy. (Illus.). iv, 28p. 1991. pap. 10.50 (*3-8055-5450-8*) S Karger.

Andriole, Vincent T. Current Infectious Disease Drugs. (Illus.). 324p. 1995. text 42.00 (*1-878132-71-7*) Current Med.

Andriole, Vincent T., ed. The Quinolones. 2nd ed. LC 97-80823. (Illus.). 441p. 1998. text 75.00 (*0-12-059514-1*) Acad Pr.

Andrioli. Cytopathology of Tumors of the Nervous System. (Illus.). 100p. 1986. text 38.00 (*88-299-0239-X*, Pub. by Piccin Nuova) Gordon & Breach.

Andrioli, G. & Rigobello, L. Cytopathology of Tumours of the Nervous System. 100p. 1986. text 34.00 (*1-57235-030-X*) Piccin Nuova.

Andriot, Donna, compiled by. Guide to U. S. Government Publications: 1997 Edition. rev. ed. 1670p. 1998. 335.00 (*1-880236-10-9*) Documents Index.

***Andriot, Laurie.** Internet Blue Pages: The Guide to Federal Government Web Sites, 2001-2002. 544p. 2000. pap. 34.95 (*0-910965-43-9*, Pub. by Info Today Inc) IPG Chicago.

Andriot, Laurie. Uncle Sam's K-12 Web: Government Internet Resources for Educators, Students & Parents. LC 99-19272. 272p. 1999. pap. 24.95 (*0-910965-32-3*) Info Today Inc.

Andriot, Laurie, compiled by. Internet Blue Pages: The Guide to Federal Government Web Sites. LC 98-40318. 368p. 1998. pap. 34.95 (*0-910965-29-3*, CyberAge Bks) Info Today Inc.

Andriote, John-Manuel. Art of Fine Cigars. LC 96-76816. (Illus.). 112p. 1996. 14.95 (*0-8212-2349-6*, Pub. by Bulfinch Pr) Little.

— Victory Deferred: How AIDS Changed Gay Life in America. LC 98-46236. 488p. 1999. 30.00 (*0-226-02049-5*) U Ch Pr.

Andris, William. Liberty Street. LC 80-51206. 460p. 1980. 14.95 (*0-9604278-0-5*) St Basil Pr.

— Nothing in Your Hands. LC 86-82253. 200p. (Orig.). 1986. pap. 6.95 (*0-9604278-1-3*) St Basil Pr.

— The World of the Fish. LC 96-69165. 318p. (Orig.). 1997. pap. 12.00 (*0-9604278-2-1*) St Basil Pr.

***Andrisani, John.** The Hogan Way: How to Apply Ben Hogan's Exceptional Swing & Shotmaking Genius to Your Own Game, LC 99-49837. 160p. 2000. 21.00 (*0-06-270236-X*) HarpC.

Andrisani, John. Short Game Magic of Tiger Woods: An Analysis of Tiger Woods' Pitching, Chipping, Sand Play & Putting Techniques. 1999. pap. 12.00 (*0-609-80420-0*) Random Hse Value.

— The Tiger Woods Way. 1999. pap. 12.00 (*0-609-80139-2*) Random Hse Value.

— The Tiger Woods' Way: Secrets of Tiger Woods' Power Swing Technique. (Illus.). 1997. pap. 18.00 (*0-614-28177-6*) Berkley Pub.

Andrisani, John, jt. auth. see Ballesteros, Seve.

Andrisani, John, jt. auth. see Couples, Fred.

Andrisani, John, jt. auth. see Harmon, Claude.

Andrisani, John, jt. auth. see McLean, Jim.

Andrisani, John, jt. auth. see Ritson, Phil.

***Andrisani, Paul J., et al, eds.** Making Government Work: Lessons from America's Governors & Mayors. LC 00-20507. 352p. 2000. 35.00 (*0-8476-9972-2*) Rowman.

Andrisano, A. O. Shaving Effects on Eccentrically Cut Gears. (Nineteen Eighty-Seven Fall Technical Meeting Ser.: Vol. 87FTM15). (Illus.). 6p. 1987. pap. text 30.00 (*1-55589-491-7*) AGMA.

Andrist. Ahora Leamos: Charlemos un Poco. 3rd ed. (College Spanish Ser.). (SPA.). (C). 1995. mass mkt. 49.95 (*0-8384-4772-4*) Heinle & Heinle.

— Charlemos un Poco. 3rd ed. (College Spanish Ser.). (SPA.). (C). 1995. text, teacher ed. 28.95 (*0-8384-4775-9*); text, teacher ed., suppl. ed. 36.95 (*0-8384-4778-3*); text, suppl. ed. 0.95 (*0-8384-5480-1*) Heinle & Heinle.

— Charlemos un Poco. 3rd ed. (College Spanish Ser.). (SPA.). (C). 1995. pap., wbk. ed. 33.95 (*0-8384-4771-6*); text 55.95 (*0-8384-4770-8*); text, teacher ed. 41.95 (*0-8384-4769-4*) Heinle & Heinle.

— The Long Death. 1995. 14.00 (*0-684-82938-X*) S&S Trade.

***Andrist.** Mares Foals & Foaling. 2000. pap. 5.95 (*0-85131-447-3*, Pub. by J A Allen) Trafalgar.

Andrist, Debra D. Deceit Plus Desire Equals Violence: A Girardian Study of the Spanish 'Comedia' (American University Studies: Romance Languages & Literature: Ser. II, Vol. 93). X, 229p. (C). 1989. text 35.95 (*0-8204-0881-6*) P Lang Pubng.

Andrist, Friedrich. Mares, Foals & Foaling. 1990. pap. 25.00 (*0-85131-053-2*, Pub. by J A Allen) St Mut.

Andrle, Robert F. & Carroll, Janet R., eds. The Atlas of Breeding Birds in New York State. LC 87-47969. (Illus.). 576p. 1988. text 42.50 (*0-8014-1691-4*); 17.95 (*0-8014-2167-5*) Cornell U Pr.

Andrle, Vladimir. A Social History of Twentieth Century Russia. 384p. 2000. text 59.50 (*0-340-52516-9*, Pub. by E A) St Martin.

— A Social History of Twentieth-Century Russia. (An Arnold Publication). 304p. 1994. pap. text 19.95 (*0-340-52515-0*, Pub. by E A) OUP.

Andrlic, Vlasta. Dictionary of Yugoslavian Political-Economics Systems Terminology: Rjecnik Terminologije Jugoslavenskog Politicko-Ekonomskog Sistema. (ENG & SER.). 144p. 1985. pap. 24.95 (*0-8288-2264-6*, F107450) Fr & Eur.

Androes, Louis C. Play - The Intentional Avoidance of Work. LC 90-70837. (Illus.). 80p. (Orig.). 1990. pap. 7.95 (*0-9626575-2-2*) Whoopee Hollow.

Androgue, Horacio J. & Wesson, Donald E. Heart Failure. (Basics in Medicine Ser.). 320p. 1994. pap. 24.95 (*0-86542-429-2*) Blackwell Sci.

Androile, Stephen J. Rapid Application Prototyping: The Storyboard Approach to User Requirements Analysis. 280p. 1993. pap. 49.95 (*0-471-55630-0*, GD4035) Wiley.

Andromeda. The Macmillan Encyclopedia of Science, 12 vols., Set. 2nd ed. LC 96-36597. 1997. 375.00 (*0-02-864556-1*, Hall Reference) Macmillan.

— The Macmillan Encyclopedia of Science, Vol. 1. 2nd rev. ed. 1997. 35.00 (*0-02-864557-X*, Hall Reference) Macmillan.

— The Macmillan Encyclopedia of Science, Vol. 2. 2nd rev. ed. 1998. 35.00 (*0-02-864558-8*, Hall Reference) Macmillan.

— The Macmillan Encyclopedia of Science, Vol. 3. 2nd rev. ed. 1997. 35.00 (*0-02-864559-6*, Hall Reference) Macmillan.

— The Macmillan Encyclopedia of Science, Vol. 4. 2nd rev. ed. 1997. 35.00 (*0-02-864560-X*, Hall Reference) Macmillan.

— The Macmillan Encyclopedia of Science, Vol. 5. 2nd rev. ed. 1997. 35.00 (*0-02-864561-8*, Hall Reference) Macmillan.

— The Macmillan Encyclopedia of Science, Vol. 6. 2nd rev. ed. 1997. 35.00 (*0-02-864562-6*, Hall Reference) Macmillan.

— The Macmillan Encyclopedia of Science, Vol. 7. 2nd rev. ed. 1997. 35.00 (*0-02-864563-4*, Hall Reference) Macmillan.

— The Macmillan Encyclopedia of Science, Vol. 8. 2nd rev. ed. 1997. 35.00 (*0-02-864564-2*, Hall Reference) Macmillan.

— The Macmillan Encyclopedia of Science, Vol. 9. 2nd rev. ed. 1997. 35.00 (*0-02-864565-0*, Hall Reference) Macmillan.

— The Macmillan Encyclopedia of Science, Vol. 10. 2nd rev. ed. 1997. 35.00 (*0-02-864566-9*, Hall Reference) Macmillan.

— The Macmillan Encyclopedia of Science, Vol. 12. 2nd rev. ed. 1997. 35.00 (*0-02-864568-5*, Hall Reference) Macmillan.

***Andromeda, Prophet.** Classification Systems: A Topographical Reference of Consciousness. Knecht, Sherry, ed. (Pathways Through Consciousness Ser.: Vol. 3). (Illus.). 289p. (Orig.). 1999. pap. text 49.95 (*1-929589-06-9*) Branching Leaf.

— Inner Work Software: The Road Home. Knecht, Sherry, ed. (Orig.). 1999. pap. 29.95 (*1-929589-08-5*) Branching Leaf.

— Mindscapes: The Virtual Reality Gamebook. Knecht, Sherry, ed. (Illus.). 85p. (Orig.). 1999. pap. 12.95 (*1-929589-09-3*) Branching Leaf.

— Path & Practice: The Road Home. Knecht, Sherry, ed. (Illus.). 188p. (Orig.). 1999. pap. 12.95 (*1-929589-01-8*) Branching Leaf.

— Pathways for Kids & Other People Too... Knecht, Sherry, ed. (Illus.). 52p. (J). (gr. 3-6). 1999. pap. 9.95 (*1-929589-03-4*) Branching Leaf.

— Pathways Through Consciousness, 4 vols. Knecht, Sherry, ed. (Illus.). (Orig.). 1999. pap. text 199.95 (*1-929589-12-3*) Branching Leaf.

— Poems, Prayers & Promises... Knecht, Sherry, ed. 56p. (Orig.). 1999. pap. 9.95 (*1-929589-10-7*) Branching Leaf.

— Principles & Practices. Knecht, Sherry, ed. (Pathways Through Consciousness Ser.: Vol. 4). (Illus.). 129p. (Orig.). 1999. pap. text 69.95 (*1-929589-07-7*) Branching Leaf.

— This Path Has Come to an End: Prophesies, 1998-2030. Knecht, Sherry, ed. 59p. (Orig.). 1999. pap. 9.95 (*1-929589-02-6*) Branching Leaf.

— Trust Arts: Keys to Travel in Virtual Reality. Knecht, Sherry, ed. (Illus.). 66p. (Orig.). 1999. pap. 9.95 (*1-929589-00-X*) Branching Leaf.

Andronescu, Serban. Bye Cadmos: A Journal of Aesthetic Analogies. (C). 5.00 (*0-917944-00-3*) Am Inst Writing Res.

— English-Rumanian Dictionary. (ENG & RUM.). 43.95 (*0-87557-064-X*) Saphrograph.

— English-Rumanian Dictionary. (ENG & RUM.). 252p. 1993. reprint ed. lib. bdg. 35.00 (*0-8288-2632-3*) Fr & Eur.

— Rumanian-English Dictionary. (ENG & RUM.). 43.95 (*0-87557-063-1*) Saphrograph.

— Rumanian-English Dictionary. (ENG & RUM.). 252p. 1993. reprint ed. lib. bdg. 35.00 (*0-8288-2630-7*) Fr & Eur.

Andronico, Michael P. Men in Groups: Insights, Interventions & Psychoeducational Work. LC 95-20968. (Measurement & Instrumentation in Psychology Ser.). 435p. 1995. pap. 29.95 (*1-55798-618-5*) Am Psychol.

Andronicos, Manolis, et al. Philip of Macedon. Hatzopoulos, Miltiades B. & Loukopoulos, Louisa D., eds. (Illus.). 254p. 1980. 60.00 (*0-89241-330-1*) Caratzas.

Andronicus, M., et al. The Greek Museums. 1981. 150.00 (*0-7855-7270-8*) St Mut.

Andronik, Catherine M. Kindred Spirit: A Biography of L. M. Montgomery, Creator of Anne of Green Gables. LC 92-25869. (Illus.). 160p. (J). (gr. 5-9). 1993. 16.00 (*0-689-31671-2*) Atheneum Yung Read.

— My Lady King Hatshepsut. LC 98-52675. (J). 2000. 17.00 (*0-689-82562-5*) Atheneum Yung Read.

— School Library Management. 4th ed. LC 97-48905. (Professional Growth Ser.). 1998. pap. 36.95 (*0-938865-66-8*) Linworth Pub.

Andronik, Cathy. Prince of Humbugs: The Life of P. T. Barnum. LC 93-36724. (Illus.). 160p. (J). (gr. 5-9). 1994. 15.95 (*0-689-31796-4*) Macmillan.

Andronikashvili, E. L. Reflections of Liquid Helium. Berman, Robert, tr. (AIP Translation Ser.). (Illus.). 1989. 60.00 (*0-88318-575-X*) Am Inst Physics.

Andronikashvili, E. L., jt. auth. see Lifshits, Evgenii M.

Andronikof-Sanglade, A., ed. Rorschachiana Vol. 23: Yearbook of the International Rorschach Society. 152p. 1999. text 38.00 (*0-88937-201-2*) Hogrefe & Huber Pubs.

***Andronikof-Sanglade, A., ed.** Rorschachiana Vol. 24: Yearbook of the International Rorschach Society. (Illus.). 188p. 2000. 38.00 (*0-88937-226-8*) Hogrefe & Huber Pubs.

Andronikoff, Betsy, et al, eds. International Yellow Pages: Paris Edition: How to Get by in Paris if You're Not a Parisian. 225p. 1999. pap. text 16.95 (*0-9666899-0-9*, Pub. by Mariposa Pr NM) Consort Bk Sales.

Andronikos, Manolis, et al. Greek Museums. (Illus.). 420p. 1975. 125.00 (*0-89241-005-1*) Caratzas.

Andronis, Constantine. Apostolos Makrakis--An Evaluation of Half a Century. 369p. (Orig.). 1966. pap. 8.95 (*0-938366-33-5*) Orthodox Chr.

Andronov, A. A., et al. Eleven Papers on Differential Equations, Two on Information Theory. LC 51-5559. (Translations Ser.: Series 2, Vol. 33). 438p. 1963. 49.00 (*0-8218-1733-7*, TRANS2/33) Am Math.

— Seven Papers on Equations Related to Mechanics & Heat. LC 51-5559. (Translations Ser.: Series 2, Vol. 75). 255p. 1968. 47.00 (*0-8218-1775-2*, TRANS2/75) Am Math.

— Theory of Oscillators. xxxii, 815p. 1987. reprint ed. pap. 19.95 (*0-486-65508-3*) Dover.

Andronov, Alexander & Vitt, A. A. Theory of Oscillators. LC 63-19610. 1966. 370.00 (*0-08-013729-6*, Pub. by Pergamon Repr) Franklin.

Andronov, Alexander, et al. Theory of Oscillators. (Illus.). 1966. 370.00 (*0-08-009981-5*, Pub. by Pergamon Repr) Franklin.

Andronova, T. Immunology Reviews Vol. 4, Pt. 1: The Structure & Immunomodulating Function of Glucosaminylmuranyl Pepties - the Thymus- & a Bone Marrow-Derived Immuno, Vol. 4. (Soviet Medical Reviews Ser.: Section D). 143p. 1992. pap. text 137.00 (*3-7186-5202-1*, Harwood Acad Pubs) Gordon & Breach.

Andropov. Speeches & Writings. 1983. 20.00 (*0-08-028177-X*, Pergamon Pr) Elsevier.

Andropov, Y. V. Speeches & Writings. 1983. pap. 11.50 (*0-08-028182-6*, Pergamon Pr) Elsevier.

Andros, George, jt. auth. see Salles-Cunha, Sergio.

Andros, Phil. Greek Ways. 159p. 1996. pap. 9.95 (*1-55583-396-9*) Alyson Pubns.

— The Joy Spot. 1995. mass mkt. 5.95 (*1-56333-301-5*, Badboy) Masquerade.

— Stud. abr. rev. ed. 212p. 1982. pap. 7.95 (*0-932870-02-3*) Alyson Pubns.

Andros, Phil, & Co. Staff. Different Strokes. 140p. 1993. reprint ed. pap. 7.95 (*1-55583-222-9*) Alyson Pubns.

Androse, R., tr. see Alessio, Piemontese.

Androsov, Sergei, et al. From the Sculptor's Hand: Italian Baroque Terracottas from the State Hermitage Museum. LC 97-78370. (Illus.). 120p. 1998. pap. 24.95 (*0-86559-158-X*) Art Inst Chi.

Androulakis, G. & Pissiotis, C., eds. European Society for Surgical Research, 18th Congress, Athens 1983: Abstracts. (Journal: European Surgical Research: Vol. 15, Suppl. 1). (Illus.). iv, 120p. 1983. pap. 39.25 (*3-8055-3781-6*) S Karger.

Androunas, Eleana. Soviet Media in Transition: Structural & Economic Alternatives. LC 93-2862. 184p. 1993. 49.95 (*0-275-94147-7*, C4147, Praeger Pubs) Greenwood.

Androus, Arthur T. Cashews & Koumboloi: The Ninety-Year Odyssey of a Greek American. 1991. pap. 12.95 (*0-933905-18-1*) Claycomb Pr.

***Androutsopoulos, Jannis K., et al.** Jugendsprache - Langue des Jeunes - Youth Language: Linguistische Und Soziolinguistische Perspektiven. (Illus.). XIII, 328p. 1998. 51.95 (*0-8204-3643-7*) P Lang Pubng.

Androvic, G. Dictionary of the Italian & Croatian Languages: Dizionario della Lingua Italiana e Croata, Vol. 1. (CRO & ITA.). 1980. 24.95 (*0-8288-1055-9*, F42510) Fr & Eur.

— Dictionary of the Italian & Croatian Languages: Dizionario della Lingue Italiana e Croata, Vol. 2. (CRO & ITA.). 1980. 27.95 (*0-8288-1638-7*, F42710) Fr & Eur.

Androvich, Bob & McAuliffe, Daniel J. California League Guide Book, 1994 Edition. (Illus.). 88p. 1994. lib. bdg. 15.00 (*0-9640859-1-7*); spiral bd. 15.00 (*0-9640859-0-9*) Circus Catch.

***Androvich, Mark.** Crash Team Racing. LC 99-67320. (Illus.). 98p. 1999. pap. 14.99 (*0-7615-2653-6*) Prima Pub.

Androwich, Ida & Burkhart, Elizabeth. Community & Home Health Nursing. LC 95-36419. (Plans of Care for Specialty Practice Ser.). 408p. (C). 1996. pap. 33.50 (*0-8273-6227-7*) Delmar.

Andrulis, Dennis P. Crisis at the Front Line: The Effects of AIDS on Public Hospitals - A Twentieth Century Fund Paper. 93p. 1989. 18.95 (*0-87078-267-3*); pap. 8.95 (*0-87078-266-5*) Century Foundation.

— Managed Care in the Inner Cities: Programs & Strategies for Providers, Plans & Communities. LC 98-56051. 1999. 41.95 (*0-7879-4623-0*) Jossey-Bass.

Andrunakievic, V. A., et al. Twelve Papers on Topology, Algebra & Number Theory. (Translations Ser.: Series 2, Vol. 52). 275p. 1966. 50.00 (*0-8218-1752-3*, TRANS2/52) Am Math.

Andrus, Amy L., ed. see David M. Kennedy Center for International Studied.

***Andrus, Carol.** Fat Free Writing: Business Writing for the Information Age. Woodbury, Debbie & Bosarge, Charlotte, eds. LC 00-104237. (Crisp 50 Minute Book Ser.). (Illus.). 108p. 2000. pap. 12.95 (*1-56052-586-X*) Crisp Pubns.

Andrus, Cecil & Connelly, Joel. Cecil Andrus: Politics Western Style. LC 98-13505. 256p. 1998. 23.95 (*1-57061-122-X*) Sasquatch Bks.

Andrus, Charles, et al, eds. Minimally Invasive Surgery: Principles & Outcomes. 416p. 1998. text 83.00 (*90-5702-261-3*, ECU107, Harwood Acad Pubs) Gordon & Breach.

Andrus, Danna G. & Tillman, Lois J. Heavenly Earth. 181p. 1997. pap. 9.95 (*0-9658226-0-5*) Creat Ideas Pr.

Andrus, David M., et al. International Marketing Management: A Reader. LC 87-73148. (Marketing Ser.). 500p. (C). 1988. pap. text 10.00 (*0-938991-22-1*) Colonial Pr AL.

Andrus, J. Russell & Mohammed, Azizali F. Trade, Finance, & Development in Pakistan. xii, 289p. 1966. 42.50 (*0-8047-0126-1*) Stanford U Pr.

Andrus, Jeff. The Neighborhood Watch: A Tracer Family Mystery. 288p. 1996. 20.50 (*0-684-19706-5*) S&S Trade.

— Tracer, Inc. 256p. 1994. text 20.00 (*0-684-19705-7*) S&S Trade.

Andrus, Jeff, ed. see Monahan, Marta.

Andrus, Jenny G., jt. auth. see Reynolds, Paula B.

Andrus, Martha W. Grambling's First Mayor, B. T. Woodard: The Man - The Movement. 60p. 1996. pap. 8.00 (*1-57502-122-6*) Morris Pubng.

Andrus, Michael J. The Brooke, Fauquier, Loudoun & Alexandria Artillery. (Virginia Regimental Histories Ser.). (Illus.). 124p. 1990. 19.95 (*0-930919-92-0*) H E Howard.

Andrus, Pat. Old Woman: Of Irish Blood. 80p. (Orig.). 1996. pap. 9.95 (*0-940880-59-8*) Open Hand.

Andrus, Regina P., jt. auth. see Peck, Eugene L.

Andrus, Ruth. A Tentative Inventory of the Habits of Children from Two to Four Years of Age. LC 77-176520. (Columbia University. Teachers College. Contributions to Education Ser.: No. 160). reprint ed. 37.50 (*0-404-55160-2*) AMS Pr.

Andrus, Silas. The Blue Laws. 119p. 1999. pap. 11.95 (*0-939883-04-X*, Pub. by Bibliopola Pr) U Pr of New Eng.

An Asterisk (*) at the beginning of an entry indicates that the title is appearing for the first time.

Andrushin, E. A., jt. auth. see Ginzburg, Vitaly L.

Andrushkiw, Vira. Lessons for Nurseries for English-Speaking Children. 2nd rev. ed.Tr. of Prohrama Zajniat u Svitlychkac Dlia Ditej. 68p. 1978. pap. 3.00 (*0-317-36111-2*) UNWLA.

Andrusia, David. Gay Europe. LC 94-35102. 304p. (Orig.). 1995. pap. 14.00 (*0-399-51910-6*, Perigee Bks) Berkley Pub.

— L A Hot & Hip-O's. 1998. pap. 10.00 (*0-7871-8010-6*, Dove Audio) NewStar Media.

— New York Hot & Hip. LC 97-32298. (Illus.). 144p. 1998. 9.95 (*0-87131-849-0*) M Evans.

Andrusia, David. The Perfect Pitch: How to Sell Yourself for Today's Job Market. LC 96-48246. 272p. (Orig.). 1997. mass mkt. 13.99 (*0-446-67294-7*, Pub. by Warner Bks) Little.

Andrusia, David, jt. auth. see Betty, Patricia.

Andrusia, David, jt. auth. see Candee, Andrea.

Andrusia, David, jt. auth. see Haskins, Rick.

Andrusko-Furphy, Kathryn T., jt. auth. see Klotz, Roger S.

Andrusyshen, C. H., ed. English-Ukrainian Dictionary. (ENG & UKR.). 1200p. 1981. reprint ed. pap. 37.50 (*0-8020-6421-3*) U of Toronto Pr.

Andrusyshen, C. H., tr. see Shevchenko, Taras.

Andrusz, Gregory. Cities after Socialism: Urban & Regional Change & Conflict in Post Socialist Societies. (Studies in Urban & Social Change). (Illus.). 356p. 1996. 72.95 (*1-55786-164-1*) Blackwell Pubs.

— Cities after Socialism: Urban & Regional Change & Conflict in Post Socialist Societies. (Studies in Urban & Social Change). (Illus.). 356p. (C). 1996. pap. 28.95 (*1-55786-165-X*) Blackwell Pubs.

— The Co-Operative Alternative in Europe. LC 98-74438. 9p. 1999. 69.95 (*1-85628-855-2*) Ashgate Pub Co.

Andry, Andrew C. & Schepp, Steven. How Babies Are Made. LC 99-944003. (Illus.). 88p. (J). 1984. reprint ed. pap. 12.95 (*0-316-04227-7*) Little.

Andryszewski, Tricia. Abortion: Rights, Options, & Choices. (Issue & Debate Ser.). 112p. (YA). (gr. 7 up). 1996. lib. bdg. 23.90 (*1-56294-573-4*) Millbrook Pr.

— The Amazing Life of Moe Berg: Catcher, Scholar, Spy. LC 95-8828. (Illus.). 128p. (YA). (gr. 7 up). 1996. lib. bdg. 22.40 (*1-56294-610-2*) Millbrook Pr.

***Andryszewski, Tricia.** Bill Bradley: A Shot at the Presidency. LC 99-28668. (Gateway Biography Ser.). 48p. (J). (gr. 2-4). 1999. 21.90 (*0-7613-1669-8*, Copper Beech Bks) Millbrook Pr.

— Bill Bradley: Scholar, Athlete, Statesman. (Gateway Biography Ser.). (Illus.). (J). 1999. 14.40 (*0-606-18278-0*) Turtleback.

Andryszewski, Tricia. Communities of the Faithful: American Religious Movements Outside the Mainstream. LC 97-1385. (Illus.). 128p. (YA). (gr. 7 up). 1997. lib. bdg. 22.40 (*0-7613-0067-8*) Millbrook Pr.

— Dust Bowl: Disaster on the Plains. LC 92-15300. (Spotlight on American History Ser.). 1993. 11.15 (*0-606-06339-0*, Pub. by Turtleback) Demco.

— The Environment & the Economy: Planting the Seeds for Tomorrow's Growth. LC 94-42396. (Issue & Debate Ser.). (Illus.). 112p. (YA). (gr. 7 up). 1995. lib. bdg. 23.90 (*1-56294-524-6*) Millbrook Pr.

***Andryszewski, Tricia.** Gay Rights. LC 99-48185. 2000. lib. bdg. write for info. (*0-7613-1568-3*) TFC Bks NY.

Andryszewski, Tricia. Immigration: Newcomers & Their Impact on the U. S. LC 94-21834. (Issue & Debate Ser.). (Illus.). 112p. (YA). (gr. 7 up). 1995. lib. bdg. 23.90 (*1-56294-499-1*) Millbrook Pr.

— Kosovo: The Splintering of Yugoslavia. LC 99-48933. (Headliners Ser.). 64p. (YA). (gr. 5-8). 1999. 23.40 (*0-7613-1750-3*) Millbrook Pr.

— The March on Washington, 1963: Gathering to Be Heard. LC 96-1217. (Spotlight on American History Ser.). (Illus.). 64p. (J). (gr. 4-6). 1996. lib. bdg. 21.90 (*0-7613-0009-0*) Millbrook Pr.

— Marjory Stoneman Douglas, Friend of the Everglades. LC 93-26731. (Gateway Green Biography Ser.). (Illus.). 48p. (J). (gr. 2-4). 1994. lib. bdg. 21.90 (*1-56294-384-7*) Millbrook Pr.

— The Militia Movement in America: Before & after Oklahoma City. LC 96-32178. (Illus.). 128p. (YA). (gr. 7 up). 1997. lib. bdg. 22.40 (*0-7613-0119-4*) Millbrook Pr.

***Andryszewski, Tricia.** The Reform Party: Ross Perot, Pat Buchanan, Jesse Ventura. LC 99-87456. (Headliners Ser.). (Illus.). 1999. lib. bdg. write for info. (*0-7613-1906-9*) Millbrook Pr.

Andryszewski, Tricia. School Prayer: A History of the Debate. LC 96-51951. (Issues in Focus Ser.). (Illus.). 104p. (YA). (gr. 6 up). 1997. lib. bdg. 20.95 (*0-89490-904-5*) Enslow Pubs.

— The Seminoles: People of the Southeast. LC 94-21819. (Native Americans Ser.). (Illus.). 64p. (J). (gr. 4-6). 1995. lib. bdg. 21.90 (*1-56294-530-0*) Millbrook Pr.

— Step by Step along the Appalachian Trail. LC 98-7304. (Step by Step Ser.). 80p. (J). (gr. 4-8). 1998. 21.90 (*0-7613-0273-5*) TFC Bks NY.

— Step by Step along the Pacific Crest Trail. LC 98-7303. (Step by Step Ser.). 80p. (J). (gr. 4-8). 1998. 21.90 (*0-7613-0274-3*) TFC Bks NY.

***Andryszewski, Tricia.** Terrorism in America. LC 99-34138. (Frontline Ser.). (J). 1999. lib. bdg. write for info. (*0-8225-2629-8*, Lerner Publctns) Lerner Pub.

Andryszewski, Tricia. What to Do about Nuclear Waste. LC 94-44662. (Illus.). 128p. (YA). (gr. 7 up). 1995. lib. bdg. 22.40 (*1-56294-577-7*) Millbrook Pr.

Andrzejczak, Krzysztof. The Writer in the Writing: Author As Hero in Postwar American Fiction. LC 98-15063. 210p. 1998. 64.95 (*1-57309-282-7*) Intl Scholars.

Andrzejewski. Oppression & Social Justice. 5th ed. 400p. (C). 1995. pap. 36.40 (*0-536-59275-6*) Pearson Custom.

Andrzejewski, B. W. Islamic Literature of Somalia. (Hans Wolff Memorial Lectures). 48p. 1983. pap. text 5.00 (*0-941934-47-0*) Indiana Africa.

Andrzejewski, B. W. & Andrzejewski, Sheila, trs. from SOM. An Anthology of Somali Poetry. LC 93-18386. 128p. 1993. 25.00 (*0-253-30462-8*); pap. 11.95 (*0-253-30463-6*) Ind U Pr.

Andrzejewski, Jerzy. Cendres et Diamant. (FRE.). 405p. 1986. pap. 17.95 (*0-7859-2047-1*, 2070377679) Fr & Eur.

Andrzejewski, Jerzy & Welsh, David J. Ashes & Diamonds. LC 96-38228. (European Classics Ser.). 1996. pap. 12.95 (*0-8101-1519-0*) Northwestern U Pr.

Andrzejewski, Julie, jt. auth. see Thompson, Karen.

Andrzejewski, Julie R. Oppression & Social Justice: Critical Frameworks. 410p. (C). 1993. 45.00 (*0-536-58474-5*) Pearson Custom.

Andrzejewski, Sheila, jt. tr. see Andrzejewski, B. W.

Andrzejewski, Susan E., ed. see Delphos, William A.

Andujar, Gloria. La Jolla. (Illus.). 1988. 9.95 (*0-938086-99-5*) Andujar Comn Tech.

Andujar, Julio. Everyday Spanish Bk. 2: Intermediate/Advanced, Bk. 2. 3rd ed. (SPA.). 174p. (C). 1996. pap., wbk. ed. 31.60 (*0-13-432791-8*) P-H.

Andujar, Julio & Dixson, Robert J. Graded Exercises in Spanish. 240p. 1987. pap. text 34.67 (*0-13-361973-7*) P-H.

Andujar, Julio I. & Dixson, Robert J. Everyday Spanish Bk. 1: Elementary/Intermediate, Bk. 1. 3rd ed. (SPA.). 208p. (C). 1996. pap., wbk. ed. 31.60 (*0-13-432774-8*) P-H.

Andujar, Julio P. Cristobal Colon: El Capricho de la Reina. LC 94-71768. (Coleccion Hispanica - Narrativa). (SPA.). 144p. (Orig.). 1994. pap. 16.00 (*0-89729-742-3*) Ediciones.

Andujar, Maria D. & Iglesias, Jose L. Mecanografia Al Dia. rev. ed. (YA). (gr. 10 up). 1977. pap. text 3.50 (*0-88345-306-1*, 18482) Prentice ESL.

Andujar, Maria D., et al. Mecanografia Al Dia. 96p. (C). 1993. pap. text 7.80 (*0-13-568684-9*) Prentice ESL.

Andujo, Emily. Appleton & Lange's Quick Review: Dental Assistant. LC 97-30650. (C). 1998. pap. 25.95 (*0-8385-1526-6*, A-1526-1) Appleton & Lange.

— Dental Assistant: Program Review & Exam Preparation. LC 96-9709. 256p. (C). 1996. pap. text 36.95 (*0-8385-1513-4*) P-H.

Andus, T., et al, eds. Inflammatory Bowel Diseases: From Bench to Bedside. (Falk Symposium Ser.: No. 96). 480p. 1997. text 240.50 (*0-7923-8728-7*) Kluwer Academic.

Anduze, A. L. Caribbean Crosswords. LC 93-70926. (Illus.). 64p. (YA). (gr. 5-12). 1993. pap. 8.95 (*0-932831-10-9*) Eastern Caribbean Inst.

— A West Indian Fish Tale (And Other Stories) 56p. 1993. pap. 8.95 (*0-932831-09-5*) Eastern Caribbean Inst.

Andvik, Erik E. A Pragmatic Analysis of Norwegian Modal Particles. LC 92-60901. (Publications in Linguistics Ser.: Vol. 113). x, 140p. 1992. pap. 11.00 (*0-88312-188-3*) S I L Intl.

Andy, B. How to Circumvent a Security Alarm in 10 Seconds or Less: An Insider's Guide to How It's Done & How to Prevent It. (Illus.). 88p. 1994. pap. 14.00 (*0-87364-777-7*) Paladin Pr.

Andy, Orlando, jt. auth. see Bhatnagar, Subhash C.

***Andy Warhol Museum Staff.** Andy Warhol Photography. Kunsthalle, Hamburger, ed. 400p. 1999. 75.00 (*3-908163-10-2*) Abbeville Pr.

Andzel, jt. auth. see Lisky.

Andzelm, J. W., jt. ed. see Labanowski, J. K.

Ane, jt. auth. see Letouzey.

Anechiarico. Pursuit Absolute Integrity. 1998. pap. text 15.00 (*0-226-02052-5*) U Ch Pr.

Anechiarico, Frank & Jacobs, James B. The Pursuit of Absolute Integrity: How Corruption Control Makes Government Ineffective. LC 96-15863. (Studies in Crime & Justice). 248p. 1996. 24.95 (*0-226-02051-7*) U Ch Pr.

Anees, Munawar. Islam & Biological Futures: Ethics, Gender & Technology. 300p. 1989. text 110.00 (*0-7201-1874-3*) Continuum.

Anees, Munawar A. & Athar, Alia N. Guide to Sira & Hadith Literature in Western Languages. (Middle East Studies. Islamic Studies). 404p. 1986. 35.00 (*0-9602920-1-2*) Kazi Pubns.

Aneja, K. R., jt. ed. see Singh, J.

Anelauskas, Valdas. Discovering America As It Is. 584p. 1999. pap. 18.95 (*0-932863-29-9*) Clarity Pr.

Aneli, J. N., et al. Structuring & Conductivity of Polmer Composites. LC 99-163019. 326p. 1999. 115.00 (*1-56072-538-9*) Nova Sci Pubs.

Anellis, Irving H. Van Heijenoort: Logic & Its History in the Work & Writings of Jean van Heijenoort. LC 94-75196. (Illus.). xvi, 341p. (Orig.). 1994. 59.95 (*1-884905-01-3*); pap. 39.95 (*1-884905-00-5*) Modern Logic.

Anellis, Irving H., ed. see Barabashev, Alexei.

Anello, Christina. Your Golden Angel. (Charming Petites Ser.). (Illus.). 80p. 1996. 4.95 (*0-88088-800-8*) Peter Pauper.

Anello, Christina, ed. For Grandma. (Charming Petites Ser.). (Illus.). 80p. 1992. 4.95 (*0-88088-754-0*) Peter Pauper.

Anello, Christina M., compiled by. Flowers for My Friend. (Charming Petites Ser.). 80p. 1992. 4.95 (*0-88088-757-5*) Peter Pauper.

Anello, Christine M. For the Bride. LC 97-220789. 80p. 1997. 4.95 (*0-88088-814-8*) Peter Pauper.

Anello, Eloy. NGOs in Latin America: Issues & Characteristics of NGOs Involved in Development. (Occasional Paper Ser.). 31p. 1991. 3.00 (*0-932288-85-5*) Ctr Intl Ed U of MA.

Anello, Marc. Master Strokes: Golf Pros on the Game. LC 99-162752. (Pocket Gift Editions Ser.). 1998. 4.95 (*0-88088-071-6*) Peter Pauper.

Anello, Marc, jt. compiled by see Vazquez, Liesl.

Anello, Rose & Shuster, Tillie. A Guide for Non-Profit Shelter Operators in New York City: Negotiating the Public Assistance System on Behalf of Homeless Adults. LC 87-401909. 98p. (Orig.). 1984. pap. 10.00 (*0-88156-031-6*) Comm Serv Soc NY.

Aneloski, Elizabeth, ed. see Anderson, Alex.

Aneloski, Elizabeth, ed. see Horton, Roberta M.

Aneloski, Elizabeth, ed. see Leone, Diana.

Aneloski, Elizabeth, ed. see McCormick, Patty.

Aneloski, Elizabeth, ed. see McDowell, Ruth B.

Aneloski, Elizabeth, ed. see Walner, Hari.

Aneloski, Elizabeth, ed. see Wells, Jean.

Aneloski, Elizabeth, ed. see Wolfrom, Joen.

Aneloski, Liz, ed. see Anderson, Alex.

Aneloski, Liz, ed. see Barickman, Amy.

Aneloski, Liz, ed. see Brackman, Barbara.

Aneloski, Liz, ed. see Brackman, Barbara Ann.

Aneloski, Liz, ed. see Hill, Wendy.

Aneloski, Liz, ed. see Laporte, Gul.

Aneloski, Liz, ed. see Laury, Jean R.

Aneloski, Liz, ed. see Miller, Margaret J.

Aneloski, Liz, ed. see Pam Bono Designs Staff.

Aneloski, Liz, ed. see Perry, Gai.

Aneloski, Liz, ed. see Walner, Hari.

Aneloski, Liz, ed. see Wolfrom, Joen.

Anema. Negotiations Game-Options: Communication Skills. (EC - HS Communication/English Ser.). 1993. pap. 18.95 (*0-538-62516-3*) S-W Pub.

— Options - Journal 1. (EC - HS Communication/English Ser.). 1993. mass mkt. 2.95 (*0-538-62154-0*) S-W Pub.

— Options - Journal 3. (EC - HS Communication/English Ser.). 1993. mass mkt. 2.95 (*0-538-62156-7*) S-W Pub.

— Options - Journal 2. (EC - HS Communication/English Ser.). 1993. mass mkt. 2.95 (*0-538-62155-9*) S-W Pub.

— Options, a Communication Skills Series, Bk. 1. LC 92-84129. (EC - HS Communication/English Ser.). 1993. mass mkt. 12.95 (*0-538-62151-6*) S-W Pub.

— Options, a Communications Skills Series, Bk. 2. LC 92-84129. (EC - HS Communication/English Ser.). 1993. mass mkt. 12.95 (*0-538-62152-4*) S-W Pub.

***Anema, Durlynn.** Louise Arner Boyd: Arctic Explorer. LC 99-59448. (Notable Americans Ser.). (Illus.). 112p. (YA). (gr. 5 up). 2000. lib. bdg. 19.95 (*1-883846-42-0*) M Reynolds.

Anema, Dyrlynn. Harriet Chalmers Adams: Explorer & Adventurer. LC 96-54642. (Notable Americans Ser.). (Illus.). 112p. (YA). (gr. 5 up). 1997. lib. bdg. 8.95 (*1-883846-18-8*) M Reynolds.

Anema-Garten, Durlynn. Effective Ministry Management: Organization the Lord's Way. (Training Ser.). 80p. 1998. pap. text 29.95 (*1-884061-23-0*) Womens Minist.

***Anemaet, Wendy.** Home Rehabilitation Guide. LC 99-40803. 1999. spiral bd. 32.95 (*0-323-00285-4*) Mosby Inc.

Anemaet, Wendy & Moffa-Trotter, Michelle. The User Friendly Home Care Handbook. 430p. 1997. text 149.00 (*0-9643582-2-0*) Learn Pubns.

Aneman, Durlynn & Sanders, Vickie. Options: A Communication Skills Series, 3 bks., Set. LC 92-84129. 1993. mass mkt. 12.95 (*0-538-62153-2*) S-W Pub.

— What Are You Saying? (Options: a Communication Skills Ser.: Bk. 2). 1994. pap. write for info. (*0-318-70141-3*) S-W Pub.

— Who Am I? (Options: a Communication Skills Ser.: Bk. 1). 1994. pap. write for info. (*0-318-70140-5*) S-W Pub.

— Who's Important to You? LC 92-84129. (Options: a Communication Skills Ser.: Bk. 3). 1994. pap. write for info. (*0-318-70142-1*) S-W Pub.

Anemark, B. R. Osseointegration in Craniofacial Reconstruction. Branemark, Per-Ingvar & Tolman, Dan E., eds. LC 98-21397. (Illus.). 337p. 1998. text 156.00 (*0-86715-337-7*) Quint Pub Co.

Aner, Karl. Die Theologie der Lessingzeit. (GER.). xi, 376p. 1976. reprint ed. write for info. (*3-487-05914-2*) G Olms Pubs.

***Aner, Walter.** Wie Wir Wirklich Waren: Erleguisse Eines Sudetendentschen Soldaten. unabridged ed. Pueschul, Rudolf, ed. & intro. by. (GER., Illus.). 179p. 1999. pap. 15.00 (*0-9663968-1-2*) RFP.

***Anerson.** Cold War in Soviet Block & Polish. 336p. 2000. pap. 65.00 (*0-8133-3783-6*, Pub. by Westview) HarpC.

Anesaki, Masaharu. Katam Karaniyam: Lectures, Essays & Studies. LC 78-72369. reprint ed. 32.50 (*0-404-17216-4*) AMS Pr.

Aneshensel, C. S. & Phelan, J. C., eds. Mental Health. LC 99-38201. (Handbooks of Sociology & Social Research Ser.). (Illus.). 600p. (C). 1999. write for info. (*0-306-46069-6*, Plenum Trade) Perseus Pubng.

Anesko, Michael, ed. see James, Henry & Howells, William Dean.

Aney, Kathleen, jt. auth. see Higbee, Paul.

***Aneziris, Charilaos.** Mystery of Knots: Computer Programming for Knot Tabulation, 20. (Series on Knots & Everything: Vol. 20). (Illus.). 1999. 55.00 (*981-02-3878-9*) World Scientific Pub.

Anfam, David. Abstract Expressionism. LC 89-50535. (World of Art Ser.). (Illus.). 1990. pap. 14.95 (*0-500-20243-5*, Pub. by Thames Hudson) Norton.

— Mark Rothko: The Works on Canvas: A Catalogue Raisonne. LC 98-25970. (Illus.). 708p. 1998. 125.00 (*0-300-07489-1*) Yale U Pr.

Anfam, David & Mancusi-Ungaro, Carol. Mark Rothko: The Chapel Commission. (Illus.). 32p. 1996. pap. 12.95 (*0-939594-38-2*, Menil Collection) Menil Found.

Anfenson, Rod. Racquetball: Teaching the Technique-The Technique of Teaching. 88p. (Orig.). 1989. pap. 8.95 (*0-317-93247-0*) R Anfenson.

Anfinsen, Christian B., et al, eds. Advances in Protein Chemistry, Vol. 47. (Illus.). 458p. 1995. text 95.00 (*0-12-034247-2*) Acad Pr.

Anfinson, Scott F. Southwestern Minnesota Archaeology: 12,000 Years in the Prairie Lake Region. LC 97-518. (Minnesota Prehistoric Archaeology Ser.: Vol. 14). (Illus.). 156p. 1997. pap. 18.00 (*0-87351-355-X*) Minn Hist.

Anfinson, Scott F., et al. Canals & American Cities: Assessing the Impact of Canals on the Course of American Urban Life. Carlisle, Ronald C., ed. & intro. by. (Illus.). 112p. 1994. pap. 15.00 (*0-930973-14-3*) H M Historical.

Anforth, Allan, jt. auth. see Sutherland, Peter.

Anfossi, Joseph. You Shall Not Commit Adultery, Nor Covet Your Neighbor's Wife, Vol. 7. (Reflections on the Commandments Ser.). 75p. 1995. pap. 2.95 (*0-8198-8804-4*) Pauline Bks.

Anfossi, Joseph & Villata, John. I am the Lord Your God, Vol. 1. (Reflections on the Commandments Ser.). 47p. 1995. pap. 2.95 (*0-8198-3671-0*) Pauline Bks.

— You Shall Not Have Strange Gods Before Me, Vol. 2. (Reflections on the Commandments Ser.). 1995. pap. 2.95 (*0-8198-8801-X*) Pauline Bks.

Anfousee, Ginette. Arthur Throws a Tantrum. (First Novels Ser.). (Illus.). 58p. (J). (gr. 1-4). 1995. mass mkt. 3.99 (*0-88780-221-4*, Pub. by Formac Publ Co); bds. 14.95 (*0-88780-222-2*, Pub. by Formac Publ Co) Formac Dist Ltd.

— Arthur's Dad. (First Novels Ser.). (Illus.). 59p. (J). (gr. 1-4). 1995. mass mkt. 3.99 (*0-88780-094-7*, Pub. by Formac Publ Co); bds. 14.95 (*0-88780-095-5*, Pub. by Formac Publ Co) Formac Dist Ltd.

— Arthur's Problem Puppy. (First Novels Ser.). (Illus.). 59p. (J). (gr. 1-4). 1995. mass mkt. 3.99 (*0-88780-276-1*, Pub. by Formac Publ Co); bds. 14.95 (*0-88780-277-X*, Pub. by Formac Publ Co) Formac Dist Ltd.

Anfousse, Ginette. Les Barricades d'Arthur. (Novels in the Premier Roman Ser.). (FRE.). 64p. (J). (gr. 2-5). 1992. pap. 8.95 (*2-89021-163-0*, Pub. by La Courte Ech) Firefly Bks Ltd.

— La Cachette. (Jiji et Pichou Ser.). (FRE., Illus.). 24p. (YA). (ps up). 1979. pap. 6.95 (*2-89021-015-4*, Pub. by La Courte Ech) Firefly Bks Ltd.

— La Chicane. (Jiji et Pichou Ser.). (FRE., Illus.). 24p. (J). (ps up). 1979. pap. 6.95 (*2-89021-017-0*, Pub. by La Courte Ech) Firefly Bks Ltd.

— Le Chien d'Arthur. (Novels in the Premier Roman Ser.). (FRE.). 64p. (J). (gr. 2-5). 1993. pap. 8.95 (*2-89021-186-X*, Pub. by La Courte Ech) Firefly Bks Ltd.

— Devine? (Jiji et Pichou Ser.). (FRE., Illus.). 24p. (J). (ps up). 1990. pap. 6.95 (*2-89021-138-X*, Pub. by La Courte Ech) Firefly Bks Ltd.

— L' Ecole. (Jiji et Pichou Ser.). (FRE., Illus.). 24p. (J). (ps up). 1983. pap. 6.95 (*2-89021-041-3*, Pub. by La Courte Ech) Firefly Bks Ltd.

— La Fete. (Jiji et Pichou Ser.). (FRE., Illus.). 24p. (J). (ps up). 1983. pap. 6.95 (*2-89021-042-1*, Pub. by La Courte Ech) Firefly Bks Ltd.

— Le Grand Reve de Rosalie. (Novels in the Roman Jeunesse Ser.). (FRE.). 96p. (J). (gr. 4-7). 1992. pap. 8.95 (*2-89021-182-7*, Pub. by La Courte Ech) Firefly Bks Ltd.

— La Grande Aventure. (Jiji et Pichou Ser.). (FRE., Illus.). 24p. (J). (ps up). 1990. pap. 6.95 (*2-89021-139-8*, Pub. by La Courte Ech) Firefly Bks Ltd.

— Le Heros de Rosalie. (Novels in the Roman Jeunesse Ser.). (FRE., Illus.). 96p. (J). (gr. 4-7). 1988. pap. 8.95 (*2-89021-075-8*, Pub. by La Courte Ech) Firefly Bks Ltd.

— L' Hiver. (Jiji et Pichou Ser.). (FRE., Illus.). 24p. (J). (ps up). 1980. pap. 6.95 (*2-89021-024-3*, Pub. by La Courte Ech) Firefly Bks Ltd.

— Je Boude. (Jiji et Pichou Ser.). (FRE., Illus.). 24p. (J). (ps up). 1986. pap. 6.95 (*2-89021-061-8*, Pub. by La Courte Ech) Firefly Bks Ltd.

— Mon Ami Pichou. (Jiji et Pichou Ser.). (FRE., Illus.). 24p. (YA). (ps up). 1979. pap. 6.95 (*2-89021-014-6*, Pub. by La Courte Ech) Firefly Bks Ltd.

— El Papa de Arturo. (Coleccion Rosa Ser.). (SPA., Illus.). 60p. (J). (gr. 5 up). 1994. pap. 5.95 (*958-07-0065-6*) Firefly Bks Ltd.

— Le Pere d'Arthur. (Novels in the Premier Roman Ser.). (FRE.). 64p. (J). (gr. 2-5). 1989. pap. 7.95 (*2-89021-112-6*, Pub. by La Courte Ech) Firefly Bks Ltd.

— Le Pere Noel. (Jiji et Pichou Ser.). (FRE., Illus.). 24p. (J). (ps up). 1993. pap. 6.95 (*2-89021-205-X*, Pub. by La Courte Ech) Firefly Bks Ltd.

— La Petite Soeur. (Jiji et Pichou Ser.). (FRE., Illus.). 24p. (J). (ps up). 1986. pap. 6.95 (*2-89021-060-X*, Pub. by La Courte Ech) Firefly Bks Ltd.

— Rosalie S'En Va-T-En Guerre. (Novels in the Roman Jeunesse Ser.). (FRE.). 96p. (J). (gr. 4-7). 1989. pap. 8.95 (*2-89021-093-6*, Pub. by La Courte Ech) Firefly Bks Ltd.

— Rosalie's Battles. Gaboriau, Linda, tr. (Rosalie Ser.). (Illus.). 96p. (J). (gr. 3-7). 1995. pap. 5.95 (*0-921556-50-0*, Pub. by Gynergy-Ragweed) U of Toronto Pr.

— Rosalie's Battles. 1996. 8.60 (*0-606-09796-1*, Pub. by Turtleback) Demco.

— Rosalie's Big Dream. (Rosalie Ser.). (Illus.). 96p. (J). (gr. 3-7). 1995. pap. 5.95 (*0-921556-52-7*, Pub. by Gynergy-Ragweed) U of Toronto Pr.

— Rosalie's Big Dream. 1996. 8.60 (*0-606-11811-X*, Pub. by Turtleback) Demco.

— Rosalie's Catastrophes. 1996. 8.70 (*0-606-09797-X*, Pub. by Turtleback) Demco.

A

A

— Le Savon. (Jiji et Pichou Ser.). (FRE., Illus.). 24p. (J). (ps up). 1980. pap. 6.95 (*2-89021-023-5*, Pub. by La Courte Ech) Firefly Bks Ltd.

— Un Terrible Secret. (Novels in the Roman Plus Ser.). (FRE.). 160p. (YA). (gr. 8 up). 1991. pap. 7.95 (*2-89021-107-X*, Pub. by La Courte Ech) Firefly Bks Ltd.

— Les Vacances de Rosalie. (Novels in the Roman Jeunesse Ser.). (FRE.). 96p. (J). (gr. 4-7). 1990. pap. 7.95 (*2-89021-116-9*, Pub. by La Courte Ech) Firefly Bks Ltd.

— La Varicelle. (Jiji et Pichou Ser.). (FRE., Illus.). 24p. (J). (ps up). 1979. pap. 6.95 (*2-89021-016-2*, Pub. by La Courte Ech) Firefly Bks Ltd.

Anft, Michael. In Service: A Documentary of the Baltimore City Firefighters. LC 87-72040. (Illus.). 158p. (Orig.). 1987. pap. 40.00 (*0-944120-00-8*) Paradigm Bks.

Anfuso, Dennis. The Winged Monkeys of Oz. (Oz Ser.). 220p. (YA). 1995. pap. 24.95 (*1-57433-000-4*) Interset Pr.

— The Winged Monkeys of Oz. (Oz Ser.). 152p. 1996. 24.95 (*1-57433-039-X*) Interset Pr.

Anfuso, Dennis & Thompson, Kevin. Fatboy & Chubbs. 62p. 1995. pap. 5.00 (*1-57433-008-X*) Interset Pr.

Anfuso, Linda. A Palette of Period Pigments. 32p. 1995. pap. 3.00 (*1-57433-011-X*) Interset Pr.

— Red Coat: And Other Poems. 16p. 1995. pap. 3.00 (*1-57433-013-6*) Interset Pr.

— Stolen Daughter: A Collection of Poems. 25p. 1995. pap. 3.00 (*1-57433-012-8*) Interset Pr.

Anfuso, Nella & Gianuario, Annibale. Le Tre Arianne di Claudio Monteverdi. LC 77-452198. (Nuova Metodologia, Studi Musicologici: No. 5). (ITA., Illus.). 37p. (Orig.). 1975. pap. 8.00 (*0-934082-14-6*, Pub. by SP Quaranta Quattro) Theodore Front.

Ang, A. H-S. The Widening World of Childhood. LC 99-16692. 2000. text 49.95 (*0-312-22668-3*) St Martin.

Ang, A. H-S., ed. Structural Design, Analysis & Testing. LC 89-6766. 1086p. 1989. pap. text 11.00 (*0-87262-700-4*, 700) Am Soc Civil Eng.

Ang, A. H-S., et al, eds. Structural Safety & Reliability, 3 vols. 2389p. 1990. text 28.00 (*0-87262-743-8*) Am Soc Civil Eng.

Ang, Alfredo H. & Tang, Wilson H. Probability Concepts in Engineering Planning & Design, Vol. 1. LC 75-5892. 424p. 1975. text 99.95 (*0-471-03200-X*) Wiley.

***Ang, Arlene.** A Perfect Night for Bloodless Love. (Illus.). 36p. 2000. pap. 4.95 (*0-9676660-7-4*, Pick Pocket Pr) Phony Lid Pubns.

Ang, Catharina Y., et al, eds. Asian Foods: Science & Technology. LC 98-83242. 550p. 1999. text 99.95 (*1-56676-736-9*) Technomic.

Ang, Conny & Cannon, Robert E. International Network of Public Libraries Vol. 6: The Role of Public Libraries in the Media Society: Electronic Media & the Evaluation of Its Use: Model Solutions for Changing & Challenging Times. LC 99-12675. (Illus.). 128p. 1999. pap. 16.00 (*0-8108-3581-9*) Scarecrow.

***Ang, Eng T.** Delightful Chinese Cooking. Bissonnette, Donald R., ed. (Illus.). 160p. 1999. pap. 13.95 (*0-9627810-6-1*) Ambrosia Pubns.

Ang, Eng T. Delightful Tofu Cooking. Bissonnette, Donald R., ed. (Illus.). 160p. 1997. pap. 12.95 (*0-9627810-1-0*) Ambrosia Pubns.

— Delightful Vietnamese Cooking. Bissonnette, Donald R., ed. (Illus.). 160p. 1997. pap. 12.95 (*0-9627810-3-7*) Ambrosia Pubns.

Ang, Eng Tie. Delightful Brazilian Cooking. (Illus.). 176p. 1993. pap. 14.95 (*0-9627810-2-9*) Ambrosia Pubns.

— Delightful Thai Cooking. (Illus.). 132p. 1990. pap. 12.95 (*0-9627810-4-5*) Ambrosia Pubns.

***Ang, Estrella K.** Biological Science. 182p. 2000. pap. text 25.00 (*0-536-02817-6*) Pearson Custom.

Ang, Ien. Desperately Seeking the Audience. 192p. (C). (gr. 13). 1991. pap. 22.99 (*0-415-05270-X*, A5068) Routledge.

— Living Room Wars. LC 95-16943. 224p. (C). 1995. pap. 22.99 (*0-415-12801-3*) Routledge.

— Living Room Wars. LC 95-16943. 224p. (C). (gr. 13). 1995. 80.00 (*0-415-12800-5*) Routledge.

— Watching Dallas. 1986. pap. 8.95 (*0-416-41640-3*) Routledge.

— Watching Dallas: Soap Opera & the Melodramatic Imagination. 224p. (C). 1985. pap. 17.99 (*0-415-04598-3*, 9781) Routledge.

Ang, Ien, jt. auth. see Chen, Kuan-Hsing.

Ang, J. K. The Beauty of Huanghuali Furniture. 92p. 1997. pap. 60.00 (*957-638-427-3*) Oriental Bk Store.

Ang, K. Kian, et al. Radiation Therapy in Pediatric Oncology. Cassady, J. Robert, ed. LC 94-2790. (Medical Radiology Ser.). 1995. 115.00 (*0-387-54105-5*) Spr-Verlag.

— Radiotherapy for Head & Neck Cancers: Indications & Techniques. LC 93-6754. (Illus.). 300p. 1993. 80.00 (*0-8121-1678-X*) Lppncott W & W.

Ang, Kiat, ed. see Favro, Brian P.

Ang, M. L., jt. auth. see Lees, F. P.

Ang, Simon S. Power-Switching Converters. (Electrical Engineering & Electronics Ser.: Vol. 93). (Illus.). 432p. 1995. text 160.00 (*0-8247-9630-6*) Dekker.

***Ang, Susan.** A New Adventure in Healthy Eating: Tofu. 1999. 12.99 (*0-9666322-2-2*) S Ang.

Ang, Susan. Secret Vegetarian Recipes from the Orient, Vol. 1. (Illus.). 34p. 1998. pap. 9.99 (*0-9666322-0-6*) S Ang.

Ang, Susan, et al. A Simple Approach to Health & Fitness, 4 vols., Vol. 2. (Illus.). 42p. 1998. 12.99 (*0-9666322-1-4*) S Ang.

Ang, Swee Hoon, jt. auth. see Kotler, Philip.

Ang, T., jt. auth. see Lasnier, F.

Ang, T. S., jt. auth. see Ylam, L.

Ang, Tom. The Art of Digital Photography. (Illus.). 160p. 1999. pap. 29.95 (*0-8174-3794-0*) Watsn-Guptill.

***Ang, Tom.** Picture Editing. 2nd ed. (Illus.). 288p. 2000. pap. 47.95 (*0-240-51618-4*, Focal) Buttrwrth-Heinemann.

Ang, Tom. Picture Editing. 2nd ed. LC 97-944. (Illus.). 240p. 2000. pap. text 36.95 (*0-240-51469-6*, Focal) Buttrwrth-Heinemann.

***Ang, Tom.** Silver Pixels: An Introduction to the Digital Darkroom. (Illus.). 128p. 2000. pap. write for info. (*0-8174-5889-1*, Amphoto) Watsn-Guptill.

— Tao of Photography: Unlock Your Creativity Using the Wisdom of the East. (Illus.). 144p. 2000. pap. 29.95 (*0-8174-6004-7*) Watsn-Guptill.

Angal, S., jt. ed. see Harris, E. L.

Angang, Hu, jt. auth. see Shaoguang, Wang.

Angaran, David M., et al. Risk Prevention Skills: Communicating for Pharmacists. iv, 83p. 1995. pap. 39.00 (*1-930548-26-5*) Tennenhouse Prof Pubns.

— Risk Prevention Skills: Record Keeping for Pharmacists. iv, 83p. 1995. pap. 39.00 (*1-930548-27-3*) Tennenhouse Prof Pubns.

Angarella. Client/Server Front End Development in Visual BASIC. 1996. write for info. (*0-201-41859-2*) Addison-Wesley.

Angarita, Ciro & Coffey, Peter. Europe & the Andean Countries: A Comparison of Economic Policies & Institutions. (Omagua Ser.). 280p. 1992. 52.00 (*0-86187-968-6*) St Martin.

***Angas, L. B.** Investment for Appreciation: Forecasting Movements in Security Prices. (Investment Greats Ser.). 344p. 2000. 29.00 (*0-273-64431-9*) F T P H.

Angaza, Mai T. Sekha-Sen Ren-A: May They Mention My Name. 50p. (Orig.). (C). 1991. pap. text 6.95 (*0-9628211-0-1*) Angaza Pubns.

Angaza, Mai T., ed. see Dixon, Sylvia W.

Ange, Daniel. Wounds Healed by Love Alone: A Charismatic Interview with St. Therese of Lisieux. Flower, Marjorie & Chariot, Elaine, trs. LC 96-76164.Tr. of Les Blessures Que Guerit l'Armour. (ENG & FRE., Illus.). 168p. (Orig.). 1996. pap. 8.95 (*0-9628088-3-0*) Laser Pr Pubs.

Angehrn, Emil. Freiheit und System Bei Hegel. (C). 1977. 157.70 (*3-11-006969-5*) De Gruyter.

— Geschichte & Identitaet. (GER.). x, 397p. 1985. 113.10 (*3-11-010122-X*) De Gruyter.

***Angel.** Algebra for College Students. 2000. pap. 29.00 (*0-13-085519-7*); pap., student ed., suppl. ed. 29.00 (*0-13-085518-9*) P-H.

Angel. Cat's Kingdom. 1999. mass mkt. 8.95 (*0-446-38969-2*, Pub. by Warner Bks) Little.

— Custom Survey Math CB. 5th ed. (C). 1997. pap. text 57.00 (*0-201-33884-X*) Addison-Wesley.

— Elementary Algebra for College Students. 4th ed. 1995. pap. text. write for info. (*0-13-367665-X*) Allyn.

— Elementary Algebra For College Students. 4th ed. 1998. text, student ed. 26.00 (*0-13-367616-1*) Allyn.

Angel. Exploring Sephardic Customs & Traditions. 7.95 (*0-88125-675-7*) Ktav.

Angel. Guide to Clast Mathematical Competency to Accompany a Survey of Mathematics with Applications. 5th ed. 396p. (C). 1996. pap. 29.06 (*0-201-59077-8*) Addison-Wesley.

— Intermediate Algebra. 4th ed. (s). 1996. pap. text, student ed. 29.33 (*0-13-235359-8*) P-H.

— Intermediate Algebra for College Students. 5th rev. ed. LC 99-14410. 758p. 1999. 83.00 (*0-13-916321-2*) P-H.

Angel. Progress in Obesity Research, No. 7. 784p. 122.00 (*0-86196-532-9*, Pub. by J Libbey Med) Bks Intl VA.

Angel. Tests & Drills in Spanish Grammar, Bk. 1. 1987. pap. text 28.00 (*0-13-911777-6*) P-H.

ANGEL, ed. Elementary & Intermediate Algebra. 1999. pap. text, student ed. 29.00 (*0-13-085513-8*); pap. text, student ed. 29.00 (*0-13-085514-6*) P-H.

— Trigonometry Supply Intermed Algebra. 5th ed. 104p. 1999. pap. text 8.00 (*0-13-016609-X*) P-H.

Angel & Porter. A Survey of Mathematics with Applications: Instructor's Solutions Manual. 5th ed. 464p. 1996. 24.00 (*0-201-80956-7*) Addison-Wesley.

Angel, et al. Equity Flex Options: A Swiss Army Knife for the Investor & Financial Engineer. (Frank J. Fabozzi Library). (Illus.). 120p. 1999. 39.00 (*1-883249-58-9*) McGraw-Hill Prof.

Angel, Allen. Angel & Porter's A Survey of Mathematics with Applications with the Trigonometry Appendix. 5th ed. 1996. 78.20 (*0-201-85762-6*) Addison-Wesley.

Angel, Allen. Computer Chapter Supplement to Accompany a Survey of Mathematics with Applications. 4th ed. 80p. (C). 1995. pap. text 3.40 (*0-201-53097-X*) Addison-Wesley.

— Macintosh Version to a Survey of Mathematics with Applications. 4th ed. (C). 1995. 0.00 (*0-201-59059-X*) Addison-Wesley.

— A Survey of Mathematics. 4th ed. 704p. (C). 1996. pap. text 65.00 (*0-201-30065-6*) Addison-Wesley.

— A Survey of Mathematics with Applications. 4th ed. 256p. (C). 1992. pap. text, student ed. 23.00 (*0-201-54996-4*) Addison-Wesley.

— A Survey of Mathematics with Applications. 5th ed. 288p. (C). 1996. pap. text, student ed. 25.00 (*0-201-80957-5*) Addison-Wesley.

— A Survey of Mathematics with Applications. 5th ed. Guardino, Karen, ed. LC 96-43388. 784p. (C). 1996. 78.00 (*0-201-84600-4*) Addison-Wesley.

— A Survey of Mathematics with Applications: With Right Triangle Trigonometry Appendix. 5th ed. Guardino, Karen, ed. LC 96-43388. 818p. (C). 1996. 86.00 (*0-201-85761-8*) Addison-Wesley.

Angel, Allen & Porter, Stuart R. A Survey of Mathematics with Applications. 4th ed. (Illus.). 800p. (C). 1992. text 59.00 (*0-201-54994-8*) Addison-Wesley.

***Angel, Allen & Porter, Stuart R.** Survey of Mathematics with Applications. 6th ed. LC 99-56911. (C). 2000. text. write for info. (*0-201-38407-8*) Addison-Wesley.

Angel, Allen R. Algebra for College Students. (C). 1999. Price not set. (*0-13-084873-5*) P-H.

— Algebra for College Students. LC 00-21573. 1024p. (C). 2000. 79.00 (*0-13-084871-9*) P-H.

— Annotated Instructor's Edition. 5th ed. LC 99-39265. (C). 1999. Price not set. (*0-13-014009-0*); Price not set. (*0-13-014011-2*); Price not set. (*0-13-022265-8*) P-H.

— Annotated Instructor's Edition. 5th ed. LC 99-51718. (C). 1999. Price not set. (*0-13-013991-2*) P-H.

— Elementary Algebra for College Students. 5th ed. LC 99-39261. 657p. (C). 1999. 83.00 (*0-13-080033-3*) P-H.

— Elementary Algebra for College Students: Early Graphing. LC 99-39265. 658p. (C). 1999. 83.00 (*0-13-011645-9*) P-H.

— Elementary & Intermediate Algebra. LC 99-51718. 936p. (C). 2000. 92.00 (*0-13-013980-7*) P-H.

Angel, Allen R. & Porter, Stuart R. A Survey of Mathematics: With Applications. 3rd ed. (Illus.). 761p. (C). 1989. text 49.50 (*0-201-13696-1*); pap. text, student ed. 18.25 (*0-201-13697-X*) Addison-Wesley.

***Angel, Allen R. & Porter, Stuart R.** A Survey of Mathematics: With Applications. 5th ed. 1999. 86.00 (*0-201-69960-5*) Addison-Wesley.

— A Survey of Mathematics with Applications: Alternate Version. 6th ed. 912p. 2000. write for info. (*0-201-70308-4*) Addison-Wesley.

Angel, Aubie, et al, eds. The Adipocyte & Obesity: Cellular & Molecular Mechanisms. LC 83-3372. (Illus.). 327p. 1983. reprint ed. pap. 101.40 (*0-608-00622-X*, 206120900007) Bks Demand.

Angel, Aubie & Frohlich, Jiri, eds. Lipoprotein Deficiency Syndromes. LC 86-16852. (Advances in Experimental Medicine & Biology Ser.: Vol. 201). (Illus.). 314p. 1986. 75.00 (*0-306-42380-4*, Plenum Trade) Perseus Pubng.

Angel, Dan & DeVault, Mike. Managing Back, Mugged by Reality. 272p. 25.00 (*1-878096-37-0*, Epigram Pr) Best E TX Pubs.

Angel, Dan & DeVault, Mike, eds. Conceptualizing 2000: Proactive Planning. 141p. (C). 1991. text 10.00 (*0-87117-226-7*, 1317) Comm Coll Pr Am Assn Comm Coll.

— Conceptualizing Two Thousand: Proactive Planning. LC 91-70258. 165p. reprint ed. pap. 51.20 (*0-608-20518-4*, 207177000002) Bks Demand.

Angel, David P. Restructuring for Innovation: The Remaking of the U. S. Semiconductor Industry. LC 93-40423. (Perspectives on Economic Change Ser.). 216p. 1994. lib. bdg. 32.50 (*0-89862-297-2*, 2297) Guilford Pubns.

Angel, Debra L. & Harney, Elisabeth E. No One Is Unemployable: Creative Solutions for Overcoming Barriers to Employment. Harney, Patricia & Wooley, Danial, eds. LC 94-12045. (Illus.). 273p. (Orig.). 1997. pap. 29.95 (*0-9657057-0-6*) WorkNet Training.

Angel, Edward. Interactive Computer Graphics: A Top down Approach with Open GL. LC 96-21656. 550p. (C). 1996. 66.00 (*0-201-85571-2*) Addison-Wesley.

***Angel, Edward.** Interactive Computer Graphics: A Top-Down Approach with OpenGL. 2nd ed. LC 99-19649. (Illus.). 613p. (C). 1999. 62.00 (*0-201-38597-X*) Addison-Wesley.

Angel, George. The Fifth Season. (Nilon Award for Fiction Ser.). 200p. 1996. 19.95 (*1-57366-015-9*); pap. 11.95 (*1-57366-016-7*) Fiction Coll.

Angel, Gilda. Sephardic Holiday Cooking: Recipes & Traditions. (Illus.). 1986. 19.95 (*0-915474-04-2*, Effective Learn) Decalogue Bks.

Angel, Hans-Ferdinand. Der Religiose Mensch in Katastrophenzeiten: Religionspadagogische Perspektiven Kollektiver Elendsphanomene. (Regensburger Studien Zur Theologie Ser.: Bd. 48). (GER.). xii, 816p. 1996. 114.95 (*3-631-48635-9*) P Lang Pubng.

Angel, Hans-Ferdinand & Hemel, Ulrich, eds. Basiskurse Im Christsein: Festschrift Zu Ehren von Wolfgang Nastainczyk. (GER.). 462p. 1992. 57.80 (*3-631-44678-0*) P Lang Pubng.

Angel, Hayyim J., ed. Seeking Good, Speaking Peace: Collected Essays of Rabbi Marc D. Angel. LC 94-10452. 1994. 25.00 (*0-88125-241-7*) Ktav.

Angel, Heather. How to Photograph Flowers. LC 97-22370. (How to Photograph Ser.). (Illus.). 128p. 1998. pap. 16.95 (*0-8117-2455-7*) Stackpole.

***Angel, Heather.** How to Photograph Water. LC 98-53196. (Illus.). 144p. 1999. pap. 19.95 (*0-8117-2461-1*) Stackpole.

Angel, Heather. Natural Visions: Creative Tips for Wildlife Photography. (Illus.). 144p. 1999. pap. 24.95 (*0-8174-4992-2*) Watsn-Guptill.

— Outdoor Photography: 101 Tips & Hints. LC 98-125195. (Magic Lantern Guides Ser.). (Illus.). 176p. (C). 1998. pap. 19.95 (*1-883403-41-3*, H 156, Silver Pixel Pr) Saunders Photo.

— Pandas: USA Edition. LC 97-42001. (WorldLife Library). (Illus.). 72p. (YA). (gr. 5 up). 1998. pap. 16.95 (*0-89658-364-3*) Voyageur Pr.

— Photographing the Natural World. LC 93-48089. (Illus.). 160p. 1994. 24.95 (*0-8069-0714-2*) Sterling.

— Photographing the Natural World. (Illus.). 160p. 1996. pap. 17.95 (*0-8069-0715-0*) Sterling.

Angel, Heather, jt. auth. see Peterson, B. Moose.

Angel, J. L. The People. LC 73-139121. (Lerna Ser.: Vol. 2). (Illus.). xi, 160p. 1971. 25.00 (*0-87661-302-4*) Am Sch Athens.

Angel, J. Lawrence, jt. ed. see Zimmerman, Michael R.

Angel, Jacqueline L. Managed Community Long-Term Care in Texas: Planning for the 21st Century. LC 97-73906. (Policy Research Project Report Ser.). 163p. 1997. pap. 16.00 (*0-89940-732-3*) LBJ Sch Pub Aff.

Angel, Jacqueline L., jt. auth. see Angel, Ronald J.

Angel, James B. Concepts of Fitness & Health. 3rd ed. (Illus.). 84p. (C). 1997. pap. text 18.95 (*0-945483-82-1*) E Bowers Pub.

Angel, James L. The Wood County Historical Church Records Survey. 56p. 1979. write for info. (*0-932690-01-7*) Ctr for Arch Collects.

Angel, Jen, ed. The Zine Yearbook, Vol. 2. (Illus.). 140p. 1998. pap. 6.00 (*0-9664829-0-5*) Become The Media.

— The Zine Yearbook, Vol. 3. (Illus.). 140p. 1999. pap. 7.00 (*0-9664829-1-3*) Become The Media.

***Angel, Jen, ed.** The Zine Yearbook, Vol. 4. (Illus.). 144p. 2000. pap. 7.00 (*0-9664829-2-1*, Pub. by Become The Media) AK Pr Dist.

Angel, John. Industrial Tribunals: Preparing & Presenting Your Case. 328p. (C). 1984. 90.00 (*0-85459-154-0*, Pub. by IPM Hse) St Mut.

Angel, John & Walden, Ian, eds. Telecommunications Law Handbook. LC 97-169319. 987p. 1997. 154.00 (*1-85431-595-1*, Pub. by Blackstone Pr) Gaunt.

Angel, Jonathan. RealMedia Complete: Streaming Audio & Video over the Web. LC 98-6440. (The Complete Reference Ser.). 800p. 1998. pap. 49.95 incl. cd-rom (*0-07-913727-X*) McGraw.

Angel-Junguito, Antonio. A Cry of Innocence: In Defense of Colombians. LC 92-44327. (Illus.). 112p. 1993. pap. 9.95 (*0-942963-31-8*) Distinctive Pub.

Angel, Juvenal L. The Complete Resume Book & Job Getter's Guide. 1990. mass mkt. 5.99 (*0-671-72564-5*) PB.

Angel, Juvenal L. & Dixson, Robert J. Tests & Drills in Spanish Grammar Bk. 2. 1987. pap. text 22.80 (*0-13-911785-7*, Prentice Hall) P-H.

Angel, Kathy C., jt. auth. see Brewer, Earl J., Jr.

Angel, Kathy C., ed. see Brewer, Earl J., Jr.

Angel, Kathy Cochran, jt. auth. see Brewer, Earl J., Jr.

Angel, L. Book of Miriam. LC 98-161894. 1997. 15.00 (*0-88962-646-4*, 734078Q) Mosaic.

Angel, Leonard. Enlightenment East & West. LC 93-39936. 388p. (C). 1994. text 22.50 (*0-7914-2053-1*) State U NY Pr.

Angel, Luz. El Arte de Leer Las Cartas Mexicanas y Espanolas: Version Moderna Expanola. 2nd rev. ed.Tr. of Spanish & Mexican Card Readings: Modern English Version. (ENG & SPA., Illus.). 146p. 1997. pap. 9.95 (*0-9644720-5-8*) L Angel.

— A Guide to Readings Using the Spanish Cards: Modern English Version. 2nd rev. ed. (Illus.). 146p. (Orig.). 1995. pap. 9.95 (*0-9644720-1-5*) L Angel.

Angel, Lyle K. & Hunter, Jim. Racing to Win, Wood Brothers Style. LC 72-91065. 158 p. 1974. write for info. (*0-668-02886-6*) Macmillan Gen Ref.

Angel, M. Marine Planktonic Ostracode. Expert-Center for Taxonomic Identification (ETI) S, ed. (World Biodiversity Database Ser.). 1998. pap. 109.00 incl. cd-rom (*3-540-14680-6*) Spr-Verlag.

Angel, M. V. Progress in Oceanography, Vol. 8. (Illus.). 296p. 1980. 125.00 (*0-08-022963-8*, Pergamon Pr) Elsevier.

Angel, M. V. & O'Brien, J. J. Progress in Oceanography, Vol. 9, Nos. 1-4. (Illus.). 246p. 1982. 125.00 (*0-08-027116-2*, Pergamon Pr) Elsevier.

Angel, M. V. & O'Brien, J. J., eds. Progress in Oceanography, Vol. 10. (Illus.). 226p. 1982. 115.00 (*0-08-029121-X*, Pergamon Pr) Elsevier.

— Progress in Oceanography, Vol. 12. (Illus.). 470p. 1984. 165.00 (*0-08-031504-6*, Pergamon Pr) Elsevier.

— Progress in Oceanography, Vol. 13. (Illus.). 520p. 1985. 175.00 (*0-08-032724-9*, Pergamon Pr) Elsevier.

Angel, Marc. Exploring the Thought of Rabbi Joseph B. Soloveitchik. LC 97-21918. 1997. 39.50 (*0-88125-578-5*) Ktav.

— Loving Truth & Peace: The Grand Religious Worldview of Rabbi Benzion Uziel. LC 98-42912. 1999. 30.00 (*0-7657-6034-7*) Aronson.

— The Orphaned Adult: Confronting the Death of a Parent. LC 86-20161. 162p. 1987. 26.95 (*0-89885-334-6*, Kluwer Acad Hman Sci) Kluwer Academic.

Angel, Marc, ed. Exploring the Thought of Rabbi Joseph B. Soloveitchik. LC 97-21918. xxvii, 346p. 1997. pap. 24.95 (*0-88125-583-1*) Ktav.

Angel, Marc D. A Sephardic Passover Haggadah. 128p. 1988. pap. 7.95 (*0-88125-145-3*) Ktav.

— Voices in Exile: A Study in Sephardic Intellectual History. 1993. 25.00 (*0-88125-370-7*) Ktav.

Angel, Marc D., ed. From Strength to Strength: Lectures from Shearith Israel. LC 97-50455. 206p. 1998. pap. 17.95 (*0-87203-152-7*) Hermon.

— Haham Gaon Memorial Volume: A Centennial Volume. LC 97-4970. (Illus.). 274p. 1997. 29.95 (*0-87203-148-9*) Hermon.

Angel, Marc D., et al. The Sephardic Journey, 1492-1992. (Illus.). 500p. 1992. pap. text. write for info. (*0-945447-03-5*) Yesh Mus.

Angel, Marc D., tr. & intro. see Papo, Eliezer.

Angel, Marie. Painting for Calligraphers. LC 83-24981. (Illus.). 128p. (C). 1984. 27.50 (*0-87951-969-X*, Pub. by Overlook Pr) Penguin Putnam.

— Painting for Calligraphers. (Illus.). 128p. 1997. 35.00 (*0-87951-804-9*, Pub. by Overlook Pr) Penguin Putnam.

Angel, Marie. An Animated Alphabet. LC 96-24222. 64p. 1996. pap. 12.95 (*1-56792-023-3*) Godine.

Angel, Myron F. The Painted Rock of California. MacDonald, Lachlan P., ed. LC 79-26494. (Illus.). 128p. 1979. reprint ed. pap. 5.95 (*0-914598-14-7*) Bear Flag Bks.

Angel, Myron F., ed. History of Nevada. LC 72-9424. (Far Western Frontier Ser.). (Illus.). 948p. 1973. reprint ed. 68.95 (*0-405-04956-0*) Ayer.

An Asterisk (*) at the beginning of an entry indicates that the title is appearing for the first time.

— History of Nevada, with Illustrations & Biographical Sketches of Its Prominent Men & Pioneers. (Illus.). 680p. 1992. reprint ed. lib. bdg. 65.00 (0-8328-2434-8) Higginson Bk Co.

Angel, Nicolas. Capsize! A Story of Survival in the North Atlantic. Wakeman, Alan, tr. from FRE. LC 81-389. (Illus.). 178p. 1981. 15.95 (0-393-03264-7) Norton.

Angel, Ralph. Neither World: Poems. LC 95-1768. 1995. 15.95 (1-881163-12-1); pap. 9.95 (1-881163-13-X) Miami Univ Pr.

Angel, Robert C. Explaining Economic Policy Failure. 1991. text 46.00 (0-231-07440-9, W4409) Col U Pr.

— Meeting the Japanese Challenge, 1969-1971: Balance of Payments Problems Force the Nixon Administration to Act. (Pew Case Studies in International Affairs). 60p. (C). 1988. pap. text 3.50 (1-56927-135-6) Geo U Inst Dplmcy.

Angel, Robert C., et al. Japan in the 1980s, VI & VII: Proceedings of the Regional Study Series. Suzman, Cedric L. & White, Peter C., eds. LC 88-61300. 1988. write for info. (0-935082-12-3) Southern Ctr Intl Stud.

Angel, Roger B. Relativity: The Theory & Its Philosophy. (Foundations & Philosophy of Science & Technology Ser.). (Illus.). 320p. 1980. 125.00 (0-08-025197-8, Pub. by Pergamon Repr) Franklin.

***Angel, Ronald J.** Who Will Care for Us? Aging & Long-Term Care in a Multicultural America. 1999. pap. text 19.00 (0-8147-0683-5) NYU Pr.

Angel, Ronald J. & Angel, Jacqueline L. Painful Inheritance: Health & the New Generation of Fatherless Families. LC 93-18788. (Life Course Studies). (Illus.). 288p. (Orig.). (C). 1994. pap. 19.95 (0-299-13964-6); lib. bdg. 55.00 (0-299-13960-3) U of Wis Pr.

— Who Will Care for Us? Aging & Long-Term Care in Multicultural America. LC 96-25333. 304p. (C). 1999. text 50.00 (0-8147-0629-0) NYU Pr.

Angel, Samuel P., jt. auth. see Scott, Samuel W.

***Angel, Schlomo.** Housing Policy Matters: A Global Analysis. (Illus.). 448p. 2000. text 49.95 (0-19-513715-9) OUP.

Angel, Tony & Greenhaigh, David. Taxation of Banks & Banking Operations. 1995. boxed set. write for info. (0-406-00735-7, UK, MICHIE) LEXIS Pub.

Angel, W. Youth Movements of the World. 1991. 130.00 (0-582-06271-3) Longman.

Angel, Warren. Yes We Can Love One Another! Catholics & Protestants Can Share a Common Faith. LC 96-94822. 143p. (Orig.). 1997. pap. 12.00 (0-9654806-0-7) Magnus Pr.

Angel, William D., ed. The International Law of Youth Rights: Source Documents & Commentary. LC 94-42242. 1995. lib. bdg. 272.00 (0-7923-3321-7) Kluwer Academic.

Angel, Y. C., ed. Anisotropy & Inhomogeneity in Elasticity & Plasticity. LC 93-71572. (AMD Ser.: Vol. 158). 61p. 1993. pap. 30.00 (0-7918-1137-9, G00781) ASME.

Angel, Yossi. English-Hebrew Dictionary of Accounting & Business Administration Terms, Vol. I. 248p. 1988. 150.00 (0-7859-9327-4) Fr & Eur.

— Hebrew/English Dictionary of Accounting & Business Administration Terms, Vol. II. (ENG & HEB.). 336p. 1988. 150.00 (0-7859-9329-0) Fr & Eur.

Angela. Aromatics. 1995. 108.00 (0-517-70138-3) Random Hse Value.

Angela, Alberto, jt. auth. see Angela, Piero.

Angela, Piero & Angela, Alberto. The Extraordinary Story of Human Origins. LC 93-9492.Tr. of Straodinaria Storia dell'Uomo. (Illus.). 328p. (C). 1993. reprint ed. 28.95 (0-87975-803-1) Prometheus Bks.

— Extraordinary Story of Life on Earth. LC 95-48159. (Illus.). 395p. 1996. 28.95 (1-57392-043-6) Prometheus Bks.

***Angela, Piero & Angela, Alberto.** Sharks: Predators of the Sea. LC 97-77495. (Illus.). 140p. 1998. 19.98 (0-7624-0354-3, Courage) Running Pr.

Angela Royal Publishing Staff. Pleasure Vessels: The Winners of the 1995 Ian St. James Awards. 1997. pap. text 12.95 (1-899860-60-6, Pub. by A Royal Pub) Red Sea Pr.

Angelakis, Andreas N. & Issar, Arie S., eds. Diachronic Climate Impacts on Water Resources: With Emphasis on the Mediterranean Region. (NATO ASI Ser.: Series 1, Vol. 36). 407p. 1995. 216.95 (3-540-60561-4) Spr-Verlag.

Angelakis, Pauline. Scarlet Author. (Illus.). 20p. 1992. pap. 4.95 (0-915992-56-6) Eastern National.

Angelakis, T., et al, eds. Wastewater Reclamation & Reuse, 1995: Selected Proceedings of the IAWQ 2nd International Symposium on Wastewater Reclamation & Reuse, Held in Iraklio, Crete, Greece, 17-20 October 1995. 492p. 1996. pap. 255.00 (0-08-042903-3, Pergamon Pr) Elsevier.

Angela's Bookshelf Publishing Staff. Choice Stories for Children. (Illus.). 144p. (J). Date not set. pap. 6.95 (1-878726-08-0) Angelas Bkshelf.

Angelas Bookshelf Publishing Staff. Choice Stories for Children. 1998. pap. text 6.95 (1-881545-99-7) Angelas Bkshelf.

Angelastro, Lynda, ed. see Chein, Edmund.

Angelbe, Hans-Peter. Dictionary of Chromatography: English, German, French, Russian: Containing about 3500 Terms. LC 84-154691. (ENG, FRE & RUS.). 132p. 1984. write for info. (3-7785-0926-8) U Pr of Amer.

Angele. Chromatography: English-German-French-Russian. 2nd ed. (FRE, GER & RUS.). 136p. 1984. 39.95 (0-7859-7245-5, 3861170000) Fr & Eur.

Angele, Gustave J., Sr. Cross-Connection & Backflow Prevention. 2nd ed. 54p. 1979. pap. 28.00 (0-89867-250-3, 20106) Am Water Wks Assn.

Angelelli, I., ed. see Frege, Gottlob.

Angelelli, Igancio & Cerezo, Maria, eds. Studies on the History of Logic: Proceedings of the III Sympoisum on the History of Logic. LC 96-5201. (Perspektiven der Analytischen Philosophie - Perspectives in Analytical Philosophy Ser.: Vol. 8). xii, 413p. (C). 1996. lib. bdg. 189.65 (3-11-014829-3, 112/96) De Gruyter.

Angelelli, Ignacio. Studies on Gottlob Frege & Traditional Philosophy. 307p. 1967. text 169.50 (90-277-0067-2, D Reidel) Kluwer Academic.

Angelelli, Ignacio, tr. see Birjukov, B. V.

Angeleri, Franco, et al, eds. Analysis of the Electrical Activity of the Brain. LC 96-27979. 372p. 1997. 195.00 (0-471-96959-1) Wiley.

Angeles, Eleanor S. & Haggerty, Edward C. Test Wise 1: Primary. (Troll Teacher Idea Bks.). (J). (gr. 1-3). 1997. pap., teacher ed. 12.95 (0-8167-4457-2) Troll Communs.

— Test Wise 2 No. 2: Intermediate. (Troll Teacher Idea Bks.). (J). (gr. 4-6). 1997. pap., teacher ed. 12.95 (0-8167-4463-7) Troll Communs.

Angeles, J., ed. Rational Kinematics. (Tracts in Natural Philosophy Ser.: Vol. 34). xii, 121p. 1989. 64.95 (0-387-96813-X) Spr-Verlag.

Angeles, J. & Kecskemethy, A., eds. Kinematics & Dynamics of Multi-Body Systems. LC 96-19724. (CISM International Centre for Mechanical Sciences Ser.: No. 360). (Illus.). 342p. 1995. pap. 97.95 (3-211-82731-5) Spr-Verlag.

Angeles, J. & Lopez-Cajun, C. S. Optimization of Cam Mechanisms. (C). 1991. lib. bdg. 145.00 (0-7923-1355-0) Kluwer Academic.

Angeles, Jorge. Fundamentals of Robotic Mechanical Systems: Theory, Methods & Algorithms. LC 96-32218. 500p. 1996. 69.95 (0-387-94540-7) Spr-Verlag.

Angeles, Jorge, ed. Computational Kinematics. (Solid Mechanics & Its Applications Ser.). 320p. (C). 1993. text 174.50 (0-7923-2585-0) Kluwer Academic.

Angeles, Jorge & Zakhariev, Evtim, eds. Computational Methods in Mechanical Systems: Mechanism Analysis, Synthesis, & Optimization. LC 98-10329. (NATO ASI Series F: Vol. 161). x, 425p. 1998. 99.00 (3-540-63939-X) Spr-Verlag.

Angeles, Peter A. Critiques of God: Making the Case Against Belief in God. LC 96-40053. 368p. 1997. pap. 22.95 (1-57392-123-8) Prometheus Bks.

— HarperCollins Dictionary of Philosophy Second Edition: In-Depth Explanations & Examples Covering More than 3,000 Entries. 2nd ed. LC 91-58546. 352p. 1992. pap. 16.00 (0-06-461026-8, Harper Ref) HarpC.

— The Problem of God: A Short Introduction. rev. ed. LC 73-85469. 166p. 1980. pap. 21.95 (0-87975-216-5) Prometheus Bks.

Angelette, Carolyn. The Cajun Pecan House Cookbook. 164p. 1989. 9.95 (0-9629822-0-2) Cajun Pecan.

Angeletti, Frank, ed. see Marvin, Joseph.

Angeletti, G. & Bjorseth, Alf, eds. Analysis of Organic Micropollutants in Water. 1984. text 200.00 (90-277-1726-5) Kluwer Academic.

— Organic Micropollutants in the Aquatic Environment. (C). 1988. text 234.00 (90-277-2738-4) Kluwer Academic.

— Organic Micropollutants in the Aquatic Environment. (C). 1991. text 257.50 (0-7923-1104-3) Kluwer Academic.

Angeletti, G. & Restelli, Giambattista, eds. Physico-Chemical Behaviour of Atmospheric Pollutants. (C). 1987. text 357.00 (90-277-2464-4) Kluwer Academic.

— Physico-Chemical Behaviour of Atmospheric Pollutants. (C). 1990. text 375.00 (0-7923-0700-3) Kluwer Academic.

Angeletti, G., jt. ed. see Bjorseth, Alf.

Angeletti, G., jt. ed. see Bjrseth, A.

Angeletti, G., jt. ed. see Versino, V.

Angeletti, Roberta. The Cave Painter of Lascaux. (Journey Through Time Ser.). (Illus.). 32p. (J). 1999. 16.95 (0-19-521558-3) OUP.

— The Minotaur of Knossos. (Journey Through Time Ser.). (Illus.). 32p. (J). (gr. 3-5). 1999. 16.95 (0-19-521557-5) OUP.

— Nefertari, Princess of Egypt. (Illus.). 32p. (YA). 1999. 16.95 (0-19-521507-9) OUP.

— Vulca the Etruscan. (Illus.). 32p. (YA). 1999. 16.95 (0-19-521506-0) OUP.

Angeletti, Ruth H., ed. Proteins: Analysis & Design. LC 98-4746. (Illus.). 362p. 1998. boxed set 99.95 (0-12-058785-8) Acad Pr.

— Techniques in Protein Chemistry. (Illus.). 640p. 1993. 63.00 (0-12-058758-0) Acad Pr.

Angelfish, Christopher. The Fish Book. LC 96-77296. (Super Shape Bks.). (Illus.). 24p. (J). (ps-k). 1997. pap. 3.29 (0-307-10094-4, 10094, Goldn Books) Gldn Bks Pub Co.

Angeli, Alberto, et al, eds. Endocrinology of Cystic Breast Disease. LC 81-86364. (Illus.). 343p. 1983. reprint ed. pap. 106.40 (0-608-00649-1, 206123700007) Bks Demand.

Angeli, Amie. The Angels' I Ching. (ACP Oracles Ser.: Vol. 4). (Illus.). 150p. Date not set. pap. 21.00 (1-891333-13-5) AngeLines Pub.

— The Angels' Tarot. (ACP Oracles Ser.: Vol. 5). (Illus.). 150p. Date not set. pap. 21.00 (1-891333-19-4) AngeLines Pub.

— The Colors in Our Lives: Working with Light Energy. (ACP Oracles Ser.: Vol. 2). (Illus.). 96p. 1999. pap. 19.50 (1-891333-03-8) AngeLines Pub.

— Crystal Creations: A Course in Working with Crystals. (Illus.). 100p. Date not set. pap. 19.50 (1-891333-07-0) AngeLines Pub.

***Angeli, Amie.** The Numbers in Our Lives: A Course in ACP Numerology. LC 97-94774. (ACP Oracles Ser.: Vol. 1). (Illus.). 96p. 1998. pap. 19.50 (1-891333-00-3) AngeLines Pub.

Angeli, Amie. Paths to Prosperity. (Illus.). 150p. Date not set. pap. 21.00 (1-891333-11-9) AngeLines Pub.

Angeli, Helen R. Dante Gabriel Rossetti. LC 76-184272. 1949. 22.00 (0-405-08206-1) Ayer.

— Pre-Raphaelite Twilight: The Story of Charles Augustus Howell. 1988. reprint ed. lib. bdg. 49.00 (0-7812-0026-1) Rprt Serv.

— Pre-Raphaelite Twilight: The Story of Charles Augustus Howell. LC 72-158494. (Illus.). 1971. reprint ed. 39.00 (0-403-01312-7) Scholarly.

— Shelley & His Friends in Italy. LC 72-3197. (Studies in Shelley: No. 25). 1972. reprint ed. lib. bdg. 75.00 (0-8383-1539-9) M S G Haskell Hse.

Angeli, Marguerite De, see De Angeli, Marguerite.

Angeli, Marguerite De, see Worth, Kathryn.

Angeli, Mark, et al. Serpent Moon: An Adventure Campaign for the Nephilum Role-Playing Game. Shirley, Sam, ed. (Nephilim Roleplaying Game Ser.). (Illus.). 128p. (Orig.). 1995. pap. 19.95 (1-56882-037-2, 3104) Chaosium.

Angeli, Massimiliano, et al. Extreme Snowboarding. (Extreme Sports Ser.). 128p. 2000. pap. 22.50 (0-7893-0222-5, Pub. by Universe) St Martin.

Angeli, Primo. Making People Respond. (Illus.). 144p. 1997. pap. 34.95 (0-942604-59-8) Madison Square.

Angeli Walls, Nina de, see Walls, Nina de Angeli.

Angelic Realm, jt. auth. see Virtue, Doreen.

***Angelica.** The Awakening: Wisdom from the Heart. 1999. pap. 8.95 (0-533-12857-9) Vantage.

Angelica, Emil & Hyman, Vincent. Coping with Cutbacks: The Nonprofit Guide to Success When Times Are Tight. LC 97-40748. (Illus.). 128p. 1997. pap. text 20.00 (0-940069-09-1) A H Wilder.

Angelica, Jade C. A Moral Emergency: Breaking the Cycle of Child Sexual Abuse. LC 93-939. 192p. (Orig.). 1993. pap. 10.95 (1-55612-617-4) Sheed & Ward WI.

Angelica, Mary. Mother Angelica's Answers, Not Promises. large type ed. 464p. 1987. pap. 16.95 (0-8027-2595-3) Walker & Co.

Angelici, Robert J., ed. Reagents for Transition Metal Complex & Organometallic Syntheses: Inorganic Synthesis, Vol. 28. (Inorganic Synthesis Ser.). 463p. 1990. 120.00 (0-471-52619-3) Wiley.

Angelides, Marios C. & Dustdar, Schahram. Multimedia Information Systems. LC 97-9412. (Multimedia Systems & Application Engineering & Computer Science Ser.). 1997. lib. bdg. 84.00 (0-7923-9915-3) Kluwer Academic.

***Angelil-Carter, Shelley.** Stolen Language? Plagiarism in Writing. 2nd ed. LC 99-87296. (Real Language Ser.). 2000. pap. write for info. (0-582-31999-4) Addison-Wesley.

Angelilli, Chris. The Christmas Snowman. LC 97-70670. (Super Shape Bks.). (Illus.). (J). (ps-k). 1997. pap. text 3.29 (0-307-10061-8, 10061, Goldn Books) Gldn Bks Pub Co.

Angelillo, Antonio. Alvaro Siza: Writings on Architecture. 1998. pap. 24.95 (88-8118-086-3) Skira IT.

Angelillo, Antonio, ed. Alvaro Siza: Writings on Architecture. (Illus.). 208p. 1999. 24.95 (88-8118-315-3, Pub. by Skira IT) Abbeville Pr.

Angelillo, Philip A. Short Bike Rides on Long Island: Rides for the Casual Cyclist. 5th ed. LC 97-44041. (Short Bike Rides Ser.). (Illus.). 176p. 1998. pap. 12.95 (0-7627-0208-7) Globe Pequot.

Angelin, Patricia, ed. see Nathan, George J.

Angelina. Song of the Soul: Notes in the Margins of Discipleship. 185p. 1999. 20.00 (0-9655558-9-5) Altarfire Pub.

Angeline, Mary. Precise Intrigues. LC 94-1789. 72p. (Orig.). 1994. pap. 12.00 (0-942996-22-4) Post Apollo Pr.

Angeline, Peter J., ed. Evolutionary Programming: 6th International Conference, EP97, Indianapolis, Indiana, U. S. A., April 13-16, 1997: Proceedings. LC 97-8373. (Lecture Notes in Computer Science Ser.). 1997. write for info. (3-540-62788-X) Spr-Verlag.

Angeline, Peter J., et al, eds. Advances in Genetic Programmings, Vol. III. (Illus.). 500p. 1999. 55.00 (0-262-01179-4, Bradford Bks) MIT Pr.

Angeline, Peter J., jt. ed. see Kinnear, Kenneth E., Jr.

Angelini, Alessandro. Piero Della Francesca. (Grandes Maestros del Arte Ser.). (SPA., Illus.). 80p. 1992. pap. 12.99 (1-878351-23-0) Riverside NY.

— Piero Della Francesca. rev. ed. Pelletti, Lisa C., tr. from ITA. (Library of Great Masters). (Illus.). 80p. 1990. pap. 14.99 (1-878351-04-4) Riverside NY.

Angelini, Diane J. & Knapp, Christine M. Case Studies in Perinatal Nursing. LC 91-25953. (Illus.). 254p. 1992. 52.00 (0-8342-0227-1, 20227) Aspen Pub.

Angelini, G. New Latin-Italian Dictionary: Nuovo Dizionario Latino-Italiano. (ITA & LAT.). 1981. 45.00 (0-8288-1030-3, F43170) Fr & Eur.

Angelini, Gianni D., et al. Arterial Conduits in Myocardial Revascularisation. 208p. 1996. text 125.00 (0-340-61024-7, Pub. by E A) OUP.

Angelini, James P., et al. Giving Credit Where Credit Is Due: A New Approach to Welfare Funding. 1995. pap. text. write for info. (1-886320-00-4) BHIFPPR.

— Tax Credits for Charitable Contributions: Alternatives, Projections & Comparisons. 1996. pap. text. write for info. (1-886320-01-2) BHIFPPR.

Angelini, Mike, tr. see Allen, Richard.

Angelini, Mike, tr. see Banthin, Richard.

Angelini, Mike, tr. see Farricielli, Susan.

Angelini, Mike, tr. see Meyers, Ron & Farricielli, Susan.

Angelini, Paolo. Coronary Artery Anomalies: A Comprehensive Approach. LC 99-10769. 1999. write for info. (0-7817-1018-9) Lppncott W & W.

Angelino, G., et al, eds. Modern Research Topics in Aerospace Propulsion: In Honor of Corrado Casci. (Illus.). 384p. 1991. 116.95 (0-387-97417-2) Spr-Verlag.

***Angelique, Janice.** Angel's Paradise. LC 99-67086. 192p. 2000. pap. 11.95 (1-56315-268-1, Pub. by SterlingHse) Natl Bk Netwk.

Angelis, Carl De, see Steen, Sara J. & De Angelis, Carl, eds.

Angelis, Georgia. The Intimate Eye. (Black Lace Ser.). 1995. mass mkt. 5.95 (0-352-33004-X, Pub. by Virgin Bks) London Brdge.

Angelis, Manlio F. De, see De Angelis, Manlio F.

Angelis, Therese De, see De Angelis, Therese.

Angelisanti, Pio Raffaele. The "New Earth" of the New Man. De Beracasa Gonzales, Bertha, tr. from SPA. (Illus.). 492p. 1978. student ed. 44.99 (0-9607590-3-4) Action Life Pubns.

Angelisanti, Raffaele, jt. auth. see Barriuso, Jose.

Angelisio, G. English in America: Dictionary of Slang. (ENG & ITA.). 1991. 125.00 (0-8288-8418-8) Fr & Eur.

Angell, Avery A. Genealogy of the Descendants of Thomas Angell, Who Settled in Providence, 1636. 210p. 1988. reprint ed. pap. 37.50 (0-8328-0127-5); reprint ed. lib. bdg. 45.50 (0-8328-0126-7) Higginson Bk Co.

Angell, Barbara. Long Turn Toward Light. (Illus.). 121p. (Orig.). 1991. pap. 10.00 (0-914946-94-3) Cleveland St Univ Poetry Ctr.

Angell, C. A., et al, eds. Structure & Dynamics of Glasses & Glass Formers. LC 97-20773. (Materials Research Society Symposium Proceedings Ser.: No. 455). 517p. 1997. text 75.00 (1-55899-359-2) Materials Res.

Angell, C. L. The Biology & Culture of Tropical Oysters. (ICLARM Studies & Reviews: No. 13). (Illus.). 42p. (Orig.). (C). 1986. pap. 6.00 (971-10-2224-9, Pub. by ICLARM) Intl Spec Bk.

Angell, Callie. Andy Warhol Museum: The Inaugural Publication. (Illus.). 188p. 1994. 40.00 (1-881616-34-7) Dist Art Pubs.

Angell, Callie, et al, contrib. by. The Andy Warhol Museum: The Inaugural Publication. LC 94-7351. 1994. 40.00 (0-88039-026-3) Mus Art Carnegie.

Angell, Carole S. Celebrations Around the World: A Multicultural Handbook. LC 96-14473. (Fulcrum Resources Bks.). (Illus.). 256p. (Orig.). 1996. pap. 19.95 (1-55591-945-6) Fulcrum Pub.

***Angell, David.** DSL for Dummies. (For Dummies Ser.). (Illus.). 384p. 2000. pap. 24.99 (0-7645-0715-X) IDG Bks.

Angell, David. Elements of E-Mail Style: Communicate Effectively Via Electronic Mail. 176p. (C). 1994. pap. text 14.95 (0-201-62709-4) Addison-Wesley.

— ISDN for Dummies. 384p. 1995. pap. 19.99 (1-56884-331-3) IDG Bks.

— ISDN for Dummies. 2nd ed. LC 96-79267. 432p. 1996. pap. 24.99 (0-7645-0064-3) IDG Bks.

— Windows Remote Access Toolkit. LC 97-13436. 512p. 1997. pap., pap. text 39.99 incl. cd-rom (0-471-19732-7) Wiley.

Angell, David & Dummies Technical Press Staff. Microsoft Internet Information Server 4 for Dummies. LC 98-84963. 384p. 1998. pap. 24.99 (0-7645-0265-4) IDG Bks.

Angell, David & Heslop, Brent. The Internet Business Companion. LC 94-20331. 256p. (C). 1994. pap. text 19.95 (0-201-40850-3) Addison-Wesley.

Angell, David, jt. auth. see Heslop, Brent.

Angell, David F. DSL for Dummies. LC 99-61342. (For Dummies Ser.). (Illus.). 360p. 1999. pap. 24.99 (0-7645-0475-4) IDG Bks.

— Mosaic for Dummies. 2nd ed. LC 96-75411. 384p. 1996. pap. 29.99 (1-56884-852-8) IDG Bks.

Angell, David F., jt. auth. see Heslop, Brent.

Angell, Frank C. Annals of Centerdale in the Town of North Providence: Its Past & Present, 1636-1909. (Illus.). 196p. 1997. reprint ed. lib. bdg. 27.00 (0-8328-6481-1) Higginson Bk Co.

Angell, George. Agricultural Options: Trading Puts & Calls in the New Grain & Livestock Futures Markets. LC 96-225117. 230p. 1990. 29.95 (0-930233-46-8, Pub. by Windsor) Natl Bk Netwk.

Angell, George. How to Triple Your Money Every Year with Stock Index Futures. 1984. 39.95 (0-930233-03-4) Windsor.

— Real-Time Proven Commodity Spreads. 1985. 72.00 (0-930233-02-6) Windsor.

— Sure-Thing Options Trading: A Money-Making Guide to the New Listed Stock & Commodity Options Markets. LC 84-6812. 288p. 1984. pap. 13.95 (0-452-26110-4, Plume) Dutton Plume.

— Winning in the Futures Markets: A Money Making Guide to Trading, Hedging & Speculating. 2nd rev. ed. 300p. 1990. per. 21.95 (1-55738-146-1, Irwn Prfssnl) McGraw-Hill Prof.

Angell, George W. & Kelley, Edward P., Jr. Handbook of Faculty Bargaining: Asserting Administrative Leadership for Institutional Progress by Preparing for Bargaining, Negotiating & Administering Contracts, & Improving the Bargaining Process. LC 76-50713. (Jossey-Bass Higher Education Ser.). 623p. reprint ed. 193.20 (0-8357-9324-9, 201723500006) Bks Demand.

Angell, Harold M. Provincial Party Financing in Quebec. LC 95-39227. 124p. 1995. lib. bdg. 29.00 (0-7618-0156-1) U Pr of Amer.

Angell, Ian O. Computer Geometric Art. (Design Library). 48p. 1985. pap. 4.95 (0-486-24855-0) Dover.

***Angell, Ian O.** The New Barbarian Manifesto: How to Survive the Information Age. 2000. 24.95 (0-7494-3151-2) Kogan Page Ltd.

Angell, Ian O. & Griffith, Gareth H. High Resolution Graphics Using FORTRAN 77. LC 86-26668. 355p. 1987. pap. text 55.95 (0-470-20773-6) Halsted Pr.

A

Angell, Israel. Diary of Colonel Israel Angell Commanding the Second Rhode Island Continental Regiment During the American Revolution, 1778-1781. Field, Edward, ed. LC 70-140852. (Eyewitness Accounts of the American Revolution Ser.). 1971. reprint ed. 16.95 (*0-405-01189-X*) Ayer.

Angell, J. R., et al. Darwinism, 4. LC 77-72191. (Contributions to the History of Psychology Ser.: Vol. IV, Pt. D, Comparative Psychology). 424p. 1977. lib. bdg. 79.50 (*0-313-26948-3*, U6948) Greenwood.

Angell, James B. The Reminiscences of James Burrill Angell. LC 79-152970. (Select Bibliographies Reprint Ser.). 1977. reprint ed. 20.95 (*0-8369-5722-9*) Ayer.

— The Reminiscences of James Burrill Angell. (American Biography Ser.). 258p. 1991. reprint ed. lib. bdg. 69.00 (*0-7812-8012-5*) Rprt Serv.

Angell, James R. American Education. LC 72-106403. (Essay Index Reprint Ser.). 1977. 26.95 (*0-8369-1440-6*) Ayer.

— Psychology: An Introductory Study of the Structure & Function of Human Consciousness. 4th ed. LC 73-2957. (Classics in Psychology Ser.). 1979. reprint ed. 36.95 (*0-405-05131-X*) Ayer.

Angell, James W. The Behavior of Money: Exploratory Studies. LC 75-85140. (Reprints of Economic Classics Ser.). xiv, 207p. 1969. reprint ed. 35.00 (*0-678-00525-7*) Kelley.

— O Susan! Looking Forward with Hope after the Death of a Child. rev. ed. LC 90-4699. 114p. 1990. reprint ed. pap. 9.95 (*0-932727-39-5*) Hope Pub Hse.

— O Susan! Looking Forward with Hope after the Death of a Child. 2nd rev. ed. LC 90-4699. 114p. 1990. reprint ed. lib. bdg. 15.95 (*0-932727-40-9*) Hope Pub Hse.

— The Romance of Preaching. LC 95-13429. 1995. 7.95 (*0-7880-0574-X*) CSS OH.

— The Theory of International Prices: History, Criticism & Restatement. LC 65-19644. (Reprints of Economic Classics Ser.). xiv, 571p. 1965. reprint ed. 57.50 (*0-678-00094-8*) Kelley.

Angell, Jeannette L. All Ground Is Holy: A Guide to the Christian Retreat. LC 92-35258. 88p. (Orig.). 1993. pap. 7.95 (*0-8192-1597-X*) Morehouse Pub.

***Angell, Joseph K.** Law of Watercourses. 7th ed. (Law Classic Ser.). 424p. 2000. pap. 34.95 (*1-893122-92-1*); pap. 34.95 (*1-893122-93-X*) Beard Bks.

Angell, Joseph K. A Treatise on the Law of Carriers of Goods & Passengers, by Land & by Water. LC 72-37694. (American Law: The Formative Years). 796p. 1972. reprint ed. 50.95 (*0-405-03991-3*) Ayer.

— A Treatise on the Law of Fire & Life Insurance. LC 76-37965. (American Law: The Formative Years). 600p. 1972. reprint ed. 39.95 (*0-405-03992-1*) Ayer.

— Treatise on the Right of Property in Tide Waters & in the Soil & Shores Thereof. 256p. 1983. reprint ed. 42.50 (*0-8377-0214-3*, Rothman) W S Hein.

Angell, Joseph K. & Ames, Samuel. A Treatise on the Law of Private Corporations, Aggregate. LC 70-37966. (American Law: The Formative Years). 600p. 1972. reprint ed. 39.95 (*0-405-03993-X*) Ayer.

***Angell, Joseph K. & Ames, Samuel.** A Treatise on the Law of Private Corporations Aggregate. 3rd ed. lv, 795p. 1999. reprint ed. 215.00 (*1-56169-563-7*) Gaunt.

Angell, Judie. The Adventures of Shirley Holmes: The Case of the Blazing Star & the Case of the King of Hearts. LC 98-36113. (Adventures of Shirley Holmes Ser.). (J). 1999. pap. 3.99 (*0-440-41503-9*) BDD Bks Young Read.

— The Buffalo Nickel Blues Band. LC 91-3793. 192p. (J). (gr. 3-7). 1991. reprint ed. pap. 3.95 (*0-689-71448-3*) Aladdin.

Angell, Judie. Ronnie & Rosey. 223p. (YA). (gr. 7 up). pap. 3.95 (*0-8072-1377-2*) Listening Lib.

Angell, M. Cathy. My Spirit Flies: Portraits & Prose of Women in Their Power. LC 96-95260. (Illus.). 96p. (Orig.). 1997. pap. 19.95 (*0-9655459-3-8*) Bay City Pr.

Angell, Madeline. A Field Guide to Berries & Berrylike Fruits. LC 80-2730. 1981. pap. 6.95 (*0-672-52695-6*) Macmillan.

Angell, Marcia. Science on Trial: The Clash of Medical Evidence & the Law in the Breast Implant Case. 288p. 1996. 27.50 (*0-393-03973-0*) Norton.

— Science on Trial: The Clash of Medical Evidence & the Law in the Breast Implant Case. LC 98-113190. 256p. 1997. pap. 13.95 (*0-393-31672-6*) Norton.

Angell, Marcia, jt. ed. see Kassirer, Jerome P.

Angell, Norman. The Great Illusion, 1933. LC 72-4264. (World Affairs Ser.: National & International Viewpoints). 316p. 1972. reprint ed. 23.95 (*0-405-04599-9*) Ayer.

Angell, Richard B. Reasoning & Logic. LC 63-16209. (Century Philosophy Ser.). (Illus.). 1964. 42.50 (*0-89197-375-3*) Irvington.

Angell, Robert. Getting into Films & Television: How to Find the Best Way In. 4th ed. (Jobs & Careers Ser.). 174p. 1997. pap. 19.95 (*1-85703-370-1*, Pub. by How To Bks) Trans-Atl Phila.

***Angell, Robert.** Getting into Films & Television: How to Spot the Opportunities & Find the Best Way In. 6th ed. (Jobs & Careers Ser.). (Illus.). 168p. 2000. pap. 14.95 (*1-85703-545-3*, Pub. by How To Bks) Midpt Trade.

Angell, Robert C. The Campus: A Study of Contemporary Undergraduate Life in the American University. Zuckerman, Harriet & Merton, Robert K., eds. LC 79-8970. (Dissertations on Sociology Ser.). 1980. reprint ed. lib. bdg. 26.95 (*0-405-12947-5*) Ayer.

— The Family Encounters the Depression. 1936. 16.50 (*0-8446-1030-5*) Peter Smith.

— The Social Integration of American Cities of More Than 100,000 Population. (Reprint Series in Social Sciences). (C). 1993. reprint ed. pap. text 5.00 (*0-8290-2810-2*, S-3) Irvington.

Angell, Robert H. A Compilation & Analysis of the 1998 Texas Constitution & the Original 1876 Text. LC 98-22975. (Studies in American History). v, 251 p. 1998. write for info. (*0-88946-099-X*) E Mellen.

Angell, Robert H., ed. A Compilation & Analysis of the 1998 Texas Constitution & the Original 1876 Text. LC 98-22975. (Studies in American History: Vol. 23). 268p. 1998. pap. 89.95 (*0-7734-8341-1*) E Mellen.

Angell, Roger. Nothing But You. LC 98-12965. 1998. pap. 15.00 (*0-375-75150-5*) Modern Lib NY.

— Stone Arbor & Other Stories. LC 79-121519. (Short Story Index Reprint Ser.). 1977. 20.95 (*0-8369-3475-X*) Ayer.

Angell, Stephen W. Bishop Henry McNeal Turner & African-American Religion in the South. LC 91-21032. (Illus.). 352p. (C). 1992. text 37.00 (*0-87049-734-0*) U of Tenn Pr.

***Angell, Stephen W. & Pinn, Anthony B., eds.** Social Protest Thought in the African Methodist Episcopal Church, 1863-1939. LC 99-6912. 392p. 2000. 50.00 (*1-57233-065-1*, Pub. by U of Tenn Pr); pap. 22.50 (*1-57233-066-X*, Pub. by U of Tenn Pr) U Ch Pr.

***Angelli, Chris, ed.** Let's Go Shopping! (J). 2000. pap. 2.99 (*0-375-80493-5*, Pub. by Random Bks Yng Read) Random.

Angelo. Introduction to Lunar Frontier. (Orbit Ser.). Date not set. write for info. (*0-89464-058-5*) Krieger.

Angelo, Anthony H., tr. see Noda, Yosiyuki, ed.

Angelo, Bonnie. First Mothers: The Women Who Shaped the Presidents. (Illus.). 464p. 2000. 27.00 (*0-688-15631-2*, Wm Morrow) Morrow Avon.

***Angelo, Eli & Bain, Joseph H.** Odysseus 2000/2001: The International Gay Travel Planner. 15th rev. ed. (Illus.). 730p. 1999. pap. 29.00 (*1-881536-05-X*, Pub. by Odysseus Ent) PDC-LPI.

Angelo, Frank. On Guard, a History of the Detroit Free Press. LC 81-1719. vi, 279 p. 1981. write for info. (*0-9605692-0-0*) Detroit Pr.

Angelo, Frank, jt. auth. see Meyers, Melanie.

Angelo, Henry. The Reminiscences of Henry Angelo. 2 vols. LC 77-81198. (Illus.). 1972. 60.95 (*0-405-08207-X*) Ayer.

— The Reminiscences of Henry Angelo, Vol. 1. 1972. 30.95 (*0-405-19035-2*) Ayer.

— The Reminiscences of Henry Angelo, Vol. 2. 1972. 30.95 (*0-405-18118-3*) Ayer.

Angelo, Ivan. The Tower of Glass. Watson, Ellen, tr. 1986. mass mkt. 3.95 (*0-380-89607-9*, Avon Bks) Morrow Avon.

Angelo, J. Champagne Syster. mass mkt. 6.95 (*0-7472-4771-4*, Pub. by Headline Bk Pub) Trafalgar.

Angelo, Jack. Hands-On Healing: A Practical Guide to Channeling Your Healing Energy. LC 97-1080. (Illus.). 256p. 1997. pap. 16.95 (*0-89281-734-8*) Inner Tradit.

— Spiritual Healing: Energy Medicine for Health & Well-Being. (Health Essentials Ser.). (Illus.). 128p. 1993. pap. 9.95 (*1-85230-219-4*, Pub. by Element MA) Penguin Putnam.

***Angelo, Jack.** Your Healing Power. 1998. pap. 14.95 (*0-7499-1906-X*, Pub. by Piatkus Bks) London Brdge.

Angelo, Jack. Your Healing Power: A Comprehensive Guide to Channelling Your Healing Energies. 256p. 1996. pap. 14.95 (*0-7499-1326-6*, Pub. by Piatkus Bks) London Brdge.

Angelo, Jennifer, et al. Assistive Technology for Rehabilitation Therapists. LC 96-19181. (Illus.). 254p. (C). 1996. pap. text 23.95 (*0-8036-0136-0*) Davis Co.

***Angelo, Joseph.** Space Technology. (Modern Technology Ser.). 424p. 2001. text 65.00 (*1-57356-335-8*) Oryx Pr.

Angelo, Joseph A. The Dictionary of Space Technology. LC 98-16419. (Illus.). 480p. 1998. 50.00 (*0-8160-3073-1*) Facts on File.

Angelo, Joseph A., Jr. & Buden, David. Space Nuclear Power. LC 84-16701. 304p. 1985. 72.50 (*0-89464-000-3*) Krieger.

Angelo, Joseph A., Jr., jt. ed. see Ginsberg, Irving W.

Angelo, Mark V. History of Saint Bonaventure University. (History Ser.). x, 251p. 1961. pap. 6.00 (*1-57659-080-1*) Franciscan Inst.

***Angelo, Michael.** Callgirls. deluxe ed. (Sexual Truths Ser.). 352p. 1998. pap. 8.99 (*0-9677874-0-8*) BlackJack Bks.

Angelo, Michael. The Sikh Diaspora: Tradition & Change in an Immigrant Community. rev. ed. Ng, Franklin, ed. LC 97-33627. (Asian Americans). (Illus.). 266p. 1997. text 65.00 (*0-8153-2985-7*) Garland.

Angelo, Rocco M. & Vladimir, Andrew M. Hospitality Today: An Introduction. 3rd rev. ed. LC 98-17570. (Illus.). 520p. (C). 1998. pap. write for info. (*0-86612-171-4*) Educ Inst Am Hotel.

— An Introduction to Hospitality Today: An Introduction. 3rd rev. ed. LC 98-17570. (Illus.). 500p. (C). 1998. pap. 61.95 (*0-86612-172-2*) Educ Inst Am Hotel.

Angelo, Sandra. Colored Pencil Drawing. LC 94-220548. (How to Draw & Paint Ser.). (Illus.). 32p. (Orig.). 1994. pap. 6.95 (*1-56010-142-3*, HT243) W Foster Pub.

— So You Thought You Couldn't Draw: Drawing Basics. (Illus.). 160p. (YA). (gr. 9-12). 1994. pap. 22.95 (*1-887882-32-4*) Discover Art.

Angelo, Sandra M. Exploring Colored Pencil. (Illus.). 160p. 1999. 25.95 (*0-87192-315-7*) Davis Mass.

***Angelo, Sharon P., et al.** Quilts: The Fabric of Friendship. LC 00-9620. 2000. pap. write for info. (*0-7643-1195-6*) Schiffer.

Angelo, Thomas A., ed. Classroom Research: Early Lessons from Success. LC 85-644763. (New Directions for Teaching & Learning Ser.: No. TL46). 1991. pap. 19.00 (*1-55542-800-2*) Jossey-Bass.

Angelo, Thomas A. & Cross, K. Patricia. Classroom Assessment Techniques: A Handbook for College Teachers. 2nd ed. LC 92-33901. (Higher & Adult Education Ser.). 448p. 1993. pap. 37.95 (*1-55542-500-3*) Jossey-Bass.

Angelo, Valenti. Golden Gate. LC 74-17918. (Italian American Experience Ser.). (Illus.). 278p. 1975. reprint ed. 19.95 (*0-405-06391-1*) Ayer.

Angeloni. Anthropology 1999-2000 Edition. 22nd ed. 1999. pap., student ed. 16.56 (*0-07-040097-0*) McGraw.

— Anthropology 1996/97. 19th annot. ed. 1996. teacher ed. 13.12 (*0-697-31509-6*, WCB McGr Hill) McGrw-H Hghr Educ.

— Anthropology 94 & 95. 17th ed. 1994. 12.74 (*1-56134-265-3*) McGraw.

— Physical Anthropology. 3rd ed. 1994. text 12.74 (*1-56134-285-8*) McGraw.

— Physical Anthropology. 4th ed. 1995. 12.74 (*1-56134-367-6*) McGraw.

— Physical Anthropology: 1999-2000 Edition. 8th ed. 1999. pap., student ed. 16.56 (*0-07-040107-1*) McGraw.

— Physical Anthropology 1996/97. 5th annot. ed. 1996. teacher ed. 13.12 (*0-697-31528-2*, WCB McGr Hill) McGrw-H Hghr Educ.

Angeloni, Elvio. Annual Editions: Anthropology, 97-98. 20th ed. 256p. (C). 1997. text. write for info. (*0-697-37201-4*) Brown & Benchmark.

— Annual Editions: Physical Anthropology, 97-98. 6th ed. 256p. (C). 1997. text. write for info. (*0-697-37341-X*, WCB McGr Hill) McGrw-H Hghr Educ.

— Anthropology: 1996-1997. annuals 19th ed. 256p. (C). 1996. text. write for info. (*0-697-31508-8*) Brown & Benchmark.

***Angeloni, Elvio.** Anthropology 2000-2001. 23rd ed. (Annual Editions Ser.). 240p. (J). 1999. pap. 16.56 (*0-07-236410-6*) McGrw-H Hghr Educ.

— Physical Anthropolgy 2000-2001. 9th ed. (Annual Editions Ser.). 240p. (C). 1999. pap. 16.56 (*0-07-236398-3*) McGrw-H Hghr Educ.

Angeloni, Elvio. Physical Anthropology, 1996-1997. annuals 5th ed. 256p. (C). 1996. text. write for info. (*0-697-31527-4*) Brown & Benchmark.

— Physical Anthropology, 98-99. 7th ed. (Annual Ser.). (Illus.). 240p. 1998. pap. text 12.25 (*0-697-39174-4*, Dshkn McG-Hill) McGrw-H Hghr Educ.

Angeloni, Elvio, ed. Annual Editions: Anthropology, 95-96. 18th rev. ed. (Illus.). 256p. (C). 1995. text 12.95 (*1-56134-346-3*, Dshkn McG-Hill) McGrw-H Hghr Educ.

— Anthropology, '98/'99. 21st ed. (Annual Ser.). (Illus.). 240p. 1998. pap. text 12.25 (*0-697-39124-8*, Dshkn McG-Hill) McGrw-H Hghr Educ.

Angeloni, Elvio, jt. auth. see Crapo, Richley.

Angeloni, Ignazio & Roovelli, Riccardo, eds. Monetary Policy & Interest Rates: Proceedings of a Conference Sponsored by Banced' Italia Centro Paolo Baffi & the Innocenzo Gasparini Institute for Economic Research (IGIER) LC 98-7081. 304p. 1998. text 79.95 (*0-312-21672-6*) St Martin.

Angeloni, Ignazio & Rovelli, Riccardo. Monetary Policy & Interest Rates: Proceedings of a Conference Sponsored by Banca D'Italia, Centro Paolo Baffi & the Innocenzo Gasparini Institute for Economic Research (IGIER) LC 98-7081. xi, 295 p. 1998. write for info. (*0-333-71647-7*, Pub. by Macmillan) St Martin.

***Angeloni, Umberto.** The Boutonniere: Style in One's Lapel. (Illus.). 96p. 2000. 25.00 (*0-7893-0388-4*, Pub. by Universe) St Martin.

Angelopoulos, Angelos. A Global Plan for Employment: A New Marshall Plan. 234p. 1983. 59.95 (*0-275-90936-0*, C0936, Praeger Pubs) Greenwood.

— The Third World & the Rich Countries: Prospects for the Year 2000. LC 72-75694. (Special Studies in International Economics & Development). 1972. text 49.50 (*0-275-28608-8*) Irvington.

Angelopoulos, Angelos & Fagen, Melvin. The Third World & the Rich Countries: Proposals to Combat the Global Economic Crisis. 158p. (C). 1993. pap. text 23.50 (*0-8191-9256-2*); lib. bdg. 48.00 (*0-8191-9240-6*) U Pr of Amer.

Angelopoulos, Angelos T. Defending Democracy: The Contribution of Greece During the Second World War. Davis, John, tr. from GRE. LC 94-74897.Tr. of From Occupation to Civil War. 232p. (Orig.). 1995. pap. text 14.00 (*0-918618-63-0*) Pella Pub.

Angelopoulos, V. & Panetta, P. V., eds. Science Closure & Enabling Technologies for Construction Class Missions. (Illus.). 151p. 1998. pap. text 10.00 (*0-9670138-0-1*) Space Sci Lab.

Angelosanto, Paul. Vampire Gangster Debutantes. (Illus.). 44p. 1998. pap. 6.00 (*1-892609-04-5*) Gracie Pub.

Angelou, Maya. All God's Children Need Traveling Shoes. 224p. 1997. 20.00 (*0-679-45774-7*) Random.

— All God's Children Need Traveling Shoes. 1987. 15.10 (*0-606-00334-7*, Pub. by Turtleback) Demco.

— All God's Children Need Traveling Shoes. LC 90-55700. 224p. 1991. pap. 10.00 (*0-679-73404-X*) Vin Bks.

— And Still I Rise. 64p. 1978. 13.00 (*0-394-50252-3*) Random.

— A Brave & Startling Truth. LC 95-32710. 32p. 1995. 10.00 (*0-679-44904-3*) Random.

— The Complete Collected Poems of Maya Angelou. LC 94-14501. 273p. (YA). (gr. 8-12). 1994. 24.00 (*0-679-42895-X*) Random.

— Even the Stars Look Lonesome. large type ed. LC 97-17317. 128p. 1997. 18.00 (*0-375-50031-6*); pap. 18.00 (*0-679-77441-6*) Random.

— Even the Stars Look Lonesome. 148p. 1998. reprint ed. pap. 10.00 (*0-553-37972-0*) Bantam.

Angelou, Maya. Gather Together in My Name. 192p. (YA). (gr. 9 up). 1985. mass mkt. 5.50 (*0-553-26066-9*) Bantam.

Angelou, Maya. Gather Together in My Name. 224p. 1997. pap. 12.00 (*0-553-37997-6*) Bantam.

— Gather Together in My Name. 224p. (YA). 1974. 20.00 (*0-394-48692-7*) Random.

— Gather Together in My Name. 1975. 10.60 (*0-606-03386-6*, Pub. by Turtleback) Demco.

— The Heart of a Woman. LC 00-2621. 272p. 1984. pap. 5.99 (*0-553-24689-5*) Bantam.

— The Heart of a Woman. 1997. 20.00 (*0-375-50072-3*); 20.00 (*0-676-53381-7*) Random.

— Heart of a Woman. 1981. 10.60 (*0-606-03806-X*, Pub. by Turtleback) Demco.

— The Heart of a Woman. large type ed. LC 97-37562. 1997. 26.95 (*1-56895-501-4*) Wheeler Pub.

— The Heart of a Woman, Vol. 4. 336p. 1997. pap. 12.00 (*0-553-38009-5*) Bantam.

— Heart of A Woman: A Flowering Career, A Growing Son, A Powerful Personal Narrative. 288p. 1997. 20.00 (*0-679-50072-3*) Random.

— The Heart of a Woman, on the Pulse. 1997. 20.00 (*0-676-53405-8*) Random.

— I Know Why the Caged Bird Sings. 304p. 1983. mass mkt. 5.50 (*0-553-27937-8*, Bantam Classics) Bantam.

— I Know Why the Caged Bird Sings. 256p. 1983. mass mkt. 5.50 (*0-553-85170-5*) Bantam.

— I Know Why the Caged Bird Sings. 1994. mass mkt. 6.99 (*0-553-54169-2*) Bantam.

— I Know Why the Caged Bird Sings. 304p. 1997. pap. 12.00 (*0-553-38001-X*) Bantam.

— I Know Why the Caged Bird Sings. Bloom, Harold, ed. LC 97-53105. (Modern Critical Interpretations Ser.). 176p. (YA). 1999. lib. bdg. 34.95 (*0-7910-4773-3*) Chelsea Hse.

— I Know Why the Caged Bird Sings. 288p. (YA). 1970. 20.00 (*0-394-42986-9*) Random.

— I Know Why the Caged Bird Sings. 1969. 10.60 (*0-606-03574-5*, Pub. by Turtleback) Demco.

— I Know Why the Caged Bird Sings; Gather Together in My Name; Singin' & Swingin' 1998. pap. 48.00 (*0-553-94104-6*) Bantam.

— I Shall Not Be Moved. LC 91-17341. 64p. 1991. pap. 9.95 (*0-553-35458-2*) Bantam.

— I Shall Not Be Moved. 64p. 1997. 15.95 (*0-679-45708-9*) Random.

— I Shall Not Be Moved. 1991. 15.15 (*0-606-01310-5*, Pub. by Turtleback) Demco.

— Just Give Me a Cool Drink of Water 'Fore I Die. large type ed. 64p. 1997. 15.00 (*0-679-45709-7*) Random.

— Kofi & His Magic. 48p. (J). (gr. 1-5). 1996. 17.00 (*0-517-70453-6*) C Potter.

— Maya Angelou: Poems. 1986. 10.60 (*0-606-03854-X*, Pub. by Turtleback) Demco.

— Maya Angelou's I Know Why the Caged Bird Sings. Bloom, Harold, ed. & intro. by. 1997. pap. text 4.95 (*0-7910-4129-8*) Chelsea Hse.

— My Painted House, My Friendly Chicken & Me. LC 93-45735. (Illus.). 48p. (J). (ps-5). 1994. 16.00 (*0-517-59667-9*) C Potter.

— My Painted House, My Friendly Chicken & Me. 48p. 1996. pap. 6.99 (*0-517-88815-7*) C Potter.

— My Painted House, My Friendly Chicken & Me. (J). 1994. 12.19 (*0-606-10885-8*, Pub. by Turtleback) Demco.

— Now Sheba Sings the Song. (Illus.). 56p. 1994. pap. 13.95 (*0-452-27143-6*, Plume) Dutton Plume.

— Oh Pray My Wings Are Gonna Fit Me Well. LC 75-10268. 80p. 1997. 15.00 (*0-679-45707-0*) Random.

— On the Pulse of Morning. LC 93-83496. 32p. 1993. pap. 6.00 (*0-679-74838-5*) Random.

— Phenomenal Woman. LC 94-27042. 32p. 1995. 10.00 (*0-679-43924-2*) Random.

***Angelou, Maya.** Phenomenal Woman. LC 99-39134. 2000. 19.95 (*0-375-50406-0*) Random.

Angelou, Maya. Poems. 224p. 1986. mass mkt. 5.50 (*0-553-85173-X*) Bantam.

— Poems. large type ed. 224p. 1997. pap. 12.00 (*0-553-37985-2*) Bantam.

— Poems: Just Give Me a Cool Drink of Water 'Fore I Diie/Oh Pray My Wings Are Gonna Fit Me Well & Still I Rise/ Shaker, Why Don't You Sin. large type ed. 224p. 1996. mass mkt. 5.99 (*0-553-25576-2*) Bantam.

— Quartet of Stories. 1993. pap. text. write for info. (*0-582-08298-6*, Pub. by Addison-Wesley) Longman.

— Selected from I Know Why the Caged Bird Sings & The Heart of a Woman. abr. ed. (Writers' Voices Ser.). (Illus.). 64p. 1989. pap. text 3.95 (*0-929631-04-8*, Signal Hill) New Readers.

Angelou, Maya. Singin' & Swingin' & Gettin' Merry Like Christmas. LC 00-3028. 256p. (gr. 8-12). 1985. mass mkt. 5.50 (*0-553-25199-6*) Bantam.

Angelou, Maya. Singin' & Swingin' & Gettin' Merry Like Christmas. 256p. 1985. mass mkt. 5.50 (*0-553-85179-9*) Bantam.

— Singin' & Swingin' & Gettin' Merry Like Christmas. 304p. 1997. pap. 12.00 (*0-553-38005-2*) Bantam.

— Singin' & Swingin' & Gettin' Merry Like Christmas. 288p. 1997. 20.00 (*0-679-45777-1*) Random.

Angelou, Maya. Singin' & Swingin' & Gettin' Merry Like Christmas. 1977. 10.60 (*0-606-01220-6*, Pub. by Turtleback) Demco.

Angelou, Maya. Voyage of the Amistad. 96p. 1999. 14.95 (*0-525-94411-7*) NAL.

Angelou, Maya. Wouldn't Take Nothing for My Journey Now. 160p. 1994. mass mkt. 5.99 (*0-553-56907-4*) Bantam.

— Wouldn't Take Nothing for My Journey Now. 160p. 1994. mass mkt. 5.50 (*0-553-85176-4*) Bantam.

— Wouldn't Take Nothing for My Journey Now. 144p. 1997. pap. 10.00 (*0-553-38017-6*) Bantam.

Angelou, Maya. Wouldn't Take Nothing for My Journey Now. LC 93-5904. 141p. 1993. 17.00 (*0-679-42743-0*) Random.

— Wouldn't Take Nothing for My Journey Now. 1993. 15.00 (*0-394-22363-2*) Random.

An Asterisk (*) at the beginning of an entry indicates that the title is appearing for the first time.

Angelou, Maya. Wouldn't Take Nothing for My Journey Now. 1994. 10.60 (*0-606-07145-8*, Pub. by Turtleback) Demco.

Angelou, Maya, jt. auth. see Braxton, Joanne M.

***Angelov, D. N., et al.** The Cerebral Perivascular Cells. Beck, F. et al, eds. LC 98-25894. (Advances in Anatomy, Embryology & Cell Biology Ser.: Vol. 147). (Illus.). xi, 90p. 1998. pap. 69.95 (*3-540-64638-8*) Spr-Verlag.

Angels of Easter Seal, Youngstown, Ohio Staff. Angels & Friends Favorite Recipes. (Illus.). 436p. 1981. 9.50 (*0-9613501-0-5*) Angels Easter.

***Angelsen, A. & Kaimowitz, D., eds.** Agricultural Technologies & Tropical Deforestation. (CABI Publishing Ser.). (Illus.). 384p. 2000. pap. text 49.95 (*0-85199-451-2*) OUP.

Angelsen, Jan E., ed. see Nautilus Publishing, Inc. Staff.

Angelsey, Zoe, ed. Listen Up! Spoken Word Poetry. LC PS615.L47 1999. 192p. 1999. pap. 12.50 (*0-345-42897-8*) Ballantine Pub Grp.

Angelsky, Oleg V., ed. International Conference on Correlation Optics, Vol. 3317. LC 98-122015. 446p. 1997. 89.00 (*0-8194-2757-8*) SPIE.

Angelson, B. The Living Dreamer: The Art of Doing It. Lindahl, Carol, ed. LC 96-78124. (Illus.). 184p. (Orig.). 1996. pap. 17.95 (*0-9651590-3-5*) Infnty Pub.

Angelucci, Eliseo. Entretenimientos Biblicos, No. 1. (SPA.). 32p. 1992. pap. 2.99 (*0-8254-1026-6*, Edit Portavoz) Kregel.

— Entretenimientos Biblicos, No. 2. (SPA.). 32p. 1992. pap. 2.99 (*0-8254-1027-4*, Edit Portavoz) Kregel.

— Entretenimientos Biblicos, No. 3. (SPA.). 32p. 1992. pap. 2.99 (*0-8254-1028-2*, Edit Portavoz) Kregel.

— Entretenimientos Biblicos, Vol. 4. (SPA.). 32p. 1996. pap. 2.99 (*0-8254-1029-0*, Edit Portavoz) Kregel.

— Entretenimientos Biblicos (Biblical Entertainment), Vol. 5. (SPA.). 32p. 1998. pap. 2.99 (*0-8254-1030-4*, Edit Portavoz) Kregel.

— Entretenimientos Biblicos (Biblical Entertainment), Vol. 6. (SPA.). 32p. 1998. pap. 2.99 (*0-8254-1031-2*, Edit Portavoz) Kregel.

Angelucci, Enzo. Les Avions Vol. 3: Seconde Guerre Mondiale, France, Allemand, Angleterre. (FRE.). 320p. 1978. text 39.95 (*0-7859-7160-2*) Fr & Eur.

— Les Avions Vol. 4: Seconde Guerre Mondiale, U. S. A., Japan, U. S. S. R. (FRE.). 320p. 1978. 39.95 (*0-7859-7161-0*, 2040125450) Fr & Eur.

— Les Avions Vol. 5: Ere des Engines a Reaction. (FRE.). 318p. 1979. 39.95 (*0-7859-7162-9*, 2040125493) Fr & Eur.

— Les Avions Vol. 6: Aviation Commerciale 1935 a 1960. (FRE.). 318p. 1981. 39.95 (*0-7859-7163-7*, 204012781X) Fr & Eur.

— Les Avions, l'Entres Deux Guerres, Vol. 2. (FRE.). 1978. 65.00 (*0-7859-3946-6*) Fr & Eur.

— Encyclopedie des Avions. (FRE.). 280p. 1978. 49.95 (*0-7859-4804-X*, M6004) Fr & Eur.

Angelucci, Enzo & Cucari, Attilio. Encyclopedie des Navires. (FRE & ITA.). 366p. 69.95 (*0-7859-0387-9*, M6005) Fr & Eur.

Angelus Press Editors, contrib. by. Determining the Future: 1941-1969. LC 98-124513. (Puritans' Progress Ser.: Vol. 5). 139p. 1997. pap. 7.95 (*0-935952-40-3*) Angelus Pr.

— Europe Crosses the Water: 1607-1770. LC 98-124513. (Puritan's Progress Ser.: Vol. 1). 145p. 1996. pap. 7.95 (*0-935952-36-5*) Angelus Pr.

— Revolution for Export, 1849-1921. LC 98-124513. (Puritans' Progress Ser.: Vol. 3). 155p. 1996. pap. 7.95 (*0-935952-38-1*) Angelus Pr.

Angelus Press Editors, ed. The End of the Beginning: 1922-1941. LC 98-124513. (Puritans' Progress Ser.: Vol. 4). 121p. 1997. pap. 7.95 (*0-935952-39-X*) Angelus Pr.

— A New Constellation, 1771-1848. LC 98-124513. (Puritans' Progress Ser.: Vol. 2). 201p. 1996. pap. 7.95 (*0-935952-35-7*) Angelus Pr.

Angelus Press Editors, ed. see Lefebvre, Marcel.

Angelus Press Editors, ed. see Quardt, Robert.

Angelus Press Editors, ed. see Robinson, Carol, et al.

Angelus, Suzann M. Chronic Fatigue Syndrome, AIDS, & Immune Dysfunction Disease: The Cause & the Cure. (Illus.). 240p. (Orig.). 1994. pap. 15.95 (*0-9640559-9-6*) Symbolic Prods.

Angenault. French Chemical Encyclopedic Dictionary. 2nd ed. Orig. Title: La Chimi Dictionnaire Encyclopedique. (FRE.). 1995. 112.50 (*2-10-002497-3*, Pub. by Dunod) IBD Ltd.

Angenault, Jacques. La Chimie: Dictionnaire Encyclopedique. 2nd ed. (FRE.). 390p. 1995. 195.00 (*0-7859-9947-7*) Fr & Eur.

— La Chimie Dictionnaire Encyclopedique. (FRE.). 450p. 1991. 135.00 (*0-7859-7711-2*, 2040198288) Fr & Eur.

Anger, et al. On Your Way. 1987. pap. text, teacher ed. 18.95 (*0-582-99875-1*, 75299) Longman.

— On Your Way (Level One) Building Basic Skills in English. (Illus.). 1987. teacher ed. 18.95 (*0-8013-0126-2*, 75790) Longman.

— On Your Way (Level Three) Building Basic Skills in English. 1987. audio 46.95 (*0-582-99878-6*, 75302) Longman.

— On Your Way (Level Two) Building Basic Skills in English. 1987. audio 46.95 (*0-582-99876-X*, 75300) Longman.

— On Your Way WB 2. 1987. pap. text, student ed. 4.87 (*0-582-90758-6*, 75262) Longman.

Anger, B. & Portenier, C. Radon Integrals: An Abstract Approach to Integration & Riesz Representation Through Function Cones. (Progress in Mathematics Ser.: Vol. 103). x, 326p. 1991. 84.00 (*0-8176-3630-7*) Birkhauser.

Anger Clinic Staff & Messer, Mitchell. Managing Anger: A Handbook of Proven Techniques. 320p. 1994. pap. text, per. 18.95 (*0-8403-9372-5*) Kendall-Hunt.

Anger, Dorothy. Other Worlds: Society Seen Through Soap Opera. LC 99-209467. 216p. 1999. pap. 16.95 (*1-55111-103-9*) Broadview Pr.

Anger, Frank D., ed. Industrial & Engineering Applications of Artificial Intelligence & Expert Systems. 696p. 1994. pap. text 128.00 (*2-88449-128-7*) Gordon & Breach.

— Spatial & Temporal Reasoning: Papers from the 1997 Workshop. (Technical Reports). (Illus.). 99p. 1998. spiral bd. 25.00 (*1-57735-044-8*) AAAI Pr.

Anger, G. Inverse Problems in Differential Equations. LC 88-43327. (Illus.). 256p. (C). 1990. text 95.00 (*0-306-43164-5*, Kluwer Plenum) Kluwer Academic.

Anger Institute Staff, jt. auth. see Messer, Mitch.

Anger, Kenneth. Hollywood Babylon. 448p. 1981. mass mkt. 7.99 (*0-440-15325-6*) Dell.

— Hollywood Babylon 2. 1999. 25.00 (*0-525-93673-4*) NAL.

— Hollywood Babylon 3. 1999. 34.95 (*0-525-93844-3*) NAL.

Anger, Per. With Raoul Wallenberg in Budapest. LC 95-289. (Illus.). 208p. 1996. reprint ed. pap. 14.95 (*0-89604-156-5*, Holocaust Library) US Holocaust.

Anger, V., jt. auth. see Feigl, F.

Anger, Y., jt. auth. see Feigl, F.

Angerbauer. Principles of DC & AC Circuits. (Electronics Technology Ser.). 1990. lab manual ed. 26.95 (*0-8273-3846-5*) Delmar.

Angerer, J. & Schaller, K. H., eds. Analyses of Hazardous Substances in Biological Materials, Vol. 2. LC 86-656024. 252p. 1988. 135.00 (*3-527-27012-4*, Wiley-VCH) Wiley.

— Analyses of Hazardous Substances in Biological Materials, Vol. 3. (Illus.). 269p. 1991. 95.00 (*3-527-27016-7*, Wiley-VCH) Wiley.

— Analyses of Hazardous Substances in Biological Materials, Vol. 4. 265p. 1994. 135.00 (*3-527-27027-2*, Wiley-VCH) Wiley.

— Analyses of Hazardous Substances in Biological Materials, Vol. 5. 280p. 1996. 135.00 (*3-527-27035-3*, Wiley-VCH) Wiley.

— Analyses of Hazardous Substances in Biological Materials, Vol. 1, Vol. 1. 2nd ed. 222p. 1992. 135.00 (*3-527-27024-8*, Wiley-VCH) Wiley.

Angerer, J., ed. see Schaller, K. H.

Angerman, Arina, et al, eds. Current Issues in Women's History. 256p. 1989. 45.00 (*0-415-00361-X*, A1696); pap. 14.95 (*0-415-00362-8*, A1700) Routledge.

Angerman, Bob. White Like She. (Illus.). 104p. 1998. pap. 12.95 (*1-56097-341-2*) Fantagraph Bks.

Angermann, H., jt. auth. see Vogel, G.

Angermeier, W. F. Evolution des Operanten Lernens. (Illus.). x, 230p. 1983. 103.50 (*3-8055-3522-8*) S Karger.

— The Evolution of Operant Learning & Memory. (Illus.). xii, 204p. 1984. text 165.25 (*3-8055-3736-0*) S Karger.

Angerpointner, T. A., ed. Operative Technique in Neonates & Infants. (Progress in Pediatric Surgery Ser.: Vol. 25). (Illus.). 150p. 1990. 124.00 (*0-387-51057-5*) Spr-Verlag.

Angerpointner, T. A., jt. ed. see Gauderer, M. W.

Angerpointner, T. A., jt. ed. see Myers, N. A.

Angerpointner, T. A., jt. ed. see Yokoyama, J.

Angers, D.A., jt. auth. see Turchenek, L. W.

Angers, JoAnn M. My Beginning Mass Book. (Illus.). 48p. (Orig.). (J). (gr. 1-4). 1978. pap. 2.95 (*0-89622-082-6*) Twenty-Third.

Angers, Marilynn M. & Angers, William P. Creating Your Own Career for Job Satisfaction. LC 82-61718. 170p. (Orig.). 1983. pap. 9.95 (*0-910793-00-X*) Marlborough Pr.

Angers, Mary. Shalom New York, 99: The Activities Guide for Young Jewish Professionals. 1998. pap. 18.00 (*0-9661659-1-8*) Shalom Ink.

Angers, Michele, jt. auth. see Kehoe, Katherine.

***Angers, Trent.** Dudley LeBlanc. 2000. pap. 9.95 (*0-925417-12-2*) Acadian Hse Pub.

— The Forgotten Hero of My Lai: The Hugh Thompson Story. LC 99-63662. (Illus.). 248p. 1999. 22.95 (*0-925417-33-5*, Pub. by Acadian Hse Pub) Forest Sales & Dist.

Angers, Trent. The Truth about the Cajuns. (Illus.). 120p. 1989. 11.95 (*0-925417-00-9*) Acadian Hse Pub.

— The Truth about the Cajuns. (Illus.). 120p. 1991. 11.95 (*0-925417-04-1*) Acadian Hse Pub.

***Angers, Trent.** Truth about the Cajuns. 2000. pap. 11.95 (*0-925417-29-7*) Acadian Hse Pub.

Angers, Trent, ed. Acadiana Profile's Cajun Cooking, Pt. 2. 192p. 1989. spiral bd. 10.00 (*0-939524-01-5*) Angers Pub.

— Acadiana Profile's Cajun Cooking, Pt. 1: From the Kitchens of South Louisiana. (Illus.). 240p. 1991. pap. 11.95 (*0-925417-03-3*) Acadian Hse Pub.

— Acadiana Profile's Cajun Cooking, Pt. 2: By the People of the Cajun Country. 193p. 1991. pap. 9.95 (*0-925417-05-X*) Acadian Hse Pub.

— Cajun Country Tour Guide & Festival Guide. (Illus.). 124p. 1991. per. 5.00 (*0-925417-07-6*) Acadian Hse Pub.

Angers, Trent, ed. The Top One-Hundred Cajun Recipes of All Time. (Illus.). 48p. (Orig.). 1995. pap. 6.95 (*0-925417-20-3*) Acadian Hse Pub.

***Angers, Trent & Backler, Martin H., eds.** The Top 50 Festivals of Cajun Country. LC 98-96818. 1999. 6.95 (*0-925417-32-7*) Acadian Hse Pub.

Angers, Trent & McDonough, Sue, eds. Acadiana Profile's Cajun Cooking, Pt. 1. (Illus.). 240p. 1988. spiral bd. 10.00 (*0-939524-02-3*) Angers Pub.

Angers, Trent, et al. The Louisiana IceGators Phenomenon. (Illus.). 56p. (Orig.). 1996. 11.95 (*0-925417-27-0*); pap. 8.95 (*0-925417-24-6*) Acadian Hse Pub.

Angers, Trent, ed. see Andelman, Bob.

Angers, Trent, ed. see Bienvenu, Marcelle.

Angers, Trent, ed. see Montagu, Ashley.

Angers, W. Thomas. Cajun Cuisine: Authentic Cajun Recipes from Louisiana's Bayou Country. McDonough, Sue, ed. (Illus.). 224p. 1985. 17.95 (*0-935619-00-3*) Beau Bayou.

Angers, William P., jt. auth. see Angers, Marilynn M.

Angerstein, Wilfried. Lexicon of Medical Radiological Engineering: Lexikon der Radiologischen Technik der Medizin. 4th ed. (GER.). 576p. 1987. 95.00 (*0-8288-1834-7*, M15430) Fr & Eur.

Anges, Aux, jt. auth. see LaTour, Pierre.

Angevine, C. D., et al, eds. The Immunochemistry & Biochemistry of Connective Tissue & Its Disease States. (Rheumatology Ser.: Vol. 3). 1970. 70.50 (*3-8055-0622-8*) S Karger.

Angevine, Erma. People--Their Power: The Rural Electric Fact Book. rev. ed. (Illus.). 196p. 1981. pap. 3.75 (*0-686-31129-9*) Natl Rural.

Angevine, Jay B., Jr. & Cotman, Carl W. Principles of Neuroanatomy. (Illus.). 393p. 1981. text 29.95 (*0-19-502885-6*) OUP.

Angevine, Jay B., Jr., jt. auth. see Nolte, John.

Anggraeni, Dewi. Journeys Through Shadows. LC 99-197401. 244p. 1998. pap. 18.95 (*0-9585805-3-2*, Pub. by Indra Pub) Intl Spec Bk.

— Parallel Forces. 197p. 1988. pap. 15.95 (*0-9587718-1-2*, Pub. by Indra Pub) Intl Spec Bk.

— The Root of All Evil. 140p. 1987. pap. 14.95 (*0-9587718-0-4*, Pub. by Indra Pub) Intl Spec Bk.

— Stories of Indian Pacific. 265p. 1992. pap. 14.95 (*0-9587718-3-9*, Pub. by Indra Pub) Intl Spec Bk.

Angha, Ghotbeddin-Mohammad. Ershad Nameh: Mirror of Self. 114p. (Orig.). 1988. 46.00 (*0-910735-30-1*); pap. 22.00 (*0-910735-29-8*) McGraw.

Angha, Hazrat M. Destination Eternity: Az Janin Ta Janan. 2nd ed. Swan, Jim, ed. Angha, Nahid, tr. from PER. (Sufism Ser.). Orig. Title: Az - Janin Ta-Janan. (Illus.). 185p. (Orig.). 1988. pap. 15.50 (*0-918437-02-4*) Intl Sufism.

Angha, Jalaleddin-Ali M. Anvare Gholoube Salekin: The Enlightened Hearts. (PER.). 456p. 1978. 110.00 (*0-910735-14-X*) MTO Printing & Pubn Ctr.

— Esharat-ol Hosseinieh. LC 86-62209. (PER.). 167p. 1986. 110.00 (*0-910735-05-0*) MTO Printing & Pubn Ctr.

— Ghoncheh Baz: Blossom of the Garden of Secret. (PER., Illus.). 108p. (Orig.). 1984. 110.00 (*0-910735-07-7*) MTO Printing & Pubn Ctr.

Angha, Mir-Ghotbeddin M. Az Janin Ta Janan. (PER.). 288p. 1987. 110.00 (*0-910735-46-8*) MTO Printing & Pubn Ctr.

— Tajaliat. (PER.). 104p. 1982. 110.00 (*0-910735-15-8*); pap. 25.00 (*0-910735-16-6*) MTO Printing & Pubn Ctr.

Angha, Molana S. The Approaching Promise. (ARA, ENG, FRE, GER & ITA.). 69p. (Orig.). 1989. pap. 13.50 (*0-8191-7403-3*) U Pr of Amer.

— Dawn. 37p. (Orig.). 1989. pap. 12.00 (*0-8191-7429-7*) U Pr of Amer.

— The Fragrance of Sufism. 107p. (Orig.). 1997. reprint ed. pap. 11.95 (*0-8191-9794-7*) U Pr of Amer.

— Ghazaliat. LC 96-14955. 198p. 1996. lib. bdg. 38.50 (*0-7618-0281-9*) U Pr of Amer.

— Ghazaliat. LC 96-14955. 173p. 1997. pap. 12.95 (*0-7618-0282-7*) U Pr of Amer.

— Manifestations of Thought. LC 88-20599. 126p. (Orig.). 1988. lib. bdg. 41.50 (*0-8191-7135-2*) U Pr of Amer.

— Manifestations of Thought. LC 88-20599. 126p. (Orig.). 1996. pap. 22.50 (*0-8191-7136-0*) U Pr of Amer.

— The Mystery of Humanity: Tranquility & Survival. 2nd ed. LC 95-441128. 86p. (Orig.). 1997. reprint ed. pap. 9.95 (*0-8191-9793-9*) U Pr of Amer.

— Peace. LC 87-63381. (ENG & PER.). 79p. 1987. pap. 11.55 (*0-910735-12-3*) MTO Printing & Pubn Ctr.

— The Secret Word. LC 88-39006. 75p. (Orig.). 1989. lib. bdg. 29.00 (*0-8191-7330-4*) U Pr of Amer.

— Sufism: The Reality of Religion. LC 98-60034. 60p. 1998. pap. 9.95 (*0-910735-80-8*) MTO Printing & Pubn Ctr.

— Whispering Moments: Inspiration. 2nd ed. LC 95-81158. (Illus.). 23p. (Orig.). 1997. reprint ed. pap. 5.00 (*0-910735-83-2*) MTO Printing & Pubn Ctr.

Angha, Nader S. Kanz-al Solouk & Raz Nameh: Wealth of Solouk & Secret Word. 4th ed. LC 84-52741. 50p. 1985. 110.00 (*0-910735-25-5*) MTO Printing & Pubn Ctr.

— Sufism. LC 95-77987. 39p. 1996. pap. 6.00 (*0-910735-98-0*) MTO Printing & Pubn Ctr.

— Sufism. (Lecture Ser.). 191p. 1997. pap. 19.95 (*0-910735-74-3*) MTO Printing & Pubn Ctr.

— Sufism & Islam. LC 95-77983. 51p. 1996. pap. 6.00 (*0-910735-97-2*) MTO Printing & Pubn Ctr.

— Sufism & Knowledge. LC 95-77986. 39p. 1996. pap. 6.00 (*0-910735-94-8*) MTO Printing & Pubn Ctr.

— Sufism & Peace. LC 95-77988. 25p. 1996. pap. 6.00 (*0-910735-96-4*) MTO Printing & Pubn Ctr.

— Sufism & Wisdom. LC 95-77982. 37p. 1996. pap. 6.00 (*0-910735-95-6*) MTO Printing & Pubn Ctr.

— Teyr-al Nader dar Sharhe Seyr-al Saer va Teyr-al Nader. LC 85-80048. (PER.). 81p. 1985. 110.00 (*0-910735-39-5*) MTO Printing & Pubn Ctr.

Angha, Nahid. The Journey: Seyr Va Soluk. 78p. (Orig.). pap. 6.50 (*0-918437-10-5*) Intl Sufism.

— The Nature of Miracle. 17p. (Orig.). 1993. pap. write for info. (*0-918437-11-3*) Intl Sufism.

— Principles of Sufism. 114p. (Orig.). 1991. pap. 8.00 (*0-918437-03-2*) Intl Sufism.

— Principles of Sufism. LC 94-29491. 128p. (Orig.). 1995. pap. 12.95 (*0-87573-061-2*) Jain Pub Co.

Angha, Nahid, tr. Selections: Poems from Khayam, Rumi, Hafez, Shah Maghsoud. 1991. pap. 14.95 (*0-918437-04-0*) Intl Sufism.

Angha, Nahid, tr. see Angha, Hazrat M.

Angha, Nahid, tr. see Maghsoud, Moulana S.

Angha, Sadegh, jt. auth. see Maghsoud, Shah.

Anghelaki-Rooke, Katerina. Beings & Things on Their Own. 46p. 1986. 18.00 (*0-918526-46-9*); pap. 10.00 (*0-918526-47-7*) BOA Edns.

Anghelaki-Rooke, Katerina, et al. Greece: The Modern Voice. LC 77-126039. (Review of National Literatures Ser.: Vol. 5, No. 2). 160p. 1975. pap. 6.95 (*0-918680-65-4*) Griffon House.

Anghelaki-Rooke, Katerina, tr. see Lekatsas, Barbara.

Anghelescu, Hermina G. & Dupuis, Elizabeth A., eds. Libraries & Culture: 25-Year Cumulative Index, 1996-1990, Vols. 1-25. 312p. (Orig.). 1995. pap. 25.00 (*0-938729-02-0*) UTX SLIS.

***Anghelides, Peter.** Frontier Worlds. (Doctor Who Ser.). 288p. 2000. mass mkt. 6.95 (*0-563-55589-0*, Pub. by BBC Bks) Genl Dist Srvs.

Anghelides, Peter. Kursaal. (Doctor Who Ser.). 1998. pap. 5.95 (*0-563-40578-3*) BBC.

***Anghileri, Julia.** Principles & Practices in Arithmetic Teaching: Innovative Approaches for the Primary Classroom. LC 00-23299. 2000. pap. write for info. (*0-335-20634-4*, Pub. by OpUniv Pr) Taylor & Francis.

Anghileri, Julia, ed. Children's Thinking in Primary Math. LC 97-127192. (Children, Teachers & Learning Ser.). 128p. 1995. pap. 29.95 (*0-304-33260-7*) Continuum.

Anghileri, Leopold J. The Role of Calcium in Biological Systems, Vol. 5. rev. ed. LC 81-155380. 304p. 1990. 153.00 (*0-8493-6284-9*, QP535) Franklin.

Anghileri, Leopold J., ed. General Processes of Radiotracer Localization, Vol. I. 272p. 1982. 110.00 (*0-685-06668-1*, CRC Reprint) Franklin.

— General Processes of Radiotracer Localization, Vol. II. 272p. 1982. 152.00 (*0-8493-6028-5*, QP519, CRC Reprint) Franklin.

Anghileri, Leopold J. & Colombetti, L. General Processes of Radiotracer Localization. LC 81-18063. (Radiotracers Biology & Medicine Ser.). 272p. 1982. 153.00 (*0-8493-6027-7*, CRC Reprint) Franklin.

Anghileri, Leopold J. & Robert, Jacques, eds. Hyperthermia in Cancer Treatment, Vol. I. 256p. 1986. 141.00 (*0-8493-6045-5*, RC271, CRC Reprint) Franklin.

— Hyperthermia in Cancer Treatment, Vol. II. 288p. 1986. 161.00 (*0-8493-6046-3*, RC271, CRC Reprint) Franklin.

— Hyperthermia in Cancer Treatment: Present Developmental State of Cancer Multistep Therapy, Vol. III. LC 85-11652. 240p. 1986. 129.00 (*0-8493-6047-1*, RC271, CRC Reprint) Franklin.

Anghileri, Leopold J. & Tuffet-Anghileri, Ann M., eds. The Role of Calcium in Biological Systems, Vol. I. 288p. 1982. 163.00 (*0-8493-6280-6*, QP535, CRC Reprint) Franklin.

— The Role of Calcium in Biological Systems, Vol. II. 240p. 1982. 138.00 (*0-8493-6281-4*, QP535, CRC Reprint) Franklin.

— The Role of Calcium in Biological Systems, Vol. III. 272p. 1982. 153.00 (*0-8493-6282-2*, QP535, CRC Reprint) Franklin.

— The Role of Calcium in Biological Systems, Vol. IV. 272p. 1987. 155.00 (*0-8493-6283-0*, QP535, CRC Reprint) Franklin.

Angi, jt. auth. see Tramotini.

Angi Ma Wong. Target: The U. S. Asian Market: A Practical Guide to Doing Business. LC 93-83449. (Illus.). 224p. (Orig.). 1993. pap. 27.50 (*0-9635906-9-3*) Pacific Herit.

— The Wind-Water Wheel: A Feng Shui Tool for Transforming Your Life. (Illus.). 6p. 1996. 19.95 (*0-9635906-7-7*) Pacific Herit.

Angier, Bradford. Field Guide to Edible Wild Plants. 1992. 28.00 (*0-8446-6527-4*) Peter Smith.

— Field Guide to Edible Wild Plants. LC 73-23042. (Illus.). 256p. 1974. pap. 16.95 (*0-8117-2018-7*) Stackpole.

— Field Guide to Medicinal Wild Plants. 320p. (C). 1992. 495.00 (*81-7002-033-6*, Pub. by Himalayan Bks) St Mut.

— Field Guide to Medicinal Wild Plants. LC 78-19112. (Illus.). 320p. 1978. pap. 18.95 (*0-8117-2076-4*) Stackpole.

— How to Stay Alive in the Woods. Orig. Title: Living off the Country. 1983. 20.75 (*0-8446-5964-9*) Peter Smith.

— How to Stay Alive in the Woods. Orig. Title: Living off the Country. (Illus.). 288p. 1998. per. 8.00 (*0-684-83101-5*) S&S Trade.

— Looking for Gold. LC 74-23258. (Illus.). 224p. 1995. pap. 16.95 (*0-8117-2034-9*) Stackpole.

— The Master Backwoodsman. 224p. 1984. pap. 5.95 (*0-449-90126-2*) Fawcett.

***Angier, Bradford.** One Acre & Security: How to Live off the Earth Without Destroying It. (Illus.). 320p. 2000. reprint ed. pap. 15.95 (*1-57223-394-X*) Willow Creek Pr.

Angier, John C. A '4-F' Goes to War: With the 100th Infantry Division. 3rd rev. ed. (World War II Memoir Ser.: Vol. 225). (Illus.). 66p. 1999. reprint ed. 21.95 (*1-57638-093-9*, M225H); reprint ed. pap. 10.95 (*1-57638-092-0*, M225S) Merriam Pr.

Angier, Natalie. The Beauty of the Beastly: New Views on the Nature of Life. 304p. 1996. pap. 14.00 (*0-395-79147-2*) HM.

— Natural Obsessions: Striving to Unlock the Deepest Secrets of the Cancer Cell. LC 99-18104. 394p. 1999. pap. 15.00 (*0-395-92472-3*) HM.

***Angier, Natalie.** Woman: An Intimate Geography. LC 99-47764. 464p. 2000. pap. 15.00 (*0-385-49841-1*, Anchor NY) Doubleday.

Angier, Natalie. Woman: An Intimate Geography. LC 98-47634. 416p. 1999. 25.00 (*0-395-69130-3*) HM.

Angier, R. H. Firearm Blueing & Browning. 160p. 1936. 18.95 (*0-8117-0610-9*) Stackpole.

Angilella, Joseph T. & Ziajka, Alan. Rediscovering Justice: Awakening World Faiths to Address World Issues: An Interfaith Conference for Youth on the Fiftieth

A

An Asterisk (*) at the beginning of an entry indicates that the title is appearing for the first time.

A

Anniversary of the Founding of the United Nations. LC 98-22229. 1133p. (YA). 1998. 19.95 (*0-9664059-0-0*); pap. write for info. (*0-9664059-1-9*) U of SF.

Angiletta, Anthony M., et al, eds. The State of Western European Studies: Implications for Collection Development. LC 84-12803. (Collection Management: Vol. 6, No. 1-2). 273p. 1984. text 49.95 (*0-86656-354-7*) Haworth Pr.

Angilette, Elizabeth. Philosopher at the Keyboard: Glenn Gould. LC 91-42986. 244p. 1992. 35.00 (*0-8108-2467-1*) Scarecrow.

Angilly, Natica. Dancing Poetry: A Workbook. Cuneo, Louis, ed. (Illus.). 1997. pap., wbk. ed. 14.95 (*0-914370-79-0*) Blue Dragon.

Angilly, Richard. Chants: A Zen Wind. (Illus.). 136p. (Orig.). 1980. pap. 11.95 (*0-931290-28-7*) Blue Dragon.

— Poems of Illumination. (Illus.). (Orig.). 1980. pap. 11.95 (*0-931290-27-9*) Blue Dragon.

Angino, Richard C. Felicita - A Private Tour. Burridge, Michael, ed. (Illus.). 128p. 1997. 35.00 (*0-9662249-0-6*) King Dr Corp.

Angiolello, Giovan M. & Mackay, Pierre A. A Fifteenth-Century Venetian's Adventures in Ottoman Lands: The Memoir of Gian-Maria Angiolello. LC 85-6177. (Near Eastern Studies, University of Washington). (ITA.). 1989. write for info. (*0-295-96264-X*) U of Wash Pr.

Angiolieri, Cecco. Cecco, As I Am & Was: The Poems of Cecco Angiolieri. Caso, Adolfo, ed. Barrett, Tracy, tr. from ITA. & contrib. by by. 140p. 1994. pap. 12.95 (*0-8283-2000-4*) Branden Bks.

Angiolillo, Paul. Mountain Biking Northern New England. LC 98-30950. (America by Mountain Bike Ser.). (Illus.). 208p. 1996. pap. 12.95 (*1-56044-432-0*) Falcon Pub Inc.

— Mountain Biking Southern New England. LC 98-49647. (Illus.). 256p. 1999. pap. 12.95 (*1-56044-748-6*) Falcon Pub Inc.

Angiolillo, Paul, ed. see Thomas, Paul.

Angiolillo, Paul F. Armed Forces' Foreign Language Teaching. 440p. 1947. 15.95 (*0-913298-57-3*) S F Vanni.

— A Criminal As Hero: Angelo Duca. LC 78-15431. xii, 212p. 1979. 29.95 (*0-7006-0184-8*) U Pr of KS.

Angiolino, Andrea. Super Sharp Pencil & Paper Games. LC 95-31719. (Illus.). 96p. 1995. pap. 5.95 (*0-8069-3884-6*) Sterling.

Angione, Genevieve. All Bisque & Half Bisque Dolls. LC 76-77265. (Illus.). 360p. 1981. reprint ed. 25.00 (*0-916838-39-0*) Schiffer.

Angione, Ronald, jt. ed. see Pyper, Diane M.

***Angiras.** Dance of the Planets - 2. (Illus.). 241p. 2000. pap. 19.95 (*0-7414-0295-5*) Buy Books.

Angiras. Dance on the Planets - The Earth. (Illus.). 284p. 1999. pap. 24.95 (*0-7414-0070-7*) Buy Books.

Anglade, Joseph. Histoire Sommaire de la Litterature Meridionale Au Moyen Age. LC 74-38486. reprint ed. 49.50 (*0-404-08343-9*) AMS Pr.

— Troubadours, Leur Vies, Leurs Oeuvre, Leur Influence. LC 78-38487. reprint ed. 49.50 (*0-404-08344-7*) AMS Pr.

Angland, Joseph, et al, eds. Antitrust Law Developments, 2 vols. 4th ed. LC 96-80282. 1876p. 1997. pap. 295.00 (*1-57073-391-0*, 503-0293, ABA Antitrust) Amer Bar Assn.

Angle. Occupational Safety & Health in the Emergency Services. LC 98-28536. 320p. 1998. pap. text 46.95 (*0-8273-8359-2*) Delmar.

— Occupational Safety & Health in the Emergency Services: Instructor's Guide. 128p. 1999. teacher ed. 24.00 (*0-8273-8360-6*) Delmar.

Angle & Harlow. Fire Service Strategies & Tactics. (Fire Science Ser.). (C). 2000. pap. 49.95 (*0-7668-1344-4*) Delmar.

— Fire Service Strategies & Tactics. (Fire Science Ser.). (C). 2001. pap., wbk. ed. 15.00 (*0-7668-1345-2*) Delmar.

***Angle, Chris.** The Nature of Aesthetics. 2nd rev. ed. 188p. 1999. pap. 14.99 (*0-9661126-0-1*) Philosophy.

— The Nature of Ethics. unabridged ed. 1997. pap. 14.99 (*0-9661126-1-X*) Philosophy.

— The Nature of Truth Consciousness & Free Will. 1997. pap. 14.99 (*0-9661126-2-8*) Philosophy.

— The Philosophical & Modular Nature of Economics. unabridged ed. 1999. pap. 14.99 (*0-9661126-3-6*) Philosophy.

Angle, Deborah K. & Buxton, Julie M. Community Living Skills Workbook for the Head-Injured Adult. LC 91-4532. 384p. 1991. 99.00 (*0-8342-0210-7*) Aspen Pub.

Angle, Kelly. One Hundred Million Dollars in Profits: An Anatomy of a Market Killing & a Realistic Trading. 1990. 50.00 (*0-930233-38-7*) Windsor.

Angle, Paul M. Bloody Williamson: A Chapter in American Lawlessness. (Prairie State Bks.). (Illus.). 350p. (C). 1992. 15.95 (*0-252-06233-7*) U of Ill Pr.

— Lincoln Memorial: A Guide to the Lincoln Memorial, District of Columbia. LC 85-600059. (Official National Park Handbook Ser.: No. 129). (Illus.). 48p. 1986. pap. 3.00 (*0-912627-28-X*, S/N 024-005-00974-4) Natl Park Serv.

— The Lincoln Reader. (History - United States Ser.). 564p. 1993. reprint ed. lib. bdg. 99.00 (*0-7812-4897-3*) Rprt Serv.

— On a Variety of Subjects. 1974. 10.00 (*0-940550-05-9*) Caxton Club.

— A Shelf of Lincoln Books: A Critical, Selective Bibliography of Lincolniana. LC 46-25256. 162p. reprint ed. pap. 50.30 (*0-608-11151-1*, 205045600083) Bks Demand.

Angle, Paul M., ed. Created Equal? The Complete Lincoln-Douglas Debates of 1858. LC 58-6885. xxx, 422p. (Orig.). 1985. pap. text 20.00 (*0-226-02085-1*) U Ch Pr.

— The Lincoln Reader. 33.95 (*0-89190-866-8*) Amereon Ltd.

— The Lincoln Reader. (Quality Paperbacks Ser.). (Illus.). 608p. 1990. pap. 16.95 (*0-306-80398-4*) Da Capo.

Angle, Paul M., ed. Abraham Lincoln, by Some Men Who Knew Him. LC 78-90601. (Essay Index Reprint Ser.). 1980. 23.95 (*0-8369-1242-X*) Ayer.

Angle, Paul M., intro. The Complete Lincoln-Douglas Debates of 1858. (Illus.). 490p. 1991. pap. 25.00 (*0-226-02084-3*) U Ch Pr.

Angle, Paul M, ed. see Connolly, James A.

Angle, Robert O. Handbook of Probate Law, 2 vols., Set. 5th rev. ed. 701p. 1988. pap. text 57.50 (*0-318-40135-5*) Lega Bks.

Angle, Susan, jt. auth. see Hiam, Alex.

Angle, W. Craig. The Great Locomotive Chase: More on the Andrews Raid & the First Medal of Honor. (Illus.). 367p. 1992. 28.57 (*0-9636029-0-X*) W C Angle. The Civil War had been under way exactly one year when on April 12, 1862, a group of Union soldiers disguised as civilians under the leadership of spy & contraband merchant, J. J. Andrews, seized the locomotive GENERAL & three boxcars twenty miles north of Atlanta, & steamed north towards Chattanooga--into American history & railroad legend. The men taking part were the first to be awarded the Medal of Honor, our nation's highest military decoration. Sixteen years in the making, THE GREAT LOCOMOTIVE CHASE combines scores of maps, photographs, & artistic plates with actual participants' accounts. Style & format satisfy the needs of specialists & general readers. "Angle has done a good job with a subject that is familiar & fun to read about"--OHIOANA QUARTERLY; "a worthy addition to the literature on the famous event"--NATIONAL RAILWAY BULLETIN; "Angle's wise use of resources keeps the text flowing smoothly...a very credible job in separating fact from myth"--THE CIVIL WAR NEWS; "a very good book--well researched but not scholarly--intimate & personal. Angle has done a fine job retelling in detail one of the most daring military exploits of the Civil War"--John M. Priest, author ANTIETAM: THE SOLDIERS' BATTLE. Order from Craig Angle, P.O. Box 347, Rouzerville, PA 17250; 1-717-762-5133.
Publisher Paid Annotation.

Angleitner, A., et al, eds. Personality Psychology in Europe Vol. 2: Current Trends & Controversies. xii, 272p. 1986. pap. 57.75 (*90-265-0597-3*) Swets.

Angleitner, A., jt. auth. see Strelau, J.

Anglesey, Debby. Battling the MSG Myth: A Survival Guide & Cookbook. Anglesey, Mike, ed. (Illus.). 1997. 19.00 (*0-9670492-0-2*) Fr Porch Prods.

Anglesey, Mike, ed. see Anglesey, Debby.

Anglesey, Zoe. Something More Than Force: Poems for Guatemala, 1971-1982. deluxe limited ed. 48p. 1982. 25.00 (*0-938566-13-X*) Adastra Pr.

— Something More Than Force: Poems for Guatemala, 1971-1982. 2nd ed. 48p. 1984. pap. 3.50 (*0-938566-21-0*) Adastra Pr.

Anglesey, Zoe, ed. Stone on Stone: Poems by Women of Diverse Heritages: Piedra Sobre Piedra: Poesia por Mujeres de Diversas Culturas. Dada, Rudolfo, tr. from ENG. LC 93-35585. (SPA.). 132p. (Orig.). (YA). (gr. 10-12). 1993. pap. 12.95 (*0-940880-48-2*) Open Hand.

— Word Up: Hope for Youth Poetry from El Centro de la Raza. (ENG, SPA & TAG.). (YA). 1992. 12.95 (*0-9633275-1-8*) El Centro de la Raza.

Anglesey, Zoe, tr. see Gander, Forrest, ed.

Anglestoff, Jack. What Would You Do If . . . ? Anecdote Joke Book. 2nd ed. (Illus.). 52p. 1995. pap. 6.95 (*0-9626963-0-7*) Acrus Pubng.

Angley, Ernest. Raptured. 50th ed. 224p. 1950. pap. 3.50 (*0-9636772-0-9*) Winston Pr OH.

— Raptured. 51st ed. 224p. 1997. pap. 3.50 (*0-9636772-2-5*) Winston Pr OH.

Angley, Wilson. A History of Fort Johnston on the Lower Cape Fear. (Illus.). vi, 150p. 1996. pap. 10.00 (*1-892444-02-X*) Southport Hist.

Angley, Wilson, et al. Sherman's March Through North Carolina: A Chronology. 129p. (Orig.). 1996. reprint ed. pap. 12.00 (*0-86526-266-7*) NC Archives.

Anglican Church of Australia Staff. A Prayer Book for Australia: Short Edition. abr. ed. 493p. 1996. 19.95 (*0-85574-190-2*, Pub. by E J Dwyer) Morehouse Pub.

***Anglican Consultative Council Staff.** Called to Be a Faithful Church in a Plural World, Sect. III. LC 98-48598. 64p. 1999. pap. 9.95 (*0-8192-1809-X*) Morehouse Pub.

— Called to Be One, Sect. IV. LC 98-48600. 80p. 1999. pap. 9.95 (*0-8192-1810-3*) Morehouse Pub.

— Called to Full Humanity, Sect. 1. LC 98-48125. 80p. 1999. pap. 9.95 (*0-8192-1807-3*) Morehouse Pub.

— Called to Live & Proclaim the Good News, Sect. II. LC 98-48599. 96p. 1999. pap. 9.95 (*0-8192-1808-1*) Morehouse Pub.

— The Communion We Share: The Official Report of the 11th Meeting of the Anglican Consultative Council, Scotland 1999. Rosenthal, James M. & Rodgers, Margaret, eds. LC 00-30551. 370p. 2000. pap. 19.95 (*0-8192-1863-4*) Morehouse Pub.

— Inter-Faith Report. LC 98-48602. 80p. 1999. pap. 9.95 (*0-8192-1811-1*) Morehouse Pub.

***Anglican Consultative Council Staff, compiled by.** The Official Report of the Lambeth Conference 1998. LC 99-12950. 544p. 1999. pap. 22.95 (*0-8192-1797-2*) Morehouse Pub.

Anglican Solitary Staff, tr. Call of Silent Love. (Cistercian Studies: No. 163). pap. 11.95 (*0-87907-663-1*) Cistercian Pubns.

Anglim, Christopher T. Annotated Catalog South Texas College of Law. LC 94-30980. xxx, 434p. 1995. 65.00 (*0-89941-902-X*, 308340) W S Hein.

— Joined in Common Enterprise: Bibliography on the History & Sources of Anglo-American Partnership Law. LC 98-48819. 1999. 74.95 (*1-57292-143-9*) Austin & Winfield.

— Labor, Employment, & the Law: A Dictionary. LC 97-20803. (Contemporary Legal Issues Ser.). 576p. 1997. lib. bdg. 45.00 (*0-87436-825-1*) ABC-CLIO.

— Special Collections Policies, Procedures & Guidelines: A Model Plan for the Management of Special Legal Collections. LC 92-37234. x, 556p. 1993. 75.00 (*0-89941-814-7*, 307570) W S Hein.

Anglim, Christopher Thomas. Religion & the Law: A Dictionary. LC 99-32889. (Contemporary Legal Issues Ser.). 450p. 1999. lib. bdg. 55.00 (*1-57607-028-X*) ABC-CLIO.

Anglim, Maryann & Allan, Walter. Kara Mia: The Story of Sudden Loss & Slow Recovery in a Teenager with Long QT Syndrome. (Illus.). 250p. (Orig.). 1997. pap. 12.95 (*0-9656501-0-3*) Seahorse Press.

Anglin, Bill A. Big Print Bible Puzzles: People, Places & Things. large type ed. Fittro, Pat, ed. 48p. 1998. pap. text 3.99 (*0-7847-0812-6*, 28-02781) Standard Pub.

Anglin, Donald L., jt. auth. see Crouse, William H.

Anglin, Douglas, et al, eds. Canada, Scandinavia & Southern Africa. (Seminar Proceedings Ser.: No. 13). 190p. 1978. write for info. (*91-7106-143-6*, Pub. by Nordic Africa) Transaction Pubs.

Anglin, Douglas G. Zambian Crisis Behaviour: Confronting Rhodesia's Unilateral Declaration of Independence, 1965-1966. (Illus.). 408p. 1994. 65.00 (*0-7735-1219-5*, Pub. by McG-Queens Univ Pr) CUP Services.

Anglin, Douglas G. & Shaw, Timothy M. Zambia's Foreign Policy: Studies in Diplomacy & Dependence. LC 79-4849. 453p. 1979. text 64.50 (*0-89158-191-X*) Westview.

Anglin, E. Warren. Seven Thunderers Utter Their Voices: History & Verse by Verse Study in the Book of Revelation of the Bible. 2nd ed. 176p. (Orig.). pap. 7.95 (*0-318-04199-5*) Total Comm Ministries.

Anglin, Gary J. Critical Issues in Instructional Technology. (Instructional Technology Ser.). 275p. 1999. 47.00 (*1-56308-497-X*) Teacher Ideas Pr.

Anglin, Gary J., ed. Instructional Technology: Past, Present & Future. 2nd ed. LC 94-41385. (Instructional Technology Ser.). xix, 431p. 1995. lib. bdg. 45.00 (*1-56308-251-9*) Libs Unl.

Anglin, James P., et al, eds. Perspectives in Professional Child & Youth Care. 359p. 1990. pap. 24.95 (*1-56024-055-5*) Haworth Pr.

— Perspectives in Professional Child & Youth Care, Pt. 1. LC 90-4051. (Child & Youth Services Ser.: Vol. 13, No. 1 & 2). 360p. 1990. text 49.95 (*0-86656-891-3*) Haworth Pr.

Anglin, Jay P. & Hamblin, William J. HCO World Hist to 1648. LC 91-55404. (College Outline Ser.). (Illus.). 480p. 1993. pap. 17.00 (*0-06-467123-2*, Harper Ref) HarpC.

Anglin, Jeremy M. Vocabulary Development: A Morphological Analysis. (Monographs of the Society for Research in Child Development: No. 238). 200p. 1993. pap. text 15.00 (*0-226-02091-6*) U Ch Pr.

***Anglin, Patty & Musser, Joe.** Acres of Hope: The Miraculous Story of One Family's Gift of Love to Children Without Hope. 288p. 1999. 19.99 (*1-57748-625-0*) Barbour Pub.

Anglin, Richard. Think Away Tension. (Illus.). 110p. (Orig.). 1988. pap. 8.95 (*0-317-91342-5*) RDA Enter.

Anglin, Ron. Forgotten Trails: Historical Sources of the Columbia's Big Bend Country. (Illus.). 256p. (Orig.). 1995. pap. 19.95 (*0-87422-116-1*) Wash St U Pr.

Anglin, W. S. Mathematics: A Concise History & Philosophy. LC 94-8075. (Undergraduate Texts in Mathematics Ser.). (Illus.). 275p. 1996. 42.95 (*0-387-94280-7*) Spr-Verlag.

— The Philosophy of Mathematics: The Invisible Art. LC 96-48604. (Studies in the History of Philosophy: Vol. 43). 260p. 1997. text 89.95 (*0-7734-8706-9*) E Mellen.

— The Queen of Mathematics: An Introduction to Number Theory. LC 94-42070. (Texts in the Mathematical Sciences Ser.: No. 8). 389p. 1995. text 173.50 (*0-7923-3287-3*) Kluwer Academic.

Anglin, W. S. & Lambek, J. The Heritage of Thales. (Undergraduate Texts in Mathematics Ser.). (Illus.). 352p. 1995. 43.95 (*0-387-94544-X*) Spr-Verlag.

Angliss, S. Science Museum Book: Communications. (Illus.). (J). mass mkt. 8.95 (*0-340-71475-1*, Pub. by Hodder & Stought Ltd) Trafalgar.

— Science Museum Book of Medicine. (Illus.). mass mkt. 8.95 (*0-340-71476-X*, Pub. by Hodder & Stought Ltd) Trafalgar.

Angliss, Sarah. Chemistry Lab: The Ultimate Chemistry Pack. (Science Lab Ser.). (Illus.). 32p. (J). (gr. 3-7). 1999. 19.95 (*1-57145-382-2*, Silver Dolph) Advantage Pubs.

***Angliss, Sarah.** The Controls: Brain & Nervous System. (Human Machine Ser.). (Illus.). 32p. (J). 1999. lib. bdg. 15.95 (*1-929298-22-6*, Pub. by Thameside Pr) Smart Apple.

Angliss, Sarah. Cosmic Journeys: A Beginner's Guide to Space & Time Travel. LC 97-41601. (Future Files Ser.). (Illus.). 32p. (J). (gr. 4-6). 1998. pap. 8.95 (*0-7613-0635-8*, Copper Beech Bks) Millbrook Pr.

— Cosmic Journeys: A Beginner's Guide to Space & Time Travel. LC 97-41601. (Future Files Ser.). (Illus.). 32p. (J). (gr. 5-7). 1998. lib. bdg. 22.40 (*0-7613-0620-X*, Copper Beech Bks) Millbrook Pr.

***Angliss, Sarah.** The Food Processor: Digestive System. (Human Machine Ser.). (Illus.). 32p. (J). 1999. lib. bdg. 15.95 (*1-929298-17-X*, Pub. by Thameside Pr) Smart Apple.

Angliss, Sarah. Future World: A Beginner's Guide to Life on Earth in the 21st Century. LC 98-4269. (Future Files Ser.). (Illus.). 32p. (J). (gr. 4-6). 1998. pap. 8.95 (*0-7613-0740-0*, Copper Beech Bks); lib. bdg. 22.40 (*0-7613-0821-0*, Copper Beech Bks) Millbrook Pr.

***Angliss, Sarah.** Gold. LC 98-46800. (Elements Ser.: Vol. 2). (Illus.). 32p. (J). (gr. 3-5). 2000. lib. bdg. 22.79 (*0-7614-0887-8*, Benchmark NY) Marshall Cavendish.

— The Human Machine, 6 vols. 32p. (J). 1999. lib. bdg. 95.70 (*1-929298-23-4*, Pub. by Thameside Pr) Smart Apple.

Angliss, Sarah. Movers & Shapers LC 99-10283. (Human Machine Ser.). (Illus.). (J). 1999. lib. bdg. write for info. (*0-382-42177-9*, New Dscvry Bks) Silver Burdett Pr.

***Angliss, Sarah.** Movers & Shapers: Muscle & Bones. (Human Machine Ser.). (Illus.). 32p. (J). 1999. lib. bdg. 15.95 (*1-929298-18-8*, Pub. by Thameside Pr) Smart Apple.

— The Outer Shell: Skin. (Human Machine Ser.). (Illus.). 32p. (J). 1999. lib. bdg. 15.95 (*1-929298-21-8*, Pub. by Thameside Pr) Smart Apple.

— The Power Pack: Cardiovascular System. 32p. (J). 1999. lib. bdg. 15.95 (*1-929298-19-6*, Pub. by Thameside Pr) Smart Apple.

— The Production Line: Reproduction & Growing Up. (Human Machine Ser.). (Illus.). 32p. (J). 1999. lib. bdg. 15.95 (*1-929298-20-X*, Pub. by Thameside Pr) Smart Apple.

***Anglo-Dutch Historical Conference Staff, et al.** The Education of a Christian Society: Humanism & the Reformation in Britain & the Netherlands. LC 99-12018. (Illus.). 1999. write for info. (*0-7546-0001-7*, Pub. by Ashgate Pub) Ashgate Pub Co.

Anglo-Swedenish Literary Foundation, London Staff. Modern Swedish Short Stories. 1977. 33.95 (*0-8369-4261-2*, 6063) Ayer.

***Anglo, Sydney.** The Martial Arts of Renaissance Europe. LC 99-89407. (Illus.). 400p. 2000. 45.00 (*0-300-08352-1*) Yale U Pr.

Anglo, Sydney. Spectacle, Pageantry, & Early Tudor Policy. 2nd ed. (Oxford-Warburg Studies). (Illus.). 410p. (C). 1997. text 89.00 (*0-19-920603-1*) OUP.

Anglo, Sydney, ed. Chivalry in the Renaissance. (Illus.). 310p. (C). 1990. 90.00 (*0-85115-264-3*) Boydell & Brewer.

Anglum, Nolan, jt. auth. see Stone, Steve.

Anglund, Joan. Bedtime Book. 48p. (J). 1997. per. 5.99 (*0-689-81702-9*) S&S Childrens.

Anglund, Joan W. Bedtime Book. (Illus.). 48p. (J). (ps-1). 1993. pap. 12.00 (*0-671-74176-4*) S&S Bks Yung.

— Childhood Is a Time of Innocence: Twentieth Anniversary Edition. 20th ed. LC 65-20974. (Illus.). 32p. (J). (gr. k up). 1984. reprint ed. 9.95 (*0-15-216952-0*, Harcourt Child Bks) Harcourt.

— Christmas Candy Book. (Illus.). (J). 1983. 5.95 (*0-915696-63-0*) Determined Prods.

— A Christmas Cookie Book. LC 77-78293. (Illus.). (J). 1982. reprint ed. 3.95 (*0-915696-07-X*) Determined Prods.

— Christmas Is Love. LC 87-35908. (Illus.). 32p. (J). (ps up). 1988. 10.00 (*0-15-200425-4*, Gulliver Bks) Harcourt.

— Do You Love Someone? LC 76-152692. (Illus.). 32p. (J). (ps up). 1971. 4.95 (*0-15-224190-6*, Harcourt Child Bks) Harcourt.

— Emily & Adam, 3 bks. Incl. Adam Book. (Illus.). 1979. Emily & Adam Book of Opposites. (Illus.). 1979. Emily Book. (Illus.). 1979. (Illus.). (J). (ps-1). 1979. 5.95 (*0-394-84254-5*, Pub. by Random Bks Yng Read) Random.

— A Friend Is Someone Who Likes You: Silver Anniversary Edition. anniversary ed. LC 58-8624. (Illus.). 32p. (J). (ps up). 1983. 9.95 (*0-15-229678-6*, Harcourt Child Bks) Harcourt.

— God Is Love. (Illus.). (J). (gr. 1 up). 5.95 (*0-317-13661-5*) Determined Prods.

— In a Pumpkin Shell. LC 60-10243. (Illus.). 32p. (J). (ps-2). 1977. pap. 6.00 (*0-15-644425-9*, Voyager Bks) Harcourt.

— In a Pumpkin Shell: A Mother Goose ABC. LC 60-10243. (Illus.). (J). (ps-2). 1960. 10.95 (*0-15-238269-0*, Harcourt Child Bks) Harcourt.

— The Jewels of the Spirit. LC 98-84164. (Little Bks.). (Illus.). 80p. 1998. 4.95 (*0-8362-6789-3*) Andrews & McMeel.

— Little Angels' Alphabet of Love. (Illus.). 32p. (J). 1997. per. 4.99 (*0-689-81145-4*) S&S Childrens.

— Little Angels' Book of Christmas. (Illus.). 32p. (J). 1997. 4.99 (*0-689-81468-2*) S&S Childrens.

— Little Book of Poems & Prayers. LC 89-5914. (Illus.). 48p. (J). 1997. mass mkt. 4.99 (*0-689-81448-8*) Atheneum Yung Read.

— Love Is a Baby. LC 91-1224. (Illus.). 32p. (J). 1992. 8.95 (*0-15-200517-X*, Harcourt Child Bks) Harcourt.

— Love Is a Special Way of Feeling: Silver Anniversary Edition. LC 84-19296. (Illus.). 32p. (J). 1985. reprint ed. 10.00 (*0-15-249724-2*, Harcourt Child Bks) Harcourt.

— Love Is Forever. LC 97-14793. (Illus.). 32p. (J). 1998. 10.00 (*0-15-201680-5*) Harcourt.

— Love One Another. LC 81-67305. (Illus.). 5.95 (*0-915696-45-2*) Determined Prods.

— Merry Christmas, Baby. LC 94-79880. (Sturdy Shape Bks.). (J). 1996. pap. text 3.99 (*0-307-12438-X*, 12438, Goldn Books) Gldn Bks Pub Co.

* An Asterisk (*) at the beginning of an entry indicates that the title is appearing for the first time.

— Morning Is a Little Child. LC 69-11592. (Illus.). (J). (gr. 4-6). 1969. 7.95 (0-15-255652-4, Harcourt Child Bks) Harcourt.

— A Mother Goose Book. Van Doren, Liz, ed. LC 90-4466. (Illus.). 32p. (J). (ps up). 1991. 7.95 (0-15-200529-3, Gulliver Bks) Harcourt.

— Nibble Nibble Mousekin: A Tale of Hansel & Gretel. LC 62-14422. (Illus.). 32p. (J). (gr. k-3). 1962. 10.95 (0-15-257400-X, Harcourt Child Bks) Harcourt.

— Nibble Nibble Mousekin: A Tale of Hansel & Gretel. LC 62-14422. (Illus.). 32p. (J). (gr. k-3). 1977. pap. 4.95 (0-15-665588-8, Voyager Bks) Harcourt.

— A Patchwork of Love. (Little Bks.). (Illus.). 80p. 1998. 4.95 (0-8362-6788-5) Andrews & McMeel.

— Peace Is a Circle of Love. LC 92-28855. (Illus.). 32p. (J). 1993. 8.95 (0-15-259922-3, Gulliver Bks) Harcourt.

— Poems of Childhood. LC 95-30937. (Illus.). 32p. 1996. 13.00 (0-15-262961-0) Harcourt.

— Prayer Is a Gentle Way of Being with God. LC 98-40504. 48p. 1999. 11.99 (0-87788-708-X, H Shaw Pubs) Waterbrook Pr.

— Rainbow Love. LC 82-70028. (Illus.). 1982. 5.95 (0-915696-51-7) Determined Prods.

— Sleepytime: Poems Prayers & Lullabies. (Illus.). 24p. (J). (ps up). 1996. per. 11.95 (0-689-80055-X) Atheneum Yung Read.

— Spring Is a New Beginning. LC 63-7892. (Illus.). 32p. (J). (ps up). 1963. 8.95 (0-15-278161-7, Harcourt Child Bks) Harcourt.

— Sweet Dreams: 3 Sleepytime Books of Poems, Prayers & Lullabes. (J). 11.95 (0-614-19250-1) Litle Simon.

— The Way of Love. 1993. 9.95 (0-679-73112-1) Random.

— What Color Is Love? LC 66-13795. (Illus.). (J). (ps-6). 1966. 3.95 (0-15-295260-8, Harcourt Child Bks) Harcourt.

***Anglund, Joan Walsh.** Be My Friend: Book & Locket. (Illus.). 32p. (J). (ps-3). 2000. 9.99 (0-689-82638-9) S&S Childrens.

— Between Friends. 2000. 4.95 (0-7407-1034-6) Andrews & McMeel.

— The Brave Cowboy. LC 00-37984. (Illus.). 40p. (J). (ps up). 2000. 6.95 (0-7407-0649-7) Andrews & McMeel.

— A Christmas Alphabet. 80p. 1999. 4.95 (0-7407-0055-3) Andrews & McMeel.

— Happy Birthday. 2000. 4.95 (0-7407-1035-4) Andrews & McMeel.

Anglund, Joan Walsh. In a Pumpkin Shell: A Mother Goose ABC. (Voyager/HBJ Bks.). 1960. 11.20 (0-606-01031-9, Pub. by Turtleback) Demco.

***Anglund, Joan Walsh.** In All Thy Ways: A Book of Bible Verses. LC 99-37753. 1999. 11.99 (0-87788-411-0, H Shaw Pubs) Waterbrook Pr.

Anglund, Joan Walsh. A Little Book of Poems & Prayers. LC 89-5914. (Illus.). 48p. (J). (ps-1). 1989. lib. bdg. 13.00 (0-671-67115-4) S&S Childrens.

***Anglund, Joan Walsh.** Love Is a Special Way of Feeling. LC 99-32782. (J). 1999. 9.95 (0-15-202358-5) Harcourt.

Anglund, Joan Walsh. My Busy Day. (Illus.). 14p. (J). (ps-k). 1999. bds. 4.99 (0-689-82023-2) S&S Childrens.

— My Busy Year. (Illus.). 14p. (J). (ps). 1999. bds. 4.99 (0-689-82024-0) S&S Childrens.

Anglund, Joan Walsh. Mother Goose Pop-Up. 16p. (J). (ps up). 1995. 11.95 (0-671-87079-3) Litle Simon.

***Anglund, Sandra M.** Small Business Policy & the American Creed. LC 99-45995. 192p. 2000. write for info. (0-275-96697-6, Praeger Pubs) Greenwood.

Angly, Edward. Oh Yeah? LC 88-82234. 64p. 1988. reprint ed. pap. 10.00 (0-87034-088-3) Fraser Pub Co.

Angnardo, Marie. 377 Simple Ways You Can Make a Difference: Practical Suggestions for Busy People. LC 94-75099. 224p. (Orig.). 1994. pap. 6.95 (0-9640406-0-3) Help Hand Pubs.

Angnostopoulos, Athan, tr. see Seferis, George.

Angoff, Allan, ed. Public Relations for Libraries: Essays in Communications Techniques, 5. LC 72-776. (Contributions in Librarianship & Information Science Ser.: No. 5). 246p. 1973. 49.95 (0-8371-6060-X, ANP/, Greenwood Pr) Greenwood.

Angoff, Allan & Dingwall, Eric J. Abnormal Hypnotic Phenomena, a Survey of Nineteenth-Century Cases Vol. 4: The United States of America, Great Britain. LC 68-85483. 190p. reprint ed. pap. 58.90 (0-8357-5007-8, 203009400022) Bks Demand.

Angoff, Allan & Shapin, Betty, eds. PSI Factors in Creativity: Proceedings of an International Conference, France, June 16-18, 1969. LC 71-140141. 1970. 16.00 (0-912328-18-5) Parapsych Foun.

Angoff, Allan, ed. see International Conference, Amsterdam Staff.

Angoff, Allan, ed. see International Conference, France Staff.

Angoff, Allan, ed. see International Conference London Staff.

Angoff, Allan, ed. see London Times Staff.

Angoff, Charles. Adventures in Heaven. LC 76-132110. (Short Story Index Reprint Ser.). 1977. 15.95 (0-8369-3667-1) Ayer.

— Emma Lazarus: Poet, Jewish Activist, Pioneer Zionist. LC 79-11570. (Illus.). 1979. pap. 2.00 (0-916790-01-0) Jewish Hist.

— Fathers of Classical Music. LC 73-84294. (Essay Index Reprint Ser.). 1977. 20.95 (0-8369-1119-9) Ayer.

— When I Was a Boy in Boston. LC 70-132111. (Short Story Index Reprint Ser.). (Illus.). 1977. 18.95 (0-8369-3668-X) Ayer.

Angoff, Charles, ed. Biology & the Future of Man: Papers by Nathan Hershey & Merril Eisenbud. LC 77-92564. (Leverton Lectures: No. 6). 52p. 1978. 14.50 (0-8386-2222-4) Fairleigh Dickinson.

— Humanities in the Age of Science. (Illus.). 272p. 1975. 29.50 (0-8386-6760-0) Fairleigh Dickinson.

— Stories from the Literary Review. LC 68-21271. 312p. 1975. 35.00 (0-8386-6899-2) Fairleigh Dickinson.

Angoff, Charles, ed. see American Mercury Staff.

Angoff, Charles, ed. see Cherry, Conrad, et al.

Angoff, Charles, ed. see Nathan, George J.

Angoff, Charles, jt. ed. see Spivak, Lawrence E.

Angoff, Charles, ed. see Wallace, Emily M., et al.

Angoff, William H. Scales, Norms, & Equivalent Scores. 1988. 6.00 (0-317-67895-7) Educ Testing Serv.

Angold, Adrian, jt. ed. see Hay, Dale F.

Angold, Michael. Byzantine Empire, 1025-1204. 2nd ed. LC 96-49085. 400p. (C). 1997. pap. 33.53 (0-582-29468-1) Longman.

***Angold, Michael.** Church & Society in Byzantium under the Comneni: 1081-1261. 620p. (C). 2000. pap. Price not set. (0-521-26986-5) Cambridge U Pr.

Angold, Michael. Church & Society in Byzantium under the Comneni, 1081-1261. 620p. (C). 1995. text 100.00 (0-521-26432-4) Cambridge U Pr.

***Angolia, J. R. & Littlejohn, David.** Labor Organizations of the Reich. deluxe ed. (Illus.). 560p. 1999. 54.95 (0-912138-76-9) Bender Pub CA.

Angolia, John R. & Hackney, Clint R. The Pour le Merite & Germany's First Aces. (Illus.). 288p. 1984. write for info. (0-9613392-0-9) Hackney Pubns.

Angotti, Charlotte. Still Crazy after All These Quilts. 36p. (Orig.). 1994. pap. 12.95 (0-929950-15-1, 118) ME Pubns.

Angotti, John. Rise up My People. pap. write for info. (1-58459-067-X, 7360) Wrld Lib Pubns.

Angotti, Karen. Lyme Disease: A Mother's Perspective. 112p. (Orig.). 1993. pap. 6.95 (0-9633902-3-6) Anarek Pubns.

Angoujard, Jean-Pierre. Metrical Structure of Arabic. (Publications in Language Sciences). iv, 200p. (Orig.). (C). 1990. pap. 106.15 (90-6765-296-2) Mouton.

Angowski, Lisa. Time off from Work: Using Sabbaticals to Enhance Your Life While Keeping Your Career on Track. 209p. 1994. pap. 14.95 (0-471-31067-0) Wiley.

Angrand, F., et al, eds. Numerical Methods for Euler Equations of Fluid Dynamics. LC 85-62674. (Proceedings in Applied Mathematics Ser.: No. 21). xii, 508p. 1985. text 56.25 (0-89871-200-9) Soc Indus-Appl Math.

Angres, Daniel H., et al. Healing the Healer: Treating the Addicted Physician. LC 98-15857. 231p. 1999. 32.50 (1-887841-15-6, Psychosocial) Intl Univs Pr.

Angresano, James. Comparative Economics. 2nd ed. LC 95-24833. 612p. 1995. 95.00 (0-13-381633-8) P-H.

— The Political Economy of Gunnar Myrdal: An Institutional Basis for the Transformation Problem. LC 97-12121. 224p. 1997. 85.00 (1-85898-530-7) E Elgar.

Angress, Werner T. Between Fear & Hope: Jewish Youth in the Third Reich. Granger, Christine, tr. (Illus.). 200p. 1988. text 41.00 (0-231-06598-1) Col U Pr.

Angrill, Muntsa C. The Big Book of Drawing & Painting the Figure. (Big Bks.). (Illus.). 192p. 1995. pap. 32.50 (0-8230-3896-3) Watsn-Guptill.

Angrisani, David P. & Goldman, Robert L. Predicting Successful Hospital Mergers & Acquisitions: A Financial & Marketing Analytical Tool. LC 96-24638. (Illus.). 132p. (C). 1997. 49.95 (0-7890-0057-1); pap. 22.95 (0-7890-0182-9) Haworth Pr.

***Angrisano, Steve.** Make a Difference: Songbook. 104p. 1998. pap. 8.95 (1-57992-001-2) OR Catholic.

Angrist, Shirley S., et al. Women After Treatment: A Study of Former Mental Patients & Their Normal Neighbors. LC 68-20043. (C). 1968. 31.00 (0-89197-471-7) Irvington.

Angrosino, Michael, jt. auth. see Crane, Julia.

Angrosino, Michael V. Documents of Interaction: Biography, Autobiography & Life History in Social Science Perspective. 128p. 1989. pap. 18.95 (0-8130-0925-1) U Press Fla.

— A Health Practitioner's Guide to the Behavioral & Social Sciences. LC 86-14642. 222p. 1986. 57.95 (0-86569-157-6, Auburn Hse) Greenwood.

— Opportunity House: Ethnographic Stories of Mental Retardation. LC 97-33813. (Ethnographic Alternatives Ser.: Vol. 2). 288p. 1997. 65.00 (0-7619-8916-1); pap. 23.95 (0-7619-8917-X) AltaMira Pr.

Angsmyr, Tore, jt. auth. see Beretta, Marco.

Angst, Jules, jt. auth. see Kline, Nathan S.

Angst-Nowik, Doris & Sloan, Jane. One-Way Ticket to Hollywood: Film Artists of Austrian & German Origin in Los Angeles. (Illus.). 107p. (Orig.). 1986. pap. 10.00 (0-318-22296-5) USC Lib Gifts.

Angstrom, M., jt. auth. see Nojd, Ruben.

Anguiano, Rabul & Galerbia Dr. J. Pilar Licona Olvera (Universidad Autobnoma de Hidalgo) Staff. Anguiano Por Anguiano: Anguiano by Anguiano. LC 98-170742. 133 p. 1997. write for info. (968-6340-59-9) Univ of Southampton.

Angulo, Carlos. Guajaro en la Arqueologia del Norte de Colombia. (SPA., Illus.). 198p. 1988. pap. 8.50 (1-877812-24-2, BR022) UPLAAP.

Angulo, Jaime de. Jaime in Taos. De Angulo, Gui, ed. (Illus.). 148p. pap. 6.95 (0-87286-165-1) City Lights.

Angulo, Jaime De, see De Angulo, Jaime.

Angulo, Maria-Elena. Magic Realism: Social Context & Discourse. LC 94-35674. (Latin American Studies: Vol. 5). (Illus.). 144p. 1995. text 35.00 (0-8153-1183-4, H1675) Garland.

Angura, Tobias O., jt. ed. see Hambly, Helen.

Angus. Mini Historias Biblicas: The German Bible Society Mini Bible Story Books. (SPA.). 1995. write for info. (0-7899-0079-3); write for info. (0-7899-0080-7); write for info. (0-7899-0081-5); write for info. (0-7899-0082-3); write for info. (0-7899-0083-1); write for info. (0-7899-0084-X); write for info. (0-7899-0085-8); write for info. (0-7899-0086-6) Editorial Unilit.

Angus & Hudson. El Barco de Pedro (Peter's Boat) (Pueblo Junto al Lago). (SPA.). 2.99 (1-56063-411-1, 493998) Editorial Unilit.

***Angus & Donahy Staff.** Dictionary of Internationa Finance. (ENG, FRE, GER, ITA & SPA.). 1998 150.00 (0-320-02120-3) Fr & Eur.

Angus, A. Great Modern European Short Stories. LC 96-96674. 1996. pap. 11.00 (0-449-91222-1) Fawcett.

Angus-Butterworth, Lionel M. Ten Master Historians. LC 69-18919. (Essay Index Reprint Ser.). 1977. 18.95 (0-8369-0000-6) Ayer.

Angus, Christopher. Reflections from Canoe Country: Paddling the Waters of the Adirondacks & Canada. LC 97-4281. (Illus.). 256p. 1997. 29.95 (0-8156-0444-0) Syracuse U Pr.

— Reflections from Canoe Country: Paddling the Waters of the Adirondacks & Canada. 196p. 1999. pap. 17.95 (0-8156-0571-4) Syracuse U Pr.

Angus, D. Contemporary American Short Stories. LC 97-153960. 1996. pap. 12.00 (0-449-91227-2) Fawcett.

***Angus, David & Mirel, Jeffery.** The Failed Promise of the American High School, 1890-1995. LC 99-17345. 1. 272p. 1999. text 58.00 (0-8077-3843-3) Tchrs Coll.

Angus, David L. & Mirel, Jeffrey. The Failed Promise of the American High School, 1890-1995 LC 99-17345. 272p. 1999. pap. text 26.95 (0-8077-3842-5) Tchrs Coll.

Angus, Douglas. The Best Short Stories of the Modern Age. 336p. (Orig.). 1987. mass mkt. 5.99 (0-449-30058-7, Prem) Fawcett.

Angus, Douglas & Angus, Sylvia, eds. Contemporary American Short Stories. 560p. 1986. mass mkt. 5.99 (0-449-30049-8, Prem) Fawcett.

***Angus, Elaine M.** The King of the Mountain. (gr. k-3). 1999. pap. 6.95 (0-533-12944-3) Vantage.

Angus, Errol W. Judgement. (Illus.). 45p. 1995. pap. 6.00 (0-9647589-0-3) GEDA Pubns.

Angus, Fay. The Gentle Art of Being There. 1991. 6.95 (0-8378-2064-2) Gibson.

Angus, Fern. Aunt Ella's Ozark Recipes. (Illus.). 66p. 1993. pap. 3.50 (0-9637913-1-1) Angus Pubns.

— Down the Wire Road in the Missouri Ozarks. (Illus.). 160p. 1992. reprint ed. pap. 10.95 (0-9637913-0-3) Angus Pubns.

— Ozark Remedies. (Ozark Ser.: No. 3). (Illus.). 64p. (Orig.). 1995. pap. 3.50 (0-9637913-3-8) Angus Pubns.

— Ozark Superstitions. (Illus.). 37p. 1993. pap. 3.00 (0-9637913-2-X) Angus Pubns.

Angus, Ian. A Border Within: National Identity, Cultural Plurality & Wilderness. LC 98-152232. 280p. 1997. text 65.00 (0-7735-1652-2, Pub. by McG-Queens Univ Pr); pap. text 22.95 (0-7735-1653-0, Pub. by McG-Queens Univ Pr) CUP Services.

— Collecting Antiques LC 79-312536. 128p. 1978. write for info. (0-7740-2570-0) Coles Publ.

***Angus, Ian.** (Dis)Figurations: Discourse/Critique/Ethics. (Phronesis Ser.). 256p. (C). 2000. 65.00 (1-85984-759-5, Pub. by Verso); pap. 20.00 (1-85984-277-1, Pub. by Verso) Norton.

— Primal Scenes of Communication: Communication Theory, Social Movements & Consumer Society. LC 99-54268. (C). 2000. pap. text 19.95 (0-7914-4666-2) State U NY Pr.

— Primal Scenes of Communication: Communication Theory, Social Movements & Consumer Society. LC 99-54268. (C). 2000. text 59.50 (0-7914-4665-4) State U NY Pr.

Angus, Ian & Langsdorf, Lenore, eds. The Critical Turn: Rhetoric & Philosophy in Postmodern Discourse. LC 92-9398. 240p. (C). 1992. pap. 16.95 (0-8093-1844-X) S Ill U Pr.

— The Critical Turn: Rhetoric & Philosophy in Postmodern Discourse. LC 92-9398. 240p. (C). 1992. 16.95 (0-8093-1843-1) S Ill U Pr.

Angus, Ian, jt. ed. see Jhally, Sut.

Angus, Ian, ed. see Orwell, George.

Angus, Ian, jt. ed. see Orwell, George.

Angus, Ian H. George Grant's Platonic Rejoinder to Heidegger: Contemporary Political Philosophy & the Question of Technology. LC 87-26332. 150p. 1987 lib. bdg. 69.95 (0-88946-715-3) E Mellen.

— Technique & Enlightment: Limits of Instrumental Reason. LC 83-27363. (Current Continental Research Ser.). 172p. (Orig.). 1984. pap. text 20.50 (0-8191-3816-9); lib. bdg. 45.00 (0-8191-3815-0) U Pr of Amer.

Angus, J. A., jt. ed. see Garland, C. J.

Angus, James, jt. auth. see Howard, David.

Angus, James T. A Respectable Ditch: A History of the Trent Severn Waterway, 1833-1920. (Illus.). 472p. 1998. pap. 19.95 (0-7735-1821-5) McG-Queens Univ Pr.

— A Respectable Ditch: The History of the Trent-Severn Waterway, 1833-1920. 472p. 1988. 44.95 (0-7735-0597-0, Pub. by McG-Queens Univ Pr) CUP Services.

Angus, Lawrence. Schooling, the School Effectiveness Movement & Educational Reform. 100p. (C). 1986. 48.00 (0-7300-0375-2, Pub. by Deakin Univ) St Mut.

Angus, Lawrence, ed. Class, Culture & Curriculum: A Study of Continuity & Change in a Catholic School. 97p. (C). 1986. 55.00 (0-7300-0374-4, Pub. by Deakin Univ) St Mut.

— Schooling for Social Order: Democracy, Equality & Social Mobility in Education. 94p. (C). 1986. 51.00 (0-7300-0397-3, Pub. by Deakin Univ) St Mut.

Angus, Lawrence B., ed. Education, Inequality & Social Identity. LC 92-42863. 1993. 75.00 (0-7507-0172-2, Falmer Pr) Taylor & Francis.

Angus Macleod, H., jt. ed. see Amra, Claude.

Angus, Margaret. The Old Stones of Kingston: Its Buildings Before 1867. LC 66-6913. (Illus.). 1980. pap. 17.95 (0-8020-6419-1) U of Toronto Pr.

Angus, Marion, ed. see Reid, George A.

Angus, Mark. Salt Lake City Underfoot: Self-Guided Tours of Historic Neighborhoods (Centennial Edition) 2nd anniversary ed. LC 96-6997. (Illus.). 220p. 1996. pap. 12.95 (1-56085-105-8) Signature Bks.

Angus, Max. The Rules of School Reform. LC 98-112940. 208p. 1997. 79.95 (0-7507-0637-6, Falmer Pr); pap. 29.95 (0-7507-0638-4, Falmer Pr) Taylor & Francis.

Angus, Murray. The Last Shall be First. 96p. (Orig.). 1991. pap. 9.95 (1-55021-064-5, Pub. by NC Ltd) U of Toronto Pr.

Angus, Raymond, jt. auth. see Brown, Ray.

Angus, Robert B. Insecta: Coleoptera, Hydrohilidae, Helophorinae. (Suesswasserfauna von Mitteleuropa Ser.: Vol. 20, No. 10-2). (GER., Illus.). 150p. 1991. pap. 100.00 (3-437-30643-X, Pub. by Gustav Fischer) Balogh.

A

Angus, Robert B. & Clark, Claudia. Math at Work, Bk. 1. LC 97-45052. 592p. 1998. pap. text 54.00 (0-13-860388-X) P-H.

— Math at Work, Bk. 2. LC 97-45052. Vol. 2. 528p. 1998. pap. text 54.00 (0-13-857442-1) P-H.

Angus, Robert B., et al. Electrical Discipline - Specific Review for the FE/EIT Exam. LC 97-22133. 80p. (Orig.). 1997. pap. 24.95 (1-888577-20-7, DSEE) Prof Pubns CA.

***Angus, Robert B., et al.** Planning, Performing, & Controlling Projects. 2nd ed. LC 99-27061. (Illus.). 290p. (C). 1999. 56.00 (0-13-099878-8) P-H.

Angus, Robert B., Jr., jt. auth. see Dearness, John L.

Angus, S. The Environment of Early Christianity. 1977. lib. bdg. 59.95 (0-8490-1778-5) Gordon Pr.

— International Thermodynamic Tables of the Fluid State, Vols. 1 & 3-4. Incl. Vol. 3. Carbon Dioxide. 1976. 179.00 (0-08-020924-6); write for info. (0-318-57472-1, Pub. by Pergamon Repr) Franklin.

Angus, S., ed. International Thermodynamic Tables of the Fluid State-6. 1979. 118.00 (0-08-022372-9, Pub. by Pergamon Repr) Franklin.

Angus, Samuel. The Environment of Early Christianity. LC 75-157322. (Select Bibliographies Reprint Ser.). 1977. reprint ed. 31.95 (0-8369-5781-4) Ayer.

— Mystery Religions. (Citadel Library of the Mystic Arts). 1989. pap. 9.95 (0-8065-1142-7, Citadel Pr) Carol Pub Group.

— The Mystery Religions. LC 74-12637. 359p. 1975. reprint ed. pap. 8.95 (0-486-23124-0) Dover.

— The Religious Quests of the Graeco-Roman World: A Study in the Historical Background of Early Christianity. LC 66-30791. 1929. 32.00 (0-8196-0196-9) Biblo.

Angus, Susan, ed. Invest Yourself: A Guide to Action. rev. ed. (Illus.). 234p. 1997. 8.00 (0-9629322-3-X) Comm Voluntary Serv & Action.

***Angus, Susan, ed.** Invest Yourself 2000: The Catalogue of Volunteer Opportunities. (Illus.). 282p. 1999. pap. 8.00 (0-9629322-4-8) Comm Voluntary Serv & Action.

Angus, Sylvia, jt. ed. see Angus, Douglas.

Angus, Vivienne. Know Yourself Through Your Cat. 192p. (Orig.). 1993. mass mkt. 4.50 (0-380-71835-9, Avon Bks) Morrow Avon.

Angustus, Patrick. Baby Father 3. 1998. pap. text 10.95 (1-874509-57-3, Pub. by X Pr) LPC InBook.

Angwin, Darice A. Feeling Good: An Alternative Approach to Health Care. 100p. (Orig.). Date not set. pap. text 9.95 (0-9648088-0-3) Sunset Intl.

***Angwin, Duncan.** Implementing Successful Post-Acquisition Management. (Management Briefings Ser.). (Illus.). 1999. pap. 157.50 (0-273-64225-1, Pub. by F T P-H) Trans-Atl Phila.

Angwin, Roselle. Creative Novel Writing. 176p. 1999. 16.95 (0-7090-6344-X, Pub. by R Hale Ltd) Seven Hills Bk.

— Riding the Dragon: Myth & the Inner Journey. LC 94-26671. 1995. pap. 11.95 (1-85230-575-4, Pub. by Element MA) Penguin Putnam.

Angyal, Andras. Foundations for a Science of Personality. LC BF0698.A5. 410p. reprint ed. pap. 127.10 (0-7837-2217-6, 205730700004) Bks Demand.

— Neurosis & Treatment: A Holistic Theory. (Psychoanalysis: Examined & Re-Examined Ser.). 328p. 1982. lib. bdg. 35.00 (0-306-79709-7) Da Capo.

Angyal, Andrew J. Lewis Thomas. (United States Authors Ser.). 176p. 1989. text 24.95 (0-8057-7536-6, TUSAS 547, Twyne) Mac Lib Ref.

— Wendell Berry. LC 95-2290. (United States Authors Ser.: Vol. TUSAS 654). 1995. 32.00 (0-8057-4628-5, Twyne) Mac Lib Ref.

Angyal, Gerald, ed. U. S. FDA Methods for the Microbiological Analysis of Selected Nutrients. 86p. 1996. pap. 39.00 (0-935584-61-7) AOAC Intl.

Anh Huong, tr. see Hanh, Thich Nhat.

Anh-Viet, Tu Dien. English-Vietnamese Dictionary. (ENG & VIE.). 1560p. 1975. 120.00 (0-7855-7165-5) St Mut.

Anhalt, Emily. Solon the Singer: Politics & Poetics. 160p. (C). 1992. text 54.00 (0-8476-7782-6); pap. text 22.00 (0-8476-7783-4) Rowman.

Anhalt, Todd S., jt. auth. see Jacobs, Paul H.

Anheier, H. K. & Toepler, S., eds. Private Funds, Public Purpose: Philanthropic Foundations in International Perspective. (Nonprofit & Civil Society Studies). (Illus.). 280p. (C). 1999. 85.00 (0-306-45946-9, Plenum Trade); pap. 37.50 (0-306-45947-7, Plenum Trade) Perseus Pubng.

Anheier, Helmut K. When Things Go Wrong: Organizational Failures & Breakdowns. LC 98-25537. 1998. pap. 21.95 (0-7619-1048-4) Sage.

— When Things Go Wrong: Organizational Failures & Breakdowns. LC 98-25537. 318p. 1999. 48.00 (0-7619-1047-6) Sage.

***Anheier, Helmut K. & Salamon, Lester M.** Nonprofit Institutions & the 1993 System of National Accounts. (Working Papers of the Johns Hopkins Comparative Nonprofit Sector Project: Vol. 25). (Illus.). 26p. 1998. pap. text 6.00 (*1-886333-30-0*) JH Univ Inst Pol Studies.

Anheier, Helmut K. & Salamon, Lester M. The Nonprofit Sector in the Developing World: A Comparative Analysis. LC 97-48661. (Johns Hopkins Nonprofit Sector Ser.). 320p. 1998. 45.00 (*0-7190-5386-2*, Pub. by Manchester Univ Pr) St Martin.

Anheier, Helmut K. & Seibel, Wolfgang. Defining the Nonprofit Sector: Germany. Salamon, Lester M., ed. & illus. by. (Working Papers of the Johns Hopkins Comparative Nonprofit Sector Project: No. 6). 35p. 1993. pap. text 6.00 (*1-886333-01-7*) JH Univ Inst Pol Studies.

Anheier, Helmut K. & Seibel, Wolfgang, eds. The Third Sector: Comparative Studies of Nonprofit Organizations. (Studies in Organization: No. 21). xiv, 413p. (C). 1990. lib. bdg. 64.95 (*3-11-011713-4*) De Gruyter.

Anheier, Helmut K., et al. The Nonprofit Sector in the United Nations System of National Accounts: Definition, Treatment, & Practice. (Working Papers of the Johns Hopkins Comparative Nonprofit Sector Project: No. 4). (Illus.). 33p. 1992. pap. text 6.00 (*1-886333-03-3*) JH Univ Inst Pol Studies.

Anheier, Helmut K., jt. auth. see Salamon, Lester M.

Anheier, Helmut K., ed. see Archambault, Edith.

Anheier, Helmut K., ed. see Atingdui, Lawrence.

Anheier, Helmut K., ed. see Barbetta, Gian P.

Anheier, Helmut K., ed. see Kandil, Amani.

Anheier, Helmut K., ed. see Kendall, Jeremy & Knapp, Matin.

Anheier, Helmut K., ed. see Kuti, Eva.

Anheier, Helmut K., ed. see Landim, Leilah.

Anheier, Helmut K., ed. see Lundstrom, Tommy & Wijkstrom, Filip.

Anheier, Helmut K., ed. see Pongsapich, Amara.

Anheier, Helmut K., ed. see Salamon, Lester M.

Anheier, Helmut K., ed. see Sen, Siddhartha.

Anheier, Helmut K., ed. see Takayoshi Amenomori.

Anheuser-Busch, Inc. Staff. The Official Collector's Guide to Anheuser-Busch Steins, Vol. 1. 244p. 1993. pap. text. write for info. (*0-9637395-0-6*) Anheuser-Busch.

Anholt, Betty. Sanibel's Story: Voices & Images from Calusa to Incorporation. LC 98-37822. 1998. write for info. (*1-57864-046-6*) Donning Co.

Anholt, C. & Anholt, L. The Best of the First Ten Years of the Labrador Quarterly. deluxe ed. (Illus.). 328p. 1995. pap. 55.00 (*0-614-04543-6*) Donald R Hoflin.

Anholt, Catherine. What Makes Me Happy? LC 94-5144. 1996. 11.19 (*0-606-10054-7*, Pub. by Turtleback) Demco.

Anholt, Catherine & Anholt, Laurence. Bear & Baby. LC 92-54581. (Illus.). 24p. (J). (ps). 1993. 5.95 (*1-56402-235-8*) Candlewick Pr.

— Catherine & Laurence Anholt's Big Book of Families. LC 97-31418. (Illus.). 32p. (J). (ps-2). 1998. 16.99 (*0-7636-0323-6*) Candlewick Pr.

— Come Back, Jack! LC 93-2885. (Illus.). 32p. (J). (ps up). 1994. 12.95 (*1-56402-313-3*) Candlewick Pr.

— Come Back, Jack! LC 93-2885. (Illus.). 32p. (J). (ps up). 1996. pap. 5.99 (*1-56402-686-8*) Candlewick Pr.

— Come Back, Jack! (J). (ps-2). reprint ed. pap. 5.99 (*0-614-15566-5*) Candlewick Pr.

Anholt, Catherine & Anholt, Laurence. First Words & Pictures. LC 95-72504. (J). 1996. write for info. (*0-7636-0041-5*) Candlewick Pr.

— Harry's Home. LC 99-16597. 32p. (J). 2000. 16.00 (*0-374-32870-6*) FS&G.

Anholt, Catherine & Anholt, Laurence. Here Come the Babies. LC 92-54584. (Illus.). 32p. (J). (ps up). 1993. 13.95 (*1-56402-209-9*) Candlewick Pr.

— Kids. LC 91-58739. (Illus.). 32p. (J). (ps up). 1994. pap. 4.99 (*1-56402-269-2*) Candlewick Pr.

— A Kiss Like This. LC 97-16452. (Illus.). 32p. (J). 1997. 12.95 (*0-7641-5068-5*) Barron.

***Anholt, Catherine & Anholt, Laurence.** Sophie & the New Baby. LC 99-50901. (Illus.). (J). (ps-1). 2000. lib. bdg. 15.95 (*0-8075-7550-X*) A Whitman.

Anholt, Catherine & Anholt, Laurence. Toddlers. LC 92-54588. (Illus.). 24p. (J). (ps). 1993. 5.95 (*1-56402-242-0*) Candlewick Pr.

— Twins, Two by Two. LC 91-71820. (Illus.). 32p. (J). (ps). 1992. 13.95 (*1-56402-041-X*) Candlewick Pr.

— Twins, Two by Two. LC 91-71820. (Illus.). 32p. (J). (ps-3). 1994. pap. 4.99 (*1-56402-397-4*) Candlewick Pr.

— What I Like. LC 97-32333. (Illus.). 32p. (J). (ps-k). 1998. pap. 5.99 (*0-7636-0585-9*) Candlewick Pr.

— What Makes Me Happy? LC 94-5144. (Illus.). 32p. (J). 1996. reprint ed. pap. 5.99 (*1-56402-828-3*) Candlewick Pr.

Anholt, Catherine, et al. The Candlewick Book of First Rhymes. LC 95-49928. (Illus.). 64p. (J). (ps-1). 1996. 17.99 (*0-7636-0015-6*) Candlewick Pr.

Anholt, L., jt. auth. see Anholt, C.

Anholt, Laurence. Billy & the Big New School. LC 98-39774. (Concept Book Ser.). (Illus.). 32p. (J). (ps-1). 1999. 15.95 (*0-8075-0743-1*) A Whitman.

— Camille & the Sunflowers. (Illus.). 32p. (J). (ps-2). 1994. 14.95 (*0-8120-6409-7*) Barron.

— Camille y Los Girasoles (Camille & the Sunflowers) (SPA., Illus.). (J). (gr. 2-4). 1997. pap. 12.95 (*1-56014-670-2*) Santillana.

— Degas & the Little Dancer. (Illus.). 32p. (J). (ps-3). 1996. 14.95 (*0-8120-6583-2*) Barron.

— Degas y la Pequena Bailarina (Degas & the Little Dancer) (SPA., Illus.). (J). (gr. 2-6). 1998. pap. 12.95 (*1-58105-122-0*) Santillana.

***Anholt, Laurence.** The Emperor's New Underwear. LC 99-32947. (Illus.). (J). 1999. pap. text. write for info. (*0-88166-347-6*) Meadowbrook.

Anholt, Laurence. The Emperor's New Underwear. (Illus.). 64p. (J). (gr. 4-6). 1999. pap. 3.95 (*0-689-83073-4*, Pub. by Meadowbrook) S&S Childrens.

***Anholt, Laurence.** The Forgotten Forest. 32p. (J). (ps-3). 1999. write for info. (*0-7112-1141-8*, Pub. by F Lincoln) Antique Collect.

— I Like Me, I Like You. LC 99-49699. (Share-a-Story Ser.). (Illus.). (J). 2000. write for info. (*0-7894-5617-6*) DK Pub Inc.

— Leonardo & the Flying Boy. 2000. 13.95 (*0-7641-5225-4*) Barron.

Anholt, Laurence. Little Red Riding Wolf. (J). (gr. 4-6). 2000. pap. 3.95 (*0-689-83293-1*) S&S Childrens.

— Picasso & the Girl with a Ponytail. LC 98-14005. (SPA., Illus.). 32p. (J). (ps-2). 1998. 13.95 (*0-7641-5031-6*) Barron.

***Anholt, Laurence.** Silly Jack & the Bean Stack. (Illus.). (J). (gr. 4-6). 1999. pap. 3.95 (*0-689-83070-X*, Pub. by Meadowbrook) S&S Childrens.

Anholt, Laurence. Stone Girl, Bone Girl: The Story of Mary Anning. LC 98-36608. (Illus.). 32p. (J). (gr. k-4). 1999. 15.95 (*0-531-30148-6*) Orchard Bks Watts.

— Summerhouse. LC 98-41959. (Illus.). (J). (ps-3). 1999. 14.95 (*0-7894-4377-5*, D K Ink) DK Pub Inc.

***Anholt, Laurence & Robins, Arthur.** Silly Jack & the Bean Stalk. LC 99-33357. (J). 1999. pap. text. write for info. (*0-88166-348-4*) Meadowbrook.

***Anholt, Laurence, et al.** Stories & Fun for the Very Young. LC 98-18028. (Illus.). 61p. (YA). (ps up). 1998. 19.99 (*0-7636-0575-1*) Candlewick Pr.

Anholt, Laurence, jt. auth. see Anholt, Catherine.

Anholt, Robert R. H. Dazzle 'em with Style: An Introduction to the Art of Oral Scientific Presentation. LC 93-50603. (C). 1994. pap. 11.95 (*0-7167-2583-5*) W H Freeman.

— Electrical & Thermal Characterization of MESFETs, HEMTs & HBTs. LC 94-36803. 1994. 110.00 (*0-89006-749-X*) Artech Hse.

***Anholt, Simon.** Another One Bites the Grass: Creating International Advertising That Makes Sense. LC 99-37987. (Adweek Ser.). 326p. 2000. 29.95 (*0-471-35488-0*) Wiley.

Anholt, Uni V. In Search of Heffalumps. (Illus.). 88p. (Orig.). pap. 2.95 (*0-9601996-0-8*) Beeberry Bks.

***Anholts, Catherine & Anholts, Laurence.** The Big Book of Families. (Illus.). 1998. pap. 9.99 (*1-58048-025-X*) Sandvik Pub.

Anholts, Laurence, jt. auth. see Anholts, Catherine.

Ani, Marimba. Yurugu: An Afrocentric Critique of European Cultural Thought & Behavior. LC 91-71027. 1994. 79.95 (*0-86543-249-X*); pap. 21.95 (*0-86543-248-1*) Africa World.

Ani, Moukhtar, jt. ed. see Stowasser, Karl.

Aniakor, Chike C. Fang. LC 96-15574. (Heritage Library of African Peoples: Set 3). (Illus.). 64p. (YA). (gr. 7-12). 1996. lib. bdg. 16.95 (*0-8239-1994-3*, D1994-3) Rosen Group.

Aniakor, Chike C., jt. auth. see Cole, Herbert M.

Aniansson, Britt H., jt. ed. see Svedin, Uno.

Anick, David. Differential Algebras in Topology. LC 93-12604. (Research Notes in Mathematics Ser.). (Illus.). 304p. (C). 1993. text 66.00 (*1-56881-001-6*) AK Peters.

Anick, Peter & Simoudis, Evangelos, eds. Case Based Reasoning & Information Retrieval: Exploring Opportunities for Technology Sharing: Papers from the 1993 Spring Symposium. (Technical Reports). (Illus.). 145p. (Orig.). (C). 1993. spiral bd. 25.00 (*0-929280-45-8*) AAAI Pr.

Anick, Peter, jt. auth. see Reiner, David.

Anies. Arabic Medium Lexicon: Mou'jam al Wasit. (ARA.). 1000p. 60.00 (*0-86685-498-3*, LDL4983, Pub. by Librairie du Liban) Intl Bk Ctr.

Anifantakis, Harry. The Diminished Mind: One Family's Extraordinary Battle with Alzheimer's: The Jean Tyler Story. large type ed. LC 92-31108. (General Ser.). 420p. 1993. 20.95 (*0-8161-5602-6*, G K Hall Lrg Type) Mac Lib Ref.

Anifowose, F. O. The Violence & Politics in Nigeria: A Case-Study of the Tiv & Yoruba. LC 79-88590. 1982. 22.95 (*0-685-03585-9*); pap. 9.95 (*0-88357-084-X*) NOK Pubs.

Anikeeff, Michael A., et al. Seniors Housing. LC 97-35809. (Research Issues in Real Estate Staff). 264p. 1997. lib. bdg. 76.00 (*0-7923-8012-6*) Kluwer Academic.

Anikiev, V. V., jt. ed. see Ilyichev, V. I.

Anikin, A. Dictionary of Economics & Finance English-Russian. (ENG & RUS.). 579p. 1993. 70.00 (*5-900428-05-2*, Pub. by St Peters) IBD Ltd.

Anikin, A. V., ed. English - Russian Dictionary of Economics & Finance. (ENG & RUS.). 589p. 1993. 59.95 (*0-8285-5455-2*) Firebird NY.

Anikin, Andrei V. English-Russian Dictionary of Economics & Finance. (ENG & RUS.). 580p. 1993. 95.00 (*0-7859-9077-1*) Fr & Eur.

— Gold: The Yellow Devil. LC 83-274. Orig. Title: Zheltyi d iavol. (RUS.). 244p. 1984. 5.95 (*0-7178-0599-9*) Intl Pubs Co.

— A Science in Its Youth. Cook, K. M., tr. from RUS. LC 78-31568. 389p. (C). 1979. pap. 3.50 (*0-7178-0503-4*) Intl Pubs Co.

Anikine, A. English-Russian Economics Dictionary. lib. bdg. 75.00 (*0-8288-2611-0*) Fr & Eur.

— English-Russian Economics Dictionary. 792p. 1981. 75.00 (*0-8288-0125-8*, F136660) Fr & Eur.

Anikonov, Yu E. Formulas in Inverse & Ill-Posed Problems. (Inverse & Ill-Posed Problems Ser.). (Illus.). 208p. 1997. 150.00 (*90-6764-216-9*, Pub. by VSP) Coronet Bks.

Anikonov, Yu. E. Multidimensional Inverse & Ill-Posed Problems for Differential Equations. (Inverse & Ill-Posed Problems Ser.). 240p. 1994. 120.00 (*90-6764-185-5*, Pub. by VSP) Coronet Bks.

Anikonov, Yu E., et al, eds. Inverse & Ill-Posed Sources Problems. (Inverse & Ill-Posed Problems Ser.). (Illus.). 244p. 1997. 147.50 (*90-6764-273-8*) Coronet Bks.

Anikpo, Mark O., jt. ed. see Shepherd, George W., Jr.

Anikst, A. Soviet Commercial Design of the Twenties. (C). 1990. 280.00 (*0-7855-4445-3*, Pub. by Collets) St Mut.

Anikst, Mikhail, ed. Soviet Commercial Design of the Twenties. (Illus.). 144p. 1991. pap. 30.00 (*1-55859-152-4*) Abbeville Pr.

Anikst, Mikhail & Turchin, V. Country Estates Around Moscow from the History of Russian Estate Culture of the 17th, 18th, & 19th Centuries. 398p. 1979. 150.00 (*0-7855-0697-7*) St Mut.

Anile, A. M. Ray Methods for Nonlinear Waves in Fluid & Plasmas. 1993. 69.95 (*0-582-02343-2*, Pub. by Addison-Wesley) Longman.

— Relativistic Fluids & Magneto-Fluids: With Applications in Astrophysics & Plasma Physics. (Cambridge Monographs on Mathematical Physics). (Illus.). 348p. (C). 1990. text 110.00 (*0-521-30406-7*) Cambridge U Pr.

Anile, A. M. & Choquet-Bruhat, Yvonne, eds. Relativistic Fluid Dynamics. (Lecture Notes in Mathematics Ser.: Vol. 1385). v, 308p. 1989. 45.95 (*0-387-51466-X*) Spr-Verlag.

Anim-Addo, Joan, ed. Framing the Word: Gender & Genre in Caribbean Women's Writing. LC 97-105031. 260p. 1997. 65.00 (*1-871177-96-0*, Pub. by Whiting & Birch); pap. 29.95 (*1-871177-91-X*, Pub. by Whiting & Birch) Paul & Co Pubs.

Animal Medical Center Staff, et al. The Complete Book of Dog Health. (Illus.). 272p. 1990. per. 15.00 (*0-87605-455-6*) Howell Bks.

Animal Production Organization Staff. Animal Quarantine in Asia & the Pacific. 309p. 1994. pap. 15.00 (*92-833-2145-6*, APO321456, Pub. by Asian Prod Organ) Bernan Associates.

Animal Rescue League Auxiliary Staff & Schuler, Rosemarie. Recipes from a Caring World. (Illus.). 236p. 1993. 15.00 (*0-9636615-0-7*) Animal Rescue.

Animaland Staff. The Animaland Cookbook, Vol. 2. LC 93-71222. (Illus.). 1993. pap. 12.95 (*0-87197-372-3*) Favorite Recipes.

Animalu, A. O. Intermediate Quantum Theory of Crystalline Solids. (Illus.). 528p. (C). 1991. reprint ed. text 90.00 (*1-878907-20-4*) TechBooks.

Animated Promotional Maps International Staff. Valley of the Sun Ultimate Golf Guide & Reference. (Illus.). 8p. 1994. 7.95 (*0-9645198-0-1*) Anim Prom Maps.

Animerica Magazine Staff. Animerica: The First Five Years: Selected Interviews with Masters of Japanese Animation. (Illus.). 175p. 1997. pap. 19.95 (*1-56931-220-6*, Cadence Bks) Viz Commns Inc.

Aniolowski, Scott, et al. The Golden Dawn. (Illus.). 192p. (Orig.). 1996. pap. 19.95 (*1-887797-02-5*) Tynes Cowan.

Aniolowski, Scott D. Return to Lovecraft Country. LC 97-90723. 242p. 1997. pap. 11.95 (*1-57502-535-3*, PO1574) Morris Pubng.

— Singers of Strange Songs: Celebration of Brian Lumley. 1997. pap. text 12.95 (*1-56882-104-2*) Chaosium.

— Ye Booke of Monsters Vol. II: The Aniolowski Collection. Sellers, Janice, ed. (Call of Cthulhu Roleplaying Game System Ser.). (Illus.). 60p. (Orig.). 1996. pap. 11.95 (*1-56882-052-6*, 2358) Chaosium.

Aniolowski, Scott D., et al. The Art of Playing Mythos: A Tome of Arcane Knowledge. (Mythos Ser.). (Illus.). 160p. (Orig.). 1996. pap. 8.95 (*1-56882-061-5*, 1304) Chaosium.

— Cthulhu's Heirs. Stratman, Thomas M., ed. & intro. by. (Call of Cthulhu Fiction Ser.). (Illus.). 270p. (Orig.). 1994. pap. 10.95 (*1-56882-013-5*, 6003) Chaosium.

Aniolowski, Scott D., ed. see Burleson, Donald R.

Aniolowski, Scott D., ed. see Campbell, Ramsey, et al.

Aniruddha. Phasestar Astrology & Natural Phenomena. Somayajulu, G. R., ed. LC 98-100484. (Illus.). 64p. (Orig.). 1995. pap. 6.95 (*0-911837-02-7*) Indus Bks.

— Sampoorna Maha Prasthanam: The Complete Book on Essentialism, Vol. I. 492p. Date not set. 49.95 (*0-911837-11-6*) Indus Bks.

— Sampoorna Maha Prasthanam: The Complete Book on Essentialism, Vol. II. 490p. Date not set. 49.95 (*0-911837-12-4*) Indus Bks.

— Sampoorna Maha Prasthanam: The Complete Book on Essentialism, Vol. III. 636p. Date not set. 63.95 (*0-911837-13-2*) Indus Bks.

— Sampoorna Maha Prasthanam: The Complete Book on Essentialism, Vol. IV. 590p. Date not set. 59.95 (*0-911837-14-0*) Indus Bks.

— Sampoorna Maha Prasthanam: The Complete Book on Essentialism, Vol. V. 405p. Date not set. 40.95 (*0-911837-15-9*) Indus Bks.

— Sampoorna Maha Prasthanam: The Complete Book on Essentialism, Vol. VI. 270p. Date not set. 26.95 (*0-911837-16-7*) Indus Bks.

— Sampoorna Maha Prasthanam: The Complete Book on Essentialism, Vol. VII. 330p. Date not set. 32.95 (*0-911837-17-5*) Indus Bks.

— Sanksjipta Maha Prasthanam: The Condensed Book on Essentialism. (Illus.). 585p. Date not set. 58.95 (*0-911837-10-8*) Indus Bks.

Anisef, Paul, ed. Learning & Sociological Profiles of Canadian High School Students: An Overview of 15-18 Year Olds & Educational Policy Implications for Dropouts, Exceptional Students, Employed Students, Immigrant Students & Native Youth. LC 93-32121. 564p. 1993. text 119.95 (*0-7734-9347-6*) E Mellen.

Anisfeld, Michael & Davis, Amy, eds. Interpharm Computer Validation Monograph Series. 1998. 298.00 (*1-57491-073-6*) Interpharm.

Anisfeld, Michael H., ed. International Biotechnology, Bulk Chemical, & Pharmaceutical GMPs. 5th expanded rev. ed. 450p. 1998. ring bd. 297.00 (*1-57491-043-4*) Interpharm.

— International Medical Device & Diagnostic GMPs. 3rd ed. 225p. 1995. ring bd. 262.00 (*0-935184-35-X*) Interpharm.

— Interpharm Guide to FDA International Inspections Vol. I: 1990-1993. 1995. ring bd. 179.00 (*1-57491-008-6*) Interpharm.

— Interpharm Master Keyword Guide to 21 CFR: 1998-1999 Edition. 610p. 1998. 99.00 (*1-57491-091-4*) Interpharm.

— Interpharm Master Keyword Guide to Twenty-One CFR: 1997-1998 Edition. 604p. 1996. pap. 99.00 (*1-57491-036-1*) Interpharm.

Anisfeld, Michael H. & Torres, Francisco, eds. FDA Warning Letters, 1996 Vol. 1: Bulk Pharmaceutical Chemicals & Finished Pharmaceuticals. (FDA Warning Letters Ser.). (Illus.). 90p. Date not set. ring bd. 194.00 (*1-57491-056-6*) Interpharm.

— FDA Warning Letters 1996 Vol. 2: Medical Devices, Medical Equipment & Diagnostic Products. (Illus.). 1997. ring bd. 194.00 (*1-57491-057-4*) Interpharm.

Anisfeld, Michael H., jt. auth. see Lyall, John.

Anisfeld, Michael H., jt. ed. see Davis, Amy.

Anisfeld, Moshe. Language Development from Birth to 3. LC 83-82493. 306p. (C). 1984. pap. text 37.50 (*0-89859-625-4*) L Erlbaum Assocs.

Anisfield, Nancy, ed. The Nightmare Considered: Critical Essays on Nuclear War Literature. LC 91-72619. 282p. (C). 1991. 35.95 (*0-87972-529-X*); pap. 18.95 (*0-87972-530-3*) Bowling Green Univ Popular Press.

— Vietnam Anthology: American War Literature. LC 87-71030. 150p. 1987. 26.95 (*0-87972-395-5*); pap. 12.95 (*0-87972-396-3*) Bowling Green Univ Popular Press.

Anishchenko, Vadim S. Dynamical Chaos: Models & Experiments: Appearance Routes & Structure of Chaos in Simple Dynamical Systems. LC 94-48586. (Nonlinear Science, Series A, Monographs & Treatises: Vol. 8). 400p. 1995. text 74.00 (*981-02-2142-8*) World Scientific Pub.

Anisimov, Evgenii V. Empress Elizabeth: Her Reign & Her Russia, 1741-1761. LC 95-237486. 276p. 1995. 35.00 (*0-87569-140-4*) Academic Intl.

— The Reforms of Peter the Great: Progress Through Coercion in Russia. Alexander, John T., tr. from RUS. LC 92-22280. (New Russian History Ser.). 344p. (gr. 13). 1993. text 81.95 (*1-56324-047-5*) M E Sharpe.

— The Reforms of Peter the Great: Progress Through Coercion in Russia. Alexander, JOhn T., tr. from RUS. LC 92-22280. (The New Russian History Ser.). 344p. (gr. 13). 1993. pap. text 32.95 (*1-56324-048-3*) M E Sharpe.

Anisimov, Mikhail A. Critical Phenomena in Liquid Crystals: A Special Issue of the Journal Molecular Crystals & Liquid Crystals. viii, 96p. 1988. pap. text 77.00 (*2-88124-268-5*) Gordon & Breach.

— Critical Phenomena in Liquids & Liquid Crystals. xvi, 431p. 1991. text 303.00 (*2-88124-806-3*) Gordon & Breach.

— Thermal Physics Reviews Vol. 3, Pt. 2: Universal Crossover Approach to Description of Thermodynamic Properties of Fluids & Fluid Mixtures, Vol. 3. (Soviet Technology Reviews Ser.: Section B). 121p. 1992. pap. text 102.00 (*3-7186-5196-3*, Harwood Acad Pubs) Gordon & Breach.

Anisimov, N. A. Compositional Methods for Communication Protocol Design: A Petri Net Approach. (Series in Computer Science). 200p. 1998. text 53.00 (*981-02-1674-2*) World Scientific Pub.

Anisimov, S. I. Instabilities in Laser-Matter Interaction. 160p. 1995. boxed set 134.95 (*0-8493-8660-8*) CRC Pr.

Anisimov, S. I., et al. Thermodynamics of the Critical State of Individual Substances: Termodinamika Kriticheskogo Sostoiamiia Individual Nykh Veshchestv. LC 94-23466. Orig. Title: Termodinamika Kriticheskogo Sostoianiia Individualnykh Veshchestv. (ENG & RUS.). 182p. 1995. 240.00 (*0-8493-9901-7*, BB9901) CRC Pr.

— Thermophysical Aspects of Meteoroid Protection in Halley's Comet Project Vega. (Thermal Physics Ser.: Vol. 2). 100p. 1989. pap. text 72.00 (*3-7186-4910-1*) Gordon & Breach.

Anisimov, V., et al. Fourteen Papers on Statistics & Probability. LC 61-9803. (Selected Translations in Mathematical Statistics & Probability Ser.: Vol. 16). 138p. 1990. text 77.00 (*0-8218-1468-0*, STAPRO/16) Am Math.

Anisimov, V. N. Carcinogenesis & Aging. 176p. 1987. 105.00 (*0-8493-6278-4*, CRC Reprint) Franklin.

— Carcinogenesis & Aging, Vol. 2. LC 86-18778. 1987. 94.00 (*0-8493-6279-2*, RC268, CRC Reprint) Franklin.

Anisimov, V. N., ed. Carcinogenesis & Aging. 2 vols., Set. LC 86-18778. 1987. 199.00 (*0-8493-6277-6*, RC268, CRC Reprint) Franklin.

***Anisimov, Vladimir I., ed.** Strong Coulomb Correlations in Electronic Structure Calculations: Beyond the Local Density Approximation. (Advances in Condensed Matter Science Ser.: Vol. 1). 320p. 1999. text 95.00 (*90-5699-131-0*) Gordon & Breach.

Aniskiewicz, Albert S., jt. auth. see Mueller, William J.

Anisovich, V. V., et al. Quark Model & High Energy Collisions. 450p. 1985. text 51.00 (*9971-966-68-9*) World Scientific Pub.

Anissimov, Myriam. Primo Levi: Tragedy of an Optimist. Cox, Steve, tr. LC 97-9904. 452p. 1999. 35.00 (*0-87951-806-5*, Pub. by Overlook Pr) Penguin Putnam.

***Anissimov, Myriam.** Primo Levi: Tragedy of an Optimist. (Illus.). 604p. 2000. pap. 18.95 (*1-58567-020-0*, Pub. by Overlook Pr) Penguin Putnam.

Anissimov, Myriam. La Soie et les Cendres. (FRE.). 438p. 1991. pap. 21.95 (*0-7859-2169-9*, 2070384047) Fr & Eur.

Anisson du Perron, J., jt. auth. see Mai-Aru.

***Aniston, Nancy.** From Mother & Daughter to Friends. LC 99-42416. 270p. 1999. 24.95 (*1-57392-772-4*) Prometheus Bks.

Anitash, Barua. Organizing & Managing Digital Product Companies. (C). 2000. text. write for info. (*0-201-32792-9*) Addison-Wesley.

Anitav, Niv, et al. Principles of Information Systems for Management. 4th ed. 704p. (C). 1994. text 69.25 (*0-697-12421-5*) Bus & Educ Tech.

Anjali, Gurani. From the Silent Depth Within Me. 101p. (Orig.). 1999. pap. 8.95 (*0-933989-03-2*) Vajra Print & Pub.

— Rtu. LC 85-50207. (Illus.). 200p. (Orig.). 1989. pap. 14.95 (*0-933989-00-8*) Vajra Print & Pub.

— Rtu: Meditational Poems. abr. ed. LC 95-10322. (Illus.). 120p. 1995. pap. 7.95 (*0-933989-05-9*) Vajra Print & Pub.

— Think on This. (Illus.). 52p. (Orig.). Date not set. pap. write for info. (*0-933989-02-4*) Vajra Print & Pub.

— Ways of Yoga. 110p. (Orig.). 1993. pap. 10.95 (*0-933989-01-6*) Vajra Print & Pub.

Anjali, Prem & Sharadananda, Swami, eds. Sri Swami Satchidananda: Portrait of a Modern Sage. (Illus.). 264p. 1997. 49.95 (*0-932040-49-7*) Integral Yoga Pubns.

Anjaria, Shailendra J., et al. Developments in International Trade Policy. (Occasional Papers: No. 16). 124p. 1982. pap. 5.00 (*1-55775-060-2*) Intl Monetary.

— Payments Arrangements & the Expansion of Trade in Eastern & Southern Africa. (Occasional Papers: No. 11). 52p. 1982. pap. 5.00 (*1-55775-079-3*) Intl Monetary.

— Trade Policy Issues & Developments. LC 85-14544. (Occasional Paper Ser.: No. 38). 161p. 1985. pap. 7.50 (*0-939934-46-9*) Intl Monetary.

Anjomani, Ardeshir, et al. Analysis of Factors Determining the Location of New Firms & Plants in Texas Counties. 291p. 1986. pap. text 7.50 (*0-936440-70-8*) U TX SUPA.

— Effects of Employment Growth in Selected Employment Centers on the Dallas-Fort Worth Metropolitan Region. (Illus.). 85p. 1983. pap. 10.00 (*0-936440-55-4*) U TX SUPA.

— Residential Mobility Patterns in Dallas-Fort Worth & San Antonio: Determinants of Move, Racial Succession & Female-Headed Households. 111p. 1985. pap. 7.50 (*0-936440-59-7*) U TX SUPA.

Anjoorian, Jason. The Beatles Japanese Record Guide. LC 93-91865. (Illus.). 228p. (Orig.). 1994. pap. 29.95 (*0-9640079-0-8*) Jason Pr MA.

Anjos, J. D., et al, eds. Instrumentation in Elementary Particle Physics. 500p. (C). 1992. text 109.00 (*981-02-0599-6*) World Scientific Pub.

Anjou, Gustave. Ulster County, New York Probate Records: In the Office of the Surrogate, & in the County Clerk's Office At Kingston, NY, Vol. I. (Illus.). 248p. (Orig.). 1992. reprint ed. pap. text 20.00 (*1-55613-704-4*) Heritage Bk.

— Ulster County, New York Probate Records, in the Office of the Surrogate at Hingston, New York, in the Surrogate's Office, New York, & in the Library of Long Island Historical Society: A Careful Abstract & Translation of Dutch & English Wills, Letters of Administration after Intestates & Inventories with Genealogical & Historical Notes, Vol. 2. 280p. 1993. reprint ed. pap. text 20.00 (*1-55613-698-6*) Heritage Bk.

Anjou, Gustave & Kelly, Arthur C. Ulster County, NY, Probate Records in the Office of the Surrogate & in the County Clerk's Office at Kingston NY: Careful Abstract & Translation of the Dutch & English Wills, Letters of Administration after Intestates & Inventories from 1665 with Genealogical & Historical Notes, & List of Dutch & Frisian Baptismal Names with Their English Equivalents. 280p. 1981. reprint ed. lib. bdg. 40.00 (*1-56012-052-5*, 51) Kinship Rhinebeck.

Anjou, Lars A. The History of the Reformation in Sweden. Mason, Henry M., tr. from SWE. LC 83-45598. reprint ed. 87.50 (*0-404-19866-X*) AMS Pr.

Anjum, Mohini, ed. Muslim Women in India. 225p. 1992. text 22.50 (*81-7027-153-3*, Pub. by Radiant Pubs) S Asia.

Anka, Darryl & Ewing, Luana. Bashar - Blueprint for Change: A Message from Our Future. (Illus.). 316p. (Orig.). 1991. pap. 13.95 (*1-56284-113-0*) New Solutions Pub.

Anka, Darryl J. Quest for Truth: 100 Insights That Could Change Your Life. Meyers, Steve, ed. & intro. by. LC 96-72629. (Illus.). xiv, 258p. 1997. pap. 22.95 (*0-9656078-1-X*) Nobul Pr.

Ankarloo, Bengt. Athlone History of Witchcraft & Magic in Europe Greece & Rome to Late Antiquity, Vol. 2. (C). 1997. text 90.00 (*0-485-89002-X*, Pub. by Athlone Pr) Humanities.

***Ankarloo, Bengt & Clark, Stuart.** Witchcraft & Magic in Europe: Ancient Greece & Rome. LC 99-26082. 408p. 1999. pap. 24.95 (*0-8122-1705-5*) U of Pa Pr.

— Witchcraft & Magic in Europe: The Eighteenth & Nineteenth Centuries. LC 99-26083. 1999. pap. 24.95 (*0-8122-1706-3*) U of Pa Pr.

— Witchcraft & Magic in Europe: The Twentieth Century. LC 99-26081. 1999. pap. 24.95 (*0-8122-1707-1*) U of Pa Pr.

Ankarloo, Bengt & Clark, Stuart, eds. Athlone History of Witchcraft & Magic in Europe Biblical & Pagan Societies, Vol. 1. (C). 1997. text 90.00 (*0-485-89001-1*, Pub. by Athlone Pr) Humanities.

***Ankarloo, Bengt & Clark, Stuart, eds.** Witchcraft & Magic in Europe: Ancient Greece & Rome. 408p. 1999. write for info. (*0-8122-3517-7*) U of Pa Pr.

— Witchcraft & Magic in Europe: The Eighteenth & Nineteenth Centuries. 376p. 1999. 55.00 (*0-8122-3518-5*) U of Pa Pr.

— Witchcraft & Magic in Europe: The Twentieth Century. 256p. 1999. write for info. (*0-8122-3519-3*) U of Pa Pr.

Ankarloo, Bengt & Henningsen, Gustav, eds. Early Modern European Witchcraft: Centres & Peripheries. (Illus.). 490p. 1993. reprint ed. pap. text 24.95 (*0-19-820388-8*) OUP.

***Ankel-Simons, Friderun.** Primate Anatomy: An Introduction. 2nd ed. LC 99-62861. (Illus.). 510p. 1999. 49.95 (*0-12-058670-3*) Acad Pr.

Ankem, S., et al, eds. Microstructure-Property Relationships of Titanium Alloys: Proceedings: Harold Margolin Symposium on Microstructure-Property Relationships of Titanium Alloys (1994: San Francisco, CA) Proceedings. LC 94-73570. (Illus.). 327p. 1995. 20.00 (*0-87339-246-9*, 2469) Minerals Metals.

***Ankem, S. & Pande, C. S., eds.** Advances in Twinning. LC 98-68627. (Illus.). 19p. 1999. 82.00 (*0-87339-430-5*, 4305) Minerals Metals.

Anken, Ralf H. & Rachmann, Hinrich. Brain Atlas of the Adult Swordtail Fish, Xiphophorus Helleri & of Certain Developmental Stages. LC 93-41657. 88p. 1994. 60.00 (*3-437-30753-3*) Balogh.

***Ankeney, Charles C.** The Breath of Life. (Illus.). v, 149p. 1999. per. 26.95 (*0-9672787-0-8*) Applied Ozone Syst.

Ankeney, Kirk, et al, eds. Bring History Alive! A Sourcebook for Teaching United States History. (Illus.). 244p. (Orig.). 1996. pap. text 17.95 (*0-9633218-5-4*) Natl Ctr Hist.

***Ankenmann, C. Gregg, et al.** Office Leasing, 2000: Drafting & Negotiating the Lease. Briggs, Donald R., ed. LC 96-83539. 236p. 2000. 72.00 (*0-7626-0401-8*, RE-30894) Cont Ed Bar-CA.

***Ankenmen, C. Gregg, et al.** Office Leasing: Drafting & Negotiating the Lease - 1/99 Update, 2 vols. Blanchette, Janis L., ed. LC 96-83539. (California Commercial Leasing Ser.). 604p. 1999. ring bd. 95.00 (*0-7626-0286-4*, RE-30893) Cont Ed Bar-CA.

***Ankeny, Rebecca Thomas.** The Story, the Teller, & the Audience in George MacDonald's Fiction. LC 00-21122. (Studies in British Literature: Vol. 44). 172p. 2000. text 79.95 (*0-7734-7728-4*) E Mellen.

Anker. Real Writer Read Every Day. 1998. pap. text 56.25 (*0-312-19564-8*) St Martin.

— Real Writing. 160p. 1998. pap. text, teacher ed. 5.00 (*0-312-13293-X*); pap. text, teacher ed. 29.00 (*0-312-13344-8*) St Martin.

***Anker.** Real Writing Documents Guide. 1999. pap. text 2.95 (*0-312-24145-3*) St Martin.

Anker. Real Writing Learning Journal. Date not set. pap. text. write for info. (*0-312-18005-5*) St Martin.

***Anker.** Real Writing Software: Writing. 1999. pap. write for info. (*0-312-15769-X*) St Martin.

Anker, Andrew. Harvard Architecture Review. 3rd ed. 25.00 (*0-262-76001-0*) MIT Pr.

***Anker, Conrad & Roberts, David.** The Lost Explorer: Finding Mallory on Mt. Everest. LC 99-46131. 192p. 1999. 21.50 (*0-684-87151-3*) S&S Trade.

***Anker, Daniel, ed.** Eiger: The Vertical Arena. LC 99-50425. (Illus.). 220p. 2000. 32.95 (*0-89886-679-0*) Mountaineers.

Anker, Deborah. Law of Asylum in the United States. 3rd rev. ed. LC 98-66970. 500p. 1998. pap. text 79.00 (*0-9665149-1-2*) Refugee Law Ctr.

Anker, Dorothy. How Children Grow & Learn: A Viewer's Guide for the Television Series The Growing Years. (Illus.). 182p. (Orig.). (C). 1988. pap. text 14.00 (*0-936339-15-2*) Circa Pr Portland.

Anker, Jean. Bird Books & Bird Art: An Outline of the Literary History & Iconography of Descriptive Ornithology. (Illus.). 251p. 1990. reprint ed. lib. bdg. 75.00 (*0-945345-36-4*) Lubrecht & Cramer.

— Bird Books & Bird Art: An Outline of the Literary History & Iconography of Descriptive Ornithology. (Illus.). 269p. 1990. reprint ed. 100.00 (*1-888262-36-2*) Martino Pubng.

— Bird Books & Bird Art: An Outline of the Literary History & Iconography of Descriptive Ornithology, Based Principally on the Collection in the University Library at Copenhagen. LC 73-17795. (Natural Sciences in America Ser.). (Illus.). 326p. 1974. reprint ed. 25.95 (*0-405-05705-9*) Ayer.

Anker, M. Basic Restaurant Theory. 1987. pap. text. write for info. (*0-582-41358-3*, Pub. by Addison-Wesley) Longman.

Anker, Nilsen. Religion & Personality Integration. (Psycholgia Religionum Ser.: No. 8). 174p. (Orig.). 1980. pap. 30.00 (*91-554-0991-1*, Pub. by Uppsala Univ Acta Univ Uppsaliensis) Coronet Bks.

***Anker, Philippe & Stroun, Maurice.** Circulating Nucleic Acids in Plasma or Serum. LC 00-27098. (Annals Ser.). 2000. write for info. (*1-57331-270-3*) NY Acad Sci.

Anker, R. Gender & Jobs: Sex Segregation of Occupations in the World. LC 98-131049. 456p. 1998. pap. 40.00 (*92-2-109524-X*) Intl Labour Office.

Anker, Richard, et al. Women's Participation in the Labour Force: A Methods Test in India for Improving Its Measurement. (Women, Work & Development Ser.: No. 16). xiv, 204p. (Orig.). 1988. pap. 24.75 (*92-2-106259-7*) Intl Labour Office.

Anker, Richard, jt. ed. see Bodrova, Valentina.

Anker, Roy M. Self-Help & Popular Religion in Early American Culture: An Interpretive Guide to Origins. LC 99-21280. (American Popular Culture Ser.). 256p. 1999. lib. bdg. 69.50 (*0-313-31136-6*) Greenwood.

— Self-Help & Popular Religion in Modern American Culture: An Interpretive Guide. LC 99-21786. (American Popular Culture Ser.). 208p. 1999. lib. bdg. 65.00 (*0-313-22249-5*, Bergin & Garvey) Greenwood.

Anker, Susan & Gallagher, Eddye S. Teaching Real Writing 2: Additional Resources. 320p. 1998. pap. text 6.66 (*0-312-15446-1*) St Martin.

Ankerberg, John. Ensenanza Falsa en la Iglesia. (Hechos Acerca de...Ser.).Tr. of False Teaching in the Church. (SPA.). 50p. 1994. pap. 3.29 (*1-56063-771-4*, 498427) Editorial Unilit.

— What Is Mary Saying? Discerning the Appearances, Messages & Devotion to the "Mother of God" 240p. Date not set. 9.99 (*1-56507-921-3*) Harvest Hse.

Ankerberg, John & Weldon. El Mito del Acto Sexual Seguro.Tr. of Myth about Safe Sex. (SPA.). pap. 9.99 (*1-56063-577-0*, 497725) Editorial Unilit.

Ankerberg, John & Weldon, John. La Astrologia. (Hechos Acerca de...Ser.).Tr. of Astrology. (SPA.). 78p. 1994. pap. 3.29 (*1-56063-769-2*, 498425) Editorial Unilit.

— Behind the Mask of Mormonism: From Its Early Schemes to Its Modern Deceptions. LC 91-38068. 492p. 1996. reprint ed. pap. 16.99 (*1-56507-443-2*) Harvest Hse.

— Catolicismo Romano. (Hechos Acerca de...Ser.).Tr. of Roman Catholicism. (SPA.). 75p. 1995. pap. 3.29 (*1-56063-515-0*, 497695) Editorial Unilit.

— Creacion vs. Evolucion. (Hechos Acerca de...Ser.).Tr. of Creation vs. Evolution. (SPA.). 70p. 1995. pap. 3.29 (*1-56063-693-9*, 497699) Editorial Unilit.

— Creation vs. Evolution: What You Need to Know. 16p. 1999. pap. 1.99 (*0-7369-0036-5*) Harvest Hse.

— Cult Watch: What You Need to Know about Spiritual Deception. LC 90-23715. 1991. pap. 14.99 (*0-89081-851-7*) Harvest Hse.

— Darwin's Leap of Faith. LC 97-40444. (Illus.). 300p. 1998. pap. 11.99 (*1-56507-657-5*) Harvest Hse.

***Ankerberg, John & Weldon, John.** Encyclopedia of Cults & New Religions. LC 99-21703. 750p. 1999. pap. 19.99 (*0-7369-0074-8*) Harvest Hse.

Ankerberg, John & Weldon, John. Encyclopedia of New Age Beliefs Bk. 1: The New Age Movement. (Defense of the Faith Ser.). (Orig.). 1996. pap. 19.99 (*1-56507-160-3*) Harvest Hse.

— Espiritus Guias. (Hechos Acerca de...Ser.).Tr. of Spirit Guides. (SPA.). 69p. 1994. pap. 3.29 (*1-56063-772-2*, 498428) Editorial Unilit.

— The Facts on Angels: Who They Are, Where They Are from & What They Do Today. LC 95-154350. ("Facts on" Ser.). 1995. pap. 3.50 (*1-56507-345-2*) Harvest Hse.

— The Facts on Astrology. LC 88-82018. (Anker Ser.). 48p. 1988. pap. 3.50 (*0-89081-715-4*) Harvest Hse.

— The Facts on Creation vs. Evolution. (Facts on Ser.). 48p. 1993. pap. 3.50 (*1-56507-152-2*) Harvest Hse.

— The Facts on False Teaching in the Church. LC 88-82015. (Anker Ser.). 48p. 1988. pap. 3.50 (*0-89081-714-6*) Harvest Hse.

— The Facts on Halloween. LC 97-159073. 48p. 1996. pap. 3.50 (*1-56507-512-9*) Harvest Hse.

— The Facts on Holistic Health & the New Medicine. (Facts on Ser.). 48p. 1992. pap. 3.50 (*0-89081-973-4*) Harvest Hse.

— The Facts on Homosexuality. LC 95-154346. ("Facts on" Ser.). 1995. pap. 3.50 (*1-56507-258-8*) Harvest Hse.

— The Facts on Islam. (Facts on Ser.). 48p. 1991. pap. 3.50 (*0-89081-913-0*) Harvest Hse.

— The Facts on Jehovah's Witnesses. (Anker Ser.) 48p. 1988. pap. 3.50 (*0-89081-733-2*) Harvest Hse.

— The Facts on Life after Death. (Facts on Ser.). 48p. 1992. pap. 3.50 (*0-89081-992-0*) Harvest Hse.

— The Facts on Near-Death Experiences. LC 96-155071. 48p. 1996. pap. 3.50 (*1-56507-455-6*) Harvest Hse.

— The Facts on Psychic Readings: A Modern Deception of Ancient Lies. LC 97-151256. 48p. 1997. pap. 3.50 (*1-56507-560-9*) Harvest Hse.

— The Facts on Rock Music. (Facts on Ser.). 48p. 1992. pap. 3.50 (*0-89081-974-2*) Harvest Hse.

— The Facts on Roman Catholicism. (Facts on Ser.). 1993. pap. 3.50 (*0-89081-995-5*) Harvest Hse.

— The Facts on Spirit Guides. LC 88-82016. (Anker Ser.). 48p. 1988. pap. 3.50 (*0-89081-713-8*) Harvest Hse.

— The Facts on the Faith Movement. (Facts on Ser.). 1993. pap. 3.50 (*0-89081-994-7*) Harvest Hse.

— The Facts on the King James Only Debate. (Facts on Booklets Ser.). 48p. 1996. pap. 3.50 (*1-56507-441-6*) Harvest Hse.

— The Facts on the Masonic Lodge. LC 88-82596. (Anker Ser.). 48p. 1988. pap. 3.50 (*0-89081-741-3*) Harvest Hse.

— The Facts on the Mormon Church. (Anker Ser.). 48p. 1991. pap. 3.50 (*0-89081-884-3*) Harvest Hse.

— The Facts on the New Age Movement. LC 88-82017. (Anker Ser.). 48p. 1988. pap. 3.50 (*0-89081-711-1*) Harvest Hse.

— The Facts on the Occult. (Anker Ser.). 1991. pap. 3.50 (*0-89081-883-5*) Harvest Hse.

— The Facts on UFOs & Other Supernatural Phenomena. (Facts on Ser.). 1992. pap. 3.50 (*0-89081-991-2*) Harvest Hse.

— Hechos Acerca de la Ensenanza Falsa en la Iglesia. (Los Hechos Acerca De Ser.).Tr. of Facts on False Teaching in the Church. (SPA.). 50p. 1994. pap. 3.29 (*0-614-27054-5*) Editorial Unilit.

— Hechos Acerca de los Espiritus Guia. (Los Hechos Acerca De Ser.).Tr. of Facts on Spirits Guide. (SPA.). 49p. 1994. pap. 3.29 (*0-614-27056-1*) Editorial Unilit.

Ankerberg, John & Weldon, John. Los Hechos Acerca de los Mormones. (Hechos Acerca de...Ser.).Tr. of Mormon Church. (SPA.). 3.29 (*1-56063-518-5*, 497693) Editorial Unilit.

Ankerberg, John & Weldon, John. Hechos Acerca de los Testigos de Jehova. (Los Hechos Acerca De Ser.).Tr. of Facts on Jehovah's Witnesses. (SPA.). 55p. 1994. pap. 3.29 (*0-614-24372-6*); pap. 3.29 (*0-614-27055-3*, 498426) Editorial Unilit.

Ankerberg, John & Weldon, John. Los Hechos Acerca del Islam. (Hechos Acerca de...Ser.).Tr. of Islam. (SPA.). 3.29 (*1-56063-692-0*, 497694) Editorial Unilit.

Ankerberg, John & Weldon, John. Knowing the Truth about Eternal Security. LC 98-171390. (Defenders Ser.). 48p. 1998. pap. 2.99 (*1-56507-794-6*) Harvest Hse.

— Knowing the Truth about the Trinity. LC 97-151385. (The Defenders Ser.). 48p. (Orig.). 1997. pap. 2.99 (*1-56507-587-0*) Harvest Hse.

— Logia Masonica. (Hechos Acerca de...Ser.).Tr. of Masonic Lodge. (SPA.). 66p. 1994. pap. 3.29 (*1-56063-774-9*, 498430); pap. 3.29 (*0-614-27053-7*) Editorial Unilit.

— El Movimiento de la Fe. (Hechos Acerca de...Ser.).Tr. of Faith Movement. (SPA.). 69p. 1995. 3.29 (*1-56063-516-9*, 497696) Editorial Unilit.

— Musica "Rock" (Hechos Acerca de...Ser.).Tr. of Rock Music. (SPA.). pap. 3.29 (*1-56063-694-7*, 497700) Editorial Unilit.

— La Nueva Era. (Hechos Acerca de...Ser.).Tr. of New Age Movement. (SPA.). 46p. 1994. pap. 3.29 (*1-56063-773-0*, 498429) Editorial Unilit.

— Ocultismo. (Hechos Acerca de...Ser.).Tr. of Occult. (SPA.). 73p. pap. 3.29 (*1-56063-517-7*, 497697) Editorial Unilit.

— Protestants & Catholics: Do They Now Agree? 1995. pap. 9.99 (*1-56507-314-2*) Harvest Hse.

— Ready with an Answer: For the Tough Questions about God. LC 96-51535. 400p. (Orig.). 1997. pap. 11.99 (*1-56507-618-4*) Harvest Hse.

— The Secret Teachings of the Masonic Lodge. pap. 14.99 (*0-8024-7695-3*, 280) Moody.

Ankerberg, John & Weldon, John. Los Testigos de Jehova. (Hechos Acerca de...Ser.).Tr. of Jehovah's Witnesses. (SPA.). 3.29 (*1-56063-770-6*, 498426) Editorial Unilit.

Ankerberg, John, et al. Steeling the Mind of America, Vol. II. Perkins, Bill, ed. & compiled by by. LC 96-69689. 224p. 1997. pap. 11.95 (*0-89221-334-5*) New Leaf.

Ankerich, Michael G. The Sound of Silence: Conversations with 16 Film & Stage Personalities who Bridged the Gap Between Silents & Talkies. LC 98-20085. (Illus.). 272p. 1998. lib. bdg. 45.00 (*0-7864-0504-X*) McFarland & Co.

Ankerl, Guy C. Beyond Monopoly Capitalism & Monopoly Socialism: Distributive Justice in a Competitive Society. 108p. 1978. 24.95 (*0-87073-938-7*) Transaction Pubs.

— Experimental Sociology of Architecture: A Guide to Theory, Research & Literature. (New Babylon Studies in the Social Sciences: No. 36). 550p. 1981. 96.15 (*90-279-3219-0*); pap. 52.35 (*90-279-3440-1*) Mouton.

Ankerman, William L., jt. auth. see Wright, Douglas B.

Ankerman, William L., jt. auth. see Wright, Douglass B.

Ankers, Arthur R. The Pater: John Lockwood Kipling His Life & Times, 1837-1911. 161p. (C). 1988. text 90.00 (*1-871044-00-6*, Pub. by Hawthorns Pubns) St Mut.

Ankersmit, F. R. The Reality Effect in the Writing of History: The Dynamics of Historiographical Topology. (Mededelingen der Koninklijke Nederlandse Akademie van Wetenschappen, Afd. Letterkunde Ser.: No. 52(1)). 1989. pap. text 17.50 (*0-444-85704-4*) Elsevier.

Ankersmit, Franklin R. Aesthetic Politics: Political Philosphy Beyond Fact & Value. LC 96-34474. (Mestizo Spaces Ser.). 1997. write for info. (*0-8047-2729-5*); pap. 19.95 (*0-8047-2730-9*) Stanford U Pr.

— History & Tropology: The Rise & Fall of Metaphor. LC 93-12081. 1994. 50.00 (*0-520-08045-9*, Pub. by U CA Pr) Cal Prin Full Svc.

— Narrative Logic: A Semantic Analysis of the Historian's Language. 274p. 1983. text 126.50 (*90-247-2731-6*) Kluwer Academic.

Ankersmit, Franklin R. & Kellner, Hans, eds. A New Philosophy of History. LC 95-11010. 300p. 1995. pap. text 19.95 (*0-226-02100-9*); lib. bdg. 55.00 (*0-226-02099-1*) U Ch Pr.

Ankerson, Dudley. Agrarian Warlord: Saturnino Cedillo & the Mexican Revolution in San Luis Potosi. LC 84-20683. 303p. 1985. 35.00 (*0-87580-101-3*) N Ill U Pr.

Anketell, Michael. Heavenly Bodies: Remembering Hollywood & Fashion's Favorite AIDS Benefit. LC 99-35239. 1999. 30.95 (*0-87833-247-2*) Taylor Pub.

***Anklam, Londa.** Jacob Sheep & More... Not Just a Coloring Book. (Illus.). 32p. (J). 2000. pap. 7.95 (*0-9701674-0-7*) Londa Signs.

Anklewicz, Larry. The Guide to Jewish Films on Video. LC 99-58433. 400p. 2000. pap. 24.95 (*0-88125-605-6*) Ktav.

— The Guide to Jewish Films on Video. LC 99-58433. 400p. 2000. 39.95 (*0-88125-618-8*) Ktav.

Ankley, Gerald T., jt. auth. see Jarvinen, Alfred W.

Ankli, Robert E. Gross Farm Revenue in Pre-Civil War Illinois. Bruchey, Stuart, ed. LC 76-39820. (Nineteen Seventy-Seven Dissertations Ser.). (Illus.). 1977. lib. bdg. 39.95 (*0-405-09901-0*) Ayer.

Ankner, William & Bivens, William E. Getting to Work: Northeast Perspectives on Rural Public Transportation & Economic Development. LC 83-72711. 98p. 1983. pap. 7.50 (*0-914193-03-1*) Coalition NE Govn.

***Ankney, Patricia A.** The Colors of His Life. Raica-Klotz, Helen, ed. (Illus.). 1999. pap. write for info. (*0-9674616-0-X*) P A Ankney.

Ankori, Zvi. Karaites in Byzantium: The Formative Years, 970-1100. LC 71-158258. (Columbia University. Studies in the Social Sciences: No. 597). reprint ed. 32.50 (*0-404-51597-5*) AMS Pr.

Ankrah, E. Maxine, jt. auth. see Long, Lynellyn D.

Ankrah, E. Maxine, ed. see Long, Lynellen D.

Ankrett, Vivienne, jt. auth. see Williams, Ian.

***Ankrum, Barbara.** I'll Remember You: Try to Remember. (Intimate Moments Ser.). 1999. mass mkt. 4.25 (*0-373-07972-9*) Silhouette.

Ankrum, Barbara. To Love a Cowboy. (Intimate Moments Ser.: No. 834). 1998. per. 3.99 (*0-373-07834-X*, 1-07834-4) Silhouette.

A

Ankrum, Betty. Raized on the Rez. (Illus.). 144p. (Orig.). 1996. pap. write for info. (*1-57579-008-4*) Pine Hill Pr.

Ankrum, Homer R. Bittersweet Years Smiling Through Tears (1920-1941) LC 93-79072. (Illus.). 414p. 1993. 23.50 (*0-89279-082-2*) Graphic Pub.

— Dogfaces Who Smiled Through Tears. LC 87-72129. 661p. 1987. text 24.95 (*0-89279-080-6*) Graphic Pub.

— Dogfaces Who Smiled Through Tears. 2nd rev. ed. LC 88-81739. 676p. 1988. reprint ed. 27.50 (*0-89279-081-4*) Graphic Pub.

Anku, Vincent. Health of the Nation: Solutions That Make Everyone a Winner. (Illus.). 144p. 1995. pap. text 9.95 (*0-9647741-0-0*) Achilles Pub.

***Anku, Vincent.** Hope-at Last-in Cancer Treatment. (Illus.). 243p. 1999. pap. 14.95 (*0-9647741-1-9*) Achilles Pub.

Ankumah, Evelyn A. The African Commission on Human & Peoples' Rights: Practices & Procedures. LC 96-4733. (Nijhoff Law Specials Ser.: No. 16). 264p. 1996. pap. 80.00 (*90-411-0130-6*) Kluwer Law Intl.

Anlezark, Mildred. Hats on Heads: The Art of Creative Millinery. (Illus.). 152p. 1992. reprint ed. pap. 17.95 (*0-86417-303-2*, Pub. by Kangaroo Pr) Seven Hills Bk.

Anliot, Sture F. The Vascular Flora of Glen Helen, Clifton Gorge & John Bryan State Park. (Biological Notes Ser.: No. 5). 1973. pap. text 6.00 (*0-86727-064-0*) Ohio Bio Survey.

Anlyan, William G., et al. The Future of Medical Education. Graves, Judy, ed. LC 72-97153. 210p. reprint ed. pap. 65.10 (*0-608-11943-1*, 202336600032) Bks Demand.

ANMC Tariff Task Group Staff. Standard Reference Tables for Metric Conversion of Transportation Tariffs. rev. ed. 90p. 1982. 19.00 (*0-686-47622-0*) Am Natl.

Anmesty International Staff. Albania: Political Imprisonment & the Law. 58p. (Orig.). 1984. pap. 3.00 (*0-86210-078-X*) Amnesty Intl USA.

Anmol Pub. Staff. Women, Society & Christianity. (C). 1995. 23.00 (*81-7488-088-7*, Pub. by Anmol) S Asia.

Ann Arbor Chapter of Jack & Jill of America, Inc. Black Children's Parents Imparting Discipline - Heritage. Hayes-Scott, Fairy C., ed. (Illus.). 204p. 1997. pap. 25.00 (*1-889743-03-8*) R Dean Pr.

Ann Arbor Public Schools Staff. Alternative Assessment. 336p. 1997. 29.95 (*0-86651-691-3*) Seymour Pubns.

Ann Arbor Publishers Editorial Staff. Manuscript Writing: Words Book 1 & 2, Bk. 1. (Manuscript Writing Words Ser.). (J). (gr. 3-6). 1994. 10.00 (*0-87879-787-4*, Ann Arbor Div) Acad Therapy.

— Manuscript Writing: Words Book 1 & 2, Bk. 2. (Manuscript Writing Words Ser.). (J). (gr. 3-6). 1994. 10.00 (*0-87879-788-2*, Ann Arbor Div) Acad Therapy.

— Symbol Discrimination Series: Books 1, 2, Bks. 1 & 2. (Illus.). 16p. (gr. k-1). 1974. write for info. (*0-318-56865-9*, Ann Arbor Div); 7.00 (*0-87879-724-6*, Ann Arbor Div); 7.00 (*0-87879-725-4*, Ann Arbor Div) Acad Therapy.

Ann Arbor Software Staff. Norton Textra Writer 2.5 with Online Handbook. (C). 1992. pap. text 36.25 (*0-393-96278-4*) Norton.

Ann Brown, Betty, ed. Expanding Circles! Women, Art & Community. LC 96-76458. (Women/Art Ser.). (Illus.). 368p. (Orig.). 1996. pap. 22.00 (*1-877675-21-0*) Midmarch Arts.

Ann C. Van Orden & Hakkarainen, T., eds. Computers in Corrosion Control Vol. 3: Expert Systems for Corrosion Control. (Illus.). 250p. 1992. pap. text 23.00 (*1-877914-41-X*) NACE Intl.

Ann, Elizabeth. Heaven's Embrace: Words of Self Discovery. LC 98-66400. (Illus.). 80p. 1998. pap. 13.95 (*0-9664156-0-4*) Lion Heart.

Ann, Fay, ed. see Nixon, Joan Lowery.

Ann-Margret & Gold, Todd. Ann-Margret: My Story. large type ed. LC 94-18046. (Orig.). 1994. 25.95 (*1-56895-104-3*) Wheeler Pub.

Ann, Martha. Goddesses: World Mythology. (Illus.). 672p. 1995. pap. 19.95 (*0-19-509199-X*) OUP.

Ann, Martha & Imel, Dorothy. Goddesses in World Mythology. LC 93-31496. (Mythology & Religion Ser.). 658p. 1993. lib. bdg. 99.00 (*0-87436-715-8*) ABC-CLIO.

Ann, Martha, et al. The Great Goddess: An Introduction to Her Many Names. rev. ed. 1993. pap. 9.95 (*0-9638567-0-7*) Our Many Names.

Ann, Nicky. LWR Series. (ENG & SPA., Illus.). 1993. 10.95 (*0-9638312-0-8*) LWR Pubs.

— The Story of Ascendeara. Wolsey, Marion, ed. (Working Bks.: Vol. 1.2). (YA). 1996. wbk. ed. 17.75 (*0-9638312-1-6*) LWR Pubs.

— The Story of Kevin Ellis & the Rainbow Fish. Magnuson, Carol, ed. (Working Bks.: Vol. 1.1). (YA). (gr. 3 up). 1993. wbk. ed. 13.75 (*0-9638312-6-7*) LWR Pubs.

— The Story of Kevin Ellis & the Rainbow Fish. Magnuson, Carol, ed. (Working Bks.: Vol. 1.1). 90p. (YA). (gr. 3 up). 1993. reprint ed. wbk. ed. 18.75 (*1-889197-06-8*) LWR Pubs.

Ann Street United Methodist Church Members. Angel Food & Deviled Crab: A Taste of Food, Local History & Artwork. 1996. pap., spiral bd. 15.95 (*0-9644721-0-4*) Ann Street Meth Ch.

Anna, Antonio L. Santa, see Santa Anna, Antonio L.

Anna, Jennifer. The Best Thing. (Illus.). 60p. (Orig.). (J). (gr. 1-4). 1997. pap. 10.95 (*1-886383-26-X*) Pride & Imprints.

***Anna, Jennifer.** My Adventure to the Enchanted Forest. (My Adventure Ser.). (Illus.). 30p. 1999. pap. 10.00 (*1-886383-72-3*, Little Blue) Pride & Imprints.

— My Adventure to the Moon. (Illus.). 20p. (J). 1999. pap. 10.00 (*1-886383-73-1*, Little Blue) Pride & Imprints.

Anna, Jennifer. Tonight I Heard the Ghost Cat. (Illus.). 30p. (J). (ps-5). 2000. pap. 11.00 (*1-886383-56-1*, Little Blue) Pride & Imprints.

***Anna, Jennifer.** Year of the Dragon. (Illus.). 60p. (J). 2000. 29.95 (*1-883573-17-3*, Little Blue) Pride & Imprints.

Anna, Levina. Ulybki I Oshibki: Povesti I Rasskazy. LC 97-30539. (RUS., Illus.). 128p. 1997. pap. 9.00 (*1-55779-104-X*) Hermitage Pubs.

Anna, Rose, pseud. A Woman's Spiritual Odyssey. 144p. (Orig.). 1991. pap. 8.95 (*0-9630561-0-7*) Rose Pub AZ.

Anna, Santa. The Eagle: The Autobiography of Santa Anna. Crawford, Ann F., ed. LC 88-19992. (Illus.). 319p. (C). 1988. reprint ed. 21.95 (*0-938349-29-5*) State House Pr.

***Anna, Susanne.** Archi-Neering: Helmut Jahn - Werner Sobek. 2000. pap. 29.95 (*3-7757-0852-9*) Gerd Hatje.

Anna, Timothy E. The Fall of the Royal Government in Peru. LC 79-9142. 305p. reprint ed. pap. 94.60 (*0-7837-6874-5*, 204670400003) Bks Demand.

— The Mexican Empire of Iturbide. LC 89-4944. xii, 286p. 1990. text 60.00 (*0-8032-1027-2*) U of Nebr Pr.

— Spain & the Loss of America. LC 82-11118. 367p. reprint ed. pap. 113.80 (*0-8357-2918-4*, 203915800011) Bks Demand.

Annabel, Russell. Adventure Is in My Blood. (Illus.). 383p. 1997. 35.00 (*1-57157-065-9*) Safari Pr.

— Adventure Is My Business. (Illus.). 340p. 1997. 35.00 (*1-57157-064-0*) Safari Pr.

— Alaskan Adventures. 369p. 1997. 35.00 (*1-57157-062-4*) Safari Pr.

— High Road to Adventure. 375p. 1998. 35.00 (*1-57157-066-7*) Safari Pr.

— Tales of a Big Game Guide. 2nd ed. (Fifty Greatest Bks.). (Illus.). 200p. 1992. reprint ed. 50.00 (*1-56416-035-1*) Derrydale Pr.

— The Way We Were. (Illus.). 369p. 1998. 35.00 (*1-57157-102-7*) Safari Pr.

Annable, Carol R., jt. auth. see Peterson, Paul M.

Annable, Toni, ed. see Sims, Bobbi.

Annacondia, Carlos. Oime Bien, Satanas! (SPA.). 1997. 9.99 (*0-88113-438-4*, B106-4384) Caribe Betania.

Annacondia, Carlos & Sawin, Gisela. Listen to Me, Satan! Cudich, Sylvia, tr. from ENG. LC 98-21052. 1999. pap. 12.99 (*0-88419-524-4*) Dake Pub.

Annadale, Ellen. The Sociology of Health & Medicine: A Critical Introduction. LC 97-45218. 250p. 1998. 62.95 (*0-7456-1357-8*); pap. 28.95 (*0-7456-1358-6*) Blackwell Pubs.

Annadananda, Swami. Swami Akhandananda. Bhattachavya, N. C., tr. from BEN. 304p. 1994. pap. 6.95 (*81-85301-04-2*, Pub. by Advaita Ashrama) Vedanta Pr.

Annala, K., ed. Fisheries & Aquaculture Research Planning Needs for Africa & West Asia: Proceedings of the Workshop Held in Cairo, Egypt September of 1995. 80p. 1997. pap. 42.00 (*971-8709-67-3*, Pub. by ICLARM) Intl Spec Bk.

Annamalai, Kalyan, et al, eds. Heat Transfer Division Vol. 2: Proceedings, ASME International Mechanical Engineering Congress & Exposition, Dallas, TX, 1997. LC 97-76718. (HTD Ser.: Vol. 352). 249p. 1997. pap. 110.00 (*0-7918-1841-1*, QC320) ASME Pr.

Annan, Gertrude L., jt. auth. see Ash, Lee.

***Annan, Kofi A., prod.** World Investment Report: 1999 Foreign Direct Investment & the Challenge of Development. (Illus.). 541p. (C). 2000. pap. text 75.00 (*0-7881-8665-5*) DIANE Pub.

Annan, Noel. Changing Enemies: The Defeat & Regeneration of Germany. (Illus.). 288p. 1997. pap. text 14.95 (*0-8014-8490-1*) Cornell U Pr.

***Annan, Noel G.** The Dons: Mentors, Eccentrics & Geniuses. LC 99-46232. 2000. 30.00 (*0-226-02107-6*) U Ch Pr.

Annan, Noel G. Leslie Stephen: His Thought & Character in Relation to His Time. Metzger, Walter P., ed. LC 76-55199. (Academic Profession Ser.). (Illus.). 1977. reprint ed. lib. bdg. 29.95 (*0-405-10028-0*) Ayer.

— Leslie Stephen: The Godless Victorian. LC 85-24714. (Illus.). 448p. 1986. pap. 17.95 (*0-226-02106-8*) U Ch Pr.

— Leslie Stephen, His Thought & Character in Relation to His Time. LC 75-30015. reprint ed. 52.50 (*0-404-14021-1*) AMS Pr.

Annan, Paul & Warner, Wayne, contrib. by. The Azusa Street Papers. (Orig.). 1997. pap. 20.00 (*0-9637090-7-0*) Togthr Hrvest.

Annan, Sampson O. & Skogan, Wesley. Drug Enforcement in Public Housing: Signs of Success in Denver. LC 93-84925. 47p. (Orig.). 1993. pap. text 18.95 (*1-884614-04-3*) Police Found.

Annand, Susan B. Making Decisions & Forming Opinions. 1997. 6.95 (*1-55708-591-9*, MCC941) McDonald Pub Co.

Annand, Harold W. Population Change & Social Continuity: Ten Years in a Coal Town. LC 85-40506. (Illus.). 144p. 1986. 32.50 (*0-941664-14-7*) Susquehanna U Pr.

Annand, Ruth & Norman, Helen. Blackstone's Guide to the Community Trade Mark. 343p. 1998. pap. 54.00 (*1-85431-580-3*, Pub. by Blackstone Pr) Gaunt.

— Blackstone's Guide to the Trade Marks Act, 1994. LC 95-126122. 422p. 1994. text 44.00 (*1-85431-384-3*, Pub. by Blackstone Pr) Gaunt.

***Annandale, Ellen & Hunt, Kate.** Gender Inequalities in Health. LC 99-30442. 1999. 27.95 (*0-335-20364-7*) OpUniv Pr.

Annandale, G. W. Reservoir Sedimentation. (Developments in Water Science Ser.: No. 29). 222p. 1987. 124.50 (*0-444-42729-5*) Elsevier.

Annandale, N. Coelenterata, Polyzoa: Freshwater Sponges, Hydroids, & Polyzoa. (Fauna of British India Ser.). (Illus.). vii, 262p. 1972. reprint ed. 20.00 (*0-88065-015-X*) Scholarly Pubns.

Annandale, Nelson. The Faroes & Iceland: Studies in Island Life. LC 77-87701. reprint ed. 42.50 (*0-404-16495-1*) AMS Pr.

Annandale, Nelson & Robinson, H. C. Fasciculi Malayenses: Anthropological & Zoological Results of an Expedition to Perak & the Siamese Malay States, 1901-1902. LC 77-87478. 1977. reprint ed. 57.50 (*0-404-16791-8*) AMS Pr.

***Annapoorna, L., ed.** New Dimensions in Indian Music, Dance & Drama. LC 98-900588. 1998. 64.00 (*81-7574-004-3*, Pub. by Sandeep Prakas) S Asia.

Annarelli, James J. Academic Freedom & Catholic Higher Education, 21. LC 86-27152. (Contributions to the Study of Education Ser.: No. 21). 257p. 1987. 59.95 (*0-313-25425-7*, ANA/, Greenwood Pr) Greenwood.

***Annarino, Alex.** The Complete Guide to Federal & State Support of Business Incubation. Hayhow, Sally, ed. 108p. 1998. pap. 35.95 (*1-887183-46-9*) NBIA.

***Annarino, Karen L.** Stepmothers & Stepdaughters: Relationships of Chance, Friendships for a Lifetime. 2000. pap. 14.95 (*1-885171-46-3*) Wldcat Canyon.

Annas, George J. Judging Medicine. LC 88-9024. (Contemporary Issues in Biomedicine, Ethics, & Society Ser.). 456p. 1988. 49.50 (*0-89603-132-2*); pap. 29.50 (*0-89603-193-4*) Humana.

— Obstetrics: Normal & Problem Pregnancies. 3rd ed. Gabbe, Steven G. et al, eds. LC 96-20732. 1348p. 1996. text 117.00 (*0-443-07690-1*) Church.

— The Rights of Patients: The Basic ACLU Guide to Patient Rights. 2nd rev. ed. LC 88-29893. 328p. 1992. 39.50 (*0-89603-182-9*) Humana.

— The Rights of Patients: The Basic ACLU Guide to Patient Rights. 2nd rev. ed. LC 88-29893. (ACLU Handbook Ser.). 312p. (C). 1989. pap. 10.95 (*0-8093-1527-0*) S Ill U Pr.

— Some Choice: Law, Medicine & the Market. LC 97-48975. 320p. 1998. text 29.95 (*0-19-511832-4*) OUP.

— Standard of Care: The Law of American Bioethics. 304p. 1997. reprint ed. pap. text 27.50 (*0-19-512006-X*) OUP.

Annas, George J. & Elias, Sherman, eds. Gene Mapping: Using Law & Ethics As Guides. (Illus.). 320p. (C). 1992. text 39.95 (*0-19-507303-7*) OUP.

Annas, George J. & Grodin, Michael A., eds. The Nazi Doctors & the Nuremberg Code: Human Rights in Human Experimentation. (Illus.). 400p. 1995. reprint ed. pap. text 24.95 (*0-19-510106-5*) OUP.

Annas, George J., jt. auth. see Law & Business Inc. Staff.

***Annas, Julia.** Ancient Philosophy: A Very Short Introduction. (Very Short Introductions Ser.). (Illus.). 128p. 2000. pap. 8.95 (*0-19-285357-0*) OUP.

Annas, Julia. Hellenistic Philosophy of Mind. LC 91-10694. 1994. pap. 16.95 (*0-520-07659-1*, Pub. by U CA Pr) Cal Prin Full Svc.

— An Introduction to Plato's Republic. 370p. (C). 1981. pap. text 19.95 (*0-19-827429-7*) OUP.

— Metaphysics: Books M & N. (Clarendon Aristotle Ser.). 240p. 1988. pap. text 32.00 (*0-19-872133-1*) OUP.

— The Morality of Happiness. 512p. 1995. pap. text 22.00 (*0-19-509652-5*) OUP.

— Oxford Studies in Ancient Philosophy Vol. IX: 1991, Vol. I. 224p. 1992. pap. 49.95 (*0-19-823991-2*) OUP.

— Platonic Ethics, Old & New. LC 98-30418. (Studies in Classical Philology - Townsend Lectures). viii, 196p. 1998. pap. write for info. (*0-8014-8517-7*) Cornell U Pr.

— Platonic Ethics, Old & New. LC 98-30418. 256p. 1999. 35.00 (*0-8014-3518-8*) Cornell U Pr.

— The Statesman. Waterfield, Robin, ed. (Cambridge Texts in the History of Political Thought Ser.). 121p. (C). 1995. pap. text 16.95 (*0-521-44778-X*) Cambridge U Pr.

Annas, Julia, ed. Oxford Studies in Ancient Philosophy Vol. III: 1985, Vol. I. 310p. 1986. pap. 29.95 (*0-19-824910-1*) OUP.

— Oxford Studies in Ancient Philosophy Vol. V: 1987, Vol. V. 272p. 1988. pap. text 39.95 (*0-19-824457-6*) OUP.

— Oxford Studies in Ancient Philosophy Vol. VI: 1988, Vol. V. 290p. 1989. pap. text 39.95 (*0-19-824835-0*) OUP.

— Oxford Studies in Ancient Philosophy Vol. VII: 1989, Vol. V. 268p. 1990. text 80.00 (*0-19-824242-5*); pap. text 39.95 (*0-19-824241-7*) OUP.

— Oxford Studies in Ancient Philosophy Vol. VIII: 1990, Vol. V. 310p. 1991. text 80.00 (*0-19-824286-7*); pap. text 39.95 (*0-19-824285-9*) OUP.

— Oxford Studies in Ancient Philosophy Vol. X: 1992, Vol. X. 304p. 1993. text 80.00 (*0-19-824047-3*) OUP.

***Annas, Julia, ed.** Voices of Ancient Philosophy: An Introductory Reader. (Illus.). 480p. 2000. pap. 29.95 (*0-19-512695-5*); text 49.00 (*0-19-512694-7*) OUP.

Annas, Julia & Barnes, Jonathan. The Modes of Scepticism: Ancient Texts & Modern Interpretations. 216p. 1985. pap. text 17.95 (*0-521-27644-6*) Cambridge U Pr.

Annas, Julia & Grimm, Robert H., eds. Oxford Studies in Ancient Philosophy: Supplementary Volume, 1988. 240p. 1989. text 75.00 (*0-19-824476-2*) OUP.

Annas, Julia, ed. see Empiricus, Sextus.

Annas, Julia, ed. see Plato.

Annas, Julia, ed. see Sextus Empiricus.

Annas, Pamela J. A Disturbance in Mirrors: The Poetry of Sylvia Plath, 89. LC 87-23653. (Contributions in Women's Studies). 192p. 1988. 45.00 (*0-313-24997-0*, ADM/, Greenwood Pr) Greenwood.

Annas, Pamela J. & Rosen, Robert C. Against the Current. LC 97-37429. (Readings for Writers Ser.). 780p. (C). 1998. pap. text 37.00 (*0-13-097924-4*) P-H.

— Literature & Society. 3rd ed. LC 99-29038. 1467p. (C). 1999. pap. text 50.67 (*0-13-012481-8*) P-H.

Annau, Zoltan, ed. Neurobehavioral Toxicology. LC 86-45452. (Johns Hopkins Series in Environmental Toxicology). (Illus.). 459p. 1986. reprint ed. pap. 142.30 (*0-608-07381-4*, 206760800009) Bks Demand.

Annau, Zoltan, jt. ed. see Eccles, Christine U.

Annaud, Jean-Jacques, et al. Seven Years in Tibet: Screenplay & Story Behind the Film. LC 97-29129. (Newmarket Pictorial Moviebook Ser.). (Illus.). 288p. 1997. 27.50 (*1-55704-342-6*, Pub. by Newmarket) Norton.

Annavarjula, Weistein. Marketing Management. (General Business Ser.). 2000. pap. 43.95 (*0-324-02737-0*) Sth-Wstrn College.

Anne Birac Consulting Staff, ed. see Jonathon, Susan.

***Anne-Johns, Michael.** Jessica Simpson. (Illus.). (J). 2000. pap. 4.95 (*0-7407-1169-5*) Andrews & McMeel.

Anne, Kristi, jt. auth. see Melhuus, Marit.

Anne, Marjorie. Making Peace Prayers in Pictures. 32p. 1986. pap. 30.00 (*0-7223-1991-6*, Pub. by A H S Ltd) St Mut.

Anne, W. Now What Do I Do for Fun? 20p. (Orig.). 1985. pap. 1.50 (*0-89486-297-9*, 1269B) Hazelden.

Annell, Lars & Torngren, Martin, eds. Nordic Transputer Applications: Proceedings of the First & Second Nordic Transputer Seminars. (Transputer & Occam Engineering Ser.). 196p. (gr. 12). 1991. pap. 70.00 (*90-5199-070-7*, Pub. by IOS Pr) IOS Press.

Annelo, Eloy & Hernandez, Joan B. Moral Leadership. 166p. 1998. pap. 16.95 (*0-9659945-1-1*) Global Classrm.

Annels, A. E., ed. Case Histories & Methods in Mineral Resource Evaluation. (Geological Society Special Publications: No. 63). (Illus.). vi, 313p. (C). 1992. 107.00 (*0-903317-79-6*, 276, Pub. by Geol Soc Pub Hse) AAPG.

Annelyse, Allen, tr. see Labaky, Mansour.

Annema, Anne-Johan. Feed-Forward Neural Networks: Vector Decomposition Analysis, Modelling & Apalog Implementation. LC 95-6884. (Kluwer International Series in Engineering & Computer Science). 256p. (C). 1995. text 103.00 (*0-7923-9567-0*) Kluwer Academic.

Annemann, Ted. Annemann's Card Magic. LC 77-75234. (Illus.). 1977. reprint ed. pap. 6.95 (*0-486-23522-X*) Dover.

Annemann, Theodore. Practical Mental Magic. (Illus.). 310p. (Orig.). 1983. pap. 8.95 (*0-486-24426-1*) Dover.

Annen, Craig. Easter Sunday. unabridged ed. (Illus.). 137p. 1998. pap. 14.95 (*1-892651-16-5*) Columbia Pubns.

Annen, Sharon, tr. see Desnos, Robert.

Annenberg. Power Place Study Guide. 3rd ed. 235p. 1999. pap. 38.95 (*0-471-35741-3*) Wiley.

***Annenberg, et al.** Fokus Deutsch: Beginning German 1. 368p. (C). 1999. 31.88 (*0-07-233664-1*); pap., student ed. 31.88 (*0-07-233665-X*) McGrw-H Hghr Educ.

— Fokus Deutsch: Beginning German 2. 368p. (C). 1999. student ed. 33.75 (*0-07-233663-3*); pap., student ed. 33.75 (*0-07-233662-5*) McGrw-H Hghr Educ.

— Fokus Deutsch: Intermediate German. 368p. (C). 1999. 35.94 (*0-07-233661-7*); student ed. 35.94 (*0-07-233660-9*) McGrw-H Hghr Educ.

Annenberg Communications Staff. Pets-R-Permitted Hotel, Motel & Kennel Directory: The Travel Resource for Pet Owners Who Travel. Nelson, M. E., ed. 222p. 1992. pap. 9.95 (*1-56471-777-1*) Annenberg.

Annenberg, Maurice. Type Foundries of America & Their Catalogs. LC 94-29933. 304p. 1994. 49.95 (*1-884718-06-X*) Oak Knoll.

Annenberg, Maurice, intro. A Typographical Journey Through the Inland Printer, 1883-1990. LC 77-89269. (C). boxed set 45.00 (*0-916526-04-6*) Maran Pub.

Anner, John, ed. Beyond Identity Politics: Emerging Social Justice Movements in Communities of Color. 200p. 1996. 40.00 (*0-89608-534-1*); pap. text 14.00 (*0-89608-533-3*) South End Pr.

Annerino, John. Adventuring in Arizona. rev. ed. (Illus.). 464p. 1996. pap. 16.00 (*0-87156-386-X*, Pub. by Sierra) Random.

— Adventuring in Arizona: The Sierra Club Travel Guide to the Grand Canyon State. LC 91-14186. (Adventure Travel Guide Ser.). (Illus.). 384p. (Orig.). 1991. pap. 15.00 (*0-87156-681-8*, Pub. by Sierra) Random.

— Apache: Sacred Path to Womanhood. LC 98-29881. (Illus.). 100p. 1998. 29.95 (*1-56924-667-X*, Pub. by Marlowe & Co) Publishers Group.

***Annerino, John.** Canyoneering. LC 98-43089. (Illus.). 160p. 1999. pap. 14.95 (*0-8117-2700-9*) Stackpole.

Annerino, John. Dead in Their Tracks: Crossing America's Desert Borderlands. LC 99-21341. (Illus.). 256p. 1999. 22.00 (*1-56858-132-7*) FWEW.

***Annerino, John.** Exploring the Desert. LC 99-17644. (Illus.). 160p. 1999. pap. 14.95 (*0-8117-2747-5*) Stackpole.

— High-Risk Photography: The Adventure Behind the Image. (Illus.). 120p. 1999. reprint ed. pap. text 18.00 (*0-7881-6833-9*) DIANE Pub.

Annerino, John. Hiking the Grand Canyon. rev. ed. LC 92-24723. (Totebook Ser.). (Illus.). 384p. (Orig.). 1997. pap. 15.00 (*0-87156-589-7*, Pub. by Sierra) Random.

***Annerino, John.** Rough Stock: The Toughest Events in Rodeo. (Illus.). 160p. 2000. 45.00 (*1-56858-177-7*, Pub. by FWEW) Publishers Group.

Annerino, John. Running Wild: An Extraordinary Adventure of the Human Spirit. 2nd ed. LC 97-39578. (Illus.). 317p. 1997. pap. text 14.95 (*1-56025-175-1*, Thunders Mouth) Avalon NY.

***Annerino, John.** Where Spirits Still Dance: The Tarahumara of the Sierra Madre. LC 99-43282. (Illus.). 128p. 1999. 27.00 (*1-56924-658-0*) Marlowe & Co.

Annerino, John, et al. Outdoors in Arizona: A Guide to Hiking & Backpacking. 5th ed. (Illus.). 136p. 2000. pap. 10.95 (*0-916179-50-8*) Ariz Hwy.

Annerl, Annemarie S., ed. see Tayler, Moi.

***Annernino, John, text.** Canyons of the Southwest: A Tour of the Great Canyon Country from Colorado to Northern... (Illus.). 160p. 2000. pap. 17.95 (*0-8165-2092-5*) U of Ariz Pr.

Annesi, James J. Enhancing Exercise Motivation Vol. 1: A Guide to Increasing Fitness Center Member Retention. (Illus.). 128p. (Orig.). 1996. pap. 19.95 (*0-9652432-0-6*, FM9601) Fitness Mgmt.

Annesley. Blank Fictions: Consumerism, Culture & the Contemporary American Novel. LC 97-45803. 1998. write for info. (*0-7453-1091-5*, Pub. by Pluto GBR) Stylus Pub VA.

— Blank Fictions: Consumerism, Culture & the Contemporary American Novel. LC 97-45803. 180p. 1998. pap. 18.95 (*0-312-21535-5*); text 55.00 (*0-312-21534-7*) St Martin.

Annesley, Noel. The Touch of the Artist: Master Drawings from the Woodner Family Collections. Grasselli, Margaret M., ed. LC 95-23191. (Illus.). 288p. 1995. 60.00 (*0-8109-3882-0*, Pub. by Abrams) Time Warner.

Annesley, Samuel. Puritan Sermons, Sixteen Fifty-Nine To Sixteen Eighty-Nine Being the Morning Exercises at Cripplegate, St. Giles in the Fields & in Southwark: By 75 Ministers of the Gospel in or Near London, with Notes & Translations by James Nichols, 6 vols., Set. Nichols, James, ed. 4200p. (C). 1981. reprint ed. lib. bdg. 150.00 (*0-940033-19-4*) R O Roberts.

***Anness Publications Staff.** Activity Box Set. abr. ed. 1999. boxed set 30.00 (*0-7548-0416-X*, Pub. by Anness Pub) Random.

— The American Practical Gardening Encyclopedia: The Complete Step-by-Step Guide to Successful Gardening, from Designing, Planning & Planting, to Year-Round Maintenance Tasks. 1999. 19.98 (*1-84038-419-0*) Random.

— Garden Book Box Set. 1999. boxed set 30.00 (*0-7548-0420-8*, Pub. by Anness Pub) Random.

Anness Publications Staff. Little Candle Book. 1999. 11.95 (*0-7548-0188-8*) Random.

***Anness Publications Staff.** The Little Wok Cookbook. 1999. 12.95 (*1-84038-400-X*, Pub. by Hermes Hse) Random.

— My Home. 1999. pap. 4.95 (*0-7548-0280-9*, Lorenz Bks) Anness Pub.

— Point & Say: Playschool Fun. (J). 2001. 10.00 (*1-85967-974-9*) Time Warner.

— Wine & Cheese Box Set. 1999. boxed set 30.00 (*0-7548-0419-4*, Pub. by Anness Pub) Random.

Anness Publications Staff, PUBL. Cats. 1999. 7.98 (*1-84038-398-4*) Random.

***Anness Publications Staff, PUBL.** Christmas Treats. 1999. 7.98 (*1-84038-399-2*) Random.

Anness Publications Staff, PUBL. Classic Cakes. 2000. 7.98 (*1-84038-022-5*) Random.

***Anness Publications Staff, PUBL.** Complete Guide to Cigars of the World. 1999. 10.95 (*0-7548-0018-0*, Lorenz Bks) Anness Pub.

Anness Publications Staff, PUBL. Country Christmas. (Illus.). 192p. 1999. 15.98 (*1-84038-377-1*) Random.

— Country Store. 1999. 15.98 (*1-84038-245-7*) Random.

***Anness Publications Staff, PUBL.** Encyclopedia of Mythology. 1999. 19.98 (*1-85967-164-0*, Lorenz Bks) Anness Pub.

Anness Publications Staff, PUBL. Encyclopedia Of Mythology. 1999. 19.98 (*1-84038-404-2*) Random.

— Encyclopedia 0f Mythology , Vol. 2. 1999. 19.98 (*1-84038-405-0*) Random.

— Essential Aromatherapy. (Illus.). 1999. 9.98 (*1-84038-406-9*) Random.

— Gingerbread. 1999. 7.98 (*1-84038-407-7*) Random.

— Karate. 1999. 14.98 (*1-84038-384-4*) Random.

— Perfect Christmas. 1999. 7.98 (*1-84038-413-1*) Random.

— Perfect Pie. 1999. 7.98 (*1-84038-411-5*) Random.

— Vegetarian Kitchen. 1999. 30.00 (*1-84038-287-2*, Pub. by Hermes Hse) Random.

— World Encyclopedia of Beer. 1999. 19.98 (*1-84038-417-4*) Random.

***Anness Publications Staff, PUBL.** World Encyclopedia of Tractors/Farm Machinery. 2000. 40.00 (*0-7548-0357-0*, Lorenz Bks) Anness Pub.

— World of Cats. 2000. 9.98 (*1-84038-115-9*) Random.

— World of Dogs. 2000. 9.98 (*1-84038-116-7*) Random.

— World of Horses. 2000. 9.98 (*1-84038-117-5*) Random.

***Anness Publishing Staff.** Babies, A Very First Picture Book. (Illus.). (J). (gr. 2-7). 2000. bds. 4.95 (*0-7548-0707-X*) Anness Pub.

— Cajun & Creole. 2000. pap. 12.95 (*0-7548-0520-4*) Anness Pub.

— Cake Decorating Bible. 2000. pap. 12.95 (*0-7548-0543-3*) Anness Pub.

— Caring for Your Dog. 2000. pap. 14.95 (*0-7548-0517-4*) Anness Pub.

— Caring for Your Horse. 2000. pap. 14.95 (*0-7548-0516-6*) Anness Pub.

— Cars-Classic Collection. 2000. boxed set 30.00 (*0-7548-0418-6*) Anness Pub.

— Containers. 2000. 13.00 (*0-7548-0539-5*) Anness Pub.

— Country Crafts, Cooking, Decorating & Flowers. (Illus.). 512p. 1998. 19.98 (*1-901289-04-4*) Anness Pub.

— Dream Desserts. 2000. pap. 12.95 (*0-7548-0438-0*) Anness Pub.

— The Encyclopedia of Herbs & Spices. (Illus.). 512p. 2000. 19.98 (*1-901289-06-0*) Anness Pub.

— Essential Plants for Every Garden. 2000. 40.00 (*0-7548-0501-8*) Anness Pub.

— Fat Free Cooks Collection. 2000. boxed set 30.00 (*0-7548-0415-1*) Anness Pub.

— Growing Fruit. 2000. pap. 12.95 (*0-7548-0452-6*) Anness Pub.

Anness Publishing Staff. Italian Cooking Encyclopedia. (Illus.). 512p. 1998. 19.98 (*1-901289-08-7*, Pub. by Hermes Hse) Random.

***Anness Publishing Staff.** Karate. 2000. pap. 11.00 (*0-7548-0523-9*) Anness Pub.

— Let's Look at Nature. (J). (-8). 2000. bds. 4.95 (*0-7548-0709-6*) Anness Pub.

— Let's Look at Patterns. (J). 2000. bds. 4.95 (*0-7548-0710-X*) Anness Pub.

— Let's Look at Pets. (J). (-7). 2000. bds. 4.95 (*0-7548-0711-8*) Anness Pub.

— Locomotives of the World. 2000. pap. 10.95 (*0-7548-0513-1*) Anness Pub.

— Main Courses. 2000. pap. 12.95 (*0-7548-0472-0*) Anness Pub.

— Men's Gift: Steam Engines. 2000. 14.95 (*0-7548-0503-4*) Anness Pub.

— Men's Gift: Tractors. 2000. 14.95 (*0-7548-0444-5*, Pub. by Anness Pub) Random.

— Messy, A Very First Picture. (J). (-7). 2000. bds. 4.95 (*0-7548-0708-8*) Anness Pub.

— Natural Beauty. 2000. pap. 19.95 (*1-84215-179-7*) Anness Pub.

— New Guide to Babycare. 2000. pap. 15.00 (*0-7548-0515-8*) Anness Pub.

— On Two Wheels. 2000. pap. 19.95 (*1-84215-203-3*) Anness Pub.

— Party Food. 2000. pap. 12.95 (*0-7548-0521-2*) Anness Pub.

— Point & Say: All About Nature. 2001. 10.00 (*1-85967-982-X*) Anness Pub.

— Quick & Easy Muffins. 1999. pap. 12.95 (*0-7548-0268-X*, Pub. by Anness Pub) Random.

— Rose Garden. 2000. pap. 12.95 (*0-7548-0464-X*) Anness Pub.

— Roses. 2000. pap. 19.95 (*0-7548-0463-1*) Anness Pub.

— Spicy Flavors. 2000. pap. 12.95 (*0-7548-0481-X*) Anness Pub.

— Taste of China. 2000. pap. 12.95 (*0-7548-0441-0*) Anness Pub.

— Taste of Indonesia. 2000. pap. 12.95 (*0-7548-0440-2*) Anness Pub.

— Taste of the Middle East. 2000. pap. 12.95 (*0-7548-0483-6*) Anness Pub.

— 30 Creative Containers: Inspirationsl Ideas For Making & Decorating Contain. 2000. 11.95 (*0-7548-0700-2*) Anness Pub.

— 30 Herbal Gifts: Enchanting Gift Ideas With Fresh & Dries Herbs. 2000. 11.95 (*0-7548-0695-2*) Anness Pub.

— Toys. (J). 2000. bds. 4.95 (*0-7548-0712-6*) Anness Pub.

— Traditional Puddings & Pies. 2000. pap. 12.95 (*0-7548-0522-0*) Anness Pub.

— Ultimate Chinese & Oriental Cookbook. (Illus.). 512p. 1998. 19.98 (*1-901289-09-5*) Anness Pub.

— Ultimate Encyclopedia of Small Pets. 2000. 35.00 (*0-7548-0597-2*) Anness Pub.

— Ultimate Low Fat Indian. 2000. pap. 12.95 (*0-7548-0482-8*) Anness Pub.

— Ultimate Wok & Stir Fry Cookbook: Over 200 Sizzling Quick-Fry Recipes from the East. (Illus.). 1997. 19.98 (*1-901289-39-7*) Hermes Hse.

— Visual Dictionary of Herbs. (Illus.). 2000. pap. 11.95 (*0-7548-0470-4*) Anness Pub.

— World Encyclopedia of Trucks. 2000. 35.00 (*0-7548-0518-2*) Anness Pub.

Anness Publishing Staff, ed. Ancient Civilizations. (Exploring History Ser.). (Illus.). 64p. (J). 1999. 12.95 (*0-7548-0211-6*, Lorenz Bks) Anness Pub.

— Ancient Weapons & Warfare. (Exploring History Ser.). (Illus.). 64p. (J). 1999. 12.95 (*0-7548-0212-4*, Lorenz Bks) Anness Pub.

— Castles. (Discovery Ser.). (Illus.). (J). 1999. 12.95 (*0-7548-0207-8*, Lorenz Bks) Anness Pub.

— Country Designs from Nature. 1999. 19.95 (*0-7548-0201-9*, Lorenz Bks) Anness Pub.

***Anness Publishing Staff, ed.** Folk Art Gifts. 1999. 11.95 (*0-7548-0178-0*, Lorenz Bks) Anness Pub.

— Garlands, Wreaths & Circles. 1999. 30.00 (*0-7548-0179-9*, Lorenz Bks) Anness Pub.

— Halloween. 1999. 11.95 (*0-7548-0180-2*, Lorenz Bks) Anness Pub.

Anness Publishing Staff, ed. Inventions. (Investigations Ser.). (Illus.). 64p. (J). 1999. 12.95 (*0-7548-0213-2*, Lorenz Bks) Anness Pub.

***Anness Publishing Staff, ed.** Pirates. (Discovery Ser.). (Illus.). (J). 1999. 12.95 (*0-7548-0208-6*, Lorenz Bks) Anness Pub.

— Tantric Sex: New Life Library. 1999. 11.95 (*0-7548-0192-6*, Lorenz Bks) Anness Pub.

Anness Publishing Staff, ed. Volcanoes. (Investigations Ser.). (Illus.). 64p. (J). 1999. 12.95 (*0-7548-0214-0*, Lorenz Bks) Anness Pub.

Anness Publishing Staff, ed. see Bright, Michael.

Anness Publishing Staff, ed. see Kerrod, Robin.

Anness Publishing Staff, ed. see Llewellyn, Claire.

Anness Publishing Staff, ed. see MacDonald, Fiona.

Anness Publishing Staff, ed. see Stotter, Michael.

Annett, Albert & Lehtinen, Alice E. History of Jaffrey, New Hampshire (Middle Monadnock) An Average Country Town in the Heart of New England, 2 vols. (Illus.). 1749p. 1997. reprint ed. lib. bdg. 169.50 (*0-8328-7137-0*) Higginson Bk Co.

Annett, Frederick A. Elevators: Electric & Electrohydraulic Elevators, Escalators, Moving Sidewalks & Ramps. (Illus.). 388p. 1989. text 65.00 (*1-886536-14-7*) Elevator Wrld.

Annett, H. & Rifkin, S. B. Guidelines for Rapid Participatory Appraisals to Assess Community Health Needs: A Focus on Health Improvements for Low-Income Urban & Rural Areas. 60p. 1995. pap. 10.80 (*0-614-32417-3*, 1930077) World Health.

Annett, H., jt. auth. see Ehrlich, Paul R.

Annette B., Natow & Heslin, Jo-Ann. The Pocket Protein Counter. 96p. 1997. per. 2.99 (*0-671-00380-1*) PB.

Annette, Natow. Iron Counter. 1993. mass mkt. 5.99 (*0-671-78324-6*) PB.

***Anniah Gowda, H. H.** Encyclopaedia of Commonwealth Literature , 2 vols. LC 99-933792. 706 p. 1998. write for info. (*81-7020-810-6*, Pub. by Cosmo Pubn) S Asia.

Annick Press Staff. Annikin Series, 4 bks. (Annikin Ser.: Vol. 10). (Illus.). (J). (ps-1). pap. write for info. (*1-55037-139-8*, Pub. by Annick) Firefly Bks Ltd.

— Annikin Series, 3 bks. (Annikin Ser.: Vol. 11). (Illus.). (J). (ps-1). pap. write for info. (*1-55037-203-3*, Pub. by Annick) Firefly Bks Ltd.

— Annikin Series, 3 bks. (Annikin Ser.: Vol. 13). (Illus.). (J). (ps-1). pap. write for info. (*1-55037-357-9*, Pub. by Annick) Firefly Bks Ltd.

— Annikin Series, 3 bks. (Annikin Ser.: Vol. 14). (Illus.). (J). (ps-1). pap. write for info. (*1-55037-387-0*, Pub. by Annick) Firefly Bks Ltd.

— Annikin Series, 3 bks. (Annikin Ser.: Vol. 3). (Illus.). (J). (ps-1). pap. write for info. (*1-55037-056-1*, Pub. by Annick) Firefly Bks Ltd.

— Annikin Series, 3 bks. (Annikin Ser.: Vol. 4). (Illus.). 32p. (J). (ps-1). pap. write for info. (*1-55037-057-X*, Pub. by Annick) Firefly Bks Ltd.

— Annikin Series, 3 bks. (Annikin Ser.: Vol. 5). (Illus.). (J). (ps-1). pap. write for info. (*1-55037-058-8*, Pub. by Annick) Firefly Bks Ltd.

— Annikin Series, 3 bks. (Annikin Ser.: Vol. 7). (Illus.). (J). (ps-1). pap. write for info. (*1-55037-060-X*, Pub. by Annick) Firefly Bks Ltd.

— Annikin Series, 3 bks. (Annikin Ser.: Vol. 8). (Illus.). (J). (ps-1). pap. write for info. (*1-55037-061-8*, Pub. by Annick) Firefly Bks Ltd.

— Annikin Series, 3 bks. (Annikin Ser.: Vol. 9). (Illus.). (J). (ps-1). pap. write for info. (*1-55037-111-8*, Pub. by Annick) Firefly Bks Ltd.

— Annikin Series, 3 bks. (Annikin Ser.: Vol. 1). (Illus.). (J). (ps-1). 1992. pap. write for info. (*1-55037-054-5* Pub. by Annick) Firefly Bks Ltd.

— Annikin Series, No. 6. (Illus.). (J). (ps-1). pap. write for info. (*1-55037-059-6*, Pub. by Annick) Firefly Bks Ltd.

Annie, Eileen. Half of the Bran Muffin Is Gone. LC 91-70408. (Illus.). 116p. (Orig.). 1991. pap. text 12.00 (*0-9616160-4-0*) Bench Pr NY.

Annie, Mama. Keli's Magic Stone. (J). 8.95 (*0-9637637-4-1*) Cleall Pubng.

Annie, Rver. Cooking on Wheels: Trailer Folks Favorite Recipes. (Illus.). 92p. 1998. reprint ed. pap. text 3.00 (*0-7881-5217-3*) DIANE Pub.

Annie Santiago De Curet. Credito Moneda y Bancos en Puerto Rico Durante el Siglo XIX. LC 89-32168. 238p. (Orig.). 1989. pap. 9.50 (*0-8477-2644-4*) U of PR Pr.

Annies, Attic. Afghan Sentiments. 1998. 19.96 (*1-57367-103-7*) Needlecrft Shop.

— Annie's Favorite Baby Projects. 1998. 19.96 (*0-9655269-3-3*) Annies Attic TX.

— Enchanting Delights. 1999. 19.96 (*1-57367-105-3*) Needlecrft Shop.

— Masterpiece Showcase. LC 98-66978. 1999. pap. 19.96 (*1-57367-104-5*) Needlecrft Shop.

Annie's Attic Inc. Staff. Crochet Private Collection. LC 98-66977. 1999. 19.96 (*1-57367-106-1*) Needlecrft Shop.

Annie's Attic Inc. Staff & Elmore, William E. More Elmore. 1994. 9.95 (*0-9641505-0-6*) Annies Attic Pr.

Annies Attic Staff. Annie's Favorite Christmas Projects. 1999. 19.96 (*0-9655269-4-1*) Annies Attic TX.

Annie's Attic Staff. Annie's Favorite Crochet Dolls. 1997. 19.96 (*0-9655269-1-7*) Annies Attic TX.

— Annie's Favorite Thread Projects. 1998. pap. 19.96 (*0-9655269-2-5*) Annies Attic TX.

Annies Attic Staff. Ultimate PC Collection. 1998. pap. text 19.96 (*1-57367-101-0*) Needlecrft Shop.

***Annie's Attic Staff, ed.** Annie's Favorite Quick & Easy Projects. (Illus.). 1999. 19.96 (*0-9655269-5-X*) Annies Attic TX.

Annikin & Munsch, Robert. Murmel, Murmel, Murmel. (Annikins Ser.: Vol. 7). (Illus.). 32p. (J). (ps-2). 1989. pap. 0.99 (*1-55037-012-X*, Pub. by Annick) Firefly Bks Ltd.

Anniko, M., ed. Endolymphatic Duct & Sac: Journal: Oto-Rhino-Laryngology, Vol. 54, No. 4, 1992. (Illus.). 60p. 1992. pap. 58.50 (*3-8055-5640-3*) S Karger.

Anniko, M. & Arnold, W., eds. Immunomorphological Analysis of the Human Inner Ear. (Journal Ser.: Vol. 57, No. 2, 1995). (Illus.). 54p. 1995. pap. 60.00 (*3-8055-6140-7*) S Karger.

Annin, B. D. & Cherepanov, G. P. Elastic-Plastic Problems. Ghojel, Jamil I., tr. from RUS. LC 88-70032. (Illus.). 250p. 1988. write for info. (*0-7918-0000-8*) ASME.

Annin, Katharine H. Country Seasons. 256p. (Orig.). 1989. pap. 9.95 (*0-9611118-3-6*) Cardamom.

Annin, Michael & Falaschetti, Dominic. Stocks, Bonds, Bills & Inflation: Valuation Edition, 1999 Yearbook. (Illus.). 300p. 1999. 120.00 (*1-882864-08-5*) Ibbotson Assocs.

***Annin, Michael & Falaschetti, Dominic.** Stocks, Bonds, Bills & Inflation: Valuation Edition 2000 Yearbook. rev. ed. (Illus.). 300p. 2000. 110.00 (*1-882864-11-5*) Ibbotson Assocs.

Annin, Michael, ed. see Ibbotson Staff.

***Anning, Angela.** Early Childhood Education. 44p. 1998. pap. 7.95 (*1-85856-090-X*, Trentham Bks) Stylus Pub VA.

Anning, Angela. The First Years at School: Education 4 to 8. 2nd ed. LC 96-33768. (Developing Teachers & Teaching Ser.). 169p. 1996. pap. 24.95 (*0-335-19690-X*) OpUniv Pr.

— A National Curriculum for the Early Years. LC 95-10789. 160p. 1995. 79.95 (*0-335-19432-X*) OpUniv Pr.

Anning, Angela, ed. A National Curriculum for the Early Years. LC 95-10789. 160p. 1995. pap. 23.95 (*0-335-19431-1*) OpUniv Pr.

Anning, Angela & Edwards, Anne. Promoting Children's Learning from Birth to Five: Developing the New Early Years Professional. LC 99-14376. 184p. 1999. pap. 23.95 (*0-335-20216-0*, Pub. by OpUniv Pr) Taylor & Francis.

Anninger, Anne. Salts of Silver, Toned with Gold. (Illus.). 176p. 1999. pap. 25.00 (*0-914630-22-9*) Houghton Lib.

Anninger, Anne, ed. Why Artists' Books? (Illus.). 32p. (Orig.). 1993. pap. 15.00 (*0-914630-12-1*) Houghton Lib.

Anninger, Anne & Stoddard, Roger, eds. Centuries of Book & Manuscripts: Collectors & Friends, Scholars & Librarians Build the Harvard College Library. (Illus.). 72p. 1992. pap. 18.00 (*0-914630-05-9*) Houghton Lib.

Annino, Joseph. How to Promote Your Own Products: Your Step-by-Step Guide to Product Success. (Illus.). 160p. 1989. 25.00 (*0-925857-00-9*) Faculty Sftware.

Anninskii, Lev, et al. Russian Culture in Transition: Selected Papers of the Working Group for the Study of Contemporary Russian Culture (1990-1991) Freidin, Gregory, ed. & intro. by. (Stanford Slavic Studies: Vol. 7). (ENG & RUS., Illus.). 323p. (Orig.). (C). 1993. pap. 30.00 (*0-933884-85-0*) Berkeley Slavic.

Annis, Daniel G. Vital Records of Londonderry, New Hampshire, 1719-1910. LC 94-78265. 328p. 1994. reprint ed. 17.50 (*0-8063-1415-X*) Clearfield Co.

Annis, David B., et al. Essays in Academic Ethics. 1992. 10.00 (*0-318-69341-0*) Soc Profs Ed.

Annis, Edward, et al. Health Care: History, Hype, & Help. 61p. 1994. 10.00 (*1-886306-11-7*) Nevada Policy.

Annis, Edward R. Code Blue: Health Care in Crisis. LC 92-44875. 288p. 1993. 21.95 (*0-89526-515-X*) Regnery Pub.

Annis, J. Lee, Jr. Howard Baker: Conciliator in an Age of Crisis. LC 94-25949. (Illus.). 304p. (Orig.). 1994. 27.95 (*1-56833-032-4*) Madison Bks UPA.

Annis, J. Lee, jt. auth. see Frist, William H.

Annis, John R. & Allen, Algernon R. An Atlas of Canine Surgery: Basic Surgical Procedures with Emphasis on the Gastrointestinal & Urogenital Systems. LC 67-29212. 235p. reprint ed. pap. 72.90 (*0-8357-5839-7*, 205541400022) Bks Demand.

Annis, Michael, ed. The Y2K Personal Survival Plan Handbook. 144p. Date not set. 15.95 (*1-882863-69-0*) Howling Dog.

Annis, Michael, ed. see Greyhawk, Gregory.

Annis, Michael, ed. & des. see Antler, et al.

Annis, Sheldon. God & Production in a Guatemalan Town. LC 87-13921. (Illus.). 213p. 1988. reprint ed. pap. 12.95 (*0-292-72742-9*) U of Tex Pr.

Annis, Sheldon, et al, eds. Poverty, Natural Resources, & Public Policy in Central America. (U. S. Third World Policy Perspectives Ser.: No. 17). 280p. (C). 1992. 32.95 (*1-56000-015-5*); pap. text 17.95 (*1-56000-577-7*) Transaction Pubs.

Annison, Michael H. & Wilford, Dan S. Trust Matters: New Directions in Health Care Leadership. LC 98-18743. (Business & Management Ser.). 160p. 1998. 29.95 (*0-7879-4389-4*) Jossey-Bass.

Anniss, Michael, jt. auth. see Musgrave, James.

Annitto, Susan. Quality Happens Through People: Why Quality Initiatives Succeed - Or Don't. (AT&T Quality Library). (Illus.). 110p. (Orig.). 1994. pap. 19.95 (*0-932764-47-9*) AT&T Customer Info.

— Shared Values: Our Common Bond. (AT&T Quality Library). (Illus.). 124p. (Orig.). 1992. pap. 24.95 (*0-932764-37-1*, 500-479A) AT&T Customer Info.

Annitto, Susan, ed. AT&T Quality Improvement Cycle. (AT&T Quality Library). (Illus.). 68p. (Orig.). 1988. pap. 29.95 (*0-932764-20-7*, 500-031) AT&T Customer Info.

Annitto, Susan, ed. see Ackerman, Roger, et al.

Annitto, Susan, ed. see Coleman, Roberta, et al.

Annitto, Susan, ed. see Wigenton, Kevin.

Annitto, Susan, ed. see Willie, Randall R.

Annixter, Paul. Devil of the Woods. LC 70-81259. (Short Story Index Reprint Ser., Vol. 1). 1977. 19.95 (*0-8369-3011-8*) Ayer.

Anno, B. Jay, jt. auth. see National Comm. on Correctional Health Care Staff.

Anno, J. N., jt. auth. see Duncan, Dan.

Anno, Masaichiro & Anno, Mitsumasa. Anno's Mysterious Multiplying Jar. 48p. (gr. k-3). 1999. pap. 6.99 (*0-698-11753-0*) Putnam Pub Group.

Anno, Mitsumasa. Anno's Alphabet. LC 73-21652. (Illus.). 64p. (J). (gr. k up). 1975. 16.00 (*0-690-00540-7*) HarpC Child Bks.

— Anno's Counting Book. LC 76-28977. (Illus.). 32p. (J). (ps-3). 1977. 15.95 (*0-690-01287-X*) HarpC Child Bks.

— Anno's Counting Book. LC 76-28977. (Illus.). 32p. (J). (ps-3). 1977. lib. bdg. 16.89 (*0-690-01288-8*) HarpC Child Bks.

— Anno's Counting Book. (J). 1977. 12.15 (*0-606-03174-X*, Pub. by Turtleback) Demco.

— Anno's Counting Book. LC 76-28977. (Trophy Picture Bk.). (Illus.). 32p. (J). (ps-3). 1986. reprint ed. pap. 6.95 (*0-06-443123-1*, HarpTrophy) HarpC Child Bks.

— Anno's Counting Book Big Book. LC 65-28977. (Trophy Picture Bk.). (Illus.). 32p. (J). (ps-3). 1992. pap. 22.95 (*0-06-443315-3*, HarpTrophy) HarpC Child Bks.

— Anno's Journey. LC 77-16336. (Illus.). 48p. (J). (ps up). 1981. 15.95 (*0-399-20762-7*, Philomel) Peng Put Young Read.

— Anno's Journey. (Illus.). 32p. (J). (ps-3). 1997. pap. 5.95 (*0-698-11433-7*, PapStar) Peng Put Young Read.

— Anno's Magic Seeds. LC 92-39309. (Illus.). (J). (ps-3). 1995. 15.99 (*0-399-22538-2*, Philomel) Peng Put Young Read.

A

***Anno, Mitsumasa.** Anno's Magic Seeds, 1 vol. (Illus.). 40p. (YA). (gr. k-4). 1999. pap. 6.99 (*0-698-11618-6*, PapStar) Peng Put Young Read.

Anno, Mitsumasa. Anno's Math Games. (Illus.). 104p. (J). (ps up). 1997. pap. 12.95 (*0-698-11671-2*, PapStar) Peng Put Young Read.

— Anno's Mysterious Multiplying Jar. LC 82-22413. (Illus.). 48p. (J). (gr. 3 up). 1983. 19.95 (*0-399-20951-4*, Philomel) Peng Put Young Read.

Anno, Mitsumasa, jt. auth. see Anno, Masaichiro.

Annobil, Ishmael F. Seven Horn Elegy. 1997. pap. 12.50 (*1-899151-00-1*) Intl Spec Bk.

Annoni, Mary. Diane's Point of View: A Doggerel Life Poem. 73p. (Orig.). 1998. pap. 19.95 (*1-891421-02-6*) Diagnostic Ctr.

Annor, Kwame P. Some Aspects of Socio-Economic & Community Factors in Planning Urban Freeways. 27p. (Orig.). 1970. pap. 2.50 (*1-55719-047-X*) U NE CPAR.

Annrachain, Maire N. & Dhiarmada, Briona N., eds. Teacs Agus Comtheacs: Gneithe de Chritic Na Gaeilge. 224p. 1998. pap. 26.95 (*1-85918-051-5*, Pub. by Cork Univ) Intl Spec Bk.

Annschild, Louise. Anatomy's Destiny: Male Behavior: Tales of Its Causes & Cures. 191p. 1995. pap. 12.00 (*0-9649540-0-1*) S B Pubng.

Annual Conf. of the Society of Plastic Eng. Staff. ANTEC 94: Plastics: Gateway to the Future, 3 vols., Set. (Illus.). 3738p. 1994. pap. 99.95 (*1-56676-165-4*) Technomic.

Annual Conference for Psychosomatic Research Staff. The Psychosomatic Approach to Prevention of Disease: Proceedings of the 20th Annual Conference for Psychosomatic Research, London, Nov. 15-16, 1976. Carruthers, M. & Priest, R., eds. 1978. pap. 26.00 (*0-08-022253-6*, Pergamon Pr) Elsevier.

Annual Conference on Magnetic Materials. Magnetism & Magnetic Materials: Proceedings of the Annual Conference on Magnetic Materials, 22nd, Pittsburgh, June 15-18, 1976. LC 76-47106. (AIP Conference Proceedings Ser.: No. 34). 1976. 19.50 (*0-88318-133-9*) Am Inst Physics.

***Annual Guides for the Arts Staff.** Annual Guides for the Arts, Millennium 1999-2000. (Illus.). 1999. pap. text 9.95 (*0-9668970-1-3*) Annual Guides Arts.

Annual Guides for the Arts Staff. Metropolitan Washington D.C. Annual Guides for the Arts 1998-1999, 1. 1999. pap. text 9.95 (*0-9668970-0-5*) Annual Guides Arts.

Annual Meeting Committee, ed. Scenario for a Magnitude 7.0 Earthquake on the Hayward Fault. (Illus.). 117p. 1996. pap. 15.00 (*0-943198-55-0*, HF-96) Earthquake Eng.

Annual Meeting of the Institute of Environmental S. The Environmental Challenge of the 70s: Proceedings of the 16th Annual Technical Meeting of the Institute of Environmental Sciences, 1970, Boston, Massachusetts. LC 62-38584. (Nineteen-Seventy Tutorial Lecture Ser.). (Illus.). 522p. 1970. pap. text 75.00 (*0-915414-10-4*) IEST.

— The Environments & Man: Proceedings of the 12th Annual Technical Meeting of the Institute of Environmental Sciences, 1966. LC 62-38584. (Illus.). 1966. pap. text 75.00 (*0-915414-06-6*) IEST.

— Hyper-Environments...Space Frontier: Proceedings of the Annual Meeting of the Institute of Environmental Sciences, 6th, 1960. (Illus.). 1960. pap. text 75.00 (*0-915414-00-7*) IEST.

— Product Improvement Through Environmental Science: Proceedings of the Annual Meeting of the Institute of Environmental Sciences, 8th, 1962. LC 62-38584. (Illus.). 1962. pap. text 75.00 (*0-915414-02-3*) IEST.

— Reliability vs. Reality: Proceedings of the Annual Meeting of the Institute of Environmental Sciences, 10th, 1964. LC 62-38584. (Illus.). 1964. pap. text 75.00 (*0-915414-04-X*) IEST.

Annual Meeting of the International Continence Soc. Proceedings of the Annual Meeting of the International Continence Society, 6th, Antwerp, Sept. 1976. Coolsaet, B., ed. (Urologia Internationalis Ser.: Vol. 33, No. 1-3). 1978. pap. 64.50 (*3-8055-2898-1*) S Karger.

Annual Meeting of the Japanese Society for Stereot. Recent Studies on the Human Thalamus: Proceedings of the Annual Meeting of the Japanese Society for Sterotactic 8, Functional Neurosurgery, 15th, Maebashi, October 1976. Gildenberg, P. L. & Ohye, Chihiro, eds. (Applied Neurophysiology Ser.: Vol. 39, No. 3-4). (Illus.). 1977. 50.50 (*3-8055-2847-7*) S Karger.

Annual of Trade Mark Design Staff. Book of American Trademarks, Vol. 7. Carter, David E., ed. LC 72-76493. (Illus.). 1980. 18.50 (*0-910158-61-4*) Art Dir.

Annual Oholo Biological Conference Staff. Methodology, Pathology & Immunology, Pt. I. Beemer, A. M. et al, eds. (Contributions to Microbiology & Immunology Ser.: Vol. 3). 1978. pap. 68.00 (*3-8055-2443-9*) S Karger.

— Specific Diseases & Therapy, Pt. II. Beemer, A. M. et al, eds. (Contributions to Microbiology & Immunology Ser.: Vol. 4). 1978. pap. 68.00 (*3-8055-2444-7*) S Karger.

Annual San Francisco Cancer Symposium Staff. Renaissance of Interstitial Brachytherapy: Proceedings of the Annual San Francisco Cancer Symposium, 12th, March 4-5, 1977. Vaeth, J. M., ed. (Frontiers of Radiation Therapy & Oncology Ser.: Vol. 12). (Illus.). 1977. 102.75 (*3-8055-2706-3*) S Karger.

Annual Technical Meeting of Institute of Environme. Environmental Technology '77: Proceedings of the 23rd Annual Technical Meeting of the Institute of Environmental Sciences, Los Angeles, April 1977. LC 62-38584. (Illus.). 437p. 1977. pap. text 75.00 (*0-915414-17-1*) IEST.

Annual Technical Meeting of the Institute of Envir. Combined Environments - Technology Interrelation: Proceedings of the Annual Technical Meeting of the Institute of Environmental Sciences, Fort Worth, Texas, April 1978. LC 62-38584. (Illus.). 511p. 1978. pap. text 75.00 (*0-915414-18-X*) IEST.

Annual West Coast Cancer Symposium Staff. Combined Effects of Chemotherapy & Radiotherapy on Normal Tissue Tolerance: Proceedings of the Annual West Coast Cancer Symposium, 13th, San Francisco, CA, March 1978. Vaeth, J. M., ed. (Frontiers of Radiation Therapy & Oncology Ser.: Vol. 13). (Illus.). 1979. 126.75 (*3-8055-2932-5*) S Karger.

— Primary Bone Cancer: The Multidiscipline Disease: Proceedings of the Annual West Coast Cancer Symposium, 10th, San Francisco, CA, September 1974. Vaeth, J. M., ed. (Frontiers of Radiation Therapy & Oncology Ser.: Vol. 10). viii, 243p. 1975. 82.75 (*3-8055-2185-5*) S Karger.

Annunziata, Jana & Jacobson-Kram, Phyllis. Solving Your Problems Together: Family Therapy for the Whole Family. LC 94-29708. (Illus.). 37p. 1994. 19.95 (*1-55798-268-6*, 4317460) Am Psychol.

Annunziata, Jane & Nemiroff, Marc A. Why Am I an Only Child? LC 98-13858. (Illus.). 36p. (J). (gr. k-2). 1998. 19.95 (*1-55798-506-5*, 441-5065) Am Psychol.

Annunziata, Jane, jt. auth. see Nemiroff, Marc A.

Annunziato, Paolo & Baldassarri, Mario, eds. Is the Economic Cycle Still Alive? Theory, Evidence, & Policies. LC 93-21104. (Central Issues in Contemporary Economic Theory & Policy Ser.). 1994. text 85.00 (*0-312-10380-8*) St Martin.

***Annuss, Hermut.** Landwirtschaftliche Groabetriebe im Transformationsprozea: Eine Untersuchung Fur das Neue Bundesland Mecklenburg-Vorpommern. (Europaische Hochschulschriften Ser.: Bd. 2553). 252p. 1999. 45.95 (*3-631-35840-7*) P Lang Pubng.

Annussek, Greg A., jt. auth. see Kessler, John F.

Annussek, Greg A., jt. auth. see Stolar, Mark.

Annwin, David, jt. auth. see Richardson, Alan.

***Ano.** From Serengeti to Silicon Valley: A Global View of Our Past, Present & Future. 199p. 1999. pap. 13.95 (*0-7414-0312-9*) Buy Books.

Ano. Mystic Dream Book: 2500 Dreams Explained. 1998. pap. 7.95 (*0-572-02411-8*, Pub. by W Foulsham) Trans-Atl Phila.

Ano, Fumio, et al. Nathaniel Hawthorne: The Introduction of an American Author's Work into Japan. (Illus.). 109p. 1993. pap. 15.00 (*0-88389-099-2*, PEMP162) Peabody Essex Mus.

Anobile, Richard J., ed. Dr. Jekyll & Mr. Hyde. (Illus.). 1976. mass mkt. 6.45 (*0-380-00450-X*, Avon Bks) Morrow Avon.

— The General. (Illus.). 1976. mass mkt. 6.45 (*0-380-00449-6*, 25817-X, Avon Bks) Morrow Avon.

Anogianakis, G., et al, eds. Advancement of Assistive Technology. LC 97-75047. (Assistive Technology Research Ser.: Vol. 3). 412p. (YA). (gr. 12). Date not set. write for info. (*90-5199-361-7*, 361-7) IOS Press.

Anokhina, I. G. English-Russian Business Dictionary-Handbook. Shimansky, M. P., ed. 424p. (C). 1992. 18.95 (*0-8285-4995-8*) Firebird NY.

— English-Russian Commercial Dictionary. (ENG & RUS.). 1992p. (C). 1992. text 120.00 (*0-569-11122-6*, Pub. by Collets) St Mut.

— English-Russian Dictionary of Commerce: Reference Guide. (ENG & RUS.). 424p. 1992. 75.00 (*0-7859-9097-6*) Fr & Eur.

***Anokwa, Kwadwo, et al.** International Communication: Issues & Cases. 2001. pap. 34.00 (*0-534-57519-6*) Thomson Learn.

Anolik, Alexander, jt. auth. see Thompson, Douglas.

Anomalous Publications Staff, ed. see LeCouturier, Jacques.

Anon. Climax in Paradise. 1997. mass mkt. 6.95 (*0-7472-5507-5*, Pub. by Headline Bk Pub) Trafalgar.

— Sensual Memoirs Edwardian Lady, Vol. 1. mass mkt. 11.95 (*0-340-66646-3*, Pub. by Hodder & Stought Ltd) Trafalgar.

Anon, jt. auth. see Abbott.

Anon, tr. see Leroux, Gaston.

Anon, C. Hit Back at the I. R. S. 1986. pap. 10.00 (*0-939856-67-0*) Tech Group.

Anon, J. B., et al. Anatomy of the Paranasal Sinuses: A Correlative Approach. (Illus.). 214p. 1996. 149.00 (*0-86577-517-6*) Thieme Med Pubs.

Anonimo. Cantar del Cid. (SPA.). 335p. 1979. 10.95 (*0-8288-7054-3*, S7513) Fr & Eur.

— Cantares de Gesta. (SPA.). 248p. 1971. 9.95 (*0-8288-7057-8*, S7500) Fr & Eur.

***Anonimo.** Kama Sutra & Ananga Ranga. (SPA.). 1998. pap. 6.95 (*84-01-45145-0*, Pub. by Plaza) Lectorum Pubns.

Anonimo. Lazarillo de Tormes. unabridged ed. (SPA.). pap. 5.95 (*84-410-0000-X*, Pub. by Bookking Intl) Distribks Inc.

— Lucas (Luke) (Biblia de Bosquejos y Sermones (The Preacher's Outline & Sermon Bible) Ser.). (SPA.). 448p. 1998. pap. 24.99 (*0-8254-1009-6*, Edit Portavoz) Kregel.

***Anonimo.** Mark. (Sermon Outline Ser.). 308p. 1998. pap. 19.99 (*0-8254-1008-8*) Kregel.

Anonimo. M.P.B. Aladino. (SPA., Illus.). (ps-3). 1997. pap. text 2.49 (*968-890-138-5*) Edit Diana.

— Poema de Mio Cid. (SPA.). pap. 12.95 (*84-206-9981-0*, Pub. by Alianza Editorial) Continental Bk.

— Poema del Cid. (SPA.). 249p. 1963. 9.95 (*0-8288-7093-4*, S7515) Fr & Eur.

— Poema Fernan Gonzalez. (SPA.). 139p. 1973. 9.95 (*0-8288-7076-4*) Fr & Eur.

— Romancero del Cid. (SPA.). 214p. 1966. 5.50 (*0-8288-7021-7*) Fr & Eur.

— Romanos (Romans) (Biblia de Bosquejos y Sermones (The Preacher's Outline & Sermon Bible) Ser.). (SPA.). 272p. 1998. pap. 19.99 (*0-8254-1012-6*, Edit Portavoz) Kregel.

Anonmio. Lazarillo de Tormes. (SPA.). pap. 15.95 (*84-376-0660-8*, Pub. by Ediciones Catedra) Continental Bk.

***Anonymous.** Arabella. 224p. 2000. mass mkt. 7.95 (*1-56201-169-3*) Blue Moon Bks.

Anonymous. Beowolf, 1 vol. LC 99-12770. 160p. 1999. mass mkt. 4.95 (*0-451-52740-2*) NAL.

***Anonymous.** Carnal Crimes of Cremorne. 1998. mass mkt. 6.95 (*0-7472-5785-X*, Pub. by Headline Bk Pub) Trafalgar.

Anonymous. Diary of a Junior Year. Vol. 3. 160p. (gr. 7-12). 1999. mass mkt. 4.99 (*0-439-08410-5*) Scholastic Inc.

***Anonymous.** Diary of a Junior Year. (Real Teens Ser.: Vol. 6). 160p. (YA). (gr. 7-12). 2000. mass mkt. 4.99 (*0-439-08413-X*) Scholastic Inc.

— An Englishwoman's Love Letters. 280p. 2000. pap. 12.00 (*1-56649-168-1*) Welcome Rain.

Anonymous. Go Ask Alice. Sparks, Beatrice, ed. LC 99-219857. 192p. (J). (gr. 7 up). 1998. per. 4.50 (*0-689-81785-1*, 870407) Aladdin.

***Anonymous.** The Heart Reader. 144p. 2000. per. 14.00 (*0-8499-1651-8*) Word Pub.

Anonymous. More Black Magic. 752p. 1997. mass mkt. 7.95 (*0-7867-0548-5*) Carroll & Graf.

— No End in Sight: A Family Survives a Repressed Memory Blast. 1997. pap. text 12.95 (*0-9641357-7-9*) Storm Peak.

— Oahspe Bible: A New Bible in the Words of Jehovih & His Angel Embassadors (1882) 1016p. 1998. reprint ed. pap. 36.00 (*0-7661-0729-9*) Kessinger Pub.

— Primary Colors: A Novel of Politics. 1998. mass mkt. 6.99 (*0-446-78840-6*) Warner Bks.

— Primary Colors: A Novel of Politics. 528p. 1996. reprint ed. mass mkt. 6.99 (*0-446-60427-5*, Pub. by Warner Bks) Little.

— Real Teens: Diary of a Junior Year, Bk. 1. Vol. 1. 160p. (YA). (gr. 7-12). 1999. mass mkt. 4.99 (*0-439-08408-3*) Scholastic Inc.

— Real Teens: Diary/Jr. Year Bk. 2. Vol. 2. 160p. (gr. 7-12). 1999. mass mkt. 4.99 (*0-439-08409-1*) Scholastic Inc.

***Anonymous.** Real Teens Mixed Display. 1999. mass mkt. 59.88 (*0-439-09276-0*) Scholastic Inc.

Anonymous. Reckoning. LC 99-475821. 208p. 1996. mass mkt. 7.95 (*1-56201-099-9*) Blue Moon Bks.

Anonymous, jt. auth. see Tyrrell, R. Emmett, Jr.

***Anonymous, Anderson A.** Finishing School. 256p. 2000. mass mkt. 7.95 (*1-56201-171-5*) Blue Moon Bks.

Anonymous, Anderson A. The 1999 Multi-Diet: Taming the Beast. LC 98-87950. (Illus.). vii, 417p. 1999. pap. 23.95 (*0-9667945-6-7*, TMD21999) Hamilton Wolcott.

***Anonymous, Anderson A.** School Life in Paris. 128p. 2000. mass mkt. 7.95 (*1-56201-172-3*) Blue Moon Bks.

Anonymous, Anonymous. At My Best: 365 Meditations for Physical, Spiritual & Emotional Well-Being. 384p. 1992. pap. 9.95 (*0-553-35337-3*) Bantam.

***Anonymous, Anonymous.** Diary of a Junior Year. (Real Teens Ser.: Vol. 4). 196p. (gr. 7-12). 2000. mass mkt. 6.99 (*0-439-08411-3*, Apple Paperbacks) Scholastic Inc.

Anosike, Benji O. All the Corporate & Legal Forms You'll Ever Need to Properly Run Your Corporation: The National Corporate Forms Kit. 250p. (Orig.). 1998. pap. text 29.95 (*0-932704-39-5*) Do It Yourself Legal Pubs.

— Before You Say "I Do" in Marriage, First Protect Yourself Legally: The National Pre-Marital Agreement Kit. rev. ed. LC 98-56537. (Illus.). 200p. 1999. pap. text 26.95 (*0-932704-34-4*) Do It Yourself Legal Pubs.

— How to Adopt a Child Without a Lawyer. rev. ed. LC 78-74123. 120p. (Orig.). 1984. pap. text 12.95 (*0-932704-00-X*) Do It Yourself Legal Pubs.

— How to Buy or Sell Your Own Home Without a Broker or Lawyer: The National Home Sale-Purchase Kit. rev. ed. LC 96-41341. (Illus.). 200p. 1997. pap. 26.95 (*0-932704-36-0*) Do It Yourself Legal Pubs.

***Anosike, Benji O.** How to Buy/Sell Your Own Home Without a Broker or Lawyer: The National Home Sale & Purchase Kit. 2nd rev. ed. LC 99-59362. 201p. 2000. pap. 28.95 (*0-932704-50-6*) Do It Yourself Legal Pubs.

Anosike, Benji O. How to Declare Your Personal Bankruptcy Without a Lawyer. rev. ed. LC 92-23829. 230p. 1992. pap. text 26.95 (*0-932704-16-6*) Do It Yourself Legal Pubs.

— How to Do Your Own Divorce Without a Lawyer. rev. ed. LC 80-65725. 82p. (Orig.). 1980. pap. text 19.95 (*0-932704-01-8*) Do It Yourself Legal Pubs.

— How To Do Your Own Divorce Without a Lawyer, Vol. 1: The New England Region Divorce Kit. (Regional Divorce Ser.). (Illus.). 210p. (Orig.). 1996. pap. 35.95 (*0-932704-18-2*) Selfhelper.

— How to Do Your Own Divorce Without a Lawyer, Vol. 10: The D. C. Area Mideast Region Divorce Kit. (Regional Divorce Ser.). (Illus.). 280p. (Orig.). 1996. pap. text 35.95 (*0-932704-27-1*) Selfhelper.

— How To Do Your Own Divorce Without a Lawyer, Vol. 2: The Northeast Region Divorce Kit. (Regional Divorce Ser.). (Illus.). 220p. (Orig.). 1996. pap. 35.95 (*0-932704-19-0*) Selfhelper.

— How To Do Your Own Divorce Without a Lawyer, Vol. 3: The Midwest Region Divorce Kit. (Regional Divorce Ser.). (Illus.). 280p. (Orig.). 1996. pap. 35.95 (*0-932704-20-4*) Selfhelper.

— How To Do Your Own Divorce Without a Lawyer, Vol. 4: The North Central Region Divorce Kit. (Regional Divorce Ser.: Vol. 4). (Illus.). 290p. (Orig.). 1996. pap. 35.95 (*0-932704-21-2*) Selfhelper.

— How To Do Your Own Divorce Without a Lawyer, Vol. 5: The North Mountain Region Divorce Kit. (Regional Divorce Ser.: Vol. 5). (Illus.). 300p. (Orig.). 1996. pap. 35.95 (*0-932704-22-0*) Selfhelper.

— How To Do Your Own Divorce Without a Lawyer, Vol. 6: The West Region Divorce Kit. (Regional Divorce Ser.: Vol. 6). (Illus.). 310p. (Orig.). 1996. pap. 36.95 (*0-932704-23-9*) Selfhelper.

— How To Do Your Own Divorce Without a Lawyer, Vol. 7: The Southwest Region Divorce Kit. (Regional Divorce Ser.: Vol. 7). (Illus.). 290p. (Orig.). 1996. pap. 35.95 (*0-932704-24-7*) Selfhelper.

— How To Do Your Own Divorce Without a Lawyer, Vol. 8: The Deep South Region Divorce Kit. (Regional Divorce Ser.: Vol. 8). 280p. (Orig.). 1996. pap. 35.95 (*0-932704-25-5*) Selfhelper.

— How to Do Your Own Divorce Without a Lawyer, Vol. 9: The Southeast Region Divorce Kit. (Regional Divorce Ser.). (Illus.). 290p. (Orig.). 1996. pap. text 35.95 (*0-932704-26-3*) Selfhelper.

— How to File for Chapter Eleven Business Bankruptcy with or Without a Lawyer. rev. ed. Orig. Title: How to File for "Chapter Eleven" Bankruptcy: Relief from Your Business Debts with or Without a Lawyer. 240p. 1992. pap. 29.95 (*0-932704-17-4*) Do It Yourself Legal Pubs.

— How to Form Your Own Chapter "S" Business Corporation. 180p. (Orig.). 1995. pap. text 23.95 (*0-932704-38-7*) Do It Yourself Legal Pubs.

— How to Form Your Own Non-Profit Corporation Without a Lawyer: The National Non-Profit Incorporation Kit. LC 95-22188. (Illus.). 190p. (Orig.). 1995. pap. text 25.95 (*0-932704-37-9*) Do It Yourself Legal Pubs.

— How to Form Your Own Profit or Non-profit Corporation Without a Lawyer LC 99-26334. 1999. pap. 25.95 (*0-932704-48-4*) Do It Yourself Legal Pubs.

— How to Form Your Own Profit or Non-Profit Corporation Without a Lawyer: The National Incorporation Kit. rev. ed. (Illus.). 190p. 1994. pap. text 23.95 (*0-932704-29-8*) Do It Yourself Legal Pubs.

— How to Legally Beat the Traffic Ticket Without a Lawyer. 90p. (Orig.). 1982. pap. text 15.95 (*0-932704-12-3*) Do It Yourself Legal Pubs.

— How to Legally Change Your Name Without a Lawyer: The National Legal Name Change Kit. 2nd ed. LC 98-27123. 1998. 24.95 (*0-932704-45-X*) Do It Yourself Legal Pubs.

— How to Legally Protect Yourself in a Gay/Lesbian & Non-Marital Cohabitation with a Cohabitation Agreement: The National Living-Together Settlement Kit. LC 99-11334. (Illus.). 160p. (Orig.). 1999. pap. 26.95 (*0-932704-44-1*) Do It Yourself Legal Pubs.

— How to Legally Reduce Your Real Estate Taxes Without a Lawyer. 100p. (Orig.). 1982. pap. 16.95 (*0-932704-11-5*) Do It Yourself Legal Pubs.

— How to Obtain Your U. S. Immigration Visa Without a Lawyer. 208p. 1990. reprint ed. pap. text 23.95 (*0-932704-10-7*) Do It Yourself Legal Pubs.

— How to Plan Your Total Estate with a Will & Living Will, Without the Lawyers' Fees: The American Will Kit. rev. ed. LC 94-26662. (Illus.). 150p. 1994. pap. text 23.95 (*0-932704-30-1*) Do It Yourself Legal Pubs.

***Anosike, Benji O.** How to Plan Your "Total" Estate with a Will & Living Will, Without the Lawyer's Fees: The American Will Kit. rev. ed. LC 99-40927. 1999. pap. 26.95 (*0-932704-49-2*) Do It Yourself Legal Pubs.

Anosike, Benji O. How to Probate, Administer & Settle an Estate Yourself Without the Lawyers' Fees: The National Probate Kit. rev. ed. LC 95-32213. (Illus.). 250p. 1995. pap. text 29.95 (*0-932704-31-X*) Do It Yourself Legal Pubs.

— How to Properly Plan Your Total Estate with a Living Trust Without the Lawyers' Fees: The National Living Trust Kit. rev. ed. LC 94-24930. (Illus.). 250p. 1994. pap. text 29.95 (*0-932704-32-8*) Do It Yourself Legal Pubs.

— How to Settle Your Own Auto Accident Claim Without a Lawyer. LC 98-4093. 1998. pap. 29.95 (*0-932704-46-8*) Do It Yourself Legal Pubs.

— How to Settle Your Own Auto Accident Claims Without a Lawyer. LC 93-4847. 250p. (Orig.). 1993. pap. 29.95 (*0-932704-13-1*) Do It Yourself Legal Pubs.

— The National Home Mortgage Qualification Kit: How to Qualify for & Obtain the Mortgage Money You Need - Guaranteed! (Illus.). 220p. (Orig.). 1997. pap. 24.95 (*0-932704-41-7*) Do It Yourself Legal Pubs.

— The National Mortgage Escrow Audit Kit: How to Audit Your Mortgage Escrow Account for Overcharges. (Illus.). 110p. (Orig.). 1996. pap. 17.95 (*0-932704-40-9*) Do It Yourself Legal Pubs.

— The National Mortgage Reduction Kit: How to Cut Your Mortgage Debt in Half & Own Your Home Fast, Free & Clear Like Magic. LC 99-44611. (Illus.). 200p. (Orig.). 2000. pap. 24.95 (*0-932704-42-5*) Do It Yourself Legal Pubs.

— Peaceful Divorce or Separation - How to Draw up Your Own Settlement Agreement with Your Spouse: The National Marital Settlement Kit. LC 97-4168. (Illus.). 125p. (Orig.). 1997. pap. 24.95 (*0-932704-43-3*) Do It Yourself Legal Pubs.

— Tenant Smart: How to Win Your Legal Tenancy Rights Without a Lawyer (New York Edition) rev. ed. (Illus.). 214p. 1998. pap. text 24.95 (*0-932704-28-X*) Do It Yourself Legal Pubs.

Anosov, D. V. Geodesic Flows on Closed Riemann Manifolds with Negative Curvature. Feder, S., tr. from RUS. LC 76-4856. (Proceedings of the Steklov Institute of Mathematics Ser.: No. 90). 239p. 1969. reprint ed. pap. 74.10 (*0-608-07821-2*, 205266600010) Bks Demand.

— Ordinary Differential Equations & Smooth Dynamical Systems. LC 98-175523. 233p. 1997. pap. text 54.50 (*3-540-61220-3*) Spr-Verlag.

Anosov, D. V., ed. Dynamical Systems with Hyperbolic Behavior. LC 94-47311. (Encyclopedia of Mathematical Sciences Ser.: Vol. 66). 1995. write for info. (*3-540-57043-8*) Spr-Verlag.

An Asterisk (*) at the beginning of an entry indicates that the title is appearing for the first time.

— Dynamical Systems with Hyperbolic Behavior. LC 94-47311. (Encyclopedia of Mathematical Sciences Ser.: Vol. 66). 1995. 107.95 (*0-387-57043-8*) Spr-Verlag.

— Twenty Lectures Delivered at the International Congress of Mathematicians in Vancouver, 1974. LC 77-9042. (Translations Ser.: Series 2, Vol. 109). 129p. 1977. reprint ed. pap. 38.00 (*0-8218-3059-7*, TRANS2/109) Am Math.

Anosov, D. V., et al, eds. Seven Papers in Applied Mathematics. LC 84-21681. (AMS Translations Ser.: Series 2, Vol. 125). 130p. 1985. text 61.00 (*0-8218-3087-2*, TRANS2/125) Am Math.

Anosov, D. V. & Arnold, V. I., eds. Dynamical Systems I, Vol. I. (Encyclopedia of Mathematical Sciences Ser.: Vol. 1). (Illus.). 250p. 1988. 97.95 (*0-387-17000-6*) Spr-Verlag.

Anosov, D. V., et al. Twenty-Four Papers on Statistics & Probability. LC 61-9803. (Selected Translations in Mathematical Statistics & Probability Ser.: Vol. 14). 296p. 1978. 80.00 (*0-8218-1464-8*, STAPRO/14) Am Math.

Anosov, D. V., ed. see Steklov Institute of Mathematics, Academy of Scien.

Anouilh, Jean. Alouette. (Folio Ser.: No. 336). (FRE.). 1963. pap. 6.95 (*2-07-036336-8*, 1153) Schoenhof.

— L' Alouette. (FRE.). 1973. pap. 10.95 (*0-8288-3618-3*, M2952); pap. 10.95 (*0-7859-1734-9*, M2952) Fr & Eur.

— L' Alouette. (FRE.). (C). 1953. pap. 7.95 (*0-8442-1747-6*, VF1747-6) NTC Contemp Pub Co.

— Anouilh: Five Plays. Fry, Christopher et al, trs. (Methuen World Dramatists Ser.). 424p. (C). 1986. pap. write for info. (*0-413-14030-X*, A0010, Methuen Drama) Methn.

— Anouilh: Five Plays, Vol. 1. 280p. 1990. pap. 10.00 (*0-374-52229-4*) FS&G.

— Antigone. (FRE.). 136p. 1975. pap. 13.95 (*0-8288-9016-1*, F81800) Fr & Eur.

— Antigone. (Table Ronde Ser.). 1975. pap. 10.95 (*2-7103-0025-7*) Schoenhof.

— Ardele: Ou, La Marguerite. (Folio Ser.: No. 1057). (FRE.). 1970. pap. 9.25 (*2-07-037057-7*) Schoenhof.

— Ardele: Ou, la Marguerite Suivi de la Valse des Toreadors. (FRE.). 256p. 1987. pap. 10.95 (*0-7859-1880-9*, 2070370577) Fr & Eur.

— Ardele: Ou, La Marquerite. (FRE.). 1970. pap. 10.95 (*0-8288-9012-9*, F81812) Fr & Eur.

— Arrestation. (FRE.). 1986. pap. 11.95 (*0-8288-3619-1*, F27470) Fr & Eur.

— L' Arrestation. (FRE.). 214p. 1986. pap. 11.95 (*0-7859-2050-1*, F27470) Fr & Eur.

— Les Avions Vol. 1: Des Origines a la Premiere Guerre Mondiale. (FRE.). 320p. 1980. pap. 12.95 (*0-7859-1922-8*, F81860) Fr & Eur.

— Becket: Or the Honor of God. Hill, Lucienne, tr. LC 95-37241.Tr. of Becket Ou, l'Honneur de Dieu. 144p. 1995. pap. 10.00 (*1-57322-508-8*, Riverhd Trade) Berkley Pub.

— Becket: Or the Honor of God. Hill, Lucienne, tr.Tr. of Becket Ou, l'Honneur de Dieu. (FRE.). (C). 1959. pap. 9.95 (*0-8442-1842-1*, VF1842-1) NTC Contemp Pub Co.

— Becket: Or the Honor of God. Hill, Lucienne, tr.Tr. of Becket Ou, l'Honneur de Dieu. 1995. 14.10 (*0-606-01489-6*, Pub. by Turtleback) Demco.

— Becket: Ou, l'Honneur De Dieu. (FRE.). 160p. 1972. pap. 10.95 (*0-7859-1709-8*, 2070361918) Fr & Eur.

— Becket: Ou, l'Honneur De Dieu. (Folio Ser.: No. 191). (FRE.). 1973. pap. 8.95 (*0-685-11038-9*, 1716) Schoenhof.

— Le Boulanger, la Boulangere et le Petit Mitron. (FRE.). 1980. pap. 10.95 (*0-7859-3563-0*, F81830) Fr & Eur.

— Cecile: Ou, L'ecole des Peres. 1954. pap. 7.95 (*0-7859-0349-6*, F81840) Fr & Eur.

— Cher Antoine: Ou l'Amour Rate. (FRE.). 1975. pap. 10.95 (*0-7859-1810-8*, 2070366979) Fr & Eur.

— Cher Antoine: Ou l'Amour Rate. (Folio Ser.: No. 697). (FRE.). 6.95 (*2-07-036697-9*) Schoenhof.

— Chers Zoiseaux. (FRE.). 192p. 1983. pap. 10.95 (*0-7859-1980-5*, 2070375102) Fr & Eur.

— Colombe. (FRE.). 1963. pap. 10.95 (*0-685-58340-6*, M2956) Fr & Eur.

— Colombe. (FRE.). 158p. 1973. pap. 10.95 (*0-7859-1729-2*, M2957) Fr & Eur.

— La Culotte. (FRE.). 183p. 1985. pap. 12.95 (*0-7859-2228-8*, 207037680X) Fr & Eur.

— Le Directeur de l'Opera. 1972. pap. 8.95 (*0-8288-9014-5*, M5849) Fr & Eur.

— Eurydice & Romeo & Jeannette. (Folio Ser.: No. 1218). (FRE.). pap. 9.95 (*2-07-037218-9*) Schoenhof.

— Fables. 1966. 27.95 (*0-7859-0350-X*, F81865) Fr & Eur.

— Fables. (Folio Ser.: No. 316). (FRE.). 1973. pap. 5.95 (*2-07-036316-3*) Schoenhof.

— La Foire d'Empoigne. 1962. pap. 7.95 (*0-7859-0351-8*, F81870) Fr & Eur.

— La Foire d'Empoigne Suivi De Cecile Ou l'Ecole Des Peres. (FRE.). 1979. pap. 10.95 (*0-7859-1886-8*, 2070371026) Fr & Eur.

— La Grotte. (FRE.). 153p. 1977. pap. 10.95 (*0-7859-2211-3*, M11010) Fr & Eur.

— L' Hurluberlu: Ou, le Reactionnaire Amoureux. (FRE.). 208p. 1959. pap. 11.95 (*0-7859-0921-4*, F81874) Fr & Eur.

— Jean Anouilh: Five Plays, Vol. 2. Incl. Ardele. 1959. Lark. 1959. Mademoiselle Colombe. 1959. Restless Heart.Tr. of Sauvage. 1959. Time Remembered.Tr. of Leocadia. 1959. (Mermaid Dramabook Ser.). 302p. (Orig.). 1959. Set pap. 6.95 (*0-8090-0713-4*) Hill & Wang.

— The Lark. 1957. pap. 5.25 (*0-8222-0634-X*) Dramatists Play.

— Leocadia. Knapp, Bettina L. & Della Fazia, Alba, eds. LC 66-17601. (FRE., Illus.). 1965. pap. text 7.95 (*0-89197-273-0*) Irvington.

— L'invitation au Chateau. 1962. pap. 11.95 (*0-7859-0352-6*, F81877) Fr & Eur.

— Medee. 1967. pap. 6.95 (*0-7859-0353-4*, F81879) Fr & Eur.

— Monsieur Barnett: Suivi de l'Orchestre. (FRE.). 160p. 1982. pap. 10.95 (*0-7859-1965-1*, 2070374262) Fr & Eur.

— Ne Reveillez Pas Madame. (FRE.). 192p. 1981. pap. 10.95 (*0-7859-1940-6*, 2070373185) Fr & Eur.

— Ne Reveillez Pas Madame. (Folio Ser.: No. 1318). (FRE.). pap. 8.95 (*2-07-037318-5*) Schoenhof.

— Nouvelles Pieces Grincantes. Incl. Boulanger. Boulangere et le Petit Mitron. Grotte. Hurluberlu: Ou, le Reactionnaire Amoureux. Orchestre. Poissons Rouges. 19.50 (*0-685-37154-9*, F81779) Fr & Eur.

— Ornifle Ou le Courant d'Air. (FRE.). 224p. 1974. pap. 10.95 (*0-7859-2206-7*, M2959) Fr & Eur.

— Ornifle Ou le Courant d'Air. (Folio Ser.: No. 545). (FRE.). 1974. pap. 8.95 (*2-07-036545-X*) Schoenhof.

— Pauvre Bitos Ou le Diner de Tetes. (Folio Ser.: No. 301). (FRE.). 1973. pap. 6.95 (*2-07-036301-5*) Schoenhof.

— Pauvre Bitos Ou le "Diner de Tetes. (FRE.). 160p. 1973. pap. 10.95 (*0-7859-1725-X*, M2960) Fr & Eur.

— Pieces Brillantes: L'invitation au chateau, Colombe, La repetition ou L'amour puni [et] L'ecole des peres. Incl. Cecile: Ou, L'ecole des Peres. Colombe. L'invitation au Chateau. Repetition Ou l'Amour Puni. 42.50 (*0-685-37149-2*, F81770) Fr & Eur.

— Pieces Costumees: L'Alouette, Becket, la Foire d'Empoigne. (FRE.). 42.95 (*0-685-37150-6*, F81772) Fr & Eur.

— Pieces Roses. Incl. Bal des Voleurs. Humulus le Muet. Leocadia. Rendez-Vous de Senlis. (FRE.). 19.50 (*0-685-37153-0*, F81777) Fr & Eur.

— Pieces Secretes. Incl. Arrestation. 1977. 24.95 Scenario. 1977. Tu Etais Si Gentil Quand Tu Etais Petit. 1977. (FRE.). 384p. 1977. 39.95 (*0-8288-9015-3*, M11237) Fr & Eur.

— Les Poissons Rouges. (FRE.). 1972. pap. 10.95 (*0-7859-1684-9*, 2070360067) Fr & Eur.

— Les Poissons Rouges. (Folio Ser.: No. 6). (FRE.). pap. 10.95 (*2-07-036006-7*) Schoenhof.

— Le Rendez-Vous de Senlis Suivi de Leocadia. (FRE.). 1973. pap. 10.95 (*0-7859-1743-8*, 2070363759) Fr & Eur.

— Le Rendez-Vous de Senlis Suivi de Leocadia. Incl. Cher Antoine. 1974. Directeur de l'Opera. 1974. Ne Reveillez Pas Madame. 1974. (FRE.). 448p. 1974. 39.95 (*0-7859-0347-X*, F81784) Fr & Eur.

— Le Rendezvous de Senlis. (Folio Ser.: No. 375). (FRE.). pap. 8.95 (*2-07-036375-9*) Schoenhof.

— La Repetition Ou l'Amour Puni. write for info. (*0-318-63588-7*, 2383) Fr & Eur.

— La Repetition Ou l'Amour Puni. (FRE.). 140p. 1973. pap. 10.95 (*0-7859-1755-1*, F81895) Fr & Eur.

— La Repetition Ou l'Amour Puni. (Folio Ser.: No. 444). (FRE.). pap. 6.95 (*2-07-036444-5*) Schoenhof.

— Ring Round the Moon. adapted ed. 1952. pap. 5.25 (*0-8222-0954-3*) Dramatists Play.

— Romin-Englez Dictionar. (FRE.). 1973. pap. 10.95 (*0-7859-3603-3*, M2956) Fr & Eur.

— Le Sauvage. (Folio Ser.: No. 874). (FRE.). pap. 10.50 (*2-07-036874-2*, 748) Schoenhof.

— La Sauvage Suivi de l'Invitation au Chateau. (FRE.). 384p. 1976. pap. 10.95 (*0-7859-3472-3*, F81898) Fr & Eur.

— Le Scenario. (FRE.). 192p. 1984. pap. 10.95 (*0-7859-2001-3*, 2070376109) Fr & Eur.

— Theatre Complet, 9 tomes. 126.95 (*0-685-11593-3*, F81760) Fr & Eur.

— Tu Etais Si Gentil Quand Tu Etais Petit. 160p. 1973. pap. 9.95 (*0-7859-0354-2*, F81900) Fr & Eur.

— Le Voyageur sans Bagage. (Folio Ser.: No. 759). (FRE.). 1961. pap. 9.25 (*2-07-036759-2*) Schoenhof.

— Le Voyageur sans Bagage: Suivi de Le Bal des Voleurs. (FRE.). (C). 1958. pap. 9.95 (*0-8442-1877-4*, VF1877-4) NTC Contemp Pub Co.

— Le Voyageur Suivi de le Bal des Voleurs. (FRE.). 219p. 1976. pap. 10.95 (*0-7859-1817-5*, 2070367592) Fr & Eur.

Anouilh, Jean, et al. Le Voyageur sans Bagage. Birckbichler, Diane W. et al, eds. (FRE.). 184p. (C). 1973. pap. text 40.50 (*0-03-088529-9*) Harcourt Coll Pubs.

Anoushiravani, Alireza, tr. see Khamenie, Ayatullah.

Anovitz, L. M., jt. ed. see Grew, E. S.

Anowitz. Clarisworks. (DA - Computer Education Ser.). 1995. pap., wbk. ed. 11.95 (*0-538-63524-X*) S-W Pub.

— Computer Dimensions - Apple, Vol. 1. (DA - Computer Education Ser.). (J). (gr. k-8). 1993. 109.25 (*0-538-63463-4*) S-W Pub.

— Computer Dimensions - DOS, Vol. 2. (DA - Computer Education Ser.). (J). (gr. k-8). 1993. 109.25 (*0-538-63466-9*) S-W Pub.

— Computer Dimensions - Mac, Vol. 1. (DA - Computer Education Ser.). (J). (gr. k-8). 1993. 109.25 (*0-538-63467-7*) S-W Pub.

— Computer Dimensions - Mac, Vol. 2. (DA - Computer Education Ser.). (J). (gr. k-8). 1993. 109.25 (*0-538-63468-5*) S-W Pub.

Anowitz, contrib. by. EIMS Appleworks. (DA - Computer Education Ser.). (J). (gr. k-8). 1993. teacher ed. write for info. (*0-538-62136-2*) S-W Pub.

— EIMS IBM Microsoft Word. (DA - Computer Education Ser.). (J). (gr. k-8). 1993. teacher ed. write for info. (*0-538-62137-0*) S-W Pub.

Anozie, F. N. Khoekhoe. LC 96-45634. (Heritage Library of African Peoples: Set 4). (Illus.). 64p. (YA). (gr. 7-12). 1996. lib. bdg. 16.95 (*0-8239-2007-0*, D2007-0) Rosen Group.

Anozie, Sunday O. Christopher Okigbo: Creative Rhetoric. LC 77-182593. (Modern African Writers Ser.). 203p. (C). 1972. pap. 14.50 (*0-8419-0117-1*, Africana) Holmes & Meier.

Anpart, Abraham. Dzovn Arhamarhets Jri Mi Katile. (One Thousand Ser.). 198p. (Orig.). 1993. pap. 10.00 (*0-9639662-4-3*) A M Karabajakyan.

***Anpo, Masakazu.** Photofunctional Zeolites: Synthesis, Characterization, Photocatalytic Reactions, Light Harvesting. LC 00-27502. 248p. 2000. lib. bdg. 79.00 (*1-56072-801-9*) Nova Sci Pubs.

Anpo, Mazakazu, ed. Surface Photochemistry. LC 95-22108. (Photoscience & Photoengineering Ser.: Vol. 1). 186p. 1996. 195.00 (*0-471-95031-9*) Wiley.

Anquetil-Duperron, A. H. Zend-Avesta, Ouvrage de Zoroastre. LC 78-60878. (Myth & Romanticism Ser.). 1904p. 1984. text 25.00 (*0-8240-3550-X*) Garland.

Anquetil, Jacques. Silk. (Illus.). 200p. 1996. 60.00 (*2-08-013616-X*, Pub. by Flammarion) Abbeville Pr.

Anquetil, P. Questions in Cost & Management Accounting. LC 95-167073. 288p. 1994. pap. write for info. (*0-409-30876-5*, MICHIE) LEXIS Pub.

***Anreus, Alejandro.** Orozco in Gringoland: The Years in New York. LC 00-9645. (Illus.). 2001. pap. write for info. (*0-8263-2068-6*) U of NM Pr.

***Anrias, David.** Adepts of the Five Elements: An Occult Survey of Past & Future Problems. (Illus.). 104p. 2000. pap. 14.95 (*1-57863-204-8*) Weiser.

Anrich, Gustav. Das Antike Mysterienwesen in Seinem Einflubauf das Christentum. (GER.). viii, 238p. 1990. reprint ed. 50.00 (*3-487-09283-2*) G Olms Pubs.

Anrig, Claudia & Plaugher, Gregory. Pediatric Chiropractic. LC 97-26950. 789p. 1998. 89.00 (*0-683-00136-1*) Lppncott W & W.

Anrig, Claudia A. & Plaugher, Gregory. Pediatric Chiropractic. LC 97-26950. 1997. write for info. (*1-68301-361-1*) Lppncott W & W.

Ansa Software Staff. The Ansa PAL Tutorial: Programming with the Paradox Application Language. 224p. 1986. pap. write for info. (*0-201-03944-3*) Addison-Wesley.

Ansa, Tina M. And You Should Know Better. 2000. 20.01 (*0-385-47600-0*) Doubleday.

— Baby of the Family. 1989. 18.95 (*0-15-110431-X*) Harcourt.

— Baby of the Family. 276p. 1991. pap. 12.00 (*0-15-610150-5*, Harvest Bks) Harcourt.

— Ugly Ways. LC 93-16395. 1993. 19.95 (*0-15-192553-4*) Harcourt.

— Ugly Ways: A Novel. LC 94-33938. 288p. 1995. pap. 13.00 (*0-15-600077-6*, Harvest Bks) Harcourt.

***Ansa, Tina M.** You Know Better. 2001. write for info. (*0-06-019779-X*) HarperTrade.

Ansa, Tina McElroy. The Hand I Fan With. LC 97-39845. 496p. 1997. pap. 11.95 (*0-385-47601-9*, Anchor NY) Doubleday.

Ansaari, M. A., tr. see Sadr, Mohammed B.

Ansah, Godfred T. A Road Map to Your Job Search: A Complete Guide to Finding & Keeping a Job. McGinnis, Richard, ed. LC 95-94458. (Illus.). 210p. 1995. 24.95 (*0-9646559-0-X*) G T Ansah.

Ansal, Jusum. As I Am: Autobiography. Ali, Masooma, tr. from HIN. LC 97-902763. 240p. (C). 1997. pap. 250.00 (*81-241-0499-9*, Pub. by Print Hse) St Mut.

Ansaldi, Michael, tr. see Llewellyn, Karl N.

Ansari. Activity-Based Management (Abm) Module. 1996. pap., student ed. 5.00 (*0-256-23787-5*) McGraw.

— The Capital Budgeting Process. 56p. 2000. pap. 5.00 (*0-07-231575-X*) McGraw.

— International Managerial Accounts. 2000. 4.00 (*0-07-027590-4*) McGraw.

— The Kaleidoscopic Nature of Costs: Cost Terms & Classifications (Module) 1997. pap. text 6.00 (*0-256-26707-3*, Irwn McGrw-H) McGrw-H Hghr Educ.

— Manufacturing Overhead Allocations. 1997. 4.00 (*0-256-26392-2*) McGrw-H Hghr Educ.

— Measuring Management Quality Cost V. 1997. pap., student ed. 5.00 (*0-256-27143-7*) McGraw.

— An Overkill of Cost Measurement. 56p. 1999. pap. 5.00 (*0-256-26394-9*) McGraw.

— Product Costing in Lean Manufacturing Operations Costing (Module) 1999. pap. text 6.00 (*0-256-26715-4*, Irwn McGrw-H) McGrw-H Hghr Educ.

— Theory Const & Throughput Acct. 48p. 1998. pap. 5.00 (*0-07-027589-0*) McGraw.

Ansari, A. Just-in-Time Purchasing. 1990. 40.00 (*0-02-900971-5*) Free Pr.

Ansari, A. A. Cooperative Management Patterns. 1990. 1990. 120.00 (*81-7041-301-X*, Pub. by Scientific Pubs) St Mut.

Ansari, Aftab A. Single-Cell Mutation Monitoring Systems: Methodologies & Applications. De Serres, Frederick J., ed. LC 84-3368. (Topics in Chemical Mutagenesis Ser.: Vol. 2). 308p. 79.50 (*0-306-41537-2*, Plenum Trade) Perseus Pubng.

Ansari, F. R. Beyond Death. 1992. pap. 1.50 (*0-935782-48-6*) Kazi Pubns.

— Foundations of Faith. 1981. pap. 3.00 (*1-56744-014-2*) Kazi Pubns.

— Islam & Christianity in the Modern World. 1991. pap. 15.50 (*1-56744-063-0*) Kazi Pubns.

— Islam & the Western Civilization. 1981. pap. 3.00 (*1-56744-075-4*) Kazi Pubns.

— Philosophy of Worship in Islam. 1991. pap. 3.00 (*1-56744-188-2*) Kazi Pubns.

— Through Science & Philosophy to Religion. 1994. pap. 2.00 (*0-933511-76-0*) Kazi Pubns.

— What Is Islam? 1991. pap. 3.00 (*0-933511-88-4*) Kazi Pubns.

Ansari, Farhad. Intl. Workshop on Fiber Optic Sensors for Construction Materials & Bridges. LC 98-60482. 276p. 1998. 189.95 (*1-56676-671-0*) Technomic.

Ansari, Farhad, ed. Applications of Fiber Optic Sensors in Engineering Mechanics: A Collection of State-of-the-Art Papers in the Application of Fiber Optic Technologies to Civil Structures. LC 93-604. 336p. 1993. 29.00 (*0-87262-895-7*) Am Soc Civil Eng.

Ansari, Farhad, et al, eds. Intelligent Civil Engineering Materials & Structures: A Collection of State-of-the-Art Papers in the Applications of Emerging Technologies to Civil Structures & Materials. LC 97-14330. 312p. 1997. 35.00 (*0-7844-0248-5*) Am Soc Civil Eng.

A

***Ansari, Farhad & American Society of Civil Engineers Staff.** Condition Monitoring of Materials & Structures. LC 00-38086. 2000. write for info. (*0-7844-0495-X*) Am Soc Civil Eng.

Ansari, Farhad & Sture, Stein, eds. Nondestructive Testing of Concrete Elements & Structures. 240p. 1992. pap. text 28.00 (*0-87262-887-6*) Am Soc Civil Eng.

Ansari, Hamied. Egypt: The Stalled Society. LC 86-14524. (SUNY Series in Near Eastern Studies). 308p. (C). 1986. text 89.50 (*0-88706-183-4*); pap. text 29.95 (*0-88706-184-2*) State U NY Pr.

Ansari, Jamal H., et al. Urban Land Management: Improving Policies & Practices in Developing Countries of Asia. LC 98-915554. xviii, 291 p. 1998. write for info. (*81-204-1284-2*) Oxford & IBH Pubng.

Ansari, Javed A., jt. auth. see Singer, Hans W.

Ansari, Khwajih A. Munajat: The Intimate Prayers. Sarfeh, Rustam, tr. from PER. LC 75-30173. (ENG.). 84p. 1975. 7.50 (*0-917220-00-5*) Khaneghah & Maktab.

***Ansari, Khyruddin Akbar.** Numerical Methods for Engineers with Mathcad. LC 99-69302. (Illus.). vi, 349p. 1999. 90.00 (*0-9645727-6-1*, Ulyssian Pubns) Pine Orchard.

Ansari-Klammer. Strategic Budgeting Pt. I: The Annual Profit & Cash Budget, Pt. 1. 1998. pap. 7.50 (*0-256-26393-0*, Irwn Prfssnl) McGraw-Hill Prof.

Ansari, M. A. Muslims & the Congress: Correspondence of Dr. M. A. Ansari. Hasan, Masud U., ed. 1979. 18.50 (*0-8364-0381-9*) S Asia.

Ansari, M. A., tr. see Al-Sadr, Ayatullah B.

Ansari, M. A., tr. see Mutahhery, Murtaza.

Ansari, M. A., tr. see Mutahhery, Murtaza, et al.

Ansari, M. A., tr. see Sadr, Muhammad B.

Ansari, M. A., tr. see Sadr, Muhammad B. & Murtaza, Mutahhery.

Ansari, M. B., ed. Frontiers in Geoscience Information: Proceedings, Geoscience Information Society Meeting, St. Louis, 1989. (Proceedings Ser.: Vol. 20). 1990. 40.00 (*0-934485-17-8*) Geosci Info.

Ansari, M. S. Supreme Court & Full Bench on Transfer of Property: Dealing with Digest of Cases, 1950-1988. (C). 1988. 165.00 (*0-7855-4746-0*) St Mut.

Ansari, Maboud. The Making of the Iranian Community in America: A Case Study of Dual Marginality, Continuity & Change. 185p. 1992. 45.00 (*0-9632600-0-6*) Pardis Pr.

Ansari, Mahfooz A. Managing People at Work: Leadership Styles & Influence Strategies. (Illus.). 218p. (C). 1990. 26.00 (*0-8039-9650-0*) Sage.

Ansari, Mark & Lark, Liz. Yoga for Beginners. LC 98-7519. 96p. 1999. pap. 18.95 (*0-06-273648-5*, Harper Ref) HarpC.

Ansari, Mary B. & Newman, Linda P. Nevada Directory of Maps & Aerial Photo Resources. LC 83-26068. (Occasional Papers: No. 11). 164p. 1984. pap. 15.00 (*0-939112-13-2*) Western Assn Map.

Ansari, Mary B., ed. see Geoscience Information Society, Meeting (24th: 198.

Ansari, Masud. Modern Hypnosis: Theory & Practice. 1950. pap. 7.95 (*0-9607984-0-4*) MAS Pr.

— Modern Hypnosis: Theory & Practice. (Illus.). 232p. (J). (gr. 5). 1982. pap. 6.95 (*0-685-05553-1*) MAS Pr.

Ansari, Max. OSHA PSM Compliance Without Going Bankrupt: The Zero-Base Strategy That Works & Saves Money. LC 97-60911. (Illus.). 274p. 1997. 50.00 (*0-9656888-1-X*) WA Indust Mgmt.

Ansari, Muhammad T. Sunan Ibn Majah, Set, Nos. I & II. 952p. (C). 1995. text 39.95 (*0-934905-63-0*) Kazi Pubns.

Ansari, Nirwan. Computational Intelligence for Optimization. LC 96-45705. 240p. (C). 1996. text 133.00 (*0-7923-9838-6*) Kluwer Academic.

Ansari, Nirwan, jt. ed. see Yuhas, Ben.

Ansari, R. & Balakrishnan, N. P. Oberonia (Orchidaceae) rev. ed. De Vogel, E. F., ed. (Orchid Monographs: Vol. 4). (Illus.). vi, 82p. 1990. pap. 25.00 (*90-71236-06-4*, Pub. by Rijksherbarium) Balogh.

***Ansari, Rashid & Tade, Moses O.** Nonlinear Model-Based Process Control. LC 99-47343. (Advances in Industrial Control Ser.). 2000. write for info. (*1-85233-213-1*) Spr-Verlag.

Ansari, S. A., et al, eds. Physics & Contemporary Needs, Vol. 20. 377p. (C). 1997. lib. bdg. 145.00 (*1-56072-435-8*) Nova Sci Pubs.

Ansari, Saghir A. Financial Intermediaries & Industrial Development. (Illus.). xii, 155p. 1998. 20.00 (*81-7024-957-0*, Pub. by APH Pubng) Nataraj Bks.

Ansari, Sarah F. Sufi Saints & State Power: The Pirs of Sind, 1843-1947. (Cambridge Asian Studies: No. 50). (Illus.). 198p. (C). 1992. text 59.95 (*0-521-40530-0*) Cambridge U Pr.

Ansari, Shahid, jt. auth. see Keating, Patrick J.

Ansari, Shahid A., et al. Target Costing: The Next Frontier in Strategic Cost Management. LC 96-31814. 240p. 1996. 50.00 (*0-7863-1053-7*, Irwn Prfssnl) McGraw-Hill Prof.

Ansari, Shahid J. Political Modernization in the Gulf. LC 99-932606. ix, 235p. 1998. write for info. (*81-7211-088-X*, Pub. by Northern Bk Centre) Nataraj Bks.

Ansari, Shahid L., et al. Measuring & Managing Environmental Costs. 32p. (C). 1996. text 7.50 (*0-256-23781-6*, Irwn McGrw-H) McGrw-H Hghr Educ.

An Asterisk (*) at the beginning of an entry indicates that the title is appearing for the first time.

— Measuring & Managing Quality Costs. 32p. (C). 1996. text 7.50 (*0-256-23785-9*, Irwn McGrw-H) McGrw-H Hghr Educ.

— Target Costing. 32p. (C). 1996. text 7.50 (*0-256-23779-4*, Irwn McGrw-H) McGrw-H Hghr Educ.

Ansari, Shukatullah. Pakistan: The Problem of India. 1997. 20.00 (*81-7169-426-8*, Commonwealth) S Asia.

Ansari, Zafar A., ed. Qur'anic Concepts of Human Psyche. (Islamization of Knowledge Ser.: No. 11). 118p. (Orig.). 1992. 12.00 (*969-462-004-X*); pap. 7.00 (*969-462-003-1*) IIIT VA.

Ansari, Zafar I., tr. see Maudoodi, Syed A.

Ansari, Zafar I., tr. see Mawdudi, S. Abul.

Ansarizadeh, M. H. & Walker, E. F. Introductory Laboratory Physics. (Illus.). 146p. (C). 1985. pap. 13.95 (*0-89641-156-7*) American Pr.

Ansary. Color Atlas of AIDS in the Tropics. (Illus.). 1989. text 85.00 (*0-7234-1567-6*) CRC Pr.

Ansary, Mir T. Afghanistan: Fighting for Freedom. LC 91-15648. (Discovering Our Heritage Ser.). (Illus.). 128p. (J). (gr. 4-6). 1991. lib. bdg. 14.95 (*0-87518-482-0*, Dillon Silver Burdett) Silver Burdett Pr.

— Columbus Day. LC 98-13721. (Holiday Histories Ser.). (J). 1998. lib. bdg. 19.92 (*0-01-575702-1*) Heinemann Lib.

***Ansary, Mir T.** Great Basin Indians. LC 99-21261. (Native Americans Ser.). (Illus.). 32p. (J). (gr. 2-4). 1999. lib. bdg. 14.95 (*1-57572-922-9*) Heinemann Lib.

***Ansary, Mir Tamim.** California Indians. LC 99-37136. (Native Americans Ser.). (Illus.). 32p. 2000. lib. bdg. write for info. (*1-57572-927-X*) Heinemann Lib.

— Columbus Day. LC 98-13721. (Holiday Histories Ser.). (Illus.). 32p. (J). (ps-3). 1999. lib. bdg. 13.95 (*1-57572-702-1*) Heinemann Lib.

Ansary, Mir Tamim. Dolls. LC 96-39413. (Cool Collections). (J). 1998. 18.50 (*1-57572-118-X*) Heinemann Lib.

***Ansary, Mir Tamim.** Eastern Woodlands Indians. LC 99-34900. (Native Americans Ser.). (Illus.). 32p. 2000. lib. bdg. write for info. (*1-57572-930-X*) Heinemann Lib.

— Holiday Histories Series, 6 bks. 32p. 1999. 119.52 (*1-57572-877-X*) Heinemann Lib.

— Labor Day. LC 98-13720. (Holiday Histories Ser.). (Illus.). 32p. (J). (ps-3). 1999. lib. bdg. 13.95 (*1-57572-703-X*) Heinemann Lib.

Ansary, Mir Tamim. Martin Luther King, Jr. Day. LC 98-14378. (Holiday Histories Ser.). (Illus.). 32p. (J). (ps-3). 1999. lib. bdg. 13.95 (*1-57572-873-7*) Heinemann Lib.

— Memorial Day. LC 98-14377. (Holiday Histories Ser.). 32p. (J). 1999. 19.92 (*1-57572-874-5*) Heinemann Lib.

***Ansary, Mir Tamim.** Northwest Coast Indians. LC 99-13517. (Native Americans Ser.). (Illus.). 32p. (J). (gr. 2-4). 1999. 14.95 (*1-57572-921-0*) Heinemann Lib.

— Plains Indians. LC 99-37137. (Illus.). 32p. 2000. lib. bdg. write for info. (*1-57572-929-6*) Heinemann Lib.

— Plateau Indians. LC 99-34897. (Illus.). 32p. 2000. lib. bdg. write for info. (*1-57572-928-8*) Heinemann Lib.

Ansary, Mir Tamim. President's Day. LC 98-14380. (Holiday Histories Ser.). 32p. (J). 1999. 19.92 (*1-57572-875-3*) Heinemann Lib.

***Ansary, Mir Tamim.** Southeast Indians. LC 99-13516. (Native Americans Ser.). (Illus.). 32p. (J). (gr. 2-4). 1999. 14.95 (*1-57572-924-5*) Heinemann Lib.

— Southwest Indians. LC 99-13518. (Native Americans Ser.). (Illus.). 32p. (J). (gr. 2-4). 1999. 14.95 (*1-57572-923-7*) Heinemann Lib.

Ansary, Mir Tamim. Stamps. LC 96-39410. (Cool Collections). (J). 1998. 18.50 (*1-57572-113-9*) Heinemann Lib.

***Ansary, Mir Tamim.** Subarctic Indians. LC 99-34899. (Native Americans Ser.). (Illus.). 32p. 2000. lib. bdg. write for info. (*1-57572-926-1*) Heinemann Lib.

Ansary, Mir Tamim. Veteran's Day. LC 98-14376. (Holiday Histories Ser.). 32p. (J). 1999. 19.92 (*1-57572-876-1*) Heinemann Lib.

Ansary, Mir Tamim, jt. auth. see Carre, Kathy.

Ansary, Mir Tamim. Arctic People. LC 99-17407. (Native Americans Ser.). (Illus.). 32p. (J). (gr. 2-4). 1999. 14.95 (*1-57572-920-2*) Heinemann Lib.

Ansary, Mir Tamim, jt. auth. see Carre, Kathy.

Ansary, Mir Tamin, jt. auth. see Carre, Kathy.

***Ansay, A. Manette.** Vinegar Hill. 256p. 1999. 24.00 (*0-688-18063-9*, Wm Morrow) Morrow Avon.

***Ansay, A. Manette.** Midnight Champagne: A Novel. LC 99-11467. 240p. 1999. 24.00 (*0-688-15244-9*, Wm Morrow) Morrow Avon.

— Midnight Champagne: A Novel. 240p. 2000. pap. 13.00 (*0-380-72975-X*) Morrow Avon.

Ansay, A. Manette. Read This & Tell Me. 142p. 1998. reprint ed. pap. 11.00 (*0-380-73077-4*, Avon Bks) Morrow Avon.

— Read This & Tell Me What It Says: Stories. LC 95-11039. 160p. 1995. 22.95 (*0-87023-988-0*) U of Mass Pr.

— River Angel. LC 97-31006. 224p. 1998. 24.00 (*0-688-15243-0*, Wm Morrow) Morrow Avon.

— River Angel: A Novel. 256p. 1999. reprint ed. pap. 12.50 (*0-380-72974-1*, Avon Bks) Morrow Avon.

***Ansay, A. Manette.** SEE 0688180639. 2000. 24.00 (*0-688-18064-7*, Wm Morrow) Morrow Avon.

Ansay, A. Manette. Sister. LC 95-52672. 224p. 1996. 24.00 (*0-688-14449-7*, Wm Morrow) Morrow Avon.

— Sister. 240p. 1997. pap. 12.50 (*0-380-72976-8*, Avon Bks) Morrow Avon.

— Vinegar Hill. LC 97-94869. 256p. 1998. pap. 13.00 (*0-380-73013-8*, Avon Bks) Morrow Avon.

— Vinegar Hill. 1999. pap. 9.95 (*0-14-023239-7*, Viking) Viking Penguin.

***Ansay, A. Manette.** Vinegar Hill. large type ed. (Basic Ser.). 2000. 30.95 (*0-7862-2511-4*) Thorndike Pr.

— Vinegar Hill: A Novel. LC 00-23383. 2000. pap. write for info. (*0-7862-2512-2*) Thorndike Pr.

— VINEGAR HILL OPRAH. Vol. 28. 240p. 2000. pap. 13.00 (*0-380-29976-3*, Avon Bks) Morrow Avon.

***Ansay, A. Manette, et al.** Tameme: New Writing from North America. Mayo, C. M., ed. & tr. by. Cadena, Agustin et al, trs.Tr. of Tameme: Nueva Literatura de Norteamerica. (SPA.). 225p. 1998. pap. 14.95 (*0-9674093-0-6*, Pub. by Tameme) Small Changes Inc.

Ansay, Tu Grul, jt. auth. see Harmathy, Attila.

Ansay, Tugrul & Wallace, Don, Jr., eds. Introduction to Turkish Law. LC 95-47267. 1996. 123.50 (*90-411-0171-3*) Kluwer Law Intl.

Ansay, Tugrul, et al. Recueil des Cours de l'Academie de Droit International de la Haye: Collected Courses of the Hague Academy of Int'l Law, Vol. 156 (1977-III) 482p. 1980. lib. bdg. 129.00 (*90-286-0600-9*) Kluwer Academic.

Ansay, Tugrul, jt. ed. see Clark, David S.

Ansay, Tugrul, jt. ed. see Dessemontet, F.

Ansbacher, Heinz L., ed. see Adler, Alfred.

***Ansbacher, Max G.** The New Options Market. 4th ed. (Trading Advantage Ser.). 336p. 2000. text 39.95 (*0-471-34880-5*) Wiley.

Ansbacher, Rowena R., ed. see Adler, Alfred.

Ansberry. Women of Troy Hill: The Back-Fence Virtues of Faith & Friendship. LC 99-47131. (Illus.). 336p. 2000. 25.00 (*0-15-100400-5*) Harcourt.

***Ansbro, George.** I Have a Lady in the Balcony: Memoirs of a Broadcaster in Radio & Television. LC 99-45416. (Illus.). 245p. 2000. boxed set 36.50 (*0-7864-0425-6*) McFarland & Co.

***Ansbro, John J.** Martin Luther King, Jr. Nonviolent Strategies & Tactics for Social Change. 2000. reprint ed. pap. 18.95 (*1-56833-169-X*, Pub. by Madison Bks UPA) Natl Bk Netwk.

Anschel, Eugene. Homer Lea, Sun Yat Sen, & the Chinese Revolution. LC 84-15999. 269p. 1984. 59.95 (*0-275-91120-9*, Praeger Pubs) Greenwood.

Anschell, Helen & Malkin, Marsha. Recipes & People of a Northwest Neighborhood. rev. ed. Malkin, Martin & Lewis, Gertrude, eds. (Illus.). 96p. 1988. reprint ed. pap. 8.95 (*0-926060-00-7*) Anschell Pub Co.

Anschuetz, Reynold J. How to Think Small Business for Big Profits. (Illus.). 126p. (Orig.). 1987. pap. text 9.95 (*0-9619358-0-4*) Confectionery World Inc.

Anschuetz, Reynold J. Born to Be Rich. 232p. (Orig.). 1988. pap. 11.95 (*0-9619358-1-2*) Confectionery World Inc.

Anschutz, Marieke. But Who Made God? pap. 10.95 (*0-86315-136-1*, 675, Pub. by Floris Bks) Anthroposophic.

— Children & Their Temperaments. pap. 10.95 (*0-86315-175-2*, 1916, Pub. by Floris Bks) Anthroposophic.

Anschutz, R. P. The Philosophy of J. S. Mill. LC 85-27075. (Illus.). 196p. 1986. reprint ed. lib. bdg. 41.50 (*0-313-25040-5*, ANPM, Greenwood Pr) Greenwood.

Anscomb, Anne. Drugs & Cosmetics for Aging Boomers: A Surging Market. LC 98-120761. 143p. 1997. 2950.00 (*1-56965-378-X*, B-111) BCC.

Anscombe, Alfred. Great Ages Assigned to Certain Irish Saints. 1996. pap. 3.00 (*0-89979-077-1*) British Am Bks.

Anscombe, Elizabeth, et al. Philosophical Writings: Descartes. 368p. (C). 1971. pap. text 10.00 (*0-02-303600-1*, Macmillan Coll) P-H.

Anscombe, F. Computing in Statistical Science Through APL. (Series in Statistics). 416p. 1981. 72.95 (*0-387-90549-9*) Spr-Verlag.

Anscombe, Frederick F. The Ottoman Gulf: The Creation of Kuwait, Saudi Arabia, & Qatar, 1870-1914. LC 97-12680. 288p. 1997. pap. 18.50 (*0-231-10839-7*); lib. bdg. 50.00 (*0-231-10838-9*) Col U Pr.

Anscombe, G. E. An Introduction to Wittgenstein's Tractatus. (Wittgenstein Studies). 180p. 1996. pap. 14.95 (*1-85506-489-8*) Bks Intl VA.

***Anscombe, G. E.** An Introduction to Wittgenstein's Tractatus. (Wittgenstein Studies). 180p. 2000. pap. text 15.00 (*1-890318-54-X*, Pub. by St Augustines Pr) U Ch Pr.

Anscombe, G. E., ed. see Wittgenstein, Ludwig Josef Johann.

Anscombe, G. E., ed. & tr. see Wittgenstein, Ludwig Josef Johann.

Anscombe, G. E., tr. see Wittgenstein, Ludwig Josef Johann.

***Anscombe, G. E. M.** Intention. 128p. 2000. pap. 14.95 (*0-674-00399-3*) HUP.

Anscombe, Isabelle. Arts & Crafts Style. (Illus.). 240p. 1996. pap. 29.95 (*0-7148-3469-6*, Pub. by Phaidon Press) Phaidon Pr.

— Arts & Crafts Style. 240p. 1997. 59.95 (*0-7148-2614-6*, Pub. by Phaidon Press) Phaidon Pr.

— Boobies, Boojums & Snarks: The Ceramic Curiosities of the Martin Brothers, 1880-1914. 59p. (Orig.). 1981. pap. 125.00 (*0-942410-04-1*) V Jordan Fine Art.

Anscombe, Roderick. The Secret Life of Laszlo, Count Dracula. LC 93-49438. 416p. 1994. 22.45 (*0-7868-6040-5*, Pub. by Hyperion) Time Warner.

***Anscombe, Roderick.** The Secret Life of Laszlo, Count Dracula. 409p. 2000. reprint ed. 25.00 (*0-7881-9294-9*) DIANE Pub.

Anscombe, Roderick. Shank. 336p. (J). 1996. 22.95 (*0-7868-6239-4*, Pub. by Hyperion) Time Warner.

— Shank. 464p. (J). 1997. reprint ed. mass mkt. 6.99 (*0-7868-8919-5*, Pub. by Hyperion) Time Warner.

Anscombre. Argumentation in Language. 1990. lib. bdg. 34.95 (*0-226-02111-4*) U Ch Pr.

Ansdell, Gary. Music for Life: Aspects of Creative Music Therapy with Adult Clients. LC 95-14419. 237p. 1995. pap. 29.95 (*1-85302-299-3*, Pub. by Jessica Kingsley) Taylor & Francis.

Ansdell, Peter, ed. see Bombeli, Karin.

Ansel, Howard, et al. Pharmaceutical Dosage Forms & Drug Delivery Systems. 6th ed. (Illus.). 530p. 1995. (*0-683-00193-0*) Lppncott W & W.

— Pharmaceutical Dosage Forms & Drug Delivery Systems. 7th ed. LC 99-17498. 676p. 1999. 48.00 (*0-683-30572-7*) Lppncott W & W.

Ansel, Howard C., et al. Pharmaceutical Dosage Forms & Drug Delivery Systems. 6th ed. LC 94-22471. 1994. write for info. (*0-683-01930-9*) Lppncott W & W.

Ansel, Howard C., jt. auth. see Stoklosa, Mitchell J.

Ansel, Talvikki. My Shining Archipelago. LC 96-45321. (Yale Series of Younger Poets). 64p. 1997. 18.00 (*0-300-07031-4*); pap. 11.00 (*0-300-07032-2*) Yale U Pr.

Ansel, Walter. Hitler & the Middle Sea. LC 77-132026. 526p. reprint ed. pap. 163.10 (*0-608-13914-9*, 202375700033) Bks Demand.

Ansel, Willits D. Boats: A Manual for Their Documentation. Lipke, Paul et al, eds. LC 94-11098. (American Association for State & Local History Book Ser.). (Illus.). 425p. (C). 1993. reprint ed. pap. 49.95 (*0-942063-17-1*) AltaMira Pr.

— The Whaleboat: A Study of Design, Construction & Use from 1850-1970. 2nd rev. ed. (Illus.). vi, 147p. 1983. 17.95 (*0-913372-40-4*) Mystic Seaport.

Ansel, Willits D., jt. auth. see Blair, Carvel H.

Anselin, Luc. Spatial Econometrics: Methods & Models. (C). 1988. lib. bdg. 171.00 (*90-247-3735-4*) Kluwer Academic.

Anselin, Luc & Florax, Raymond, eds. New Directions in Spatial Econometrics. LC 95-31116. (Advances in Spatial Science Ser.). (Illus.). 420p. 1995. 119.00 (*3-540-60020-5*) Spr-Verlag.

Ansell. Oceanography Marine Biology: An Annual Review, Vol. 33. (Illus.). 500p. 1995. 150.00 (*1-85728-363-5*, Pub. by UCL Pr Ltd) Taylor & Francis.

Ansell, Alan D., ed. Oceanography & Marine Biology: An Annual Review. LC 98-150574. 599p. 1997. 165.00 (*1-85728-716-9*) Taylor & Francis.

Ansell, Alan D., et al, eds. Oceanography & Marine Biology: An Annual Review, Vol. 31. 640p. 1993. 150.00 (*1-85728-085-7*, Pub. by UCL Pr Ltd) Taylor & Francis.

— Oceanography & Marine Biology: An Annual Review, Vol. 32. 624p. 1994. 150.00 (*1-85728-236-1*, Pub. by UCL Pr Ltd) Taylor & Francis.

— Oceanography & Marine Biology: An Annual Review, Vol. 34. 600p. 1996. 160.00 (*1-85728-581-6*, Pub. by UCL Pr Ltd) Taylor & Francis.

Ansell, Amy. New Right, New Racism: Race & Reaction in the United States & Great Britain. LC 97-14583. 352p. (C). 1998. text 40.00 (*0-8147-0656-8*) NYU Pr.

— Unraveling the Right: The New Conservatism in American Thought & Politics. (C). 1998. pap. 19.95 (*0-8133-3147-1*) Westview.

Ansell, Amy E. Unraveling the Right: The New Conservatism in American Thought & Politics. LC 98-9569. 272p. (C). 1998. text 75.00 (*0-8133-3146-3*, Pub. by Westview) HarpC.

Ansell, Anthony E. Managing for Quality in the Financial Services Industry. LC 92-39843. (Strategic Management of Financial Institutions Ser.). 360p. 1993. mass mkt. 84.95 (*0-412-47300-3*) Chapman & Hall.

Ansell, Barbara M. & White, Patricia H. Paediatric Rheumatology Update. Woo, Patricia et al, eds. (Illus.). 222p. 1990. 65.00 (*0-19-261860-1*) OUP.

Ansell, Brian, et al. Lonely Planet Diving & Snorkeling Guide to Vanuatu. LC 94-23351. (Diving & Snorkeling Guides Ser.). 96p. 1995. pap. 14.95 (*1-55992-080-7*, Pisces Books) Lonely Planet.

Ansell, Dorothy, jt. auth. see Griffin, William V.

Ansell, Dorothy I. The New Making It on Your Own. 2nd rev. ed. Cauldwell, Samuel M. & Insley, Jeannette R., eds. (Illus.). 92p. (YA). (gr. 7-12). 1995. spiral bd. 25.00 (*1-878848-55-0*, 237) Natl Res Ctr.

***Ansell, Dorothy I. & Kroner, Mark J.** Operation: Independence. (Illus.). 55p. 1998. spiral bd. 25.00 (*1-878848-52-6*, 240) Natl Res Ctr.

Ansell, Dorothy I. & Morse, Joan M., eds. Creative Life Skill Activities. (Illus.). 143p. 1994. spiral bd. 25.00 (*1-878848-54-2*, 238) Natl Res Ctr.

Ansell, G. B., jt. ed. see Hanin, Israel.

Ansell, George. The Floor Trader's Confidential Handbook. 1987. pap. 15.00 (*0-930233-17-4*) Windsor.

Ansell, George, ed. Imaging Drug Reactions & Toxic Hazards. 3rd ed. (Illus.). 352p. 1997. text 90.00 (*0-412-55590-5*, Pub. by E A) OUP.

Ansell, George S., et al, eds. Oxide Dispersion Strengthening: Proceedings of a Symposium, Bolton Landing, New York, June 27-29, 1966. LC 67-26577. (Metallurgical Society Conference Ser.: Vol. 47). 922p. reprint ed. pap. 200.00 (*0-608-11366-2*, 200153500079) Bks Demand.

Ansell, I. D. Atlas of Male Reproductive System Pathological. (Current Histopathology Ser.). 1985. text 274.00 (*0-85200-327-7*) Kluwer Academic.

Ansell, J. I. & Phillips, M. J. Practical Methods for Reliability Data Analysis. (Oxford Statistical Science Ser.: No. 14). (Illus.). 256p. 1994. text 65.00 (*0-19-853664-X*) OUP.

Ansell, Jack E. Anticoagulation Therapy Management Manual. LC 97-6378. 1997. 195.00 (*0-8342-0878-4*, S443) Aspen Pub.

— Handbook of Hemostatis & Thrombosis. (Illus.). 130p. 1986. 28.95 (*0-316-04331-1*, Little Brwn Med Div) Lppncott W & W.

Ansell, Judith. His Sheltering Arms. large type ed. 288p. 1995. 23.99 (*0-263-14176-4*, Pub. by Mills & Boon) Ulverscroft.

Ansell, Kharalambos. Male & Female Created He Them. Date not set. pap. 6.00 (*1-879038-84-6*, 9054) Synaxis Pr.

Ansell, M. F. Rodd's Chemistry of Carbon Compounds, Suppl. Vol 3F, (Partial) G. 2nd ed. 290p. 1984. 226.00 (*0-444-42269-2*, I-479-83) Elsevier.

— Rodd's Chemistry of Carbon Compounds Vol. 4, Pt. IJ: Heterocyclic Compounds. 2nd ed. 552p. 1989. 511.25 (*0-444-87322-8*) Elsevier.

— Rodd's Chemistry of Carbon Compounds-Heterocyclic Compounds Vol. 4, Pt. A: Three, Four & Five-Membered Compounds, Vol. 4A. 540p. 1984. suppl. ed. 383.50 (*0-444-42397-4*) Elsevier.

— Supplements to the 2nd Edition of Rodd's Chemistry of Carbon Compounds Vol. IV, Pt. L: Fused-Ring Heterocyclic Compounds Containing Three or More Nitrogen Atoms; Purines & Related Ring Systems; Nucleosides; Nucleotides & Nucleic Acids; Pteridines, Alloxazines, Flavins & Related Compounds. 276p. 1988. 228.00 (*0-444-42978-6*) Elsevier.

— Supplements to the 2nd Edition of Rodd's Chemistry of Carbon Compounds Vol. IV, Pt. F: Six-Membered Heterocyclic Compounds with a Single Nitrogen Atom in the Ring; Pyridine, Polymethylenepyridines, Quinoline, Isoquinoline & Their Derivatives. 252p. 1987. 208.75 (*0-444-42821-6*) Elsevier.

— Supplements to the 2nd Edition of Rodd's Chemistry of Carbon Compounds Vol. IV, Pt. G: Six-Membered Ring Compounds Where the Hetero-Atom is Phosphorus, Arsenic, Antimony or Bismuth. 460p. 1987. 370.50 (*0-444-42897-6*) Elsevier.

Ansell, M. F., ed. Rodd's Chemistry of Carbon Compounds. 2nd ed. 320p. 1995. suppl. ed. 229.25 (*0-444-82260-7*) Elsevier.

— Rodd's Chemistry of Carbon Compounds, 2 pts. in 1, Suppl. Vol. 1 C & D. 464p. 1973. 286.00 (*0-444-41072-4*) Elsevier.

— Rodd's Chemistry of Carbon Compounds, 2 pts. in 1, Suppl. Vol. 1 A & B. xvi,268p. 1975. 204.00 (*0-444-40972-6*) Elsevier.

— Rodd's Chemistry of Carbon Compounds, 2 pts. in 1, Suppl. Vol. 2 A & B. 424p. 1974. 286.00 (*0-444-41133-X*) Elsevier.

— Rodd's Chemistry of Carbon Compounds, 3 pts. in 1, Suppl. Vol. 2, Pts. C-E. 318p. 1974. 226.00 (*0-444-41135-6*) Elsevier.

— Rodd's Chemistry of Carbon Compounds, Suppl. Vols. 3 B & C. 358p. 1981. 286.00 (*0-444-42017-7*) Elsevier.

— Rodd's Chemistry of Carbon Compounds, Suppl. Vols. 3, Pts. D-F. 424p. 1982. 286.00 (*0-444-42088-6*) Elsevier.

— Rodd's Chemistry of Carbon Compounds Pt. A: Aromatic Compounds, Vol. 3, Pt. A. 2nd ed. 438p. 1983. 286.00 (*0-444-42150-5*) Elsevier.

— Rodd's Chemistry of Carbon Compounds Vol. 4 - Suppls. Heterocyclic Compounds, Part E: Six-Membered Monoheterocyclic Compounds Containing Oxygen, Sulphur, Selenium, Tellurium, Silicon, Germanium, Tin, Lead or Iodine as the Hetero-atom. 2nd ed. 640p. 1990. 466.25 (*0-444-88611-7*) Elsevier.

— Supplement to the Second Edition of Rodd's Chemistry of Carbon Compounds, Vol. 1, Pts F & G. 404p. 1983. 286.00 (*0-444-42183-1*) Elsevier.

— Supplements to the 2nd Edition of Rodd's Chemistry of Carbon Compounds: Supplement to Vol. 1: Aliphatic Compounds; Part E: Unsaturated Acyclic Hydrocarbons, Trihydric Alcohols, Their Oxidation Products & Derivatives. 1983. 279.50 (*0-444-42236-6*) Elsevier.

— Supplements to the 2nd Edition of Rodd's Chemistry of Carbon Compounds Vol. 4: Heterocyclic Compounds. 272p. 1987. 233.50 (*0-444-42792-9*) Elsevier.

— Supplements to the Second Edition of Rodd's Chemistry of Carbon Compounds: Supplement to Vol. IV: Heterocyclic Compounds, Part B: Five-Membered Heterrocyclic Compounds with a Single Hetero-Atom in the Ring; Alkaloids, Dyes & Pigments. 318p. 1985. 259.25 (*0-444-42485-7*) Elsevier.

— Supplements to the Second Edition of Rodd's Chemistry of Carbon Compounds, Vol. III: Aromatic Compounds; Part H: Polycarbocyclic Compounds with More Than Thirteen Atoms in the Fused-Riding System. 140p. 1988. 128.00 (*0-444-42989-1*) Elsevier.

— Supplements to the Second Edition of Rodd's Chemistry of Carbon Compounds - Volume IV: Heterocyclic Compounds; Part K. 626p. 1989. 476.75 (*0-444-87399-6*) Elsevier.

Ansell, M. F. & Pattenden, G. Saturated Heterocyclic Chemistry, Vol. 2. LC 72-83454. 1974. 47.00 (*0-85186-532-1*) Am Chemical.

— Saturated Heterocyclic Chemistry, Vol. 3. LC 72-83454. 1975. 43.00 (*0-85186-562-3*) Am Chemical.

— Saturated Heterocyclic Chemistry, Vol. 4. LC 72-83454. 1977. 77.00 (*0-85186-592-5*) Am Chemical.

— Saturated Heterocyclic Chemistry, Vol. 5. LC 72-83454. 1978. 66.00 (*0-85186-622-0*) Am Chemical.

Ansell, M. F., jt. ed. see Coffey, S.

Ansell, M. O., jt. auth. see Arif, I. M.

Ansell, Maggi, ed. see Shane, Victor.

Ansell, Martin R. Oil Baron of the Southwest: Edward L. Doheny & the Development of the Petroleum Industry in California & Mexico. LC 97-37567. 302p. 1998. text 62.50 (*0-8142-0749-9*) Ohio St U Pr.

Ansell, Mary. Dogs & Men. LC 70-142257. (Short Story Index Reprint Ser.). 1977. 17.95 (*0-8369-3741-4*) Ayer.

Ansell, Nicholas J. The Woman Will Overcome the Warrior: A Dialogue with the Christian - Feminist Theology of Rosemary Radford Ruether. 395p. (C). 1994. pap. text 32.50 (*0-8191-9546-4*); lib. bdg. 64.50 (*0-8191-9545-6*) U Pr of Amer.

An Asterisk (*) at the beginning of an entry indicates that the title is appearing for the first time.

Ansell-Pearson, Keith. Deleuze & Philosophy: The Difference Engineer. LC 96-36570. (Warwick Studies in European Philosophy Ser.). 288p. (C). 1997. 85.00 (*0-415-14269-5*); pap. 25.99 (*0-415-14270-9*) Routledge.
— Germinal Life: The Difference & Repetition of Deleuze. LC 98-41197. 2000. 75.00 (*0-415-18350-2*); pap. 24.99 (*0-415-18351-0*) Routledge.
— An Introduction to Nietzsche As Political Thinker: The Perfect Nihilist. LC 93-5504. 263p. (C). 1994. pap. text 16.95 (*0-521-42721-5*) Cambridge U Pr.
— Nietzsche Contra Rousseau: A Study of Nietzsche's Moral & Political Thought. 302p. (C). 1991. text 59.95 (*0-521-41173-4*) Cambridge U Pr.
***Ansell-Pearson, Keith.** Nihilism Now. LC 99-88249. 2000. text 59.95 (*0-312-23209-8*) St Martin.
Ansell-Pearson, Keith. The Transhuman Condition: A Report on Machines, Technics & Evolution. LC 96-20530. 224p. (C). 1997. 70.00 (*0-415-15434-0*); pap. 20.99 (*0-415-15435-9*) Routledge.
Ansell-Pearson, Keith & Caygill, Howard, eds. The Fate of the New Nietzsche. (Avebury Series in Philosophy). 336p. 1993. 87.95 (*1-85628-409-3*, Pub. by Avebury) Ashgate Pub Co.
Ansell-Pearson, Keith, ed. see Nietzsche, Friedrich Wilhelm.
Ansell, Rod & Percy, Rachel. To Fight the Wild. LC 85-22023. (Illus.). 156p. (YA). (gr. 7 up). 1986. 12.95 (*0-15-289068-8*, Harcourt Child Bks) Harcourt.
Ansell, S. E. Sac Metroscan. 35p. (Orig.). 1994. pap. 10.95 (*0-9640436-0-2*) Quad As Elect.
Ansello, Edward F. & Eustis, Nancy N., eds. Aging & Disabilities: Seeking Common Ground. LC 92-28829. (Generations & Aging Ser.). 204p. 1992. pap. text 23.95 (*0-89503-108-6*) Baywood Pub.
Ansello, Edward F. & Rose, Thomas. Aging & Lifelong Disabilities: Partnership for the Twenty First Century: Wingspread Report. (C). 1989. pap. 10.00 (*0-924840-00-5*) E Lewis Found.
Ansello, Edward F., et al. Partners: Building Inter-System Cooperation in Aging with Developmental Disabilities. LC 97-80588. (Illus.). 92p. 1997. pap. text 10.00 (*0-9664705-0-8*) VA Ctr on Aging.
Ansello, Edward F., jt. auth. see Janicki, Matthew P.
Anselm, Abbot of BEC. The Letters of Saint Anselm of Canterbury. Frohlich, Walter, tr. from LAT. (Cistercian Studies: Vol. 2). (Illus.). 1993. 42.95 (*0-87907-897-9*) Cistercian Pubns.
***Anselm, Marcus, et al.** Intellectual Property & Media Law Companion. 3rd ed. (Companion Ser.). 225p. 1999. pap. 40.00 (*1-85431-918-3*, Pub. by Blackstone Pr) Gaunt.
Anselm, Marcus, et al. Intellectual Property & Media Law Companion, 1998/99. 221p. 1998. pap. 56.00 (*1-85431-863-2*) Gaunt.
Anselm, Marcus, jt. auth. see Bleakley, Alasdair.
Anselm of Canterbury. Anselm of Canterbury - The Major Works. Davies, Brian & Evans, Gill, eds. LC 97-50479. (Oxford World's Classics Ser.). 544p. 1998. pap. 11.95 (*0-19-282525-9*) OUP.
— The De Grammatico of St. Anselm: The Theory of Paronymy. LC 64-17066. (Notre Dame, University Publications in Mediaeval Studies Ser.: No. 18). 188p. reprint ed. pap. 58.30 (*0-608-30654-1*, 202206900024) Bks Demand.
Anselm, Saint of Canterbury. Anselm of Canterbury: Why God Became Man. Hopkins, Jasper & Richardson, Herbert W., eds. 105p. (C). 1980. pap. 39.95 (*0-88946-009-4*) E Mellen.
— Anselm of Canterbury Vol. I: Monologion, Proslogion, Debate with Gaunilo, & a Meditation on Human Redemption, Vol. 1. Hopkins, Jasper, ed. Richardson, Herbert W., tr. LC 74-19840. (LAT.). 161p. 1974. lib. bdg. 79.95 (*0-88946-000-0*) E Mellen.
— Anselm of Canterbury Vol. II: Philosophical Fragments; De Grammatico; on Truth; Freedom of Choice; the Fall of the Devil; the Harmony of the Foreknowledge, the Predestination, & the Grace of God with Free Choice, Vol. 2. Hopkins, Jasper & Richardson, Herbert W., trs. LC 74-19840. (LAT.). 237p. 1976. lib. bdg. 109.95 (*0-88946-250-X*) E Mellen.
— Anselm of Canterbury Vol. III: Two Letters Concerning Roscelin; the Incarnation of the Word; Why God Became a Man; the Virgin Conception & Original Sin; the Procession of the Holy Spirit; Three Letters on the Sacraments, Vol. 3. Hopkins, Jasper & Richardson, Herbert W., trs. LC 74-19840. (LAT.). 265p. 1976. lib. bdg. 109.95 (*0-88946-350-6*) E Mellen.
— The Letters of Saint Anselm of Canterbury, Vol. 3. 2nd ed. Frohlich, Walter, tr. from LAT. (Cistercian Studies). 1994. 42.95 (*0-87907-742-5*) Cistercian Pubns.
— Monologion & Proslogion: With the Replies of Gaunilo & Anselm. Williams, Thomas, tr. from LAT. LC 95-47275. (Hackett Classics Ser.). 192p. (Orig.). (C). 1996. pap. text 7.95 (*0-87220-297-6*); lib. bdg. 34.95 (*0-87220-298-4*) Hackett Pub.
Anselme, Jean-Pierre, ed. N-Nitrosamines. LC 79-12461. (ACS Symposium Ser.: No. 101). 1979. 29.95 (*0-8412-0503-5*) Am Chemical.
— N-Nitrosamines. LC 79-12461. (ACS Symposium Ser.: Vol. 101). 214p. 1979. reprint ed. pap. 66.40 (*0-608-03096-1*, 206354900007) Bks Demand.
Anselment, Raymond A. Betwixt Jest & Earnest: Marprelate, Milton, Marvell, Swift & the Decorum of Religious Ridicule. LC 79-12498. 215p. reprint ed. pap. 66.70 (*0-8357-7152-0*, 202644600049) Bks Demand.
— Loyalist Resolve: Patient Fortitude in the English Civil War. LC 87-40514. 240p. 1989. 36.50 (*0-87413-338-6*) U Delaware Pr.
— The Realms of Apollo: Literature & Healing in Seventeenth-Century England. LC 94-46922. 1995. 47.50 (*0-87413-553-2*) U Delaware Pr.
Anselmi, Dina & Law, Anne L. Questions of Gender: Perspectives & Paradoxes. LC 97-31723. 800p. 1997. pap. 36.88 (*0-07-006017-7*) McGraw.
Anselmi, William. Elusive Margins: Consuming Media, Ethnicity & Culture. LC 97-70437. 180p. 1997. pap. 15.00 (*1-55071-042-7*) Guernica Editions.
— Mediating Culture: The Politics of Representation - Essays. 217p. 1994. pap. 15.00 (*0-920717-85-3*) Guernica Editions.
Anselmino, Isi & Predazzi, E. Diquarks II. LC 94-204573. 304p. 1994. text 86.00 (*981-02-1676-9*) World Scientific Pub.
Anselmino, Luciano & Pilat, Bianca. Man Ray's Graphic Work: Catalogue Raisonne, 2 vols., Set, Vols. 1 & 2. (ITA., Illus.). 1984. 250.00 (*1-55660-087-9*) A Wofsy Fine Arts.
Anselmino, M. & Predazzi, E., eds. Diquarks. 308p. (C). 1989. text 86.00 (*9971-5-0880-X*) World Scientific Pub.
— Diquarks III: Proceedings of the Workshop Villa Gualino, Torino, Italy 28-30 October 1996. 264p. 1998. 68.00 (*981-02-3635-2*) World Scientific Pub.
Anselmo Book Committee Staff. Victoria Creek Neighbors. 832p. 45.00 (*0-9615586-9-5*) Loup Valley.
Anselmo, Franz. Early Childhood Development: PrebirthThrough Age Eight. 2nd ed. LC 94-13382. 576p. (C). 1994. pap. text 64.00 (*0-02-303607-9*, Macmillan Coll) P-H.
Anselmo, Peter. Ayurvedic Secrets to Longevity & Total Health. 320p. (C). 1996. pap. text 13.95 (*0-13-156465-X*) P-H.
Anselmo, Thomas, et al. Thinking Writing College. (C). 1997. 34.60 (*0-673-39245-7*) Addson-Wesley Educ.
Anselone, Philip M. Nonlinear Integral Equations. LC 64-17771. (U. S. Army Mathematics Research Center Publication Ser.: No. 11). 390p. reprint ed. pap. 120.90 (*0-608-30938-9*, 201020500068) Bks Demand.
Anselone, Philip M. & Lee, John W. Multivariable Calculus Engineer Preliminary. alternate ed. LC 95-33009. 577p. (C). 1995. pap. text 50.67 (*0-13-045279-3*) P-H.
Ansen, Alan. Contact Highs: Selected Poems, 1957-1987. LC 89-7768. 240p. 1989. pap. 11.95 (*0-916583-45-7*) Dalkey Arch.
Ansert, jt. auth. see Hagen.
Anshakov, A. S. & Fedorchenko, A. I., eds. High Velocity Acceleration of Macrobodies: Theory, Practice & Perspectives. 337p. (C). 1994. lib. bdg. 145.00 (*1-56072-194-4*) Nova Sci Pubs.
Anshaw, Carol. Aquamarine. 208p. 1997. pap. 11.00 (*0-395-87755-5*, Mariner Bks) HM.
— Aquamarine. 197p. 1993. pap. 10.00 (*0-671-79586-4*, WSP) PB.
— Seven Moves. 224p. 1997. pap. 11.00 (*0-395-87756-3*, Mariner Bks) HM.
Ansheim, Lester, jt. auth. see Berelson, Bernard.
Anshel, Iris, jt. auth. see Goldfeld, Dorian.
Anshel, Jeffrey. Smart Medicine for Your Eyes: A Guide to Safe & Effective Relief of Common Eye Disorders. LC 98-51713. 224p. 1998. pap. 17.95 (*0-89529-870-8*, Avery) Penguin Putnam.
— Visual Ergonomics in the Workplace. LC 98-140511. 160p. 1997. pap. 28.95 (*0-7484-0658-1*, Pub. by Tay Francis Ltd) Taylor & Francis.
Anshel, Mark H. Sport Psychology: From Theory to Practice. 3rd ed. 432p. (C). 1997. pap. text 53.00 (*0-13-776584-3*) Allyn.
Anshel, Mark H., ed. see Hamill, Joseph, et al.
Anshel, Michael & Gewirtz, W., eds. Mathematics of Information Processing. LC 85-26693. (Proceedings of Symposia in Applied Mathematics Ser.: Vol. 34). 233p. 1986. pap. 37.00 (*0-8218-0086-8*, PSAPM/34) Am Math.
Anshen, Frank, jt. auth. see Frank, Francine.
Anshen, Melvin & Bach, George L., eds. Management & Corporations, 1985. LC 75-4938. 253p. 1975. reprint ed. lib. bdg. 65.00 (*0-8371-8051-1*, ANMC, Greenwood Pr) Greenwood.
Anshen, Ruth N. The Rebirth of Thought: Light from the East. 128p. (Orig.). 1998. 19.95 (*1-55921-169-5*) Moyer Bell.
Anshen, Ruth N., ed. Beyond Victory. LC 75-156605. (Essay Index Reprint Ser.). 1977. reprint ed. 20.95 (*0-8369-2303-0*) Ayer.
— Mid-East-World Center: Yesterday, Today & Tomorrow. LC 78-20183. (Science & Culture Ser.). xiv, 386p. 1975. reprint ed. lib. bdg. 65.00 (*0-8154-0508-1*) Cooper Sq.
— Our Emergent Civilization. LC 70-134048. (Essay Index Reprint Ser.). 1977. 23.95 (*0-8369-2101-1*) Ayer.
Anshen, Ruth N., ed. see Cavalieri, Liebe F.
Anshen, Ruth N., ed. see Delgado, Jose M.
Anshen, Ruth N., ed. see Lovell, Bernard & Bank, Jodrell.
Anshen, Ruth N., ed. see Newell, Norman D.
ANSI Staff. Recommended Practice; File Format for Storage & Exchange of Image; Bi-Level Image File Format: ANSI/AIIM MS53-1993, Pt. 1. 55p. 1993. pap. 52.00 (*0-89258-257-X*, MS53) Assn Inform & Image Mgmt.
ANSI/ISA Staff. Application of Safety Instrumented Systems for the Process Industries: S84.01. (Safety Ser.). 1996. 80.00 (*1-55617-590-6*, S84.01) ISA.
— Area Classification in Hazardous, Classified, Dust Locations: S12.10. rev. ed. 1988. reprint ed. pap. 30.00 (*1-55617-095-5*, S12.10) ISA.
— Batch Control System Models & Terminology: S88.01. 1995. pap. 95.00 (*1-55617-562-0*, S88.01) ISA.
— Control Valve Aerodynamic Noise Prediction: S75.17. 1989. pap. 25.00 (*1-55617-207-9*, S75.17) ISA.
— Control Valve Capacity Test Procedure: S75.02. (Control Valves Ser.). 1996. 25.00 (*1-55617-621-X*, S75.02) ISA.
— Environmental Conditions for Process Measurement & Control Systems: Mechanical Influences S71.03. (Environmental Conditions Ser.). 1995. 25.00 (*1-55617-576-0*, S71.03) ISA.
— Face-to-Face Dimensions for Buttweld-End Globe-Style Control Valves: ANSI Class 4500, S75.14. 1993. pap. 25.00 (*1-55617-479-9*, S75.14) ISA.
— Face-to-Face Dimensions for Buttweld-End Globe-Style Control Valves: ANSI Classes 150, 300, 600, 900, 1500 & 2500, S75.15. 1993. pap. 25.00 (*1-55617-480-2*, S75.15) ISA.
— Face-to-Face Dimensions for Flanged Globe-Style Control Valve Bodies: ANSI Classes 125, 150, 250, 300 & 600, S75.03. 1992. pap. 25.00 (*1-55617-316-4*, S75.03) ISA.
— Face-to-Face Dimensions for Flanged Globe-Style Control Valve Bodies: ANSI Classes 900, 1500 & 2500, S75.16. 1993. pap. 25.00 (*1-55617-481-0*, S75.16) ISA.
— Face-to-Face Dimensions for Flangeless Control Valves: ANSI Classes 150, 300, 600, 900, 1500 & 2500, S75.04. 1995. pap. 25.00 (*1-55617-569-8*, S75.04) ISA.
— Face-to-Face Dimensions for Separable Flanged Globe-Style Control Valves: ANSI Classes 150, 300 & 600, S75.20. 1993. pap. 25.00 (*1-55617-313-X*, S75.20) ISA.
— Face-to-Face Dimensions for Socket Weld-End & Screwed-End Globe-Style Control Valves: ANSI Classes 150, 300, 600, 900, 1500, & 2500, S75.12. 1993. pap. 25.00 (*1-55617-478-0*, S75.12) ISA.
— Fieldbus Standard for Use in Industrial Control Systems, Part 2: Physical Layer Specification & Service Definition S50.02. 93p. 1993. pap. 70.00 (*1-55617-317-2*, S50-02) ISA.
— Fossil Fuel Plant Steam Temperature Control System: Drum Type S77.44. 1995. pap. 55.00 (*1-55617-544-2*, S77.44) ISA.
— Fossil-Fuel Power Plant Feedwater Control System - Drum-Type: S77.42. 1987. pap. 30.00 (*1-55617-048-3*, S77.42) ISA.
— Fossil Fuel Power Plant Human Machine Interface: TR77.60.04. (Fossil Fuel Power Plants Ser.). 1996. 40.00 (*1-55617-609-0*, TR77.60.04) ISA.
— Fossil Fuel Power Plant Instrument Piping: S77.70. 1995. pap. 40.00 (*1-55617-543-4*, S77.70) ISA.
— Fossil Fuel Power Plant Simulators: Functional Requirements S77.20. 1993. pap. 40.00 (*1-55617-494-2*, S77.20) ISA.
— Fossil Fuel Power Plant Unit - Plant Demand Development, Drum Type: S77.43. 1993. pap. 40.00 (*1-55617-495-0*, S77.43) ISA.
— Graphic Symbols for Process Displays: S5.5. 1985. pap. 40.00 (*0-87664-935-5*, S5.5) ISA.
— Hydrostatic-Testing of Control Valves: S75.19. (Control Valves Ser.). 1995. 40.00 (*1-55617-580-9*, S75.19) ISA.
— Identification of Emergency Shutdown Systems & Controls That Are Critical to Maintaining Safety in Process Industries: S91.01. 1995. pap. 25.00 (*1-55617-570-1*, S91.01) ISA.
— Inherent Flow Characteristic & Rangeability of Control Valves: ISA Standard S75.11. 1985. pap. 25.00 (*0-87664-835-9*, S75.11) ISA.
— Instrument Loop Diagrams: S5.4. rev. ed. 1989. reprint ed. pap. 25.00 (*1-55617-227-3*, S5.4) ISA.
— Manufacturing Message Specification: Companion Standard for Process Control S72.02. 1993. pap. 95.00 (*1-55617-519-1*, S72.02) ISA.
— Nonincendive Electrical Equipment for Use in Class I & II, Division 2 & Class III, Divisions I & 2 Hazardous: S12.12. 1994. pap. 55.00 (*1-55617-518-3*, S12.12) ISA.
— Qualifications & Certification of Instrumentation & Control Technicians in Nuclear Facilities: S67.14. 1994. pap. 40.00 (*1-55617-524-8*, S67.14) ISA.
— Quality Standard for Instrument Air: S7.0.01. (Pneumatics & Instrument Air Ser.). 1996. 80.00 (*1-55617-605-6*, S7.0.01) ISA.
— Safety Requirements for Electrical Equipment for Measurement, Control, & Laboratory Use: S82.02.02. (Safety Ser.). 1996. 30.00 (*1-55617-607-4*, S82.02.02) ISA.
— Safety Requirements for Electrical Equipment for Measurement, Control, & Laboratory Use: S82.02.04. (Safety Ser.). 1996. 25.00 (*1-55617-608-2*, S82.02.04) ISA.
— Safety Standard for Electrical & Electronic Test, Measuring, Controlling & Related Equipment (Electrical & Electronic Test & Measuring Equipment) S82.03. (Safety Ser.). 1988. pap. 25.00 (*1-55617-102-1*, S82.03) ISA.
— Setpoints for Nuclear Safety-Related Instrumentation: S64.04, Pt. I. 1994. pap. 40.00 (*1-55617-534-5*, S67.04) ISA.
— Setpoints for Sequenced Actions: TR67.04.08. (Nuclear Facilities Ser.). 1996. 40.00 (*1-55617-591-4*, TR67.04.08) ISA.
— Software Interface for CEMS Relative Accuracy Test Audit Data: TR77.81.05. 1995. pap. 30.00 (*1-55617-571-X*, S77.81.05) ISA.
— Transducer & Transmitter Installation for Nuclear Safety Applications, 1994: S67.01. Date not set. 40.00 (*1-55617-542-6*) ISA.
— Wiring Practices for Hazardous Classified Locations Instrumentation Pt. 1: Intrinsic Safety RP12.6. 1995. pap. 55.00 (*1-55617-545-0*, RP12.6) ISA.
Ansky, S. The Dybbuk. Engel, S. Morris, tr. from YID. LC 79-63047. (Illus.). 1979. reprint ed. pap. 8.95 (*0-89526-904-X*) Regnery Pub.
Ansky, S. & Neugroschel, Joachim, trs. The Dybuk & or Between Two Worlds. LC 97-48351. 96p. (Orig.). 1997. pap. 12.95 (*1-55936-137-9*) Theatre Comm.
***Ansky, Sherry & Elon, Beth.** The Food of Israel: Authentic Recipes from the Land of Milk & Honey. LC 99-50252. (Illus.). 144p. 2000. 18.95 (*962-593-268-2*, Pub. by Periplus) Tuttle Pubng.
Ansley, Clive. The Heresy of Wu Han: His Play "Hai Jui's Dismissal" & Its Role on China's Cultural Revolution. LC 73-24463. 133p. reprint ed. pap. 41.30 (*0-608-11010-8*, 201411200090) Bks Demand.
Ansley, Delight. Good Ways. rev. ed. LC 59-14674. (Illus.). (J). (gr. 7-11). 1959. 11.25 (*0-690-33757-4*) HarpC Child Bks.
Ansley, Frank. Trucks at Work: A Counting Pop-up. LC 98-114641. (Illus.). 12p. (J). (ps-1). 1997. per. 12.95 (*0-689-81736-3*) S&S Childrens.
***Ansley, John H.** Valley Forge: Triumph of Spirit. 2000. pap. write for info. (*0-9666304-0-8*) J Ansley Inc.
Ansley, Leslie J., ed. Friend of a Friend: Inspiring Stories of Black America's Quest to Improve the Lives of Its Children. 136p. 1996. pap. 7.95 (*0-9653887-0-0*) Nat Assn Blck.
Ansley, Norman & Abrams, Stanley. The Polygraph Profession. LC HV8078.A6. 56p. reprint ed. pap. 30.00 (*0-608-12943-7*, 202468100038) Bks Demand.
Ansley, Norman & Pumphrey, Jane, eds. Justice & the Polygraph: A Collection of Cases. LC K 5477.. 80p. reprint ed. pap. 30.00 (*0-7837-3159-0*, 204282500006) Bks Demand.
Ansley, Norman, et al. Truth & Science: A Bibliography. 2nd ed. 1997. 15.00 (*0-317-01466-8*) Am Polygraph.
***Ansley, Robert B., et al.** Smith, Currie & Hancock LLP's Common Sense Construction Law. 2nd ed. LC 00-26832. 2000. write for info. (*0-471-39090-9*) Wiley.
Ansley, Robert E., Jr. Discrimination in Housing. (CPL Bibliographies Ser.: No. 13). 75p. 1979. pap. 10.00 (*0-86602-013-6*, Sage Prdcls Pr) Sage.
Anslim. Beyond Sexuality: Feminism, Men's Liberation, Gender & Power, Sexuality, Class & Economics. (Illus.). 115p. (Orig.). 1994. pap. 10.00 (*0-948984-24-4*, Pub. by Phoenix Pr) AK Pr Dist.
Anslinger, H. J. & Tompkins, William F. The Traffic in Narcotics. Grob, Gerald N., ed. LC 80-1211. (Addiction in America Ser.). 1981. reprint ed. lib. bdg. 33.95 (*0-405-13567-X*) Ayer.
***Anslyn, Dougherty.** Modern Physical & Organic Chemistry. (Chemistry Ser.). 2001. 77.00 (*0-534-37721-1*) Brooks-Cole.
Ansmann, Albert, ed. see Laser Radar Conference Staff.
Ansoff, H. Igor. Management Laureates: A Collection of Autobiographical Essays, Vol. 1. Bedeian, Arthur G., ed. LC 92-34213. 416p. 1992. 86.25 (*1-55938-469-7*) Jai Pr.
— The New Corporate Strategy. rev. ed. LC 87-23266. 288p. 1988. 29.95 (*0-471-62950-2*) Wiley.
Ansoff, H. Igor, et al, eds. From Strategic Planning to Strategic Management. LC 74-20598. (Illus.). 267p. reprint ed. pap. 82.80 (*0-8357-4607-0*, 203754000008) Bks Demand.
Ansoff, H. Igor, et al. Acquisition Behavior of U. S. Manufacturing Firms, 1946-1965. LC 79-163771. (Illus.). 160p. reprint ed. pap. 49.60 (*0-7837-6193-7*, 204591500009) Bks Demand.
Ansoff, Igor. La Estrategia en la Practica Empresarial. 2nd ed. (SPA.). 576p. (C). 1997. pap. text 32.00 (*0-201-62580-6*) Addison-Wesley.
Ansoff, Igor, et al. Implanting Strategic Management. 2nd ed. 500p. 1991. pap. 32.00 (*0-13-451881-0*) P-H.
Ansolabehere, Stephen. Going Negative. 256p. 1997. pap. 14.95 (*0-684-83711-0*) S&S Trade.
Ansolabehere, Stephen & Iyengar, Shanto. Going Negative: How Political Advertisements Shrink & Polarize the Electorate. LC 95-563. 1996. write for info. (*0-02-900732-1*) Free Pr.
— Going Negative: How Political Advertisements Shrink & Polarize the Electorate. (Illus.). 272p. 1996. 23.50 (*0-684-82284-9*) Free Pr.
Ansolabehere, Stephen, et al. The Media Game: American Politics in the Television Age. LC 92-21876. (New Topics in Politics Ser.). 248p. (C). 1992. pap. text 30.13 (*0-02-359965-0*, Macmillan Coll) P-H.
Anson. Longman Handbook: Modern Language Association(Update) 862p. (C). 1999. 41.00 (*0-321-04966-7*) Addson-Wesley Educ.
— Longman Handbook for Writers: Document Guide. (C). 1997. pap. text 10.00 (*0-673-97976-8*) Addison-Wesley.
Anson. Longman Handbook for Writers & Readers. 252p. (C). 1997. pap. text, wbk. ed. 26.73 (*0-673-98552-0*) Addison-Wesley.
Anson. Longman Handbook for Writers & Readers. (C). 1997. pap. text 13.00 (*0-673-98570-9*) Addison-Wesley.
— Longman Handbook for Writers & Readers. (C). 1997. pap. text. write for info. (*0-321-40006-2*) Addson-Wesley Educ.
— Longman Handbook for Writers & Readers. LC 97-154701. (C). 1997. pap. text. write for info. (*0-321-40007-0*) Addson-Wesley Educ.
— The Longman Handbook for Writers & Readers. 2nd ed. LC 99-30574. 979p. (C). 1999. 41.00 (*0-321-05804-6*) Addison-Wesley.
— Longman Handbook for Writers & Readers: MAC. (C). 1997. pap. text 14.80 (*0-673-98571-7*) Addison-Wesley.
— Longman Handbook for Writers & Readers-Answer Key. (C). 1997. pap. text 12.00 (*0-673-97974-1*) Addison-Wesley.
***Anson.** Longman Writers Companion. 1999. pap. 30.67 (*0-201-67713-X*) Addison-Wesley.
— The Longman Writer's Companion. LC 99-36017. 471p. (C). 1999. spiral bd. 35.00 (*0-8013-3157-9*) Longman.
Anson & Schwegler. The Longman Handbook for UIC Writers & Readers. (C). 1998. text 34.67 (*0-201-45657-5*) Addison-Wesley.
***Anson & Schwegler.** The Longman Handbook for Writers & Readers with MLA Updates. 1999. pap. text 36.00 (*0-201-57608-2*) Addison-Wesley.
Anson, Adrian C. A Ball Player's Career - Cap Anson. 31.95 (*0-8488-1540-8*) Amereon Ltd.

A

Anson, Audrey M. Breast Cancer - Treatments & Therapy Including Drugs: Index of New Information. 145p. 1997. 47.50 (0-7883-1578-1); pap. 44.50 (0-7883-1579-X) ABBE Pubs Assn.

***Anson, Bert.** The Miami Indians. (Civilization of the American Indian Ser.: Vol. 103). (Illus.). 352p. 1999. pap. 25.95 (0-8061-3197-7) U of Okla Pr.

Anson, Bert. Miami Indians. LC 74-108793. (Civilization of the American Indian Ser.: Vol. 103). (Illus.). 363p. reprint ed. 112.60 (0-8357-9735-X, 201619100002) Bks Demand.

Anson Bicentennial Committee. Anson. LC 98-86556. (Images of America Ser.). 1998. write for info. (0-7524-1259-0) Arcadia Publng.

Anson, Brian. Rolfing: Stories of Personal Empowerment. 2nd ed. LC 98-17150. (Illus.). 400p. 1998. pap. 22.95 (1-55643-293-3) North Atlantic.

Anson, Chris M., et al, eds. Writing Across the Curriculum: An Annotated Bibliography, 13. LC 93-29897. (Bibliographies & Indexes in Education Ser.: No. 13). 192p. 1993. lib. bdg. 65.00 (0-313-25960-7, Greenwood Pr) Greenwood.

Anson, Chris M. & Beach, Richard. Journals in the Classroom: Writing to Learn. 216p. (YA). (gr. 8-12). 1995. pap. text 32.95 (0-926842-33-1) CG Pubs Inc.

Anson, Chris M. & Schwegler, Robert A. The Longman Handbook for Writers & Readers. LC 96-2037. (C). 1997. text 31.75 (0-673-98550-4) Longman.

Anson, Chris M. & Wilcox, Dennis L. Field Guide to Writing. 208p. (C). 1997. pap. text 26.73 (0-06-040292-X) Addson-Wesley Educ.

— Field Guide to Writing. (C). 1997. text 11.00 (0-06-500614-3) Addson-Wesley Educ.

Anson, Chris M., jt. auth. see Farris, Christine.

Anson, Chris M., jt. ed. see Farris, Christine.

Anson, Denis K. Alternate Computer Access: A Guide to Selection. LC 96-32687. (Illus.). 280p. (C). 1996. pap. 29.95 (0-8036-0137-9) Davis Co.

Anson, Doris C., tr. see Maritain, Jacques.

Anson, Edward. How to Prepare & Write Your Employee Handbook. 2nd ed. LC 88-23334. 330p. 1988. 79.95 (0-8144-1140-1) AMACOM.

Anson, Edward M. A Civilization Primer. 3rd ed. 144p. (C). 1993. pap. text 26.00 (0-15-500261-9, Pub. by Harcourt Coll Pubs) Harcourt.

— A Civilization Primer. 4th ed. LC 97-72808. 144p. (C). 1997. 24.00 (0-15-502328-4, Pub. by Harcourt Coll Pubs) Harcourt.

Anson, Jack L. & Marchesani, Robert A., eds. Baird's Manual of American College Fraternities. 20th ed. 1000p. 1991. 59.95 (0-9637159-0-9) Bairds Manual.

Anson, John, et al. Ethnicity & Politics in Bulgaria & Israel. 272p. 1993. 66.95 (1-85628-621-5, Pub. by Avebry) Ashgate Pub Co.

***Anson, Margaret.** Personal Recollections of the Use of the Rod. 240p. 2000. mass mkt. 7.95 (1-56201-188-X, Pub. by Blue Moon Bks) Publishers Group.

Anson, Mark J. Accounting & Taxation of Derivative Instruments. 200p. 1999. 150.00 (1-883249-69-4) McGraw.

— Credit Derivatives. (Illus.). 190p. 1999. 58.00 (1-883249-61-9) F J Fabozzi.

Anson, Maud. Life's a Jubilee. large type ed. 349p. 1979. 27.99 (0-7089-0289-8) Ulverscroft.

Anson, Melanie D. Olmsted's Sudbrook - The Making of a Community. Kessler, Barry, ed. LC 97-61916. (Illus.). 1998. pap. 24.95 (0-9661031-0-6) Sudbrook Park.

Anson, R. W. Basic Cartography. 2nd ed. 160p. 1997. pap. text 52.95 (0-7506-3216-X) Buttrwrth-Heinemann.

Anson, R. W., ed. Basic Cartography for Students & Technicians, Vol. 2. 144p. 1989. text 92.00 (1-85166-249-9) Elsevier.

Anson, R. W. & Oremling, Ferdinand J., Jr., eds. Basic Cartography: For Students & Technicians - Exercise Manual. 288p. 1991. pap. text 52.95 (1-85166-590-0) Elsevier.

Anson, R. W. & Ormeling, Ferdinand J. Basic Cartography: For Students & Technicians, Vol. 3. (Illus.). 144p. (C). 1996. pap. 47.95 (0-7506-2702-6) Buttrwrth-Heinemann.

Anson, R. W. & Ormeling, Ferdinand J., eds. Basic Cartography for Students & Technicians, Vol. 1. 2nd ed. LC 93-35427. 212p. 1994. text 158.00 (0-08-042343-4, Pergamon Pr) Elsevier.

— Basic Cartography for Students & Technicians, Vol. 1. 2nd ed. LC 93-35427. (Illus.). 228p. 1994. pap. text 52.95 (0-08-042344-2, Pergamon Pr) Elsevier.

Anson, Robert S. Best Intentions: The Education & Killing of Edmund Perry. LC 87-45938. 224p. 1988. pap. 12.00 (0-394-75707-6) Vin Bks.

— Exile: The Unquite Oblivion of Richard M. Nixon. 1985. pap. 8.95 (0-671-60566-6) S&S Trade.

— War News: A Young Reporter in Indochina. 317p. 1989. 19.95 (0-685-28399-2) S&S Trade.

Anson, Ronald J., jt. ed. see Rist, Ray C.

Anson, Suzan. Bone Appetit! Gourmet Cooking for Your Dog. (Illus.). 288p. (Orig.). 1989. pap. 9.95 (0-942257-13-8) New Chapter Pr.

Anson, Tom. The Bountymen. large type ed. 244p. pap. 18.99 (0-7089-5412-X) Ulverscroft.

— Jailbird. large type ed. 224p. 1999. pap. 18.99 (0-7089-5514-2, Linford) Ulverscroft.

Anson, Tom. Plague of Gunfighters. large type ed. (Linford Western Library Ser.). 256p. 1997. pap. 16.99 (0-7089-5130-9, Linford) Ulverscroft.

Anson-Weber, Joan. The Gate of the Year. 60p. (Orig.). 1993. pap. 6.95 (0-9636264-0-X) J Anson-Weber.

— Snuffles. LC 94-38154. (Illus.). 32p. (J). (ps-7). 1994. 14.95 (0-87797-262-1) Cherokee.

Anson, William R. Anson's Law of Contract. 25th ed. Guest, Anthony G., ed. 1980. pap. write for info. (0-19-876069-8) OUP.

***Ansons, Alec M. & Davis, Helen.** Diagnosis & Management of Ocular Motility Disorders. 3rd rev. ed. (Illus.). 568p. 2000. 160.00 (0-632-04798-4) Blackwell Sci.

***Ansorge, Peter.** From Liverpool to Los Angeles. 256p. 1998. pap. 14.95 (0-571-17912-6) Faber & Faber.

Ansorge, Siegfried, et al, eds. Cellular Peptidases in Immune Functions & Diseases: Proceedings of an International Conference Held in Magdeburg, Germany, November 3-5, 1996. LC 97-21524. (Advances in Experimental Medicine & Biology Ser.: Vol. 421). 350p. (C). 1997. text 95.00 (0-306-45616-8, Kluwer Plenum) Kluwer Academic.

Ansorge, Siegfried, jt. auth. see Langner, Jhurgen.

Ansorge, Wilhelm, et al, eds. DNA Sequencing Strategies: Automated & Advanced Approaches. LC 96-9932. 202p. 1996. pap. 64.95 (0-471-13683-2) Wiley.

Anspach, Kenneth. Environmental Law & Insurance Handbook, 1997. (Clark Boardman Callaghan Environmental Law Ser.). 1997. pap. 140.00 (0-8366-1113-6) West Group.

Anspach, L. E. & Coutanche, A. M. Dictionary of Anglo-Belgian Law. 181p. 1988. reprint ed. 35.00 (0-8377-1905-4, Rothman) W S Hein.

Anspach, Ralph. The Billion Dollar Monopoly Swindle: During a David & Goliath Battle, the Inventor of the Anti-Monopoly Game Uncovers the Secret History of Monopoly. unabridged ed. LC 98-186436. 230p. 1998. pap. 15.00 (0-9666497-0-2) R Anspach.

Anspach, Renee R. Deciding Who Lives: Fateful Choices in the Intensive-Care Nursery. 1993. 45.00 (0-520-05268-4, Pub. by U CA Pr) Cal Prin Full Svc.

— Deciding Who Lives: Fateful Choices in the Intensive-Care Nursery. 1997. pap. text 17.95 (0-520-21213-4, Pub. by U CA Pr) Cal Prin Full Svc.

Anspacher, Abraham S. Tiglath Pileser Third. LC 70-158263. (Columbia University. Contributions to Oriental History & Philology Ser.: No. 5). reprint ed. 39.50 (0-404-50535-X) AMS Pr.

Anspacher, Louis K. Shakespeare As Poet & Lover. LC 73-9528. (Studies in Shakespeare: No. 24). 1973. reprint ed. lib. bdg. 75.00 (0-8383-1701-4) M S G Haskell Hse.

Anspacher, Stephen J., ed. see American Institute of Certified Public Accountants.

Anspaugh & Ezell. Teaching Today's Health. 5th ed. LC 97-22719. 600p. 1997. 60.00 (0-205-27413-7) P-H.

Anspaugh, David J. Wellness Concepts & Applications. 3rd ed. 1996. 403.75 (0-8151-0973-3) Mosby Inc.

— Wellness Concepts & Applications. 4th ed. LC 99-461819. 1999. 22.00 (0-07-039329-X) McGraw.

Ansprenger, Franz. The Dissolution of Colonial Empires. 336p. 1989. 45.00 (0-415-00838-7); pap. 16.95 (0-415-03143-5) Routledge.

Anstall, H. & Williams, B. Orthodox Worship: A Living Continuity with the Synagogue, the Temple & the Early Church. 1990. pap. 12.95 (0-937032-72-7) Light&Life Pub Co MN.

Anstall, Harold B. & Blylock, Robert C. Practical Aspects of the Transfusion Service. LC 95-40102. 335p. 1996. pap. 55.00 (0-89189-396-2) Am Soc Clinical.

Anstall, Harold B., et al. Managing Hazards in the Transfusion Service. 212p. 1993. 47.00 (0-89189-324-5) Am Soc Clinical.

Anstall, Kharalahbos. Aspects of Theosis. 27p. Date not set. pap. 4.00 (1-879038-72-2, 9042) Synaxis Pr.

Ansted, A. A Dictionary of Sea Terms. 3rd ed. (Illus.). 360p. 1985. text 35.00 (0-85174-481-8, Pub. by Brown Son & Ferguson) Sheridan.

Anstee, David J., jt. auth. see Issitt, Peter D.

Anstein Holtet, Jan & Egeland, Alv, eds. The Polar Cusp. (NATO Advanced Study Institutes Series C, Mathematical & Physical Sciences). 1985. text 195.50 (90-277-1923-3) Kluwer Academic.

Ansteinsson, J. English - Norwegian Technical Dictionary. 5th ed. (ENG & NOR.). 541p. 1991. 106.50 (82-7028-492-0) IBD Ltd.

— English-Norwegian Technical Dictionary. (ENG & NOR.). 541p. 1991. 89.95 (0-7859-7456-3, 8270284920) Fr & Eur.

— English-Norwegian Technical Dictionary. 5th ed. (ENG & NOR.). 461p. 1991. 79.95 (0-8288-6912-X, M1571) Fr & Eur.

— Norwegian-English Technical Dictionary. rev. ed. (ENG & NOR.). 223p. 1985. 125.00 (0-7859-7137-8) Fr & Eur.

— Norwegian-English Technical Dictionary. 3rd ed. (ENG & NOR.). 1990. 88.00 (0-7859-8965-X) Fr & Eur.

— Norwegian-English Technical Dictionary. 4th ed. (ENG & NOR.). 514p. 1994. 125.00 (0-8288-0647-0, M8480) Fr & Eur.

Ansteinsson, J. & Reiersen, Olav. Norwegian-English Technical Dictionary. 4th rev. ed. 514p. 1994. 85.00 (82-7028-496-3) IBD Ltd.

Anstendig, Linda & Hicks, David. Writing Through Literature. LC 95-34512. 1034p. 1995. pap. text 54.00 (0-02-303564-1, Macmillan Coll) P-H.

***Anstett, Tim.** Honorable Work: A Process for Achieving Success & Satisfaction in Your Work. LC 99-49371. 192p. 2000. pap. 14.95 (0-940262-97-5, Lindisfarne) Anthroposophic.

Anstey. Atlantic Slave Trade & British Abolition. 456p. 1993. 79.95 (0-7512-0112-X) Ashgate Pub Co.

Anstey, A. Boundary Disputes & How to Resolve Them. 72p. (C). 1990. pap. text 85.00 (0-85406-463-X, Pub. by R-I-C-S Bks) St Mut.

Anstey, A., ed. Party Walls & What to Do with Them. 127p. (C). 1988. text 75.00 (0-85406-496-6, Pub. by R-I-C-S Bks) St Mut.

Anstey, Christopher. The New Bath Guide: or The Memoirs of the B-R-D Family. iv, 173p. 1989. reprint ed. 50.00 (3-487-09132-1) G Olms Pubs.

Anstey, Henry, ed. Munimenta Academica: or Documents Illustrative of Academical Life & Studies at Oxford, 2 vols. (Rolls Ser.: No. 50). 1974. reprint ed. 140.00 (0-8115-1109-X) Periodicals Srv.

Anstey, John. Anstey's Abbeys. 120p. (C). 1987. text 60.00 (0-85406-337-4, Pub. by Surveyors Pubns) St Mut.

— Party Walls & What to Do with Them. 128p. (C). 1988. text 80.00 (0-85406-413-3, Pub. by Surveyors Pubns) St Mut.

— Rights of Light & How to Deal with Them. 114p. (C). 1988. text 85.00 (0-85406-412-5, Pub. by Surveyors Pubns) St Mut.

Anstey, M. Employee Participation & Workplace Forums. 216p. 1998. pap. 35.00 (0-7021-3907-6, Pub. by Juta & Co) Intl Spec Bk.

***Anstey, Mark.** Managing Change: Negotiating Conflict. 2nd ed. 399p. 1999. pap. 37.95 (0-7021-5066-5, Pub. by Juta & Co) Intl Spec Bk.

Anstey, Mark. Negotiating Conflict: Insights & Skills for Negotiators & Peacemakers. 401p. 1991. pap. text 44.00 (0-7021-2612-8, Pub. by Juta & Co) Intl Spec Bk.

— Practical Peacemaking: A Mediator's Handbook. 178p. 1993. pap. 24.00 (0-7021-2966-6, Pub. by Juta & Co) Intl Spec Bk.

Anstey, N. A., ed. see Jenyon, Malcolm K. & Fitch, Albert A.

Anstey, Nigel A. Seismic Prospecting Instruments Vol. 1: Signal Characteristics & Instrument Specifications. 2nd rev. ed. (Geoexploration Monographs: No. 3). (Illus.). x, 154p. 1981. 32.00 (3-443-13303-7, Pub. by Gebruder Borntraeger) Balogh.

***Anstey, Peter R.** The Philosophy of Robert Boyle. LC 99-59382. (Studies in Seventeenth-Century Philosophy). 2000. write for info. (0-415-22429-2) Routledge.

Anstey, Robert L., jt. ed. see Erwin, Douglas H.

Anstey, Roger. Britain & the Congo in the Nineteenth Century. LC 81-20224. (Illus.). 260p. 1982. reprint ed. lib. bdg. 69.50 (0-313-23366-7, ANBC, Greenwood Pr) Greenwood.

Anstey, Sandra, ed. Critical Writings on R. S. Thomas. 2nd rev. ed. 235p. 1993. 35.00 (1-85411-062-4, Pub. by Seren Bks) Dufour.

Anstey, Sandra, ed. see Thomas, R. S.

Anstey, Vera. The Economic Development of India. Wilkins, Mira, ed. LC 76-29760. (European Business Ser.). (Illus.). 1977. reprint ed. lib. bdg. 57.95 (0-405-09775-1) Ayer.

Anstie, Francis E. Stimulants & Narcotics: Their Mutual Relations. Grob, Gerald N., ed. LC 80-1212. (Addiction in America Ser.). 1981. reprint ed. lib. bdg. 38.95 (0-405-13568-8) Ayer.

Anstin, Margaret G. Voyage: A Chartbook for Career Life Planning. 192p. (C). 1996. pap. text, per. 21.95 (0-8403-2204-6) Kendall-Hunt.

Anstotz, Christoph, et al. Peter Singer in Deutschland: Zur Gefahrdung der Diskussionsfreiheit in der Wissenschaft eine Kommentierte Dokumentation. (GER.). vii, 425p. 1997. 69.95 (3-631-48014-8) P Lang Pubng.

Anstrother, F. C., ed. Old Polish Legends (Gift Edition) (Illus.). 66p. 1997. 11.95 (0-7818-0521-X) Hippocrene Bks.

Anstrumer, Richard. Are You Really Listening? (Illus.). 32p. 1999. pap. 15.00 (1-890234-06-0) High Gain Pr.

Anstruther, Godfrey. The Seminary Priests - A Dictionary of the Secular Clergy of England, 1660-1715, Vol. 3. 1976. pap. 18.50 (0-85597-116-9) Attic Pr.

— The Seminary Priests - A Dictionary of the Secular Clergy of England Vol. 2: Early Stuarts, 1603-1659. 1975. 18.50 (0-85597-082-0) Attic Pr.

Anstruther-Thomson, Clementina. Art & Man. LC 74-93314. (Essay Index Reprint Ser.). 1977. 27.95 (0-8369-1270-5) Ayer.

— Art & Man: Essays & Fragments. LC 74-93314. (Essay Index Reprint Ser.). (Illus.). 371p. reprint ed. lib. bdg. 21.00 (0-8290-0470-X) Irvington.

Anstruthor, Godfrey. The Seminary Priests - A Dictionary of the Secular Clergy of England Vol. 1: Elizabeth, 1558-1603. 448p. 1968. 18.50 (0-87921-059-1) Attic Pr.

— The Seminary Priests - A Dictionary of the Secular Clergy of England, 1718-1800, Vol. 4. LC 76-441910. 367p. 1977. pap. 18.50 (0-85597-118-5) Attic Pr.

Antai-O. Psychiatric Nursing. 1995. 125.00 (0-7216-6225-0) Harcourt.

Antai-Otong. Psychiatric Mental Health Nursing Care Plans. (C). 2002. pap. 27.75 (0-7668-1141-7) Thomson Learn.

***Antai-Otong.** Psychiatric Nursing: Biological & Behavior Concepts. (C). 2002. pap. 47.25 (0-7668-1712-1) Delmar.

Antai-Otong, Deborah, ed. Psychiatric Nursing: Biological & Behavioral Concepts. (Illus.). 1995. teacher ed. write for info. (0-7216-4925-4, W B Saunders Co) Harcrt Hlth Sci Grp.

— Psychiatric Nursing: Biological & Behavioral Concepts, Assessment & Medications Booklet. (Illus.). (C). 1995. pap. text. write for info. (0-7216-6231-5, W B Saunders Co) Harcrt Hlth Sci Grp.

Antaki, Charles. Explaining & Arguing: The Social Organizations of Accounts. 222p. 1994. 45.00 (0-8039-8605-X); pap. 14.99 (0-8039-8606-8) Sage.

Antaki, Charles, ed. Analysing Everyday Explanation: A Casebook of Methods. 256p. (C). 1988. text 45.00 (0-8039-8139-2); pap. text 17.95 (0-8039-8140-6) Sage.

Antaki, Charles & Brewin, Chris R., eds. Attributions & Psychological Change: Application of Attributional Theories to Clinical & Educational Practice. LC 81-71575. (Illus.). 1982. text 103.00 (0-12-058780-7) Acad Pr.

Antaki, Charles & Widdicombe, Sue. Identities in Talk. LC 98-60740. 224 p. 1998. write for info. (0-7619-5061-3) Sage.

Antal, David, tr. see Glaeser, Bernhard.

Antal, David R., jt. auth. see Kossuth, Karen C.

Antal, Frederick. Florentine Painting & Its Social Background. (Studies in Art History Paperbacks). (Illus.). 576p. 1986. pap. 26.50 (0-674-30668-6) Belknap Pr.

Antal, John. Armor Attacks: The Tank Platoon: An Interactive Exercise in Small-Unit. 331p. 1991. reprint ed. pap. 19.95 (0-89141-383-9, Pub. by Presidio Pr) Natl Bk Netwk.

***Antal, John.** Proud Legions. (Illus.). 389p. 2000. mass mkt. 6.99 (0-515-12784-1, Jove) Berkley Pub.

Antal, John. Proud Legions. LC 98-45437. (Illus.). 368p. 1999. 24.95 (0-89141-667-6, Pub. by Presidio Pr) Natl Bk Netwk.

Antal, John F. Combat Team - The Captains' War: An Interactive Exercise in Company-Level Command in Battle. LC 98-9324. 384p. 1998. pap. 17.95 (0-89141-635-8) Presidio Pr.

— Infantry Combat - The Rifle Platoon: An Interactive Exercise in Small-Unit Tactics & Leadership. LC 95-30. (Illus.). 304p. 1995. pap. 18.95 (0-89141-536-X) Presidio Pr.

Antal-Mokos, Zoltan. Privatisation, Politics & Economic Performance in Hungary. LC 97-15775. 248p. (C). 1998. text 59.95 (0-521-59339-5) Cambridge U Pr.

Antal, Paul, tr. see Lagarce, Jean-Luc.

Antalffy, Gyula. Basic Problems of State & Society. 188p. (C). 1974. 35.00 (963-05-0010-8, Pub. by Akade Kiado) St Mut.

Antalffy, Les, et al, eds. High Pressure Technology 1997: Proceedings ASME Pressure Vessels & Piping Conference (1997, Orlando, FL) LC 97-72853. (PVP Ser.: Vol. 344). 91p. 1997. pap. 72.00 (0-7918-1560-9) ASME.

Antall, J. Pictorial History of European Medicine & Pharmaceutics. 1981. 55.00 (0-7855-1605-0) St Mut.

***Antall, Richard C.** Witnesses to Calvary: Reflections on the Seven Last Words of Jesus. LC 99-75030. 160p. 2000. pap. 8.95 (0-87973-340-3) Our Sunday Visitor.

Antao, B. & Rutenbar, R. A., eds. Computer-Aided Design of Analog Integrated Circuits. 400p. 1999. 99.95 (0-7803-1150-7, PC5621-QOE) Inst Electrical.

Antao, Brian N., ed. Modeling & Simulation of Mixed Analog-Digital Systems. LC 96-8201. (Kluwer International Series in Engineering & Computer Science). 136p. (C). 1996. text 103.00 (0-7923-9738-X) Kluwer Academic.

Antar, Basil N. & Nuotio-Antar, Vappu S. Fundamentals of Low Gravity Fluid Dynamics & Heat Transfer. LC 93-11613. 320p. 1993. boxed set 147.95 (0-8493-8913-5) CRC Pr.

Antar, Johanna, jt. auth. see Edeiken, Louise.

Antas, Luiz M. Dicionario de Termos Tecnicos Ingles-Portugues. 5th ed. (ENG & POR.). 1980. pap. 110.00 (0-685-65229-7, F11375) Fr & Eur.

— Dicionario de Termos Tecnicos Portugues-Ingles. 3rd ed. (ENG & POR.). 335p. 1991. pap. 75.00 (0-7859-0346-1, F60022) Fr & Eur.

Antas, Mendes L. Dictionary of Technical Terms: English-Portuguese. (ENG & POR.). 952p. 1980. 150.00 (0-8288-3964-6) Fr & Eur.

— Dictionary of Technical Terms: Portuguese-English. (ENG & POR.). 335p. 1983. 150.00 (0-8288-4021-0) Fr & Eur.

Antcliff, A. J., jt. auth. see Kerridge, G. H.

Antczak. Presenting Young Adult Science Fiction. 1998. 22.95 (0-8057-4152-6, Twyne) Mac Lib Ref.

Antczak-Bouckoms, et al. Clinical Research As the Basis of Clinical Practice. Vig, Katherine D. & Vig, Peter S., eds. (Craniofacial Growth Ser.: Vol. 25). (Illus.). 222p. 1991. 55.00 (0-929921-21-6) UM CHGD.

Antczak, Frederick J. Thought & Character: The Rhetoric of Democratic Education. LC 85-2430. (Illus.). 250p. 1985. reprint ed. pap. 77.50 (0-608-00026-4, 206079200006) Bks Demand.

Antczak, Janice. Science Fiction: The Mythos of a New Romance. Hannigan, Jane Anne, ed. LC 84-14726. (Diversity & Direction in Children's Literature Ser.). 233p. 1985. 38.50 (0-918212-43-X) Neal-Schuman.

Antek, Samuel. This Was Toscanini. 1980. 34.50 (0-8149-0018-6) Random.

Antel, Jack P., et al. Clinical Neuroimmunology. LC 97-2678. (Illus.). 1997. 195.00 (0-86542-411-X) Blackwell Sci.

Antelava, H. G. Abbreviated Turkish-Russian Dictionary of New Words. (RUS & TUR.). 95p. 1978. pap. 19.95 (0-8288-4859-9, M9054) Fr & Eur.

Antell, Karen, ed. see Richardson, Kathy.

Antelman, Gordon. Elementary Bayesian Statistics. Madansky, Albert & McCulloch, Robert, eds. LC 97-14359. 480p. 1997. 120.00 (1-85898-504-8) E Elgar.

Antelman, Marvin S. The Encyclopedia of Chemical Electrode Potentials. 302p. 1982. 79.50 (0-306-40903-8, Plenum Trade) Perseus Pubng.

Antelme, Robert. The Human Race. Haight, Jeffrey & Mahler, Annie, trs. from FRE. LC 91-61532. 304p. 1991. 29.95 (0-910395-77-2) Marlboro Pr.

— The Human Race. Haight, Jeffrey & Mahler, Annie, trs. 312p. 1998. pap. 16.95 (0-8101-6061-7, Marlboro) Northwestern U Pr.

Antelo, Lisa, jt. auth. see Wyse, Lois.

Antelo-Suarez, Sandra. Space of Time. 1994. pap. 17.50 (1-879128-07-1) Americas Soc.

Antenucci, John C., et al. Geographic Information Systems: A Guide to the Technology. (Illus.). 204p. 1991. text 62.95 (0-442-00756-6) Chapman & Hall.

Antes, G. & Eggemann, F. Small Bowel Radiology. (Illus.). 210p. 1988. 139.00 (0-387-15263-6) Spr-Verlag.

An Asterisk (*) at the beginning of an entry indicates that the title is appearing for the first time.

A

Antes, H. & Panagiotopoulos, P. D. The Boundary Integral Approach to Static & Dynamic Contact Problems: Equality & Inequality Methods. LC 92-25605. (International Series of Numerical Mathematics: Vol. 108). xv, 307p. 1992. 137.00 (*0-8176-2592-5*, Pub. by Birkhauser) Princeton Arch.

Antes, Peter, jt. auth. see Graf, Peter.

Antes, Richard S., et al. Federal Income Taxation of Life Insurance Companies, 3 vols., Set. 1984. ring bd. 630.00 (*0-8205-1693-7*) Bender.

Antes, Richard S., jt. auth. see Lerner, Herbert J.

Antheil, George. Bad Boy of Music. LC 81-1169. (Illus.). 378p. 1981. lib. bdg. 45.00 (*0-306-76084-3*) Da Capo.

— Bad Boy of Music. LC 90-3331. (Illus.). 378p. 1990. reprint ed. pap. 14.95 (*0-573-60604-8*) S French Trade.

— Bad Boy of Music: Music Book Index. 295p. 1993. reprint ed. lib. bdg. 79.00 (*0-7812-9585-8*) Rprt Serv.

Anthenat, Kathy S. Fantastic Family Gatherings: Tried & True Ideas for Large & Small Family Reunions. (Illus.). 198p. (Orig.). 1995. pap. text 29.00 (*0-7884-0229-3*) Heritage Bk.

Antherjanam, Lalithambika. Cast Me Out If You Will. Krishnankutty, Gita, tr. & intro. by. LC 97-32979. 194p. 1998. pap. 11.95 (*1-55861-188-6*) Feminist Pr.

— Cast Me Out If You Will. Krishnankutty, Gita, tr. & intro. by. LC 97-32979. 194p. 1998. lib. bdg. 28.00 (*1-55861-187-8*) Feminist Pr.

Anthes, Richard A. Meteorology. 7th ed. LC 96-17574. 214p. (C). 1996. pap. text 43.00 (*0-13-231044-9*) P-H.

— Tropical Cyclones: Their Evolution, Structure & Effects. (Meteorological Monograph: Vol. 19, No. 41). (Illus.). 208p. 1982. 40.00 (*0-933876-54-8*) Am Meteorological.

Anthes, Richard A., jt. auth. see Cotton, William R.

Anthes, William L., et al. How to Make Adoption an Affordable Option. (Illus.). 76p. 1999. reprint ed. pap. text 20.00 (*0-7881-7584-X*) DIANE Pub.

***Anthias, Flora & Lazaridis, Gabriella, eds.** Into the Margins: Migration & Exclusion in Southern Europe. (Perspectives on Europe Ser.). 222p. 1999. text 65.95 (*1-84014-116-6*, Pub. by Ashgate Pub) Ashgate Pub Co.

Anthias, Floya. Ethnicity, Class, Gender & Migration: Greek Cypriots in Britain. (Research in Ethnic Relations Ser.). 166p. 1992. 61.95 (*1-85628-038-1*, Pub. by Avebry) Ashgate Pub Co.

Anthias, Floya & Kelly, Michael P., eds. Sociological Debates: Thinking about "The Social" LC 97-189290. 454p. (C). 1996. pap. 29.00 (*1-874529-55-8*, Pub. by Greenwich Univ Pr) NYU Pr.

***Anthias, Floya & Lazaridis, Gabriella, eds.** Gender & Migration in Southern Europe: Women on the Move. (Mediterranea Ser.). 224p. 2000. 65.00 (*1-85973-231-3*, Pub. by Berg Pubs); pap. 19.50 (*1-85973-236-4*, Pub. by Berg Pubs) NYU Pr.

Anthias, Floya & Yuval-Davis, Nira. Racialized Boundaries: Race, Nation, Gender, Colour & Class & the Anti-Racist Struggle. 240p. (C). 1993. pap. 22.99 (*0-415-10388-6*) Routledge.

Anthimos. Ecumenism or Truth: The Reply of the Orthodox Church to Roman Catholic Overtures on Reunion. 1990. pap. 1.95 (*0-89981-117-5*) Eastern Orthodox.

— Reply of the Orthodox Church to Roman Catholic Overtures on Reunion. enl. rev. ed. 64p. 1986. pap. 2.00 (*0-913026-62-X*) St Nectarios.

Anthimus. On the Observance of Foods. Grant, Mark, ed. Orig. Title: De Observatione Ciborum. 142p. 1996. pap. 20.00 (*0-907325-75-0*, Pub. by Prospect) Food Words.

Anthimus, jt. auth. see Holy Synod of the Ecumenical Patriarchate Staff.

Anthologia Graeca Selections. Poems from the Greek Anthology, in English Paraphrase. Fitts, Dudley, tr. LC 78-13574. 141p. 1978. reprint ed. lib. bdg. 49.50 (*0-313-21017-9*, AGPG, Greenwood Pr) Greenwood.

***Anthology of Teen Essays Staff.** Aids Why Should I Care? Teens Across America Speak Out. rev. ed. Starr, Robert, ed. 288p. (YA). (gr. 9-12). 1999. pap., teacher ed. 16.95 (*0-9673441-0-7*, Pub. by People Taking) Alamo Sq Dist.

Anthology of Winning Poets Staff. A Book of the Year 1995. Ottenstein, Claire & Poetry Society of Texas Staff, eds. (Illus.). 224p. (Orig.). 1995. pap. 7.50 (*1-878149-33-4*) Counterpoint Pub.

Anthology Staff. Bad Dreams/Good Dreams: A Collection of New Short Fiction. LC 94-72715. 248p. (Orig.). 1995. pap. 9.95 (*1-885884-13-3*) Cormorant Pr.

— China Anthology: Seventy Years of Shanghai "Tiffin" Perspectives. Tsuan, Victor T. & Chung, Charles C., eds. LC 96-84511. 160p. (Orig.). 1996. pap. 25.00 (*0-9639310-2-4*) COMPASS Bks.

— Joyful Noise. Kempher, Ruth M., ed. (Friendly Creatures Ser.: Vol. 2). (Illus.). 112p. (Orig.). 1996. pap. write for info. (*1-888832-00-2*) Kings Estate.

— Portfolio: Essays for Critical Thinking & Writing. Scanlan, Patrick, ed. LC 99-193995. 290p. 1998. pap. text 24.95 (*0-917962-44-3*) T H Peek.

Anthology-64 Staff. Christmas Blues: Behind the Holiday Mask: an Anthology. Gatuskin, Zelda L. et al, eds. LC 95-79549. (Illus.). 352p. 1995. pap. 15.00 (*0-938513-18-4*) Amador Pubs.

Antholt, Charles H. Getting Agriculture Ready for the 21st Century in Asia: Technical Change & Institutional Modernization in Agriculture. LC 93-14540. (Technical Paper, 0253-7494; Asia Technical Department Ser.: No. 217). 55p. 1994. pap. 22.00 (*0-8213-2510-8*, 12510) World Bank.

Anthon, Charles. The Works of Charles Anthon, 1797-1867, Set. 1987. reprint ed. lib. bdg. 600.00 (*0-685-18598-2*) Rprt Serv.

Anthoney, Terence R. Neuroanatomy & the Neurologic Exam: A Thesaurus of Synonyms, Similar-Sounding Non-Synonyms, & Terms of Variable Meaning. LC 93-13864. 656p. 1993. boxed set 131.95 (*0-8493-8631-4*, QM541) CRC Pr.

Anthoni, U., jt. auth. see Christophersen, C.

Anthonioz, Genevieve de Gaulle. The Dawn of Hope: A Memoir of Ravensbruck & Beyond. LC 99-38018. 128p. 1999. 14.95 (*1-55970-498-5*, Pub. by Arcade Pub Inc) Time Warner.

Anthony. Human Resource Management. 3rd ed. LC 98-87427. (C). 1998. text 81.00 (*0-03-022377-6*) Harcourt Coll Pubs.

Anthony, et al. Vaya!, Level 2. 1992. pap. 23.95 (*0-17-439157-9*) Heinle & Heinle.

Anthony, Albert S., jt. ed. see Brinton, Daniel G.

Anthony, Alberta P., jt. auth. see Kahananui, Dorothy M.

Anthony, Alfred K. Woe Is Me. 48p. 1999. pap. write for info. (*0-9672186-0-8*, 001) Passport Pr.

Anthony, Allen. Columbus, KY As the Nation's Capital: Legend or Near Reality? (Illus.). 170p. (Orig.). 1994. pap. 14.95 (*0-9625865-1-X*, Pub. by River Microstudies) Herveys Bklink.

— River at the Door: Unusual Experiences in Remote Areas. (Illus.). 143p. 1987. reprint ed. 13.95 (*0-9625865-0-1*, Pub. by River Microstudies) Herveys Bklink.

Anthony, Ann, jt. ed. see Adams, Carolyn E.

Anthony, Anne. Orienteering Handbook. (Illus.). 48p. 1981. pap. 5.95 (*0-88839-047-5*) Hancock House.

Anthony, Becky. Western Images, Vol. 2. (Illus.). 60p. 1998. pap. 10.50 (*1-56770-436-0*) S Scheewe Pubns.

***Anthony, Bendell.** Never in Anger. 1999. 40.00 (*0-7528-1796-5*, Pub. by Orion Pubng Grp) Trafalgar.

Anthony, Bertha W. Williams Vol. II: Roger Williams of Providence, R. I. (Illus.). 213p. 1991. reprint ed. pap. 31.00 (*0-8328-2194-2*); reprint ed. lib. bdg. 41.00 (*0-8328-2193-4*) Higginson Bk Co.

Anthony, Bertha W. & Weeden, Harriett W. Williams: Roger Williams of Providence, R. I. (Illus.). 220p. 1991. reprint ed. pap. 34.00 (*0-8328-2192-6*); reprint ed. lib. bdg. 44.00 (*0-8328-2191-8*) Higginson Bk Co.

Anthony, Brian & Edmonds, Andy. Smile When the Raindrops Fall: The Story of Charley Chase. LC 97-25443. (Filmmakers Ser.). 283p. 1997. 49.95 (*0-8108-3377-8*) Scarecrow.

***Anthony, C.** My Son, My Son. 1998. text 35.00 (*0-7195-5416-0*, Pub. by John Murray) Trafalgar.

Anthony, C. L. Touch Wood: A Play. 128p. 1934. 9.95 (*0-910278-67-9*) Boulevard.

Anthony, Camille, jt. auth. see Anthony, William A.

Anthony, Carl S. America's Most Influential First Ladies. rev. ed. LC 92-18444. (Profiles Ser.). (Illus.). 160p. (YA). (gr. 5-12). 1997. lib. bdg. 18.95 (*1-881508-00-5*) Oliver Pr MN.

— As We Remember Her: Jacqueline Kennedy Onassis in the Words of Her Friends & Family. LC 96-47518. (Illus.). 384p. 1997. 30.00 (*0-06-017690-3*) HarpC.

— First Ladies, Vol. 1. LC 91-41976. (Illus.). 688p. 1992. pap. 17.00 (*0-688-11272-2*, Quil) HarperTrade.

— First Ladies, Vol. 2. 1993. pap. 17.00 (*0-688-12575-1*, Quil) HarperTrade.

***Anthony, Carl S.** Florence Harding: The First Lady, the Jazz Age & the Death of America's Most Scandalous President. (Illus.). 672p. 1999. reprint ed. pap. 17.00 (*0-688-16975-9*, Quil) HarperTrade.

Anthony, Carl Sferrazza. Florence Harding: The First Lady, the Jazz Age, & the Death of America's Most Scandalous President. LC 97-49955. (Illus.). 544p. 1998. 30.00 (*0-688-07794-3*, Wm Morrow) Morrow Avon.

***Anthony, Carl Sierrazza.** America's First Families: An Inside View of 200 Years of Private Life in the White House. (Illus.). 2000. pap. 18.00 (*0-684-86442-8*, Touchstone) S&S Trade Pap.

Anthony, Carmen. Getting Married after 40: Advice & Inspiration from 100 Women Who Found Good Men & Happy Marriages. LC 98-31837. 256p. 1999. pap. 12.95 (*1-58062-115-5*) Adams Media.

Anthony, Carol K. Guide to the I Ching. 3rd rev. ed. 336p. 1988. pap. 14.95 (*0-9603832-4-7*) Anthony Pub Co.

— Love, an Inner Connection: Based on Principles Drawn from the I Ching. 168p. (Orig.). 1993. pap. 12.95 (*0-9603832-6-3*) Anthony Pub Co.

— The Other Way: Meditation Experiences Based on the I Ching. 288p. (Orig.). 1990. pap. 12.95 (*0-9603832-5-5*) Anthony Pub Co.

***Anthony, Carol K.** The Philosophy of the I Ching 2nd exp. ed. LC 99-198017. xi, 216 p. 1998. write for info. (*0-9603832-2-0*) Anthony Pub Co.

Anthony, Carol K., ed. see Gottner-Abendroth, Heide, et al.

Anthony, Catherine H. Connoisseur's Collection of 6" Quilt Blocks. LC 97-6512. (Illus.). 80p. 1997. reprint ed. pap. text 6.95 (*0-486-29674-1*) Dover.

Anthony, Catherine P., jt. auth. see Thibodeau, Gary A.

Anthony, Charles L. Genealogy of the Anthony Family from 1495 to 1904, Traced from William Anthony. (Illus.). 379p. 1988. reprint ed. pap. 57.00 (*0-8328-0129-1*); reprint ed. lib. bdg. 65.00 (*0-8328-0128-3*) Higginson Bk Co.

Anthony, Christopher, ed. Bacterial Energy Transduction. 517p. 1988. text 104.00 (*0-12-058815-3*) Acad Pr.

Anthony, Christopher, ed. see Hart, Jo & Edelstein, David.

Anthony, Constance G. Mechanization & Maize: Agriculture & the Politics of Technology Transfer in East Africa. (Political Economy of International Change Ser.). 192p. 1988. text 44.00 (*0-231-06596-5*) Col U Pr.

***Anthony, David, ed.** I Found It! Vol. 1: Evidence of the Human Condition. unabridged ed. (Illus.). 144p. 1999. pap. 9.95 (*0-9667339-1-6*) PULP WA.

Anthony, Denis. Health on the Internet. LC 96-15920. 240p. (Orig.). 1996. pap. text 29.95 (*0-632-04072-6*, Pub. by Blckwll Scitfc UK) Blackwell Sci.

— Understanding Advanced Statistics: A Guide for Nurses & Health Care Researchers. LC 98-3310. 1999. write for info. (*0-443-05933-0*, W B Saunders Co) Harcrt Hlth Sci Grp.

Anthony, Diana. The Ornamental Vegetable Garden. (Illus.). 120p. 1999. pap. 19.95 (*1-894020-55-3*) Warwick Publ.

Anthony, Dick, jt. auth. see Robbins, Thomas.

Anthony, Don. A Strategy for British Sport. 1980. 55.00 (*0-7735-0531-8*, Pub. by McG-Queens Univ Pr) CUP Services.

Anthony, Dorothy. Legendary Bells Vol. II: World of Bells. (Illus.). 50p. (Orig.). 1997. pap. 13.95 (*0-9607944-9-2*) World of Bells.

Anthony, Dorothy M. Bell Tidings. (Illus.). 52p. 1987. 9.95 (*0-9607944-4-1*) World of Bells.

— More Bell Lore. (World of Bells Ser.). (Illus.). 1993. ring bd. 11.95 (*0-9607944-7-6*) World of Bells.

— World of Bells, Vol. 5. (Illus.). 50p. 1984. 8.95 (*0-9607944-3-3*) World of Bells.

***Anthony, E.** A Friend Indeed. 48p. (J). 1999. pap. 8.50 (*1-890622-71-0*) Leathers Pub.

Anthony, E., jt. auth. see Snelling, Henry H.

Anthony, E. J., jt. auth. see Foulkes, S. H.

Anthony, E. James & Benedek, Therese, eds. Depression & Human Existence. 568p. 1975. 30.00 (*0-316-04371-0*) Little.

— Parenthood: Its Psychology & Psychopathology. 648p. 1996. pap. 60.00 (*0-7657-0012-3*) Aronson.

— Parenthood: Its Psychology & Psychopathology. LC 75-112005. 650p. 1970. 33.00 (*0-316-04370-2*, Little Brwn Med Div) Lppncott W & W.

Anthony, E. James & Cohler, Bertram J., eds. The Invulnerable Child. LC 86-27120. (Psychiatry Ser.). 432p. 1987. lib. bdg. 49.00 (*0-89862-227-1*) Guilford Pubns.

Anthony, E. James & Gilpin, Doris C., eds. Clinical Faces of Childhood, Set, Vol. I & II. LC 94-72350. 608p. 1994. pap. 75.00 (*1-56821-332-8*) Aronson.

— Clinical Faces of Childhood Volume I: The Oppositional Child, The Inhibited Child, The Depressed Child. LC 94-72350. 272p. 1994. pap. text 25.00 (*1-56821-334-4*) Aronson.

— Clinical Faces of Childhood Volume II: The Hysterical Child, The Anxious Child, The Borderline Child. LC 94-72350. 336p. 1994. pap. text 25.00 (*1-56821-335-2*) Aronson.

Anthony, Earl. Spitting in the Wind. LC 89-24310. 208p. 1990. pap. 18.95 (*0-915677-45-8*) Roundtable Pub.

Anthony, Earl & Taylor, Dawson. Winning Bowling. LC 77-75718. (Winning Ser.). (Illus.). 194p. 1977. pap. 10.95 (*0-8092-7791-3*) NTC Contemp Pub Co.

— Winning Bowling. (Illus.). 208p. 1994. pap. 12.95 (*0-8092-3526-9*, 352690, Contemporary Bks) NTC Contemp Pub Co.

Anthony, Edd. Healing Life's Journey. 132p. (C). 1992. student ed. 10.95 (*1-881586-04-9*) Canticle Cass.

— A Time for Prayer: Daily Prayer Journal. (Illus.). 212p. 1993. student ed. 10.95 (*1-881586-05-7*) Canticle Cass.

Anthony, Edward. Thy Rod & Staff: New Light on the Flagellatory Impulse. (Illus.). 323p. 1996. pap. 14.95 (*0-349-10709-2*) Trafalgar.

Anthony, Edward F., ed. see Ohio Math Project, Inc. Staff.

Anthony, Edwin. The 21st Century Pedigree Handbook. 1998. 75.00 (*0-9662925-0-2*) E C Anthony.

Anthony, Elizabeth. Airbrushing for Nails. (NAILS). 128p. 1997. pap. 29.95 (*1-56253-270-7*) Thomson Learn.

Anthony, Elwyn J., et al, eds. The Child in His Family, Vol. 4. LC RJ0499.. 685p. reprint ed. pap. 200.00 (*0-608-08144-2*, 205518100011) Bks Demand.

Anthony, Evelyn. Bloodstones. 384p. 1996. mass mk. 7.99 (*0-552-14241-7*) Bantam.

— Bloodstones. large type ed. LC 95-14158. 655p. 1995. 25.95 (*0-7862-0458-3*) Thorndike Pr.

— Exposure. large type ed. LC 94-7548. 486p. 1994. lib. bdg. 23.95 (*0-8161-7429-6*, G K Hall Lrg Type) Mac Lib Ref.

— The French Bride. large type ed. 432p. 1991. reprint ed. lib. bdg. 21.95 (*1-56054-315-9*) Thorndike Pr.

— The Legacy. LC 98-17591. 361 p. 1998. write for info. (*0-7540-2118-1*) Chivers N Amer.

***Anthony, Evelyn.** Mission to Malaspiga. large type ed. LC 00-35833. 370p. 2000. lib. bdg. 27.95 (*1-58547-042-2*) Ctr Point Pubg.

Anthony, Evelyn. The Relic. large type ed. (General Ser.). 376p. 1992. pap. 16.95 (*0-8161-5380-9*, G K Hall Lrg Type) Mac Lib Ref.

— The Scarlet Thread. large type ed. LC 90-22836. 658p. 1991. lib. bdg. 15.95 (*1-56054-994-7*) Thorndike Pr.

— The Scarlet Thread. large type ed. LC 90-22836. 658p. 1991. reprint ed. lib. bdg. 20.95 (*1-56054-096-6*) Thorndike Pr.

Anthony, Evelyn. The Tamarind Seed. 1995. 32.00 (*0-09-108040-1*, Pub. by Ebury Pr) Random.

Anthony, F. Patt, jt. auth. see Honeycutt, Fred L., Jr.

Anthony, Farid R. Questions & Answers on Immigration in Britain. LC 97-112132. 192p. 1996. pap. 26.50 (*0-7146-4272-X*, Pub. by F Cass Pubs) Intl Spec Bk.

— Questions & Answers on Immigration in Britain. LC 97-112132. 163p. 1996. 35.00 (*0-7146-4781-0*, Pub. by F Cass Pubs) Intl Spec Bk.

Anthony, Francis. Love Chef Cooks Pasta. LC 97-48319. (Illus.). 224p. 1998. 20.00 (*0-688-14969-3*, Hearst) Hearst Commns.

Anthony, G. H. Tavistock, Launceston & Princetown Railways. 104p. (C). 1985. 39.00 (*0-85361-223-4*) St Mut.

Anthony, Gary. Dirty Talk: Diary of a Phone Sex Mistress. LC 97-32602. 336p. 1998. 25.95 (*1-57392-188-2*) Prometheus Bks.

Anthony, Gene. The Summer of Love. 170p. 1995. 19.95 (*0-86719-421-9*) Last Gasp.

Anthony, Geraldine. A Vision of Service: Celebrating the Sisters of Charity. LC 97-20334. 304p. 1997. pap. 16.95 (*1-55612-972-6*, LL1972) Sheed & Ward WI.

Anthony, Gloria M. Echoes in a Shell. LC 74-77317. 1974. pap. 2.95 (*0-913748-04-8*) Orovan Bks.

Anthony, Govinda. Management Control Systems. 9th ed. LC 97-21861. 1997. text 44.12 (*0-256-16878-4*, Irwn McGrw-H) McGrw-H Hghr Educ.

Anthony, Greg. The Science Project Worksheet System. unabridged ed. 55p. (J). (gr. 5-10). 1999. 15.95 (*1-891022-03-2*) Showboard.

Anthony, Ian. The Future of the Defence Industries in Central & Eastern Europe. (SIPRI Research Reports: No. 7). (Illus.). 152p. 1994. pap. text 28.00 (*0-19-829189-2*) OUP.

Anthony, Ian. The Future of the Defence Industries in Central & Eastern Europe. (SIPRI Research Reports: No. 7). (Illus.). 152p. 1994. 45.00 (*0-19-829184-1*) OUP.

— The Naval Arms Trade. (SIPRI Strategic Issue Papers). (Illus.). 232p. 1990. text 38.00 (*0-19-829137-X*) OUP.

Anthony, Ian, ed. Arms Trade Regulations. (SIPRI Publication Ser.). (Illus.). 272p. 1991. text 59.00 (*0-19-829158-2*) OUP.

— Russia & the Arms Trade. (Illus.). 318p. 1998. text 65.00 (*0-19-829278-3*) OUP.

Anthony, J. & Kaye, P. Notes for the DRCOG. 3rd ed. (Illus.). 215p. 1995. pap. write for info. (*0-443-04713-8*) Church.

Anthony, James. French Baroque Mast. rev. ed. 1997. pap. 15.95 (*0-393-30356-X*) Norton.

— Twisted Metal 2: Unauthorized Game Secrets. LC 97-65237. 96p. 1997. per. 12.99 (*0-7615-1081-8*) Prima Pub.

Anthony, James R. French Baroque Music from Beaujoyeulx to Rameau. LC 96-38352. 1997. 39.95 (*1-57467-021-2*, Amadeus Pr) Timber.

Anthony, James R., ed. see Lalande, Michel R.

Anthony, James R., ed. see Pignolet De Monteclair, Michel.

***Anthony, Jay.** Children's Country Trilogy. (Illus.). 39p. (J). (gr. 3-6). 2000. pap. 5.95 (*0-533-13059-X*) Vantage.

Anthony, Joby M., ed. In Eves' Circles. (Notes Ser.: Vol. 34). 220p. 1994. pap. text 8.00 (*0-88385-088-5*, NTE-34) Math Assn.

Anthony, John. Derbyshire. (Country Guide Ser.: Vol. 6). (Illus.). 56p. 12.50 (*0-7478-0048-0*) Shire Pubns.

— Discovering Period Gardens. 1989. pap. 25.00 (*0-7478-0168-1*, Pub. by Shire Pubns) St Mut.

***Anthony, John.** Discovering Period Gardens. (Handbook Ser.: No. 129). (Illus.). 112p. 1999. pap. 9.50 (*0-7478-0340-4*, Pub. by Shire Pubns) Parkwest Pubns.

Anthony, John. Joseph Paxton. (Lifelines Ser.: No. 21). (Illus.). 48p. 1989. pap. 7.50 (*0-85263-208-8*, Pub. by Shire Pubns) Parkwest Pubns.

— The Renaissance Garden in Britain. (Garden History Ser.: No. 4). (Illus.). 96p. 1989. pap. 10.50 (*0-7478-0130-4*, Pub. by Shire Pubns) Parkwest Pubns.

— Sandbag, Stage Left: or One Dead Dolly. 80p. 1996. pap. 5.00 (*0-87440-031-7*) Bakers Plays.

Anthony, John D. Historical & Cultural Dictionary of the Sultanate of Oman & the Emirates of Eastern Arabia. LC 76-42216. (Historical & Cultural Dictionaries of Asia Ser.: No. 9). 144p. 1976. 21.00 (*0-8108-0975-3*) Scarecrow.

— U. S. - Arab Relations: The Iran-Iraq War & the Gulf Cooperation Council, No. 12. (Orig.). 1984. pap. 2.00 (*0-916729-10-9*) Natl Coun Arab.

Anthony, John W., et al. Handbook of Mineralogy Vol. 2: Silica, Silicates. 904p. 1995. text 144.00 (*0-9622097-1-6*) Mineral Data Pub.

— Handbook of Mineralogy Vol. 3: Halides, Hydroxides, Oxides. 628p. 1997. 100.00 (*0-9622097-2-4*) Mineral Data Pub.

***Anthony, John W., et al.** Handbook of Mineralogy Vol. 4: Arsenates, Phosphates, Vanadates. 680p. 2000. 108.00 (*0-9622097-3-2*) Mineral Data Pub.

Anthony, John W., et al. Handbook of Mineralogy, Vol. 1: Elements, Sulfides, Sulfosalts. 588p. 1990. text 94.00 (*0-9622097-0-8*) Mineral Data Pub.

— The Mineralogy of Arizona. 3rd ed. Wilson, Wendell E., ed. LC 94-18765. (Illus.). 508p. 1995. pap. 37.00 (*0-8165-1555-7*) U of Ariz Pr.

— The Mineralogy of Arizona. 3rd ed. Wilson, Wendell E., ed. LC 94-18765. (Illus.). 508p. 1995. 77.00 (*0-8165-1579-4*) U of Ariz Pr.

Anthony, Joseph. The Dandelion Seed. (Illus.). 36p. (J). (ps-5). 1997. 16.95 (*1-883220-66-1*); pap. 7.95 (*1-883220-67-X*) Dawn CA.

***Anthony, Joseph.** Dandelion Seed. 1999. pap. text 15.65 (*0-613-06547-6*) Econo-Clad Bks.

— In a Nutshell. LC 99-12165. 36p. (J). (ps-5). 1999. 16.95 (*1-883220-99-8*) Dawn CA.

Anthony, Joseph. In a Nutshell. LC 99-12165. (Sharing Nature with Children Book Ser.). (Illus.). 32p. (J). (ps-5). 1999. pap. 7.95 (*1-883220-98-X*) Dawn CA.

— Kiplinger's Working for Yourself. 2nd ed. rev. (Illus.). 343p. 1995. pap. 15.00 (*0-8129-2645-5*) Kiplinger Bks.

***Anthony, Joseph A.** Dandelion Seed. 1999. 13.40 (*0-606-16436-7*, Pub. by Turtleback) Demco.

***Anthony, Joseph M.** Blood God. 364p. 2000. pap. 19.95 (*0-595-09344-2*) iUniversecom.

Anthony, Juliette, jt. auth. see Farmer, Steven.

Anthony, K. H., ed. see Seventh International Symposium on Continuum Model.

Anthony, Katharine S. Louisa May Alcott. LC 77-2388. 304p. 1977. reprint ed. lib. bdg. 35.00 (*0-8371-9552-7*, ANLMA, Greenwood Pr) Greenwood.

— Margaret Fuller: A Psychological Biography. (BCL1-PS American Literature Ser.). 223p. 1992. reprint ed. lib. bdg. 79.00 (*0-7812-6818-4*) Rprt Serv.

Anthony, Kenny. The Legal Framework of Education in the Organization of Eastern Caribbean States (OECS) LC 93-44090. (Coleccion Interamer Ser.: No. 35). 1994. write for info. (*0-8270-3301-X*) OAS.

A

*__Anthony, Kitty.__ The King's Castles. 101p. (J). (ps-3). 2000. pap. 7.99 (*0-85151-777-3*) Banner of Truth.
Anthony, L. J., ed. see Line, Maurice B.
Anthony, Laura. Baby Business. 1997. per. 3.25 (*0-373-19240-1*, 1-19240-0) Silhouette.
— Bride of a Texas Trueblood. 1998. per. 3.50 (*0-373-19285-1*, 1-19285-5) Silhouette.
— Honey of a Husband. (Romance Ser.). 1998. per. 3.50 (*0-373-19322-X*, 1-19322-6) Silhouette.
— I Married the Boss! Loving the Boss. (Romance Ser.: No. 1372). 1999. per. 3.50 (*0-373-19372-6*, 1-19372-1) Silhouette.
— Look-Alike Bride. (Surprise Brides Ser.). 1997. per. 3.25 (*0-373-19220-7*, 1-19220-2) Silhouette.
— Raleigh & the Rancher. (Romance Ser.). 1995. per. 2.99 (*0-373-19092-1*, 1-19092-5) Silhouette.
— Second Chance Family. 1995. per. 2.99 (*0-373-19119-7*, 1-19119-6) Silhouette.
— Stranded with a Tall, Dark Stranger. (Romance Ser.: No. 1340). 1998. per. 3.50 (*0-373-19340-8*, 1-19340-8) Silhouette.
— The Stranger's Surprise. 1997. per. 3.25 (*0-373-19260-6*, 1-19260-8) Silhouette.
— The Twenty-Four-Hour Groom. (Romance Ser.: No. 1393). 1999. mass mkt. 3.50 (*0-373-19393-9*, 1-19393-7) Silhouette.
— Undercover Honeymoon. (Romance Ser.: No. 1166). 1996. per. 3.25 (*0-373-19166-9*, 1-19166-7) Silhouette.
*__Anthony, Laurie.__ Have a Great One! A Homeless Man's Story. 198p. 1999. pap. 12.95 (*0-9675298-0-8*) Anthony Pubs.
Anthony, Lillian S., jt. auth. see Sieben, J. Kenneth.
Anthony, Louise. Love in Camera. (Rainbow Romances Ser.). 160p. 1993. 14.95 (*0-7090-4890-4*) Parkwest Pubns.
— Venetian Rhapsody. (Lythway Adult Ser.). 176p. 1991. 18.95 (*0-7451-1376-1*, G K Hall Lrg Type) Mac Lib Ref.
Anthony, M. H., jt. auth. see Biggs, Norman L.
*__Anthony, Maggy.__ Jung's Circle of Women: The Valkyries. 2nd rev. ed. LC 99-22623. Orig. Title: Valkyries. (Illus.). 144p. 1999. pap. 18.95 (*0-89254-044-3*) Nicolas-Hays.
Anthony, Maggy. Valkyries: The Women Around Jung. 1993. pap. 14.95 (*1-85230-187-2*, Pub. by Element MA) Penguin Putnam.
Anthony, Margaret, ed. American Cancer Society's Healthy Eating Cookbook. LC 99-47049. (Illus.). 216p. 1999. 24.00 (*0-944235-14-X*) Am Cancer NY.
Anthony, Marie. Coming to Life Again. LC 95-73233. xii, 62p. 1996. pap. 14.95 (*0-9647540-0-2*) D Sawicki.
*__Anthony, Mark.__ Beyond the Pale: Book One of the Last Rune. (Last Run Ser.: Bk. 1). 1999. mass mkt. 6.99 (*0-553-57934-7*) Bantam.
Anthony, Mark. Dogism. LC 98-96362. v, 228p. 1998. 23.00 (*0-9665738-6-2*); pap. 12.00 (*0-9665738-0-3*) Trendsettaz.
— Escape from the Undermountain. (Forgotten Realms Nobles Ser.: Bk. 3). 1996. pap. 5.99 (*0-7869-0477-1*, Pub. by TSR Inc) Random.
*__Anthony, Mark.__ The Keep of Fire. 2000. mass mkt. 6.99 (*0-553-57932-0*) Bantam.
Anthony, Mark. The Keep of Fire: Book Two of the Last Rune. LC 99-15685. 480p. 1999. pap. 14.95 (*0-553-37956-9*) Bantam.
— Kindred Spirits. LC 90-71494. (DragonLance Meetings Sextet: Vol. 1). (Illus.). 320p. (Orig.). 1991. pap. 5.99 (*1-56076-069-9*, Pub. by TSR Inc) Random.
— Urban Massacre. 2nd rev. ed. LC 98-96361. v, 246p. 1998. 23.00 (*0-9665738-7-0*); pap. 12.00 (*0-9665738-1-1*) Trendsettaz.
— Vanishing Republic: How Can We Save the American Dream? LC 96-112864. 384p. 1996. 24.97 (*0-9646138-0-8*) M Anthony Commun.
*__Anthony, Martin & Bartlett, Peter.__ Neural Network Learning: Theoretical Foundations. LC 98-53260. 416p. (C). 1999. 59.95 (*0-521-57353-X*) Cambridge U Pr.
Anthony, Martin, jt. ed. see Shawe-Taylor, John.
*__Anthony, Martin M. & Swinson, Richard P.__ The Shyness & Social Anxiety Workbook: Proven Techniques for Overcoming Your Fears. 216p. 2000. pap., wbk. ed. 15.95 (*1-57224-216-7*, Pub. by New Harbinger) Publishers Group.
Anthony, Meredith, et al. One Hundred One Reasons Why We're Doomed: A Cynic's Guide to What's Left of the Future. 128p. (Orig.). 1993. pap. 7.50 (*0-380-77188-8*, Avon Bks) Morrow Avon.
Anthony, Michael. All That Glitters. (Caribbean Writers Ser.). 202p. (C). 1983. pap. 7.95 (*0-435-98034-3*, 98034, Pub. by Heinemann) Lubrecht & Cramer.
— All That Glitters. 208p. 1997. pap. 10.95 (*0-435-98945-6*) Heinemann.
— Cricket in the Road. (Caribbean Writers Ser.). 143p. (C). 1973. pap. 7.95 (*0-435-98032-7*, 98032) Heinemann.
— The Games Were Coming. (Caribbean Writers Ser.). 107p. (C). 1977. pap. 7.95 (*0-435-98033-5*, 98033) Heinemann.
— Historical Dictionary of Trinidad & Tobago. (Latin American Historical Dictionaries Ser.: No. 26). 672p. 1997. 84.00 (*0-8108-3173-2*) Scarecrow.
— In the Heat of the Day. (Caribbean Writers Ser.). 192p. 1996. pap. 11.95 (*0-435-98944-8*) Heinemann.
— In the Heat of the Day. 1996. pap. 10.95 (*0-614-97782-7*) Heinemann.
— The Year in San Fernando. (Caribbean Writers Ser.). 137p. (C). 1970. pap. 7.95 (*0-435-98031-9*, 98031) Heinemann.
— Year in San Fernando. LC 97-219570. (Caribbean Writers Ser.). 1997. pap. 10.95 (*0-435-98943-X*) Heinemann.
Anthony, Michael & Griffiths, Gareth. Green Days by the River. (Caribbean Writers Ser.). 192p. (C). 1985. pap. 7.95 (*0-435-98030-0*, 98030) Heinemann.
*__Anthony, Michael A.__ Nec Answers. LC 99-35502. 523p. 1999. pap. 34.95 (*0-07-134494-2*) McGraw.
Anthony, Michael D. Dark Provenance. large type ed. 528p. 1995. 27.99 (*0-7089-3324-6*) Ulverscroft.
— Midnight Come. LC 98-46678. 304p. 1999. text 22.95 (*0-312-20058-7*) St Martin.
*__Anthony, Michael J., ed.__ Foundations of Ministry: An Introduction to Christian Education for a New Generation. LC 91-42034. 400p. (C). 1998. pap. 14.99 (*0-8010-2166-9*, Bridgept Bks) Baker Bks.
Anthony, Michael P., jt. auth. see Korwin, Alan.
Anthony, Michelle & McLaughlin, Dennis R. The Gigantic Book of Games for Youth Ministry, Vol. 1. LC 98-29467. 320p. 1998. pap. 21.99 (*0-7644-2113-1*) Group Pub.
Anthony, Mitch, jt. auth. see West, Scott.
Anthony, N. C., jt. auth. see Schelpe, E. A.
*__Anthony, Nathan & Gardner, Robert.__ The Bombing of Pearl Harbor in American History. LC 00-8455. (Illus.). 2000. write for info. (*0-7660-1126-7*) Enslow Pubs.
Anthony of Sourozh. God & Man. 2nd ed. 125p. 1983. reprint ed. pap. text 8.95 (*0-88141-024-1*) St Vladimirs.
Anthony of Taize, tr. see Ch'on Sang Pyong.
Anthony of Taize, tr. see So Chong-Ju.
Anthony, Patricia. Brother Termite. 272p. 1995. mass mkt. 5.99 (*0-441-00187-4*) Ace Bks.
— Cold Allies. 304p. 1994. mass mkt. 5.99 (*0-441-00018-5*) Ace Bks.
— Cold Allies. LC 92-16195. 1993. 21.95 (*0-15-118503-4*) Harcourt.
— Conscience of the Beagle. 256p. (Orig.). 1995. mass mkt. 5.50 (*0-441-00262-5*) Ace Bks.
— Cradle of Splendor. LC 95-21212. 304p. (Orig.). 1996. 22.95 (*0-441-00301-X*) Ace Bks.
— Cradle of Splendor. 304p. (Orig.). 1997. reprint ed. mass mkt. 5.99 (*0-441-00426-1*) Ace Bks.
— Eating Memories. 367p. 1998. mass mkt. 6.50 (*0-441-00556-X*) Ace Bks.
— Eating Memories. LC 98-167400. 334p. pap. 15.00 (*1-882968-17-4*) Old Earth Bks.
— Flanders. LC 97-33120. 384p. 1998. 23.95 (*0-441-00528-4*) Ace Bks.
*__Anthony, Patricia.__ Flanders. 2000. pap. text 13.95 (*0-425-17293-7*) Berkley Pub.
Anthony, Patricia. God's Fires. LC 96-31430. 384p. 1997. 22.95 (*0-441-00407-5*) Ace Bks.
— God's Fires. 1998. mass mkt. 6.50 (*0-441-00537-3*) Ace Bks.
— Happy Policeman. 1996. mass mkt. 5.99 (*0-441-00321-4*) Ace Bks.
— Happy Policeman. LC 93-42949. 288p. 1994. 21.95 (*0-15-138478-9*) Harcourt.
Anthony, Patricia & Jacobson, Stephen L. Helping At-Risk Students: What Are the Educational & Financial Costs? 320p. 1992. pap. 32.95 (*0-8039-6049-2*, 4208) Corwin Pr.
Anthony, Patricia, jt. ed. see Ward, James G.
Anthony, Paul. The Fragile Peace. 320p. 1996. 29.95 (*1-85756-292-5*, Pub. by Janus Pubng) Paul & Co Pubs.
Anthony, Peter. Managing Culture. LC 93-25316. (Managing Work & Organizations Ser.). 112p. 1994. pap. 34.95 (*0-335-09788-X*) OpUniv Pr.
Anthony, Peter P. Recent Advances in Histopathology, Vol. 17. (Orig.). (C). 1998. pap. text 77.00 (*0-443-05766-4*) Harcourt.
Anthony, Peter P. & MacSween, Roderick N., eds. Recent Advances in Histopathology 15. (Illus.). 257p. (Orig.). 1992. pap. text 72.00 (*0-443-04519-4*) Church.
Anthony, Piers. Alien Plot. 256p. 1993. mass mkt. 4.99 (*0-8125-3072-1*, Pub. by Tor Bks) St Martin.
— And Eternity. LC 00-1508. (Incarnations of Immortality Ser.: 7). 384p. 1991. mass mkt. 6.99 (*0-380-75286-7*, Avon Bks) Morrow Avon.
— Balook. 1997. mass mkt. 5.99 (*0-441-00398-2*) Ace Bks.
— Battle Circle. 544p. 1978. mass mkt. 5.99 (*0-380-01800-4*, Avon Bks) Morrow Avon.
— Bearing an Hourglass. (Incarnations of Immortality Ser.: Bk. 2). 384p. 1985. mass mkt. 6.99 (*0-345-31315-1*, Ballantine) Ballantine Pub Grp.
— Bearing an Hourglass. (Incarnations of Immortality Ser.). 1985. 11.05 (*0-606-00252-9*, Pub. by Turtleback) Demco.
— Being a Green Mother. (Incarnations of Immortality Ser.: Bk. 5). 1988. mass mkt. 5.95 (*0-345-32223-1*, Del Rey) Ballantine Pub Grp.
— Bio of A Space Tyrant, 4 vols., Set. 1986. pap., boxed set 14.00 (*0-380-75246-8*, Avon Bks) Morrow Avon.
— Blue Adept. 336p. 1987. mass mkt. 5.95 (*0-345-35245-9*, Del Rey) Ballantine Pub Grp.
— But What of Earth? (Illus.). 256p. 1989. mass mkt. 4.95 (*0-8125-3098-5*, Pub. by Tor Bks) St Martin.
— But What of Earth? A Novel Rendered Into a Bad Example. 1989. 10.05 (*0-606-11177-8*, Pub. by Turtleback) Demco.
— Castle Roogna. 336p. 1987. mass mkt. 5.95 (*0-345-35048-0*, Del Rey) Ballantine Pub Grp.
— Castle Roogna. (Magic of Xanth Ser.). 1979. 11.05 (*0-606-02463-8*, Pub. by Turtleback) Demco.
— The Caterpillar's Question. Farmer, Philip Jose, ed. 272p. 1995. mass mkt. 5.99 (*0-441-00213-7*) Ace Bks.
— Centaur Aisle. (Magic of Xanth Ser.). 304p. 1987. mass mkt. 5.95 (*0-345-35246-7*, Del Rey) Ballantine Pub Grp.
— Centaur Aisle. 304p. 24.00 (*0-7278-5127-6*) Severn Hse.
— Centaur Aisle. (Magic of Xanth Ser.). 1979. 11.05 (*0-606-02462-X*, Pub. by Turtleback) Demco.
— Chaining the Lady. (Cluster Ser.: No. 2). 1978. pap. 3.50 (*0-380-01779-2*, Avon Bks) Morrow Avon.
— Chaos Mode. 368p. 1995. mass mkt. 5.99 (*0-441-00132-7*) Ace Bks.
— Cluster. (Cluster Ser.: No. 1). 256p. 1977. pap. 3.95 (*0-380-01755-5*, Avon Bks) Morrow Avon.
— The Continuing Xanth Saga. LC 96-41490. 736p. 1997. 13.99 (*0-517-18337-4*) Random Hse Value.
— Crewel Lye: A Caustic Yarn. LC 84-90936. 320p. 1987. mass mkt. 5.95 (*0-345-34599-1*, Del Rey) Ballantine Pub Grp.
Anthony, Piers. Crewel Lye: A Caustic Yarn. (Magic of Xanth Ser.). 1984. 11.05 (*0-606-02461-1*, Pub. by Turtleback) Demco.
— The Dastard. 2000. text 24.95 (*0-312-86900-2*) St Martin.
Anthony, Piers. Dead Morn. 1994. 11.09 (*0-606-06313-7*, Pub. by Turtleback) Demco.
Anthony, Piers. Demons Don't Dream. Vol. 16. 352p. 1994. mass mkt. 5.99 (*0-8125-3483-2*, Pub. by Tor Bks) St Martin.
Anthony, Piers. Demons Don't Dream, 16. (Xanth Ser.). 1994. 11.09 (*0-606-11249-9*, Pub. by Turtleback) Demco.
— Dragon on a Pedestal. 320p. Date not set. pap. 5.95 (*0-345-34936-9*) Carol Pub Group.
— Dragon on a Pedestal. (Magic of Xanth Ser.). 1983. 11.05 (*0-606-02477-8*, Pub. by Turtleback) Demco.
— Dragon's Gold. (Orig.). 1991. mass mkt. 4.99 (*0-8125-1384-3*, Pub. by Tor Bks) St Martin.
— Executive. (Bio of a Space Tyrant Ser.: No. 4). 336p. 1985. mass mkt. 4.50 (*0-380-89834-9*, Avon Bks) Morrow Avon.
*__Anthony, Piers.__ Executive: Bio of a Space Tyrant, Vol. 4. LC 99-91255. 2000. 25.00 (*0-7388-0698-6*); pap. 18.00 (*0-7388-0699-4*) Xlibris Corp.
Anthony, Piers. Faun & Games. LC 97-19362. Vol. 21. 320p. 1997. text 23.95 (*0-312-86162-1*) St Martin.
— Faun & Games. LC 97-19362. 340p. 1998. mass mkt. 6.99 (*0-8125-5511-2*, Pub. by Tor Bks) St Martin.
— For Love of Evil. (Incarnations of Immortality Ser.: 6). 336p. 1990. mass mkt. 6.99 (*0-380-75285-9*, Avon Bks) Morrow Avon.
— Fractal Mode. 336p. 1992. mass mkt. 5.99 (*0-441-25126-9*) Ace Bks.
— Geis of the Gargoyle. 320p. 1995. 22.95 (*0-312-85391-2*) Tor Bks.
— Geis of the Gargoyle. 1995. 5.99 (*0-8125-3485-9*, Pub. by Tor Bks) St Martin.
— Geis of the Gargoyle. (Xanth Ser.). 1995. 11.09 (*0-606-11360-6*, Pub. by Turtleback) Demco.
Anthony, Piers. Ghost. 1987. pap. 3.95 (*0-8125-3127-2*, Pub. by Tor Bks) St Martin.
Anthony, Piers. Ghost. 288p. 1992. mass mkt. 3.99 (*0-8125-2088-2*, Pub. by Tor Bks) St Martin.
— Ghost. 1992. 9.09 (*0-606-11367-3*, Pub. by Turtleback) Demco.
— Golem in the Gears. (Xanth Ser.). 1986. 11.05 (*0-606-01025-4*, Pub. by Turtleback) Demco.
Anthony, Piers. Hard Sell. 272p. 1993. mass mkt. 4.99 (*0-441-31748-0*) Ace Bks.
Anthony, Piers. Hard Sell. LC 90-70209. 187p. 1990. 18.95 (*0-9623712-1-1*) Tafford Pub.
— Harpy Thyme. (Magic of Xanth Ser.). 1995. 11.09 (*0-606-11439-4*, Pub. by Turtleback) Demco.
— Harpy Thyme, No. 17. (Xanth Ser.: bk. 17). 352p. 1995. mass mkt. 5.99 (*0-8125-3484-0*, Pub. by Tor Bks) St Martin.
— Hasan. LC 77-24589. (Illus.). 190p. 1977. pap. 21.00 (*0-89370-215-3*) Millefleurs.
— Hasan. 1991. mass mkt. 3.99 (*0-8125-1348-7*, Pub. by Tor Bks) St Martin.
*__Anthony, Piers.__ Heaven Cent. 352p. 2000. mass mkt. 6.99 (*0-8125-7498-2*) Tor Bks.
— Heaven Cent. (Illus.). (J). 2000. 12.34 (*0-606-18643-3*) Turtleback.
Anthony, Piers. Hope of Earth. LC 96-53954. 384p. 1997. text 24.95 (*0-312-86340-3*) St Martin.
— Hope of Earth. (Geodyssey Saga Ser.). 1998. 11.09 (*0-606-13488-3*, Pub. by Turtleback) Demco.
— Hope of Earth, Vol. 1. 1998. mass mkt. 6.99 (*0-8125-7111-8*, Pub. by Tor Bks) St Martin.
Anthony, Piers. Isle of Woman, 1. (Geodyssey Saga Ser.). 1994. 11.09 (*0-606-13527-8*, Pub. by Turtleback) Demco.
Anthony, Piers. Isle of Woman, Vol. 1. (Geodyssey Ser.: No. 1). 480p. 1994. mass mkt. 5.99 (*0-8125-3366-6*, Pub. by Tor Bks) St Martin.
— Juxtaposition. 352p. 1987. mass mkt. 5.95 (*0-345-34934-2*, Del Rey) Ballantine Pub Grp.
— Killobyte. 320p. 1994. mass mkt. 5.50 (*0-441-44425-3*) Ace Bks.
— Killobyte. (J). 1993. 10.60 (*0-606-05900-8*, Pub. by Turtleback) Demco.
— Kirlian Quest. (Cluster Ser.: No. 3). 320p. 1978. pap. 3.50 (*0-380-01778-4*, Avon Bks) Morrow Avon.
— Letters to Jenny. Riggs, Alan, ed. 288p. 1994. pap. 4.99 (*0-8125-2282-6*, Pub. by Tor Bks) St Martin.
— Macroscope. 480p. 1976. mass mkt. 4.95 (*0-380-00209-4*, Avon Bks) Morrow Avon.
— Man from Mundania. 352p. 1989. mass mkt. 5.99 (*0-380-75289-1*, Avon Bks) Morrow Avon.
— Mercenary. (Bio of a Space Tyrant Ser.: Vol. II). 384p. 1984. mass mkt. 4.50 (*0-380-87221-8*, Avon Bks) Morrow Avon.
*__Anthony, Piers.__ Mercenary: Bio of a Space Tyrant, Vol. 2. LC 99-91253. 1999. 25.00 (*0-7388-0694-3*); pap. 18.00 (*0-7388-0695-1*) Xlibris Corp.
— MerCycle. 352p. 1992. mass mkt. 5.99 (*0-441-52562-8*) Ace Bks.
Anthony, Piers. Muse of Art Vol. 4: Geodyssey. LC 99-12905. 448p. 1999. 26.95 (*0-312-86896-0*, Pub. by Tor Bks) St Martin.
Anthony, Piers. Mute. 448p. (Orig.). 1981. mass mkt. 4.50 (*0-380-77578-6*, Avon Bks) Morrow Avon.
Anthony, Piers. Night Mare. LC 82-90817. (Magic of Xanth Ser.). 320p. 1987. mass mkt. 6.99 (*0-345-35493-1*, Del Rey) Ballantine Pub Grp.
— Night Mare. (Magic of Xanth Ser.). (J). 1982. 12.09 (*0-606-02597-9*, Pub. by Turtleback) Demco.
— Ogre, Ogre. LC 82-6659. (Magic of Xanth Ser.). 320p. 1987. mass mkt. 5.95 (*0-345-35492-3*, Del Rey) Ballantine Pub Grp.
Anthony, Piers. Ogre, Ogre. (Magic of Xanth Ser.). (J). 1982. 11.05 (*0-606-02599-5*, Pub. by Turtleback) Demco.
Anthony, Piers. Omnivore. 1978. pap. 3.95 (*0-380-00262-0*, Avon Bks) Morrow Avon.
— On a Pale Horse. (Incarnations of Immortality Ser.: Bk. 1). 336p. 1986. mass mkt. 5.95 (*0-345-33858-8*, Del Rey) Ballantine Pub Grp.
— On a Pale Horse. (Incarnations of Immortality Ser.: Bk. 1). 1983. 11.05 (*0-606-02598-7*, Pub. by Turtleback) Demco.
— Orn. 1978. pap. 3.95 (*0-380-00266-3*, Avon Bks) Morrow Avon.
— Out of Phaze. 488p. 1989. mass mkt. 6.50 (*0-441-64465-1*) Ace Bks.
Anthony, Piers. Ox. 1976. pap. 3.95 (*0-380-00461-5*, Avon Bks) Morrow Avon.
Anthony, Piers. Phaze Doubt. 1991. mass mkt. 5.99 (*0-441-66263-3*) Ace Bks.
Anthony, Piers. Phaze Doubt. (Illus.). 1991. write for info. (*0-450-54814-7*, Pub. by New Eng Lib); pap. write for info. (*0-450-54815-5*, Pub. by New Eng Lib) Trafalgar.
Anthony, Piers. Politician. (Bio of a Space Tyrant Ser.: No. 3). 352p. 1985. mass mkt. 4.99 (*0-380-89685-0*, Avon Bks) Morrow Avon.
*__Anthony, Piers.__ Politician: Bio of a Space Tyrant, Vol. 3. LC 99-91254. 2000. 25.00 (*0-7388-0696-X*); pap. 18.00 (*0-7388-0697-8*) Xlibris Corp.
Anthony, Piers. Pornucopia. 188p. 27.95 (*0-8488-1594-7*) Amereon Ltd.
— Pornucopia. 188p. 1998. lib. bdg. 29.95 (*1-56723-120-9*) Yestermorrow.
— Prostho Plus. 224p. 1986. reprint ed. pap. 2.95 (*0-8125-3116-7*, Pub. by Tor Bks) St Martin.
Anthony, Piers. Race Against Time. 256p. 1986. reprint ed. pap. write for info. (*0-8125-3101-9*, Pub. by Tor Bks) St Martin.
— Reality Check. LC 00-190719. 181p. 2000. 25.00 (*0-7388-1954-9*); pap. 18.00 (*0-7388-1955-7*) Xlibris Corp.
Anthony, Piers. Refugee. (Bio of a Space Tyrant Ser.: Vol. I). 320p. 1983. mass mkt. 4.50 (*0-380-84194-0*, Avon Bks) Morrow Avon.
*__Anthony, Piers.__ Refugee: Bio of a Space Tyrant, Vol. 1. LC 99-91252. 2000. 25.00 (*0-7388-0692-7*); pap. 18.00 (*0-7388-0693-5*) Xlibris Corp.
Anthony, Piers. The Ring. 295p. 1989. reprint ed. pap. 3.95 (*0-8125-0104-7*, Pub. by Tor Bks) St Martin.
— Rings of Ice. 192p. 1974. pap. 3.50 (*0-380-00036-9*, Avon Bks) Morrow Avon.
— Robot Adept. 1989. mass mkt. 5.99 (*0-441-73118-X*) Ace Bks.
— Roc & a Hard Place. 320p. 1995. 23.95 (*0-312-85392-0*) Tor Bks.
— Roc & a Hard Place. 1996. mass mkt. 5.99 (*0-614-20532-8*) Tor Bks.
Anthony, Piers. Roc & a Hard Place. LC 95-30306. 1996. 11.09 (*0-606-11804-7*, Pub. by Turtleback) Demco.
Anthony, Piers. Roc & a Hard Place, Vol. 1. LC 95-30306. 1996. mass mkt. 5.99 (*0-8125-3486-7*, Pub. by Tor Bks) St Martin.
— Shade of the Tree. (Illus.). 352p. 1987. pap. 3.95 (*0-8125-3103-5*, Pub. by Tor Bks) St Martin.
— Shame of Man. 512p. 1995. mass mkt. 6.99 (*0-8125-5091-9*, Pub. by Tor Bks) St Martin.
— Shame of Man. 1995. 11.09 (*0-606-13772-6*, Pub. by Turtleback) Demco.
— The Source of Magic. 336p. 1987. mass mkt. 5.95 (*0-345-35058-8*, Del Rey) Ballantine Pub Grp.
Anthony, Piers. Source of Magic. (Magic of Xanth Ser.). (J). 1979. 11.05 (*0-606-02647-9*, Pub. by Turtleback) Demco.
Anthony, Piers. A Spell for Chameleon. LC 77-1666. (The Wizards of Fantasy Promotion). 352p. 1987. mass mkt. 3.99 (*0-345-34753-6*, Del Rey) Ballantine Pub Grp.
Anthony, Piers. A Spell for Chameleon. (Magic of Xanth Ser.). (J). 1977. 11.05 (*0-606-02492-1*, Pub. by Turtleback) Demco.
Anthony, Piers. Split Infinity. 368p. 1987. mass mkt. 5.95 (*0-345-35491-5*, Del Rey) Ballantine Pub Grp.
— Statesman. (Bio of a Space Tyrant Ser.: No. 5). 320p. 1986. mass mkt. 4.99 (*0-380-89835-7*, Avon Bks) Morrow Avon.
*__Anthony, Piers.__ Statesman: Bio of a Space Tyrant, Vol. 5. LC 99-91256. 2000. 25.00 (*0-7388-0700-1*); pap. 18.00 (*0-7388-0701-X*) Xlibris Corp.
Anthony, Piers. Steppe. 256p. (Orig.). 1992. reprint ed. mass mkt. 3.99 (*0-8125-1922-1*, Pub. by Tor Bks) St Martin.
— Tarot. 1987. pap. 9.95 (*0-441-79841-1*) Ace Bks.
— Tatham Mound. 528p. 1992. mass mkt. 5.99 (*0-380-71309-8*, Avon Bks) Morrow Avon.
— Total Recall. 1990. mass mkt. 4.50 (*0-380-70874-4*, Avon Bks) Morrow Avon.
— Triple Detente. 256p. (Orig.). 1988. pap. 3.95 (*0-8125-3129-9*, Pub. by Tor Bks) St Martin.
— Unicorn Point. (Apprentice Adept Fantasy Ser.: No. 6). 1990. mass mkt. 5.99 (*0-441-84563-0*) Ace Bks.
— Vale of the Vole. 336p. 1987. mass mkt. 5.99 (*0-380-75287-5*, Avon Bks) Morrow Avon.
*__Anthony, Piers.__ Vale of the Vole. (Xanth Ser.). 352p. 2000. mass mkt. 6.99 (*0-8125-7496-6*, Pub. by Tor Bks) St Martin.

An Asterisk (*) at the beginning of an entry indicates that the title is appearing for the first time.

A

Anthony, Piers. Vale of the Vole. (J). 1987. 11.09 (*0-606-03669-5*, Pub. by Turtleback) Demco.

— Virtual Mode. 1991. mass mkt. 6.50 (*0-441-86503-8*) Ace Bks.

— Viscous Circle. (Cluster Ser.: No. 5). 272p. 1982. mass mkt. 4.50 (*0-380-79897-2*, Avon Bks) Morrow Avon.

— Volk. LC 98-96125. 335 p. 1998. 25.00 (*0-9663501-0-3*); pap. 15.00 (*0-7388-0040-6*) Xlibris Corp.

Anthony, Piers. Wielding a Red Sword. (Incarnations of Immortality Ser.: Bk. 4). 320p. 1987. mass mkt. 5.95 (*0-345-32221-5*, Del Rey) Ballantine Pub Grp.

Anthony, Piers. With a Tangled Skein. (Incarnations of Immortality Ser.: No. 3). 1986. mass mkt. 6.99 (*0-345-31885-4*, Del Rey) Ballantine Pub Grp.

— With a Tangled Skein. (Incarnations of Immortality Ser.: Bk. 3). (J). 1985. 11.05 (*0-606-03298-3*, Pub. by Turtleback) Demco.

— X #11: Heaven Cent. 336p. (Orig.). 1988. mass mkt. 5.99 (*0-380-75288-3*, Avon Bks) Morrow Avon.

Anthony, Piers. Xanth: Isle of View, Bk. 13. (Xanth Ser.: No. 13). 352p. 1990. mass mkt. 6.99 (*0-380-75947-0*, Avon Bks) Morrow Avon.

— Xanth: Question Quest, Bk. 14. 368p. 1991. mass mkt. 5.99 (*0-380-75948-9*, Avon Bks) Morrow Avon.

— Xanth: The Color of Her Panties, Bk. 15. (Xanth Ser.: No. 15). 352p. 1992. mass mkt. 5.99 (*0-380-75949-7*, Avon Bks) Morrow Avon.

— Xone of Contention. LC 99-22200. 304p. 1999. text 24.95 (*0-312-86691-7*, Pub. by Tor Bks) St Martin.

— Xone of Contention. 2000. mass mkt. 6.99 (*0-8125-5523-6*) Tor Bks.

Anthony, Piers. Yon Ill Wind. LC 96-16216. 320p. 1996. 23.95 (*0-312-86227-X*) St Martin.

— Yon Ill Wind. (Xanth Ser.). 352p. 1997. mass mkt. 6.99 (*0-8125-5510-4*, Pub. by Tor Bks) St Martin.

***Anthony, Piers.** Zombie Lover, 48 vols. LC 98-23526. 341p. 1999. mass mkt. 6.99 (*0-8125-5512-0*, Pub. by Tor Bks) St Martin.

Anthony, Piers. Zombie Lover, No. 22. LC 98-23526. Vol. 22. 304p. 1998. 23.95 (*0-312-86690-9*, Pub. by Tor Bks) St Martin.

***Anthony, Piers & Brady, Judy.** Dream a Little Dream: A Tale of Myth & MoonShine. 1999. mass mkt. 6.99 (*0-8125-6490-1*, Pub. by Tor Bks) St Martin.

Anthony, Piers & Brady, Julie. Dream a Little Dream: A Tale of Myth & MoonShine. LC 98-46147. 304p. 1999. 23.95 (*0-312-86466-3*, Pub. by Tor Bks) St Martin.

Anthony, Piers & Fuentes, Roberto. Dead Morn. 352p. 1994. mass mkt. 5.99 (*0-441-00052-5*) Ace Bks.

Anthony, Piers & Fuentes, Roberto. Dead Morn. LC 90-70957. 265p. 1990. 19.95 (*0-9623712-2-X*) Tafford Pub.

Anthony, Piers & Gilliam, Richard, eds. Tales from the Great Turtle. 352p. 1995. mass mkt. 5.99 (*0-8125-3490-5*, Pub. by Tor Bks) St Martin.

Anthony, Piers & Hall, Frances. Piers Anthony's Pretender. 320p. 1993. mass mkt. 4.99 (*0-8125-2396-2*, Pub. by Tor Bks) St Martin.

— Pretender: Science Fiction. LC 79-317. (Illus.). 159p. 1979. pap. 19.00 (*0-89370-230-7*) Millefleurs.

Anthony, Piers & Kornwise, Robert. Through the Ice. 1992. mass mkt. 5.99 (*0-671-72113-5*) Baen Bks.

Anthony, Piers & Lackey, Mercedes. If I Pay Thee Not in Gold. LC 93-21473. 416p. 1993. 20.00 (*0-671-72175-5*) Baen Bks.

— If I Pay Thee Not in Gold. 416p. 1994. mass mkt. 5.99 (*0-671-87623-6*) Baen Bks.

***Anthony, Piers & Leming, Ron.** The Gutbucket Quest. 288p. 2000. 23.95 (*0-312-86463-9*, Pub. by Tor Bks) St Martin.

Anthony, Piers & Margroff, Robert E. Chimaera's Copper. 320p. 1991. mass mkt. 4.95 (*0-8125-0915-3*, Pub. by Tor Bks) St Martin.

— Mouvar's Magic. 320p. 1993. mass mkt. 4.99 (*0-8125-1982-5*, Pub. by Tor Bks) St Martin.

— Orc's Opal. 1991. mass mkt. 4.99 (*0-8125-1177-8*) Tor Bks.

— Serpent's Silver, Vol. 2. 320p. 1989. mass mkt. 4.95 (*0-8125-0257-4*, Pub. by Tor Bks) St Martin.

Anthony, Piers & Nye, Jody Lynn. Visual Guide to Xanth. 240p. 1989. pap. 15.00 (*0-380-75749-4*, Avon Bks) Morrow Avon.

Anthony, Piers & Pickover, Clifford A. Spider Legs. LC 97-29854. 304p. 1997. text 22.95 (*0-312-86465-5*) St Martin.

— Spider Legs. 1999. mass mkt. 5.99 (*0-8125-6489-8*, Pub. by Tor Bks) St Martin.

***Anthony, Piers & Taeusch, Jo Anne.** The Secret of Spring. LC 99-89921. 256p. 2000. 22.95 (*0-312-86464-7*, Pub. by Tor Bks) St Martin.

Anthony, Piers & Tella, Alfred. The Willing Spirit. LC 96-29211. 1996. 22.95 (*0-312-86266-0*, Pub. by Tor Bks) St Martin.

— The Willing Spirit, Vol. 1. 1998. mass mkt. 6.99 (*0-8125-7146-0*, Pub. by Tor Bks) St Martin.

Anthony, Piers, et al. Quest for the Fallen Star. LC 98-14560. 416p. 1998. 25.95 (*0-312-86409-4*, Pub. by Tor Bks) St Martin.

— Quest for the Fallen Star. 688p. 1999. mass mkt. 6.99 (*0-8125-6485-5*, Pub. by Tor Bks) St Martin.

Anthony, R., jt. auth. see Cousins, E. F.

Anthony, R. J. The Manufacture & Use of the Functional Foot Orthosis. (Illus.). xiv, 220p. 1991. 172.25 (*3-8055-5298-X*) S Karger.

Anthony, Ray. Talking to the Top: Executive's Guide to Career-Making Presentations. (Illus.). 331p. 1999. text 20.00 (*0-7881-5997-6*) DIANE Pub.

Anthony, Ray & Kushner, Malcolm. High Octane Selling: Boost Your Creative Power to Close More Sales. LC 95-21036. 144p. 1995. pap. 16.95 (*0-8144-7898-0*) AMACOM.

Anthony, Rebecca & Roe, Gerald. The Curriculum Vitae Handbook: How to Present & Promote Your Academic Career. 2nd rev. ed. LC 98-7277. 176p. 1998. pap. 15.95 (*0-945213-26-3*) Rudi Pub.

— 101 Grade A Resumes for Teachers. 2nd ed. LC 97-29628. 184p. 1998. pap. 10.95 (*0-7641-0129-3*) Barron.

Anthony, Rebecca J. & Roe, Gerald. From Contact to Contract. rev. ed. 84p. (C). 1994. pap. text 11.99 (*0-945819-75-7*) Sulzburger & Graham Pub.

— Over Forty & Looking for Work? A Guide for the Unemployed, Underemployed, & Unhappily Employed. 180p. 1990. pap. 7.95 (*1-55850-870-8*) Adams Media.

Anthony, Richard. How to Perform Your Own Urinalysis Without a Doctor for Under Fifty Cents. (Illus.). pap. 10.00 (*0-916976-00-9*) P I Industries.

Anthony, Robert. Dr. Robert Anthony's Advanced Formula for Total Success. Levanthal, Sallye, ed. 176p. (Orig.). 1997. mass mkt. 4.99 (*0-425-10804-X*) Berkley Pub.

— Doing What You Love, Loving What You Do: The Ultimate Key to Permanent Happiness & Financial... 1991. pap. 12.00 (*0-425-12738-9*) Berkley Pub.

***Anthony, Robert.** Essentials of Accounting. 7th ed. LC 99-27566. 214p. (C). 1999. pap. 42.00 (*0-201-61540-1*, Prentice Hall) P-H.

Anthony, Robert. Fifty Ideas That Can Change Your Life. 1987. pap. 4.99 (*0-425-10421-4*) Berkley Pub.

— How to Make a Fortune from Public Speaking. 1988. mass mkt. 4.99 (*0-425-11327-2*) Berkley Pub.

— How to Make the Impossible Possible: Turning Your Life Around Through Possibility Thinking. 1996. pap. 12.00 (*0-425-14955-2*); pap. 12.00 (*0-425-14978-1*) Berkley Pub.

— A Review of Essentials of Accounting. 5th rev. ed. LC 94-25150. (C). 1995. pap. text 22.00 (*0-201-88121-7*) Addison-Wesley.

***Anthony, Robert.** Review of Essentials of Accounting. 7th ed. LC 99-34139. 179p. (C). 1999. pap. 25.00 (*0-201-61541-X*, Prentice Hall) P-H.

Anthony, Robert. Think. 480p. 1985. pap. 4.50 (*0-425-08747-6*) Berkley Pub.

— Think Again. 480p. 1986. pap. 4.50 (*0-425-09572-X*) Berkley Pub.

— Think & Win. 80p. (Orig.). 1992. pap. 4.50 (*0-425-13468-7*) Berkley Pub.

— Think Big (Think, Think, & Win, Think Again, Think Together) (Orig.). 1999. pap. 10.00 (*0-425-16866-2*) Berkley Pub.

— Think On. 1988. pap. 4.50 (*0-425-11186-5*) Berkley Pub.

— The Ultimate Secrets of Total Self-Confidence. 1986. mass mkt. 5.99 (*0-425-10170-3*) Berkley Pub.

Anthony, Robert, et al. Evaluating Literacy: A Perspective for Change. LC 91-11368. 186p. (C). 1991. pap. text 23.00 (*0-435-08589-1*, 08589) Heinemann.

Anthony, Robert H. Teach Yourself Essentials of Accounting: Version 5.0 (For Macintosh) 2nd ed. (C). 1996. 37.95 (*0-201-82382-9*) Addison-Wesley.

Anthony, Robert N. Essentials Accounting with Cash Flow. (C). 1992. pap. 29.25 (*0-201-50894-X*) Addison-Wesley.

— Essentials of Accounting. 3rd ed. LC 81-17557. (Accounting Ser.). (Illus.). 192p. (C). 1982. pap. text 20.50 (*0-201-00006-7*) Addison-Wesley.

— Essentials of Accounting. 4th ed. (Accounting Ser.). (Illus.). (C). 1988. pap. text 27.95 (*0-201-00017-2*) Addison-Wesley.

— Essentials of Accounting. 6th ed. LC 96-34147. 1p. (C). 1996. pap. text 40.00 (*0-201-84866-X*) Addison-Wesley.

— Financial Accounting in Nonbusiness Organizations: An Exploratory Study of Conceptual Issues. LC 78-58734. (Financial Accounting Standards Board Research Report Ser.). (Illus.). 205p. (Orig.). 1978. pap. 5.00 (*0-910065-02-0*) Finan Acct Found.

— Fundamentals of Management Accounting. 2nd ed. (C). 1977. 18.95 (*0-256-01896-0*, Irwn McGrw-H) McGrw-H Hghr Educ.

Anthony, Robert N. Management Control Function. 260p. 1988. 27.96 (*0-07-103201-0*) McGraw.

Anthony, Robert N. Management Control Systems. 10th ed. 2000. 69.74 (*0-07-231635-7*) McGraw.

— A Review of Essentials of Accounting. (Illus.). (C). 1988. pap. text 26.95 (*0-201-05905-3*) Addison-Wesley.

— A Review of Essentials of Accounting. 6th ed. LC 96-34146. 192p. (C). 1996. pap. text 28.00 (*0-201-44278-7*) Addison-Wesley.

— Should Business & Non-Business Accounting Differ? 1989. 14.95 (*0-07-103202-9*) McGraw.

— Think Together. 80p. (Orig.). 1995. pap. 4.50 (*0-425-15046-1*) Berkley Pub.

Anthony, Robert N. & Govindarajan, Vijay. Management Control Systems. 8th ed. LC 93-48215. (Irwin Series in Graduate Accounting). 888p. (C). 1994. text 74.85 (*0-256-13154-6*, Irwn McGrw-H) McGrw-H Hghr Educ.

Anthony, Robert N. & Graham-Walker, Ross. Essentials of Accounting: A Reference Guide. LC 84-6469. (C). 1985. pap. text. write for info. (*0-201-10234-X*) Addison-Wesley.

Anthony, Robert N. & Herzlinger, Regina. Management Control in Nonprofit Organizations. 2nd ed. (C). 1980. 64.95 (*0-256-02326-3*, Irwn McGrw-H) McGrw-H Hghr Educ.

Anthony, Robert N. & Young, David W. Management Control in Nonprofit Organizations. 5th ed. LC 93-18016. 944p. (C). 1993. text 72.35 (*0-256-08642-7*, Irwn McGrw-H) McGrw-H Hghr Educ.

— Management Control in Nonprofit Organizations. 6th ed. LC 98-7083. 888p. 1998. 89.06 (*0-256-25532-6*) McGraw.

Anthony, Robert N., et al. Accounting, Text & Cases. 10th ed. LC 98-7755. (Irwin Graduate Accounting Ser.). xxxii, 951p. 1998. write for info. (*0-256-21840-4*, Irwn Prfssnl) McGraw-Hill Prof.

— CPS Accounting Principles & Finance: Essentials of Accounting & Finance. 7th ed. 516p. (C). 1995. 32.95 (*0-256-21385-2*, Irwn McGrw-H) McGrw-H Hghr Educ.

Anthony, Rock. Some of My Best Friends Are Losers. Hamilton, Hazel, ed. 204p. 1998. pap. 11.93 (*0-9661686-0-7*) L T A Bks.

Anthony, Rosalind. The Model's Black Book to Success. 100p. 1994. pap. text 15.00 (*0-9640693-0-X*) Lord & Jediah.

Anthony, Ruth, ed. see Vernon, Geraldine J.

Anthony Schools Corporation Staff. California Insurance Code & Ethics Prelicense Course. 102p. (Orig.). 1992. pap. text 20.00 (*0-941833-42-9*) Anthony Schools.

— Environmental Issues & Obligations. 2nd ed. (Continuing Education in Real Estate Ser.). (Illus.). 416p. (Orig.). 1995. pap. text 25.00 (*0-941833-50-X*) Anthony Schools.

— Real Estate Terms & Definitions Wordbook. (Real Estate License Course Ser.). 48p. (Orig.). 1994. pap. text 8.00 (*0-941833-47-X*) Anthony Schools.

Anthony, Scott. For Now or Forever: The Dating Process Which Leads to a Happy & Lasting Marriage. 123p. 1999. pap. 12.95 (*0-9666115-4-3*, Our Ladys Pr) Eureka Pub.

***Anthony, Scott.** Juggling & Comedy for Entertaining Children. LC 98-93288. (Illus.). 64p. 1998. pap. 7.95 (*0-9666115-0-0*, Maladast) Eureka Pub.

— A Marriage Repair Manual. 64p. 1999. pap. 7.95 (*0-9666115-5-1*, Our Ladys Pr) Eureka Pub.

***Anthony, Sensei Mark.** Tao of Golf, Set. DeBonis, Todd, ed. 40p. 1999. pap. 29.95 (*0-9678094-0-1*) Tao of Golf.

Anthony, Sharon L., ed. see Towns, Elmer L.

Anthony, Stan. Farm & Ranch Safety Management. (Agriculture Ser.). 1995. teacher ed. 12.75 (*0-8273-6538-1*) Delmar.

Anthony, Stan. Farm & Ranch Safety Management. LC 94-13136. (Illus.). 224p. 1995. pap. 26.95 (*0-8273-6537-3*) Delmar.

Anthony, Sterling. Cookie Cutter. LC 99-42027. 336p. 1999. 24.99 (*0-345-42604-5*) Ballantine Pub Grp.

***Anthony, Sterling.** Cookie Cutter. 2000. pap. 14.00 (*0-345-43568-0*) Ballantine Pub Grp.

Anthony, Steven, jt. auth. see Santangelo, Nick.

Anthony, Susan B. An Account of the Proceedings on the Trial of Susan B. Anthony on the Charge of Illegal Voting at the Presidential Election in Nov. 1872. LC 74-3923. (Women in America Ser.). 220p. 1976. reprint ed. 21.95 (*0-405-06072-6*) Ayer.

Anthony, Susan C. Addition Facts in Five Minutes a Day. (Math Facts in Five Minutes a Day Ser.). 88p. (Orig.). 1995. teacher ed., spiral bd. 11.95 (*1-879478-05-6*, 056) Instr Res Co.

— Dictation Resource Book. 90p. 1999. teacher ed., per. 12.95 (*1-879478-21-8*, 137) Instr Res Co.

— Division Facts in Five Minutes a Day. (Math Facts in Five Minutes a Day Ser.). 88p. (Orig.). (J). (gr. 4-6). 1995. teacher ed., spiral bd. 11.95 (*1-879478-08-0*, 080) Instr Res Co.

— Facts Plus: An Almanac of Essential Information. 4th rev. ed. LC 98-73287. (Illus.). 250p. (J). (gr. 3-8). 1999. pap. 15.95 (*1-879478-19-6*, 196) Instr Res Co.

— Facts Plus Activity Book. 2nd rev. ed. (Illus.). 182p. 1995. teacher ed., spiral bd. 19.95 (*1-879478-11-0*, 110) Instr Res Co.

— Homophones Resource Book. 172p. (J). (gr. 1-8). 1995. teacher ed., per. 15.95 (*1-879478-14-5*, 145) Instr Res Co.

— Multiplication Facts in Five Minutes a Day. (Math Facts in Five Minutes a Day Ser.). 120p. 1999. reprint ed. teacher ed., per. 13.95 (*1-879478-22-6*, 072) Instr Res Co.

— Spelling Plus: 1000 Words Toward Spelling Success. 2nd rev. ed. 170p. 1999. teacher ed., per. 19.95 (*1-879478-20-X*, 048) Instr Res Co.

— Subtraction Facts in Five Minutes a Day. (Math Facts in Five Minutes a Day Ser.). 88p. (Orig.). (J). (gr. 2-4). 1995. teacher ed., spiral bd. 11.95 (*1-879478-06-4*, 064) Instr Res Co.

Anthony, Suzanne. Haiti: Major World Nations. (Major World Nations Ser.). (Illus.). 144p. (YA). (gr. 5 up). 1999. lib. bdg. 19.95 (*0-7910-4759-8*) Chelsea Hse.

— West Indies: Major World Nations. (Major World Nations Ser.). (Illus.). 144p. (YA). (gr. 5 up). 1999. lib. bdg. 19.95 (*0-7910-4772-5*) Chelsea Hse.

Anthony, T. M. The Bellamy Solution: The Way Out. 141p. (Orig.). 1982. pap. 5.95 (*0-88286-153-0*) C H Kerr.

Anthony, T. Mitchel. Suicidio - Suicide: Como Saber Cuando Su Adolescente/Riesgo - Knowing When Your Teen Is at Risk. (SPA.). 218p. 1995. write for info. (*1-56063-851-6*) Editorial Unilit.

Anthony, Thomas A. Kelmin's Tower. Boire, Suzzane, ed. 250p. (Orig.). 1992. 19.95 (*0-9630915-0-6*); pap. 4.95 (*0-9630915-1-4*) Rising Sun NH.

Anthony, Tony. Life Is War but You Can Win: A Vietnam Veteran's Survival Guide for Everyone. LC 93-80045. (Illus.). 96p. (Orig.). 1994. pap. 5.95 (*0-9630976-1-X*) Morgin Pr.

Anthony, Valerie, jt. auth. see Davidson, Scooter T.

Anthony, W. S. Cotton Ginners Handbook. 337p. (Orig.). 1995. per. 28.00 (*0-16-045369-0*, Agriculture Dept) USGPO.

Anthony, W. S. & Mayfield, William D., eds. Cotton Ginners Handbook. (Illus.). 337p. (Orig.). (C). 1995. pap. text 50.00 (*0-7881-2420-X*) DIANE Pub.

Anthony, Warner, Jr. Business Uses of Life Insurance. Vol. IN1. text 82.00 (*0-8205-2407-7*) Bender.

Anthony, William. Bill Anthony's Greatest Hits: Drawings 1963-1987. LC 87-80709. (Illus.). 84p. 1988. 20.00 (*0-912330-62-7*) Jargon Soc.

— Bill Anthony's Greatest Hits: Drawings 1963-1987. limited ed. LC 87-80709. (Illus.). 84p. 1988. 100.00 (*0-912330-63-5*) Jargon Soc.

***Anthony, William.** War Is Swell: A Kid's Idiotic Vision of WW II. (Illus.). 126p. 2000. 25.00 (*1-889195-39-1*, Pub. by Smart Art Pr) RAM Publications.

Anthony, William A. The Art of Napping. (Illus.). 112p. (Orig.). 1997. pap. 9.95 (*0-943914-82-5*) Larson Pubns.

— Community Support Systems: Lessons for Managed Care. 49p. 1996. pap. text 18.95 (*1-878512-05-6*) Boston Univ Ctr Psy Rehab.

Anthony, William A. & Anthony, Camille. The Art of Napping at Work. (Illus.). 112p. 1999. pap. 10.95 (*0-943914-95-7*) Larson Pubns.

Anthony, William A. & Spaniol, LeRoy, eds. Readings in Psychiatric Rehabilitation. LC 94-72719. 552p. (C). 1994. pap. text 34.95 (*1-878512-02-1*) Boston Univ Ctr Psy Rehab.

Anthony, William A., et al. Psychiatric Rehabilitation. LC 89-62415. 283p. 1990. text 39.95 (*1-878512-00-5*) Boston Univ Ctr Psy Rehab.

Anthony, William A., jt. ed. see Farkas, Marianne D.

Anthony, William P. Management: Competencies & Incompetencies. LC 79-25171. 604p. (C). 1981. text. write for info. (*0-201-00085-7*) Addison-Wesley.

— Participative Management. LC 77-83035. 1978. pap. text. write for info. (*0-201-00253-1*) Addison-Wesley.

— Practical Strategic Planning: A Guide & Manual for Line Managers. LC 85-9489. (Illus.). 217p. 1985. 62.95 (*0-89930-102-9*, ANT/, Greenwood Pr) Greenwood.

— Strategic Human Resource Management. 2nd ed. (C). 1995. text 86.00 (*0-03-012887-0*) Harcourt Coll Pubs.

Anthony, William P., et al. Envisionary Management: A Guide for Human Resources Professionals in Management. LC 87-7373. 220p. 1988. 57.95 (*0-89930-257-2*, AYE/, Quorum Bks) Greenwood.

Anthor, Cecilia L., tr. see Abbate, Matthew & Wagner, Allison, eds.

Anti-Defamation League of B'nai B'rith Staff, jt. auth. see Balch Institute for Ethnic Studies Staff.

***Anti-Defamation League Staff.** Closing the Book of Hate. 32p. 2000. pap. text 9.95 (*0-439-21121-2*) Scholastic Inc.

***Antia, Bassey Edem, ed.** Terminology & Language Planning: An Alternative Framework of Practice & Discourse. LC 99-86614. (Terminology & Lexicography Research & Practice Ser.: Vol. 2). xxiv, 261p. 2000. 79.00 (*1-55619-771-3*) J Benjamins Pubng Co.

Antia, F. P. & Abraham, Philip. Clinical Dietetics & Nutrition. 4th ed. 540p. 1998. text 65.00 (*0-19-564165-5*) OUP.

Antia, Noshir H. & Shetty, Vanaja P., eds. The Peripheral Nerve in Leprosy & Other Neuropathies. LC 98-124923. (Illus.). 300p. 1997. text 85.00 (*0-19-563429-2*) OUP.

Antia, Noshir H., et al. The Surgical Management of Deformities in Leprosy & Other Peripheral Neuropathies. (Illus.). 172p. 1993. text 45.00 (*0-19-563058-0*) OUP.

Anticancer-Symposium Staff, et al. Application of Cancer Chemotherapy: Proceedings of the 10th International Congress, Zurich, September 1977. Schoenfeld, H., ed. (Antibiotics & Chemotherapy Ser.: Vol. 24). (Illus.). 1978. 64.50 (*3-8055-2831-0*) S Karger.

— Fundamentals in Cancer Chemotherapy: Proceedings of the 10th International Congress, Zurich, September 1977. (Antibiotics & Chemotherapy Ser.: Vol. 23). (Illus.). 1978. 76.75 (*3-8055-2830-2*) S Karger.

Antico, Paul. Interactive Isolation. (Plagued by Thought Ser.). (Illus.). 32p. 1998. spiral bd. 6.95 (*0-9663577-0-1*) Creative Antics.

***Anticouni, Marilyn D., et al.** California Durable Powers of Attorney: March 2000 Update. Gerber, Mary, ed. LC 96-83298. 736p. 2000. 59.00 (*0-7626-0413-1*) Cont Ed Bar-CA.

— Drafting California Revocable Living Trusts: 11/96 Update. 3rd ed. Gerber, Mary & Sanders, Carol, eds. LC 94-69872. 310p. 1996. ring bd. 67.00 (*0-7626-0043-8*, ES-32182) Cont Ed Bar-CA.

Antieau, Chester James. Commentaries on the Constitution of the United States: Including 1967 Supplement. LC 98-84629. xi,416, 103p. 1998. reprint ed. 65.00 (*1-57588-443-7*, 311750) W S Hein.

— The Higher Laws: Origins of Modern Constitutional Law. LC 93-45712. viii, 208p. 1994. 45.00 (*0-89941-862-7*, 308070) W S Hein.

— Intended Significance of the Fourteenth Amendment. LC 96-53564. x, 412p. 1997. 65.00 (*1-57588-275-2*, 310900) W S Hein.

— Local Government Law, 6 vols. 2nd ed. LC 97-29353. 1997. ring bd. 1040.00 (*0-8205-1020-3*) Bender.

— Modern Constitutional Law, 2 vols. LC 69-19951. 170.00 (*0-318-11982-X*) West Group.

— Modern Constitutional Law, 2 vols. 1993. suppl. ed. 52.50 (*0-317-04342-0*) West Group.

Antieau, Chester James & Rich, William J. Modern Constitutional Law. LC 97-76525. 1997. write for info. (*0-7620-0194-1*) West Group.

Antieau, Chester James, et al. Current Constitutional Issues: A Symposium. LC 77-153885. (Symposia on Law & Society Ser.). 1971. reprint ed. lib. bdg. 25.00 (*0-306-70154-5*) Da Capo.

***Antier, Jean Jacques.** Charles De Foucauld, Vol. 1. 1999. pap. 17.95 (*0-89870-756-0*) IGNA Books.

Antigua Staff. Antigua Giant Print Bible. large type ed. (SPA.). 1990. 39.99 (*0-311-48724-6*) Baptist Spanish.

Antikainen, Ari, et al. Living in a Learning Society: Life-Histories, Identities, & Education. (Knowledge, Identity & School Life Ser.: No. 4). 125p. 1996. 85.00 (*0-7507-0497-7*, Falmer Pr); 27.95 (*0-7507-0498-5*, Falmer Pr) Taylor & Francis.

Antill, Ellen, ed. see Williams, Robert A.

Antill, James M. & Woodhead, Ronald W. Critical Path Methods in Construction Practice. 4th ed. LC 89-35471. 448p. 1990. 120.00 (*0-471-62057-2*) Wiley.

A

Antill, Nicholas, jt. auth. see Arnott, Robert.

*Antill, Nick & Arnott, Robert. Valuing Oil & Gas Companies. 2000. 170.00 (1-85573-451-6, Pub. by Woodhead Pubng) Am Educ Systs.

Antilla, Gary D. Pickers Is a Thief: A Story about Shoplifting. LC 96-79868. (Illus.). 16p. (J). (gr. 3-6). 1997. pap. 5.95 (1-57543-027-4) Mar Co Prods.

Antillano, Laura. Diana en la Tierra Wayuu.Tr. of Diana in a Foreign Land. (SPA., Illus.). 121p. (J). (gr. 5-7). 1994. pap. 7.95 (958-24-0180-X, Pub. by Santillana) T R Bks.

Antilles, Kem. Highest Score. (Star Trek: Deep Space Nine Ser.: No. 8). (J). (gr. 3-6). 1996. pap. 3.99 (0-671-89936-8) S&S Trade.

Antilogus, Pierre. Europe, Peut-On Vraiment Faire Confiance a des Etrangers? Premier Dictionnaire du Chauvanisme Francais. (FRE.). 188p. 1989. pap. 36.95 (0-7859-8165-9, 2869302436) Fr & Eur.

Antimirov, M. Y., et al, eds. Complex Variables. LC 97-47110. (Illus.). 476p. 1998. text 69.95 (0-12-059545-1) Acad Pr.

Antimirov, M. Ya., et al. Applied Integral Transforms. LC 92-38114. (CRM Monograph Ser.: No. 2). 265p. 1993. text 29.00 (0-8218-6998-1, CRMM/2) Am Math.

Antin, Alan J., jt. auth. see Antin, H. Brad.

Antin, David. Selected Poems, 1963-1973. (Sun & Moon Classics Ser.: No. 10). 431p. (Orig.). 1990. pap. 13.95 (1-55713-058-2) Sun & Moon CA.

— Talking. pap. 3.50 (0-686-09756-4) Kulchur Foun.

— Tuning. LC 84-3446. 288p. (Orig.). 1984. pap. 12.50 (0-8112-0894-X, NDP570, Pub. by New Directions) Norton.

— What It Means to Be Avant-Garde. LC 93-9189. 256p. (Orig.). 1993. pap. 15.95 (0-8112-1238-6, NDP760, Pub. by New Directions) Norton.

Antin, David, et al. Coherence. Wellman, Don, ed. Waldrop, Rosmarie, tr. (Illus.). 208p. 1981. pap. 6.95 (0-942030-01-X) O ARS.

Antin, David, tr. see Dorrie, Heinrich.

Antin, Eleanor. Being Antinova. LC 83-72104. (Illus.). 88p. 1983. pap. 10.00 (0-937122-11-4) Astro Artz Eighteenth St.

— Eleanora Antinova Plays. (Illus.). 254p. (Orig.). 1994. pap. 12.95 (1-55713-057-4) Sun & Moon CA.

*Antin, Eleanor. Man Without a World: A Silent Film with English Subtitles Supposedly Made in 1928 by the Imaginary Film Director Yevgeny Antinov. 76p. 2000. pap. 10.95 (1-892295-81-4) Green Integer.

*Antin, H. Brad & Antin, Alan J. The Entrepreneur's Guide to Common Sense Marketing. 209p. 1999. pap. 17.95 (0-9637232-1-9) Mktg Group.

Antin, H. Brad & Antin, Alan J. Secrets from the Lost Art of Common Sense Marketing. (Illus.). 192p. (Orig.). 1992. pap. 14.95 (0-9637232-0-0) Mktg Group.

Antin, Mary. From Plotzk to Boston. LC 74-104404. reprint ed. lib. bdg. 22.50 (0-8398-0060-6) Irvington.

— From Plotzk to Boston. Sarna, Jonathan D., ed. LC 85-40728. (Masterworks of Modern Jewish Writing Ser.). 175p. 1986. reprint ed. pap. 6.95 (0-910129-45-2) Wiener Pubs Inc.

— The Promised Land. Baxter, Annette K., ed. LC 79-8768. (Signal Lives Ser.). 1980. reprint ed. lib. bdg. 48.49 (0-405-12818-5) Ayer.

— The Promised Land. (History - United States Ser.). 373p. 1993. reprint ed. lib. bdg. 89.00 (0-7812-4849-3) Rprt Serv.

— The Promised Land. 2nd ed. LC 84-42936. 397p. 1985. reprint ed. pap. 123.10 (0-7837-8159-8, 204786400008) Bks Demand.

Antin, Mary, jt. auth. see Wells, Rosemary.

Antin, Parker & Weiss, Phyllis W. Himalayan Odyssey: The Perilous Trek to Western Nepal. (C). 1992. 36.00 (0-7855-0183-5, Pub. by Ratna Pustak Bhandar) St Mut.

Antin, Tony. Great Print Advertising: Creative Approaches, Strategies, & Tactics. LC 92-27820. 256p. 1993. 39.95 (0-471-55713-7) Wiley.

Antinarella, Joseph C., jt. auth. see Wolfe, Denny.

Antinello, Lauren. Is That You, Lizzy Lou? 24p. (J). 1999. 1.99 (0-679-89382-2) Random.

— It's Your Bed, Fred! 24p. (J). 1999. 1.99 (0-679-89383-0) Random.

Antink, Suzanne L. & Tingey, Richard. C++ Advanced Placement Test. (DG - Computer Programming Ser.). 1998. text, wbk. ed. 46.95 (0-538-66576-9) S-W Pub.

— C++ Advanced Placement Text. (DG - Computer Programming Ser.). 1998. pap., wbk. ed. 12.95 (0-538-66577-7) S-W Pub.

Antink, Suzanne L., jt. auth. see Tingey, Richard.

*Antinori, Deborah. Journey Through Pet Loss, Set. 18p. 1998. pap. 24.95 incl. audio (0-9668848-0-9, Pub. by YokoSpirit) Penton Overseas.

Antinori, Deborah, et al. Pet Loss Symposiums: Delta Society Conference Lecture Summaries & Writings on Pet Owner's Grief, Bereavement Therapy & Human Nature, 1996-1998. 56p. 1999. reprint ed. pap. 15.00 (1-889785-07-5) Delta Soc.

Antinucci, Francesco. Cognitive Structure & Development in Nonhuman Primates. 272p. (C). 1989. pap. 36.50 (0-8058-0544-3); text 69.95 (0-8058-0242-8) L Erlbaum Assocs.

Antioch Staff. Antioch Review Anthology. Bixler, Paul, ed. LC 79-117752. (Essay Index Reprint Ser.). 1977. 27.95 (0-8369-1782-0) Ayer.

Antion, Thomas. Do It Yourself Over the Hill Birthday Parties. (Illus.). 32p. (Orig.). 1990. pap. 6.95 (0-926395-05-X) Anchor Maryland.

— Making Money in the Novelty Telegram Business. 1990. 49.95 (0-926395-02-5) Anchor Maryland.

— Wake 'em Up! How to Use Humor & Other Professional Techniques to Create Alarmingly Good Business Presentations. LC 96-86293. (Illus.). 336p. (Orig.). 1997. pap. 24.95 (0-926395-12-2) Anchor Maryland.

Antiphon & Andocides. Antiphon & Andocides. Gagarin, Michael & MacDowell, Douglas M., trs. from GRE. LC 97-21207. (Oratory of Classical Greece Ser.). 174p. 1998. 35.00 (0-292-72808-5, GAGANT); pap. 16.95 (0-292-72809-3, GAGANP) U of Tex Pr.

*Antiporda, Enrico. The Band of Gypsies. LC 99-90592. iii, 202p. 2000. pap. 13.95 (0-9672793-0-5, BOG11500, Pub. by Blue Owl Ed) IPG Chicago.

Antipov, E. V. & Marezio, M. Crystal Chemistry of Superconducting Copper Mixed Oxides & Related Phases: Relationship Between Structure & Superconductivity. 400p. 1999. text 78.00 (981-02-2432-X, SCipPrc-B2904) World Scientific Pub.

Antiquarian Catalogues Staff. Prints & Illustrated Books Six Centuries. (Illus.). 56p. 1974. 12.50 (0-915346-21-4) A Wofsy Fine Arts.

Antique Airplane Association Staff. Classic Airplanes of the Thirties - Aircraft of the Roaring Twenties. Gilbert, James B., ed. LC 79-7238. (Flight: Its First Seventy-Five Years Ser.). (Illus.). 1980. reprint ed. lib. bdg. 19.95 (0-405-12153-9) Ayer.

Antique Collectors Club. Alfredo De Vido Architects. (Master Architect Ser.). 1998. 59.95 (1-875498-76-1) Images Aust AT.

*Antique Collectors Club Staff. Akoun: International Auction Art 1998. 1890p. 1999. 65.00 (2-85917-250-5) Edits Amateur.

Antique Collectors Club Staff. Building Design Partnership. 80p. 1999. pap. text 29.95 (1-86470-045-9) Images.

— Cats & Kittens at Play: The Art of Henriette Ronner-Knip, 1821-1909. LC 98-182590. (Illus.). 80p. 1998. 19.50 (1-85149-282-8) Antique Collect.

— The Dictionary of British Art Vol. 5: British Artists 1880-1940. 572p. 1976. 89.50 (0-902028-36-7) Antique Collect.

— Educational Spaces: A Pictorial Review, 1. 1998. 45.00 (1-86470-013-0) Images.

— Gwathmey Siegel & Associates. 1998. 59.95 (1-875498-74-5) Images Aust AT.

— Hok. 256p. 1999. 59.95 (1-86470-022-X) Images.

— House Design: Regina Pizzinni/Leon Luxemburg. 1998. pap. text 19.95 (1-86470-002-5) Images.

*Antique Collectors Club Staff. Houses by the Sea. 1998. pap. text 24.95 (2-7450-0001-2) Telleri Edit.

Antique Collectors Club Staff. Kwan Architects, 2. (Monograph Ser.). 1997. pap. text 19.95 (1-875498-84-2) Images Aust AT.

Antique Collectors Club Staff. Kwan Architects, 3. 1997. pap. text 19.95 (1-875498-85-0) Images Aust AT.

Antique Collectors Club Staff. Old Clocks & Watches & Their Makers. 3rd ed. (Illus.). 520p. 1978. reprint ed. 69.50 (0-902028-69-3) Antique Collect.

*Antique Collectors Club Staff. Outstanding Bar & Restaurant Designs. (Illus.). 1998. pap. 24.95 (2-7450-0011-X) Telleri Edit.

Antique Collectors Club Staff. The Royal Society of British Artists, 1824-1893. 620p. 1975. 89.50 (0-902028-35-9) Antique Collect.

— Sailing Stories & Poems. (Illus.). 120p. (J). 1998. 24.95 (1-85149-703-X) Antique Collect.

*Antique Collectors Club Staff. Transport Spaces: A Pictorial Review. 1998. 45.00 (1-86470-012-2, Pub. by Images) Antique Collect.

Antique Collectors Club Staff. Watch & Clock Encyclopedia. 1994. 39.00 (0-7198-0170-2, Pub. by R Hale Ltd) Seven Hills Bk.

Antique Collectors Club Staff, jt. auth. see Andrews, John.

Antiseri, Dario. Weak Thought & Its Strength. LC 95-83039. (Avebury Series on Philosophy). 144p. 1996. 61.95 (1-85972-257-1, Pub. by Avebury) Ashgate Pub Co.

Antitrust Law Section Members. Antitrust Discovery Handbook Supplement. 1983. student ed. 45.00 (0-685-10021-9); pap. 19.00 (0-685-10020-0, 503-0045) Amer Bar Assn.

— Criminal Antitrust Litigation Manual. LC 83-71753. 655p. 1983. 55.00 (0-89707-107-7, 503-0049) Amer Bar Assn.

— Merger Case Digest, 1982. 756p. 1984. 40.00 (0-685-10016-2, 503-0053) Amer Bar Assn.

— Refusals to Deal & Exclusive Distributorships. 64p. 1983. pap. 20.00 (0-685-10017-0, 503-0047) Amer Bar Assn.

Antle. Economics of Agriculture Vol. 2: Essays on Agricultural Economics in Honor of D. Gale Johnson. (C). 1995. 59.95 (0-226-40175-8) U Ch Pr.

— Financial Accounting. (AB - Accounting Principles Ser.). (C). 2000. pap. write for info. (0-538-84671-2) S-W Pub.

Antle, et al. Student Workbook: Study Guide for Financial Accounting. (SWC-Accounting Ser.). (C). 2000. pap. 19.00 (0-324-02369-3) Thomson Learn.

Antle, John M. Choice & Efficiency in Food Safety Policy. (Studies in Agricultural Policy). 118p. 1995. 29.95 (0-8447-3902-2) Am Enterprise.

— Pesticide Policy, Production Risk, & Producer Welfare. LC 88-14120. 134p. 1988. pap. 16.95 (0-915707-39-X) Resources Future.

*Antle, John M. & Smith, Vincent H. The Economics of World Wheat Markets. LC 99-16709. (CABI Publishing Ser.). 300p. 2000. text 110.00 (0-85199-360-5) OUP.

Antle, John M., et al. Agriculture, Trade, & the Environment: The Impact of Liberalisation on Sustainable Development. LC 98-13466. 272p. 1999. 90.00 (1-85898-783-0) E Elgar.

Antle, John M., jt. ed. see Capalbo, Susan M.

Antle, John M., ed. see Johnson, David G.

Antle, Martine. Theatre et Poesie Surrealistes: Vitrac et la Scene Virtuelle. LC 88-60341. (FRE., Illus.). 136p. 1988. lib. bdg. 22.95 (0-917786-61-0) Summa Pubns.

Antle, Nancy. Beautiful Land. 1997. pap. 4.99 (0-14-036808-6) Viking Penguin.

— The Good Bad Cat. Gregorich, Barbara, ed. (Start to Read! Ser.). (Illus.). 16p. (J). (gr. k-2). 1985. pap. 2.29 (0-88743-012-0, 06012) Sch Zone Pub Co.

— The Good Bad Cat. Gregorich, Barbara, ed. (Start to Read! Ser.). (Illus.). 32p. (J). (ps-3). 1993. pap. 3.99 (0-88743-410-X, 06062) Sch Zone Pub Co.

— Hard Times. 1999. pap. 3.99 (0-14-036253-3, Viking) Viking Penguin.

*Antle, Nancy. Lost in the War. (Illus.). 144p. (YA). (gr. 6-12). 2000. pap. 4.99 (0-14-130836-2, PuffinBks) Peng Put Young Read.

Antle, Nancy. Ordinary Albert. 1998. 16.00 (0-207-19047-X) HarpC.

— Ordinary Albert. 1998. pap. 6.95 (0-207-19158-1) HarpC.

*Antle, Nancy. Playing Solitaire. LC 99-30704. (Illus.). 112p. (YA). 2000. 16.99 (0-8037-2406-3, Dial Yng Read) Peng Put Young Read.

— Sam's Wild West Christmas. LC 99-47057. (Illus.). 40p. (J). (ps-3). 2000. 13.99 (0-8037-2199-4, Dial Yng Read) Peng Put Young Read.

Antle, Nancy. Sam's Wild West Show: Level 3. (Puffin Easy-to-Read Program Ser.). 40p. (J). (gr. 1-4). 1998. pap. 3.99 (0-14-130133-3, PuffinBks) Peng Put Young Read.

— Tough Choices. 1999. pap. 3.99 (0-14-036388-2, Viking) Viking Penguin.

Antler, et al. Stiletto2: The Disinherited. deluxe ed. Annis, Michael, ed. & des. by. (Illus.). 300p. 1992. pap., per. 21.50 (1-882863-02-X) Howling Dog.

Antler, Joyce. Journey Home. LC 96-39280. 1997. 27.00 (0-684-83444-8) Free Pr.

— Journey Home. 1997. 24.95 (0-02-900735-6) Free Pr.

— The Journey Home: How Jewish Women Shaped Modern America. LC 98-4191. 1998. pap. 16.00 (0-8052-1101-2) Schocken.

Antler, Joyce, ed. America & I: Short Stories by American Jewish Women Writers. LC 89-78237. 368p. 1991. pap. 17.50 (0-8070-3607-2) Beacon Pr.

— Talking Back: Images of Jewish Women in American Popular Culture. LC 97-15874. (Brandeis Series in American Jewish History, Culture, & Life). (Illus.). 315p. 1998. text 45.00 (0-87451-841-5) U Pr of New Eng.

*Antler, Joyce, ed. Talking Back: Images of Jewish Women in American Popular Culture. LC 97-15874. (Brandeis Series in American Jewish History, Culture, & Life). (Illus.). 315p. 1998. pap. 22.95 (0-87451-842-3) U Pr of New Eng.

Antler, Joyce & Biklen, Sari K., eds. Changing Education: Women As Radicals & Conservators. LC 89-35030. (SUNY Series, Feminist Theory in Education). 388p. (C). 1990. text 89.50 (0-7914-0233-9); pap. text 29.95 (0-7914-0234-7) State U NY Pr.

Antler, Stephen, ed. Child Abuse & Child Protection: Policy & Practice. LC 82-80767. (Readings in Social Work Ser.). 182p. (Orig.). reprint ed. pap. 56.50 (0-7837-5369-1, 204513300005) Bks Demand.

*Antlhov, Hans & Ngo, Tak W. The Cultural Construction of Politics in Asia. LC 99-37896. 1999. text 59.95 (0-312-22828-7) St Martin.

*Antliff, Allan. Anarchist Modernism. 1999. 40.00 (0-226-02103-3); pap. text 25.00 (0-226-02104-1) U Ch Pr.

*Antliff, Mark. A Cubism Reader. 1998. pap. text 18.00 (0-226-02110-6); lib. bdg. 45.00 (0-226-02109-2) U Ch Pr.

Antliff, Mark. Inventing Bergson: Cultural Politics & the Parisian Avant-Garde. LC 92-13264. (Illus.). 256p. (C). 1993. text 45.00 (0-691-03202-5, Pub. by Princeton U Pr) Cal Prin Full Svc.

*Antliff, Mark, et al. Rethinking Images Between the Wars: New Perspectives in Art History. 220p. 1999. 42.00 (87-7289-523-3, Pub. by Mus Tusculanum) Paul & Co Pubs.

Antliff, Mark, jt. auth. see Affron, Matthew.

Antlo-Suarez, Sandra, ed. see Acker, Kathy, et al.

Antlov, Hans. Exemplary Centre, Administrative Periphery: Rural Leadership & the New Order on Java. LC 95-115100. (SIAS Monographs: No. 68). 200p. (C). 1996. pap. text 35.00 (0-7007-0293-8, Pub. by Curzon Pr Ltd) UH Pr.

Antlov, Hans & Cederroth, Sven. Leadership on Java: Gentle Hints, Authoritarian Rule. (SIAS Monographs: No. 16). 260p. (C). 1996. pap. text 40.00 (0-7007-0295-4, Pub. by Curzon Pr Ltd) UH Pr.

Antlov, Hans & Ngo, Tak-Wing. The Cultural Construction of Politics in Asia. (Democracy in Asia Ser.: Vol. 2). 288p. (C). 1999. text 45.00 (0-7007-0612-7, Pub. by Curzon Pr Ltd) UH Pr.

Antlov, Hans & Tonnesson, Stein, eds. Imperial Policy & South East Asian Nationalism. (SIAS Studies in Asian Topics: No. 19). 336p. (C). 1996. text 45.00 (0-7007-0319-5, Pub. by Curzon Pr Ltd) UH Pr.

Antlov, Hans, jt. auth. see Tonnesson, Stein.

Antman, Dani, jt. auth. see Barr, Vilma.

Antman, Elliott M. & Rutherford, John D. Coronary Care Medicine. 1986. text 161.50 (0-89838-788-4) Kluwer Academic.

Antman, Karen H., jt. auth. see Armitage, James O.

Antman, Karen H., jt. ed. see Armitage, James O.

Antman, Stuart S. Nonlinear Problems of Elasticity. LC 94-25684. (Applied Mathematical Sciences: 107). 750p. 1994. 69.95 (0-387-94199-1) Spr-Verlag.

Antman, Stuart S., et al, eds. Analysis & Continuum Mechanics. (Illus.). 840p. 1989. 106.95 (0-387-50917-8, 2819) Spr-Verlag.

— Metastability & Incompletely Posed Problems. (IMA Volumes in Mathematics & Its Applications Ser.: Vol. 3). (Illus.). 367p. 1986. 69.95 (0-387-96462-2) Spr-Verlag.

Antoce, Oana-Arina, jt. auth. see Takahashi, Katsutada.

Antoch, J., ed. Computational Aspects of Model Choice. (Contributions to Statistics Ser.). (Illus.). viii, 286p. 1992. 90.00 (0-387-91436-6) Spr-Verlag.

Antochiw, Michel, compiled by. Bibliography of the Mayan Language in Yucatan. LC 96-79443. (Illus.). 154p. (Orig.). (C). 1997. pap. text 20.00 (0-911437-69-X) Labyrinthos.

Antoft, M. L., tr. see Resch, H. & Beck, E.

Antognetti, et al. Bioelectronics: A Handbook of Devices & Mechanisms in Electronics & Biology. LC 97-51529. 416p. 1998. 89.50 (0-07-003174-6) McGraw.

Antognetti, Paolo. Neural Networks Vol. 2: Concepts, Application & Implementations, Vol. 2. 1991. text 52.60 (0-13-612763-0) P-H.

Antognetti, Paolo, ed. Process & Device Simulation for MOS-VLSI Circuits. 1983. text 255.50 (90-247-2824-X) Kluwer Academic.

Antognetti, Paolo, et al, eds. Design Systems for VLSI Circuits: Logic Synthesis & Silicon Comiletion. (C). 1987. pap. text 138.00 (90-247-3562-9) Kluwer Academic.

*Antohi, Sorin. Between Past & Future: The Revolutions of 1989 & Their Aftermath. LC 99-86119. 2000. pap. text 28.95 (963-9116-71-8) Ctrl Europ Univ.

Antoine, Andre. Memories of the Theatre-Libre. Albright, H. D., ed. Carlson, Marvin, tr. LC 64-8734. (Books of the Theatre: No. 5). (Illus.). 1964. 19.95 (0-87024-034-X) U of Miami Pr.

Antoine, Charles. Church & Power in Brazil. Nelson, Peter, tr. LC 72-93341. 287p. reprint ed. pap. 89.00 (0-8357-8847-4, 203347700086) Bks Demand.

Antoine, Charles, ed. see Perez Esquivel, Adolfo.

Antoine, Fabrice. French-English - English-French Vocabulary of Civil Engineering. 64p. 1988. pap. 17.50 (2-85608-027-8) IBD Ltd.

— French-English - English-French Vocabulary of Road Construction Machinery & Equipment. 72p. 1989. pap. 20.00 (2-85608-033-2) IBD Ltd.

— Vocabulaire des Travaux Publiques: Anglais-Francais, Francais-Anglais. (ENG & FRE.). 55p. 1988. pap. 35.00 (0-7859-3913-X, 2856080278) Fr & Eur.

— Vocabulaires des Engins et Materials de Chantiers: Anglais-Francais, Francais-Anglais. (ENG & FRE.). 64p. 1989. pap. 35.00 (0-7859-3916-4) Fr & Eur.

Antoine, Heloise. Curious Kids Go on Vacation: Another Big Book of Words. Holifield, Vicky, tr. LC 96-42511. (Big Book of Words). (Illus.). 26p. (J). (ps-k). 1996. 13.95 (1-56145-143-6) Peachtree Pubs.

— Curious Kids Go to Preschool: Another Big Book of Words. LC 96-7260. (Big Book of Words: Bk. 2). (Illus.). 26p. (J). (ps up). 1996. 13.95 (1-56145-129-0) Peachtree Pubs.

Antoine, J. P., et al. Quantization & Infinite-Dimensional Systems. LC 94-44822. (Lecture Notes in Physics: Vol. 248). (Illus.). 300p. (C). 1995. text 95.00 (0-306-44834-3, Kluwer Plenum) Kluwer Academic.

— Quantization, Coherent States, & Complex Structures: Proceedings of the Thirteenth Workshop on Geometric Methods in Physics Held in Bialowieza, Poland, July 9-15, 1994. (Illus.). 312p. (C). 1996. text 110.00 (0-306-45214-6, Kluwer Plenum) Kluwer Academic.

Antoine, Jacques C. Jean Price-Mars & Haiti. (Illus.). 225p. (C). 1981. 28.00 (0-914478-55-9, Three Contnts); pap. 14.95 (0-914478-56-7, Three Contnts) L Rienner.

Antoine, Jean-Pierre & Tirapegui, Enrique, eds. Colloquium on Functional Integration Theory & Applications: Functional Integration Theory & Applications. LC 80-21935. 365p. 1980. reprint ed. pap. 113.20 (0-608-05400-3, 206586900006) Bks Demand.

Antoine, Louis B. Ah les Femmes! 257p. 25.95 (0-7541-1119-9, Pub. by Minerva Pr) Unity Dist.

Antoine, Louis B. Lone Survivor: Judge, Jury, & Executioner. 1998. pap. 12.95 (0-533-12846-3) Vantage.

*Antoine, Marie-Claire. French Together. LC 00-26850. (For the Car Ser.). (FRE.). 48p. (ps-3). 2000. 14.95 (0-609-60652-2) Liv Lang.

— Italian Together. LC 00-26851. (For the Car Ser.). (ITA.). 48p. (ps-3). 2000. 14.95 (0-609-60651-4) Liv Lang.

Antoine, Nabil. Don't Worry Mom-I Can Take Care of Myself: A Little Person's Guide to a Big Person's World. 60p. 1994. reprint ed. pap. 12.95 (1-880979-00-4) Alert Pubns & Video.

Antoine, Rose-Marie B. Commonwealth Caribbean Law & Legal Systems. LC 99-168464. (Commonwealth Caribbean Law Ser.). xiiii, 346 p. 1999. write for info. (1-85941-423-0) Cavendish Pubng.

Antoine, Theodore J. S., see St. Antoine, Theodore J.

*Antoinette, Jeanne Marie. Circle of Tears: The Spiritual Phenomenon of Elian Gonzalez. LC 00-104446. 253p. 2000. pap. 16.00 (1-58776-060-6, Mystic Oracle Bks) Vivisphere.

Antokol, Norm, jt. auth. see Nudell, Mayer.

Antokol, Norman, jt. auth. see Nudell, Mayer.

Antokoletz, Elliott. Bela Bartok: A Guide to Research. 2nd ed. Marco, Guy A., ed. LC 96-39298. (Composer Resource Manuals Ser.: Vol. 40). 536p. 1997. text 75.00 (0-8153-2088-4) Garland.

— The Music of Bela Bartok: A Study of Tonality & Progression in Twentieth Century Music. LC 82-17352. (Illus.). 472p. (C). 1984. pap. 22.50 (0-520-06747-9, Pub. by U CA Pr) Cal Prin Full Svc.

— Twentieth Century Music. 512p. (C). 1991. text 48.00 (0-13-934126-9) P-H.

*Antokoletz, Elliott, et al, eds. Bartok Perspectives: Man, Composer & Ethnomusicologist. LC 99-22696. (Illus.). 352p. 2000. text 65.00 (0-19-512562-2) OUP.

Antol Kiss, Zersammeugestellt Von, see Von Antol Kiss, Zersammeugestellt.

Antol, Marie N. Healing Teas: How to Prepare & Use Teas to Maximize Your Health. LC 95-20039. (Illus.). 256p. Date not set. pap. 12.95 (0-89529-707-8, Avery) Penguin Putnam.

An Asterisk (*) at the beginning of an entry indicates that the title is appearing for the first time.

*Antol, Marie Nadine. The Incredible Secrets of Vinegar: The Quintessential Guide to the History, Lore, Varieties & Healthful Benefits of Vinegar. LC 99-46570. 192p. 2000. pap. 11.95 (1-58333-005-4, Avery) Penguin Putnam.

*Antol, Nikki. The Mustard Book: The Quintessential Guide to History, Lore, Varieties & Curiosities of Mustard. 224p. 1999. pap. 11.95 (0-89529-920-8, Avery) Penguin Putnam.

Antol, Nikki, ed. see Fischer, William L.

Antola, Esko, jt. ed. see Rosas, Allan.

Antolik, Michael. ASEAN & the Diplomacy of Accommodation. LC 89-49026. 216p. (gr. 13). 1990. text 70.95 (0-87332-630-X, East Gate Bk) M E Sharpe.

Antolin, Fernando N. Lygdamus: Corpus Tibullianum III, 1-6: Lygdami Elegiarum Liber. LC 95-20759. (Mnemosyne, Bibliotheca Classica Batava Ser.: Vol. 154). 1996. 202.50 (90-04-10210-8) Brill Academic Pubs.

Antolin, Francisco. Los Espacios en Juan Rulfo. LC 91-72253. (SPA.). 148p. 1991. 19.00 (0-89729-604-4) Ediciones.

Antolinez Quijano, Crescencio. Legal & Management Dictionary: Fachwoerterbuch fur Recht und Verwaltung. 2nd ed. (GER & SPA.). 427p. 1983. 150.00 (0-8288-0979-8, M7398) Fr & Eur.

Antolini, Renzo, et al, eds. Transport in Biomembranes: Model Systems & Reconstitution. LC 82-12364. (Illus.). 288p. 1982. reprint ed. pap. 89.30 (0-608-00648-3, 206123600007) Bks Demand.

Antolovich, Renato. Successful Sex for Men. 96p. 1998. pap. 9.00 (0-8059-4433-8) Dorrance.

Antolovich, S. D., ed. see International Symposium on Superalloys Staff.

Anton. Applied Finite Math. 5th ed. (C). 1997. pap. text 76.50 (0-15-517761-3) Harcourt Coll Pubs.

— Calculus, Vol. 3. 6th ed. 463p. 1998. pap. 43.95 incl. cd-rom (0-471-24349-3) Wiley.

*Anton. Calculus , Vol. 3. 6th ed. 1999. pap. text 50.50 (0-471-37097-5) Wiley.

— Calculus: A New Horizon, Vol. 1. 6th ed. 592p. 1997. pap. 58.95 (0-471-24331-0) Wiley.

— Calculus: A New Horizon, Vol. 2. 6th ed. 512p. 1998. pap. 43.95 (0-471-24348-5) Wiley.

Anton. Calculus: Selected Chapters. 80p. 1998. pap. text 9.00 (0-471-32385-3) Wiley.

— Calculus: Student Solutions Manual & Mathematica Manual, set. 5th ed. 1901p. 1995. pap. text 97.00 (0-471-14629-3) Wiley.

— Calculus Brief with Mathematical Dynamic Set. 5th ed. 800p. 1995. text 139.95 (0-471-12797-3) Wiley.

Anton. The Calculus Companion. 5th ed. 768p. 1995. pap. 48.95 (0-471-10678-X) Wiley.

Anton. Differential Equations with Boundary Value Problems. (Mathematics Ser.). 2000. mass mkt. 72.95 (0-534-26328-3) Brooks-Cole.

*Anton. Elementary Linear Algebra. 8th ed. LC 99-44926. 588p. 1999. text 102.95 (0-471-17055-0) Wiley.

— Elementary Linear Algebra Applications. 8th ed. LC 99-44870. 822p. 1999. text 102.95 (0-471-17052-6) Wiley.

Anton. Linear Algebra to Accompany Calculus with Analytics. 160p. 1995. pap. text, suppl. ed. 17.95 (0-471-10677-1) Wiley.

— Modeling & Lab Manual for Differential Equations. (Mathematics Ser.). 2002. mass mkt. 32.95 (0-534-34130-6) Brooks-Cole.

— Occupational Safety Health Management. 2nd ed. 1989. student ed. 28.12 (0-07-002109-0) McGraw.

*Anton. Public Goods. 416p. 2000. 68.00 (0-8133-6617-8, Pub. by Westview) HarpC.

Anton. Student Solutions Manual to Accompany Calculus with Analytics. 315p. 1995. pap. 34.95 (0-471-10591-0) Wiley.

*Anton, et al. Public Goods. 416p. 2000. pap. 25.00 (0-8133-6618-6, Pub. by Westview) HarpC.

Anton, jt. auth. see Prada.

Anton, Carole, jt. auth. see Anton, Douglas.

Anton, Christine. Selbstreflexivitat der Kunsttheorie in den Kunstlernovellen des Realismus. (North American Studies in Nineteenth-Century German Literature). 227p. 1998. 46.95 (0-8204-3854-5) P Lang Pubng.

*Anton, Corey. Selfhood & Authenticity. (C). 2001. pap. text 16.95 (0-7914-4900-9) State U NY Pr.

— Selfhood & Authenticity. (C). 2001. text 49.50 (0-7914-4899-1) State U NY Pr.

Anton, D. L., et al, eds. Intermetallic Matrix Composites Vol. 194: Symposium Proceedings Ser. 441p. 1990. text 17.50 (1-55899-083-6) Materials Res.

Anton, Danilo J. Ciudades en Riesgo. 1997. pap. 15.00 (0-88936-788-4, Pub. by IDRC Bks) Stylus Pub VA.

— Diversidad, Globalizacion y los Caminos de la Naturaleza. (SPA.). 302p. 2000. pap. 17.95 (0-88936-885-6, Pub. by IDRC Bks) Stylus Pub VA.

Anton, Danilo J. Diversity, Globalization & the Ways of Nature. LC 96-117709. 234p. 1995. pap. 16.00 (0-88936-724-8, Pub. by IDRC Bks) Stylus Pub VA.

— Thirsty Cities: Urban Environments & Water Supply in Latin America. 200p. 1993. pap. write for info. (0-88936-666-7) IDRC Bks.

Anton, Debra, jt. auth. see Anton, Glenn.

*Anton, Douglas & Anton, Carole. ISO 9000 Survival Guide. unabridged ed. Hall, Al, ed. (Illus.). 56p. 1999. pap. 5.95 (0-9672170-0-8) AEM Cons Grp.

Anton, Francisco J., tr. see Pratt, Richard.

*Anton, Frank. Why Didn't You Get Me Out? A POW'S Nightmare in Vietnam. (Illus.). 256p. 2000. mass mkt. 6.99 (0-312-97488-4, St Martins Paperbacks) St Martin.

Anton, G. Haberkamp De, see Haensch, Guenther & De Anton, G. Haberkamp.

Anton, G. Haberkamp De, see De Anton, G. Haberkamp.

Anton, Glenn & Anton, Debra. Who Shares Your Birthday? Famous Birthdays Listed for Each Day of the Year. LC 94-18202. 176p. 1994. pap. 12.95 (0-9637195-2-1, Kingsley Pr) Anton Enterprises.

Anton, H. Elementary Linear Algebra. 7th ed. 520p. 1994. pap., student ed. 36.95 (0-471-30622-3) Wiley.

Anton, H. J., ed. Control of Cell Proliferation & Differentiation During Regeneration. (Monographs in Developmental Biology: Vol. 21). (Illus.). x, 246p. 1988. 192.25 (3-8055-4737-4) S Karger.

Anton, Harley, jt. auth. see Bader, Carol.

*Anton, Howard. Calculus: A New Horizon. 6th ed. LC 98-13917. 1312p. 1998. text 122.95 (0-471-15306-0) Wiley.

— Calculus: A New Horizon. 6th ed. 560p. 1998. pap., student ed. 40.95 (0-471-24628-X) Wiley.

— Calculus: A New Horizon, 2. 6th ed. 224p. 1998. pap. text, student ed. 14.00 (0-471-24623-9) Wiley.

Anton, Howard. Calculus: A New Horizon, Brief Edition. 6th ed. LC 98-14809. 758p. 1998. text 99.95 (0-471-15307-9) Wiley.

— Calculus: With Analytic Geometry, 1 vol. 4th ed. 1994. cd-rom 52.95 (0-471-55803-6) Wiley.

— Calculus with Analytic Geometry. 5th ed. 1136p. 1994. text 112.95 (0-471-59495-4) Wiley.

Anton, Howard. Calculus with Analytic Geometry, 1. 5th ed. LC 94-36646. 800p. 1994. text 90.95 (0-471-07653-8) Wiley.

Anton, Howard. Calculus with Analytic Geometry & Linear Algebra Supplement to Accompany Calculus with Analytic Geometry Fifth Edition & Graphing Calculator Survival Guide to Accompany Calculus 5th ed. 1320p. 1996. text 151.90 (0-471-17766-0) Wiley.

— Elementary Linear Algebra. 7th ed. LC 93-28546. 640p. 1993. text 95.95 (0-471-58742-7) Wiley.

— Elementary Linear Algebra. 7th ed. 570p. 1994. text 56.00 incl. 3.5 ld (0-471-00828-1) Wiley.

— Linear Algebra: With Applications Chapter, Set. 7th ed. 570p. 1994. pap. text 47.50 (0-471-01562-8) Wiley.

— Linear Algebra Applications. 7th ed. 864p. 1994. text 58.00 (0-471-07276-1) Wiley.

— Multivariable Calculus. 5th ed. LC 95-32954. 409p. 1995. pap. 80.95 (0-471-13909-2) Wiley.

*Anton, Howard & Rorres, Chris. Elementary Linear Algebra. 8th ed. 720p. 2000. pap., student ed. 39.95 (0-471-38248-5) Wiley.

Anton, Howard & Rorres, Chris. Elementary Linear Algebra: Applications Version. 7th ed. 864p. 1994. text 99.95 (0-471-58741-9) Wiley.

Anton, Howard & Rorres, Chris. Elementary Linear Algebra: Applications Version, Textbook & Student Solutions Manual. 1544p. 1995. pap. text 130.90 (0-471-15439-3) Wiley.

Anton, Howard, et al. Applied Finite Mathematics. 5th ed. 624p. (C). 1991. text 77.50 (0-15-502942-8, Pub. by SCP) Harcourt.

— Elementary Linear Algebra Applications & Linear Algebra with Maple Set. 864p. 1995. pap. text 124.90 (0-471-13834-7) Wiley.

— Elementary Linear Algebra with Applications. 7th ed. 680p. 1994. pap. text, student ed. 25.00 (0-471-30896-X) Wiley.

Anton, J. Spanish with Ease. Smellie, John, tr. from FRE. (With Ease Ser.). (SPA., Illus.). 479p. 1987. 24.95 (2-7005-0131-4, Pub. by Assimil) Distribks Inc.

Anton, Jim. Wise & Wacky Proverbs: The Truth Behind Everyday Sayings. (Illus.). 128p. 1996. pap. 6.95 (0-8069-8485-6) Sterling.

Anton, John. Critical Humanism As a Philosophy of Culture: The Case of E. P. Papanoutos. (Modern Greek History & Culture Ser.). 1981. 10.00 (0-935476-07-5) Nostos Bks.

— Customer Relationship Management: Making Hard Decisions with Soft Numbers. LC 95-33737. 183p. (C). 1996. 49.00 (0-13-438474-1) P-H.

*Anton, John. Last-He: The Last He-Man. LC 00-190409. 210p. 2000. 25.00 (0-7388-1657-4); pap. 18.00 (0-7388-1658-2) Xlibris Corp.

Anton, John P. Categories & Experience: Essays on Aristotelian Themes. (Studies in the Humanities & the Social Sciences). 346p. (Orig.). (C). 1996. pap. 17.00 (1-883058-02-3, Dowling College) Global Pubns.

— The Poetry & Poetics of Constantine P. Cavafy: Aesthetic Visions of Sensual Reality. LC 95-233198. (Greek Poetry Archives Ser.: Vol. 1). 387p. 1995. text 74.00 (3-7186-5551-9, Harwood Acad Pubs); pap. text 27.00 (3-7186-5552-7, Harwood Acad Pubs) Gordon & Breach.

Anton, John P., ed. Science & the Sciences in Plato. LC 78-13418. 144p. 1997. 35.00 (0-88206-301-4) Caravan Bks.

— Upward Panic: The Autobiography of Eva Palmer-Sikelianos, Vol. 4. (Choreography & Dance Studies). 252p. 1993. text 36.00 (3-7186-5264-1) Gordon & Breach.

Anton, John P., intro. Upward Panic: The Autobiography of Eva Palmer-Sikelianos, Vol. 4. (Choreography & Dance Studies). 252p. 1993. pap. text 19.00 (3-7186-5310-9) Gordon & Breach.

Anton, John P. & Preus, Anthony, eds. Essays in Ancient Greek Philosophy II. LC 69-14648. 541p. (C). 1984. text 29.50 (0-87395-623-0) State U NY Pr.

— Essays in Ancient Greek Philosophy III: Plato. LC 69-14648. 358p. (C). 1989. text 29.50 (0-88706-916-9) State U NY Pr.

— Essays in Ancient Greek Philosophy IV: Aristotle's Ethics. LC 69-14648. 290p. (C). 1991. text 29.50 (0-7914-0654-7) State U NY Pr.

Anton, John P., jt. ed. see Preus, Anthony.

Anton, Jon. Callcenter Management: By the Numbers. 1997. pap. 44.95 (1-55753-112-9) Purdue U Pr.

— Listening to the Voice of the Customer. LC 97-67089. 152p. 1997. pap. 39.95 (0-915910-43-8) Customer Srv Grp.

*Anton, Jon & Gustin, David. Call Center Benchmarking: Deciding If Good Is Good Enough. LC 00-27224. 2000. write for info. (1-55753-215-X, Ichor Busn Bks) Purdue U Pr.

*Anton, Jon, et al. Call Center Performance Enhancement Using Simulation & Modeling. LC 99-41758. (Customer Access Management Ser.). 1999. pap. 44.95 (1-55753-182-X) Purdue U Pr.

Anton, Kelly & Barnhart, Rochelle. QuarkXPress 4 Complete. 900p. 1999. 45.00 (1-56830-412-9) Hayden.

*Anton, Kelly K. Using Quarkxpress 4. LC 98-84535 (Using... Ser.). 1998. pap. 29.99 (0-7897-1659-3) Que.

Anton, Klaus, jt. ed. see Berger, Claire.

*Anton, Linda Hunt. Never to Be a Mother: A Guide for All Women Who Didn't - Or Couldn't - Have Children. 197p. 2000. reprint ed. text 18.00 (0-7881-6945-9) DIANE Pub.

Anton, Liz & Dooley, Beth. It's the Berries! Exotic & Common Recipes. Oxley, Constance, ed. LC 87-45580. (Illus.). 160p. (Orig.). 1988. pap. 9.95 (0-88266-425-5, Garden Way Pub) Storey Bks.

— It's the Berries! Exotic & Common Recipes. Oxley, Constance, ed. LC 87-45580. (Illus.). 160p. (Orig.). 1988. 15.95 (0-88266-424-7, Garden Way Pub) Storey Bks.

— Recipes from Massachusetts: With Love. (Illus.). 250p. (Orig.). 1985. spiral bd. 13.95 (0-913703-07-9) Strawberry Pt.

*Anton, Mauricio. Big Cats & Their Fossil Relatives: An Illustrated Guide to Their Evolution & Natural History. (Illus.). 2000. pap. text 17.95 (0-231-10229-1) Col U Pr.

Anton, Mauricio & Turner, Alan. The Big Cats & Their Fossil Relatives: An Illustrated Guide to Their Evolution & Natural History. LC 96-3969. (Illus.). 1996. 39.95 (0-231-10228-3) Col U Pr.

Anton, Peter J. Naturalism & Historical Understanding: Essays on the Philosophy of John Hermann Randall, Jr. LC 67-63753. 235p. reprint ed. pap. 72.90 (0-608-10167-2, 201095700072) Bks Demand.

Anton, R. F. The Pharmacology of Alcohol Abuse. Kranzler, Henry R., ed. LC 94-28586. (Handbook of Experimental Pharmacology Ser.: 114). 1994. 471.95 (0-387-57425-6) Spr-Verlag.

Anton, Shari. By King's Decree. (Historical Ser.: No. 401). 1998. per. 4.99 (0-373-29001-2, 1-29001-4) Harlequin Bks.

— By Queen's Grace. (Historical Ser.: Bk. 493). 2000. mass mkt. 4.99 (0-373-29093-4, 1-29093-1) Harlequin Bks.

*Anton, Shari. Conqueror. (Knights of the Black Rose Ser.). 2000. per. 4.99 (0-373-29107-8) Harlequin Bks.

Anton, Shari. Emily's Captain. (March Madness Ser.). 1997. per. 4.99 (0-373-28957-X, 1-28957-8) Harlequin Bks.

— Lord of the Manor. (Historical Ser.: Vol. 434). 1998. per. 4.99 (0-373-29034-9, 1-29034-5) Harlequin Bks.

*Anton, Ted. Bold Science: Seven Scientists Who Are Changing Our World. LC 00-21596. 256p. 2000. text 24.95 (0-7167-3512-1) W H Freeman.

Anton, Ted. Eros, Magic, & the Murder of Professor Culianu. LC 96-9432. 296p. 1996. 24.95 (0-8101-1396-1) Northwestern U Pr.

Anton, Thomas J. Administered Politics: Elite Political Culture in Sweden. 1980. lib. bdg. 86.50 (0-89838-025-1) Kluwer Academic.

— American Federalism & Public Policy: How the System Works. 320p. (C). 1988. 37.95 (0-87722-577-X) Temple U Pr.

— Federal Aid to Detroit. LC 82-74099. 55p. 1983. pap. 8.95 (0-8157-0437-2) Brookings.

— Occupational Safety & Health Management. 2nd ed. 432p. (C). 1989. 88.44 (0-07-002108-2) McGraw.

Anton, Uwe, ed. see Dick, Philip K.

Anton, William. Adonde Va el Agua? Curriculum Concepts Staff, ed. (Discovery Links Ser.).Tr. of Where Does the Water Go?. (SPA., Illus.). 16p. 1998. pap., teacher ed. 16.50 (1-56784-797-8) Newbridge Educ.

Anton, William T., Jr. & Kesse, Bruce. Forgotten Coins of the North American Colonies. rev. ed. LC 92-71449. (Illus.). 112p. 1992. 50.00 (0-87341-210-9, FG01) Krause Pubns.

Antonacci, Gary. Optimal Commodity Investing. 1983. pap. 35.00 (0-930233-20-4) Windsor.

Antonacci, Mark. The Resurrection of the Shroud: New Scientific, Medical & Archeological Evidence. LC 99-46809. (Illus.). 340p. 2000. 21.95 (0-87131-890-3) M Evans.

Antonacci, Patricia & Hedley, Carolyn N., eds. Natural Approaches to Reading & Writing. 216p. (C). 1994. text 73.25 (0-89391-750-8); pap. text 39.50 (0-89391-922-5) Ablx Pub.

Antonaccio, Carla M. An Archaeology of Ancestors: Tomb Cult & Hero Cult in Early Greece. (Greek Studies: Interdisciplinary Approaches). 315p. (C). 1994. pap. text 26.95 (0-8476-7942-X); lib. bdg. 64.00 (0-8476-7941-1) Rowman.

*Antonaccio, Egidio. First Aid for a Woman's Soul. (Charming Petites Ser.). 80p. 2000. 4.95 (0-88088-397-9) Peter Pauper.

*Antonaccio, Maria. Picturing the Human: The Moral Thought of Iris Murdoch. LC 99-41886. 272p. 2000. 35.00 (0-19-513171-1) OUP.

Antonaccio, Maria & Schweiker, William, eds. Iris Murdoch & the Search for Human Goodness. 296p. 1996. pap. text 18.95 (0-226-02113-0) U Ch Pr.

— Iris Murdoch & the Search for Human Goodness. LC 96-12925. 266p. 1996. lib. bdg. 48.00 (0-226-02112-2) U Ch Pr.

Antonaccio, Michael J., ed. Cardiovascular Pharmacology. LC 90-8549. (Illus.). 572p. 1990. reprint ed. pap. 177.40 (0-608-07224-9, 206744900009) Bks Demand.

Antonacopoulos, Nicolaus. Six Language Dictionary of Fish, Crustaceans & Molluscs & Products. (ENG, FRE, GER, ITA & LAT.). 640p. 1997. 295.00 (0-7859-9671-0) Fr & Eur.

Antonak, Richard F. & Livneh, Hanoch. The Measurement of Attitudes Toward People with Disabilities: Methods, Psychometrics & Scales. (Illus.). 326p. 1988. pap., spiral bd. 40.95 (0-398-06008-8) C C Thomas.

— The Measurement of Attitudes Toward People with Disabilities: Methods, Psychometrics & Scales. (Illus.). 326p. (C). 1988. text 62.95 (0-398-05404-5) C C Thomas.

A

Antonak, Richard F., jt. auth. see Livneh, Hanoch.

Antonakes, Michael, tr. see Kazantzakis, Nikos.

Antonakos. Application Programming in Structured C. (C). 1997. write for info. (0-13-378282-4, Macmillan Coll) P-H.

— Digital Data Communications. 56p. (C). 2000. 77.00 (0-02-303605-2, Macmillan Coll) P-H.

Antonakos. Simulations for Op Amps Using PSpice. 112p. (C). 1997. pap. 46.00 incl. disk (0-13-632449-5) P-H.

Antonakos, James L. An Introduction to the Intel Family of Microprocessors: Utilizing the 80x86 Microprocessor Family. 3rd ed. LC 97-46893. 768p. (C). 1998. 105.67 (0-13-893439-8) P-H.

— Microcomputer Repair. 3rd ed. LC 98-24766. 693p. 1998. pap. text 90.00 (0-13-893454-1) P-H.

— Pentium Microprocessor. LC 96-43995. 539p. (C). 1996. 106.00 (0-02-303614-1, Macmillan Coll) P-H.

— Simulations for Digital Electronics Using Electronic Workbench. 120p. (C). 1999. pap. text 42.00 (0-13-646423-8, Macmillan Coll) P-H.

*Antonakos, James L. Simulations for Digital Electronics Using Electronic Workbench. 260p. 2002. pap. 36.00 (0-13-646431-9) P-H.

— Simulations for Electric Circuits Using Electronic Workbench. 260p. 2000. pap. 36.00 (0-13-646449-1) P-H Intl.

Antonakos, James L. Simulations for Electric Circuits Using Pspice. 260p. (C). 2002. pap. 36.00 (0-13-646456-4) P-H.

*Antonakos, James L. Simulations for Electronic Devices Using Electronic Workbench. 260p. 2000. pap. text 37.33 (0-13-646464-5, Prentice Hall) P-H.

— Simulations for Electronic Devices Using Pspice. 260p. 2000. pap. text 37.33 (0-13-646472-6, Prentice Hall) P-H.

— Simulations for Operational Amplifiers Using Electronics Workbench. LC 97-200930. 108p. (C). 1997. pap. text 50.00 incl. disk (0-13-632464-9) P-H.

— Simulations for Transistors Using Electronic Workbench. 260p. 2000. pap. text 37.33 (0-13-632456-8, Prentice Hall) P-H.

— Simulations for Transistors Using Pspice. 260p. 2000. pap. text 37.33 (0-13-632472-X, Prentice Hall) P-H.

Antonakos, James L. The 68000 Microprocessor: Hardware & Software Principles & Applications. 4th ed. LC 97-46805. 602p. (C). 1998. 105.00 (0-13-668120-4) P-H.

*Antonakos, James L. Structured BASIC Applied to Technology. 4th ed. LC 98-50032. (Illus.). 339p. 1999. pap. text 77.00 incl. disk (0-13-081139-4) P-H.

*Antonakos, James L. & Dixon, Alan C. A Practical Approach to Digital Electronics. LC 99-26192. (Illus.). 376p. (C). 1999. text 76.00 incl. audio compact disk (0-13-727595-1, Macmillan Coll) P-H.

*Antonakos, James L. & Mansfield, Kenneth. Microcomputer Hardware, Software & Troubleshooting for Engineering & Technology Students. LC 99-58000. (Illus.). 616p. (C). 2000. pap. text 81.00 incl. audio compact disk (0-13-011466-9) P-H.

Antonakos, James L. & Mansfield, Kenneth C., Jr. Application Programming in Structured C. LC 95-41076. 623p. (C). 1995. pap. text 86.00 (0-13-356684-6) P-H.

Antonakos, James L. & Mansfield, Kenneth C. Introduction to Computers for Technology Students. LC 99-27117. (Illus.). 752p. (C). 1999. pap. text 73.00 incl. audio compact disk (0-13-227786-7, Macmillan Coll) P-H.

— Introduction to Microsoft Windows for Technology & Engineering Students. LC 99-48940. (Illus.). 544p. (C). 2000. pap. text 66.00 incl. audio compact disk (0-13-227497-3, Macmillan Coll) P-H.

— Reference Guide to C & C++ LC 98-10914. 200p. (C). 1998. pap. 48.00 (0-13-956376-8) P-H.

— Visual Basic for Technology & Engineering Students. (C). 2000. pap. 53.00 (0-13-442344-5, Macmillan Coll) P-H.

*Antonakos, James L., et al. Sructured C for Engineering & Technology. 4th ed. LC 00-24618. 896p. 2000. pap. 78.00 incl. disk (0-13-020682-2) P-H.

Antonakos, James L., jt. auth. see Adamson, Thomas A.

Antonakos, James L., jt. auth. see Mansfield, Kenneth C.

Antonaya, A. L., jt. ed. see Premchand, A.

*Antone, Harvey & Elm, Demus. The Oneida Creation Story. Lounsbury, Floyd G., ed. Gick, Bryan, tr. LC 00-24446. 178p. 2000. pap. 12.00 (0-8032-6742-8) U of Nebr Pr.

Antone, Susan. Picture the Blues. (Illus.). 1990. pap. 22.95 (0-932117-13-9) Osborne Enterps.

Antonelli, Alfredo P. The Best of Italian Music: All New Piano/Vocal Sheet Music Arrangements. 1997. pap. 14.95 (1-56922-014-X) Creat Cncpts.

Antonelli, Cristiano. The Dynamics of Technological Change. LC 98-35407. (Frontiers of Political Economy Ser.). 288p. (C). (gr. 13). 1998. 85.00 (0-415-19052-5, D6099) Routledge.

— The Economics of Localized Technological Change & Industrial Dynamics. LC 94-18130. (Economics of Science, Technology & Innovation Ser.: Vol. 3). 1995. lib. bdg. 136.00 (0-7923-2910-4) Kluwer Academic.

Antonelli, Cristiano, ed. The Economics of Information Networks. (Illus.). viii,478p. 1982. 147.00 (*0-444-88642-7*, North Holland) Elsevier.
— New Information Technology & Industrial Change: The Italian Case. (C). 1988. lib. bdg. 130.50 (*90-277-2747-3*) Kluwer Academic.
Antonelli, Cristiano, et al. The Economics of Industrial Modernization. (Illus.). 182p. 1992. pap. text 44.95 (*0-12-059630-X*) Acad Pr.
Antonelli, Gilberto & De Liso, Nicola. Economics of Structural & Technological Change. LC 97-213719. (Industrial Economic Strategies for Europe Ser.). 328p. (C). 1997. 85.00 (*0-415-16238-6*) Routledge.
Antonelli, J. P. The Maltese Dog Scrapbook, Vol. I. (Illus.). 168p. 1998. 32.00 (*0-8059-4253-X*) Dorrance.
***Antonelli, Joseph A.** Power Supervising: Correcting Job Performance. Antonelli, Sally W., ed. v, 71p. 1998. 12.95 (*0-9672586-0-X*) Mgmt Support.
Antonelli, Judith S. In the Image of God: A Feminist Commentary on the Torah. LC 95-15872. 608p. 1996. 50.00 (*1-56821-438-3*) Aronson.
— In the Image of God: A Feminist Commentary on the Torah. LC 95-15872. 608p. 1997. pap. 40.00 (*0-7657-9952-9*) Aronson.
Antonelli, P. L. The Theory of Sprays & Finsler Spaces with Applications in Physics & Biology. LC 93-37463. (Fundamental Theories of Physics Ser.). 324p. (C). 1993. text 196.50 (*0-7923-2577-X*) Kluwer Academic.
Antonelli, P. L., ed. Lagrange & Finsler Geometry: Applications to Physics & Biology. (Fundamental Theories of Physics Ser.). 292p. (C). 1996. text 144.00 (*0-7923-3873-1*) Kluwer Academic.
Antonelli, P. L. & Bradbury, R. H. Volterra-Hamilton Models in the Ecology & Evolution of Colonial Organisms. Vol. 2. 250p. 1996. text 38.00 (*981-02-2450-8*, BMBae-B2922) World Scientific Pub.
***Antonelli, Paola & Schneider, Christiane.** Jorge Pardo. (Illus.). 48p. 1999. 25.00 (*0-9619760-6-3*) Fabric Workshop Inc.
Antonelli, Peter L. Fundamentals of Finslerian Diffusion with Applications. LC 98-46914. (Fundamental Theories of Physics Ser.). 13p. 1999. write for info. (*0-7923-5511-3*) Kluwer Academic.
Antonelli, Peter L. & Lackey, Bradley C. The Theory of Finslerian Laplacians & Applications. LC 98-31128. 1998. write for info. (*0-7923-5313-7*) Kluwer Academic.
Antonelli, Sally W., ed. see Antonelli, Joseph A.
Antonellis, James. A Journalist Looks at the Lord's Prayer. 144p. (C). 1996. pap. 39.95 (*0-85439-384-6*, Pub. by St Paul Pubns) St Mut.
Antonello, Jean. How to Become Naturally Thin by Eating More. 1991. mass mkt. 5.99 (*0-380-76442-3*, Avon Bks) Morrow Avon.
Antonello, Stephen J. Social Skills Development: Practical Strategies for Adolescents & Adults with Developmental Disabilities. LC 95-21050. 384p. (C). 1995. pap. text 76.00 (*0-205-17411-6*) Allyn.
Antonette, Josiane. Whispers of the Soul: Journeys to the Other Side of Life. LC 98-92955. (Illus.). xii, 144p. 1998. pap. 12.95 (*0-9664552-9-0*) J Antonette.
Antonette, Leslie. The Rhetoric of Diversity & the Traditions of American Literary Study: Critical Multiculturalism in English. LC 98-9531. (Critical Studies in Education & Culture). 160p. 1998. 49.95 (*0-89789-546-0*, Bergin & Garvey) Greenwood.
Antonetty, Evelina L., ed. The Genoveva De Arteaga Papers. (Finding Aid Ser.). (Illus.). 14p. (C). 1992. reprint ed. pap. text 5.00 (*1-878483-21-8*) Hunter Coll CEP.
— The Jesus Colon Papers. (Finding Aid Ser.). (Illus.). 37p. (C). 1991. reprint ed. pap. text 5.00 (*1-878483-20-X*) Hunter Coll CEP.
— The Pura Belpre Papers. (Finding Aid Ser.). 23p. 1992. reprint ed. pap. text 5.00 (*1-878483-19-6*) Hunter Coll CEP.
— The Records of United Bronx Parents, Inc. (Finding Aid Ser.). (Illus.). 15p. (C). 1992. reprint ed. pap. text 5.00 (*1-878483-23-4*) Hunter Coll CEP.
Antonevich, A., et al. Functional Differential Equations II: C*-Applications. 400p. 1998. ring bd. 120.00 (*0-582-10049-6*, Chap & Hall CRC) CRC Pr.
— Functional Differential Equations II Pt. 2: Equations with Discontinuous Coefficients & Boundary Value Problems. 432p. 1998. ring bd. 160.00 (*0-582-30269-2*, LM0612, Chap & Hall CRC) CRC Pr.
Antonevich, Anatolij. Linear Functional Equations: Operator Approach. Muzafarov, Victory & Iacob, Andrei, trs. from RUS. (Operator Theory, Advances, & Applications Ser.: Vol. 83). 1995. write for info. (*0-8176-2931-9*) Birkhauser.
— Linear Functional Equations: Operator Approach. Muzafarov, Victory & Iacob, Andrei, trs. from RUS. (Operator Theory, Advances, & Applications Ser.: Vol. 83). 192p. 1996. 123.00 (*3-7643-2931-9*) Birkhauser.
Antonevich, Anatolij, jt. auth. see Lebedev, A. V.
Antongini, Tom. D'Annunzio. LC 75-37327. (Select Bibliographies Reprint Ser.). 1977. reprint ed. 34.95 (*0-8369-6676-7*) Ayer.
Antongnetti, P., et al, eds. Microarchitecture of VLSI Computers. 1985. text 184.00 (*90-247-3202-6*) Kluwer Academic.
Antoni, Brian. Paradise Overdose. 320p. 1994. 21.00 (*0-671-88426-3*) S&S Trade.
— Paradise Overdose. LC 96-9581. 256p. 1997. reprint ed. pap. 12.00 (*0-8021-3487-4*, Grove) Grove-Atltic.
Antoni, Carlo. From History to Sociology. LC 98-25655. (Max Weber Classic Monographs). 1998. write for info. (*0-415-17452-X*) Routledge.
Antoni, F. & Staub, M. Renal Biopsy in Glomerular Diseases: Clinical Histological, Immunohistological & Electro-Microscopic Studies. 164p. (C). 1978. 55.00 (*963-05-1562-8*, Pub. by Akade Kiado) St Mut.
Antoni, F., jt. auth. see Laszlo, F. A.
Antoni, F. De, see De Antoni, F.
Antoni, Klaus. Shinto und die Konzeption des Japanischen Nationalwesens (Kokutai) Der Religiose Traditionalismus in Neuzeit und Moderne Japans. (Handbook of Oriental Studies: No. 8, Pt. 5). 336p. 1998. 97.50 (*90-04-10316-3*) Brill Academic Pubs.
Antoni, Michael H., et al. Stress Management for HIV: Clinical Validation & Intervention Manual. Kristeller, Jean, ed. LC 97-9633. (Behavioral Medicine - from Research to Practice). 300p. 1996. pap. write for info. (*0-8058-2246-1*) L Erlbaum Assocs.
Antoni, Pietro D. & Bassani, Giovanni B. The Masses. Schnoebelen, Anne, ed. (Seventeenth-Century Italian Sacred Music Ser.: Vol. 10). 272p. 1999. 125.00 (*0-8153-2416-2*) Garland.
Antoni, Robert. Divina Trace. 436p. 1992. 22.95 (*0-87951-445-0*, Pub. by Overlook Pr) Penguin Putnam.
— Divina Trace. 436p. 1993. pap. 13.95 (*0-87951-485-X*, Pub. by Overlook Pr) Penguin Putnam.
Antoni, Robert & Morrow, Bradford, eds. Conjunctions Vol. 27: The Archipelago, New Writing from & about the Caribbean. 360p. 1996. pap. text 12.00 (*0-941964-43-4*) Conjunctions.
Antoni, Robert, jt. ed. see Morrow, Bradford.
Antoni, Thomas. Drives Dictionary, German/English-English/German. (ENG & GER.). 800p. 1996. 250.00 (*0-7859-9533-1*) Fr & Eur.
Antonia, Kita. Autobiography of a Young One. 86p. (Orig.). 1994. pap. 12.00 (*1-887116-00-1*) Saxon West Pubns.
— Compositions in Two Languages. (Illus.). 142p. (Orig.). 1993. pap. 12.00 (*1-887116-01-X*) Saxon West Pubns.
— Interviews in Tucson: Preparing a Television Show for Public Access. (Illus.). 125p. (Orig.). 1994. pap. 12.00 (*1-887116-05-2*) Saxon West Pubns.
— Issues, Expressed in English & in Spanish. Scrivner, Antonia V., ed. (SPA.). 88p. (Orig.). 1995. pap. 12.00 (*1-887116-12-5*) Saxon West Pubns.
— Pensamientos. (SPA.). 108p. (Orig.). 1994. pap. 15.00 (*1-887116-07-9*) Saxon West Pubns.
— The Wee Book. (Illus.). 32p. (Orig.). (J). (gr. k-3). 1995. pap. 12.00 (*1-887116-17-6*) Saxon West Pubns.
Antonia, Nina. New York Dolls: Too Much. (Illus.). 208p. 1998. pap. text 17.95 (*0-7119-6777-6*) Music Sales.
— The One & Only: Peter Berrett - Homme Fatale. 1999. pap. 17.95 (*0-946719-16-0*) Interlink Pub.
Antoniades, Anthony C. Architecture & Allied Design: An Environmental Design Perspective. (Illus.). 512p. 1993. per. 48.95 (*0-8403-5820-2*) Kendall-Hunt.
Antoniades, Anthony C. Poetics Architecture Design: Theory of Design. 320p. 1992. pap. 39.95 (*0-471-28530-7*, VNR) Wiley.
Antoniades, Anthony C. Poetics of Architecture. 1992. pap. 32.95 (*0-442-01330-2*, VNR) Wiley.
Antoniades, Harry N., ed. Hormones in Human Blood: Detection & Assay. 811p. 1976. 85.00 (*0-674-40635-4*, ANHH) HUP.
Antonian, Armen. Toward a Theory of Eurocommunism: The Relationship of Eurocommunism to Eurosocialism, 166. LC 86-19395. (Contributions in Political Science Ser.: No. 166). 199p. 1987. 52.95 (*0-313-25295-5*, ATT/, Greenwood Pr) Greenwood.
***Antonich, Michael.** Corvette Black Book, 1953-2001. (Illus.). 144p. 2000. pap. 14.95 (*0-933534-47-7*, 130596AE, Pub. by M Bruce Assocs) Motorbooks Intl.
Antonick, Michael. California Screamin' The Glory Days of Corvette Road Racing. (Illus.). 160p. 1990. pap. 19.95 (*0-933534-31-0*) M Bruce Assocs.
— Camaro White Book, 1967-1997. (Camaro White Bks.). (Illus.). 128p. 1996. pap. 12.95 (*0-933534-40-X*) M Bruce Assocs.
— Corvette Black Book, 1953-2000. (Illus.). 144p. 1999. pap. 14.95 (*0-933534-46-9*, Pub. by M Bruce Assocs) Motorbooks Intl.
— Illustrated Camaro Buyer's Guide. 3rd ed. (Illustrated Buyer's Guide Ser.). (Illus.). 176p. 1994. pap. 17.95 (*0-87938-895-1*) MBI Pubg.
— Illustrated Corvette Buyer's Guide. 4th ed. LC 97-10370. (Illustrated Buyer's Guide Ser.). (Illus.). 176p. 1997. pap. 17.95 (*0-7603-0250-2*) MBI Pubg.
— Secrets of Corvette Detailing. 2nd ed. (Illus.). 128p. 1999. pap. 19.95 (*0-933534-44-2*) M Bruce Assocs.
***Antonides.** Case Studies in Consumer Behavior. LC 98-54170. 180p. (C). 1999. pap. 32.95 (*0-471-98781-6*) Wiley.
Antonides, G., ed. see Raaij, W. F. van.
Antonides, Gerrit. The Lifetime of a Durable Good. (C). 1990. lib. bdg. 160.00 (*0-7923-0574-4*) Kluwer Academic.
— Psychology in Economics & Business. 360p. 1991. lib. bdg. 145.00 (*0-7923-1375-5*) Kluwer Academic.
— Psychology in Economics & Business: An Introduction to Economic Psychology. 2nd ed. LC 96-19922. 430p. 1996. lib. bdg. 172.00 (*0-7923-4107-4*) Kluwer Academic.
Antonides, Gerrit & VanRaaij, W. Fred. Consumer Behaviour: A European Perspective. LC 97-31193. 642p. 1999. pap. 49.95 (*0-471-97513-3*) Wiley.
Antonides, Gerrit, et al. Advances in Economic Psychology. LC 96-3081. 334p. 1997. 135.00 (*0-471-97087-5*) Wiley.
Antonimo. Mateo 1 (1:1 - 16:12) (Matthew 1 (1:1 - 16:12) (Biblia de Bosquejos y Sermones (The Preacher's Outline & Sermon Bible) Ser.). (SPA.). 336p. 1997. pap. 19.99 (*0-8254-1006-1*, Edit Portavoz) Kregel.
— Mateo 2 (16:13 - 28:20) (Matthew 2 (16:13 - 28:20) (Biblia de Bosquejos y Sermones (The Preacher's Outline & Sermon Bible) Ser.). (SPA.). 272p. 1997. pap. 19.99 (*0-8254-1007-X*, Edit Portavoz) Kregel.
***Antonine, Marie-Claire.** Learn Spanish Together. (For the Car Ser.). (SPA.). 48p. (ps-3). 2000. 14.95 (*0-609-60650-6*) Liv Lang.
Antonini, Eraldo, jt. ed. see Colowick, Sidney P.
Antonini, Gustavo A., et al. Population & Energy: A Systems Analysis of Resource Utilization in the Dominican Republic. LC 75-2495. (Latin American Monographs: Vol. 14). (Illus.). 189p. 1975. reprint ed. pap. 58.60 (*0-608-04501-2*, 206524600001) Bks Demand.
Antonini, Orlando. Getting a Business Loan: Your Step-by-Step Guide. Manber, Beverly, ed. LC 92-54353. (Small Business & Entrepreneurship Ser.). 196p. 1993. pap. 15.95 (*1-56052-164-3*) Crisp Pubns.
Antonini, Orlando & Collay, Casey. The Loan Book: Complete Step by Step Guide to Getting a Personal or Business Loan. (Small Business Ser.). 185p. (Orig.). 1990. pap. 19.95 (*0-318-50011-6*) El Dorado Pr.
***Antonino, Carmella.** Beyond the Wedding Vows: Circumstances, Choices, & Consequences of an Extramarital Affair. LC 99-69662. 192p. 2000. pap. 17.95 (*1-58501-061-8*, Pub. by CeShore Pubg) Natl Bk Netwk.
Antoninus. Robinson Jeffers: Fragments of an Older Fury. 1970. 7.50 (*0-685-04672-9*) Oyez.
Antonio de Alarcon, Pedro. El Capitan Veneno: El Sombrero de Tres Picos. (SPA.). 9.95 (*0-8288-2548-3*, S9860) Fr & Eur.
Antonio De Guevara, Fray. Epistolas Familiares, 2 vols. Cossio, Jose Maria de, ed. (SPA.). 938p. 1968. 200.00 (*0-614-00112-9*) Elliots Bks.
Antonio De Villena, Luis. Leonardo Da Vinci: Una Biografia. LC 93-205010. (Memoria de La Historia Ser.). (Illus.). 1998. pap. 15.95 (*84-08-00284-8*) Planeta.
Antonio de Yturriaga, Jose. Straits Used for International Navigation: A Spanish Perspective. 388p. (C). 1991. lib. bdg. 142.00 (*0-7923-1141-8*) Kluwer Academic.
Antonio, Fausto, ed. see Matrullo, Fondano.
Antonio, Gene. AIDS: Rage & Reality: Why Silence Is Deadly. 336p. (Orig.). 1992. pap. 19.95 (*0-9634774-3-9*) Anchor Bks.
— AIDS - Zmowa Milczenia. Szacki, Jacek, tr. from ENG. (POL.). 190p. (Orig.). 1992. pap. text 8.50 (*0-9632313-1-6*) Global Comm Netwk.
— The AIDS Cover-Up? The Real & Alarming Facts about AIDS. 2nd ed. LC 86-81935. 267p. (Orig.). 1986. pap. 9.95 (*0-89870-129-5*) Ignatius Pr.
Antonio, Goubaud C. The Guajxaquip Bats, an Indian Ceremony of Guatemala. (Illus.). 27p. 1986. reprint ed. pap. 4.25 (*0-913129-23-2*) La Tienda.
Antonio, Jose. Diets Drive Me Nuts: Sensible Solutions for Lasting Fitness. LC 98-71005. 76p. 1998. pap. 12.95 (*1-58151-010-1*) BookPartners.
Antonio, Lamar. Chistes Centellantes. (SPA.). 1997. pap. text 6.98 (*968-403-381-8*) Selector.
***Antonio Marcos, Duarte, Jr.** Risk Management & Asset Management. 250p. 2000. 70.00 (*1-883249-74-0*) F J Fabozzi.
Antonio, Robert J. & Glassman, Ronald M., eds. A Weber-Marx Dialogue. LC 85-3148. xxii, 336p. 1985. 35.00 (*0-7006-0265-8*); pap. 16.95 (*0-7006-0312-3*) U Pr of KS.
Antonio, Salgado. Canciones Infantiles. (SPA.). (ps-3). 1997. pap. text 8.98 (*968-403-439-3*) Selector.
Antonio, Thomas M., ed. see Sabuco, John J.
Antonio-Villarreal, Jose. The Fifth Horseman. 2nd ed. LC 83-72426. xxvi, 410p. 1984. pap. 19.00 (*0-916950-49-2*) Biling Rev-Pr.
Antonio y Bas Peired, Carlos, jt. auth. see Jonch, Cuspinera.
Antonioli, Donald A., et al. Diagnostic Surgical Pathology. 3rd ed. Sternberg, Stephen S., ed. 2,784p. 399.00 (*0-7817-1930-5*) Lppncott W & W.
Antonioni, David, jt. auth. see Aldag, Ramon J.
Antonioni, Michelangelo. Architecture of Vision: Writings & Interviews on Cinema. 350p. 1996. 36.95 (*1-56886-012-9*) Marsilio Pubs.
— The Architecture of Vision: Writings & Interviews on Cinema. 350p. 1996. pap. 19.95 (*1-56886-016-1*) Marsilio Pubs.
— Unfinished Business: Screenplays, Scenarios & Ideas. LC 98-29373. 350p. 1998. pap. text 19.95 (*1-56886-051-X*) Marsilio Pubs.
Antonioni, Michelangelo, et al. The Passenger. (Illus.). 192p. (Orig.). 1986. pap. 6.95 (*0-936839-52-X*) Applause Theatre Bk Pubs.
Antoniotti, Walter. Economics. (Quick Notes Learning System Ser.). (Illus.). 128p. (Orig.). (C). 1993. pap. text 9.95 (*0-9632772-1-9*) Twen Frst Cent Lrn.
— Financial Accounting. 2nd rev. ed. (Quick Notes Learning System Ser.). 242p. (C). 1994. pap. text 14.95 (*0-9632772-2-7*) Twen Frst Cent Lrn.
— Financial Accounting: Lecture Notes & Practice Set. (Quick Learn Ser.). 112p. (Orig.). (C). 1991. pap. text 9.95 (*0-9632772-0-0*) Twen Frst Cent Lrn.
— Financial Accounting for Owners, Managers, & Administrators. rev. ed. 51p. 1998. pap. 7.95 (*0-9632772-4-3*) Twen Frst Cent Lrn.
— Financial Accounting Practice Sets: Peachtree Edition. rev. ed. (Quick Notes Learning System Ser.). 42p. 1999. pap. 9.95 (*0-9632772-3-5*) Twen Frst Cent Lrn.
— Statistics. 2nd rev. ed. (Quick Notes Learning System Ser.). (Illus.). 265p. (C). 1998. pap. text 19.95 (*0-9632772-5-1*) Twen Frst Cent Lrn.
Antoniotti, Walter, jt. auth. see Cohen, Pamela.
***Antoniou.** Digital Filters. 3rd ed. 2001. text 77.00 (*0-07-239340-8*) McGraw.
Antoniou. Digital Filters Analysis Design. 2nd ed. 1994. teacher ed. 75.31 (*0-07-002122-8*) McGraw.
Antoniou, Andreas. Digital Filters. 2nd ed. 689p. (C). 1993. 97.50 (*0-07-002121-X*) McGraw.
Antoniou, Andreas, jt. auth. see Lu, Wu-Sheng.
Antoniou, G., et al, eds. Learning & Reasoning with Complex Representations: PRICAI '96 Workshops on Reasoning with Incomplete & Changing Information & on Inducing Complex Representations, Cairns, Australia, August 26-30, 1996, Selected Papers. LC 98-18108. (Lecture Notes in Artficial Intelligence Ser.: Vol. 1359). x, 283p. 1998. pap. 49.00 (*3-540-64413-X*) Spr-Verlag.
Antoniou, G. Oint Artificial Intelligence Conference Staff & Slaney, J. K. Advanced Topics in Artificial Intelligence 11th Australian Joint Conference on Artificial Intelligence, Ai'98 Brisbane, Australia, July 13-17, 1998. LC 98-46040. (Lecture Notes in Artificial Intelligence Ser.). 1998. pap. 55.00 (*3-540-65138-1*) Spr-Verlag.
Antoniou, Grigoris. Nonmonotonic Reasoning. (Artificial Intelligence Ser.). (Illus.). 275p. 1997. 39.50 (*0-262-01157-3*) MIT Pr.
Antoniou, Grigoris, jt. ed. see Plant, Robert.
Antoniou, Ioannis & Lambert, F. J., eds. Solitons & Chaos. (Research Reports in Physics). (Illus.). xvi, 333p. 1991. 75.95 (*0-387-54389-9*) Spr-Verlag.
***Antoniou, Ioannis & Lumer, Gunter.** Generalized Functions, Operator Theory, & Dynamical Systems, 399. LC 98-50688. (C&H/CRC Research Notes in Mathematics Series). 392p. 1999. per. 84.95 (*0-8493-0619-1*, Chap & Hall CRC) CRC Pr.
Antoniou, Jim. Cities Then & Now. 1999. 15.99 (*0-7858-1115-X*) Bk Sales Inc.
***Antoniou, Jim.** Historic Cairo: A Walk Through the Islamic City. LC 99-895676. (Illus.). 96p. 1999. pap. text 16.95 (*977-424-497-4*, Pub. by Am Univ Cairo Pr) Col U Pr.
***Antoniou, Laura.** Academy: Tales of the Marketplace. (Marketplace Ser.). 2000. pap. 13.95 (*0-9645960-3-2*) Mystic Rose.
— Marketplace. 2000. pap. 13.95 (*0-9645960-4-0*) Mystic Rose.
Antoniou, Laura. The Marketplace. 2nd ed. 1998. mass mkt. 7.95 (*1-56333-602-2*, Rhinoceros) Masquerade.
***Antoniou, Laura.** Slave. (Marketplace Ser.). 2000. pap. 13.95 (*0-9645960-5-9*) Mystic Rose.
Antoniou, Laura. Some Women. 2nd ed. (Orig.). 1997. reprint ed. mass mkt. 7.95 (*1-56333-573-5*, Rhinoceros) Masquerade.
***Antoniou, Laura.** Trainer. (Marketplace Ser.). 2000. pap. 13.95 (*0-9645960-6-7*) Mystic Rose.
Antoniou, Laura, ed. By Her Subdued. (Orig.). 1995. mass mkt. 6.95 (*1-56333-281-7*, Rhinoceros) Masquerade.
— Leatherwomen. (Orig.). 1998. mass mkt. 6.95 (*1-56333-598-0*, Rosebud) Masquerade.
— Looking for Mr. Preston. 1995. 23.95 (*1-56333-288-4*, R Kasak Bks) Masquerade.
— No Other Tribute: Erotic Tales of Women in Submission. 2nd ed. 1997. mass mkt. 7.95 (*1-56333-603-0*, Rhinoceros) Masquerade.
Antoniou, S., jt. ed. see Elnashai, A. S.
Antonious, Laura. The Catalyst. 1998. mass mkt. 6.95 (*1-56333-621-9*) Masquerade.
Antoniov, Laura. The Slave. 2nd ed. 1998. mass mkt. 7.95 (*1-56333-601-4*, Rhinoceros) Masquerade.
Antoniov, Laura, ed. Leatherwoman III: The Clash of the Cultures. 1998. mass mkt. 6.95 (*1-56333-619-7*, Rosebud) Masquerade.
Antonius, George. The Arab Awakening. 1976. lib. bdg. 250.00 (*0-8490-1444-1*) Gordon Pr.
— The Arab Awakening: The Story of the Arab National Movement. 482p. 2000. text 110.00 (*0-7103-0673-3*) Col U Pr.
Antonius, George. The Arab Awakening: The Story of the Arab National Movement. 156p. 1969. 29.95 (*0-86685-000-7*, LDL0007) Intl Bk Ctr.
Antonius, Marcus Aurelius. The Meditations of Marcus Aurelius Antoninus: And a Selection from the Letters of Marcus & Fronto. Farquharson, A. S. L., tr. (Oxford's World Classics Ser.). 224p. 1998. pap. 8.95 (*0-19-283907-1*) OUP.
Antoniv, V. F., jt. auth. see Pogosov, V. S.
Antonoff, Andrea, ed. see Chogyam, Ngakpa.
Antonoff, Stanley J., et al. The "J" Book - Justice for All. 1998. pap. 5.00 (*0-89214-016-X*) Intl Dyslexia.
Antonoff, Steven. The College Finder: Choosing the School That's Right for You. rev. ed. LC 98-45525. 484p. 1999. pap. 15.95 (*0-449-00389-2*) Fawcett.
Antonoff, Steven R. College Match: A Blueprint for Choosing the Best School for You! 6th ed. 1999. pap. 8.00 (*1-57509-048-1*) Octameron Assocs.
Antonoff, Steven R. & Friedemann, Marie A. College Match: A Blueprint for Choosing the Best School for You! 5th ed. (Illus.). 132p. 1997. pap. 8.00 (*1-57509-025-2*) Octameron Assocs.
Antonopoulos, A. A. Biotechnological Advances in Processing Municipal Wastes for Fuels & Chemicals. LC 86-31144. (Illus.). 488p. 1987. 45.00 (*0-8155-1122-1*) Noyes.
Antonopoulou, T. The Homilies of the Emperor Leo VI. LC 97-5794. (Medieval Mediterranean Ser.: No. 14). 272p. 1997. 110.50 (*90-04-10814-9*, NLG 150) Brill Academic Pubs.
Antonov, A. N. Physiology & Pathology of the Newborn. (SRCD M Ser.: Vol. 10, No. 2). 1945. 25.00 (*0-527-01535-0*) Periodicals Srv.
Antonov, A. N., et al. Nucleon Correlations in Nuclei. LC 92-27020. (Series in Nuclear & Particle Physics). 1993. 141.95 (*0-387-55911-6*) Spr-Verlag.
Antonov, N. R. Khram Bozhij i Tserkovnija Sluzhbi.Tr. of Temple of God & Church Services. 300p. 1983. reprint ed. pap. text 10.00 (*0-317-30284-1*) Holy Trinity.
***Antonov, Roumen.** Antonov: My Story. (Illus.). 176p. 1999. pap. write for info. (*0-9534186-0-X*, Pub. by Read) Vine Hse Dist.
Antonov, V. K. Chemistry of Proteolysis. 496p. 1992. 412.95 (*0-387-54736-3*) Spr-Verlag.

An Asterisk (*) at the beginning of an entry indicates that the title is appearing for the first time.

Antonov, V. N., jt. auth. see Nemoshkalenko, V. V.
Antonov, Vladimir, et al. OKB Sukhoi: A History of the Design Bureau & Its Aircraft. (Illus.). 300p. 1996. 59.95 (*1-85780-012-5*) Specialty Pr.
Antonova, Irina. Pushkin Museum of Fine Arts, Moscow: Painting. (Illus.). 184p. (C). 1988. text 90.00 (*0-569-09109-8*, Pub. by Collets) St Mut.
— The Pushkin State Museum of Fine Arts. (FRE & RUS.). 1981. 116.00 (*0-7855-1655-7*) St Mut.
Antonovich, Michael P. FoxPro 2 Programming Guide. Leventhal, Lance A., ed. LC 91-53064. (Lance A. Leventhal Microtrend Ser.). 624p. (Orig.). 1992. pap. 29.95 (*0-915391-48-1*) Slawson Comm.
— FoxPro 2.5 for Windows Programming Guide. Leventhal, Lance A., ed. LC 93-16743. (Lance A. Leventhal Microtrend Ser.). 650p. (Orig.). 1993. pap. 34.95 (*0-915391-80-5*) Slawson Comm.
— Special Edition Using Visual FoxPro 5. LC 96-70614. 960p. 1996. 59.99 (*0-7897-0885-X*) Que.
Antonovics, Janis, jt. ed. see Futuyma, Douglas J.
Antonovitz, Susan, ed. see Schweitzer, Carole D.
Antonovskii, M. Ja, et al. Topological Semifields & Their Applications to General Topology. LC 77-11046. (Translations Ser.: Series 2, Vol. 106). 142p. 1977. reprint ed. pap. 34.00 (*0-8218-3056-2*, TRANS2/106) Am Math.
Antonovsky, Aaron, ed. Health & Health Care in Israel: Studies of Israeli Society, Vol. 5. 400p. 1990. 44.95 (*0-88738-308-4*); pap. 24.95 (*0-88738-824-8*) Transaction Pubs.
Antonovych. Pathology of Systemic Lupus. (Illus.). 175p. 1995. pap. text 35.00 (*1-881041-23-9*) Am Registry Path.
Antonovych, Marc, ed. see Mijakovs'kyj, Volodymyr.
***Antons, Christoph.** Intellectual Property Law in Indonesia. LC 00-42663. (Max Planck Series on Asian Intellectual Property Law). 2000. write for info. (*90-411-9803-2*) Kluwer Law Intl.
Antonsanti, Hector M. Antecedentes Historicos del Cooperativismo: Del Profetismo Etico Religioso al Socialismo Utopica. Bauza, Carmen M., ed. (SPA.). 245p. (Orig.). 1986. 13.50 (*0-934885-01-X*) Edit Nosotros.
Antonsen, Elmer H. & Hock, Hans Henrich, eds. Staefcraeft: Studies in Germanic Linguistics. Selected Papers from the First & Second Symposium on Germanic Linguistics. LC 91-24743. (Current Issues in Linguistic Theory Ser.: Vol. 79). viii, 217p. 1991. 56.00 (*1-55619-134-0*) J Benjamins Pubng Co.
Antonsen, Elmer H., ed. see Grimm, Wilhelm K.
Antonsen, Elmer H., tr. see Makaev, E. A.
Antonsen, Lasse, jt. auth. see Romer, Jorgen.
Antonsen, T. M., jt. auth. see Freund, H. P.
Antonson, Belinda. Learning about the World Through Geography. Cox, Art, ed. (Illus.). 80p. 1997. pap. 8.95 (*1-889931-05-5*) Bayou Printing Inc.
Antonson, Joan M. & Hanable, William S. Alaska's Heritage, Set. LC 84-72718. (Alaska Historical Commission Studies in History: No. 133). (Illus.). (Orig.). (YA). (gr. 10-12). 1986. text 37.00 (*0-943712-18-1*) Alaska Hist.
Antonsson, Erik K. Fuzzy Sets in Engineering Design & Configuration. Sebastian, Hans-Juergen, ed. LC 96-30566. (International Series in Intelligent Technologies). 304p. (C). 1996. text 151.50 (*0-7923-9802-5*) Kluwer Academic.
Antontsev, S. N., ed. Energy Methods in Continuum Mechanics. 184p. (C). 1996. text 129.00 (*0-7923-4229-1*) Kluwer Academic.
Antontsev, S. N., et al, eds. Free Boundary Problems in Continuum Mechanics: International Conference on Free-Boundary Problems in Continuum Mechanics, Novosibirsk, July 16-19, 1991. LC 92-32867. ix, 358p. 1992. 122.00 (*0-8176-2784-7*) Birkhauser.
Antonuc, jt. auth. see Knipscheer, C. P.
Antonucci, E. & Page, D. E., eds. The Sun & Its Role in the Heliosphere: Proceedings of the E2.2 Symposium of COSPAR Scientific Commission E Which Was Held During the Thirty-First COSPAR Scientific Assembly, Birmingham, U. K., 14-21 July, 1996. 138p. 1997. pap. 100.50 (*0-08-043296-4*, Pergamon Pr) Elsevier.
Antonucci, E. & Shea, M. A., eds. The Sun & Its Atmosphere: Proceedings of the EZ.1 Symposium of COSPAR Scientific Commission E Which Was Held During the 31st COSPAR Scientific Assembly, Birmingham, U. K., 14-21 July, 1996. (Advances in Space Research Ser.: 20/12). 204p. 1997. pap. 100.50 (*0-08-043309-X*, Pergamon Pr) Elsevier.
Antonucci, E. & Somov, Boris V., eds. Solar Corona & Solar Wind: Proceedings of Symposium 9 of the COSPAR Twenty-Eighth Plenary Meeting held in The Hague, The Netherlands, 25 June-6 July 1990. (Advances in Space Research Ser.: Vol. 11). (Illus.). 418p. 1991. pap. 156.50 (*0-08-041141-X*, Pergamon Pr) Elsevier.
Antonucci, Francis J. & Whitman, Robert. After Death Tax Planning: Minimizing Tax Liabilities. 2nd rev. ed. LC 99-60281. 204p. 1999. 110.00 (*0-8318-0790-3*, B790) Am Law Inst.
Antonucci, Mark, jt. auth. see DeMatteis, Bob.
Antonucci, Michael, ed. see Antonucci, Thomas & Historical Briefs, Inc. Staff.
Antonucci, Michael, ed. see Historical Briefs, Inc. Staff.
Antonucci, Thomas. Battle of Britain, 2 vols., Vol. I. 1991. 19.95 (*0-89677-054-0*) Hist Briefs.
Antonucci, Thomas & Historical Briefs, Inc. Staff. WW II in Baltimore. Antonucci, Michael, ed. 176p. 1993. pap. 19.95 (*0-89677-051-6*) Hist Briefs.
Antonucci, Thomas, ed. see Historical Briefs, Inc. Staff.
Antonvich, Michael. Debugging & Maintaining FoxPro Applications. Leventhal, Lance A., ed. LC 92-32253. (Lance A. Leventhal Microtrend Ser.). 500p. (Orig.). 1992. pap. 34.95 (*0-915391-73-2*) Slawson Comm.
Antony, jt. auth. see Simon.
Antony-Black, Jenifer, jt. ed. see Walker, Moira.
Antony, Gerhard. Gear Vibration - Investigation of the Dynamic Behavior or One Stage Epicyclic Gears. (Nineteen Eighty-Eight Fall Technical Meeting Ser.: Vol. 88FTM12). (Illus.). 9p. 1988. pap. text 30.00 (*1-55589-517-4*) AGMA.
***Antony, Jiju & Kaye, Mike.** Experimental Quality: A Strategic Approach to Achieve & Improve Quality LC 99-37333. 1999. write for info. (*0-412-81440-4*, Kluwer Plenum) Kluwer Academic.
Antony, Judith. Where Time Becomes Space. 147p. 1978. 4.95 (*0-8199-0699-9*, Frncscn Herld) Franciscan Pr.
***Antony, Louise.** A Mind of One's Own. 2nd ed. 416p. 2001. pap. 25.00 (*0-8133-6607-0*, Pub. by Westview) HarpC.
***Antony, Martin M. & Swinson, Richard P.** Phobic Disorders & Panic in Adults: A Guide to Assessment & Treatment. LC 00-38094. 2000. write for info. (*1-55798-696-7*) Am Psychol.
Antony, Martin M. & Swinson, Richard P. When Perfect Isn't Good Enough: Strategies for Coping with Perfectionism. LC 98-66704. 208p. 1998. pap. 13.95 (*1-57224-124-1*) New Harbinger.
Antony of Choziba. The Life of Saint George of Choziba & The Miracles of the Holy Mother of God at Choziba. Vivian, Tim & Athnassakis, Apostolos N., trs. from GRE. 130p. 1994. 64.95 (*1-883255-59-7*) Intl Scholars.
Antony, Peter D. The Conduct of Industrial Relations. 336p. (C). 1977. 60.00 (*0-85292-157-8*) St Mut.
Antony, Richard T. Principles of Data Fusion Automation. LC 95-15178. 470p. 1995. 105.00 (*0-89006-760-0*) Artech Hse.
***Antoon, Alia Y. & Tompkins, Denise M.** A Parent's Quick Reference to Baby's Health: Birth to Age 5. 2000. pap. 18.95 (*0-7373-0492-8*, Pub. by Lowell Hse) NTC Contemp Pub Co.
Antopol, Justine & Kusnet, Jack, eds. Modern Banking Forms. rev. ed. 1992. suppl. ed. 80.75 (*0-7913-0910-X*); suppl. ed. 83.25 (*0-7913-0990-8*) Warren Gorham & Lamont.
— Modern Banking Forms, 3 vols, Set. rev. ed. 1992. 260.00 (*0-88262-549-7*) Warren Gorham & Lamont.
Antopol, Justine, jt. auth. see Kusnet, Jack.
Antos, George J., et al, eds. Catalytic Naphtha Reforming: Science & Technology. (Chemical Industries Ser.: Vol. 61). (Illus.). 528p. 1994. text 195.00 (*0-8247-9236-X*) Dekker.
Antos, Joseph, et al. The Colorado River Through Glen Canyon Before Lake Powell: Historic Photo Journal 1872-1964. Inskip, Eleanor, ed. LC 97-79089. (Illus.). 96p. 1995. pap. 25.00 (*0-9648078-0-7*) Inskip Ink.
— The Colorado River Through Glen Canyon Before Lake Powell: Historic Photo Journal 1872-1964. limited ed. Inskip, Eleanor, ed. LC 97-79089. (Illus.). 96p. 1995. 150.00 (*0-9648078-1-5*) Inskip Ink.
Antos, Joseph, jt. auth. see Hamilton, Douglas.
Antosiewicz, Mike. New Techniques for Aligning & Maintaining Large Ring Gears. (Technical Papers: Vol. P159.04A). (Illus.). 11p. 1981. pap. text 30.00 (*1-55589-207-8*) AGMA.
Antosik, P. & Kaminski, A., eds. Generalized Functions & Convergence. 396p. (C). 1990. text 92.00 (*981-02-0183-4*) World Scientific Pub.
Antosik, P. & Schwartz, C. Matrix Methods in Analysis. (Lecture Notes in Mathematics Ser.: Vol. 1113). iv, 114p. 1985. 29.95 (*0-387-15185-0*) Spr-Verlag.
Antosz, Lynn, ed. see Aspen Reference Group Staff.
Antoszewski, Andrzej, jt. auth. see Cordell, Karl.
Antoucci, Thomas, ed. see Historical Briefs, Inc. Staff.
Antoulas, A. C., ed. Mathematical Systems Theory: The Influence of R. E. Kalman. (Illus.). 528p. 1991. 228.95 (*0-387-52994-2*) Spr-Verlag.
Antoun, Richard T. Arab Village: A Social Structural Study of a Transjordanian Peasant Community. LC 70-633555. (Indiana University Social Science Ser.: Vol. 29). 208p. reprint ed. pap. 64.50 (*0-8357-5704-8*, 205602200044) Bks Demand.
— Low-Key Politics: Local-Level Leadership & Change in the Middle East. LC 77-19018. (Illus.). 285p. (C). 1979. text 19.50 (*0-87395-373-8*) State U NY Pr.
— Muslim Preacher in the Modern World: A Jordanian Case Study in Comparative Perspective. LC 88-21482. 305p. 1989. reprint ed. pap. 94.60 (*0-608-02938-6*, 206400400008) Bks Demand.
Antoun, Richard T. & Quataert, Donald, eds. Syria: Society, Culture, & Polity. LC 90-10251. (SUNY Series in Middle Eastern Studies). 144p. (C). 1991. text 24.50 (*0-7914-0713-6*) State U NY Pr.
Antranikian, G. & Scheper, T., eds. Biotechnology of Extremophiles. (Advances in Biochemical Engineering/Biotechnology Ser.: Vol. 61). (Illus.). 214p. 1998. 130.00 (*3-540-63817-2*) Spr-Verlag.
Antreassian, Alice. Armenian Cooking Today. rev. ed. LC 75-28680. (Illus.). xxix, 189p. 1989. reprint ed. ring bd. 22.00 (*0-934728-20-8*) D O A C.
Antreassian, Alice & Jebejian, Mariam. Classic Armenian Recipes: Cooking Without Meat. LC 81-10961. (Illus.). 350p. 1981. ring bd. 24.95 (*0-935102-05-1*) D O A C.
— Classic Armenian Recipes: Cooking Without Meat. (Illus.). 1994. pap. 19.95 (*0-941567-39-7*) D O A C.
Antreassian, Antranig. Kerezman Yev Harutiune. (ARM.). 1985. write for info. (*0-936893-00-1*) Baikar.
— Tebi Mayramoud. LC 89-91382. (ARM.). 1989. write for info. (*0-936893-05-2*) Baikar.
Antreassian, Elise, ed. see Koushagian, Torkom.
Antreassian, Jack, tr. see Zohrab, Krikor.
Antreasyan, Agustin, tr. see Bittner, Wolfgang.
Antreasyan, Agustin, tr. see De Beer, Hans.
Antreasyan, Agustin, tr. see Weninger, Brigitte.
Antrei, Albert C., ed. see Sanpete County Commission.
***Antrei, Albert C. T. & Roberts, Allen D.** A History of Sanpete County. LC 98-61326. (Illus.). 1999. write for info. (*0-913738-42-5*) Utah St Hist Soc.
Antrews, Grant. Legacies. 1997. mass mkt. 7.95 (*1-56333-587-5*, Rhinoceros) Masquerade.
— My Darling Dominatrix. 3rd ed. (Orig.). 1997. reprint ed. mass mkt. 7.95 (*1-56333-566-2*, Rhinoceros) Masquerade.
— Rogue's Gallery. 1997. mass mkt. 6.95 (*1-56333-522-0*, Rhinoceros) Masquerade.
— Submissions. (Orig.). 1998. mass mkt. 7.95 (*1-56333-618-9*, Rhinoceros) Masquerade.
Antrich, J. & Usher, S., eds. Xenophon: The Persian Expedition. (Bristol Greek Texts Ser.). (GRE., Illus.). 200p. 1978. pap. 18.95 (*0-906515-11-4*, Pub. by Brist Class Pr) Focus Pub-R Pullins.
Antrim. The Varificationist. 1998. write for info. (*0-517-70311-4*) Random Hse Value.
Antrim, Angela. The Yorkshire Wold Rangers. 120p. 1981. 40.00 (*0-907033-06-7*) St Mut.
Antrim, David. The Hundred Brothers. 1998. pap. 12.00 (*0-679-76942-0*) Crown Pub Group.
Antrim, Donald. The Verificationist. LC 99-31383. 192p. 2000. 21.00 (*0-375-40822-3*) Knopf.
— The Verificationist. 2001. 12.00 (*0-679-76943-9*) McKay.
Antrim, Eleanor S. Thanks Again, God. 1980. pap. 3.50 (*0-913342-29-7*) Barclay Pr.
Antrim, Harriet S. Records of the Antrim Family of America. (Illus.). 232p. 1988. reprint ed. lib. bdg. 43.00 (*0-8328-0132-1*) Higginson Bk Co.
Antrim, Harry T. T. S. Eliot's Concept of Language: A Study of Its Development. LC 76-634405. (University of Florida Humanities Monographs: No. 35). 84p. reprint ed. pap. 30.00 (*0-7837-4967-8*, 204463300004) Bks Demand.
Antrim History Commitee. Parades & Promenades: History of Antrim, N. H. LC 76-30841. (Illus.). 1977. 15.00 (*0-914016-39-3*) Phoenix Pub.
Antrim, Joshua. History of Champaign & Logan Courties, from Their First Settlement. (Illus.). 460p. 1997. reprint ed. lib. bdg. 49.50 (*0-8328-6297-5*) Higginson Bk Co.
Antrim, William. Advertising. 2nd ed. Dorr, Eugene L., ed. (Occupational Manuals & Projects in Marketing Ser.). (Illus.). (gr. 11-12). 1978. text 15.43 (*0-07-002114-7*) McGraw.
Antrobus, Augustine M. History of Des Moines County, Iowa & Its People, Vol. 1. (Illus.). 556p. 1994. reprint ed. lib. bdg. 56.00 (*0-8328-3815-2*) Higginson Bk Co.
— History of Des Moines County, Iowa & Its People, Vol. 2. (Illus.). 537p. 1994. reprint ed. lib. bdg. 54.00 (*0-8328-3816-0*) Higginson Bk Co.
Antrobus, Edmund. Britain Nineteen Eighty-Five. Fisher, Robert C., ed. (Fisher Annotated Travel Guides Ser.). 320p. 1984. 12.95 (*0-8116-0069-6*) NAL.
— London, 1985. Fisher, Robert C., ed. (Fisher Annotated Travel Guides Ser.). 128p. 1984. pap. 8.95 (*0-8116-0018-1*) NAL.
Antrobus, John. Hitler in Liverpool & Other Plays: One Orange for the Baby & Up in the Hyde. (Orig.). 1984. pap. 9.95 (*0-7145-3898-1*) Riverrun NY.
— Ronnie & the Flying Fitted Carpet. (J). 1995. pap. 9.95 (*0-86051-822-1*, Robson-Parkwest) Parkwest Pubns.
— Ronnie & the High Rise. (J). 1995. 9.95 (*0-86051-821-3*, Robson-Parkwest) Parkwest Pubns.
— Trixie & Baba. 93p. 1969. 16.95 (*0-910278-10-5*) Boulevard.
— Why Bournemouth? 1988. pap. 12.95 (*0-7145-0641-9*) Riverrun NY.
Antrobus, John & Bertini, Mario, eds. The Neuropsychology of Sleep & Dreaming. 336p. 1992. text 79.95 (*0-8058-0925-2*) L Erlbaum Assocs.
Antrobus, John, jt. ed. see Ellman, Steven J.
Antrobus, Robert. The Square of Sevens. 3rd ed. Stevenson, E. Irenaeus, ed. (Astro-Cards Reprints Ser.). 97p. 1996. reprint ed. pap. text 13.00 (*1-885500-07-6*, AR5) Astro-Cards.
— Square of Sevens: A Rare 18th Century Work of Genuine Gypsy Card Reading. 104p. 1998. reprint ed. pap. 14.95 (*1-56459-466-1*) Kessinger Pub.
***Antsaklis, P., et al, eds.** Hybrid Systems V. LC 99-28214. (Lecture Notes in Computer Science Ser.: Vol. 1567). x, 445p. 1999. pap. 73.00 (*3-540-65643-X*) Spr-Verlag.
Antsaklis, Pano J., et al, eds. Hybrid Systems. LC 97-27813. (Lecture Notes in Computer Science Ser.: Vol. 1273). x, 405p. pap. 67.00 (*3-540-63358-8*) Spr-Verlag.
Antsaklis, Panos, et al, eds. Hybrid Systems II. (Lecture Notes in Computer Science Ser.: Vol. 999). 569p. 1995. 87.00 (*3-540-60472-3*) Spr-Verlag.
Antsaklis, Panos & Michel, Anthony. Linear Systems. LC 97-3753. 688p. (C). 1997. 100.31 (*0-07-041433-5*) McGraw.
Antsaklis, Panos J. & Passino, Kevin M., eds. An Introduction to Intelligent & Autonomous Control. LC 92-18192. (C). 1992. text 171.50 (*0-7923-9267-1*) Kluwer Academic.
Antsaklis, Panos J., jt. auth. see Moody, John O.
Antsiferov, E. G. Energy Reviews Vol. 6, Pt. 1: New Mathematical Programming Algorithms & Their Applications to Energy Problems, Vol. 6. (Soviet Technology Reviews Ser.: Section A). 125p. 1992. pap. text 164.00 (*3-7186-5359-1*, Harwood Acad Pubs) Gordon & Breach.
Antsiferov, V. V. & Smirnov, G. I. Coherent Radiation Processes in Plasma. 250p. 1995. pap. 111.00 (*1-898326-16-9*, Pub. by CISP) Balogh.
— Physics of Solid State Lasers. 250p. 1995. pap. 111.00 (*1-898326-17-7*, Pub. by CISP) Balogh.
Antsis, Boris. Galaxy & Atom: As above, So Below. LC 90-83957. 51p. (C). 1991. pap. 10.00 (*0-911971-54-8*) Effect Pub.
Anttalainen, Tarmo. Introduction to Telecommunications Network Engineering: Telecommunications Network Technology. LC 98-41082. 1998. 79.00 (*0-89006-984-0*) Artech Hse.
Anttila, Arto. Analogy. (Trends in Linguistics, Studies & Monographs: No. 10). 1977. 47.70 (*90-279-7975-8*) Mouton.
Anttila, E. Ellen. The Eagle & Other Poems. (Illus.). 1992. per. 10.00 (*0-934616-46-9*) Valkyrie Pub Hse.
Anttila, Elizabeth K. English Oral Production. 116p. 1980. pap. 6.00 (*0-8477-3333-5*) U of PR Pr.
— English Structure Exercises. 104p. (C). 1978. reprint ed. pap. 1.50 (*0-8477-3300-9*) U of PR Pr.
Anttila, Harry. Pradikate und Satzmodelle in Zeitungstexten. (Studies in the Humanities & Social Sciences: Bd. 12). (GER.). 569p. 1996. 88.95 (*3-631-31105-2*) P Lang Pubng.
***Anttila, Raimo.** Greek & Indo-European Etymology in Action. (Current Issues in Linguistic Theory Ser.: Vol. 200). 2000. write for info. (*1-55619-978-3*) J Benjamins Pubng.
Anttila, Raimo. Historical & Comparative Linguistics. LC 88-36035. (Current Issues in Linguistic Theory Ser.: Vol. 6). xvi, 460p. (C). 1989. reprint ed. 74.00 (*90-272-3556-2*); reprint ed. pap. 27.95 (*90-272-3557-0*) J Benjamins Pubng Co.
Anttila, Raimo & Brewer, Warren A. Analogy: A Basic Bibliography. (Library & Information Sources in Linguistics: No.1). xiv, 50p. 1977. 29.00 (*90-272-0992-8*) J Benjamins Pubng Co.
Anttila, Stan T. Aspects of Macro-Sociological Methodology. (Studia Sociologica Upsaliensia: No. 36). 126p. (Orig.). 1993. pap. 36.00 (*91-554-3054-6*) Coronet Bks.
Antunes, Antonio L. Act of the Damned. Zenith, Richard, tr. from POR. 256p. 1996. reprint ed. pap. 12.00 (*0-8021-3476-9*, Grove) Grove-Atltic.
— An Explanation of the Birds: A Novel. Zenith, Richard, tr. from POR. LC 91-4471. 272p. 1995. pap. 11.00 (*0-8021-3420-3*, Grove) Grove-Atltic.
— Fado Alexandrino: A Novel. Rabassa, Gregory, tr. from POR. LC 91-4471. 512p. 1995. pap. 14.00 (*0-8021-3421-1*, Grove) Grove-Atltic.
Antunes, J. Lobo, jt. ed. see Cohadon, F.
Antunes, Jose E. Liability of Corporate Groups: Autonomy & Control in Parent-Subsidiary Relationships in U. S., German & EEC Law: An International & Comparative Perspective. LC 93-42436. (Studies in Transnational Economic Law: Vol. 10). 1994. 178.50 (*90-6544-785-7*) Kluwer Law Intl.
Antunovich, John D., jt. auth. see Ritter, Beverly L.
Antush, John, ed. Recent Puerto Rican Theatre: Five Plays from New York. LC 90-32908. 256p. 1991. pap. 11.00 (*1-55885-019-8*, Pub. by Arte Publico) Empire Pub Srvs.
Antwerp, Emily S. Van, see Van Antwerp, Emily S.
Antwerp, Margaret A. Van, see Van Antwerp, Margaret A., ed.
Antwerpen, Marie Van, see Van Antwerpen, Marie.
Antwi-Akowoah, Thomas. Lingala-English - English-Lingala Dictionary & Phrasebook. LC 96-17266. 120p. (Orig.). 1996. pap. 11.95 (*0-7818-0456-6*) Hippocrene Bks.
Antworth, Evan L. PC-Kimmo: A Two-Level Processor for Morphological Analysis. (Occasional Publications in Academic Computing: No. 16). 280p. 1990. pap. 24.00 (*0-88312-639-7*) S I L Intl.
***Antworth, Terrance.** Death from the Sea. LC 98-90947. 1999. pap. 7.95 (*0-533-12998-2*) Vantage.
***Antyufeev, V. S.** Monte Carlo Method for Solving Inverse Problems of Radiation Transfer. (Illus.). 202p. 2000. 132.50 (*90-6764-320-3*, Pub. by Uppsala Universitet) Coronet Bks.
Antze, Paul & Lambek, Michael, eds. Tense Past: Cultural Essays in Trauma & Memory. LC 95-26249. 272p. (C). 1996. 80.00 (*0-415-91562-7*); pap. 23.99 (*0-415-91563-5*) Routledge.
Antzelevitch, Charles, et al, eds. The Brugada Syndrome. LC 99-19225. (Clinical Approaches to Tachyarrhythmias Ser.: Vol. 10). (Illus.). 112p. 1999. pap. 21.00 (*0-87993-434-4*) Futura Pub.
Anuff, Ed. The Java Sourcebook. 498p. 1996. pap. 29.95 (*0-471-14859-8*) Wiley.
Anuff, Joey & Cox, Ana M., eds. Suck: Worst-Case Scenarios in Media, Culture, Advertising & the Internet. LC 97-29753. (Illus.). 224p. (Orig.). 1997. pap. 14.95 (*1-888869-27-5*) Wired Bks.
***Anuff, Joey & Wolf, Gary.** Dumb Money: Adventures of a Day Trader. LC 99-56973. 240p. 2000. 23.95 (*0-375-50388-9*) Random.
Anuman, Rajadhon P. Life & Ritual in Old Siam: Three Studies of Thai Life & Customs. Gedney, William J., ed. LC 78-23833. (Illus.). 109p. 1979. reprint ed. lib. bdg. 49.75 (*0-313-21193-0*, ARLF, Greenwood Pr) Greenwood.
Anundsen, Kristin, jt. auth. see Shaffer, Carolyn R.
***Anundson, Thomas.** A&O Forestry (And Outdoor Enthusiast) Handbook, Vol. II. rev. ed. (Illus.). 45p. 2000. pap. 12.00 (*0-9678890-0-6*) T Anundson.
Anunobi, Fredoline O. The Implications of Conditionality: The International Monetary Fund & Africa. 362p. (C). 1992. 59.50 (*0-8191-8794-1*); pap. text 34.50 (*0-8191-8795-X*) U Pr of Amer.
— International Dimensions of African Political Economy: Trends, Challenges, & Realities. 590p. (Orig.). (C). 1994. pap. text 56.50 (*0-8191-9691-6*); lib. bdg. 76.50 (*0-8191-9690-8*) U Pr of Amer.

A

A

Anupam, Sanyal, et al, eds. Power Generation Conference: Environmental Control/Fuels & Combustion Technologies/Nuclear Engineering, Proceedings. LC 96-78524. 688p. 1997. pap. 170.00 (0-7918-1577-3) ASME.

Anupindi. Managing Business Process Flow. 1998. 19.25 (0-07-232496-1) McGraw.

— Managing Business Process Flows. 2nd ed. 328p. 1998. pap. text 31.20 (0-536-01357-8) S&S Trade.

Anupindi, et al. Manager Business Process Flows. LC 98-30746. 267p. 1999. pap. text 37.60 (0-13-907775-8) P-H.

Anurag, Ma Y., ed. see Osho.

Anurag, Ma Yoga, ed. see Osho.

Anuras, Sinn, ed. Motility Disorders of the Gastrointestinal Tract: Principles & Practice. LC 92-14367. (Illus.). 479p. 1992. reprint ed. pap. 148.50 (0-608-07229-X, 206745400009) Bks Demand.

Anuruddha, Acariya, jt. auth. see Bodhi, Bhikkhu.

Anusavice. Phillip's Science of Dental Mat. 10th ed. 656p. 1996. text 61.95 (0-7216-5741-9, W B Saunders Co) Harcrt Hlth Sci Grp.

Anusavice, Kenneth J., ed. Quality Evaluation of Dental Restorations. (Illus.). 424p. 1989. text 106.00 (0-86715-202-8) Quint Pub Co.

Anuskiewicz, J. Michael. How to Protect Yourself Against the Fast-Approaching Depression. 40p. (Orig.). 1988. pap. 9.95 (0-685-44273-X) Gemini Pr.

— How to Survive Our Savage Society: A Self-Help Guide to Smart Living. LC 78-55863. 1978. pap. 4.95 (0-9601690-1-6) Gemini Pr.

Anuszkiewicz, Richard. Anuskiewicz OpArt. (Illus.). 119p. 1999. pap. 45.00 (3-7757-0671-2) Gerd Hatje.

Anuta, Michael J. East Prussians from Russia: Bound with Supplement to East Prussians from Russia. (Illus.). 293p. 1999. pap. 27.50 (0-8063-1437-0) Clearfield Co.

Anutoshen, D., ed. see Osho.

Anvik, Orville. Stand by Faith or Not at All. LC 96-61544. 368p. (Orig.). 1996. pap. 12.99 (1-883893-65-8) WinePress Pub.

Anwandter, Patty, ed. see Hamilton, Marian.

Anwar, Ali M. UNESCO Field Mission Reports on Muslim Countries: An Annotated Biliography. 1995. 34.00 (0-7069-9860-X, Pub. by Vikas) S Asia.

Anwar, B., jt. auth. see Yaqin, Anwarul.

Anwar, Chairil. The Voice of the Night: Complete Poetry & Prose of Chairil Anwar. Raffel, Burton, tr. from IND. LC 92-37868. (Monographs in International Studies, Southeast Asia Ser.: No. 89). 196p. (Orig.). (C). 1993. pap. text 20.00 (0-89680-170-5) Ohio U Pr.

Anwar, Dewi F. Indonesia in ASEAN: Foreign Policy & Regionalism. LC 94-29486. 1994. text 59.95 (0-312-12419-8) St Martin.

Anwar, Medhi. Test Yourself Electric Circuits. LC 97-25148. (Test Yourself Ser.). (Illus.). 96p. (C). 1996. pap. 12.95 (0-8442-2354-9, 23549) NTC Contemp Pub Co.

Anwar, Mohamed Sami. Be & Equational Sentences in Egyptian Colloquial Arabic. (Studies in Language Companion: No. 2). vi, 128p. 1979. 33.00 (90-272-3001-3, SLCS 2) J Benjamins Pubng Co.

Anwar, Muhammad. Between Cultures: Continuity & Change in the Lives of Young Asians. LC 97-18727. (Illus.). 232p. (C). 1998. 85.00 (0-415-04647-5); pap. 25.99 (0-415-04648-3) Routledge.

— From Legislation to Integration. LC 99-26812. 2000. text 69.95 (0-312-22574-1) St Martin.

— Modelling Interest-Free Economy: A Study in Macro-Economics & Development. LC 87-82481. (Islamization of Knowledge Ser.: No. 4). 140p. (Orig.). (C). 1987. text 15.75 (0-912463-78-3); pap. text 8.00 (0-912463-11-2) IIIT VA.

— Race & Politics. 256p. 1986. 32.50 (0-422-79840-1, 9913, Pub. by Tavistock) Routldge.

Anwar, Muhammad, jt. auth. see Shah, Nasra M.

Anwar, Raja. Terrorist Prince. 1997. 25.00 (1-85984-886-9) Routledge.

Anwar, Rebecca A., ed. Emergency Medicine Residencies. (Emergency Health Services Review Ser.: Vol. 1, No. 1). 129p. 1981. pap. text 19.95 (0-917724-57-7) Haworth Pr.

Anway, Carol A., jt. auth. see Anway, Joseph H.

Anway, Carol L. Daughters of Another Path: Experiences of American Women Choosing Islam. LC 95-90490. 224p. 1995. pap. 13.95 (0-9647169-0-9) Yawna Pubns.

Anway, Joseph H. & Anway, Carol A. Adventures in a New Land. 216p. 1987. pap. 19.00 (0-8309-0487-5) Herald Pub Hse.

Anwer, M. Modelling Interest-Free Economy. 1992. pap. 12.95 (1-56744-142-4) Kazi Pubns.

Anxo, Dominique, et al, eds. Work Patterns & Capital Utilization: An International Comparative Study. LC 94-39862. 1995. lib. bdg. 140.00 (0-7923-3263-6) Kluwer Academic.

Any, Carol. Boris Eikhenbaum: Voices of a Russian Formalist. (Illus.). 270p. (C). 1993. 42.50 (0-8047-2229-3) Stanford U Pr.

***Anyabolu, Oliver I.** Nigeria Past to the Present. 2000. pap. text. write for info. (0-9663234-1-6) Classic Publ.

Anyane-Ntow, Kwabena, ed. International Handbook of Accounting Education & Certification. LC 91-42895. (Illus.). 588p. 1992. 151.00 (0-08-041372-2, Pergamon Pr) Elsevier.

Anyanechi, Marie C. Constructivism: A New Method of Teaching Science. LC 98-60014. (Sunscholars Ser.). (Illus.). 1998. pap., teacher ed. write for info. (1-889218-11-1) Sungai Bks.

Anyanwu, Longy & LeBel, Phillip, eds. Promoting Equity Markets in Africa, Vol. 9. unabridged ed. LC 98-103755. 106p. (Orig.). 1997. pap. 9.50 (0-944572-08-1) MSU Ctr Econ Res Africa.

Anyanwu, Rose-Juliet. Aspects of Igbo Grammar: Phonetics, Phonology, Morphology & the Tonology of Nouns. 200p. 1997. pap. text 25.95 (3-8258-3233-3) Transaction Pubs.

Anyaoku, Emeka. The Missing Headlines: Selected Speeches. LC 98-144389. (Illus.). 352p. 1997. 36.95 (0-85323-812-X, Pub. by Liverpool Univ Pr); pap. 22.95 (0-85323-822-7, Pub. by Liverpool Univ Pr) Intl Spec Bk.

Anyi, G. Arbor Hars, see Hars Anyi, G. Arbor.

Anyi, Wang. Brocade Valley. McDougall, Bonnie S. & Maiping, Chen, trs. from CHI. LC 92-18529. 128p. (Orig.). 1992. 17.95 (0-8112-1224-6, Pub. by New Directions) Norton.

Anyidoho, Kofi. Ancestral Logic & Caribbean Blues. LC 91-75601. 24.95 (0-86543-264-3); pap. 9.95 (0-86543-265-1) Africa World.

— The Word Behind Bars & the Paradox of Exile. LC 97-16003. 288p. 1997. 59.95 (0-8101-1392-9); pap. 19.95 (0-8101-1393-7) Northwestern U Pr.

Anyidoho, Kofi, et al, eds. Beyond Survival: African Literature & the Search for New Life. LC 99-15525. (ALA Annuals Ser.: No. 5). 350p. 1998. 69.95 (0-86543-708-4); pap. 19.95 (0-86543-709-2) Africa World.

Anyike, James C. African American Holidays: A Historical Research & Resource Guide to Cultural Celebrations. 85p. (C). 1991. pap. text 7.95 (0-9631547-0-2) Pop Truth.

Anylan, William G, jt. ed. see Yaggy, Duncan.

Anyon, George J. Entrepreneurial Dimensions of Management. LC 73-622. 1973. text 9.95 (0-915180-12-X) Harrowood Bks.

Anyon, Jean. Ghetto Schooling: A Political Economy of Urban Educational Reform. LC 97-26507. 240p. (Orig.). 1997. 45.00 (0-8077-3663-5); pap. 18.95 (0-8077-3662-7) Tchrs Coll.

Anysas, J. A., jt. auth. see Melford, S. J.

Anyumba, G. Kisumu Town, Kenya: History of the Built Form, Planning & Environment. (Housing & Urban Policy Studies: No. 10). 390p. 1995. pap. 77.50 (90-407-1067-8, Pub. by Delft U Pr) Coronet Bks.

Anzai, Shigeo & Ogura, Yasuyuki, photos by. Isamu Noguchi: Space of Akari & Stone. LC 86-13623. (Illus.). 100p. (Orig.). 1986. pap. 24.95 (0-87701-405-1) Chronicle Bks.

Anzai, Tetsuo, ed. Shakespeare in Japan. LC 99-193160. 332p. 1999. 99.95 (0-7734-8214-8) E Mellen.

Anzai, Y., et al, eds. Symbiosis of Human & Artifact, 2 vols. (Advances in Human Factors/Ergonomics Ser.: Vol. 20 A-B). 2296p. 1995. 441.00 (0-444-81795-6, North Holland) Elsevier.

Anzai, Yuichiro. Pattern Recognition & Machine Learning. (Illus.). 407p. 1992. text 94.00 (0-12-058830-7) Acad Pr.

Anzald, Antonio. Fantasia: Worlds of Magic, Mystery & Fantasy; Man's Imagination at Work. 192p. 1996. 27.50 (88-7301-051-2, Pub. by Gremese Intl) Natl Bk Netwk.

Anzaldo, Armando A. En la Frontera de la Vida: Los Virus. (Ciencia para Todos Ser.). (SPA.). pap. 6.99 (968-16-4811-0, Pub. by Fondo) Continental Bk.

***Anzaldua, Gloria.** Borderlands - La Frontera: The New Mestiza. LC 99-22546. 1999. 39.50 (1-879960-57-5, Pub. by Aunt Lute Bks) Consort Bk Sales.

— Borderlands - La Frontera: The New Mestiza. 2nd ed. LC 99-22546. 251p. 1999. pap. text 13.95 (1-879960-56-7, Pub. by Aunt Lute Bks) SPD-Small Pr Dist.

Anzaldua, Gloria. Friends from the Other Side: Amigos del Otro Lado. LC 92-34384. 1993. 12.15 (0-606-09303-6, Pub. by Turtleback) Demco.

— Friends from the Other Side (Amigos del Otro Lado) LC 92-34384. (Illus.). 32p. (YA). (gr. 1 up). 1993. 14.95 (0-89239-113-8) Childrens Book Pr.

— Friends from the Other Side (Amigos del Otro Lado) LC 92-34384. (ENG & SPA., Illus.). 28p. (YA). (ps-3). 1995. pap. 6.95 (0-89239-130-8) Childrens Book Pr.

***Anzaldua, Gloria.** Interviews/Entrevistas. Keating, AnaLouise, ed. LC 99-55530. 320p. 2000. pap. 18.99 (0-415-92504-5); text 75.00 (0-415-92503-7) Routledge.

Anzaldua, Gloria. Prietita & the Ghost Woman (Prietita y la Llorona) (Illus.). 32p. (J). (gr. 2-4). 1996. 19.90 (0-516-20000-3) Childrens.

— Prietita & the Ghost Woman (Prietita y la Llorona) LC 95-37573. (ENG & SPA., Illus.). (YA). (ps-3). 1996. 15.95 (0-89239-136-7) Childrens Book Pr.

Anzaldua, Gloria, ed. Making Face, Making Soul - Haciendo Caras: Creative & Critical Perspectives by Feminists of Color. LC 90-9428. 448p. 1990. lib. bdg. 25.95 (1-879960-11-7) Aunt Lute Bks.

— Making Face, Making Soul - Haciendo Caras: Creative & Critical Perspectives by Feminists of Color. LC 90-9428. 448p. 1990. pap. 17.95 (1-879960-10-9) Aunt Lute Bks.

Anzaldua, Gloria, jt. ed. see Moraga, Cherrie.

Anzaldua, Mike. Mexican American Literature: A Preliminary Bibliography of Literary Criticism. (Latin American Curriculum Units for Junior & Community Colleges Ser.). vii, 29p. (Orig.). (C). 1980. pap. text 3.95 (0-86728-004-2) U TX Inst Lat Am Stud.

Anzaldua, Mike M., Jr. & Pierce, James A. First Steps: Grammar & Guided Composition for Basic Writing Students. 2nd ed. 200p. 1980. pap. text, student ed. 17.95 (0-89641-034-X) American Pr.

Anzaldua, Ricardo, jt. ed. see Cornelius, Wayne A.

Anzaldua, Ricardo, jt. ed. see Maxfield, Sylvia.

***Anzalone, Christopher A., ed.** Encyclopedia of Supreme Court Quotations. LC 99-41504. 416p. 2000. text 79.95 (0-7656-0485-X) M E Sharpe.

***Anzalone, Joseph E., Jr.** Carpitis' Honor. 350p. 1998. pap. 16.95 (0-9666577-1-3) Joseph E Anzalone.

Anzalone, Stephen & McLaughlin, Stephen. Making Literacy Work: The Specific Literacy Approach. (Illus.). 73p. 1983. pap. 4.00 (0-932288-73-1) Ctr Intl Ed U of MA.

Anzar, Naosherwan. The Beloved: The Life & Work of Meher Baba. rev. ed. LC 83-13540. (Illus.). 160p. 1983. pap. 12.00 (0-913078-47-6) Sheriar Pr.

— Presence. 90p. (Orig.). 1992. pap. 9.95 (0-9613907-2-7) Beloved Bks.

Anzar, Naosherwan, ed. The Best of the Glow: A Fifteen Year Retrospective, Vol. 1. LC 84-23518. 208p. (Orig.). 1984. pap. 8.95 (0-913078-54-9) Sheriar Pr.

Anzen, Bjorn, tr. see Momen, Karl.

Anzenberger, Regina M. Regina Maria Anzenberger: Presents 20 Photographs. (Illus.). 208p. 1997. 55.00 (3-908162-73-4) Dist Art Pubs.

Anzetti, Tony. Typhon's Children. 329p. 1999. mass mkt. 5.99 (0-345-41871-9, Del Rey) Ballantine Pub Grp.

Anzhi, Zhang. A History of Chinese Painting. (Illus.). 244p. 1992. 75.00 (0-8351-2798-2) China Bks.

Anziano, Michael C., et al. Approaches to Preschool Curriculum. LC 94-6686. 1994. text 37.50 (0-02-802096-0); teacher ed. write for info. (0-02-802097-9) Glencoe.

Anzick, William, ed. & illus. see Deutsch, Alina.

Anzieu, Didier. Freud's Self-Analysis. LC 86-14924. 1986. 92.50 (0-8236-2045-X) Intl Univs Pr.

— A Skin for Thought: Interviews with Gilbert Tarrab on Psychology & Psychoanalysis. 176p. 1990. pap. text 28.00 (0-946439-86-9, Pub. by H Karnac Bks Ltd) Other Pr LLC.

— Thought: From the Skin to the Thinking Ego. 160p. 1996. pap. 32.95 (1-85302-401-5, Pub. by Jessica Kingsley) Taylor & Francis.

Anzieu, Didier, ed. Psychic Envelopes. 280p. 1990. pap. text 29.00 (0-946439-60-5, Pub. by H Karnac Bks Ltd) Other Pr LLC.

Anzilotti, Gloria I. Four English-Italian Stories: Experiments in Translation. LC 84-23351. (Edward Sapir Monographs in Language, Culture & Cognition: No. 11). (ENG & ITA.). viii, 84p. (Orig.). 1983. pap. 18.00 (0-933104-16-2) Jupiter Pr.

Anzilotti, Gloria I., et al, trs. from ITA. New Italian Women: A Collection of Short Fiction. LC 89-45539. 218p. (Orig.). 1989. pap. 14.95 (0-934977-16-X) Italica Pr.

Anzlowar, Rajka, ed. see Pharmaco Medical Doc., Inc. Staff.

Anzovin, Steven, ed. Our Future in Space. (Reference Shelf Ser.: Vol. 63, No. 2). 175p. 1991. pap. 25.00 (0-8242-0812-9) Wilson.

— Preserving the World Ecology, 6 vols. (Reference Shelf Ser.: Vol. 62, No. 1). 175p. 1990. pap. 25.00 (0-8242-0790-4) Wilson.

***Anzovin, Steven & Podell, Janet. Famous First Facts: International Edition. LC 99-86869. (Famous First Facts Series). 1000p. 2000. 115.00 (0-8242-0958-3) Wilson.**

Famous First Facts, International Edition Destined to become as indispensable to historians, librarians, teachers, students & general readers as the acclaimed American-based classic, the international Edition lists thousands of inventions, discoveries & first happenings from a global perspective. To order: H.W.Wilson - 1-800-367-6770 (1-717-588-8400 outside U.S. & Canada); custserv@hwwilson.com, or visit www.hwwilson.com. *Publisher Paid Annotation.*

–Famous First Facts about American Politics. (Famous First Facts Series). 700p. 2000. 105.00 (0-8242-0971-0) Wilson.

Provides 4,000 entries on firsts in national state & local politics. To order: H.W.Wilson - 1-800-367-6770 (1-718-588-8400 outside U.S. & Canada) *Publisher Paid Annotation.*

Anzovin, Steven & Podell, Janet. Old Worlds to New: The Age of Exploration & Discovery. LC 92-19264. 296p. 1993. 44.00 (0-8242-0838-2) Wilson.

Anzovin, Steven, jt. ed. see Podell, Janet.

Anzueto, Antonio. Contemporary Diagnosis & Management of Bronchitis. (Illus.). 135p. (C). 1999. pap. 28.95 (1-884065-33-3, Hndbks Hlth Care) Assocs in Med.

Anzulovic, Branimir. Heavenly Serbia: From Myth to Genocide. LC 98-40143. 256p. 1999. 24.95 (0-8147-0671-1) NYU Pr.

***Anzulovic, Branimir.** Heavenly Serbia: From Myth to Genocide: From Myth to Genocide LC 98-40143. 233 p. 1999. pap. write for info. (0-8147-0672-X) NYU Pr.

***Ao, Lee.** Martyrs' Shrine: The Reform Movement of 1898 in China. (Illus.). 312p. 2000. 35.00 (0-19-592438-X) OUP.

A'o, Lono K. Don't Drink the Water: The Essential Guide to Our Contaminated Water & What You Can Do about It. 2nd rev. ed. Tinkle, Susan, ed. LC 98-66190. (Illus.). 107p. 1998. pap. 11.95 (0-9628882-9-X) Kali Pr.

***AOA Staff.** Self Study Course for Paraoptometric Certification. 2nd ed. Jameson, Mary, ed. LC 96-30878. (Illus.). 358p. 2000. pap. text 50.00 (0-7506-7266-8) Buttrwrth-Heinemann.

Aoahan, Miriam. The Family Connection: Understanding Your Loved Ones. (Miriam Aoahan Handbook Ser.). 245p. 1995. 12.95 (1-56871-072-0) Targum Pr.

Aodha, Michael O. Seumas O'Kelly's the Weaver's Grave. (New Abbey Theatre Ser.). 1984. pap. 2.95 (0-912262-81-8) Proscenium.

Aoe, Jun-ichi, ed. Computer Algorithms: String Pattern Matching Strategies. LC 93-40355. 296p. 1994. pap. 49.00 (0-8186-5462-7) IEEE Comp Soc.

Aoki, A., et al, eds. New Horizons in Low Dimensional Electron Systems: A Festschrift in Honour of Professor H. Kamimura. 488p. (C). 1992. text 287.50 (0-7923-1302-X) Kluwer Academic.

Aoki, Byron Yl. Evaluation, Stabilization & Transport of the Critically Ill Child. (Illus.). 512p. (C). (gr. 13). 1992. pap. text 42.95 (0-8151-0114-7, 22560) Mosby Inc.

Aoki, Haruo. Nez Perce Dictionary. LC 93-11792. (Publications in Linguistics: Vol. 122). 1993. 155.00 (0-520-09763-7, Pub. by U CA Pr) Cal Prin Full Svc.

Aoki, Haruo, et al. Basic Structures in Japanese. (JPN.). 480p. (C). 1984. pap. text 60.00 (4-469-22062-0) Asian Humanities.

Aoki, Hideki, ed. see Segawa, K. & Takahashi, K.

***Aoki, Hideo, et al, eds.** Physics Meets Mineralogy: Condensed Matter Physics in Geosciences. LC 99-86299. (Illus.). 432p. 2000. write for info. (0-521-64342-2) Cambridge U Pr.

Aoki, Hideo, jt. auth. see Kamimura, Hiroshi.

Aoki, Hideo, tr. see Kawabe, Seiji.

Aoki, Hiroyuki. Shintaido: An Art of Movement & Life Expression. Thompson, Michael & Ito, Haruyoshi, trs. from JPN. LC 82-80496. (Illus.). 120p. 1991. reprint ed. pap. 20.00 (0-942634-00-4) Shintaido.

***Aoki, Hiroyuki.** Total Stick Fighting: Shintaido Bojutsu. LC 99-88170. (Illus.). 140p. 1999. 25.00 (4-7700-2383-9, Pub. by Kodansha Intl) Kodansha.

Aoki, Hisako. Santa's Favorite Story. 2nd ed. LC 82-60895. (Pixies Ser.). (Illus.). 28p. (J). (ps up). 1991. reprint ed. 4.95 (0-88708-153-3, Picture Book Studio) S&S Childrens.

Aoki, Hisako & Gantschev, Ivan. Santa's Favorite Story. LC 82-60895. (Illus.). 32p. (J). (ps-3). 1997. per. 5.99 (0-689-81723-1) S&S Childrens.

***Aoki, K.** Nonlinear Dynamics & Chaos in Semiconductors. 1999. 149.00 (0-7503-0514-2); pap. text 59.00 (0-7503-0515-0) IOP Pub.

Aoki, K., ed. Essential Hypertension, No. 2. (Illus.). 416p. 1990. 176.00 (0-387-70044-7) Spr-Verlag.

Aoki, K. & Kobayashi, M., eds. Present & Future of High-Energy Physics: Proceedings of the 5th Nishinomiya-Yukawa Memorial Symposium on Theoretical Physics, Nishinomiya City, Japan, October 25-26, 1990. (Proceedings in Physics Ser.: Vol. 65). (Illus.). ix, 233p. 1992. 97.95 (0-387-55283-9) Spr-Verlag.

Aoki, K., jt. ed. see Ohta, T.

Aoki, Kaye. Manual for the Lawyer's Assistant (NALS) 3rd ed. 1200p. (C). 1994. pap. text. write for info. (0-314-04069-2) West Pub.

— NALS - Manual for the Lawyer's Assistant. 3rd ed. 333p. (C). 1994. pap. text, teacher ed. write for info. (0-314-04912-6); pap. text, student ed. write for info. (0-314-04849-9) West Pub.

— NALS - Teacher's Manual to Accompany the Career Legal Secretary. 3rd ed. 363p. 1993. pap. text, teacher ed. 11.95 (0-314-02924-9) West Pub.

— NALS - The Career Legal Secretary: Student Study Guide & Work Project. 3rd ed. 291p. 1993. pap. text 11.95 (0-314-02914-1) West Pub.

Aoki, Kaye, jt. auth. see National Association of Legal Secretary Staff.

Aoki, Keith & Epps, Garrett. The Accidental Law Student: A Graphic Introduction to Law School. (Critical America Ser.). 184p. 1999. pap. 15.95 (0-8147-0655-X); text 45.00 (0-8147-0654-1) NYU Pr.

Aoki, Kiyoshi. Ethical Dilemmas in Health & Development. 1994. 82.50 (4-7622-7764-9, Pub. by Jap Sci Soc Pr) Intl Spec Bk.

Aoki, M., jt. ed. see Patrick, Hugh T.

Aoki, Masahiko. The Co-Operative Game Theory of the Firm. (Illus.). 1984. pap. 13.95 (0-685-09581-9) OUP.

— The Co-Operative Game Theory of the Firm. (Illus.). 1986. 21.00 (0-19-877268-8) OUP.

***Aoki, Masahiko.** Information, Corporate Governance & Institutional Diversity: Competitiveness in Japan, the USA, & the Transitional Economies. 208p. 2000. 29.95 (0-19-829703-3) OUP.

Aoki, Masahiko. Information, Incentives & Bargaining in the Japanese Economy. (Illus.). 332p. (C). 1990. pap. text 33.95 (0-521-38681-0) Cambridge U Pr.

— Optimal Control & System Theory in Dynamic Economic Analysis. (Dynamic Economics Ser.: Vol. 1). 402p. 1976. write for info. (0-7204-8603-3, North Holland) Elsevier.

— State Space Modeling of Time Series. (Illus.). 330p. 1986. 69.00 (0-387-17256-4) Spr-Verlag.

— State Space Modeling of Time Series. (Universitext Ser.). (Illus.). xi, 314p. 1987. pap. 25.00 (0-387-17257-2) Spr-Verlag.

— State Space Modeling of Time Series. enl. rev. ed. (Illus.). xviii, 323p. 1990. pap. 32.00 (0-387-52870-9) Spr-Verlag.

— State Space Modeling of Time Series. 2nd enl. rev. ed. (Illus.). xviii, 323p. 1990. 79.95 (0-387-52869-5) Spr-Verlag.

Aoki, Masahiko, ed. The Firm As a Nexus of Treaties. (Advanced Studies in the Social Sciences). 368p. (C). 1989. text 45.00 (0-8039-8244-5); pap. text 18.95 (0-8039-8245-3) Sage.

Aoki, Masahiko & Dore, Ronald, eds. The Japanese Firm: Sources of Competitive Strength. (Illus.). 422p. 1996. pap. text 32.00 (0-19-829215-5) OUP.

***Aoki, Masahiko & Saxonhouse, Gary R., eds.** Finance, Governance & Competitiveness in Japan. LC 99-59051. (Japan Business & Economics Ser.). 288p. 2000. text 66.00 (0-19-829721-1) OUP.

Aoki, Masahiko, et al. The Role of Government in East Asian Economic Development: Comparative Institutional Analysis. (Illus.). 432p. 1998. reprint ed. pap. text 24.95 (0-19-829491-3) OUP.

An Asterisk (*) at the beginning of an entry indicates that the title is appearing for the first time.

Aoki, Masanao. New Approaches to Macroeconomic Modeling: Evolutionary Stochastic Dynamics, Multiple Equilibria, & Externalities As Field Effects. (Illus.). 303p. (C). 1996. text 59.95 (*0-521-48207-0*) Cambridge U Pr.

— New Approaches to Macroeconomic Modeling: Evolutionary Stochastic Dynamics, Multiple Equilibria, & Externalities As Field Effects. (Illus.). 306p. (C). 1998. reprint ed. pap. text 19.95 (*0-521-63769-4*) Cambridge U Pr.

— Optimization of Stochastic Systems: Topics in Discrete-Time Dynamics. 2nd ed. (Economic Theory, Econometrics & Mathematical Economics Ser.). 400p. 1989. text 104.00 (*0-12-058851-X*) Acad Pr.

Aoki, Mashiko, jt. auth. see Kim, Hyung-Ki.

Aoki, Michiko Y. Records of Wind & Earth: A Translation of Fudoki, with Introduction & Commentaries. LC 96-36340. 1996. 36.00 (*0-924304-32-4*) Assn Asian Studies.

Aoki, Michiko Y. & Dardess, Margaret B., eds. As the Japanese See It: Past & Present. LC 81-11526. 328p. 1981. pap. text 14.00 (*0-8248-0760-X*) UH Pr.

Aoki, N., ed. Dynamical Systems & Applications. (Advanced Series in Dynamical Systems: Vol. 4). 256p. (C). 1988. text 81.00 (*9971-5-0499-5*) World Scientific Pub.

— The Study of Dynamical Systems. (Advanced Series in Dynamical Systems: Vol. 7). 244p. (C). 1989. text 74.00 (*981-02-0040-4*) World Scientific Pub.

Aoki, N. & Hiraide, K. Topological Theory of Dynamical Systems: Recent Advances. LC 94-11678. (North-Holland Mathematical Library: No. 52). 424p. 1994. 142.50 (*0-444-89917-0*, North Holland) Elsevier.

***Aoki, Toshiuao.** Pikachu's Day. (Pokemon Tales Ser.: No. 4). (Illus.). 18p. (J). (ps-k). 1999. bds. 4.95 (*1-56931-386-5*, Pub. by Viz Commns Inc) Publishers Group.

Aoki, Y., ed. Deuteron Involving Reactions & Polarization Phenomena: Proceedings of the Tsukuba International Workshop, Tsukuba, Japan, August 22-23, 1985. 400p. 1986. text 99.00 (*9971-5-0008-6*) World Scientific Pub.

Aon Consulting, Inc. Staff. 1996 CUES Compensation Manual. 15th rev. ed. 161p. 1996. pap. 119.00 (*1-889394-13-0*) Credit Union Execs.

Aon, Miguel Antonio & Cortassa, Sonia. Dynamic Biological Organization: Its Fundamentals as Applied to Cellular Systems. LC 96-86752. 584p. 1997. write for info. (*0-412-79890-5*) Kluwer Academic.

***Aone.** Staffing Management & Methods: Tools & Techniques for Nursing Leaders. Fralic, Maryann F., ed. 2000. pap. 32.95 (*1-55648-284-1*) AHPI.

***Aone & Fralic, Maryann F.** Staffing Management & Methods: Tools & Techniques for Nursing Leaders. 2000. pap. 32.95 (*0-7879-5536-1*) Jossey-Bass.

Aono, Toshihiro, ed. see Serono Symposia, U. S. A. Staff.

Aoolloni, Ignazio & Cerami, Pietro. Impossible Poems: Italian Antipoetry. 118p. 1983. 50.00 (*0-89304-660-4*) Cross-Cultrl NY.

AORN Staff. AORN Patient Classification Instrument for Perioperative Nursing. rev. ed. Applegeet, Carol, ed. 50p. (Orig.). 1993. pap. text 25.00 (*0-939583-83-6*) Assn Oper Rm Nurses.

— Core Curriculum for the RN First Assistant. rev. ed. Rothrock, Jane C. et al, eds. (Illus.). 220p. 1994. pap. text 43.75 (*0-939583-86-0*) Assn Oper Rm Nurses.

— Optimizing Resources: A Manager's Guide to Success. 107p. (Orig.). 1993. pap. text 43.75 (*0-939583-82-8*) Assn Oper Rm Nurses.

— Standards, Recommended Practices & Guidelines 1998: With Official AORN Statements. 341p. 1998. pap. text 48.75 (*1-888460-00-8*) Assn Oper Rm Nurses.

***Aosen, Larry.** Postcards of North Dakota. (Postcard History Ser.). 1999. pap. 18.99 (*0-7385-0161-1*) Arcadia Publng.

Aoshima, Hitoshi. A Collection of Ceramic Works: A Communication of Tool for the Dental Office & Laboratory. (Illus.). 92p. 1992. text 64.00 (*4-87417-386-1*) Quint Pub Co.

AOTA Staff. Clinical Education & Supervision: An Instructional Guide. 350p. (C). 1991. ring bd. 225.00 incl. VHS (*0-910317-65-8*) Am Occup Therapy.

— 1998 Reference Guide to the Occupational Therapy Code of Ethics. rev. ed. 58p. 1999. pap. 20.00 (*1-56900-113-8*, 1139) Am Occup Therapy.

— Occupational Therapy Practice Guidelines for Adults with Alzheimer's Disease. (AOTA Practice Guidelines Ser.). (Illus.). 21p. 1999. pap. 22.00 (*1-56900-133-2*, 1191) Am Occup Therapy.

***AOTA Staff.** Occupational Therapy Practice Guidelines for Adults with Alzheimer's Disease. (AOTA Practice Guidelines Ser.). (Illus.). 2000. pap. write for info. (*1-56900-146-4*) Am Occup Therapy.

AOTA Staff. Occupational Therapy Practice Guidelines for Adults with Carpal Tunnel Syndrome. (AOTA Practice Guidelines Ser.). (Illus.). 13p. 1999. pap. 22.00 (*1-56900-121-9*, 1188) Am Occup Therapy.

***AOTA Staff.** Occupational Therapy Practice Guidelines for Adults with Carpal Tunnel Syndrome. (AOTA Practice Guidelines Ser.). (Illus.). 2000. pap. write for info. (*1-56900-147-2*) Am Occup Therapy.

— Occupational Therapy Practice Guidelines for Adults with Hip Fracture Replacement. (AOTA Practice Guidelines Ser.). (Illus.). 2000. pap. write for info. (*1-56900-148-0*) Am Occup Therapy.

AOTA Staff. Occupational Therapy Practice Guidelines for Adults with Hip Fracture/Replacement. (AOTA Practice Guidelines Ser.). (Illus.). 11p. 1999. pap. 22.00 (*1-56900-122-7*, 1153) Am Occup Therapy.

— Occupational Therapy Practice Guidelines for Adults with Low Back Pain. (AOTA Practice Guidelines Ser.). (Illus.). 15p. 1999. pap. 22.00 (*1-56900-123-5*, 1155) Am Occup Therapy.

***AOTA Staff.** Occupational Therapy Practice Guidelines for Adults with Low Back Pain. (AOTA Practice Guidelines Ser.). (Illus.). 2000. pap. write for info. (*1-56900-149-9*) Am Occup Therapy.

AOTA Staff. Occupational Therapy Practice Guidelines for Adults with Low Vision. (AOTA Practice Guidelines Ser.). (Illus.). 25p. 1999. pap. 22.00 (*1-56900-124-3*, 1192) Am Occup Therapy.

***AOTA Staff.** Occupational Therapy Practice Guidelines for Adults with Low Vision. (AOTA Practice Guidelines Ser.). (Illus.). 2000. pap. write for info. (*1-56900-150-2*) Am Occup Therapy.

— Occupational Therapy Practice Guidelines for Adults with Mood Disorders. (AOTA Practice Guidelines Ser.). (Illus.). 2000. pap. write for info. (*1-56900-142-1*) Am Occup Therapy.

AOTA Staff. Occupational Therapy Practice Guidelines for Adults with Neurodegenerative Diseases. (AOTA Practice Guidelines Ser.). (Illus.). 19p. 1999. pap. 22.00 (*1-56900-125-1*, 1194) Am Occup Therapy.

***AOTA Staff.** Occupational Therapy Practice Guidelines for Adults with Rheumatoid Arthritis. (AOTA Practice Guidelines Ser.). (Illus.). 2000. pap. write for info. (*1-56900-152-9*) Am Occup Therapy.

AOTA Staff. Occupational Therapy Practice Guidelines for Adults with Schizophrenia. (AOTA Practice Guidelines Ser.). (Illus.). 25p. 1999. pap. 22.00 (*1-56900-126-X*, 1189) Am Occup Therapy.

***AOTA Staff.** Occupational Therapy Practice Guidelines for Adults with Schizophrenia. (AOTA Practice Guidelines Ser.). (Illus.). 2000. pap. write for info. (*1-56900-153-7*) Am Occup Therapy.

AOTA Staff. Occupational Therapy Practice Guidelines for Adults with Spinal Cord Injury. (AOTA Practice Guidelines Ser.). (Illus.). 33p. 1999. pap. 22.00 (*1-56900-129-4*, 1154) Am Occup Therapy.

***AOTA Staff.** Occupational Therapy Practice Guidelines for Adults with Spinal Cord Injury. (AOTA Practice Guidelines Ser.). (Illus.). 2000. pap. write for info. (*1-56900-154-5*) Am Occup Therapy.

AOTA Staff. Occupational Therapy Practice Guidelines for Adults with Stroke. (AOTA Practice Guidelines Ser.). (Illus.). 15p. 1999. pap. 22.00 (*1-56900-127-8*, 1152) Am Occup Therapy.

***AOTA Staff.** Occupational Therapy Practice Guidelines for Adults with Stroke. (AOTA Practice Guidelines Ser.). (Illus.). 2000. pap. write for info. (*1-56900-155-3*) Am Occup Therapy.

AOTA Staff. Occupational Therapy Practice Guidelines for Adults with Traumatic Brain Injury. (AOTA Practice Guidelines Ser.). (Illus.). 18p. 1999. pap. 22.00 (*1-56900-128-6*, 1151) Am Occup Therapy.

***AOTA Staff.** Occupational Therapy Practice Guidelines for Adults with Traumatic Brain Injury. (AOTA Practice Guidelines Ser.). (Illus.). 2000. pap. write for info. (*1-56900-156-1*) Am Occup Therapy.

AOTA Staff. Occupational Therapy Practice Guidelines for Attention-Deficit/Hyperactivity Disorders. (AOTA Practice Guidelines Ser.). (Illus.). 13p. 1999. pap. 22.00 (*1-56900-130-8*, 1159) Am Occup Therapy.

***AOTA Staff.** Occupational Therapy Practice Guidelines for Attention-Deficit/Hyperactivity Disorders. (AOTA Practice Guidelines Ser.). (Illus.). 2000. pap. write for info. (*1-56900-157-X*) Am Occup Therapy.

AOTA Staff. Occupational Therapy Practice Guidelines for Cerebral Palsy. (AOTA Practice Guidelines Ser.). (Illus.). 13p. (Orig.). 1999. pap. 22.00 (*1-56900-131-6*, 1156) Am Occup Therapy.

***AOTA Staff.** Occupational Therapy Practice Guidelines for Cerebral Palsy. (AOTA Practice Guidelines Ser.). (Illus.). (Orig.). 2000. pap. write for info. (*1-56900-158-8*) Am Occup Therapy.

AOTA Staff. Occupational Therapy Practice Guidelines for Chronic Pain. (AOTA Practice Guidelines Ser.). (Illus.). 15p. 1999. pap. 22.00 (*1-56900-132-4*, 1193) Am Occup Therapy.

***AOTA Staff.** Occupational Therapy Practice Guidelines for Chronic Pain. (AOTA Practice Guidelines Ser.). (Illus.). 2000. pap. write for info. (*1-56900-159-6*) Am Occup Therapy.

AOTA Staff. Occupational Therapy Practice Guidelines for Substance Use Disorders. (AOTA Practice Guidelines Ser.). (Illus.). 23p. 1999. pap. 22.00 (*1-56900-134-0*, 1190) Am Occup Therapy.

***AOTA Staff.** Occupational Therapy Practice Guidelines for Substance Use Disorders. (AOTA Practice Guidelines Ser.). (Illus.). 2000. pap. write for info. (*1-56900-160-X*) Am Occup Therapy.

AOTA Staff. Occupational Therapy Practice Guidelines for Tendon Injuries. (AOTA Practice Guidelines Ser.). (Illus.). 13p. 1999. pap. 22.00 (*1-56900-135-9*, 1157) Am Occup Therapy.

***AOTA Staff.** Occupational Therapy Practice Guidelines for Tendon Injuries. (AOTA Practice Guidelines Ser.). (Illus.). 2000. pap. write for info. (*1-56900-161-8*) Am Occup Therapy.

AOTA Staff. Occupational Therapy Practice Guidelines for Young Children with Delayed Development. (AOTA Practice Guidelines Ser.). (Illus.). 15p. 1999. pap. 22.00 (*1-56900-136-7*, 1158) Am Occup Therapy.

***AOTA Staff.** Occupational Therapy Practice Guidelines for Young Children with Delayed Development. (AOTA Practice Guidelines Ser.). (Illus.). 2000. pap. write for info. (*1-56900-162-6*) Am Occup Therapy.

AOTA Staff. Occupational Therapy Quick Coding Guide. (Illus.). 20p. 1999. pap. 18.00 (*1-56900-115-4*, 1199) Am Occup Therapy.

***AOTA Staff.** Occupational Therapy Services for Children & Youth under the Individuals with Disabilities Education Act. 2nd ed. (Illus.). 1999. pap. write for info. (*1-56900-137-5*) Am Occup Therapy.

AOTA Staff, ed. Managed Care: A Sourcebook for Occupational Therapy. LC 96-227563. 160p. (Orig.). 1996. pap. text 35.00 (*1-56900-046-8*, 1161) Am Occup Therapy.

— Mental Health Service Delivery Guidelines. 176p. (Orig.). 1996. pap. text 25.00 (*1-56900-037-9*, 1135) Am Occup Therapy.

***Aoude, Ibrahim G., ed.** The Ethnic Studies Story: Politics & Social Movements in Hawaii--Essays in Honor of Marion Kelly. (Social Process in Hawaii Ser.). 352p. 1999. pap. text 20.00 (*0-8248-2244-7*) UH Pr.

Aoufi, Rabah. Digital Control Systems. 56p. (C). 2001. 58.00 (*0-02-303651-6*, Macmillan Coll) P-H.

Aoumiel. Green Witchcraft: Folk Magic, Fairy Lore & Herb Craft. LC 96-16406. (Illus.). 288p. (Orig.). 1999. pap. 12.95 (*1-56718-690-4*, K-690-4) Llewellyn Pubns.

Aoun, Joseph & Li, Yen-Hui A. Syntax of Scope. LC 92-30929. (Linguistic Inquiry Monographs: Vol. 21). (Illus.). 190p. 1993. 37.50 (*0-262-01133-6*); pap. text 18.95 (*0-262-51068-5*) MIT Pr.

Aoyagi, Akiko, ed. Bibliography of Soy Fiber - Okara (Soymilk Pulp), Soy Bran (Ground Hulls), & Soy Isolate Fiber: 468 References from 1716 to 1989, Partially Annotated. (Bibliographies of Soya Ser.). 105p. (Orig.). 1989. spiral bd. 53.00 (*0-933332-64-5*) Soyfoods Center.

— Bibliography of Soy Protein Isolates, Concentrates, & Textured Soy Protein Products: 2,528 References from 1883 to 1989. (Bibliographies of Soya Ser.). 328p. (Orig.). 1989. spiral bd. 164.00 (*0-933332-63-7*) Soyfoods Center.

— Bibliography of Soya in Latin America: 1,520 References from 1880 to 1989. (Bibliographies of Soya Ser.). 215p. (Orig.). 1989. spiral bd. 108.00 (*0-933332-62-9*) Soyfoods Center.

— Bibliography of Soya in the Indian Subcontinent (South Asia) 1,118 References from 1679 to 1989. (Bibliographies of Soya Ser.). 180p. (Orig.). 1989. spiral bd. 90.00 (*0-933332-61-0*) Soyfoods Center.

— Maketing Tofu Second Generation Products: Varieties & Okara Products (1977-1985) Labels, Ads, Posters & Other Graphics. 205p. 1988. spiral bd. 82.00 (*0-933332-31-9*) Soyfoods Center.

— Marketing Miso & Soy Sauce: Labels, Ads, Posters & Other Graphics. (Marketing Soyfoods Ser.). 148p. 1988. spiral bd. 59.20 (*0-933332-35-1*) Soyfoods Center.

— Marketing Soymilk & Soymilk Products: Labels, Ads, Posters & Other Graphics. (Marketing Soyfoods Ser.). 174p. 1988. spiral bd. 69.60 (*0-933332-34-3*) Soyfoods Center.

— Marketing Tempeh & Tempeh Products: Labels, Ads, Posters & Other Graphics. (Marketing Soyfoods Ser.). 175p. 1988. spiral bd. 70.00 (*0-933332-33-5*) Soyfoods Center.

— Marketing Tofu: Labels, Ads, Posters & Other Graphics. (Marketing Soyfoods Ser.). 180p. (Orig.). 1988. spiral bd. 71.00 (*0-933332-30-0*) Soyfoods Center.

— Marketing Tofu Second Generation Products: Labels, Ads, Posters & Other Graphics. (Marketing Soyfoods Ser.). 176p. 1988. spiral bd. 70.40 (*0-933332-32-7*) Soyfoods Center.

— Marketing Tofutti & Other Soy Ice Creams: Labels, Articles, Ads, Posters & Other Graphics. (Marketing Soyfoods Ser.). 214p. 1985. pap., spiral bd. 75.00 (*0-933332-37-8*) Soyfoods Center.

Aoyagi, Akiko, jt. auth. see Shurtleff, William.

Aoyagi, Akiko, jt. auth. see Shurtlell, William.

Aoyagi, Akiko, jt. compiled by see Shurtleff, William.

Aoyagi, Y., et al, eds. Microcrystalline Semiconductors: Materials Science & Devices. (Materials Research Society Symposium Proceedings Ser.: Vol. 283). 951p. 1993. text 79.00 (*1-55899-178-6*) Materials Res.

***Aoyama, Atsuko.** Toward a Virtuous Circle: A Nutrition Review of the Middle East & North Africa. LC 99-35061. (Health, Nutrition, & Population Ser.). 124p. 1999. pap. 25.00 (*0-8213-4557-5*, 14557) World Bank.

Aoyama, Miyuki, jt. ed. see Lowitz, Leza.

Aoyama, Sara, tr. see Sakai, Kazuo & Ide, Nakana.

Aoyama, Shundo. Zen Seeds: Reflections of a Female Priest. Bennage, Patricia D., tr. 168p. 1992. pap. 5.95 (*4-333-01478-6*, Pub. by Kosei Pub Co) Tuttle Pubng.

Aoyama, Yuko & Teitz, Michael B. Small Business Policy in Japan & the United States: A Comparative Analysis of Objectives & Outcomes. LC 96-77878. (Policy Papers in International Affairs). (Illus.). 1996. pap. text 8.25 (*0-87725-544-X*) U of Cal IAS.

***Aozzola.** Get Started with Windows 98. (C). 1998. pap. 26.95 (*0-7600-5951-9*) Thomson Learn.

ap Gwilym, Dafydd. Houses of Leaves: Poems by Dafydd Ap Gwilyn. aut. limited abr. ed. Bromwich, Rachel, tr. LC 97-132180. (Illus.). 59p. 1993. 150.00 (*0-907664-31-8*, Pub. by Old Stiles) St Mut.

Ap Gwilyn, Gwynn & Ap Gwilyn, Ifor, eds. The Hymns of Wales: Fifty Favorites. 1996. pap. 17.95 (*0-86243-369-X*, Pub. by Y Lolfa) Intl Spec Bk.

Ap Gwilyn, Ifor, jt. ed. see Ap Gwilyn, Gwynn.

AP Professional Staff. Crawford's Directory of City Connections, 1998 Edition. 1999. pap. 435.00 (*0-906247-98-5*) Kogan Page Ltd.

— Oliver's Guide to the City of London, 1998 Edition. 1999. pap. 125.00 (*0-906247-93-4*) Kogan Page Ltd.

AP Staff. Directory of Management Consultants in the UK: 1998 Edition. 1999. pap. text 150.00 (*0-906247-90-X*) Kogan Page Ltd.

***APA Automated Clearing House Committee.** The Guide to Successful Direct Deposit. 12th rev. ed. O'Toole, Michael P., ed. (Illus.). 300p. 2000. 55.95 (*1-930471-05-X*, 0300) American Payroll.

APA Committee on Managed Care. Utilization Management: A Handbook for Psychiatrists. LC 91-47117. 65p. 1992. pap. text 9.95 (*0-89042-235-4*, 2235) Am Psychiatric.

APA Committee on Psychiatry & Mental Health in Sch. Psychiatric Consultation in Schools: A Report of the American Psychiatric Association. LC 93-6913. 96p. 1993. text 9.95 (*0-89042-243-5*, 2243) Am Psychiatric.

APA Ethics Committee. Opinions of the Ethics Committee on the Principles of Medical Ethics with Annotations Especially Applicable to Psychiatry. 56p. 1995. pap. text 3.00 (*0-89042-139-0*, 2139) Am Psychiatric.

Apa, Ma P., ed. see Osho.

APA, Office of Research Staff, ed. American Psychiatric Association Practice Guidelines: Includes Psychiatric Evaluation of Adults, Eating Disorders, Bipolar Disorder, Etc. LC 96-213131. 361p. 1996. pap. text 46.50 (*0-89042-306-7*, 2306) Am Psychiatric.

APA Productions Staff, ed. France. (Insight Guides Ser.). 1986. pap. 6.95 (*0-13-330856-1*) S&S Trade.

APA Staff. Quick Reference to the Diagnostic Criteria from DSM-IV. 358p. 1994. pap. text 23.00 (*0-89042-063-7*, 2063) Am Psychiatric.

APA Staff, ed. American Psychiatric Association Practice Guidelines: Includes Psychiatric Evaluation of Adults, Eating Disorders, Bipolar Disorder, Etc. LC 96-213131. 361p. 1996. text 56.95 (*0-89042-305-9*, 2305) Am Psychiatric.

— The Directory of the American Psychological Association, 1997. 2110p. 1997. 70.00 (*1-55798-423-9*) Am Psychol.

APA Task Force on Models of Practice in Geriatric. Selected Models of Practice in Geriatric Psychiatry: A Task Force Report of the American Psychiatric Association. LC 92-48940. 82p. 1993. 12.95 (*0-89042-239-7*, 2239) Am Psychiatric.

Apacki, Carol. Energize! Barr, Linda & Harrington, Christine, eds. (Illus.). 155p. (J). (gr. k-12). 1991. pap. text 14.95 (*1-56095-059-5*) Quest Intl.

Apacki, Carol & Barr, Linda. Cambios y Desafios: Descubre Lo Mejor Que Hay en Ti. Facundo Santiago, Blanca, tr. (Skills for Adolescence Ser.). (SPA., Illus.). 228p. (J). (gr. 6-8). 1992. pap. text 5.76 (*1-56095-078-1*) Quest Intl.

Apacki, Carol, et al. Ana & Quentin Go to School. (Illus.). 24p. (J). (gr. k-2). 1993. pap. text 12.95 (*1-56095-080-3*) Quest Intl.

— A Bright Day for Everyone. (Illus.). 24p. (J). (gr. k-2). 1993. pap. text 12.95 (*1-56095-084-6*) Quest Intl.

— Changes & Challenges: Becoming the Best You Can Be. (Skills for Adolescence Ser.). (Illus.). 228p. (J). (gr. 6-8). 1992. pap. text 5.76 (*1-56095-073-0*) Quest Intl.

— Mariko Wears Her Thinking Cap. (Illus.). 24p. (J). (gr. k-2). 1993. pap. text 12.95 (*1-56095-083-8*) Quest Intl.

— Michael's Decision. (Illus.). 24p. (J). (gr. k-2). 1993. pap. text 12.95 (*1-56095-082-X*) Quest Intl.

— Q-Bear's Book of Rhymes & Songs - Grade One. (Illus.). 32p. (J). (gr. 1-2). 1993. pap. text 12.95 (*1-56095-095-1*) Quest Intl.

— Q-Bear's Book of Rhymes & Songs - Kindergarten. (Illus.). 32p. (J). (gr. k-1). 1993. pap. text 12.95 (*1-56095-094-3*) Quest Intl.

— The Surprising Years: Understanding Your Changing Adolescent. 3rd ed. Hambrecht, Dale, ed. (Skills for Adolescence Ser.). (Illus.). 72p. 1992. pap. text 3.95 (*1-56095-070-6*) Quest Intl.

— Turnabout's Fair Play. (Illus.). 24p. (J). (gr. k-2). 1993. pap. text 12.95 (*1-56095-081-1*) Quest Intl.

Apagyi, Barnabas, et al, eds. Inverse & Algebraic Quantum Scattering Theory: Proceedings of a Conference Held at Lake Balaton, Hungary, 3-7 September 1997. LC 97-19501. (Lecture Notes in Physics Ser.: No. 488). xv, 385p. 1997. 79.00 (*3-540-63021-X*) Spr-Verlag.

Apan, Valeria. How to Play Romanian Panpipe. Miller, Miamon, ed. (Illus.). 49p. (C). 1991. pap., student ed. 20.00 incl. audio (*0-9626468-1-4*) Fuge Imaginea.

Apanasov, Boris, et al, eds. Topology '90: Proceedings of the Research Semester in Low Dimensional Topology at Ohio State University. LC 92-16406. (Ohio State Mathematical Research Institute Publications: Vol. 1). xii, 457p. (C). 1992. lib. bdg. 69.95 (*3-11-012598-6*) De Gruyter.

Apanasov, Boris N., et al, eds. Geometry, Topology & Physics: Proceedings ofthe First Brazil-USA Workshop Held in Campinas, Brazil, June 30-July 7, 1996. LC 97-35550. 348p. 1997. 128.95 (*3-11-015594-X*) De Gruyter.

Aparicio, A., et al, eds. Stellar Astrophysics for the Local Group: A First Step to the Universe: VIII Canary Islands Winter School of Astrophysics. LC 97-52718. (Cambridge Contemporary Astrophysics Ser.). (Illus.). 610p. (C). 1998. 74.95 (*0-521-63255-2*) Cambridge U Pr.

Aparicio, Angel. Cinco Poetisas Cubanas, 1935-1969: Mercedes Garcia Tuduri, Pura del Prado, Teresa M. Rojas, Rita Geada y Ana Rosa Nunez. (SPA.). pap. 9.00 (*0-89729-055-0*) Ediciones.

Aparicio, Angel, ed. see De Balboa, Silvestre.

Aparicio, Angel, ed. see Zenea, Juan C.

Aparicio, Eduardo. 101 Spanish Proverbs: Understanding Spanish Language & Culture Through Common Sayings. LC 97-69973. (ENG & SPA., Illus.). 160p. 1998. pap. 6.95 (*0-8442-7227-2*, 72272) NTC Contemp Pub Co.

Aparicio, Eduardo, tr. see Klaus, Sandra.

Aparicio, Frances R. Listening to Salsa: Gender, Latin Popular Music, & Puerto Rican Cultures. LC 97-9121. (Music - Culture Ser.). (Illus.). 302p. 1998. pap. 19.95 (*0-8195-6308-0*, Wesleyan Univ Pr) U Pr of New Eng.

— Versiones, Interpretaciones, Creaciones: Instancias de la Traduccion Literaria en Hispanoamerica en el Siglo XX. LC 90-85355. (SPA.). 196p. 1991. pap. text 15.00 (*0-935318-18-6*) Edins Hispamerica.

Aparicio, Frances R., ed. Latino Voices. LC 93-42893. (Writers of America Ser.). (Illus.). 144p. (YA). (gr. 7 up). 1994. lib. bdg. 23.90 (*1-56294-388-X*) Millbrook Pr.

Aparicio, Frances R., tr. see Miller, Yvette E., ed.

Aparicio, Francis R. & Chavez-Silverman, Susana, eds. Tropicalizations: Transcultural Representations of Latinidad. LC 97-558. (Rencounters with Colonialism Ser.). (Illus.). 238p. 1997. pap. 19.95 (0-87451-817-2) U Pr of New Eng.

Aparicio, J., jt. ed. see Aldama, A. A.

Aparicio-Laurencio, Angel. Los Dias Cubanos de Hernan Cortes y Su Lucha Por un Ideal. (SPA.). 40p. (Orig.). 1988. pap. 5.00 (84-86662-09-5) Ediciones.

Aparicio Laurencio, Angel. Es Heredia el Primer Escritor Romantico en Lengua Espanola? (SPA.). 1988. pap. 6.00 (0-89729-515-3) Ediciones.

Aparicio, Manuel, IV, jt. ed. see Levine, Daniel S.

Aparicio, Rambon, jt. auth. see Harwood, John L.

Aparis, Fina, tr. see Clymer, R. S.

Aparvary, Leslie. A Legionnaire's Journey. (Illus.). 324p. (Orig.). 1989. pap. 17.95 (0-920490-93-X) Temeron Bks.

Apastamba, jt. auth. see Leggett, Trevor.

Apatiki, E., et al. Whangaperegaaghmeng (All about Me) (ESK.). 74p. 1981. pap. 5.00 (0-933769-87-3) Alaska Native.

Apatow, Robert. The Spiritual Art of Dialogue: Mastering Communication for Personal Growth, Relationships, & the Workplace. 224p. 1998. 22.00 (0-89281-674-0, Inner Trad) Inner Tradit.

Apblett, William R., Jr., ed. see Symposium on Shell & Tube Heat Exchangers Staff.

APCI Staff. European Design Guide. 672p. 1995. pap. 84.95 (0-566-07721-3, Pub. by Gower) Ashgate Pub Co.

APCTP Winter School Staff, et al. Dualities in Gauge & String Theories: Proceedings of APCTP Winter School, Sorak Mountain Resort, Korea, 17-28 February, 1997. LC 98-8803. 420p. 1998. 88.00 (981-02-3586-0) World Scientific Pub.

Apczynski. Intellectual Journey. 466p. 1998. pap. text 35.75 (0-536-01405-1) Pearson Custom.

Apczynski, John V. Doers of the Word: Toward a Foundational Theology Based on the Thought of Michael Polanyi. LC 76-51640. (American Academy of Religion. Dissertation Ser.: No. 18). 214p. reprint ed. pap. 66.40 (0-7837-5471-X, 20452360005) Bks Demand.

Apczynski, John V., ed. Foundations of Religious Literacy. 186p. (C). 1986. reprint ed. pap. text 23.00 (0-8191-5617-5) U Pr of Amer.

— Theology & the University, Vol. 33. 290p. (Orig.). (C). 1990. pap. text 25.00 (0-8191-7473-4); lib. bdg. 46.50 (0-8191-7472-6) U Pr of Amer.

APEC Committee on Trade & Investment. A Blueprint for Apec Customs Modernization: Working with Business for a Faster, Better Border. LC 97-944113. 25p. 1997. write for info. (0-662-26133-X) Can7 Govern Pub.

APEC Industrial Science & Technology Working Group Staff. Guidebook to Industrial Science & Technology Policies in Selected APEC Economies, 1997. LC 98-945505. 74 p. 1997. write for info. (981-00-8871-X) Miscell Pubs.

APEC Roundtable on "Best Practices" in Infrastructure Development Staff. APEC Roundtable on "Best Practices" in Infrastructure Development: Conference Summary & Case Studies. LC 97-945712. 284p. 1996. write for info. (981-00-8349-1) Miscell Pubs.

APEC Telecommunications Working Group. Practical Manual for Network Planning, 1997. LC 97-944112. 165p. 1997. write for info. (981-00-9291-1) AgBe Pub.

— Teleports Project. LC 97-945716. 42p. 1995. write for info. (981-00-5451-3) AgBe Pub.

APEC Telecommunications Working Group Staff. APEC EDI Pilot on Electronic Commerce. LC 97-945663. 1995. write for info. (981-00-6736-4, Pub. by AgBe Pub) Balogh.

APEC Tourism Working Group Staff. A Tourism Training Manual for Tourism Administrators in the Asia-Pacific Region. LC 97-945741. 1996. write for info. (981-00-7374-7) Miscell Pubs.

Apeitos, Stacey. Princess Priscilla. (Illus.). 32p. 1998. pap. 6.95 (0-207-18198-5) HarpC.

Apel, D. Scott, ed. Philip K. Dick: The Dream Connection. 2nd ed. LC 87-60689. reprint ed. pap. 14.95 (1-886404-03-8, 1886404038) Permanent San Jose.

Apel, D. Scott, jt. auth. see Wilson, Robert A.

Apel, Dieter & Pharaoh, Timothy M. Transport Concepts in European Cities. (Avebury Studies in Green Research). 320p. 1996. 87.95 (1-85972-094-3, Pub. by Avebry) Ashgate Pub Co.

Apel, Dora, jt. ed. see Hofmann, Irene.

Apel, Emanuel. European Monetary Integration 1958-2002. LC 97-21643. 240p. (C). 1998. 85.00 (0-415-11432-2); pap. 25.99 (0-415-11433-0) Routledge.

Apel, Eric. Friends Forever: A Pop-Up Book with Mailer. LC 99-185723. 5p. 1998. 5.95 (1-888443-14-6, Pop-Up Pr) Intervisual Bks.

Apel, James M. Small Voices: Heralds of Wonder in Everyday Life. LC 94-68164. 208p. (Orig.). 1994. pap. 8.95 (0-9642782-9-4) Sparrow Press.

Apel, John R. Principles of Ocean Physics. (International Geophysics Ser.). 520p. 1987. text 135.00 (0-12-058865-X); pap. text 73.00 (0-12-058866-8) Acad Pr.

Apel, John R., jt. ed. see Garland, G. D.

Apel, John R., ed. see Seeber, G.

Apel, Karl-Otto. Charles Peirce: From Pragmatism to Pragmaticism. 1995. pap. 17.95 (1-57392-603-5) Prometheus Bks.

Apel, Karl-Otto. Charles S. Peirce: From Pragmatism to Pragmaticism. Krois, John M., tr. from GER. 286p. (C). 1995. pap. 17.50 (0-391-03895-8) Humanities.

— Karl-Otto Apel - Selected Essays Vol. 2: Ethics & the Theory of Rationality, 2 vols., vol. 2. Mendieta, Eduardo, ed. & intro. by. 377p. (C). 1996. text 65.00 (0-391-03869-9) Humanities.

— Towards a Transformation of Philosophy. LC 98-8230. (Studies in Philosophy). xxxviii, 308p. 1998. 35.00 (0-87462-619-6) Marquette.

— Understanding & Explanation: A Transcendental Pragmatic Perspective. Warnke, Georgia, tr. from GER. (Studies in Contemporary German Social Thought). 320p. 1984. 37.50 (0-262-01079-8) MIT Pr.

— Understanding & Explanation: A Transcendental Pragmatic Perspective. Warnke, Georgia, tr. from GER. (Studies in Contemporary German Social Thought). 320p. 1988. pap. text 16.50 (0-262-51041-3) MIT Pr.

Apel, Karl-Otto, jt. auth. see Griffioen, Sander.

Apel, Lorelei. Dealing with Weapons in School & at Home, 6 vols., Set. (Conflict Resolution Library). (Illus.). 24p. (J). (gr. k-4). 1996. lib. bdg. 15.93 (0-8239-2327-4, PowerKids) Rosen Group.

Apel, Max & Luds, Peter. Philosophiches Woerterbuch. 6th ed. (Sammlung Goeschen Ser.: No. 2202). (GER.). (C). 1980. pap. 12.95 (3-11-006729-3) De Gruyter.

***Apel, Melanie A.** Let's Talk about Feeling Confused. LC 00-36711. (Let's Talk about Library). (Illus.). (J). 2000. write for info. (0-8239-5623-7, PowerKids) Rosen Group.

***Apel, Melanie Ann.** Careers in Information Science. LC 00-28592. (Illus.). (YA). 2000. pap. write for info. (0-8239-2892-6, PowerKids) Rosen Group.

— Cocaine & Your Nose: The Incredibly Disgusting Story. LC 00-20210. (Incredibly Disgusting Drugs Ser.). (Illus.). (J). 2000. lib. bdg. 17.95 (0-8239-3251-6) Rosen Group.

— Let's Talk about Feeling Lonely. LC 00-23838. 2000. write for info. (0-8239-5620-2, PowerKids) Rosen Group.

— Let's Talk about Feeling Worried. LC 00-24769. (Let's Talk about Library). (Illus.). (J). 2000. write for info. (0-8239-5622-9, PowerKids) Rosen Group.

— Let's Talk about Living with Your Single Dad. LC 99-88251. (Let's Talk Library). 2000. lib. bdg. write for info. (0-8239-5619-9) Rosen Group.

Apel, Otto F. & Apel, Pat. M*A*S*H: An Army Surgeon in Korea. LC 98-15170. (Illus.). 256p. 1998. 25.00 (0-8131-2070-5) U Pr of Ky.

Apel, Pat, jt. auth. see Apel, Otto F.

Apel, Willi. Editions, Historical: In His Harvard Dictionary of Music. 1993. reprint ed. lib. bdg. 89.00 (0-7812-9693-5) Rprt Serv.

— French Secular Music of the Late 14th Century. (Medieval Academy Bks.: No. 55). 1962. reprint ed. 25.00 (0-910956-29-4) Medieval Acad.

— Gregorian Chant. LC 57-10729. (Illus.). 540p. 1958. 49.95 (0-253-32650-8) Ind U Pr.

— Gregorian Chant. LC 57-10729. Vol. 601. (Illus.). 540p. 1958. pap. 22.50 (0-253-20601-4) Ind U Pr.

— Harvard Dictionary of Music. 2nd enl. rev. ed. LC 68-21970. (Illus.). 953p. 1968. 62.00 (0-674-37501-7) Belknap Pr.

— The History of Keyboard Music to 1700. Tischler, Hans, tr. LC 79-135015. 896p. 1972. 89.95 (0-253-32795-4) Ind U Pr.

— The History of Keyboard Music to 1700. Tischler, Hans, tr. & rev. by. LC 79-135015. 896p. 1997. pap. 49.95 (0-253-21141-7) Ind U Pr.

— Italian Violin Music of the Seventeenth Century. Binkley, Thomas, ed. LC 88-45503. (Music: Scholarship & Performance Ser.). (Illus.). 320p. 1990. 19.95 (0-253-30683-3) Ind U Pr.

— Masters of the Keyboard: A Brief Survey of Pianoforte Music. LC 47-12245. 335p. reprint ed. pap. 103.90 (0-7837-4135-9, 205795800011) Bks Demand.

— Notation of Polyphonic Music, 900-1600. 5th ed. LC 61-12067. (Medieval Academy Bks.: No. 38). 1961. 28.00 (0-910956-15-4) Medieval Acad.

— Periodicals, Musical: In His Harvard Dictionary of Music. 567p. 1993. reprint ed. lib. bdg. 99.00 (0-7812-9684-6) Rprt Serv.

— Sources, Musical, Prior to 1450: In His Harvard Dictionary of Music. 1993. reprint ed. lib. bdg. 89.00 (0-7812-9696-X) Rprt Serv.

Apel, Willi & Daniel, Ralph. The Harvard Brief Dictionary of Music. 342p. 1996. 9.98 (1-56731-097-4, MJF Bks) Fine Comms.

Apel, Willi, jt. ed. see Davison, Archibald T.

Apel, William. Harvard Brief Dictionary of Music. 1991. mass mkt. 5.99 (0-671-73747-3, WSP) PB.

***Apel, William D.** Silent Conversations: Reading the Bible in Good Company. LC 99-59130. 176p. 2000. pap. 15.00 (0-8170-1320-2) Judson.

Apelbaum, Shiffy. Moshe Mendel the Mitzva Maven & His Amazing Mitzva Quest. LC 94-4118. (J). 1994. 13.95 (0-87306-662-6) Feldheim.

Apelgren, Keith N. & Dean, Richard E. Enteral Feeding in Long Term Care. LC 90-60436. 125p. 1990. pap. 22.95 (0-944496-13-X) Precept Pr.

Apelian, Diran & Szekely, J., eds. Plasma Processing & Synthesis of Materials III Vol. 190: Symposium Proceedings Ser. 355p. 1991. text 17.50 (1-55899-079-8) Materials Res.

Apelian, Diran & Szekely, Julian, eds. Plasma Processing & Synthesis of Materials II. (Materials Research Society Symposium Proceedings Ser.: Vol. 98). 1987. text 17.50 (0-931837-65-0) Materials Res.

Apelian, Diran, ed. see Metallurgical Society of AIME Staff.

Apelian, Edward, jt. ed. see Boghigian, Apo.

Apello, Tim. Ally Mcbeal. write for info. (0-06-107591-4) HarpC.

Apelman, Maja & King, Julie. Exploring Everyday Math: Ideas for Students, Teachers, & Parents. LC 93-8737. (Illus.). 232p. (J). 1993. pap. text 25.00 (0-435-08341-4, 08341) Heinemann.

Apeloig, Y., jt. ed. see Rappoport, Z.

Apelt, Brian. Steel Town Story. (Illus.). 160p. (Orig.). 1995. pap. write for info. (0-614-07231-X) J Szilagyi.

Apelt, H. P. Reading Knowledge in German for Art Historians & Archaeologists: An English-German Course in Art History & Archaeology. 2nd ed. 152p. 1991. pap. 35.95 (3-503-03025-5) Adlers Foreign Bks.

Apelt, Mary L. Diccionario de Ciencias. 2nd rev. ed. (SPA.). 277p. 1990. 95.00 (0-8288-0775-2, M15754) Fr & Eur.

— German-English Dictionary: Art History-Archaeology. 2nd ed. (ENG & GER.). 1990. pap. 56.00 (0-7859-8962-5) Fr & Eur.

— Meyers Enzyklopaedisches Lexikon Vol. 4: Bes-Buc und 1 Nachtrag. (ENG & GER.). 240p. 1987. 95.00 (0-8288-0774-4, F56700) Fr & Eur.

— Reading Knowledge in German. (ENG & GER.). 152p. 1984. pap. 34.95 (0-7859-7457-1, 3503022872) Fr & Eur.

Apelt, Mary L., et al. Grammatik a la Carte 1: Answer Key. (GER.). 50p. (C). 1993. pap. text 9.00 (3-425-05993-9, Pub. by Verlag Moritz Diesterweg) Intl Bk Import.

— Grammatik a la Carte 1: Answer Key. (GER.). 50p. (C). 1997. pap. text 10.00 (3-425-25993-8, Pub. by Verlag Moritz Diesterweg) Intl Bk Import.

— Grammatik a la Carte 1: Practice Book for the German Elementary Grammar. (Basic Learner Ser.). (GER., Illus.). 188p. 1995. pap. 18.00 (3-425-05991-2, Pub. by Verlag Moritz Diesterweg) Intl Bk Import.

— Grammatik a la Carte 1: Practice Book for the German Elementary Grammar. (Basic Learner Ser.). (GER., Illus.). 188p. 1997. pap. 19.00 (3-425-25991-1, Pub. by Verlag Moritz Diesterweg) Intl Bk Import.

— Grammatik a la Carte 2: Key Book. (GER.). 64p. (C). 1995. pap. text 9.00 (3-425-05994-7, Pub. by Verlag Moritz Diesterweg) Intl Bk Import.

— Grammatik a la Carte 2: Key Book. (GER.). 64p. (C). 1997. pap. text 10.00 (3-425-25994-6, Pub. by Verlag Moritz Diesterweg) Intl Bk Import.

— Grammatik a la Carte 2: Practice Book for the German Elementary Grammar. (Advanced Learner Ser.). (GER., Illus.). 190p. (C). 1994. pap. text 20.75 (3-425-05992-0, Pub. by Verlag Moritz Diesterweg) Intl Bk Import.

— Grammatik a la Carte 2: Practice Book for the German Elementary Grammar. (Advanced Learner Ser.). (GER., Illus.). 190p. (C). 1997. pap. text 23.50 (3-425-25992-X, Pub. by Verlag Moritz Diesterweg) Intl Bk Import.

Apelt, Otto. Platonische Aufsatze. LC 75-13251. (History of Ideas in Ancient Greece Ser.). (GER.). 1976. reprint ed. 21.95 (0-405-07288-0) Ayer.

Apeltauer, Von E. Grundlagen des Erst- und Fremd-Sprachenerwerbs. (GER.). 168p. 1997. pap. 11.25 (3-468-49658-3) Langenscheidt.

Apen, John, ed. The Gold Book: Classics & Antiques, 1897-1942, Vol. 18, No. 2. 100p. 1996. ring bd. 20.00 (1-57033-031-X) Gold Bk GA.

— The Gold Book: Classics & Antiques, 1897-1942: April-September 1997, Vol. 18, No. 1. 100p. 1997. ring bd. 20.00 (1-57033-030-1) Gold Bk GA.

— The Gold Book: Contemporary Vehicles, 1981-1996: May-June 1997, Vol. 18, No. 3. 250p. 1997. ring bd. 20.00 (1-57033-038-7) Gold Bk GA.

— The Gold Book: Contemporary Vehicles, 1981-1996: November-December 1997, Vol. 18, No. 6. 250p. 1997. ring bd. 20.00 (1-57033-041-7) Gold Bk GA.

— The Gold Book: Contemporary Vehicles, 1981-1996: September-October 1997, Vol. 18, No. 5. 250p. 1997. ring bd. 20.00 (1-57033-040-9) Gold Bk GA.

— The Gold Book: Older Vehicles 1945-1980: April-May-June 1997, Vol. 18, No. 2. 195p. Date not set. ring bd. 20.00 (1-57033-033-6) Gold Bk GA.

— The Gold Book: Older Vehicles 1945-1980: July-August-September 1997, Vol. 18, No. 3. 195p. 1997. ring bd. 20.00 (1-57033-034-4) Gold Bk GA.

— The Gold Book: Older Vehicles 1945-1980: October-November-December 1997, Vol. 18, No. 4. 195p. 1997. ring bd. 20.00 (1-57033-035-2) Gold Bk GA.

— The Gold Book - Classics & Antiques 1897-1942: October - March 1998-99. 100p. 1998. ring bd. 20.00 (1-57033-043-3) Gold Bk GA.

— The Gold Book - Classics & Antiques 1897-1942 Vol. 19, No. 1: April - September 1998. 100p. 1998. ring bd. 20.00 (1-57033-042-5) Gold Bk GA.

— The Gold Book - Contemporary Vehicles 1981-1996 Vol. 19, No. 1: January - February 1998. 250p. 1997. ring bd. write for info. (1-57033-048-4) Gold Bk GA.

— The Gold Book - Contemporary Vehicles 1981-1996 Vol. 19, No. 2: March - April 1998. 250p. 1998. ring bd. 20.00 (1-57033-049-2) Gold Bk GA.

— The Gold Book - Contemporary Vehicles 1981-1996 Vol. 19, No. 3: May - June 1998. 250p. 1998. ring bd. 20.00 (1-57033-050-6) Gold Bk GA.

— The Gold Book - Contemporary Vehicles 1981-1996 Vol. 19, No. 4: July - August 1998. 250p. 1998. ring bd. 20.00 (1-57033-051-4) Gold Bk GA.

— The Gold Book - Contemporary Vehicles 1981-1996 Vol. 19, No. 5: September - October 1998. 250p. 1998. ring bd. 20.00 (1-57033-052-2) Gold Bk GA.

— The Gold Book - Contemporary Vehicles 1981-1996 Vol. 19, No. 6: November - December 1998. 250p. 1998. ring bd. write for info. (1-57033-053-0) Gold Bk GA.

— The Gold Book - Older Vehicles, 1945-1980 Vol. 19, No. 1: January - February - March 1998. 170p. 1997. ring bd. 20.00 (1-57033-044-1) Gold Bk GA.

— The Gold Book - Older Vehicles, 1945-1980 Vol. 19, No. 2: April - May - June 1998. 170p. 1998. ring bd. write for info. (1-57033-045-X) Gold Bk GA.

— The Gold Book - Older Vehicles, 1945-1980 Vol. 19, No. 3: July - August - September 1998. 170p. 1998. ring bd. 20.00 (1-57033-046-8) Gold Bk GA.

— The Gold Book - Older Vehicles, 1945-1980 Vol. 19, No. 4: October - November - December 1998. 170p. 1998. ring bd. 20.00 (1-57033-047-6) Gold Bk GA.

Apen, John & Keating, Patrick, eds. The Gold Book: Contemporary Vehicles, 1981-1996: July-August 1997, Vol. 18, No. 4. 250p. 1997. ring bd. 20.00 (1-57033-039-5) Gold Bk GA.

Apena, Adeline. Colonization, Commerce & Entrepreneurship in Nigeria: The Western Delta, 1914-1960. LC 96-19237. (Society & Politics in Africa Ser.: No. 2). (Illus.). XXXIII, 229p. (C). 1997. text 47.95 (0-8204-3131-1) P Lang Pubng.

Apena Taiyewo Ogunade. Three Yoruba Divination Systems & Ebo. LC 94-67072. (Illus.). 84p. (Orig.). 1996. pap. 14.50 (1-881549-05-4) Oluweri Pubns.

Apenehouse Productions Staff, jt. auth. see Packaged Facts Staff.

***Apenszlak, Jacob, et al, eds.** The Black Book of Polish Jewry: An Account of the Martyrdom of Polish Jewry Under the Nazi Occupation. LC 99-68816. (Illus.), 400p. 2000. reprint ed. pap. 30.00 (1-930423-02-0, 83750) Brohan Pr.

Aper, Janet. Buy a Car on Your Terms. 16p. (Orig.). 1996. pap. write for info. (0-9654011-0-3) Marketier.

Aper, Jeffrey, jt. auth. see Bogue, E. Grady.

Apers, P. M., et al, eds. Advances in Database Technology - EDBT '96: 5th International Conference on Extending Database Technology, Avignion, France, March 1996 Proceedings. LC 96-17668. (Lecture Notes in Computer Science Ser.: Vol. 1057). 636p. 1996. pap. 94.00 (3-540-61057-X) Spr-Verlag.

Apers, P. M., et al. Multimedia Databases in Perspective. LC 96-52104. 400p. 1997. pap. 49.95 (3-540-76109-8) Spr-Verlag.

***Aperture Books Staff.** 160. (Illus.). 80p. 2000. pap. 18.50 (0-89381-925-5) Aperture.

Aperture Foundation Inc. Staff. Crossing Borders: Contemporary Czech & Slovak Photography, Vol. 152. (Aperture Ser.: No. 152). (Illus.). 80p. 1998. pap. 27.95 (0-89381-816-X) Aperture.

— Rio de Luz, Vol. 153. (Aperture Ser.: No. 153). (Illus.). 80p. 1998. pap. 27.95 (0-89381-813-5) Aperture.

Aperture Foundation Staff. India: A Celebration of Independence, 1947-1997. LC 96-80164. 1997. 76.00 (0-89381-695-7) Aperture.

— Photographs of Manuel Alvarez Bravo: His Life's Work. 1997. 53.00 (0-89381-721-X) Aperture.

***Aperture Staff.** Aperture 158 Time, Vol. 158. (Illus.). 80p. 2000. pap. 18.50 (0-89381-898-4) Aperture.

Aperture Staff. Aperture 133 on Location, No. 133. 1993. pap. text 27.95 (0-89381-561-6) Aperture.

— Explorations. 1999. pap. text 18.50 (0-89381-952-2) Aperture.

— Optical Allusions. 1999. pap. text 18.50 (0-89381-858-5) Aperture.

— Our Town: Aperture, Issue 127. 1992. pap. 27.95 (0-89381-521-7) Aperture.

Aperyan, V. Manpower Resources & Population under Socialism: Socialism Today. 198p. 1979. 40.00 (0-317-53795-4, Pub. by Collets) St Mut.

Apes, William. Eulogy on King Phillip. Dexter, Lincoln A., ed. LC 85-91530. (Illus.). 100p. 1985. reprint ed. pap. text 5.50 (0-9601210-3-X) L A Dexter.

— The Works of William Apes, Set. 1987. reprint ed. lib. bdg. write for info. (0-318-62095-2) Rprt Serv.

Apess, William. On Our Own Ground: The Complete Writings of William Apess, a Pequot. LC 91-27750. (Native Americans of the Northeast Ser.). 432p. (C). 1992. pap. 20.95 (0-87023-770-5); lib. bdg. 50.00 (0-87023-766-7) U of Mass Pr.

— "A Son of the Forest" & Other Writings by William Apess, a Pequot. O'Connell, Barry, ed. LC 97-20126. 176p. 1997. pap. 15.95 (1-55849-107-4) U of Mass Pr.

Apesteguia, Raul, jt. auth. see Reid, James.

Apetaur, M., ed. The Dynamics of Vehicles on Roads & on Tracks: Proceedings of the 10th IAVSD Symposium. (Vehicle System Dynamics Ser.: Vol. 17). xiv, 578p. 1988. 100.00 (90-265-0898-0) Swets.

Apfel, Iris B. Dragon Threads: Court Costumes of the Celestial Kingdom. Price, Mary S., ed. LC 92-36266. (Illus.). 44p. (Orig.). 1992. pap. 12.95 (0-932828-28-0) Newark Mus.

Apfel, Necia H. Orion, the Hunter. LC 94-44268. (Illus.). 48p. (J). (gr. 4-7). 1995. 16.95 (0-395-68962-7, Clarion Bks) HM.

Apfel, Patrick J., jt. auth. see Tortorici, Marianne R.

Apfel, Roberta J. & Fisher, Susan M. To Do No Harm: DES & the Dilemmas of Modern Medicine. LC 83-16803. (Illus.). 204p. 1984. 37.50 (0-300-03192-0) Yale U Pr.

— To Do No Harm: DES & the Dilemmas of Modern Medicine. LC 83-16803. (Illus.). 204p. 1986. pap. 16.00 (0-300-03619-1, Y-560) Yale U Pr.

Apfel, Roberta J. & Simon, Bennett, eds. Minefields in Their Hearts: The Mental Health of Children in War & Communal Violence. LC 96-10976. 256p. 1996. 37.50 (0-300-06570-1) Yale U Pr.

Apfel, Stuart C., ed. Clinical Applications of Neurotrophic Factors. LC 97-1334. 250p. 1997. text 89.00 (0-397-51782-3) Lppncott W & W.

Apfelbaum, Jim, jt. auth. see Puett, Barbara.

Apfelbaum, Jonathan D. EMS Field Protocal Manual. (Illus.). 300p. 1998. spiral bd. 24.95 (1-56930-091-7) Skidmore Roth Pub.

Apfelbaum, Marian & Perlemuter, Leon. Practical Dictionary of Diet & Nutrition: Dictionnaire Pratique de Dietetique et de Nutrition. (FRE.). 736p. 1981. 150.00 (0-8288-1298-5, M15571) Fr & Eur.

Apfelberg, David B., ed. Atlas of Cutaneous Laser Surgery. (Illus.). 496p. 1991. text 215.00 (0-88167-764-7) Lppncott W & W.

An Asterisk (*) at the beginning of an entry indicates that the title is appearing for the first time.

— Evaluation & Installation of Surgical Laser Systems. (Illus.). 340p. 1986. 133.00 (*0-387-96385-5*) Spr-Verlag.

Apfelberg, David B., jt. auth. see Alster, Tina S.

Apfelberg, Hank. Effective Supervision in the Small or Medium Size Printing Plant: A How-to Guide from Graphic Services Publications. (Illus.). 90p. (C). 1993. text 14.95 (*1-882602-03-X*) Graphic Srvs.

Apfelberg, Herschel L. & Apfelberg, Michael. Implementing Quality Management in the Graphic Arts. LC 95-75372. (Illus.). 350p. 1995. text 75.00 (*0-88362-177-0*, 1320) GATFPress.

Apfelberg, Michael, jt. auth. see Apfelberg, Herschel L.

***Apfeld, Michael B.** Contract Law in Wisconsin. 2nd ed. LC 00-36563. 2000. write for info. (*1-57862-046-5*) State Bar WI.

Apfeld, Michael B., et al. Contract Law in Wisconsin. LC 95-135. 675p. 1995. ring bd. 125.00 (*0-945574-72-X*) State Bar WI.

Apfestadt, Marc. Musical PC. 1991. pap. 19.95 (*0-9623397-8-4*) Midi Amer.

Apffel, Helmut, et al. Die Verfassungsdebatte bei Herodot & Politisches Denken bei Herodot & Frauenemuncipation in Athen, 3 vols. Vlastos, Gregory, ed. LC 78-14603. (Morals & Law in Ancient Greece Ser.). 1979. reprint ed. lib. bdg. 21.95 (*0-405-11574-1*) Ayer.

Apffel-Marglin. Spirit Regeneration, Vol. 1. 1998. pap. text 25.00 (*1-85649-548-5*, Pub. by Zed Books) St Martin.

— Spirit Regeneration: Andean Culture Confronting Western Notions of Development, Vol. 1. 288p. 1998. text 65.00 (*1-85649-547-7*) St Martin.

Apffel-Marglin, Frederique & Marglin, Stephen A., eds. Decolonizing Knowledge: From Development to Dialogue. (WIDER Studies in Development Economics). (Illus.). 406p. 1996. text 75.00 (*0-19-828884-0*) OUP.

***Apgar, Cheryl.** The Creative K-1 Classroom Vol. 3351: Making & Managing a Playful Learning Environment. Johnson, Kristine, ed. (Illus.). 224p. 1999. pap. text 17.98 (*1-57471-634-4*, 3351) Creat Teach Pr.

Apgar, Garry, et al. The Newspaper in Art. LC 97-181483. (Illus.). 232p. 1996. 75.00 (*0-923910-05-0*) NMV.

Apgar, Kathryn. Overcoming Relationship Addiction: A Workshop for Women Who Love Too Much. LC 90-39462. (Workshop Models for Family Life Education Ser.). 94p. 1991. pap. 15.95 (*0-87304-239-5*) Manticore Pubs.

Apgar, William C., Jr., et al. The Housing Outlook: 1980-1990. LC 85-16738. 190p. 1985. 55.00 (*0-275-90193-9*, C0193, Praeger Pubs) Greenwood.

Apgar, William C., Jr., jt. auth. see Kain, John F.

APHA Project Task Force Staff. Healthy Communities Two Thousand: Model Standards. 3rd ed. 470p. 1991. 35.00 (*0-87553-204-7*) Am Pub Health.

Aphek, Edna & Tobin, Yishai. The Semiotics of Fortune - Telling. LC 89-35950. (Foundations of Semiotics Ser.: No. 22). vii, 216p. 1990. 74.00 (*90-272-3294-6*) J Benjamins Pubng Co.

— The Semiotics of Fortune Telling. LC 89-35950. (Foundations of Semiotics Ser.: No. 22). vii, 216p. 1990. pap. 27.95 (*1-55619-091-3*) J Benjamins Pubng Co.

Aphek, Edna, jt. auth. see Haramati, Shlomo.

Aphra, Behn. Oroonako & Other Stories. (Cloth Bound Pocket Ser.). 320p. 1999. 7.95 (*3-8290-0902-X*, 520665) Konemann.

Aphraates, Saint. Prayer. 1993. pap. 1.00 (*0-89981-072-1*) Eastern Orthodox.

Aphrodite. Para Excitarlas, 39 Fantasias Sexuales. 1997. pap. text 11.98 (*968-419-067-0*) Grijalbo Edit.

Apicella, Raymond. Journeys into Luke: 16 Lessons of Exploration & Discovery. 63p. 1992. pap. 5.95 (*0-86716-144-2*) St Anthony Mess Pr.

— Journeys into Mark: 16 Lessons of Exploration & Discovery. 60p. 1990. pap. text 4.95 (*0-86716-112-4*) St Anthony Mess Pr.

— Journeys into Matthew: 18 Lessons of Exploration & Discovery. 80p. (Orig.). 1996. pap. 7.95 (*0-86716-183-3*, B1833) St Anthony Mess Pr.

Apicella, Vincent, et al. The Concise Guide to Type Identification. (Illus.). 176p. 1990. pap. 24.95 (*0-8306-3449-5*, 3449) McGraw-Hill Prof.

Apicius. Concordantia Apiciana. (GER.). vi, 542p. 1995. write for info. (*3-487-09890-3*) G Olms Pubs.

— Cookery & Dining in Imperial Rome. Vehling, Joseph D., ed. & tr. by. from LAT. LC 77-89410. Orig. Title: Apicius De Re Coquinaria. 301p. 1977. pap. 8.95 (*0-486-23563-7*) Dover.

APICS Bucks-Mont. Chapter Staff. Material Requirements Planning Training Aid. 62p. 1979. 40.00 (*0-935406-10-7*) Am Prod & Inventory.

— Planeacion de los Requerimentos de Material.Tr. of Material Requirements Planning. (SPA.). 87p. (Orig.). 1994. pap. 40.00 (*1-55822-113-1*) Am Prod & Inventory.

APICS Milwaukee Chapter Staff. Shop Floor Controls Training Aid. 30p. 1979. 35.00 (*0-935406-08-5*) Am Prod & Inventory.

APICS Production Activity Control Committee of the, ed. Production Activity Control Reprints. rev. ed. LC 88-82787. (Illus.). 169p. 1993. pap. 21.00 (*1-55822-039-9*) Am Prod & Inventory.

APICS T. A. Sig. Software Requirements Evaluation Guide for Manufacturing Planning Control Systems Symposium. 50p. (Orig.). 1994. pap. 30.00 (*1-55822-115-8*) Am Prod & Inventory.

Apidta, Tingba. The Hidden History of Massachusetts: A Guide for Black Folks. (Hidden Histories of America Ser.: No. 1). 64p. 1995. pap. 5.95 (*1-892705-01-X*) Reclamation Projct.

— The Hidden History of New York: A Guide for Black Folks. (Hidden Histories of America Ser.: No. 3). (Illus.). 160p. 1998. pap. 9.95 (*1-892705-00-1*) Reclamation Projct.

— The Hidden History of Washington, D. C. A Guide for Black Folks. (Hidden Histories of America Ser.: No. 2). (Illus.). 80p. 1995. pap. 8.95 (*1-892705-02-8*) Reclamation Projct.

Apilado, Vincent P. Finance Management. Date not set. pap. text, teacher ed. write for info. (*0-314-34706-2*) West Pub.

Apinwall, Mark, jt. auth. see Greenwood, Justin.

***Apio, Alani.** Kamau. (Illus.). 64p. 2000. pap. 10.00 (*0-9674183-1-3*) Palila Bks.

Apirion, D. Processing of RNA. LC 82-22834. 360p. 1983. 203.00 (*0-8493-6510-4*, CRC Reprint) Franklin.

Apisdorf, Shimon. Chanukah: Eight Nights of Light, Eight Gifts for the Soul. LC 99-218285. (Illus.). 112p. 1997. pap. 12.00 (*1-881927-15-6*) Leviathan OH.

— The One Hour Purim Primer: Everything a Family Needs to Understand, Celebrate & Enjoy Purim. pap. 7.95 (*1-881927-04-0*) Leviathan OH.

— Passover Survival Kit. rev. ed. 160p. 1997. 16.95 (*1-881927-10-5*) Leviathan OH.

— Rosh Hashanah Yom Kippur Survival Kit. rev. ed. LC 99-226253. 1997. 14.95 (*1-881927-14-8*) Leviathan OH.

— Survival Kit Family Haggadah: Everything a Family Needs to Create An Enjoyable, Educational Experience. LC 99-218908. 95p. 1997. pap. text 8.95 (*1-881927-11-3*) Leviathan OH.

Apisdorf, Shimon, jt. auth. see Braverman, Nachum.

Apisson, Barbara, jt. auth. see McQueen-Williams, Morvyth.

Apkarian, A. V. & Ayapetian, eds. Application Of The Theory of Metabolic Regulation to Pain. LC 96-78412. 340p. (YA). (gr. 12). 1998. 88.00 (*90-5199-306-4*, 306-4) IOS Press.

Apkarian, P. A., jt. ed. see Spekreijse, H.

Apkarian-Russe, Pamela E. More Halloween Collectibles: Anthropomorphic Vegetables & Fruits of Halloween. LC 98-86161. 160p. 1998. pap. 29.95 (*0-7643-0658-8*) Schiffer.

Apkarian-Russell, Pamela. Around Swanzey. LC 97-112555. (Images of America Ser.). 1996. pap. 16.99 (*0-7524-0427-X*) Arcadia Publng.

— Halloween: An American Holiday. LC 97-7410. 192p. 1997. pap. 29.95 (*0-7643-0281-7*) Schiffer.

Apkarian-Russell, Pamela E. A Collector's Guide to Salem Witchcraft & Souvenirs. LC 97-80136. (Illus.). 128p. 1998. pap. 19.95 (*0-7643-0425-9*) Schiffer.

***Apkarian-Russell, Pamela E.** Halloween; Collectible Decorations & Games. (Illus.). 176p. 2000. pap. 29.95 (*0-7643-1027-5*) Schiffer.

— Washday Collectibles. (Illus.). 160p. 2000. pap. 29.95 (*0-7643-1128-X*) Schiffer.

Aplan, F. F., et al, eds. Solution Mining Symposium, 1974: Proceedings of a Symposium, 103rd AIME Annual Meeting, Dallas, Texas, Feb. 25-27, 1974. LC 73-94005. 479p. reprint ed. pap. 148.50 (*0-608-14264-6*, 201742200005) Bks Demand.

Aplet, Greg, et al, eds. Defining Sustainable Forestry. LC 93-8389. (Illus.). 320p. 1993. text 55.00 (*1-55963-233-X*); pap. text 30.00 (*1-55963-234-8*) Island Pr.

Aplevich, J. D. The Essentials of Linear State-Space Systems. LC 99-13831. 320p. 1999. text 86.95 (*0-471-24133-4*) Wiley.

— Implicit Linear Systems. (Lecture Notes in Control & Information Sciences: Vol. 152). (Illus.). xii, 188p. 1991. 38.95 (*0-387-53537-3*) Spr-Verlag.

Apley, A. Graham & Solomon, Louis. Concise System of Orthopaedics & Fractures. 2nd ed. (Illus.). 360p. 1994. pap. text 37.50 (*0-7506-1767-5*) Buttrwrth-Heinemann.

APLIC International Staff. Association for Population-Family Planning Libraries & Information Centers-International (APLIC-I) Union List of Serials. Zimmerman, Michael F., ed. & compiled by by. LC 95-3107. (Special Publication Ser.: No. 7). 1995. write for info. (*0-933438-22-2*) APLIC Intl.

— Proceedings of the Eighteenth Annual Conference. Vanderlin, Jane & Barrow, William, eds. LC 76-643241. 129p. (Orig.). 1986. pap. 15.00 (*0-933438-11-7*) APLIC Intl.

— Proceedings of the 17th Annual Conference. Turner, Carann G., ed. LC 76-643241. 121p. (Orig.). 1985. pap. 15.00 (*0-933438-10-9*) APLIC Intl.

— Proceedings of the 13th Annual Conference. Burns, Adele B., ed. LC 76-643241. 157p. 1980. pap. 13.00 (*0-933438-05-2*) APLIC Intl.

***Aplin, A. C., et al, eds.** Muds & Mudstones: Physical & Fluid-Flow Properties. (Special Publication Ser.: No. 158). 200p. 1999. 108.00 (*1-86239-044-4*, Pub. by Geol Soc Pub Hse) AAPG.

Aplin, Geoff & Payne, Chris. Staff Supervision in Services for Sensory Impaired Children & Adults: A European Perspective. 1994. pap. 70.00 (*0-902789-92-9*, Pub. by Natl Inst Soc Work) St Mut.

Aplin, Graeme. Australians & Their Environment: An Introduction to Environmental Studies. LC 98-207515. (Illus.). 552p. 1998. pap. text 65.00 (*0-19-553960-5*) OUP.

Aplin, Graeme, ed. A Difficult Infant: Sydney Before Macquarie. 1988. pap. 24.95 (*0-86840-171-4*, Pub. by New South Wales Univ Pr) Intl Spec Bk.

Aplin, Graeme, et al. Global Environmental Crises: An Australian Perspective. 2nd ed. LC 98-199809. (Illus.). 408p. 1999. pap. text 45.00 (*0-19-550827-0*) OUP.

Aplin, J. D., jt. ed. see Denker, H. W.

Aplin, Rebecca. Spice Girls: Giving You Everything. (Illus.). 64p. (Orig.). pap. 12.95 (*1-873884-95-8*, VX06000, Pub. by UFO Books) Music Sales.

Aplon, Roger. By Dawn's Early Light at One Hundred Twenty Miles Per Hour. 1983. 12.95 (*0-931848-58-X*); pap. 9.95 (*0-931848-57-1*) Dryad Pr.

— It's Mother's Day. LC 96-83443. 100p. (Orig.). 1996. pap. 12.95 (*0-9651329-0-0*) Barracuda Pr.

— Stiletto. 1976. pap. 8.95 (*0-931848-14-8*) Dryad Pr.

Apmyrddin, Mair, jt. auth. see Brake, Phylip.

APN Publishers, tr. see Gorbachev, Mikhail S.

APO Seminar on Forestry Resources Management. Perspectives on Forestry Resources Management: Report of an APO Seminar, 17-27 October 1995, Tokyo, Japan. LC 98-155144. 275p. 1997. write for info. (*92-833-2198-7*) Asian Prod Organ.

APO Staff. APO Productivity Journal: Spring 1993. 229p. 1993. pap. 23.00 (*92-833-4001-9*, APO0019, Pub. by Asian Prod Organ) Bernan Associates.

— APO Productivity Journal: Summer 1996. 229p. 1996. pap. 23.00 (*92-833-4005-1*, APO96, Pub. by Asian Prod Organ) Bernan Associates.

— Rural Land Use in Asia & the Pacific. 391p. 1993. pap. 15.00 (*92-833-2134-0*, APO1340, Pub. by Asian Prod Organ) Bernan Associates.

Apodaca, Alice O. Lilliputian. Johnston, Linda, ed. (Illus.). 34p. (Orig.). (J). (gr. 4). 1996. pap. text. write for info. (*0-9630505-1-6*) A O Apodaca.

Apodaca, Anthony A. & Gritz, Larry. Advanced RenderMan: Beyond the Companion. Barsky, Brian A., ed. LC 99-88455. (Computer Graphics & Geometric Modeling Ser.). 400p. (C). 1999. pap. 44.95 (*1-55860-618-1*, Pub. by Morgan Kaufmann) Harcourt.

Apodaca, Paul, jt. auth. see Labbe, Armand J.

***Apogee Books Publishing Company Staff.** Apollo 12. (NASA Mission Reports). (Illus.). 256p. 1999. pap. 16.95 (*1-896522-54-8*, Apogee Books) CN06.

— Space Toys of the 60s: An Illustrated Collector's Guide to Major Matt Mason: Mattel's Man in Space. (Illus.). 160p. 1999. pap. 19.95 (*1-896522-37-8*, Apogee Books) CN06.

***Apogee Books Staff.** Apollo 9: The NASA Mission Reports. (Illus.). 240p. 1999. pap. text 14.95 (*1-896522-51-3*, Apogee Books) CN06.

— Apollo 10: The NASA Mission Reports, 4. (Illus.). 240p. 1999. pap. text 14.95 (*1-896522-52-1*, Apogee Books) CN06.

— Friendship 7: The NASA Mission Reports, 3. (Illus.). 216p. 1999. pap. text 14.95 (*1-896522-60-2*, Apogee Books) CN06.

Apogee Training & Development Staff, Yi Quiz, ed. The Palaeobiogeography of China. (Biogeography Ser.: No. 8). (Illus.). 384p. 1994. text 125.00 (*0-19-854671-8*) OUP.

Apogee Training Staff, jt. auth. see Martinson, T.

***Apol, Laura.** Falling into Grace. 95p. 1998. pap. 10.25 (*0-932914-42-X*) Dordt Coll Pr.

Apol, Laura, ed. see Stafford, William.

Apol, Laura J. Falling into Grace. (Orig.). 1998. pap. 10.25 (*0-932914-36-5*) Dordt Coll Pr.

Apol, Philip. Acts: Bursting the Boundaries. (Revelation Ser.). 64p. (Orig.). 1996. pap., teacher ed. 6.75 (*1-56212-187-1*); pap., student ed. 4.95 (*1-56212-186-3*) CRC Pubns.

Apole, Russell A. Trails from Steppingstones to Kerbstones. LC 66-4453. (Bernice P. Bishop Museum Special Publications: No. 53). (Illus.). 85p. reprint ed. pap. 30.00 (*0-608-17286-3*, 203032200068) Bks Demand.

Apolinarski, Ingrid, jt. auth. see Gerlach, Peter.

Apolinsky, Harold, jt. auth. see Welch, Stewart H., III.

Apolito, Paolo. Apparitions of the Madonna at Oliveto Citra: Local Visions & Cosmic Drama. Christian, William A., Jr., tr. from ITA. LC 98-20833. 288p. 1998. 49.50 (*0-271-01795-3*) Pa St U Pr.

Apollinaire, Guillaume. Alcools. Rees, Garnet, ed. (French Poets Ser.). (FRE & ENG.). 192p. (C). 1975. pap. 12.50 (*0-485-12708-3*, Pub. by Athlone Pr) Humanities.

— Alcools. (FRE.). (C). 1920. pap. 11.95 (*0-8442-1794-8*, VF1794-8) NTC Contemp Pub Co.

— Alcools: Poems. Revell, Donald, tr. LC 95-2294. (Wesleyan Poetry Ser.). (ENG & FRE.). 185p. 1995. pap. 15.95 (*0-8195-1228-1*, Wesleyan Univ Pr) U Pr of New Eng.

— Alcools, le Bestaire: Vitam Impendere Amori. (Poesie Ser.). (FRE.). 1971. pap. 9.95 (*2-07-030007-2*) Schoenhof.

— Alcools, le Bestiare Vitam Impendere Amori. (FRE.). 192p. 1971. pap. 11.95 (*0-7859-2753-0*, F82040) Fr & Eur.

— Anecdotiques. (FRE.). 336p. 1955. pap. 39.95 (*0-7859-1099-9*, 2070202097) Fr & Eur.

***Apollinaire, Guillaume.** Bestiary: or The Parade of Orpheus. Karmel, Pepe, tr. (Pocket Paragon Ser.). (Illus.). 64p. 2000. reprint ed. pap. 14.95 (*1-56792-142-6*) Godine.

Apollinaire, Guillaume. Calligrammes. (FRE.). 192p. 1970. pap. 11.95 (*0-7859-2754-9*, F82072) Fr & Eur.

— Calligrammes. (Poesie Ser.). (FRE.). 1964. pap. 9.95 (*2-07-030008-0*) Schoenhof.

— Calligrammes: Poems of Peace & War (1913-1916) Greet, Anne H., tr. from FRE. & notes by. (ENG & FRE.). 525p. 1991. pap. 19.95 (*0-520-07390-8*, Pub. by U CA Pr) Cal Prin Full Svc.

— Les Diables Amoureux. (FRE.). 384p. 1981. pap. 12.95 (*0-7859-3465-0*, 2070354458) Fr & Eur.

— L' Enchanteur Pourrissant. Burgos, ed. (Coll. Paralogue). (FRE.). 16.95 (*0-8288-9017-X*, F82122) Fr & Eur.

— L' Enchanteur Pourrissant: Les Mamelles de Tiresias: Couleur du Temps. (FRE.). 246p. 1972. pap. 16.95 (*0-7859-1146-4*, F82122) Fr & Eur.

Apollinaire, Guillaume. Enchanteur Pourrissant. Les Mamelles de Tiresias. Couleir de Temps. (Poesie Ser.). (FRE.). 1972. pap. 13.95 (*2-07-031948-2*) Schoenhof.

Apollinaire, Guillaume. Les Exploits d'un Jeune Don Juan. (FRE.). 67p. 1991. 32.95 (*0-8288-9019-6*, 2277128759) Fr & Eur.

— La Femme Assise. (Imaginaire Ser.). (FRE.). pap. 9.95 (*2-07-028612-6*) Schoenhof.

— La Femme Assise. Chronique de France et d'Amerique: Moeurs et Merveilles du Temps Lanka. (FRE.). 152p. 1979. pap. 13.95 (*0-7859-2742-5*, 2070286126) Fr & Eur.

— Le Flaneur des Deux Rives: Contemporaines Pittoresques. (FRE.). 1975. pap. 10.95 (*0-7859-2844-8*, 2070353389) Fr & Eur.

— Flesh Unlimited. Lykiard, Alexis, tr. (Velvet Ser.: Vol. 4). 192p. (Orig.). 1995. pap. 15.95 (*1-871592-56-9*) Creation Books.

— Le Guetteur Melancolique: Poemes Retrouves. (FRE.). 256p. 1982. pap. 14.95 (*0-7859-2756-5*, 2070300102) Fr & Eur.

— Le Guetteur Melancolique: Poemes Retrouves. (Poesie Ser.). (FRE.). 11.95 (*2-07-020207-0*) Schoenhof.

— The Heresiarch & Co. Hall, Remy I., tr. from FRE.Tr. of L'Heresiarque et Cie. 172p. (Orig.). 1991. reprint ed. pap. 13.95 (*1-878972-03-0*) Exact Change.

— L' Heresiarque et Cie. (FRE.). 286p. 1988. pap. 12.95 (*0-7859-3145-7*, F82170) Fr & Eur.

— Lettres a Lou. (FRE.). 528p. 1990. pap. 28.95 (*0-7859-2942-8*, 2070718549) Fr & Eur.

— Lettres a Sa Marraine (1915-1918) pap. 8.95 (*0-685-37173-5*) Fr & Eur.

Apollinaire, Guillaume. Oeuvres en Prose, Tome 1. deluxe ed. (Pleiade Ser.). (FRE.). 1988. 80.95 (*2-07-010828-7*) Schoenhof.

— Oeuvres en Prose, Tome 2. deluxe ed. (Pleiade Ser.). (FRE.). 1991. 119.95 (*2-07-011216-0*) Schoenhof.

— Oeuvres en Prose Completes, Vol. 1. deluxe ed. (Pleiade Ser.). (FRE.). 1584p. 1993. 110.00 (*0-8288-3416-4*, M4806) Fr & Eur.

— Oeuvres en Prose Completes, Vol. 2. deluxe ed. Decaudin, Michel, ed. (FRE.). 1872p. 1991. lib. bdg. 195.00 (*0-7859-3899-0*, 2070112160) Fr & Eur.

Apollinaire, Guillaume. Oeuvres en Proses Completes, Vol. 3. (FRE.). 1617p. 1993. 195.00 (*0-7859-7573-X*) Fr & Eur.

Apollinaire, Guillaume. Oeuvres Poetiques. deluxe ed. Adema & Decaudin, eds. (Pleiade Ser.). (FRE.). 1957. 71.95 (*2-07-010015-4*) Schoenhof.

— Oeuvres Poetiques Completes, Vol. 1. deluxe ed. (Pleiade Ser.). (FRE.). 1344p. 1956. 110.00 (*0-8288-3417-2*, F82020) Fr & Eur.

Apollinaire, Guillaume. Les Onze Mille Verges: The Amorous Adventures of Prince Mony Vibescu. Rootes, Nina, tr. 127p. 1992. pap. 17.95 (*0-7206-0735-3*, Pub. by P Owen Ltd) Dufour.

— Poemes a Lou. II y A. (FRE.). 266p. 1969. pap. 11.95 (*0-7859-2755-7*, F82220) Fr & Eur.

— Poemes a Lou. II y A. Decaudin, ed. (Poesie Ser.). pap. 9.95 (*2-07-030009-9*) Schoenhof.

— The Poet Assassinated. Josephson, Matthew, tr. (Illus.). 158p. 1999. reprint ed. pap. 13.95 (*1-878972-29-4*, Pub. by Exact Change) SPD-Small Pr Dist.

— Le Poete Assassine. 12.50 (*0-685-37175-1*) Fr & Eur.

— Le Poete Assassine. (Poesie Ser.). (FRE.). pap. 15.95 (*2-07-032179-7*) Schoenhof.

— Selected Poems. expanded ed. Bernard, Oliver, tr. & intro. by. (FRE & ENG.). 158p. 1994. pap. 18.95 (*0-85646-155-5*, Pub. by Anvil Press) Dufour.

— Selected Writings of Apollinaire. rev. ed. Shattuck, Roger, tr. from FRE. LC 72-145928. 1971. pap. 13.95 (*0-8112-0003-5*, NDP310, Pub. by New Directions) Norton.

***Apollinaire, Guillaume & Aragon, Louis.** Flesh Unlimited: 3 Surrealist/Erotic Novellas. 224p. 2000. 13.95 (*1-84068-015-6*, Pub. by Creation Bks) Subterranean Co.

Apollinaris, Sidonius. Concordantia in Sidonii Apollinaris Carmina. Christiansen, Peder G. & Holland, James E., eds. (Alpha-Omega, Reihe A Ser.: Bd. CXII). (GER.). 256p. 1993. write for info. incl. 3.5 hd (*3-487-09684-6*) G Olms Pubs.

Apollodorus. The Library of Greek Mythology. Hard, Robin, tr. & intro. by. (Oxford World's Classics Ser.). (Illus.). 336p. 1999. pap. 10.95 (*0-19-283924-1*) OUP.

Apollon, Marlene R. Haitian Trivia: English, Haitian Creole & French. Vilsaint, Fequiere, ed. 75p. 1988. pap. 7.50 (*1-881839-65-6*) Educa Vision.

Apollon, Willy & Feldstein, Richard, eds. Lacan, Politics, Aesthetics. LC 94-10967. (SUNY Series in Psychoanalysis & Culture). (Illus.). 341p. (C). 1996. text 59.50 (*0-7914-2371-9*); pap. text 19.95 (*0-7914-2372-7*) State U NY Pr.

Apolloni, Ignazio. Advertise Poems: Italian Antipoems. (Illus.). 80p. 1978. 10.00 (*0-89304-652-3*) Cross-Cultrl NY.

***Apollonio, Marco, et al, eds.** Vertebrate Mating Systems. 430p. 2000. 98.00 (*981-02-4260-3*) World Scientific Pub.

***Apollonio, Spencer, ed.** The Last of the Cape Horners: Firsthand Accounts from the Final Days of the Commercial Tall Ships. 2000. 26.95 (*1-57488-283-X*) Brasseys.

Apollonius. On Cutting off a Ratio. Macierowski, Edward, tr. from ARA. (Illus.). 160p. 1987. lib. bdg. 30.00 (*0-931267-00-5*) Golden Hind Pr.

Apollonius of Perga. Conics. Densmore, Dana, ed. Taliaferro, R. Catesby, tr. from GEC. LC 98-87076. (Illus.). 318p. (C). 1998. pap. text 23.95 (*1-888009-05-5*); lib. bdg. 42.00 (*1-888009-04-7*) Grn Lion Pr.

Apollonius, Rhodius. Apollonii Rhodii Argonautica. Frankel, Herman, ed. 292p. 1986. text 29.95 (*0-19-814559-4*) OUP.

— Argonautica. (Loeb Classical Library: No. 1). 448p. 1912. 18.95 (*0-674-99001-3*) HUP.

A

— The Argonautica of Apollonius Rhodius, Bk. III. Connor, W. R., ed. LC 78-18578. (Greek Texts & Commentaries Ser.). (ENG & GRE.). 1979. reprint ed. lib. bdg. 22.95 (*0-405-11421-4*) Ayer.

— Jason & the Golden Fleece: The Argonautica. Hunter, Richard, tr. & intro. by. (Oxford World's Classics Ser.). (Illus.). 210p. 1998. reprint ed. pap. 9.95 (*0-19-283583-1*) OUP.

— The Voyage of the Argo. Rieu, Emil V., tr. & intro. by. (Classics Ser.). 224p. 1959. pap. 12.95 (*0-14-044085-2*, Penguin Classics) Viking Penguin.

Apollonius Sophista. Lexicon Homericum. iv, 195p. 1967. reprint ed. 50.00 (*0-318-71996-7*) G Olms Pubs.

Apolonja, Kojder M. Marynia, Don't Cry: Memoirs of Two Polish-Canadian Families. LC 96-132578. (Illus.). 208p. 1995. pap. 24.94 (*0-919045-65-0*) Multicult Hist.

Apolzon, Linda R. Stray Cat. Kemnitz, Myrna, ed. LC 97-216294. 110p. (J). (gr. 7-8). 1996. pap. 9.99 (*0-88092-329-6*) Royal Fireworks.

Aponick, Kathleen. Near the River's Edge. 34p. 1995. pap. 7.95 (*0-944754-27-9*) Pudding Hse Pubns.

Aponte, Gladys. Fundamentos y Aplicaciones de Mathematicas Basicas. (SPA.). 496p. (C). 1992. pap. text 24.33 (*0-201-51874-0*) Addison-Wesley.

Aponte, Gladys, et al. Curso Individualizado de Matematicas Basicas: Aritmetica, Algebra Elemental & Algebra Intermedia. LC 84-20838. (SPA.). 356p. (C). 1984. pap. text 15.00 (*0-8477-2638-X*) U of PR Pr.

— Curso Individualizado de Matematicas Basicas Vol. II: Algebra Elemental. (SPA.). 126p. 1987. pap. 5.50 (*0-8477-2640-1*) U of PR Pr.

— Curso Individualizado de Matematicas Basicas Vol. III: Algebra Intermedia. (SPA.). 152p. 1986. pap. 6.00 (*0-8477-2641-X*) U of PR Pr.

Aponte, Harry J. Bread & Spirit: Therapy with the New Poor--Diversity of Race, Culture & Values. 256p. 1994. 27.00 (*0-393-70176-X*) Norton.

***Aponte, Joseph F. & Wohl, Julian, eds.** Psychological Intervention & Cultural Diversity. 2nd ed. LC 99-37811. 320p. 1999. 66.67 (*0-205-29474-X*) Allyn.

Aponte, Maria. Quimica Organica: Manual de Laboratorio Escala Micro, Primera Parte. rev. ed. 141p. (C). 1992. pap. text 24.95 (*1-881375-01-3*) Libreria Univ.

— Quimica Organica: Manual de Laboratorio Escala Micro Primera Parte. 2nd ed. 175p. (C). 1994. pap. text 24.95 (*1-881375-17-X*) Libreria Univ.

— Quimica Organica: Manual de Laboratorio Escala Micro, Segunda Parte. rev. ed. 183p. (C). 1994. pap. text 24.95 (*1-881375-02-1*) Libreria Univ.

Aponte, Maria A. & Rivera, Zwinda L. Quimica Organica: Manual de Laboratorio Escala Micro Segunda Parte. 2nd ed. (Illus.). 196p. (C). 1996. pap. text 24.95 (*1-881375-21-8*) Libreria Univ.

Aponte, Marines. Las Instituciones Depositarias en Puerto Rico. (SPA.). 90p. 1995. pap. write for info. (*0-929441-78-8*) Pubns Puertorriquenas.

Aponte, Olimpia Colon, see Colon Aponte, Olimpia.

Aponte, Paul. Expression Obsession. (SPA & ENG., Illus.). 80p. (Orig.). 1999. pap. 9.95 (*1-891571-02-8*) Easy Break.

Aposhyan, Susan. Natural Intelligence: Body-Mind Intergration & Human Development. 196p. 1998. pap. 19.95 (*0-683-30599-9*) Lppncott W & W.

Apostle, Hippocrates G. Mathematics as a Science of Quantities. LC 91-91162. 95p. 1991. text 25.00 (*0-911589-12-0*) Peripatetic.

Apostle, Hippocrates G., ed. see Aristotle.

Apostle, Hippocrates G., tr. see Aristotle.

Apostle, Hippocrates G., tr. & comment see Aristotle.

Apostle, Richard & Barrett, Gene. Emptying Their Nets: Small Capital & Rural Industrialization in the Fishing Industry of Nova Scotia. (Illus.). 544p. 1991. text 65.00 (*0-8020-5894-9*); pap. text 24.95 (*0-8020-6831-6*) U of Toronto Pr.

Apostle, Richard A. Community, State & Market on the North Atlantic Rim: Challenges to Modernity in the Fishers. LC 99-173166. (Illus.). 464p. 1998. text 60.00 (*0-8020-0745-7*) U of Toronto Pr.

Apostle, Richard A. & Raymond, Boris. Librarianship & the Information Paradigm. LC 96-40043. 192p. 1997. 32.00 (*0-8108-3273-9*) Scarecrow.

Apostles for Triumph Staff. En el Fin Mi Inmaculado Corazon Triunfara. Martinez, Edie, tr. LC 94-66337. (SPA.). 84p. 1994. pap. 3.00 (*1-882972-28-7*) Queenship Pub.

Apostol, Jane. El Alisal: Where History Lingers. LC 94-76725. (Illus.). 100p. 1994. pap. 12.95 (*0-914421-12-3*) Hist Soc So CA.

— The Historical Society of Southern California: A Centennial History. LC 91-73248. (Illus.). 170p. 1991. 45.00 (*0-914421-04-2*) Hist Soc So CA.

— Museums along the Arroyo: A History & Guide. LC 95-82227. (Illus.). 139p. (Orig.). (C). 1996. pap. 13.95 (*0-914421-17-4*) Hist Soc So CA.

— Painting with Light: A Centennial History of the Judson Studios. LC 97-73289. xii, 138p. 1997. write for info. (*0-914421-20-4*) Hist Soc So CA.

Apostol, Tom M. Calculus: Multi-Variable Calculus & Linear Algebra with Applications, Vol. 2, Multi-Variable Calculus and Linear Algebra. 2nd ed. 704p. (C). 1969. text 122.95 (*0-471-00007-8*) Wiley.

— Calculus: One-Variable Calculus with an Introduction to Linear Algebra, Vol. 1, One-Variable Calculus with an Introduction. 2nd ed. 688p. (C). 1967. text 122.95 (*0-471-00005-1*) Wiley.

— Introduction to Analytic Number Theory. (Undergraduate Texts in Mathematics Ser.). (Illus.). 370p. (C). 1995. 54.95 (*0-387-90163-9*) Spr-Verlag.

— Linear Algebra: A First Course with Applications to Differential Equations. LC 96-37131. (Illus.). 368p. 1997. 84.95 (*0-471-17421-1*) Wiley.

— Mathematical Analysis: A Modern Approach to Advanced Calculus. 2nd ed. LC 72-11473. 492p. (C). 1974. 106.00 (*0-201-00288-4*, Health Sci) Addison-Wesley.

— Modular Functions & Dirichlet Series in Number Theory. 2nd ed. (Graduate Texts in Mathematics Ser.: Vol. 41). (Illus.). 216p. 1997. 49.95 (*0-387-97127-0*) Spr-Verlag.

Apostol, Tom M., et al, eds. A Century of Calculus, 1894-1968, Pt. I. (Raymond W. Brink Selected Mathematical Papers). 500p. 1992. pap. text 18.00 (*0-88385-205-5*, CALC/1) Math Assn.

Apostol, Virgil J., jt. auth. see Evangelista, Cornelio H.

Apostolakis, G., ed. see NATO Advanced Study Institute on Synthesis & Analysis.

***Apostoli, Andrew.** The Trilogy on the Holy Spirit. Incl. Advocate: The Spirit of Truth: In the Life of the Individual Christian. LC 98-46618. 160p. 1999. pap. 9.95 (*0-8189-0780-0*); Comforter: The Spirit of Joy. O'Connor, John Cardinal, pref. LC 95-3954. 1995. pap. 7.95 (*0-8189-0734-7*); Gift of God: The Holy Spirit. Groeschel, Benedict J., pref. LC 94-4450. 1994. pap. 9.95 (*0-8189-0703-7*); 1999. Set pap. 24.95 (*0-8189-0825-4*) Alba.

Apostoli, Andrew. When God Asks for an Undivided Heart: Choosing Celibacy in Love & Freedom. LC 95-37944. 208p. 1995. pap. 7.95 (*0-8198-8272-0*) Pauline Bks.

Apostolic Fathers. Works of Apostolic Fathers, 2 vols. Incl. Vol. 1. Clement, Ignatius, Polycarp, Didache, Barnabas. 420p. 1912. 19.95 (*0-674-99027-7*); Vol. 2. Shepherd of Hermas, Martyrdom of Polycarp, Epistle to Diognetus. 402p. 1913. 19.95 (*0-674-99028-5*); (Loeb Classical Library: Nos. 24-25). write for info. (*0-318-53223-9*) HUP.

Apostolici, Patres. Concordantia in Patres Apostolicos Vol. 1: Concordantia in Epistulam Ad Diognetum. Urban, Angel, ed. (Alpha-Omega, Reihe A Ser.: Bd. CXXXV). (GER.). 212p. 1993. 80.00 incl. 3.5 hd (*3-487-09726-5*) G Olms Pubs.

Apostolico, A., et al, eds. Combinatorial Pattern Matching: Fourth Annual Symposium, CPM 93, Padova, Italy, June 1993, Proceedings. LC 93-28891. (Lecture Notes in Computer Science Ser.: Vol. 684). viii, 265p. 1993. 44.95 (*0-387-56764-X*) Spr-Verlag.

Apostolico, A. & Galil, Zvi, eds. Combinatorial Algorithms on Words. (NATO Asi Series F: Vol. 12). viii, 361p. 1985. 100.95 (*0-387-15227-X*) Spr-Verlag.

Apostolico, A. & Hein, J., eds. Combinatorial Pattern Matching: Proceedings, 8th Annual Symposium, CPM 97, Aarhus, Denmark, June-July 1997. (Lecture Notes in Computer Science Ser.: Vol. 1264). viii, 277p. pap. 50.00 (*3-540-63220-4*) Spr-Verlag.

Apostolico, A., et al. Combinatorial Pattern Matching: Third Annual Symposium, Tucson, Arizona, U. S. A., April 29-May 1, 1992, Proceedings. LC 92-31070. 1992. 47.00 (*0-387-56024-6*) Spr-Verlag.

Apostolico, Alberto & Galil, Zvi, eds. Pattern Matching Algorithms. LC 96-49602. (Illus.). 400p. 1997. text 75.00 (*0-19-511367-5*) OUP.

Apostolides, Alex. Juarez: Miracle of the North. (Illus.). 144p. 1991. 39.95 (*0-944551-04-1*) Sundance Pr TX.

Apostolides, Marianne. Inner Hunger: A Young Woman's Struggle Through Anorexia & Bulimia. LC 97-49805. 192p. 1998. 22.00 (*0-393-04590-0*) Norton.

***Apostolidis, Paul.** Stations of the Cross: Adorno & Christian Right Radio. LC 99-87368. 312p. 2000. lib. bdg. 54.95 (*0-8223-2504-7*) Duke.

— Stations of the Cross: Adorno & Christian Right Radio. LC 99-87368. 312p. 2000. pap. 18.95 (*0-8223-2541-1*) Duke.

***Apostolo, Giorgio & Massimello, Giovanni.** Italian Aces of World War 2. (Aircraft of the Aces Ser.: Vol. 34). (Illus.). 96p. 2000. pap. 17.95 (*1-84176-078-1*, 130584AE, Pub. by Ospry) Motorbooks Intl.

Apostoloci, Patres. Concordantia in Patres Apostolicos Pars III: Primae Epistulae Clementis Romani Ad Corinthios Concordantiae. Urban, Angel, ed. (Alpha-Omega, Reihe A Ser.: Bd. CLXIV). (GER.). 450p. 1996. write for info. (*3-487-10044-4*) G Olms Pubs.

Apostolon, Billy. Evangelistic Sermon Outlines. (Sermon Outline Ser.). 48p. 1979. pap. 4.99 (*0-8010-0144-7*) Baker Bks.

— Preach the Word. (Sermon Outline Ser.). 64p. 1958. pap. 4.99 (*0-8010-0039-4*) Baker Bks.

— Special Days & Occasions. (Sermon Outline Ser.). 64p. (gr. 13). 1959. pap. 4.99 (*0-8010-0007-6*) Baker Bks.

Apostolopoulos, I., jt. auth. see Gentithes, J.

***Apostolopoulos, Nick, et al.** Professional Site Server 3.0 Personalization & Membership. 1000p. 1999. pap. text 59.99 (*1-86100-269-6*) Wrox Pr Inc.

Apostolopoulos, Yiorgis & Leivadi, Stella, eds. Sociology of Tourism: Theoretical & Empirical Investigations. 376p. (C). 1996. 85.00 (*0-415-13508-7*) Routledge.

***Apostolopoulos, Yiorgos, et al.** Mediterranean Tourism: Facets of Socioeconomic Development & Cultural Change. LC 00-32822. 2000. write for info. (*0-415-18023-6*) Routledge.

Apostolos-Cappadona, Diane. The Dictionary of Christian Art. (Illus.). 380p. (C). 1994. 24.95 (*0-8264-0779-X*) Continuum.

— Dictionary of Christian Art. LC 98-13846. 376p. 1997. pap. 24.95 (*0-8264-1065-0*) Continuum.

— Dictionary of Women in Religious Art. LC 97-46632. (Illus.). 464p. 1998. reprint ed. pap. 18.95 (*0-19-512098-1*) OUP.

— Encyclopedia of Women in Religious Art. LC 96-41647. (Illus.). 352p. 1996. 44.50 (*0-8264-0915-6*) Continuum.

— The Spirit & the Vision: The Influence of Christian Romanticism on the Development of 19th-Century American Art. LC 94-7797. (Academy Ser.). 246p. (C). 1995. 39.95 (*1-55540-974-1*, 010184); pap. 24.95 (*1-55540-975-X*, 010184) OUP.

Apostolos-Cappadona, Diane, ed. Art, Creativity & the Sacred: An Anthology in Religion & Art. rev. ed. LC 98-19078. (Illus.). 352p. 1995. pap. 24.95 (*0-8264-0829-X*) Continuum.

Apostolos-Cappadona, Diane & Ebersole, Lucinda, eds. Women, Creativity & the Arts. (Illus.). 240p. 1995. pap. 19.95 (*0-8264-0831-1*) Continuum.

Apostolos-Cappadona, Diane, tr. see Eliade, Mircea.

Apostolos-Paul Refenes, et al. Decision Technologies for Computational Finance: Proceedings of the 5th International Conference Computational Finance. LC 98-41134. (Advances in Computational Management Science Ser.). 10p. 1998. 159.95 (*0-7923-8308-7*) Kluwer Academic.

Apostolou, Anna. A Murder in Macedon. LC 97-14781. 256p. 1997. text 21.95 (*0-312-16939-6*) St Martin.

— A Murder in Macedon. 272p. 1998. mass mkt. 5.99 (*0-312-96792-6*) St Martin.

— A Murder in Thebes. LC 98-28727. 240p. 1998. text 21.95 (*0-312-19585-0*) St Martin.

— A Murder in Thebes: A Mystery of Alexander the Great. 240p. 1999. mass mkt. 5.99 (*0-312-97278-4*) St Martin.

Apostolou, Barbara. Keys to Investing in Common Stocks. 2nd ed. 1995. pap. 4.95 (*0-8120-9004-7*) Barron.

Apostolou, Barbara & Alleman, Francine. Internal Audit Sampling. Campbell, Lee A., ed. 135p. 1991. pap. 20.00 (*0-89413-241-5*, A835) Inst Inter Aud.

***Apostolou, Barbara & Apostolou, Nicholas G.** Keys to Investing in Common Stocks. 3rd ed. LC 99-42080. (Business Keys Ser.). 160p. 2000. 7.95 (*0-7641-1301-1*) Barron.

Apostolou, John L. & Greenberg, Martin H., eds. The Best Japanese Science Fiction Stories. LC 97-25052. 176p. 1997. pap. 10.00 (*1-56980-124-X*) Barricade Bks.

Apostolou, Nicholas G. Keys to Business & Personal Financial Statements. (Barron's Business Keys Ser.). 160p. 1991. pap. 4.95 (*0-8120-4622-6*) Barron.

— Keys to Conservative Investments. 2nd ed. LC 95-42798. (Barron's Business Keys Ser.). (Orig.). 1996. pap. 4.95 (*0-8120-9006-3*) Barron.

— Keys to Investing in Options & Futures. 2nd ed. LC 95-18424. (Barron's Business Keys Ser.). 1995. pap. 4.95 (*0-8120-9005-5*) Barron.

***Apostolou, Nicholas G.** Keys to Investing in Options & Futures. 3rd ed. LC 99-56821. (Business Keys Ser.). 180p. 2000. pap. 7.95 (*0-7641-1303-8*) Barron.

— Keys to Understanding the Financial News. 3rd ed. 2000. pap. write for info. (*0-7641-1308-9*, Pub. by Barron) Prodn Assocs.

Apostolou, Nicholas G. & Crumbley, D. Larry. Keys to Understanding the Financial News. 2nd ed. LC 93-23233. (Barron's Business Keys Ser.). 1994. pap. 4.95 (*0-8120-1694-7*) Barron.

Apostolou, Nicholas G., jt. auth. see Apostolou, Barbara.

Apotheker, Nan, tr. see Garaudy, Roger.

App, August J. Lancelot in English Literature. LC 65-21392. (Arthurian Legend & Literature Ser.: No. 1). (C). 1969. reprint ed. lib. bdg. 75.00 (*0-8383-0504-0*) M S G Haskell Hse.

App, Austin J. History's Most Terrifying Peace. 1986. lib. bdg. 250.00 (*0-87700-877-9*) Revisionist Pr.

— Morgenthau Era Letters. 1986. 250.00 (*0-87700-878-7*) Revisionist Pr.

App, Linda H. Nurturing Happiness: Natural Ways to Relieve & Prevent Depression. LC 97-90954. 200p. 1997. pap. 11.95 (*0-9659879-5-7*) Windmill Pr Alex.

App, Urs. Master Yunmen: From the Record of the Chan Master "Gate-of-the-Clouds" De Angelis, Paul, ed. LC 93-42824. (Illus.). 256p. 1994. pap. 13.00 (*1-56836-005-3*) Kodansha.

APPA Staff & Lilly Endowment, Inc. Staff. Today's Challenge to Tomorrow's Vision: A Study of Facilities Conditions at Schools of Theology. (Illus.). 97p. 1991. pap. 35.00 (*0-913359-65-3*) APPA VA.

Appachana, Anjana. Incantations & Other Stories. 180p. 1992. pap. 12.95 (*0-8135-1828-8*); text 32.00 (*0-8135-1827-X*) Rutgers U Pr.

Appadorai, Angadipuram. Contemporary India: Essays in Domestic & Foreign Policy. 251p. (C). 1988. 18.50 (*81-7003-087-0*, Pub. by S Asia Pubs) S Asia.

— Indian Political Thinking in the Twentieth Century: An Introduction Survey. 228p. 1987. 15.00 (*81-7003-074-9*, Pub. by S Asia Pubs) S Asia.

Appadorai, Angadipuram, ed. Select Documents on India's Foreign Policy & Relations, Vol. 2. 1986. 42.00 (*0-19-561496-8*) OUP.

— Select Documents on India's Foreign Policy & Relations, 1947-72, Vol. 1. 1983. 49.95 (*0-19-561309-0*) OUP.

— Status of Women in South Asia. LC 75-38654. 1976. reprint ed. 23.95 (*0-89201-026-6*) Zenger Pub.

Appadurai, Arjun. The Anthropology of Consumption: A Transnational Perspective. (C). 1994. pap. text 15.95 (*0-8133-0963-8*) Westview.

***Appadurai, Arjun.** Globalization. (Illus.). 300p. 2000. pap. 12.00 (*0-8223-6472-7*) Duke.

Appadurai, Arjun. Modernity at Large: Cultural Dimensions of Globalization. (Public Worlds Ser.: Vol. 1). 224p. (C). 1996. pap. 18.95 (*0-8166-2793-2*) U of Minn Pr.

Appadurai, Arjun. Space Identity Uncertainty. 1997. 24.95 (*0-226-02115-7*) U Ch Pr.

Appadurai, Arjun. Worship & Conflict under Colonial Rule: A South Indian Case. LC 80-24508. (Cambridge South Asian Studies: No. 27). 276p. reprint ed. pap. 78.70 (*0-608-15688-4*, 2031614) Bks Demand.

Appadurai, Arjun, ed. The Social Life of Things: Commodities in Cultural Perspective. (Illus.). 352p. 1988. pap. text 20.95 (*0-521-35726-8*) Cambridge U Pr.

Appadurai, Arjun, et al, eds. Gender, Genre & Power in South Asian Expressive Traditions. LC 91-2711. (South Asian Regional Studies & Publications of the American Folklore Society). 464p. (C). 1991. text 49.95 (*0-8122-3082-5*); pap. text 23.95 (*0-8122-1337-8*) U of Pa Pr.

Appalachia Educational Laboratory Staff & Winefordner, David. Worker Trait Group Guide. rev. ed. 495p. 1988. 23.95 (*1-55631-119-2*) Chron Guide.

Appalachian Land Ownership Task Force Staff. Who Owns Appalachia? Landownership & Its Impact. LC 82-40173. 260p. reprint ed. pap. 80.60 (*0-608-17873-X*, 203270500080) Bks Demand.

Appalachian Mountain Club Book Staff. Maine: Acadia National Park. (AMC Trail Maps Ser.). Date not set. pap. text 3.95 (*1-878239-23-6*) AMC Books.

Appalachian Mountain Club Staff. AMC River Guide: Massachusetts, Connecticut, Rhode Island. 2nd ed. 1990. pap. 11.95 (*0-87823-900-6*) Am Soc Eng Ed.

— Maine Mountain Guide. 8th rev. ed. LC 99-21954. (Illus.). 1999. pap. 18.95 (*1-878239-74-0*) AMC Books.

— Massachusetts & Rhode Island Trail Guide. 7th rev. ed. (Illus.). 384p. 1995. pap. 16.95 (*1-878239-39-2*) AMC Books.

***Appalachian Mountain Club Staff, ed.** AMC River Guide: Massachusetts - Connecticut - Rhode Island. 3rd ed. (Illus.). 2000. pap. 14.95 (*1-878239-75-9*) AMC Books.

Appalachian Studies Staff. Contemporary Appalachia: In Search of a Usuable Past: Proceedings of the Appalachian Studies, 9th Annual Conference. Ross, Carl, ed. 1987. pap. 10.95 (*0-913239-49-6*) Appalach Consortium.

Appaluccio, Robert. New Jersey Homeowner's Guide to Property Tax Appeals. Vanzini, Mark, ed. 35p. 1998. pap. 29.95 (*0-9673269-0-7*) Insight Mktg.

***Appaluccio, Robert.** New Jersey Homeowner's Guide to Property Tax Appeals. 2nd rev. ed. Vanzini, Mark, ed. (Illus.). 48p. 2000. pap. 11.95 (*0-9673269-1-5*) Insight Mktg.

Appanah, Simmathiri, jt. auth. see D'Silva, Emmanuel.

Apparao, Ankaraboyina. Developments in Geoelectrical Methods. (Illus.). 314p. (C). 1997. text 74.00 (*90-5410-707-3*, Pub. by A A Balkema) Ashgate Pub Co.

Apparao, K. M. Composition of Cosmic Radiation. x, 86p. 1975. text 171.00 (*0-677-03770-8*) Gordon & Breach.

Appasamy, A. J. & Streeter, Burnett H. The Sadhu: A Study in Mysticism & Practical Religion. rev. ed. 264p. (C). 1987. 17.50 (*0-8364-2097-7*, Pub. by Mittal Pubs Dist) S Asia.

Appasamy, Jaya. Indian Paintings on Glass. (Illus.). 75p. 1980. 35.95 (*0-318-36337-2*) Asia Bk Corp.

Appasamy, Paul, et al. Social Exclusion from a Welfare Rights Perspective in India. LC 97-145269. x, 133p. 1996. pap. 20.25 (*92-9014-575-7*) Intl Labour Office.

APPC Staff, et al. Proceedings of a Workshop on Coconut Shell Carbonization/Waste Heat Recovery, Colombo, Sri Lanka, September 1989. 69p. 1991. pap. 30.00 (*0-85954-279-3*, Pub. by Nat Res Inst) St Mut.

Appea, Pamela, ed. see St. Clair, Barbara.

***Appel.** Cults in America. rev. ed. 1998. pap. 12.95 (*0-8050-5727-7*) St Martin.

Appel. On the Birth of Your Child. LC 99-36065. 1999. text 11.95 (*0-312-20690-9*) St Martin.

Appel, Alfred, Jr., ed. see De Forest, John W.

Appel, Alfred, Jr., ed. see Nabokov, Vladimir.

Appel, Allan, ed. A Portable Apocalypse: A Quotable Companion to the End of the World. LC 98-41789. 272p. 1999. pap. 12.00 (*1-57322-714-5*, Riverhd Trade) Berkley Pub.

Appel, Allan & New York Botanical Garden Staff. Plants & People: A Walk Through a World of Plants at the Enid A. Haupt Conservatory. LC 96-54479. 1997. pap. 10.00 (*0-89327-425-9*) NY Botanical.

***Appel, Allen.** Dogs Guide for Pups. LC 00-35252. (Illus.). 128p. 2000. text 11.95 (*0-312-26212-4*) St Martin.

Appel, Allen. From Father to Son: Wisdom for the Next Generation. 12th ed. LC 96-48915. (Illus.). 128p. 1993. text 9.95 (*0-312-09814-6*) St Martin.

— High Holiday Sutra. LC 97-15992. 192p. (Orig.). 1997. pap. 13.95 (*1-56689-065-9*) Coffee Hse.

— The Squire of East Hampton: The Life of Evan M. Frankel. LC 89-80476. (Illus.). 280p. 1989. write for info. (*0-9622459-0-9*) Jewish Ctr Hamptons.

— Thanks, Dad. LC 96-48918. 1997. text 9.95 (*0-312-15221-3*) St Martin.

Appel, Allen, jt. auth. see Roberts, Craig.

Appel, Andrew W. Compiling with Continuations. (Illus.). 272p. (C). 1991. text 47.95 (*0-521-41695-7*) Cambridge U Pr.

— Modern Compiler Implementation in C. LC 97-31089. (Illus.). 554p. (C). 1997. text 54.95 (*0-521-58390-X*) Cambridge U Pr.

— Modern Compiler Implementation in Java. LC 97-31090. (Illus.). 558p. (C). 1997. text 54.95 (*0-521-58388-8*) Cambridge U Pr.

— Modern Compiler Implementation in ML. LC 97-31091. (Illus.). 548p. (C). 1997. text 54.95 (*0-521-58274-1*) Cambridge U Pr.

Appel, Benjamin. Shepherd of the Sun. (Illus.). (J). (gr. 5 up). 1961. 10.95 (*0-8392-3033-8*) Astor-Honor.

Appel, C. Jeff, jt. auth. see Ganson, Harriet C.

Appel, Carl L. Provenzalische Chrestomathie, Mit Abriss der Formenlehre & Glossar. 6th ed. LC 71-38488. reprint ed. 27.50 (*0-404-08345-5*) AMS Pr.

— Provenzalische Lautlehre: Mit Einer Karte. LC 80-2165. (Provenzalische Chrestomathie Ser.). reprint ed. 37.50 (*0-404-19027-8*) AMS Pr.

— Die Singweisen Bernarts Von Ventadorn nach den Handschriften mitgeteilt. LC 80-2171. reprint ed. 32.50 (*0-404-19002-2*) AMS Pr.

— Der Trobador Uc Brunec Oder Brunenc in: Abhandlungen Herrn Prof. Adolf Tobler. LC 80-2177. 1981. reprint ed. 17.50 (*0-404-19003-0*) AMS Pr.

Appel, David. Workers' Compensation Insurance Pricing. (S. S. Huebner International Ser.). 1988. 53.50 (*0-89838-268-8*) Huebner Foun Insur.

Appel, David, et al. Principles of Workers Compensation Claims. 2nd ed. Jones, James R., ed. LC 98-71633. 311p. 1998. pap. text 41.00 (*0-89462-125-4*, 3402) IIA.

Appel, David, jt. ed. see Borba, Philip S.

Appel, David, jt. ed. see Worrall, John D.

Appel, David N. & Billings, Ronald F., eds. Oak Wilt Perspectives: The Proceedings of the National Oak Wilt Symposium. (Illus.). 320p. (Orig.). (C). 1995. pap. text 30.00 (*0-9644015-0-9*) Info Develop.

Appel, Dee. I Thought of You Today. (Illus.). 22p. 1998. pap. 3.95 (*0-9654957-1-X*) Heartfelt Lines-Mailbox Memories.

— Tiny Tea, a Friendship Gift. (Illus.). 22p. (Orig.). 1996. pap. 6.95 (*0-9654957-0-1*) Heartfelt Lines-Mailbox Memories.

Appel, Frederic C. Encyclopedie de la Femme, 2: Son Corps. (FRE.). 144p. 24.95 (*0-7859-0388-7*, M6006) Fr & Eur.

Appel, Fredrick. Nietzsche Contra Democracy. LC 98-27125. 160p. 1998. 29.95 (*0-8014-3424-6*) Cornell U Pr.

Appel, Gabriela & Dechert, Hans W., eds. A Case for Psycholinguistic Cases. LC 91-13230. viii, 195p. 1991. 35.00 (*1-55619-120-0*) J Benjamins Pubng Co.

Appel, Gabriela, jt. ed. see Lantolf, James P.

Appel, Georgius. De Romanorum Precationibus. LC 75-10628. (Ancient Religion & Mythology Ser.). 1976. reprint ed. 22.95 (*0-405-07004-7*) Ayer.

Appel, Gerald. Winning Market Systems. 1989. 49.95 (*0-930233-33-6*) Windsor.

— Winning Market Systems: Eighty Three Ways to Beat the Market. 232p. 1986. reprint ed. pap. 39.95 (*0-934380-12-0*, 175) Traders Pr.

Appel, Gerald & Hitschler, Fred. Stock Market Trading Systems. LC 79-55228. 208p. 1990. reprint ed. 45.00 (*0-934380-16-3*, 7) Traders Pr.

Appel, Gersion. The Concise Code of Jewish Law, Vol. 1. 1991. 22.95 (*0-88125-298-0*) Ktav.

— The Concise Code of Jewish Law: A Guide to Prayer & Religious Observance on the Sabbath, Vol. 2. 1989. 22.95 (*0-88125-314-6*) Ktav.

— The Concise Code of Jewish Law: Daily Prayers & Religious Observances in the Life-Cycle of the Jew, Vol. 1. 22.95 (*0-87068-298-9*) Ktav.

— A Philosophy of Mizvot. 1995. pap. 16.95 (*0-87068-250-4*) Ktav.

Appel, Jens C. & Gentry, F. Bruce. The Complete Probate Kit. 256p. 1991. pap. 29.95 (*0-471-53492-7*) Wiley.

Appel, Jens C., 3rd, jt. auth. see Gentry, F. Bruce.

Appel, John. Francisco Jose de Caldas: A Scientist at Work in Nueva Granada. LC 94-71521. (Transactions Ser.: Vol. 84, Pt. 5). (Illus.). 200p. (C). 1994. pap. 20.00 (*0-87169-845-5*, T845-APJ) Am Philos.

Appel, John & Appel, Selma. Pat-Riots to Patriots: American Irish in Caricature & Comic Art. Caltrider, Sue & Fitzgerald, Ruth D., eds. (Illus.). 32p. (Orig.). 1990. pap. text 5.95 (*0-944311-03-2*) MSU Museum.

Appel, John J. Immigrant Historical Societies in the United States, 1880-1950. Cordasco, Francesco, ed. LC 80-838. (American Ethnic Groups Ser.). 1981. lib. bdg. 47.95 (*0-405-13402-9*) Ayer.

***Appel, John W.** Who's in Charge? Autonomy & Mental Disorder. 160p. 2000. 18.95 (*1-58244-071-9*) Rutledge Bks.

Appel, Joseph H. Business Biography of John Wanamaker. reprint ed. lib. bdg. 71.50 (*0-404-00365-6*) AMS Pr.

Appel, Karel. Psychopathological Art, 1948-1950. (Illus.). 1998. 120.00 (*3-906127-52-4*, Pub. by Gachnang & Springer) Dist Art Pubs.

— Psychopathological Notebook: Drawings & Gouaches 1948-1950. 200p. 1999. pap. text 65.00 (*3-906127-57-5*) Gachnang & Springer.

Appel, Kenneth I., et al, eds. Contributions to Group Theory. LC 84-18454. (Contemporary Mathematics Ser.: Vol. 33). 517p. 1984. pap. 58.00 (*0-8218-5035-0*, CONM/33) Am Math.

***Appel, Kenneth J.** It Takes Two.Com: A Psychological & Spiritual Guide to Finding Love on the Internet Personals. 1999. pap. 19.95 (*0-9677323-0-1*) Tara Ent NV.

Appel, L. Fruit & Vegetable Lexicon: Lexique des Fruits et Legumes. (ENG, FRE & LAT.). 124p. 1982. pap. 9.95 (*0-8288-0067-7*, M6007) Fr & Eur.

Appel, Libby. Mask Characterization: An Acting Process. LC 81-9157. 136p. (Orig.). (C). 1982. pap. 17.95 (*0-8093-1039-2*) S Ill U Pr.

Appel, M. J., ed. Virus Infections of Carnivores. (Virus Infections of Vertabrates Ser.: Vol. 1). 500p. 1987. 316.50 (*0-444-42709-0*) Elsevier.

Appel, M. J. & Gillespie, J. H. Canine Distemper Virus. LC 02-79603. (Virology Monographs: Vol. 11). (Illus.). 159p. 1972. 45.00 (*0-387-81059-5*) Spr-Verlag.

Appel, Margaret A., jt. ed. see McNamara, J. Regis.

Appel, Marsha C. Illustration Index, Vol. IV. LC 79-26091. 468p. 1980. lib. bdg. 50.00 (*0-8108-1273-8*) Scarecrow.

— Illustration Index VIII, 1992-1996. LC 98-15585. (Illus.). 480p. 1998. 65.00 (*0-8108-3484-7*) Scarecrow.

— Illustration Index V: 1977-1981. LC 83-15201. 421p. 1984. 50.00 (*0-8108-1656-3*) Scarecrow.

— Illustration Index VI: 1982 - 1986. LC 88-18207. 541p. 1988. 60.00 (*0-8108-2146-X*) Scarecrow.

— Illustration Index VII, 1987-1991. LC 93-5153. 503p. 1993. 65.00 (*0-8108-2659-3*) Scarecrow.

Appel, Marty. Joe DiMaggio. (Baseball Legends Ser.). (Illus.). 64p. (J). (gr. 3 up). 1990. lib. bdg. 15.95 (*0-7910-1164-X*) Chelsea Hse.

— Slide, Kelly, Slide: The Wild Life & Times of Mike "King" Kelly. LC 98-55703. (Illus.). 244p. 1999. pap. 14.95 (*1-57886-003-2*) Scarecrow Trade.

— Slide, Kelly, Slide: The Wild Life & Times of Mike "King" Kelly, Baseball's First Superstar. LC 94-49546. (American Sports History Ser.: No. 3). (Illus.). 244p. 1996. 32.50 (*0-8108-2997-5*) Scarecrow.

— Yogi Berra. (Baseball Legends Ser.). (Illus.). 64p. (J). (gr. 3 up). 1992. lib. bdg. 15.95 (*0-7910-1169-0*) Chelsea Hse.

Appel, Marty, jt. auth. see King, Larry.

Appel, Marty, jt. auth. see Seaver, Tom.

Appel, Odette M., jt. auth. see Sobieszek, Robert A.

Appel, Paul P., ed. Homage to Sherwood Anderson. LC 77-105304. 212p. 1970. lib. bdg. 15.00 (*0-911858-02-4*) Appel.

Appel, Paul P., pref. Sacco-Vanzetti Case: A Transcript of the Record of the Trial of Nicola Sacco & Bartolomeo Vanzetti in the Courts of Massachusetts & Subsequent Proceedings, 1920-27, 6 vols. 2nd ed. (Illus.). 6400p. 1969. 500.00 (*0-911858-01-6*) Appel.

Appel, Rene. Immigrant Children Learning Dutch: Sociolinguistic & Psycholinguistic Aspects of Second-Language Acquisition. viii, 198p. (Orig.). (C). 1984. pap. text 46.15 (*3-11-013272-9*) Mouton.

Appel, Rene & Muysken, Pieter. Language Contact & Bilingualism. 224p. 1995. pap. text 24.95 (*0-7131-6491-3*, Pub. by E A) St Martin.

Appel, Rosaire. Mabel in Her Twenties. (Illus.). 1992. 18.95 (*0-932511-43-0*); pap. 8.95 (*0-932511-44-9*) Fiction Coll.

— TransiT: A Novel. 133p. 1993. 18.95 (*0-932511-70-8*); pap. 8.95 (*0-932511-71-6*) Fiction Coll.

Appel, Selma, jt. auth. see Appel, John.

Appel, Sergio, tr. see Rodecker, Stephen B. & Quon-Warner, Maryanna.

Appel, Shannon, et al. Chronicle of the Awakenings: New Past Lives & Rules Expansions. Shirley, Sam, ed. & illus. by. Bridges, John, illus. (Nephilim Role Playing Game Ser.). 96p. (Orig.). 1995. pap. 16.95 (*1-56882-035-6*, 3102) Chaosium.

— The Cthulhu for President, 1996: Why Settle for the Lesser Evil? (Illus.). (Orig.). 1996. pap. 14.95 (*1-56882-067-4*, 5113) Chaosium.

— Nephilim Gamemaster's Companion: Indispensable Resources for the Nephilim Gamemaster. (Nephilim Role Playing Game Ser.). (Illus.). 96p. (Orig.). 1996. pap. 14.95 (*1-56882-066-6*, 3106) Chaosium.

Appel, Sherry C. Thanks, Mom. LC 96-48917. 1997. text 9.95 (*0-312-15222-1*) St Martin.

— Wisdom from the Kitchen: From Mother to Daughter. LC 97-39801. 1998. text 10.95 (*0-312-18099-3*) St Martin.

Appel, Sherry Conway. From Mother to Daughter: Wisdom from the Kitchen. 1998. 65.70 (*0-312-18329-1*) St Martin.

Appel, Stephen. Positioning Subjects: Psychoanalysis & Critical Educational Studies. LC 96-3624. (Critical Studies in Education & Culture: No. 1064-8615). 240p. 1996. 59.95 (*0-89789-442-1*, Bergin & Garvey) Greenwood.

Appel, Stephen, ed. Psychoanalysis & Pedagogy. LC 98-38307. (Critical Studies in Education & Culture). 208p. 1999. 55.00 (*0-89789-502-9*, Bergin & Garvey) Greenwood.

Appel, Ted. Jose Marti: Cuban Revolutionary & Poet. (Hispanics of Achievement Ser.). (Illus.). 120p. (YA). (gr. 5 up). 1992. lib. bdg. 19.95 (*0-7910-1246-8*) Chelsea Hse.

Appel, Theodore. Life & Work of John Williamson Nevin. LC 71-83409. (Religion in America, Ser. 1). 1970. reprint ed. 39.95 (*0-405-00203-3*) Ayer.

Appel, Toby A. The Cuvier-Geoffroy Debate: French Biology in the Decades Before Darwin. (Monographs in the History & Philosophy of Biology). (Illus.). 321p. 1987. text 60.00 (*0-19-504138-0*) OUP.

***Appel, Toby A.** Shaping Biology: The National Science Foundation & American Biological Research, 1952-1975. LC 99-89620. 408p. 2000. 42.50 (*0-8018-6321-X*) Johns Hopkins.

Appel, Vibeke, jt. ed. see Dollerup, Cay.

Appel, Walter. Alco Official Color Photography. LC 98-66810. (Illus.). 128p. 1998. 49.95 (*1-58248-006-0*) Morning NJ.

***Appel, Walter.** Trackside along the B & O with Ed Griffith. (Illus.). 128p. 1999. 54.95 (*1-58248-036-2*) Morning NJ.

Appel, Wendy S., et al. Working Together: Producing Synergy by Honoring Diversity. Arien, Angeles, ed. Palazchenko, Pavel, tr. LC 97-67417. (Illus.). 274p. 1998. 28.75 (*1-886710-02-3*, Pub. by New Leaders) Natl Bk Netwk.

Appel, Willa. Cults in America: Programmed for Paradise. LC 82-15538. 216p. 1995. pap. 9.95 (*0-8050-0524-2*, Owl) H Holt & Co.

Appel, Willa, jt. ed. see Schechner, Richard.

Appel, William. Whisper...He Might Hear You. 256p. 1992. reprint ed. mass mkt. 4.50 (*1-55817-641-1*, Pinncle Kensgtn) Kensgtn Pub Corp.

— Widowmaker. LC 94-15362. 1994. 19.95 (*0-8027-3193-7*) Walker & Co.

Appelbaum. Sociology: A Brief Introduction/With a Global Reader. (C). 1997. pap. text 46.00 (*0-673-98520-2*) Addison-Wesley.

— Traditional Chinese Designs. (Design Library). (Illus.). 48p. (Orig.). pap. 5.95 (*0-486-25347-3*) Dover.

Appelbaum, A. & Dawson, L. R., eds. Infrared Detectors - Materials, Processing, & Devices. LC 94-21607. (Symposium Proceedings Ser.: Vol. 299). 343p. 1994. text 60.00 (*1-55899-195-6*) Materials Res.

Appelbaum, Arlene. Start Your New Business Now! 164p. 1997. pap., per. 48.00 (*1-885750-04-8*, SB97) Visions Communs.

Appelbaum, Barbara. Guide to Environmental Protection of Collections. (Illus.). 271p. (C). 1991. text 39.00 (*0-932087-16-7*) Sound View Pr.

Appelbaum, Barbara, ed. Art & Archaeology Technical Abstracts, 2 vols. Incl. Vol. 2. Brown, Jessica S., ed. 1184p. 1997. pap. Not sold separately (*0-89236-407-6*, Getty Conservation Inst); Vol. 1. Brown, Jerssica S., ed. 1232p. 1997. pap. Not sold separately (*0-89236-408-4*, Getty Conservation Inst); 70.00 (*0-614-31339-2*, Getty Conservation Inst) J P Getty Trust.

Appelbaum, D. A. Navigation Rules, International-Inland. (Illus.). 212p. 1998. pap. text 40.00 (*0-7881-3951-7*) DIANE Pub.

***Appelbaum, David.** An Alchemist at Heart: Poems, 1993-1996. LC 00-38367. 2000. pap. write for info. (*1-930337-00-0*) Codhill Pr.

— The Delay of the Heart. (C). 2000. pap. text 19.95 (*0-7914-4768-5*) State U NY Pr.

— The Delay of the Heart. (C). 2000. text 59.50 (*0-7914-4767-7*) State U NY Pr.

Appelbaum, David. Disruption. LC 95-40494. 186p. (C). 1996. text 59.50 (*0-7914-2797-8*); pap. text 19.95 (*0-7914-2798-6*) State U NY Pr.

— Everyday Spirits. LC 92-32009. 195p. (C). 1993. text 48.50 (*0-7914-1583-X*); pap. text 16.95 (*0-7914-1584-8*) State U NY Pr.

— On Count. Schultz, Patricia, ed. LC 89-33518. (Poetry Ser.: Vol. 5). 88p. 1989. pap. 14.95 (*0-88946-889-3*) E Mellen.

— The Sawn Bench: Poems. LC 92-19966. 72p. 1993. pap. 14.95 (*0-7734-9517-7*, Mellen Poetry Pr) E Mellen.

— The Stop. LC 94-48098. (SUNY Series in Western Esoteric Traditions). 154p. (C). 1995. text 44.50 (*0-7914-2381-6*); pap. text 16.95 (*0-7914-2382-4*) State U NY Pr.

— Voice. LC 89-35228. 155p. (C). 1990. text 59.50 (*0-7914-0287-8*); pap. text 19.95 (*0-7914-0288-6*) State U NY Pr.

***Appelbaum, David, ed.** The Illustrated Encyclopedia of World Philosophy. (Illus.). 2000. pap. text 29.95 (*1-86204-228-4*, Pub. by Element MA) Penguin Putnam.

Appelbaum, David, jt. ed. see Needleman, Jacob.

Appelbaum, Diana. Cocoa Ice. LC 96-40365. (Illus.). 56p. (J). (gr. k-4). 1997. 16.95 (*0-531-30040-4*); lib. bdg. 17.99 (*0-531-33040-0*) Orchard Bks Watts.

— Giants in the Land. LC 92-26526. (Illus.). 32p. (J). 1993. 17.00 (*0-395-64720-7*) HM.

***Appelbaum, Diana.** Giants in the Land. (Illus.). 32p. (YA). 2000. pap. 6.95 (*0-618-03305-X*) HM.

Appelbaum, Diana K. The Glorious Fourth: An American Holiday, an American History. LC 88-30881. 190p. 1989. reprint ed. pap. 58.90 (*0-608-02810-X*, 206387700007) Bks Demand.

Appelbaum, E. Sociology. (C). 1997. text 22.00 (*0-06-502577-6*) Addison-Wesley.

Appelbaum, Eileen. Back to Work: Determinants of Women's Successful Re-entry. LC 81-8008. 158p. 1981. 45.00 (*0-86569-076-6*, Auburn Hse) Greenwood.

Appelbaum, Eileen & Batt, Rosemary. The New American Workplace: Transforming Work Systems in the United States. LC 93-31201. 256p. 1994. pap. text 18.95 (*0-87546-319-3*, ILR Press) Cornell U Pr.

Appelbaum, Eileen & Schettkat, Ronald. Labor Market Adjustments to Structural Change & Technological Progress. LC 90-14230. (Illus.). 264p. 1990. 65.00 (*0-275-93376-8*, C3376, Praeger Pubs) Greenwood.

Appelbaum, Eileen & Young, Lowell S. Macroeconomics & the Financial System. 3rd ed. LC 97-70708. 295p. (C). 1997. text 41.00 (*0-89463-075-X*) Am Inst FCPCU.

***Appelbaum, Eileen, et al.** Manufacturing Advantage: Why High Performance Work Systems Pay Off. LC 99-48690. 2000. pap. 19.95 (*0-8014-8655-6*) Cornell U Pr.

Appelbaum, Elie, jt. auth. see Scheffman, David T.

***Appelbaum, Henry.** Studies in Intelligence: A Collection of Articles on the Historical, Operational, Doctrinal & Theoretical Aspects of Intelligence, Winter 1999- 2000. 103p. 2000. pap. 11.00 (*0-16-059090-6*) USGPO.

Appelbaum, Irwyn. The World According to Beaver. rev. ed. (Illus.). 340p. 1998. reprint ed. pap. 14.95 (*1-57500-052-0*, Pub. by TV Bks) HarpC.

Appelbaum, Judith. How to Get Happily Published, Fifth Edition: Complete & Candid Guide, A. 5th ed. LC 97-41128. 400p. 1998. pap. 14.00 (*0-06-273509-8*) HarpC.

Appelbaum, Judith & Janovic, Florence. Writer's Workbook. 71p. 1991. pap. 9.95 (*0-916366-69-3*, Pub. by Pushcart Pr) Norton.

Appelbaum, Neil. Is There a Hole in Your Head? (Illus.). (J). (gr. k-3). 1963. 8.95 (*0-8392-3012-5*) Astor-Honor.

Appelbaum, Paul S. Almost a Revolution: Mental Health Law & the Limits of Change. 248p. 1994. text 45.00 (*0-19-506880-7*) OUP.

— Law & the Disordered: The Consequences of Reform in Mental Health Law. 1994. write for info. (*0-318-72284-4*) OUP.

Appelbaum, Paul S. & Gutheil, Thomas G. Clinical Handbook of Psychiatry & the Law. 2nd ed. 408p. 1991. 59.00 (*0-683-00237-6*) Lppncott W & W.

Appelbaum, Paul S., jt. auth. see Grisso, Thomas.

Appelbaum, Paul S., jt. auth. see Gutheil, Thomas G.

Appelbaum, Peter M. Popular Culture, Educational Discourse, & Mathematics. LC 94-46206. (SUNY Series, Education & Culture: Critical Factors in the Formation of Character & Community in American Life). 309p. (C). 1995. text 57.50 (*0-7914-2269-0*); pap. text 18.95 (*0-7914-2270-4*) State U NY Pr.

Appelbaum, Richard P. Karl Marx. (Masters of Social Theory Ser.: Vol. 7). 160p. (C). 1988. text 48.00 (*0-8039-2579-4*); pap. text 19.95 (*0-8039-2580-8*) Sage.

— S/G Sociology. 2nd ed. (C). 1997. pap. text, student ed. 21.00 (*0-673-98184-3*) Addison-Wesley.

Appelbaum, Richard P., ed. A Global Reader to Accompany Sociology: A Brief Introduction. 192p. (C). 1997. 29.40 (*0-673-97777-3*) Addison-Wesley.

— Student Guide to Sociology: Brief. 256p. (C). 1997. pap. text, student ed. 19.00 (*0-673-98395-1*) Addison-Wesley.

Appelbaum, Richard P. & Chambliss, William J. Sociology. 575p. (C). 1997. pap. 66.00 (*0-06-500813-8*) Addson-Wesley Educ.

— Sociology. 2nd ed. LC 96-24447. 704p. (C). 1997. 74.00 (*0-673-98140-1*) Longman.

— Sociology: A Brief Introduction. LC 96-35566. (C). 1997. pap. 48.00 (*0-673-98279-3*, GoodYrBooks) Addson-Wesley Educ.

Appelbaum, Richard P. & Henderson, Jeffrey, eds. States & Development in the Pacific Rim. (Illus.). 320p. (C). 1992. 49.95 (*0-8039-4034-3*); pap. 22.95 (*0-8039-4035-1*) Sage.

Appelbaum, Richard P., jt. auth. see Gilderbloom, John I.

Appelbaum, S., jt. auth. see Dore, Gustave.

Appelbaum, Samuel. Chtcheglov: Poems. 80p. 1998. pap. 10.00 (*1-878580-62-0*) Asylum Arts.

— Judea Capta. LC 94-78916. 64p. (Orig.). 1995. pap. 8.95 (*1-878580-61-2*) Asylum Arts.

Appelbaum, Stanley. The Chicago World's Fair of Eighteen Ninety-Three: A Photographic Record. (Illus.). 116p. (Orig.). 1980. pap. 9.95 (*0-486-23990-X*) Dover.

— The Hollywood Musical: A Picture Quiz Book. (Illus.). 126p. (Orig.). 1978. pap. 5.95 (*0-486-23008-2*) Dover.

— Introduction to French Poetry. 192p. 1991. pap. 5.95 (*0-486-26711-3*) Dover.

***Appelbaum, Stanley.** Nineteenth-Century French Short Stories: Contes et Nouvelles Franpcais du Xixe Siecle. LC 99-47448. 2000. pap. 9.95 (*0-486-41126-5*) Dover.

Appelbaum, Stanley, ed. English Romantic Poetry: An Anthology. LC 97-177016. 256p. (Orig.). 1998. pap. text 2.00 (*0-486-29282-7*) Dover.

— French Satirical Drawings from "L'Assiette au Beurre" LC 77-84742. (Illus.). 184p. 1978. pap. 8.95 (*0-486-23583-1*) Dover.

— Great Actors & Actresses of the American Stage in Historic Photographs: 332 Portraits from 1850-1950. (Performing Arts: Drama, Film & Dance Ser.). (Illus.). 144p. (Orig.). 1984. pap. 10.95 (*0-486-24555-1*) Dover.

— Great German Poems of the Romantic Era - Beruhmte Gedichte der Deutschen Romantik: A Dual-Language Book. LC 94-29812. (ENG & GER.). 272p. (Orig.). 1995. pap. text 8.95 (*0-486-28497-2*) Dover.

— Peg O'My Heart & Other Favorite Song Hits, 1912 & 1913. 176p. 1989. pap. 12.95 (*0-486-25998-6*) Dover.

— Scenes from the Nineteenth-Century Stage in Advertising Woodcuts. (Pictorial Archive Ser.). (Illus.). 152p. 1977. pap. 10.95 (*0-486-23434-7*) Dover.

Appelbaum, Stanley, ed. Five Great German Short Stories: Funf Deutsche Meistererzahlungen: A Dual-Language Book. LC 92-42992. (ENG & GER.). 240p. (Orig.). 1993. pap. 7.95 (*0-486-27619-8*) Dover.

— Simplicissimus: One-Hundred Eighty Satirical Drawings from the Famous German Weekly. LC 74-79171. (Illus.). 172p. 1975. 14.95 (*0-486-23099-6*) Dover.

Appelbaum, Stanley, et al, eds. Great Drawings & Illustrations from Punch 1841-1901: 192 Works by Leech, Keene, du Maurier, May & 21 Others, Vol. 901. (Illus.). 144p. (Orig.). 1981. pap. 7.95 (*0-486-24110-6*) Dover.

***Appelbaum, Stanley, tr.** Medieval Tales & Stories. 2000. pap. 9.95 (*0-486-41407-8*) Dover.

Appelbaum, Stanley & Barbaresi, Nina. Easy French Crossword Puzzles. (FRE.). (J). 1993. pap. 1.00 (*0-486-27451-9*) Dover.

Appelbaum, Stanley & Camner, James. Stars of the American Musical Theater in Historic Photographs: 361 Portraits from the 1860s to 1950. (Illus.). 170p. 1981. pap. 13.95 (*0-486-24209-9*) Dover.

Appelbaum, Stanley, jt. auth. see Hesse, Hermann.

Appelbaum, Stanley, ed. see Durer, Albrecht.

Appelbaum, Stanley, ed. see Posada, Jose G.

Appelbaum, Stanley, ed. & tr. see Kafka, Franz.

Appelbaum, Stanley, ed. & tr. see La Fontaine, Jean de.

Appelbaum, Stanley, ed. & tr. see Moliere.

Appelbaum, Stanley, tr. see Amman, Jost & Sachs, Hans.

Appelbaum, Stanley, tr. see Balzac, Honore de.

Appelbaum, Stanley, tr. see Brahms, Johannes.

Appelbaum, Stanley, tr. see Cocteau, Jean.

Appelbaum, Stanley, tr. see Gide, Andre.

Appelbaum, Stanley, tr. see Grosz, George.

Appelbaum, Stanley, tr. see Kafka, Franz.

Appelbaum, Stanley, tr. see Pirandello, Luigi.

Appelbaum, Stanley, tr. see Schubert, Franz.

Appelbaum, Stanley, tr. see Schumann, Robert.

Appelbaum, Stanley, tr. & comment see Mann, Thomas.

Appelbaum, Stanley, tr. & intro. see Hesse, Hermann.

***Appelbaum, Stephen.** Evocativeness: Moving & Persuasive Interventions in Psychotherapy. LC 00-28853. 9200p. 2000. 40.00 (*0-7657-0246-0*) Aronson.

Appelbaum, Stephen A. Effecting Change in Psychotherapy. LC 81-65786. 256p. 1995. pap. 45.00 (*1-56821-600-9*) Aronson.

— The Mystery of Healing: Journeys Through Alternative Medicine. LC 98-38700. 288p. 1998. pap. 16.95 (*1-57129-062-1*) Brookline Bks.

— A Psychoanalyst Explores the Alternate Therapies: Out in Inner Space. LC 93-73987. 552p. 1994. pap. 50.00 (*1-56821-168-6*) Aronson.

A

An Asterisk (*) at the beginning of an entry indicates that the title is appearing for the first time.

Appelbaum, Steven. Stress Management for Health Care Professionals. LC 80-25213. 487p. 1981. text 85.00 (0-89443-332-6) Aspen Pub.

Appelbaun, Stanley, tr. & intro. see De Cervantes Saavedra, Miguel.

Appelbe. C++ 2000. pap. text, teacher ed., suppl. ed. write for info. (0-13-104225-4) P-H.

Appelbee, Evelyn C. A Way of Going & Other Poems LC 99-167019. vi, 143 p. 1998. write for info. (0-9626347-5-1) Harp & Quill Pr.

Appelbee, Evelyn C. & Newton, Violette. Letters from Two Women: Poems. 25p. (Orig.). 1990. pap. write for info. (0-9626347-0-0) Harp & Quill Pr.

Appeldorn, Claudia, jt. ed. see Cammermeyer, Margarethe.

Appelfeld, Aharon. The Age of Wonders. Bilu, Dalya, tr. from HEB. LC 81-47318. 270p. 1981. reprint ed. pap. 11.95 (0-87923-798-8) Godine.

— Badenheim 1939. Bilu, Dalya, tr. from HEB. LC 80-66192. 160p. 1980. pap. 11.95 (0-87923-799-6) Godine.

— Beyond Despair: Three Lectures & a Conversation with Philip Roth. Green, Jeffrey M., tr. from HEB. LC 93-34763. 128p. 1994. 17.50 (0-88064-150-9) Fromm Intl Pub.

— The Conversion. Green, Jeffrey M., tr. LC 98-18169. 240p. 1998. 22.00 (0-8052-4153-1) Schocken.

— The Conversion: A Novel. 240p. 1999. pap. 12.00 (0-8052-1098-9) Schocken.

— For Every Sin. Green, Jeffrey M., tr. LC 89-40486. 1990. pap. 9.95 (0-679-72758-2) Vin Bks.

— For Every Sin. Green, Jeffrey M., tr. from HEB. 176p. 1996. reprint ed. pap. 11.00 (0-8021-3446-7, Grove) Grove-Atltic.

— The Healer. LC 89-25847. 224p. 1994. pap. 11.00 (0-8021-3357-6, Grove) Grove-Atltic.

— The Immortal Bartfuss. LC 87-23111. 138p. 1994. pap. 11.00 (0-8021-3358-4, Grove) Grove-Atltic.

— The Iron Tracks. Green, Jeffrey M., tr. from HEB. LC 97-27982. 1998. 21.00 (0-8052-4158-2) Schocken.

— The Iron Tracks. 208p. 1999. pap. 12.00 (0-8052-1099-7) Schocken.

— Katerina. Green, Jeffrey M., tr. LC 93-1520. (ENG & HEB.). 1994. pap. 11.00 (0-393-31110-4) Norton.

— Laish. 1999. write for info. (0-8052-4159-0); pap. write for info. (0-8052-1100-4) Schocken.

— The Retreat. Bilu, Dalya, tr. from HEB. LC 97-28634. 1998. pap. 13.00 (0-8052-1096-2) Schocken.

— To the Land of the Cattails. 148p. 1994. pap. 11.00 (0-8021-3359-2, Grove) Grove-Atltic.

— Tzili. Bilu, Dalya, tr. from HEB. 192p. 1996. reprint ed. pap. 11.00 (0-8021-3455-6, Grove) Grove-Atltic.

— Unto the Soul. Green, Jeffery M., tr. LC 97-28619. 1998. pap. 13.00 (0-8052-1097-0) Schocken.

Appelhof, Mary. Nomad Shelves. (Illus.). 14p. (Orig.). 1977. pap. 3.50 (0-942256-02-6, Flower Pr) Flowerfield Ent.

— Vermicomposting: Selected Articles. 32p. 1982. pap. 10.00 (0-942256-04-2, Flower Pr) Flowerfield Ent.

— Workshop on the Role of Earthworms in the Stabilization of Organic Residues: Proceedings, Vol. I. LC 81-65289. 340p. 1981. pap. 25.00 (0-939294-07-9, TD-772-W6-1981) Beech Leaf.

— Worms Eat My Garbage. LC 82-242012. (Illus.). (Orig.). 1982. pap. 9.95 (0-942256-03-4, Flower Pr) Flowerfield Ent.

— Worms Eat My Garbage: How to Set up & Maintain a Worm Composting System. 2nd rev. ed. LC 82-242012. (Illus.). 176p. (Orig.). 1997. pap. 12.95 (0-942256-10-7) Flowerfield Ent.

Appelhof, Mary, et al. Worms Eat Our Garbage: Classroom Activities for a Better Environment. (Illus.). 232p. (Orig.). (J). (gr. 4 up). 1993. pap., student ed. 21.95 (0-942256-05-0) Flowerfield Ent.

Appell. Atlas of Female Urologic Surgery. 1997. 125.00 (0-397-51528-6, A0738) Lppncott W & W.

Appell, Clara & Appell, Morey L. Glenn Learns to Read. 2nd ed. LC 87-62285. (Illus.). 64p. (J). (ps-2). 1987. reprint ed. pap. 8.25 (0-943501-00-8) M L Appell.

Appell, David & Balido, Paul. Hot! International: Love & Sex in 7 Languages. LC 95-78892. 320p. (Orig.). 1995. pap. 12.95 (1-885948-17-4) Babelcom.

— Hot! International/Gay: Love & Sex in 7 Languages. LC 95-78895. 320p. (Orig.). 1995. pap. 12.95 (1-885948-18-2) Babelcom.

— Hot! International/Lesbian: Love & Sex in 7 Languages. 320p. (Orig.). 1996. pap. 12.95 (1-885948-19-0) Babelcom.

— Hot! Spanish: For Guys & Girls. 2nd ed. 160p. (Orig.). 1995. pap. 9.95 (1-885948-22-0) Babelcom.

— Hot! Spanish: For Guys & Guys. 2nd ed. 160p. (Orig.). 1995. pap. 9.95 (1-885948-23-9) Babelcom.

Appell, David, et al. Hot! French for Guys & Girls: A Phrasebook for Love & Sex. (ENG & FRE.). 160p. (Orig.). 1998. pap. 9.95 (1-885948-25-5) Babelcom.

— Hot! French for Guys & Guys: A Gay Phrasebook for Love & Sex. (ENG & FRE.). 160p. (Orig.). Date not set. pap. 9.95 (1-885948-26-3) Babelcom.

Appell, Don. Lullaby. 1954. pap. 5.25 (0-8222-0707-9) Dramatists Play.

Appell, George N. & Wright, Leigh R., eds. The Status of Social Science Research in Borneo. LC H 0062.5.B66. (Cornell University, Southeast Asia Program, Data Paper Ser.: No. 109). 134p. reprint ed. pap. 41.60 (0-8357-3681-4, 203640500003) Bks Demand.

***Appell, J., ed.** Recent Trends in Nonlinear Analysis: Festschrift Dedicated to Alfonso Vignoli on the Occasion of His Sixtieth Birthday. (Progress in Nonlinear Differential Equations & Their Applications Ser.: Vol. 40). 272p. 2000. 92.00 (3-7643-6292-8, Pub. by Birkhauser) Spr-Verlag.

***Appell, Jhurgen, et al.** Partial Integral Operators & Integro-Differential Equations. LC 00-22902. (Monographs & Textbooks in Pure & Applied Mathematics). 2000. write for info. (0-8247-0396-0) Dekker.

Appell, Jhurgen, jt. auth. see Vignoli, Alfonso.

Appell, Morey L. John Dewey: Pattern for Adventuring. LC 88-63323. 83p. (Orig.). 1988. pap. 8.50 (0-943501-01-6) M L Appell.

Appell, Morey L., jt. auth. see Appell, Clara.

Appell, Paul, et al. Theorie des Fonctions Algebriques et Leurs Integrales, Vol. 1. 3rd ed. LC 72-114210. 1977. text 49.50 (0-8284-0285-X) Chelsea Pub.

— Theorie des Fonctions Algebriques et Leurs Integrales, Vol. II. LC 72-114210. text 49.50 (0-8284-0299-X) Chelsea Pub.

***Appell, Rodney A., ed.** Voiding Dysfunction: Diagnosis & Treatment. (Current Clinical Urology Ser.). 336p. 2000. 99.50 (0-89603-659-6) Humana.

Appell, Scott D. Pansies. LC 99-19215. 1999. text 15.00 (1-56799-771-6) M Friedman Pub Grp Inc.

***Appell, Scott D., ed.** Landscaping Indoors: Bringing the Outside Inside. (Twenty-First Century Gardening Ser.: Vol. 165). (Illus.). 112p. 2000. pap. 9.95 (1-889538-18-3, Pub. by Bklyn Botanic) IPG Chicago.

***Appell, Scott D., intro.** Lilies. LC 99-53774. (Illus.). 176p. 2000. 40.00 (1-56799-936-0, Friedman-Fairfax) M Friedman Pub Grp Inc.

— Tulips. LC 99-19216. (Illus.). 176p. 1999. text 40.00 (1-56799-747-3) M Friedman Pub Grp Inc.

Appell, Thomas. Can You Sing a High "C" Without Straining? 2nd ed. (Illus.). 122p. 1992. per. 39.95 incl. audio compact disk (0-9632339-2-0) Vocal Dynam.

Appella, Ettore, jt. ed. see Atassi, M. Zouhair.

Appellof, Marian, ed. Everything You Ever Wanted to Know about Oil Painting. (Illus.). 256p. 1993. pap. 29.95 (0-8230-1606-4) Watsn-Guptill.

— Everything You Ever Wanted to Know about Watercolor. (Illus.). 400p. (Orig.). (C). 1992. pap. 29.95 (0-8230-5649-X) Watsn-Guptill.

Appelman, jt. auth. see Lewin.

Appelman, Bernard R., jt. ed. see Rex, Janet.

Appelman, D. Ralph. The Science of Vocal Pedagogy: Theory & Application, Tape 3. LC 67-10107. 1967. 8.95 (0-253-35114-6) Ind U Pr.

Appelman, D. Ralph, jt. auth. see Appleman, D. Ralph.

Appelo, C. A. J. & Postma, D. Geochemistry, Groundwater & Pollution. (Illus.). 500p. (C). 1993. pap. 50.00 (90-5410-106-7, Pub. by A A Balkema) Ashgate Pub Co.

Appelqvist, Orjan, ed. see Myrdal, Gunnar.

***Appelrath, Hans-Jurgen & Ritter, J.** SAP R/3 Implementation: Methods & Tools. LC 00-28521. (SAP Excellence Ser.). (Illus.). xii, 200p. 2000. 44.95 (3-540-66863-2) Spr-Verlag.

Appels, A. D. Behavioral Observations in Cardiovascular Research. 130p. 1991. 49.00 (90-265-1036-5) Swets.

Appels, A. D. & Falger, P., eds. The Role of Psychosocial Factors in the Pathogenesis of Coronary Heart Disease, 1980. (Journal: Psychotherapy & Psychosomatics: Vol. 34, No. 2-3). (Illus.). iv, 160p. 1981. pap. 35.75 (3-8055-2286-X) S Karger.

Appels, A. D., jt. ed. see Steptoe, Andrew.

Appels, R., jt. auth. see Gustafson, J. P.

Appels, R., jt. ed. see Skerritt, J. H.

Appels, Rudi, et al. Chromosome Biology. LC 97-15812. x424p. 1998. write for info. (0-412-02601-5) Kluwer Academic.

Appelstein, Charles D. The Gus Chronicles: Reflections from an Abused Kid. 144p. (Orig.). 1994. pap. 12.95 (0-945653-05-0) A E Trieschman.

— No Such Thing As a Bad Kid: Understanding & Responding to the Challenging Behavior of Troubled Children & Youth. LC 97-74764. 304p. 1998. pap. 19.95 (0-9659836-0-9) Gifford Schl.

Appelt. Incredible Meetings for Kids. 32p. (J). (ps-1). 15.95 (0-06-028622-9); pap. 5.95 (0-06-443609-8); pap. text 15.89 (0-06-028623-7) HarpC Child Bks.

Appelt. Rain Dance. 24p. (J). (ps up). 9.95 (0-694-01291-2) HarpC.

Appelt, Douglas E. Planning English Sentences. (Studies in Natural Language Processing). (Illus.). 181p. (C). 1992. pap. text 19.95 (0-521-43803-9) Cambridge U Pr.

***Appelt, Erna & Jarosch, Monica, eds.** Combatting Racial Discrimination. 256p. 2000. 65.00 (1-85973-308-5, Pub. by Berg Pubs) NYU Pr.

***Appelt, Glenn D. & Sinclair, Jennifer.** Nature's Medicine Chest: A Sampler. (Illus.). 84p. 2000. pap. 12.95 (1-930509-00-6) Lorelei.

Appelt, Jennifer & Torey, Allysa. The Magnolia Bakery Cookbook: Baking the Old-Fashioned Way. LC 99-37070. (Illus.). 128p. 1999. 24.50 (0-684-85910-6) S&S Trade.

Appelt, Kathi. Bat Jamboree. LC 95-35383. (Illus.). 32p. (J). 1996. 15.93 (0-688-13883-7, Wm Morrow) Morrow Avon.

Appelt, Kathi. Bat Jamboree. LC 95-35383. (Illus.). 32p. (J). (ps-3). 1996. 16.00 (0-688-13882-9, Wm Morrow) Morrow Avon.

— Bat Jamboree. (Illus.). 24p. (J). (ps-3). 1998. mass mkt. 4.95 (0-688-16167-7, Wm Morrow) Morrow Avon.

— Bats on Parade. LC 98-23603. (Illus.). 32p. (YA). (ps-3). 1999. 16.00 (0-688-15665-7, Wm Morrow) Morrow Avon.

***Appelt, Kathi.** Bats on Parade. LC 98-23603. (Illus.). 32p. (YA). (ps up). 1999. 15.93 (0-688-15666-5, Wm Morrow) Morrow Avon.

Appelt, Kathi. Bayou Lullaby. LC 94-16639. (Illus.). 40p. (J). (ps-3). 1995. 16.00 (0-688-12856-4, Wm Morrow) Morrow Avon.

— Bayou Lullaby. LC 94-16639. (Illus.). 40p. (J). (ps up). 1995. lib. bdg. 15.93 (0-688-12857-2, Wm Morrow) Morrow Avon.

— Bubba & Beau. 2002. write for info. (0-15-202060-8) Harcourt.

***Appelt, Kathi.** Bubbles, Bubbles. (Growing Tree Ser.). 24p. (J). 2001. 9.95 (0-694-01458-3, HarpFestival) HarpC Child Bks.

Appelt, Kathi. Cowboy Dreams. LC 98-18316. (Illus.). 32p. (J). (gr. k-2). 1999. lib. bdg. 14.89 (0-06-027764-5) HarpC Child Bks.

— Cowboy Dreams. LC 98-18316. (Illus.). 32p. (J). (ps-2). 1999. 14.95 (0-06-027763-7, HarpTrophy) HarpC Child Bks.

— Elephants Aloft. LC 92-4231. (Illus.). 40p. (J). (ps-3). 1993. 13.95 (0-15-225384-X, Harcourt Child Bks) Harcourt.

— Elephants Aloft. LC 92-4231. (Illus.). 36p. (J). 1997. reprint ed. pap. 6.00 (0-15-201556-6, Harcourt Child Bks) Harcourt.

***Appelt, Kathi.** Hushabye, Baby Blue. (Growing Tree Ser.). (Illus.). 14p. (YA). (ps up). 2000. 5.95 (0-694-01341-2, HarpFestival) HarpC Child Bks.

Appelt, Kathi. I See the Moon. LC 96-33232. (Illus.). 24p. (J). 1997. 15.00 (0-8028-5118-5, Eerdmans Bks) Eerdmans.

— Just People & Paper - Pen - Poem: A Young Writer's Way to Begin. (Writers & Young Writers Ser.). (Orig.). (YA). 1996. pap. 11.95 (1-888842-02-4) Absey & Co.

— Just People & Paper - Pen - Poem: A Young Writer's Way to Begin. (Writers & Young Writers Ser.: Vol. 1). (Illus.). 91p. (Orig.). (YA). 1997. pap. 11.95 (1-888842-07-5, 1020) Absey & Co.

***Appelt, Kathi.** Kissing Tennessee: And Other Stories from the Stardust Dance. LC 99-50505. 128p. (YA). (gr. 7-12). 2000. 15.00 (0-15-202249-X, Harcourt Child Bks) Harcourt.

Appelt, Kathi. Oh My Baby, Little One. LC 99-6363. (Illus.). 32p. (J). (ps-k). 2000. 16.00 (0-15-200041-0) Harcourt.

Appelt, Kathi. The Packhorse Librarians. (J). 16.95 (0-06-029135-4, Wm Morrow); lib. bdg. 16.89 (0-06-029244-X, Wm Morrow) Morrow Avon.

— Red & Ginger. 2002. write for info. (0-15-201980-4) Harcourt.

Appelt, Kathi. Someone's Come to Our House. LC 98-46965. (Illus.). 24p. (J). (ps-3). 1999. 16.00 (0-8028-5144-4, Eerdmans Bks) Eerdmans.

Appelt, Kathi. The Thunderherd. (Illus.). (J). 1996. 16.00 (0-688-13263-4, Wm Morrow) Morrow Avon.

Appelt, Kathi. Toddler Two-Step. LC 98-75697. (Growing Tree Ser.). (Illus.). 24p. (J). (ps up). 2000. 9.95 (0-694-01244-0, HarpFestival) HarpC Child Bks.

— Watermelon Day. LC 95-38200. (Illus.). 32p. (J). (ps-2). 1995. 14.95 (0-8050-2304-6) H Holt & Co.

— Watermelon Day. (J). 1996. 14.95 (0-8050-4582-1) H Holt & Co.

Appelt, Kathi A. Bats Around the Clock. LC 99-15502. (Illus.). 32p. (J). (gr. k-5). 2000. 15.95 (0-688-16469-2, Wm Morrow); lib. bdg. 15.89 (0-688-16470-6, Wm Morrow) Morrow Avon.

Appelt, Krysztof, jt. ed. see Clendeninn, Neil J.

Appelt, W. Document Architecture in Open Systems: The ODA Standard. (Illus.). x, 350p. 1991. 87.95 (0-387-54539-5) Spr-Verlag.

Appendini, Kirsten A. De, see De Appendini, Kirsten A.

Appenzeller, Herb. Managing Sports & Risk Management Strategies. LC 92-72046. (Illus.). 220p. (C). 1993. 39.95 (0-89089-504-X) Carolina Acad Pr.

— Risk Management in Sport: Issues & Strategies. 1997. text. write for info. (0-89089-665-8) Carolina Acad Pr.

Appenzeller, Herb, ed. Risk Management in Sport: Issues & Strategies. LC 97-77686. 444p. 1998. per. 29.95 (0-89089-666-6) Carolina Acad Pr.

Appenzeller, Herb, et al. Sports & the Law. (Illus.). 200p. (J). 1984. mass mkt. 26.75 (0-314-79386-0) West Pub.

Appenzeller, Herb, jt. auth. see Lewis, Guy.

Appenzeller, Herb, ed. see Appenzeller, Thomas.

Appenzeller, Herb, ed. see Fried, Gil B.

Appenzeller, Herb, ed. see Fried, Gil & Miller, Lori.

Appenzeller, I., jt. auth. see Muller, Edith Alice.

Appenzeller, I., ed. see Fridman, A. M. & Gor'kavyi, N. N.

Appenzeller, I., ed. see Rohlfs, K. & Wilson, T.

Appenzeller, I., ed. see Wilson, T. & Huettemeister, S.

Appenzeller, Immo, ed. Highlights of Astronomy. (International Astronomical Union Highlights Ser.). (C). 1995. pap. text 119.00 (0-7923-3554-6); lib. bdg. 310.00 (0-7923-3553-8) Kluwer Academic.

— Reports on Astronomy: Transactions of the International Atronomical Union, Vol. XXIII-A. 1997. text 211.00 (0-7923-4540-1) Kluwer Academic.

— Transactions of the International Astronomical Union Vol. XXIIB: Proceedings of the Twenty-Second General Assembly The Hague '1994. (International Astronomical Union Transactions Ser.: Vol. 22b). 944p. (C). 1996. lib. bdg. 287.00 (0-7923-3842-1) Kluwer Academic.

Appenzeller, Immo & Jordan, C., eds. Circumstellar Matter. (C). 1987. pap. text 87.00 (90-277-2512-8); lib. bdg. 208.50 (90-277-2511-X) Kluwer Academic.

Appenzeller, L., et al, eds. Evolution of Galaxies Astronomical Observations. (Lecture Notes in Physics Ser.: Vol. 333). x, 391p. 1989. 61.95 (0-387-51315-9) Spr-Verlag.

Appenzeller, O., ed. Health Aspects of Endurance Training. (Medicine & Sport Science Ser.: Vol. 12). 1978. 41.75 (3-8055-2960-0) S Karger.

Appenzeller, O. & Oribe, E. The Autonomic Nervous System. 5th enl. rev. ed. 992p. 1997. pap. 126.00 (0-444-82761-7) Elsevier.

Appenzeller, Otto & Oribe, Emilio. The Autonomic Nervous System: An Introduction to Basic & Clinical Concepts. 5th ed. LC 97-24. (Vasc Infections of Vertebrates Ser.: 1). 922p. 1997. 258.50 (0-444-82546-0) Elsevier.

Appenzeller, Otto, tr. see Mumenthaler, Mark.

***Appenzeller, Thomas.** Youth Sport & the Law: A Guide to Legal Issues. Appenzeller, Herb, ed. LC 99-88424. 216p. 2000. pap. 19.95 (0-89089-663-1) Carolina Acad Pr.

Appere, G. Dialogue with God. 1994. pap. 4.99 (0-85234-133-4, Pub. by Evangelical Pr) P & R Pubng.

Appere, Guy. Mystery of Christ (Colossians) (Welwyn Commentary Ser.). 1984. pap. 8.99 (0-85234-180-6, Pub. by Evangelical Pr) P & R Pubng.

Apperley, Charles J. Aus Alten Zeiten (Nimrods Tagebuch) (Documenta Hippologica Ser.). (GER.). xvi, 245p. 1992. reprint ed. 50.00 (3-487-08161-X) G Olms Pubs.

Apperley, Dawn. Animal Moves. LC 98-65815. (Illus.). 12p. (J). (gr. k-3). 1999. 9.95 (0-316-04902-6) Little.

— Animal Noises. LC 98-65814. (Illus.). 12p. (J). (gr. k-3). 1999. 9.95 (0-316-04912-3) Little.

***Apperley, Dawn.** Best Tea Party Ever! (Jewel Sticker Stories Ser.). (Illus.). 24p. (J). (ps-3). 2000. pap. 3.99 (0-448-42161-5, G & D) Peng Put Young Read.

Apperley, Dawn. Nighty-Night. LC 98-66851. (Illus.). 8p. (J). (ps). 1999. 5.95 (0-316-60427-5) Little.

— Noah's Ark: With Press-Out Ark & Animals Play Set. 20p. (J). 1998. pap. 6.95 (1-86233-021-2) Sterling.

— Wakey-Wakey. LC 98-66849. (Illus.). 8p. (J). (ps). 1999. 5.95 (0-316-60504-2) Little.

Apperley, Dawn, jt. auth. see Burns, Kate.

Apperley, Mark, jt. ed. see Grundy, John.

Apperson. Dictionary of Proverbs. (Reference Library). 352p. 1997. pap. 6.95 (1-85326-321-4, 3214WW, Pub. by Wrdsworth Edits) NTC Contemp Pub Co.

Apperson, Carl, jt. auth. see Chauvin, William.

Apperson, G. L. A Jane Austen Dictionary. LC 68-24894. (Studies in Fiction: No. 34). 1969. reprint ed. lib. bdg. 75.00 (0-8383-0909-7) M S G Haskell Hse.

***Apperson, G. L., ed.** The Wordsworth Dictionary of Proverbs: A Lexicon of Folklore & Traditional Wisdom. 721p. 1999. reprint ed. pap. text 20.00 (0-7881-6532-1) DIANE Pub.

Apperson, Linda. Stage Managing & Theatre Etiquette: A Basic Guide. LC 98-20546. (Illus.). 128p. 1998. pap. 12.95 (1-56663-201-3, Pub. by I R Dee); text 24.95 (1-56663-200-5, Pub. by I R Dee) Natl Bk Netwk.

Appia, Adolphe. Music & Art of the Theatre. Hewitt, Barnard, ed. LC 62-20172. (Books of the Theatre: No. 3). 1962. pap. 19.95 (0-87024-018-8) U of Miami Pr.

Appia, Adolpho. The Work of Living Art & Man Is the Measure of All Things. 1962. 19.95 (0-87024-305-5) U of Miami Pr.

Appia, Tracy, ed. see Chekwas, Sam.

Appiah, Joseph. Joe Appiah: The Life of an African Patriot. LC 90-7386. 400p. 1990. 55.00 (0-275-93672-4, C3672, Praeger Pubs) Greenwood.

Appiah-Kubi, Kofi. Man Cures, God Heals: Religion & Medical Practice among the Akans of Ghana. LC DT0510.43.A5. (Illus.). 189p. 1981. reprint ed. pap. 58.60 (0-608-00248-8, 206075100006) Bks Demand.

Appiah-Kubi, Kofi & Torres, Sergio, eds. African Theology En Route: Papers from the Pan African Conference of Third World Theologians, December 17-23, 1977, Accra, Ghana. LC 78-10604. 224p. reprint ed. pap. 69.50 (0-8357-8792-3, 203346100086) Bks Demand.

Appiah, Kwame Anthony. In My Father's House: Africa in the Philosophy of Culture. 232p. 1992. pap. 12.95 (0-685-49797-6) OUP.

— In My Father's House: Africa in the Philosophy of Culture. 256p. 1993. pap. text 16.95 (0-19-506852-1) OUP.

***Appiah, Kwame Anthony.** Richard Wright. Gates, Henry Louis, Jr., ed. & intro. by. LC 92-45754. (Literary Ser.). 476p. 1999. 24.95 incl. 5.25 hd (1-56743-014-7, Amistad) HarperTrade.

Appiah, Kwame Anthony. Transition: The Anniversary Issue. 1998. pap. 18.00 (0-8223-6458-1) Duke.

Appiah, Kwame Anthony, et al, eds. Transition, Issue 69. 245p. 1996. pap. 10.00 (0-8223-6439-5) Duke.

— Transition 73: The White Issue, Vol. 7, No. 1. 217p. 1998. pap. 10.00 (0-8223-6442-5) Duke.

Appiah, Kwame Anthony, intro. Early African-American Classics. 608p. 1990. mass mkt. 6.95 (0-553-21379-2) Bantam.

Appiah, Kwame Anthony & Gates, Henry Louis, Jr., eds. Identities. 466p. 1995. pap. text 19.95 (0-226-28439-5); lib. bdg. 37.50 (0-226-28438-7) U Ch Pr.

Appiah, Kwame Anthony & Gutmann, Amy. Color Conscious: The Political Morality of Race. 200p. 1996. pap. text 13.95 (0-691-05909-8, Pub. by Princeton U Pr) Cal Prin Full Svc.

— Color Conscious: The Political Morality of Race. LC 96-21573. 232p. 1996. text 29.95 (0-691-02661-0, Pub. by Princeton U Pr) Cal Prin Full Svc.

Appiah, Kwame Anthony, jt. auth. see Gates, Henry Louis, Jr.

Appiah, Kwame Anthony, jt. ed. see Gates, Henry Louis, Jr.

Appiah, Peggy. Tales of an Ashanti Father. LC 88-19059. (Night Lights Ser.). (Illus.). 160p. (J). (gr. 2-6). 1989. reprint ed. pap. 7.95 (0-8070-8313-5) Beacon Pr.

Appian. Appianus - Concordantia in Appianum, 3 vols., Set. Famerie, Etienne, ed. (Alpha-Omega, Reihe A Ser.: Bd. CXXXIII). (GER.). xxx, 2150p. 1993. 800.00 (3-487-09660-9) G Olms Pubs.

— Roman History, 4 vols. No. 2-5. 19.95 (0-318-53178-X) HUP.

Appiano, Len, ed. see Carrozzi, Craig J.

An Asterisk (*) at the beginning of an entry indicates that the title is appearing for the first time.

Appic Master Planning Committee, ed. Master Planning Reprints. LC 86-72586. 164p. 1993. pap. 21.00 (*1-55822-040-2*) Am Prod & Inventory.

Appice, Carmine. The Updated Realistic Rock Drum Method. (Illus.). 76p. (Orig.). 1979. pap. 7.95 (*0-89705-012-6*) Almo Pubns.

Appier, Janis. Policing Women: The Sexual Politics of Law Enforcement & the LAPD. LC 97-9965. (Critical Perspectives on the Past Ser.). 256p. 1998. 59.95 (*1-56639-559-3*); pap. 19.95 (*1-56639-560-7*) Temple U Pr.

Appignanesi, Lisa. Dream of Innocence. 1996. pap. 5.99 (*0-614-98078-X*, Onyx) NAL.

Appignanesi, Lisa, jt. ed. see Maitland, Sara.

Appignanesi, Richard. Freud for Beginners. LC 79-1891. 160p. 1990. pap. 11.00 (*0-679-72509-1*) McKay.

***Appignanesi, Richard.** Introducing Lenin & the Russian Revolution. (Illus.). 176p. 2000. pap. 10.95 (*1-84046-156-X*) Totem Bks.

Appignanesi, Richard & Garratt, Chris. Introducing Postmodernism. LC 95-60971. (Illus.). 176p. pap. 9.95 (*1-874166-21-8*, Pub. by Totem Bks) Natl Bk Netwk.

Appius & Virginia. Appius & Virginia. LC 70-133632. (Tudor Facsimile Texts. Old English Plays Ser.: No. 47). reprint ed. 49.50 (*0-404-53347-7*) AMS Pr.

Appl. Ammonia. LC 99-211214. 310p. 1999. 179.95 (*3-527-29593-3*) Wiley.

Appl, Cynthia. Heinrich Schirmbeck & the Two Cultures: A Post-War German Writer's Approach to Science & Literature. LC 96-53922. (Studies on Themes & Motifs in Literature: Vol. 34). VIII, 160p. (C). 1998. text 39.95 (*0-8204-3737-9*) P Lang Pubng.

Applause. Womenswork. 1991. 10.95 (*0-936830-29-8*) Saurian Pr.

***Applbaum, Arthur I.** Ethics for Adversaries: The Morality of Roles in Public & Professional Life. 288p. 2000. pap. 16.95 (*0-691-05739-7*) Princeton U Pr.

***Applbaum, Arthur Isak.** Ethics for Adversaries: The Morality of Roles in Public & Professional Life. LC 98-32010. 1999. 29.95 (*0-691-00712-8*, Pub. by Princeton U Pr) Cal Prin Full Svc.

Apple Barn & Cider Mill Inc Staff. Apple Barn Cookbook, 2. LC 98-74336. 1999. 15.98 (*0-9611508-3-1*) Apple Barn.

Apple Barn Staff. Apple Barn Cookbook. (Illus.). 1983. pap. 6.95 (*0-9611508-2-3*) Apple Barn.

Apple Computer, Inc. Staff. Apple CD-ROM Handbook: A Guide to Planning, Creating, & Producing a CD-ROM. 160p. (C). 1992. cd-rom 19.95 (*0-201-63230-6*) Addison-Wesley.

Apple Computer Inc. Staff. Apple Computer Inc. Japan Inside Macintosh, Vols. 1 & 2. (C). 1988. text. write for info. (*0-201-41680-8*) Addison-Wesley.

— Apple Computer Japan Inc. Vol. 3: Inside MacIntosh. (C). 1989. pap. text. write for info. (*0-201-41681-6*) Addison-Wesley.

Apple Computer, Inc. Staff. Apple Guide Complete: Designing & Developing Onscreen Assistance. 592p. 1995. pap. text 39.95 (*0-201-48334-3*) Addison-Wesley.

Apple Computer, Inc. Staff. Apple II Guides Toolbox Reference, Vol. 3. 1088p. 1990. pap. text 39.95 (*0-201-55019-9*) Addison-Wesley.

— Apple IIgs GS-OS Reference. 528p. 1990. pap. text 28.95 (*0-201-55020-2*) Addison-Wesley.

Apple Computer, Inc. Staff. Apple IIgs ProDOS 16 Reference: Includes System Loader. 208p. 1987. 29.95 (*0-201-17754-4*) Addison-Wesley.

Apple Computer, Inc. Staff. Apple Imagewriter II Technical Reference Manual. 1987. 19.95 (*0-201-17766-8*) Addison-Wesley.

Apple Computer Inc. Staff. Apple Japan: Hypercd Stck Des. (C). 1990. pap. text. write for info. (*0-201-50974-1*) Addison-Wesley.

Apple Computer, Inc. Staff. Apple Numerics Manual. 304p. 1986. pap. text 29.95 (*0-201-17741-2*) Addison-Wesley.

Apple Computer Inc. Staff. Apple II & Apple IIc Technical Reference Manual. 2nd ed. 1987. text 24.95 (*0-201-17752-8*) Addison-Wesley.

Apple Computer, Inc. Staff. Apple IIgs Hardware Reference. 256p. 1987. 24.95 (*0-201-17743-9*) Addison-Wesley.

— Apple IIgs Hardware Reference. 2nd ed. 1989. pap. text 26.95 (*0-201-52389-2*) Addison-Wesley.

— AppleScript Finder Guide. LC 94-16208. 176p. (C). 1994. pap. text 19.95 (*0-201-40910-0*) Addison-Wesley.

— AppleScript Scripting Additions Guide: English Dialect. LC 93-40357. 144p. (C). 1993. pap. text 18.95 (*0-201-40736-1*) Addison-Wesley.

— BASIC Programming with ProDOS. 296p. 1985. pap. text 29.95 (*0-201-17721-8*) Addison-Wesley.

— Cyberdog Programmer's Kit. LC 96-15566. 416p. (C). 1996. pap. text 39.95 (*0-201-18375-7*) Addison-Wesley.

Apple Computer Inc. Staff. Demystifying Multimedia. 1994. pap. write for info. (*0-201-62625-X*) Addison-Wesley.

— Designing Cards & Drivers. 2nd ed. (C). 1992. pap. text. write for info. (*0-201-55667-5*) Addison-Wesley.

Apple Computer, Inc. Staff. Designing Cards & Drivers for the Macintosh Family. 3rd ed. 672p. (C). 1992. pap. text 29.95 (*0-201-60855-3*) Addison-Wesley.

— Elec Gd Mac Hum Interfc. (C). 1994. pap. 49.95 incl. cd-rom (*0-201-40916-X*) Addison-Wesley.

— Gt Mac Family Hardware. 2nd ed. 560p. (C). 1990. pap. text 26.95 (*0-201-52405-8*) Addison-Wesley.

— Guide to Macintosh Software Localization. 352p. (C). 1992. pap. text 24.95 (*0-201-60856-1*) Addison-Wesley.

— Human Interface Guidelines: The Apple Desktop Interface. (Apple Technical Library). 1987. pap. text 14.95 (*0-201-17753-6*) Addison-Wesley.

— Hypercard IIgs Script Language Guide. 432p. 1991. pap. text 24.95 (*0-201-57766-6*) Addison-Wesley.

— Hypercard IIgs Script Language Guide. 2nd ed. 1990. pap. 26.95 (*0-201-57081-5*) Addison-Wesley.

— Hypercard Script Language Guide. 320p. 1988. 22.95 (*0-201-17632-7*) Addison-Wesley.

Apple Computer Inc. Staff. Hypercard Script Language Guide: Japanese Edition. 2nd ed. (JPN.). (C). 1992. pap. text. write for info. (*0-201-55671-5*) Addison-Wesley.

Apple Computer, Inc. Staff. Image Writer II Technical Reference Manual. write for info. (*0-318-60212-1*) Addison-Wesley.

Apple Computer Inc. Staff. Inside Appletalk: Japanese Edition. 2nd ed. (JPN.). (C). 1992. pap. text. write for info. (*0-201-55672-3*) Addison-Wesley.

Apple Computer, Inc. Staff. Inside Macintosh, Vols. I-III. 1240p. 1985. text 79.95 (*0-201-17737-4*) Addison-Wesley.

— Inside Macintosh: AOCE Application Interfaces. LC 94-16207. 1376p. 1994. pap. text 44.95 (*0-201-40848-1*) Addison-Wesley.

— Inside Macintosh: AOCE Service Access Modules. LC 94-7195. 480p. (C). 1994. pap. text 29.95 (*0-201-40846-5*) Addison-Wesley.

— Inside Macintosh: Devices. 2nd ed. 560p. (C). 1994. pap. text 29.95 (*0-201-62271-8*) Addison-Wesley.

— Inside Macintosh: Files. 2nd ed. 544p. (C). 1992. pap. text 29.95 (*0-201-63244-6*) Addison-Wesley.

— Inside Macintosh: Interapplication Communication. 1008p. (C). 1993. pap. text 36.95 (*0-201-62200-9*) Addison-Wesley.

— Inside Macintosh: Networking. 2nd ed. 592p. (C). 1994. pap. text 29.95 (*0-201-62269-6*) Addison-Wesley.

Apple Computer, Inc. Staff. Inside Macintosh: Opendoc Programmer's Guide. 688p. 1995. pap. text 44.95 (*0-201-47954-0*) Addison-Wesley.

Apple Computer, Inc. Staff. Inside Macintosh: Operating System Utilities. 2nd ed. 400p. (C). 1994. pap. text 28.95 (*0-201-62270-X*) Addison-Wesley.

— Inside Macintosh: PowerPC Numerics. LC 93-51248. 352p. (C). 1994. pap. text 28.95 (*0-201-40728-0*) Addison-Wesley.

— Inside Macintosh: QuickDraw GX Graphics. LC 94-1843. 672p. (C). 1994. pap. text 31.95 (*0-201-40673-X*) Addison-Wesley.

— Inside Macintosh: QuickDraw GX Objects. 656p. (C). 1994. pap. text 31.95 (*0-201-40675-6*) Addison-Wesley.

— Inside Macintosh: QuickDraw GX Printing. LC 94-17336. 416p. (C). 1994. pap. text 28.95 (*0-201-40677-2*) Addison-Wesley.

— Inside Macintosh: QuickDraw GX Printing Extensions & Drivers. LC 93-49875. 512p. (C). 1994. pap. text 29.95 (*0-201-40678-0*) Addison-Wesley.

— Inside Macintosh: QuickDraw GX Programmer's Overview. 304p. (C). 1994. pap. text 24.95 (*0-201-40847-3*) Addison-Wesley.

— Inside Macintosh: QuickTime. 736p. (C). 1993. pap. text 29.95 (*0-201-62201-7*) Addison-Wesley.

— Inside Macintosh: Sound. 2nd ed. 512p. (C). 1994. pap. text 29.95 (*0-201-62272-6*) Addison-Wesley.

— Inside Macintosh: X-Ref. 3rd ed. 320p. (C). 1995. pap. text 19.95 (*0-201-48330-0*) Addison-Wesley.

— Inside the Macintosh Communications Toolbox. 368p. (C). 1991. pap. text 26.95 (*0-201-57775-5*) Addison-Wesley.

— Laserwriter Reference. 184p. (C). 1988. 19.95 (*0-201-19258-6*) Addison-Wesley.

— MacBugs Reference & DeBugging Guide: For MacBugs Version 6.2. 464p. (C). 1991. pap. text 26.95 (*0-201-56767-9*) Addison-Wesley.

— Macintosh Human Interface Guidelines. 416p. (C). 1992. pap. text 29.95 (*0-201-62216-5*) Addison-Wesley.

— MacIntosh Technology in the Common Hardware Reference Platform. 224p. (C). 1995. pap. text 43.95 (*1-55860-393-X*) Morgan Kaufmann.

— Macintosh User Reference. 1994. pap. text. write for info. (*0-201-62279-3*) Addison-Wesley.

— Macsbug Reference & Debugging Guide: For Macsbug 6.2. 1991. pap. 34.95 incl. disk (*0-201-56768-7*) Addison-Wesley.

— Making It Macintosh. (C). 1993. pap. 39.95 incl. cd-rom (*0-201-62626-8*) Addison-Wesley.

Apple Computer, Inc. Staff. Newton Programmer's Guide. 944p. 1996. pap. text 50.95 (*0-201-47947-8*) Addison-Wesley.

Apple Computer, Inc. Staff. Newton 2.0 User Interface Guidelines. LC 96-20168. 320p. (C). 1996. pap. text 29.95 (*0-201-48838-8*) Addison-Wesley.

— OpenDoc Cookbook. 208p. (C). 1996. pap. text 24.95 (*0-201-47956-7*) Addison-Wesley.

— PRODOS 8TECH REF MNL DSK. 1985. 29.95 (*0-201-17757-9*) Addison-Wesley.

— Resedit Reference. 192p. 1991. pap. 29.95 incl. disk (*0-201-57768-2*) Addison-Wesley.

— ResEdit Reference: For ResEdit Version 2.1. 192p. (C). 1991. pap. text 19.95 (*0-201-57767-4*) Addison-Wesley.

Apple Computer Inc. Staff. Resedit Reference 2.1: Japanese Edition. 2nd ed. (JPN.). (C). 1992. pap. text. write for info. (*0-201-55682-0*) Addison-Wesley.

Apple Computer, Inc. Staff. Speaking of Networks: A Glossary for Network Users. 224p. 1989. pap. 14.95 (*0-201-51761-2*) Addison-Wesley.

— Technical Introduction to the Apple IIgs. 160p. 1987. pap. 9.95 (*0-201-17742-0*) Addison-Wesley.

— Technical Introduction to the Macintosh Family. (Illus.). 160p. 1987. pap. 19.95 (*0-201-17765-X*) Addison-Wesley.

— 3D Graphics Programming: Macintosh. 496p. 1995. pap. 39.95 incl. cd-rom (*0-201-48926-0*) Addison-Wesley.

Apple Computer, Inc. Staff, et al. PowerPC Microprocessor Common Hardware Reference Platform: A System Architecture. LC 95-49032. 309p. (C). 1996. pap. text 43.95 (*1-55860-394-8*) Morgan Kaufmann.

Apple Computer Staff. Advanced Color Imaging on the Mac OS. 352p. 1995. pap. 36.95 (*0-201-48949-X*) Pearson Custom.

Apple Computers Inc. Staff. Apple Inside MacIntosh: Quicktime Components (Japanese Edition) (JPN.). (C). 1994. pap. text. write for info. (*0-201-42074-0*) Addison-Wesley.

— Apple Inside MacIntosh: Text (Japanese Edition) (JPN.). (C). 1994. pap. text. write for info. (*0-201-42075-9*) Addison-Wesley.

Apple, D. J., jt. auth. see Naumann, Gottfried O.

Apple, Daniel K., et al, eds. Learning Through Problem Solving. (Illus.). 394p. (C). 1992. pap. text 40.00 (*1-878437-20-8*) Pac Crest Soft.

Apple, Daniel K. & Merten, Cyndie. Math & Graphing Skills. 89p. (C). 1992. 20.00 incl. 3.5 hd (*0-87843-721-5*) Pac Crest Soft.

Apple, Daniel K. & PCS Associates Staff. Faculty PC: SOLVE, 3 vols., Set. (Orig.). (C). 1990. pap. text 60.00 (*1-878437-35-6*) Pac Crest Soft.

Apple, Daniel K., jt. auth. see PCS Associates Staff.

Apple, Daniel K., ed. see Krumsieg, Karl & Baehr, Marie.

Apple, Daniel K., ed. see Marten, Cyndie.

Apple, David, compiled by. I Take Thee to Be My Spouse: Bible Study for Newlyweds. 142p. 1992. pap. text 9.95 (*0-7673-2552-4*, LifeWay Press) LifeWay Christian.

Apple, David F., Jr. Physical Fitness: A Guide for Individuals with Spinal Cord Injury. (Illus.). 110p. (Orig.). 1996. pap. text 30.00 (*0-7881-3364-0*) DIANE Pub.

Apple, David F., Jr. & Hayes, Wilson C., eds. Prevention of Falls & Hip Fractures in the Elderly. 148p. 1994. pap. 45.00 (*0-89203-101-8*) Amer Acad Ortho Surg.

Apple, David J. & Rabb. Ocular Pathology. 5th ed. LC 97-41914. (Illus.). 718p. (C). (gr. 13). 1997. text 189.00 (*0-8151-0592-4*, 27523) Mosby Inc.

***Apple, David J., et al.** Foldable Intraocular Lenses: Clinicopathologic Correlations & Complications. (Illus.). 300p. 2000. 95.00 (*1-55642-435-3*) SLACK Inc.

Apple, Gary, jt. see Kauffman, Dorothy.

Apple, Glenn R., jt. auth. see Heyl, Richard E.

Apple, Hope, jt. auth. see Jacob, Merle A.

Apple, Hope, jt. auth. see Jacob, Merle L.

Apple, Jacki. Doing It Right in L. A. Self-Producing for the Performing Artist. Durland, Steven, ed. LC 90-82053. (Illus.). 136p. (Orig.). 1990. pap., wbk. ed. 12.00 (*0-937122-13-0*) Fringe Fest LA.

Apple, James G., et al. Manual for Cooperation Between State & Federal Courts. 251p. (C). 1998. pap. text 35.00 (*0-7881-7472-X*) DIANE Pub.

Apple, James M. Plant Layout & Materials Handling. LC 90-48718. 496p. (C). 1991. reprint ed. lib. bdg. 59.50 (*0-89464-545-5*) Krieger.

Apple, Jody L. Hermeneutical Agnosticism: A Critique of Subjectivism in Biblical Interpretation. LC 84-62067. 195p. (Orig.). 1985. pap. 7.95 (*0-931247-00-4*) New Testament Christ Pr.

Apple, Karen, et al. Master Plan for the City of Litchfield Park. (Illus.). 105p. 1993. pap. text 100.00 (*1-884320-04-X*); pap. text 35.00 (*1-884320-03-1*) ASU Herberger Ctr.

Apple, Lindsey. Cautious Rebel: A Biography of Susan Clay Sawitzky. LC 97-3112. (Illus.). 360p. 1997. 35.00 (*0-87338-579-9*) Kent St U Pr.

Apple, Lindsey, et al, eds. Scott County, Kentucky: A History. LC 93-87203. 496p. 1993. text 28.50 (*0-9639910-0-0*) Scott County Hist.

Apple, Loyal E. & May, Marianne. Distance Vision & Perceptual Training: A Concept for Use in the Mobility Training of Low Vision Clients. LC 70-155919. 23p. reprint ed. pap. 30.00 (*0-608-16856-4*, 202734600055) Bks Demand.

Apple, M. Sue. Principles & Practice of Interventional Cardiology. LC 99-38188. 380p. 1998. pap. text 42.95 (*0-7817-1020-0*) Lppncott W & W.

Apple, Mali, ed. see Bloomer, Anne M.

Apple, Mali, ed. see Charles, R., et al.

Apple, Mali, ed. see Lappan, Glenda, et al.

Apple, Mali, ed. see Marks-Tarlow, Terry.

Apple, Mali, ed. see McIntosh, Margaret E. & Draper, Roni J.

Apple, Mali, ed. see Rockwell, Robert E., et al.

Apple, Mali, ed. see Winnett, David A., et al.

Apple, Margot. Brave Martha. LC 97-42616. (Illus.). 32p. (J). (gr. k-3). 1999. 15.00 (*0-395-59422-7*) HM.

Apple, Margot, et al. Read . . . Set . . . Read & Laugh: A Funny Treasury for Beginning Readers. LC 94-32535. 144p. (J). (ps-3). 1995. 17.95 (*0-385-32119-8*) BDD Bks Young Read.

Apple, Margot, jt. auth. see Crunk, Tony.

Apple, Margot, jt. auth. see Shaw, Nancy.

***Apple, Mary.** A Maze of Secrets. 2000. mass mkt. 5.96 (*1-55279-004-5*) Picasso Publ.

Apple, Max. I Love Gootie: My Grandmother's Story. LC 97-32318. 244p. 1998. 24.00 (*0-446-52074-8*, Pub. by Warner Bks) Little.

***Apple, Max.** I Love Gootie: My Grandmother's Story. 256p. 2000. mass mkt. 13.95 (*0-446-67597-0*) Warner Bks.

Apple, Max. I Love Gootie: My Grandmother's Story. large type ed. LC 98-20074. 340p. 1998. 26.95 (*0-7838-0274-9*, G K Hall Lrg Type) Mac Lib Ref.

— Roommates: My Grandfather's Story. 256p. 1995. mass mkt. 5.99 (*0-446-60200-0*, Pub. by Warner Bks) Little.

— Roommates: My Grandfather's Story. large type ed. LC 94-39795. 312p. 1995. pap. 19.95 (*0-7862-0366-8*) Thorndike Pr.

***Apple, Michael.** The Hamlyn Encyclopedia of Family Health: Diagnosis & Treatments for More Than 2000 Ailments, Using Orthodox & Complimentary Medicine. (Illus.). 2000. 45.00 (*0-600-59254-5*, Pub. by Hamlyn Publishing Group Ltd) Sterling.

Apple, Michael W. Cultural Politics & Education. LC 95-36212. (John Dewey Lectures: Vol. 5). 176p. (C). 1996. text 40.00 (*0-8077-3504-3*); pap. text 18.95 (*0-8077-3503-5*) Tchrs Coll.

— Education & Power. 2nd rev. ed. LC 95-541. 248p. (C). 1995. pap. 19.99 (*0-415-91310-1*) Routledge.

— Education & Power: Reproduction & Contradiction in Education. LC 81-19920. 218p. 1982. 29.50 (*0-7100-0977-1*, Routledge Thoemms); pap. 10.95 (*0-7448-0030-7*, Routledge Thoemms) Routledge.

— Ideology & Curriculum. 2nd rev. ed. 224p. (C). 1990. pap. 20.99 (*0-415-90266-5*, A4281) Routledge.

— Official Knowledge: Democratic Education in a Conservative Age. LC 92-35829. 240p. (C). (gr. 13). 1993. pap. 19.99 (*0-415-90749-7*, B0262) Routledge.

***Apple, Michael W.** Power, Meaning & Identity: Essays in Critical Educational Studies. LC 98-53525. (Counterpoints Ser.: Vol. 109). ix, 252p. (C). 1999. pap. text 29.95 (*0-8204-4427-8*) P Lang Pubng.

Apple, Michael W. Teachers & Texts: A Political Economy of Class & Gender Relations in Education. 272p. (C). 1988. pap. 20.99 (*0-415-90074-3*) Routledge.

Apple, Michael W. & Beane, James A., eds. Democratic Schools. LC 95-7784. 1995. pap. 17.95 (*0-87120-241-7*, 195052) ASCD.

Apple, Michael W. & Christian-Smith, Linda K. The Politics of the Textbook. 296p. (C). 1991. pap. 17.99 (*0-415-90223-1*) Routledge.

Apple, Michael W., et al. Educational Evaluation: Analysis & Responsibility. LC 73-17611. 1974. 39.00 (*0-8211-0011-4*) McCutchan.

Apple, Michael W., jt. ed. see Beyer, Landon E.

Apple, Michael W., jt. ed. see Bromley, Hank.

Apple, Michael W., jt. ed. see Carlson, Dennis.

Apple Press Staff & Fisher, Charles, eds. Education & Technology: Reflections on a Decade of Experience in the Classroom. LC 96-10105. (Education Ser.). 350p. 1996. 29.95 (*0-7879-0238-1*) Jossey-Bass.

Apple Press Staff & Gooden, Andrea. Computers in the Classroom: How Teachers & Students Are Using Technology to Transfrom Learning. 1996. 26.00 (*0-7879-0262-4*) Jossey-Bass.

Apple, Rima & Golden, Janet L., eds. Mothers & Motherhood: Readings in American History. LC 97-15670. (Women & Health Ser.). 1997. pap. text 21.95 (*0-8142-0739-1*) Ohio St U Pr.

Apple, Rima D. Mothers & Medicine: A Social History of Infant Feeding, 1890-1950. LC 87-40137. (Wisconsin Publications in the History of Science & Medicine). (Illus.). 280p. 1987. pap. text 18.95 (*0-299-11484-8*) U of Wis Pr.

— Vitamania: Vitamins in American Culture. LC 95-43281. (Health & Medicine in American Society Ser.). (Illus.). 280p. (C). 1996. pap. text 18.95 (*0-8135-2278-1*) Rutgers U Pr.

Apple, Rima D., ed. Women, Health & Medicine in America: A Historical Handbook. LC 90-2719. 600p. 1990. text 20.00 (*0-8240-8447-0*, 483) Garland.

— Women, Health, & Medicine in America: A Historical Handbook. LC 91-20496. (Illus.). 580p. (Orig.). 1992. reprint ed. pap. text 18.95 (*0-8135-1766-4*) Rutgers U Pr.

Apple, Rima D. & Golden, Janet L., eds. Mothers & Motherhood: Readings in American History. LC 97-15670. (Women & Health Ser.). 605p. 1997. text 60.00 (*0-8142-0738-3*) Ohio St U Pr.

Apple, Russell A., ed. see Nordhoff, Charles.

Apple, Terri. Making Money in Voice-Overs: Winning Strategies to a Successful Career in Commercials, Cartoons & Radio. LC 98-45809. 225p. 1998. pap. 16.95 (*1-58065-011-2*, Pub. by Lone Eagle Pub) Natl Bk Netwk.

Apple Tree Graphics Staff, ed. see Egge, Joe.

Apple, W. Michael & Weis, Lois, eds. Ideology & Practice in Schooling. 320p. 1983. pap. 22.95 (*0-87722-313-0*) Temple U Pr.

Apple, Wynolia C., jt. auth. see Chandler, Lizzie G.

Applebaum & Diamond, eds. The Impact of Gender on Transference & Countertransference. (Psychoanalytic Inquiry Ser.: Vol. 13, No. 2). 1993. 20.00 (*0-88163-943-5*) Analytic Pr.

Applebaum, Charles, jt. auth. see Schachter, Robert C.

Applebaum, David. Probability & Information: An Integrated Approach. (Illus.). 225p. (C). 1996. text 74.95 (*0-521-55507-8*); pap. text 26.95 (*0-521-55528-0*) Cambridge U Pr.

— Vision of Hume. 144p. 1996. pap. 10.95 (*1-85230-850-8*, Pub. by Element MA) Penguin Putnam.

— Vision of Kant. (Element Masters of Philosophy Ser.). 1995. pap. 10.95 (*1-85230-624-6*, Pub. by Element MA) Penguin Putnam.

Applebaum, Edward L., ed. Reader in Technical Services. LC 72-87717. 266p. 1983. lib. bdg. 59.95 (*0-313-24048-5*, ZRP/, Greenwood Pr) Greenwood.

Applebaum, Herbert. The American Work Ethic & the Changing Work Force: An Historical Perspective, 52. LC 97-49999. (Contributions in Labor Studies: Vol. 52). 248p. 1998. 59.95 (*0-313-30677-X*, Greenwood Pr) Greenwood.

— Colonial American at Work. LC 96-20772. 342p. 1996. lib. bdg. 49.50 (*0-7618-0431-5*) U Pr of Amer.

— Construction Workers, U. S. A., 54. LC 99-22093. (Contributions in Labor Studies: No. 54). 248p. 1999. 59.95 (*0-313-30937-X*, GM937, Greenwood Pr) Greenwood.

A

An Asterisk (*) at the beginning of an entry indicates that the title is appearing for the first time.

A

Applebaum, Herbert, ed. Perspectives in Cultural Anthropology. LC 86-19168. 614p. (C). 1987. pap. text 23.95 (0-88706-439-6) State U NY Pr.

— Work in Market & Industrial Societies. LC 83-9267. (SUNY Series in the Anthropology of Work). 315p. (C). 1984. pap. text 18.95 (0-87395-811-X) State U NY Pr.

***Applebaum, Julie.** Fun with the Family in Hawaii: Hundreds of Ideas for Day Trips with the Kids. 3rd ed. (Fun with the Family Ser.). (Illus.). 2000. pap. 12.95 (0-7627-0821-2) Globe Pequot.

Applebaum, Julie. Fun with the Family in Hawaii: Hundreds of Ideas for Daytrips with the Kids. 2nd ed. LC 98-20768. (Fun with the Family Ser.). Orig. Title: Hawaii: Family Adventure Guide. (Illus.). 256p. 1998. pap. 12.95 (0-7627-0283-4) Globe Pequot.

Applebaum, Paul S., et al, eds. Trauma & Memory: Clinical & Legal Controversies. (Illus.). 568p. 1997. text 59.50 (0-19-510065-4) OUP.

Applebaum, Robert & Austin, Carol. Long-Term Care Case Management: Design & Evaluation. LC 90-9483. 192p. 1990. 29.95 (0-8261-6430-7) Springer Pub.

***Applebaum, Robert A., et al, eds.** Assessing Satisfaction in Health & Long-Term Care: Practical Approaches to Hearing the Voices of Consumers. LC 99-42882. (Illus.). 144p. 2000. pap. text 30.95 (0-8261-1305-2) Springer Pub.

Applebaum, Samuel. The Art & Science of String Performance. LC 86-3487. (Illus.). 240p. (Orig.). 1986. pap. 16.95 (0-88284-352-4, 2336) Alfred Pub.

— String Builder Bk. 2: Violin. Proctor, Thom, ed. (Belwin Course for Strings Ser.). 32p. (C). 1960. pap. text 5.50 (0-7692-1774-5, EL01550) Wrner Bros.

— String Builder - Viola Bk. 1: Belwin Course for Strings. 32p. (YA). 1960. pap. text 5.50 (0-7692-1553-X, EL01545) Wrner Bros.

Applebaum, Samuel & Paradise, Paul, eds. The Best of Mozart, Violin II for String Quartet or String Orchestra. (YA). (gr. 6-12). Date not set. pap. 5.95 (0-7692-0342-6, EL03244) Wrner Bros.

Applebaum, Sharon, jt. auth. see Hirschmann, Linda.

Applebaum, Stanley & Barbaresi, Nina. Easy Spanish Crossword Puzzles. (SPA.). (J). 1993. pap. 1.00 (0-486-27452-7) Dover.

Applebaum, Stanley, tr. see Revault, Jacques.

***Applebaum, Wilbur.** Encyclopedia of the Scientific Revolution: From Copernicus to Newton. LC 00-25149. (Reference Library of the Humanities). 2000. write for info. (0-8153-1503-1) Garland.

Applebee, Arthur N. The Child's Concept of Story. 224p. 1997. pap. text 16.50 (0-226-02120-3, Midway Reprint) U Ch Pr.

— The Child's Concept of Story: Ages Two to Seventeen. LC 77-8309. (Midway Reprint Ser.). 219p. reprint ed. pap. 67.90 (0-608-08044-6, 206900900002) Bks Demand.

— Contexts for Learning to Write: Studies of Secondary School Instruction. Farr, Marcia, ed. LC 84-6428. (Writing Research Ser.: Vol. 1). 240p. 1984. pap. 39.50 (0-89391-283-2); text 73.25 (0-89391-225-5) Ablx Pub.

— Curriculum As Conversation: Transforming Traditions of Teaching & Learning. 160p. 1996. pap. 14.00 (0-226-02123-8) U Ch Pr.

— Curriculum As Conversation: Transforming Traditions of Teaching & Learning. 1998. lib. bdg. 34.95 (0-226-02121-1) U Ch Pr.

Applebee, Arthur N., jt. auth. see Langer, Judith A.

Appleberg, Marilyn J. I Love Los Angeles Guide. 3rd ed. LC 93-20200. (Illus.). 244p. 1993. pap. 11.00 (0-02-097242-3) Macmillan.

— I Love San Francisco Guide. 224p. 1990. pap. 9.95 (0-02-041512-5) Macmillan.

***Appleberg, Marilyn J.** Romantic N. Y. 165 Romantic Things to See & Do in New York. rev. ed. 200p. 2000. pap. 12.00 (0-9677659-0-0, Pub. by Apple Ink) Koen Bk Distributors.

Applebey, George. A Practical Guide to the Small Claims Court: A Guide to Suing & Defending. 223p. 1994. pap. 150.00 (0-85459-767-0, Pub. by Tolley Pubng) St Mut.

Applebome, Peter. Dixie Rising: How the South is Shaping American Values, Politics, & Culture. LC 96-16080. 385p. 1996. 25.00 (0-8129-2653-6, Times Bks) Crown Pub Group.

— Dixie Rising: How the South is Shaping American Values, Politics, & Culture. LC 97-27787. 1997. pap. 13.00 (0-15-600550-6) Harcourt.

***Applebome, Peter.** Scout's Honor. 2001. write for info. (0-15-100592-3) Harcourt.

Applebroog, Ida, et al. Applebroog. (Illus.). 63p. 1987. pap. 20.00 (0-914661-05-1) Feldman Fine Arts.

— Ida Applebroog: Nothing Personal, Paintings 1987-1997. LC 97-24150. (Illus.). 128p. 1997. 35.00 (0-88675-052-0) Corcoran.

Appleby. Handbook for Psychology. LC 97-127559. 117p. (C). 1997. pap. text 18.00 (0-673-98455-9) Addison-Wesley.

— Programming Languages. 1991. teacher ed. 27.50 (0-07-002574-6) McGraw.

— Programming Manual: C Mini-Manual. 2nd ed. 1996. 18.25 (0-07-005320-0) McGraw.

Appleby, Amy. America's All-Time Favorite Songs: Over 200 Best-Loved Songs in One Volume. LC 95-750798. (Illus.). 398p. 1991. pap. 24.95 (0-8256-1230-6) Music Sales.

Appleby, Amy. Childrens Song Classics Library. LC 93-727717. (Illus.). 240p. 1996. pap. 19.95 (0-8256-1358-2) Omnibus NY.

— The Harp Styles of Bob Dylan. (Illus.). 80p. 1992. pap. 14.95 (0-8256-1341-8, AM87516) Music Sales.

— The Library of Children's Piano Pieces. (Library Of...). 240p. pap. 19.95 (0-8256-1455-4, AM 92874) Omnibus NY.

***Appleby, Amy.** The Library of Christmas Songs. (Illus.). 258p. (J). 1999. pap. 19.95 (0-8256-1704-9, AM948850, Pub. by Omnibus NY) Music Sales.

Appleby, Amy. The Library of Easy Guitar Classics. 238p. 1997. pap. text 19.95 (0-8256-1617-4, AMN943239) Music Sales.

— The Library of Piano Classics, Vol. 2. (Library Of...). 300p. pap. 19.95 (0-8256-1377-9, AM 91728) Omnibus NY.

— The Library of Ragtime & Early Blues Piano. LC 96-704233. (Library Of...). 240p. (Orig.). 1995. pap. 21.95 (0-8256-1458-9, AM 92877) Omnibus NY.

— Start Reading Music. (Illus.). 64p. 1992. pap. 5.95 (0-8256-1246-2, AM80219) Music Sales.

— You Can Play Piano. (You Can...Ser.). (Illus.). 92p. pap. 17.95 incl. audio compact disk (0-8256-1516-X, AM 932349) Music Sales.

— You Can Write a Song LC 96-157132. 67p. 1995. write for info. (0-7119-5211-6) Music Sales.

Appleby, Amy, compiled by. The Library of Irish Music. 239p. 1998. pap. 19.95 (0-8256-1653-0) Music Sales.

— The Library of Piano Favorites. 240p. 1997. pap. text 19.95 (0-8256-1613-1, AM943195, Amsco Music) Music Sales.

Appleby, Amy, ed. The Complete Holiday Celebration. 1994. 19.95 (0-8256-1428-7, AM91477) Omnibus NY.

***Appleby, Amy, ed.** The Library of Folk Songs. 239p. 1999. pap. text 19.95 (0-8256-1770-7, AM961521) Music Sales.

— The Piano Bench of Classical Music. 399p. 1999. pap. text 27.95 (0-8256-1769-3, AM961510) Music Sales.

***Appleby, Amy & Gibbons, Vanessa, eds.** Easiest Book of Piano Favorites. 239p. 1999. pap. text 19.95 (0-8256-1761-8, AM960399) Omnibus NY.

Appleby, Amy & Pickow, Peter. The Songwriter's Companion. (Illus.). 48p. 1992. pap. 5.95 (0-8256-1347-7, AM90164) Music Sales.

— You Can Play Harmonica. (You Can...Ser.). (Illus.). 64p. pap. 17.95 incl. audio compact disk (0-8256-1517-8, AM 932350) Omnibus NY.

Appleby, Amy & Rekon, Peter, compiled by. The Library of Songs & Arias. rev. ed. (Library Of...). 240p. Date not set. 21.95 (0-8256-1389-2, AM91735) Music Sales.

Appleby, B. L. Elsevier's Dictionary of Commercial Terms & Phrases. (ENG, FRE, GER, SPA & SWE., Illus.). 1092p. 1984. 323.00 (0-444-42270-6, I-251-84) Elsevier.

— Elsevier's Dictionary of Commercial Terms & Phrases. (ENG, FRE, GER, SPA & SWE.). 1084p. 1984. 495.00 (0-8288-9256-3, M15101) Fr & Eur.

Appleby, Brenda M. Responsible Parenthood: Decriminalizing Contraception in Canada. 320p. 1999. text 60.00 (0-8020-4374-7); pap. text 24.95 (0-8020-8189-4) U of Toronto Pr.

Appleby, Bruce C., jt. ed. see McCracken, Nancy M.

Appleby, Carol, jt. auth. see Redding, Noel.

Appleby, Charles A., et al, eds. Intelligence & Arms Control: Challenges in Strategic Nuclear Force Monitoring. 224p. (C). 1999. pap. 34.95 (0-8133-8323-4) Westview.

Appleby, David P. Heitor Villa-Lobos: A Bio-Bibliography. 9. LC 87-28042. (Bio-Bibliographies in Music Ser.: No. 9). 372p. 1988. lib. bdg. 65.00 (0-313-25346-3, AHV/, Greenwood Pr) Greenwood.

— The Music of Brazil. LC 82-13613. (Illus.). 223p. reprint ed. pap. 69.20 (0-608-08650-9, 206917300003) Bks Demand.

Appleby, Derek & McCann, Maurice. Eclipses. (Illus.). 288p. 1985. pap. 14.95 (0-85030-481-4, Pub. by Aqrn Pr) HarpC.

Appleby, Doris. Programming Languages: Paradigm & Practice. (C). 1991. text 48.50 (0-07-557904-9) McGraw.

— Programming Languages: Paradigm & Practice - Ada Mini-Manual. (C). 1991. pap. text 20.00 (0-07-002578-9) McGraw.

— Programming Languages: Paradigm & Practice - Turbo Pascal Mini-Manual. (C). 1991. mass mkt. 17.74 (0-07-002575-4) McGraw.

Appleby, Doris & Vandekopple, Julius. Programming Languages: Paradigm & Practice. 2nd ed. LC 96-36525. (Illus.). 444p. (C). 1996. pap. 64.06 (0-07-005315-4) McGraw.

Appleby, Drew C. Abnormal Psychology: Case Studies. LC 97-170068. 250p. (C). 1997. pap. text 43.00 (0-673-99662-X, GoodYrBooks) Addson-Wesley Educ.

Appleby, Ellen. Elmo Saves Christmas. (Illus.). 24p. (J). (ps-3). 1997. pap. 3.25 (0-679-88765-2, Pub. by Random Bks Yng Read) Random.

— Goodnight, Elmo. 12p. (J). 1999. 7.99 (0-679-89405-5, Pub. by Random Bks Yng Read) Random.

— The Three Billy-Goats Gruff. (Easy-to-Read Folktales Ser.). (Illus.). 32p. (J). (ps-3). 1985. pap. 2.99 (0-590-41121-7) Scholastic Inc.

— The Three Billy-Goats Gruff. (J). (ps-3). 1993. 19.95 (0-590-71393-0) Scholastic Inc.

— The Three Billy Goats Gruff. (FRE.). (J). pap. 6.99 (0-590-71770-7) Scholastic Inc.

Appleby, Ellen. Three Billy-Goats Gruff: A Norwegian Folktale. (Easy-to-Read Folktale Ser.). (J). 1984. 8.19 (0-606-03937-6, Pub. by Turtleback) Demco.

Appleby, Ellen. Trois Barbichu Les, Big Bk. large type ed. (FRE.). (J). 29.99 (0-590-71769-3) Scholastic Inc.

Appleby, Ellen. A Merry Scary Halloween. (Chubby Board Bks.). 16p. (J). (ps up). 1990. bds. 3.95 (0-671-70721-3) Litle Simon.

— Peek-a-Boo. LC 90-218986. 16p. (J). (ps-k). 1990. 3.95 (0-671-70722-1) Litle Simon.

Appleby, Ellen, jt. auth. see Benjamin, Alan.

Appleby, George & Anastas, Jeane. Not Just a Passing Phase: Social Work with Gay, Lesbian & Bisexual People. LC 97-37962. 496p. 1998. 52.00 (0-231-10322-0); pap. 29.00 (0-231-10323-9) Col U Pr.

Appleby, H. By Gods Grace Alone. 1996. pap. 3.99 (0-946462-01-1, Pub. by Evangelical Pr) P & R Pubng.

Appleby, H. J., ed. see Burroughs, Jeremiah.

Appleby, H. J., ed. see Owen, John.

Appleby, Jerry & VanDyne, Glen. The Church is in a Stew: Developing Multi-Congregational Churches. 144p. (Orig.). 1990. pap. 9.99 (0-8341-1357-0) Beacon Hill.

Appleby, John. Financing Healthcare in the Nineteen Nineties. (State of Health Ser.). 160p. 1992. pap. 37.95 (0-335-09776-6) OpUniv Pr.

— To Tell the Truth. 1997. pap. 9.99 (0-946462-42-9, Pub. by Evangelical Pr) P & R Pubng.

Appleby, John, ed. Fuel Cells: Trends in Research & Applications. 300p. 1987. 104.00 (0-89116-625-4) Hemisp Pub.

Appleby, John, ed. see Spring, Gardiner.

Appleby, Joyce. Capitalism & a New Social Order: The Republican Version of the 1790's. (Anson G. Phelps Lectureship on Early American History Ser.). 132p. (C). 1984. pap. text 16.00 (0-8147-0583-9) NYU Pr.

— Liberalism & Republicanism in the Historical Imagination. 351p. (C). 1992. 45.00 (0-674-53012-8); pap. 23.50 (0-674-53013-6) HUP.

Appleby, Joyce, et al, eds. Knowledge & Postmodernism in Historical Perspective. LC 95-35192. 600p. (C). 1995. pap. 28.99 (0-415-91383-7) Routledge.

— Knowledge & Postmodernism in Historical Perspective. LC 95-35192. 600p. (C). (gr. 13). 1995. 80.00 (0-415-91382-9) Routledge.

***Appleby, Joyce, et al.** The American Journey. LC 97-221486. (Illus.). 1998. student ed. write for info. (0-02-823218-6) Glencoe.

Appleby, Joyce, et al. The American Journey. LC 97-221486. 1998. teacher ed. write for info. (0-02-821787-X) Glencoe.

— Telling the Truth about History. 336p. 1995. pap. 13.95 (0-393-31286-0, Norton Paperbks) Norton.

Appleby, Joyce, ed. see Jefferson, Thomas.

Appleby, Joyce, ed. see Smith, Margaret B.

Appleby, Joyce O. Economic Thought & Ideology in Seventeenth-Century England. LC 77-85527. 298p. 1978. reprint ed. pap. 92.40 (0-608-02945-9, 206401100008) Bks Demand.

***Appleby, Joyce O.** Inheriting the Revolution: The First Generation of Americans. LC 99-49787. (Illus.). 320p. 2000. 26.00 (0-674-00236-9) HUP.

Appleby, Joyce O., ed. Recollections of the Early Republic: Selected Autobiographies. LC 96-48086. (Illus.). 300p. 1997. text 47.50 (1-55553-302-7); pap. text 17.95 (1-55553-301-9) NE U Pr.

Appleby, Kathleen. Paivi. (Illus.). 12p. 1999. pap. 15.00 (0-9672237-0-9, 1022) V A Pubg.

— PAIVI BEE For the Light Bos. (Illus.). 10p. 1999. ring bd. 35.00 (0-9672237-1-7, 1023) V A Pubg.

Appleby, Kristyn S. & Tarver, Joanne. Medical Records Review. 1. 3rd ed. LC 98-49309. 656p. 1998. boxed set 98.65 (0-7355-0337-0) Panel Pubs.

***Appleby, Lois, et al.** Postgraduate Psychiatry: Clinical & Scientific Foundations. 2nd ed. (Illus.). 624p. 2000. pap. 50.00 (0-7506-3503-7) Buttrwrth-Heinemann.

Appleby, Martha & Morton, Larry. Follow Me: A Self-Guide to Playing Electronic Keyboards. 40p. 1989. pap. text 19.95 incl. audio (0-8497-9346-7, WP173) Kjos.

***Appleby, Michael C.** What Should We Do about Animal Welfare? LC 99-35003. 160p. 1999. pap. text 29.95 (0-632-05066-7, Pub. by Blckwell Science) Iowa St U Pr.

Appleby, Michael C. & Hughes, Barry O., eds. Animal Welfare. LC 97-12578. 336p. 1997. pap. text 45.00 (0-85199-180-7) OUP.

Appleby, Paul H. Citizens As Sovereigns. LC 62-10727. 224p. reprint ed. pap. 69.50 (0-608-14040-6, 202237800026) Bks Demand.

Appleby, Pauline. How to Work with Dogs: A Practical Guide for Everyone. 128p. 1995. pap. 19.95 (1-85703-134-2, Pub. by How To Bks) Trans-Atl Phila.

***Appleby, Pauline.** Organizing a Conference: How to Plan & Run an Outstanding & Effective Event. (Illus.). 144p. (Orig.). 1999. pap. 19.95 (1-85703-382-5, Pub. by How To Bks) Trans-Atl Phila.

— Working with Dogs: How to Spot the Jobs & Get Qualified for Them. 2nd ed. (Illus.). 128p. (Orig.). 1999. pap. 19.95 (1-85703-468-6, Pub. by How To Bks) Trans-Atl Phila.

Appleby, R. C. Modern Business Administration. 401p. (C). 1987. 140.00 (0-7855-5687-7, Pub. by Inst Pur & Supply) St Mut.

— Modern Business Administration. 401p. (C). 1988. 100.00 (0-7855-3776-7, Pub. by Inst Pur & Supply) St Mut.

— Modern Business Administration. 401p. (C). 1989. 135.00 (0-7855-4631-6, Pub. by Inst Pur & Supply) St Mut.

Appleby, R. Scott. The Ambivalence of the Sacred: Religion, Violence, & Reconciliation. LC 99-32597. (Carnegie Commission on Preventing Deadly Conflict Ser.). 448p. 1999. pap. 24.95 (0-8476-8555-1); text 69.00 (0-8476-8554-3) Rowman.

— Church & Age Unite! The Modernist Impulse in American Catholicism. LC 90-50976. (Studies in American Catholicism: Vol. 11). (C). 1991. text 34.50 (0-268-00782-9) U of Notre Dame Pr.

— Religious Fundamentalisms & Global Conflict. Hoepli, Nancy L., ed. LC 94-70363. (Headline Ser.: No. 301). (Illus.). 80p. (Orig.). 1994. pap. 5.95 (0-87124-157-9) Foreign Policy.

Appleby, R. Scott, ed. Spokesmen for the Despised: Fundamentalist Leaders of the Middle East. LC 96-20600. 424p. 1996. pap. 19.95 (0-226-02125-4) U Ch Pr.

— Spokesmen for the Despised: Fundamentalist Leaders of the Middle East. LC 96-20600. 424p. 1996. lib. bdg. 55.00 (0-226-02124-6) U Ch Pr.

Appleby, R. Scott, jt. auth. see Marty, Martin E.

Appleby, R. Scott, ed. see Marty, Martin E.

Appleby, R. Scott, jt. ed. see Marty, Martin E.

Appleby, R. Scott, jt. ed. see Weaver, Mary J.

Appleby, Robert C. Modern Business Administration. 6th ed. 512p. 1994. pap. 52.50 (0-273-60282-9, Pub. by Pitman Pub) Trans-Atl Phila.

Appleby, Ruth. Pocket Guide to Menopause. LC 99-37388. Orig. Title: Menopause - The Common Sense Approach. 96p. 2000. pap. 6.95 (1-58091-012-2) Crossing Pr.

***Appleby, Steven.** Alien Invasion: The Complete Guide to Having Children. 2000. 17.95 (1-58234-077-3) Bloomsbury Pubg.

— The Truth about Love. 2000. 17.95 (1-58234-065-X) Bloomsbury Pubg.

Appleduck, Cosmo. American Bluegrass Country Cookbook. 100p. spiral bd. 22.95 (0-911505-08-3) Lifecraft.

— Cosmo Appleduck's Kitchen Fun Cooking School. 1984. 39.95 (0-911505-27-X) Lifecraft.

— Happy Home Cookbook. 1997. pap. 22.95 (0-911505-16-4) Lifecraft.

— Ignorance Almanac 1997-98: What You Know Ain't So. annuals 19.95 (0-911505-15-6) Lifecraft.

— Kitchen Fun Cookbook, Vol. 1. 1984. 22.95 (0-911505-13-X) Lifecraft.

— Kitchen Fun Cookbook, Vol. 2. 1984. 22.95 (0-911505-26-1) Lifecraft.

— My Cookbook . . . Where All Your Favorite Recipes Live: Do-It-Yourself Cookbook. 1982. spiral bd. 19.95 (0-911505-06-7) Lifecraft.

— Unlimited Credit . . . The Credit Builder Sourcebook. (Unlimit Your Life Ser.: Vol. 5). 19.95 (0-911505-05-9) Lifecraft.

***Applefield, David.** Frank 16/17. 1998. pap. text 14.95 (2-913053-00-9, Pub. by Anglophone) Midpt Trade.

Applefield, David. Once Removed. LC 96-931076. 1997. pap. 15.95 (0-88962-622-7) Mosaic.

— Paris Anglophone: The Directory of English Speaking Paris. 4th ed. 1996. pap. 14.95 (2-84096-046-X, Pub. by Parigramme Edits) Midpt Trade.

— Paris Inside Out: The Insider's Handbook to Life in Paris. 5th ed. LC 99-56913. 380p. 1999. pap. 19.95 (0-7627-0594-9) Globe Pequot.

Appleford, Annie. M Is for Mitten: The Michigan Alphabet Book. LC 99-33497. (Illus.). 32p. 1999. 15.95 (1-886947-73-2) Sleepng Bear.

Appleford, Steve. The Rolling Stones: It's Only Rock & Roll: Song by Song. (Illus.). 256p. 1999. reprint ed. pap. text 20.00 (0-7881-6412-0) DIANE Pub.

Applegarth. Organelle Diseases. 688p. 1997. text 150.00 (0-412-54910-7, Pub. by E A) OUP.

***Applegarth, Adrienne.** Female Sexuality: Contemporary Engagements. Bassin, Donna, ed. LC 97-34280. (Illus.). 528p. 1998. 60.00 (0-7657-0081-6) Aronson.

Applegarth, Albert C. Quakers in Pennsylvania. LC 78-63813. (Johns Hopkins University. Studies in the Social Sciences. Thirtieth Ser. 1912: 8-9). reprint ed. 27.50 (0-404-61076-5) AMS Pr.

Applegarth, Allen. Florida Fishing: Florida's Complete Saltwater Fishing Guide. Voshardt, Robin, ed. (Illus.). 176p. (Orig.). 1997. pap. 9.95 (0-941072-25-8) Southern Herit.

***Applegarth, Ginger.** Wake up & Smell the Money: Fresh Starts at Any Age & Any Season of Your Life. 384p. 2000. pap. 13.95 (0-14-028855-4) Penguin Putnam.

Applegarth, Michael. How to Take a Training Audit. 128p. (C). 1991. pap. 45.00 (0-7494-0429-9, Pub. by IPM Hse) St Mut.

Applegarth, Mike, jt. auth. see Posner, Keith.

Applegarth, Virginia & Whitaker, Leslie. Wake Up & Smell the Money: Fresh Starts at Any Age & Any Season of Your Life. LC 98-53707. (Illus.). 336p. 1999. 24.95 (0-670-87397-7) Viking Penguin.

Applegate. Elements of Medical Terminology. 1994. 46.50 incl. audio (0-8273-6552-7) Delmar.

— How to Eat Away Heart Disease & High Blood Pressure. (C). 1999. text 26.95 (0-13-918491-0, Macmillan Coll) P-H.

Applegate. Introduction to Nutrition. pap. text. write for info. (1-57259-189-7) Worth.

— Nutrition: Principles & Practices. 2002. pap. text. write for info. (0-7167-3727-2) W H Freeman.

— Nutrition for Today. 2002. pap. text, student ed. write for info. (0-7167-3954-2) W H Freeman.

Applegate. Slides to Sectional Anatomy Learning Section. 1991. 520.00 (0-7216-3239-4, W B Saunders Co) Harcrt Hlth Sci Grp.

Applegate, Adrietta A. & Applegate, Hixon. On to Oregon. 117p. 1973. 16.95 (0-87770-117-2) Ye Galleon.

Applegate, April & Overton, Valerie. The Elements of Medical Terminology Instructor's Guide. 218p. 1994. 20.00 (0-8273-6674-4) Delmar.

Applegate, April, et al. The Elements of Medical Terminology. LC 93-32985. 388p. (C). 1994. pap. 44.95 (0-8273-6406-7) Delmar.

Applegate, Bergen, tr. see Verlaine, Paul M.

Applegate, Brandon K., jt. ed. see Cullen, Francis T.

Applegate, Celia. A Nation of Provincials: The German Idea of Heimat. LC 89-20522. 273p. 1990. 55.00 (0-520-06394-5, Pub. by U CA Pr) Cal Prin Full Svc.

Applegate, Debbie. Breach of Faith. 30.00 (0-06-019473-1); pap. 17.50 (0-06-093263-5) HarpC.

An Asterisk (*) at the beginning of an entry indicates that the title is appearing for the first time.

Applegate, Edd. Journalistic Advocates & Muckrakers: Three Centuries of Crusading Writers. LC 97-11662. 227p. 1997. lib. bdg. 39.95 (*0-7864-0365-9*) McFarland & Co.

— Literary Journalism: A Biographical Dictionary of Writers & Editors. LC 96-7142. 352p. 1996. lib. bdg. 89.50 (*0-313-29949-8*, Greenwood Pr) Greenwood.

— Personalities & Products: A Historical Perspective on Advertising in America, 53. LC 97-26893. (Contributions to the Study of Mass Media & Communications: Vol. 53). 192p. 1998. 57.95 (*0-313-30364-9*, Greenwood Pr) Greenwood.

— Print & Broadcast Journalism: A Critical Examination. LC 96-14725. 224p. 1996. 57.95 (*0-275-95333-5*, Praeger Pubs) Greenwood.

Applegate, Edd, ed. The Ad Men & Women: A Biographical Dictionary of Advertising. LC 93-28040. 424p. 1994. lib. bdg. 85.00 (*0-313-27801-6*, Greenwood Pr) Greenwood.

Applegate, Edd, jt. auth. see Kelly, Gary.

Applegate, Edd, jt. ed. see Kelly, Gary.

Applegate, Edith J. The Anatomy & Physiology Learning System: Textbook. LC 93-44258. 1994. write for info. (*0-7216-6835-6*, W B Saunders Co) Harcrt Hlth Sci Grp.

— The Anatomy & Physiology Learning System: Textbook. LC 93-44258. (Illus.). 507p. 1994. pap. text 32.50 (*0-7216-6635-3*, A0242, W B Saunders Co); pap. text, wbk. ed. 17.95 (*0-7216-6638-8*, W B Saunders Co) Harcrt Hlth Sci Grp.

— The Anatomy & Physiology Learning System: Textbook. (Illus.). 1995. pap., teacher ed. write for info. (*0-7216-6636-1*, W B Saunders Co) Harcrt Hlth Sci Grp.

— The Anatomy & Physiology Learning System: Textbook. LC 99-51568. (Illus.). 545p. 2000. pap. text. write for info. (*0-7216-8020-8*, W B Saunders Co) Harcrt Hlth Sci Grp.

— The Anatomy & Physiology Learning System: Textbook, Textbook/Workbook Package. (Illus.). 507p. 1994. text, wbk. ed. 45.00 (*0-7216-5903-9*, W B Saunders Co) Harcrt Hlth Sci Grp.

Applegate, Edith J. The Anatomy/Physiology Learning System Examaster. 2nd ed. Date not set. write for info. (*0-7216-8784-9*, W B Saunders Co) Harcrt Hlth Sci Grp.

Applegate, Edith J. The Sectional Anatomy Learning System: Concepts & Applications. (Illus.). 600p. 1991. teacher ed. write for info. (*0-7216-3240-8*, W B Saunders Co) Harcrt Hlth Sci Grp.

— The Sectional Anatomy Learning System: Concepts & Applications, 2 vols. (Illus.). 1991. text 61.50 (*0-7216-3269-6*, W B Saunders Co) Harcrt Hlth Sci Grp.

Applegate, Edward C. Advertising: Concepts, Strategies & Issues. 352p. 1993. per. 34.95 (*0-8403-8345-2*) Kendall-Hunt.

Applegate, Francis. Indian Stories from the Pueblo. (Illus.). 198p. 1990. pap. 10.00 (*0-87380-153-9*) Popular E Commerce.

Applegate, Frank. Indian Stories from the Pueblos. LC 93-47398. (Illus.). 178p. 1929. reprint ed. pap. 10.95 (*1-55709-227-3*) Applewood.

Applegate, Frank G. Indian Stories from the Pueblos: Tales of New Mexico & Arizona. (Beautiful Rio Grande Classics Ser.). 198p. 1990. reprint ed. pap. 10.00 (*0-87380-138-5*) Popular E Commerce.

Applegate, Gary. Happiness; It's Your Choice: The Skill Development Theory for Successful Change. (Illus.). 1985. 15.00 (*0-9614987-0-6*) Beringer Pub.

Applegate, George. Complete Book of Dowsing: The Definitive Guide to Finding Underground Water. LC 97-33663. 256p. 1998. 24.95 (*1-86204-142-3*, Pub. by Element MA) Penguin Putnam.

Applegate, Helen. Anchor in the Storm. 142p. 1988. pap. 7.99 (*0-9615534-1-3*) YWAM Pub.

Applegate, Hixon, jt. auth. see Applegate, Adrietta A.

Applegate, Howard L. Coca-Cola a History in Photographs 1930-1969: Photographs from the Archives Department the Coca-Cola Company. LC 95-82100. (Photo Archive Ser.). (Illus.). 128p. 1996. pap. 24.95 (*1-882256-46-8*) Iconografix.

— Coca-Cola Its Vehicles in Photographs 1930-1969: Photographs from the Archives Department of the Coca-Cola Company. LC 95-82101. (Photo Archive Ser.). (Illus.). 128p. 1996. pap. 24.95 (*1-882256-47-6*) Iconografix.

Applegate, Howard L., ed. Dodge Trucks 1929-1947 Photo Archive. LC 95-77485. (Photo Archive Ser.). (Illus.). 128p. 1995. pap. 29.95 (*1-882256-36-0*) Iconografix.

— Studebaker 1946-1958 Photo Archive. LC 94-79320. (Photo Archive Ser.). (Illus.). 144p. 1995. pap. 29.95 (*1-882256-25-5*) Iconografix.

— Studebaker 1933-1942 Photo Archive. LC 94-79319. (Photo Archive Ser.). (Illus.). 144p. 1995. pap. 29.95 (*1-882256-24-7*) Iconografix.

— Studebaker Trucks 1941-1964 Photo Archive. LC 95-77493. (Photo Archive Ser.). (Illus.). 128p. 1995. pap. 29.95 (*1-882256-41-7*) Iconografix.

— Studebaker Trucks 1927-1940 Photo Archive. LC 95-77494. (Photo Archive Ser.). (Illus.). 128p. 1995. pap. 29.95 (*1-882256-40-9*) Iconografix.

Applegate, James L., jt. auth. see Waldhart, Enid S.

Applegate, James L., jt. ed. see Sypher, Howard E.

Applegate, Jane. 201 Great Ideas for Your Small Business. LC 97-52249. (Small Business Ser.). 400p. 1998. pap. 14.95 (*1-57660-050-5*, Pub. by Bloomberg NJ) Norton.

Applegate, Jeffrey S. & Bonovitz, Jennifer M. The Facilitating Partnership: A Winnicottian Approach for Social Workers & Other Helping Professionals. LC 94-49143. 296p. 1995. 55.00 (*1-56821-494-4*) Aronson.

Applegate, Jill, ed. see Petralia, Joseph F.

Applegate, John S. The U. N. Peace Imperative. 1992. 16.95 (*0-533-10113-1*) Vantage.

Applegate, Joseph P. The Eternal Privilege. 148p. (C). 1988. 45.00 (*0-7212-0778-2*, Pub. by Regency Pr GBR) St Mut.

Applegate, Joseph R. An Outline of the Structure of Shila. LC 58-13941. viii, 71p. (C). 1971. reprint ed. pap. 3.00 (*0-87950-252-5*) Spoken Lang Serv.

***Applegate, K. A.** L' Alerte. 2nd ed. (Animorphs Ser.: No. 16).Tr. of Warning. (FRE.). (J). (gr. 3-7). 1999. pap. text 12.95 (*2-07-052191-5*) Distribks Inc.

Applegate, K. A. The Alien. LC 49-245410. (Animorphs Ser.: No. 8). 159p. (J). (gr. 3-7). 1997. pap. 4.99 (*0-590-99728-9*) Scholastic Inc.

Applegate, K. A. The Alien. (Animorphs Ser.: No. 8). (J). (gr. 3-7). 1997. 9.09 (*0-606-11050-X*, Pub. by Turtleback) Demco.

Applegate, K. A. The Andalite Chronicles. (Animorphs Ser.). (J). (gr. 3-7). 1997. pap. text 4.99 (*0-590-10971-5*, Little Apple) Scholastic Inc.

Applegate, K. A. The Andalite Chronicles. (Animorphs Ser.). (J). (gr. 3-7). 1997. 11.34 (*0-606-12617-1*) Turtleback.

Applegate, K. A. The Andalites Gift. (Animorphs: No. 1). (J). (gr. 3-7). 1997. mass mkt. 4.99 (*0-590-21304-0*) Scholastic Inc.

Applegate, K. A. The Andalites Gift. (Animorphs: No. 1). (J). (gr. 3-7). 1997. 9.09 (*0-606-11052-6*, Pub. by Turtleback) Demco.

Applegate, K. A. The Android. LC 49-245380. (Animorphs Ser.: No. 10). (Illus.). 170p. (J). (gr. 4-7). 1997. pap. text 4.99 (*0-590-99730-0*) Scholastic Inc.

— The Android. (Animorphs Ser.: No. 10). (J). (gr. 3-7). 1997. 9.09 (*0-606-11047-X*, Pub. by Turtleback) Demco.

— Animorphs. (Animorphs Ser.). (J). (gr. 3-7). 1998. pap. 143.64 (*0-590-51066-5*) Scholastic Inc.

***Applegate, K. A.** Animorphs, 6 bks. large type ed. Incl. Conspiracy. large type ed. 160p. (J). (gr. 4 up). 2000. lib. bdg. 21.27 (*0-8368-2754-6*); Prophecy. large type ed. 160p. (J). (gr. 4 up). 2000. lib. bdg. 21.27 (*0-8368-2757-0*); Separation. large type ed. 160p. (J). (gr. 4 up). 2000. lib. bdg. 21.27 (*0-8368-2759-7*); 160p. (J). (gr. 4 up). 2000. Set lib. bdg. 127.62 (*0-8368-2753-8*) Gareth Stevens Inc.

Applegate, K. A. Animorphs Series Boxed Set: The Change; The Unknown; The Escape; The Warning. (Animorphs Ser.: Nos. 13-16). (J). (gr. 3-7). 1998. pap., boxed set 15.96 (*0-590-28434-7*, Apple Paperbacks) Scholastic Inc.

Applegate, K. A. Animorphs Series Boxed Set: The Invasion; The Visitor; The Encounter; The Message, 4 vols. (Animorphs Ser.). (J). (gr. 3-7). 1997. pap., boxed set 15.96 (*0-590-38187-3*) Scholastic Inc.

— Animorphs Series Boxed Set: The Predator; The Capture; The Stranger; The Alien, 4 vols. (Animorphs Ser.). (J). (gr. 3-7). 1997. boxed set 19.96 (*0-590-90725-5*) Scholastic Inc.

— Animorphs Series Boxed Set: The Secret; The Android; The Forgotten; The Reaction. (Animorphs Ser.: Nos. 9-12). (J). (gr. 3-7). 1997. pap. text 19.96 (*0-590-35020-X*) Scholastic Inc.

Applegate, K. A. Animorphs Series Boxed Set: The Threat; The Solution; The Pretender; The Suspicion. (Animorphs Ser.: Nos. 21-24). (J). (gr. 3-7). 1998. pap. text 19.96 (*0-590-28543-2*) Scholastic Inc.

***Applegate, K. A.** Animorphs Series Boxed Set: The Underground; The Decision; The Departure; The Discovery. (Animorphs Ser.: Nos. 17-20). (J). (gr. 3-7). 1998. pap., boxed set 15.96 (*0-590-28497-5*, Apple Paperbacks) Scholastic Inc.

— Animorphs Series Boxed Set: The Weakness; The Arrival; The Hidden; The Other. (Animorphs Ser.: No. 37-40). (Illus.). (J). (gr. 3-7). 2000. pap., boxed set 19.96 (*0-439-10688-5*, Apple Paperbacks) Scholastic Inc.

— The Arrival. (Animorphs Ser.: No. 38). (Illus.). 160p. (J). (gr. 4-7). 2000. pap. 5.99 (*0-439-10677-X*, Apple Paperbacks) Scholastic Inc.

— Arrival. (Animorphs Ser.: Vol. 38). (Illus.). (J). 2000. 10.34 (*0-606-18509-7*) Turtleback.

Applegate, K. A. The Attack. (Animorphs Ser.: No. 26). 145p. (J). (gr. 3-7). 1999. pap. 4.99 (*0-590-76259-1*) Scholastic Inc.

***Applegate, K. A.** Back to Before. (Animorphs: No. 4). (Illus.). 240p. (J). (gr. 3-7). 2000. pap. 5.99 (*0-439-17307-8*) Scholastic Inc.

— Back to Before. (Animorphs: Vol. 4). (Illus.). (J). 2000. 11.34 (*0-606-18513-5*) Turtleback.

— Brave the Betrayal, Vol. 8. (Everworld Ser.: Vol. 8). (Illus.). 208p. (YA). (gr. 7-12). 2000. mass mkt. 4.99 (*0-590-87854-9*) Scholastic Inc.

Applegate, K. A. The Capture. LC 49-242330. (Animorphs Ser.: No. 6). 154p. (J). (gr. 4-7). 1997. pap. 4.99 (*0-590-62982-4*) Scholastic Inc.

Applegate, K. A. The Capture. (Animorphs Ser.: No. 6). (J). (gr. 3-7). 1997. 9.09 (*0-606-10742-8*, Pub. by Turtleback) Demco.

Applegate, K. A. The Change. (Animorphs Ser.: No. 13). 162p. (J). (gr. 4-7). 1997. pap. 4.99 (*0-590-49418-X*, Little Apple) Scholastic Inc.

Applegate, K. A. The Change. (Animorphs Ser.: No. 13). (J). (gr. 3-7). 1997. 10.34 (*0-606-12619-8*) Turtleback.

— The Conspiracy. (Animorphs Ser.: No. 31). (J). (gr. 3-7). 1999. pap. 4.99 (*0-439-07031-7*) Scholastic Inc.

— The Conspiracy. (Animorphs Ser.: No. 31). (Illus.). (J). (gr. 3-7). 1999. 10.34 (*0-606-16928-8*) Turtleback.

— Deception, Vol. 46. (Illus.). (J). 2000. pap. 4.99 (*0-439-11520-5*) Scholastic Inc.

Applegate, K. A. The Decision. (Animorphs Ser.: No. 18). 168p. (J). (gr. 4-7). 1998. pap. text 4.99 (*0-590-49441-4*, Apple Paperbacks) Scholastic Inc.

***Applegate, K. A.** The Decision. (Animorphs Ser.: No. 18). (J). (gr. 3-7). 1998. 9.09 (*0-606-13138-8*, Pub. by Turtleback) Demco.

Applegate, K. A. The Departure. (Animorphs Ser.: No. 19). 159p. (J). (gr. 4-7). 1998. pap. text 4.99 (*0-590-49451-1*, Apple Paperbacks) Scholastic Inc.

***Applegate, K. A.** The Departure. (Animorphs Ser.: No. 19). (J). (gr. 3-7). 1998. 9.09 (*0-606-13139-6*, Pub. by Turtleback) Demco.

— Discover the Destroyer. (Everworld Ser.: No. 5). (Illus.). 192p. (YA). (gr. 7-12). 2000. mass mkt. 6.99 (*0-590-87762-3*) Scholastic Inc.

Applegate, K. A. The Discovery. (Animorphs Ser.: No. 20). 153p. (J). (gr. 3-7). 1998. pap. 4.99 (*0-590-49637-9*, Apple Paperbacks) Scholastic Inc.

— The Discovery. (Animorphs Ser.: No. 20). (J). (gr. 3-7). 1998. 9.09 (*0-606-13140-X*, Pub. by Turtleback) Demco.

— Elfangor's Secret. (Animorphs: No. 3). 208p. (J). (gr. 3-7). 1999. pap. 5.99 (*0-590-03639-4*) Scholastic Inc.

Applegate, K. A. The Encounter. (Animorphs Ser.: No. 3). 157p. (J). (gr. 4-7). 1996. pap. 4.99 (*0-590-62979-4*) Scholastic Inc.

Applegate, K. A. The Encounter. (Animorphs Ser.: No. 3). (J). (gr. 3-7). 1996. 9.09 (*0-606-09004-5*, Pub. by Turtleback) Demco.

— The Escape. (Animorphs Ser.: No. 15). 170p. (J). (gr. 4-7). 1998. pap. text 4.99 (*0-590-49424-4*) Scholastic Inc.

***Applegate, K. A.** The Escape. (Animorphs Ser.: No. 15). (J). (gr. 3-7). 1998. 10.09 (*0-606-12876-X*) Turtleback.

Applegate, K. A. The Experiment. (Animorphs Ser.: No. 28). 139p. (J). (gr. 3-7). 1999. mass mkt. 4.99 (*0-590-76261-3*) Scholastic Inc.

— The Exposed. (Animorphs Ser.: No. 27). 154p. (J). (gr. 4-7). 1999. pap. 4.99 (*0-590-76260-5*) Scholastic Inc.

***Applegate, K. A.** The Extreme. (Animorphs Ser.: No. 25). (J). (gr. 3-7). 1999. pap. text 179.64 (*0-439-04365-4*) Scholastic Inc.

Applegate, K. A. The Extreme. (Animorphs Ser.: No. 25). 146p. (J). (gr. 4-7). 1999. pap. 4.99 (*0-590-76258-3*) Scholastic Inc.

***Applegate, K. A.** Familiar. (Animorphs Ser.: Vol. 41). (Illus.). (J). 2000. 10.34 (*0-606-18512-7*) Turtleback.

— Fear the Fantastic. (Everworld Ser.: Vol. 6). (Illus.). 208p. (J). (gr. 7-12). 2000. mass mkt. 4.99 (*0-590-87764-X*) Scholastic Inc.

— Fear the Fantastic. (Illus.). (J). 2000. 10.34 (*0-606-18540-2*) Turtleback.

Applegate, K. A. The First Journey. (Animorphs: No. 1). 115p. (J). (gr. 3-7). 1999. pap. 4.99 (*0-439-06164-4*) Scholastic Inc.

— The Forgotten. LC 49-245390. (Animorphs Ser.: No. 11). 162p. (J). (gr. 4-7). 1997. pap. text 4.99 (*0-590-99732-7*) Scholastic Inc.

— The Forgotten. (Animorphs Ser.: No. 11). (J). (gr. 3-7). 1997. 9.09 (*0-606-11048-8*, Pub. by Turtleback) Demco.

***Applegate, K. A.** Gateway to the Gods. (Everworld Ser.: Vol. 7). (Illus.). 208p. (J). (gr. 7-12). 2000. mass mkt. 4.99 (*0-590-87766-6*) Scholastic Inc.

Applegate, K. A. The Haunted Palace. LC 93-70936. (Little Mermaid Novels Ser.). (Illus.). 80p. (J). (gr. 1-4) 1993. pap. 2.95 (*1-56282-503-8*, Pub. by Disney Pr) Time Warner.

***Applegate, K. A.** The Hidden. (Animorphs Ser.: No 39). 160p. (J). (gr. 4-7). 2000. mass mkt. 4.99 (*0-439-10678-8*) Scholastic Inc.

Applegate, K. A. The Hork-Bajir Chronicles. LC 98-7324. (Animorphs Ser.). 206p. (J). (gr. 4-7). 1998. 12.95 (*0-439-04291-7*) Scholastic Inc.

— The Hork-Bajir Chronicles. (Animorphs Ser.). 206p. (J). (gr. 4-7). 1999. pap. 4.99 (*0-590-03646-7*, Pub. by Scholastic Inc) Penguin Putnam.

— The Hork-Bajir Chronicles. deluxe ed. (Animorphs Ser.). (J). (gr. 3-7). 1998. 12.95 (*0-590-38198-9*) Scholastic Inc.

— The Illusion. (Animorphs Ser.: No. 33). (J). (gr. 3-7). 1999. pap. 4.99 (*0-439-07033-3*, Pub. by Scholastic Inc) Penguin Putnam.

***Applegate, K. A.** The Illusion. large type ed. (Animorphs Ser.: No. 33). 160p. (J). (gr. 4 up). 2000. lib. bdg. 21.27 (*0-8368-2755-4*) Gareth Stevens Inc.

Applegate, K. A. In the Time of Dinosaurs. (Animorphs: No. 2). (J). (gr. 3-7). 1998. pap. text 4.99 (*0-590-95615-9*, Apple Paperbacks) Scholastic Inc.

— In the Time of Dinosaurs. (Animorphs: No. 2). (J) (gr. 3-7). 1998. 9.09 (*0-606-13142-6*, Pub. by Turtleback) Demco.

***Applegate, K. A.** Inside the Illusion, Vol. 9. (Everworld Ser.: Vol. 9). (Illus.). 208p. (J). (gr. 8-12). 2000. mass mkt. 4.99 (*0-590-87855-7*) Scholastic Inc.

Applegate, K. A. The Invasion. (Animorphs Ser.: No 1). (Illus.). 144p. (J). (gr. 4-7). 1996. pap. text 4.99 (*0-590-62977-8*) Scholastic Inc.

— The Invasion. (Animorphs Ser.: No. 1). (J). (gr. 3-7). 1996. 9.09 (*0-606-09002-9*, Pub. by Turtleback) Demco.

— L' Invasion. (Animorphs Ser.: No. 1).Tr. of The Invasion. (FRE.). (J). (gr. 3-7). 1999. pap. text 4.99 (*0-439-05602-0*) Scholastic Inc.

***Applegate, K. A.** The Journey. (Animorphs Ser.: No. 42). (Illus.). 144p. (J). (gr. 4-7). 2000. pap. 4.99 (*0-439-11516-7*) Scholastic Inc.

— Journey. (Animorphs Ser.: Vol. 42). (Illus.). (J). 2000. 10.34 (*0-606-18860-6*) Turtleback.

Applegate, K. A. Land of Loss. (Everworld Ser.: No 2). 208p. (YA). (gr. 7-12). 1999. pap. 4.99 (*0-590-87751-8*, Pub. by Scholastic Inc) Penguin Putnam.

— The Message. (Animorphs Ser.: No. 4). 151p. (J). (gr. 4-7). 1996. pap. text 4.99 (*0-590-62980-8*) Scholastic Inc.

***Applegate, K. A.** The Message. (Animorphs Ser.: No. 4). (J). (gr. 3-7). 1999. pap. text 4.99 (*0-439-08783-X*) Scholastic Inc.

Applegate, K. A. Le Message. (Animorphs Ser.: No. 4).Tr. of Message. (FRE.). (J). (gr. 3-7). 1996. 9.09 (*0-606-10126-8*, Pub. by Turtleback) Demco.

***Applegate, K. A.** Message. (Animorphs Ser.: Vol. 39). (Illus.). (J). 2000. 10.34 (*0-606-18510-0*) Turtleback.

— The Mutation. (Animorphs Ser.: No. 36). (Illus.). 142p. (J). (gr. 4-7). 1999. mass mkt. 4.99 (*0-439-10675-3*) Scholastic Inc.

— Mutation. (Animorphs Ser.: Vol. 36). (Illus.). (J). 1999. 10.34 (*0-606-18507-0*) Turtleback.

— The Next Passage. (Animorphs: No. 2). (Illus.). 128p. (J). (gr. 3-7). 2000. mass mkt. 4.99 (*0-439-14263-6*) Scholastic Inc.

— Next Passage. (Illus.). (J). 2000. 10.34 (*0-606-18506-2*) Turtleback.

— Other. (Animorphs Ser.: Vol. 40). (Illus.). (J). 2000. 10.34 (*0-606-18511-9*) Turtleback.

Applegate, K. A. The Predator. LC 49-117690. (Animorphs Ser.: No. 5). 152p. (J). (gr. 4-7). 1996. pap. 4.99 (*0-590-62981-6*) Scholastic Inc.

— The Predator. (Animorphs Ser.: No. 5). (J). (gr. 3-7). 1996. 9.09 (*0-606-10127-6*, Pub. by Turtleback) Demco.

— The Pretender. (Animorphs Ser.: No. 23). 154p. (J). (gr. 3-7). 1998. pap. 4.99 (*0-590-76256-7*, Pub. by Scholastic Inc) Penguin Putnam.

***Applegate, K. A.** The Prophecy. (Animorphs Ser.: No. 34). 141p. (J). (gr. 4-7). 1999. pap. 4.99 (*0-439-07034-1*, Pub. by Scholastic Inc) Penguin Putnam.

— The Proposal. (Animorphs Ser.: No. 35). (J). (gr. 3-7). 1999. mass mkt. 4.99 (*0-439-07035-X*, Pub. by Scholastic Inc) Penguin Putnam.

Applegate, K. A. The Reaction. (Animorphs Ser.: No. 12). 152p. (J). (gr. 4-7). 1997. pap. 4.99 (*0-590-99734-3*) Scholastic Inc.

— The Reaction. (Animorphs Ser.: No. 12). (J). (gr. 3-7). 1997. 10.09 (*0-606-12618-X*) Turtleback.

***Applegate, K. A.** Realm/Reaper: Enter the Enchanted, Vol. 4. (Everworld Ser.: 4). 173p. (gr. 7-12). 1999. mass mkt. 4.99 (*0-590-87760-7*) Scholastic Inc.

— The Reunion. (Animorphs Ser.: No. 30). 156p. (J). (gr. 4-7). 1999. pap. 4.99 (*0-590-76263-X*) Scholastic Inc.

— Revelation. (Animorphs Ser.: Vol. 45). (Illus.). 160p. (gr. 4-7). 2000. pap. text 4.99 (*0-439-11519-1*) Scholastic Inc.

— Revelation. (Animorphs Ser.: Vol. 45). (Illus.). (J). 2000. 10.34 (*0-606-18863-0*) Turtleback.

— Search for Senna. (Everworld Ser.: No. 1). 208p. (YA). (gr. 7-12). 1999. pap. 4.99 (*0-590-87743-7*, Pub. by Scholastic Inc) Penguin Putnam.

Applegate, K. A. The Secret. LC 49-245420. (Animorphs Ser.: No. 9). 158p. (J). (gr. 4-7). 1997. 4.99 (*0-590-99729-7*) Scholastic Inc.

Applegate, K. A. The Secret. (Animorphs Ser.: No. 9). (J). (gr. 3-7). 1997. 9.09 (*0-606-11051-8*, Pub. by Turtleback) Demco.

Applegate, K. A. The Separation. (Animorphs Ser.: No. 32). 158p. (J). (gr. 3-7). 1999. pap. 4.99 (*0-439-07032-5*, Pub. by Scholastic Inc) Penguin Putnam.

— The Sickness. (Animorphs Ser.: No. 29). 152p. (J). (gr. 4-7). 1999. pap. 4.99 (*0-590-76262-1*) Scholastic Inc.

— The Solution. (Animorphs Ser.: No. 22). 152p. (J). (gr. 3-7). 1998. pap. 4.99 (*0-590-76255-9*, Pub. by Scholastic Inc) Penguin Putnam.

— The Stranger. LC 49-245400. (Animorphs Ser.: No. 7). 163p. (J). (gr. 3-7). 1997. pap. 4.99 (*0-590-99726-2*) Scholastic Inc.

Applegate, K. A. The Stranger. (Animorphs Ser.: No. 7). (J). (gr. 3-7). 1997. 9.09 (*0-606-11049-6*, Pub. by Turtleback) Demco.

Applegate, K. A. The Suspicion. (Animorphs Ser.: No. 24). (J). (gr. 3-7). 1998. pap. text 179.64 (*0-590-63052-0*) Scholastic Inc.

— The Suspicion. (Animorphs Ser.: no. 24). 155p. (J). (gr. 3-7). 1998. pap. text 4.99 (*0-590-76257-5*) Scholastic Inc.

***Applegate, K. A.** The Test. (Animorphs Ser.: No. 43). (Illus.). 144p. (J). (gr. 4-7). 2000. pap. text 4.99 (*0-439-11517-5*) Scholastic Inc.

— Test. (Animorphs Ser.: Vol. 43). (Illus.). (J). 2000. 10.34 (*0-606-18861-4*) Turtleback.

Applegate, K. A. The Threat. (Animorphs Ser.: No. 21). (J). (gr. 3-7). 1998. 10.09 (*0-606-13141-8*, Pub. by Turtleback) Demco.

— The Underground. (Animorphs Ser.: No. 17). 167p. (J). (gr. 3-7). 1998. pap. text 4.99 (*0-590-49436-8*, Little Apple) Scholastic Inc.

— The Underground. (Animorphs Ser.: No. 17). (J). (gr. 3-7). 1998. 9.09 (*0-606-13137-X*, Pub. by Turtleback) Demco.

***Applegate, K. A.** Unexpected. (Animorphs Ser.: Vol. 44). (Illus.). (J). 2000. pap. 4.99 (*0-439-11518-3*) Scholastic Inc.

— Unexpected. (Animorphs Ser.: Vol. 44). (Illus.). (J). 2000. 10.34 (*0-606-18862-2*) Turtleback.

Applegate, K. A. The Unknown. (Animorphs Ser.: No. 14). 166p. (J). (gr. 4-7). 1998. pap. text 4.99 (*0-590-49423-6*, Apple Paperbacks) Scholastic Inc.

***Applegate, K. A.** The Unknown. (Animorphs Ser.: No. 14). (J). (gr. 3-7). 1998. 9.09 (*0-606-12875-1*, Pub. by Turtleback) Demco.

— El Visitante. (Animorphs Ser.: No. 2).Tr. of Visitor. (SPA., Illus.). 192p. (J). (gr. 3-7). 1999. pap. text 4.99 (*0-439-07163-1*) Scholastic Inc.

Applegate, K. A. The Visitor. (Animorphs Ser.: No. 2). (Illus.). 144p. (J). (gr. 3-7). 1996. pap. 4.99 (*0-590-62978-6*) Scholastic Inc.

— The Visitor. (Animorphs Ser.: No. 2). (J). (gr. 3-7). 1996. 9.09 (*0-606-09003-7*, Pub. by Turtleback) Demco.

— Visser. LC 99-31359. (Animorphs Ser.). (J). (gr. 3-7). 1999. 12.95 (*0-439-08764-3*) Scholastic Inc.

— The Warning. (Animorphs Ser.: No. 16). 151p. (J). (gr. 3-7). 1998. pap. text 4.99 (*0-590-49430-9*, Apple Paperbacks) Scholastic Inc.

— The Warning. (Animorphs Ser.: No. 16). (J). (gr. 3-7). 1998. 9.09 (*0-606-13136-1*, Pub. by Turtleback) Demco.

A

***Applegate, K. A.** The Weakness. (Animorphs Ser.: No. 37). 160p. (J). (gr. 3-7). 2000. pap. 5.99 (*0-439-10676-1*, Apple Paperbacks) Scholastic Inc.

— Weakness. (Animorphs Ser.: Vol. 37). (Illus.). (J). 2000. 10.34 (*0-606-18508-9*) Turtleback.

***Applegate, Katherine.** Aaron Lets Go. (Making Out Ser.: No. 14). 176p. (YA). (gr. 7-12). 1999. mass mkt. 3.99 (*0-380-80870-6*, Avon Bks) Morrow Avon.

— Aisha Goes Wild. (Making Out Ser.: No. 8). 192p. (YA). (gr. 7-12). 1999. mass mkt. 3.99 (*0-380-80219-8*, Avon Bks) Morrow Avon.

— Always Loving Zoey. LC 99-95317. (Making Out Ser.: No. 22). 192p. (YA). (gr. 7-12). 2000. mass mkt. 3.99 (*0-380-81311-4*, Avon Bks) Morrow Avon.

Applegate, Katherine. Beaches Boys & Betrayal. (Summer Ser.: No. 6). (YA). (gr. 7 up). 1996. per. 3.99 (*0-671-51040-1*) PB.

***Applegate, Katherine.** Ben Takes a Chance. (Making Out Ser.: No. 11). 192p. (YA). (gr. 7-12). 1999. mass mkt. 3.99 (*0-380-80867-6*, Avon Bks) Morrow Avon.

— Ben's in Love. (Making Out Ser.: No. 4). 208p. (YA). (gr. 7-12). 1998. mass mkt. 3.99 (*0-380-80214-7*, Avon Bks) Morrow Avon.

Applegate, Katherine. The Boyfriend Mix-Up. LC 93-72888. (Little Mermaid Novels Ser.: No. 10). (Illus.). 80p. (J). (gr. 1-4). 1994. pap. 3.50 (*1-56282-642-5*, Pub. by Disney Pr) Little.

— Christmas with All the Trimmings: Original Stories & Crafts from Mickey Mouse & Friends. LC 93-74420. (Illus.). 64p. (J). 1994. 12.95 (*0-7868-3003-4*, Pub. by Disney Pr) Little.

***Applegate, Katherine.** Claire Can't Lose. (Making Out Ser.: No. 12). 176p. (YA). (gr. 7-12). 1999. mass mkt. 3.99 (*0-380-80868-4*, Avon Bks) Morrow Avon.

— Claire Gets Caught. (Making Out Ser.: No. 5). 208p. (YA). (gr. 7-12). 1998. mass mkt. 3.99 (*0-380-80215-5*, Avon Bks) Morrow Avon.

Applegate, Katherine. Climb Aboard If You Dare! Stories from the Pirates of the Caribbean. (Illus.). 80p. (J). (gr. 2-6). 1996. pap. 3.50 (*0-7868-4061-7*, Pub. by Disney Pr) Time Warner.

— Climb Aboard If You Dare: Stories from the Pirates of the Caribbean. (Illus.). 80p. (J). (gr. 2-6). 1996. lib. bdg. 13.89 (*0-7868-5033-7*, Pub. by Disney Pr) Little.

***Applegate, Katherine.** Don't Forget Lara. LC 99-96356. (Making Out Ser.: No. 25). 176p. (YA). (gr. 7-12). 2000. mass mkt. 3.99 (*0-380-81529-X*, Avon Bks) Morrow Avon.

— Don't Tell Zoey. (Making Out Ser.: No. 13). 176p. (YA). (gr. 7-12). 1999. mass mkt. 3.99 (*0-380-80869-2*, Avon Bks) Morrow Avon.

— Enter the Enchanted, Vol. 3. (Everworld Ser.: Vol. 3). 169p. (J). (gr. 7-12). 1999. mass mkt. 4.99 (*0-590-87754-2*) Scholastic Inc.

— Falling for Claire. LC 99-69743. (Making Out Ser.: No. 27). 176p. (YA). (gr. 7-12). 2000. mass mkt. 3.99 (*0-380-81531-1*) Morrow Avon.

— Jake Finds Out. (Making Out Ser.: No. 2). 224p. (YA). (gr. 7-12). 1998. reprint ed. mass mkt. 3.99 (*0-380-80212-0*, Avon Bks) Morrow Avon.

Applegate, Katherine. July's Promise. (YA). (gr. 7 up). 1995. per. 3.99 (*0-671-51031-2*, Archway) PB.

— June Dreams. (YA). (gr. 7 up). 1995. per. 3.99 (*0-671-51030-4*, Archway) PB.

***Applegate, Katherine.** Kate Finds Love. (Making Out Ser.: No. 19). 176p. (YA). (gr. 7-12). 1999. mass mkt. 3.99 (*0-380-81121-9*, Avon Bks) Morrow Avon.

Applegate, Katherine. King Triton, Beware! LC 93-71030. (Little Mermaid Novels Ser.). (Illus.). 80p. (J). (gr. 1-4). 1993. pap. 2.95 (*1-56282-502-X*, Pub. by Disney Pr) Time Warner.

***Applegate, Katherine.** Lara Gets Even. LC 98-94950. (Making Out Ser.: No. 16). (Illus.). 176p. (YA). (gr. 7-12). 1999. mass mkt. 3.99 (*0-380-80872-2*, Avon Bks) Morrow Avon.

— Lara Gets Lucky. LC 99-95488. (Making Out Ser.: No. 23). 176p. (YA). (gr. 7-12). 2000. mass mkt. 3.99 (*0-380-81527-3*, Avon Bks) Morrow Avon.

— Lucas Gets Hurt. (Making Out Ser.: No. 7). 192p. (YA). (gr. 7-12). 1998. mass mkt. 3.99 (*0-380-80217-1*, Avon Bks) Morrow Avon.

— Never Trust Lara. LC 99-94488. (Making Out Ser.: No. 20). 176p. (YA). (gr. 7-12). 2000. mass mkt. 3.99 (*0-380-81309-2*, Avon Bks) Morrow Avon.

— Nina Shapes Up. (Making Out Ser.: No. 10). 192p. (YA). (gr. 7-12). 1999. mass mkt. 3.99 (*0-380-80743-2*, Avon Bks) Morrow Avon.

— Nina Won't Tell. (Making Out Ser.: No. 3). 224p. (YA). (gr. 7-12). 1998. reprint ed. mass mkt. 3.99 (*0-380-80213-9*, Avon Bks) Morrow Avon.

— Now Zoey's Alone. LC 99-96352. (Making Out Ser.: No. 24). 176p. (YA). (gr. 7-12). 2000. mass mkt. 5.95 (*0-380-81528-1*, Avon Bks) Morrow Avon.

Applegate, Katherine. Rays, Romance & Rivalry, vol. 5. (Summer Ser.). (YA). (gr. 7 up). 1996. per. 3.99 (*0-671-51039-8*) PB.

— Sand, Surf & Seduction. (Summer Ser.: No. 4). (J). (gr. 7 up). 1996. mass mkt. 3.99 (*0-671-51037-1*) S&S Trade.

— Sharing Sam. (Love Stories Ser.). 192p. (YA). (gr. 7-12). 1995. mass mkt. 4.50 (*0-553-56660-1*) Bantam.

— Summer Special Edition: Spring Break Special Edition. (YA). (gr. 7 up). 1996. per. 3.99 (*0-671-51041-X*, Archway) PB.

— Summer: August Magic. (YA). (gr. 7 up). 1995. per. 3.99 (*0-671-51032-0*, Archway) PB.

— Summer Special Christmas Edition. 208p. (YA). (gr. 7 up). 1996. mass mkt. 3.99 (*0-671-51042-8*) PB.

— Tales from Agrabah: Seven Original Stories of Aladdin & Jasmine. LC 94-71484. (Illus.). 96p. (J). (gr. 1-4). 1995. 14.95 (*0-7868-3023-9*, Pub. by Disney Pr); 14.89 (*0-7868-5038-8*, Pub. by Disney Pr) Little.

***Applegate, Katherine.** Trouble with Aaron. LC 99-95192. (Making Out Ser.: No. 21). 176p. (YA). (gr. 7-12). 2000. mass mkt. 3.99 (*0-380-81310-6*) Morrow Avon.

— Two-Timing Aisha. (Making Out Ser.: No. 17). 176p. (YA). (gr. 7-12). 1999. mass mkt. 3.99 (*0-380-81119-7*, Avon Bks) Morrow Avon.

— What Zoey Saw. (Making Out Ser.: No. 6). 208p. (YA). (gr. 7-12). 1998. mass mkt. 3.99 (*0-380-80216-3*, Avon Bks) Morrow Avon.

— Who Loves Kate? (Making Out Ser.: No. 15). 176p. (YA). (gr. 7-12). 1999. mass mkt. 3.99 (*0-380-80871-4*, Avon Bks) Morrow Avon.

Applegate, Katherine. The World's Best Jinx McGee. 80p. (Orig.). (J). (gr. 2). 1992. pap. 2.99 (*0-380-76728-7*, Avon Bks) Morrow Avon.

***Applegate, Katherine.** Zoey Comes Home. LC 99-69744. (Making Out Ser.: No. 28). 176p. (YA). (gr. 7-12). 2000. mass mkt. 3.99 (*0-380-81532-X*) Morrow Avon.

— Zoey Fools Around. (Making Out Ser.: No. 1). 272p. (YA). (gr. 7-12). 1998. reprint ed. mass mkt. 3.99 (*0-380-80211-2*, Avon Bks) Morrow Avon.

— Zoey Plays Games. (Making Out Ser.: No. 9). 192p. (YA). (gr. 7-12). 1999. mass mkt. 3.99 (*0-380-80742-4*, Avon Bks) Morrow Avon.

— Zoey Speaks Out. (Making Out Ser.: No. 18). 192p. (YA). (gr. 7-12). 1999. mass mkt. 3.99 (*0-380-81120-0*, Avon Bks) Morrow Avon.

— Zoey's Broken Heart. LC 99-69742. (Making Out Ser.: No. 26). 176p. (YA). (gr. 7-12). 2000. mass mkt. 3.99 (*0-380-81530-3*, Avon Bks) Morrow Avon.

Applegate, Katherine, et al. See You in September. 125p. (Orig.). (J). (gr. 7-10). 1995. mass mkt. 3.99 (*0-380-78088-7*, Avon Bks) Morrow Avon.

***Applegate, Katherine A.** Brave the Betrayal. (Illus.). (J). 2000. 10.34 (*0-606-18541-0*) Turtleback.

— Discover the Destroyer. (Illus.). (J). 1999. 10.34 (*0-606-18539-9*) Turtleback.

— Gateway to the Gods. (Illus.). (J). 2000. 10.34 (*0-606-18872-X*) Turtleback.

***Applegate, Liz.** 101 Miracle Foods That Heal Your Heart. (Illus.). 2000. pap. 12.00 (*0-7352-0169-2*) PH Pr.

Applegate, Liz. Power Foods: High-Performance Nutrition for High-Performance People. 304p. 1994. pap. 14.95 (*0-87596-219-X*) Rodale Pr Inc.

Applegate, Lloyd R. A Life of Service: William Augustus Newell. (Illus.). (Orig.). 1994. pap. 10.00 (*0-941965-08-2*) Ocean Cnty Hist.

***Applegate, Lynda M., et al.** Corporate Information Systems Management: Text & Cases. 5th ed. LC 98-54098. 1999. write for info. (*0-07-290283-3*) McGrw-H Hghr Educ.

— Corporate Information Systems Management: The Challenge of Managing in an Information Age. 5th ed. LC 98-53862. 360p. 1999. pap. 52.50 (*0-07-290282-5*) McGraw.

Applegate, Lynda M., et al. Corporate Information Systems Management: The Issues Facing Senior Executives. 4th rev. ed. 320p. (C). 1995. text 40.95 (*0-256-18213-2*, Irwn McGrw-H) McGrw-H Hghr Educ.

Applegate, R. B., et al. The Journal of California Anthropology. fac. ed. (Malki Museum, Journal of California Anthropology Ser.: Vol. 2:1). 148p. (C). 1975. reprint ed. pap. text 16.25 (*1-55567-765-7*) Coyote Press.

Applegate, Rex. Combat Use of the Double-Edged Fighting Knife. (Illus.). 48p. 1993. pap. 8.00 (*0-87364-735-1*) Paladin Pr.

— Kill or Get Killed. (Illus.). 400p. 1976. text 39.95 (*0-87364-084-5*) Paladin Pr.

Applegate, Rex & Janich, Michael. Bullseyes Don't Shoot Back! The Complete Textbook of Point Shooting for Close Quarters Combat. LC 99-164966. (Illus.). 120p. 1998. pap. 22.00 (*0-87364-957-5*) Paladin Pr.

Applegate, Rex, jt. auth. see Melson, Chuck.

Applegate, Robert. General Care & Maintenance of Milk Snakes. 71p. 1992. pap. text 11.50 (*1-882770-19-6*) Adv Vivarium.

Applegate, Shannon. Skookum. 1996. 22.95 (*1-884961-09-6*) LEO Prods.

Applegate, Shannon & O'Donnell, Terence, eds. Talking on Paper: An Anthology of Oregon Letters & Diaries. (Oregon Literature Ser.: Vol. 6). (Illus.). 352p. (Orig.). 1994. pap. 21.95 (*0-87071-378-7*); text 35.95 (*0-87071-377-9*) Oreg St U Pr.

Applegate, Stan. Natchez under-the-Hill. LC 98-43051. (Illus.). 186p. (YA). (gr. 3-7). 1999. pap. 8.95 (*1-56145-191-6*, 51916) Peachtree Pubs.

***Applegate, Stanley.** The Devil's Highway. LC 98-22720. (Illus.). 224p. (YA). (gr. 3-7). 1998. pap. 8.95 (*1-56145-184-3*, Peachtree) Peachtree Pubs.

Applegate, Tom. Sergeant Savage: The Adventures of John Savage: A Man Called Squad Leader. (Illus.). 166p. 1996. pap. 16.95 (*1-887617-50-7*); lib. bdg. 55.00 (*1-887617-51-5*) Sitton & Assocs.

Applegeet, Carol, ed. see AORN Staff.

Applehans, Wayne, et al. Managing Knowledge: A Practical Web Based Approach. LC 98-43437. (Addison-Wesley Information Technology Ser.). 128p. (C). 1998. pap. text 29.95 (*0-201-43315-X*) Addison-Wesley.

Appleman, ed. see Darwin, Charles.

Appleman & Dellacorte Staff. AIDS: Lessons from the First Decade. 176p. (C). 1992. pap. text 31.95 (*0-8403-7206-X*) Kendall-Hunt.

Appleman, Bernard R. Expanding Metropolitan Highways: Implications for Air Quality & Energy Use, Vol. 245. LC 95-4464. (Special Report Ser.: No. 245). 387p. 1995. pap. 32.00 (*0-309-06107-5*) Natl Res Coun.

Appleman, Bernard R., et al, eds. Lead Paint Removal: Proceedings of SSPC Symposium Held February 29-March 1, 1988, Arlington, VA. (Illus.). 209p. 1988. pap. text 40.00 (*0-938477-34-X*) SSPC.

Appleman, Bernard R. & Bruno, Joseph A., Jr. Evaluation of the Effectiveness of Wet Abrasive Blast Cleaning Methods of Surface Preparation. (Illus.). 185p. 1986. pap. text 40.00 (*0-938477-15-3*) SSPC.

Appleman, Bernard R. & Busse, J. G., eds. Techniques for Long-Term Protection of Steel Structures: Proceedings of SSPC Symposium, Feb. 1986. (Illus.). 238p. 1986. pap. text 40.00 (*0-938477-23-4*, SSPC 86-01) SSPC.

Appleman, Bernard R. & Hower, Harold E. Surface Preparation: The State of the Art. 234p. 1985. pap. text 40.00 (*0-938477-06-4*) SSPC.

Appleman, Bernard R. & Smith, L. M. Removal of Lead-Based Bridge Paints: Report on FHWA Workshop. 113p. 1988. pap. text 40.00 (*0-938477-35-8*) SSPC.

Appleman, Bernard R., et al. Protective Coatings for Weathering Steel Tower Joints. (Illus.). 61p. 1987. pap. text 40.00 (*0-938477-32-3*, 87-03) SSPC.

Appleman, Bernard R., jt. ed. see Rex, Janet.

Appleman, D. Ralph & Appelman, D. Ralph. The Science of Vocal Pedagogy: Soprano & Mezzo-Soprano, Tape 1. LC 67-10107. 1967. 7.95 incl. audio (*0-253-35112-X*) Ind U Pr.

— The Science of Vocal Pedagogy: Tenor & Bass, Tape 2. LC 67-10107. 1967. 7.95 incl. audio (*0-253-35113-8*) Ind U Pr.

Appleman, Dan. Dan Appleman's Developing ActiveX Components with Visual Basic 5.0. LC 98-159772. 768p. 1997. 49.99 (*1-56276-510-8*, Ziff-Davis Pr) Que.

— Dan Appleman's Visual Basic 5.0 Programmer's Guide to the Windows 32 API. 1584p. 1997. pap. text 59.99 incl. cd-rom (*1-56276-446-2*, Ziff-Davis Pr) Que.

— Dan Appleman's WIN 32 API Puzzle Book & Tutorial for Visual Basic Programmers. 400p. 1999. pap. 39.95 (*1-893115-01-1*) APress L P.

***Appleman, Dan.** How Computer Programming Works. 2nd ed. LC 00-25265. (Illus.). 225p. 2000. pap. 24.99 (*1-893115-23-2*, Pub. by APress L P) Spr-Verlag.

Appleman, Dan. PC Magazine Visual Basic Programmers Guide to Windows API. (Programming Ser.). 1056p. 1993. pap. 34.95 incl. disk (*1-56276-073-4*, Ziff-Davis Pr) Que.

Appleman, Daniel. Developing COM/ActiveX Components with Visual Basic. 6th ed. LC 98-85903. 850p. 1998. pap. 49.99 (*1-56276-576-0*, Ziff-Davis Pr) Que.

Appleman, Diane & McClear, Johanna. Teacher, the Children Are Here: A Guide for Teachers of the Elementary Grades. (Illus.). 180p. (Orig.). 1988. pap. 9.95 (*0-673-38001-7*, GoodYrBooks) Addson-Wesley Educ.

Appleman, Earl. Inland Marine Insurance: An Interpretation of the Policies. LC 95-77928. xi, 221p. 1995. reprint ed. 55.00 (*0-89941-977-1*, 308820) W S Hein.

Appleman, Harlene & Shapiro, Jane. A Seder for Tu B'Shevat. (Illus.). 32p. (J). (ps up). 1984. pap. 3.95 (*0-930494-39-3*) Kar-Ben.

Appleman, John A. Appleman on Insurance Law & Practice, 57 vols. Date not set. text 2800.00 (*0-318-57508-6*, 63130, MICHIE) LEXIS Pub.

— Military Tribunals & International Crimes. LC 76-152589. (Illus.). 421p. 1972. reprint ed. lib. bdg. 75.00 (*0-8371-6022-7*, APMT, Greenwood Pr) Greenwood.

Appleman-Jurman, Alicia. Alicia: My Story. 448p. 1989. mass mkt. 6.99 (*0-553-28218-2*) Bantam.

Appleman, Marjorie. Against Time. (Illus.). 32p. (Orig.). (C). 1994. pap. text 5.00 (*1-878173-38-3*) Birnham Wood.

Appleman, Philip. Darwin's Ark: Poems. LC 83-49412. (Illus.). 103p. 1984. reprint ed. pap. 32.00 (*0-608-01045-6*, 205935300001) Bks Demand.

— New & Selected Poems, 1956-1996. 280p. 1996. 38.00 (*1-55728-419-9*); pap. 22.00 (*1-55728-420-2*) U of Ark Pr.

Appleman, Philip, ed. Darwin. 2nd ed. (Critical Editions Ser.). (Illus.). (C). 1979. pap. text 13.00 (*0-393-95009-3*) Norton.

Appleman, Philip, ed. see Darwin, Charles.

Appleman, Philip, ed. see Malthus, Thomas Robert.

Appleman, Rich & Viola, Joseph. Chord Studies for Electric Bass. 144p. 1987. per. 14.95 (*0-634-01646-6*) H Leonard.

Appleman, Roy. Lewis & Clark: Historic Places Associated with Their Transcontinental Exploration (1804-1806) 2nd ed. (Illus.). 484p. (C). 1993. reprint ed. pap. text 14.95 (*0-931056-09-8*) Jefferson Natl.

Appleman, Roy E. Disaster in Korea: The Chinese Confront MacArthur. LC 88-28133. (Military History Ser.: No. 11). (Illus.). 472p. 1989. 39.95 (*0-89096-344-4*) Tex A&M Univ Pr.

— East of Chosin: Entrapment & Breakout in Korea, 1950. LC 86-22184. (Texas A&M University Military History Ser.: Vol. 2). (Illus.). 416p. 1998. reprint ed. pap. 17.95 (*0-89096-465-3*) Tex A&M Univ Pr.

— Escaping the Trap: The U. S. Army X Corps in Northeast Korea, 1950. LC 89-4987. (Military History Ser.: No. 14). (Illus.). 432p. 1989. 39.95 (*0-89096-395-9*) Tex A&M Univ Pr.

— Ridgway Duels for Korea. LC 89-48499. (Military History Ser.: No. 18). (Illus.). 688p. 1990. 39.50 (*0-89096-432-7*) Tex A&M Univ Pr.

— United States Army in World War 2: War in the Pacific, Okinawa, the Last Battle. LC 49-45742. (Illus.), 529p. 1995. boxed set 29.00 (*0-16-001907-9*) USGPO.

Appleman, Roy E. United States Army in World War 2, War in the Pacific: Okinawa, the Last Battle. 556p. 1995. pap. 32.00 (*0-16-061318-3*) USGPO.

Appler, Charles R. Appler Family History. 280p. 1994. reprint ed. pap. 44.00 (*0-8328-4048-3*); reprint ed. lib. bdg. 54.00 (*0-8328-4047-5*) Higginson Bk Co.

Appler, Tom Y. Medical & International Cooperation of Local & World Health Problems: Index of New Information. 1998. 47.50 (*0-7883-1806-3*); pap. 44.50 (*0-7883-1807-1*) ABBE Pubs Assn.

Appleseth, Cindy, jt. auth. see Lapchick, Mike.

Appleton. Anesthesiology Continuing Education. (C). 1999. write for info. (*0-8385-0100-1*) Appleton & Lange.

***Appleton.** Primary Care Hiv Aids Site. 1999. text 2500.00 (*0-8385-8144-7*) Appleton & Lange.

Appleton & Lange Staff. Basic & Clinical Pharmacology. 8th ed. (C). 2000. 41.95 (*0-8385-0598-8*) Appleton & Lange.

***Appleton & Lange Staff, ed.** Health Assessment & Promotion Strategies. 7th ed. (C). 2000. text 45.95 (*0-8385-3688-3*) Appleton & Lange.

— Medical First: Comprehensive First Repsonder. (C). 1999. text 25.00 (*0-8385-6430-5*) Appleton & Lange.

— Medical First: Comprehensive First Responder. (C). 1999. text 29.95 (*0-8385-6433-X*); text 40.00 (*0-8385-6431-3*); spiral bd. 25.00 (*0-8385-6432-1*) Appleton & Lange.

— Medical Medicine: Comprehensive Paramedical Care. (C). 2000. text 25.00 (*0-8385-6413-5*); text 24.95 (*0-8385-6415-1*); text 29.95 (*0-8385-6416-X*) Appleton & Lange.

Appleton, A. D. Superconducting D. C. Machines. 1984. write for info. (*0-318-57806-9*) Elsevier.

Appleton, A. S., jt. auth. see Bodsworth, Colin.

Appleton, Andrew M. & Ward, Daniel S., eds. State Party Profiles: A 50-State Guide to Development, Organization, & Resources. LC 96-25500. 388p. (YA). 1997. text 98.00 (*1-56802-150-X*) Congr Quarterly.

Appleton, Arthur E. Environmental Labelling Programmes. LC 98-106464. 280p. 1998. text 180.00 (*90-411-0715-0*) Kluwer Law Intl.

Appleton, Barbara, jt. auth. see Appleton, Richard.

Appleton, Bonnie L. Container Nursery Design. 122p. 1986. pap. 14.95 (*1-887632-53-0*) Amer Nurseryman Pub.

— Landscape Rejuvenation: Remodeling the Home Landscape. Clarkson, Sarah M., ed. LC 87-42970. (Illus.). 144p. (Orig.). 1988. pap. 10.95 (*0-88266-496-4*, Garden Way Pub) Storey Bks.

— Landscape Rejuvenation: Remodeling the Home Landscape. Clarkson, Sarah M., ed. LC 87-42970. (Illus.). (Orig.). 1988. 19.95 (*0-88266-495-6*, Garden Way Pub) Storey Bks.

Appleton, Bonnie L. & Scheider, Alfred F. Trees, Shrubs, & Vines. (Rodale's Successful Organic Gardening Ser.). (Illus.). 1993. pap. 14.95 (*0-87596-562-8*) Rodale Pr Inc.

***Appleton, Brian W.** Cleaning up in Your Service Business. 200p. 2000. pap. 17.95 (*1-55571-537-0*, Pub. by PSI Resch) Midpt Trade.

Appleton, C. M. Yuk It up with Urkel! 64p. (J). (ps-3). 1992. pap. 2.95 (*0-590-45745-4*) Scholastic Inc.

— Yuk It up with Urkel! Hilarious Urkel Jokes, Silly Sayings, Riotous Riddles, Far-Out Facts. 1992. 8.15 (*0-606-01985-5*, Pub. by Turtleback) Demco.

Appleton, Christopher. A Guide to the Freshwater Molluscs of Southern Africa. LC 97-137048. (Illus.). 80p. 1996. pap. 21.25 (*0-86980-919-9*, Pub. by Univ Natal Pr) Intl Spec Bk.

Appleton, Cyril. The Fourth Market. LC 96-178620. 380p. 1995. pap. write for info. (*1-85863-720-1*, Pub. by Minerva Pr) Unity Dist.

Appleton, Daniel S. Probe: The Principles of Business Engineering: A Management Guide for High-Involvement Change. (Illus.). 268p. (Orig.). pap. 34.95 (*0-9642954-0-7*) D Appleton.

Appleton, George. The Pocket Oxford Book of Prayer. 128p. 1989. pap. 14.00 (*0-19-122441-3*) OUP.

Appleton, George. Reflections from a Life of Prayer: Meditations & Prayers. 160p. 1995. pap. 10.95 (*0-687-85004-5*) Intl Pubs Mktg.

Appleton, George, ed. The Oxford Book of Prayer. (Illus.). 416p. 1985. 35.00 (*0-19-213222-9*) OUP.

— The Oxford Book of Prayer. (Illus.). 416p. 1989. pap. 14.95 (*0-19-282108-3*) OUP.

Appleton, Helen, ed. Do It Herself: Women & Technical Innovation. LC 96-142081. 310p. 1995. pap. 29.95 (*1-85339-287-1*, Pub. by Intermed Tech) Stylus Pub VA.

Appleton, Ian. Buildings for the Performing Arts: A Design & Development Guide. rev. ed. LC 95-20185. (Illus.). 160p. 1996. text 95.00 (*0-7506-1276-2*, Butterwrth Archit) Buttrwrth-Heinemann.

Appleton, J. D., et al, eds. Environmental Geochemistry & Health: With Special Reference to Developing Countries. (Geological Society Special Publication Ser.: No. 113). (Illus.). 272p. 1996. 98.00 (*1-897799-64-0*, 354, Pub. by Geol Soc Pub Hse) AAPG.

Appleton, J. D., jt. auth. see Seddon, Edmund.

Appleton, Jay. The Experience of Landscape. rev. ed. 1996. text 140.00 (*0-471-96233-3*) Wiley.

— The Experience of Landscape. rev. ed. LC 96-1681. 296p. 1996. pap. 59.95 (*0-471-96235-X*) Wiley.

— How I Made the World: Shaping a View of Landscape. (Illus.). 255p. 1995. pap. 25.00 (*0-85958-620-0*, Pub. by Univ of Hull Pr) Paul & Co Pubs.

— The Symbolism of Habitat: An Interpretation of Landscape in the Arts. LC 89-24811. (Jessie & John Danz Lectures). (Illus.). 104p. 1990. 17.50 (*0-295-96940-7*) U of Wash Pr.

Appleton, Jo Ann. Instructor's Kit for FLMI 280. rev. ed. (FLMI Insurance Education Program Ser.). 302p. spiral bd. 200.00 (*1-57974-031-6*, Pub. by Life Office) PBD Inc.

Appleton, Jo Ann, et al. Customer Service in Insurance: Improving Your Skills. 2nd rev. ed. LC 98-67192. (Associate, Customer Service Program Ser.). 284p. pap. text 49.95 (*1-57974-060-X*, Pub. by Life Office) PBD Inc.

— Prep Pak for FLMI 310. (FLMI Insurance Education Program Ser.). 247p. 1998. spiral bd. 24.00 (*1-57974-052-9*) Life Office.

— Prep Pak for FLMI 320. 2nd rev. ed. (FLMI Insurance Education Program Ser.). 211p. spiral bd. 24.00 (*1-57974-009-X*, Pub. by Life Office) PBD Inc.

An Asterisk (*) at the beginning of an entry indicates that the title is appearing for the first time.

Appleton, JoAnn S. Instructor's Kit for FLMI 310: Life & Health Insurance Law. (FLMI Insurance Education Program Ser.). spiral bd. 200.00 (*1-57974-021-9*, Pub. by Life Office) PBD Inc.

***Appleton, JoAnn S.** Instructor's Kit for FLMI 290. rev. ed. (FLMI Insurance Education Progam Ser.). (C). 2000. spiral bd. 200.00 (*1-57974-086-3*, Pub. by Life Office) PBD Inc.

Appleton, JoAnn S. & Hartley, Iris F. Instructor's Kit for FLMI 361. (FLMI Insurance Education Program Ser.). ring bd. 200.00 (*0-939921-87-1*, Pub. by Life Office) PBD Inc.

— Instructor's Kit for FLMI 301: Insurance Administration. (FLMI Insurance Education Program Ser.). ring bd. 200.00 (*0-939921-96-0*, Pub. by Life Office) PBD Inc.

Appleton, Jon. Twenty-First Century Musical Instruments: Hardware & Software. LC 89-82244. (I.S.A.M. Monographs: No. 29). (Illus.). 44p. (Orig.). 1990. pap. 12.00 (*0-914678-32-9*) Inst Am Music.

Appleton Jr., Thomas H., et al, eds. Kentucky: Land of Tomorrow. LC 98-226808. 254 p. 1998. 39.95 (*0-916968-25-1*) Kentucky Hist.

Appleton, Ken. Teaching Science: Exploring the Issues. ix, 180p. 1997. pap. 24.95 (*1-875998-17-9*, Pub. by Central Queensland) Accents Pubns.

Appleton, Leroy H. American Indian Design & Decoration. Orig. Title: Indian Art of the Americas. (Illus.). 1990. 23.00 (*0-8446-0007-5*) Peter Smith.

— American Indian Design & Decoration. Orig. Title: Indian Art of the Americas. (Illus.). 279p. 1971. reprint ed. pap. 10.95 (*0-486-22704-9*) Dover.

Appleton, Lilla E. A Comparative Study of the Play Activities of Adult Savages & Civilized Children. LC 75-35062. (Studies in Play & Games). 1976. reprint ed. 17.95 (*0-405-07913-3*) Ayer.

Appleton, Lulu, jt. auth. see Geller, Uri.

Appleton, Marguerite. A Portrait Album of Four RI Leaders. 1978. 12.00 (*0-932840-00-0*) RI Hist Soc.

Appleton, Michael & Henschell, Todd. At Home with Terminal Illness. LC 94-9604. 1994. pap. text 20.80 (*0-13-299843-2*) P-H.

***Appleton, Nancy.** Curse of Louis Pasteur. 1999. pap. 11.95 (*0-9672337-0-4*) Choice Pubns CA.

Appleton, Nancy. Healthy Bones: What You Should Know about Osteoporosis. 160p. (Orig.). pap. 8.95 (*0-89529-462-1*, Avery) Penguin Putnam.

— Healthy Bones: What You Should Know about Osteoporosis. 160p. (Orig.). Date not set. pap. 9.95 (*0-89529-800-7*, Avery) Penguin Putnam.

— Healthy Bones: What You Should Know about Osteoporosis. (Orig.). 1999. mass mkt. 6.95 (*0-89529-899-6*, Avery) Penguin Putnam.

— Lick the Sugar Habit: How to Break Your Sugar Addiction Naturally. 2nd ed. LC 96-8296. 272p. (Orig.). 1996. mass mkt. 5.95 (*0-89529-695-0*, Avery) Penguin Putnam.

— Lick the Sugar Habit: How to Break Your Sugar Addiction Naturally. 2nd ed. 272p. (Orig.). 1997. pap. 11.95 (*0-89529-768-X*, Avery) Penguin Putnam.

Appleton, Richard & Appleton, Barbara. The Cambridge Dictionary of Australian Places. (Illus.). 368p. (C). 1993. text 69.95 (*0-521-39506-2*) Cambridge U Pr.

Appleton, Richard, ed. see Brown, Robin.

Appleton, Richard E. & Baldwin, Tony, eds. Management of Brain-injured Children. (Illus.). 270p. 1998. pap. text 39.95 (*0-19-262793-7*) OUP.

Appleton, Richard E., jt. auth. see Hopkins, Anthony.

Appleton-Smith, Laura. It is Halloween! (Illus.). (J). (ps-3). Date not set. pap. 8.95 (*0-9658246-4-0*, Bks To Remember) Flyleaf Pubg.

Appleton-Smith, Laura. Jen's Best Gift Ever. LC 98-96630. (J). (ps-3). 17.95 (*0-9658246-2-4*, Bks To Remember) Flyleaf Pubg.

— Meg & Jim's Sled Trip. LC 98-96631. (Illus.). (J). (ps-3). 17.95 (*0-9658246-0-8*, Bks To Remember) Flyleaf Pubg.

Appleton, Susan F., jt. auth. see Weisberg, D. Kelly.

Appleton, Thomas G. The Works of Thomas Gold Appleton, 1812-1884, Set. 1987. reprint ed. lib. bdg. 500.00 (*0-685-18599-0*) Rprt Serv.

Appleton, Thomas H., jt. auth. see Smith, John D.

Appleton, Victor. The Alien Probe. (Tom Swift Ser.: No. 3). (J). (gr. 3-7). 20.95 (*0-88411-464-3*) Amereon Ltd.

— The Astral Fortress. (Tom Swift Ser.: No. 5). (J). (gr. 3-7). 20.95 (*0-88411-461-9*) Amereon Ltd.

— The City in the Stars. (Tom Swift Ser.). (J). (gr. 3-7). 20.95 (*0-88411-463-5*) Amereon Ltd.

— Cyborg Kickboxer. Greenberg, Ann, ed. (Tom Swift Ser.: No. 3). 160p. (YA). (gr. 7 up). 1991. per. 2.95 (*0-671-67825-6*, Archway) PB.

— Fire Biker. Greenberg, Anne, ed. (Tom Swift Ser.: No. 9). 160p. (YA). (gr. 7 up). 1992. mass mkt. 2.99 (*0-671-75652-4*, Archway) PB.

— The Invisible Force. Barish, Wendy, ed. (Tom Swift Ser.: No. 10). 192p. (J). (gr. 3-7). 1983. 8.50 (*0-671-43958-8*) S&S Trade.

— Mutant Beach. Greenberg, Anne, ed. (Tom Swift Ser.: No. 11). 160p. (Orig.). (YA). (gr. 7 up). 1992. pap. 2.99 (*0-671-75657-5*, Archway) PB.

— The Negative Zone. Greenberg, Anne, ed. (Tom Swift Ser.: No. 2). 176p. (YA). (gr. 7 up). 1991. per. 2.95 (*0-671-67824-8*, Archway) PB.

— The Rescue Mission. (Tom Swift Ser.: No. 6). (J). (gr. 3-7). 20.95 (*0-88411-458-9*) Amereon Ltd.

— Terror on the Moons of Jupiter. (Tom Swift Ser.: No. 2). (J). (gr. 3-7). 20.95 (*0-88411-460-0*) Amereon Ltd.

— Tom Swift & His Airship. LC 92-29496. (Tom Swift Ser.: No. 3). 216p. (J). (gr. 3-7). 1992. 14.95 (*1-55709-177-3*) Applewood.

Appleton, Victor. Tom Swift & His Airship. (Tom Swift Ser.: No. 3). (J). (gr. 3-7). Date not set. pap. write for info. (*1-57646-203-X*) QVision.

Appleton, Victor. Tom Swift & His Electric Rifle. (Tom Swift Ser.: No. 10). (J). (gr. 3-7). 1998. lib. bdg. 18.95 (*1-56723-020-2*) Yestermorrow.

— Tom Swift & His Electronic Electroscope. (J). (gr. 5-6). 20.95 (*0-88411-462-7*) Amereon Ltd.

— Tom Swift & His Motor Boat. LC 92-29497. (Tom Swift Ser.: No. 2). 212p. (J). (gr. 3-7). 1992. 14.95 (*1-55709-176-5*) Applewood.

Appleton, Victor. Tom Swift & His Motor Boat. (Tom Swift Ser.: No. 2). (J). (gr. 3-7). Date not set. pap. write for info. (*1-57646-202-1*) QVision.

Appleton, Victor. Tom Swift & His Motor Cycle. LC 92-28649. (Tom Swift Ser.: No. 1). 206p. (J). (gr. 3-7). 1992. 14.95 (*1-55709-175-7*) Applewood.

Appleton, Victor. Tom Swift & His Motor Cycle. (Tom Swift Ser.: No. 1). (J). (gr. 3-7). Date not set. pap. write for info. (*1-57646-201-3*) QVision.

Appleton, Victor. Tom Swift & His Photo Telephone. (Tom Swift Ser.: No. 17). (J). (gr. 3-7). 1998. lib. bdg. 18.95 (*1-56723-022-9*) Yestermorrow.

— Tom Swift & His Space Solatron. (J). (gr. 5-6). 20.95 (*0-88411-457-0*) Amereon Ltd.

Appleton, Victor. Tom Swift & His Submarine Boat. (Tom Swift Ser.: No. 4). (J). (gr. 3-7). Date not set. pap. write for info. (*1-57646-204-8*) QVision.

Appleton, Victor. Tom Swift & His Triphibian Atomicar. (Tom Swift Jr. Ser.). (J). (gr. 5-6). 20.95 (*0-88411-459-7*) Amereon Ltd.

— Tom Swift in the Caves of Ice. (Tom Swift Ser.: No. 8). (J). (gr. 3-7). 1998. lib. bdg. 18.95 (*1-56723-021-0*) Yestermorrow.

— The War in Outer Space. (Tom Swift Ser.: No. 4). (J). (gr. 3-7). 19.95 (*0-88411-465-1*) Amereon Ltd.

Appleton, Wanda H., jt. auth. see Randolph, Gretchen L.

Appleton-Weber, Sarah, tr. see Teilhard De Chardin, Pierre.

Appleton, William. Practical Clinical Psychopharmacology. 3rd ed. 224p. 1988. pap. 33.00 (*0-683-00239-2*) Lppncott W & W.

Appleton, William S. Ancestry of Priscilla Baker, Who Lived 1674-1731, & Was Wife of Isaac Appleton, of Ipswich. 143p. 1988. reprint ed. pap. 21.50 (*0-8328-0163-1*); reprint ed. lib. bdg. 31.50 (*0-8328-0162-3*) Higginson Bk Co.

***Appleton, William S.** Prozac & the New Antidepressants: What You Need to Know about Prozac, Zoloft, Paxil, Luvox, Wellburtin, Effexor, Serzone, Selexa, St. John's Wart & Others. LC 99-44963. (Illus.). 2000. pap. 13.95 (*0-452-28164-4*, Plume) Dutton Plume.

Appleton, William S., intro. The Fifth Psychoactive Drug Usage Guide. 105p. (C). 1991. pap. text 19.95 (*0-933171-00-5*) Phys Postgrad.

Appleton, William W., ed. see Cibber, Colley.

Appleton, William W., ed. see Hill, Aaron & Popple, William.

Appletree Press Staff. Ireland: The Complete Guide & Road Atlas. 6th ed. (Illus.). 128p. 1998. pap. text 19.95 (*0-7627-0248-6*) Globe Pequot.

— Scotland: The Complete Guide & Road Atlas. (Illus.). 128p. 1999. pap. text 19.95 (*0-7627-0581-7*, Pub. by Apletree Pr) Globe Pequot.

Applewhaite, Charles. Tennis. LC 96-37858. (Know the Sport Ser.). (Illus.). 48p. 1997. pap. 5.95 (*0-8117-2836-6*) Stackpole.

Applewhaite, Charles & Moss, Bill. Tennis. (Skills of the Game Ser.). (Illus.). 128p. 1996. pap. 19.95 (*1-85223-899-2*, Pub. by Crolwood) Trafalgar.

***Applewhite, Ashton.** Cutting Loose: Why Women Who End Their Marriages Do So Well. 302p. 2000. text 24.00 (*0-7881-6769-3*) DIANE Pub.

Applewhite, Ashton. Cutting Loose: Why Women Who End Their Marriages Do So Well. 320p. 1998. pap. 13.00 (*0-06-092888-3*) HarpC.

— Thinking Positive: Words of Inspiration, Encouragement & Validation for People with AIDS & Those Who Care for Them. 1995. pap. 9.00 (*0-684-80266-X*, Fireside) S&S Trade Pap.

Applewhite, Ashton, et al. And I Quote: The Definitive Collecton of Quotes, Sayings, & Jokes for the Contemporary Speechmaker. 544p. 1992. text 25.95 (*0-312-06897-2*) St Martin.

Applewhite, D., tr. see Villarejo, F. J.

Applewhite, E. J. Washington Itself: An Informal Guide to the Capital of the United States. 2nd ed. (Illus.). 368p. 1993. reprint ed. pap. 14.95 (*1-56833-008-1*) Madison Bks UPA.

Applewhite, Edgar J., jt. auth. see Fuller, R. Buckminster.

Applewhite, Harriet B. Political Alignment in the French National Assembly, 1789-1791. LC 92-32493. 304p. (C). 1993. text 45.00 (*0-8071-1751-X*) La State U Pr.

Applewhite, Harriet B. & Levy, Darline G., eds. Women & Politics in the Age of the Democratic Revolution. LC 90-10738. (Illus.). 308p. (C). 1993. pap. text 19.95 (*0-472-06413-4*, 06413) U of Mich Pr.

Applewhite, James. Daytime & Starlight. LC 97-7076. 64p. 1997. pap. 11.95 (*0-8071-2150-9*); text 19.95 (*0-8071-2149-5*) La State U Pr.

— Following Gravity. LC 80-21578. (Associated Writing Programs Series for Contemporary Poetry). 67p. 1980. text 10.95 (*0-8139-0885-X*) U Pr of Va.

— Foreseeing the Journey: Poems. LC 82-17165. 64p. 1983. pap. 30.00 (*0-7837-8518-6*, 204932700011) Bks Demand.

— Lessons in Soaring. LC 88-3148. 64p. 1989. pap. 6.95 (*0-8071-1540-1*); text 15.95 (*0-8071-1539-8*) La State U Pr.

— Ode to the Chinaberry Tree & Other Poems. LC 85-19707. 62p. 1986. reprint ed. pap. 30.00 (*0-608-00861-3*, 206165200010) Bks Demand.

Applewhite, Karen M. On the Road to Nowhere: A History of Greer, Arizona, 1879-1979. 2nd ed. (Illus.). 122p. reprint ed. pap. text 7.95 (*0-9603472-0-8*) Applewhite.

Applewhite, Richard C. Clear Your Credit & Get Out of Debt: Five Easy Steps. LC 93-94163. 160p. (Orig.). 1994. pap. 8.95 (*1-884148-25-5*) JaCee Pubng.

Applewhite, Ronald, jt. auth. see Wofford, Thomas.

Applewhite, Stephen Z. Cultural Competence in Social Work. (C). 1997. pap. text. write for info. (*0-8013-1545-X*) Addison-Wesley.

Applewhite, Steven R., ed. Hispanic Elderly in Transition: Theory, Research, Policy & Practice, 9. LC 87-37563. (Contributions to the Study of Aging Ser.: No. 9). 250p. 1988. 65.00 (*0-313-24478-2*, AHE/, Greenwood Pr) Greenwood.

Applewhite, Thomas H., ed. Proceedings of the World Conference on Biotechnology for the Fats & Oils Industry. 364p. 1988. 40.00 (*0-935315-20-9*) Am Oil Chemists.

— Proceedings of the World Conference on Lauric Oils: Sources, Processing & Applications. (Illus.). 192p. 1994. lib. bdg. 135.00 (*0-935315-56-X*, PCWC94) Am Oil Chemists.

— Proceedings of the World Conference on Oilseed Technology & Utilization. LC 93-3191. (Illus.). 512p. 1993. lib. bdg. 130.00 (*0-935315-45-4*, PCWC92) Am Oil Chemists.

— Proceedings of the World Congress on Vegetable Protein Utilization in Human Foods & Animal Feedstuffs. 588p. 1989. 130.00 (*0-935315-25-X*) Am Oil Chemists.

— World Conference on Biotechnology for the Fats & Oils Industry. (Illus.). 216p. (C). 1988. lib. bdg. 40.00 (*0-935315-21-7*, PCWC87) Am Oil Chemists.

— The World Conference on Oleochemicals. 336p. (C). 1991. 130.00 (*0-935315-34-9*) Am Oil Chemists.

Applewhite, Wayne A. Back to the Basics: A Handbook for Success in America. (Illus.). xvii, 119p. 1998. pap. 15.95 (*0-9662737-0-2*) Metanoic Perspect.

Applewood. Harper's Weekly: November 10, 1860-May 4, 1861, Deluxe Edition. 1999. 49.95 (*1-55709-862-X*, Pub. by Applewood) Consort Bk Sales.

***Applewood Books Staff.** Beadle's Dime Song Book. 72p. 2000. pap. 5.95 (*1-55709-552-3*) Applewood.

— Beadle's Dime Song Book. (Illus.). 72p. (J). 2000. pap. 5.95 (*1-55709-553-1*) Applewood.

— Beadle's Dime Union Song Book. (Illus.). 72p. 2000. pap. text 5.95 (*1-55709-551-5*) Applewood.

Applewood Books Staff. Buckaroos: Sitting Bull, Indian Sign Language & Calamity Jane. (Illus.). (J). 1995. pap. text 90.00 (*1-55709-364-4*) Applewood.

***Applewood Books Staff.** Floral Birthday Book. (Illus.). 272p. 2000. pap. 12.95 (*1-55709-385-7*) Applewood.

— Greetings from Apple Country. (Illus.). 32p. 2000. pap. 9.95 (*1-55709-480-2*) Applewood.

— Greetings from Old California. (Illus.). 32p. 2000. pap. 9.95 (*1-55709-481-0*) Applewood.

— Harper's Weekly: A Journal of Civilization, November 9, 1861-May 3, 1862. (Illus.). 2000. 49.95 (*1-55709-866-2*) Applewood.

Applewood Books Staff. Harper's Weekly: May, 1860-November 1861. deluxe ed. 1999. 75.00 (*1-55709-863-8*, Pub. by Applewood) Consort Bk Sales.

***Applewood Books Staff.** Inaugural Addresses of the Presidents of the United States, Vol. 1. 160p. 2000. pap. 14.95 (*1-55709-503-5*) Applewood.

— Inaugural Addresses of the Presidents of the United States, Vol. 2. 160p. 2000. pap. 14.95 (*1-55709-504-3*) Applewood.

Applewood Books Staff, ed. Animal Tracks. (Wonderlings Ser.). (Illus.). 32p. (Orig.). (J). (ps up). 1996. pap. 1.50 (*1-55709-378-4*) Applewood.

— Bird Songs. (Wonderlings Ser.). (Illus.). 32p. (Orig.). (J). (ps up). 1996. pap. 1.50 (*1-55709-376-8*) Applewood.

— Leaves. (Wonderlings Ser.). (Illus.). 32p. (Orig.). (J). (ps up). 1996. pap. 1.50 (*1-55709-381-4*) Applewood.

— Nature Journal. (Wonderlings Ser.). (Illus.). 32p. (J). (ps up). 1996. pap. 1.50 (*1-55709-377-6*) Applewood.

— On Insects. (Wonderlings Ser.). (Illus.). 32p. (Orig.). (J). (ps up). 1996. pap. 1.50 (*1-55709-380-6*) Applewood.

— Stars. (Wonderlings Ser.). (Illus.). 32p. (J). (ps up). 1996. pap. 1.50 (*1-55709-379-2*) Applewood.

— Wonderlings: Itty Bitty Nature Books. 1996. pap. 90.00 (*1-55709-375-X*) Applewood.

Appley, Dee G. & Winder, Alvin E. T-Groups & Therapy Groups in a Changing Society. LC 73-10934. (Jossey-Bass Behavioral Science Ser.). 232p. reprint ed. 72.00 (*0-8357-9350-8*, 201391300088) Bks Demand.

Appley, M. H. & Trumbull, R. A. Dynamics of Stress: Physiological, Psychological, & Social Perspectives. LC 86-25175. (Illus.). 360p. (C). 1986. 65.00 (*0-306-42252-2*, Plenum Trade) Perseus Pubng.

Appley, Mortimer H. & Maher, Winifred B. Social & Behavioral Sciences: Report of the Project 2061 Phase I. LC 89-101. 56p. 1989. pap. 8.00 (*0-87168-346-6*, 89-05S) AAAS.

Appleyard. Guide to the Identification of Animal Fibres. (C). 1978. 125.00 (*0-7855-4578-6*, Pub. by British Textile Tech) St Mut.

— International Economics. 4th ed. 2000. 66.25 (*0-07-231514-8*) McGraw.

— International Economics: Payments, Exchange Rates, & Macro Policy. LC 98-167671. 1997. text 39.60 (*0-256-17165-3*, Irwn McGrw-H) McGrw-H Hghr Educ.

Appleyard, et al. Conversion of Ukraine: The Continuing Story. Laszok, Anthony A. & Stoutenberger, Joseph, eds. 56p. (Orig.). 1988. pap. write for info. (*0-923635-00-9*) Ukrain Cath Diocese Parma.

Appleyard, Bryan. Brave New Worlds: Staying Human in the Genetic Future. LC 98-10243. 173p. 1998. 23.95 (*0-670-86989-9*, Viking) Viking Penguin.

Appleyard Communication Staff, ed. see Murphy, Bert.

Appleyard Communications Staff, ed. see Murphy, Bert.

Appleyard, David & Appleyard, David L. Colloquial Amharic: A Complete Language Course. (Colloquials Ser.). 336p. (C). (gr. 13). 1995. 55.00 incl. audio (*0-415-10005-4*, B4037) Routledge.

Appleyard, David L. Colloquial Amharic: A Complete Language Course. LC 95-5029. (Colloquials Ser.). 336p. (C). (gr. 13). 1995. pap. 24.99 (*0-415-10003-8*, B4029); audio 29.99 (*0-415-10004-6*, B4033) Routledge.

Appleyard, David L., jt. auth. see Appleyard, David.

Appleyard, Dennis R. International Economics. 3rd ed. 1997. text 55.80 (*0-256-17243-9*) McGraw.

— International Economics. 3rd ed. 1997. pap., student ed., wbk. ed. 23.75 (*0-256-17244-7*) McGraw.

Appleyard, Dennis R. & Cobb, Steven. International Economics. 2nd ed. 360p. (C). 1995. text, wbk. ed. 21.25 (*0-256-15401-5*, Irwn McGrw-H) McGrw-H Hghr Educ.

Appleyard, Dennis R. & Field, Alfred J., Jr. International Economics. 2nd ed. LC 94-19843. 656p. (C). 1994. text 69.75 (*0-256-14365-X*, Irwn McGrw-H) McGrw-H Hghr Educ.

Appleyard, Dennis R. & Field, Alfred J. International Economics. 3rd ed. LC 97-35040. 1997. 70.00 (*0-256-17163-7*, Irwn Prfssnl) McGraw-Hill Prof.

Appleyard, Dennis R. & Field, Alfred J., Jr. International Economics: Payments, Exchange Rates & Macro Policy. 2nd ed. LC 94-19842. 328p. (C). 1994. text 49.50 (*0-256-16192-5*, Irwn McGrw-H) McGrw-H Hghr Educ.

Appleyard, Dennis R. & Field, Alfred J. International Economics: Payments, Exchange Rates & Macro Policy. 3rd ed. LC 97-36817. 376p. 1997. pap. 60.31 (*0-07-109322-2*) McGraw.

Appleyard, Dennis R. & Field, Alfred J., Jr. International Economics: Trade Theory & Policy. 2nd ed. LC 94-19841. 424p. (C). 1994. text 49.50 (*0-256-16193-3*, Irwn McGrw-H) McGrw-H Hghr Educ.

Appleyard, Donald, ed. The Conservation of European Cities. (Illus.). 1979. 57.50 (*0-262-01057-7*) MIT Pr.

Appleyard, H. M. Guide to the Identification of Animal Fibres. 124p. 1982. 100.00 (*0-7855-7312-7*) St Mut.

Appleyard, J. A. Becoming a Reader: The Experience of Fiction from Childhood to Adulthood. 238p. (C). 1991. text 49.95 (*0-521-38364-1*) Cambridge U Pr.

— Becoming a Reader: The Experience of Fiction from Childhood to Adulthood. 238p. (C). 1994. pap. text 16.95 (*0-521-46756-X*) Cambridge U Pr.

Appleyard, John. De Luna. 1977. lib. bdg. 5.95 (*0-686-22981-9*) Appleyard Agency.

Appleyard, John, ed. see Dunlap, Deborah.

***Appleyard, Reginald, ed.** The Arab Region. (Emigration Dynamics in Developing Countries Ser.: Vol. 4). 290p. 1999. text 74.95 (*1-84014-552-8*, Pub. by Ashgate Pub) Ashgate Pub Co.

Appleyard, Reginald, ed. Emigration Dynamics in Developing Countries No. 3: Mexico, Central America & the Caribbean. LC 98-73509. 13p. 1999. text 74.95 (*1-84014-551-X*) Ashgate Pub Co.

— Emigration Dynamics of Developing Countries Vol. 1: Sub-Saharan Africa. LC JV9480.E55 1998. (Emigration Dynamics in Developing Countries Ser.). 3p. (C). 1998. text 72.95 (*1-84014-554-4*, Pub. by Ashgate Pub) Ashgate Pub Co.

— Emmigration Dynamics in Developing Countries Vol. 2: South Asia. LC 98-73509. 308p. 1999. text 67.95 (*1-84014-553-6*, Pub. by Ashgate Pub) Ashgate Pub Co.

Appleyard, Reginald T. The Ten Pound Immigrants. 192p. 1988. 60.00 (*1-85283-220-7*, Pub. by Boxtree) St Mut.

Appleyard, Reginald T. & Manford, Toby. The Beginning. 239p. 1980. 21.50 (*0-85564-146-0*, Pub. by Univ of West Aust Pr) Intl Spec Bk.

***Appleyard, Reginald T., et al.** Emigration Dynamics in Developing Countries LC 98-73509. 1998. write for info. (*1-84014-566-8*) Ashgate Pub Co.

Appleyard, Rollo. Pioneers of Electrical Communication. LC 68-54322. (Essay Index Reprint Ser). 1977. 26.95 (*0-8369-0156-8*) Ayer.

Appleyard, S. F. Marine Electronic Navigation. 2nd ed. 600p. (C). 1988. 110.00 (*0-415-06600-X*) Routledge.

Application Automation Div. Staff. Automation for Injection Molding. 1985. 5.00 (*0-910447-03-9*) Application Eng Corp.

Application Engineering Corporation Staff. Engineering & Application Manual for AEC Companies: Material Handling Division. 214p. (C). 1982. 80.00 (*0-910447-02-0*) Application Eng Corp.

— Engineering & Application Manual for AEC Companies: Size Reduction Division. 100p. (C). 1982. 80.00 (*0-910447-01-2*) Application Eng Corp.

— Engineering & Application Manual for AEC Companies: Water Division. 165p. 1981. 80.00 (*0-910447-00-4*) Application Eng Corp.

Application of Computers & Operations Research in. Application of Computers & Operations Research in the Minerals Industry: 17th International Symposium. Johnson, Thys B. & Barnes, Randal J., eds. LC 82-70116. (Illus.). 816p. 1982. reprint ed. pap. 200.00 (*0-7837-9181-X*, 204988000003) Bks Demand.

Applications of Computers & Operations Research in. Application of Computers & Operations Research in the Mineral Industry: 23rd International Symposium. Kim, Y. C., ed. LC 91-68323. (Illus.). 998p. 1992. reprint ed. pap. 200.00 (*0-7837-9182-8*, 204988100003) Bks Demand.

Applications of Holography in Mechanics Symposium. Applications of Holography in Mechanics: Symposium, University of Southern California, 1971. Gottenberg, W. G., ed. LC 78-172086. 94p. reprint ed. pap. 30.00 (*0-8357-5668-8*, 201684200005) Bks Demand.

Applied Biomathematics Staff. Cluster Analysis in Space & Time. 278p. 1990. 490.00 (*1-884977-06-5*); teacher ed. 980.00 (*1-884977-07-3*) Applied Biomath.

A

Applied Continuum Mechanics Symposium Staff. Proceedings of the Applied Continuum Mechanics Symposium, Vienna, 1974. Zeman, J. L. & Ziegler, Franz, eds. LC 74-12227. (Illus.). vii, 221p. 1974. 33.00 (*0-387-81260-1*) Spr-Verlag.

Applied Management Engineering Staff & Rush, Sean C. Managing the Facilities Portfolio. 100p. 1991. 37.00 (*0-915164-59-0*) NACUBO.

Applied Mathematics Symposium Staff. Applications of Nonlinear Partial Differential Equations in the Mathematical Physics. Finn, R., ed. LC 65-18255. (Proceedings of Symposia in Applied Mathematics Ser.: Vol. 17). 234p. 1965. text 36.00 (*0-8218-1317-X*, PSAPM/17) Am Math.

— Applied Probability. MacColl, L. A., ed. LC 50-1183. (Proceedings of Symposia in Applied Mathematics Ser.: Vol. 7). 104p. 1957. text 31.00 (*0-8218-1307-2*, PSAPM/7) Am Math.

— Calculus of Variations & Its Applications. LC 50-1183. (Proceedings of the Symposium in Applied Mathematics Ser., Chicago, 1956: Vol.8). 153p. 1958. reprint ed. pap. 42.00 (*0-8218-1308-0*, PSAPM/8) Am Math.

— Combinatorial Analysis. Bellman, R. & Hall, M., Jr., eds. LC 50-1183. (Proceedings of Symposia in Applied Mathematics Ser.: Vol. 10). 311p. 1960. reprint ed. pap. 49.00 (*0-8218-1310-2*, PSAPM/10) Am Math.

— Electromagnetic Theory. Taub, A. H. et al, eds. LC 50-1183. (Proceedings of Symposia in Applied Mathematics Ser.: Vol. 2). 91p. 1950. text 26.00 (*0-8218-1302-1*, PSAPM/2) Am Math.

— Experimental Arithmetic, High Speed Computing & Mathematics: Proceedings. Metropolis, N. C. et al, eds. LC 63-17582. (Proceedings of Symposia in Applied Mathematics Ser.: Vol. 15). 396p. 1963. pap. 38.00 (*0-8218-1315-3*, PSAPM/15) Am Math.

— Fluid Dynamics. Martin, M. H., ed. LC 50-1183. (Proceedings of Symposia in Applied Mathematics Ser.: Vol. 4). 186p. 1953. pap. 35.00 (*0-8218-1304-8*, PSAPM/4) Am Math.

— The Influence of Computing on Mathematical Research & Education. La Salle, Joseph P., ed. LC 74-5166. (Proceedings of Symposia in Applied Mathematics Ser.: Vol. 20). 205p. 1974. text 52.00 (*0-8218-1326-9*, PSAPM/20) Am Math.

— Magneto-Fluid & Plasma Dynamics: Proceedings. Grad, H., ed. LC 66-20436. (Proceedings of Symposia in Applied Mathematics Ser.: Vol. 18). 293p. 1967. pap. 34.00 (*0-8218-1318-8*, PSAPM/18) Am Math.

— Numerical Analysis. Curtiss, J. H., ed. LC 50-1183. (Proceedings of Symposia in Applied Mathematics Ser.). 303p. 1956. text 49.00 (*0-8218-1306-4*, PSAPM/6) Am Math.

— Orbit Theory. Birkhoff, Garrett D. & Langer, R. E., eds. LC 50-1183. (Proceedings of Symposia in Applied Mathematics Ser.). 195p. 1959. text 35.00 (*0-8218-1309-9*, PSAPM/9) Am Math.

Applied Mathematics Symposium Staff, et al. Elasticity. Churchill, R. V., ed. LC 50-1183. (Proceedings of Symposia in Applied Mathematics Ser.: Vol. 3). 233p. 1950. reprint ed. pap. 50.00 (*0-8218-1303-X*, PSAPM/3) Am Math.

— Nonlinear Problems in Mechanics of Continua. Reissner, Eric, ed. LC 50-1183. (Proceedings of Symposia in Applied Mathematics Ser.). 219p. 1949. text 31.00 (*0-8218-1301-3*, PSAPM/1) Am Math.

Applied Mechanics, Bioengineering & Fluids Enginee. Computer Methods for Nonlinear Solids & Structural Mechanics. Atluri, Satya N. & Perrone, Nicholas, eds. LC 83-71307. (AMD Ser.: Vol. 54). (Illus.). 270p. reprint ed. pap. 83.70 (*0-8357-6068-5*, 205681200089) Bks Demand.

— Numerical Methods for Fluid Transient Analysis: Presented at Applied Mechanics, Bioengineering & Fluids Engineering Conference, Houston, Texas, June 20-22, 1983. Martin, C. S. & Chaudhry, M. Hanif, eds. LC 83-71317. (FED Ser.: Vol. 4). 87p. pap. 30.00 (*0-7837-0202-7*, 204049800017) Bks Demand.

Applied Mechanics Conference Staff. Propagation of Shock Waves in Solids: Presented at the Applied Mechanics Conference, Salt Lake City, Utah, June 14-17, 1976. LC 76-12662. (American Society of Mechanical Engineers, Applied Mechanics Division Ser.: Vol. 17). 122p. reprint ed. pap. 37.90 (*0-608-12667-5*, 202418500035) Bks Demand.

Applied Research & Development Institute Internati. Nonprofit Compensation & Benefits Practices. LC 97-35611. (Nonprofit Law, Finance, & Management Ser.). 224p. 1998. 59.95 (*0-471-18089-0*) Wiley.

Applied Social Psychology Annual Staff. Applied Social Psychology Annual, 4 vols., 2. LC 80-645341. 294p. pap. 91.20 (*0-8357-8474-6*, 203474200002) Bks Demand.

— Applied Social Psychology Annual, 4 vols., 3. LC 80-645341. 304p. pap. 94.30 (*0-8357-8475-4*, 203474200003) Bks Demand.

— Applied Social Psychology Annual, 4 vols., 4. LC 80-645341. 280p. pap. 86.80 (*0-8357-8476-2*, 203474200004) Bks Demand.

— Applied Social Psychology Annual, 4 vols., 5. LC 80-645341. 288p. pap. 89.30 (*0-8357-8477-0*, 203474200005) Bks Demand.

Applin, David. Key Science: Biology. (Illus.). 384p. (Orig.). 1994. pap. 33.00 (*0-7487-1676-9*, Pub. by S Thornes Pubs); pap., teacher ed. 33.00 (*0-7487-1722-6*, Pub. by S Thornes Pubs) Trans-Atl Phila.

— Key Science: Biology Extension File. 256p. 1998. pap. 130.00 (*0-7487-3004-4*, Pub. by S Thornes Pubs) Trans-Atl Phila.

— Key Science - Biology. 2nd ed. (Illus.). 448p. (YA). (gr. 9-11). 1998. pap. 29.50 (*0-7487-3007-9*, Pub. by S Thornes Pubs) Trans-Atl Phila.

Applin, E. A., jt. auth. see Cole, W. S.

***Appling, J. William, ed.** Integrated Health Care: Lessons Learned. 398p. 1999. pap. 67.00 (*1-56829-096-9*) Med Group Mgmt.

Appling, Jeffrey R. Discover Chemistry. 2nd ed. (Chemistry Ser.). 1998. pap. 44.40 (*0-534-36134-X*) Brooks-Cole.

— Math Survival Guide: Tips for Science Students. LC 94-223785. 140p. 1994. pap. 28.95 (*0-471-03103-8*) Wiley.

Appling, Mary Ann. Making Memories: Ideas for Family Missions Involvement. Gross, Karen, ed. 91p. (Orig.). 1993. pap. text 6.95 (*1-56309-077-5*, N934109, New Hope) Womans Mission Union.

Appold, Hans, et al. Technology of the Metal Trade. (C). 1987. pap. 16.00 (*81-224-0029-9*) S Asia.

Appolis, Keith U. From Fragmentation to Wholeness: The Black South African Family under Seige. 198p. (Orig.). (C). 1995. pap. text 27.50 (*0-7618-0132-4*); lib. bdg. 51.50 (*0-7618-0131-6*) U Pr of Amer.

Appollo, Annette. The Last One Home. LC 98-42116. 288p. 1999. 24.00 (*0-06-019208-9*) HarpC.

— The Last One Home. 400p. 2000. mass mkt. 6.99 (*0-06-109721-7*) HarpC.

— The Last One Home. large type ed. LC 99-28425. 470p. 1999. pap. 26.95 (*0-7862-2069-4*) Mac Lib Ref.

Appollo, Ken. Humble Work & Mad Wanderings: Street Life in the Machine Age. (Illus.). 108p. 1997. 19.95 (*1-887694-03-X*) C Mautz Pubng.

Appraisal Institute (U. S.) Staff. Viewpoints: A Collection of Papers Presented at the Appraisal Institute 1997 National Summer Conference. LC 97-38001. 1997. write for info. (*0-922154-43-0*) Appraisal Inst.

Appraisal Institute (U.S.) Staff, jt. auth. see Harrison, Frank E.

Appraisal Institute Staff. The Appraisal of Real Estate. 11th ed. LC 96-41019. (Illus.). 816p. 1996. 49.50 (*0-922154-35-X*) Appraisal Inst.

***Appraisal Institute Staff.** Appraising Residential Properties. 3rd ed. LC 99-45746. 454p. 1999. write for info. (*0-922154-57-0*) Appraisal Inst.

Appraisal Institute Staff. An Atlas of American Real Estate Appraisers. (Illus.). 180p. 1997. spiral bd. 15.00 (*0-922154-38-4*, 0661M) Appraisal Inst.

— Real Estate Market Analysis: Supply & Demand Factors. 1993. 25.00 (*0-922154-14-7*) Appraisal Inst.

Appraisal Institute Staff & Rayburn, William B. Exam Preparation for Residential Appraiser Certification. 287p. 1991. pap. text 37.95 (*0-7931-0112-3*, 1556-1301) Dearborn.

Appraisal Institute Staff, ed. see Akerson, Charles B.

Apprey, Maurice & Stein, Howard F. Intersubjectivity, Projective Identification & Otherness. LC 92-47242. 304p. 1993. 39.95 (*0-8207-0247-1*) Duquesne.

Apprey, Maurice, jt. auth. see Stein, Howard F.

Apprey, Maurice, tr. see Politzer, Georges.

Apps, D. A., jt. ed. see Tipton, Keith F.

Apps, D. K., ed. Essays in Biochemistry, Vol. 31. (Illus.). 150p. (C). 1996. pap. text 30.00 (*1-85578-019-4*, Pub. by Portland Pr Ltd) Ashgate Pub Co.

Apps, F. R., tr. see Ishio, H. & Shimada, S., eds.

Apps, F. R., tr. see Motooka, Tohru & Kitsuregawa, Masaru.

Apps, F. R., tr. see Yoshiaki Shirai & Jun-ichi Tsujii.

Apps, Jerold W. Leadership for the Emerging Age. (Higher & Adult Education Ser.). 272p. 1994. text 32.95 (*0-7879-0036-2*) Jossey-Bass.

— Mastering the Teaching of Adults. LC 91-3362. 160p. (C). 1991. lib. bdg. 22.50 (*0-89464-558-7*) Krieger.

— Study Skills for Today's College Student. 256p. 1990. pap. 23.93 (*0-07-002464-2*) McGraw.

***Apps, Jerold W.** Symbols: Viewing a Rural Past. LC 99-69674. (Illus.). 200p. 2000. pap. 16.95 (*0-942495-97-7*) Palmer Pubns Inc.

Apps, Jerold W. Teaching from the Heart. LC 95-37271. (Professional Practices in Adult Education & Human Resource Development Ser.). 140p. (C). 1996. 22.50 (*0-89464-940-X*) Krieger.

— Toward a Working Philosophy of Adult Education. LC 73-7425. (Occasional Papers). 65p. 1973. pap. 5.00 (*0-87060-059-1*, OCP 36) Syracuse U Cont Ed.

Apps, Jerold W., jt. ed. see Boyd, Robert D.

Apps, Jerry. Barns of Wisconsin. rev. ed. LC 77-5472. (Illus.). 152p. 1995. pap. 18.95 (*0-915024-48-9*) Trails Media.

— Breweries of Wisconsin. LC 92-10591. (North Coast Bks.). (Illus.). 272p. 1992. pap. 19.95 (*0-299-13374-5*) U of Wis Pr.

— Cheese: The Making of a Wisconsin Tradition. LC 98-12317. (Illus.). 248p. 1998. pap. 18.95 (*0-942495-80-2*) Palmer Pubns Inc.

— One-Room Country Schools: History & Recollections from Wisconsin. LC 96-7046. (Illus.). 240p. 1996. pap. 18.95 (*0-942495-53-5*) Palmer Pubns Inc.

— Rural Wisdom: Time-Honored Values of the Midwest. LC 97-1138. (Illus.). 128p. 1997. pap. 14.95 (*0-942495-63-2*) Palmer Pubns Inc.

— Skiing into Wisconsin: A Celebration of Winter. (Illus.). 270p. (Orig.). 1985. pap. 10.95 (*0-9606240-7-4*) Pearl-Win.

— When Chores Were Done: Boyhood Stories. LC 98-48776. (Illus.). 200p. 1999. pap. 16.95 (*0-942495-84-5*) Palmer Pubns Inc.

— The Wisconsin Traveler's Companion Vol. 1: A Guide to Country Sights. McBride, Elizabeth, ed. LC 97-60686. (Illus.). 208p. (Orig.). 1997. pap. 16.95 (*0-915024-56-X*) Trails Media.

Apps, John A. & Tsang, Chin-Fu, eds. Deep Injection Disposal of Hazardous & Industrial Waste: Scientific & Engineering Aspects. (Illus.). 775p. 1996. text 149.95 (*0-12-060060-9*) Acad Pr.

Apps, Michael J. Boreal Forests & Global Change: Conference on Boreal Forests & Global Change, Held in Saskatoon, Saskatchewan, Canada, September 25-30, 1994. Wisniewski, Joe & Price, David T., eds. LC 95-34349. 536p. (C). 1995. text 260.00 (*0-7923-3665-8*) Kluwer Academic.

Apps, Michael J. & Price, David T., eds. Forest Ecosystems, Forest Management & the Global Carbon Cycle. LC 95-48092. (NATO ASI Series I: Vol. 40). (Illus.). 454p. 1996. 219.00 (*3-540-60684-X*) Spr-Verlag.

Apps, Peter. Wild Ways: Field Guide to the Behavior of Southern African Mammals. (Illus.). 198p. pap. 14.95 (*1-86812-373-1*) Menasha Ridge.

Apps, Rod & Goacher, David. The Monetary & Financial System. 450p. 1990. pap. 125.00 (*0-85297-355-1*, Pub. by Chartered Bank) St Mut.

Appu, P. S. Land Reforms in India: A Survey of Policy, Legislation & Implementation. 1998. 40.00 (*81-259-0233-3*, Pub. by Vikas) S Asia.

Appy, Christian G. Cold War Constructions: The Political Culture of United States Imperialism, 1945-1966. LC 99-37754. (Culture, Politics & the Cold War Ser.). 328p. 2000. text 60.00 (*1-55849-217-8*) U of Mass Pr.

— Working-Class War: American Combat Soldiers & Vietnam. LC 92-18318. xii, 365p. (C). 1993. 55.00 (*0-8078-2057-1*); pap. 18.95 (*0-8078-4391-1*) U of NC Pr.

Appy, Christian G., ed. Cold War Constructions: The Political Culture of United States Imperialism, 1945-1966. LC 99-37754. (Culture, Politics & the Cold War Ser.). 328p. 2000. pap. text 18.95 (*1-55849-218-6*) U of Mass Pr.

Aprahamian, Francis, ed. see Pentz, Mike & Shott, Milo.

Aprahamian, Francis, jt. ed. see Swann, Brenda.

***Aprahmian, Peter.** Mexican Style Source Book: Creative Ideas for Enhancing Your Space. (Illus.). 144p. 2000. 29.95 (*0-7893-0402-3*) Universe.

Aprajita, Upali. Culture & Development: Dongrias of Niyamgiri. LC 94-900264. (C). 1994. 34.00 (*81-210-0329-6*, Pub. by Inter-India Pubns) S Asia.

Apraku, Kofi K. African Emigres in the United States: A Missing Link in Africa's Social & Economic Development. LC 90-24130. 192p. 1991. 52.95 (*0-275-93799-2*, C3799, Praeger Pubs) Greenwood.

— Outside Looking In: An African Perspective on American Pluralistic Society. LC 94-12349. 144p. 1996. 47.95 (*0-275-94207-4*, Praeger Pubs) Greenwood.

***Apraxine, Pierre.** La Divine Contesse: Photographs of the Countess de Castiglione. (Illus.). 192p. 2000. 24.95 (*0-300-08509-5*) Yale U Pr.

***Apresjan, Juri Derenick.** Systematic Lexicography. Windle, Kevin, tr. 320p. 2000. text 90.00 (*0-19-823780-4*) OUP.

Apresjan, Yuri D. English-Russian Dictionary of Synonyms. (ENG & RUS.). 544p. 1980. 29.95 (*0-8288-0788-4*, M15176) Fr & Eur.

— Principles & Methods of Contemporary Structural Linguistics. Crockett, Dina B., tr. from DUT. LC 72-94441. (Janua Linguarum, Ser. Minor: No. 144). (Illus.). 349p. (Orig.). 1973. pap. text 65.40 (*90-279-2386-8*) Mouton.

Apresjan, Yuri D., jt. ed. see Mednikova, E. M.

Apresyan, L. A. & Kravtsov, Yu A. Radiation Transfer: Statistical & Wave Aspects. 448p. 1996. text 84.00 (*2-88124-920-5*) Gordon & Breach.

April, Ernest W. Anatomy. 9th ed. (Basic Sciences: Pretest Self Assessment & Review Ser.). (Illus.). 1998. pap. 18.95 (*0-07-052683-4*) McGraw-Hill HPD.

— Clinical Anatomy. 3rd ed. LC 96-1552. (National Medical Series for Independent Study). (Illus.). 670p. 1997. pap. 27.00 (*0-683-06199-2*) Lppncott W & W.

— NMS Anatomy. 2nd ed. (National Medical Ser.). 610p. 1990. 26.00 (*0-683-06200-X*) Lppncott W & W.

April, Susan, et al. French Class: French Canadian-American Writings on Identity, Culture, & Place. (Illus.). 64p. 1999. pap. 12.00 (*0-931507-11-1*) Loom Pr.

April, Tom. Taste Missouri Wine Country. 150p. 1991. spiral bd. 11.95 (*0-9631456-0-6*) MO River Trad.

Aprile, Dianne. The Abbey of Gathsemani - Place of Peace & Paradox: 150 Years in the Life of America's Oldest Trappist Monastery. (Illus.). 248p. 1998. 39.95 (*0-9642802-1-3*) Trout Lily Pr.

***Aprile, Dianne.** Making a Heart for God: A Week Inside a Catholic Monastery. 2000. 21.95 (*1-893361-14-4*) SkyLight Paths.

Aprile, Dianne. The Things We Don't Forget: Views from Real Life. 364p. 1994. pap. 12.95 (*0-9642802-0-5*) Trout Lily Pr.

Aprill, Arnold, jt. auth. see Frank, Daniel B.

Aprill, Dennis. Paths Less Traveled: The Adirondack Experience for Walkers, Hikers & Climbers of All Ages. LC 98-65509. (Illus.). 150p. (YA). (gr. 9-12). 1998. pap. 14.95 (*0-9632476-6-2*) Pinto Pr.

***Aprill, Dennis.** Paths Less Traveled: The Adirondack Experience for Walkers, Hikers & Climbers of All Ages. 2nd rev. ed. (Illus.). 231p. 1999. pap. 16.95 (*0-9632476-9-7*) Pinto Pr.

Aprill, Dennis, ed. Good Fishing in the Adirondacks: From Lake Champlain to the Streams of Tug Hill. 2nd rev. ed. LC 98-52993. (Backcountry Guides Ser.). (Illus.). 233p. 1999. pap. 16.00 (*0-88150-452-1*, Pub. by Countryman) Norton.

Aprill, Dennis, jt. auth. see Chapman, William K.

ApRoberts, Ruth. The Biblical Web. LC 94-782. 200p. 1994. text 42.50 (*0-472-10494-2*, 10494) U of Mich Pr.

APS Judges Accreditation Committee Staff & Bauer, William H., eds. Manual of Philatelic Judging. 3rd rev. ed. 120p. 1990. pap. 8.50 (*0-318-41175-X*) Am Philatelic Society.

APSA Staff, ed. The American Political Science Association Membership Directory, 1997-1999. rev. ed. 312p. (C). 1980. pap. text 45.00 (*1-878147-25-0*) Am Political.

— Directory of Undergraduate Political Science Faculty, 1996-1998. 5th rev. ed. (C). 1996. 24.00 (*1-878147-22-6*) Am Political.

Apsan, Howard N. ISO 14000: Understanding the Emerging Global Environmental Standards Program Strategies for Legal, International & Financial Issues. Date not set. 59.95 (*1-56670-258-5*, L1258) Lewis Pubs.

Apseloff, Glen, jt. auth. see Apseloff, Stanford.

Apseloff, Marilyn F. Elizabeth George Speare. (Twayne's United States Authors Ser.: No. 541). 170p. 1992. 23.95 (*0-8057-7636-2*) Macmillan.

Apseloff, Marilyn F., compiled by. They Wrote for Children Too: An Annotated Bibliography of Children's Literature by Famous Writers for Adults, 20. LC 89-2194. (Bibliographies & Indexes in World Literature Ser.: No. 20). 216p. 1989. lib. bdg. 65.00 (*0-313-25981-X*, ACL/) Greenwood.

Apseloff, Stanford & Apseloff, Glen. The Ultimate Diet Tool Kit: Ohio Distinctive Software Guide to Diet & Nutrition. 250p. (Orig.). 1994. pap. 8.95 (*0-9647934-0-7*) OH Distinct Pub.

Apseloff, Stanford, ed. see Shearer, Tamara S.

ApSimon, Helen, et al, eds. Acid Rain in Europe: Counting the Cost. 192p. 1997. pap. 40.00 (*1-85383-443-2*, Pub. by Escan Pubns) Island Pr.

ApSimon, Hugh. Educating Evelyn: Conversations on the Curious Laws of Rubber Bridge. LC 98-116490. 112p. 1998. pap. 12.95 (*0-86140-389-4*, Pub. by Smyth) Dufour.

Apsimon, John W. The Total Synthesis of Natural Products, Vol. 9. 544p. 1992. 215.00 (*0-471-55189-9*) Wiley.

Apsimon, John W., ed. The Total Synthesis of Natural Products, 9 vols. 5106p. 1992. 1495.00 (*0-471-58083-X*) Wiley.

— The Total Synthesis of Natural Products, Vol. 1. LC 72-4075. 624p. 1973. 180.00 (*0-471-03251-4*) Wiley.

— The Total Synthesis of Natural Products, Vol. 2. 768p. 1973. 180.00 (*0-471-03252-2*) Wiley.

— The Total Synthesis of Natural Products, Vol. 3. 566p. 1977. 180.00 (*0-471-02392-2*) Wiley.

— The Total Synthesis of Natural Products, Vol. 4. LC 72-4075. (Total Synthesis of Natural Products Ser.). 610p. 1981. 180.00 (*0-471-05460-7*) Wiley.

— The Total Synthesis of Natural Products, Vol. 5. (Total Synthesis of Natural Products Ser.). 550p. 1983. 180.00 (*0-471-09808-6*) Wiley.

— The Total Synthesis of Natural Products, Vol. 6. LC 72-4075. (Total Synthesis of Natural Products Ser.). 291p. 1984. 140.00 (*0-471-09900-7*) Wiley.

— The Total Synthesis of Natural Products, Vol. 8. 720p. 1992. 250.00 (*0-471-54507-4*) Wiley.

Apsley, Brenda. Colors & Numbers. (I Can Learn Ser.). (Illus.). 24p. (J). (ps-2). 1994. 1.95 (*1-56293-511-9*, McClanahan Book) Learn Horizon.

Apsley, John W., II. The Genesis Effect: Spearheading Regeneration with Wild Blue Green Algae, Vol. 1. LC 96-84804. 96p. (Orig.). 1996. pap. 7.95 (*0-945704-01-1*) Genesis Comns.

Apstein, C. Die Pyrocysteen der Plankton-Expedition der Humboldt-Stiftung. 1971. reprint ed. 15.00 (*3-7682-0807-9*) Lubrecht & Cramer.

Apstein, C., jt. ed. see Brandt, K.

Apt, Alan, ed. see Metzelaar, Lawrence C. & Fox.

Apt, Alan, ed. see Miller, Nancy E.

Apt, Alan, ed. see Thorne, Michael.

Apt, Bryan. Case of the Missing Detective: Mystery down Under. LC 95-80394. (Illus.). 18p. (J). (gr. 1-4). 1995. pap. text 2.99 (*0-9649055-0-7*) Harper Benton.

Apt, Charles. A Book of Special Days. 1992. 16.00 (*0-614-01773-4*) Gibson.

Apt, K. R., et al, eds. Logic Programming Languages: Constraints, Functions, & Objects. LC 92-46899. (Logic Programming Ser.). (Illus.). 225p. 1993. 35.00 (*0-262-01134-4*) MIT Pr.

Apt, K. R. & Olderog, F. R. Verification of Sequential & Concurrent Programs. Gries, David, ed. (Texts & Monographs in Computer Science). xvi, 441p. 1991. 59.95 (*0-387-97532-2*) Spr-Verlag.

Apt, K. R., jt. auth. see Olderog, Ernst R.

Apt, Krzysztof & Turini, Franco, eds. Meta-Logics & Logic Programming. (Logic Programming Ser.). (Illus.). 350p. (C). 1995. 44.00 (*0-262-01152-2*) MIT Pr.

Apt, Krzysztof R., et al, eds. The Logic Programming Paradigm: A 25-year Perspective. LC 99-18481. (Artificial Intelligence Ser.). xiv, 457p. 1999. 62.00 (*3-540-65463-1*) Spr-Verlag.

Apt, L. Louis-Philippe de Segur: An Intellectual in a Revolutionary Age. (International Archives of the History of Ideas Ser.: No. 25). 173p. 1969. lib. bdg. 71.50 (*90-247-0201-1*, Pub. by M Nijhoff) Kluwer Academic.

Apt, Nana. Coping with Old Age in a Changing Africa: Social Change & the Elderly Ghanian. 176p. 1996. 66.95 (*1-85972-024-2*, Pub. by Avebry) Ashgate Pub Co.

Apt, Nana A., et al, eds. Maintaining the Momentum of Beijung: The Contribution of African Gender NGOs. LC 98-72625. (University of North London Voices in Development Management Ser.). 234p. 1998. text 59.95 (*1-85972-483-3*, Pub. by Avebry) Ashgate Pub Co.

APTA Staff, contrib. by. Financial Assistance. (Resource Guide Ser.). 87p. 1999. pap. 15.50 (*1-887759-27-1*, P-62) Am Phys Therapy Assn.

— Guidelines for Evaluating Functional Capacity. 12p. 1998. pap. 10.00 (*1-887759-29-8*, P-147) Am Phys Therapy Assn.

— Guidelines for Programs for Injured Workers: Work Conditioning & Work Hardening. 12p. 1994. pap. 10.00 (*1-887759-30-1*, P-114) Am Phys Therapy Assn.

— Guidelines for Recognizing & Providing Care for Victims of Domestic Violence. 36p. 1997. pap. 15.00 (*1-887759-31-X*, P-138) Am Phys Therapy Assn.

An Asterisk (*) at the beginning of an entry indicates that the title is appearing for the first time.

— Healing the Generations: A History of Physical Therapy & the American Physical Therapy Association. 256p. 1995. 79.95 (*1-887759-33-6*, APTA-20) Am Phys Therapy Assn.

— Hydrotherapy/Therapeutic Pool Infection Control Guidelines. 30p. 1994. pap. 15.00 (*1-887759-34-4*, P-112) Am Phys Therapy Assn.

— In Touch: Topics in Physical Therapy, a Refresher. 1997. pap. 209.00 (*1-887759-37-9*, Ref-1) Am Phys Therapy Assn.

— International Opportunities in Physical Therapy. 103p. 1997. pap. 12.50 (*1-887759-49-2*, I-01) Am Phys Therapy Assn.

— A Normative Model of Physical Therapist Professional Education: Version 97. 250p. 1997. pap. 55.95 (*1-887759-38-7*, E-33) Am Phys Therapy Assn.

— Patient Satisfaction Instruments: A Compendium. 96p. 1995. pap. 29.95 (*1-887759-40-9*, P-127) Am Phys Therapy Assn.

— Peer Assistance/Impaired Provider Program: A Model. 59p. 1994. pap. 15.00 (*1-887759-41-7*, P-111) Am Phys Therapy Assn.

— Physical Therapists Facing Changing Organizational Structures. 165p. 1996. pap. 18.50 (*1-887759-43-3*, P-126) Am Phys Therapy Assn.

— Self-Assessment Tools for Physical Therapists: Cardiopulmonary. 1997. pap. 14.00 (*1-887759-45-X*, E-34) Am Phys Therapy Assn.

— Self-Assessment Tools for Physical Therapists: Clinical Electrophysiologic. 1997. pap. 14.00 (*1-887759-55-7*, E-35) Am Phys Therapy Assn.

— Self-Assessment Tools for Physical Therapists: Geriatric. 1997. pap. 14.00 (*1-887759-56-5*, E-36) Am Phys Therapy Assn.

— Self-Assessment Tools for Physical Therapists: Neurologic. 1997. pap. 14.00 (*1-887759-57-3*, E-37) Am Phys Therapy Assn.

— Self-Assessment Tools for Physical Therapists: Orthopaedic. 1997. pap. 14.00 (*1-887759-58-1*, E-38) Am Phys Therapy Assn.

— Self-Assessment Tools for Physical Therapists: Pediatric. 1997. pap. 14.00 (*1-887759-59-X*, E-39) Am Phys Therapy Assn.

— Self-Assessment Tools for Physical Therapists: Sports Physical Therapy. 1997. pap. 14.00 (*1-887759-60-3*) Am Phys Therapy Assn.

— Women's Issues. 192p. 1998. pap. 18.50 (*1-887759-46-8*, P-119) Am Phys Therapy Assn.

*__Apte, D. G.__ Book of Indian Shells. LC 98-915482. (Illus.). 162p. 1999. 19.95 (*0-19-564783-1*) OUP.

Apte, D. G., jt. auth. see Dadape, E. V.

Apte, Helen J. Heart of a Wife: The Diary of a Southern Jewish Woman. Rosenbaum, Marcus D., ed. LC 98-21416. (Illus.). 224p. 1998. 55.00 (*0-8420-2745-9*, SR Bks); pap. 17.95 (*0-8420-2746-7*, SR Bks) Scholarly Res Inc.

*__APTE, Inc. Staff.__ Internet Coach for Microsoft Internet Explorer 4.0 Workbook. (Illus.). 28p. 1999. spiral bd. 19.95 (*1-889651-49-4*) APTE.

— Internet Coach Puzzle Builder Teacher's Guide. (Illus.). Date not set. teacher ed., spiral bd. 42.95 (*1-889651-46-X*) APTE.

— Internet Coach Solution Facilitator's Manual. (Illus.). teacher ed., spiral bd. write for info. (*1-889651-51-6*) APTE.

— Internet Coach Solution Workbook: For Netscape Navigator & Communicator. (Illus.). 1999. spiral bd., wbk. ed. write for info. (*1-889651-47-8*) APTE.

— Internet Coach Solution Workbook for Microsoft Internet Explorer. (Illus.). spiral bd., wbk. ed. write for info. (*1-889651-48-6*) APTE.

APTE, Inc. Staff. Teacher's Guide for Internet Coach for Net Safety. (Illus.). Date not set. spiral bd. 10.00 (*1-889651-25-7*) APTE.

— Teacher's Guide for Liftoff to Lizard Island: Internet Coach. (Illus.). 65p. 1997. spiral bd. 10.00 (*1-889651-31-1*) APTE.

— Teacher's Guide for Mission to Planet X: Internet Coach (Version 2.0) (Illus.). 48p. 1997. spiral bd. 10.00 (*1-889651-30-3*) APTE.

— Teacher's Guide for Search for the Black Rhino: Internet Coach. (Illus.). x, 57p. 1997. spiral bd. 10.00 (*1-889651-32-X*) APTE.

Apte, James. First Nights. LC 75-86854. 311p. 1972. 24.95 (*0-405-18121-3*) Ayer.

*__APTE Staff.__ Internet Coach for Netscape Navigator & Communicator Workbook. (Illus.). 28p. 1999. spiral bd. 19.95 (*1-889651-50-8*) APTE.

— Mission to Planet X: Internet Coach. 2nd rev. ed. (Illus.). 81p. 1999. spiral bd. 25.00 (*1-889651-53-2*) APTE.

APTE Staff. Teacher's Guide for Field Trap: Internet Coach. (Illus.). 50p. 1999. spiral bd. 25.00 (*1-889651-39-7*) APTE.

APTE Staff, ed. Search for the Black Rhino: Internet Coach. (YA). (gr. 4-12). 1997. pap., lab manual ed. 179.95 incl. cd-rom (*1-889651-20-6*) APTE.

Apte, Stuart C. Stu Apte's Fishing in the Florida Keys & Flamingo. 6th ed. (Illus.). 80p. 1995. pap. 6.95 (*0-89317-062-3*) Windward Pub.

Apte, U. M. The Sacrament of Marriage in Hindu Society. 25p. 1978. 19.95 (*0-318-36842-0*) Asia Bk Corp.

*__Apte, Vama Shivaram.__ Practical Sanskrit-English Dictionary. 1998. 40.00 (*81-208-1568-8*) Motilal Bnarsidass.

Apte, Vaman S. English-Sanskrit, Student's Dictionary. 3rd ed. (ENG & SAN.). 501p. 1991. 20.75 (*81-208-0299-3*) IBD Ltd.

— The Practical Sanskrit-English Dictionary. rev. ed. 112p. 1987. 95.00 (*0-8288-1779-0*, M14250) Fr & Eur.

— Student's English-Sanskrit Dictionary. 501p. 1987. reprint ed. 12.50 (*0-685-19385-3*, Pub. by Motilal Bnarsidass); reprint ed. pap. 9.50 (*81-208-0300-0*, Pub. by Motilal Bnarsidass) S Asia.

— The Student's Guide to Sanskrit Composition: Being a Treatise on Sanskrit Syntax. 404p. 1995. 12.00 (*81-86339-20-5*, Pub. by Eastern Bk Linkers) Nataraj Bks.

— Student's Sanskrit-English Dictionary. 1987. 59.95 (*0-8288-1778-2*, M7830); 59.95 (*0-8288-4022-9*, F43360) Fr & Eur.

— Student's Sanskrit-English Dictionary: Containing Appendices on Sanskrit Prosody & Important Literary & Geographical Names in the Ancient History of India. 2nd ed. (ENG & SAN.). 664p. (C). 1993. reprint ed. text 24.00 (*81-208-0044-3*, Pub. by Motilal Bnarsidass) S Asia.

Apte, Vasudeo G. Concise Sanskrit-English Dictionary. 366p. 1986. reprint ed. 17.50 (*0-685-17531-6*, Pub. by Motilal Bnarsidass); reprint ed. 14.00 (*81-208-0151-2*, Pub. by Motilal Bnarsidass) S Asia.

— Concise Sanskrit-English Dictionary. 1998. reprint ed. pap. 12.00 (*81-208-0152-0*) Motilal Bnarsidass.

Apted, J., jt. auth. see Eaglestone, Frank N.

Apted, M. J. & Westerman, R. E., eds. Scientific Basis for Nuclear Waste Management XI. (Symposium Proceedings Ser.: Vol. 112). 1988. text 17.50 (*0-931837-80-4*) Materials Res.

Aptekar, Ken, et al. Ken Aptekar: Talking to Pictures. LC 97-34488. (Illus.). 1997. write for info. (*0-88675-053-9*) Corcoran.

Aptekar, Lewis. Environmental Disasters in Global Perspective. LC 93-12836. (Reference Ser.). 208p. 1993. 26.95 (*0-8161-7381-8*, Hall Reference); 16.95 (*0-8161-1608-3*, Hall Reference) Macmillan.

— The Psychological Process of Adjusting to Natural Disasters. 45p. (Orig.). (C). 1993. pap. text 25.00 (*1-56806-972-3*) DIANE Pub.

— Street Children of Cali. LC 87-34234. (Illus.). xxi, 272p. 1988. text 44.95 (*0-8223-0834-7*) Duke.

Apter. Continental Drift. 1999. pap. text 19.00 (*0-226-02350-8*); lib. bdg. 49.00 (*0-226-02349-4*) U Ch Pr.

— The Legitimization of Violence. 448p. 1998. pap. text 20.00 (*0-8147-0649-5*) NYU Pr.

Apter. Pas de Vacances pour le Commissaire. text 3.95 (*0-88436-908-0*) EMC-Paradigm.

Apter, Andrew. Black Critics & Kings: The Hermeneutics of Power in Yoruba Society. (Illus.). 298p. 1992. pap. text 19.95 (*0-226-02343-5*); lib. bdg. 46.00 (*0-226-02342-7*) U Ch Pr.

Apter-Cragnolino, Aida. Espejos Naturalistas: Ideologia y Representacion en la Novela Argentina (1884-1919) (Wor(l)ds of Change Ser.: Vol. 11). (SPA.). X, 187p. (C). 1999. text 44.95 (*0-8204-2690-3*) P Lang Pubng.

Apter, David E. Choice & the Politics of Allocation: A Developmental Theory. LC 70-151566. 222p. reprint ed. pap. 68.90 (*0-8357-8713-3*, 203366300087) Bks Demand.

— A Comparative Method for the Study of Politics. (Reprint Series in Social Sciences). (C). 1993. reprint ed. pap. text 5.00 (*0-8290-3379-3*, PS-8) Irvington.

— Ghana in Transition. 2nd rev. ed. LC 63-3161. (Illus.). 462p. reprint ed. pap. 143.30 (*0-608-11815-X*, 201001300071) Bks Demand.

— Political Change. 245p. 1973. 32.50 (*0-7146-2941-3*, BHA-02941, Pub. by F Cass Pubs); pap. 19.50 (*0-7146-4012-3*, BHA-00097, Pub. by F Cass Pubs) Intl Spec Bk.

— The Political Kingdom in Uganda: A Study in Bureaucratic Nationalism. 3rd ed. LC 97-13495. 498p. (C). 1997. 59.50 (*0-7146-4696-2*, Pub. by Irish Acad Pr); pap. 27.50 (*0-7146-4234-7*, Pub. by Irish Acad Pr) Intl Spec Bk.

— The Politics of Modernization. LC JF0051.A7. (Phoenix Bks.). (Illus.). 503p. reprint ed. pap. 156.00 (*0-608-18231-1*, 205663900078) Bks Demand.

— Rethinking Development: Modernization, Dependency, & Post-Modern Politics. 312p. (C). 1987. text 49.95 (*0-8039-2971-4*); pap. text 25.00 (*0-8039-2972-2*) Sage.

Apter, David E., ed. The Legitimization of Violence. 448p. (C). 1997. text 55.00 (*0-8147-0648-7*) NYU Pr.

Apter, David E. & Rosberg, Carl G. Political Development & the New Realism in Sub-Saharan Africa. LC 93-2428. 1994. pap. text 19.50 (*0-8139-1480-9*) U Pr of Va.

Apter, David E. & Saich, Tony. Revolutionary Discourse in Mao's Republic. LC 94-4421. (Illus.). 423p. 1994. text 58.50 (*0-674-76779-9*, APTREV); pap. text 25.95 (*0-674-76780-2*, APTREX) HUP.

Apter, David E. & Sawa, Nagayo. Against the State. (Illus.). 296p. 1986. pap. 17.00 (*0-674-00921-5*) HUP.

— Against the State: Politics & Social Protest in Japan. LC 83-15338. (Illus.). 296p. 1984. 37.50 (*0-674-00920-7*) HUP.

Apter, David E., jt. auth. see Andrain, Charles F.

Apter, David E., ed. see Qing, Dai.

Apter-Desselles, Mitzi & Komaki, Judith L. Effective Supervision. (People & Organizations Ser.). (Illus.). 296p. (C). (gr. 13). 1998. 85.00 (*0-415-09873-4*, B4120) Routledge.

Apter, Emily. Andre Gide: And the Codes of Homotextuality. (Stanford French & Italian Studies: Vol. 48). 174p. 1987. pap. 56.50 (*0-915838-64-8*) Anma Libri.

— Feminizing the Fetish: Psychoanalysis & Narrative Obsession in Turn-of-the-Century France. Pietz, William, ed. LC 91-55067. (Illus.). 296p. 1991. text 45.00 (*0-8014-2653-7*); pap. text 17.95 (*0-8014-9952-6*) Cornell U Pr.

Apter, Emily & Pietz, William, eds. Fetishism As Cultural Discourse. LC 92-31984. 416p. 1993. 47.50 (*0-8014-2522-0*); pap. text 18.95 (*0-8014-9757-4*) Cornell U Pr.

Apter, M. F., et al, eds. Reversal Theory: Applications & Development. 212p. (C). 1985. text 39.95 (*0-906449-74-X*) L Erlbaum Assocs.

Apter, Michael J. Reversal Theory: Motivation, Emotion & Personality. 224p. 1989. 45.00 (*0-415-01581-2*) Routledge.

Apter, Michael J., jt. auth. see Svebak, Sven.

Apter, Michael J., jt. auth. see Svebek, Sven.

Apter, Michael J., jt. ed. see Kerr, J. H.

Apter, Millie, jt. auth. see Brody, Lora A.

Apter, Ronnie. A Bilingual Edition of the Love Songs of Bernart de Ventadorn in Occitan & English: Sugar & Salt. Herman, Mark, tr. from PRO. LC 99-20076. (Studies in Medieval Literature: Vol. 17). xvii, 307p. 1999. text 99.95 (*0-7734-8009-9*) E Mellen.

Apter, Ronnie & Herman, Mark, trs. from FRE. Reader's Digest Bible for Children: Timeless Stories from the Old & New Testaments. LC 95-7993. (Reader's Digest Ser.).Tr. of Bible: les Belles Histoires de l'Ancien et du Nouveau Testament. (Illus.). 165p. (J). (gr. 4-6). 1995. 19.95 (*0-89577-815-7*) Rdrs Digest.

Apter, T. E. Virginia Woolf: A Study of Her Novels LC 79-317982. viii, 167p. 1979. write for info. (*0-333-23979-2*) Macmillan.

Apter, Terri. Altered Loves: Mothers & Daughters During Adolescence. 288p. 1991. pap. 10.00 (*0-449-90631-0*, Columbine) Fawcett.

Apter, Terri. The Confident Child: Raising a Child to Try, Learn, & Care. LC 96-36180. 224p. (C). 1997. 23.00 (*0-393-04058-5*) Norton.

Apter, Terri. The Confident Child: Raising Children to Believe in Themselves. 272p. 1998. reprint ed. pap. 11.95 (*0-553-37986-0*) Bantam.

— Secret Paths: Women in the New Midlife. 352p. 1997. pap. 15.00 (*0-393-31500-2*) Norton.

— Working Women Don't Have Wives: Professional Success in the 1990s. LC 95-1554. 1995. pap. 16.95 (*0-312-12560-7*) St Martin.

*__Apter, Terri & Josselson, Ruthellen.__ Best Friends: The Pleasures & Perils of Girls' & Women's Friendships. 320p. 1999. reprint ed. pap. 12.00 (*0-609-80472-3*, Three Riv Pr) Crown Pub Group.

Aptheker, Bettina. Big Business & the American University. 1966. pap. 0.40 (*0-87898-009-1*) New Outlook.

— The Morning Breaks: The Trial of Angela Davis. 2nd ed. LC 98-52220. 1999. pap. 16.95 (*0-8014-8597-5*) Cornell U Pr.

— Tapestries of Life: Women's Work, Women's Consciousness, & the Meaning of Daily Experience. LC 88-26715. 312p. 1989. pap. 18.95 (*0-87023-659-8*) U of Mass Pr.

— Woman's Legacy: Essays on Race, Sex, & Class in American History. LC 81-23137. 192p. 1982. pap. 15.95 (*0-87023-365-3*) U of Mass Pr.

Aptheker, Bettina, ed. see Aptheker, Herbert.

Aptheker, Herbert. Abolitionism: A Revolutionary Movement. (Social Movements Past & Present Ser.). 224p. 1989. 26.95 (*0-8057-9702-5*, Twyne); pap. 15.95 (*0-8057-9730-0*, Twyne) Mac Lib Ref.

— Afro-American History: The Modern Era. 1971. reprint ed. pap. 10.95 (*0-8065-0362-9*, Citadel Pr) Carol Pub Group.

— American Negro Slave Revolts. 50th anniversary ed. LC 83-7063. 428p. 1993. pap. 9.95 (*0-7178-0605-7*) Intl Pubs Co.

— American Revolution, 1763-1783. LC 60-9948. 340p. (C). 1960. pap. 4.95 (*0-7178-0005-9*) Intl Pubs Co.

— Anti-Racism in U. S. History: The First Two Hundred Years. LC 91-24177. 264p. 1993. pap. 19.95 (*0-275-94808-0*, Praeger Pubs) Greenwood.

— Anti-Racism in U. S. History: The First Two Hundred Years, 143. LC 91-24177. (Contributions in American History Ser.: No. 143). 264p. 1992. 59.95 (*0-313-28199-8*, ARU, Greenwood Pr) Greenwood.

— Colonial Era. 2nd ed. LC 59-11215. 158p. 1966. pap. 2.25 (*0-7178-0033-4*) Intl Pubs Co.

— Czechoslovakia & Counter-Revolution: Why the Socialist Countries Intervened. 1969. pap. 0.35 (*0-87898-032-6*) New Outlook.

— A Documentary History of the Negro People in the United States Vol. 1: From Colonial Times to 1910. 15.00 (*0-8065-0346-7*, Citadel Pr) Carol Pub Group.

— A Documentary History of the Negro People in the United States Vol. 3: From the Emergence of the A. A. A. C. P. to the Beginning of the New Deal. 752p. (C). reprint ed. pap. 14.95 (*0-8065-1006-4*, Citadel Pr) Carol Pub Group.

— A Documentary History of the Negro People in the United States Vol. 3: 1932-1945. 640p. 1974. 17.50 (*0-8065-0438-2*, Citadel Pr) Carol Pub Group.

— A Documentary History of the Negro People in the United States Vol. 4: From the Beginning of the New Deal to the End of the Second World War (1933-1945) 607p. 1990. reprint ed. pap. 14.95 (*0-8065-1007-2*, Citadel Pr) Carol Pub Group.

— A Documentary History of the Negro People in the United States Vol. 7: From the Alabama Protest. 424p. 1994. pap. 16.95 (*0-8065-1532-5*, Citadel Pr) Carol Pub Group.

— Early Years of the Republic, 1783-1793. 2nd ed. LC 76-40213. 177p. 1990, pap. 5.95 (*0-7178-0471-2*) Intl Pubs Co.

— Herbert Aptheker's Afro-American History: The Modern Era. 256p. 1986. reprint ed. pap. 10.95 (*0-8065-1005-6*, Citadel Pr) Carol Pub Group.

— The Nature of Democracy, Freedom & Revolution. 2nd ed. LC 67-20076. 128p. 1981. pap. 2.95 (*0-7178-0137-3*) Intl Pubs Co.

— Racism, Imperialism, & Peace. Berlowitz, Marvin J. & Morgan, Carol E., eds. LC 87-2984. (Studies in Marxism: Vol. 21). 210p. 1987. 22.95 (*0-930656-49-0*); pap. 9.95 (*0-930656-50-4*) MEP Pubns.

— To Be Free: Studies in American Negro History. 256p. 1992. pap. 9.95 (*0-8065-1257-1*, Citadel Pr) Carol Pub Group.

— To Be Free: Studies in American Negro History. LC 48-5693. 256p. reprint ed. pap. 79.40 (*0-608-13361-2*, 202554400044) Bks Demand.

— The Unfolding Drama: Studies in U. S. History by Herbert Aptheker. Aptheker, Bettina, ed. LC 78-21025. 188p. 1979. pap. 3.50 (*0-7178-0501-8*) Intl Pubs Co.

A

Aptheker, Herbert, ed. A Documentary History of the Negro People in the United States Vol. 2: From the Reconstruction Years to the Founding of the National Association for the Advancement of Colored People, 1910. 1989. reprint ed. pap. 14.95 (*0-8065-0167-7*, 160, Citadel Pr) Carol Pub Group.

— A Documentary History of the Negro People in the United States Vol. 2: 1910-1932. 832p. 1973. 17.50 (*0-8065-0355-6*, Citadel Pr) Carol Pub Group.

— A Documentary History of the Negro People in the United States Vol. 5: From the End of the Second World War to the Korean War. 420p. 1993. pap. 16.95 (*0-8065-1421-3*, Citadel Pr) Carol Pub Group.

— A Documentary History of the Negro People in the United States Vol. 6: From the Korean War to the Emergence of Martin Luther King, Jr. 388p. 1993. pap. 16.95 (*0-8065-1431-0*, Citadel Pr) Carol Pub Group.

Aptheker, Herbert, ed. see Du Bois, W. E. B.

Apthorp, William F. Musicians & Music-Lovers. 1972. 59.95 (*0-8490-0684-8*) Gordon Pr.

— Musicians & Music-Lovers: And Other Essays. LC 74-39633. (Essay Index Reprint Ser.). 1977. reprint ed. 23.95 (*0-8369-2736-2*) Ayer.

— The Opera, Past & Present. LC 72-4148. (Select Bibliographies Reprint Ser.). 1977. reprint ed. 21.95 (*0-8369-6870-0*) Ayer.

Apthorpe, Raymond, ed. People Planning & Development Studies: Some Reflections on Social Planning. 168p. 1970. 45.00 (*0-7146-2582-5*, BHA-02582, Pub. by F Cass Pubs) Intl Spec Bk.

Apthorpe, Raymond & Casper, Des, eds. Arguing Development Policy: Frames & Discourses. 178p. (Orig.). (C). 1996. pap. 19.50 (*0-7146-4294-0*, Pub. by F Cass Pubs) Intl Spec Bk.

Apthorpe, Raymond, ed. see Stefaniszyn, Bronislaw.

Aptowitzer, Victor. Das Schriftwort in der Rabbinischen Literatur. rev. ed. (Library of Biblical Studies). 1970. 50.00 (*0-87068-005-6*) Ktav.

Aptowitzer, Victor, et al. Abhandlungen zur Erinnerung an Hirsch Perez Chajes. LC 07-7163. (Jewish Philosophy, Mysticism & History of Ideas Ser.). 1980. reprint ed. lib. bdg. 66.95 (*0-405-12237-3*) Ayer.

Aptroot, Andre. Fungi & Lichens: Pyxinaceae (Lichens) Goerts-van-Rijn, A. R. A., ed. (Flora of the Guianas Ser.: Series E, Fascicle 1). (Illus.). 53p. 1987. pap. 30.00 (*3-87429-272-X*, 030509, Pub. by Koeltz Sci Bks) Lubrecht & Cramer.

— A Monograph of the Pyrenulaceae (Excluding Anthracothecium & Pyrenula) & the Requienellaceae, with Notes on the Pleomassariaceae, the Trypetheliaceae & Mycomicrothelia (Lichenized & Non-Lichenized Ascomycetes) Wirth, Volkmar et al, eds. (Bibliotheca Lichenologica: Vol. 44). (GER., Illus.). 178p. 1991. pap. 53.00 (*3-443-58023-8*, Pub. by Gebruder Borntraeger) Balogh.

Aptroot, Andre, et al, eds. Lichens & Lichenicolous Fungi from New Guinea. (Bibliotheca Lichenologica Ser.: Vol. 64). (Illus.). 220p. 1997. 94.40 (*3-443-58043-2*, Pub. by Gebruder Borntraeger) Balogh.

Apts, David W. The Back Book. (Illus.). 42p. (C). 1988. pap. text 6.50 (*0-685-24275-7*) Amer Back School.

— Back Facts. 2nd ed. (SPA., Illus.). 28p. (C). 1981. pap. text 3.50 (*0-685-24276-5*) Amer Back School.

— Back Injury Prevention Handbook. 208p. 1991. lib. bdg. 75.00 (*0-87371-419-9*, L419) Lewis Pubs.

Apulee. L' Ane d'Or Ou les Metamorphoses. (FRE.). 320p. 1975. pap. 10.95 (*0-7859-1794-2*, 2070366294) Fr & Eur.

Apuleius. The Golden Ass. (Classics of World Literature Ser.). pap. 5.95 (*1-85326-460-1*, 4601WW, Pub. by Wrdsworth Edits) NTC Contemp Pub Co.

Apuleius, Lucius. Apologia Sive Pro Se de Magia Liber. (Illus.). lxvi, 208p. 1983. reprint ed. 57.20 (*3-487-01463-7*) G Olms Pubs.

Apuleius, Lucius. Apuleius on the God of Socrates. Taylor, Thomas, tr. (LAT.). 1984. reprint ed. pap. 7.95 (*0-916411-25-7*) Holmes Pub.

Apuleius, Lucius. Cupid & Psyche. Balme, Maurice G. & Morwood, James H., eds. (Illus.). 80p. 1976. pap. text 18.95 (*0-19-912047-1*) OUP.

— Cupid & Psyche. Kenney, Edwin J., ed. (Greek & Latin Classics - Imperial Library). (Illus.). 253p. (C). 1991. text 65.00 (*0-521-26038-8*); pap. text 22.95 (*0-521-27813-9*) Cambridge U Pr.

— The Golden Ass. Lindsay, Jack, tr. LC 62-1610. 256p. (C). 1962. pap. 9.95 (*0-253-20036-9*, MB 36) Ind U Pr.

— The Golden Ass. Walsh, P. G., tr. (Oxford World's Classics Ser.). (Illus.). 332p. 1999. pap. 11.95 (*0-19-283888-1*) OUP.

— Golden Ass. (Loeb Classical Library: No. 44). 14.50 (*0-685-02128-9*) HUP.

— Golden Ass. LC 99-178805. 320p. 1998. pap. 15.99 (*0-14-043590-5*, Penguin Classics) Viking Penguin.

— Metamorphoses, Vol. I. Hanson, J. Arthur, tr. (Loeb Classical Library: Nos. 44 & 453). 371p. 1990. text 19.95 (*0-674-99049-8*) HUP.

— Metamorphoses, Vol. II. Hanson, J. Arthur, tr. (Loeb Classical Library: Nos. 44 & 453). 377p. 1990. text 19.95 (*0-674-99498-1*) HUP.

— Metamorphoses, Vols. I & II. Hanson, J. Arthur, tr. Nos. 44 & 453. 1989. text. write for info. (*0-318-65540-3*) HUP.

— Opera Omnia, 2 vols., Set. xc, 1820p. 1968. reprint ed. 498.00 (*0-318-71066-8*) G Olms Pubs.

Apuleius, Lucius. The Story of Cupid & Psyche: As Related by Apuleius. Purser, Louis C., ed. (College Classical Ser.). cviii, 155p. (C). 1983. reprint ed. pap. text 17.50 (*0-89241-111-2*); reprint ed. lib. bdg. 32.50 (*0-89241-359-X*) Caratzas.

Apuleius, Madaurensis. Apologia & Florida of Apuleius of Madaura. Butler, H. E., tr. LC 72-95084. 238p. 1970. reprint ed. lib. bdg. 39.75 (*0-8371-3066-2*, APAF, Greenwood Pr) Greenwood.

— Golden Ass of Apuleius. Adlington, William, tr. LC 78-158265. (Tudor Translations Ser.: No. 4). reprint ed. 57.50 (*0-404-51851-6*) AMS Pr.

Apurvananda, Swami. Acharya Shankara. 362p. 1985. pap. 7.95 (*0-87481-529-0*, Pub. by Ramakrishna Math) Vedanta Pr.

Apurvananda, Swami, compiled by. Swami Vijanananda: A Short Life & Spiritual Discourses. 173p. 1987. pap. 3.50 (*0-87481-547-9*, Pub. by Ramakrishna Math) Vedanta Pr.

Apurvananda, Swami, jt. auth. see Roshan.

Apuzzo. Brain Surgery. 1998. write for info. incl. cd-rom (*0-443-07822-X*) Church.

Apuzzo, Michael L. Surgery of the Third Ventricle. 2nd ed. LC 96-29699. 1200p. 1997. 250.00 (*0-683-00249-X*) Lppncott W & W.

Apuzzo, Michael L., ed. Brain Surgery: Complication Avoidance & Management, 2 vols. (Illus.). 2616p. 1992. text 525.00 (*0-443-08709-1*) Church.

Apuzzo, Robert. Bottles of Old New York: A Pictorial Guide to Early New York City Bottles, 1680-1925. LC 93-92793. (Illus.). 176p. (Orig.). 1994. pap. 19.95 (*0-9629913-1-7*) R & L Pub.

— New York City's Buried Past: A Guide to Excavated New York City's Revolutionary War Artifacts 1776-1783. 2nd ed. (Illus.). 164p. (Orig.). 1992. pap. 24.95 (*0-9629913-0-9*) R & L Pub.

Aqil-Hossain, Barlas M., tr. see Sa'di.

Aqil, Moinuddin & Khalidi, Omar, eds. Deccan Ka Ahad-i Islami. (Monograph Ser.: No. 5). (URD.). 109p. 1994. pap. 10.00 (*0-930811-04-6*) Haydarabad Hist Soc.

Aqu, Dr., ed. see Crenshaw, Vernita Y.

Aqua, E. N. & Whitman, C. I. Modern Developments in Powder Metallurgy Vol. 15: Principles & Processes. LC 66-5483. (Illus.). 864p. 1985. 29.00 (*0-918404-64-9*) Metal Powder.

Aqua, E. N. & Whitman, C. I., eds. Modern Developments in Powder Metallurgy Vol. 16: Ferrous & Nonferrous Materials. LC 66-5483. (Illus.). 784p. 1985. 29.00 (*0-918404-65-7*) Metal Powder.

— Modern Developments in Powder Metallurgy Vol. 17: Special Materials. LC 66-5483. (Illus.). 944p. 1985. 29.00 (*0-918404-66-5*) Metal Powder.

Aqua Group Staff. Contract Administration. 8th ed. LC 96-14442. (Illus.). 144p. 1996. pap. text 26.95 (*0-632-03847-0*) Blackwell Sci.

— Pre-Contract Practice for the Building Team. 8th rev. ed. LC 92-12075. (Illus.). 128p. 1992. pap. 32.95 (*0-632-02817-3*) Blackwell Sci.

***AQUA Group Staff.** Tenders & Contracts for Building 3rd ed. LC 99-34759. 1999. write for info. (*0-632-04277-X*) Blackwell Sci.

***Aquarius, Gruzian.** The Bible of Pro Football: Here is the Key for You to Be the Winner. LC 99-62929. 280p. 1999. pap. 18.95 (*1-56167-551-2*) Am Literary Pr.

Aquauo-Quezada, Sergio, jt. ed. see Bailey, John.

Aqued, Ahmed. The Constitutional Law of Algeria: Texts & Contents. (C). 1987. 95.00 (*0-7855-6538-8*, Pub. by Royston Ltd) St Mut.

Aqued, Ahmed, ed. The Constitutional Law of Algeria: Texts & Contents. (C). 1987. 175.00 (*0-7855-6871-9*, Pub. by Royston Ltd) St Mut.

Aquien, Michele. Dictionnaire de Poetique. (FRE.). 344p. 1993. pap. 22.95 (*0-7859-5627-1*, 2253063622) Fr & Eur.

Aquila, August J. Breaking the Paradigm: New Approaches to Pricing Accounting Services. LC 95-24715. 1995. 31.00 (*0-87051-171-8*) Am Inst CPA.

Aquila, August J., et al. CPA Firm Merger Strategies That Work. LC 93-43015. 120p. 1994. text 50.00 (*0-7863-0126-0*, Irwn Prfssnl) McGraw-Hill Prof.

Aquila, Frank. Course Outline Education Law. 1998. pap. text 24.50 (*0-87457-300-9*) Casenotes Pub.

Aquila, Philip L., et al. Home Front Soldier: The Story of a G. I. & His Italian-American Family During World War II. LC 98-4321. 1999. pap. text 21.95 (*0-7914-4076-1*) State U NY Pr.

Aquila, Ralph. Manifestations: Poems & Aphorisms by Ralph Aquila. 1997. pap. write for info. (*1-57553-507-6*) Watermrk Pr.

— Pathetique - Poetical Sketches by Ralph Aquila. 1998. pap. write for info. (*1-57553-839-3*) Watermrk Pr.

Aquila, Richard. Home Front Soldier: The Story of a G. I. & His Italian American Family During World War II. LC 98-4321. (Illus.). 288p. (C). 1999. text 65.50 (*0-7914-4075-3*) State U NY Pr.

— The Iroquois Restoration: Iroquois Diplomacy on the Colonial Frontier, 1701- 1754. LC 82-13539. (Illus.). 287p. reprint ed. pap. 89.00 (*0-608-16051-2*, 203318100084) Bks Demand.

— The Iroquois Restoration: Iroquois Diplomacy on the Colonial Frontier, 1701-1754. LC 97-18524. (Illus.). ix, 285p. 1997. pap. text 15.00 (*0-8032-5932-8*, Bison Books) U of Nebr Pr.

— That Old Time Rock & Roll: A Chronicle of an Era, 1954-1963. 375p. 1989. 25.00 (*0-02-870082-1*, Schirmer Books) Mac Lib Ref.

***Aquila, Richard.** That Old-Time Rock & Roll: A Chronicle of an Era, 1954-1963. LC 00-28679. (Illus.). 432p. 2000. reprint ed. pap. 21.95 (*0-252-06919-6*) U of Ill Pr.

Aquila, Richard, ed. Wanted Dead or Alive: The American West in Popular Culture. LC 95-32476. (Illus.). 296p. 1996. 29.95 (*0-252-02224-6*) U of Ill Pr.

— Wanted Dead or Alive: The American West in Popular Culture. LC 95-32476. 1996. pap. write for info. (*0-252-06527-1*) U of Ill Pr.

Aquila, Richard E. Matter in Mind: A Study of Kant's Transcendental Deduction. LC 88-45387. (Studies in Phenomenology & Existential Philosophy). 262p. 1989. 36.95 (*0-253-33712-7*) Ind U Pr.

— Representational Mind: A Study of Kant's Theory of Knowledge. LC 83-47918. (Studies in Phenomenology & Existential Philosophy). 224p. 1984. 31.50 (*0-253-35005-0*) Ind U Pr.

Aquilano, Nicholas & Chase, Richard B. Fundamentals of Operations Management: Select Chapters. (C). 1994. pap. text 24.50 (*0-256-18449-6*, Irwn McGrw-H) McGrw-H Hghr Educ.

— Fundamentals of Operations Management, International. (C). 1991. text, student ed. 32.50 (*0-256-11399-8*, Irwn McGrw-H) McGrw-H Hghr Educ.

Aquilano, Nicholas, et al. Fundamentals of Operations Management. 2nd ed. LC 94-14029. 688p. (C). 1994. text 67.95 (*0-256-13219-4*, Irwn McGrw-H); text, student ed. 25.62 (*0-256-13876-1*, Irwn McGrw-H) McGrw-H Hghr Educ.

— Fundamentals of Operations Management. 2nd ed. (C). 1996. text, student ed. 67.95 (*0-256-23780-8*, Irwn McGrw-H) McGrw-H Hghr Educ.

Aquilano, Nicholas, jt. auth. see Chase, Richard.

Aquilano, Nicholas J., jt. auth. see Chase, Richard B.

Aquilar, Teri, et al, eds. Tierra Norte: A Collection of Works from North Tejas. (Illus.). 39p. (Orig.). 1994. pap. 6.00 (*0-913983-12-8*) M & A Edns.

Aquilar, Victor. Axiomatic Theory of Economics. LC 95-48994. 277p. (C). 1998. text 80.00 (*1-56072-296-7*) Nova Sci Pubs.

Aquilera-Navarro, V. C., ed. Condensed Matter Theories, Vol. 5. LC 87-656591. (Illus.). 406p. 1990. 145.00 (*0-306-43509-8*, Plenum Trade) Perseus Pubng.

Aquilia, Michael G. & Markisz, John A. Technical Magnetic Resonance Imaging. 287p. (C). 1996. pap. 37.50 (*0-8385-8836-0*, A8836-7, Apple Lange Med) McGraw.

Aquilina, Alfred P. MacKenzie: Yesterday & Beyond. (Illus.). 204p. 1981. pap. 7.95 (*0-88839-083-1*) Hancock House.

Aquilina, J. Maltese Complete Course, 2 cass. (Teach Yourself Ser.). 240p. 1977. pap. 25.95 incl. audio (*0-8442-3866-X*, 686189) NTC Contemp Pub Co.

— Teach Yourself Maltese. (Illus.). 240p. 1995. pap. 14.95 (*0-8442-3697-7*, Teach Yrslf) NTC Contemp Pub Co.

Aquilina, LaVada B. Unsung Heroes: Combat Nurses & Army Wives. LC 95-62217. (Illus.). 208p. (Orig.). 1996. pap. 12.95 (*0-9636577-3-9*) Trego-Hill.

Aquilina, Michael J. & Stubna, Kris D. What Catholics Believe: A Pocket Catechism. LC 98-67817. 111p. 1999. pap. 5.95 (*0-87973-574-0*) Our Sunday Visitor.

Aquilina, Mike. The Fathers of the Church: An Introduction to the First Christian Teachers. LC 98-67816. 240p. 1999. pap. 10.95 (*0-87973-689-5*) Our Sunday Visitor.

***Aquilina, Mike.** The Way of the Fathers: Praying with the Early Christians. LC 99-75028. 208p. 2000. pap. 10.95 (*0-87973-334-9*) Our Sunday Visitor.

Aquilina, Mike, ed. Talking to Youth about Sexuality: A Parent's Guide. LC 84-62159. 64p. 1995. pap. 4.95 (*0-87973-716-6*, 716) Our Sunday Visitor.

***Aquilina, Mike & Flaherty, Regis J.** The How to Book of Catholic Devotions: Everything You Need to Know but No One Ever Taught You. 272p. 2000. pap. 12.95 (*0-87973-415-9*) Our Sunday Visitor.

Aquilina, Mike, jt. ed. see Scott, David.

Aquilina, Patrick. Timely Topics. 335p. (J). 1993. mass mkt. 25.95 (*0-8384-4200-5*) Heinle & Heinle.

Aquilino, Vincent M., jt. auth. see Conlon, Steven D.

Aquilonius, S. M. & Gillberg, P. G., eds. Cholinergic Neurotransmission: Functional & Clinical Aspects. (Progress in Brain Research Ser.: No. 84). 516p. 1990. 210.00 (*0-685-39431-X*) Elsevier.

Aquin de Chateau-Lyon, Pierre-Louis D'. Siecle Litteraire de Louis XV: Ou Lettres sur les Hommes Celebres, 2 vols., 1 bk. LC 76-43913. (Music & Theatre in France in the 17th & 18th Centuries Ser.). reprint ed. 57.50 (*0-404-60156-1*) AMS Pr.

Aquin, Hubert. The Antiphonary. Brown, Alan, tr. from FRE. 196p. 1973. reprint ed. 9.95 (*0-88784-426-X*, Pub. by Hse of Anansi Pr) Genl Dist Srvs.

Aquinaco, Carmen, tr. see Baro, Joan.

***Aquinas, Thomas, Saint.** The Aquinas Catechism: A Simple Explanation of the Catholic Faith by the Church's Greatest Theologian. Orig. Title: The Three Greatest Prayers & God's Greatest Gifts. 336p. 2000. pap. 17.95 (*1-928832-10-5*) Sophia Inst Pr.

— The Aquinas Prayer Book: The Prayers & Hymns of St. Thomas Aquinas. rev. ed. Anderson, Robert & Moser, Johann, eds. & trs. by. Orig. Title: Devoutly I Adore Thee. 128p. 2000. pap. 11.95 (*1-928832-14-8*) Sophia Inst Pr.

Aquinas, Thomas, Saint. Aurora Consurgens, a Document Attributed to Thomas Aquinas on the Problem of Opposites in Alchemy. Von Franz, Marie-Louise, ed. Hull, R. F. C., tr. LC 65-10405. 571p. reprint ed. pap. 177.10 (*0-8357-5884-2*, 205159800097) Bks Demand.

— Basic Writings of Saint Thomas Aquinas, 2 vols., Set. Pegis, Anton C., ed. Incl. Vol. I. LC 97-26330. 1151p. (C). 1997. reprint ed. pap. 39.95 (*0-87220-380-8*); Vol. I. LC 97-26330. 1151p. 1997. reprint ed. lib. bdg. 79.00 (*0-87220-381-6*); Vol. II. LC 97-26330. 1211p. (C). 1997. reprint ed. pap. 39.95 (*0-87220-382-4*); Vol. II. LC 97-26330. 1211p. (C). 1997. reprint ed. lib. bdg. 79.00 (*0-87220-383-2*); LC 97-26330. (Classics Ser.). 2362p. (C). 1997. reprint ed. 75.00 (*0-87220-384-0*); reprint ed. 149.00 (*0-87220-385-9*) Hackett Pub.

— Catena Aurea (The Golden Chain) A Commentary on the Four Gospels - Collected Out of the Works of the Fathers by St. Thomas Aquinas, 4 vols. Newman, John Henry, tr. & pref. by. Incl. Vol. I. St. Matthew. 1028p. 1997. Not sold separately (*1-901157-41-5*, Pub. by St Austin); Vol. II. St. Mark. 355p. 1997. 145.00 (*1-901157-42-3*, Pub. by St Austin); Vol. III. St. Luke. 811p. 1997. Not sold separately (*1-901157-43-1*, Pub. by St Austin); Vol. IV. St. John. 631p. 1997. Not sold separately (*1-901157-44-X*, Pub. by St Austin); Set per. 145.00 (*1-901157-40-7*, Pub. by St Austin) St Augustines Pr.

— The Childhood of Christ. (Summa Theologiae Ser.: Vol. 52). 1973. 10.00 (*0-07-002027-2*) McGraw.

***Aquinas, Thomas, Saint.** The Commandments of God. (Saint Joseph Picture Bks.). (Illus.). 32p. (J). (gr. 1-6). 1999. pap. 1.25 (*0-89942-517-8*, 514) Catholic Bk Pub.

Aquinas, Thomas, Saint. A Commentary on Aristotle's De Anima. Foster, Kenelm & Humphries, Silvester, trs. from LAT. (Aristotelian Commentary Ser.). 298p. (C). 1995. pap. 30.00 (*1-883357-11-X*) Dumb Ox Bks.

— A Commentary on Aristotle's De Anima. Foster, Kenelm & Humphries, Silvester, trs. from LAT. (Aristotelian Commentary Ser.: xxii, 276). 298p. (C). 1995. 70.00 (*1-883357-10-1*) Dumb Ox Bks.

***Aquinas, Thomas, Saint.** A Commentary on Aristotle's De Anima. Pasnau, Robert, tr. from ENG. LC 98-35986. (Library of Medieval Philosophy). 452p. 1999. 50.00 (*0-300-07420-4*) Yale U Pr.

Aquinas, Thomas, Saint. Commentary on Aristotle's Metaphysics. rev. unabridged ed. Rowan, John P., tr. from LAT. (Aristotelian Commentary Ser.). 870p. (C). 1995. text 90.00 (*1-883357-60-8*); pap. text 40.00 (*1-883357-61-6*) Dumb Ox Bks.

— Commentary on Aristotle's Nicomachecys Ethics. (Thomas Aquinas's Aristotelian Commentaries Ser.). 900p. 1993. pap. text 35.00 (*1-883357-51-9*) Dumb Ox Bks.

— Commentary on Aristotle's Nicomaheau. (Thomas Aquinas's Aristotelian Commentaries Ser.). 900p. 1993. text 85.00 (*1-883357-50-0*) Dumb Ox Bks.

— Commentary on Aristotle's Physics. Blackwell, Richard J. et al, trs. (Aristotelian Commentary Ser.). 670p. 1998. text 85.00 (*1-883357-75-6*); pap. text 40.00 (*1-883357-76-4*) Dumb Ox Bks.

— Commentary on the Book of Causes. Guagliardo, Vincent A. et al, trs. LC 95-22559. (Thomas Aquinas in Translation Ser.: Vol. 1). 193p. 1996. 26.95 (*0-8132-0843-2*); pap. 16.95 (*0-8132-0844-0*) Cath U Pr.

— Commentary on the Gospel of St. John, Pt. I. Weisheipl, James A., ed. Larcher, Fabian R., tr. from LAT. LC 66-19306. (Aquinas Scripture Ser.: Vol. 4). (Illus.). 512p. 1980. 35.00 (*0-87343-031-X*) Magi Bks.

— Commentary on the Gospel of St. John, Pt. II. Larcher, Fabian R., tr. from LAT. (Aquinas Scripture Ser.: Vol. 5). 570p. 1999. 25.00 (*1-879007-40-1*) St Bedes Pubns.

— Disputed Questions on Virtue. McInerny, Ralph, tr. from LAT. & pref. by. LC 98-20702. Orig. Title: Quaestio Disputata de Virtutibus in Communi & Quaestio Disputata de Virtutibus Cardinalibus. 316p. 1999. 25.00 (*1-890318-20-5*) St Augustines Pr.

Aquinas, Thomas, Saint. Fear & Anger. (Summa Theologiae Ser.: Vol. 21). 1965. 10.00 (*0-07-001996-7*) McGraw.

Aquinas, Thomas, Saint. The Gifts of the Spirit. (Summa Theologiae Ser.: Vol. 24). 1975. 10.95 (*0-07-001999-1*) McGraw.

— God & Creation. Baumgarth, William P. & Regan, Richard J., trs. from LAT. LC 92-63002.Tr. of Summa theologica. 49.50 (*0-940866-27-7*) U Scranton Pr.

— God's Greatest Gifts: The Commandments & the Sacraments. LC 91-42376. Orig. Title: De Decem Praeceptis & De Scaramentis Ecclesiae. 132p. 1997. reprint ed. pap. 14.95 (*0-918477-53-0*) Sophia Inst Pr.

— Homilies of St. Thomas Aquinas. Ashley, John M., ed. 213p. 1996. reprint ed. text 24.95 (*0-912141-25-5*) Roman Cath Bks.

— The Human Constitution. Regan, Richard J., tr. & intro. by. LC 96-49915. (C). 1997. 24.95 (*0-940866-62-5*); pap. 19.95 (*0-614-25166-4*) U Scranton Pr.

— Introduction to Saint Thomas Aquinas. Pegis, Anton C., ed. (Modern Library College Editions). 690p. (C). 1965. pap. 7.50 (*0-07-553653-6*, T74) McGraw.

— An Introduction to the Metaphysics of St. Thomas Aquinas. LC 97-8643. 137p. (Orig.). 1997. pap. 9.95 (*0-89526-420-X*, Gateway Editions) Regnery Pub.

— Law & Political Theory. (Summa Theologiae Ser.: Vol. 28). 1966. 10.00 (*0-07-002003-5*) McGraw.

— Light of Faith: The Compendium of Theology. LC 93-6793. 428p. 1998. reprint ed. pap. 22.95 (*0-918477-67-0*) Sophia Inst Pr.

— The Literal Exposition of Job: A Scriptual Commentary Concerning Providence. Damico, Anthony, tr. LC 88-31855. (American Academy of Religion, Classics in Religious Studies). 496p. 1989. 62.95 (*1-55540-291-7*, 01-05-07); pap. 41.95 (*1-55540-292-5*) OUP.

Aquinas, Thomas, Saint. Make Room for Danny. 1992. pap. 15.95 (*1-55927-187-6*) Audio Renaissance.

Aquinas, Thomas, Saint. Meditations for Lent. Hughes, Philip, tr. 141p. 1999. reprint ed. 16.95 (*0-912141-68-9*) Roman Cath Bks.

— On Charity. Kendzierski, Lottie H., tr. (Medieval Philosophical Texts in Translation Ser.: No. 10). 1960. pap. 15.00 (*0-87462-210-7*) Marquette.

— On Evil. Oesterle, John A., tr. from LAT. LC 94-44961. (C). 1995. text 49.95 (*0-268-03700-0*) U of Notre Dame Pr.

— On Faith & Reason. Brown, Stephen F., ed. & intro. by. LC 98-50833. 320p. (C). 1999. pap. 10.95 (*0-87220-456-1*); lib. bdg. 34.95 (*0-87220-457-X*) Hackett Pub.

— On Human Nature. Hibbs, Thomas S., ed. & intro. by. LC 98-50832. Orig. Title: Sentencia Libri De Anima/Summa Theologica. 224p. (C). 1999. pap. 9.95 (*0-87220-454-5*); lib. bdg. 34.95 (*0-87220-455-3*) Hackett Pub.

— On Law, Morality, & Politics. Regan, Richard J. & Baumgarth, William P., eds. LC 87-28272. (HPC Classics Ser.). 316p. (C). 1988. 32.95 (*0-87220-032-9*); pap. 8.95 (*0-87220-031-0*) Hackett Pub.

— On Spiritual Creatures. Fitzpatrick, Mary C., tr. (Medieval Philosophical Texts in Translation Ser.: No. 5). 1949. pap. 15.00 (*0-87462-205-0*) Marquette.

— On the Unity of the Intellect Against the Averroists. Zedler, Beatrice H., ed. LC 68-28029. (Medieval Philosophical Texts in Translation Ser.: No. 19). 1968. pap. 10.00 (*0-87462-219-0*) Marquette.

— The Philosophy of Thomas Aquinas: Introductory Readings. Martin, Christopher, ed. (Croom Helm Philosophy Ser.). 256p. (C). 1988. pap. 25.99 (*0-415-00296-6*) Routledge.

— Political Ideas of St. Thomas Aquinas: Representative Selections. Bigongiari, Dino, ed. (Library of Classics: No. 15). 255p. 1997. pap. 15.95 (*0-684-83641-6*) Hafner.

— Questions on the Soul. Robb, James H., tr. LC 84-61636. (Medieval Philosophical Texts in Translation Ser.). 1984. 25.00 (*0-87462-226-3*) Marquette.

— Quodlibetal Questions 1 & 2. Edwards, Sandra, tr. from LAT. & intro. by. viii, 128p. pap. 12.00 (*0-88844-276-9*) Brill Academic Pubs.

— Readings in the Summa Theologiae. Jordan, Mark D., tr. from LAT. LC 89-40753. 208p. (C). 1990. pap. text 15.00 (*0-268-01503-1*) U of Notre Dame Pr.

— St. Thomas Aquinas on Politics & Ethics. Sigmund, Paul E., ed. & tr. by. (Critical Editions Ser.). (C). 1987. pap. 11.25 (*0-393-95243-6*) Norton.

— Selected Philosophical Writings. McDermott, Timothy, tr. & selected by by. (Oxford World's Classics Ser.). 488p. 1998. pap. 13.95 (*0-19-283585-8*) OUP.

— Selected Writings. McInerny, Ralph, ed. & tr. by. from LAT. LC 99-180304. 450p. 1999. pap. 14.95 (*0-14-043632-4*) Penguin Putnam.

— Selected Writings of St. Thomas Aquinas. Goodwin, Robert P., tr. Incl. On Being & Essence. LC 65-26529. 1965. pap. On Free Choice. LC 65-26529. 1965. pap. On the Virtues in General. LC 65-26529. 1965. pap. Principles of Nature. LC 65-26529. 1965. pap. LC 65-26529. (Orig.). 1965. Set pap. 4.00 (*0-672-60469-8*, LLA217) Macmillan.

— The Sermon-Conferences of St. Thomas Aquinas on the Apostles' Creed. Ayo, Nicholas, ed. & intro. by. LC 87-40620. 176p. 1989. pap. text 18.50 (*0-268-01729-8*) U of Notre Dame Pr.

— A Shorter Summa: The Most Essential Philosophical Passages of St. Thomas Aquinas' Summa Theologica. Kreeft, Peter, ed. & comment by. LC 92-75065. 162p. (C). 1993. pap. 10.95 (*0-89870-438-3*) Ignatius Pr.

— Some Question about Evil (De Malo) Davies, Brian, ed. Regan, Richard J., tr. 488p. (C). 2002. pap. text 16.95 (*0-19-509183-3*) OUP.

— Summa Contra Gentiles: Providence, Bk. 3. LC 75-19883. 1976. pap. 11.50 (*0-268-01686-0*); pap. 11.50 (*0-268-01688-7*) U of Notre Dame Pr.

— A Summa of the Summa: The Essential Philosophical Passages of St. Thomas Aquinas' Summa Theologica Edited & Explained for Beginners. Kreeft, Peter, ed. LC 90-81772. 539p. (Orig.). 1990. pap. 24.95 (*0-89870-300-X*) Ignatius Pr.

— Summa Theologiae: A Concise Translation. McDermott, Timothy, ed. 652p. 1989. 54.95 (*0-87061-211-5*) Chr Classics.

— Summa Theologiae: A Concise Translation. McDermott, Timothy, ed. LC 91-73302. 652p. 1991. pap. 34.95 (*0-87061-210-7*) Chr Classics.

— The Summa Theologica, 5 vols., Set. LC 81-68580. 3104p. 1981. reprint ed. pap. 155.00 (*0-87061-069-4*, 6904) Chr Classics.

— Summa Theologica, 5 vols., Set. LC 81-68580. 3104p. 1998. reprint ed. 225.00 (*0-87061-063-5*, 6903) Chr Classics.

— The Sunday Sermons of the Great Fathers, 4 vols., Set. Toal, M. F., ed. & tr. by. LC 96-44004. 1844p. 1996. reprint ed. 129.95 (*1-886412-14-6*) Preserv Press.

— The Sunday Sermons of the Great Fathers, 4 Vols., Vol. 1. Toal, M. F., ed. & tr. by. LC 96-44004. 1996. write for info. (*1-886412-15-4*) Preserv Press.

— The Sunday Sermons of the Great Fathers, 4 Vols., Vol. 2. Toal, M. F., ed. & tr. by. LC 96-44004. 1996. write for info. (*1-886412-16-2*) Preserv Press.

— The Sunday Sermons of the Great Fathers, 4 Vols., Vol. 3. Toal, M. F., ed. & tr. by. LC 96-44004. 1996. write for info. (*1-886412-17-0*) Preserv Press.

— The Sunday Sermons of the Great Fathers, 4 Vols., Vol. 4. Toal, M. F., ed. & tr. by. LC 96-44004. 1996. write for info. (*1-886412-18-9*) Preserv Press.

— Thomas Aquinas - Gifts of the Spirit: Selected Spiritual Writings. 2nd ed. Ashley, Benedict M., ed. Rzeczkoski, Matthew, tr. (Profiles Ser.). 144p. (Orig.). 1995. pap. 9.95 (*1-56548-071-6*) New City.

— Thomas Aquinas's Earliest Treatment of the Divine Essence Bk. 1, Distinction 8: Scriptum Super Libros Sententiarum. Macierowski, Edward M., tr. from LAT. & contrib. by by. (Episteme Ser.). 140p. (Orig.). (C). 1997. pap. 17.00 (*1-883058-22-8*, Episteme) Global Pubns.

— The Three Greatest Prayers: Commentaries on the Lord's Prayer, the Hail Mary, & the Apostles' Creed. LC 87-12661. 209p. 1997. reprint ed. pap. 14.95 (*0-918477-52-2*) Sophia Inst Pr.

— Treatise on Happiness. Oesterle, John A., tr. LC 83-17091. 224p. (C). 1983. pap. 11.50 (*0-268-01849-9*, 85-18490) U of Notre Dame Pr.

— The Treatise on Law: Summa Theologiae, I-II; QQ. 90-97. Henle, R. J., tr. from LAT. LC 92-56861. (Notre Dame Studies in Law & Contemporary Issues: Vol. 4). (C). 1993. text 40.50 (*0-268-01880-4*) U of Notre Dame Pr.

— The Treatise on Law: Summa Theologiae, I-II; 88-90-97. Henle, R. J., tr. from LAT. LC 92-56861. (Notre Dame Studies in Law & Contemporary Issues: Vol. 4). (C). 1993. pap. text 23.00 (*0-268-01881-2*) U of Notre Dame Pr.

— Treatise on Law: Summa Theologica, Questions 90-97. 116p. (Orig.). 1996. pap. 9.95 (*0-89526-705-5*, Gateway Editions) Regnery Pub.

— Treatise on Man. Anderson, James F., tr. LC 81-6631. 178p. 1981. lib. bdg. 38.50 (*0-313-22186-3*, TATM, Greenwood Pr) Greenwood.

— Treatise on the Virtues. Oesterle, John A., tr. LC 84-10691. 171p. (C). 1984. pap. 11.50 (*0-268-01855-3*) U of Notre Dame Pr.

— Truth, 3 vols., Set. Mulligan, Robert W. et al, trs. from LAT. LC 94-29598.Tr. of Quaestiones Disputatae de Veritate. 1525p. (C). 1994. lib. bdg. 135.00 (*0-87220-270-4*) Hackett Pub.

— The Ways of God. LC 95-36706. 92p. (Orig.). 1995. pap. 5.50 (*0-918477-30-1*) Sophia Inst Pr.

Aquinas, Thomas, Saint & Regan, Richard J. The Ultimate Human Goal: Human Acts & Virtue. LC 99-11402. 1999. write for info. (*0-940866-77-3*); pap. write for info. (*0-940866-78-1*) U Scranton Pr.

Aquinas, Thomas, Saint & Saint Albertus Magnus. Albert & Thomas: Selected Writings. Tugwell, Simon, ed. & tr. by. (Classics of Western Spirituality Ser.). 1988. pap. 27.95 (*0-8091-3022-X*) Paulist Pr.

Aquinas, Thomas, Saint & Windeatt, Mary F. The Story of the Dumb Ox. LC 92-82033. (Illus.). 81p. (J). 1993. reprint ed. pap. 6.00 (*0-89555-420-8*) TAN Bks Pubs.

***Aquinas, Thomas, Saint, et al.** An Exposition of the on the Hebdomads of Boethius. LC 00-37883. (Thomas Aquinas in Translation Ser.). 2001. pap. write for info. (*0-8132-0995-1*) Cath U Pr.

Aquinas, Thomas, Saint, jt. auth. see Murphy, Richard T.

Aquino, Consuelo De Jesus, see De Jesus Aquino, Consuelo.

Aquino, Fran De, see De Aquino, Fran.

Aquino, James, ed. see Cook, Sharon T.

Aquino, James, ed. see Cook, Sharon Touhy.

Aquino, James, ed. see Young, Natalie B.

Aquino, John T., compiled by. Waste Age & Recycling Times' Recycling Handbook. LC 95-14479. 304p. 1995. lib. bdg. 75.00 (*1-56670-068-X*, L1068) Lewis Pubs.

Aquino, Maria P. Our Cry for Life: Feminist Theology from Latin America - Nuestra Clamor por la Vida. Livinstone, Dinah, tr. from SPA. LC 93-33087. 200p. 1993. reprint ed. pap. 18.00 (*0-88344-895-5*) Orbis Bks.

Aquino, Maria P. & Goizueta, Roberto S., eds. Theology - Expanding the Borders Vol. 43: The Annual Publication of the College Theology Society. 352p. 1998. pap. 14.95 (*0-89622-933-5*) Twenty-Third.

Aquino, Marifi, jt. auth. see Rankin, Jimmie R.

Aquino, Modesto S., jt. ed. see Corral, G. Herrera.

Aquino, Thomas F. Taiwanese Firms in Southeast Asia: Networking Across Borders. Tain-Jy Chen, ed. LC 98-13904. (New Horizons in International Business Ser.). 288p. 1998. 85.00 (*1-85898-746-6*) E Elgar.

Aquino, Tracey. Essential Evidence. Bourne, Nicholas, ed. (Essential Law Ser.). 180p. 1996. pap. write for info. (*1-85941-145-2*, Pub. by Cavendish Pubng) Gaunt.

Aquino, Tracy. Family Law. (Questions & Answers Ser.). 291p. 1995. 18.00 (*1-874241-33-3*, Pub. by Cavendish Pubng) Gaunt.

Aquino, Vicente F. A Practical Guide in Handling Your Own Traffic Cases in Honolulu. pap. 7.95 (*0-681-27238-4*) Booklines Hawaii.

Aquirre, Adalberto & Baker, David V., eds. Structured Inequality in the United States: Discussions on the Continuing Significance of Race, Ethnicity. LC 99-34388. 416p. 1999. pap. text 32.20 (*0-13-097403-X*) P-H.

Aquirre, Adalberto, et al. Race, Racism & the Death Penalty in the United States. (Illus.). 130p. (C). 1991. text 29.95 (*0-9628916-5-7*) Vande Vere.

Aquisap, A. C., et al, contrib. by. Asian Fisheries Science: A Profile. (Asian Fisheries Society Spec. Publications: No. 6). 45p. 1991. pap. write for info. (*971-8709-04-5*, Pub. by ICLARM) Intl Spec Bk.

Aqvist & Mullock, Philip. Causing Harm: A Logico - Legal Study. (Foundations of Communication & Cognition Ser.). xx, 353p. (C). 1989. lib. bdg. 134.65 (*3-11-011510-7*) De Gruyter.

AR/GE Kunst Bozen, ed. see Niedermayr, Walter.

Ara, Charles. The Grass Is Greener Where It's Watered: All A's of Successful Relationships. rev. ed. 1991. pap. 12.95 (*0-9630928-0-4*) EJ Pub.

Ara, Shabeen. Old Age among Slum Dwellers. (C). 1994. 16.00 (*81-7003-179-6*, Pub. by S Asia Pubs) S Asia.

Arab Business Laws Staff, ed. see El-Alami, D.

Arab, L., et al. Ernaehrung und Gesundheit. (Beitraege zur Infusionstherapie und Klinische Ernaehrung Ser.: Band 7). (GER., Illus.). xii, 204p. 1981. pap. 28.75 (*3-8055-2384-X*) S Karger.

Arab Maritime Academy Staff. A Comprehensive Maritime Dictionary: English-French-Arabic. (ARA, ENG & FRE.). 568p. 1989. 65.00 (*0-86685-509-2*, LDL5092, Pub. by Librairie du Liban) Intl Bk Ctr.

Arab Mothers Club Members. Simple Pleasures. (Illus.). 190p. 1998. 16.95 (*0-9662196-0-0*) Arab Mothers Club.

Arab Women Union Staff. Sahtain, Middle East Cookbook. (Illus.). 312p. 1995. vinyl bd. 19.95 (*0-86685-036-8*, AWUO36-8, Pub. by Librairie du Liban) Intl Bk Ctr.

Arabaki, Touraj. Baku Documents Vol. 1: A Complete Catalogue of Persian, Azeri, Ottoman & Arabic Newspapers. 224p. 1995. text 95.00 (*1-85043-836-6*, Pub. by I B T) St Martin.

Arabasz, Walter J., ed. A Guide to Reducing Losses from Future Earthquakes in Utah - Consensus Document: Concensus Document. (Miscellaneous Publication Ser.: Vol. 91-1). (Illus.). 30p. 1991. pap. 5.00 (*1-55791-310-2*, MP-91-1) Utah Geological Survey.

Arabasz, Walter J., et al. Evaluation of Seismicity Relevant to the Proposed Siting of a Superconducting Supercollider (SEC) in Tooele County, Utah. (Miscellaneous Publication Ser.: Vol. 89-1). (Illus.). 107p. 1989. pap. 8.50 (*1-55791-301-3*, MP-89-1) Utah Geological Survey.

***Arabella, Seymour.** Sins of the Mother. 2000. pap. 8.95 (*0-553-40483-0*, Pub. by Transworld Publishers Ltd) Trafalgar.

Arabian Horse Trust Editors, ed. Beyond Oats: A Horse Lover's Cookbook. LC 89-16901. 1994. pap. text 10.00 (*0-87197-257-3*) Favorite Recipes.

Arabian, Jack H. Comp Integ Electro Manual. (Manufacturing Engineering & Materials Processing Ser.: No. 31). (Illus.). 560p. 1989. text 215.00 (*0-8247-7849-9*) Dekker.

Arabian Nights Staff. The Tale of Aladdin & the Wonderful Lamp. LC 91-814. (Illus.). 32p. (J). (gr. k-3). 1992. lib. bdg. 14.95 (*0-8234-0938-4*) Holiday.

Arabie, P., et al. Clustering & Classification. LC 96-156758. 555p. 1996. text 109.00 (*981-02-1287-9*); vdisk 61.00 (*981-02-1354-9*) World Scientific Pub.

Arabie, Phipps, et al. Three-Way Scaling & Clustering. (Quantitative Applications in the Social Sciences Ser.: Vol. 65). 92p. (C). 1987. pap. text 10.95 (*0-8039-3068-2*) Sage.

Arabnia, H. R. Transputer Research & Applications 7: Proceedings of the 7th Conference of the North American Transputer Users Group, Oct 23-25, 1994, Athens, GA. LC 94-78470. (Transputer & Occam Engineering Ser.: Vol. 42). 349p. (gr. 12). 1994. pap. 99.00 (*90-5199-187-8*) IOS Press.

Arabnia, Hamid R., ed. Proceedings of the International Conference on Imaging Science, Systems, & Technology, 1997: C. I. S. S. T. '97. 565p. (C). 1997. pap. text 80.00 (*0-9648666-9-2*) C S R E A.

— Proceedings of the International Conference on Parallel & Distributed Processing Techniques & Applications. 900p. (Orig.). 1995. pap. text 100.00 (*0-9648666-0-9*) C S R E A.

— Proceedings of the International Conference on Parallel & Distributed Processing Techniques & Applications, 1997: P. D. P. T. A. '97, 3 vols. Incl. Vol. I. 617p. (Orig.). (C). 1997. pap. text 70.00 (*0-9648666-5-X*); Vol. II. 611p. (Orig.). (C). 1997. pap. text 70.00 (*0-9648666-6-8*); Vol. III. 578p. (Orig.). (C). 1997. pap. text 70.00 (*0-9648666-7-6*); 200.00 (*0-9648666-8-4*) C S R E A.

Arabnia, Hamid R., ed. Proceedings of the International Conference on Parallel & Distributed Processing Techniques & Applications-96, 3 vols. Incl. Vol. III. 573p. (Orig.). 1996. pap. text 70.00 (*0-9648666-3-3*); Vol. II. 508p. (Orig.). (C). 1996. pap. text 70.00 (*0-9648666-2-5*); Vol. I. 590p. (Orig.). (C). 1996. pap. text 70.00 (*0-9648666-1-7*); (P. D. P. T. A. Ser.). 210.00 (*0-9648666-4-1*) C S R E A.

Arac, Jonathan. Commissioned Spirits: The Shaping of Social Motion in Dickens, Carlyle, Melville, & Hawthorne. 216p. 1989. text 52.50 (*0-231-07116-7*); pap. text 18.50 (*0-231-07117-5*) Col U Pr.

— Huckleberry Finn As Idol & Target: The Functions of Criticism in Our Time. LC 97-15550. (Wisconsin Project on American Writers Ser.). 264p. 1997. pap. 18.95 (*0-299-15534-X*) U of Wis Pr.

Arac, Jonathan, ed. After Foucault Humanistic Knowledge, Postmodern Challenges. 224p. (Orig.). (C). 1988. pap. text 16.00 (*0-8135-1330-8*) Rutgers U Pr.

— Postmodernism & Politics. LC 85-28835. (Theory & History of Literature Ser.: Vol. 28). 224p. (Orig.). 1986. pap. 14.95 (*0-8166-1468-7*) U of Minn Pr.

Arac, Jonathan, et al, eds. The Yale Critics: Deconstruction in America. LC 83-1127. (Theory & History of Literature Ser.: No. 6). 260p. reprint ed. pap. 80.60 (*0-7837-2979-0*, 205747500006) Bks Demand.

Arac, Jonathan & Johnson, Barbara, eds. Consequences of Theory. LC 90-32670. (Selected Papers from the English Institute; 1982-83, New Ser.: No. 14). 256p. 1990. pap. text 14.95 (*0-8018-4045-7*) Johns Hopkins.

Arac, Jonathan & Ritvo, Harriet, eds. Macropolitics of Nineteenth-Century Literature: Nationalism, Exoticism, Imperialism. LC 94-41318. (New Americanists Ser.). 328p. 1995. pap. text 17.95 (*0-8223-1612-9*) Duke.

— Macropolitics of Nineteenth-Century Literature: Nationalism, Exoticism, Imperialism. LC 90-44874. (New Cultural Studies). 320p. (C). 1991. text 39.95 (*0-8122-8208-6*) U of Pa Pr.

Arac, Jonathan, ed. see Cappetti, Carla.

Arach, Abdeljabar. Foderalismus in Deutschland und Regionalisierung in Marokko: Politische Perspektiven Institutionelle und Rechtliche Rahmenbedingungen im Landervergleich. (Europaische Hochschulschriften: Reihe 31: Bd. 319). (GER., Illus.). 271p. 1996. pap. 51.95 (*3-631-30641-5*) P Lang Pubng.

Arachchige-Don, Neville S. Patterns of Community Structure in Colombo, Sri Lanka: An Investigation of Contemporary Urban Life in South Asia. 310p. (C). 1994. lib. bdg. 42.50 (*0-8191-9606-1*) U Pr of Amer.

***Aracil, J., et al, eds.** Stability Issues in Fuzzy Control. (Studies in Fuzziness & Soft Computing: 44). viii, 390p. 2000. (*3-7908-1277-3*) Spr-Verlag.

Arackal, Joseph J. Twenty-Two Gathering Prayers: Praying in Inclusive Language. 120p. (Orig.). 1992. pap. 8.95 (*1-55612-560-7*) Sheed & Ward WI.

Arackel, Joseph J. Psalms in Inclusive Language. 216p. (Orig.). 1993. pap. 12.95 (*0-8146-2024-8*) Liturgical Pr.

Arad, Gulie N. Passing into History: Nazism & the Holocaust Beyond Memory. Date not set. 39.95 (*0-253-30021-5*); pap. 25.00 (*0-253-30026-6*) Ind U Pr.

***Arad, Gulie Neeman.** America, Its Jews & the Rise of Nazism. LC 00-38910. (Jewish Literature & Culture Ser.). (Illus.). 2000. 35.00 (*0-253-33809-3*) Ind U Pr.

Arad, Ron. The International Design Yearbook 9, Vol. 9. (International Design Yearbooks Ser.). (Illus.). 240p. 1994. 80.00 (*1-55859-831-6*) Abbeville Pr.

Arad, Yitzhak. Belzec, Sobibor, Treblinka: The Operation Reinhard Death Camps. LC 85-45883. (Illus.). 448p. 1987. text 39.95 (*0-253-34293-7*) Ind U Pr.

***Arad, Yitzhak.** Belzec, Sobibor, Treblinka: The Operation Reinhard Death Camps. (Illus.). 448p. 1999. pap. 18.95 (*0-253-21305-3*) Ind U Pr.

Arad, Yitzhak. Ghetto in Flames. 1980. 35.00 (*0-87068-753-0*) Ktav.

— Ghetto in Flames. LC 80-50198. (Illus.). 500p. 1982. pap. 14.95 (*0-89604-043-7*, Holocaust Library) US Holocaust.

— The Partisan. LC 78-71299. (Illus.). 288p. 1979. 9.95 (*0-89604-010-0*, Holocaust Library) US Holocaust.

Arad, Yitzhak, et al, compiled by. The Einsatzgruppen Reports: Selections from the Official Dispatches of the Nazi Death Squads' Campaign Against the Jews. 1988. 19.95 (*0-89604-057-7*, Holocaust Library); pap. 12.95 (*0-89604-058-5*, Holocaust Library) US Holocaust.

Arad, Z. & Herzog, M., eds. Products of Conjugacy Classes in Groups. (Lecture Notes in Mathematics Ser.: Vol. 1112). v, 244p. 1985. 37.95 (*0-387-13916-8*) Spr-Verlag.

Arader, Graham, III, intro. The Redoute Album: Bouquets & Lilies. (Illus.). 340p. 1991. 95.00 (*0-87951-439-6*, Pub. by Overlook Pr) Penguin Putnam.

Arafat. Diwan of Hassan Ibn Thabit, Vols. I & II. 1971. 96.00 (*0-906094-30-5*, Pub. by Aris & Phillips) David Brown.

Arafat, Ibtihaj S. & Allen, Donald E. Thinking about Population: An Introduction to Modern Demography. LC 94-78415. 400p. (Orig.). 1995. text 48.95 (*1-882289-28-5*); pap. text 34.95 (*1-882289-27-7*) Gen Hall.

Arafat, Karim W. Classical Zeus: A Study in Art & Literature. (Oxford Monographs on Classical Archaeology). (Illus.). 286p. 1990. 130.00 (*0-19-814912-3*) OUP.

— Pausanias' Greece: Ancient Artists & Roman Rulers. 262p. (C). 1996. text 64.95 (*0-521-55340-7*) Cambridge U Pr.

Arafiles, Claribell & Arafiles, Clarissa M. Dumpty Humbug - Science Landmark. 96p. (J). (gr. 4-9). 1998. pap. 9.95 (*1-881539-19-9*) Tabby Hse Bks.

Arafiles, Clarissa M., jt. auth. see Arafiles, Claribell.

Arafune, J., ed. 7th Workshop on Grand Unification - ICOBAN '86: Proceedings of Workshop, Toyama, Japan, April 16-18, 1986. 572p. 1987. pap. 49.00 (*9971-5-0131-7*); text 131.00 (*9971-5-0130-9*) World Scientific Pub.

Aragaki, Sayako, tr. from JPN. Agam Beyond the Visible: Yaacov Agam & Jewish Art. 1997. pap. text 18.95 (*965-229-113-7*, Pub. by Gefen Pub Hse) Gefen Bks.

Aragdao-Lagergren, Aida. Working Children in the Informal Sector in Managua. LC 97-184950. (Geografia Region Studies). 311 p. 1997. write for info. (*91-506-1201-8*) Coronet Bks.

Araghi, Gayle, ed. see Bundy, Mary Lee.

Aragno, Anna. Symbolization: Proposing a Developmental Paradigm for a New Psychoanalytic Theory of Mind. LC 97-15905. 432p. 1997. 65.00 (*0-8236-6294-2*) Intl Univs Pr.

Aragnostatos, G., ed. see Kuo, T. T., et al.

Arago, Francois. Biographies of Distinguished Scientific Men. Smyth, W. H. et al, trs. LC 72-39662. (Essay Index Reprint Ser.). 1977. reprint ed. 58.95 (*0-8369-2737-0*) Ayer.

Arago, M. Historical Eloge of James Watt. LC 74-26247. (History, Philosophy & Sociology of Science Ser.). 1975. reprint ed. 23.95 (*0-405-06577-9*) Ayer.

Aragon, Alvaro Cubillo De, see Cubillo De Aragon, Alvaro.

Aragon, Clyde J. The PC Affair: A Comic Mystery of Murder, Mayhem, & Data Processing. LC 96-92977. 160p. (Orig.). 1997. pap. 7.95 (*0-9648641-1-8*) Cliff Zone Bks.

— Tales of Delight & Shame. LC 95-92560. 176p. (Orig.). 1996. pap. 9.95 (*0-9648641-0-X*) Cliff Zone Bks.

Aragon, Francisco, tr. see Alarcon, Francisco X.

Aragon, Francisco, tr. see Garcia Lorca, Federico.

Aragon, George A., jt. auth. see Viscione, Jerry A.

Aragon, Jack. Work Force: Construction Humor. LC 92-80790. (Illus.). 94p. 1992. pap. 5.95 (*0-9632697-0-4*) VJAK Corp.

Aragon, James R. Shipmaster's Handbook on Ship's Business. 2nd ed. LC 87-47998. 283p. 1988. text 24.00 (*0-87033-378-X*) Cornell Maritime.

Aragon, Jane Chelsea. Salt Hands. (Picture Puffin Ser.). 1994. 11.19 (*0-606-05991-1*, Pub. by Turtleback) Demco.

Aragon, Laurie W., ed. The Elementary Mathematician Pull-Out Book. (Illus.). 72p. (J). (gr. k-6). 1994. pap. 8.99 (*0-912843-34-9*, 4003) COMAP Inc.

Aragon, Laurie W., ed. see Martin, Paula & Carss, Marjorie.

***Aragon, Lorraine V.** Fields of the Lord: Animism, Christian Minorities & State Development in Indonesia. LC 99-58189. 2000. pap. 21.95 (*0-8248-2303-6*) UH Pr.

***Aragon, Lorraine V. & Russell, Susan D., eds.** Structuralism's Transformations: Order & Revision in Indonesian & Malaysian Societies. LC 99-68149. (Illus.). lxii, 402p. 1999. 24.95 (*1-881044-21-1*) ASU Prog SE Asian.

Aragon, Louis. The Adventures of Telemachus. Hubert, Renee R. & Hubert, Judd D., trs. from FRE. 160p. 1997. pap. text 13.95 (*1-878972-23-5*) Exact Change.

— The Adventures of Telemachus. Hubert, Renee Riese & Hubert, Judd D., trs. from FRE. LC 87-18208. (French Modernist Library). xxx, 102p. 1988. text 40.00 (*0-8032-1021-3*) U of Nebr Pr.

— Anicet ou le Panorama, Vol. 3. (FRE.). 288p. 1972. pap. 10.95 (*0-7859-2865-0*, F82562) Fr & Eur.

— Aurelien: Le Monde Reel. (FRE.). 697p. 1986. pap. 20.95 (*0-7859-2039-0*, 2070377504) Fr & Eur.

— Beaux Quartiers. (Folio Ser.: No. 241). (FRE.). 624p. 1965. pap. 13.95 (*2-07-036241-8*) Schoenhof.

— Les Beaux Quartiers: Le Monde Reel. (Monde Reel Ser.). (FRE.). 640p. 1989. reprint ed. pap. 17.95 (*0-7859-1714-4*, 2070362418) Fr & Eur.

— Chagall l'Admirable. (D. L. M. Ser.: No. 198). (FRE., Illus.). 32p. 1972. 450.00 (*1-55660-090-9*) A Wofsy Fine Arts.

— Cloches de Bale. (Folio Ser.: No. 791). (FRE.). pap. 10.95 (*2-07-036791-6*) Schoenhof.

— Les Cloches de Bales: Le Monde Reel. (FRE.). 437p. 1978. pap. 13.95 (*0-7859-1825-6*, 2070367916) Fr & Eur.

— Le Creve-Coeur. (Poesie Ser.). (FRE.). pap. 9.95 (*2-07-032189-4*) Schoenhof.

— Irene's Cunt. Lykiard, Alexis, tr. from FRE. (Velvet Ser.: No. 7). 96p. (Orig.). 1996. pap. 12.95 (*1-871592-54-2*) Creation Books.

— La Libertinage. (FRE.). 283p. 1977. pap. 17.95 (*0-7859-2750-6*, 2070297748) Fr & Eur.

— The Libertine. Levy, Jo, tr. from FRE. 160p. 1993. pap. 11.95 (*0-7145-4020-X*) Riverrun NY.

— La Mise a Mort. (FRE.). 256p. 1978. pap. 16.95 (*0-7859-1728-4*, 2070363147) Fr & Eur.

— La Mise a Mort. (Folio Ser.: No. 314). (FRE.). pap. 12.95 (*2-07-036314-7*) Schoenhof.

— Le Mouvement Perpetuel - Feu de Joie: Ecritures Automatique. (FRE.). 1970. pap. 10.95 (*0-8288-3811-9*, 2070300129) Fr & Eur.

— Le Mouvement Perpetuel & Feu de Joie et Ecritures Automatiques. (Poesie Ser.). (FRE.). pap. 7.95 (*2-07-030012-9*) Schoenhof.

— Le Nouveau Creve-Coeur. (FRE.). 192p. 1980. pap. 12.95 (*0-8288-3810-0*, 2070321894) Fr & Eur.

— Paris Peasant. Taylor, Simon W., tr. from FRE. 224p. (Orig.). 1993. reprint ed. pap. 15.95 (*1-878972-10-3*) Exact Change.

— Le Paysan de Paris. (FRE.). 256p. 1978. pap. 10.95 (*0-7859-1824-8*, 2070367827) Fr & Eur.

— Le Paysan de Paris. (Folio Ser.: No. 782). (FRE.). pap. 8.95 (*2-07-036782-7*) Schoenhof.

— Les Poetes. (FRE.). 256p. 1976. pap. 14.95 (*0-7859-3463-4*, 2070321614) Fr & Eur.

— Le Roman Inacheve. (FRE.). 1978. pap. 14.95 (*0-7859-3462-6*, 2070300110) Fr & Eur.

— Le Roman Inacheve. (Poesie Ser.). (FRE.). pap. 9.95 (*2-07-030011-0*) Schoenhof.

— Traite de Style. (FRE.). 1980. pap. 16.95 (*0-7859-3377-8*, 207020989X) Fr & Eur.

— Treatise on Style. Waters, Alyson, tr. from FRE. & intro. by. LC 90-12894. (French Modernist Library). Orig. Title: Traite du Style. xx, 119p. 1991. text 40.00 (*0-8032-1024-8*) U of Nebr Pr.

Aragon, Louis & Cocteau, Jean. Conversations on the Dresden Gallery. Scarfe, Francis, tr. from FRE. LC 81-6640. (Illus.). 288p. 1982. 65.00 (*0-8419-0730-7*) Holmes & Meier.

Aragon, Louis, jt. auth. see Apollinaire, Guillaume.

Aragon, Luis Cardoza y, see Cardoza y Aragon, Luis.

Aragon, Margo, jt. auth. see Axtell, Horace.

Aragon, Rafael & Loschcke, Eberhard. Die Kircher der Armen in Nicaragua: Geschichte und Perspektiven. (Wurzburger Studien Zur Fundamentaltheologie Ser.: Bd. 20). (GER.). 176p. 1996. 38.95 (*3-631-48669-3*) P Lang Pubng.

Aragon, Randall, jt. auth. see Memory, John M.

Aragon-Salamanca, A., jt. auth. see Maddox, S.

Aragon, Virginia. Through the Darkness to the Dawn. 47p. 1997. 19.95 (*0-9661759-0-5*) Ariz Lib.

Aragon y Ulibarri, Daniel. Devil's Hatband: A Story about a People's Struggle Against Land Theft & Racism. LC 98-49982. 288p. 1999. 29.95 (*0-86534-284-9*) Sunstone Pr.

Aragone, C., ed. Relativity, Cosmology, Topological Mass & Supergravity: Proceedings of the 4th Silarg Symposium on Gravity, Gauge Theories & Supergravity, USB Campus, Caracas, Dec. 5-11, 1982. 304p. 1984. text 89.00 (*9971-950-95-2*) World Scientific Pub.

Aragones, Juan E. Veinte Anos de Teatro Espanol (1960-1980) LC 87-60874. (SPA.). 301p. 1987. pap. 35.00 (*0-89295-043-9*) Society Sp & Sp-Am.

Aragones, Sergio. Aragones' More Mad Pantomimes. 192p. 1988. mass mkt. 3.95 (*0-446-34715-9*, Pub. by Warner Bks) Little.

— Incurably Mad. (Illus.). 1989. mass mkt. 3.50 (*0-446-35813-4*, Pub. by Warner Bks) Little.

— Mad As a Hatter. 192p. (Orig.). 1987. mass mkt. 3.95 (*0-446-34741-8*, Pub. by Warner Bks) Little.

— Mad As Usual. 192p. 1990. mass mkt. 3.50 (*0-446-35860-6*, Pub. by Warner Bks) Little.

— Mad-ly Yours. 1989. mass mkt. 3.95 (*0-446-35815-0*, Pub. by Warner Bks) Little.

— Mad Menagerie. 1989. mass mkt. 3.50 (*0-446-35419-8*, Pub. by Warner Bks) Little.

An Asterisk (*) at the beginning of an entry indicates that the title is appearing for the first time.

— Mad Pantomimes. 192p. 1987. mass mkt. 3.99 (*0-446-34397-8*, Pub. by Warner Bks) Little.

— Mad's Sergio Aragones on Parade. (Illus.). 160p. (Orig.). 1982. mass mkt. 6.95 (*0-446-37369-9*) Warner Bks.

— More Mad Marginals. 192p. 1988. mass mkt. 3.50 (*0-446-35245-4*, Pub. by Warner Bks) Little.

— Sergio Aragones Is Totally Mad. 1991. mass mkt. 3.99 (*0-446-35979-3*, Pub. by Warner Bks) Little.

— Sergio Aragones Louder Than Words. (Illus.). 160p. (YA). (gr. 7 up). 1998. pap. 12.95 (*1-56971-343-X*) Dark Horse Comics.

— Sergio Aragones' Next Mad Book. 1992. mass mkt. 3.99 (*0-446-36368-5*, Pub. by Warner Bks) Little.

— Shootin' Mad. (Mad Ser.). (Illus.). 192p. (Orig.). 1989. mass mkt. 3.50 (*0-446-35993-9*, Pub. by Warner Bks) Little.

— Viva Mad! (Illus.). 192p. (Orig.). 1989. mass mkt. 3.95 (*0-446-35817-7*, Pub. by Warner Bks) Little.

***Aragones, Sergio & Evanier, Mark.** The Groo Houndbook. (Illus.). 96p. 1999. pap. 9.95 (*1-56971-385-5*, Pub. by Dark Horse Comics) Penguin Putnam.

Aragones, Sergio & Evanier, Mark. Sergio Aragones' Groo: The Most Intelligent Man in the World. 112p. (YA). (gr. 7 up). 1999. pap. 9.95 (*1-56971-294-8*) Dark Horse Comics.

***Aragones, Sergio & Evanier, Mark.** Sergio Aragones Groo & Rufferto. 112p. 2000. pap. 9.95 (*1-56971-447-9*, Pub. by Dark Horse Comics) Penguin Putnam.

Aragones, Sergio & Zone, Ray. Aragones 3-D. (Illus.). 64p. (Orig.). (YA). (gr. 9-12). 1989. pap. 4.95 (*0-925300-00-4*) Three-D Zone.

Aragunde, Rafael. Sobre Lo Universitario y la Universidad de Puerto Rico. (SPA.). 200p. 1996. pap. write for info. (*0-929441-79-6*) Pubns Puertorriquenas.

Arahamson, Royce L., jt. auth. see Pickle, Hal B.

Arahood, Dale A. Bank Performance Bonus Plans: 1999 State of the Art Report. (Illus.). 206p. 1988. pap. 89.00 (*0-9638047-1-5*, Incentive Comp) D Arahood & Assocs.

— Community Bank Incentive Compensation Plans. (Illus.). 184p. 1989. pap. 99.00 (*0-9638047-2-3*, Incentive Comp) D Arahood & Assocs.

— Employee Incentive Plans: Retail & Branch Banking. (Illus.). 169p. 1991. pap. 99.00 (*0-9638047-3-1*, Incentive Comp) D Arahood & Assocs.

— How to Design & Install Management Incentive Compensation Plans. rev. ed. LC 94-94223. 190p. 1996. pap. 129.00 (*0-9638047-0-7*) D Arahood & Assocs.

— How to Design Sale Bonus Plans, Vol. 1. (Illus.). 200p. 1997. pap. 129.00 (*0-9638047-6-6*) D Arahood & Assocs.

— Installing Management Incentive Bonus Plans. rev. ed. LC 94-94223. (Illus.). 150p. (Orig.). 1996. pap. 109.00 (*0-9638047-5-8*) D Arahood & Assocs.

Arai, Hakuseki. Told Round a Brushwood Fire: The Autobiography of Arai Hakuseki. LC DS0872.A7A31. (Princeton Library of Asian Translations). (Illus.). 359p. reprint ed. pap. 111.30 (*0-8357-4046-3*, 203673600005) Bks Demand.

Arai, K., jt. ed. see Crookall, David.

Arai, Keisuke, jt. auth. see Sekine, Kenichi.

Arai, Keisuke, jt. auth. see Sekine, Ken'ichi.

Arai, Keisuke, jt. auth. see Sekine, Kenichi.

Arai, Kenji. Cartoon Illustration. (Illus.). 456p. 1993. pap. 49.95 (*4-7661-0721-7*, Pub. by Graphic-Sha) Bks Nippan.

Arai, Kiyoshi, jt. ed. see Crookall, David A.

Arai, Munehito, jt. auth. see Kuwajima, Kunihiro.

Arai, Paula K. R. Women Living Zen: Japanese Soto Buddhist Nuns. LC 98-17675. (Illus.). 272p. 1999. text 39.95 (*0-19-512393-X*) OUP.

Arai, S. The Economics of Education: An Analysis of College-Going Behaviour. 216p. 1998. 95.00 (*4-431-70224-5*) Spr-Verlag.

Arai, Shinya. Shoshaman: A Tale of Corporate Japan. Mulhern, Chieko, tr. from JPN. (Voices from Asia Ser.: No. 3). 232p. 1991. pap. 16.95 (*0-520-07142-5*, Pub. by U CA Pr) Cal Prin Full Svc.

Arai, Tomie & Yee, Lydia. Double Happiness. LC 98-71319. 64p. 1998. write for info. (*0-917535-25-1*) Bronx Mus.

Arai, Tosh & Ariarajah, S. Wesley, eds. Spirituality in Interfaith Dialogue. LC BV4501.2.S69. 120p. 1989. reprint ed. pap. 37.20 (*0-7837-9830-X*, 206055900005) Bks Demand.

Arai, Toshihiro, et al. Mesoscopic Materials & Clusters: Their Physical & Chemical Properties. LC 99-17748. (Series in Cluster Physics). 470p. 1999. 129.00 (*3-540-64884-4*) Spr-Verlag.

Arai, Toshikazu, tr. see Ikeyama, Eikichi.

Arai, Toshikazu, tr. see Sakakibara, Tokuso, et al.

Arai, Yoishi. The World Airports: International Airports & Their Commercial Facilities. (Illus.). 172p. 1996. 69.95 (*4-7858-0039-9*, Pub. by Shotenkenchiku-Sha) Bks Nippan.

Araia, Ghelawdewos. Ethiopia: The Political Economy of Transition. LC 94-24368. 246p. (C). 1995. pap. text 29.50 (*0-8191-9770-X*); lib. bdg. 53.00 (*0-8191-9769-6*) U Pr of Amer.

Araico, Susana H. La Ironia en Tragedias de Calderon. 1984. 25.00 (*0-916379-18-3*) Scripta.

Araim, Amer S. Intergovernmental Commodity Organizations & the New International Economic Order. LC 90-31187. 256p. 1991. 55.00 (*0-275-93405-5*, C3405, Praeger Pubs) Greenwood.

Araji, Sharon K. Sexually Aggressive Children: Coming to Understand Them. LC 97-4819. 264p. 1997. text 48.00 (*0-8039-5175-2*); pap. text 22.95 (*0-8039-5176-0*) Sage.

— Society: An Alaskan Perspective. 512p. (C). 1996. pap. text 33.95 (*0-7872-1898-7*) Kendall-Hunt.

Arak, Jonathan. Cracking the New York City Specialized Sciences High School Admission Test. 1999. pap. 15.95 (*0-375-75347-8*) Random.

Arak, T. & Zaitsev, A. Uniform Limit Theorems for Sums of Independent Random Variables. LC 88-10443. (Proceedings of the Steklov Institute of Mathematics Ser.: Vol. 174). 222p. 1988. reprint ed. pap. 124.00 (*0-8218-3118-6*, STEKLO/174) Am Math.

Arakawa, K., et al, eds. ACE Inhibitors at the Kidney. (Journal: Nephron: Vol. 54, Supl. 1, 1990). (Illus.). iv, 100p. 1990. pap. 43.50 (*3-8055-5180-0*) S Karger.

Arakawa, Yoichi. Great Jazz Riffs for Guitar. 30p. pap., pap. text 17.95 incl. cd-rom (*0-89524-943-X*, 02503467, Pub. by Cherry Lane) H Leonard.

Arakawa, Yoichi. Guitar Chords & Accompaniment: Learn Guitar Chords & Various Accompaniment Styles Step by Step! (Illus.). 125p. (YA). 1999. pap. text 14.95 (*1-891370-00-6*, SSM00760, Pub. by Six Strings) Music Sales.

***Arakawa, Yoichi.** Jazz Guitar Chords & Accompaniment. 125p. 2000. pap. text 15.95 (*1-891370-07-3*, SSM00761) Six Strings.

— More Guitar Chords & Accompaniment: Take a Step up in Your Chord Vocabulary & Accompaniment Skills! (Illus.). 89p. 1999. pap. 14.95 (*1-891370-01-4*, SSM00761, Pub. by Six Strings) Music Sales.

— 101 Basic: Blue Scales for Guitar. (Illus.). 29p. 1999. pap. 6.95 (*1-891370-05-7*, SSM00765, Pub. by Six Strings) Music Sales.

— 101 Basic: Guitar Chords. (Illus.). 29p. 1999. pap. 6.95 (*1-891370-02-2*, SSM00762, Pub. by Six Strings) Music Sales.

Arakawa, Yoichi. 101 Basic: Major Pentatonic Scales for Guitar. (Illus.). 29p. 1999. pap. 6.95 (*1-891370-04-9*, SSM00764, Pub. by Six Strings) Music Sales.

***Arakawa, Yoichi.** 101 Basic: Minor Pentatonic Scales for Guitars. (Illus.). 32p. 1999. pap. 6.95 (*1-891370-03-0*, SSM00763, Pub. by Six Strings) Music Sales.

— 101 Basic Reading for Guitar. (Illus.). 37p. 1999. pap. 6.95 (*1-891370-06-5*, SSM00766, Pub. by Six Strings) Music Sales.

Arakawa, Yoichi, ed. A Fingerstyle Christmas. 40p. (YA). pap. text 9.95 (*0-89524-947-2*, 02506920, Pub. by Cherry Lane) H Leonard.

Arakelian, Mary. Orra Phelps, M. D. Adirondack Naturalist & Mountaineer. (Illus.). 2000. 30.00 (*0-925168-66-1*) North Country.

Arakelian, Sourene. The Violin: Precepts & Observations of a Luthier. 88p. 1981. pap. 24.95 (*0-933224-36-2*, I047) Bold Strummer Ltd.

Arakhov, V. I. Protective Coatings on Metals, Vol. 12. 1986. 42.50 (*0-8364-2275-9*, Pub. by Oxford IBH) S Asia.

Araki, et al, eds. Structure & Properties & Multiphase Polymeric Materials. LC 97-52811. (Illus.). 480p. 1998. text 185.00 (*0-8247-0142-9*) Dekker.

Araki, Chiyo. Origami for Christmas. LC 82-80736. (Illus.). 140p. 1987. pap. 19.00 (*0-87011-807-2*) Kodansha.

— Origami in the Classroom, Bk. 1. LC 65-13412. (Illus.). 40p. (J). (gr. 1 up). 1968. bds. 14.95 (*0-8048-0452-4*) Tuttle Pubng.

— Origami in the Classroom, Bk. 2. LC 65-13412. (Illus.). 40p. (J). (gr. 1 up). 1968. bds. 14.95 (*0-8048-0453-2*) Tuttle Pubng.

Araki, Gary. Netware Professional's Toolkit. 450p. (gr. 10 up). 1999. pap. 39.95 incl. audio compact disk (*1-889671-11-8*) Advice Pr.

Araki, H., et al, eds. Current Topics in Operator Algebras: Satellite Conference of ICM-90, Japan, 16-20 August 1990. 448p. (C). 1991. text 104.00 (*981-02-0651-8*) World Scientific Pub.

— Operator Algebras & Their Connections with Topology & Ergodic Theory. (Lecture Notes in Mathematics Ser.: Vol. 1132). vi, 594p. 1985. 65.95 (*0-387-15643-7*) Spr-Verlag.

Araki, H., et al. Subfactors: Proceedings of the Taniguchi Symposium on Operator Algebras. 304p. 1994. text 74.00 (*981-02-1803-6*) World Scientific Pub.

Araki, H., jt. auth. see Aizenman, M.

Araki, H., jt. ed. see Aizenman, M.

Araki, Hirohiko. Baoh, Vol. 2. (Illus.). 176p. 1995. pap. 14.95 (*1-56931-088-2*) Viz Commns Inc.

— Boah, Volume One, Vol. 1. (Illus.). 184p. 1995. pap. 14.95 (*1-56931-097-1*) Viz Commns Inc.

***Araki, Huzihiro.** Mathematical Theory of Quantum Fields. LC 99-41253. 101. 248p. 2000. text 100.00 (*0-19-851773-4*) OUP.

Araki, Huzihiro, et al, eds. Quantum & Non-Commutative Analysis: Past, Present, & Future Perspectives. LC 93-31537. (Mathematical Physics Studies: Vol. 16). 468p. (C). 1993. text 264.50 (*0-7923-2532-X*) Kluwer Academic.

Araki, Huzihiro & Kadison, Richard V. Mappings of Operator Algebras. (Progress in Mathematics Ser.: Vol. 84). 300p. 1990. 64.00 (*0-8176-3476-2*) Birkhauser.

Araki, J., tr. see Inoue, Yasushi.

Araki, James T., tr. see Brazell, Karen.

Araki, James T., tr. see Muraoka, Tsunetsugu.

Araki, K., ed. RIMS Symposia on Software Science & Engineering II. (Lecture Notes in Computer Science Ser.: Vol. 220). xi, 323p. 1986. 39.00 (*0-387-16470-7*) Spr-Verlag.

***Araki, K., et al, eds.** IFM 99: Proceedings of the 1st International Conference on Integrated Formal Methods, York, 28-29 June 1999. LC 99-29060. (Illus.). xiv, 477p. 1999. pap. 119.00 (*1-85233-107-0*, Pub. by Spr-Verlag) Spr-Verlag.

Araki, Nancy K. & Horii, Jane. Matsuri: Festival Japanese American Celebrations & Activities. (Illus.). (Orig.). (J). 1985. reprint ed. pap. 9.95 (*0-89346-019-2*) Heian Intl.

Araki, Nobuyoshi. Araki: Tokyo Lucky Hole. (Klutz Ser.). (Illus.). 700p. 1997. pap. 29.95 (*3-8228-8189-9*) Taschen Amer.

***Araki, Nobuyoshi.** Nobuyoshi Araki: Araki in Wein, 2 Vols. 1999. 65.00 (*4-7713-0316-9*) Dist Art Pubs.

— Nobuyoshi Araki: Taipei. 1999. 120.00 (*4-7713-0324-X*) Dist Art Pubs.

Araki, Nobuyoshi. Shikijyo: Sexual Desire. (Illus.). 168p. 1997. 55.00 (*3-908162-44-0*) Dist Art Pubs.

— Tokyo Novelle. 1997. 35.00 (*3-89322-853-5*, Pub. by Edition Cantz) Dist Art Pubs.

Araki, Nobuyoshi, jt. auth. see Goldin, Nan.

Araki, S. Behavioral Medicine. x382p. 1992. 164.50 (*0-444-89253-2*) Elsevier.

Araki, Takeo, ed. Liquid Membranes: Chemical Applications. 232p. 1990. lib. bdg. 225.00 (*0-8493-5314-9*, QP562) CRC Pr.

Arakin, V. D. English-Russian Dictionary. (ENG & RUS.). 606p. (C). 1987. 110.00 (*0-569-09278-7*, Pub. by Collets) St Mut.

Arakin, V. D., et al. Dictionary of Common Words. (ENG & RUS.). 567p. 1981. 17.95 (*0-8288-1226-8*, F60770) Fr & Eur.

— English - Russian Dictionary. 12th rev. ed. 608p. (C). 1987. 16.95 (*0-8285-1956-0*) Firebird NY.

— English-Russian Dictionary. 11th ed. (ENG & RUS.). 1980. 39.95 (*0-8288-1227-6*, M9107) Fr & Eur.

Aral, Mustafa M. Ground Water Modeling in Multilayer Aquifers: Steady Flow. (Illus.). 192p. 1990. lib. bdg. 159.00 (*0-87371-304-4*, L304) Lewis Pubs.

— Ground Water Modeling in Multilayer Aquifers: Unsteady Flow. (Illus.). 240p. 1990. lib. bdg. 159.00 (*0-87371-305-2*, L305) Lewis Pubs.

Aral, Mustafa M., ed. Advances in Groundwater Pollution Control & Remediation: Proceedings of the NATO Advanced Study Institute, Antalya, Turkey, May 20-June 1, 1995. LC 95-48406. (NATO ASI Series: Partnership Sub-Series 2: Environment: Vol. 9). 624p. (C). 1996. text 320.50 (*0-7923-3926-6*) Kluwer Academic.

Araluce, Jose R., tr. see Nicholson, Robert.

Araluce, Jose R., tr. see Nicholson, Robert & Watts, Claire.

Aram, John D., jt. auth. see Westin, Alan F.

Aram, Joseph, jt. auth. see Watson, James T.

Aramanovic, I. G. & Sneddon, Ian N. Mathematical Analysis: Differentiation & Integration. LC 64-8051. (International Series of Monographs on Pure & Applied Mathematics: No. 81). 1965. 152.00 (*0-08-011011-8*, Pub. by Pergamon Repr) Franklin.

Arambulo, ed. Parasitic Zoonoses: Section C, 3 vols., Vol. I. (CRC Handbook Series in Zoonoses). 400p. 1982. 208.00 (*0-8493-2916-7*, RC113, CRC Reprint) Franklin.

— Parasitic Zoonoses: Section C, 3 vols., Vol. II. (CRC Handbook Series in Zoonoses). 360p. 1982. 207.00 (*0-8493-2917-5*, CRC Reprint) Franklin.

— Parasitic Zoonoses: Section C, 3 vols., Vol. III. (CRC Handbook Series in Zoonoses). 384p. 1982. 195.00 (*0-8493-2918-3*, CRC Reprint) Franklin.

Arambulo, Hector & Jenkins, Connie. How to Create & Manage Effective Support Teams. Bultema, Patrick et al, eds. (Illus.). 170p. (Orig.). pap. write for info. (*1-57125-016-6*) Help Desk Inst.

***Arambulo, K.** Strengthening the Supervision of the International Covenant on Economic, Social & Cultural Rights: Theoretical & Procedural Aspects. (School of Human Rights Research Ser.: Vol. 3). 468p. 1999. 90.00 (*90-5095-058-2*, Pub. by Intersentia Uitgevers) Intl Spec Bk.

Arambulo, Primo, III, et al, eds. Primates of the Americas: Strategies for Conservation & Sustained Use in Biomedical Research: Proceedings of the First Ordinary Meeting, Regional Primatology Committee for the Americas (CORP-1), Battelle Seattle Conference Center, October 29-31, 1990. LC 93-16987. 336p. 1993. pap. 34.95 (*0-935470-73-5*) Battelle.

Arams, Frank R. Infrared-to-Millimeter Wavelength Detectors. LC 78-189396. (Modern Frontiers in Applied Science Ser.). 378p. reprint ed. pap. 117.20 (*0-8357-4177-X*, 202716500054) Bks Demand.

Aran, Aitor, ed. see Conroy, Joseph.

Aran, J. M. & Dauman, R., eds. Tinnitus, 1991: Proceedings of the Fourth International Tinnitus Seminar, Bordeaux, France, August 27-30, 1991. LC 92-49982. (Illus.). 575p. 1992. lib. bdg. 168.50 (*90-6299-087-8*, Pub. by Kugler) Kugler Pubns.

Aran, Robin. The Secret Skater: A Winner Family Sports Mystery. LC 96-35659. (Winning Readers Ser.). (J). 1996. write for info. (*1-879852-52-7*) Univ Tampa.

Arana, Alice A. & Arana, Oswaldo. Que tal? An Introductory Course. 4th ed. (C). 1995. pap., wbk. ed. 29.38 (*0-07-017958-1*) McGraw.

***Arana, Alice A., et al.** Que Tal? 5th ed. 192p. (C). 1998. pap., wbk. ed. 28.75 (*0-07-013683-1*) McGrw-H Hghr Educ.

— Que Tal? 5th ed. (Illus.). 192p. (C). 1998. pap., wbk. ed., lab manual ed. 28.75 (*0-07-013684-X*) McGrw-H Hghr Educ.

Arana de Love, Francisca. Diccionario de Interjecciones Espanol-Ingles-Espanol. (ENG & SPA.). 1985. 19.95 (*0-8288-2324-3*, S10647) Fr & Eur.

Arana, George W., et al. Handbook of Psychiatric Drug Therapy. 3rd ed. LC 95-1489. 240p. 1995. pap. text 34.00 (*0-316-04946-8*) Lppncott W & W.

Arana, George W., jt. auth. see Hyman, Steven E.

Arana, Oswaldo, jt. auth. see Arana, Alice A.

Arana Perez, I. Vascos en America. (Gran Enciclopedia de Espana y America Ser.). (SPA., Illus.). 1989. 200.00 (*84-87053-14-9*) Elliots Bks.

Arana, Raul M. Proyecto Coatlan, Area Tonatico-Pilcaya. 243p. 1990. pap. 14.00 (*968-6068-72-4*, IN029) UPLAAP.

Arana, Soto. Diccionario de Medicos Puertorriquenos Que Se Man Distinguico Fuera de la Medicina. (SPA.). 22.50 (*0-8288-8094-8*, S5070) Fr & Eur.

Aranaboldi, Mario Antonio. Jean Claude Pondevie: Soft-tech Architecture. 1999. pap. text 25.00 (*88-7838-074-1*) L'Arca IT.

Aranadez, Richard, tr. see Masseron, Alexandre.

Arancibia, Jose L. De Zayas y, see Y Almeida, Luis E. & De Zayas y Arancibia, Jose L.

Arancibia, Rene, tr. see Mackay, W. P.

Arancibia, Rene, tr. see Moody, et al.

Arand, Charles P. Testing the Boundaries: Windows to Lutheran Identity. LC 95-36697. (Concordia Scholarship Today Ser.). 1995. 18.00 (*0-570-04839-7*, 12-3276) Concordia.

Arand, Louis A., tr. see Kuasten, J. & Plumpe, J., eds.

Aranda. Diccionario De Terminos Legales (Dictonary/Legal Terms) (SWC-Business Law Ser.). Date not set. 56.40 (*0-314-09029-0*) Sth-Wstrn College.

— Diccionario De Terminos Legalses (Dict/Legal Terms) (SWC-Business Law Ser.). Date not set. 55.40 (*0-314-09030-4*) Sth-Wstrn College.

— Dictionary of Legal Terms. Date not set. pap. text 9.00 (*0-314-03554-0*) West Pub.

***Aranda-Alvarad, Belen.** Latina Beauty: A Get - Gorgeous Guide For Every Mujer. (Illus.). 224p. 2000. 29.95 (*0-7868-6669-1*, Pub. by Hyperion) Time Warner.

Aranda, Charles. Dichos: Sayings & Proverbs from the Spanish. rev. ed. LC 77-78611. (ENG & SPA., Illus.). 32p. 1983. pap. 4.95 (*0-913270-47-4*) Sunstone Pr.

Aranda, Eileen K. Teams: Structure, Process, Culture, & Politics. LC 98-2936. 176p. (C). 1998. pap. text 29.40 (*0-13-494584-0*) P-H.

Aranda, Fernando Molina, see Molina Aranda, Fernando.

Aranda, Francisco. Luis Bunuel: A Critical Biography. Robinson, David, ed. LC 76-7621. 1976. reprint ed. lib. bdg. 35.00 (*0-306-70754-3*) Da Capo.

— Luis Bunuel: A Critical Biography. Robinson, David, ed. LC 76-7621. (Illus.). 327p. 1976. reprint ed. pap. 11.95 (*0-306-80028-4*) Da Capo.

Aranda, J. V., jt. ed. see Vert, P.

Aranda, Josefina, jt. auth. see Fox, Jonathan.

Aranda, Linda. Three Nativity Plays for Christmas. 25p. (Orig.). 1994. pap. 6.95 (*1-57514-233-3*, 6004) Encore Perform Pub.

Aranda, M., tr. see Descartes, Rene.

Aranda Regules, J. M. Nuevas Perspectivas en Atencion Primaria de Salud. (SPA.). 399p. 1994. pap. 31.50 (*84-7978-114-9*, Pub. by Ediciones Diaz) IBD Ltd.

Araneo, A. Les Cloches de Bales (Le Monde Reel) (SPA.). 287p. 1989. 39.95 (*0-7859-6405-3*, 8486761115) Fr & Eur.

Arangio-Ruis, V. & Olivieri, A. Inscriptiones Graecae Sicilae et Infimae Italiae Ad Ius Pertinentes. 289p. 1980. 30.00 (*0-89005-321-9*) Ares.

Arangio-Ruiz, G. U. N. Declaration on Friendly Relations & the System of Sources of International Law. 354p. 1979. lib. bdg. 64.50 (*90-286-0149-X*) Kluwer Academic.

Arangno, Deborah. Schaum's Outline of Abstract Algebra. LC 98-53077. (Illus.). 256p. 1999. pap. 15.95 (*0-07-006995-6*, Schaums Outlne) McGraw-Hill Prof.

Arangno, Deborah, jt. auth. see Knepell, Peter.

Arango. Schaum's Advanced Calculus. 2nd ed. LC 99-53281. 2000. pap. 15.95 (*0-07-135019-5*) McGraw.

Arango, Alfredo, tr. see Brito, Alan.

Arango, Ariel C. Dirty Words. 1996. 40.00 (*1-56821-799-4*) Aronson.

— Dirty Words: Psychoanalytic Insights. LC 89-6745. 240p. 1989. 40.00 (*0-87668-855-5*) Aronson.

Arango, Felipe M. Los Aborigenes de la Cuenca de Santiago de Cuba. LC 97-60083. (Coleccion Cuba y Sus Jueces Ser.). (SPA., Illus.). 293p. (Orig.). 1997. pap. 24.95 (*0-89729-829-2*, 829-2) Ediciones.

Arango, Guillermo. Remembrance of a Time Just Past - Memoris De un Pasado in Mediato: Poetry. Linden Lane Press Staff, ed. Harter, Hugh A., tr. from SPA. 96p. (Orig.). pap. 13.00 (*0-685-65348-X*) Linden Ln Pr.

Arango, Joaquin, jt. auth. see Baldwin-Edwards, Martin.

Arango, Jorge V. Coloquio del Azogamiento. (SPA.). 112p. (Orig.). 1988. pap. 8.00 (*0-917049-18-7*) Saeta.

***Arango, Manuel Antonio.** Contribucion al Estudio de la Obra Dramatica de Sor Juana Ines de la Cruz. (Currents in Comparative Romance Languages & Literatures Ser.: No. 84). (SPA.). 392p. (C). 2000. text 62.95 (*0-8204-4423-5*) P Lang Pubng.

Arango, Polly E., et al. Touring New Mexico. LC 94-16724. 414p. (C). 1995. pap. 19.95 (*0-8263-1622-0*) U of NM Pr.

Arango, Ramon E. Spain: Democracy Regained. 2nd ed. (Nations of the Modern World Ser.). (C). 1996. pap. 34.00 (*0-8133-2915-9*, Pub. by Westview) HarpC.

Aranjo, Carl. Guitar Guru: The Chord Book, Your Guide for Success. 1997. pap. text 12.95 (*1-56922-159-6*) Creat Cncpts.

Aranjo, Karl. Guitar Scale Guru Scale Book: Your Guide for Success! 1997. pap. text 14.95 (*1-56922-186-3*) Creat Cncpts.

Arano, Luisa C. The Medieval Health Handbook: Tacuinum Sanitatis. Ratti, Oscar & Westbrook, Adele, trs. from ITA. LC 75-21725. (Illus.). 156p. 1992. reprint ed. pap. 20.00 (*0-8076-1277-4*, Pub. by Braziller) Norton.

Aranovich, Raul, et al, eds. Proceedings of the Thirteenth West Coast Conference on Formal Linguistics Vol. 13 (WCCFL 13) Proceedings of the West Coast Conference on Formal Linguistics. 1995. pap. 26.95 (*1-881526-76-3*) CSLI.

Aranow, Edward R. & Einhorn, Herbert A. Tender Offers for Corporate Control. LC 72-10557. 352p. 1973. text 110.50 (*0-231-03671-X*) Col U Pr.

Aranson, I. S., et al. Multidimensional Strange Attractors & Turbulence, Vol. 8. (Mathematical Physics Reviews Ser.: SSR Sec. C, Vol. 8, Pt. 5). ii, 88p. 1989. pap. text 107.00 (*3-7186-4868-7*) Gordon & Breach.

Aranson, Peter H., ed. Supreme Court Economic Review, Vol. 1. 250p. 1994. reprint ed. lib. bdg. 60.00 (*0-913969-66-4*) Univ Pub Assocs.

— Supreme Court Economic Review, Vol. 2. 300p. 1994. reprint ed. lib. bdg. 60.00 (*0-913969-67-2*) Univ Pub Assocs.

Aranson, S. K. & Zhuzhoma, E. V. Introduction to the Qualitative Theory of Dynamical Systems on Surfaces. LC 96-19197. (Translations of Mathematical Monographs: Vol. 153). 325p. 1996. text 129.00 (*0-8218-0369-7*, MMONO/153) Am Math.

Arant, Bruce. Easy Living: One Story Designs. 2nd ed. 104p. 1995. reprint ed. pap. text 7.95 (*0-9647658-5-3*) Design Basics.

Arant, Bruce, ed. see Brown, Joyce.

Arant, Bruce, ed. see Shea, Carol Stratman.

Arant, Bruce, jt. ed. see Shea, Carol Stratman.

Arant, Bruce, ed. see Stratman Shea, Carol.

Arant, Olive G. Magic: The Cookbook of the Junior League of Birmingham. 5th ed. LC 81-85953. 348p. 1982. 14.95 (*0-9607810-0-5*) Jr League Birm.

Arant, Patricia. Compositional Techniques of the Russian Oral Epic, the Bylina. LC 90-36860. (Harvard Dissertations in Folklore & Oral Literature Ser.). 214p. 1990. reprint ed. text 20.00 (*0-8240-2962-3*) Garland.

Arant, Patricia M. Russian for Reading. 214p. 1981. pap. text 16.95 (*0-89357-086-9*) Slavica.

***Arant, Wendi & Mosely, Pixie Anne, eds.** Library Outreach, Partnerships & Distance Education: Reference Librarians at the Gateway. LC 00-21759. 304p. 2000. 59.95 (*0-7890-0842-4*) Haworth Pr.

***Arant, Wendi & Mosley, Pixey Anne, eds.** Library Outreach, Partnerships & Distance Education: Reference Librarians at the Gateway. LC 00-21759. 304p. 2000. pap. text 24.95 (*0-7890-0953-6*) Haworth Pr.

Arantes, E. R. De, see Tasso, C. & De Arantes, E. R., eds.

Arany, A. Laszlo. Phonological System of a Hungarian Dialect: An Introduction to Structural Dialectology. LC 67-63039. (Uralic & Altaic Ser.: Vol. 85). 184p. 1967. reprint ed. pap. text 13.00 (*0-87750-034-7*) Res Inst Inner Asian Studies.

Arany, Lynne & Hobson, Archie. Little Museums: Over 1,000 Small & Not-So-Small American Showplaces. LC 97-9406. (Illus.). 464p. 1998. pap. text 17.95 (*0-8050-4823-5*, Owl) H Holt & Co.

Arany-Makkai, Agnes. Russian Idioms. LC 96-84562. 1996. pap. text 6.95 (*0-8120-9436-0*) Barron.

— 2001 Russian & English Idioms. LC 96-80252. (Two Thousand One Idioms Ser.). 608p. 1997. pap. text 14.95 (*0-8120-9532-4*) Barron.

Aranya. A Journey to the Center: A Guidebook to Enlightenment. 120p. (Orig.). 1988. 25.00 (*0-922644-00-4*); pap. 12.95 (*0-922644-01-2*) Winterhaven Pr.

Aranya, Hariharananda. Samkhya-Sutras of Pancasikha & the Samkhyatattvalcka. 1977. 12.50 (*0-89684-313-0*, Pub. by Motilal Bnarsidass) S Asia.

Aranza, Jacob. Making a Love That Lasts: How to Find Love Without Settling for Sex. 2nd rev. ed. LC 96-43157. 140p. (YA). 1996. pap. 9.99 (*1-56955-019-0*, Vine Bks) Servant.

Araoz, Daniel L. The New Hypnosis in Sex Therapy: Cognitive-Behavioral Methods for Clinicians. LC 97-34484. 208p. 1998. pap. 40.00 (*0-7657-0137-5*) Aronson.

Araoz, Daniel L. & Bleck, Robert T. Sexual Joy Through Self-Hypnosis. Orig. Title: Hypnosex. (Illus.). 1991. reprint ed. audio 15.95 (*0-930298-00-4*) Westwood Pub Co.

Araoz, Daniel L. & Carrese, Marie A. Solution-Oriented Brief Therapy for Adjustment Disorders: A Guide for Providers under Managed Care. (Mental Health Practice under Managed Care Ser.; No. 3). 176p. 1996. pap. text 21.95 (*0-87630-790-X*) Brunner-Mazel.

Araoz, Daniel L. & Negley-Parker, Esther. The New Hypnosis in Family Therapy. LC 87-25960. 304p. 1988. text 35.95 (*0-87630-491-9*) Brunner-Mazel.

Arapovic, Rudolf, ed. see Ciliga, Ante.

Arapura, J. G. Gnosis & the Question of Thought in Vedanta. 332p. 1986. lib. bdg. 184.00 (*90-247-3061-9*, Pub. by M Nijhoff) Kluwer Academic.

— Hermeneutical Essays on Vedantic Topics. 207p. 1986. 17.50 (*81-208-0183-0*, Pub. by Motilal Bnarsidass) S Asia.

— Religion As Anxiety & Tranquility: An Essay in Comparative Phenomenology of the Spirit. (Religion & Reason Ser.: No. 5). 1973. 29.25 (*90-279-7180-3*) Mouton.

Ararbanel, Andrew. Loving Madly/Loving Sanely. LC 96-79080. 224p. 1997. 22.00 (*1-57566-161-6*, Knsington) Kensgtn Pub Corp.

Aras, Bulent. Palestinian-Israeli Peace Process & Turkey. LC 98-5134. 1998. 65.00 (*1-56072-549-4*) Nova Sci Pubs.

Aras, Bulent, jt. auth. see Croissont, Michael P.

Arasanayagam, Jean. Reddened Water Flows Clear: Poems from Sri Lanka. 143p. (Orig.). 1991. pap. 21.00 (*0-948259-96-5*, Pub. by Forest Bks) Dufour.

Arasaratnam, Sinnappah. Ceylon & the Dutch, 1600-1800: External Influences & Internal Change in Early Modern Sri Lanka. (Collected Studies Ser.: CS525). 352p. 1996. text 113.95 (*0-86078-579-3*, Pub. by Variorum) Ashgate Pub Co.

— Maritime Commerce & English Power: Southeast India, 1750-1800. 1996. write for info. (*81-207-1814-3*) Sterling Pubs.

— Maritime Commerce & English Power: Southeast India, 1750-1800. LC 96-33879. 336p. 1996. 83.95 (*0-86078-610-2*, Pub. by Variorum) Ashgate Pub Co.

— Maritime India in the Seventeenth Century. (Illus.). 304p. 1994. text 27.00 (*0-19-563424-1*) OUP.

— Maritime Trade, Society & European Influence in South Asia, 1600-1800. (Collected Studies: No. CS471). 320p. 1995. 106.95 (*0-86078-452-5*, Pub. by Variorum) Ashgate Pub Co.

— Merchants, Companies & Commerce on the Coromandel Coast, 1650-1740. (Illus.). 400p. 1987. 32.00 (*0-19-561873-4*) OUP.

Arasaratnam, Sinnappah & Rya, Aniruddha. Masulipatnam & Cambay: A History of 2 Port-Towns, 1500-1800. LC 94-907524. (C). 1994. text 34.00 (*81-215-0646-8*, Pub. by M Manoharial) Coronet Bks.

Arase, David. Buying Power: The Political Economy of Japanese Foreign Aid. LC 94-34471. 307p. 1995. lib. bdg. 58.00 (*1-55587-497-9*) L Rienner.

Arashvili, N. G., ed. Breast Cancer: An Annotated Guide to the Current Literature. annot. ed. 202p. 1995. pap. text 95.00 (*1-56072-112-X*) Nova Sci Pubs.

— National Health Care: An Annotated Guide to the Current Literature. annot. ed. 204p. 1994. pap. text 95.00 (*1-56072-113-8*) Nova Sci Pubs.

***Araskog, Rand V.** The ITT Wars. LC 99-47573. 1999. pap. write for info. (*1-893122-38-7*) Beard Bks.

Arasse, Daniel. Leonardo Da Vinci. (Illus.). 560p. 1998. 40.00 (*1-56852-198-7*, Konecky & Konecky) W S Konecky Assocs.

— Vermeer: Faith in Painting. 208p. 1994. pap. text 18.95 (*0-691-02930-X*, Pub. by Princeton U Pr) Cal Prin Full Svc.

— Vermeers Ambition. (Illus.). 224p. 1996. text 40.00 (*3-364-00327-0*) Gordon & Breach.

Arasteh, A. R. Creativity in the Life Cycle, 2 vols. Incl. Vol. 1. Annotated Bibliography. 1968. Vol. 2. Interpretative Account of Creativity in Childhood, Adolescence & Adulthood. 1968. 1968. 75.00 (*90-04-00103-4*) Brill Academic Pubs.

Arasteh, Josephine, jt. ed. see Hetherington, E. Mavis.

***Arastoopour, Hamid.** Advanced Technologies for Fluid-Particle Systems. LC 99-47818. (AICHE Symposium Ser.). 1999. write for info. (*0-8169-0815-X*) Am Inst Chem Eng.

Arastoopour, Hamid & Chen, John C. Fluidization & Fluid Particle Systems: Recent Research & Development. LC 98-36294. (AICHE Symposium Ser.). 1998. 90.00 (*0-8169-0774-9*) Am Inst Chem Eng.

Arasu, K. T., et al, eds. Groups, Difference Sets, & the Monster: Proceedings of a Special Research Quarter at the Ohio State University, Spring 1993. (Ohio State University Mathematical Research Institute Publications: Vol. 4). xiii, 461p. 1995. lib. bdg. 89.95 (*3-11-014791-2*) De Gruyter.

Arat, Yesim. The Patriarchal Paradox: Women Politicians in Turkey. LC 88-45715. 160p. 1989. 29.50 (*0-8386-3347-1*) Fairleigh Dickinson.

Arat, Yesim, et al. Challenges to Democracy in the Middle East. LC 96-48610. 160p. (Orig.). (C). 1997. pap. text 15.95 (*1-55876-149-7*) Wiener Pubs Inc.

Arat, Zehra F., ed. Deconstructing Images of the 'Turkish Woman' LC 97-42319. 320p. 1998. text 55.00 (*0-312-17544-2*) St Martin.

Arata, Esther S. More Black American Playwrights: A Bibliography. LC 78-15231. 335p. 1978. lib. bdg. 31.50 (*0-8108-1158-8*) Scarecrow.

Arata, Luis O. The Festive Play of Fernando Arrabal. LC 81-51020. (Studies in Romance Languages: No. 25). 112p. 1982. 15.00 (*0-8131-1451-9*) U Pr of Ky.

Arata, Stephen. Fictions of Loss in the Victorian Fin de Siecle: Identity & Empire. LC 96-3489. 246p. (C). 1996. text 54.95 (*0-521-56352-6*) Cambridge U Pr.

Aratani, Mariko, jt. auth. see Hirshfield, Jane.

Araten, Harry. Essential Jewish Trivia Book for Kids. 96p. (J). (gr. 2-8). 1997. pap. text 12.95 (*0-943706-29-7*) Pitspopany.

***Araten, Harry.** Welcome, Baby! A Personal Record Book. 1998. 14.95 (*0-8246-0403-2*) Jonathan David.

Araten, Rachel. Jacob Sarna: Here & There. 180p. 1992. pap. 8.95 (*965-229-074-2*, Pub. by Gefen Pub Hse) Gefen Bks.

— Three Children: Orphan Survivors in Israel. 152p. 1993. pap. 8.95 (*965-229-091-2*, Pub. by Gefen Pub Hse) Gefen Bks.

— Yes, We Came Home. LC 96-104787. 120p. 1995. pap. text 9.95 (*965-229-141-2*, Pub. by Gefen Pub Hse) Gefen Bks.

Araten, Rachel S. Strands of a Plait-Singly. LC 98-12257. 128p. 1998. pap. 9.95 (*965-229-181-1*, Pub. by Gefen Pub Hse) Gefen Bks.

Aratis. Fifteen Sayings of Jesus. 16p. 1997. pap. 5.00 (*0-938075-70-5*, Permanence Pr) Ocean View Bks.

— Genesis & the Self. 16p. 1997. pap. 5.00 (*0-938075-69-1*, Permanence Pr) Ocean View Bks.

— How to Meditate. 16p. 1997. pap. 2.00 (*0-938075-71-3*, Permanence Pr) Ocean View Bks.

— Plain Understanding. 8p. (Orig.). 1994. pap. 2.00 (*0-938075-57-8*) Ocean View Bks.

— The Unity of All Religions & Atheism. 8p. (Orig.). 1995. pap. 2.00 (*0-938075-66-7*) Ocean View Bks.

Arato, Andrew. Civil Society, Constitution, & Legitimacy. LC 99-55368. 352p. 1998. pap. 21.95 (*0-8476-8772-4*); text 72.00 (*0-8476-8771-6*) Rowman.

— From Neo-Marxism to Democratic Theory: Essays on the Critical Theory of Soviet-Type Societies. LC 91-21128. 362p. (gr. 13). 1993. text 74.95 (*0-87332-882-5*) M E Sharpe.

Arato, Andrew & Gebhardt, Eike, eds. The Essential Frankfurt School Reader. LC 82-8063. 560p. (Orig.). 1982. pap. 27.50 (*0-8264-0194-5*) Continuum.

Arato, Andrew, jt. auth. see Cohen, Jean L.

Arato, Andrew, jt. auth. see Rosenfeld, Michel.

Arato, Andrew, jt. ed. see Feher, Ferenc.

***Arato, Christine A. & Eleey, Patrick L.** Safety Moored at Last: Cultural Landscape Report for New Bedford Whaling National Historical Park. LC 00-35139. (Cultural Landscape Publications). (Illus.). 2000. write for info. (*0-912627-66-2*) Natl Park Serv.

Arato, M. Linear Stochastic Systems with Constant Coefficients: A Statistical Approach. (Lecture Notes in Control & Information Sciences: Vol. 45). 309p. 1982. 33.95 (*0-387-12090-4*) Spr-Verlag.

Arato, M. & Kusnirenko, A. G. Thirty-Two Papers on Statistics & Probability. LC 61-9803. (Selected Translations in Mathematical Statistics & Probability Ser.: Vol. 10). 314p. 1972. 50.00 (*0-8218-1460-5*, STAPRO/10) Am Math.

Arato, M. & Varga, L. Mathematical Models in Computer Systems. 1981. pap. 170.00 (*963-05-2945-9*, Pub. by Akade Kiado) St Mut.

Arato, M., et al. Topics in the Theoretical Bases & Applications of Computer Science: Proceedings of the 4th Hungarian Computer Science Conference, Gyor, Hungary, July 8-10, 1985. 513p. (C). 1986. 162.00 (*963-05-4242-0*, Pub. by Akade Kiado) St Mut.

— Twenty Papers on Statistics & Probability. LC 61-9803. (Selected Translations in Mathematical Statistics & Probability Ser.: Vol. 13). 298p. 1973. 75.00 (*0-8218-1463-X*, STAPRO/13) Am Math.

Aratow, Paul. 100 Years of Erotica: A Photographic Portfolio of Mainstream American Culture from 1845 to 1945. LC 99-30837. 128p. 1999. pap. text 24.95 (*1-58008-087-1*) Ten Speed Pr.

Aratus. Aratus: Index Verborum in Arati Phaenomena. Campbell, Malcolm, ed. (Alpha-Omega, Reihe A Ser.: Vol. XC). (GER.). v, 96p. 1988. 50.00 (*3-487-09016-3*) G Olms Pubs.

— Phaenomena. Kidd, Douglas, ed. & tr. by. LC 96-44962. (Classical Texts & Commentaries Ser.: Vol. 34). 614p. (C). 1997. text 100.00 (*0-521-58230-X*) Cambridge U Pr.

— Phaenomena. Maass, Ernst, ed. xxvi, 100p. 1964. 36.00 (*3-296-10500-X*) G Olms Pubs.

— Sky Signs: Aratus' Phaenomena. Lombardo, Stanley, tr. from GRE. & intro. by. 100p. 1983. 20.00 (*0-938190-15-6*) North Atlantic.

Aratyn, Henrik. Supersymmetry & Integrable Models: Proceedings of a Workshop Held at Chicago, IL, 12-14 June, 1997. LC 97-51611. (Lecture Notes in Physics Ser.: Vol. 502). 1998. write for info. (*3-540-63976-1*) Spr-Verlag.

Araujo, A. DePina, see DePina Araujo, A.

Araujo, Americo C. Portuguese Fluency & Culture One. (Illus.). xv, 217p. 1989. text 26.95 (*1-881495-00-0*) DAC Pubs.

— Portuguese Fluency & Culture One: Testing - Activities Program. (Illus.). 85p. 1991. ring bd. 49.95 (*1-881495-01-9*) DAC Pubs.

— Portuguese Fluency & Culture Two: Continuemos (Illus.). x, 332p. 1991. text 28.95 (*1-881495-02-7*); text 28.95 (*1-881495-10-8*) DAC Pubs.

Araujo, C. B. De, see De Araujo, C. B.

Araujo, Frank P. Nekane, the Lamina & the Bear: A Tale of the Basque Pyrenees. LC 93-84620. (Toucan Tales Ser.: Vol. 1). (Illus.). 32p. (J). (gr. 1 up). 1993. 16.95 (*1-877810-01-0*, NEKA) Rayve Prodns.

— The Perfect Orange: A Tale from Ethiopia. LC 94-67524. (Toucan Tales Ser.: Vol. 2). (Illus.). 32p. (J). (ps-8). 1994. 16.95 (*1-877810-94-0*, ORAN) Rayve Prodns.

Araujo, G. L., jt. ed. see Luque, Antonio.

Araujo, Jess J. The Law & Your Legal Rights: A Bilingual Guide To Everyday Legal Issues - Un Manual Bilingue Para Asuntos Legal. LC 98-21982.Tr. of Law & Your Legal Rights. (SPA & ENG.). 288p. 1998. pap. 16.00 (*0-684-83970-9*) S&S Trade.

Araujo, Juan S., tr. see Campbell, Ross.

Araujo, Juan S., tr. see Cho, Paul Y. & Manzano, R. Whitney.

Araujo, Juan S., tr. see Cunningham, Loren & Rogers, Janice.

Araujo, Juan S., tr. see Duewel, Wesley L.

Araujo, Juan S., tr. see MacDonald, Gordon.

Araujo, Juan S., tr. see McDowell, Josh.

Araujo, Juan S., tr. see Smalley, Gary & Scott, Steve.

Araujo, Juan S., tr. see Swindoll, Charles R.

Araujo, Karen L., jt. auth. see Roberts, Paul C.

Araujo-Lima, Carlos & Goulding, Michael. So Fruitful a Fish: Ecology, Conservation & Aquaculture of the Amazon's Tambaqui. LC 96-45658. (Biology & Resource Management in the Tropics Ser.). 1997. 45.00 (*0-231-10830-3*) Col U Pr.

Araujo, Luis. Vanzetti. Zatlin, Phyllis, ed. Lessing, Mary Alice, tr. from SPA. LC 98-73881. (Contemporary Spanish Plays Ser.: Vol. 16). (Illus.). x, 38p. 1999. pap. 8.00 (*1-888463-08-2*) Estreno.

Araujo, Orlando. Miguel Vicente Pata Caliente (Hot-Footed Miquel Vicente)Tr. of Hot-Footed Miguel Vicente. (SPA., Illus.). 48p. (J). (gr. 3 up). Date not set. 11.95 (*980-257-102-4*, Pub. by Ediciones Ekare) Kane-Miller Bk.

Arauz, Rachel, et al. Masterpieces of Twentieth-Century Art at the Philadelphia Museum of Art. (Illus.). 160p. 1999. write for info. (*0-87633-133-9*) Phila Mus Art.

— Twentieth Century Painting & Sculpture in the Philadelphia Museum of Art. (Illus.). 160p. 2000. pap. write for info. (*0-87633-132-0*) Phila Mus Art.

Arav, Monique, tr. see Al-Rawi, Rosina-Fawzia.

Arav, N., et al, eds. Mass Ejection from Active Galactic Nuclei: Proceedings of a Workshop Held at the Carnegie Observatories in Pasadena, California, February 19-21, 1997. (ASP Conference Series Proceedings: Vol. 128). 328p. 1997. 34.00 (*1-886733-48-1*) Astron Soc Pacific.

Arav, Rami, jt. ed. see Freund, E. Richard.

Arava, Douglas A., jt. auth. see Chia, Mantak.

Arava, Douglas Abrams, jt. auth. see Chia, Mantak.

Aravamudan, Srinivas. Tropicopolitans: Colonialism & Agency, 1688-1804. LC 98-23374. (Post-Contemporary Interventions Ser.). 1999. write for info. (*0-8223-2283-8*); pap. 20.95 (*0-8223-2315-X*) Duke.

Arave, C. W., jt. auth. see Albright, J. L.

***Arave, Larry.** Key Notes: Amateur Radio Personal Notebook. (Illus.). 160p. 2000. 6.95 (*0-9677641-0-6*) Micrographics.

Arax, Mark. In My Father's Name: A Family, a Town, a Murder. LC 97-15507. 1997. per. 14.00 (*0-671-01002-6*, PB Trade Paper) PB.

Arax, Mark & Wartzman, Rick. The Cotton King: J. B. Boswell & the Making of a Secret American Empire. 2000. write for info. (*0-316-04904-2*) Little.

***Araya, Belainesh.** Counseling in an Eritrean Context. LC 00-39043. 2000. write for info. (*1-56902-129-5*) Red Sea Pr.

Araya, Braulio & Chester, Sharon R. The Birds of Chile: A Field Guide. (Illus.). 400p. (C). 1993. pap. 24.95 (*0-9638511-0-1*) Wander Albatross.

Araya, Victorio. God of the Poor: The Mystery of God in Latin American Liberation Theology. Barr, Robert R., tr. from SPA. LC 87-7808. 223p. 1987. reprint ed. pap. 69.20 (*0-7837-9834-2*, 206056300005) Bks Demand.

Arayama, Yuko & Mourdoukoutas, Panos. China Against Herself: Innovation or Imitation in Global Business? LC 98-35747. 152p. 1999. 55.00 (*1-56720-245-4*, Quorum Bks) Greenwood.

***Arayama, Yuko & Mourdoukoutas, Panos.** The Rise & Fall of Abacus Banking in Japan & China. LC 99-46055. 208p. 2000. 59.95 (*1-56720-324-8*, Quorum Bks) Greenwood.

***Arazi, Albert, et al, eds.** Israel Oriental Studies 19: Compilation & Creation in Adab & Luga (in Memory of Naphtali Kinberg) 499p. 1999. text 59.50 (*1-57506-045-0*) Eisenbrauns.

Arazi, Benjamin. A Commonsense Approach to Theory of Error-Correcting Codes. 1988. 28.00 (*0-262-01098-4*) MIT Pr.

Arazy, Jonathan & Friedman, Y. Contractive Projections in C Sub 1 & C to Infinity. LC 77-28610. (Memoirs Ser: No. 13/200). 165p. 1978. pap. 22.00 (*0-8218-2200-4*, MEMO 13/200) Am Math.

— Contractive Projections in C(Sub P) LC 91-36296. (Memoirs Ser.: No. 95/459). 134p. 1992. pap. 26.00 (*0-8218-2515-1*, MEMO 95/459) Am Math.

Arazy, Jonathan & Friedman, Yaakov. Contractive Projections in C1 & Coo. LC 77-28610. (American Mathematical Society, Memoirs Ser.: No. 200). 180p. reprint ed. pap. 55.80 (*0-7837-4420-X*, 204416500012) Bks Demand.

Arb, F. I., jt. auth. see Irukwu, J. O.

Arbabi, Freydoon. Structural Analysis & Behavior. 592p. (C). 1991. text 71.50 (*0-07-002143-0*); pap. text, teacher ed. 27.50 (*0-07-002146-5*) McGraw.

Arbaczewski, Carol, jt. auth. see Johnson, Corky.

Arban, Jean B. Complete Conservatory Method for Trumpet (Cornet) or E-Flat Alto, B-Flat Tenor, Baritone, Euphonium & B-Flat Bass in Treble Clef. Goldman, Edwin F. & Smith, Walter M., eds. 350p. (Orig.). (J). 1936. pap. 25.95 (*0-8258-0010-2*, 021) Fischer Inc NY.

Arbarbanel, Henry D. & Young, W. R., eds. General Circulation of the Ocean. (Topics in Atmospheric & Oceanographic Sciences Ser.). (Illus.). 305p. 1986. 132.95 (*0-387-96354-5*) Spr-Verlag.

Arbarello, E., et al. Geometry of Algebraic Curves, Vol. 1. (Grundlehren der Mathematischen Wissenschaften Ser.: Vol. 267). (Illus.). xvi, 387p. 1984. 94.95 (*0-387-90997-4*) Spr-Verlag.

Arbatov, Alexei, et al, eds. Managing Conflict in the Former Soviet Union: Russian & American Perspectives. LC 97-11343. (CSIA Studies in International Security). (Illus.). 550p. 1997. pap. text 27.50 (*0-262-51093-6*) MIT Pr.

Arbatov, Alexei G. Lethal Frontiers: A Soviet View of Nuclear Strategy, Weapons, & Negotiations. Lee, Kent D., tr. LC 88-15538. 313p. 1988. 59.95 (*0-275-93017-3*, C3017, Praeger Pubs) Greenwood.

Arbatov, Alexei G., ed. The Security Watershed: Disarmament & Security Yearbook, 1991-1992. (Science & Global Security Monograph Ser.: Vol. 2). 664p. 1993. text 101.00 (*2-88124-551-X*) Gordon & Breach.

Arbatov, Alexei G. & Miller, Steven E., eds. Taming Armageddon? Revising the U. S./Russian Nuclear Relationship. (CSIA Studies in International Security: No. 8). (Illus.). 350p. Date not set. pap. text 17.95 (*0-262-51085-5*) MIT Pr.

— Taming Armageddon? Revising the U. S./Russian Nuclear Relationship. (CSIA Studies in International Security: No. 8). (Illus.). 350p. 1997. 39.95 (*0-262-01149-2*) MIT Pr.

***Arbdeya, Jesus.** The Cuban Counterrevolution. Betancourt, Rafael, tr. (Research in International Studies : Vol. 33). 368p. (C). 2000. pap. text 26.00 (*0-89680-214-0*, Ohio U Ctr Intl) Ohio U Pr.

Arbeau, Thoinot. Orchesographie. 104p. 1989. reprint ed. 80.00 (*3-487-06697-1*) G Olms Pubs.

Arbeau, Thoinot. Orchesography. Sutton, Julia, ed. Evans, Mary S., tr. (Illus.). 266p. 1966. pap. 6.00 (*0-486-21745-0*) Dover.

Arbeeny, Cynthia. Therapeutic Approaches to the Treatment of Obesity. DiClemente, Susan C., ed. LC 98-227256. (Illus.). 300p. 1997. spiral bd. write for info. (*1-57936-062-9*, 963) IBC USA.

Arbeille, Ph., et al, eds. Fetal Hypoxia. LC 99-32279. (Progress in Obstetric & Gynecological Sonography Ser.). (Illus.). 146p. 1999. 78.00 (*1-85070-012-5*) Prthnon Pub.

Arbeit, Behorde, ed. Epidemiologisches Untersuchungsprogramm Bille-Siedlung. (Illus.). 714p. 1997. pap. 95.95 (*3-631-30040-9*) P Lang Pubng.

A

Arbeit, J., et al. AIDS Ninety Summary: A Practical Synopsis of the VI International Conference. (Illus.). 350p. (Orig.). 1991. pap. 85.00 (*0-924236-05-1*) Phila Scis Group.
— AIDS 91 Summary: A Practical Synopsis of the VII International Conference. (Illus.). 350p. 1992. pap. 85.00 (*0-924236-07-8*) Phila Scis Group.
Arbeit, Wendy. Baskets in Polynesia. LC 89-20656. (Illus.). 136p. (Orig.). 1990. pap. 19.95 (*0-8248-1281-6*, Kolowalu Bk) UH Pr.
— Tapa in Tonga. (Illus.). 32p. (Orig.). 1995. pap. text 9.00 (*0-8248-1727-3*) Palm Frond Prods.
— What Are Fronds For? LC 85-13940. (Illus.). 110p. (Orig.). 1985. pap. 14.95 (*0-8248-0999-8*, Kolowalu Bk) UH Pr.
Arbeiter, Jean S., jt. auth. see Marcus, Norman J.
Arbeiter, Solomon, et al. Forty Million Americans in Career Transition: The Need for Information. 64p. 1978. pap. 4.50 (*0-87447-050-1*, 237403) College Bd.
***Arbeitman, Y. L.** The Asia Minor Connexion: Studies on the Pre-Greek Languages in Memory of Charles Carter. xii, 244p. 1999. 52.00 (*90-429-0798-3*, Pub. by Peeters Pub) Bks Intl VA.
Arbeitman, Yoel L., ed. Fucus: A Semitic-Afrasian Gathering in Remembrance of Albert Ehrman. LC 87-34477. (Current Issues in Linguistic Theory Ser.: Vol. 58). xvi, 530p. (C). 1988. 115.00 (*90-272-3552-X*) J Benjamins Pubng Co.
Arbeitman, Yoel L. & Bomhard, Allan R., eds. Bono Homini Donum: Essays in Historical Linguistics in Memory of J. Alexander Kerns, Set, Vol. 1-xvi, 557-Vol. 2-viii, 518. (Current Issues in Linguistic Theory Ser.: No. 16). 1981. 194.00 (*90-272-3507-4*) J Benjamins Pubng Co.
Arbeitsgemeinschaft der Katholisch-Theoligischen, ed. Handbuch der Katholisch-Theologischen Bibliotheken: Bundesrepublik Deutschland und West-Berlin. 3rd ed. (GER.). 176p. 1991. lib. bdg. 85.00 (*3-598-10919-9*) K G Saur Verlag.
Arbel. Medicinal Plants Col. Book. 1998. pap. 2.95 (*0-486-27462-4*) Dover.
Arbel, Ami. Exploring Interior-Point Linear Programming: Algorithms & Software. LC 93-15937. (Foundations of Computing Ser.). (Illus.). 208p. 1993. pap. text 40.00 (*0-262-51073-1*) MIT Pr.
Arbel, Benjamin. Intercultural Contacts in the Medieval Mediterranean. 320p. (C). 1996. 49.50 (*0-7146-4714-4*, Pub. by F Cass Pubs); pap. 24.50 (*0-7146-4260-6*, Pub. by F Cass Pubs) Intl Spec Bk.
— Trading Nations: Jews & Venetians in the Early-Modern Eastern Mediterranean. (Brill's Series in Jewish Studies: Vol. 14). 1995. 85.00 (*90-04-10057-1*) Brill Academic Pubs.
Arbel, Benjamin, et al, eds. Latins & Greeks in the Eastern Mediterranean after 1204. 256p. 1989. text 35.00 (*0-7146-3372-0*, Pub. by F Cass Pubs) Intl Spec Bk.
Arbel, Ilil. Favorite Roses Coloring Book. (Illus.). 32p. (J). (gr. 1-3). 1989. pap. 2.95 (*0-486-25845-9*) Dover.
— Witchcraft. 125p. (Orig.). (YA). (gr. 7-12). 1996. pap. 6.95 (*1-57515-092-1*) PPI Pubng.
Arbel, Llil. Favorite Wildflowers Coloring Book. (Illus.). (J). (gr. k-3). 1991. pap. 2.95 (*0-486-26729-6*) Dover.
Arbel, Rachel, jt. auth. see Magal, Lily, pseud.
Arbelaez, Jorge, tr. see Henrichsen, Walter A.
Arbelbide, Sylvia J., et al, eds. Evaluation of Environmental Impact Statement Alternatives by the Science Integration Team, Vol. I. 554p. 1998. reprint ed. 61.40 (*0-89904-717-3*, Ecosytems Resrch); reprint ed. pap. 56.40 (*0-89904-718-1*, Ecosytems Resrch) Crumb Elbow Pub.
Arbelbide, Sylvia J., jt. ed. see Quigley, Thomas M.
***Arbell, Mordechai, compiled by.** Spanish & Portuguese Jews in the Caribbean & the Guianas: A Bibliography. (Illus.). 160p. 1999. 17.50 (*0-916617-52-1*) J C Brown.
Arbelo, William. Mas Alla de Mis Fuerzas. LC 88-82056. (Coleccion Cuba y sus Jueces). (SPA., Illus.). 100p. (Orig.). 1989. pap. 9.95 (*0-89729-502-1*) Ediciones.
Arbena, Joseph, et al. Regionalism & the Musical Heritage of Latin America. (Latin American Curriculum Units for Junior & Community Colleges Ser.). v, 84p. (Orig.). (C). 1980. pap. text 4.95 (*0-86728-006-9*) U TX Inst Lat Am Stud.
Arbena, Joseph L., compiled by. An Annotated Bibliography of Latin American Sport: Pre-Conquest to the Present, 17. LC 89-37527. (Bibliographies & Indexes in World History Ser.: No. 17). 337p. 1989. lib. bdg. 85.00 (*0-313-25495-8*, ABS, Greenwood Pr) Greenwood.
***Arbena, Joseph L., compiled by.** Latin American Sport: An Annotated Bibliography, 1988-1998, 3. LC 99-11260. (Bibliographies & Indexes on Sports History Ser.: Vol. 3). 264p. 1999. lib. bdg. 75.00 (*0-313-29611-1*) Greenwood.
Arbena, Joseph L., ed. Sport & Society in Latin America: Diffusion, Dependency, & the Rise of Mass Culture, 20. LC 87-32271. (Contributions to the Study of Popular Culture Ser.: No. 20). 171p. 1988. 45.00 (*0-313-24774-9*, ARS/) Greenwood.
Arbenz, Peter, et al, eds. High Performance Algorithms for Structured Matrix Problems. 203p. 1998. 95.00 (*1-56072-594-X*) Nova Sci Pubs.
Arber, Agnes. Monocotyledons: A Morphological Study. (Illus.). 1961. reprint ed. 64.00 (*3-7682-0074-4*) Lubrecht & Cramer.
Arber, Edward. Transcripts of the Registers of the Worshipful Company of Stationers, 1554-1640 & 1640-1708, 3 vols. 1967. 24.50 (*0-8446-1449-1*) Peter Smith.
Arber, Edward, ed. The Dunbar Anthology, Fourteen Hundred One to Fifteen Hundred Eight A. D. (British Anthologies Ser.). 312p. 1985. reprint ed. lib. bdg. 49.00 (*0-932051-23-5*) Rprt Serv.
— The Dunbar Anthology, Fourteen Hundred One to Fifteen Hundred Eight A.D. (British Anthologies Ser.). 312p. 1985. reprint ed. lib. bdg. 69.00 (*0-7812-0854-8*) Rprt Serv.
— English Reprints, 8 vols. LC 71-158266. reprint ed. 676.00 (*0-404-00420-2*) AMS Pr.
— English Scholar's Library of Old & Modern Works, 5 vols. in 4. LC 75-158267. reprint ed. 365.00 (*0-404-00430-X*) AMS Pr.
Arber, Edward, ed. see Addison, Joseph.
Arber, Edward, ed. see Ascham, Roger.
Arber, Edward, ed. see Earle, John.
Arber, EDward, ed. see Gascoigne, George.
Arber, Edward, ed. see Googe, Barnabe.
Arber, Edward, ed. see Latimer, Hugh.
Arber, Edward, ed. see Lever, Thomas.
Arber, Edward, ed. see Lyly, John.
Arber, Edward, ed. see Naunton, Robert.
Arber, Edward, ed. see Selden, John.
Arber, Edward, ed. see Udall, Nicholas.
Arber, Edward, ed. see Villiers, George.
Arber, Edward, ed. see Webbe, William.
Arber, Edward, tr. see Habington, William.
Arber, Edward, tr. see Howell, James.
Arber, Sara & Attias-Donfut, Claudine. The Myth of Generational Conflict: The Family & State in Ageing Societies LC 99-28669. (ESA Studies in European Society). 1999. write for info. (*0-415-20770-3*) Routledge.
Arber, Sara & Evandrou, Maria, eds. Ageing, Independence & the Life Course. 256p. 1993. pap. 27.00 (*1-85302-180-6*) Taylor & Francis.
Arber, Sara & Ginn, Jay. Gender & Later Life: A Sociological Analysis of Resources & Constraints. (Illus.). 248p. 1992. 69.95 (*0-8039-8396-4*); pap. 19.95 (*0-8039-8397-2*) Sage.
Arber, Sara & Ginn, Jay, eds. Connecting Gender & Ageing: A Sociological Approach. LC 95-14729. 212p. 1995. 114.95 (*0-335-19471-0*); pap. 33.95 (*0-335-19470-2*) OpUniv Pr.
Arber, W., ed. Current Topics in Microbiology & Immunology, Vol. 72. LC 15-12910. (Illus.). 200p. 1976. 60.00 (*0-387-07564-X*) Spr-Verlag.
— Current Topics in Microbiology & Immunology, Vol. 78. LC 15-12910. (Illus.). 1977. 66.00 (*0-387-08499-1*) Spr-Verlag.
Arber, W., et al, eds. Current Topics in Microbiology & Immunology, 86. (Illus.). 1979. 55.00 (*0-387-09432-6*) Spr-Verlag.
— Current Topics in Microbiology & Immunology, 87. (Illus.). 1980. 52.00 (*0-387-09433-4*) Spr-Verlag.
— Current Topics in Microbiology & Immunology, Vol. 62. LC 73-17985. (Illus.). 170p. 1973. 49.00 (*0-387-06598-9*) Spr-Verlag.
— Current Topics in Microbiology & Immunology, Vol. 63. LC 73-20915. (Illus.). 230p. 1974. 69.00 (*0-387-06599-7*) Spr-Verlag.
— Current Topics in Microbiology & Immunology, Vol. 64. LC 74-3541. (Illus.). 190p. 1974. 65.00 (*0-387-06713-2*) Spr-Verlag.
— Current Topics in Microbiology & Immunology, Vol. 65. LC 15-12910. (Illus.). 165p. 1974. 65.00 (*0-387-06774-4*) Spr-Verlag.
— Current Topics in Microbiology & Immunology, Vol. 66. LC 15-12910. (Illus.). 130p. 1974. 45.00 (*3-540-06831-7*) Spr-Verlag.
— Current Topics in Microbiology & Immunology, Vol. 67. LC 15-12910. (Illus.). iv, 162p. 1974. 55.00 (*3-540-06838-4*) Spr-Verlag.
— Current Topics in Microbiology & Immunology, Vol. 76. LC 15-12910. (Illus.). 1977. 54.00 (*3-540-08238-7*) Spr-Verlag.
— Current Topics in Microbiology & Immunology, Vol. 77. LC 15-12910. (Illus.). 1977. 61.00 (*0-387-08401-0*) Spr-Verlag.
— Current Topics in Microbiology & Immunology, Vol. 82. LC 15-12910. (Illus.). 1978. 53.00 (*0-387-08981-0*) Spr-Verlag.
— Current Topics in Microbiology & Immunology, Vol. 83. LC 15-12910. (Illus.). 1978. 55.00 (*0-387-09034-7*) Spr-Verlag.
— Current Topics in Microbiology & Immunology, Vol. 85. (Illus.). 1979. 67.00 (*0-387-09410-5*) Spr-Verlag.
— Current Topics in Microbiology & Immunology, Vol. 90. (Illus.). 147p. 1980. 76.00 (*0-387-10181-0*) Spr-Verlag.
— Current Topics in Microbiology & Immunology, Vol. 91. (Illus.). 250p. 1981. 100.00 (*0-387-10722-3*) Spr-Verlag.
Arber, W., et al. Current Topics in Microbiology & Immunology, Vol. 75. LC 15-12910. (Illus.). 1976. 54.00 (*3-540-08013-9*) Spr-Verlag.
— Current Topics in Microbiology & Immunology, Vol. 79. LC 15-12910. 1978. 73.00 (*0-387-08587-4*) Spr-Verlag.
Arber, Werner, et al. Genetic Manipulation: Impact on Man & Society. LC 83-26166. 304p. 1984. text 52.95 (*0-521-26417-0*) Cambridge U Pr.
Arberry, A. J., tr. see Iqbal, Muhammad.
Arberry, A. J., tr. see Rumi, Jalal Al-Din.
Arberry, A. J., tr. see Yarshater, Ehsan, ed.
Arberry, Arthur J. Aspects of Islamic Civilization As Depicted in the Original Texts. 416p. 1967. pap. text 19.95 (*0-472-06130-5*, 06130, Ann Arbor Bks) U of Mich Pr.
— Aspects of Islamic Civilization As Depicted in the Original Texts. LC 77-673. 408p. 1977. reprint ed. lib. bdg. 35.00 (*0-8371-9494-6*, ARAI, Greenwood Pr) Greenwood.
— Classical Persian Literature. LC 94-134343. 464p. (C). 1994. reprint ed. pap. 37.50 (*0-7007-0276-8*, Pub. by Curzon Pr Ltd) Paul & Co Pubs.
— The Doctrine of the Sufis. 1986. 16.95 (*0-935782-76-1*) Kazi Pubns.
— FitzGerald's Salaman & Absal: A Study. LC 57-6828. (University of Cambridge Oriental Studies). 216p. reprint ed. pap. 61.60 (*0-608-12321-8*, 2024406) Bks Demand.
— The Koran Interpreted. 360p. 1996. pap. 17.95 (*0-614-21057-7*, 701) Kazi Pubns.
— The Koran Interpreted. 358p. 1964. pap. 17.00 (*0-02-083260-5*) Macmillan.
— The Koran Interpreted. 708p. 1996. per. 18.00 (*0-684-82507-4*) S&S Trade.
— A Maltese Anthology. LC 75-8831. 280p. 1975. reprint ed. lib. bdg. 39.75 (*0-8371-8112-7*, ARMA, Greenwood Pr) Greenwood.
— Oriental Essays. LC 95-163904. 220p. (C). 1996. 65.00 (*0-7007-0289-X*, Pub. by Curzon Pr Ltd) Paul & Co Pubs.
— Revelation & Reason in Islam. LC 80-1936. (BCL Ser. I & II). reprint ed. 32.50 (*0-404-18952-0*) AMS Pr.
— Shiraz, Persian City of Saints & Poets. LC 60-8752. (Centers of Civilization Ser.: No.2). (Illus.). 191p. reprint ed. pap. 59.30 (*0-608-11726-9*, 201619200002) Bks Demand.
Arberry, Arthur J., ed. Arabic Poetry: A Primer for Students. LC 65-11206. 183p. reprint ed. pap. 52.20 (*0-8357-5706-4*, 2024405) Bks Demand.
— Notes on Iqbal's Asrar-i Khudi. 46p. 1996. pap. 4.00 (*0-614-21234-0*, 909) Kazi Pubns.
— Religion in the Middle East: Three Religions in Concord & Conflict, Vol. 2: Islam. LC 76-11080. 764p. reprint ed. pap. 180.00 (*0-608-15689-2*, 2031615) Bks Demand.
Arberry, Arthur J., ed. The Koran. (World's Classics Ser.). 688p. 1983. pap. (*0-19-281628-4*) OUP.
Arberry, Arthur J., tr. Discourses of Rumi. 286p. (C). 1993. pap. 25.00 (*0-7007-0274-1*, Pub. by Curzon Pr Ltd) Paul & Co Pubs.
— Fifty Poems of Hafiz. 220p. (C). 1947. pap. 21.50 (*0-7007-0275-X*, Pub. by Curzon Pr Ltd) Paul & Co Pubs.
— Tales from the Masnavi. 300p. (C). 1961. pap. 25.00 (*0-7007-0273-3*, Pub. by Curzon Pr Ltd) Paul & Co Pubs.
Arberry, Arthur J., tr. see Al-Mutanabbi & Abu al-Tayyib Ahmad ibn al-Husan.
Arberry, Arthur J., tr. see Ibn-Hazm, Ali ibn Ahmad.
Arberry, Arthur J., tr. see Kalabadhi, Muhammed.
Arberry, Arthur J., tr. see Rumi, Jalal Al-Din.
Arbesmann, Rudolph, tr. see Tertullian.
Arbetman & McMahon. A Course in Street Law. 4th ed. (Unknown Planning Family Ser.). 1990. text 41.00 (*0-314-68197-3*) West Pub.
Arbetman, et al. California Supplement, Street Law: A Course in Practical Law. 4th ed. 1990. pap. 46.25 (*0-314-69565-6*) Thomson Learn.
— Streetlaw, Select Court Cases: A Course in Precent Law. 5th ed. 1994. pap. 22.50 (*0-314-04522-8*) West Pub.
Arbetman, Lee P. Law Lesson Plans. Date not set. write for info. (*0-314-04649-6*) West Pub.
***Arbetman, Lee P.** Street Law: A Course in Practical Law. 6th ed. 1999. pap. 41.00 (*0-538-42694-2*) Sth-Wstrn College.
— Street Law: A Course in Practical Law. 6th ed. 1999. pap., wbk. ed. 21.00 (*0-538-42695-0*) Sth-Wstrn College.
— Street Law: A Course in Practical Law. 6th ed. 2000. 44.50 (*0-538-43106-7*) Sth-Wstrn College.
Arbetman, Lee P. Trials of American History. Date not set. pap. text, teacher ed. 15.95 (*0-314-90077-2*) West Pub.
Arbetman, Lee P. & Mcmahon. Street Law: A Course in Practical Law. 5th ed. 1994. mass mkt., wbk. ed. 19.50 (*0-314-04523-6*) West Pub.
Arbetman, Lee P. & McMahon, Edward T. Street Law: A Course in Practical Law. 6th ed. 1999. mass mkt. 36.75 (*0-314-14077-8*) West Pub.
Arbetman, Lee P. & Roe, Richard L. Great Trials in American History: Civil War to the Present. (Illus.). 209p. (Orig.). 1985. mass mkt. 26.75 (*0-314-80461-7*) West Pub.
Arbetman, Lee P., et al. Street Law: A Course in Practical Law. 4th ed. 1990. mass mkt. 46.50 (*0-314-68198-1*) West Pub.
Arbetman, Lee P., et al. Street Law: A Course in Practical Law. 5th ed. 1994. pap. 41.00 (*0-314-02935-4*) Thomson Learn.
— Street Law: A Course in Practical Law. 6th ed. 2000. pap. 44.50 (*0-538-43105-9*) Sth-Wstrn College.
Arbetman, Marina & Kugler, Jacek, eds. Political Capacity & Economic Behavior. LC 98-157765. (Political Economy of Global Interdependence Ser.). 352p. (C). 1997. pap. 29.00 (*0-8133-3364-4*, Pub. by Westview) HarpC.
Arbetslivsinstitutet (Sweden) Staff, jt. auth. see Ennals, J. R.
Arbett, Lorenzo. Kicking the Depression Habit: Bouncing Back Chasing the Blues Away. (Orig.). 1986. pap. 10.95 (*0-941122-01-8*) Lorenzo Prema.
Arbia, Giuseppe. Spatial Data Configuration in Statistical Analysis of Regional Economic & Related Problems. (C). 1989. lib. bdg. 148.50 (*0-7923-0284-2*) Kluwer Academic.
Arbib, Michael A. Brains, Machines & Mathematics. 2nd ed. (Illus.). 310p. 1990. 52.95 (*0-387-96539-4*) Spr-Verlag.
— In Search of the Person: Philosophical Explorations in Cognitive Science. LC 85-14152. 176p. 1986. pap. 15.95 (*0-87023-500-1*); lib. bdg. 25.00 (*0-87023-499-4*) U of Mass Pr.
— Metaphorical Brain 2: Neural Networks & Beyond. 2nd ed. LC 88-27877. 458p. 1989. 145.00 (*0-471-09853-1*) Wiley.
Arbib, Michael A., ed. The Handbook of Brain Theory & Neural Networks. LC 94-44408. 1995. 185.00 (*0-262-01148-4*, Bradford Bks) MIT Pr.
— The Handbook of Brain Theory & Neural Networks. (Illus.). 1136p. 1998. pap. text 75.00 (*0-262-51102-9*, Bradford Bks) MIT Pr.
Arbib, Michael A., et al, eds. Visual Structures & Integrated Functions. (Research Notes in Neural Computing Ser.: Vol. 3). (Illus.). xii, 441p. 1991. pap. 53.00 (*0-387-54241-8*) Spr-Verlag.
Arbib, Michael A. & Amari, S., eds. Dynamic Interactions in Neural Networks: Models & Data. (Research Notes in Neural Computing Ser.: Vol. 1). (Illus.). viii, 280p. 1988. 76.95 (*0-387-96893-8*) Spr-Verlag.
Arbib, Michael A. & Hesse, Mary B. The Construction of Reality. (Illus.). 304p. 1986. text 80.00 (*0-521-32689-3*) Cambridge U Pr.
Arbib, Michael A., et al. Natural & Artificial Parallel Computation. Robinson, J. Alan, ed. 1990. 44.00 (*0-262-01120-4*) MIT Pr.
— Neural Organization: Structure, Function & Dynamics. LC 96-44543. 328p. 1997. 62.50 (*0-262-01159-X*, Bradford Bks) MIT Pr.
Arbib, Michael A., jt. auth. see Alagic, S.
Arbib, Michael A., jt. auth. see Manes, Ernest G.
Arbib, Michael A., jt. ed. see Ewert, Jorg-Peter.
Arbib, Michael A., ed. see Hanson, Allen R.
Arbib, Michael A., ed. see Zhou, Y. T. & Chellappa, R.
Arbib, Robert S., Jr. Lord's Woods. LC 73-139373. 219p. 1971. 6.95 (*0-393-08639-9*) Norton.
Arbingast, Stanley A. & Hezlep, William L. Atlas of Central America. LC 78-64336. (Illus.). (Orig.). 1979. pap. 18.00 (*0-87755-262-2*) Bureau Busn TX.
Arbingast, Stanley A., et al. Atlas of Mexico. rev. ed. LC 75-11269. (Illus.). 1975. pap. 20.00 (*0-87755-187-1*) Bureau Busn TX.
***Arbinger Institute Staff.** Leadership & Self-Deception: Getting Out of the Box. LC 99-86442. 175p. 2000. 22.00 (*1-57675-094-9*, Pub. by Berrett-Koehler) Publishers Group.
Arbiter, Nathaniel, ed. Seventh International Mineral Processing Congress: Proceedings, 1965. xii, 612p. 1965. pap. text 195.00 (*0-677-10695-5*) Gordon & Breach.
Arbiter, Nathaniel & Han, K. N. Gold: Advances in Precious Metals Recovery: A Special Issue of the Journal Mineral Processing & Extractive Metallurgy Review. vi, 232p. 1990. text 123.00 (*2-88124-397-5*) Gordon & Breach.
Arbiter, Nathaniel, jt. ed. see Somasundaran, P.
Arbiter, Petronius. Petronius: Cena Trimalchionis. rev. ed. Cutt, Thomas, ed. LC 73-105090. (Wayne State University Classical Texts Ser.). 135p. reprint ed. pap. 41.90 (*0-7837-3644-4*, 204351300009) Bks Demand.
— The Satyricon. rev. ed. Sullivan, J. P., tr. & intro. by. LC 87-107609. (Illus.). 240p. 1986. pap. 18.99 (*0-14-044489-0*, Penguin Classics) Viking Penguin.
Arbitter, Elizabeth, et al. Collecting Figural Tape Measures: With Price Guide. LC 95-24050. (Illus.). 128p. (Orig.). 1995. pap. 19.95 (*0-88740-866-4*) Schiffer.
Arblaster, Anthony. Democracy. LC 87-18130. (Concepts in Social Thought Ser.). 119p. (Orig.). 1988. pap. 11.95 (*0-8166-1665-5*) U of Minn Pr.
— Democracy. 2nd ed. Parkin, Frank, ed. (Concepts in the Social Sciences Ser.). 128p. (Orig.). 1994. 9.00 (*0-335-19300-5*); pap. 2.00 (*0-335-19299-8*) OpUniv Pr.
— Democracy. 2nd ed. LC 94-9589. (Concepts in Social Thought Ser.). (Orig.). 1994. pap. 14.95 (*0-8166-2601-4*) U of Minn Pr.
— Viva la Liberta! Politics in Opera. 1997. pap. 18.00 (*0-86091-618-9*, Pub. by Verso) Norton.
Arblay, Frances D'O. Memoirs of Dr. Burney, Arranged from His Own Manuscripts, from Family Papers, & from Personal Recollections, 3 vols., Set. LC 78-37680. reprint ed. 210.00 (*0-404-56704-5*) AMS Pr.
Arble, William C. & Murphy, Dennis J. Extinguishing Silo Fires. 4th rev. ed. (Farm Safety Ser.). (Illus.). 12p. 1989. pap. text. write for info. (*0-935817-05-0*, NRAES-18) NRAES.
Arbnor, Ingeman & Bjerke, Bjorn. Methodology for Creating Businesss Knowledge. 2nd ed. LC 96-25244. 1996. 65.00 (*0-7619-0449-2*); pap. 32.00 (*0-7619-0450-6*) Sage.
Arbocz, Johann, et al. Buckling & Post-Buckling, Vol. 288. (Lecture Notes in Physics Ser.). vii, 246p. 1987. 37.95 (*0-387-18312-4*) Spr-Verlag.
Arbogast, Bradley W. & Taylor, Robert N. Molecular Mechanisms of Pre-Eclampsia. LC 96-39273. (Medical Intelligence Unit Ser.). 1996. 99.00 (*1-57059-397-3*) Landes Bioscience.
Arbogast, Doyle. Wounded Warriors: A Time for Healing. LC 95-168938. 330p. (Orig.). 1995. pap. 22.00 (*0-9645066-0-2*) Little Trtle.
Arbogast, Gary & Kizer, David. Case Study Workbook for Physical Education Teacher Preparation. 174p. (C). 1996. pap. text, wbk. ed. 26.95 (*0-7872-2845-1*) Kendall-Hunt.
Arbogast, Nicole, jt. auth. see Bray, Lindsay.
Arbogast, Susanne L., jt. auth. see Moss, Kathy.
Arboleda, Alba, et al. Outer Space Adventures. (BrainBooster Ser.). (Illus.). 32p. (J). (gr. 3 up). 1986. 6.95 (*0-88679-462-5*) Educ Insights.
Arboleda, Teja. In the Shadow of Race: Growing up As a Multiethnic, Multicultural, & "Multiracial" American. LC 98-16200. 256p. 1998. write for info. (*0-8058-2574-6*) L Erlbaum Assocs.
— In the Shadow of Race: Growing up as a Multiethnic, Multicultural & "Multiracial" American. LC 98-16200. 280p. 1998. pap. 24.50 (*0-8058-2575-4*) L Erlbaum Assocs.

Arboleya, Jesus. Havana-Miami: The U. S.-Cuba Migration Conflict. 72p. 1996. pap. 8.95 (*1-875284-91-5*) Ocean Pr NJ.

Arbon, Beverly, jt. auth. see Spencer, Carolyn.

Arbon, Beverly, jt. auth. see Spencer, Carolyn M.

Arbon, E. R., et al. The Practice of Aviation Safety: Observations from Flight Safety Foundation Safety Audits. LC TL0553.5. 45p. reprint ed. pap. 30.00 (*0-7837-7031-6*, 204684600004) Bks Demand.

Arbon, Lee. They Also Flew: The Enlisted Pilot Legacy, 1912-1942. LC 91-32814. (Illus.). 288p. 1992. 32.00 (*1-56098-108-3*) Smithsonian.

— They Also Flew: The Enlisted Pilot Legacy, 1912-1942. (Illus.). 288p. 1998. pap. 17.95 (*1-56098-837-1*) Smithsonian.

Arbona, Guillermo, et al. Health Objectives for the Developing Society: Responsibility of Individual, Physician, & Community. Long, E. Croft, ed. LC 65-19451. 179p. reprint ed. pap. 55.50 (*0-608-11986-5*, 20234210033) Bks Demand.

Arbor, Ann. Spelling. (C). Date not set. pap. write for info. (*0-393-95837-X*) Norton.

Arbor, Ann, jt. auth. see Windfuhr, Gernot L.

Arboreda, Alejandro. El Mito de Edipoen la Tragedia Barroca Espanola Vol. 5: No Hay Resistencia a los Hados. LC 92-46060. (Iberica Ser.: Vol. 5). (SPA.). 219p. (C). 1995. text 49.95 (*0-8204-1833-1*) P Lang Pubng.

Arboretum, Arnold. Arnold Arboretum: Inventory of Living Collections. (Illus.). 220p. (Orig.). pap. 20.00 (*1-878297-02-3*) Arnold Arboretum.

Arbour, Basil. The Final Gift: A New Way of the Cross. (Illus.). 64p. 1981. reprint ed. 2.95 (*0-86683-647-0*) Harper SF.

— Time Out: Prayers for Busy People. 96p. 1985. 3.95 (*0-86683-828-7*) Harper SF.

***Arbour, Keith.** Benjamin Franklin's First Government Printing Pt. 5: The Pennsylvania General Loan Office Mortgage Register of 1729 & Subsequent Franklin Mortgage Registers & Bonds. LC 99-52095. (Transactions of the American Philosophical Society Ser.: Vol. 89). 1999. pap. 15.00 (*0-87169-895-1*) Am Philos.

Arbour, Shirley E. Dark Triangle. 176p. 1997. mass mkt. 4.99 (*1-55197-139-9*) Picasso Publ.

Arbroath Abbey Staff. Liber S. Thome de Aberbrothoc, 2 vols. Innes, Cosmo N. & Chalmers, Patrick, eds. LC 79-158268. (Bannatyne Club, Edinburgh. Publications: No. 86). reprint ed. 210.00 (*0-404-52815-5*) AMS Pr.

Arbuckle. WinAmos 3.6. 1996. 465.00 incl. disk (*1-56321-196-3*) L Erlbaum Assocs.

Arbuckle, jt. auth. see Siems, Tom.

Arbuckle, Elisabeth S., ed. Harriet Martineau in the London Daily News: Selected Contributions, 1852-1866. LC 93-22864. 472p. 1994. text 30.00 (*0-8153-0835-3*, H1600) Garland.

Arbuckle, Gerald A. Earthing the Gospel: An Introduction Handbook for the Pastoral Worker. LC 89-77599. 1990. pap. 20.00 (*0-88344-643-X*) Orbis Bks.

— From Chaos to Mission: Refounding Religious Life Formation. 288p. (Orig.). 1997. pap. text 19.95 (*0-8146-2463-4*, Liturg Pr Bks) Liturgical Pr.

***Arbuckle, Gerald A.** Healthcare Ministry: Refounding the Mission in Tumultuous Times. LC 99-16139. 376p. 2000. pap. 34.95 (*0-8146-2570-3*) Liturgical Pr.

Arbuckle, Gerald A. Out of Chaos: Refounding Religious Congregations. LC 88-11969. 208p. 1988. pap. 12.95 (*0-8091-3004-1*) Paulist Pr.

— Refounding the Church: Dissent for Leadership. LC 93-19668. 288p. 1993. pap. 20.00 (*0-88344-896-3*) Orbis Bks.

— Strategies for Growth in Religious Life. LC 86-17359. 240p. (Orig.). 1986. pap. 11.95 (*0-8189-0505-0*) Alba.

— Strategies for Growth in Religious Life. (Orig.). (C). 1988. 39.00 (*0-85439-160-6*, Pub. by St Paul Pubns) St Mut.

Arbuckle, Gerald L. & Fleming, David L. Religious Life: Rebirth Through Conversion. 142p. (Orig.). (C). 1990. text 60.00 (*0-85439-341-2*, Pub. by St Paul Pubns) St Mut.

Arbuckle, J. Gordon, et al. Emergency Planning & Community Right-to-Know Act Handbook: A Handbook Covering SARA Title III Law & Regulations. 4th ed. 192p. 1992. pap. text 79.00 (*0-86587-272-4*) Gov Insts.

Arbuckle, J. W. Front Seat in Hell. (Illus.). 335p. 1991. 19.95 (*0-932807-53-4*) Overmountain Pr.

Arbuckle, J. W. & Shook, Alan C. The Mountain Goat. (Illus.). 135p. 1992. pap. 12.95 (*0-932807-64-X*) Overmountain Pr.

Arbuckle, James. A Collection of Letters & Essays on Several Subjects, Lately Published in the Dublin Journal, 2 vols. in 1. (Anglistica & Americana Ser.: Vol. 154). xv, 895p. 1980. reprint ed. 190.00 incl. 3.5 hd (*3-487-05662-3*) G Olms Pubs.

Arbuckle, James L. Amos for Windows: Analysis of Moment Structures Version 3.5 (Program & Manual) (Illus.). iv, 557p. 1995. 465.00 incl. disk (*1-886744-00-9*); 45.00 (*1-886744-01-7*) SmallWaters.

— Amos for Windows: Analysis of Moment Structures Version 3.6 (Manual) rev. ed. (Illus.). iv, 600p. 1996. pap. text 49.00 (*1-886744-03-3*) SmallWaters.

— Amos 3.51. 1996. 465.00 incl. disk (*1-56321-193-9*) L Erlbaum Assocs.

Arbuckle, James L. & Liothke, Werner. Amos for Windows: Analysis of Moment Structures Version 3.6 Program & Manual. rev. ed. (Illus.). 600p. pap. text 465.00 (*1-886744-02-5*) SmallWaters.

Arbuckle, Kathy. The Bible Promise Book for Preschoolers. (Illus.). 96p. (J). 1996. 4.97 (*1-55748-892-4*) Barbour Pub.

— Bible Word Games. (J). 1999. pap. 1.39 (*1-57748-598-X*) Barbour Pub.

— Jumbo Bible Coloring Fun, Vol. 4. (Jumbo Bible Coloring Bks.). (Illus.). 384p. (J). (ps-2). 1998. pap. 4.97 (*1-57748-359-6*) Barbour Pub.

***Arbuckle, Katrina & Group Publishing Staff.** PointMaker Object Lessons for Youth Ministry. LC 99-58642. (Illus.). 109p. 2000. pap. 14.99 (*0-7644-2196-4*) Group Pub.

Arbuckle, Mary A. Kerr. Joseph Kerr of Ballygoney & His Descendants. (Illus.). 188p. 1997. reprint ed. pap. 28.00 (*0-8328-9407-9*); reprint ed. lib. bdg. 38.00 (*0-8328-9406-0*) Higginson Bk Co.

Arbuckle, Nancy, ed. see Brandies, Monica.

Arbuckle, Nancy, ed. see Haas, Carhy.

Arbuckle, Nancy, ed. see Haas, Cathy.

Arbuckle, Nancy, ed. see Hildebrand, Ron, et al.

Arbuckle, Nancy, ed. see Tekulsky, Mathew.

Arbuckle, Scott. Zeb, the Cow's on the Roof Again! And Other Tales of Early Texas Dwellings. LC 96-8489. (Illus.). 120p. (J). (gr. 4-8). 1996. 14.95 (*1-57168-102-7*, Eakin Pr) Sunbelt Media.

Arbur, Rosemarie. Marion Zimmer Bradley. Schlobin, Roger C., ed. LC 85-2721. (Starmont Reader's Guide Ser.: Vol. 27). ii, 138p. 1985. lib. bdg. 29.00 (*0-916732-96-7*) Millefleurs.

Arbury, Jim, et al. The Complete Book of Plant Propagation. LC 97-208316. (Illus.). 224p. 1997. 29.95 (*1-56158-234-4*, 070355) Taunton.

***Arbury, Steve.** Radford University Art Museum Selections from the Permanent Collection. LC 99-61489. 96p. 1999. write for info. (*0-9633654-5-2*) Radford U Fnd.

***Arbus, Amy.** The Inconvenience of Being Born. LC 99-60867. (Illus.). 72p. 1999. 24.95 (*1-881270-35-1*) FotoFolio.

Arbus, Diane. Diane Arbus. LC 94-74494. (Illus.). 112p. 1995. 76.00 (*0-89381-623-X*) Aperture.

— Diane Arbus: An Aperture Monograph. (Illus.). 184p. 1972. 76.00 (*0-912334-40-1*) Aperture.

Arbus, Doon, jt. auth. see Avedon, Richard.

Arbuthmot, John. The History of John Bull. Bower, Alan W. & Erickson, Robert A., eds. (Oxford English Texts Ser.). (Illus.). 1976. 78.00 (*0-19-812719-7*) OUP.

Arbuthnot, F. F. Arabic Authors. 262p. 1984. 200.00 (*1-85077-091-3*, Pub. by Darf Pubs Ltd) St Mut.

Arbuthnot, F. F., jt. auth. see Burton, Richard.

Arbuthnot, F. F., tr. see Archer, W. G., ed.

Arbuthnot, F. F., jt. tr. see Burton, Richard.

Arbuthnot, Nancy P. American Artist in World War 2. 66p. (C). 1996. text 32.40 (*0-536-59430-9*) Pearson Custom.

Arbuthnot, Nancy P. Mexico Shining: Versions of Aztec Songs. (Illus.). 120p. (Orig.). 1995. 25.00 (*0-89410-785-2*, Three Contnts); pap. 12.00 (*0-89410-786-0*, Three Contnts) L Rienner.

Arbuthnott, G. W. & Emson, P. C., eds. Chemical Signaling in the Basal Ganglia. LC 93-1791. (Progress in Brain Research Ser.: 99). (Illus.). 370p. 1993. 246.00 (*0-444-81562-7*) Elsevier.

Arbuthnott, Gordon W., jt. ed. see Meredith, Gloria E.

Arbuzov, Aleksei. The Promise. Nicolaeff, Ariadne, tr. 1998. pap. 5.25 (*0-8222-0921-7*) Dramatists Play.

Arc en reve centre d'architecture, jt. auth. see Koolhaas, Rem.

Arc, Joan O. & Carver, Wayne. A Child's Christmas in Utah. 1998. 10.00 (*0-939394-07-3*) Blck Willw Pr.

— I'm a Stranger Here Myself: 21 Poems. 1998. 10.00 (*0-939394-05-7*) Blck Willw Pr.

Arca. Infopower Practice & Infostar Uses. 1985. pap. 16.95 (*0-89599-108-X*) Smithsonian Bks.

Arca, Emil & Pamel, Gregory J., eds. The Triumph of the American Spirit: The Presidential Speeches of Ronald Reagan. 362p. 1984. 9.95 (*0-685-57961-1*) Natl Repro Corp.

Arcama Group Staff. America by Mail. 240p. (Orig.). 1990. pap. 14.95 (*0-380-76175-0*, Avon Bks) Morrow Avon.

Arcana, Judith. Grace Paley's Life Stories: A Literary Biography. (Illus.). 304p. (C). 1993. text 29.95 (*0-252-01945-8*) U of Ill Pr.

— Grace Paley's Life Stories: A Literary Biography. 304p. 1994. pap. text 15.95 (*0-252-06447-X*) U of Ill Pr.

Arcand, Bernard. The Jaguar & the Anteater: Pornography & the Modern World. Grady, Wayne, tr. from FRE.Tr. of Jaguar et le Tamanoir. 286p. 1999. reprint ed. pap. text 15.00 (*0-7881-6210-1*) DIANE Pub.

— The Jaguar & the Anteater: Pornography Degree Zero. Grady, Wayne, tr. 320p. (gr. 13). 1993. 30.00 (*0-86091-446-1*, B2502, Pub. by Verso) Norton.

***Arcand, Tim.** A Father's Handbook. LC 98-91115. 151p. 2000. pap. 7.95 (*0-533-13052-2*) Vantage.

Arcane Book Company Staff. The Arcane Formulas: Mental Alchemy. 109p. 1969. reprint ed. spiral bd. 10.00 (*0-7873-0038-1*) Hlth Research.

— The Arcane Formulas or Mental Alchemy (1909) 110p. 1996. reprint ed. pap. 9.95 (*1-56459-858-6*) Kessinger Pub.

Arcangelo, Virginia. Weaver & Koehler's Programmed Mathematics of Drugs & Solutions. 5th ed. (Illus.). 160p. 1992. pap. text 18.95 (*0-397-54918-0*) Lppncott W & W.

***Arcangelo, Virginia Poole.** Programmed Mathematics of Drugs & Solutions. 6th ed. 224p. 1999. pap. text 19.95 Lppncott W & W.

Arcangelo, Virginia Poole & Petersen, Andrew. Pharmacotherapeutics for Advanced Practice. 992p. pap. text. write for info. (*0-7817-1876-7*) Lppncott W & W.

Arcario, Paul J. & ABC Staff. HealthWatch. (ABC News Intermediate ESL Video Library). (Illus.). 160p. (C). 1994. pap. text 27.93 (*0-13-501172-8*) P-H.

Arcario, Paul J., jt. ed. see Stempleski, Susan.

Arcaro, Janice. Creating Quality in the Classroom. 152p. 1995. per. 44.95 (*1-884015-57-3*) St Lucie Pr.

Arcaro, Janice, ed. see Arcaro, Jerome.

Arcaro, Jerome. Team Performance Model. unabridged ed. Arcaro, Janice, ed. (Illus.). 133p. 1998. 29.95 (*0-9664672-0-5*) Galileo Qual.

Arcaro, Jerome S. The Baldridge Award for Education: How to Measure & Document Quality Improvement. 160p. (Orig.). 1995. per. 49.95 (*1-884015-75-1*) St Lucie Pr.

— Teams in Education: Creating an Integrated Approach. 120p. (Orig.). 1995. per. 44.95 (*1-884015-52-2*) St Lucie Pr.

— TQM Facilitator's Guide. (Illus.). 216p. (Orig.). 1997. per. 44.95 (*1-57444-089-6*) St Lucie Pr.

Arcaro, Jerry. President's Quality Award Program Self-Assessment Process for Federal, State & Local Government. LC 97-206857. (Illus.). 260p. 1997. lib. bdg. 125.00 (*1-57444-167-1*) St Lucie Pr.

— Quality in Education: An Implementation Handbook. LC 94-46378. 192p. 1995. boxed set 49.95 (*1-884015-58-1*) St Lucie Pr.

***Arcaro, Thomas & Torke, Kyle.** Dead Triathletes Speak: Voices from the Middle of the Pack. 166p. 1999. pap. 13.95 (*0-9674540-0-X*) T Arcaro.

Arcarti, Kristnya. Spiritual Healing: A Beginner's Guide. (Illus.). 96p. 1997. pap. 11.95 (*0-340-67416-4*, Pub. by Headway) Trafalgar.

***Arcarti, Kristyna.** Beginners Guide to Chinese Horoscopes. (Guides for Beginners Ser.). (Illus.). 96p. 1999. mass mkt. 11.95 (*0-340-74250-X*, Pub. by Headway) Trafalgar.

— Beginners Guide to Numerology. (Guides for Beginners Ser.). (Illus.). 96p. 1999. mass mkt. 11.95 (*0-340-74247-X*, Pub. by Headway) Trafalgar.

— Beginners Guide to Tarot. 1999. pap. 11.95 (*0-340-73751-4*) Headway.

Arcarti, Kristyna. Chinese Horoscopes for Beginners. (Headway Guide for Beginners Ser.). (Illus.). 96p. 1996. mass mkt. 11.95 (*0-340-64804-X*, Pub. by Headway) Trafalgar.

— Gems & Crystals for Beginners. (Headway Guide for Beginners Ser.). (Illus.). 128p. 1995. pap. 11.95 (*0-340-60883-8*, Pub. by Headway) Trafalgar.

— The Healing Powers of Plants: A Beginner's Guide. (Beginner's Guide Ser.). (Illus.). 96p. 1998. pap. 11.95 (*0-340-71148-5*, Pub. by Hodder & Stought Ltd) Trafalgar.

***Arcarti, Kristyna.** I Ching: A Beginner's Guide. (Headway Guides for Beginners Ser.). (Illus.). 96p. 2000. pap. 11.95 (*0-340-77205-0*, Pub. by Headway) Trafalgar.

Arcarti, Kristyna. I Ching for Beginners. (Headway Guide for Beginners Ser.). (Illus.). 192p. 1995. pap. 11.95 (*0-340-62080-3*, Pub. by Headway) Trafalgar.

— Interpreting Signs & Symbols. (Beginner's Guide Ser.). (Illus.). 96p. 1997. pap. 11.95 (*0-340-68827-0*, Pub. by Headway) Trafalgar.

— The Language of Flowers: A Beginner's Guide. (Illus.). 96p. 1997. pap. 11.95 (*0-340-69781-4*, Pub. by Headway) Trafalgar.

— Love Signs for Beginners. (Headway Guide for Beginners Ser.). (Illus.). 96p. 1996. mass mkt. 11.95 (*0-340-64805-8*, Pub. by Headway) Trafalgar.

— Numerology for Beginners. (Headway Guide for Beginners Ser.). 108p. 1995. pap. 11.95 (*0-340-59551-5*, Pub. by Headway) Trafalgar.

— Palmistry. (For Beginners Ser.). (Illus.). 103p. 1995. pap. 11.95 (*0-340-59552-3*, Pub. by Headway) Trafalgar.

— Runes for Beginners. (Headway Guide for Beginners Ser.). (Illus.). 112p. 1995. pap. 11.95 (*0-340-62081-1*, Pub. by Headway) Trafalgar.

***Arcarti, Kristyna.** Spiritual Healing: A Beginner's Guide. (Headway Guides for Beginners Ser.). (Illus.). 96p. 2000. pap. 11.95 (*0-340-74259-3*, Pub. by Headway) Trafalgar.

Arcarti, Kristyna. Star Signs. (For Beginners Ser.). (Illus.). 103p. 1995. pap. 11.95 (*0-340-59553-1*, Pub. by Headway) Trafalgar.

— Tarot for Beginners. (Headway Guide for Beginners Ser.). (Illus.). 89p. 1995. pap. 11.95 (*0-340-59550-7*, Pub. by Headway) Trafalgar.

Arce. Curriculum: A Child's Perspective. (Education). 1999. pap. 39.50 (*0-534-55755-4*) Wadsworth Pub.

***Arce, Alberto.** Anthropology, Development, & Modernities: Exploring Discourses, Counter-tendencies, & Violence. LC 98-54357. 1999. write for info. (*0-415-20499-2*) Routledge.

— Anthropology, Development, & Modernities: Exploring Discourses, Counter-Tendencies, & Violence. LC 98-54357. 1999. pap. write for info. (*0-415-20500-X*) Routledge.

Arce, Carmen V. El Libro de los Afectos Culinarios. 1996. pap. text. write for info. (*1-56758-042-4*) Edit Cultl.

Arce de Vazquez, Margot. Garcilaso De la Vega: Contribucion Al Estudio De la Lirica Espanola Del Siglo XVI. 4th ed. (UPREX, Estudios Literarios Ser.: No. 43). 195p. (C). 1975. pap. 1.50 (*0-8477-0043-7*) U of PR Pr.

Arce De Vazquez, Margot, et al. Lecturas Puertorriquenas - Prosa. 1966. 14.95 (*0-87751-011-3*) E Torres & Sons.

Arce de Vazquez, Margot, ed. see Pales Matos, Luis.

Arce, Eva M. Curriculum for Young Children. LC 99-11642. 246p. 2000. 25.95 (*0-7668-1278-2*) Delmar.

Arce, G. H. De, see De Arce, G. H.

Arce, Gallego. Arrigoitia: Lecturas Puertorriquenas-Poesia. 1966. 14.95 (*0-87751-006-7*) E Torres & Sons.

Arce, Gary. Defying Gravity: High Adventure on Yosemite's Walls. LC 95-31974. 194p. 1995. pap. 24.95 (*0-89997-185-7*) Wilderness Pr.

Arce, Hector, jt. auth. see Minnelli, Vincente.

Arceivala, S. J. Wastewater Treatment & Disposal: Engineering & Ecology in Pollution Control. LC 81-1521. (Pollution Engineering & Technology Ser.: Vol. 15). (Illus.). 904p. reprint ed. pap. 200.00 (*0-608-18335-0*, 203301200082) Bks Demand.

***Arcel, Harvey.** On Stage with the Igor System: Is This Our Future? (Illus.). 435p. 2000. pap. 39.95 (*1-930002-04-1*) I&L Pubs.

Arcellana, Francisco. The Mats. LC 98-35719. (Illus.). 32p. (J). (ps-4). 1999. 13.95 (*0-916291-86-3*) Kane-Miller Bk.

Arcelli, C., et al, eds. Advances in Visual Form Analysis: Proceedings of the Third International Workshop in Visual Form Capri, Italy 28-30 May, 1997. LC 98-180626. 760p. 1998. 118.00 (*981-02-3258-6*) World Scientific Pub.

Arcelli, C., et al. Visual Form: Analysis & Recognition. (Illus.). 656p. (C). 1992. 135.00 (*0-306-44185-3*, Plenum Trade) Perseus Pubng.

Arcelli, Carlo, et al, eds. Aspects of Visual Form Processing: Proceedings of the Second International Workshop on Visual Form. LC 94-31172. 632p. 1994. text 162.00 (*981-02-2011-1*) World Scientific Pub.

***Arcelli, Enrico.** Soccer Nutritian. (Illus.). 120p. 1999. pap. 10.95 (*1-890946-17-6*) Reedswain.

***Arcelli, Enrico & Ferretti, Ferretto.** Soccer Fitness Training. (Illus.). 146p. 1999. pap. 12.95 (*1-890946-21-4*) Reedswain.

Arcenaux, Claude, ed. see Electron Microscopy Society Staff.

Arceneaux, Pamela D. & Travis, Jessica. Preservation Guide No. 5: Books. LC 84-106237. (Illus.). ii, 14p. (Orig.). 1989. pap. 3.95 (*0-917860-27-6*) Historic New Orleans.

Arceneaux, Therese. Where Music Lives. LC 99-475893. 32p. 1999. pap. 9.95 (*1-886094-94-2*) Chicago Spectrum.

Arceneaux, William. No Spark of Malice: The Murder of Martin Begnaud. LC 99-15677. (Illus.). 360p. 1999. 34.95 (*0-8071-2447-8*) La State U Pr.

Arcese, Peter, jt. ed. see Sinclair, A. R.

Arch Books Staff. Abraham, Sarah & Isaac. LC 97-136040. 1997. pap. 1.99 (*0-570-07529-7*, 59-1502) Concordia.

***Arch Books Staff.** Bright Light, Saul's Sight. (Arch Bks.). (Illus.). 16p. (J). (gr. k-4). 1998. pap. text 1.99 (*0-570-07552-1*, 59-1525GJ) Concordia.

— Down Through the Roof. (Arch Books Ser.). (Illus.). 16p. (J). (gr. k-4). 1999. pap. text 11.94 (*0-570-07562-9*) Concordia.

— God's Fire for Elijah. (Arch Bks.). (Illus.). 16p. (J). (gr. k-4). 1998. pap. text 1.99 (*0-570-07550-5*, 59-1523GJ) Concordia.

— The Good Shepherd. (Arch Bks.). (Illus.). 16p. (J). (gr. k-4). 1998. pap. text 1.99 (*0-570-07551-3*, 59-1524GJ) Concordia.

— Jailhouse Rock. (Arch Books Ser.). (Illus.). 16p. (J). (gr. k-4). 1999. pap. text 11.94 (*0-570-07563-7*) Concordia.

Arch Books Staff. Jesus & the Family Trip. LC 98-228008. (Illus.). 16p. (J). (gr. k-4). 1998. pap. 1.99 (*0-570-07547-5*) Concordia.

— Jesus Calms the Storm: Matthew 8:23-27; Mark 4:35-41. (Illus.). 24p. (J). (ps-3). 1994. pap. 1.99 (*0-570-09045-8*, 59-1468) Concordia.

— Mary & Martha's Dinner Guest. 16p. (J). (gr. k-4). 1998. pap. 1.99 (*0-570-07548-3*) Concordia.

— My Christmas Prayer Book. LC 98-228009. (Illus.). 16p. (J). (gr. k-5). 1998. pap. 1.99 (*0-570-07546-7*) Concordia.

— My Happy Easter Book. LC 96-132987. (Arch Bks.). (Illus.). (J). (gr. k-4). 1996. 1.99 (*0-570-07520-3*, 59-1493) Concordia.

— Noah's 2-by-2 Adventure. LC 97-228735. 1997. 1.99 (*0-570-07538-6*) Concordia.

— Samson: Judges 13-16. (J). (ps-3). 1994. pap. 1.99 (*0-570-09042-3*, 59-1465) Concordia.

— Seeds That Grew & Grew. LC 97-221920. 1997. 1.99 (*0-570-07539-4*, 59-1512) Concordia.

— The Seeds That Grew to Be a Hundred & The Day the Little Children Came. Concordia Publishing House Staff, ed. LC 98-220272. (J). (ps-3). 1998. pap. 13.00 incl. audio (*0-570-06836-3*, 59KM2133) Concordia.

— Shepard's Christmas. LC 98-101854. 1997. 1.99 (*0-570-07540-8*, 59-1513) Concordia.

***Arch Books Staff.** The Springy, Slingy Sling. (Arch Bks.). (Illus.). 16p. (J). (gr. k-4). 1998. pap. text 1.99 (*0-570-07549-1*, 59-1522GJ) Concordia.

— Surprise in Disguise. (Arch Books Ser.). (Illus.). 16p. (J). (gr. k-4). 1999. pap. text 11.94 (*0-570-07564-5*) Concordia.

— Tried & True Job. (Arch Books Ser.). (Illus.). 16p. (J). (gr. k-4). 1999. pap. text 11.94 (*0-570-07561-0*) Concordia.

Arch Books Staff. The Very First Lord's Supper. LC 97-133945. (Illus.). 16p. (J). (ps-4). 1997. pap. 2.00 (*0-570-07528-9*, 59-1501) Concordia.

— What's for Lunch? LC 97-223929. 1997. 1.99 (*0-570-07537-8*, 59-1510) Concordia.

Arch, Dave. All New Tricks for Trainers: 57 Tricks & Techniques to Grab & Hold the Attention of Any Audience. 1998. pap. text 24.95 (*0-87425-448-5*) HRD Press.

Arch, Dave. First Impressions Lasting Impressions: Openings & Closings You Can Count On! 80p. pap. 24.95 (*0-7879-5122-6*, Pfffr & Co) Jossey-Bass.

— Red Hot Handouts! Taking the Ho Hum out of Handouts. 192p. 39.95 (*0-7879-5118-8*, Pfffr & Co) Jossey-Bass.

— Showmanship for Presenters: 49 Proven Training Techniques from Professional Performers. 144p. pap. 29.95 (*0-7879-5119-6*, Pfffr & Co) Jossey-Bass.

— Tricks for Trainers: 57 Tricks & Teasers Guaranteed to Add Magic to Your Presentation, Vol. 1. 34.95 (*0-7879-5116-1*, Pfffr & Co) Jossey-Bass.

— Tricks for Trainers: 57 Tricks & Teasers Guaranteed to Add Magic to Your Presentation, Vol. 2. 192p. 34.95 (*0-7879-5117-X*, Pfffr & Co) Jossey-Bass.

A

A

*Arch, Dave, et al. One-on-One Training: How to Effectively Train One Person at a Time. LC 99-6639. 141p. 2000. 24.95 (0-7879-5143-9, Pfffr & Co) Jossey-Bass.

Arch, Dave, jt. auth. see Meiss, Rich.

Arch, Dave, jt. auth. see Pike, Robert W.

Arch, Davey, jt. auth. see Duncan, Barbara R.

Arch, E. L. Inheritance Taxes. (Information Services Ser.). 1987. 425.00 (0-685-07446-3) P-H.

Arch, John C., ed. Technology in the Schools: Equity & Funding. 56p. 1986. pap. 6.95 (0-8106-1535-5) NEA.

Arch, Stephen C. Authorizing the Past: The Rhetoric of History in Seventeenth-Century New England. LC 94-8729. 256p. 1994. lib. bdg. 32.00 (0-87580-188-9) N Ill U Pr.

Arch, Stephen Carl, ed. see Allen, Ethan.

Archaeological Institute of America Staff. Entrance to the Athenian Acropolis Before Mnesicles. 162p. 1994. boxed set 40.00 (0-8403-9391-1) Kendall-Hunt.

Archaeology Data Service Staff. Guides to Good Practice: GIS. 100p. (Orig.). 1999. pap. 18.00 (1-900188-69-4, Pub. by Oxbow Bks) David Brown.

Archaeometry of Glass Sessions Staff, et al. Scientific Research in Early Chinese Glass: Proceedings of the Archaeometry of Glass Sessions of the 1984 International Symposium on Glass, Beijing, September 7, 1984, with Supplementary Papers. LC 92-192550. ix, 212 p. 1991. 55.00 (0-87290-126-2) Corning.

Archakov, I. A. & Bachmanova, G. I. Cytochrome P-450 & Active Oxygen. 320p. 1990. 145.00 (0-85066-805-0, Pub. by Tay Francis Ltd) Taylor & Francis.

Archambault, jt. auth. see Corbeil.

Archambault, Alan. Civil War Coloring Book. (Illus.). (J). (gr. 4-7). 1985. pap. 4.95 (0-88388-047-4) Bellerophon Bks.

— Paper Soldiers of the Civil War. (Illus.). (J). (gr. 1-9). 1992. pap. 4.95 (0-88388-152-7) Bellerophon Bks.

Archambault, Alan, jt. auth. see Canon, Jill.

Archambault, Alan H. A Sketchbook of the Confederate Infantryman. (Illus.). Date not set. pap. write for info. (1-57747-058-3) Thomas Publications.

— A Sketchbook of the Union Infantryman. LC 99-60261. (Historical Sketchbook Ser.). 80p. 1999. pap. 10.00 (1-57747-047-8) Thomas Publications.

Archambault, Ariane, jt. auth. see Corbeil, Jean C.

Archambault, Ariane, jt. auth. see Corbeil, Jean-Claude.

Archambault, Ariane, jt. compiled by see Corbeil, Jean-Claude.

Archambault, Edith. Defining the Nonprofit Sector: France. Salamon, Lester M. & Anheier, Helmut K., eds. (Working Papers of the Johns Hopkins Comparative Nonprofit Sector Project: No. 7). (Illus.). 24p. 1993. pap. text 6.00 (1-886333-05-X) JH Univ Inst Pol Studies.

— The Nonprofit Sector in France. (Johns Hopkins Non-Profit Sector Ser.). 200p. 1997. text 27.95 (0-7190-4904-0, Pub. by Manchester Univ Pr) St Martin.

— Nonprofit Sector in France: C Edition. Salamon, Lester M. & Anheier, Helmut K., eds. (Johns Hopkins Non-Profit Sector Ser.). 200p. 1997. text 45.00 (0-7190-4903-2, Pub. by Manchester Univ Pr) St Martin.

Archambault, Florence. Occupied Japan Collectibles. LC 91-67013. (Illus.). 208p. 1992. text 49.95 (0-88740-378-6) Schiffer.

*Archambault, Florence. Occupied Japan for the Home. (Illus.). 160p. 2000. pap. 24.95 (0-7643-1133-6) Schiffer.

*Archambault, Francois. 15 Seconds. 96p. 2000. pap. 14.95 (0-88922-427-7, Pub. by Talonbks) SPD-Small Pr Dist.

Archambault, John. Beautiful Feast for a Big King Cat. LC 92-32331. 1994. 10.15 (0-606-09061-4, Pub. by Turtleback) Demco.

Archambault, John. The Birth of a Whale. (Illus.). 48p. (J). (gr. 1-3). 1996. 14.95 (0-382-39565-4, Silver Pr NJ); lib. bdg. 15.95 (0-382-39566-2, Silver Pr NJ) Silver Burdett Pr.

— The Birth of a Whale. (Illus.). (J). (gr. 2). 1996. 5.00 incl. audio (0-382-39568-9) Silver Burdett Pr.

— Birth of a Whale. (Illus.). 48p. (J). (gr. 2). 1996. pap. 19.95 incl. audio (0-382-39569-7) Silver Burdett Pr.

— Fox & the Chicken. (Illus.). (J). 1998. 14.95 (0-382-39647-2, Silver Pr NJ); 19.95 (0-382-39662-6, Silver Pr NJ) Silver Burdett Pr.

Archambault, John & Martin, Bill, Jr. A Beautiful Feast for a Big King Cat. LC 92-32331. (Illus.). 32p. (J). (ps-3). 1994. 14.95 (0-06-022903-9) HarpC Child Bks.

— A Beautiful Feast for a Big King Cat: New Edition. LC 92-32331. (Trophy Picture Bk.). (Illus.). 32p. (J). (ps-3). 1996. pap. 5.95 (0-06-443460-5, HarpTrophy) HarpC Child Bks.

*Archambault, John & Plummer, David. Chicka Chicka Boom Boom, No. 2360. (Happy Song Sing - Alongs Ser.). (Illus.). 64p. (J). (ps-3). 1999. pap. 12.98 incl. audio (1-57471-549-6) Creat Teach Pr.

— Counting Kittens. Cernek, Kim, ed. (Happy Song Sing-Alongs Ser.: Vol. 2356). (Illus.). 64p. (J). (gr. k-7). 1999. pap. 12.98 incl. cd-rom (1-57471-637-9) Creat Teach Pr.

Archambault, John & Plummer, David. Counting Kittens. LC 96-7576. (Illus.). 1996. pap. 5.95 (0-382-39651-0, Silver Pr NJ) Silver Burdett Pr.

— Counting Kittens. LC 96-7576. (Illus.). (J). 1996. 15.95 (0-382-39649-9, Silver Pr NJ) Silver Burdett Pr.

— Counting Kittens, No. 2361. Cernek, Kim, ed. (Happy Song Sing - Alongs Ser.). (Illus.). 64p. (J). (ps-3). 1999. pap. 12.98 (1-57471-550-X) Creat Teach Pr.

— The Fox & the Chicken. LC 96-7577. (Illus.). (J). 1996. pap. 5.95 (0-382-39648-0, Silver Pr NJ); lib. bdg. 15.95 (0-382-39646-4, Silver Pr NJ) Silver Burdett Pr.

— Grandmother's Garden. LC 96-3469. (Illus.). 32p. (J). 1997. lib. bdg. 15.95 (0-382-39652-9) Silver Burdett Pr.

— Grandmother's Garden. LC 96-3469. (Illus.). 32p. (J). (ps-3). 1997. 13.95 (0-382-39653-7) Silver Burdett Pr.

— Grandmother's Garden: A/Read-ALong Story Tape. LC 96-3469. (Illus.). 32p. (J). 1996. 19.95 incl. audio (0-382-39664-2) Silver Burdett Pr.

— I Love the Mountains: A Traditional Song. LC 97-37806. (Illus.). (J). 1998. write for info. (0-382-42132-9); pap. 22.00 (0-382-42133-7) Silver Burdett Pr.

*Archambault, John & Plummer, David. I'm a Can-Do Kid. Cernek, Kim, ed. (Happy Song Sing-Alongs Ser.: Vol. 2357). (Illus.). 64p. (J). 1999. pap. 12.98 (1-57471-638-7) Creat Teach Pr.

Archambault, John & Plummer, David. I'm a Can Do Kid, No. 2362. Cernek, Kim, ed. (Happy Song Sing - Alongs Ser.). (Illus.). 64p. (J). (ps-3). 1999. pap. 12.98 (1-57471-551-8) Creat Teach Pr.

Archambault, John, jt. auth. see Martin.

Archambault, John, jt. auth. see Martin, Bill, Jr.

Archambault, John, jt. auth. see Plummer, David.

Archambault, Lise, tr. see Carlson, Daniel J.

Archambault, Marie T. Retreat with Black Elk: Living in the Sacred Hoop. 112p. 1998. pap. text 7.95 (0-86716-271-6) St Anthony Mess Pr.

*Archambault, Matthew. The Happy Hoppy Frog. LC 99-41923. (Gabe & Critters Ser.). (Illus.). 32p. (J). (ps-3). 2000. 9.99 (0-7814-3342-8) Chariot Victor.

Archambault, Matthew, jt. auth. see Freeman, Becky.

Archambault, Paul J. A Monk's Confession: The Memoirs of Guibert of Nogent. LC 95-11479.Tr. of De Vita Sua. 248p. 1995. pap. 14.95 (0-271-01482-2) Pa St U Pr.

— Seven French Chroniclers: Witnesses to History. LC 73-16652. 170p. reprint ed. pap. 52.70 (0-608-06976-0, 206718400009) Bks Demand.

Archambault, Paul J. & Guibert of Nogent. A Monk's Confession: The Memoirs of Guibert of Nogent. LC 95-11479.Tr. of De Vita Sua. 248p. 1995. 40.00 (0-271-01481-4) Pa St U Pr.

Archambault, Paul J., ed. see Crenne, Helisenne D.

Archambault, Reginald D., ed. & intro. see Dewey, John.

Archambault, Richard. The McMaster Family Workbook. 110p. (Orig.). 1996. pap. text 14.95 (0-940139-38-3) Consortium RI.

*Archambault, Richard. The McMaster Family Workbook. 2nd rev. ed. 178p. (Orig.). 2000. pap. text, wbk. ed. 18.95 (0-940139-54-5) Consortium RI.

Archambault, Richard. The McMaster Family Workbook: One-Parent Family. rev. ed. 154p. 1997. pap. text, wbk. ed. 17.95 (0-940139-48-0) Consortium RI.

— The McMaster Family Workbook: Two-Parent Family. rev. ed. 154p. 1997. pap. text, wbk. ed. 17.95 (0-940139-47-2) Consortium RI.

Archambault, Richard C. Child Development Workbook. 118p. 1999. text 17.95 (0-940139-51-0) Consortium RI.

Archambeau, Robert. Word Play Place: Essays on the Poetry of John Matthias. LC 98-19478. 272p. 1998. text 39.95 (0-8040-1008-0) Swallow.

Archambeault, Bob & Gibbs, Mardie. CICS - ESA Version 3.0: Architecture & Problem Detection. 506p. 1994. 50.00 (0-07-002744-7) McGraw.

Archambeault, James. The Gift of Pleasant Hill: Shaker Community in Kentucky. LC 91-19274. (Illus.). 160p. (Orig.). 1991. 29.95 (0-9629116-0-7) Plsnt Hill KY.

Archambeault, James, photos by. Kentucky III. LC 98-51957. (Illus.). 144p. 1999. 39.95 (1-55868-409-3) Gr Arts Ctr Pub.

Archambeault, Marci. A Step Beyond. Bell, Barbara, ed. LC 99-70085. 292p. 1999. pap. 14.95 (1-888861-07-X) Quest MA.

Archangeli, Diana B. & Langendoer, D. Terence, eds. Optimality Theory. LC 97-16853. 250p. (Orig.). (C). 1997. 72.95 (0-631-20225-0); pap. 29.95 (0-631-20226-9) Blackwell Pubs.

Archangeli, Diana B. & Pulleyblank, Douglas. Grounded Phonology. LC 93-8873. (Current Studies in Linguistics: Vol. 25). 502p. 1994. 60.00 (0-262-01137-9) MIT Pr.

Archangelsky, Boris, jt. auth. see Lein, Anatoly.

Archangelsky, Miguel. Studies on the Biology, Ecology & Systematics of the Immature Stages of New World Hydrophiloidea. LC 97-76268. (Bulletin New Ser.: Vol. 12, No. 1). (Illus.). 207p. 1997. pap. text 25.00 (0-86727-126-4) Ohio Bio Survey.

Archard, Cary, ed. Alun Lewis: Collected Poems. 206p. 1995. 27.00 (1-85411-011-X, Pub. by Seren Bks) Dufour.

*Archard, Cary, ed. Mr. Roopratna's Chocolates: Winning Stories of the Rhys Davies Prize. 160p. 1999. pap. 17.95 (1-85411-267-8, Pub. by Seren Bks) Dufour.

Archard, Cary, ed. Poetry Wales: 25 Years. 280p. (Orig.). (YA). (gr. 10-12). 1990. pap. 17.95 (1-85411-031-4, Pub. by Seren Bks) Dufour.

Archard, Cary, jt. auth. see Abse, Dannie.

Archard, David. Children: Rights & Childhood. LC 92-2464. (Ideas Ser.). 224p. (C). 1993. pap. 22.99 (0-415-08252-8, B0294) Routledge.

— Marxism & Existentialism: The Political Philosophy of Satre & Merlean-Ponty. (Modern Revivals in Philosophy Ser.). 142p. 1992. 56.95 (0-7512-0051-4, Pub. by Gregg Revivals) Ashgate Pub Co.

— Sexual Consent. LC 98-113389. 200p. (C). 1997. pap. text 24.00 (0-8133-3082-3, Pub. by Westview) HarpC.

Archard, David, ed. Philosophy & Pluralism. (Royal Institute of Philosophy Supplements Ser.: No. 40). 219p. (C). 1996. pap. text 22.95 (0-521-56750-5) Cambridge U Pr.

Archard, G. D., tr. see Basov, N. G., ed.

Archard, Geoffrey C., tr. see Arifov, Ubai A., ed.

Archard, Geoffrey D., tr. see Sirota, N. N.

Archard, Michel. Representation of Cognitive Structures: Syntax & Semantics of French Sentential Complements. LC 98-18504. (Cognitive Lingusitics Research Ser.: No. 11). 377p. 1998. 105.35 (3-11-015760-8) De Gruyter.

Archarel, Chuck. Building Bass Lines. (National Guitar Workshop Arts Ser.). 1998. pap. 19.95 incl. audio compact disk (0-88284-922-0, 18406) Alfred Pub.

Archbald, Doug A. & Newmann, Fred M. Beyond Standardized Testing: Assessing Authentic Academic Achievement in the Secondary School. 73p. (Orig.). (C). 1988. pap. 9.00 (0-88210-214-1) Natl Assn Principals.

Archbald, Elizabeth. Fifty Images of Ancient Greece. (Orig.). 1990. pap. 7.95 (0-913412-23-6) Brandon Hse.

Archbald, Robert W. Built-in Test. 442p. 1990. pap. text 65.00 (0-9625300-0-X) Fellows Pub.

Archbishop Averky. On the Situation of the Orthodox Christian in the Contemporary World. 12p. (Orig.). 1984. pap. 2.00 (0-912927-12-7, X012) St John Kronstadt.

Archbishop Averky Taushev. Rukovodstvo k Izuchjeniju Svjashchennago Pisanija Novago Zavjeta- Tchetvjerojevangelija.Tr. of A/Guide for Study of the Holy Scriptures of the New Testament-The Four Gospels. 345p. 1974. pap. text 12.00 (0-317-29299-4) Holy Trinity.

— Rukovodstvo Po Gomiletike.Tr. of Handbook for Homiletics. 110p. 1961. pap. text 5.00 (0-317-30276-0) Holy Trinity.

— Visokopreosvjashennij Theofan, Arkhiepiskop Poltavsky i Perejaslavsky.Tr. of His Eminance Theophan, Archbishop of Poltava & Perejaslavl. 88p. 1974. pap. 5.00 (0-317-29284-6) Holy Trinity.

Archbishop Nikon Rklitsky, ed. Zhizneopisanie i Tvorenije Blazhennejshago Antonia, Mitropolita Kievskago i Galitzkago, v 17 tomakh. 17 vols.Tr. of Life & Works of His Beatitude Anthony, Metropolitan of Kiev & Galitch. 6000p. 1971. pap. 200.00 (0-317-29015-0) Holy Trinity.

Archbishop of York, et al. More Points of View. LC 69-18933. (Essay Index Reprint Ser.). 1977. 17.95 (0-8369-0048-0) Ayer.

Archbishop Paul of Finland. The Feast of Faith: An Invitation to the Love Feast of the Kingdom of God. Williams, Esther, tr. from FIN. LC 88-11360. 112p. (Orig.). 1988. pap. 8.95 (0-88141-072-1) St Vladimirs.

Archbishop Theophan of Poltava. Archbishop Theophan of Poltava: Selected Letters Together with a Memorial Address. Janda, Antonina L., tr. from RUS. 80p. (Orig.). 1989. pap. 4.50 (0-912927-31-3, X031) St John Kronstadt.

Archbishop Vitaly Maximenko. Motivi Moijej Zhizni.Tr. of Motives of My Life. 205p. 1955. pap. 7.00 (0-317-29054-1) Holy Trinity.

*Archbishop's Commission. Future of the Greek Language. 110p. 1999. pap. 4.95 (1-58438-014-4, Pub. by Greek Orth) BookWorld.

*Archbold, John Frederick. A Summary of the Laws of England. 4 vols. 879p. 2000. reprint ed. 230.00 (1-56169-604-8) Gaunt.

Archbold, Lawrence. Style & Structure in the Praeludia of Dietrich Buxtehude. LC 85-1064. (Studies in Musicology: No. 82). (Illus.). 357p. reprint ed. pap. 110.70 (0-8357-1646-5, 207034500087) Bks Demand.

Archbold, Lawrence & Peterson, William J., eds. French Organ Music: From the Revolution to Franck & Widor, Vol. 5. LC 99-30297. (Eastman Studies in Music: Vol. 1071-9989). (Illus.). 320p. 1999. pap. 24.95 (1-58046-071-2, Pub. by Univ Rochester Pr) Boydell & Brewer.

Archbold, Richard & Rand, Austin L. New Guinea Expedition, Fly River Area, 1936-1937. LC 75-32797. (Illus.). reprint ed. 52.50 (0-404-14100-5) AMS Pr.

Archbold, Rick. Deep-Sea Explorer: The Story of Robert Ballard, Discoverer of the Titanic. (J). (gr. 6). 1995. 9.28 (0-395-73272-7) HM.

— Deep-Sea Explorer: The Story of Robert Ballard, Discoverer of the Titanic. large type ed. 174p. 43.50 (0-614-20584-0, L-38210-00 APHB) Am Printing Hse.

— Ken Marschall's Art of Titanic: An Illustrated History. LC 98-41433. (Illus.). 176p. 1998. 40.00 (0-7868-6455-9, Pub. by Hyperion) Time Warner.

Archbold, Rick & McCauley, Dana. Last Dinner on the Titanic: Menus & Recipes from the Great Liner. LC 96-47057. (Illus.). 128p. 1997. 24.45 (0-7868-6303-X, Pub. by Hyperion) Time Warner.

Archbold, Rick, jt. auth. see Ballard, Robert Duane.

Archbold, Rick, jt. auth. see Bateman, Robert.

Archbold, Tim. Who's There? Over 400 Knock-Knock Jokes. (Illus.). (J). (gr. 2-7). 1995. 3.95 (1-85697-570-3) LKC.

Archbold, William A., ed. Twentieth-Century Essays & Addresses. LC 78-128202. (Essay Index Reprint Ser.). 1977. 20.95 (0-8369-1861-4) Ayer.

Archdale, F. A. Elementary Radiesthesia & the Use of the Pendulum. 32p. 1996. spiral bd. 10.00 (0-7873-0039-X) Hlth Research.

Archdall, Mervyn, ed. see Lodge, John.

Archdeacon, H. C. & Ellsworth, Ken, eds. Track Cyclopedia. 1985. 10th ed. (Illus.). 1985. 39.95 (0-911382-02-X) Simmons-Boardman.

Archdeacon, Henry. Historia Anglorum. Greenway, Diana, ed. & tr. by. (Oxford Medieval Texts Ser.). (Illus.). 1,072p. 1997. text 195.00 (0-19-822224-6) OUP.

Archdeacon, Thomas J. Becoming American: An Ethnic History. LC 82-48691. 320p. 1984. pap. 18.95 (0-02-900980-4) Free Pr.

— Correlation & Regression Analysis: A Historian's Guide. LC 92-56927. (Illus.). 374p. (Orig.). (C). 1994. pap. text 24.95 (0-299-13654-X) U of Wis Pr.

Archdeacon, Tim. Amplifiers: U. S. Markets, Materials & Opportunities, 1991-1994 Analysis. 125p. 1992. 1800.00 (1-883742-00-5) Allied Busn.

— Crystal Oscillators - U. S. Markets, Applications, & Competitors: 1993-1998 Analysis & Forecasts. 100p. 1994. pap. text 1900.00 (1-878218-45-X) World Info Tech.

— Medium & High Voltage Electrical Insulators, 1991-1996 Analysis: North American Markets, Technologies & Opportunities. (Illus.). 125p. (Orig.). 1991. pap. 1800.00 (1-878218-16-6) World Info Tech.

— Oscillators, North American Markets, Applications & Competitors: 1992-1996 Analysis. 250p. 1900.00 (1-883742-02-1) Allied Busn.

— Telecommunications Outside Plant Products - U. S. Markets, End-Users & Competitors: 1991-1996 Analysis. (Illus.). 260p. 1992. pap. text 2400.00 (1-878218-25-5) World Info Tech.

— U. S. Crystal Oscillator Markets, Technologies, & Opportunities: 1991-1996 Analysis. (Illus.). 175p. 1991. pap. text 1800.00 (1-878218-21-2) World Info Tech.

Archdeacon, Tim, ed. see Carter, Don.

Archdeacon, Tim, ed. see Fuertes, Andy.

Archdeacon, Tim, ed. see Fuertes, Andy & Sweet, Bill.

Archdeacon, Tim, ed. see Hirschhurn, Stuart.

Archdeacon, Tim, ed. see Katz, Jake.

Archdeacon, Tim, ed. see Simon, Sean G. & Hebner, Paul.

Archdiocese of Baltimore Staff, ed. The Papal Visit: Pope John Paul II in Baltimore. LC 95-71402. (Illus.). 128p. 1995. 39.95 (1-885938-01-2) Cathdrl Fndtn Pr.

Archdiocese of Detroit Staff. Come Holy Spirit: Practical Prayer Services for Parish Meetings. LC 96-9294. 112p. 1996. pap. 11.95 (0-87793-592-0) Ave Maria.

Archdiocese of Milwaukee Staff. Milwaukee Symposia for Church Composers: A Ten Year Report. 16p. 1992. pap. 4.95 (0-912405-43-0, Pastoral Press) OR Catholic.

Archdiocese of Sao Paulo Staff. Torture in Brazil: A Shocking Report on the Pervasive Use of Torture by Brazilian Military Governments, 1964-1979. rev. ed. Dassin, Joan, ed. Wright, Jamie, tr. from POR. LC 98-13511. Orig. Title: Brasil: Nunca Mais (Brazil: Never Again). 268p. 1998. pap. 15.95 (0-292-70484-4, CATTOP) U of Tex Pr.

Archduke Rudolph of Austria. Archduke Rudolph of Austria: Forty Variations on a Theme by Beethoven; Sonata in F Minor for Violin & Piano. Kagan, Susan, ed. (Recent Researches in Music of the 19th & Early 20th Centuries Ser.: Vol. RRN21). (Illus.). xiv, 136p. 1992. pap. 50.00 (0-89579-275-3) A-R Eds.

Archell, Doug. NetWare 3.12 System Administration. LC 94-67942. 1994. 27.99 (1-56529-925-6) Que.

Archenhold, W. F., jt. auth. see Treloar, L. R.

Archenti, Augustine & Pedrini, Arnold. Every Day with Saint Francis de Sales: Teachings & Examples from the Life of the Saint. Klauder, Francis J., ed. Cornell, Wallace L., tr. from ITA. LC 85-72838. Orig. Title: Buon Giorno. (Illus.). xii, 379p. (Orig.). 1997. reprint ed. pap. 13.00 (0-89944-082-7, 082-7) Salesiana Pubs.

Archer. College Macroeconomics. (C). 1996. pap. text, student ed. write for info. (0-201-82901-0) Addison-Wesley.

— Extraordinary Measures. (C). 1998. text 50.00 (0-15-501357-2) Harcourt Coll Pubs.

— Imperial Glass. (Illus.). 1995. reprint ed. pap. 14.95 (0-89145-074-2, 1008) Collector Bks.

Archer & Marshall. Your Food & Health: A Study Guide for Man's Food. 4th ed. 234p. (C). 1998. spiral bd. 39.95 (0-7872-5114-3) Kendall-Hunt.

Archer, Jr., et al. The Expositor's Bible Commentary, Vol. 7. 1986. 37.99 (0-88469-194-2) BMH Bks.

Archer, A. A., et al, eds. Man's Dependence on the Earth: The Role of Geosciences in the Environment. (Illus.). xiii, 216p. 1987. text 41.00 (3-510-65128-6, Pub. by E Schweizerbartsche) Balogh.

Archer, A. C. The Man with the Thorn in His Flesh. pap. 4.99 (0-88019-146-5) Schmul Pub Co.

Archer, A. J. Car Living: How to Make It a Successful, Sane, Safe Experience. LC 99-93722. 72p. 1999. pap. 15.95 (0-9649573-1-0) Touchstone Advent.

Archer, A. Jane. Teaching Organics: Fun Activities for Home & School. (Illus.). 128p. (J). 1999. pap. 15.95 (0-9649573-2-9) Touchstone Advent.

— What to Do When the Stock Market Falls: Learn from the Financial Experts Who Saw It Coming. LC 95-90960. 128p. (Orig.). 1996. pap. 12.95 (0-9649573-0-2) Touchstone Advent.

Archer, Alan. The Aston Martin. (C). 1989. pap. 25.00 (0-85263-980-5, Pub. by Shire Pubns) St Mut.

Archer, Alan W. The Lichen Genus Pertusaria in Australia. (Bibliotheca Lichenologica Ser.: Vol. 69). (Illus.). 249p. 1997. 76.70 (3-443-58048-3, Pub. by Gebruder Borntraeger) Balogh.

Archer, B. A., tr. see Chuvin, Pierre.

Archer, Beth, tr. see Chastel, Andre.

*Archer, Bill, ed. Background Material & Data on Programs Within the Jurisdiction of the Committee on Ways & Means: 1998 Green Book, Overview of Entitlement Programs. (Illus.). 1492p. 1999. pap. text 95.00 (0-7881-8155-6) DIANE Pub.

*Archer, Bill & Roth, William V., Jr., eds. Analysis of Proposed Tax & Savings Incentives for Higher Education. 96p. (C). 1999. reprint ed. pap. text 20.00 (0-7881-7611-0) DIANE Pub.

— Impact on Individuals & Families of Replacing the Federal Income Tax: House Committee on Ways & Means. (Illus.). 135p. (C). 2000. reprint ed. pap. text 25.00 (0-7881-8511-X) DIANE Pub.

Archer, Bill, jt. ed. see Roth, William.

*Archer, Bob. U. S. Air Force. (Illus.). 176p. 2000. pap. 29.95 (1-85780-102-4, Pub. by Midland Pubng) Specialty Pr.

*Archer, Bob & Jurden, Dan. Creating Visual FoxPro Applications with Visual FoxExpress. Feltman, Mike, ed. 400p. 2000. pap. 49.95 (1-930919-03-4) Hentzenwerke.

Archer, C. Black & White Skin Diseases. (Illus.). 320p. 1995. 165.00 (0-632-02529-8) Blackwell Sci.

Archer, C., adapted by. The Angry Intruder. LC 95-4806. (Christy Fiction Ser.: Vol. 3). 128p. (J). (gr. 5-9). 1995. mass mkt. 4.99 (0-8499-3688-8) Tommy Nelson.

— The Bridge to Cutter Gap. LC 95-13127. (Christy Fiction Ser.: Vol. 1). 128p. (J). (gr. 5-9). 1995. mass mkt. 4.99 (*0-8499-3686-1*) Tommy Nelson.
— Brotherly Love. LC 97-11071. (Christy Fiction Ser.: Vol. 12). 128p. (Orig.). (YA). (gr. 5-8). 1997. mass mkt. 4.99 (*0-8499-3963-1*) Tommy Nelson.
— Christy's Choice. (Christy Fiction Ser.: Vol. 6). 128p. (Orig.). (YA). (gr. 5-8). 1996. mass mkt. 4.99 (*0-8499-3919-4*) Tommy Nelson.
— Family Secrets. (Christy Fiction Ser.: Vol. 8). (Illus.). 128p. (Orig.). (YA). (gr. 5-8). 1996. mass mkt. 4.99 (*0-8499-3959-3*) Tommy Nelson.
— Goodbye, Sweet Prince. LC 97-532. (Christy Fiction Ser.: Vol. 11). 128p. (Orig.). (J). (gr. 5-9). 1997. pap. 4.99 (*0-8499-3962-3*) Tommy Nelson.
— Midnight Rescue. LC 95-13160. (Christy Fiction Ser.: Vol. 4). 128p. (J). (gr. 5-9). 1995. mass mkt. 4.99 (*0-8499-3689-6*) Tommy Nelson.
— Mountain Madness. adapted ed. LC 96-38918. (Christy Fiction Ser.: Vol. 9). 128p. (Orig.). (J). (gr. 5-9). 1997. mass mkt. 4.99 (*0-8499-3960-7*) Tommy Nelson.
— The Princess Club. LC 96-26806. (Christy Fiction Ser.: No. 7). 128p. (J). (gr. 5-9). 1996. pap. text 4.99 (*0-8499-3958-5*) Tommy Nelson.
— The Proposal. LC 95-53078. (Christy Fiction Ser.: Vol. 5). 128p. (J). (gr. 5-9). 1995. mass mkt. 4.99 (*0-8499-3918-6*) Tommy Nelson.
— Stage Fright. LC 96-45388. (Christy Fiction Ser.: Vol. 10). (Illus.). 128p. (J). (gr. 5-9). 1997. mass mkt. 4.99 (*0-8499-3961-5*) Tommy Nelson.

Archer, C. & Kincaid, B., adapted by. Silent Superstitions. LC 95-13126. (Christy Fiction Ser.: Vol. 2). 128p. (J). (gr. 5-9). 1995. mass mkt. 4.99 (*0-8499-3687-X*) Tommy Nelson.

Archer, C., jt. ed. see Cerio, Rino.

Archer, Carine, ed. Estate Planning Practice: December 1993 Update, Set, Vols. 1 & 2. LC 86-7314. 420p. 1993. 99.00 (*0-88124-681-6*, ES-30854) Cont Ed Bar-CA.
— Estate Planning, 1989. LC 82-640282. 495p. 1990. text 80.00 (*0-88124-184-9*, ES-31280) Cont Ed Bar-CA.
— Estate Planning, 1990. LC 82-64082. 406p. 1991. pap. text 90.00 (*0-88124-349-3*, ES-31600) Cont Ed Bar-CA.

Archer, Carine, ed. see Depper, Estelle M.

Archer, Carine, ed. see Depper, Estelle M., et al.

Archer, Carine, ed. see Johnstone, William S., Jr., et al.

Archer, Carine, ed. see Kellogg, Irving.

Archer, Carol. Living with Strangers in the U. S. A. Communicating Beyond Culture. 128p. (C). 1990. pap. text 28.60 (*0-13-538620-9*) P-H.

***Archer, Caroline.** Parenting the Child Who Hurts: The First Steps. LC 99-41636. 1999. pap. 19.95 (*1-85302-801-0*) Jessica Kingsley.
— Parenting the Child Who Hurts: The Next Steps, Vol. 2. LC 99-41637. 1999. pap. 24.95 (*1-85302-802-9*) Jessica Kingsley.

***Archer, Catherine.** Bride of Spring. (Historical Ser.: Vol. 514). 2000. per. 4.99 (*0-373-29114-0*) Harlequin Bks.

Archer, Catherine. Fire Song: 10th Anniversary Promotion. anniversary ed. (Historical Ser.: Vol. 426). 1998. per. 4.99 (*0-373-29026-8*, 1-29026-1) Harlequin Bks.
— Lady Thorn. (Historical Ser.). 1997. per. 4.99 (*0-373-28953-7*, 1-28953-7) Harlequin Bks.
— Lord Sin. 1997. per. 4.99 (*0-373-28979-0*, 1-28979-2) Harlequin Bks.
— Velvet Bond. LC 96-342. (Historical Ser.). 299p. 1995. per. 4.50 (*0-373-28882-4*, 1-28882-8) Harlequin Bks.
— Velvet Touch. (Historical Ser.). 1996. per. 4.99 (*0-373-28922-7*, 1-28922-2) Harlequin Bks.
— Winter's Bride. (Historical Ser.). 1999. per. 4.99 (*0-373-29077-2*, 1-29077-4) Harlequin Bks.

***Archer, Charles W., et al, eds.** Biology of the Synovial Joint. (Illus.). 654p. 1998. text 70.00 (*90-5702-327-X*, Harwood Acad Pubs) Gordon & Breach.

Archer, Cheryl. Snow Watch: Experiments, Activities & Things to Do with Snow. unabridged ed. (Illus.). 56p. (J). (gr. 3-6). 1994. pap. 9.95 (*1-55074-190-X*, Pub. by Kids Can Pr) Genl Dist Srvs.

Archer, Chris. Alien Blood. (Mindwarp Ser.: No. 2). (YA). (gr. 6-8). 1997. pap. 3.99 (*0-671-01483-8*, Minstrel Bks) PB.
— Alien Blood. (Mindwarp Ser.: No. 2). (YA). (gr. 6-8). 1997. 9.09 (*0-606-12771-2*, Pub. by Turtleback) Demco.
— Alien Scream. (Mindwarp Ser.: No. 3). (YA). (gr. 6-8). 1997. pap. 3.99 (*0-671-01484-6*, Minstrel Bks) PB.
— Alien Terror. (Mindwarp Ser.: No. 1). (YA). (gr. 6-8). 1997. pap. 3.99 (*0-671-01482-X*) PB.
— Alien Terror. (Mindwarp Ser.: No. 1). (J). (gr. 3-6). 1997. 9.09 (*0-606-12770-4*, Pub. by Turtleback) Demco.
— Face the Fear. (Mindwarp Ser.: No. 8). (YA). (gr. 4-7). 1998. pap. 3.99 (*0-671-02168-0*, Minstrel Bks) PB.
— Flash Forward. (Mindwarp Ser.: No. 7). (YA). (gr. 6-8). 1998. pap. 3.99 (*0-671-02167-2*, Minstrel Bks) PB.
— Meltdown. (Mindwarp Ser.: No. 10). (YA). (gr. 6-8). 1999. pap. 3.99 (*0-671-02170-2*, Minstrel Bks) PB.
— Out of Time. (Mindwarp Ser.: No. 9). 144p. (YA). (gr. 4-7). 1998. pap. 3.99 (*0-671-02169-9*, Minstrel Bks) PB.
— Second Sight. (Mindwarp Ser.: No. 4). (YA). (gr. 4-7). 1998. pap. 3.99 (*0-671-01485-4*) PB.
— Shape-Shifter. (Mindwarp Ser.: No. 5). (YA). (gr. 6-8). 1998. pap. 3.99 (*0-671-01486-2*, Minstrel Bks) PB.

***Archer, Christon, et al, eds.** The Wars of Independence in Spanish America. LC 99-45128. (Jaguar Books on Latin America: No. 20). 384p. 2000. 55.00 (*0-8420-2468-9*, SR Bks) Scholarly Res Inc.
— The Wars of Independence in Spanish America. LC 99-45128. (Jaguar Books on Latin America: No. 20). (Illus.). 384p. 2000. pap. 18.95 (*0-8420-2469-7*, SR Bks) Scholarly Res Inc.

Archer, Christon, jt. ed. see Travers, Timothy.

Archer, Clive. International Organizations. (Key Concepts in International Relations Ser.: No. 1). 160p. (Orig.). 1983. pap. text 17.95 (*0-04-320157-1*) Routledge.
— International Organizations. 2nd ed. LC 91-39334. 208p. (Orig.). (C). 1992. pap. 25.99 (*0-415-07837-7*, A7467) Routledge.
— Organizing Europe: The Institutions of Integration. 2nd ed. LC 93-23351. (An Arnold Publication). (Illus.). 320p. 1998. pap. text 22.00 (*0-340-59039-4*, Pub. by E A) OUP.

Archer, Clive, ed. The Soviet Union & Northern Waters. 288p. 1988. lib. bdg. 52.50 (*0-415-00489-6*) Routledge.

Archer, Clive & Butler, Fiona. The European Union: Structure & Process. 2nd ed. 256p. 1997. pap. 29.95 (*1-85567-304-5*) Bks Intl VA.
— European Union: Structure & Process. 2nd ed. 256p. 1996. pap. 21.95 (*0-312-12769-3*) St Martin.

Archer, Clive & Main, John, eds. Scotland's Voice in International Affairs. 160p. 1980. 55.00 (*0-7735-0512-1*, Pub. by McG-Queens Univ Pr) CUP Services.

Archer, Clive & Scrivener, David, eds. Northern Waters: Resources & Security Issues. 256p. 1986. 61.00 (*0-389-20657-1*, N8215) B&N Imports.

Archer, Clive, jt. ed. see Jonson, Lena.

Archer, Colleen R. Riding High. 73p. (YA). (gr. 9-12). 1986. 7.95 (*0-920806-39-2*, Pub. by Penumbra Pr) U of Toronto Pr.

Archer, Dane & Gartner, Rosemary. Violence & Crime in Cross-National Perspective. LC 83-21700. 342p. 1987. pap. 20.00 (*0-300-04023-7*) Yale U Pr.

Archer, Daniel & Bullock, Walter. Mr. Barry's Etchings. 1950. pap. 5.25 (*0-8222-0779-6*) Dramatists Play.

Archer, Darrell. Christmas Piano. 32p. 1986. pap. 5.95 (*0-87166-075-X*, 94116) Mel Bay.

Archer, Dennis, et al. 96 Ways You Can Save Taxes in '96: Washington Edition. 128p. (Orig.). Date not set. pap. 9.95 (*1-888303-00-X*) Loopholes Pr.

Archer, Don, ed. Child Support Performance & Incentive Act of 1998: Report of the Committee on Ways & Means, U. S. House of Representatives. 62p. (C). 1999. pap. text 20.00 (*0-7881-7843-1*) DIANE Pub.

Archer, Doug. Iowa Agriculture. (History of Iowa Ser.). (Illus.). 56p. (Orig.). (YA). (gr. 9 up). 1988. pap. text 1.50 (*0-924702-04-4*) Grn Valley Area.

Archer, Douglas L., jt. auth. see Marshall, Maurice.

Archer, E. C. & Pemberton, LeRoy A. Typing Skill Drills. 1973. pap. text 6.95 (*0-89420-103-4*, 143000) Natl Book.

Archer, Earnest R. Influence & Motivation: A Managerial Perspective. (Illus.). 321p. (C). 1987. text 19.95 (*0-925628-00-X*) Wesley Cabot & Keith Pub.

Archer, Edgar G., ed. see Letterman, Jonathan & Clements, Bennett A.

Archer, Elayne, jt. auth. see Pincus, Fred L.

Archer, Ellen. Darling. 352p. 1996. mass mkt. 4.99 (*0-8217-5235-9*, Zebra Kensgtn) Kensgtn Pub Corp.
— Taboo. large type ed. (Black Satin Romance Ser.). 336p. 1996. 27.99 (*1-86110-013-2*) Ulverscroft.
— Tiger Lil. 288p. 1997. mass mkt. 4.99 (*0-8217-5644-3*, Zebra Kensgtn) Kensgtn Pub Corp.

Archer, Emma & Turner, B. L., III. Introduction to the Human Dimensions of Global Change. (Active Learning Modules on the Human Dimensions of Global Change Ser.). (Illus.). 132p. (C). 1997. pap., teacher ed. 20.00 (*0-89291-239-1*); pap., student ed., wbk. ed. 8.75 (*0-89291-240-5*) Assn Am Geographers.

Archer, Ethel. The Whirlpool. 1993. reprint ed. 27.50 (*1-55818-215-2*, First Impress) Holmes Pub.

Archer, Francis B. Gambia Colony & Protectorate: An Official Handbook. 342p. 1967. reprint ed. 45.00 (*0-7146-1139-5*, BHA-01139, Pub. by F Cass Pubs) Intl Spec Bk.

Archer, Fred. Benedict's Pool. 2000. 29.95 (*0-7509-2135-8*) Sutton Pub Ltd.
— The Cuckoo Pen: Tales of English Village Life Between the Wars. LC 97-187146. (Illus.). 160p. 1997. pap. 14.95 (*0-7509-1288-X*, Pub. by Sutton Pub Ltd) Intl Pubs Mktg.
— Farmers, Craftsmen & Music Makers: Life in a Worcestershire Village Between the Wars. (Illus.). 192p. 1994. 26.95 (*0-7509-0572-7*, Pub. by Sutton Pub Ltd) Intl Pubs Mktg.
— Fred Archer, Farmer's Son: Life As a Farmer's Son. large type ed. (Reminiscence Ser.). 23.95 (*1-85695-161-8*, Pub. by ISIS Lrg Prnt) Transaction Pubs.
— Hawthorn Farm. (Illus.). 160p. 1998. pap. 29.95 (*0-7509-1472-6*, Pub. by Sutton Pub Ltd) Intl Pubs Mktg.
— Muddy Boots & Sunday Suits. large type ed. (Reminiscence Ser.). 23.95 (*1-85695-104-9*, Pub. by ISIS Lrg Prnt) Transaction Pubs.
— The Secrets of Bredon Hill: A Country Chronicle. large type ed. 1998. 24.95 (*0-7531-5046-8*, Pub. by ISIS Lrg Prnt) T T Beeler.
— Sir Lionel. (Illus.). 339p. 1980. 12.95 (*0-86595-005-9*) Gift Pubns.
— The Tibblestone Hundred: A Journey Through an English Village. (Illus.). 160p. 1996. 26.95 (*0-7509-1256-1*, Pub. by Sutton Pub Ltd) Intl Pubs Mktg.

Archer, Fred, et al. Engineering Statics. 2nd ed. 240p. 1998. pap. text 49.95 (*0-86840-425-X*) Intl Spec Bk.

Archer, Fred C. & Stewart, Jeffrey R., Jr. Model Office Practice Set. 2nd ed. 1975. text 12.96 (*0-07-002306-9*) McGraw.

Archer, Fred C., Jr., et al. Accounts Payable Practice Set. 1969. text 12.96 (*0-07-002196-1*) McGraw.

Archer, Fred C., et al. Accounts Receivable Practice Set. 1970. text 12.96 (*0-07-002195-3*) McGraw.
— Office Cashiering Practice Set. 1969. text 12.96 (*0-07-002167-8*) McGraw.
— Stock Control Practice Set. 1969. text 12.96 (*0-07-002176-7*) McGraw.

Archer, Frederick M. Working for the Lord Like the Devil: A Look at Institutionalized Christianity. 102p. (Orig.). 1990. pap. 7.95 (*0-9625823-0-1*) Archer Pub.

Archer, Gail, ed. see Strozzi, Barbara.

***Archer, Geoffrey.** Skydancer. large type ed. LC 99-43729. (Thorndike Mystery Ser.). 1999. 25.95 (*0-7862-2226-3*) Mac Lib Ref.

Archer, Gleason L., Jr. Big Business & Radio. LC 76-161133. (History of Broadcasting: Radio to Television Ser.). 1976. reprint ed. 40.95 (*0-405-03558-6*) Ayer.

Archer, Gleason L. Dictionary of Biblical Manners & Customs. LC 96-22775. (Counterpoints Ser.). 1996. 39.99 (*0-310-21270-7*) Zondervan.

Archer, Gleason L., Jr. An Encyclopedia of Bible Difficulties. 480p. 1982. 24.99 (*0-310-43570-6*, 11252) Zondervan.

Archer, Gleason L. Ethical Obligations of the Lawyer. 367p. 1981. reprint ed. 37.50 (*0-8377-0207-0*, Rothman) W S Hein.

Archer, Gleason L., Jr. History of Radio to 1926. LC 72-161132. (History of Broadcasting: Radio to Television Ser.). (Illus.). 1975. reprint ed. 30.95 (*0-405-03557-8*) Ayer.

Archer, Gleason L. Resena Critica de una Introduccion al Antiguo Testamento.Tr. of Survey of Old Testament Introduction. (SPA.). 576p. 1982. pap. 16.99 (*0-8254-1033-9*, Edit Portavoz) Kregel.
— Survey of the Old Testament Introduction. 1996. pap. 29.99 (*0-8024-8201-5*) Moody.
— Three Views on the Rapture: Pre, Mid or Post-Tribulation? LC 96-22775. (Counterpoints Ser.). 272p. 1996. pap. 14.99 (*0-310-21298-7*) Zondervan.

Archer, Gleason L., et al, eds. The Illustrated Children's Bible. (Illus.). 300p. (J). (ps-6). 1993. 15.99 (*0-529-07657-8*, WICB) World Publng.

Archer, Gleason L., ed. see Hill, Gary.

Archer, Gordon, jt. auth. see Crossley, Kent B.

Archer, Helen M. Tales, Rhymes & Other Stuff. unabridged ed. Wegeng, Lana & Adams, Paul, eds. (Illus.). 131p. 1997. pap. 13.50 (*0-9659454-1-3*) Columbia Pubns.

Archer-Hind, Richard D., ed. see Plato.

Archer, Horace R., ed. Rare Book Collections: Some Theoretical & Practical Suggestions for Use by Librarians & Students, 27. LC 81-13311. (ACRL Monograph: No. 27). 128p. 1982. reprint ed. lib. bdg. 55.00 (*0-313-23226-1*, ARRB) Greenwood.

Archer, J., jt. auth. see Dowdy, J.

Archer, J. Clark & Shelley, Fred M. American Electoral Mosaics. LC 85-26810. (Resource Publications in Geography). (Orig.). 1986. pap. text 15.00 (*0-89291-195-6*) Assn Am Geographers.

Archer, J. Clark & Taylor, Peter J. Section & Party: A Political Geography of American Presidential Elections from Andrew Jackson to Ronald Reagan. LC 81-182752. (Geographical Research Studies: No. 4). (Illus.). 285p. reprint ed. pap. 88.40 (*0-8357-3529-X*, 203421100089) Bks Demand.

Archer, J. Clark, jt. auth. see Shelley, Fred M.

Archer, Jack H., et al. The Public Trust Doctrine & the Management of America's Coasts. LC 93-48759. 208p. 1994. lib. bdg. 35.00 (*0-87023-898-1*) U of Mass Pr.

Archer, James, Jr. & Cooper, Stewart. Counseling & Mental Health Services on Campus: A Handbook of Contemporary Practices. LC 98-22390. (Education Ser.). 496p. 1998. 39.95 (*0-7879-1026-0*) Jossey-Bass.

Archer, Jane. The Blue Goose B & B. LC 95-35261. 1995. pap. 5.00 (*0-88734-347-3*) Players Pr.
— Caught in the Act. LC 90-53079. 1991. pap. 6.00 (*0-88734-222-1*) Players Pr.

***Archer, Jane.** Exploring Texas Natural Habitats with Children. (Illus.). 300p. 2000. pap. 18.95 (*1-55622-783-3*, Rep of TX Pr) Wordware Pub.

Archer, Jane. Lady Besieged: Playscript. LC 90-53080. (Orig.). 1990. pap. 6.00 (*0-88734-221-3*) Players Pr.
— Maverick Moon. 1997. per. 5.99 (*0-671-53708-3*, Pocket Books) PB.
— One Sharp & Two Flats. LC 90-53338. (Orig.). 1990. pap. 5.00 (*0-88734-319-8*) Players Pr.
— Out of the West. 1996. mass mkt. 5.99 (*0-671-53710-5*) PB.

***Archer, Jane.** Texas Indian Myths & Legends. (Illus.). 1999. pap. 18.95 (*1-55622-725-6*, Rep of TX Pr) Wordware Pub.

Archer, Jeanne S., jt. auth. see Taylor, Dan.

Archer, Jeanne S., jt. auth. see Taylor, Don.

Archer, Jeff. Strike Four: Adventures in European Baseball. White, Colin et al, eds. (Illus.). 250p. (Orig.). 1995. pap. 12.50 (*0-9625006-7-4*) White-Boucke.
— Theater in a Squared Circle: The Mystique of Professional Wrestling. Boucke, Rick & Carlson, Linda, eds. (Illus.). 446p. 1999. pap. 18.50 (*1-888580-06-2*) White-Boucke.

Archer, Jeffrey. Aftershock. (Mindwarp Ser.: No. 6). (YA). (gr. 6-8). 1998. pap. 3.99 (*0-671-01487-0*) PB.
— As the Crow Flies. 800p. 1992. mass mkt. 7.50 (*0-06-109934-1*, Harp PBks) HarpC.
— Beyond Reasonable Doubt. LC 90-144519. (Illus.). 55p. 1989. 8.95 (*0-573-01676-3*) S French Trade.
— The Eleventh Commandment. LC 98-3670. 368p. 1998. 26.00 (*0-06-019150-3*) HarpC.
— The Eleventh Commandment. large type ed. LC 98-28861. 548p. 1998. 30.00 (*0-7862-1592-5*) Thorndike Pr.
— The Eleventh Commandment. large type ed. LC 98-28861. 548p. 1999. pap. 30.00 (*0-7862-1593-3*) Thorndike Pr.
— The Eleventh Commandment: A Novel. 448p. 1999. mass mkt. 7.99 (*0-06-101331-5*) HarpC.

***Archer, Jeffrey.** The Eleventh Commandment: Jarvis,&Martin, Set. abr. ed. 1998. audio. write for info. (*0-694-51973-1*, 696013, Pub. by HarperAudio) Lndmrk Audiobks.

Archer, Jeffrey. First Among Equals. 496p. 1993. mass mkt. 6.99 (*0-06-100716-1*, Harp PBks) HarpC.
— The Fourth Estate. 752p. 1997. mass mkt. 7.50 (*0-06-109203-7*, Harp PBks) HarpC.
— The Fourth Estate. large type ed. LC 96-31421. 1996. 28.95 (*0-7838-1912-9*, G K Hall Lrg Type) Mac Lib Ref.
— The Fourth Estate. large type ed. LC 96-31421. 793p. 1997. pap. 26.95 (*0-7838-1913-7*, G K Hall Lrg Type) Mac Lib Ref.

Archer, Jeffrey. The Fourth Estate: Jarvis,&Martin, Set. abr. ed. 1996. audio 25.00 (*0-694-51689-9*, 694095) HarperAudio.

Archer, Jeffrey. Honor Among Thieves. LC 92-56224. 480p. 1994. mass mkt. 6.99 (*0-06-109204-5*) HarpC.
— Kane & Abel: Kane & Abel. 592p. 1993. mass mkt. 7.50 (*0-06-100712-9*, Harp PBks) HarpC.
— A Matter of Honor. 368p. 1993. mass mkt. 6.50 (*0-06-100713-7*, Harp PBks) HarpC.
— Not a Penny More, Not a Penny Less. 320p. 1994. mass mkt. 6.50 (*0-06-100735-8*, Harp PBks) HarpC.
— Not a Penny More, Not a Penny Less. 1990. per. 4.50 (*0-671-69353-0*) PB.
— The Prodigal Daughter. 496p. 1993. mass mkt. 7.50 (*0-06-100714-5*, Harp PBks) HarpC.
— The Proprietors. 1995. 25.00 (*0-614-96259-5*) HarpC.
— A Quiver Full of Arrows. 224p. 1993. mass mkt. 5.50 (*0-06-100715-3*, Harp PBks) HarpC.

***Archer, Jeffrey.** A Quiver Full of Arrows: Jeffrey Archer. LC 00-42578. 2000. write for info. (*0-7862-2685-4*) Thorndike Pr.
— Selected Stories: Jarvis,&Martin, Set. 1998. audio 25.00 (*0-694-52056-X*) HarperAudio.

Archer, Jeffrey. Shall We Tell the President? 288p. 1987. mass mkt. 5.50 (*0-671-63305-8*) PB.
— Shall We Tell the President. 336p. 1999. mass mkt. 6.99 (*0-06-101370-6*) HarpC.
— Twelve Red Herrings. 384p. 1995. mass mkt. 6.50 (*0-06-109365-3*, Harp PBks) HarpC.
— A Twist in the Tale. 1991. pap. text. write for info. (*0-582-06022-2*, Pub. by Addison-Wesley) Longman.
— A Twist in the Tale. 256p. 1994. mass mkt. 5.99 (*0-06-100717-X*, Harp PBks) HarpC.

***Archer, Jeffrey & Bainbridge, Simon, eds.** Fools, Knaves, & Heroes: Great Political Short Stories. 245p. 1998. reprint ed. 20.00 (*0-7881-7392-8*) DIANE Pub.

***Archer, Jennifer.** Body & Soul. 368p. 1999. mass mkt. 5.50 (*0-505-52334-5*, Pub. by Dorchester Pub Co) CMG.

Archer, John. Crop Nutrition & Fertilizer Use. 2nd ed. 278p. 1988. 34.95 (*0-85236-175-0*, Pub. by Farming Pr) Diamond Farm Bk.
— The Nature of Grief: The Evolution & Psychology of Reactions to Loss. LC 98-20134. (Illus.). 336p. (C). 1999. 90.00 (*0-415-17857-6*); pap. 31.99 (*0-415-17858-4*) Routledge.
— Winning at Poker: An Expert's Guide. 1978. 10.00 (*0-87980-362-2*) Wilshire.
— Winning at Twenty-One. 1977. reprint ed. pap. 10.00 (*0-87980-328-2*) Wilshire.

Archer, John, ed. Male Violence. 352p. (C). 1993. pap. 27.99 (*0-415-08962-X*) Routledge.

Archer, John & Browne, Kevin, eds. Human Aggression: Naturalistic Approaches. LC 89-183537. 300p. reprint ed. pap. 93.00 (*0-608-20308-4*, 207156100002) Bks Demand.

Archer, John & Lloyd, Barbara. Sex & Gender. (Illus.). 286p. 1985. pap. text 19.95 (*0-521-31921-8*) Cambridge U Pr.

Archer, John, jt. auth. see Lydenberg, Harry M.

Archer, John, jt. ed. see Browne, Kevin D.

Archer, John C. Faiths Men Live By. LC 79-156606. (Essay Index Reprint Ser.). 1977. reprint ed. 28.95 (*0-8369-2266-2*) Ayer.
— Mystical Elements in Mohammed. LC 80-26396. (Yale Oriental Series: Researches: No. 11 Pt. 1; All Published). reprint ed. 39.50 (*0-404-60281-9*) AMS Pr.

Archer, John E. By a Flash & a Scare: Incendiarism, Animal Maiming, & Poaching in East Anglia, 1815-1870. (Illus.). 296p. 1990. 85.00 (*0-19-820177-X*) OUP.

***Archer, John E.** Social Unrest & Popular Protest in England, 1780-1840. (New Studies in Economic & Social History). (Illus.). 128p. 2001. write for info. (*0-521-57216-9*); pap. write for info. (*0-521-57656-3*) Cambridge U Pr.

Archer, John M. Sovereignty & Intelligence: Spying & Court Culture in the English Renaissance. LC 92-30593. 216p. 1993. 37.50 (*0-8047-2079-7*) Stanford U Pr.

Archer, John M., jt. ed. see Burt, Richard.

Archer, John S. & Wall, Colin G. Petroleum Engineering: Principles & Practice. (Illus.). 350p. 1986. pap. text 85.50 (*0-86010-715-9*) G & T Inc.
— Petroleum Engineering: Principles & Practice. (Illus.). 350p. 1986. lib. bdg. 152.00 (*0-86010-665-9*) G & T Inc.

Archer, Jules. Breaking Barriers: The Feminist Revolution from Susan B. Anthony to Margaret Sanger to Betty Friedan. LC 90-42043. (Epoch Biographies Ser.). 1996. 11.09 (*0-606-09103-3*, Pub. by Turtleback) Demco.
— Breaking Barriers: The Feminist Revolution from Susan B. Anthony to Margaret Sanger to Betty Friedan. (Illus.). 207p. (J). 1998. reprint ed. text 15.00 (*0-7881-5195-9*) DIANE Pub.
— Children of War: Growing up in Nicaragua. LC 89-78456. 1990. write for info. (*0-15-217335-8*) Harcourt.
— Earthquake! LC 90-45370. (Nature's Disasters Ser.). (Illus.). 48p. (J). (gr. 5-6). 1991. lib. bdg. 16.95 (*0-89686-593-2*) Silver Burdett Pr.

A

An Asterisk (*) at the beginning of an entry indicates that the title is appearing for the first time.

A

— A House Divided: The Lives of Ulysses S. Grant & Robert E. Lee. 192p. (J). (gr. 3-7). 1995. 14.95 (0-590-48325-0) Scholastic Inc.
— A House Divided: The Lives of Ulysses S. Grant & Robert E. Lee. LC 93-38886. 208p. (J). (gr. 3-7). 1997. 3.99 (0-590-46102-8) Scholastic Inc.
— A House Divided, the Lives of Ulysses S. Grant & Robert E. Lee. (Scholastic Biography Ser.). (J). 1997. 9.09 (0-606-11481-5, Pub. by Turtleback) Demco.
— Hurricane! LC 90-45369. (Nature's Disasters Ser.). (Illus.). 48p. (J). (gr. 5-6). 1991. lib. bdg. 12.95 (0-89686-597-5, Crstwood Hse) Silver Burdett Pr.
— The Incredible Sixties: The Stormy Years That Changed America. LC 85-16421. (Illus.). 223p. (J). (gr. 7 up). 1986. 17.95 (0-15-238298-4, Harcourt Child Bks) Harcourt.
— Special Interests: How Lobbyists Influence Our Legislation. LC 96-27076. 144p. (YA). (gr. 7 up). 1997. lib. bdg. 23.90 (0-7613-0060-0) Millbrook Pr.
— Superspies: The Secret Side of Government. LC 77-72640. (J). (gr. 7). 1977. pap. 7.95 (0-440-08136-X) Delacorte.
— They Had a Dream: The Civil Rights Struggle, from Frederick Douglass to Marcus Garvey to Martin. (Epoch Biographies Ser.). 1996. 11.09 (0-606-09964-6, Pub. by Turtleback) Demco.
— They Had a Dream: The Civil Rights Struggle from Frederick Douglass to Marcus Garvey to Martin Luther King, Jr., & Malcolm X. (Illus.). 272p. (YA). (gr. 5 up). 1996. pap. 6.99 (0-14-034954-5, PuffinBks) Peng Put Young Read.
— Tornado! LC 90-45373. (Nature's Disasters Ser.). (Illus.). 48p. (J). (gr. 5-6). 1991. lib. bdg. 12.95 (0-89686-594-0, Crstwood Hse) Silver Burdett Pr.
— Winners & Losers: How Elections Work in America. LC 83-18368. (Illus.). 240p. (YA). (gr. 7 up). 1984. 14.95 (0-15-297945-X, Harcourt Child Bks) Harcourt.

Archer, Julian P. The First International in France - 1864-1872: Its Origins, Theories, & Impact. LC 97-33153. 376p. (C). 1997. 62.00 (0-7618-0887-6) U Pr of Amer.
Archer, Keith. Political Choices & Electoral Consequences: A Study of Organized Labour & the New Democratic Party. 128p. (C). 1990. text 60.00 (0-7735-0744-2, Pub. by McG-Queens Univ Pr) CUP Services.
Archer, Keith & Whitehorn, Alan. Political Activists: Ndp In Convention. 320p. 1998. pap. text 29.95 (0-19-541145-5) OUP.
***Archer, Keith & Young, Lisa, eds.** Regionalism & Party Politics in Canada. 224p. 2000. pap. 22.00 (0-19-541599-X) OUP.
Archer, Kenneth. Roerich. (Great Painters Ser.). (Illus.). 176p. 1999. 40.00 (1-85995-483-9) Parkstone Pr.
Archer, Laird. Athens Journal 1940-1941: The Graeco-Italian & the Graeco-German Wars & the German Occupation. 113p. 1983. pap. text 35.95 (0-89126-122-2) MA-AH Pub.
Archer, Laird, ed. Balkan Tragedy. rev. ed. 575p. 1983. pap. text 67.95 (0-89126-120-6) MA-AH Pub.
Archer, Leonie J. Exhausting Our Options. 132p. 1992. 29.95 (0-948061-72-3, P7483) PennWell Bks.
Archer, Leonie J., et al, eds. Women in Ancient Societies: An Illusion of the Night. LC 93-31197. (Illus.). 308p. (C). 1994. pap. 19.99 (0-415-90882-5) Routledge.
***Archer, Lucy.** Architecture in Britain & Ireland. LC 99-490309. 1999. text 55.00 (1-86046-701-6) FS&G.
— Architecture in Britain & Ireland, 600-1500: Saxon, Norman, & Medieval. (Illus.). 228p. 1999. pap. 40.00 (1-86046-404-1, Pub. by Harvill Press) FS&G.
Archer, M. B. Archer. Genealogical History of the Archer Family, from the Time of the Settlement of James Archer 1st to the 5th Generation, 1803-1919. 100p. 1997. reprint ed. pap. 17.00 (0-8328-7291-1); reprint ed. lib. bdg. 27.00 (0-8328-7290-3) Higginson Bk Co.
Archer, Madeline. The Illustrated Bartsch Vol. 28, Commentary: Italian Masters of the Sixteenth Century. (Illus.). 1995. lib. bdg. 149.00 (0-89835-127-8) Abaris Bks.
Archer, Margaret S. Culture & Agency: The Place of Culture in Social Theory. rev. ed. 380p. (C). 1996. pap. text 25.95 (0-521-56441-7) Cambridge U Pr.
— Realist Social Theory: The Morphogenetic Approach. (Illus.). 366p. (C). 1995. text 59.95 (0-521-48176-7); pap. text 20.95 (0-521-48442-1) Cambridge U Pr.
— Social Origins of Educational Systems: The University Edition. abr. ed. LC 83-51281. (Illus.). 238p. reprint ed. pap. 73.80 (0-8357-4738-7, 203765800009) Bks Demand.
***Archer, Martin.** Daze of Our Lives: State of the Art 19th Century Humor. (Illus.). 80p. 2000. 9.95 (0-9701844-0-9) Proudfoot Pr.
Archer, Mary. From Solar Photons to Electrons & Molecules. (Series on Photoconversion of Solar Energy: Vol. 1). 500p. 1999. 86.00 (1-86094-149-4, Pub. by Imperial College) World Scientific Pub.
***Archer, Mary D. & Hill, R., eds.** Photoconversion: Clean Electricity from Photovoltaics. (Series on Photoconversion of Solar Energy: Vol. 2). 670p. 1999. 98.00 (1-86094-161-3) Imperial College.
Archer, Michael. Art since 1960. LC 96-61018. (World of Art Ser.). (Illus.). 224p. (Orig.). 1997. pap. 14.95 (0-500-20298-2, Pub. by Thames Hudson) Norton.
Archer, Michael. Delftware: The Tin-Glazed Earthenware of the British Isles. A Catalogue of the Collection in the Victoria & Albert Museum. (Illus.). 772p. 1997. 207.00 (0-11-290499-8, Pub. by Statnry Office) Balogh.
***Archer, Michael, et al.** Liam Gillick. Kalthoff, Brigitte, tr. from GER. (Illus.). 168p. 2000. pap. 25.00 (0-9671802-3-6) Lukas & Sternberg.
Archer, Mildred. Company Paintings: Indian Paintings of the British Period. (Illus.). 240p. 1992. 45.00 (0-944142-17-6, Pub. by Mapin Pubng) Antique Collect.
Archer, Mildred, ed. The Raffles Drawings. (Oxford in Historical Reprints Ser.). (Illus.). 1979. 55.00 (0-19-580317-5) OUP.
Archer, Mildred, et al. A Journey to Hindoostan: The Graphic Art of British India, 1780-1860. (Illus.). 72p. 13.95 (0-918386-37-3) W Benton Mus.
— Treasures from India: The Clive Collection at Powis Castle. LC 87-12234. (Illus.). 144p. 1987. 25.00 (0-941533-01-8, NAB) I R Dee.
Archer, Myrtle. In the Wilderness. rev. ed. LC 85-73737. 220p. (J). 1986. reprint ed. pap. 6.95 (0-9615263-0-0) Ames Pub Co.
Archer, N. & Burch, M. Pediatric Cardiology: An Introduction. (Illus.). 256p. 1999. text 65.00 (0-412-73450-8, Pub. by E A) OUP.
Archer, N. P., ed. The Sufi Mystery. 2nd ed. 218p. 1988. 25.00 (0-900860-79-0, Pub. by Octagon Pr) ISHK.
Archer, Nathan. Predator: Cold War. 272p. 1997. mass mkt. 4.99 (0-553-57493-0, Spectra) Bantam.
— Predator: Concrete Jungle. 320p. 1995. mass mkt. 4.99 (0-553-56557-5, Spectra) Bantam.
— Ragnarok. (Star Trek Ser.: No. 3). 1995. mass mkt. 5.99 (0-671-52044-X) PB.
— Valhalla. Ordover, John, ed. (Star Trek: No. 10). 288p. (Orig.). 1995. mass mkt. 5.50 (0-671-88115-9) PB.
Archer, Nathan, jt. auth. see Busiek, Kurt.
Archer, Nuala. From a Mobile Home. LC 95-156784. 131p. 1995. pap. 15.95 (1-897648-59-6, Pub. by Poolbeg Pr) Dufour.
— Pan/Ama. (Shot Works Ser.). 24p. 1992. pap. 3.00 (0-87376-070-0) Red Dust.
— Whale on the Line. 42p. 1981. 16.95 (0-904011-21-6) Dufour.
Archer, Nuala, jt. auth. see McGuckian, M.
Archer, Nuala, ed. see Rankine, Claudia.
***Archer, Pat.** Therapeutic Sports Massage. 200p. 2001. pap. text 30.00 (1-55642-480-9) SLACK Inc.
Archer, Peter. The Christian Calendar & the Gregorian Reform. LC 41-15354. (Illus.). 136p. reprint ed. pap. 42.20 (0-7837-5586-4, 204537900005) Bks Demand.
Archer, Peter & Lord Reay. Freedom at Stake. LC 67-15647. (Background Ser.). 1967. 18.95 (0-8023-1118-0) Dufour.
Archer, Phil. The Heart of England. (Radio Times Around Britain Guides Ser.). (Illus.). 96p. 1994. 8.95 (0-563-36952-3, Pub. by BBC) Parkwest Pubns.
Archer, Phillip, jt. auth. see Kimbrough, Dan.
Archer, R. D. The Official Monogram U. S. Army Air Service & Air Corps Aircraft Color Guide, 1908-1941, Vol. 1. Hitchcock, T. H., ed. LC 94-76072. (Illus.). 241p. 1995. 54.95 (0-914144-46-4) Monogram Aviation.
Archer, R. Douglas & Saarlas, Maido. An Introduction to Aerospace Propulsion. LC 95-33012. 608p. (C). 1996. text 75.00 (0-13-120496-3) P-H.
Archer, R. L. Secondary Education in the Nineteenth Century. 363p. 1966. reprint ed. 30.00 (0-7146-1446-7, BHA-01446, Pub. by F Cass Pubs) Intl Spec Bk.
Archer, R. R. Growth Stresses & Strains in Trees. (Wood Science Ser.). (Illus.). 305p. 1986. 171.95 (0-387-16406-5) Spr-Verlag.
Archer, R. R., jt. auth. see Lardner, Thomas J.
Archer, R. Wayne. Fast & Loose with Mother Goose & Other Stuff. (Illus.). 50p. 1995. pap. 2.00 (0-9648622-5-5) Pine Grve Pr.
Archer, Raymond L. Muhammadan Mysticism in Sumatra. LC 77-87487. (Royal Asiatic Society, Malayan Branch. Journal Ser.: Vol. 15). reprint ed. 27.50 (0-404-16695-4) AMS Pr.
Archer, Rebecca. Little Bo-Peep, Incl. 2 puppets. LC 97-71902. (Hand Puppet Bks.). 16p. (J). (ps). 1998. 12.95 (0-448-41742-1, G & D) Peng Put Young Read.
— Old Mother Hubbard, Incl. 2 puppets. LC 97-71901. (Hand Puppet Bks.). 16p. (J). (ps). 1998. 12.95 (0-448-41743-X, G & D) Peng Put Young Read.
Archer, Richard P. Concept Spelling Student Workbook, No. 4. 69p. 1979. 10.00 (0-935276-00-9) Concept Spelling.
— Concept Spelling's: Language Awareness Workbook. (Concept Spelling Ser.). 56p. (Orig.). (J). (gr. 4-12). 1982. 10.00 (0-935276-06-8) Concept Spelling.
— Concept Spelling's: The Secrets of Spelling-Cassette-Workbook. (Concept Spelling Ser.). 30p. (J). (gr. 5-12). 1982. student ed. 20.00 (0-935276-07-6) Concept Spelling.
— Introduction to Concept Spelling Teacher's Guide. 48p. (Orig.). 1980. teacher ed. 5.00 (0-935276-02-5); 10.00 (0-935276-01-7) Concept Spelling.
— The Shortcut to Reading. 29p. 1983. 10.00 (0-317-02255-5) Concept Spelling.
Archer, Richard P., ed. Concept Spelling Teacher's Manual. 132p. 1979. 50.00 (0-935276-03-3) Concept Spelling.
Archer, Robert. Archer & Sylvester Families: A History Written in 1870. (Illus.). 29p. 1996. reprint ed. pap. 6.00 (0-8328-5358-5); reprint ed. lib. bdg. 16.00 (0-8328-5357-7) Higginson Bk Co.
— The Pervasive Image: The Role of Analogy in the Poetry of Ausias March. LC 85-13360. (Purdue University Monographs in Romance Languages: No. 17). xii, 220p. 1985. pap. 54.00 (0-915027-56-9) J Benjamins Pubng Co.
Archer, Robert D. Airliners at LAX - Los Angeles International Airport 1956-1976: Los Angeles International Airport, 1956-1976. Proctor, Jon, ed. (Illus.). 120p. 1997. pap. 24.95 (0-9626730-6-4, 2600) World Transport.
***Archer, Robert D.** Edwards Air Force Base Open House at the USAF Flight Test Center 1957-1966: A Photo Chronicle of Aircraft Displayed LC 98-86278. (Military History Ser.). 232 p. 1999. write for info. (0-7643-0689-8) Schiffer.
Archer, Robert D. & Archer, Victor G. USAAF Aircraft Markings & Camouflage, 1941-1947: The History of USAAF Aircraft Markings, Insignia, Camouflage & Colors. LC 96-71971. 352p. 1997. 79.95 (0-7643-0246-9) Schiffer.
Archer, Robert F. Lehigh Valley Railroad. LC 93-61333. (Illus.). 372p. 1993. 44.95 (0-911581-29-4) Heimburger Hse Pub.
Archer, Robert P. MMPI-A: Assessing Adolescent Psychopathology. 472p. (C). 1992. text 39.95 (0-8058-1113-3) L Erlbaum Assocs.
— MMPI-A: Assessing Adolescent Psychopathology. 2nd ed. 512p. (C). 1996. 39.95 (0-8058-2343-3) L Erlbaum Assocs.
Archer, Robert P., et al. MMPI-A Casebook. LC 94-5851. 223p. 1994. pap. 33.00 (0-911907-14-9) Psych Assess.
Archer, Robin. Economic Democracy: The Politics of Feasible Socialism. (Illus.). 280p. 1995. text 55.00 (0-19-827891-8) OUP.
— Economic Democracy: The Politics of Feasible Socialism. (Illus.). 276p. 1999. pap. text 24.95 (0-19-829538-3) OUP.
Archer, Rodney & Jones, Powell. The Harlot's Curse. (Illus.). 59p. (Orig.). 1990. pap. 10.00 (1-870615-01-8, Pub. by Preston Ed) Players Pr.
Archer, Ron. On Teams. 156p. 1996. text 19.95 (0-7863-0498-7, Irwn Prfssnl) McGraw-Hill Prof.
Archer, Rosemary. The Versatile Arabian Horse. 1996. text 90.00 (0-85131-669-7, Pub. by J A Allen) Trafalgar.
Archer, Rowena E., ed. Crown, Government & People in the Fifteenth Century. (Fifteenth Century Ser.: No. 2). 256p. 1996. 72.00 (0-7509-0588-3, Pub. by Sutton Pub Ltd) Intl Pubs Mktg.
Archer, Rowena E. & Walker, Simon, eds. Rulers & Ruled in Late Medieval England: Essays Presented to Gerald Harriss. LC 95-49415. 1995. 60.00 (1-85285-133-3) Hambledon Press.
Archer, S. N. Adaptive Mechanisms in the Ecology of Vision. LC 98-31125. 1998. 335.00 (0-7923-5319-6) Kluwer Academic.
Archer, Sally L. Interventions for Adolescent Identity Development. LC 93-38497. (Focus Editions Ser.: Vol. 169). 272p. (C). 1994. text 59.95 (0-8039-4188-9); pap. text 26.00 (0-8039-4189-7) Sage.
***Archer-Shaw, Petrine.** Negrophilia: Avant-Garde Paris & Black Culture in the 1920s. LC 99-69806. (Interplay Ser.). (Illus.). 208p. 2000. pap. 24.95 (0-500-28135-1, Pub. by Thames Hudson) Norton.
Archer, Stanley. W. Somerset Maugham: A Study of the Short Fiction. LC 92-42071. (Twayne's Studies in Short Fiction: No. 44). 152p. 1993. 29.00 (0-8057-0856-1) Macmillan.
Archer, Stephen M. Junius Brutus Booth: Theatrical Prometheus. LC 91-25725. (Illus.). 320p. (C). 1992. 36.95 (0-8093-1766-4) S Ill U Pr.
***Archer, Steve.** Rangeland Desertification. LC 99-52310. (Advances in Vegetation Science Ser.). 1999. write for info. (0-7923-6071-0) Kluwer Academic.
Archer, Steve. Stay Right Here. 1998. 10.99 (0-7684-0173-9); 15.99 (0-7684-0172-0) Destiny Image.
— Willis O'Brien: Special Effects Genius. LC 92-50950. (Illus.). 239p. 1998. per. 20.00 (0-7864-0573-2, McFarland Cls) McFarland & Co.
***Archer, Susan D.** Leader's Guide for Churches: Your Blended Family's Road Map. (Illus.). 48p. 2000. pap. 12.95 (0-9668670-2-5) Together Pubg.
— Your Blended Family's Road Map: A Step-by-Step Guide for Blending Your Stepfamily. LC 99-90756. Orig. Title: Your Stepfamily's Road Map. (Illus.). 170p. 1999. pap. 15.95 (0-9668670-1-7) Together Pubg.
Archer, T. & Nilsson, L. G., eds. Aversion, Avoidance & Anxiety: Perspectives on Aversively Motivated Behavior. 512p. (C). 1988. text 99.95 (0-8058-0132-4) L Erlbaum Assocs.
Archer, Ted. Recollections of a Rambling Life. 358p. (C). 1990. 90.00 (0-86439-074-2, Pub. by Boolarong Pubns) St Mut.
Archer, Thomas A. The Crusade of Richard I, 1189-1992. LC 76-29828. reprint ed. 65.00 (0-404-15408-5) AMS Pr.
Archer, Thomas A. & Kingsford, Charles L. The Crusades: The Story of the Latin Kingdom of Jerusalem. LC 76-29833. reprint ed. 84.50 (0-404-15409-3) AMS Pr.
Archer, Thomas P., et al. Morning Report: Internal Medicine. LC 99-33659. (Illus.). 240p. 1999. pap. text 42.50 (0-07-006692-2) McGraw-Hill HPD.
Archer, Timothy, et al. Desire High Heels Red Wine: A Gay & Lesbian Anthology. LC 95-218202. 96p. 1997. pap. 9.99 (1-895837-26-X) Insomniac.
***Archer, Tom.** Teach Yourself Visual InterDev 6 in 24 Hours. (Teach Yourself Ser.). 450p. 1999. pap. text 24.99 (0-672-31642-0) Sams.
Archer, Trevor & Hansen, Stefan, eds. Behavioral Biology: Neuroendocrine Axis. 288p. 1991. text 69.95 (0-8058-0790-X) L Erlbaum Assocs.
Archer, Trevor, jt. ed. see Nilsson, L. G.
Archer, Trevor, jt. ed. see Sagvolden, Terje.
Archer, Victor G., jt. auth. see Archer, Robert D.
Archer, W. G. Blue Grove. LC 72-7219. (Select Bibliographies Reprint Ser.). 1977. reprint ed. 24.95 (0-8369-6920-0) Ayer.
— Love Songs of Vidyapati. 1987. 14.00 (81-208-0291-8, Pub. by Motilal Bnarsidass) S Asia.
Archer, W. G., ed. The Kama Sutra of Vatsyayana. Burton, Richard & Arbuthnot, F. F., trs. 296p. 1999. reprint ed. pap. text 17.00 (0-7881-6303-5) DIANE Pub.
Archer, Walter, jt. auth. see Garrison, D. R.
Archer, Wesley L. Industrial Solvents Handbook. (Illus.). 328p. 1996. text 155.00 (0-8247-9718-3) Dekker.
Archer, William. English Dramatists of To-Day. (Works of William Archer). 387p. 1985. reprint ed. 69.00 (0-7812-0850-5) Rprt Serv.
— English Dramatists of Today. 1976. reprint ed. 39.00 (0-403-06038-9, Regency) Scholarly.
— Henry Irving: Actor & Manager: A Critical Study. (Works of William Archer). 108p. reprint ed. lib. bdg. 59.00 (0-932051-21-9) Rprt Serv.
— Henry Irving, Actor & Manager. LC 70-107156. 1970. reprint ed. 59.00 (0-403-00468-3) Scholarly.
— The Old Drama & the New: An Essay in Re-Valuation. 1972. 26.95 (0-405-18113-2, 1320) Ayer.
— The Old Drama & the New: An Essay in Re-Valuation. (BCL1-PR English Literature Ser.). 396p. 1992. reprint ed. lib. bdg. 89.00 (0-7812-7075-8) Rprt Serv.
— Poets of the Younger Generation. LC 76-120572. (BCL Ser. I). reprint ed. 76.50 (0-404-00367-2) AMS Pr.
— Poets of the Younger Generation. (BCL1-PR English Literature Ser.). 564p. 1992. reprint ed. lib. bdg. 99.00 (0-7812-7092-8) Rprt Serv.
— Poets of the Younger Generation. LC 72-8574. 564p. reprint ed. 12.00 (0-403-00240-0) Scholarly.
— The Theatrical "World" LC 77-82818. 1972. reprint ed. 24.95 (0-405-08211-8, Pub. by Blom Pubns); reprint ed. 24.95 (0-405-08210-X, Pub. by Blom Pubns) Ayer.
— Through Afro-America. (Works of William Archer). xvi, 295p. reprint ed. 49.00 (0-932051-75-8) Rprt Serv.
Archer, William, ed. see Ibsen, Henrik.
Archer, William, tr. see Ibsen, Henrik.
Archer, William, tr. see Kielland, Alexander L.
***Archer-Wills, Anthony.** Designing Water Gardens: A Unique Approach. (Illus.). 2000. 27.95 (1-84091-156-5) Conran Octopus.
Archer-Wills, Anthony. The Water Gardener. LC 92-44565. (Illus.). 192p. 1993. 45.00 (0-8120-6332-5) Barron.
Arches National Park Intrepretive Staff. Road Guide: Arches National Park. Anderson, Peter, ed. (Illus.). 32p. 1992. 2.00 (0-937407-03-8) Canyonlands.
***Archestratos of Gela Staff.** Archestratos of Gela Text, Translation & Commentary: Greek Culture & Cuisine in the Fourth Century BCE. Olson, S. Douglas & Sens, Alexander, eds. LC 99-16102. 336p. 2000. text 80.00 (0-19-924008-6) OUP.
Archestratus, et al. The Life of Luxury: Europe's Oldest Cookery Book. (GRE., Illus.). 110p. 1994. pap. 17.00 (0-907325-53-X, Pub. by Prospect) Food Words.
Archetti, Eduardo, et al, eds. Latin America. (Sociology of "Developing Societies" Ser.). 320p. (Orig.). 1987. 26.00 (0-85345-685-2, Pub. by Monthly Rev) NYU Pr.
Archetti, Eduardo P. Guinea Pigs. Napolitano, Valentina & Worsley, Peter, trs. LC 97-202415. 1997. 55.00 (1-85973-114-7, Pub. by Berg Pubs); pap. 19.50 (1-85973-119-8, Pub. by Berg Pubs) NYU Pr.
Archetti, Eduardo P. Masculinities: An Anthropology of Football, Polo & Tango. LC 99-229403. 224p. 1999. pap. 19.50 (1-85973-266-6, Pub. by Berg Pubs) NYU Pr.
***Archetti, Eduardo P.** Masculinities: An Anthropology of Football, Polo & Tango. LC 99-229403. 224p. 1999. 55.00 (1-85973-261-5, Pub. by Berg Pubs) NYU Pr.
Archetti, Eduardo P., ed. Exploring the Written: Anthropology & the Multiplicity of Writing. 342p. 1994. 22.00 (82-00-03937-4) Scandnvan Univ Pr.
Archetti, F., et al, eds. Operations Research Models in Flexible Manufacturing Systems. (CISM Ser.: Vol. 306). (Illus.). vii, 305p. 1989. 75.95 (0-387-82099-X) Spr-Verlag.
— Stochastic Programming. (Lecture Notes in Control & Information Sciences: Vol. 76). v, 285p. 1985. 40.95 (0-387-16044-2) Spr-Verlag.
Archetto, Macia & Owens, Jessie A. Francesco Portinaro il Terzo Libro di Madrigali a Cinque et Sei Voci. LC 89-755341. (Italian Madrigal Sixteenth Century Ser.: Vol. 23). 302p. 1990. text 30.00 (0-8240-5523-3) Garland.
Archi, Alfonso. Five Tablets from the Southern Wing of Palace G-Ebla. (Mesopotamian Studies: No. 5-2). (Illus.). 38p. (C). 1993. pap. text 13.00 (0-89003-277-7) Undena Pubns.
Archiati, Pietro. From Christianity to Christ. Barton, Matthew, tr. from GER. 128p. 1996. 15.95 (0-904693-83-X, Pub. by Temple Lodge) Anthroposophic.
— Giving Judas a Chance: The Vision & Venture of Weaving Many Lives. unabridged ed. Bailey, Joseph, ed. xi, 238p. 1999. pap. 13.00 (1-893843-00-9, 001) Sprtl Sci.
***Archiati, Pietro.** Great Religions: Pathways to Our Innermost Being. Wehrle, Pauline, tr. 192p. 1998. pap. 19.95 (1-902636-01-5, Pub. by Temple Lodge) Anthroposophic.
Archiati, Pietro. Reincarnation in Modern Life: Towards a New Christian Awareness. 1998. pap. 14.95 (0-904693-88-0, Pub. by Temple Lodge) Anthroposophic.
Archibald, Alasdair N. The Acquisition of Discourse Proficiency: A Study of the Ability of German School Students to Produce Written Texts in English as a Foreign Language. (Illus.). 299p. 1994. pap. 52.95 (3-631-47831-3) P Lang Pubng.
Archibald, Allene, et al. The Historic Mission Inn. Moore, Barbara, ed. 120p. 1998. text. write for info. (0-9666914-0-7) Fnds Mission Inn.
Archibald, Catherine. Hawk's Lady. 304p. (Orig.). 1997. mass mkt. 4.99 (0-8439-4312-2, Leisure Bks) Dorchester Pub Co.
***Archibald, Catherine.** Loving Charity. 320p. 2000. mass mkt. 4.99 (0-8439-4704-7, Leisure Bks) Dorchester Pub Co.
Archibald, Chestina M., ed. Say Amen! The African-American Family's Book of Prayers. (Illus.). 384p. 1998. pap. 12.95 (0-452-27729-9, Plume) Dutton Plume.

An Asterisk (*) at the beginning of an entry indicates that the title is appearing for the first time.

Archibald, Chestina Mitchell. Secrets of the Psalms. 336p. 1999. pap. text 13.00 (*0-425-17043-8*) Berkley Pub.

Archibald, Christal, et al. Discourses in Dialect: 10 New Black Poets. 111p. (Orig.). 1992. pap. 6.95 (*1-886986-00-2*) Blackface Bks.

Archibald, Colin & Kwok, Paul, eds. Research in Computer & Robot Vision. LC 94-45576. 432p. 1995. text 109.00 (*981-02-2134-7*) World Scientific Pub.

Archibald, Colin & Petriu, Emil, eds. Advances in Machine Vision: Strategies & Applications. LC 92-19672. (Series in Computer Science: Vol. 32). 380p. 1992. text 81.00 (*981-02-0976-2*) World Scientific Pub.

Archibald, Dale. Dale Archibald's Using Computers. (Illus.). 160p. (Orig.). 1986. pap. 8.95 (*0-937819-00-X*) Archibald Pub.

Archibald, David. Water Gardens: A Firefly Gardener's Guide. Patton, Mary, ed. (Illus.). 96p. 1996. pap. text 10.95 (*1-895565-96-0*) Firefly Bks Ltd.

Archibald, Douglas N. John Butler Yeats. LC 71-125792. (Irish Writers Ser.). 103p. 1975. pap. 1.95 (*0-8387-7733-3*) Bucknell U Pr.

— Yeats. LC 86-14492. (Irish Studies). 296p. 1983. reprint ed. pap. 91.80 (*0-608-06983-3*, 206719100009) Bks Demand.

Archibald, Douglas N., ed. see Yeats, William Butler.

Archibald, E. H. Dictionary of Sea Painters. 3rd ed. (Illus.). 576p. 1989. 89.50 (*1-85149-047-7*) Antique Collect.

— The Dictionary of Sea Painters of Europe & America. (Illus.). 576p. 1999. 89.50 (*1-85149-269-0*) Antique Collect.

Archibald, Elizabeth. Apollonius of Tyre: Medieval & Renaissance Themes & Variations. 264p. (C). 1991. 75.00 (*0-85991-316-3*) Boydell & Brewer.

Archibald, Elizabeth & Edwards, A. S., eds. A Companion to Malory. 280p. (Orig.). 1999. reprint ed. pap. 29.95 (*0-85991-520-4*, DS Brewer) Boydell & Brewer.

Archibald, Erika. Sudanese Family. (Journey Between Two Worlds Ser.). 1997. pap. text 8.95 (*0-8225-9753-5*) Lerner Pub.

— A Sudanese Family. (Journey Between Two Worlds Ser.). (Illus.). (J). (gr. 3-6). 1997. pap. 8.95 (*0-614-28838-X*, First Ave Edns) Lerner Pub.

Archibald, Erika, jt. auth. see Maple, Terry L.

Archibald, G. C. Information, Incentives & the Economics of Control. (Illus.). 189p. (C). 1992. text 52.95 (*0-521-33045-9*) Cambridge U Pr.

Archibald, J. David. Dinosaur Extinction & the End of an Era: What the Fossils Say. (Illus.). 240p. 1996. pap. 24.50 (*0-231-07625-8*) Col U Pr.

Archibald, J. F., jt. auth. see Bawden, W. F.

Archibald, James K., jt. auth. see Sandler, Paul M.

Archibald, Janet S., jt. auth. see Mills, Thomas S.

Archibald, John. Language Learnability & L2 Phonology: The Acquisition of Metrical Parameters. LC 93-31917. (Studies in Theoretical Psycholinguistics: Vol. 19). 220p. (C). 1993. text 146.00 (*0-7923-2486-2*) Kluwer Academic.

— Second Language Phonology. LC 98-23347. (Language Acquisition & Language Disorders (LALD) Ser.: No. 17). xii, 313p. 1998. 59.00 (*1-55619-781-0*) J Benjamins Pubng Co.

Archibald, John, ed. Phonological Acquisition & Phonological Theory. 224p. 1995. text 49.95 (*0-8058-1352-7*) L Erlbaum Assocs.

— Second Language Acquisition & Linguistic Theory. LC 99-16612. (Illus.). 352p. (C). 2000. text 64.95 (*0-631-20591-8*); pap. text 29.95 (*0-631-20592-6*) Blackwell Pubs.

Archibald, Katherine. Wartime Shipyard: A Study in Social Disunity. Stein, Leon, ed. LC 77-70478. (Illus.). 1977. reprint ed. lib. bdg. 25.95 (*0-405-10152-X*) Ayer.

— Wartime Shipyard: A Study in Social Disunity. LC 76-7621. (FDR & the Era of the New Deal Ser.). 1976. reprint ed. 27.50 (*0-306-70802-7*) Da Capo.

Archibald, Liliana, tr. see Klyuchevsky, Vasili.

***Archibald, Linda R.** Sunshine in My Soul: Discovering the Magic in Everyday Life. LC 99-16925. 1999. write for info. (*1-57345-555-5*) Deseret Bk.

***Archibald, Mark.** Mechanical Engineering Design with Pro/Engineer Release 2000i. (Illus.). 353p. 2000. pap. 59.95 (*1-58503-019-8*, SDC Pubns) Schroff Dev Corp.

Archibald, Norman. Heaven High, Hell Deep: Nineteen Seventeen to Nineteen Eighteen. Gilbert, James B., ed. LC 79-7231. (Flight: Its First Seventy-Five Years Ser.). 1980. reprint ed. lib. bdg. 31.95 (*0-405-12147-4*) Ayer.

Archibald, R. A Semicentennial History of the American Mathematical Society (1888-1938), Set. (Procsemi Ser.: Vol. 1). 262p. 1988. reprint ed. pap. 90.00 (*0-8218-0128-7*, SEMISET) Am Math.

— A Semicentennial History of the American Mathematical Society (1888-1938), Vol. 1. 262p. 1988. reprint ed. text 52.00 (*0-8218-0118-X*, HMREPRINT) Am Math.

Archibald, R. E. The Diatoms of the Sundays & Great Fish Rivers in the Eastern Cape Province of South Africa. (Bibliotheca Diatomologica Ser.: Vol. 1). 432p. 1983. text 115.00 (*3-7682-1365-X*) Lubrecht & Cramer.

Archibald, Raymond. Carlyle's First Love. LC 72-3374. (English Literature Ser.: No. 33). (Illus.). 1972. reprint ed. lib. bdg. 75.00 (*0-8383-1535-6*) M S G Haskell Hse.

Archibald, Raymond C. A Semicentennial History of the American Mathematical Society: Eighteen Hundred Eighty-Eight to Nineteen Hundred Thirty-Eight; with Biographies & Bibliographies Odents, 2 vols., Set. Cohen, I. Bernard, ed. LC 79-7947. (Three Centuries of Science in America Ser.). (Illus.). 1980. reprint ed. lib. bdg. 60.95 (*0-405-12528-3*) Ayer.

— A Semicentennial History of the American Mathematical Society, 1888-1938, Vol. 1. 1980. 30.95 (*0-405-12618-2*) Ayer.

Archibald, Robert R. The Economic Aspects of the California Missions. (Monograph Ser.). 1978. 30.00 (*0-88382-063-3*) AAFH.

— History & Memory. (Copper Dome Monograph Ser.). 16p. (C). 1998. pap. 5.00 (*1-890551-02-3*) SMSU.

— A Place to Remember: Using History to Build Community. LC 99-6261. (AASLH Ser.). 200p. 1999. 59.00 (*0-7619-8942-0*); pap. 22.95 (*0-7619-8943-9*) AltaMira Pr.

Archibald, Russell D. Managing High Tech Programs & Projects. LC 91-25865. 400p. 1992. 107.50 (*0-471-51327-X*) Wiley.

Archibald, Sandra O., jt. auth. see McCorkle, Chester O.

Archibald, Sarah, jt. auth. see Odden, Allan.

***Archibald, Theodore.** Marriage: God's Wonderful Gift of Love. 2000. pap. text 12.95 (*0-7880-0990-7*) CSS OH.

Archibald, Theodore. The Winding Path to America. LC 95-83307. 148p. 1996. pap. 8.95 (*0-7880-0654-1*, Fairway Pr) CSS OH.

Archibald, Tracy, jt. auth. see Graber, Jan.

Archibald, W. Peter. Marx & the Missing Link: Human Nature. LC 89-1978. 292p. (C). 1992. pap. 18.50 (*0-391-03754-4*) Humanities.

Archibald, Z. H. The Odrysian Kingdom of Thrace: Orpheus Unmasked. LC 97-22110. (Oxford Monographs on Classical Archaeology). (Illus.). 394p. 1998. text 150.00 (*0-19-815047-4*) OUP.

Archibald, Zofia. Discovering the World of the Ancient Greeks. (Illus.). 192p. 1991. 29.95 (*0-8160-2614-9*) Facts on File.

Archiband, W. R., jt. ed. see Darling, Laura.

Archibecque, Orlando, jt. auth. see Alive, Camila.

Archibugi. Associative Economy LC 99-32866. 1999. text 69.95 (*0-312-22380-3*) St Martin.

Archibugi. Towards a European Urban Systems Concept & Strategies. 65.95 (*1-84014-586-2*) Ashgate Pub Co.

Archibugi, Daniele, et al, eds. Innovation Policy in a Global Economy. (Illus.). 300p. (C). 1999. text 69.95 (*0-521-63327-3*); pap. text 24.95 (*0-521-63361-3*) Cambridge U Pr.

— Re-Imagining Political Community: Studies in Cosmopolitan Democracy. LC 98-60721. 352p. 1998. 22.95 (*0-8047-3535-2*) Stanford U Pr.

Archibugi, Daniele & Held, David, eds. Cosmopolitan Democracy: An Agenda for a New World Order. LC 94-44706. 1995. pap. 24.95 (*0-7456-1381-0*, Pub. by Polity Pr) Blackwell Pubs.

Archibugi, Daniele & Michie, Jonathan, eds. Technology, Globalisation & Economic Performance. 321p. (C). 1997. text 59.95 (*0-521-55392-X*); pap. text 20.95 (*0-521-55642-2*) Cambridge U Pr.

— Trade, Growth & Technical Change. 296p. (C). 1998. text 64.95 (*0-521-55393-8*); pap. text 22.95 (*0-521-55641-4*) Cambridge U Pr.

Archibugi, Daniele & Pianta, Mario. The Technological Specialization of Advanced Countries: A Report to the EEC on International Science & Technology Activities. LC 92-8629. 1992. lib. bdg. 132.00 (*0-7923-1750-5*) Kluwer Academic.

Archibugi, F. & Nijkamp, Peter, eds. Economy & Ecology: Towards Sustainable Development. (C). 1989. lib. bdg. 214.50 (*0-7923-0477-2*) Kluwer Academic.

Archibugi, Franco. The Ecological City & the City Effect: Essays on the Urban Planning Requirements for the Sustainable City. LC 97-74456. (Studies in Green Research). (Illus.). 252p. 1998. text 69.95 (*1-85972-653-4*, Pub. by Ashgate Pub) Ashgate Pub Co.

Archidocese of Dublin Staff. Pastoral Guidelines on Infant Baptism. 1993. pap. 24.95 (*1-85390-001-X*, Pub. by Veritas Pubns) St Mut.

Archie, Barbara, ed. see Jones, Charles.

Archie Conference Staff. The Integration of Geology, Geophysics, Petrophysics, & Petroleum Engineering in Reservoir Delineation, Description, & Management: Proceedings of the First Archie Conference, Held October 22-25, 1990, in Houston, Texas, U. S. A. LC 91-191329. (Illus.). 451p. 1991. reprint ed. pap. 139.90 (*0-608-04229-3*, 206498600012) Bks Demand.

Archie, M. Environmental Education Materials: Guidelines for Excellence. 24p. text 10.00 (*1-884008-41-0*) NAAEE.

Archie, Michele. Clean Water: Taking Care of Unfinished Business. (Environmental Issues Forums Ser.). (Illus.). 48p. (Orig.). pap. 6.00 (*1-884008-21-6*) Kendall-Hunt.

— Grant Funding for Your Environmental Education Program: Strategies & Options. (Illus.). 30p. (Orig.). 1993. pap. 9.00 (*1-884008-09-7*) NAAEE.

— The Wetlands Issue: What Should We Do with Our Bogs, Swamps & Marshes? (Environmental Issues Forums Ser.: Vol. 2). (Illus.). 46p. (Orig.). 1992. pap. 6.00 (*1-884008-00-3*) Kendall-Hunt.

Archie, Peter B. & Alberg, Tom A. Going Private & Corporate Securities Repurchases. 2nd ed. (Corporate Practice Ser.: No. 7-2nd). 1986. 92.00 (*1-55871-256-9*) BNA.

Archie, Ralph. Beware the Night. mass mkt. write for info. (*0-312-97689-5*) St Martin.

Archilla, Aurelio A. The Theology of History & Apologetic Historiography in Heinrich Bullinger: Truth in History. LC 92-11975. 344p. 1992. lib. bdg. 99.95 (*0-7734-9828-1*) E Mellen.

Archilla, Rodrigo. Sectarismo o Cristianismo?Tr. of Sectism or Christianism?. (SPA.). 1990. 4.50 (*0-685-74982-7*, 498476) Editorial Unilit.

Archilla, Rogelio. Certeza y Seguridad.Tr. of Assurance & Security. (SPA.). 144p. 1992. pap. 3.99 (*1-56063-399-9*, 498549) Editorial Unilit.

— Creencia y Conciencia - Belief & Consciousness. (SPA.). 82p. 1995. write for info. (*1-56063-664-5*) Editorial Unilit.

— Participantes - Participant. (SPA.). 150p. 1995. write for info. (*1-56063-696-3*) Editorial Unilit.

— Sectarismo o Cristianismo?Tr. of Sectism or Christianism. (SPA.). 1991. pap. 1.50 (*1-56063-122-8*, 498476) Editorial Unilit.

— Somos Diferentes: Contextualizacion Cultural.Tr. of We Are Different. (SPA.). 92p. 1992. pap. 3.99 (*1-56063-112-0*, 498404) Editorial Unilit.

— La Virgen Maria.Tr. of Virgin Mary. (SPA.). 101p. 1995. 3.99 (*1-56063-663-7*, 497723) Editorial Unilit.

Archilochus & Semonides. Greek Elegy, Iambus, & Anacreontea, 2 vols., 2. (Loeb Classical Library: No. 258-259). 15.50 (*0-674-99285-7*) HUP.

Archimandrite Anthony Yamshcikov, ed. Sovremennost' v svjetje Slova Bozhija - Slove i Rechi Arkiepiskopa Averkija, 4 vols.Tr. of Comtemporaneity in Light of the Word of God - the Works & Writings of Archbishop Averky. 2100p. 1976. 89.00 (*0-317-29057-6*); pap. 69.00 (*0-317-29058-4*) Holy Trinity.

Archimandrite C. Karambelas & Archimandrite Ioannicius. Contemporary Ascetics of Mount Athos, Vol. 2. St. Xenia Skete, tr. from GRE. LC 91-68395. (Illus.). 358p. (Orig.). 1992. 30.00 (*0-938635-57-3*) St Herman Pr.

Archimandrite I. Balan & Balan, Ioanichie. Romanian Patericon: Saints of the Romanian Orthodox Church. McCarthy, Brigid, tr. from RUM. LC 95-72085. (Third-Eighteenth Centuries Ser.: Vol. I). (RUM., Illus.). 504p. 1996. pap. 20.00 (*0-938635-97-2*) St Herman Pr.

Archimandrite Ioannicius, jt. auth. see Archimandrite C. Karambelas.

Archimandrite Lazarus Moore, tr. see Brianchianinov, Ignatius.

Archimandrite Sophrony. Saint Silouan the Athonite. 504p. 34.95 (*0-9512786-8-1*, 001849) Conciliar Pr.

Archimault, Charles. The New Year Ceremony at Basak (South Laos) Boas, Simone B., tr. from FRE. 137p. 1988. reprint ed. pap. 20.00 (*0-923135-03-0*) Dalley Bk Service.

Archimbaud, Michel. Francis Bacon: In Conversation with Michel Archimbaud. LC 94-144673. (Illus.). 192p. (Orig.). (C). 1994. pap. 14.95 (*0-7148-2983-8*, Pub. by Phaidon Press) Phaidon Pr.

Archimbaud, Nicholas D. The Louvre: Portrait of a Museum. LC 98-17163. 336p. 1998. 60.00 (*1-55670-625-1*) Stewart Tabori & Chang.

Archimedes. Archimedes in the Middle Ages, Vol. 3, P1-2. Claggett, Marshall, ed. LC 62-7218. (ENG & LAT.). 302p. reprint ed. pap. 93.70 (*0-7837-6706-4*, 204633900031) Bks Demand.

— Archimedes in the Middle Ages, Vol. 3, P3. Claggett, Marshall, ed. LC 62-7218. (ENG & LAT.). 958p. reprint ed. pap. 200.00 (*0-7837-6707-2*, 204633900033) Bks Demand.

— Archimedes in the Middle Ages, Vol. 3, P4. Claggett, Marshall, ed. LC 62-7218. (ENG & LAT.). 340p. reprint ed. pap. 105.40 (*0-7837-6708-0*, 204633900034) Bks Demand.

— Archimedes in the Middle Ages, Vol. 4, P1. Claggett, Marshall, ed. LC 62-7218. (ENG & LAT.). 469p. reprint ed. pap. 145.40 (*0-7837-6709-9*, 204633900041) Bks Demand.

— Archimedes in the Middle Ages, Vol. 4, P2. Claggett, Marshall, ed. LC 62-7218. (ENG & LAT.). 106p. reprint ed. pap. 32.90 (*0-7837-6710-2*, 204633900042) Bks Demand.

— Archimedes in the Middle Ages, Vol. 5, P1-4. Claggett, Marshall, ed. LC 62-7218. (ENG & LAT.). 613p. reprint ed. pap. 190.10 (*0-7837-6711-0*, 204633900051) Bks Demand.

— Archimedes in the Middle Ages, Vol. 5, P5. Claggett, Marshall, ed. LC 62-7218. (ENG & LAT.). 118p. reprint ed. pap. 36.60 (*0-7837-6712-9*, 204633900055) Bks Demand.

Archipelag. Abnormal Psychology Case Studies. (C). 1998. 77.50 (*0-15-503092-2*) Harcourt Coll Pubs.

— Lectureactive Users Guide. (C). 1995. pap. text 33.50 (*0-03-018073-2*) Harcourt Coll Pubs.

***Architects & Publishers Arco Staff.** How to Decorate with Blue. 2000. pap. 24.95 (*84-8185-247-3*) Arco Edit.

— Imaginative & Affordable Studios. 2000. pap. 24.95 (*84-8185-246-5*) Watsn-Guptill.

— The Kitchen. 2000. pap. 19.95 (*84-8185-244-9*) Watsn-Guptill.

Architects, Designers & Planners for Social Respon, contrib. by. Quonset Huts on the River Styx: The Bomb Shelter Design Book. 72p. 1988. pap. 12.95 (*1-55643-027-2*) North Atlantic.

Architects' Emergency Committee. Great Georgian Houses of America, 2 vols., Vol. 2. (Illus.). 520p. 1970. reprint ed. pap. 15.95 (*0-486-22492-9*) Dover.

— Great Georgian Houses of America, 2 vols., Vol.1. (Illus.). 520p. 1970. reprint ed. pap. 15.95 (*0-486-22491-0*) Dover.

Architectural Design Editors. A House for Today: An Architectural Design Profile. (Illus.). 80p. 1987. pap. 19.95 (*0-312-00713-2*) St Martin.

Architectural Design Special Issue Staff. British Architecture. (Academy Editions Ser.). (Illus.). 240p. 1983. pap. 29.95 (*0-312-10035-3*) St Martin.

Architectural History Foundation Staff, jt. ed. see Fondation Le Corbusier Staff.

Architectural League of New York Staff, jt. auth. see Pancoast, Douglas.

Architectural Monograph Staff. Foster Associates: Architectural Monograph. 1992. 55.00 (*0-312-07242-2*) St Martin.

— Foster Associates: Architectural Monograph, Vol. 20. 1992. pap. 38.00 (*0-312-07146-9*) St Martin.

— Robert Stern: Architectural Monograph, Vol. 17. 1992. 55.00 (*0-312-07147-7*) St Martin.

***Architecture Foundation Staff.** New Architects: A Guide To Britains Best Young Architectural Practices,new.. 2000. 39.95 (*1-86154-018-3*) Abrams.

Architecture Technology Corporation Staff. IBM Token-Ring Product Guide. 298p. 1991. 165.00 (*1-85617-103-5*, Pub. by Elsvr Adv Tech) Elsevier.

— IBM Token-Ring Report & Reference. x, 178p. 1991. 400.00 (*1-85617-129-9*, Pub. by Elsvr Adv Tech) Elsevier.

Architekturgalerie Luzern Staff. Jean Nouvel-Luzern: Concert Hall Konzertsaal Salle De Concert Luzern. (Illus.). 112p. 1999. pap. 35.00 (*3-7643-5995-1*, Pub. by Birkhauser) Princeton Arch.

Architekturgalerie Luzern Staff, ed. Peter Zumthor: Drei Konzepte. (Illus.). 84p. 1997. pap. 35.00 (*3-7643-5744-4*, Pub. by Birkhauser) Princeton Arch.

— Peter Zumthor: Three Concepts. LC 97-39815. (Illus.). 84p. 1997. pap. 35.00 (*3-7643-5745-2*, Pub. by Birkhauser) Princeton Arch.

Archiv, Bauhaus. Bauhaus: 1919-1933. LC 99-461714. 1998. 24.99 (*3-8228-7627-5*) Taschen Amer.

Archive Editions Staff. Military Handbooks of Arabia, 1913-1917, 10 vols., Set. (Illus.). 5140p. (C). 1988. reprint ed. lib. bdg. 1495.00 (*1-85207-080-3*, Pub. by Archive Editions) N Ross.

— Persian Gulf Administration Reports, 1837-1957, 11 vols., Set. 7500p. (C). 1986. reprint ed. lib. bdg. 2495.00 (*1-85207-010-2*, Pub. by Archive Editions) N Ross.

— The Persian Gulf Gazette & Supplements, 1953-1972, 6 vols., Set. 3900p. (C). 1987. reprint ed. lib. bdg. 995.00 (*1-85207-090-0*, Pub. by Archive Editions) N Ross.

Archives, Jean P., ed. see Tryphon, Anastasia & Voneche, Jacques.

Archives of American Art Staff. Archives of American Art Collection of Exhibition Catalogs. 1979. 175.00 (*0-8161-1531-1*, G K Hall & Co) Mac Lib Ref.

Archives of American Art Staff, intro. The Card Catalog of the Manuscript Collections of the Archives of American Art: 1981-84 Supplement. LC 84-20203. 542p. 1985. lib. bdg. 75.00 (*0-8420-2235-X*) Scholarly Res Inc.

Archives Research Ltd. Staff. The Bahrain Government Annual Reports, 1924-1970, 8 vols. (Illus.). 4000p. (C). 1986. reprint ed. lib. bdg. 1495.00 (*1-85207-040-4*, Pub. by Archive Editions) N Ross.

— Islands & Maritime Boundaries of the Gulf, 1798-1960, 20 vols., Set. 11000p. (C). 1987. text 15000.00 (*0-7855-2613-7*, Pub. by Archive Res Ltd) St Mut.

— La Nation Arabe, 1930-1938, 4 vols., Set. 2400p. (C). 1987. text 1600.00 (*0-7855-5291-X*, Pub. by Archive Res Ltd) St Mut.

— The Middle East Intelligence Handbooks, 1943-1946, 5 vols., Set. (Illus.). 3178p. (C). 1987. reprint ed. lib. bdg. 995.00 (*1-85207-060-9*, Pub. by Archive Editions) N Ross.

— Neglected Arabia - Arabia Calling, 1892-1962, 8 vols., Set. 4600p. (C). 1988. reprint ed. lib. bdg. 995.00 (*1-85207-110-9*, Pub. by Archive Editions) N Ross.

— The Persian Gulf Historical Summaries, 1907-1953, 5 vols., Set. (Illus.). 92p. (C). 1987. reprint ed. lib. bdg. 395.00 (*1-85207-105-2*, Pub. by Archive Editions) N Ross.

— The Persian Gulf Pilot, 1864-1932, 8 vols., Set. 2600p. (C). 1989. reprint ed. lib. bdg. 395.00 (*1-85207-180-X*, Pub. by Archive Editions) N Ross.

— Persian Gulf Trade Reports, 1905-1940, 8 vols., Set. 3250p. (C). 1987. reprint ed. lib. bdg. 995.00 (*1-85207-050-1*, Pub. by Archive Editions) N Ross.

— Political Diaries of the Persian Gulf, 1904-1965, 20 vols. (C). 1987. text 11000.00 (*0-318-68197-8*, Pub. by Archive Res Ltd) St Mut.

— Political Diaries of the Persian Gulf, 1904-1965, 24 vols., Set. 13000p. (C). 1990. reprint ed. lib. bdg. 3995.00 (*1-85207-250-4*, Pub. by Archive Editions) N Ross.

Archives Research Ltd. Staff, ed. The Buraimi Memorials, 1955, 5 vols., Set. (Illus.). 2100p. (C). 1987. reprint ed. lib. bdg. 995.00 (*1-85207-070-6*, Pub. by Archive Editions) N Ross.

Archondo-Callao, Rodrigo S. & Faiz, Asif. Estimating Vehicle Operating Costs. LC 93-37219. (Technical Papers: Vol. 234). 96p. 1994. pap. 24.00 (*0-8213-2677-5*, 12677) World Bank.

Archpriest Boris Molchanov. Antikhrist.Tr. of Antichrist. 24p. 1976. pap. 1.00 (*0-317-29128-9*) Holy Trinity.

— Epokha Apostasii.Tr. of Epoch of Apostasy. 24p. 1976. pap. 1.00 (*0-317-29125-4*) Holy Trinity.

Archpriest Kyrill Zaits. Tserkov' Boga Ahivago, Stolp i Utverzhdjenije Istini.Tr. of Church of the Living God, Piller & Affirmation of Truth. 92p. 1956. pap. 2.00 (*0-317-29113-0*) Holy Trinity.

Archpriest Michael Bogoslovsky. Prigotovlenije k Ispovjedi i Blagogvejnomy Prithashcheniju Svijatikh Khristvikh Tajin.Tr. of Preporation for Confession & the Receiving of the Holy Mysteries. 169p. reprint ed. pap. 8.00 (*0-317-29105-X*) Holy Trinity.

Archpriest Michael Kheraskov & Athanasiev, D. Rukovodstvo k Izucheniju Svijashchennago Pisanija Vjetkhago Zavjeta, 3 vols.Tr. of A/Guide for Study of the Holy Scriptures of the Old Testament. 942p. reprint ed. pap. text 32.00 (*0-317-29295-1*) Holy Trinity.

Archpriest Mitrophan Znosko-Borovsky. Iz Missionersko-Pastirskoj Dejatel'nosti na Nivje Khristovoj v Emigratsii.Tr. of From My - Missionary-Pastoral Activities in Christ's Field in the Immigration. 320p. 1985. pap. 12.00 (*0-317-29117-3*) Holy Trinity.

Archuleta, Hank, jt. auth. see Bennett, William H.

Archuleta, Margaret. Fifth Biennial Native American Fine Arts Invitational, December 7, 1991-August 30, 1992: Lance Belanger, Susie Bevins-Ericsen-Qimmiqsak, Jeffrey Chapman, S. Ruth Cuthand, James Joe, Anthony Jojola, George Littlechild, Dan Viets Lomahaftewa,

A

An Asterisk (*) at the beginning of an entry indicates that the title is appearing for the first time.

A

Jolene Rickard, Gail Tremblay, Lauren Wuttunee, Phil Young. (Illus.). 40p. (Orig.). 1991. pap. 4.95 (*0-934351-33-3*) Heard Mus.

— The Fourth Biennial Native American Fine Arts Invitational, October 21, 1989-Spring 1990. LC 90-113577. (Illus.). 32p. (Orig.). 1989. pap. 5.00 (*0-934351-03-1*) Heard Mus.

— The Heard Museum 6th Native American Fine Arts Invitational, September 24, 1994-October 1, 1995: Norman Akers, Rebecca Gloria-Jean Baird, Rebecca Belmore, Susan A. Point, Duane Slick, Bently Spang. Gully, Anne, ed. LC 94-78496. (Illus.). 26p. (Orig.). 1994. pap. 5.95 (*0-934351-45-7*) Heard Mus.

Archuleta, Margaret & Strickland, Rennard, eds. Shared Visions: Native American Painters & Sculptors in the Twentieth Century. 2nd ed. LC 92-50853. (Illus.). 112p. (Orig.). 1993. pap. 20.00 (*1-56584-069-0*, Pub. by New Press NY) Norton.

Archuleta, Margaret, et al. Mayan Life: Source & Symbol: The Paintings of Nicolas Reanda Quieju. LC 96-28449. 1996. write for info. (*0-934351-55-4*) Heard Mus.

— Red River Crossings: Contemporary Native American Artists Respond to Peter Rindisbacher (1806-1834) (Illus.). 60p. (Orig.). Date not set. pap. 15.00 (*1-884692-04-4*) Swiss Inst.

***Archuleta, Margaret, et al.** Remembering Our Indian Schools. LC 00-32012. 2000. write for info. (*0-934351-62-7*) Heard Mus.

Archwamety, Teara. Data Analysis: Using IBM PC Computers. rev. ed. 156p. (Orig.). 1995. 45.00 incl. disk (*1-878276-36-0*) Educ Systs Assocs Inc.

— Data Analysis: Using Macintosh Computers. 329p. (Orig.). (C). 1994. student ed. 45.00 incl. disk (*1-878276-50-6*) Educ Systs Assocs Inc.

Archway Paperbacks Editorial Staff, ed. Most Wanted Holiday Hunks, Vol. 1. (J). 1998. mass mkt. 7.99 (*0-671-02665-8*) S&S Trade.

Archway Paperbacks Staff, ed. Hunks & Kisses. (Illus.). (YA). 1999. 7.99 (*0-671-02807-3*, PB Trade Paper) PB.

Archway Press, Inc. Staff. Complete Book of Affordable Homes. 1994. pap. 8.95 (*1-882697-01-4*) Archway Pr.

— Five: A Biography. 1999. mass mkt. 4.99 (*0-671-03639-4*, Archway) PB.

Archway Staff. The Essential Angel: A Poster Book, 1. (Illus.). 32p. (gr. 4-7). 1999. per. 7.99 (*0-671-03653-X*, Archway) PB.

— Ghost Stories. (J). (gr. 3 up). 1990. mass mkt. 2.95 (*0-671-73695-7*, Archway) PB.

ARCIC II Staff. Salvation & the Church: An Agreed Statement by the Second Anglican-Roman Catholic International Commission. (Lambeth Study Papers). 30p. 1987. pap. 1.40 (*0-88028-063-8*, 884) Forward Movement.

Arcidiacono, Giuseppe. Projective Relativity Cosmology & Gravitation. 295p. 1986. pap. text 60.00 (*0-911767-39-8*) Hadronic Pr Inc.

Arcidiacono, Michael J. & Maier, Eugene. Picturing Algebra, Unit IX. (Math & the Mind's Eye Ser.). (Illus.). 88p. (C). 1993. teacher ed., ring bd. 10.00 (*1-886131-21-X*, ME9) Math Lrning.

Arcidiacono, Michael J., et al. Seeing Symmetry, Unit X. (Math & the Mind's Eye Ser.). (Illus.). 81p. (C). 1996. text, teacher ed. 10.00 (*1-886131-22-8*, ME10) Math Lrning.

Arcidiacono, Michael J., jt. auth. see Shaughnessy, Michael.

***Arcieri, Anthony & Green, Marianne.** Majoring in Success: Building Your Career While Still in College. 128p. 1999. pap. 8.00 (*1-57509-046-5*) Octameron Assocs.

***Arciero, Susan.** Nantucket 1, (2), 3. large type ed. LC 99-91977. (Illus.). (J). (ps). 2000. 7.95 (*0-9677548-2-8*) Pigtail Pub MD.

Arcilla, A. S., et al, eds. Coastal Dynamics, 1994: Proceedings of an International Conference on the Role of the Large-Scale Experiments in Coastal Research, Universitat Politecnica de Catalunya, Barcelona, Spain, February 21-25, 1994. LC 94-5424. 1000p. 1994. 76.00 (*0-7844-0043-1*) Am Soc Civil Eng.

— Computer Modelling in Ocean Engineering 91: Proceedings of the Second International Conference, Barcelona, 30 September-4 October 1991. (Illus.). 580p. (C). 1991. text 136.00 (*90-5410-024-9*, Pub. by A A Balkema) Ashgate Pub Co.

***Arcilla, Jose S.** An Introduction to Philippine History. 4th enl. ed. 152p. 1999. pap. text 8.00 (*971-550-261-X*, Pub. by Ateneo de Manila Univ Pr) UH Pr.

Arcilla, Rene. For the Love of Perfection: Richard Rorty & Liberal Education. LC 94-20981. 224p. (C). 1994. pap. 19.99 (*0-415-91051-X*, B4156) Routledge.

Arcilla, Rene V. For the Love of Perfection: Richard Rorty & Liberal Education. LC 94-20981. 224p. (C). (gr. 13). 1994. 70.00 (*0-415-91050-1*, B4152) Routledge.

Arciniegas, German. America Ladina. (SPA.). 432p. 1993. 27.99 (*968-16-4208-2*, Pub. by Fondo) Continental Bk.

Arciniegas, German, et al. Secrets of El Dorado: Colombia. (Illus.). 240p. 1992. 65.00 (*0-252-01914-8*) U of Ill Pr.

Arciniegas, Triunfo. Los Casibandidos Que Casi Se Roban el Sol (The Almost Bandits Who Almost Steal the Sun, & Other Stories) (SPA.). 40p. (J). (gr. 5-6). 1991. pap. 5.99 (*968-16-3670-8*, Pub. by Fondo) Continental Bk.

Arcipreste de Hita. Libro de Buen Amor. (SPA.). 7.95 (*84-241-5640-4*) E Torres & Sons.

— Libro de Buen Amor. (Nueva Austral Ser.: No. 9). (SPA.). pap. 12.95 (*84-239-1809-2*) Elliots Bks.

Arciszewski, Tomasz & Rossman, Lewis A., eds. Knowledge Acquisition in Civil Engineering. LC 91-41435. 232p. 1992. pap. text 5.00 (*0-87262-864-7*) Am Soc Civil Eng.

Arckens-Keustermans, Ingrid M., jt. auth. see Keustermans, Jozef A.

Arclais De Montamy, Didier D. Traite des Couleurs pour la Peinture en Email et Sur la Porcelaine. lii, 287p. 1981. reprint ed. 71.00 (*3-487-07062-6*) G Olms Pubs.

Arceneaux, Lynette, et al. Tastefully Yours. 3rd ed. (Illus.). 148p. 1992. reprint ed. 2.95 (*0-9637140-0-7*) Tstefully Yours.

Arco. Civil Service Handbook. 14th ed. (Arco Civil Service Ser.). 272p. 1999. pap. text 12.95 (*0-02-863541-8*, Arco) Macmillan Gen Ref.

— College Admissions. (Unofficial Guides Ser.). 416p. 1999. pap. text 16.95 (*0-02-863547-7*, Arco) Macmillan Gen Ref.

— Nursing School & Allied Health Entrance Exams. 15th ed. (Arco Nursing & Allied Health Programs Ser.). 432p. 1999. pap. text 16.95 (*0-02-863542-6*, Arco) Macmillan Gen Ref.

— Postal Exams Handbook. 5th ed. 272p. 1999. pap. text 12.95 (*0-02-863538-8*, Arco) Macmillan Gen Ref.

— TOEFL Supercourse, Vol. 2. 3rd ed. 1995. pap. 5.25 (*0-02-860567-5*) Free Pr.

***Arco Editorial.** The Homeschooler's Guide to Transcripts & Portfolios with CD-ROM. 320p. 1999. pap. text 19.95 (*0-02-863738-0*) Macmillan.

***Arco Editorial, ed.** Arco EMT-Basic Exams. (Illus.). 272p. 2000. pap. 12.95 (*0-02-863759-3*, Arco) Macmillan Gen Ref.

ARCO Editorial Board Staff. ACT, 2000 Edition, with CD. 2000th ed. LC 99-61614. (Arco ACT). (Illus.). 720p. 1999. pap. 14.95 incl. cd-rom (*0-02-863239-7*, Arc) IDG Bks.

— Allied Health Professions. 176p. 1993. per. 18.00 (*0-671-84708-2*, Arc) IDG Bks.

— Arco Praxis I/PPST. 3rd ed. LC 96-176971. 208p. 1996. 15.95 (*0-02-861078-4*) Macmillan.

***ARCO Editorial Board Staff.** Bar Decors. (Illus.). 2001. pap. 29.95 (*84-8185-266-X*) Arco Edit.

ARCO Editorial Board Staff. The Best of Monarch Notes, Vol. 1. 1995. pap. 15.00 (*0-671-51903-4*) S&S Trade.

— The Best of Monarch Notes, Vol. 2. 1995. pap. 15.00 (*0-671-51904-2*) S&S Trade.

***ARCO Editorial Board Staff.** Big Book of Drawing & Painting. (Illus.). 2000. 39.95 (*84-8185-231-7*) Arco Edit.

— Big Book of Environmental Design. (Illus.). 2000. pap. 39.95 (*84-8185-234-1*) Arco Edit.

— Big Book of Twenty-Five Houses. (Illus.). 2000. pap. 39.95 (*84-8185-232-5*) Arco Edit.

ARCO Editorial Board Staff. Building Details. (Details in Architecture Ser.). (Illus.). 108p. 1998. pap. text 19.95 (*0-8230-7188-X*) Watsn-Guptill.

— Classical Furniture. (Illus.). 208p. 1998. 55.00 (*0-8230-6606-1*) Watsn-Guptill.

— Clerical Exams Handbook. 2nd ed. 224p. 1996. 14.95 (*0-02-861056-3*) Macmillan.

— A Commercial Truck Driver's Guide to Driver Licensing. 512p. 1990. pap. 24.95 (*0-13-152258-2*) P-H.

***ARCO Editorial Board Staff.** European Architecture. (Illus.). 2000. pap. 39.95 (*84-8185-233-3*) Arco Edit.

ARCO Editorial Board Staff. House Details. (Details in Architecture Ser.). (Illus.). 108p. 1998. pap. text 19.95 (*0-8230-7185-5*) Watsn-Guptill.

***ARCO Editorial Board Staff.** International Beach Houses. (Illus.). 2000. pap. 29.95 (*84-8185-237-6*) Arco Edit.

— Landscape Artists. (Illus.). 2000. pap. 29.95 (*84-8185-236-8*) Arco Edit.

— Master the MAT 2001: Miller Analogies Test. 702p. 2000. pap. 15.95 (*0-7645-6144-8*) IDG Bks.

ARCO Editorial Board Staff. New Modern Furniture Design. (Illus.). 208p. 1998. 55.00 (*0-8230-7194-4*) Watsn-Guptill.

***ARCO Editorial Board Staff.** New Projects. 2000. pap. 39.95 (*84-8185-235-X*) Arco Edit.

ARCO Editorial Board Staff. Peripheral Parks, 3. (Urban Spaces Ser.). (Illus.). 256p. 1997. 80.00 (*84-8185-007-1*) Watsn-Guptill.

— Restaurant Details. (Details in Architecture Ser.). (Illus.). 108p. 1998. pap. text 19.95 (*0-8230-7186-3*) Watsn-Guptill.

***ARCO Editorial Board Staff.** School of Drawing. (Illus.). 2000. pap. 24.95 (*84-8185-228-7*) Arco Edit.

— Start Learning Oil Painting. (Illus.). 2000. pap. 24.95 (*84-8185-230-9*) Arco Edit.

— Storage: Shelves & Cupboards: Practical Library of Home Decoration. (Illus.). 2001. pap. 19.95 (*84-8185-262-7*) Arco Edit.

— TOEFL Supercourse, Vol. 3. 3rd ed. 1995. pap. text 5.45 (*0-02-861167-5*, Arc) IDG Bks.

ARCO Editorial Board Staff. Urban Space Details. (Details in Architecture Ser.). (Illus.). 108p. 1998. pap. text 19.95 (*0-8230-7187-1*) Watsn-Guptill.

***ARCO Editorial Board Staff.** Urban Spaces: Streets, Squares & Parks. (Illus.). 2001. 29.95 (*84-8185-272-4*) Arco Edit.

ARCO Editorial Board Staff. Urban Spaces I: Streets & Squares. (Urban Spaces Ser.). (Illus.). 256p. 1997. 80.00 (*84-8185-005-5*) Watsn-Guptill.

— Urban Spaces II: Urban Parts. (Urban Spaces Ser.). (Illus.). 256p. 1997. 80.00 (*84-8185-006-3*) Watsn-Guptill.

***ARCO Editorial Board Staff.** Watercolor Fundamentals. (Illus.). 2000. pap. 24.95 (*84-8185-229-5*) Arco Edit.

ARCO Editorial Board Staff, ed. Arco Praxis I/PPST. 4th ed. 240p. 1998. pap. text 15.95 (*0-02-862462-9*, Arc) IDG Bks.

— PPST: Pre-Professional Skills Test. 224p. 1991. pap. 14.00 (*0-13-691130-7*, Arco) Macmillan Gen Ref.

— Unofficial Guide to Studying Abroad. 416p. 1999. pap. text 14.95 (*0-02-863700-3*) S&S Trade.

***ARCO Editorial Board Staff & Turlington, Shannon R., eds.** Field Guide to Colleges. 992p. 1999. pap. 24.95 incl. cd-rom (*0-02-863325-3*, Arco) Macmillan Gen Ref.

ARCO Editorial Board Staff & Vedral, Joyce L. TOEFL Supercourse, Vol. 1. 3rd ed. 1995. pap. 5.25 (*0-02-860566-7*) Free Pr.

ARCO Editorial Board Staff, et al. Automobile Technician Certification Tests: National Institute for Automotive Service Excellence Exam. 3rd ed. LC 93-34094. 208p. 1994. per. 16.95 (*0-671-87071-8*) IDG Bks.

***Arco Editorial Staff.** Arco Master the AP Biology Exam. 2000. pap. 15.99 (*0-7645-6180-4*) IDG Bks.

— Arco Special Agent, Deputy U.S. Marshal. 10th ed. 224p. 2000. pap. 19.99 (*0-7645-6104-9*) IDG Bks.

— How to Become a U. S. Citizen. 3rd ed. 176p. 2000. pap. 12.95 (*0-7645-6097-2*) IDG Bks.

— Law Enforcement Exams. 4th ed. 224p. 2000. pap. 12.95 (*0-7645-6099-9*) IDG Bks.

— Master the SSAT & ISEE 2001. (Illus.). 702p. 2000. pap. 13.95 (*0-7645-6145-6*) IDG Bks.

— Master the TOEFL 2001. 720p. 2000. pap. 16.95 (*0-7645-6146-4*) IDG Bks.

Arco Editorial Staff. Oliver Twist. (C). 3.95 (*0-671-00824-2*, Arco) Macmillan Gen Ref.

— Siddhartha. 1973. 3.95 (*0-671-00922-2*, Arco) Macmillan Gen Ref.

Arco Editorial Staff, ed. Monarch Notes on Faulkner's Sound & the Fury. 4.50 (*0-671-00613-4*, Arco) Macmillan Gen Ref.

***Arco Editorial Team Staff.** Drawing. 2000. pap. 19.95 (*84-8185-249-X*) Watsn-Guptill.

— Watercolor. 2000. pap. 19.95 (*84-8185-248-1*, Pub. by Arco Edit) Watsn-Guptill.

Arco, Hearst Books International Staff. The Architecture of Minimalism. (Illus.). 192p. 1998. pap. 39.95 (*0-8230-6149-3*, Whitney Lib) Watsn-Guptill.

— The Architecture of Museums. (Illus.). 192p. 1998. pap. 39.95 (*0-8230-6131-0*, Whitney Lib) Watsn-Guptill.

Arco, Jose Nunez del, see Nunez del Arco, Jose, ed.

***Arco Publishing Co. Staff.** Master the GRE 2001. (Arco GRE). 704p. 2000. pap. 13.95 (*0-7645-6119-7*) IDG Bks.

— Master the LSAT 2001. (Arco LSAT Ser.). 448p. 2000. pap. 16.95 (*0-7645-6121-9*) IDG Bks.

— Master the SAT & PSAT 2001. (Arco SAT & PSAT Ser.). 672p. 2000. pap. 12.95 (*0-7645-6120-0*) IDG Bks.

***Arco Publishing Staff.** Absolute Decoration. 2000. pap. 29.95 (*84-8185-224-4*) Arco Edit.

— Master the ACT 2001. (Arco ACT Ser.). 608p. 2000. pap. 13.95 (*0-7645-6117-0*) IDG Bks.

— Master the Catholic High School Entrance Examinations 2001. 408p. 2000. pap. 13.95 (*0-7645-6081-6*) IDG Bks.

— Master the GMAT 2001. 560p. 2000. pap. 13.95 (*0-7645-6118-9*) IDG Bks.

***Arco Staff.** Arco NCLEX LPN Certification Exams. (Illus.). 432p. 2000. pap. 14.95 (*0-02-863778-X*, Arco) Macmillan Gen Ref.

— Teach Yourself the ACT in 24 Hours. 2000th ed. LC 99-461856. (Illus.). 439p. 1999. pap. 14.95 (*0-02-863679-1*, Arc) IDG Bks.

Arco Torres, Miguel. Diccionario de Derecho Civil. (SPA.). 1504p. 1984. 275.00 (*0-7859-3358-1*, 8470162578) Fr & Eur.

Arcocha, Juan. Los Banos de Canela. LC 88-80055. (Coleccion Caniqui). (SPA.). 119p. (Orig.). 1988. pap. 9.95 (*0-89729-476-9*) Ediciones.

Arcodia, Charles. Stories for Sharing: With Themes & Discussion Starters for Teachers & Speakers. 1992. pap. 8.95 (*0-85574-348-4*, Pub. by E J Dwyer) Morehouse Pub.

Arcos, Joseph C., et al, eds. Chemical Induction of Cancer: Modulation & Combination Effects: An Inventory of the Many Factors Which Influence Carcinogenesis. LC 94-29782. 1994. write for info. (*3-7643-3766-4*) Birkhauser.

— Chemical Induction of Cancer: Modulation & Combination Effects: An Inventory of the Many Factors Which Influence Carcinogenesis. LC 94-29782. 725p. 1995. 132.00 (*0-8176-3766-4*) Birkhauser.

Arctic Audubon Society Staff, compiled by. Birds of Alaska Coloring Book. (ENG.). 40p. (J). 1981. pap. 4.00 (*1-57833-097-1*) Todd Commns.

Arctic Institute of North America, Montreal Editor. Catalogue of the Library of the Arctic Institute of North America, First Supplement, 1. 1971. 160.00 (*0-8161-0830-7*, G K Hall & Co) Mac Lib Ref.

— Catalogue of the Library of the Arctic Institute of North America, Third Supplement. 1980. 520.00 (*0-8161-1162-6*, G K Hall & Co) Mac Lib Ref.

Arcucci, Daniel, jt. auth. see Cantor, Andres.

***Arcudi, John.** I Love New York: Gen 13. DeSantis, Eric, ed. (Illus.). 112p. 1999. pap. text 9.95 (*1-56389-543-9*, Pub. by DC Comics) Time Warner.

Arcudi, John. The Mask. deluxe limited ed. (Illus.). 1995. boxed set 99.95 (*1-56971-056-2*) Dark Horse Comics.

— The Mask: Strikes Back. unabridged ed. (Illus.). 128p. (Orig.). (YA). (gr. 9 up). 1996. pap. 17.95 (*1-56971-168-2*) Dark Horse Comics.

— The Mask Returns. (Illus.). 1993. pap. 14.95 (*1-56971-021-X*) Dark Horse Comics.

Arcudi, John & Mahnke, Doug. The Mask Collection. (Illus.). 152p. 1993. pap. 14.95 (*1-878574-50-7*) Dark Horse Comics.

Arcudi, John, et al. Barb Wire. unabridged ed. (Illus.). 96p. (Orig.). 1996. pap. 8.95 (*1-56971-139-9*) Dark Horse Comics.

— Predator: Big Game. unabridged ed. Schutz, Diana, ed. (Predator Ser.). (Illus.). 96p. (YA). (gr. 7 up). 1996. pap. 20.95 (*1-56971-166-6*) Dark Horse Comics.

Arcudi, John, jt. auth. see Willis, Damon.

Arcuri, Lorraine. Symbol Articulation. (Illus.). 406p. 1996. spiral bd. 34.00 (*1-884135-28-5*) Mayer-Johnson.

***Arcus, Sam George.** Deja Views of an Aging Orphan: Growing Up in the Hebrew National Orphan Home. LC 00-190573. 2000. 25.00 (*0-7388-1846-1*); pap. 18.00 (*0-7388-1847-X*) Xlibris Corp.

Arcus, Margaret E., et al, eds. Handbook of Family Life Education. LC 93-26637. (Handbook of Family Life Education Ser.: Vol. 1). 1993. 46.00 (*0-8039-4294-X*) Sage.

— Handbook of Family Life Education, Vol. 2: The Practice of Family Life Education, Vol. 2. (C). 1993. text 39.95 (*0-8039-4295-8*) Sage.

Arczynski, Joanne. Sexual Positions for the Knee Patient. (Illus.). 47p. 1996. pap. text 9.95 (*0-9650561-0-4*) Sex Life.

Ard, Ben N., Jr. Living Without Guilt & or Blame: Conscience, Superego & Psychotherapy. 2nd ed. LC 89-35194. (American University Studies: Psychology: Ser. VIII, Vol. 19). 143p. 1989. text 30.50 (*0-8204-1124-8*) P Lang Pubng.

— Rational Sex Ethics. (American University Studies: Philosophy: Ser. V, Vol. 73). XXVIII, 219p. (C). 1989. text 35.50 (*0-8204-0857-3*) P Lang Pubng.

— The Sexual Realm in Long-Term Marriages: A Longitudinal Study Following Marital Partners over Twenty Years. LC 90-42211. 196p. 1990. lib. bdg. 79.95 (*0-7734-9982-2*) E Mellen.

— Solving Sexual Problems in the 1990's. (American University Studies: Psychology: Ser. VIII, Vol. 15). XIV, 302p. (C). 1989. text 44.95 (*0-8204-1061-6*) P Lang Pubng.

Ard, Ben N., Jr., ed. Counseling & Psychotherapy: Classics on Theories & Issues, 2 vols. LC 93-390. 274p. 1993. pap. text 39.95 (*0-7734-9932-6*); pap. text 39.95 (*0-7734-9934-2*) E Mellen.

Ard, Ben Neal, Jr. A Glossary & Bibliography of Rational-Emotive Therapy Concepts. LC 93-16905. 152p. 1993. 39.95 (*1-880921-30-8*); pap. 24.95 (*1-880921-19-7*) Austin & Winfield.

Ard, Linda & Pitts, Mabel. Room to Grow - How to Create Quality Early Childhood Environments. rev. ed. Parks, Louise, ed. (Illus.). 24p. (C). Date not set. 22.00 (*0-9640108-1-X*) TX Assoc Educ.

Ard, M. D, jt. ed. see Haines, Duane E.

Ard, Patricia M., ed. & intro. see Mann, Mary Peabody.

Ardagh, A. Business Law of Australia Workbook. 2nd ed. 296p. 1994. pap. 35.00 (*0-409-31036-0*, Austral, MICHIE) LEXIS Pub.

— Butterworths Student Companions: Administration Law. 2nd ed. 1994. pap. 18.00 (*0-409-30863-3*, A.T., MICHIE) LEXIS Pub.

Ardagh, Arjuna, ed. Keep Quiet! 200p. (Orig.). 1994. pap. 12.00 (*0-9638022-1-6*) Avadhuta Fnd.

Ardagh, Arjuna N. Relaxing into Clear Seeing: Interactive Tools in the Service of Self-Awakening. Bodian, Stephan, ed. LC 97-91936. (Illus.). xvi, 368p. 1998. pap. 18.95 (*1-890909-15-7*) Self X.

***Ardagh, Arjuna Nick.** How about Now? Satsang with Arjuna. Bishop, Kate, ed. 190p. 1999. pap. text 15.00 (*1-890909-63-7*) Self X.

Ardagh, John. Germany. (C). 1989. 25.00 (*1-85368-049-4*, Pub. by New5 Holland) St Mut.

— Germany & the Germans: New Edition - The United Germany in the Mid-1990s. 624p. 1996. pap. 14.95 (*0-14-025266-5*, Penguin Bks) Viking Penguin.

— Ireland & the Irish. LC 96-151596. 480p. 1995. pap. 13.95 (*0-14-017160-6*) Viking Penguin.

Ardagh, John & Jones, Colin. Cultural Atlas of France. (Cultural Atlas Ser.). (Illus.). 240p. 1991. 45.00 (*0-8160-2619-X*) Facts on File.

Ardagh, Philip. African Myths & Legends. LC 98-2673. (J). 1999. 19.95 (*0-382-42000-4*, Dillon Silver Burdett); pap. 9.95 (*0-382-42001-2*, Dillon Silver Burdett) Silver Burdett Pr.

— Ancient Egyptian Myths & Legends. LC 98-50437. (J). 1999. lib. bdg. write for info. (*0-382-42002-0*) Silver Burdett Pr.

— Ancient Greek Myths & Legends. LC 97-39531. (J). 1999. write for info. (*0-382-39996-X*); pap. write for info. (*0-382-39997-8*) Silver Burdett Pr.

— Celtic Myths & Legends. LC 98-29804. 1999. 23.00 (*0-382-42006-3*, Dillon Silver Burdett); pap. 13.00 (*0-382-42007-1*, Dillon Silver Burdett) Silver Burdett Pr.

— Chinese Myths & Legends. LC 98-43664. 1999. 23.00 (*0-382-42008-X*, Dillon Silver Burdett) Silver Burdett Pr.

— Norse Myths & Legends. LC 97-29439. (Illus.). (J). 1999. 23.00 (*0-382-39994-3*, Dillon Silver Burdett); pap. write for info. (*0-382-39995-1*, Dillon Silver Burdett) Silver Burdett Pr.

— North American Myths & Legends. LC 97-47440. (J). 1999. 23.00 (*0-382-39998-6*, Dillon Silver Burdett); pap. write for info. (*0-382-39999-4*, Dillon Silver Burdett) Silver Burdett Pr.

— South American Myths & Legends. LC 98-34231. (J). 1998. 17.25 (*0-382-42004-7*, Dillon Silver Burdett) Silver Burdett Pr.

Ardal, Pall S. Passion & Value in Hume's Treatise. 2nd ed. 222p. 1990. pap. 28.50 (*0-85224-641-2*, Pub. by Edinburgh U Pr) Col U Pr.

***Ardalan, Abol.** Economic & Financial Analysis for Engineering & Project Management. LC 99-65999. 242p. 1999. text 59.95 (*1-56676-832-2*) Technomic.

***Ardalan, Hayde.** Milton. (Illus.). 40p. 2000. 7.95 (*0-8118-2762-3*) Chronicle Bks.

— Milton's Christmas. LC 00-8932. (Illus.). (J). 2000. pap. write for info. (*0-8118-2842-5*) Chronicle Bks.

Ardalan, Nader & Bakhtiar, Laleh. The Sense of Unity: The Sufi Tradition in Persian Architecture. LC 72-92278. (Illus.). xx, 172p. 1979. pap. 35.95 (*0-226-02560-8*) U Ch Pr.

Ardalan, Nader, jt. auth. see Bakhtiar, Laleh.

Ardanaz, Francisco X. Alerta, el Protestantismo de los Ex-Sacerdotes. LC 86-83109. (SPA.). 117p. (Orig.). 1987. pap. write for info. (*0-89729-429-7*) Ediciones.

Ardant Du Picq, Charles J. Battle Studies: Ancient & Modern Battle. Greely, John N. & Cotton, Robert C., trs. LC 83-45691. reprint ed. 27.00 (*0-404-20006-0*) AMS Pr.

Ardary, Doug. The Pub Crawler's Guide to Montana's Small Town Taverns: A Field Guide to 365 Taverns in Montana's Smallest Communities. LC 96-93006. (Illus.). x, 392p. (Orig.). 1997. pap. 14.95 (*0-9655981-0-1*, 0101) Pub Crawler.

Ardayfio, David D. Fundamentals of Robotics. (Mechanical Engineering Ser.: Vol. 57). (Illus.). 448p. 1987. text 175.00 (*0-8247-7440-X*) Dekker.

Ardeberg, Arne L., ed. Optical Telescopes of Today & Tomorrow, Vol. 2871. LC 97-175314. 1401p. 1997. 195.00 (*0-8194-2268-1*) SPIE.

Ardell, Donald. 14 Days to Wellness: The Easy, Effective & Fun Way to Optimum Health & Total Well-Being. 2nd rev. ed. LC 98-42405. 224p. 1999. pap. 14.00 (*1-57731-028-4*) New Wrld Lib.

Ardell, Donald & Tager, Mark J. Planning for Wellness: A Guidebook for Achieving Optimal Health. 3rd ed. 112p. 1988. per. 16.95 (*0-8403-5031-7*) Kendall-Hunt.

Ardell, Donald B. The Book of Wellness: A Secular Approach to Spirituality, Meaning & Purpose. LC 96-13490. 268p. 1996. 23.95 (*1-57392-083-5*) Prometheus Bks.

— High Level Wellness. LC 77-10993. 384p. 1986. reprint ed. pap. 9.95 (*0-89815-162-7*) Ten Speed Pr.

Ardell, Jeffrey L., jt. ed. see Armour, John A.

Ardema, M. D., ed. Singular Perturbations in Systems & Control. (CISM Courses & Lectures: Vol. 280). (Illus.). 337p. 1983. 51.95 (*0-387-81751-4*) Spr-Verlag.

Ardemagni, Enrica J., ed. Text & Concordance of Biblioteca Nacional, MS2147: Compendio de Cirugia. (Medieval Spanish Medical Texts Ser.: No. 24). (SPA.). 10p. 1988. 10.00 incl. fiche (*0-940639-23-8*) Hispanic Seminary.

Ardemagni, Enrica J., et al, eds. Text & Concordance of Biblioteca Nacional Manuscript 18052, Visita y consejo de medicos. (Medieval Spanish Medical Texts Ser.: No. 3). 8p. 1988. 10.00 incl. fiche (*0-942260-54-6*) Hispanic Seminary.

Ardemagni, Enrica J., ed. see Chirino, Alfonso.

Ardemagni, Enrica J., ed. see Chirino, Alfonso, et al.

Ardemagni, Enrica J., ed. see Lanfranc De Milan, Guido.

Arden. Antony & Cleopatra. Maynard, ed. 1985. pap. 8.95 (*0-415-02680-6*) Routledge.

— Measure for Measure. 1985. pap. 8.95 (*0-416-49630-X*) Routledge.

— Poems. 1985. pap. 8.95 (*0-416-27870-1*) Routledge.

***Arden, Andrea.** Dog Friendly, Dog Training. 160p. 1999. text 17.95 (*1-58245-009-9*) Howell Bks.

Arden, Andrea. Train Your Dog the Lazy Way. (Lazy Way Ser.). 224p. 1998. pap. 12.95 (*0-87605-180-8*) Macmillan Gen Ref.

Arden, Caroline. Getting the Donkey Out of the Ditch: The Democratic Party in Search of Itself, 224. LC 88-10253. (Contributions in Political Science Ser.: No. 224). 188p. 1988. 55.00 (*0-313-25838-4*, AGD/, Greenwood Pr) Greenwood.

Arden, Celeste. The Dreams of Fair Women. 220p. 1988. mass mkt. 4.50 (*0-8216-5028-9*, Pub. by Blue Moon Bks) Publishers Group.

— Fantasy Hunters. 234p. 1990. mass mkt. 4.95 (*0-929654-29-3*, Pub. by Blue Moon Bks) Publishers Group.

Arden, Christopher. Dictionnaire des Calories. (FRE.). 192p. 1990. pap. 12.95 (*0-7859-7983-2*, 2732841307) Fr & Eur.

Arden, Dan, ed. see Cummings, Connie.

Arden, Darlene. The Irrepressible Toy Dog. LC 97-15941. 192p. 1997. 17.95 (*0-87605-649-4*) Howell Bks.

Arden, Eugene. Collected Works of Eugene Arden. (Illus.). 112p. (Orig.). 1990. write for info. (*0-933691-03-3*) U Mich-Dearborn.

Arden Group Staff & Martin, James. A Breakthrough in Making Computers Friendly: The Macintosh Computer. (Illus.). 320p. 1985. pap. 26.95 (*0-685-10930-5*); text 44.00 (*0-13-081589-6*) P-H.

Arden, Harvey, ed. Noble Red Man: Lakota Wisdomkeeper Mathew King. 128p. 1994. 16.95 (*1-885223-01-3*) Beyond Words Pub.

Arden, Harvey & Wall, Steve. Travels in a Stone Canoe: The Return to the Wisdomkeepers. LC 98-19189. (Illus.). 320p. 1998. 25.00 (*0-684-80094-2*) Simon & Schuster.

— Wisdomkeepers: Meetings with Native American Spiritual Elders. LC 90-83550. (Earthsong Collection). (Illus.). 144p. 1990. 39.95 (*0-941831-55-8*) Beyond Words Pub.

— Wisdomkeepers: Meetings with Native American Spiritual Elders. LC 90-83550. (Earthsong Collection). (Illus.). 144p. 1991. pap. 24.95 (*0-941831-66-3*) Beyond Words Pub.

Arden, Harvey, jt. auth. see Peltier, Leonard F.

Arden, Harvey, ed. see King, Mathew.

Arden, Harvey, ed. see Peltier, Leonard.

Arden, Heather M. The Roman de la Rose: An Annotated Bibliography. LC 93-15492. (Medieval Bibliographies Ser.: Vol. 8). 416p. 1993. text 20.00 (*0-8240-5799-6*, H1358) Garland.

— The Romance of the Rose. (World Authors Ser.: No. 791). 144p. 1987. 32.00 (*0-8057-6645-6*, Twyne) Mac Lib Ref.

Arden House Conference Staff. Use of Personnel in Child Welfare Agencies: Proceedings of the Arden House Conference, October 1966. Fradkin, Helen, ed. 1966. 2.00 (*0-686-16767-8*) Univ Bk Serv.

Arden, James, jt. auth. see Arden, John.

Arden, John. Arden: Plays One. 448p. pap. write for info. (*0-413-68800-3*, A0703, Methuen Drama) Methn.

— Arden: Plays Two. pap. write for info. (*0-413-68810-0*, A0704, Methuen Drama) Methn.

— John Arden: Plays One. Incl. Armstrong's Last Goodnight. 1978. Serjeant Musgrave's Dance. 1978. Workhouse Donkey. 1978. 1978. Set pap. 4.95 (*0-394-17061-X*, B415) Grove-Atltic.

— Pearl. 80p. 1995. pap. 9.95 (*0-413-40100-6*, A0207) Heinemann.

***Arden, John & Arden, James.** Advertising Law: 1999 Year in Review. Zale, William, ed. 2000. pap. 85.00 (*0-8080-0477-8*) CCH INC.

Arden, John & D'Arcy, Margaretta. Arden-D'Arcy: Plays One. (Methuen World Dramatists Ser.). 432p. (Orig.). (C). 1991. pap. 15.95 (*0-413-64940-7*, AO564, Methuen Drama) Methn.

— The Business of Good Government. (Methuen Young Drama Ser.). 54p. (C). 1984. pap. write for info. (*0-413-53460-X*, A0043, Methuen Drama) Methn.

— The Royal Pardon. 109p. (C). 1988. pap. write for info. (*0-413-33410-4*, A0249, Methuen Drama) Methn.

— Whose Is the Kingdom? A Nine-Part Radio Series. 212p. (Orig.). (C). 1988. pap. write for info. (*0-413-18710-1*, AO337, Methuen Drama) Methn.

Arden, John, et al. Best Radio Plays of 1982: BBC Giles Cooper Award Winners. 149p. 1988. write for info. (*0-413-52540-6*, A0027, Methuen Drama) Methn.

Arden, John B. Consciousness, Dreams, & Self: A Transdisciplinary Approach. 204p. 1996. 28.50 (*1-887841-01-6*, BN 61043, Psychosocial) Intl Univs Pr.

— Science, Theology & Consciousness: The Search for Unity. LC 97-18723. 208p. 1998. 55.00 (*0-275-96032-3*, Praeger Pubs) Greenwood.

Arden, John Boghosian. Consciousness, Dreams & Self: A Transdisciplinary Approach. 210p. 1999. pap. 25.95 (*1-887841-21-0*, 61044, Psychosocial) Intl Univs Pr.

Arden, Judith. Golden Promises. large type ed. 1995. pap. 18.99 (*1-85389-566-0*, Dales) Ulverscroft.

Arden, Kelvin J. & Whalen, William J. Your Guide to Effective Publications: A Handbook for Campus Publications Professionals. 167p. 1991. pap. 24.00 (*0-89964-282-9*, 20022) Coun Adv & Supp Ed.

Arden, Lynie. The Work-at-Home Sourcebook: How to Find "At-Home" Work That's Right for You. 7th ed. (Work-At-Home Sourcebook Ser.). (Illus.). 304p. 1999. pap. 19.95 (*0-911781-16-1*, 0995, Pub. by Live Oak Pubns) Publishers Group.

***Arden, Lynie, et al.** 101 Best Dot.coms to Start: The Essential Sourcebook of Startup Wisdom, Financial Tips & Inside Secrets for Building a Business on the Internet. LC 00-39774. 544p. 2000. 17.95 (*0-7679-0604-7*) Broadway BDD.

— The 220 Best Franchises to Buy. 3rd ed. LC 99-57644. 496p. 2000. pap. 17.95 (*0-7679-0546-6*) Broadway BDD.

Arden, M. & Burley, S. Solar World Congress, 1991: ISES Solar World Congress, 6 vols., Set. 1992. 1586.00 (*0-08-041690-X*, Pub. by Pergamon Repr) Franklin.

Arden, Margaret. Midwifery of the Soul: A Holistic Perspective on Psychoanalysis. 200p. 1998. 50.00 (*1-85343-389-6*, Pub. by Free Assoc Bks); pap. 21.50 (*1-85343-391-8*, Pub. by Free Assoc Bks) NYU Pr.

Arden, Marianne M., jt. auth. see Dowling, Barbara T.

Arden, Mary. Luck. LC 72-4425. (Short Story Index Reprint Ser.). 1977. reprint ed. 21.95 (*0-8369-4167-5*) Ayer.

Arden, Nicky. African Spirits Speak: A Woman's Journey into the Healing Tradition of the Sangoma. LC 98-52092. 272p. 1999. 14.95 (*0-89281-752-6*, Destiny Bks) Inner Tradit.

— The Spirits Speak: One Woman's Mystical Journey Into the African Spirit World. LC 95-37708. 89p. 1995. 22.50 (*0-8050-4207-5*) H Holt & Co.

Arden, Richard L. & Truelson, John M. Microvascular Free Flaps in Head & Neck Reconstruction. LC 97-36821. (Monograph Ser.). (Illus.). 130p. 1998. pap. text 60.00 (*1-56772-057-9*, 5206265) AAO-HNS.

Arden, Robert, jt. auth. see Zahra, Peter.

Arden, T. Harelquin's Dance. text 35.00 (*0-575-06517-6*, Pub. by V Gollancz) Trafalgar.

Arden, Yves. Telephone Cards. LC 95-131365. (Album Ser.: No. 304). 1999. pap. 4.75 (*0-7478-0253-X*, Pub. by Shire Pubns) Parkwest Pubns.

Ardener, Shirley, ed. Defining Females: The Nature of Women in Society. 2nd ed. LC 92-39823. (Cross-Cultural Perspectives on Women Ser.). 216p. 1993. pap. 19.50 (*0-85496-727-3*, Pub. by Berg Pubs) NYU Pr.

— Persons & Powers of Women in Diverse Cultures. (Illus.). 224p. 1992. pap. 19.50 (*0-85496-866-0*, Pub. by Berg Pubs) NYU Pr.

— Persons & Powers of Women in Diverse Cultures. (Illus.). 224p. 1992. 49.50 (*0-85496-744-3*, Pub. by Berg Pubs) NYU Pr.

— Women & Space: Ground Rules & Social Maps. 2nd rev. ed. 240p. 1993. pap. 19.50 (*0-85496-728-1*, Pub. by Berg Pubs) NYU Pr.

Ardener, Shirley, et al, eds. Money-Go-Rounds: The Importance of ROSCA's for Women. (Cross-Cultural Perspectives on Women Ser.). 320p. 1995. 47.50 (*0-85496-832-6*) Berg Pubs.

— Money-Go-Rounds: The Importance of ROSCAs for Women. (Cross-Cultural Perspectives on Women Ser.). 320p. 1996. pap. 19.50 (*1-85973-170-8*, Pub. by Berg Pubs) NYU Pr.

Ardener, Shirley, jt. auth. see Agbasiere, Joseph Therese.

Ardener, Shirley, jt. auth. see Agbasieri, Joseph-Theresa.

***Ardenne, Paul.** Christian Hauvette. (Illus.). 144p. 2000. pap. 49.95 (*3-7643-6233-2*) Birkhauser.

Ardenne, Von, see Von Ardenne.

Arder, F., jt. ed. see Allgower, M.

Ardery, Julia S. The Temptation: Edgar Tolson & the Genesis of Twentieth-Century Folk Art. LC 97-23897. (Illus.). 376p. 1998. 49.95 (*0-8078-2397-X*); pap. 19.95 (*0-8078-4700-3*) U of NC Pr.

Ardery, Julia S., ed. see Garland, Jim.

Ardery, Mrs. William B. Kentucky (Court & Other) Records Vol. II: Wills, Deeds, Orders, Suits, Church Minutes, Marriages, Old Bibles & Tombstone Records. LC 65-24115. 257p. 1999. reprint ed. 22.50 (*0-8063-0510-X*) Genealog Pub.

Ardery, Philip. Bomber Pilot: A Memoir of World War II. (Illus.). 280p. 1978. pap. 18.00 (*0-8131-0866-7*) U Pr of Ky.

— Heroes & Horses: Tales of the Bluegrass. (Illus.). 128p. 1996. 22.50 (*0-8131-1992-8*) U Pr of Ky.

Ardery, William B. Kentucky Court & Other Records Vol. 1: Early Wills & Marriages, Old Bible Records & Tombstone Inscriptions. LC 65-24115. 206p. 1999. reprint ed. 20.00 (*0-8063-0005-1*) Genealog Pub.

Ardila, A. & Ostrosky-Solis, F. Brain Organization of Language & Cognitive Processes. LC 89-16051. (Critical Issues in Neuropsychology Ser.). (Illus.). 276p. (C). 1989. text 54.00 (*0-306-43169-6*, Kluwer Plenum) Kluwer Academic.

Ardila, A., et al. Neuropsychological Evaluation of the Spanish Speaker. (Critical Issues in Neuropsychology Ser.). (Illus.). 216p. (C). 1994. text 37.50 (*0-306-44149-7*, Kluwer Plenum) Kluwer Academic.

***Ardila, Alfredo, ed.** Assessment of Spanish-Speaking Populations: A Special Issue of Applied Neuropsychology. 2000. pap. write for info. (*0-8058-9759-3*) L Erlbaum Assocs.

Ardila, Alfredo & Ostosky-Solis, Peggy. The Right Hemisphere: Neurology & Neuropsychology. (Monographs in Neuroscience). xvi, 278p. 1984. text 235.00 (*2-88124-103-4*) Gordon & Breach.

Ardila, Alfredo, jt. auth. see Benson, D. F.

Ardila, Patricia, et al, eds. Nuestra Voz: Poblacion y Desarrollo: Perspectiva de Latinamerica y el Caribe. (SPA., Illus.). 44p. (C). 1994. pap. text 5.95 (*1-879358-05-0*) Panos Inst.

Ardila, Patricia, et al. We Speak for Ourselves: Population & Development: Voices from Latin America & the Caribbean. (Illus.). 44p. 1994. pap. 5.95 (*1-879358-04-2*) Panos Inst.

Ardila, Patricia, tr. see Foreman, Martin & De Salazar, Annelise H.

Ardila, R., jt. auth. see Bunge, Mario.

Ardin, William. Plain Dealer. 224p. 1998. 24.00 (*0-7278-5288-4*) Severn Hse.

Ardin, William. Plain Dealer. large type ed. 352p. 31.99 (*0-7089-4044-7*) Ulverscroft.

Ardinger, Barbara. Goddess Meditations. LC 98-39623. (Illus.). 256p. 1999. pap. 17.95 (*1-56718-034-5*) Llewellyn Pubns.

***Ardinger, Barbara.** Practicing the Presence of the Goddess: Everyday Rituals to Personal Power. (Illus.). 128p. 2000. 16.00 (*1-57731-173-6*, Pub. by New Wrld Lib) Publishers Group.

Ardinger, Barbara. A Woman's Book of Rituals & Celebrations. 2nd rev. ed. LC 91-42162. 240p. 1995. pap. 11.95 (*1-880032-57-0*) New Wrld Lib.

Ardinger, Barbara, ed. see Pogosian, Barbara.

Ardinger, Rick, jt. ed. see Studebaker, William.

Ardis, Ann. New Women, New Novels: Feminism & Early Modernism. LC 90-35039. 225p. (Orig.). (C). 1990. text 40.00 (*0-8135-1581-5*); pap. text 15.00 (*0-8135-1582-3*) Rutgers U Pr.

Ardis, Marcia M. Sing Alongs: Helping Children Learn to Read. large type ed. (Illus.). 96p. (J). (ps-2). 1999. pap. 9.95 (*0-9667936-0-9*, 122) Literacy Links.

Ardis, Patrick M. & Comer, Michael J. Risk Management: Computers, Fraud & Insurance. (C). 1986. 240.00 (*0-7855-4235-3*, Pub. by Witherby & Co) St Mut.

Ardis, Susan. Library Without Walls: Plug in & Go. LC 93-47261. 216p. 1994. pap. 36.00 (*0-87111-422-4*) SLA.

ARdissino, Diegoi, et al, eds. Drug Evaluation in Angina Pectoris. LC 94-12345. (Developments in Cardiovascular Medicine Ser.: Vol. 158). 288p. (C). 1994. text 133.50 (*0-7923-2897-3*) Kluwer Academic.

Ardisson, Thierry. Louis the Twentieth. (FRE.). 249p. 1988. pap. 11.95 (*0-7859-2083-8*, 2070379124) Fr & Eur.

Ardist, J. M., et al. Interstitial & Intracavitary Thermoradiotherapy. Seegenschmiedt, Michael H. & Sauer, Rolf, eds. LC 93-13822. (Medical Radiology Ser.). 1993. 305.00 (*0-387-55670-2*) Spr-Verlag.

Arditi. Genealogy of Manners. LC 98-23581. 304p. 1998. pap. text 17.00 (*0-226-02584-5*); lib. bdg. 35.00 (*0-226-02583-7*) U Ch Pr.

Arditi, Aries, et al, eds. Vision into the Future - Toward a Low-Vision Research Agenda: Pisart Tenth-Anniversary Scientific Symposium. 68p. (Orig.). 1991. pap. 10.00 (*0-9603444-9-7*) Lighthouse NYC.

***Arditi, Benjamin.** Polemicization. LC 99-41201. 157p. 1999. pap. text 18.50 (*0-8147-0689-4*) NYU Pr.

***Arditi, Benjamin & Valentine, Jeremy.** Polemicization. LC 99-41201. (Taking on the Political Ser.). 192p. 1999. text 55.00 (*0-8147-0688-6*) NYU Pr.

Arditi, Luigi. My Reminiscences. LC 77-5500. (Music Reprint Ser.). (Illus.). 1977. reprint ed. lib. bdg. 39.50 (*0-306-77417-8*) Da Capo.

Ardito, Carlo, tr. see De Filippo, Eduardo.

***Ardito, Stefano.** History of the Great Mountaineering Adventures. (Illus.). 304p. 2000. 48.00 (*0-89886-722-3*) Mountaineers.

Ardito, Stefano. Mont Blanc: Discovery & Conquest of the Giant of the Alps. Milan, A. B., tr. from ITA. LC 97-223132. (Illus.). 228p. 1997. 48.00 (*0-89886-519-0*) Mountaineers.

Arditti, Fred D. Derivatives: A Comprehensive Resource for Options, Futures, Interest Rate Swaps & Mortgage Securities. LC 95-31894. (Financial Management Association Survey & Synthesis Ser.). 416p. 1996. 60.00 (*0-87584-560-6*) Harvard Busn.

Arditti, Joseph. Fundamentals of Orchid Biology. LC 91-32733. 704p. 1992. 195.00 (*0-471-54906-1*) Wiley.

Arditti, Joseph, ed. Orchid Biology: Reviews & Perspectives, Vol. III. LC 76-25648. (Comstock Bk.). (Illus.). 416p. 1983. text 72.50 (*0-8014-1512-8*) Cornell U Pr.

— Orchid Biology: Reviews & Perspectives, Vol. IV. LC 76-25648. (Comstock Bk.). (Illus.). 352p. 1987. text 72.50 (*0-8014-1777-5*) Cornell U Pr.

— Orchid Biology: Reviews & Perspectives, Vol. V. (Illus.). 432p. 1991. 58.00 (*0-88192-170-X*) Timber.

— Orchid Biology Vol. 6: Reviews & Perspectives, Vol. 6. 610p. 1994. 195.00 (*0-471-54907-X*, Wiley-Liss) Wiley.

Arditti, Joseph & Ernst, Robert. Micropropagation of Orchids. LC 91-40768. 696p. 1993. 195.00 (*0-471-54905-3*) Wiley.

Arditti, Joseph & Pridgeon, Alec M., eds. Orchid Biology Vol. 7: Reviews & Perspectives, Vol. VII. 424p. 1997. text 220.50 (*0-7923-4516-9*) Kluwer Academic.

Arditti, Leon. The Will to Live: 2 Brothers in Auschwitz. LC 96-67119. 200p. 1997. 18.95 (*0-88400-186-5*, Pub. by Schreiber Pub) Natl Bk Netwk.

Arditti, Michael. The Celibate. LC 96-52198. 341p. 1997. 24.00 (*1-56947-089-8*) Soho Press.

— The Celibate. 2000. pap. 13.00 (*1-56947-184-3*) Soho Press.

***Arditti, Michael.** Easter. 2000. pap. 13.99 (*1-900850-34-6*) Arcadia Bks.

Arditti, Michael. Pagan's Father. LC 96-12308. 436p. 1996. 24.00 (*1-56947-062-6*) Soho Press.

— Pagan's Father. 416p. 2000. pap. 14.00 (*1-56947-183-5*) Soho Press.

***Arditti, Rita.** Searching for Life: The Grandmothers of the Plaza de Mayo & the Disappeared Children of Argent. LC 98-46637. 270p. 1999. pap. 17.95 (*0-520-21570-2*, Pub. by U CA Pr) Cal Prin Full Svc.

Arditti, Rita. Searching for Life: The Grandmothers of the Plaza de Mayo & the Disappeared Children of Argentina. LC 98-46637. 270p. 1999. 45.00 (*0-520-21113-8*, Pub. by U CA Pr) Cal Prin Full Svc.

Arditti, Rita, et al, eds. Science & Liberation. 398p. write for info. (*0-919618-97-9*); pap. write for info. (*0-919618-96-0*) Black Rose.

Ardittis, Solon, ed. The Politics of East-West Migration. LC 93-48290. 1994. text 69.95 (*0-312-12140-7*) St Martin.

Arditty, H. J., jt. ed. see Ezekiel, S.

Ardizzi, Maria. Made in Italy, Vol. 10. 2nd rev. ed. Castrilli, Anna Maria, tr. from ITA. 246p. 1999. pap. 8.00 (*1-55071-054-0*) Guernica Editions.

***Ardizzi, Maria.** Women & Lovers: A Novel. 144p. 2000. pap. 13.00 (*1-55071-115-6*, Pub. by Guernica Editions) Paul & Co Pubs.

Ardizzone, E., et al, eds. Trends in Artificial Intelligence: 2nd Congress of the Italian Association for Artificial Intelligence, AI-IA Palermo, Italy, October 29-31, 1991 Proceedings. (Lecture Notes in Artificial Intelligence: Vol. 549). xiv, 479p. 1991. 47.95 (*0-387-54712-6*) Spr-Verlag.

***Ardizzone, Edward.** Little Tim & the Brave Sea Captain. LC 99-33894. 48p. (YA). 2000. 16.00 (*0-688-17678-X*) Morrow Avon.

— Tim & Charlotte. LC 99-47454. (Illus.). 48p. (YA). (ps-3). 2000. 15.95 (*0-688-17680-1*) Morrow Avon.

— Tim & Ginger. 2000. 15.89 (*0-06-029207-5*) HarpC.

— Tim & Ginger. LC 00-20136. (Illus.). 48p. (J). (ps up). 2000. 15.95 (*0-688-17676-3*) Morrow Avon.

— Tim in Danger. 2000. 15.89 (*0-06-029206-7*) HarpC.

— Tim in Danger. LC 00-20136. (Illus.). 48p. (J). (ps up). 2000. 15.95 (*0-688-17675-5*) Morrow Avon.

— Tim to the Rescue. LC 99-47251. (Illus.). 48p. (YA). (ps-3). 2000. 15.95 (*0-688-17679-8*) Morrow Avon.

— Tim's Friend Towser. LC 00-20137. (Illus.). 48p. (J). (ps up). 2000. 15.95 (*0-688-17677-1*) Morrow Avon.

— Tims Friend Towser. 2000. 15.89 (*0-06-029205-9*) HarpC.

Ardizzone, Maria L., ed. & intro. see Pound, Ezra.

***Ardizzone, Matthew.** The Mazurkas Collection. 72p. 1999. 10.95 (*0-7866-4937-2*, 98096) Mel Bay.

Ardizzone, Tony. In the Garden of Papa Santuzzu. LC 99-22963. 368p. 1999. text 24.00 (*0-312-20307-1*, Picador USA) St Martin.

***Ardizzone, Tony.** In the Garden of Papa Santuzzu. 352p. 2000. pap. 14.00 (*0-312-26341-4*) St Martin.

Ardizzone, Tony. Larabi's Ox: Stories of Morocco. LC 92-5306. (Illus.). 250p. 1992. pap. 13.00 (*0-915943-72-7*) Milkweed Ed.

— Taking It Home: Stories from the Neighborhood. LC 95-11027. (Sunsinger Bks. - Illinois Short Fiction). 152p. 1996. 12.95 (*0-252-06483-6*) U of Ill Pr.

Ardle, W. H., et al. Xplore: An Interactive Statistical Computing Environment. LC 94-41488. (Statistics & Computing Ser.). 387p. 1995. 60.95 (*0-387-94429-X*) Spr-Verlag.

Ardley, Brigette & Ardley, Neil. Skin, Hair & Teeth. (How Our Bodies Work Ser.). (Illus.). 48p. (J). (gr. 5-8). 1988. lib. bdg. 12.95 (*0-382-09706-8*) Silver Burdett Pr.

Ardley, Gavin. The Common Sense Philosophy of James Oswald. (Illus.). 150p. 1981. 29.00 (*0-08-025717-8*, Pergamon Pr) Elsevier.

Ardley, Neil. Electricity. LC 91-4963. (Way It Works Ser.). (Illus.). 48p. (J). (gr. 8-9). 1999. text 22.00 (*0-02-705665-1*, Mac Bks Young Read) S&S Childrens.

— Heat. LC 91-29057. (Way It Works Ser.). (Illus.). 48p. (YA). (gr. 6 up). 1992. text 22.00 (*0-02-705666-X*, Mac Bks Young Read) S&S Childrens.

— How Things Work. LC 97-13112. (Techno Guides Ser.). (J). 1997. write for info. (*0-7894-2031-7*) DK Pub Inc.

A

An Asterisk (*) at the beginning of an entry indicates that the title is appearing for the first time.

A

— Jets. LC 97-13111. (Techno Guides Ser.). (J). 1997. write for info. (0-7894-2244-1) DK Pub Inc.

***Ardley, Neil.** Music. (Eyewitness Books). (Illus.). 2000. 19.99 (0-7894-6561-2) DK Pub Inc.

— Music. (Eyewitness Books). (Illus.). (J). (gr. 4-7). 2000. 15.95 (0-7894-5828-4) DK Pub Inc.

— Science. (Concise Encyclopedias Ser.). 192p. (YA). (gr. 5-9). 2000. pap. text 5.95 (0-7894-6107-2, D K Ink) DK Pub Inc.

Ardley, Neil. The Science Book of Air. 32p. 1991. mass mkt. 12.50 (0-385-25296-X) Doubleday.

— The Science Book of Air. LC 90-36103. (Illus.). 29p. (J). (gr. 2-5). 1991. 9.95 (0-15-200578-1); 9.95 (0-15-200576-5) Harcourt.

— Science Book of Electricity. 32p. 1991. 12.50 (0-385-25323-0) Doubleday.

— Science Book of Electricity. LC 90-48030. (Illus.). 29p. (J). (ps-3). 1991. 9.95 (0-15-200583-8, Harcourt Child Bks) Harcourt.

— Science Book of Electricity. 1993. pap. text 11.00 (0-15-365406-6) Harcourt Schl Pubs.

— Science Book of Energy. LC 91-18094. (Illus.). 28p. (J). (gr. 2-5). 1992. 9.95 (0-15-200611-7, Harcourt Child Bks) Harcourt.

— The Science Book of Gravity. 32p. 1992. 12.50 (0-385-25387-7) Doubleday.

— The Science Book of Gravity. LC 92-3413. (Illus.). 28p. (J). 1992. 9.95 (0-15-200621-4, Gulliver Bks) Harcourt.

— The Science Book of Gravity. 1993. pap. text 11.00 (0-15-365415-5) Harcourt Schl Pubs.

— Science Book of Light. 32p. 1991. mass mkt. 12.50 (0-385-25297-8) Doubleday.

— Science Book of Light. LC 90-36102. (Illus.). 29p. (J). (gr. 2-5). 1991. 9.95 (0-15-200577-3) Harcourt.

— Science Book of Magnets. 32p. 1991. 12.50 (0-385-25322-2) Doubleday.

— Science Book of Magnets. LC 90-48028. (Illus.). 29p. (J). (ps-3). 1991. 9.95 (0-15-200581-1, Harcourt Child Bks) Harcourt.

— The Science Book of Motion. 32p. 1992. 12.50 (0-385-25384-2) Doubleday.

— The Science Book of Motion. LC 92-3412. (Illus.). 28p. (J). (ps-3). 1992. 9.95 (0-15-200622-2, Gulliver Bks) Harcourt.

— The Science Book of Numbers. 32p. 1992. 12.50 (0-385-25385-0) Doubleday.

— Science Book of Sound. 32p. 1991. 12.50 (0-385-25321-4) Doubleday.

— Science Book of Sound. 1993. pap. text 11.00 (0-15-365404-X) Harcourt Schl Pubs.

— Science Book of the Senses. LC 91-20587. (Illus.). 28p. (J). (gr. 2-5). 1992. 9.95 (0-15-200614-1, Harcourt Child Bks) Harcourt.

— Science Book of Things That Grow. LC 90-48097. (Illus.). 29p. (J). (ps-3). 1991. 9.95 (0-15-200586-2, Harcourt Child Bks) Harcourt.

— Science Book of Water. 32p. 1991. mass mkt. 12.50 (0-385-25294-3) Doubleday.

— Science Book of Water. LC 90-37176. (Illus.). 29p. (J). (gr. 4-7). 1991. 9.95 (0-15-200575-7) Harcourt.

— Science Book of Water. 1993. pap. text 11.00 (0-15-365400-7) Harcourt Schl Pubs.

— The Science Book of Weather. 32p. 1992. 12.50 (0-385-25386-9) Doubleday.

— A Young Person's Guide to Music: A Listener's Guide, Incl. audio CD. LC 95-19595. (Illus.). 80p. (J). (gr. 4-9). 1995. 24.95 (0-7894-0313-7, 5-70667) DK Pub Inc.

Ardley, Neil, jt. auth. see Ardley, Brigette.

Ardley, Neil, jt. auth. see Farndon, John.

Ardley, Suzanne. Bathroom. LC 98-11907. (Home Design Workbook Ser.). 1999. 12.95 (0-7894-3526-8) DK Pub Inc.

***Ardley, Suzanne.** Kitchen Planner: Hundreds of Great Ideas for Your New Kitchen. LC 99-24934. (Illus.). 112p. 1999. spiral bd. 29.95 (0-8118-2517-5) Chronicle Bks.

— The Time-Life Book of Home Design Techniques. (Illus.). 256p. 2001. 29.95 (0-7370-0321-9) Time-Life Educ.

Ardman, Carol, jt. auth. see Fishman, Loren.

Ardman, Harvey. The Woman's Day Book of Weddings. LC 82-4236. 1982. write for info. (0-672-52729-4) Macmillan.

***Ardo, Zsuzsanna.** Hungary. (Culture Shock! Ser.). 2000. pap. 12.95 (1-55868-530-8) Gr Arts Ctr Pub.

Ardoin, John. Callas at Julliard: The Master Classes. LC 98-17773. (Illus.). 300p. 1998. pap. 19.95 (1-57467-042-5, Amadeus Pr) Timber.

— The Callas Legacy. 1979. 3.95 (0-684-16343-8, Scribners Ref) Mac Lib Ref.

— The Callas Legacy: A Biography of a Career. rev. ed. (Illus.). 256p. 1982. 5.50 (0-684-17450-2, Scribners Ref) Mac Lib Ref.

— The Callas Legacy: The Complete Guide to Her Recordings on Compact Disc. 4th ed. (Illus.). 254p. 1995. pap. 22.95 (0-931340-90-X, Amadeus Pr) Timber.

— The Furtwangler Record. LC 93-32503. (Illus.). 388p. 1994. 32.95 (0-931340-69-1, Amadeus Pr) Timber.

— Master Classes: Callas at Juilliard. 1997. pap. text 16.00 (1-880909-60-X) Baskerville.

Ardoin, John, ed. see Philadelphia Orchestra Association Staff.

Ardoin, Robert B. Louisiana Census Records: Avoyelles & St. Landr. 114p. 1995. reprint ed. pap. 14.00 (0-8063-0446-4, 151) Clearfield Co.

— Louisiana Census Records Vol. II: Iberville, Natchitoches. 216p. 1995. reprint ed. pap. 21.50 (0-8063-0507-X, 152) Clearfield Co.

Ardolina, Rosemary M. Old Calvary Cemetery - New Yorkers Carved in Stone. (Illus.). 549p. (Orig.). 1996. pap. 76.00 (0-7884-0453-9, A615) Heritage Bk.

Ardolino, Frank R. Apocalypse & Armada in Kyd's Spanish Tragedy. LC 94-25542. (Sixteenth Century Essays & Studies (SCE&S): Vol. 29). 187p. 1995. 40.00 (0-940474-31-X, SCJP) Truman St Univ.

Ardon, Patricia. Post-War Reconstruction in Central America: Lessons from El Salvador, Guatemala, & Nicaragua. Eade, Deborah, tr. from SPA. & adapted by by. (Oxfam Working Papers Ser.). 120p. 1998. pap. 15.95 (0-85598-405-8, Pub. by Oxfam Pub) Stylus Pub VA.

***Ardone, Armin Vito.** Entwicklung Einzelstaatlicher und Multinationaler Treibhausgasminderungsstrategien Fur die Bundesrepublik Deutschland Mit Hilfe von Optimierenden Energie- und Stofffluamodellen. xiii, 305p. 1999. 52.95 (3-631-35288-3) P Lang Pubng.

Ardonin, Claude D., ed. Museums & Archaeology in West Africa. LC 98-209036. (Illus.). 163p. (Orig.). 1997. pap. text 26.95 (1-56098-785-5) Smithsonian.

Ardouin, Claude D. & Arinze, Emmanuel, eds. Museums & the Community in West Africa. LC 95-68002. (Illus.). 144p. 1995. pap. text 26.95 (1-56098-611-5) Smithsonian.

***Ardouin, Claude Daniel, et al.** Museums & History in West Africa. LC 99-38643. (Illus.). 192p. 2000. pap. 29.95 (1-56098-805-3) Smithsonian.

Ardouin, D., ed. Corinne '90. 484p. (C). 1990. text 101.00 (981-02-0317-9) World Scientific Pub.

Ardouin, D., jt. auth. see Aichelin, J.

***Ardovino, Joan, et al.** Multiple Measures: Accurate Ways to Assess Student Achievement. LC 00-21527. (Illus.). (J). 2000. write for info. (0-7619-7680-9) Corwin Pr.

Ardrade, Juan Jose. After the Battle of the Alamo: Documents Published by General Juan Jose Andrade on the Evacuation of San Antonio de Bejar, Texas, May 1836. LC 97-60854. (Illus.). 60p. 1997. mass mkt. 9.99 (0-9624727-9-4) LaVillita Pubns.

Ardrey. LC-MS: An Introduction. 350p. 1996. 115.00 (3-527-28633-0, Wiley-VCH) Wiley.

Ardrey, ed. Pharmaceutical Mass Spectra. 1985. 100.00 (0-85369-172-X, Pub. by Pharmaceutical Pr) Rittenhouse.

Ardrey, Robert. Plays of Three Decades: Thunder Rock, Jeb, Shadow of Heroes. LC 67-19963. 255p. 1968. 18.95 (0-910278-89-X) Boulevard.

— Sing Me No Lullaby. 1955. pap. 5.25 (0-8222-1032-0) Dramatists Play.

— The Territorial Imperative: A Personal Inquiry into the Animal Origins of Property & Nations. Turner, Philip, ed. LC 96-45037. 400p. 1997. reprint ed. pap. 16.00 (1-56836-144-0, Kodansha Globe) Kodansha.

— Thunder Rock. 1946. pap. 5.25 (0-8222-1146-7) Dramatists Play.

Ardrey, Robert L. American Agricultural Implements, a Review of Invention & Development in the Agricultural Implement Industry of the United States Pt. 1: General History of Invention & Improvement, Pt. 2 - Pioneer Manufacturing Centers, 2 pts. LC 72-5028. (Technology & Society Ser.). (Illus.). 240p. 1972. reprint ed. 23.95 (0-405-04681-2) Ayer.

Ardsma, Gerald E. A New Approach to the Chronology of Biblical History from Abraham to Samuel. LC 95-95068. 112p. 1995. pap. 24.95 (0-9647665-0-7) Aardsma Res & Pub.

Arduini, A. Principles of Eidetics: Outline of a Theory. xii, 251p. 1991. 99.00 (0-387-54506-9) Spr-Verlag.

Arduini, D., et al, eds. Fetal Cardiac Function. (Illus.). 140p. (C). 1994. text 78.00 (1-85070-467-8) Prthnon Pub.

Arduini, Paolo & Teruzzi, Giorgio. Simon & Schuster's Guide to Fossils. (Nature Guide Ser.). (Illus.). 320p. 1987. pap. 14.00 (0-671-63132-2, Fireside) S&S Trade Pap.

Ardura, Ernesto. America en el Horizonte: Una Perspectiva Cultural. LC 79-54965. (Coleccion de Estudios Hispanicos - Hispanic Studies Collection). (SPA., Illus.). 161p. (Orig.). 1981. pap. 10.95 (0-89729-240-5) Ediciones.

— Cuba y Su Destino Historico. LC 88-83552. (Coleccion Cuba y sus Jueces). (SPA., Illus.). 291p. (Orig.). 1989. pap. 15.00 (0-89729-518-8) Ediciones.

Ardus, D. A. & Champ, M. A., eds. EEZ-Resources: Technology Assessment. Ser. 570p. 1990. 168.00 (0-7923-0954-5) Kluwer Academic.

— EEZ-Resources: Technology Assessment, Vol. 1: Assessment & Utilization. 1990. lib. bdg. 118.50 (0-7923-0952-9) Kluwer Academic.

— EEZ-Resources: Technology Assessment, Vol. 2: Subsea Work Systems & Technologies. 1990. lib. bdg. 145.00 (0-7923-0953-7) Kluwer Academic.

Ardus, D. A. & Green, C. D., eds. Safety in Offshore Drilling: The Roll of Shallow Gas Surveys. (C). 1990. text 160.00 (0-7923-0889-1) Kluwer Academic.

Ardus, D. A., jt. auth. see McQuillan, Robert.

Ardzrooni, Leon, jt. auth. see Veblen, Thorstein B.

Ardzrooni, Leon, ed. see Veblen, Thorstein B.

Are, Thomas L. Israeli Peace - Palestinian Justice: Liberation Theology & the Peace Process. 220p. (Orig.). 1994. pap. 14.95 (0-932863-15-9) Clarity Pr.

— Please Don't Ask Me to Sing in the Choir. 120p. (Orig.). 1985. pap. 8.95 (0-916642-28-3, 905) Hope Pub.

Area Staff. Diccionario de Fisica. (SPA.). 676p. 1990. pap. write for info. (0-7859-6435-5, 8487606016) Fr & Eur.

Arebi, Saddeka. Women & Words in Saudi Arabia: The Politics of Literary Discourse. 357p. 1994. 57.50 (0-231-08420-X); pap. 20.50 (0-231-08421-8) Col U Pr.

Arecchi, Angelo V., ed. Illumination & Source Engineering, Vol. 3428. LC 99-169808. 1998. 48.00 (0-8194-2883-3) SPIE.

— Photometric Engineering of Sources & Systems. 24p. 1997. pap. 59.00 (0-8194-2562-1) SPIE.

Arecchi, F. T. & Harison, R. G., eds. Selected Papers on Optical Chaos. LC 92-46456. (Milestone Ser.: Vol. MS 75/HC). 1993. 45.00 (0-8194-1217-1) SPIE.

Arecchi, F. T. & Harrison, R. G. Instabilities & Chaos in Quantum Optics. (Synergetics Ser.: Vol. 34). (Illus.). 270p. 1987. 72.95 (0-387-17282-3) Spr-Verlag.

Arecchi, F. T. & Harrison, Robert G., eds. Optical Chaos. 736p. 1994. pap. 50.00 (0-8194-1216-3) SPIE.

Arecchi, F. T. & Schulz-Dubois, E. O., eds. Laser Handbook ,Volumes 1 & 2, Vols. 1 & 2. xxxii, 1948p. 1988. reprint ed. 504.50 (0-7204-0213-1, North Holland) Elsevier.

Arechavaleta, Ma. D. Soto de, see Dahlgren, Barbro & Soto de Arechavaleta, Ma. D., eds.

Arechiga, H., jt. ed. see Valverde-Rodriguez, C.

Arechiga, Joseph. The Twin Peaks of 1999 Vol. I: A Stock Market Forecast for 1999. Arechiga, William K., ed. 54p. 1998. pap. 49.95 (0-9670000-0-9) Josephs.

Arechiga, William K. Think, Do & Read. 1999. pap. text 14.95 (1-56822-672-1) Instruct Fair.

Arechiga, William K., ed. see Arechiga, Joseph.

Areco, Amelia. El Cocuyo y la Mora.Tr. of Firefly & the Raspberry. (SPA.). 36p. (J). (gr. 1-4). 1995. pap. 6.95 (980-257-042-7, Pub. by Ediciones Ekare) Kane-Miller Bk.

Areeda, Phillip & Kaplow, Louis. Antitrust Analysis: Problems, Text, Cases. 5th ed. LC 97-27101. 1100p. 1997. boxed set 62.00 (1-56706-566-X) Aspen Law.

Areeda, Phillip E. Antitrust, Vol. 1. 1978. 125.00 (0-316-05046-6, Aspen Law & Bus) Aspen Pub.

— Antitrust, Vol. 2. 1978. 110.00 (0-316-05048-2, Aspen Law & Bus) Aspen Pub.

— Antitrust, Vol. 2. rev. ed. 1994. 125.00 (0-316-05084-9, Aspen Law & Bus) Aspen Pub.

— Antitrust, Vol. 2A. 2nd ed. 1994. 125.00 (0-316-05085-7, Aspen Law & Bus) Aspen Pub.

— Antitrust, Vol. 3. 1978. 125.00 (0-316-05049-0, Aspen Law & Bus) Aspen Pub.

— Antitrust, Vol. 4. 1980. 125.00 (0-316-05051-2) Aspen Pub.

— Antitrust, Vol. 5. 1980. 125.00 (0-316-05054-7, Aspen Law & Bus) Aspen Pub.

— Antitrust, Vol. 6. 1985. 125.00 (0-316-05062-8, Aspen Law & Bus) Aspen Pub.

— Antitrust, Vol. 7. 1985. 125.00 (0-316-05063-6, Aspen Law & Bus) Aspen Pub.

— Antitrust, Vol. 8. 1989. 125.00 (0-316-05071-7, Aspen Law & Bus) Aspen Pub.

— Antitrust, Vol. 9. 1991. 125.00 (0-316-05078-4, Aspen Law & Bus) Aspen Pub.

— Antitrust, Vol. 10. 1995. 135.00 (0-316-05034-2) Aspen Pub.

— Antitrust Law: An Analysis of Antitrust Principles & Their Application. 1989. write for info. (0-318-63272-1, Aspen Law & Bus) Aspen Pub.

— Antitrust, 1995. 1995. 325.00 (0-316-05094-6, Aspen Law & Bus) Aspen Pub.

— Antitrust '94. 1994. pap. text, lib. bdg. 16.50 (0-316-05036-9) Little.

— Temp FM-EM, Nos. 1-9. 1991. 40.00 (0-316-05079-2) Little.

— Temp FM/EM. 1994. lib. bdg. 45.00 (0-316-05017-2) Little.

Areeda, Phillip E. & Kaplow, Louis. Antitrust Analysis: Problems, Text, Cases. 4th ed. 1250p. 1988. 55.00 (0-316-05037-7) Aspen Pub.

Areeda, Phillip E. & Turner, Donald. Antitrust Law: An Analysis of Antitrust Law Principles & Their Application, Vols. I-VII. 5149p. 1985. boxed set 1895.00 (0-316-05052-0, Aspen Law & Bus) Aspen Pub.

Areen, Judith. Family Law, 1997 Supplement to Cases & Materials On. 3rd ed. (University Casebook Ser.). 350p. 1997. pap. text. write for info. (1-56662-539-4) Foundation Pr.

Areen, Judith C. Family Law: Cases & Materials. 3rd ed. (University Casebks.). 1720p. 1992. text 48.95 (0-88277-982-6) Foundation Pr.

— Family Law: Cases & Materials. 3rd ed. 424p. 1992. pap. text, teacher ed. write for info. (1-56662-045-7) Foundation Pr.

— Family Law: 1995 Supplement to Cases & Materials On. 3rd ed. (University Casebook Ser.). 344p. (C). 1995. pap. text 12.95 (1-56662-235-2) Foundation Pr.

Areen, Judith C., et al. Law Science & Medicine. (University Casebook Ser.). 276p. 1996. pap. text. write for info. (1-56662-447-9) Foundation Pr.

— Law, Science & Medicine. LC 84-8181. (University Casebook Ser.). 1494p. (C). 1990. reprint ed. text 44.50 (0-88277-179-5) Foundation Pr.

— Law, Science & Medicine. 2nd ed. Gostin, Lawrence, ed. LC 96-13106. (University Casebook Ser.). 1846p. 1996. text. write for info. (1-56662-338-3) Foundation Pr.

— Law, Science & Medicine: 1988 Supplement. (University Casebook Ser.). 395p. 1990. reprint ed. pap. text 14.50 (0-88277-702-5) Foundation Pr.

Aref, Hassan & El Nashie, M. S., eds. Chaos Applied to Fluid Mixing. 370p. 1995. 107.50 (0-08-042028-1, Pergamon Pr) Elsevier.

Areglado, Ronald J., et al. Learning for Life: Creating Classrooms for Self-Directed Learning. (Illus.). 184p. 1996. 55.95 (0-8039-6385-8); pap. 24.95 (0-8039-6386-6) Corwin Pr.

Arehart, G. B. & Hulston, J. R., eds. Water-Rock Interaction: Proceedings of the 9th International Symposium - WRI-9, Taupo, New Zealand 30 March-3 April, 1998. LC 99-496400. (Illus.). 1020p. (C). 1998. text 146.00 (90-5410-942-4, Pub. by A A Balkema) Ashgate Pub Co.

Arehart, Lynda & Torrie, Margaret. Understanding HIV-AIDS: A Workbook Suitable for Mainstreamed Students. LC 90-71077. (Contemporary Parenting Choices Ser.). (Illus.). 47p. reprint ed. pap. 30.00 (0-608-09061-1, 206969500005) Bks Demand.

Arehart, Lynda L. & Torrie, Margaret. Understanding HIV-AIDS: A Workbook Suitable for Mainstreamed Students. (Contemporary Parenting Choices Ser.). (Illus.). 48p. (YA). (gr. 9-12). 1990. pap. text, teacher ed. 8.95 (0-8138-1619-X) Iowa St U Pr.

Areilza, Jose M. Paisajes y Semblanzas. (Nueva Austral Ser.: No. 64). (SPA.). 1991. pap. text 29.95 (84-239-1856-4) Elliots Bks.

Arellano, E. Ramirez De, see Ramirez de Arellano, E., ed.

Arellano, Enrique R. De, see De Arellano, Enrique R.

***Arellano, Fay L., tr.** Delaware Trails: Some Tribal Records, 1842-1907. 527p. 1998. reprint ed. pap. 55.00 (0-8063-4664-7, Pub. by Clearfield Co) ACCESS Pubs Network.

Arellano, Ignacio, ed. see Molina, Tirso de.

Arellano, Maria, jt. auth. see Schwalm, Nancy.

Arellano, Richard G. & Allen, Alexandra. Export Potential: Mexico Special Research Study. 31p. 1979. 10.00 (0-942286-02-2) Intl Mktg.

Arellano, Susan, ed. see Lustbader, Wendy.

Arellanos, Lita C., tr. see Elovson, Allana.

Arem, Cynthia. Conquering Math Anxiety: A Self-Help Workbook. LC 92-18880. 1992. mass mkt. 12.00 (0-534-18876-1) Brooks-Cole.

Arem, Joel E. Descubre Dinosaurios. University of Mexico City Staff, tr. (Descubre - Spanish Ser.).Tr. of Discover Dinosaurs. (SPA., Illus.). 48p. (J). (gr. 3-6). 1995. lib. bdg. 16.95 (1-56674-049-5, HTS Bks) Forest Hse.

— Descubre Rocas y Minerales. University of Mexico City Staff, tr. (Descubre - Spanish Ser.).Tr. of Discover Rocks & Minerals. (SPA., Illus.). 48p. (J). (gr. 3-6). 1993. lib. bdg. 16.95 (1-56674-051-7, HTS Bks) Forest Hse.

— Gems & Jewelry. 2nd ed. LC 92-72086. (Illus.). 186p. 1992. reprint ed. pap. 13.25 (0-945005-09-1) Geoscience Pr.

— Rocks & Minerals. LC 91-74106. (Illus.). 160p. (YA). 1991. reprint ed. pap. 13.25 (0-945005-06-7) Geoscience Pr.

Arem, Ridha. The Thyroid Solution: A Mind-Body Program for Beating Depression & Regaining Your Emotional & Physical Health. (Illus.). 389p. 1999. 24.00 (0-345-42919-2) Ballantine Pub Grp.

***Arem, Ridha.** The Thyroid Solution: A Mind-Body Program for Beating Depression & Regaining Your Emotional & Physical Health. 400p. 2000. pap. 16.00 (0-345-42920-6) Ballantine Pub Grp.

Arem, T. Z. The Story of Reb Baruch Ber Lebowitz: The Kamenitzer Rosh Yeshiba - Rabbi Baruch Ber Leibowitz & His Successor, Rabbi Reuven Grozovsky. (ArtScroll Youth Ser.). (Illus.). 128p. (YA). (gr. 6-12). pap. 8.99 (0-89906-804-9, RBBP) Mesorah Pubns.

Arem, T. Z., jt. auth. see Roberts, M.

Arem, T. Z., ed. see Bergman, Tzvi.

Arem, T. Z., ed. see Rabinovitch, M.

Arem, T. Z., ed. see Rosenberg, A. Y.

Aremu & Steifel. A Magical Musical Celebration/Kwanzaa. 1997. pap. 19.95 (0-936073-26-8) Gumbs & Thomas.

Aremv, Olaleye, jt. auth. see Stevick, Earl W.

***Arena, Hector Facundo.** Linux - Guia del Administrador en Espanol: Linux - Administrator's Guide in Spanish. deluxe ed. (Manuales Compumagazine Ser.). (SPA., Illus.). 288p. 2000. pap. 19.90 incl. cd-rom (987-526-035-5, Pub. by MP Ediciones) Downtown Bk.

Arena, Jay M. & Bachar, Miriam. Child Safety Is No Accident: A Parents' Handbook of Emergencies. LC 77-80346. xi, 296p. 1978. text 24.95 (0-8223-0390-6) Duke.

Arena, Jay M., ed. see Davidson, Wilburt C.

Arena, Jillayne. Step Back from the Exit: 45 Reasons to Say No to Suicide. LC 95-94711. 1996. pap. text 10.00 (0-9647340-0-1) Zebulon Pr.

Arena, John. Diagnostic Spelling Potential Test (DSPT) 1982. student ed. 23.00 (0-87879-305-4) Acad Therapy.

— How to Write an I.E.P. 1989 Edition. 128p. 1989. pap. text 10.00 (0-87879-072-1) Acad Therapy.

Arena, L. A. Language Proficiency: Defining, Teaching, & Testing. (Topics in Language & Linguistics Ser.). (Illus.). 210p. (C). 1990. 65.00 (0-306-43710-4, Plenum Trade) Perseus Pubng.

Arena, Louis A. Linguistics & Composition: A Method to Improve Expository Writing Skills. LC 75-34100. 212p. reprint ed. pap. 65.80 (0-7837-6304-2, 204601900010) Bks Demand.

Arena, R. & Longhi, Christian, eds. Markets & Organization. LC 97-50107. (Illus.). vi, 697p. 1998. pap. 99.00 (3-540-63810-5) Spr-Verlag.

Arena, Susan, jt. auth. see Hein, Morris.

Arenal, Electa, tr. see De la Cruz, Sor Juana Ines.

Arenal, Electra & Schlau, Stacey, eds. Untold Sisters: Hispanic Nuns in Their Own Works. Powell, Amanda, tr. LC 88-34947. (Illus.). 464p. 1989. reprint ed. pap. 143.90 (0-608-04147-5, 206488000011) Bks Demand.

Arenas, Alberto, jt. auth. see Marcel, Mario.

Arenas, Alberto, jt. ed. see Marcel, Mario.

Arenas, Miguel A., jt. auth. see Salazar Chavez, Gerardo A.

Arenas, Reinaldo. Adios a Mama: De la Habana a Nueva York. LC 96-83114. (Coleccion Caniqui). (SPA.). 175p. (Orig.). 1996. pap. 19.00 (0-89729-791-1) Ediciones.

— El Asalto. LC 90-86232. 141p. 1991. 16.00 (0-89729-596-X) Ediciones.

— The Assault. Hurley, Andrew, tr. from SPA. 160p. 1995. pap. 10.95 (0-14-015718-2, Penguin Bks) Viking Penguin.

— Before Night Falls: A Memoir. Koch, Dolores M., tr. 336p. 1994. reprint ed. pap. 11.95 (0-14-015765-4, Penguin Bks) Viking Penguin.

— Celestino Antes del Alba. 2nd ed. LC 95-60529. (Coleccion Caniqui). (SPA.). 215p. 1996. pap. 18.00 (0-89729-772-5) Ediciones.

An Asterisk (*) at the beginning of an entry indicates that the title is appearing for the first time.

— El Color del Verano. LC 90-86229. (Coleccion Caniqui). (SPA.). 446p. (Orig.). 1991. pap. 29.00 (*0-89729-595-1*) Ediciones.

— El Color del Verano. (Orig.). 1999. pap. 9.95 (*0-14-015719-0*) Viking Penguin.

— The Color of Summer or The New Garden of Earthly Delight. Hurley, Andrew, tr. LC 99-55698. 448p. 2000. 28.95 (*0-670-84065-3*) Viking Penguin.

— The Doorman. LC 90-28775. 208p. 1995. pap. 10.00 (*0-8021-3405-X*, Grove) Grove-Atltic.

— Farewell to the Sea. 432p. 1987. pap. 11.95 (*0-14-006636-5*, Penguin Bks) Viking Penguin.

— Graveyard of the Angels. MacAdam, A., tr. 128p. 1987. pap. 3.95 (*0-380-75075-9*, Avon Bks) Morrow Avon.

— The Ill-Fated Peregrinations of Fray Servando. Hurley, Andrew, tr. 272p. 1987. pap. 7.95 (*0-380-75074-0*, Avon Bks) Morrow Avon.

— La Loma del Angel. LC 95-60528. (Coleccion Caniqui). (SPA.). 140p. (Orig.). 1995. reprint ed. pap. 16.00 (*0-89729-519-6*) Ediciones.

— Old Rosa & the Brightest Star. LC 88-21421. 106p. 1995. pap. 10.00 (*0-8021-3406-8*, Grove) Grove-Atltic.

— The Palace of the White Skunks. Hurley, Andrew, tr. 368p. 1993. pap. 12.50 (*0-14-009792-9*, Penguin Bks) Viking Penguin.

— Persecucion: Cinco Piezas de Teatro Experimental. LC 86-80353. (Coleccion Teatro). (SPA.). 67p. (Orig.). 1986. pap. 7.95 (*0-89729-391-6*) Ediciones.

— El Portero. LC 89-82738. (Coleccion Caniqui). (SPA.). 158p. (Orig.). 1990. pap. 16.00 (*0-89729-560-9*) Ediciones.

— Singing from the Well. 224p. 1988. pap. 7.95 (*0-14-009444-X*, Penguin Bks) Viking Penguin.

— Viaje a la Habana. LC 89-85397. (Coleccion Caniqui). (SPA.). 158p. (Orig.). 1990. pap. 16.00 (*0-89729-544-7*) Ediciones.

Arenas, Roberto & Estrada, Roberto. Tropical Dermatology. LC 99-10905. (Vademecum Ser.). 316p. 2000. spiral bd. 45.00 (*1-57059-493-7*) Landes Bioscience.

Arenas, Shelley. Seattle Baby Resource Guide. 2nd ed. Hazen, Kari & Smith, Troy M., eds. (Illus.). 340p. (Orig.). 1996. 10.95 (*0-9633777-5-2*) Im Expecting.

Arenas, Shelley & Hazen, Kari. Seattle Baby Resource Guide. (Illus.). 340p. (Orig.). 1995. pap. 10.95 (*0-9633777-3-6*) Im Expecting.

Arenau, jt. auth. see Anderson.

Arenberg, Gerald S., et al. Preventing Missing Children. 128p. (Orig.). 1984. pap. 6.95 (*0-936320-21-4*) Compact Books.

— Preventing Missing Children: A Parental Guide to Child Security. 128p. 1987. pap. 3.95 (*0-380-70429-3*, Avon Bks) Morrow Avon.

Arenberg, I. Kaufman, ed. Dizziness & Balance Disorders: An Interdisciplinary Approach to Diagnosis, Therapy Treatment & Rehabilitation. LC 93-38841. (Illus.). 1993. lib. bdg. 223.00 (*90-6299-100-9*, Pub. by Kugler) Kugler Pubns.

Arenberg, I. Kaufman & Graham, Malcolm D. Treatment Options for Meniere's Disease: Endolymphatic Sac Surgery - Do It or Don't Do It. LC 98-12943. (Illus.). 300p. 1998. 160.95 (*1-56593-734-1*, 1428) Thomson Learn.

Arend, Anthony C. Pursuing a Just & Durable Peace: John Foster Dulles & International Organization, 212. LC 87-37552. (Contributions in Political Science Ser.: No. 212). 253p. 1988. 59.95 (*0-313-25637-3*, ADJ/, Greenwood Pr) Greenwood.

***Arend, Anthony Clark.** Legal Rules & International Society. LC 98-44260. 224p. 1999. 35.00 (*0-19-512710-2*); pap. 17.95 (*0-19-512711-0*) OUP.

Arend, H. & Hulliger, J., eds. Crystal Growth in Science & Technology. LC 89-28393. (NATO ASI Ser.: Vol. 210). (Illus.). 438p. (C). 1989. text 162.00 (*0-306-43393-1*, Kluwer Plenum) Kluwer Academic.

Arend, Liana P. & Hillwood Museum & Gardens Staff. Sevres Porcelain at Hillwood. LC 98-9972. 1998. pap. write for info. (*0-9654958-5-X*) Hillwood Mus.

Arend, Liana P., jt. auth. see Odom, Anne.

Arend, Scott. Skipper Barbie's Little Sister: Identification & Value Guide. LC 98-161247. 1998. pap. text 19.95 (*1-57432-062-9*, 5059) Collector Bks.

Arend, Walter. Problemata, Forschungen Zur Klassischen Philologie, Heft 7: Die Typischen Szenen Bei Homer. x, 162p. 1975. 50.00 (*3-296-10550-6*) G Olms Pubs.

Arendal, Laura. America Online Amazing Secrets. LC 97-81250. 368p. 1998. pap. text 19.99 (*0-7821-2229-9*) Sybex.

Arendale, David R., jt. auth. see Martin, Deanna C.

Arendale, David R., jt. ed. see Martin, Deanna C.

Arendell, Terry. Fathers & Divorce. LC 94-42213. 288p. 1995. text 54.00 (*0-8039-7188-5*); pap. text 26.00 (*0-8039-7189-3*) Sage.

— Mothers & Divorce: Legal, Economic, & Social Dilemmas. 320p. (C). 1986. pap. 15.95 (*0-520-06215-9*, Pub. by U CA Pr) Cal Prin Full Svc.

Arendell, Terry, ed. Contemporary Parenting: Challenges & Issues. LC 97-4678. (Understanding Families Ser.: Vol. 9). 344p. 1997. 49.95 (*0-8039-7268-7*) Sage.

Arender, Barney. Barney's Book on the Olympic Peninsula: A Compendium for Motorists & Hikers of All Major Roads & Trails. LC 90-91668. (Illus.). 376p. (Orig.). 1991. pap. 18.95 (*1-878903-00-4*) Nosado Pr.

— Barney's Book on the Olympic Peninsula: A Compendium for Motorists & Hikers of All Major Roads & Trails. 2nd ed. (Illus.). 352p. (Orig.). 1993. pap. 19.95 (*1-878903-06-3*) Nosado Pr.

— Barney's Portable Book on the Southeastern Olympic Peninsula: A Small Compendium for Motorists & Hikers of All Major Roads & Trails. LC 91-90280. (Illus.). xiii, 78 p. (Orig.). 1991. pap. 8.95 (*1-878903-01-2*) Nosado Pr.

Arendonk, J. A. van, see Korver, S., ed.

Arendonk, J. A. van, see Korver, S. & Van Arendonk, J. A., eds.

Arendonk, J. A. van, see Van Arendonk, J. A.

Arendrup, Birthe, et al, eds. China in the 1980s & Beyond. (Illus.). 174p. (C). 1996. pap. text 16.00 (*0-7007-0174-5*, Pub. by Curzon Pr Ltd) UH Pr.

Arends. Feel Free Folio. 1997. pap. 12.95 (*0-7601-1784-5*) Brentwood Music.

***Arends, Carolyn.** Living the Questions. 200p. 2000. pap. 9.99 (*0-7369-0226-0*) Harvest Hse.

Arends, Charles B. Polymer Toughening. (Plastics Engineering Ser.: Vol. 30). (Illus.). 432p. 1996. text 185.00 (*0-8247-9474-5*) Dekker.

Arends, J. F. Die Einheit der Polis: Eine Studie Uber Platons Staat. LC 88-7310. (Mnemosyne Ser.: Supplement 106). (GER.). xxiv, 482p. (Orig.). 1988. pap. 134.00 (*90-04-08785-0*) Brill Academic Pubs.

Arends, Jacques, ed. The Early Stages of Creolization. LC 95-50435. (Creole Language Library: No. 13). xvi, 297p. 1994. 75.00 (*1-55619-167-7*) J Benjamins Pubng Co.

Arends, Jacques, et al, eds. Pidgins & Creoles: An Introduction. LC 94-24286. (Creole Language Library: No. 15). xv, 412p. 1995. pap. 29.95 (*1-55619-170-7*); lib. bdg. 79.00 (*1-55619-169-3*) J Benjamins Pubng Co.

Arends, Jane H., jt. auth. see Arends, Richard I.

***Arends, Marthe.** Genealogy on CD-ROM. LC 99-73351. (Illus.). 266p. 1999. pap. 29.95 incl. cd-rom (*0-8063-1623-3*) Genealog Pub.

Arends, Marthe. Genealogy Software Guide. LC 98-73250. 269p. 1998. pap. 24.95 (*0-8063-1581-4*) Genealog Pub.

***Arends, Marthe.** The Lion's Shadow. (Illus.). 330p. 1999. mass mkt. 6.99 (*1-929613-05-9*) Avid MI.

Arends, Richard. Learning to Teach. 4th ed. LC 97-36997. 576p. 1997. pap. 63.75 (*0-07-006282-X*) McGraw.

Arends, Richard, et al. Exploring Teaching. LC 97-29508. 512p. 1997. pap. 51.88 (*0-07-003045-6*) McGraw.

Arends, Richard I. Classroom Instruction & Management. LC 96-22930. 307p. (C). 1996. pap. 31.25 (*0-07-003082-0*) McGraw.

— Exploring Teaching. 2nd ed. 2000. 40.50 (*0-07-232180-6*) McGraw.

— Learning to Teach. 3rd ed. LC 93-11851. (C). 1993. text 70.50 (*0-07-002599-1*) McGraw.

— Learning to Teach. 5th ed. 2000. 47.00 (*0-07-232164-4*) McGraw.

Arends, Richard I. & Arends, Jane H. Systems Change Strategies in Educational Settings. LC 77-22315. (New Vistas in Counseling Ser.: Vol. III). 120p. 1977. 32.95 (*0-87705-310-3*, Kluwer Acad Hman Sci) Kluwer Academic.

Arends, T., ed. see Hemoglobin Symposium Staff.

***Arendse, Margot.** Couture Bridalwear Design: Fashion (or Pattern?) Layout & Design. (Illus.). 2000. pap. 23.95 (*1-57488-274-0*) Brasseys.

Arendt. Essays in Understanding. 1996. pap. 12.95 (*0-15-600195-0*) Harcourt.

— Kreise. (College German Ser.). (C). 1992. student ed. 19.95 incl. audio (*0-8384-3572-6*) Heinle & Heinle.

— Kreise. (College German Ser.). (C). 1993. suppl. ed. 17.95 (*0-8384-3585-8*) Heinle & Heinle.

Arendt. Kreise-chapter 13-15 Of Workbook. (Collge German). (C). 1993. mass mkt., wbk. ed. 17.95 (*0-8384-5375-9*) Heinle & Heinle.

Arendt. Kreise-chapter 13-15 Of Text. (Collge German). (GER.). (C). 1993. mass mkt. 21.95 (*0-8384-5408-9*) Heinle & Heinle.

— Kreise-Sample. (Collge German). (C). 1992. wbk. ed. write for info. (*0-8384-3779-6*) Heinle & Heinle.

Arendt & Baumann. Kreise. (College German Ser.). (GER.). (C). 1992. mass mkt., suppl. ed. 36.95 (*0-8384-3932-2*) Heinle & Heinle.

***Arendt, Elizabeth A., et al.** Orthopaedic Knowledge Update. LC 99-26597, 1999. write for info. (*0-89203-205-7*) Amer Acad Ortho Surg.

Arendt, F., ed. Contaminated Soil '93: Fourth International KfK-TNO Conference on Contaminated Soil, 3-7 May 1993, Berlin, Germany, 2 vols., Set. (Soil & Environment Ser.). (C). 1993. lib. bdg. 662.00 (*0-7923-2328-9*) Kluwer Academic.

Arendt, F., et al, eds. Contaminated Soil, 1990, 2 vols. (C). 1990. text 633.50 (*0-7923-1058-6*) Kluwer Academic.

Arendt, Germaine D., et al. Kreise. (C). 1992. mass mkt. 58.95 (*0-8384-3573-4*) Heinle & Heinle.

Arendt, Hannah. Between Past & Future. 320p. 1993. pap. 13.95 (*0-14-018650-6*, Penguin Classics) Viking Penguin.

— Correspondence, 1926-1969. 1992. 49.95 (*0-15-107887-4*) Harcourt.

— Crises of the Republic. LC 72-187703. 252p. 1972. pap. 13.00 (*0-15-623200-6*, Harvest Bks) Harcourt.

— Diccionario de Derecho Civil, Vol. 1. (SPA.). 484p. 1991. pap. 16.95 (*0-7859-1677-6*, 2070326217) Fr & Eur.

— Eichmann in Jerusalem. 1983. 24.75 (*0-8446-5977-0*) Peter Smith.

— Eichmann in Jerusalem: A Report on the Banality of Evil. 320p. 1994. pap. 13.95 (*0-14-018765-0*, Penguin Classics) Viking Penguin.

— Human Condition. LC 58-5535. 340p. 1970. pap. 16.00 (*0-226-02593-4*, P361) U Ch Pr.

— The Human Condition. 1990. 27.00 (*0-8446-6183-X*) Peter Smith.

— Human Condition. 2nd ed. LC 98-17015. 1998. pap. 16.00 (*0-226-02598-5*); lib. bdg. 45.00 (*0-226-02599-3*) U Ch Pr.

Arendt, Hannah. Imperialism. LC 66-22273. Orig. Title: Origins of Totalitarianism Pt. 2. 201p. 1968. reprint ed. pap. 12.00 (*0-15-644200-0*, Harvest Bks) Harcourt.

Arendt, Hannah. Lectures on Kant's Political Philosophy. Beiner, Ronald S., ed. LC 82-4817. 192p. 1982. 17.50 (*0-226-02594-2*) U Ch Pr.

— Lectures on Kant's Political Philosophy. Beiner, Ronald S., ed. LC 82-4817. 184p. 1989. pap. text 13.00 (*0-226-02595-0*) U Ch Pr.

— The Life of the Mind. LC 80-25403. 300p. 1981. pap. 15.00 (*0-15-651992-5*, Harvest Bks) Harcourt.

— Love & Saint Augustine. Scot, Joanna V. & Stark, Judith C., eds. LC 95-12866.Tr. of Libesbegrieff bei Augustine. 254p. 1995. 22.50 (*0-226-02596-9*) U Ch Pr.

— Love & Saint Augustine. Scot, Joanna V. & Stark, Judith C., eds. LC 95-12866.Tr. of Libesbegrieff bei Augustine. 234p. 1998. pap. 16.00 (*0-226-02597-7*) U Ch Pr.

Arendt, Hannah. Men in Dark Times. LC 68-24381. 288p. 1970. reprint ed. pap. 15.00 (*0-15-658890-0*, Harvest Bks) Harcourt.

Arendt, Hannah. On Revolution. 352p. 1991. pap. 13.95 (*0-14-018421-X*, Penguin Classics) Viking Penguin.

— On Revolution. LC 82-6266. 343p. 1982. reprint ed. lib. bdg. 69.50 (*0-313-23493-0*, AROR, Greenwood Pr) Greenwood.

— On Violence. LC 74-95867. 114p. (C). 1970. reprint ed. pap. 8.00 (*0-15-669500-6*, Harvest Bks) Harcourt.

— The Origins of Totalitarianism. LC 68-3757. 574p. 1973. pap. 17.00 (*0-15-670153-7*, HB244, Harvest Bks) Harcourt.

— Rahel Varnhagen: The Life of a Jewess. Weissberg, Liliane, ed. Winston, Richard & Winston, Clara, trs. from GER. LC 97-6484. (Illus.). 416p. 1997. 29.95 (*0-8018-5587-X*) Johns Hopkins.

***Arendt, Hannah.** Rahel Varnhagen: The Life of a Jewess. (Illus.). 2000. pap. text 18.95 (*0-8018-6335-X*) Johns Hopkins.

Arendt, Hannah. Thinking, Vol. 1. 1978. 12.50 (*0-685-73339-4*) Harcourt.

Arendt, Hannah. Totalitarianism. LC 66-22273. Orig. Title: Origins of Totalitarianism Pt. 3. 222p. 1968. reprint ed. pap. 13.00 (*0-15-690650-3*, Harvest Bks) Harcourt.

Arendt, Hannah. Willing, Vol. 2. 1978. 12.50 Harcourt.

***Arendt, Hannah & Baehr, P. R.** The Portable Hannah Arendt. LC 99-38487. 2000. pap. 16.95 (*0-14-026974-6*) Penguin Putnam.

***Arendt, Hans-Jurgen.** Gustav Theodor Fechner: Ein Deutscher Naturwissenschaftler und Philosoph Im 19. Jahrhundert. (Daedalus - Europaisches Denken in Deutscher Philosophie Ser.). 285p. 1999. 48.95 (*3-631-35337-5*) P Lang Pubng.

Arendt, Randall. Rural by Design: Maintaining Small Town Character. LC 93-71517. (Illus.). 441p. (Orig.). 1994. pap. 49.95 (*0-918286-85-9*, Planners Press); lib. bdg. 86.00 (*0-918286-86-7*, Planners Press) Am Plan Assn.

Arendt, Randall G. Conservation Design for Subdivisions: A Practical Guide to Creating Open Space Networks. LC 96-20454. 160p. (Orig.). (C). 1996. pap. text 37.50 (*1-55963-489-8*) Island Pr.

Arendt, T., jt. ed. see Gertz, H. J.

Arendt, William F. Midnights of the Soul: From Normandy to the Rhineland, the Personal War of a WWII Infantry Platoon Leader Told in Compelling & Bloody Details. LC 98-65169. (Illus.). 191p. 1998. pap. 11.90 (*0-9640235-1-2*) PRA.

Arendzen, J. P. Purgatory & Heaven. (Canterbury Ser.). 1990. reprint ed. pap. 5.00 (*0-89555-045-8*) TAN Bks Pubs.

Arengo-Jones, Peter. Queen Victoria in Switzerland. (Illus.). 160p. 1999. 24.95 (*0-7090-6460-8*, Pub. by R Hale Ltd) Seven Hills Bk.

***Arengo, Sue.** The Enormous Turnip. (Illus.). 24p. 1998. pap. 4.95 (*0-19-422002-8*) OUP.

— The Gingerbread Man Beginner Level 2. (Illus.). 24p. 1999. pap. 4.95 (*0-19-422022-2*) OUP.

Arengo, Sue. Snow White & the Seven Dwarfs. (Illus.). 32p. 1996. pap. text 4.95 (*0-19-422010-9*) OUP.

— A Taste of Murder. 4th ed. (Illus.). 32p. 1998. pap. text 4.95 (*0-19-421970-4*) OUP.

***Arengo, Sue.** The Three Billy-Goats: Beginner Level 1. (Illus.). 24p. 1998. pap. 4.95 (*0-19-422003-6*) OUP.

— The Town Mouse & the Country Mouse Beginner Level 2. (Illus.). 24p. 1999. pap. 4.95 (*0-19-422021-4*) OUP.

Arenhovel, H. & Sanzone, M. Photodisintegration of the Deuteron: A Review of Theory & Experiment. (Few-Body Systems Ser.: Suppl. 3). 192p. 1991. 100.95 (*0-387-82276-3*) Spr-Verlag.

Arenhovel, H., jt. auth. see Schmitt, K. M.

Arenibia, Ariel D., ed. see International Symposium on Plant Genetic Engineering Staff.

Arens & Loebbecke. Auditing. 7th rev. ed. 848p. (C). 1997. text 94.00 (*0-13-649385-8*) P-H.

— S/G Auditing. 7th rev. ed. 352p. (C). 1997. pap. text, student ed. 33.00 (*0-13-790759-1*) P-H.

***Arens, Alvin A.** Auditing: An Integrated Approach. 8th ed. 791p. 1999. 98.00 (*0-13-082735-5*) P-H.

Arens, Alvin A. & Kerr, David S. Integrated Audit Practice Case. 265p. (Orig.). (C). 1993. pap. text 29.95 (*0-912503-09-2*) Armond-Dalton.

***Arens, Alvin A. & Loebbecke, James K.** Auditing, an Integrated Approach. 8th ed. LC 99-46401. 1999. write for info. (*0-13-084192-7*) P-H.

Arens, Alvin A. & Ward, D. Dewey. Systems Understanding Aid. 4th ed. Orig. Title: Systems Understanding Aid for Auditing. (Illus.). 148p. (Orig.). (C). 1995. pap. text 22.95 (*0-912503-10-6*) Armond-Dalton.

Arens, Alvin A., et al. Systems Understanding Aid - Microcomputer Version. 3rd ed. 160p. (Orig.). (C). 1989. pap. text 12.00 incl. disk (*0-912503-08-4*) Armond-Dalton.

Arens, Alvin A., jt. auth. see Swaffar, Janet K.

Arens, Axel, text. James Dean: Photographs. (Schirmer's Visual Library). (Illus.). 136p. 1993. pap. 10.95 (*0-393-30897-9*) Norton.

Arens, Donald E., et al. Practical Lessons in Endodontic Surgery. (Illus.). 216p. 280.00 incl. VHS (*0-86715-336-9*) Quint Pub Co.

Arens, Donald E., et al. Practical Lessons in Endodontic Surgery. LC 98-15844. (Illus.). 216p. 1998. spiral bd. 82.00 (*0-86715-333-4*) Quint Pub Co.

Arens, Edmund. Christopraxis: A Theology of Action. Hoffmeyer, John F., tr. from GER. LC 95-2302. 184p. 1995. pap. 19.00 (*0-8006-2746-6*, 1-2746, Fortress Pr) Augsburg Fortress.

Arens, Egmont, jt. auth. see Sheldon, Roy.

Arens, Katherine. Austria & Other Margins: Reading Culture. LC 96-27663. (GERM Ser.). xiv, 263p. 1997. 65.00 (*1-57113-109-4*) Camden Hse.

— Functionalism & Fin de Siecle: Fritz Mauthner's Critique of Language. (Stanford German Studies: Vol. 23). 304p. (C). 1984. text 29.00 (*0-8204-0201-X*) P Lang Pubng.

— Structures of Knowing. 440p. (C). 1989. lib. bdg. 175.00 (*0-7923-0009-2*, Pub. by Kluwer Academic) Kluwer Academic.

Arens, Katherine, jt. ed. see Johns, Jorun B.

Arens, Richard & Lasswell, Harold D. In Defense of Public Order: The Emerging Field of Sanction Law. LC 84-27979. 314p. 1985. reprint ed. lib. bdg. 69.50 (*0-313-24732-3*, ARDP, Greenwood Pr) Greenwood.

Arens, Ursula & British Nutrition Foundation Staff. Oral Health - Diet & Other Factors: The Report of the British Nutrition Foundation's Task Force. LC 98-39770. 240p. 1999. 139.50 (*0-444-50025-1*) Elsevier.

Arens, W. The Man-Eating Myth: Anthropology & Anthropophagy. (Illus.). 220p. 1980. pap. text 13.95 (*0-19-502793-0*) OUP.

Arens, W., ed. A Century of Change in Eastern Africa. (World Anthropology Ser.). xii, 310p. 1976. 44.65 (*90-279-7879-4*) Mouton.

Arens, William F. Contemporary Advertising. 6th ed. 656p. (C). 1995. text 69.95 (*0-256-18257-4*, Irwn McGrw-H) McGrw-H Hghr Educ.

— Contemporary Advertising. 7th ed. 736p. (C). 1998. 83.13 (*0-256-26253-5*) McGraw.

Arens, William F., jt. auth. see Bovee, Courtland L.

***Arensberg, Ann.** Group Sex. 192p. 2000. pap. 14.00 (*0-345-43817-5*, Ballantine) Ballantine Pub Grp.

— Incubus. 336p. 2000. pap. 14.00 (*0-345-43816-7*, Ballantine) Ballantine Pub Grp.

Arensberg, Ann. Incubus. LC 98-41732. 326p. 1999. 24.00 (*0-394-55696-8*) Knopf.

***Arensberg, Ann.** Sister Wolf. 224p. 2000. pap. 14.00 (*0-345-43818-3*) Ballantine Pub Grp.

Arensberg, Conrad. The Irish Countryman: An Anthropological Study. 200p. (C). 1988. reprint ed. pap. text 11.50 (*0-88133-401-4*) Waveland Pr.

Arensberg, Conrad M. The Irish Countryman: An Anthropological Study. 1990. 18.75 (*0-8446-1031-3*) Peter Smith.

Arensberg, Conrad M. & Kimball, S. T. Culture & Community. 1990. 16.50 (*0-8446-1544-7*) Peter Smith.

Arensberg, Conrad M. & Niehoff, Arthur H. Introducing Social Change: A Manual for Community Development. 2nd ed. LC 78-14936. 269p. 1971. lib. bdg. 30.95 (*0-202-01072-4*) Aldine de Gruyter.

Arensberg, Mary, ed. The American Sublime. LC 85-31824. 218p. (C). 1986. pap. text 24.95 (*0-88706-190-7*) State U NY Pr.

Arensberg, S. & Dennis, D. Rules of Warfare: Silent Death Annex Book. (Silent Death - The Next Millennium Ser.). (Illus.). 32p. 1997. pap. 12.00 (*1-55806-279-3*, 7218) Iron Crown Ent Inc.

Arensberg, Walter C. The Burial of Francis Bacon & His Mother in the Lichfield Chapter House. 60p. (Orig.). 1992. reprint ed. pap. 12.95 (*1-56459-113-1*) Kessinger Pub.

Arensen, Jonathan E. Mice Are Men: Language & Society among the Murle of Sudan. LC 92-73535. (International Museum of Cultures Ser.: Vol. 27). 384p. 1992. pap. 27.00 (*0-88312-606-0*) S I L Intl.

— Sticks & Straw: Comparative house forms in Southern Sudan & Northern Kenya. LC 81-50907. (International Museum of Cultures Publications: No. 13). (Illus.). 140p. (Orig.). 1983. pap. 12.00 (*0-88312-164-6*) S I L Intl.

Arensky. Arensky: Complete Piano Works I. 1999. pap. 7.95 (*963-9155-45-4*) Kone Music.

Arensman, Robert M. Pediatric Surgery. (Vademecum Ser.). 2000. spiral bd. 45.00 (*1-57059-499-6*) Landes Bioscience.

Arensman, Robert M., ed. Pediatric Trauma: Initial Care of the Injured. LC 95-3117. (Illus.). 288p. 1995. text 75.00 (*0-7817-0260-7*) Lppncott W & W.

Arensman, Robert M. & Cornish, J., eds. Extracorporeal Life Support. (Illus.). 416p. 1992. 125.00 (*0-86542-197-8*) Blackwell Sci.

Arensmeyer, Lynn, ed. see Flynn, J. T.

***Arenson-Bell.** Understanding Cultures of the United States. 250p. (C). 2000. spiral bd. 42.95 (*0-7872-6925-5*) Kendall-Hunt.

***Arenson, Carole L.** Boots, the Church Cat. (Illus.). 34p. (Orig.). (J). (ps-2). 1998. reprint ed. pap. 15.95 (*1-929187-12-2*, CGBK63, Pub. by Choristers) Lorenz Corp.

Arenson, David & Werden, Marilyn. Got Milk? The Cookbook: The Feel Good Cookbook for Closet Milk Lovers. 1998. per. 18.00 (*0-7615-1551-8*) Prima Pub.

Arenson, David, jt. auth. see Werden, Marilyn.

Arenson, Gloria. Born to Spend: How to Overcome Compulsive Spending. 224p. 1991. pap. 9.95 (*0-07-001652-6*) McGraw.

A

A

— A Substance Called Food: How to Understand, Control, & Recover from Addictive Eating. 2nd ed. 256p. 1989. pap. 11.95 (*0-8306-3430-4*) McGraw-Hill Prof.

— A Substance Called Food: How to Understand, Control & Recover from Addictive Eating. 2nd ed. 294p. 1989. pap. 12.95 (*0-07-156827-1*) McGraw.

Arenson, Gregory K., ed. see New York State Bar Association Staff.

Arenson, Herbert. The Lodge at Lake Annabel. 88p. 1998. 14.95 (*1-890622-22-2*) Leathers Pub.

Arenson, Joseph T., et al. New York Practice Guide: Probate & Estate Administration, 2 vols. 1985. ring bd. 385.00 (*0-8205-1522-1*) Bender.

***Arenson, Lauren.** Learn by Doing: A Hands-on Approach for Physical Anthropology. 250p. (C). 1999. spiral bd. 43.95 (*0-7872-6291-9*) Kendall-Hunt.

***Arenson, Roberta.** One, Two, Skip a Few! First Number Rhymes. (Illus.). 32p. (J). (ps-2). 2000. pap. 6.99 (*1-84148-130-0*) Barefoot Bks NY.

Arenson, Roberta. A Caribbean Counting Book. 24p. (J). (ps-3). 1996. 13.95 (*0-395-77944-8*) HM.

***Arenson, Roberta.** Manu & the Talking Fish. 32p. (J). (ps-3). 2000. 15.95 (*1-84148-032-0*) Barefoot Bks NY.

Arenson, Roberta. One, Two, Skip a Few! First Number Rhymes. 32p. (J). (ps-2). 1998. 15.95 (*1-901223-99-X*) Barefoot Bks NY.

Arenson, Ronald L. & Friedenberg, Richard M. S - Car Ninety: Computer Applications to Assist Radiology. 774p. 1990. 99.00 (*0-88372-005-1*) CRC Pr.

Arent, Emma. The Relation of the State to Private Education in Norway: A Study of the Historical Development of State Regulations Governing the Various Types of Private Education in Norway. LC 74-176522. (Columbia University. Teachers College. Contributions to Education Ser.: No. 235). reprint ed. 37.50 (*0-404-55235-8*) AMS Pr.

Arent, Leonora. Electric Franchises in New York City. LC 70-77999. (Columbia University. Studies in the Social Sciences: No. 201). reprint ed. 29.50 (*0-404-51201-1*) AMS Pr.

Arent, Ruth P. Building Trust with Children Who Hurt: A One-to-One At-Risk Prevention Program for Counselors & Teachers. 224p. 1991. text 29.95 (*0-87628-191-9*) Ctr Appl Res.

Arentz, Dick. The Grand Tour. (Illus.). 40p. 30.00 (*3-923922-62-0*) Nazraeli Pr.

— Platinum & Palladium Printing. LC 99-28233. 184p. 1999. pap. text 29.95 (*0-240-80377-9*, Focal) Buttrwrth-Heinemann.

Arentz, Dick & Thompson, Ian. Four Corners Country. LC 86-11397. (Illus.). 112p. 1994. reprint ed. pap. 29.95 (*0-8165-1435-6*) U of Ariz Pr.

Areola, Oldsegun. Ecology of Natural Resources in Nigeria. 187p. 1991. 75.95 (*1-85628-175-2*, Pub. by Avebry) Ashgate Pub Co.

Ares-Grief, Sophie, jt. auth. see Grief, Samuel N.

Ares, Jacques d'. Encyclopedie de l'Esoterisme, 5 vols. (FRE.). 1975. pap. 125.00 (*0-8288-5876-4*, M6008) Fr & Eur.

Ares, Marcy, et al. Caracteristicas Nacionales de la Literatura Cubana. (Patronato Ramon Guiteras Intercultural Center Ser.). (SPA.). 92p. (Orig.). 1985. pap. 6.95 (*0-89729-404-1*) Ediciones.

Ares, Mercedes. Diario de un Caracol. LC 86-83092. (Coleccion Espejo de Paciencia). (SPA.). 28p. (Orig.). 1987. pap. 6.00 (*0-89729-422-X*) Ediciones.

Arese, Francesco. A Trip to the Prairies & in the Interior of North America 1837-1838 Travel Notes. LC 74-12556. (Illus.). 216p. 1974. reprint ed. lib. bdg. 42.00 (*0-8154-0496-4*) Cooper Sq.

Aresenault, Jane & Cedor, Jean. Guided Meditations for Youth on Personal Themes. unabridged ed. Stamschror, Robert, ed. (Quiet Place Apart Ser.). (YA). (gr. 9-12). 1995. audio 7.95 (*0-88489-354-5*) St Marys.

— Guided Meditations for Youth on Personal Themes. unabridged ed. Stamschror, Robert, ed. (Quiet Place Apart Ser.). (Illus.). 48p. (YA). (gr. 9-12). 1995. pap. 9.95 incl. audio (*0-88489-347-2*) St Marys.

Areskoug, S., et al, eds. Off-Road Transportation & Soil-Working: Means to Promote Development & Operations. 120p. 1985. pap. 33.00 (*0-08-031652-2*, Pergamon Pr) Elsevier.

Areson, Todd W., jt. ed. see Whicker, Marcia L.

Aresta, M. & Forti, G., eds. Carbon Dioxide As a Source of Carbon: Chemical & Biochemical Uses. (C). 1987. text 218.00 (*90-277-2544-6*) Kluwer Academic.

Aresta, M. & Schloss, J. V., eds. Enzymatic & Model Carboxylation & Reduction Reactions for Carbon Dioxide Utilization. (C). 1990. text 221.50 (*0-7923-0871-9*) Kluwer Academic.

Arestis, Phililp, ed. Method, Theory & Policy in Keynes Vol. 3: Essays in Honour of Paul Davidson. LC 97-25912. 272p. 1998. 85.00 (*1-85898-626-5*) E Elgar.

Arestis, Philip. Money, Pricing, Distribution & Economic Integration. LC 96-3465. 240p. 1997. text 69.95 (*0-312-16532-3*) St Martin.

— The Post-Keynesian Approach to Economics: An Alternative Analysis of Economic Theory & Policy. (New Directions in Modern Economics Ser.). 336p. 1992. 90.00 (*1-85278-154-8*) E Elgar.

— The Post-Keynesian Approach to Economics: An Alternative Analysis of Economic Theory & Policy. (New Directions in Modern Economics Ser.). 336p. 1994. pap. 30.00 (*1-85898-013-5*) E Elgar.

Arestis, Philip, ed. Employment, Economic Growth, & the Tyranny of the Market Vol. 2: Essays in Honour of Paul Davidson. LC 96-5866. 256p. 1996. 85.00 (*1-85898-313-4*) E Elgar.

— Keynes, Money, & the Open Economy: Essays in Honour of Paul Davidson, Vol. 1. LC 96-15345. 224p. 1996. 85.00 (*1-85898-312-6*) E Elgar.

— Money & Banking Issues for the Twenty-First Century: Essays in Honour of Stephen Frowen. LC 93-17301. 319p. 1993. text 79.95 (*0-312-09994-0*) St Martin.

— Post-Keynesian Monetary Economics: New Approaches to Financial Modelling. (New Directions in Modern Economics Ser.). 320p. 1988. text 95.00 (*1-85278-046-0*) E Elgar.

Arestis, Philip, et al, eds. Capital Controversy, Post Keynesian Economics & the History of Economic Thought: Essays in Honor of Geoff Harcourt. (Routledge Frontiers of Political Economy Ser.: Vol. 6). 482p. (C). 1996. 125.00 (*0-415-13391-2*) Routledge.

Arestis, Philip & Chick, Victoria, eds. Finance, Development & Structural Change: Post-Keynesian Perpectives. (Post-Keynesian Economics Study Group). 336p. 1995. 95.00 (*1-85278-656-6*) E Elgar.

Arestis, Philip & Kitromilides, Yiannis, eds. Theory & Policy in Political Economy: Essays in Pricing, Distribution & Growth. (New Directions in Modern Economics Ser.). (Illus.). 328p. 1990. text 95.00 (*1-85278-205-6*) E Elgar.

Arestis, Philip & Marshall, Mike, eds. The Political Economy of Full Employment: Conservationism, Corporatism & Institutional Change. 296p. 1995. 95.00 (*1-85278-880-1*) E Elgar.

Arestis, Philip & Palma, Gabriel, eds. Markets, Unemployment, & Economic Policy: Essays in Honour of Geoff Harcourt, Vol. 2. LC 97-155047. (Illus.). 576p. (C). 1997. 125.00 (*0-415-13390-4*) Routledge.

Arestis, Philip & Sawyer, Malcolm C. A Biographical Dictionary of Dissenting Economists. 656p. 1992. text 190.00 (*1-85278-331-1*) E Elgar.

***Arestis, Philip & Sawyer, Malcolm C.** A Biographical Dictionary of Dissenting Economists. 2nd ed. LC 00-34824. 2000. write for info. (*1-85898-560-9*) E Elgar.

Arestis, Philip & Sawyer, Malcolm C., eds. The Elgar Companion to Radical Political Economy. LC 93-29063. 512p. 1994. 160.00 (*1-85278-460-1*) E Elgar.

— The Political Economy of Central Banking. LC 98-12817. 256p. 1998. 85.00 (*1-85898-742-3*) E Elgar.

Aresty, Jeffrey M., jt. auth. see Silkenat, James R.

Aretha, David. The Michigan Wolverines Football Team. LC 98-25727. (Great Sports Teams Ser.). 48p. (J). (gr. 4-10). 1999. lib. bdg. 18.95 (*0-7660-1101-1*) Enslow Pubs.

— The Montreal Canadiens Hockey Team. LC 97-21308. (Great Sports Teams Ser.). (Illus.). 48p. (J). (gr. 4-10). 1998. lib. bdg. 18.95 (*0-7660-1022-8*) Enslow Pubs.

Aretha, David. The Seattle SuperSonics Basketball Team. LC 98-19228. (Great Sports Teams Ser.). (Illus.). 48p. (YA). (gr. 4-10). 1999. lib. bdg. 18.95 (*0-7660-1102-X*) Enslow Pubs.

***Aretha, David.** The Seattle SuperSonics Basketball Team. LC 98-19228. (Great Sports Teams Ser.). (Illus.). 48p. (YA). (gr. 4-10). 1999. pap. 9.95 (*0-7660-1754-0*) Enslow Pubs.

Aretino, Lionardo B., jt. auth. see Boccaccio, Giovanni.

Aretino, Pietro. Aretino's Dialogues. Rosenthal, Raymond, tr. from ITA. 384p. 1994. pap. 16.95 (*0-941419-96-7*) Marsilio Pubs.

— La Comedia De la Corte: El Caballerizo. Chiclana, Angel, ed. & tr. by. (Nueva Austral Ser.: No. 74). (SPA.). 1991. pap. text 24.95 (*84-239-1874-2*) Elliots Bks.

Aretino, Pietro, jt. auth. see Ariosto, Ludovico.

***Arettam, Joanna.** Dharma Beads: Making & Using Your Own Buddhist Malas. LC 00-22896. (Illus.). 2000. write for info. (*1-58290-033-7*, Pub. by Jrny Editions) Tuttle Pubng.

Aretxaga, Begona. Shattering Silence: Women, Nationalism, & Political Subjectivity in Northern Ireland. LC 97-4176. 208p. 1997. text 49.50 (*0-691-03755-8*, Pub. by Princeton U Pr); pap. text 14.95 (*0-691-03754-X*, Pub. by Princeton U Pr) Cal Prin Full Svc.

Aretz, H. Thomas. Pathology of Cardiovascular Disease. 650p. 1997. text 125.00 (*0-397-51455-7*) Lppncott W & W.

Arewa, Caroline Shola, see Shola Arewa, Caroline.

Arewa, Erastus O. A Classification of the Folktales of the Northern East African Cattle Area by Types. Dorson, Richard M., ed. LC 80-7234. (Folklore of the World Ser.). 1981. lib. bdg. 31.95 (*0-405-13302-2*) Ayer.

Arey, James B. Cardiovascular Pathology in Infants & Children. (Illus.). 392p. 1984. text 145.00 (*0-7216-1395-0*, W B Saunders Co) Harcrt Hlth Sci Grp.

Arey, June B. The Purpose, Financing & Governance of Museums: Three Conferences on Present & Future Issues. 1978. pap. text 2.50 (*0-932676-01-4*) Spring Hill.

Arey, Richard. Twin Cities Bicycling: Fred's Best Guide to Twin Cities Bicycling. (Illus.). 128p. (Orig.). 1995. pap. 14.50 (*0-9620918-1-2*) MN Outdoors Pr.

Arey, Richard F. Twin Cities Bicycling. expanded rev. ed. (Illus.). 144p. 1998. pap. 15.95 (*0-9620918-4-7*) MN Outdoors Pr.

— Twin Cities Summer Recreation. (Illus.). 1999. pap. 16.75 (*0-9620918-3-9*) MN Outdoors Pr.

— Twin Cities Winter Recreation. (Illus.). 128p. 1996. pap. 14.95 (*0-9620918-2-0*) MN Outdoors Pr.

Arey, T. J. Radio Monitoring: The How-To Guide. LC 95-81300. (Illus.). 336p. (Orig.). 1997. pap. 19.95 (*1-56866-101-0*) Index Pub Grp.

Arey, Velma. The Grand Art Tour. 18p. (Orig.). 1994. pap. write for info. (*1-885206-02-X*, Iliad Pr) Cader Pubng.

Arezzo, Diana, et al. Early Violence Prevention: Tools for Teachers of Young Children. LC 94-69779. (Illus.). 198p. 1995. pap. text 8.00 (*0-935989-65-X*, 325) Natl Assn Child Ed.

Arffa, Robert C. Grayson's Diseases of the Cornea. 4th ed. LC 97-18628. (Illus.). 784p. (C). (gr. 13). 1997. text 199.00 (*0-8151-3654-4*, 30969) Mosby Inc.

Arffman, Francis. Ages Ago. 1998. pap. write for info. (*1-57553-832-6*) Watermrk Pr.

Arfken, Cynthia L. & Evans, David, eds. Asthma Management in Minority Children: Practical Insights for Clinicians, Researchers & Public Health Planners. (Illus.). 60p. (C). 1997. reprint ed. pap. text 20.00 (*0-7881-4594-0*) DIANE Pub.

Arfken, George B. Mathematical Methods for Physics. 4th ed. 1995. pap. text 42.00 (*0-12-059816-7*) Acad Pr.

Arfken, George B. & Weber, Hans-Jurgen, eds. Mathematical Methods for Physicists. 4th ed. (Illus.). 1029p. 1995. text 73.00 (*0-12-059815-9*) Acad Pr.

Arford, Joanne M. & Burnside, Judy D. Advanced Microsoft Word 2000: Desktop Publishing: Instructor's Guide, CD Rom Package. 69.00 incl. cd-rom (*0-7638-0247-6*) EMC-Paradigm.

— Advanced Microsoft Word 2000: Desktop Publishing: Text with CD Rom. 640p. 41.95 incl. cd-rom (*0-7638-0246-8*) EMC-Paradigm.

Arford, Joanne Marschke, jt. auth. see Rutkosky, Nita H.

***Argabright, Dave & Doty, Brad.** Still Wide Open. 288p. 1999. 29.95 (*1-891390-03-1*) Witness Prods.

Argabright, Loren N. & De Lamadrid, J. G. Almost Periodic Measures. LC 90-31823. (Memoirs Ser.: No. 85/428). 219p. 1990. pap. 28.00 (*0-8218-2490-2*, MEMO/85/428) Am Math.

Argabright, Loren N. & De Lamadrid, Jesus G. Fourier Analysis of Unbounded Measures on Locally Compact Abelian Groups. LC 74-6499. (Memoirs Ser.: Vol. 1\145). 53p. 1974. pap. 17.00 (*0-8218-1845-7*, MEMO/1/145) Am Math.

Argaman, Shmuel. The Captivity of Maharam. LC 90-83947. (Illus.). 120p. (J). (gr. 3-5). 1990. 11.95 (*1-56062-045-5*); pap. 8.95 (*0-685-46904-2*) CIS Comm.

Argan, G. C. Canova. 400p. 1987. pap. 39.95 (*0-941419-75-4*, Eridanos Library) Marsilio Pubs.

Argan, G. C., et al. Antonio Canova. LC 92-82649. (Illus.). 400p. 1992. 65.00 (*0-941419-72-X*) Marsilio Pubs.

Argan, Giulio C. Dusan Dzamonja Croatian Sculptor. 206p. 1981. 25.00 (*0-614-08447-4*) Ragusan Pr.

— The Renaissance City. LC 70-90409. (Planning & Cities Ser.). (Illus.). 128p. 1969. pap. 9.95 (*0-8076-0521-2*) Braziller.

Argan, Guilio C. & Contardi, Bruno. Michelangelo Architect. Grayson, Marion L., tr. from ITA. LC 92-38117. (Illus.). 388p. 1993. 125.00 (*0-8109-3638-0*, Pub. by Abrams) Time Warner.

Arganbright, Deane. Practical Handbook of Spreadsheet Curves & Geometric Constructions. LC 93-7960. 224p. 1993. boxed set 94.95 (*0-8493-8938-0*, QA483) CRC Pr.

Arganbright, Nancy, jt. auth. see Weekley, Dallas A.

Arganbright, Nancy, jt. auth. see Weekly.

Arganda, Antonio, ed. The Ethical Dimension of Financial Institutions & Markets. (Studies in Economic Ethics & Philosophy). (Illus.). 263p. 1995. 98.00 (*3-540-59209-1*) Spr-Verlag.

Arganian, Lillian. Stan Kenton: The Man & His Music. (Illus.). 220p. (Orig.). 1989. pap. 22.50 (*0-9621116-0-0*) Artistry Pr.

Argardizzo, Carmen. Children in Action. 144p. (C). 1992. pap. 18.75 (*0-13-131467-X*) P-H.

Argauer, Robert J., jt. auth. see White, Charles E.

***Argay, Melissa Ann.** A Day in the Life of Francis. LC 00-91175. (World as Francis Knows It Ser.). (Illus.). 22p. (J). (ps). 2000. write for info. (*0-9679664-0-X*) Chosn Collec.

Arge, Erlend, et al, eds. Modern Software Tools for Scientific Computing. LC 97-6613. 385p. 1997. 69.95 (*0-8176-3974-8*) Birkhauser.

Arge, Erlend, et al. Modern Software Tools for Scientific Computing. LC 97-6613. 380p. 1997. write for info. (*3-7643-3974-8*) Birkhauser.

ARGEMA Staff. Anchoring of Floating Structures: Design Guides for Offshore Structures. (Design Guides for Offshore Structures Ser.: Vol. 2). 248p. (C). 1990. 420.00 (*2-7108-0572-3*, Pub. by Edits Technip) Enfield Pubs NH.

— Offshore Pile Design: Design Guides for Offshore Structures. Le Tirant, Pierre, ed. (Design Guides for Offshore Structures Ser.: Vol. 3). (Illus.). 324p. (C). 1992. 490.00 (*2-7108-0614-2*, Pub. by Edits Technip) Enfield Pubs NH.

Argent, George, et al. Accepted Names in Rhododendron Section Vireya. ii, 40p. 1996. pap. 12.00 (*1-872291-56-2*, Pub. by Royal Botanic Edinburgh) Balogh.

Argent, H. Keeping the Doors Open: A Review of Post-Adoption Services. (C). 1989. 39.00 (*0-903534-75-4*, Pub. by Brit Ag for Adopt & Fost) St Mut.

Argent, Hedi. See You Soon: Contact with Children Looked after by Local Authorities. 210p. 1995. 55.00 (*1-873868-30-8*) BAAF.

Argent, Hedi & Kerrane, Ailie, eds. Taking Extra Care: Respite, Shared & Permanent Care for Children with Disabilities. 96p. 1997. pap. 65.00 (*1-873868-38-3*) BAAF.

Argent, Jeanne. The Complete Step-by-Step Guide to Home Sewing. LC 89-27169. (Illus.). 240p. 1990. pap. 24.95 (*0-8019-8080-1*) Krause Pubns.

Argent, Kerry & Trinca, Rod. One Woolly Wombat. (Illus.). 32p. (J). (ps-1). 1987. reprint ed. pap. 6.95 (*0-916291-10-3*) Kane-Miller Bk.

Argent, Leanne, jt. auth. see Wignell, Edel.

Argent, Mark, ed. Recollections of R. J. S. Stevens: An Organist in Georgian London. (Music in Georgian & Victorian Society Ser.). 212p. (C). 1992. 36.95 (*0-8093-1790-7*) S Ill U Pr.

Argent, Sally & Loedolff, Jeanette. Discovering Indigenous Forests at Kirstenbosch: Colonialism & Comparative Religion in Southern Africa. LC 98-108983. (Illus.). 128p. 1997. pap. 69.95 (*1-919713-12-3*, U Pr W Africa) Intl Scholars.

Argent, Yvonne, jt. auth. see Marriot, Paul.

Argente del Castillo, Baldomero, tr. see George, Henry.

Argente, J. & Attanasio, A., eds. International Symposium on Endocrinology & Development: 14th Symposium, Palma de Mallorca, November 1995. (Journal: Hormone Research Ser.: Vol. 45, Suppl. 1, 1996). (Illus.). iv, 74p. 1996. pap. 33.25 (*3-8055-6322-1*) S Karger.

Argentesi, F., et al, eds. Mathematical & Statistical Methods in Nuclear Safeguards, Vol. 2. (Ispra Courses on Nuclear Engineering & Technology Ser.). xii, 446p. 1983. text 404.00 (*3-7186-0124-9*) Gordon & Breach.

Argenteuil Symposium Staff. The Role of Receptors in Biology & Medicine: Proceedings of the Ninth Argenteuil Symposium, Brussels, Belgium, 1984. Gotto, Antonio M., Jr. & O'Malley, Bert W., eds. LC 85-23389. 233p. 1986. reprint ed. pap. 72.30 (*0-608-00375-1*, 206108800007) Bks Demand.

Argenti, John. Practical Corporate Planning. 3rd ed. 434p. 1989. pap. 14.99 (*0-415-09100-4*) Routledge.

— Your Organization: What Is It For? Challenging Traditional Organizational Aims. LC 92-43398. 1993. 24.95 (*0-07-707799-7*) McGraw.

Argenti, Paul A. Corporate Communication. LC 93-1310. 224p. (C). 1993. text 33.50 (*0-256-05705-2*, Irwn McGrw-H) McGrw-H Hghr Educ.

— Corporate Communication. 2nd ed. LC 97-36694. (C). 1997. text 53.00 (*0-256-21723-8*, Irwn Prfssnl) McGraw-Hill Prof.

— Fast Forward MBA Pocket Reference. LC 96-40006. 338p. 1997. pap. 12.95 (*0-471-14595-5*) Wiley.

Argenti, Philip P. The Occupation of Chios by the Genoese & Their Administration of the Island, 1346-1566, 3 vols., Set. LC 78-63339. (Crusades & Military Orders Ser.: Second Series). reprint ed. 120.00 (*0-404-17000-5*) AMS Pr.

Argentieri, Michael, ed. see ECRI Staff.

Argentine, Cindy C. Vermont Act 250 Handbook: A Guide to State & Regional Land Use Regulation. 2nd rev. ed. (Illus.). xviii, 264p. 1999. pap. 32.95 (*1-882934-03-2*) Putney Pr.

Argentini, Paul. Elements of Style for Screenwriters: The Essential Manual for Writers of Screenplays. LC 98-22446. 1998. pap. text 11.95 (*1-58065-003-1*) Lone Eagle Pub.

Argentini, Paul, jt. auth. see Boland, Robert.

Argerami, Omar, jt. auth. see Dales, Richard C.

Argeri, Saul A. Dictionary of Commercial & Business Law: Diccionario de Derecho Comercial y de la Empresa. (ENG & SPA.). 398p. 1982. pap. 42.50 (*0-8288-1527-5*, S40508) Fr & Eur.

Argerion, Milton & McCarty, Dennis. Treating Alcoholism & Drug Abuse among Homeless Men & Women: Nine Community Demonstration Grants. LC 90-4301. (Alcoholism Treatment Quarterly Ser.: Vol. 7, No. 1). (Illus.). 164p. 1990. text 39.95 (*0-86656-992-8*) Haworth Pr.

Argers, Helen. The Gilded Lily. 320p. 1998. text 23.95 (*0-312-18571-5*) St Martin.

— Noblesse Oblige. large type ed. LC 94-45659. 424p. 1995. reprint ed. lib. bdg. 22.95 (*0-7838-1230-2*, G K Hall Lrg Type) Mac Lib Ref.

Argersinger, Jo Ann E. Toward a New Deal in Baltimore: People & Government in the Great Depression. LC 87-21767. (Illus.). xix, 284p. (C). 1988. 49.95 (*0-8078-1769-4*) U of NC Pr.

Argersinger, Jo Anne. Making the Amalgamated: Gender, Ethnicity & Class in the Baltimore Clothing Industry, 1899-1939. LC 98-9922. (Studies in Industry & Society). 248p. 1999. 39.95 (*0-8018-5989-1*) Johns Hopkins.

Argersinger, Peter H. The Limits of Agrarian Radicalism: Western Populism & American Politics. LC 94-23556. 312p. 1995. 29.95 (*0-7006-0702-1*) U Pr of KS.

— Structure, Process & Party: Essays in American Political History. LC 91-9567. 240p. (C). (gr. 13). 1991. text 70.95 (*0-87332-798-5*) M E Sharpe.

Arges, George S. Estimated Useful Lives of Depreciable Hospital Assets. LC 98-159897. xix, 42p. 1998. pap. text 30.00 (*1-55648-227-2*) AHPI.

Argeseanu, Liviu. Riding the Dragon: A Taoist Meditation Guide. 2nd ed. LC 95-94551. (Illus.). 144p. (Orig.). 1996. pap. 19.95 (*0-9646988-9-7*) Apollo Pr NY.

Argetsinger, Gerald S. Ludvig Holberg's Comedies. LC 82-5796. (Illus.). 208p. 1983. 20.95 (*0-8093-1058-9*) S Ill U Pr.

Argetsinger, Gerald S., tr. see Holberg, Ludvig.

Argetsinger, Jerry. Unfortunate Courtship of Brian Tanner. 1998. pap. 2.50 (*1-57514-331-3*, 3116) Encore Perform Pub.

***Argetsinger, Kathryn.** Students' Handbook of Latin Grammar. 1999. pap. 12.95 (*0-941051-94-3*) Focus Pub-R Pullins.

Argez, Samuel. Historia, Indice, y Prologo de la Revista: La Palabra y el Hombre (1957-1970) (SPA.). (Orig.). 1982. pap. write for info. (*0-89729-315-0*) Ediciones.

Arghandawi, A. A. British Imperialism & Afghanistan's Struggle for Independence, 1914-1921. 414p. 1990. reprint ed. 37.50 (*81-215-0452-X*, Pub. by M Manoharial) Coronet Bks.

Arghyrou, M. G., jt. auth. see Mourmouras, I. A.

Argila, Carl. Transitioning to Object Technology: A 12 Step Approach. (C). 2000. text 36.00 (*0-13-491945-9*) P-H.

Argilan, Mae. Grace under Fire. 175p. (Orig.). 1997. pap. 9.95 (*0-9659308-8-2*) Erica Hse.

Argiles, Josep M. Ubiquitin & Disease. (Molecular Biology Intelligence Unit Series). 174p. 1998. 99.00 (*1-57059-545-3*) Landes Bioscience.

Argiriou, Steven L. Concealed Handgun Carry Techniques. LC 99-188370. (Illus.). viii, 160p. 1998. pap. text 19.99 (*0-9667029-0-5*) POLICE Train Syst.

Argiro, Patricia R. Branching: Selected Essays by Patricia Regan Argiro. 304p. 1999. pap. 14.95 (*0-9659960-1-8*) Prase Pr.

An Asterisk (*) at the beginning of an entry indicates that the title is appearing for the first time.

— Toward Sunset: Poems & Drawings by Patricia Regan Argiro. LC 97-92427. (Illus.). 72p. 1997. pap. 27.00 (*0-9659960-0-X*) Prase Pr.

Argisle, Bethany, ed. see Light Years Ahead Productions Staff.

Argo, Burnis & Ruth, Kent. Oklahoma Historical Tour Guide. Wilson, D. Ray, ed. LC 91-70305. (Illus.). 355p. 1991. 19.95 (*0-916445-34-8*); pap. 15.00 (*0-916445-31-3*) Crossroads Comm.

Argo, Tracy M. Dare to Remember. 98p. (Orig.). 1996. pap. 8.95 (*0-614-20174-8*) T M Argo Pubns.

Argon, A. S., ed. Topics in Fracture & Fatigue. (Illus.). 346p. 1992. 119.95 (*0-387-97833-X*) Spr-Verlag.

Argon, A. S., jt. auth. see McClintock, F. A.

Argon, A. S., jt. auth. see McClintock, Frank A.

Argonne National Laboratory Staff. Environmental Consequences of & Control Processes for Energy Technologies. LC 90-30717. (Pollution Technology Review Ser.: No. 181). (Illus.). 453p. 1990. 56.00 (*0-8155-1231-7*) Noyes.

— Thermal Energy Storage: Design & Installation (1983 Edition) (Illus.). 365p. 1983. reprint ed. lib. bdg. 125.00 (*0-89934-213-2*, BT921) Bus Tech Bks.

Argonne National Laboratory Staff & AEC Technical Information Center Staff. Reactor Physics Constants. 2nd ed. 859p. 1963. pap. 91.00 (*0-87079-337-3*, ANL-5800); fiche 9.00 (*0-87079-497-3*, ANL-5800) DOE.

***Argos, V. P. & Shohov, Tatiana, eds.** Sexual Harassment: Analyses & Bibliography. 257p. 1999. 49.00 (*1-56072-711-X*) Nova Sci Pubs.

Argos Vergara Staff. Diccionario de Derecho Civil, Vol. 2. (SPA.). 384p. 1987. pap. 95.00 (*0-7859-6280-8*, 8477090289) Fr & Eur.

— Diccionario Empresarial Stanford, 5 vols., Set. (SPA.). 384p. 1987. pap. 95.00 (*0-7859-6274-3*, 8477090203) Fr & Eur.

— Diccionario Enciclopedico Illustrado Vol. 8: Piramo-S.A. (SPA.). 4552p. 1984. 595.00 (*0-7859-6182-8*, 8471785633) Fr & Eur.

— Diccionario Enciclopedico Argos-Vergara, 12 vols. (SPA.). 1984. 59.95 (*0-7859-6191-7*, 8471785730) Fr & Eur.

— Diccionario Enciclopedico Argos-Vergara, Vol. 2. (SPA.). 444p. 1984. 59.95 (*0-7859-6486-X*, 847178565X) Fr & Eur.

— Diccionario Enciclopedico Argos-Vergara, Vol. 3. (SPA.). 444p. 1984. 59.95 (*0-7859-6184-4*, 8471785668) Fr & Eur.

— Diccionario Enciclopedico Argos-Vergara, Vol. 4. (SPA.). 444p. 1984. 59.95 (*0-7859-6185-2*, 8471785676) Fr & Eur.

— Diccionario Enciclopedico Argos-Vergara, Vol. 5. (SPA.). 444p. 1984. 59.95 (*0-7859-6186-0*, 8471785684) Fr & Eur.

— Diccionario Enciclopedico Argos-Vergara, Vol. 6. (SPA.). 444p. 1984. 59.95 (*0-7859-6187-9*, 8471785692) Fr & Eur.

— Diccionario Enciclopedico Argos-Vergara, Vol. 7. (SPA.). 444p. 1984. 59.95 (*0-7859-6188-7*, 8471785706) Fr & Eur.

— Diccionario Enciclopedico Argos-Vergara, Vol. 7. (SPA.). 3860p. 1990. 1495.00 (*0-7859-6281-6*, 8477090815) Fr & Eur.

— Diccionario Enciclopedico Argos-Vergara, Vol. 8. (SPA.). 444p. 1984. 59.95 (*0-7859-6189-5*, 8471785714) Fr & Eur.

— Diccionario Enciclopedico Argos-Vergara, Vol. 8. (SPA.). 304p. 1990. 125.00 (*0-7859-6282-4*, 8477090823) Fr & Eur.

— Diccionario Enciclopedico Argos-Vergara, Vol. 9. (SPA.). 444p. 1984. 59.95 (*0-7859-6190-9*, 8471785722) Fr & Eur.

— Diccionario Enciclopedico Argos-Vergara, Vol. 9. (SPA.). 324p. 1990. 125.00 (*0-7859-6290-5*, 8477090912) Fr & Eur.

— Diccionario Enciclopedico Illustrado: Comicios-Es, Vol. 3 (SPA.). 384p. 1987. pap. 95.00 (*0-7859-6275-1*, 8477090211) Fr & Eur.

— Diccionario Enciclopedico Illustrado Vol. 2: Bayaceto-Co. (SPA.). 384p. 1987. pap. 95.00 (*0-7859-6276-X*, 8477090238) Fr & Eur.

— Diccionario Enciclopedico Illustrado Vol. 3: Comicios-Es. (SPA.). 384p. 1987. pap. 95.00 (*0-7859-6277-8*, 8477090246) Fr & Eur.

— Diccionario Enciclopedico Illustrado Vol. 4: Espana-Grand Bretagne. (SPA.). 384p. 1987. pap. 95.00 (*0-7859-6278-6*, 8477090254) Fr & Eur.

— Diccionario Enciclopedico Illustrado Vol. 5: Gran Bretan. (SPA.). 384p. 1987. pap. 95.00 (*0-7859-6279-4*, 8477090262) Fr & Eur.

— Diccionario Enciclopedico Illustrado Vol. 6: Lanzarot-M. (SPA., Illus.). 384p. 1987. pap. 95.00 (*0-7859-6439-8*, 8777090270) Fr & Eur.

— Diccionario Enciclopedico Illustrado Vol. 7: Munataner-P. (SPA.). 1984. 695.00 (*0-8288-2011-2*, S50444) Fr & Eur.

— Diccionario Enciclopedico Illustrado Vol. 9: Salt-Tripo, Vol. 1. (SPA.). 448p. 1984. 59.95 (*0-7859-6183-6*, 8471785641) Fr & Eur.

— Diccionario Enciclopedico Illustrado Vol. 10: Tripolitan. (SPA., Illus.). 384p. 1987. pap. 95.00 (*0-7859-6492-4*, 847709022X) Fr & Eur.

— Diccionario Enciclopedico Ilustrado Argos Vergara, 12 vols. (SPA.). 1990. 125.00 (*0-7859-6291-3*, 8477090920) Fr & Eur.

— Diccionario Enciclopedico Ilustrado Argos Vergara, Vol. 10. (SPA.). 324p. 1990. 125.00 (*0-685-70608-7*, 8477090912) Fr & Eur.

— Diccionario Enciclopedico Ilustrado Argos Vergara Vol. 2: Avellaneda-Carol I. (SPA.). 328p. 1990. 125.00 (*0-7859-6285-9*, 8477090866) Fr & Eur.

— Diccionario Enciclopedico Ilustrado Argos Vergara Vol. 3: Carol II-Desideratum. (SPA.). 332p. 1990. 125.00 (*0-7859-6286-7*, 8477090874) Fr & Eur.

— Diccionario Enciclopedico Ilustrado Argos Vergara Vol. 4: Desierto-Faceta. (SPA.). 324p. 1990. 125.00 (*0-7859-6287-5*, 8477090882) Fr & Eur.

— Diccionario Enciclopedico Ilustrado Argos Vergara Vol. 5: Facial-Hannibal. (SPA.). 320p. 1990. 125.00 (*0-7859-6288-3*, 8477090890) Fr & Eur.

— Diccionario Enciclopedico Ilustrado Argos Vergara Vol. 6: Hannon-Lazaro. (SPA.). 320p. 1990. 125.00 (*0-7859-6289-1*, 8477090904) Fr & Eur.

— Diccionario Enciclopedico Ilustrado Argos Vergara Vol. 10: Redova-Sobreperico. (SPA.). 324p. 1990. 125.00 (*0-7859-6283-2*, 8477090831) Fr & Eur.

— Diccionario Enciclopedico Ilustrado Argos Vergara Vol. 11: Sobrequilla-Uzcudun. (SPA., Illus.). 340p. 1990. 125.00 (*0-7859-6493-2*, 847709084X) Fr & Eur.

— Diccionario Enciclopedico Ilustrado Argos Vergara Vol. 12: V-Zworikin. (SPA.). 328p. 1990. 125.00 (*0-7859-6284-0*, 8477090858) Fr & Eur.

— Diccionario Enciclopedico Ilustrado Argos Vergara, Vol. 1: Avellaneda. (SPA.). 296p. 1990. 125.00 (*0-7859-6292-1*, 8477090939) Fr & Eur.

— Enciclopedia Panoramica, 7 vols., Set. 2nd ed. (SPA.). 1004p. 1975. 225.00 (*0-8288-5872-1*, S50446) Fr & Eur.

Argosy. Best Short Stories Argosy, Vol. I. 25.95 (*0-8488-1538-6*) Amereon Ltd.

***Argote, Linda.** Organizational Learning: Creating, Retaining & Transferring Knowledge. LC 98-51375. 1999. write for info. (*0-7923-8420-2*) Kluwer Academic.

Argote De Molina, Gonzalo. Nobleza Del Andalucia. (Textos y Estudios Clasicos De las Literaturas Hispanicas Ser.). xx, 696p. 1975. reprint ed. 290.00 (*3-487-05607-0*) G Olms Pubs.

Argoul, P. IUTAM Symposium on Variations of Domains & Free-Boundary Problems in Solid Mechanics: Proceedings of the Iutam Symposium Held in Paris, France, 22-25 April, 1997. LC 98-44223. 338p. 1998. 165.00 (*0-7923-5450-8*) Kluwer Academic.

Argubright, John. Bible Believers Archaeology: Historical Evidence That Proves the Bible. (Illus.). 120p. 1997. pap. write for info. (*1-57502-502-7*, PO1491) Morris Pubng.

Argue, Derry. Pointers & Setters. (Illus.). 192p. 1993. 40.00 (*1-85310-239-3*, Pub. by Swan Hill Pr) Voyageur Pr.

***Argue, John.** Parkinson's Disease & the Art of Moving. (Illus.). 176p. 2000. pap. text 15.95 (*1-57224-183-7*) New Harbinger.

Argue, Madeleine, et al. Review for the Graduate Record Examination. 350p. (C). 1996. pap. text 15.95 (*1-56030-011-6*) Comex Systs.

Argue, Theodora D. Practicing Daily Prayer in the Orthodox Christian Life. 1989. pap. 4.95 (*0-937032-64-6*) Light&Life Pub Co MN.

Arguedas, Jose M. Deep Rivers. Barraclough, Frances H., tr. from SPA. LC 77-26243. (Texas Pan American Ser.). 264p. 1978. pap. 13.95 (*0-292-71533-1*) U of Tex Pr.

— Yawar Fiesta. Barraclough, Frances H., tr. from SPA. LC 84-19625. (Texas Pan American Ser.). 224p. 1985. 22.50 (*0-292-79601-3*); pap. 12.95 (*0-292-79602-1*) U of Tex Pr.

***Arguedas, Jose Maria.** The Fox from up above & the Fox from down Below. Ortega, Julio, ed. Barraclough, Frances Horning, tr. 320p. 2000. pap. 19.95 (*0-8229-5718-3*); text 45.00 (*0-8229-4117-1*) U of Pittsburgh Pr.

Arguelles, Gonzalez E. Un Golodrino no Compone Primavera. LC 84-80618. (Coleccion Caniqui). (SPA.). 221p. (Orig.). 1984. pap. 9.95 (*0-89729-350-9*) Ediciones.

Arguelles, Hugo. Teatro - Arguelles, Vol. II. (SPA.). 16.99 (*968-16-4567-7*, Pub. by Fondo) Continental Bk.

— Teatro Vario - Arguelles, Vol. I. (SPA.). 16.99 (*968-16-4566-9*, Pub. by Fondo) Continental Bk.

Arguelles, Ivan. Baudelaire's Brain. (Illus.). 56p. (Orig.). 1988. pap. 3.00 (*0-945085-08-7*) Sub Rosa.

— Captive of the Vision of Paradise. 75p. 1982. pap. 8.75 (*0-915868-02-4*) Hartmus Pr.

***Arguelles, Ivan.** City of Angels. 52p. 1999. pap. 7.00 (*0-937013-94-3*, Pub. by Potes Poets) SPD-Small Pr Dist.

— Daya Karo: Two Songs. 25p. 1999. pap. 6.00 (*1-892280-05-1*) Luna Bisonte.

Arguelles, Ivan. Enigma & Variations: Paradise Is Persian for Park. 96p. (Orig.). 1996. pap. 8.95 (*1-880766-11-6*) Pantograph Pr.

— Hapax Legomenon. 69p. (Orig.). 1993. pap. 8.95 (*1-880766-04-3*) Pantograph Pr.

— The Invention of Spain. 62p. 1978. pap. 7.50 (*0-685-49042-4*) Cross-Cultrl NY.

— The Invention of Spain. 1978. pap. 2.50 (*0-917402-07-3*) Downtown Poets.

— Looking for Mary Lou: Illegal Syntax. LC 88-92723. (Illus.). 169p. (Orig.). 1989. pap. 35.00 (*0-9621676-0-6*) Rock Steady Pr.

— Madonna. LC 98-213529. 23p. 1998. pap. 5.00 (*1-57141-043-0*) Runaway Spoon.

— Nailed to the Coffin of Life. Glazier, Loss P., ed. (Oxyura Jamaicensis Rubida Monographs in Poetry: No. 1). (Illus.). 1985. pap. 3.50 (*0-910697-03-5*) Ruddy Duck Pr.

— Pieces of the Bone - Text Still There. (Illus.). 28p. 1987. pap. 3.00 (*0-318-23467-X*) Skydog OR.

— That Goddess. 104p. 1991. pap. 8.95 (*1-880766-00-0*) Pantograph Pr.

Arguelles, Ivan & Berry, Jake. Purisima Sex Addict, No. II. 23p. 1997. pap. 7.00 (*0-935350-64-0*) Luna Bisonte.

Arguelles, Ivan & Foley, Jack. New Poetry from California: Dead/Requiem. (Illus.). 127p. 1998. pap. 9.95 (*1-880766-16-7*) Pantograph Pr.

Arguelles, Jose. Arcturus Probe. 1996. pap. 14.95 (*0-929385-75-6*) Light Tech Pubng.

— Charles Henry & the Formation of a Psychophysical Aesthetic. LC 72-189026. 209p. reprint ed. pap. 64.80 (*0-608-09261-4*, 205406300002) Bks Demand.

— The Mayan Factor: Path Beyond Technology. LC 87-960. (Illus.). 224p. 1987. pap. 16.00 (*0-939680-38-6*) Bear & Co.

— Surfers of the Zuvuya: Tales of Intergalactic Travel. 2nd ed. LC 88-18091. 180p. (Orig.). 1988. pap. 15.00 (*0-939680-55-6*) Bear & Co.

— The Transformative Vision: Reflections on the Nature & History of Human Expression. (Illus.). 364p. (C). 1992. reprint ed. pap. 14.95 (*0-9631750-0-9*) Muse Pubns.

Arguelles, Jose A. Charles Henry & the Formation of a Psychophysical Aesthetic. LC 72-189026. x, 20(p. 1974. pap. text 3.25 (*0-226-02758-9*) U Ch Pr.

Arguelles, Maria Del Pilar, see Del Pilar Arguelles, Maria.

Arguelles, Marilla, ed. Extracts from Pelican Bay. 8(p. (Orig.). 1995. pap. 8.95 (*1-880766-10-8*) Pantograph Pr.

***Arguelles, Tony.** Web Professionals Comprehensive Guide. 2000. pap., student ed. 39.99 (*0-13-027091-1*) P-H.

Arguello, Antonio. The Death of the Last Dragon. Fox, Deborah, ed. LC 96-84286. (Illus.). (Orig.). (J). 1997. pap. write for info. (*0-9651976-0-3*) Dragon Ink.

***Arguerta, Manlio.** A Place Called Milagro de la Paz. Miller, Michael B., tr. LC 99-86710. 203p. 2000. pap. 15.95 (*1-880684-68-3*) Curbstone.

Argueta, Jorge. Corazon del Barrio. 28p. (Orig.). 1994. pap. 4.00 (*0-916397-29-7*) Manic D Pr.

Argueta, Manlio. Cuzcatlan: Where the Southern Sea Beats. Hansen, Clark, tr. 255p. 1987. pap. 8.95 (*0-679-74253-0*) Vin Bks.

— Little Red Riding Hood in the Red Light District. Hood, Edward W., tr. from SPA. LC 99-86170. 238p. 1998. pap. 14.95 (*1-880684-32-2*) Curbstone.

— The Magic Dogs of the Volcanoes. 1995. 13.00 (*0-606-09582-9*, Pub. by Turtleback) Demco.

— Magic Dogs of the Volcanoes (Los Perros Magicos de los Volcanes) (ENG & SPA., Illus.). 32p. (J). (gr. 1 up). 1995. pap. 7.95 (*0-89239-129-4*) Childrens Book Pr.

— One Day of Life. LC 90-50213. (Vintage International Ser.). 224p. 1991. pap. 13.00 (*0-679-73243-8*) Vin Bks.

Argueta, Manlio, et al. Magic Dogs of the Volcanoes (Los Perros Magicos de los Volcanes) LC 90-2254. (ENG & SPA., Illus.). 32p. (YA). (ps-3). 1990. 14.95 (*0-89239-064-6*) Childrens Book Pr.

Argueta, Nelson Stanley. El Hijo del Sol. (SPA.). 180p. 1997. pap. text 6.98 (*968-409-569-4*) Edit Diana.

Argullol, Rafael. Lampedusa. (SPA.). 140p. 1981. pap. 5.50 (*84-85859-09-X*, 2002) Ediciones Norte.

Argus. Argus de l'Autographe et du Manuscrit. (FRE.). 130p. 1992. 125.00 (*0-8288-7226-0*, 2765404984) Fr & Eur.

— Argus du Livre de Collection: Repertoire Bibliographique, 1992. (FRE.). 852p. 1992. 350.00 (*0-8288-7225-2*, 2765404976) Fr & Eur.

Argus, George W. Genus Salix (Salicaceae) in the Southeastern United States. Anderson, Christiane, ed. LC 85-26871. (Systematic Botany Monographs: Vol. 9). (Illus.). 170p. (Orig.). 1986. pap. 20.00 (*0-912861-09-6*) Am Soc Plant.

— Infrageneric Classification of Salix (Salicaceae) in the New World. Anderson, Christiane, ed. (Systematic Botany Monographs: Vol. 52). (Illus.). 121p. 1997. pap. 15.00 (*0-912861-52-5*) Am Soc Plant.

Argy, Fred. Australia at the Crossroads: Radical Free Market or a Progressive Liberalism? LC 99-179900. 304p. 1998. pap. 24.95 (*1-86448-669-4*, Pub. by Allen & Unwin Pty) Paul & Co Pubs.

Argy, Victor. Exchange-Rate Management in Theory & Practice. LC 82-12015. (Studies in International Finance: No. 50). 92p. 1982. pap. text 13.50 (*0-88165-221-0*) Princeton U Int Finan Econ.

— International Macroeconomics: Theory & Policy. LC 93-4621. 258p. (C). 1994. pap. 32.99 (*0-415-09823-8*) Routledge.

— International Macroeconomics: Theory & Policy. LC 93-4621. (Illus.). 285p. (C). (gr. 13). 1994. 150.00 (*0-415-09822-X*) Routledge.

Argy, Victor & De Grauwe, Paul, eds. Choosing an Exchange Rate Regime: The Challenge for Smaller Industrial Counties. LC 89-48328. v, 391p. 1990. pap. 19.50 (*1-55775-133-1*) Intl Monetary.

Argy, Victor & Stein, Leslie. The Japanese Economy. LC 96-21387. (Illus.). 379p. (C). 1996. text 60.00 (*0-8147-0659-2*) NYU Pr.

Argy, Victor, et al. Exchange-Rate Regimes for a Small Economy in a Multi-Country World. LC 89-26966. (Studies in International Finance: No. 67). 46p. 1990. pap. text 13.50 (*0-88165-239-3*) Princeton U Int Finan Econ.

Argyle, Carolyn. How to Start & Run a Home Day-Care Business. LC 96-29585. (Illus.). 192p. 1997. pap. 10.95 (*0-8065-1852-9*, Citadel Pr) Carol Pub Group.

Argyle, Michael. Bodily Communication. 2nd ed. LC 75-18679. xii, 363p. (Orig.). 1988. 55.00 (*0-8236-0551-5*) Intl Univs Pr.

***Argyle, Michael.** Psychology & Religion: Introduction. LC 99-16956. 320p. 1999. pap. write for info. (*0-415-18907-1*) Routledge.

— Psychology & Religion: Introduction. LC 99-16956. 304p. (C). 2000. text. write for info. (*0-415-18906-3*) Routledge.

Argyle, Michael. The Psychology of Happiness. pap. 14.95 (*0-317-65255-9*) Routledge.

Argyle, Michael. Psychology of Interpersonal Behaviour. 1994. pap. 17.95 (*0-14-017274-2*, Pub. by Pnguin Bks Ltd) Trafalgar.

Argyle, Michael. The Psychology of Social Class. LC 93-3445. 256p. (C). 1993. pap. 25.99 (*0-415-07955-1*, A9838) Routledge.

— The Scientific Study of Social Behavior. LC 73-13021. (Illus.). 239p. 1974. reprint ed. lib. bdg. 59.75 (*0-8371-7108-3*, ARSS, Greenwood Pr) Greenwood.

— Social Interaction. 1973. pap. 16.95 (*0-422-75480-3*, Pub. by Tavistock) Routldge.

— The Social Psychology of Everyday Life. (Illus.). 352p. (Orig.). (C). 1992. pap. 25.99 (*0-415-01072-1*, A6660) Routledge.

Argyle, Michael. Social Psychology of Leisure. 1996. pap. 17.95 (*0-14-023887-5*, Pub. by Pnguin Bks Ltd) Trafalgar.

Argyle, Michael, ed. Experiments in Social Interaction. (Benchmark Ser.). 336p. 1993. 79.95 (*1-85521-371-0*, Pub. by Dartmth Pub) Ashgate Pub Co.

Argyle, Michael & Colman, Andrew M., eds. Social Psychology Long. LC 95-18119. (Essential Psychology Ser.). 110p. (C). 1995. pap. text 18.00 (*0-582-27804-X*) Addison-Wesley.

Argyle, Michael, jt. auth. see Beit-Hallahmi, Benjamin.

Argyle, Michael, jt. auth. see Furnham, Adrian.

Argyle, Michael, jt. auth. see Rutter, Derek R.

Argyle Municipality Historical & Genealogical Society, jt. auth. see Crowell, Peter M.

Argyll & the Islands Enterprise Staff. Dunoon & Cowal Business Directory, 1994. 112p. (C). 1993. pap. write for info. (*1-874640-60-2*, Pub. by Argyll Pubng) St Mut.

Argyll, Archibald C. Letters from Archibald, Earl of Argyll, to John, Duke of Lauderdale. Sinclair, George & Sharpe, C. K., eds. LC 75-38489. (Bannatyne Club, Edinburgh: Publications: No. 33). reprint ed. 49.50 (*0-404-52739-6*) AMS Pr.

Argyll Publishing Staff & Save the Children Staff. Fair Start. (Illus.). 80p. 1994. pap. write for info. (*1-874640-26-2*, Pub. by Argyll Pubng) St Mut.

Argyraki, Mary, tr. see Yatromanolakis, Yoryis.

Argyres, E., et al, eds. Elementary Particle Physics: Proceedings of the Third Hellenic School, Corfu, Greece, September 13-30, 1989. 804p. 1990. text 137.00 (*981-02-0355-1*) World Scientific Pub.

Argyres, E. & Zoupanos, G. Elementary Particle Physics: Proceedings of the 2nd Hellenic School Sept. 1-20, 1985, Corfu, Greece. 640p. 1986. text 138.00 (*9971-5-0206-2*, PH-P344) World Scientific Pub.

Argyris, Chris. Behind the Front Page: Organizational Self-Renewal in a Metropolitan Newspaper. LC 73-22558. (Jossey-Bass Behavioral Science Ser.). 325p. reprint ed. pap. 100.80 (*0-8357-4695-X*, 205235000008) Bks Demand.

— The Individual & Organization: Some Problems of Mutual Adjustment. (Reprint Series in Social Sciences). (C). 1993. reprint ed. pap. text 5.00 (*0-8290-4072-2*, PS-10) Irvington.

— Integrating the Individual & the Organization. 405p. 1990. pap. 24.95 (*0-88738-803-5*) Transaction Pubs.

— Integrating the Individual & the Organization. LC 64-13209. 342p. reprint ed. pap. 106.10 (*0-608-10852-9*, 201929600011) Bks Demand.

— Intervention Theory & Method: A Behavioral Science View. LC 79-114331. (Business Ser.). (C). 1970. text 27.00 (*0-201-00342-2*) Addison-Wesley.

— Knowledge for Action: A Guide to Overcoming Barriers to Organizational Change. LC 92-42861. (Management Ser.). 329p. 1993. text 35.45 (*1-55542-519-4*) Jossey-Bass.

— Leadership, Learning, Change & Commitment: How Managers Can Know When They're Getting Good Advice & When They're Not. LC 99-32358. (Illus.). 272p. 2000. 27.50 (*0-19-513286-6*) OUP.

— On Organizational Learning. 480p. 1995. pap. text 30.95 (*1-55786-663-5*) Blackwell Pubs.

— On Organizational Learning. LC 98-54396. 560p. 1999. 72.95 (*0-631-21308-2*) Blackwell Pubs.

***Argyris, Chris.** On Organizational Learning. 2nd ed. LC 98-54396. 1999. pap. text 39.95 (*0-631-21309-0*) Blackwell Pubs.

Argyris, Chris. Organization of a Bank: Study of the Nature of Organization & the Fusion Process. Stein, Leon, ed. LC 77-70479. 1977. reprint ed. lib. bdg. 29.95 (*0-405-10153-8*) Ayer.

— Overcoming Organizational Defenses. 180p. 1990. 70.00 (*0-205-12338-4*, H23385) Allyn.

— Strategy, Change & Defensive Routines. LC 85-584. 368p. 1986. text 28.00 (*0-273-02329-2*, HarpBusn) HarpInfo.

Argyris, Chris & Schon, Donald A. Theory in Practice: Increasing Professional Effectiveness. LC 74-3606. (Jossey-Bass Series in Higher Education). 240p. reprint ed. pap. 74.40 (*0-7837-2513-2*, 204267200006) Bks Demand.

— Theory in Practice: Increasing Professional Effectiveness. LC 74-3606. (Classics Ser.). 260p. 1992. reprint ed. pap. 28.95 (*1-55542-446-5*) Jossey-Bass.

Argyris, Chris, et al. Action Science: Concepts, Methods, & Skills for Research & Intervention. LC 85-45051. (Social & Behavioral Science Ser.). 500p. 1985. 46.95 (*0-87589-665-0*) Jossey-Bass.

Argyris, Chris, jt. ed. see Cooper, Cary L.

Argyris, J. H. Introduction to the Finite Element Method. 1984. write for info. (*0-318-57807-7*, North Holland) Elsevier.

Argyris, J. H. & Mlejnek, H. P., eds. Dynamics of Structures: Proceedings of the 2nd World Conference, Stuttgart, Germany, 27-31 Aug., 1990. (Texts on Computational Mechanics Ser.: Vol. 5). 606p. 1991. 212.00 (*0-444-89045-9*, North Holland) Elsevier.

Argyris, John, et al. An Exploration of Chaos: An Introduction for Natural Scientists & Engineers. LC 94-11680. (Texts on Computational Mechanics Ser.: Vol. VII). 772p. 1994. 281.50 (*0-444-82002-7*, North Holland); pap. 111.00 (*0-444-82003-5*, North Holland) Elsevier.

A

An Asterisk (*) at the beginning of an entry indicates that the title is appearing for the first time.

Argyris, John, jt. auth. see Tenek, Lazarus T.

Argyros, Alexander J. A Blessed Rage for Order: Deconstruction, Evolution & Chaos. (Illus.). 376p. (C). 1992. text 52.50 (*0-472-10221-4*, 10221) U of Mich Pr.

Argyros, Ellen. Without Any Check of Proud Reserve: Sympathy & Its Limits in George Eliot's Novels. LC 97-39301. (Studies in Nineteenth-Century British Literature). 244p. 1999. 52.95 (*0-8204-3677-1*) P Lang Pubng.

***Argyros, Ioannis K.** Advances in the Efficiency of Computational Methods & Applications. 560p. 2000. pap. 42.00 (*981-02-4349-9*) World Scientific Pub.

— Advances in the Efficiency of Computational Methods & Applications. LC 00-33367. (Illus.). 560p. 2000. 84.00 (*981-02-4336-7*) World Scientific Pub.

Argyros, Ioannis K. Polynomial Operator Equations in Abstract Spaces & Applications. LC 98-6373. 592p. 1998. boxed set 94.95 (*0-8493-8702-7*) CRC Pr.

Argyros, Ioannis K., jt. auth. see Szidarovszky.

Argyros, S. & Longstaff, W. Atomic Boolean Subspace Lattices & Applications to the Theory of Bases. LC 91-7545. (MEMO Ser.: Vol. 91/445). 94p. 1991. pap. 20.00 (*0-8218-2511-9*, MEMO/91/445) Am Math.

Argyrou, Vassos. Tradition & Modernity in the Mediterranean: The Wedding As Symbolic Struggle. (Studies in Social & Cultural Anthropology: Vol. 101). (Illus.). 220p. (C). 1996. text 49.95 (*0-521-56095-0*) Cambridge U Pr.

Argyroudi-Akoyunoglou, J. H. Regulation of Choloroplast Biogenesis. (NATO ASI Ser.: Vol. 226). (Illus.). 644p. (C). 1992. text 155.00 (*0-306-44184-5*, Kluwer Plenum) Kluwer Academic.

Argyroudi-Akoyunoglou, Joan H. & Senger, H. The Chloroplast: From Molecular Biology to Biotechnology. LC 98-55185. (NATO ASI Ser.). 16p. 1999. write for info. (*0-7923-5576-8*) Kluwer Academic.

Argyrous, George. Statistics for Social Research. 336p. 1997. 79.95 (*0-7329-3936-4*, Pub. by Macmill Educ); pap. 39.95 (*0-7329-3939-9*, Pub. by Macmill Educ) Paul & Co Pubs.

Arhangel'skii, A. V., ed. General Topology II, Vol. 50. Lysko, J. M., tr. (Encyclopedia of Mathematical Sciences Ser.). 263p. 1995. reprint ed. 107.95 (*0-387-54695-2*) Spr-Verlag.

Arhangel'skii, A. V. & Gamkrelidze, R. V., eds. General Topology III: Paracompactness, Metrization, Coverings. Gould, G. G., tr. from RUS. (Encyclopedia of Mathematical Sciences Ser.: Vol. 51). 236p. 1995. 118.95 (*0-387-54698-7*) Spr-Verlag.

Arhar, Joanne, ed. Research in Middle Level Education Vol. 15, No. 2, Vol. 15, No. 1. 84p. (C). 1991. pap. text 14.00 (*1-56090-062-8*) Natl Middle Schl.

Arhem, Kaj. Makuna: Portrait of an Amazonian People. LC 98-13898. 192p. 1998. 34.95 (*1-56098-874-6*) Smithsonian.

***Arhem, Peter.** Disorder Versus Order in Brain Function Essays in Theoretical Neurobiology. 1999. 46.00 (*981-02-4008-2*) World Scientific Pub.

Arhem, Peter, et al, eds. Matter Matters? Vol. X: On the Material Basis of the Cognitive Activity of Mind. LC 96-52744. (Illus.). 240p. 1997. 44.95 (*3-540-61776-0*) Spr-Verlag.

Arhin, Kwame. West African Traders in Ghana in the Nineteenth & Twentieth Centuries. LC 79-40716. (Legon History Ser.). 160p. reprint ed. pap. 49.60 (*0-8357-3586-9*, 203447100090) Bks Demand.

Arhin, Kwame, ed. The Life & Work of Kwame Nkrumah. LC 93-30706. 395p. 1993. reprint ed. 49.95 (*0-86543-395-X*); reprint ed. pap. 16.95 (*0-86543-396-8*) Africa World.

Arhin, Kwame, et al. Marketing Boards in Tropical Africa. (Monographs from the African Studies Centre, Leiden). (Illus.). 350p. 1985. 69.50 (*0-7103-0109-X*) Routledge.

Arhipov, Sergei, jt. auth. see Orthodox Church in America Staff.

Arhiri, Emmanuel. Unequal Exchange: A Study of the Imperialism of Trade. LC 78-158920. 493p. reprint ed. pap. 152.90 (*0-7837-3924-9*, 204377200010) Bks Demand.

Arhmad, Navzeir & Siddiqi, Iqtidar H. Islamic Heritage in the South Asian Subcontinent. LC 98-917271. 1998. write for info. (*81-86782-29-X*) S Asia.

Ari & Hauser. Healing, NIV. gif. ed. (God's Light Ser.). 160p. 1998. 9.99 (*0-310-97338-4*, Zondervan Gifts) Zondervan.

Ari, Mark. Shoemaker's Tale. 240p. 1993. 19.00 (*0-939010-38-0*); pap. 10.00 (*0-939010-39-9*) Zephyr Pr.

ARI Staff & PES Staff. Study Guide to the ARI-GAMA Competency in HVACR, 1987-1988. 80p. (C). 1987. pap. text, student ed. 8.60 (*0-13-855636-9*) P-H.

Aria, Barbara & Gon, Russell E. Spirit of the Chinese Character: Gifts from the Heart. 96p. 1992. 14.95 (*0-8118-0142-X*) Chronicle Bks.

Aria, Barbara, jt. auth. see Tobin, Phyllis Z.

Ariadne, Patricia A. Women Dreaming-into-Art: Seven Artists Who Create from Dreams. LC 98-6622. (Illus.). 256p. 1998. pap. 14.95 (*1-880090-69-4*) Galde Pr.

Ariail, Robert B., jt. auth. see Warner, Deborah J.

Arian, Asher. The Elections in Israel: Nineteen Sixty-Nine. 311p. 1969. 44.95 (*0-87855-237-5*) Transaction Pubs.

— The Second Republic: Politics in Israel. LC 97-5247. (Illus.). 432p. (C). 1997. pap. text 29.95 (*1-56643-052-6*, Chatham House Pub) Seven Bridges.

— Security Threatened: Surveying Israeli Opinion on Peace & War. (Studies in Political Psychology & Public Opinion). (Illus.). 320p. (C). 1995. text 64.95 (*0-521-48314-X*) Cambridge U Pr.

— Security Threatened: Surveying Israeli Opinion on Peace & War. (Studies in Political Psychology & Public Opinion). (Illus.). 320p. (C). 1995. pap. text 23.95 (*0-521-49925-9*) Cambridge U Pr.

***Arian, Asher, ed.** The Elections in Israel 1996. LC 98-42749. (SUNY Series in Israeli Studies). (Illus.). 317p. (C). 1999. pap. text 25.95 (*0-7914-4238-1*) State U NY Pr.

Arian, Asher & Shamir, Michal, eds. The Elections in Israel, 1996. LC 98-42749. (SUNY Series in Israeli Studies). 448p. (C). 1999. text 75.50 (*0-7914-4237-3*) State U NY Pr.

— The Elections in Israel, 1992. LC 93-49761. (SUNY Series in Israeli Studies). 326p. (C). 1994. text 64.50 (*0-7914-2175-9*); pap. text 21.95 (*0-7914-2176-7*) State U NY Pr.

Arian, Edward. The Unfilled Promise: Public Subsidy of the Arts in America. 120p. 1993. pap. 14.95 (*1-56639-083-4*) Temple U Pr.

— The Unfulfilled Promise: Public Subsidy of the Arts in America. 120p. (C). 1989. 24.95 (*0-87722-612-1*) Temple U Pr.

***Ariano, Marjorie.** Receptor Localization: Laboratory Methods & Procedures. LC 97-17105. (Receptor Biochemistry & Methodology Ser.). 264p. 1998. 165.00 (*0-471-16571-9*) Wiley.

Ariano, Marjorie. Receptor Localization: Laboratory Methods & Procedures. LC 97-17105. (Receptor Biochemistry & Methodology Ser.). 250p. 1998. pap. 84.95 (*0-471-19524-3*) Wiley.

Arianoutsou, Margarita, ed. Plant-Animal Interactions in Mediterranean-Type Ecosystems. LC 93-6345. (Tasks for Vegetation Science Ser.). 184p. (C). 1994. text 156.00 (*0-7923-2470-6*) Kluwer Academic.

Ariarajah, S. Wesley. The Bible & People of Other Faiths. LC 88-26773. 87p. (Orig.). reprint ed. pap. 30.00 (*0-608-20204-5*, 207146300012) Bks Demand.

Ariarajah, S. Wesley, jt. ed. see Arai, Tosh.

Ariaratnam, S. T., et al, eds. Stochastic Structural Dynamics: Progress in Theory & Applications. 376p. 1988. ring bd. 208.95 (*1-85166-211-1*, Chap & Hall CRC) CRC Pr.

Arias, Alfonso M., jt. ed. see Bate, Michael.

Arias, Arnold. Dimension Doors. (Illus.). 64p. (Orig.). 1987. pap., per. write for info. (*0-318-67009-7*) Paradise Planet.

— The Iridescent Dimension. 1976. per. 2.50 (*0-9602374-0-2*) Paradise Planet.

Arias, Arturo. After the Bombs. Zatz, Asa, tr. from SPA. LC 90-81428. 221p. (Orig.). 1990. 19.95 (*0-915306-88-3*); pap. 10.95 (*0-915306-89-1*) Curbstone.

Arias, Claire C. & Sawdy, Herald. Window Base Primer. (Trainers' Signature Ser.). 399p. 1992. pap. 29.95 (*1-880663-39-2*) Ellipsys Intl.

Arias, Claire C., ed. see Hart, Anne.

Arias, Claire C., ed. & illus. see Lienhard, Janet.

Arias, David. Spanish Cross in Georgia. 242p. (C). 1994. lib. bdg. 45.00 (*0-8191-9700-9*) U Pr of Amer.

Arias de la Cruz, Manual. Diccionario de Americanismos (Dictionary of Americanisms)Tr. of Dictionary of Americanisms. (SPA.). 572p. 1980. 24.95 (*0-8288-0778-7*, S39789) Fr & Eur.

Arias, Enrique A. Alexander Tcherepnin: A Bio-Bibliography, 8. LC 87-31441. (Bio-Bibliographies in Music Ser.: No. 8). 276p. 1989. lib. bdg. 59.95 (*0-313-25318-8*, ARA/, Greenwood Pr) Greenwood.

Arias, Enrique A., et al, eds. A Compendium of American: Essays in Honor of John F. Ohl. 416p. 1999. text 69.95 (*0-8101-1536-0*) Northwestern U Pr.

Arias, Enrique A., ed. see De Vivanco, Sebastian.

***Arias, Enrique Alberto.** Comedy in Music: A Historical Bibliographical Resource Guide. LC 99-46020. 2000. lib. bdg. write for info. (*0-313-29980-3*) Greenwood.

Arias, Esther. El Clamor De Mi Pueblo: Desde el Cautiverio En America Latina. fac. ed. LC 81-4816. (Illus.). 167p. 1994. pap. 51.80 (*0-7837-7707-8*, 204746600007) Bks Demand.

Arias, Fernando. Practical Guide to High-Risk Pregnancy & Delivery. 2nd ed. (Illus.). 496p. (C). (gr. 13). 1992. pap. text 62.00 (*0-8016-0057-X*, 00057) Mosby Inc.

Arias, Harmodio. Panama Canal: A Study in International Law & Diplomacy. LC 79-111707. (American Imperialism: Viewpoints of United States Foreign Policy, 1898-1941 Ser.). 1977. reprint ed. 18.95 (*0-405-02001-5*) Ayer.

Arias, Irwin M., et al, eds. The Liver: Biology & Pathobiology. 3rd ed. LC 93-23602. 1664p. 1994. text 289.00 (*0-7817-0133-3*) Lppncott W & W.

Arias, J. M., et al, eds. Nuclear Physics at the Borderlines: Proceedings of the Fourth International Summer School, Sponsored by the Universidad Hispano-Americana, Santa Maria de la Rapida, La Rapida, Huelva, Spain, June 17-29, 1991. (Research Reports in Physics). (Illus.). xii, 268p. 1992. 79.95 (*0-387-55074-7*) Spr-Verlag.

Arias, Jorge R., jt. auth. see Penny, Norman D.

Arias, Jorge R., jt. ed. see Stycos, J. Mayone.

Arias, Jose M., et al, eds. Many-Body Theory of Correlated Fermion Systems: Proceedings of the VI Hispalensis International School Oromana, Seville, Spain 9-21 June, 1997. LC 99-170956. 330p. 1998. 78.00 (*981-02-3383-3*) World Scientific Pub.

Arias, Jose M., ed. see Fifth La Rabida International Summer School on Nuc.

***Arias, Juan.** Fernando Savater: El Arte De Vivir. 1999. pap. 19.95 (*84-08-02996-7*) Planeta.

Arias, Juan. The God I Don't Believe In. Berrett, Paul, tr. LC 73-76766. (Priority Bks.). 208p. 1973. reprint ed. pap. 64.50 (*0-608-15023-1*, 205216900048) Bks Demand.

***Arias, Juan.** Jose Saramago: El Amor Posible, Vol. 1. (Colecion Documento Ser.). (SPA.). 1998. 18.95 (*84-08-02480-9*) Planeta Edit.

— Paulo Coelho Las Confesiones del Peregrino. 1999. pap. 19.95 (*84-08-02956-8*) Planeta Edit.

***Arias, Kathleen Meehan.** Quick Reference to Outbreak Investigation & Control in Health Care Facilities. LC 99-33381. 339p. 1999. pap. 59.00 (*0-8342-1179-3*) Aspen Pub.

Arias-Klein, Marta, ed. see Klein, Irving J.

Arias, M. Beatriz & Casanova, Ursula, eds. Bilingual Education: Policy, Practice, & Research. (National Society for the Study of Education Publication Ser.: No. 92, Pt. 2). 262p. (C). 1993. 24.95 (*0-226-60160-9*) U Ch Pr.

Arias, M. Pombo. Manual de Pediatria Practica. 4th ed. (SPA.). 693p. 1992. 37.50 (*84-7978-055-X*, Pub. by Ediciones Diaz) IBD Ltd.

Arias, Miguel, ed. Palabra de Dios 1999. (SPA.). 1998. pap. 7.00 (*1-56854-220-8*, SAHW99) Liturgy Tr Pubns.

Arias-Misson, Alain. The Mind Crime of August Saint: A Novel. 420p. 1993. 22.95 (*0-932511-78-3*); pap. 11.95 (*0-932511-79-1*) Fiction Coll.

Arias, Mortimer & Johnson, Alan. The Great Commission: Biblical Models for Evangelism. 160p. (Orig.). 1992. pap. 12.95 (*0-687-15784-6*) Abingdon.

Arias, Oscar. The Struggle for Peace. Darst, David H., ed. (International Albert Schweitzer Lecture Ser. at Yale University). (Illus.). 12p. (Orig.). (C). pap. text 3.50 (*1-885007-01-9*) A Schweitzer.

— The Struggle for Peace: An Inaugural Lecture. (Lecture Ser.). (Illus.). 49p. (Orig.). 1990. pap. 3.25 (*1-881157-00-8*) In Ctr Global.

Arias, Ramon A. Festividades Satanicas/Apariencia Inofensiva. (Serie Realidades - Realities Ser.).Tr. of Satanic Festivities/Harmless Appearance. (SPA.). 31p. 1985. pap. 1.99 (*1-56063-119-8*, 498145) Editorial Unilit.

***Arias, Robert.** Apology: A New Age Meditation. LC 99-91585. 1999. 25.00 (*0-7388-0910-1*); pap. 18.00 (*0-7388-0911-X*) Xlibris Corp.

Arias, Ron. The Road to Tamazunchale. LC 86-70700. (Chicano Classics - Clasicos Chicanos Ser.: No. 3). (Illus.). 134p. 1997. pap. 10.00 (*0-916950-70-0*) Biling Rev-Pr.

Arias, Toby & Frassanito, Elaine. Fiesta Mexicana. 7th ed. (Illus.). 92p. 1982. pap. 7.95 (*0-9609942-0-3*) T & E Ent.

Ariasingam, David L., jt. auth. see Patrinos, Harry A.

Ariass, Glaurys, jt. auth. see Ariass, Helsa.

Ariass, Helsa & Ariass, Glaurys. Save Pennies, Bank Millions: Accelerate Financial Growth on a Modest Income. LC 98-92854. (Illus.). x, 157p. 1998. pap. 10.99 (*0-9664584-0-0*) Ariass Fortune.

Ariav, Gad, jt. auth. see Ginzberg, Michael J.

Arichea, Daniel C. & Hatton, Howard A. A Handbook on Paul's Letters to Timothy & to Titus. LC 95-31605. (UBS Handbook Ser.). viii, 336p. 1995. pap. 8.99 (*0-8267-0168-X*, 105623) Untd Bible Soc.

— A Handbook on the Letter from Jude & the Second Letter from Peter. LC 93-18768. (UBS Handbook Ser.). viii, 188p. 1993. pap. 16.99 (*0-8267-0172-8*, 105035) Untd Bible Soc.

Arichea, Daniel C. & Nida, Eugene A. A Handbook on Paul's Letter to the Galatians. LC 92-20511. (UBS Handbook Ser.). Orig. Title: A Translator's Handbook on Paul's Letter to the Galatians. vii, 176p. 1976. pap. 12.99 (*0-8267-0163-9*, 102690) Untd Bible Soc.

— A Handbook on the First Letter from Peter. LC 94-5553. (UBS Handbook Ser.). Orig. Title: Translators Handbook on the First Letter from Peter. vii, 190p. 1980. pap. 13.99 (*0-8267-0171-X*, 102728) Untd Bible Soc.

Arick, Martin R. Data Communications: Concepts & Systems. LC 84-62291. (Illus.). 279p. (Orig.). reprint ed. pap. 86.50 (*0-7837-0588-3*, 204093200019) Bks Demand.

— The Essential Guide to TCP/IP Commands. LC 95-41515. 265p. 1996. pap. 24.95 (*0-471-12569-5*) Wiley.

— The TCP/IP Companion: A Guide for the Common User. 272p. 1993. pap. 29.95 (*0-471-55631-9*, GD4663) Wiley.

— UNIX C Shell Desk Reference. 224p. 1993. pap. 44.95 (*0-471-55680-7*, GD3234) Wiley.

— UNIX3 for DOS Users. LC 95-14629. 256p. 1995. pap. 34.99 (*0-471-04988-3*) Wiley.

Arico, Diane, ed. William Shakespeare's Romeo & Juliet. LC 98-36178. (Illus.). 40p. (YA). (gr. 5-8). 1999. 16.99 (*0-8037-2462-4*, Dial Yng Read) Peng Put Young Read.

Arico, Diane, ed. see Armstrong, Jennifer.

Arico, Diane, ed. see Crocker, Chris.

Arico, Diane, ed. see Keene, Carolyn & Dixon, Franklin W.

Arico, Diane, ed. see Maloney, Peter & Zekauskas, Felicia.

Arico, Diane, ed. see Matthews, Gordon.

Arico, Diane, ed. see Mayer, Marianna.

Arico, Diane, ed. see McGee, Eddie.

Arico, Diane, ed. see Rotsler, William.

Arico, Diane, ed. see Schur, Maxine R.

Arico, Diane, ed. see Wise, William.

Arico, Santo L. Oriana Fallaci: The Woman & the Myth. LC 97-14420. 320p. 1998. 29.95 (*0-8093-2153-X*) S Ill U Pr.

— Rousseau's Art of Persuasion in "La Nouvelle Heloise" 212p. (Orig.). (C). 1994. pap. text 28.50 (*0-8191-9618-5*); lib. bdg. 51.00 (*0-8191-9617-7*) U Pr of Amer.

Arico, Santo L., ed. Contemporary Women Writers in Italy: A Modern Renaissance. LC 89-28436. 248p. (C). 1990. lib. bdg. 32.50 (*0-87023-710-1*) U of Mass Pr.

Aricola, Johann Friedrich. Introduction to the Art of Singing. Baird, Julianne C., ed. 308p. 1995. text 69.95 (*0-521-45428-X*) Cambridge U Pr.

Arid, Forbes. Aerodynamics for Racing & Performance Cars. LC 96-49347. 144p. 1997. pap. 17.95 (*1-55788-267-3*, HP Books) Berkley Pub.

***Arida.** Quantum City. (Illus.). 160p. 2001. pap. 37.95 (*0-7506-5012-5*, Architectural Pr) Buttrwrth-Heinemann.

Arida, Carol. Christian Expressions, Bk. 1. LC 94-94273. (Illus.). 110p. (Orig.). 1997. 5.00 (*1-885493-00-2*) C Arida Christian.

— Christian Expressions, Bk. 2. LC 94-94273. (Illus.). 110p. (Orig.). 1997. pap. 5.00 (*1-885493-01-0*) C Arida Christian.

— Christian Expressions, Bk. 3. LC 94-94273. (Illus.). 110p. (Orig.). 1997. pap. 5.00 (*1-885493-02-9*) C Arida Christian.

— Christian Expressions, Bk. 4. LC 94-94273. (Illus.). 110p. (Orig.). 1997. pap. 5.00 (*1-885493-03-7*) C Arida Christian.

— Christian Expressions, Bk. 5. LC 94-94273. (Illus.). 110p. (Orig.). 1997. 5.00 (*1-885493-04-5*) C Arida Christian.

— Christian Expressions, Bk. 6. LC 94-94273. (Illus.). 110p. (Orig.). 1997. pap. 5.00 (*1-885493-05-3*) C Arida Christian.

— Christian Expressions, Bk. 7. LC 94-94273. (Illus.). 110p. (Orig.). 1997. pap. 5.00 (*1-885493-06-1*) C Arida Christian.

— Christian Expressions, Bk. 8. LC 94-94273. (Illus.). 110p. (Orig.). 1997. pap. 5.00 (*1-885493-07-X*) C Arida Christian.

— Christian Expressions, Bk. 9. LC 94-94273. (Illus.). 110p. (Orig.). 1997. pap. 5.00 (*1-885493-08-8*) C Arida Christian.

— Christian Expressions, Vol. 10. LC 94-94273. (Illus.). 110p. (Orig.). 1997. pap. 5.00 (*1-885493-09-6*) C Arida Christian.

— Christian Expressions, Vol. 11. LC 94-94273. (Illus.). 110p. (Orig.). 1997. pap. 5.00 (*1-885493-10-X*) C Arida Christian.

— Christian Expressions, Vol. 12. LC 94-94273. (Illus.). 110p. (Orig.). 1997. pap. 5.00 (*1-885493-11-8*) C Arida Christian.

— Christian Expressions, Vol. 13. LC 94-94273. (Illus.). 110p. (Orig.). 1997. pap. 5.00 (*1-885493-12-6*) C Arida Christian.

— Christian Expressions, Vol. 14. LC 94-94273. (Illus.). 110p. (Orig.). 1997. pap. 5.00 (*1-885493-13-4*) C Arida Christian.

— Christian Expressions, Vol. 15. LC 94-94273. (Illus.). 110p. (Orig.). 1997. pap. 5.00 (*1-885493-14-2*) C Arida Christian.

— Christian Expressions, Vol. 16. LC 94-94273. (Illus.). 110p. (Orig.). 1997. pap. 5.00 (*1-885493-15-0*) C Arida Christian.

— Christian Expressions, Vol. 17. LC 94-94273. (Illus.). 110p. (Orig.). 1997. pap. 5.00 (*1-885493-16-9*) C Arida Christian.

— Christian Expressions, Vol. 18. LC 94-94273. (Illus.). 110p. (Orig.). 1997. pap. 5.00 (*1-885493-17-7*) C Arida Christian.

— Christian Expressions, Vol. 19. LC 94-94273. (Illus.). 110p. (Orig.). 1997. pap. 5.00 (*1-885493-18-5*) C Arida Christian.

— Christian Expressions, Vol. 20. LC 94-94273. (Illus.). 110p. (Orig.). 1997. pap. 5.00 (*1-885493-19-3*) C Arida Christian.

— Christian Expressions, Vol. 21. LC 94-94273. (Illus.). 110p. (Orig.). 1997. pap. 5.00 (*1-885493-20-7*) C Arida Christian.

***Aridas, Chris.** The Catholic Funeral: The Church's Ministry of Hope. LC 98-11271. 160p. 1998. pap. 9.95 (*0-8245-1750-4*, Crsrd) Crossroad NY.

Aridas, Chris. Your Catholic Wedding: A Complete Plan-Book. rev. ed. LC 97-565. 192p. 1997. pap. 8.95 (*0-8245-1675-3*, Pub. by Crossroad NY) Natl Bk Netwk.

Aride, J., et al, eds. Physical Chemistry of Solid State Materials: REMCES VI. (Advanced Materials Research Ser.: Vols. 1-2). (Illus.). 694p. (C). 1995. 216.00 (*3-908450-05-5*, Pub. by Scitec Pubns) Enfield Pubs NH.

Aridjis. Memorias del Nuevo Mundo. 1996. 26.95 (*0-15-158872-4*) Harcourt.

Aridjis, Homero. Antologia. 107p. 1976. 9.95 (*0-8288-7484-0*) Fr & Eur.

Aridjis, Homero. Antologia Poetica, 1960-1994. (SPA.). 503p. 1994. pap. 15.99 (*968-16-4296-1*) Fondo.

Aridjis, Homero. En Quien Piensas Cuando Haces el Amor? (Who Do You Think of When Make Love?) (SPA.). 1996. 14.95 (*0-679-76850-5*) Vin Bks.

***Aridjis, Homero.** 1492: Vida y Tiempos de Juan C. de Castilla. 4th ed. 317p. 1998. pap. 7.99 (*968-16-5534-6*) Fondo CA.

Aridjis, Homero. Gran Teatro Del Fin Del Mundo (Great Theater of the World's End) (SPA.). 293p. 1994. pap. 13.99 (*968-16-4149-3*, Pub. by Fondo) Continental Bk.

— La Leyenda de Los Soles. (SPA.). 1993. pap. text 12.99 (*968-16-3952-9*) Fondo.

— Mirandola Dormir (Watching Her Sleep) Persefone, 2 vols. in 1. (SPA.). 295p. 1992. pap. 17.99 (*968-16-3932-4*, Pub. by Fondo) Continental Bk.

— EL Poeta Nino (The Child Poet) (SPA.). 175p. 1984. pap. 6.99 (*968-16-1655-3*, Pub. by Fondo) Continental Bk.

— Tiempo de Angeles (Time of Angels) 2nd ed. (SPA., Illus.). 165p. 1997. 52.99 (*968-16-5028-X*, Pub. by Fondo) Continental Bk.

Aridjis, Homero, et al. Many Mountains Moving, Vol. 3, No. 1. (Illus.). 1996. pap. 6.50 (*1-886976-06-6*) Many Mntns.

Arie, Staal. Hawthorne's Narrative Art. 1976. lib. bdg. 250.00 (*0-87700-250-9*) Revisionist Pr.

Arie, Tom, ed. Health Care of the Elderly: Essays in Old Age Medicine. LC 81-81354. 240p. reprint ed. pap. 74.40 (*0-608-14635-8*, 202582500046) Bks Demand.

Arieff, Allen I., ed. Hypoxia, Metabolic Acidosis & the Circulation. (Clinical Physiology Series - An American Physiological Society Book). (Illus.). 232p. 1992. text 59.50 (*0-19-506062-8*, 10045) OUP.

An Asterisk (*) at the beginning of an entry indicates that the title is appearing for the first time.

Arieff, Allen I. & DeFronzo, Ralph A. Fluid, Electrolyte & Acid-Base Disorders. 2nd ed. LC 95-19811. 946p. 1995. text 179.00 (*0-443-08774-1*) Church.

Arieff, Allen I. & DeFronzo, Ralph A., eds. Fluid, Electrolyte, & Acid-Base Disorders, Vol. 1. LC 84-11392. (Illus.). 728p. reprint ed. pap. 200.00 (*0-7837-6826-5*, 204665700001) Bks Demand.

— Fluid, Electrolyte, & Acid-Base Disorders, Vol. 2. LC 84-11392. (Illus.). 654p. reprint ed. pap. 200.00 (*0-7837-6827-3*, 204665700002) Bks Demand.

Ariel. Alchemy of Love. 272p. 1999. 5.95 (*0-7407-0094-4*) Andrews & McMeel.

— Aquarius Mini Edition. 1999. 4.95 (*0-8362-7879-8*) Andrews & McMeel.

— Aries Mini Edition. 1999. 4.95 (*0-8362-7880-1*) Andrews & McMeel.

***Ariel.** The Bride's Book of Weddings. (Illus.). 80p. 1999. 4.95 (*0-7407-0058-8*) Andrews & McMeel.

Ariel. Cancer Mini Edition. (Women's Astrology Library). 1999. 4.95 (*0-8362-7882-8*) Andrews & McMeel.

— Capricorn Mini Edition. (Women's Astrology Library). 1999. 4.95 (*0-8362-7883-6*) Andrews & McMeel.

— A Celebration of Kwanzaa. 80p. 1999. 4.95 (*0-7407-0059-6*) Andrews & McMeel.

***Ariel.** Confirmation: A Treasury of Faith. 80p. 1999. 4.95 (*0-7407-0063-4*) Andrews & McMeel.

— Eve's Wisdom: The Goddess Within. (Illus.). 272p. 1999. 5.95 (*0-7407-0098-7*) Andrews & McMeel.

— Finding Our Selves. LC 99-60620. (Illus.). 80p. 1999. 4.95 (*0-7407-0064-2*) Andrews & McMeel.

— For My Bridesmaid. 80p. 1999. 4.95 (*0-7407-0065-0*) Andrews & McMeel.

— For My Granddaughter, with Love. LC 99-60631. (Illus.). 80p. 1999. 4.95 (*0-7407-0066-9*) Andrews & McMeel.

— Garth Brooks: Hitting the High Notes. LC 99-60623. (Illus.). 80p. 1999. 4.95 (*0-7407-0067-7*) Andrews & McMeel.

Ariel. Gemini Mini Edition. (Women's Astrology Library). 1999. 4.95 (*0-8362-7885-2*) Andrews & McMeel.

***Ariel.** Grandfathers: A Celebration. 80p. 1999. 4.95 (*0-7407-0068-5*) Andrews & McMeel.

Ariel. Happy 30th Birthday Mini Edition: A Book of Wit & Wisdom. 1999. 4.95 (*0-8362-7886-0*) Andrews & McMeel.

***Ariel.** It's a Boy: A Book of Quotations. (Illus.). 80p. 1999. 4.95 (*0-7407-0070-7*) Andrews & McMeel.

— It's a Girl: A Book of Quotations. 80p. 1999. 4.95 (*0-7407-0071-5*) Andrews & McMeel.

— Kindred Spirits: A Book of Friendship. (Illus.). 272p. 1999. 5.95 (*0-7407-0099-5*) Andrews & McMeel.

Ariel. Leo Mini Edition. (Women's Astrology Library). 1999. 4.95 (*0-8362-7889-5*) Andrews & McMeel.

— Libra Mini Edition. (Women's Astrology Library). 1999. 4.95 (*0-8362-7890-9*) Andrews & McMeel.

***Ariel.** Martin Luther King Jr. Dream of Freedom. (Illus.). 80p. 1999. 4.95 (*0-7407-0072-3*) Andrews & McMeel.

— Mother Earth, Father Sky: Native American Wisdom. LC 99-60617. (Illus.). 80p. 1999. 4.95 (*0-7407-0073-1*) Andrews & McMeel.

— The Numerology of Birthdays. 272p. 1999. 5.95 (*0-7407-0100-2*) Andrews & McMeel.

— Pickup Trucks. 80p. 1999. 4.95 (*0-7407-0075-8*) Andrews & McMeel.

Ariel. Puff Daddy. 1999. 4.95 (*0-8362-8183-7*) Andrews & McMeel.

***Ariel.** Qi Gong: The Energy of Harmony & Healing. 272p. 1999. 5.95 (*0-7407-0101-0*) Andrews & McMeel.

Ariel. Sagittarius: Mini Edition. (Women's Astrology Library). 1999. 4.95 (*0-8362-7892-5*) Andrews & McMeel.

— Scorpio Mini Edition. (Women's Astrology Library). 1999. 4.95 (*0-8362-7893-3*) Andrews & McMeel.

***Ariel.** The Secret Life of Cats. 272p. 1999. 5.95 (*0-7407-0102-9*) Andrews & McMeel.

— The Spirit of Daughters. (Illus.). 272p. 1999. 5.95 (*0-7407-0097-9*) Andrews & McMeel.

— The Spirit of Mothers. 272p. 1999. 5.95 (*0-7407-0104-5*) Andrews & McMeel.

— The Spirit of Sisters. 272p. 1999. 5.95 (*0-7407-0103-7*) Andrews & McMeel.

— Sun, Moon & Stars: A Guide to Astrology. 272p. 1999. 5.95 (*0-7407-0105-3*) Andrews & McMeel.

— Sweet Sixteen. LC 99-60627. (Illus.). 80p. 1999. 4.95 (*0-7407-0076-6*) Andrews & McMeel.

Ariel. Taurus Mini Edition. (Women's Astrology Library). 1999. 4.95 (*0-8362-7894-1*) Andrews & McMeel.

— Titanic: Mini Edition. 1999. 4.95 (*0-8362-8184-5*) Andrews & McMeel.

***Ariel.** Uncommon Wisdom. (Illus.). 272p. 1999. 5.95 (*0-7407-0108-8*) Andrews & McMeel.

Ariel. Virgo Mini Edition. (Women's Astrology Library). 1999. 4.95 (*0-8362-7896-8*) Andrews & McMeel.

— Welcome to the World: All about Babies. 272p. 1999. 5.95 (*0-7407-0095-2*) Andrews & McMeel.

***Ariel.** What Girlfriends Do. (Illus.). 64p. 1999. 7.95 (*0-7407-0109-6*) Andrews & McMeel.

Ariel, jt. auth. see Andrews & McMeel Staff.

Ariel Books Staff. Acceptance: The Little Books of Virtue. LC 95-60373. (Illus.). 80p. 1995. 4.95 (*0-8362-3122-8*) Andrews & McMeel.

— All Things Chocolate: A Cookbook. (Illus.). 80p. 1994. 4.95 (*0-8362-3061-2*, Arie Bks) Andrews & McMeel.

— America: Of Thee I Sing. (Illus.). 374p. 1995. pap. 4.95 (*0-8362-0715-7*, Arie Bks) Andrews & McMeel.

— American Dolls. LC 96-125813. (Illus.). 80p. 1995. 4.95 (*0-8362-3127-9*, Arie Bks) Andrews & McMeel.

— The American West of Frederic Remington. (Illus.). 80p. 1994. 4.95 (*0-8362-3060-4*) Andrews & McMeel.

— An Angel Is... (Illus.). 80p. 1995. 4.95 (*0-8362-3133-3*, Arie Bks) Andrews & McMeel.

— Angels. (Illus.). 32p. 1993. 4.95 (*0-8362-3042-6*, Arie Bks) Andrews & McMeel.

— Angels. LC 97-164359. 128p. 1996. 3.95 (*0-8362-0981-8*, Arie Bks) Andrews & McMeel.

— Angels: Messengers of Grace. LC 97-221479. 128p. 1997. 6.95 (*0-8362-2946-0*, Arie Bks) Andrews & McMeel.

— Anthology of Black Folk Wit, Wisdom, & Sayings. LC 93-73365. (Illus.). 80p. 1994. 4.95 (*0-8362-3064-7*, Arie Bks) Andrews & McMeel.

— Aquarius. (Tiny Tomes Ser.). 128p. 1997. 3.95 (*0-8362-2658-5*, Arie Bks) Andrews & McMeel.

— Aquarius: Your Sun-&-Moon Guide to Love & Life. 374p. (Orig.). 1997. pap. 5.95 (*0-8362-3552-5*, Arie Bks) Andrews & McMeel.

— Aries. (Tiny Tomes Ser.). 128p. 1997. 3.95 (*0-8362-2659-3*, Arie Bks) Andrews & McMeel.

— Aries: Your Sun-&-Moon Guide to Love & Life. (Illus.). 374p. 1997. pap. text 5.95 (*0-8362-3553-3*, Arie Bks) Andrews & McMeel.

— The Art of the Cigar: Bands & Box Labels. LC 97-198464. (Tiny Tomes Ser.). 128p. 1997. 3.95 (*0-8362-2662-3*, Arie Bks) Andrews & McMeel.

— Astrology: A Sun Guide. 128p. 1996. 3.95 (*0-8362-0988-5*, Arie Bks) Andrews & McMeel.

— The Astrology Book. LC 96-132394. (Illus.). 48p. 1995. 6.95 (*0-8362-4742-6*) Andrews & McMeel.

— Babies. LC 97-163262. 128p. 1996. 3.95 (*0-8362-0975-3*, Arie Bks) Andrews & McMeel.

— Babies: A Pop-Up Book. LC 99-163145. (Tiny Tomes Ser.). (Illus.). 12p. 1997. 3.95 (*0-8362-2952-5*, Arie Bks) Andrews & McMeel.

— Baker Street Companion. 128p. 1996. 3.95 (*0-8362-1008-5*, Arie Bks) Andrews & McMeel.

— The Ballet Paintings of Degas. (Illus.). 80p. 1994. 4.95 (*0-8362-3059-0*) Andrews & McMeel.

— Baseball: A Book of Quips & Quotes. (Illus.). 80p. 1995. 4.95 (*0-8362-3112-0*, Arie Bks) Andrews & McMeel.

— Beagles. LC 96-83359. 80p. 1996. 4.95 (*0-8362-2108-7*, Arie Bks) Andrews & McMeel.

— The Beatles. (Illus.). 80p. 1993. 4.95 (*0-8362-3046-9*, Arie Bks) Andrews & McMeel.

— Beatrix Potter. 128p. 1996. 3.95 (*0-8362-0993-1*, Arie Bks) Andrews & McMeel.

— Beauty & the Beast - Gift Book. (Illus.). 80p. (J). (ps-3). 1993. 4.95 (*0-8362-3036-1*, Arie Bks) Andrews & McMeel.

— Believing in Ourselves: A Celebration of Women. 128p. 1996. 3.95 (*0-8362-0986-9*, Arie Bks) Andrews & McMeel.

***Ariel Books Staff.** Believing in Ourselves: The Wisdom of Women. (Quote-a-Page Ser.). (Illus.). 2001. 9.95 (*0-7407-0444-3*) Andrews & McMeel.

Ariel Books Staff. Ben Franklin. 128p. 1996. 3.95 (*0-8362-1018-2*, Arie Bks) Andrews & McMeel.

— Birds & Birding. LC 97-164239. 128p. 1996. 3.95 (*0-8362-1016-6*, Arie Bks) Andrews & McMeel.

— Birthday Book: A Treasury for Men. (Illus.). 128p. 1996. 3.95 (*0-8362-0966-4*, Arie Bks) Andrews & McMeel.

— Birthday Book: A Treasury for Women. 128p. 1996. 3.95 (*0-8362-0965-6*, Arie Bks) Andrews & McMeel.

— Birthday Celebrations. LC 94-198529. (Illus.). 16p. 1994. 4.95 (*0-8362-3051-5*) Andrews & McMeel.

— The Book of Beer. LC 96-85941. 80p. 1997. 4.95 (*0-8362-2639-9*, Arie Bks) Andrews & McMeel.

— Book of Gardens. 128p. 1996. 3.95 (*0-8362-0987-7*, Arie Bks) Andrews & McMeel.

— A Book of Love. LC 93-73371. (Illus.). 80p. 1994. 4.95 (*0-8362-3065-5*, Arie Bks) Andrews & McMeel.

— Book of Psalms. 128p. 1996. 3.95 (*0-8362-1007-7*, Arie Bks) Andrews & McMeel.

— Boxers. LC 96-85906. 80p. 1997. 4.95 (*0-8362-2640-2*, Arie Bks) Andrews & McMeel.

— Brides. 128p. 1996. 3.95 (*0-8362-0976-1*, Arie Bks) Andrews & McMeel.

— Butterflies. 128p. 1996. 3.95 (*0-8362-0992-3*, Arie Bks) Andrews & McMeel.

— Cancer: Your Sun-&-Moon Guide to Love & Life. 374p. (Orig.). 1997. pap. 5.95 (*0-8362-3556-8*, Arie Bks) Andrews & McMeel.

— Capricorn. (Tiny Tomes Ser.). 128p. 1997. 3.95 (*0-8362-2661-5*, Arie Bks) Andrews & McMeel.

— Capricorn: Your Sun-&-Moon Guide to Love & Life. 374p. (Orig.). 1997. pap. 5.95 (*0-8362-3557-6*, Arie Bks) Andrews & McMeel.

— Cars with Fins. LC 96-85938. 80p. 1997. 4.95 (*0-8362-2642-9*, Arie Bks) Andrews & McMeel.

— Cat Chat: A Treasury of Feline Quips & Quotes. LC 97-208769. 128p. 1997. 6.95 (*0-8362-2948-7*, Arie Bks) Andrews & McMeel.

***Ariel Books Staff.** Cat Talk: A Book of Quotations. (Quote-a-Page Ser.). 2001. 9.95 (*0-7407-0983-6*) Andrews & McMeel.

Ariel Books Staff. Cat Talk: A Quote Book for Cat Lovers. (Illus.). 374p. 1995. pap. 5.95 (*0-8362-0707-6*, Cader Bks) Andrews & McMeel.

— Cats. 128p. 1996. 3.95 (*0-8362-0983-4*, Arie Bks) Andrews & McMeel.

— Cats: A Feline Potpourri. (Illus.). 80p. 1992. 4.95 (*0-8362-3002-7*, Arie Bks) Andrews & McMeel.

— Cats: A Pop-Up Book. LC 99-163128. (Tiny Tomes Ser.). (Illus.). 12p. 1997. 3.95 (*0-8362-2954-1*, Arie Bks) Andrews & McMeel.

— Cats: Those Wonderful Creatures. LC 94-198269. (Illus.). 16p. 1994. 4.95 (*0-8362-3052-3*, Arie Bks) Andrews & McMeel.

— Champagne. LC 97-164363. 128p. 1996. 3.95 (*0-8362-1015-8*, Arie Bks) Andrews & McMeel.

— Christmas: A Season of Traditions. LC 96-119838. (Illus.). 48p. 1995. 6.95 (*0-8362-4741-8*) Andrews & McMeel.

— Christmas Angels: A Pop-Up Book. (Illus.). 16p. (J). (ps-3). 1994. 4.95 (*0-8362-3090-6*, Arie Bks) Andrews & McMeel.

— Christmas Carol. 128p. 1996. 3.95 (*0-8362-1013-1*, Arie Bks) Andrews & McMeel.

— The Christmas Paintings of Norman Rockwell. (Illus.). 40p. 1993. 4.95 (*0-8362-3038-8*) Andrews & McMeel.

— Cigar Book: Up in Smoke! LC 96-85937. 80p. 1997. 4.95 (*0-8362-2643-7*, Arie Bks) Andrews & McMeel.

— Cinderella. (Illus.). 80p. (J). (ps-3). 1993. 4.95 (*0-8362-3034-5*, Arie Bks) Andrews & McMeel.

— Cocker Spaniels. LC 96-85936. 80p. 1997. 4.95 (*0-8362-2644-5*, Arie Bks) Andrews & McMeel.

— Common Sense: A Book of Wit & Wisdom. LC 96-85933. 80p. 1997. 4.95 (*0-8362-2645-3*, Arie Bks) Andrews & McMeel.

— Compassion: The Little Books of Virtue. (Illus.). 80p. 1995. 4.95 (*0-8362-3124-4*) Andrews & McMeel.

— Cookies, Cakes, & Pies. (Illus.). 80p. 1993. 4.95 (*0-8362-3032-9*) Andrews & McMeel.

— Country: The Music of America. (Illus.). 80p. 1995. 4.95 (*0-8362-3113-9*) Andrews & McMeel.

— Dachshunds. LC 96-83365. 1996. 4.95 (*0-8362-2109-5*, Arie Bks) Andrews & McMeel.

— Dinosarus. 128p. 1996. 3.95 (*0-8362-1004-2*, Arie Bks) Andrews & McMeel.

— The Dog Book. (Illus.). 40p. 1995. 6.95 (*0-8362-4736-1*) Andrews & McMeel.

— Dogs. (Illus.). 80p. 1992. 4.95 (*0-8362-3017-5*, Arie Bks) Andrews & McMeel.

— Dogs. LC 97-164368. 128p. 1996. 3.95 (*0-8362-0984-2*, Arie Bks) Andrews & McMeel.

— Ducks: A Dabbler's Miscellany. LC 97-198493. (Tiny Tomes Ser.). 128p. 1997. 3.95 (*0-8362-2663-1*, Arie Bks) Andrews & McMeel.

— Elvis. (Illus.). 80p. 1993. 4.95 (*0-8362-3045-0*) Andrews & McMeel.

— Elvis: A Tribute to the King. LC 99-162720. 1998. pap. text 6.95 (*0-8362-5234-9*, Arie Bks) Andrews & McMeel.

— Encouragement. (Illus.). 40p. 1995. 6.95 (*0-8362-4743-4*) Andrews & McMeel.

— Faith & Inspiration. 128p. 1996. 3.95 (*0-8362-0985-0*, Arie Bks) Andrews & McMeel.

— Fantastic Baseball Quiz Book. LC 96-83550. 374p. (Orig.). 1997. pap. 5.95 (*0-8362-1511-7*) Andrews & McMeel.

— Fashion: Bustles to Bikinis. 128p. 1996. 3.95 (*0-8362-0996-6*, Arie Bks) Andrews & McMeel.

— Fishing: An Angler's Miscellany. (Illus.). 80p. 1995. 4.95 (*0-8362-3117-1*) Andrews & McMeel.

— Flowers. LC 94-198266. (Illus.). 16p. 1994. 4.95 (*0-8362-3053-1*) Andrews & McMeel.

— Fly Fishing: Life Is but a Stream. LC 96-85931. 80p. 1997. 4.95 (*0-8362-2646-1*, Arie Bks) Andrews & McMeel.

— Folk Art. 128p. 1996. 3.95 (*0-8362-1017-4*, Arie Bks) Andrews & McMeel.

— For a New Mother. (Illus.). 80p. 1995. 4.95 (*0-8362-3128-7*, Arie Bks) Andrews & McMeel.

— For a Special Friend. (Illus.). 80p. 1992. 4.95 (*0-8362-3000-0*, Arie Bks) Andrews & McMeel.

— For Father with Love. 128p. 1996. 3.95 (*0-8362-0971-0*, Arie Bks) Andrews & McMeel.

— For Mom with Love: A Book of Quotations. LC 97-71544. 1998. pap. text 5.95 (*0-8362-3558-4*, Arie Bks) Andrews & McMeel.

— For Mother with Love. 128p. 1996. 3.95 (*0-8362-0970-2*, Arie Bks) Andrews & McMeel.

— For My Daughter. (Illus.). 80p. 1993. 4.95 (*0-8362-3028-0*, Arie Bks) Andrews & McMeel.

— For My Daughter. LC 96-229827. 48p. 1996. 6.95 (*0-8362-1527-3*, Arie Bks) Andrews & McMeel.

— For My Daughter: A Treasury of Love & Wisdom. LC 98-120214. (Illus.). 128p. 1997. pap. text 5.95 (*0-8362-3623-8*, Arie Bks) Andrews & McMeel.

— For My Daughter with Love. 128p. 1996. 3.95 (*0-8362-0972-9*, Arie Bks) Andrews & McMeel.

— For My Father. LC 97-102008. 48p. 1996. 6.95 (*0-8362-1528-1*, Arie Bks) Andrews & McMeel.

— For My Sister. LC 96-85951. 48p. 1996. 6.95 (*0-8362-1530-3*, Arie Bks) Andrews & McMeel.

— For My Sister: Reflections on Life, Love & Sisterhood. LC 96-85951. 374p. (Orig.). 1997. pap. 5.95 (*0-8362-2592-9*, Arie Bks) Andrews & McMeel.

— Friend to Friend: Reflections on Friendship. LC 98-121343. (Illus.). 128p. 1997. pap. text 5.95 (*0-8362-3624-6*, Arie Bks) Andrews & McMeel.

***Ariel Books Staff.** Friends Forever: A Book of Quotations. (Quote-a-Page Ser.). 2001. 9.95 (*0-7407-0984-4*) Andrews & McMeel.

Ariel Books Staff. Friendship. LC 97-164366. 128p. 1996. 3.95 (*0-8362-0968-0*, Arie Bks) Andrews & McMeel.

— Friendship: What You Mean to Me. LC 94-198643. (Illus.). 16p. 1994. 4.95 (*0-8362-3055-8*) Andrews & McMeel.

— A Gardener's Miscellany. LC 95-198427. (Illus.). 48p. 1995. 6.95 (*0-8362-4735-3*, Arie Bks) Andrews & McMeel.

— Gargoyles. LC 96-83363. 1996. 4.95 (*0-8362-1517-6*, Arie Bks) Andrews & McMeel.

— Gemini. (Tiny Tomes Ser.). 128p. 1997. 3.95 (*0-8362-2666-6*) Andrews & McMeel.

— Gemini: Your Sun-&-Moon Guide to Love & Life. 374p. (Orig.). 1997. pap. 5.95 (*0-8362-3560-6*, Arie Bks) Andrews & McMeel.

— Gems. 128p. 1996. 3.95 (*0-8362-0999-0*, Arie Bks) Andrews & McMeel.

— German Shepherds. LC 96-83362. 1996. 4.95 (*0-8362-1518-4*, Arie Bks) Andrews & McMeel.

— Ghosts. 128p. 1996. 3.95 (*0-8362-0998-2*, Arie Bks) Andrews & McMeel.

— Go for the Gold: Thoughts on Achieving Your Personal Best. (Illus.). 374p. 1995. pap. 5.95 (*0-8362-0709-2*) Andrews & McMeel.

***Ariel Books Staff.** Go for the Gold: Thoughts on Achieving Your Personal Best. (Quote-a-Page Ser.). 2001. 9.95 (*0-7407-0939-9*) Andrews & McMeel.

Ariel Books Staff. Golden Retrievers. LC 96-83361. 1996. 4.95 (*0-8362-2110-9*, Arie Bks) Andrews & McMeel.

— Golf. 128p. 1996. 3.95 (*0-8362-0982-6*, Arie Bks) Andrews & McMeel.

— Golf: A Pop-Up Book. LC 98-194749. (Tiny Tomes Ser.). (Illus.). 12p. 1997. 3.95 (*0-8362-2956-8*, Arie Bks) Andrews & McMeel.

— Golf: Par for the Course A Book of Quips & Quotes. LC 97-221458. 128p. 1997. 6.95 (*0-8362-2949-5*, Arie Bks) Andrews & McMeel.

— Good Advice for a Happy Life. (Illus.). 374p. 1995. pap. 4.95 (*0-8362-0716-5*) Andrews & McMeel.

— Goodness: The Little Books of Virtue. (Illus.). 80p. 1995. 4.95 (*0-8362-3125-2*) Andrews & McMeel.

— Grace: The Little Books of Virtue. LC 95-60375. (Illus.). 80p. 1995. 4.95 (*0-8362-3123-6*) Andrews & McMeel.

— Grandmothers. (Illus.). 80p. 1992. 4.95 (*0-8362-3005-1*) Andrews & McMeel.

— Grandmothers. 128p. 1996. 3.95 (*0-8362-0974-5*, Arie Bks) Andrews & McMeel.

— The Great Divide: Men & Women at the Edge of the Gender Gap. (Illus.). 374p. 1995. pap. 4.95 (*0-8362-0717-3*) Andrews & McMeel.

— Happy Birthday! A Book of Wit & Wisdom. LC 97-221493. 128p. 1997. pap. 6.95 (*0-8362-2947-9*, Arie Bks) Andrews & McMeel.

— Happy Birthday! A Pop-Up Book. LC 98-194673. (Tiny Tomes Ser.). (Illus.). 12p. 1997. 3.95 (*0-8362-2953-3*, Arie Bks) Andrews & McMeel.

— The Heart's Song: Reflections on Love. (Illus.). 374p. 1995. pap. 5.95 (*0-8362-0718-1*, Arie Bks) Andrews & McMeel.

— Heart's Witness: A Wedding Book. (Illus.). 48p. 1995. 6.95 (*0-8362-4745-0*, Arie Bks) Andrews & McMeel.

— Herbs. 128p. 1996. 3.95 (*0-8362-1005-0*, Arie Bks) Andrews & McMeel.

— Here Comes the Bride: Wit & Wisdom on Weddings. LC 98-140888. (Illus.). 128p. 1997. pap. text 5.95 (*0-8362-3626-2*, Arie Bks) Andrews & McMeel.

— Heritage: An African-American Quote Book. LC 96-230490. 48p. 1996. 6.95 (*0-8362-1526-5*, Arie Bks) Andrews & McMeel.

— Horror-Scopes: Your Day-to-Day Guide to Disasters, Defeats & Despair. LC 97-80444. 1998. pap. text 5.95 (*0-8362-3554-1*, Arie Bks) Andrews & McMeel.

— Horse. 128p. 1996. 3.95 (*0-8362-1019-0*, Arie Bks) Andrews & McMeel.

— Hummingbirds. LC 97-164235. 125p. 1996. 3.95 (*0-8362-0991-5*, Arie Bks) Andrews & McMeel.

— Irish. (Illus.). 80p. 1993. 4.95 (*0-8362-3031-0*, Arie Bks) Andrews & McMeel.

— Irish. 128p. 1996. 3.95 (*0-8362-0979-6*, Arie Bks) Andrews & McMeel.

— Jack & the Beanstalk. (Illus.). 80p. (J). (ps-3). 1993. 4.95 (*0-8362-3035-3*, Arie Bks) Andrews & McMeel.

— Jackie. LC 96-83370. 1996. 4.95 (*0-8362-1519-2*, Arie Bks) Andrews & McMeel.

— Jingle Bells: A Pop-Up Book. (Illus.). 16p. (J). (ps-3). 1995. 4.95 (*0-8362-0018-7*, Arie Bks) Andrews & McMeel.

— The Joys of the Garden. (Illus.). 80p. 1992. 4.95 (*0-8362-3010-8*, Arie Bks) Andrews & McMeel.

— Kindness: The Little Books of Virtue. (Illus.). 80p. 1995. 4.95 (*0-8362-3120-1*) Andrews & McMeel.

— Labrador Retrievers. LC 96-83371. 1996. 4.95 (*0-8362-1520-6*, Arie Bks) Andrews & McMeel.

— Leo. (Tiny Tomes Ser.). 128p. 1997. 3.95 (*0-8362-2667-4*, Arie Bks) Andrews & McMeel.

— Leo: Your Sun-&-Moon Guide to Love & Life. 374p. (Orig.). 1997. pap. 5.95 (*0-8362-3561-4*, Arie Bks) Andrews & McMeel.

— Libra. (Tiny Tomes Ser.). 128p. 1997. 3.95 (*0-8362-2668-2*, Arie Bks) Andrews & McMeel.

— Libra: Your Sun-&-Moon Guide to Love & Life. 374p. (Orig.). 1997. pap. 5.95 (*0-8362-3562-2*, Arie Bks) Andrews & McMeel.

— Life of Saint Francis of Assisi. LC 97-164228. 128p. 1996. 3.95 (*0-8362-1012-3*, Arie Bks) Andrews & McMeel.

— Life Stinks: A Wry Look at Hopelessness, Despair, & Disaster. (Illus.). 80p. 1995. 4.95 (*0-8362-3114-7*) Andrews & McMeel.

— A Little Book of Angels. (Illus.). 16p. 1995. pap. 4.95 (*0-8362-0365-8*, Arie Bks) Andrews & McMeel.

— The Little Book of Christmas Carols. (Illus.). 16p. 1993. 4.95 (*0-8362-3041-8*, Arie Bks) Andrews & McMeel.

— A Little Book of Saints. LC 95-60371. (Illus.). 80p. 1995. pap. 4.95 (*0-8362-3129-5*, Arie Bks) Andrews & McMeel.

— A Little Christmas Cookbook. (Illus.). 16p. 1993. 4.95 (*0-8362-3039-6*, Arie Bks) Andrews & McMeel.

— Love. 128p. 1996. 3.95 (*0-8362-0969-9*, Arie Bks) Andrews & McMeel.

— Love. LC 99-163154. (Tiny Tomes Ser.). 12p. 1997. 3.95 (*0-8362-2957-6*) Andrews & McMeel.

***Ariel Books Staff.** Love Is Patient & Kind: St. Paul's Letter: 1 Corinthians 13. 2000. pap. 4.95 (*0-7407-1036-2*) Andrews & McMeel.

Ariel Books Staff. Love Love Love. LC 97-193805. 12p. 1997. 4.95 (*0-8362-2945-2*, Arie Bks) Andrews & McMeel.

— Marilyn Monroe. (Illus.). 80p. 1995. 4.95 (*0-8362-3115-5*, Arie Bks) Andrews & McMeel.

— Marriage. (Illus.). 80p. 1992. 4.95 (*0-8362-3007-8*, Arie Bks) Andrews & McMeel.

— Merry Christmas. 128p. 1996. 3.95 (*0-8362-0967-2*, Arie Bks) Andrews & McMeel.

— The Moon. LC 97-164372. 128p. 1996. 3.95 (*0-8362-1002-6*, Arie Bks) Andrews & McMeel.

— Mother Goose's Nursery Rhymes. (Illus.). 80p. (J). 1992. 4.95 (*0-8362-3024-8*) Andrews & McMeel.

— Mothers. (Illus.). 80p. 1992. 4.95 (*0-8362-3008-6*, Arie Bks) Andrews & McMeel.

— Mothers: A Pop-Up Book. LC 99-163151. (Tiny Tomes Ser.). 12p. 1997. 3.95 (*0-8362-2958-4*, Arie Bks) Andrews & McMeel.

— Moving Forward, Keeping Still: The Gateway to Eastern Wisdom. LC 96-85947. 374p. (Orig.). 1997. pap. 5.95 (*0-8362-2593-7*, Arie Bks) Andrews & McMeel.

— Mutts. LC 96-83369. 1996. 4.95 (*0-8362-2111-7*, Arie Bks) Andrews & McMeel.

— Nature: The Beauty & the Wonder. (Illus.). 80p. 1994. 4.95 (*0-8362-3062-0*, Arie Bks) Andrews & McMeel.

— The 1960s. LC 93-73362. (Illus.). 80p. 1994. 4.95 (*0-8362-3063-9*) Andrews & McMeel.

— The 1960s: Words of a Decade. 374p. 1995. pap. 4.95 (*0-8362-0713-0*) Andrews & McMeel.

— Noah's Ark. LC 96-85803. (Little Bks.). (Illus.). 80p. 4.95 (*0-8362-2648-8*, Arie Bks) Andrews & McMeel.

— Oh, Brother! LC 96-85926. 80p. 1997. 4.95 (*0-8362-2641-0*, Arie Bks) Andrews & McMeel.

— On Being Christian. (Illus.). 374p. 1995. pap. 4.95 (*0-8362-0720-3*, Arie Bks) Andrews & McMeel.

— On the Wings of Angels. LC 95-197054. (Illus.). 48p. 1995. 6.95 (*0-8362-4730-2*, Arie Bks) Andrews & McMeel.

— Patience: The Little Books of Virtue. (Illus.). 80p. 1995. 4.95 (*0-8362-3119-8*) Andrews & McMeel.

— Pisces. (Tiny Tomes Ser.). 128p. 1997. 3.95 (*0-8362-2669-0*, Arie Bks) Andrews & McMeel.

— Pisces: Little Birth Sign. (Illus.). 80p. 1994. 4.95 (*0-8362-3076-0*, Arie Bks) Andrews & McMeel.

— Pisces: Mini Edition. (Women's Astrology Library). 1999. 4.95 (*0-8362-7891-7*) Andrews & McMeel.

— Pisces: Your Sun-&-Moon Guide to Love & Life. 374p. (Orig.). 1997. pap. 5.95 (*0-8362-3563-0*, Arie Bks) Andrews & McMeel.

— Play Ball: Quotes on America's Favorite Pastime. (Illus.). 374p. 1995. pap. 4.95 (*0-8362-0721-1*, Arie Bks) Andrews & McMeel.

— Poodles. LC 96-85911. 80p. 1997. 4.95 (*0-8362-2649-6*, Arie Bks) Andrews & McMeel.

— Positive Thoughts: Living Your Life to the Fullest. (Illus.). 374p. 1995. pap. 5.95 (*0-8362-0723-8*) Andrews & McMeel.

— Puppy Love. LC 96-85921. 80p. 1997. 4.95 (*0-8362-2651-8*, Arie Bks) Andrews & McMeel.

— Really Redneck. LC 98-232363. 1998. pap. text 6.95 (*0-8362-5235-7*, Arie Bks) Andrews & McMeel.

— Reflections on Faith & Inspiration. LC 96-132874. (Illus.). 40p. 1995. 6.95 (*0-8362-4744-2*) Andrews & McMeel.

— Rose. 128p. 1996. 3.95 (*0-8362-1011-5*, Arie Bks) Andrews & McMeel.

— Rottweilers. LC 96-83366. 1996. 4.95 (*0-8362-1521-4*, Arie Bks) Andrews & McMeel.

— Sagittarius. (Tiny Tomes Ser.). 128p. 1997. 3.95 (*0-8362-2670-4*, Arie Bks) Andrews & McMeel.

— Sagittarius: Little Birth Sign. (Illus.). 80p. 1994. 4.95 (*0-8362-3077-9*, Arie Bks) Andrews & McMeel.

— Sagittarius: Your Sun-&-Moon Guide to Love & Life. 374p. (Orig.). 1997. pap. 5.95 (*0-8362-3564-9*, Arie Bks) Andrews & McMeel.

— Scorpio. (Tiny Tomes Ser.). 128p. 1997. 3.95 (*0-8362-2671-2*, Arie Bks) Andrews & McMeel.

— Scorpio: Little Birth Sign. (Illus.). 80p. 1994. 4.99 (*0-8362-3078-7*) Andrews & McMeel.

— Scorpio: Your Sun-&-Moon Guide to Love & Life. 374p. (Orig.). 1997. pap. 5.95 (*0-8362-3565-7*, Arie Bks) Andrews & McMeel.

— Serenity. LC 93-73374. (Illus.). 80p. 1994. 4.95 (*0-8362-3081-7*) Andrews & McMeel.

— Sex, Sex, Sex. (Illus.). 80p. 1995. 4.95 (*0-8362-3116-3*, Arie Bks) Andrews & McMeel.

— Sisters. 128p. 1996. 3.95 (*0-8362-0973-7*, Arie Bks) Andrews & McMeel.

— Smitten with Kittens. LC 96-85916. 80p. 1997. 4.95 (*0-8362-2652-6*, Arie Bks) Andrews & McMeel.

***Ariel Books Staff.** Sophy V. 2000. pap. 11.95 (*0-89804-605-X*, Pub. by Ariel GA) Alliance Bk Co.

Ariel Books Staff. The South. (Illus.). 80p. 1995. 4.95 (*0-8362-3131-7*) Andrews & McMeel.

— The Spiritual Life: A Book of Reflections. LC 95-76439. (Illus.). 374p. 1995. pap. 4.95 (*0-8362-0724-6*) Andrews & McMeel.

— Success: A Book of Wit & Wisdom. LC 96-83367. 1996. 4.95 (*0-8362-1522-2*, Arie Bks) Andrews & McMeel.

— Take Me Out to the Ball Game: A Book of History, Hits, & Heroes. (Illus.). 48p. 1995. 6.95 (*0-8362-4732-9*, Arie Bks) Andrews & McMeel.

— Tarot: It's in the Cards! LC 96-85927. 80p. 1997. 4.95 (*0-8362-2653-4*, Arie Bks) Andrews & McMeel.

— Tattoos. LC 96-83368. 1996. 4.95 (*0-8362-1523-0*, Arie Bks) Andrews & McMeel.

— Taurus. (Tiny Tomes Ser.). 128p. 1997. 3.95 (*0-8362-2672-0*, Arie Bks) Andrews & McMeel.

— Taurus: Your Sun-&-Moon Guide to Love & Life. 374p. (Orig.). 1997. pap. 5.95 (*0-8362-3566-5*, Arie Bks) Andrews & McMeel.

— Teddy Bear Book. LC 96-83375. 1996. 4.95 (*0-8362-1524-9*, Arie Bks) Andrews & McMeel.

— Teddy Bears. 128p. 1996. 3.95 (*0-8362-0997-4*, Arie Bks) Andrews & McMeel.

— Thank You. 128p. 1996. 3.95 (*0-8362-0978-8*, Arie Bks) Andrews & McMeel.

— Thank You: Thoughts on Gratitude & Friendship. LC 98-120208. (Illus.). 128p. 1997. pap. text 5.95 (*0-8362-3625-4*, Arie Bks) Andrews & McMeel.

— Thoughts for a Sunny Day. (Illus.). 16p. 1994. 4.95 (*0-8362-3056-6*) Andrews & McMeel.

— Tied Flies: The Fisherman's Companion. LC 97-198482. (Tiny Tomes Ser.). 128p. 1997. 3.95 (*0-8362-2665-8*, Arie Bks) Andrews & McMeel.

— Trains. 128p. 1996. 3.95 (*0-8362-0995-8*, Arie Bks) Andrews & McMeel.

— A Tribute to Mothers: Reflections on Motherhood. LC 97-221487. 128p. 1997. 5.95 (*0-8362-2951-7*, Arie Bks) Andrews & McMeel.

— U. S. Animal Stamps. 128p. 1996. 3.95 (*0-8362-0989-3*, Arie Bks) Andrews & McMeel.

— Unicorns. (Illus.). 80p. 1992. 4.95 (*0-8362-3020-5*) Andrews & McMeel.

— Vampires. LC 96-83374. 1996. 4.95 (*0-8362-1525-7*) Andrews & McMeel.

— Victorians. 128p. 1996. 3.95 (*0-8362-1003-4*, Arie Bks) Andrews & McMeel.

— Virgo. (Tiny Tomes Ser.). 128p. 1997. 3.95 (*0-8362-2673-9*, Arie Bks) Andrews & McMeel.

— Virgo: Little Birth Sign. (Illus.). 80p. 1994. 4.99 (*0-8362-3080-9*) Andrews & McMeel.

— Virgo: Your Sun-&-Moon Guide to Love & Life. 374p. (Orig.). 1997. pap. 5.95 (*0-8362-3567-3*, Arie Bks) Andrews & McMeel.

— Wagging Their Tongues: A Canine Compendium. LC 96-85943. 374p. (Orig.). 1997. pap. 5.95 (*0-8362-2591-0*, Arie Bks) Andrews & McMeel.

— The Wedding Book. (Illus.). 80p. 1992. 4.95 (*0-8362-3011-6*, Arie Bks) Andrews & McMeel.

— Wedding Sentiments. LC 94-198262. (Illus.). 16p. 1994. 4.95 (*0-8362-3057-4*, Arie Bks) Andrews & McMeel.

— Whales. 128p. 1996. 3.95 (*0-8362-1010-7*, Arie Bks) Andrews & McMeel.

***Ariel Books Staff.** What Love Is. (Illus.). (J). 2000. pap. 7.95 (*0-7407-1083-4*) Andrews & McMeel.

Ariel Books Staff. What Women Say about Men. (Illus.). 80p. 1993. 4.95 (*0-8362-3030-2*, Arie Bks) Andrews & McMeel.

— Witches. LC 97-164210. 128p. 1996. 3.95 (*0-8362-1009-3*, Arie Bks) Andrews & McMeel.

— With All My Heart: Reflections on Love. LC 97-221471. 128p. 1997. 6.95 (*0-8362-2950-9*, Arie Bks) Andrews & McMeel.

— Witty Women: Wise, Wicked & Wonderful Words. LC 93-73357. (Illus.). 80p. 1994. 4.95 (*0-8362-3067-1*, Arie Bks) Andrews & McMeel.

— A Women's Journey: Reflections of Life, Love & Happiness. (Illus.). 374p. 1995. pap. 5.95 (*0-8362-0742-4*) Andrews & McMeel.

— Zen. (Illus.). 80p. 1995. 4.95 (*0-8362-3132-5*) Andrews & McMeel.

Ariel Books Staff, ed. Fantastic Football Quiz Book. LC 96-83549. 374p. (Orig.). 1996. pap. 5.95 (*0-8362-1512-5*) Andrews & McMeel.

— Hidden Meaning of Birthdays. LC 96-83360. 374p. (Orig.). 1996. pap. 5.95 (*0-8362-1516-8*, Arie Bks) Andrews & McMeel.

— Mucho Macho: Tough Talk for Tough Guys. LC 96-83358. 374p. (Orig.). 1996. pap. 5.95 (*0-8362-1514-1*, Arie Bks) Andrews & McMeel.

Ariel Books Staff & Henry, O. The Gift of the Magi: A Classic Christmas Tale. LC 96-119834. (Illus.). 40p. 1995. 6.95 (*0-8362-4739-6*) Andrews & McMeel.

Ariel Books Staff & Mars, Julie. Dalmatians. LC 96-83364. 1996. 4.95 (*0-8362-2112-5*, Arie Bks) Andrews & McMeel.

Ariel Books Staff & Nickerson, Arlene. The Spiritual Season: Reflections on Christmas. (Illus.). 16p. 1995. 4.95 (*0-8362-3134-1*) Andrews & McMeel.

Ariel, David S. The Mystic Quest: An Introduction to Jewish Mysticism. LC 88-10431. 256p. 1988. 30.00 (*0-87668-928-4*) Aronson.

***Ariel, David S.** Spiritual Judaism: Restoring Heart & Soul to Jewish Life. LC 98-12594. 256p. (J). 1998. 21.45 (*0-7868-6306-4*, Pub. by Hyperion) Time Warner.

Ariel, David S. What Do Jews Believe? The Spiritual Foundations of Judaism. 304p. 1996. reprint ed. pap. 13.00 (*0-8052-1059-8*) Schocken.

Ariel, I. M. & Cahan, Anthony C. Treatment of Precancerous Lesions & Early Breast Cancer: Diagnosis & Management. 416p. 1993. 89.00 (*0-683-00255-4*) Lppncott W & W.

Ariel, I. M., jt. ed. see Ragaz, J.

Ariel Institute Staff. Ariel Chumash. 1997. 29.95 (*0-87306-842-4*) Feldheim.

Ariel, Joan, et al. Women's Legal Rights in the United States: A Selective Bibliography. LC 85-15733. 64p. reprint ed. pap. 30.00 (*0-7837-6154-6*, 204587600008) Bks Demand.

Ariel, Shlomo. Culturally Competent Family Therapy: A General Model. LC 99-11269. (Contributions in Psychology Ser.). 272p. 1999. pap. 24.95 (*0-275-96655-0*, Praeger Pubs) Greenwood.

— Culturally Competent Family Therapy: A General Model, 37. LC 99-11269. (Contributions in Psychology Ser.: Vol. 37). 272p. 1999. 65.00 (*0-313-31079-3*) Greenwood.

***Ariel, Sunny.** Shalom My Love: The Story of a True Love that Bridges Heaven & Earth, 1. 191p. 1998. pap. 16.95 (*0-932482-90-2*) Blue Feather.

***Ariel, Yaakov.** Evangelizing the Chosen People: Missions to the Jews in America, 1880 - 2000. (H. Eugene & Lillian Youngs Lehman Series). 384p. 2000. lib. bdg. 49.95 (*0-8078-2566-2*) U of NC Pr.

— Evangelizing the Chosen People: Missions to the Jews in America, 1880-2000. (H. Eugene & Lillian Youngs Lehman Ser.). 384p. 2000. pap. 19.95 (*0-8078-4880-8*) U of NC Pr.

Ariel, Yoav. Kung-Tsung-Tzu: A Study & Translation of Chapters 15-23, with a Reconstruction of the "Hsiao Erh-ya" Dictionary. LC 95-45180. (Sinica Leidensia Ser.: No. 35). 1995. 72.00 (*90-04-09992-1*) Brill Academic Pubs.

— Kung-Tsung-Tzu: The Kung Family Masters' Anthology: A Study & Translation of Chapters 1-10, 12-14. LC 88-22521. (Princeton Library of Asian Translations). (Illus.). 232p. 1989. reprint ed. pap. 72.00 (*0-608-06421-1*, 206663400008) Bks Demand.

Ariel, pseud. My Best Friend Mini Edition. 1999. 4.95 (*0-8362-8172-1*) Andrews & McMeel.

Arieli, Mordecai. The Occupational Experience of Residential Child & Youth Care Workers: Caring & Its Discontents. LC 97-7841. (Child & Youth Services Monograph Ser.: Vol. 18, No. 2). 125p. (C). 1997. 39.95 (*1-56024-784-3*); pap. 14.95 (*0-7890-0306-6*) Haworth Pr.

Arielli, A. D. Grisons. (Panorama Bks.). (FRE., Illus.). 62p. 4.95 (*0-685-23347-2*) Fr & Eur.

Arielweehawk, ed. see DeFrain, Judith.

Arielweehawk, ed. see DeFrain, Judith, et al.

Arien, Angeles, ed. see Appel, Wendy S., et al.

Arieno, Marlene A. Victorian Lunatics: A Social Epidemiology of Mental Illness in Mid-Nineteenth-Century England. LC 88-43163. (Illus.). 144p. 1989. 32.50 (*0-945636-03-2*) Susquehanna U Pr.

Ariens, Michael S. & Destro, Robert A. Religious Liberty in a Pluralistic Society. LC 96-9431. 1020p. 1996. 80.00 (*0-89089-653-4*) Carolina Acad Pr.

Arienti, M., et al. Dioxin-Containing Wastes: Treatment Technologies. LC 88-17858. (Pollution Technology Review Ser.: No. 160). (Illus.). 243p. 1989. 39.00 (*0-8155-1181-7*) Noyes.

Aries, A. B., tr. see Fridman, A. M. & Polyachenko, V. I.

Aries, A. B., tr. see Fridman, A. M. & Polyachenko, V. L.

Aries, A. B., tr. see Ibragimov, I. A. & Rozanov, Yuri A.

Aries, A. B., tr. see Morozov, V. A.

Aries, Anthony, et al. Busy Signals from the Holy City. (Illus.). 70p. (Orig.). 1988. pap. 4.50 (*0-945085-06-0*) Sub Rosa.

Aries, Philippe. Centuries of Childhood. 1965. pap. 17.00 (*0-394-70286-7*) Random.

— Centuries of Childhood: A Social History of Family Life. 1965. pap. text 8.95 (*0-07-553689-7*) McGraw.

— The Hour of Our Death. Weaver, Helen, tr. (Illus.). 702p. 1991. pap. 22.50 (*0-19-507364-9*) OUP.

— Images of Man & Death. Lloyd, Janet, tr. from FRE. LC 85-768. (Illus.). 288p. 1985. 46.00 (*0-674-44410-8*) HUP.

— Western Attitudes Toward Death: From the Middle Ages to the Present. Ranum, Patricia M., tr. from FRE. LC 73-19340. (Symposia in Comparative History Ser.). (Illus.). 122p. 1974. pap. 12.95 (*0-8018-1762-5*) Johns Hopkins.

Aries, Philippe, et al, eds. A History of Private Life Vol. 1: From Pagan Rome to Byzantium. Goldhammer, Arthur, tr. from FRE. LC 86-18286. (Illus.). 688p. 1987. 39.95 (*0-674-39975-7*) Belknap Pr.

— A History of Private Life Vol. 1: From Pagan Rome to Byzantium. Goldhammer, Arthur, tr. from FRE. (Illus.). 688p. (Orig.). 1992. pap. 19.95 (*0-674-39974-9*) Belknap Pr.

— A History of Private Life Vol. 3: Passions of the Renaissance. Goldhammer, Arthur, tr. 1989. pap. 19.95 (*0-674-40002-X*) Belknap Pr.

Aries, Philippe, jt. ed. see Duby, Georges.

Aries, Ruby. Dream & Play with Us: Come Share Tim's & Lisa's Adventures & Learn How to Play Their Games. Loft, Randi, ed. (Illus.). 115p. (Orig.). (J). (gr. k-4). 1990. pap. 14.95 (*0-9626570-5-0*) Perk-Lo Pk Prodns.

Arieti, James A. Discourses on the First Book of Herodotus. LC 95-14368. 240p. (C). 1995. pap. text 22.95 (*0-8226-3039-7*); lib. bdg. 59.50 (*0-8226-3038-9*) Littlefield.

— Interpreting Plato: The Dialogues as Drama. 280p. 1991. pap. text 27.95 (*0-8476-7663-3*); lib. bdg. 69.50 (*0-8476-7662-5*) Rowman.

Arieti, James A. & Crossett, John M., trs. Longinus: On the Sublime. LC 84-25435. (Texts & Studies in Religion: Vol.21). 275p. 1985. lib. bdg. 89.95 (*0-88946-554-1*) E Mellen.

Arieti, James A., jt. ed. see Stump, Donald V.

***Arieti, Silvano.** The Parnas: A Scene from the Holocaust. LC 99-41323. (Illus.). xii, 147p. 2000. pap. 14.95 (*0-9664913-0-0*, Pub. by Paul Dry Bks) IPG Chicago.

Arieti, Silvano. Understanding & Helping the Schizophrenic: A Guide for Family & Friends. LC 94-77917. 252p. 1995. pap. text 28.50 (*1-56821-269-0*) Aronson.

Arieti, Silvano. Understanding & Helping the Schizophrenic: A Guide for Family & Friends. 222p. 1993. reprint ed. pap. text 32.95 (*1-85575-063-5*, Pub. by H Karnac Bks Ltd) Brunner-Mazel.

Arieti, Silvano & Chrzanowski, Gerard, eds. New Dimensions in Psychiatry: A World Review. LC 74-16150. 460p. reprint ed. pap. 142.60 (*0-608-30499-9*, 201195100080) Bks Demand.

— New Dimensions in Psychiatry: A World Review, Vol. 2. rev. ed. LC 74-16150. 523p. 1977. reprint ed. pap. 162.20 (*0-7837-3423-9*, 205774400008) Bks Demand.

Ariew. Cara a Cara Software. 1987. write for info. (*0-318-66661-8*) Heinle & Heinle.

Ariew. C'Est a Dire: Introductory French. annot. ed. (FRE.). (C). 1989. text, teacher ed. 43.50 (*0-8384-1695-0*) Thomson Learn.

Ariew. Premiers Echanges. 2nd ed. (College French Ser.). (FRE.). (C). 1993. student ed., suppl. ed. 13.95 incl. audio (*0-8384-4433-4*) Heinle & Heinle.

— Premiers Echanges. 2nd ed. (College French Ser.). (C). 1993. mass mkt., suppl. ed. 36.95 (*0-8384-4439-3*) Heinle & Heinle.

— Premiers Echanges. 2nd ed. (College French Ser.). (C). 1993. mass mkt., suppl. ed. 28.95 (*0-8384-4437-7*) Heinle & Heinle.

— Premiers Echanges. 2nd ed. (College French Ser.). (FRE.). (C). 1993. suppl. ed., lab manual ed. 28.95 incl. audio (*0-8384-4434-2*) Heinle & Heinle.

— Premiers Echanges. 2nd ed. (College French Ser.). (FRE.). (C). 1993. mass mkt., suppl. ed. 21.95 (*0-8384-4438-5*) Heinle & Heinle.

Ariew, jt. auth. see Nerenz, Anne.

Ariew, Robert. Par Ici: Echanges Intermediaires. annot. ed. (FRE.). (C). 1993. text, teacher ed. 51.16 incl. audio (*0-669-35189-X*) HM Trade Div.

Ariew, Robert & Nerenz, Anne. ARIEW PAR ICI 2C W/CASSETTE. (FRE.). 448p. (C). 1993. 38.36 incl. audio (*0-669-32596-1*) HM Trade Div.

— ARIEW PAR ICI 4C (PB) W/CASSE. (FRE.). 484p. (C). 1993. pap. text 49.96 incl. digital audio (*0-669-35187-3*) HM Trade Div.

— Par Ici: Echanges Intermediaires. (FRE.). 448p. (C). 1993. pap. text 36.36 (*0-669-24885-1*); pap. text 34.36 (*0-669-24887-8*); pap. text, teacher ed. 2.66 (*0-669-24889-4*) HM Trade Div.

— Par Ici: Echanges Intermediaires. annot. ed. (FRE.). 448p. (C). 1993. teacher ed. 39.56 incl. audio (*0-669-32597-X*) HM Trade Div.

— Par Ici: Exchanges Intermediaires. (FRE.). 448p. (C). 1993. audio 31.16 (*0-669-24890-8*); audio 7.16 (*0-669-32595-3*) HM Trade Div.

— Par Ici: Lectures et Videos. (FRE.). 224p. (C). 1995. pap. text 38.36 (*0-669-24888-6*) HM Trade Div.

— Premiers Exchanges. 2nd ed. LC 92-40946. (C). 1993. 60.95 (*0-8384-4443-1*) Heinle & Heinle.

— Premiers Exchanges. 2nd ed. LC 92-40946. (C). 1993. mass mkt., student ed. 36.95 (*0-8384-4432-6*) Heinle & Heinle.

Ariew, Robert, jt. auth. see Bragger, Jeannette D.

***Ariew, Roger.** Descartes & the Last Scholastics. LC 99-11953. (Illus.). 240p. 1999. 42.50 (*0-8014-3603-6*) Cornell U Pr.

Ariew, Roger, et al, eds. Descartes' "Meditations" Background Source Materials. LC 97-49942. (Philosophical Texts in Context Ser.). 224p. (C). 1998. pap. 18.95 (*0-521-48579-7*); text 54.95 (*0-521-48126-0*) Cambridge U Pr.

Ariew, Roger & Grene, Marjorie. Descartes & His Contemporaries: Objections & Replies. LC 94-6453. 270p. 1995. pap. text 17.95 (*0-226-02630-2*) U Ch Pr.

Ariew, Roger & Grene, Marjorie, eds. Descartes & His Contemporaries: Objections & Replies. LC 94-6453. 270p. 1995. lib. bdg. 45.00 (*0-226-02629-9*) U Ch Pr.

***Ariew, Roger & Watkins, Eric.** Readings in Modern Philosophy, 2 vols. LC 00-38860. 2000. write for info. (*0-87220-532-0*) Hackett Pub.

Ariew, Roger & Watkins, Eric, eds. Modern Philosophy: An Anthology of Primary Sources. LC 98-34866. 968p. (C). 1998. pap. 29.95 (*0-87220-440-5*); lib. bdg. 49.95 (*0-87220-441-3*) Hackett Pub.

Ariew, Roger, jt. ed. see Barker, Peter.

Ariew, Roger, ed. see Descartes, Rene.

Ariew, Roger, ed. see Duhem, Pierre M.

Ariew, Roger, ed. see Leibniz, Gottfried Wilhelm & Clarke, Samuel.

Ariew, Roger, ed. & tr. see Leibniz, Gottfried Wilhelm.

Ariew, Roger, tr. see Duhem, Pierre.

Ariew, Roger, tr. see Leibniz, Gottfried Wilhelm.

Arif, A., ed. Adverse Health Consequences of Cocaine Abuse. (ENG & RUS.). 47p. 1987. pap. text 9.00 (*92-4-156107-6*, 1150272) World Health.

Arif, A. & Hughes, P. Drug Use Among Non-Student Youth. (WHO Offset Publications: No. 60). 58p. 1981. 5.00 (*92-4-170060-2*) World Health.

Arif, A. & Westmeyer, J. Manual of Drug & Alcohol Abuse: Guidelines for Teaching in Medical & Health Institutions. LC 88-22414. (Illus.). 350p. (C). 1988. text 65.00 (*0-306-42890-3*, Kluwer Plenum) Kluwer Academic.

Arif, A., et al. Drug Dependence: A Methodology for Evaluating Treatment & Rehabilitation. (Offset Publications: No. 98). 67p. 1987. pap. text 12.00 (*92-4-170098-X*, 1120098) World Health.

Arif, A, jt. auth. see Edwards, G.

Arif Al-Arif. Bedouin Love, Law & Legend, Dealing Exclusively with the Badu of Beersheba. LC 79-180318. (Mid-East Studies). (Illus.). reprint ed. 37.50 (*0-404-56213-2*) AMS Pr.

Arif, Awni & Westermeyer, Joseph, eds. Methadone Maintenance in the Management of Opioid Dependence: An International Review. LC 89-78368. 128p. 1990. 47.95 (*0-275-93392-X*, C3392, Praeger Pubs) Greenwood.

Arif, I. M. & Ansell, M. O. Libyan Civil Code. (Libya Past & Present Ser.: Vol. 4). 1976. 95.00 (*0-902675-00-1*). Oleander Pr.

— Libyan Revolution: A Sourcebook of Legal & Historical Documents, Vol. 1, Sept. 1, 1969 to Aug. 30, 1970. (Libya Past & Present Ser.: Vol. 1). 1970. 45.00 (*0-902675-10-9*) Oleander Pr.

Arif, Iftikhar. Twelfth Man. LC 89-80342. 91p. 1989. pap. 16.95 (*0-948259-49-3*) Dufour.

***Arif, K. M.** Khaki Shadows: The Pakistan Army 1947-1997. (Illus.). 670p. 2000. text 26.00 (0-19-579396-X) OUP.

Arif, Khalid M. Working with Zia: Pakistan Power Politics, 1977-1988. (Illus.). 456p. 1995. text 45.00 (0-19-577570-8) OUP.

Arif, Nasr M. Nazariyat Al-siyasah Al-mugarana: Mugaraba Epitimologiat. large type ed. LC 96-46876. (ARA.). 414p. 1998. pap. text 10.00 (0-9661494-1-6) SISS.

— Nazariyat Al-siyasah Al-mugarana: Mugaraba Epitimologiat. large type ed. LC 96-46876. (ARA.). 414p. (C). 1998. 15.00 (0-9661494-0-8) SISS.

— Nazariyat al Tanmiyah al Siyasiyah al Mu'asirah - Contemporary Theories of Political Development: Dirasah Naqdiyah Muqaranah fi Daw' al Manzur al Hadari al Islami - Islamic Viewpoint. 2nd ed. LC 91-44547. (Silsilat al Rasa'il al Jami'iyah Ser.: No. 6). (ARA.). 481p. 1992. 18.00 (1-56564-017-9); pap. 12.00 (1-56564-018-7) IIIT VA.

Ariff, Mohamed. The Malaysian Economy: Pacific Connections. (South-East Asian Social Science Monographs). (Illus.). 236p. 1991. text 45.00 (0-19-588564-3) OUP.

— The Role of ASEAN in the Uruguay Round: Opportunities & Constraints. LC 92-42718. 1993. pap. 9.95 (1-55815-249-0) ICS Pr.

Ariff, Mohamed, ed. The Pacific Economy Growth & External Stability. 372p. 1991. 44.95 (1-86373-036-2, Pub. by Allen & Unwin Pty); pap. 29.95 (1-86373-035-4, Pub. by Allen & Unwin Pty) Paul & Co Pubs.

***Ariff, Mohamed & Khalid, Ahmed M.** Liberalization, Growth & the Asian Financial Crisis: Lessons for Developing & Transitional Economies in Asia. 544p. 2000. 120.00 (1-85898-839-X) E Elgar.

Ariffin, A., et al. Diabetes & Primary Eye Care. (Modern Optometry Ser.). (Illus.). 224p. 1992. 70.00 (0-632-03142-5) Blackwell Sci.

Arifov, Ubai A., ed. Secondary Emission & Structural Properties of Solids. Archard, Geoffrey C., tr. LC 78-157931. 154p. reprint ed. pap. 47.80 (0-608-30725-4, 202068300018) Bks Demand.

Ariga, Chieko. Jenda Kaitai No Kiseki: Bungaku, Seido, Bunka. (JPN.). 245p. (Orig.). 1996. pap. 22.00 (0-9654892-0-5) US-Japan Wom Ctr.

Ariga, Eiko, tr. see Okura, Nagatsune.

***Ariga, Kenn, et al.** Internal Labour Markets in Japan. (Illus.). 320p. (C). 2000. text 69.95 (0-521-64240-X) Cambridge U Pr.

Arigazin, A. K., et al. Santilli's Generalization of Galilei's & Einstein's Relativities. (Illus.). 388p. (Orig.). 1992. pap. text 70.00 (0-911767-56-8) Hadronic Pr Inc.

Arihood, Wayne. Imaginals: What in the World Is a Clockodile? A Moosepaper? A Caterputer. They're All Imaginals. Eichenbaum, Ken, ed. (Illus.). 40p. (J). (gr. k-6). 1998. lib. bdg. 15.95 (0-9620271-8-9) Litterati Bks.

Arijon, Daniel. Grammar of the Film Language. (Illus.). 640p. 1991. reprint ed. pap. 24.95 (1-879505-07-X) Silman James Pr.

***Arikawa, S. & Furukawa, Keoichi.** Discovery Science: Proceedings of the 2nd International Conference, DS'99, Tokyo, Japan, December 6-8, 1999. rev. ed. LC 99-52991. (Lecture Notes in Computer Science Ser.: Vol. 1721). xi, 374p. 1999. pap. 62.00 (3-540-66713-X) Spr-Verlag.

***Arikawa, Setsuo.** Discovery Science: First International Conference, DS, 98, Fukuoka, Japan, December 14-16, 1998, Proceedings, 153. LC 98-51763. (Lecture Notes in Artificial Intelligence). 1998. pap. write for info. (3-540-65390-2) Spr-Verlag.

Arikawa, Setsuo, et al, eds. Algorithmic Learning Theory II: Proceedings of ALT'91, Tokyo, October 23-25, 1991. LC 92-53256. 320p. 1992. 88.00 (90-5199-088-X, Pub. by IOS Pr) IOS Press.

Arikawa, Setsuo & Jantke, K. P., eds. Algorithmic Learning Theory: Proceedings of the 4th International Workshop on Analogical & Inductive Inference, AII'94, & 5th International Workshop on Algorithmic Learning Theory, ALT'94, Reinhardsbrunn Castle, Germany, October 10-15, 1994. LC 94-36692. (Lecture Notes in Computer Science: Lecture Notes in Artificial Intelligence: Vol. 872). xiv, 575p. 1994. 79.95 (3-540-58520-6) Spr-Verlag.

Arikawa, Setsuo & Jantke, Klaus P., eds. Algorithmic Learning Theory. LC 94-36692. (Lecture Notes in Computer Science, Lecture Notes in Artificial Intelligence: Vol. 872). 1994. write for info. (0-387-58520-6) Spr-Verlag.

Arikawa, Setsuo, jt. auth. see Sharma, Arum K.

Arikoo, K., ed. Central Asia. (C). 1995. 36.00 (81-241-0303-8, Pub. by Har-Anand Pubns) S Asia.

Arima, A., et al, eds. Asia-Pacific Physics Conference: Proceedings of the First, 2 vols., 1. 1984. write for info. (9971-978-00-8) World Scientific Pub.

— Asia-Pacific Physics Conference: Proceedings of the First, 2 vols., Set. 1984. 140.00 (0-317-01258-4) World Scientific Pub.

Arima, A. & Eguchi, T. Group Theoretical Methods in Physics: Proceedings of the 20th International Colloquium. 544p. 1995. text 116.00 (981-02-2087-1) World Scientific Pub.

Arima, A., jt. auth. see Iachello, F.

***Arima, Elaine.** The Kids 'N' Clay Ceramics Book: Handbuilding & Wheel-Throwing Projects from the Kids 'N' Clay Pottery Studio. LC 99-45683. (Illus.). 128p. (YA). (gr. k up). 2000. pap. 16.95 (1-883672-89-9) Tricycle Pr.

Arima, Eugene Y. Inuit Kayaks in Canada: A Review of Historical Records & Construction. (Mercury Ser.: No. 110). (Illus.). 244p. 1988. pap. 14.95 (0-660-10764-3, Pub. by CN Mus Civilization) U of Wash Pr.

Arima, Eugene Y., et al. Between Ports Alberni & Renfrew: Notes on West Coast Peoples. (Mercury Ser.: CES No. 121). (Illus.). 328p. 1991. pap. 19.95 (0-660-12912-4, Pub. by CN Mus Civilization) U of Wash Pr.

Arima, Masataka, et al, eds. The Developing Brain & Its Disorders: Proceedings of the 4th Annual Symposium on Development Disabilities, "Biological Aspects in the Pathogenesis of Developmental Disabilities," November 3-5, 1983, Tokyo. (Illus.). viii, 314p. 1985. 139.25 (3-8055-4010-8) S Karger.

Arima, Phlip. Beneath the Beauty. 80p. pap. 9.99 (1-895837-36-7) Insomniac.

— Damaged. LC 98-175166. 112p. 1998. pap. text 9.99 (1-895837-21-9) Insomniac.

Arima, Phlip, et al. Playing in the Asphalt Garden: An Anthology. LC 95-189170. 128p. pap. 14.99 (1-895837-20-0) Insomniac.

Arima, Takashi. Journey to the Real: Selected Poems of Takashi Arima. Hikihara, Tadeo & Kuzell, John M., eds. & trs. by. from JPN. LC 92-31599. (Illus.). 160p. 1993. pap. 9.95 (0-8348-0276-7) Weatherhill.

Arima, Tatsuo. The Failure of Freedom: A Portrait of Modern Japanese Intellectuals. LC 74-82292. (Harvard East Asian Ser.: No. 39). 315p. reprint ed. pap. 97.70 (0-608-30750-5, 200642800059) Bks Demand.

Ariman, Teoman, et al, eds. Recent Advances in Lifeline Earthquake Engineering. LC 87-72298. 245p. 1987. 49.00 (0-931215-71-4) Computational Mech MA.

Ariman, Teoman & Veziroglu, T. Nejat, eds. Particulate & Multiphase Processes, 3 vols., Set. (Illus.). 2236p. 1987. 730.00 (0-89116-636-X) Hemisp Pub.

Ariman, Teoman, ed. see National Congress on Pressure Vessels & Piping Sta.

Arimany Coma, Miguel. Catalan-Castilian (Spanish), Castilian (Spanish)-Catalan Dictionary: Diccionari Usual Catala-Castella-Catala. (CAT & SPA.). 958p. 1983. 59.95 (0-8288-1756-1, S50361) Fr & Eur.

— Diccionari Actual Il Iustrat de la Llengua Catalana. 431p. 1983. 14.95 (0-8288-1754-5, S40318) Fr & Eur.

— Diccionari Escolar Catala Arimany, 3 vols. in 1. 7th ed. (CAT.). 1418p. 1983. 59.95 (0-8288-2081-3, S50049) Fr & Eur.

— Diccionari Escolar Valencia, 3 vols. in 1. (CAT.). 310p. 1980. pap. 12.95 (0-8288-2082-1, S50050) Fr & Eur.

— Diccionari Manual Castella-Catala. 2nd ed. (CAT.). 413p. 1975. 24.95 (0-8288-5798-9, S50358) Fr & Eur.

— Diccionari Manual Catala-Castella. 2nd ed. (CAT.). 535p. 1975. 35.00 (0-8288-5799-7, S50357) Fr & Eur.

— Diccionari Manual Catala-Castella i Castella-Catala. 9th ed. (CAT.). 956p. 1976. 39.95 (0-8288-5803-9, S50360) Fr & Eur.

— Dictionary of the Undersea World: Enciclopedia Del Mundo Submarino. 2nd ed. (ENG & SPA.). 711p. 1981. 75.00 (0-8288-1582-8, S23069) Fr & Eur.

— Practical Catalan-Castilian, Castilian-Catalan Dictionary: Diccionari Practic Catila-Castella-Catala. 9th ed. 232p. 1981. pap. 14.95 (0-7859-4940-2) Fr & Eur.

Arimany Coma, Miquel. Diccionari Basic Catala-Castella, Castella-Catala. 9th ed. (CAT & SPA.). 390p. 1975. pap. 9.95 (0-8288-5797-0, S50359) Fr & Eur.

Arimes, Tom, ed. HVAC & Chemical Resistance Handbook for the Engineer & Architect. LC 94-71613. (Illus.). 1650p. 1994. lib. bdg. 100.00 (0-9640967-0-6) BCT.

Arimilli, R. V., jt. ed. see Prasad, V.

Arimoto, Michel M. A Six Million Dollar Man's Trading Advice: The Secrets of Successfully Trading Futures & Stocks. (Illus.). 140p. (Orig.). (C). 1993. pap. 39.12 (0-317-05741-3) Clermont NY.

Arimoto, Suguru. Control Theory of Nonlinear Mechanical Systems. (Oxford Engineering Science Ser.: Vol. 48). (Illus.). 290p. 1996. text 100.00 (0-19-856291-8) OUP.

Arimura, Akira & Said, Sami I. Vip, Pacap, & Related Peptides: Second International Symposium. LC 96-39419. (Annals of the New York Academy of Sciences Ser.). 1997. 135.00 (0-89766-983-5); pap. 135.00 (0-89766-984-3) NY Acad Sci.

Arinaga, Esther Kwon, jt. ed. see Raywid, Mary Anne.

Arinc, Emel, et al, eds. Molecular & Applied Aspects of Oxidative Drug Metabolizing Enzymes. LC 98-44331. (NATO ASI Ser.: 303). (Illus.). 302p. (C). 1999. text 127.50 (0-306-46048-3) Plenum.

— Molecular Aspects of Monooxygenases & Bioactivation of Toxic Compounds. (NATO ASI Ser.: Vol. 202). (Illus.). 508p. (C). 1991. text 180.00 (0-306-43823-2, Kluwer Plenum) Kluwer Academic.

— Molecular Aspects of Oxidative Drug Metabolizing Enzymes: Their Signigicance in Environmental Toxicology, Chemical Carcinogenesis & Health. LC 94-47314. (NATO ASI Series H: Cell Biology: Vol. 90). 1995. 291.95 (3-540-58856-6) Spr-Verlag.

Arinc, Faruk & Diller, Kenneth R., eds. Heat & Mass Transfer in Biological & Medical Engineering. LC 98-39012. (Annals of the New York Academy of Sciences Ser.: Vol. 858). 319p. 1998. 120.00 (1-57331-172-3); pap. 120.00 (1-57331-173-1) NY Acad Sci.

Aring, Charles D. The Understanding Physician: Writings of Charles D. Aring, M. D. enl. rev. ed. LC 73-143496. 220p. reprint ed. pap. 68.20 (0-608-16518-2, 202765000055) Bks Demand.

Aringhi, Paolo. The Catacombs of Rome: Roma Subterranea Houissing, 2 vols. (Printed Sources of Western Art Ser.). (LAT., Illus.). 1981. reprint ed. pap., boxed set 160.00 (0-915346-61-3) A Wofsy Fine Arts.

Arino, O., et al, eds. Advances in Mathematical Population Dynamics - Molecules, Cells & Man: Proceedings of the 4th International Conference on Mathematical Population Dynamics, Rice University, Houston, TX, 23-27 May 1995. LC 98-205920. (Series in Mathematical Biology & Medicine). 800p. 1997. 128.00 (981-02-3176-8) World Scientific Pub.

Arino, Ovide, et al, eds. Mathematical Population Dynamics: Proceedings of the Second International Conference. (Lecture Notes in Pure & Applied Mathematics Ser.: Vol. 131). (Illus.). 808p. 1991. pap. text 215.00 (0-8247-8424-3) Dekker.

Arinoldo, Carl. How to Control Your Eating. 151p. 1998. pap. 17.95 (1-56072-584-2, Nova Kroshka Bks) Nova Sci Pubs.

Arintero, John G. Mystical Evolution, 2 vols., I. Aumann, Jordan, tr. from SPA. LC 78-62254. Orig. Title: La Evolucion Mistica. 1979. reprint ed. pap. write for info. (0-89555-072-5) TAN Bks Pubs.

— Mystical Evolution, 2 vols., II. Aumann, Jordan, tr. from SPA. LC 78-62254. Orig. Title: La Evolucion Mistica. 1979. reprint ed. pap. write for info. (0-89555-073-3) TAN Bks Pubs.

— Mystical Evolution, 2 vols., Set. Aumann, Jordan, tr. from SPA. LC 78-62254. Orig. Title: La Evolucion Mistica. 1979. reprint ed. pap. 36.00 (0-89555-071-7) TAN Bks Pubs.

Arintero, Juan G. Song of Songs: A Mystical Exposition. Valender, James & Morales, Jose L., trs. 571p. 1992. reprint ed. pap. 20.00 (0-89555-485-2, 1049) TAN Bks Pubs.

Arinze, Emmanuel, jt. ed. see Ardouin, Claude D.

Arinze, Francis. Meeting Other Believers: The Risks & Rewards of Interreligious Dialogue. LC 98-65358. 112p. 1998. pap. 7.95 (0-87973-949-5) Our Sunday Visitor.

Arion, V. Y. Physicochemical Aspects of Medicine Reviews: Thymic Peptides As Immunoregulators, with Special Reference to T-Activin, Vol. 2. (Soviet Medical Reviews Ser.: Vol. 2, Pt. 3). iv, 64p. 1989. pap. text 69.00 (3-7186-4965-9) Gordon & Breach.

Ariosto, Ludovico. Ariostos Seven Planets Governing Italie. LC 76-57350. (English Experience Ser.: No. 770). 1977. reprint ed. lib. bdg. 20.00 (90-221-0770-1) Walter J Johnson.

— Cinque Canti. Sheers, Alexander & Quint, David, trs. LC 94-45611. (Biblioteca Italiana Ser.: No. 8).Tr. of Five Cantos. (ITA & ENG.). 368p. 1996. pap. 19.95 (0-520-20009-8, Pub. by U CA Pr) Cal Prin Full Svc.

— Cinque Canti. Sheers, Alexander & Quint, David, trs. LC 94-45611. (Biblioteca Italiana Ser.: No. 8).Tr. of Five Cantos. (ITA & ENG.). 368p. (C). 1996. 55.00 (0-520-20007-1, Pub. by U CA Pr) Cal Prin Full Svc.

— The Comedies of Ariosto. Beame, Edmond M. & Sbrocchi, Leonard G., eds. LC 74-5739. 368p. reprint ed. pap. 114.10 (0-608-16359-7, 202720900054) Bks Demand.

— Five Cantos. Morgan, Leslie Z., tr. from ITA. LC 90-3041. (Library of World Literature in Translation: Vol. 3). Orig. Title: Cinque Canti. 158p. 1992. text 15.00 (0-8240-2989-5) Garland.

— Orlando Furioso. Waldman, Guido, tr. & intro. by. (Oxford World's Classics Ser.). 656p. 1999. pap. 16.95 (0-19-283677-3) OUP.

— Orlando Furioso: An English Translation with Introductions, Notes & Index by Allan Gilbert, 2 vols. (C). 1954. 45.00 (0-913298-31-X) S F Vanni.

— Orlando Furioso: The Frenzy of Orlando: A Romantic Epic, Vol. 1. Reynolds, Barbara, tr. from ITA. & intro. by. (Classics Ser.). 832p. 1975. pap. 16.95 (0-14-044311-8, Penguin Classics) Viking Penguin.

— Orlando Furioso in English Heroical Verse. Harrington, John, tr. LC 77-25638. (English Experience Ser.: No. 259). (Illus.). 424p. 1970. reprint ed. 75.00 (90-221-0259-9) Walter J Johnson.

— Sir John Harington's Translation of Orlando Furioso. LC PQ4582.E5A35. (Centaur Classics Ser.). 591p. reprint ed. pap. 183.30 (0-8357-6653-5, 203532200094) Bks Demand.

Ariosto, Ludovico & Aretino, Pietro. Three Renaissance Comedies. Cairns, Christopher, ed. LC 91-42459. (Illus.). 366p. 1991. lib. bdg. 99.95 (0-7734-9450-2) E Mellen.

Ariosto, Ludovico & Trissino, Giovanni Giorgio. Two Renaissance Plays: Ariosto, 'Il Negromante' & Trissino, 'Sofonisba' Corrigan, Beatrice, ed. & intro. by. (Italian Texts Ser.). (ITA.). 184p. (C). 1975. pap. 11.00 (0-685-07670-9, Pub. by Manchester Univ Pr) St Martin.

Ariosto, Ludovico, et al. Archivio Delle Similitudini. (Archivio Delle Similitudini - ASIM Ser.: Vol. 1). (GER.). x, 478p. 1993. write for info. (3-487-09795-8) G Olms Pubs.

— Le Rime, 2 vols. 692p. 1995. write for info. (3-487-10056-8) G Olms Pubs.

Ariotti, Piero, ed. see Bronowski, Jacob.

Aripu, Lawrence. Stories That Make the World: Oral Literature of the Indian Peoples of the Inland Northwest, Vol.218. 1999. pap. text 14.95 (0-8061-3131-4) U of Okla Pr.

Aris, A., jt. auth. see Van Alphen, J.

Aris, Michael. Hidden Treasures & Secret Lives: A Study of Pemalingpa (1450-1521) & the Sixth Dalai Lama (1683-1706) 240p. 1989. 45.00 (0-7103-0328-9) Routledge.

— The Raven Crown: The Origins of Buddhist Monarchy in Bhutan. (Illus.). 160p. 1995. 29.95 (0-906026-32-6, Pub. by Serindia) Weatherhill.

Aris, Michael, ed. see Richardson, Hugh.

Aris, Michael, ed. see Richardson, Hugh E.

Aris, Pepita. Flavor of Andalusia. 96p. 1996. 9.98 (0-7858-0580-X) Bk Sales Inc.

***Aris, Pepita.** Spanishwoman's Kitchen. (Illus.). 2000. pap. 21.95 (1-84188-016-7) Seven Dials.

Aris, Philippe A. A History of Private Life Vol. V: Riddles of Identity in Modern Times. Duby, Georges et al, eds. Goldhammer, Arthur, tr. (Illus.). 736p. (C). 1991. 39.95 (0-674-39979-X) Belknap Pr.

Aris, Reinhold. History of Political Thought in Germany, 1789-1815. 414p. 1965. reprint ed. 37.50 (0-7146-1546-3, Pub. by F Cass Pubs) Intl Spec Bk.

Aris, Rosemary. Trade Unions & the Management of Industrial Conflict. LC 97-26516. 224p. 1998. text 65.00 (0-312-17761-5) St Martin.

Aris, Rutherford. Elementary Chemical Reactor Analysis. LC 99-47132. 366p. 1999. pap. text 14.95 (0-486-40928-7) Dover.

— Mathematical Modeling: A Chemical Engineer's Perspective. LC 98-89644. (Illus.). 479p. 1999. text 99.95 (0-12-604585-2) Acad Pr.

— Mathematical Modelling Techniques. (Illus.). 288p. 1995. reprint ed. pap. 9.95 (0-486-68131-9) Dover.

— The Mathematical Theory of Diffusion & Reaction in Permeable Catalysts, 2 vols., Set. Incl. Vol. 1. Theory of the Steady State. (Illus.). 460p. 1975. text 95.00 (0-19-851931-1); Vol. 2. Questions of Uniqueness, Stability, & Transient Behaviour. 232p. 1975. 85.00 (0-19-851942-7); (Illus.). 692p. (C). 1975. 150.00 (0-19-519829-8) OUP.

— Vectors Tensors & the Basic Equations. 300p. 1990. pap. 9.95 (0-486-66110-5) Dover.

Aris, Rutherford, et al, eds. Springs of Scientific Creativity: Essays on Founders of Modern Science. LC 82-23715. 353p. 1983. reprint ed. pap. 109.50 (0-608-00784-6, 205933300010) Bks Demand.

Aris, Rutherford & Varma, Arvind, eds. The Mathematical Understanding of Chemical Engineering Systems: Selected Papers of Neal R. Amundson. LC 79-40686. (Illus.). 1980. 370.00 (0-08-023836-X, Pub. by Pergamon Repr) Franklin.

Arisa, Miguel, tr. see Moreton, Daniel.

***Arisawa, Hiroshi & Catarci, Tiziana.** Advances in Visual Information Management - Visual Database Systems. (International Federation for Information Processing Ser.). 424p. 2000. 180.00 (0-7923-7835-0) Kluwer Academic.

Arisman, Marshall. Sacred Monkey Man. Spurlock, J. David, ed. (Tales from the Edge Ser.). (Illus.). 52p. 1998. pap. 4.00 (1-887591-01-X) Vanguard Prodns.

Arisman, Marshall, jt. ed. see Heller, Steven.

Ariss, Robert & Dowsett, Gary. Against Death: The Practice of Living with AIDS. 208p. 1997. text 32.00 (90-5699-563-4); pap. text 14.00 (90-5699-564-2) Gordon & Breach.

Aristide, Jean-Bertrand. Dignity. Coates, Carrol F., tr. & afterword by by. LC 95-42660. 210p. (C). 1996. 35.00 (0-8139-1674-7) U Pr of Va.

Aristide, Jean-Bertrand. Eyes of the Heart: Seeking a Path for the Poor in the Age of Globalization. 75p. Date not set. pap. write for info. (1-56751-186-4) Common Courage.

— Eyes of the Heart: Seeking a Path for the Poor in the Age of Globalization. 96p. 2000. 9.00 (1-56751-187-2, Pub. by Common Courage) LPC InBook.

Aristide, Jean-Bertrand. In the Parish of the Poor: Writings from Haiti. LC 90-42004. 1990. pap. 14.00 (0-88344-682-0) Orbis Bks.

Aristide, Jean-Bertrand & Wargny, Christophe. Aristide: An Autobiography. Maloney, Linda M., tr. LC 92-34558. 213p. reprint ed. pap. 66.10 (0-608-20257-6, 207151600012) Bks Demand.

***Aristide, Jean-Bertrand, et al.** Media's Dark Age: The Rise & Fall of Western Journalism. LC 99-52468. 1999. write for info. (0-9656916-5-9) Intl Action Ctr.

Aristides. Aristides, Vol. 1. Behr, C. A., tr. (Loeb Classical Library: No. 458). 594p. 1973. text 19.95 (0-674-99505-8) HUP.

Aristides, P. Aelius. The Complete Works: P. Aelius Aristides. Behr, Charles Allison, tr. LC 81-196975. 1981. write for info. (90-04-06384-6) Brill Academic Pubs.

— Quae Supersunt Omnia, 2 vols., Set. Keil, Bruno, ed. xlii, 472p. 1958. 130.00 (3-296-10200-0) G Olms Pubs.

Aristides, P. Aelius, jt. auth. see Behr, Charles.

Aristigueta, Maria P. Managing for Results in State Government. LC 98-23643. 192p. 1999. 55.00 (1-56720-246-2, Quorum Bks) Greenwood.

Ariston, H. J. Decide! LC 83-80421. (Illus.). 56p. (Orig.). 1983. pap. 5.95 (0-935344-01-2) Jupiter Bks.

— Reality. LC 83-80423. 60p. (Orig.). 1983. pap. 5.95 (0-935344-03-9) Jupiter Bks.

— Win! LC 83-80422. 80p. (Orig.). 1983. pap. 5.95 (0-935344-02-0) Jupiter Bks.

Aristophanes. The Acharnians. Landes, William-Alan, ed. LC 97-50506. 36p. 1998. pap. 7.00 (0-88734-811-4) Players Pr.

— The Acharnians of Aristophanes. Connor, W. R., ed. LC 78-18610. (Greek Texts & Commentaries Ser.). (ENG & GRE.). 1979. reprint ed. lib. bdg. 30.95 (0-405-11450-8) Ayer.

— Aristophanes: Acharnians. Sommerstein, Alan H., ed. (Classical Texts Ser.: Vol. 1). 1980. 59.99 (0-85668-167-9, Pub. by Aris & Phillips); pap. 28.00 (0-85668-172-5, Pub. by Aris & Phillips) David Brown.

— Aristophanes: Birds. Sommerstein, Alan H., ed. (Classical Texts Ser.: Vol. 6). 1987. pap. 32.00 (0-85668-288-8, Pub. by Aris & Phillips) David Brown.

— Aristophanes: Birds, Lysistrata, Assembly-Women, Wealth. Halliwell, Stephen, ed. & tr. by. 378p. 1997. text 85.00 (0-19-814993-X) OUP.

***Aristophanes.** Aristophanes: Birds, Lysistrata, Women at the Thesmophoria. (Loeb Classical Library). 624p. 2000. 19.95 (0-674-99587-2) HUP.

Aristophanes. Aristophanes: Clouds. Sommerstein, Alan H., ed. (Classical Texts Ser.: Vol. 3). 1980. 59.99 (0-85668-209-8, Pub. by Aris & Phillips); pap. 28.00 (0-85668-210-1, Pub. by Aris & Phillips) David Brown.

Aristophanes. Aristophanes: Frogs. Sommerstein, Alan H., ed. & tr. by. (Classical Texts Ser.). 200p. 1997. 59.99 (0-85668-647-6, Pub. by Aris & Phillips); pap. 32.00 (0-85668-648-4, Pub. by Aris & Phillips) David Brown.

Aristophanes. Aristophanes: Frogs. 414p. 1994. pap. text 28.00 (0-19-815005-9) OUP.

A

— Aristophanes: Frogs. Stanford, W. G., ed. (GRE.). 270p. (C). 1983. reprint ed. pap. 29.95 (0-86292-115-5, Pub. by Brist Class Pr) Focus Pub-R Pullins.
— Aristophanes: Knights. Sommerstein, Alan H., ed. (Classical Texts Ser.: Vol. 2). 1981. 59.99 (0-85668-177-6, Pub. by Aris & Phillips); pap. 28.00 (0-85668-178-4, Pub. by Aris & Phillips) David Brown.
— Aristophanes: Lysistrata. Sommerstein, Alan H., ed. (Classical Texts Ser.: Vol. 7). 1990. pap. 28.00 (0-85668-458-9, Pub. by Aris & Phillips) David Brown.
— Aristophanes: Lysistrata. Sommerstein, Alan H., ed. (Classical Texts Ser.: Vol. 7). 1992. 59.99 (0-85668-457-0, Pub. by Aris & Phillips) David Brown.
— Aristophanes: Peace. Sommerstein, Alan H., ed. (Classical Texts Ser.: Vol. 5). 1985. 59.99 (0-85668-262-4, Pub. by Aris & Phillips); pap. 28.00 (0-85668-263-2, Pub. by Aris & Phillips) David Brown.
— Aristophanes: Peace. Olson, S. Douglas, ed. 408p. 1999. text 92.00 (0-19-814081-9) OUP.
— Aristophanes: Plays One. 264p. (C). 1993. pap. 11.95 (0-413-66900-9, A0667, Methuen Drama) Methn.
— Aristophanes: Plays Two. 384p. (C). 1993. pap. 11.95 (0-413-66910-6, A0679, Methuen Drama) Methn.
— Aristophanes: Thesmophoriazusae. Sommerstein, Alan H., ed. (Classical Texts Ser.: Vol. 8). 59.99 (0-85668-558-5, Pub. by Aris & Phillips); pap. 28.00 (0-85668-559-3, Pub. by Aris & Phillips) David Brown.
— Aristophanes: Wasps. Sommerstein, Alan H., ed. (Classical Texts Ser.: Vol. 4). 1983. 59.99 (0-85668-212-8, Pub. by Aris & Phillips); pap. 28.00 (0-85668-213-6, Pub. by Aris & Phillips) David Brown.
— Aristophanes Vol. I: Clouds, Wasps, Birds. Meineck, Peter, tr. from GRE. & notes by. LC 98-37824. (Classics Ser.). 480p. (C). 1998. pap. text 12.95 (0-87220-360-3); lib. bdg. 37.95 (0-87220-361-1) Hackett Pub.
— Aristophanes Plutos, with Commentary. Connor, W. R., ed. LC 78-18582. (Greek Texts & Commentaries Ser.). (GER., Illus.). 1979. reprint ed. lib. bdg. 39.95 (0-405-11425-7) Ayer.
— Assembly of Women. Mayhew, Robert, tr. & intro. by. LC 96-52486. 124p. 1997. pap. 8.95 (1-57392-133-5) Prometheus Bks.
— The Birds. LC 99-25512. (Thrift Editions Ser.). 64p. 1999. text 1.50 (0-486-40886-8) Dover.
— Birds: Greek Text with Introduction & Commentary. Dunbar, Nan, ed. & comment by. 552p. 1998. pap. text, student ed. 35.00 (0-19-872177-3) OUP.
— Birds & Other Plays. Halliwell, Stephen, ed. (Oxford World's Classics Ser.). 384p. 1999. pap. 9.95 (0-19-282408-2) OUP.
***Aristophanes.** Clouds. Meineck, Peter, tr. from GRE. LC 99-58753. 160p. (C). 2000. pap. 5.95 (0-87220-516-9); lib. bdg. 19.95 (0-87220-517-7) Hackett Pub.
Aristophanes. The Clouds. Landes, S. H., tr. LC 96-36107. 55p. (Orig.). 1996. pap. 7.00 (0-88734-286-8) Players Pr.
— The Clouds. Starkie, W. J., tr. from GRE. 420p. (Orig.). 1911. reprint ed. lib. bdg. 67.50 (0-685-13326-5, Pub. by AM Hakkert) Coronet Bks.
— Complete Plays of Aristophanes. 512p. 1984. mass mkt. 5.95 (0-553-21343-1, Bantam Classics) Bantam.
— Ecclesiazusae. Ussher, R. G., ed. (College Classical Ser.). (GRE.). xlviii, 259p. 1986. reprint ed. pap. text 20.00 (0-89241-435-9) Caratzas.
— Four Major Plays, Aristophanes: The Acharnians, the Birds, the Clouds, Lysistrata. (Airmont Classics Ser.). (YA). (gr. 11 up). 1968. mass mkt. 2.95 (0-8049-0189-9) Airmont.
— Frogs. 266p. 1997. text 70.00 (0-19-872175-7) OUP.
— Frogs. Landes, William-Alan, ed. Mila, R. L., tr. LC 95-38083. 32p. 1995. pap. 6.00 (0-88734-282-5) Players Pr.
— Frogs. abr. ed. Dover, Kenneth, ed. & comment by. LC 96-16386. 268p. 1997. pap. text, student ed. 26.00 (0-19-815071-7) OUP.
— Frogs: Aristophanes; One-Act Adaptation. (Illus.). 32p. 1965. pap. 3.25 (0-88680-060-9) I E Clark.
— Frogs: Aristophanes; One-Act Adaptation - Director's Script. (Illus.). 32p. 1965. pap. 10.00 (0-88680-061-7) I E Clark.
— The Frogs - Musical. 127p. 1975. pap. 5.95 (0-87129-657-8, F05) Dramatic Pub.
— The Knights. Frere, John H., tr. from GRE. LC 92-53876. 70p. (Orig.). 1992. pap. 7.00 (0-88734-255-8) Players Pr.
— The Knights, the Peace, the Birds, the Assembly Women Wealth. Barrett, David & Sommerstein, Alan H., trs. (Classics Ser.). 336p. 1978. pap. 10.95 (0-14-044332-0, Penguin Classics) Viking Penguin.
Aristophanes. Lysistrata. Sutherland, Donald, tr. (C). 1997. pap. text 13.40 (0-8102-0031-7) Addson-Wesley Educ.
Aristophanes. Lysistrata. Date not set. lib. bdg. 17.95 (0-8488-1953-5) Amereon Ltd.
— Lysistrata. Neuburg, Matt, ed. & tr. by. (Crofts Classics). 128p. 1992. pap. text 4.95 (0-88295-127-0) Harlan Davidson.
— Lysistrata. Rudall, Nicholas, tr. from GRE. (Plays for Performance Ser.). 65p. 1991. pap. 7.95 (0-929587-57-X, Pub. by I R Dee); lib. bdg. 15.95 (0-929587-61-8, Pub. by I R Dee) Natl Bk Netwk.
— Lysistrata. Parker, Douglass, ed. & tr. by. 128p. 1970. mass mkt. 5.99 (0-451-62495-5, Ment) NAL.
— Lysistrata. Landes, William-Alan, ed. Landes, S. H., tr. 14p. 1995. pap. 7.00 (0-88734-345-7) Players Pr.
— Lysistrata. unabridged ed. 64p. 1994. pap. text 1.00 (0-486-28225-2) Dover.
— Lysistrata & Other Plays. Sommerstein, Alan H., tr. (Classics Ser.). 256p. 1973. pap. 12.99 (0-14-044287-1, Penguin Classics) Viking Penguin.
— Lysistrate. Von Wilamowitz-Moellendorff, Ulrich, ed. ii, 223p. 1964. 50.00 (3-296-10600-6) G Olms Pubs.
***Aristophanes.** New Class, Clouds, Birds. LC 98-8446. 1999. 40.00 (0-8122-3501-0) U of Pa Pr.
Aristophanes. New Comedy. 256p. 1993. pap. 15.95 (0-413-67180-1, A0681, Methuen Drama) Methn.
— Peace. unabridged ed. Landes, William-Alan, ed. Landes, S. H., tr. LC 98-10740. 55p. (Orig.). 1998. pap. 7.00 (0-88734-781-9) Players Pr.
— Peace of Aristophanes. Webb, Robert, tr. from GRE. LC 64-22630. 107p. reprint ed. pap. 33.20 (0-608-15495-4, 202968400063) Bks Demand.
— Scholia Graeca in Aristophanem. Dubner, Friedrich, ed. xxxi, 726p. 1969. reprint ed. 160.00 (0-318-70855-8) G Olms Pubs.
— Theatre Complet Tome I, Tome I. (FRE.). 509p. 1987. pap. 15.95 (0-7859-2233-4, 207037789X) Fr & Eur.
— Theatre Complet Tome II, Tome II. (FRE.). 511p. 1987. pap. 15.95 (0-7859-2056-0, 2070377903) Fr & Eur.
— Three Comedies: The Birds, the Clouds, the Wasps. Arrowsmith, William, ed. (Illus.). 408p. 1969. pap. text 14.95 (0-472-06153-4, 06153, Ann Arbor Bks) U of Mich Pr.
— Wasps. 356p. 1988. reprint ed. pap. 24.95 (0-19-814465-2) OUP.
Aristophanes & Daitz, Stephen G. Aristophanes' Birds. unabridged ed. (Living Voice of Greek & Latin Ser.). 93p. pap. 39.95 incl. audio (0-88432-117-7, S23670) Audio-Forum.
Aristophanes & Plautus. Birds & the Brothers Menaechmus. Arnott, Peter D., ed. & tr. by. (Crofts Classics Ser.). 128p. 1958. pap. text 4.95 (0-88295-004-5) Harlan Davidson.
— The Clouds & the Pot of Gold. Arnott, Peter D., ed. & tr. by. (Crofts Classics Ser.). 128p. 1967. pap. text 4.95 (0-88295-005-3) Harlan Davidson.
***Aristophanes., et al.** Lysistrata: The Sex Strike. (Absolute Classics Ser.). 96p. 2000. pap. 16.95 (0-9536757-0-X) Theatre Comm.

Aristophanes, jt. auth. see Henderson, Jeffrey.

Aristos. Diccionario Ilustrado de la Lengua Espanola. (SPA.). 640p. 24.95 (0-7859-0881-1, S12234) Fr & Eur.
Aristotle. Aragonese Version of the Secreto Secretorum. (Dialect Ser.: No. 3). Date not set. 12.00 (0-942260-30-9) Hispanic Seminary.
— Aristote: Traite de l'ame, 2 vols. Rodier, G., tr. (Classical Studies). (FRE & GRE.). reprint ed. lib. bdg. 85.00 (0-89197-662-0) Irvington.
— Aristote: Traite de l'ame, 2 vols., 1. Rodier, G., tr. (Classical Studies). (FRE & GRE.). reprint ed. lib. bdg. 45.50 (0-697-00045-1) Irvington.
— Aristote: Traite de l'ame, 2 vols., 2. Rodier, G., tr. (Classical Studies). (FRE & GRE.). reprint ed. lib. bdg. 42.50 (0-697-00046-X) Irvington.
— Aristoteles - Metaphysica: Index Verborum, Listes de Frequence, Releves Statistiques. Delatte, Louis et al, eds. (Alpha-Omega, Reihe A Ser.: Bd. XLII). (GER.). xiii, 521p. 1984. 130.00 (3-487-07559-8) G Olms Pubs.
— Aristoteles - Schriften zur Aristotelischen Ethik. Muller-Goldingen, Christian, ed. (Olms GW Studien: Bd. 7). (GER.). 504p. 1988. 80.00 (3-487-09037-6) G Olms Pubs.
— Aristotelis Ethica Eudemia. Walzer, R. R. & Mingay, J. M., eds. (Oxford Classical Texts Ser.). (Illus.). 182p. 1991. text 32.00 (0-19-814575-6) OUP.
— Aristotle: Introductory Readings. Irwin, Terence & Fine, Gail, trs. LC 96-9317. (Classics Ser.). 386p. (C). 1996. pap. 9.95 (0-87220-339-5); lib. bdg. 34.95 (0-87220-340-9) Hackett Pub.
***Aristotle.** Aristotle: Nicomachean Ethics. Crisp, Roger, ed. (Cambridge Texts in the History of Philosophy Ser.). 180p. (C). 2000. 44.95 (0-521-63221-8); pap. 12.95 (0-521-63546-2) Cambridge U Pr.
Aristotle. Aristotle: On Sleep & Dreams. 2nd ed. Gallop, David, ed. & tr. by. from GRE. (Classical Texts Ser.). 1996. reprint ed. 59.99 (0-85668-674-3, Pub. by Aris & Phillips); reprint ed. pap. 28.00 (0-85668-675-1, Pub. by Aris & Phillips) David Brown.
— Aristotle: Selections. Fine, Gail & Irwin, Terence H., trs. LC 95-31470. 650p. (C). 1995. pap. 19.95 (0-915145-67-7); lib. bdg. 49.95 (0-915145-68-5) Hackett Pub.
— Aristotle Bks. I & II: On the Heavens. Leggatt, Stuart, ed. & tr. by. from GRE. (Classical Texts Ser.). 272p. 1995. 59.99 (0-85668-662-X, Pub. by Aris & Phillips); pap. 28.00 (0-85668-663-8, Pub. by Aris & Phillips) David Brown.
Aristotle. Aristotle on Fallacies. Poste, Edward, tr. & notes by. LC 86-29570. Orig. Title: Sophistici Elenchi. 252p. 1987. reprint ed. 35.00 (0-8240-6930-7) Garland.
Aristotle. Aristotle on Sleep & Dreams: A Text & Translation. Gallop, David, ed. & tr. by. 200p. 1990. 29.95 (0-921149-60-3) Broadview Pr.
***Aristotle.** Aristotle's Constitution of Athens (Aristotelous Athenaion Politeia) A Revised Text with an Introduction Critical & Explanatory Notes Testimonia & Indices. 1912. rev. ed. LC 99-23952. (GRE & ENG.). 2000. 75.00 (1-58477-004-X) Lawbk Exchange.
Aristotle. Aristotle's Physics: A Collection of Essays. Judson, Lindsay, ed. 296p. 1995. pap. text 24.00 (0-19-823602-6) OUP.
— Art of Poetry: A Greek View of Poetry & Drama. LC 83-45409. reprint ed. 37.50 (0-404-20007-9) AMS Pr.
— The Athenian Constitution. Rhodes, P. J., tr. & intro. by. LC 85-103504. (Classics Ser.). 208p. (C). 1984. pap. 9.95 (0-14-044431-9, Penguin Classics) Viking Penguin.
— Atheniensium Respublica. Kenyon, Frederic G., ed. (Oxford Classical Texts Ser.). 1920. text 14.95 (0-19-814506-3) OUP.
— Basic Works of Aristotle. McKeon, Richard P., ed. 1941. 45.00 (0-394-41610-4) Random.
— Categories & Propositions. Apostle, Hippocrates G., tr. & comment by. LC 80-80777. (Apostle Translations of Aristotle's Works: Vol. 3). Orig. Title: De Interpretatione. 157p. 1980. 25.00 (0-9602870-4-3); pap. 15.00 (0-9602870-5-1) Peripatetic.
— The Complete Works of Aristotle: The Revised Oxford Translation, 2 Vols., Set. Barnes, Jonathan, ed. LC 82-5317. (Bollingen Ser.: Vol. LXXI, No. 2). 3762p. 1983. text 85.00 (0-691-09950-2, Pub. by Princeton U Pr) Cal Prin Full Svc.
— Constitution of Athens. 2nd enl. rev. ed. LC 78-155630. (BCL Ser.: No. 1). reprint ed. 36.50 (0-404-00368-0) AMS Pr.
— Constitution of Athens. 2nd rev. ed. LC 72-9302. (Philosophy of Plato & Aristotle Ser.). (ENG & GRE.). 1974. reprint ed. 25.95 (0-405-04857-2) Ayer.
— De Anima. Hen, Zerahyah, tr. (Aristoteles Semitico-Latinus Ser.: No. 6). (HEB.). viii, 198p. 1993. 97.00 (90-04-09937-9, NLG135) Brill Academic Pubs.
— De Anima. Hicks, R. D., tr. LC 91-60431. (Great Books in Philosophy). 103p. 1991. pap. 6.95 (0-87975-610-1) Prometheus Bks.
— De Anima. Lawson-Tancred, Hugh, tr. & intro. by. (Penguin Classics Ser.). 256p. 1987. pap. 12.95 (0-14-044471-8, Penguin Classics) Viking Penguin.
— De Anima. Hicks, Robert Drew, tr. & intro. by. LC 75-13252. (History of Ideas in Ancient Greece Ser.). 1980. reprint ed. 47.95 (0-405-07289-9) Ayer.
— De Anima. Hicks, R. D., tr. & intro. by. lxxxiv, 626p. 1990. reprint ed. 160.00 incl. 3.5 hd (3-487-09368-5) G Olms Pubs.
— De Anima With Passages from Book I, Bks. II-III. rev. ed. Hamlyn, David W., tr. from GRE. & intro. by. (Clarendon Aristotle Ser.). 212p. (C). 1993. pap. text 23.00 (0-19-824085-6) OUP.
— De Anima Libri Tres. (GER.). xliii, 224p. 1970. reprint ed. 55.00 incl. 3.5 hd (0-318-70447-1) G Olms Pubs.
— De Animalibus: Michael Scot's Arabic-Latin Translation. Van Oppenraaij, Aafke M., ed. Scot, Michael, tr. LC 92-4288. (Aristoteles Semitico-Latinus Ser.: Vol. 5). (LAT.). xxvii, 504p. 1992. 189.00 (90-04-09603-5) Brill Academic Pubs.
— De Animalibus Pt. 2, Bks. XI-XIV: Parts of Animals. Scot, Michael, tr. from ARA. (Aristoteles Semitico-Latinus Ser.: Vol. 10). 600p. 1998. 161.00 (90-04-11070-4) Brill Academic Pubs.
— De Arte Poetica Liber. (GER.). xxix, 298p. 1964. reprint ed. pap. 70.00 incl. 3.5 hd (0-318-70448-X) G Olms Pubs.
— De Arte Poetica Liber. Vahlen, Johannes, ed. xxix, 298p. 1964. reprint ed. pap. 28.00 incl. 3.5 hd (0-318-70859-0) G Olms Pubs.
— De Partibus Animalium, Book I, & De Generatione Animalium, Book I with Passages from Book II, 1-3. rev. ed. Balme, D. M., tr. & notes by. (Clarendon Aristotle Ser.). 190p. 1992. pap. text 29.95 (0-19-875128-1) OUP.
— De Poetica Liber. (Documenta Semiotica Ser. 2). (GER.). 357p. 1976. reprint ed. 95.00 (3-487-05859-6) G Olms Pubs.
— De Sensu & De Memoria. Ross, George R., tr. LC 72-9301. (Philosophy of Plato & Aristotle Ser.). (ENG & GRE.). 1979. reprint ed. 21.95 (0-405-04856-4) Ayer.
— Dichtkunst. (Documenta Semiotica Ser. 2). (GER.). xx, 421p. 1973. reprint ed. 95.00 incl. 3.5 hd (3-487-04767-5) G Olms Pubs.
— The Ethics of Aristotle. Burnet, John, ed. LC 72-9282. (Philosophy of Plato & Aristotle Ser.). (ENG & GRE.). 1974. reprint ed. 44.95 (0-405-04833-5) Ayer.
— The Ethics of Aristotle, 2 vols. 4th ed. LC 72-9289. (Philosophy of Plato & Aristotle Ser.). (ENG & GRE., Illus.). 1974. reprint ed. 64.95 (0-405-04839-4) Ayer.
— The Ethics of Aristotle: The Nicomachean Ethics. rev. ed. Thomson, J. A. K., tr. 384p. 1955. pap. 10.95 (0-14-044055-0, Penguin Classics) Viking Penguin.
— Eudemian Ethics, Set. 2nd ed. Woods, Michael, tr. LC 92-15172. (Clarendon Aristotle Ser.: Bks. I, II, & VIII). 224p. 1992. pap. text 32.00 (0-19-824020-1, Clarendon Pr) OUP.
— The Fifth Book of the Nicomachaen Ethics of Aristotle. Jackson, Henry, ed. LC 72-9294. (Philosophy of Plato & Aristotle Ser.). (ENG & GRE.). 1980. reprint ed. 18.95 (0-405-04845-9) Ayer.
— A Guided Tour of Selections from Aristotle's Nicomachean Ethics. Biffle, Christopher, ed. LC 90-45138. vii, 167p. (C). 1991. pap. text 14.95 (0-87484-895-4, 895) Mayfield Pub.
— History of Animals, Bks. VII-X. Balme, D. M., ed. & tr. by. (Loeb Classical Library: No. 439). 605p. 1992. 18.95 (0-674-99483-3) HUP.
— Introduction to Aristotle. McKeon, Richard P., ed. (Modern Library College Editions). 667p. (C). 1965. pap. 7.50 (0-07-553652-8, T73) McGraw.
— Introduction to Aristotle. 19th ed. McKeon, Richard P., ed. & intro. by. LC 92-50208. 728p. 1992. 19.95 (0-679-60027-2) Modern Lib NY.
— Metafisica. Cancel, Miguel, ed. Azcarate, Patricio D., tr. (Nueva Austral Ser.: No. 27). (SPA.). 1991. pap. text 24.95 (84-239-1827-0) Elliots Bks.
— Metaphysics. Sachs, Joe, tr. & intro. by. 366p. (C). 1999. text 45.00 (1-888009-02-0); pap. text 24.95 (1-888009-03-9) Grn Lion Pr.
— Metaphysics. LC 99-461806. 560p. 1999. pap. 11.95 (0-14-044619-2, PuffinBks) Peng Put Young Read.
— Metaphysics. Hope, Richard, tr. 416p. 1952. pap. text 15.95 (0-472-06042-2, 06042, Ann Arbor Bks) U of Mich Pr.
— Metaphysics. Apostle, Hippocrates G., tr. & comment by. LC 79-88598. (Apostle Translations of Aristotle's Works: Vol. 1). 498p. 1979. reprint ed. 40.00 (0-9602870-0-0); reprint ed. pap. 20.00 (0-9602870-1-9) Peripatetic.
— Metaphysics. McMahon, John H., tr. LC 91-60430. (Great Books in Philosophy). 322p. (C). 1991. reprint ed. pap. 9.95 (0-87975-671-3) Prometheus Bks.
— Metaphysics, 2 vols. rev. ed. Ross, W. David, ed. 1,064p. 1924. text 170.00 (0-19-814107-6) OUP.
— Metaphysics, Bks. VII-X. Furth, Montgomery, tr. from GRE. LC 84-19159. (HPC Classics Ser.). 166p. (C). 1985. pap. 10.95 (0-915145-90-1); lib. bdg. 29.95 (0-915145-89-8) Hackett Pub.
— Metaphysics Book Beta & Book Kappa. Madigan, Arthur, tr. & comment by. LC 99-26129. (Clarendon Aristotle Ser.). 232p. 2000. text 60.00 (0-19-875105-2, Clarendon Pr); pap. text 24.95 (0-19-875106-0, Clarendon Pr) OUP.
— Metaphysics Books Gamma, Delta & Epsilon. 2nd ed. Kirwan, Christopher, tr. & notes by. LC 93-18390. (Clarendon Aristotle Ser.). 264p. (C). 1993. pap. text 28.00 (0-19-824087-2, Clarendon Pr) OUP.
— Metaphysics Books Zeta & Eta. Bostock, David, tr. & comment by. (Clarendon Aristotle Ser.). 318p. 1994. 65.00 (0-19-823946-7, Clarendon Pr); pap. text 28.00 (0-19-823947-5, Clarendon Pr) OUP.
— Meteorologicorum Libri Quattuor. (GER.). xlvii, 234p. 1967. reprint ed. 70.00 (0-318-70449-8) G Olms Pubs.
— A New Aristotle Reader. Ackrill, J. L., ed. 600p. 1987. pap. 18.95 (0-691-02043-4, Pub. by Princeton U Pr) Cal Prin Full Svc.
Aristotle. Nichomachean Ethics. (Classics of World Literature Ser.). 1997. pap. 5.95 (1-85326-461-X, 461XWW, Pub. by Wrdsworth Edits) NTC Contemp Pub Co.
Aristotle. Nicomachean Ethics. Chase, D. P., tr. LC 97-39242. (Thrift Editions Ser.). 256p. 1998. pap. 2.00 (0-486-40096-4) Dover.
Aristotle. Nicomachean Ethics. Rackham, H., tr. (Loeb Classical Library: No. 73). 684p. 1926. 18.95 (0-674-99081-1) HUP.
Aristotle. The Nicomachean Ethics. Ross, David, tr. & intro. by. (Oxford World's Classics Ser.). 320p. 1998. pap. 8.95 (0-19-283407-X) OUP.
Aristotle. Nicomachean Ethics. Ramsauer, Gottfried, ed. & comment by. LC 86-29529. 1987p. 1987. reprint ed. 80.00 (0-8240-6901-3) Garland.
Aristotle. Nicomachean Ethics. 2nd ed. Apostle, Hippocrates G., ed. LC 84-60009. (Apostle Translations of Aristotle's Works: Vol. 6). 372p. 1984. reprint ed. pap. 19.00 (0-911589-03-1) Peripatetic.
Aristotle. Nicomachean Ethics. 2nd ed. Apostle, Hippocrates G., ed. LC 84-60009. (Apostle Translations of Aristotle's Works: Vol. 6). 372p. 1991. reprint ed. 40.00 (0-911589-02-3) Peripatetic.
— Nicomachean Ethics. 2nd rev. ed. Irwin, Terence, tr. from GRE. LC 99-26709. 480p. (C). 2000. pap. 9.95 (0-87220-464-2); lib. bdg. 34.95 (0-87220-465-0) Hackett Pub.
Aristotle. Nicomachean Ethics, Bks. 8-11. Pakaluk, Michael, tr. from GEC. & comment by. LC 98-37479. (Clarendon Aristotle Ser.). 254p. 1999. text 65.00 (0-19-875103-6, Clarendon Pr); pap. text 19.95 (0-19-875104-4, Clarendon Pr) OUP.
— Nicomachean Ethics, Vol. 6. Greenwood, L. H., tr. LC 72-9290. (Philosophy of Plato & Aristotle Ser.). (ENG & GRE.). 1977. reprint ed. 18.95 (0-405-04842-4) Ayer.
— Nicomachean Ethics: Aristotle. Ostwald, Martin, ed. 352p. (C). 1962. pap. text 10.00 (0-02-389530-6, Pub. by P-H) S&S Trade.
***Aristotle.** On Aristotles's "Physics 8.6-10" (Ancient Commentators on Aristotle Ser.). 2000. 55.00 (0-8014-3787-3) Cornell U Pr.
Aristotle. On Coming-to-Be & Passing-Away (De Generatione et Corruptione) rev. ed. (GER.). xxxviii, 303p. 1982. reprint ed. lib. bdg. 70.00 (3-487-02901-4) G Olms Pubs.
— On Interpretation. (Loeb Classical Library). (ENG & GRE.). (C). write for info. (0-318-53020-1) HUP.
— On Poetry & Style. Grube, G. M. A., tr. & intro. by. LC 58-13827. (HPC Classics Ser.). 144p. (C). 1989. reprint ed. 21.95 (0-87220-073-6); reprint ed. pap. 6.95 (0-87220-072-8) Hackett Pub.
— On Rhetoric: A Theory of Civil Discourse. Kennedy, George A., tr. & intro. by. 368p. (C). 1992. pap. text 19.95 (0-19-506487-9) OUP.
— On the Art of Poetry. Bywater, Ingram & Murray, Gilbert, trs. 96p. 1920. pap. text 16.95 (0-19-814110-6) OUP.
— On the Constitution of Athens. 2nd ed. Poste, E., tr. & anno. by. xiv, 172p. 1993. reprint ed. 36.00 (0-8377-2520-8, Rothman) W S Hein.
— On the Heavens. Guthrie, W. K., tr. (Loeb Classical Library: No. 338). 420p. 1939. 18.95 (0-674-99372-1) HUP.
Aristotle. On the Parts of the Animals. Ogle, William, tr. & intro. by. LC 86-29613. 263p. 1987. reprint ed. 40.00 (0-8240-6925-0) Garland.
Aristotle. On the Soul. Apostle, Hippocrates G., tr. & comment by. LC 81-86481. (Apostle Translations of Aristotle's Works: Vol. 5). Orig. Title: De Anima. 225p. (C). 1981. pap. 15.00 (0-9602870-9-4); text 30.00 (0-9602870-8-6) Peripatetic.
— Opera Omnia, 5 vols. Dubnerum, F., tr. from LAT. (GER.). lvii, 3590p. 1973. reprint ed. 1185.00 (3-487-05019-6) G Olms Pubs.
— Organum, Hoc est Libri Omnes Ad Logicam Pertinentes, Graece et Latine. (GER.). 895p. 1967. reprint ed. write for info. (0-318-70450-1) G Olms Pubs.
— Organum, Hoc Est, Libri Omnes Ad Logicam Pertinentes, Graece et Latine. 895p. 1967. reprint ed. write for info. (0-318-70862-0) G Olms Pubs.
— Otot Ha-Shamayim: Samuel Ibn Tibbon's Hebrew Version of Aristotle's Meteorology: A Critical Edition. Fontaine, Resianne, tr. & intro. by. LC 94-48198. (Aristoteles Semitico-Latinus Ser.: Vol. 8). 1995. 114.50 (90-04-10258-2) Brill Academic Pubs.

An Asterisk (*) at the beginning of an entry indicates that the title is appearing for the first time.

— Physics. 166p. 1998. pap. 13.95 (0-9665678-3-8) Buy Books.

— Physics. Ross, W. David, ed. 1936. 135.00 (0-19-814109-2) OUP.

— Physics. 382p. 1999. pap. 9.95 (0-19-283586-6) OUP.

— Physics. Hope, Richard, tr. LC 61-5498. (Illus.). 256p. reprint ed. pap. 79.40 (0-8357-6443-5, 203581400097) Bks Demand.

— Physics. Apostle, Hippocrates G., ed. LC 80-80037. (Apostle Translations of Aristotle's Works: Vol. 2). 386p. 1980. reprint ed. pap. text 18.00 (0-9602870-3-5) Peripatetic.

— Physics, Bk. 8. Graham, Daniel W., tr. from GEC. & comment by. LC 98-49448. 227p. 1999. pap. text 24.95 (0-19-824092-9) OUP.

— Physics, Bk. 8. Graham, Daniel W., tr. from GEC. & comment by. LC 98-49448. Bk. VIII. 229p. 1999. text 70.00 (0-19-824091-0) OUP.

— Physics, Bks. III & IV. Hussey, Edward, tr. & notes by. (Clarendon Aristotle Ser.). (Illus.). 274p. 1983. pap. text 29.95 (0-19-872069-6, Clarendon Pr) OUP.

— The Pocket Aristotle. Kaplan, Justin E., ed. 400p. 1983. mass mkt. 5.99 (0-671-46377-2, WSP) PB.

— The Poetics. LC 94-5113. 342p. 1981. pap. text 26.00 (0-19-814024-X) OUP.

— The Poetics. MacLeish, Kenneth, tr. from GRE. LC 99-18986. (Dramatic Contexts Ser.). 64p. 1999. pap. 9.95 (1-55936-170-0, Pub. by Theatre Comm) Consort Bk Sales.

— The Poetics. Else, Gerald F., tr. LC 94-5113. 136p. 1967. pap. text 11.95 (0-472-06166-6, 06166) U of Mich Pr.

— Poetics. Janko, Richard, tr. from GRE. & notes by. LC 94-5113. (Classics Ser.). 261p. (Orig.). (C). 1987. pap. 9.95 (0-87220-033-7); lib. bdg. 34.95 (0-87220-034-5) Hackett Pub.

— Poetics. Butcher, S. H., tr. from GRE. (Mermaid Dramabook Ser.). 118p. (Orig.). 1961. pap. 6.00 (0-8090-0527-1) Hill & Wang.

— Poetics. Hutton, James, tr. from GRE. & intro. by. (Illus.). 120p. (Orig.). (C). 1982. pap. 11.25 (0-393-95216-9) Norton.

— Poetics. Buckley, Theodore, tr. LC 92-33258. (Great Books in Philosophy). 77p. (Orig.). 1992. pap. 5.95 (0-87975-776-0) Prometheus Bks.

— Poetics. Heath, Malcolm, tr. & intro. by. LC 97-138026. 144p. (Orig.). 1997. pap. 10.95 (0-14-044636-2) Viking Penguin.

— Poetics. Fyfe, W. Hamiltin et al, eds. Halliwell, Stephen et al, trs. LC 94-5113. (Loeb Classical Library: No. 199). 500p. 1995. text 18.95 (0-674-99563-5, L199) HUP.

— Poetics. Baxter, John & Atherton, J. P., eds. Whalley, George, tr. from GEC. & comment by. 224p. 1997. 55.00 (0-7735-1611-5, Pub. by McG-Queens Univ Pr); pap. 19.95 (0-7735-1612-3, Pub. by McG-Queens Univ Pr) CUP Services.

— Poetics. Halliwell, Stephen, ed. LC 86-4299. 381p. 1986. pap. 118.20 (0-608-05227-2, 206576400001) Bks Demand.

— Poetics. Halliwell, Stephen, ed. & intro. by. LC 98-36373. 384p. 1999. pap. text 22.00 (0-226-31394-8) U Ch Pr.

— Poetics. Butcher, S. H., ed. LC 96-47116. (Thrift Editions Ser.). (Illus.). 64p. (Orig.). 1997. reprint ed. pap. 1.00 (0-486-29577-X) Dover.

— La Poetique d'Aristote. Dacier, Andre, tr. & comment by.Tr. of Poetics. xxxii, 527p. 1976. reprint ed. 130.00 (3-487-05591-0) G Olms Pubs.

— The Politics. Lord, Carnes, tr. from GRE. LC 84-215. (Illus.). vi, 290p. (C). 1985. pap. 13.50 (0-226-02669-8) U Ch Pr.

— Politics. Rackham, H., tr. (Loeb Classical Library: No. 264). 712p. 1932. 18.95 (0-674-99291-1) HUP.

— Politics. Reeve, C. D. C., tr. from GRE. & intro. by. LC 97-46398. (Classics Ser.). 384p. (C). 1998. pap. 8.95 (0-87220-388-3); lib. bdg. 34.95 (0-87220-389-1) Hackett Pub.

— Politics. Barker, Ernest, tr. from GEC. LC 98-215869. (Oxford World's Classics Ser.). (Illus.). 470p. 1998. pap. 10.95 (0-19-283393-6) OUP.

— Politics. Gerson, Lloyd P. & Apostle, Hippocrates G., trs. from GEC. LC 86-60430. (Apostle Translations of Aristotle's Works: Vol. 7). 399p. 1986. pap. 17.00 (0-911589-05-8) Peripatetic.

— Politics. Ellis, William, tr. LC 86-70378. (Great Books in Philosophy). 259p. 1986. pap. text 7.95 (0-87975-346-3) Prometheus Bks.

— Politics, Bks. I & II. Saunders, Trevor J., tr. & comment by. (Clarendon Aristotle Ser.). 210p. 1996. text 55.00 (0-19-824892-X); pap. text 18.95 (0-19-824894-6) OUP.

— Politics, Bks. I[00ad]IV. rev. ed. LC 75-13363. (History of Ideas in Ancient Greece Ser.: Bks. 1-5). (ENG & GRE.). 1976. reprint ed. 56.95 (0-405-07291-0) Ayer.

— Politics, Bks. III & IV. Robinson, Richard, tr. & comment by. LC 97-158552. (Clarendon Aristotle Ser.). 186p. 1996. text 46.00 (0-19-823591-7) OUP.

— Politics, Bks. III & IV. Robinson, Richard, tr. & intro. by. LC 97-158552. (Clarendon Aristotle Ser.). 186p. 1996. pap. text 19.95 (0-19-823592-5) OUP.

— Politics, Bks. VII & VIII. Kraut, Richard, tr. & comment by. LC 97-11500. (Clarendon Aristotle Ser.). 240p. 1998. text 58.00 (0-19-875113-3, Clarendon Pr); pap. text 24.00 (0-19-875114-1) OUP.

— Politics, Vols. 5-6. Keyt, David, tr. from GEC. & comment by. LC 98-43637. 284p. 1999. text 72.00 (0-19-823535-6) OUP.

— Politics, Vols. 5-6 Keyt, David, tr. from GEC. & comment by. LC 98-43637. (Illus.). 284p. 1999. pap. text 19.95 (0-19-823536-4) OUP.

— The Politics: Aristotle. rev. ed. Sinclair, T. A., tr. & intro. by. (Classics Ser.). 512p. 1981. pap. 12.95 (0-14-044421-1, Penguin Classics) Viking Penguin.

— The Politics & the Constitution of Athens. 2nd rev. ed. Everson, Stephen, ed. LC 96-28275. (Cambridge Texts in the History of Political Thought Ser.). 325p. (C). 1996. pap., student ed. 10.95 (0-521-48400-6); pap., student ed. 29.95 (0-521-48243-7) Cambridge U Pr.

— The Politics of Aristotle. Phillips Simpson, Peter L., tr. & intro. by. LC 96-30395. 1997. 45.00 (0-8078-2327-9) U of NC Pr.

— The Politics of Aristotle. Phillips Simpson, Peter L., tr. & intro. by. LC 96-30395. 336p. (C). (gr. 13). 1997. pap. 14.95 (0-8078-4637-6) U of NC Pr.

— The Politics of Aristotle, 4 vols. LC 72-9297. (Philosophy of Plato & Aristotle Ser.). (ENG & GRE.). 1973. reprint ed. 169.95 (0-405-04848-3) Ayer.

— The Politics of Aristotle, 4 vols., 1. LC 72-9297. (Philosophy of Plato & Aristotle Ser.). (ENG & GRE.). 1976. reprint ed. 42.95 (0-405-04849-1) Ayer.

— The Politics of Aristotle, 4 vols., Vol. 2. LC 72-9297. (Philosophy of Plato & Aristotle Ser.). (ENG & GRE.). 1976. reprint ed. 42.95 (0-405-04850-5) Ayer.

— The Politics of Aristotle, 4 vols., Vol. 3. LC 72-9297. (Philosophy of Plato & Aristotle Ser.). (ENG & GRE.). 1976. reprint ed. 42.95 (0-405-04851-3) Ayer.

— The Politics of Aristotle, 4 vols., Vol. 4. LC 72-9297. (Philosophy of Plato & Aristotle Ser.). (ENG & GRE.). 1976. reprint ed. 42.95 (0-405-04852-1) Ayer.

— Poridat de las Poridades. Kasten, Lloyd A., ed. 94p. 1957. pap. 4.00 (0-942260-00-7) Hispanic Seminary.

— Posterior Analytics. Apostle, Hippocrates G., tr. & comment by. LC 81-80233. (Apostle Translations of Aristotle's Works: Vol. 4). 328p. (C). 1981. 35.00 (0-9602870-6-X); pap. 17.00 (0-9602870-7-8) Peripatetic.

— Posterior Analytics. 2nd ed. Barnes, Jonathan, tr. & comment by. (Clarendon Aristotle Ser.). (Illus.). 326p. (C). 1994. 60.00 (0-19-824088-0, 6050); pap. text 26.00 (0-19-824089-9) OUP.

— Posterior Analytics, Bks. 1 & 2. Forster, E. S. & Tredennick, Hugh, trs. (Loeb Classical Library: No. 391). (ENG & GRE.). (C). 15.50 (0-674-99430-2) HUP.

— Prior Analytics. Smith, Robin, ed. & tr. by. from GRE. LC 88-39877. (HPC Classics Ser.). 320p. (C). 1989. pap. 16.95 (0-87220-064-7) Hackett Pub.

— Prior Analytics. Smith, Robin, tr. from GRE. & intro. by. LC 88-39877. (HPC Classics Ser.). 320p. (C). 1989. lib. bdg. 37.95 (0-87220-065-5) Hackett Pub.

*Aristotle. The Problemata Physica Attributed to Aristotle: The Arabic Version of Hunain ibn Ishaq & the Hebrew Version of Moses ibn Tibbon. Filius, L. S., ed. LC 99-17460. (ARA & ENG.). 902p. 1999. 294.50 (90-04-11483-1) Brill Academic Pubs.

Aristotle. Psychology. LC 75-13253. (History of Ideas in Ancient Greece Ser.). (ENG & GRE.). 1976. reprint ed. 30.95 (0-405-07290-2) Ayer.

— The Rhetoric & Poetics of Aristotle. (Modern Library College Editions). 250p. (C). 1984. pap. text. write for info. (0-07-554602-7) McGraw.

— The Rhetoric of Aristotle, 2 vols. Sandys, John E., ed. LC 72-9304. (Philosophy of Plato & Aristotle Ser.). (ENG & GRE.). 1980. reprint ed. 66.95 (0-405-04858-0) Ayer.

— Secreta Secretorum. Copland, Robert, tr. LC 71-26095. (English Experience Ser.: No. 220). 72p. 1970. reprint ed. 20.00 (90-221-0220-3) Walter J Johnson.

— Selected Works. 3rd ed. Gerson, Lloyd P. & Apostle, Hippocrates G., trs. LC 91-62514. 723p. 1991. 45.00 (0-911589-14-7) Peripatetic.

— Selected Works. 3rd ed. Apostle, Hippocrates G. & Gerson, Lloyd P., eds. LC 91-62514. 723p. 1991. pap. text 20.00 (0-911589-13-9) Peripatetic.

— Topics With Excerpts from Related Texts, Bks. I & VIII. Smith, Robin, tr. & comment by. (Clarendon Aristotle Ser.). (Illus.). 242p. 1997. pap. text 32.00 (0-19-823942-4) OUP.

— Topics With Excerpts from Related Texts, Bks. I & VIII. Smith, Robin, tr. & comment by. (Clarendon Aristotle Ser.: Bks. 1 & 8). (Illus.). 242p. 1997. text 69.00 (0-19-823945-9) OUP.

— Treatise on Rhetoric. Buckley, Theodore, tr. from GRE. LC 95-11390. (Great Books in Philosophy). 277p. 1995. pap. 7.95 (0-87975-976-3) Prometheus Bks.

— The Works of Aristotle: The Famous Philosopher. LC 73-20613. (Sex, Marriage & Society Ser.). (Illus.). 268p. 1974. reprint ed. 23.95 (0-405-05792-X) Ayer.

*Aristotle & Jowett, Benjamin. Politics. LC 00-31841. (Thrift Editions Ser.). 2000. pap. write for info. (0-486-41424-8) Dover.

Aristotle & Michael of Ephesus. On the Movement & Progression of Animals: Aristotle & Michael of Ephesus. Preus, Anthony, tr. & intro. by. (Studien und Materialien Zur Geschichte der Philosophie Ser.: Vol. XXII). 209p. 1981. 50.70 (3-487-07073-1) G Olms Pubs.

Aristotle, et al. Aristotle & Xenophon on Democracy & Oligarchy. Moore, J. M., tr. & intro. by. LC 75-322050. 320p. 1975. 4.25 (0-7011-2060-6) Chatto & Windus.

— Imagination & Creativity. Potter, Clifton W., Jr., ed. LC 95-40504. (Lynchburg College Symposium Readings Ser.). 1995. pap. text. write for info. (0-7618-0127-8) U Pr of Amer.

— Poetics. LC 89-64029. (Apostle Translations of Aristotle's Works: Vol. 8). 167p. 1990. pap. 12.00 (0-911589-09-0) Peripatetic.

Aristotle, jt. auth. see Heidegger, Martin.

Aritonang, Jan S. Missions Schools in Batakland, Indonesia, 1861-1940. Boehlke, Robert R., ed. & tr. by. LC 93-41413. (Studies in Christian Mission: Vol. 10). 450p. 1993. 124.50 (90-04-09967-0, NLG190) Brill Academic Pubs.

Ariyama, J., jt. auth. see Sai, J.

Ariyan, Stephan. The Hand Book, Vol. 4. pap. 29.95 (0-9666930-0-0) RE Pubg CT.

Ariyavatkul, Dawn R. Understanding the Revelation. LC 94-72421. 1995. 8.95 (0-8158-0506-3) Chris Mass.

Ariyoshi, George R. With Obligation to All. LC 96-39505. (Illus.). 208p. 1997. text 20.00 (0-8248-1941-1) Ariyoshi Fnd.

*Ariyoshi, Rita. Hawaii: A Century of Travel Experience in Every Guide. (National Geographic Traveler Ser.). (Illus.). 2000. pap. 22.95 (0-7922-7944-1) Natl Geog.

Ariyoshi, Rita. Maui on My Mind. (Illus.). 256p. 1988. 39.95 (0-935180-16-8) Mutual Pub HI.

Ariyoshi, Sawako. The Doctor's Wife. Hironaka, Wakako & Kostant, Ann S., trs. from JPN. LC 80-85380. 184p. (C). 1992. reprint ed. pap. 10.00 (0-87011-465-4) Kodansha.

— The Kabuki Dancer: A Novel of the Beginnings of Kabuki. Brandon, James R., tr. 288p. 1994. 25.00 (4-7700-1783-9) Kodansha.

— The River Ki. Tahara, Mildred, tr. from JPN. LC 79-66240. 248p. 1982. pap. 10.00 (0-87011-514-6) Kodansha.

*Ariza, et al. Theories & Practices in ESOL. 295p. (C). 2000. per. 53.95 (0-7872-7187-X) Kendall-Hunt.

Ariza, Maria E., et al. Environmental Metal Pollutants, Reactive Oxygen Intermediaries & Genotoxicity: Molecular Approaches to Determine Mechanisms of Toxicity. LC 98-55187. 1999. write for info. (0-7923-8448-2) Kluwer Academic.

Ariza, Rene. Cuentos Breves y Brevisimos. Lorenzo, Alejandro, ed. LC 94-70348. (Coleccion Caniqui). (SPA., Illus.). 125p. Date not set. pap. write for info. (0-89729-728-8) Ediciones.

Arizaga, Lavora S. Exercising Your Legal Rights. (Orig.). 1983. pap. text 2.00 (0-915757-01-X) League Women Voters TX.

Arize, Augustine C. & Bonitsis, Theologos H., eds. Keynesian & Monetary Approaches to Managing Disequilibrium in Balance of Payments Accounts, 203. LC 98-15330. (Contributions in Economics & Economic History Ser.: Vol. 203). 280p. 2000. 69.50 (0-313-30826-8, Greenwood Pr) Greenwood.

Arize, Francis. Christian-Muslim Relations in the Twenty-First Century. (Occasional Papers Ser.). iii, 18p. 1998. pap. 3.95 (1-929218-04-4) Georgetwn U Ctr Muslim.

Arizmendi, Yareli, tr. see Gonzalez-Rubio, Javier.

Arizona Heart Institute Foundation Staff. The Arizona Heart Institute Foundation Cookbook: A Renaissance in Good Eating. 576p. 1993. pap. 19.95 (0-9635767-1-2) AZ Heart Inst.

Arizona Highways. Tombstone Chronicles: Tough Folks, Wild Times. 1998. pap. text 7.95 (0-916179-76-1) Ariz Hwy.

*Arizona Highways Staff. Wild West Assortment. 2000. pap. 7.95 (5-550-03093-4, Chambers LKC) LKC.

Arizona Highways Staff & West Group Editors. West's Arizona Revised Statutes. LC 99-162173. 1998. write for info. (0-314-23794-1) West Pub.

Arizona Highways Staff, jt. auth. see Tallon, James.

Arizona. Insurance Dept, et al. Arizona Circular Letters: Containing Circular Letters & Selected Orders of the Department of Insurance, & Selected Attorney General's Opinions. LC 97-69283. (Illus.). 1997. write for info. (0-89246-482-8) NILS Pub.

Arizona-Sonora Desert Museum (Tucson, Ariz.) Staff, jt. auth. see Lazaroff, David W.

Arizona-Sonora Desert Museum Staff. A Natural History of the Sonoran Desert. LC 99-33675. 650p. 1999. 55.00 (0-520-22029-3, Pub. by U CA Pr) Cal Prin Full Svc.

*Arizona-Sonora Desert Museum Staff. A Natural History of the Sonoran Desert. LC 99-33675. 650p. 1999. pap. 24.95 (0-520-21980-5, Pub. by U CA Pr) Cal Prin Full Svc.

Arizona State University Art Museum Staff. Art under Duress: El Salvador, 1980-Present. LC 94-47049. (ENG & SPA., Illus.). 128p. 1995. 36.00 (0-9644646-0-8) Ariz St U Art Mus.

Arizona State University Staff. Learning Media Design. 1997. pap. text 85.00 (1-57576-278-1) Que Educ & Trng.

Arizona State University Staff, et al. Soil Treatability Pilot Studies to Design & Model Soil Aquifer Treatment Systems. LC 97-17617. 1997. write for info. (0-89867-911-7, 90731) Am Water Wks Assn.

Arizona's Senior Adults Staff. Star in the Window: Reminiscences of the Years 1941-1945 & the Personal Impact of World War II. Smith, Nadine L. et al, eds. LC 95-25960. (Illus.). 154p. (Orig.). 1995. pap. write for info. (0-9617772-5-7) Scottsdale Cmnty Coll.

Arizpe, Lourdes, et al, eds. Population & the Environment: Rethinking the Debate. LC 94-2805. 352p. (C). 1994. pap. text 75.00 (0-8133-8843-0, Pub. by Westview) HarpC.

Arizpe, Lourdes, et al. Culture & Global Change: Social Perceptions of Deforestation in the Lacandona Rain Forest in Mexico. LC 95-44333. 128p. (C). 1996. text 47.50 (0-472-10652-X, 10652); pap. text 18.95 (0-472-08348-1, 08348) U of Mich Pr.

Arizpe, Victor, ed. see Santos, Francisco.

*Arizzoli-Clementel, Pierre. Views & Plans of the Petit Trianon at Versailles. 1998. 120.00 (2-909838-30-7) Antique Collect.

Arjat, Gillean S., jt. auth. see Wilson, Rebecca.

Arjava, Antti. Women & Law in Late Antiquity. 316p. 1998. reprint ed. pap. text 24.95 (0-19-815233-7) OUP.

Arjomand, Said A. Revolution & Counter-Revolution. 300p. (C). 1990. pap. text 14.95 (0-226-02686-8); lib. bdg. 34.95 (0-226-02683-3) U Ch Pr.

— The Shadow of God & the Hidden Imam: Religion, Political Order & Societal Change in Shiite Iran from the Beginning to 1890. LC 83-27196. (Publications of the Center for Middle Eastern Studies: No. 17). 368p. reprint ed. pap. 114.10 (0-608-09262-2, 205406400002) Bks Demand.

— The Shadow of God & the Hidden Inam: Religion, Political Order, & Societal Change in Shi'ite Iran from the Beginning to 1890. LC 83-27196. (Publications of the Center for Middle Eastern Studies: No. 17). (Illus.). xii, 356p. 1992. lib. bdg. 28.00 (0-226-02782-1) U Ch Pr.

— The Shadow of God & the Hidden Inam: Religion, Political Order, & Societal Change in Shi'ite Iran from the Beginning to 1890. LC 83-27196. (Publications of the Center for Middle Eastern Studies: No. 17). (Illus.). xii, 368p. (C). 1997. pap. text 18.00 (0-226-02784-8) U Ch Pr.

— The Turban for the Crown: The Islamic Revolution in Iran. 283p. 1998. pap. text 12.00 (0-7881-5235-1) DIANE Pub.

— The Turban for the Crown: The Islamic Revolution in Iran. (Studies in Middle Eastern History). 304p. 1989. pap. 13.95 (0-19-504258-1) OUP.

Arjomand, Said A., ed. Authority & Political Culture in Shi'ism. LC 87-10064. 393p. (C). 1988. text 67.50 (0-88706-638-0); pap. text 24.95 (0-88706-639-9) State U NY Pr.

— The Political Dimensions of Religion. LC 92-28757. (SUNY Series in Near Eastern Studies). 293p. (C). 1993. text 64.50 (0-7914-1557-0); pap. text 21.95 (0-7914-1558-9) State U NY Pr.

Arjona, Gloria, tr. see Galdos, Benito Perez.

Arjona-Tseng, Etilvia. A Bibliography of Pedagogy & Research in Interpretation & Translation. (Technical Report Ser.: No. 4). 128p. 1993. pap. text 10.00 (0-8248-1572-6) Sec Lang Tching.

Arjonillo, Rolando B., Jr. Conjugal Love & the Ends of Marriage, No. 23, Vol. 619. No. 23. xi, 373p. 1998. 54.95 (3-907597-92-3) P Lang Pubng.

— Conjugal Love & the Ends of Marriage: A Study of Dietrich von Hildebrand & Herbert Doms in the Light of the Pastoral Constitution "Gaudium et Spes" (European University Studies: Series 23, Vol. 619). xi, 373p. 1998. pap. 54.95 (3-906759-79-2) P Lang Pubng.

— Conjugal Love & the Ends of Marriage: A Study of Dietrich von Hildebrand & Herbert Doms in the Light of the Pastoral Constitution Gaudium et Spes. LC 98-20782. (European University Studies, Series 23: Series 23, Vol. 619). XI, 373p. (C). 1998. pap. text 54.95 (0-8204-3432-9) P Lang Pubng.

Arjouni, Jakob. And Still Drink More! Hollo, Anselm, tr. from GER. LC 94-32004. 156p. 1994. 16.95 (0-88064-161-4) Fromm Intl Pub.

— Happy Birthday, Turk! Hollo, Anselm, tr. from GER. LC 93-23518. 160p. 1993. 19.95 (0-88064-148-7) Fromm Intl Pub.

— One Death to Die: A Kayankaya Mystery. Hollo, Anselm, tr. from GER. LC 96-18593. (Kayankaya Mysteries Ser.). 192p. 1997. reprint ed. pap. 21.95 (0-88064-170-3) Fromm Intl Pub.

Arjunan, Krishman & Keong, Chee. Lipton & Hertzberg's Understanding Company Law in Hong Kong. LC 96-207799. 550p. 1996. pap. 80.00 (0-455-21422-0, Pub. by Cavendish Pubng) Gaunt.

*Arjunan, Palanisamy, et al. Advances in Olefin Polymerization: Emerging Frontiers. LC 99-47688. (ACS Symposium Ser.: 749). (Illus.). 224p. 1999. text 120.00 (0-8412-3614-3, Pub. by Am Chemical) OUP.

Ark, Bart Van, see Wagner, Karin, ed.

Ark, Bart Van, see Crafts, Nick, ed.

Ark, Dan Vander. Fit to Follow. 103p. pap., teacher ed. 20.10 (0-930265-78-5) CRC Pubns.

— Fit to Follow. (Illus.). 114p. pap. 11.25 (0-930265-77-7) CRC Pubns.

— Honest to God. (Illus.). 100p. pap., student ed. 11.25 (0-930265-40-8) CRC Pubns.

— Honest to God Manual. 109p. pap. 20.10 (0-930265-41-6) CRC Pubns.

— Live It! 99p. pap. 20.10 (0-930265-69-6) CRC Pubns.

— Live It! (Illus.). 111p. pap., student ed. 11.25 (0-930265-68-8) CRC Pubns.

Ark, James W. Van, see Hethcote, Herbert W. & Van Ark, James W.

Ark, Laurine. Writing from the Exterior Dramatic Perspective: A New Vision for Literature. Stoumen, Tatiana, ed. LC 95-83137. 170p. (Orig.). 1996. pap. 24.95 (0-9648009-1-8) Ft Tryon Pr.

Ark, O. J. English-Norwegian Military Dictionary. 459p. 1985. 95.00 (0-8288-1907-6, M15809) Fr & Eur.

Arkadie, Brain Van, see Havnevik, Kjell J. & Van Arkadie, Brain, eds.

Arkadievich, Gordin Y. Lev Tolstoi I Russkaia Istoriia. LC 92-23259. (RUS.). 152p. (Orig.). 1992. pap. 12.00 (1-55779-057-4) Hermitage Pubs.

Arkangeliskii, A. V. & Ponomarev, V. I. Fundamentals of General Topology. 1984. text 236.00 (90-277-1355-3) Kluwer Academic.

*Arkansas & NILS Publishing Company. Arkansas Insurance Laws. LC 98-65069. 1999. write for info. (0-89246-493-3) NILS Pub.

Arkansas Department of Planning Staff. Arkansas Natural Area Plan. (Illus.). xvii, 248p. (Orig.). 1974. pap. 11.95 (0-912456-07-8) Ozark Soc Bks.

Arkansas International Center Staff & CTIR Staff. Building Community: West African Style. (J). (gr. 6-9). 1994. ring bd. 35.95 incl. sl. (0-614-06470-8) U of Denver Teach.

Arkansas Supreme Court Committee on Criminal Jury. Arkansas Model Jury Instructions - Criminal, 2 vols., Set. 2nd ed. 1994. spiral bd. 140.00 (1-55834-143-9, MICHIE) LEXIS Pub.

Arkansas Symphony Orchestra Society Guild Staff, ed. Concerts in the Kitchen. 300p. 1980. spiral bd. 9.95 (0-9615625-0-1) AR Symphony Orch.

*Arkansas Times Staff, ed. Almanac of Arkansas History. 208p. 2000. 18.95 (0-87483-598-4) August Hse.

A

***Arkava, Mort.** Hiking the Anaconda-Pintler Wilderness. (Illus.). 139p. 2000. pap. 14.95 (*0-9677518-0-2*) M Arkava.

— Hiking the Bitterroots. 2nd rev. ed. LC 98-92401. (Illus.). 122p. 1998. pap. 12.95 (*0-9677518-1-0*) M Arkava.

Arkava, Mort, jt. auth. see Russell, John.

Arkebauer, James. Going Public: Everything You Need to Know to Take Your Company Public or Invest in an IPO or DPO. 3rd ed. LC 97-48651. 361p. 1998. pap. text 29.95 (*0-7931-2835-8*) Dearborn.

Arkebauer, James B. Leading Edge Business Planning for Entrepreneurs. LC 98-52091. 1999. pap. text 22.95 (*1-57410-117-X*) Dearborn.

— The McGraw-Hill Guide to Writing a High-Impact Business Plan: A Proven Blueprint for First-Time Entrepreneurs. LC 94-21739. 1994. 32.95 (*0-07-003059-6*); pap. 17.95 (*0-07-003060-X*) McGraw.

Arkelian, John. Northern Shadows: An Illustrated Guide to Canadian Vampires. (Illus.). 1998. pap. text 14.95 (*1-55082-209-8*, Pub. by Quarry Pr) LPC InBook.

Arkell, Anthony J. A History of the Sudan: From the Earliest Times to 1821. LC 73-13413. (Illus.). 252p. 1974. reprint ed. lib. bdg. 38.50 (*0-8371-7129-6*, ARHS, Greenwood Pr) Greenwood.

— Prehistory of the Nile Valley. LC 76-361917. (Handbuch Der Orientalistik Ser.). ix, 55 p. 1975. 36.00 (*90-04-04397-7*) Brill Academic Pubs.

Arkell, Julie. Classic Rum. (Classic Drinks Ser.). (Illus.). 1999. 16.95 (*1-85375-298-3*, Pub. by Prion) Trafalgar.

***Arkell, Julie.** New World Wines: The Complete Guide. (Illus.). 224p. 2000. 39.95 (*0-304-35160-1*, Pub. by Cassell) Sterling.

Arkell, W. J., jt. auth. see Sandford, Kenneth S.

***Arkenberg, Rebecca N., et al.** The Art of Renaissance Europe: Resource for Educators. LC 00-37992. (Illus.). 2000. write for info. (*0-87099-953-2*) Metro Mus Art.

Arkenbout, Gerard J. Melt Crystallization Technology. LC 94-60013. 400p. 1995. pap. text 99.95 (*1-56676-181-6*) Technomic.

Arkeryd, L. Nonequilibrium Problems in Many-Particle Systems: Lectures Given at the 3rd Session of the Centro Internazionale Metematico Estive held in Montecatini, Italy, June 1992. LC 93-5230. (Lecture Notes in Mathematics Ser.: Vol. 1551). 1993. 37.95 (*0-387-56945-6*) Spr-Verlag.

Arkeryd, L., et al. Nonstandard Analysis: Theory & Applications: Lectures Given at the NATO Advanced Study Institute, Nonstandard Analysis & Its Applications, at the International Centre for Mathematical Sciences, Edinburgh, July 1996. LC 97-14127. (NATO ASI Series. Series C, Mathematical & Physical Sciences). 1997. text 197.50 (*0-7923-4586-X*) Kluwer Academic.

Arkes. Psychological Theories of Motivation. (Psychology Ser.). 1977. mass mkt. 19.50 (*0-8185-0216-9*) Brooks-Cole.

Arkes, Hadley. First Things: An Inquiry into the First Principles of Morals & Justice. LC 85-43267. 480p. 1986. text 65.00 (*0-691-07702-9*, Pub. by Princeton U Pr); pap. text 18.95 (*0-691-02247-X*, Pub. by Princeton U Pr) Cal Prin Full Svc.

— The Return of George Sutherland: Restoring a Jurisprudence of Natural Rights. 312p. 1994. pap. text 18.95 (*0-691-01628-3*, Pub. by Princeton U Pr) Cal Prin Full Svc.

— The Return of George Sutherland: Restoring a Jurisprudence of Natural Rights. LC 94-219. 312p. (C). 1994. text 45.00 (*0-691-03472-9*, Pub. by Princeton U Pr) Cal Prin Full Svc.

Arkfeld, Michael R. The Digital Practice of Law: A Practical Reference Applying Technology Concepts to the Practice of Law. 4th rev. ed. LC 98-94865. (Digital Practice Ser.). (Illus.). xv, 350p. 1999. pap. text 49.95 (*0-9669347-0-9*, 0001) Law Partner.

Arkham, Candice. Deadly Friendship. large type ed. (Linford Mystery Library). 1991. pap. 16.99 (*0-7089-7074-5*) Ulverscroft.

Arkham House Staff, ed. see Ruber, Peter A.

Arkhangel'skii, A. V. Topological Function Spaces. (C). 1991. text 137.50 (*0-7923-1531-6*) Kluwer Academic.

Arkhipov, Andrey. Po Tu Styoronu Sambationa: Etiudy o Russko-Evreiskikh Kul'turnykh, Iasykovykh i Literaturnykh Kontaktakh V V-XVI Vekakh. (Monuments of Early Russian Literature Ser.: Vol. 9). (RUS.). 296p. (Orig.). 1995. pap. 20.00 (*1-57201-011-8*) Berkeley Slavic.

Arkhipov, Andrey & Polinskaya, Irene, eds. Issledovaniia Po Slavianskomu Fol'kloru I Narodnoi Kul'ture. (Studies in Slavic Folklore & Folk Culture: Vol. 2). (RUS.). 162p. 1997. pap. text 15.00 (*1-57201-031-2*) Berkeley Slavic.

— Issledovaniia Po Slavianskomu Fol'klory I Narodnoi Kul'ture. (Studies in Slavic Folklore & Folk Culture: Vol. 1). (RUS.). 140p. 1997. pap. text 15.00 (*1-57201-030-4*) Berkeley Slavic.

Arkhipova, Irina R. Drosophila Retrotransposons. Lyubomirskaya, Nataliya V. et al, eds. LC 94-44104. (Molecular Biology Intelligence Unit Ser.). 134p. 1995. 69.00 (*1-57059-192-X*) Landes Bioscience.

Arkhiv, Rossiiskii G. Tsentral'nyi Gosudarstvennyi Arkhiv Sovetskii Armii Putevoditel'v Dvukh Tomakh, Tom I. Kariaveva, T. F. & Stegantsev, M. V., eds. (RUS.). 422p. 1991. 59.95 (*1-879944-02-2*) East View Pubns.

— Tsentral'nyi Gosudarstvennyi Arkhiv Sovetskii Armii, Putevoditel'v Dvukh Tomakh, Tom II. Kariaveva, T. F. & Stegantsev, M. V., eds. (RUS.). 531p. 1993. 59.95 (*1-879944-03-0*) East View Pubns.

Arkhurst, Joyce C. Adventures of Spider: West African Folk Tales. (J). 1992. 13.15 (*0-606-02228-7*, Pub. by Turtleback) Demco.

Arkin. Stochastic Models of Control & Economic Dynamics. LC 96-37173. 216p. 1987. 114.00 (*0-12-062080-4*) Acad Pr.

***Arkin, Alan.** Cassie Loves Beethoven. 170p. (J). 2000. lib. bdg. 15.49 (*0-7868-2489-1*, Pub. by Disney Pr) Little.

Arkin, Alan. Cassie Loves Beethoven. 176p. (J). 2000. 16.99 . (*0-7868-0564-1*) Little.

— The Lemming Condition. LC 75-6296. (Illus.). 64p. (J). (gr. 4 up). 1976. 13.00 (*0-06-020133-9*) HarpC Child Bks.

— The Lemming Condition. LC 89-7418. 64p. 1989. pap. 9.00 (*0-06-250048-1*, Perennial) HarperTrade.

— The Lemming Condition. (J). 1976. 14.20 (*0-606-04266-0*, Pub. by Turtleback) Demco.

— One Present from Flekman's. LC 98-20346. (Illus.). 32p. (J). (gr. k-3). 1999. 15.95 (*0-06-024530-1*); lib. bdg. 14.89 (*0-06-024531-X*) HarpC Child Bks.

— Tony's Hard Work Day. LC 76-183161. (Illus.). 32p. (J). (gr. k-3). 1972. 12.95 (*0-06-020137-1*) HarpC Child Bks.

Arkin, Anthony D. Captain Hawaii. LC 94-2683. 256p. (YA). (gr. 6-9). 1997. pap. 3.95 (*0-06-440583-4*, HarpTrophy) HarpC Child Bks.

Arkin, Arthur M. Sleep-Talking: Psychology & Psychophysiology. LC 81-3300. (Illus.). 640p. 1982. text 99.95 (*0-89859-031-0*) L Erlbaum Assocs.

Arkin, Ed. Creative Chord Substitutions. Stang, Aaron, ed. 124p. (C). 1985. pap. text 15.00 (*0-7692-1287-5*, PMP00047) Wrner Bros.

Arkin, Elaine B. & Funkhouser, Judith E., eds. Communicating about Alcohol & Other Drugs: Strategies for Reaching Populations at Risk. (Illus.). 402p. (Orig.). (C). 1996. reprint ed. pap. text 45.00 (*0-7881-2967-8*) DIANE Pub.

Arkin, Frieda. Complete Book of Kitchen Wisdom. 1993. 9.98 (*0-88365-823-2*) Galahad Bks.

— The Essential Kitchen Gardener. (Illus.). 346p. 1995. pap. 14.95 (*0-8050-1650-3*, Owl) H Holt & Co.

— Essential Kitchen Gardner. 1996. 10.98 (*0-88365-939-5*) Galahad Bks.

Arkin, G. F. & Taylor, H. M., eds. Modifying the Root Environment to Reduce Crop Stress. LC 81-69116. 420p. 1981. text 44.50 (*0-916150-40-2*, M1481) Am Soc Ag Eng.

Arkin, Linda, ed. Spotlight on Turkey: Continuity & Change. 200p. (C). 1992. ring bd. 30.00 (*0-944675-49-2*) Amer Forum.

Arkin, Lois & Crenshaw, Richard. Sustainable Cities: Concepts & Strategies for Eco-City Development. Walter, Bob et al, eds. LC 92-90568. (Illus.). 354p. (Orig.). 1992. pap. text 20.00 (*0-9633511-0-9*) Eco-Home Media.

Arkin, Lois, jt. auth. see Cohen, Lottie.

***Arkin, Michael B. & Laskin, Franklin T.** From the Depth of the Mines Came the Law: A History of the Bench & Bar of Calaveras County. (Illus.). 160p. 2000. pap. 15.95 (*1-884995-16-0*) Word Dancer.

Arkin, Ronald C. Behavior-Based Robotics. LC 97-18389. (Complex Adaptive Systems Ser.). (Illus.). 464p. 1998. 52.50 (*0-262-01165-4*, Bradford Bks) MIT Pr.

Arkin, Stanley S. & Dudley, Earl C. Business Crime: Criminal Liability of the Business Community, 7 vols. 1981. ring bd. 1380.00 (*0-8205-1265-6*) Bender.

Arkin, Stephen, ed. see Weiss, Daniel.

Arkin, V. I., et al, eds. Stochastic Optimization. (Lecture Notes in Control & Information Sciences: Vol. 81). (Illus.). 770p. 1986. 118.95 (*0-387-16659-9*) Spr-Verlag.

Arkin, William M. Research Guide to Current Military & Strategic Affairs. 232p. 1981. 19.95 (*0-89758-032-X*); pap. 9.95 (*0-89758-025-7*) Inst Policy Stud.

— Taking Stock: Worldwide Deployments, 1998. 1998. pap. 20.00 (*1-893340-14-7*) Natl Resources Defense Coun.

— The U. S. Military Online: A Directory for Internet Access to the Department of Defense. LC 97-11163. 256p. (Orig.). 1997. pap. 29.95 (*1-57488-143-4*) Brasseys.

— The U. S. Military Online: A Directory for Internet Access to the Department of Defense. 2nd ed. LC 98-22207. (Illus.). 256p. (Orig.). 1998. pap. 32.95 (*1-57488-178-7*) Brasseys.

Arkin, William M., et al, eds. The Encyclopedia of the U. S. Military. 1072p. 1990. text 39.95 (*0-88730-215-7*, HarpBusn) HarpInfo.

Arkin, William M. & Norris, Robert S. The Internet & the Bomb: A Research Guide to Policy & Information about Nuclear Weapons. 159p. 1997. pap. 19.95 (*1-893340-16-3*) Natl Resources Defense Coun.

Arking, Robert. Biology of Aging: Observations & Principles. 2nd ed. LC 98-4247. (Illus.). (C). 1998. text 62.95 (*0-87893-043-4*) Sinauer Assocs.

Arkins, Anne & Harrell, Gary. Watchmen on the Walls: Praying Character into Your Child. 112p. 1998. 12.99 (*1-57673-373-4*, Multnomah Bks) Multnomah Pubs.

Arkins, Brian. Builders of My Soul. 1990. lib. bdg. 69.00 (*0-389-20913-9*) B&N Imports.

***Arkins, Brian.** Greek & Roman Themes in Joyce. LC 99-40752. (Studies in Irish Literature Ser.). 1999. write for info. (*0-7734-8035-8*) E Mellen.

— An Interpretation of the Poems of Catullus. LC 99-43722. (Studies in Classics: Vol. 11). 148p. 1999. text 69.95 (*0-7734-7890-6*) E Mellen.

Arkins, Brian. Sexuality in Catullus. (Altertumswissenschaftliche Texte und Studien: Vol. 8). 272p. 1982. 37.70 (*3-487-07277-7*) G Olms Pubs.

***Arkins, Diane C.** Halloween: Romantic Art & Customs of Yesteryear. (Illus.). 2000. pap. 5.95 (*1-56554-835-3*) Pelican.

— Halloween: Romantic Arts & Customs of Yesteryear. (Illus.). 2000. 19.95 (*1-56554-712-8*) Pelican.

Arkinson, David R. Hope Springs Eternal: Surviving a Chronic Illness. LC 98-10631. 200p. 1999. pap. 12.95 (*0-87604-408-9*, 502) ARE Pr.

Arkinstall, Steve, jt. ed. see Watson, Steve.

Arkkelin, Daniel, jt. auth. see Veitch, Russell.

Arkle, Bill. Transformation: The Poetry of Spiritual Consciousness. 180p. (C). 1988. pap. 40.00 (*0-947612-28-9*, Pub. by Rivelin Grapheme Pr) St Mut.

Arkle, P. The Railway Cat & the Ghost. (Illus.). (J). mass mkt. 6.95 (*0-340-69993-0*, Pub. by Hodder & Stought Ltd) Trafalgar.

— Railway Cat on the Run. (Illus.). (J). 1996. mass mkt. 6.95 (*0-340-67287-0*, Pub. by Hodder & Stought Ltd) Trafalgar.

— Railway Cat's Secret. (Illus.). (J). 1996. mass mkt. 7.95 (*0-340-67288-9*, Pub. by Hodder & Stought Ltd) Trafalgar.

***Arkless, Jan.** The Bride's Guide: How to Arrange a Wonderful Wedding. (Illus.). 160p. 2001. pap. 7.95 (*0-7160-2048-3*, Pub. by Elliot RW Bks) Midpt Trade.

— How to Boil an Egg: . . . And 184 Other Simple Recipes for One. 2nd ed. (Illus.). 192p. 2001. pap. 8.95 (*0-7160-2073-4*, Pub. by Elliot RW Bks) Midpt Trade.

Arkoff, Abe. The Illuminated Life. LC 94-9590. 464p. 1994. pap. text 63.00 (*0-205-15008-X*) Allyn.

— Psychology & Personal Growth. 3rd ed. 1987. text 36.00 (*0-205-10533-5*, H05333) Allyn.

— Psychology & Personal Growth. 3rd ed. 1987. pap. text, wbk. ed. 34.00 (*0-205-10534-3*, H0534-1) Allyn.

Arkoff, Abe & Goud, Nelson. Psychology & Personal Growth. 5th ed. LC 96-40313. 375p. 1997. pap. 63.00 (*0-205-26102-7*) Allyn.

Arkoff, Sam & Trubo, Richard. Flying Through Hollywood by the Seat of My Pants. (Illus.). 304p. 1992. 18.95 (*1-55972-107-3*, Birch Ln Pr) Carol Pub Group.

***Arkoff, Samuel Z.** Flying Through Hollywood by the Seat of My Pants. (Illus.). 256p. 2000. pap. 20.00 (*1-887664-39-4*, Pub. by Midnght Marquee Pr) Koen Bk Distributors.

Arkon, Nicholas. Basic Guide to 1A2 Key Telephone Installation. rev. ed. LC 73-85629. (ABC of the Telephone Ser.: Vol. 15). (Illus.). 84p. (C). 1988. pap. 24.95 (*1-56016-014-4*) ABC TeleTraining.

Arkou-Tewia, Rose E. Stories from Africa: Tsie Na Atsie. (Illus.). 80p. (J). 1993. pap. 14.95 (*0-904693-45-7*, Pub. by Temple Lodge) Anthroposophic.

Arkoun, Mohammed. Rethinking Islam. 139p. 1996. 59.95 (*0-614-21447-5*, 1075); pap. 19.95 (*0-614-21446-7*, 1075); pap. 3.95 (*0-614-21445-9*, 1411) Kazi Pubns.

— Rethinking Islam: Common Questions, Uncommon Answers. 160p. (C). 1994. pap. 26.00 (*0-8133-2294-4*, Pub. by Westview) HarpC.

Arkow, Phil, jt. auth. see Ascione, Frank R.

Arkowitz, Hal & Messer, Stanley, eds. Psychoanalytic Therapy & Behavior Therapy: Is Integration Possible? 370p. 1984. 62.50 (*0-306-41578-X*, Plenum Trade) Perseus Pubng.

Arksey, Hilary. RSI & the Experts: The Construction of Medical Knowledge. LC 98-230629. vii, 286 p. 1998. pap. 26.95 (*1-85728-813-0*) UCL Pr Ltd.

— RSI & the Experts: The Construction of Medical Knowledge. LC 98-230629. 1999. 75.00 (*1-85728-864-5*) UCL Pr Ltd.

Arksey, Neil. Surfer's Result. (Illus.). 128p. (J). pap. 7.95 (*0-14-130206-2*, Pub. by Pnguin Bks Ltd) Trafalgar.

Arkun, Y., et al. Model Based Process Control. (IFAC Workshop Ser.: Vol. 82). 465p. 1989. 94.00 (*0-08-035735-0*, Pergamon Pr) Elsevier.

Arkun, Y., jt. auth. see Shah, S. L.

Arkush, Allan. Moses Mendelssohn & the Enlightenment. LC 93-39401. (SUNY Series in Judaica: Hermeneutics, Mysticism, & Religion). 304p. (C). 1994. text 64.50 (*0-7914-2071-X*); pap. text 21.95 (*0-7914-2072-8*) State U NY Pr.

Arkush, Allan, tr. see Mendelssohn, Moses.

Arkush, Allan, tr. see Scholem, Gershom.

***Arkush, Brooke.** Archaeological Investigations at Mosquito Willie Rockshelter & Lower Lead Mine Hills Cave, Great Salt Lake Desert, Utah. (Archives of Great Basin Prehistory Ser.: Vol. 2). (Illus.). 149p. (C). 1998. pap. text 16.25 (*1-55567-751-7*) Coyote Press.

Arkush, Brooke S. The Archaeology of CA-Mno-2122: A Study of Pre-Contact & Post-Contact Lifeways among the Mono Basin Paiute. LC 95-3282. (Publications in Anthropology: Vol. 31). 1995. pap. 48.00 (*0-520-09793-9*, Pub. by U CA Pr) Cal Prin Full Svc.

Arkush, Brooke S., jt. auth. see Sutton, Mark.

***Arkush, Michael.** Fairways & Dreams: 25 of the World's Greatest Golfers & the Fathers Who Inspired Them. LC 98-11090. (Illus.). 166p. 1998. 18.95 (*1-55853-597-7*) Rutledge Hill Pr.

— I Remember Payne Stewart: Personal Memories of Golf's Most Dapper Champion by the People Who Knew Him Best. 192p. 2000. 18.95 (*1-58182-082-8*, Cumberland Hearthside) Cumberland Hse.

Arkush, Michael. Rush. 1993. mass mkt. 4.99 (*0-380-77539-5*, Avon Bks) Morrow Avon.

— Tim Allen Laid Bare: Unauthorized. (Orig.). 1995. mass mkt. 5.99 (*0-380-78260-X*, Avon Bks) Morrow Avon.

Arkush, R. David. Fei Xiaotong & Sociology in Revolutionary China. (East Asian Monographs: No. 98). 409p. (C). 1981. 30.00 (*0-674-29815-2*) HUP.

Arkush, R. David & Lee, Leo O., eds. Land Without Ghosts: Chinese Impressions of America from the Mid-Nineteenth Century to the Present. 1989. pap. 17.95 (*0-520-08424-1*, Pub. by U CA Pr) Cal Prin Full Svc.

Arkwright, Richard. The Queen Anne's Gate Mystery: A Novel, 2 vols. LC 75-32733. (Literature of Mystery & Detection Ser.). 1976. reprint ed. 41.95 (*0-405-07863-3*) Ayer.

Arky, Ronald A. & Kettyle, William M. Endocrine Pathophysiology: A Problem-Oriented Approach. LC 98-18408. (Illus.). 250p. 1998. pap. text 26.95 (*0-397-51376-3*) Lppncott W & W.

Arland, Marcel. Terre Natale. (FRE.). 256p. 1972. pap. 10.95 (*0-7859-1715-2*, 2070362507) Fr & Eur.

— Zelie dans le Desert. (FRE.). 160p. 1974. pap. 10.95 (*0-7859-1774-8*, 2070365344) Fr & Eur.

Arland, Marcel, ed. see Marivaux, Pierre Carlet de Chamblain de.

Arlandson, James M. Women, Class, & Society in Early Christianity: Models from Luke-Acts. LC 96-48298. 238p. (C). 1997. 24.95 (*1-56563-181-1*) Hendrickson MA.

Arlart, Ingolf P., et al, eds. Magnetic Resonance Angiography. LC 95-31126. (Medical Radiology Ser.). 1995. (*3-540-56896-4*) Spr-Verlag.

— Magnetic Resonance Angiography. (Medical Radiology, Diagnostic Imaging & Radiation Oncology Ser.). (Illus.). 440p. 1995. 239.00 (*0-387-56896-4*) Spr-Verlag.

Arlaud, G., et al, eds. International Complement Workshop, 12th Abstracts, Chamonix, September 1987. (Journal: Complement & Inflammation: Vol. 4, No. 3-4). iv, 132p. 1987. pap. 77.50 (*3-8055-4674-2*) S Karger.

Arlaud, Odile. Dictionnaire pour Rever, S'Amuser et Chanter. 1991. write for info. (*0-7859-7673-6*, 2036515150) Fr & Eur.

Arledge, Amy A., jt. ed. see McBride, William M.

Arledge, G., ed. see Richards, C.

Arledge, Rick & Friedman, David. Dynamic Fund-Raising Projects. 153p. 1992. ring bd. 50.00 (*0-944496-35-0*) Precept Pr.

Arlee, Johnny. Over a Century of Moving to the Drum: Salish Indian Celebrations on the Flathead Indian Reservation. Bigart, Robert, ed. LC 99-52175. (Illus.). 104p. 1998. pap. 14.95 (*0-917298-57-8*) MT Hist Soc.

Arlen, jt. auth. see Marcove, Ralph C.

Arlen, Alice. In the Maine Woods: An Insider's Guide to Traditional Maine Sporting Camps. 2nd ed. LC 98-3276. (Illus.). 280p. 1998. reprint ed. pap. 17.00 (*0-88150-417-3*, Pub. by Countryman) Norton.

— In the Maine Woods: The Insider's Guide to Traditional Maine Sporting Camps. Lyons, Lisa, ed. 296p. 1994. pap. 14.95 (*0-9640901-0-4*) AJ & Co.

***Arlen, Alice.** She Took to the Woods: Louise Dickinson Rich, a Biography. 176p. 2000. pap. 14.95 (*0-89272-483-8*) Down East.

Arlen, Karen, et al. Days of Gold: Songs of the California Gold Rush. (Illus.). 99p. 1998. pap. 20.00 (*0-9648362-5-4*) Calicanto Assocs.

Arlen, Karen W., et al. They Came Singing: Songs from California's History. 3rd ed. (Illus.). ii, 110p. (J). (gr. 3-8). 1995. pap. 20.00 (*0-9648362-2-X*) Calicanto Assocs.

Arlen, Michael J. Ghost Stories. Reginald, R. & Menville, Douglas A., eds. LC 75-46249. (Supernatural & Occult Fiction Ser.). 1976. reprint ed. lib. bdg. 17.95 (*0-405-08109-X*) Ayer.

— The Green Hat. 1992. reprint ed. lib. bdg. 18.95 (*0-89966-961-1*) Buccaneer Bks.

— Living Room War. Thompson, Robert J., ed. LC 97-3070. (Television Ser.). xii, 242p. 1997. reprint ed. pap. 17.95 (*0-8156-0466-1*) Syracuse U Pr.

— London Venture. Van Thal, Herbert, ed. 1968. pap. 4.95 (*0-304-92614-0*) Dufour.

— Passage to Ararat. LC 95-81171. 300p. 1996. reprint ed. pap. 15.00 (*1-886913-05-6*) Ruminator Bks.

— The View from Highway 1: Essays on Television. Thompson, Robert J., ed. LC 97-1277. (Television Ser.). 293p. 1997. reprint ed. pap. 17.95 (*0-8156-0467-X*) Syracuse U Pr.

Arlen, Myron & Marcove, Ralph C. Surgical Management of Soft Tissue Sarcomas. (Illus.). 344p. 1987. text 142.00 (*0-7216-1399-3*, W B Saunders Co) Harcrt Hlth Sci Grp.

Arlen, Shelley. The Cambridge Ritualists: An Annotated Bibliography of the Works by & about Jane Ellen Harrison, Gilbert Murray, Francis M. Cornford, & Arthur Bernard Cook. LC 90-47304. (Illus.). 424p. 1990. 47.50 (*0-8108-2373-X*) Scarecrow.

***Arlena-Kai.** Hypnosis of a Lover. 1999. pap. 10.00 (*0-9677615-0-6*) A Lopez.

Arler, Finn & Svenning, Ingeborg. Cross-Cultural Protection of Nature & the Environment. LC 98-184861. 248p. 1998. 30.50 (*87-7838-347-1*, Pub. by Odense Univ) Intl Spec Bk.

Arles, Siga. Theological Education for the Mission of the Church in India, 1847-1987: Theological Education in Relation to the Identification of the Task of Mission & the Development of Ministries in India, 1947-1987. LC 91-31294. (Illus.). XX, 558p. 1992. 67.00 (*3-631-44129-0*) P Lang Pubng.

Arlett, Robert. Epic Voices: Inner & Global Impulse in the Contemporary American & British Novel. LC 95-49127. 192p. 1996. 33.50 (*0-945636-81-4*) Susquehanna U Pr.

***Arlette, Joan.** Maybe, Molly & Must-Be-Red. (Illus.). 8p. (J). (ps-5). 1998. mass mkt. 7.00 (*0-9700121-0-1*, 001) Light Years.

Arley, Catherine. Tantalus. 1982. pap. 5.25 (*0-8222-1110-6*) Dramatists Play.

Arlidge, A. Fraud. 448p. 1985. 80.00 (*0-08-039163-X*) Macmillan.

Arlie, Jean-Pierre. Commodity Thermoplastics: Technical & Economic Characteristics. (Illus.). 112p. (C). 1991. 195.00 (*2-7108-0591-X*, Pub. by Edits Technip) Enfield Pubs NH.

Arlie, Jean-Pierre, ed. Synthetic Rubbers: Processes & Economic Data. 128p. (C). 1992. pap. 220.00 (*2-7108-0619-3*, Pub. by Edits Technip) Enfield Pubs NH.

Arlien-Soborg, Peter. Solvent Neurotoxicity. 400p. 1991. lib. bdg. 195.00 (*0-8493-6234-2*, RC347) CRC Pr.

An Asterisk (*) at the beginning of an entry indicates that the title is appearing for the first time.

Arlin, Mary A. Esquisse de l'Histore de l'Harmonie. (Harmonologia Ser.: No. 7).Tr. of An English-Language Translation of the Francois-Joseph Fetis History of Harmony. (FRE.). 1994. lib. bdg. 54.00 (*0-945193-51-3*) Pendragon NY.

Arlin, Mary I., et al. Music Sources: A Collection of Excerpts & Complete Movements. 2nd ed. 592p. (C). 1989. pap. text 50.00 (*0-13-608282-3*) P-H.

Arlin, Stephen. Raw Power! Building Strength & Muscle Naturally. large type ed. (Illus.). 136p. 1998. pap. 11.95 (*0-9653533-1-1*) Maul Bros.

Arlin, Stephen, et al. Nature's First Law: The Raw-Food Diet. 2nd rev. ed. 232p. (Orig.). 1996. pap. 14.95 (*0-9653533-0-3*) Maul Bros.

Arlin, Stephen, ed. see Halfmoon, Hygeia.

Arlin, Stephen, ed. see Wolfe, David.

Arling, Emanie S. The Terrible Siren: Victoria Woodhull (1838-1927) LC 72-2587. (American Women Ser.: Images & Realities). (Illus.). 478p. 1978. reprint ed. 29.95 (*0-405-04474-7*) Ayer.

Arling, Harry J. Trombone Chamber Music. 2nd ed. Glover, Stephen L., ed. LC 83-19669. (Brass Research Ser.: No. 8). 1983. reprint ed. pap. text 10.00 (*0-914282-29-8*) Brass Pr.

Arlinger, Stig. Practical Audiometry Manual, Vol. 1. 226p. 1989. 64.50 (*1-56593-554-3*, 0002) Singular Publishing.

— Practical Audiometry Manual, Vol. 2. 248p. 1991. pap. 64.50 (*1-56593-555-1*, 0003) Singular Publishing.

Arlinghaus, Ralph B., jt. auth. see Deisseroth.

Arlinghaus, Sandra L. An Atlas of Steiner Networks. (Monographs: No. 9). (Illus.). 84p. (Orig.). (C). 1989. pap. 15.95 (*1-877751-18-9*); pap. text 15.95 (*1-877751-19-7*) Inst Math Geo.

— Down the Mail Tubes: The Pressured Postal Era, 1853-1984. (Monographs: No. 2). (Illus.). 79p. (Orig.). (C). 1986. pap. 15.95 (*1-877751-04-9*); pap. text 15.95 (*1-877751-05-7*) Inst Math Geo.

— Essays on Mathematical Geography, No. I. (Monographs: No. 3). (Illus.). 167p. (Orig.). (C). 1986. pap. 15.95 (*1-877751-06-5*); pap. text 15.95 (*1-877751-07-3*) Inst Math Geo.

— Essays on Mathematical Geography, No. II. (Monographs: No. 5). (Illus.). 95p. (Orig.). (C). 1987. pap. 15.95 (*1-877751-10-3*); pap. text 15.95 (*1-877751-11-1*) Inst Math Geo.

— Essays on Mathematical Geography III. (Monographs: No. 14). (Orig.). 1991. pap. 15.95 (*1-877751-50-2*) Inst Math Geo.

Arlinghaus, Sandra L. Practical Handbook of Digital Mapping Concepts & Terminology. 352p. 1994. boxed set 104.95 (*0-8493-0131-9*, GA139) CRC Pr.

Arlinghaus, Sandra L., ed. Solstice Vol. 1, No. 1: An Electronic Journal of Geography & Mathematics. (Illus.). 50p. (Orig.). 1990. pap. 5.00 (*1-877751-51-0*) Inst Math Geo.

— Solstice IV. (Monographs: No. 17). 1993. pap. 15.95 (*1-877751-55-3*) Inst Math Geo.

— Solstice III. (Monographs: No. 16). 1992. pap. 15.95 (*1-877751-54-5*) Inst Math Geo.

— Solstice II. (Monographs: No. 15). 1991. pap. 15.95 (*1-877751-53-7*) Inst Math Geo.

Arlinghaus, Sandra L., et al, eds. Handbook of Practical Curve Fitting. LC 94-10118. 272p. 1994. boxed set 78.95 (*0-8493-0143-2*) CRC Pr.

Arlinghaus, Sandra L. & Griffith, Daniel A., eds. Practical Handbook of Spatial Statistics. 336p. 1995. boxed set 84.95 (*0-8493-0132-7*, 132) CRC Pr.

Arlinghaus, Sandra L. & Nystuen, John D. Environmental Effects on Bus Durability. (Institute of Mathematical Geography, Monographs: No. 11). (Illus.). 104p. (Orig.). 1989. reprint ed. pap. 15.95 (*1-877751-40-5*); reprint ed. pap. text 15.95 (*1-877751-41-3*) Inst Math Geo.

— Mathematical Geography & Global Art: The Mathematics of David Barr's "Four Corners Project" (Monographs: No. 1). (Illus.). 78p. (Orig.). (C). 1986. pap. 15.95 (*1-877751-02-2*); pap. text 15.95 (*1-877751-03-0*) Inst Math Geo.

Arlinghaus, William C. The Classification of Minimal Graphs with Given Abelian Automorphism Group. LC 85-13537. (MEMO Ser.: No. 57/330). 86p. 1985. pap. 18.00 (*0-8218-2331-0*, MEMO/57/330) Am Math.

Arlington County Genealogical Society Staff, compiled by. Graveyards of Arlington County, Virginia. 144p. 1985. pap. text 15.00 (*0-915156-54-7*) Natl Genealogical.

Arlington, Lewis C. Chinese Drama. LC 65-19614. (Illus.). 1972. reprint ed. 46.95 (*0-405-08212-6*) Ayer.

ARLIS-NA Staffing Standards Task Force. Staffing Standards for Art Libraries & Visual Resources Collections. (Occasional Papers: No. 11). 16p. (Orig.). 1995. pap. 7.50 (*0-942740-16-5*) Art Libs Soc.

Arliss, Edward, ed. see Crowley, Aleister.

Arliss, G. Picturegoers Who's Who & Encyclopedia of the Screen. 608p. 1976. lib. bdg. 300.00 (*0-8490-0837-9*) Gordon Pr.

Arliss, Laurie P. & Borisoff, Deborah. Women & Men Communicating: Challenges & Changes. LC 92-71051. 224p. (C). 1993. pap. text 33.00 (*0-03-074656-6*, Pub. by Harcourt Coll Pubs) Harcourt.

Arlock, Eli, tr. see Zeldovich, Ya B. & Novikov, I. D.

***Arlosoroff, Saul.** Community Water Supply. 2nd ed. 320p. 1999. pap. 40.00 (*1-85339-383-5*, Pub. by Intermed Tech) Stylus Pub VA.

Arlotto, Anthony. Introduction to Historical Linguistics. LC 80-6309. 284p. (C). 1981. reprint ed. pap. text 21.00 (*0-8191-1460-X*) U Pr of Amer.

Arlov, Pamela. Wordsmith: A Guide to College Writing. LC 99-13468. 532p. (C). 1999. pap. text 39.80 (*0-13-628355-1*, Macmillan Coll) P-H.

Arlow, Jacob A. Legacy of Sigmund Freud. LC 56-9746. 1956. 35.00 (*0-8236-2980-5*) Intl Univs Pr.

— Psychoanalysis: Clinical Theory & Practice. LC 91-20811. 450p. (C). 1991. 65.00 (*0-8236-5202-5*) Intl Univs Pr.

Arlow, Jacob A., ed. Selected Writings of Bertram D. Lewin, M. D. LC 72-94802. (Illus.). 608p. 1973. 25.00 (*0-911194-02-9*) Psych Qtly.

Arlow, Jacob A. & Brenner, Charles. Psychoanalytic Concepts & the Structural Theory. LC 64-16190. (Journal of the American Psychoanalytic Association Monograph Ser.: No. 3). 216p. (Orig.). 1964. 32.50 (*0-8236-5060-X*) Intl Univs Pr.

Arlt, Gustave O., ed. see Werfel, Franz.

Arlt, Lenelis, jt. auth. see Kruse, Lenelis.

Arlt, Lisa E. Smoke & Mirrors. rev. ed. (Temptation Ser.: Vol. 680). 1998. per. 3.75 (*0-373-25780-5*, 1-25780-7) Harlequin Bks.

Arlt, Roberto. The Seven Madmen. Caistor, Nick, tr. 256p. 1998. pap. 14.99 (*1-85242-592-X*) Serpents Tail.

Arlt, Roberto, jt. auth. see Martinez, Victoria J.

Arlt, W., jt. auth. see Eckermann, Reiner.

Arluke, Arnold & Sanders, Clinton R. Regarding Animals. LC 95-43062. (Animals, Culture & Society Ser.). 256p. (C). 1996. pap. 18.95 (*1-56639-441-4*); lib. bdg. 69.95 (*1-56639-440-6*) Temple U Pr.

Arluke, Arnold, jt. auth. see Gritzer, Glenn.

Arluke, Arnold, jt. auth. see Levin, Jack.

ARMA Conference Speakers Staff. Proceedings of the ARMA International Annual Conference, 39th (Toronto) 906p. 1994. pap. 30.00 (*0-933887-50-7*, A4579) ARMA Intl.

— Proceedings of the ARMA International 40th Annual Conference (Nashville) 582p. 1995. pap. 30.00 (*0-933887-55-8*, A4582) ARMA Intl.

— Proceedings of the 42nd ARMA International Conference (Chicago) 692p. 1997. pap. 60.00 (*0-933887-75-2*, A4585) ARMA Intl.

ARMA International Staff. Alphabetic Filing Rules. 2nd ed. 38p. 1995. pap. 29.00 (*0-933887-58-2*) ARMA Intl.

***ARMA International Staff.** ARMA 1998 Salary & Compensation Survey. 136p. 1998. pap. 50.00 (*0-933887-81-7*) ARMA Intl.

ARMA International Staff. Converting from a Manual System to an Automated System: A Guideline. 15p. 1992. pap. 32.00 (*0-933887-44-2*, A4548) ARMA Intl.

— Criteria for Developing - Evaluating Records Management Software. 10p. 1990. pap. 27.00 (*0-933887-37-X*, A4518) ARMA Intl.

— Developing & Operating a Records Retention Program: A Guideline. 86p. 1986. pap. 30.00 (*0-933887-18-3*, A4520) ARMA Intl.

— E. L. F. - Eliminate Legal-Size Files: A Guideline. 8p. 1991. pap. 8.00 (*0-933887-38-8*, A4547) ARMA Intl.

***ARMA International Staff.** Essential Elements of Local Government Legislation. 2nd ed. 1999. pap. write for info. (*0-933887-86-8*) ARMA Intl.

ARMA International Staff. Filing Procedures: A Guideline. 26p. 1989. pap. 30.00 (*0-933887-33-7*, A4532) ARMA Intl.

— An Introduction to Records & Information Management: Home Study Course. 2nd ed. 344p. 1992. ring bd. 365.00 (*0-933887-25-6*, A4590) ARMA Intl.

— Job Descriptions: A Guideline. 40p. 1991. pap. 28.00 (*0-933887-12-4*, A4541) ARMA Intl.

— Numeric Filing: A Guideline. 14p. 1989. pap. 29.00 (*0-933887-32-9*, A4531) ARMA Intl.

— Records Center Operations: A Guideline. 51p. 1986. 27.00 (*0-933887-11-6*, A4540) ARMA Intl.

— Subject Filing: A Guideline. 47p. 1988. pap. 38.00 (*0-933887-29-9*, A4546) ARMA Intl.

— Vital Records: A Guideline. 2nd ed. 29p. 1993. pap. 19.00 (*0-933887-14-0*, A4543) ARMA Intl.

ARMA International's Utilities Industry Staff. Records Retention Resource Guidelines for the U. S. Based Gas Utilities. 56p. 1997. pap. 45.00 (*0-933887-66-3*, A4566) ARMA Intl.

Arma, Tom, photos by. Animal Time! (Illus.). 18p. (J). (ps-3). 1994. bds. 5.99 (*0-448-40437-0*, G & D) Peng Put Young Read.

— Baby Bugs. (Illus.). 12p. (J). (ps-3). 1996. bds. 5.99 (*0-448-41141-5*, G & D) Peng Put Young Read.

— Dress-Up Time! (Illus.). 18p. (J). (ps-3). 1994. bds. 5.95 (*0-448-40438-9*, G & D) Peng Put Young Read.

— Funny Farm. (Illus.). 12p. (J). (ps-3). 1996. bds. 5.99 (*0-448-41138-5*, G & D) Peng Put Young Read.

— Little Grown-Ups. (Illus.). 18p. (J). (ps up). 1995. bds. 4.95 (*0-448-40093-6*, G & D) Peng Put Young Read.

— TykeOsaurs. (Illus.). 18p. (J). (ps up). 1995. bds. 5.99 (*0-448-40092-8*, G & D) Peng Put Young Read.

— Water Babies. LC 96-79293. (Illus.). 14p. (J). (ps-3). 1997. bds. 5.99 (*0-448-41567-4*, G & D) Peng Put Young Read.

— Zoo Crew. LC 96-79292. (Illus.). 14p. (J). (ps-3). 1997. bds. 5.99 (*0-448-41142-3*, G & D) Peng Put Young Read.

Armacost, George H. High School Principals' Annual Reports. LC 78-176523. (Columbia University. Teachers College. Contributions to Education Ser.: No. 807). reprint ed. 37.50 (*0-404-55807-0*) AMS Pr.

Armacost, Michael H. Friends or Rivals? The Insider's Account of U. S.-Japan Relations. LC 95-25480. (Illus.). 241p. 1996. 28.00 (*0-231-10488-X*) Col U Pr.

Armagost, James, jt. auth. see Robinson, Lila W.

Armah, Ayi Kwei. The Beautiful Ones Are Not Yet Born. (African Writers Ser.). 183p. (Orig.). (C). 1989. pap. 9.95 (*0-435-90540-6*, 90540) Heinemann.

Armajani & Ricks. Middle East. 3rd ed. 448p. (C). 2001. pap. 38.67 (*0-13-976010-5*) P-H.

Armajani, Babak, et al. A Model for the Reinvented Higher Education System. 1994. 10.00 (*0-614-13562-1*) SHEEO.

Armajani, Siah. Bridge Book. limited ed. (Illus.). 21p. 1991. lib. bdg. 250.00 (*1-879832-17-8*) MN Ctr Book Arts.

Armajo, Charlotte. Desert Dance. (Let Me Read Ser.). (Illus.). 16p. (J). (ps-2). 1995. 2.95 (*0-673-36280-9*, GoodYrBooks) Addson-Wesley Educ.

Armalinskii, Mikhail, tr. & intro. see Pushkin, Aleksandr.

Armalinskii, Mikhail, pseud. Dobrovolniye Priznaniya - Vinuzhdennaya Perepiska (Voluntary Confessions - Forced Correspondence) LC 90-26739. (RUS.). 312p. (Orig.). 1997. reprint ed. pap. 15.00 (*0-916201-03-0*) M I P Co.

— Gonimoye Chudo.Tr. of Expelling the Miracle. (RUS.). 130p. (Orig.). 1996. pap. 9.00 (*0-916201-20-1*) M I P Co.

— Majatnik. 2nd ed. LC 84-90582. (RUS.). 130p. (Orig.). 1984. pap. 4.00 (*0-916201-01-5*) M I P Co.

— Muskulistaya Smert; Raskazi. (RUS.). 150p. (Orig.). 1984. pap. 6.00 (*0-916201-00-7*, 83-63508) M I P Co.

— Persuaded Passions. 74p. 1980. pap. 5.00 (*0-935090-03-7*) Almanac Pr.

— Po Obye Storoni Orgasma. LC 88-90891. (RUS.). 150p. 1988. pap. 10.00 (*0-916201-04-X*) M I P Co.

— Towards Myself. 110p. 1981. pap. 7.00 (*0-935090-05-3*) Almanac Pr.

— Vplotnuyu. LC 94-18382.Tr. of Close To. (RUS.). 100p. (Orig.). 1994. pap. 9.00 (*0-916201-16-3*) M I P Co.

— Zhizneopisaniye Mgnovenia.Tr. of Chronicle of a Moment. (RUS.). 90p. (Orig.). 1997. pap. 8.00 (*0-916201-21-X*) M I P Co.

Armalinskii, Mikhail, pseud, ed. Russkeye Bestizhie Poslovitsi i Pogovorki - Russian Shameless Proverbs & Sayings. 2nd expanded rev. ed. (RUS.). 95p. (Orig.). 1995. pap. 6.00 (*0-916201-18-X*) M I P Co.

Armalinskii, Mikhail, pseud, ed. Detskii Eroticheskii Folklore - Children's Erotic Folklore. LC 95-17353. (RUS., Illus.), 92p. (Orig.). 1995. pap. 6.00 (*0-916201-17-1*) M I P Co.

Armaly, B. F., ed. see AIAA-ASME Joint Thermophysics & Heat Transfer Conf.

Armaly, B. F., jt. ed. see Blackwell, B. F.

Armaly, B. F., jt. ed. see Simoneau, R. J.

Arman, David & Arman, Linda. First Supplement to Historical Staffordshire: An Illustrated Check List. (Illus.). 1977. pap. 20.00 (*0-915438-01-1*) Oakland Pr.

— Historical Staffordshire: Illustrated Checklist. LC 74-18756. (Illus.). 258p. 1975. 40.00 (*0-915438-00-3*) Oakland Pr.

— Transfer Printed Creamware & Pearlware for the American Market, 1760-1860. (Anglo-American Ceramics Ser.: Pt. I). (Illus.). 300p. 1998. 90.00 (*0-915438-02-X*) Oakland Pr.

Arman, Florence & Wooldridge, Glen. The Rogue: A River to Run. LC 81-52732. (Illus.). 1982. pap. 16.95 (*0-9607260-0-4*) Wildwood Pr.

Arman, Linda, jt. auth. see Arman, David.

Arman, Mike. Motorcycle Electrics Without Pain. (Illus.). 1980. pap. 11.00 (*0-933078-03-X*) M Arman.

Arman, Mike & Bolender, John. Unauthorized Flat Rate Schedule for Harley Davidson Motorcycles, 1984. 1986. ring bd. 8.00 (*0-933078-13-7*, H-D FLATRATE 30) M Arman.

Arman, Mike & Heinrichs, Kurt. Harley Davidson Special Tools: Where to Get Them, How to Use Them. (Illus.). 64p. 1982. pap. text 8.00 (*0-933078-07-2*) M Arman.

— What Fits What on Harley Davidson Nineteen Thirty-Six to Nineteen Eighty-Three. 6th ed. (Illus.). 1983. pap. 8.00 (*0-933078-11-0*) M Arman.

Arman, Mike, ed. see Geokan, Mike.

***Arman, Miriam Jaskierowicz.** The Voice: A Spiritual Approach to Singing, Speaking & Communicating. (Illus.). 160p. 1999. per. 14.95 (*0-9674181-0-0*) Music Visions.

Armand. Understanding Soc Stdnt Wkbk. (C). 1997. pap. text 16.67 (*0-201-32237-4*) Addison-Wesley.

Armand, Alain. Reunion Creole - French Dictionary Dictionnaire Kreole Reunion-Francais. (CRP & FRE.). 399p. 1987. pap. 105.00 (*0-8288-1094-X*, M970) Fr & Eur.

Armand, Aram A. Pathway of Existence: Quatrains. LC 92-33844. (ARM.). 172p. 1992. pap. 15.00 (*0-9628715-4-0*) Blue Crane Bks.

Armand, Barton L. The Roots of Horror in the Fiction of H. P. Lovecraft. (Illus.). 1977. 45.00 (*0-911499-04-0*) Ultramarine Pub.

Armand, M. Solid State Ionics III. Nazri, Gholam-Abbas et al, eds. (Materials Research Society Symposium Proceedings Ser.: Vol. 293). 471p. 1993. text 79.00 (*1-55899-188-3*) Materials Res.

Armand, N. N., jt. ed. see Kolchanova, V. P.

Armand, Octavio. Refractions. Maier, Carol, tr. from SPA. LC 95-212008. 232p. (Orig.). 1994. pap. 15.00 (*0-930829-21-2*) Lumen Inc.

Armand, R. Paul St., see St. Armand, R. Paul.

Armand, Richard, et al. The Management Revolution: Management Consultancy & Computer-aided Decision Making. LC 72-190063. xvi, 319p. 1972. write for info. (*0-356-03928-5*) Janes Info Group.

Armander & Skipwith, Ashkain. The Son of a Duck Is a Floater. (Illus.). 90p. 1995. 16.95 (*0-86685-526-2*, Pub. by Stacey Intl) Intl Bk Ctr.

Armando, Davide. David Armando. (Illus.). 128p. 1997. 49.95 (*3-908162-64-5*) Dist Art Pubs.

Armando, Vega Gil. Colmos Pelados. (SPA.). 1997. pap. text 6.98 (*968-403-920-4*) Selector.

Armanel, C. Parler des Bouches-du-Rhone. (FRE.). 105p. 1993. 34.95 (*0-320-03042-3*) Fr & Eur.

Armanet, J. & Becquer, Gustavo A. Annales des Mines: Lexique Technique Allemand-Francais. (FRE & GER.). 344p. 1951. 19.95 (*0-8288-6881-6*, M6011) Fr & Eur.

***Armani, Eddy.** The Real T: My 22 Years with Tina Turner. (Illus.). 256p. 1999. 26.00 (*1-85782-183-1*, Pub. by Blake Publng) Seven Hills Bk.

Armanias, E. A., ed. Composite Materials Vol. 6: Fatigue & Fracture. 577p. 1997. text 129.00 (*0-8031-2411-2*) ASTM.

Armanini, A. & Michiue, Masanori. Recent Developments on Debris Flows. LC 96-30076. (Lecture Notes in Earth Sciences Ser.). 1997. 78.00 (*3-540-62466-X*) Spr-Verlag.

Armanino, C., et al, eds. Chemometrics & Species Identification. (Topics in Current Chemistry Ser.: Vol. 141). (Illus.). 190p. 1987. 103.95 (*0-387-17308-0*) Spr-Verlag.

Armanios, E. A., ed. Fracture of Composites. (Key Engineering Materials: 120-121). (Illus.). 612p. 1996. text 166.00 (*0-87849-725-0*, Pub. by Trans T Pub) Enfield Pubs NH.

— Interlaminar Fracture of Composites. 340p. 1989. text 133.00 (*0-87849-590-8*, Pub. by Trans T Pub) Enfield Pubs NH.

Armanno, Frank, Sr. How to Succeed in Slimness Without Really Trying: The Eat Anything Desired Invention for the Overweight or Diabetic. (Illus.). 1999. pap. 7.95 (*0-9671820-2-6*) Prog Time Corp.

— Lotto Cipher Book Game: A Journey into Alphanumeric Time! (Illus.). 48p. 1992. pap. 5.95 (*0-9671820-0-X*) Prog Time Corp.

— Poetic Time Scroll's: A Journey into Sentimental Time! (Illus.). 48p. 1999. pap. 7.95 (*0-9671820-1-8*) Prog Time Corp.

***Armanno, Venero.** Gabriella's Book of Fire: A Novel. (Illus.). 2001. 23.95 (*0-7868-6597-0*, Pub. by Hyperion) Time Warner.

***Armanno, Vince.** Firehead 2001. 14.95 (*0-7868-8510-6*, Pub. by Disney Pr) Time Warner.

***Armannsson, Halldor, ed.** Geochemistry of the Earth's Surface: Proceedings of the 5th International Symposium, Reykjavik, 15-20 August, 1999. (Illus.). 580p. 1999. text 125.00 (*90-5809-073-6*) A A Balkema.

Armantrout, N. B., compiled by. Glossary of Aquatic Habitat Inventory Terminology, 2 vols. LC 98-87146. (Illus.). 152p. 1998. spiral bd. 30.00 (*1-888569-11-5*, 550.25P) Am Fisheries Soc.

Armantrout, Neal B., ed. The Condition of Major Aquatic Habitats Theme 1: Proceedings of the World Fisheries Congress, Athens, Greece. 400p. 1995. text 105.00 (*1-886106-12-6*) Science Pubs.

Armantrout, Rae. Made to Seem. (New American Poetry Ser.: No. 20). 64p. 1995. pap. 9.95 (*1-55713-220-8*) Sun & Moon CA.

— Necromance. (New American Poetry Ser.: No. 7). 56p. 1991. pap. 8.95 (*1-55713-096-5*) Sun & Moon CA.

— Precedence: Poems. 48p. 1985. pap. 5.00 (*0-930901-24-X*) Burning Deck.

***Armantrout, Rae.** Pretext, Vol. 45. 2000. pap. 9.95 (*1-892295-39-3*) Green Integer.

Armantrout, Rae. True, Vol. 3. 63p. 1998. pap. 12.95 (*1-891190-03-2*) Atelos.

Armarego, W. L. & Perrin, D. D. Purification of Laboratory Chemicals. 4th ed. 512p. 2000. reprint ed. pap. text 74.95 (*0-7506-3761-7*, TD1050) Buttrwrth-Heinemann.

Armas, Armando De, see De Armas, Armando.

Armas Barea, Calixto A., jt. auth. see Ruda, Jose Maria.

Armas, Daniel. Dictionary of Guatamalan Popular Expressions: Diccionario de al Espresion Popular Guatemalteca. (SPA.). 438p. 1982. 45.00 (*0-8288-2029-5*, S15747) Fr & Eur.

Armas, Jose, ed. see Menendez, Enrique C.

Armas, Jose, jt. ed. see Ramos, Luis A.

Armas, Jose, ed. see Vento, Arnold C.

Armas, O. Rodriquez, et al, eds. Fertility & Sterility: Progress in Research & Practice: The Official Proceedings of the XIV World Congress on Fertility & Sterility, Caracas, November 1992. LC 93-46623. (International Congress, Symposium, & Seminar Ser.: Vol. 5). 599p. 1994. 125.00 (*1-85070-501-1*) Prthnon Pub.

Armata Bianca Staff. Armata Bianca. LC 99-203043. 24p. 1973. write for info. (*1-882972-94-5*) Queenship Pub.

Armatage, Kay, et al, eds. Gendering the Nation: Canadian Women's Cinema. 350p. 1999. text 70.00 (*0-8020-4120-5*); pap. text 21.95 (*0-8020-7964-4*) U of Toronto Pr.

Armatas, James P., jt. auth. see Lundberg, Donald E.

Armattoe, Raphael E., jt. auth. see Wiegraebe, P.

Armayor, O. Kimball. Herodotus' Autopsy of the Fayoum: Lake Moeris & the Labyrinth of Egypt. xiv, 160p. (C). 1985. 47.00 (*90-70265-07-9*, Pub. by Gieben) J Benjamins Pubng Co.

Armbrecht. Image International, Vol. 5, No. 2. 1993. pap. 20.00 (*0-8058-9999-5*) L Erlbaum Assocs.

Armbrecht, H. J., et al, eds. Endocrine Function & Aging. (Illus.). xxi, 236p. 1989. 80.95 (*0-387-97007-X*) Spr-Verlag.

— Nutritional Intervention in the Aging Process. (Illus.). 330p. 1984. 87.00 (*0-387-96025-2*) Spr-Verlag.

Armbrester, Margaret E. Samuel Ullman & "Youth" The Life, the Legacy. LC 92-37414. (Judaic Studies). 168p. (C). 1993. 24.95 (*0-8173-0685-4*) U of Ala Pr.

Armbrust, Betty J. & Bradley, Hugh H. Practical Real Estate Math. 2nd ed. 306p. (Orig.). (C). 1995. pap. text 32.67 (*0-13-777707-8*) P-H.

Armbrust, Walter. Mass Culture & Modernism in Egypt. (Studies in Social & Cultural Anthropology: No. 102). (Illus.). 286p. (C). 1996. pap. text 20.95 (*0-521-48492-8*) Cambridge U Pr.

— Mass Culture & Modernism in Egypt. (Cambridge Studies in Social & Cultural Anthropology: No. 102). (Illus.). 286p. (C). 1996. text 59.95 (*0-521-48147-3*) Cambridge U Pr.

***Armbrust, Walter.** Mass Mediations. LC 99-43224. 325p. 2000. 55.00 (*0-520-21925-2*, Pub. by U CA Pr) Cal Prin Full Svc.

A

A

— Mass Mediations: New Approaches to Popular Culture in the Middle East & Beyond. LC 99-43224. 325p. 2000. pap. 24.95 (*0-520-21926-0*, Pub. by U CA Pr) Cal Prin Full Svc.

Armbruster. Introduction to Operating Systems. (DC - Introduction to Computing Ser.). 1996. pap. 30.95 (*0-7895-0684-X*) Course Tech.

Armbruster, Ann. The American Flag. (First Bks.). (Illus.). 64p. (J). (gr. 5-8). 1991. lib. bdg. 22.00 (*0-531-20045-0*) Watts.

— Floods. LC 96-14599. (First Books-Natural Disasters). 64p. (J). (gr. 4-6). 1996. lib. bdg. 21.00 (*0-531-20239-9*) Watts.

— Geography: Great Lakes, 6 vols. 1999. 126.00 (*0-516-29972-7*) Childrens.

— Lake Erie. LC 96-2028. (True Bk.). (Illus.). 48p. (J). 1996. lib. bdg. 21.00 (*0-516-20011-9*) Childrens.

— Lake Erie. (True Bks.). 48p. (J). 1997. pap. 6.95 (*0-516-26102-9*) Childrens.

— Lake Huron. LC 96-2026. (True Bk.). (Illus.). 48p. (J). 1996. lib. bdg. 21.00 (*0-516-20012-7*) Childrens.

— Lake Huron. (True Bks.). 48p. (J). 1997. pap. 6.95 (*0-516-26103-7*) Childrens.

— Lake Michigan. LC 96-2029. (True Bk.). (Illus.). 48p. (J). 1996. lib. bdg. 21.00 (*0-516-20013-5*) Childrens.

— Lake Michigan. (True Bks.). 48p. (J). 1997. pap. 6.95 (*0-516-26104-5*) Childrens.

— Lake Ontario. LC 96-2081. (True Bk.). (Illus.). 48p. (J). 1996. lib. bdg. 21.00 (*0-516-20014-3*) Childrens.

— Lake Ontario. (True Bks.). 48p. (J). 1997. pap. 6.95 (*0-516-26105-3*) Childrens.

— Lake Superior. LC 96-2027. (True Bk.). (Illus.). 48p. (J). 1996. lib. bdg. 21.00 (*0-516-20015-1*) Childrens.

— Lake Superior. (True Bks.). 48p. (J). 1997. pap. 6.95 (*0-516-26106-1*) Childrens.

— The Life & Times of Miami Beach. LC 94-11572. 224p. 1995. 45.00 (*0-394-57052-9*) Knopf.

— St. Lawrence Seaway. LC 96-2086. (True Bk.). 48p. (J). (gr. 3-5). 1996. lib. bdg. 21.00 (*0-516-20016-X*) Childrens.

— St. Lawrence Seaway. (True Bks.). 48p. (J). 1997. pap. 6.95 (*0-516-26114-2*) Childrens.

— Wildfires. LC 96-13551. (First Books-Science). 64p. (J). 1996. lib. bdg. 22.00 (*0-531-20250-X*) Watts.

Armbruster, Ann & Taylor, Elizabeth A. Tornadoes. (First Bks.). (Illus.). 64p. (J). (gr. 5-8). 1993. pap. 6.95 (*0-531-15666-4*) Watts.

***Armbruster, Bonnie B.** Understanding the Ira's Standards. (C). 2000. pap. write for info. (*0-321-06395-3*) Addison-Wesley.

Armbruster, Carl, ed. see Liszt, Franz.

Armbruster, Carol. Publishing & Readership in Revolutionary France & America: A Symposium at the Library of Congress, Sponsored by the Center for the Book & the European Division, 4. LC 92-38070. (Beta Phi Mu Monograph: No. 4). 240p. 1993. 52.95 (*0-313-28793-7*, GM8793) Greenwood.

Armbruster, D., jt. auth. see Rand, R. H.

Armbruster, David B. & Red Wing Business Systems Staff. Introduction to Agricultural Accounting. (Orig.). Date not set. pap. 19.95 (*0-87265-011-1*) Red Wing Busn.

Armbruster, David L., jt. auth. see Zenkovsky, Serge A.

Armbruster, Dieter. Ordinary Differential Equations. (C). 1997. pap. text, lab manual ed. write for info. (*0-201-82476-0*) Addison-Wesley.

Armbruster, Dieter, jt. auth. see Kostelich, Eric J.

Armbruster, Dieter, jt. auth. see Kostelch, Eric J.

Armbruster, Judith. Bamboo & Other Things: Techniques of Oriental Brush Painting. LC 90-92085. (Illus.). 83p. (Orig.). 1999. pap. text 12.95 (*0-9619502-1-8*) Maple Tree Studio.

Armbruster, Kurt. Orphan Road: The Railroad Comes to Seattle, 1853-1911. LC 99-37058. (Illus.). 280p. 1999. 39.95 (*0-87422-185-4*) Wash St U Pr.

— Orphan Road: The Railroad Comes to Seattle, 1853-1911. LC 99-37058. (Illus.). 280p. 1999. pap. 29.95 (*0-87422-186-2*) Wash St U Pr.

Armbruster, Kurt E. Whistle down the Valley: One Hundred Years of Green River Railroading. LC 91-61795. (Illus.). 78p. (Orig.). 1991. pap. 10.95 (*0-9629725-3-3*) NW Railway Loco Pres.

Armbruster, W. Michael. Hugs & Other Wonderful Stuff. LC 97-91703. (Illus.). 120p. 1997. pap. 12.00 (*1-57502-471-3*, P01409) Morris Pubng.

Armed Forces Institute of Pathology Staff. AFIP Laboratory Methods in Histotechnology. 1992. 35.00 (*1-881041-00-X*) Am Registry Path.

— Pathology of the Head & Neck. (C). 1992. 700.00 incl. disk (*1-56815-011-3*) Mosby Inc.

Armed Forces Institute of Pathology Staff, jt. auth. see American Registry of Pathology Staff.

Armel, Aliette. Marguerite Duras. (FRE.). 152p. 1998. pap. 49.95 (*2-86808-117-7*) Intl Scholars.

Armel, Jack. Entropic Spacetime Theory. LC 96-28661. (Series on Knots & Everything). 1996. write for info. (*981-02-2842-2*) World Scientific Pub.

Armel, L. Robert Dictionnaire des Rimes, Assonances. (FRE.). 697p. 1998. 69.95 (*0-320-00394-9*) Fr & Eur.

Armellini, Sylvia, ed. see Armellini, Toby J.

***Armellini, Toby J.** What You Should Know About Radiation. Armellini, Sylvia & Dobkins, Eve, eds. 112p. (C). 2000. pap. 9.95 (*0-9675953-0-4*) Armellini.

Armen, Harry, ed. see American Society of Mechanical Engineers Staff.

Armen, M. A. The Hanging of Father Miguel. large type ed. LC 90-35641. 220p. 1990. lib. bdg. 14.95 (*1-56054-008-7*) Thorndike Pr.

Armendariz, Abe L., jt. auth. see Gonzales, Frank.

Armendariz de Aghion, Beatriz & Williamson, John. The G-7's Joint & Several Blunder. LC 93-20501. (Essays in International Finance Ser.: No. 189). 28p. 1993. pap. 10.00 (*0-88165-096-X*) Princeton U Int Finan Econ.

Armendariz, M. Luisa. Chiapas, una Radiografia. (SPA.). 18.99 (*968-16-4515-4*, Pub. by Fondo) Continental Bk.

Armengol, Arturo C. Gran Diccionario Cuyas Ingles-Espanol, Spanish-English. 10th ed. (ENG & SPA.). 1648p. 1988. write for info. (*0-7859-5079-6*) Fr & Eur.

***Armengol, Carmen G., et al.** The Consumer Oriented Neuropsychological Report. LC 99-50125. 1999. write for info. (*0-911907-35-1*) Psych Assess.

Armengol, Norma C., tr. see Brock, Charles.

Armenian, Haroutune K. & Shapiro, Sam, eds. Epidemiology & Health Services. LC 97-856. (Illus.). 284p. 1997. text 45.00 (*0-19-509359-3*) OUP.

Armenian, Haroutune K., jt. ed. see Zurayk, Huda G.

Armenini, Giovanni B. De'veri Precetti Della Pittura Libri Tre. 232p. 1971. reprint ed. 65.00 (*0-318-71578-3*) G Olms Pubs.

***Armenise, Mario N., et al, eds.** Optical Devices & Methods for Microwave/Millimeter Wave & Frontier Applications, Vol. 3464. LC 99-193803. 1998. 80.00 (*0-8194-2919-8*) SPIE.

Armenise, Mario N., jt. ed. see Najafi, S. I.

Armens, Sven. In the Vernacular: A Secular Mass in C-Minor. 596p. (Orig.). 1990. 19.95 (*0-944266-03-7*) Maecenas Pr.

Armentano, Dominick T. Antitrust: The Case for Repeal. 2nd rev. ed. xviii, 112p. 1999. pap. 9.95 (*0-945466-25-0*) Ludwig von Mises.

— Antitrust & Monopoly: Anatomy of a Policy Failure. 2nd ed. LC 96-14806. (Studies in Political Economy). 292p. 1996. reprint ed. pap. 19.95 (*0-945999-62-3*) Independent Inst.

— Antitrust Policy: The Case for Repeal. 78p. 1986. pap. 3.00 (*0-932790-58-5*) Cato Inst.

Armenti, Angelo, Jr., ed. The Physics of Sports. 360p. 1992. 35.00 (*0-88318-946-1*) Am Inst Physics.

Armento. Elementary Middle Schools. (C). 1996. pap. text. write for info. (*0-8013-0172-6*) Addison-Wesley.

— Elementary Middle Schools. (C). 1996. pap. text 0.50 (*0-8013-0205-6*) Longman.

Armento, Amira, tr. see Byrne, Hugh, et al.

***Armento, Beverly J.** A More Perfect Union. 21st ed. LC 98-234526. (Social Studies). xvii, 767 p. 1999. write for info. (*0-395-93072-3*) HM.

Armentrout, Barbara, ed. see Goddard, Greg.

Armentrout, David. The Biggest. LC 96-20862. (Fascinating Facts Ser.). 1996. 14.60 (*1-57103-126-X*) Rourke Pr.

— Boating. LC 98-18413. (Outdoor Adventures Ser.). 1998. (*1-57103-201-0*) Rourke Pr.

— Camping. LC 98-18417. (Outdoor Adventures Ser.). 1998. (*1-57103-202-9*) Rourke Pr.

— Climbing. LC 98-18419. (Outdoor Adventures Ser.). 1998. (*1-57103-203-7*) Rourke Pr.

— The Fastest. LC 96-25730. (Fascinating Facts Ser.). 1996. lib. bdg. 14.60 (*1-57103-127-8*) Rourke Pr.

— The Firsts. LC 96-23843. (Fascinating Facts Ser.). 1996. lib. bdg. 14.60 (*1-57103-128-6*) Rourke Pr.

— Fishing. LC 98-4289. (Outdoor Adventures Ser.). 1998. (*1-57103-204-5*) Rourke Pr.

— Gymnastics. LC 97-13005. (Sports Challenge Ser.). 24p. (J). (gr. 3-7). 1997. lib. bdg. 18.60 (*1-55916-221-X*) Rourke Bk Co.

— Hiking. LC 98-18418. (Outdoor Adventures Ser.). 1998. (*1-57103-205-3*) Rourke Pr.

— Hunting. LC 98-4290. (Outdoor Adventures Ser.). 1998. (*1-57103-206-1*) Rourke Pr.

— In-Line Skating. LC 97-13006. (Sports Challenge Ser.). 24p. (J). (gr. 3-7). 1997. lib. bdg. 18.60 (*1-55916-222-8*) Rourke Bk Co.

— The Longest. LC 96-26509. (Fascinating Facts Ser.). 1996. lib. bdg. 14.60 (*1-57103-129-4*) Rourke Pr.

— Martial Arts. LC 97-12421. (Sports Challenge Ser.). 24p. (J). (gr. 3-7). 1997. lib. bdg. 18.60 (*1-55916-217-1*) Rourke Bk Co.

— Moto Cross. LC 97-12420. (Sports Challenge Ser.). 24p. (J). (gr. 3-7). 1997. lib. bdg. 18.60 (*1-55916-218-X*) Rourke Bk Co.

— Mounting Biking. LC 97-12419. (Sports Challenge Ser.). 24p. (J). (gr. 3-7). 1997. lib. bdg. 18.60 (*1-55916-219-8*) Rourke Bk Co.

— The Smallest. LC 96-20858. (Fascinating Facts Ser.). 1996. lib. bdg. 14.60 (*1-57103-130-8*) Rourke Pr.

— Snowboarding. LC 97-12418. (Sports Challenge Ser.). 24p. (J). (gr. 3-7). 1997. lib. bdg. 18.60 (*1-55916-220-1*) Rourke Bk Co.

— The Tallest. LC 96-23861. (Fascinating Facts Ser.). 1996. lib. bdg. 14.60 (*1-57103-131-6*) Rourke Pr.

***Armentrout, David & Armentrout, Patricia.** China. LC 00-29075. (Treasures from the Past Ser.). (Illus.). 2000. write for info. (*1-55916-288-0*) Rourke Bk Co.

Armentrout, David & Armentrout, Patricia. Classical. LC 99-14249. (Sounds of Music Ser.). 24p. 1999. lib. bdg. write for info. (*0-86593-534-3*) Rourke Corp.

— Country. LC 99-14251. (Sounds of Music Ser.). 24p. 1999. lib. bdg. write for info. (*0-86593-535-1*) Rourke Corp.

— Cranes. LC 95-3979. (Heavy Equipment Discovery Library). 24p. (J). (gr. k-4). 1995. lib. bdg. 15.93 (*1-55916-133-7*) Rourke Bk Co.

— Diggers. LC 95-3978. (Heavy Equipment Discovery Library). 24p. (J). (gr. k-4). 1995. lib. bdg. 15.93 (*1-55916-134-5*) Rourke Bk Co.

— Drill. LC 94-47277. (Learning about Tools Discovery Library). 24p. (J). (gr. k-4). 1995. lib. bdg. 15.93 (*1-55916-117-5*) Rourke Bk Co.

— Earth Movers. LC 95-3975. (Heavy Equipment Discovery Library). 24p. (J). (gr. k-4). 1995. lib. bdg. 15.93 (*1-55916-131-0*) Rourke Bk Co.

***Armentrout, David & Armentrout, Patricia.** Egypt. LC 00-29074. (Treasures from the Past Ser.). (Illus.). 2000. write for info. (*1-55916-289-9*) Rourke Bk Co.

Armentrout, David & Armentrout, Patricia. Farm Machinery. LC 95-3977. (Heavy Equipment Discovery Library). 24p. (J). (gr. k-4). 1995. lib. bdg. 15.93 (*1-55916-135-3*) Rourke Bk Co.

***Armentrout, David & Armentrout, Patricia.** Folk. LC 99-20059. (Sounds of Music Ser.). 24p. 1999. 55.01 (*0-86593-532-7*) Rourke Corp.

— Greece. LC 00-29078. (Treasures from the Past Ser.). (Illus.). 2000. write for info. (*1-55916-291-0*) Rourke Bk Co.

Armentrout, David & Armentrout, Patricia. Hammer. LC 94-46472. (Learning about Tools Discovery Library). 24p. (J). (gr. k-4). 1995. lib. bdg. 15.93 (*1-55916-121-3*) Rourke Bk Co.

— Hockey... Leagues & Tournaments. LC 98-28438. 48p. 1998. lib. bdg. (*1-57103-220-7*) Rourke Pr.

— Hockey... Play by the Rules. LC 98-27371. (Hockey Ser.). 48p. (J). 1998. lib. bdg. (*1-57103-221-5*) Rourke Pr.

— Hockey... The Basics of the Game. LC 98-27532. (Hockey Ser.). 48p. (J). 1998. lib. bdg. (*1-57103-219-3*) Rourke Pr.

— Hockey... The Players. LC 98-28404. 48p. 1998. lib. bdg. 22.60 (*1-57103-223-1*) Rourke Pr.

— Hockey... The Rink & Equipment. LC 98-28437. (Hockey Ser.). 48p. (J). 1998. lib. bdg. (*1-57103-222-3*) Rourke Pr.

— Hockey... Training & Fitness. LC 98-28403. (Hockey Ser.). 48p. (J). 1998. (*1-57103-224-X*) Rourke Pr.

***Armentrout, David & Armentrout, Patricia.** Italy. LC 00-29077. (Treasures from the Past Ser.). (Illus.). 2000. write for info. (*1-55916-292-9*) Rourke Bk Co.

— Jazz & Blues. LC 99-20060. (Sounds of Music Ser.). 24p. (J). 1999. lib. bdg. write for info. (*0-86593-533-5*) Rourke Corp.

— Mexico. LC 00-29080. (Treasures from the Past Ser.). (Illus.). 2000. write for info. (*1-55916-290-2*) Rourke Bk Co.

Armentrout, David & Armentrout, Patricia. Pliers. LC 94-46473. (Learning about Tools Discovery Library). 24p. (J). (gr. k-4). 1995. lib. bdg. 15.93 (*1-55916-120-5*) Rourke Bk Co.

***Armentrout, David & Armentrout, Patricia.** Rap. LC 99-20058. (Sounds of Music Ser.). 24p. (J). 1999. lib. bdg. write for info. (*0-86593-531-9*) Rourke Corp.

Armentrout, David & Armentrout, Patricia. Road Builders. LC 95-3976. (Heavy Equipment Discovery Library). 24p. (J). (gr. k-4). 1995. lib. bdg. 15.93 (*1-55916-136-1*) Rourke Bk Co.

***Armentrout, David & Armentrout, Patricia.** Rock. LC 99-14250. (Sounds of Music Ser.). 24p. 1999. lib. bdg. write for info. (*0-86593-536-X*) Rourke Corp.

Armentrout, David & Armentrout, Patricia. Saw. LC 94-46475. (Learning about Tools Discovery Library). 24p. (J). (gr. k-4). 1995. lib. bdg. 15.93 (*1-55916-122-1*) Rourke Bk Co.

— Screwdriver. LC 94-46471. (Learning about Tools Discovery Library). 24p. (J). (gr. k-4). 1995. lib. bdg. 15.93 (*1-55916-119-1*) Rourke Bk Co.

***Armentrout, David & Armentrout, Patricia.** Spain. LC 00-29076. (Treasures from the Past Ser.). (Illus.). 2000. write for info. (*1-55916-293-7*) Rourke Bk Co.

Armentrout, David & Armentrout, Patricia. Work Trucks. LC 95-3980. (Heavy Equipment Discovery Library). 24p. (J). (gr. k-4). 1995. lib. bdg. 15.93 (*1-55916-132-9*) Rourke Bk Co.

— Wrench. LC 94-45590. (Learning about Tools Discovery Library). 24p. (J). (gr. k-4). 1995. lib. bdg. 15.93 (*1-55916-118-3*) Rourke Bk Co.

***Armentrout, David P.** Heart Cry! God's Prescription for Depression. LC 99-23612. 148p. 2000. pap. 14.95 (*1-57249-159-0*, Ragged Edge) White Mane Pub.

Armentrout, Don S. & Slocum, Robert B. Documents of Witness: A History of the Episcopal Church 1782-1985. xviii, 652 p. 1994. 45.95 (*0-89869-237-7*) Church Pub Inc.

***Armentrout, Donald S. & Slocum, Robert Boak.** An Episcopal Dictionary of the Church: A User-friendly Reference for Episcopalians. LC 99-58545. 1999. write for info. (*0-89869-211-3*) Church Pub Inc.

Armentrout, Donald S., ed. see DuBose, William P.

Armentrout, Douglas. Canvas in the Mirror. LC 96-97033. 64p. (Orig.). 1996. pap. 11.95 (*0-9655113-0-8*) Creative Lure.

Armentrout, Ginger. Community Based Nursing. LC 97-45780. 250p. (C). 1998. pap. 26.95 (*0-8385-1522-3*, A-1522-0) Appleton & Lange.

Armentrout, J. Michael, jt. auth. see Doman, Glenn.

Armentrout, J. Michael, jt. ed. see Winn, R. D.

Armentrout, John M., ed. Pacific Northwest Cenozoic Biostratigraphy. LC 80-82937. (Geological Society of America, Special Paper: No. 184). (Illus.). 178p. reprint ed. pap. 55.20 (*0-8357-6841-4*, 203552900095) Bks Demand.

Armentrout, Patricia. American Currency. LC 96-3458. (Money Ser.). (J). 1996. lib. bdg. 14.60 (*1-57103-122-7*) Rourke Pr.

— Caves. LC 96-2894. (Earthly Oddities Ser.). 1996. 17.27 (*1-57103-152-9*) Rourke Pr.

— Extreme Machines... In Space. LC 98-24063. (Extreme Machines Ser.). (J). 1998. (*1-57103-214-2*) Rourke Pr.

— Extreme Machines... In the Air. LC 98-20293. (Extreme Machines Ser.). (J). 1998. (*1-57103-215-0*) Rourke Pr.

— Extreme Machines... On Ice & Snow. LC 98-24064. (Extreme Machines Ser.). (J). 1998. (*1-57103-210-X*) Rourke Pr.

— Extreme Machines... On Land. LC 98-20294. (Extreme Machines Ser.). (J). 1998. (*1-57103-211-8*) Rourke Pr.

— Extreme Machines... On Water. LC 98-20295. (Extreme Machines Ser.). (J). 1998. (*1-57103-212-6*) Rourke Pr.

— Extreme Machines... Under the Sea. LC 98-24065. (Extreme Machines Ser.). (J). 1998. (*1-57103-213-4*) Rourke Pr.

— The Gulf Stream. LC 96-2893. (Earthly Oddities Ser.). 1996. lib. bdg. 14.60 (*1-57103-153-7*) Rourke Pr.

— The History of Money. LC 96-4575. (Money Ser.). (Illus.). (J). 1996. lib. bdg. 14.60 (*1-57103-118-9*) Rourke Pr.

— Hot Springs & Geysers. LC 96-2892. (Earthly Oddities Ser.). 1996. lib. bdg. 17.27 (*1-57103-154-5*) Rourke Pr.

— How Money Is Made. LC 96-4566. (Money Ser.). (Illus.). (J). 1996. lib. bdg. 14.60 (*1-57103-119-7*) Rourke Pr.

— The Inclined Plane. LC 97-15150. (Simple Machines Ser.). (J). 1997. 17.27 (*1-57103-176-6*) Rourke Pr.

— The Lever. LC 97-15149. (Simple Machines Ser.). (J). 1997. lib. bdg. 17.27 (*1-57103-177-4*) Rourke Pr.

— Lights in the Sky. LC 96-2881. (Earthly Oddities Ser.). 1996. 17.27 (*1-57103-155-3*) Rourke Pr.

— Money Around the World. LC 96-4564. (Money Ser.). (Illus.). (J). 1996. lib. bdg. 14.60 (*1-57103-123-5*) Rourke Pr.

— The Ozone Layer. LC 96-2883. (Earthly Oddities Ser.). 1996. lib. bdg. 17.27 (*1-57103-156-1*) Rourke Pr.

— Paying Without Money. LC 96-4568. (Money Ser.). (Illus.). (J). 1996. lib. bdg. 14.60 (*1-57103-121-9*) Rourke Pr.

— Protecting Money. LC 96-3457. (Money Ser.). (Illus.). (J). 1996. lib. bdg. 14.60 (*1-57103-120-0*) Rourke Pr.

— The Pulley. LC 97-15148. (Simple Machines Ser.). (J). 1997. lib. bdg. 17.27 (*1-57103-178-2*) Rourke Pr.

— The Screw. LC 97-15152. (Simple Machines Ser.). (J). 1997. lib. bdg. 17.27 (*1-57103-179-0*) Rourke Pr.

— Waves & Tides. LC 96-2882. (Earthly Oddities Ser.). 1996. lib. bdg. 17.27 (*1-57103-157-X*) Rourke Pr.

— The Wedge. LC 97-15158. (Simple Machines Ser.). (J). 1997. lib. bdg. 17.27 (*1-57103-181-2*) Rourke Pr.

— The Wheel. LC 97-15151. (Simple Machines Ser.). (J). 1997. lib. bdg. 17.27 (*1-57103-180-4*) Rourke Pr.

Armentrout, Patricia, jt. auth. see Armentrout, David.

Armentrout, Steve. Cellular Decompositions of Three-Manifolds that Yield Three-Manifolds. LC 52-42839. (Memoirs Ser.). 72p. 1971. pap. 16.00 (*0-8218-1807-4*, MEMO/1/107) Am Math.

Armentrout, Steve, et al, eds. Collected Papers of R. H. Bing, 2 pts. LC 88-14445. 1654p. 1988. text 188.00 (*0-8218-0117-1*, CWORKS/1) Am Math.

Armentrout, Vivienne N., ed. see Rabeler, Richard K.

Armer, Alan A. Directing Television & Film. 337p. (C). 1985. mass mkt. 23.00 (*0-534-05202-9*) Wadsworth Pub.

— Writing the Screenplay: TV & Film. 272p. (C). 1987. mass mkt. write for info. (*0-534-08292-0*) Wadsworth Pub.

— Writing the Screenplay: TV & Film. 2nd ed. LC 92-12141. 314p. (C). 1992. 32.50 (*0-534-16668-7*) Wadsworth Pub.

Armer, G. S. T. Fire, Static & Dynamic Tests of Building Structures. 101st ed. LC 97-132428. (Illus.). 296p. (C). 1997. 125.00 (*0-419-21680-4*, E & FN Spon) Routledge.

Armer, Michael. African Social Psychology: Review & Annotated Bibliography. LC 74-23711. (African Bibliography Ser.: Vol. 2). 400p. 1975. 45.00 (*0-8419-0164-3*, Africana) Holmes & Meier.

Armerding, Carl E. Judges. (Biblical Commentary Ser.: Vol. 8). Date not set. 29.99 (*0-8499-0207-X*) Word Pub.

Armerding, Hudson T. The Heart of Godly Leadership. LC 92-6453. 224p. 1992. 15.99 (*0-89107-675-1*) Crossway Bks.

Armes, Ethel. The Story of Coal & Iron in Alabama. LC 73-1988. (Big Business; Economic Power in a Free Society Ser.). (Illus.). 1973. reprint ed. 44.95 (*0-405-05072-0*) Ayer.

Armes, Ethel, ed. Nancy Shippen: Her Journal. LC 68-21204. 1972. 24.95 (*0-405-08213-4*, Pub. by Blom Pubns) Ayer.

Armes, Keith, et al. State & Nation in Multi-Ethnic Societies: The Breakup of Multinational States. 1992. 39.95 (*0-685-61137-X*, Pub. by Manchester Univ Pr) St Martin.

Armes, Keith, jt. auth. see Armes, Pat.

Armes, N. J., et al. The Laboratory Culture & Development of Helicoverpa Armigera. 1992. pap. 25.00 (*0-85954-325-0*, Pub. by Nat Res Inst) St Mut.

***Armes, Pat & Armes, Keith.** Collector's Guide to Lady Figurine Planters. (Illus.). 160p. 2000. pap. 29.95 (*0-7643-1073-9*) Schiffer.

Armes, Roy. The Films of Alain Robbe-Grillet. (Purdue University Monographs in Romance Languages: Vol. 6). x, 216p. 1981. 55.00 (*90-272-1716-5*) J Benjamins Pubng Co.

— Third World Film Making & the West. (Orig.). (C). 1987. pap. 24.95 (*0-520-05690-6*, Pub. by U CA Pr) Cal Prin Full Svc.

***Armesto.** Truth. LC 99-49472. 1999. text 23.95 (*0-312-24253-0*) St Martin.

Armesto, jt. auth. see Wilson.

Armesto, Antonio. Atlantic Houses. (Illus.). 144p. Date not set. 50.00 (*84-252-1666-4*) Watsn-Guptill.

Armesto, Felipe F. The European Opportunity. (Expanding World Ser.: No. 2). 384p. (C). 1995. text 124.95 (*0-86078-501-7*, Pub. by Variorum) Ashgate Pub Co.

Armesto, Felipe F., ed. The Global Opportunity. (Expanding World Ser.: No. 1). 352p. 1995. 124.95 (*0-86078-500-9*, Pub. by Variorum) Ashgate Pub Co.

Armesto, Fernandez. Millennium. (Illus.). 816p. 1996. per. 18.00 (*0-684-82536-8*) S&S Trade.

An Asterisk (*) at the beginning of an entry indicates that the title is appearing for the first time.

Armey, Dick. The Flat Tax: A Citizen's Guide to the Facts on What It Will Do for You, Your Country & Your Pocketbook. 160p. 1996. pap. 10.00 (*0-449-91095-4*) Fawcett.

— The Freedom Revolution: The New Republican House Majority Leader Tells Why Big Government Failed, Why Freedom Works, & How We Will Rebuild America. 318p. 24.95 (*0-89526-469-2*) Regnery Pub.

Armey, Joe. Harvest of Contempt. LC 95-3109. (Illus.). viii, 132p. (Orig.). 1995. pap. 12.00 (*0-86663-209-3*) Ide Hse.

Armfield, Ben, ed. see Grinberg, Anatoly.

Armfield, Ben, ed. see Grinberg, Frada.

Armfield, Ben, ed. see Kresin, Vladimir.

Armfield, Ben, ed. see Shlapentokh, Vladimir.

Armfield, Follin, ed. see Chapman, Elwood N.

Armfield, Follin, ed. see Finch, Lloyd.

Armfield, Follin, ed. see Forzley, Michele.

Armfield, Follin, ed. see Thompkins, Neville C.

Armfield, Follin, ed. see Viale, J. David.

Armfield, Mike. Valley of the Sun Golf Guide. 1993. pap. 12.95 (*0-9634127-0-1*) Golf Guys.

Armi, Anna M., tr. see Petrarca, Francesco.

Armi, C. Edson. The Art of American Car Design: The Profession & Personalities. LC 86-43251. (Illus.). 312p. 1988. 42.50 (*0-271-00479-7*) Pa St U Pr.

— The Headmaster of Chartres & the Origins of Gothic Sculpture. LC 92-45891. (Illus.). 256p. (C). 1994. 65.00 (*0-271-01050-9*) Pa St U Pr.

— Masons & Sculptors in Romanesque Burgundy: The New Aesthetic of Cluny III, 2 vols. LC 82-42784. (Illus.). 384p. 1984. 87.50 (*0-271-00338-3*) Pa St U Pr.

Armie, Robin L. Mom's Metal Men. 181p. mass mkt. 4.99 (*1-55197-367-7*) Picasso Publ.

***Armijo, Anthony J.** Writing-Craftsmanships: A Powerful Writing System You Can Easily Master. (Illus.). 196p. 2000. pap. 24.95 (*0-9679150-0-7*) ACPA Pr.

Armijo, Moses A., jt. auth. see Harcharik, Kathleen.

Armijos, Jack, jt. ed. see Severns, Rudy.

***Armilla, Jose.** Negotiate with Feng Shui: Enhance Your Skills in Diplomacy, Business & Relationships. 2001. pap. 12.95 (*1-56718-038-8*) Llewellyn Pubns.

Armin Kranzhoff, Jorg. Arado: History of an Aircraft Company. Theriault, Ray, tr. from GER. LC 97-65441. 168p. 1997. 35.00 (*0-7643-0293-0*) Schiffer.

Armin, Robert. Two Maids of Moreclacke. LC 77-133634. (Tudor Facsimile Texts. Old English Plays Ser.: No. 127). reprint ed. 49.50 (*0-404-53427-9*) AMS Pr.

Arminas, David & Tennison, Ted. Edmonton: The Untold Story. LC 98-14772. (Illus.). 221p. 1998. 39.00 (*1-885352-86-7*) Community Comm.

Arminas, David, et al. Edmonton, the Untold Story. LC 98-14772. 1998. pap. write for info. (*1-885352-87-5*) Community Comm.

Arminger, G., et al, eds. Handbook of Statistical Modeling for the Social & Behavioral Sciences. (Illus.). 614p. (C). 1994. 65.00 (*0-306-44805-X*, Plenum Trade) Perseus Pubng.

Armington, David. The Living Classroom: Writing, Reading, & Beyond. LC 97-69846. (Illus.). 233p. 1997. pap. 9.00 (*0-935989-83-8*) Natl Assn Child Ed.

Armington, Kevin, jt. auth. see Timour, Karin.

Armington, Stan. Lonely Planet Bhutan. (Illus.). 256p. 1998. pap. 19.95 (*0-86442-483-3*) Lonely Planet.

— Lonely Planet Trekking en Himalaya-Nepal. 6th ed. (FRE., Illus.). 372p. 1994. 22.95 (*2-84070-023-9*) Lonely Planet.

— Lonely Planet Trekking in the Nepal Himalaya: A Walking Guide. 7th ed. (Illus.). 400p. 1997. pap. 17.95 (*0-86442-511-2*) Lonely Planet.

— Trek to Mustang. (C). 1992. 30.00 (*0-7855-0217-3*, Pub. by Ratna Pustak Bhandar) St Mut.

Arminio, Joseph A. Precedent for Peace: Ancient China's Strategy & a Plan for the Prevention of World War. LC 96-77902. (Illus.). 400p. 1996. per. write for info. (*0-9644991-0-X*) Intrepid Pr.

Arminius, James. The Works of James Arminius: London Edition, 3. 2280p. (YA). (gr. 10). 1977. reprint ed. 89.95 (*0-8010-0206-0*) Baker Bks.

Armisen, P., tr. see Malgorn, Guy.

Armistead, Anne. Camp Waldemar: The Oral History of Doris Johnson. LC 98-75196. (Illus.). x, 94p. 1998. pap. 15.00 (*0-934955-36-0*) Watercress Pr.

Armistead, Bob. Warrior Forrest. (Illus.). 268p. 1998. text 24.00 (*0-9660098-0-0*) B Armistead.

***Armistead, Colin.** Knowledge Management. 1999. pap. 37.95 (*0-304-70604-3*) Continuum.

Armistead, Colin & Kiely, Julia, eds. Effective Organisations: Looking to the Future. 254p. 1997. 99.50 (*0-304-70262-5*) Continuum.

Armistead, Colin G. & Clark, Graham. Outstanding Customer Service: Implementing the Best Ideas from Around the World. LC 93-29974. 300p. 1993. 25.00 (*1-55623-629-8*, Irwn Prfssnl) McGraw-Hill Prof.

Armistead, Colin G. & Teare, Richard. Services Management: New Directions & Perspectives. (Illus.). 304p. 1996. 100.00 (*0-304-33624-6*) Continuum.

Armistead, Jack M., ed. The First English Novelists: Essays in Understanding. LC 85-3153. (Tennessee Studies in Literature: Vol. 29). 329p. 1985. text 36.00 (*0-87049-468-6*) U of Tenn Pr.

***Armistead, Jeanne.** FTCE Social Studies High School. (C). 2000. per. 22.50 (*1-58197-074-9*) XAM.

— PRAXIS Social Studies High School. (Praxis Ser.). (C). 2000. per. 22.50 (*1-58197-016-1*) XAM.

Armistead, John. Cruel As the Grave: A Sheriff Bramlett Mystery. 256p. 1996. 21.00 (*0-7867-0303-2*) Carroll & Graf.

— A Homecoming for Murder: A Sheriff Bramlett Mystery. 272p. 1995. 19.95 (*0-7867-0197-8*) Carroll & Graf.

— A Legacy of Vengeance. 256p. 1994. 19.95 (*0-7867-0059-9*) Carroll & Graf.

***Armistead, John.** The $66 Summer. (Illus.). 240p. (J). (gr. 3-8). 2000. 15.95 (*1-57131-626-4*, Pub. by Milkweed Ed); pap. 6.95 (*1-57131-625-6*, Pub. by Milkweed Ed) Publishers Group.

Armistead, M. Kathryn. God-Images: In the Healing Process. 144p. 1995. pap. 17.00 (*0-8006-2586-2*, 1-2586) Augsburg Fortress.

Armistead, Samuel G. The Spanish Tradition in Louisiana. 274p. 1991. 22.00 (*0-936388-51-X*); pap. 15.00 (*0-936388-48-X*) Juan de la Cuesta.

Armistead, Samuel G. & Silverman, Joseph H., eds. Judeo-Spanish Ballads from Bosnia. LC 76-131487. (Folklore & Folklife, Haney Ser.). (Illus.). 139p. reprint ed. pap. 43.10 (*0-8357-9747-3*, 201942000011) Bks Demand.

— Judeo-Spanish Ballads from New York: Collected by Mair Jose Bernardete. LC 80-28714. 1982. 45.00 (*0-520-04348-0*, Pub. by U CA Pr) Cal Prin Full Svc.

Armistead, Samuel G., et al. Folk Literature of the Sephardic Jews Vol. III: Judeo-Spanish Ballads from Oral Tradition, II Carolingian Ballads, 1: Roncesvalles. LC 84-24145. 375p. 1990. 55.00 (*0-520-06572-7*, Pub. by U CA Pr) Cal Prin Full Svc.

Armistead, Wilson S. Five Hundred Thousand Strokes for Freedom. LC 77-83953. (Black Heritage Library Collection). 1977. 31.95 (*0-8369-8504-4*) Ayer.

— Negro Is a Man. LC 74-89427. (Black Heritage Library Collection). 1977. 44.95 (*0-8369-8505-2*) Ayer.

— Tribute for the Negro. (Black Heritage Library Collection). 1977. 43.95 (*0-8369-8503-6*) Ayer.

Armit, Ian. The Archeology of Skye & the Western Isles. (Illus.). 288p. 1996. 25.00 (*0-7486-0640-8*, Pub. by Edinburgh U Pr) Col U Pr.

— Excavations at Cnip, West Lewis, 1988. 41p. 1988. pap. 7.50 (*0-614-21844-6*) David Brown.

— Excavations at Loch Olabhat, N. Uist, 1988. 39p. 1988. pap. 7.50 (*0-614-21845-4*) David Brown.

— Excavations at Loch Olabhat, North Uist, 1986. 19p. 1986. pap. 6.00 (*0-614-21840-3*) David Brown.

— Excavations at Loch Olabhat, North Uist, 1987. 34p. 1987. pap. 6.00 (*0-614-21843-8*) David Brown.

— The Loch Olabhat Project, 1989. 40p. 1990. pap. 7.50 (*0-614-21847-0*) David Brown.

Armit, Ian. Scotland's Hidden History. (Illus.). 176p. 1999. 29.99 (*0-7524-1400-3*, Pub. by Tempus Pubng) Arcadia Pubing.

***Armit, Ian.** Scotland's Hidden History. (Illus.). 176p. 1999. pap. 19.99 (*0-7524-1474-7*, Pub. by Tempus Pubng) Arcadia Publng.

Armit, Ian, ed. Beyond the Brochs: Changing Perspectives on the Atlantic Scottish Iron Age. (Illus.). 288p. 1991. 65.00 (*0-7486-0197-X*, Pub. by Edinburgh U Pr) Col U Pr.

Armitage, Aileen. Annabella. large type ed. LC 97-28639. 392p. 1997. 21.95 (*0-7862-1225-X*) Thorndike Pr.

— Cambermere. 224p. 1996. 22.00 (*0-7278-5110-1*) Severn Hse.

— Cambermere. large type ed. LC 96-52556. 348p. 1997. pap. 20.95 (*0-7862-1024-9*) Thorndike Pr.

***Armitage, Aileen.** The Dark Arches. 2000. pap. 10.95 (*0-552-14453-3*, Pub. by Transworld Publishers Ltd) Trafalgar.

Armitage, Aileen. The Dark Arches. large type ed. LC 97-14281. 497p. 1997. pap. 20.95 (*0-7862-1129-6*) Thorndike Pr.

— A Dark Moon Raging. large type ed. (Magna Large Print Ser.). 445p. 1997. 27.99 (*0-7505-0941-4*) Ulverscroft.

— Hawkrise. large type ed. (Magna Large Print Ser.). 339p. 1996. 27.99 (*0-7505-0942-2*, Pub. by Mgna Lrg Print) Ulverscroft.

— Hawksmoor. large type ed. (Magna Large Print Ser.). 631p. 1996. 27.99 (*0-7505-0943-0*, Pub. by Mgna Lrg Print) Ulverscroft.

— Hunter's Moon. large type ed. (Magna Large Print Ser.). (Illus.). 450p. 1996. 27.99 (*0-7505-0951-1*) Ulverscroft.

— Jason's Dominion. 192p. 22.00 (*0-7278-5203-5*) Severn Hse.

***Armitage, Aileen.** The Jericho Years. 2000. pap. 8.95 (*0-552-14049-X*, Pub. by Transworld Publishers Ltd) Trafalgar.

Armitage, Aileen. Mallory Keep. 288p. 1998. 24.00 (*0-7278-5308-2*) Severn Hse.

— The Radley Curse. 256p. 1999. 24.00 (*0-7278-2222-5*, Pub. by Severn Hse) Chivers N Amer.

— The Radley Curse. large type ed. LC 98-35737. 1999. 21.95 (*0-7862-1275-6*) Thorndike Pr.

— The Seamstress. 192p. 1999. 24.00 (*0-7278-5410-0*, Pub. by Severn Hse) Chivers N Amer.

Armitage, Aileen. A Theft of Honour. 224p. 25.00 (*0-7278-5558-1*) Severn Hse.

Armitage, Aileen. Touchstone. large type ed. (Magna Large Print Ser.). 384p. 1996. 27.99 (*0-7505-0950-3*, Pub. by Mgna Lrg Print) Ulverscroft.

— Winter Serpent. 1999. 25.00 (*0-7278-5475-5*) Severn Hse.

Armitage, Allan M. Armitage's Garden Perennials: A Color Encyclopedia. LC 99-30800. (Illus.). 324p. 2000. 49.95 (*0-88192-435-0*) Timber.

— Bedding Plants: Prolonging Shelf Performance: Postproduction Care & Handling. LC 92-45175. (Postproduction Ser.). (Illus.). 71p. (C). 1993. pap. 19.95 (*0-9626796-6-6*, B012) Ball Pub.

— Herbaceous Perennial Plants: A Treatise on Their Identification, Culture & Garden Attributes. 2nd ed. (Illus.). 1141p. 1997. pap. text 56.80 (*0-87563-723-X*) Stipes.

— Herbaceous Perennial Plants: A Treatise on Their Identification, Culture & Garden Attributes. 2nd ed. (Illus.). 1141p. (C). 1997. 69.80 (*0-87563-810-4*) Stipes.

— Ornamental Bedding Plants. (CAB International Publication Ser.: 4). 186p. 1994. pap. text 40.00 (*0-85198-901-2*) OUP.

— Specialty Cut Flowers: The Production of Annuals, Perennials, Bulbs, & Woody Plants for Fresh & Dried Cut Flowers. LC 92-34463. (Illus.). 392p. 1993. 39.95 (*0-88192-225-0*) Timber.

Armitage, Allan M., ed. see Larson, Roy A.

Armitage-Amato. Ecrire en Anglais. (ENG & FRE.). 191p. 1992. 22.95 (*0-7859-0970-2*, 2098863209) Fr & Eur.

Armitage, Andrew. Social Welfare in Canada Revisited: Facing up to the Future. 3rd ed. LC 96-221323. 220p. 1996. pap. text 38.00 (*0-19-541204-4*) OUP.

***Armitage, Andrew.** Your Voice: How to Enrich It & Develop It for Speaking, Acting & ... (Illus.). 128p. 2001. pap. 6.95 (*0-7160-2003-3*, Pub. by Elliot RW Bks) Midpt Trade.

Armitage, Andy. Teaching & Training in Post-Compulsory Education. LC 98-14516. 246p. 1998. pap. 29.95 (*0-335-20067-2*) OpUniv Pr.

Armitage, Angus. World of Copernicus. 22.95 (*0-8488-0908-4*) Amereon Ltd.

Armitage, Barri. Double Helix. LC 93-7012. 72p. 1993. 10.00 (*0-931846-42-0*) Wash Writers Pub.

Armitage, Barri, ed. see Balbo, Ned C.

Armitage, Christopher. Anne Wilkinson & Her Works. (Canadian Author Studies). 40p. (C). 1989. pap. text 9.95 (*1-55022-012-8*, Pub. by ECW) Genl Dist Srvs.

Armitage, Christopher M. Sir Walter Raleigh: An Annotated Bibliography. LC 87-40134. 252p. 1987. reprint ed. pap. 78.20 (*0-608-03183-6*, 206363600007) Bks Demand.

Armitage, Christopher M., ed. Sir Walter Raleigh: An Annotated Bibliography. LC 87-40134. xiii, 236p. 1988. 22.50 (*0-8078-1757-0*) U of NC Pr.

***Armitage, David.** The Ideological Origins of the British Empire. LC 99-87438. (Ideas in Context Ser.: Vo. 59). 260p. (C). 2000. text Price not set. (*0-521-59081-7*); pap. text Price not set. (*0-521-78978-8*) Cambridge U Pr.

Armitage, David, ed. Theories of Empire, 1450-1800 (Expanding World Ser.: No. 20). 388p. 1998. text 125.95 (*0-86078-516-5*, Pub. by Variorum) Ashgate Pub Co.

Armitage, David, et al, eds. Milton & Republicanism. (Ideas in Context Ser.: No. 35). (Illus.). 296p. (C). 1996. text 59.95 (*0-521-55178-1*) Cambridge U Pr.

— Milton & Republicanism. LC 99-162521. (Ideas in Context Ser.: No. 35). (Illus.). 296p. (C). 1998. pap. 22.95 (*0-521-64648-0*) Cambridge U Pr.

Armitage, David, jt. auth. see Armitage, Ronda.

Armitage, David, ed. see Bolingbroke, Henry.

Armitage, Edward N., jt. auth. see Wildsmith, J. A.

Armitage, Edward N., jt. ed. see Wildsmith, J. A.

Armitage, F. B. & Burley, J. Pinus Kesiya. 1980. 50.00 (*0-85074-030-4*) St Mut.

Armitage, George T. A Brief History of Hawaii. 1973. pap. 2.50 (*0-930492-04-8*) Hawaiian Serv.

Armitage, Ian M., jt. ed. see Handschumacher, Robert E.

Armitage, J. G. 75th Jubilee Conference on the Helium-4: Proceedings of the Jubilee Conference, St. Andrew, Scotland, Aug. 1-5, 1983. 232p. 1984. 41.00 (*9971-966-23-9*) World Scientific Pub.

Armitage, J. P. & Lackie, J. M., eds. Biology of the Chemotactic Response. (Society for General Microbiology Symposium Ser.: No. 46). 420p. (C). 1991. text 125.00 (*0-521-40313-8*) Cambridge U Pr.

Armitage, James O. & Antman, Karen H. High-Dose Cancer Therapy: Pharmacology, Hematopoietins, Stem Cells. (Illus.). 840p. 1992. 160.00 (*0-683-00254-6*) Lppncott W & W.

— High-Dose Cancer Therapy: Pharmacology, Hematopoietins, Stem Cells. 2nd ed. (Illus.). 925p. 1995. (*0-683-00262-7*) Lppncott W & W.

— High Dose Cancer Therapy: Pharmacology, Hematopoietins, Stem Cells. 3rd ed. LC 99-33655. 951p. 1999. text 150.00 (*0-683-30654-5*) Lppncott W & W.

Armitage, James O. & Antman, Karen H., eds. High-Dose Cancer Therapy: Pharmacology, Hematopoietins, Stem Cells. 2nd ed. LC 94-46701. 1995. 150.00 (*0-683-02627-5*) Lppncott W & W.

***Armitage, James O., et al.** Text Atlas of Lymphomas. 207p. 1999. 135.00 (*1-85317-705-9*) Martin Dunitz.

Armitage, John. History of Brazil, from the Period of the Arrival of the Braganza Family in 1808, to the Abdication of Don Pedro the First in 1831, 2 vols., Set. LC 78-128438. 1836. 145.00 (*0-404-00440-7*) AMS Pr.

Armitage, John & Brackenbury, Mark. Norwegian Cruising Guide. 2nd ed. (Illus.). 200p. 1996. 39.50 (*0-7136-4115-0*) Sheridan.

Armitage, Kate, et al. For Citrus Only. (Illus.). 160p. (Orig.). 1994. pap. 9.95 (*0-9642590-0-1*) Four Citrus Only.

Armitage, Katie & Lee, John. Nineteenth Century Houses in Lawrence, Kansas. rev. ed. LC 90-70831. (Illus.). 71p. 1991. pap. 8.95 (*0-913689-29-7*) Spencer Muse Art.

Armitage, M. J. & Mason, R. A. Air Power in the Nuclear Age. 2nd ed. LC 82-17551. 334p. reprint ed. pap 103.60 (*0-8357-6354-4*, 203562900096) Bks Demand.

Armitage, Margaret. More Than Skin Deep. 1988. pap. 4.95 (*9971-972-67-0*) OMF Bks.

Armitage, Merle. Dance Memoranda. Corle, Edwin, ed. LC 78-76890. (Essay Index Reprint Ser.). 1977. 44.95 (*0-8369-0001-4*) Ayer.

— Dance Memoranda. Corle, Edwin & Bamman, Catherine, eds. LC 78-76890. (Essay Index Reprint Ser.). (Illus.). 200p. reprint ed. lib. bdg. 42.00 (*0-8290-0836-5*) Irvington.

— George Gershwin, Man & Legend. LC 75-117324. (Biography Index Reprint Ser.). 1980. 29.95 (*0-8369-8016-6*) Ayer.

— Igor Stravinsky. Corle, Edwin, ed. LC 77-84295. (Essay Index Reprint Ser.). 1977. 34.95 (*0-8369-1120-2*) Ayer.

— Merle Armitage: Book Designer. (Illus.). 32p. 1963. pap. 7.50 (*0-87959-117-X*) U of Tex H Ransom Ctr.

Armitage, Merle, ed. George Gershwin. LC 94-37445. (Illus.). 261p. 1995. pap. 16.95 (*0-306-80615-0*) Da Capo.

— Martha Graham: The Early Years. LC 78-17608. (Series in Dance). (Illus.). 1978. reprint ed. pap. 12.95 (*0-306-80084-5*); reprint ed. lib. bdg. 25.00 (*0-306-79504-3*) Da Capo.

— Schoenberg: Articles by Arnold Schoenberg, Erwin Stein & Others, 1929-1937. LC 79-106709. 319p. 1977. reprint ed. lib. bdg. 65.00 (*0-8371-3439-0*, ARSC) Greenwood.

— Schoenberg: Articles by Arnold Schoenberg, Erwin Stein & Others, 1929-1937. LC 79-106709. 1977. reprint ed. fiche 11.80 (*0-8371-9600-0*) Greenwood.

— Schoenberg: Articles by Arnold Schoenberg, Erwin Stein & Others, 1929-1937. LC 79-106709. 1977. reprint ed. fiche 20.65 (*0-8371-9599-3*) Greenwood.

— Schoenberg: Nineteen Twenty-Nine to Nineteen Thirty-Seven. LC 77-157360. (Select Bibliographies Reprint Ser.). 1980. reprint ed. 23.95 (*0-8369-5783-0*) Ayer.

Armitage, Michael. Unmanned Aircraft. Mason, R. A., ed. (Air Power: Aircraft, Weapons Systems & Technology Ser.: Vol. 3). (Illus.). 137p. 1988. 40.00 (*0-08-034743-6*, Pub. by Brasseys); 25.00 (*0-08-034744-4*, Pub. by Brasseys) Brasseys.

Armitage, Michael, jt. auth. see Cantwell, James R.

***Armitage, Oliver C. P.** Fox Tales. LC 98-88357. 210 P. ;p. 1998. write for info. (*0-9667989-0-2*) Sharp Printng.

Armitage, P. & Berry, G. Statistical Methods in Medical Research. 3rd ed. LC 93-22118. (Illus.). 640p. 1994. 69.95 (*0-632-03695-8*, Pub. by Blckwll Scitfc UK) Blackwell Sci.

***Armitage, Peter & Colton, Ted, eds.** Encyclopedia of Biostatistics, 6 vols. LC 98-10160. 4898p. 1998. text 2750.00 (*0-471-97576-1*) Wiley.

Armitage, Peter & David, Herbert A., eds. Advances in Biometry. LC 96-12147. (Series in Probability & Statistics). 496p. 1996. 99.95 (*0-471-16018-0*) Wiley.

Armitage, Richard & Taylor, John. Out & About: A Travel & Transport Guide. (C). 1989. 30.00 (*0-86242-092-X*, Pub. by Age Concern Eng) St Mut.

Armitage, Robert B. The Law of Breathing & Chest Development. 170p. 1996. reprint ed. spiral bd. 13.00 (*0-7873-0040-3*) Hlth Research.

***Armitage, Ronda.** Family Violence. LC 99-26786. (J). 1999. 27.12 (*0-7398-1371-4*) Raintree Steck-V.

Armitage, Ronda. Lighthouse Keeper. (J). Date not set. pap. text. write for info. (*0-05-004387-0*) Addison-Wesley.

Armitage, Ronda & Armitage, David. Harry Hates Shopping! LC 92-27945. (Hello Reader! Ser.). (Illus.). 32p. (J). (gr. 1-3). 1993. pap. 3.50 (*0-590-45886-8*) Scholastic Inc.

***Armitage, Shelley.** Bones Incandescent: The Pajarito Journals of Peggy Pond Church. 2001. 32.95 (*0-89672-438-7*) Tex Tech Univ Pr.

Armitage, Shelley. Kewpies & Beyond: The World of Rose O'Neil. LC 94-11421. (Studies in Popular Culture). (Illus.). 224p. 1994. pap. text 18.95 (*0-87805-711-0*) U Pr of Miss.

— Peggy Pond Church. LC 93-70136. (Western Writers Ser.: No. 108). (Illus.). 52p. 1993. pap. 4.95 (*0-88430-107-9*) Boise St U W Writ Ser.

— Women's Work: Essays in Cultural Studies. LC 95-6180. (Locust Hill Literary Studies: No. 15). (Illus.). 311p. (C). 1995. lib. bdg. 32.00 (*0-933951-58-2*) Locust Hill Pr.

Armitage, Simon. Zoom. LC 89-82482. 80p. (Orig.). 1990. pap. 14.95 (*1-85224-078-4*, Pub. by Bloodaxe Bks) Dufour.

***Armitage, Simon & Gill, Peter.** Eclipse/Friendly Fire. (Connections Ser.). (Illus.). 112p. (YA). 2000. pap. 17.95 (*0-7487-4290-5*, Pub. by S Thornes Pubs) Trans-Atl Phila.

***Armitage, Simon, et al.** The Poetry Quartets, Vol. 1. 1999. (*1-85224-468-2*, Pub. by Bloodaxe Bks) Dufour.

Armitage-Smith, George. Free-Trade Movement & Its Results. LC 77-95061. (Select Bibliographies Reprint Ser.). 1977. 29.95 (*0-8369-5063-1*) Ayer.

Armitage, Susan & Jameson, Elizabeth, eds. The Women's West. LC 86-14672. (Illus.). 336p. 1987. 35.00 (*0-8061-2043-6*); pap. 17.95 (*0-8061-2067-3*) U of Okla Pr.

Armitage, Susan, jt. ed. see Jameson, Elizabeth.

Armitage, Yvonne N. Paradise Preserves. LC 87-32710. (Illus.). 126p. (Orig.). 1988. pap. 7.95 (*0-916630-63-3*) Pr Pacifica.

Armitstead, K. A., et al, contrib. by. Macromolecules: Synthesis, Order & Advanced Properties. (Advances in Polymer Science Ser.: Vol. 100). (Illus.). xi, 422p. 1992. 200.00 (*0-387-54490-9*) Spr-Verlag.

Armitt, Lucie. Contemporary Women's Fiction. LC 99-36163. 200p. 1999. text 49.95 (*0-312-22666-7*) St Martin.

— Theorising the Fantastic. LC 96-21671. (Interrogating Texts Ser.). (Illus.). 230p. 1996. pap. text 19.95 (*0-340-60587-1*) OUP.

— Theorising the Fantastic. LC 96-21671. (Interrogating Texts Ser.). (Illus.). 230p. 1996. text 65.00 (*0-340-67726-0*) OUP.

Armleder, John. John Armleder. (Illus.). 64p. 1988. 30.00 (*0-929445-00-7*) D Greenidge Editions.

Armogathe, J. R. Theologia Cartesiana. (International Archives of the History of Ideas Ser.: No. 84). 157p. 1977. lib. bdg. 126.50 (*90-247-1869-4*, Pub. by M Nijhoff) Kluwer Academic.

Armold. A Essentials of Gob. (C). 1998. pap. text. write for info. (*0-03-022428-4*) Harcourt Coll Pubs.

A

An Asterisk (*) at the beginning of an entry indicates that the title is appearing for the first time.

A

Armold, Chris. Steel Pots: History of America's Steel Combat Helmets. LC 98-121012. (Illus.). 272p. 1997. 47.95 (*0-912138-70-X*) Bender Pub CA.

Armon, Carmel. ALS 1996 & Beyond: New Hopes & Challenges - Manual for Patients, Families & Friends. 2nd rev. ed. (Illus.). 18p. 1996. pap. write for info. (*0-9655186-0-4*) Loma Lnda U Neur.

Armon, Cheryl, jt. auth. see Richards, Francis A.

Armon-Jones, Claire. Varieties of Affect. (Studies in Philosophy). 200p. 1992. text 50.00 (*0-8020-2823-3*) U of Toronto Pr.

Armona, Jose A. De, see De Armona, Jose A.

Armond, Elizabeth De, see De Armond, Elizabeth.

Armond, Gary E. De, see De Armond, Garry E.

Armond Marchant, Alexander N. De, see De Armond Marchant, Alexander N.

Armond, Robert N. De, see Atwood, Evangeline & De Armond, Robert N., compiled by.

Armond, Steve de, see Kunzle-Watson, Karin.

Armond, Steve de, see Kunzle-Watson, Karin & De Armond, Steve.

***Armoni, Adi, ed.** Healthcare Information Systems: Challenges of the New Millennium. LC 99-52784. (Illus.). 300p. (C). 2000. pap. 69.95 (*1-878289-62-4*) Idea Group Pub.

Armony, Ariel C. Argentina, the United States, & the Anti-Communist Crusade in Central America. LC 96-8612. (Monographs in International Studies, Southeast Asia Ser.: No. 26). 250p. (Orig.). 1997. pap. text 26.00 (*0-89680-196-9*) Ohio U Pr.

Armony, Ariel C., jt. auth. see Walker, Thomas W.

Armony, Ariel C., jt. ed. see Walker, Thomas W.

Armor, David J. The American School Counselor: A Case Study in the Sociology of Professions. LC 68-58127. 228p. 1969. 22.00 (*0-87154-069-X*) Russell Sage.

— Forced Justice: School Desegregation & the Law. (Illus.). 288p. 1995. text 60.00 (*0-19-509012-8*) OUP.

— Forced Justice: School Desegregation & the Law. (Illus.). 288p. 1996. reprint ed. pap. 19.95 (*0-19-511135-4*) OUP.

Armor, David J. & Peiser, Brett M. Competition in Education: A Case Study of Interdistrict Choice. Ciffolillo, Kathryn, ed. LC 97-11432. (Pioneer Papers: No. 12). 185p. (Orig.). 1997. pap. 15.00 (*0-929930-17-7*) Pioneer Inst.

Armor de Comos. Notes from the Netshed. (Illus.). 256p. 1997. pap. 17.95 (*1-55017-172-0*) Harbour Pub Co.

Armor, John C. The Six O'Clock Man. 272p. (Orig.). 1988. pap. 12.95 (*0-87651-995-8*) Southern U Pr.

— Why Terms Limits? Because They Have It Coming. LC 95-161615. 176p. 1994. pap. 9.95 (*0-915463-70-9*) Jameson Bks.

Armor, John C., jt. auth. see Wright, Peter.

Armor, John N., ed. Environmental Catalysis. LC 93-51098. (ACS Symposium Ser.: No. 552). 467p. 1994. text 110.00 (*0-8412-2851-5*, Pub. by Am Chemical) OUP.

Armor, Joyce. What You Don't Know about Having Babies. (Illus.). 1997. 6.00 (*0-671-57682-8*) S&S Trade.

— What You Don't Know about Having Babies: The Pregnancy Question & Answer Book. LC 97-20567. 1997. write for info. (*0-88166-292-5*) Meadowbrook.

Armor, Murray. Building Your Own Home. 1988. pap. write for info. (*1-85327-007-5*, Pub. by Prism Pr) Assoc Pubs Grp.

— Building Your Own Home. 11th ed. 1989. pap. write for info. (*1-85327-028-8*, Pub. by Prism Pr) Assoc Pubs Grp.

Armor, Reginald C. Ernest Holmes: The Man. 128p. 1977. pap. 7.95 (*0-911336-66-4*) Sci of Mind.

— The Magic of Love. LC 67-14304. 120p. (Orig.). 1992. pap. 10.95 (*0-917849-14-0*, 0500) Sci of Mind.

***Armor, Reginald C.** That Was Ernest: The Story of Ernest Holmes & the Religious Science Movement. Vergara, Arthur, ed. LC 98-74806. (Illus.). 176p. 1999. pap. 10.95 (*0-87516-712-8*) DeVorss.

Armor, William. Lives of the Governors of Pennsylvania with the . . . 500p. 1985. reprint ed. lib. bdg. 69.00 (*0-932051-37-5*) Rprt Serv.

Armour, Andrew J., ed. Asia & Japan: The Search for Modernization & Identity. LC 85-9029. 169p. (C). 1985. text 36.00 (*0-485-11261-2*, Pub. by Athlone Pr) Humanities.

Armour, Audrey M., ed. The Siting of Locally Unwanted Land Uses: Towards a Cooperative Approach. (Progress in Planning Ser.: No. 35). (Illus.). 80p. 1991. pap. 54.00 (*0-08-040788-9*, Pergamon Pr) Elsevier.

Armour, D. J. Felsted Preparatory School: The First 100 Years, 1895-1995. LC 95-6401. (Illus.). 99p. (C). 1995. text 39.95 (*0-485-11482-8*, Pub. by Athlone Pr) Humanities.

Armour, David, ed. see Eustice, Sally.

Armour, David A. Fort Michilimackinac Sketch Book. (Illus.). 64p. (Orig.). 1975. pap. 2.95 (*0-911872-16-7*) Mackinac St Hist Pks.

— Historic Mill Creek. (Illus.). 62p. 1996. pap. 8.95 (*0-911872-66-3*) Mackinac St Hist Pks.

— 100 Years at Mackinac: A Centennial History of the Mackinac Island State Park Commission 1895-1995. LC 96-622027. (Illus.). 138p. 1995. 29.95 (*0-911872-63-9*) Mackinac St Hist Pks.

Armour, David A., ed. Treason at Michilimackinac? The Proceedings of a General Court Martial Held at Montreal in October 1768 for the Trial of Major Robert Rogers. LC 67-81179. (Illus.). 103p. 1967. pap. 6.00 (*0-911872-32-9*) Mackinac St Hist Pks.

Armour, David A. & Widder, Keith R. At the Crossroads: Michilimackinac During the American Revolution. (Illus.). 249p. 1978. 19.95 (*0-911872-24-8*) Mackinac St Hist Pks.

Armour, David A., ed. see Dunnigan, Brian L.

Armour, David A., ed. see Hamilton, T. M.

Armour, David A., ed. see Heldman, Donald P. & Minnerly, William L.

Armour, David A., ed. see Henry, Alexander.

Armour, David A., ed. see Porter, Phil.

Armour, David A., ed. see Stone, Lyle M.

Armour, E. A., jt. ed. see Humberston, John W.

Armour, Ellen T. Deconstruction. 1999. pap. text 18.00 (*0-226-02690-6*) U Ch Pr.

— Deconstruction, Feminist Theology, & the Problem of Difference: Subverting the Race/Gender Div. LC 98-48860. 264p. 1999. lib. bdg. 45.00 (*0-226-02689-2*) U Ch Pr.

***Armour, Frank & Miller, Granville.** Advanced Use Case Modeling: Software Systems, 1. 304p. 2000. pap. 34.95 (*0-201-61592-4*) Addison-Wesley.

Armour, J. & Ogbourne, C. P., eds. Bovine Ostertagiasis: A Review & Annotated Bibliography. 93p. (C). 1996. pap. 29.95 (*0-85198-495-9*) OUP.

Armour, Joan, ed. see McGraw, Marjie.

Armour, Jody D. Negrophobia & Reasonable Racism: The Hidden Costs of Being Black in America. LC 96-51306. (Critical America Ser.). 1997. text 25.00 (*0-8147-0640-1*) NYU Pr.

Armour, Jody David. Negrophobia & Reasonable Racism: The Hidden Costs of Being Black in America. 2000. pap. 17.95 (*0-8147-0670-3*) NYU Pr.

***Armour, John.** Death of a Doctor. 296p. 2000. 18.99 (*0-7089-5718-8*) Ulverscroft.

— Murder in Hawthorn. large type ed. 256p. pap. 18.99 (*0-7089-5418-9*) Ulverscroft.

Armour, John. The Sun Devils. large type ed. (Linford Western Library). 304p. 1992. pap. 16.99 (*0-7089-7173-3*) Ulverscroft.

Armour, John A. & Ardell, Jeffrey L., eds. Neurocardiology. LC 93-41500. (Illus.). 456p. (C). 1994. text 75.00 (*0-19-507304-5*) OUP.

Armour, Joyce. Pregnant Pauses. 256p. 1995. mass mkt. 4.99 (*0-7860-0137-2*) Kensgtn Pub Corp.

Armour, Kathleen R. Physical Education: Teachers' Lives & Careers. LC 98-185973. 1998. 79.00 (*0-7507-0818-2*, Falmer Pr); pap. 25.95 (*0-7507-0817-4*, Falmer Pr) Taylor & Francis.

Armour, Leslie. Being & Idea: Development of Some Themes in Spinoza & Hegel. (Philosophische Texte und Studien: Vol. 26). (GER.). xxii, 185p. 1992. 35.00 (*3-487-09513-0*) G Olms Pubs.

— Infini Rien: Pascal's Wager & the Human Paradox. LC 92-27762. (Journal of the History of Philosophy Monograph Ser.). 136p. (C). 1993. pap. 20.95 (*0-8093-1839-3*) S Ill U Pr.

Armour, Leslie & Trott, Elizabeth. The Faces of Reason: An Essay on Philosophy & Culture in English Canada 1850-1950. 574p. (C). 1995. reprint ed. pap. 34.95 (*0-88920-255-9*) W Laurier U Pr.

Armour, Margaret-Ann. Handbook of Hazardous Laboratory Chemicals: Information & Disposal. 352p. 1991. lib. bdg. 121.95 (*0-8493-0265-X*, 265BK) CRC Pr.

— Hazardous Laboratory Chemicals Disposal Guide. 2nd ed. LC 96-2428. 592p. 1996. spiral bd. 104.95 (*1-56670-108-2*) CRC Pr.

Armour, Maureen W. Poetry, the Magic Language: Children Learn to Read & Write It. xvii, 215p. 1994. pap. text 17.50 (*1-56308-033-8*) Teacher Ideas Pr.

Armour, Michael C. Newcomer's Guide to the Bible: Themes & Timelines. LC 99-30558. 300p. 1999. pap. 17.99 (*0-89900-859-3*) College Pr Pub.

— Orca Song. LC 94-927. (Smithsonian Oceanic Collection). (Illus.). 32p. (J). (ps-2). 1994. 15.95 (*1-56899-069-3*) Soundprints.

— Orca Song. unabridged ed. LC 94-927. (Smithsonian Oceanic Collection). (Illus.). 32p. (J). (ps-2). 1994. 19.95 incl. audio (*1-56899-073-1*) Soundprints.

— Orca Song, Incl. large toy. LC 94-927. (Smithsonian Oceanic Collection). (Illus.). 32p. (J). (ps-2). 1994. 29.95 (*1-56899-071-5*) Soundprints.

— Orca Song, Micro-Book. LC 94-927. (Smithsonian Oceanic Collection). (Illus.). 32p. (J). (ps-2). 1994. 4.95 (*1-56899-070-7*) Soundprints.

— Orca Song, Micro-Book, incl. small toy. LC 94-927. (Smithsonian Oceanic Collection). (Illus.). 32p. (J). (ps-2). 1994. 9.95 (*1-56899-072-3*) Soundprints.

— Puma Range. (Smithsonian Wild Heritage Collection). (Illus.). 32p. (J). (ps-3). 1995. pap. 4.95 (*1-56899-202-5*) Soundprints.

— Puma Range. (Smithsonian Wild Heritage Collection). 1994. 10.15 (*0-606-08047-3*, Pub. by Turtleback) Demco.

— Puma Range, Incl. 6" toy. (Smithsonian Wild Heritage Collection). (Illus.). 32p. (J). (gr. k-3). 1995. pap. 15.95 (*1-56899-208-4*) Soundprints.

Armour, Michael C. & Browning, Don. Systems-Sensitive Leadership: Empowering Diversity Without Polarizing the Church. LC 95-2490. 1995. pap. 12.99 (*0-89900-736-8*) College Pr Pub.

***Armour, Michael C. & Browning, Don.** Systems-Sensitive Leadership: Empowering Diversity Without Polarizing the Church. 2nd ed. LC 00-31604. 2000. pap. write for info. (*0-89900-814-3*) College Pr Pub.

Armour, Mike. You Are Not Your Own: Becoming God's Steward. (Small Group Studies). 39p. 1997. pap. 4.99 (*0-89900-701-5*, T96-701-5) College Pr Pub.

Armour, Peter. Dante's Griffin & the History of the World: A Study of the Earthly Paradise (Purgatorio, Cantos xxiv-xxxiii) (Illus.). 340p. 1989. text 75.00 (*0-19-815816-5*) OUP.

— The Door of Purgatory: A Study of Multiple Symbolism in Dante's Purgatorio. 1984. 49.95 (*0-19-815787-8*) OUP.

Armour, Peter. Stop That Pickle! LC 92-903544. (Illus.). 32p. (J). 1993. 16.00 (*0-395-66375-X*) HM.

Armour, Richard. Anyone for Insomnia? A Playful Look at Sleeplessness. LC 82-9996. 128p. (Orig.). 1982. pap. 4.95 (*0-912800-69-0*) Woodbridge Pr.

— Armoury of Light Verse. 1962. pap. 5.95 (*0-8283-1424-1*, 25) Branden Bks.

— Educated Guesses: Light-Serious Suggestions for Parents & Teachers. LC 82-17670. 192p. (Orig.). 1983. pap. 5.95 (*0-88007-127-3*) Woodbridge Pr.

— Golf Is a Four-Letter Word: The Intimate Confessions of a Hooked Slicer. LC 92-45798. (Illus.). 128p. 1993. reprint ed. pap. 12.95 (*1-55821-222-1*) Burford Bks.

— Our Presidents: From George Washington to Ronald Reagan. rev. ed. LC 82-23762. (Illus.). 96p. 1983. 9.95 (*0-88007-133-8*); pap. 5.95 (*0-88007-134-6*) Woodbridge Pr.

Armour, Richard & Gurney, Eric. Richard Armour's Punctured Poems: Famous First & Infamous Second Lines. LC 82-10989. (Illus.). 96p. 1982. pap. 3.95 (*0-912800-55-0*) Woodbridge Pr.

Armour, Robert A. Film: A Reference Guide. LC 79-6566. (American Popular Culture Ser.). 251p. 1980. lib. bdg. 59.95 (*0-313-22241-X*, AFR/, Greenwood Pr) Greenwood.

— God & Myths of Ancient Egypt. 1986. pap. 17.00 (*977-424-113-4*, Pub. by Am Univ Cairo Pr) Col U Pr.

***Armour, Rollin Stely.** Anabaptist Baptism: A Representative Study. 214p. 1998. pap. 20.00 (*1-57910-158-5*) Wipf & Stock.

Armour-Thomas, Eleanor & Gopaul-McNicol, Sharon-Ann. Assessing Intelligence: Applying a Biocultural Model. LC 97-45335. (Ethnic Minority Psychology Ser.). 264p. 1998. 30.00 (*0-7619-0520-0*); pap. 13.99 (*0-7619-0521-9*) Sage.

Armour, Tommy. Classic Golf Tips. 1994. 19.95 (*1-56943-009-8*) NTC Contemp Pub Co.

— Classic Golf Tips. LC 95-23058. (Illus.). 176p. 1995. pap. 10.00 (*0-8092-3342-8*) NTC Contemp Pub Co.

— How to Play Your Best Golf All the Time. 18.95 (*0-89190-272-4*) Amereon Ltd.

— How to Play Your Best Golf All the Time. 1995. per. 11.00 (*0-684-81379-3*, Fireside) S&S Trade Pap.

— How to Play Your Best Golf All the Time. rev. ed. (Classics of Golf Ser.). (Illus.). 150p. 1985. 28.00 (*0-940889-02-1*) Classics Golf.

— A Round of Golf with Tommy Armour. LC 92-39124. (Illus.). 160p. 1993. reprint ed. pap. 13.95 (*1-55821-217-5*) Burford Bks.

Armpriester, K. E. Do Your Own Wiring. LC 91-18970. (Illus.). 128p. 1991. pap. 12.95 (*0-8069-8472-4*) Sterling.

Armpriester, K. E. & Bremer, B. A. The Homeowner's Guide to Carpentry & Cabinetry. LC 90-22206. (Illus.). 256p. (Orig.). 1990. pap. 16.95 (*0-8069-7298-X*) Sterling.

— The Homeowner's Guide to Carpentry & Cabinetry. (Illus.). 246p. (Orig.). 1990. pap. 12.95 (*1-55654-059-0*) Times Mir Mag Bk Div.

Armpriester, K. E. & Favorite, Mary J. Fifty Storage Projects for the Home. LC 89-11553. (Illus.). 247p. 1989. pap. 14.95 (*0-8069-5798-0*) Sterling.

Arms. Bio Art - Biology. 3rd ed. (C). 1994. pap. text 40.00 (*0-03-097835-1*, Pub. by Harcourt Coll Pubs) Harcourt.

— BIO: JOURNEY/LIFE 2/E (SCH ED) 2nd ed. (C). 1991. text 80.00 (*0-03-072617-4*) Harcourt Coll Pubs.

— Bioart - Biology. 4th ed. (C). 1995. 35.50 (*0-03-007522-X*, Pub. by Harcourt Coll Pubs) Harcourt.

— Biologie, Vol. 1. (C). 1991. pap. write for info. (*0-03-998306-4*) Harcourt Coll Pubs.

— Biologie, Vol. 2. (C). 1991. pap. write for info. (*0-03-998292-0*) Harcourt Coll Pubs.

— Biology. 4th ed. (C). 1995. student ed. 110.50 (*0-03-016833-3*) Harcourt.

— Biology. 4th ed. (C). 1995. text 97.00 (*0-03-050003-6*, Pub. by Harcourt Coll Pubs) Harcourt.

— Biology. 4th ed. (C). 1995. pap. text, teacher ed. 32.00 (*0-03-005688-8*) Harcourt Coll Pubs.

— Biology. 4th ed. (C). 1995. pap. text, teacher ed., suppl. ed. 37.50 (*0-03-005692-6*, Pub. by Harcourt Coll Pubs) Harcourt.

— Biology. 4th ed. (C). 1995. pap. text, student ed. 26.00 (*0-03-005689-6*, Pub. by Harcourt Coll Pubs) Harcourt.

— Biology: A Journey into Life. (C). 1989. text 80.00 (*0-03-031352-X*) Harcourt Coll Pubs.

— Biology: A Journey into Life. 3rd ed. (C). 1993. pap. text, teacher ed. 40.00 (*0-03-006774-X*, Pub. by Harcourt Coll Pubs) Harcourt.

— Biology: A Journey into Life. 3rd ed. (C). 1994. pap. text 80.00 (*0-03-098796-2*, Pub. by Harcourt Coll Pubs) Harcourt.

— Biology: A Journey into Life. 3rd ed. (C). 1994. 288.00 (*0-03-006777-4*, Pub. by Harcourt Coll Pubs) Harcourt.

— Biology: A Journey into Life. 3rd ed. (C). 1994. pap. text, student ed. 27.50 (*0-03-097829-7*, Pub. by Harcourt Coll Pubs) Harcourt.

— Biology: A Journey into Life. 3rd ed. (C). 1994. pap. text, student ed. 33.75 (*0-03-097828-9*) Harcourt Coll Pubs.

— Biology: A Journey into Life. 4th ed. (C). 1997. pap. text 55.75 (*0-03-011208-7*) Harcourt.

— Biology: A Journey into Life, Vol. 2. 3rd ed. (C). 1994. pap. text 58.50 (*0-03-003149-4*, Pub. by Harcourt Coll Pubs) Harcourt.

— Biology: Journey into Life. 2nd ed. (C). 1991. pap. text, teacher ed. 34.00 (*0-03-047454-X*) Harcourt Coll Pubs.

— Biology: Journey into Life. 3rd ed. (C). 1994. text 90.50 (*0-03-010253-7*) Harcourt Coll Pubs.

— Biology: The Journey Through Life. (C). 1988. pap. text, teacher ed., lab manual ed. 34.00 (*0-03-012839-0*) Harcourt Coll Pubs.

— Biology Journey into Life. 3rd ed. (C). 1994. text 91.00 (*0-03-076704-0*, Pub. by Harcourt Coll Pubs) Harcourt.

— Discover Magazine - Biology. 4th ed. (C). 1993. pap. text 11.50 (*0-03-005079-0*, Pub. by Harcourt Coll Pubs) Harcourt.

— Enviromental Science. 2nd ed. (C). 1994. text 82.00 (*0-03-001821-8*) Harcourt Coll Pubs.

— Environmental Concerns Quarterly. (C). 1994. pap. text 33.75 (*0-03-014999-1*) Harcourt Coll Pubs.

— Environmental Science. (C). 1990. pap. text, teacher ed. 34.00 (*0-03-007179-8*) Harcourt Coll Pubs.

— Environmental Science. (C). 1990. text 74.00 (*0-03-053614-6*) Harcourt Coll Pubs.

— Environmental Science. 2nd ed. (C). 1994. pap. text, teacher ed., suppl. ed. 33.75 (*0-03-072822-3*) Harcourt Coll Pubs.

— Environmental Science: Northwest. 2nd ed. (C). 1993. 82.00 (*0-03-003659-3*) Harcourt.

— Environmental Science: Southeast. 2nd ed. (C). 1993. 82.00 (*0-03-003642-9*) Harcourt.

— Environmental Science: Southwest. 2nd ed. (C). 1993. 82.00 (*0-03-003658-5*) Harcourt.

— Holt Environmental Science. 1996. text 75.00 (*0-03-095400-2*) Holt R&W.

— Oht - Biology: A Journey Into Life 3e. 3rd ed. (C). 1994. pap. text 288.00 (*0-03-097834-3*) Harcourt.

— PE Biology 4/E. 95th ed. (C). 1995. text 93.00 (*0-03-015434-0*) Harcourt Coll Pubs.

***Arms Bzdak, Meredith.** Public Sculpture in New Jersey: Monuments to Collective Identity. LC 98-55319. 220p. 1999. pap. 22.00 (*0-8135-2700-7*) Rutgers U Pr.

Arms, Caroline, et al, eds. Enabling Access in Digital Libraries: A Report on a Workshop on Access Management. LC 99-222916. (Illus.). 36p. 1999. pap. 15.00 (*1-887334-64-5*) Coun Lib & Info.

Arms, Caroline R., ed. Campus Strategies for Libraries & Electronic Information. (Illus.). 404p. 1989. text 41.95 (*1-55558-036-X*, EY-C185E-DP, Digital DEC) Buttrwrth-Heinemann.

Arms, George. The Fields Were Green: A New View of Bryant, Whittier, Holmes, Lowell, & Longfellow, with a Selection of Their Poems. xii, 246p. 1953. 35.00 (*0-8047-0443-0*) Stanford U Pr.

Arms, George, jt. ed. see Gibson, William M.

Arms, George, ed. see Howells, Elinor M.

Arms, George, ed. see Howells, William Dean.

Arms, Karen. Biology: Journey of Life. 2nd ed. (C). 1991. pap. text 40.50 (*0-03-076679-6*, Pub. by Harcourt Coll Pubs) Harcourt.

— Environmental Science. 2nd ed. 546p. (C). 1993. pap. text 77.50 (*0-03-098569-2*) SCP.

Arms, Karen, ed. Brief Dictionary of Biology & Environmental Sciences. (Illus.). 128p. (Orig.). (C). 1992. pap. text 4.95 (*0-9629275-1-1*) Halfmoon Pub.

Arms, Karen G., et al. Cultural Diversity & Families. 224p. (C). 1992. text. write for info. (*0-697-16410-1*) Brown & Benchmark.

Arms, Marsha E., jt. auth. see Arms, William T.

Arms, Myron. Cathedral of the World: Sailing Notes for a Blue Planet. LC 98-27557. 176p. 1999. 21.95 (*0-385-49269-3*, Anchor NY) Doubleday.

***Arms, Myron.** Cathedral of the World: Sailing Notes for a Blue Planet. 176p. 2000. pap. 12.00 (*0-385-49476-9*, Anchor NY) Doubleday.

Arms, Myron. Cathedral of the World: Sailing Notes for a Blue Planet. LC 99-26566. 1999. 25.95 (*0-7838-8647-0*) Thorndike Pr.

— Riddle of the Ice. 288p. 1999. pap. 12.95 (*0-385-49093-3*) Doubleday.

***Arms, Myron.** Riddle of the Ice: A Scientific Adventure into the Arctic. LC 97-26104. 288p. 1998. 22.95 (*0-385-49092-5*, Anchor NY) Doubleday.

Arms, Phil. Promise Keepers: Another Trojan Horse: They Really Are Breaking down the Walls. LC 96-71761. 416p. 1997. 25.95 (*1-890058-00-9*); pap. 15.95 (*1-890058-01-7*) P Arms Minist.

Arms, Richard, Jr. Arms Index. (Illus.). 100p. 1998. 39.95 (*1-883272-15-7*) Traders Lib.

— Profits in Volume: Equivolume Charting. (Illus.). 158p. 1999. 39.95 (*1-883272-25-4*) Traders Lib.

Arms, Richard W. Trading Without Fear: Eliminating Emotional Decisions with Arms Trading. LC 96-10229. 288p. 1996. 59.95 (*0-471-13748-0*) Wiley.

Arms, Richard W., Jr. Volume Cycles in the Stock Market: Market Timing Through Equivolume Charting. rev. ed. (University Ser.). (Illus.). 148p. 1994. reprint ed. 39.95 (*1-885439-00-8*) Equis International.

Arms, Suzanne. Adoption: A Handful of Hope. enl. rev. ed. LC 88-13861. (Illus.). 320p. 1995. pap. 14.95 (*0-89087-551-0*) Celestial Arts.

— Immaculate Deception II: Myth, Magic, & Birth. 302p. 1995. pap. 14.95 (*0-89087-633-9*) Celestial Arts.

— Seasons of Change: Growing Through Pregnancy & Birth. LC 94-76629. (Illus.). 184p. (Orig.). 1994. pap. 14.95 (*1-882308-58-1*) Kivaki Pr.

Arms, Thomas S. Encyclopedia of the Cold War. (Illus.). 640p. 1994. 70.00 (*0-8160-1975-4*) Facts on File.

Arms, W. Y., et al. A Practical Approach to Computing. fac. ed. LC 75-15787. 365p. pap. 113.20 (*0-7837-7375-7*, 204718500005) Bks Demand.

Arms, William T. & Arms, Marsha E. History of Leyden, MA 1676-1959. (Illus.). 220p. 1997. reprint ed. lib. bdg. 32.00 (*0-8328-5959-1*) Higginson Bk Co.

Arms, William Y. Digital Libraries. LC 99-14773. (Digital Libraries & Electronic Publishing). 519p. 2000. 45.00 (*0-262-01180-8*) MIT Pr.

Armsby, Leonora W. Musicians Talk. LC 76-99679. (Essay Index Reprint Ser.). 1977. 21.95 (*0-8369-1338-8*) Ayer.

Armsstrong, A. H., tr. see Stauffer, Dietrich & Stanley, H. Eugene.

Armstead, jt. auth. see NBPA Staff.

Armstead, H. Christopher. Geothermal Energy: Its Past, Present & Future Contributions to the Energy Needs to Man. 2nd ed. LC 83-337. 1983. 59.95 (*0-419-12220-6*, NO. 6824, E & FN Spon) Routledge.

***Armstead, Jeanne.** ExCet Social Sciences High School. (ExCet Teacher Certification Ser.). (C). 1999. per. 22.50 (*1-58197-112-5*) XAM.

Armstead, Karen, et al. Fresh Ink No. One: A Collection by Thirteen Bay Area Poets. 82p. 1989. pap. 4.00 (*1-883348-00-5*) Fresh Ink.

Armstead, Lloyd D. Whitewater Rafting in North America: More Than 100 Rafting Adventures in the U. S. & Canada. 2nd rev. ed. LC 96-47037. (Illus.). 288p. 1997. pap. 16.95 (*0-7627-0083-1*) Globe Pequot.

Armstead, Myra Beth Young. "Lord, Please Don't Take Me in August" African Americans in Newport & Saratoga Springs. LC 98-58092. 1999. 39.95 (*0-252-02485-0*) U of Ill Pr.

***Armstead, Myra Beth Young.** "Lord, Please Don't Take Me in August" African Americans in Newport & Saratoga Springs. LC 98-58092. (Illus.). 208p. 1999. pap. 16.95 (*0-252-06801-7*) U of Ill Pr.

Armster, Linda, ed. see New York Times Staff.

Armstong, Charlotte. The Unsuspected. 1990. reprint ed. lib. bdg. 15.95 (*0-89968-474-2*) Buccaneer Bks.

Armstong, Ray. X-Ray Astronomy, Including a Catalogue & Bibliography of Galactic X-Ray Sources: Proceedings of the 21st Plenary Meeting, Innsbruck, Austria, 1978. Baity, W. A. & Peterson, L. E., eds. (Illus.). 1979. 76.00 (*0-08-023418-6*, Pergamon Pr) Elsevier.

Armstron, H., jt. auth. see Trew, A. J.

Armstrong. Baby Brother Jesus. 1990. 8.90 (*0-687-02342-4*) Abingdon.

— Career Paths: A Guide to Jobs in Criminal Justice. 3rd ed. 2000. pap. 14.80 (*0-13-096278-3*) P-H.

Armstrong. Drew & the Filthy Rich Kid. 96p. (J). (gr. 2-5). pap. 4.25 (*0-06-442070-1*) HarpC Child Bks.

Armstrong. From Versailles to Maastricht. LC 96-10360. 336p. 1996. text 59.95 (*0-312-16116-6*) St Martin.

— General Biology. 74p. (C). 1996. pap. text 10.40 (*0-536-59577-1*) Pearson Custom.

— General Biology 1. 3rd ed. 120p. 1998. pap. text 8.00 (*0-536-01303-9*) Pearson Custom.

***Armstrong.** General Biology 1. 4th ed. 114p. 1999. pap. text 11.20 (*0-536-02684-X*) Pearson Custom.

Armstrong. Governance Single European Market. LC 97-20798. 288p. 1998. 79.95 (*0-7190-4456-1*, Pub. by Manchester Univ Pr); pap. 27.95 (*0-7190-4457-X*, Pub. by Manchester Univ Pr) St Martin.

— Management. 5th ed. 144p. (C). 1997. pap. text 20.63 (*0-673-98021-9*) Addson-Wesley Educ.

— Marketing. 4th ed. 1996. pap. text, teacher ed. write for info. (*0-13-252850-9*) Allyn.

— Marketing. 4th ed. 1996. pap. text, teacher ed. write for info. (*0-13-252909-2*) Allyn.

***Armstrong.** Sci-Fi Aesthetics. 96p. 1998. pap. 45.95 (*0-471-97855-8*) Wiley.

Armstrong, ed. Patternmaking for Fashion Design. 2nd ed. 814p. (C). 1997. reprint ed. 80.00 (*0-673-98026-X*) Addison-Wesley.

***Armstrong & Baron.** Job Evaluation Handbook 1995. 416p. 2000. pap. 56.95 (*0-8464-5099-2*) Beekman Pubs.

Armstrong & Fildes. Industrial Development. (Progress in Planning Ser.). 1988. pap. 28.00 (*0-08-036879-4*, Pergamon Pr) Elsevier.

Armstrong & Jarvis. The Earth: Home of Humanity. 1990. pap. text. write for info. (*0-582-87099-2*, Pub. by Addison-Wesley) Longman.

Armstrong, jt. auth. see Baron.

Armstrong, jt. auth. see Orazem.

Armstrong, ed. see Pike, et al.

Armstrong, Marian. I Knew You'd Come: A Collection of Devotional Readings. Ulmer, Louise, ed. 168p. 1998. pap. 10.00 (*0-941367-05-3*) Peach Blossom Pubns.

Armstrong, A., jt. auth. see Krasnosel'Skii, M. M.

Armstrong, A. H. An Introduction to Ancient Philosophy. 3rd ed. LC 81-3731. (Quality Paperback Ser.: No. 418). 260p. (C). 1981. reprint ed. pap. 14.95 (*0-8226-0418-3*) Littlefield.

— Works, 7 vols., 2. (Loeb Classical Library: No. 440-445, & 468). 312p. 1966. text 19.95 (*0-674-99486-8*) HUP.

— Works, 7 vols., 3. (Loeb Classical Library: No. 440-445, & 468). 426p. 1967. text 19.95 (*0-674-99487-6*) HUP.

Armstrong, A. H., ed. Classical Mediterranean Spirituality: Egyptian, Greek, Roman. (World Spirituality Ser.: Vol. 15). 496p. 1986. 49.50 (*0-8245-0764-9*) Crossroad NY.

Armstrong, A. H., tr. Works, 7 vols., 1. (Loeb Classical Library: No. 440-445, & 468). 364p. 1966. text 19.95 (*0-674-99484-1*) HUP.

— Works, 7 vols., 4. (Loeb Classical Library: No. 440-445, & 468). 452p. 1967. text 18.95 (*0-674-99488-4*) HUP.

— Works, 7 vols., 5. (Loeb Classical Library: No. 440-445, & 468). 332p. 1967. text 19.95 (*0-674-99489-2*) HUP.

— Works, 7 vols., 6. (Loeb Classical Library: No. 440-445, & 468). 379p. 1988. text 19.95 (*0-674-99490-6*) HUP.

— Works, 7 vols., 7. (Loeb Classical Library: No. 440-445, & 468). 352p. 1988. text 19.95 (*0-674-99515-5*) HUP.

Armstrong, A. Hilary. Expectations of Immortality in Late Antiquity. LC 87-60376. (Aquinas Lectures: No. 51). 70p. (C). 1987. 15.00 (*0-87462-154-2*) Marquette.

— Hellenic & Christian Studies. (Collected Studies: No. CS324). 330p. 1990. text 109.95 (*0-86078-273-5*, Pub. by Variorum) Ashgate Pub Co.

— Plotinian & Christian Studies. (Collected Studies: No. CS102). 384p. (C). 1979. reprint ed. lib. bdg. 112.95 (*0-86078-047-3*, Pub. by Variorum) Ashgate Pub Co.

Armstrong, A. Hilary & Smith, Gerard. The Philosophy of Being. LC 61-5281. 400p. 1961. pap. 20.00 (*0-87462-530-0*) Marquette.

***Armstrong, A. Joseph.** Trout Unlimited Guide to Pennsylvania Limestone Streams. (Illus.). 2000. pap. 14.95 (*0-8117-2944-3*) Stackpole.

Armstrong, A. Joseph. Trout Unlimited's Guide to Pennsylvania Limestone Streams. LC 91-34271. (Illus.). 256p. 1992. 22.95 (*0-8117-1651-1*) Stackpole.

Armstrong, Alan. Off in Zora. 120p. (Orig.). 1997. pap. 12.95 (*1-879923-13-0*) Booksellers Pub.

— Regards, Rodeo: The Mariner Dog of Cassis. LC 99-46029. (Illus.). 176p. 1999. pap. 15.00 (*1-880158-25-6*, Pub. by J N Townsend) A C Hood.

Armstrong, Alan, ed. The Economy of Kent, 1640-1914. LC 95-38023. (Kent History Project Ser.: Vol. 3). (Illus.). 352p. (C). 1996. 75.00 (*0-85115-582-0*, Boydell Pr) Boydell & Brewer.

Armstrong, Alexandra & Donahue, Mary R. On Your Own: A Widow's Passage to Emotional & Financial Well-Being. 377p. 1999. reprint ed. text 25.00 (*0-7881-6190-3*) DIANE Pub.

***Armstrong, Alexandra & Donahue, Mary R.** On Your Own: A Widow's Passage to Emotional & Financial Well-Being. 3rd ed. 392p. 2000. pap. 17.95 (*0-7931-3727-6*, 56087503) Dearborn.

Armstrong, Alison. The Joyce of Cooking: Food & Drink in James Joyce's Dublin. LC 85-14772. (Illus.). 272p. 1986. 24.95 (*0-930794-85-0*) Station Hill Pr.

— The Joyce of Cooking: Food & Drink in James Joyce's Dublin. 2nd ed. 1989. reprint ed. pap. text 15.95 (*0-88268-081-1*) Station Hill Pr.

***Armstrong, Alison & Casement, Charles.** The Child & the Machine: How Computers Put Our Children's Education at Risk. LC 00-29122. 256p. 2000. pap. 16.00 (*0-87659-210-8*, Robins Ln Pr) Gryphon Hse.

Armstrong, Alison, ed. see Yeats, William Butler.

Armstrong, Amatullah. And the Sky Is Not the Limit: An Australian Woman's Spiritual Journey Within the Traditions. 170p. 1996. pap. 17.00 (*0-614-21251-0*, 1375); pap. 17.00 (*0-614-21384-3*, 1375) Kazi Pubns.

— Letters Inside the Journey. 206p. 1996. pap. 17.00 (*0-614-21302-9*, 1398) Kazi Pubns.

— The Water of Life. 78p. 1996. pap. 24.00 (*0-614-21377-0*, 1420) Kazi Pubns.

Armstrong, Angela, tr. see Rashed, Roshdi.

Armstrong, Annabel. Marvena: Paintings & Works on Paper. (Illus.). 36p. 1990. pap. 15.00 (*0-8150-0015-4*) Wittenborn Art.

— Nicolas Tarkhoff: A Retrospective Exhibition. (Illus.). 64p. 1989. pap. 20.00 (*0-8150-0014-6*) Wittenborn Art.

Armstrong, Anne. Unconditional Surrender. LC 73-22633. 304p. (C). 1974. reprint ed. lib. bdg. 35.00 (*0-8371-7042-7*, ARUS, Greenwood Pr) Greenwood.

Armstrong, April O. Tales Christ Told. LC 90-34304. 264p. 1990. reprint ed. pap. 9.95 (*0-932506-82-8*) St Bedes Pubns.

Armstrong, Arthur G., jt. auth. see Hagel, John, 3rd.

Armstrong, B. Bodacious Borders. (Illus.). 68p. (J). 1992. pap. 9.95 (*0-88160-214-0*, LW208) Learning Wks.

— Build a Doodle, No. 1. (Holiday & Art Ser.: No. 1). (Illus.). 32p. (J). (ps-4). 1985. pap. 3.95 (*0-88160-124-1*, LW133) Learning Wks.

— Build a Doodle, No. 2. (Holiday & Art Ser.: No. 2). (Illus.). 32p. (J). (ps-4). 1985. pap. 3.95 (*0-88160-125-X*, LW34) Learning Wks.

Armstrong, B. H. & Nicholls, R. W. Emission, Absorption & Transfer of Radiation in Heated Atmospheres. 319p. (C). 1972. 148.00 (*0-08-016774-8*, Pub. by Pergamon Repr) Franklin.

Armstrong, Barbra K. Index to the 1800 Census of New York. 432p. 1996. reprint ed. pap. 36.50 (*0-8063-1070-7*, 155) Clearfield Co.

Armstrong, Barry L. & Murphy, James B. The Natural History of Mexican Rattlesnakes. Collins, Joseph T., ed. (Special Publications: No. 5). (Illus.). 88p. (Orig.). 1979. pap. 6.00 (*0-89338-010-5*) U KS Nat Hist Mus.

Armstrong, Barry L., jt. auth. see Murphy, James B.

Armstrong, Beth. For Whom Doth the Bell Toll? LC 91-60649. 68p. (Orig.). 1991. pap. 8.95 (*0-88100-073-6*) Natl Writ Pr.

— My Four Lives. LC 89-61703. (Illus.). 164p. 1989. pap. 15.95 (*0-88100-064-7*) Natl Writ Pr.

Armstrong, Betsy R., jt. auth. see Williams, Knox.

Armstrong, Bev. Great Books I Have Read. 1998. pap. 8.95 (*0-88160-287-6*) Learning Wks.

Armstrong, Beverley. Language of Love. 44p. (Orig.). 1996. pap. 7.95 (*0-7880-0671-1*, Fairway Pr) CSS OH.

Armstrong, Beverly. Build a Doodle Circus. (Holiday & Art Ser.). (Illus.). 32p. (J). (ps-4). 1986. pap. 3.95 (*0-88160-133-0*, LW138) Learning Wks.

— Build a Doodle City. (Enrichment & Gifted Ser.). (Illus.). 32p. (J). (ps-4). 1986. pap. 3.95 (*0-88160-132-2*, LW136) Learning Wks.

— Build a Doodle Farm. (Holiday & Art Ser.). (Illus.). 32p. (J). (ps-4). 1986. pap. 3.95 (*0-88160-130-6*, LW135) Learning Wks.

— Build a Doodle Ocean. (Holiday & Art Ser.). (Illus.). 32p. (J). (ps-4). 1986. pap. 3.95 (*0-88160-131-4*, LW137) Learning Wks.

— Dinosaur Detective. (Skill Builder Ser.). (Illus.). 32p. (J). (ps-3). 1979. pap. 4.95 (*0-88160-075-X*, LW808) Learning Wks.

— Have Fun Following Directions. (Skill Builder Ser.). (Illus.). 32p. (J). (gr. 1-3). 1979. pap., student ed. 4.95 (*0-88160-077-6*, LW810) Learning Wks.

— Insects. (Science Mini Units Ser.). (Illus.). 48p. (J). (gr. 2-5). 1990. pap. 6.95 (*0-88160-192-6*, LW151) Learning Wks.

— Lively Listening. (Skill Builder Ser.). (Illus.). 32p. (J). (gr. 4-6). 1981. pap., student ed. 4.95 (*0-88160-080-6*, LW 813) Learning Wks.

— Superdoodle Dinosaurs. LC 92-74102. (Illus.). (J). (gr. 3 up). 1993. pap. 4.95 (*0-88160-223-X*, LW301) Learning Wks.

— Superdoodle Endangered Animals. LC 93-80434. (Illus.). 32p. (J). (gr. 1-6). 1994. pap. 4.95 (*0-88160-228-0*, LW323) Learning Wks.

— Superdoodle Insects. LC 96-77883. (Illus.). 32p. (J). (gr. 1-6). 1996. pap. 4.95 (*0-88160-295-7*, LW365) Learning Wks.

— Superdoodle Pets. LC 96-77884. (Illus.). 32p. (J). (gr. 1-6). 1996. pap. 4.95 (*0-88160-296-5*, LW366) Learning Wks.

— Superdoodles Mammals. LC 92-74100. (Illus.). (J). (gr. 1-6). 1993. pap. 4.95 (*0-88160-219-1*, LW303) Learning Wks.

— Superdoodles Marine Life. LC 93-80432. (Illus.). 32p. (J). (gr. 1-6). 1994. pap. 4.95 (*0-88160-227-2*, LW322) Learning Wks.

— Superdoodles Rain Forest. LC 92-74101. (Illus.). (J). (gr. 1-6). 1993. pap. 4.95 (*0-88160-218-3*, LW302) Learning Wks.

— Superdoodles Reptiles. LC 93-80433. (Illus.). 32p. (J). (gr. 1-6). 1994. pap. 4.95 (*0-88160-229-9*, LW324) Learning Wks.

— Superdoodles Sports. LC 92-74098. (Illus.). (J). (gr. 1-6). 1993. pap. 4.95 (*0-88160-221-3*, LW305) Learning Wks.

— Superdoodles Zoo Animals. LC 93-80431. (Illus.). 32p. (J). (gr. 1-6). 1994. pap. 4.95 (*0-88160-230-2*, LW325) Learning Wks.

— Who's Following Directions? (Skill Builder Ser.). (Illus.). 32p. (J). (gr. 4-7). 1979. pap., student ed. 4.95 (*0-88160-072-5*, LW 805) Learning Wks.

— Who's Listening? (Skill Builder Ser.). (Illus.). 32p. (J). (gr. 1-3). 1981. pap., student ed. 4.95 (*0-88160-079-2*, LW 812) Learning Wks.

— The Writing Rhino. (Illus.). 56p. (J). (gr. 1-3). 1995. pap. 5.95 (*0-88160-269-8*, LW108) Learning Wks.

— The Writing Warthog. (Illus.). 56p. (J). (gr. 4-6). 1995. pap. 6.95 (*0-88160-243-4*, LW338) Learning Wks.

Armstrong, Bill, jt. auth. see Parker, Noel.

Armstrong, Bob. Getting Started in Powerboating. 2nd ed. LC 97-164721. 1995. pap. text 17.95 (*0-07-003095-2*) Intl Marine.

Armstrong, Bob, ed. Florida Cruising Directory, 1999-2000. (Illus.). 188p. 1999. pap. 12.50 (*0-9625102-9-7*) Waterways Etc.

— Florida Cruising Directory, 2000/2001. (Illus.). 188p. 2000. pap. 12.50 (*1-928864-00-7*) Waterways Etc.

Armstrong, Brent R. LLC Revolution: LLCs vs. S Corporations. 144p. 1995. pap. write for info. (*0-9645073-0-7*) Hamilton Sq Pr.

Armstrong, Brian, contrib. by. Airports '95: Airport Engineering Innovation, Best Practices & the Environment. (National Conference Proceedings 95 Ser.: Vol. 7). (Illus.). 314p. 1995. pap. 110.50 (*0-85825-630-4*, Pub. by Inst Engrs Aust-EA Bks) Accents Pubns.

Armstrong, Brian, ed. Calvinus Sincerioris Religionis Vindex: Calvin as Protector of the Purer Religion. LC 97-10433. (Sixteenth Century Essays & Studies: No. 38). (Illus.). 333p. 1997. 45.00 (*0-940474-40-9*, SCJP) Truman St Univ.

Armstrong, Brian G. Calvinism & the Amyraut Heresy: Protestant Scholasticism & Humanism in Seventeenth-Century France. LC 72-84949. 354p. reprint ed. pap. 109.80 (*0-8357-4741-7*, 203766100009) Bks Demand.

Armstrong, Brian H. Legal Liability & Malpractice in Health Sciences: Index of New Information with References. 150p. 1996. 47.50 (*0-7883-0814-9*); pap. 44.50 (*0-7883-0815-7*) ABBE Pubs Assn.

Armstrong-Brown. Fundamental Techniques of Chemistry. 116p. (C). 1998. spiral bd. 28.95 (*0-7872-5406-1*, 41540601) Kendall-Hunt.

— Techniques of Chemistry II. 118p. (C). 1999. spiral bd. 26.95 (*0-7872-5716-8*, 41571601) Kendall-Hunt.

***Armstrong, Bruce.** Discover Nova Scotia Historic Sites. (Nova Scotia Travel Guide Ser.). (Illus.). 112p. 2000. pap. 10.95 (*1-55109-254-9*) Nimbus Publ.

Armstrong, Bruce. Sable Island. (Illus.). 210p. 1995. pap. 14.95 (*0-88780-058-0*, Pub. by Formac Publ Co) Formac Dist Ltd.

Armstrong, Bruce, et al. Principles of Exposure Measurement in Epidemiology. (Monographs in Epidemiology & Biostatistics: No. 21). (Illus.). 360p. 1994. reprint ed. pap. text 59.95 (*0-19-262020-7*) OUP.

Armstrong, C. The Charlotte Armstrong Treasury. 30.95 (*0-88411-576-3*) Amereon Ltd.

Armstrong, C. A. England, France & Burgundy in the Fifteenth Century. 450p. (C). 1983. 60.00 (*0-907628-13-3*) Hambledon Press.

Armstrong, C. F. Hymns for Little Children. 1977. lib. bdg. 59.95 (*0-8490-2030-1*) Gordon Pr.

Armstrong, C. J. World Databases in Biosciences & Pharmacology. LC 96-42191. 1325p. 1996. 200.00 (*1-85739-068-7*) Bowker-Saur.

— World Databases in Company Information. LC 96-186648. 1700p. 1996. 325.00 (*1-85739-195-0*) Bowker-Saur.

— World Databases in Social Sciences. LC 96-148588. 1200p. 1995. 235.00 (*1-85739-116-0*) Bowker-Saur.

Armstrong, C. J., ed. World Databases in Agriculture. LC 96-139611. (World Databases Ser.). 1142p. 1995. 250.00 (*1-85739-043-1*) Bowker-Saur.

— World Databases in Chemistry. 1200p. 1995. 235.00 (*1-85739-101-2*) Bowker-Saur.

— World Databases in Geography & Geology. 1272p. 1995. 200.00 (*1-85739-111-X*) Bowker-Saur.

— World Databases in Humanities. (World Databases Ser.). 1200p. 1996. 250.00 (*1-85739-048-2*) Bowker-Saur.

— World Databases in Industry. LC 94-43151. (World Databases Ser.). 852p. 1994. 165.00 (*1-85739-185-3*) Bowker-Saur.

— World Databases in Management. LC 94-24953. (World Database Ser.: Vol. 3). 1200p. 1995. 165.00 (*1-85739-190-X*) Bowker-Saur.

— World Databases in Patents. 750p. 1995. 165.00 (*1-85739-106-3*) Bowker-Saur.

— World Databases in Physics-Mathematics. (World Databases Ser.). 1300p. 1995. 200.00 (*1-85739-038-5*) Bowker-Saur.

***Armstrong, C. J. & Large, Andrew, eds.** Manual of Online Search Strategies, 3 vols. 3rd ed. LC 00-25154. 1088p. 2000. 400.00 (*0-566-07990-9*, Pub. by Ashgate Pub) Ashgate Pub Co.

Armstrong, C. J. & Large, J. A. CD-ROM Information Products: An Evaluation Guide & Directory. (Illus.). 470p. 1990. lib. bdg. 84.95 (*0-566-03626-6*, Pub. by Gower) Ashgate Pub Co.

***Armstrong, C. J. & Large, J. A.** Manual of Online Search Strategies, 3 vols. 3rd ed. LC 00-25154. 2000. write for info. (*0-566-08305-1*, Pub. by Gower) Ashgate Pub Co.

Armstrong, Campbell. Concert of Ghosts. large type ed. 464p. 1994. 27.99 (*0-7089-3126-X*) Ulverscroft.

***Armstrong, Campbell.** I Hope You Have a Good Life: A Memoir. 256p. 2000. 22.00 (*0-609-60531-3*) Crown Pub Group.

Armstrong, Campbell. Jig. 1989. mass mkt. 4.95 (*0-671-66524-3*) PB.

— Jigsaw. 1996. pap. 8.99 (*0-552-14168-2*) Bantam.

— Jigsaw. 352p. 1997. mass mkt. 5.99 (*0-7860-0412-6*, Pinncle Kensgtn) Kensgtn Pub Corp.

Armstrong, Carmen L. Designing Assessment in Art. 216p. (Orig.). 1994. pap. text 25.00 (*0-937652-71-7*, 203) Natl Art Ed.

— Including Aesthetics in Art Curriculum Planning. (Illus.). xx, 350p. 1999. pap. text. write for info. (*0-9670402-0-5*) A B A F A.

Armstrong, Carol. Scenes in a Library: Reading the Photograph in the Book, 1843-1875. LC 98-18193. (Illus.). 572p. 1998. 45.00 (*0-262-01169-7*) MIT Pr.

***Armstrong, Carol.** Wild Birds: Designs for Applique & Quilting. Kuhn, Barb & MacFarland, Sara, eds. LC 99-6920. (Illus.). 80p. 2000. pap. 22.95 (*1-57120-087-8*, 10204, Pub. by C & T Pub) Watsn-Guptill.

Armstrong, Carol. Wildflowers: Designs for Applique & Quilting. Nelson, Annie & Roberts, Diana, eds. LC 97-39822. (Illus.). 96p. 1998. pap. 22.95 (*1-57120-045-2*, 10169) C & T Pub.

Armstrong, Carol A. Gifts & Bequests: On the Occasion of the Welcoming of a New Child. (Illus.). 15p. (Orig.). 1996. pap. 7.95 (*0-9615599-1-8*) Tatnic Pr.

Armstrong, Carol M. Odd Man Out: Readings of the Work & Reputation of Edgar Degas. (Illus.). 310p. 1991. 46.00 (*0-226-02695-7*) U Ch Pr.

Armstrong, Carole. Lives & Legends of the Saints: With Paintings from the Great Art Museums of the World. LC 94-43009. (Illus.). 45p. (YA). (gr. 5 up). 1995. 17.00 (*0-689-80277-3*) S&S Bks Yung.

— My Van Gogh Art Museum: A Sticker Book of Paintings. (Illus.). 16p. (J). (gr. 1-5). 1996. pap. 11.95 (*0-399-23012-2*, Philomel) Peng Put Young Read.

***Armstrong, Carole.** Tour of Western Art. (Illus.). 16p. (J). (ps-3). 1999. pap. text 9.99 (*0-7112-0886-7*) F Lincoln.

— Van Gogh: My Sticker Art Gallery. (Illus.). (YA). (gr. 2 up). 1999. pap. text 9.99 (*0-7112-1055-1*) F Lincoln.

Armstrong, Carole. Women of the Bible: An Inspirational Volume Celebrating the Women of the Bible. LC 97-17059. (Illus.). 48p. (J). 1998. per. 18.00 (*0-689-81728-2*) S&S Trade.

Armstrong, Carole & Peppin, Anthea. All My Own Work! Adventures in Art. (Illus.). 48p. (J). (gr. 2 up). 1993. pap. 6.95 (*0-8120-1755-2*) Barron.

Armstrong, Carolyn T. Leather & Lace No. 6: Honeysuckle Love. 1983. mass mkt. 2.50 (*0-686-82614-0*, Zebra Kensgtn) Kensgtn Pub Corp.

Armstrong, Cecil F. A Century of Great Actors, 1750-1950. 1972. 24.95 (*0-405-09134-6*, 116) Ayer.

— Shakespeare to Shaw: Studies in the Life's Work of Six Dramatists of the English Stage. LC 68-8435. (Essay Index Reprint Ser.). 1977. 23.95 (*0-8369-0157-6*) Ayer.

— Shakespeare to Shaw: Studies in the Life's Work of Six Dramatists of the English Stage. LC 70-95402. (BCL Ser.: No. 1). reprint ed. 20.00 (*0-404-00383-4*) AMS Pr.

— Shakespeare to Shaw: Studies in the Life's Work of Six Dramatists of the English Stage. (BCL1-PR English Literature Ser.). 330p. 1992. reprint ed. lib. bdg. 89.00 (*0-7812-7076-6*) Rprt Serv.

Armstrong, Cedric V., jt. auth. see Fathi, Eli T.

Armstrong, Charles W., Jr. A Study Guide to Gary North's Liberating Planet Earth. 84p. 1991. pap. 5.95 (*0-930464-42-7*) Inst Christian.

Armstrong, Charles W., jt. auth. see Drowatzky, John W.

Armstrong, Charlotte. The Balloon Man. 1988. 22.95 (*0-8488-0419-8*) Amereon Ltd.

— Catch As Catch Can. 1990. mass mkt. 3.50 (*0-8217-3126-2*, Zebra Kensgtn) Kensgtn Pub Corp.

— Charlotte's Table: Down Home Cooking from an Uptown Girl. LC 97-22335. 288p. 1998. 23.00 (*0-88001-545-4*) HarpC.

— A Dram of Poison. reprint ed. lib. bdg. 18.95 (*0-88411-565-8*) Amereon Ltd.

— A Dram of Poison. 1994. reprint ed. lib. bdg. 24.95 (*1-56849-253-7*) Buccaneer Bks.

— Dream of Fair Woman. 256p. 1992. mass mkt. 3.99 (*0-8217-3964-6*, Zebra Kensgtn) Kensgtn Pub Corp.

— The Dream Walker. 320p. 1992. mass mkt. 3.99 (*0-8217-3908-5*, Zebra Kensgtn) Kensgtn Pub Corp.

— Lay on, MacDuff! 224p. 1993. mass mkt. 3.99 (*0-8217-4037-7*, Zebra Kensgtn) Kensgtn Pub Corp.

A

— Mischief. LC 87-82448. 148p. 1987. reprint ed. pap. 4.95 (*0-930330-72-2*) Intl Polygonics.

— The Turret Room. reprint ed. lib. bdg. 18.95 (*0-88411-566-6*) Amereon Ltd.

— The Unsuspected. reprint ed. lib. bdg. 19.95 (*0-88411-567-4*) Amereon Ltd.

Armstrong, Cheri, ed. Did You Really Fall into a Vat of Anchovies? Games & Activities. 96p. 1993. pap. text 18.95 (*1-877673-18-8*, VAT) Cottonwood Pr.

Armstrong, Chris & Large, Andy. Manual of Online Search Strategies. 2nd ed. (Professional Librarian Ser.). 200p. 1992. 65.00 (*0-8161-1992-9*, Hall Reference) Macmillan.

***Armstrong, Chris J., ed.** Staying Legal: A Guide to Issues & Practice for Users & Publishers of Electronic Resources. 277p. 1999. 110.00 (*1-85604-276-6*, LAP42766, Pub. by Library Association) Bernan Associates.

Armstrong, Christa, tr. see Lorenz, Juliane, ed.

Armstrong, Christine M. The Moralizing Prints of Cornelis Anthonisz. LC 88-34199. (Illus.). 321p. reprint ed. pap. 99.60 (*0-608-06414-9*, 206662700008) Bks Demand.

Armstrong, Christopher. Blue Skies & Boiler Rooms: Buying & Selling Securities in Canada, 1870-1940. LC 98-129965. (Illus.). 472p. 1997. text 39.95 (*0-8020-4184-1*) U of Toronto Pr.

— Evelyn Underhill: Eighteen Seventy-Five to Nineteen Forty-One: An Introduction to Her Life & Writing. LC 75-33401. 327p. reprint ed. 101.40 (*0-8357-9127-0*, 201285900083) Bks Demand.

— The Politics of Federalism: Ontario's Relations with the Federal Government 1867-1942. (Ontario Historical Studies). 316p. 1981. text 30.00 (*0-8020-2434-3*) U of Toronto Pr.

Armstrong, Christopher & Nelles, H. V. Monopoly's Moment: The Organization & Regulation of Canadian Utilities 1830-1930. 408p. (C). 1988. pap. 19.95 (*0-8020-6709-3*); text 47.50 (*0-8020-2671-0*) U of Toronto Pr.

— Southern Exposure: Canadian Promoters in Latin America & the Caribbean, 1896-1930. (Illus.). 391p. (C). 1988. text 40.00 (*0-8020-2660-5*) U of Toronto Pr.

Armstrong, Cindy. Raising Awareness. 128p. 1999. pap. 13.00 (*0-8059-4538-5*) Dorrance.

Armstrong, Cindy, jt. auth. see Rosenberg, Albert.

Armstrong, Clay M., jt. ed. see Oxford, Gerry S.

Armstrong, Curtis. Echoes from the Heart. LC 97-67922. 1997. mass mkt., per. 10.95 (*1-889131-17-2*) CasAnanda.

Armstrong, D. Mammals of the Canyon Country. (Illus.). 263p. 2.95 (*0-614-05154-1*) Canyonlands.

Armstrong, D., et al. The Old Church Slavonic Translation of the Andron Hagion Biblos in the Edition of Nikolas Van Wijk. Van Schooneveld, C. H., ed. (Slavistic Printings & Reprintings Ser.: No. 1). 310p. 1975. text 172.35 (*90-279-3196-8*) Mouton.

Armstrong, D. A., et al, eds. The Effects of Aging & Environment on Vision. (Illus.). 232p. (C). 1991. text 114.00 (*0-306-43920-4*, Kluwer Plenum) Kluwer Academic.

Armstrong, D. M. Cambridge History of Later Greek & Early Medieval Philosophy. 726p. 1967. text 130.00 (*0-521-04054-X*) Cambridge U Pr.

— A Combinatorial Theory of Possibility. (Cambridge Studies in Philosophy). (Illus.). 176p. (C). 1989. text 64.95 (*0-521-37427-8*) Cambridge U Pr.

— The Mind-Body Problem: An Opinionated Introduction. LC 99-19443. (Focus Ser.). 184p. 1999. mass mkt. 20.00 (*0-8133-9057-5*) Westview.

***Armstrong, D. M.** The Mind-Body Problem: An Opinionated Introduction. LC 99-19443. (Focus Ser.). 184p. 1999. 60.00 (*0-8133-9056-7*) Westview.

Armstrong, D. M. Universals: An Opinionated Introduction. 160p. (C). 1989. pap. 22.00 (*0-8133-0772-4*, Pub. by Westview) HarpC.

— What Is a Law of Nature? (Studies in Philosophy). 192p. 1985. pap. text 22.95 (*0-521-31481-X*) Cambridge U Pr.

— A World of States of Affairs. (Cambridge Studies in Philosophy). 298p. (C). 1997. text 59.95 (*0-521-58064-1*) Cambridge U Pr.

Armstrong, D. M., et al. Dispositions: A Debate. Crane, Tim, ed. & intro. by. 208p. (C). 1996. 75.00 (*0-415-14432-9*) Routledge.

Armstrong-Dailey, Ann & Goltzer, Sarah Z., eds. Hospice Care for Children. LC 92-48937. (Illus.). 320p. 1993. text 50.00 (*0-19-507312-6*) OUP.

Armstrong, Daniel, tr. see Polivanov, E. D.

Armstrong, Daniel W., jt. ed. see Hinze, Willie L.

Armstrong, Dave. God's Gunslinger. large type ed. (Linford Western Library). 256p. 1996. pap. 16.99 (*0-7089-7876-2*, Linford) Ulverscroft.

***Armstrong, David.** Herbs That Work: A Consumer's Guide to the Scientific Evidence. (Illus.). 250p. 2000. pap. 12.95 (*1-56975-211-7*, Pub. by Ulysses Pr) Publishers Group.

Armstrong, David. Horace. 177p. (C). 1989. 37.50 (*0-300-04579-4*) Yale U Pr.

— Less Than Kind. large type ed. (Linford Mystery Large Print Ser.). 336p. 1998. pap. 17.99 (*0-7089-5262-3*, Linford) Ulverscroft.

— Night's Black Agents. large type ed. (Linford Mystery Library). 352p. 1998. pap. 17.99 (*0-7089-5214-3*, Linford) Ulverscroft.

— Revolution & World Order: The Revolutionary State in International Society. LC 92-40619. 338p. (C). 1993. text 65.00 (*0-19-827528-5*, Clarendon Pr) OUP.

— Russian Lacquer Boxes. (C). 1992. text 110.00 (*0-569-23751-3*, Pub. by Collets) St Mut.

— Silver Cord: Photographs. (Illus.). 128p. 1997. 45.00 (*3-931141-48-9*) Dist Art Pubs.

— Until Dawn Tomorrow. large type ed. (Linford Mystery Large Print Ser.). 368p. 1997. pap. 16.99 (*0-7089-5166-X*) Ulverscroft.

Armstrong, David & Goldstein, Erik, eds. The End of the Cold War. 219p. 1991. text 35.00 (*0-7146-3419-0*, Pub. by F Cass Pubs) Intl Spec Bk.

Armstrong, David & Grace, John. Research Methods & Audit in General Practice. 2nd ed. (Oxford General Practice Ser.: No. 29). (Illus.). 228p. 1995. pap. text 49.50 (*0-19-262454-7*) OUP.

***Armstrong, David & Grace, John.** Research Methods & Audit in General Practice. 3rd ed. (Oxford General Practice Ser.). (Illus.). 208p. 2000. pap. text 59.95 (*0-19-263191-8*) OUP.

Armstrong, David & Rossie, Sandra S., eds. Ion Channel Regulation. (Advances in Second Messenger & Phosphoprotein Research Ser.). 480p. 1998. text 125.00 (*0-397-51847-1*) Lppncott W & W.

Armstrong, David & Sievers, Burkhard, eds. Discovering Social Meanings & Social Dreaming Vol. 1: Essays in Honour of Gordon Lawrence, Vol. 1. 1998. pap. 29.95 (*1-899209-06-9*, Pub. by Process Pr) Intl Spec Bk.

— Discovering Social Meanings & Social Dreaming Vol. 2: Essays in Honour of Gordon Lawrence, Vol. 2. 1998. pap. 29.95 (*1-899209-07-7*, Pub. by Process Pr) Intl Spec Bk.

Armstrong, David, et al. Group Relations: An Introduction. 1998. pap. 24.95 (*1-899209-09-3*, Pub. by Process Pr) Intl Spec Bk.

Armstrong, David, jt. auth. see Savage, Tom.

Armstrong, David A. Bullets & Bureaucrats: The Machine Gun & the United States Army, 1861-1916, 29. LC 81-7226. (Contributions in Military History Ser.: No. 29). (Illus.). 239p. 1982. 55.00 (*0-313-23029-3*, ABU, Greenwood Pr) Greenwood.

Armstrong, David E. Alcohol & Altered States in Ancestor Veneration Rituals of Zhou Dynasty China & Iron Age Palestine: A New Approach to Ancestor Rirual. LC 98-22819. 164p. 1998. text 79.95 (*0-7734-8360-8*) E Mellen.

Armstrong, David F. Original Signs: Gesture, Sign & the Sources of Language. LC 98-49671. (Illus.). 181p. 1999. text 39.95 (*1-56368-075-0*) Gallaudet Univ Pr.

Armstrong, David F., et al. Gesture & the Nature of Language. 270p. (C). 1995. pap. text 20.95 (*0-521-46772-1*) Cambridge U Pr.

Armstrong, David G. & Henson, Kenneth T. Teaching Today: An Introduction to Education. 5th ed. LC 96-20386. 373p. (C). 1996. 71.00 (*0-13-382177-3*) P-H.

Armstrong, David G. & Henson, Kenneth T. Teaching Today: An Introduction to Education. 5th ed. 1997. 71.00 (*0-13-027992-7*) P-H.

Armstrong, David G., et al. Instructional Skills Handbook. LC 77-25986. (Illus.). 320p. 1978. 39.95 (*0-87778-102-8*) Educ Tech Pubns.

— Secondary Education: An Introduction. 4th ed. LC 97-3421. 472p. 1997. pap. text, teacher ed. 62.00 (*0-13-496498-5*) P-H.

***Armstrong, David G., et al.** Teaching Today: An Introduction to Education. 6th ed. LC 99-88678. 496p. 2000. pap. 52.00 (*0-13-022680-7*) P-H.

Armstrong, David G., jt. auth. see Savage, Tom V.

Armstrong, David L. & Rossie, Sandra S. Advances in Second Messenger & Phosphoprotein Research Vol. 33: Ion Channel Regulation. (Illus.). 344p. 1999. 99.95 (*0-12-036133-7*) Acad Pr.

Armstrong, David L., et al. Riverside: Restoration of a Way of Life. (Illus.). 1998. write for info. (*0-9607612-9-2*) Cty of Jffrsn KY.

Armstrong, David M. Mammals of the Canyon Country. (Illus.). 263p. (Orig.). (C). 1982. pap. 3.95 (*0-937407-01-1*) Canyonlands.

— Managing by Storying Around. 249p. 1995. pap. 14.00 (*0-9648027-1-6*) D M Armstrong.

— A Materialist Theory of the Mind. 2nd ed. LC 93-19013. (International Library of Philosophy). 400p. (C). 1993. pap. 27.99 (*0-415-10031-3*, B2456) Routledge.

— Once Told, They're Gold: Stories to Enliven & Enrich the Workplace. (Illus.). 320p. 1998. pap. 16.00 (*0-9648027-2-4*) D M Armstrong.

Armstrong, Debra, jt. ed. see Fisher, Jack C.

Armstrong, Dennis L. The Seven Voyages of Sindbad the Snail. LC 96-86559. (Illus.). 80p. (Orig.). (J). (gr. 4-6). 1996. pap. 7.50 (*0-9654326-0-2*) Cupcake Pr.

Armstrong, Derek L. & Yu, Kam W. The Persona Principle: How to Succeed in Business with Image-Marketing. (Illus.). 256p. 1996. 24.50 (*0-684-80268-6*) S&S Trade.

***Armstrong, Derek Lee & Yu, Kam W.** The Persona Principle: How to Succeed in Business with Image-Marketing. (Illus.). 240p. 2000. reprint ed. 25.00 (*0-7881-9253-1*) DIANE Pub.

***Armstrong, Diana.** Adopt a Missionary: Ministering to Those Who Minister on the Mission Field. LC 99-63456. 144p. 1999. pap. 12.95 (*1-57921-195-X*, Pub. by WinePress Pub) BookWorld.

Armstrong, Diana. Cooking for My Friends: Casual Healthy Entertaining. 200p. 1998. pap. 17.95 (*0-9664650-0-8*) Culinary Prods.

***Armstrong, Diane.** Mosaic: A Chronicle of Five Generations. LC 99-487959. 1998. write for info. (*0-09-183713-8*) Trafalgar.

***Armstrong, Diane G.** The Retirement Nightmare: How to Save Yourself from Your Heirs & Protectors. LC 99-87527. 420p. 2000. pap. 22.95 (*1-57392-796-1*) Prometheus Bks.

***Armstrong, Dianne.** Home Again, Home Again, Jiggety Jig: 16 True Stories of Lost Pets That Overcame Incredible Odds Before Finding Their Way Back to the Loving Arms of Their Owners. (Illus.). 2000. pap. 7.95 (*0-9671779-0-1*) Dianne Armstrong.

Armstrong, Doc. Got the Beer Iced Down! Cowboy & Folk Rhymes (a la Louisiane) LC 94-90142. (Illus.). 48p. (Orig.). 1994. pap. 8.00 (*0-9641227-3-1*) Wafer Creek.

Armstrong, Don. I Flew Them First. (Orig.). 1994. pap. 24.95 (*0-614-12911-7*) Champlin Museum.

— The Lloyd Shaw Foundation Recreational Dance Program. 133p. (C). 1985. pap. text 20.00 (*0-915213-01-X*) L Shaw Found.

Armstrong, Donald. Book Publishing: A Working Guide. 1979. 15.00 (*0-918464-20-X*) D Armstrong.

***Armstrong, Donald.** Free Radical & Antioxidant Protocols. LC 98-16172. (Methods in Molecular Biology Ser.: Vol. 108). (Illus.). 480p. 1998. 89.50 (*0-89603-472-0*) Humana.

Armstrong, Donald. Strategies for Success in Small Business. (Illus.). 1977. text 10.00 (*0-918464-15-3*) D Armstrong.

***Armstrong, Donald.** What Do You Say That I Am? 1999. pap. text 14.00 (*0-8028-4746-3*) Eerdmans.

Armstrong, Donald, ed. Free Radicals in Diagnostic Medicine: A Systems Approach to Laboratory Technology, Clinical Correlations & Antioxidant Therapy, Vol. 366. LC 95-3634. (Advances in Experimental Medicine & Biology Ser.: Vol. 366). 480p. (C). 1995. text 125.00 (*0-306-44981-1*, Kluwer Plenum) Kluwer Academic.

Armstrong, Donald, 3rd, ed. The Truth about Jesus. 150p. 1998. pap. 12.00 (*0-8028-4598-3*) Eerdmans.

Armstrong, Donald, et al, eds. Free Radicals in Molecular Biology, Aging, & Disease. LC 84-16102. (Aging Ser.: No. 27). (Illus.). 433p. 1984. reprint ed. pap. 134.30 (*0-608-05776-2*, 205974100007) Bks Demand.

***Armstrong, Douglas, et al.** Accessing the Past: The Iroquois Gas Transmission System Pipeline Archaeological Collection: Technical Synthesis, with Goals & Recommendations for Collections Management. (Syracuse University Archaeological Research Center Publications: Vol. 11). (Illus.). vii, 100p. 1999. 20.00 (*1-929436-00-9*) S U Archaeological.

Armstrong, Douglas, jt. auth. see Rosenoer, Jonathan.

Armstrong, Douglas H. The Road to Santiago: A Pilgrimage, Past & Present. LC 94-181267. (American University Studies, Series XXI, Regional Studies: Vol. 13). 1997. write for info. (*0-8204-2542-7*) P Lang Pubng.

Armstrong, Douglas V. The Old Village & the Great House: An Archaeological & Historical Examination of Drax Hall Plantation, St. Ann's Bay, Jamaica. (Blacks in the New World Ser.). (Illus.). 424p. 1990. text 44.95 (*0-252-01617-3*) U of Ill Pr.

Armstrong, E. F. & Armstrong, Sara. In a Copper Kettle. 15th ed. (Illus.). 1958. pap. 4.95 (*0-87315-019-8*) Golden Bell.

Armstrong, Edward A. The Emperor Charles V, 2 vols., Set. LC 83-45652. reprint ed. 155.00 (*0-404-19800-7*) AMS Pr.

— Italian Studies. Ady, C. M., ed. LC 67-30172. (Essay Index Reprint Ser.). 1977. 23.95 (*0-8369-0158-4*) Ayer.

— Shakespeare's Imagination: A Study of the Psychology of Association & Inspiration. LC 63-8165. 236p. 1982. reprint ed. pap. 73.20 (*0-608-02691-3*, 206334400004) Bks Demand.

— St. Francis, Nature Mystic: The Derivation & Significance of the Nature Stories in the Franciscan Legend. LC 74-149949. (Hermeneutics, Studies in the History of Religions: No. 2). (Illus.). 296p. reprint ed. pap. 91.80 (*0-608-18042-4*, 202903600058) Bks Demand.

— The Wren. (Natural History Ser.: No. 59). (Illus.). 24p. pap. 5.25 (*0-7478-0160-6*, Pub. by Shire Pubns) Parkwest Pubns.

Armstrong, Edward A., ed. see Penn, William.

Armstrong, Edward C. Authorship of the Vengement Alixandre & of the Venjance Alixandre. (Elliott Monographs: Vol. 19). 1926. pap. 25.00 (*0-527-02622-0*) Periodicals Srv.

— French Metrical Versions of Barlaam & Josaphat. (Elliott Monographs: Vol. 10). 1922. 25.00 (*0-527-02614-X*) Periodicals Srv.

— Marshall Elliot, a Retrospect. (Elliott Monographs: Vol. 15). 1923. pap. 25.00 (*0-527-02618-2*) Periodicals Srv.

Armstrong, Edward J. Penitence: A True Story. Stevens, Gifford, ed. (Illus.). 352p. 1994. pap. 19.95 (*0-9642473-0-5*) L Madden Assocs.

Armstrong, Elizabeth, et al. Peter Fischli & David Weiss: In a Restless World. (Illus.). 128p. (Orig.). 1996. pap. 19.95 (*0-935640-51-7*) Walker Art Ctr.

— Tyler Graphics: The Extended Image. (Illus.). 256p. 1987. 19.98 (*0-89659-750-4*) Abbeville Pr.

— Tyler Graphics: The Extended Image. (Illus.). 256p. 1996. 19.98 (*0-89659-772-5*) Abbeville Pr.

***Armstrong, Elizabeth Ann.** Multiplying Identities. 1999. pap. text 18.00 (*0-226-02694-9*); lib. bdg. 40.00 (*0-226-02693-0*) U Ch Pr.

Armstrong, Ellis L. & Rosen, Howard. Effective Emergency Response: The Salt Lake Valley Floods of 1983, 1984 & 1985. (Illus.). 58p. 1986. pap. text 30.00 (*1-882102-02-9*) Pub Works Hist Soc.

Armstrong, Emma P. James K. Polk Cookbook. Pryor, Harold, ed. LC 78-60329. (Illus.). 254p. 1978. pap. 8.95 (*0-9607668-0-4*) James K Polk.

Armstrong, Eric. Growing-Up & Ducking Down. 210p. 1999. write for info. (*1-86106-275-3*, Pub. by Minerva Pr) Unity Dist.

— JBuilder "X" Bible. LC 97-74812. (Bible Ser.). 864p. 1998. pap. 49.99 incl. cd-rom (*0-7645-3114-X*) IDG Bks.

— Jim & Heidi. 193p. 1997. write for info. (*1-86106-400-4*, Pub. by Minerva Pr) Unity Dist.

Armstrong, Ernest S. ORACLS: A Design System for Linear Multivariable Control. (Control & Systems Theory Ser.: Vol. 10). (Illus.). 256p. 1980. text 135.00 (*0-8247-1239-0*) Dekker.

Armstrong, Este & Falk, Dean, eds. Primate Brain Evolution: Methods & Concepts. LC 81-21150. 346p. (C). 1982. 79.50 (*0-306-40914-3*, Plenum Trade) Perseus Pubng.

Armstrong, Esther. Let God Comfort You. 16p. 1996. pap. 1.50 (*0-88243-936-7*) Gospel Pub.

Armstrong, Felicity & Barton, Len, eds. Disability, Human Rights & Education: Cross Cultural Perspectives. LC 99-13640. 237p. 1999. pap. 31.95 (*0-335-20457-0*) Taylor & Francis.

Armstrong, Fiona, et al. Getting Ready for the World of Work. (Illus.). 1980. text 13.96 (*0-07-002517-7*) McGraw.

— Housing Needs, Renting a Place to Live. 1979. text 13.96 (*0-07-047301-3*) McGraw.

— A Realistic Job Search. (Lifeworks Ser.). (Illus.). 1980. text 13.96 (*0-07-002518-5*) McGraw.

— The Reality of Work & Promotion. (Illus.). 208p. 1980. text 13.96 (*0-07-002519-3*) McGraw.

— Realizing What's Available in the World of Work. (Lifeworks Ser.). (Illus.). 1979. text 13.96 (*0-07-002516-9*) McGraw.

— You & the World of Work. (Lifeworks Ser.). (Illus.). 1979. text 13.96 (*0-07-002515-0*) McGraw.

Armstrong, Foster, et al. A Guide to Cleveland's Sacred Landmarks. LC 91-30918. (Illus.). 344p. 1992. pap. 28.00 (*0-87338-454-7*) Kent St U Pr.

Armstrong, Franette. Beyond Glasses! The Consumer's Guide to Laser Vision Correction. LC 97-140161. (Illus.). 368p. (Orig.). 1997. pap. 19.95 (*0-9656505-0-2*) U C Books.

— Beyond Glasses! The Consumer's Guide to Laser Vision Correction. 2nd rev. ed. LC 98-60581. (Illus.). 384p. (Orig.). 1998. pap. 19.95 (*0-9656505-3-7*) U C Books.

Armstrong, Frank A. The Connected Company: Streamlining Management for More Sales & Profit. Stein, Toby, ed. (Illus.). 165p. 1999. 23.95 (*0-9648563-8-7*); pap. 14.95 (*0-9648563-9-5*) Arrowhead CA.

Armstrong, Frank H. Payoff Artillery - W. W. II: The Wide-Ranging Combat of the Battalion that Fought under Five Armies & Eight Divisions in the European Theatre. LC 93-71275. (Illus.). 208p. 1994. 21.00 (*0-9632448-1-7*) Bull Run VT.

Armstrong, Frank H., ed. The 1st Cavalry Division & Their 8th Engineers in Korea: America's Silent Generation at War. LC 96-85022. (Illus.). 320p. 1997. 24.95 (*0-9632448-2-5*) Bull Run VT.

— Unit History 283rd Field Artillery Battalion. 2nd rev. ed. (Illus.). 91p. 1995. pap. text 17.95 (*0-9632448-3-3*) Bull Run VT.

Armstrong, Frank H. & Oates, Marguerite. Window Seat: An Aerial Perspective of America's Forests with General Enlightenment for Civic Leaders. LC 92-138582. 163p. (Orig.). 1992. pap. 10.00 (*0-9632448-0-9*) Bull Run VT.

Armstrong, Frank N. Food Processing & Its Industry: Index of New Information for Reference & Research. 160p. 1997. 47.50 (*0-7883-1330-4*); pap. 44.50 (*0-7883-1331-2*) ABBE Pubs Assn.

Armstrong, Frankie & Pearson, Jenny. As Far As the Eye Can Sing: The Autobiography of Frankie Armstrong. pap. 13.95 (*0-7043-4294-4*, Pub. by Womens Press) Trafalgar.

Armstrong, Fred C. Our Economic Predicament in Perspective. LC 77-91219. 1978. 10.00 (*0-87212-100-3*) Libra.

Armstrong, Frederick H. London: The Forest City: An Illustrated History of London, Canada. LC 86-23434. 336p. 1986. 29.95 (*0-89781-180-1*) Am Historical Pr.

Armstrong, G. Cyril, jt. tr. see Tredennick, H.

Armstrong, Gale. Cottage Holidaying in Britain: The Complete Guide to the Most Economic & Memorable Holiday in England, Whales, & Scotland. LC 94-70762. (Illus.). 351p. (Orig.). 1995. pap. 16.95 (*0-9644325-5-2*) Classic Media.

Armstrong, Gary. Football Hooligans: Knowing the Score. LC 98-128792. (Explorations in Anthropology Ser.). 320p. 1998. 55.00 (*1-85973-952-0*, Pub. by Berg Pubs); pap. 19.50 (*1-85973-957-1*, Pub. by Berg Pubs) NYU Pr.

***Armstrong, Gary, told to.** Marketing: An Introduction. 5th ed. LC 99-35215. 596p. 1999. 64.00 (*0-13-012771-X*) S&S Trade.

Armstrong, Gary & Douglas, Derek. Jethart's Here! The Gary Armstrong Story. (Illus.). 224p. 1996. 34.95 (*1-85158-727-6*, Pub. by Mainstream Pubng) Trafalgar.

Armstrong, Gary & Giulianotti, Richard, eds. Entering the Field: New Perspectives on World Football. LC 97-202754. (Illus.). 256p. 1997. 55.00 (*1-85973-193-7*, Pub. by Berg Pubs); pap. 19.50 (*1-85973-198-8*, Pub. by Berg Pubs) NYU Pr.

Armstrong, Gary, jt. auth. see Kotler, Philip.

Armstrong, Gary, jt. auth. see Norris, Clive.

Armstrong, Gene. Early Tigers. (Illus.). 61p. 1995. pap. 9.00 (*0-944920-18-7*) Bellowing Ark Pr.

Armstrong, Geoff, ed. View from the Bridge. 176p. 1993. 75.00 (*0-85292-541-7*, Pub. by IPM Hse) St Mut.

***Armstrong, George.** The Rothschild Money Trust. 229p. 1998. pap. 7.00 (*0-9600358-0-X*) CPA Bk Pub.

Armstrong, George, jt. auth. see Darst, Paul.

Armstrong, George A., Jr. The Incidents. 304p. Date not set. pap. 10.95 (*1-57087-448-4*) Prof Pr NC.

Armstrong, George D. Christian Doctrine of Slavery. LC 69-16595. 148p. 1969. reprint ed. lib. bdg. 38.50 (*0-8371-0892-6*, ARC&) Greenwood.

— A Discussion on Slaveholding. LC 72-6454. (Black Heritage Library Collection). 1977. reprint ed. 16.95 (*0-8369-9155-9*) Ayer.

— The Summer of the Pestilence: A History of the Ravages of the Yellow Fever in Norfolk, Virginia A. D. 1855. 3rd ed. LC 94-67855. 76p. 1995. pap. 10.00 (*1-57000-037-9*) W S Dawson.

An Asterisk (*) at the beginning of an entry indicates that the title is appearing for the first time.

Armstrong, George M., Jr. Law & Market Society in Mexico. LC 88-25934. 173p. 1989. 57.95 (0-275-93117-X, C3117, Praeger Pubs) Greenwood.
— Louisiana Landlord & Tenant Law. 16th ed. 400p. 1994. ring bd. 120.00 (0-614-05887-2, MICHIE) LEXIS Pub.
— Louisiana Landlord & Tenant Law, 1987-1993. 400p. 1989. suppl. ed. 55.00 (0-250-42071-6, MICHIE) LEXIS Pub.
— The Soviet Law of Property. 1984. lib. bdg. 72.50 (90-247-2864-9) Kluwer Academic.
Armstrong, George R., jt. auth. see Guthrie, John A.
Armstrong, George W. The Rothschild Money Trust. 1988. lib. bdg. 250.00 (0-87700-370-X) Revisionist Pr.
Armstrong, Gloria & Hansen, Merrily. Right at Home: Family Experiences for Building Literacy. 1992. text 9.95 (0-201-81367-X) Addison-Wesley.
Armstrong, Gloria & Jillson, Katherine. Reading Books for Math: A Study Guide. Friedland, J. & Kessler, R., eds. (Novel-Ties Ser.). 1993. pap. text, student ed. 20.95 (1-56982-027-9) Lrn Links.
Armstrong, Gordon. Crime & the Justice System in America: An Encyclopedia. Schmalleger, Frank M., ed. LC 96-10748. 312p. 1997. lib. bdg. 65.00 (0-313-29409-7, Greenwood Pr) Greenwood.
— Scary Stories. 1996. pap. 10.95 (0-921368-63-1) Blizzard Publ.
Armstrong, Gordon S. Samuel Beckett, W. B. Yeats, & Jack Yeats: Images & Words. LC 87-48015. (Illus.). 272p. 1990. 42.50 (0-8387-5141-5) Bucknell U Pr.
Armstrong, Gregory, ed. see Roads, Michael J.
Armstrong, Gregory, ed. see Roman, Sanaya & Packer, Duane.
Armstrong, Gregory, ed. see Silva, Jose & Stone, Robert B.
Armstrong, H. C. Grey Wolf: Mustafa Kemal: An Intimate Study of a Dictator. LC 72-8397. (Select Bibliographies Reprint Ser.). 1977. reprint ed. 25.95 (0-8369-6962-6) Ayer.
— Lord of Arabia: An Intimate Study of a King. LC 96-41813. (The Kegan Paul Arabia Library). 306 p. 1997. 110.00 (0-7103-0568-0, Pub. by Kegan Paul Intl) Col U Pr.
Armstrong, Hamilton F., jt. auth. see Dulles, Allen W.
***Armstrong-Hand, Martha.** Learning to Be a Doll Artist. LC 99-66913. 138p. 1999. 19.95 (1-893625-04-4, MAHD) Scott Pubns MI.
***Armstrong-Hansche, Melissa & MacQueen, Neal.** Workshop Rotation: A New Model for Sunday School. LC 99-46804. (Illus.). 72p. 2000. pap. 8.95 (0-664-50110-9, Pub. by Geneva Press) Presbyterian Pub.
Armstrong, Harold C. Gray Wolf: Mustafa Kemal, an Intimate Study of a Dictator. LC 75-180317. (Mid-East Studies). reprint ed. 37.50 (0-404-56212-4) AMS Pr.
Armstrong, Harry & Wilk, Tom. New Jersey Firsts: The Famous, Infamous & Quirky of the Garden State. LC 98-55151. (Illus.). 176p. 1999. pap. 9.95 (0-940159-45-7) Camino Bks.
***Armstrong, Harry C.** Obsessed to Fly. 1999. pap. 7.95 (0-533-13177-4) Vantage.
***Armstrong, Harvey W. & Taylor, Jim.** Regional Economics & Policy. 400p. 2000. 79.95 (0-631-21657-X); pap. 44.95 (0-631-21713-4) Blackwell Pubs.
Armstrong, Harvey W. & Taylor, Jim, eds. The Economics of Regional Policy. LC 99-49221. (International Library of Critical Writings in Economics). 489p. 2000. 190.00 (1-84064-008-1) E Elgar.
Armstrong, Hayward. Bases para la Educacion Cristiana.Tr. of Basis for Christian Education. (SPA.). 190p. (Orig.). 1989. pap., teacher ed. 10.50 (0-311-11048-7) Casa Bautista.
Armstrong, Helen. Taking Care: A Response to Children, Adults & Abuse for Churches & Other Faith Communities. 59p. 1998. pap., spiral bd. 19.95 (1-874579-85-7, Pub. by Natl Childrens Bur) Paul & Co Pubs.
Armstrong, Helen J. Patternmaking. 2nd ed. (C). 1997. 63.67 (0-06-501789-7) Addson-Wesley Educ.
Armstrong, Helen J. Patternmaking for Fashion Design. 3rd ed. LC 99-43802. 821p. (C). 1999. 67.00 (0-321-03423-6, Prentice Hall) P-H.
— Patternmaking For Fashion Design. 3rd ed. (C). 2000. text. write for info. (0-321-03424-4) Addson-Wesley Educ.
Armstrong, Helen J., jt. ed. see Armstrong, O. V.
Armstrong, Helene H . Francis Bacon: The Spear Shaker. (Illus.). 210p. (Orig.). 1987. 17.95 (0-9616288-0-4) Golden Gate SF.
Armstrong-Helouvry, Brian. Control of Machines with Friction. (C). 1991. text 98.00 (0-7923-9133-0) Kluwer Academic.
— Introduction to Electrical Engineering. LC 94-15502. (C). 1995. pap. text, student ed., lab manual ed. 14.60 (0-02-304156-0, Macmillan Coll) P-H.
Armstrong, Hugh, jt. auth. see Armstrong, Pat.
Armstrong, Hugo & Gross, Dick. Tricontinental: The Rise & Fall of a Merchant Bank. 384p. 1995. 39.95 (0-522-84658-0, Pub. by Melbourne Univ Pr) Paul & Co Pubs.
Armstrong, I. M., ed. Geostatistical Simulations: Proceedings of the Geostatistical Simulation Workshop, Fontainebleau, France, 27-28 May 1993. 268p. (C). 1994. text 136.00 (0-7923-2732-2) Kluwer Academic.
Armstrong-Ingram, Jackson R. Written in Light: Abdu'l-Baha & the American Baha'i Community, 1895-1921. LC 98-27349. 1998. 35.00 (1-890688-02-9) Kalimat.
Armstrong-Ingram, R. Jackson. Studies in Babi & Baha'i History, Vol. 4: Music, Devotions, & Mashriq'l-Adkhar, Vol. 4. (Illus.). 1988. 32.50 (0-933770-62-6); pap. 22.50 (0-933770-77-4) Kalimat.
***Armstrong, Irene.** God's Wheel Turns Slowly. 140p. 2000. pap. text 12.95 (0-9661337-3-0) Son-Kin.
Armstrong, Irene. Out of the Soil. Hanners, Doreen, ed. 130p. 1998. pap. 10.95 (0-9661337-1-4) Son-Kin.
***Armstrong, Irene.** Poems Galore/Inspirational Writings. 70p. 2000. pap. 8.95 (0-9661337-2-2) Son-Kin.
Armstrong, Irene. Under His Shadow. 170p. 1997. pap. 10.95 (0-9661337-0-6, PO1828) Son-Kin.
Armstrong, Isabel. Victorian Poetry. 560p. (C). 1996. pap. 27.99 (0-415-14425-6) Routledge.
Armstrong, Isobel. Language As Living Form in Nineteenth Century Poetry. LC 83-2815. 234p. (C). 1982. text 44.00 (0-389-20293-2, 07128) B&N Imports.
***Armstrong, Isobel.** The Radical Aesthetic. 272p. 2000. text 59.95 (0-631-22052-6, Pub. by Blackwell Publishers) Blackwell Pubs.
— The Radical Aesthetic. 272p. 2000. pap. text 24.95 (0-631-22053-4, Pub. by Blackwell Pubs) Blackwell Pubs.
Armstrong, Isobel. Victorian Poetry: Poetry, Poetics, Politics. LC 92-2451. (Critical History of Victorian Poetry Ser.). 512p. (C). (gr. 13). 1993. 90.00 (0-415-03016-1, B0703) Routledge.
Armstrong, Isobel, et al, eds. Nineteenth-Century Women Poets: An Oxford Anthology. 872p. 1998. pap. text 19.95 (0-19-818483-2) OUP.
Armstrong, Isobel, ed. see Bradford, Richard.
Armstrong, Isobel, ed. see Bronfen, Elisabeth.
Armstrong, Isobel, ed. see Bygrave, Stephen.
Armstrong, Isobel, ed. see Conradi, Peter J.
Armstrong, Isobel, ed. see Davies, Stevie.
Armstrong, Isobel, ed. see Dennis, Barbara & Skittoa, David.
Armstrong, Isobel, ed. see Flint, Kate.
Armstrong, Isobel, ed. see Holt, Michael.
Armstrong, Isobel, ed. see Larrissy, Edward.
Armstrong, Isobel, ed. see McDonagh, Josephine.
Armstrong, Isobel, ed. see Msiska, Mpalive.
Armstrong, Isobel, ed. see Parker, Kenneth.
Armstrong, Isobel, ed. see Priestman, Martin.
Armstrong, Isobel, ed. see Ridgman, Jeremy.
Armstrong, Isobel, ed. see Rigney, Jim.
Armstrong, Ivy Claudette. Native Dawta: Poems. LC 98-194521. 63 p. 1995. write for info. (976-625-072-3) Kingston Pub.
Armstrong, J. Condition Monitoring: An Introduction to Its Application in Building Services. (C). 1986. pap. 25.00 (0-86022-108-3, Pub. by Build Servs Info Assn) St Mut.
— The Effect of Maintenance on Boiler Efficiency. (C). 1983. pap. 25.00 (0-86022-181-4, Pub. by Build Servs Info Assn) St Mut.
— Energy & Maintenance Costs. (C). 1983. 50.00 (0-86022-121-0, Pub. by Build Servs Info Assn) St Mut.
— Fault Finding Procedures in the Building Service Industry. (C). 1986. pap. 25.00 (0-86022-193-8, Pub. by Build Servs Info Assn) St Mut.
— Guidelines for Building Services: Operating & Maintenance Manuals. (C). 1984. 50.00 (0-86022-122-9, Pub. by Build Servs Info Assn) St Mut.
— Inspection of Building Services Plant & Equipment: A Review of Current Practice. (C). 1986. pap. 120.00 (0-86022-148-2, Pub. by Build Servs Info Assn) St Mut.
— Maintenance Management: Results of a Survey. (C). 1981. pap. 25.00 (0-86022-130-X, Pub. by Build Servs Info Assn) St Mut.
— Planned Maintenance & the Use of Computers. (C). 1991. pap. 60.00 (0-86022-127-X, Pub. by Build Servs Info Assn) St Mut.
Armstrong, J. & Jones, S. Business Documents: Their Origins, Sources & Uses in Historical Research. 224p. 1987. text 110.00 (0-7201-1846-8) Continuum.
Armstrong, J. & Taylor, P. Low-Cost Condition Monitoring for Engineering Services. 160p. 1988. text 50.00 (0-419-14450-1, E & FN Spon) Routledge.
Armstrong, J. H. Operating & Maintenance Manuals for Building Services Installations. (C). 1990. pap. 100.00 (0-86022-179-2, Pub. by Build Servs Info Assn) St Mut.
Armstrong, J. M. Company Staff. The Biographical Encyclopedia of Kentucky: Of the Dead & Living Men of the Ninteenth Century. 1978. reprint ed. 42.50 (0-89308-193-0) Southern Hist Pr.
Armstrong, J. T. & Porter, J. R., eds. Microbeam Analysis: Proceedings of the 27th Annual MAS Meeting in Los Angeles, CA, July 1993. 298p. 1993. pap. 50.00 (1-56081-659-7, Wiley-VCH) Wiley.
Armstrong, J. T., jt. ed. see Winnewisser, G.
Armstrong, J. W., jt. ed. see Paull, R. E.
Armstrong, Jack & Wilson, Delores. Boulangerie! A Pocket Guide to Paris's Famous Bakeries. LC 99-14772. (Illus.). 176p. 1999. text 9.95 (1-58008-065-0) Ten Speed Pr.
Armstrong, James. Captivating Cats. (Illus.). 88p. 1991. pap. 14.95 (1-55912-150-5) CEDCO Pub.
— From the Underside: Evangelism from a Third World Vantage Point. LC 81-9509. 109p. (Orig.). reprint ed. pap. 33.80 (0-8357-8885-7, 203356200086) Bks Demand.
— Monument in a Summer Hat: (Poems) (New Issues Press Poetry Ser.). 64p. 1999. 22.00 (0-932826-77-6, Pub. by WMU Poetry & Prose) Partners Pubs Grp.
***Armstrong, James.** Monument in a Summer Hat: (Poems) (New Issues Press Poetry Ser.). 64p. 1999. pap. 12.00 (0-932826-78-4, Pub. by WMU Poetry & Prose) Partners Pubs Grp.
***Armstrong, James & Gray, F.** Vhdl Design Representation & Synthesis. 2nd ed. LC 99-56533. 672p. (C). 2000. 75.00 (0-13-021670-4) P-H.
Armstrong, James & Gray, Gail. Structured Logic Design with VHDL. 400p. 1993. text 67.00 (0-13-855206-1) P-H.
***Armstrong, James C., Jr.** UNIX Secrets. 2nd ed. LC 99-30197. (Illus.). 1200p. 1999. pap. 39.99 incl. cd-rom (0-7645-3320-7) IDG Bks.
Armstrong, James C., jt. auth. see Taylor, Dave.
Armstrong, James D., jt. auth. see DeVita, Philip R.
Armstrong, James D., jt. ed. see DeVita, Philip R.
***Armstrong, James E.** Escape: An American Airman's Escape From Hitler's Fortress. (War - Non Fiction). (Illus.). 224p. 2000. pap. 19.95 (1-885354-08-8) Honoribus Pr.
Armstrong, James E. La Salle Co. Life of a Woman Pioneer: As Illustrated in the Life of Elsie Strawn Armstrong, 1789-1871; Part I, Her Personal History; Part Two, Short Accounts of Important Events in Pioneer Times. (Illus.). 124p. 1997. reprint ed. pap. 18.00 (0-8328-6640-7); reprint ed. lib. bdg. 28.00 (0-8328-6639-3) Higginson Bk Co.
Armstrong, James W. History of Leesburg & Plain Township. (Illus.). 194p. 1997. reprint ed. lib. bdg. 27.50 (0-8328-6658-X) Higginson Bk Co.
Armstrong, James W., jt. auth. see Sarafino, Edward P.
Armstrong, Jane. A National Assessment of Achievement & Participation of Women in Mathematics: Final Report. 236p. 1979. write for info. (0-318-59921-X, 10-MA-60) Natl Assessment.
Armstrong, Janice G., jt. auth. see Wilson, John.
***Armstrong, Jeanette.** Whispering in Shadows. 248p. 1999. pap. 15.95 (0-919441-99-8, Pub. by Theytus Bks) Orca Bk Pubs.
***Armstrong, Jeanette & Grauer, Lally, eds.** Anthology of Native Poetry in Canada. 300p. 2000. pap. text 17.95 (1-55111-200-0) Broadview.
***Armstrong, Jeannette.** Demythologizing the Romance of Conquest, 100. LC 99-58882. (Contributions to the Study of World Literature Ser.: Vol. 100). 144p. 2000. 49.95 (0-313-31067-X, Greenwood Pr) Greenwood.
Armstrong, Jeannette C. Slash. 3rd rev. ed. 256p. (YA). (gr. 8-12). 1985. pap. 8.95 (0-919441-29-7, Pub. by Theytus Bks) Orca Bk Pubs.
Armstrong, Jeannette C., ed. Looking at the Words of Our People: An Anthology of First Nation Literary Criticism. 216p. 1993. pap. 10.95 (0-919441-52-1, Pub. by Theytus Bks) Orca Bk Pubs.
Armstrong, Jeannette C., jt. auth. see Cardinal, Douglas J.
Armstrong, Jeannette C., jt. auth. see Marchand, Barb.
Armstrong, Jeff, jt. auth. see Owen, Michael G.
Armstrong, Jeffrey. Seventy Five Lightbulb Jokes. (Illus.). 152p. (Orig.). 1993. pap. text 4.50 (1-883532-02-7) Carmel Bay.
Armstrong, Jenice S., ed. see Poole, Daaimah S.
Armstrong, Jennifer. Black-Eyed Susan. 1997. 10.09 (0-606-12892-1, Pub. by Turtleback) Demco.
— Black-Eyed Susan. (Illus.). 128p. (J). (gr. 2-6). 1997. reprint ed. pap. 4.99 (0-679-88556-0, Pub. by Knopf Bks Yng Read) Random.
— Chin Yu Min & the Ginger Cat. (Illus.). 32p. (J). (ps-4). 1996. pap. 6.99 (0-517-88549-2) Crown Pub Group.
— Chin Yu Min & the Ginger Cat. 1996. 11.19 (0-606-08714-1, Pub. by Turtleback) Demco.
***Armstrong, Jennifer.** Dear Mr. President: Theodore Roosevelt: Letters from a Young Coal Miner. LC 99-462099. (Dear Mr. President Ser.: Vol. 1). (Illus.). 128p. (J). (gr. 4-7). 2001. 8.95 (1-890817-27-9, Pub. by Winslow Pr) Publishers Group.
— Dear Mr. President: Thomas Jefferson: Letters from a Philadelphia Bookworm. LC 00-20528. (Dear Mr. President Ser.: Vol. 2). (Illus.). 128p. (J). (gr. 4-7). 2001. 8.95 (1-890817-30-9, Pub. by Winslow Pr) Publishers Group.
Armstrong, Jennifer. The Dreams of Mairhe Mehan. (J). 1996. 18.00 (0-679-88152-2) McKay.
Armstrong, Jennifer. The Dreams of Mairhe Mehan. 1997. 10.09 (0-606-12925-1, Pub. by Turtleback) Demco.
Armstrong, Jennifer. The Dreams of Mairhe Mehan. 128p. (J). (gr. 6-9). 1997. reprint ed. mass mkt. 4.99 (0-679-88557-9, Pub. by Knopf Bks Yng Read) Random.
***Armstrong, Jennifer.** Endurance: The True Story of the Shackleton Expedition to the Antarctic. LC 99-37450. (Illus.). 32p. (YA). (ps up). 2000. lib. bdg. 18.99 (0-517-80092-6) Crown Pub Group.
Armstrong, Jennifer. Fantastic Failure: A True Story. (J). 18.00 (0-679-88897-7, Pub. by Random Bks Yng Read); lib. bdg. 19.99 (0-679-98897-1, Pub. by Random Bks Yng Read) Random.
— Foolish Gretel. (Stepping Stone Book: Children of America Ser.). 1997. 9.19 (0-606-11340-1, Pub. by Turtleback) Demco.
— Kenji & Little Mouse Boy. (J). 1998. pap. 3.99 (0-679-88279-0); lib. bdg. 11.99 (0-679-98279-5) Random Bks Yng Read.
— Lili the Brave. LC 97-11219. (Children of America Ser.). (Illus.). 80p. 1997. lib. bdg. 11.99 (0-679-97286-2) Random.
Armstrong, Jennifer. Lili the Brave, 2. (Children of America Ser.). (J). 1997. 9.19 (0-606-12655-4, Pub. by Turtleback) Demco.
Armstrong, Jennifer. Mary Mehan Awake. LC 97-6465. 160p. (J). (gr. 5-9). 1997. 18.00 (0-679-88276-6, Pub. by Knopf Bks Yng Read) Random.
— Mary Mehan Awake. (J). (gr. 6-11). 1998. pap. 4.99 (0-679-89265-6, Pub. by Random Bks Yng Read) Random.
— Patrick at Bat. (Illus.). (J). 1997. pap. 3.99 (0-679-87787-8) Random.
— Patrick Doyle Is Full of Blarney. LC 95-24754. (First Stepping Stone Bks.). (Illus.). (J). (gr. 1-4). 1996. lib. bdg. 17.99 (0-679-97285-4, Pub. by Random Bks Yng Read) Random.
— Patrick Doyle Is Full of Blarney. (Stepping Stone Books/Fourth of July Ser.). (Illus.). (J). (gr. 1-4). 1997. pap. 3.99 (0-614-28934-3) Random Bks Yng Read.
Armstrong, Jennifer. Patrick Doyle Is Full of Blarney. (Stepping Stone Bks.). (J). 1997. 9.19 (0-606-11725-3, Pub. by Turtleback) Demco.
Armstrong, Jennifer. Pierre's Dream. LC 98-36179. (Illus.). (J). 1999. lib. bdg. 15.89 (0-8037-2460-8, Dial Yng Read) Peng Put Young Read.
— Pierre's Dream. Arico, Diane, ed. LC 98-36179. (Illus.). 32p. (J). (ps-3). 1999. 15.99 (0-8037-1700-8, Dial Yng Read) Peng Put Young Read.
— Pockets. LC 97-10962. (Illus.). (J). (gr. 1-6). 1998. lib. bdg. 18.99 (0-517-70927-9, Pub. by Crown Bks Yng Read) Random.
— Pockets. LC 97-10962. (J). (gr. 1-6). 1998. 17.00 (0-517-70926-0) Random.
— Reading Group Guide to The Dreams of Mairhe Mehan. (YA). 1997. pap. 1.00 (0-676-76074-0) Random.
— Saint Wolf. 1999. write for info. (0-679-89486-1); lib. bdg. 18.99 (0-679-99486-6) Knopf.
***Armstrong, Jennifer.** Shipwreck at the Bottom of the World: The Extraordinary True Story of Shackleton & the Enduran. 120p. (gr. 4-7). 2000. pap. 9.95 (0-375-81049-8) Knopf.
Armstrong, Jennifer. Shipwreck at the Bottom of the World: The Extraordinary True Story of Shackleton & the Endurance. LC 97-52063. (J). (gr. 4-7). 1998. lib. bdg. 19.99 (0-517-80014-4, Crown) Crown Pub Group.
— Shipwreck at the Bottom of the World: The Extraordinary True Story of Shackleton & the Endurance. LC 97-52063. 144p. (YA). (gr. 5-8). 1998. 18.00 (0-517-80013-6, Crown) Crown Pub Group.
— The Snowball. LC 94-48883. (Early Step into Reading Ser.). (J). (ps-3). 1996. pap. 3.99 (0-679-86444-X) Random.
— The Snowball. LC 94-48883. (Early Step into Reading Ser.). (J). (ps-3). 1996. lib. bdg. 11.99 (0-679-96444-4) Random.
Armstrong, Jennifer. The Snowball. LC 94-48883. (Early Step into Reading Ser.). (J). (ps-k). 1996. 9.19 (0-606-11853-5, Pub. by Turtleback) Demco.
— Spirit of Endurance: The True Story of the Shackleton Expedition to the Antarctic. LC 99-37450. (Illus.). 32p. (J). (ps up). 2000. 16.95 (0-517-80091-8, Pub. by Crown Bks Yng Read) Random.
Armstrong, Jennifer. Steal Away. 224p. (J). (gr. 3-7). 1993. pap. 3.99 (0-590-46921-5, Apple Paperbacks) Scholastic Inc.
— Steal Away. (J). 1992. 9.60 (0-606-05623-8, Pub. by Turtleback) Demco.
— Sunshine, Moonshine. LC 94-34992. (Early Step into Reading Ser.). (Illus.). 32p. (J). (ps-1). 1997. pap. 3.99 (0-679-86442-3) Random.
— Sunshine, Moonshine. LC 94-34992. (Early Step into Reading Ser.). (Illus.). (J). (gr. 1-4). 1997. lib. bdg. 11.99 (0-679-96442-8) Random.
Armstrong, Jennifer. Sunshine, Moonshine. LC 94-34992. (Early Step into Reading Ser.). (J). (ps-k). 1997. 9.19 (0-606-11939-6, Pub. by Turtleback) Demco.
Armstrong, Jennifer. Wild Rose Inn. (J). 1994. mass mkt. 3.95 (0-553-54154-4) BDD Bks Young Read.
Armstrong, Jennifer, jt. auth. see Opdyke, Irene Gut.
Armstrong, Jill. Uganda's AIDS Crisis: Its Implications for Development. LC 95-37063. (Discussion Paper Ser.: No. 298). 108p. 1995. pap. 22.00 (0-8213-3437-9) World Bank.
Armstrong, Joe. Concurrent Programming in ERLANG. 2nd ed. 358p. 1996. pap. 52.00 (0-13-508301-X) P-H.
Armstrong, Joe E. Tales of a Fledging Homestead. LC 84-25389. (Illus.). 110p. (Orig.). 1985. pap. 7.95 (0-930079-00-0) Misty Hill Pr.
Armstrong, John. The Art of Preserving Health: A Poem. Kastenbaum, Robert J., ed. LC 78-22185. (Aging & Old Age Ser.). 1979. reprint ed. lib. bdg. 17.95 (0-405-11803-1) Ayer.
— Can Fallen Pastors Be Restored? The Church's Response to Sexual Misconduct. pap. 11.99 (0-8024-1412-5, 105) Moody.
— The Catholic Mystery: Understanding the Beliefs & Practices of Modern Catholicism. LC 99-22974. 200p. 1999. pap. 9.99 (0-7369-0103-5) Harvest Hse.
— Five Evangelists. 1996. 10.99 (1-85792-157-7, Pub. by Christian Focus) Spring Arbor Dist.
***Armstrong, John.** Move Closer: An Intimate Philosophy of Art. (Illus.). 224p. 2000. 25.00 (0-374-10596-0) FS&G.
Armstrong, John. The Solo & Ensemble Singer. Busch, Brian, ed. (Illus.). 48p. (Orig.). (C). 1995. pap. text, teacher ed. 12.95 (0-89724-988-7, SVB9601); pap. text, student ed. 3.95 (0-89724-989-5, SVB9601S) Wrner Bros.
— Track Planning for Realistic Operation. 3rd rev. ed. LC 63-5732. (Illus.). 144p. (YA). (gr. 6 up). 1979. per. 18.95 (0-89024-227-5, 12148, Kalmbach Books) Kalmbach.
— When God Moves: Preparing Your Heart for True Revival. LC 98-12644. 220p. 1998. pap. 10.99 (1-56507-868-3) Harvest Hse.
Armstrong, John, ed. Coastal & Short Sea Shipping. LC 96-27867. (Studies in Transport History). 208p. 1996. 61.95 (1-85928-301-2, Pub. by Scolar Pr) Ashgate Pub Co.
Armstrong, John & Malacinski, George M., eds. Developmental Biology of the Axolotl. (Illus.). 336p. 1989. text 95.00 (0-19-505073-8) OUP.
Armstrong, John A. Ideology, Politics, & Government in the Soviet Union. 4th ed. (Illus.). 256p. (C). 1986. reprint ed. pap. text 24.50 (0-8191-5405-9) U Pr of Amer.

An Asterisk (*) at the beginning of an entry indicates that the title is appearing for the first time.

— Nations Before Nationalism. LC 81-12988. 447p. reprint ed. pap. 138.60 (*0-7837-0287-6*, 204060800018) Bks Demand.

— Ukrainian Nationalism. 3rd ed. xviii, 271p. 1990. lib. bdg. 45.00 (*0-87287-755-8*) Libs Unl.

Armstrong, John B. Factory under the Elms: A History of Harrisville, New Hampshire 1774-1969. LC 85-21674. (Illus.). 1985. 15.00 (*0-937474-07-X*) Am Textile Hist.

Armstrong, John H. The Compromised Church: The Present Evangelical Crisis. LC 98-22534. 1998. 19.99 (*1-58134-006-0*) Crossway Bks.

— Un Escrutinio de Roma: Guia para Entender las Creencias y Practicas de los Catolicos Romanos. (SPA.). 144p. 1997. pap. 6.99 (*0-8254-1036-3*, Edit Portavoz) Kregel.

— The Railroad What It Is What It Does: The Introduction to Railroading. 3rd ed. (Illus.). 270p. 1996. reprint ed. pap. 28.95 (*0-911382-04-6*) Simmons-Boardman.

Armstrong, John H., ed. The Coming Evangelical Crisis: Current Challenges to the Authority of Scripture & the Gospel. LC 96-204850. 269p. 1997. pap. 12.99 (*0-8024-7738-0*, 117) Moody.

Armstrong, John M., ed. see Michigan University, Institute of Science & Techno.

Armstrong, John W. The Water of Life. 136p. (C). 1971. pap. 19.95 (*0-8464-1060-5*) Beekman Pubs.

— The Water of Life. 111p. 1971. pap. 11.95 (*0-85032-052-6*, Pub. by C W Daniel) Natl Bk Netwk.

Armstrong, Joseph & Williamson, Margaret. Building of The Mother Church. (Illus.). 169p. 1980. pap. 18.95 (*0-87510-347-2*) Writings of Mary Baker.

***Armstrong, Joshua.** The Seekers: A Bounty Hunter's Story. 336p. 2000. 24.00 (*0-06-019343-3*) HarpC.

Armstrong, Joshua. The Seekers: A Bounty Hunter's Story. Date not set. pap. 14.00 (*0-06-093160-4*, Perennial) HarperTrade.

Armstrong, Judith M. The Christesen Romance. LC 96-213069. 248p. 1997. pap. 29.95 (*0-522-84731-5*, Pub. by Melbourne Univ Pr) Paul & Co Pubs.

Armstrong, K. M. & Curry, Bob. The Civil War Through the Camera. (Illus.). 256p. 1994. pap. text 31.00 (*0-7884-0078-9*) Heritage Bk.

***Armstrong, Karen.** The Battle for God: Fundamentalism in Judaism, Christianity & Islam. LC 99-34022. 448p. 2000. 27.50 (*0-679-43597-2*) Knopf.

— Buddha: A Penguin Life. 2001. 19.95 (*0-670-89193-2*, Viking) Viking Penguin.

— Freedom from Fear: The Complete Guide to Personal Safety for Women. (Illus.). 113p. 1999. pap. text 12.00 (*0-7881-6649-2*) DIANE Pub.

— The History of God: The 4000- Year Quest of Judaism, Christianity & Islam: Armstrong,&Karen, Set. abr. ed. 1994. audio 25.00 (*0-694-51503-5*, 692226, Pub. by HarperAudio) Lndmrk Audiobks.

Armstrong, Karen. History of God: The 4000-Year Quest of Judaism, Christianity & Islam. 496p. 1994. reprint ed. pap. 15.00 (*0-345-38456-3*) Ballantine Pub Grp.

— In the Beginning: A New Interpretation of Genesis. 208p. 1997. pap. 12.00 (*0-345-40604-4*) Ballantine Pub Grp.

— In the Beginning: A New Interpretation of Genesis. 1996. 20.00 (*0-614-19810-0*); 20.00 (*0-614-20419-4*) Knopf.

— In the Beginning: A New Interpretation of Genesis. 192p. 1996. 20.00 (*0-679-45089-0*) McKay.

***Armstrong, Karen.** Islam: A Short History. LC 00-25285. 144p. 2000. 19.95 (*0-679-64040-1*) Modern Lib NY.

Armstrong, Karen. Jerusalem: One City, Three Faiths. 1997. pap. 17.50 (*0-345-39168-3*) Ballantine Pub Grp.

— Jerusalem: One City, Three Faiths. 544p. 1996. 30.00 (*0-679-43596-4*) Knopf.

Armstrong, Karen. Jerusalem: One City, Three Faiths, Set. 1996. audio 25.00 (*0-694-51716-X*, 628175) HarperAudio.

Armstrong, Karen. Muhammad: A Biography of the Prophet. 290p. 1996. 14.95 (*0-614-21088-7*, 806) Kazi Pubns.

— Muhammad: A Biography of the Prophet. rev. ed. LC 91-55407. 288p. 1993. pap. 14.00 (*0-06-250886-5*, Pub. by Harper SF) HarpC.

— Through the Narrow Gate. large type ed. 544p. 1983. 27.99 (*0-7089-0941-8*) Ulverscroft.

Armstrong, Karen, ed. Shifting Ground & Cultured Bodies: Postcolonial Gender Relations in Africa & India. LC 99-14681. 152p. 1999. 45.00 (*0-7618-1388-8*); pap. 24.50 (*0-7618-1389-6*) U Pr of Amer.

Armstrong, Katherine. Studying Shakespeare: A Practical Guide. 1998. pap. text 23.00 (*0-13-786788-3*) P-H.

Armstrong, Katherine & Atkin, Graham. Studying Shakespeare: A Practical Guide. 1997. pap. text 23.00 (*0-13-486788-2*) Aspen Law.

Armstrong, Kathie & Harvey, Chet. Adirondack Mountain Club Canoe Guide to the Central Hudson & Delaware Watersheds, Set, Vol. 4. Freeman, Mark, ed. LC 96-34248. (Adirondack Mountain Club Canoe Guide Ser.). (Illus.). 256p. (Orig.). 2000. pap. 16.95 (*0-935272-78-X*) ADK Mtn Club.

Describes over sixty of the best white, quick & flat water paddle trips the upper the upper & central Hudson region has to offer. Covers major rivers & tributries from the Newcomb-North Hudson area to Kingston & from Herkimer in the west-central portion of the Adirondacks east to the New England states. Includes the many inviting waterways in & around the Capital District. Details launch sites & how to get to them, scenery & points of interest, difficulty levels, special cautions, paddling distances & takeouts. Numerous age maps. To order contact: Adirondack Mountain Club, 814 Goggins Rd., Lake George, NY 12845 or call 800-395-8080. *Publisher Paid Annotation.*

Armstrong, Kathryn, jt. auth. see Adams, Tom.

Armstrong, Keith. Care & Repair of Advanced Composite Structures. LC 97-35791. xxiv, 552p. 1998. 69.00 (*0-7680-0047-5*, R-174) Soc Auto Engineers.

— Visual Pathways to the Inner Self. (Illus.). 295p. (C). 1996. text 35.00 (*1-879528-17-7*); pap. text 19.95 (*1-879528-16-9*) Ed Studies Pr.

Armstrong, Keith, jt. auth. see Williams, Tim.

Armstrong, Ken. No Amateur Did This: What Is the Truth about the Oklahoma City Bombing? large type ed. (Illus.), 192p. (Orig.). 1997. 19.95 (*0-9657155-0-7*) Blckeye Pr.

Armstrong, Kenneth A. Regulation, Deregulation, Re-regulation: The Paradoxed Of Eu Governance. 1999. pap. text 20.00 (*0-7494-2995-X*, Kogan Pg Educ) Stylus Pub VA.

Armstrong, Kenneth D. Choosing Your Homebuilt. 2nd ed. (Illus.). 384p. (Orig.). 1993. pap. 19.95 (*0-932579-26-4*) Butterfield Pr.

Armstrong, Kevin B. Methylphenate HCL (Ritalin) Index of New Information with Authors, Subjects & References. 131p. 1997. 47.50 (*0-7883-1252-9*); pap. 44.50 (*0-7883-1253-7*) ABBE Pubs Assn.

***Armstrong, Kristin.** Lance Armstrong: The Race of His Life. (All Aboard Reading Ser.). (Illus.). (J). 2000. 13.89 (*0-448-42415-0*, Planet Dexter) Peng Put Young Read.

— Lance Armstrong: The Race of His Life. (All Aboard Reading Ser.). (Illus.). 48p. (J). (gr. 4-7). 2000. pap. 3.99 (*0-448-42407-X*, Planet Dexter) Peng Put Young Read.

***Armstrong, Lance & Jenkins, Sally.** It's Not about the Bike: My Journey Back to Life. LC 00-35612. (Illus.). 288p. 2000. 24.95 (*0-399-14611-3*) Putnam Pub Group.

***Armstrong, Lance, et al.** The Lance Armstrong Performance Program: Seven Weeks to the Perfect Ride. (Illus.). 256p. 2000. pap. 15.95 (*1-57954-270-0*) Rodale Pr Inc.

***Armstrong, Lawrence E.** Performing in Extreme Environments: Training & Working in Intense Heat, Frigid Cold, under Water, High Altitude, Air Pollution. LC 99-38795. 344p. 2000. 19.95 (*0-88011-837-7*) Human Kinetics.

Armstrong, Leroy & Denny, J. O. Financial California: An Historical Review of the Beginnings & Progess of Banking in the State. Bruchey, Stuart, ed. LC 80-1131. (Rise of Commercial Banking Ser.). 1981. reprint ed. lib. bdg. 28.95 (*0-405-13632-3*) Ayer.

Armstrong, Lilias E. The Phonetic & Tonal Structure of Kikuyu. LC 41-22752. (Illus.). 382p. reprint ed. pap. 118.50 (*0-8357-3210-X*, 205708000010) Bks Demand.

Armstrong, Linda. Armstrong Naming Test. (Illus.). (Orig.). 1996. pap. 150.00 (*1-56593-779-1*, 1520) Singular Publishing.

— Pendragon's Brave Rider. 126p. (J). (gr. 6-8). 1998. pap. 9.95 (*1-57532-172-6*) Press-Tige Pub.

Armstrong, Linda, jt. auth. see Hastings, Pattie B.

Armstrong, Lindsay. Accidental Nanny: (Nanny Wanted!) (Presents Ser.: Vol. 1986). 1998. per. 3.75 (*0-373-11986-0*, 1-11986-6) Harlequin Bks.

— Casada con Su Enemigo: When Enemies Marry. (Bianca Ser.). (SPA.). 1996. per. 3.50 (*0-373-33378-1*, 1-33378-0) Harlequin Bks.

— Dangerous Deceiver. (Presents Ser.). 1997. per. 3.50 (*0-373-11874-0*, 1-11874-4) Harlequin Bks.

— A Dangerous Lover. (Presents Ser.). 1993. per. 2.89 (*0-373-11546-6*, 1-11546-8) Harlequin Bks.

— Dark Captor. (Presents Ser.). 1993. per. 2.99 (*0-373-11569-5*, 1-11569-0) Harlequin Bks.

— Dark Captor. large type ed. 285p. 1992. reprint ed. 18.95 (*0-263-12835-0*) Mac Lib Ref.

— A Difficult Man. 1994. per. 2.99 (*0-373-11693-4*, 1-11693-8) Harlequin Bks.

— The Director's Wife. (Presents Ser.: No. 439). 1992. pap. 2.89 (*0-373-11439-7*, 1-11439-6) Harlequin Bks.

— En Brazos de un Seductor. (SPA.). 1997. per. 3.50 (*0-373-33409-5*, 1-33409-3) Harlequin Bks.

— Having His Babies: Expecting! (Presents Ser.: No. 2057). 1999. per. 3.75 (*0-373-12057-5*, 1-12057-5) Harlequin Bks.

***Armstrong, Lindsay.** Having His Babies: Expecting! large type ed. 1999. 21.95 (*0-263-16203-6*, Pub. by Mills & Boon) Ulverscroft.

Armstrong, Lindsay. He's My Husband! (Presents Ser.: Bk. 2040). 1999. per. 3.75 (*0-373-12040-0*, 1-12040-1) Harlequin Bks.

***Armstrong, Lindsay.** He's My Husband! large type ed. 1999. 25.99 (*0-263-15931-0*, Pub. by Mills & Boon) Ulverscroft.

Armstrong, Lindsay. El Hombre de Mi Vida - The Man of My Life. (SPA.). 1997. per. 3.50 (*0-373-33412-5*, 1-33412-7) Harlequin Bks.

— Leave Love Alone. (Presents Ser.). 1992. per. 2.89 (*0-373-11487-5*, 1-11487-5) Harlequin Bks.

— Marriage Ultimatum. (Presents Ser.: Bk. 2075). 2000. per. 3.75 (*0-373-12075-3*, 1-12075-7) Harlequin Bks.

***Armstrong, Lindsay.** Marriage Ultimatum. large type ed. (Thorndike Harlequin Romance Ser.). 2000. 22.95 (*0-263-16366-0*) Mills & Boon.

Armstrong, Lindsay. Married for Real. (Presents Ser.: No. 1925). 1997. per. 3.50 (*0-373-11925-9*, 1-11925-4) Harlequin Bks.

— Married for Real. large type ed. (Mills & Boon Large Print Ser.). 288p. 1997. 23.99 (*0-263-14991-9*) Ulverscroft.

— The Marrying Game. large type ed. 1990. lib. bdg. 18.95 (*0-263-12351-0*) Mac Lib Ref.

— A Marrying Man? 1998. per. 3.75 (*0-373-18695-9*, 1-18695-6, Mira Bks) Harlequin Bks.

— A Marrying Man? large type ed. (Harlequin Romance Ser.). 1997. 20.95 (*0-263-15119-0*) Mac Lib Ref.

— A Masterful Man. LC 96-255. 189p. 1995. per. 3.25 (*0-373-11770-1*, 1-11770-4) Harlequin Bks.

— One More Night. large type ed. 1990. reprint ed. lib. bdg. 18.95 (*0-263-12259-X*) Mac Lib Ref.

***Armstrong, Lindsay.** Outback Mistress. (Presents Ser.). 2000. mass mkt. 3.99 (*0-373-12124-5*, 1-12124-3) Harlequin Bks.

— Outback Mistress. large type ed. 1999. 25.99 (*0-263-16053-X*, Pub. by Mills & Boon) Ulverscroft.

Armstrong, Lindsay. Playboy Lover. (Australians Ser.: Vol. 5). 1998. per. 4.50 (*0-373-82575-7*) Harlequin Bks.

— Se Necesita Amor: Accidental Nanny. (Bianca Ser.: Vol. 121).Tr. of Love Is Needed. 1998. per. 3.50 (*0-373-33471-0*, 1-33471-3) Harlequin Bks.

— The Seduction Stakes. (Presents Ser.). 1994. per. 2.99 (*0-373-11626-8*, 1-11626-8) Harlequin Bks.

— Tendre et Rebelle. (Azur Ser.: No. 730). (FRE.). 1998. mass mkt. 3.50 (*0-373-34730-8*, 1-34730-1) Harlequin Bks.

— Trial by Marriage. LC 96-3725. 186p. 1996. per. 3.50 (*0-373-11798-1*, 1-11798-5) Harlequin Bks.

— Trial by Marriage. large type ed. (Harlequin Romance Ser.). 287p. 1995. 20.95 (*0-263-14149-7*) Mac Lib Ref.

— An Unsuitable Wife. (Presents Ser.). 1995. per. 2.99 (*0-373-11713-2*, 1-11713-4) Harlequin Bks.

— An Unsuitable Wife. large type unabridged ed. (Harlequin Ser.). 1994. lib. bdg. 19.95 (*0-263-13893-3*, Pub. by Mills & Boon) Ulverscroft.

— An Unusual Affair. (Presents Ser.). 1993. per. 2.99 (*0-373-11593-8*, 1-11593-0) Harlequin Bks.

— Unwilling Mistress. 1994. per. 2.99 (*0-373-11656-X*, 1-11656-5) Harlequin Bks.

— Unwilling Mistress. large type ed. (Harlequin Ser.). 1994. lib. bdg. 19.95 (*0-263-13773-2*) Thorndike Pr.

— Vengeance ou Provocation. (Azur Ser.). 1999. mass mkt. 3.50 (*0-373-34765-0*, 1-34765-7) Harlequin Bks.

— When Enemies Marry . . . (Presents Ser.). 1998. per. 3.75 (*0-373-11946-1*, 1-11946-0) Harlequin Bks.

— When Enemies Marry. large type ed. 288p. 1995. 23.99 (*0-263-14315-5*, Pub. by Mills & Boon) Ulverscroft.

— Wildcat Wife. 1999. per. 4.50 (*0-373-82582-X*, 1-82582-7, Harlequin) Harlequin Bks.

— Wildcat Wife. large type ed. (Mills & Boon Large Print Ser.). 288p. 1998. 24.99 (*0-263-15559-5*, Pub. by Mills & Boon) Ulverscroft.

Armstrong, Lindsay, ed. see Jordan, Penny & Leclaire, Day.

***Armstrong, Louis.** Louis Armstrong, in His Own Words. Brothers, Thomas, ed. (Illus.). 304p. 2001. pap. 14.95 (*0-19-514046-X*) OUP.

— Louis Armstrong, in His Own Words: Selected Writings. Brothers, Thomas, ed. LC 99-17040. (Illus.). 302p. 1999. 25.00 (*0-19-511958-4*) OUP.

Armstrong, Louis. Satchmo: My Life in New Orleans. (Illus.). 248p. 1988. pap. 11.95 (*0-306-80276-7*) Da Capo.

Armstrong, Louise. And They Call It Help: The Psychiatric Policing of America's Children. 1996. pap. write for info. (*0-201-62692-6*) Addison-Wesley.

— Kiss Daddy Goodnight. 1987. pap. 5.99 (*0-685-67638-2*) PB.

— Kiss Daddy Goodnight: 10 Years Later. rev. ed. 1988. mass mkt. 5.99 (*0-671-68056-0*) PB.

— Of Sluts & Bastards: A Feminist Decodes the Child Welfare Debate. 336p. (C). 1995. pap. 18.95 (*1-56751-066-3*); lib. bdg. 29.95 (*1-56751-067-1*) Common Courage.

— Satchmo My Life in New Orleans: My Life in New Orleans. 240p. reprint ed. lib. bdg. 39.00 (*0-685-14803-3*) Rprt Serv.

— Swing That Music. LC 93-21594. (Illus.). 200p. 1993. reprint ed. pap. 12.95 (*0-306-80544-8*) Da Capo.

— We Too Are the People. LC 78-137155. (Poverty U. S. A. Historical Record Ser.). 1971. reprint ed. 38.95 (*0-405-03093-2*) Ayer.

Armstrong, Luanne. Annie. LC 96-115930. 336p. (Orig.). 1995. pap. 12.95 (*1-896095-00-3*) Polstar Bk.

***Armstrong, Luanne & Woodend, Dorothy.** Maggie & Shine. 90p. (J). (gr. 4-6). 1999. pap. 6.95 (*1-895836-67-0*, Tesseract) Bk Collective.

Armstrong, M. George Borrow. LC 74-6381. (English Literature Ser.: No. 33). 1974. lib. bdg. 55.00 (*0-8383-1963-7*) M S G Haskell Hse.

Armstrong, M., jt. ed. see Matheron, G.

Armstrong, M. A. Basic Topology. rev. ed. (Undergraduate Texts in Mathematics Ser.). (Illus.). 250p. 1997. reprint ed. 39.95 (*0-387-90839-0*) Spr-Verlag.

— Groups & Symmetry. (Undergraduate Texts in Mathematics Ser.). (Illus.). 175p. 1997. 39.95 (*0-387-96675-7*) Spr-Verlag.

Armstrong, M. C. Pilot Ladder Safety. (C). 1987. 50.00 (*0-85174-499-0*) St Mut.

— Practical Ship Handling. (C). 1987. 60.00 (*0-85174-387-0*) St Mut.

Armstrong, M. C., jt. auth. see Hume, C. W.

Armstrong, Malcom, jt. auth. see Davies, Don.

Armstrong, Margaret. Basic Linear Geostatistics. LC 98-34424. (Illus.). 160p. 1998. pap. 29.95 (*3-540-61845-7*) Spr-Verlag.

Armstrong, Margaret D. Tales from an Irish Wake. LC 89-25798. 256p. 1990. 19.95 (*0-912526-45-9*) Lib Res.

Armstrong, Mark. Lonely Planet Melbourne. 2nd ed. (Illus.). 312p. 1997. pap. 12.95 (*0-86442-386-1*) Lonely Planet.

— Lonely Planet Queensland: Australia Guide. (Illus.). 672p. 1996. pap. 17.95 (*0-86442-318-7*) Lonely Planet.

Armstrong, Mark, ed. Communications Law & Policy in Australia. (Butterworths Australia Ser.). write for info. (*0-409-49375-9*, MICHIE) LEXIS Pub.

Armstrong, Mark, et al. Regulatory Reform: Economic Analysis & British Experience. 400p. 1994. 45.00 (*0-262-01143-3*) MIT Pr.

Armstrong, Mark, jt. auth. see Cowan, Simon.

Armstrong, Mark, jt. auth. see McClymont, David.

Armstrong, Marsha. Core Bibliography on Technology & Social Change in Foreign Cultures. (Reports on Technology & Social Change). 133p. 1973. 10.00 (*0-945271-22-0*) ISU-CIKARD.

Armstrong, Martin D. Bazaar & Other Stories. LC 71-106242. (Short Story Index Reprint Ser.). 1977. 20.95 (*0-8369-3278-1*) Ayer.

— Puppet Show. LC 71-163020. (Short Story Index Reprint Ser.). 1977. reprint ed. 16.95 (*0-8369-3934-4*) Ayer.

— Sir Pompey & Madame Juno: And Other Tales. LC 75-163021. (Short Story Index Reprint Ser.). 1977. reprint ed. 19.95 (*0-8369-3935-2*) Ayer.

Armstrong, Mary. Arabic-English Dictionary of Legal Terms. (ARA & ENG.). (C). 1988. 350.00 (*0-7855-6537-X*) St Mut.

Armstrong, Mary F. & Ludlow, Helen W. Hampton & Its Students. Fenner, Thomas P., ed. LC 75-149862. (Black Heritage Library Collection). 1977. 27.95 (*0-8369-8744-6*) Ayer.

— Hampton & Its Students. LC 71-132385. reprint ed. 31.50 (*0-404-07234-8*) AMS Pr.

Armstrong, Mary W., jt. auth. see Armstrong, Richard B.

Armstrong, Mary Willems, jt. auth. see Armstrong, Richard B.

Armstrong, Matthew, jt. auth. see Rubin, William S.

Armstrong, Matthew, tr. see Meyer-Abich, Klaus M.

Armstrong, Michael. After the Zap. 256p. 1987. pap. 2.95 (*0-445-20438-9*) Warner Bks.

— Agviq. 1990. mass mkt. 4.50 (*0-445-20848-1*) Warner Bks.

— Closely Observed Children: The Diary of a Primary Classroom. (Chameleon Education Ser.). (Illus.). 224p. (Orig.). 1981. 12.95 (*0-906495-04-0*); pap. 5.95 (*0-906495-21-0*) Writers & Readers.

— Collected Poems, 1961-1996. 1997. pap. 19.95 (*3-7052-0117-4*, Pub. by Poetry Salzburg) Intl Spec Bk.

***Armstrong, Michael.** Employee Reward. 2000. pap. 59.95 (*0-8464-5043-7*) Beekman Pubs.

Armstrong, Michael. Growing Through the Day. (Orig.). pap. text 4.00 (*0-317-67321-1*) In Tradition Pub.

— Handbook Of Human Resource Management Practice, 7th Ed. 7th ed. 1999. pap. text 39.95 (*0-7494-2964-X*, Kogan Pg Educ) Stylus Pub VA.

— A Handbook of Management Techniques. 2nd ed. (Illus.). 576p. (C). 1993. text 59.95 (*0-89397-387-4*) Nichols Pub.

— How to Be an Even Better Manager: A Complete A-Z of Proven Techniques & Essential Skills--Reveals the Secrets of Successful Managers. 4th rev. ed. 328p. 1995. pap. 37.95 (*0-89397-440-4*, Pub. by Kogan Pg) Nichols Pub.

— Management Processes & Functions. 250p. (C). 1990. 95.00 (*0-85292-438-0*, Pub. by IPM Hse) St Mut.

***Armstrong, Michael.** Managing Activities. 320p. 2000. pap. 47.95 (*0-8464-5110-7*) Beekman Pubs.

Armstrong, Michael. Managing People: A Practical Guide For Line Managers. 1999. pap. text 24.95 (*0-7494-2612-8*) Kogan Page Ltd.

— Managing Reward Systems. LC 92-29885. (Managing Work & Organizations Ser.). 176p. 1993. 122.00 (*0-335-15767-X*) OpUniv Pr.

— Personnel & the Bottom Line. 256p. (C). 1989. 150.00 (*0-85292-421-6*, Pub. by IPM Hse) St Mut.

***Armstrong, Michael.** Rewarding Teams. 96p. 2000. pap. 29.99 (*0-8464-5182-4*) Beekman Pubs.

Armstrong, Michael. Using the HR Consultant Achieving Results - Adding Value. 160p. 1993. pap. 120.00 (*0-85292-546-8*, Pub. by IPM Hse) St Mut.

Armstrong, Michael, ed. The Human Resource Management Yearbook, 1989. 400p. (C). 1988. 120.00 (*1-85091-746-9*) St Mut.

Armstrong, Michael & Baron, Angela. The Job Evaluation Handbook. 416p. 1995. pap. 60.00 (*0-85292-581-6*, Pub. by IPM Hse) St Mut.

Armstrong, Michael & Baron, Angela, eds. Performance Management: The New Realities. 320p. 1998. pap. 57.00 (*0-85292-727-4*, Pub. by IPM Hse) St Mut.

Armstrong, Michael & Long, Phil. The Reality of Strategic HRM. 224p. (C). 1994. pap. 40.00 (*0-85292-563-8*, Pub. by IPM Hse) St Mut.

Armstrong, Michael & Murlis, Helen. Reward Management: A Handbook of Remuneration, Strategy & Practice. 600p. 1993. pap. 175.00 (*0-7494-1009-4*, Pub. by IPM Hse) St Mut.

— Reward Management: A Handbook of Salary Administration. 592p. (C). 1991. pap. 100.00 (*0-7494-0220-2*, Pub. by IPM Hse) St Mut.

— Reward Management: A Handbook of Salary Administration. 550p. (C). 1988. 150.00 (*1-85091-335-8*) St Mut.

Armstrong, Michael, jt. auth. see Brown, Duncan.

Armstrong, Michael, ed. see Tolstoy, Leo.

Armstrong, Michael L. Electrocardiagrams: A Systematic Method of Reading Them. 5th ed. (Illus.). 328p. pap. 38.00 (*0-07-470248-3*) McGraw-Hill Prof.

Armstrong, Milton, ed. see Robinson, Maxx.

Armstrong, Mimi. Calligraphic Designs. (International Design Library). (Illus.). 48p. (Orig.). 1983. pap. 6.95 (*0-88045-031-2*) Stemmer Hse.

Armstrong, Missy & Lauzen, Sara. Community Integration Program. 2nd ed. (Illus.). 321p. 1994. pap. 50.00 (*1-882883-09-8*, B245) Idyll Arbor.

Armstrong, Missy & Lauzen, Sara. Community Integration Program. 2nd ed. 321p. 1994. ring bd. 50.00 (*1-882883-03-9*, B245) Idyll Arbor.

Armstrong, Moses. Orthodox Christian Alphabet Coloring Book. 35p. (J). (gr. k-3). Date not set. pap. 5.00 (1-879038-45-5, 9013) Synaxis Pr.

Armstrong, Moses K. Early Empire Builders of the Great West. LC 72-2557. (Select Bibliographies Reprint Ser.). 1977. reprint ed. 31.95 (0-8369-6846-8) Ayer.

Armstrong, Moses K. History & Resources of Dakota, Montana & Idaho. 62p. 1967. 9.95 (0-87770-104-0); pap. 5.95 (0-87770-031-1) Ye Galleon.

Armstrong, Myrna L., ed. Telecommunications for Health Professionals: Providing Successful Distance Education & Telehealth. LC 97-52155. (Illus.). 352p. 1998. 48.95 (0-8261-9840-6) Springer Pub.

Armstrong, Nancy. Desire & Domestic Fiction: A Political History of the Novel. 320p. 1990. reprint ed. pap. text 19.95 (0-19-506160-8) OUP.

***Armstrong, Nancy.** Fiction in the Age of Photography: The Legacy of British Realism. LC 99-35660. 331p. 2000. 29.95 (0-674-29930-2) HUP.

Armstrong, Nancy. Navajo Children. (Indian Culture Ser.). (J). (gr. 2-6). 1975. pap. 1.95 (0-89992-037-3) Coun India Ed.

— Navajo Long Walk. 88p. (J). (gr. 4-9). 1983. pap. 5.95 (0-89992-083-7) Coun India Ed.

— Navajo Long Walk. (Council for Indian Education Ser.). (Illus.). 128p. (J). (gr. 4-8). 1994. pap. 8.95 (1-879373-56-4) Roberts Rinehart.

Armstrong, Nancy & Tennenhouse, Leonard. The Imaginary Puritan: Literature, Intellectual Labor, & the Origins of Personal Life. (New Historicism: Studies in Cultural Poetics: No. 21). (C). 1992. 50.00 (0-520-07756-3, Pub. by U CA Pr) Cal Prin Full Svc.

— The Imaginary Puritan: Literature, Intellectual Labor, & the Origins of Personal Life. 275p. (C). 1994. pap. 18.95 (0-520-08643-0, Pub. by U CA Pr) Cal Prin Full Svc.

Armstrong, Nancy & Tennenhouse, Leonard, eds. Ideology of Conduct: Essays on Literature & the History of Sexuality. 45.00 (0-416-38590-7); pap. 13.95 (0-416-38600-8) Routledge.

— The Violence of Representation: Literature & the History of Violence. 240p. 1989. 45.00 (0-415-01447-6, A1582); pap. 16.95 (0-415-01448-4, A1586) Routledge.

Armstrong, Nancy, et al. The Heritage. (J). (gr. 3-6). 1977. 1.95 (0-89992-065-9) Coun India Ed.

Armstrong, Neil. New Directions in Physical Education: Change & Innovation. (Cassell Education Ser.). (Illus.). 256p. (Orig.). 1996. pap. 35.00 (0-304-33449-9) Continuum.

Armstrong, Neil, ed. New Directions in Physical Education Vol. 2: Physical Education Association of Great Britain & Northern Ireland. LC 90-31892. (Illus.). 221p. reprint ed. pap. 68.60 (0-608-20817-5, 207191600002) Bks Demand.

Armstrong, Neil, et al, eds. Children & Exercise XIX: Promoting Health & Well-Being. LC 98-205524. (Illus.). 584p. (C). (gr. 13). 1997. 120.00 (0-419-22100-X, D5577, E & FN Spon) Routledge.

Armstrong, Neil & Sparkes, Andrew C. Issues in Physical Education. 256p. 1991. 85.00 (0-304-32413-2); pap. 35.00 (0-304-32432-9) Weidner & Sons.

***Armstrong, Neil & Van Mechelen, Willem, eds.** Paediatric Exercise Science & Medicine. (Illus.). 480p. 2000. text 129.50 (0-19-262977-8) OUP.

Armstrong, Neil & Wellsman, Joanne. Young People & Physical Activity. LC 96-26617. (Illus.). 384p. 1996. pap. text 59.50 (0-19-262659-0) OUP.

Armstrong, Neil, ed. see New Directions in Physical Education Staff.

Armstrong, O. V. & Armstrong, Helen J., eds. Prayer Poems. LC 72-86793. (Granger Index Reprint Ser.). 1977. 18.95 (0-8369-6094-7) Ayer.

Armstrong, P. & Wastie, M. L. Diagnostic Imaging. 3rd ed. (Illus.). 456p. 1992. 75.00 (0-632-03093-3) Blackwell Sci.

Armstrong, Pam. Young Explorer's Guide to Undersea Life. LC 96-1051. (Illus.). 60p. (J). (gr. k-4). 1996. 16.95 (1-878244-10-8) Monterey Bay Aquarium.

Armstrong, Pam, ed. Sea Searcher's Handbook: Activities from the Monterey Bay Aquarium. LC 96-27100. (Illus.). 224p. (J). (ps-12). 1996. pap. 16.95 (1-878244-15-9) Monterey Bay Aquarium.

Armstrong, Pat. Labour Pains: Women's Work in Crisis. 2nd ed. 250p. reprint ed. pap. 10.95 (0-88961-091-6, Pub. by Womens Pr) LPC InBook.

***Armstrong, Pat, et al, contrib. by.** Universal Health Care: What the United States Can Learn from the Canadian Experience. (Illus.). 176p. 1999. reprint ed. pap. 14.95 (1-56584-515-3, Pub. by New Press NY) Norton.

Armstrong, Pat & Armstrong, Hugh. Wasting Away: The Undermining of Canadian Health Care. LC 96-220755. 244p. 1996. pap. text 24.95 (0-19-541070-X) OUP.

Armstrong, Pat, et al. Universal Health Care: What the United States Can Learn from the Canadian Experience. LC 97-41011. 192p. 1998. 24.00 (1-56584-410-6, Pub. by New Press NY) Norton.

Armstrong, Patricia. Kate. LC 96-517. 299p. 1995. per. 3.75 (0-373-70665-0, 1-70665-4) Harlequin Bks.

Armstrong, Patricia, ed. Critique: Review of the Department of State's Country. (Reports on Human Rights Practices for 1992 Ser.). 445p. (Orig.). 1993. pap. text 19.50 (0-934143-60-9) Lawyers Comm Human.

Armstrong, Patricia, jt. ed. see Black, George.

Armstrong, Patricia, ed. see Frazier, Carolyn Casey.

Armstrong, Patrick H. The Changing Landscape: The History & Ecology of Man's Impact on East Anglia. 144p. (C). 1988. 30.00 (0-900963-53-0, Pub. by T Dalton) St Mut.

— Charles Darwin in Western Australia: A Young Scientist's Perception of an Environment. 88p. 1994. pap. 12.95 (0-85564-237-8, Pub. by Univ of West Aust Pr) Intl Spec Bk.

Armstrong, Patrick H., ed. Darwin's Desolate Islands: A Naturalist in the Falklands 1833 to 1834. 160p. 1990. 75.00 (0-948251-55-7, Pub. by Picton) St Mut.

Armstrong, Patrick H. & Martin, Geoffrey J., eds. Geographers: Biobibliographical Studies, Vol. 19. (Illus.). 192p. 1999. 80.00 (0-7201-2377-1) Continuum.

— Geographers Vol. 10: Biobibliographical Studies, Vol. 18. 272p. 1998. 85.00 (0-7201-2339-9) Continuum.

Armstrong, Patrick H., jt. ed. see Martin, Geoffrey J.

Armstrong, Paul B. The Challenge of Bewilderment: Understanding & Representation in James, Conrad, & Ford. LC 87-6683. 320p. (C). 1987. text 42.50 (0-8014-1949-2) Cornell U Pr.

— Conflicting Readings: Variety & Validity in Interpretation. LC 89-37186. xvi, 192p. 1990. 37.50 (0-8078-1895-X) U of NC Pr.

— Journey with My Jesus. (Illus.). 84p. 1993. pap. 3.95 (0-933704-97-6) Dawn Pr.

— The Phenomenology of Henry James. LC 82-24713. 256p. reprint ed. pap. 79.40 (0-7837-2465-9, 204261800005) Bks Demand.

Armstrong, Paul B., ed. see Forster, E. M.

Armstrong, Paul J. & Poss, Jeffery S., eds. Space, Movement, & Light: The Architecture of Jack Sherman Baker, FAIA. (Illus.). 110p. 1997. pap. 30.00 (0-9660146-1-8) U IL Schl Archit.

Armstrong, Peg. I-Openers. LC 81-82584. (Illus.). (Orig.). 1981. pap. 6.95 (0-686-35731-0) Guadalupe River Pr.

Armstrong, Perry A. The Sauks & the Black Hawk War. LC 76-43643. (Illus.). reprint ed. 57.50 (0-404-15478-6) AMS Pr.

***Armstrong, Peter.** Ancient & Medieval Modelling Masterclass. (Illus.). 128p. 2000. 24.95 (1-84176-007-2, Pub. by Ospry) Motorbooks Intl.

Armstrong, Peter. Risings. 53p. 1988. reprint ed. pap. 11.95 (1-870612-00-0, Pub. by Enitha Pr) Dufour.

Armstrong, Peter & Wastie, M. L., eds. Diagnostic & Interventional Radiology in Surgical Practice. LC 96-86529. (Companion Series to Bailey & Love's Short Practice of Surgery). (Illus.). 608p. 1997. text 100.00 (0-412-61960-1, Pub. by E A) OUP.

Armstrong, Peter & Wastie, Marin L. Diagnostic Imaging. 4th ed. LC 97-23281. 460p. 1998. 79.95 (0-86542-696-1) Blackwell Sci.

Armstrong, Peter, et al. Imaging Diseases of the Chest. 2nd ed. LC 94-5302. (Illus.). 992p. (C). (gr. 13). 1994. text 230.00 (0-8151-0011-6, 23755) Mosby Inc.

***Armstrong, Peter S.** Opening Gambits: The First Session of Psychotherapy. LC 99-41431. 1999. 40.00 (0-7657-0241-X) Aronson.

Armstrong, Philip. A More Perfect Legacy: A Portrait of Brother Ephrem O'Dwyer, C. S. C., 1888-1978. LC 94-15933. (C). 1995. text 34.50 (0-268-01414-0) U of Notre Dame Pr.

***Armstrong, Philip.** Shakespeare's Visual Regime: Tragedy, Psychoanalysis & the Gaze. LC 00-33324. 2000. write for info. (0-312-23557-7) St Martin.

Armstrong, Philip N. Data Rearrangement & Real-Time Computation. LC 93-18544. 120p. 1993. pap. text 15.00 (0-8330-1340-8, MR-113-OSD/AF) Rand Corp.

Armstrong, Piers. Third World Literary Fortunes: Brazilian Culture & Its International Reception. LC 98-43783. 264p. 1999. 41.50 (0-8387-5404-X) Bucknell U Pr.

Armstrong, R. & Osborne, B., eds. Echoes of the Sea: Scotland & the Sea - An Anthology. LC 99-216239. 1998. pap. 19.95 (0-86241-783-X, Pub. by Canongate Books) Interlink Pub.

***Armstrong, R. D., ed.** Blood on the Floor. unabridged ed. (Little Red Books Ser.). (Illus.). 44p. 1999. pap. 5.00 (1-929878-13-3) Lummox.

— Eyes Like Mingus. (Little Red Books Ser.). (Illus.). 48p. 1999. pap. 5.00 (1-929878-10-9) Lummox.

Armstrong, R. D., ed. see Constantine, Brendan & Buck, Janet.

Armstrong, R. D., ed. see Holstad, Scott C.

Armstrong, R. D., ed. see International Meeting on Solid Electrolytes Staff.

Armstrong, R. D., ed. see Niditch, B. Z.

Armstrong, R. D., ed. see Taylor, William, Jr.

Armstrong, R. F. & Salmon, J. B., eds. Critical Care Cases. (Illus.). 242p. 1997. pap. text 49.50 (0-19-262583-7) OUP.

Armstrong, R. M. Sugar Land, Texas & the Imperial Sugar Company. (Illus.). 200p. 1991. 26.95 (0-9629314-0-3) Imperial Holly.

Armstrong, R. W., et al, eds. Structure & Properties of Energetic Materials. (Materials Research Society Symposium Proceedings Ser.: Vol. 296). 387p. 1993. text 17.50 (1-55899-191-3) Materials Res.

Armstrong, Rachel, ed. Sci-Fi Aesthetics. (Art & Design Ser.: Vol. 56). (Illus.). 96p. 1997. pap. 29.95 (1-85490-528-7) Academy Ed UK.

Armstrong, Ralph. Christianity & Change. LC 89-61930. 256p. (Orig.). 1990. pap. 16.95 (1-55612-308-6) Sheed & Ward WI.

Armstrong, Regis, ed. Francis & Clare. (Franciscan Classics). 2000. pap. 12.95 (1-56548-131-3) New City.

Armstrong, Regis J. Clare of Assisi: Early Documents. (Clare Resources Ser.). 434p. 1994. 35.00 (1-57659-073-9); pap. 25.00 (1-57659-117-4) Franciscan Inst.

— St. Francis of Assisi: Writings for a Gospel Life. 240p. 1996. pap. 39.95 (0-85439-484-2, Pub. by St Paul Pubns) St Mut.

Armstrong, Regis J., et al, eds. The Founder: Francis of Assisi: Early Documents, Vol. 2. Hellmann, Wayne J. et al, trs. from ITA. (Francis of Assisi: Early Documents Ser.). (Illus.). 638p. 2000. pap. 29.95 (1-56548-112-7) New City.

— The Founder: Francis of Assisi: Early Documents, Vol. 2. Hellmann, Wayne J. et al, trs. from ITA. LC 99-18776. (Francis of Assisi: Early Documents Ser.: Vol. 2). (Illus.). 638p. 2000. 49.00 (1-56548-113-5) New City.

— The Prophet: Francis of Assisi: Early Documents, Vol. 3. Hellmann, Wayne J. et al, trs. from ITA. 638p. 1999. 49.00 (1-56548-115-1) New City.

— The Prophet: Francis of Assisi: Early Documents, Vol. 3. Hellmann, Wayne J. et al, trs. from ITA. (Francis of Assisi: Early Documents Ser.). (Illus.). 638p. 2001. pap. 29.95 (1-56548-114-3) New City.

— The Saint: Francis of Assisi: Early Documents. Hellmann, Wayne J. et al, trs. from ITA. LC 99-18776. (Francis of Assisi: Early Documents Ser.). (Illus.). 640p. 1999. 49.00 (1-56548-111-9) New City.

— The Saint: Francis of Assisi: The Early Documents. Hellmann, Wayne J. et al, trs. from ITA. LC 99-18776. (Francis of Assisi: Early Documents Ser.: Vol. 1). (Illus.). 640p. 1999. pap. 29.95 (1-56548-110-0) New City.

Armstrong, Regis J. & Brady, Ignatius C., eds. Francis & Clare: The Complete Works. (Classics of Western Spirituality Ser.). 1983. pap. 17.95 (0-8091-2446-7) Paulist Pr.

Armstrong, Regis J. & Brady, Ignatius C., trs. True Joy: The Wisdom of Francis & Clare. LC 96-12041. (Spiritual Samplers Ser.). 96p. (Orig.). 1996. pap. 1.95 (0-8091-3672-4) Paulist Pr.

Armstrong, Regis J. & Milland, Pacelli. Towards the Discovery of Clare of Assisi: Clare Formed by Francis. (Clare Centenary Ser.). 172p. 1992. pap. 8.00 (1-57659-077-1) Franciscan Inst.

— Towards the Discovery of Clare of Assisi: Fraternal Life, Vol. IV. (Clare Centenary Ser.). 364p. 1992. pap. 10.00 (1-57659-074-7) Franciscan Inst.

Armstrong, Regis J. & Millane, Pacelli. Towards the Discovery of Clare of Assisi: Clare Discovers the Love of God in the Church, Vol. II. (Clare Centenary Ser.). 188p. 1992. pap. 10.00 (1-57659-076-3) Franciscan Inst.

— Towards the Discovery of Clare of Assisi: Clare's Form of Gospel Life, Vol. III. (Clare Centenary Ser.). 188p. 1992. pap. 9.00 (1-57659-075-5) Franciscan Inst.

***Armstrong, Richard.** Billy Wilder, American Film Realist. (Illus.). 172p. 2000. 32.00 (0-7864-0821-9) McFarland & Co.

Armstrong, Richard. Carnegie International 1995. 256p. 1996. 45.00 (0-88039-028-X) Mus Art Carnegie.

— Iowa Artists, 1994. LC 94-71532. (Illus.). 44p. 1994. pap. 12.00 (1-879003-11-2) Edmundson.

— Kim MacConnel: Collection Applied Design. 8p. 1976. 3.00 (0-686-99808-1) Mus Contemp Art.

— The Modern Chair: Its Origins & Evolution. LC 77-84973. (Illus.). 62p. 1977. pap. 7.00 (0-934418-05-5) Mus Contemp Art.

— Richard Anuszkiewicz. LC 76-43241. (Illus.). 40p. 1976. 10.00 (0-686-99811-1) Mus Contemp Art.

Armstrong, Richard & Baker, Kenneth. Jack Tworkov: Paintings, 1928-1982. (Illus.). 168p. 1987. pap. 19.95 (0-943836-08-5) Penn Acad Art.

— Jack Tworkov: Paintings, 1928-1982. (Illus.). 168p. 1987. pap. 21.95 (0-295-96499-5) U of Wash Pr.

Armstrong, Richard & Schjeldahl, Peter. Ellen Phelan: From the Lives of Dolls. LC 92-82616. (Illus.). 36p. 1992. 15.00 (0-929597-02-8) UMass Univ Gallery.

Armstrong, Richard, jt. ed. see Fahey, Joseph J.

Armstrong, Richard B. & Armstrong, Mary W. The Movie List Book: A Reference Guide to Film Themes, Settings & Series. LC 89-43692. 400p. 1990. lib. bdg. 36.50 (0-89950-240-7) McFarland & Co.

***Armstrong, Richard B. & Armstrong, Mary Willems.** Encyclopedia of Film Themes, Settings & Series. (Illus.). 288p. 2000. boxed set 75.00 (0-7864-0893-6) McFarland & Co.

***Armstrong, Richard D.** Who's Who in e-Commerce Fulfillment? Armstrong's Guide to eFulfillment Services Providers. 166p. 2000. spiral bd. 225.00 (1-891645-05-6) Armstrong & Assocs.

Armstrong, Richard D. Who's Who in Logistics? Armstrong's Guide to Third Party Logistics Services Providers. 6th rev. ed. 385p. 1998. spiral bd. 245.00 (1-891645-02-1) Armstrong & Assocs.

— Who's Who in Logistics? Armstrong's Guide to Third Party Logistics Services Providers, 2 vols. 7th ed. 414p. 1999. 245.00 (1-891645-03-X) Armstrong & Assocs.

***Armstrong, Richard D.** Who's Who in Logistics? Armstrong's Guide to Third Party Logistics Services Providers, 2 vols. 8th ed. 391p. 2000. spiral bd. 245.00 (1-891645-06-4) Armstrong & Assocs.

— Who's Who in Logistics Software? Armstrong's Guide to Supply Chain Management Systems. 117p. 1999. 149.00 (1-891645-04-8) Armstrong & Assocs.

Armstrong, Richard L. Eleventh Virginia Cavalry. (Virginia Regimental Histories Ser.). (Illus.). 210p. 1989. 19.95 (0-930919-68-8) H E Howard.

— Nineteenth & Twentieth Virginia Cavalry. (Virginia Regimental Histories Ser.). (Illus.). 260p. 1994. 19.95 (1-56190-061-3) H E Howard.

— Seventh Virginia Cavalry. (Virginia Regimental Histories Ser.). (Illus.). 259p. 1993. 19.95 (1-56190-040-0) H E Howard.

— Twenty-Fifth Virginia Infantry & Ninth Battalion Virginia Infantry. (Virginia Regimental Histories Ser.). (Illus.). 263p. 1990. 19.95 (1-56190-007-9) H E Howard.

— Twenty-Sixth Virginia Cavalry. (Virginia Regimental Histories Ser.). (Illus.). 151p. 1995. 19.95 (1-56190-074-5) H E Howard.

Armstrong, Richard N. Red Army Legacies: Essays on Forces, Capabilities & Personalities. LC 95-67622. (Illus.). 320p. 1995. 24.95 (0-88740-805-2) Schiffer.

— Red Army Tank Commanders: The Armored Guards. LC 93-87474. (Illus.). 475p. 1994. 24.95 (0-88740-581-9) Schiffer.

— The Rhetoric of David O. McKay: Mormon Prophet. LC 93-17292. (American University Studies: Theology & Religion: Ser. VII, Vol. 92). VI, 136p. (C). 1994. text 35.95 (0-8204-2293-2) P Lang Pubng.

Armstrong, Richard N., ed. Red Army Combat Orders: Combat Regulations for Tank & Mechanized Forces 1944. Welsh, Joseph G., tr. 163p. 1991. text 42.50 (0-7146-3401-8, Pub. by F Cass Pubs) Intl Spec Bk.

Armstrong, Richard N., et al, eds. Winter Warfare: Red Army Orders & Experiences. Welsh, Joseph G., tr. LC 96-29933. (Soviet Study of War Ser.: No. 8). (Illus.). 192p. (C). 1997. 45.00 (0-7146-4699-7, Pub. by F Cass Pubs); pap. 19.50 (0-7146-4237-1, Pub. by F Cass Pubs) Intl Spec Bk.

Armstrong, Richard S. Faithful Witnesses Minicourse. 2nd rev. ed. Graham, Mary, ed. 120p. 1997. pap. 9.00 (1-57153-012-6) Curriculm Presbytrn KY.

— If I Do Say So Myself: More Thoughts about Faith & Life. 1997. pap. 9.95 (0-7880-0918-4, Fairway Pr) CSS OH.

Armstrong, Richard Stoll. Enough, Already! And Other Church Rhymes. 1993. pap. 8.95 (1-55673-544-8, Fairway Pr) CSS OH.

— Faithful Witnesses: A Course in Evangelism for Presbyterian Laity. LC 87-23661. 108p. (Orig.). 1987. pap., teacher ed. 12.95 (0-664-24076-3) Westminster John Knox.

— Now, That's a Miracle! Reflections on Faith & Life. LC 96-7630. (Illus.). 1996. 9.25 (0-7880-0762-9) CSS OH.

— Service Evangelism. LC 78-26701. 198p. 1979. pap. 16.95 (0-664-24252-9) Westminster John Knox.

Armstrong, Rob. Golfing in Ireland: The Most Complete Guide for Adventurous Golfers. LC 96-35418. (Illus.). 176p. 1997. pap. 17.95 (1-56554-194-4) Pelican.

***Armstrong, Rob.** Golfing in Ireland: The Most Complete Guide for Adventurous Golfers. 2nd ed. LC 99-54587. (Illus.). 256p. 2000. pap. 19.95 (1-56554-726-8) Pelican.

Armstrong, Rob. Golfing the Virginias. LC 99-12558. (Illus.). 208p. 1999. 34.95 (1-56554-273-8) Pelican.

Armstrong, Robb. Drew & the Bub Daddy Showdown. LC 95-30004. (Trophy Chapter Bk.). (Illus.). 96p. (J). (gr. 2-5). 1996. pap. 4.25 (0-06-442030-2, HarpTrophy) HarpC Child Bks.

— Drew & the Bub Daddy Showdown. LC 95-30004. 1996. 9.15 (0-606-09217-X, Pub. by Turtleback) Demco.

— Drew & the Filthy Rich Kid. (Illus.). 96p. (J). (gr. 2-5). Date not set. lib. bdg. 13.89 (0-06-026660-0) HarpC Child Bks.

— Drew & the Filthy Rich Kid. (Illus.). 96p. (J). (gr. 2-5). 1997. pap. 3.95 (0-06-443434-6, HarpTrophy) HarpC Child Bks.

— Drew & the Homeboy Question. LC 96-41319. (Illus.). 80p. (J). (gr. 5-7). 1997. pap. 4.25 (0-06-442047-7, HarpTrophy) HarpC Child Bks.

— Drew & the Homeboy Question. LC 96-41319. (Illus.). 80p. (J). (gr. 2-5). 1997. lib. bdg. 14.89 (0-06-027527-8) HarpC Child Bks.

***Armstrong, Robb.** Got Game? LC 98-70472. (Patrick's Pals Ser.: No. 3). (Illus.). 96p. (J). (gr. 2-7). 1998. mass mkt. 3.99 (0-06-107069-6) HarpC.

— In Your Face! LC 98-70305. (Patrick's Pals Ser.: No. 2). (Illus.). 96p. (J). (gr. 2-7). 1998. mass mkt. 3.99 (0-06-107068-8) HarpC.

Armstrong, Robb. Jump Start. LC 97-71628. (Illus.). 128p. (Orig.). 1997. pap. 9.95 (0-8362-3661-0) Andrews & McMeel.

***Armstrong, Robb.** Large & in Charge. (Patrick's Pals Ser.: No. 7). (Illus.). 96p. (J). (gr. 2-7). 1999. pap. 3.99 (0-06-107073-4) HarpC.

— Runnin' with the Big Dawgs. LC 97-78009. (Patrick's Pals Ser.: No. 1). (Illus.). 96p. (J). (gr. 2-7). 1998. mass mkt. 3.99 (0-06-107067-X) HarpC Child Bks.

— Schoolin' LC 98-70474. (Patrick's Pals Ser.: No. 5). (Illus.). 96p. (J). (gr. 2-7). 1999. mass mkt. 3.99 (0-06-107071-8) HarpC.

Armstrong, Robb. Stuffin' It! LC 98-70473. (Patrick's Pals Ser.: No. 4). (Illus.). 89p. (J). (gr. 2-7). 1998. mass mkt. 3.99 (0-06-107070-X) HarpC.

— Trashmaster. LC 98-73301. (Patrick's Pals Ser.: No. 6). (Illus.). 96p. (J). (gr. 2-7). 1999. mass mkt. 3.99 (0-06-107072-6, HarpEntertain) Morrow Avon.

Armstrong, Robert. Gardener's Source Guide (GSG) 64p. 1991. pap. 9.95 (0-9700148-0-5) Gardeners Src Gde.

Armstrong, Robert & Shenk, Janet. El Salvador: The Face of Revolution. LC 82-80688. 285p. 1982. 35.00 (0-89608-138-9); pap. 12.00 (0-89608-137-0) South End Pr.

Armstrong, Robert, jt. auth. see Dreizler, Bob.

Armstrong, Robert, jt. auth. see Murray, William J.

Armstrong, Robert C. Just Before the Dawn: Life & Work of Ninomiya Sontoku. LC 78-72370. reprint ed. 42.50 (0-404-17217-2) AMS Pr.

— Light from the East: Studies in Japanese Confucianism. 1974. lib. bdg. 300.00 (0-87968-134-9) Krishna Pr.

Armstrong, Robert D. Nevada Printing History: A Bibliography of Imprints & Publications, 1858-1880. LC 81-7422. (Illus.). 428p. 1982. 50.00 (0-87417-063-X) U of Nev Pr.

— Nevada Printing History: A Bibliography of Imprints & Publications, 1881-1890. LC 88-33955. (Illus.). 408p. 1982. 50.00 (0-87417-124-5) U of Nev Pr.

Armstrong, Robert H. Alaska's Birds: A Guide to Selected Species. LC 93-51034. (Pocket Guides Ser.). (Illus.). 124p. (Orig.). 1996. pap. 14.95 (0-88240-455-5, Alaska NW Bks) Gr Arts Ctr Pub.

***Armstrong, Robert H.** Alaska's Natural Wonders: A Guide to the Phenomena of the Far North. (Alaska Pocket Guide Ser.). (Illus.). 96p. 2000. pap. 12.95 (0-88240-526-8) Gr Arts Ctr Pub.

A

Armstrong, Robert H. & Newby, Leroy W. Angel on Our Wing. (Illus.). 360p. 24.95 (*0-9632257-0-7*) R H Armstrong.

Armstrong, Robert J. United States Decennial Life Tables For 1989- 91, V. 1, No. 1, United States Life Tables. 37p. 1997. pap. 4.00 (*0-16-061475-9*) USGPO.

Armstrong, Robert L. Metaphysics & British Empiricism. LC 78-109602. 187p. reprint ed. pap. 58.00 (*0-8357-8671-4*, 205682700091) Bks Demand.

Armstrong, Robert P. Ghana Country Assistance Review: A Review of Development Effectiveness. LC 95-41383. (Operations Evaluation Studies). 160p. 1996. pap. 22.00 (*0-8213-3465-4*) World Bank.

Armstrong, Rodney. Critical Care Cases. (Illus.). 242p. 1997. text 51.00 (*0-19-262584-5*) OUP.

Armstrong, Rodney F. Anaesthetic Algorithms. (Illus.). 92p. 1996. text 81.00 (*0-19-262596-9*) OUP.

Armstrong, Rodney F., et al. Anaesthetic Algorithms. (Illus.). 92p. 1996. pap. text 39.50 (*0-19-262595-0*) OUP.

Armstrong, Roger. Beginning Jewelry: A Notebook for Design & Technique. 2nd ed. (Illus.). 1992. 19.95 (*0-89863-156-4*) Star Pub CA.

— Comic Strips. (How to Draw & Paint Ser.). (Illus.). 32p. (Orig.). 1990. pap. 6.95 (*1-56010-050-8*, HT220) W Foster Pub.

— Wax & Casting: A Notebook of Process & Technique. (Illus.). 160p. 1988. pap. 19.95 (*0-89863-038-X*) Star Pub CA.

Armstrong, Roger, jt. auth. see Kelly, Graham.

Armstrong, Roger W. U. S. A. the Hard Way: An Autobiography of a B-17 Crew Member. Stone, Ken, ed. LC 90-64463. (Illus.). 350p. 1991. reprint ed. pap. 15.95 (*0-9629161-1-0*) Quail Hse.

***Armstrong, Ronald.** Mungo's City: A Glasgow Anthology. 400p. 2000. pap. 25.95 (*1-84158-025-2*, Pub. by Birlinn Ltd) Dufour.

Armstrong, Ronald, jt. auth. see Osborne, Brian D.

Armstrong, Ruth G. Sisters under the Sari. LC 63-22164. 508p. reprint ed. pap. 157.50 (*0-608-11635-1*, 202276500029) Bks Demand.

Armstrong, Ruth M. The Kachins of Burma. Lee, Don, ed. LC 97-61418. (Illus.). 194p. 1997. 42.50 (*0-939758-37-7*) Eastern Pr.

Armstrong, Ruth W. Cycle of Seasons in Corrales: A History. LC 88-12232. (Illus.). 96p. (Orig.). 1988. pap. 8.95 (*0-86534-124-9*) Sunstone Pr.

Armstrong, S., jt. auth. see Hawthorn, P.

Armstrong, S., jt. auth. see Royston, E.

Armstrong, Samantha, ed. see Stott, Bill.

Armstrong, Sara, jt. auth. see Armstrong, E. F.

Armstrong, Scott & Grier, Peter. Strategic Defense Initiative: Splendid Defense or Pipe Dream? LC 86-80312. (Headline Ser.: No. 275). (Illus.). 64p. (Orig.). 1985. pap. 5.95 (*0-87124-103-X*) Foreign Policy.

Armstrong, Scott, jt. auth. see Niland, Kurt R.

Armstrong, Scott, jt. auth. see Woodward, Bob.

Armstrong, Shawn, ed. see Georgeva, Vasila D.

***Armstrong-Smith, Michael.** Oracle Discoverer Handbook. (Illus.). 2000. pap. 44.99 (*0-07-212635-3*) Osborne-McGraw.

Armstrong, Stephen V. & Terrell, Timothy P. Thinking Like a Writer: A Lawyer's Guide to Effective Writing & Editing. LC 92-15739. 1992. 29.95 (*0-87632-898-2*) West Group.

Armstrong, Steve & Thompson, Gail. Facing up to Radical Change in Universities & Colleges. 192p. 1997. pap. 25.00 (*0-7494-2129-0*, Kogan Pg Educ) Stylus Pub VA.

Armstrong, Susan, ed. Using Large Corpora. (Illus.). 300p. 1994. 40.00 (*0-262-51082-0*, Bradford Bks) MIT Pr.

Armstrong, Susan J., jt. auth. see Botzler, Richard G.

Armstrong, T. E. & Moyer, J. H. Armstrong: History of the Armstrong Family, 980-1939, & Genealogy of David Armstrong & Sarah Harris Armstrong, 1746-1939. 270p. 1993. reprint ed. pap. 43.00 (*0-8328-3638-9*); reprint ed. lib. bdg. 53.00 (*0-8328-3637-0*) Higginson Bk Co.

Armstrong, Teasdale, Schlafly & Staff, et al. Missouri Environmental Law Handbook. 3rd rev. ed. 436p. 1997. pap. text 95.00 (*0-86587-574-X*, 574) Gov Insts.

Armstrong, Terry A., et al, eds. A Reader's Hebrew-English Lexicon of the Old Testament, Vol. 4. 224p. 1988. 16.95 (*0-310-37000-0*, 6296) Zondervan.

— A Reader's Hebrew-English Lexicon of the Old Testament: Genesis-II Kings. (ENG & HEB.). 1984. 16.95 (*0-310-37040-X*, 6291) Zondervan.

Armstrong, Terry A., et al. A Reader's Hebrew-English Lexicon of the Old Testament: Isaiah-Malachi, Vol. 3. 208p. 1986. 16.95 (*0-310-37010-8*, 6293) Zondervan.

Armstrong, Thom. Politics, Diplomacy, & Intrigue in the Early Republic: The Cabinet Career of Robert Smith, 1801-1811. 240p. (C). 1991. pap. text, per. 32.95 (*0-8403-7055-5*) Kendall-Hunt.

— Readings in American History: The Age of Exploration to Reconstruction, Vol. 1. 240p. (C). 1993. per. 32.95 (*0-8403-8486-6*) Kendall-Hunt.

— Readings in American History Vol. II: Reconstruction to Watergate. 288p. (C). 1990. per. 28.95 (*0-8403-5894-6*) Kendall-Hunt.

***Armstrong, Thomas.** ADD/ADHD Alternatives in the Classroom. LC 99-6861. 1999. pap. 11.95 (*0-87120-359-6*) ASCD.

Armstrong, Thomas. Awakening Your Child's Natural Genius: Enhancing Your Child's Curiosity, Creativity & Learning Ability. LC 90-21074. 288p. 1991. pap. 14.95 (*0-87477-608-2*, Tarcher Putnam) Putnam Pub Group.

***Armstrong, Thomas.** In Their Own Way: Discovering & Encouraging Your Child's Multiple Intelligences. rev. ed. 288p. 2000. pap. 13.95 (*1-58542-051-4*, Tarcher Putnam) Putnam Pub Group.

Armstrong, Thomas. In Their Own Way: Discovering & Encouraging Your Child's Personal Learning Style. 224p. 1988. pap. 11.95 (*0-87477-466-7*, Tarcher Putnam) Putnam Pub Group.

Armstrong, Thomas. Inteligencias en el Salon de Clases (Multiple Intelligences in the Classroom) LC 95-37991. (SPA., Illus.). 185p. 1995. pap. 17.95 (*0-87120-256-5*) ASCD.

— Multiple Intelligences in the Classroom. 2nd ed. (Illus.). 140p. 2000. pap. 22.95 (*0-87120-376-6*) ASCD.

Armstrong, Thomas. The Myth of the A. D. D. Child: 50 Ways to Improve Your Child's Behavior & Attention Span Without Drugs, Labels or Coercion. 320p. 1997. pap. 13.95 (*0-452-27547-4*, Plume) Dutton Plume.

— The Radiant Child. LC 85-40409. 220p. 1988. pap. 8.95 (*0-8356-0600-7*, Quest) Theos Pub Hse.

— Seven Kinds of Smart: Identifying & Developing Your Many Intelligences. LC 99-34423. 1999. pap. 12.95 (*0-452-28137-7*, Plume) Dutton Plume.

Armstrong, Thomas, contrib. by. Awakening Genius in the Classroom. LC 98-19666. 81p. 1998. pap. 10.95 (*0-87120-302-2*, 198033) ASCD.

Armstrong, Thomas J. & Lackey, Ellen A. Cumulative Trauma Disorders of the Hand & Wrist: An Ergonomics Guide. (Ergonomics Guide Ser.). (Illus.). 24p. (Orig.). 1994. pap. text 8.00 (*0-932627-56-0*, 181-ER-94) Am Indus Hygiene.

Armstrong, Tim. American Bodies: History of the Physique. (SAP Literature Ser.). 178p. 1996. 33.00 (*1-85075-753-4*, Pub. by Sheffield Acad); pap. 19.95 (*1-85075-790-9*, Pub. by Sheffield Acad) CUP Services.

— Colour Perception: A Practical Approach to Colour Theory. 1993. pap. 14.95 (*0-906212-74-X*, Pub. by Tarquin Pubns) Parkwest Pubns.

***Armstrong, Tim.** Haunted Hardy: Poetry, History, Memory. LC 00-33323. 2000. pap. write for info. (*0-312-23692-1*) St Martin.

Armstrong, Tim. Make Moving Patterns: How to Make Optical Illusions of Your Own. (Illus.). pap. 12.95 (*0-906212-26-X*, Pub. by Tarquin Pubns) Parkwest Pubns.

— Modernism, Technology, & the Body: A Cultural Study. LC 97-8815. (Illus.). 318p. (C). 1998. text 59.95 (*0-521-59004-3*); pap. text 19.95 (*0-521-59997-0*) Cambridge U Pr.

— Thomas Hardy: Selected Poems. LC 92-44541. (Annotated Texts Ser.). 1994. pap. 26.95 (*0-685-72541-3*, 79857) Longman.

Armstrong, Tim, ed. American Bodies: Cultural Histories of the Physique. LC 96-21578. 212p. (C). 1996. text 55.00 (*0-8147-0657-6*); pap. text 20.00 (*0-8147-0658-4*) NYU Pr.

Armstrong, Tim & Hardy, Thomas. Thomas Hardy Selected Poems: Longman Annotated Texts. annot. ed. (Annotated Texts Ser.). (C). 1994. pap. text 37.50 (*0-582-04061-2*) Longman.

Armstrong, Tim, ed. see Hardy, Thomas.

Armstrong, Tom. Active Template Library: A Developer's Guide. LC 98-10611. 416p. 1998. pap. 39.99 (*1-55851-580-1*, M&T Bks) IDG Bks.

— ActiveX Developers Sourcebook. 1997. pap. text 49.95 incl. cd-rom (*0-07-006213-7*) McGraw.

Armstrong, Tom. ActiveX Developers Sourcebook. LC 97-33284. (Illus.). 551p. 1997. pap., pap. text 49.95 incl. cd-rom (*0-07-913228-6*) McGraw.

— ATL Developer's Guide. 2nd ed. (Illus.). 600p. 2000. pap. text 39.99 (*0-7645-4683-X*) IDG Bks.

Armstrong, Tom C. Bytes & Bites: With a Bark or Two for Good Measure. LC 93-73192. 56p. (Orig.). 1993. pap. 5.99 (*0-9638661-0-9*) AD HOC Bks.

— Gift Rap. 64p. 1997. pap. 5.99 (*0-9638661-3-3*) AD HOC Bks.

— Loving Words: And Gentle Barbs from Cupid's Arrow. LC 95-80286. 60p. (Orig.). 1995. pap. 5.99 (*0-9638661-1-7*) AD HOC Bks.

— Word Whys from the Would Pile: or Tom C.'s Short Ease. 64p. (Orig.). 1992. pap. 5.99 (*0-9638661-2-5*) AD HOC Bks.

— Work in Words: A Poetry Chapman's Chapbook. 44p. (Orig.). 1993. pap. 3.25 (*0-9636452-0-X*) AD HOC Bks.

Armstrong, Tom C., jt. auth. see Deitschmann, Craig.

Armstrong, Tony, ed. Breaking the Ice: Rapprochement Between East & West Germany, the United States & China, & Israel & Egypt. LC 93-9862. 1993. pap. text 13.95 (*1-878379-26-7*) US Inst Peace.

Armstrong, Troy L., ed. Intensive Interventions with High-Risk Youths: Promising Approaches in Juvenile Probation & Parole. 457p. 1991. pap. 30.00 (*0-9606960-7-5*, Criminal Justice) Willow Tree NY.

Armstrong, Troy L., jt. auth. see Altschuler, David M.

Armstrong, Vicki. A Dragon Drinks Just One Drop. (Beginning Sounds Readers Ser.). (Illus.). 32p. (J). (gr. 1-6). 1990. student ed. 5.99 (*0-933367-01-5*) See the Sounds.

— Pigs Pet People. (Beginning Sounds Readers Ser.). (Illus.). (J). (ps-4). 1985. student ed. 5.99 (*0-933367-00-7*) See the Sounds.

Armstrong, Victoria L. Statistics for Social Sciences. LC 94-18819. 576p. 1994. 65.00 (*0-13-101320-3*) P-H.

Armstrong, Virgil. The Armstrong Report: They Need Us, We Don't Need Them. 147p. (Orig.). 1989. pap. 7.95 (*0-925390-07-0*) Armstrong Assocs.

— The Assassination of General George Armstrong Custer: The True Story Behind the Battle of the Little Big Horn. Whitman, Patricia, ed. 300p. (YA). (gr. 9-12). 1990. pap. write for info. (*0-925390-22-4*) Armstrong Assocs.

— The Twelve Women Apostles, Bk. 1. Whitman, Beth, ed. 300p. (Orig.). 1990. pap. 9.99 (*0-925390-15-1*) Armstrong Assocs.

Armstrong, Virginia I., ed. I Have Spoken: American History Through the Voices of the Indians. LC 74-150755. xxii, 206p. 1971. pap. 15.95 (*0-8040-0530-3*) Swallow.

Armstrong, Vivien. Close Call. 1994. lib. bdg. 20.00 (*0-7278-4708-2*) Severn Hse.

— Dead in the Water. 224p. 1999. 25.00 (*0-7278-2229-2*, Pub. by Severn Hse) Chivers N Amer.

***Armstrong, Vivien.** Dead in the Water. large type ed. 352p. 2000. 20.99 (*1-84137-016-9*, Pub. by Mgna Lrg Print) Ulverscroft.

— Fool's Gold. 224p. 26.00 (*0-7278-5531-X*) Severn Hse.

Armstrong, Vivien. Sleight of Hand. large type ed. 383p. 1993. 27.99 (*0-7505-0518-4*) Ulverscroft.

— The Wrong Road. 224p. 1997. 24.00 (*0-7278-5283-3*) Severn Hse.

Armstrong, W. Prayer-Hymns: A New & Different Hymnal for Church & Home. LC 73-101347. pap. write for info. (*0-686-08988-X*) Gonzaga U Pr.

Armstrong, W. Clinton. Armstrong. Genealogical Record of the Descendants of Nathan Armnstrong, Early Settler of Warren Co., NJ, with Sketches of Family History. 201p. 1996. reprint ed. pap. 31.00 (*0-8328-5378-X*) Higginson Bk Co.

— Armstrong. Genealogical Record of the Descendants of Nathan Armstrong, Early Settler of Warren Co., NJ, with Sketches of Family History. 201p. 1996. reprint ed. lib. bdg. 41.00 (*0-8328-5377-1*) Higginson Bk Co.

— Wildrick: John Wildrick of New Jersey, 1707-1793; Genealogy of the Descendants of His Son George Wildrick. (Illus.). 67p. 1993. reprint ed. pap. 14.00 (*0-8328-3432-7*); reprint ed. lib. bdg. 24.00 (*0-8328-3431-9*) Higginson Bk Co.

Armstrong, W. G. A Record of the Opera in Philadelphia. LC 74-27327. reprint ed. 41.50 (*0-404-12853-X*) AMS Pr.

Armstrong, Wallace E. Rossel Island: An Ethnological Study. LC 75-32798. reprint ed. 54.00 (*0-404-14101-3*) AMS Pr.

Armstrong, Wally. In His Grip: Insights on God & Golf, Supersaver Edition. 1998. 12.99 (*0-8499-5450-9*) Word Pub.

Armstrong, Wally, jt. auth. see Sheard, James L.

Armstrong, Wally, jt. auth. see Sheard, Jim.

Armstrong, Walter. Lawrence. LC 70-100531. (BCL Ser.: No. 2). (Illus.). reprint ed. 54.50 (*0-404-00385-0*) AMS Pr.

Armstrong, Walter, ed. see Perrot, Georges.

Armstrong, Warren B. For Courageous Fighting & Confident Dying: Union Chaplains in the Civil War. LC 98-21026. (Modern War Studies). (Illus.). 192p. 1998. 24.95 (*0-7006-0912-1*) U Pr of KS.

Armstrong, Warwick & McGee, Terence. Theatres of Accumulation: Studies in Asian & Latin America Urbanization. 320p. 1985. text 40.00 (*0-416-78570-0*, 9706); pap. text 14.95 (*0-416-39800-6*, 9528) Routledge.

Armstrong-West, jt. auth. see Balliet.

Armstrong-West, Suzan. The Color of Leadership: Research Findings of African American Science. LC 99-179012. 82p. 1998. per. 38.95 (*0-7872-5370-7*, 41537001) Kendall-Hunt.

***Armstrong-West, Suzan.** Shaping a Life: Douglass College First Year Course. 3rd ed. 210p. (C). 1999. ring bd. 34.95 (*0-7872-6473-3*, 41647301) Kendall-Hunt.

Armstrong-West, Suzan, jt. auth. see Balliet, Barbara.

***Armstrong-Wickell, Janet.** Teach Yourself Quilting. (Teach Yourself Crafts Ser.). 128p. 2000. pap. 14.95 (*0-658-00494-8*, 004948) NTC Contemp Pub Co.

Armstrong, William. Romantic World of Music. LC 71-90602. (Essay Index Reprint Ser.). 1977. 21.95 (*0-8369-1271-3*) Ayer.

— Some Practical Problems in Demand Management: The Stamp Memorial Lecture Delivered Before The University of London on 26 November 1968. LC 71-412421. (Stamp Memorial Lectures). 20p. 1969. write for info. (*0-485-16423-X*) Humanities.

Armstrong, William, ed. see King, Cecil.

***Armstrong, William A. & Davis, Don.** Calculus & Applications. LC 99-56124. 622p. 1999. 93.33 (*0-13-754904-0*) P-H.

Armstrong, William C. Axford - the Axfords of Oxford, NJ: A Genealogy Beginning in 1725. (Illus.). 78p. 1994. reprint ed. pap. 16.00 (*0-8328-4190-0*); reprint ed. lib. bdg. 26.00 (*0-8328-4189-7*) Higginson Bk Co.

— Kerr Clan of New Jersey, Beginning with Walter Kerr of Freebold & Ending with Other Related Lines. (Illus.). 196p. 1997. reprint ed. pap. 29.50 (*0-8328-9405-2*); reprint ed. lib. bdg. 39.50 (*0-8328-9404-4*) Higginson Bk Co.

— Kirkpatrick. Capt. John Kirkpatrick of New Jersey, 1739-1822, & His Sisters, Mrs. Joseph Linn & Mrs. Stephen Roy. (Illus.). 81p. 1997. reprint ed. pap. 16.00 (*0-8328-9439-7*); reprint ed. lib. bdg. 26.00 (*0-8328-9438-9*) Higginson Bk Co.

Armstrong, William C., ed. see Darrow, A. P.

Armstrong, William E. Purser's Handbook. LC 65-21748. 288p. 1966. reprint ed. pap. 89.30 (*0-7837-9069-4*, 204981800003) Bks Demand.

Armstrong, William H. Effective Introduction of Evidence in California. Russell, Linda W., ed. LC 89-82625. 236p. 1996. ring bd. 52.00 (*0-88124-994-7*, CP-31355) Cont Ed Bar-CA.

Armstrong, William H. Effective Introduction of Evidence in California: December 1991 Update. Harris, Anne, ed. LC 89-82625. 265p. 1991. ring bd. 40.00 (*0-88124-453-8*, CP-31351) Cont Ed Bar-CA.

— Effective Introduction of Evidence in California: January 1993 Update. Dworin, Christopher D., ed. LC 89-82625. 178p. 1993. ring bd. 41.00 (*0-88124-582-8*, CP-31352) Cont Ed Bar-CA.

***Armstrong, William H.** Major McKinley: William McKinley & the Civil War. LC 99-48531. 248p. 2000. 18.00 (*0-87338-657-4*) Kent St U Pr.

Armstrong, William H. Red-Tape & Pigeon-Hole Generals. Arner, Frederick B., ed. LC 97-47436. (Illus.). 384p. 1998. reprint ed. 34.95 (*1-883522-15-3*, Rockbridge) Howell Pr VA.

— Sounder. LC 70-85030. (Illus.). 128p. (YA). (gr. 4-7). 1969. lib. bdg. 15.89 (*0-06-020144-4*) HarpC Child Bks.

— Sounder. LC 70-85030. (Illus.). 128p. (YA). (gr. 4-7). 1969. 15.95 (*0-06-020143-6*) HarpC Child Bks.

— Sounder. (J). 1972. 10.05 (*0-606-04962-2*, Pub. by Turtleback) Demco.

— Sounder. large type ed. (LRS Large Print Cornerstone Ser.). (Illus.). 230p. (YA). (gr. 6-12). 1999. lib. bdg. 27.95 (*1-58118-054-3*, 22768) LRS.

— Sounder. LC 70-85030. (Trophy Bk.). (Illus.). 128p. (YA). (gr. 4-7). 1972. reprint ed. pap. 5.95 (*0-06-440020-4*, HarpTrophy) HarpC Child Bks.

— Sounder Ri. LC 88-45956. 128p. (YA). (gr. 4-7). 1989. reprint ed. mass mkt. 6.00 (*0-06-080975-2*, P 975, Perennial) HarperTrade.

— Sour Land. LC 70-135783. (Trophy Bk.). 128p. (YA). (gr. 7 up). 1976. reprint ed. pap. 4.95 (*0-06-440074-3*, HarpTrophy) HarpC Child Bks.

— Study Is Hard Work: The Most Accessible & Lucid Text Available on Acquiring, & Keeping Study Skills Throughout a Lifetime. 160p. (YA). (gr. 8-12). 1995. pap. 11.95 (*1-56792-025-X*) Godine.

— Study Tactics. 272p. (gr. 10-12). 1983. pap. text 8.95 (*0-8120-2590-3*) Barron.

— Trueno. 1996. 16.05 (*0-606-13875-7*, Pub. by Turtleback) Demco.

— Trueno (Sounder) 1996. pap. text 10.95 (*84-241-3187-8*) Lectorum Pubns.

— Warrior in Two Camps: Ely S. Parker, Union General & Seneca Chief. (Iroquois Bks.). (Illus.). 256p. 1990. pap. text 16.95 (*0-8156-2495-6*) Syracuse U Pr.

Armstrong, William H., et al. A Pocket Guide to Study Tips. 3rd ed. LC 96-19015. 290p. 1997. pap. 6.95 (*0-8120-9812-9*) Barron.

Armstrong, William J., jt. auth. see Grossnick, Roy A.

Armstrong, William M. E. L. Godkin & American Foreign Policy: 1865-1900. LC 77-9534. 1977. reprint ed. lib. bdg. 69.50 (*0-8371-9711-2*, ARGA, Greenwood Pr) Greenwood.

Armstrong, William N. Around the World with a King. (Illus.). 320p. 1995. mass mkt. 5.95 (*1-56647-017-X*) Mutual Pub HI.

— Around the World with a King. (Pacific Basin Bks.). 320p. 1988. pap. 14.95 (*0-7103-0291-6*) Routledge.

Armstrong, Zella. The History of Hamilton County & Chattanooga, Tennessee, Vol. 1. (Illus.). 604p. 1993. reprint ed. 32.50 (*0-932807-91-7*) Overmountain Pr.

— The History of Hamilton County & Chattanooga, Tennessee, Vol. 2. (Illus.). 456p. 1994. reprint ed. 29.95 (*0-932807-99-2*) Overmountain Pr.

— Notable Southern Families, Vol. 1. 247p. 1997. reprint ed. pap. 25.00 (*0-8063-4725-2*, Pub. by Clearfield Co) ACCESS Pubs Network.

***Armstrong, Zella.** Notable Southern Families, Vol. III. 369p. 2000. reprint ed. pap. 32.50 (*0-8063-4889-5*, Pub. by Clearfield Co) ACCESS Pubs Network.

— Notable Southern Families, Vol. V. 611p. 2000. reprint ed. pap. 48.50 (*0-8063-4891-7*, Pub. by Clearfield Co) ACCESS Pubs Network.

Armstrong, Zella. Notable Southern Families Vol. II: Genealogies of the Families of Bean, Boone, Borden, Bryan, Carter, Davis, Donaldson, Hardwick, Haywood, Holliday, Hollingsworth, Houston, Johnston, Kelton, Magill, Rhea, Montgomery, Shelby, Vance, Wear, & Williams. 377p. 1997. reprint ed. pap. 32.50 (*0-8063-4726-0*, Pub. by Clearfield Co) ACCESS Pubs Network.

***Armstrong, Zella.** Notable Southern Families Vol. 4: The Sevier Family: Antecedents & Emigration; William Sevier, the Emigrant, & His Descendants; Valentine Sevier, the Emigrant, & His Descendants; Joanna Goode Sevier, Wife of Younger Landrum, Jr., & Her Descendants; Governor John Sevier & His Descendants. 325p. 2000. reprint ed. pap. 28.00 (*0-8063-4890-9*) Clearfield Co.

Armstrong, Zella. Twenty-Four Hundred Tennessee Pensioners: Revolution & War of 1812. LC 75-971. 121p. 1996. reprint ed. pap. 9.00 (*0-8063-0665-3*) Genealog Pub.

Armstrongand, N. A. & James, K. C. Pharmaceutical Experimental Design & Interpretation. LC 97-131175. 300p. 1996. 125.00 (*0-7484-0436-8*) Taylor & Francis.

Armstrongs Golf Log, Wally. Wally Armstrong Golf Log. (Illus.). 144p. 1994. pap. 13.95 (*1-885198-00-0*) Sports Log Pubs.

Army Air Force Historical Office Staff. The Official Pictorial History of the AAF. Gilbert, James B., ed. LC 79-7273. (Flight: Its First Seventy-Five Years Ser.). (Illus.). 1980. reprint ed. lib. bdg. 31.95 (*0-405-12384-1*) Ayer.

Armytage, Gee & Seabrook, Mike, eds. Turf Accounts: A Prize Racing Anthology. 208p. 1996. pap. 19.95 (*0-85493-247-X*, Pub. by V Gollancz) Trafalgar.

Armytage, Livingston. Educating Judges: Towards a New Model of Continuing Judicial Learning. LC 96-18259. 238p. 1996. 107.00 (*90-411-0256-6*) Kluwer Law Intl.

Armytage, W. H. Civil Universities: Aspects of a British Tradition. LC 76-55207. (Academic Profession Ser.). (Illus.). 1977. reprint ed. lib. bdg. 28.95 (*0-405-10031-0*) Ayer.

— Four Hundred Years of English Education. 2nd ed. LC 78-85709. 365p. pap. 104.10 (*0-608-30535-9*, 2051488) Bks Demand.

An Asterisk (*) at the beginning of an entry indicates that the title is appearing for the first time.

Arn, Charles. How to Start a New Service: Your Church Can Reach New People. LC 97-1377. 272p. 1997. pap. 17.99 (*0-8010-9037-7*) Baker Bks.

Arn, Charles, jt. auth. see Arn, Win.

Arn, Joseph V. & Titlow, Paula H. Records Management for an Information Age. 416p. 1991. teacher ed. 14.95 (*0-8273-3552-0*) Delmar.

***Arn, Mary-Jo, ed.** Charles d'Orleans in England, 1415-1440. LC 00-25693. (Illus.). 288p. 2000. 75.00 (*0-85991-580-8*) Boydell & Brewer.

Arn, Mary-Jo, ed. Fortunes Stabilnes: Charles of Orleans's English Book of Love: A Critical Edition. LC 94-44657. (Medieval & Renaissance Texts & Studies: Vol. 138). (Illus.). 640p. 1994. 45.00 (*0-86698-147-0*, MR138) MRTS.

Arn, Win. Catch the Age Wave: A Handbook for Effective Ministry with Senior Adults. LC 99-24414. 184p. (Orig.). 1999. pap. 16.99 (*0-8341-1800-9*) Beacon Hill.

Arn, Win & Arn, Charles. The Master's Plan for Making Disciples: Every Christian an Effective Witness through an Enabling Church. 2nd ed. LC 97-35109. 176p. 1998. pap. 10.99 (*0-8010-9051-2*) Baker Bks.

Arnaboldi, M., et al, eds. The 2nd Stromlo Symposium: The Nature of Elliptical Galaxies: Proceedings of a Symposium Held at the Australian Academy of Science, Canberra, Australia, August 26-30, 1996. (ASP Conference Series Proceedings: Vol. 116). 572p. 1997. 34.00 (*1-886733-36-8*) Astron Soc Pacific.

Arnade, Peter J. Realms of Ritual: Burgundian Ceremony & Civic Life in Late Medieval Ghent. LC 96-15632. 1996. text 47.50 (*0-8014-3098-4*, Comstock Pub) Cornell U Pr.

Arnado, Elena. Gran Libro de La Mujer. 1998. 34.95 (*84-7880-868-X*) Planeta.

Arnadottir, Gudrun. The Brain & Behavior: Assessing Cortical Dysfunction Through ADL. (Illus.). 336p. (C). (gr. 13). 1990. text 47.95 (*0-8016-0334-X*, 00334) Mosby Inc.

Arnaiz, Rosario R. Las Toxinas Ambientales y Sus Efectos. (Ciencia para Todos Ser.). (SPA.). pap. 6.99 (*968-16-4368-2*, Pub. by Fondo) Continental Bk.

***Arnaiz-Villena, Antonio, et al.** Prehistoric Iberia: Genetics, Anthropology & Linguistics. LC 00-22850. 2000. write for info. (*0-306-46364-4*, Kluwer Plenum) Kluwer Academic.

Arnakis, G. G. Stillman: American Consul in a Cretan War. rev. ed. 146p. 1966. 10.00 (*0-318-12222-7*); pap. 8.00 (*0-318-12223-5*) Ad Council.

Arnakis, G. G., ed. Howe: A Historical Sketch of the Greek Revolution, Pts. 1 & 2. 251p. 1966. 10.00 (*0-317-34059-X*); pap. 8.00 (*0-317-34060-3*) Ctr Neo Hellenic.

— Return to Mount Athos. 171p. 1968. 9.00 (*0-317-34062-X*); pap. 6.00 (*0-317-34063-8*) Ctr Neo Hellenic.

— Stillman: Articles & Despatches from Crete. LC 76-9149. 138p. 1976. 10.00 (*0-317-34064-6*); pap. 7.00 (*0-317-34065-4*) Ctr Neo Hellenic.

Arnakis, G. G. & Demetracopoulou, E., eds. Jarvis: His Journal & Related Documents. 282p. 1965. 8.00 (*0-317-34061-1*) Ctr Neo Hellenic.

Arnakis, G. G. & Demetracopoulou, E., eds. Historical Texts of the Greek Revolution from the Papers of George Jarvis. 98p. 1967. 10.00 (*0-317-34057-3*); pap. 6.00 (*0-317-34058-1*) Ctr Neo Hellenic.

Arnakis, George G. & Proussis, Costas M., eds. Neo-Hellenika III. 1978. pap. 25.00 (*0-932242-00-6*) Ctr Neo Hellenic.

Arnaktauyok, Germaine. Harpoon of the Hunter: Markoosie. 84p. 1970. 44.95 (*0-7735-0102-9*, Pub. by McG-Queens Univ Pr) CUP Services.

— Harpoon of the Hunter: Markoosie. 84p. 1974. pap. 10.95 (*0-7735-0232-7*, Pub. by McG-Queens Univ Pr) CUP Services.

Arnal, D., jt. ed. see Michel, R.

Arnal, Oscar L. Ambivalent Alliance: The Catholic Church & the Action Francaise, 1899-1939. LC 84-21961. 270p. 1985. reprint ed. pap. 83.70 (*0-608-00896-6*, 206169000010) Bks Demand.

Arnal, William E. & Desjardins, Michel, eds. Whose Historical Jesus? (Studies in Christianity & Judaism: Vol. 7). vi, 337p. 1997. pap. 27.95 (*0-88920-295-8*) W Laurier U Pr.

Arnaldez. Collection to ICC Arbitral Awards 1991-1995/Recuel des Sentences Artibrates de La, Vol. CIAA 3. 1997. 227.50 (*90-411-0414-3*) Kluwer Law Intl.

Arnaldez, J. J., et al, comments. Collection of Arbitral Awards, 1991-1995. 672p. (C). 1997. text 235.00 (*92-842-0207-8*, 553) ICC Pub.

Arnaldez, Jean-Jacques, jt. ed. see Derains, Yves.

***Arnaldez, Roger.** Averroes: A Rationalist in Islam. Streight, David, tr. from FRE. 184p. 2000. 34.95 (*0-268-02007-8*, Pub. by U of Notre Dame Pr) Chicago Distribution Ctr.

Arnaldez, Roger. Three Messengers for One God. Schlabach, Gerald W. et al, trs. from FRE. LC 93-42512. (C). 1995. text 34.50 (*0-268-01885-5*) U of Notre Dame Pr.

***Arnaldez, Roger & Streight, David.** Averroes: A Rationalist in Islam. 184p. 2000. pap. 21.95 (*0-268-02008-6*, Pub. by U of Notre Dame Pr) Chicago Distribution Ctr.

Arnaldi, B., et al, eds. Computer Animation & Simulation '98: Proceedings of the Eurographics Workshop in Lisbon, Portugal, August 31-September 1, 1998. (Eurographics Ser.). (Illus.). 130p. 1999. pap. 59.95 (*3-211-83257-2*) Spr-Verlag.

Arnaldi De Olmeda, Cecilia. Concha Melendez: Vida y Obra. 186p. (C). 1972. 3.50 (*0-8477-3107-3*); pap. 2.50 (*0-8477-3108-1*) U of PR Pr.

— La Individualizacion de la Ensenanza: Consideraciones y Proceso. LC 76-1904. (Illus.). 124p. (Orig.). 1977. pap. 3.00 (*0-8477-2733-5*) U of PR Pr.

Arnaldo, Alicia, et al. Aprenda Ingles Facil y Rapido: English the Fast & Fun Way for Spanish Speakers. 2nd rev. ed. (Barron's Fast & Fun Way Ser.). (ENG & SPA., Illus.). 288p. 1999. pap. 14.95 (*0-7641-0622-8*) Barron.

— Aprenda Ingles Facil y Rapido: English the Fast & Fun Way for Spanish Speakers, 4 cass., Set. 2nd rev. ed. (ENG & SPA., Illus.). 288p. 1999. pap., boxed set 39.95 incl. audio (*0-7641-7289-1*) Barron.

Arnaldo, D. & Dente, Anita. Learn English the Fast & Fun Way. (Barron's Fast & Fun Way Ser.).Tr. of Learn English the Fast & Fun Way for Spanish Speakers. (SPA & ENG.). 304p. 1990. pap. 14.95 (*0-8120-4364-2*) Barron.

Arnall, Ellis G. The Shore Dimly Seen. (History - United States Ser.). 312p. 1993. reprint ed. lib. bdg. 89.00 (*0-7812-4917-1*) Rprt Serv.

Arnall, Franklin M. The Padlock Collector: Illustrations & Prices of 2800 Padlocks of the Past 100 Years. 6th ed. LC 96-84415. (Illus.). 284p. 1996. pap. 21.95 (*0-914638-05-X*) Collctr Clrmnt.

— The Padlock Collector: 100 Years of Padlocks. 5th ed. LC 87-72771. (Illus.). 190p. 1988. pap. 14.95 (*0-914638-04-1*) Collctr Clrmnt.

Arnall, Richard E. Essentials of Customer Service: A Workbook for Improving Customer Service. 56p. 1995. 9.95 (*0-9642114-2-4*) Busn Systs.

— Essentials of Customer Service: Workshop Presentation Guide. 46p. 1995. 49.95 (*0-9642114-3-2*) Busn Systs.

***Arnall, William & Varey, Simon.** The Case of Opposition Stated, Between the Craftsman & the People, 1731. LC 99-28771. (British Ideas & Issues, 1660-1820 Ser.). 1999. write for info. (*0-404-59653-3*) AMS Pr.

***Arnand, S. C. & Raj, G. D., eds.** Encyclopaediac Dictionary of Physics, 5 vols. 1560p. 1998. pap. 1000.00 (*81-7041-409-1*, Pub. by Print Hse) St Mut.

Arnander, Primrose & Shipwith. Apricots Tomorrow & Other Arab Sayings. (ARA & ENG.). 1991. 16.95 (*0-86685-563-7*, Pub. by Stacey Intl) Intl Bk Ctr.

Arnander, Primrose & Skipwith, Ashkhain. Apricots Tomorrow. (Illus.). 90p. 1993. boxed set 16.95 (*0-905743-57-1*, Pub. by Stacey Intl) Intl Bk Ctr.

— The Son of a Duck Is a Floater. (Illus.). 90p. 1995. boxed set 16.95 (*0-905743-41-5*, Pub. by Stacey Intl) Intl Bk Ctr.

Arnandez, Richard, et al. So Favored by Grace: Education in the Time of John Baptist de La Salle. Colhocker, Lawrence, ed. LC 90-62775. (Lasallian Resources: Vol. 2). (Illus.). xvi, 193p. 1990. pap. 15.00 (*0-944808-06-9*) Lasallian Pubns.

Arnandez, Richard, tr. see Blain, Jean-Baptiste.

Arnandez, Richard, tr. see De La Salle, John B.

Arnandez, Richard, tr. see De Lubac, Henri.

Arnandez, Richard, tr. see Gjergji, Lush.

Arnandez, Richard, tr. see Leclerc, Eloi.

Arnandez, Richard, tr. see Manteau-Bonamy, H. M.

Arnandez, Richard, tr. see Martini, Carlo M.

Arnaoutoglou, Ilias. Ancient Greek Laws: A Sourcebook. LC 97-25557. (Illus.). 192p. (C). 1998. 65.00 (*0-415-14984-3*); pap. 21.99 (*0-415-14985-1*) Routledge.

Arnar, Anna S. Encyclopedism from Pliny to Borges. LC 90-50215. (Illus.). 68p. 1990. pap. 5.00 (*0-943056-12-8*) Univ Chi Lib.

Arnason. History of Modern Art. 4th ed. 1998. text 57.95 (*0-13-227323-3*) P-H.

Arnason, David. The Dragon & the Dry Goods Princess: Fractured Prairie Tales. 133p. 1997. pap. 11.95 (*0-88801-187-3*, Pub. by Turnstone Pr) Genl Dist Srvs.

— The Happiest Man in the World: And Other Stories. 164p. 1989. pap. 13.95 (*0-88922-269-X*, Pub. by Talonbks) Genl Dist Srvs.

— If Pigs Could Fly: More Fractured Prairie Tales. 175p. 1997. pap. 14.95 (*0-88801-202-0*, Pub. by Turnstone Pr) Genl Dist Srvs.

— The Pagan Wall. LC 92-246771. 304p. (Orig.). 1992. pap. 16.95 (*0-88922-312-2*, Pub. by Talonbks) Genl Dist Srvs.

Arnason, David & Arnason, Vincent, eds. The New Icelanders: A North American Community. (Illus.). 125p. 1997. pap. 14.95 (*0-88801-186-5*, Pub. by Turnstone Pr) Genl Dist Srvs.

Arnason, Eleanor. Daughter of the Bear King. 256p. (Orig.). 1987. pap. 3.50 (*0-380-75109-7*, Avon Bks) Morrow Avon.

— Ring of Swords. 384p. 1994. pap. 13.95 (*0-312-89016-8*) Orb NYC.

— A Woman of the Iron People Pt. 1: In the Light of Sigma Draconis. 256p. 1992. mass mkt. 4.99 (*0-380-75637-4*, Avon Bks) Morrow Avon.

— A Woman of the Iron People Pt. 2: Changing Women. 288p. 1992. mass mkt. 4.99 (*0-380-75638-2*, Avon Bks) Morrow Avon.

Arnason, H. Horvard & Diamonstein, Barbaralee. Robert Motherwell: New & Revised. (Illus.). 252p. 1982. 95.00 (*0-8109-1333-X*, Pub. by Abrams) Time Warner.

Arnason, H. Horvard & Prather, Marla. History of Modern Art: Painting, Sculpture, Architecture & Photography. 4th ed. LC 96-49408. (Illus.). 856p. 1997. 75.00 (*0-8109-3439-6*, Pub. by Abrams) Time Warner.

Arnason, J. Ohann. Social Theory & Japanese Experience: The Dual Civilization. LC 97-25795. (Japanese Studies). 1997. 110.00 (*0-7103-0485-4*, Pub. by Kegan Paul Intl) Col U Pr.

Arnason, J. T. Icelandic Legends, 2 vols., Set. Powell, G. E., tr. LC 78-67683. (Folktale Ser.). (Illus.). reprint ed. 75.00 (*0-404-16050-6*) AMS Pr.

Arnason, J. T., et al, eds. Insecticides of Plant Origin. LC 89-85. (ACS Symposium Ser.: No. 387). 224p. 1989. 49.95 (*0-8412-1569-3*, Pub. by Am Chemical) OUP.

— Insecticides of Plant Origin. LC 89-85. (ACS Symposium Ser.: No. 387). (Illus.). 224p. 1989. reprint ed. pap. 69.50 (*0-608-03142-9*, 206359500007) Bks Demand.

Arnason, Johann P., jt. ed. see Sugimoto, Yoshio.

Arnason, John T., et al, eds. Phytochemistry of Medicinal Plants: Proceedings of the Thirty-Fourth Annual Meeting of the Phytochemical Society of North America Held in Mexico City, Mexico, August 15-19, 1994, Vol. 29. LC 95-39616. (Recent Advances in Phytochemistry Ser.: Vol. 29). (Illus.). 372p. 1995. 105.00 (*0-306-45181-6*, Kluwer Plenum) Kluwer Academic.

Arnason, Jon Yard & Fletcher, Ian M., eds. Practitioner's Guide to Cross-Border Insolvencies, 2 vols. LC 99-48141. 2000. ring bd. 300.00 (*0-379-01280-4*, 0517011) Oceana.

Arnason, R. The Icelandic Fisheries: Evolution & Management of a Fishing Industry. (Fishing News Bks.). 192p. 1994. 80.00 (*0-85238-210-3*) Blackwell Sci.

Arnason, Ragnar, et al, eds. Essays on the Economics of Migratory Fish Stocks. (Studies in Contemporary Economics). (Illus.). viii, 197p. 1991. 47.95 (*0-387-54362-7*) Spr-Verlag.

Arnason, Sia, et al. Legal Rights of the Elderly: Everything You & Your Family Need to Know about Government Benefits, Health Care, Social Security, Veteran's Benefits, Medicare & Medicaid, & Guardianship. 319p. 1995. pap. 15.95 (*0-87224-079-7*, K1-1500) PLI.

Arnason, Vincent, jt. ed. see Arnason, David.

Arnau, Eduard, jt. auth. see Parramon Studios Staff.

Arnau, Edward & Tenllado, Antonio Munzo. The Skeletal System. (Invisible World Ser.). (Illus.). 32p. (J). (gr. 4 up). 1995. lib. bdg. 15.95 (*0-7910-3151-9*) Chelsea Hse.

Arnau, Frank. Universal Film Lexicon. 1972. 69.95 (*0-8490-1246-5*) Gordon Pr.

Arnau, J. Sanchez, ed. Debt & Development. LC 82-431. 337p. 1982. 65.00 (*0-275-90756-2*, C0756, Praeger Pubs) Greenwood.

Arnaud, A. French-English Selling-Words: Les Mots-Vendeurs. 128p. 1989. pap. 40.00 (*2-85608-032-4*) IBD Ltd.

Arnaud, A. J. & Kingdom, Elizabeth. Women's Rights & the Rights of Man. (Enlightenment Rights & Revolution Ser.: No. 5). 1990. pap. text 38.00 (*0-08-040923-7*, Pub. by Aberdeen U Pr) Macmillan.

Arnaud, Alain. Les Mots-Vendeurs: Francais-Anglais. (ENG & FRE.). 122p. 1989. pap. 59.95 (*0-7859-3915-6*, 2856080324) Fr & Eur.

Arnaud, Andre-Jean, et al. Dictionnaire Encyclopedique de Theorie et de Sociologie du D. 2nd ed. (FRE.). 1993. write for info. (*0-7859-8640-5*, 227500601X) Fr & Eur.

Arnaud, Bridger & Assoc. Staff, tr. see Isherwood, Judith.

Arnaud, Claude. Chamfort: A Biography. Dusinberre, Deke, tr. LC 91-31913. (Illus.). 374p. 1992. 27.50 (*0-226-02697-3*) U Ch Pr.

Arnaud, Jean F. Diccionario de la Electronica. 3rd ed. (SPA.). 368p. 1976. pap. 9.95 (*0-8288-5592-7*, S14211) Fr & Eur.

***Arnaud, Linda.** The Artful Chicken: Delightful Recipes & Charming Collectibles. LC 00-22965. (Illus.). 2000 29.95 (*1-58479-022-9*) Stewart Tabori & Chang.

***Arnaud, Michel, photos by.** Nashville: The Pilgrims of Guitar Town. LC 99-57641. (Illus.). 176p. 2000. 27.50 (*1-55670-989-7*) Stewart Tabori & Chang.

Arnaud, Nicole & Dofny, Jacques. Nationalism & the National Question. Williams, Penelope, tr. from FRE. 133p. 1977. 38.99 (*0-919618-46-4*, Pub. by Black Rose); pap. 9.99 (*0-919618-45-6*, Pub. by Black Rose) Consort Bk Sales.

Arnaud, Noel, ed. see Jarry, Alfred.

Arnaud, Rene. Second Republic & Napoleon Third. LC 70-158271. reprint ed. 57.50 (*0-404-50799-9*) AMS Pr.

Arnaudet, Martin C. & Barrett. Paragraph Development. 2nd ed. 208p. (C). 1990. pap. text 33.00 (*0-13-648502-2*) P-H.

Arnaudet, Martin L. & Barrett, Mary Ellin. Approaches to Academic Reading & Writing. (Illus.). 288p. (C). 1984. pap. text 30.00 (*0-13-043679-8*) P-H.

***Arnaudo, Gianni.** Gianni Arnaudo: Opacity & Transparency. 2000. pap. 25.00 (*88-7838-079-2*) L'Arca IT.

Arnaudon, Jean-Claude. Dictionnaire du Blues. (FRE.). 296p. 1978. 59.95 (*0-8288-5191-3*, M6646) Fr & Eur.

Arnaudova, Olga, ed. see Open Linguistics Forum Staff.

Arnauld, Antoine. The Arraignment of the Whole Societie of Jesuites in Fraunce: Holden-the Twelfth & Thirteenth of July, 1594. LC 79-84084. (English Experience Ser.: No. 904). 68p. 1979. reprint ed. lib. bdg. 15.00 (*0-902210-90-4*) Walter J Johnson.

— On True & False Ideas with Arnauld's New Objections to Descartes' Meditations & Descartes' Replies. Kremer, Elmar J., tr. LC 89-77476. (Studies in the History of Philosophy: Vol. 16). 232p. 1990. lib. bdg. 89.95 (*0-88946-287-9*) E Mellen.

Arnauld, Antoine & Lancelot, Claude. Grammaire Generale et Raisonnee. 138p. 1973. reprint ed. write for info. (*3-487-04418-8*) G Olms Pubs.

Arnauld, Antoine & Nicole, Pierre. Antoine Arnauld & Pierre Nicole: Logic or the Art of Thinking. Buroker, Jill V., ed. (Cambridge Texts in the History of Philosophy Ser.). 319p. (C). 1996. text 59.95 (*0-521-48249-6*); pap. text 18.95 (*0-521-48394-8*) Cambridge U Pr.

— La Logique ou l'Art de Penser. 389p. 1970. reprint ed. 95.00 (*0-318-71313-6*) G Olms Pubs.

Arnault. Satellite Monitoring of the Earth's Surface & Atmosphere 16-10. (Advances in Space Research Ser.: 16). 194p. 1995. pap. 97.75 (*0-08-042635-2*, Pergamon Pr) Elsevier.

Arnautov, V. I., et al. Introduction to the Theory of Topological Rings & Modules. LC 95-41065. (Monographs & Textbooks in Pure & Applied Mathematics: No. 197). (Illus.). 584p. 1995. text 175.00 (*0-8247-9323-4*, QA251) Dekker.

Arnavas, Donald P. & Ruberry, William J. Government Contract Guidebook & Supplement. 2nd ed. (Government Contract Text Ser.). 500p. 1994. ring bd. 175.00 (*0-318-19473-2*) Fed Pubns Inc.

Arnaz, Desi, Jr. A Book. 1994. reprint ed. lib. bdg. 45.95 (*1-56849-254-5*) Buccaneer Bks.

Arnberg, Lenore. Raising Children Bilingually: The Pre-School Years. 1987. 59.00 (*0-905028-71-6*, Pub. by Multilingual Matters); pap. 29.50 (*0-905028-70-8*, Pub. by Multilingual Matters) Taylor & Francis.

Arnberger, Leslie P. Flowers of the Southwest Mountains. rev. ed. Priehs, T. J., ed. LC 81-86380. (Illus.). 144p. 1983. pap. 9.95 (*0-911408-61-4*) SW Pks Mnmts.

Arnbjerg-Nielsen, K., et al, eds. Use of Historical Rainfall Series for Hydrological Modelling. 210p. 1998. pap. 159.00 (*0-08-043387-1*) Elsevier.

Arnborg, S., et al, eds. Algorithm Theory SWAT '98: 6th Scandinavian Workshop on Alforithm Theory, Stockholm, Sweden, July 8-10, 1998. Proceedings. (Lecture Notes in Computer Science Ser.: Vol. 1432). ix, 347p. 1998. pap. 59.00 (*3-540-64682-5*) Spr-Verlag.

Arndal, Steffen, ed. see Sorensen, Bengt A.

Arndorfer, Elizabeth, et al. Who Decides? A State-by-State Review of Abortion & Reproductive Rights. 7th ed. (Illus.). 156p. (C). 1998. pap. text 45.00 (*0-7881-7481-9*) DIANE Pub.

Arnds, Peter O. Wilhelm Raabe's "Der Hungerpastor" & Charles Dickens's "David Copperfield" Intertextuality of Two Bildungsromane. LC 96-12947. (North American Studies in Nineteenth-Century German Literature: Vol. 20). XI, 191p. (C). 1997. 44.95 (*0-8204-3321-7*) P Lang Pubng.

Arndt, Alice. Seasoning Savvy: How to Cook with Herbs, Spices & Other Flavorings. LC 99-20217. (Illus.). 268p. 1999. pap. 24.95 (*1-56022-032-5*, Haworth Herbal Pr) Haworth Pr.

— Seasoning Savvy: How to Cook with Herbs, Spices & Other Flavorings. LC 99-20217. (Illus.). 268p. 1999. lib. bdg. 59.95 (*1-56022-031-7*, Haworth Herbal Pr) Haworth Pr.

Arndt, Andreas. Cutaneous Medicine & Surgery. (Illus.). 400p. 1995. text 425.00 (*0-7216-6333-8*, W B Saunders Co) Harcrt Hlth Sci Grp.

— Cutaneous Medicine & Surgery. (Illus.). 400p. 1996. text 595.00 (*0-7216-6332-X*, W B Saunders Co); text 495.00 (*0-7216-6331-1*, W B Saunders Co) Harcrt Hlth Sci Grp.

— Manual Derm Asia, No. 4. 1988. 10.95 (*0-316-05179-9*, Little Brwn Med Div) Lppncott W & W.

— Manual Derm ISE, No. 4. 1988. 15.95 (*0-316-05178-0*) Little.

Arndt, Andreas & Virmond, Wolfgang. Friedrich Daniel Ernst Schleiermacher Kritische Gesamtausgabe: Funfte Abteilung (Briefwechsel und Biographische Dokumente) Band 5: Briefwechsel 1801-1802 (Briefe 1005-1244) 450p. 1999. 174.00 (*3-11-016218-0*) De Gruyter.

Arndt, Andreas & Virmond, Wolfgang, eds. Friedrich Daniel Ernst Schleiermacher: Kritische Gesamtausgabe. (Briefwechsel, 1799-1800 Ser.: Bd. 3). (GER.). cxxvi, 585p. (C). 1992. lib. bdg. 267.70 (*3-11-011021-0*) De Gruyter.

— Schleiermachers Briefwechsel, Verzeichnis, Nebst Einer Liste Seiner Vorlesungen. (GER.). vii, 337p. (C). 1992. lib. bdg. 98.50 (*3-11-013189-7*) De Gruyter.

Arndt, Andreas, ed. see Schleiermacher, Friedrich Daniel Ernst.

Arndt, Andreas, ed. see Virmond, Wolggang.

Arndt, Barbara T. Dorothea Schlote & Her Family: A Rememberance. LC 89-91444. (Illus.). 120p. (Orig.). 1989. pap. 25.00 (*0-685-26936-1*) B E Arndt.

— The Timms of Waterloo County. (Illus.). 100p. (Orig.). 1991. pap. 45.00 (*0-9623606-1-9*) B E Arndt.

Arndt, Bruno. Der Ubergang Vom Mittelhochdeutschen Zum Neuhochdeutschen in der Sprache der Breslauer Kanzlei. (GER.). 118p. 1977. reprint ed. write for info. (*3-487-06169-4*) G Olms Pubs.

Arndt, Chris, jt. auth. see Hyser, Raymond.

Arndt, Christian O. & Everett, Samuel, eds. Education for a World Society: 11th Yearbook of John Dewey Society. LC 72-142603. (Essay Index Reprint Ser.). 1977. reprint ed. 23.95 (*0-8369-2383-9*) Ayer.

Arndt, David. How to Shoot & Sell Sports Photography. LC 98-72742. (Illus.). 120p. 1999. pap. 29.95 (*0-936262-72-9*) Amherst Media.

— Make Money with Your Camera. (Illus.). 128p. 1999. pap. 29.95 (*0-936262-84-2*) Amherst Media.

***Arndt, David Neil.** How to Buy & Sell Used Cameras. (Illus.). 112p. 2000. pap. 19.95 (*1-58428-035-2*, Pub. by Amherst Media) IPG Chicago.

— Innovative Techniques for Wedding Photographers. (Illus.). 120p. 2000. pap. 29.95 (*1-58428-025-5*) Amherst Media.

Arndt-Dietrich, Ilona B. Naehrstoffbilanz Des Woelfersheimer Sees (Hessen), Eines Durch Abwaerme und Abwassereinleitung Beemflussten Gewaessers. (Dissertationes Botanicae Ser.: Band 142). (GER., Illus.). viii, 166p. 1989. pap. 42.00 (*3-443-64051-6*, Pub. by Gebruder Borntraeger) Balogh.

Arndt, Elizabeth E., jt. auth. see Albu, Susan H.

Arndt, Ernst. Das Verhaltnis der Verstandeserkenntnis Zur Sinnlichen in der Vorsokratischen Philosophie. (Abhandlungen Zur Philosophie und Ihrer Geschichte Ser.: Bd. 31). 57p. 1975. reprint ed. 20.00 (*3-487-05636-4*) G Olms Pubs.

Arndt, Ernst M. Gedichte. (GER.). vi, 314p. 1992. 49.80 (*3-615-00004-8*, Pub. by Weidmann) Lubrecht & Cramer.

Arndt, Guenter, intro. International Conference on Manufacturing Engineering, 5th, 1990: ICME-90, Vols. 1 & 2. (Illus.). 562p. (Orig.). 1990. pap. 115.25 (*0-85825-501-4*, Pub. by Inst Engrs Aust-EA Bks) Accents Pubns.

A

Arndt, H. W. Asian Diaries with Photographs by Hedda Morrison. (Asia-Pacific Monographs: No. 2). (Illus.). 284p. 1987. text 45.00 (*9971-68-125-0*, Pub. by Chopmen Singapore) Advent Bks Div.
— Economic Development: The History of an Idea. LC 86-25108. viii, 218p. (C). 1987. reprint ed. 20.95 (*0-226-02720-1*) U Ch Pr.
— Economic Development: The History of an Idea. LC 86-25108. 226p. (C). 1989. reprint ed. pap. text 10.95 (*0-226-02722-8*) U Ch Pr.
— Economic Lessons of the Nineteen Thirties. 314p. 1963. 35.00 (*0-7146-1204-9*, BHA-01204, Pub. by F Cass Pubs) Intl Spec Bk.
— The Economic Lessons of the Nineteen Thirties. (Modern Revivals in Economic History Ser.). 320p. 1993. 61.95 (*0-7512-0065-4*, Pub. by Gregg Revivals) Ashgate Pub Co.
— Essays in International Economics 1944-1994. 400p. 1996. text 87.95 (*1-85972-394-2*, Pub. by Avebry) Ashgate Pub Co.
— Essays on Development in a Liberal Economic Order. LC 92-34710. (Occasional Papers: No. 35). 1992. pap. 9.95 (*1-55815-237-7*) ICS Pr.
— The Indonesian Economy: Collected Papers. 290p. 1986. text 50.00 (*0-317-43150-1*, Pub. by Chopmen Singapore) Advent Bks Div.
— The Rise & Fall of Economic Growth: A Study in Contemporary Thought. LC 83-24185. vi, 162p. 1984. pap. text 9.95 (*0-226-02717-1*) U Ch Pr.
Arndt, Hans J. West Germany: Politics of Non-Planning. LC 66-17524. (National Planning Ser.: No. 8). 186p. reprint ed. pap. 57.70 (*0-608-13884-3*, 202039400017) Bks Demand.
Arndt, Hans W. Methodo Scientifica Pertractatum: Mos geometricus und Kalkuelbegriff in der Philosophischen Theorienbildung des 17. und 18. (Quellen und Studien zur Philosophie: Vol. 4). 1971. 89.25 (*3-11-003942-7*) De Gruyter.
Arndt, Helmut & Muller-Holtz, Henner. Schulerfahrungen - Lebenserfahrungen Anspruch und Wirklichkeit von Bildung und Erziehung Heute: Reformpadagogik Auf dem Prufstand 2., Unveranderte Auflage. 2nd ed. (Erziehungskonzeptionen und Praxis Ser.: Bd. 31). (GER.). 213p. 1996. 25.95 (*3-631-30622-9*) P Lang Pubng.
Arndt, Herman. Why Did Jesus Fast? 87p. (Orig.). 1996. reprint ed. pap. 11.00 (*0-7873-0041-1*) Hlth Research.
Arndt, Horst & Janney, Richard W. InterGrammar: Toward an Integrative Model of Verbal, Prosodic & Kinesic Choices in Speech. xvi, 458p. (C). 1987. lib. bdg. 165.40 (*0-89925-331-8*) Mouton.
Arndt, Jack R. & Coons, Stephen J., eds. Continuing Education in Pharmacy. LC 87-71365. (Illus.). 374p. (C). 1987. text 40.00 (*0-937526-13-4*) AACP Alexandria.
***Arndt, Jorg.** Pi - Unleashed. 250p. 2000. pap. text 39.95 (*3-540-66572-2*) Spr-Verlag.
Arndt, Jurgen, et al. Jazz und Avantgarde. (Musikwissenschaftliche Arbeiten Ser.: Bd. 5). (GER.). 274p. 1997. write for info. (*3-487-10563-2*) G Olms Pubs.
Arndt, Karl J. Economy on the Ohio, 1826-1834. The Harmony Society During the Period of Its Greatest Power & Influence & Its Messianic Crisis. LC 84-648. (ENG & GER., Illus.). 1056p. 1984. 50.00 (*0-937640-03-4*) Harmony Soc.
— George Rapp's Harmony Society: 1785-1847. rev. ed. LC 72-147267. (Illus.). 713p. 1975. 65.00 (*0-8386-7888-2*) Fairleigh Dickinson.
— George Rapp's Separatists: 1700-1803. LC 80-82896.Tr. of Georg Rapps Separatisten. (ENG & GER., Illus.). 480p. 1980. 50.00 (*0-937640-00-X*) Harmony Soc.
— George Rapp's Successors & Material Heirs: 1847-1916. LC 76-147268. (Illus.). 445p. 1975. 60.00 (*0-8386-7889-0*) Fairleigh Dickinson.
— George Rapp's Years of Glory: Economy on the Ohio, 1834-1847 Oekonomie am Ohio. XXXII, 1163p. (C). 1987. text 193.00 (*0-8204-0481-0*) P Lang Pubng.
Arndt, Karl J., ed. see Kaufmann, Peter & Emerson, Ralph Waldo.
Arndt, Karl J., ed. see Sealsfield, Charles, pseud.
Arndt, Katherine L., tr. see Len'kov, V. D., et al.
Arndt, Kathy, ed. see Alekseev, A. I.
Arndt, Kenneth A. Manual of Dermatologic Therapeutics: With Essentials of Diagnosis. 6th ed. 400p. spiral bd. 39.95 (*0-7817-2170-9*) Lppncott W & W.
Arndt, Kenneth A. Manual of Dermatological Therapeutics. 3rd ed. 1983. 19.50 (*0-316-05181-0*, Little Brwn Med Div) Lppncott W & W.
Arndt, Kenneth A., et al, eds. Cutaneous Laser Therapy: Principles & Methods. LC 82-17379. (Wiley-Medical Publication). (Illus.). 255p. reprint ed. pap. 79.10 (*0-8357-8630-7*, 203505400092) Bks Demand.
Arndt, Kenneth A. & Dover, Jeffrey S., eds. Cutaneous Laser Surgery. LC 97-3099. (Illus.). 432p. 1997. text 126.00 (*0-316-05177-2*) Lppncott W & W.
Arndt, Kenneth A., et al. Manual of Dermatologic Therapeutics. 5th ed. LC 94-24451. 382p. 1995. spiral bd. 38.00 (*0-316-05175-6*) Lppncott W & W.
— Primary Care Dermatology, 2 vols. Fletcher, Judy, ed. LC 96-44227. (Illus.). 352p. 1997. pap. text 49.95 (*0-7216-6096-7*, W B Saunders Co) Harcrt Hlth Sci Grp.
Arndt, Laurel L. Before I Write. (Step Ahead Workbooks Ser.). (Illus.). 32p. (J). (ps). 1997. pap., wbk. ed. 2.19 (*0-307-03596-4*, 03596) Gldn Bks Pub Co.
Arndt, Marianne. Nurses' Medication Errors: An Interpretative Study of Experiences. LC 95-167614. (Illus.). XVIII, 408p. 1994. pap. 59.95 (*3-631-47209-9*) P Lang Pubng.
Arndt, N. T., ed. see Nisbet, Evan G.
Arndt, P. & Luettig, G. W., eds. Mineral Resources' Extraction, Environmental Protection & Land-Use Planning in the Industrial & Developing Countries. x, 338p. (C). 1987. pap. text 59.00 (*3-510-65132-4*, Pub. by E Schweizerbartsche) Balogh.
Arndt, R. E., et al, eds. Advancements in Aerodynamics, Fluid Mechanics, & Hydraulics. 1026p. 1986. 96.00 (*0-87262-539-7*) Am Soc Civil Eng.
— Bubble Noise & Cavitation Erosion in Fluid Systems 1993. LC 93-73593. 129p. pap. 40.00 (*0-7918-1040-2*) ASME.
Arndt, R. E. & Prosperetti, A., eds. Aeration Technology. LC 94-71359. (Fluid Engineering Division Conference Ser.: Vol. 187). 67p. 1994. pap. 25.00 (*0-7918-1370-3*) ASME.
Arndt, Richard T. & Rubin, David L., eds. The Fulbright Difference, 1948-1992. LC 92-28068. (Fulbright Association Ser.). 490p. (C). 1993. text 49.95 (*1-56000-085-6*) Transaction Pubs.
Arndt, Richard T., jt. ed. see Rubin, David L.
Arndt, Rick. The Real Victory. 160p. 1998. pap. 7.99 (*0-570-05068-5*) Concordia.
Arndt, Roger E., ed. see American Society of Mechanical Engineers Staff, et al.
Arndt, Roger E., jt. ed. see George, William K.
Arndt, Roger E., jt. ed. see Swift, Walter L.
Arndt, Stephen W., tr. see Dante Alighieri.
Arndt, Sven & Milner, Chris, eds. Global Trade Policy, 1997. (World Economy Ser.). 224p. 1998. pap. text 33.95 (*0-631-20759-7*) Blackwell Pubs.
Arndt, Sven W. The World Economy: Global Trade Policy, 1996. 1997. pap. text 33.95 (*0-631-20348-6*) Blackwell Pubs.
Arndt, Sven W., ed. The Political Economy of Austria. LC 82-11661. (AEI Symposia Ser.: No. 82D). (Illus.). 240p. reprint ed. pap. 74.40 (*0-8357-4524-4*, 203738500008) Bks Demand.
Arndt, Sven W. & Richardson, J. David, eds. Real-Financial Linkages among Open Economies. 216p. 1987. 27.50 (*0-262-01096-8*) MIT Pr.
Arndt, U., et al. Inventory of Air Pollution Effects in Baden-Wurttemberg. (C). 1988. 24.00 (*81-7087-026-7*, Pub. by Oxford IBH) S Asia.
Arndt, Ulrich W. & Willis, B. T. Single Crystal Diffractometry. LC 66-13637. (Cambridge Monographs on Physics). 355p. reprint ed. pap. 101.20 (*0-608-12317-X*, 2024404) Bks Demand.
Arndt, Uwe. Theologie Als Weltordnung: Zur Frage des Gesellschaftsentwurfs in der Theologie Thomas Muntzers. (Europaische Hochschulschriften Ser.: Reihe 31, Bd. 329). (GER.). 188p. 1997. 42.95 (*3-631-31927-4*) P Lang Pubng.
Arndt, Walter, tr. see Busch, Wilhelm.
Arndt, Walter, tr. see Goethe, Johann Wolfgang Von.
Arndt, Walter, jt. tr. see Hoisington, Sona S.
Arndt, Walter, tr. see Johnson, Uwe.
Arndt, Walter, tr. see Konwicki, Tadeusz.
Arndt, Walter, tr. see Pushkin, Aleksandr.
Arndt, Walter, tr. see Rilke, Rainer Maria.
Arndt, Walter, tr. see Rilke, Rainer Maria, et al.
Arndt, Walter, tr. see Walser, Robert.
Arndt, Walter, tr. & intro. see Pushkin, Aleksandr.
Arndt, Walter W., tr. see Heine, Heinrich.
Arndt, Wilhelm & Tangl, Michael. Schrifttafeln zur Erlernung der Lateinischen Palaeographie. 64p. 1976. reprint ed. 145.00 (*3-487-05940-1*) G Olms Pubs.
Arndt, William B., Jr. Gender Disorders & the Paraphilias. 500p. 1991. 62.50 (*0-8236-2150-2*) Intl Univs Pr.
Arndt, William F., tr. see Bauer, Walter, et al, eds.
Arne, Paul H., jt. auth. see Yates, John C.
Arnebeck, Bob. Through a Fiery Trial: Building Washington, 1790-1800. (Illus.). 732p. 1991. 29.95 (*0-8191-7832-2*) Madison Bks UPA.
— Through a Fiery Trial: Building Washington, 1790-1800. 1994. pap. 16.95 (*1-56833-027-8*) Madison Bks UPA.
Arneheim, Rudolf. The Split & the Structure: Twenty-Eight Essays. 125p. 1996. 45.00 (*0-520-20477-8*, Pub. by U CA Pr); pap. 15.95 (*0-520-20478-6*, Pub. by U CA Pr) Cal Prin Full Svc.
Arneil, Barbara. John Locke & America: The Defense of English Colonialism. 240p. 1996. text 59.00 (*0-19-827967-1*, Clarendon Pr) OUP.
— Politics & Feminism: An Introduction. LC 98-29203. 325p. 1999. pap. 62.95 (*0-631-19812-1*); pap. 29.95 (*0-631-19813-X*) Blackwell Pubs.
Arneil, Steve & Keaveny, Liam. Teach Yourself Karate. (Illus.). 190p. 1995. pap. 9.95 (*0-8442-3927-5*, Teach Yrslf) NTC Contemp Pub Co.
Arnell, Nigel W. Global Warming, River Flows & Water Resources. LC 96-35032. 234p. 1996. 64.95 (*0-471-96599-5*) Wiley.
Arnell, Peter. Made in Brooklyn: A Visual Diary. (Illus.). 134p. 1996. write for info. (*0-9631817-9-3*) Sidney Pr.
— O Wonderful, Wonderful & Most Wonderful, Wonderful! Again Wonderful . . . 96p. 1992. write for info. (*0-9631817-0-X*) Sidney Pr.
— O Wonderful, Wonderful & Most Wonderful, Wonderful! Again Wonderful . . . (Illus.). 90p. 1992. pap. write for info. (*0-9631817-1-8*) Sidney Pr.
Arner, Frederick B. Mutiny at Brandy Station: The Last Battle of the Hooker Brigade: A Controversial Army Reorganization, Courts Martial, & the Bloody Days That Followed. LC 93-73405. (Illus.). 210p. 1993. 29.95 (*0-9638523-4-5*) Bates & Blood.
Arner, Frederick B., ed. see Armstrong, William H.
Arner, George B. Consanguineous Marriages in the American Population. LC 74-77992. (Columbia University. Studies in the Social Sciences: No. 83). reprint ed. 37.50 (*0-404-51083-3*) AMS Pr.
Arner, Robert D. Dobson's Encyclopedia: The Publisher, Text, & Publication of America's First Britannica, 1789-1803. LC 91-17624. (Illus.). 320p. (C). 1991. text 45.00 (*0-8122-3092-2*) U of Pa Pr.
***Arner, Timothy.** Re-Entry Review of Arithmetic & Preparation for Algebra. 284p. (C). 1999. pap. text 42.95 (*0-7872-6520-9*) Kendall-Hunt.
Arneri-Georgijev. English for Doctors, Medical Students: English to Serbian - Romanized. 4th ed. (ENG & SER.). 318p. 1997. 95.00 (*0-320-00050-8*) Fr & Eur.
Arneric, Stephen P. & Brioni, Jorge D., eds. Neuronal Nicotinic Receptors: Pharmacology & Therapeutic Opportunities. LC 98-17280. 421p. 1998. 185.00 (*0-471-24743-X*) Wiley.
Arnesen, Anna M., ed. see Lawrence, Loretta N.
***Arnesen, Eric.** Brotherhoods of Color: Black Railroad Workers & the Struggle for Equality. 659p. 2001. 39.95 (*0-674-00319-5*) HUP.
Arnesen, Eric. Waterfront Workers of New Orleans: Race, Class, & Politics, 1863-1923. LC 93-33057. (Illus.). 384p. 1994. reprint ed. pap. text 15.95 (*0-252-06377-5*) U of Ill Pr.
Arnesen, Eric, et al. Labor Histories: Class, Politics, & the Working Class Experience. LC 97-45358. (Working Class in American History Ser.). 400p. 1998. text 49.95 (*0-252-02407-9*); text 19.95 (*0-252-06710-X*) U of Ill Pr.
Arnesen, Peter J. The Medieval Japanese Daimyo: The Ouchi Family's Rule of Suo & Nagato. LC 79-10337. (Yale Historical Publications: Miscellany: No. 122). 256p. reprint ed. pap. 79.40 (*0-7837-2781-X*, 204317300006) Bks Demand.
Arnesen, Peter J., ed. The Auto Industry Ahead: Who's Driving? LC 89-506. (Michigan Papers in Japanese Studies: No. 18). x, 131p. 1989. pap. 9.00 (*0-939512-36-X*) U MI Japan.
— Is There Enough Business to Go Around? Overcapacity in the Auto Industry. LC 87-30006. (Michigan Papers in Japanese Studies: No. 16). x, 121p. 1988. pap. 9.00 (*0-939512-35-1*) U MI Japan.
— The Japanese Competition: Phase 2. LC 86-31756. (Michigan Papers in Japanese Studies: No. 15). xii, 126p. 1987. 17.00 (*0-939512-30-0*); pap. 9.00 (*0-939512-31-9*) U MI Japan.
Arneson, Charles, jt. auth. see Colin, Patrick L.
Arneson, Christina. How to Aggravate a Man Every Time. LC 99-15774. 144p. 1999. pap. 6.95 (*1-58062-214-3*) Adams Media.
Arneson, D. J. Bats: A Nature-Fact Book. (Nature-Fact Bks.). (Illus.). 32p. (J). 1992. pap. 2.50 (*1-56156-147-9*) Kidsbks.
— Fun & Funny April Fool's Jokes & Riddles. (Illus.). 64p. 1992. pap. 2.95 (*0-8125-1642-7*, Pub. by Tor Bks) St Martin.
— The Human Body. (Nature-Fact Bks.). (Illus.). 32p. (J). 1991. pap. 2.50 (*1-56156-024-3*) Kidsbks.
— Incredible Insects. (Nature-Fact Bks.). (Illus.). 24p. (Orig.). (J). 1990. pap. 2.50 (*0-942025-20-2*) Kidsbks.
— Martin Luther King Poster Book. (Illus.). 6p. (J). 1992. pap. 2.95 (*1-56156-161-4*) Kidsbks.
— Rocks & Minerals. (Nature Fact Book). (Illus.). 32p. (Orig.). (J). 1990. pap. 2.50 (*0-942025-90-3*) Kidsbks.
— Toxic Cops. LC 90-13102. (Venture Bks.). (Illus.). 112p. (YA). (gr. 7-12). 1991. lib. bdg. 24.00 (*0-531-12525-4*) Watts.
Arneson, D. J. & Bruce, Maureen L. The EMT Handbook of Emergency Care. LC 65-8592. (Illus.). 320p. 1986. text 19.00 (*0-397-54595-9*, Lippncott) Lppncott W & W.
Arneson, D. J., ed. see London, Jack.
Arneson, Dave. Mugshots One: The Case of the Pacific Clipper. Loomis, Rick, ed. (Illus.). 80p. 1991. pap. 8.95 (*0-940244-41-1*) Flying Buffalo.
Arneson, Pat, jt. auth. see Arnett, Ronald C.
Arneson, Richard J., ed. Liberalism, 3 vols., Set. (Schools of Thought in Politics Ser.: Vol. 2). 2016p. 1992. 680.00 (*1-85278-348-6*) E Elgar.
***Arness, Christine.** Wedding Chimes, Assorted Crimes. LC 99-50008. (Romance Ser.). 1999. 24.95 (*0-7862-2316-2*) Five Star.
Arnet, Carroll. Night Perimeter: New & Selected Poems, 1958-1990. 1991. pap. 9.95 (*0-912678-81-X*) Greenfld Rev Lit.
***Arnet, Gary F.** Dentists: Making Hiring Decisions on More Than a Gut Feeling: A Comprehensive Plan to Finding & Keeping the Best Employee. 217p. 1999. pap. 49.95 (*0-9674136-0-5*) New Horizon Pubns.
Arnett. American Insects. 2nd ed. 1998. 39.95 (*1-57444-185-X*) St Lucie Pr.
Arnett, Benjamin H., jt. auth. see Ashley, James M.
Arnett, Bishop, ed. see Bell, James M.
Arnett, Carlen, et al, eds. The Four Way Reader #2, No. 2. LC 95-61377. 400p. Date not set. pap. 16.95 (*1-884800-05-X*) Four Way Bks.
Arnett, Chris. The Terror of the Coast: Land Alienation & Colonial War on Vancouver Island & the Gulf Islands, 1849-1863. 352p. 1999. pap. 15.95 (*0-88922-318-1*, Pub. by Talonbks) Genl Dist Srvs.
Arnett, David. Supernovae & Nucleosynthesis: An Investigation of the History of Matter, from the Big Bang to the Present. (Princeton Series in Astrophysics). 496p. 1996. text 89.50 (*0-691-01148-6*, Pub. by Princeton U Pr); pap. text 39.50 (*0-691-01147-8*, Pub. by Princeton U Pr) Cal Prin Full Svc.
Arnett, Edward M. & Kent, Allen, eds. Computer-Based Chemical Information. LC 72-95840. (Books in Library & Information Science: No. 4). (Illus.). 239p. reprint ed. pap. 74.10 (*0-7837-0901-3*, 204120600019) Bks Demand.
Arnett, Eric, ed. Nuclear Weapons & Arms Control in South Asia after the Test Ban. (SIPRI Research Reports Ser.: No. 14). (Illus.). 108p. 1998. text 47.50 (*0-19-829412-3*); pap. text 24.50 (*0-19-829411-5*) OUP.
Arnett, Eric H. Gunboat Diplomacy & the Bomb: Nuclear Proliferation & the U. S. Navy. LC 89-32274. 194p. 1989. 57.95 (*0-275-93345-8*, C3345, Praeger Pubs) Greenwood.
— Sea-Launched Cruise Missiles & U. S. Security. LC 90-27515. 224p. 1991. 57.95 (*0-275-93716-X*, C3716, Praeger Pubs) Greenwood.
Arnett, Eric H., ed. Implementing the Comprehensive Test Ban. (SIPRI Research Reports: No. 8). 144p. 1995. text 42.00 (*0-19-829188-4*); pap. text 28.00 (*0-19-829187-6*) OUP.
— Military Capacity & the Risk of War: China, India, Pakistan & Iran. LC 96-30040. (A SIPRI Publication). (Illus.). 382p. 1997. text 65.00 (*0-19-829281-3*) OUP.
— Nuclear Weapons after the Comprehensive Test Ban: Implications for Modernization & Proliferation. LC 96-222615. (SIPRI Publication). (Illus.). 160p. 1996. text 39.95 (*0-19-829194-9*) OUP.
Arnett, Grace M. Empowering Health Care Consumers through Tax Reform. LC 99-21949. 320p. 1999. pap. text 27.95 (*0-472-06716-8*, 06716) U of Mich Pr.
***Arnett, Grace M., ed.** Empowering Health Care Consumers through Tax Reform. LC 99-21949. (Illus.). 320p. (C). 1999. text 39.50 (*0-472-09716-4*, 09716) U of Mich Pr.
Arnett, Joe A. Painting Sumptuous Vegetables, Fruits & Flowers in Oil. LC 97-22334. (Illus.). 128p. 1998. 27.99 (*0-89134-770-4*, North Lght Bks) F & W Pubns Inc.
Arnett, Judd. Lessons Learned During a Wasted Youth: Selected Writings by Judd Arnett. 376p. (Orig.). 1995. pap. 17.95 (*0-9625276-1-0*) T P Stewart Pub.
Arnett, Kirk P. & Marshall, Leisa L. Instructor's Manual to Accompany Lawlor, Computer Information Systems. 3rd ed. 308p. (C). 1994. pap. text 95.25 (*0-03-098192-1*) Dryden Pr.
Arnett, Kirk P. & Weir, Ronald L. Computer Information Systems. 3rd ed. 287p. (C). 1994. pap. text, student ed. 30.00 (*0-03-098193-X*) Dryden Pr.
Arnett, Kirk P., et al. Policy Expert: A Supplement for Courses in Business Policy & Strategic Management. 3rd ed. (C). 1992. text 29.56 incl. 5.25 hd (*0-395-63003-7*) HM.
— Policy Expert: A Supplement for Courses in Business Policy & Strategic Management. 3rd ed. (C). 1992. text 29.56 incl. 3.5 hd (*0-395-63004-5*) HM.
***Arnett, Matthew Flint.** Network Management Suites Unraveled: How to Reduce Your Network Management Costs. 2000. pap. 39.95 (*1-55860-660-2*) Morgan Kaufmann.
Arnett, Peter. Arnett: Live from the Battlefield. (Illus.). 400p. 1994. 23.00 (*0-671-75586-2*) S&S Trade.
Arnett, Robert. India Unveiled. LC 96-85065. (Illus.). viii, 215p. 1996. 45.00 (*0-9652900-7-7*) Atman Pr.
— India Unveiled. 2nd rev. ed. LC 98-73037. (Illus.). 224p. 1999. 45.00 (*0-9652900-3-4*) Atman Pr.
Arnett, Ronald C. Dialogic Education: Conversation about Ideas & Between Persons. LC 49-45964. 267p. (C). 1997. pap. 19.95 (*0-8093-2131-9*) S Ill U Pr.
— Dwell in Peace: Applying Nonviolence to Everyday Relationships. LC 79-24639. 156p. 1980. reprint ed. pap. 48.40 (*0-608-02151-2*, 206282000004) Bks Demand.
Arnett, Ronald C. & Arneson, Pat. Dialogic Civility in a Cynical Age: Community, Hope & Interpersonal Relationships. LC 99-26607. (SUNY Series in Communication Studies). 352p. (C). 1999. text 62.50 (*0-7914-4325-6*); pap. text 20.95 (*0-7914-4326-4*) State U NY Pr.
Arnett, Ronald C., jt. auth. see Longenecker, Stephen L.
Arnett, Ronald C., jt. ed. see Makau, Josina M.
***Arnett, Ross H.** American Insects: A Handbook of the Insects of America North of Mexico. 2nd ed. LC 00-22172. (Illus.). 2000. 99.95 (*0-8493-0212-9*) CRC Pr.
Arnett, Ross H. & Jacques, Richard, Jr. Simon & Schuster's Guide to Insects. (Illus.). 1981. per. 15.00 (*0-671-25014-0*) S&S Trade.
Arnett, Ross H., et al. Beetles. 2nd ed. (Pictured Key Nature Ser.). 424p. (C). 1980. text. write for info. (*0-697-04776-8*, WCB McGr Hill) McGrw-H Hghr Educ.
Arnett, Ross H., Jr., et al. The Insect & Spider Collections of the World. 220p. 1986. spiral bd. 75.00 (*90-04-08192-5*) Lubrecht & Cramer.
Arnett, Ross H., Jr., ed. see Jolivet, Pierre.
Arnett, Ross H., Jr., ed. see Mockford, Edward L.
Arnett, T., jt. auth. see Henderson, B.
Arnett, W. D., et al, eds. Cosmogonical Processes: Proceedings of the Symposium Held in Boulder, Colorado, March 1985. 310p. 1986. lib. bdg. 115.00 (*90-6764-054-9*, Pub. by VSP) Coronet Bks.
Arnett, W. David & Truran, James W., eds. Nucleosynthesis: Challenges & New Developments. LC 85-1160. (Illus.). x, 308p. 1985. pap. text 21.00 (*0-226-02788-0*) U Ch Pr.
— Nucleosynthesis: Challenges & New Developments. LC 85-1160. (Illus.). x, 308p. 1995. lib. bdg. 43.50 (*0-226-02787-2*) U Ch Pr.
— Nucleosynthesis: Challenges & New Developments. LC 85-1160. (Illus.). 316p. reprint ed. pap. 98.00 (*0-608-09263-0*, 205406500002) Bks Demand.
Arnett, W. David, ed. see Zeldovich, Ya B. & Novikov, I. D.
Arnett, W. E. Santayana & the Sense of Beauty. 1984. 16.00 (*0-8446-0458-5*) Peter Smith.
Arnett, Willard E. Religion & Judgment: An Essay on the Method & Meaning of Religion. LC 66-11680. (Century Philosophy Ser.). 1966. 52.50 (*0-89197-377-X*) Irvington.
Arnett, Willard E., ed. Modern Reader in the Philosophy of Religion. LC 66-20470. (Century Philosophy Ser.). 1966. 42.50 (*0-89197-482-2*) Irvington.

Arnette, Charles B. History of the East Main Street Church of Christ. (Illus.). 1988. write for info. (*0-318-64362-6*) C B Arnette.

Arnette, Earl, et al. Maryland: A New Guide to the Old Line State. 2nd ed. LC 98-46982. 631p. 1999. pap. 22.50 (*0-8018-5980-8*) Johns Hopkins.

— Maryland: A New Guide to the Old Line State. 2nd ed. LC 98-46982. (Illus.). 631p. 1999. 45.00 (*0-8018-5979-4*) Johns Hopkins.

***Arnette, Joe & Hickox, George.** Training Retrievers & Spaniels to "Hunt 'em Up!" LC 99-88304. 250p. 2000. 24.95 (*0-89272-450-1*, Silver Quill Pr) Down East.

Arnette, Nick. The Encyclopedia of Dude. (Illus.). 64p. (Orig.). 1991. pap. 3.95 (*0-9630130-9-2*, TX 438-457) N Arnette Enter.

Arney, Angela. The Second Wife. (Scarlet Ser.). 1998. mass mkt. 3.99 (*1-85487-998-7*, Pub. by Scarlet Bks) London Brdge.

***Arney, Angela.** The Second Wife. large type ed. 480p. 1999. 31.99 (*0-7505-1403-5*, Pub. by Mgna Lrg Print) Ulverscroft.

— Secrets. large type ed. 480p. 1999. 31.99 (*0-7505-1402-7*, Pub. by Mgna Lrg Print) Ulverscroft.

Arney, David. Exploring Calculus with Derive. 176p. (C). 1991. pap. text 14.00 (*0-201-52839-8*) Addison-Wesley.

Arney, David C. Derive Lab Manual for Differential Equations. (C). 1991. pap. text 22.00 (*0-201-57886-7*) Addison-Wesley.

— Differential Equations with Derive. 284p. (Orig.). (C). 1993. pap. text 22.95 (*0-9623629-3-X*) MathWare.

Arney, David C., ed. Interdisciplinary Lively Application Projects. LC 97-70504. (Classroom Resource Materials Ser.). 206p. (Orig.). (C). 1997. pap. text, suppl. ed. 29.95 (*0-88385-706-5*) Math Assn.

Arney, Shelly, jt. auth. see Keith, Pat.

Arney, William R. Experts in the Age of Systems. LC 90-23501. 254p. 1991. reprint ed. pap. 78.80 (*0-608-07273-7*, 206750100009) Bks Demand.

— Power & the Profession of Obstetrics. LC 82-8410. (Illus.). xii, 304p. (C). 1983. lib. bdg. 30.00 (*0-226-02728-7*) U Ch Pr.

— Power & the Profession of Obstetrics. LC 82-8410. (Illus.). xii, 290p. (C). 1993. pap. text 10.95 (*0-226-02729-5*) U Ch Pr.

Arney, William R. & Bergen, Bernard J. Medicine & the Management of Living: Taming the Last Great Beast. LC 83-24380. (Illus.). x, 216p. 1984. 23.95 (*0-226-02792-9*) U Ch Pr.

Arney, William R., jt. auth. see Finkel, Donald L.

***Arney, William Ray.** Thoughts Out of School. LC 99-53754. (Counterpoints: Vol. 133). 232p. (C). 2000. pap. text 29.95 (*0-8204-4876-1*) P Lang Pubng.

Arnez, Janez A. Gabrovskov Dnevnik: Msgr Gabrovsek's Diary, 1941-1945. (Studia Slovenica Ser.: Vol. 18). (SLV.). 112p. 1997. pap. 8.00 (*0-614-25685-2*) Studia Slovenica.

Arnez, John A. A Slovenian Community in Bridgeport, CT. LC 73-170467. (Studia Slovenica, Special Ser.). 96p. 1971. 7.00 (*0-686-28388-0*) Studia Slovenica.

— Slovenian Lands & Their Economies, 1848-1873. LC 83-116220. (Studia Slovenica Ser.: No. 15). 321p. 1983. pap. 20.00 (*0-938616-16-1*) Studia Slovenica.

Arnez, John A., intro. Slovenian Letters by Missionaries in America, 1851-1874. (Studia Slovenica, Special Ser.: No.4). 230p. 1984. pap. 12.00 (*0-318-01454-8*) Studia Slovenica.

Arnez, Nancy L. Moll Flanders Notes. (Cliffs Notes Ser.). 80p. 1969. pap. 4.95 (*0-8220-0854-8*, Cliff) IDG Bks.

Arnfield, et al. Environmental Science: Global Ecosystems under Stress. 4th ed. 362p. (C). 1998. per. 55.95 (*0-7872-5211-5*, 41521101) Kendall-Hunt.

***Arnfield, Edwin, et al.** Environmental Science: A Field & Laboratory Manual. 248p. (C). 1999. spiral bd. 38.95 (*0-7872-6290-0*, 41629002) Kendall-Hunt.

ARNHA Publication Committee, ed. see Ball, Terri.

Arnhart, Larry. Aristotle on Political Reasoning: A Commentary on the "Rhetoric" LC 81-11330. 230p. 1981. pap. 15.00 (*0-87580-537-X*) N Ill U Pr.

— Darwinian Natural Right: The Biological Ethics of Human Nature. LC 97-49287. (SUNY Series in Philosophy & Biology). 332p. (C). 1998. text 74.50 (*0-7914-3693-4*); pap. text 24.95 (*0-7914-3694-2*) State U NY Pr.

— Political Questions: Political Philosophy from Plato to Rawls. 2nd ed. 406p. (C). 1993. pap. text 21.95 (*0-88133-728-5*) Waveland Pr.

Arnheim. Athletic Training. 8th ed. 1993. 13.75 (*0-697-40347-5*, WCB McGr Hill) McGrw-H Hghr Educ.

— Deportiva Fisioterapia y Entrenamiento Aletico. 2nd ed. (SPA.). 1994. 50.00 (*84-8086-073-1*) Mosby-Doyma Libros.

— Essential Athletic Training. 4th ed. LC 98-35782. 608p. 1998. pap. 48.75 (*0-07-092125-3*) McGraw.

— Essentials of Athletic Training. 3rd ed. 1995. teacher ed. (*0-8151-0396-4*) Mosby Inc.

— Princeton's Athletic Training Lab Manual. 1999. 22.66 (*0-8151-2383-3*) McGraw.

Arnheim, Daniel D. Athletic Training: A Study & Laboratory. 2nd ed. (C). (gr. 13). 2000. text 13.12 (*0-8016-0331-5*, 00331) Mosby Inc.

— Dance Injuries: Their Prevention & Care. 3rd ed. LC 90-53353. (Illus.). 240p. 1991. reprint ed. pap. 19.95 (*0-87127-146-X*, Dance Horizons) Princeton Bk Co.

— Essentials of Athletic Training. 4th ed. 608p. 1998. 57.81 (*0-07-232537-2*) McGraw.

— Principles of Athletic Training. 10th ed. 1999. 10.31 (*0-07-236104-2*) McGraw.

Arnheim, Daniel D. & Prentice, William E. Principles of Athletics Training. 10th ed. LC 99-20214. (Illus.). 864p. 1999. 54.50 (*0-07-109255-2*) McGraw-Hill HPD.

Arnheim, Louise & Webb, Lee, eds. A Health Care Agenda for the States. 150p. 1985. 10.95 (*0-89788-083-8*) CPA Washington.

Arnheim, Michael. British Constitutional Law: A Guide for Practicing Lawyers. 1800p. 1998. text 149.00 (*0-471-96917-6*) Wiley.

— Drafting Settlements of Disputes: A Guide for Litigators. 181p. 1994. pap. 150.00 (*0-85459-756-5*, Pub. by Tolley Pubng) St Mut.

Arnheim, Michael & Campbell, Tom D., eds. Common Law. (International Library of Essays in Law & Legal Theory). 500p. (C). 1994. lib. bdg. 150.00 (*0-8147-0625-8*) NYU Pr.

Arnheim, Rudolf. Art & Visual Perception: A Psychology of the Creative Eye, the New Version. enl. rev. ed. LC 73-87587. 508p. 1997. pap. 22.50 (*0-520-02613-6*, Pub. by U CA Pr) Cal Prin Full Svc.

— Dynamics of Architectural Form. LC 76-19955. (Illus.). 1977. pap. 18.95 (*0-520-03551-8*, Pub. by U CA Pr) Cal Prin Full Svc.

— Entropy & Art: An Essay on Disorder & Order. LC 71-128585. (Illus.). 1971. pap. 14.95 (*0-520-02617-9*, Pub. by U CA Pr) Cal Prin Full Svc.

— Film As Art. LC 57-10496. 1957. pap. 13.95 (*0-520-00035-8*, Pub. by U CA Pr) Cal Prin Full Svc.

— Film Essays & Criticism. Benthien, Brenda, tr. from GER. LC 96-35969. (Wisconsin Studies in Film). 264p. 1997. 54.00 (*0-299-15260-X*); pap. 19.95 (*0-299-15264-2*) U of Wis Pr.

— The Genesis of a Painting: Picasso's Guernica. LC 62-20637. (Illus.). 1980. reprint ed. pap. 22.50 (*0-520-04266-2*, Pub. by U CA Pr) Cal Prin Full Svc.

— Kunst und Sehen: Eine Psychologie des Schopeferischen Auges. 2nd ed. (Illus.). (C). 1978. 55.40 (*3-11-006682-3*) De Gruyter.

— New Essays on the Psychology of Art. (Illus.). 348p. 1986. pap. 18.95 (*0-520-05554-3*, Pub. by U CA Pr) Cal Prin Full Svc.

— Parables of Sun Light: Observations on Psychology, the Arts & the Rest. 379p. 1989. pap. 16.95 (*0-520-06536-0*, Pub. by U CA Pr) Cal Prin Full Svc.

— The Power of the Center: The New Version. (Illus.). 256p. 1988. pap. 17.95 (*0-520-06242-6*, Pub. by U CA Pr) Cal Prin Full Svc.

— Radio. LC 73-161151. (History of Broadcasting: Radio to Television Ser.). (Illus.). 1976. reprint ed. 28.95 (*0-405-03570-5*) Ayer.

— Thoughts on Art Education. LC 89-26831. (Occasional Paper Ser.: Vol. 2). (Illus.). 68p. 1990. pap. 15.00 (*0-89236-163-8*, Pub. by J P Getty Trust) OUP.

— To the Rescue of Art: Twenty-Six Essays. LC 91-9038. (Illus.). 243p. 1992. 55.00 (*0-520-07458-0*, Pub. by U CA Pr); pap. 18.95 (*0-520-07459-9*, Pub. by U CA Pr) Cal Prin Full Svc.

— Toward a Psychology of Art: Collected Essays. LC 66-10692. 1966. pap. 17.95 (*0-520-02161-4*, Pub. by U CA Pr) Cal Prin Full Svc.

— Visual Thinking. LC 71-76335. (Illus.). 345p. 1980. reprint ed. pap. 17.95 (*0-520-01871-0*, Pub. by U CA Pr) Cal Prin Full Svc.

Arnheim, Rudolf, intro. Radio: The Psychology of an Art of Sound. LC 73-164504. (Cinema Ser.). 1972. reprint ed. lib. bdg. 39.50 (*0-306-70291-6*) Da Capo.

Arnheim, Rudolf, et al. Simon Dinnerstein: Paintings & Drawings. LC 99-72755. (Illus.). 126p. 2000. pap. 35.00 (*0-9650485-4-3*, Pub. by Phoenix Intl AR) Hudson Hills.

Arnheim, Rudolph, et al. Julian Stanczak: Color = Form: A Conversation Between Julian Stanczak & Rudolph Arnheim. LC 93-71309. (Illus.). 28p. 1998. pap. 4.00 (*0-9636721-0-X*) Dennos Mus.

Arnholz, Jim, intro. New Mexico on My Mind. LC 90-80038. (America on My Mind Ser.). (Illus.). 120p. 1990. 29.95 (*1-56044-034-1*) Falcon Pub Inc.

Arnich, Julian. Diccionario Maritimo. 4th ed. (SPA.). 472p. 1991. 55.00 (*0-7859-5829-0*, S12232) Fr & Eur.

Arniches, Carlos. Diccionario Ilustrado de la Lengua Espanola. (SPA.). 67p. 1964. 5.95 (*0-8288-7100-0*, S8718) Fr & Eur.

Arnim, Achim V. Isabelle d'Egypte et Autres Recits. (FRE.). 416p. 1983. pap. 18.95 (*0-7859-4506-7*) Fr & Eur.

Arnim, Bettine Von, see Von Arnim, Bettine.

Arnim Grimm, Giseta Von, see Von Arnim, Bettine & Von Arnim Grimm, Giseta.

Arnim, Hans F. Von, see Von Arnim, Hans F.

Arnim, J. Von. Stoicorum Veterum Fragmenta, 4 vols., Set. (Classical Studies). (GRE & LAT.). 1054p. 1986. reprint ed. lib. bdg. 180.00 (*0-89197-950-6*) Irvington.

— Stoicorum Veterum Fragmenta, 4 vols., Vols. 1 & 2. (Classical Studies). (GRE & LAT.). 1054p. 1986. reprint ed. lib. bdg. 88.50 (*0-8290-1775-5*) Irvington.

— Stoicorum Veterum Fragmenta, 4 vols., Vols. 3 & 4. (Classical Studies). (GRE & LAT.). 1054p. 1986. reprint ed. lib. bdg. 88.50 (*0-8290-1776-3*) Irvington.

Arnim, Maximilian. Index Verborum a Philone Byzantio in Mechanicae Syntaxis Libris Quarto Quintoque Adhibitorum. viii, 90p. 1966. reprint ed. 25.00 (*0-318-70869-8*) G Olms Pubs.

Arnison, Christine. Do You Take This... Name? The Brides' Complete Guide to Choosing & Changing Her Name. (Illus.). 96p. (Orig.). 1997. pap. 14.95 (*1-56167-379-X*) Am Literary Pr.

Arnison, Jim. The Million Pound Strike. 86p. 1971. pap. 14.95 (*0-8464-0631-4*) Beekman Pubs.

Arnison, Nancy, et al. Medical Testimony on Victims of Torture: A Physician's Guide to Political Asylum Cases. 46p. 1991. pap. text 7.00 (*1-879707-02-0*) Phy Human Rights.

Arnn, Larry P. A Primer in Political Economy. (Occasional Paper of the Study of Statesmanship & Political Philosophy: No. 1). 18p. (C). 1982. pap. text 2.00 (*0-930783-07-7*) Claremont Inst.

Arnn, Larry P. & Jeffrey, Douglas A., eds. Moral Ideas for America. 149p. (Orig.). (C). pap. text 6.95 (*0-930783-21-2*) Claremont Inst.

Arnn, Larry P., et al. Primer in Soviet Government. (Claremont Paper: No. 10). 58p. (Orig.). 1987. pap. text 3.00 (*0-317-61646-3*) Claremont Inst.

Arno, Iris Hiskey. I Love You, Dad. 1998. 8.70 (*0-606-13507-3*, Pub. by Turtleback) Demco.

— I Love You, Mom. 1998. 8.70 (*0-606-13508-1*, Pub. by Turtleback) Demco.

Arno, Andrew. The World of Talk on a Fijian Island: An Ethnography of Law & Communicative Causation. Dervin, Brenda, ed. LC 92-21909. (Communication & Information Science Ser.). 152p. (C). 1993. pap. 39.50 (*0-89391-961-6*); text 73.25 (*0-89391-866-0*) Ablx Pub.

***Arno, Iris H.** I Like a Snack on an Iceberg. LC 99-71482. (Growing Tree Ser.). (Illus.). 24p. (ps up). 1999. 9.95 (*0-694-01176-2*) HarpC Child Bks.

Arno, Iris H. I Love You, Dad. (Illus.). 32p. (J). (ps-3). 1998. pap. 3.50 (*0-8167-4526-9*) Troll Communs.

— I Love You, Mom. LC 97-152368. (Illus.). 32p. (J). (ps-3). 1998. pap. 3.50 (*0-8167-4440-8*) Troll Communs.

Arno, John. From Cradle to Grave: A Dying Profession. 209p. (Orig.). (C). 1994. pap. 12.95 (*0-9641621-0-5*) Everlasting.

***Arno, Jon.** Trees: An Explore Your World Handbook. LC 00-29449. (Illus.). 192p. 2000. pap. 14.95 (*1-56331-840-7*, Pub. by Discovery) Random.

Arno, Jon. The Woodworkers Visual Handbook: From Standards to Styles, from Tools to Techniques: the Ultimate Guide to Every Phase of Woodworking. LC 99-24914. 1999. write for info. (*0-7621-0224-1*) RD Assn.

Arno, Owen G. Once for the Asking: Manuscript Edition. 1964. pap. 13.00 (*0-8222-0850-4*) Dramatists Play.

— Two Short Plays by Owen G. Arno. 1964. pap. 5.25 (*0-8222-0867-9*) Dramatists Play.

Arno, Paula V., tr. see Champe, Gertrud G., ed.

Arno Press Staff. Judaism & Christianity: Selected Accounts, 1892-1962. LC 73-2212. (Jewish People; History, Religion, Literature Ser.). 1975. 29.95 (*0-405-05276-6*) Ayer.

Arno Press Staff & Silk, Leonard, eds. The Poetry of Industry: Two Literary Reactions to the Industrial Revolution 1755-1757. LC 70-38474. (Evolution of Capitalism Ser.). 1972. reprint ed. 21.95 (*0-405-04131-4*) Ayer.

— Religious Attitudes Toward Usury: Two Early Polemics. LC 79-38471. (Evolution of Capitalism Ser.). 1979. 28.95 (*0-405-04135-7*) Ayer.

Arno, Richard, tr. see Gozo, Yoshimasu.

Arno, Roger. The Story of Space & Rockets. (Illus.). (J). (gr. 5). 1978. pap. 4.95 (*0-88388-063-6*) Bellerophon Bks.

Arno, Sholomo & Borisute, Moshe, trs. The Rishon Transliterated Hagada: The Complete Hebrew Text with English Translation & Transliteration in Linear Format. (Illus.). 116p. (Orig.). 1995. pap. text. write for info. (*1-880880-08-3*) Israeli Trad.

Arno, Stephen F. Discovering Sierra Trees. (Discovering Sierra Ser.). (Illus.). 89p. (Orig.). 1973. pap. 5.00 (*0-939666-04-9*) Yosemite Assn.

— Northwest Trees. LC 77-82369. (Illus.). 238p. 1977. 30.00 (*0-916890-55-4*) Mountaineers.

— Northwest Trees. LC 77-82369. (Illus.). 238p. 1990. pap. 12.95 (*0-916890-50-3*) Mountaineers.

— Timberline: Mountain & Arctic Forest Frontiers. LC 84-14844. (Illus.). 304p. (Orig.). 1984. pap. 16.95 (*0-89886-085-7*) Mountaineers.

Arno, Stephen F., jt. ed. see Hardy, Colin C.

Arnobius. Index Arnobianus. Berkowitz, Luci, ed. xv, 761p. 1967. 160.00 (*0-318-71071-4*) G Olms Pubs.

Arnold. Bruising Apothecary: Images of Pharmacy & Medicine in Health Care. 1989. pap. 22.00 (*0-85369-223-8*, Pub. by Pharmaceutical Pr) Rittenhouse.

***Arnold.** Casebook Introduction for Materials Management. 144p. 2000. pap. 26.67 (*0-13-973223-3*) P-H.

Arnold. Cats & Yammerings. 1994. pap. 12.50 (*0-940168-35-9*) Boxwood.

— Earth. 2nd ed. (C). 1989. write for info. (*0-7167-2017-5*) W H Freeman.

***Arnold.** Economic & Pop Culture-Economics in Our Times. 2nd ed. 2000. pap. 10.95 (*0-538-43091-5*) Sth-Wstrn College.

— Economic Connections in History: Economics in Our Times. 2nd ed. 2000. pap. write for info. (*0-538-43089-3*) Sth-Wstrn College.

Arnold. Economic Graph Exercises. 1996. mass mkt. write for info. (*0-314-08819-9*) West Pub.

***Arnold.** Economic Math Review Practice: Economics in Our Times. 2nd ed. 2000. pap. 10.95 (*0-538-43090-7*) Sth-Wstrn College.

Arnold. Economics. 3rd ed. (SWC-Economics Ser.). Date not set. 57.40 (*0-314-09268-4*) Sth-Wstrn College.

— Economics. 3rd ed. Date not set. pap. text, teacher ed. write for info. (*0-314-09035-5*); pap. text, teacher ed. write for info. (*0-314-09034-7*) West Pub.

— Economics: Graphing Exercise. 3rd ed. 1996. pap. 6.00 (*0-314-09002-9*) West Pub.

— Economics in Our Times. rev. ed. (Principles of Economics Ser.). 1998. pap. 55.00 (*0-538-42619-5*) S-W Pub.

***Arnold.** Economics in Our Times. 2nd ed. 2000. pap. 10.95 (*0-538-43084-2*); pap. 10.95 (*0-538-43085-0*); pap. 10.95 (*0-538-43087-7*) Sth-Wstrn College.

— Economics in Our Times. 2nd ed. 2002. pap. 62.75 (*0-538-43101-6*) Sth-Wstrn College.

— Economics in Our Times: Texas Teacher's Resources. 2nd ed. 2002. pap. 53.00 (*0-538-43083-4*) Sth-Wstrn College.

— Economics in Our Times Casebook. 2nd ed. 2000. pap. 10.95 (*0-538-43086-9*) Sth-Wstrn College.

Arnold. Economics on the Internet: Exercises & Activities. 3rd ed. 1996. pap. 9.50 (*0-314-20142-4*) Thomson Learn.

***Arnold.** Graphing Exercises in Economics. 5th ed. (SWC-General Business Ser.). 2000. pap. 16.75 (*0-324-05799-7*) Sth-Wstrn College.

Arnold. A Guide Dog Puppy Grows Up. (J). 1997. pap. 7.00 (*0-15-201557-4*, Harcourt Child Bks) Harcourt.

— How to Think Like an Economist. 5th ed. 2000. pap. 850.00 (*0-324-01575-5*) Thomson Learn.

— Jazz Saxophone Scale & Chord Improvisation. 1990. 6.95 (*0-685-32221-1*, K789) Hansen Ed Mus.

— Macroeconomics. 3rd ed. 1996. pap., student ed. 17.75 (*0-314-08937-3*) West Pub.

Arnold. Math for Computer Science. 2nd ed. 350p. 1996. pap. 61.00 (*0-13-234717-2*) P-H.

Arnold. Media Writer. 1995. teacher ed., wbk. ed. 13.43 (*0-697-29406-4*, WCB McGr Hill) McGrw-H Hghr Educ.

— Miniature Harmonica. (Illus.). 1995. pap. 14.95 (*0-940168-30-8*) Boxwood.

***Arnold.** Monteverdi. 256p. 2000. pap. 17.95 (*0-19-816465-3*) OUP.

— Primary Sources in Economics: Economics in Our Times. 2nd ed. 2000. pap. 11.95 (*0-538-43088-5*) Sth-Wstrn College.

Arnold. Resource Center Update 1997: Economics in Out Times. (Principles of Economics Ser.). 1998. mass mkt. 9.95 (*0-538-42340-4*) S-W Pub.

— Student's Guide to Basic French. 2nd ed. 1980. pap. text 23.28 (*0-88334-021-6*, 76043) Longman.

— Teachers' Teaming Handbook. LC 97-68444. (C). 1997. pap. text 35.50 (*0-15-503072-8*, Pub. by Harcourt Coll Pubs) Harcourt.

— Very First Flute Duets. 1990. 6.95 (*0-685-32135-5*, H606) Hansen Ed Mus.

— Very First Flute Method. 1990. 6.95 (*0-685-32136-3*, H607) Hansen Ed Mus.

— Visual Test 6 Bible. LC QA76.76.T48A764 1999. (Illus.). 720p. 1998. pap. 49.99 (*0-7645-3255-3*) IDG Bks.

***Arnold.** Web Tutor on Webct to Microeconomics. 5th ed. 2000. pap. 19.00 (*0-324-06575-2*) Sth-Wstrn College.

Arnold. Year of Full Moons. 2000. text 23.95 (*0-312-19965-1*) St Martin.

Arnold, et al, eds. Singularities of Differentiable Maps. (Monographs in Mathematics: No. 83, Vol. II). 400p. 1988. 120.50 (*0-8176-3185-2*) Birkhauser.

Arnold & Scott. Starting Points. Date not set. pap. text. write for info. (*0-582-55483-7*, Pub. by Addison-Wesley) Longman.

Arnold, et al. Singularities of Differentiable Maps, Vol. 1. (Monographs in Mathematics). 1985. 86.50 (*0-8176-3187-9*) Birkhauser.

Arnold, jt. auth. see Pearce.

Arnold, Jane. Affect in Language Learning. LC 98-30812. (Cambridge Language Teaching Library). (Illus.). 360p. 1999. 69.95 (*0-521-65041-0*) Cambridge U Pr.

— Affect in Language Learning. LC 98-30812. (Cambridge Language Teaching Library). (Illus.). 360p. (C). 1999. pap. 26.95 (*0-521-65963-9*) Cambridge U Pr.

Arnold, A. Let There Be a Forest. 95p. 1986. pap. 125.00 (*81-7089-097-7*, Pub. by Intl Bk Distr) St Mut.

— Pearls of the Faith. 1996. pap. 4.00 (*0-933511-97-3*) Kazi Pubns.

Arnold, A., et al, eds. CAAP '90: Fifteenth Colloquium on Trees in Algebra & Programming Copenhagen, Denmark, May 15-18, 1990 Proceedings. (Lecture Notes in Computer Science Ser.: Vol. 431). vi, 285p. 1990. 32.70 (*0-387-52590-4*) Spr-Verlag.

Arnold, A., et al. Construction & Analysis of Transition Systems with MEC. 200p. 1994. text 48.00 (*981-02-1922-9*) World Scientific Pub.

Arnold, A. J. Paul Valery & His Critics. LC 72-12808. (Studies in French Literature: No. 45). 1972. reprint ed. lib. bdg. 75.00 (*0-8383-1590-9*) M S G Haskell Hse.

Arnold, A. J., ed. see Depestre, Rene.

Arnold, A. J., ed. see Glissant, Edouard.

Arnold, A. J., ed. see Oyono-Mbia, Guillaume, et al.

Arnold, A. James. Modernism & Negritude: The Poetry & Poetics of Aime Cesaire. LC 80-29007. 329p. (C). 1981. 39.95 (*0-674-58057-5*) HUP.

Arnold, A. James, ed. A History of Literature in the Caribbean Vol. 3: Cross-Cultural Studies. (Comparative History of Literature in European Languages Ser.: No. 12). xviii, 381p. 1997. lib. bdg. 120.00 (*1-55619-603-2*) J Benjamins Pubng Co.

— Monsters, Tricksters & Sacred Cows: Animal Tales & American Identities. (New World Studies). 1996. pap. text 18.50 (*0-8139-1646-1*) U Pr of Va.

— Monsters, Tricksters & Sacred Cows: Animal Tales & American Identities. (New World Studies). 291p. (C). 1996. text 45.00 (*0-8139-1645-3*) U Pr of Va.

Arnold, A. James, et al, eds. A History of Literature in the Caribbean Vol. 1: Hispanic & Francophone Regions. LC 94-3353. (Comparative History of Literatures in European Languages Ser.: No. 10). xviii, 579p. 1994. lib. bdg. 150.00 (*1-55619-601-6*) J Benjamins Pubng Co.

Arnold, A. James, ed. see Fantoure, Alioum.

Arnold, A. James, ed. see Juminer, Bertene.

Arnold, A. P., ed. Hormones & Neural Development. (Journal Ser.: Vol. 18, No. 1-2, 1996). (Illus.). 138p. 1996. pap. 78.25 (*3-8055-6340-X*) S Karger.

Arnold, Adolf W. A Boy Without Toys. LC 99-70095. (Illus.). 240p. 2000. pap. 24.95 (*1-57197-157-2*) Pentland Pr.

Arnold, Alan. The AS/400 as a Business Solution. 1998. pap. 59.00 (*0-9663375-1-4*) AS-Four Hundr Pr.

— Developing Your AS/400 Internet Strategy: A Guide to

A

Business Solutions Created Through This Powerful Partnership. LC 96-45827. 248p. 1997. pap. 45.00 (*1-882419-54-5*) News Four-Hund.

Arnold, Alan, et al. Mastering AS/400 Performance. LC 96-25347. 259p. (Orig.). 1996. pap. 45.00 (*1-882419-49-9*) News Four-Hund.

Arnold, Alan, ed. see Zeitler, Bill, et al.

Arnold, Albert G. Work Motivation & Change in Eastern Europe LC 99-184277. (WTM Ser.). 76p. 1998. write for info. (*90-407-1773-7*) Coronet Bks.

Arnold, Alison, ed. South Asia: The Indian Subcontinent. (Encyclopedia of World Music Ser.: Vol. 5). (Illus.). 1004p. 1999. 195.00 (*0-8240-4946-2*, H1191) Garland.

Arnold, Alvin L. The Arnold Encyclopedia of Real Estate. 2nd ed. LC 93-20335. 610p. 1993. 245.95 (*0-471-58102-X*) Wiley.

— Real Estate Investor's Deskbook. annuals 2nd rev. ed. LC 87-50237. 825p. (C). 1987. suppl. ed. 145.00 (*0-88712-825-4*) Warren Gorham & Lamont.

— Real Estate Syndication Manual: Investment, Tax & Marketing Strategies. 580p. (C). 1992. 135.00 (*0-88712-176-4*) Warren Gorham & Lamont.

Arnold, Alvin L. & Kove, Myron. Real Estate Professionals Tax Guide. 500p. 1996. 140.00 (*0-7913-2647-0*) Warren Gorham & Lamont.

Arnold, Alvin L., et al. Modern Real Estate & Mortgage Forms Checklists. annuals 712p. 1979. ring bd., suppl. ed. 130.00 (*0-88262-280-3*) Warren Gorham & Lamont.

Arnold, Andrea. Fear of Food: Environmentalist Scams, Media Mendacity, & the Law of Disparagement. Gottlieb, Alan, ed. LC 90-3495. 184p. (Orig.). 1990. pap. 9.95 (*0-939571-08-0*) Free Enter Pr.

Arnold, Andrew. Endocrine Neoplasms. LC 96-49030. (Cancer Treatment & Research Ser.). 786p. 1997. text 412.50 (*0-7923-4354-9*) Kluwer Academic.

***Arnold, Angela.** Inner Scripts: Hidden Patterns & Secret Reasons Why We Act the Way We Do. 396p. 1998. pap. 22.50 (*0-9525539-7-X*, Pub. by Waterweaver Pr) Trans-Atl Phila.

— A Psychological Zodiac: The Roots of Self & Society. 384p. 1995. pap. 22.50 (*0-9525539-3-7*, Pub. by Waterweaver Pr) Trans-Atl Phila.

Arnold, Ann. Gamblers & Gangsters: Fort Worth's Jacksboro Highway in the 40s & 50s. LC 98-28262. (Illus.). 208p. 1998. pap. 18.95 (*1-57168-250-3*, Eakin Pr) Sunbelt Media.

Arnold, Anthony. Afghanistan's Two-Party Communism: Parcham & Khalq. (Publication Ser.: No. 279). 242p. 1983. pap. 4.38 (*0-8179-7792-9*) Hoover Inst Pr.

— The Fateful Pebble: Afghanistan's Role in the Fall of the Soviet Empire. 225p. 1998. text 30.00 (*0-7881-5836-8*) DIANE Pub.

— Rhythm & Touch: An Introduction to Craniosacral Therapy. LC 95-22042. (Illus.). 156p. (Orig.). 1995. pap. 15.95 (*0-914732-35-8*) Bro Life Inc.

— Suisun Marsh History: Hunting & Saving a Wetland. (Illus.). 258p. 1996. 39.95 (*1-880710-40-4*); pap. 23.35 (*1-880710-04-8*) Monterey Pacific.

Arnold, Arlene. Colorcards: A Guide to Your Inner Knowing. 60p. 1995. ring bd. 20.00 (*0-9649990-0-5*) Transform WA.

***Arnold, Arlene.** ColorCards: Inner Guidance Made Simple Through the Vibration of Color. 2nd rev. enl. ed. 7p. 2000. pap. 29.95 (*0-9649990-1-3*) Transform WA.

Arnold, Armin. Casar Von Arx: Briefe an den Vater. (GER.). 182p. 1982. 12.00 (*3-261-05000-4*) P Lang Pubng.

Arnold, Armin, ed. see Arnold-Schuster, Ingrid.

Arnold, Arnold. Antique Paper Dolls, 1915-1920, Vol. 181. (J). 1975. pap. 4.95 (*0-486-23176-3*) Dover.

— Pictures & Stories from Forgotten Children's Books. (Illus.). 170p. (Orig.). (J). (gr. k-6). 1969. pap. 11.95 (*0-486-22041-9*) Dover.

Arnold, Arthur J. Victory at Plattsburg: The British Invasion of New York - 1814. 216p. 2000. pap. write for info. (*0-925168-74-2*) North Country.

Arnold, B., et al. Conditionally Specification of Statistical Models. LC 99-30378. (Statistics Ser.). 432p. 1999. 74.95 (*0-387-98761-4*) Spr-Verlag.

Arnold, B. E. Conflict Across the Strait: A Battery Commander's Story of Kent's Defences 1939-1945. 174p. 1984. 39.00 (*0-906124-06-9*, Pub. by Regency Pr GBR) St Mut.

Arnold-Baker, Charles. Companion to British History. 1408p. (C). 1998. 150.00 (*0-415-18582-3*) Routledge.

— Local Council Administration. 4th ed. 1994. write for info. (*0-406-04821-5*, U.K., MICHIE) LEXIS Pub.

Arnold, Barbara J. & Welch, Maureen. The Job of Finding a Job: An Employment Guide for Librarians & Information Specialists. 31p. 1993. pap. 11.50 (*0-936442-19-0*) U Wis Sch Lib.

Arnold, Barbara J., ed. see Conference on Periodical Publishing in Wisconsin,, et al.

Arnold, Barry. Records: Probability & Statistics. (Wiley Ser. in Probability & Statistics). 312p. 1998. 89.95 (*0-471-08108-6*) Wiley.

Arnold, Barry, ed. see Sellers, James.

Arnold, Barry C. Majorization & the Lorenz Order: Brief Introduction. (Lecture Notes in Statistics Ser.: Vol. 43). vi, 122p. 1987. 42.95 (*0-387-96592-0*) Spr-Verlag.

Arnold, Barry C. & Balakrishnan, N. Relations, Bounds & Approximations for Order Statistics. (Lecture Notes in Statistics Ser.: Vol. 53). ix, 173p. 1989. 39.95 (*0-387-96975-6*) Spr-Verlag.

Arnold, Barry C., et al. Conditionally Specified Distributions. Berger, J. O. et al, eds. (Lecture Notes in Statistics Ser.: Vol. 73). 160p. 1992. 48.95 (*0-387-97794-5*) Spr-Verlag.

— A First Course in Order Statistics. (Probability & Mathematical Statistics Ser.). 304p. 1992. 109.95 (*0-471-57416-3*) Wiley.

Arnold, Ben. Music & War: A Research & Information Guide. LC 93-24938. (Music Research & Information Guides Ser.: Vol. 17). (Illus.). 464p. 1993. text 20.00 (*0-8153-0826-4*, H1581) Garland.

***Arnold, Ben, et al.** The Exploits of Ben Arnold: Indian Fighter, Gold Miner, Cowboy, Hunter & Army Scout. LC 99-27498. (Western Frontier Library). 336p. 1999. 22.95 (*0-8061-3105-5*) U of Okla Pr.

Arnold, Benjamin. Count & Bishop in Medieval Germany: A Study of Regional Power, 1100-1350. LC 91-24938. (Middle Ages Ser.). (Illus.). 232p. (C). 1992. text 39.95 (*0-8122-3084-1*) U of Pa Pr.

— Count & Bishop in Medieval Germany: A Study of Regional Power, 1100-1350. LC 91-24938. (Middle Ages Ser.). 230p. reprint ed. pap. 71.30 (*0-608-07303-2*, 206753100009) Bks Demand.

— Medieval Germany, 500-1300: A Political Interpretation. LC 97-184168. 224p. 1997. pap. text 19.95 (*0-8020-8053-7*) U of Toronto Pr.

— Medieval Germany, 500-1300: A Political Interpretation. LC 97-184168. 247p. 1997. text 55.00 (*0-8020-4191-4*, DD114) U of Toronto Pr.

Arnold, Benjamin W. History of the Tobacco Industry in Virginia from 1860 to 1894. LC 78-63855. (Johns Hopkins University. Studies in the Social Sciences. Thirtieth Ser. 1912: 1-2). reprint ed. 27.50 (*0-404-61111-7*) AMS Pr.

***Arnold, Bess.** Union Pacific: Crossing Sherman Hill & Other Railroad Stories. (Illus.). 80p. 1999. pap. 19.95 (*0-942035-51-8*) South Platte.

Arnold, Bess. Wyoming - Along the Union Pacific Corridor. Acton, Avis, ed. LC 96-205974. (Illus.). 69p. 1996. pap. 7.95 (*0-9627412-1-3*) ABC Pub.

Arnold, Beth E., jt. auth. see Malinowski, Michael J.

Arnold, Betty J. Poisonous Plants. LC 77-9240. 141p. 1978. pap. 10.00 (*0-9670441-0-3*) Terra.

Arnold, Beverly J., jt. auth. see Keppie, Lawrence J.

Arnold, Bill. Emily Dickinson's Secret Love: Mystery "Master" Behind Poems, Vol. 1. LC 98-66885. (Illus.). 230p. 1998. pap. 19.95 (*1-892582-00-7*) PPB Pr.

Arnold, Bill T. Encountering the Book of Genesis. (Encountering Biblical Studies Ser.). (Illus.). 240p. (C). (gr. 13). 1998. 24.99 (*0-8010-2177-4*) Baker Bks.

Arnold, Bill T. & Beyer, Bryon E. Encountering the Old Testament: A Christian Survey. Elwell, Walter A., ed. LC 98-18612. (Encountering Biblical Studies). (Illus.). 512p. (C). 1997. 49.99 (*0-8010-2176-6*) Baker Bks.

Arnold, Bill T., jt. ed. see Baker, David W.

Arnold, Bion J. Report on the Improvement & Development of the Transportation Facilities of San Francisco. LC 73-11900. (Metropolitan America Ser.). (Illus.). 510p. 1974. reprint ed. 46.95 (*0-405-05383-5*) Ayer.

Arnold-Biucchi, Carmen. The Randazzo Hoard 1980 & Sicilian Chronology in the Early Fifth Century B. C. LC 92-193886. (Numismatic Studies: Vol. 18). 100p. 1990. reprint ed. pap. 31.00 (*0-608-03364-2*, 206407600008) Bks Demand.

— Randazzo Hoard Nineteen Eighty & Sicilian Chronology in the Early Fifth Century B.C. (ANSNS Ser.: No. 18). (Illus.). 77p. 1989. 50.00 (*0-89722-227-X*) Am Numismatic.

Arnold, Bob. American Train Letters. rev. ed. Koller, James, ed. LC 94-32001. 256p. (Orig.). 1995. pap. 10.00 (*0-940556-08-1*) Coyote.

— Beautiful Swimmers: A Tale. 68p. 1998. pap. 8.00 (*0-9620575-3-3*) Origin Pr.

— By Heart: Pages from a Lost Vermont. Corman, Cid, ed. LC 90-45956. 96p. (Orig.). 1991. pap. 8.00 (*0-9620575-1-7*) Origin Pr.

— Country/City: A Year at the River. LC 98-65542. (Illus.). 288p. 1998. 31.95 (*0-9663489-0-7*); pap. 19.95 (*0-9663489-1-5*) Kingfisher Pr.

— Engine Trouble. 32p. 1998. pap. 7.50 (*0-9620575-6-8*) Origin Pr.

— On Stone: A Builder's Notebook. Corman, Cid, ed. (Illus.). 96p. (Orig.). 1988. pap. text 15.00 (*0-9620575-0-9*) Origin Pr.

***Arnold, Bob.** Once in Vermont. LC 99-73467. 128p. 1999. pap. 13.50 (*0-917788-74-5*, Pub. by Gnomon Pr) SPD-Small Pr Dist.

Arnold, Bob. Steelhead & the Floating Line. LC 96-136102. (Illus.). 181p. 1995. pap. 15.95 (*1-57188-040-2*) F Amato Pubns.

— Steelhead Water. 300p. 1993. 24.95 (*1-878175-60-2*) F Amato Pubns.

— This Romance, a Further Notebook on Rural Life, Building, Love & a Son. Corman, Cid, ed. LC 91-46046. 112p. (Orig.). 1992. pap. 8.00 (*0-9620575-2-5*) Origin Pr.

Arnold, Brian J. & McIntyre, Michael J. International Tax Primer. 150p. 1995. pap. 30.00 (*90-411-0959-5*) Kluwer Law Intl.

Arnold, Bruce. Chord Workbook for Guitar: Chords & Chord Progressions, Vol. 1. 2nd ed. (Illus.). 165p. 1996. pap. 31.50 (*0-9648632-1-9*) Muse Eek.

— Chord Workbook for Guitar: Chords & Chord Progressions, Vol. 2. 2nd ed. (Illus.). 175p. (C). 1997. pap. text 31.50 (*0-9648632-3-5*) Muse Eek.

— Comping Styles: Funk Bass. 120p. (C). 1999. pap. text 31.50 (*1-890944-08-4*) Muse Eek.

— Comping Styles: Funk Guitar. 60p. (C). 1999. pap. text 25.00 (*1-890944-07-6*) Muse Eek.

— Concise History of Irish Art. rev. ed. 1985. 19.95 (*0-500-18090-3*, Pub. by Thames Hudson) Norton.

***Arnold, Bruce.** Contemporary Rhythms. 120p. (C). 1999. pap. 31.50 (*1-890944-27-0*) Muse Eek.

Arnold, Bruce. How the GATT Affects the U. S. Antidumping & Countervailing-Duty Policy. (Illus.). 85p. (Orig.). (C). 1994. pap. text 35.00 (*0-7881-1288-0*) DIANE Pub.

— Independence, Vol. 1. 51p. 1997. pap. text 20.00 (*1-890944-00-9*) Muse Eek.

— Irish Art. LC 89-51262. (World of Art Ser.). 1989. pap. 14.95 (*0-500-20148-X*, Pub. by Thames Hudson) Norton.

— Jack Yeats. LC 98-19116. (Illus.). 416p. 1998. 45.00 (*0-300-07549-9*) Yale U Pr.

— Mainie Jellett & the Modern Movement in Ireland. (Illus.). 244p. (C). 1992. 70.00 (*0-300-05463-7*) Yale U Pr.

— Music Theory Workbook for Guitar: Intervals & Chords, Vol. 1: Intervals & Chords. (Illus.). 194p. 1997. pap. 31.50 (*0-9648632-4-3*) Muse Eek.

— Music Theory Workbook for Guitar Vol. 2: Scale Construction & Application. (Illus.). 215p. 1999. pap., wbk. ed. 31.50 (*0-9648632-5-1*) Muse Eek.

— Odd Meters: Music Sight Reading Exercises, Vol. 1. (Illus.). 150p. 1997. pap. 31.50 (*0-9648632-9-4*) Muse Eek.

— Rhythm Primer: Music Sight Reading Exercises. 61p. (C). 1998. pap. text 20.00 (*1-890944-03-3*) Muse Eek.

— Rhythms: Music Sight Reading Exercises, Vol. 1. (Illus.). 150p. 1997. pap. 31.50 (*0-9648632-7-8*) Muse Eek.

— Rhythms: Music Sight Reading Exercises, Vol. 2. (Illus.). 150p. 1997. pap. 31.50 (*0-9648632-8-6*) Muse Eek.

— Rhythms Vol. 3: Music Sight Reading Exercises, Vol. 3. 102p. (C). 1998. pap. text 31.25 (*1-890944-04-1*) Muse Eek.

— Right Hand Technique for Guitar. (Illus.). 175p. (Orig.). 1997. pap. 31.50 (*0-9648632-6-X*) Muse Eek.

— Single String Studies: Bass Clef, Vol. 1. 65p. (C). 1997. pap. text 20.00 (*1-890944-02-5*) Muse Eek.

— Single String Studies: Bass Clef, Vol. 2. 65p. (C). 1998. pap. text 20.00 (*1-890944-06-8*) Muse Eek.

— Single String Studies: Mastering the Guitar Fretboard, Vol. 1. 91p. (C). 1997. pap. text 20.00 (*1-890944-01-7*) Muse Eek.

— Single String Studies Vol. 2: Mastering the Guitar Fretboard, Vol. 2. 91p. (C). 1998. pap. text 20.00 (*1-890944-05-X*) Muse Eek.

***Arnold, Bruce.** Swift: An Illustrated Life. LC 99-490272. (Illus.). 2000. pap. 16.95 (*1-901866-39-4*, Pub. by Lilliput Pr) Irish Bks Media.

Arnold, Bruce, jt. auth. see Steward, James Christen.

***Arnold, Bruce E.** A Big Metronome. 118p. (C). 1999. pap. 45.00 incl. audio (*1-890944-37-8*) Muse Eek.

— Doing Time with the Blues. 40p. (C). 1999. pap. 20.00 incl. audio (*1-890944-17-3*) Muse Eek.

— Doing Time with the Blues, Vol. 2. 40p. (C). 1999. pap. 20.00 incl. audio (*1-890944-18-1*) Muse Eek.

— Doing Time with 32 Bars. 39p. (C). 1999. pap. 20.00 incl. audio (*1-890944-22-X*) Muse Eek.

Arnold, Bruce E. Ear Training: One Note Advanced Level. 6p. 1999. pap. text 20.00 (*1-890944-14-9*) Muse Eek.

— Ear Training: One Note Beginning Level. 6p. 1999. pap. text 20.00 (*1-890944-12-2*) Muse Eek.

— Ear Training: One Note Intermediate Level. 6p. 1999. pap. text 20.00 (*1-890944-13-0*) Muse Eek.

***Arnold, Bruce E.** A Fanatic's Guide to Ear Training & Sight Singing. 58p. (C). 1999. pap. 31.50 incl. audio (*1-890944-19-X*) Muse Eek.

— Key Note Recognition. 7p. (C). 1999. pap. 20.00 incl. audio (*1-890944-30-0*) Muse Eek.

Arnold, Bruce E. Lines: Sight Reading & Sight Singing Exercises. 120p. 1999. pap. text 31.50 (*1-890944-09-2*) Muse Eek.

Arnold, Bryan. Towards the Sun: A Poetic Journey. (Illus.). 121p. (Orig.). 1989. 20.00 (*0-9622511-0-0*); pap. 15.00 (*0-9622511-1-9*) Asgard Pub.

Arnold, C. D. The Dinosaur Plays. LC 83-8446. (Gay Play Script Ser.). (Illus.). 73p. 1984. pap. 6.95 (*0-935672-09-5*) T n T Class.

Arnold, C. J. The Archaeology of the Early Anglo-Saxon Kingdoms. 224p. (C). 1988. lib. bdg. 59.95 (*0-415-00349-0*, A2385) Routledge.

— An Archaeology of the Early Anglo-Saxon Kingdoms. 224p. 1989. 17.95 (*0-415-03248-2*, A3235) Routledge.

— An Archaeology of the Early Anglo-Saxon Kingdoms. 2nd ed. LC 96-28369. (Illus.). 280p. (C). 1997. 85.00 (*0-415-15635-1*); pap. 29.99 (*0-415-15636-X*) Routledge.

Arnold, C. P., jt. auth. see Arrillaga, J.

Arnold, Carolina. Children of the Settlement Houses. LC 97-43555. (Picture the American Past Ser.). (Illus.). 48p. (J). (gr. 3-6). 1998. 22.60 (*1-57505-242-3*, Carolrhoda) Lerner Pub.

Arnold, Caroline. African Animals. LC 96-16964. (Illus.). 48p. (J). 1997. 16.95 (*0-688-14115-3*, Wm Morrow); lib. bdg. 15.93 (*0-688-14116-1*, Wm Morrow) Morrow Avon.

— The Ancient Cliff Dwellers of Mesa Verde. (Illus.). 64p. (J). (gr. 3-6). 1992. 16.00 (*0-395-56241-4*, Clarion Bks) HM.

***Arnold, Caroline.** Ancient Cliff Dwellers of Mesa Verde. (Illus.). 64p. (gr. 4-7). 2000. pap. 6.95 (*0-618-05149-X*, Clarion Bks) HM.

— Australian Animals. LC 99-52378. 48p. (J). 2000. 15.89 (*0-688-16767-5*) Morrow Avon.

— Australian Animals. LC 99-52378. (Illus.). 48p. (J). (gr. k-3). 2000. 15.95 (*0-688-16766-7*) Morrow Avon.

— Baby Whale Rescue: The True Story of J. J. (Illus.). (J). 1999. 11.40 (*0-606-18663-8*) Turtleback.

Arnold, Caroline. Bat. LC 95-35228. (Illus.). 48p. (J). 1996. 16.00 (*0-688-13726-1*, Wm Morrow) Morrow Avon.

Arnold, Caroline. Bat. LC 95-35228. (Illus.). 48p. (J). 1996. 15.89 (*0-688-13727-X*, Wm Morrow) Morrow Avon.

Arnold, Caroline. Bobcats. LC 96-35084. (Early Bird Nature Bks.). (Illus.). (J). 1997. lib. bdg. 19.93 (*0-8225-3021-X*, Lerner Publctns) Lerner Pub.

— Cats. LC 98-38206. (Early Bird Nature Bks.). (Illus.). 48p. (J). (gr. 2-3). 1999. 22.60 (*0-8225-3032-5*, Lerner Publctns) Lerner Pub.

— Cats: In from the Wild. LC 92-32986. (Illus.). (J). (gr. 4-6). 1993. lib. bdg. 19.95 (*0-87614-692-2*, Carolrhoda) Lerner Pub.

— Cats: In from the Wild. (Illus.). 48p. (J). 1995. pap. 7.95 (*0-87614-962-X*) Lerner Pub.

Arnold, Caroline. City of the Gods: Mexico's Ancient City of Teotihuacan. (Illus.). 48p. 1994. 14.95 (*0-395-66584-1*, Clarion Bks) HM.

Arnold, Caroline. Coping with Natural Disasters. (J). (gr. 5 up). 1988. 13.95 (*0-8027-6716-8*); lib. bdg. 14.85 (*0-8027-6717-6*) Walker & Co.

***Arnold, Caroline.** Did You Hear That? Animals with Super Hearing. LC 00-38369. (Illus.). 2001. pap. write for info. (*1-57091-405-2*) Charlesbridge Pub.

Arnold, Caroline. Dinosaur Mountain. LC 88-30218. 48p. (J). (ps-3). 1990. 15.95 (*0-89919-693-4*, Pub. by Ticknor & Fields) HM.

— Dinosaurs All Around: An Artist's View of the Prehistoric World. LC 92-5726. (Illus.). 48p. (J). (gr. 3-6). 1993. 14.95 (*0-395-62363-4*, Clarion Bks) HM.

— Dinosaurs All Around: An Artist's View of the Prehistoric World. (Illus.). 48p. (J). (gr. 3-6). 1997. pap. 6.95 (*0-395-86620-0*, Clarion Bks) HM.

Arnold, Caroline. Dinosaurs Down Under: And Other Fossils from Australia. LC 89-32783. 1990. 12.15 (*0-606-06325-0*, Pub. by Turtleback) Demco.

Arnold, Caroline. Dinosaurs down Under: And Other Fossils from Australia. 48p. (J). (gr. 4-7). 1994. pap. 6.95 (*0-395-69119-2*, Clarion Bks) HM.

— Fireflies. LC 93-30439. (Illus.). 32p. (J). (gr. 1-4). 1994. pap. 3.95 (*0-590-46944-4*) Scholastic Inc.

— Fox. (Illus.). (J). 1996. write for info. (*0-614-08107-6*, Wm Morrow); write for info. (*0-614-08108-4*, Wm Morrow); 16.00 (*0-688-13728-8*, Wm Morrow); lib. bdg. 15.93 (*0-688-13729-6*, Wm Morrow) Morrow Avon.

— A Guide Dog Puppy Grows Up. LC 90-5154. (Illus.). 48p. (J). (gr. 1 up). 1991. 16.95 (*0-15-232657-X*) Harcourt.

— Hawk Highway in the Sky: Watching Raptor Migration. LC 95-51213. (Illus.). 48p. (J). 1997. 18.00 (*0-15-200868-3*) Harcourt.

— Heart Disease. LC 90-33609. (Venture Bks.). (Illus.). 112p. (YA). (gr. 7-12). 1990. lib. bdg. 22.50 (*0-531-10884-8*) Watts.

— House Sparrows Everywhere. (Nature Watch Bks.). (Illus.). 48p. (J). (gr. 2-5). 1992. lib. bdg. 19.95 (*0-87614-696-5*, Carolrhoda) Lerner Pub.

— Killer Whale. LC 93-33668. (Illus.). 48p. (J). (gr. 2 up). 1994. 17.00 (*0-688-12029-6*, Wm Morrow) Morrow Avon.

Arnold, Caroline. Killer Whale. LC 93-33668. (Illus.). 48p. (J). (gr. 2 up). 1994. 14.93 (*0-688-12030-X*, Wm Morrow) Morrow Avon.

Arnold, Caroline. Koala. 1992. 10.90 (*0-606-01342-3*, Pub. by Turtleback) Demco.

— Lion. LC 94-23880. (More Animal Favorites ser.). (Illus.). 48p. (J). (gr. 2 up). 1995. lib. bdg. 15.93 (*0-688-12693-6*, Wm Morrow) Morrow Avon.

— Mealtime for Zoo Animals. LC 97-43099. (Illus.). 32p. (J). (gr. k-2). 1999. 21.27 (*1-57505-286-5*, Carolrhoda) Lerner Pub.

— Mealtime for Zoo Animals. LC 97-43099. 32p. (J). (gr. k-2). 1999. 9.95 (*1-57505-389-6*, Carolrhoda) Lerner Pub.

***Arnold, Caroline.** Megalodon: Giant Shark of the Prehistoric World. LC 99-86991. (Illus.). 32p. (J). (gr. 4-7). 2000. 15.00 (*0-395-91419-1*, Clarion Bks) HM.

Arnold, Caroline. Mother & Baby Zoo Animals. LC 98-15749. (Zoo Animals Ser.). (Illus.). 32p. (J). (gr. k-2). 1999. 21.27 (*1-57505-285-7*, Carolrhoda) Lerner Pub.

***Arnold, Caroline.** Mother & Baby Zoo Animals. LC 98-15749. (Zoo Animals Ser.). 32p. (J). (gr. k-2). 1999. 9.95 (*1-57505-390-X*, Carolrhoda) Lerner Pub.

Arnold, Caroline. El Nino: Stormy Weather for People & Wildlife. LC 98-4826. 48p. (J). (gr. 3-6). 1998. 16.00 (*0-395-77602-3*, Clarion Bks) HM.

— Noisytime for Zoo Animals. LC 98-24376. (Illus.). 32p. (J). (gr. k-2). 1999. 21.27 (*1-57505-289-X*, Carolrhoda) Lerner Pub.

***Arnold, Caroline.** Noisytime for Zoo Animals. LC 98-24376. (Zoo Animals Ser.). 32p. (J). (gr. k-2). 1999. 9.95 (*1-57505-392-6*, Carolrhoda) Lerner Pub.

Arnold, Caroline. On the Brink of Extinction: The California Condor. 1993. 14.20 (*0-606-12461-6*) Turtleback.

— On the Brink of Extinction: The California Condor. abr. ed. LC 92-14914. (Illus.). 48p. (J). (gr. 3-7). 1993. 17.95 (*0-15-257990-7*, Gulliver Bks) Harcourt.

***Arnold, Caroline.** Ostriches. LC 99-45703. (Early Bird Nature Ser.). (Illus.). 32p. (J). (ps-3). 2000. 22.60 (*0-8225-3044-9*, Lerner Publctns) Lerner Pub.

Arnold, Caroline. Ostriches & Other Flightless Birds. (Nature Watch Bks.). (Illus.). 48p. (J). (gr. 2-5). 1990. lib. bdg. 19.95 (*0-87614-377-X*, Carolrhoda) Lerner Pub.

— Pele: The King of Soccer. Mathews, V., ed. LC 91-33557. (First Bks.). (Illus.). 64p. (J). (gr. 3-6). 1992. lib. bdg. 22.00 (*0-531-20077-9*) Watts.

— Playtime for Zoo Animals. LC 98-24380. (Zoo Animals Ser.). (Illus.). 32p. (J). (gr. k-2). 1999. 21.27 (*1-57505-287-3*, Carolrhoda) Lerner Pub.

***Arnold, Caroline.** Playtime for Zoo Animals. LC 98-24380. (Zoo Animals Ser.). 32p. (J). (gr. k-2). 1999. 9.95 (*1-57505-391-8*, Carolrhoda) Lerner Pub.

Arnold, Caroline. Reindeer. LC 93-12981. (Illus.). (J). (gr. 4-7). 1993. pap. 3.95 (*0-590-46943-6*) Scholastic Inc.

— Rhino. LC 94-23904. (More Animal Favorites Ser.). (Illus.). 48p. (J). (gr. 2 up). 1995. 16.00 (*0-688-12694-4*, Wm Morrow) Morrow Avon.

An Asterisk (*) at the beginning of an entry indicates that the title is appearing for the first time.

— Saving the Peregrine Falcon. LC 84-15576. (Nature Watch Bks.). (Illus.). 48p. (J). (gr. 2-5). 1985. pap. 7.95 (*0-87614-523-3*, Carolrhoda) Lerner Pub.

— Sea Lion. LC 93-27007. (Illus.). 48p. (J). 1994. 15.00 (*0-688-12027-X*, Wm Morrow) Morrow Avon.

— Sea Turtles. LC 93-6353. (Illus.). 32p. (J). (gr. 1-4). 1994. pap. 3.95 (*0-590-46945-2*) Scholastic Inc.

— Shockers of the Sea: And Other Electric Animals. LC 98-7035. (Illus.). 32p. (J). (ps-4). 1999. 15.95 (*0-88106-873-X*); pap. 6.95 (*0-88106-874-8*) Charlesbridge Pub.

— Sleepytime for Zoo Animals. LC 98-24377. (Zoo Animals Ser.). (Illus.). 32p. (J). (gr. k-2). 1999. 21.27 (*1-57505-290-3*, Carolrhoda) Lerner Pub.

***Arnold, Caroline.** Sleepytime for Zoo Animals. LC 98-24377. (Zoo Animals Ser.). 32p. (J). (gr. k-2). 1999. 9.95 (*1-57505-393-4*, Carolrhoda) Lerner Pub.

Arnold, Caroline. South American Animals. LC 98-7669. (Illus.). 48p. (J). 1999. 16.00 (*0-688-15564-2*, Wm Morrow) Morrow Avon.

***Arnold, Caroline.** South American Animals. LC 98-7669. (Illus.). 48p. (J). 1999. lib. bdg., lab manual ed. 15.93 (*0-688-15565-0*, Wm Morrow) Morrow Avon.

Arnold, Caroline. Splashtime for Zoo Animals. LC 98-24378. (Illus.). 32p. (J). (gr. k-2). 1998. 21.27 (*1-57505-288-1*, Carolrhoda) Lerner Pub.

***Arnold, Caroline.** Splashtime for Zoo Animals. LC 98-24378. (Zoo Animals Ser.). (Illus.). 32p. (J). (ps-2). 1999. 9.95 (*1-57505-394-2*, Carolrhoda) Lerner Pub.

Arnold, Caroline. Stone Age Farmers Beside the Sea: Scotland's Prehistoric Village of Skara Brae. LC 96-20021. (Illus.). 48p. (J). (gr. 3-6). 1997. 15.95 (*0-395-77601-5*, Clarion Bks) HM.

— Stories in Stone: Rock Art Pictures by Early Americans. (Illus.). 48p. (J). (gr. 3-6). 1996. 15.95 (*0-395-72092-3*) HM.

— The Terrible Hodag. (Illus.). 30p. (J). (ps-3). 1989. 14.95 (*0-15-284750-2*) Harcourt.

— Through the Year with - Prairie Dogs. LC 92-38283. (Illus.). 32p. (J). (gr. 2-7). 1993. pap. 3.95 (*0-590-46946-0*) Scholastic Inc.

Arnold, Caroline. Trapped in Tar: Fossils from the Ice Age. 1987. 12.15 (*0-606-04832-4*, Pub. by Turtleback) Demco.

Arnold, Caroline. Tule Elk. (Nature Watch Bks.). (Illus.). 48p. (J). (gr. 2-5). 1989. lib. bdg. 14.95 (*0-87614-343-5*, Carolrhoda) Lerner Pub.

— A Walk by the Seashore. Brook, Bonnie, ed. (First Facts: Natural Sciences Ser.). (Illus.). 32p. (J). (ps-1). 1990. pap. 2.95 (*0-382-24648-9*) Silver Burdett Pr.

— A Walk by the Seashore. Brook, Bonnie, ed. (First Facts: Natural Sciences Ser.). (Illus.). 32p. (J). (ps-1). 1990. lib. bdg. 6.95 (*0-671-68662-3*, Silver Pr NJ) Silver Burdett Pr.

— A Walk in the Desert. Brook, Bonnie, ed. (First Facts: Natural Sciences Ser.). (Illus.). 32p. (J). (ps-1). 1990. pap. 4.95 (*0-382-24649-7*) Silver Burdett Pr.

— A Walk in the Desert. Brook, Bonnie, ed. (Illus.). 32p. (J). (ps-1). 1990. lib. bdg. 6.95 (*0-671-68664-X*, Silver Pr NJ) Silver Burdett Pr.

— A Walk in the Woods. Brook, Bonnie, ed. (First Facts: Natural Sciences Ser.). (Illus.). 32p. (J). (ps-1). 1990. pap. 4.95 (*0-382-24650-0*); lib. bdg. 6.95 (*0-671-68661-5*, Silver Pr NJ) Silver Burdett Pr.

— A Walk on the Great Barrier Reef. (Nature Watch Bks.). (Illus.). 48p. (J). (gr. 2-5). 1988. lib. bdg. 14.95 (*0-87614-285-4*, Carolrhoda) Lerner Pub.

— A Walk up a Mountain. Brook, Bonnie, ed. (First Facts: Natural Sciences Ser.). (Illus.). 32p. (J). (ps-1). 1990. pap. 4.95 (*0-382-24651-9*, Silver Pr NJ); lib. bdg. 9.95 (*0-671-68663-1*, Silver Pr NJ) Silver Burdett Pr.

— Watch Out for Sharks! (Illus.). 48p. (J). (gr. 3-6). 1994. pap. 8.95 (*0-395-69941-X*, Clarion Bks) HM.

Arnold, Caroline. Watch Out for Sharks! 1991. 12.15 (*0-606-08351-0*, Pub. by Turtleback) Demco.

Arnold, Caroline. Watching Desert Wildlife. LC 93-48076. (Nature Watch Bks.). (Illus.). (J). (gr. 2-5). 1994. lib. bdg. 19.95 (*0-87614-841-0*, Carolrhoda) Lerner Pub.

Arnold, Caroline. Zebra. (J). 1993. 11.15 (*0-606-05716-1*, Pub. by Turtleback) Demco.

Arnold, Caroline. Zebra. LC 87-1503. (Illus.). 48p. (J). (gr. 2-5). 1993. reprint ed. pap. 5.95 (*0-688-12273-6*, Wm Morrow) Morrow Avon.

***Arnold, Caroline & Hewett, Richard.** Baby Whale Rescue: The True Story of J. J. LC 98-31229. (Illus.). 32p. (J). (gr. 3-8). 1999. 15.95 (*0-8167-4961-2*) BrdgeWater.

— Baby Whale Rescue: The True Story of J. J. (Illus.). 32p. (ps-3). 2000. pap. 5.95 (*0-8167-5653-8*) Bridgewater Pub.

***Arnold, Catherine.** Class Action. 1999. mass mkt. 6.99 (*0-451-19869-7*, Sig) NAL.

Arnold, Catherine. Due Process. 368p. 1996. mass mkt. 5.99 (*0-451-18614-1*, Sig) NAL.

— Wrongful Death. 352p. 1999. mass mkt. 6.99 (*0-451-19593-0*, Sig) NAL.

Arnold, Chandler. Read with Me: Student Volunteers, Starting Early Childhood Literacy Programs. 51p. 1997. pap. 6.00 (*0-16-063642-6*) USGPO.

Arnold, Charles. Climate Inside Lava Tubes. 56p. 1996. pap. 10.00 (*1-886168-08-3*) ABC Pubng.

— Ritual Body Art: Drawing the Spirit. LC 98-163514. (Illus.). 160p. (Orig.). 1997. pap. 14.95 (*0-919345-74-3*) Phoenix WA.

Arnold, Chesty. Standby Arnold. 104p. 1992. pap. 5.00 (*0-9634288-0-2*) R M C Arnold.

— Standby Arnold. rev. ed. (Illus.). 116p. 1994. pap. 9.95 (*0-9634288-1-0*) R M C Arnold.

Arnold, Chirley. The Bet. LC 96-20483. (Values for Young Women Ser.). 170p. (YA). 1996. pap. 7.95 (*1-56236-450-2*, Pub. by Aspen Bks) Origin Bk Sales.

Arnold, Chirley. Double Trouble: A Novel. 160p. (YA). pap. 7.95 (*1-56236-454-5*, Pub. by Aspen Bks) Origin Bk Sales.

Arnold, Christopher. A Nontechnical Explanation of the 1994 NEHRP Recommended Provisions. (Illus.). 82p. 1997. reprint ed. pap. text 25.00 (*0-7881-4698-X*) DIANE Pub.

Arnold, Christopher & Mahoney, Michael, eds. Seismic Considerations for Communities at Risk. (Illus.). 114p. 1998. reprint ed. pap. text 30.00 (*0-7881-4237-2*) DIANE Pub.

***Arnold, Christopher & Nathe, Sarah K., eds.** Past, Present & Future Issues in Earthquake Engineering: 50th Anniversary Special Commemorative Volume. (Illus.). 207p. 1998. pap. 40.00 (*0-943198-64-X*, AM-98) Earthquake Eng.

***Arnold, Christopher, et al.** Lessons Learned over Time. (Illus.). 118p. 1998. pap. 15.00 (*0-943198-67-4*, 99-01) Earthquake Eng.

Arnold, Claude G. The Orchestra on Record, 1896-1926: An Encyclopedia of Orchestral Recordings Made by the Acoustical Process, 73. LC 97-2740. (Discographies Ser.: Vol. 173). 728p. 1997. lib. bdg. 135.00 (*0-313-30099-2*, Greenwood Pr) Greenwood.

Arnold, Clinton E. The Colossian Syncretism: The Interface between Christianity & Folk Belief at Colossae. 384p. 1996. pap. text 19.99 (*0-8010-2092-1*) Baker Bks.

— Powers of Darkness: Principalities & Powers in Paul's Letters. LC 91-33075. 234p. (Orig.). 1992. pap. 13.99 (*0-8308-1336-5*, 1336) InterVarsity.

— 3 Crucial Questions about Spiritual Warfare. LC 97-8642. (Three Crucial Questions Ser.). 224p. 1997. pap. 11.99 (*0-8010-5784-1*) Baker Bks.

Arnold, Corinna, jt. auth. see Selby, Nick.

Arnold, Corliss R. Organ Literature: A Comprehensive Survey, 2 vols. 3rd ed. 1995. 110.00 (*0-8108-2970-3*) Scarecrow.

— Organ Literature: A Comprehensive Survey, Vol. 1. 3rd ed. 398p. 1995. 55.00 (*0-8108-2964-9*) Scarecrow.

— Organ Literature: A Comprehensive Survey, Vol. 2. 3rd ed. 922p. 1995. 85.00 (*0-8108-2965-7*) Scarecrow.

Arnold, Craig. Euterpe: Diaries, Letters & Logs of the "Star of India" As a British Emigrant Ship. (Illus.). 1988. pap. 22.00 (*0-944580-06-8*) Maritime Mus Assn.

— Medea: The Classic Steam Yacht. LC 94-18961. (Illus.). 228p. (Orig.). 1994. pap. 22.00 (*0-944580-08-4*) Maritime Mus Assn.

— Shells. LC 98-31256. (Younger Poets Ser.: Vol. 93). 79p. 1999. 18.00 (*0-300-07909-5*); pap. 11.00 (*0-300-07910-9*) Yale U Pr.

Arnold, Curtis M. Curtis Arnold's PPS Trading System: A Proven Method for Consistently Beating the Market. 225p. 1996. 47.50 (*1-55738-877-6*, Irwn Prfssnl) McGraw-Hill Prof.

— How to Pick a Winning Trading System. (Illus.). 250p. 1998. 39.95 incl. cd-rom (*0-07-006666-3*) McGraw.

— Timing the Market: How to Profit in Bull & Bear Markets with Technical Analysis. 2nd rev. ed. 250p. 1995. text 24.95 (*1-55738-496-7*, Irwn Prfssnl) McGraw-Hill Prof.

— Your Personal Computer Can Make You Rich in Stocks & Commodities. LC 83-51498. (Illus.). 300p. 14.95 (*0-9613048-0-4*) M D Weiss Pub.

Arnold, Cynthia, et al. Sustainable Agriculture Directory of Expertise. 3rd ed. 400p. (Orig.). 1997. pap. text 50.00 (*0-7881-3830-8*) DIANE Pub.

***Arnold, D.** Abelian Groups & Representations of Finite Partially Ordered Sets. Borwein, J. J. & Borwein, P., eds. LC 99-87081. (CMS Books in Mathematics: 2). 232p. 2000. 79.95 (*0-387-98982-X*) Spr-Verlag.

Arnold, D., et al. Parallel Computing & Applications (Transputers), '93. LC 93-80962. (Transputer & Occam Engineering Ser.: Vol. 37). 392p. (YA). (gr. 12). 1992. 98.00 (*90-5199-149-5*, Pub. by IOS Pr) IOS Press.

Arnold, D. B., et al, eds. Graphics & Communications: Proceedings of an International Workshop Breuberg, FRG, October 15-17, 1990. (Eurographic Seminars Ser.). (Illus.). viii, 274p. 1991. 82.95 (*0-387-54001-6*) Spr-Verlag.

Arnold, D. B. & Bono, P. R. Cgm & Cgi: Metafile & Interface Standards for Computer Graphics (Symbolic Computation Computer Graphics---Systems & Applications) (Symbolic Computation Ser.). (Illus.). xxiii, 279p. 1988. 66.95 (*0-387-18950-5*) Spr-Verlag.

Arnold, Dana. Georgian Villa. 1999. pap. text 22.95 (*0-7509-2022-X*) Bks Intl VA.

***Arnold, Dana.** Metropolis & Its Image: Constructing Identities for London, 1750-1950. LC 99-56077. (Art History Special Issues Ser.). 184p. 2000. pap. 22.95 (*0-631-21667-7*) Blackwell Pubs.

Arnold, Dana, ed. The Georgian Country House: Architecture, Landscape & Society. LC 99-494969. (Illus.). 224p. 1999. 49.95 (*0-7509-1590-0*, Pub. by Sutton Pub Ltd) Intl Pubs Mktg.

— The Georgian Villa. (Illus.). 192p. 1996. 44.95 (*0-7509-1020-8*, Pub. by Sutton Pub Ltd) Intl Pubs Mktg.

Arnold, Danny R., et al. Business Strategy & Policy, 3 vols. 3rd ed. (C). 1991. pap. text. write for info. (*0-395-43367-3*) HM Soft Schl Col Div.

— Strategic Retail Management. LC 82-8852. 752p. 1983. text. write for info. (*0-201-10085-1*) Addison-Wesley.

Arnold, Darryl. How to Find a Job. 80p. 1995. pap. 14.95 (*1-57087-032-2*) Prof Pr NC.

Arnold, Dave. Vintage John Deere: Early History & the Two-Cylinder Years, 1837-1960. LC 94-31815. (Illus.). 112p. 1997. pap. 17.95 (*0-89658-348-1*) Voyageur Pr.

Arnold, David. Colonizing the Body: State Medicine & Epidemic Disease in Nineteenth-Century India. LC 92-25623. (C). 1993. 55.00 (*0-520-08124-2*, Pub. by U CA Pr); pap. 22.50 (*0-520-08295-8*, Pub. by U CA Pr) Cal Prin Full Svc.

— The Congress in Tamiland: Nationalist Politics in South India, Nineteen Nineteen to Nineteen Thirty-Seven. 1977. 12.00 (*0-88386-958-5*) S Asia.

— The Handbook of Brand Management. LC 92-31025. (Economist Bks.). 1993. 27.50 (*0-201-63279-9*) Addison-Wesley.

— Intermediate Algebra. (C). 1998. text. write for info. (*0-201-58655-X*) Addison-Wesley.

— Intermediate Algebra: A Discovery Approach, Preliminary Edition. (Illus.). 864p. (C). 1994. ring bd. 43.00 (*0-201-62873-2*) Addison-Wesley.

— A New Owner's Guide to Beagles. (Illus.). 160p. 1998. 12.95 (*0-7938-2785-X*, JG136) TFH Pubns.

Arnold, David. Police Power & Colonial Rule, Madras, 1859-1947. LC 86-900007. 277p. 1987. 29.95 (*0-19-561893-9*) OUP.

Arnold, David. The Problem of Nature: Environment, Culture & European Expansion. LC 96-2054. (New Perspectives on the Past Ser.). 224p. 1996. 60.95 (*0-631-17732-9*) Blackwell Pubs.

— The Problem of Nature: Environment, Culture & European Expansion. LC 96-2054. (New Perspectives on the Past Ser.). (Illus.). 224p. 1996. pap. 22.95 (*0-631-19021-X*) Blackwell Pubs.

***Arnold, David.** Science, Technology & Medicine in Colonial India. (New Cambridge History of India Ser.: Vol. III:5). (Illus.). 228p. (C). 2000. text 59.95 (*0-521-56319-4*) Cambridge U Pr.

Arnold, David. Tides & Currents. 64p. (C). 1990. text 59.00 (*0-906754-24-0*, Pub. by Fernhurst Bks) St Mut.

Arnold, David & Guha, Ramachandra, eds. Nature, Culture, Imperialism: Essays on the Environmental History of South Asia. (Studies in Social Ecology & Environmental History). (Illus.). 388p. 1997. pap. text 17.95 (*0-19-564075-6*) OUP.

Arnold, David & Robb, Peter, eds. Institutions & Ideologies: A School of Oriental & African Studies South Asia Reader. (Collected Papers on South Asia: No. 10). 320p. (C). 1996. text 48.00 (*0-7007-0283-0*, Pub. by Curzon Pr Ltd); pap. text 26.95 (*0-7007-0284-9*, Pub. by Curzon Pr Ltd) UH Pr.

Arnold, David, jt. auth. see Polkinghorne, John C.

Arnold, David A., ed. see Lowenstein, Bill.

Arnold, David D., jt. ed. see Aziz, Abdul.

Arnold, David M. & Rangaswamy, K. M. Abelian Groups & Modules: Proceedings of the International Conference at Colorado Springs. LC 96-23964. (Lecture Notes in Pure & Applied Mathematics Ser.: Vol. 182). (Illus.). 432p. 1996. pap. text 175.00 (*0-8247-9789-2*) Dekker.

Arnold, David O. Computers & Society: Impact! (C). 1991. pap. text 47.74 (*0-07-557812-3*) McGraw.

Arnold, David S. & Plant, Jeremy F. Public Official Associations & State & Local Government: A Bridge Across One Hundred Years. (C). 1993. lib. bdg. 45.00 (*0-913969-65-6*) Univ Pub Assocs.

Arnold, Dean A. American Economic Enterprises in Korea, 1895-1939. Bruchey, Stuart & Bruchey, Eleanor, eds. (American Business Abroad Ser.). (Illus.). 1976. 47.95 (*0-405-09264-4*) Ayer.

Arnold, Dean E. Ceramic Theory & Cultural Process. New Studies in Archaeology). (Illus.). 288p. 1988. pap. text 30.95 (*0-521-27259-9*) Cambridge U Pr.

— Ecology & Ceramic Production in an Andean Community. LC 92-34658. (New Studies in Archaeology). (Illus.). 310p. (C). 1993. text 74.95 (*0-521-43289-8*) Cambridge U Pr.

Arnold, Dean E., jt. auth. see Neuenswander, Helen L.

Arnold, Denis. Italian Baroque Mast. rev. ed. 1997. pap. 16.95 (*0-393-30360-8*) Norton.

— Oxford Encyclopedic Dictionary of Music: French Edition, 2 vols., Set. (FRE.). 2400p. 1988. pap. 95.00 (*0-8288-7288-0*, 2221900243) Fr & Eur.

Arnold, Denis, ed. The New Oxford Companion to Music, 2 vols., Set. (Illus.). 2,032p. 1983. 185.00 (*0-19-311316-3*) OUP.

Arnold, Denis & Arnold, Elsie. The Oratorio in Venice. (Royal Musical Association Monographs: Vol. 2). 118p. 1993. 24.95 (*0-947854-01-0*) U Ch Pr.

Arnold, Denis, ed. see Marenzio, Luca.

Arnold, Dieter. Building in Egypt: Pharaonic Stone Masonry. (Illus.). 336p. 1997. reprint ed. pap. 35.00 (*0-19-511374-8*) OUP.

— Lexikon der Aegyptischen Baukunst. (GER.). 352p. 1994. 150.00 (*0-7859-8453-4*, 3760810993) Fr & Eur.

***Arnold, Dieter.** The Pyramid Complex of Senwosret III at Dahshur Architectural Studies. LC 00-35505. 2000. write for info. (*0-87099-956-7*) Metro Mus Art.

Arnold, Dieter. The South Cemeteries of Lisht Vol. 1: The Pyramid of Senwosret I. (Metropolitan Museum of Art Egyptian Expedition Publications: No. 22). (Illus.). 156p. 1989. 75.00 (*0-87099-506-5*) Metro Mus Art.

— Temples of the Last Pharaohs. LC 99-24117. (Illus.). 384p. 1999. 49.95 (*0-19-512633-5*) OUP.

***Arnold, Dorothea.** Egyptian Art in the Age of the Pyramids. (Illus.). 536p. 1999. 90.00 (*0-8109-6543-7*, Pub. by Abrams) Time Warner.

Arnold, Dorothea & Metropolitan Museum of Art (New York, N. Y.) Staff. When the Pyramids Were Built: Egyptian Art in the Age of the Pyramids LC 99-33287. 1999. write for info. (*0-87099-909-5*) Metro Mus Art.

Arnold, Dorothea & Metropolitan Museum of Art Staff. The Royal Women of Amarna: Images of Beauty from Ancient Egypt. LC 96-34517. 1996. pap. 29.95 (*0-87099-818-8*) Metro Mus Art.

Arnold, Dorothy M. Where Is the Light. 244p. (C). 1988. 55.00 (*0-85335-236-4*, Pub. by Stuart Titles Ltd) St Mut.

Arnold, Doug, et al, eds. Essays on Grammatical Theory & Universal Grammar. (Illus.). 314p. 1989. text 69.00 (*0-19-824216-6*) OUP.

— Essays on Grammatical Theory & Universal Grammar. (Illus.). 316p. 1991. reprint ed. pap. text 35.00 (*0-19-824897-0*, 12347) OUP.

Arnold, Douglas M. A Republican Revolution: Ideology & Politics in Pennsylvania, 1776-1790. (Outstanding Studies in Early American History). 388p. 1989. reprint ed. 25.00 (*0-8240-6171-3*) Garland.

Arnold, Douglas R. Congress & the Bureaucracy: A Theory of Influence. LC 78-65493. (Studies in Political Science: No. 28). (Illus.). 251p. 1980. reprint ed. pap. 17.00 (*0-300-02592-0*) Yale U Pr.

Arnold, Duane W. Early Episcopal Career of Anthanasius of Alexandria. LC 90-45796. (Christianity & Judaism in Antiquity Ser.: Vol. 6). 256p. (C). 1991. 29.00 (*0-268-00925-2*) U of Notre Dame Pr.

— Prayers of the Martyrs. 144p. 1991. 12.99 (*0-310-31450-X*) Zondervan.

Arnold, Duane W. & Bright, Pam, eds. De Doctrina Christiana: A Classic of Western Culture. LC 94-15772. (Studies in Judaism & Christianity: No. 9). (C). 1995. text 40.50 (*0-268-00874-4*) U of Notre Dame Pr.

Arnold, Duane W. & Fry, George. Francis: The Call to Conversion. 144p. 1988. 12.95 (*0-310-52060-6*, 12831) Zondervan.

Arnold, E. J. Selected Short Stories. Hornsey, A. W., ed. 1964. 3.35 (*0-08-010714-1*, Pergamon Pr); pap. 3.45 (*0-08-010713-3*, Pergamon Pr) Elsevier.

Arnold, Eberhard. Eberhard Arnold: A Testimony to the Church Community from His Life & Writings. 2nd ed. LC 73-11605. 120p. 1973. 5.00 (*0-87486-112-8*) Plough.

— God's Revolution: Justice, Community, & the Coming Kingdom. 2nd ed. Yoder, John Howard & Bruderhof Staff, eds. Orig. Title: God's Revolution: The Witness of Eberhard Arnold. 224p. 1997. pap. 12.00 (*0-87486-091-1*) Plough.

— The Individual & World Need. LC 92-30196.Tr. of Der Einzelne und Die Weltnot. 84p. 1993. 4.00 (*0-87486-052-0*) Plough.

***Arnold, Eberhard.** Innerland: A Guide into the Heart of the Gospel. 2nd rev. ed. LC 99-13145. 424p. 1999. pap. 14.00 (*0-87486-978-1*) Plough.

Arnold, Eberhard. Salt & Light: Living the Sermon on the Mount. 4th ed. 184p. 1998. pap. 12.00 (*0-87486-099-7*) Plough.

Arnold, Eberhard, ed. The Early Christians: In Their Own Words. 4th rev. ed. Plough Publishing House Staff, tr. from GER. LC 97-36585. (Illus.). 379p. 1998. pap. 20.00 (*0-87486-095-4*) Plough.

Arnold, Eberhard & Merton, Thomas. Why We Live in Community: With Two Interpretive Talks by Thomas Merton. Bruderhof, ed. 88p. 1995. pap. 8.00 (*0-87486-068-7*) Plough.

***Arnold, Edward J.** The Development of the Radical Right in France: From Boulanger. LC 00-21256. 288p. 2000. text 59.95 (*0-312-23165-2*) St Martin.

Arnold, Edward V. Rigveda. LC 73-139172. (Popular Studies in Mythology, Romance & Folklore: No. 9). reprint ed. 27.50 (*0-404-53509-7*) AMS Pr.

— Roman Stoicism. LC 76-169750. (Select Bibliographies Reprint Ser.). 1977. reprint ed. 39.95 (*0-8369-5970-1*) Ayer.

— Roman Stoicism. LC 76-169750. 468p. reprint ed. 26.50 (*0-8290-0494-7*) Irvington.

Arnold, Edward V., ed. see Hitopadesa.

Arnold, Edwin. The Book of Good Counsels. (Illus.). 162p. 1986. reprint ed. 14.00 (*0-8364-1761-5*, Pub. by Manohar) S Asia.

— Hindu Literature (1900) 470p. 1998. reprint ed. pap. 22.00 (*0-7661-0640-3*) Kessinger Pub.

— The Light of Asia. 1997. pap. 7.95 (*81-7059-136-8*, 7603, Quest) Theos Pub Hse.

— The Light of Asia. 239p. 1995. reprint ed. pap. 19.95 (*1-56459-496-3*) Kessinger Pub.

***Arnold, Edwin.** The Light of Asia: Being the Life & Teaching of Guatama, Prince of India & founder of Buddhism, 3. LC 99-80174. 208p. 2000. write for info. (*1-893766-13-6*) Aeon Pub Co.

Arnold, Edwin. The Light of Asia: The Life & Teaching of Gautama Buddha. xi, 238p. 1977. 6.00 (*0-938998-17-X*) Theosophy.

— Pearls of Faith (1883) 320p. 1998. reprint ed. pap. 24.95 (*0-7661-0243-2*) Kessinger Pub.

— Pearls of the Faith. 368p. 1984. 250.00 (*1-85077-004-2*, Pub. by Darf Pubs Ltd) St Mut.

— Poems (1880) 246p. 1998. reprint ed. pap. 19.95 (*0-7661-0239-4*) Kessinger Pub.

— Poets of Greece. LC 70-39680. (Essay Index Reprint Ser.). 1977. reprint ed. 23.95 (*0-8369-2738-9*) Ayer.

— The Secret of Death with Some Collected Poems (1886) 250p. 1998. reprint ed. pap. 19.95 (*0-7661-0244-0*) Kessinger Pub.

— Song Celestial: A Poetic Version of the Bhagavad Gita. 1975. reprint ed. pap. 5.95 (*0-8356-0418-7*, Quest) Theos Pub Hse.

***Arnold, Edwin.** The Song Celestial or Bhagavad-Gita: Being a Discourse Between Arjuna, Prince of India & the Supreme Being Under the Form of Krishna. 3. LC 99-80175. 160p. 2000. write for info. (*1-893766-14-4*) Aeon Pub Co.

Arnold, Edwin. Wandering Words. LC 75-39660. (Essay Index Reprint Ser.). (Illus.). 1977. reprint ed. 30.95 (*0-8369-2739-7*) Ayer.

Arnold, Edwin, contrib. by. The Song Celestial or Bhagavad-Gita (1885) 200p. 1998. reprint ed. pap. 17.95 (*0-7661-0249-1*) Kessinger Pub.

Arnold, Edwin, tr. Bhagavadgita. LC 93-1448. (Thrift Editions Ser.). (Illus.). 112p. 1993. pap. 1.50 (*0-486-27782-8*) Dover.

— Song Celestial: Bhagavad-Gita. 176p. 1985. reprint ed. 6.50 (*0-87612-210-1*) Self Realization.

A

An Asterisk (*) at the beginning of an entry indicates that the title is appearing for the first time.

Arnold, Edwin & Huebener, Theodore. Foreign Language Careers. 1988. text 13.95 (*0-8442-6202-1*, VGM Career) NTC Contemp Pub Co.

— Foreign Language Careers. 1995. pap. text 10.95 (*0-8442-6204-8*, VGM Career) NTC Contemp Pub Co.

Arnold, Edwin, tr. see Swoboda, Jorg.

Arnold, Edwin L. Gulliver of Mars. 1976. lib. bdg. 12.95 (*0-89968-173-5*, Lghtyr Pr) Buccaneer Bks.

— Lepidus the Centurion: A Roman of Today. Reginald, R. & Melville, Douglas, eds. LC 77-84196. (Lost Race & Adult Fantasy Ser.). 1978. reprint ed. lib. bdg. 29.95 (*0-405-10954-7*) Ayer.

— Lieut. Gulliver Jones: His Vacation. LC 74-15947. (Science Fiction Ser.). 304p. 1975. reprint ed. 25.95 (*0-405-06273-7*) Ayer.

Arnold, Edwin P. Phra the Phoenician. 1976. lib. bdg. 12.95 (*0-89968-174-3*, Lghtyr Pr) Buccaneer Bks.

Arnold, Edwin T., ed. Conversations with Erskine Caldwell. LC 87-27682. (Literary Conversations Ser.). xxiii, 312 p. 1988. pap. 15.95 (*0-87805-344-1*) U Pr of Miss.

— Erskine Caldwell Reconsidered. LC 89-49307. (Southern Quarterly Ser.). 120p. 1990. text 20.00 (*0-87805-432-4*) U Pr of Miss.

Arnold, Edwin T. & Luce, Dianne C., eds. Perspectives on Cormac McCarthy. 2nd rev. ed. LC 98-36319. 224p. 1998. pap. 18.00 (*1-57806-105-9*); text 40.00 (*1-57806-104-0*) U Pr of Miss.

Arnold, Edwin T. & Trouard, Dawn. Reading Faulkner: Sanctuary. LC 96-3478. (Reading Faulkner Ser.). 256p. (C). 1996. 45.00 (*0-87805-873-7*); pap. 17.50 (*0-87805-874-5*) U Pr of Miss.

Arnold, Edwin T. & Williamson, J. W., eds. Interviewing Appalachia: The Appalachian Journal Interviews, 1978-1992. LC 93-28428. (Illus.). 448p. (C). 1994. pap. text 22.50 (*0-87049-822-3*); lib. bdg. 45.00 (*0-87049-821-5*) U of Tenn Pr.

Arnold, Eleanor, ed. Voices of American Homemakers. LC 92-21509. (Illus.). 304p. (Orig.). (C). 1993. 26.50 (*0-253-12986-9*) Ind U Pr.

***Arnold, Elizabeth.** Brainticklers: Beyond Y2K: Questions for the New Millennium & the Year 3000. 1999. pap. 9.95 (*0-9675731-0-6*) Brainticklers.

Arnold, Elizabeth. The Reef. LC 98-17505. 1999. pap. 12.00 (*0-226-02737-6*); lib. bdg. 28.00 (*0-226-02736-8*) U Ch Pr.

Arnold, Elizabeth & Boggs, Kathleen. Interpersonal Relationships: Professional Communication Skills for Nurses. 2nd ed. LC 93-48584. (Illus.). 608p. 1994. pap. text 30.50 (*0-7216-6684-1*, W B Saunders Co) Harcrt Hlth Sci Grp.

Arnold, Elizabeth & Boggs, Kathleen U., eds. Interpersonal Relationships: Professional Communication Skills for Nurses. 2nd ed. (Illus.). 608p. 1995. pap., teacher ed. write for info. (*0-7216-6685-X*, W B Saunders Co) Harcrt Hlth Sci Grp.

Arnold, Elizabeth N. & Boggs, Kathleen U. Interpersonal Relationships: Professional Communication Skills for Nurses. 3rd ed. Wood, Terri, ed. LC 98-38372. (Illus.). 525p. (C). 1999. pap. text. write for info. (*0-7216-8103-4*, W B Saunders Co) Harcrt Hlth Sci Grp.

Arnold, Elizabeth N., jt. auth. see Carson, Verna B.

Arnold, Elizabeth N., jt. ed. see Carson, Verna B.

***Arnold, Ellen.** Brilliant Brain Banishes Boredom. (Illus.). 32p. 2000. pap. 10.00 (*1-56976-115-9*, 1144) Zephyr Pr AZ.

— Brilliant Brain Battles Bad Guys. (Illus.). 32p. (J). (gr. k-7). 2000. pap. 10.00 (*1-56976-111-6*, 1140) Zephyr Pr AZ.

Arnold, Ellen. Brilliant Brain Becomes Brainy. (Illus.). 44p. (J). (ps-5). 1997. 13.95 (*1-888633-04-2*) Arncraft.

***Arnold, Ellen.** Brilliant Brain Selects Spelling Strategies. (Illus.). 32p. 2000. pap. 10.00 (*1-56976-113-2*, 1142) Zephyr Pr AZ.

— Magnificent Mind Listens Mindfully. (Illus.). 32p. 2000. pap. 10.00 (*1-56976-112-4*, 1141) Zephyr Pr AZ.

— Magnificent Mind Magnifies Meaning When Reading. (Illus.). 32p. 2000. pap. 10.00 (*1-56976-114-0*) Zephyr Pr AZ.

— Magnificent Mind Masters Multiplication. (Illus.). 32p. 2000. pap. 10.00 (*1-56976-116-7*, 1145) Zephyr Pr AZ.

— MI Strategies for Kids: Featuring Brilliant Brain & Magnificent Mind. (Illus.). 80p. 2000. pap. 21.00 (*1-56976-110-8*, 1146) Zephyr Pr AZ.

Arnold, Ellen. The MI Strategy Bank. LC 98-43674. (Illus.). 96p. (J). (gr. k-12). 1998. pap. 18.00 (*1-56976-097-7*) Zephyr Pr AZ.

***Arnold, Ellen L., ed.** Conversations with Leslie Marmon Silko. (Literary Conversations Ser.). 224p. 2000. pap. 18.00 (*1-57806-301-9*); lib. bdg. 45.00 (*1-57806-300-0*) U Pr of Miss.

Arnold, Elliott. Blood Brother. LC 78-26788. x, 454p. 1979. reprint ed. pap. 13.95 (*0-8032-5901-8*, Bison Books) U of Nebr Pr.

— The Time of the Gringo. 626p. reprint ed. lib. bdg. 30.95 (*0-88411-180-6*) Amereon Ltd.

Arnold, Elsie, jt. auth. see Arnold, Denis.

Arnold, Emma S. Emma: Through It All. Munro, Sarah, ed. LC 95-79507. (Illus.). 214p. (Orig.). 1995. pap. 6.95 (*1-883602-09-2*) Atlantic Digital.

***Arnold, Emmy.** A Joyful Pilgrimage: My Life in Community. 2nd rev. ed. Plough Publishing House Staff, ed. Orig. Title: Torches Together. (Illus.). 184p. 1999. pap. 14.00 (*0-87486-956-0*) Plough.

***Arnold, Eric.** Darth Maul's Revenge. (Star Wars). (J). 2000. pap. 3.99 (*0-375-80432-3*, Pub. by Random Bks Yng Read) Random.

— Darth Maul's Revenge. (Star Wars Ser.). (Illus.). 48p. (J). (ps-3). 2000. 11.99 (*0-375-90432-8*) Random Bks Yng Read.

Arnold, Eric. Day in the Life of a Baseball Player: Mo Vaughn. 1996. 10.15 (*0-606-09183-1*, Pub. by Turtleback) Demco.

— Jokes You Shouldn't Tell a Dog! (Illus.). 64p. (J). (gr. 4-6). 1999. per. 2.99 (*0-689-83094-7*) Aladdin.

***Arnold, Eric.** Jokes You Shouldn't Tell a Dog. (Illus.). (J). 1999. 8.34 (*0-606-17926-7*) Turtleback.

Arnold, Eric. Jokes You Shouldn't Tell a Ghost! (Illus.). 64p. (J). (gr. 4-6). 1999. per. 2.99 (*0-689-83007-6*) Aladdin.

***Arnold, Eric.** Jokes You Shouldn't Tell a Ghost. (Illus.). (J). 1999. 8.34 (*0-606-17927-5*) Turtleback.

Arnold, Eric. Volcanoes! LC 96-49778. 1997. lib. bdg. 11.99 (*0-679-98641-3*) Random.

— Volcanoes! Mountains of Fire. LC 96-49778. 1997. pap. 3.99 (*0-679-88641-9*) Random.

— Volcanoes! Mountains of Fire. (Step into Reading Ser.: A Step 3 Book). (J). (gr. 2-3). 1997. 9.19 (*0-606-12041-6*, Pub. by Turtleback) Demco.

***Arnold, Eric & Taggart, Sean.** Jokes You Shouldn't Tell Your Teacher. LC 99-18088. (J). 1999. pap. 2.99 (*0-689-82698-2*) Aladdin.

Arnold, Eric A., Jr., ed. A Documentary Survey of Napoleonic France. LC 93-27114. 412p. (Orig.). (C). 1993. pap. text 39.50 (*0-8191-9291-0*) U Pr of Amer.

Arnold, Eric A., ed. A Documentary Survey of Napoleonic France: A Supplement. 136p. (C). 1995. lib. bdg., suppl. ed. 28.50 (*0-7618-0059-X*) U Pr of Amer.

Arnold, Eric H. A Day in the Life of a Baseball Player. LC 96-140818. (Illus.). 32p. (J). (gr. k-3). 1996. pap. 4.95 (*0-590-54350-4*) Scholastic Inc.

Arnold, Erik & Guy, Ken. Parallel Convergence: National Strategies in Information Technology. LC 86-16954. 228p. 1986. 49.95 (*0-89930-226-2*, ADC/, Quorum Bks) Greenwood.

Arnold, Ethan L. Arnold Family Record: 323 Years in America, a Record of Some of the Descendants of William Arnold & His Son Benedict Arnold of R. I., & His Grandson, Benedict Arnold, Jr., 1635-1958. (Illus.). 101p. 1997. reprint ed. pap. 18.00 (*0-8328-7295-4*); reprint ed. lib. bdg. 28.00 (*0-8328-7294-6*) Higginson Bk Co.

Arnold, Ethel. Platonics: 1894 Edition. Roberts, Marie M., ed. (Her Write His Name Ser.). 160p. 1996. reprint ed. pap. 24.95 (*1-85506-385-1*) Bks Intl VA.

Arnold, Eugene. Big Water: Range Boundaries - Unknown. (Illus.). 130p. 1997. pap. 6.95 (*1-879630-42-7*, Wind Canyon Bks) Wind Canyon.

— Big Water: Revenge - Bounty. (Illus.). 150p. 1998. pap. 6.95 (*1-891118-26-9*, Wind Canyon Bks) Wind Canyon.

Arnold, Eugene D., Jr., et al. Trip Generation, Vols. 1, 2 & 3. 6th rev. ed. Pena, Michelle V., ed. LC 97-47441. (Illus.). 1700p. 1997. text 205.00 (*0-935403-09-4*, IR-016D) Inst Trans Eng.

Arnold, Eunice. Teach Yourself Torchon Lace: Six Basic Lessons in Bobbin Lace with Workcards. 1980. pap. 15.00 (*0-903585-08-1*) Robin & Russ.

Arnold, F. C. Gesammelte Lichenologische Schriften Vol. 1: Die Lichenen des Fraenkischen Juras. 385p. 1985. reprint ed. lib. bdg. 160.00 (*3-7682-1442-7*) Lubrecht & Cramer.

— Gesammelte Lichenologische Schriften. Incl. Vol. 3. Lichenologische Ausfluege in Tirol., 30 pts. & register 1971. 120.00 (*3-7682-0707-2*); 1971. write for info. (*0-318-54140-8*) Lubrecht & Cramer.

Arnold, Fayette F., III, jt. auth. see National Association of Review Appraisers & Mortga.

Arnold, Felix. The South Cemeteries of Lisht Vol. 2: The Control Notes & Team Marks. (Metropolitan Museum of Art Egyptian Expedition Publications: No. 23). (Illus.). 204p. 1990. 75.00 (*0-87099-551-0*) Metro Mus Art.

Arnold, Francena H. Not My Will. pap. 9.99 (*0-8024-3831-8*, 232) Moody.

Arnold, Frank A. Let's Take a Trip. (Illus.). 135p. 1998. write for info. (*0-7541-0040-5*, Pub. by Minerva Pr) Unity Dist.

***Arnold, Frank J.** Suggested Readings in the Holy Bible. LC 97-91221. 2000. pap. 9.95 (*0-533-12601-0*) Vantage.

Arnold, Frank S. Economic Analysis of Environmental Policy & Regulation. 264p. 1994. text 50.95 (*0-471-00084-1*) Wiley.

Arnold, Fred A. An Account of the English Homes of Three Early "Proprietors" of Providence, Wm. Arnold, Stukeley Westcott & Wm. Carpenter. (Illus.). 43p. 1997. reprint ed. pap. 9.00 (*0-8328-6484-6*) Higginson Bk Co.

Arnold, Frederic, jt. auth. see Hartmann, Erich.

Arnold, Frederick. Turning Points in Life. LC 72-4480. (Essay Index Reprint Ser.). 1977. reprint ed. 24.95 (*0-8369-2934-9*) Ayer.

Arnold, Frederick C. Stepping into College English. 4th ed. 264p. 1988. pap. 9.50 (*0-933704-63-1*) Dawn Pr.

Arnold, Frederick C., jt. auth. see Terry, John R.

Arnold, Fredric. Door Knob Five Two. (Illus.). 274p. 1984. 25.00 (*0-914961-00-4*) S E Maxwell.

Arnold, Gary. Entering the 5th Dimension. unabridged ed. (Illus.). 1998. pap. 12.95 (*1-57867-354-2*) Windhorse Corp.

— How to Get to Heaven in 21 Days or Less. (Illus.). 1998. pap. 12.95 (*1-57867-340-2*) Windhorse Corp.

— Positive Thoughts for Successful Living. unabridged ed. LC 97-90384. (Illus.). 239p. 1999. pap. write for info. (*1-57867-032-2*) Windhorse Corp.

— Speaking with Your Guardian Angel. unabridged ed. (Illus.). 1998. pap. 12.95 (*1-57867-323-2*) Windhorse Corp.

— The Tao Zooo. unabridged ed. (Illus.). 160p. 1997. pap. 16.95 (*1-57867-368-2*) Windhorse Corp.

— Uni-Versa-Visa: Paradoxical, Resolution, the Art of Resolving Opposites. unabridged ed. LC 97-90382. (Illus.). 196p. 1998. 21.95 (*1-57867-028-4*); pap. 16.95 (*1-57867-029-2*) Windhorse Corp.

— The Way of Life. unabridged ed. LC 96-90728. (Illus.). 176p. 1997. pap. write for info. (*1-57867-001-2*) Windhorse Corp.

***Arnold, Gary & Arnold, Gary N.** The Way of Life: Tao Te' Ching, 2. unabridged ed. 1999. pap. 16.95 incl. audio (*1-57867-002-0*) Windhorse Pubns.

Arnold, Gary J. The Washington Gladden Collection: An Inventory to the Microfilm Edition. 235p. 1972. 3.00 (*0-318-03209-0*) Ohio Hist Soc.

Arnold, Gary N. Radical Enlightenment for the CEO. 185p. 1999. pap. text 16.95 (*1-57867-497-2*) Windhorse Corp.

— Way of Life: Tao Te Ching, 2. 1999. audio. write for info. (*1-57867-003-9*) Windhorse Pubns.

Arnold, Gary N., jt. auth. see Arnold, Gary.

Arnold, Genevieve. Connections & Contradictions: Modern & Contemporary Art from Atlanta Collections. LC 99-213573. 16p. 1998. pap. 4.00 (*0-9638169-9-3*) M C Carlos Mus.

— Progressive Sound Game. 1973. text 3.00 (*0-686-09405-0*) Expression.

— Sound & Articulation Game. 1973. text 3.00 (*0-686-09406-9*) Expression.

— Sound Ladder Game. 1973. text 3.00 (*0-686-09404-2*) Expression.

— Speech-O, a Phonetic Game. 1973. text 4.25 (*0-686-09407-7*) Expression.

Arnold, Geoffrey. A Short-Title Catalogue of Books Printed in Hungary Before 1850. (Catalogues of the British Library Collections). 329p. 1994. 120.00 (*0-7123-0313-8*, Pub. by B23tish Library) U of Toronto Pr.

Arnold, George T. Fundamentals of Journalistic Writing & Editing. 272p. (C). 1995. text 20.35 (*0-697-14731-2*) Brown & Benchmark.

— Media Writer's Handbook. 100p. (C). 1996. text 12.50 (*0-697-29405-6*) Brown & Benchmark.

— Media Writer's Handbook: A Guide to Common Writing & Editing Problems. 2nd ed. LC 99-25514. 288p. 1999. pap. 30.00 (*0-697-35501-2*) McGraw.

Arnold, Gina. Kiss This: Punk in the Present Tense. LC 97-19811. (Illus.). 224p. 1997. pap. 11.95 (*0-312-15521-2*) St Martin.

— On the Road to Nirvana. (Illus.). 224p. (Orig.). 1993. pap. 13.95 (*0-312-09376-4*) St Martin.

Arnold, Gladys. One Woman's War: A Canadian Reporter With the Free French. (Illus.). 222p. 1988. mass mkt. 4.95 (*0-88780-154-4*, Pub. by Formac Publ Co) Formac Dist Ltd.

Arnold, Glen. Corporate Financial Management. 896p. 1998. pap. 67.50 (*0-273-63078-4*, Pub. by Pitman Pub) Trans-Atl Phila.

***Arnold, Gordon B.** The Politics of Faculty Unionization: The Experience of Three New England Universities. 2000. write for info. (*0-89789-716-1*, Bergin & Garvey) Greenwood.

Arnold, Gottfried. Unparteiische Kirchen- und Ketzerhistorie vom Anfang des Neuen Testaments bis auf das Jahr Christi, 1688, 2 vols. (GER.). 2690p. 1999. reprint ed. 980.00 (*3-487-01671-0*, Pub. by G Olms Verlag) Lubrecht & Cramer.

Arnold, Graham. Lotus. LC 99-185217. (Sutton's Photographic History of Railways Ser.). (Illus.). 160p. 1998. pap. 21.95 (*0-7509-1865-9*, Pub. by Sutton Pub Ltd) Intl Pubs Mktg.

Arnold, Guy. Historical Dictionary of Aid & Development Organizations. LC 95-12561. (International Organizations Ser.: No. 10). 216p. 1996. 32.50 (*0-8108-3040-X*) Scarecrow.

— Historical Dictionary of Civil Wars in Africa. LC 98-53946. (Historical Dictionaries of War, Revolution & Civil Unrest Ser.: Vol. 12). 376p. 1999. 75.00 (*0-8108-3633-5*) Scarecrow.

— The Maverick State: Libya & the New World Order. LC 96-7827. (Global Issues Ser.). 224p. 1997. 89.50 (*0-304-33366-2*); pap. 18.95 (*0-304-33367-0*) Continuum.

— Mercenaries. LC 99-18562. 198p. 1999. text 65.00 (*0-312-22203-3*) St Martin.

***Arnold, Guy.** The New South Africa. LC 00-33322. 2000. write for info. (*0-312-23517-8*) St Martin.

Arnold, Guy. Resources of the Third World. 448p. 1997. lib. bdg. 75.00 (*1-57958-014-9*) Fitzroy Dearborn.

— The Third World Handbook. LC 90-63741. (Illus.). 221p. 1991. 59.95 (*1-55862-149-0*) St James Pr.

— The Third World Handbook. 2nd ed. (Reference Ser.). (Illus.). 224p. 1994. 30.00 (*0-304-32837-5*) Continuum.

— Third World Handbook. 2nd rev. ed. (Illus.). 400p. 1994. lib. bdg. 45.00 (*1-884964-12-5*) Fitzroy Dearborn.

— Wars in the Third World since 1945. 2nd ed. 672p. 1995. 180.00 (*0-304-33086-8*) Continuum.

***Arnold, Guy, ed.** World Strategic Highways. (Illus.). 250p. 1999. 55.00 (*1-57958-186-2*) Fitzroy Dearborn.

Arnold, H. J. Astrophotography: An Introduction. LC 94-42325. (Sky & Telescope Observer's Guides Ser.). (Illus.). 192p. 1995. pap. 18.95 (*0-933346-73-5*) Sky Pub.

— Photographer of the World: A Biography of Herbert Ponting. LC 75-156270. (Illus.). 176p. 1975. 18.50 (*0-8386-7959-5*) Fairleigh Dickinson.

Arnold, H. J., et al, eds. The Photographic Atlas of the Stars: The Whole Sky in 50 Plates & Maps. (Illus.). 224p. 1996. 63.00 (*0-7503-0378-6*) IOP Pub.

Arnold, H. J., et al. The Photographic Atlas of the Stars. unabridged ed. (Illus.). 224p. 1997. 59.95 (*0-913135-31-3*, 18549) Kalmbach.

***Arnold, H. J. P.** Eclipse '99: Capture It on Film. LC 99-11882. viii, 56p. 1999. 10.00 (*0-7503-0619-X*) IOP Pub.

***Arnold, H. J. P., et al.** The Photographic Atlas of the Stars. LC 97-162455. (Illus.). 220p. 1999. 31.95 (*0-7503-0654-8*) IOP Pub.

Arnold, H. R. Atlas of Amphibians & Reptiles in Britain. (ITE Research Publication Ser.: No. 10). 44p. 1995. pap. 18.00 (*0-11-701824-4*, Pub. by Statnry Office) Balogh.

— Atlas of Mammals in Britain. LC 98-129662. (Illus.). 144p. 1993. pap. 25.00 (*0-11-701667-5*, HM16675, Pub. by Statnry Office) Balogh.

Arnold, H. V. Danielson Historical Memoir of the West or Brooklyn Side, Danielson, Connecticut: A Specimen of Village Annals or Common-Place Local History. With 1996 Index by Marcella Pasay. 173p. 1997. reprint ed. pap. 21.50 (*0-8328-5632-0*); reprint ed. lib. bdg. 29.50 (*0-8328-5631-2*) Higginson Bk Co.

— Early History of Ransom County, Including References to Sargent County, 1835-1885. 74p. 1995. reprint ed. pap. 15.00 (*0-8328-4715-1*) Higginson Bk Co.

Arnold, H. V., ed. History of Danielson to the Year 1882. With 1996 Index by Marcella Pasay. 237p. 1997. reprint ed. pap. 27.00 (*0-8328-5634-7*); reprint ed. lib. bdg. 35.00 (*0-8328-5633-9*) Higginson Bk Co.

***Arnold, Hap.** The Secret of Council Hill. (Illus.). iv, 134p. (J). (gr. 2-6). 2000. pap. 7.99 (*0-9700809-0-5*) Pyxis Pr Ky.

Arnold, Harriett. Antioch: A Place of Christians. LC 93-60521. (Illus.). 132p. (Orig.). 1993. 18.95 (*0-936029-29-3*); pap. 12.95 (*0-936029-30-7*) Western Bk Journ.

Arnold, Harrison H. & Chambers, Rae D. Root, Leaf, Bud & Berry: A Collection of Plants from Central Pennsylvania. (Illus.). 176p. (Orig.). 1993. pap. 10.00 (*1-887315-07-1*) Centre Cty Hist Soc.

Arnold, Harry L., Jr., et al. Andrews' Diseases of the Skin: Clinical Dermatology. 8th ed. (Illus.). 1058p. 1990. text 153.00 (*0-7216-2424-3*, W B Saunders Co) Harcrt Hlth Sci Grp.

Arnold, Helen. Australia. LC 95-15225. (Postcards From Ser.). (J). 1995. lib. bdg. 21.40 (*0-8172-4010-1*) Raintree Steck-V.

— Australia. LC 95-15225. (Postcards From Ser.). 32p. (J). (gr. 2-4). 1996. pap. text 4.95 (*0-8172-4231-7*) Raintree Steck-V.

— Egypt. LC 95-52954. (Postcards From Ser.). (Illus.). (J). 1996. lib. bdg. 21.40 (*0-8172-4017-9*) Raintree Steck-V.

— France. LC 95-10118. (Postcards from Ser.). (J). 1995. lib. bdg. 21.40 (*0-8172-4004-7*) Raintree Steck-V.

— France. LC 95-10118. (Postcards From Ser.). (Illus.). 32p. (J). (gr. 2-4). 1996. pap. text 4.95 (*0-8172-4225-2*) Raintree Steck-V.

— Great Britain. LC 95-15828. (Postcards From Ser.). (J). 1995. lib. bdg. 21.40 (*0-8172-4005-5*) Raintree Steck-V.

— Great Britain. LC 95-15828. (Postcards From Ser.). (Illus.). 32p. (J). (gr. 2-4). 1996. pap. text 4.95 (*0-8172-4226-0*) Raintree Steck-V.

— Ireland. LC 95-52927. (Postcards From Ser.). (Illus.). 32p. (J). (gr. 1-4). 1996. lib. bdg. 21.40 (*0-8172-4026-8*) Raintree Steck-V.

— Ireland. (Postcards from... Ser.). 1998. pap. 4.95 (*0-8172-6217-2*) Raintree Steck-V.

***Arnold, Helen.** Italy. (Postcards from... Ser.). (Illus.). (J). 2000. pap. 4.95 (*0-8172-6223-7*) Raintree Steck-V.

Arnold, Helen. Kenya. LC 95-52928. (Postcards From Ser.). (Illus.). (J). 1996. lib. bdg. 21.40 (*0-8172-4024-1*) Raintree Steck-V.

— Mexico. LC 95-7595. (Postcards from Ser.). (YA). 1995. lib. bdg. 21.40 (*0-8172-4012-8*) Raintree Steck-V.

— Mexico. LC 95-7595. (Postcards From Ser.). (Illus.). 32p. (J). (gr. 2-4). 1996. pap. text 4.95 (*0-8172-4233-3*) Raintree Steck-V.

— Of Ebony & Alabaster. LC 95-75751. 96p. (Orig.). (YA). (gr. 9 up). 1996. pap. 9.95 (*1-884242-90-1*) Multicult Pubns.

— Postcards from Germany. LC 95-16215. (Postcards From Ser.). (J). 1995. lib. bdg. 21.40 (*0-8172-4008-X*) Raintree Steck-V.

— Postcards from Germany. LC 95-16215. (Postcards from... Ser.). (Illus.). 32p. (J). (gr. 2-4). 1995. pap. 4.95 (*0-8172-4229-5*) Raintree Steck-V.

— Russia. LC 95-8100. (Postcards from Ser.). (J). 1995. lib. bdg. 21.40 (*0-8172-4006-3*) Raintree Steck-V.

— Russia. LC 95-8100. (Postcards From Ser.). (Illus.). 32p. (J). (gr. 2-4). 1996. pap. 4.95 (*0-8172-4227-9*) Raintree Steck-V.

— Spain. LC 95-10300. (Postcards from...Ser.). (J). 1995. lib. bdg. 21.40 (*0-8172-4009-8*) Raintree Steck-V.

— Spain. LC 95-10300. (Illus.). 32p. (J). (gr. 2-4). 1995. lib. bdg. 21.40 (*0-8172-4230-9*) Raintree Steck-V.

— The West Indies. LC 96-3497. (Postcards From Ser.). (Illus.). (J). 1997. lib. bdg. 21.40 (*0-8172-4021-7*) Raintree Steck-V.

Arnold, Helen S. & Denley, Nick. Tallahatchie County, Mississippi Cemetery Records. LC 99-214369. 348p. 1998. pap. 38.00 (*1-885480-26-1*) Pioneer Pubng.

— Tallahatchie County, Mississippi Marriage Records. 495p. 1999. pap. 48.00 (*1-885480-31-8*) Pioneer Pubng.

— Veterans of Tallahatchie County, Mississippi. LC 99-214350. 111p. 1998. pap. 10.00 (*1-885480-23-7*) Pioneer Pubng.

Arnold, Henri. Jumble Classics, Vol. 6. (Jumble Classic Ser.). (Illus.). 1994. reprint ed. pap. 3.95 (*1-56943-043-8*) NTC Contemp Pub Co.

— The Super Jumble Puzzle Book. (Illus.). 224p. (Orig.). 1991. pap. 8.95 (*0-941263-23-1*) NTC Contemp Pub Co.

— Trees in Urban Design. 2nd ed. LC 92-11127. 1993. text 46.95 (*0-442-00889-9*, VNR) Wiley.

Arnold, Henri & Lee, Bob. Jumble for Kids, Vol. 4. (Jumble for Kids Ser.). (Illus.). (J). (gr. 2-6). pap. 3.95 (*0-941263-96-7*) NTC Contemp Pub Co.

Arnold, Henry F. Trees in Urban Design. 2nd ed. 197p. 1992. 59.95 (*0-471-28444-0*, VNR) Wiley.

Arnold, Henry H. Global Mission. LC 70-169404. (Literature & History of Aviation Ser.). 1972. reprint ed. 37.95 (*0-405-03750-3*) Ayer.

Arnold, Hilary. Heaven & Earth: A Jacob's Ladder Book. LC 94-74280. (Illus.). 24p. (J). (gr. 2 up). 1995. 12.95 (*0-7868-0141-7*, Pub. by Hyprn Child) Little.

Arnold, Horace L., Jr. The Complete Cost-Keeper: Some Original Systems of Shop Cost-Keeping or Factory Accounting Together with an Exposition of the Advantages of Account Keeping by Means of Cards. Chandler, Alfred D., ed. LC 79-7530. (History of Management Thought & Practice Ser.). 1980. reprint ed. lib. bdg. 40.95 (*0-405-12313-2*) Ayer.

Arnold, Horace L. & Faurote, Fay L. Ford Methods & the Ford Shops. LC 72-5029. (Technology & Society Ser.). (Illus.). 450p. 1977. reprint ed. 42.95 (*0-405-04682-0*) Ayer.

Arnold, Howard P. European Mosaic. LC 72-39709. (Essay Index Reprint Ser.). 1977. reprint ed. 20.95 (*0-8369-2740-0*) Ayer.

— The Washington Medal. 1976. 3.00 (*0-89073-040-7*, 138) Boston Public Lib.

Arnold, Hugh. Small-Business Consulting. 110p. (Orig.). (C). 1994. pap. text 16.00 (*0-9639974-0-8*) Arnold Bks.

***Arnold, Hugo.** Outdoor Feasts. (Illus.). 160p. 1999. 29.95 (*1-85626-284-7*, Pub. by Cathie Kyle) Trafalgar.

Arnold, Isaac N. A Centennial Offering, Being a Brief History of Cooperstown, with a Biographical Sketch of James Fenimore Cooper, Together with Other Interesting Local Facts & Data. Shaw, S. M., ed. 240p. 1997. reprint ed. lib. bdg. 33.50 (*0-8328-6123-5*) Higginson Bk Co.

— History of Abraham Lincoln: And Overthrow of Slavery. LC 72-154069. (Black Heritage Library Collection). 1977. 37.95 (*0-8369-8780-2*) Ayer.

— The Life of Abraham Lincoln. LC 94-17449. xvi, 471p. 1994. pap. 14.95 (*0-8032-5924-7*, Bison Books) U of Nebr Pr.

— The Life of Benedict Arnold. Kohn, Richard H., ed. LC 78-22373. (American Military Experience Ser.). 1980. reprint ed. lib. bdg. 33.95 (*0-405-11851-1*) Ayer.

Arnold, Issac N. The Works of Isaac Newton Arnold, 1815-1884, Set. 1987. reprint ed. lib. bdg. 600.00 (*0-685-18603-2*) Rprt Serv.

Arnold, J. How to Play Blues Harp Today. 1990. 6.95 (*0-685-32192-4*, H656) Hansen Ed Mus.

Arnold, J. & Pearson, G., eds. Computer Applications in Nursing Education & Practice. 400p. (C). 1992. 29.95 (*0-88737-522-7*) Natl League Nurse.

Arnold, J., jt. auth. see Fisher, J.

Arnold, J. Douglas. Awesome Sega Genesis Secrets. (Gaming Mastery Ser.: No. 1). (Illus.). 256p. (Orig.). (J). 1992. pap. 9.95 (*0-9624676-4-2*, GV1469.3) Sandwich Islands.

— Awesome Sega Genesis Secrets. (Gaming Mastery Ser.: No. 2). (Illus.). 288p. (Orig.). 1992. pap. 9.95 (*0-9624676-5-0*) Sandwich Islands.

— Awesome Super Nintendo Secrets. (Gaming Mastery Ser.). (Illus.). 320p. (Orig.). 1993. pap. 11.95 (*0-9624676-6-9*) Sandwich Islands.

— Clocktower II: The Struggle Within Official Survival Guide. 1998. pap. text 12.95 (*1-884364-28-4*) Sandwich Islands.

***Arnold, J. Douglas.** Digimon Collector's Guide. (Illus.). 2000. pap. 12.95 (*1-884364-52-7*) Sandwich Islands.

Arnold, J. Douglas. Nintendo 64 Survival Guide. 1997. pap. text 14.95 (*1-884364-45-4*) Sandwich Islands.

***Arnold, J. Douglas.** Pokemon Gold & Silver Japanese Translation Guide. (Illus.). (J). 2000. pap. 12.95 (*1-884364-51-9*) Sandwich Islands.

Arnold, J. Douglas. Star Fox 64 Survival Guide. 176p. 1997. pap. 12.95 (*1-884364-41-1*) Sandwich Islands.

***Arnold, J. Douglas, ed.** Furby Trainer's Guide. (Illus.). 962p. 1999. pap. 11.95 (*1-884364-42-X*) Sandwich Islands.

Arnold, J. Douglas, ed. Yoshi Story 64 Players Guide. (Gaming Mastery Ser.). 224p. (Orig.). 1997. pap. 12.95 (*1-884364-43-8*) Sandwich Islands.

***Arnold, J Douglas & Brokaw, Brian.** Pokemon Trading Card Game Player's Guide. (Illus.). 144p. (YA). 1999. pap. 12.95 (*1-884364-50-0*, Pub. by Sandwich Islands) Login Pubs Consort.

Arnold, J. Douglas & Elies, Mark. Castlevania 64 Survival Guide: For Nintendo 64. (Illus.). 1998. pap. 14.95 (*1-884364-27-6*) Sandwich Islands.

— Castlevania Survival Guide: Symphony of the Night. (Gaming Mastery Ser.). (Illus.). 144p. (Orig.). 1997. pap. 12.95 (*1-884364-36-5*) Sandwich Islands.

***Arnold, J. Douglas & Elies, Mark.** Furby Official Trainer's Guide. (Illus.). 144p. 1999. pap. text 12.95 (*1-884364-26-8*) Sandwich Islands.

Arnold, J. Douglas & MacDonald, Mark. Final Fantasy VII Guide. (Gaming Mastery Ser.). 180p. 1997. pap. 14.95 (*1-884364-48-9*) Sandwich Islands.

Arnold, J. Douglas & Meston, Zach. Atari Jaguar: Official Gamer's Guide. (Gaming Mastery Ser.). (Illus.). 240p. (Orig.). 1995. pap. 16.95 (*1-884364-13-6*) Sandwich Islands.

— Awesome Sega Genesis Secrets. (Gaming Mystery Ser.: No. 3). (Illus.). 320p. (Orig.). 1993. pap. 11.95 (*0-9624676-3-4*) Sandwich Islands.

— Awesome Super Nintendo Secrets 3. (Gaming Mastery Ser.). 320p. 1994. pap. 11.95 (*0-9624676-8-5*) Sandwich Islands.

— Lunar: Official Guide. (Gaming Mastery Ser.). (Illus.). 136p. (Orig.). 1994. pap. 11.95 (*1-884364-00-4*) Sandwich Islands.

— Lunar, Eternal Blue: Official Strategy Guide. (Gaming Mastery Ser.). (Illus.). 220p. (Orig.). 1995. pap. 16.95 (*1-884364-07-1*) Sandwich Islands.

— Mario 64 Survival Guide. (Gaming Mastery Ser.). (Illus.). 160p. (Orig.). 1996. pap. 12.95 (*1-884364-19-5*) Sandwich Islands.

— Mortal Kombat III: Player's Guide. (Gaming Mastery Ser.). (Illus.). 128p. (Orig.). 1995. pap. 12.95 (*1-884364-14-4*) Sandwich Islands.

— Nintendo 64 Survival Guide, Vol. 2. LC 98-60566. (Nintendo 64 Survival Guides). 1998. pap. 9.95 (*1-884364-34-9*) Sandwich Islands.

— 3DO Game Secrets. (Gaming Mastery Ser.). (Illus.). 256p. (Orig.). 1995. pap. 14.95 (*1-884364-17-9*) Sandwich Islands.

— Yoshi's Island Strategy Guide. (Gaming Mastery Ser.). (Illus.). 240p. (Orig.). 1995. pap. 12.95 (*1-884364-21-7*) Sandwich Islands.

Arnold, J. Douglas, et al. Awesome Super Nintendo Secrets 4, No. 4. (Gaming Mastery Ser.). (Illus.). 320p. (Orig.). 1995. pap. 13.95 (*1-884364-06-3*) Sandwich Islands.

Arnold, J. Douglas, jt. auth. see Brokaw, Brian.

Arnold, J. Douglas, jt. auth. see Meston, Zach.

Arnold, J. Douglas, ed. see Sandwich Islands Publishing Staff.

Arnold, J. E. & Dewees, Peter A., eds. Tree Management in Farmer Strategies: Responses to Agricultural Intensification. (Illus.). 304p. 1995. 115.00 (*0-19-858414-8*) OUP.

Arnold, J. E. & Dewees, Peter E., eds. Farms, Trees & Farmers: Responses to Agricultural Intensification. 304p. 1997. pap. 34.00 (*1-85383-484-X*, Pub. by Escan Pubns) Island Pr.

Arnold, J. E., jt. auth. see Goldberg, S. K.

Arnold, J. Heinrich. Discipleship: Living for Christ in the Daily Grind. Bruderhof Staff, ed. LC 94-33910. 301p. 1994. pap. 16.00 (*0-87486-066-0*) Plough.

— Discipleship (Uchenichestvo) Michka, Nikolas & Michka, Vera, eds. Zadorozhny, Tatiana, tr. from ENG. (RUS.). 231p. (Orig.). 1995. pap. write for info. (*1-885024-02-9*) Slavic Christian.

— Freedom from Sinful Thoughts. 2nd ed. LC 97-31609. 133p. 1997. pap. 8.00 (*0-87486-094-6*) Plough.

Arnold, J. N., ed. see Chase, D., et al.

Arnold, J. O., jt. auth. see Galley, H.

Arnold, J. R. & Clive, Lloyd. Principios de Manejo de Materials: Principles of Materials Management. (SPA.). (Orig.). 1996. pap., teacher ed. 400.00 (*0-614-24998-8*); pap., student ed. 30.00 (*0-614-24999-6*) Am Prod & Inventory.

***Arnold, J. R. Tony & Chapman, Stephen N.** Introduction to Materials Management. 4th ed. 480p. 2000. 80.00 (*0-13-014490-8*, Prentice Hall) P-H.

Arnold, J. S., jt. ed. see Pirrie, S. R.

Arnold, J. Tony. Introduction to Materials Management. 3rd ed. LC 97-30065. 454p. (C). 1997. 86.00 (*0-13-862087-3*) P-H.

Arnold, Jackie S. Kinship Is a Relative Thing. LC 85-71444. (Illus.). 60p. (Orig.). 1985. pap. 4.95 (*0-9615458-0-1*) Arnold Assocs.

Arnold, James. Ardennes 1944: Hitler's Last Gamble in the West. (Campaign Ser.: No. 5). (Illus.). 96p. pap. 14.95 (*0-85045-959-1*, 9504, Pub. by Ospry) Stackpole.

— Chickamauga 1863. (Campaign Ser.: No. 17). (Illus.). 96p. pap. 14.95 (*1-85532-263-3*, 9516, Pub. by Ospry) Stackpole.

***Arnold, James.** Gettysburg-Confederate: The Army of Northern Virginia July 2, 1863. (Illus.). 96p. 1999. pap. 19.95 (*1-85532-855-0*) Ospry.

Arnold, James. Gettysburg-Confederate: The Army of Northern Virginia July 3, 1863. 1999. pap. 19.95 (*1-85532-860-7*) Ospry.

***Arnold, James.** Gettysburg-Union: The Army of the Potomac July 2, 1863. Vol. 7. (Illus.). 96p. 1999. pap. 19.95 (*1-85532-856-9*) Ospry.

Arnold, James. Gettysburg-Union: The Army of the Potomac July 3, 1863. 1999. pap. 19.95 (*1-85532-861-5*) Ospry.

Arnold, James & Wiener, Roberta. Operation Overlord: Omaha Beach & Pointe du Hoc. (Order of Battle Ser.). (Illus.). 32p. 1994. pap. 10.95 (*1-898994-02-1*) Stackpole.

— Operation Overlord: Utah Beach & the U. S. Airborne Divisions. (Order of Battle Ser.). (Illus.). 32p. 1994. pap. 10.95 (*1-898994-03-X*) Stackpole.

— Union: The Army of the Potomac. (Order of Battle Ser.: Vol. 2). (Illus.). 96p. 1999. pap. text 19.95 (*1-85532-833-X*, Pub. by Ospry) Stackpole.

Arnold, James A. Vital Record of Rhode Island, 1636-1850 - Births, Marriages & Deaths: A Family Register for the People, Newspaper Vitals, Vol. X. 640p. 1997. pap. 61.00 (*1-58211-108-1*) Quintin Pub RI.

— Vital Record of Rhode Island, 1636-1850 - Births, Marriages & Deaths: A Family Register for the People, Newspaper Vitals, Vol. XI. 640p. 1997. pap. 64.00 (*1-58211-109-X*) Quintin Pub RI.

— Vital Record of Rhode Island, 1636-1850 - Births, Marriages & Deaths: A Family Register for the People, Newspaper Vitals, Vol. XIII. 717p. 1997. pap. 62.00 (*1-58211-111-1*) Quintin Pub RI.

— Vital Record of Rhode Island, 1636-1850 - Births, Marriages & Deaths: A Family Register for the People, Newspaper Vitals, Vol. XIV. 717p. 1997. pap. 70.00 (*1-58211-112-X*) Quintin Pub RI.

— Vital Record of Rhode Island, 1636-1850 - Births, Marriages & Deaths: A Family Register for the People, Newspaper Vitals, Vol. XV. 650p. 1997. pap. 65.00 (*1-58211-113-8*) Quintin Pub RI.

— Vital Record of Rhode Island, 1636-1850 - Births, Marriages & Deaths: A Family Register for the People, Newspaper Vitals, Vol. XVI. 650p. 1998. pap. 65.00 (*1-58211-114-6*) Quintin Pub RI.

— Vital Record of Rhode Island, 1636-1850 - Births, Marriages & Deaths Vol. III: A Family Register for the People. 687p. 1997. pap. 65.00 (*1-58211-107-3*) Quintin Pub RI.

— Vital Records of Rhode Island, 1636-1850, First Series Births, Marriage & Deaths Vol. 20: A Family Register for the People. 730p. 1997. pap. 58.00 (*1-58211-117-0*) Quintin Pub RI.

— Vital Records of Rhode Island to 1850, Warwick. 2000. pap. 23.95 (*1-58211-074-3*) Quintin Pub RI.

— Vital Records of Rhode Island to 1850, East Greenwich. 2000. pap. 18.95 (*1-58211-075-1*) Quintin Pub RI.

— Vital Records of Rhode Island to 1850, West Greenwich. 2000. pap. 11.95 (*1-58211-076-X*) Quintin Pub RI.

— Vital Records of Rhode Island to 1850, Coventry. 2000. pap. 11.95 (*1-58211-077-8*) Quintin Pub RI.

— Vital Records of Rhode Island to 1850, Providence. 2000. pap. 30.95 (*1-58211-078-6*) Quintin Pub RI.

— Vital Records of Rhode Island to 1850, Cranston. 2000. pap. 5.95 (*1-58211-079-4*) Quintin Pub RI.

— Vital Records of Rhode Island to 1850, Johnston. 2000. pap. 5.95 (*1-58211-080-8*) Quintin Pub RI.

— Vital Records of Rhode Island to 1850, Scituate. 2000. pap. 5.95 (*1-58211-083-2*) Quintin Pub RI.

Arnold, James A. & Wiener, Roberta. The American West: Living the Frontier Dream. (Illus.). 192p. 1997. 29.95 (*0-8117-0977-9*) Stackpole.

Arnold, James K., jt. auth. see Lundin, Stephen C.

Arnold, James N. Arthur Aylsworth & His Descendants in America, with Notes, Historical & Genealogical, Relating to the Family, from Early English Records. (Illus.). 632p. 1988. reprint ed. pap. 95.00 (*0-8328-0147-X*); reprint ed. lib. bdg. 105.00 (*0-8328-0146-1*) Higginson Bk Co.

— The Narragansett Historical Register, Vol. 5. 368p. (Orig.). 1996. reprint ed. pap. 28.00 (*0-7884-0510-1*, A660) Heritage Bk.

— The Narragansett Historical Register (R1) 404p. 1996. reprint ed. pap. 30.50 (*0-7884-0511-X*, A661) Heritage Bk.

— Vital Record of Cranston, Johnston & North Providence, Rhode Island. (Vital Record of Rhode Island Ser.: Vol. 2, Pts. 2, 3 & 4). 138p. 1983. reprint ed. lib. bdg. 14.00 (*0-912606-12-6*) Hunterdon Hse.

— Vital Record of Providence, Rhode Island. (Vital Record of Rhode Island Ser.: Vol. 2, Pt. 1). 304p. 1988. lib. bdg. 21.00 (*0-912606-31-2*) Hunterdon Hse.

— Vital Record of Warwick, Rhode Island. (Vital Record of Rhode Island Ser.: Vol. 1, Pt. 1). 234p. 1983. reprint ed. lib. bdg. 16.00 (*0-912606-11-8*) Hunterdon Hse.

— Vital Record of (West Greenwich), 1636-1850: Births, Marriages & Deaths. 109p. 1997. reprint ed. pap. 15.00 (*0-8328-6491-9*) Higginson Bk Co.

— Vital Records of (Westerly), 1636-1850: Births, Marriages & Deaths. 152p. 1997. reprint ed. pap. 21.00 (*0-8328-6492-7*) Higginson Bk Co.

Arnold, James N., ed. The Narragansett Historical Register Vol. 1: A Magazine. 333p. 1994. pap. 28.50 (*1-55613-967-5*) Heritage Bk.

— The Narragansett Historical Register, Vol. 1. 336p. (Orig.). 1994. pap. text 26.00 (*0-7884-0141-6*) Heritage Bk.

— The Narragansett Historical Register, Vol. 3. (Illus.). 336p. (Orig.). 1994. pap. 25.00 (*0-7884-0098-3*) Heritage Bk.

— Narragansett Historical Register, Vol. 7. xlvi, 432p. 1996. reprint ed. pap. 25.00 (*0-7884-0535-7*, A662) Heritage Bk.

— The Narragansett Historical Register, Vol. 8. xxxiv, 352p. (Orig.). 1996. pap. 28.00 (*0-7884-0536-5*, A663) Heritage Bk.

— Narragansett Historical Register, Vol. 9. iv, 200p. 1996. reprint ed. pap. 18.50 (*0-7884-0537-3*, A664) Heritage Bk.

— The Narragansett Historical Register Vol. 2: A Magazine Devoted to the Antiquities, Genealogy & Historical Matter Illustrating the History of the State of RI & Providence Plantations. (Illus.). 339p. 1994. reprint ed. pap. text 25.00 (*0-7884-0026-6*) Heritage Bk.

Arnold, James R. The Armies of U. S. Grant. (Illus.). 320p. (Orig.). 1996. pap. 19.95 (*1-85409-374-6*, Pub. by Arms & Armour) Sterling.

***Arnold, James R.** Battle of the Bulge. 2000. pap. 17.95 (*1-84176-027-7*) Ospry.

Arnold, James R. Grant Wins the War: Decision at Vicksburg. LC 96-53871. 387p. 1997. 30.00 (*0-471-15727-9*) Wiley.

***Arnold, James R.** Jeff Davis's Own: Cavalry, Comanches & the Battle for the Texas Frontier. LC 00-21316. (Illus.). 400p. 2000. 30.00 (*0-471-33364-6*) Wiley.

— Marengo & Hohenlinden: Napoleon's Rise to Power. (Illus.). x, 301p. 1999. 34.00 (*0-9670985-0-5*) Napoleon Bks.

Arnold, James R. Napoleon Conquers Austria: The 1809 Campaign for Vienna. LC 94-44177. 280p. 1995. 55.00 (*0-275-94694-0*, Praeger Pubs) Greenwood.

— Tet-Offensive, 1968. (Campaign Ser.: No. 4). (Illus.). 96p. 1990. pap. 14.95 (*0-85045-960-5*, 9503, Pub. by Ospry) Stackpole.

Arnold, Janet. Patterns of Fashion, 1860 to 1940 Vol. 2: Englishwomen's Dresses & Their Construction. 3rd rev. ed. LC 76-189820. (Illus.). 88p. 1977. pap. 34.95 (*0-89676-027-8*, Costume & Fashion Pr) QSMG Ltd.

— Patterns of Fashion, 1560-1620: The Art & Construction of Clothes for Men & Women. (Illus.). 128p. 1985. pap. 39.95 (*0-89676-083-9*, Costume & Fashion Pr) QSMG Ltd.

— Patterns of Fashion, 1660-1860 Vol. 1: Englishwomen's Dresses & Their Construction. 3rd rev. ed. LC 76-189820. (Illus.). 76p. 1977. pap. 34.95 (*0-89676-026-X*, Costume & Fashion Pr) QSMG Ltd.

Arnold, Janis. Daughters of Memory. 378p. 1991. 16.95 (*0-945575-68-8*) Algonquin Bks.

— Daughters of Memory. (Front Porch Paperback Ser.). 378p. 1999. pap. 9.95 (*1-56512-031-0*) Algonquin Bks.

— Excuse Me for Asking. (Front Porch PB Ser.). 364p. 1997. pap. 10.95 (*1-56512-172-4*, 72172) Algonquin Bks.

Arnold, Jay. A Chord Guide to Pop Music. 1967. pap. 11.95 (*0-8256-4167-5*, AM10596) Music Sales.

— Easy Flute Solos or Duets, EFS102. (Illus.). 144p. 1960. pap. 14.95 (*0-8256-2102-X*, AM40411) Music Sales.

— Flute Solos, EFS38. (Illus.). 192p. 1968. pap. 14.95 (*0-8256-2038-4*, AM40197) Music Sales.

— Oboe Solos, EFS99. (Illus.). 160p. 1958. pap. 14.95 (*0-8256-2099-6*, AM40387) Music Sales.

— Selected Trumpet Solos, EFS42. (Illus.). 128p. 1960. pap. 15.95 (*0-8256-2042-2*, AM40213) Music Sales.

Arnold, Jay, ed. Elementary Clarinet Solos. (Illus.). 192p. 1997. pap. 16.95 (*0-8256-2033-3*, AM40171) Music Sales.

— Elementary Trumpet Solos, EFS32. (Illus.). 128p. 1942. pap. 15.95 (*0-8256-2032-5*, AM40163) Music Sales.

Arnold, Jay, selected by. Clarinet Solos, EFS28. (Illus.). 192p. 1987. pap. 14.95 (*0-8256-2028-7*, AM40155) Music Sales.

Arnold, Jean. The I of Me Now: Poems by Jean Arnold. LC 88-28236. 96p. (Orig.). 1988. 14.95 (*0-944266-00-2*); pap. 8.95 (*0-944266-01-0*) Maecenas Pr.

— Walking on Cork: Poems. 96p. (Orig.). 1991. 14.95 (*0-944266-10-X*); pap. 8.95 (*0-944266-11-8*) Maecenas Pr.

Arnold, Jeanne. Amy Asks a Question: Grandma, What's a Lesbian. LC 96-32240. (Illus.). 64p. (J). (gr. 4 up). 1997. 10.95 (*0-941300-28-5*) Mother Courage.

Arnold, Jeanne E. Craft Specialization in the Prehistoric Channel Islands, California. (UC Publications in Anthropology: Vol. 18). (Orig.). 1987. 45.00 (*0-520-09726-2*, Pub. by U CA Pr) Cal Prin Full Svc.

Arnold, Jeanne E., ed. Emergent Complexity: The Evolution of Intermediate Societies. LC 95-53050. (Archaeological Ser.: No. 9). (Illus.). 128p. 1996. 40.00 (*1-879621-21-5*); pap. 24.00 (*1-879621-20-7*) Intl Mono Prehstry.

***Arnold, Jeanne Louise.** Sir Bumpety Bump. (J). 2000. pap. 5.95 (*0-533-13320-3*) Vantage.

Arnold, Jeannette, ed. Cat Calls. 111p. (C). 1992. pap. 35.00 (*0-9518743-1-4*, Pub. by Fox Pr) St Mut.

Arnold, Jeffrey. The Big Book on Small Groups. LC 91-37115. 264p. (Orig.). 1992. pap. 12.99 (*0-8308-1377-2*, 1377) InterVarsity.

— Discovering the Bible for Yourself. LC 92-34566. (Illus.). 151p. (Orig.). 1993. pap. 8.99 (*0-8308-1387-X*, 1387) InterVarsity.

— Seven Tools for Building Effective Groups. 95p. 1997. pap. 8.00 (*1-57683-020-9*) NavPress.

— Seven Traits of a Successful Leader. 95p. 1997. pap. 8.00 (*1-57683-019-5*) NavPress.

— Small Group Outreach: Turning Groups Inside Out. LC 98-18567. 120p. 1998. pap. 8.99 (*0-8308-1170-2*, 1170) InterVarsity.

— Small Group Starter Kit. (LifeGuide Bible Studies). 64p. (Orig.). 1995. pap., wbk. ed. 4.99 (*0-8308-1073-0*, 1073) InterVarsity.

— Starting Small Groups: Building Communities That Matter. Miller, Herb, ed. LC 98-112702. (Leadership Insight Ser.). 168p. 1997. pap. 13.95 (*0-687-01856-0*) Abingdon.

Arnold, Jeffrey. What We Believe. (Pilgrimage Ser.). 79p. 1997. pap. 6.00 (*1-57683-071-3*) NavPress.

***Arnold, Jeffrey, et al.** Field-Programmable Custom Computing Technology: Architecture, Tools & Applications. 140p. 2000. 130.00 (*0-7923-7803-2*) Kluwer Academic.

Arnold, Jennifer, et al, eds. Sociolinguistic Variation: Data, Theory, & Analysis. 552p. (C). 1996. pap. 29.95 (*1-57586-038-4*) CSLI.

— Sociolinguistic Variation: Data, Theory, & Analysis. Selected Papers from NWAV23 at Stanford. 552p. (C). 1996. text 64.95 (*1-57586-039-2*) CSLI.

Arnold, Jennifer T., jt. auth. see Gianoulis, Deborah.

***Arnold, Jerry L.** Die Makers Handbook. (Illus.). 224p. 2000. pap. 27.95 (*0-8311-3132-2*) Indus Pr.

Arnold, Jerry L. & Diamond, Michael A. Corporate Financial Policies: A Review & Analysis of Existing Literature. LC 89-85782. 103p. (Orig.). 1989. pap. 20.00 (*0-910586-75-6*, 083-89) Finan Exec.

Arnold, Jerry L., et al. The Impact of Electronic Technology at the S. E. C. An Analysis of Policies Governing the Content & Dissemination of Corporate Disclosures. (Second Financial Reporting Institute Topical Issues Study Ser.: No. 1). 107p. (Orig.). 1987. pap. 20.00 (*0-9618802-0-1*) U SCA Sch Acct.

Arnold, Jerry L., jt. auth. see Keller, Earl C.

Arnold, Jesse C., jt. auth. see Milton, J. Susan.

***Arnold, Jo.** Go, Go Putt Putt Go! LC 00-100699. (Illus.). 24p. (J). (ps-2). 2000. 5.99 (*1-57064-945-6*, 73112, Humongous Bks) Lyrick Pub.

— Putt-Putt the Great Pet Chase. LC 00-100698. (Illus.). 24p. (J). (ps-2). 2000. pap. 3.99 (*1-57064-944-8*, 73111, Humongous Bks) Lyrick Pub.

Arnold, Joan, jt. auth. see Sheinfeld Gorin, Sherri.

Arnold, Joan, ed. see Plaskow, Judith.

Arnold, Joan H., jt. auth. see Gemma, Penelope B.

Arnold, Johann C. I Tell You a Mystery: Life, Death, & Eternity. rev. ed. LC 96-44035. (Illus.). 176p. 1996. pap. 12.00 (*0-87486-083-0*) Plough.

— A Plea for Purity: Sex, Marriage & God. 2nd rev. expanded ed. LC 98-33914. 224p. 1998. pap. 12.00 (*0-87486-960-9*) Plough.

***Arnold, Johann C.** Setenta Veces Siete: Reconciliacion en Neustra Sociedad. Palmer, Juan S. & Berrios, Luz, trs.Tr. of Seventy Times Seven: The Power of Forgiveness. (SPA.). 152p. 1999. pap. 9.00 (*0-87486-977-3*, Pub. by Plough) Spring Arbor Dist.

***Arnold, Johann Christoph.** Cries from the Heart: Stories of Struggle & Hope. LC 99-14692. (Illus.). 240p. 2000. pap. 10.00 (*0-87486-980-3*) Plough.

A

Arnold, Johann Christoph. Drained: Stories of People Who Wanted More. LC 99-18719. 152p. 1999. pap. 8.00 (0-87486-970-6) Plough.

***Arnold, Johann Christoph.** Endangered: Your Child in a Hostile World. 160p. 2000. pap. 10.00 (0-87486-997-8, Pub. by Plough) Spring Arbor Dist.

— Un Llamado a la Pureza. (SPA.). 1997. pap. write for info. (950-724-671-1) Lumen ARG.

— Un Llamada a la Pureza: El Sexo, el Matrimonio y Dios. (SPA.). 2000. pap. 12.00 (0-87486-994-3) Plough.

— Seeking Peace: Notes & Conversations Along the Way. LC 99-89716. 2000. pap. 12.95 (0-452-28186-5, Plume) Dutton Plume.

Arnold, Johann Christoph. Seeking Peace: Notes & Conversations along the Way. 264p. 1998. 15.00 (0-87486-958-7) Plough.

***Arnold, Johann Christoph.** Why Forgive? LC 99-50827. 192p. 2000. 17.00 (0-87486-992-7) Plough.

***Arnold, Johann Christoph, ed.** Eberhard Arnold: Writings Selected with an Introduction. LC 99-87489. (Modern Spiritual Masters Ser.). 140p. 2000. pap. 14.00 (1-57075-304-0) Orbis Bks.

Arnold, John. Managing Careers into the 21st Century. LC 97-198284. 272p. 1997. pap. 29.95 (1-85396-317-8, Pub. by P Chapman) Taylor & Francis.

— Medieval Music. (Topics in Music Ser.). (Illus.). 48p. 1985. pap. text 11.95 (0-19-321332-X) OUP.

— The Quality of Mercy: A Fresh Look at the Sacrament of Reconciliation. 128p. (C). 1996. pap. 39.95 (0-85439-433-8, Pub. by St Paul Pubns) St Mut.

Arnold, John, ed. Visions of Teaching & Learning: Eighty Exemplary Middle Level Projects. 150p. (Orig.). (C). 1990. pap. text 14.00 (1-56090-048-2) Natl Middle Schl.

Arnold, John & Turley, Stuart. Accounting for Management Decisions. 3rd ed. LC 95-35467. 1996. 56.50 (0-13-308818-9) P-H.

Arnold, John, et al. Work Psychology: Understanding Human Behaviour in the Workplace. 3rd ed. (Financial Times Ser.). 525p. (Orig.). 1998. pap. 62.50 (0-273-62868-2, Pub. by F T P-H) Natl Bk Netwk.

Arnold, John, jt. ed. see Attwood, Bain.

Arnold, John D. When the Sparks Fly: Resolving Conflicts in Your Organization. (Illus.). 236p. 1999. text 23.00 (0-7881-5992-5) DIANE Pub.

***Arnold, John H.** History: A Very Short Introduction. LC 99-57694. (Very Short Introductions Ser.). (Illus.). 144p. 2000. pap. 8.95 (0-19-285352-X) OUP.

Arnold, John P. & Kernkamp, Howard H. One Hundred Years of Progress: The History of Veterinary Medicine in Minnesota. Boyd, Thomas H., ed. (Illus.). 260p. (C). 1994. 45.00 (0-9641872-0-5) MN Veterinary.

Arnold, Joseph L. Maryland: Old Line to New Prosperity. LC 85-6416. 256p. 1985. 24.95 (0-89781-147-X) Am Historical Pr.

***Arnold, Judith.** L' Aventure d'une Vie. (Amours d'Aujourd'Hui Ser.: No. 341). (FRE.). 1999. mass mkt. 5.50 (0-373-38341-X, 1-38341-3, Harlequin French) Harlequin Bks.

Arnold, Judith. Barefoot in the Grass. 1996. per. 3.99 (0-373-70715-0, 1-70715-7) Harlequin Bks.

***Arnold, Judith.** Birthright, Vol.924. (Superromance Ser.). 2000. mass mkt. 4.50 (0-373-70924-2) Harlequin Bks.

Arnold, Judith. Change of Life. (Family Continuity Program Ser.: No. 19). 1999. per. 4.50 (0-373-82167-0, 1-82167-7) Harlequin Bks.

— Courting Trouble. 1997. per. 3.50 (0-373-25751-1, 1-25751-8) Harlequin Bks.

***Arnold, Judith.** Cry Uncle. 2000. mass mkt. 4.50 (0-373-82207-3, 1-82207-1) Harlequin Bks.

Arnold, Judith. Cry Uncle: (Family Man) LC 95-7065. (Superromance Ser.). 299p. 1995. per. 3.75 (0-373-70634-0, 1-70634-0) Harlequin Bks.

***Arnold, Judith.** Dr. Dad. (Superromance Ser.: Vol. 894). 2000. mass mkt. 4.50 (0-373-70894-7) Harlequin Bks.

Arnold, Judith. Father of Two. (Superromance Ser.: No. 771). 1998. per. 3.99 (0-373-70771-1) Harlequin Bks.

— Flashfire. (Superromance Ser.). 1993. per. 3.50 (0-373-70559-X, 1-70559-9) Harlequin Bks.

— Found: One Son: Finders, Keepers. 1999. per. 4.25 (0-373-70856-4, No. 1-70856-9) Harlequin Bks.

— Found: One Wife (Finders, Keepers) (Superromance Ser.). 1998. per. 4.25 (0-373-70809-2, 1-70809-8) Harlequin Bks.

***Arnold, Judith.** Her Secret Lover. (Temptation Ser.: No. 755). 1999. per. 3.75 (0-373-25855-0, 1-25855-7) Harlequin Bks.

Arnold, Judith. Just Like Romeo & Juliet. (American Romance Ser.). 1993. mass mkt. 3.39 (0-373-16482-3, 1-16482-1) Harlequin Bks.

— The Lady in the Mirror: Bachelor Arms. LC 95-22363. 218p. 1995. per. 3.25 (0-373-25661-2) Harlequin Bks.

— Legacy of Secrets. (Delta Justice Ser.). 1998. per. 4.50 (0-373-82571-4) Harlequin Bks.

— Married to the Man (Reunited) (Superromance Ser.). 1996. per. 3.99 (0-373-70684-7, 1-70684-5) Harlequin Bks.

— The Marrying Type. 1994. mass mkt. 3.50 (0-373-16553-6, 1-16553-9) Harlequin Bks.

— Oh, You Beautiful Doll. (American Romance Ser.). 1993. per. 3.50 (0-373-16496-3, 1-16496-1) Harlequin Bks.

— One Good Turn. (American Romance Ser.: No. 378). 1991. per. 2.95 (0-373-16378-9) Harlequin Bks.

— One Good Turn. large type ed. 327p. 1991. reprint ed. lib. bdg. 18.95 (1-56054-219-5) Thorndike Pr.

— The Parent Plan. 1994. mass mkt. 3.50 (0-373-70581-6, 1-70581-3) Harlequin Bks.

— Private Lies. (American Romance Ser.). 1994. per. 3.50 (0-373-16524-2, 1-16524-0) Harlequin Bks.

— A Stranger's Baby. (Weddings by DeWilde Ser.). 1996. per. 4.50 (0-373-82543-9, 1-82543-9) Harlequin Bks.

— Timeless Love. LC 96-3483. 217p. 1995. per. 3.25 (0-373-25665-5, 1-25665-0) Harlequin Bks.

— Trust Me. (American Romance Ser.: No. 431). 1992. per. 3.39 (0-373-16431-9, 1-16431-8) Harlequin Bks.

***Arnold, Judith.** Le Verdict de l'Amour. 1999. mass mkt. 3.99 (0-373-37533-6) Silhouette.

Arnold, Judith. The Wrong Bride: By the Year 2000: Revenge. (Superromance Ser.: No. 830). 1999. per. 4.25 (0-373-70830-0, 1-70830-4, Harlequin) Harlequin Bks.

Arnold, Judith, et al. Mom, Apple Pie . . . & the Fourth of July, 3 bks. in 1. 1998. per. 5.99 (0-373-20149-4, 1-20149-0) Harlequin Bks.

— Research Writing in the Information Age. LC 98-17326. 282p. 1998. spiral bd. 23.00 (0-205-26211-2) Allyn.

Arnold, Julie W. Art Criticism As Narrative Vol. 13: Diderot's Salon de 1767, Vol. 13. (The Ages of Revolution & Romanticism Ser.). XI, 161p. (C). 1996. text 42.95 (0-8204-2662-8) P Lang Pubng.

Arnold, June. The Cook & the Carpenter: A Novel by the Carpenter. (The Cutting Edge: Lesbian Life & Literature Ser.). 230p. (C). 1995. pap. text 16.50 (0-8147-0631-2) NYU Pr.

— The Cook & the Carpenter: A Novel by the Carpenter. (The Cutting Edge: Lesbian Life & Literature Ser.). 230p. (C). 1995. text 42.50 (0-8147-0628-2) NYU Pr.

— Sister Gin. LC 89-7926. 240p. 1989. pap. 12.95 (1-55861-010-3) Feminist Pr.

Arnold, K. Wirschaftsgeographie in Stichworten. 239p. 1992. 25.00 (3-443-03102-1, Pub. by Gebruder Borntraeger) Balogh.

Arnold, K., et al. Normandy. LC 94-68179. (Illustrated Travel Guides from Thomas Cook Ser.). (Illus.). 192p. (Orig.). 1994. pap. 12.95 (0-8442-9090-4, Passprt Bks) NTC Contemp Pub Co.

Arnold, K. P. Vom Sofakissen Zum Stadtebau. (GER., Illus.). 500p. 1992. text 68.00 (3-364-00252-5) Gordon & Breach.

Arnold, Karen. Border Crossings. 56p. (Orig.). 1998. pap. 10.00 (1-891043-01-3) Perry Pubng.

***Arnold, Karen.** Playing Grandma's Games. LC 00-190332. (Illus.). 160p. 2000. pap. 11.95 (1-890437-47-6) Western Reflections.

Arnold, Karen D., jt. ed. see Subotnik, Rena F.

Arnold, Karen S., ed. see Cunningham, Bill.

Arnold, Karl W., jt. auth. see Karrer, Pierre A.

Arnold, Kathleen, et al. Coming Home to Door: Vignettes & Recipes Celebrating the 100th Anniversary of the Door County Literary Guild. LC 98-94136. 152p. 1998. pap. 15.95 (1-891609-05-X) Home Brew Pr.

***Arnold, Kathy.** Essential Madrid. (AAA Essential Guides Ser.). (Illus.). 128p. 2000. pap. 8.95 (0-658-00375-5, 003755, Passprt Bks) NTC Contemp Pub Co.

Arnold, Kathy. Florida Charming Small Hotels. (Charming Small Hotel Guides Ser.). (Illus.). 176p. (Orig.). 1996. pap. 12.95 (1-55650-757-7) Hunter NJ.

— London. 2nd ed. LC 94-67812. (Illustrated Travel Guides from Thomas Cook Ser.). (Illus.). 192p. 1994. pap. 12.95 (0-8442-9047-5, Passprt Bks) NTC Contemp Pub Co.

***Arnold, Kathy.** London. 4th ed. (Illustrated Travel Guides Ser.). (Illus.). 2000. pap. 14.95 (0-658-01074-3, Passprt Bks) NTC Contemp Pub Co.

Arnold, Kathy. Passport's Illustrated Guide to Normandy. 2nd ed. LC 98-67245. (Passport's Illustrated Travel Guides Ser.). (Illus.). 192p. 2000. pap. 14.95 (0-8442-1151-6, 11516, Passprt Bks) NTC Contemp Pub Co.

***Arnold, Kathy.** Passport's Illustrated Guides to Turkey. (Illus.). 192p. 2000. pap. write for info. (0-658-00150-7, Passprt Bks) NTC Contemp Pub Co.

Arnold, Kathy & Wade, Paul. The Loire Valley. (Thomas Cook Illustrated Guides Ser.). (Illus.). 192p. (Orig.). 1996. pap. 12.95 (0-8442-9102-1, 91021, Passprt Bks) NTC Contemp Pub Co.

***Arnold, Kathy & Wade, Paul.** The National Geographic Traveler Florida. LC 99-39976. 272p. 1999. per. 22.95 (0-7922-7432-6) Natl Geog.

Arnold, Katya. The Adventures of Snowwoman. LC 98-16227. (Illus.). 32p. (J). (ps-3). 1998. lib. bdg. 15.95 (0-8234-1390-X) Holiday.

— Katya's Book of Mushrooms. LC 95-52598. (J). 1997. 16.95 (0-8050-4136-2) H Holt & Co.

***Arnold, Katya.** Me Too! Two Small Stories about Small Animals. LC 99-16696. (Illus.). 32p. (J). (ps-1). 2000. 15.95 (0-8234-1483-3) Holiday.

— That Apple is Mine! (Illus.). 32p. (ps-1). 2000. 15.95 (0-8234-1629-1) Holiday.

Arnold, Katya. Baba Yaga: A Russian Folktale. LC 92-38199. 32p. (J). (ps-3). 1996. pap. 6.95 (1-55858-593-1, Pub. by North-South Bks NYC) Chronicle Bks.

— Duck, Duck, Goose? LC 96-54856. 32p. (J). (gr. k-3). 1997. 15.95 (0-8234-1296-2) Holiday.

Arnold, Keith. Preserving Texas' Natural Heritage, No. 31. (Policy Research Project Report Ser.). 40p. 1978. pap. 3.00 (0-89940-627-0) LBJ Sch Pub Aff.

***Arnold, Ken.** Embedded Controller Hardware Design. (Illus.). 320p. 2000. pap. 49.95 incl. cd-rom (1-878707-52-3, Pub. by LLH Tech Pub) IPG Chicago.

Arnold, Ken. Gifts from the Heart: A Celebration of Service to Women, Their Families & the Community. Handy, William R., ed. (Illus.). 80p. 1999. pap. 24.95 (0-9663673-2-4) ASR Philan.

— The Java Programming Language. 2nd ed. LC 97-43181. 464p. (C). 1997. pap. text 39.95 (0-201-31006-6) Addison-Wesley.

***Arnold, Ken.** Jini Specification. LC 99-22850. 400p. 1999. pap. text 39.95 (0-201-61634-3) Addison-Wesley.

Arnold, Ken. Practical Java. (C). 2001. pap. 29.95 (0-201-31005-8) Addison-Wesley.

Arnold, Ken & Gosling, James. The Java Programming Language. (Java Ser.). 352p. 1996. pap. text 36.95 (0-201-63455-4) Addison-Wesley.

***Arnold, Ken & Gosling, James.** The Java Programming Language. 3rd ed. 352p. 2000. pap. 37.95 (0-201-70433-1) Addison-Wesley.

Arnold, Ken & Peyton, John. The C User's Guide to ANSIC. (Illus.). 144p. (C). 1992. pap. text 27.95 (0-201-56331-2) Addison-Wesley.

Arnold, Ken & Stewart, Maurice. Design of Oil-Handling Systems & Facilities. LC 86-345. (Surface Production Operations Ser.: Vol. 1). (Illus.). 432p. 1986. reprint ed. pap. 134.00 (0-608-07946-4, 206791900012) Bks Demand.

Arnold, Ken & Stewart, Maurice, Jr. Surface Production Operations, Vol. 1. 2nd ed. LC 97-38110. 443p. 1998. 115.00 (0-88415-821-7, 5821) Gulf Pub.

— Surface Production Operations, Vol. 2. 2nd ed. 550p. 1998. 115.00 (0-88415-822-5, 5822) Gulf Pub.

Arnold, Ken, et al. SanFrancisco Lifecycle Programming Techniques. LC 99-50064. 240p. (C). 1999. pap. text 39.95 (0-201-61658-0) Addison-Wesley.

Arnold, Kenneth L. & Holler, Michael. Quality Assurance: Philosophies, Methods, & Technologies. 1995. teacher ed. 12.21 (0-02-802334-X) Glencoe.

Arnold, Kenneth & Palmer, Ray. The Coming of the Saucers. (Illus.). 192p. 1996. reprint ed. pap. 18.95 (0-9644997-1-1) Legend Pr.

Arnold, Kenneth J. California Civil Actions: Pleading & Practice, 5 vols., Set. 1983. ring bd. 930.00 (0-8205-1115-3) Bender.

Arnold, Kenneth L. The Manager's Guide to ISO 9000. LC 94-4413. 384p. 1994. 35.00 (0-02-901035-7) Free Pr.

Arnold, Kenneth L. & Holler, Michael. Quality Assurance: Philosophies, Methods & Technologies. LC 94-20426. 1994. 69.12 (0-02-802333-1) Glencoe.

Arnold, Kevin D., et al. Passing the Ohio Ninth Grade Proficiency. (Illus.). 304p. (Orig.). (J). (gr. 7-12). 1996. reprint ed. pap. 15.95 (1-884183-06-9) Englfld & Arnold.

Arnold, Klaves, ed. Johannes Trithemius: In Praise of Scribes. Behrendt, Roland, tr. 125p. 1974. 7.50 (0-87291-066-0) Coronado Pr.

Arnold, Krstyn E., jt. auth. see McManus, Catherine O.

Arnold, Krystyn E. & McManus, Catherine O. The Lazy Cook: From Lobster to Brats - Recipes of the New England, Mid-Atlantic & Great Lakes States Made Easy. LC 96-45962. 1997. pap. 12.95 (1-57090-051-5) Alexander Dist.

Arnold, Krystyn E., jt. auth. see McManus, Catherine O.

Arnold, L. Random Dynamical Systems. LC 98-27207. (Monographs in Mathematics). (Illus.). 625p. 1998. 89.00 (3-540-63758-3) Spr-Verlag.

Arnold, L., et al, eds. Lyapunov Exponents: Proceedings of a Conference Held in Oberwolfach, FRG, May 28-June 2, 1990. (Lecture Notes in Mathematics Ser.: Vol. 1486). viii, 365p. 1991. 65.95 (0-387-54662-6) Spr-Verlag.

Arnold, L. & Kotelenz, P., eds. Stochastic Space-Time Models & Limit Theories. (Mathematics & Its Applications Ser.). 1985. text 155.50 (90-277-2038-X) Kluwer Academic.

Arnold, L. & Wihstutz, V., eds. Lyapunov Exponents. (Lecture Notes in Mathematics Ser.: Vol. 1186). vi, 374p. 1986. 63.95 (0-387-16458-8) Spr-Verlag.

Arnold, L., et al. Dynamical Systems: Lectures Given at the 2nd Session of the Centro Internazionale Matematico Estivo (C. I. M. E.) Held in Montecatini Terme, Italy, June 13-22, 1994. Johnson, R., ed. LC 95-22024. (Lecture Notes in Mathematics Ser.: Vol. 1609). 1995. write for info. (0-387-60047-7) Spr-Verlag.

— Dynamical Systems: Lectures Given at the 2nd Session of the Centro Internazionale Matematico Estivo (C.I.M.E.) Held in Montecatini Terme, Italy, June 13-22, 1994. Dold, A. & Takens, F., eds. (Lecture Notes in Mathematics Ser.: Vol. 1609). 329p. 1995. pap. 62.95 (3-540-60047-7) Spr-Verlag.

Arnold, L. Eugene. Contemporary Diagnosis & Management of Attention Deficit/Hyperactivity Disorder. (Illus.). 200p. 2000. pap. 29.95 (1-884065-53-8, Hndbks Hlth Care) Assocs in Med.

Arnold, L. Eugene, ed. Childhood Stress. LC 90-30510. (Series in Child Mental Health). 624p. 1990. 175.00 (0-471-50868-3) Wiley.

Arnold, L. M. History of the Origin of All Things. unabridged ed. 460p. 1993. pap. 5.00 (0-9664031-0-X) Christ Age Pr.

Arnold, L. W. & Luckey, E. Z. Arnold - Luckey Family Ties: Authorized History & Genealogy Complete. (Illus.). 168p. 1991. reprint ed. pap. 25.00 (0-8328-2048-2); reprint ed. lib. bdg. 35.00 (0-8328-2047-4) Higginson Bk Co.

Arnold, L. Walker. Legend of Old Faithful. LC 86-50716. 364p. 1986. 12.95 (0-931117-05-4) Univ Pub.

— Out of the Night. 384p. 1987. 15.95 (0-931117-08-9) Univ Pub.

Arnold, Larry & Nevius, Sandy. The Reiki Handbook. 4th ed. 160p. 1982. pap. 13.50 (0-9625500-1-9) PSI Pr PA.

Arnold, Larry E. Ablaze! The Mysterious Fires of Spontaneous Human Combustion. LC 95-34593. (Illus.). 512p. 1996. 24.95 (0-87131-789-3) M Evans.

Arnold, Lauren. Princely Gifts & Papal Treasures: The Franciscan Mission to China & Its Influence on the Art of the West, 1250-1350. (Illus.). 175p. 1999. 49.95 (0-9670628-0-2) Desiderata Pr.

Arnold, Lawrence J. The Restoration Land Settlement in Co. Dublin, 1660-88. (Illus.). 224p. 1993. 45.00 (0-7165-2503-8, Pub. by Irish Acad Pr) Intl Spec Bk.

Arnold, Lee E., Jr. Commercial Investment Real Estate: Marketing & Brokerage Management, Bk. 1. 2nd ed. 332p. 1991. text 50.25 (0-13-151440-7) P-H.

— Commercial-Investment Real Estate: Marketing & Management, Bk. 1. Gerth, Dawn M., ed. LC 82-62949. (Illus.). 250p. text 24.95 (0-913652-53-9, BK 161) Realtors Natl.

— Commercial Investment Real Estate Bk. 2: Policies & Procedures. 2nd ed. (Illus.). 248p. 1986. pap. text 18.40 (0-13-152737-1) P-H.

Arnold, Linda. Bureaucracy & Bureaucrats in Mexico City, 1742-1835. LC 88-17226. 202p. 1988. 35.00 (0-8165-1068-7) U of Ariz Pr.

***Arnold, Lisa A. & Glover, Linda J.** Co-Treat with Confidence: Joint Activities for SLP's & OT's. 194p. 1999. spiral bd. 34.95 (0-7606-0302-2) LinguiSystems.

***Arnold, Lois Embree.** Pine Tree Quilts: Perfect Patchwork Piecing. (Illus.). 144p. 2000. pap. 25.95 (1-57432-749-6, Am Quilters Soc) Collector Bks.

***Arnold, Lorna & Pyne, Katherine.** Britain & the H-Bomb. LC 00-36898. 2000. pap. write for info. (0-312-23518-6) St Martin.

Arnold, Louis. The Israeli Countdown to Eternity. LC 85-81082. 160p. 1985. pap. 5.95 (0-931117-03-8) Univ Pub.

Arnold, Louisa T. Tennis Ticklers: Tennis Poems to Make You Laugh. (Illus.). 80p. 1994. 16.95 (0-9641835-0-1) Tengo Pubng.

Arnold, Lucinda K., jt. compiled by see Grabowski, John J.

Arnold, Luis, ed. Flamenco Styling for the Latin American Dances. (Ballroom Dance Ser.). 1986. lib. bdg. 250.00 (0-8490-3365-9) Gordon Pr.

— Flamenco Styling for the Latin American Dances. (Ballroom Dance Ser.). 1985. lib. bdg. 250.00 (0-87700-871-X) Revisionist Pr.

Arnold, Lyle. The Protection Formula: Thinking Like a Cop. Lippman, Paul, ed. LC 95-72860. (Illus.). 166p. (Orig.). 1996. pap. 12.95 (0-9650241-7-2) Philippi Pubng.

Arnold, Lynda. Angels of Love: Celebrating Diversity & Adoption. (Illus.). 32p. (YA). (gr. k-1). 1998. 18.95 (1-892073-00-5) Dream Pub.

— My Mommy Has AIDS: Angels of Love: Celebrating Diversity & Adoption. (Illus.). 32p. (J). (gr. k-5). 1998. 18.95 (1-892073-01-3) Dream Pub.

Arnold, M. H., ed. Agricultural Research for Development: The Hamulonge Contribution. LC 75-31400. 375p. reprint ed. pap. 106.90 (0-8357-5271-2, 2024411) Bks Demand.

***Arnold, Madelyn.** Bird-Eyes. 240p. 2000. pap. 12.95 (0-312-26294-9) St Martin.

Arnold, Magda B. Memory & the Brain. 544p. 1984. text 99.95 (0-89859-290-9) L Erlbaum Assocs.

Arnold, Malcolm. Rainy Sunday. Krentz, Linda S., ed. 157p. 1991. 37.50 (0-9628256-0-3) Swegal & Son.

Arnold, Malcolm, jt. auth. see Swegal, Franz B.

Arnold, Marc, jt. auth. see LeMesuier, Charles.

Arnold, Marc, jt. auth. see LeMesurier, Charles.

Arnold, Marc, jt. ed. see LeMesurier, Charles.

Arnold, Margaret. How to Use Numerology for Career Success. LC 96-9054. (How to Ser.). (Illus.). 128p. (Orig.). 1996. mass mkt. 4.99 (1-56718-039-6) Llewellyn Pubns.

***Arnold, Margaret.** Love Numbers. 2000. 7.99 (0-517-16184-2) Crown Pub Group.

Arnold, Margaret. Love Numbers: How to Use Numerology to Make Love Count. LC 97-40972. (Illus.). 272p. (Orig.). 1999. pap. 9.95 (1-56718-040-X) Llewellyn Pubns.

***Arnold, Margaret.** Numerologia (Compatibilidad y Amistad) (ENG & SPA.). 240p. 2000. pap. 9.95 (1-56718-041-8, Llewellyn Esp) Llewellyn Pubns.

Arnold, Margot, pseud. The Cape Cod Caper. (Penny Spring & Sir Toby Glendower Mystery Ser.). 192p. 1988. pap. 7.95 (0-88150-116-6, Foul Play) Norton.

— The Cape Cod Conundrum. (Penny Spring & Sir Toby Glendower Mystery Ser.). 224p. 1994. reprint ed. pap. 7.95 (0-88150-293-6, Foul Play) Norton.

— The Catacomb Conspiracy. (Penny Spring & Sir Toby Glendower Mystery Ser.). 240p. 1993. pap. 7.95 (0-88150-255-3, Foul Play) Norton.

— Death of a Voodoo Doll. 220p. 1989. reprint ed. pap. 6.95 (0-88150-132-8, Foul Play) Norton.

— Death on the Dragon's Tongue. (Penny Spring & Sir Toby Glendower Mystery Ser.). 224p. 1990. reprint ed. pap. 7.95 (0-88150-158-1, Foul Play) Norton.

— Dirge for a Dorset Druid. (Penny Spring & Sir Toby Glendower Mystery Ser.). 240p. 1993. 20.00 (0-88150-266-9, Foul Play) Norton.

— Dirge for a Dorset Druid. (Penny Spring & Sir Toby Glendower Mystery Ser.). 240p. 1995. pap. 7.95 (0-88150-334-7, Foul Play) Norton.

— Exit Actors, Dying. (Penny Spring & Sir Toby Glendower Mystery Ser.). 176p. 1988. reprint ed. pap. 7.95 (0-88150-115-8, Foul Play) Norton.

— Lament for a Lady Laird. (Penny Spring & Sir Toby Glendower Mystery Ser.). 224p. 1990. reprint ed. pap. 6.95 (0-88150-159-X, Foul Play) Norton.

— The Menehune Murders. (Penny Spring & Sir Toby Glendower Mystery Ser.). 260p. 1991. pap. 7.95 (0-88150-196-4, Foul Play) Norton.

— The Midas Murders. (Penny Spring & Sir Toby Glendower Mystery Ser.). 224p. 1995. 20.00 (0-88150-340-1, Foul Play) Norton.

— The Midas Murders. 224p. 1997. pap. 7.95 (0-88150-394-0) Norton.

— The Officer's Woman. large type ed. 1982. 27.99 (0-7089-8018-X, Charnwood) Ulverscroft.

— Toby's Folly. (Penny Spring & Sir Toby Glendower Mystery Ser.). 256p. 1992. pap. 7.95 (0-88150-228-6, Foul Play) Norton.

— Zadok's Treasure. (Penny Spring & Sir Toby Glendower Mystery Ser.). 192p. 1989. reprint ed. pap. 7.95 (0-88150-133-6, Foul Play) Norton.

Arnold, Marilyn. Desert Song. 1998. 14.95 (1-57734-254-2, 01113348) Covenant Comms.

— Pure Love: Readings on Enduring Virtues. LC 97-23499. xxii, 519p. 1997. 24.95 (1-57345-239-4) Deseret Bk.

An Asterisk (*) at the beginning of an entry indicates that the title is appearing for the first time.

*Arnold, Marilyn. Song of Hope. LC 99-24549. 1999. 15.95 (1-57734-429-4, 01113836) Covenant Comms.

Arnold, Marilyn. Sweet Is the Word: Reflections on the Book of Mormon. LC 96-12275. 1996. pap. 15.95 (1-55503-925-1, 01112325) Covenant Comms.

— Willa Cather: A Reference Guide. (Reference Guides to Literature Ser.). 490p. (C). 1986. 45.00 (0-8161-8654-5, Hall Reference) Macmillan.

Arnold, Marion. Women & Art in South Africa. LC 96-38342. (Illus.). 232p. 1997. text 39.95 (0-312-16586-2) St Martin.

*Arnold, Mark. Administering Apache. (Illus.). 600p. 2000. pap. 44.99 (0-07-212291-9) McGrw-H Intl.

Arnold, Mark G. Verilog Digital Computer Design: Algorithms to Hardware. LC 98-20107. 592p. (C). 1998. 78.00 (0-13-639253-9) P-H.

Arnold, Mark W. & Preble, Kevin. Trading on Tomorrow's Headlines: How to Make Extraordinary Profits by Following the Stock Purchases. (Illus.). 134p. (Orig.). 1994. pap. 39.95 (0-9650256-0-8) TTH Inc.

*Arnold, Marsha D. The Bravest of Us All. LC 99-34170. (Illus.). (J). 2000. 15.99 (0-8037-2409-8, Dial Yng Read) Peng Put Young Read.

Arnold, Marsha D. The Chicken Salad Club. LC 97-19375. (Illus.). 32p. (J). (ps-3). 1998. 15.89 (0-8037-1916-7, Dial Yng Read) Peng Put Young Read.

— Heart of a Tiger. LC 94-17126. (Illus.). 32p. (J). (ps-3). 1995. 16.99 (0-8037-1695-8, Dial Yng Read) Peng Put Young Read.

— The Pumpkin Runner. LC 97-26666. (Illus.). (J). 1998. 15.89 (0-8037-2125-0, Dial Yng Read) Peng Put Young Read.

— Quick, Quack, Quick. LC 94-38054. (Step into Reading Ser.: A Step 1 Book). (Illus.). 32p. (J). (ps-4). 1996. pap. 3.99 (0-679-87243-4) Random.

— Quick, Quack, Quick. (Step into Reading Ser.: A Step 1 Book). (J). (ps-1). 1996. 8.94 (0-606-09775-9, Pub. by Turtleback) Demco.

Arnold, Martha, jt. ed. see Silkworth, Cynthia.

Arnold, Marti. Alaska, Uncle Jim & Me. Lesko, Marian, ed. (Illus.). 146p. (Orig.). (J). (gr. 6 up). 1983. pap. 5.95 (0-912683-00-7) Fireweed.

Arnold, Mary. The Fussy Angel. LC 95-70500. (LambTime Bks.). (Illus.). 32p. (Orig.). (J). (ps-2). 1995. 11.95 (1-883937-35-3, 35-3) Bethlehem ND.

— Pregnancy Diary: A Christian Mother's Reflections. LC 95-79887. 156p. (Orig.). 1996. pap. 9.95 (0-89870-564-9) Ignatius Pr.

Arnold, Mary, ed. see Evers, Yvonne M.

Arnold, Mary E. & Reed, Mabel. In the Land of the Grasshopper Song: Two Women in the Klamath River Indian Country in 1908-09. LC 80-12556. (Illus.). iv, 329p. 1980. reprint ed. pap. 11.95 (0-8032-6703-7, Bison Books) U of Nebr Pr.

Arnold, Mary E., ed. see Hill, Kathleen T. & Hill, Gerald N.

Arnold, Mary-Kim. Preventing Unknown Barriers from Creeping into Your Treatment. (Orig.). 1995. pap. 39.95 (1-884937-32-2) Manisses Communs.

Arnold, Marylyn, et al, eds. A Reader's Companion to the Fiction of Willa Cather. LC 92-42434. 880p. 1993. lib. bdg. 115.00 (0-313-28767-8, GR8767, Greenwood Pr) Greenwood.

Arnold, Matthew. Civilization in the United States: First & Last Impressions of America. 192p. 1977. 18.95 (0-8369-6871-9) Ayer.

— The Complete Prose Works of Matthew Arnold: Culture & Anarchy, 5. Super, R. H., ed. 586p. 1965. text 59.50 (0-472-11655-X, 11655) U of Mich Pr.

— The Complete Prose Works of Matthew Arnold: Democratic Education, 2. Super, R. H., ed. 430p. 1962. text 59.50 (0-472-11652-5, 11652) U of Mich Pr.

— The Complete Prose Works of Matthew Arnold: English Literature & Irish Politics, 9. Super, R. H., ed. 494p. 1973. text 59.50 (0-472-11659-2, 11659) U of Mich Pr.

— The Complete Prose Works of Matthew Arnold: Essays Religious & Mixed, 8. Super, R. H., ed. 560p. 1972. text 59.50 (0-472-11658-4, 11658) U of Mich Pr.

— The Complete Prose Works of Matthew Arnold: Lectures & Essays in Criticism, 3. Super, R. H., ed. 596p. 1962. text 59.50 (0-472-11653-3, 11653) U of Mich Pr.

— The Complete Prose Works of Matthew Arnold: On the Classical Tradition, 1. Super, R. H., ed. 290p. 1960. text 59.50 (0-472-11651-7, 11651) U of Mich Pr.

— The Complete Prose Works of Matthew Arnold: Philistinism in England & America, 10. Super, R. H., ed. 622p. 1974. text 59.50 (0-472-11660-6, 11660) U of Mich Pr.

— The Complete Prose Works of Matthew Arnold: Schools & Universities on the Continent, 4. Super, R. H., ed. 446p. 1964. text 59.50 (0-472-11654-1, 11654) U of Mich Pr.

— Culture & Anarchy. 282p. (C). 1932. pap. text 19.95 (0-521-09103-9) Cambridge U Pr.

— Culture & Anarchy. Lipman, Samuel, ed. LC 93-2427. (Rethinking the Western Tradition Ser.). 289p. 1994. reprint ed. pap. 16.00 (0-300-05867-5) Yale U Pr.

— Culture & Anarchy. Lipman, Samuel, ed. LC 93-2427. (Rethinking the Western Tradition Ser.). 289p. 1994. reprint ed. 37.50 (0-300-05866-7) Yale U Pr.

— Culture & Anarchy: 1869 Edition. Stern, Jeffrey, ed. & intro. by. (Classics in Education Ser.). 326p. 1996. reprint ed. 80.00 (1-85506-265-8) Bks Intl VA.

— Culture & Anarchy & Other Writings. Collini, Stefan, ed. (Cambridge Texts in the History of Political Thought Ser.). 282p. (C). 1993. pap. text 11.95 (0-521-37796-X) Cambridge U Pr.

— Discourses in America. reprint ed. lib. bdg. 59.00 (0-7812-0319-8) Rprt Serv.

— Discourses in America. LC 76-131610. 1970. reprint ed. 25.00 (0-403-00497-7) Scholarly.

— Dover Beach & Other Poems. LC 93-23660. 80p. (Orig.). 1994. pap. 1.50 (0-486-28037-3) Dover.

— God & the Bible: A Review of Objections to "Literature & Dogma" LC 75-129382. reprint ed. 38.50 (0-404-00386-9) AMS Pr.

— The Letters of Matthew Arnold, 1848-1888, 2 vols., Set. (BCL1-PR English Literature Ser.). 1992. reprint ed. lib. bdg. 150.00 (0-7812-7424-9) Rprt Serv.

— The Letters of Matthew Arnold, 1848-1888, 2 vols., Set. Russell, George W., ed. LC 04-13997. 1969. reprint ed. 59.00 (0-403-00141-2) Scholarly.

— The Letters of Matthew Arnold, 1866-1870. Lang, Cecil Y., ed. (Victorian Literature & Culture Ser.: Vol. 3). 544p. 1998. 60.00 (0-8139-1765-4) U Pr of Va.

— The Letters of Matthew Arnold, 1860-1865, Vol. II. Lang, Cecil Y., ed. (Victorian Literature & Culture Ser.). 560p. (C). 1997. text 60.00 (0-8139-1706-9) U Pr of Va.

— Literature & Dogma: An Essay Towards a Better Apprehension of the Bible. LC 78-126650. 1970. reprint ed. 38.50 (0-404-00387-7) AMS Pr.

— Matthew Arnold & the Education of the New Order: A Selection of Arnold's Writings on Education. Smith, Peter & Summerfield, Geoffrey, eds. LC 69-10433. (Cambridge Texts & Studies in the History of Education). 268p. reprint ed. pap. 76.40 (0-608-12175-4, 2024533) Bks Demand.

*Arnold, Matthew. On the Study of Celtic Literature & on Translating Homer. 320p. 1998. reprint ed. pap. 24.95 (0-7661-0436-2) Kessinger Pub.

Arnold, Matthew. On Translating Homer. LC 78-136411. (BCL Ser.: No. 2). reprint ed. 27.50 (0-404-00388-5) AMS Pr.

— Selected Poems & Prose. Allott, Miriam, ed. 296p. 1993. pap. 7.95 (0-460-87392-X, Everyman's Classic Lib) Tuttle Pubng.

— Stakeholder Negotiations: Exercise in Sustainable Development. 184p. (C). 1995. text 16.25 (0-256-18806-8, Irwn McGrw-H) McGrw-H Hghr Educ.

— The Works of Matthew Arnold, 15 vols. LC 72-113544. (BCL Ser.: No. 1). reprint ed. 810.00 (0-404-00450-4) AMS Pr.

— Works of Matthew Arnold, 15 vols. reprint ed. lib. bdg. 900.00 (0-7812-0170-5) Rprt Serv.

— Works of Matthew Arnold, 15 vols. LC 70-107157. 1970. reprint ed. 40.00 (0-685-74309-8) Scholarly.

— Works of Matthew Arnold, 15 vols., Set. LC 70-107157. 1970. reprint ed. 395.00 (0-403-00201-X) Scholarly.

— The Yale Manuscript. 236p. 1989. text 55.00 (0-472-10105-6, 10105) U of Mich Pr.

Arnold, Matthew & Day, Robert. The Next Bottom Line: Making Sustainable Development Tangible. LC 98-88622. (Illus.). 64p. 1998. pap. 20.00 (1-56973-283-3) World Resources Inst.

Arnold, Matthew, ed. see Burke, Edmund.

Arnold, Matthias. Toulouse-Lautrec. 1994. pap. 9.99 (3-8228-9641-1) Taschen Amer.

— Toulouse-Lautrec. (SPA.). 1996. pap. 9.99 (3-8228-0211-5) Taschen Amer.

Arnold, Maureen M., jt. auth. see Novick, Barbara Z.

Arnold, Melvin T. Essentials of General, Organic & Biochemistry. 640p. (C). 1999. text. write for info. (0-03-005648-9) SCP.

— Essentials of General Organic & Biochemistry. teacher ed. write for info. (0-03-005649-7) SCP.

— Essentials of General Organic Biochemistry. 100p. pap. write for info. (0-03-005687-X) SCP.

Arnold, Michael L. Natural Hybridization & Evolution. LC 96-26496. (Oxford Series in Ecology & Evolution). (Illus.). 232p. 1997. text 75.00 (0-19-509974-5); pap. text 40.00 (0-19-509975-3) OUP.

Arnold, Mike. Crazy Picnic Game. (Crazy Games Ser.). (J). (gr. 1 up). 1996. pap. 2.95 (0-8431-3870-X, Price Stern) Peng Put Young Read.

Arnold, Mit. Supported Employment for Persons with Developmental Disabilities. 126p. 1992. pap. 23.95 (0-398-06009-6); text 33.95 (0-398-05780-X) C C Thomas.

Arnold, Morris, et al. Arkansas Before the Americans. Davis, Hester A., ed. (Research Ser.). (Illus.). 153p. 1991. pap. 10.00 (1-56349-070-6, RS40) AR Archaeol.

Arnold, Morris L. Soliloquies of Shakespeare: A Study in Technic. LC 78-58273. reprint ed. 37.50 (0-404-00389-3) AMS Pr.

Arnold, Morris S. Colonial Arkansas, 1686-1804: A Social & Cultural History. (Illus.). 232p. 1993. pap. 22.00 (1-55728-317-6) U of Ark Pr.

*Arnold, Morris S. The Rumble of a Distant Drum: The Quapaw & Old World Newcomers, 1673-1804. LC 99-51769. (Illus.). 336p. 2000. 35.00 (1-55728-590-X) U of Ark Pr.

Arnold, Morris S. Unequal Laws unto a Savage Race: European Legal Traditions in Arkansas, 1686-1836. LC 84-168. (Illus.). 262p. 1985. pap. 14.00 (0-938626-76-0) U of Ark Pr.

— Year Books Of Richard II: Richard II 1378-1379. (Ames Foundation Publications: Vol. 1). (FRE, LAT & ENG.). xl,124,151p. 1975. 60.00 (1-893606-00-7) W S Hein.

Arnold, N. Scott. The Philosophy & Economics of Market Socialism: A Critical Study. LC 93-31714. (Illus.). 320p. 1994. text 70.00 (0-19-508827-1) OUP.

Arnold, N. Scott, et al. Philosophy Then & Now: An Introductory Text with Classic Readings. LC 97-47396. 720p. 1998. 69.95 (1-55786-741-0); pap. 39.95 (1-55786-742-9) Blackwell Pubs.

Arnold, N. Xavier. The Genocide Files. 2nd ed. LC 96-90572. 332p. 1997. reprint ed. 16.95 (0-9651007-0-7, 021-99) Tana Lake.

Arnold, Nick. Blood, Bones & Body Bits. (Horrible Science Ser.). (J). (gr. 5-9). 1998. pap. text 3.99 (0-590-13859-6, Point) Scholastic Inc.

— Chemical Chaos. (Horrible Science Ser.). (J). (gr. 5-9). 1998. pap. 3.99 (0-590-10885-9) Scholastic Inc.

— Disgusting Digestion. (Horrible Science Ser.). 160p. (gr. 7-12). 1999. pap. 4.50 (0-439-04362-X) Scholastic Inc.

— Fatal Forces. (Horrible Science Ser.). 160p. (gr. 7-12). 1999. pap. 4.50 (0-439-04363-8) Scholastic Inc.

— Horrible Science Mixed Display. 1999. pap. text 54.00 (0-439-05989-5) Scholastic Inc.

*Arnold, Nick. Medicine. (Future Tech Ser.). (Illus.). 32p. (J). 1999. lib. bdg. 15.95 (1-929298-39-0, Pub. by Thameside Pr) Smart Apple.

Arnold, Nick. Nasty Nature. (Horrible Science Ser.). (Illus.). 159p. (YA). (gr. 5-9). 1998. pap. 3.99 (0-590-21677-2) Scholastic Inc.

— Ugly Bugs. (J). (gr. 5-9). 1998. pap. text 3.99 (0-590-13858-8, Point) Scholastic Inc.

Arnold, Nick. Volcano, Earthquake & Hurricane. LC 96-32760. (Remarkable World Ser.). (Illus.). 48p. (J). (gr. 4 up). 1997. lib. bdg. 24.26 (0-8172-4540-5) Raintree Steck-V.

Arnold, Nick. Voyages of Exploration. (Remarkable World Ser.). (Illus.). 48p. (YA). (gr. 3-8). 1995. lib. bdg. 24.26 (1-56847-368-0) Raintree Steck-V.

Arnold, Nick, et al. Sticker Activity Atlas. (Illus.). 8p. (J). pap. 9.99 (0-590-24921-5) Scholastic Inc.

Arnold, Norman R. & Frumker, Sanford C. Occlusal Treatment: Preventive & Corrective Occlusal Adjustment. LC 75-1306. 174p. reprint ed. pap. 54.00 (0-608-17754-7, 205650000069) Bks Demand.

Arnold, Oren. Pancho Villa: The Mexican Centaur. LC 76-29143. 1979. 20.00 (0-916620-06-9) Portals Pr.

— Thunder in the Southwest: Echoes from the Wild Frontier. LC 52-4324. 246p. reprint ed. pap. 76.30 (0-608-13724-3, 205550800023) Bks Demand.

Arnold, P. Ultimate Encyclopedia of Boxing. 208p. 1996. 19.98 (0-7858-0641-5) Bk Sales Inc.

Arnold Palmer Golf Academy Staff. Arnold Palmer Golf Journal: A Personal Handbook of Practice, Performance, & Progress. (Illus.). 144p. 1997. 17.95 (1-57243-172-5) Triumph Bks.

Arnold, Patrick M. Gibeah: The Search for a Biblical City. (Journal for the Study of the Old Testament Supplement Ser.: Vol. 79). 200p. 1990. 57.50 (1-85075-223-0, Pub. by Sheffield Acad) CUP Services.

— Wildmen, Warriors, & Kings: Masculine Spirituality & the Bible. 240p. 1992. pap. 13.95 (0-8245-1252-9) Crossroad NY.

Arnold, Paul. Wisdom of the Guides: Rocky Mountain Trout Guides Talk Fly Fishing. LC 99-164795. (Illus.). 150p. 1998. 24.95 (1-57188-128-X) F Amato Pubns.

Arnold, Paul, jt. auth. see Watson, Delmar.

Arnold, Paul A., ed. see Braddock Communications Staff.

Arnold, Peri E. Making the Managerial Presidency: Comprehensive Reorganization Planning, 1905-1996. 2nd ed. LC 97-52290. (Studies in Government & Public Policy). 456p. 1998. 50.00 (0-7006-0893-1); pap. 25.00 (0-7006-0894-X) U Pr of KS.

Arnold, Peter. Bulbs in Bloom: Tubers, Corms, & Rhizomes. LC 99-42673. (Illus.). 132p. 1999. 24.95 (1-57145-645-7, Laurel Glen Pub) Advantage Pubs.

— Making Direct Mail Work: How to Boost Your Profits with Effective Direct Mail Promotion. (Illus.). 144p. 1999. pap. 19.95 (1-85703-297-7, Pub. by How To Bks) Trans-Atl Phila.

Arnold, Peter, jt. auth. see Hugman, Barry J.

Arnold, Peter, jt. auth. see Wallach, Ellen J.

Arnold, Peter J. Education, Movement & the Curriculum: A Philosophic Enquiry. 1990. write for info. (0-318-66776-2) Taylor & Francis.

Arnold, Peter-Klaus. Dresdner Porzellan Geschichte Einer Manufaktur. (GER., Illus.). 80p. 1996. pap. text 16.50 (90-5705-005-6) Gordon & Breach.

Arnold, Philip J., III. Domestic Ceramic Production & Spatial Organization: A Mexican Case Study in Ethnoarchaeology. (New Studies in Archaeology). (Illus.). 194p. (C). 1991. text 74.95 (0-521-39199-7) Cambridge U Pr.

Arnold, Philip J., III, jt. auth. see Stark, Barbara.

Arnold, Philip P. Eating Landscape: Aztec & European Occupation of Tzalocan. LC 99-10880. (Mesoamerican Worlds Ser.). (Illus.). 287p. 1999. 45.00 (0-87081-578-0) Univ Pr Colo.

Arnold, Phillip G., jt. auth. see McCaw, John B.

Arnold, Phillip G., jt. auth. see McCraw, John B.

Arnold, Phyllis, jt. auth. see Fresquez, Margarit.

Arnold, R., ed. Somatostatin Analogues: Basic & Clinical Perspectives Meeting, Sorrento, November, 1995. (Journal Digestion Ser.: Vol. 57, Suppl. 1, 1996). (Illus.). vi, 120p. 1996. pap. 50.50 (3-8055-6337-X) S Karger.

Arnold, R. B. A First Physics Course. (Illus.). 256p. (C). 1994. pap. 19.95 (0-85950-119-1, Pub. by S Thornes Pubs) Trans-Atl Phila.

Arnold, R. Douglas. The Logic of Congressional Action. 293p. (C). 1992. reprint ed. pap. 20.00 (0-300-05659-1) Yale U Pr.

Arnold, R. Douglas, et al, eds. Framing the Social Security Debate: Values, Politics, & Economics. LC 98-25429. 200p. 1998. pap. 19.95 (0-8157-0153-5) Brookings.

Arnold, R. E., tr. see Fischer, P. C., ed.

Arnold, R. G., ed. Electronuclear Physics with Internal Targets: Proceedings of the Topical Conference SLAC, California, U. S. A., 9-12 Jan. 1989. 316p. (C). 1990. text 151.00 (9971-5-0888-5) World Scientific Pub.

Arnold, R. Keith, et al. View from the Top: Forest Service Research. Steen, Harold K., ed. LC 93-46520. xiv, 365p. 1994. pap. 16.95 (0-89030-049-6) Forest Hist Soc.

Arnold, R. Steven. How to Survive a Jewish Mother. Carle, Cliff, ed. (Illus.). 144p. 1996. pap. 6.95 (1-57644-005-2) CCC Pubns.

Arnold, Ree K., jt. auth. see Chepko, Steveda F.

Arnold, Rhodes. The B-24-PB4Y in Combat: The World's Greatest Bomber. (Illus.). 185p. 1990. 10.00 (0-9619253-3-7) Pima Paisano.

Arnold, Rhodes, ed. Foul Weather Front Vol. 1: A History of Air Operations in the North Pacific. (Illus.). 348p. 1995. pap. 20.00 (0-9619253-4-5) Pima Paisano.

Arnold, Richard. Disaster Recovery Plan. 144p. 1993. pap. 119.99 (0-471-55696-3) Wiley.

— The English Hymn: Studies in a Genre. LC 93-50230. XIII, 254p. (C). 1995. text 35.95 (0-8204-2485-4) P Lang Pubng.

Arnold, Richard, ed. English Hymns of the Eighteenth Century: An Anthology. LC 91-19805. (American University Studies: English Language & Literature: Ser. IV, Vol. 127). 546p. (C). 1992. text 58.95 (0-8204-1674-6) P Lang Pubng.

Arnold, Richard A. Ecological Studies of Six Endangered Butterflies (Lepidoptera, Lycaenidae) Island Biogeography, Patch Dynamics, & the Design of Habitat Preserves. LC 83-3566. (University of California Publications in Entomology: No. 99). 173p. 1983. pap. 53.70 (0-7837-7464-8, 204918600010) Bks Demand.

Arnold, Richard D. Letters of Richard D. Arnold, M. D., 1808-1876. Shryock, Richard H., ed. LC 71-115999. (Duke University. Trinity College Historical Society. Historical Papers: Nos. 18-19). reprint ed. 30.00 (0-404-51768-4) AMS Pr.

Arnold, Richard L. Scene Technology. 3rd ed. LC 93-16748. 384p. 1993. 69.00 (0-13-501073-X) P-H.

Arnold, Richard S., Jr., et al. Capitalizing & Protecting New Businesses. Hagelstein, Marie, ed. LC 97-65861. (California Business Start-Up Ser.). 654p. 1997. ring bd. 150.00 (0-7626-0062-4, BU-32940) Cont Ed Bar-CA.

Arnold, Richard W. Keys to Soil Taxonomy. 7th ed. 644p. (C). 1997. pap. text 60.00 (0-7881-3989-4) DIANE Pub.

Arnold, Rick. Demystifying ISDN. LC 97-30544. 1997. pap. text 24.95 (1-55622-573-3) Wordware Pub.

Arnold, Rita E., jt. auth. see Cannatella, Mary M.

Arnold, Robert. Education Administrators: One Hundred Eight Billion Dollar Managers. 176p. (Orig.). (C). 1993. pap. text 26.00 (0-8191-9248-1); lib. bdg. 42.50 (0-8191-9247-3) U Pr of Amer.

— Hoosier Autumn: The Remarkable Story of Indiana University's 1945 Football Championship Team. LC 96-76829. 150p. 1996. 22.95 (1-878208-86-1); pap. 15.95 (1-878208-85-3) Guild Pr IN.

Arnold, Robert & Bohner, Shawn. Software Change Impact Analysis. LC 95-52098. 392p. 1996. pap. 45.00 (0-8186-7384-2, BPO7384) IEEE Comp Soc.

Arnold, Robert, jt. auth. see Tannenbaum, Peter.

Arnold, Robert F., ed. see Hernick, James L.

Arnold, Robert H. Interpretation of Airphotos & Remotely Sensed Imagery. LC 96-25112. 262p. (C). 1996. spiral bd. 50.00 (0-02-303924-8, Macmillan Coll) P-H.

Arnold, Robert S. Software Reengineering. LC 92-41597. 688p. 1993. 79.00 (0-8186-3272-0, 3272) IEEE Comp Soc.

Arnold, Roger A. Economics. LC 93-32249. 1994. text, student ed. write for info. (0-314-02938-9) West Pub.

— Economics. LC 93-32249. 1994. pap., student ed. 53.00 (0-314-02901-X) West Pub.

Arnold, Roger A. Economics. 4th ed. LC 97-37733. (HB - Economics Ser.). (C). 1997. pap. 92.95 (0-538-88043-0) S-W Pub.

Arnold, Roger A. Economics. 4th ed. (HB - Economics Ser.). (C). 1997. mass mkt. 22.95 (0-538-88051-1) S-W Pub.

*Arnold, Roger A. Economics. 5th ed. LC 00-36551. 2000. write for info. (0-324-01745-6) Sth-Wstn College.

Arnold, Roger A. Economics, 2e. 2nd ed. Perlee, Clyde, ed. (SWC-Economics). 836p. (C). 1992. mass mkt. 63.75 (0-314-88424-6) West Pub.

— Economics. 3/e. 3rd ed. (SWC-Economics). 876p. (C). 1996. pap. 64.25 (0-314-06589-X) West Pub.

— Macroeconomics. 4th ed. LC 97-37734. (HD - Intermediate Macroeconomics Ser.). (C). 1997. mass mkt. 67.95 (0-538-88045-7); mass mkt. 19.95 (0-538-88052-X) S-W Pub.

*Arnold, Roger A. Macroeconomics. 5th ed. LC 00-36552. 2000. write for info. (0-324-01747-2) Sth-Wstn College.

Arnold, Roger A. Macroeconomics, 2e. 2nd ed. Perlee, Clyde, ed. (SWC-Economics). 508p. (C). 1992. pap. 47.25 (0-314-88425-4) West Pub.

— Microeconomics. 3rd ed. 570p. (C). 1996. mass mkt. 70.95 (0-314-06969-0) West Pub.

Arnold, Roger A. Microeconomics. 4th ed. LC 97-37701. (HC - Intermediate Microeconomics Ser.). (C). 1997. pap. 67.95 (0-538-88044-9) S-W Pub.

Arnold, Roger A. Microeconomics. 4th ed. (HC - Intermediate Microeconomics Ser.). (C). 1997. mass mkt., student ed. 19.95 (0-538-88050-3) S-W Pub.

— Microeconomics, 2e. 2nd ed. Perlee, Clyde, ed. (SWC-Economics). 525p. (C). 1992. pap. 47.25 (0-314-88423-8) West Pub.

Arnold, Roland, ed. Bibliographie der Veroffentlichungen von S. B. Liljegren. (Essays & Studies on English Language & Literature: Vol. 16). 1972. reprint ed. pap. 25.00 (0-8115-0214-7) Periodicals Srv.

— Bibliographie II der Veroffentlichungen von S. B. Liljegren. (Essays & Studies on English Language & Literature: Vol. 22). 1972. reprint ed. pap. 25.00 (0-8115-0220-1) Periodicals Srv.

— Bibliographie III der Veroffentlichungen von S. B. Liljegren. (Essays & Studies on English Language & Literature: Vol. 26). 1972. reprint ed. pap. 25.00 (0-8115-0224-4) Periodicals Srv.

Arnold, Ron. Eco Terror: The Violent Agenda to Save Nature - The World of the Unabomber. 336p. (Orig.). 1997. pap. 16.95 (0-939571-18-8) Free Enter Pr.

A

— Ecology Wars. (Free Enterprise Battle Bks.). 180p. 1987. 14.95 (*0-939571-00-5*) Free Enter Pr.

— Ecology Wars: Environmentalism As if People Mattered. 182p. (Orig.). 1993. pap. 14.95 (*0-939571-14-5*) Free Enter Pr.

— The Grand Prairie Years. 2nd ed. (Illus.). 722p. 1987. 19.95 (*0-936783-01-X*) Merril Pr.

***Arnold, Ron.** Undue Influence: Wealthy Foundations, Grant Driven Environmental Groups & Zealous Bureaucrats That Control Your Future. LC 99-43093. (Illus.). 284p. 1999. pap. 16.95 (*0-939571-20-X*) Free Enter Pr.

Arnold, Ron & Gottlieb, Alan. Trashing the Economy: How Runaway Environmentalism Is Wrecking America. 672p. (Orig.). 1993. pap. 19.95 (*0-939571-13-7*) Free Enter Pr.

— Trashing the Economy: How Runaway Environmentalism Is Wrecking America. 2nd ed. 670p. (Orig.). 1994. pap. 19.95 (*0-939571-17-X*) Free Enter Pr.

Arnold, Ron, jt. auth. see Gottlieb, Alan.

Arnold, Ron, ed. see Bennett, Michael.

Arnold, Ron, ed. see Fulda, Joseph S.

Arnold, Ron, ed. see Gottlieb, Alan.

Arnold, Ron, ed. see Hage, Wayne.

Arnold, Ron, ed. see Hummel, Don.

Arnold, Ron, ed. see Hummel, Don & Hummel, Eugenia.

Arnold, Ron, ed. see Jacobson, Ken.

Arnold, Ron, ed. see Pendley, William P.

Arnold, Ron, ed. see Soderberg, K. A. & Durette, Jackie.

Arnold, Roslyn. Writing Development: Magic in the Brain. (English, Language & Education Ser.). 160p. 1991. pap. 34.95 (*0-335-15195-7*) OpUniv Pr.

Arnold, Ruthie, jt. auth. see Freeman, Becky.

Arnold, Sam. How I Learned to Talk with Bears. (Illus.). 64p. (Orig.). Date not set. pap. 7.50 (*0-914454-04-8*) Fur Pr.

Arnold, Sam'l P. Eating up the Santa Fe Trail. (Illus.). 180p. 1990. pap. 17.50 (*0-87081-187-8*) Univ Pr Colo.

Arnold, Samuel J. No More Bedwetting: How to Help Your Child Stay Dry. LC 97-21709. 192p. 1997. pap. 12.95 (*0-471-14690-0*) Wiley.

Arnold, Samuel P. The Fort Cookbook: The New Foods of the Old West from the Denver Restaurant. LC 97-35766. (Illus.). 320p. 1997. 30.00 (*0-06-017567-2*) HarpC.

— Frying Pans West. write for info. (*0-914454-03-X*) Fur Pr.

Arnold, Sandra. Hijo del Sol. (Leyendas del Mundo Ser.).Tr. of Child of the Sun. (SPA., Illus.). 32p. (Orig.). (J). (gr. 2-6). 1996. pap. 4.95 (*0-8167-4173-5*) Troll Communs.

Arnold, Sandra M. Alicia Alonso: First Lady of the Ballet. LC 93-18098. 104p. (YA). (gr. 7 up). 1993. 14.95 (*0-8027-8242-6*); lib. bdg. 15.85 (*0-8027-8243-4*) Walker & Co.

Arnold, Sandra Martin. Child of the Sun: A Cuban Legend. (Legends of the World Ser.). 1995. 9.15 (*0-606-07363-9*, Pub. by Turtleback) Demco.

Arnold-Schuster, Ingrid. Ich Habe Niemals eine Zeile Geschrieben, Wenn Sie Mir Fern War. Arnold, Armin et al, eds. (Kanadische Studien Zur Deutschen Sprache und Literatur Ser.: Bd. 43). 227p. 1998. pap. 36.95 (*3-906760-03-0*) P Lang Pubng.

Arnold-Sommerfeld-Institut FHUR Mathematische Physik Staff, jt. auth. see Doebner, H. D.

Arnold, Stephanie. The Creative Spirit: An Introduction to Theatre. LC 97-31810. xxii, 426p. 1998. pap. text 46.95 (*1-55934-717-1*) Mayfield Pub.

***Arnold, Stephanie.** The Creative Spirit: An Introduction to Theatre. 2nd ed. LC 00-55050. 2000. write for info. (*0-7674-1703-8*) Mayfield Pub.

Arnold, Stephen & Nitecki, Andre, eds. Culture & Development in Africa. LC 89-81234. (Comparative Studies in African-Caribbean Literature Ser.). 365p. (C). 1990. 45.00 (*0-86543-145-0*); pap. 14.95 (*0-86543-146-9*) Africa World.

Arnold, Stephen, jt. ed. see Parker, Carolyn.

Arnold, Stephen D. Industrial Hygiene Laboratory Manual. 90p. 1996. write for info. (*0-944111-13-0*) Natl Environ Health.

Arnold, Stephen H., ed. Critical Perspectives on Mongo Beti. LC 97-14267. 453p. 1998. lib. bdg. 59.95 (*0-89410-586-8*, Three Contnts) L Rienner.

Arnold, Stephen H., ed. see Ngate, Jonathan.

Arnold, Stephen H., ed. see Priebe, Richard K.

Arnold, Steven. Epiphanies. (Illus.). 96p. 1987. 50.00 (*0-942642-33-3*) Twelvetrees Pr.

Arnold, Sue. Burma Quest. 256p. 1996. text 40.00 (*0-340-41609-2*, Pub. by Hodder & Stought Ltd) Trafalgar.

Arnold, Suzanne, et al. Ready or Not: Your Retirement Planning Guide 2000. 27th ed. 2000. pap. 10.95 (*1-882548-06-X*) Manpower Ed Inst.

Arnold, Sylvia. Wild Flowers of the North York Moors National Park. 120p. 1986. 50.00 (*0-907033-42-3*) St Mut.

Arnold, T. W. The Old & New Testaments in Muslim Religious Art. (British Academy, London, Schweich Lectures on Biblical Archaeology Series, 1930). 1974. reprint ed. pap. 25.00 (*0-8115-1270-3*) Periodicals Srv.

— Preaching of Islam. 19.50 (*1-56744-185-8*) Kazi Pubns.

— The Preaching of Islam. 480p. 1986. 300.00 (*1-85077-132-4*, Pub. by Darf Pubs Ltd) St Mut.

— The Preaching of Islam: A History of the Propogation of the Muslim Faith. 1990. reprint ed. 15.00 (*81-85395-60-8*, Pub. by Low Price) S Asia.

— Prescribed Prayer Made Simple. 770p. 1996. pap. 10.50 (*0-614-21473-4*, 978) Kazi Pubns.

Arnold, Tedd. Five Ugly Monsters. LC 94-36991. (Cartwheel Books Story Corner Ser.). (Illus.). 24p. (J). (ps-1). 1995. 6.95 (*0-590-22226-0*) Scholastic Inc.

— Green Wilma. LC 91-31501. (Illus.). 32p. (J). (ps-3). 1993. 16.99 (*0-8037-1313-4*, Dial Yng Read) Peng Put Young Read.

— Green Wilma. 1998. 11.19 (*0-606-12958-8*, Pub. by Turtleback) Demco.

— Green Wilma. 32p. (J). (ps-2). 1998. pap. 5.99 (*0-14-056362-8*) Viking Penguin.

— Huggly & the Toy Monster. LC 98-24834. (Monsters under the Bed Ser.). (J). 1998. pap. 3.50 (*0-590-11761-0*) Scholastic Inc.

***Arnold, Tedd.** Huggly & the Toy Monster. (Huggly Ser.). (Illus.). 32p. (ps-3). 1999. pap. 3.25 (*0-439-10270-7*) Scholastic Inc.

Arnold, Tedd. Huggly & the Toy Monster. LC 98-24834. (Monsters under the Bed Ser.). (Illus.). 32p. (J). (ps-3). 1999. pap. 3.25 (*0-590-91821-4*, Pub. by Scholastic Inc) Penguin Putnam.

— Huggly Gets Dressed. LC 97-18777. (Monster under the Bed Ser.). (Illus.). 24p. (J). 1997. 2.99 (*0-590-11759-9*) Scholastic Inc.

— Huggly Gets Dressed. (Monster under the Bed Ser.). (Illus.). 24p. (J). 1998. pap. text 8.95 (*0-590-91819-2*, Cartwheel) Scholastic Inc.

***Arnold, Tedd.** Huggly Gets Dressed. (Illus.). 24p. (ps-1). 1999. pap. 3.25 (*0-439-10268-5*) Scholastic Inc.

— Huggly Goes to School. (Monster under the Bed Ser.). (Illus.). 32p. (J). (ps-3). 2000. pap. 3.25 (*0-439-13499-4*, Cartwheel) Scholastic Inc.

Arnold, Tedd. Huggly Takes a Bath. LC 97-21414. (Monster under the Bed Ser.). (Illus.). 24p. (J). (gr. k-2). 1998. 2.99 (*0-590-11760-2*) Scholastic Inc.

— Huggly Takes a Bath. (Monster under the Bed Ser.). (Illus.). 32p. (J). (gr. k-2). 1999. 15.95 (*0-590-91820-6*) Scholastic Inc.

***Arnold, Tedd.** Huggly Takes a Bath. (Illus.). 24p. (ps-1). 1999. pap. 3.25 (*0-439-10269-3*) Scholastic Inc.

— Huggly's Pizza. LC 94-45341. (Illus.). 32p. (J). (ps-3). 2000. pap. 3.25 (*0-439-13498-6*, Cartwheel) Scholastic Inc.

Arnold, Tedd. My First Drawing Book. LC 87-134510. (My First Bks.). (Illus.). 16p. (J). (ps-3). 1986. pap. 5.95 (*0-89480-350-6*, 1350) Workman Pub.

— No Jumping on the Bed! LC 86-13501. (Illus.). 32p. (J). (ps-2). 1987. 16.99 (*0-8037-0038-5*, Dial Yng Read) Peng Put Young Read.

— No Jumping on the Bed! LC 86-13501. (Illus.). 32p. (J). (ps-3). 1996. pap. 5.99 (*0-14-055839-X*, PuffinBks) Peng Put Young Read.

Arnold, Tedd. No Jumping on the Bed! LC 86-13501. (J). 1996. 10.19 (*0-606-09691-4*, Pub. by Turtleback) Demco.

Arnold, Tedd. No More Water in the Tub! Sequel To: No Jumping on the Bed! (Picture Puffin Ser.). (J). (ps-3). 1998. pap. 5.99 (*0-14-056430-6*, PuffinBks) Peng Put Young Read.

— Parts. LC 96-28552. (Illus.). 32p. (J). (ps-3). 1997. 15.99 (*0-8037-2040-8*, Dial Yng Read) Peng Put Young Read.

***Arnold, Tedd.** Parts. (Illus.). 32p. (J). (ps-3). 2000. pap. 5.99 (*0-14-056533-7*, PuffinBks) Peng Put Young Read.

Arnold, Tedd. The Twin Princes. LC 97-2216. (J). 1998. 15.99 (*0-8037-1417-3*, Dial Yng Read) Peng Put Young Read.

Arnold, Tedd. Actions. (Nursery Rhyme Concept Bks.). 16p. (J). (ps). 1992. pap. 3.95 (*0-671-77824-2*) Litle Simon.

— Bialosky's Bedside Books. 16p. (J). (ps). 1996. bds. 10.95 (*0-7611-0447-X*) Workman Pub.

— Colors. (Nursery Rhyme Concept Bks.). 16p. (J). (ps). 1992. pap. 3.95 (*0-671-77825-0*) Litle Simon.

— Opposites. (Nursery Rhyme Concept Bks.). 16p. (J). (ps). 1992. pap. 3.95 (*0-671-77823-4*) Litle Simon.

— Sounds. (Nursery Rhyme Concept Bks.). 16p. (J). (ps). 1992. pap. 3.95 (*0-671-77826-9*) Litle Simon.

Arnold, Tedd, jt. illus. see Capucilli, Alyssa.

Arnold, Thomas. An Introduction to Politics & Political Inquiry. LC 97-214665. 208p. (C). 1997. per. 57.95 (*0-7872-3883-X*, 41388301) Kendall-Hunt.

— Observations on the Nature, Kinds, Causes, & Prevention of Insanity: Containing Observations on the Nature, & Various Kinds of Insanity & the Appearances on Dissection, 2 vols. 2nd ed. LC 75-16680. (Classics in Psychiatry Ser.). 1976. reprint ed. 56.95 (*0-405-07412-3*) Ayer.

Arnold, Thomas, ed. Henrici Huntendunensis Historia Anglorum: The History of the English by Henry, Archdeacon of Huntingdon, from 55-1154, 8 bks. (Rolls Ser.: No. 74). 1969. reprint ed. 70.00 (*0-8115-1142-1*) Periodicals Srv.

— Memorials of St. Edmund's Abbey, 3 vols. (Rolls Ser.: No. 96). 1974. reprint ed. 210.00 (*0-8115-1175-8*) Periodicals Srv.

— Symeonis Monachi Opera Omnia, 2 vols., Set. Incl. Vol. 1. Historia Ecclesiae Dunelmensis. 1974. (*0-8115-1143-X*); Vol. 2. Historia Regum. 1974. (*0-8115-1144-8*); (Rolls Ser.: No. 75). 1974. reprint ed. 140.00 (*0-685-10007-3*) Periodicals Srv.

Arnold, Thomas, jt. auth. see Goldwasser, Dan L.

Arnold, Thomas C. Words & Deeds: Language & the Practice of Political Theory. LC 92-38025. (Major Concepts in Politics & Political Theory Ser.: Vol. 2). VII, 154p. (C). 1993. text 39.95 (*0-8204-1836-6*) P Lang Pubng.

Arnold, Thomas W. The Preaching of Islam: A History of Propagation of the Muslim Faith. LC 72-180319. (Mid-East Studies). reprint ed. 47.50 (*0-404-56214-0*) AMS Pr.

Arnold, Thurman W. The Bottlenecks of Business. LC 72-2363. (FDR & the Era of the New Deal Ser.). 352p. 1973. reprint ed. lib. bdg. 42.50 (*0-306-70470-6*) Da Capo.

— The Folklore of Capitalism. LC 79-26573. 400p. 1980. reprint ed. lib. bdg. 75.00 (*0-313-22199-5*, ARFC, Greenwood Pr) Greenwood.

— Voltaire & the Cowboy: The Letters of Thurman Arnold. Gressley, Gene M., ed. LC 76-15772. (Illus.). 576p. reprint ed. pap. 178.60 (*0-8357-5519-3*, 203513500093) Bks Demand.

Arnold, Thurman W., et al. The Future of Democratic Capitalism. LC 77-142631. (Essay Index Reprint Ser.). 1977. reprint ed. 15.95 (*0-8369-2395-2*) Ayer.

Arnold, Tim. Natural History from A to Z: A Terrestrial Sampler. LC 88-26879. (Illus.). 64p. (J). (gr. 5-9). 1991. lib. bdg. 15.95 (*0-689-50467-5*) McElderry Bks.

— The Winter Mittens. LC 88-2736. (Illus.). 32p. (J). (gr. 3-6). 1988. lib. bdg. 13.95 (*0-689-50449-7*) McElderry Bks.

Arnold, Tim. The Three Billy Goats Gruff. LC 92-23992. 32p. (J). (ps-3). 1993. lib. bdg. 14.95 (*0-689-50575-2*) McElderry Bks.

Arnold, Tim, ed. see Levine, Melvin D.

Arnold, Tom. Patent Alternative Dispute Resolution Handbook. (IP Ser.). 1991. pap. 110.00 (*0-87632-775-7*) West Group.

Arnold, V. & Monastyrsky, M., eds. Developments in Mathematics: The Moscow School. (Illus.). 304p. (C). 1993. ring bd. 89.95 (*0-412-45270-7*) Chapman & Hall.

***Arnold, V. I.** The Arnoldfest: Proceedings of a Conference in Honour of V. I. Arnold for His 60th Birthday. Bierstone, Edward et al, eds. LC 99-45778. (FIC Ser.: Vol. 24). 555p. 2000. 100.00 (*0-8218-0945-8*) Am Math.

Arnold, V. I. Arnold-Gelfand Mathematical Seminars: Geometry & Singularity Theory. LC 96-3542. (ENG & FRE.). 1996. write for info. (*3-7643-3883-0*) Birkhauser.

— Catastrophe Theory. 2nd rev. ed. (Illus.). 120p. 1987. pap. 17.00 (*0-387-16199-6*) Spr-Verlag.

— Catastrophe Theory. 3rd rev. ed. Wassermann, G. S. & Thomas, R. K., trs. from RUS. LC 92-9633. (Illus.). 144p. 1994. 32.95 (*0-387-54811-4*) Spr-Verlag.

— Geometrical Methods in the Theory of Ordinary Differential Equations. 2nd ed. (Grundlehren Ser.: Vol. 250). (Illus.). 365p. 1996. 59.95 (*0-387-96649-8*) Spr-Verlag.

Arnol'd, V. I. Huygens & Barrow, Newton & Hooke: Pioneers in Mathematical Analysis & Catastrophe Theory from Involutes to Quasi-Crystalls. 128p. 1990. 24.50 (*0-8176-2383-3*) Birkhauser.

Arnold, V. I. Mathematical Aspects of Classical & Celestial Mechanics. 2nd ed. 291p. 1997. pap. text 54.50 (*3-540-61224-6*) Spr-Verlag.

— Mathematical Methods in Classical Mechanics. (Graduate Texts in Mathematics Ser.: Vol. 60). (Illus.). 1978. 39.00 (*0-387-90314-3*) Spr-Verlag.

— Mathematical Methods of Classical Mechanics. 2nd ed. (Graduate Texts in Mathematics Ser.: Vol. 60). (Illus.). 520p. 1997. text 49.95 (*0-387-96890-3*) Spr-Verlag.

— Ordinary Differential Equations. (Illus.). 270p. (C). 1978. pap. text 25.00 (*0-262-51018-9*) MIT Pr.

Arnol'd, V. I. Ordinary Differential Equations. Cooke, R., tr. from RUS. (Universitext Ser.). (Illus.). xiv, 322p. 1997. text 59.95 (*0-387-54813-0*) Spr-Verlag.

Arnold, V. I. Singularities of Caustics & Wave Fronts. (Mathematics & Its Applications, Soviet Ser.). 280p. 1990. text 166.50 (*0-7923-1038-1*) Kluwer Academic.

Arnol'd, V. I. Theory of Singularities & Its Applications. LC 90-45636. (Advances in Soviet Mathematics Ser.: Vol. 1). 333p. 1990. text 130.00 (*0-8218-4100-9*, ADVSOV/1) Am Math.

Arnold, V. I. Theory of Singularities & Its Applications. (Lezione Fermiane Ser.). (Illus.). 74p. (C). 1991. pap. text 25.95 (*0-521-42280-9*) Cambridge U Pr.

— Topological Invariants of Plane Curves & Caustics. LC 94-16254. (University Lectures: Vol. 5). 60p. 1994. pap. 15.00 (*0-8218-0308-5*, ULECT/5) Am Math.

Arnold, V. I., ed. Arnold-Gelfand Mathematical Seminars: Geometry & Singularity Theory. LC 96-3542. 300p. 1997. 89.50 (*0-8176-3883-0*) Birkhauser.

— Dynamical Systems III: Mathematical Aspects of Classical & Celestial Mechanics. Iacob, A., tr. from RUS. (Encyclopedia of Mathematical Sciences Ser.: Vol. 3). xiv, 291p. 1993. 113.95 (*0-387-57241-4*) Spr-Verlag.

— Dynamical Systems 8: Singularity Theory 2 Applicationis. (Encyclopedia of Mathematical Sciences Ser.: Vol. 39). 235p. 1993. 118.95 (*0-387-53376-1*) Spr-Verlag.

— Singularities & Bifurcations. LC 91-640741. (Advances in Soviet Mathematics Ser.: Vol. 21). 262p. 1994. text 100.00 (*0-8218-0237-2*, ADVSOV/21) Am Math.

Arnol'd, V. I., et al, eds. Dynamical Systems IV: Symplectic Geometry & Its Applications. 2nd ed. Wassermann, G. & Dzhamay, A., trs. (Encyclopaedia of Mathematical Sciences Ser.: Vol. 4). (Illus.). 330p. 1998. 98.00 (*3-540-62635-2*) Spr-Verlag.

Arnold, V. I., et al, eds. Singularities: The Brieskorn Anniversary Volume. LC 98-18099. (Progress in Mathematics Ser.: Vol. 162). 488p. 1998. 98.00 (*3-7643-5913-7*) Spr-Verlag.

Arnol'd, V. I. & Gamkrelidze, R. V., eds. Dynamical Systems Five: Bifurcation Theory & Catastrophe Theory. Kazarinoff, Nicholas D., tr. from RUS. (Encyclopedia of Mathematical Sciences Ser.: Vol. 5). (Illus.). 280p. 1994. 75.95 (*0-387-18173-3*) Spr-Verlag.

Arnold, V. I. & Monastyrsky, M., eds. Developments in Mathematics: The Moscow School. LC 92-38106. 1993. write for info. (*0-04-124527-X*) Chapman & Hall.

Arnold, V. I. & Novikov, S. P., eds. Dynamical Systems IV. (Encyclopedia of Mathematical Sciences Ser.: Vol. 4). (Illus.). 295p. 1994. 69.00 (*0-387-17003-0*, 1780) Spr-Verlag.

Arnol'd, V. I. & Novikov, S. P., eds. Dynamical Systems VII: Integrable Systems, Nonholonomic Dynamical Systems. Reyman, A. & Semenov-Tian-Shansky, M. A., trs. from RUS. (Encyclopedia of Mathematical Sciences Ser.: Vol. 16). (Illus.). 350p. 1993. write for info. (*3-540-18176-8*) Spr-Verlag.

Arnold, V. I. & Novikov, S. P., eds. Integrable Systems, Nonholonomic Dynamical Systems. LC 92-24315. 1993. 113.95 (*0-387-18176-8*) Spr-Verlag.

Arnold, V. I., et al. Dynamical Systems III. Iacob, A., tr. from RUS. (Encyclopedia of Mathematical Sciences Ser.: Vol. 3). 320p. 1987. 59.00 (*0-387-17002-2*) Spr-Verlag.

Arnol'd, V. I., et al. Dynamical Systems VI: Singularity Theory I. Iacob, A., tr. from RUS. (Encyclopedia of Mathematical Sciences Ser.: Vol. 6). (Illus.). 256p. 1993. 118.95 (*0-387-50583-0*) Spr-Verlag.

Arnold, V. I., et al. Eleven Papers on Analysis. LC 51-5559. (Translations Ser.: Series 2, Vol. 53). 284p. 1966. 50.00 (*0-8218-1753-1*, TRANS2/53) Am Math.

Arnol'd, V. I., et al. Fourteen Papers on Functional Analysis & Differential Equations. LC 51-5559. (Translations Ser. 2: Vol. 61). 311p. 1967. 52.00 (*0-8218-1761-2*, TRANS2/61) Am Math.

Arnold, V. I., et al. Fourteen Papers Translated from the Russian. LC 87-17526. (Translations Ser. 2: Vol. 137). 129p. 1987. 58.00 (*0-8218-3113-5*, TRANS2/137) Am Math.

Arnol'd, V. I., et al. Seventeen Papers on Analysis. LC 51-5559. (Translations Ser.: Series 2, Vol. 28). 344p. 1963. 38.00 (*0-8218-1728-0*, TRANS2/28) Am Math.

Arnold, V. I., et al. Singularities of Differentiable Maps. (Monographs in Mathematics: Vol. 83). 492p. 1988. 39.00 (*3-7643-3185-2*) Birkhauser.

Arnol'd, V. I., et al. Singularity Theory I. (Illus.). 245p. 1998. reprint ed. pap. 49.95 (*3-540-63711-7*) Spr-Verlag.

— Thirteen Papers on Functional Analysis & Differential Equations. LC 51-5559. (Translations Ser.: Series 2, Vol. 79). 269p. 1969. 49.00 (*0-8218-1779-5*, TRANS2/79) Am Math.

Arnold, V. I., jt. ed. see Anosov, D. V.

Arnold, Vladimir I. Topological Methods in Hydrodynamics. LC 97-10079. 398p. 1997. 59.95 (*0-387-94947-X*) Spr-Verlag.

***Arnold, Vladimir I., et al, eds.** Pseudoperiodic Topology. LC 91-640741. (TRANS2 Ser.: Vol. 197). 179p. 2000. 85.00 (*0-8218-2094-X*) Am Math.

Arnold, Vladimir I., ed. see International Mathematical Union Staff.

Arnold, W. Lexikon der Psychologie: Lexicon of Psychology, 3 vols. (GER.). 1306p. 1980. 495.00 (*0-8288-2207-7*, M7234) Fr & Eur.

Arnold, W., et al, eds. Immunodeficient Animals: Models for Cancer Research. (Beitraege Zur Onkologie, Contributions to Oncology Ser.: Vol. 51, 1996). (Illus.). xiv, 230p. 1996. 160.00 (*3-8055-6270-5*) S Karger.

— Inner Ear Biology, Selected Papers from the 22nd Workshop, Wuerzburg, September 1985: Journal: ORL, Vol. 48, No. 2. (Illus.). 80p. 1986. pap. 42.75 (*3-8055-4268-2*) S Karger.

Arnold, W., jt. ed. see Anniko, M.

Arnold, W., jt. ed. see Ferlito, A.

Arnold, W. D. Oakfield: or Fellowship in the East: Or, Fellowship in the East. xi, 442p. reprint ed. 59.00 (*0-932051-74-X*) Rprt Serv.

Arnold, W. H. Arnold Family. 210p. 1996. reprint ed. pap. 33.50 (*0-8328-5376-3*); reprint ed. lib. bdg. 43.50 (*0-8328-5375-5*) Higginson Bk Co.

Arnold, W. T. Roman Provincial Administration. 298p. 1974. pap. 20.00 (*0-89005-027-9*) Ares.

Arnold, W. Vincent. The Illusion of Victory: Fascist Propaganda & the Second World War. LC 92-27579. (American University Studies: Vol. 130). VIII, 270p. (C). 1998. text 45.95 (*0-8204-1895-1*) P Lang Pubng.

***Arnold, Wally & Marlis, Stefanie.** Illuminations: Living by Candlelight. LC 00-40499. (Illus.). 2000. write for info. (*0-8118-3072-1*) Chronicle Bks.

Arnold, Walter, jt. ed. see Briggs, Andrew.

Arnold, Wesley E. Amplenomics Ample for All Can Be Created: Workable Solutions & Practical Insights into the Problems of Our Time. 224p. (Orig.). 1984. pap. 6.00 (*0-915935-00-7*) W Arnold.

— Basic Esperanto Quick International Understanding in One-Tenth the Time with International Words. 104p. (Orig.). 1992. pap. 5.98 (*0-915935-11-2*) W Arnold.

— Basic International Language Quick International Understanding in One-Tenth the Time Using International Words. 104p. (Orig.). 1993. pap. 5.98 (*0-915935-12-0*) W Arnold.

— The Easiest Language & the Runners up from University Research. LC 93-90939. (Orig.). 1993. pap. 5.98 (*0-915935-18-X*) W Arnold.

— Esperanto Pocket Dictionary of American English to Esperanto with over 40,000 Total Words. (ESP.). (Orig.). 1991. pap. 5.98 (*0-915935-10-4*) W Arnold.

— Esperanto the International Language Concise Up-to-Date Information with References. (ESP.). 152p. (Orig.). 1995. pap. 5.98 (*0-915935-21-X*) W Arnold.

— Esperanto to English Pocket Dictionary with 10,500 Entries. (ESP.). 85p. (Orig.). 1995. pap. 5.98 (*0-915935-20-1*) W Arnold.

— Esperanto Vest Pocket Fifteen Thousand Seven Hundred Word Eng-Eo Dictionary. (ESP.). 80p. (Orig.). 1991. pap. 5.98 (*0-915935-09-0*) W Arnold.

Arnold, Wilfred N. Vincent Van Gogh: Chemicals, Crises, & Creativity. LC 92-13130. (Illus.). x, 322p. 1992. 34.50 (*0-8176-3616-1*) Birkhauser.

Arnold, Wilfred N., ed. Yeast Cell Envelopes: Biochemistry, Biophysics, & Ultrastructure, Vol. I. 144p. 1981. 83.00 (*0-8493-5965-1*, QK617, CRC Reprint) Franklin.

— Yeast Cell Envelopes: Biochemistry, Biophysics, & Ultrastructure, Vol. II. 192p. 1981. 107.00 (*0-8493-5966-X*, QK617, CRC Reprint) Franklin.

Arnold, William D. & Lyden, John P. Musculoskeletal Injuries. (Illus.). 800p. 1987. text. write for info. (*0-07-044994-5*) McGraw.

Arnold, William E. & McClure, Lynne. Communication Training & Development. 2nd rev. ed. LC 96-133969. 196p. (C). 1995. pap. text 14.95 (*0-88133-877-X*) Waveland Pr.

An Asterisk (*) at the beginning of an entry indicates that the title is appearing for the first time.

Arnold, William H. French Diction for Singers & Speakers. LC 74-27328. reprint ed. 32.50 (*0-404-12854-8*) AMS Pr.

Arnold, William J., ed. see Nebraska Symposium on Motivation Staff.

Arnold, William T. The Roman System of Provincial Administration: To the Accession of Constantine the Great. 3rd ed. Bouchier, E. S., ed. LC 79-179501. (Select Bibliographies Reprint Ser.). 1977. reprint ed. 34.95 (*0-8369-6630-9*) Ayer.

— Roman System of Provincial Administration to the Accession of Constantine the Great. 288p. reprint ed. lib. bdg. 59.00 (*0-7812-0730-4*) Rprt Serv.

Arnold, William V. Introduction to Pastoral Care. LC 81-16092. 222p. 1982. pap. 22.95 (*0-664-24400-9*) Westminster John Knox.

— Pastoral Responses to Sexual Issues. LC 93-10750. 176p. 1993. pap. 15.00 (*0-664-25450-0*) Westminster John Knox.

Arnold, William W. & Plas, Jeanne M. The Human Touch: Today's Most Unusual Program for Productivity & Profit. LC 92-36817. 288p. 1993. 22.95 (*0-471-57291-8*) Wiley.

Arnold, Willus J. The Black Nazi. LC 81-20526. 1984. 22.95 (*0-87949-198-1*) Ashley Bks.

Arnold, Z. Douglas, ed. Metal Gear Solid Survival Guide. (Illus.). 144p. 1998. pap. 12.95 (*1-884364-31-4*) Sandwich Islands.

Arnold, Zach M. Miniature Thermoplastics Sculpture. 232p. (Orig.). 1996. pap. 14.95 (*0-940168-39-1*) Boxwood.

— Musical Punstruments. (Illus.). 287p. 1994. pap. 14.95 (*0-940168-28-6*) Boxwood.

Arnoldi, Kathrine. The Amazing True Story of a Teenage Single Mom. LC 98-14230. (Illus.). 176p. (YA). 1998. text 14.95 (*0-7868-6420-6*, Pub. by Hyperion) Time Warner.

Arnol'di, L. V., et al. Mesozoic Coleoptera. (Illus.). 297p. 1991. 72.00 (*90-73348-05-6*, Pub. by Backhuys Pubs) Balogh.

Arnoldi, Mary Jo. Playing with Time: Art & Performance in Central Mali. LC 94-38744. (Traditional Arts of Africa Ser.). (Illus.). 256p. 1995. text 29.95 (*0-253-30900-X*) Ind U Pr.

Arnoldi, Mary Jo, et al, eds. African Material Culture. LC 95-40501. (African Systems of Thought Ser.). 384p. 1996. pap. text 24.50 (*0-253-21037-2*) Ind U Pr.

Arnoldi, Mary Jo & Kreamer, Christine M. Crowning Achievements: African Arts of Dressing the Head. (Exhibition Ser.). (Illus.). 192p. 1995. 50.00 (*0-930741-42-0*); pap. 29.00 (*0-930741-43-9*) UCLA Fowler Mus.

Arnoldi, Mary Jo, et al. Beauty in the Blade. (Illus.). 36p. 1998. pap. 15.00 (*0-914489-19-4*) Univ Miss-KC Art.

Arnoldi, Mary Jo, jt. auth. see Anderson, M.

Arnolds, Eef. Ecology & Coenology of Macrofungi in Grasslands & Moist Heathlands in Drenthe, the Netherlands, Pt. 3 Taxonomy. (Bibliotheca Mycologica Ser.: Vol. 90). (Illus.). 510p. (Orig.). 1982. lib. bdg. 160.00 (*3-7682-1346-3*) Lubrecht & Cramer.

— Ecology & Coenology of Macrofungi in Grasslands & Moist Heathlands in Drenthe, the Netherlands Pt. 1: Introduction & Synecology. (Bibliotheca Mycologica Ser.: Vol. 83). (Illus.). 410p. 1981. text 100.00 (*3-7682-1314-5*) Lubrecht & Cramer.

Arnoldsche. A Century of Design: Staatliches Museum, Munich. LC 97-105563. 256p. 1997. 75.00 (*3-925369-59-7*, Pub. by Arnoldsche Art Pubs) Antique Collect.

— On Jewelry & Gems: Contemporary Jewelry & Gem Design at the Department of Gem & Jewelry Design of the Fachhochschule Idar-Oberstein, Germany. (ENG & GER., Illus.). 168p. 1997. 75.00 (*3-925369-62-7*, Pub. by Arnoldsche Art Pubs) Antique Collect.

***Arnoldsche.** Picasso's Ladies: Jewellery by Wendy Ramshaw. 1999. 75.00 (*3-925369-80-5*) Arnoldsche Art Pubs.

Arnoldsche Art Publications Staff. Beauty, Function & Art: Danner Award 1996. (Illus.). 152p. 1997. 59.50 (*3-925369-60-0*, Pub. by Arnoldsche Art Pubs) Antique Collect.

— Plastics & Design. (Illus.). 162p. 1997. 75.00 (*3-925369-72-4*, Pub. by Arnoldsche Art Pubs) Antique Collect.

***Arnoldsche Art Publications Staff.** Schon und Provokane (Beautiful & Provocative) (GER & ENG., Illus.). 2000. 60.00 (*3-925369-93-7*) Arnoldsche Art Pubs.

Arnoldsche Publishers Staff. Design Innovations 1997: The Handsaw, Tool of the Future. 1997. pap. text 29.00 (*3-925369-73-2*, Pub. by Arnoldsche Art Pubs) Antique Collect.

— Schmucken, the Art of Adornment: Jewelry & Tableware, 1965-1995. 1997. 75.00 (*3-925369-50-3*, Pub. by Arnoldsche Art Pubs) Antique Collect.

Arnoldson, Torild W. Parts of the Body in Older Germanic & Scandinavian. LC 71-158274. (Chicago. University. Germanic Studies: No. 2). reprint ed. 37.50 (*0-404-50282-2*) AMS Pr.

Arnoldssen, T. C., jt. auth. see Nunnelley, L. L.

Arnon, Arie. Thomas Tooke: Pioneer of Monetary Theory. 224p. 1990. 80.00 (*1-85278-204-8*) E Elgar.

— Thomas Tooke: Pioneer of Monetary Theory. LC 90-35606. 208p. (C). 1991. text 52.50 (*0-472-10199-4*, 10199) U of Mich Pr.

Arnon, Arie, et al. The Palestinian Economy: Between Imposed Integration & Voluntary Separation. LC 97-26555. (Social, Economic & Political Studies of the Middle East & Asia: No. 60). (Illus.). 288p. 1997. 79.50 (*90-04-10538-7*) Brill Academic Pubs.

Arnon, Isaac. Agriculture in Dry Lands: Principles & Practice. LC 92-12960. (Developments in Agricultural & Managed-Forest Ecology Ser.: Vol. 26). xii,980p. 1992. 441.00 (*0-444-88912-4*) Elsevier.

Arnon, Itzhak. Modernization of Agriculture in Developing Countries: Resources, Potentials & Problems. LC 80-41588. (Environmental Monographs & Symposia). (Illus.). 589p. 1981. reprint ed. pap. 182.60 (*0-608-17338-X*, 202979400065) Bks Demand.

— Modernization of Agriculture in Developing Countries: Resources, Potentials & Problems. 2nd fac. ed. LC 87-6288. (Environmental Monographs & Symposia). (Illus.). 650p. 1987. pap. 200.00 (*0-7837-7668-3*, 204742100007) Bks Demand.

Arnon, R. Synthetic Vaccines, 2 vols., Set. 1987. reprint ed. 203.00 (*0-8493-4658-4*, CRC Reprint) Franklin.

Arnon, Ruth. Synthetic Vaccines, Vol. I. 168p. 1987. 101.00 (*0-8493-4659-2*, CRC Reprint) Franklin.

— Synthetic Vaccines, Vol. II. 176p. 1987. 103.00 (*0-8493-4660-6*, CRC Reprint) Franklin.

***Arnone, Marilyn P. & Small, Ruth V.** WWW Motivation Mining: Finding Treasures for Teaching Evaluation Skills, Grades 1-6. (Professional Growth Ser.). (Illus.). 241p. 1999. pap. 39.95 (*0-938865-88-9*) Linworth Pub.

Arnone, Marilyn P., jt. auth. see Small, Ruth V.

Arnone, Miles. High Performance Machining. LC 98-28907. 298p. 1998. 59.95 (*1-56990-246-1*) Hanser-Gardner.

Arnone, Terry, jt. auth. see Lovisi, Gary.

Arnopoulos, P. Sociophysics: A General Theory of Natural & Cultural Systems. 390p. (C). 1994. lib. bdg. 115.00 (*1-56072-108-1*) Nova Sci Pubs.

Arnopoulos, Paris. Cosmopolitics: Public Policy of Outer Space. LC 97-72804. 250p. 1997. pap. 18.00 (*1-55071-046-X*) Guernica Editions.

***Arnopoulos, Paris.** Exopolitics: Polis - Ethnos - Cosmos: Classical Theories & Praxis of Foreign Affairs. 280p. 1999. lib. bdg. 49.00 (*1-56072-662-8*) Nova Sci Pubs.

Arnopoulos, Sheila M. Voices from French Ontario. 319p. 1982. 55.00 (*0-7735-0405-2*, Pub. by McG-Queens Univ Pr); pap. 24.95 (*0-7735-0406-0*, Pub. by McG-Queens Univ Pr) CUP Services.

— Voices from French Ontario. LC 83-185309. 215p. reprint ed. pap. 66.70 (*0-7837-6898-2*, 204672800003) Bks Demand.

Arnopoulos, Sheila M. & Clift, Dominique. The English Fact in Quebec. 2nd ed. LC 84-98406. 263p. 1983. 55.00 (*0-7735-0413-3*, Pub. by McG-Queens Univ Pr) CUP Services.

— The English Fact in Quebec. 2nd ed. LC 84-98406. 263p. 1993. pap. 22.95 (*0-7735-0414-1*, Pub. by McG-Queens Univ Pr) CUP Services.

— The English Fact in Quebec. 2nd ed. LC 84-673478. 263p. reprint ed. pap. 81.60 (*0-7837-2624-4*, 204297400006) Bks Demand.

Arnosky. One Day in Crinkle Canyon. 1999. per. 5.99 (*0-689-81599-9*) S&S Childrens.

— One Day in Crinkle Canyon. (J). 1999. per. 14.00 (*0-689-81598-0*) S&S Childrens.

Arnosky, James. Crinkleroot's Guide to Knowing Animal Habitats. LC 96-19226. (Illus.). 32p. (J). (ps-5). 1997. 13.00 (*0-689-80583-7*) S&S Childrens.

— Crinkleroot's Preserving Wildlife. (J). 1999. per. 13.00 (*0-689-80474-1*) S&S Childrens.

Arnosky, Jim. All about Deer. (Illus.). 32p. (ps-4). 1999. mass mkt. 5.99 (*0-439-05874-0*) Scholastic Inc.

— All about Owls. LC 94-10422. (Illus.). 32p. (J). (ps-3). 1995. 15.95 (*0-590-46790-5*, Scholastic Hardcover) Scholastic Inc.

***Arnosky, Jim.** All About Owls. (Illus.). 32p. (ps-4). 1999. pap. text 5.99 (*0-439-05852-X*) Scholastic Inc.

Arnosky, Jim. All about Turkeys. LC 97-34716. (Illus.). 32p. (J). (ps-5). 1998. 15.95 (*0-590-48147-9*, Pub. by Scholastic) Scholastic Inc.

— All about Turkeys. LC 97-34716. 1998. pap. write for info. (*0-590-69780-3*) Scholastic Inc.

Arnosky, Jim. All about Turtles. LC 99-29657. (J). Date not set. pap. write for info. (*0-590-69781-1*) Scholastic Inc.

— All about Turtles. LC 99-29657. (Illus.). 32p. (J). (ps-3). 2000. 15.95 (*0-590-48149-5*, Scholastic Ref) Scholastic Inc.

Arnosky, Jim. All Night near the Water. (Illus.). 32p. (J). (ps-1). 1999. pap. 5.99 (*0-698-11565-1*, PapStar) Peng Put Young Read.

— Arnosky's Ark: Beginning a New Century with Old Friends. LC 98-54601. (Illus.). 32p. (J). (ps-3). 1999. per. 15.95 (*0-7922-7112-2*, Pub. by Natl Geog) S&S Trade.

***Arnosky, Jim.** Big Jim & the White-Legged Moose. LC 98-21309. (J). 1999. 15.89 (*0-688-10865-2*, Wm Morrow) Morrow Avon.

Arnosky, Jim. Big Jim & the White-Legged Moose. LC 98-21309. (Illus.). 32p. (J). (ps-3). 1999. 16.00 (*0-688-10864-4*, Wm Morrow) Morrow Avon.

— Book of Animal Tracking. LC 88-15353. (Crinkleroot Ser.). (Illus.). 48p. (J). (gr. k-5). 1989. 14.95 (*0-02-705851-4*) S&S Bks Yung.

— Climbing Crinkle Mountain. (J). Date not set. per. 5.99 (*0-689-81601-4*) S&S Childrens.

— Climbing Crinkle Mountain. (J). 2001. 14.00 (*0-689-81600-6*) S&S Childrens.

***Arnosky, Jim.** Crinkleroot's Guide to Knowing Animal Habitats. (Illus.). 2000. pap. 5.99 (*0-689-83538-8*) Aladdin.

Arnosky, Jim. Crinkleroot's Guide to Knowing Butterflies & Moths. LC 95-9408. (Crinkleroot Ser.). (Illus.). 32p. (J). (ps-5). 1996. 15.00 (*0-689-80587-X*) S&S Bks Yung.

— Crinkleroot's Guide To Knowing the Birds. LC 91-38234. (Crinkleroot Ser.). (Illus.). 32p. (J). (ps-5). 1992. 15.00 (*0-02-705857-3*) S&S Bks Yung.

— Crinkleroot's Guide to Knowing the Birds. (Aladdin Picture Bks.). 1997. 11.19 (*0-606-11225-1*, Pub. by Turtleback) Demco.

— Crinkleroot's Guide to Knowing the Birds: Crinkleroot. LC 91-38234. (Illus.). 32p. (J). 1997. mass mkt. 5.99 (*0-689-81532-8*) Aladdin.

— Crinkleroot's Guide to Knowing the Trees. LC 91-18651. (Crinkleroot Ser.). (Illus.). 40p. (J). (ps-5). 1992. 15.00 (*0-02-705855-7*) S&S Bks Yung.

— Crinkleroot's Guide to Walking in Wild Places. LC 89-38427. (Crinkleroot Ser.). (Illus.). 32p. (J). (gr. k-5). 1993. mass mkt. 5.95 (*0-689-71753-9*) Aladdin.

— Crinkleroot's Guide to Walking in Wild Places. LC 89-38427. (Crinkleroot Ser.). (Illus.). 32p. (J). (gr. k-5). 1990. 15.00 (*0-02-705842-5*) S&S Bks Yung.

— Crinkleroot's Nature Almanac. LC 98-27191. (Illus.). 64p. (J). (gr. 1-7). 1999. 16.00 (*0-689-80534-9*) S&S Bks Yung.

— Crinkleroot's 25 Birds Every Child Should Know. LC 92-36059. (Illus.). 32p. (J). (ps-3). 1993. lib. bdg. 14.00 (*0-02-705859-X*, Bradbury S&S) S&S Childrens.

— Crinkleroot's Twenty-Five More Animals Every Child Should Know. LC 93-7584. (Illus.). 32p. (J). (ps-3). 1994. mass mkt. 12.95 (*0-02-705846-8*, Bradbury S&S) S&S Childrens.

— Crinkleroot's Visit to Crinkle Cove. (Crinkleroot Ser.). (Illus.). 32p. (J). 1999. pap. 5.99 (*0-689-81603-0*) Aladdin.

— Crinkleroot's 25 Fish Every Child Should Know. LC 92-39381. (Illus.). 32p. (J). (ps-3). 1993. lib. bdg. 12.95 (*0-02-705844-1*, Bradbury S&S) S&S Childrens.

— Deer at the Brook. LC 84-12239. (Illus.). 32p. (J). (ps-3). 1986. lib. bdg. 15.93 (*0-688-04100-0*) Lothrop.

— Drawing from Nature. 1987. 14.15 (*0-606-03568-0*, Pub. by Turtleback) Demco.

— Every Autumn Comes the Bear. (Illus.). 32p. (J). (ps-3). 1996. pap. 5.99 (*0-698-11405-1*, PapStar) Peng Put Young Read.

— Every Autumn Comes the Bear. LC 92-30515. 1996. 11.15 (*0-606-10177-2*, Pub. by Turtleback) Demco.

— Flies in the Water, Fish in the Air: A Personal Introduction to Fly Fishing. LC 92-19433. (Illus.). 96p. 1992. pap. 13.95 (*0-88150-246-4*, Pub. by Countryman) Norton.

— Freshwater Fish & Fishing. 1982. 8.95 (*0-590-07799-6*) Scholastic Inc.

— I Was Born in a Tree & Raised by Bees. LC 88-6121. (Crinkleroot Ser.). (Illus.). 48p. (J). (gr. k-5). 1988. reprint ed. 13.95 (*0-02-705841-7*) S&S Bks Yung.

— Little Lions. LC 96-49837. (Illus.). 32p. (J). 1998. 15.99 (*0-399-22944-2*, G P Putnam) Peng Put Young Read.

— Long Spikes. (Illus.). 96p. (J). (gr. 3-7). 1992. 13.00 (*0-395-58830-8*, Clarion Bks) HM.

— Manatee Morning. LC 99-39430. (J). 2000. per. 14.00 (*0-689-81604-9*) S&S Childrens.

***Arnosky, Jim.** Manatee Morning. (J). 2001. per. 5.99 (*0-689-81605-7*) S&S Childrens.

Arnosky, Jim. Mouse Letters: A Very First Alphabet Book. (Illus.). 48p. 1999. teacher ed. 4.95 (*0-395-55386-5*, Clarion Bks) HM.

— Mouse Numbers: A Very First Counting Book. (Illus.). 1999. teacher ed. 4.95 (*0-395-55006-8*) HM.

— Nearer Nature. LC 95-43954. (Illus.). 176p. (YA). (gr. 6 up). 1996. 18.00 (*0-688-12213-2*) Lothrop.

— Otters under Water. (Illus.). 32p. (J). (ps-1). 1992. 14.95 (*0-399-22339-8*, G P Putnam) Peng Put Young Read.

***Arnosky, Jim.** Otters under Water, 1 vol. 1999. pap. 5.99 (*0-698-11556-2*) Putnam Pub Group.

Arnosky, Jim. Rabbits & Raindrops. 32p. (J). 1997. 15.99 (*0-399-22635-4*, G P Putnam) Peng Put Young Read.

Arnosky, Jim. Raccoons & Ripe Corn. (Reading Rainbow Bks.). (J). 1991. 10.15 (*0-606-00709-1*, Pub. by Turtleback) Demco.

Arnosky, Jim. Raccoons & Ripe Corn. LC 87-4243. (Illus.). 32p. (J). (ps up). 1991. reprint ed. mass mkt. 4.95 (*0-688-10489-4*, Wm Morrow) Morrow Avon.

***Arnosky, Jim.** The Rattlesnake Dance. LC 99-21634. (Illus.). 32p. (J). 2000. 15.99 (*0-399-22755-5*, G P Putnam) Peng Put Young Read.

Arnosky, Jim. Sketching Outdoors in Spring. LC 86-2308. (Illus.). 48p. (J). (gr. 4 up). 1987. 12.95 (*0-688-06284-9*) Lothrop.

— Sketching Outdoors in Summer. LC 87-29728. (J). (gr. 5 up). 1988. 12.95 (*0-688-06286-5*) Lothrop.

— Watching Desert Wildlife. LC 98-13189. (Illus.). 32p. (J). (gr. 4-6). 1998. 15.95 (*0-7922-7304-4*, Pub. by Natl Geog) S&S Trade.

— Watching Water Birds. LC 97-7594. (Illus.). 32p. (J). (gr. 1-7). 1997. 16.00 (*0-7922-7073-8*, Pub. by Natl Geog) S&S Trade.

— Wild & Swampy. LC 99-52381. (Illus.). 32p. (J). (gr. 1-5). 2000. 15.95 (*0-688-17119-2*, Wm Morrow); lib. bdg. 15.89 (*0-688-17120-6*, Wm Morrow) Morrow Avon.

— The Wild Coast. 1924. write for info. (*0-688-17117-6*, Wm Morrow); lib. bdg. write for info. (*0-688-17118-4*, Wm Morrow) Morrow Avon.

— The Wild Desert. 1924. write for info. (*0-688-17123-0*, Wm Morrow) Morrow Avon.

— The Wild Plains. 1924. write for info. (*0-688-17121-4*, Wm Morrow); lib. bdg. write for info. (*0-688-17122-2*, Wm Morrow) Morrow Avon.

Arnosky, Jim, ed. Crinkleroot's Visit to Crinkle Cove. LC 97-39456. (Illus.). 32p. (J). (ps-3). 1998. mass mkt. 14.00 (*0-689-81602-2*) S&S Childrens.

Arnot. Crossword Puzzles for Dummies, Vol. 4. (For Dummies Ser.). 208p. 1999. pap. 9.99 (*0-7645-5142-6*) IDG Bks.

— Crossword Puzzles for Dummies, Vol. 5. (For Dummies Ser.). 192p. 1999. pap. 9.99 (*0-7645-5143-4*) IDG Bks.

Arnot, Bob. The Breast Cancer Prevention Diet: The Powerful Foods, Supplements & Drugs That Can Combat Breast Cancer. rev. ed. LC 96-15419. 288p. 1999. pap. 14.95 (*0-316-05109-8*) Little.

— The Breast Cancer Prevention Diet: The Powerful Foods, Supplements & Drugs That Can Save Your Life. 272p. 1998. 24.00 (*0-316-05114-4*) Little.

— The Breast Cancer Prevention Diet: The Powerful Foods, Supplements & Drugs That Can Save Your Life. large type ed. 1999. 29.95 (*0-7838-8563-6*) Thorndike Pr.

— Controlling Soviet Labour: Experimental Change from Brezhnev to Gorbachev. LC 87-32364. 328p. (gr. 13). 1988. text 85.95 (*0-87332-470-6*) M E Sharpe.

— Dr. Bob Arnot's Guide to Turning Back the Clock. 416p. 1996. pap. 14.00 (*0-316-05174-8*) Little.

— Dr. Bob Arnot's Revolutionary Weight Control Program. 320p. 1998. pap. 13.95 (*0-316-05167-5*) Little.

***Arnot, Bob.** The Prostate Cancer Protection Plan: The Foods, Supplements, & Drugs That Could Save Your Life. 352p. 2000. 24.95 (*0-316-05153-5*) Little.

Arnot, David, jt. ed. see Turner, Mervyn.

Arnot, Frederick L. Collision Processes in Gases. LC 50-12768. (Methuen's Monographs on Physical Subjects). 116p. reprint ed. pap. 36.00 (*0-608-30844-7*, 201314800085) Bks Demand.

Arnot, Frederick S. Garenganze: or Seven Years' Pioneer Mission Work in Central Africa. 2nd rev. ed. (Illus.). 276p. 1969. 47.50 (*0-7146-1860-8*, BHA-01860, Pub. by F Cass Pubs) Intl Spec Bk.

Arnot, Hugo. A Collection & Abridgement of Celebrated Criminal Trials in Scotland: From A. D. 1536 to 1784. LC 99-61966. xxiii, 400p. 1999. reprint ed. 127.50 (*1-56169-507-6*) Gaunt.

Arnot, Hugo, contrib. by. A Collection & Abridgement of Celebrated Criminal Trials in Scotland from A. D. 1536 to 1784. x, 440p. 1998. reprint ed. 136.50 (*1-56169-439-8*) Gaunt.

Arnot, Madeleine, ed. Race & Gender: Equal Opportunities Policies in Education. 158p. 1985. 31.95 (*0-08-032675-7*, M110, M115, M12, Pergamon Press) Buttrwrth-Heinemann.

***Arnot, Madeleine & Dillabough, Jo-Anne.** Challenging Democracy: Feminist Perspectives on the Education of Citizens. LC 00-30438. 2000. pap. write for info. (*0-415-20316-3*) Routledge.

Arnot, Madeleine & Weiler, Kathleen. Feminism & Social Justice in Education: International Perspectives. LC 93-8940. 1993. 85.00 (*0-7507-0101-3*, Falmer Pr); pap. 34.95 (*0-7507-0102-1*, Falmer Pr) Taylor & Francis.

Arnot, Madeleine, et al. Closing the Gender Gap: Postwar Education & Social Change. LC 99-25731. 200p. 1999. pap. 24.95 (*0-7456-1884-7*, Pub. by Polity Pr); text 59.95 (*0-7456-1883-9*, Pub. by Polity Pr) Blackwell Pubs.

Arnot, Michelle. Crossword Puzzles for Dummies. LC 97-81240. (For Dummies Ser.). 336p. 1998. pap. 16.99 (*0-7645-5067-5*) IDG Bks.

— 101 Crossword Puzzles, Vol. 2. (For Dummies Ser.). 192p. 1998. pap. 9.99 (*0-7645-5110-8*) IDG Bks.

— 101 Crossword Puzzles, Vol. 3. (For Dummies Ser.). 192p. 1998. pap. 9.99 (*0-7645-5111-6*) IDG Bks.

— 101 Crossword Puzzles for Dummies, Vol. 1. (For Dummies Ser.). 192p. 1998. pap. 9.99 (*0-7645-5068-3*) IDG Bks.

Arnot, Paul, jt. auth. see Doney, Dennis.

Arnot, Phil. The High Sierra: John Muir's Range of Light. LC 95-51712. (Illus.). 256p. (Orig.). 1996. pap. 12.95 (*1-884550-06-1*) Wide World-Tetra.

— Point Reyes: Secret Places & Magic Moments. 3rd rev. ed. LC 88-50274. (Illus.). 224p. 1992. pap. 9.95 (*0-933174-84-5*) Wide World-Tetra.

— Yosemite Valley: Secret Places & Magic Moments. (Illus.). 198p. (Orig.). 1992. pap. 9.95 (*0-933174-82-9*) Wide World-Tetra.

Arnot, Phil & Monroe, Elvira. Exploring Point Reyes: A Guide to Point Reyes National Seashore. 7th rev. ed. LC 98-216720. (Illus.). 256p. 1998. pap. 10.95 (*1-884550-15-0*) Wide World-Tetra.

— Run for Your Life. 1977. pap. 3.95 (*0-933174-01-2*) Wide World-Tetra.

***Arnot, Robert.** The Biology of Success. LC 99-36050. 288p. 2000. 24.95 (*0-316-05161-6*) Little.

— The Biology of Success. 288p. 2001. pap. 14.95 (*0-316-05129-2*) Little.

Arnot, Robert. The Biology of Sucess. 320p. 2000. 24.95 Little.

***Arnot, Robert.** The Breast Cancer Reduction Cookbook. 1999. write for info. (*0-316-05133-0*, Little Brwn Med Div) Lppncott W & W.

Arnot, Robert B. Dr. Bob Arnot's Program for Perfect Weight Control for Men & Women. LC 96-40190. 320p. (gr. 8). 1997. 23.95 (*0-316-05172-1*) Little.

Arnot, Robert P. The Miners: One Union, One Industry: A History of the National Union of Mineworkers, 1939-1946. LC 78-40603. 240p. reprint ed. pap. 74.40 (*0-608-14647-1*, 202330600032) Bks Demand.

— The Miners - In Crisis & War: A History of the Miner's Federation of Great Britain from 1930 Onwards. 451p. 1961. 49.50 (*0-678-08024-0*) Kelley.

— William Morris, the Man & the Myth. LC 76-107. 131p. 1976. reprint ed. lib. bdg. 59.50 (*0-8371-8652-8*, ARWM, Greenwood Pr) Greenwood.

Arnot, Susie. Indonesia. LC 95-52958. (Worldfocus Ser.). 1998. 18.50 (*1-57572-075-2*) Heinemann Lib.

Arnot, William. Studies in Proverbs. LC 78-6014. (Reprint Library). Orig. Title: Laws From Heaven for Life on Earth. 584p. 1986. reprint ed. pap. 18.99 (*0-8254-2123-3*, Kregel Class) Kregel.

Arnote, Ralph. Fallen Idols. 320p. 1992. mass mkt. 4.99 (*0-8125-1612-5*) Tor Bks.

— False Promises. 352p. (Orig.). 1995. pap. 5.99 (*0-8125-5043-9*) Forge NYC.

***Arnote, Ralph.** The Fast Lane. 2000. mass mkt. 6.99 (*0-8125-4035-2*) Forge NYC.

Arnote, Ralph. Fatal Secrets. 448p. (Orig.). 1994. mass mkt. 4.99 (*0-8125-3451-4*) Tor Bks.

— Hong Kong, China. 1997. mass mkt. 6.99 (*0-8125-4289-4*, Pub. by Tor Bks) St Martin.

A

— A Rage in Paradise. LC 96-52690. 288p. 1997. text 23.95 (*0-312-86198-2*) St Martin.

— A Rage in Paradise. 288p. 1999. mass mkt. 5.99 (*0-8125-6263-1*, Pub. by Tor Bks) St Martin.

— Weekenders' Club. 1996. mass mkt. 5.99 (*0-8125-3880-3*) Forge NYC.

Arnothy, Christine. I Am Fifteen: And I Don't Want to Die. 128p. (J). (gr. 7 up). 1986. pap. 3.99 (*0-590-44630-4*) Scholastic Inc.

Arnothy, Christine. I Am Fifteen--And I Don't Want to Die. (J). 1956. 9.09 (*0-606-03103-0*, Pub. by Turtleback) Demco.

Arnott, D. W. The Nominal & Verbal System of Fula. LC 77-18225. 469p. reprint ed. pap. 145.40 (*0-8357-3967-8*, AU0040100005) Bks Demand.

***Arnott, Dave.** Corporate Cults: The Insidious Lure of the All-Consuming Organization. LC 99-39967. 240p. 1999. 23.95 (*0-8144-0493-6*) AMACOM.

***Arnott, David & Fitzgerald, Maureen.** Marketing Communications Classics. 256p. 1999. pap. 21.99 (*1-86152-507-9*) ITBP.

Arnott, Jake. The Long Firm. LC 99-26932. 345p. 1999. 25.00 (*1-56947-169-X*) Soho Press.

Arnott, Joanne. Breasting the Waves: On Writing & Healing. LC PR9199.3.A65 Z46 199. 152p. 1995. pap. 12.95 (*0-88974-049-6*, Pub. by Press Gang Pubs) LPC InBook.

— Ma MacDonald. (Illus.). 24p. (J). pap. 5.95 (*0-88961-180-7*, Pub. by Womens Pr) LPC InBook.

— My Grass Cradle. 72p. 1993. pap. 10.95 (*0-88974-048-8*, Pub. by Press Gang Pubs) LPC InBook.

— Wiles of Girlhood. 1991. pap. 9.50 (*0-88974-034-8*, Pub. by Press Gang Pubs) LPC InBook.

Arnott, JoAnne, ed. see Puckett, Dale & Dibble, Peter.

Arnott, John. The Father's Blessing: A Refreshing Move of God That Is Shaking Toronto-& the World. LC 95-68309. 1995. pap. 12.99 (*0-88419-404-3*) Creation House.

— La Importancia del Perdon. Bremer, Enrique, tr.Tr. of Importance of Forgiveness. (SPA.). 34p. 1998. pap. 3.00 (*1-885630-49-2*) HLM Producciones.

Arnott, John & Destiny Images Staff. An Audience of One. 14.99 incl. audio compact disk (*0-7684-0085-6*) Destiny Image.

Arnott, Kathleen. African Myths & Legends. (Oxford Myths & Legends Ser.). (Illus.). 220p. (YA). (gr. 5-12). 1990. pap. 12.95 (*0-19-274143-8*) OUP.

— African Myths & Legends. (J). 1989. 18.05 (*0-606-02878-1*, Pub. by Turtleback) Demco.

***Arnott, Kathleen.** Tales from Africa. (Illus.). 224p. (YA). 2000. pap. 12.95 (*0-19-275079-8*) OUP.

***Arnott, Margaret A. & Raab, Charles D.** The Governance of Schooling: Comparative Studies of Devolved Management. LC 99-57255. 2000. write for info. (*0-415-19538-1*) Routledge.

Arnott, Margaret L. Gender & Crime in Modern Europe. 1999. pap. text 26.95 (*0-8153-3413-3*) Garland.

Arnott, Margaret L., ed. Gastronomy: The Anthropology of Food & Food Habits. (World Anthropology Ser.). (Illus.). xvi, 365p. 1976. 41.55 (*90-279-7739-9*) Mouton.

Arnott, Marilyn S., ed. see Symposium on Fundamental Cancer Research Staff.

Arnott, Peter D. Greek Scenic Conventions in the Fifth Century B.C. LC 78-5950. 147p. 1978. reprint ed. lib. bdg. 35.00 (*0-313-20401-2*, ARGS, Greenwood Pr) Greenwood.

— Public & Performance in the Greek Theatre. 224p. 1989. 45.00 (*0-415-02914-7*, A3036) Routledge.

— Public & Performance in the Greek Theatre. 224p. (C). 1991. pap. 24.99 (*0-415-06299-3*, A5383) Routledge.

Arnott, Peter D., jt. auth. see Reinert, Otto.

Arnott, Peter D., jt. auth. see Walton, J. Michael.

Arnott, Peter D., ed. & tr. see Aristophanes & Plautus.

Arnott, Peter D., ed. & tr. see Sophocles.

Arnott, Peter D., tr. see Euripides.

Arnott, Richard, ed. Regional & Urban Economics, Pts. 1 & 2. 1997. text 150.00 (*3-7186-5410-5*, ECU192, Harwood Acad Pubs) Gordon & Breach.

Arnott, Richard & Vickrey, William, eds. Public Economics: Selected Papers. (Illus.). 570p. 1997. pap. text 29.95 (*0-521-59763-3*) Cambridge U Pr.

Arnott, Robert & Antill, Nicholas. Oil & Gas Equities: Evaluation & Trading. (International Equities Ser.). 272p. 1994. 170.00 (*1-85573-119-3*, Pub. by Woodhead Pubng) Am Educ Systs.

Arnott, Robert, jt. auth. see Antill, Nick.

Arnott, Robert D. & Fabozzi, Frank J., eds. Active Asset Allocation: State-of-the-Art Portfolio Policies, Strategies & Tactics. rev. ed. (Institutional Investor Publications). 430p. 1992. text 70.00 (*1-55738-237-9*, Irwn Prfssnl) McGraw-Hill Prof.

Arnott, Steve, jt. auth. see Slater, Lisa C.

Arnott, Struther, et al, eds. Molecular Biophysics of the Extracellular Matrix. LC 84-6640. 189p. 1984. 89.50 (*0-89603-051-2*) Humana.

***Arnott, W. G.** Menander. (Loeb Classical Library: Vol. 3). 2000. text 19.95 (*0-674-99584-8*) HUP.

Arnott, W. G., tr. Comedies. (Loeb Classical Library: No. 132). 582p. 1979. text 18.95 (*0-674-99147-8*) HUP.

Arnott, W. Geoffrey, ed. from GRE. Menander, Vol. II. (Loeb Classical Library: No. 459). 528p. 1996. 19.95 (*0-674-99506-6*) HUP.

Arnott, W. Geoffrey, ed. see Alexis, Andre.

Arnoudse, Donald M. & Tyson, Nancy J., eds. End-User Computing Management. 1992. ring bd. 568.00 (*0-87769-309-9*) Warren Gorham & Lamont.

Arnoudt, Peter J. The Imitation of the Sacred Heart of Jesus. LC 79-112463. 1992. reprint ed. pap. 15.00 (*0-89555-012-1*) TAN Bks Pubs.

Arnouil, Eduardo, ed. see Cervantes, Carmen M.

Arnould. Geology & Confinement of Toxic Waste, Vol. 1. 400p. 1993. 142.00 (*90-5410-331-0*) Ashgate Pub Co.

— Geology & Confinement of Toxic Waste, Vol. 2. 1995. 142.00 (*90-5410-332-9*) Ashgate Pub Co.

Arnould & Beaumarchis, eds. Beaumarchais: Le Marriage de Figaro. (Bristol French Texts Ser.). (FRE.). 190p. 1992. pap. 18.95 (*1-85399-317-4*, Pub. by Brist Class Pr) Focus Pub-R Pullins.

Arnould, Arthur. Histoire Populaire et Parlementaire de la Commune de Paris. LC 75-158275. reprint ed. 55.00 (*0-404-07117-1*) AMS Pr.

Arnould, Caroline. Les Arcs Romains de Jerusalem: Architecture, Decor et Urbanisme. (Novum Testamentum et Orbis Antiquus Ser.: Vol. 35). (FRE., Illus.). 315p. 1997. text 68.75 (*3-7278-1141-2*, Pub. by Ed Univ Fri) Eisenbrauns.

Arnould, Dominique. Guerre et Paix Dans la Poesie Greque. rev. ed. Connor, W. R., ed. LC 80-2639. (Monographs in Classical Studies). 1981. lib. bdg. 64.95 (*0-405-14027-4*) Ayer.

***Arnould, Eric & Scott, Linda, eds.** Advances in Consumer Research Vol. 26: Proceedings of the 1998 Conference. 1999. 59.00 (*0-915552-42-6*) Assn Consumer Res.

Arnould, M., et al, eds. Tours Symposium on Nuclear Physics III. (AIP Conference Proceedings Ser.: Vol. 425). (Illus.). 661p. 1998. 175.00 (*1-56396-749-9*) Am Inst Physics.

Arnould, M. & Zubini, F. English-French Dictionary of Oil Field Terminology. (ENG & FRE.). 267p. 1981. 69.95 (*0-8288-0695-0*, M10277) Fr & Eur.

Arnould, Marcel & Come, Michele B., eds. Geology & Confinement of Toxic Wastes: Proceedings of the International Symposium Geoconfine, Montpellier, France, June 1993. (Illus.). 808p. 1995. text 226.00 (*90-5410-330-2*, Pub. by A A Balkema) Ashgate Pub Co.

Arnould, Richard J., et al, eds. Competitive Approaches to Health Care Reform. LC 93-1603. 384p. 1993. pap. text 36.00 (*0-87766-604-0*) Urban Inst.

Arnould-Taylor, W. E. Principles & Practice of Physical Therapy. 3rd ed. (Illus.). 224p. 1991. pap. 29.50 (*0-7487-1250-X*, Pub. by S Thornes Pubs) Trans-Atl Phila.

— A Textbook of Anatomy & Physiology. 3rd ed. (Illus.). 112p. 1999. pap. 22.50 (*0-7487-3634-4*, Pub. by S Thornes Pubs) Trans-Atl Phila.

— A Textbook of Holistic Aromatherapy: The Use of Essential Oils Treatments. 2nd ed. 104p. 1992. pap. 26.50 (*0-7487-1551-7*, Pub. by S Thornes Pubs) Trans-Atl Phila.

Arnould-Taylor, W. E., jt. auth. see Howard, George.

Arnout, J. The Antiphospholipid Syndrome. NO. 92. 109p. (Orig.). 1994. pap. 47.50 (*90-6186-635-9*, Pub. by Leuven Univ) Coronet Bks.

Arnoux, Jean-Claude. The Ultimate Water Garden Book. (Illus.). 216p. 1996. 39.95 (*1-56158-159-3*, 070288) Taunton.

Arnov, Boris. Fish Florida Saltwater. (Illus.). 232p. 1991. pap. 12.95 (*0-88415-002-X*, 5002) Gulf Pub.

***Arnove, Anthony, ed.** Iraq under Siege: The Deadly Impact of Sanctions & War. LC 00-21052. 224p. 2000. 40.00 (*0-89608-620-8*, Pub. by South End Pr) Consort Bk Sales.

— Iraq under Siege: The Deadly Impact of Sanctions & War. LC 00-21052. (Illus.). 224p. 2000. pap. 16.00 (*0-89608-619-4*, Pub. by South End Pr) Consort Bk Sales.

Arnove, R. F. & Graff, H. J. National Literacy Campaigns: Historical & Comparative Perspectives. LC 87-10873. (Illus.). 332p. (C). 1987. 69.50 (*0-306-42458-4*, Plenum Trade) Perseus Pubng.

Arnove, Robert F. Education & Revolution in Nicaragua. LC 86-8187. 172p. 1986. 49.95 (*0-275-92138-7*, C2138, Praeger Pubs) Greenwood.

Arnove, Robert F., et al, eds. Emergent Issues in Education: Comparative Perspectives. LC 91-4328. (SUNY Series, Frontiers in Education). 363p. (C). 1992. text 69.50 (*0-7914-1031-5*); pap. text 24.95 (*0-7914-1032-3*) State U NY Pr.

Arnove, Robert F. & Torres, Carlos A., eds. Comparative Education: The Dialectic of the Global & the Local. LC 98-52849. 550p. (C). 1999. 65.00 (*0-8476-8460-1*); pap. 35.00 (*0-8476-8461-X*) Rowman.

Arnovick, Leslie K. The Development of Future Constructions in English: The Pragmatics of Modal & Temporal Shall & Will in Middle English. LC 90-6027. (Berkeley Insights in Linguistics & Semiotics Ser.: Vol. 2). (Illus.). 215p. (C). 1990. text 52.95 (*0-8204-0646-5*) P Lang Pubng.

***Arnovick, Leslie K.** Diachronic Pragmatics: Seven Case Studies in English Illocutionary Development. LC 99-36345. (Pragmatics & Beyond New Ser.: Vol. 68). xii, 196p. 2000. 65.00 (*1-55619-946-5*) J Benjamins Pubng Co.

Arnow, Bruce A., jt. auth. see Taylor, C. Barr.

***Arnow, David.** Introduction to Programming Using Java: An Object-Oriented Approach. LC 97-78122. (Illus.). 765p. (C). 1998. pap. text 68.00 (*0-201-31184-4*) Addison-Wesley.

Arnow, David. Introduction to Programming with Java. 736p. (C). 1998. pap. text. write for info. (*0-201-35750-X*) Addison-Wesley.

***Arnow, David & Weiss, Gerald.** Supplement: Introduction To Programming Using Java. 1999. cd-rom. write for info. (*0-201-61281-X*) Addison-Wesley.

Arnow, E. Earle. Food Power: A Doctor's Guide to Common Sense Nutrition. LC 75-185419. (Illus.). 305p. 1972. text 32.95 (*0-911012-37-0*) Burnham Inc.

Arnow, Harriet S. Old Burnside. (Illus.). 148p. 1996. pap. 12.00 (*0-8131-0860-8*) U Pr of Ky.

***Arnow, Harriette.** The Dollmaker. 608p. 1999. mass mkt. 6.99 (*0-380-00947-1*, Avon Bks) Morrow Avon.

Arnow, Harriette, jt. auth. see Center for Learning Network Staff.

***Arnow, Harriette S.** Between the Flowers. LC 99-6812. 448p. 1999. 34.95 (*0-87013-535-X*) Mich St U Pr.

Arnow, Harriette S. Flowering of the Cumberland. LC 96-11178. (Illus.). xxviii, 443p. (C). 1996. pap. 17.95 (*0-8032-5928-X*, Bison Books) U of Nebr Pr.

— Hunter's Horn. rev. ed. LC 97-44492. 375p. 1997. pap. 18.95 (*0-87013-437-X*) Mich St U Pr.

Arnow, Harriette Simpson. Seedtime on the Cumberland. LC 95-34152. (Illus.). 451p. 1996. pap. 16.95 (*0-8032-5926-3*, Bison Books) U of Nebr Pr.

Arnow, Jan. Teaching Peace: How to Raise Children in Harmony Without Prejudice, Fear or Violence. LC 95-8712. 272p. 1995. pap. 12.00 (*0-399-52155-0*, Perigee Bks) Berkley Pub.

Arnow, Pat, ed. Drive-Through South: From Teen Cruising to Hospital Scams, Seven Award-Winning Journalists Offer a Tour of the Rapidly Changing Region. (Southern Exposure Ser.). (Illus.). 64p. (Orig.). (C). 1994. pap. 5.00 (*0-943810-62-0*) Inst Southern Studies.

— Eminent Domain: Taking Land...in the National Defense to Power Urban America for Recreation & Tourism & the "Wise Use" Movement. (Southern Exposure Ser.). (Illus.). 64p. (Orig.). (C). 1995. pap. 5.00 (*0-943810-64-7*) Inst Southern Studies.

— Image of the South: Hillbillies, Black Republicans, & Whatever Happened to Southern Democrats? (Southern Exposure Ser.). (Illus.). 64p. (Orig.). (C). 1995. pap. 5.00 (*0-943810-63-9*) Inst Southern Studies.

— Southern Journalism Awards. (Southern Exposure Ser.). (Illus.). 64p. (Orig.). (C). 1996. pap. 5.00 (*0-943810-67-1*) Inst Southern Studies.

— Targeting Youth: Child Labor, Tobacco & Kids, School Tracking. (Southern Exposure Ser.). (Illus.). 64p. (Orig.). (C). 1995. pap. 5.00 (*0-943810-65-5*) Inst Southern Studies.

Arnow, Pat & Piedmont Peace Project Staff, eds. Falling Apart/Coming Together: Will Our Differences Overcome Us? (Southern Exposure Ser.). (Illus.). 64p. (Orig.). (C). 1996. pap. 5.00 (*0-943810-66-3*) Inst Southern Studies.

Arnow, Pat, jt. ed. see Bates, Eric R.

Arnowich & Svoronos. Fundamentals of Lab Chemistry. 3rd ed. 168p. (C). 1991. pap. 31.20 (*0-536-58118-5*) Pearson Custom.

Arnowich, Beatrice & Tietjen, John. Chemistry Laboratory Experiments, vol. 2. 2nd rev. ed. 262p. (C). 1990. text 59.00 (*0-536-57707-2*) Pearson Custom.

Arnowich, Beatrice & Wong, Peter. Chemistry Laboratory Experiments, vol. 1. 2nd rev. ed. (C). 1990. text 34.80 (*0-536-57706-4*) Pearson Custom.

Arnowitt, R., et al, eds. Hot Nuclei: The Texas A & M Symposium on Hot Nuclei: Texas A & M University. 516p. (C). 1988. text 125.00 (*9971-5-0548-7*) World Scientific Pub.

— Strings '90. 548p. (C). 1991. pap. 35.00 (*981-02-0313-6*); text 98.00 (*981-02-0312-8*) World Scientific Pub.

Arnowitt, R., jt. auth. see Duff, Michael J.

Arnowitz. Blue Venture: Enviromental Science. (Ms - Middle School Science Ser.). 1999. 21.95 (*0-538-66218-2*) S-W Pub.

— Computer Dimension - Apple, Vol. 2. (DA - Computer Education Ser.). (J). (gr. k-8). 1993. 109.25 (*0-538-63464-2*) S-W Pub.

— Computer Dimensions: Apple. (DA - Computer Education Ser.). (J). (gr. k-8). 1993. pap., wbk. ed. 11.95 (*0-538-63157-0*) S-W Pub.

— Computer Dimensions: Appleworks I. (DA - Computer Education Ser.). (J). (gr. k-8). 1993. pap., wbk. ed. 11.95 (*0-538-63154-6*) S-W Pub.

— Computer Dimensions: IBM. (DA - Computer Education Ser.). (J). (gr. k-8). 1993. pap., wbk. ed. 11.95 (*0-538-63158-9*) S-W Pub.

— Computer Dimensions: Mac. (DA - Computer Education Ser.). 1993. pap. 11.95 (*0-538-63159-7*) S-W Pub.

— Computer Dimensions: Mac MS-Works. (DA - Computer Education Ser.). (J). (gr. k-8). 1993. pap., wbk. ed. 11.95 (*0-538-63156-2*) S-W Pub.

— Computer Dimensions - DOS, Vol. 1. (DA - Computer Education Ser.). (J). (gr. 8). 1993. 109.25 (*0-538-63465-0*) S-W Pub.

— Computer Dimensions Student Workbook Wordbook. (DA - Computer Education Ser.). (J). (gr. k-8). 1993. pap. 11.95 (*0-538-63523-1*) S-W Pub.

— Computer Visions. (DA - Computer Education Ser.). (J). (gr. k-8). 1993. pap., student ed., suppl. ed. 10.95 (*0-538-62535-X*); pap., student ed., wbk. ed. 10.95 (*0-538-62533-3*); pap., student ed., wbk. ed. 10.95 (*0-538-62537-6*) S-W Pub.

— Computer Visions. (DA - Computer Education Ser.). (J). (gr. k-8). 1993. pap., wbk. ed. 10.95 (*0-538-62536-8*) S-W Pub.

— Computer Visions EIMS Literacy Apple Volume. (DA - Computer Education Ser.). (J). (gr. k-8). 1993. 147.95 (*0-538-62855-3*) S-W Pub.

— Computer Visions EIMS Literacy MS-DOS Volume. (DA - Computer Education Ser.). (J). (gr. k-8). 1993. 147.95 (*0-538-62856-1*) S-W Pub.

Arnowitz, contrib. by. Computer Dimensions Training Binder, Vol. 1. (DA - Computer Education Ser.). (J). (gr. k-8). 1993. 76.95 (*0-538-63141-4*) S-W Pub.

Arnowitz Productions Inc., Staff. Microsoft Works 3 for Windows Student Resource Guide. (DA - Computer Education Ser.). (J). (gr. k-8). 1995. text 11.95 (*0-538-64336-6*) S-W Pub.

— Microtools 3.0 DOS Student Resource Guide. (DA - Computer Education Ser.). (J). (gr. k-8). 1995. text 11.95 (*0-538-64333-1*) S-W Pub.

Arnowitz Studios Inc., Staff. Blue Venture: Environmental Science. (MS - Middle School Science Ser.). 1997. pap., wbk. ed. 14.95 (*0-538-66215-8*) S-W Pub.

Arnowitz Studios Inc. Staff. Clarisworks 3.0 Student Resource Guide: Computer Dimensions. (DA - Computer Education Ser.). 1996. pap. 11.95 (*0-538-65627-1*) S-W Pub.

Arnowitzno. Computer Dimensions. (Da - K-8 Computer Education Ser.). 1993. teacher ed. 76.95 (*0-538-63145-7*) S-W Pub.

Arnowtizno. Computer Dimensions: IBM MS-Works. (DA - Computer Education Ser.). (J). (gr. k-8). 1993. pap., wbk. ed. 11.95 (*0-538-63155-4*) S-W Pub.

Arns, Betsy. The Survival Guide to School-Age Child Care. (Illus.). 254p. (Orig.). (C). 1988. pap. text 19.95 (*0-317-93309-4*) Schl-Age Wkshops Pr.

— Training School Age Child Care Teachers. 284p. 1991. 135.00 (*0-9622108-1-1*) Schl-Age Wkshops Pr.

Arnsberger, David & Booker, John. Spamarama - The Cookbook. Santacroce, Clare, ed. (Illus.). 128p. 1998. 19.95 (*0-9662073-0-0*) D Arnsberger.

Arnsdorf, Morton, et al. Clinical Cardiac Electrophysiology. Date not set. text. write for info. (*0-7817-0145-7*) Lppncott W & W.

Arnson, Bob, jt. auth. see Hyman, Michael.

Arnson, Carol, ed. see Frost, Joyce H.

***Arnson, Cynthia.** Comparative Peace Processes in Latin America LC 99-17745. 1999. 19.95 (*0-8047-3589-1*) Stanford U Pr.

Arnson, Cynthia. Crossroads: Congress, the President, & Central America, 1976-1992. 336p. 1993. reprint ed. 50.00 (*0-271-01099-1*); reprint ed. pap. 17.95 (*0-271-01098-3*) Pa St U Pr.

***Arnson, Cynthia J., ed.** Comparative Peace Processes in Latin America. LC 99-17745. 493p. 1999. 49.50 (*0-8047-3588-3*) Stanford U Pr.

Arnsparger, Arleen, jt. auth. see Ledell, Marjorie.

Arnsparger, Bill. Arnsparger's Coach Defense Football. LC 98-206065. 424p. 1998. boxed set 34.95 (*1-57444-162-0*) St Lucie Pr.

Arnst, Dennis, et al. Managing Managed Care: A Practical Guide for Audiologists & Speech-Language Pathologists. 150p. 1994. pap. text 40.00 (*0-910329-82-6*, 0111906) Am Speech Lang Hearing.

Arnsteen, Katy K. Abraham & Isaac. LC 96-27838. (KidScripts Ser.). (Illus.). 24p. (Orig.). (J). (gr. 2-5). 1997. pap. 3.95 (*0-8198-0766-4*) Pauline Bks.

— Deborah. LC 96-37083. (KidScripts Ser.). (Illus.). 160p. (Orig.). (J). (gr. 2-5). 1997. pap. 3.95 (*0-8198-1874-7*) Pauline Bks.

— Jonah, the Whale & the Vine. LC 96-37086. (KidScripts Ser.). (Illus.). 24p. (Orig.). (J). (gr. 2-5). 1997. pap. 3.95 (*0-8198-3967-1*) Pauline Bks.

— Joseph & the Dreams. LC 96-27840. (KidScripts Ser.). (Illus.). 24p. (Orig.). (J). (gr. 2-5). 1997. pap. 3.95 (*0-8198-3965-5*) Pauline Bks.

— Joshua, God's General. LC 96-37084. (KidScripts Ser.). (Illus.). 24p. (Orig.). (J). (gr. 2-5). 1997. pap. 3.95 (*0-8198-3966-3*) Pauline Bks.

— Moses. LC 96-37085. (KidScripts Ser.). (Illus.). 24p. (Orig.). (J). (gr. 2-5). 1997. pap. 3.95 (*0-8198-4793-3*) Pauline Bks.

— Naomi & Ruth. LC 96-27839. (KidScripts Ser.). (Illus.). 24p. (Orig.). (J). (gr. 2-5). 1997. pap. 3.95 (*0-8198-5134-5*) Pauline Bks.

— Queen Esther. LC 96-27844. (KidScripts Ser.). (Illus.). 24p. (Orig.). (J). (gr. 2-5). 1997. pap. 3.95 (*0-8198-6207-X*) Pauline Bks.

Arnstein, Barbara. What's Your Excuse? 1991. 4.98 (*1-55521-645-5*) Bk Sales Inc.

Arnstein, Bennett. Three-D Paper Ornaments & Calendars. 1988. pap. 9.95 (*0-9620058-0-0*) B Arnstein.

Arnstein, Bennett, jt. auth. see Gurkewitz, Rona.

Arnstein, Bennett, jt. auth. see Simon, Lewis.

Arnstein, H. R. & Cox, R. H. Protein Biosynthesis: In Focus. (In Focus Ser.). (Illus.). 128p. (C). 1992. pap. text 19.95 (*0-19-963040-2*) OUP.

Arnstein, Peter M., jt. auth. see Shervington Ball, Adrian.

Arnstein, Walter L. Britain Yesterday & Today: 1830 to the Present. 7th ed. 520p. (C). 1996. pap. text 28.36 (*0-669-39719-9*) HM Trade Div.

— Protestant vs. Catholic in Mid-Victorian England: Mr. Newdegate & the Nuns. LC 81-11451. 288p. 1982. text 28.00 (*0-8262-0354-X*) U of Mo Pr.

— Recent Historians of Great Britain: Essays on the Post-1945 Generation. LC 90-4478. 217p. 1990. reprint ed. pap. 67.30 (*0-608-00114-7*, 206087900006) Bks Demand.

Arnstein, Walter L., ed. Sources & Problems in British History since 1688, 2 Vols. 2nd ed. (Past Speaks Ser.: Vol. II). 427p. (C). 1993. pap. text 25.96 (*0-669-24602-6*) HM Trade Div.

Arnstein, Walter L., jt. auth. see Wilcox, William B.

Arnstein, Walter L., jt. auth. see Willcox, William B.

Arnstein, William E. & Gilabert, Frank. Direct Costing. LC 79-54827. 288p. reprint ed. pap. 89.30 (*0-608-11090-6*, 202261500028) Bks Demand.

***Arnstine, Barbara & Futernick, Ken, eds.** Raising the Bar: Standards & Tests in California[0012]s High Schools: A Town Hall Meeting. 89p. 2000. reprint ed. pap. text 20.00 (*0-7881-8792-9*) DIANE Pub.

Arnstine, Donald. Democracy & the Arts of Schooling. LC 95-4243. 304p. (C). 1995. pap. text 24.95 (*0-7914-2722-6*) State U NY Pr.

Arnston. dBASE IV Concepts Exercises & Applications. (DF - Computer Applications Ser.). (C). 1995. pap. 27.95 (*0-538-70600-7*) S-W Pub.

Arnts, Douglas R. You Say You Want a Revolution? 50p. 1995. pap. text 18.95 (*0-9648923-0-8*) Abailard Pub.

Arntsen, Steve. Coast. 242p. (Orig.). 1997. pap. 12.95 (*1-880298-25-2*) Viridiana.

Arntson. Concepts & Applications for Desktop Publishing. (DF - Computer Applications Ser.). (C). pap. 19.25 (*0-538-70400-4*) S-W Pub.

An Asterisk (*) at the beginning of an entry indicates that the title is appearing for the first time.

Arntson, jt. auth. see Moore.

Arntson, Amy E. Graphic Design Basics. 3rd ed. LC 97-70871. 240p. (C). 1997. pap. text 56.00 (*0-03-018734-6*, Pub. by Harcourt Coll Pubs) Harcourt.

***Arntz, Claudia.** Molekularbiologische Untersuchungen zur Alkaloidsynthese bei Claviceps. (Bibliotheca Mycologica: Band 176). (Illus.). vi, 145p. 1999. 53.00 (*3-443-59078-0*, Pub. by Gebruder Borntraeger) Balogh.

Arntz, James & Wilson, Thomas S. Julie Andrews. (Illus.). 240p. 1995. pap. 24.95 (*0-8092-3267-7*) NTC Contemp Pub Co.

Arntz, Reiner. Einfuhrung In die Terminologiearbeit. (Studien Zu Sprache und Technik Ser.: Vol. 2). xi, 344p. 1991. 30.00 (*3-487-07235-1*) G Olms Pubs.

— Textlinguistik und Fachsprache. (GER.). 1997. write for info. (*3-487-09145-3*) G Olms Pubs.

Arntz, Wilhelm F. Catalogue of Catalogues Raisonnes of Twentieth Century Artists, 1945-83, 2 vols. (GER., Illus.). 1984. pap. 150.00 (*1-55660-206-5*) A Wofsy Fine Arts.

Arntz, Wolf E. & Fahrbach, Eberhard. El Nino (The El Nino Effect) Climatico de la Naturaleza (A Climate Experiment of Nature) (Ciencia para Todos Ser.). (SPA.). 312p. 1996. pap. 26.99 (*968-16-5042-5*, Pub. by Fondo) Continental Bk.

Arntzen, C. J. & Staehelin, L. Andrew, eds. Photosynthesis III. (Encyclopedia of Plant Physiology Ser.: Vol. 19). (Illus.). 810p. 1986. 415.95 (*0-387-16140-6*) Spr-Verlag.

Arntzen, Charles J. & Ritter, Ellen M., eds. Encyclopedia of Agriculture Science, 4 vols., I. (Illus.). 1994. text 163.00 (*0-12-226671-4*) Acad Pr.

— Encyclopedia of Agriculture Science, 4 vols., II. (Illus.). 1994. text 163.00 (*0-12-226672-2*) Acad Pr.

— Encyclopedia of Agriculture Science, 4 vols., III. (Illus.). 1994. text 163.00 (*0-12-226673-0*) Acad Pr.

— Encyclopedia of Agriculture Science, 4 vols., IV. (Illus.). 1994. text 163.00 (*0-12-226674-9*) Acad Pr.

— Encyclopedia of Agriculture Science, 4 vols., Set. (Illus.). 2744p. 1994. text 625.00 (*0-12-226670-6*) Acad Pr.

Arntzen, Charles J., ed. see DuPont - UCLA Symposium on Molecular Strategies fo.

Arntzen, Helmut, et al, eds. Albert Bloch: Artistic & Literary Perspectives. LC 96-77614. (Illus.). 176p. 1997. 49.95 (*3-7913-1777-6*, Pub. by Prestel) te Neues.

Arntzen, J., et al, eds. International Trade & Sustainable Development. (Illus.). 172p. 1993. pap. text 23.50 (*90-5383-145-2*, Pub. by VU Univ Pr) Paul & Co Pubs.

Arntzen, Lucile S., jt. auth. see Williams, Leslie A.

Arntzen, Sonja, ed. from JPN. The Kagero Diary: A Woman's Autobiographical Text from Tenth-Century Japan. LC 97-15880. (Michigan Monograph Series in Japanese Studies: No. 19). Orig. Title: Kagero Nikki. (Illus.). 415p. 1997. 56.95 (*0-939512-80-7*) U MI Japan.

Arntzen, Sonja, ed. from JPN. The Kagero Diary: A Woman's Autobiographical Text from Tenth-Century Japan. LC 97-15880. (Michigan Monograph Series in Japanese Studies: No. 19). Orig. Title: Kagero Nikki. (Illus.). 415p. 1997. pap. 19.95 (*0-939512-81-5*) U MI Japan.

Arntzen, Sonya, tr. from JPN. Ikkyu & the Crazy Cloud Anthology. 230p. 1987. 32.50 (*0-86008-340-3*, Pub. by U of Tokyo) Col U Pr.

***Arnull, Anthony.** The European Union & Its Court of Justice. LC 99-38499. 1999. write for info. (*0-19-829881-1*) OUP.

— The European Union & Its Court of Justice. LC 99-38499. (Oxford European Community Law Library Ser.). 680p. 2000. write for info. (*0-19-825898-4*) OUP.

Arnup, Katherine. Education for Motherhood: Advice for Mothers in Twentieth Century Canada. (Illus.). 336p. (C). 1994. text 50.00 (*0-8020-2861-6*); pap. text 18.95 (*0-8020-7361-1*) U of Toronto Pr.

Arnup, Katherine, ed. Lesbian Parenting. LC 95-188265. 432p. 1995. pap. 16.95 (*0-921881-33-9*) LPC InBook.

Arnup, Katherine, et al, eds. Delivering Motherhood: Maternal Ideologies & Practices in the 19th & 20th Centuries. LC 89-10297. (Illus.). 348p. reprint ed. pap. 107.90 (*0-608-20309-2*, 207156200002) Bks Demand.

Arnush, Craig. Teach Yourself Borland C++ 5 in 21 Days. 3rd ed. (Illus.). 864p. 1995. 39.99 (*0-672-30756-1*) Sams.

Arnush, Michael. A Guide to Graduate Programs in Ancient History. 80p. 1998. pap. 10.50 (*0-941690-77-6*) Regina Bks.

Arny. Exploring Astronomy. 2nd ed. 1997. 67.50 (*0-07-561112-0*) McGraw.

— Exploring Astronomy. 2nd ed. LC 99-14026. 1999. pap. text 47.50 (*0-07-228249-5*) McGraw.

Arny, Linda Ray. The Search for Data in the Physical & Chemical Sciences. LC 83-20376. 158p. reprint ed. pap. 49.00 (*0-7837-1181-6*, 204171000023) Bks Demand.

***Arny, Thomas.** Explorations: An Introduction to Astronomy. 2nd ed. (C). 1999. student ed. 16.88 (*0-07-232734-0*) McGrw-H Hghr Educ.

Arny, Thomas T. Explorations. 656p. (C). 1997. per. write for info. (*0-07-114023-9*, WCB McGr Hill) McGrw-H Hghr Educ.

— Explorations: An Introduction to Astronomy. (C). 1994. text. write for info. (*0-8151-0059-0*, WCB McGr Hill) McGrw-H Hghr Educ.

***Arny, Thomas T.** Explorations: An Introduction to Astronomy with Interactive CD-ROM. 2nd ed. 1998. teacher ed. 20.00 (*0-697-39617-7*, WCB McGr Hill) McGrw-H Hghr Educ.

Arnzen, Herausgegeben von Rudiger. Aristoteles' de Anima: Eine Verlorene Spatantike Paraphrase in Arabischer und Persischer Uberlieferung. unabridged ed. 825p. 1997. 241.50 (*90-04-10699-5*) Brill Academic Pubs.

Arnzen, Michael. Pa. Public Utility Commission: January 1996 to December 1996, Vol. 86. Leming, Shirley, ed. 681p. Date not set. write for info. (*0-8182-0235-1*) Commonweal PA.

Arnzen, Michael A. Paratabloids. (Illus.). 45p. 1999. pap. write for info. (*1-893816-04-4*) Ozark Tri.

Aro, H. & Niinikoski, J., eds. European Society for Surgical Research (ESSR), 28th Congress, Turku - Finland, May 1993 Abstracts. (Journal: European Surgical Research: Vol. 25, Suppl. 1, 1993). (Illus.). xii, 124p. 1993. pap. 41.75 (*3-8055-5794-9*) S Karger.

***Aro, Hiroshi.** Futaba-kun Change! A Whole New You. Bennett, Stephen R. & Hofmann, Mark, eds. Kimura, Kuni, tr. from JPN. (Illus.). 1999. pap. 15.95 (*1-929090-00-5*, GNFC01) Studio Ironcat.

— Futaba-Kun Change: Who Wears the Pants. Bennett, Stephen R. & Hofmann, Mark, eds. Bennett, Kevin, tr. from JPN. (Illus.). 194p. 1999. pap. 15.95 (*1-929090-01-3*, GNFC 02) Studio Ironcat.

Aro, Kauko, tr. see Linder, Leo & Dromberg, D. A.

Aro, Kauko I., tr. see Oesch, Herbert.

Aro, Kauko I., tr. see Ossa, Mikka.

Aroa, J. C. & Kalra, J. S., eds. All India Banking Law Judgments, 1940-1987, 8 vols. (C). 1990. 80.00 (*0-89771-235-8*) St Mut.

Arobateau, Red J. Black Biker. 1998. mass mkt. 6.95 (*1-56333-624-3*, Rosebud) Masquerade.

— Boy's Night Out. (Orig.). 1996. mass mkt. 6.50 (*1-56333-463-1*, Rosebud) Masquerade.

— Dirty Pictures. 1995. mass mkt. 6.95 (*1-56333-345-7*, Rosebud) Masquerade.

— Laughter of the Witch: And Other Known Poems. (Series 1A). 48p. (Orig.). (C). 1995. pap. 15.00 (*0-934172-40-4*) WIM Pubns.

— Lucy & Mickey. (Orig.). 1995. mass mkt. 6.95 (*1-56333-311-2*, Hard Candy) Masquerade.

— Rough Trade. (Orig.). 1996. mass mkt. 6.50 (*1-56333-470-4*, Rosebud) Masquerade.

— Satan's Best. 1997. mass mkt. 6.50 (*1-56333-539-5*, Rosebud) Masquerade.

— Street Fighter. (Orig.). 1997. mass mkt. 6.95 (*1-56333-583-2*, Rosebud) Masquerade.

— Where the Word Is No. 1998. mass mkt. 7.95 (*1-56333-674-X*, Hard Candy) Masquerade.

Aroca, Jose M., et al. Complex Analytic Desingularization. LC 97-43567. (Ergebnisse der Mathematik und Ihrer Grenzgebiete Ser.). 1997. write for info. (*4-431-70025-0*) Spr-Verlag.

— Complex Analytic Desingularization. LC 97-43567. (Ergebnisse der Mathematik und Ihrer Grenzgebiete Ser.). 1998. 119.00 (*4-431-70218-0*) Spr-Verlag.

Arocena, Fausto. Diccionario Maritimo. (SPA.). 215p. 1963. pap. 19.95 (*0-7859-6053-8*, 8470250159) Fr & Eur.

Arockisamy, M. Expert System Application: Design, Construction & Maintenance of Structures. 176p. 1992. lib. bdg. 59.95 (*0-8493-4217-1*, TA345) CRC Pr.

***Arogundade, Ben.** Black Beauty: A History & Celebration. (Illus.). 192p. 2000. 39.95 (*1-56025-276-6*, Thunders Mouth) Avalon NY.

Arogyaswamy, Bernard. The Asian Miracle, Myth & Mirage: The Coming Economic Slowdown. LC 97-41002. 160p. 1998. 55.00 (*1-56720-127-X*, Quorum Bks) Greenwood.

Arogyaswamy, Bernard & Simmons, Ron. Value-Directed Management Organizations, Customers, & Quality. LC 92-1749. 248p. 1993. 59.95 (*0-89930-797-3*, AQY, Quorum Bks) Greenwood.

Arogyaswamy, R. N. Geotechnical Application in Civil Engineering. (Illus.). 313p. (C). 1992. text 91.00 (*90-5410-208-X*, Pub. by A A Balkema) Ashgate Pub Co.

Arois, Marcia M. Family Literacy: Easy Ways for Families to Read & Write Together. large type ed. (Illus.). 96p. (J). (ps-3). 1999. pap. 9.95 (*0-9667936-1-7*, 123) Literacy Links.

Arokiasamy, Charles-Maria V., et al. The TBI Annual Research Index. 400p. 1993. pap. 29.95 (*1-878205-01-3*) St Lucie Pr.

Arokiasamy, Charles-Maria V., ed. see McMorrow, Debra B. & Moss, Gregory R.

***Arolin, Marianna.** Here in My Garden. 1999. pap. write for info. (*1-58235-349-2*) Watermrk Pr.

Arom, Kit V., jt. ed. see Emery, Robert W.

***Aromatico, Andrea.** Alchemy: The Great Secret. LC 99-37575. (Discoveries Ser.). 144p. 2000. pap. 12.95 (*0-8109-2889-2*, Pub. by Abrams) Time Warner.

Aromatorio, Dave, jt. auth. see Dixon, Ramon.

Arome Interactive Staff. Food & Wine: An Italian Passion. (Art de la Table Ser.). (Illus.). 160p. 1996. 24.95 incl. cd-rom (*1-887675-48-5*) Arome Pub.

Aromolaran, Adebisi T. Wise Sayings for Boys & Girls. (Illus.). 100p. (Orig.). (YA). (gr. 7-12). 1994. pap. text 9.95 (*0-9635862-0-3*) Meroe Pub.

— Wise Sayings for Boys & Girls. (Illus.). 100p. (Orig.). 1994. text 16.95 (*0-9635862-1-1*) Meroe Pub.

— The Wise Sayings Manual: A Users Guide to & a Student's Workbook for Wise Sayings. 190p. 1997. pap. text, wbk. ed. 17.95 (*0-9635862-2-X*) Meroe Pub.

Aromolaran, Adebisi T., ed. & intro. see Oladele, Folasade.

***Aron.** History of the 20th Century. 2000. 32.00 (*0-465-00407-5*, Pub. by Basic); pap. 16.00 (*0-465-00408-3*, Pub. by Basic) HarpC.

Aron. SPSS 6.1 Statistics. 1997. pap. text, student ed. 20.40 (*0-13-651951-2*) P-H.

— Statistics for Psycholgy. 2nd ed. LC 98-7802. 643p. (C). 1998. 81.00 (*0-13-914078-6*) P-H.

— Statistics for Psychology. 2nd ed. 1998. pap. text, student ed. 23.45 (*0-13-959982-7*) P-H.

Aron, Adrianne, ed. see Martin-Baro, Ignacio.

Aron, Alex. Inside ActiveX. LC 97-4199. 800p. 1997. pap. text 49.99 incl. cd-rom (*1-56205-658-1*) New Riders Pub.

Aron, Arthur. Free Ourselves: Forgotten Goals of the Revolution. (Illus.). 64p. (Orig.). 1972. pap. 3.25 (*0-87810-018-0*) Times Change.

Aron, Arthur & Aron, Elaine N. Love & the Expansion of Self. (Clinical & Community Psychology Ser.). 420p. 1986. pap. 29.95 (*0-89116-459-6*) Hemisp Pub.

Aron, Bill, et al. Creation Out of Clay: The Ceramic Art & Writings of Brother Thomas. LC 99-20377. 220p. 1999. 80.00 (*0-8028-3870-7*) Eerdmans.

Aron, Carl, et al. Class Actions: Law & Practice with Forms, 1987-1988, Set. 200.00 (*0-685-24487-3*) West Group.

Aron, Cindy Sondik. Working at Play: A History of Vacations in the United States. LC 98-25552. (Illus.). 336p. 1999. 35.00 (*0-19-505584-5*) OUP.

Aron, Elaine N. The Highly Sensitive Person. LC 97-1937. 272p. 1997. pap. 15.00 (*0-553-06218-2*) Broadway BDD.

— The Highly Sensitive Person: How to Thrive When the World Overwhelms You. 256p. 1996. 21.95 (*1-55972-350-5*, Birch Ln Pr) Carol Pub Group.

— The Highly Sensitive Person: How to Thrive When the World Overwhelms You. 274p. 1999. reprint ed. 32.95 (*0-7351-0073-X*) Replica Bks.

***Aron, Elaine N.** The Highly Sensitive Person in Love: How Your Relationships Can Thrive When the World Overwhelms You. LC 99-54965. 288p. 2000. 25.00 (*0-7679-0335-8*) Broadway BDD.

Aron, Elaine N. The Highly Sensitive Person's Workbook. 336p. 1999. pap., wbk. ed. 17.50 (*0-7679-0337-4*) Broadway BDD.

— Statistics for Behavioral & Social Sciences. LC 96-41285. 329p. 1996. pap. text 69.00 (*0-13-458902-5*) P-H.

Aron, Elaine N., jt. auth. see Aron, Arthur.

Aron, Elana. Obstacle Illusions. LC 92-70695. 176p. 1992. 13.95 (*1-56062-123-0*); pap. 10.95 (*1-56062-124-9*) CIS Comm.

Aron, Gert. The Halo of the Jungle: A Story of Emigration from Nazi Germany to the Ecuadorian Jungle. unabridged ed. Aron, Jean J., tr. from GER.Tr. of Heiligenschein des Urwald. (Illus.). 130p. 1999. pap. 12.00 (*0-9670597-0-4*) Aron Pubns.

***Aron, Isa.** Becoming a Congregation of Learners: Learning as a Key to Revitalizing Congregational Life. 2000. pap. 19.95 (*1-58023-089-X*) Jewish Lights.

Aron, Jean J. The Short Hiker: Small Green Circles. 3rd rev. ed. LC 99-228206. (Illus.). 208p. 1999. pap. 12.00 (*0-9670597-1-2*) Aron Pubns.

Aron, Jean J., tr. see Aron, Gert.

Aron, Jean-Paul. Art of Eating in France: Manners & Menus in the 19th Century. 1975. 32.00 (*0-7206-0493-1*) Dufour.

— The Office. Ward, Matthew & Ilton, Irene, trs. from FRE. 144p. (Orig.). 1983. pap. text 8.95 (*0-913745-03-0*) Ubu Repertory.

Aron, Joan. Licensed to Kill? The Nuclear Regulatory Commission & the Shoreham Power Plant. LC 97-21163. 200p. 1998. pap. 18.95 (*0-8229-5649-7*); text 45.00 (*0-8229-4044-2*) U of Pittsburgh Pr.

Aron, Joel D. Program Development Process Pt. I: The Individual Programmer. (IBM Systems Programming Ser.). (Illus.). 280p. 1974. text. write for info. (*0-201-14451-4*) Addison-Wesley.

— The Program Development Process Pt. II: The Programming Team. LC 74-2847. (Illus.). 704p. 1983. text. write for info. (*0-201-14463-8*) Addison-Wesley.

Aron, Laudan, et al. Serving Children with Disabilities: A Systematic Look at the Programs. (Urban Institute Ser.). 201p. 1996. pap. 59.95 (*1-85972-352-7*, Pub. by Avebry) Ashgate Pub Co.

Aron, Laudan Y., et al. Serving Children with Disabilities: A Systematic Look at the Programs. 202p. 1996. pap. text 24.50 (*0-87766-651-2*); lib. bdg. 55.50 (*0-87766-650-4*) Urban Inst.

Aron, Leah, ed. see Chiarella, Gail.

***Aron, Leon.** Yeltsin: A Revolutionary Life. LC 99-45222. (Illus.). 896p. 2000. 35.00 (*0-312-25185-8*, Thomas Dunne) St Martin.

Aron, Leon & Jensen, Kenneth M., eds. The Emergence of Russian Foreign Policy. LC 94-3625. 1994. pap. text 19.95 (*1-878379-36-4*) US Inst Peace.

Aron, Lewis. A Meeting of Minds: Mutuality in Psychoanalysis. (RPBS Ser.: Vol. 4). 320p. 1996. 42.50 (*0-88163-159-0*) Analytic Pr.

Aron, Lewis & Anderson, Frances S., eds. Relational Perspectives on the Body. LC 98-19363. (Relational Perspectives Ser.: No. 12). 352p. 1998. 49.95 (*0-88163-230-9*) Analytic Pr.

Aron, Lewis & Harris, Adrienne, eds. The Legacy of Sandor Ferenczi. LC 93-6594. 320p. 1996. reprint ed. 49.95 (*0-88163-149-3*) Analytic Pr.

Aron, Lewis, jt. ed. see Mitchell, Stephen A.

Aron, Michael. Governor's Race: A TV Reporter's Chronicle of the 1993 Florio-Whitman Campaign. LC 93-37996. (Illus.). 288p. (Orig.). 1994. pap. 14.95 (*0-8135-2072-X*) Rutgers U Pr.

Aron, Paul. Ben: The Alien Bird. Auswaks, Alex, tr. from DAN. LC 98-22726. 1999. write for info. (*965-229-183-8*, Pub. by Gefen Pub Hse) Gefen Bks.

— Unsolved Mysteries of American History. large type ed. LC 98-51851. (American History Ser.). 1999. 26.95 (*0-7838-8517-2*, G K Hall Lrg Type) Mac Lib Ref.

— Unsolved Mysteries of American History: An Eye-Opening Journey Through 500 Years of Disappearances & Baffling Discoveries. LC 97-7319. (Illus.). 240p. 1997. 22.95 (*0-471-15369-9*) Wiley.

— Unsolved Mysteries of American History: An Eye-Opening Journey Through 500 Years of Discoveries. 225p. 1998. pap. 14.95 (*0-471-28368-1*) Wiley.

***Aron, Paul.** Unsolved Mysteries of History: An Eye-Opening Investigation into the Most Baffling Events of All Time. 240p. 2000. 24.95 (*0-471-35190-3*) Wiley.

Aron, Raymond. The Century of Total War. LC 81-40. 379p. 1981. reprint ed. lib. bdg. 59.75 (*0-313-22852-3*, ARCT, Greenwood Pr) Greenwood.

— Culture & Its Creators: Essays in Honor of Edward Shils. Ben-David, Joseph & Clark, Terry N., eds. LC 76-610. 335p. Date not set. reprint ed. pap. 103.90 (*0-608-21005-6*, 205453300003) Bks Demand.

— Estudios Sociologicos. Ferran, Rosendo, tr. (Nueva Austral Ser.: No. 97). (SPA.). 1991. pap. text 34.95 (*84-239-1897-1*) Elliots Bks.

— German Sociology. Coser, Lewis A. & Powell, Walter W., eds. Bottomore, Mary & Bottomore, Thomas B., trs. LC 79-6983. (Perennial Works in Sociology). 1980. reprint ed. lib. bdg. 16.95 (*0-405-12083-4*) Ayer.

— The Great Debate: Theories of Nuclear Strategy. Pawel, Ernst, tr. from FRE. LC 81-495. 265p. 1981. reprint ed. lib. bdg. 65.00 (*0-313-22851-5*, ARGR, Greenwood Pr) Greenwood.

— The Great Debate: Theories of Nuclear Strategy. Pawel, Ernst, tr. from FRE. 278p. 1985. reprint ed. pap. text 25.50 (*0-8191-4564-5*) U Pr of Amer.

— History, Truth, Liberty: Selected Writings of Raymond Aron. Draus, Franciszek, ed. Krance, Charles, tr. LC 85-8590.Tr. of Fr.. 386p. 1986. 33.00 (*0-226-02800-3*) U Ch Pr.

— In Defense of Decadent Europe. LC 95-50133. 297p. 1996. pap. text 24.95 (*1-56000-894-6*) Transaction Pubs.

— Main Currents in Sociological Thought: Durkheim, Pareto, Weber. 360p. 1998. pap. text 24.95 (*0-7658-0436-0*) Transaction Pubs.

— Main Currents in Sociological Thought Vol. 1: Montesquieu, Comte, Marx, Tocqueville, & the Sociologists & the Revolution of 1848. LC 97-30354. 374p. 1998. pap. 24.95 (*0-7658-0401-8*) Transaction Pubs.

— Memoirs: Fifty Years of Political Reflection. Holoch, George, tr. from FRE. LC 89-7621. 509p. 1989. 49.95 (*0-8419-1113-4*) Holmes & Meier.

— Memoirs: Fifty Years of Political Reflection. Holoch, George, tr. from FRE. LC 89-7621. 510p. 1997. pap. 24.00 (*0-8419-1114-2*) Holmes & Meier.

— On War. Kilmartin, Terence, tr. 164p. 1985. reprint ed. pap. text 19.50 (*0-8191-4565-3*) U Pr of Amer.

— The Opium of the Intellectuals. Kilmartin, Terence, tr. from FRE. LC 77-7400. 324p. 1977. lib. bdg. 69.50 (*0-8371-9672-8*, AROI, Greenwood Pr) Greenwood.

***Aron, Raymond.** The Opium of the Intellectuals. rev. ed. 467p. 2000. pap. 39.95 (*0-7658-0700-9*) Transaction Pubs.

Aron, Raymond. Peace & War: A Theory of International Relations. LC 81-14296. 838p. 1981. reprint ed. 89.50 (*0-89874-391-5*) Krieger.

— Politics & History. Conant, Miriam B., ed. 304p. 1984. reprint ed. pap. 24.95 (*0-87855-944-2*) Transaction Pubs.

— Social Structure & the Ruling Class, Pt. I. (Reprint Series in Sociology). (C). 1993. reprint ed. pap. text 10.00 (*0-8290-2779-3*, S-4) Irvington.

— Thinking Politically: A Liberal in the Age of Ideology. (Orig.). 1996. pap. 24.95 (*0-614-20823-8*) Transaction Pubs.

— Thinking Politically: A Liberal in the Age of Ideology. LC 96-38935. 340p. (Orig.). 1997. pap. text 24.95 (*1-56000-934-9*) Transaction Pubs.

Aron, Raymond & Heckscher, August. Diversity of Worlds. LC 72-12631. 178p. 1973. reprint ed. lib. bdg. 65.00 (*0-8371-6686-1*, ARDW, Greenwood Pr) Greenwood.

Aron, Robert. A Boy Named Jesus: How the Early Years Shaped His Life. LC 97-9424. Orig. Title: Jesus of Nazareth: The Hidden Years. (Illus.). 240p. 1997. pap. 14.00 (*1-56975-119-6*) Ulysses Pr.

Aron, Roberto, et al. Trial Communication Skills. 2nd ed. LC 96-6406. (Trial Practice Ser.). (Illus.). 1996. ring bd. write for info. (*0-07-172600-4*) West Group.

Aron, Stephen. How the West Was Lost: The Transformation of Kentucky from Daniel Boone to Henry Clay. (Illus.). 272p. 1996. 32.50 (*0-8018-5296-X*) Johns Hopkins.

— How the West Was Lost: The Transformation of Kentucky from Daniel Boone to Henry Clay. (Illus.). 272p. 1999. pap. text 16.95 (*0-8018-6198-5*) Johns Hopkins.

Arond, Miriam & Pauker, Samuel L. The First Year of Marriage: What to Expect, What to Accept, & What You Can Change for a Lasting Marriage. 432p. 1991. mass mkt. 6.50 (*0-446-34662-4*, Pub. by Warner Bks) Little.

Arone, Cathleen. Sea Babies: And Their Friends. (Illus.). 32p. (J). (ps-3). 1997. 15.95 (*0-915009-56-0*) World Leis Corp.

Aroner, Miriam. Giraffes Aren't Half As Fat. LC 94-2046. (Illus.). 32p. (J). (gr. k-3). 1995. lib. bdg. 20.90 (*1-56294-484-3*) Millbrook Pr.

— Kingdom of Singing Birds. (J). 1993. 11.15 (*0-606-05396-4*, Pub. by Turtleback) Demco.

Aroner, Miriam & Haas, Shelly O. The Kingdom of Singing Birds. LC 92-39382. (J). (gr. 1-5). 1993. 13.95 (*0-929371-43-7*); pap. 5.95 (*0-929371-44-5*) Kar-Ben.

Aroney-Sine, Christine. Survival of the Fittest: Keeping Healthy in Travel & Service. 1994. 9.95 (*0-912552-88-3*) MARC.

Aronhime, Peter B. & Stephenson, F. W., eds. Analog Signal Processing. LC 94-33388. 104p. (C). 1994. text 106.00 (*0-7923-9510-7*) Kluwer Academic.

Aronica, Michele T. Beyond Charismatic Leadership: The New York Catholic Worker Movement. 224p. 1987. 34.95 (*0-88738-168-5*) Transaction Pubs.

A

Aronica, Paul. A Man Sent by God. 2nd ed. 32p. 1988. reprint ed. pap. 1.50 (0-89944-134-3, 134-3) Salesiana Pubs.

Aronica, Paul, tr. see St. John Bosco.

Aronie, Nancy S. Writing from the Heart: Tapping the Power of Your Inner Voice. 256p. (J). 1998. pap. 13.45 (0-7868-8287-5, Pub. by Hyperion) Time Warner.

Aronna, Michael. Pueblos Enfermos: The Discourse of Illness in the Turn-of-the-Century Spanish & Latin American Essay. LC 99-42034. No. 262. 160p. 1999. pap. 27.50 (0-8078-9266-1) U of NC Pr.

Aronne-Amestoy, Lida. Utopia, Paraiso e Historia: Inscripciones del Mito en Garcia Marquez, Rulfo y Cortazar. LC 85-30723. (Purdue University Monographs in Romance Languages: Vol. 19). xi, 167p. 1986. pap. 41.00 (0-915027-68-2) J Benjamins Pubng Co.

Aronne, Louis J. Weigh Less, Live Longer: Dr. Lou Aronne's "Getting Healthy" Plan. (Illus.). 292p. 1997. pap. 14.95 (0-471-23948-8) Wiley.

— Weigh Less, Live Longer: Dr. Lou Aronne's "Getting Healthy" Plan for Permanent Weight Control. (Illus.). 304p. 1995. 22.95 (0-471-58112-7) Wiley.

Aronne, Louis J. & Graver, Fred. Weigh Less, Live Longer: Dr. Lou Aronne's "Getting Healthy" Plan. 304p. 1996. pap. 5.99 (0-471-17695-8) Wiley.

***Aronoff.** Contemporary Linguisitics: An Introduction. 4th ed. 2000. pap. text. write for info. (0-312-24738-9) St Martin.

Aronoff. Contemporary Linguistics. 3rd ed. 688p. 1996. pap. text 50.95 (0-312-13749-4) St Martin.

Aronoff, jt. auth. see Baskin.

Aronoff, B. R. Dead Man Walking: A Matter of Time. LC 90-84185. 300p. (Orig.). 1991. pap. 10.95 (1-879027-00-3) Eagle Red Bluff.

Aronoff, Carol, jt. auth. see Nydahl, Ole.

Aronoff, Carol A., ed. see Nydahl, Ole.

Aronoff, Craig, jt. auth. see Baskin, Otis W.

Aronoff, Craig E., et al, eds. Family Business Sourcebook II. 2nd rev. ed. 600p. 1996. 69.00 (0-9651011-0-X) Busn Owner Res.

Aronoff, Craig E. & Ward, John L. Another Kind of Hero: Preparing Successors for Leadership. 3rd ed. (Family Business Leadership Ser.: No. 3). (Illus.). 66p. 1992. reprint ed. pap. 14.95 (0-9651011-3-4) Busn Owner Res.

— Family Business Compensation. 2nd ed. (Family Business Leadership Ser.: No. 5). (Illus.). 65p. 1993. reprint ed. pap. 14.95 (0-9651011-5-0) Busn Owner Res.

— Family Business Governance: Maximizing Family & Business Potential. 2nd ed. (Family Business Leadership Ser.: No. 8). (Illus.). 60p. 1996. reprint ed. pap. 14.95 (0-9651011-8-5) Busn Owner Res.

— Family Business Succession: The Final Test of Greatness. 8th ed. (Family Business Leadership Ser.: No. 1). (Illus.). 50p. 1992. reprint ed. pap. 14.95 (0-9651011-1-8) Busn Owner Res.

— Family Meetings: How to Build a Stronger Family & a Stronger Business. 4th ed. (Family Business Leadership Ser.: No. 2). (Illus.). 51p. 1992. reprint ed. pap. 14.95 (0-9651011-2-6) Busn Owner Res.

— How to Choose & Use Advisors: Getting the Best Professional Family Business Advice. 2nd ed. (Family Business Leadership Ser.: No. 6). 69p. 1994. reprint ed. pap. 14.95 (0-9651011-6-9) Busn Owner Res.

— Making Sibling Teams Work: The Next Generation. (Family Business Leadership Ser.: Vol. 10). (Illus.). 72p. 1997. pap. 14.95 (1-891652-00-1) Busn Owner Res.

— Preparing Your Family Business for Strategic Change, Vol. 9. (Family Business Leadership Ser.). (Illus.). 70p. 1997. pap. 14.95 (0-9651011-9-3) Busn Owner Res.

Aronoff, Craig E. & Ward, John L., eds. Contemporary Entrepreneurs. 450p. 1992. lib. bdg. 95.00 (1-55888-315-0) Omnigraphics Inc.

Aronoff, Craig E., et al. Financing Transitions: Managing Capital & Liquidity in the Family Business. 2nd ed. (Family Business Leadership Ser.: Vol. 7). (Illus.). 62p. 1995. reprint ed. pap. 14.95 (0-9651011-7-7) Busn Owner Res.

Aronoff, Daisy P. ABC Bible & Holiday Stories. (Illus.). 58p. (J). (ps-7). 1992. reprint ed. pap. 15.95 (1-878612-28-X) Sunflower Co.

Aronoff, Daisy P. & Forster, Sarabess A. God Is Now Here--for the New Age Religious Family. (Illus.). 80p. 1990. pap. 15.95 (1-878612-00-X) Sunflower Co.

Aronoff, Frances W. Move with the Music. LC 81-24070. 133p. 1982. ring bd. 15.95 (0-9602590-1-5) Turning Wheel Pr.

— Music & Young Children: Expanded Edition. LC 72-75917. 224p. 1979. reprint ed. pap. text 13.95 (0-9602590-0-7) Turning Wheel Pr.

Aronoff, George R., et al. Drug Prescribing in Renal Failure: Dosing Guidelines for Adults. 4th ed. LC 98-44099. 176p. (C). 1999. pap. text 28.00 (0-943126-76-2) Amer Coll Phys.

Aronoff, Gerald M., ed. Evaluation & Treatment of Chronic Pain. 2nd rev. ed. (Illus.). 608p. 1992. 99.00 (0-683-00261-9) Lppncott W & W.

— Evaluation & Treatment of Chronic Pain. 3rd ed. LC 98-22557. 749p. 1998. 120.00 (0-683-30149-7) Lppncott W & W.

Aronoff, Joel, et al, eds. The Emergence of Personality. 272p. 1987. 35.95 (0-8261-6120-0) Springer Pub.

Aronoff, Joel & Wilson, John P. Personality in the Social Process. 408p. 1985. text 79.95 (0-89859-526-6) L Erlbaum Assocs.

Aronoff, Mark. Morphology by Itself: Items & Inflectional Classes. LC 93-20543. (Linguistic Inquiry Monographs: Vol. 22). (Illus.). 275p. 1993. 40.00 (0-262-01136-0); pap. text 20.00 (0-262-51072-3) MIT Pr.

Aronoff, Mark, ed. Morphology Now. LC 90-22725. (SUNY Series in Linguistics). 227p. (C). 1992. text 67.50 (0-7914-0815-9) State U NY Pr.

Aronoff, Mark, et al, eds. Language Sound & Structure. (Illus.). 360p. 1984. 49.50 (0-262-01074-7) MIT Pr.

Aronoff, Mark & Kean, Mary-Louise, eds. Juncture. (Studia Linguistica et Philological Ser.: Vol. 7). 144p. 1980. pap. 56.50 (0-915838-46-X) Anma Libri.

***Aronoff, Mark & Rees-Miller, Janie, eds.** The Handbook of Linguistics. LC 99-87401. (Handbooks in Linguistics Ser.). (Illus.). 832p. 2000. text 124.95 (0-631-20497-0) Blackwell Pubs.

Aronoff, Myron J. Israeli Visions & Divisions. 250p. 1989. 44.95 (0-88738-255-X) Transaction Pubs.

— Israeli Visions & Divisions. 178p. (C). 1991. 24.95 (0-88738-897-3) Transaction Pubs.

— Power & Ritual in the Israel Labor Party: A Study in Political Anthropology. rev. ed. LC 92-13466. (Comparative Politics Ser.). 288p. (C). (gr. 13). 1993. text 75.95 (1-56324-105-6); pap. text 35.95 (1-56324-106-4) M E Sharpe.

Aronoff, Myron J., ed. Cross Currents in Israeli Culture & Politics. (Political Anthropology Ser.: Vol. IV). 115p. (C). 1984. text 39.95 (0-88738-010-7); pap. text 24.95 (0-87855-811-X) Transaction Pubs.

— The Frailty of Authority. (Political Anthropology Ser.: Vol. 5). 221p. (Orig.). 1985. 39.95 (0-88738-091-3); pap. text 21.95 (0-88738-634-2) Transaction Pubs.

— Ideology & Interest: The Dialectic of Politics. LC 79-92197. (Political Anthropology Ser.: Vol. 1). 217p. 1980. text 39.95 (0-87855-371-1) Transaction Pubs.

— Religion & Politics. (Political Anthropology Ser.: Vol. III). 145p. 1983. 39.95 (0-87855-459-9) Transaction Pubs.

Aronoff, Myron J., et al, eds. State Formation & Political Legitimacy. (Political Anthropology Ser.: Vol. 6). 340p. 1987. 39.95 (0-88738-161-8) Transaction Pubs.

***Aronoff, Myron Joel.** The Spy Novels of John Le Carre: Balancing Ethics & Politics. LC 98-43405. 356p. 1998. text 49.95 (0-312-21482-0) St Martin.

Aronoff, Phyllis, tr. see Atwood, Margaret & Beaulieu, Victor-Levy.

Aronoff, Phyllis, tr. see Coulon, Jocelyn.

Aronoff, Phyllis, tr. see Lamoureux.

Aronoff, Phyllis, tr. see Robin, Regine.

Aronoff, Stepen C. Advances in Pediatric Infectious Diseases, Vol.14. (Illus.). 320p. (C). (gr. 13). 1998. text 83.00 (0-8151-0961-X, 29140) Mosby Inc.

Aronoff, Stephen C. Advances in Pediatric Infectious Disease, Vol. 15. 400p. 1999. text 79.95 (0-8151-0958-X) Mosby Inc.

Aronofsky, Darren. PI. (Illus.). 160p. 1999. pap. 14.00 (0-571-20042-7) Faber & Faber.

***Aronofsky, Darren.** Requiem for a Dream. (Illus.). 128p. 2000. pap. 14.00 (0-571-20631-X) Faber & Faber.

Aronofsky, Julius S., et al. Managerial Planning with Linear Programming: In Process Industry Operations. LC 78-2848. (Illus.). 395p. reprint ed. pap. 122.50 (0-608-11455-3, 205539900017) Bks Demand.

Aronov, A., et al, eds. High Temperature Superconductivity & Localization Phenomena: Proceedings of the International Conference, Moscow, Russia, 11-15 May 1991. (Progress in High Temperature Superconductivity Ser.: Vol. 32). 800p. 1992. text 137.00 (981-02-1004-3) World Scientific Pub.

Aronovici, Carol. Housing the Masses. 1977. 23.95 (0-8369-7128-0, 7962) Ayer.

Aronovitz, Avis. Gardening Around Atlanta. 1998. pap. text 18.00 (0-9656345-0-7) Eldorado Pub.

Aronovitz, David. Ballantine Books: The First Decade. 107p. 1987. 25.00 (0-9618295-0-8) Bailiwick Bks.

Aronow, jt. ed. see Tresch.

Aronow, Edward, et al. The Rorschach Technique: Content, Interpretation, & Application. 2nd ed. 256p. (C). 1994. 43.00 (0-205-14912-X, Longwood Div) Allyn.

Aronow, Michael. Don Aronow: The King of Thunderboat Row. Rodengen, Jeffrey L., ed. (Illus.). 144p. 1994. 39.95 (0-945903-22-7) Write Stuff Syndicate.

Aronow, Wilbert S., ed. see Stemmer, Edward A.

Aronowicz, Annette. Freedom from Ideology: Secrecy in Modern Expression. (Modern European History Ser.). 288p. 1988. text 15.00 (0-8240-8066-1) Garland.

— Jews & Christians on Time & Eternity: Charles Peguy's Portrait of Bernard-Lazare. LC 97-19076. (Stanford Studies in Jewish History & Culture). 180p. 1998. 35.00 (0-8047-3005-9) Stanford U Pr.

Aronowitz. Education & the American Future. 250p. Date not set. 60.00 (0-8133-2809-8) Westview.

Aronowitz, Eugene, ed. Prevention Strategies for Mental Health. LC 82-24133. 1982. pap. 9.95 (0-88202-139-7, Prodist) Watson Pub Intl.

Aronowitz, Eugene & Bromberg, Eleanor M., eds. Mental Health & Aging. LC 86-22684. 1986. pap. 6.95 (0-88135-051-6) Watson Pub Intl.

— Mental Health & Long-Term Physical Illness. 96p. 1984. pap. 6.95 (0-88135-001-X, N Watson) Watson Pub Intl.

Aronowitz, Eugene & Sussman, Robert, eds. Issues in Community Mental Health: Youth. LC 87-29074. 1987. pap. 6.95 (0-88135-052-4) Watson Pub Intl.

***Aronowitz, Marguerite.** Maternity Ward: Final Flight of a WWII Liberator. LC 98-91721. (Illus.). 164p. 1998. pap. 14.95 (0-9666615-0-8) Pine Castle.

Aronowitz, Robert A. Making Sense of Illness: Science, Society & Disease. (Studies in the History of Medicine Ser). 283p. (C). 1999. pap. text 17.95 (0-521-55825-5) Cambridge U Pr.

— Making Sense of Illness: Studies in Twentieth Century Medical Thought. LC 97-9805. (Studies in the History of Medicine). 282p. (C). 1998. 29.95 (0-521-55234-6) Cambridge U Pr.

Aronowitz, Stanley. The Crisis in Historical Materialism: Class, Politics, & Culture in Marxist Theory. LC 80-29488. 345p. 1981. 79.50 (0-275-90578-0, C0578, Praeger Pubs) Greenwood.

— The Crisis in Historical Materialism: Class, Politics & Culture in Marxist Theory. 2nd ed. 288p. 1990. pap. 18.95 (0-8166-1836-4) U of Minn Pr.

— Dead Artists, Live Theories, & Other Cultural Problems. 256p. (C). (gr. 13). 1993. pap. 20.99 (0-415-90738-1, A9974) Routledge.

— Death & Rebirth of American. 232p. (C). 1996. 75.00 (0-415-91240-7); pap. 19.99 (0-415-91241-5) Routledge.

— False Promises: The Shaping of American Working Class Consciousness. LC 91-24168. 516p. 1991. text 49.95 (0-8223-1181-X); pap. text 19.95 (0-8223-1198-4) Duke.

***Aronowitz, Stanley.** From the Ashes of the Old: American Labor & America's Future. LC 98-18998. 264p. 2000. pap. 16.50 (0-465-00409-1) Basic.

Aronowitz, Stanley. From the Ashes of the Old: American Labor & America's Future. LC 98-18998. 230p. 1998. 25.00 (0-395-88132-3) HM.

— Honor America: The Nature of Fascism, Historic Struggles Against It & a Strategy for Today. 32p. (Orig.). 1970. pap. 1.95 (0-87810-011-3) Times Change.

— The Knowledge Factory: Dismantling the Corporate University & Creating True Higher Learning. LC 99-34355. 224p. 2000. 25.00 (0-8070-3122-4) Beacon Pr.

— The Politics of Identity: Class, Culture, Social Movements. 288p. (C). 1992. pap. 19.99 (0-415-90437-4, A5748) Routledge.

— Roll over Beethoven: The Return of Cultural Strife. LC 92-56898. 291p. (C). 1993. pap. 22.95 (0-8195-6262-9, Wesleyan Univ Pr) U Pr of New Eng.

— Science As Power: Discourse & Ideology in Modern Society. LC 88-4782. xii, 384p. (Orig.). 1988. pap. 18.95 (0-8166-1659-0) U of Minn Pr.

— Working Class Hero: A New Strategy for Labor. LC 84-11018. 229p. 1984. reprint ed. pap. 12.95 (0-915361-13-2) Lambda Pubs.

Aronowitz, Stanley, et al, eds. Technoscience & Cyberculture: A Cultural Study. LC 95-22528. (Illus.). 288p. (C). 1995. pap. 19.99 (0-415-91176-1, C0244) Routledge.

Aronowitz, Stanley & Cutler, Jonathan, eds. Post Work: Wages of Cybernation. LC 97-26548. 288p. 1997. pap. 19.99 (0-415-91783-2) Routledge.

— Post Work: Wages of Cybernation. LC 97-26548. 288p. (C). 1997. 75.00 (0-415-91782-4) Routledge.

Aronowitz, Stanley & DiFazio, William. The Jobless Future. LC 94-14102. 1994. text 34.95 (0-8166-2193-4) U of Minn Pr.

— The Jobless Future: Sci-Tech & the Dogma of Work. 408p. 1995. pap. 17.95 (0-8166-2194-2) U of Minn Pr.

Aronowitz, Stanley & Giroux, Henry A. Education Still under Siege. 2nd ed. LC 93-15183. (Critical Studies in Education & Culture). 256p. 1993. pap. 21.95 (0-89789-311-5, G311, Bergin & Garvey) Greenwood.

— Education under Siege. 2nd ed. LC 93-15183. (Critical Studies in Education & Culture). 256p. 1993. 65.00 (0-89789-310-7, H310, Bergin & Garvey) Greenwood.

— Postmodern Education: Politics, Culture, & Social Criticism. 192p. (C). 1990. pap. 15.95 (0-8166-1880-1) U of Minn Pr.

Aronowitz, Stanley, jt. auth. see Poster, Mark.

Aronowitz, Vivienne, jt. auth. see Turner, Stephanie.

Arons, Arnold B. A Guide to Introductory Physics. LC 89-22653. 360p. 1990. text 68.95 (0-471-51341-5) Wiley.

— Homework & Test Questions for Introductory Physics Teaching. 279p. 1994. pap. 46.95 (0-471-30931-1) Wiley.

— Introductory Physics Teaching Set: With Homework & Test Questions. 621p. 1995. text. write for info. (0-471-08691-6) Wiley.

— Teaching Introductory Physics. LC 96-16838. 816p. 1996. text 73.95 (0-471-13707-3) Wiley.

Arons, Henry. New Master Course in Hypnotism. 223p. 1997. pap. 8.95 (0-87505-420-X) Borden.

Arons, Katie & Shannon, Jacqueline. Sexy at Any Size: The Real Woman's Guide to Dating & Romance. LC 98-48293. 256p. 1999. pap. 12.00 (0-684-85415-5, Fireside) S&S Trade Pap.

Arons, Linda J. Art Projects Made Easy: Recipes for Fun. (Illus.). xv, 165p. (J). (gr. 1-6). 1995. pap. text 16.00 (1-56308-342-6) Teacher Ideas Pr.

Arons, Raymond A. New Economic Health Care: Drugs Case Mix & Patients' Length of Stay. LC 84-6831. 256p. 1984. 55.00 (0-275-91421-6, C1421, Praeger Pubs) Greenwood.

Arons, Rick. EuroMarketing: A Strategic Planner for Selling into the New Europe. 250p. 1991. per. 37.50 (1-55738-201-8, Irwn Prfssnl) McGraw-Hill Prof.

— God Is Missing . . . & They Think We Did It! Addressing Our Doubts about God & Judaism. (Rediscovering Jewish Philosophy Ser.). (Illus.). 180p. 1998. pap. 15.00 (0-9667019-0-9) BSD Pr.

Arons, Stephen. Compelling Belief: The Culture of American Schooling. LC 85-28818. 240p. 1986. reprint ed. pap. 16.95 (0-87023-524-9) U of Mass Pr.

— Short Route to Chaos: Conscience, Community, & the Re-Constitution of American Schooling. LC 96-51512. 232p. 1997. pap. 16.95 (1-55849-078-7); lib. bdg. 40.00 (1-55849-077-9) U of Mass Pr.

Aronsen, Lawrence R. American National Security & Economic Relations with Canada, 1945-1954. LC 96-53611. 240p. 1997. 67.95 (0-275-95891-4, Praeger Pubs) Greenwood.

Aronsfeld, C. C. The Text of the Holocaust: A Documentation of the Nazis' Extermination Propaganda from 1919-45. LC 85-351. 107p. 1985. 20.00 (0-916288-17-X); pap. 12.00 (0-916288-18-8) Micah Pubns.

Aronsfeld, Caesar C. The Ghosts of Fourteen Ninety-Two. (Conference on Jewish Social Studies). 1979. text 10.00 (0-910430-00-4, JS0004, Conf Jewsh Soc Studies) Col U Pr.

Aronsohn, Ernst. You Can't Catch Trout with a Broomstick: The Unorthodox & Unauthorized Views of a Contemporary Jew. 32p. 1997. pap. 7.00 (0-8059-4209-2) Dorrance.

Aronson. Existentialism. 1998. 22.95 (0-8057-8612-0, Twyne) Mac Lib Ref.

— Readings about the Social Animal. 1998. pap. text 23.95 (0-7167-3313-7) W H Freeman.

— Readings on a Social Animal. (C). 1991. pap. text 17.60 (0-7167-2272-0) W H Freeman.

***Aronson.** Running Out of People to Hate. 2001. pap. text. write for info. (1-57259-939-1, Pub. by Worth) St Martin.

Aronson. Social Animal Imagine. 8th ed. 1998. pap. 16.00 (0-7167-3439-7) W H Freeman.

— Social Animal Text & Readings, Vol. 1. 1991. 30.40 (0-7167-2304-2) W H Freeman.

— Social Psychology. 3rd ed. 224p. (C). 1998. pap. text, student ed. 22.00 (0-321-02440-0) Addson-Wesley Educ.

— Social Psychology, Vol. 1. (C). 1992. lib. bdg. 175.00 (0-8147-0610-X) NYU Pr.

— Social Psychology, Vol. 2. (C). 1992. lib. bdg. 175.00 (0-8147-0611-8) NYU Pr.

— Social Psychology, Vol. 3. (C). 1992. lib. bdg. 175.00 (0-8147-0612-6) NYU Pr.

— Social Psychology & Social Psychiatry Study Guide Local: 1st Edition. (C). 1997. text, student ed. 111.00 (0-201-38224-5) Addison-Wesley.

Aronson, jt. auth. see Bartow, Gary.

Aronson, jt. ed. see Kimmel, Michael S.

Aronson, Alex. Studies in Twentieth-Century Diaries: The Concealed Self. LC 90-21050. (Studies in Comparative Literature: Vol. 12). 135p. 1991. lib. bdg. 69.95 (0-88946-385-9) E Mellen.

Aronson, Andrew C. & Boughner, Robert. Catullus & Horace. 1988. pap. text 14.88 (0-582-36750-6, 72526) Longman.

Aronson, Armand. Christian Sing-Along Guitar, Bk. 1. large type ed. Ward, Ronald, ed. LC 96-92839. (Illus.). 56p. 1997. spiral bd. 7.95 (1-889844-00-4) Christian Sing-Along.

Aronson, Armand. Christian Sing-Along Guitar & Tape One, Vol. 1. 1997. 16.95 incl. audio (1-889844-03-9) Christian Sing-Along.

***Aronson, Arnold.** American Avant-Garde Theatre. LC 00-32215. (Theatre Production Studies). (Illus.). 2000. write for info. (0-415-24139-1) Routledge.

Aronson, Arnold. American Set Design. LC 84-72626. (Illus.). 182p. 1985. reprint ed. pap. 22.95 (0-930452-39-9) Theatre Comm.

— The History & Theory of Environmental Scenography. LC 81-11677. (Theater & Dramatic Studies: No. 3). 296p. reprint ed. pap. 84.40 (0-8357-1224-9, 2070641) Bks Demand.

***Aronson, Arnold E.** Aronson's Neurosciences Pocket Lectures: Speech, Language, Voice. LC 99-40696. 382p. 1999. pap. 54.95 (0-7693-0060-X) Singular Publishing.

Aronson, Arnold E. Clinical Voice Disorders. 3rd ed. (Illus.). 398p. 1990. text 49.00 (0-86577-337-8) Thieme Med Pubs.

Aronson, Bernard & Breck, Richard, eds. ISHM Proceedings, 1989. 600p. 1989. 70.00 (0-930815-23-8) Intl Soc Hybrid.

Aronson, Billy. Betting on Forever. (Illus.). 144p. (J). (gr. 4-7). 1996. 17.95 (0-07-006107-6); pap. 10.95 (0-07-005829-6) McGraw.

— Eclipses. LC 95-48847. (First Bks.). 64p. (J). 1996. lib. bdg. 22.00 (0-531-20238-0) Watts.

— Eclipses: Nature's Blackouts. (First Bks.). 64p. (J). 1997. pap. 6.95 (0-531-15810-1) Watts.

— A Journey to the Center of the Earth: Wishbone Classic Series #9. (Wishbone Classics Ser.). 1996. 9.09 (0-606-10975-7, Pub. by Turtleback) Demco.

— Meteors. LC 95-48846. (First Bks.). 64p. (J). 1996. lib. bdg. 22.00 (0-531-20242-9) Watts.

— Meteors: The Truth Behind Shooting Stars. (First Bks.). 64p. (J). 1997. pap. 6.95 (0-531-15813-6) Watts.

— Romeo & Juliet. (Wishbone Classics Ser.). 1996. 9.09 (0-606-10366-X, Pub. by Turtleback) Demco.

— Scientific Goofs. LC 94-4492. (Illus.). 80p. (J). (gr. 3-7). 1995. pap. 7.95 (0-7167-6553-5) W H Freeman.

Aronson, Bradley, jt. auth. see Zeff, Robin L.

Aronson, Charles N. The Big House. LC 74-81876. (Illus.). 288p. (C). 1974. 20.00 (0-915736-04-7) C N Aronson.

— Eagle in a Butterfly Net. LC 74-22641. (Eagle Ser.: No. 1). (Illus.). 652p. 1975. 16.00 (0-915736-05-5); pap. 10.00 (0-915736-06-3) C N Aronson.

— Free Enterprise. LC 78-73546. (Eagle Ser.: No. 5). (Illus.). (C). 1979. 25.00 (0-915736-15-2); pap. 18.00 (0-915736-16-0) C N Aronson.

— In the Labor Pool. LC 77-78227. (Eagle Ser.: No. 4). (Illus.). 1977. 12.00 (0-915736-13-6); pap. 8.00 (0-915736-14-4) C N Aronson.

— Into Man. LC 76-44030. (Eagle Ser.: No. 3). 1977. 18.00 (0-915736-11-X); pap. 12.00 (0-915736-12-8) C N Aronson.

— Mud & Dust. LC 76-5966. (Eagle Ser.: No. 2). (Illus.). 1976. 16.00 (0-915736-09-8); pap. 10.00 (0-915736-10-1) C N Aronson.

— Positioneering. (Illus.). 347p. (C). 1969. 20.00 (0-915736-01-2) C N Aronson.

— Regimen for Weight Control in Retired Couples & Others Who Want to Control Weight Happily. LC 73-88985. (Illus.). (C). 1973. 5.00 (0-915736-03-9) C N Aronson.

— Sculptured Hyacinths. (Illus.). (C). 1973. 20.00 (0-915736-02-0) C N Aronson.

An Asterisk (*) at the beginning of an entry indicates that the title is appearing for the first time.

— The Writer Publisher. LC 75-36854. (C). 1976. 10.00 (*0-915736-07-1*); pap. 7.00 (*0-915736-08-X*) C N Aronson.

Aronson, Dan R. The City Is Our Farm: Seven Migrant Ijebu Yoruba Families. 2nd ed. 224p. 1978. pap. text 21.95 (*0-87073-563-2*) Transaction Pubs.

Aronson, David. Jewish Way of Life. 1957. 5.00 (*0-8381-1107-6*) USCJE.

Aronson, Diane & Resolve Staff. Resolving Infertility: Understanding the Options & Choosing Solutions When You Want to Have a Baby. 384p. 1999. 27.50 (*0-06-273522-5*) HarpC.

Aronson, E., jt. auth. see Lindzey, Gardner.

Aronson, E. A., et al. Satellites & Forecasting of Solar Radiation. Bahm, Raymond E., ed. LC 80-70943. (International Solar Energy Society, American Section, Workshop Ser.). 1982. pap. text 32.50 (*0-89553-026-0*) Am Solar Energy.

Aronson, Elliot. Age of Propaganda: The Everyday Use & Abuse of Persuasion. 320p. (C). 1991. pap. text 14.95 (*0-7167-2211-9*) W H Freeman.

***Aronson, Elliot.** Nobody Left to Hate: Teaching Compassion after Columbine. 2000. 19.95 (*0-7167-4132-6*) W H Freeman.

Aronson, Elliot. The Social Animal. rev. ed. 496p. (C). 1991. pap. text 18.40 (*0-7167-2166-X*) W H Freeman.

— The Social Animal. 6th rev. ed. 496p. (C). 1991. text 26.40 (*0-7167-2165-1*) W H Freeman.

— The Social Animal. 7th ed. (Illus.). 528p. (C). 1994. pap. text 36.95 (*0-7167-2618-1*) W H Freeman.

— The Social Animal. 7th ed. 1997. 39.00 (*0-7167-3196-7*) W H Freeman.

— The Social Animal. 7th ed. 2000. 37.00 (*0-7167-2733-1*) W H Freeman.

— The Social Animal. 8th ed. 1998. pap. text 34.95 (*0-7167-3312-9*) W H Freeman.

— Social Psychology: Professional. 2nd ed. (C). 1997. pap. text 9.00 (*0-321-40170-0*) Addson-Wesley Educ.

Aronson, Elliot & Pratkanis, Anthony R., eds. Social Psychology, 3 vols. (International Library of Critical Writings in Economics). 1993. 500.00 (*1-85278-422-9*) E Elgar.

— Social Psychology, 3 vols. (International Library of Critical Writings in Business History). 1800p. (C). 1993. lib. bdg. 525.00 (*0-8147-0609-6*) NYU Pr.

Aronson, Elliot, et al. Methods of Research in Social Psychology. 2nd ed. 376p. (C). 1989. 72.19 (*0-07-002466-9*) McGraw.

— Social Psychology. LC 93-43017. (C). 1997. 71.00 (*0-06-040294-6*) Addson-Wesley Educ.

— Social Psychology: 3/e. 3rd ed. LC 98-20751. 704p. (C). 1998. 81.00 (*0-321-02435-4*, Prentice Hall) P-H.

Aronson, Elliot, jt. auth. see Pratkanis, Anthony R.

Aronson, Elliot, jt. ed. see Lindzey, Gardner.

Aronson, Elliot, tr. see Peterkops, Raimonds.

Aronson, Elliott, jt. auth. see Pratkanis, Anthony R.

Aronson, Elyse F. Mz Goose & Her Wonderful Rhymes: They Make You Happy All of the Time. (Illus.). 56p. (J). (ps-3). 2000. pap. 12.95 incl. audio (*0-9669510-1-8*, Pub. by Good Things) Penton Overseas.

Aronson, Elyse G., ed. see Hertzman, Monica N.

Aronson, Geoffrey. Israel, Palestinians & the Intifada: Creating Facts on the West Bank. 372p. 1989. 29.95 (*0-7103-0336-X*) Routledge.

— Settlements & Israel-Palestinian Negotiations: An Overview. 57p. 1996. pap. 4.95 (*0-88728-263-6*) Inst Palestine.

Aronson, Harvey B. Love & Sympathy in Theravada Buddhism. viii, 127p. 1986. 12.00 (*81-208-0049-4*, Pub. by Motilal Bnarsidass) S Asia.

Aronson, Helene D. Easy Ayurvedic Menus & Recipes. 145p. (Orig.). 1986. pap. 10.00 (*0-939753-11-1*); lib. bdg. 21.50 (*0-939753-10-3*) Sunrise Lodge Prods.

Aronson, Howard I. Georgian: A Reading Grammar. rev. ed. (Illus.). 526p. 1990. reprint ed. pap. text 28.95 (*0-89357-207-1*) Slavica.

— A Reading Georgian Grammar. rev. ed. 580p. pap. 99.50 incl. audio (*0-88432-704-3*, SGG150) Audio-Forum.

Aronson, Howard I., ed. Non-Slavic Languages of the U. S. S. R. Papers from the 4th Conference. (Illus.). 309p. (Orig.). 1994. pap. 24.95 (*0-89357-250-0*) Slavica.

Aronson, Howard I., jt. auth. see Getzoff, Steven.

Aronson, I. Michael. Troubled Waters: The Origins of the 1881 Anti-Jewish Pogroms in Russia. LC 90-33957. (Russian & East European Studies Ser.). 286p. 1991. text 49.95 (*0-8229-3656-9*) U of Pittsburgh Pr.

Aronson, J. K. An Account of the Foxglove & Its Medical Uses 1785-1985. (Illus.). 420p. 1986. text 45.00 (*0-19-261501-7*) OUP.

— Side Effects of Drugs Annual: A Worldwide Yearly Survey of New Data & Trends, Vol. 21. 590p. 1998. 227.00 (*0-444-82818-4*) Elsevier.

***Aronson, J. K.** Side Effects of Drugs Annual Vol. 22: A Worldwide Yearly Survey of New Data & Trendes. (Illus.). 600p. 1999. 203.00 (*0-444-50092-8*) Elsevier.

Aronson, J. K., ed. Annual 20, Side Effects Drugs, 1997, Vol. 20. 564p. 1997. 224.00 (*0-444-82532-0*, North Holland) Elsevier.

Aronson, J. K. & Van Boxtel, C. J., eds. Annual 19, Side Effects Drugs, 1995. 532p. 1996. 210.00 (*0-444-82531-2*) Elsevier.

— Side Effects of Drugs Annual, 18. 558p. 1995. 233.50 (*0-444-81939-8*) Elsevier.

— Side Effects of Drugs Annual 17: A Worldwide Yearly Critical Survey of New Data & Trends. 648p. 1994. 228.00 (*0-444-82005-1*) Elsevier.

Aronson, J. K., et al. ABC of Monitoring Drug Therapy. 48p. 1993. pap. text 18.00 (*0-7279-0791-3*, Pub. by BMJ Pub) Login Brothers Bk Co.

Aronson, J. K., jt. auth. see Dukes, M. N.

Aronson, J. K., jt. ed. see Dukes, M. N.

Aronson, J. Richard & Schwartz, Eli, eds. Management Policies in Local Government Finance. 3rd ed. LC 87-2658. (Municipal Management Ser.). 449p. 1987. 39.95 (*0-87326-075-9*) Intl City-Cnty Mgt.

— Management Policies in Local Government Finance. 4th ed. LC 96-13387. (Municipal Management Ser.). 455p. 1996. 41.95 (*0-87326-108-9*) Intl City-Cnty Mgt.

Aronson, J. Richard, et al. Financing State & Local Governments. 4th ed. LC 85-48207. (Studies in Government Finance). 265p. 1986. 16.95 (*0-8157-5518-X*) Brookings.

Aronson, J. Richard, jt. ed. see Thornton, Robert F.

Aronson, Jake. Two Hundred Eighty-Nine Most Asked Questions on Condominiums Answered. 224p. 1984. pap. 4.95 (*0-913428-39-6*) Landfall Pr.

Aronson, James. Deadline for the Media: Today's Challenges to Press, TV & Radio. LC 72-179640. 348p. 1975. pap. 2.95 (*0-672-52115-6*, Bobbs) Macmillan.

— The Press & the Cold War. exp. ed. 352p. 1990. 33.00 (*0-85345-805-7*, Pub. by Monthly Rev); pap. 16.00 (*0-85345-806-5*, Pub. by Monthly Rev) NYU Pr.

Aronson, James, jt. auth. see Blondel, Jacques.

Aronson, Jason Inc., Staff. An Authoritative Guide to Books in Psychotherapy, Set. 144p. 1996. pap. 2.00 (*0-7657-0112-X*) Aronson.

Aronson, Jason, Inc. Staff, ed. Psychotherapist's Book Guide. 208p. 1994. pap. 3.95 (*1-56821-277-1*) Aronson.

Aronson, Jay, jt. auth. see Turban, Efraim.

Aronson, Jay E. & Zionts, Stanley, eds. Operations Research: Methods, Models, & Applications, 7. LC 95-42161. (IC2 Management & Management Science Ser.: No. 7). 400p. 1998. 69.50 (*1-56720-027-3*, Quorum Bks) Greenwood.

Aronson, Jay E., jt. auth. see Turban, Efraim.

Aronson, Jerrold L., et al. Realism Rescued: How Scientific Progress Is Possible. 234p. 1995. text 49.95 (*0-8126-9288-8*); pap. text 18.95 (*0-8126-9289-6*) Open Court.

Aronson, Jodi. The Dictionary of Managed Behavioral Health Care: "A" Is for "Access" LC 97-17437. 50p. 1997. pap. 9.95 (*0-87630-846-9*) Brunner-Mazel.

— Inside Managed Care: Family Therapy in a Changing Environment. 160p. 1996. pap. 19.95 (*0-87630-818-3*) Brunner-Mazel.

Aronson, Jodi C., jt. auth. see O'Reilly, James T.

Aronson, Jonathan. Negotiating to Launch Negotiations: Getting Trade in Services onto the GATT Agenda. (Pew Case Studies in International Affairs). 50p. (C). 1992. pap. text 3.50 (*1-56927-125-9*) Geo U Inst Dplmcy.

Aronson, Jonathan, jt. auth. see Cowhey, Peter F.

Aronson, Jonathan D. & Cowhey, Peter F. When Countries Talk: International Trade in Telecommunications Services. (American Enterprise Institute Trade in Services Ser.). 368p. 1988. text 32.95 (*0-88730-284-X*, HarpBusn) HarpInfo.

Aronson, Joseph. Encyclopedia of Furniture. rev. ed. (Illus.). 496p. 1961. 30.00 (*0-517-03735-1*, Crown) Crown Pub Group.

***Aronson, Joyce.** The Use of the Telephone in Psychotherapy. 2000. write for info. (*0-7657-0268-1*) Aronson.

Aronson, Julie Z. Stop the Clock: Ending the Tyranny of Time in Education Policy Perspectives on Time & Learning. (Illus.). 39p. (C). 1998. reprint ed. pap. text 15.00 (*0-7881-7483-5*) DIANE Pub.

Aronson, Kristin. To Eat Flesh They Are Willing Are Their Spirits Weak? Vegetarians Who Return to Meat. LC 96-92415. 352p. (Orig.). 1996. 18.95 (*0-9626169-3-1*) Pythago Bks.

Aronson, Larry. HTML 3.0 Manual of Style. 2nd ed. LC 96-121378. 216p. 1995. 24.95 (*1-56276-352-0*, Ziff-Davis Pr) Que.

— HTML 3.2 Manual of Style. 3rd ed. LC 97-221034. 408p. 1997. pap. text 29.99 incl. cd-rom (*1-56276-529-9*) Que.

Aronson, Lynn & Simon, Elizabeth. Bowlfood Cookbook: Over 200 Dazzling & Eclectic Recipes from the Restaurant Lola Bowla. LC 99-17895. (Illus.). 256p. 1999. 20.95 (*0-7611-0002-4*, 10002) Workman Pub.

Aronson, M. I., et al. Litigation-Evidence & Procedure. 4th ed. 1988. 83.00 (*0-409-49507-7*, AT, MICHIE); pap. 105.00 (*0-409-49508-5*, AT, MICHIE) LEXIS Pub.

Aronson, Marc. Art Attack: A Short Cultural History of the Avant-Garde. LC 97-22372. (Illus.). 160p. (J). (gr. 5 up). 1998. 20.00 (*0-395-79729-2*, Clarion Bks) HM.

Aronson, Marc & Meltzer, Ellen. Day by Day: The Eighties, 2 vols. LC 94-26632. 1659p. 1994. 195.00 (*0-8160-1592-9*) Facts on File.

Aronson, Mark & Franklin, Nicola. Review of Administrative Action. lxvii, 720p. 1987. 130.00 (*0-455-20721-6*, Pub. by LawBk Co); pap. 94.50 (*0-455-20722-4*, Pub. by LawBk Co) Gaunt.

Aronson, Mark D. & Delbanco, Thomas L. Manual of Clinical Evaluation. (Brown Spiral Manual Ser.). (Illus.). 350p. 1988. 31.95 (*0-316-05210-8*, Little Brwn Med Div) Lppncott W & W.

***Aronson, Martin.** Jesus & Lao Tzu: The Parallel Sayings. 2000. 19.00 (*1-56975-224-9*) Ulysses Pr.

Aronson, Melissa. Building Communication Partnerships with Parents. (Professional's Guide Ser.). (Illus.). 80p. 1995. pap., teacher ed. 9.95 (*1-55734-846-4*) Tchr Create Mat.

Aronson, Merry & Spetner, Don. The Public Relations Writer's Handbook. LC 98-7627. 1998. 20.95 (*0-7879-4570-6*) Jossey-Bass.

Aronson, Milton, ed. see Gold, Andrew.

Aronson, Miriam K., ed. Understanding Alzheimer's Disease: What It Is, How to Cope with It, Future Directions. (Illus.). 380p. 1998. reprint ed. text 17.00 (*0-7881-5582-2*) DIANE Pub.

Aronson, Miriam K., et al, eds. The Acting-Out Elderly: Issues for Helping Professionals. LC 82-23430. (Advanced Models & Practice in Aged Care Ser.: No. 1). 132p. 1983. text 39.95 (*0-917724-76-3*) Haworth Pr.

Aronson, Miriam K. & Post, Donna C., eds. Reshaping Dementia Care: Issues in Nursing Home Care. 176p. 1994. 35.00 (*0-8039-5159-0*); pap. 16.95 (*0-8039-5160-4*) Sage.

Aronson, Morton J. & Scharfman, Melvin A., eds. Psychotherapy: The Analytic Approach. LC 92-13540. 400p. 1992. 60.00 (*0-87668-508-4*) Aronson.

Aronson, Myra, ed. Trade & Investment in the Asia - Pacific Region: Experts Debate Japan-U. S. Issues. 128p. (C). 1996. text 25.00 (*0-8147-0641-X*) NYU Pr.

Aronson, Nathan N., Jr., ed. see Mononen, Iikka.

Aronson, R. B., jt. auth. see Drago, Raymond J.

Aronson, Robert H. The Law of Evidence in Washington. 2nd ed. LC 93-22768. 560p. 1993. spiral bd. 105.00 (*0-250-40718-3*, MICHIE) LEXIS Pub.

— The Law of Evidence in Washington. 3rd ed. 751p. 1998. lib. bdg. 125.00 (*0-327-00901-2*, 8281811) LEXIS Pub.

Aronson, Robert H. & Weckstein, Donald T. Professional Responsibility in a Nutshell. 2nd ed. (Nutshell Ser.). 514p. (C). 1991. reprint ed. pap. 23.50 (*0-314-83121-5*) West Pub.

Aronson, Robert H., et al. Problems, Cases & Materials in a Professional Responsibility: Problems, Cases, & Materials. 2nd ed. LC 95-30769. (American Casebook Ser.). 525p. (C). 1995. teacher ed. 50.50 (*0-314-06468-0*) West Pub.

— Professional Responsibility, Problems, Cases & Materials. LC 84-27029. (American Casebook Ser.). 745p. 1988. reprint ed. teacher ed., student ed. write for info. (*0-314-39543-1*); reprint ed. text 42.50 (*0-314-87537-9*) West Pub.

— Washington Objections at Trial. 200p. 1992. pap. 39.50 (*0-88063-825-7*, MICHIE) LEXIS Pub.

Aronson, Robert L. Self Employment: A Labor Market Perspective. (Cornell Studies in Industrial & Labor Relations: No. 24). 168p. (Orig.). 1991. text 32.50 (*0-87546-175-1*, ILR Press); pap. text 13.95 (*0-87546-176-X*, ILR Press) Cornell U Pr.

Aronson, Ronald. After Marxism. 322p. 1994. pap. text 18.95 (*0-89862-416-9*) Guilford Pubns.

— Sartre's Second Critique. LC 86-30707. 271p. reprint ed. pap. 84.10 (*0-608-08045-4*, 206901000002) Bks Demand.

— Sartre's Second Critique: An Explanation & Commentary. LC 86-30707. xviii, 254p. (C). 1987. pap. text 16.95 (*0-226-02805-4*) U Ch Pr.

— Stay Out of Politics: A Philosopher Views South Africa. LC 89-20291. 178p. 1990. pap. text 18.00 (*0-226-02803-8*); lib. bdg. 38.50 (*0-226-02801-1*) U Ch Pr.

Aronson, Ronald, ed. see Sartre, Jean-Paul.

Aronson, Ronald, ed. see Van Den Hoven, Adrian.

Aronson, Shlomo. The Beginnings of the Gestapo System. 80p. 1969. boxed set 32.95 (*0-87855-203-0*) Transaction Pubs.

— Conflict & Bargaining in the Middle East: As Israeli Perspective. LC 77-10967. (Illus.). 464p. 1978. reprint ed. pap. 143.90 (*0-608-07380-6*, 206760700009) Bks Demand.

— Israel's Nuclear Options. (CISA Working Papers: No. 7). 37p. (Orig.). 1977. pap. 15.00 (*0-86682-006-X*) Ctr Intl Relations.

— The Politics & Strategy of Nuclear Weapons in the Middle East: Opacity, Theory, & Reality, 1960-1991 - An Israeli Perspective. LC 91-46244. (SUNY Series in Israeli Studies). 398p. (C). 1992. pap. text 24.95 (*0-7914-1208-3*) State U NY Pr.

— Sadat's Initiative & Israel's Response: The Strategy of Peace & the Strategy of Strategy. (Research Note Ser.: Vol. 4). 1978. reprint ed. pap. 10.00 (*0-86682-035-3*) Ctr Intl Relations.

Aronson, Stephanie, intro. Resources for Reproductive Rights Research. LC 93-77744. (Orig.). 1993. pap. write for info. (*1-878428-10-1*) Inst Womens Policy Rsch.

***Aronson, Steven M. L., contrib. by.** Dogs. LC 99-178402. (Fandex Family Field Guides Ser.). 1998. pap. 9.95 (*0-7611-0758-4*) Workman Pub.

Aronson, Steven M. L., contrib. by. Trees. LC 99-178273. 1998. pap. 9.95 (*0-7611-1204-9*) Workman Pub.

Aronson, Tara. Simplify Your Household: Less-Stress Solutions for Efficient Home Management. LC 98-5190. (Simple Life Bks.). (Illus.). 144p. 1998. 17.95 (*0-7621-0066-4*, Pub. by RD Assn) Penguin Putnam.

Aronson, Tara, ed. see Stephens, Stephanie.

Aronson, Theo. Grandmama of Europe: The Crowned Descendants of Queen Victoria. LC 73-15044. (Illus.). 384p. 1974. 12.95 (*0-672-51723-X*, Bobbs) Macmillan.

Aronson, Trudy. English Grammar Digest. 224p. (C). 1984. pap. text 33.60 (*0-13-281014-X*) P-H.

***Aronson, Virginia.** Abigail Van Buren: Ann Landers. LC 99-50097. (Women of Achievement Ser.). (Illus.). 112p. 2000. pap. text 9.95 (*0-7910-5298-2*) Chelsea Hse.

— Abigail Van Buren/Ann Landers: Advice Columnists. LC 99-50097. (Women of Achievement Ser.). (Illus.). 112p. 1999. 19.95 (*0-7910-5297-4*) Chelsea Hse.

— Celestial Healing: Close Encounters That Cure. 288p. 1999. mass mkt. 6.99 (*0-451-19884-0*) NAL.

Aronson, Virginia. Dave Thomas. (Overcoming Adversity Ser.). (Illus.). 128p. (gr. 5-9). 1999. pap. 9.95 (*0-7910-5303-2*) Chelsea Hse.

— Drew Barrymore. LC 99-34256. (Overcoming Adversity Ser.). (Illus.). 128p. (gr. 5-9). 1999. pap. 9.95 (*0-7910-5307-5*) Chelsea Hse.

— Drew Barrymore. LC 99-34256. (Overcoming Adversity Ser.). (Illus.). 128p. 1999. 19.95 (*0-7910-5306-7*) Chelsea Hse.

***Aronson, Virginia.** Ethan Allan. (Revolutionary War Leaders Ser.). 2000. 18.95 (*0-7910-5974-X*) Chelsea Hse.

— Everything You Need to Know about Breast Health. LC 00-8726. 2000. lib. bdg. write for info. (*0-8239-3224-9*, PowerKids) Rosen Group.

— History of Motown. (African-American Achievers Ser.). 2000. 19.95 (*0-7910-5814-X*) Chelsea Hse.

— Influenza Pandemic of 1918-1919. (Great Disasters Ser.). (Illus.). 128p. (YA). (gr. 5 up). 2000. write for info. (*0-7910-5263-X*) Chelsea Hse.

— Jennifer Love Hewitt. LC 99-35561. (Galaxy of Superstars Ser.). (Illus.). 64p. (YA). (gr. 3). 1999. pap. 9.95 (*0-7910-5498-5*) Chelsea Hse.

Aronson, Virginia. Jennifer Love Hewitt. LC 99-35561. (Galaxy of Superstars Ser.). (Illus.). 64p. (J). 1999. 17.95 (*0-7910-5497-7*) Chelsea Hse.

***Aronson, Virginia.** Venus & Serena Williams. LC 00-23019. 2000. 17.95 (*0-7910-5799-2*) Chelsea Hse.

— Venus & Serena Williams. (Illus.). 2000. pap. 7.95 (*0-7910-6158-2*) Chelsea Hse.

Aronson, Virginia. Venus Williams. (Galaxy of Superstars Ser.). (Illus.). 64p. (YA). (gr. 3 up). 1999. 16.95 (*0-7910-5153-6*) Chelsea Hse.

Aronson, Virginia & Stare, Frederick J. RX Executive Diet. 1986. pap. 9.75 (*0-8158-0424-5*) Chris Mass.

Aronson, Virginia, jt. auth. see Haller, Henry.

Aronsson, Bertil & Lundstrohm, Torsten. Borides, Silicides, & Phosphides: A Critical Review of Their Preparation, Properties & Crystal Chemistry. LC 65-8351. 138p. reprint ed. pap. 42.80 (*0-8357-7354-X*, 201314900085) Bks Demand.

***Aronsson, Lars.** Development of Sustainable Tourism. (Illus.). 2000. 82.95 (*0-304-70691-4*); pap. 33.95 (*0-304-70692-2*) Continuum.

Aronsson, Thomas, et al. Welfare Measurement, Sustainability & Green National Accounting: A Growth Theoretical Approach. LC 96-23170. (New Horizons in Environmental Economics Ser.). 192p. 1997. 90.00 (*1-85898-485-8*) E Elgar.

Aronstein, David C. & Piccirillo, Albert C. Have Blue & the F-117A: Evolution of the Stealth Fighter. LC 97-15440. 350p. 1997. 54.95 (*1-56347-245-7*) AIAA.

Aronstein, David C., et al. Advanced Tactical Fighter to F-22 Raptor: Origins of the 21st Century Air Dominance Fighter. LC 98-27265. 308p. 1998. pap. write for info. (*1-56347-282-1*) AIAA.

Aronstein, David C., jt. auth. see Piccirillo, Albert C.

Aronstein, David M. & Thompson, Bruce J., eds. HIV & Social Work: A Practitioner's Guide. LC 97-21867. (Illus.). 586p. 1998. 69.95 (*0-7890-0180-2*, Harrington Park) Haworth Pr.

— HIV & Social Work: A Practitioner's Guide. LC 97-21867. (Illus.). 586p. (C). 1998. pap. 24.95 (*1-56023-906-9*, Harrington Park) Haworth Pr.

Aronwald, Benecia. Things You Can Be. LC 97-67185. (J). 1998. 6.99 (*0-679-88284-7*, Pub. by Random Bks Yng Read) Random.

— Things You Can Give. 1997. 6.99 (*0-679-88287-1*) Random.

— Things You Should Save. LC 96-17617. 1997. 6.99 (*0-679-88285-5*) Random Hse Value.

Aronwicz, Annette, tr. see Levinas, Emmanuel.

Arora. Banking Law in Europe. 78.95 (*1-85521-584-5*) Ashgate Pub Co.

Arora & Verney, eds. Multiple Identities in a Single State. (C). 1995. 40.00 (*81-220-0414-8*, Pub. by Konark Pubs) S Asia.

Arora, jt. ed. see Grove.

Arora, A. & Kalra, K. All India Banking Law Judgments, 1990, Vol. 3. (C). 1990. 83.00 (*0-89771-236-6*) St Mut.

— Supreme Court on Full Bench Motor Vehicle & Compensation Cases, 1950-1990. (C). 1990. 120.00 (*0-89771-192-0*) St Mut.

Arora, A. & Malhotra, M. Law of Compulsory - Voluntary Retirement & Registration, Ion Government & Public Sector. (C). 1990. 100.00 (*0-89771-294-3*) St Mut.

Arora, A. & Sachdeva, S. Law Relating to Suspension of Employees, Officers - Workmen, in Banks. (C). 1990. 55.00 (*0-89771-293-5*) St Mut.

— Service Condition of Workmen in Banks with Supplement. (C). 1990. 60.00 (*0-89771-292-7*) St Mut.

Arora, A. K., et al, eds. Ordering & Phase Transitions in Charged Colloids. LC 95-30600. (Complex Fluids & Fluid Microstructures Ser.). (Illus.). 400p. 1996. 125.00 (*1-56081-917-0*, Wiley-VCH) Wiley.

Arora, A. K. & Tata, B. V., eds. Ordering & Phase Transitions in Charged Colloids. 361p. 1996. 169.00 (*0-471-18630-9*) Wiley.

Arora, A. S. Digest of Wills Cases, 1900-1988. (C). 1988. 140.00 (*0-7855-4734-7*) St Mut.

Arora, Anand. The Women Elite of India. 225p. 1990. text 32.50 (*0-685-31264-X*, Pub. by Radiant Pubs) S Asia.

Arora, Anu. Practical Banking & Building Society Law. 430p. 1997. pap. 54.00 (*1-85431-628-1*, Pub. by Blackstone Pr) Gaunt.

Arora, Ashish, et al, eds. Chemicals & Long-Term Economic Growth: Insights from the Chemical Industry. LC 97-28674. 564p. 1998. 79.95 (*0-471-18247-8*, Wiley-Interscience) Wiley.

Arora, Balveer & Mukherji, Nirmal, eds. Federalism in India. (C). 1992. 37.50 (*0-7069-5970-1*, Pub. by Vikas) S Asia.

***Arora, D. K., ed.** Advances in Plant Morphology & Anatomy, 5 vols. 1864p. 1998. pap. 1750.00 (*81-7488-145-X*, Pub. by Print Hse) St Mut.

Arora, D. K., et al, eds. Handbook of Applied Mycology, Vol. 1: Soil & Plants. (Illus.). 736p. 1991. text 235.00 (*0-8247-8380-8*) Dekker.

Arora, David. All That the Rain Promises & More... A Hip Pocket Guide to Western Mushrooms. (Illus.). 236p. (Orig.). 1991. pap. 17.95 (*0-89815-388-3*) Ten Speed Pr.
— Mushrooms Demystified. 2nd rev. ed. (Illus.). 959p. 1986. pap. 39.95 (*0-89815-169-4*) Ten Speed Pr.
Arora, Dayanand. Investment Banking in Japan: Retrospect & Prospects. (European University Studies: Economics & Management: Ser. 5, Vol. 1141). (Illus.). XVII, 170p. 1991. pap. 47.00 (*3-631-43191-0*) P Lang Pubng.
— Japanese Financial Institutions in Europe: International Competitiveness of Japanese Banks & Securities Companies. (Advances in Finance, Investment, & Banking Ser.: Vol. 1). (Illus.). 304p. 1995. text 114.00 (*0-444-82142-2*, North Holland) Elsevier.
Arora, Dilip K., et al, eds. Handbook of Applied Mycology, Vol. 2: Humans, Animals & Insects. (Illus.). 800p. 1991. text 235.00 (*0-8247-8435-9*) Dekker.
— Handbook of Applied Mycology, Vol. 3: Foods & Feeds. (Illus.). 640p. 1991. text 235.00 (*0-8247-8491-X*) Dekker.
— Handbook of Applied Mycology, Vol. 4: Fungal Biotechnology. (Illus.). 1144p. 1991. text 235.00 (*0-8247-8501-0*) Dekker.
Arora, Dilip K., et al, eds. Mycotoxins in Ecological Systems. (Handbook of Applied Mycology Ser.: Vol. 5). (Illus.). 464p. 1991. text 235.00 (*0-8247-8551-7*) Dekker.
Arora, G., tr. see Kondrat'ev, K. Ya.
Arora, G. L. Bruchidae (Coleoptera) of Northwest India. (Oriental Insects Monographs: No. 7). 1977. 30.00 (*1-877711-17-9*) Assoc Pubs FL.
Arora, Gomti. Social Structure & Fertility. (C). 1990. 27.50 (*81-85135-50-9*) S Asia.
Arora, J. C. All India Banking Law Judgments, 1940-1987. (C). 1987. 160.00 (*0-7855-6127-7*) St Mut.
— All India Banking Law Judgments, 1940-1987. (C). 1989. 170.00 (*0-7855-3719-8*) St Mut.
Arora, Jasbir S. Introduction to Optimum Design. (Illus.). 625p. (C). 1988. 98.13 (*0-07-002460-X*) McGraw.
Arora, Jasbir S., ed. Guide to Structural Optimization. LC 96-30071. (ASCE Manuals & Reports on Engineering Practice: No. 90). 360p. 1997. 66.00 (*0-7844-0220-5*) Am Soc Civil Eng.
Arora, K. C. Indian Nationalist Movement in Britain, 1930-1949. (C). 1992. 28.00 (*81-210-0292-3*, Pub. by Inter-India Pubns) S Asia.
Arora, N. MOSFET Models for VLSI Circuit Simulation: Theory & Practice. (Computational Microelectronics Ser.). (Illus.). 632p. 1993. 238.95 (*0-387-82395-6*) Spr-Verlag.
Arora, Neena. Nayantara Sahgal & Doris Lessing: A Feminist Study in Comparison. 1991. text 25.00 (*81-85218-31-5*, Pub. by Prestige) Advent Bks Div.
Arora, P. N. & Bagga, P. C. A Text Book of Coordinate Geometry. 260p. 1989. pap. 25.00 (*81-209-0206-8*, Pub. by Pitambar Pub) St Mut.
Arora, Poonam, jt. auth. see Alamgir, Mohivddin.
Arora, R. & Mosch, W. High Voltage Insulation Engineering: Behaviour of Dielectrics - Their Properties & Applications. 1995. write for info. (*81-224-0619-X*, Pub. by Wiley Estrn) Franklin.
Arora, R. K., jt. auth. see Mathur, M. V.
Arora, R. K., jt. auth. see Mehrotra, R. C.
Arora, Ramesh K. & Raghavulu, C. V., eds. Values in Administration. 1990. text 27.50 (*81-7045-017-9*, Pub. by Assoc Pub Hse) Advent Bks Div.
Arora, Ranjana, jt. auth. see Grover, Verinder.
Arora, Ranjana, jt. ed. see Grover, Verinder.
Arora, S. C. President's Rule in Indian States. 1990. 32.50 (*81-7099-234-6*, Pub. by Mittal Pubs Dist) S Asia.
Arora, S. C. & Kumar, Ramesh. A Text Book of Calculus. 548p. 1997. pap. 95.00 (*81-209-0170-3*, Pub. by Pitambar Pub) St Mut.
Arora, S. P. & Soni, T. S. Advanced Cost Accounting - Problems & Solutions. 864p. 1990. 110.00 (*81-209-0010-3*, Pub. by Pitambar Pub) St Mut.
— Cost Accounting - Principles, Practice & Problems. 873p. 1990. pap. 48.00 (*81-209-0007-3*, Pub. by Pitambar Pub) St Mut.
Arora, Shirley. Proverbial Comparisons & Related Expressions in Spanish: Recorded in Los Angeles, California. LC 75-46053. (University of California Publications, Folklore Studies: No. 29). 530p. reprint ed. pap. 164.30 (*0-608-13908-4*, 202120800021) Bks Demand.
***Arora, Subhash Chander.** Strategies to Combat Terrorism: A Study of Punjab. LC 99-939394. 204p. 1999. 24.00 (*81-241-0610-X*, Pub. by Har-Anand Pubns) Nataraj Bks.
Arora, Sudhir, jt. auth. see Adams, Henry G.
Aros, Andrew A. Actor's Guide to the Talkies, 1965-1974. LC 77-21589. 781p. 1977. 55.50 (*0-8108-1052-2*) Scarecrow.
— Broadway & Hollywood Too. LC 80-67670. 60p. 1980. pap. 6.50 (*0-932352-04-9*) Applause Pubns.
— Elvis Presley: His Films, & Music. LC 79-55876. (Vinyl Gold Ser.: No. 1). 75p. (Orig.). 1980. pap. 6.50 (*0-932352-01-4*) Applause Pubns.
— The Latin Music Handbook. LC 78-59987. (Illus.). 1978. pap. 6.50 (*0-932352-00-6*) Applause Pubns.
— The Latin Music Yearbook, 1980. (Vinyl Gold Ser.: No. 2). (Orig.). 1980. pap. 6.50 (*0-932352-02-2*) Applause Pubns.
— A Title Guide to the Talkies, Nineteen Seventy-Five Through Nineteen Eighty-Four. LC 85-27682. 355p. 1986. 37.00 (*0-8108-1868-X*) Scarecrow.
— A Title Guide to the Talkies, Nineteen Sixty-Four to Nineteen Seventy-Four. LC 76-40451. 344p. 1977. 37.00 (*0-8108-0976-1*) Scarecrow.
Aros, Andrew A., jt. auth. see Pearson, John C.
Aros, J. W., ed. Balancing the Budget. LC 96-6130. (Reference Shelf Ser.: Vol. 68, No. 2). 1996. pap. 25.00 (*0-8242-0887-0*) Wilson.
Aros, Robert & Ternan, Rob. Beyond Courage: Shipwrecked & Adrift, One Family Fights to Survive. Buchanan, Paul, ed. (Illus.). 272p. 1994. pap. 15.95 (*0-9638704-1-6*) Shore Pubng.
— Beyond Courage: Shipwrecked & Adrift, One Family Fights to Survive. Buchanan, Paul, ed. (Illus.). 272p. 1995. 22.95 (*0-9638704-0-8*) Shore Pubng.
Arostegui, Martin C. Twilight Warriors. (Special Warfare Ser.). 352p. 1998. mass mkt. 6.99 (*0-312-96493-5*) St Martin.
— Twilight Warriors: Inside the World's Special Forces. LC 96-37352. 1997. 24.95 (*0-312-15234-5*) St Martin.
Arougheti, Paul J. Radical Zionism: The Emergence of the Radical Zionist Movement, 1968-1972. (Illus.). 130p. 1997. pap. 10.00 (*0-932270-21-2*) Spencer Pr.
Arouin, Aaron. Seeking Wisdom: Collected Essays on the Human Condition. (Illus.). 103p. 1995. pap. 20.00 (*1-57074-291-X*) Greyden Pr.
Aroul, G., tr. see Paz, Octavio.
Aroutunova, Bayara. Lives in Letters Princess Zinaida Volkonskaya & Her Correspondence. (ENG & FRE., Illus.). 224p. 1994. 24.95 (*0-89357-251-9*) Slavica.
Arowolo, O. & Ekanem, I. Population & Development Planning: An Integrated Approach. 300p. 1992. 49.95 (*0-89388-228-3*); pap. 35.95 (*0-89388-229-1*) Okpaku Communications.
Arozarena, M. M., et al. Stabilization & Solidification of Hazardous Wastes. 390p. 1990. 109.00 (*0-8155-1245-7*) Noyes.
Arozarena, Marcelino, jt. auth. see Guirao, Ramon.
Arozena, Steven. Best Books for Public Libraries: The 10,000 Top Fiction & Nonfiction Titles. 840p. 1992. 75.00 (*0-8352-3073-2*) Bowker.
Arp, Bill, pseud. Bill Arp, So Called: Side Show of the Southern Side of the War. LC 72-158277. (Illus.). reprint ed. 39.50 (*0-404-00213-7*) AMS Pr.
— Bill Arp's Peace Papers. LC 79-158276. (Illus.). reprint ed. 39.50 (*0-404-00405-9*) AMS Pr.
Arp, Claudia. Almost 13 LC 85-29735. 256 p. 1986. write for info. (*0-8407-5493-0*) Nelson Comm.
— Big Book of Family Fun: Year-Round Creative Activities. 1994. pap. 12.99 (*0-7852-8200-9*) Nelson.
Arp, Claudia & Arp, David. The Second Half of Marriage: Facing the Eight Challenges of Every Long-Term Marriage. 256p. 1997. pap. 12.99 (*0-310-21935-3*) Zondervan.
Arp, Claudia, jt. auth. see Arp, David.
***Arp, Dave.** Fighting for Your Empty Nest Marriage. LC 00-9169. (Psychology Ser.). 2000. 25.00 (*0-7879-5222-2*) Jossey-Bass.
Arp, David. Quiet Whispers from God's Heart for Couples. 128p. 1999. pap. text 12.99 (*0-8499-5484-3*) World Pubns.
Arp, David & Arp, Claudia. Family Moments: Making an Investment with a Priceless Return. LC 98-50333. 1999. 4.97 (*1-56955-092-1*) Servant.
— Fifty-Two Dates for You & Your Mate. LC 92-20484. 1993. pap. 7.99 (*0-8407-3435-2*) Nelson.
— Love Life for Parents: How to Have Kids & a Sex Life Too. LC 97-39951. 1997. pap. 10.99 (*0-310-20715-0*) Zondervan.
— Marriage Moments: Heart to Heart Times to Deepen Your Love. LC 98-15318. 178p. 1998. 9.97 (*1-56955-091-3*, Vine Bks) Servant.
— Suddenly They're Thirteen. LC 99-18213. 1999. pap. 12.99 (*0-310-22788-7*) HarpC.
— Where the Wild Strawberries Grow. LC 96-5115. (Illus.). 224p. 1996. 16.99 (*0-7814-0291-3*) Chariot Victor.
Arp, David, jt. auth. see Arp, Claudia.
Arp, H. C., et al. Progress in New Cosmologies: Beyond the Big Bang. (Illus.). 376p. (C). 1994. text 110.00 (*0-306-44635-9*, Kluwer Plenum) Kluwer Academic.
Arp, Halton C. Quasars, Redshifts & Controversies. LC 87-80290. (Illus.). 208p. 1987. 19.95 (*0-941325-00-8*) Interstellar Media.
— Seeing Red: Redshifts, Cosmology & Academic Science. LC 98-497. (Illus.). 306p. 1999. pap. (*0-9683689-0-5*) C Roy Keys.
Arp, Halton C. & Madore, Barry F. A Catalogue of Southern Peculiar Galaxies & Associations Vol. 1: Positions & Descriptions. (Illus.). 216p. 1987. text 95.00 (*0-521-33086-6*) Cambridge U Pr.
Arp, Halton C. & Madore, Barry F. A Catalogue of Southern Peculiar Galaxies & Associations Vol. 2: Selected Photographs. (Illus.). 288p. 1987. text 105.00 (*0-521-33087-4*) Cambridge U Pr.
Arp, Hans. Isms of Art. (GER, FRE & ENG., Illus.). 60p. 1996. 30.00 (*1-56898-069-8*) Princeton Arch.
Arp, Hans, et al, eds. Plastique, Nos. 1[00ad]5. LC 74-91379. (Contemporary Art Ser.). 1970. reprint ed. 15.95 (*0-405-00725-6*) Ayer.
Arp, Hans, jt. auth. see Lissitzky, El.
Arp, J. Hans. Arp: Collected French Writings. Neugroschel, Joachim, tr. from FRE. Orig. Title: Jours Effeuillantes. (Illus.). 704p. (C). pap. 18.95 (*0-7145-0854-3*) Riverrun NY.
Arp, Thomas R. Perrine's Literature: Structure, Sound & Sense. 7th ed. LC 97-72035. 1552p. (C). 1997. text 47.50 (*0-15-503822-2*, Pub. by Harcourt Coll Pubs) Harcourt.
Arp, Thomas R. & Perrine, Laurence. Perrine's Story & Structure. 9th ed. LC 97-72036. 624p. (C). 1997. pap. text 34.00 (*0-15-503721-8*, Pub. by Harcourt Coll Pubs) Harcourt.
Arp, Thomas R., jt. auth. see Perrine, Laurence.
ARPA Staff. Human Language Technology: Proceedings of the 1994 Conference. 478p. (C). 1994. pap. text 50.00 (*1-55860-357-3*) Morgan Kaufmann.
— Human Language Technology Workshop Proceedings. 436p. (C). 1998. pap. text 50.00 (*1-55860-324-7*) Morgan Kaufmann.
— Image Understanding: Proceedings of the 23rd Workshop 1994. 1647p. (C). 1998. pap. text 85.00 (*1-55860-338-7*) Morgan Kaufmann.
— Spoken-Language Technology: Proceedings of the 1994 Conference. 153p. (C). 1998. pap. text 40.00 (*1-55860-358-1*) Morgan Kaufmann.
— Spoken-Language Technology: Proceedings of the 1995 Conference. 305p. (C). 1998. pap. text 50.00 (*1-55860-374-3*) Morgan Kaufmann.
ARPA Staff, ed. Message Understanding: Evaluation & Conference: Proceedings of the 3rd-6th DARPA Workshops. 413p. (Orig.). (C). 1996. pap. text 40.00 (*1-55860-402-2*) Morgan Kaufmann.
— Spoken Language Systems Technology (SL'96) 187p. (Orig.). (C). 1998. pap. text 50.00 (*1-55860-422-7*) Morgan Kaufmann.
— Tipster Text Program. 492p. (Orig.). (C). 1996. pap. text 55.00 (*1-55860-426-X*) Morgan Kaufmann.
Arpaci, V. A., jt. ed. see Avedisian, C. T.
Arpaci, V. S., jt. ed. see Bayazitoglu, Y.
Arpaci, Vedat S. Introduction to Heat Transfer. LC 99-53323. 611p. 2000. 100.00 (*0-13-391061-X*) P-H.
— Microsales of Turbulence: Heat & Mass Transfer Correlations. 211p. 1997. text 33.00 (*90-5699-565-0*) Gordon & Breach.
Arpad, Joseph J. & Lincoln, Kenneth R. Buffalo Bill's Wild West. LC 73-106990. (Wild & Woolly West Ser.: No. 19). (Illus.). (Orig.). 1971. pap. 3.00 (*0-910584-62-1*) Filter.
Arpad, Joseph J., ed. see Crockett, David.
Arpad, V. Multilingual Dictionary of Foundry. (ENG, FRE, GER, HUN & RUS.). 435p. 1978. 95.00 (*0-8288-6153-6*) Fr & Eur.
***Arpaia, Joseph & Rapgay, Lobsang.** Tibetan Wisdom for Western Life. LC 99-28487. 372p. 1999. pap. 14.95 (*1-58270-013-3*, Pub. by Beyond Words Pub) Publishers Group.
Arpaio, Joe & Sherman, Len. America's Toughest Sheriff: How We Can Win the War Against Crime. (Illus.). xxii, 262 p. 1996. 22.95 (*1-56530-202-8*, Pub. by Summit TX) BookWorld.
Arpajian, Scott. How to Use HTML 3.0. 7th ed. 240p. 1996. pap. 24.99 (*1-56276-390-3*, Ziff-Davis Pr) Que.
— How to Use HTML 3.2. 2nd ed. 1997. 24.99 (*1-56276-561-2*) Que.
Arpan, Jeffrey S. International Business. (Opportunities In . . . Ser.). (Illus.). 160p. pap. 11.95 (*0-8442-4424-4*, 44244, VGM Career) NTC Contemp Pub Co.
— International Business. 128p. 1993. pap. 7.95 (*0-8442-8679-6*, VGM Career) NTC Contemp Pub Co.
— International Business. (Opportunities in...Ser.). (Illus.). 160p. 1994. 14.95 (*0-8442-4423-6*, 44236, VGM Career) NTC Contemp Pub Co.
— Opportunities in International Business Careers. (Illus.). 160p. 1991. 13.95 (*0-8442-6516-0*, VGM Career) NTC Contemp Pub Co.
— Opportunities in International Business Careers. (Illus.). 160p. 1993. pap. 10.95 (*0-8442-6517-9*, VGM Career) NTC Contemp Pub Co.
Arpan, Jeffrey S. & AlHashim, Dhia D. International Dimensions Of Accounting. Ricks, David A., ed. LC 83-18747. (SWC-Management). 240p. (C). 1984. mass mkt. 15.75 (*0-534-01467-4*) PWS Pubs.
Arpan, Jeffrey S., et al. Hallmarks of Successful International Business Programs. (Occasional Papers on International Educational Exchange: No. 25). 32p. 1988. pap. 4.00 (*1-882036-00-X*) Coun Intl Ed.
— International Business Education in the 1990s: A Global Survey. 310p. 1993. 10.00 (*0-9634394-1-3*) AACSB.
Arpante, Barbara A. The Recovery of a Cancer Patient: A Personal Diary. Melenski, Aaron, ed. (Illus.). 54p. (Orig.). 1992. pap. text 7.95 (*0-9625313-2-4*) Mntn Pr MA.
Arpe, Curt. Das Ti Nv Eivai Bei Aristoteles. LC 75-13254. (History of Ideas in Ancient Greece Ser.). (GER.). 1976. reprint ed. 21.95 (*0-405-07292-9*) Ayer.
Arpee, Leon. The Armenian Awakening. (Works of Leon Arpee). xi, 234p. 1985. reprint ed. 69.00 (*0-932051-67-7*) Rprt Serv.
Arpels, John C., jt. auth. see Kenley, Joan.
Arpey, Christopher, et al, eds. Cutaneous Surgery: An Illustrated & Practical Approach. LC 96-34920. (Illus.). 350p. 1996. text 99.00 (*0-07-069619-5*) McGraw-Hill HPD.
***Arpi, Claude.** The Fate of Tibet: When Big Insects Eat Small Insects. 432p. 1999. 35.00 (*81-241-0638-X*, Pub. by Har-Anand Pubns) Nataraj Bks.
Arpi, Erik. A Troll Wedding: The Troll Children's Search for the Magic Wedding Flower. Engen, Kari & Gracey, Kirsten, trs. from SWE. LC 92-60297. (Illus.). 30p. (J). (ps-5). 1992. 12.95 (*1-881278-00-X*) M S Pr.
Arpin, Maurice. La Fortune Litteraire de Paul Nizan: Une Analyse des Deux Receptions Critiques de Son Oeuvre. (Publications Universitaires Europeennes Ser.: Series 13, Vol. 204). (FRE.). xvi, 310p. 1995. 54.95 (*3-906752-86-0*, Pub. by P Lang) P Lang Pubng.
Arponen, A. Chinese-Finnish Dictionary: Kina-Suomi Sanakirja. (CHI & FIN.). 485p. 1985. 125.00 (*0-8288-1004-4*, M2843) Fr & Eur.
Arponen, Annikki. Chinese to Finnish Dictionary. (CHI & FIN.). 484p. 1985. 95.00 (*0-320-00075-3*) Fr & Eur.
Arponen, J. S., et al, eds. Condensed Matter Theories, Vol. 3. LC 87-656591. (Illus.). 414p. 1988. 125.00 (*0-306-42829-6*, Plenum Trade) Perseus Pubng.
Arps, Louisa W. Denver in Slices: A Historical Guide to the City. LC 83-11058. (Illus.). 263p. 1998. reprint ed. pap. 21.95 (*0-8040-0841-8*) Swallow.
Arps, R. B. & Pratt, W. K., eds. Image Processing & Interchange: Implementation & Systems. 1992. 20.00 (*0-8194-0813-1*, 1659) SPIE.
Arquelles, Jose. Earth Ascending: An Illustrated Treatise on Law Governing Whole Systems. 3rd ed. LC 83-20052. (Illus.). 170p. 1996. reprint ed. pap. 24.00 (*0-939680-45-9*) Bear & Co.
Arquembourg, P. C. Immunoelectrophoresis Theory, Methods, Identification, Interpretation. 2nd rev. ed. (Illus.). ix, 104p. 1975. 53.25 (*3-8055-2136-7*) S Karger.
Arquette, Cliff. Here's Charlie Weaver, Mamma & Mt. Idy. Buscher, Sherri, ed. 200p. 1989. reprint ed. pap. 9.95 (*0-942936-18-3*) Lincoln-Herndon Pr.
Arquette, Kerry, ed. see Haglund, Jill.
***Arquette, Kerry.** Daddy Promises. (Illus.). 32p. 1999. 15.00 (*0-570-05554-7*, 56-1971) Concordia.
Arquette, Kerry. What Did You Do Today? LC 98-17230. 2001. write for info. (*0-15-201414-4*) Harcourt.
Arquette, Kerry, jt. auth. see Gerbrandt, Michele.
Arquette, Mardiningsih. She Child. (Illus.). 32p. (Orig.). 1982. pap. 4.00 (*0-9605594-1-8*) Monkey Man.
Arquie, Louis. Hi, How Are You Doing? Guide to Spoken American for French Speakers. (ENG & FRE.). 301p. 1992. pap. 39.95 (*0-7859-0994-X*, 2227067152) Fr & Eur.
Arquilevic, Gabriel. Shiloh. (Literature Units Ser.). (Illus.). 48p. 1996. pap., wbk. ed. 7.95 (*1-55734-566-X*) Tchr Create Mat.
Arquilevich, Gabriel. Fairview's Guide to Composition & Essay Writing. 103p. 1999. pap. text 15.00 (*0-9649042-1-7*) G Arquilevich.
***Arquilevich, Gabriel.** How to Write an Essay: Grades 6-8. (Illus.). 48p. 1999. pap., teacher ed. 7.95 (*1-57690-491-1*, TCM 2491) Tchr Create Mat.
Arquilevich, Gabriel. Writing for 100 Days: A Student-Centered Approach to Composition & Creative Writing. 105p. 1995. pap. text. write for info. (*0-9649042-0-9*) G Arquilevich.
Arquilevich, Gabriel, et al. World Religions. (Interdisciplinary Units Ser.). 1995. pap. text 21.95 (*1-55734-624-0*) Tchr Create Mat.
Arquilevich, Gabriel, ed. see Rouse, Toni.
Arquilevich, Gabriel, ed. see Smith, J. L.
Arquilla, John. Dubious Battles: Aggression, Defeat, & the International System. 277p. 1992. 75.00 (*0-8448-1734-1*, Crane Russak); pap. 45.00 (*0-8448-1736-8*, Crane Russak) Taylor & Francis.
Arquilla, John, ed. From Troy to Entebbe: Special Operations in Ancient & Modern Times. LC 95-45702. 392p. 1996. pap. text 19.95 (*0-7618-0186-3*); lib. bdg. 39.50 (*0-7618-0185-5*) U Pr of Amer.
Arquilla, John & Ronfeldt, David. The Advent of Netwar. (Illus.). 135p. 1996. pap. text 15.00 (*0-8330-2414-0*, MR-789-OSD) Rand Corp.
— The Emergence of Noopolitik: Toward An American Information Strategy. LC 99-10120. 99p. 1999. pap. 15.00 (*0-8330-2698-4*, MR-1033-OSD) Rand Corp.
Arquilla, John & Ronfeldt, David F., eds. In Athena's Camp: Preparing for Conflict in the Information Age. LC 97-31571. (Illus.). 526p. 1997. pap. 20.00 (*0-8330-2514-7*, MR-880-OSD/RC) Rand Corp.
Arquin, Florence. Diego Rivera, the Shaping of An Artist, 1889-1921. LC 71-108795. (Illus.). 171p. reprint ed. pap. 53.10 (*0-608-11268-2*, 201619300002) Bks Demand.
Arra, R. Power Surfcasting. 1991. pap. 12.95 (*1-55821-112-8*) Lyons Pr.
Arrabal, Fernando. L' Architecte et l'Empereur de l'Assyrie. (FRE.). 320p. 1986. pap. 16.95 (*0-7859-3639-4*, 2267007869) Fr & Eur.
— Baal Babylone. 172p. pap. 13.95 (*0-8288-9021-8*, F83452) Fr & Eur.
— The Body-Builder's Book of Love. Zatlin, Phyllis, ed. Mans, Lorenzo, tr. from FRE. LC 98-73220. (Contemporary Spanish Plays Ser.: Series 15). (Illus.). 1999. pap. 8.00 (*1-888463-05-8*) Estreno.
— Le Cimetiere des Voitures. (FRE.). 192p. 1972. pap. 10.95 (*0-8288-9025-0*, FA783) Fr & Eur.
— Le Grand Ceremonial: Ceremonie pour un Noir Assassine: Le Jardin des Delices: Bestialite Erotique, Vol. 3. (FRE.). 684p. 1986. pap. 18.95 (*0-7859-3190-2*, 2264007842) Fr & Eur.
— Guernica & Other Plays. Wright, Barbara, tr. from FRE. Incl. Labyrinth. 1969. Picnic on the Battlefield. 1969. Tricycle. 1969. 1969. Set pap. 4.95 (*0-394-17318-X*, E521) Grove-Atltic.
— Guernica & Other Plays: The Labyrinth, The Tricycle, Picnic on the Battlefield, & They Put Handcuffs on the Flowers, The Architect & the Emperor of Assyria, Garden of Delights. LC 86-80293. 392p. 1986. pap. 14.00 (*0-8021-5122-1*, Grove) Grove-Atltic.
— Isabelle d'Egypte et Autres Recits. 200p. 1970. pap. 10.95 (*0-8288-9023-4*, FA784) Fr & Eur.
— Jeunes Barbares de'aujourd'hui. (FRE.). 48p. 1975. pap. 9.95 (*0-7859-5369-8*) Fr & Eur.
— Lettre au General Franco. (FRE.). 192p. 1984. pap. 16.95 (*0-7859-4708-6*, F83490) Fr & Eur.
— Pic-Nic - Elrticiclo - El Laberinto. (SPA.). 269p. 1985. 14.95 (*0-8288-7047-0*, S31240) Fr & Eur.
— La Pierre de la Folie: Poemes. (FRE.). 111p. 1969. pap. 15.95 (*0-7859-3181-3*, F83452) Fr & Eur.
— La Pierre de la Folie: Poemes. 1970. pap. 9.95 (*0-686-54461-7*) Fr & Eur.
— Teatro Bufo (Robame un Billoncito, Apertura, Orangutan, Punk y Punk y Colegram) Torres Monreal, Francisco, ed. (Nueva Austral Ser.: No. 18). (SPA.). 1991. pap. text 24.95 (*84-239-1818-1*) Elliots Bks.
— Theatre: Avec: Le Ciel et la Mer, la Grande Revue du 20e Siecle, Vol. 9. 261p. 1969. 15.95 (*0-686-54468-4*) Fr & Eur.

An Asterisk (*) at the beginning of an entry indicates that the title is appearing for the first time.

A

An Asterisk (*) at the beginning of an entry indicates that the title is appearing for the first time.

A

Arrigo, Joseph A. The Grace & Grandeur of Natchez Homes. LC 94-10729. (Illus.). 128p. 1994. pap. 19.95 (*0-89658-226-4*) Voyageur Pr.
— Historic Baton Rouge Coloring Book. (Illus.). 32p. (J). (gr. k-3). 1999. pap. 3.25 (*1-56554-421-8*) Pelican.
— Historic Natchez Homes Coloring Book. (Illus.). (ps-3). 1997. pap. text 3.25 (*1-56554-315-7*) Pelican.
— Steamboats on the River Coloring Book. (Illus.). (J). (ps-3). 1997. pap. text 3.25 (*1-56554-316-5*) Pelican.
Arrigo, Kevin R., jt. auth. see Lizotte, Michael P.
Arrigo, Mary & Hargreaves, Connie. When I Visit Yosemite. (Illus.). 43p. (Orig.). (J). (ps). pap. 2.95 (*0-318-21253-6*) Arrigo CA.
Arrigo, Sal, Jr. Beyond Bingo 2: More Innovative Programs for the New Senior. LC 98-84291. 64p. 1998. pap. 12.95 (*0-910251-96-7*, BYB101) Venture Pub PA.
Arrigo, Sal, Jr., et al. Beyond Bingo: Innovative Programs for the New Senior. LC 92-82884. (Illus.). 62p. 1992. pap. 12.95 (*0-910251-58-4*) Venture Pub PA.
Arrigoitia, Luis De, see Gallego, Laura & De Arrigoitia, Luis.
Arrigoitia, Luis De, see De Arrigoitia, Luis.
Arrigon, James R. Mental Equitation: A Guide to Interdisciplinary Horsemanship. LC 98-47580. (Illus.). 144p. 1999. 24.95 (*1-57779-010-3*) Alpine Pubns.
Arrigoni, Edward. Exploring Nature Safely. 2nd ed. (Illus.). 272p. 1988. pap. 11.95 (*0-943805-00-7*) Nature Safe Consults.
— A Nature Walk to Ka'ena Point. (Illus.). 1978. pap. 1.50 (*0-914916-30-0*) Ku Paa.
Arrigoni, Enrico. Freedom: My Dream. 440p. 1985. pap. 14.95 (*0-88189-002-2*) West World Pr.
— The Totalitarian Nightmare. 280p. 1982. reprint ed. pap. 8.95 (*0-88189-001-4*) West World Pr.
Arrigoni, Patricia. Harpo, the Baby Harp Seal. Falken, Linda & Bollow, Janet, eds. LC 94-90107. (Illus.). 32p. (J). (gr. 2-5). 1995. 16.95 (*0-9625468-8-7*) Trvl Pubs Intl.
— Making the Most of Marin. 1990. pap. 15.95 (*0-9625468-9-5*) Trvl Pubs Intl.
***Arrigoni, Patricia.** Making the Most of Marin: A Northern California Guide. 3rd rev. ed. Dana, Carroll, ed. (Illus.). 400p. 2000. pap. 19.95 (*0-9625468-7-9*, Pub. by Trvl Pubs Intl) Sunbelt Pubns.
Arrigoni, Rena. Casa Angelica: Arlene's Legacy. LC 97-4744. 122p. 1997. pap. 11.95 (*0-8263-1809-6*) U of NM Pr.
Arrigucci, Mario, et al, eds. Country Guides: Basic Information on Trademark Registration Worldwide. 208p. 1996. pap. 62.95 (*0-939190-21-4*) Intl Trademark.
Arrillaga, J. Computer Modelling of Electric Power. text. write for info. (*0-471-87249-0*) Wiley.
Arrillaga, J. High Voltage Direct Current Transmission. 2nd ed. (Power Ser.: No. 29). 311p. 1998. 90.00 (*0-85296-941-4*, PO029) INSPEC Inc.
Arrillaga, J. Power System Harmonic Analysis. LC 97-309. 382p. 1997. 149.95 (*0-471-97548-6*) Wiley.
Arrillaga, J. & Arnold, C. P. Computer Analysis of Power Systems. LC 90-39424. 376p. 1990. pap. 195.00 (*0-471-92760-0*) Wiley.
Arrillaga, J. & Smith, B. C. AC/DC Power System Analysis. (Power Ser.: No. 27). 406p. 1998. 90.00 (*0-85296-934-1*, PO027) INSPEC Inc.
Arrillaga, J., et al. Power System Harmonics. LC 84-22097. 348p. reprint ed. pap. 107.90 (*0-7837-0110-1*, 204038700016) Bks Demand.
***Arrillaga, J., et al.** Power System Quality Assessment. LC 99-38990. 400p. 2000. text 120.00 (*0-471-98865-0*) Wiley.
Arrillaga-Torrens, Rafael. Filosofia Griega: Introduccion al Pensamiento Moderno. 2nd ed. 632p. 1978. 7.50 (*84-292-5103-0*) U of PR Pr.
Arrillaga Torrens, Rafael. Sonar y Hacer. LC 76-56437. (Coleccion Mente y Palabra). 176p. 1977. 5.00 (*0-8477-0546-3*); pap. 4.00 (*0-8477-0547-1*) U of PR Pr.
Arrindell, Willem A., jt. auth. see Hofstede, Geert H.
Arrington & Stronstad. Full Life Bib Comm Nt. LC 98-51044. 1999. 39.99 (*0-310-20118-7*) Zondervan.
Arrington, B. T. The Medal of Honor at Gettysburg. (Illus.). 60p. (Orig.). 1996. pap. 9.95 (*0-939631-92-X*) Thomas Publications.
Arrington, Cedric. The Truth about Blacks & Whites Vol. 1: A Biblical Perspective. 125p. 1997. pap. 60.00 (*0-9661116-0-5*) Comalco Pub.
Arrington, Christian & Duffy, Mary. Celebration! Arts & Crafts for Festivals & Traditions Observed in the U. S. A. Arrington, Doris, ed. (Illus.). 100p. (Orig.). 1997. pap. 23.95 (*1-885762-02-X*, 971) Abbeygate Pr.
Arrington, Diane. Seventh Sense: A Collection of True Unsolved Mysteries from the Animal World. LC 96-13167. (Illus.). 224p. 1996. 14.95 (*0-87605-683-4*) Howell Bks.
Arrington, Doris, ed. see Arrington, Christian & Duffy, Mary.
***Arrington, Frances.** Bluestem. LC 99-53726. (Illus.). 144p. (YA). (gr. 5-9). 2000. 16.99 (*0-399-23564-7*, G P Putnam) Peng Put Young Read.
Arrington, French L. Christian Doctrine: A Pentecostal Perspective, Vol. 1. 1992. pap. 15.99 (*0-87148-199-5*) Pathway Pr.
— Christian Doctrine: A Pentecostal Perspective, Vol. 2. 279p. 1993. 15.99 (*0-87148-200-2*) Pathway Pr.
— Christian Doctrine: A Pentecostal Perspective, Vol. 3. 277p. 1994. 15.99 (*0-87148-204-5*) Pathway Pr.
Arrington, H. J. The Heart of a Friendship: An East African Folktale. LC 96-42238. (Illus.). 32p. (J). 1997. 14.95 (*1-56554-224-X*) Pelican.
Arrington, James. Aunt Pearl's Personal Pointers on How to "Farley-Up" Your Very Own Family Reunion: Family Reunion Book. LC 98-16694. 1998. pap. 10.95 (*1-57345-380-3*) Deseret Bk.
Arrington, James, et al. The Trail of Dreams: A Musical. 1997. pap. 5.00 (*1-57514-296-1*, 0029) Encore Perform Pub.
Arrington, John, jt. ed. see Greenfield, George B.
Arrington, Jud K., ed. Public Cemeteries of Sumter County, Alabama, 1834-1972: A Geneaological Listing. LC 98-66417. (Regional History Ser.: Vol. 4). 480p. 1998. 27.00 (*0-942979-48-6*) Livingston AL.
Arrington, Jud K., jt. auth. see Stegall, Joseph F.
Arrington, Kenna & Parrish, Joan. Spectacular Spelling. (Illus.). 105p. (J). (gr. k-2). 1996. pap. write for info. (*0-9656478-0-3*) Finger Works.
Arrington, Kenna, jt. auth. see Parrish, Joan.
Arrington, L. R. & Kelley, Kathleen C. Domestic Rabbit Biology & Production. LC 76-10173. 1976. 19.95 (*0-8130-0537-X*) U Press Fla.
Arrington, Lael. Worldproofing Your Kids: Helping Moms Prepare Their Kids to Navigate Today's Turbulent Times. LC 97-11017. 304p. 1997. pap. 12.99 (*0-89107-956-4*) Crossway Bks.
Arrington, Lance & Fogel, Wayne. Dealing with Change, Vol. 1. (Illus.). 158p. 1999. 29.95 (*0-9671470-0-X*) Arrington Grp.
Arrington, Leonard. History of Idaho. LC 92-36968. 996p. 1995. pap. 39.95 (*0-89301-176-2*) U of Idaho Pr.
Arrington, Leonard J. Adventures of a Church Historian. Leonard J. Arrington. LC 97-33895. 1998. write for info. (*0-252-02381-1*) U of Ill Pr.
— Brigham Young: American Moses. LC 85-24533. (Illus.). 544p. 1986. 17.95 (*0-252-01296-8*) U of Ill Pr.
— David Eccles: Pioneer Western Industrialist. LC 75-2093. (Illus.). 310p. reprint ed. pap. 96.10 (*0-7837-6213-5*, 204593700009) Bks Demand.
— Faith & Intellect As Partners in Mormon History. (Leonard J. Arrington Mormon History Lecture Ser.: No. 1). 40p. 1996. pap. 5.95 (*0-87421-213-8*) Utah St U Pr.
— Great Basin Kingdom: Economic History of the Latter-Day Saints, 1830-1900. LC 93-2943. 534p. 1993. reprint ed. pap. 14.95 (*0-87480-420-5*) U of Utah Pr.
— Utah's Audacious Stockman, Charlie Redd. LC 94-18758. (Illus.). 296p. reprint ed. pap. 91.80 (*0-608-08569-3*, 206909200002) Bks Demand.
Arrington, Leonard J., pref. The Presidents of the Church. LC 85-31117. 460p. 1993. reprint ed. pap. 11.95 (*0-87579-683-4*) Deseret Bk.
Arrington, Leonard J. & Alley, John R., Jr. Harold F. Silver: Western Inventor, Businessman & Civic Leader. LC 92-4195. 260p. 1992. reprint ed. 80.60 (*0-7837-9253-0*, 204999300004) Bks Demand.
Arrington, Leonard J. & Bitton, Davis. The Mormon Experience: A History of the Latter-Day Saints. 2nd ed. (Illus.). 456p. 1992. 16.95 (*0-252-06236-1*) U of Ill Pr.
Arrington, Leonard J. & Hansen, Gary B. The Richest Hole on Earth: A History of the Bingham Copper Mine. LC 63-64592. (Utah State University. Monograph Ser.: Vol. 11, No. 1). 103p. (Orig.). reprint ed. pap. 32.00 (*0-8357-7908-4*, 203633600002) Bks Demand.
Arrington, Leonard J., et al. Building the City of God: Community & Cooperation among the Mormons. 2nd ed. (Illus.). 520p. 1992. 16.50 (*0-252-06235-3*) U of Ill Pr.
Arrington, Leonard J., jt. auth. see Bartholomew, Rebecca.
Arrington, Lewis R. & Kelley, K. C. Domestic Rabbit Biology & Production. LC 76-10173. (Illus.). 238p. 1976. reprint ed. pap. 73.80 (*0-608-04472-5*, 206521700001) Bks Demand.
Arrington, Melvin S., Jr., tr. see De Jesus, Carolina M.
Arrington, Robert L. The Blackwell Companion to the Philosophers. LC 98-7599. (Blackwell Companions to Philosophy Ser.). 600p. 1998. 89.95 (*1-55786-845-X*) Blackwell Pubs.
— Rationalism, Realism, & Relativism: Perspectives in Contemporary Moral Epistemology. LC 89-42874. 344p. 1989. pap. text 18.95 (*0-8014-9563-6*) Cornell U Pr.
— Western Ethics: An Historical Introduction. LC 97-8618. 448p. (C). 1997. text 68.95 (*0-631-19415-0*); pap. text 29.95 (*0-631-19416-9*) Blackwell Pubs.
Arrington, Robert L. & Glock, Hans-Johann, eds. Wittgenstein & Quine. LC 95-25913. 304p. (C). 1996. 75.00 (*0-415-09676-6*) Routledge.
Arrington, Stephen. The Expedition & Diving Operations Handbook. 124p. (C). 1994. 12.95 (*0-941332-40-3*, D623) Best Pub Co.
Arrington, Stephen L. High on Adventure: Stories of Good, Clean, Spine-Tingling Fun. LC 94-74568. 160p. (Orig.). 1995. pap. 9.99 (*1-56384-082-0*) Huntington Hse.
— High on Adventure II: Dreams Becoming Reality, No. II. LC 95-81878. 160p. 1996. pap. 9.99 (*1-56384-115-0*) Huntington Hse.
— High on Adventure III: Building the Dream Machine. LC 97-60875. 160p. 1997. pap. 9.99 (*1-56384-144-4*, Vital Issue Pr) Huntington Hse.
— Journey into Darkness: Nowhere to Land. LC 91-72961. 224p. (Orig.). 1992. pap. 10.99 (*1-56384-003-0*) Huntington Hse.
Arrington, Veneta B., ed. see Mitchell, Alvan.
Arrington, Vera, ed. see Harrell, Angie.
***Arrioja-Dechert, Aurora.** Compendium of Veterinary Products. 5th ed. 1999. pap. 89.95 (*1-889750-10-7*) Nrth Amer Compendiums.
Arrioja-Dechert, Aurora, ed. Compendium of Veterinary Products. 4th ed. 1452p. 1997. pap. 85.00 (*1-889750-00-X*) Nrth Amer Compendiums.
Arriola, Gustavo M., jt. auth. see Harvey, Robert C.
Arrison, Sonia, jt. auth. see Gibbins, Roger.
Arrison, Thomas S., ed. see National Research Council Staff.
Arrive, Michel. Linguistics & Psychoanalysis: Freud, Saussure, Hjelmslev, Lacan & Others. LC 92-8213. (Semiotic Crossroads Ser.: No. 4). xvi, 180p. 1992. 56.00 (*1-55619-338-6*) J Benjamins Pubng Co.
Arrivi, Francisco. Via Poetica. LC 77-25892. 1978. 5.00 (*0-8477-3222-3*); pap. text 4.00 (*0-8477-3223-1*) U of PR Pr.
Arrizabalaga, Jon, et al. The Great Pox: The French Disease in Renaissance Europe. LC 96-23453. 368p. 1997. 37.50 (*0-300-06934-0*) Yale U Pr.
Arrizabalaga, P., jt. auth. see Valter, K.
Arrizon, Alicia. Latina Performance: Traversing the Stage. LC 99-11577. (Illus.). 272p. 1999. text 39.95 (*0-253-33508-6*) Ind U Pr.
***Arrizon, Alicia.** Latina Performance: Traversing the Stage. LC 99-11577. (Unnatural Acts Ser.). (Illus.). 218p. 1999. pap. 18.95 (*0-253-21285-5*) Ind U Pr.
Arro, Emily, et al. Competitive & Business Intelligence: Leveraging Information for Action. Elliott, Susan, ed. (Illus.). 51p. 1997. spiral bd. 395.00 (*1-928593-01-1*) Am Prodtv Qual.
— Managing Competitive Intelligence Knowledge in a Global Economy. Elliott, Susan K., ed. (Illus.). 93p. 1998. spiral bd. 495.00 (*1-928593-08-9*) Am Prodtv Qual.
Arroba, Tanya & James, Kim. Pressure at Work. 208p. 1989. pap. 11.95 (*0-07-084931-5*) McGraw.
Arroba, Tanya, jt. auth. see Bell, Lesley.
Arroba, Tanya, jt. auth. see James, Kim.
Arrogave, Guillermo, et al, eds. Methodologies for Monitoring & Evaluating Vitamin A Deficiency Intervention Programs. LC 89-83358. 66p. 1989. pap. text 3.50 (*0-944398-04-9*) ILSI.
Arrol, John. The Arrol, Arroll & Arrell Families. 800p. 1994. 20.00 (*0-9639687-0-X*) J Arrol.
— Arrol Biographies. (Illus.). (Orig.). 1994. pap. 9.99 (*0-9639687-2-6*) J Arrol.
Arrom, Josbe Juan, jt. auth. see Panbe, Rambon.
Arrom, Jose Juan, ed. see Pane, Fray Ramon.
Arrom, Silvia M. The Women of Mexico City, 1790-1857. xvi, 384p. (C). pap. 17.95 (*0-8047-2095-9*) Stanford U Pr.
— The Women of Mexico City, 1790-1857. LC 83-51324. (Illus.). 400p. 1985. 49.50 (*0-8047-1233-6*) Stanford U Pr.
Arrom, Silvia M. & Ortoll, Servando, eds. Riots in the Cities: Popular Politics & the Urban Poor in Latin America, 1765-1910. LC 95-25920. (Latin American Silhouettes Ser.). 248p. 1996. 45.00 (*0-8420-2580-4*); pap. 17.95 (*0-8420-2581-2*) Scholarly Res Inc.
***Arrom, Silvia Marina.** Containing the Poor: The Mexico City Poor House, 1774-1871. LC 00-29396. (Illus.). 408p. 2000. write for info. (*0-8223-2561-6*) Duke.
— Containing the Poor: The Mexico City Poor House, 1774-1871. LC 00-29396. (Illus.). 408p. 2000. lib. bdg. 59.95 (*0-8223-2527-6*) Duke.
Arron, Deborah. What Can You Do with a Law Degree? A Lawyer's Guide to Career Alternatives Inside, Outside & Around the Law. 4th rev. ed. LC 96-49539. 400p. (Orig.). 1997. pap. 29.95 (*0-940675-46-3*) Niche Pr.
Arron, Deborah L. & Guyol, Deborah. The Complete Guide to Contract Lawyering: What Every Lawyer & Law Firm Needs to Know about Temporary Legal Services. 2nd ed. 317p. (Orig.). 1999. pap. 34.95 (*0-940675-45-5*) Niche Pr.
Arronet, Nikola'i I. Motile Muscle & Cell Models. LC 72-88884. (Studies in Soviet Science). 202p. reprint ed. pap. 62.70 (*0-608-13734-0*, 202068500018) Bks Demand.
Arrons, J., et al, eds. Particle Acceleration Mechanics in Astrophysics. LC 79-55844. (AIP Conference Proceedings Ser.: No. 56). (Illus.). 425p. 1979. lib. bdg. 22.00 (*0-88318-155-X*) Am Inst Physics.
Arronson, Susan A. Trade Is Everybody's Business. LC 95-42266. 64p. (YA). (gr. 7-12). 1996. pap. 5.95 (*0-932765-72-6*) Close Up Fnd.
— Trade Is Everybody's Business: Teacher's Guide. Sass, Charles, ed. LC 95-42266. 40p. 1996. pap., teacher ed. 5.95 (*0-614-08835-6*) Close Up Fnd.
Arrossi, Silvina, et al. Funding Common Initiatives. 1994. 30.00 (*1-85383-204-9*, Pub. by Escan Pubns) Island Pr.
Arrow. Crazy Charlie. 1980. pap. 3.95 (*0-09-924130-7*) Arrow Bks.
Arrow, et al. Benefit-Cost Analysis in Environmental, Health, & Safety Regulation. LC 97-105693. 1996. pap. 9.95 (*0-8447-7066-3*) Am Enterprise.
***Arrow, D.** Idol Rough with the Smooth. 240p. 1998. mass mkt. 15.99 (*0-352-33292-1*) Virgin Pr.
Arrow, Dennis W. Oklahoma Tribal Court Reports, Vol. 3. 1996. 75.00 (*0-9641790-2-4*) OCU Native Amer.
Arrow, Dennis W., ed. Oklahoma Tribal Court Reports, Vol. 1. 612p. 1994. 75.00 (*0-9641790-0-8*) OCU Native Amer.
Arrow, Dennis W., ed. Oklahoma Tribal Court Reports, Vol. 2. 584p. 1995. 75.00 (*0-9641790-1-6*) OCU Native Amer.
Arrow, G. J. Coleoptera: Clavicornia, Erotylidae, Languriidae & Endomychidae. (Fauna of British India Ser.). (Illus.). xvi, 416p. 1976. reprint ed. 25.00 (*0-88065-016-8*) Scholarly Pubns.
— Coleoptera: Lamellicornia, Cetoniinae, & Dynastinae. (Fauna of British India Ser.). (Illus.). xiv, 328p. 1976. reprint ed. 25.00 (*0-88065-017-6*) Scholarly Pubns.
— Coleoptera: Lamellicornia, Coprinae, Pt. III. (Fauna of British India Ser.). (Illus.). xii, 452p. 1977. reprint ed. 25.00 (*0-88065-019-2*) Scholarly Pubns.
— Coleoptera: Lamellicornia, Rutelinae, Desmonoycinae & Euchirinae. (Fauna of British India Ser.). (Illus.). xiv, 400p. 1974. reprint ed. 50.00 (*0-88065-018-4*) Scholarly Pubns.
— Coleoptra, Lamellicornia, Lucanidae & Passalidae. 274p. 1976. reprint ed. write for info. (*0-88065-020-6*, Pub. by Today Tomorrow) Scholarly Pubns.
***Arrow, Holly, et al.** Small Groups as Complex Systems: Formation, Coordination, Development & Adaptation. LC 99-50490. 2000. write for info. (*0-8039-7230-X*) Sage.
Arrow, K. J. & Hahn, F. H. General Competitive Analysis. (Advanced Textbooks in Economics Ser.: Vol. 12). xii,452p. 1991. 81.25 (*0-444-85497-5*, North Holland) Elsevier.
Arrow, Kenneth Joseph. Collected Papers of Kenneth J. Arrow Vol. 3: Individual Choice under Certainty & Uncertainty, Vol. 3. (Illus.). 288p. 1984. 36.00 (*0-674-13762-0*) Belknap Pr.
— Collected Papers of Kenneth J. Arrow Vol. 4: The Economics of Information, Vol. 4. (Illus.). 296p. 1994. 40.50 (*0-674-13763-9*) Belknap Pr.
— Collected Papers of Kenneth J. Arrow Vol. 5: Production & Capital, Vol. 5. (Illus.). 496p. 1985. 45.00 (*0-674-13777-9*) Belknap Pr.
— Collected Papers of Kenneth J. Arrow Vol. 6: Applied Economics, Vol. 6. (Illus.). 280p. 1985. 36.00 (*0-674-13778-7*) Belknap Pr.
— Collected Papers of Kenneth J. Arrow Vols. 1 & 2: Social Choice & Justice; General Equilibrium, 1. 240p. 1983. 33.50 (*0-674-13760-4*) HUP.
— Collected Papers of Kenneth J. Arrow Vols. 1 & 2: Social Choice & Justice; General Equilibrium, Vol. 2. 320p. 1983. 43.50 (*0-674-13761-2*) HUP.
— Handbook of Mathematical Economics. Intriligator, Michael D., ed. (Handbooks in Economics Ser.: No. 1). 396p. 1981. 110.00 (*0-444-86126-2*) Elsevier.
— Handbook of Mathematical Economics, Vol. II. Intriligator, Michael D., ed. 692p. 1986. 110.00 (*0-444-86127-0*) Elsevier.
— Handbook of Mathematical Economics, Vol. III. Intriligator, Michael D., ed. (Illus.). 468p. 1986. 110.00 (*0-444-86128-9*) Elsevier.
— The Limits of Organization. (Fels Center of Government Ser.). 86p. (C). 1974. pap. text 9.25 (*0-393-09323-9*) Norton.
***Arrow, Kenneth Joseph.** Rational Foundations Economic Behavior. LC 95-7828. 379p. 1999. pap. 27.95 (*0-312-22566-0*) St Martin.
Arrow, Kenneth Joseph. Social Choice & Individual Values. 2nd ed. (Cowles Foundation Monograph Ser.: No. 12). 1970. pap. 14.00 (*0-300-01364-7*, Y233) Yale U Pr.
— What Does the Present Owe the Future? An Economic & Ethical Perspective on Climate Changes. 12p. 1996. 7.50 (*0-910153-12-4*) E T Woolf.
Arrow, Kenneth Joseph, ed. Issues in Contemporary Economics Vol. 1: Markets & Welfare. (International Economic Association Book Ser.). 260p. (C). 1991. text 100.00 (*0-8147-0598-7*) NYU Pr.
Arrow, Kenneth Joseph, et al, eds. Barriers to Conflict Resolution. 450p. 1995. 35.00 (*0-393-03737-1*) Norton.
— Education in a Research University. LC 96-10877. 408p. 1996. 60.00 (*0-8047-2595-0*) Stanford U Pr.
— Social Choice Re-Examined: Proceedings of the IEA Conference Held at Schloss Hernstein, Berndorf, Near Vienna, Austria, 2 vols., Vol. 2. LC 95-11796. (IEA Conference Ser.: No. 116-117). 256p. 1997. text 65.00 (*0-312-12741-3*) St Martin.
— Social Choice Re-Examined: Proceedings of the IEA Conference Held at Schoss Hernstein, Berndorf, near Vienna, Austria, Vol. 1. LC 95-11796. (IEA Conference Ser.: No. 116). 224p. 1997. text 65.00 (*0-312-12739-1*) St Martin.
Arrow, Kenneth Joseph & Hahn, F. H. General Competitive Analysis. (Advanced Textbooks in Economics Ser.: Vol. 12). 452p. 1977. 66.50 (*0-7204-0750-8*, North Holland) Elsevier.
Arrow, Kenneth Joseph & Hurwicz, Leonid, eds. Studies in Resource Allocation Process. LC 76-9171. (Illus.). 576p. 1977. text 99.95 (*0-521-21522-6*) Cambridge U Pr.
Arrow, Kenneth Joseph & Kurz, Mordecai. Public Investment, the Rate of Return, & Optimal Fiscal Policy. LC 73-108380. 248p. reprint ed. pap. 76.90 (*0-608-16182-9*, 202562700045) Bks Demand.
Arrow, Kenneth Joseph, ed. see Stanford Symposium on Mathematical Methods in the.
Arrow Staff. Arrow Cambridge Pocket Street Directory with Maps. 1995. pap. 4.95 (*1-55751-502-6*) Arrow Map.
— Arrow Rhode Island Street Map Atlas. 1997. 14.95 (*1-55751-405-4*) Arrow Map.
***Arrow Staff.** Arrow Street Guide of Boston, MA. 1999. 10.95 (*1-55751-003-2*) Arrow Map.
Arrow Staff. Arrow Street Guide of Greater Springfield, MA. 1996. 10.95 (*1-55751-504-2*) Arrow Map.
— Arrow Zip Code Directory. 640p. 2000. pap. 6.95 (*0-913450-85-5*) Arrow Map.
— Greater Boston Street Map Atlas. 1998. 14.95 (*1-55751-391-0*) Arrow Map.
— Greater Boston Street Map Atlas - Laminated. 1998. 39.95 (*1-55751-409-7*) Arrow Map.
Arrow Staff. New Hampshire City & Town Atlas. 1992. 12.95 (*1-55751-441-0*) Arrow Map.
Arrow Staff. Official Arrow Street Map Atlas Metro Worcester, MA. 1999. 12.95 (*0-913450-97-9*) Arrow Map.
— Official Arrow Street Map Atlas of Cape Cod. 1997. 13.95 (*1-55751-407-0*) Arrow Map.
***Arrow Staff.** Official Arrow Street Map Atlas of Central/Eastern, CT. 2000. 16.95 (*1-55751-445-3*) Arrow Map.
Arrow Staff. Official Arrow Street Map Atlas of Eastern, MA. 1999. 19.95 (*1-55751-401-1*) Arrow Map.
— Official Arrow Street Map Atlas of Middlesex County, MA. 1999. 11.95 (*1-55751-403-8*) Arrow Map.

An Asterisk (*) at the beginning of an entry indicates that the title is appearing for the first time.

— Official Arrow Street Map Atlas of Western, MA. LC 95-675710. 1998. 13.95 (*0-913450-83-9*) Arrow Map.

Arrowood, Charles F. The Taxation of the United Kingdom. (Works of Charles Flinn Arrowood). vi, 180p. 1985. reprint ed. lib. bdg. 39.00 (*0-685-10502-4*) Rprt Serv.

— Thomas Jefferson & Education in a Republic. 1988. reprint ed. lib. bdg. 49.00 (*0-7812-0210-8*) Rprt Serv.

Arrowood, Charles F., ed. Thomas Jefferson & Education in a Republic. LC 79-136406. (BCL Ser.: No. 1). reprint ed. 20.00 (*0-404-00406-7*) AMS Pr.

— Thomas Jefferson & Education in a Republic. (History - United States Ser.). 184p. 1992. reprint ed. lib. bdg. 69.00 (*0-7812-6141-4*) Rprt Serv.

— Thomas Jefferson & Education in a Republic. LC 70-131611. 1970. reprint ed. 49.00 (*0-403-00498-5*) Scholarly.

Arrowood, Clinton, jt. auth. see Elliott, Donald.

Arrowood, David & Cirrito, William. Area Lighting: Solar Electric Area Lighting. 144p. 1993. 49.95 (*0-9636559-0-6*) Photocomm.

Arrowood, Katy O. A Woman's Recipe for Life: A Nurturing Approach Throughout Womenhood from Adolescence to Aging. (Illus.). 205p. 1996. 21.95 (*0-9655351-0-X*) Lifetime Books.

Arrowsmith, Alexandra, ed. see Lanting, Frans.

***Arrowsmith-Brown, Nicholas.** Prutkys Travels to Ethiopia & Other Countries. 1998. 52.95 (*0-904180-30-1*) Ashgate Pub Co.

Arrowsmith-Brown, Nicholas. Setting up Your Own Pony Stud. 132p. 1990. pap. 21.00 (*0-85131-386-8*, Pub. by J A Allen) St Mut.

Arrowsmith, D. K. & Place, C. H. Introduction to Dynamical Systems. (Illus.). 431p. (C). 1990. pap. text 44.95 (*0-521-31650-2*) Cambridge U Pr.

Arrowsmith, D. K. & Place, C. M. Dynamical Systems: Differential Equations, Maps & Chaotic Behavior. (Chapman & Hall Mathematics Ser.). 320p. (C). 1992. text 45.00 (*0-412-39070-1*, A6964) Chapman & Hall.

Arrowsmith, James, ed. An Analysis of Drapery & the Upholsterers' Accelerator: A Reprint of Two Rare 19th Century Drapery Manuals in the Winterthur Library 19th Century: Landmarks in Design. (Nineteenth Century: Landmarks in Design Ser.: Vol. 1). (Illus.). 166p. 1993. reprint ed. 27.50 (*0-926494-03-1*) Acanthus Pr.

Arrowsmith, Joseph. The Reformation: A Comedy Acted at the Dukes Theater. LC 92-23808. (Augustan Reprints Ser.: Nos. 237-238). 1986. reprint ed. 21.50 (*0-404-70237-6*, PR3316) AMS Pr.

Arrowsmith, Keith. Bush Paths. 177p. (C). 1989. text 60.00 (*1-872795-24-2*, Pub. by Pentland Pr) St Mut.

Arrowsmith, Pat. Many Are Called. 1998. pap. text 10.99 (*0-906500-59-1*) Onlywomen Pr.

Arrowsmith, Richard S. The Prelude to the Reformation: A Study of English Church Life from the Age of Wycliffe to the Breach with Rome. LC 83-45573. reprint ed. 57.50 (*0-404-19891-0*) AMS Pr.

Arrowsmith, Sandy, ed. Lachapelle Land: Photographs by David LaChapelle. LC 96-14275. (Illus.). 150p. 1996. 50.00 (*0-684-83302-6*) Callaway Edns.

Arrowsmith, Sue & Davies, Arwel. Public Procurement: Global Revolution. LC 98-29820. (International Economic Development Law Ser.). 1998. 91.00 (*90-411-9662-5*) Kluwer Law Intl.

Arrowsmith, William. Antonioni: The Poet of Images. 208p. 1995. text 25.00 (*0-19-509270-8*) OUP.

— Four Comedies: Lysistrata, the Congresswomen, the Acharnians, the Frogs. (Illus.). 432p. 1969. pap. text 14.95 (*0-472-06152-6*, 06152, Ann Arbor Bks) U of Mich Pr.

Arrowsmith, William, et al, eds. Four Plays by Aristophanes: The Clouds, the Frogs, the Birds, Lysistrata. 1984. pap. 11.95 (*0-452-00717-8*, Mer) NAL.

Arrowsmith, William, tr. Cyclops & Heracles. LC 56-6639. write for info. U Ch Pr.

— Hecuba. LC 55-5787. write for info. U Ch Pr.

— Orestes. LC 55-5787. 1968. write for info. U Ch Pr.

— The Satyricon. 1983. pap. 12.95 (*0-452-01005-5*, Mer) NAL.

Arrowsmith, William, ed. see Aristophanes.

Arrowsmith, William, ed. see Nietzsche, Friedrich Wilhelm.

Arrowsmith, William, tr. see Euripides.

Arrowsmith, William, tr. see Leslie, Alfred, ed.

Arrowsmith, William, tr. see Montale, Eugenio.

Arrowsmith, William, tr. see Pavese, Cesare.

Arrowsmith, William, tr. & notes see Montale, Eugenio.

Arrowsmith, William, tr. & pref. see Montale, Eugenio.

Arroy Center Staff, jt. auth. see Shukiar, Herbert J.

Arroyave, G., et al. Lignes de Conduite pour l'Erradication de la Deficience en Vitamine A Et De la Xerophtalmie. Vincent, Marc, tr. (FRE., Illus.). 83p. (Orig.). 1984. pap. text 3.50 (*0-935368-38-8*) ILSI.

Arroyave, G., ed. see Bauernfeind, J. Christopher.

Arroyave, Guillermo, tr. see Bothwell, Thomas H. & Carlton, Robert W.

Arroyave, Guillermo, tr. see Dallman, Peter R., et al.

Arroyo, Alan A., jt. auth. see Selig, W. George.

***Arroyo, Alfred.** Francisca & the Boys. LC 99-93740. 1999. 17.95 (*0-533-13141-3*) Vantage.

Arroyo, Anita. America en Su Literatura. 2nd ed. LC 77-3041. (Illus.). 676p. 1978. 12.00 (*0-8477-3175-8*); pap. text 9.60 (*0-8477-3182-0*) U of PR Pr.

— Cuentos Del Caribe. LC 91-77116. (Coleccion Caniqui). (SPA.). 64p. (Orig.). 1992. pap. 9.95 (*0-89729-630-3*) Ediciones.

— El Grillo Grunon: Cuentos para Chicos y Grandes. LC 84-13199. (Ninos y Letras Ser.). (SPA., Illus.). 122p. (Orig.). (J). (gr. 1-6). 1984. pap. 5.50 (*0-8477-3527-3*) U of PR Pr.

— Jose Antonio Saco: Su Influencia en la Cultura y en las Ideas Politicas de Cuba. LC 88-80744. (Coleccion Cuba y sus Jueces). (SPA.). 157p. (Orig.). 1989. pap. 12.00 (*0-89729-483-1*) Ediciones.

— Narrativa Hispanoamericana Actual: America y Sus Problemas. LC 79-19468. (Coleccion Mente y Palabra). v, 435p. (C). 1980. 15.00 (*0-8477-0562-5*); pap. 12.00 (*0-8477-0563-3*) U of PR Pr.

— Las Pequenas Muertes. LC 91-77115. (Coleccion Caniqui). (SPA.). 144p. (Orig.). 1992. pap. 16.00 (*0-89729-629-X*) Ediciones.

Arroyo Center Staff, jt. auth. see Fuller, Graham E.

Arroyo Center Staff, jt. auth. see Moore, Nancy Y.

Arroyo Center Staff, jt. auth. see Wong, Carolyn.

Arroyo, Ciriaco M. Celestina & Castilian Humanism at the End of the Fifteenth Century. LC 94-40654. (Medieval & Renaissance Texts & Studies: No. 3). 44p. 1994. 7.95 (*0-86698-144-6*, PCM3) Pegasus Pr.

Arroyo, Ciriaco M., ed. Ortega y Gasset: Un Humanista Para Nuestro Tiempo. (Monografias De ALDEEU Ser.). (SPA.). 176p. (C). 1992. pap. 22.00 (*0-9626630-2-6*) Spanish Profs Amer.

Arroyo De La Cuesta, Felipe. Grammar of the Mutsun Language Spoken at the Mission of San Juan Bautista Alta California. LC 76-158278. (Library of American Linguistics: Vol. 4). reprint ed. 42.75 (*0-404-50984-3*) AMS Pr.

Arroyo de la Cuesta, Felipe. Vocabulary or Phrase Book of the Mutsun Language of Alta California. (Library of American Linguistics: Vol. 8). (CAT.). reprint ed. 42.75 (*0-404-50988-6*) AMS Pr.

Arroyo, Elsa & Ortiz, Julia C. Leer para Escribir: Antologia de Lecturas para Practicar los Procesos de la Redaccion. 4th ed. (SPA.). 448p. (C). 1996. reprint ed. pap. text 16.95 (*1-56328-065-5*) Edit Plaza Mayor.

Arroyo, Hiram V. & Cerqueira, Maria T. La Promocion de la Salud y la Educacion para la Salud en America Latina: Un Analisis Sectorial. 330p. 1997. pap. 16.95 (*0-8477-0295-2*) U of PR Pr.

Arroyo, Ignacio. International Maritime Conventions. 1600p. 1991. 260.00 (*90-6544-440-8*) Kluwer Law Intl.

Arroyo, Ignacio, ed. Yearbook Maritime Law, Vol. 1. 528p. 1986. 165.00 (*90-6544-254-5*) Kluwer Law Intl.

— Yearbook Maritime Law, Vol. 2. 468p. 1987. 104.00 (*90-6544-311-8*) Kluwer Law Intl.

— Yearbook Maritime Law, Vol. 3. 428p. 1988. 106.00 (*90-6544-361-4*) Kluwer Law Intl.

— Yearbook Maritime Law, Vol. 4. 522p. 1990. 103.00 (*90-6544-464-5*) Kluwer Law Intl.

Arroyo, Imna. Why Goats Smell Bad: And Other Stories from Benin. LC 97-30935. xvii, 138p. (J). (gr. 3-6). 1998. lib. bdg. 19.95 (*0-208-02469-7*, Linnet Bks) Shoe String.

Arroyo, Isabel Guiterrez Del, see Guiterrez Del Arroyo, Isabel.

***Arroyo, Jose.** Action/Spectacle Cinema. (Sight & Sound Reader Ser.). 1999. pap. 19.95 (*0-85170-757-2*) British Film Inst.

Arroyo, Luis A., tr. see Hall, Robert W.

Arroyo, Luis L. & Rios-Bustamante, Antonio. Cinco de Mayo: Symbol of National Self Determination. (Illus.). 200p. 1990. 40.00 (*0-685-38355-5*) Floricanto Pr.

Arroyo, Mary T. The Systematics of the Legume Genus Harpalyce: Leguminosae Lotodeae. LC 66-6394. (Memoirs Ser.: Vol. 26, No. 4). (Illus.). 144p. 1976. pap. 16.00 (*0-89327-001-6*) NY Botanical.

Arroyo, Mary T. K., et al, eds. Ecology & Biogeography of Mediterranean Ecosystems in Chile, California & Australia. LC 94-3097. (Ecological Studies: Vol. 108). 1994. 105.00 (*0-387-94266-1*) Spr-Verlag.

Arroyo, Mike A., jt. auth. see Ward, Michael K.

Arroyo-Ortiz, Nelson. Versos de Amor. (ENG & SPA.). 50p. (Orig.). 1992. pap. 5.95 (*0-9634872-0-5*) Blue Sky TX.

Arroyo, Rane. Columbus's Orphan. 62p. (Orig.). 1993. pap. 7.95 (*1-878116-17-7*) JVC Bks.

— The Naked Thief. 30p. (Orig.). 1997. pap. 8.00 (*0-932616-57-7*) Brick Hse Bks.

— Pale Ramon. LC 98-7789. 96p. 1998. pap. 13.00 (*0-944072-94-1*) Zoland Bks.

— The Singing Shark. 88p. (Orig.). 1996. pap. 9.00 (*0-927534-61-4*) Biling Rev-Pr.

***Arroyo, Robert, Jr. & Wynne, Robert.** Call the Sun Down. O'Halloran, Jamie, ed. 32p. 1999. pap. 5.00 (*0-9670715-4-2*) Valley Contemp.

Arroyo, Roberto. Rape, the Crime I Did Not Commit . . . Today Is the Day of Your Miracle. 100p. (Orig.). 1995. pap. text 5.99 (*0-9630423-6-X*) R A Aviles.

— Truant Light. 48p. 1998. pap. 6.00 (*1-890887-07-2*) Mille Grazie.

Arroyo, Rose E. Incrustada en la Pena. Williams, Karen, ed.Tr. of Adhered to the Rock: Experiencing the Silence of God. (SPA.). 96p. 1998. pap. 8.00 (*0-8358-0839-4*, UR839) Upper Room Bks.

Arroyo, Santana. Hustle into Death. large type ed. 352p. 1995. 27.99 (*0-7089-3215-0*) Ulverscroft.

Arroyo, Sidney L., ed. see Payne, R. E.

Arroyo, Stephen. Astrology, Karma & Transformation: The Inner Dimensions of the Birth Chart. 2nd rev. ed. (Illus.). 269p. 1992. pap. 14.95 (*0-916360-54-7*) CRCS Pubns CA.

— Astrology, Psychology & the Four Elements: An Energy Approach to Astrology & Its Use in the Counseling Arts. LC 75-27828. 200p. (Orig.). 1975. pap. 14.00 (*0-916360-01-6*) CRCS Pubns CA.

— Exploring Jupiter: The Astrological Key to Progress, Prosperity & Potential. McEnerney, Barbara, ed. (Illus.). 316p. (Orig.). 1995. pap. 14.95 (*0-916360-58-X*) CRCS Pubns CA.

— Practicing the Cosmic Science: Key Insights in Modern Astrology. 2nd rev. ed. LC 99-28073. 210p. 1999. pap. 13.95 (*0-916360-62-8*) CRCS Pubns CA.

— Relationships & Life Cycles: Astrological Patterns of Personal Experience. 2nd rev. ed. (Illus.). 240p. 1993. pap. 14.00 (*0-916360-55-5*) CRCS Pubns CA.

— Stephen Arroyo's Chart Interpretation Handbook: Guidelines for Understanding the Essentials of the Birth Chart. Marshall, Jerilynn, ed. 188p. (Orig.). 1989. pap. 10.95 (*0-916360-49-0*) CRCS Pubns CA.

Arroyo, Stephen & Greene, Liz. New Insights in Modern Astrology. 2nd rev. ed. Orig. Title: The Jupiter - Saturn Conference Lectures. 212p. 1991. pap. 14.95 (*0-916360-47-4*) CRCS Pubns CA.

Arroyo, Vicente, et al. Ascites & Renal Dysfunction in Liver Disease: Pathogenesis, Diagnosis & Treatment. LC 98-37812. (Illus.). xiii, 568p. 1999. 125.00 (*0-632-04342-3*) Blackwell Sci.

Arrubla, Gerardo, jt. auth. see Henao, Jesus M.

Arruda, Ayda I., ed. see Brazilian Conference on Mathematical Logic Staff.

Arruda, J. A. & Kurtzman, N. A., eds. Disorders of Tubular Transport: Physiologic & Clinical Correlations. (Journal: Mineral & Electrolyte Metabolism Ser.: Vol. 5, Nos. 2-4). (Illus.). 144p. 1981. pap. 91.50 (*3-8055-2515-X*) S Karger.

Arrudnada, Benito. The Economics of Audit Quality: Private Incentives & the Regulation of Audit & Non-Audit Services. LC 99-13938. 1999. write for info. (*0-7923-8473-3*) Kluwer Academic.

Arrupe, Pedro. Challenge to Religious Life Today: Selected Letters & Addresses--I. Aixala, Jerome, ed. LC 79-87603. xii, 297p. 1979. 3.50 (*0-912422-45-9*); 3.00 (*0-912422-44-0*) Inst Jesuit.

— In Him Alone Is Our Hope: Texts on the Heart of Christ (1965-1983) Aixala, Jerome, ed. Ganss, G. E. et al, trs. from SPA. LC 83-80037. (Selected Letters & Addresses of - Series IV). xvi, 164p. 1984. pap. 6.00 (*0-912422-87-4*) Inst Jesuit.

— Justice with Faith Today: Selected Letters & Addresses--II. Aixala, Jerome, ed. LC 80-229. xvi, 320p. 1980. 4.00 (*0-912422-51-3*); pap. 3.50 (*0-912422-50-5*) Inst Jesuit.

— One Jesuit's Spiritual Journey: Autobiographical Conversations with Jean-Claude Dietsch, S. J. Bradley, Ruth, tr. LC 84-81990. Orig. Title: Itineraire d'un Jesuite. Entretiens avec Jean-Claude Dietsch, S. J.. xiv, 160p. 1986. 10.00 (*0-912422-69-6*); 8.00 (*0-912422-68-8*) Inst Jesuit.

— Other Apostolates Today: Selected Letters & Addresses - III. Aixala, Jerome, ed. LC 81-80741. xvi, 365p. 1981. 4.50 (*0-912422-81-5*); pap. 4.00 (*0-912422-80-7*) Inst Jesuit.

Arruti, Maria O., tr. see Broger, Achim.

Arruti, Maria O., tr. see Heuck, Sigrid.

***Arruza, Tony, photos by.** Miami. LC 00-26018. (Citylife Pictorial Guides Ser.). (Illus.). 96p. 2000. pap. 16.95 (*0-89658-498-4*) Voyageur Pr.

Arruza, Tony, photos by. The Smithsonian Guides to Natural America: The Southeast - South Carolina, Georgia, Alabama, Florida. (Illus.). 1997. pap. 19.95 (*0-679-76480-1*) Random.

Ars, B., ed. Congenital External & Middle Ear Malformations: Management. LC 92-49672. (Illus.). 80p. 1992. 31.50 (*90-6299-086-X*, Pub. by Kugler) Kugler Pubns.

— Inner Ear Partition. (Illus.). xi, 56p. (Orig.). 1998. pap. 36.00 (*90-6299-149-1*) Kugler Pubns.

Ars, B. & Van Cauwenberge, P., eds. Middle Ear Structures, Organogenesis & Congenital Defects. LC 91-12019. (Illus.). 98p. 1991. pap. text 34.50 (*90-6299-074-6*, Pub. by Kugler) Kugler Pubns.

Ars, Bernard & Ars-Piret, Nicole. Tympano-Ossicular, Allograft Tympanoplasty: A Manual of Techniques. (Illus.). 55p. 1993. pap. text 26.00 (*90-6299-093-2*, Pub. by Kugler) Kugler Pubns.

Ars-Piret, Nicole, jt. auth. see Ars, Bernard.

Arsac, Jacques. Foundations of Programming. Duncan, Fraser, tr. (APIC Studies in Data Processing: No. 20). 1985. text 78.00 (*0-12-064460-6*) Acad Pr.

Arsan, Emmanuelle. Emmanuelle. Bair, Lowell, tr. 224p. 1994. pap. 11.00 (*0-8021-3069-0*, Grove) Grove-Atltic.

Arsanes. Orations of Arsanes Agaynst Philip: Of the Embassadors of Venice. LC 70-26068. (English Experience Ser.: No. 233). 164p. 1970. reprint ed. 20.00 (*90-221-0233-5*) Walter J Johnson.

Arscott, David. Explore Sussex. 128p. 1987. 30.00 (*0-86368-014-3*) St Mut.

Arscott, David, jt. auth. see Skinner, Archie.

Arscott, David, jt. auth. see Swinfen, Warden.

Arscott, F. & Khabaza, I. M. Tables of Lame Polynomials. (Mathematical Tables Ser.). 172.00 (*0-08-009739-1*, Pub. by Pergamon Repr) Franklin.

Arscott, F. & Sneddon, Ian N. Periodic Differential Equations: Introduction to Mathieu Lame & Allied Functions. LC 62-8703. (International Series of Monographs on Pure & Applied Mathematics: Vol. 66). 1964. 131.00 (*0-08-009984-X*, Pub. by Pergamon Repr) Franklin.

Arsdale, Barb Van, see Van Arsdale, Barb, ed.

Arsdale, Jay Van, see Van Arsdale, Jay.

Arsdale, Peter W. Van, see Van Arsdale, Peter W., ed.

Arsdale, William G. Van, see Van Arsdale, William G.

Arsdell, Robert Van, see Van Arsdell, Robert.

Arsdol, Ted Van, see Hatheway, John Shadrach & Van Arsdol, Ted.

ARSEM Staff. Design Guides for Offshore Structures: Welded Tubular Joints. 352p. 1987. 500.00 (*2-7108-0530-8*, Pub. by Edits Technip) Enfield Pubs NH.

Arsenault, Henri & Sheng, Yunlong. An Introduction to Optical Computing. (Tutorial Texts in Optical Engineering Ser.: Vol. TT 8). 140p. 1992. 20.00 (*0-8194-0825-5*) SPIE.

***Arsenault, Idamay Michaud.** Worcester's Union Station: The Monument & the Memories. LC 99-68270. 139p. 2000. pap. 21.95 (*0-9646439-1-X*) Ambasdr Bks.

Arsenault, Jane. Forging Nonprofit Alliances: A Comprehensive Guide to Enhancing Your Mission. LC 98-7508. (Nonprofit & Public Administration Ser.). 198p. 1998. 25.95 (*0-7879-1003-1*) Jossey-Bass.

Arsenault, Jane & Cedor, Jean. Guided Meditations for Youth on Sacramental Life. unabridged ed. Stamschror, Robert P. & Stamschror, Robert, eds. (Quiet Place Apart Ser.). (Illus.). 40p. (YA). (gr. 9-12). 1993. pap. 8.95 incl. audio (*0-88489-308-1*) St Marys.

— Guided Meditations for Youth on Sacramental Life. unabridged ed. (Quiet Place Apart Ser.). (YA). (gr. 9-12). 1993. audio 7.95 (*0-88489-309-X*) St Marys.

***Arsenault, Mark, et al.** Enemies of San Angelo. (Illus.). 96p. 1999. pap. 16.00 (*1-890305-13-8*) Gold Rush.

Arsenault, Mark, jt. auth. see Lidbert, Paul A.

Arsenault, Mark, ed. see Bryant, Anthony J.

Arsenault, Mark, ed. see Crocker, Jim, et al.

Arsenault, Mark, ed. see Long, Steven, et al.

Arsenault, Mark, ed. see Sweeney, Patrick, et al.

Arsenault, R. J., jt. auth. see Taya, M.

Arsenault, R. J., ed. see ASM International Materials Science Div., Science.

Arsenault, Ray, ed. see Simmons, Glen & Ogden, Laura.

Arsenault, Raymond. St. Petersburg & the Florida Dream, 1888-1950. LC 96-3863. (Illus.). 1996. reprint ed. pap. write for info. (*0-8130-1446-8*) U Press Fla.

— St. Petersburg & the Florida Dream, 1888-1950. (Illus.). 360p. (C). 1996. reprint ed. 34.95 (*0-8130-1442-5*) U Press Fla.

— The Wild Ass of the Ozarks: Jeff Davis & the Social Bases of Southern Politics. LC 87-25461. 352p. (C). 1988. pap. 19.50 (*0-87049-569-0*) U of Tenn Pr.

Arsenault, Theresa. Wings at the Window. (Illus.). 112p. (Orig.). 1992. pap. 10.00 (*0-9633836-0-4*) Brass Oaks Pubns.

Arsene, Grigore. Linear Operators in Function Spaces: 12th International Conference on Operator Theory, 1988. (Operator Theory Ser.: No. 43). 350p. 1989. 137.00 (*0-8176-2343-4*) Birkhauser.

— Operators in Indefinite Metric Spaces, Scattering Theory & Other Topics. (Operator Theory Ser.: No. 24). 380p. 1987. 113.50 (*0-8176-1843-0*) Birkhauser.

Arsene, Grigore, ed. Advances in Invariant Subspaces & Other Results of Operator Theory. (Operator Theory Ser.: No. 17). 376p. 1986. 122.00 (*0-8176-1763-9*) Birkhauser.

— Dilation Theory, Toeplitz Operators, & Other Topics. (Operator Theory Ser.: No. 11). 400p. (C). 1983. text 65.95 (*3-7643-1516-4*) Birkhauser.

Arsene, Grigore & Vasilescu, F. H., eds. Special Classes of Linear Operators & Other Topics. (Operator Theory Ser.: No. 28). 322p. 1988. 129.00 (*0-8176-1970-4*) Birkhauser.

***Arseneau, Mary, et al, eds.** The Culture of Christina Rossetti: Female Poetics & Victorian Contexts. LC 98-49443. (Illus.). 368p. 1999. 39.95 (*0-8214-1243-4*) Ohio U Pr.

***Arseneault, David M.** Basketball: The Running Game. (Illus.). 68p. 1998. pap. write for info. (*1-890946-00-1*) Reedswain.

Arsen'ev, Nicolai S. We Beheld His Glory. Ewer, Mary A., tr. LC 76-113545. reprint ed. 37.50 (*0-404-00407-5*) AMS Pr.

Arsenian, Seth. Bilingualism & Mental Development. LC 75-176525. (Columbia University. Teachers College. Contributions to Education Ser.: No. 712). reprint ed. 37.50 (*0-404-55712-0*) AMS Pr.

Arseniev, A.A. Mathematical Theory of Kinetic Equations. 1999. 55.00 (*981-02-3717-0*) World Scientific Pub.

Arseniev, Nicholas. Mysticism & the Eastern Church. LC 96-27837. 173p. 1979. pap. 11.95 (*0-913836-55-9*) St Vladimirs.

— Revelation of Life Eternal: An Introduction to the Christian Message. 144p. 1964. pap. 8.95 (*0-913836-00-1*) St Vladimirs.

— Russian Piety. 143p. 1964. pap. 9.95 (*0-913836-21-4*) St Vladimirs.

Arseniev, V. K. Dersu the Trapper. Burr, Malcolm, tr. (Illus.). 352p. 1996. reprint ed. 25.00 (*0-929701-50-X*); reprint ed. pap. 16.00 (*0-929701-49-6*) McPherson & Co.

Arsenijevic, N. S. German-Serbocroatian Electrotechnical Dictionary. (CRO, GER & SER.). 150p. 1971. 24.95 (*0-8288-6460-8*, M9633) Fr & Eur.

Arsenis, William, tr. see Messinis, Dimosthenis.

Arsenjev, D. G., et al. Adaptive Methods of Calculus Mathematics & Mechanics Stochastic Variant. LC 98-7861. 400p. 1998. 78.00 (*981-02-3501-1*) World Scientific Pub.

Arshad, Muhammed, jt. ed. see Frankenberger, W. T.

Arshadi, Nasser. The Law & Finance of Corporate Insider Trading: Theory & Evidence. LC 93-19386. 184p. (C). 1993. lib. bdg. 104.50 (*0-7923-9360-0*) Kluwer Academic.

Arshadi, Nasser & Karels, Gordon V. Modern Financial Intermediaries & Markets. LC 96-23952. 501p. (C). 1996. 98.00 (*0-13-119470-4*) P-H.

Arshady, R., et al. Polymer Synthesis. (Advances in Polymer Science Ser.: Vol. 111). (Illus.). 234p. 1994. 136.95 (*0-387-57198-1*) Spr-Verlag.

Arshady, Reza, ed. Desk Reference of Functional Polymers: Syntheses & Applications. LC 96-39093. (ACS Professional Reference Bk.). 832p. 1997. text 195.00 (*0-8412-3469-8*, Pub. by Am Chemical) OUP.

Arsham, Gary, jt. auth. see Lowe, Ernest.

Arshed, Aneela Khalid. The Bounty of Allah: Daily Readings from the Koran & Islamic Tradition. LC 99-35104. 1999. 19.95 (*0-8245-1823-3*) Crossroad NY.

A

Arshi, P. S. Sikh Architecture in the Punjab. 1986. 70.00 (*0-8364-1945-6*, Pub. by Intellect Pub Hse) S Asia.

Arshinov, Peter. History of the Makhnovist Movement 1918-1921. Perlman, Lorraine & Perlman, Fredy, trs. from RUS. 284p. (Orig.). (C). 1987. pap. 10.00 (*0-900384-40-9*) Left Bank.

Arshy, Ziba, et al. Kurdistan. (Illus.). 139p. 1991. 45.00 (*0-7103-0448-X*, A6718) Routledge.

Arslan, Mehdi & Rajan, Janaki, eds. Communalism in India: Challenge & Response. (C). 1994. text 21.00 (*81-7304-073-7*, Pub. by Manohar) S Asia.

***Arslan, Orhan.** Neuroanatomical Basis of Clinical Neurology. (Illus.). 350p. 2001. 98.00 (*1-85070-578-X*) Prthnon Pub.

Arslanian, G. T. Russian-Arabic Medical Dictionary. (ARA & RUS.). 622p. 1983. 49.95 (*0-8288-1158-X*, M15440) Fr & Eur.

Arslanian, Richard. The Rocking Chair. LC 98-90487. 1998. pap. 6.95 (*0-533-12814-5*) Vantage.

Arslanov, M. M., et al, eds. Algebra & Analysis: Proceedings of the International Centennial Chebotarev Conference Held in Kazan, Russia, June 5-11, 1994. LC 95-49558. viii, 163p. (C). 1996. lib. bdg. 128.95 (*3-11-014803-X*) De Gruyter.

***Arslanov, Marat & Lempp, Steffen, eds.** Recursion Theory & Complexity: Proceedings of the Kazan '97 Workshop, Kazan, Russia, July 14-19, 1997. LC 99-32783. 1999. 168.00 (*3-11-016587-2*) De Gruyter.

Arson-Dizzo, Nina, jt. ed. see Earle, Ann M.

Arson, I. S., et al. Eighteen Papers on Logic & Theory of Functions. (Translations Ser.: Series 2, Vol. 83). 283p. 1970. 45.00 (*0-8218-1783-3*, TRANS2/83) Am Math.

Arson, Noyan & Satterfield, Naomi L. Sanfield, Inc. A Computerized Audit Case. 2nd ed. 170p. (C). 1994. pap., text 30.85 incl. disk (*0-256-12909-6*, Irwn McGrw-H) McGrw-H Hghr Educ.

Arsone, Sarah. Zen & the Art of Changing Diapers. 2nd ed. (Illus.). 63p. (Orig.). 1993. pap. text 8.95 (*0-9632721-0-1*) S Arsone.

***Arsov, R.** Environmental Protection Technologies for Coastal Areas II. (Water Science & Technology Ser.: No. 39-8). 214p. 1999. pap. 163.00 (*0-08-042808-8*, Pergamon Pr) Elsevier.

Arsov, R., et al, eds. Environment Protection Technologies for Coastal Areas: Selected Proceedings of the Black Sea Regional Conference on Environmental Protection Technologies for Coastal Areas, held in Varna, Bulgaria, 13-15 June 1995. (Water Science & Technology Ser.: Vol. 32). 226p. 1996. pap. text 111.00 (*0-08-042883-5*, Pergamon Pr) Elsevier.

Arsove, Maynard & Leutwiler, Heinz. Algebraic Potential Theory. LC 79-24384. (Memoirs of the American Mathematical Society Ser.: Vol. 23/226). 130p. 1983. reprint ed. pap. 18.00 (*0-8218-2226-8*, MEMO/23/226) Am Math.

Arsove, Maynard G. & Johnson, Guy, Jr. A Conformal Mapping Technique for Infinitely Connected Regions. LC 52-42839. (Memoirs Ser.: No. 1/91). 56p. 1970. pap. 16.00 (*0-8218-1291-2*, MEMO 1/91) Am Math.

Arsuaga De Vila, Maria. Manual De Espanol, 2. rev. ed. LC 80-36752. 253p. (C). 1980. 5.00 (*0-8477-3165-0*) U of PR Pr.

— Manual De Espanol, Set. rev. ed. LC 80-36752. 253p. (C). 1980. 15.00 (*0-8477-3177-4*) U of PR Pr.

— Manual De Espanol, Vol. 1, Pt. 1. rev. ed. LC 80-36752. 253p. (C). 1980. 5.00 (*0-8477-3195-2*) U of PR Pr.

— Manual De Espanol, Vol. 1, Pt. 2. rev. ed. LC 80-36752. 253p. (C). 1980. 5.00 (*0-8477-3196-0*) U of PR Pr.

Art. International Politics: Enduring Concepts & Contemporary Issues. 5th ed. LC 99-41205. 559p. (C). 1999. pap. text 46.00 (*0-321-00525-2*) Addson-Wesley Educ.

Art Associates, Inc. Staff. The Art Associates Architectural Presentation Desk Reference. (Illus.). 50p. (C). 1989. 21.95 (*0-685-29360-2*) Art Assocs.

Art, Brad. Ethics & the Good Life: A Text with Readings. LC 93-6669. 520p. (C). 1993. 38.00 (*0-534-17653-4*) Wadsworth Pub.

— What Is the Best Life? An Introduction to Ethics. 310p. (C). 1992. 27.75 (*0-534-17652-6*) Wadsworth Pub.

Art Calenders Editors. Making a Living As an Artist. LC 98-10803. (Art Calendar Guide Ser.). 1998. pap. 17.95 (*1-55821-729-0*) Lyons Pr.

Art, Clip & Landtroop, Belinda A. Whispers of Love. (Illus.). 24p. 1997. 6.99 (*0-9658553-0-9*) Whispers TN.

Art Direction Magazine Editors, intro. Creativity, One. LC 59-14827. (Creativity Ser.: Vol. 1). (Illus.). 288p. 1972. 20.00 (*0-910158-02-9*) Art Dir.

Art Direction Staff, jt. ed. see Barron, Don.

Art Directors Club., Inc. Staff. The 76th Art Directors Annual. 76th ed. (Illus.). 560p. 1997. 70.00 (*2-88046-340-8*, Rotovision) Watsn-Guptill.

Art Directors Club, New York Staff. Creativity: An Examination of the Creative Process, 3rd Communications Conference, Smith, Paul, ed. LC 77-167306. (Essay Index Reprint Ser.). 1977. reprint ed. 35.95 (*0-8369-2578-5*) Ayer.

— Symbology: The Use of Symbols in Visual Communications, 4th Communications Conference, Whitney, Elwood, ed. LC 70-167307. (Essay Index Reprint Ser.). 1977. reprint ed. 39.95 (*0-8369-2579-3*) Ayer.

Art Directors Club of Europe Staff. Best of European Design & Advertising. (Illus.). 128p. pap. 29.95 (*0-9531000-1-4*, Pub. by Art Directors Club) Bks Nippan.

Art Directors Club of New York Staff. The Sixty-First Art Directors Annual. Solomon, Miriam L., ed. (Illus.). 672p. 1982. 39.95 (*0-937414-02-6*) ADC Pubns.

— Sixty-Second Art Directors Annual. Solomon, Miriam L., ed. (Illus.). 816p. 1983. 39.95 (*0-937414-03-4*) ADC Pubns.

— Sixty-Third Art Directors Annual. Soloman, Miriam L., ed. (Illus.). 516p. 1984. 39.95 (*0-937414-04-2*) ADC Pubns.

***Art Directors Club Staff.** Best of European Design & Advertising. 8th ed. (Illus.). 180p. 2000. 55.00 (*1-85669-181-0*) L King Pubng.

Art Directors Club Staff, ed. Best Of European Design, 1. 7th ed. (Illus.). 192p. 1999. 49.95 (*1-85669-155-1*, Pub. by L King Pubng) Bks Nippan.

Art Education for the Blind, Inc. Staff & Gerson, Paula L. Baroque Art in the Seventeenth Century: Art History Through Touch & Sound: A Multisensory Guide for the Blind & Visually Impaired. 65p. (Orig.). 1997. 125.00 incl. audio (*1-890116-00-9*) OpticalTouch Sys.

Art, Edwards, jt. illus. see Haskins, Jennifer L.

Art Gallery California State University, Fullerton & McAlpine, Barbara. Emerson Woelffer: Profile of the Artist 1947-1981. (Orig.). 1982. pap. write for info. (*0-935314-00-8*) CSU Art Gallery.

***Art Glass Originals Studio Staff.** Stained Glass for the First Time. LC 99-53580. (Illus.). 112p. 2000. 19.95 (*0-8069-6829-X*, Chapelle) Sterling.

Art Guys Group Staff, jt. auth. see Oldham, Todd.

Art, Henry W. Creating a Wildflower Meadow. (Country Wisdom Bulletins Ser.: Vol. 102). 1988. pap. 2.95 (*0-88266-511-1*) Storey Bks.

— A Garden of Wildflowers: One Hundred One Native Species & How to Grow Them. LC 85-45163. (Illus.). 304p. 1986. pap. 18.95 (*0-88266-405-0*, Garden Way Pub) Storey Bks.

— A Garden of Wildflowers: One Hundred One Native Species & How to Grow Them. LC 85-45163. (Illus.). 304p. 1986. 22.50 (*0-88266-404-2*, Garden Way Pub) Storey Bks.

— The Wildflower Gardener's Guide: California, Desert Southwest, & Northern Mexico Edition. Burns, Deborah, ed. LC 89-45741. (Wildflower Gardener's Guide Ser.: No. 2). (Illus.). 192p. (Orig.). 1990. pap. 14.95 (*0-88266-565-0*, Garden Way Pub) Storey Bks.

— The Wildflower Gardener's Guide: Midwest, Great Plains & Canadian Prairies Edition. Burns, Deborah, ed. LC 90-55865. (Illus.). 200p. 1991. pap. 18.95 (*0-88266-668-1*) Storey Bks.

— The Wildflower Gardener's Guide: Northeast, Mid-Atlantic, Lake States, & Eastern Canada Edition. LC 86-45713. (Illus.). 192p. 1987. 19.95 (*0-88266-450-6*, Garden Way Pub); pap. 18.95 (*0-88266-439-5*, Garden Way Pub) Storey Bks.

— The Wildflower Gardener's Guide: Pacific Northwest, Rocky Mountain, & Western Canada Edition. Burns, Deborah, ed. LC 89-46017. (Wildflower Gardener's Guide Ser.: No. 3). (Illus.). 192p. 1990. 22.95 (*0-88266-585-5*, Garden Way Pub) Storey Bks.

Art, Henry W., ed. The Dictionary of Ecology & Environmental Science. LC 92-38526. (Reference Bks.). (Illus.). 640p. 1995. 60.00 (*0-8050-2079-9*); pap. 19.95 (*0-8050-3848-5*) H Holt & Co.

Art In-Forms Staff, ed. see Ullom, A. Thomas.

Art In-Forms Staff, ed. see Ullom, M. Madeline.

Art in General Staff. Annual: Art in General, 1992-1993. (Illus.). 112p. (Orig.). 1993. pap. write for info. (*1-883967-00-7*) Art in General.

Art Institute of Chicago Staff. The Art Institute of Chicago Museum Studies: Mary Reynolds & the Spirit of Surrealism. (Museum Studies: Vol. 22, No. 2). (Illus.). 104p. 1996. pap. 14.95 (*0-86559-135-0*) Art Inst Chi.

— The Art Institute of Chicago Museum Studies: Rooted in Chicago: Fifty Years of Textile Design Traditions. (Museum Studies: Vol. 23, No. 1). (Illus.). 96p. 1997. pap. 14.95 (*0-86559-148-2*) Art Inst Chi.

— The Art Institute of Chicago Museum Studies: The Prairie School: Design Vision for the Midwest. (Museum Studies: Vol. 21, No. 2). (Illus.). 112p. 1995. pap. 15.95 (*0-86559-141-5*) Art Inst Chi.

***Art Institute of Chicago Staff.** Impressionism. (Eyewitness Books). 64p. (J). (gr. 4-7). 2000. 15.95 (*0-7894-5583-8*, D K Ink) DK Pub Inc.

Art Institute of Chicago Staff, ed. The Burnham Index to Architectural Literature. LC 89-16850. 532p. 1990. text 95.00 (*0-8240-2661-6*) Garland.

— The Burnham Index to Architectural Literature, Vol. 2. LC 89-16850. 518p. 1990. text 95.00 (*0-8240-2662-4*) Garland.

— The Burnham Index to Architectural Literature, Vol. 3. LC 89-16850. 510p. 1990. text 95.00 (*0-8240-2663-2*) Garland.

— The Burnham Index to Architectural Literature, Vol. 4. LC 89-16850. 508p. 1990. text 95.00 (*0-8240-2664-0*) Garland.

— The Burnham Index to Architectural Literature, Vol. 5. LC 89-16850. 506p. 1990. text 95.00 (*0-8240-2665-9*) Garland.

— The Burnham Index to Architectural Literature, Vol. 6. LC 89-16850. 514p. 1990. text 95.00 (*0-8240-2666-7*) Garland.

— The Burnham Index to Architectural Literature, Vol. 7. LC 89-16850. 514p. 1990. text 95.00 (*0-8240-2667-5*) Garland.

— The Burnham Index to Architectural Literature, Vol. 8. LC 89-16850. 516p. 1990. text 95.00 (*0-8240-2668-3*) Garland.

— The Burnham Index to Architectural Literature, Vol. 9. LC 89-16850. 578p. 1990. text 95.00 (*0-8240-2669-1*) Garland.

— The Burnham Index to Architectural Literature, Vol. 10. LC 89-16850. 658p. 1990. text 95.00 (*0-8240-2670-5*) Garland.

Art Institute of Chicago Staff & Joachim, Harold. French Drawings & Sketchbooks of the Nineteenth Century, 2 vols., Vol. 1. LC 78-23641. 132p. 1979. lib. bdg. 90.00 (*0-226-68796-1*, CVL 25) U Ch Pr.

— French Drawings & Sketchbooks of the Nineteenth Century, 2 vols., Vol. 2. LC 78-23641. 140p. 1979. lib. bdg. 120.00 (*0-226-68798-8*, CVL 26) U Ch Pr.

— French Drawings of the Sixteenth & Seventeenth Centuries. LC 77-9417. 40p. 1977. lib. bdg. 28.50 (*0-226-68794-5*) U Ch Pr.

— Italian Drawings of the Eighteenth & Nineteenth Centuries. LC 79-19721. (Illus.). 104p. 1980. lib. bdg. 54.00 (*0-226-68803-8*) U Ch Pr.

— Italian Drawings of the Fifteenth, Sixteenth, & Seventeenth Centuries. LC 79-14276. (Chicago Visual Library: No. 31). (Illus.). 202p. 1995. lib. bdg. 96.00 (*0-226-68801-1*) U Ch Pr.

Art Institute of Chicago Staff & Speyer, A. James. 20th Century European Paintings. LC 80-18785. (Illus.). 299p. 1981. lib. bdg. 72.00 (*0-226-68804-6*) U Ch Pr.

Art-Journal Staff. Crystal Palace Exhibition Illustrated Catalogue: London, 1851. Orig. Title: Art-Journal Illustrated Catalogue. (Illus.). 426p. 1970. reprint ed. pap. 16.95 (*0-486-22503-8*) Dover.

Art Libraries Society of North America Staff. Current Issues in Fine Arts Collection Development. (Occasional Papers: 3). 36p. (Orig.). 1984. pap. 7.50 (*0-942740-03-3*) Art Libs Soc.

Art, Pam, ed. see Bubel, Mike & Bubel, Nancy.

Art, Pam, ed. see Damerow, Gail.

Art, Pam, ed. see Hill, Cherry.

Art, Pam, ed. see Macunovich, Janet.

Art, Pam, ed. see Osborne, Robert A.

Art, Pam, ed. see Saddington, Marianne.

Art, Pam, ed. see Whitehead, Jeffrey.

Art, Pam, ed. see Yost, Harry.

Art, Pat, ed. see Hobson, Phyllis.

Art, Robert. Politics among the Ungoverned: International Relations in the Modern World. 528p. (C). 2001. pap. 30.00 (*0-02-303991-4*, Macmillan Coll) P-H.

Art, Robert J. & Waltz, Kenneth N., eds. The Use of Force: Military Power & International Politics. 4th ed. 620p. (C). 1993. pap. text 23.95 (*0-8191-8864-6*) U Pr of Amer.

— The Use of Force: Military Power & International Politics. 5th ed. LC 99-29075. 608p. 1999. pap. 26.95 (*0-8476-9554-9*); text 75.00 (*0-8476-9553-0*) Rowman.

Art Services International Staff, jt. auth. see Bautze, J.

Art Services International Staff, jt. auth. see Rogers, J. M.

Art Services International Staff, jt. auth. see Sweeney, Jane.

Art Staff. Index to Art Periodicals. 1980. 1155.00 (*0-8161-1304-1*, G K Hall & Co) Mac Lib Ref.

— Index to Art Periodicals, Supplement 1. 1980. suppl. ed. 170.00 (*0-8161-1311-4*, G K Hall & Co) Mac Lib Ref.

Art, Suzanne S. Beulah & the Feast. 32p. (J). (gr. 4-6). 1998. pap. text 2.95 (*0-9656557-5-X*) Pemblewick Pr.

— Cindie Ellis. 24p. (J). (gr. 4-6). 1998. pap. text 2.95 (*0-9656557-6-8*) Pemblewick Pr.

— The Cotton Blend Horse. 24p. (J). (gr. 4-6). 1998. pap. text 2.95 (*0-9656557-2-5*) Pemblewick Pr.

— Early Times: The Story of Ancient Egypt. rev. ed. (Illus.). 128p. (Orig.). (J). (gr. 5-8). 1993. pap. text 11.00 (*1-877653-24-1*, 12) Wayside Pub.

— Early Times: The Story of Ancient Greece. rev. ed. (Illus.). 224p. (J). (gr. 5-8). 1994. pap. text 14.67 (*1-877653-26-8*, 13) Wayside Pub.

— Early Times: The Story of Ancient Rome. (Illus.). 192p. (Orig.). (J). (gr. 5-8). 1995. pap. text 14.00 (*1-877653-23-3*, 14) Wayside Pub.

— Early Times: The Story of the Middle Ages. (Illus.). 192p. (Orig.). (J). (gr. 6-9). 1995. pap. text 16.00 (*1-877653-30-6*, 30) Wayside Pub.

— Early Times: West Meets East - the Travels of Alexander. (Illus.). 199p. (YA). (gr. 5-8). 1996. pap. text 14.67 (*1-877653-43-8*, 81) Wayside Pub.

— The Hatfelds & the McGoos. 24p. (J). (gr. 4-6). 1998. pap. text 2.95 (*0-9656557-4-1*) Pemblewick Pr.

— Joe Knight & the Seven Serfs. 32p. (J). (gr. 4-6). 1998. pap. text 2.95 (*0-9656557-3-3*) Pemblewick Pr.

— Quintet: Five Lively Plays for Kids. LC 99-216315. 134p. (J). (gr. 4-6). 1998. 12.95 (*0-9656557-1-7*) Pemblewick Pr.

***Art, Suzanne S.** The Story of the First Americans Bk. I: Ancient Times. (Illus.). 184p. (J). (gr. 5-6). 1999. pap. text 10.95 (*0-9656557-7-6*) Pemblewick Pr.

Art, Suzanne S. The Story of the Renaissance. (Illus.). 232p. (YA). (gr. 7-12). 1997. 12.95 (*0-9656557-0-9*) Pemblewick Pr.

***Art, Suzanne Strauss.** Native America on the Eve of Conquest. (Story of the First Americans Ser.: Vol. 2). (Illus.). 232p. (YA). (gr. 6-9). 2000. 12.95 (*0-9656557-9-2*) Pemblewick Pr.

Artacho-Kintziger, Zenaida, ed. And Tears No More: A Misty Rose Collection. Glasgwyn, Margaret E. & Del Rosso, Mario, trs. LC 92-91014. (Illus.). 64p. (Orig.). 1992. pap. 5.95 (*0-9633485-0-7*) M R Arts & Poetry.

Artaega, Robert F. Building of the Arch. 28p. 1967. pap. 4.95 (*0-931056-05-5*) Jefferson Natl.

Artal-Bartolo, Enrique. Forme de Jordan de la Monodromie des Singularites Supersisolees de Surfaces. LC 94-4141. (Memoirs of the American Mathematical Society Ser.: Vol. 109, No. 525). 84p. 1994. 31.00 (*0-8218-2587-9*, MEMO/109/525C) Am Math.

Artal-Mittelmark, Raul, et al. Exercise in Pregnancy. 2nd ed. (Illus.). 352p. 1990. 69.00 (*0-683-00258-9*) Lppncott W & W.

Artale, Angelo. Rings in Auctions Vol. X: An Experimental Approach, Vol. 447. LC 96-46237. (Lecture Notes in Economics & Mathematical Systems Ser.). (Illus.). 172p. 1997. pap. 49.00 (*3-540-61930-5*) Spr-Verlag.

Artalejo, Lucrecia. La Mascara y el Maranon: La Identidad Nacional Cubana. LC 91-76552. (Coleccion Cuba y sus Jueces). (SPA.). 196p. (Orig.). 1992. pap. 19.95 (*0-89729-626-5*) Ediciones.

Artalejo, M. R., jt. auth. see Hanus, Michael.

Artalejo, Mario R., jt. auth. see Levi, Giorgio.

Artan, Nazik, jt. auth. see Orhon, Derin.

Artaud, Antonin. Antonin Artaud: Selected Writings. Sontag, Susan, ed. Weaver, Helen, tr. 720p. (Orig.). (C). 1988. pap. text 19.95 (*0-520-06443-7*, Pub. by U CA Pr) Cal Prin Full Svc.

— Artaud: Collected Works, 6 vols., Vol. 1. Hamilton, Alastair & Corti, Victor, trs. (FRE.). (Orig.). pap. 13.95 (*0-7145-0170-0*) Riverrun NY.

— Artaud: Collected Works, 6 vols., Vol. 2. Hamilton, Alastair & Corti, Victor, trs. (FRE.). (Orig.). pap. 13.95 (*0-7145-0172-7*) Riverrun NY.

— Artaud: Collected Works, 6 vols., Vol. 3. Hamilton, Alastair & Corti, Victor, trs. (FRE.). (Orig.). pap. 13.95 (*0-7145-0779-2*) Riverrun NY.

— Artaud: Collected Works, 6 vols., Vol. 4. Hamilton, Alastair & Corti, Victor, trs. (FRE.). (Orig.). pap. 13.95 (*0-7145-0623-0*) Riverrun NY.

— Artaud: Collected Works, 6 vols., Vol. 5. Hamilton, Alastair & Corti, Victor, trs. (FRE.). (Orig.). pap. 13.95 (*0-7145-3660-1*) Riverrun NY.

— Artaud: Collected Works, 6 vols., Vol. 6. Hamilton, Alastair & Corti, Victor, trs. (FRE.). (Orig.). pap. 13.95 (*0-7145-3656-3*) Riverrun NY.

— Artaud: Four Texts. Eshleman, Clayton, tr. from FRE. (Illus.). 100p. 1982. 16.95 (*0-915572-57-5*); pap. 6.95 (*0-915572-56-7*) Panjandrum.

— Artaud Anthology. 2nd rev. ed. Hirschman, Jack, ed. LC 65-12730. 1965. pap. 14.95 (*0-87286-000-0*) City Lights.

— Messages Revolutionnaires. (Idees Ser.). (FRE.). 1979. pap. 8.95 (*2-07-035411-3*) Schoenhof.

— Mexico - Viaje Al Pais de Los Tarahumaras (Mexico & Voyage to the Land of the Tarahumaras) (SPA.). 381p. 1984. 9.99 (*968-16-1572-7*, Pub. by Fondo) Continental Bk.

— Le Moine. (FRE.). 1975. reprint ed. pap. 13.95 (*0-7859-1808-6*, 2070366901) Fr & Eur.

— Oeuvres Completes, Vol. 11. (FRE.). 368p. 1974. pap. 29.95 (*0-8288-9027-7*, 2070289672) Fr & Eur.

— L' Ombilic de Limbes & Correspondance Avec Jacques Riviere, le Pese-Nerfs, Fragments d'un Journal d'Enfer, l'Art et la Mot, Etc. (Poesie Ser.). (FRE.). 256p. 1968. pap. 9.95 (*2-07-030019-6*) Schoenhof.

— Poete Noir et Autres Textes. (ENG & FRE.). 64p. 1966. pap. 9.95 (*0-7859-5319-1*) Fr & Eur.

— Les Tarahumaras. (Folio Essais Ser.: No. 52). (FRE.). 217p. 1963. 9.95 (*2-07-032402-8*) Schoenhof.

— The Theater & Its Double. Richards, Mary C., tr. from FRE. 176p. 1988. pap. 11.00 (*0-8021-5030-6*, Grove) Grove-Atltic.

— Le Theatre et Son Double. (Folio Essais Ser.: No. 14). (FRE.). 256p. 1971. 9.95 (*2-07-032301-3*) Schoenhof.

— Le Theatre et Son Double: Le Theatre de Seraphin. (FRE.). 251p. 1985. pap. 12.95 (*0-7859-2795-6*, 2070323013) Fr & Eur.

— Watchfriends & Rack Screams: Works from the Final Period, 1945-48. Eshleman, Clayton & Bador, Bernard, eds. & trs. by. from FRE. 354p. 1995. pap. 17.95 (*1-878972-18-9*) Exact Change.

Artaud, Antonin & Gonzague-Frick, Louis de. Probetes et Prophetes. 1976. 9.95 (*0-686-53836-6*) Fr & Eur.

Artaud-Wild, Sabine M. Simply Nutritious: Recipes & Recommendations to Reduce Your Risk of Cancer. LC 86-71576. 182p. 1987. lib. bdg. 6.00 (*0-9617128-0-5*); spiral bd. 8.00 (*0-9617128-1-3*) Amer Cancer Soc OR.

Arteaga, Alfred. Cantos. (Illus.). 49p. 1991. pap. 7.95 (*0-9624536-2-5*) Chusma Hse.

— Chicano Poetics: Heterotexts & Hybridities. LC 97-12730. (Cambridge Studies in American Literature & Culture Ser.: Vol. 109). 202p. (C). 1997. text 54.95 (*0-521-57370-X*); pap. text 17.95 (*0-521-57492-7*) Cambridge U Pr.

— House with the Blue Bed. LC 97-26875. 128p. (Orig.). 1997. pap. 12.95 (*1-56279-106-0*) Mercury Hse Inc.

***Arteaga, Alfred.** Red. 104p. 2000. pap. 10.00 (*0-927534-94-0*) Biling Rev-Pr.

Arteaga, Alfred, ed. An Other Tongue: Nation & Ethnicity in the Linguistic Borderlands. LC 93-45755. 336p. 1994. text 54.95 (*0-8223-1458-4*); pap. text 18.95 (*0-8223-1462-2*) Duke.

Arteaga, Deborah L. Obviation in Romance: Diachronic & Synchronic Perspectives. 218p. (C). 1994. lib. bdg. 39.50 (*0-8191-9767-X*) U Pr of Amer.

Arteaga, Gertrudis G. De Avellaneda y, see De Avellaneda y Arteaga, Gertrudis G.

Arteaga, Patricia. Beginning Algebra. 586p. (C). spiral bd. 66.00 (*0-7872-6244-7*) Kendall-Hunt.

Arteaga, Robert. Building of the Arch. rev. ed. Pepple, Ted, ed. (Illus.). 1995. pap. 6.95 (*0-931056-12-8*) Jefferson Natl.

Arteca, G. A., et al. Large Order Perturbation Theory & Summation Methods in Quantum Mechanics. (Lecture Notes in Chemistry Ser.: Vol. 53). (Illus.). xi, 644p. 1990. 94.95 (*0-387-52847-4*) Spr-Verlag.

Artedi, P. Genera Piscium: Emendata & Aucta. 1967. reprint ed. 225.00 (*3-7682-0190-2*) Lubrecht & Cramer.

— Ichthyolgia. Linnaeus, Carl, ed. 1961. reprint ed. 120.00 (*3-7682-0082-5*) Lubrecht & Cramer.

Artel, Linda & Wengraf, Susan. Positive Images: A Guide to 400 Non-Sexist Films for Young People. LC 75-46089. 1976. pap. 10.00 (*0-912932-03-1*) Booklegger Pubng.

Artell, M. Hidden Pictures. (J). 1994. pap. 1.00 (*0-486-28153-1*) Dover.

Artell, Mike. Awesome Alphabet. (J). 1998. pap. 9.95 (*0-673-58647-2*) Addison-Wesley.

— Big Long Animal Song. 2nd ed. (Let Me Read Ser.). (Illus.). 8p. (J). (ps). 1994. text 2.95 (*0-673-36190-X*, GoodYrBooks) Addson-Wesley Educ.

An Asterisk (*) at the beginning of an entry indicates that the title is appearing for the first time.

— Classroom Cartooning: For the Artistically Challenged. 192p. (J). (gr. k-6). 1996. pap. 12.95 (*0-673-36208-6*, GoodYrBooks) Addson-Wesley Educ.
— Gran Cancion de los Animales. 3rd ed. Ada, Alma F., tr. (Let Me Read, Level 1 Ser.).Tr. of Big Long Animal Song. (SPA., Illus.). 8p. (J). (ps-k). 1995. bds. 2.95 (*0-673-36290-6*, GoodYrBooks) Addson-Wesley Educ.
— How to Create Picture Books. (Illus.). 96p. 1994. pap. 9.95 (*1-878279-62-9*, MM1983) Monday Morning Bks.
— Little Giant Book of Tongue Twisters. LC 99-21361. 351p. (J). 1999. write for info. (*0-8069-0951-X*) Sterling.
— Maze Fun. (Illus.). (J). 1995. pap. 1.00 (*0-486-28788-2*) Dover.
***Artell, Mike.** Petite Rouge Riding Hood: The Cajun Retelling of the Classic Folktale. LC 99-87550. (Illus.). (J). 2001. write for info. (*0-8037-2514-0*, Dial Yng Read) Peng Put Young Read.
— Sports Hidden Pictures. 1998. pap. 1.00 (*0-486-40147-2*) Dover.
Artell, Mike. Starry Skies: Questions, Facts, & Riddles about the Universe. LC 98-114308. (Illus.). 96p. (J). 1997. pap. text 12.95 (*0-673-36350-3*, GoodYrBooks) Addson-Wesley Educ.
— Weather Whys. 96p. (Orig.). (J). (gr. k up). 1995. pap. 12.95 (*0-673-36173-X*, GoodYrBooks) Addson-Wesley Educ.
— Writing Start-Ups. (Ten-Minute Ser.). (Illus.). 96p. (Orig.). (J). (gr. 3-6). 1997. pap. 10.95 (*1-57612-002-3*, MM2030) Monday Morning Bks.
Artell, Mike & Schiller, Pam. The Earth & Me: A Kid's Guide to Ecology, Pre-Gr. 2. (Illus.). 144p. (Orig.). 1994. pap. 12.95 (*0-673-36135-7*, GoodYrBooks) Addson-Wesley Educ.
Artell, Mike & Schiller, Pam. Parties Kids Love: Great New Party Ideas for Birthdays, Holidays, or Just Fun. 1996. pap. 12.95 (*0-673-36229-9*, GoodYrBooks) Addson-Wesley Educ.
Artell, Mike, jt. auth. see Schiller, Pam.
Artemidorus. Oneirocritica: The Interpretation of Dreams by Artemidorus. White, Robert J., tr. from GRE. 270p. 1990. reprint ed. pap. 36.50 (*0-944558-03-8*) Original Bks.
Artemiev, S. S. & Averina, T. A. Numerical Analysis of Systems of Ordinary & Stochastic Differential Equations. (Illus.). 184p. 1997. 129.50 (*90-6764-250-9*, Pub. by VSP) Coronet Bks.
Artemis, Deuce, et al. Feeding the Crow. Bright, Susan, ed. (New Voices Ser.: Vol. 12). 220p. (Orig.). 1998. pap. 17.95 (*0-911051-26-0*) Plain View.
Artemis Staff. Lexikon des Mittelalters: Lexicon of the Middle Ages. (GER.). 1977. pap. 3500.00 (*0-8288-5492-0*, M7206) Fr & Eur.
Artemyev, V. E. Geochemistry of Organic Matter in River-Sea System. 190p. 1996. text 114.50 (*0-7923-4030-2*) Kluwer Academic.
Artenstein, Jeffrey. Moving: A Parent-Child Manual. 1990. pap. 9.95 (*0-8125-0579-4*, Pub. by Tor Bks) St Martin.
— Runaways: In Their Own Words, Vol. 1. 1990. text 16.95 (*0-312-93132-8*) St Martin.
— Runaways: In Their Own Words: Kids Talking about Living... 128p. 1995. mass mkt. 3.99 (*0-8125-1354-1*, Pub. by Tor Bks) St Martin.
— We Grow up Fast Nowadays: Conversations with a New Generation. 204p. 1991. 19.95 (*0-929923-46-4*) Lowell Hse.
— We Grow up Fast Nowadays: Conversations with a New Generation. 192p. 1993. pap. 12.95 (*1-56565-020-4*) Lowell Hse.
— We Grow up Fast Nowadays: Conversations with America's Youth. 1991. 19.95 (*0-929923-69-3*) Lowell Hse.
Artenstein, Michael, ed. see Kehl, Mark.
Artenstein, Michael, ed. see Pearce, Q. L.
Artenstein, Michael, ed. see Tung, Angela.
Arter. Scandinavian Politics Today. 2000. pap. text 24.95 (*0-7190-5133-9*, Pub. by Manchester Univ Pr) St Martin.
Arter, Christine, et al. Visual Impairment: Access to Education for Children & Young People. Mason, Heather & McCall, Stephen, eds. LC 98-102232. 400p. 1997. pap. 34.95 (*1-85346-412-0*, Pub. by David Fulton) Taylor & Francis.
Arter, David. The Nordic Parliaments: A Comparative Analysis. LC 84-9803. 432p. 1985. text 35.00 (*0-312-57767-2*) St Martin.
— Parties & Democracy in the Post-Soviet Republics: The Case of Estonia. 304p. 1996. 81.95 (*1-85521-466-0*, Pub. by Dartmth Pub) Ashgate Pub Co.
— The Politics of European Integration in the Twentieth Century. LC 93-18110. 316p. 1993. 72.95 (*1-85521-216-1*, Pub. by Dartmth Pub); pap. text 29.95 (*1-85521-255-2*, Pub. by Dartmth Pub) Ashgate Pub Co.
— Scandinavian Politics Today. 1999. text 79.95 (*0-7190-5132-0*) St Martin.
Arter, Dennis R. Quality Audits for Improved Performance. 2nd ed. LC 93-46980. 119p. 1994. 32.00 (*0-87389-263-1*, H0844) ASQ Qual Pr.
Arter, Jared M. Echoes from a Pioneer Life. LC 72-170688. (Black Heritage Library Collection). 1977. reprint ed. 18.95 (*0-8369-8877-9*) Ayer.
***Arter, Judith A. & McTighe, Jay.** Scoring Rubrics in the Classroom: Using Performance Criteria for Assessing & Improving Student Performance. LC 00-9504. (Experts in Assessment Ser.). 2000. pap. write for info. (*0-7619-7575-6*) Corwin Pr.
Arter, Judith A., jt. ed. see Blum, Robert E.
Arterberry, Martha E., jt. auth. see Kellman, Philip J.
Arterburn, David R., ed. Calculus Three Exam File. (Exam File Ser.). 282p. 1986. pap. 19.50 (*0-910554-63-3*) Engineering.
Arterburn, Jerry. How Will I Tell My Mother? A True Story of One Man's Battle with Homosexuality & AIDS. rev. ed. 1990. pap. 8.99 (*0-8407-9578-5*) Nelson.
Arterburn, Stephen. Addicted to "Love" Understanding Dependencies of the Heart, Romance, Relationships, & Sex. 310p. 1996. pap., student ed. 12.99 (*0-89283-930-9*, Vine Bks) Servant.
— Cuando el Sexo se Vuelve una Adiccion. (Serie Enfoque a la Familia - Focus on the Family Ser.).Tr. of When Sex Becomes an Addiction. (SPA.). 32p. 1993. pap. 1.99 (*1-56063-435-9*, 497441) Editorial Unilit.
***Arterburn, Stephen.** 5-Minute New Testament. 400p. 2000. pap. text 9.99 (*0-8423-7356-X*) Tyndale Hse.
Arterburn, Stephen. Gentle Eating Workbook: Achieve Permanent Weight Loss Through Gradual Life Changes. 1997. pap. text 15.99 (*0-7852-7520-7*) Nelson.
— God of Second Chances. 1999. pap. text 5.99 (*1-56179-717-0*) Focus Family.
— My Spiritual Journey: New Testament. LC 96-109302. 857p. 1995. pap. 14.99 (*0-8423-4501-9*) Tyndale Hse.
— Parent's Guide to Top 10 Dangers Teens Face. 332p. 1999. mass mkt. 5.99 (*1-56179-689-1*) Focus Family.
***Arterburn, Stephen.** Restore the Passion: A Journal for Spiritual Renewal. 1998. 9.99 (*0-8423-6051-4*) Tyndale Hse.
Arterburn, Stephen. Ways to Say I Love You to Those You Love the Most. 288p. 1994. 6.98 (*0-88365-858-5*) Galahad Bks.
— Winning at Work Without Losing at Love. LC 94-33977. 1995. 18.99 (*0-8407-9703-6*) Nelson.
Arterburn, Stephen & Burns, Jim. Steering Them Straight: A Parental Plan for Conquering Today's Temptations. LC 95-30774. 1995. pap. 10.99 (*1-56179-406-6*) Focus Family.
— When Love Is Not Enough. LC 92-14651. 1992. 14.99 (*1-56179-098-2*) Focus Family.
***Arterburn, Stephen & Felton, Jack.** More Jesus, Less Religion: Moving from Rules to Relationship. LC 99-55258. 224p. 2000. pap. 12.95 (*1-57856-250-3*) Waterbrook Pr.
Arterburn, Stephen & Neal, Connie. The Emotional Freedom Workbook: Take Control of Your Life & Experience Emotional Strength. LC 97-210044. 288p. (Orig.). 1997. pap. 15.99 (*0-7852-7918-0*) Nelson.
***Arterburn, Stephen & Rinck, Meg J.** Avoiding Mr. Wrong (And What to Do If You Didn't) Ten Men Who Will Ruin Your Life. 256p. 2000. 16.99 (*0-7852-6889-8*) Nelson.
Arterburn, Stephen & Stoop, David. Seven Keys to Spiritual Renewal. LC 98-21899. 1998. 13.97 (*0-8423-5885-4*) Tyndale Hse.
— The Twelve Step Life Recovery Devotional. 384p. 1991. pap. 9.99 (*0-8423-4753-4*) Tyndale Hse.
Arterburn, Stephen & Wilkins, Rob. Surprised by God. LC 96-43831. 1997. 16.99 (*1-56179-465-1*) Focus Family.
***Arterburn, Stephen, et al.** Every Man's Battle: Winning the War on Sexual Temptation One Victory at a Time. LC 00-22845. 224p. 2000. pap. 12.95 (*1-57856-368-2*) Waterbrook Pr.
Arterburn, Stephen, et al. Gentle Eating. 256p. 1996. mass mkt. 5.99 (*0-7852-7501-0*) Nelson.
— Safe Places: Finding Security in the Passages of Your Life. LC 97-12990. 256p. 1997. 16.99 (*0-7852-7867-2*) Nelson.
Arterton, F. Christopher. Teledemocracy: Can Technology Protect Democracy? LC 86-17447. (Sage Library of Social Research: No. 165). 224p. 1987. reprint ed. pap. 69.50 (*0-608-01486-9*, 205953000001) Bks Demand.
Artes, Joan C., et al. Structurally Stable Quadratic Vector Fields. LC 98-4217. (Memoirs of the American Mathematical Society Ser.: Vol. 134, No. 639). 108p. 1998. pap. 40.00 (*0-8218-0796-X*, MEMO/134/639) Am Math.
Artes, Matilde. Cronica de una Desaparicion: La Lucha de una Abuela de Plaza de Mayo. LC 97-211872. (Espasa Hoy Ser.). (SPA.). 1997. 22.95 (*84-239-7756-0*) Espasa Calpe.
Arteseros, Sally, ed. American Voices: Best Short Fiction by Contemporary Authors. LC 92-30087. 400p. 1993. pap. 12.00 (*0-671-78315-7*, WSP) PB.
Artexim. Dictionar de Mecanica. (FRE & RUM.). 1980. write for info. (*0-8288-2161-5*, M15837) Fr & Eur.
— German-Rumanian Dictionary of Metallurgy: Dictionar de Metalurgie German-Roman. (GER.). 1981. write for info. (*0-8288-1924-6*, M15844) Fr & Eur.
Arth, Marvin & Ashmore, Helen. Newsletter Editor's Desk Book. 2nd rev. ed. LC 80-83042. (Illus.). 168p. 1980. pap. 9.95 (*0-938270-00-1*) Parkway Pr Ltd.
— The Newsletter Editor's Desk Book. 3rd ed. LC 81-83398. 188p. 1984. pap. 11.50 (*0-938270-03-6*) Parkway Pr Ltd.
Arth, Michael E. Michael E. Arth Introspective Nineteen Seventy-Two to Nineteen Eighty-Two. LC 83-80162. (Illus.). 256p. 1983. 29.95 (*0-912467-00-2*) G Apple Pubg Co.
— Michael E. Arth Introspective Nineteen Seventy-Two to Nineteen Eighty-Two. limited ed. LC 83-80162. (Illus.). 256p. 1983. 295.00 (*0-912467-01-0*) G Apple Pubg Co.
Arthanari, T. S. & Dodge, Yadolah. Mathematical Programming in Statistics. LC 80-21637. 431p. reprint ed. pap. 133.70 (*0-7837-2840-9*, 205763200006) Bks Demand.
— Mathematical Programming in Statistics Paper. (Wiley Classics Library). 432p. 1993. pap. 84.95 (*0-471-59212-9*) Wiley.
Arther, Richard O. The Scientific Investigator. (Illus.). 248p. 1976. 43.95 (*0-398-00055-7*) C C Thomas.
Arthey, David & Dennis, Colin, eds. Vegetable Processing. 279p. 1991. lib. bdg. 130.00 (*1-56081-081-5*, Wiley-VCH) Wiley.
Arthos, John. On the Poetry of Spenser & the Form of Romances. LC 77-119951. (Select Bibliographies Reprint Ser.). 1977. 19.95 (*0-8369-5394-0*) Ayer.
Arthos, John, pref. Dante, Michelangelo, & Milton. LC 78-32053. 124p. 1979. reprint ed. lib. bdg. 49.50 (*0-313-20979-0*, ARDA, Greenwood Pr) Greenwood.
Arthos, John, ed. see Shakespeare, William.
Arthrell, William G., ed. Heart's Cargo. (Illus.). 64p. 1996. reprint ed. pap. 8.00 (*1-880834-30-8*) Cleveland St Univ Poetry Ctr.
Arthritis Center & Dept. Nutrition Sciences, Univ. The Essential Arthritis Cookbook: Kitchen Basics for People with Arthritis, Fibromyalgia & Other Chronic Pain & Fatigue. Hachfeld, Linda & Winchester, Faith, eds. LC 95-80010. (Illus.). 288p. 1995. 24.95 (*0-9620471-6-3*, 170) Appletree MN.
Arthritis Center Staff. The Essential Arthritis Cookbook: Kitchen Basics for People with Arthritis, Fibromyalgia & Other Chronic Pain & Fatigue. University of Alabama at Kimingham Staff et al, eds. 288p. Date not set. 16.00 (*1-891011-01-4*) Appletree MN.
Arthritis Foundation Editors. Understanding Arthritis: What It Is, How To Treat it, How to Cope with It. (Illus.). 290p. 1986. pap. 12.00 (*0-684-18736-1*) S&S Trade.
Arthritis Foundation of New South Wales Staff. The Arthritis Handbook. 2nd ed. 187p. 1996. pap. 30.00 (*0-8036-0376-2*) Davis Co.
Arthritis Foundation Staff. Arthritis 101: Answers to Your Questions about Arthritis. 176p. (Orig.). 1997. pap. 11.95 (*1-56352-380-9*) Longstreet.
Arthritis Foundation Staff. Health Organizer: A Personal Health-Care Record. LC 98-66369. 148p. 1998. pap. 14.95 (*0-912423-18-8*) Arthritis Found.
— Living Better with Arthritis. (Illus.). (Orig.). 1996. write for info. (*0-912423-11-0*) Arthritis Found.
— Living Better with Fibromyalgia. (Illus.). (Orig.). 1996. pap. write for info. (*0-912423-10-2*) Arthritis Found.
— Raising a Child with Arthritis: A Parent's Guide. LC 98-66377. 200p. 1998. pap. 14.95 (*0-912423-19-6*) Arthritis Found.
— 250 Tips for Making Life with Arthritis Easier. 128p. (Orig.). 1997. pap. 9.95 (*1-56352-381-7*) Longstreet.
***Arthritis Foundation Staff.** Walk With Ease: Your Guide to Walking For Better Health, Improved Fitness & Less Pain. 1999. pap. 8.95 (*0-912423-22-6*) Arthritis Found.
Arthritis Foundation Staff. Your Personal Guide to Living Well with Fibromyalgia. LC 96-79811. (Illus.). 160p. (Orig.). 1997. pap. 14.95 (*1-56352-382-5*) Longstreet.
Arthritis Foundation Staff, ed. Toward Healthy Living: A Wellness Journal. 144p. 1998. 14.95 (*1-56352-453-8*) Longstreet.
Arthritis Foundation Staff, ed. see Klippel, John H., et al.
Arthritis Society Alberta Division Staff. The Real World of Engineering: Case History, No. 59. 81p. 3.50 (*0-614-05228-9*, CHN05905913.5M) ASFE.
Arthur. Aspirations & Self Assertions. (C). 1999. write for info. (*0-415-01105-1*) Routledge.
— Desktop Publishing. Date not set. text. write for info. (*0-314-01410-1*) West Pub.
— Morality & Moral Controver. 5th ed. LC 98-33679. (C). 1998. pap. text 39.80 (*0-13-914128-6*) S&S Trade.
— Patience of Hope. 1997. pap. 10.99 (*0-85234-385-X*, Pub. by Evangelical Pr) P & R Pubng.
Arthur, et al. Computer Skills Resource Guide, PFS: 1st Choice Rev Prntg. abr. ed. 1991. pap. 27.25 (*0-314-84673-5*) Thomson Learn.
— Strategic Reading for Regents' Reading Exams. 3rd ed. 200p. (C). 2000. per. 37.95 (*0-7872-7078-4*) Kendall-Hunt.
Arthur, et al. Teaching & Learning History: History Teachers in the Making. LC 97-47456. 1998. pap. 27.95 (*0-335-19825-2*) OpUniv Pr.
— Teaching & Learning History: History Teachers in the Making. LC 97-47456. 164p. 1998. 89.00 (*0-335-19826-0*) Taylor & Francis.
Arthur, John R., jt. ed. see Berman, Lonny E.
Arthur, A. S., tr. see Gladkov, Fyodor V.
***Arthur, Alex.** Shell. (Eyewitness Books). (Illus.). (J). (gr. 4-7). 2000. 19.99 (*0-7894-6558-2*) DK Pub Inc.
— Shell. (Eyewitness Books). (J). (gr. 4-7). 2000. 15.95 (*0-7894-5830-6*) DK Pub Inc.
Arthur, Alex. Shell. LC 88-13449. (Eyewitness Books). (Illus.). 64p. (J). (gr. 5 up). 1989. lib. bdg. 18.99 (*0-394-92256-5*, Pub. by Knopf Bks Yng Read) Random.
Arthur Andersen & Co. Staff & Pilko Associates Staff. Principles of Environmental Health & Safety Management. West, Gordon A. & Michaud, Ronald W., eds. 335p. 1995. pap. text 69.00 (*0-86587-478-6*) Gov Insts.
Arthur, Anne. Minnesota's State Parks: How to Get There - What to Do - Where to Do It. 280p. 1998. pap. 14.95 (*1-885061-51-X*) Adventure Pubns.
Arthur, Anthony. Tailor King: The Rise & Fall of the Anabaptist Kingdom of Munster. LC 99-35866. 256p. 1999. text 24.95 (*0-312-20515-5*) St Martin.
Arthur, Bev & Arthur, Martin. Mama's Boy. LC 86-14348. (Illus.). 216p. (Orig.). 1986. pap. 9.95 (*0-89407-054-1*) Strawberry Hill.
Arthur-Bird, Kay. Come Walk in My Ways: 1 & 2 Kings & 2 Chronicles. LC 97-18322. (International Inductive Study Ser.). 176p. (Orig.). 1997. pap. 5.99 (*1-56507-707-5*) Harvest Hse.
Arthur, Bonnie. Unicorns in Soft Sculpture, Bk. 1. (Illus.). (Orig.). 1982. pap. 3.50 (*0-941284-14-X*) J Shaw Studio.
Arthur, C. J. In the Hall of Mirrors: Some Problems of Commitment in a Religiously Plural World: The Gifford Research Fellowship Lectures for 1985, Delivered at St Mary's College, University of St. Andrews LC 87-108697. (Christian Studies Ser.). xiii, 172 p. 1986. write for info. (*0-264-67090-6*, Pub. by A R Mowbray) Cassell & Continuum.
— Religious Pluralism: A Metaphorical Approach. LC 99-56327. 292p. 2000. 16.95 (*1-888570-54-7*) Davies Grp.
Arthur, C. J., ed. see Marx, Karl.
Arthur, C. J., ed. see Marx, Karl & Engels, Friedrich.
***Arthur, Charles.** Haiti in Focus: A Guide to the People, Politics & Culture. (Illus.). 2000. pap. 12.95 (*1-56656-359-3*) Interlink Pub.
***Arthur, Charles B. & Dash, Michael, eds.** A Haiti Anthology: Libete. LC 99-22454. (Illus.). 280p. 1999. pap. text 19.95 (*1-55876-230-2*) Wiener Pubs Inc.
— A Haiti Anthology: Libete. LC 99-22454. (Illus.). 280p. (C). 1999. text 39.95 (*1-55876-229-9*) Wiener Pubs Inc.
Arthur, Chris. Irish Nocturnes. Herbert, Gigi, ed. LC 99-29840. (Illus.). 256p. 1999. pap. 14.99 (*1-888570-49-0*) Davies Grp.
Arthur, Chris, ed. Biting the Bullet: Some Personal Reflections on Religious Education. 194p. (C). 1990. pap. text 40.00 (*0-7152-0635-4*) St Mut.
Arthur, Christ. Biting the Bullet: Some Personal Reflections on Religious Education. 194p. (C). 1992. pap. 59.00 (*0-7855-6825-5*, Pub. by St Andrew) St Mut.
Arthur, Christopher J., ed. Engels Today: A Centenary Appreciation. 256p. 1996. text 59.95 (*0-312-16013-5*) St Martin.
Arthur, Christopher J. & Reuten, Geert, eds. The Circulation of Capital: Essays on Vol. 2 of Marx's "Capital", Vol. 2. LC 97-28027. 256p. 1998. text 65.00 (*0-312-21025-6*) St Martin.
Arthur, D. Aid to Career Decisions. 267p. 1991. pap. text 18.95 (*0-9632164-0-6*) Windsong Pub.
Arthur D. Little, Inc. Staff. Electric Vehicle Thermal Management for Cold Weather Operation (Oct.-1994) (Electric Vehicle Information Ser.: Vol. 15). (Illus.). 60p. 1996. pap. 75.00 (*0-89934-269-8*, BT042); lib. bdg. 105.00 (*0-89934-270-1*, BT942) Bus Tech Bks.
Arthur D. Little, Inc. Staff, et al. Civil Aviation Development: A Policy & Operation Analysis. LC 70-185656. (Special Studies in U. S. Economic, Social & Political Issues). 1980. reprint ed. 52.50 (*0-89197-697-3*) Irvington.
Arthur D. Little Staff & CommerceNet Staff. The iMarket. 1997. pap. 29.95 (*0-614-28495-3*) McGraw-Hill Prof.
Arthur, Daniel & Keiper, Ronald R. Renfrew Park: A Pennsylvania German Farmstead. LC 87-91942. (Illus.). 160p. 1988. 14.95 (*0-9618407-0-6*) Daniel W Arthur.
Arthur, David, et al. Mental Health Nursing. (Illus.). 260p. 1992. write for info. (*0-7295-1209-6*) Bailliere Tindall.
Arthur, David, jt. auth. see Arthur, Kay.
Arthur, Diane. The Complete Human Resources Writing Guide. LC 96-50445. 384p. 1997. 55.00 (*0-8144-0325-5*) AMACOM.
— Managing Human Resources in Small & Mid-Sized Companies. 2nd ed. LC 95-412. 352p. 1995. 59.95 (*0-8144-0277-1*) AMACOM.
— Recruiting, Interviewing, Selecting & Orienting New Employees. 2nd ed. 350p. 1991. 49.95 (*0-8144-5007-5*) AMACOM.
— Recruiting, Interviewing, Selecting & Orienting New Employees. 3rd ed. LC 98-16733. 400p. 1998. 59.95 (*0-8144-0401-4*) AMACOM.
Arthur, Donald, jt. auth. see Varnay, Astrid.
Arthur, Dorothy. Modeling in Clay. (Illus.). 128p. 1993. reprint ed. pap. 29.95 (*1-889250-03-1*) Gentle Br.
Arthur, Dorothy. Modelling in Clay: And other Materials. (Illus.). 128p. 1997. pap. text. write for info. (*90-5703-921-4*, Harwood Acad Pubs) Gordon & Breach.
Arthur, Elisabeth. Come the Winter. large type ed. (Linford Romance Library). 1991. pap. 16.99 (*0-7089-7103-2*) Ulverscroft.
Arthur, Eric. Barn: Vanishing Landmark in North America. 1989. 19.98 (*0-88486-020-5*) Arrowood Pr.
Arthur, Eric R. Toronto: No Mean City. 3rd ed. 336p. 1986. 47.50 (*0-8020-5668-7*); pap. 22.95 (*0-8020-6587-2*) U of Toronto Pr.
Arthur, Ernie, jt. auth. see Perry, Larry.
Arthur, Frank. Another Mystery in Suva. large type ed. 1991. 27.99 (*0-7089-2528-6*) Ulverscroft.
— Confession to Murder. large type ed. 1991. 27.99 (*0-7089-2422-0*) Ulverscroft.
— Murder in the Tropic Night. large type ed. 1990. pap. 16.99 (*0-7089-6997-6*, Linford) Ulverscroft.
— The Throbbing Dark. large type ed. 1990. pap. 16.99 (*0-7089-6993-3*) Ulverscroft.
— Who Killed Netta Maul? large type ed. (Large Type Ser.). 480p. 1994. 27.99 (*0-7089-2999-0*) Ulverscroft.
***Arthur, Gary.** The Arthur NCE Exam Study Guide. 500p. 1999. student ed., ring bd. 250.00 (*1-887617-73-6*) St Bart Pr Ltd.
***Arthur, Gary, et al.** The Arthur NCE Exam Study Guide. 500p. 1999. student ed. 250.00 (*1-887617-68-X*) St Bart Pr Ltd.
Arthur, George, tr. see Poincare, Raymond.
Arthur, George C. From Phelps to Gielgud. LC 77-91472. 1972. reprint ed. 23.95 (*0-405-08214-2*, Pub. by Blom Pubns) Ayer.
— From Phelps to Gielgud: Reminiscences of the Stage Through Sixty-Five Years. LC 67-23174. (Essay Index Reprint Ser.). 1977. reprint ed. 20.95 (*0-8369-0160-6*) Ayer.
Arthur, Gibbs L., Jr. & Swanson, Carl D. Confidentiality & Privileged Communication, Vol. 6. rev. ed. 78p. (C). 1995. pap. text 18.95 (*1-55620-105-2*, 72306) Am Coun Assn.
Arthur, Gwendolyn A. Nutrition God's Way. 96p. 1987. pap. 4.25 (*0-88144-115-5*) Christian Pub.
***Arthur, Gwendolyn A.** The Truth vs. the Lie: God's Way vs. Man's Way. 88p. 1999. pap. write for info. (*0-9672864-0-9*) Fishers of Men Pubn.

A

An Asterisk (*) at the beginning of an entry indicates that the title is appearing for the first time.

A

***Arthur, Heidi & Pollock, Jane.** New York's 50 Best Fun-Filled Family Getaways. (Illus.). 128p. 2000. pap. 12.00 (*1-885492-92-8*) City & Co.

Arthur, Heidi, et al. Who Knew Raising Kids in New York Could Be This Easy? From Playgrounds to Preschools, Strollers to Sneakers, Eateries to Excursions . . . Everything a Manhattan Parent Needs to Know. LC 97-35284. 176p. 1998. pap. 13.95 (*0-312-18222-8*) St Martin.

***Arthur, Helen.** Malt Whisky. (Evergreens Ser.). 1998. 16.99 (*3-8228-7572-4*) Benedikt Taschen.

Arthur, Helen. Single Malt Whiskey Companion: A Connoisseur's Guide. LC 97-3201. 256p. 1997. 24.95 (*0-02-861780-0*, Pub. by Macmillan) S&S Trade.

— Single Malt Whisky. (Illus.). 80p. 1998. 7.99 (*0-7858-1027-7*) Bk Sales Inc.

***Arthur, Helen.** The Single Malt Whisky Companion: A Connoisseur's Guide. (Illus.). 256p. 1999. reprint ed. text 25.00 (*0-7881-6665-4*) DIANE Pub.

— Whisky: The Water of Life - Uisge Beatha. (Illus.). 224p. 2000. 39.95 (*1-55209-425-1*) Firefly Bks Ltd.

Arthur, J. R., ed. Asian Fish Health Bibliography & Abstracts No. 1: Southeast Asia. 252p. 1992. per. write for info. (*971-8709-30-4*, Pub. by ICLARM) Intl Spec Bk.

Arthur, James. Retracing Kipp Trails. 72p. (Orig.). 1997. pap. 12.95 (*1-887804-10-2*, News-Argus) Cent Mont Pubng.

— Schools & Community: The Communitarian Agenda in Education. LC 99-39367. 165p. 1999. pap. 28.95 (*0-7507-0954-5*, Pub. by Falmer Pr UK) Taylor & Francis.

Arthur, James & Bailey, Richard With. Schools & Community: The Communitarian Agenda in Education. LC 99-39367. 160p. 1999. 74.00 (*0-7507-0955-3*, Pub. by Falmer Pr UK) Taylor & Francis.

Arthur, James & Clozel, Laurent. Simple Algebras, Base Change, & the Advanced Theory of the Trace Formula. LC 88-22560. (Annals of Mathematics Studies: No. 120). (Illus.). 244p. reprint ed. pap. 75.70 (*0-608-06432-7*, 206664500008) Bks Demand.

***Arthur, James & Phillips, Robert.** Issues in History Teaching. LC 99-35738. 272p. 1999. write for info. (*0-415-20669-3*) Routledge.

Arthur, James J. Fowler: Annals of the Fowler Family, with Branches in Virginia, North Carolina, South Carolina, Tennessee, Kentucky, Alabama, Mississippi, California & Texas. (Illus.). 327p. 1993. reprint ed. pap. 51.00 (*0-8328-3099-2*); reprint ed. lib. bdg. 61.00 (*0-8328-3098-4*) Higginson Bk Co.

Arthur James Ltd. Staff. Swann's Way. 280p. (C). 1993. 59.00 (*0-85305-329-4*, Pub. by Arthur James) St Mut.

Arthur James Ltd. Staff & Cooke, Christopher H. Health Is for God. 100p. 1988. 30.00 (*0-7855-1739-1*) St Mut.

Arthur, Jean. Hellroaring: Fifty Years on the Big Mountain. LC 96-61579. (Illus.). 88p. 1996. pap. 29.95 (*0-9645477-8-3*) Whitefish Ed.

***Arthur, Jean.** Montana: The Best Cross-Country Ski & Snowshoe Trails. (Winter Trails Ser.). (Illus.). 2000. pap. 14.95 (*0-7627-0730-5*) Globe Pequot.

Arthur, Jean. Timberline: And a Century of Skiing on Mt. Hood. LC 98-89155. (Illus.). 104p. 1998. pap. 21.95 (*0-9645477-0-8*) Whitefish Ed.

Arthur, Jean, jt. auth. see Arthur, Lindsay G.

Arthur, Jeffrey L., jt. auth. see Lawrence, Kenneth D.

Arthur, Jett C., ed. Cellulose & Fiber Science Developments: A World View. LC 77-22540. (American Chemical Society Symposium Ser.: No. 50). 296p. reprint ed. pap. 91.80 (*0-608-10053-6*, 201994100015) Bks Demand.

Arthur, Jett C., Jr., ed. Polymers for Fibers & Elastomers. LC 84-14635. (ACS Symposium Ser.: No. 260). (Illus.). 444p. 1984. reprint ed. pap. 137.70 (*0-608-03137-2*, 206359000007) Bks Demand.

— Polymers or Fibers & Elastomers. LC 84-14635. (Symposium Ser.: No. 260). 434p. 1984. lib. bdg. 76.95 (*0-8412-0859-X*) Am Chemical.

— Textile & Paper Chemistry & Technology, No. 49. LC 77-7938. 1977. 30.95 (*0-8412-0377-6*) Am Chemical.

Arthur, Jett C., Jr., ed. see American Chemical Society, International Developme.

Arthur, Joe. Justice for All: The Story of Thurgood Marshall. 1995. 8.60 (*0-606-07757-X*, Pub. by Turtleback) Demco.

Arthur, John. Realist Watercolors. (Illus.). 32p. 1990. pap. 9.95 (*0-911209-41-7*) Palmer Mus Art.

— Robert Cottingham: A Print Retrospective, 1972-1986. LC 86-61945. (Illus.). 72p. (Orig.). 1986. pap. text 21.95 (*0-934306-07-9*) Springfield.

Arthur, John & Shapiro, Amy, eds. Color Classidentity: The New Politics of Race. 240p. (C). 1996. pap. text 25.00 (*0-8133-3115-3*, Pub. by Westview) HarpC.

Arthur, John & Shaw, William H. Justice & Economic Distribution. 2nd ed. LC 90-48333. 304p. (C). 1991. pap. text 39.60 (*0-13-514241-5*) P-H.

— Readings in the Philosophy of Law. 2nd ed. 640p. 1993. pap. text 72.00 (*0-13-753849-9*) P-H.

***Arthur, John & Shaw, William H.** Readings in the Philosophy of Law. 3rd ed. LC 00-26709. 688p. 2000. pap. 56.00 (*0-13-027741-X*) P-H.

Arthur, John & Shaw, William H. Social & Political Philosophy. 560p. (C). 1991. pap. text 34.60 (*0-13-753799-9*) P-H.

***Arthur, John, et al.** Green Woods & Crystal Waters: The American Landscape Tradition. LC 99-38336. (Illus.). 176p. 1999. pap. 30.00 (*0-86659-021-8*) Philbrook Mus Art.

***Arthur, John A.** Invisible Sojourners: African Immigrant Diaspora in the United States. LC 99-54445. 2000. write for info. (*0-275-96759-X*, Praeger Pubs) Greenwood.

Arthur, John P. History of Watauga Co., with Sketches of Prominent Families. (Illus.). 363p. 1998. reprint ed. lib. bdg. 42.50 (*0-8328-9617-9*) Higginson Bk Co.

— History of Watauga County, North Carolina. (Illus.). 443p. 1986. reprint ed. 37.50 (*0-89308-001-2*) Southern Hist Pr.

— A History of Watauga County, North Carolina with Sketches of Prominent Families. (Illus.). 378p. 1992. reprint ed. 24.95 (*0-932807-66-6*) Overmountain Pr.

— Western North Carolina: A History from 1730-1913. (Illus.). 679p. 1996. 37.50 (*1-57072-062-2*) Overmountain Pr.

***Arthur, John Preston.** Western North Carolina: A History 1730-1913, 2 vols. (Illus.). 736p. 1999. reprint ed. pap. 48.00 (*0-7884-1280-9*, A673) Heritage Bk.

Arthur, Joseph. How I Conquered My Parents: Memoirs from a Part-Time Angel. 208p. 1998. pap. 14.95 (*1-886094-84-5*) Chicago Spectrum.

***Arthur, Judith Carmel.** Antoni Gaudi. 1999. 14.95 (*1-85868-747-0*, Pub. by Carlton Bks Ltd) Natl Bk Netwk.

— Philippe Starck. 1999. text 14.95 (*1-85868-738-1*, Pub. by Carlton Bks Ltd) Natl Bk Netwk.

Arthur, Julia, jt. auth. see Arthur, Stephen.

Arthur, K. Con Amor Eterno.Tr. of With an Everlasting Love. (SPA.). 1996. pap. 7.99 (*0-8297-0482-5*) Vida Pubs.

— Dios Estas Ahi?Tr. of God Are You There?. (SPA.). 208p. 1995. pap. 9.99 (*0-8297-0459-0*) Vida Pubs.

— He Aqui Que Jesus Viene!Tr. of Behold Jesus Is Coming. (SPA.). 1996. pap. 7.99 (*0-8297-1507-X*) Vida Pubs.

— Respaesta de Dios Relociones.Tr. of God's Answers, Relationships & Passions. (SPA.). 1996. pap. 6.99 (*0-8297-1506-1*) Vida Pubs.

— Senor Esename a Orar en 28 Diaz.Tr. of Lord, Teach Me to Pray in 28 Days. (SPA.). 128p. 7.95 (*0-8297-0460-4*) Vida Pubs.

— Senor, Sana Mis Heridas.Tr. of Lord, Heal My Hurts. (SPA.). 240p. 1995. pap. 10.99 (*0-8297-1984-9*) Vida Pubs.

— Victoria y No Derrota.Tr. of Choosing Victory over Defeat. (SPA.). 1996. pap. 6.99 (*0-8297-1505-3*) Vida Pubs.

Arthur, Karl. All... the Little Bitches. LC 98-68711. 306p. 1999. 28.95 (*1-893660-24-9*, 9908001-H) Ravenhawk.

Arthur, Kateryna, jt. auth. see Acheson, James M.

Arthur, Katherine. Keep My Heart Forever. (Romance Ser.: No. 181). 1992. per. 2.89 (*0-373-03181-5*, 1-03181-4) Harlequin Bks.

— One More Secret. large type ed. 277p. 1993. 27.99 (*0-7505-0573-7*, Pub. by Mgna Lrg Print) Ulverscroft.

— Reluctant Lover. 1993. per. 2.99 (*0-373-03282-X*, 1-03282-0) Harlequin Bks.

Arthur, Kay. As Silver Refined: Learning to Embrace Life's Disappointments. LC 98-229108. 288p. 1998. 19.95 (*1-57856-004-7*) Waterbrook Pr.

***Arthur, Kay.** As Silver Refined: Learning to Embrace Life's Disappointments. 288p. 1999. pap. 12.95 (*1-57856-064-0*) Waterbrook Pr.

Arthur, Kay. As Silver Refined Study Guide: Learning to Embrace Life's Disappointments. 96p. 1998. pap., student ed. 6.95 (*1-57856-058-6*) Waterbrook Pr.

— Behold, Jesus Is Coming! Capstone Publishers Staff, tr. from CHI. (Illus.). 145p. (Orig.). 1996. pap. 4.99 (*1-888655-62-3*) Precept Ministries.

— Beloved: From God's Heart to Yours. LC 94-10728. 1994. 17.99 (*1-56507-198-0*) Harvest Hse.

***Arthur, Kay.** Boy, Have I Got Problems! James. (Discover 4 Yourself Inductive Bible Studies for Kids). 128p. (J). 2000. pap. 8.99 (*0-7369-0148-5*) Harvest Hse.

Arthur, Kay. The Call to Follow Jesus. LC 93-33926. (International Inductive Study Ser.). (Orig.). 1994. pap. 4.99 (*1-56507-221-9*) Harvest Hse.

— The Call to Follow Jesus. Capstone Publishers Staff, tr. from CHI. (Illus.). 78p. (Orig.). 1996. pap. 4.99 (*1-888655-58-5*) Precept Ministries.

— Choosing Victory, Overcoming Defeat. Capstone Publishers Staff, tr. from CHI. 114p. (Orig.). 1996. pap. 4.99 (*1-888655-59-3*) Precept Ministries.

— Choosing Victory, Overcoming Defeat: Joshua, Judges, Ruth, Parchment. rev. ed. (International Inductive Study Ser.). (Orig.). 1995. reprint ed. pap. 4.99 (*1-56507-304-5*) Harvest Hse.

— The Covenant God Study Guide: Learning to Trust Him. 112p. 1999. pap., student ed. 6.95 (*1-57856-184-1*) Waterbrook Pr.

***Arthur, Kay.** Discovering True Worship. (International Inductive Study Ser.). 160p. 2000. pap. 6.99 (*0-7369-0358-5*) Harvest Hse.

Arthur, Kay. Ensename Tus Caminos. Capstone Publishers Staff, tr. from CHI.Tr. of Teach Me Your Ways. (SPA.). 161p. (Orig.). 1996. pap. 6.99 (*1-888655-57-7*) Precept Ministries.

— Free from Bondage God's Way (Galatians-Ephesians) LC 94-19165. (International Inductive Study Ser.). 1994. pap. 4.99 (*1-56507-205-7*) Harvest Hse.

— God, Are You There? Do You Care? Do You Know about Me? LC 94-6872. 1994. pap. 9.99 (*1-56507-239-1*) Harvest Hse.

— God, Are You There? Do You Care? Do You Know about Me? Capstone Publishers Staff, tr. from CHI. (Illus.). 235p. 1995. pap. 8.99 (*1-888655-63-1*) Precept Ministries.

— God's Answers for Relationships & Passions. Capstone Publishers Staff, tr. from CHI. (Illus.). 114p. (Orig.). 1996. pap. 4.99 (*1-888655-60-7*) Precept Ministries.

— God's Answers for Relationships & Passions: 1 & 2 Corinthians. (International Inductive Study Ser.). (Orig.). 1995. pap. 5.99 (*1-56507-303-7*) Harvest Hse.

— God's Blueprint for Bible Prophecy: Daniel. (International Inductive Study Ser.). (Orig.). 1995. pap. 5.99 (*1-56507-317-7*) Harvest Hse.

Arthur, Kay. God's Time Machine: Daniel. (Discover 4 Yourself Bible Studies for Kids Ser.). 128p. (J). Date not set. pap. 8.99 (*0-7369-0147-7*) Harvest Hse.

Arthur, Kay. The Holy Spirit Unleashed in You. Capstone Publishers Staff, tr. from CHI. 104p. (Orig.). 1996. pap. 4.99 (*1-888655-56-9*) Precept Ministries.

— The Holy Spirit Unleashed in You: Acts. LC 94-25522. (International Inductive Study Ser.). 1994. pap. 4.99 (*1-56507-245-6*) Harvest Hse.

— How to Study Your Bible: The Lasting Reward of the Inductive Approach. LC 93-31606. 1994. pap. 9.99 (*1-56507-173-5*) Harvest Hse.

***Arthur, Kay.** How to Study Your Bible for Kids. 128p. (J). 2000. pap. 8.99 (*0-7369-0362-3*) Harvest Hse.

Arthur, Kay. Israel, My Beloved. 450p. 1997. pap. 12.99 (*1-56507-624-9*) Harvest Hse.

— Liberados de la Esclavitud. Capstone Publishers Staff, tr. from CHI.Tr. of Free from Bondage God's Way. 87p. 1996. pap. 4.99 (*1-888655-61-5*) Precept Ministries.

— Liberados de la Esclavitud. (International Inductive Study Ser.).Tr. of Free from Bondage God's Way. (SPA.). 1996. pap. 5.99 (*0-8297-1503-7*) Vida Pubs.

— Llamado a Siquir a Cristo. (International Inductive Study Ser.).Tr. of Call to Follow Jesus. (SPA.). 80p. 1995. pap. 5.99 (*0-8297-1502-9*) Vida Pubs.

— Lord, Heal My Hurts. 280p. 1996. pap. 12.99 (*0-88070-879-4*, Multnomah Bks) Multnomah Pubs.

— Lord, Heal My Hurts. Capstone Publishers Staff, tr. from CHI. 280p. 1996. pap. 9.95 (*1-888655-55-0*) Precept Ministries.

— Lord, I Need Grace to Make It. 252p. 1996. pap. 12.99 (*0-88070-881-6*, Multnomah Bks) Multnomah Pubs.

— Lord, I Need Grace to Make It. Capstone Publishers Staff, tr. from CHI. 247p. 1996. pap. 9.95 (*1-888655-52-6*) Precept Ministries.

— Lord, I Want to Know You. 219p. (Orig.). 1996. pap. 12.99 (*0-88070-880-8*, Multnomah Bks) Multnomah Pubs.

— Lord, I Want to Know You. Capstone Publishers Staff, tr. from CHI. 219p. (Orig.). 1995. pap. 9.99 (*1-888655-53-4*) Precept Ministries.

Arthur, Kay. Lord, I Want to Love You More: A Daily Inspirational Calendar. 384p. (gr. 10). 1993. spiral bd. 11.99 (*0-8007-7138-9*) Revell.

Arthur, Kay. Lord, I'm Torn Between Two Masters. LC 96-15067. 264p. 1996. pap. 12.99 (*0-88070-886-7*, Multnomah Bks) Multnomah Pubs.

— Lord, Is It Warfare? 350p. 1996. pap. 12.99 (*0-88070-882-4*, Multnomah Bks) Multnomah Pubs.

— Lord, Is It Warfare? Teach Me to Stand. Capstone Publishers Staff, tr. from CHI. 339p. (Orig.). 1996. pap. 10.95 (*1-888655-54-2*) Precept Ministries.

— Lord, Only You Can Change Me. 244p. 1996. pap. 12.99 (*0-88070-878-6*, Multnomah Bks) Multnomah Pubs.

— Lord, Teach Me to Pray in 28 Days. LC 94-29310. 1995. pap. 8.99 (*1-56507-252-9*) Harvest Hse.

— Lord, Teach Me to Pray in 28 Days. Capstone Publishers Staff, tr. from CHI. 159p. 1996. pap. 3.95 (*1-888655-51-8*) Precept Ministries.

— Lord Teach Me to Pray in 28 Days. large type ed. LC 96-22272. 172p. 1996. pap. 13.95 (*0-8027-2706-9*) Walker & Co.

— Lord, Where Are You When Bad Things Happen? 238p. 1996. pap. 12.99 (*0-88070-883-2*, Multnomah Bks) Multnomah Pubs.

— Lord, Where Are You When Bad Things Happen? Capstone Publishers Staff, tr. from CHI. 270p. 1996. pap. 8.99 (*1-888655-50-X*) Precept Ministries.

***Arthur, Kay.** A Marriage Without Regrets: International Edition. 250p. 2000. pap. 11.99 (*0-7369-0440-9*) Harvest Hse.

Arthur, Kay. A Marriage Without Regrets: Your Life Together As God Intended. LC 99-14080. 250p. 2000. 18.99 (*1-56507-451-3*) Harvest Hse.

***Arthur, Kay.** A Marriage Without Regrets Study Guide. 144p. 2000. pap., student ed. 6.99 (*0-7369-0439-5*) Harvest Hse.

Arthur, Kay. A Moment with God. 1998. 14.99 (*1-56507-995-7*) Harvest Hse.

— My Savior, My Friend: A Daily Devotional. 1995. 17.99 (*1-56507-351-7*) Harvest Hse.

— Our Covenant God: Learning to Trust Him. LC 99-11808. 288p. 1999. 19.95 (*1-57856-182-5*); pap. 12.95 (*1-57856-261-9*) Waterbrook Pr.

— Plan Divino Perfecto Profecia Biblica.Tr. of God's Blueprint for Prophecy. (SPA.). 7.95 (*0-8297-1508-8*) Vida Pubs.

— A Sanctuary for Your Soul. LC 98-14674. (Illus.). 48p. 1999. 12.99 (*1-56507-946-9*) Harvest Hse.

***Arthur, Kay.** Search My Heart, O God: 365 Appointments with God. 416p. 1999. 15.95 (*1-57856-274-0*) Waterbrook Pr.

Arthur, Kay. Teach Me Your Ways (The Pentateuch) LC 93-33925. (International Inductive Study Ser.). 1994. pap. 6.99 (*1-56507-204-9*) Harvest Hse.

— To Know Him by Name. 143p. 1995. 21.99 (*0-88070-733-X*, Multnomah Bks) Multnomah Pubs.

***Arthur, Kay.** Wandering Woolly. 40p. (J). 2000. 14.95 (*1-57856-158-2*) Waterbrook Pr.

— With an Everlasting Love. 144p. 1999. 12.99 (*0-7369-0127-2*) Harvest Hse.

Arthur, Kay & Arthur, David. Behold, Jesus Is Coming! Revelation. (International Inductive Study Ser.). (Orig.). 1995. pap. 5.99 (*1-56507-318-5*) Harvest Hse.

***Arthur, Kay & Domeij, Scoti.** Portuguese Wrong Way, Jonah. Leite, Eleni, tr. (Discover 4 Yourself Series for Children). (Illus.). 97p. (J). 1999. 7.99 (*1-888655-71-2*) Precept Ministries.

— Wrong Way, Jonah! Book of Jonah. (Discover 4 Yourself Ser.). 80p. 1999. pap. 7.99 (*0-7369-0203-1*) Harvest Hse.

***Arthur, Kay & Guest, Lisa.** Digging up the Past Pt. 1: Genesis 1-11. (Discover 4 Yourself Inductive Bible Studies for Kids). 128p. (J). 2000. pap. 8.99 (*0-7369-0374-7*) Harvest Hse.

Arthur, Kay & Lawson, David. That I May Know Him: Philippians & Colossians. LC 98-36529. (International Inductive Study Ser.). 120p. 1998. pap. 5.99 (*1-56507-931-0*) Harvest Hse.

Arthur, Kay & Shearer, Cyndy. Jesus in the Spotlight Pt. 1: John 1-10. (Discover 4 Yourself Ser.). 80p. 1999. pap. 8.99 (*0-7369-0119-1*) Harvest Hse.

Arthur, Kay & Vereen, Bob. Standing Firm in These Last Days: First & Second Thessalonians. (International Inductive Study Ser.). 120p. 1996. pap. 4.99 (*1-56507-387-8*) Harvest Hse.

Arthur, Kay, et al. Can a Busy Christian Develop Her Spiritual Life? Answers to Questions Women Ask About... LC 94-27806. 224p. 1994. pap. 9.99 (*1-55661-518-3*) Bethany Hse.

— Desiring God's Own Heart: Samuel, Kings, Chronicles. LC 96-40300. (International Inductive Study Ser.). 156p. 1997. pap. 5.99 (*1-56507-385-1*) Harvest Hse.

***Arthur, Kay, et al.** Genesis 1: In the Beginning, God... (Illus.). 203p. 1999. 19.50 (*1-888655-64-X*) Precept Ministries.

— Genesis 2: The Fall, the Flood & the Nations. (Illus.). 305p. 1999. 19.50 (*1-888655-65-8*) Precept Ministries.

Arthur, Kay, et al. Jesus--Awesome Power, Awesome Love Pt. 2: John 11-16. (Discover 4 Yourself Inductive Bible Studies for Kids). 128p. (J). 2000. pap. 8.99 (*0-7369-0144-2*) Harvest Hse.

***Arthur, Kay, et al.** Living with Discernment in the End Times. (International Inductive Study Ser.). 128p. 2000. pap. 5.99 (*0-7369-0446-8*) Harvest Hse.

Arthur, Kay, et al. Overcoming Fear & Discouragement. LC 99-21976. (International Inductive Study Ser.). 156p. 1999. 5.99 (*1-56507-702-4*) Harvest Hse.

— Walking in Power, Love & Discipline. LC 99-57269. (International Inductive Study Ser.). 120p. 2000. pap. 5.99 (*1-56507-703-2*) Harvest Hse.

Arthur, Kevyn A. The View from Belmont. LC 98-111041. 230p. 1997. pap. 14.95 (*1-900715-02-3*, Pub. by Peepal Tree Pr) Paul & Co Pubs.

Arthur, Linda. Reading Test: Georgia Regents' 2nd ed. 232p. (C). 1996. pap. text 29.95 (*0-7872-2187-2*) Kendall-Hunt.

***Arthur, Linda & Dallas, Mark.** Reading for College: Georgia Reading Exams. 310p. (C). 1999. per. 36.95 (*0-7872-6151-3*, 41615101) Kendall-Hunt.

***Arthur, Linda B.** Aloha Attire; Hawaiian Dress in the Twentieth Century. (Illus.). 192p. 1999. 49.95 (*0-7643-1015-1*) Schiffer.

Arthur, Linda Boynton. Religion, Dress & the Body. 224p. 1999. pap. 19.50 (*1-85973-297-6*) Berg Pubs.

***Arthur, Linda Boynton, ed.** Religion, Dress & the Body. (Dress, Body, Culture Ser.). (Illus.). 224p. 1999. 65.00 (*1-85973-292-5*, Pub. by Berg Pubs) NYU Pr.

— Undressing Religion: Commitment & Conversion from a Cross-Cultural Perspective. (Dress, Body, Culture Ser.). (Illus.). 224p. 2001. 65.00 (*1-85973-475-8*, Pub. by Berg Pubs); pap. 19.50 (*1-85973-480-4*, Pub. by Berg Pubs) NYU Pr.

Arthur, Linda L. & Mills, Michael T. Making the Most of Your Southern Experience. 208p. (C). 1996. text 28.20 (*0-536-59277-2*) Pearson Custom.

Arthur, Lindsay G. & Arthur, Jean. Twin Cities Uncovered: The Arthur Family. LC 94-48650. 296p. 1995. pap. 16.95 (*1-55622-388-9*, Seaside Pr) Wordware Pub.

Arthur, Lois, jt. auth. see Nolasco, Rob.

Arthur, Lowell J. Attracting Romance: The Secrets to Successful Relationships. LC 92-6891. (Illus.). 208p. 1992. pap. 14.95 (*0-942963-20-2*) Distinctive Pub.

— Attracting Romance: The Secrets to Successful Relationships. (Illus.). 201p. 1992. pap. 15.95 (*1-884180-10-8*) LifeStar.

— The Beginner's Guide to TQM: TQM Made Easy. (QI Coloring Bks.). 48p. 1999. pap., student ed. 9.95 (*1-884180-04-3*) LifeStar.

— Improving Software Quality: An Insider's Guide to TQM. LC 92-23057. 320p. 1992. 69.99 (*0-471-57804-5*) Wiley.

— Love Map Playbook: Charting Your Course to a Loving Relationship. 32p. 1995. student ed. 12.95 (*1-884180-07-8*) LifeStar.

— Measuring Programmer Productivity & Software Quality. LC 84-13176. (Wiley-Interscience Publications). 310p. reprint ed. pap. 96.10 (*0-7837-2381-4*, 204006700006) Bks Demand.

— The QI Coloring Book Instructor Guide: Quantum Improvements Made Easy. (QI Coloring Bks.). (Illus.). 188p. 1997. student ed., ring bd. 39.95 (*1-884180-06-X*) LifeStar.

— The QI Coloring Book Macros for Excel: Graphing Made Easy. (Illus.). 32p. 1999. pap. 59.95 (*1-884180-09-4*) LifeStar.

— The Quality Improvement Book of Bows & Arrows: Quality Planning Made Easy. (QI Coloring Bks.). 48p. 1999. pap., student ed. 9.95 (*1-884180-03-5*) LifeStar.

— The Quality Improvement Coloring Book: Problem Solving Made Easy. (QI Coloring Bks.). 48p. 1999. student ed. 9.95 (*1-884180-01-9*) LifeStar.

— The Quality Improvement Connect-the-Dots Book: SPC Made Easy. (QI Coloring Bks.). 48p. 1999. pap., student ed. 9.95 (*1-884180-02-7*) LifeStar.

Arthur, Lowell J. Rapid Evolutionary Development: Requirements, Prototyping & Software Creation. LC 91-16670. (Series in Software Engineering Practice). 240p. 1991. 59.99 (*0-471-53633-4*) Wiley.

An Asterisk (*) at the beginning of an entry indicates that the title is appearing for the first time.

Arthur, Lowell J. Software Evolution: A Software Maintenance Challenge. LC 87-20972. 272p. 1988. 67.95 (*0-471-62871-9*) Wiley.
— TQM Basics. (C). 1997. pap. text. write for info. (*0-201-63487-2*) Addison-Wesley.
Arthur, Lowell J. & Burns, Edward N. UNIX Shell Programming. 30th ed. 462p. 1994. pap. 39.99 (*0-471-59941-7*) Wiley.
Arthur, Lowell J., et al. UNIX Shell Programming. 4th ed. LC 97-11528. 528p. 1997. pap. 44.99 (*0-471-16894-7*) Wiley.
Arthur, Lowell J., jt. auth. see Engel, Gregory.
***Arthur, Lowell Jay.** Six Sigma Simplified. (QI Coloring Bks.). 128p. 2000. pap. 29.95 (*1-884180-13-2*) LifeStar.
Arthur, M. Navy. text 45.00 (*0-340-68469-0*, Pub. by Hodder & Stought Ltd) Trafalgar.
Arthur, Malcolm, tr. see Perrault, Charles.
Arthur, Margy, jt. auth. see Dever, Pat.
Arthur, Martin, jt. auth. see Arthur, Bev.
Arthur, Mavis E. & Caruso, James R. Video Editing & Post Production. 400p. (C). 1992. pap. text 28.95 (*0-13-946575-8*) P-H.
Arthur, Max. The Busby Babes: Men of Magic. (Illus.). 200p. 1998. pap. 17.95 (*1-84018-069-2*, Pub. by Mainstream Pubng) Trafalgar.
— True Glory/Royal Navy: Jutland to Today. (Illus.). 400p. 1995. 39.95 (*0-340-62301-2*, Pub. by Hodder & Stought Ltd) Trafalgar.
— True Glory/Royal Navy: Jutland to Today. large type ed. (Isis Large Print Ser.). 1997. 29.95 (*0-7531-5430-7*) T T Beeler.
Arthur, Michael A. Stable Isotopes in Sedimentary Geology. LC QE0501.4.N9. (Society of Economic Paleontologists & Mineralogists, Special Publication Ser.: No. 10). (Illus.). 458p. reprint ed. pap. 142.00 (*0-608-15489-X*, 202967600062) Bks Demand.
Arthur, Michael A., jt. ed. see Dean, Walter E.
Arthur, Michael B., et al, eds. Handbook of Career Theory. (Illus.). 572p. (C). 1989. pap. text 47.95 (*0-521-38944-5*) Cambridge U Pr.
Arthur, Michael B. & Rousseau, Denise M., eds. The Boundaryless Careers: A New Employment Principal for a New Organizational Era. (Illus.). 408p. 1996. text 49.95 (*0-19-510014-X*) OUP.
Arthur, Michael B., et al. Working with Careers: Understanding What We Apply & Applying What We Understand. (C). 1983. text 22.50 (*0-914383-00-0*); pap. text 19.00 (*0-914383-01-9*) CU Ctr Career Res.
Arthur, Michael J. & Bailey, Bryan L. Complete Conditioning for Football. LC 97-38483. (Illus.). 296p. 1998. pap. 16.95 (*0-88011-521-1*, PART0521) Human Kinetics.
Arthur, Nigel & Hardy, Clive. The Free Polish Armed Forces Nineteen Forty to Nineteen Forty-Seven: A Pictorial History. (Illus.). 288p. (C). 1989. 70.00 (*1-85563-015-X*, Pub. by Quoin Pub Ltd) St Mut.
Arthur, Patti T. A Sacrament of Holy Communion: A Study Guide for Young People. (Illus.). 16p. 1999. pap. 4.75 (*0-7880-1351-3*) CSS OH.
— Stand up, Sit down, Sing, Pray: Why We Do What We Do in Lutheran Worship. (Illus.). 28p. 1999. pap. 6.25 (*0-7880-1352-1*) CSS OH.
Arthur, Paul. Romans in Northern Campania: Settlement & Land-Use Around the Massico & the Garigliano Basin. (British School at Rome Archaeological Monographs). (Illus.). 137p. 1991. pap. 54.00 (*0-904152-15-4*, Pub. by British Schl Rome) David Brown.
— Wayfinding: People, Signs & Architecture. 238p. 1992. 58.00 (*0-07-551016-2*) McGraw.
Arthur Purdy Stout Society Centennial Symposium on. Proceedings of the Arthur Purdy Stout Society Centennial Symposium on Neoplasia. Sternberg, Stephen S., ed. LC RD0057.. (American Journal of Surgical Pathology Ser.: Vol. 10). (Illus.). 119p. 1986. reprint ed. pap. 36.90 (*0-608-00663-7*, 206121600007) Bks Demand.
***Arthur, Randall.** Betrayal: A Novel. LC 99-12077. 1999. pap. text 12.99 (*0-8499-3738-9*) Word Pub.
Arthur, Randall. Jordan's Crossing. 320p. 1993. pap. 10.99 (*0-88070-582-5*, Multnomah Bks) Multnomah Pubs.
***Arthur, Randall.** Wisdom Hunter. 323p. 1999. pap. 11.99 (*1-57673-230-4*) Multnomah Pubs.
Arthur, Richard. Gangs & Schools. 1992. pap. 16.95 (*1-55691-036-3*, 363) Learning Pubns.
Arthur, Richard L., tr. see Arthur, Rose H.
Arthur, Robert. The Mystery of the Green Ghost. Hitchcock, Alfred, ed. (Three Investigators Ser.: No. 4). (Illus.). 160p. (J). (gr. 3-7). 1985. pap. 3.99 (*0-394-86404-2*, Pub. by Random Bks Yng Read) Random.
— The Mystery of the Screaming Clock. (Three Investigators Ser.: No. 9). (J). (gr. 3-7). 1999. pap. 3.99 (*0-679-82173-2*, Pub. by Random Bks Yng Read) Random.
— The Mystery of the Vanishing Treasure. Hitchcock, Alfred, ed. LC 99-197945. (Three Investigators Ser.: No. 5). (Illus.). (J). (gr. 3-7). 1985. pap. 3.99 (*0-394-86405-0*, Pub. by Random Bks Yng Read) Random.
— The Mystery of the Whispering Mummy. Hitchcock, Alfred, ed. LC 99-192344. (Three Investigators Ser.: No. 3). (Illus.). 160p. (J). (gr. 3-7). 1985. pap. 3.99 (*0-394-86403-4*, Pub. by Random Bks Yng Read) Random.
— The Secret of Skeleton Island. Hitchcock, Alfred, ed. LC 99-169376. (Three Investigators Ser.: No. 6). (Illus.). (J). (gr. 3-7). 1985. pap. 3.99 (*0-394-86406-9*, Pub. by Random Bks Yng Read) Random.
Arthur, Robert A. The Seven Year Itch. 1956. pap. 5.25 (*0-8222-1017-7*) Dramatists Play.
***Arthur, Robert B.** Land Management Agencies: Revenue Sharing Payments to States & Counties. (Illus.). 72p. (C). 1999. pap. text 20.00 (*0-7881-7731-1*) DIANE Pub.
***Arthur, Robert P.** Crazy Horse in Heaven. 320p. 2000. 22.95 (*0-9669930-1-2*, Pub. by Stonehall Pubg) BookMasters.
— Horse Hammock Point. Johnston, Ann Louise, tr. 100p. 2000. pap. 37.95 (*0-9669930-3-9*) Stonehall Pubg.
Arthur, Robert P. Hymn to the Chesapeake. Adams, Joseph D., ed. LC 93-83822. (Illus.). xii, 76p. (Orig.). 1996. reprint ed. pap. 14.95 (*1-880016-12-5*) Road Pubs.
Arthur, Rose H. The Wisdom Goddess: Feminine Motifs in Eight Nag Hammadi Documents. Arthur, Richard L., tr. (Illus.). 256p. (Orig.). 1984. lib. bdg. 49.50 (*0-8191-4171-2*) U Pr of Amer.
Arthur, Ross G., ed. Three Arthurian Romances: Poems from Medieval France. (Everyman Paperback Classics Ser.). 288p. (Orig.). (C). 1996. pap. 7.50 (*0-460-87577-9*, Everyman's Classic Lib) Tuttle Pubng.
Arthur, Ross G., tr. Amadas & Ydoine. LC 93-2715. (Library of Medieval Literature: Vol. 95B).Tr. of Amadas et Ydoine. (ENG & FRE.). 144p. 1993. text 10.00 (*0-8240-4030-9*) Garland.
— Jaufre: An Occitan Arthurian Romance. LC 91-45059. (Library of Medieval Literature: Vol. 88B). 248p. 1992. text 19.00 (*0-8153-0406-4*) Garland.
Arthur, Ross G., tr. see Margolis, Maxine L. & Murphy, Martin F., eds.
Arthur, S. The Story of the West Florida Rebellion. 1977. 30.00 (*0-87511-148-3*) Claitors.
***Arthur, Shirley M.** Surviving Teen Pregnancy: Your Choices, Dreams & Decisions. 1999. 20.25 (*0-8335-7401-9*) Econo-Clad Bks.
— Surviving Teen Pregnancy: Your Choices, Dreams, & Decisions. rev. ed. Lindsay, Jeanne W., ed. LC 95-33735. (Illus.). 192p. (YA). (gr. 6-12). 1996. pap. 11.95 (*1-885356-06-4*) Morning Glory.
Arthur, Stanley C. Old New Orleans: Walking Tours of the French Quarter. rev. ed. Dore, Susan C., ed. LC 89-31668. (Illus.). 160p. 1990. pap. 8.95 (*0-88289-740-3*) Pelican.
***Arthur, Stanley C. & de Kernion, George C.** Old Families of Louisiana. 432p. 1999. reprint ed. pap. 36.50 (*0-8063-4688-4*, Pub. by Clearfield Co) ACCESS Pubs Network.
Arthur, Stephen & Arthur, Julia. Your Life & Times. 50p. 1994. reprint ed. pap. 8.95 (*0-8063-1194-0*, 180) Genealog Pub.
Arthur, Stephen E., et al. The Attorney's Guide to the Seventh Circuit Court of Appeals. 2nd ed. LC 96-41510. 500p. 1996. ring bd. 95.00 (*0-945574-89-4*) State Bar WI.
Arthur, Sue. Evaluation of the 1995 Changes to Disability Working Allowance: A Survey Carried Out on Behalf of the Department of Social Security. LC 98-235683. (In-House Report Ser.). 1997. write for info. (*1-85197-830-5*) Dept of Social Security.
Arthur, Thomas. Bond Financing. 3rd ed. (Corporate Practice Ser.: No. 13). 1992. ring bd. 95.00 (*1-55871-286-0*) BNA.
Arthur, Timothy. The Hand but Not the Heart. LC 78-104405. 1987. reprint ed. pap. text 7.95 (*0-8290-2124-8*); reprint ed. lib. bdg. 21.75 (*0-8398-0061-4*) Irvington.
Arthur, Timothy S. Cast Adrift. (Works of Timothy Shay Arthur). 1989. reprint ed. lib. bdg. 90.00 (*0-7812-1805-5*) Rprt Serv.
— Hidden Wings & Other Stories. LC 72-137719. (American Fiction Reprint Ser.). 1977. reprint ed. 19.95 (*0-8369-7018-7*) Ayer.
— The Lady at Home. (Works of Timothy Shay Arthur). 1989. reprint ed. lib. bdg. 79.00 (*0-7812-1798-9*) Rprt Serv.
— Lights & Shadows of Real Life. (Works of Timothy Shay Arthur). 1989. reprint ed. lib. bdg. 79.00 (*0-685-44733-2*) Rprt Serv.
— The Maiden. (Works of Timothy Shay Arthur). 1989. reprint ed. lib. bdg. 79.00 (*0-7812-1799-7*) Rprt Serv.
— Marriage & Single: or Marriage & Celibacy Contrasted. (Works of Timothy Shay Arthur). 1989. reprint ed. lib. bdg. 79.00 (*0-685-27488-8*) Rprt Serv.
— Pride & Prudence: or The Married Sisters. (Works of Timothy Shay Arthur). 1989. reprint ed. lib. bdg. 79.00 (*0-7812-1800-4*) Rprt Serv.
— Riches Have Wings: A Tale for the Rich & Poor. LC 77-137720. (American Fiction Reprint Ser.). 1977. reprint ed. 19.95 (*0-8369-7019-5*) Ayer.
— Six Nights with the Washingtonians. (Works of Timothy Shay Arthur). 1989. reprint ed. lib. bdg. 79.00 (*0-685-27473-X*) Rprt Serv.
— Sowing the Wind & Other Stories. LC 77-137721. (American Fiction Reprint Ser.). 1977. reprint ed. 19.95 (*0-8369-7020-9*) Ayer.
— Sparing to Spend. (Works of Timothy Shay Arthur). 1989. reprint ed. lib. bdg. 79.00 (*0-7812-1801-2*) Rprt Serv.
— The Strike at Tivoli Mills. (Works of Timothy Shay Arthur). 1989. reprint ed. lib. bdg. 79.00 (*0-7812-1807-1*) Rprt Serv.
— Sunshine at Home & Other Stories. LC 77-137722. (American Fiction Reprint Ser.). 1977. reprint ed. 20.95 (*0-8369-7021-7*) Ayer.
***Arthur, Timothy S.** Ten Nights in a Bar-Room & What I Saw There. 240p. 2000. pap. 14.95 (*1-55709-508-6*) Applewood.
Arthur, Timothy S. Ten Nights in a Barroom & What I Saw There. (Works of Timothy Shay Arthur). 1989. reprint ed. lib. bdg. 79.00 (*0-7812-1802-0*) Rprt Serv.
— Three Years in a Mantrap. (Works of Timothy Shay Arthur). 1989. reprint ed. lib. bdg. 79.00 (*0-7812-1804-7*) Rprt Serv.
— Woman to the Rescue. (Works of Timothy Shay Arthur). 1989. reprint ed. lib. bdg. 79.00 (*0-7812-1806-3*) Rprt Serv.
— The Works of Timothy Shay Arthur, 1809-1885, Set. 1987. reprint ed. lib. bdg. 500.00 (*0-685-18605-9*) Rprt Serv.
Arthur, Vivian. The Infinite Economy: How We Can All Be Rich. (Orig.). 1993. pap. 8.95 (*0-9630804-1-5*) Apollo NM.
Arthur, W. Living Beneath Our Dreams. French, William A., ed. 100p. (Orig.). 1988. pap. 5.95 (*0-317-89767-5*) Circadian Pr.
Arthur, W. Brian. The Economy as a Complex Evolving System. LC 97-37913. (Santa Fe Institute Ser.). (C). 1997. 60.00 (*0-201-95988-7*) Addison-Wesley.
— Economy As an Evolving Complex System II. LC 97-37913. (Proceedings: Vol. 27). 1997. pap. 35.00 (*0-201-32823-2*) Addison-Wesley.
— Increasing Returns & Path Depenedence in the Economy. (Economics, Cognition, & Society Ser.). 224p. (C). 1994. pap. 21.95 (*0-472-06496-7*, 06496) U of Mich Pr.
Arthur, Wallace. Mechanisms of Morphological Evolution: A Combined Genetic, Developmental & Ecological Approach. LC 83-16993. (Illus.). 291p. reprint ed. pap. 90.30 (*0-7837-1882-9*, 204208300001) Bks Demand.
— The Origin of Animal Body Plans: A Study in Evolutionary Developmental Biology. (Illus.). 352p. (C). 1997. text 74.95 (*0-521-55014-9*) Cambridge U Pr.
— The Origin of Animal Body Plans: A Study in Evolutionary Developmental Biology. (Illus.). 352p. (C). 2000. pap. write for info. (*0-521-77928-6*) Cambridge U Pr.
Arthur, William. An Etymological Dictionary of Family & Christian Names: With an Essay on Their Derivation & Import. LC 89-63009. 300p. 1990. reprint ed. lib. bdg. 42.00 (*1-55888-839-X*) Omnigraphics Inc.
Arthur, William J. A Financial Planning Model for Private Colleges: A Research Report. LC 72-92879. 132p. reprint ed. pap. 41.00 (*0-608-16124-1*, 201780700008) Bks Demand.
Arthur, Zinn & Hornsey, Pat. Shooting Superstars: Me, My Camera, & the Show-Biz Legends. (Illus.). 240p. (C). 1989. 24.95 (*0-685-27244-3*) Artique Pr.
Arthurs, A. M. Probability Theory. (Library of Mathematics). 88p. 1973. ring bd. 29.95 (*0-7100-4359-7*, Chap & Hall CRC) CRC Pr.
Arthurs, H. W. Collective Bargaining by Public Employee Unions in Canada: Five Models. LC 70-634394. (Comparative Studies in Public Employment Labor Relations Ser.). 1971. 10.00 (*0-87736-005-7*); pap. 5.00 (*0-87736-006-5*) U of Mich Inst Labor.
— Without the Law: Administrative Justice & Legal Pluralism in 19th-Century England. 328p. 1985. text 35.00 (*0-8020-5654-7*) U of Toronto Pr.
Arthurs, H. W., et al. Labour Law & Industrial Relations in Canada. 4th ed. LC 93-42426. 1993. 144.00 (*90-6544-777-6*) Kluwer Law Intl.
— Labour Law & Industrial Relations in Canada. 4th ed. 340p. 1993. pap. 54.00 (*0-409-91620-X*, MICHIE) LEXIS Pub.
Arthurs, Harry W., jt. auth. see Stager, David A.
***Arthurs, Jane & Grant, Ian, eds.** Crash Cultures. 280p. 2000. 60.00 (*1-85343-492-2*, Pub. by Free Assoc Bks); pap. 25.00 (*1-85343-493-0*, Pub. by Free Assoc Bks) Intl Spec Bk.
Arthurson, Ian. The Perkin Warbeck Conspiracy, 1491-1499. (Illus.). 256p. 1998. pap. 19.95 (*0-7509-1610-9*, Pub. by Sutton Pub Ltd) Intl Pubs Mktg.
Arthursson, Elizabeth. The Year of the Rams. large type ed. 1991. 27.99 (*0-7089-2546-4*) Ulverscroft.
***Arthus-Bertrand, Yann.** Earth from Above. LC 99-23917. (Illus.). 408p. 1999. 65.00 (*0-8109-3267-9*, Pub. by Abrams) Time Warner.
Arthus-Bertrand, Yann. Good Breeding LC 99-11062. 180p. 1999. 49.50 (*0-8109-4132-5*, Pub. by Abrams) Time Warner.
— New York from the Air. LC 98-26701. (Illus.). 160p. 1998. 45.00 (*0-8109-3692-5*, Pub. by Abrams) Time Warner.
Arthus, Gothard. Dialogues in the English & Malaiane Languages. Spalding, A., tr. LC 74-80160. (English Experience Ser.: No. 640). 1974. reprint ed. 20.00 (*90-221-0640-3*) Walter J Johnson.
Arthus, Mark G. Integrated Compliance & Total Risk Management: Creating a Bankwide Compliance System That Works. 250p. (C). 1994. text 50.00 (*1-55738-397-9*, Irwn Prfssnl) McGraw-Hill Prof.
Artiaga, Lucio & Davis, Lloyd D. Algorithms & Their Computer Solutions. LC 71-181581. (Merrill Mathematics Ser.). xii, 367 p. 1972. write for info. (*0-675-09151-9*) Mrrill.
Artial Order Methods in Verification Staff, et al. Partial Order Methods in Verification: Workshop on Partial Order Methods in Verification, July 24-26, 1996, Princeton University. LC 96-48739. (Dimacs Series in Discrete Mathematics & Theoretical Computer Science: Vol. 29). 403p. 1997. text 85.00 (*0-8218-0579-7*, DIMACS/29) Am Math.
Artiba, A., et al. Introduction to Intelligent Simulation: The Rao Language. LC 98-21507. 516p. 1998. write for info. (*0-7923-8176-9*) Kluwer Academic.
Artibise, A. Borderlands: Essays in Canadian-American Relations. Lecker, Robert, ed. 328p. (C). 1991. pap. text 45.00 (*1-55022-133-7*, Pub. by ECW) Genl Dist Srvs.
Artibise, A. F. Winnipeg: A Social History of Urban Growth, 1874-1914. (Illus.). 400p. 1975. 44.95 (*0-7735-0202-5*, Pub. by McG-Queens Univ Pr) CUP Services.
Artibise, Alan F., ed. Interdisciplinary Approaches to Canadian Society: A Guide to the Literature. 164p. (C). 1990. 65.00 (*0-7735-0763-9*, Pub. by McG-Queens Univ Pr); pap. 24.95 (*0-7735-0788-4*, Pub. by McG-Queens Univ Pr) CUP Services.
Article 19 (Organization) Staff. Information Freedom & Censorship: World Report, 1991 - Article 19 International Centre for Censorship. LC 91-27214. 487p. reprint ed. pap. 151.00 (*0-608-08897-8*, 206953200004) Bks Demand.
— The Press under Siege: Censorship in Indonesia. LC 95-126155. ii, 31 p. 1994. write for info. (*1-870798-62-7*) Article Nineteen.
Article 19 (Organization) Staff, jt. auth. see Committee to Protect Journalist Staff.
Article 19 Staff, jt. auth. see Thompson, Mark.
Articola, George A. Partial Differential Equations & Boundary Value Problems with Maple V. LC 97-48543. (Illus.). 628p. (C). 1998. pap. text 44.95 (*0-12-064475-4*) Morgan Kaufmann.
Artieda, Julio, jt. ed. see Pastor, Maria A.
Artificial Intelligence Conference Staff. Agents & Multi-Agent Systems: Formalisms, Methodologies & Applications: Based on the AI '97 Workshops on Commonsense Reasoning, Intelligent Agents, & Distributed Artificial Intelligence, Perth, Australia, November 30-December 1, 1997. Pagnucco, Maurice et al, eds. LC 98-29400. (Lecture Notes in Artificial Intelligence Ser.: Vol. 1441). xii, 241p. 1998. pap. 49.00 (*3-540-64769-4*) Spr-Verlag.
Artificial Ventilation Symposium Staff. Proceedings of the Artificial Ventilation Symposium, Paris, 1969. Minkowski, A. et al, eds. (Biology of the Neonate Ser.: Vol. 16, No. 1-3). 1970. pap. 52.25 (*3-8055-0755-0*) S Karger.
Artigal, Josep M. The Catalan Immersion Program: A European Point of View. DiPietro, Robert J., ed. (Second Language Learning Ser.: Vol. 4). 128p. (C). 1991. text 73.25 (*0-89391-747-8*) Ablx Pub.
Artigas De Sierra, Ione M. Las Bodas del Gallo Perico (On the Way to the Wedding) (Superbks./Superlibros). (SPA.). (J). (gr. k-1). pap. 6.95 (*0-88272-489-4*) Santillana.
— Las Bodas del Gallo Perico (On the Way to the Wedding) (Superbks./Superlibros). (J). (gr. k-1). 1989. pap. 6.95 (*0-88272-491-6*) Santillana.
— Las Bodas del Gallo Perico (On the Way to the Wedding), Big Book. (Superbks./Superlibros). (SPA.). (J). (gr. k-1). 21.95 (*0-88272-488-6*) Santillana.
— Las Bodas del Gallo Perico (On the Way to the Wedding), Big Book. (Superbks./Superlibros). (J). (gr. k-1). 1989. 21.95 (*0-88272-490-8*) Santillana.
— La Chivita del Cebollar (The Goat in the Onion Patch) (Superbks./Superlibros). (J). (gr. k-1). 21.95 (*0-88272-486-X*); pap. 6.95 (*0-88272-487-8*) Santillana.
— La Chivita del Cebollar (The Goat in the Onion Patch), Big Book. (Superbks./Superlibros). (SPA.). (J). (gr. k-1). 21.95 (*0-88272-484-3*) Santillana.
Artigas, J., et al, eds. The Central Nervous System in AIDS. (Illus.). 250p. 1993. write for info. (*3-540-55839-X*) Spr-Verlag.
***Artigas, Mariano.** The Ethical Nature of Karl Popper's Theory of Knowledge: Including Popper's Unpublished Comments on Bartley & Critical Rationalism. LC 99-17014. (Illus.). 153p. (C). 1999. pap. text 26.95 (*0-8204-4606-8*) P Lang Pubng.
— The Mind of the Universe: The Current Worldview & Our Image of God. LC 99-37740. 475p. 1999. 22.95 (*1-890151-32-7*) Templeton Fnd.
Artigaud, Frank, jt. auth. see Doroy, Jean Francois.
Artigue, Ray J., jt. auth. see Matera, Frances R.
Artiles, Alfredo J. & Duran, Grace Z., eds. Reducing Disproportionate Representation of Culturally Diverse Students in Special & Gifted Education. LC 97-17073. 98p. (Orig.). 1997. pap. text 26.95 (*0-86586-297-4*, P5219) Coun Exc Child.
Artiles, Alfredo J. & Hallahan, Daniel P., eds. Special Education in Latin America: Experiences & Issues. LC 95-14429. 312p. 1995. 69.50 (*0-275-94667-3*, Praeger Pubs) Greenwood.
Artiles, Alfredo J. & Trent, Stanley C., eds. Building a Knowledge Base on Culturally Diverse Students with Learning Disabilities: The Need to Enrich Research with a Sociocultural Perspective. 65p. 1997. pap. write for info. (*0-8058-9874-3*) L Erlbaum Assocs.
Artime, Rafael, et al. Havana's City of Marble: The Necropolis of Colon.Tr. of Ciudad de Marmol de la Habana: La Necropolis de Colon. (SPA., Illus.). 148p. 1998. pap. 40.00 (*0-9665841-0-4*) Perennial Pr.
***Artimo Publishing Staff.** Viktor & Rolf. (Illus.). 150p. 1999. pap. 50.00 (*90-75380-16-X*, 920263, Pub. by Artimo Fnd) Dist Art Pubs.
Artimovich, Patricia, et al, eds. Stars, Stripes & Statutes: A Compendium of State Flag & Related Laws. 68p. (Orig.). 1992. pap. 4.95 (*0-934021-25-2*) Natl Flag Foun.
Artin, E. Algebraic Numbers & Algebraic Functions. xiv, 350p. 1967. pap. text 168.00 (*0-677-00635-7*) Gordon & Breach.
— Geometric Algebra. (Classics Library). 224p. 1988. pap. 84.95 (*0-471-60839-4*) Wiley.
Artin, Emil. Collected Papers. Lang, Serge A. & Tate, J. T., eds. (Illus.). 576p. 1988. 95.95 (*0-387-90686-X*) Spr-Verlag.
Artin, Emil & Milgram, Arthur N. Galois Theory: Lectures Delivered at the University of Notre Dame. unabridged ed. LC 97-51372. (Notre Dame Mathematical Lectures: No. 2). (Illus.). 86p. 1998. reprint ed. pap. 4.95 (*0-486-62342-4*) Dover.

An Asterisk (*) at the beginning of an entry indicates that the title is appearing for the first time.

A

Artin, M. & Mumford, D., eds. Oscar Zariski - Collected Papers Vol. 2: Holomorphic Functions & Linear Systems. (Mathematicians of Our Time Ser.). 1973. 60.00 (*0-262-01038-0*) MIT Pr.

Artin, Michael. Algebra. 672p. 1995. 89.33 (*0-13-004763-5*, 540201) P-H.

Artin, Michael, et al, eds. Duration & Change: Fifty Years at Oberwolfach. LC 94-28935. 1994. 108.95 (*0-387-57214-7*) Spr-Verlag.

— Duration & Change: Fifty Years at Oberwolfach. LC 94-28935. 1994. write for info. (*3-540-57214-7*) Spr-Verlag.

Artin, Michael & Mazur, Barry. Etale Homotopy. LC 75-88710. (Lecture Notes in Mathematics Ser.: Vol. 100). (Orig.). 1986. 39.95 (*0-387-04619-4*) Spr-Verlag.

Artin, Michael & Mumford, David, eds. Contributions to Algebraic Geometry in Honor of Oscar Zariski. LC 79-88169. (Illus.). 524p. reprint ed. pap. 162.50 (*0-8357-6602-0*, 203524700094) Bks Demand.

Artin, Michael & Tate, John, eds. Arithmetic, Vol. 1. (Progress in Mathematics Ser.). 350p. 1983. 60.50 (*0-8176-3132-1*) Birkhauser.

— Geometry: Papers Dedicated to I. R. Shafarevich on the Occasion of His Sixtieth Birthday, Vol. 2. (Progress in Mathematics Ser.: No. 36). 450p. 1991. 60.50 (*0-8176-3133-X*) Birkhauser.

Artin, Tom. The Allegory of Adventure: Reading Chretien's "Erec & Yvain" LC 73-687. 264p. 1974. 18.00 (*0-8387-1257-6*) Bucknell U Pr.

Artingstall, Kathryn. Practical Aspects of Munchausen by Proxy & Munchausen Syndrome Investigation. LC 98-13159. (Practical Aspects of Criminal & Forensic Investigation Ser.). 384p. 1998. boxed set 74.95 (*0-8493-8162-2*, 8162) CRC Pr.

Artinian, Barbara M. & Conger, Margaret M., eds. Integrating Theory & Practice: The Intersystem Model. LC 96-45795. 358p. 1997. 52.00 (*0-8039-5558-8*); pap. 24.95 (*0-8039-5559-6*) Sage.

Artinian, Vrej-Armen, ed. Historical Atlas of Armenia. LC 86-675028. (Illus.). 1987. pap. 25.00 (*0-9617933-0-9*) Armenian Natl Educ.

Artino, Ralph. Introduction to Boolean Algebra for Computer Scientists & Engineers. 80p. (C). 1994. per. 14.95 (*0-8403-6750-3*) Kendall-Hunt.

Artino, Ralph A., et al. Contest Problem Book IV: Annual High School Examinations 1973-1982. LC 82-51076. (New Mathematical Library: No. 29). 184p. 1983. pap. text 13.00 (*0-88385-629-8*, NML-29) Math Assn.

Artino, Ralph A., jt. auth. see Barros-Neto, Jose.

Artis. Aspirations to Manifestations: From the Womb to the Void. LC 93-8430. 106p. 1993. pap. 13.50 (*0-938493-20-5*) Hulogosi Inc.

Artis, Denise. Odour Nuisances & Their Control. 1984. pap. 90.00 (*0-7219-1000-9*, Pub. by Scientific) St Mut.

Artis, Denise & Houghton, John T. SWOT Land Law. 190p. (C). 1990. 80.00 (*1-85431-053-4*, Pub. by Blackstone Pr) St Mut.

— SWOT Land Law. 4th ed. 202p. 1995. pap. 22.00 (*1-85431-383-5*, Pub. by Blackstone Pr) Gaunt.

— SWOT Land Law. 5th ed. 205p. 1998. pap. 24.00 (*1-85431-806-3*, Pub. by Blackstone Pr) Gaunt.

Artis Inc. Staff, jt. auth. see Wyatt, Nancy Fitzpatrick.

Artis, M. J. & Miller, M. H., eds. Essays in Fiscal & Monetary Economics. 1981. 45.00 (*0-19-829001-2*) OUP.

Artis, M. J., jt. auth. see Taylor, M. P.

Artis, Michael, ed. The U. K. Economy. 14th ed. (Illus.). 408p. 1996. pap. text 35.00 (*0-19-877511-3*) OUP.

***Artis, Michael J., et al, eds.** The Euro. LC 99-54586. 344p. 2000. 100.00 (*0-415-21710-5*) Routledge.

Artis, Mike J. & Lee, Norman, eds. The Economics of the European Union: Policy & Analysis. 2nd ed. LC 97-8966. (Illus.). 458p. 1997. pap. text 39.95 (*0-19-877560-1*) OUP.

— The Economics of the European Union: Policy & Analysis. 2nd ed. LC 97-8966. (Illus.). 458p. (C). 1997. text 92.00 (*0-19-877561-X*) OUP.

Artis, Nellie T., jt. ed. see Finger, J. Michael.

***Artisien-Maksimenko, Patrick.** Multinationals in Eastern Europe. LC 99-54921. 304p. 2000. 75.00 (*0-312-23131-8*) St Martin.

Artiss, David. Theodor Storm: Studies in Ambivalence. Symbol & Myth in his Narrative Fiction. (German Language & Literature Monographs: No. 5). xix, 215p. 1978. 52.00 (*90-272-0965-0*) J Benjamins Pubng Co.

Artiss, Kenneth L. Mistake Making: The Addiction to Shame. LC 93-3020. (Illus.). 302p. (C). 1993. text 22.50 (*0-9615865-1-6*) Psych Bks.

— Mistake Making: With Sections on Stuttering & Psychotherapy. 298p. 1996. pap. text 34.50 (*0-7618-0309-2*) U Pr of Amer.

— Therapeutic Studies. (C). 1986. text 22.50 (*0-9615865-0-8*) Psych Bks.

Artist Consortium Staff. SoHo Guide. 118p. 1995. 10.00 (*1-886016-01-1*) SoHo Prtnship.

— Soho Journal, 94-95. Bergman-Ungar, Robert, ed. (Journal Ser.). 176p. 1994. pap. 20.00 (*1-886016-00-3*) SoHo Prtnship.

Artist, J. William. Far East Trade & Tourism: Is Colorado Serious? (Issue Papers: No. 15-87). 8p. 1987. pap. text 8.00 (*1-57655-014-1*) Independ Inst.

Artistic Creations Staff, ed. see Wilson, Stephanie E.

Artists' Services Staff. Sektor. (Illus.). 256p. (Orig.). Date not set. 39.00 (*3-931126-07-2*, Pub. by Die Gestalten); pap. 32.99 (*3-931126-08-0*, Pub. by Die Gestalten) Consort Bk Sales.

Artl, Karen A., ed. see Hafer, Todd.

Artley, Alexandra, ed. Artist, Architect & Patron. (Illus.). 96p. 1980. 22.50 (*0-85139-075-7*) Eastview.

Artley, Bob. A Book of Chores: As Remembered by a Former Kid. Gruchow, Paul, ed. LC 89-84032. (Illus.). 100p. 1989. reprint ed. pap. 12.95 (*0-8138-1069-8*) Iowa St U Pr.

— Cartoons: From the Newspaper Series Memories of a Former Kid. (Illus.). 192p. 1988. reprint ed. pap. 12.95 (*0-8138-1068-X*) Iowa St U Pr.

— Cartoons II: From the Newspaper Series Memories of a Former Kid. (Illus.). 190p. 1988. pap. 12.95 (*0-8138-1067-1*) Iowa St U Pr.

— Country Christmas: As Remembered by a Former Kid. LC 94-13179. (Illus.). 40p. 1994. 16.95 (*0-8138-2778-7*) Iowa St U Pr.

— A Country School: Marion No. 7. LC 89-15516. (Illus.). 104p. (Orig.). 1989. pap. 12.95 (*0-8138-1077-9*) Iowa St U Pr.

— Country Things. LC 94-21239. (Illus.). 136p. 1994. pap. 12.95 (*0-8138-2650-0*) Iowa St U Pr.

— Ginny: A Love Remembered. LC 93-1485. (Illus.). 278p. 1993. 24.95 (*0-8138-2104-5*) Iowa St U Pr.

— Living with Cows. (Illus.). 104p. (Orig.). 1996. pap. 14.95 (*0-8138-2648-9*) Iowa St U Pr.

— Memories of a Former Kid. LC 79-1908. (Illus.). 96p. 1978. pap. 12.95 (*0-8138-1070-1*) Iowa St U Pr.

— More Country Things. LC 95-22049. (Illus.). 152p. (Orig.). 1995. pap. 12.95 (*0-8138-2451-6*) Iowa St U Pr.

***Artley, Bob.** Once upon a Farm. LC 00-26270. (Illus.). 2000. 21.95 (*1-56554-753-5*) Pelican.

Artlip, Mary A., et al. The New American Family: Tools for Strengthening Step-Families. LC 92-81392. 272p. 1993. pap. 10.95 (*0-914984-44-6*) Starburst.

Artman, Charles E. Food Costs & City Consumers. LC 70-76687. (Columbia University. Studies in the Social Sciences: No. 280). reprint ed. 20.00 (*0-404-51280-1*) AMS Pr.

Artman, E Townsend. Toasters, 1909-1960. (Illus.). 176p. 1996. pap. 29.95 (*0-88740-956-3*) Schiffer.

Artman, Fran, jt. auth. see Artman, John.

Artman, John. Ancient Greece. (Gifted Learning Ser.). 64p. (J). (gr. 4-8). 1991. 8.99 (*0-86653-583-7*, GA1310) Good Apple.

— Ancient Rome. (Gifted Learning Ser.). 64p. (J). (gr. 4-8). 1991. 8.99 (*0-86653-638-8*, GA1343) Good Apple.

— Collectible Correctibles. (Illus.). 64p. (J). (gr. 4-8). 1984. student ed. 8.99 (*0-86653-214-5*, GA 559) Good Apple.

— Cowboys: An Activity Book. 64p. (J). (gr. 4 up). 1982. 8.99 (*0-86653-068-1*, GA 417) Good Apple.

— Daily Doses of Thinking for Fall: September, October, November. (Illus.). 96p. (J). (gr. 3-9). 1998. pap. text 5.95 (*1-56490-078-9*, Turning Two Thousand) G Grimm Assocs.

— Explorers. (Illus.). 64p. (YA). (gr. 4 up). 1986. 8.99 (*0-86653-340-0*, GA 796) Good Apple.

— Good Apple & Reading Fun. 144p. (J). (gr. 3-7). 1981. 13.99 (*0-86653-046-0*, GA 278) Good Apple.

— Great Explorers. (Illus.). 16p. (J). (gr. 5-8). 1997. teacher ed. 15.95 (*1-56490-033-9*) G Grimm Assocs.

— Indians: An Activity Book. 64p. (J). (gr. 4 up). 1981. 8.99 (*0-86653-012-6*, GA 240) Good Apple.

— Insights. 112p. (J). (gr. 4-8). 1989. 12.99 (*0-86653-511-X*, GA1096) Good Apple.

— Native Americans. (Illus.). 16p. (J). (gr. 5-8). 1997. teacher ed. 15.95 (*1-56490-032-0*) G Grimm Assocs.

— Pioneers. (Illus.). 64p. (J). (gr. 4 up). 1987. pap. 8.99 (*0-86653-401-6*, GA 1027) Good Apple.

— Slanguage. 80p. (J). (gr. 4 up). 1980. 9.99 (*0-916456-60-9*, GA 175) Good Apple.

Artman, John & Artman, Fran. Daily Doses of Nostalgia Fall. (Illus.). 192p. (Orig.). 1996. pap. text 12.95 (*1-56490-019-3*) G Grimm Assocs.

— Daily Doses of Nostalgia Spring. (Illus.). 192p. (Orig.). 1996. pap. text 12.95 (*1-56490-021-5*) G Grimm Assocs.

— Daily Doses of Nostalgia Summer. (Illus.). 192p. (Orig.). 1996. pap. text 12.95 (*1-56490-022-3*) G Grimm Assocs.

— Daily Doses of Nostalgia Winter. (Illus.). 192p. (Orig.). 1996. pap. text 12.95 (*1-56490-020-7*) G Grimm Assocs.

Artman, John & Grimm, Gary. The Basic Needs of Man. (Illus.). 48p. (J). (gr. 3-9). 1998. pap. text 7.95 (*1-56490-075-4*, Turning Two Thousand) G Grimm Assocs.

— Understanding a Millennium. (Illus.). 48p. (J). (gr. 3-9). 1998. pap. text 7.95 (*1-56490-077-0*, Turning Two Thousand) G Grimm Assocs.

— Writing to the Future. (Illus.). (J). (gr. 3-9). 1998. pap. text 7.95 (*1-56490-076-2*, Turning Two Thousand) G Grimm Assocs.

Artman, John, jt. auth. see Grimm, Gary.

Artman, John H. The Write Stuff! (Illus.). 64p. (J). (gr. 4-8). 1985. student ed. 8.99 (*0-86653-273-0*, GA 681) Good Apple.

Artman, L. P., Jr. Key West Guided Tour: Thirty-Two Points of Interest with Illustrations & Maps. (Illus.). 1975. pap. 3.00 (*1-880661-16-0*) L P Artman.

— Key West History. 52p. 1969. pap. 7.00 (*1-880661-09-8*) L P Artman.

Artman, Michael. Developmental Changes in Myocardial Inotropic Responsiveness. (Medical Intelligence Unit Ser.). 118p. 1994. 99.00 (*1-57059-127-X*, LN9127) Landes Bioscience.

Artmann, B. Euclid: The Creation of Mathematics. (Illus.). 307p. 1999. 49.95 (*0-387-98423-2*) Spr-Verlag.

Artmann, Benno. The Concept of Number: From Quaternions to Monads & Topological Fields. 1988. text 52.95 (*0-470-21323-X*) P-H.

Artmann, H. C. The Quest for Dr. U. Green, Malcolm, tr. from GER. 120p. Date not set. reprint ed. pap. 14.99 (*0-947757-56-2*) Serpents Tail.

Artmann, Joseph, et al. Issues & Technology in the Management of Impacted Wildlife: Proceedings of a National Symposium (1982) 250p. 1984. pap. 25.00 (*0-916055-01-9*) Thorne Eco Inst.

Artmov, A. P. Rocket & Artillery Technology. (GER & RUS.). 1982. 65.00 (*0-8288-1909-2*, M15457) Fr & Eur.

Artner, Stephen J. A Change of Course: The West German Social Democrats & NATO, 1957-1961, 127. LC 84-15786. (Contributions in Political Science Ser.: No. 127). 242p. 1985. 59.95 (*0-313-24701-3*, ACC/, Greenwood Pr) Greenwood.

Artobolevskiy, S. S. Regional Policy in Europe. 300p. 1995. pap. text 39.95 (*1-85302-308-6*) Taylor & Francis.

Artof, Sue. Don't Smoke the Joists! 1995. 9.95 (*0-930030-62-1*) ProStar Pubns.

Artof, Susan, ed. see Druxman, Michael B.

Artof, Susan D. Boat Naming Made Simple: The Complete Book. 3rd rev. ed. LC 99-10787. (Boating Made Simple Ser.). (Illus.). 196p. 1999. pap. 12.95 (*1-889198-06-4*) Ctr Pr CA.

— The Little Book of No: Secrets for Success. LC 96-20324. (Psycho Silly Act Bk.). (Orig.). pap. 7.95 (*0-9626888-6-X*) Ctr Pr CA.

— Sailing: A Parent's Handbook for Junior Sailing. LC 94-70066. (Boating Made Simple Ser.). (Illus.). 120p. (Orig.). 1993. pap. 10.95 (*0-9626888-3-5*) Ctr Pr CA.

— Writing for Pleasure: Use of Personal Writing for Personal Growth. 2nd ed. 224p. 1992. 12.95 (*0-9626888-1-9*) Ctr Pr CA.

Artola Gallego, Miguel. Historia de Espana No. 32: La Espana de Fernando VII: La Guerra de Independencia y los Origenes del Regimen Constitucional. 1036p. 1992. 189.50 (*84-239-4980-X*) Elliots Bks.

Artos, Allen. Arthur: The King of Light. (Illus.). 100p. (Orig.). 1986. pap. 8.00 (*0-934852-29-4*) Lorien Hse.

— The Astrolabe: And Other Phenomenal Wonders. (Illus.). 40p. 1996. pap. 6.00 (*0-934852-43-X*) Lorien Hse.

— Jonah. 52p. (Orig.). 1984. pap. 3.50 (*0-934852-24-3*) Lorien Hse.

***Artress, Lauren.** The Sand Labyrinth: Meditation at Your Fingertips. LC 00-27046. 2000. pap. 44.95 (*1-885203-99-3*) Jrny Editions.

Artress, Lauren. Walking a Sacred Path: Rediscovering the Labyrinth As a Spiritual Tool. 1996. pap. 11.00 (*1-57322-547-9*, Riverhd Trade) Berkley Pub.

Arts. Gammer Gurton's Needle in Three Acts. (Illus.). 44p. 1970. pap. 4.00 (*0-88680-066-8*) I E Clark.

— Gammer Gurton's Needle in Three Acts: Director's Script. (Illus.). 44p. 1970. 10.00 (*0-88680-067-6*) I E Clark.

Arts, Bas. Political Influence of Global NGOs: Case Studies on the Climate & Biodiversity Conventions. 300p. 1998. pap. 29.95 (*90-5727-012-9*, Pub. by Intl Bks) Paul & Co Pubs.

Arts Council of England Staff, jt. auth. see Ridgman, Jeremy.

Arts Council Of Great Britain. Pictorial History of Shakespearean Production in England, 1576-1946. Byrne, M. St. Clare, ed. LC 70-109640. (Select Bibliographies Reprint Ser.). 1977. 13.95 (*0-8369-5249-9*) Ayer.

Arts Council Staff, jt. auth. see Thomas, Peter.

Arts, Herwig. God, the Christian & Human Suffering. 104p. (Orig.). 1993. pap. 7.95 (*0-8146-2100-7*) Liturgical Pr.

Arts Inc. Staff. The Greater Los Angeles Arts Resource Directory: And Arts & Education Guide. 4th rev. ed. LC 99-72384. 280p. 1999. pap. 19.95 (*0-9664318-0-4*) Arts Inc Calif.

***Arts, Karin.** Integrating Human Rights into Development Cooperation: The Case of the Lombe Convention. LC 00-24914. 472p. 2000. 133.00 (*90-411-1356-8*) Kluwer Law Intl.

***Arts, Karin & Thomasma, David C.** Integrating Human Rights into Development Cooperation: The Case. 472p. 2000. pap. 133.00 (*90-411-1357-6*) Kluwer Law Intl.

Arts Leisure Staff. Christmas with Southern Living Cookbook , Vol. 3. 1999. 29.95 (*0-8487-1895-X*) Oxmoor Hse.

— Cooking Light: Annual Recipies, 1999 Edition. (Illus.). 368p. 1999. 34.95 (*0-8487-1801-1*) Oxmoor Hse.

— Fabric Lovers Holiday Creations. 1999. pap. 14.95 (*0-8487-1909-3*) Oxmoor Hse.

— Quick Cozy Flannel Quilts. 64p. 1999. pap. 9.95 (*0-8487-1948-4*) Oxmoor Hse.

— Quick Quilts from Your Scrap Bag. 144p. 1999. pap. 19.95 (*0-8487-1907-7*) Oxmoor Hse.

Arts, M. T. & Wainman, B. Lipids in Freshwater Ecosystems. (Illus.). 384p. 1998. 69.95 (*0-387-98505-0*) Spr-Verlag.

Arts, P. L. Tetsubin. (Illus.). 582p. 1987. 39.50 (*90-72370-01-5*, Pub. by Bamboo Pub) Antique Collect.

Arts, W., ed. see Raaij, W. F. van.

Arts, Wilhelmus A. & Halman, Loek. New Directions in Quantitative Comparative Sociology. LC 99-21487. (International Studies in Sociology & Social Anthropology Ser.). 1999. write for info. (*90-04-11411-4*) Brill Academic Pubs.

Artsimovich, L. A. A Physicist's ABC on Plasma. 124p. 1985. 39.75 (*0-7855-1183-0*, Pub. by Collets); pap. 30.00 (*0-7855-2959-4*, Pub. by Collets) St Mut.

— Physicist's ABC on Plasma. 124p. (C). 1978. 40.00 (*0-7855-4968-4*, Pub. by Collets) St Mut.

Artson, Bradley S. It's a Mitzvah! Step-by-Step to Jewish Living. Siegel, Adam, ed. (Illus.). 256p. (Orig.). 1995. pap. 18.00 (*0-87441-585-3*) Behrman.

Artsruni, Thomas. History of the House of Artsrunik. Thomson, Robert W., ed. & tr. by. LC 85-3228. (Byzantine Texts in Translation Ser.). 416p. reprint ed. pap. 129.00 (*0-608-10563-5*, 207118300009) Bks Demand.

— History of the House of Artsrunik. LC 91-12987. (Classical Armenian Texts Ser.). 372p. 1991. reprint ed. 60.00 (*0-88206-074-0*) Caravan Bks.

Artsybashev, Mikhail P. Millionaire. Pinkerton, Percy, tr. LC 78-103491. (Short Story Index Reprint Ser.). 1977. 20.95 (*0-8369-3233-1*) Ayer.

— Tales of the Revolution. Pinkerton, Percy, tr. 1977. 19.95 (*0-8369-4168-3*) Ayer.

Artto, E. Cash-Based Profitability & Financing of Industries: A Study of Finland & Sweden. 158p. 1981. text 46.50 (*91-22-00442-4*) Coronet Bks.

Artto, Karlos A., jt. ed. see Kahkonen, Kalle.

Artucio, Alejandlo, jt. auth. see Fragoso, Heleno C.

Artucio, Alejandro. A Breach of Impurity: The Trial for the Murder of Jesuits in El Salvador Report of the Trial Observer of the International Commission of Jurists. LC 92-26144. (Illus.). 89p. Date not set. reprint ed. pap. 30.00 (*0-608-20636-9*, 207207200003) Bks Demand.

— The Trial of Macias in Equatorial Guinea: The Story of a Dictatorship. LC DT0620.8.A78. 70p. reprint ed. pap. 30.00 (*0-608-18110-2*, 203270900081) Bks Demand.

Artuk, Simone L. Une Descente aux Enfers: Images de la Mort et de la Destruction dans "Les Chants de Maldoror" de Lautreamont. (Publications Universitaires Europeennes Ser.: Series 13, Vol. 206). (FRE.). 148p. 1995. 28.95 (*3-906754-10-3*, Pub. by P Lang) P Lang Pubng.

Artus, P., et al. International Macroeconomic Modelling for Policy Decisions. 1986. lib. bdg. 164.00 (*90-247-3201-8*) Kluwer Academic.

Artusi, Giovanni M. L' Arte Del Contraponto. 80p. 1969. reprint ed. write for info. (*0-318-71579-1*) G Olms Pubs.

Artusi, Pellegrino. Art of Eating Well: An Italian Cookbook. Phillips, Kyle, tr. (Illus.). 384p. 1996. 29.95 (*0-679-43056-3*) Random.

— Science in the Kitchen & the Art of Eating Well. 750p. (C). 1997. 32.50 (*1-56886-040-4*); pap. 19.95 (*1-56886-039-0*) Marsilio Pubs.

Artusio, Joseph F., Jr., jt. auth. see Yao, Fun-Sun F.

Artuso, Anthony. Drugs of Natural Origin: Economic & Policy Aspects of Discovery, Development, & Marketing. LC 97-19503. (Illus.). 201p. (C). 1997. pap. 24.95 (*0-7890-0414-3*, Pharmctl Prods) Haworth Pr.

— Drugs of Natural Origin: Economic & Policy Aspects of Discovery, Development, & Marketing. LC 97-19503. (Illus.). 201p. (C). 1997. 39.95 (*0-7890-0123-3*, Pharmctl Prods) Haworth Pr.

Artuso, R., et al. Chaos, Order & Patterns. (NATO ASI Ser.: Vol. 280). (Illus.). 296p. (C). 1992. text 110.00 (*0-306-44080-6*, Kluwer Plenum) Kluwer Academic.

Artwick, Bruce A. Microcomputer Displays, Graphics, & Animation. LC 84-61429. (Illus.). 384p. (C). 1985. pap. 31.95 (*0-13-580226-1*) P-H.

— Microcomputer Interfacing. 1980. text 45.00 (*0-13-580902-9*) P-H.

Artwohl, Alexis, jt. auth. see Christensen, Loren.

***Artymiak, Jacek.** Applixware 5 for Linux. LC 99-89902. (Illus.). 912p. 2000. 39.99 (*0-7645-3403-3*) IDG Bks.

Artymiak, Jacek. Teach Yourself SED & AWK in 24 Hours. (Teach Yourself Ser.). 400p. 1999. pap. 24.99 (*0-672-31737-0*) Sams.

Artyunyan, N. K. & Zevin, A. A. Design of Structures Considering Creep. (Illus.). 258p. (C). 1997. text 110.00 (*90-5410-280-2*, Pub. by A A Balkema) Ashgate Pub Co.

Artz, Frederick B. The Enlightenment in France. LC 68-21503. 176p. 1968. pap. 12.00 (*0-87338-032-0*) Kent St U Pr.

— From the Renaissance to Romanticism: Trends in Style in Art, Literature, & Music 1300-1830. LC 62-20021. 1965. pap. text 10.00 (*0-226-02838-0*) U Ch Pr.

— The Mind of the Middle Ages: An Historical Survey: A. D. 200-1500. 3rd rev. ed. LC 79-16259. 600p. 1980. reprint ed. pap. text 28.00 (*0-226-02840-2*, P859) U Ch Pr.

Artz, Joan W., ed. see Hudson, Howard P.

Artz, Ken, ed. see Nimzowitsch, Aron.

Artz, Lee. Communication Practices & Democratic Society. LC 98-133325. 350p. (C). 1997. per. 45.95 (*0-7872-4420-1*, 41442001) Kendall-Hunt.

***Artz, Lee & Murphy, Bren Ortega.** Cultural Hegemony in the United States. LC 00-8363. (Foundations of Populat Culture Ser.). 2000. pap. write for info. (*0-8039-4503-5*) Sage.

Artz, Nancy, ed. 301 Great Customer Service Ideas from America's Most Innovative Small Companies. 352p. 1998. pap. 14.95 (*1-880394-33-2*) Thomson Learn.

***Artz, Sibylle.** Feeling As a Way of Knowing: A Practical Guide for Working with Emotional Experience. (Illus.). 108p. 1999. pap. 12.55 (*1-895579-34-1*, Pub. by Trifolium Inc) ACCESS Pubs Network.

Artz, Sibylle. Sex, Power, & the Violent School Girl. LC 98-32007. 192p. 1999. pap. 24.95 (*0-8077-3854-9*) Tchrs Coll.

Artz, Thomas R., jt. auth. see Pierce, Gregory F.

Artzner, Darrah, et al. A Systematic Illustrated Guide to Fossil Organic-Walled Dinoflagellate Genera. (Illus.). 120p. pap. 16.57 (*0-88854-237-2*) Brill Academic Pubs.

Artzrouni, M. The Demographic Modelling of the HIV-AIDS Epidemic. 76p. 1992. pap. text 147.00 (*2-88124-567-6*) Gordon & Breach.

Artzt, Alice. The Art of Practicing. 1993. pap. 13.95 (*0-933224-17-6*, T/08) Bold Strummer Ltd.

Artzt, Alice F. & Newman, Claire M. How to Use Cooperative Learning in the Mathematics Classroom. 2nd ed. LC 97-26980. (Illus.). 81p. 1997. pap. 13.95 (*0-87353-437-9*) NCTM.

***ARUCC Staff.** A Warm Wlcome? Recruitment & Admission of International Students to Canadian Universities : Policies, Procedures & Capacity. LC 99-198732. 1998. write for info. (*0-88876-196-1*) AUCC.

Aruchamy, A., ed. Photoelectrochemistry & Photovoltaics of Layered Semiconductors. (C). 1992. text 185.00 (*0-7923-1556-1*) Kluwer Academic.

Aruego, Jose. Look What I Can Do. (J). 1988. 10.15 (*0-606-03608-3*, Pub. by Turtleback) Demco.

An Asterisk (*) at the beginning of an entry indicates that the title is appearing for the first time.

Aruego, Jose. Look What I Can Do! LC 87-21743. (Illus.). 32p. (J). (ps-1). 1988. reprint ed. mass mkt. 4.95 (*0-689-71205-7*) Aladdin.
— Rockabye Crocodile: A Folktale from the Philippines. (J). 1993. 10.15 (*0-606-05569-X*, Pub. by Turtleback) Demco.
Aruego, Jose. We Hide, You Seek. LC 78-13638. (Illus.). 32p. (J). (ps-3). 1979. 15.89 (*0-688-84201-1*, Grenwillow Bks) HarpC Child Bks.
Aruego, Jose. We Hide, You Seek. LC 78-13638. (Illus.). 32p. (J). (ps-3). 1988. mass mkt. 4.95 (*0-688-07815-X*, Wm Morrow) Morrow Avon.
Aruego, Jose. We Hide, You Seek. (J). 1979. 10.15 (*0-606-03951-1*, Pub. by Turtleback) Demco.
Aruego, Jose & Dewey, Ariane. Rockabye Crocodile. LC 92-24587. 32p. (J). (ps up). 1993. mass mkt. 4.95 (*0-688-12333-3*, Wm Morrow) Morrow Avon.
Aruego, Jose, jt. auth. see Dewey, Ariane.
Aruego, Jose, jt. illus. see Dewey, Ariane.
***Arulanandan, Kandiah, et al.** Computer Simulation of Earthquake Effects: Proceedings of Sessions of Geo-Denver 2000. LC 00-42141. (Geotechnical Special Publications). 2000. write for info. (*0-7844-0523-9*) Am Soc Civil Eng.
Arulanandan, Kandish. Verification of Numerical Procedures, Vol. 1. 1231p. 1993. 123.00 (*90-5410-361-2*) Ashgate Pub Co.
— Verification of Numerical Procedures, Vol. 2. 1994. 123.00 (*90-5410-362-0*) Ashgate Pub Co.
Arulanandan, Kandish, et al, eds. Verification of Numerical Procedures for the Analysis of Soil Liquefaction Problems: Proceedings of the International Conference, Davis, California, October 1993, 2 vols. (Illus.). 2000p. (C). 1994. text 180.00 (*90-5410-360-4*, Pub. by A A Balkema) Ashgate Pub Co.
Arulkumaran, Sabaratnam, jt. auth. see Gibo, D. M.
Arulpragasam, Jehan & Sahn, David E. Economic Transition in Guinea: Implications for Growth & Poverty. LC 96-9056. 221p. 1996. 45.00 (*0-8147-0664-9*) NY Acad Sci.
Arulpragasam, Jehan, jt. auth. see Sahn, David E.
Arulselvam, M. Law Relating to Cheque & Its Dishonour. (C). 1990. 70.00 (*0-89771-282-X*) St Mut.
— Law Relating to Limitation. (C). 1990. 50.00 (*0-89771-252-8*) St Mut.
***Arum, Richard & Beattie, Irene R.** The Structure of Schooling: Readings in the Sociology of Schooling. LC 99-24017. x, 516p. 1999. pap. text 39.95 (*0-7674-1070-X*, 1070-X) Mayfield Pub.
Arumugam, R., jt. auth. see Minford, Adrian.
Arun & Dasa, Anadi K. Understanding AIDS. 1987. 11.95 (*0-318-36373-9*) Asia Bk Corp.
***Aruna, Augustine S.** Caffeine Fact & Fallacy: Effects & Uses as a Medicine, Food & Beverage Ingredient & as a Flavoring Agent, 2 bks. Coe, Mary E., ed. 80p. 1998. pap. 18.95 (*0-9677721-2-5*) Global Pubng Net.
— NonPrescription (OTC) Medications: Counseling Guidelines on the Safe Use of Over-the-Counter Medicines. Padron, Victor A., ed. 168p. 1997. pap. text 23.50 (*0-9677721-1-7*) Global Pubng Net.
— Synchronism of Common Over-the-Counter Herbals & Western Medicines: Role of the Clinician in Consumer Counseling. 137p. 1998. pap. text 15.95 (*0-9677721-0-9*) Global Pubng Net.
Arunachalam, P. Sketches of Ceylon History. (C). 1993. reprint ed. text 10.00 (*81-206-0800-3*, Pub. by Asian Educ Servs) S Asia.
Arunachalam, V. S. & Roman, O. V., eds. Powder Metallurgy - Recent Applications. (C). 1989. 42.00 (*81-204-0424-6*, Pub. by Oxford IBH) S Asia.
Arundale. Lotus Fire. 1976. 23.95 (*0-8356-7502-5*) Theos Pub Hse.
Arundale, Francesca. Idea of Rebirth Including a Translation of an Essay on Reincarnation by Karl Heckl (1890) 156p. 1998. reprint ed. pap. 17.95 (*0-7661-0585-7*) Kessinger Pub.
Arundale, George S. Kundalini: An Occult Experience. 1997. pap. 5.25 (*81-7059-101-5*) Theos Pub Hse.
— Mount Everest: Its Spiritual Attainment (1933) 198p. 1998. reprint ed. pap. 17.95 (*0-7661-0237-8*) Kessinger Pub.
Arundale, Justin. Getting Your Scottish & National Vocational Qualifications: A Guide for Candidates in the Library & Information Sector. 2nd ed. 120p. 1997. pap. 17.00 (*1-85604-289-8*, LAP42898, Pub. by Library Association) Bernan Associates.
Arundel, John. Sewage & Industrial Effluent Treatment 2nd ed. LC 99-33304. 2000. write for info. (*0-632-05356-9*) Blackwell Sci.
— Sewage & Industrial Effluent Treatment: A Practical Guide. LC 95-659. 256p. 1995. 75.00 (*0-632-03898-5*) Blackwell Sci.
Arundell, Dennis. The Critic at the Opera: Contemporary Comments on Opera in London Over Three Centuries. LC 79-25062. (Music Reprint Ser.: 1980). (Illus.). 1980. reprint ed. lib. bdg. 45.00 (*0-306-76026-6*) Da Capo.
Arundell, Dennis D. Henry Purcell. LC 72-109614. (Select Bibliographies Reprint Ser.). 1977. 15.95 (*0-8369-5223-5*) Ayer.
— Henry Purcell. 135p. 1990. reprint ed. lib. bdg. 59.00 (*0-7812-9079-1*, 10079) Rprt Serv.
Arundell, Francis V. Discoveries in Asia Minor: Including a Description of the Ruins of Several Ancient Cities, Especially Antioch of Pisidia, 2 vols. in 1. (Illus.). xxx, 797p. 1975. reprint ed. lib. bdg. 135.00 (*3-487-05440-X*) G Olms Pubs.
Arundell, Lucy. Living with Grandma. (C). 1989. text 35.00 (*0-948929-06-5*) St Mut.
Arundhati, P. Brahmanism Jainism & Buddhism in Andhra Desa. (C). 1990. text 84.00 (*81-85067-30-9*) S Asia.
— Royal Life in Manasollasa. LC 94-905948. (C). 1995. 62.00 (*81-85067-89-9*, Pub. by Sundeep Prak) S Asia.
Aruny, John E., jt. ed. see Kandarpa, Krishna.
Aruoma, Okezie I., ed. Free Radicals in Tropical Diseases. LC 92-48845. xxii, 281p. 1993. text 114.00 (*3-7186-5261-7*) Gordon & Breach.
Aruoma, Okezie I. & Halliwell, Barry, eds. Free Radicals & Food Additives. 350p. 1991. 90.00 (*0-85066-766-6*, Pub. by Tay Francis Ltd) Taylor & Francis.
Aruoma, Okezie I., jt. auth. see Halliwell, Barry.
Aruona, Okezie I., jt. ed. see Cuppett, Susan L.
ARUP Associates Staff, ed. see Patkau Architects Staff.
Arup, Christopher. Innovation, Policy, & Law: Australia & the International High Technology Economy. LC 92-34686. 348p. (C). 1993. text 64.95 (*0-521-43003-8*) Cambridge U Pr.
***Arup, Christopher.** The New World Trade Organization Agreements: Globalizing Law Through Services & Intellectual Property. (Cambridge Studies in Law & Society). 336p. 2000. 54.95 (*0-521-77355-5*) Cambridge U Pr.
Arup, Christopher. Science, Law, & Society. (Orig.). (C). pap. 19.95 (*1-86324-014-4*, Pub. by LaTrobe Univ) Intl Spec Bk.
Arup, H. & Parkins, R. N. Stress Corrosion Research, No. 30. (NATO Advanced Study Institute Ser.). 279p. 1979. text 99.50 (*90-286-0647-5*) Kluwer Academic.
Arup, Jens, tr. see Ibsen, Henrik.
Arup, Prem, tr. see Osho.
Aruri, N., et al. Reagan & the Middle East. (Monographs: No. 17). 95p. (Orig.). 1983. pap. text 5.50 (*0-937694-59-2*) Assn Arab-Amer U Grads.
***Aruri, Naseer & Shuraydi, Mohammad A., eds.** Revising Culture, Reinventing Peace: The Influence of Edward W. Said. 2000. pap. 17.95 (*1-56656-357-7*) Interlink Pub.
Aruri, Naseer H. The Obstruction of Peace: The U. S., Israel & the Palestinians. 350p. 1995. text 29.95 (*1-56751-055-8*) Common Courage.
— The Obstruction of Peace: The U. S., Israel & the Palestinians. 350p. 1995. pap. text 18.95 (*1-56751-054-X*) Common Courage.
— The Sinai Accord As a Phase of the U. S. Containment Policy. (Occasional Papers: No. 2). 7p. (C). 1976. pap. 1.00 (*0-937694-41-X*) Assn Arab-Amer U Grads.
Aruri, Naseer H., ed. Middle East Crucible: Studies on the Arab-Israeli War of October 1973. (Monographs: No. 6). 479p. 1975. 15.00 (*0-914456-10-5*); pap. 7.95 (*0-914456-11-3*) Assn Arab-Amer U Grads.
— Occupation: Israel over Palestine. 2nd rev. ed. (Monographs: No. 18). 728p. 1989. pap. 29.00 (*0-937694-64-9*) Assn Arab-Amer U Grads.
Aruri, Naseer H. & AbuKhalil, As'ad. Amal & the Palestinians: Understanding the Battle of the Camps. Hagopian, Elaine C., ed. LC 85-18636. (Arab World Issues Occasional Papers: No. 9). 33p. 1985. pap. 4.00 (*0-937694-71-1*) Assn Arab-Amer U Grads.
Arutiunov, Serghei, jt. ed. see Holloman, Regina E.
Arutyunian, R. V. Thermal Physics Reviews Vol. 3, Pt. 1: Thermohydrodynamic Models of Laser Irradiation of Metals, Vol. 3. (Soviet Technology Reviews Ser.: Section B). 174p. 1990. text 101.00 (*3-7186-5071-1*, Harwood Acad Pubs) Gordon & Breach.
— Thermal Physics Reviews Vol. 4, Pt. 2: Interaction of Intense Laser Radiation with Matter, Vol. 4. (Soviet Technology Reviews Ser.: Section B). 65p. 1992. pap. text 84.00 (*3-7186-5216-1*, Harwood Acad Pubs) Gordon & Breach.
Arutyunyan, R. M., jt. auth. see Gebhart, E.
Arvan. Understanding Architecture. 1995. pap. text 65.00 (*0-13-190828-6*, Prentice Hall) P-H.
Arvanitakis, Froso, jt. auth. see Arvanitakis, Kleanthis.
Arvanitakis, Kleanthis & Arvanitakis, Froso. Communicate in Greek 1A Exercises. 3rd rev. ed. (Communicate in Greek Ser.). (GRE.). 56p. 1997. pap. text 9.25 (*960-8464-11-0*, Pub. by Deltos Pubns) Cosmos.
— Communicate in Greek 1B Exercises. 3rd rev. ed. (Communicate in Greek Ser.). (GRE.). 51p. 1997. pap. text 9.25 (*960-8464-12-9*, Pub. by Deltos Pubns) Cosmos.
— Communicate in Greek 1 Textbook. 3rd rev. ed. (Communicate in Greek Ser.). (GRE., Illus.). 316p. 1997. pap. text 26.50 (*960-8464-08-0*, Pub. by Deltos Pubns) Cosmos.
— Communicate in Greek 3 Exercises. 3rd rev. ed. (Communicate in Greek Ser.). (GRE.). 58p. 1997. pap. text 9.25 (*960-8464-06-4*, Pub. by Deltos Pubns) Cosmos.
— Communicate in Greek 3 Textbook. 3rd rev. ed. (Communicate in Greek Ser.). (GRE., Illus.). 276p. 1997. pap. text 26.50 (*960-8464-05-6*, Pub. by Deltos Pubns) Cosmos.
— Communicate in Greek 2A Exercises. 3rd rev. ed. (Communicate in Greek Ser.). (GRE.). 49p. 1997. pap. text 9.25 (*960-8464-02-1*, Pub. by Deltos Pubns) Cosmos.
— Communicate in Greek 2B Exercises. 3rd rev. ed. (Communicate in Greek Ser.). (GRE.). 58p. 1997. pap. text 9.25 (*960-8464-03-X*, Pub. by Deltos Pubns) Cosmos.
— Communicate in Greek 2 Textbook. 3rd rev. ed. (Communicate in Greek Ser.). (GRE., Illus.). 275p. 1997. pap. text 26.50 (*960-8464-00-5*, Pub. by Deltos Pubns) Cosmos.
Arvaniti, Amalia, jt. ed. see Connell, Bruce.
Arvanitis, Jim. Mu Tau Pankration Vol. 1: Concepts & Skills of "All-Powers" Combat. (Illus.). 200p. (Orig.). 1997. pap. 40.00 (*0-614-30247-1*) Spartan Pubns.
— Mu Tau Pankraton: Concepts & Skills of "All-Powers" Combat. 198p. 1997. pap. 29.95 (*0-9657442-0-5*) Spartan Pubns.
Arvastson, Gosta & Lindqvist, Mats, eds. The Story of Progress. (Studia Ethnologica Upsaliensia: No. 17). 95p. (Orig.). 1996. 36.00 (*91-554-3817-2*) Coronet Bks.
Arvedson. Pediatric Swallowing & Feeding. 1997. 6[illegible].00 (*0-7616-1741-8*) Commun Skill.
Arvedson, Joan C. Pediatric Videofluoroscopic Swallow Studies: A Professional Manual with Caregiver Guidelines. 1998. pap. text 69.00 (*0-12-785064-3*) Acad Pr.
Arvedson, Joan C. & Brodsky, Linda, eds. Pediatric Swallowing & Feeding: Assessment & Management. LC 92-49930. (Early Childhood Intervention Ser.). (Illus.). 486p. (Orig.). (C). 1992. pap. 59.95 (*1-56593-069-X*, 0376) Thomson Learn.
Arvedson, Joan C. & Lefton-Greif, Maureen A. Pediatric Videofluoroscopic Swallow Studies: A Professional Manual with Caregiver Guidelines. LC 98-5487. 1998. 69.00 (*0-7616-3228-X*) Commun Skill.
Arvedson, Joan C. & Rogers, Brian T. Pediatric Dysphagia: Management Challenges for the School-Based Speech-Language Pathologist. 1998. 110.00 incl. VHS (*1-58041-018-9*, 0112094) Am Speech Lang Hearing.
Arvedson, Joan C., et al. Pediatric Dypshagia: Assessment & Intervention Considerations for Children & Young Adults. 157p. 1998. 72.00 incl. audio (*1-58041-021-9*, 0112156) Am Speech Lang Hearing.
Arvedson, Lennart, et al. Economics & Values. 136p. 1986. pap. text 44.00 (*0-317-54518-3*) Coronet Bks.
Arveson. Operator Algebras & Operator Theorys. 1992. pap. 47.95 (*0-582-09358-9*, Pub. by Addison-Wesley) Longman.
Arveson, William. Operator Algebras & Operator Theory: Proceedings of the OATE 2 Conference, Romania, 1989. Mishchenko, A. S. et al, eds. LC 92-234313. (Pitman Research Notes in Mathematics Ser.: Vol. 271). 228p. reprint ed. pap. 70.70 (*0-608-08053-5*, 206901800002) Bks Demand.
Arveson, William B. Continuous Analogues of Fock Space. LC 89-6998. (Memoirs Ser.: Vol. 80/409). 66p. 1989. pap. 18.00 (*0-8218-2472-4*, MEMO 80/409) Am Math.
— An Invitation to C-Algebras. LC 76-3656. 1976. 39.00 (*0-387-90176-0*) Spr-Verlag.
— Ten Lectures on Operator Algebras. LC 84-9222. (CBMS Regional Conference Series in Mathematics: No. 55). 93p. 1984. reprint ed. pap. 22.00 (*0-8218-0705-6*, CBMS/55) Am Math.
Arveson, William B. & Douglas, R., eds. Operator Theory - Operator Algebras & Applications. LC 90-33771. (Proceedings of Symposia in Pure Mathematics Ser.: Vol. 51). 1025p. 1990. text 190.00 (*0-8218-1486-[illegible]*, PSPUM/51) Am Math.
Arvetis, Chris & Palmer, Carole. Deserts. LC 93-502. (Where Are We? Ser.). (Illus.). (J). 1993. 3.95 (*0-528-83574-2*) Rand McNally.
— Forests. LC 93-500. (Where Are We? Ser.). (Illus.). (J). 1993. 3.95 (*0-528-83573-4*) Rand McNally.
— Lakes & Rivers. LC 93-499. (Where Are We? Ser.). (Illus.). (J). 1993. 3.95 (*0-528-83572-6*) Rand McNally.
— Oceans & Seas. LC 93-33674. (Where Are We? Ser.). (Illus.). (J). 1994. 3.95 (*0-528-83675-7*) Rand McNally.
— Swamps & Marshes. LC 93-33675. (Where Are We? Ser.). (Illus.). (J). (gr. 4 up). 1994. 3.95 (*0-528-83676-5*) Rand McNally.
Arvey, Michael. The End of the World: Opposing Viewpoints. LC 92-15101. (Great Mysteries Ser.). (Illus.). 112p. (J). (gr. 5-8). 1992. lib. bdg. 22.45 (*0-89908-096-0*) Greenhaven.
— Miracles: Opposing Viewpoints. LC 90-39156. (Great Mysteries Ser.). (Illus.). 112p. (J). (gr. 5-8). 1990. lib. bdg. 22.45 (*0-89908-084-7*) Greenhaven.
Arvey, Richard D. Fairness in Selecting Employees. LC 78-74678. 1979. pap. text 9.50 (*0-201-00070-9*) Addison-Wesley.
— Fairness in Selecting Employees. 3rd ed. 320p. (C). 2000. pap. text. write for info. (*0-201-34597-8*) Addison-Wesley.
Arvey, Verna. In One Lifetime. 2nd ed. 280p. 1984. 20.00 (*1-877873-12-8*); pap. 9.00 (*1-877873-13-6*) Master-Player Lib.
Arvey, Verna. In One Lifetime: A Biography of William Grant Still. LC 83-24226. (Illus.). 280p. 1984. pap. 12.00 (*0-938626-36-1*) U of Ark Pr.
Arvey, Verna, jt. auth. see Still, Judith A.
Arvidson, Lucy. Alaawich. 1978. pap. 3.00 (*0-939046-01-6*) Malki Mus Pr.
***Arvidson, P. Sven & Abdian, Geoffrey.** The Behavioral Elements: Teacher's Guide for Grades 11-12. Ourcharacter.com Technical Advisory Committee, ed. (Illus.). 101p. 1999. spiral bd. 24.95 (*1-930567-08-1*, Ourcharacter.com) Axios Pubng Corp.
— The Behavioral Elements: Teacher's Guide for Grades 7-8. Ourcharacter.com Technical Advisory Committee, ed. (Illus.). 93p. 1999. spiral bd. 24.95 (*1-930567-06-5* Ourcharacter.com) Axios Pubng Corp.
— The Behavioral Elements: Teacher's Guide for Grades 9-10. Ourcharacter.com Technical Advisory Committee, ed. (Illus.). 91p. 1999. spiral bd. 24.95 (*1-930567-07-3*, Ourcharacter.com) Axios Pubng Corp.
— The Character Circle: Teacher's Guide for Grades K-4. Ourcharacter.com Technical Advisory Committee, ed. (Illus.). 87p. 1999. spiral bd. 24.95 (*1-930567-04-9* Ourcharacter.com) Axios Pubng Corp.
— The Character Club Parent's Manual (for Ages 5-9) Ourcharacter.com Technical Advisory Committee, ed. (Illus.). 79p. 1999. spiral bd. 24.95 (*1-930567-09-X* Ourcharacter.com) Axios Pubng Corp.
— Introduction to the Behavioral Elements: Teacher's Guide for Grades 5-6. Ourcharacter.com Technical Advisory Committee, ed. (Illus.). 93p. 1999. spiral bd. 24.95 (*1-930567-05-7*, Ourcharacter.com) Axios Pubng Corp.
— Introduction to the Behavioral Elements Parent's Manual (for Ages 10-13) Ourcharacter.com Technical Advisory Committee, ed. (Illus.). 83p. 1999. spiral bd. 24.95 (*1-930567-10-3*, Ourcharacter.com) Axios Pubng Corp.
Arvidson, P. Sven, jt. auth. see Abdian, Geoffrey.
Arvidson, P. Sven, jt. auth. see Davis-Floyd, Robbie.
Arvidson, Rose C. Cordova: The First Seventy-Five Years. LC 84-80040. (Illus.). 98p. 1984. pap. 11.95 (*0-9607358-3-6*) Fathom Pub.
Arvidsson, Claes & Blomqvist, Lars E. Symbols of Power: The Esthetics of Political Legitimation in the Soviet Union & Eastern Europe. (Illus.). 185p. 1987. 57.50 (*91-22-00843-8*) Coronet Bks.
Arvidsson, Fredrik, photos by. The Kathmandu Valley. LC 98-7451. 1998. 49.95 (*1-57062-404-6*, Pub. by Shambhala Pubns) Random.
***Arvigo, Rosita.** Rainforest Home Remedies. 2000. pap. 17.00 (*0-06-251637-X*, Pub. by Harper SF) HarpC.
Arvigo, Rosita & Balick, Michael J. Rain-Forest Remedies: 100 Healing Herbs of Belize. 2nd rev. ed. LC 93-80280. 336p. (Orig.). 1998. pap. 15.95 (*0-914955-13-6*) Lotus Pr.
Arvigo, Rosita & Epstein, Nadine. Sastun: One Woman's Apprenticeship with a Maya Healer & their Efforts to Save the Vanishing Tradition of Rainforest Medicine. LC 93-37439. 208p. 1995. pap. 15.00 (*0-06-250259-X*, Pub. by Harper SF) HarpC.
Arvikar, R. & Seireg, Ali A. Biomechanical Analysis of the Musculoskeletal Structure for Medicine & Sports. 700p. 1989. 120.00 (*0-89116-423-5*) Hemisp Pub.
***Arvin, Ann & Gershon, Anne, eds.** Varicella-Zoster Virus: Virology & Clinical Management. (Illus.). 544p. (C). 2000. write for info. (*0-521-66024-6*) Cambridge U Pr.
Arvin, E., ed. Biological Degradation of Organic Chemical Pollutants in Biofilm Systems: Selected Proceedings of the International Specialized Research Seminar, Copenhagen, Denmark, Held May 19-21, 1994. (Water Science & Technology Ser.: 31). (Illus.). 282p. 1995. pap. 122.50 (*0-08-042645-X*, Pergamon Pr) Elsevier.
— Degradation, Retention & Dispersion of Pollutants in Groundwater: Proceedings of the IAWPRC Seminar Held in Copenhagen, Denmark, 12-14 September 1984. LC 82-645900. 432p. 1985. pap. 48.00 (*0-08-033658-2*, Pub. by PPL) Elsevier.
Arvin, Neil C. Eugene Scribe & the French Theatre, 1815-1860. LC 67-13422. 1972. 20.95 (*0-405-08216-9*, Pub. by Blom Pubns) Ayer.
Arvin, Newton. Hawthorne. (BCL1-PS American Literature Ser.). 303p. 1992. reprint ed. lib. bdg. 89.00 (*0-7812-6722-6*) Rprt Serv.
— Herman Melville. LC 72-7818. (Illus.). 316p. 1973. reprint ed. pap. 5.95 (*0-8371-8952-7*, ARHPB) Greenwood.
— Longfellow: His Life & Work. LC 77-1342. 338p. 1977. reprint ed. lib. bdg. 65.00 (*0-8371-9505-5*, ARLO, Greenwood Pr) Greenwood.
Arvin, Newton, ed. see Hawthorne, Nathaniel.
***Arvin, Reed.** The Will. LC 00-26012. 2000. 25.00 (*0-7432-0148-5*) Scribner.
Arvin, Reed. The Wind in the Wheat. 1996. mass mkt. 5.99 (*0-7852-7360-3*) Nelson.
***Arvin, Reed, ed.** Getting Started in Christian Music. LC 99-43231. 350p. 2000. pap. 17.99 (*0-7369-0267-8*) Harvest Hse.
Arvind, D. K., et al, eds. Eighth Workshop on Parallel & Distributed Simulation (PADS '94) Proceedings of the 8th Workshop, Edinburgh, Scotland, 1994. 200p. 1994. pap. 80.00 (*1-56555-027-7*, PADS-94) Soc Computer Sim.
Arvind, V., et al, eds. Foundations of Software Technology & Theoretical Computer Science: 18th Conference, Chennai, India, December 17-19, 1998. (Lecture Notes in Computer Science Ser.: Vol. 1530). xii, 369p. 1998. pap. 59.00 (*3-540-65384-8*) Spr-Verlag.
Arvio, Sarah, tr. see Marcelo, J. J.
Arvizu, Steven F., jt. auth. see Saravia-Shore, Marietta.
Arvo, James. Graphics Gems. 1994. 49.95 (*0-12-064881-4*) Morgan Kaufmann.
— Graphics Gems, No. 2. 1994. text 59.00 (*0-12-064481-9*) Morgan Kaufmann.
Arvold, Bridget & Cromwell, Peter. Knottedness. (Illus.). 48p. pap. text 11.99 (*0-614-05326-9*, GM 6654) COMAP Inc.
Arwady, Joseph W. & Gayeski, Diane M. Using Video: Interactive & Linear Designs. LC 88-31105. (Techniques in Training & Performance Development Ser.). (Illus.). 190p. 1989. 39.95 (*0-87778-199-0*) Educ Tech Pubns.
Arwady, Joseph W., ed. see Spitzer, Dean R.
Arwas. Alphonse Mucha, Vol. 1. 1986. 19.95 (*0-312-02141-0*) St Martin.
Arwas, Victor. Alphonse Mucha: Master of Art Nouveauwor. 1986. pap. 15.00 (*0-312-02142-9*) St Martin.
— Art Deco. rev. ed. (Illus.). 316p. 1998. 75.00 (*0-8109-1926-5*, Pub. by Abrams) Time Warner.
***Arwas, Victor.** Art Deco. rev. ed. (Illus.). 316p. 2000. 34.98 (*0-8109-8199-8*, Pub. by Abrams) Time Warner.
Arwas, Victor. Art Deco Sculpture. (Illus.). 252p. 1992. 75.00 (*0-312-08345-9*) Academy Ed UK.
— Art Deco Sculpture. (Illus.). 116p. 1985. pap. 11.95 (*0-312-05251-0*) St Martin.
— Art of Glass. (Illus.). 112p. 1997. 40.00 (*0-8478-2054-8*, Pub. by Rizzoli Intl) St Martin.
***Arwas, Victor.** The Art of Glass. 112p. 1999. 35.00 (*1-901092-00-3*) Andreas Papadakis.
Arwas, Victor, et al. Alphonse Mucha: The Spirit of Art Nouveau. LC 97-43743. (Illus.). 400p. 1998. 65.00 (*0-300-07419-0*) Yale U Pr.
Arweck, Elisabeth B. & Clarke, Peter. New Religious Movements in Western Europe: An Annotated Bibliography, 41. LC 96-44066. (Bibliographies & Indexes in Religious Studies: Vol. 41). 328p. 1997. lib. bdg. 95.00 (*0-313-24324-7*, Greenwood Pr) Greenwood.

A

A

***Arwidsson, Greta & Berg, Gosta.** The Mastermyr Find: A Viking Age Tool Chest from Gotland. (Illus.). 90p. 2000. reprint ed. pap. 17.95 (*0-9650755-1-6*) Larson Publng.

Arwill, ed. Persuasion As Intervention: Reclaiming Rhetoric As a Civic Art. (C). 1999. text. write for info. (*0-321-01593-2*) Addson-Wesley Educ.

Arwine, David K., jt. auth. see McHugh, Michael J.

Arx, J. A. von. The Genera of Fungi Sporulating in Pure Culture. 3rd rev. ed. (Illus.). 410p. 1981. lib. bdg. 125.00 (*3-7682-0693-9*) Lubrecht & Cramer.

Arx, Jeffrey P. Von, see Von Arx, Jeffrey P.

Ary. Introduction to Research in Education. 5th ed. (C). 1995. pap. text, teacher ed. 30.00 (*0-15-503111-2*) Harcourt Coll Pubs.

Ary, D., jt. auth. see Suen, H. K.

Ary, Daniel. Middle School Math Challenge. (Middle School Math Ser.). (Illus.). 136p. (J). (gr. 5-8). 1996. pap. 9.95 (*0-88160-267-1*, LW1018) Learning Wks.

Ary, Donald, et al. Introduction to Research in Education. 5th ed. LC 94-73499. 590p. (C). 1995. text 88.50 (*0-15-500982-6*) Harcourt.

Ary Group, Inc. Staff. We Shoot Every Third Salesperson . . . The Second One Just Left. LC 97-73553. 128p. 1997. per. 18.95 (*0-7872-4167-9*) Kendall-Hunt.

Ary, S. The Oxford Book of Wild Flowers: Pocket Edition. (Illus.). 240p. 1976. pap. 9.95 (*0-19-910013-6*) OUP.

Arya, jt. auth. see Pandey.

Arya, Atam P. Elementary Modern Physics. LC 73-1466. (C). 1974. text 33.56 (*0-201-00304-X*) Addison-Wesley.

Arya, Atam Parkash. Introduction to Classical Mechanics. 2nd ed. LC 97-16622. 712p. 1997. 100.00 (*0-13-505223-8*) P-H.

Arya, Bob. Thirty Seconds to Air: A Field Reporter's Guide to Live Television Reporting. LC 99-14529. (Illus.). 246p. 1999. pap. text 27.95 (*0-8138-2579-2*) Iowa St U Pr.

Arya, C. Design of Structural Elements: Concrete, Steelwork, Masonry, & Timber Design to British Standards & Eurocodes. LC 93-32219. (Illus.). 384p. (C). 1994. pap. 39.99 (*0-419-17620-9*, E & FN Spon) Routledge.

Arya, D. K. & Sharma, R. C., eds. Management Issues & Operational Planning for India's Borders. write for info. (*0-318-71687-9*, Pub. by Promilla) Nataraj Bks.

Arya, H. C. Advancing Frontiers: Plant Sciences. (C). 1986. text 140.00 (*0-7855-0109-6*, Pub. by Scientific Pubs) St Mut.

— Advancing Frontiers Plant Sciences. 305p. (C). 1985. 60.00 (*0-7855-2271-9*, Pub. by Scientific) St Mut.

Arya, H. C., et al. Advancing Frontiers Plant Sciences. 305p. (C). 1986. 270.00 (*81-85046-10-7*, Pub. by Scientific) St Mut.

Arya, Jagdish C. & Lardner, Robin W. Mathematical Analysis. 4th ed. 1993. pap. text, student ed. 22.00 (*0-13-564295-7*) P-H.

— Mathematical Analysis for Business, Economics & the Life & Social Sciences. 4th ed. 880p. (C). 1992. 70.00 (*0-13-564287-6*) P-H.

— Mathematics for the Biological Sciences. LC 78-13424. (Illus.). 705p. 1979. 96.00 (*0-13-562439-8*) P-H.

Arya, K. S., jt. auth. see Yadav, K. C.

Arya, Krishna S. Swami Dayananda Sarswati. 355p. 1987. 23.00 (*81-85054-22-3*, Pub. by Manohar) S Asia.

Arya, O. P. & Hart, C. A., eds. Sexually Transmitted Infections & Kids in the Tropics. LC 98-23327. (CAB International Publication Ser.). 400p. 1998. 110.00 (*0-85199-262-5*) OUP.

Arya, Pandit U. & Lih, D. Philosophy of Hatha Yoga. 2nd ed. LC 84-19790. 95p. 1985. pap. 8.95 (*0-89389-088-X*) Himalayan Inst.

— Superconscious Meditation. LC 78-102982. 150p. 1978. pap. 12.95 (*0-89389-035-9*) Himalayan Inst.

— Yoga Sutras of Patanjali: With the Exposition of Vyasa: A Translation & Commentary. LC 85-7570. Vol. I. 493p. (C). 1986. pap. 16.95 (*0-89389-092-8*) Himalayan Inst.

Arya, Pandit Usharbudh. Meditation & the Art of Dying. LC 78-78252. 179p. 1979. pap. 12.95 (*0-89389-056-1*) Himalayan Inst.

Arya, Pandit Usharbudh & Lih, D. God. LC 79-88824. 162p. 1979. pap. 12.95 (*0-89389-060-X*) Himalayan Inst.

— Mantra & Meditation. LC 81-84076. 237p. 1981. pap. 14.95 (*0-89389-074-X*) Himalayan Inst.

***Arya, Pasang Y.** Dictionary of Tibetan Materia Medica. Gyatso, Yonten, ed. 310p. 1998. pap. 200.00 (*81-208-1567-X*, Pub. by Motilal Bnarsidass) St Mut.

Arya, Prem Singh. Vegetable Growing in Hills. 439p. 1997. pap. 250.00 (*81-7533-056-2*, Pub. by Print Hse) St Mut.

Arya, Pyare L. Structure, Policies & Growth Prospects of Nigeria. LC 92-46730. (African Studies: Vol. 29). 164p. 1993. text 79.95 (*0-7734-9252-6*) E Mellen.

Arya, S. Pal. Air Pollution Meteorology & Dispersion. LC 97-35738. (Illus.). 320p. (C). 1998. text 79.95 (*0-19-507398-3*) OUP.

— Introduction to Micrometeorology. (International Geophysics Ser.). 410p. 1988. text 70.00 (*0-12-064490-8*) Acad Pr.

Arya-Sura. The Gatnkamala: Or, Garland of Birth-Stories. Muller, F. Max, ed. Speyer, J. C., tr. from SAN. LC 78-72371. reprint ed. 49.50 (*0-404-17218-0*) AMS Pr.

Arya, Suresh C., et al. Design of Structures & Foundations for Vibrating Machines. LC 78-56171. 190p. 1979. 39.00 (*0-87201-294-8*, 1294) Gulf Pub.

— Design of Structures & Foundations for Vibrating Machines. LC 78-56171. (Illus.). 208p. 1979. reprint ed. pap. 64.50 (*0-608-07941-3*, 206791400012) Bks Demand.

Aryai, Sia. ABCs. (Baby Bright Board Bks.). (Illus.). 10p. (J). (ps). 1997. pap. 5.95 (*1-56565-851-5*, 08515W, Pub. by Lowell Hse Juvenile) NTC Contemp Pub Co.

— Baby Bright Board Books: ABC's. (Illus.). 20p. (J). 1993. 5.95 (*1-56565-049-2*) Lowell Hse.

— Baby Bright Board Books: Colors. (Illus.). 20p. (J). 1993. 5.95 (*1-56565-050-6*) Lowell Hse.

— Baby Bright Board Books: Shapes. (Illus.). 20p. (J). 1993. 5.95 (*1-56565-051-4*) Lowell Hse.

— Shapes. (Baby Bright Board Bks.). (Illus.). 10p. (J). (ps). 1997. pap. 5.95 (*1-56565-852-3*, 08523W, Pub. by Lowell Hse Juvenile) NTC Contemp Pub Co.

Aryai, Sia, photos by. Colors. (Baby Bright Board Bks.). (Illus.). 10p. (J). (ps). 1997. bds. 5.95 (*1-56565-850-7*, 08507W, Pub. by Lowell Hse Juvenile) NTC Contemp Pub Co.

— 123s. (Baby Bright Board Bks.). (Illus.). 10p. (J). (ps). bds. 5.95 (*1-56565-824-8*, 08248W, Pub. by Lowell Hse Juvenile) NTC Contemp Pub Co.

Aryal, Deepak, ed. Nepal's Who's Who. 1997. pap. 130.00 (*0-7855-7464-6*, Pub. by Ratna Pustak Bhandar) St Mut.

Aryan Books International Staff, ed. see Waddell.

Aryan, K. C. Basis of Decorative Element in Indian Art. (Illus.). 141p. 1981. 37.00 (*81-900002-8-4*, Pub. by Rekha Prakashn) Nataraj Bks.

— The Cultural Heritage of Punjab, 3000 B. C. to 1947 A. D. (Illus.). 149p. 1983. 37.00 (*81-900002-9-2*, Pub. by Rekha Prakashn) Nataraj Bks.

— Indian Folk Bronzes. (Illus.). 143p. 1991. 57.00 (*81-900003-5-7*, Pub. by Rekha Prakashn) Nataraj Bks.

— Unknown Pahari Wall Paintings in North India. (Illus.). 122p. 1992. 37.00 (*81-900003-6-5*, Pub. by Rekha Prakashn) Nataraj Bks.

***Aryan, K. C. & Aryan, Subhashini.** The Aryans: History of Vedic Period LC 98-908473. 268p. 1998. write for info. (*81-900003-9-X*, Pub. by Rekha Prakashn) S Asia.

Aryan, K. C. & Aryan, Subhashini. Hanuman: Art, Mythology & Folklore. LC 94-906518. (Illus.). 186p. (C). 1994. 69.00 (*81-900003-7-3*, Pub. by Rekha Prakashn) Nataraj Bks.

Aryan, S. A Catalogue of Indian Folk & Tribal Art in the Collection of Home of Folk Art, Museum of Folk, Tribal & Neglected Art. (Illus.). 12p. 1990. 18.00 (*81-85304-28-9*, Pub. by Rekha Prakashn) Nataraj Bks.

Aryan, Subhashini. Crafts of Himachal Pradesh. LC 89-80993. (Living Traditions of India Ser.). (Illus.). 168p. 1994. 65.00 (*0-944142-46-X*) Grantha.

— Folk Embroidery of Himachal Pradesh. 82p. 1992. 24.95 (*1-881338-24-X*) Nataraj Bks.

Aryan, Subhashini & Gupta, R. K. Crafts of Himachal Pradesh. (Illus.). 168p. 1993. 65.00 (*81-85822-05-0*, Pub. by Mapin Pubng) Antique Collect.

Aryan, Subhashini, jt. auth. see Aryan, K. C.

Aryangat, Ajikumar. The MCAT Chemistry Book. (Illus.). 496p. (C). 1999. pap. 29.95 (*1-889057-12-6*) Nova Pr.

***Aryangat, Ajikumar.** The MCAT Practice Book. (Illus.). 450p. (C). 2000. 29.95 (*1-889057-16-9*) Nova Pr.

Aryanpur. The Concise Persian-English Dictionary. (ENG & PER.). 1986. 39.95 (*0-8288-1736-7*, F107970) Fr & Eur.

— The Pocket Persian-English Dictionary. (ENG & PER.). 1049p. 1986. 24.95 (*0-8288-1121-0*, F98990) Fr & Eur.

Aryanpur-Kashani, Abbas & Aryanpur-Kashani, Manoochehr. The Combined New Persian-English & English-Persian Dictionary. LC 85-61402. 688p. 1986. 39.95 (*0-939214-29-6*); lib. bdg. 49.95 (*0-939214-28-8*) Mazda Pubs.

— English-Persian Collegiate Dictionary, 2 vols., Set. (Illus.). xv, 2584p. (C). 1992. lib. bdg. 69.00 (*1-56859-010-5*) Mazda Pubs.

Aryanpur-Kashani, Manoochehr, jt. auth. see Aryanpur-Kashani, Abbas.

Aryasura. The Marvelous Companion: Life Stories of the Buddha. LC 83-15023. (Tibetan Translation Ser.: Vol. 10). (Illus.). 250p. 1983. 40.00 (*0-913546-88-7*); pap. 19.95 (*0-913546-89-5*) Dharma Pub.

Aryeetey-Attoh, Samuel. Geography of Sub-Saharan Africa. LC 96-36108. 379p. (C). 1996. 67.00 (*0-13-375684-X*) P-H.

Aryeetey, Ernest & Nissanke, Machiko. Financial Integration & Development. (Routledge Studies in Development Economics: Vol. 11). 304p. (C). 1998. 90.00 (*0-415-18081-3*) Routledge.

***Aryeetey, Ernest, et al.** Economic Reforms in Ghana: The Myth & the Mirage. LC 00-30621. 2000. pap. write for info. (*0-86543-844-7*) Africa World.

Aryeetey, Ernest, et al. Financial Market Fragmentation & Reforms in Sub-Saharan Africa. LC 96-53413. (Technical Paper Ser.: No. 356). 64p. 1997. pap. 22.00 (*0-8213-3861-7*, 13861) World Bank.

— Supply & Demand for Finance of Small Enterprises in Ghana. LC 94-27214. (Discussion Paper Ser.: No. 251). 126p. 1994. pap. 22.00 (*0-8213-2964-2*, 12964) World Bank.

Arzans de Orsua y Vela, Bartolome. Tales of Potosi. Padden, R. C., ed. LC 74-6574. 243p. reprint ed. pap. 75.40 (*0-7837-0367-8*, 204068900018) Bks Demand.

Arzen, K. E., ed. Computer Software Structures Integrating AI-KBS Systems in Process Control: IFAC Workshop, Lund, Sweden, 10-12 August, 1994. LC 94-39392. (Illus.). 232p. 1994. pap. 87.50 (*0-08-042360-4*, Pergamon Pr) Elsevier.

Arzhakov, M. S., et al, eds. Structural & Mechanical Properties of Glassy Polymers. LC 97-191094. 295p. (C). 1997. lib. bdg. 145.00 (*1-56072-434-X*) Nova Sci Pubs.

Arzola de Calero, Eva. Observaciones Astronomicas. LC 86-7068. (Illus.). x, 75p. 1992. pap. 5.00 (*0-8477-2327-5*) U of PR Pr.

Arzoomanian, Raffi. Four Plays. LC 80-13309. 1980. 12.50 (*0-933706-18-9*); pap. 5.95 (*0-933706-19-7*) Ararat Pr.

Arzoumanian, Alexander. Beyond-Physics: A Velocity Theory. LC 91-67797. 100p. (C). 1992. 12.95 (*0-9601206-2-9*) Persepolis NJ.

Arzruni, Sahan. A Treasury of Armenian Chants. (Illus.). 1994. 25.00 incl. audio (*0-934728-26-7*) D O A C.

Arzt, Donna E. Refugees into Citizens: Palestinians & the End of the Arab-Israeli Conflict. 232p. 1996. pap. 18.95 (*0-87609-194-X*) Coun Foreign.

Arzt, Edya, tr. see Schachter, Helene & Wise, Maureen, eds.

Arzt, Max, jt. auth. see Silverman, Morris.

Arzt, Noam H. The Business of Higher Education: The American University & Its Banking Function. rev. ed. LC 95-37226. (Financial Sector of the American Economy Ser.). (Illus.). 172p. 1995. text 20.00 (*0-8153-2241-0*) Garland.

Arzt, Peter. Bedrohtes Christsein: Zu Eigenart und Funktion Eschatologisch Bedrohlicher Propositionen in Den Echten Paulusbriefen. (Beitrage zur Biblischen Exegese und Theologie Ser.: Bd. 26). (GER.). 294p. 1992. 50.80 (*3-631-45097-4*) P Lang Pubng.

***Arzt-Wegman, Dita.** Nostradamus' Dream Interpretations. Orig. Title: Umfangreiches Agyptisches Traum-Deutungs Buch by Nostradamus. (Illus.). 175p. 1999. pap. 14.95 (*0-9686022-0-7*, Pub. by VPI1) Allnce Hse.

Arzumanov, S. D. & Akhrori, K. A. Russian - Tadzhik Dictionary. Asimova, M. S., ed. (RUS.). 1280p. 1985. 42.95 (*0-8285-5402-1*) Firebird NY.

AS, Harmen R. Vantional Conference on High Perform. High Performance Networking: IFIP TC-6 Eighth International Conference on High Performance Networking (HPN '98), Vienna, Austria, September 21-25, 1998. LC 98-37275. 1998. write for info. (*0-412-84660-8*) Chapman & Hall.

As-Sadr, Muhammad B. Our Philosophy. Inati, Shams, tr. 480p. 1988. text 57.50 (*0-7103-0179-0*) Routledge.

As-Saffar, Muhammad. Disorienting Encounters: Travels of a Moroccan Scholar in France in 1845-1846, the Voyage of Muhammad As-Saffar. Miller, Susan G., tr. & intro. by. (Comparative Studies on Muslim Societies: Vol. 14). (C). 1992. 45.00 (*0-520-07461-0*, Pub. by U CA Pr); pap. 15.95 (*0-520-07462-9*, Pub. by U CA Pr) Cal Prin Full Svc.

As-Samarra'i, Ibrahim. Al Fara'id: Gems from the Arabic Classical Dictionaries - Arabic Dictionary. (ARA.). 1984. 19.95 (*0-86685-357-X*) Intl Bk Ctr.

***As-Sulami.** Early Sufi Women: Dhikr an-Niswa al-Muta 'Abbitdat as-Sufiyyat. Cornell, Rkia, tr. LC 99-67569. 270p. 2000. pap. 24.95 (*1-887752-06-4*, Pub. by Fons Vitae) Words Distrib.

Asa, Ariel. Sefer Yehoshua. Fruchter, Yaakov, ed. (Illus.). 88p. 1996. wbk. ed. 6.00 (*1-878895-17-6*, A375) Torah Umesorah.

Asa, Leland F. The Psychology of Religious Commitment & Development. 190p. (C). 1995. pap. text 28.50 (*0-8191-9839-0*); lib. bdg. 51.50 (*0-8191-9838-2*) U Pr of Amer.

Asa, Lucille M. Recollections of Great Memories. (Illus.). 40p. 1996. 9.00 (*0-8059-3969-5*) Dorrance.

ASA Staff. Aircraft Log: #ASA-SA-1. rev. ed. (Logbook Ser.). 64p. 1998. pap. 5.95 (*1-56027-164-7*, ASA-SA-1) ASA Inc.

— Avionics Log: #ASA-SA-V. (Logbook Ser.). 64p. 1992. pap. 5.95 (*1-56027-057-8*, ASA-SA-V) ASA Inc.

— Certified Flight Instructor Test Prep 2000: #TP-CFI-00. rev. ed. (Test Prep 2000 Ser.). (Illus.). 440p. 1999. pap. 19.95 (*1-56027-345-3*, ASA-TP-CFI-99) ASA Inc.

— Commercial Pilot Test Prep 2000: TP-C-00. rev. ed. (Test Prep 2000 Ser.). (Illus.). 338p. 1999. pap. 16.95 (*1-56027-346-1*, ASA-TP-C-99) ASA Inc.

— Engine Log: #ASA-SE-1. rev. ed. (Logbook Ser.). 62p. 1998. pap. 5.95 (*1-56027-165-5*, ASA-SE-1) ASA Inc.

— Engine Log: #ASA-SE-2. rev. ed. (Logbook Ser.). 95p. 1998. 9.95 (*1-56027-326-7*, ASA-SE-2) ASA Inc.

— Flight Schedule: #ASA-FS-KT. (Logbook Ser.). 60p. 1992. 34.95 (*1-56027-109-4*, ASA-FS-KT) ASA Inc.

— Propeller Log: #ASA-SP-L. rev. ed. (Logbook Ser.). (Illus.). 20p. 1998. pap. 4.95 (*1-56027-202-3*, ASA-SP-L) ASA Inc.

— Standard Pilot Log, Black: #ASA-SP-30. rev. ed. (Logbook Ser.). 68p. 1998. 6.95 (*1-56027-328-3*, ASA-SP-30) ASA Inc.

— Standard Pilot Log Blue. (Logbook Ser.). 110p. 1985. 10.95 (*1-56027-090-X*) ASA Inc.

— Standard Pilot Log, Blue: #ASA-SP-57. rev. ed. (Logbook Ser.). 110p. 1998. 10.95 (*1-56027-330-5*, ASA-SP-57) ASA Inc.

— Standard Pilot Log, Red: #ASA-SP-40. rev. ed. (Logbook Ser.). 206p. 1998. 9.95 (*1-56027-329-1*, ASA-SP-40) ASA Inc.

— Standard Pilot Master Log: #ASA-SP-6. rev. ed. (Logbook Ser.). 278p. 1998. 24.95 (*1-56027-327-5*, ASA-SP-6) ASA Inc.

ASA Staff, ed. Aircraft Log: #ASA-SA-2. (Logbook Ser.). 94p. 1991. 9.95 (*1-56027-117-5*, ASA-SA-2) ASA Inc.

— Flight Engineer Test Prep, 2000: #TP-FE-00. rev. ed. (Test Prep 2000 Ser.). (Illus.). 338p. 1999. pap. 29.95 (*1-56027-344-5*, ASA-TP-FE-99) ASA Inc.

— Instrument Rating Test Prep 2000: #TP-I-00. rev. ed. (Test Prep 2000 Ser.). 326p. 1999. pap. 19.95 (*1-56027-343-7*, ASA-TP-I-99) ASA Inc.

ASA Staff, ed. see Holmes, Harold J.

ASA Staff, ed. see Newton, Dennis W.

ASA Staff, ed. see U. S. Army Staff.

Asa, Sylvia L., jt. auth. see Kovacs, Kalman.

Asaad, Ghazi. Hallucinations in Clinical Psychiatry: A Guide for Mental Health Professionals. LC 90-2125. (Clinical Psychiatry Monographs: No. 2). 160p. 1990. text 29.95 (*0-87630-592-3*) Brunner-Mazel.

— Psychosomatic Disorders: Theoretical & Clinical Aspects, No. 7. (Basic Principles into Practice Ser.: Vol.67). 147p. 1996. pap. text 21.95 (*0-87630-803-5*) Brunner-Mazel.

— Understanding Mental Disorders Due to Medical Conditions or Substance Abuse: What Every Therapist Should Know, No. 3. LC 94-11620. (Basic Principles into Practice Ser.: Vol. 3). (Illus.). 172p. 1995. pap. text 22.95 (*0-87630-751-9*) Brunner-Mazel.

Asaaro, Catherine. Primary Inversion. 1996. mass mkt. 5.99 (*0-8125-5023-4*, Pub. by Tor Bks) St Martin.

Asaba, Neil. Coast Guard: Challenges for Addressing Budget Constraints. (Illus.). 77p. 1998. pap. text 20.00 (*0-7881-4750-1*) DIANE Pub.

Asachenkov, Alexander, et al, eds. Disease Dynamics: Systems & Control: Foundations & Applications. LC 93-40316. (Illus.). xv, 316p. 1993. 92.00 (*0-8176-3692-7*) Birkhauser.

***Asacker, Tom.** Sandbox Wisdom: Revolutionize Your Brand with the Genius of Childhood. 125p. 2000. 19.95 (*0-9677528-0-9*) Eastside Pub NH.

Asad, M. N. Muslims of Sri Lanka under the British Rule. (C). 1993. 22.00 (*81-7013-099-9*, Pub. by Navarang) S Asia.

Asad, Muhammad. Islam & Politics. 12p. (Orig.). 1988. pap. 3.00 (*1-56744-301-X*) Kazi Pubns.

— Islam at the Crossroads. 104p. (Orig.). 1996. 19.95 (*0-614-21425-4*, 571) Kazi Pubns.

— Islam at the Crossroads. 104p. (Orig.). 1982. 8.95 (*0-317-52459-3*) New Era Publns MI.

— Islam at the Crossroads. 102p. (Orig.). 1934. reprint ed. 16.00 (*0-939660-15-6*, Pub. by Dar Al-Andalus) Threshold CA.

— Message of the Quran. 1000p. (Orig.). 1996. 55.00 (*0-614-21062-3*, 779) Kazi Pubns.

— Message of the Quran. 998p. (Orig.). 1980. 49.95 (*0-317-52456-9*) New Era Publns MI.

— The Principles of State: Government in Islam. 108p. 1961. reprint ed. 18.00 (*0-939660-11-3*, Pub. by Dar Al-Andalus) Threshold CA.

— The Principles of State & Government. 107p. (Orig.). 1980. pap. 9.95 (*0-317-52457-7*) New Era Publns MI.

— The Principles of State & Government in Islam. 110p. 1996. 19.95 (*0-614-21498-X*, 985) Kazi Pubns.

— The Road to Mecca. 374p. (Orig.). 1996. 15.95 (*0-614-21476-9*, 1087) Kazi Pubns.

— The Road to Mecca. 380p. (Orig.). 1981. 14.95 (*0-317-52460-7*) New Era Publns MI.

— The Road to Mecca. (Illus.). 375p. (Orig.). 1954. reprint ed. 25.00 (*0-939660-13-X*, Pub. by Dar Al-Andalus) Threshold CA.

— Sahih Al-Bukhari: The Early Years. 306p. (Orig.). 1981. 24.95 (*0-317-52458-5*) New Era Publns MI.

— This Law of Ours. 195p. 1996. 21.95 (*0-614-21449-1*, 1229) Kazi Pubns.

Asad, Muhammad, tr. see Al-Bukhari, Sahih.

Asad, Talal. Genealogies of Religion: Discipline & Reasons of Power in Christianity & Islam. LC 93-21831. 296p. (C). 1993. text 60.00 (*0-8018-4631-5*) Johns Hopkins.

Asad, Talal, ed. Anthropology & the Colonial Encounter. LC 73-12199. (C). 1974. pap. 17.50 (*0-391-00391-7*) Humanities.

Asad, Talal & Owen, Roger, eds. The Middle East. LC 83-42527. (Sociology of "Developing Societies" Ser.). 240p. 1983. pap. 14.00 (*0-85345-637-2*, Pub. by Monthly Rev) NYU Pr.

Asada, Bin. SEA Robot Design. 288p. 1996. 140.00 (*0-471-16303-1*) Wiley.

Asada, Carol. Conscious Eating: Dietless. LC 97-66409. 1997. pap. 14.95 (*0-89716-752-X*, Peanut Btr Pubng) Elton-Wolf Pub.

Asada, Haruhiko, jt. auth. see Slotine, Jean-Jacques E.

Asada, K., ed. see Sixth International Conference on Superoxide & Sup.

***Asada, Mineko.** Rice Bowl Recipes: Over 100 Tasty One-Dish Meals. 2000. pap. 18.00 (*4-88996-048-1*, Pub. by Japan Pubn Trad) Bks Nippan.

***Asada, Minoru, et al, eds.** Robocup-98: Robot Soccer World Cup II. LC 99-39843. (Lecture Notes in Computer Science Ser.: Vol. 1604). xi, 509p. 1999. pap. 59.95 (*3-540-66320-7*) Spr-Verlag.

Asada, Teruhiko. The Night of a Thousand Suicides: The Japanese Outbreak at Cowra. LC 75-597929. 125p. 1970. write for info. (*0-207-12052-8*) Consort Bk Sales.

Asada, Toshi, ed. Earthquake Prediction Techniques: Their Application in Japan. Ohnuki, Masako, tr. LC 82-185347. (Illus.). 333p. 1982. reprint ed. pap. 103.30 (*0-608-01194-0*, 206188300001) Bks Demand.

Asada, Y., jt. auth. see Rao, K. R.

Asada, Y., jt. ed. see Rao, K. R.

Asada, Y., jt. ed. see Swindeman, R. W.

Asadi, Murlene Wallace. Stenoscript ABC Shorthand: Text. rev. ed. 161p. 21.50 (*1-56118-454-3*) EMC-Paradigm.

Asadorian, William, jt. auth. see Seyfried, Vincent.

Asadorian, William, jt. auth. see Seyfried, Vincent F.

Asadour, Zabel. The Bride. Parlakian, Nishan, tr. 1987. 6.95 (*0-918680-37-9*) Griffon House.

Asaduddin, M., jt. ed. see Hasan, Mushirul.

Asady, Raad A. & Narayanan, Ajit. Inheritance Networks for Artificial Intelligence. 320p. (Orig.). 1994. pap. text 29.95 (*1-871516-32-3*, Pub. by Intellect) Cromland.

ASAE Research Staff. Association Management Companies Compensation & Benefits Study. (Management Research Ser.). (Illus.). x, 42p. 1997. pap. 125.00 (*0-88034-129-7*) Am Soc Assn Execs.

— Association Meeting Trends. (Management Research Ser.). (Illus.). xi, 184p. 1999. pap. 90.00 (*0-88034-152-1*) Am Soc Assn Execs.

— Association Publishing Operations, 1998. (Management Research Ser.). (Illus.). xvii, 277p. 1998. pap. 115.00 (*0-88034-147-5*) Am Soc Assn Execs.

ASAE Staff. Association Management Companies: Business Operations Report. (Management Research Ser.). (Illus.). xiii, 32p. 1998. pap. 125.00 (*0-88034-142-4*) Am Soc Assn Execs.

An Asterisk (*) at the beginning of an entry indicates that the title is appearing for the first time.

*ASAE Standards Committee Staff, ed. ASAE Standards 1999. LC 54-14360. (Illus.). 1015p. 1999. text 158.50 (1-892769-05-0) Am Soc Ag Eng.

Asafev, Boris V. A Book about Stravinsky. French, Richard F., tr. LC 82-4810. (Russian Music Studies: No. 5). 315p. reprint ed. pap. 97.70 (0-8357-1320-2, 207060500005) Bks Demand.

*Asafu-Adjaye, John. Enviornmental Economics for Non-Economists. 250p. 2000. 48.00 (981-02-4013-9) World Scientific Pub.

*Asagiri, Yu. Midnight Panther Vol. 1: I'll Love You to Death. 160p. 1998. pap. 15.95 (1-56219-908-0, CMX 06071) Central Pk Media.

— Midnight Panther Vol. 2: Feline Fanatics. (Illus.). 160p. 1999. pap. 15.95 (1-56219-914-5, CMX 06072) Central Pk Media.

— Midnight Panther Vol. 3: School Daze Yearbook. (Illus.). 120p. 1999. pap. 15.95 (1-56219-915-3, CMX 06073) Central Pk Media.

— Midnight Panther Vol. 4: Feudal Fantasy. (Illus.). 160p. 1999. pap. 15.95 (1-56219-916-1, CMX 06074) Central Pk Media.

Asahara, Yashiyuki, jt. auth. see Yamane, Masayuki.

Asahi, Isamu. Origami Greeting Cards: A Guide to Making Unique, Attractive Cards for Any Occasion. Tomita, Yuko S., tr. (Illus.). 32p. (Orig.). 1990. pap. 7.95 (0-8048-1587-9) Tuttle Pubng.

— Origami Monsters. (Illus.). 32p. 1992. pap. 8.95 (0-8048-1867-3) Tuttle Pubng.

Asahina & Shigiya, R., eds. Physiological Adaptability & Nutritional Status of the Japanese B, Vol. 4. (Japan International Biological Program Synthesis Ser.). 250p. 1975. 50.00 (0-86008-214-8, Pub. by U of Tokyo) Col U Pr.

Asai, David J., et al, eds. Methods in Cell Biology, Vol. 37: Antibodies in Cell Biology. (Illus.). 452p. 1993. text 104.00 (0-12-564137-0) Acad Pr.

*Asai, David J. & Forney, James D., eds. Methods in Cell Biology Vol. 62: Tetrahymena Thermophila. 650p. 1999. 125.00 (0-12-544164-9) Acad Pr.

— Tetrahymena Thermophila. (Methods in Cell Biology Ser.). 650p. 1999. 79.95 (0-12-064525-4) Acad Pr.

Asai, K. Fuzzy Systems for Information Processing. LC 94-73404. (gr. 12). 1995. 77.00 (90-5199-206-8) IOS Press.

— Fuzzy Systems for Management. LC 94-78471. (gr. 12). 1995. 71.00 (90-5199-188-6) IOS Press.

Asai, Susan M. Nomai Dance Drama: A Surviving Spirit of Medieval Japan, 47. LC 98-14243. (Contributions to the Study of Music & Dance Ser.: Vol. 47). 280p. 1999. 65.00 (0-313-30698-2, Greenwood Pr) Greenwood.

Asaithambi. Numerical Analysis: Theory & Practice. (C). 1995. text 87.50 (0-03-030983-2) Harcourt Coll Pubs.

Asaka, Tetsuichi & Ozeki, Kazuo, eds. Handbook of Quality Tools: The Japanese Approach. 1997. pap. 30.00 (1-56327-138-9) Productivity Inc.

Asaka, Yuho, tr. see Jackins, Harvey.

*Asakae, Bedu. Ghana in Search of Political Changes. LC 99-97516. 2000. pap. 7.95 (0-533-13424-2) Vantage.

Asakawa, Bruce. California Gardener's Guide: The What, Where, When, How & Why of Gardening in California. (Illus.). 424p. 2000. pap. 19.95 (1-888608-43-9) Cool Springs Pr.

Asakura, Reiji. Revolutionaries at Sony: The Making of the Sony Playstation & the Visionaries Who Conquered the World of Video Games. 256p. 2000. 19.95 (0-07-135587-1) McGraw.

*Asakura, T., et al, eds. International Trends in Optics & Photonics: ICO IV. LC 99-17027. (Optical Sciences Ser.: Vol. 74). (Illus.). 400p. 1999. 112.00 (3-540-65897-1) Spr-Verlag.

Asakura, T., ed. see Gu, Min.

Asakura, Tetsuo, jt. auth. see Ando, I.

Asakura, Toshimitsu, jt. ed. see Jutamulia, Suganda.

*Asala, Jason. Poe, Vol. 1. (Illus.). 128p. 1998. pap. 14.95 (1-57989-018-0) Sirius Ent.

Asala, Joanne. Celtic Folklore Cooking. LC 98-3993. (Illus.). 264p. 1999. pap. 17.95 (1-56718-044-2) Llewellyn Pubns.

— Fairy Tales of the Slav Peasants & Herdsmen. 158p. 1994. pap. 12.95 (0-941016-99-4) Penfield.

— The Green Knight: A Tale of Ancient Britain - Arthurian Romance about Sir Gawain & the Green Knight. (Illus.). 64p. (J). (gr. 3). 1992. pap. 6.95 (1-880954-00-1) Kalevala Bks.

*Asala, Joanne. Legends of the Rhine. Reichmann, Eberhardt et al, eds. (Illus.). 128p. 2000. pap. 12.95 (1-57216-040-3) Penfield.

Asala, Joanne, compiled by. Czech Proverbs. 63p. 1994. pap. 10.95 (1-57216-010-1) Penfield.

— Norwegian Proverbs: Selected from the Tales of Peter Christian Asbjornsen & Jorgen Moe. 63p. 1994. pap. 10.95 (0-941016-97-8) Penfield.

— Polish Proverbs. 1995. pap. 10.95 (1-57216-011-X) Penfield.

— Proverbs from North: Words of Wisdom-Vikings. 63p. 1994. pap. 10.95 (1-57216-022-5) Penfield.

— Swedish Proverbs. 63p. 1994. pap. 10.95 (0-941016-98-6) Penfield.

Asala, Joanne, contrib. by. Trolls Remembering Norway. 167p. 1994. pap. 12.95 (1-57216-000-4) Penfield.

Asala, Joanne, ed. Recipes from Ireland. 1995. spiral bd. 6.95 (1-57216-017-9) Penfield.

— Ukrainian Recipes. 140p. 1996. spiral bd. 6.95 (1-57216-019-5) Penfield.

— Whistling Jigs to the Moon: Tales of Irish & Scottish Pipers - Folklore about Bagpipers. 144p. (Orig.). 1993. pap. 9.95 (1-880954-02-8) Kalevala Bks.

Asala, Joanne, retold by. Scandinavian Ghost Stories: And Other Tales of the Supernatural. LC 95-69794. 1995. pap. 12.95 (1-57216-015-2) Penfield.

Asala, Joanne & Ekman, Marlene. Celtic Tales of the Strange. LC 97-17802. (Illus.). 96p. 1998. 6.95 (0-8069-9671-4) Sterling.

Asala, Joanne, jt. ed. see Goree, Sue R.

Asala, Joanne E., ed. And No One Would Eat Tomatoes: An Iowa City Anthology. (Illus.). 158p. 1993. pap. text 10.00 (1-880954-04-4) Kalevala Bks.

Asali, K. J. Jerusalem in History. LC 89-16000. (Illus.). 328p. 2000. pap. 18.95 (1-56656-304-6, Olive Branch Pr) Interlink Pub.

Asali, K. J., ed. Jerusalem in History: From 300 BC to 1996 AD. LC 96-16435. 312p. 1996. pap. 34.00 (0-7103-0559-1, Pub. by Kegan Paul Intl) Col U Pr.

Asali, K. J., pref. Jerusalem in History. LC 89-16000. (Illus.). 192p. 1990. 19.95 (0-940793-44-X, Olive Branch Pr) Interlink Pub.

Asalone, Anthony J. Love Affair with God. Date not set. pap. write for info. (0-9673212-1-2) Gods Love Pub.

*Asalone, Anthony J. Love Letters from God. xii, 142p. 1999. pap. 12.99 (0-9673212-0-4) Gods Love Pub.

Asalone, Anthony J. What if Love Happens: A Magnificent President. Date not set. pap. write for info. (0-9673212-2-0) Gods Love Pub.

Asals, Frederick. Flannery O'Connor: The Imagination of Extremity. LC 81-10513. 288p. 1986. reprint ed. pap. 18.00 (0-8203-0839-0) U of Ga Pr.

— The Making of Malcolm Lowry's "Under the Volcano" LC 96-2221. x, 476p. 1996. 85.00 (0-8203-1826-4) U of Ga Pr.

*Asals, Frederick & Tiessen, Paul, eds. Darkness That Murmured: Essays on Malcolm Lowry & the Twentieth Century. 264p. 1999. 45.00 (0-8020-4462-X) U of Toronto Pr.

Asals, Heather, jt. auth. see Stanwood, Paul G.

Asama, H., et al, eds. Distributed Autonomous Robotic Systems 2. (Illus.). xvi, 472p. 1996. 159.50 (4-431-70190-7) Spr-Verlag.

Asamen, Joy K. & Berry, Gordon L., eds. Research Paradigms, Television & Social Behavior. LC 97-21129. 480p. 1997. 62.00 (0-7619-0654-1); pap. 28.95 (0-7619-0655-X) Sage.

Asamen, Joy K., jt. ed. see Berry, Gordon L.

Asami, H., et al. Distributed Autonomous Robotic Systems. LC 94-37490. 1995. 149.00 (0-387-70147-8) Spr-Verlag.

Asamiya, Kia. Gunhed: Gun Unit - Heavy Elimination Device. Horibuchi, Seiji, ed. Fujii, Satoru, tr. from JPN. (Illus.). 136p. (Orig.). (YA). (gr. 10 up). 1991. pap. 14.95 (0-929279-14-X) Viz Commns Inc.

*Asamiya, Kia. Kia Asamiya Sketchbook. Masuda, Mutsumi et al, trs. from JPN. (Illus.). 64p. 1999. pap. 5.00 (1-56219-921-8, CMX 625) Central Pk Media.

— Silent Mobius, No. 4. (Illus.). (J). 2000. pap. 15.95 (1-56931-472-1, Viz Comics) Viz Commns Inc.

— Silent Mobius, Vol. 1. Vol. 1. (Illus.). 256p. 1999. pap. text 16.95 (1-56931-364-4) Viz Commns Inc.

— Silent Mobius, Vol. 2. Vol. 2. (Illus.). 248p. 1999. pap. text 16.95 (1-56931-367-9) Viz Commns Inc.

Asamiya, Kia. Silent Mobius, Vol. 3. (Illus.). 248p. 1999. pap. text 16.95 (1-56931-370-9) Viz Commns Inc.

— Steam Detectives. (Illus.). 200p. 1999. pap. text 15.95 (1-56931-317-2, Viz Comics) Viz Commns Inc.

*Asamiya, Kia. Steam Detectives , Vol. 2. 1999. pap. 15.95 (1-56931-405-5) Viz Commns Inc.

Asamoah, Yvonne W., ed. Innovations in Delivering Culturally Sensitive Social Work Services: Challenges for Practice & Education. LC 96-51968. (Journal of Multicultural Social Work Monograph Ser.: Vol. 4, No. 4). 160p. (C). 1997. 39.95 (1-56024-812-2) Haworth Pr.

Asamoto, Bruce, ed. Fourier Transform Ion Cyclotron Resonance Mass Spectrometry: Analytical Applications. 306p. 1991. 105.00 (0-471-18734-8) Wiley.

Asamoto, Bruce, ed. Fourier Transform Ion Cyclotron Resonance Mass Spectrometry: Analytical Applications. 306p. 1991. text 69.50 (0-89573-767-1, Wiley-VCH) Wiley.

Asan, E., contrib. by. The Proceedings of the 6th International Symposium on Artificial Heart & Assist Devices, July 30-31, 1996 Tokyo, Japan No. 6. LC 97-41992. (Illus.). xx, 524p. 1998. 260.00 (4-431-70209-1) Spr-Verlag.

Asana, Ana, et al. Attacks on the Press in 1995: A Worldwide Survey. (Illus.). 300p. 1996. pap. 30.00 (0-944823-15-7) Comm to Protect Jrnlists.

Asanami, Soichiro & Kasazaki, Yasunori. Expert Third Molar Extractions. (Illus.). 109p. 1990. text 42.00 (4-87417-308-X) Quint Pub Co.

Asanga. Abhidharmasamuccaya. Walpola, Rahula & Webb, Sara-Boin, trs. (Illus.). 480p. 2000. 70.00 (0-89581-941-4) Asian Humanities.

— On Knowing Reality: The Tattvartha Chapter of Asanga's Bodhisattvabhumi. Willis, Janice D., tr. & comment by. LC 79-16047. 216p. reprint ed. pap. 67.00 (0-608-17356-8, 202982500065) Bks Demand.

Asanga & Jnanagarbha. Two Commentaries on the Samdhinirmocana-Sutra by Asanga & Jnanagarbha. Powers, John, tr. LC 92-520. (Studies in Asian Thought & Religion: Vol. 13). 156p. 1992. lib. bdg. 69.95 (0-7734-9477-4) E Mellen.

Asani, Ali S. The Bujh Niranjan: An Ismaili Mystical Poem. (Orig.). 1992. pap. 14.95 (0-932885-08-X) Harvard CMES.

— The Harvard Collection of Ismaili Literature in Indic Languages: A Descriptive Catalog & Finding Aid. 640p. (C). 1992. 105.00 (0-8161-0560-X, G K Hall & Co) Mac Lib Ref.

Asani, Ali S. & Abdel-Malek, Kamal. Celebrating Muhammad: Images of the Prophet in Popular Muslim Poetry. Denny, Frederick, ed. LC 95-10341. (Studies in Comparative Religion). 150p. 1996. text 34.95 (1-57003-050-2) U of SC Pr.

Asano, Kazutoshi, jt. ed. see Crowley, Joseph M.

Asano, Naruyoshi & Kato, Y. Algebraic & Spectral Methods for Nonlinear Wave Equations. LC 89-13199. (Pitman Monographs & Surveys in Pure & Applied Mathematics: Vol. 49). 436p. 1990. reprint ed. pap. 135.20 (0-608-03587-4, 206441000009) Bks Demand.

Asano, Shuzo, ed. Structure of the Transition Zone. (Advances in Earth & Planetary Sciences Ser.: No. 8). 184p. 1980. text 107.50 (90-277-1149-6) Kluwer Academic.

Asano, T., et al, eds. Algorithms: International Symposium SIGAL '90, Tokyo, Japan, August 16-18, 1990 Proceedings. (Lecture Notes in Computer Science Ser.: Vol. 450). viii, 479p. 1990. 46.00 (0-387-52921-7) Spr-Verlag.

— Algorithms & Computation Vol. X: Proceedings, 7th International Symposium, ISAAC '96, Osaka, Japan, December 16-18, 1996. (Lecture Notes in Computer Science Ser.: Vol. 1178). 448p. 1996. pap. 75.00 (3-540-62048-6) Spr-Verlag.

Asano, T., et al. Acute Aneurysm Surgery. (Illus.). 300p. 1987. 175.00 (0-387-81987-8) Spr-Verlag.

*Asano, Takao, et al, eds. Computing & Combinatorics: Proceedings, 5th Annual International Conference, COCOON'99, Tokyo, Japan, July 26-28, 1999. LC 99-36296. (Lecture Notes in Computer Science Ser.: Vol. 1627). xiv, 494p. 1999. pap. 79.00 (3-540-66200-6) Spr-Verlag.

Asano, Takashi, ed. Wastewater Reclamation & Reuse. LC 97-62550. (Water Quality Management Library: Vol. 10). xxxvii, 1528p. 1998. 159.95 (1-56676-620-6) Technomic.

Asano, Takashi, jt. auth. see Pettygrove, G. Stuart.

Asano, Yasuhiro. Cyberscapes: Computer Graphics from the Yagi Studio. (Illus.). 84p. 1994. 24.95 (4-8381-0126-0, Pub. by Mitsumura Suiko Shoin) Bks Nippan.

Asanov, A. & Atamanov, E. R. Nonclassical & Inverse Problems for Pseudoparabolic Equations. (Inverse & Ill-Posed Problems Ser.). (Illus.). 156p. 1997. 125.00 (90-6764-235-5, Pub. by VSP) Coronet Bks.

Asanov, G. S. Finsler Geometry, Relativity & Gauge Theories. 1985. text 237.50 (90-277-1960-8) Kluwer Academic.

Asante. Traditions. 1997. 40.00 (0-02-503511-8) Free Pr.

— Wilderness. 1995. 22.50 (0-684-19608-5) S&S Trade.

Asante, Clement E. Press Freedom & Development: A Research Guide & Selected Bibliography, 11. LC 97-21983. (Bibliographies & Indexes in Mass Media & Communications Ser.: 11). 232p. 1997. lib. bdg. 75.00 (0-313-29994-3, Greenwood Pr) Greenwood.

— The Press in Ghana: Problems & Prospects. 230p. (C). 1995. lib. bdg. 42.50 (0-7618-0167-7) U Pr of Amer.

Asante-Dauh, D. Kofi. Hazardous Waste Risk Assessment. 400p. 1993. lib. bdg. 95.00 (0-87371-570-5, L570) Lewis Pubs.

Asante-Duah. International Trade in Hazardous Wastes. 224p. (C). 1998. 75.00 (0-419-21890-4, E & FN Spon) Routledge.

Asante-Duah, D. Kofi. Management of Contaminated Site Problems. LC 95-11258. 432p. 1995. lib. bdg. 85.00 (1-56670-079-5, L1079) Lewis Pubs.

— Managing Contaminated Sites: Problem Diagnosis & Development of Site Restoration. LC 96-25954. 254p. 1997. 145.00 (0-471-96633-9) Wiley.

— Risk Assessment in Environmental Management: A Guide for Managing Chemical Contamination Problems. LC 98-16174. 536p. 1998. 190.00 (0-471-98147-8) Wiley.

Asante, Emmanuel. Toward an African Christian Theology of the Kingdom of God: The Kingship of Onyame. LC 94-11493. 212p. 1995. text 89.95 (0-7734-2291-9) E Mellen.

Asante, Kariamu W., jt. auth. see Asante, Molefi K.

Asante, Kariamu W., jt. ed. see Asante, Molefi K.

Asante, Molefi K. African American History: A Journey of Liberation. LC 98-221248. xvi, 485p. 1995. 43.00 (1-56256-903-1) Peoples Pub Grp.

— The Afrocentric Idea. LC 86-30046. 232p. 1988. pap. 14.95 (0-87722-573-7) Temple U Pr.

— The Afrocentric Idea. rev. ed. LC 97-40735. 256p. 1998. text 59.95 (1-56639-594-1); pap. text 16.95 (1-56639-595-X) Temple U Pr.

— Afrocentricity: The Theory of Social Change. 2nd ed. LC 87-72779. x, 126 p. (Orig.). 1990. reprint ed. pap. 9.95 (0-86543-067-5) Africa World.

— The Book of African Names. LC 91-72493. 64p. 1991. 24.95 (0-86543-254-6); pap. 9.95 (0-86543-255-4) Africa World.

— Kemet, Afrocentricity & Knowledge. 1992. reprint ed. 35.00 (0-86543-188-4); reprint ed. pap. 16.95 (0-86543-189-2) Africa World.

— Love Dances. LC 95-71324. (Illus.). 80p. 1996. pap. text 9.95 (0-9635245-9-3) Sungai Bks.

— Malcolm X As Cultural Hero & Other Afrocentric Essays. LC 93-21330. 185p. 1993. 39.95 (0-86543-401-8); pap. 12.95 (0-86543-402-6) Africa World.

*Asante, Molefi K. The Painful Demise of Eurocentrism: An Afrocentric Response to Critics LC 99-20777. 1999. 19.95 (0-86543-743-2) Africa World.

Asante, Molefi K. The Scream of Blood: Desettlerism in Southern Africa. LC 98-60018. (Sunscholars Ser.). 112p. 1998. pap. 14.95 (1-889218-15-4) Sungai Bks.

Asante, Molefi K., et al, eds. Handbook of Intercultural Communication. LC 78-2468. (Illus.). 479p. reprint ed. pap. 148.50 (0-8357-4730-1, 203764600009) Bks Demand.

— Handbook of International & Intercultural Communication. 620p. (C). 1989. pap. 34.00 (0-8039-5868-4); text 69.95 (0-8039-3202-2) Sage.

Asante, Molefi K. & Abarry, Abu S., eds. African Intellectual Heritage: A Book of Sources. LC 96-33807. 828p. (C). 1996. 79.95 (1-56639-402-3); pap. text 29.95 (1-56639-403-1) Temple U Pr.

Asante, Molefi K. & Asante, Kariamu W. African Culture: The Rhythms of Unity, 81. LC 84-9015. (Contributions in Afro-American & African Studies: No. 81). (Illus.). 270p. 1985. 59.95 (0-313-24404-9, ASA/, Greenwood Pr) Greenwood.

Asante, Molefi K. & Asante, Kariamu W., eds. African Culture: The Rhythms of Unity. LC 89-84609. 280p. (C). 1989. pap. 14.95 (0-86543-134-5) Africa World.

Asante, Molefi K. & Mattson, Mark T. Historical & Cultural Atlas of African Americans. 208p. 1992. 28.00 (0-02-897029-2) Macmillan.

Asante, Molefi K. & Mattson, Mart T. The African American Atlas: Black History & Culture: An Illustrated Reference. 2nd ed. LC 98-25556. 1998. 34.95 (0-02-864985-0) Macmillan.

*Asante, Molefi K. & Muntaquim, Renee. The African American Book of Names & Their Meanings. LC 98-221225. 67p. 1999. 15.00 (1-56256-921-X) Peoples Pub Grp.

Asante, Molefi K. & Vandi, Abdulai S., eds. Contemporary Black Thought: Alternative Analysis in Social & Behavioral Science. LC 80-15186. (Sage Focus Editions Ser.: No. 26). 302p. 1980. reprint ed. pap. 93.70 (0-608-01117-7, 205942100001) Bks Demand.

Asante, Molefi K., jt. auth. see Mattson, Mark T.

Asante, Molefi K., jt. auth. see Ziegler, Dhyana.

Asante, S. K. African Development: Adebayo Adedeji's Alternative Strategies. 248p. 1991. 70.00 (0-905450-49-3, Pub. by H Zell Pubs) Seven Hills Bk.

— Pan-African Protest: West Africa & the Italo-Ethiopian Crisis, 1934-1941. LC 78-312713. (Legon History Ser.). 260p. reprint ed. pap. 80.60 (0-608-13164-4, 202523100043) Bks Demand.

— The Political Economy of Regionalism in Africa: The Case of the Economic Community of West African States. LC 85-16740. 286p. 1985. 69.50 (0-275-90194-7, C0194, Praeger Pubs) Greenwood.

— Regionalism & Africa's Development: Expectations, Reality, & Challenges. LC 97-18971. 206p. 1997. text 65.00 (0-312-17697-X) St Martin.

Asantewa, Doris. Strategic Planning Basics for Special Libraries. LC 92-13276. (Illus.). 65p. reprint ed. pap. 30.00 (0-608-07555-8, 205265500009) Bks Demand.

Asanuma, Hiroshi. The Motor Cortex. LC 88-43160. 202p. 1989. reprint ed. pap. 62.70 (0-608-04671-X, 206539200004) Bks Demand.

Asanuma, Toshioo, jt. auth. see Murauchi, Sadanori.

Asaoka, Koji. Chitin-Chitosan - The Choice Food Supplement for over 10,000 Physicians in Japan. Kai, Mutsuoki, tr. LC 96-90069. (Orig.). 1996. pap. 14.95 (0-533-11879-4) Vantage.

ASAP World Consultancy Staff. Administering SAP R/3: MM-Material Management Module. LC 97-69807. 448p. 1997. pap. 49.99 (0-7897-1502-3) Que.

*ASAP World Consultancy Staff. Administering SAP R/3: The Production & Planning Module. (Illus.). 1999. 49.99 (0-7897-2274-7) Que.

ASAP World Consultancy Staff. Administering SAP R/3: FI-Finance & CO-Control Modules. LC 97-80938. 496p. 1998. pap. text 49.99 (0-7897-1548-1) Que.

— Administering Sap R/3: SD-Sales & Distribution Module. LC 98-85891. 1998. 49.99 (0-7897-1755-7) Que.

*ASAP World Consultancy Staff, et al. Administering SAP R/3: The HR-Human Resources Module. LC 98-89573. 390p. 1999. 49.99 (0-7897-1756-5) Que.

Asar, A. Entura: A Galactic Awareness Workbook. (Illus.). 53p. (Orig.). 1997. pap., wbk. ed. 12.95 (1-890186-00-7) StarGate Pub.

Asar Jubal, J. The Black Truth. 232p. 1991. write for info. (0-9634292-0-5) Black Truth.

Asard, Erik & Bennett, W. Lance. Democracy & the Marketplace of Ideas: Communication & Government in Sweden & the United States. (Illus.). 259p. (C). 1997. text 59.95 (0-521-56336-4); pap. text 18.95 (0-521-56525-1) Cambridge U Pr.

Asard, Erik, jt. ed. see Lunden, Rolf.

*Asard, Han, ed. Plasma Membrane Redox Systems & Their Role in Biological Stress & Disease. LC 98-31686. 332p. 1998. 180.00 (0-7923-5467-2) Kluwer Academic.

Asare, Bediako. Rebel. (African Writers Ser.). 156p. (C). 1969. pap. 8.95 (0-435-90059-5, 90059) Heinemann.

Asare, Meshack. Cat in Search of a Friend. LC 86-10583.Tr. of Die Katze sucht sich einen Freund. (Illus.). 32p. (J). (ps-5). 1986. 10.95 (0-916291-07-3) Kane-Miller Bk.

— Cat in Search of a Friend. LC 88-71622.Tr. of Die Katze sucht sich einen Freund. (Illus.). 32p. (J). (ps-3). 1988. reprint ed. pap. 6.95 (0-86543-107-8) Africa World.

*Asaro, Catherine. Ascendant Sun. LC 99-89166. 384p. 2000. 24.95 (0-312-86824-3, Pub. by Tor Bks) St Martin.

Asaro, Catherine. Catch the Lightning. 1997. mass mkt. 5.99 (0-8125-5102-8, Pub. by Tor Bks) St Martin.

— The Last Hawk. 1998. mass mkt. 6.99 (0-8125-5110-9, Pub. by Tor Bks) St Martin.

*Asaro, Catherine. The Phoenix Code. 2000. mass mkt. 5.99 (0-553-58154-6) Bantam.

— The Quantum Rose. 2000. text 25.95 (0-312-89062-1) St Martin.

— The Radiant Seas. LC 98-7979. 512p. 1998. text 26.95 (0-312-86714-X) St Martin.

— The Radiant Seas. 512p. 1999. mass mkt. 6.99 (0-8125-8036-2, Pub. by Tor Bks) St Martin.

Asaro, Catherine. The Veiled Web. 368p. 1999. mass mkt. 5.99 (0-553-58151-1) Bantam.

Asaro, R. A., jt. ed. see Benson, D. J.

Asatani, K. Introduction to B-ISDN. LC 96-3340. 272p. 1997. 115.00 (0-471-96766-1) Wiley.

Asato, Andrew, jt. auth. see Fuller, Rose.

*Asato, Dennis. A Dolphin Day in Hawaii. large type ed. (Illus.). 50p. (J). (ps-1). 1999. 12.00 (0-9653971-8-1, Pub. by Anoai Pr) Booklines Hawaii.

A

A

Asatrian, Garnik, ed. Acta Kurdica, 1995, Vol. 2. 1995. 65.00 (*0-7007-0469-8*, Pub. by Curzon Pr Ltd) Paul & Co Pubs.

Asatrian, Garnik, et al, eds. Acta Kurdica, 1994 Vol. 1: International Journal of Kurdish & Iranian Studies. 260p. (C). 1994. pap. 65.00 (*0-7007-0324-1*, Pub. by Curzon Pr Ltd) Paul & Co Pubs.

Asawa, Paige P., jt. auth. see Junge, Maxine B.

Asay, Carlos E. Family Pecan Trees: Planting a Legacy of Faith at Home. LC 92-15838. 254p. 1992. 12.95 (*0-87579-608-7*) Deseret Bk.

— The Seven M's of Missionary Service. 1996. 12.95 (*1-57008-287-1*) Bookcraft Inc.

Asay, Chuck. Asay Doodles Goes to Town. LC 95-18141. (Editorial Cartoonists Ser.). (Illus.). 160p. 1995. pap. 8.95 (*1-56554-142-1*) Pelican.

Asay, Diane, ed. see Shiba, Shoji, et al.

Asay, Diane, ed. see Uchimaru, Kiyoshi, et al.

Asay, Karol. Gray Head & Long Hair. 1988. 24.95 (*0-8488-0221-7*); pap. 14.95 (*0-8488-0241-1*) Amereon Ltd.

Asay, Karol, intro. Camp Talk: The Very Private Letters of Captain Frederick W. Benteen of the 7th U. S. Calvalry to His Wife, 1871-1888. (Illus.). 1985. 36.95 (*0-8488-0001-X*, J M C & Co) Amereon Ltd.

Asay, Roger, jt. auth. see Davis, Rebecca.

Asayesh, Gelareh. Saffron Sky: A Life Between Iran & America. LC 99-27889. 224p. 1999. 24.00 (*0-8070-7210-9*) Beacon Pr.

***Asayesh, Gelareh.** Saffron Sky: A Life Between Iran & American. 2000. pap. 14.00 (*0-8070-7211-7*) Beacon Pr.

Asayesh, Gelareh, ed. see Melaville, Atelia I. & Blank, Martin J.

Asbach, Charles & Schermer, Victor C. Object Relations, the Self & the Group: A Conceptual Paradigm. 288p. 1987. 55.00 (*0-7100-9839-1*, Routledge Thoemms) Routledge.

Asbach, Olaf. Kritische Gesellschaftstheorie und Historische Praxis: Entwicklungen der Kritischen Theorie Bei Max Horkheimer, 1930-1942 - 43. (GER.). 336p. 1997. 57.95 (*3-631-31766-2*) P Lang Pubng.

Asbe, Michael & Counsell, Lynne. Insider Trading. 2nd ed. 275p. 1993. 120.00 (*0-85459-815-4*, Pub. by Tolley Pubng) St Mut.

Asbee, Sue. Flann O'Brien. (Twayne's English Authors Ser.: No. 485). 160p. 1991. 22.95 (*0-8057-7001-1*) Macmillan.

— Virginia Woolf. (Life & Works Ser.: Set II). (Illus.). 112p. (YA). (gr. 7 up). 1990. lib. bdg. 18.95 (*0-86593-019-8*) Rourke Corp.

Asbell, Bernard. The Senate Nobody Knows. LC 80-8928. 480p. 1978. reprint ed. pap. 148.80 (*0-608-05923-4*, 206625900008) Bks Demand.

Asbell, Bernard, ed. Mother & Daughter: The Letters of Eleanor & Anna Roosevelt. LC 88-16572. 366p. 1988. pap. 9.95 (*0-88064-108-8*) Fromm Intl Pub.

Asbell, Bernard, jt. auth. see Vough, Clair F.

Asbell, Riva Lee. Evaluation & Management Coding: A Comprehensive Guide for Ophthalmology. (Illus.). 35p. 1997. pap. write for info. incl. audio, cd-rom (*1-929196-02-4*) Am Opthlmc Admin.

Asberg, M., jt. ed. see Jenike, Michael A.

Asbery, David, jt. auth. see Wayans, Damon.

Asbjornsen, Jan, jt. auth. see Arrants, Cheryl.

Asbjornsen, Peter C. Tales from the Fjeld. Dasent, George W., tr. LC 69-13232. (Illus.). 1972. reprint ed. 23.95 (*0-405-08217-7*) Ayer.

— The Three Billy Goats Gruff. LC 96-42349. (Illus.). 24p. (J). (ps up). 1998. 9.95 (*0-694-01033-2*) HarpC.

Asbjornsen, Peter C. & Moe, J. E. The Man Who Kept House. LC 91-37599. (Illus.). 32p. (J). (ps-3). 1992. 13.95 (*0-689-50560-4*) McElderry Bks.

— The Three Billy Goats Gruff. LC 57-5265. (Illus.). 32p. (J). (ps-3). 1991. reprint ed. pap. 6.00 (*0-15-690150-1*) Harcourt.

Asbjornsen, Peter C. & Moe, Jorgen. Norwegian Folk Tales. 192p. 1982. pap. 14.00 (*0-394-71054-1*) Pantheon.

Asbjornsen, Peter C., et al. East o' the Sun & West o' the Moon & Other Fairy Tales. LC 96-26351. (Children's Thrift Editions Ser.). (Illus.). 96p. (Orig.). (J). 1996. pap. text 1.00 (*0-486-29439-0*) Dover.

Asbjrnsen, Peter C. Easy Work! An Old Tale. LC 97-28184. (Illus.). 32p. (J). (gr. k-3). 1998. lib. bdg. 15.95 (*0-8234-1349-7*) Holiday.

Asbraf, Mary. Political Verse & Song from Britain & Ireland. 1976. 12.95 (*0-8464-0731-0*) Beekman Pubs.

***Asbridge, Thomas S.** The Creation of the Principality of Antioch, 1098-1130. 242p. 2000. 75.00 (*0-85115-661-4*) Boydell & Brewer.

***Asbridge, Thomas S. & Edgington, Susan B., trs.** Walter the Chancellor's the Antiochene Wares: A Translation & Commentary. LC 99-72047. (Crusade Texts in Translation Ser.: Vol. 4). 230p. 1999. 61.95 (*1-84014-263-4*, Pub. by Ashgate Pub) Ashgate Pub Co.

Asbrink, L., jt. auth. see Lindholm, E.

Asbury, Arthur K., et al, eds. Diseases of the Nervous System: Clinical Neurobiology, 2 vols. 2nd ed. (Illus.). 1780p. 1991. text 335.00 (*0-7216-3208-4*, W B Saunders Co) Harcrt Hlth Sci Grp.

— Sensory Neuropathies. LC 94-47263. (Illus.). 220p. 1995. 86.95 (*3-211-82642-4*) Spr-Verlag.

Asbury, Arthur K. & Thomas, P. K., eds. Peripheral Nerve Disorders 2, Vol. 2. LC 95-11157. (Blue Books of Practical Neurology: Vol. 15). 352p. 1995. text 100.00 (*0-7506-1765-9*) Buttrwrth-Heinemann.

Asbury, Carl & Asbury, Linda. When They Say You Are Going to Die. LC 96-108591. 112p. 1995. pap. 7.99 (*0-89274-784-6*, HH-784) Harrison Hse.

Asbury, Francis. Heart & Church. 1979. pap. 4.99 (*0-88019-036-1*) Schmul Pub Co.

Asbury, Greg & McDonald, Elvin. Rainforests to Flowers - Gardens on Java. Smith, Judy, ed. (Illus.). 112p. 1996. 24.95 (*0-9654003-0-1*) Mitra Publns.

Asbury, Henry. Reminiscences of Quincy, Containing Historical Events, Anecdotes, Matters Concerning Old Settlers & Old Times. (Illus.). 224p. 1995. reprint ed. lib. bdg. 29.50 (*0-8328-4682-1*) Higginson Bk Co.

Asbury, Herbert. The Barbary Coast. 1992. reprint ed. lib. bdg. 75.00 (*0-7812-5000-5*) Rprt Serv.

— Gangs of New York. 400p. 1994. pap. 12.95 (*1-56924-991-1*) Marlowe & Co.

***Asbury, Herbert.** Gangs of New York: An Informal History of the Underworld. (Illus.). 2000. pap. 14.95 (*1-56025-275-8*, Thunders Mouth) Avalon NY.

Asbury, Herbert. Great Illusion: An Informal History of Prohibition. LC 68-8051. (Illus.). 344p. 1968. reprint ed. lib. bdg. 69.50 (*0-8371-0008-9*, ASGI, Greenwood Pr) Greenwood.

— Suckers Progress: An Informal History of Gambling in America from the Colonies to Canfield. LC 69-14909. (Criminology, Law Enforcement, & Social Problems Ser.: No. 51). (Illus.). 1969. reprint ed. 25.00 (*0-87585-051-0*) Patterson Smith.

Asbury, Herbert & Craige, Betty J. Gem of the Prairie: An Informal History of the Chicago Underworld. 2nd ed. LC 86-8631. xxx, 416p. 1986. reprint ed. pap. 16.00 (*0-87580-534-5*) N Ill U Pr.

Asbury, Kelly A. Bonnie's Blue House. LC 96-21715. (J). 1995. 7.95 (*0-8050-4022-6*) H Holt & Co.

— Rusty's Red Vacation. LC 96-21712. (J). 1995. 7.95 (*0-8050-4021-8*) H Holt & Co.

***Asbury, Kelly A.** Where Is Snowy's Nose? (Illus.). 14p. (J). (ps-3). 2000. 6.99 (*0-8431-7627-X*, G & D) Peng Put Young Read.

Asbury, Kelly A. Yolanda's Yellow School. LC 96-21714. (J). 1995. 7.95 (*0-8050-4023-4*) H Holt & Co.

Asbury, Linda, jt. auth. see Asbury, Carl.

Asbury, Martha, ed. see Gallagher, Francis.

***Asbury, Stephen.** Enterprise Linux at Work: How to Build 10 Distributed Applications for Your Organizations. LC 99-59493. 448p. 2000. pap. text 49.99 incl. cd-rom (*0-471-36349-9*) Wiley.

Asbury, Stephen & Weiner, Scott R. Developing Java Enterprise Applications. LC 98-55106. 800p. 1999. pap. 59.99 incl. cd-rom (*0-471-32756-5*) Wiley.

Asbury, Stephen, et al. CGI How-To: The Definitive CGI Scripting Problem-Solver. (Illus.). 576p. 1996. 39.99 (*1-57169-028-X*) Sams.

— Perl 5 How-To. 2nd ed. LC 97-20245. 928p. 1997. 49.99 (*1-57169-118-9*) Sams.

Asbury, Stephen, jt. auth. see Weiner, Scott.

ASCA Staff. A Guide to Report Writing for Consulting Arborists. Abeyta, Dorthy, ed. (Illus.). 142p. (Orig.). 1995. pap. 60.00 (*1-881956-11-3*) Int Soc Arboricult.

Ascani, E., et al, eds. Osteosynthesis in Spinal Surgery. (Progress in Spinal Pathology Ser.: Vol. 4). (Illus.). 185p. 1990. 62.95 (*0-387-82150-3*) Spr-Verlag.

Ascanio, Pam. White Men Don't Have Juju: An American Couple's Adventure Through Africa from the Forbidden Zone to Timbuktu. LC 91-51220. (Illus.). 345p. (Orig.). 1992. pap. 12.95 (*1-879360-12-8*) Noble Pr.

ASCAP Staff. ASCAP's 50 Most Performed Songs of the 90's. 19.95 (*0-7692-9160-0*) Warner Bros.

Ascari, Rosalia C., jt. auth. see Killiam, Marie-Therese.

***Ascari, Rosalia Colombo & Pozzi, Grazia Viva, eds.** Il Testo: Lo Stile dell'analisi dello Stile. 384p. 1998. pap. 54.95 (*1-57292-010-6*) Austin & Winfield.

ASCD Improving Student Achievement Research Panel. Educating Everybody's Children: Diverse Teaching Strategies for Diverse Learners - What Research & Practice Say about Improving Achievement. Cole, Robert W. et al, eds. LC 95-7075. 1995. pap. 25.95 (*0-87120-237-9*) ASCD.

ASCE Boston Civil Engineers Section Structural Gro, jt. auth. see ASCE Structures Congress Staff.

ASCE, Boston Society of Civil Engineers Staff. Integrated Water Resources Planning for the 21st Century: Proceedings of the 22nd Annual Conference, Cambridge, MA, May 7-11, 1995. ASCE, Water Resource Planning & Management Divisio & Domenica, Michael F., eds. LC 95-15111. 1204p. 1995. pap. 119.00 (*0-7844-0081-4*) Am Soc Civil Eng.

ASCE Committee on Compression Members Staff. Bibliography of Steel Columns. 214p. 1990. pap. text 6.00 (*0-87262-780-2*) Am Soc Civil Eng.

ASCE Committee on Engineering Management, Aug. 197. The Civil Engineer's Role in Productivity in the Construction Industry, 2 vols., Set. 402p. 1976. pap. 5.00 (*0-87262-075-1*) Am Soc Civil Eng.

ASCE Committee on Masonry & Reinforced Concrete St. Design of Cylindrical Concrete Shell Roofs. LC 54-312. (ASCE Manual of Engineering Practice Ser.: No. 31). (Illus.). 185p. pap. 57.40 (*0-8357-6657-8*, 203532600094) Bks Demand.

ASCE Composite Steel Deck Slabs Standards Committe. ANSI-ASCE 3-84 Specifications for the Design & Construction of Composite Slabs & Commentary on Specifications for the Design & Construction of Composite Slabs. 56p. 1985. 15.00 (*0-87262-470-6*) Am Soc Civil Eng.

ASCE Conference, Aerospace Division, 1980. Civil Engineering Applications of Remote Sensing. Kiefer, Ralph W., ed. LC 80-67879. 199p. 1980. pap. 21.00 (*0-87262-253-3*) Am Soc Civil Eng.

ASCE Conference, Hydraulics Division, 1980. Computer & Physical Modeling in Hydraulic Engineering. Ashton, George, ed. LC 80-67878. 500p. 1980. pap. 43.00 (*0-87262-252-5*) Am Soc Civil Eng.

ASCE, Engineering Mechanics Division Staff & University of Colorado, Boulder, Department of Civ. Engineering Mechanics: Proceedings of the Tenth Conference Sponsored by the Engineering Mechanics Division of the ASCE & the Department of Civil, Environmental & Architectural Engineering of the University of Colorado at Boulder, Boulder, Colorado, May 21-24, 1995, 2 vols. Sture, Stein, ed. LC 95-15188. 1448p. 1995. pap. 149.00 (*0-7844-0083-0*, ASCE Press) Am Soc Civil Eng.

ASCE, Environmental Engineering Division, Committe. Quality of Ground Water: Guidelines for Selection & Application of Frequently Used Models - A Report on the State-of-the-Art. LC 96-21049. (ASCE Manual & Report of Engineering Practice: No. 85). 160p. 1996. pap. 48.00 (*0-7844-0137-3*) Am Soc Civil Eng.

ASCE Environmental Engineering Division Staff, jt. auth. see ASCE Geotechnical Engineering Division Staff.

ASCE Geotechnical Engineering Division Staff & ASCE Environmental Engineering Division Staff. Geoenvironment 2000: Characterization, Containment, Remediation, & Performance in Environmental Geotechnics: Proceedings, 2 vols. Acar, Yalcin B. & Daniel, David E., eds. LC 95-1420. (Geotechnical Special Publications: No. 46). 1856p. 1995. pap. 154.00 (*0-7844-0074-1*) Am Soc Civil Eng.

ASCE National Convention, Environmental Analysis R. Appropriate Technology in Resource Conservation & Recovery. Gunnerson, Charles G. & Kalbermatten, John M., eds. LC 80-65304. 218p. 1980. pap. 5.00 (*0-87262-035-2*) Am Soc Civil Eng.

ASCE Pipeline Division, New Orleans, March, 1981. Underground Plastic Pipe. Schrock, B. J., ed. LC 81-65630. 553p. 1981. pap. 6.00 (*0-87262-265-7*) Am Soc Civil Eng.

ASCE, Pipeline Division Staff, et al. Advances in Underground Pipeline Engineering II: Proceedings of the Second International Conference, Bellevue, Washington, June 25-28, 1995. Jeyapalan, Jey K. & Jeyapalan, Menaka, eds. LC 95-19043. 876p. 1995. 82.00 (*0-7844-0093-8*) Am Soc Civil Eng.

ASCE Press Staff. Hydraulic Design of Flood Control Channels. LC 95-10050. (U. S. Army Corps of Engineers Adapted Technical Engineering & Design Guides Ser.: Vol. 10). 128p. 1995. 39.00 (*0-7844-0067-9*, ASCE Press) Am Soc Civil Eng.

***ASCE Specialty Conference on Performance Confirmation of Constructed Geotechnical Facilities Staff, et al.** Performance Confirmation of Constructed Geotechnical Facilities: Proceedings of Sessions of ASCE Specialty Conference On Performance Confirmation of Constructed Geotechnical Facilities: April 9-12, 2000, Amherst, Massachusetts. LC 00-24611. 2000. write for info. (*0-7844-0486-0*) Am Soc Civil Eng.

ASCE Staff, ed. Settlement Analysis. LC 94-37791. (Adapted Technical Engineering & Design Guides from the U.S. Corp of Army Engineers Ser.: Vol. 9). 136p. 1994. 39.00 (*0-7844-0021-0*) Am Soc Civil Eng.

ASCE Staff, et al. Residential Streets. 2nd ed. 90p. 1990. pap. text 23.95 (*0-87420-700-2*, R07) Urban Land.

ASCE Staff, jt. auth. see ACSM Staff.

ASCE, Structural Division, Committee on Wood, Task, ed. Classic Wood Structures. 256p. 1989. pap. text 23.00 (*0-87262-739-X*) Am Soc Civil Eng.

ASCE Structures Congress Staff & ASCE Boston Civil Engineers Section Structural Gro. Restructuring: American & Beyond: Proceedings: ASCE Structures Congress (13th: 1995: Boston, Mass.) Sanayei, Masoud, ed. LC 95-3639. 1936p. 1995. pap. 187.00 (*0-7844-0076-8*) Am Soc Civil Eng.

ASCE Task Committee on Hydrographic Investigations. Measurement of Hydrographic Parameters in Large Sand-Bed Streams from Boats. 84p. 1983. pap. 14.00 (*0-87262-354-8*) Am Soc Civil Eng.

ASCE Technical Council on Ocean Engineering, Dec. Civil Engineering in the Oceans II. 1277p. 1970. 7.00 (*0-87262-018-2*) Am Soc Civil Eng.

ASCE, Water Resource Planning & Management Divisio, ed. see ASCE, Boston Society of Civil Engineers Staff.

ASCE, Waterway, Port, Coastal & Ocean Division, Co. Wave Forces on Inclined & Vertical Wall Structures: Task Committee on Forces on Inclined & Vertical Wall Structures of the Committee on Waves & Wave Forces of the Waterway, Port, Coastal & Ocean Engineering Division. LC 95-8330. 408p. 1995. 39.00 (*0-7844-0080-6*) Am Soc Civil Eng.

Ascencio, Juan A., jt. ed. see Bowen, David.

Ascended Master Bob. The I AM Discourses. LC 87-20624. (Saint Germain Ser.: Vol. 12). (Illus.). 236p. 1987. 25.00 (*1-878891-52-9*) St Germain Press Inc.

Ascended Masters Discourses. I Am the Open Door. 3rd ed. (Illus.). 85p. 1989. reprint ed. pap. text 6.95 (*0-9619770-5-1*) Pearl Publishing.

— Step by Step We Climb to Freedom, Vol. 2. LC 88-18011. (Step by Step Ser.). (Illus.). 200p. 1990. reprint ed. pap. 9.95 (*0-9619770-2-7*) Pearl Publishing.

Ascended Masters Discourses Staff. Step by Step We Climb, Vol. 1. rev. ed. LC 88-18012. (Step by Step Ser.). (Illus.). 225p. 1990. reprint ed. pap. 9.95 (*0-9619770-1-9*) Pearl Publishing.

Ascended Masters Staff. Ascended Master Discourses. LC 85-1778. (Saint Germain Ser.: Vol. 6). (Illus.). 337p. 1937. 26.00 (*1-878891-28-6*) St Germain Press Inc.

— I Am the Open Door. 2nd ed. Mt. Shasta, Peter, ed. & pref. by. 96p. 1987. reprint ed. pap. 6.95 (*0-9617951-0-7*) Peter Mt Shasta.

Ascensao, J. L., et al, eds. Molecular Biology of Erythropoiesis. (Advances in Experimental Medicine & Biology Ser.: Vol. 271). (Illus.). 240p. 1989. 79.50 (*0-306-43532-2*, Plenum Trade) Perseus Pubng.

Ascenzi, Joseph. Handbook of Disinfectants & Antiseptics. (Illus.). 312p. 1995. text 145.00 (*0-8247-9524-5*) Dekker.

Asch. Bear Scare. (J). 1998. 12.95 (*0-13-071283-3*) S&S Childrens.

— Feminism & Bioethics. 1997. 22.95 (*0-8057-9761-0*, Twyne) Mac Lib Ref.

— Government & the Marketplace. 3rd ed. (C). 1996. text. write for info. (*0-03-097626-X*) Harcourt Coll Pubs.

— Thirty Years War, 1618 to 1648. LC 96-41029. 224p. 1997. text 49.95 (*0-312-16584-6*) St Martin.

Asch, jt. auth. see Lunden.

Asch, A. Concertino: Upper Intermediate. 16p. 1994. pap. 4.95 (*0-7935-3159-4*, 00290455) H Leonard.

— Concertino No. 2: Solo Piano, 2 Pianos, or Solo Piano with Orchestra. 12p. 1995. pap. 4.95 (*0-7935-3759-2*, 00290473) H Leonard.

Asch, Adrienne, jt. ed. see Fine, Michelle.

Asch, Adrienne, jt. ed. see Parens, Erik.

Asch, Berta & Mangus, A. R. Farmers on Relief & Rehabilitation. LC 78-165678. (Research Monographs). 1971. reprint ed. lib. bdg. 27.50 (*0-306-70340-8*) Da Capo.

Asch, Beth J. Designing Military Pay: Contributions & Implications of the Economics Literature. LC 93-16003. 1993. pap. text 13.00 (*0-8330-1391-2*, MR-161-FMP) Rand Corp.

— Military Support for Youth Development: An Exploratory Analysis. LC 94-24606. 51p. (Orig.). 1995. pap. text 7.50 (*0-8330-1588-5*, MR-497-A/RC) Rand Corp.

— Reserve Supply in the Post-Desert Storm Recruiting Environment. LC 93-15861. 1993. pap. 13.00 (*0-8330-1382-3*, MR-224) Rand Corp.

Asch, Beth J. & Dertouzos, James N. Educational Benefits vs. Enlistment Bonuses: A Comparison of Recruiting Options. LC 94-39723. 62p. (Orig.). 1995. pap. text 15.00 (*0-8330-1603-2*, MR-302-OSD) Rand Corp.

Asch, Beth J. & Hosek, James R. Military Compensation: Trends & Policy Options. LC 99-230327. v, 50p. 1999. pap. 6.00 (*0-8330-2742-5*, DB-273-OSD) Rand Corp.

Asch, Beth J. & Karoly, Lynn A. The Role of the Job Counselor in the Military Enlistment Process. LC 93-36448. 1993. pap. 13.00 (*0-8330-1451-X*, MR-315-P&R) Rand Corp.

Asch, Beth J. & Orvis, Bruce R. Recent Recruiting Trends & Their Implications: Preliminary Analysis & Recommendations. 46p. 1995. pap. text 7.50 (*0-8330-1628-8*, MR-549-A/OSD) Rand Corp.

Asch, Beth J. & Warner, John T. A Policy Analysis of Alternative Military Retirement Systems. LC 94-28238. 1994. pap. 15.00 (*0-8330-1565-6*, MR-465-OSD) Rand Corp.

— Separation & Retirement Incentives in the Civil Service: A Comparison of Federal Employees Retirement System & the Civil Services Retirement System. LC 98-51689. 81p. 1999. pap. 15.00 (*0-8330-2689-5*, MR-986-OSD) Rand Corp.

— A Theory of Military Compensation & Personnel Policy. LC 94-16956. 1994. pap. 15.00 (*0-8330-1544-3*, MR-439-OSD) Rand Corp.

***Asch, Beth J., et al.** Attracting College-Bound Youth into the Military: Toward the Development of New Recruiting Policy Options. LC 98-52212. (Illus.). vxii, 46p. 1999. pap. 7.50 (*0-8330-2702-6*, MR-98405D) Rand Corp.

Asch, Beth J., et al. Reforming the Military Retirement System. LC 96-37426. 81p. 1998. pap. 15.00 (*0-8330-2463-9*, MR-748) Rand Corp.

Asch, Beth J., jt. auth. see Oken, Carole.

Asch, Bonnie B., jt. auth. see Ip, Margot M.

Asch, Connie. Indian Designs. 64p. 1985. pap. 5.95 (*0-918080-25-8*, Rio Nuevo) Treas Chest Bks.

— Indians of the Americas Coloring Book. (Illus.). 32p. (Orig.). (J). (gr. k-6). 1987. pap. 3.50 (*0-918080-33-9*) Treas Chest Bks.

— Tohono O'Odham (Papago) Indian Coloring Book. rev. ed. (Illus.). 32p. (Orig.). (J). (gr. 1-6). 1983. reprint ed. pap. 3.50 (*0-918080-60-6*) Treas Chest Bks.

Asch, David L. The Middle Woodland Population of the Lower Illinois Valley. LC 82-101264. (Scientific Papers: No. 1). (Illus.). 112p. 1976. 7.50 (*0-942118-00-6*); pap. 4.50 (*0-942118-01-4*) Ctr Amer Arche.

Asch, Devin, jt. auth. see Asch, Frank.

Asch, F. Moon Cloud. (J). 1998. 10.95 (*0-13-600552-7*) P-H.

Asch, Frank. Baby Bird's First Nest. LC 97-32653. (Illus.). 32p. (J). 1999. 14.00 (*0-15-201726-7*) Harcourt.

— Barnyard Lullaby. LC 96-44987. 40p. (J). (ps-1). 1998. 15.00 (*0-689-81363-5*) Aladdin.

— Bear Shadow. LC 82-18250. (Illus.). 32p. (J). (ps-k). 1988. pap. 4.95 (*0-671-66866-8*) S&S Bks Yung.

— Bear Shadow. (Big Bks.). (J). (gr. 6 up). 1992. pap. 19.95 (*0-590-72736-2*) Scholastic Inc.

— Bear Shadow. (J). 1985. 10.15 (*0-606-03727-6*, Pub. by Turtleback) Demco.

— Bear's Bargain. LC 85-6355. (Illus.). 32p. (J). (gr. k-4). 1989. pap. 4.95 (*0-671-67838-8*) S&S Bks Yung.

— Bear's Bargain. (Big Bks.). (J). (ps-3). 1992. 19.95 (*0-590-72698-6*) Scholastic Inc.

— Bears Bargain. (J). 1989. 10.15 (*0-606-04167-2*, Pub. by Turtleback) Demco.

— Cactus Poems. LC 96-50351. (Illus.). 48p. (gr. 3-5). 1998. 18.00 (*0-15-200676-1*) Harcourt.

— The Earth & I. LC 93-237. (Illus.). 32p. (J). (ps-2). 1994. 15.00 (*0-15-200443-2*, Gulliver Bks) Harcourt.

— Good Night, Baby Bear. LC 96-39178. (Illus.). 32p. (J). (ps-1). 1998. 14.00 (*0-15-200836-5*, Gulliver Bks) Harcourt.

— Goodbye House. LC 85-19263. (Illus.). 32p. (J). (ps-3). 1989. pap. 4.95 (*0-671-67927-9*) Litle Simon.

— Hands Around Lincoln School. LC 92-31246. 144p. (J). (gr. 4-7). 1994. 13.95 (*0-590-44149-3*) Scholastic Inc.

— Hands Around Lincoln School. 1994. 8.60 (*0-606-07606-9*, Pub. by Turtleback) Demco.

— Happy Birthday, Moon. LC 88-6569. (Illus.). 32p. (J). (gr. k-4). 1982. pap. 15.00 (*0-671-66454-9*) Litle Simon.

An Asterisk (*) at the beginning of an entry indicates that the title is appearing for the first time.

— Happy Birthday, Moon. LC 88-6569. (Illus.). 32p. (J). (gr. k-4). 1985. pap. 4.95 (*0-671-66455-7*) Litle Simon.

— Happy Birthday, Moon. (J). 1982. 10.15 (*0-606-00658-3*, Pub. by Turtleback) Demco.

***Asch, Frank.** Happy Birthday Moon. (Illus.). (J). (ps-3). 1999. 15.00 (*0-689-83543-4*) S&S Childrens.

Asch, Frank. I Can Blink Like an Owl. unabridged ed. (Illus.). 12p. (J). 1997. bds. 4.95 (*1-55074-380-5*, Pub. by Kids Can Pr) Genl Dist Srvs.

— I Can Roar Like a Lion. unabridged ed. (Illus.). 12p. (J). 1997. bds. 4.95 (*1-55074-382-1*, Pub. by Kids Can Pr) Genl Dist Srvs.

— Just Like Daddy. (Illus.). 32p. (J). (gr. k-4). 1984. pap. 4.95 (*0-671-66457-3*) S&S Bks Yung.

— The Last Puppy. LC 80-215. (Illus.). 32p. (J). (ps-3). 1989. pap. 4.95 (*0-671-66687-8*) S&S Bks Yung.

— The Last Puppy. (J). 1980. 10.15 (*0-606-04264-4*, Pub. by Turtleback) Demco.

— Moonbear Book & Bear. (Moonbear Ser.). (Illus.). (J). (ps-k). 1994. 16.95 (*0-671-89555-9*) Litle Simon.

***Asch, Frank.** Moonbear's Bargain. (Moonbear Ser.). (J). (gr. k-3). 2000. per. 5.99 (*0-689-83516-7*) Aladdin.

Asch, Frank. Moonbear's Books. (Moonbear Ser.). (Illus.). 14p. (J). (ps-k). 1993. 3.95 (*0-671-86744-X*) Litle Simon.

— Moonbear's Canoe. LC 94-160067. (Moonbear Ser.). (Illus.). 14p. (J). (ps-k). 1993. pap. 3.95 (*0-671-86745-8*) Litle Simon.

— Moonbear's Dream. LC 98-24133. (Moonbear Ser.). (Illus.). 32p. (J). (ps-k). 1999. per. 15.00 (*0-689-82244-8*) S&S Bks Yung.

— Moonbear's Friend. LC 94-127052. (Moonbear Ser.). (Illus.). 14p. (J). (ps-k). 1993. pap. 3.95 (*0-671-86746-6*) Litle Simon.

***Asch, Frank.** Moonbear's Pet. (Moonbear Ser.). (J). (gr. k-3). 2000. per. 5.99 (*0-689-83580-9*) Aladdin.

Asch, Frank. Moonbear's Pet. (Moonbear Ser.). (J). (ps-k). 1997. 15.00 (*0-614-29069-4*) S&S Childrens.

— Moonbear's Pet. LC 95-30011. (Moonbear Ser.). (Illus.). 32p. (J). (ps-k). 1997. 15.00 (*0-689-80794-5*) S&S Childrens.

— Moonbear's Pet. LC 95-30011. (Moonbear Ser.). (Illus.). 32p. (J). (ps-1). 2000. per. 4.99 (*0-689-82094-1*) S&S Childrens.

***Asch, Frank.** Moonbear's Shadow. (Moonbear Ser.). (J). (ps-k). 2000. per. 5.99 (*0-689-83519-1*) Aladdin.

— Moonbear's Skyfire. (Moonbear Ser.). (J). (ps-k). 2000. per. 5.99 (*0-689-83545-0*) Aladdin.

— Mooncake. (Moonbear Ser.). (J). (gr. k-3). 2000. per. 5.99 (*0-689-83517-5*) Aladdin.

Asch, Frank. Mooncake. (Moonbear Ser.). (Illus.). 32p. (J). (ps-k). 1986. pap. 4.95 (*0-671-66451-4*) S&S Trade.

Asch, Frank. Mooncake. (Moonbear Ser.). (J). (ps-k). 1983. 10.15 (*0-606-02840-4*, Pub. by Turtleback) Demco.

— Moondance. (Moonbear Ser.). (Illus.). (J). (ps-k). 1999. pap. 12.25 (*0-7857-3558-5*) Econo-Clad Bks.

Asch, Frank. Moondance. LC 92-12358. (Moonbear Ser.). (Illus.). 32p. (J). (ps-k). 1993. 12.95 (*0-590-45487-0*) Scholastic Inc.

— Moondance. LC 92-12358. (Moonbear Ser.). (J). (ps-3). 1994. pap. 3.95 (*0-590-45488-9*) Scholastic Inc.

Asch, Frank. Moondance. LC 92-12358. (Moonbear Ser.). (J). (ps-k). 1993. 9.15 (*0-606-06578-4*, Pub. by Turtleback) Demco.

— Moongame. (Moonbear Ser.). (J). (ps-k). 2000. per. 5.99 (*0-689-83518-3*) Aladdin.

— Moongame. (Moonbear Ser.). (Illus.). (J). (ps-k). 1999. pap. 12.20 (*0-8085-9171-1*) Econo-Clad Bks.

Asch, Frank. Moongame. (Moonbear Ser.). (Illus.). 32p. (J). (ps-k). 1987. pap. 4.95 (*0-671-66453-0*) S&S Bks Yung.

— Moongame. (Moonbear Ser.). (J). (ps-k). 1992. 19.95 (*0-590-72624-2*) Scholastic Inc.

— One Man Show. LC 97-7626. (Meet the Author Ser.). (Illus.). 32p. (J). (gr. 2-5). 1997. 14.95 (*1-57274-095-7*, 717) R Owen Pubs.

— Sawgrass Poems: A View of the Everglades. LC 95-22762. (Illus.). 52p. (J). (gr. k-4). 1996. 18.00 (*0-15-200180-8*, Gulliver Bks) Harcourt.

— Skyfire. LC 88-3193. (Illus.). 32p. (J). (gr. k-4). 1988. pap. 4.95 (*0-671-66861-7*) Litle Simon.

— Skyfire. 1990. 10.15 (*0-606-03920-1*, Pub. by Turtleback) Demco.

— Song of the North. LC 97-50161. (Illus.). 32p. (J). 1999. 16.00 (*0-15-201258-3*) Harcourt.

— The Sun Is My Favorite Star. LC 98-46383. (Illus.). 32p. (J). (ps-3). 2000. 15.00 (*0-15-202127-2*, Harcourt Child Bks) Harcourt.

— Water. LC 93-47967. (Gulliver Green Book Ser.). (Illus.). 32p. (J). (ps-2). 1995. 15.00 (*0-15-200189-1*, Gulliver Bks) Harcourt.

***Asch, Frank.** Water. (Illus.). 32p. (J). 2000. pap. 6.00 (*0-15-202348-8*, Voyager Bks) Harcourt.

Asch, Frank. Ziggy Piggy & the Three Little Pigs. (Illus.). 32p. (J). (ps-2). 1998. 14.95 (*1-55074-515-8*, Pub. by Kids Can Pr) Genl Dist Srvs.

***Asch, Frank & Asch, Devin.** Baby Duck's New Friend. LC 00-8189. (J). 2001. write for info. (*0-15-202257-0*) Harcourt.

Asch, Frank & Vagin, Vladimir. Dear Brother. 32p. (J). (gr. 1-4). 1992. 13.95 (*0-590-43107-2*, Scholastic Hardcover) Scholastic Inc.

— Insects from Outer Space. LC 93-26876. (Illus.). 32p. (J). (gr. k-3). 1995. 14.95 (*0-590-45489-7*) Scholastic Inc.

Asch, Jan. Games for Global Awareness. (Illus.). 80p. (J). (gr. 2-5). 1994. 10.99 (*0-86653-792-9*, GA1486) Good Apple.

Asch, Lisa. Tanzania. 2nd ed. (Passport's Regional Guides of Africa Ser.). (Illus.). 192p. 1997. pap. 19.95 (*0-8442-8962-0*, 89620, Passprt Bks) NTC Contemp Pub Co.

Asch, Michael. Home & Native Land: Aboriginal Rights & the Canadian Constitution. 166p. 1984. pap. 16.95 (*0-7748-0472-6*) U of Wash Pr.

Asch, Michael, ed. Aboriginal & Treaty Rights in Canada: Essays on Law, Equality, & Respect for Difference. LC 97-175369. 288p. 1997. 65.00 (*0-7748-0580-3*) U of Wash Pr.

Asch, Moses & Lomax, Alan. The Leadbelly Songbook. (Illus.). 96p. 1962. pap. 12.95 (*0-8256-0042-1*, OK62224, Oak) Music Sales.

Asch, Nathan. Pay Day. (Proletarian Literature Ser.). xxxiii, 280p. 1990. reprint ed. lib. bdg. 38.00 (*1-55888-268-5*) Omnigraphics Inc.

Asch, Peter. Consumer Safety Regulation: Putting a Price on Life & Limb. (Illus.). 190p. 1988. text 60.00 (*0-19-504972-1*) OUP.

Asch, Peter & Quandt, Richard E. Racetrack Betting: The Professor's Guide to Strategies. LC 91-13947. 206p. 1991. pap. 19.95 (*0-275-94103-5*, B4103, Praeger Pubs) Greenwood.

Asch, Ricardo H., et al, eds. Gamete Physiology. (Serono Symposia, USA Ser.). (Illus.). 366p. (C). 1990. text 65.00 (*1-878601-02-4*) Serono Symposia USA.

Asch, Richard H. & Studd, John W., eds. Progress in Reproductive Medicine, Vol. 2. (Illus.). 304p. 1995. 65.00 (*1-85070-574-7*) Prthnon Pub.

Asch, Sholem. Children of Abraham: The Short Stories of Sholem Asch. Samuel, Maurice, tr. LC 74-152934. (Short Story Index Reprint Ser.). 1977. reprint ed. 30.95 (*0-8369-3792-9*) Ayer.

— East River. 438p. 1983. reprint ed. pap. 8.95 (*0-88184-014-9*) Carroll & Graf.

— Kiddush Ha-Shem: An Epic of 1648. Learsi, Rufus, tr. LC 74-27960. (Modern Jewish Experience Ser.). 1975. reprint ed. 23.95 (*0-405-06691-0*) Ayer.

— Mother. Ausubel, Nathan, tr. LC 73-114047. (BCL Ser.: No. 1). reprint ed. 35.00 (*0-404-00408-3*) AMS Pr.

— Mottke the Thief. LC 73-98807. 314p. 1970. reprint ed. lib. bdg. 65.00 (*0-8371-2953-2*, ASMO, Greenwood Pr) Greenwood.

— The Nazarene. 704p. 1996. reprint ed. pap. 15.95 (*0-7867-0379-2*) Carroll & Graf.

— Sabbatai Zevi. Whyte, Florence & Noyes, George R., trs. LC 74-3622. (Illus.). 131p. 1974. reprint ed. lib. bdg. 59.75 (*0-8371-7449-X*, ASSZ, Greenwood Pr) Greenwood.

— Tales of My People. Levin, Meyer, tr. LC 75-128752. (Short Story Index Reprint Ser.). 1977. 23.95 (*0-8369-3609-4*) Ayer.

Asch, Sholem & Samual, Maurice. Children of Abraham: The Short Stories of Sholem Asch. LC 74-152934. (Short Story Index Reprint Ser.). 433p. 1982. reprint ed. lib. bdg. 26.50 (*0-8290-0827-6*) Irvington.

Asch, Solomon E., ed. see Kohler, Wolfgang.

Asch, Timothy, et al. Yanomamo Film Study Guide. Seaman, Gary, ed. (Illus.). 220p. (Orig.). (C). 1993. pap. 15.00 (*1-878986-10-4*) Ethnographics Pr.

Aschaffenburg, Gustav. Crime & Its Repression. Albrecht, Adalbert, tr. LC 68-55767. (Criminology, Law Enforcement, & Social Problems Ser.: No. 11). 1968. reprint ed. 26.00 (*0-87585-011-1*) Patterson Smith.

Ascham, Anthony. Of the Confusions & Revolutions of Governments. LC 75-33731. 226p. 1975. lib. bdg. 50.00 (*0-8201-1161-9*) Schol Facsimiles.

Ascham, Roger. Letters of Roger Ascham. Vos, Alvin, ed. & tr. by. from LAT. Hatch, Maurice, tr. from LAT. 322p. (C). 1989. 52.95 (*0-8204-0205-2*) P Lang Pubng.

— The Scholemaster. Mayor, John E., ed. LC 75-161717. reprint ed. 31.50 (*0-404-00409-1*) AMS Pr.

— The Scholemaster: Or, Plaine & Perfite Way of Teachyng Children the Latin Tong. LC 68-54609. (English Experience Ser.: No. 15). 134p. 1968. reprint ed. 60.00 (*90-221-0015-4*) Walter J Johnson.

— The Scholemaster: 1570 Edition. Stern, Jeffrey, ed. & intro. by. (Classics in Education Ser.). 80p. 1996. reprint ed. 65.00 (*1-85506-266-6*) Bks Intl VA.

— Toxophilus, 1545. 1988. reprint ed. lib. bdg. 49.00 (*0-7812-0203-5*) Rprt Serv.

— Toxophilus, 1545. Arber, Edward, ed. LC 73-131612. 1971. reprint ed. 29.00 (*0-403-00499-3*) Scholarly.

— Whole Works, 3 vols. in 4 pts., Set. Giles, J. A., ed. LC 70-121837. reprint ed. 265.00 (*0-404-00490-3*) AMS Pr.

Aschan. The Man Whom Women Loved. mass mkt. write for info. (*0-312-90055-4*) Tor Bks.

Aschauer, David A. How Big Should the Public Capital Stock Be? (Public Policy Brief Highlights Ser.: Vol. 43A). (Illus.). 6p. 1998. pap. write for info. (*0-941276-52-X*) J Levy.

— How Big Should the Public Capital Stock Be? The Relationship Between Public Capital & Economic Growth. (Public Policy Brief Ser.: Vol. 43). (Illus.). 36p. 1998. pap. write for info. (*0-941276-51-1*) J Levy.

Aschbacher, M. Overgroups of Sylow Subgroups in Sporadic Groups. LC 86-1040. (Memoirs of the AMS Ser.: Vol. 60/343). 235p. 1986. pap. 29.00 (*0-8218-2344-2*, MEMO/60/343) Am Math.

Aschbacher, M., et al, eds. Geometries & Groups. (C). 1988. text 260.00 (*90-277-2623-X*) Kluwer Academic.

***Aschbacher, Michael.** Finite Group Theory. 2nd ed. LC 99-55693. (Illus.). 336p. (C). 2000. text 74.95 (*0-521-78145-0*); pap. text 32.95 (*0-521-78675-4*) Cambridge U Pr.

Aschbacher, Michael. Sporadic Groups. (Cambridge Tracts in Mathematics Ser.: No. 104). (Illus.). 328p. (C). 1994. text 57.95 (*0-521-42049-0*) Cambridge U Pr.

— 3-Transposition Groups. (Tracts in Mathematics Ser.: No. 124). (Illus.). 267p. (C). 1996. text 54.95 (*0-521-57196-0*) Cambridge U Pr.

Aschbrenner, Angela M. Effective Meetings & Boundary Breakers. (Successful Ideas Ser.). (Illus.). 80p. (Orig.). 1990. pap. 10.00 (*1-880662-03-5*) A M Aschbrenner.

— Effective Time Management & Goal Setting. (Successful Ideas Ser.). (Illus.). 68p. (Orig.). 1990. pap. 10.00 (*1-880662-01-9*) A M Aschbrenner.

— Fundraising & Financial Accountability. (Successful Ideas Ser.). (Illus.). 40p. (Orig.). 1990. pap. 10.00 (*1-880662-02-7*) A M Aschbrenner.

— Motivational Sayings. (Successful Ideas Ser.). 60p. 1990. pap. 10.00 (*1-880662-04-3*) A M Aschbrenner.

***Aschbumer, Steve.** Kevin Garnett: Scratching the Surface. (SuperStar Series: Vol. 4). 96p. (J). 1999. pap. 4.95 (*1-58261-178-5*, Pub. by Sprts Pubng) Partners-West.

Asche, Catherine, ed. see Liquorman, Wayne.

Asche, D. An Introduction to Groups. (Illus.). 100p. 1989. pap. 39.00 (*0-85274-377-7*); disk 270.00 (*0-85274-378-5*) IOP Pub.

Asche, Florian. Das Product Placement Im Kinospielfilm. (GER.). 156p. 1996. 35.95 (*3-631-30254-1*) P Lang Pubng.

Ascheid, Gerd, jt. auth. see Meyr, Heinrich.

Aschenbach, B., ed. Astrophysics at FUV & EUV Wavelengths: Proceedings of the Topical Meeting of the COSPAR Interdisciplinary Scientific Commission E (Meeting E3) of the COSPAR 28th Plenary Meeting Held in The Hague, The Netherlands, 25 June-6 July, 1990. (Advances in Space Research Ser.: Vol. 1). 240p. 1991. pap. 156.50 (*0-08-041841-4*, Pergamon Pr) Elsevier.

Aschenbach, Bernd, et al. The Invisible Sky: ROSAT & the Age of X-Ray Astronomy. LC 97-34139. 1998. write for info. (*0-387-98343-0*) Copernicus Systs.

— The Invisible Sky: ROSAT & the Age of X-Ray Astronomy. Jenkner, Helmut, tr. LC 97-34139. (Illus.). 184p. 1997. 40.00 (*0-387-94928-3*) Spr-Verlag.

Aschenbrenner, Caralee. Please Don't Quote Me, Vol. 1. (Illus.). 344p. 1994. 32.00 (*0-9647651-0-1*) Straddle Creek.

Aschenbrenner, Dorothy J. Down Sunnyside Lane: Memories & Recipes. Yoder, Nelson, ed. & illus. by. 145p. 1992. text. write for info. (*0-9619439-1-2* D J Aschenbrenner.

Aschenbrenner, Erich. Oriental Rugs Vol. 2: Persian. (Illus.). 268p. 1981. 69.50 (*0-907462-12-X*) Antique Collect.

Aschenbrenner, Gerald. Jack, the Seal & the Sea. (Illus.). 30p. (J). (gr. 2-5). 1988. pap. 4.95 (*0-382-09986-9*); lib. bdg. 12.95 (*0-382-09985-0*) Silver Burdett Pr.

Aschenbrenner, Joyce & Collins, Lloyd R., eds. Processes of Urbanism: A Multidisciplinary Approach. (World Anthropology Ser.). xiv, 424p. 1978. 58.50 (*90-279-7620-1*) Mouton.

Aschenbrenner, Judge Peter S. Alaska Commercial Landlord Manual. 34.95 incl. disk (*1-891623-03-6*) Todd Commns.

Aschenbrenner, Karl. Analysis of Appraisive Characterization. 200p. 1983. text 155.50 (*90-277-1452-5*, D Reidel) Kluwer Academic.

— Coherence in Art. 1985. lib. bdg. 184.00 (*90-277-1959-4*) Kluwer Academic.

— A Companion to Kant's Critique of Pure Reason: Transcendental Aesthetic & Analytic. LC 83-6889. 334p. (Orig.). (C). 1983. pap. text 26.00 (*0-8191-3230-6*) U Pr of Amer.

— The Concepts of Criticism. LC 74-80523. (Foundations of Language Supplementary Ser.: No. 20). 540p. 1974. text 249.00 (*90-277-0482-1*) Kluwer Academic.

— The Concepts of Value: Foundations of Value Theory. LC 70-159651. (Foundations of Language Supplementary Ser.: No. 12). 462p. 1971. text 184.00 (*90-277-0185-7*) Kluwer Academic.

Aschenbrenner, Karl, tr. see Bochenski, Innocentius.

Aschenbrenner, Peter J. The Alaska Nonprofit Corporation Manual. LC 98-61221. 145 p. 1998. pap. 24.95 (*1-891623-00-1*, ALO1145, Americas Law) Wildenshaw Pub.

Aschenbrenner, Peter S. Thoroughly Modern Landlord. pap. 59.95 incl. disk (*1-891623-01-X*, Americas Law) Wildenshaw Pub.

Aschenbrunner, Jurgen. Lexikon Lokaler Netzwerke: Fachbegriffe. (GER.). 232p. 1992. 95.00 (*0-7859-8692-8*, 377234691x) Fr & Eur.

Aschengram, Ann & Seage. Essentials of Epidemiology in Public Health. 275p. 2000. 45.00 (*0-8342-0626-7*) Aspen Pub.

Ascher. Writing Repair Shop. (J). 1993. pap. 13.95 (*0-8384-3411-8*) Heinle & Heinle.

Ascher & Straus. Red Moon-Red Lake. 32p. (Orig.) 1984. pap. 3.00 (*0-917061-21-7*) Top Stories.

Ascher, A., et al, eds. The Mutual Effects of the Islamic & Judeo-Christian Worlds: The East European Pattern. LC 77-90629. (Studies on Society in Change: No. 3). 1979. write for info. (*0-930888-00-6*) Brooklyn Coll Pr.

Ascher, Abraham. Pavel Axelrod & the Development of Menshevism. LC 72-78423. (Russian Research Center Studies: No. 70). 435p. reprint ed. pap. 134.90 (*0-7837-3842-0*, 204366400010) Bks Demand.

— The Revolution of 1905: Russia in Disarray. LC 87-26657. (Illus.). xvi, 424p. 1988. 65.00 (*0-8047-1436-3*) Stanford U Pr.

— The Revolution of 1905: Authority Restored. LC 87-26697. 472p. (C). 1992. 65.00 (*0-8047-1972-1*) Stanford U Pr.

— The Revolution of 1905: Authority Restored. xvi, 444p. 1994. pap. 18.95 (*0-8047-2328-1*) Stanford U Pr.

Ascher, Abraham, et al, eds. The Mutual Effects of the Islamic & Judeo-Christian Worlds: The East European Pattern. 244p. (C). 1986. reprint ed. lib. bdg. 45.00 (*0-8191-5564-0*) U Pr of Amer.

Ascher, Allen. Think about Editing: A Grammar Guide. 334p. (J). 1996. mass mkt. 27.95 (*0-8384-3976-4*) Heinle & Heinle.

Ascher, Allen, ed. see Heyer, Sandra.

Ascher, Barbara Lazear. Dancing in the Dark: Romance, Yearning & the Search for the Sublime. LC 98-51506. 256p. 1999. 24.00 (*0-06-017442-0*) HarpC.

***Ascher, Barbara Lazear.** Isn't It Romantic: Finding the Magic in Everyday Life. 256p. 2000. pap. 13.00 (*0-06-093247-3*, Cliff Street) HarperTrade.

Ascher, Barbara Lazear. Landscape Without Gravity: A Memoir of Grief. LC 92-28088. 158p. 1993. 20.00 (*1-883285-10-0*) Delphinium.

— Landscape Without Gravity: A Memoir of Grief. 158p. 1999. reprint ed. pap. text 10.00 (*0-7881-6287-X*) DIANE Pub.

Ascher, Carol. The Flood: A Novel. LC 96-27245. 184p. 1996. reprint ed. pap. 11.95 (*1-880684-43-8*) Curbstone.

Ascher, Carol, et al, eds. Between Women: Biographers, Novelists, Critics, Teachers, & Artists Write about Their Work on Women. LC 93-13009. 525p. (C). 1993. reprint ed. pap. 26.99 (*0-415-90770-5*, B0658) Routledge.

Ascher, Carol, et al. Free to Choose: The False Promise of School Privatization. LC 96-32848. 144p. 1996. 9.95 (*0-87078-399-8*) Century Foundation.

Ascher, David, jt. auth. see Lutz, Mark.

Ascher, H. Statistical Analysis of Repairable Systems Reliability. (Statistics Ser.). Date not set. write for info. (*0-8247-9333-1*) Dekker.

Ascher, Harold & Feingold, Harry. Repairable Systems Reliability Modeling, Inference, Misconceptions & Their Causes. (Lecture Notes in Statistics Ser.: Vol. 7). (Illus.). 240p. 1984. text 75.00 (*0-8247-7276-8*) Dekker.

Ascher, K. R. S., jt. ed. see Navon, A.

Ascher, Katherine. Taking Control of Your Office Records: A Managers Guide. LC 83-6133. (Professional Librarian Ser.). 264p. 1986. 25.00 (*0-8161-1883-3*, Hall Reference) Macmillan.

Ascher, L. Michael, ed. Therapeutic Paradox. LC 89-11999. 385p. 1989. lib. bdg. 46.50 (*0-89862-393-6*) Guilford Pubns.

Ascher, M. Ethnomathematics: A Multicultural View of Mathematical Ideas. LC 90-48677. 300p. (C). (gr. 13). 1991. ring bd. 58.95 (*0-534-14880-8*, Chap & Hall CRC) CRC Pr.

— Ethnomathematics: A Multicultural View of Mathematical Ideas. (Illus.). 203p. (C). (gr. 13). 1994. per. 41.95 (*0-412-98941-7*, Chap & Hall CRC) CRC Pr.

Ascher, Marcia & Ascher, Robert. Mathematical Fallacies & Paradoxes. LC 97-15386. 224p. 1997. reprint ed. pap. text 7.95 (*0-486-29664-4*) Dover.

— Mathematics of the Incas: Code of the Quipu. LC 96-47494. (Illus.). 176p. 1997. reprint ed. pap. text 11.95 (*0-486-29554-0*) Dover.

Ascher, Maria L., tr. see Yourcenar, Marguerite.

Ascher, Mark L. Federal Income Taxation of Trusts & Estates: Cases, Problems & Materials. 2nd ed. LC 96-85847. 539p. 1996. boxed set 75.00 (*0-89089-656-9*) Carolina Acad Pr.

Ascher, P., et al, eds. Glutamate, Cell Death & Memory. (Research & Perspectives in Neurosciences Ser.: Vol. 1). (Illus.). 160p. 1991. 56.95 (*0-387-54134-9*) Spr-Verlag.

Ascher, P. & Selverston, Allen I., eds. Cellular & Molecular Mechanisms: Report of the Dahlem Workshop on Cellular & Molecular Mechanisms Underlying Higher Neural Functions, Berlin, 1993, February 28-March 5. LC 93-46293. (Life Sciences Research Reports: Vol. 54). 344p. 1994. 290.00 (*0-471-94304-5*) Wiley.

Ascher, Robert, jt. auth. see Ascher, Marcia.

***Ascher, Sheila.** ABC Street. 120p. 2001. pap. 10.95 (*1-892295-85-7*) Green Integer.

Ascher, Steven & Pincus, Edward. The Filmmaker's Handbook: A Comprehensive Guide for the Digital Age. rev. ed. LC 98-41665. 448p. 1999. pap. 18.95 (*0-452-27957-7*) NAL.

Ascher-Straus. Letter to an Unknown Woman. deluxe ed. (Treacle Story Ser.: No. 6). (Illus.). 48p. 1979. 12.50 (*0-914232-21-5*) McPherson & Co.

— The Menaced Assassin. 2nd ed. LC 89-8343. 128p. 1989. pap. 9.00 (*0-929701-03-8*) McPherson & Co.

— The Other Planet. LC 88-4991. 256p. 1988. 15.95 (*0-914232-93-2*) McPherson & Co.

— Red Moon - Red Lake. LC 88-23017. 128p. 1988. 16.00 (*0-914232-96-7*); pap. 8.00 (*0-914232-97-5*) McPherson & Co.

Ascher, Susan, jt. ed. see Lang, Erich K.

Ascher, Susan M., jt. auth. see Evans, Stephen R.

Ascher-Svanum, Haya & Krause, Audrey A. Psychoeducational Groups for Patients with Schizophrenia: A Guide for Practitioners. LC 90-14474. 308p. 1991. 93.00 (*0-8342-0197-6*) Aspen Pub.

Ascher, Uri M. & Petzold, Linda R. Computer Methods for Ordinary Differential Equations & Differential-Algebraic Equations. LC 98-21535. (Miscellaneous Titles in Applied Mathematics Ser.: Vol. 61). (Illus.). xvii, 314p. 1998. pap. text 36.50 (*0-89871-412-5*, BKOT0061) Soc Indus-Appl Math.

Ascher, Uri M., et al. Numerical Solution of Boundary Value Problems for Ordinary Differential Equations. LC 95-33340. (Classics in Applied Mathematics Ser.: Vol. 13). xxv, 595p. 1995. pap. 42.50 (*0-89871-354-4*, CL13) Soc Indus-Appl Math.

Ascher, William. Scheming for the Poor: The Politics of Redistribution in Latin America. LC 83-12866. (Illus.). 360p. 1984. 43.00 (*0-674-79085-5*) HUP.

***Ascher, William.** Why Governments Waste Natural Resources: Political Economy of Resource Policy Failures in Developing Countries. LC 98-51020. 328p. 1999. write for info. (*0-8018-6095-4*); pap. 17.95 (*0-8018-6096-2*) Johns Hopkins.

***Ascher, William & Miroviktlskakila, N. S.** The Caspian Sea: A Quest for Environmental Security. LC 00-26281. (NATO Science Series 2, Environmental Security). 2000. write for info. (*0-7923-6218-7*) Kluwer Academic.

A

***Ascher, William & Mirovitskaya, Natalia.** The Caspian Sea: A Quest for Environmental Security. 380p. 2000. pap. 66.00 (*0-7923-6219-5*) Kluwer Academic.

Ascher, William L. Communities & Sustainable Forestry in Developing Countries. LC 94-29702. 1994. pap. 19.95 (*1-55815-419-1*) ICS Pr.

— A Report of the International Commission for Central American Recovery & Development. Hubbard, Ann, ed. LC 89-1475. 148p. 1989. text 40.95 (*0-8223-0897-5*); pap. text 16.95 (*0-8223-0933-5*) Duke.

Ascher, William L. & Healy, Robert G. Natural Resource Policymaking in Developing Countries: Environment, Economic Growth, & Income Distribution. LC 90-2743. 239p. (Orig.). (C). 1990. pap. text 19.95 (*0-8223-1049-X*) Duke.

Ascher, William L. & Hubbard, Ann. Central American Recovery & Development, Vol. II. LC 89-7695. (Illus.). 448p. 1989. text 88.00 (*0-8223-0905-X*); pap. text 45.95 (*0-8223-1002-3*) Duke.

***Ascheri, Mario, et al.** Legal Consulting in the Civil Law Tradition. LC 99-56417. (Studies in Comparative Legal History). 1999. write for info. (*1-882239-11-3*) Robbins Collection.

Ascherman, Kurt & San Marco, Jim. Coaching Kids to Play Soccer. 144p. 1987. per. 9.00 (*0-671-63936-6*, Fireside) S&S Trade Pap.

***Aschermann, Arla.** MCSE Networking Essentials for Dummies. 2nd ed. LC 99-63442. (For Dummies Ser.). 384p. 1999. pap. 29.99 incl. cd-rom (*0-7645-0614-5*) IDG Bks.

Aschermann, Arla. Winds in the Cornfields of Early Pueblo County: Ghost Towns & Settlements, 1787-1872. 2nd ed. (Illus.). 72p. 1988. pap. 5.00 (*0-915617-15-3*) Pueblo Co Hist Soc.

***Aschersleben, Gisa, et al.** Cognitive Contributions to the Perception of Spatial & Temporal Events. LC 99-49978. (Advances in Psychology Ser.). 1999. write for info. (*0-444-50325-0*) Elsevier.

***Ascherson, Neal.** Berlin: A Century of Change. (Illus.). 98p. 2000. pap. 25.00 (*3-7913-2299-0*) Prestel Pub NY.

Ascherson, Neal. Black Sea. LC 95-19722. 304p. 1995. 23.00 (*0-8090-3043-8*) Hill & Wang.

— Black Sea. (Illus.). 320p. 1996. pap. 13.00 (*0-8090-1593-5*) Hill & Wang.

— Games with Shadows. 1989. pap. 12.95 (*0-09-173018-X*) Constable & Co.

***Aschheim, Eve.** Eve Aschheim: Paintings & Drawings. (Illus.). 2000. pap. 25.00 (*3-931135-39-X*) Hard Pr MA.

Aschheim, Joseph. Techniques of Monetary Control. LC 61-7804. (Illus.). 176p. reprint ed. pap. 54.60 (*0-608-18266-4*, 203298700082) Bks Demand.

Aschheim, K. W., jt. auth. see Dale, B.

Aschheim, Steven E. Brothers & Strangers: The East European Jew in German & German Jewish Consciousness, 1800-1923. LC 81-69812. (Mark H. Ingraham Prize). (Illus.). 364p. 1983. pap. text 19.95 (*0-299-09114-7*) U of Wis Pr.

Aschheim, Steven E. Brothers & Strangers: The East European Jew in German & German Jewish Consciousness, 1800-1923. LC 81-69812. 347p. reprint ed. pap. 107.60 (*0-608-09841-8*, 206922900003) Bks Demand.

— Culture & Catastrophe: German & Jewish Confrontations with National Socialism & Other Crises. LC 95-2924. 240p. (C). 1996. text 45.00 (*0-8147-0639-8*) NYU Pr.

— Culture & Catastrophe: German & Jewish Confrontations with National Socialism & Other Crises. LC 95-2924. (C). 1997. pap. text 20.00 (*0-8147-0642-8*) NYU Pr.

***Aschheim, Steven E.** In Times of Crisis: Essays on European Culture, Germans & Lews. 2000. 59.95 (*0-299-16860-3*); pap. 22.95 (*0-299-16864-6*) U of Wis Pr.

Aschheim, Steven E. The Nietzsche Legacy in Germany, 1890-1990. (Weird & Horrible Library: No. 2). (Illus.). 337p. (C). 1992. pap. 18.95 (*0-520-08555-8*, Pub. by U CA Pr) Cal Prin Full Svc.

Aschieris, Rochelle, jt. auth. see Hallberg, Edmond C.

Aschiero, Hipolito F. Diccionario de Homofonos Castellaros. (SPA.). 120p. 1975. 22.50 (*0-8288-5809-8*, S33053) Fr & Eur.

Aschkenasy, Nehama. Eve's Journey: Feminine Images in Hebraic Literary Tradition. LC 94-30739. 286p. 1994. reprint ed. pap. text 18.95 (*0-8143-2553-X*) Wayne St U Pr.

Aschkenes, Anna M., jt. auth. see Karasik, Gary.

Aschkensay, Nehama. Woman at the Window: Biblical Tales of Oppression & Escape. LC 98-14988. 256p. 1998. text 39.95 (*0-8143-2626-9*) Wayne St U Pr.

— Woman at the Window: Biblical Tales of Oppression & Escape. LC 98-14988. 1998. pap. text 18.95 (*0-8143-2627-7*) Wayne St U Pr.

Aschleitner, Friedrich, et al. Thomas Herzog: Design Center Linz. 132p. 1995. pap. 45.00 (*3-7757-0524-4*) Dist Art Pubs.

Aschliman, Kathryn. Growing Toward Peace. LC 93-18505. 320p. (Orig.). 1993. pap. 15.99 (*0-8361-3602-0*) Herald Pr.

Aschmann, Lisa. 500 Songwriting Ideas (For Brave & Passionate People) LC 97-71391. 112p. 1997. pap. 9.95 (*0-918371-15-5*, HL00330299, MixBooks) Intertec Pub.

Aschmann, Richard P. Proto Witotoan. LC 93-60089. (Publications in Linguistics Ser.: Vol. 114). viii, 168p. 1993. pap. 17.00 (*0-88312-189-1*) S I L Intl.

Aschner, Katherine. The Word Processing Handbook: A Step-by-Step Guide to Automating Your Office. LC 82-3. (Professional Librarian Ser.). (Illus.). 193p. 1986. 25.00 (*0-86729-018-8*, Hall Reference) Macmillan.

Aschner, Michael & Kimbelberg, Harold K., eds. The Role of Glia in Neurotoxicity. 384p. 1996. boxed set 199.95 (*0-8493-4792-0*, 4792) CRC Pr.

Aschoff, Frank. Der Theologische Weg Johann Friedrich Kleukers (1749-1827) (Europaische Hochschulschriften Ser.: Reihe 23, Bd. 436). (GER.). IX, 350p. 1991. 61.80 (*3-631-44253-X*) P Lang Pubng.

Aschoff, Jurgen, ed. Biological Rhythms. LC 80-21037. (Handbook of Behavioral Neurobiology Ser.: Vol. 4). 582p. 1981. 115.00 (*0-306-40585-7*, Plenum Trade) Perseus Pubng.

Aschwanden, Charles R., ed. see Aschwanden, Maria.

Aschwanden, Charles R., ed. see Aschwanden, Richard J. & Aschwanden, Maria.

Aschwanden, Maria. Challenging a Humanist. Aschwanden, Richard J. & Aschwanden, Charles R., eds. 160p. (Orig.). 1986. pap. 4.95 (*0-913071-03-X*) Rama Pub Co.

— Congratulations, America. Aschwanden, Richard J., ed. 176p. 1987. reprint ed. pap. 4.95 (*0-913071-06-4*) Rama Pub Co.

— Faithfully Yours. Aschwanden, Richard J., ed. (Illus.). 135p. 1989. pap. 4.95 (*0-913071-08-0*) Rama Pub Co.

— Grow, Eat, Drink Herbs. Aschwanden, Richard J., ed. 54p. (Orig.). 1988. pap. 5.00 (*0-913071-07-2*) Rama Pub Co.

— If Men Were Men. Aschwanden, Richard J. & Aschwanden, Charles R., eds. 127p. (Orig.). 1984. pap. 4.95 (*0-913071-02-1*) Rama Pub Co.

— Space Defenders Do. Aschwanden, Richard J. et al, eds. 126p. (Orig.). 1987. pap. 4.95 (*0-913071-04-8*) Rama Pub Co.

Aschwanden, Maria, jt. auth. see Aschwanden, Richard J.

Aschwanden, Richard J. The Way: A Walk with Paul, the Apostle. 156p. (Orig.). 1990. pap. 5.00 (*0-913071-09-9*) Rama Pub Co.

Aschwanden, Richard J. & Aschwanden, Maria. Escaping Collusion. 90p. (Orig.). 1983. reprint ed. pap. 4.50 (*0-913071-01-3*) Rama Pub Co.

— A Time of Personal Regeneration. Aschwanden, Charles R., ed. 60p. 1984. pap. 3.40 (*0-913071-00-5*, TX1-202-40) Rama Pub Co.

Aschwanden, Richard J., ed. see Aschwanden, Maria.

***Aschwer, Hermann.** Triathlon Training: From Novice to Ironman. 1998. pap. text 19.95 (*3-89124-515-7*) Meyer & Meyer.

***ASCI Staff.** ACSI Elementary Mathematics - Student: Grade Two - Life in the Air - Supplemental Exercises. (Enabling Educators Ser.). (Illus.). iv, 112p. (J). (gr. 2-3). 1999. student ed. 17.95 (*1-58331-193-9*) Assn Christ Sch.

Asci, Sue, ed. see Viglione, Steve.

***Ascione, Frank J.** Basic Skills in Scientific Literature Evaluation: Critiquing Clinical Drug Trials. 150p. (C). 2000. pap. 30.00 (*1-58212-008-0*) Am Pharm Assn.

Ascione, Frank J., et al. Principles of Drug Information & Scientific Literature Evaluation. LC 93-41705. 236p. (C). 1994. pap. text 30.00 (*0-914768-52-2*, T169) Am Pharm Assn.

***Ascione, Frank R.** Child Abuse, Domestic Violence & Animal Abuse: Linking the Circles of Compassion for Prevention & Intervention. LC 98-48878. 1998. 54.95 (*1-55753-142-0*) Purdue U Pr.

Ascione, Frank R. & Arkow, Phil. Child Abuse, Domestic Violence & Animal Abuse: Linking the Circles of Compassion for Prevention & Intervention. LC 98-48878. 480p. 1999. pap. 27.95 (*1-55753-143-9*) Purdue U Pr.

Ascione, Frank R., jt. auth. see Lockwood, Randall.

ASCLA Staff. Standards & Guidelines of Service for the Library of Congress Network of Libraries for the Blind & Physically Handicapped, 1995. 48p. 1995. 12.00 (*0-8389-7797-9*) ASCLA.

Asclepiades Staff, et al. Asclepiades of Samos & Leonidas of Tarentum: The Poems. LC 99-21625. 1999. pap. 30.00 (*0-86516-456-8*) Bolchazy-Carducci.

ASCLS Staff. Optimizing Light Microscopy for Biological & Clinical Laboratories. LC 97-207224. 208p. 1997. per. 24.95 (*0-7872-3538-5*) Kendall-Hunt.

Ascol, Thomas K. From the Protestant Reformation to the Southern Baptist Convention Vol. 1: What Hath Geneva to Do with Nashville. (Founder Heritage Ser.: Vol. 1). 15p. (Orig.). 1996. pap. 2.40 (*0-9654955-0-7*) Founders Pr.

Ascoli, Albert R. Ariosto's Bitter Harmony: Crisis & Evasion in the Italian Renaissance. LC 86-8881. 445p. reprint ed. pap. 138.00 (*0-608-06367-3*, 206672800008) Bks Demand.

Ascoli, Albert R. & Kahn, Victoria, eds. Machiavelli & the Discourse of Literature. (Illus.). 312p. 1993. 49.95 (*0-8014-2870-X*); pap. text 19.95 (*0-8014-8109-0*) Cornell U Pr.

Ascoli, Mario, ed. Luteinizing Hormone Receptors & Actions. 248p. 1985. 142.00 (*0-8493-5674-1*, QP572, CRC Reprint) Franklin.

Ascoli, Max, ed. see Reporter.

Ascoli, Max, ed. & tr. see Mussolini, Benito.

Ascone, Teresa. We're All Artists: Watercolor for Everyone. (Illus.). 148p. (C). 1994. pap., otabind 21.95 (*1-883724-00-7*) Alaskan Portfolio.

Ascott, Roy, ed. Reframing Consciousness: Consequences of Art Through Technology. 352p. 1999. 49.95 (*1-84150-013-5*, Pub. by Intellect) Intl Spec Bk.

***Ascough, Richard S.** New Proclamation Year c. 2000-2001: Advent Through Holy Week. LC 00-35467. 2000. 25.00 (*0-8006-4244-9*, Fortress Pr) Augsburg Fortress.

Ascough, Richard S. What Are They Saying about the Formation of Pauline Churches? LC 97-32986. (What Are They Saying about . . . Ser.). 176p. 1998. pap. 9.95 (*0-8091-3768-2*) Paulist Pr.

Ascroft, G. & Slater, Roger. Quantitative Techniques in a Business Context. (Business in Context Ser.). 416p. 1995. pap. 29.95 (*0-412-37570-2*) Chapman & Hall.

Ascroft, Joseph R. Participatory Communication: Working for Change & Development. White, Shirley A. et al, eds. LC 93-34804. (Communication & Human Values Ser.). 1994. pap. 24.95 (*0-8039-9143-6*) Sage.

— Participatory Communication: Working for Change & Development. White, Shirley A. et al, eds. LC 93-34804. (Communication & Human Values Ser.). 436p. 1994. 52.00 (*0-8039-9142-8*) Sage.

***ASD Staff.** High School Driver's Ed: Annotated Teacher's Edition. annot. ed. 576p. 1999. teacher ed. write for info. (*0-7668-0303-1*) Delmar.

— License to Drive - Alabama State Specific Text. LC 99-22615. 560p. 1999. 41.95 (*0-7668-0312-0*) Delmar.

Ase-Berit & Strandskogen, Rolf. Norsk for Utlendinger. 6 cass., Set, Vol. 1. (NOR.). pap. text 125.00 incl. audio (*0-88432-147-9*, AFNW01) Audio-Forum.

Ase-Berit & Strandskogen, Rolf. Norwegian Norsk Fonetikk for Utlendinger (Norwegian Phonetics), 4 cass., Set. (Norwegian Phonetics Ser.). 210p. pap. text 75.00 incl. audio (*0-88432-148-7*, AFNW98) Audio-Forum.

Asean Staff. ASEAN at 30. LC 97-943653. 101 p. :p. 1997. write for info. (*979-8080-26-2*, NIPI Bks) Natl Intermedia.

ASEAN/U. S. Coastal Resources Management Staff. The Coastal Environmental Profile of South Johore, Malaysia. (ICLARM Technical Reports: No. 24). 65p. 1991. per. write for info. (*971-10-2278-8*, Pub. by ICLARM) Intl Spec Bk.

— The Integrated Management Plan for Segara Anakan-Cilacap, Central Java, Indonesia. (ICLARM Technical Reports: No. 34). 100p. 1992. per. write for info. (*971-8709-20-7*, Pub. by ICLARM) Intl Spec Bk.

Asedillo, Rebecca C. & Williams, B. David. The Sari-Sari Store: A Philippine Scrapbook. (Illus.). 80p. (Orig.). 1989. pap. 4.95 (*0-377-00195-3*) Friendship Pr.

Asedillo, Rebecca C. & Williams, B. David, eds. Rice in the Storm: Faith in Struggle in the Philippines. 1989. pap. 6.95 (*0-377-00192-9*) Friendship Pr.

ASEE Staff. 1996 ASEE Membership Handbook. 421p. 1996. spiral bd. 30.00 (*0-87823-153-6*, HANDBK 96) Am Soc Eng Ed.

Aseev, G. G. Electrolytes, Equilibria in Solutions & Phase Equilibria: Calculation of Multicomponent Systems & Experimental Data on the Activities of Water, Vapor Pressures, & Osmotic Coefficients. LC 98-30446. 1998. write for info. (*1-56700-122-X*) Begell Hse.

— Electrolytes, Interparticle Interactions: Theory, Calculation Methods, & Experimental Data. Shakhlevich, Kirill, tr. from ENG. LC 97-51375. 753p. 1998. write for info. (*1-56700-100-9*) Begell Hse.

— Electrolytes, Properties of Solutions: Methods for Calculation of Multicomponent Systems & Experimental Data on Thermal Conductivity & Surface Tension. Shakhlevich, Kirill, tr. LC 97-52399. 1998. 275.56 (*1-56700-106-8*) Begell Hse.

— Electrolytes, Transport Phenomena: Methods for Calculation of Multicomponent Solutions & Experimental Data on Viscosities & Diffusion Coefficients. Gorin, Stanislav N., tr. from RUS. LC 98-16114. 549p. 1998. write for info. (*1-56700-104-1*) Begell Hse.

Aseev, Iu S. Architecture of Ancient Kiev. 159p. 1982. 35.00 (*0-7855-1493-7*) St Mut.

Aseev, Nikolai, et al. Liren' (RUS.). 40p. (C). 1989. reprint ed. pap. 7.00 (*0-933884-70-2*) Berkeley Slavic.

Asefa, Sisay, ed. Economic Decision Making: Private & Public Decisions. LC 84-25162. 126p. 1985. reprint ed. pap. 39.10 (*0-608-00088-4*, 206085300006) Bks Demand.

— World Food & Agriculture: Economic Problems & Issues. LC 88-29044. 144p. 1988. text 19.00 (*0-88099-067-8*); pap. text 9.00 (*0-88099-066-X*) W E Upjohn.

Asefa, Sisay & Huang, Wei-Chiao. Human Capital & Economic Development. LC 94-22612. 164p. 1994. text 33.00 (*0-88099-148-8*); pap. text 14.00 (*0-88099-147-X*) W E Upjohn.

Asekoff, L. S. Dreams of a Work. 80p. 1994. 18.95 (*0-914061-47-X*) Orchises Pr.

— North Star. LC 96-19975. 96p. 1997. 20.00 (*0-914061-57-7*) Orchises Pr.

Aseltine, Gwen P. Letters to Virgins. LC 79-65034. 1979. pap. 3.95 (*0-917182-13-8*) Triumph Pub.

Aseltine, Lorraine. First Grade Can Wait. Tucker, Kathleen, ed. LC 87-26457. (Albert Whitman Concept Bks.). (Illus.). 32p. (J). (ps-2). 1988. lib. bdg. 13.95 (*0-8075-2451-4*) A Whitman.

Aseltine, Lorraine, et al. I'm Deaf, & It's Okay. LC 85-26446. (Albert Whitman Concept Bks.). (Illus.). 40p. (J). (gr. 1-4). 1986. lib. bdg. 13.95 (*0-8075-3472-2*) A Whitman.

Asem, Ebenzer, jt. auth. see Gupta, Kanhaya L.

***Asen.** Root of Deception. 480p. 1998. mass mkt. 5.99 (*0-553-57516-3*, Crimeline) Bantam.

Asen, Eia. Family Therapy for Everyone: How to Get the Best Out of Living Together. (Illus.). 224p. 1997. pap. 17.50 (*0-563-37054-8*, BBC-Parkwest) Parkwest Pubns.

***Asen, Eia & Jones, E.** Systemic Therapy with Depression in Couples. 160p. 2000. pap. 24.00 (*1-85575-221-2*, Pub. by H Karnac Bks Ltd) Other Pr LLC.

Asencio. Tes Curativos Mexicanos. (SPA.). 1997. pap. text 7.98 (*968-403-813-5*) Selector.

Asencio, Diego & Asencio, Nancy. Our Man Is Inside. 288p. 1983. 17.00 (*0-316-05294-9*) Little.

Asencio, Nancy, jt. auth. see Asencio, Diego.

Asendorf, Christoph. Batteries of Life: On the History of Things & Their Perception in Modernity. Reneau, Don, tr. LC 92-15011. (Weimar & Now Ser.: Vol. 4). 1993. 45.00 (*0-520-06573-5*, Pub. by U CA Pr) Cal Prin Full Svc.

Asendorpf, Jens, jt. ed. see Rubin, Kenneth H.

Asendorpf, Jens B. & Valsiner, Jaan, eds. Framing Stability & Change: An Investigation into Methodological Reasoning. 336p. (C). 1991. text 58.00 (*0-8039-3807-1*); pap. text 26.00 (*0-8039-3808-X*) Sage.

Asenjo. Separation Processes in Biotechnology. (Bioprocess Technology Ser.: Vol. 9). (Illus.). 840p. 1990. text 235.00 (*0-8247-8270-4*) Dekker.

Asenjo, Bernardo R., et al. Diccionario de Marketing. 3rd ed. (SPA.). 168p. 1990. pap. 35.00 (*0-7859-4919-4*) Fr & Eur.

Asenjo, F. G. In-Between: An Essay on Categories. (Current Continental Research Ser.). 182p. 1988. 50.00 (*0-8191-6922-6*); pap. 22.50 (*0-8191-6923-4*) U Pr of Amer.

Asenjo, Federico. Fiestas of San Juan. (Puerto Rico Ser.). 1979. lib. bdg. 59.95 (*0-8490-2917-1*) Gordon Pr.

Asenjo, Juan A. & Andrews, Barbara A., eds. Recombinant DNA Biotechnology III: The Integration of Biological & Engineering Sciences. LC 96-7239. (Annals of the New York Academy of Sciences Ser.: Vol. 782). 569p. 1996. 160.00 (*0-89766-961-4*); pap. 160.00 (*0-89766-962-2*) NY Acad Sci.

Asenjo, Juan A. & Hong, Juan, eds. Separation, Recovery, & Purification in Biotechnology: Recent Advances & Mathematical Modeling. LC 86-10833. (ACS Symposium Ser.: No. 314). (Illus.). 226p. 1986. 60.95 (*0-8412-0978-2*) Am Chemical.

— Separation, Recovery, & Purification in Biotechnology: Recent Advances & Mathematical Modeling. LC 86-10833. (ACS Symposium Ser.: Vol. 314). 240p. 1986. reprint ed. pap. 74.40 (*0-608-03519-X*, 206423800008) Bks Demand.

Asenjo, Juan A. & Merchuk, J. C. Bioreactor System Design. LC 94-35424. (Bioprocess Technology Ser.: Vol. 21). (Illus.). 648p. 1994. text 225.00 (*0-8247-9002-2*) Dekker.

Asenkova, Natalia. Krasnaia Liliia - Red Lily. LC 96-41305. (RUS.). 136p. (Orig.). 1996. pap. 9.00 (*1-55779-094-9*) Hermitage Pubs.

Asenkova, Natalya. Na Fone Kormil'tsa (On the Background of a Provider) LC 97-6960. (RUS.). 120p. 1997. 9.00 (*1-55779-096-5*) Hermitage Pubs.

Asensi, Manuel, jt. auth. see Miller, J. Hillis.

***Asensio Cerver, Francisco.** Home Furniture Design of the New Century. (Illus.). 2000. pap. 24.95 (*84-8185-227-9*) Arco Edit.

— New Concepts in House Interiors. (Illus.). 2000. pap. 24.95 (*84-8185-226-0*) Arco Edit.

— New European Architecture. LC 99-198853. (Colour Collection Ser.). 159p. 1997. write for info. (*84-8185-016-0*, Pub. by Arco Edit) Watson Guptill.

— One Thousand Practical Ideas for Decorating the Home. 2000. pap. 29.95 (*84-8185-243-0*) Watsn-Guptill.

***Asensio, Manuel.** Sold Short: A Stock Crusader in a Short-Seller Suit. 240p. 2000. text 29.95 (*0-471-38338-4*) Wiley.

Asente, Paul, et al. X Window System Toolkit: A Complete Programmer's Guide & Specification. 2nd ed. LC 97-39173. 1000p. 1998. pap. 99.95 (*1-55558-178-1*, Digital DEC) Buttrwrth-Heinemann.

Aseshananda, Swami. Glimpses of a Great Soul: The Life of Swami Saradananda. 320p. (Orig.). 1982. pap. 7.95 (*0-87481-039-6*) Vedanta Pr.

ASET Committee. Guidelines on Intraoperative Electroencephalography for Technologists. 20p. 1998. pap. 15.00 (*1-57797-033-0*) ASET.

***ASET Committee.** Policies & Procedures for the Electroneurodiagnostic Laboratory. 150p. 1999. spiral bd. 80.00 (*1-57797-039-X*) ASET.

— Review Questions in Intraoperative Monitoring. 48p. 1999. spiral bd. 24.00 (*1-57797-036-5*) ASET.

— Review Questions in Nerve Conduction Studies. 60p. 1999. spiral bd. 24.00 (*1-57797-038-1*) ASET.

— Review Questions in Polysomnography. (Illus.). 64p. 1999. spiral bd. 24.00 (*1-57797-037-3*) ASET.

ASET Staff. Evoked Potentials, 3 vols. Incl. Bk. I. Concepts & Somatosensory. American END Society Committee. (Illus.). iv, 152p. 1998. per. 24.00 (*1-57797-018-7*); Bk. II. Visual. American END Society Staff. (Illus.). iv, 122p. 1998. spiral bd. 24.00 (*1-57797-019-5*); Bk. III. Auditory. American Journal of END Technology Staff & American END Society Committee. (Illus.). iv, 178p. 1998. spiral bd. 24.00 (*1-57797-020-9*); 1994. Set spiral bd. 69.00 (*1-57797-017-9*) ASET.

ASET Staff, et al. Sleep. 4th rev. ed. (Illus.). iv, 144p. 1998. spiral bd. 25.00 (*1-57797-015-2*) ASET.

ASET Task Force Staff. Preparing for END Board Exams: Study Tools & Survival Tips. (Illus.). iv, 236p. 1996. per. 57.00 incl. VHS (*1-57797-021-7*); per. 28.00 (*1-57797-022-5*) ASET.

Aseyev, Georgiy G. & Zaitsev, Ivan D. Volumetric Properties of Electrolyte Solutions: Estimation Methods & Experimental Data. LC 96-27714. 1996. write for info. (*1-56700-072-X*) Begell Hse.

Aseyev, Georgiy G., jt. ed. see Zaytsev, Ivan D.

Aseyev, Gergiy G. Thermal Property of Electrolyte Solutions, Methods for Calculation of Multicomponent Systems & Experimental Data. LC 96-45116. 498p. 1996. 120.00 (*1-56700-076-2*) Begell Hse.

Asfahani, R., ed. see International Symposium on Low-Carbon Steels for t.

Asfahani, Riad, ed. Accelerated Cooling/Direct Quenching of Steels. LC 97-73646. 240p. 1997. 104.00 (*0-87170-607-5*, 6632) ASM.

Asfahani, Riad, et al, eds. High Strain Rate Behavior of Refractory Metals & Alloys: Proceedings of a Symposium Sponsored by the Refractory Metals Committee & the Structural Materials Division, Held During the 1991, TMS Fall Meeting, Cincinnati Ohio. LC 91-68509. (Illus.). 323p. 1992. pap. 100.20 (*0-608-04882-8*, 206557400004) Bks Demand.

An Asterisk (*) at the beginning of an entry indicates that the title is appearing for the first time.

Asfahl, C. Ray. Industrial Safety & Health Management. 4th ed. LC 98-35475. 474p. 1998. 92.00 (*0-13-895350-3*) P-H.
— Robots & Manufacturing Automation. 2nd ed. LC 91-32355. 512p. (C). 1992. text 100.95 (*0-471-55391-3*) Wiley.
Asfahl, C. Ray, ed. OSHA Standards Digest. 162p. 1985. pap. 49.95 (*0-945709-04-8*) New Cent Media.
***Asfour, Amal & Williamson, Paul.** Gainsborough's Vision. (Illus.). 320p. 1999. 75.95 (*0-85323-874-X*, Pub. by Liverpool Univ Pr) Intl Spec Bk.
Asfour, Edmund Y. Syria: Development & Monetary Policy. LC 59-13357. (Middle Eastern Monographs: No. 1). (Illus.). 164p. 1959. pap. 5.95 (*0-674-86190-6*) HUP.
Asfour, John, tr. see Al-Maghut, Muhammad.
Asfour, Mohammad. Arabic in Three Months. LC 98-31746. (Hugo's Simplified Language Course Ser.). 256p. (Orig.). 1999. pap. 14.95 (*0-7894-4398-8*) DK Pub Inc.
Asgar, Jack. The Organizational Role of Supervisors. 94p. 1989. write for info. (*0-9622797-0-6*) Practical Mgmt.
***Asgeirsson, J. Ma., et al.** From Quest to Q: Festschrift James M. Robinson. 2000. 68.50 (*90-429-0771-1*, Pub. by Peeters Pub) Bks Intl VA.
Asghar Ali Engineer, ed. Delhi Meerut Riots. (C). 1987. 26.00 (*81-202-0198-1*, Pub. by Ajanta) S Asia.
— Status of Women in Islam. (C). 1987. 17.50 (*81-202-0190-6*, Pub. by Ajanta) S Asia.
Ash. Chemical Manufacturers Directory of Trade Names. 1997. 195.00 (*1-890595-03-9*) Ashgate Pub Co.
Ash. Chemical Tradename Dictionary. 1993. 85.00 (*0-07-586376-6*) McGraw.
***Ash.** Handbook of Adhesive Chemicals & Compounding. 1999. 250.00 (*1-890595-15-2*) Ashgate Pub Co.
— Handbook of Fillers Extenders & Diluents. 1998. 195.00 (*1-890595-13-6*) Ashgate Pub Co.
— Handbook of Food Packaging Chemicals & Materials. 1999. 250.00 (*1-890595-11-X*) Ashgate Pub Co.
— Handbook of Green Chemicals. 1998. 225.00 (*1-890595-09-8*) Ashgate Pub Co.
— Handbook of Industrial Chemical Additives. 1998. 495.00 (*1-890595-06-3*) Ashgate Pub Co.
— Handbook of Industrial Surfactants 3rd Edition. 450.00 (*1-890595-21-7*) Ashgate Pub Co.
Ash. Leather Machzor: Yom Kippur. 49.99 (*0-89906-687-9*, MAYL-A); 49.99 (*0-89906-690-9*, MSYL-A) Mesorah Pubns.
— Writing in Between. LC 99-12662. 1999. text 45.00 (*0-312-21483-9*) St Martin.
Ash & Dauija. Plan or Not to Plan. 320p. 2000. 49.00 (*0-13-095192-7*) S&S Trade.
***Ash, C. J. & Knight, J.** Computable Structures & the Hyperarithmetical Hierarchy. LC 00-34103. (Studies in Logic & the Foundations of Mathematics). 2000. write for info. (*0-444-50072-3*) Elsevier.
***Ash, Deborah Rebeck.** Riding Past Grief: A Daughter's Journey. LC 00-130333. 120p. 2000. 12.95 (*1-882792-92-0*) Proctor Pubns.
Ash, A., et al. Smooth Compactification of Locally Symmetric Varieties. LC 75-38142. (Lie Groups: History, Frontiers & Applications Ser.: No. 4). 340p. 1975. 35.00 (*0-915692-12-0*, 991600061) Math Sci Pr.
Ash, A. S., ed. see Milton, John.
Ash, A. S., ed. see Plato.
Ash, Agnes. Palm Beach Sketchbook. (Great Places Ser.). (Illus.). 144p. 1988. 32.00 (*0-923078-01-0*) Olendorf Graph.
Ash, Andrew, ed. The Future of Tropical Savannas: An Australian Perspective. (Illus.). 178p. (Orig.). 1996. pap. 59.95 (*0-643-05784-6*, Pub. by CSIRO) Accents Pubns.
Ash, Annalee. Whispering of Angels: Affirmations for the Child in Your Life. LC 98-73904. (Illus.). 72p. (J). 1999. 14.95 (*1-57174-128-3*) Hampton Roads Pub Co.
Ash, Anthony L. The Acts of the Apostles, Pt. 1. LC 79-632639. 175p. 1984. 12.95 (*0-915547-24-4*) Abilene Christ U.
— Commentary on Jeremiah & Lamentations. LC 86-72834. 500p. 1987. 17.95 (*0-915547-94-5*) Abilene Christ U.
— The Gospel According to Luke, Pt. 1. LC 72-77838. 1984. 12.95 (*0-915547-20-1*) Abilene Christ U.
— The Gospel According to Luke, Pt. 2. LC 75-77838. 1984. 12.95 (*0-915547-21-X*) Abilene Christ U.
— Psalms. LC 79-67300. 1984. 17.95 (*0-915547-42-2*) Abilene Christ U.
***Ash, Betty.** The Gulf War: How It Hit Home. 52p. 2000. pap. 10.00 (*0-8059-4952-6*) Dorrance.
Ash, Carol. The Probability Tutoring Book: Intuitive Essentials to Engineers & Scientists & Everyone Else! LC 92-53183. 480p. 1996. pap. 39.95 (*0-7803-1051-9*, PP2881) Inst Electrical.
Ash, Carol & Ash, Robert B. The Calculus Tutoring Book. 544p. 1993. pap. 39.95 (*0-7803-1044-6*, PP1776) Inst Electrical.
Ash, Carol, jt. auth. see Ash, Robert B.
Ash, Caroline. The Garden Planner & Record Book. 80p. 1997. 17.95 (*0-7894-1472-4*) DK Pub Inc.
***Ash, Carolyn.** Timeless Skin; Healthy Skin for a Lifetime. 2000. pap. text 14.95 (*0-9670240-0-5*) Splash Pub.
Ash, Carolyn. Working with African American Families: A Guide to Resources. 100p. 1994. ring bd. 35.00 (*1-885429-08-8*) Family Resource.
Ash, Constance. Not of Woman Born, 1 vol. 288p. 1999. mass mkt. 6.99 (*0-451-45681-5*) NAL.
Ash, Daniel. Basic Diesel Operation & Maintenance. LC 84-730280. 1984. student ed. 7.00 (*0-8064-0199-0*, 475) Bergwall.
— Six Point Two Diesel Engine Explained. (Orig.). 1985. student ed. write for info. (*0-8064-0201-6*, 476) Bergwall.
Ash, David. Essential Bulgaria. (Essential Travel Guides Ser.). (Illus.). 128p. 1994. pap. 7.95 (*0-8442-8901-9*, Passprt Bks) NTC Contemp Pub Co.
Ash, David & Werlinger, Caren J. Exercises for Health Promotion: A Prescriptive Approach. LC 96-49908. 288p. 1997. 59.00 (*0-8342-0869-5*) Aspen Pub.
Ash, E. A. & Paige, E. G. Rayleigh Wave Theory & Application. (Wave Phenomena Ser.: Vol. 2). (Illus.). x, 360p. 1985. 89.95 (*0-387-15933-9*) Spr-Verlag.
Ash, Edward C. Dogs: Their History & Development, 2 vols., 1. LC 72-79945. 1972. 30.95 (*0-405-08219-3*, Pub. by Blom Pubns) Ayer.
— Dogs: Their History & Development, 2 vols., 2. LC 72-79945. 1972. 27.95 (*0-405-08220-7*, Pub. by Blom Pubns) Ayer.
— Dogs: Their History & Development, 2 vols., Set. LC 72-79945. (Illus.). 812p. 1972. 55.95 (*0-405-08218-5*, Pub. by Blom Pubns) Ayer.
Ash, Ehiel & Strittmatter, Robert. Accounting in the Soviet Union. LC 90-24129. 208p. 1992. 65.00 (*0-275-93069-6*, C3069, Praeger Pubs) Greenwood.
Ash, Ehiel, ed. Soviet Cost-Accounting in the Machine-Building & Metal-Working Sector (Theory & Practice) Selected Papers with Analysis. Nobel, Erika D., ed. Talmy, Vladimir, tr. from RUS. (Illus.). 200p. (Orig.). 1988. pap. text 100.00 (*1-55831-071-1*) Delphic Associates.
Ash, Eric. Sir Frederick Sykes & the Air Revolution, 1912-1918. LC 98-22294. (Studies in Air Power). 286p. 1999. 59.50 (*0-7146-4828-0*, Pub. by F Cass Pubs); pap. 24.50 (*0-7146-4382-3*, Pub. by F Cass Pubs) Intl Spec Bk.
Ash, F. Close Up. mass mkt. 6.95 (*0-7472-4779-X*, Pub. by Headline Bk Pub) Trafalgar.
— Indecent. mass mkt. 6.95 (*0-7472-4269-0*, Pub. by Headline Bk Pub) Trafalgar.
— Undercover. mass mkt. 6.95 (*0-7472-4499-5*, Pub. by Headline Bk Pub) Trafalgar.
Ash, Fenton. A Trip to Mars. LC 74-15948. (Science Fiction Ser.). (Illus.). 326p. 1975. reprint ed. 26.95 (*0-405-06274-5*) Ayer.
Ash-Geisler, Viki, jt. ed. see Immroth, Barbara F.
Ash, Gerald R. Dynamic Routing in Telecommunications Networks. LC 97-42105. (Telecommunications Ser.). (Illus.). 752p. 1998. 85.00 (*0-07-006414-8*) McGraw.
Ash, H. B., tr. On Agriculture. (Loeb Classical Library: No. 283). 570p. 1972. 18.95 (*0-674-99313-6*) HUP.
Ash, Harrison B., tr. De Re Rustica, 3 vols., 1. (Loeb Classical Library: No. 361, 407, 408). 496p. 1941. 18.95 (*0-674-99398-5*) HUP.
Ash, I. A., jt. ed. see Ash, M. B.
Ash, Irene, ed. Chemical Tradename Dictionary. LC 92-35154. 530p. 1992. 95.00 (*1-56081-625-2*, Wiley-VCH) Wiley.
— Industrial Chemical Thesaurus: Chemical to Tradename Reference & Tradename to Chemical Cross Reference & Manufacturers Directory, 2 vols. 2nd ed. LC 92-22095. 1312p. 1992. 295.00 (*1-56081-615-5*, Wiley-VCH) Wiley.
Ash, Irene, jt. auth. see Ash, M.
Ash, Irene, jt. auth. see Ash, Michael.
Ash, Irene, jt. compiled by see Ash, Michael.
Ash, Irene, jt. ed. see Ash, Michael.
Ash, J., jt. auth. see Cambie, R. C.
Ash, J. S. & Miskell, J. E. Birds of Somalia. LC 98-180617. (Illus.). 336p. 1998. write for info. (*1-873403-58-5*) HEL1.
Ash, James L., Jr. Protestantism & the American University: An Intellectual Biography of William Warren Sweet. LC 82-10629. (Illus.). 180p. 1982. 15.95 (*0-87074-183-7*) SMU Press.
Ash, Jayne. Clipping, Trimming & Plaiting. (Illus.). 96p. 1996. pap. 17.95 (*1-85223-907-7*, Pub. by Cro1wood) Trafalgar.
Ash, Jennifer. Tropical Style: Private Palm Beach. (Illus.). 180p. 1998. 45.00 (*1-55859-489-2*) Abbeville Pr.
Ash, Jennifer & Brott, Armin A. The Expectant Father: Facts, Tips & Advice for Dads-to-Be. LC 94-41096. (Illus.). 224p. 1995. pap. 10.95 (*1-55859-690-9*) Abbeville Pr.
Ash, Jennifer, jt. auth. see Brott, Armin A.
Ash, Joan. Catch Me a Nightingale. large type ed. (General Ser.). (Illus.). 416p. 1993. 11.50 (*0-7089-2853-6*) Ulverscroft.
Ash, Joel D. Potpourri of the Mind: A Collection of Poems in the Limerick Style. LC 97-92589. 109p. 1997. 20.00 (*0-9664047-0-X*) Old Pine Bks.
— A Sojourn in Limerick: Poetic Limericks Visited Once Again. deluxe ed. LC 98-92237. 109p. 1999. 20.00 (*0-9664047-1-8*) Old Pine Bks.
***Ash, John.** The Anatolikon. 2000. 35.95 (*1-58498-011-7*); pap. 14.95 (*1-58498-010-9*) Talisman Hse.
Ash, John. A Byzantine Journey. 330p. Date not set. 25.00 (*0-614-32363-0*) Random.
— From the Earth to the Table: John Ash's Wine Country Cuisine. 1999. pap. 16.95 (*0-452-27841-4*, Plume) Dutton Plume.
— Grammatical Institutes. LC 79-15248. (American Linguistics Ser.). 216p. 1979. reprint ed. 50.00 (*0-8201-1339-5*) Schol Facsimiles.
Ash, John. The Poet's Grandmother. (Illus.). (C). text. write for info. (*0-472-09644-3*); pap. text. write for info. (*0-472-06644-7*) U of Mich Pr.
Ash, John, contrib. by. Jane Wilson: Fischbach Gallery: September 30-October 23, 1993; Arnot Art Museum: November 13, 1993-January 9, 1994. (Illus.). 50p. (Orig.). 1993. 10.00 (*0-9626097-3-0*) Fischbach Gal.
Ash, John & Goldstein, Sid. American Game Cooking: A Contemporary Guide to Preparing Farm-Raised Game Birds & Meats. (Illus.). 304p. 1993. pap. 20.00 (*0-201-62468-0*) Addison-Wesley.
— From the Earth to the Table: John Ash's Wine Country Cuisine. (Illus.). 448p. 1995. 33.95 (*0-525-94000-6*, Dutt) Dutton Plume.
Ash, John & Miskell, John. Birds of Somalia. (Illus.). 304p. 1998. 65.00 (*0-300-07456-5*) Yale U Pr.
Ash, John, et al. Terence Main: Terrestrial Tale. LC 96-83582. (Illus.). 80p. (Orig.). 1996. pap. write for info. (*0-9651328-0-3*) Art Et Industrie.
Ash, John, jt. auth. see Turner, Louis.
Ash, Juliet & Wilson, Elizabeth, eds. Chic Thrills: A Fashion Reader. LC 92-36413. (C). 1993. 19.95 (*0-520-08339-3*, Pub. by U CA Pr) Cal Prin Full Svc.
Ash, Juliet & Wright, Lee. Components of Dress: Design, Marketing & Image. (Illus.). 144p. 1988. pap. 15.95 (*0-415-00648-1*); lib. bdg. 45.00 (*0-415-00647-3*) Routledge.
Ash, Jutta. Only a Cat. (Illus.). 32p. (J). (ps-1). 1998. 17.95 (*0-86264-738-X*, Pub. by Andersen Pr) Trafalgar.
Ash, Lawrence R. & Orihel, Thomas C. Atlas of Human Parasitology. LC 89-17988. 1997. 300.00 (*0-89189-436-5*) Am Soc Clinical.
Ash, Lawrence R. & Orihel, Thomas C. Atlas of Human Parasitology. 4th ed. LC 97-2149. 424p. 1997. text 155.00 (*0-89189-399-7*, 16-7-004-00) Am Soc Clinical.
— Parasites: A Guide to Laboratory Procedures & Identification. LC 86-32179. (Illus.). 328p. 1987. text 15.00 (*0-89189-231-1*) Am Soc Clinical.
— Parasites in Human Tissues. (Illus.). 300p. 1995. 165.00 (*0-89189-379-2*) Am Soc Clinical.
Ash, Lawrence R., et al. Bench Aids for the Diagnosis of Intestinal Parasites. (CHI, ENG, FRE & SPA.). 20p. 1994. pap. text 31.50 (*92-4-154476-7*, 1150417) World Health.
Ash, Lee. Subject Collections, 2 vols. 7th rev. ed. 2466p. 1993. 275.00 (*0-8352-3141-0*) Bowker.
Ash, Lee & Annan, Gertrude L. Serial Publications Containing Medical Classics. 2nd ed. 1979. 35.00 (*0-9603990-0-3*) Antiquarium.
***Ash, Linda.** Design Teams for School Change: A Cyberprojects Approach. LC 98-61809. 150p. 1999. 26.95 (*1-57517-154-6*) SkyLght.
Ash, Lori, ed. see Lischner, Ray.
***Ash, Lorraine.** Monroe: Character in Time: The U. S. Presidents. Cox, R. David & Kuhens, Brian, eds. 44p. 1999. 5.95 (*1-929403-12-7*) History Proj.
— Tyler: Character in Time: The U. S. Presidents. Cox, R. David & Kuhens, Brian, eds. 31p. 1998. 5.95 (*1-929403-06-2*) History Proj.
Ash, M. & Ash, Irene. Encyclopedia of Industrial Chemical Additives, Vol. 2, G-O. 1984. 105.00 (*0-8206-0308-2*) Chem Pub.
— Formulary of Detergents & Other Cleaning Agents. 348p. 1998. reprint ed. pap. 55.00 (*0-8206-0369-4*) Chem Pub.
Ash, M., Jr., jt. auth. see Ramfjord, Sigurd P.
Ash, M. B. & Ash, I. A., eds. Handbook of Plastic Compounds, Elastomers & Resins: An International Guide by Category, Tradename, Composition & Supplier. 872p. 1991. 299.00 (*0-471-18830-1*) Wiley.
Ash, Major M., Jr. Wheeler's Atlas of Tooth Form. 5th ed. (Illus.). 158p. 1984. text 51.00 (*0-7216-1277-6*, W B Saunders Co) Harcrt Hlth Sci Grp.
— Wheeler's Dental Anatomy, Physiology & Occlusion. 7th ed. (Illus.). 490p. 1992. text 54.00 (*0-7216-4374-4*, W B Saunders Co) Harcrt Hlth Sci Grp.
Ash, Major M., jt. auth. see Ramfjord, Sigurd P.
Ash, Marinell. Thinking with Both Hands: Sir Daniel Wilson in the Old World & the New. Hulse, Elizabeth, ed. 392p. 1999. text 50.00 (*0-8020-4443-3*) U of Toronto Pr.
***Ash, Mary Kay.** Mary Kay. 3rd ed. 224p. 2005. pap. 8.00 (*0-06-092601-5*) HarpC.
Ash, Mary Kay. Mary Kay: You Can Have It All. 1996. 16.95 (*0-7615-0342-0*) Prima Pub.
Ash, Mary Kay. Mary Kay: You Can Have It All. 272p. 1996. pap., per. 13.00 (*0-7615-0647-0*) Prima Pub.
Ash, Mary Kay. Mary Kay: You Can Have It All: Practical Advice for Doing Well by Doing Good. LC 95-12582. 272p. 1995. 22.95 (*0-7615-0162-2*) Prima Pub.
— Mary Kay - You Can Have It All: Lifetime Wisdom from America's Foremost Woman Entrepreneur. 258p. 1998. text 23.00 (*0-7881-5294-7*) DIANE Pub.
— Mary Kay on People Management. LC 84-40254. 208p. 1985. mass mkt. 3.95 (*0-446-32974-6*, Pub. by Warner Bks) Little.
Ash, Maureen, jt. auth. see Fox, M.
Ash, Maurice, et al. Sharpham Miscellany: Essays in Spirituality & Ecology. 192p. 1995. pap. 14.95 (*0-9518298-0-7*, Pub. by Buddhist Pub) Assoc Pubs Grp.
Ash, Mel. Beat Spirit: The Way of the Beat Writers As a Living Experience. LC 97-14662. (Illus.). 336p. 1997. pap. 15.95 (*0-87477-880-8*, Tarcher Putnam) Putnam Pub Group.
***Ash, Mel.** Sacred Remedies for the Soul. 2000. pap. 14.00 (*0-7352-0134-X*) PH Pr.
Ash, Mel. Shaving the Inside of Your Skull: Crazy Wisdom for Discovering Who You Really Are. LC 96-20618. (Illus.). 256p. (Orig.). 1997. pap. 15.95 (*0-87477-841-7*, Tarcher Putnam) Putnam Pub Group.
— The Zen of Recovery. LC 92-14154. 240p. (Orig.). 1993. pap. 15.95 (*0-87477-706-2*, Tarcher Putnam) Putnam Pub Group.
Ash, Michael & Ash, Irene. Chemical Tradename Dictionary. 529p. 1997. 165.00 (*0-471-18857-3*) Wiley.
— Formulary of Paints & Other Coatings, Vol. 1. 427p. 1978. reprint ed. pap. text 50.00 (*0-8206-0348-1*) Chem Pub.
— Gardner's Chemical Synonyms & Trade Names. 1994. cd-rom 250.00 (*0-566-07559-8*, Pub. by Gower); 3.5 hd 250.00 (*0-566-07557-1*, Pub. by Gower) Ashgate Pub Co.
— Gardner's Chemical Synonyms & Trade Names. 10th ed. 1994. 195.00 (*0-566-07491-5*, Pub. by Gower) Ashgate Pub Co.
— Handbook of Cosmetics & Personal Care Additives. 986p. 1994. 335.00 (*0-566-07470-2*, Pub. by Gower) Ashgate Pub Co.
— Handbook of Food Additives. (Gower Chemical Reference Ser.). 1014p. 1995. text 335.00 (*0-566-07592-X*, Pub. by Gower) Ashgate Pub Co.
— Handbook of Industrial Chemical Additives: An International Guide by Product, Trade Name Function & Supplier. 859p. 1991. 299.00 (*0-471-72022-4*, Wiley-VCH) Wiley.
— Handbook of Industrial Chemical Additives: An International Guide by Product, Tradename, Function, & Supplier. 872p. 1991. 195.00 (*1-56081-521-3*, Wiley-VCH) Wiley.
— Handbook of Industrial Surfactants: An International Guide to More Than 21,000 Products by Trade Name, Composition, Function & Manufacturer. 2nd ed. LC 96-29925. 1997. 450.00 (*0-566-07892-9*, Pub. by Gower) Ashgate Pub Co.
— Handbook of Paint & Coating Raw Materials Vol. 1: An International Guide to More Than 11,000 Products by Trade Name, Chemical Function, & Manufacturer. 1016p. 1996. 295.00 (*0-566-07824-4*, Pub. by Gower) Ashgate Pub Co.
— Handbook of Paint & Coating Raw Materials Vol. 2: An International Guide to More Than 11,000 Products by Trade Name, Chemical Function, & Manufacturer. 605p. 1996. 195.00 (*0-566-07823-6*, Pub. by Gower) Ashgate Pub Co.
— Handbook of Water Treatment Chemicals: An International Guide to More Than 3,400 Products by Trade Name, Composition, Function & Manufacturer. (Chemical Reference Ser.). 700p. 1996. text 325.00 (*0-566-07801-5*, Pub. by Gower) Ashgate Pub Co.
— Index of Antimicrobials: An International Guide to More Than 1,600 Products by Trade Name, Chemical, Application, & Manufacturer. (Chemical Reference Ser.). 608p. 1996. text 175.00 (*0-566-07816-3*, Pub. by Gower) Ashgate Pub Co.
— Index of Antioxidants & Antiozonants: An International Guide to More Than 1,200 Products by Trade Name, Chemical, Application & Manufacturer. LC 96-35859. (Chemical Reference Ser.). 600p. 1997. text 175.00 (*0-566-07883-X*, Pub. by Gower) Ashgate Pub Co.
— Index of Flame Retardants: An International Guide to More Than 1,000 Products by Trade Name, Chemical, Application, & Manufacturer. LC 96-44253. (Chemical Reference Ser.). 600p. 1997. text 175.00 (*0-566-07885-6*, Pub. by Gower) Ashgate Pub Co.
— Index of Solvents: An International Guide to More Than 1,700 Products by Trade Name, Chemical, Application, & Manufacturer. (Chemical Reference Ser.). 400p. 1996. text 175.00 (*0-566-07884-8*, Pub. by Gower) Ashgate Pub Co.
Ash, Michael & Ash, Irene. Industrial Chemical Thesaurus, 2 vols., Vol. 2. 2nd ed. 1288p. 1997. 425.00 (*0-471-18893-X*, Wiley-VCH) Wiley.
Ash, Michael & Ash, Irene. Industrial Surfacants Electronic Handbook. 1994. 325.00 incl. cd-rom (*0-566-07506-7*, Pub. by Gower) Ashgate Pub Co.
— Landscape Construction Vol. 2: Roads, Paving & Drainage, 3 vols. 266p. 1996. text 86.95 (*0-566-09042-2*, Pub. by Gower) Ashgate Pub Co.
Ash, Michael & Ash, Irene, compiled by. Handbook of Paint & Coating Raw Materials Vols. 1 & 2: Trade Name Products; Chemical Products Dictionary with Trade Name Cross-Reference, 2 vols., Set. 1350p. 1996. 475.00 (*0-566-07787-6*, Pub. by Gower) Ashgate Pub Co.
— Handbook of Pharmaceutical Additives: An International Guide to More Than 5,500 Products by Trade Name, Chemical, Function, & Manufacturer. 1132p. 1996. 395.00 (*0-566-07596-2*, Pub. by Gower) Ashgate Pub Co.
— Handbook of Plastic & Rubber Additives: An International Guide to More Than 13,000 Products by Trade Name, Composition, Function, & Manufacturer. LC 95-3822. 1322p. 1995. 395.00 (*0-566-07594-6*, Pub. by Gower) Ashgate Pub Co.
Ash, Michael & Ash, Irene, eds. Conditioners, Emollients, & Lubricants. (What Every Chemical Technologist Wants to Know About...Ser.: Vol. IV). 400p. 1990. text 80.00 (*0-8206-0330-9*) Chem Pub.
— Dispersants, Solvents, & Solubilizers. (What Every Chemical Technologist Wants to Know About...Ser.: Vol. II). 478p. 1988. 80.00 (*0-8206-0327-9*) Chem Pub.
— Handbook of Plastic Compounds, Elastomers & Resins: An International Guide by Category, Tradename, Composition, & Supplier. 872p. 1992. 195.00 (*1-56081-553-1*, Wiley-VCH) Wiley.
— Plasticizers, Stabilizers & Thickeners. (What Every Chemical Technologist Wants to Know About...Ser.: Vol. III). 422p. 1989. 80.00 (*0-8206-0329-5*) Chem Pub.
— Resins. (What Every Chemical Technologist Wants to Know About...Ser.: Vol. V). 392p. 1990. 80.00 (*0-8206-0331-7*) Chem Pub.
— Specialty Chemicals Source Book, 2 vols. LC 97-66347. (Synapse Chemical Library). 2463p. 1997. 395.00 (*1-890595-00-4*) Ashgate Pub Co.
Ash, Mitchell G. Gestalt Psychology in German Culture, 1890-1967: Holism & the Quest for Objectivity. (Studies in the History of Psychology). (Illus.). 527p. (C). 1996. text 59.95 (*0-521-47540-6*) Cambridge U Pr.
— Gestalt Psychology in German Culture, 1890-1967: Holism & the Quest for Objectivity. (Studies in the History of Psychology). (Illus.). 527p. (C). 1998. pap. 24.95 (*0-521-64627-8*) Cambridge U Pr.
Ash, Mitchell G. & Lankowski, Carl, eds. German Universities: Past & Future: Crisis or Renewal? LC 96-52552. (Policies & Institutions: Vol. 1). 288p. (C). 1997. 39.00 (*1-57181-070-6*) Berghahn Bks.

A

Ash, Mitchell G. & Sollner, Alfons, eds. Forced Migration & Scientific Change: Emigre German-Speaking Scientists & Scholars after 1933. (Publications of the German Historical Institute, Washington, D.C.). (Illus.). 319p. (C). 1996. text 74.95 (*0-521-49741-8*) Cambridge U Pr.

Ash, Nancy, et al. Watermarks in Rembrandt's Prints. LC 97-31832. 1998. 45.00 (*0-89468-233-4*) Natl Gallery Art.

Ash, Nancy, jt. auth. see Fletcher, Shelley.

***Ash, Narain Roy.** Third World in the Age of Globalisation. 1999. text 59.95 (*1-85649-795-X*) Zed Books.

— Third World in the Age of Globalisation: Requiem of New Agenda? 1999. pap. 19.95 (*1-85649-796-8*) Zed Books.

***Ash, Niema.** Touching Tibet. (Illus.). 288p. 2000. pap. 14.95 (*0-9530575-5-0*, Pub. by Travellerseye Ltd) Midpt Trade.

Ash, Paul. Southern Africa: A Bradt Rail Guide. LC 98-28278. (Illus.). 280p. 1998. pap. 18.95 (*1-898323-72-0*, Pub. by Bradt Pubns) Globe Pequot.

***Ash, Paul S.** David, Solomon & Egypt: A Reassessment. (Journal for the Study of the Old Testament Supplement Ser.: No. 297). 160p. 1999. 46.50 (*1-84127-021-0*, Pub. by Sheffield Acad) CUP Services.

Ash, Pauline. Doctor Arnold's Ambition. large type ed. 1990. 27.99 (*0-7089-2196-5*) Ulverscroft.

— The Much-Loved Nurse. large type ed. 1990. 27.99 (*0-7089-2148-5*) Ulverscroft.

— Nurse for the Season. large type ed. (Linford Romance Library). 320p. 1986. pap. 6.95 (*0-7089-6169-X*, Linford) Ulverscroft.

Ash, Peter F. & Robinson, Edward E. Basic College Mathematics: A Calculator Approach. LC 80-15352. (Illus.). 544p. 1981. write for info. (*0-201-00091-1*) Addison-Wesley.

Ash, Philip, ed. Volunteers for Mental Health. LC 73-10368. 1973. 31.00 (*0-8422-5121-9*) Irvington.

Ash, Renata. Relax: 200 Ways to Achieve Calm in Mind & Body. (Style Ser.). 1999. pap. text 9.99 (*1-84100-138-4*) Quadrillion Media.

Ash, Rene L. The Motion Picture Film Editor. LC 74-4072. 193p. 1974. 29.00 (*0-8108-0718-1*) Scarecrow.

***Ash, Rhiannon.** Ordering Anarchy: Leaders & Armies in Tacitus' "Histories" LC 99-47172. 246p. 1999. text 49.50 (*0-472-11113-2*, 11113) U of Mich Pr.

Ash, Rhiannon. Roman Colosseum. LC 97-10020. (Mystery History Ser.). (Illus.). (J). 1997. 9.95 (*0-7613-0625-0*, Copper Beech Bks) Millbrook Pr.

— Roman Colosseum. LC 97-10020. (Mystery History of a--Ser.). (Illus.). 32p. (YA). (gr. 3 up). 1997. lib. bdg. 23.90 (*0-7613-0613-7*, Copper Beech Bks) Millbrook Pr.

Ash, Richard N., jt. auth. see Ley, Beth M.

***Ash, Robert.** Hong Kong in Transition. 2000. text 75.00 (*0-312-23354-X*) St Martin.

Ash, Robert. Information Theory. 352p. 1990. pap. 10.95 (*0-486-66521-6*) Dover.

— Real Analysis: With Basic Metric Space Topology. LC 92-53187. (Illus.). 232p. (C). 1992. text 79.95 (*0-7803-0408-X*, PC0304-6) Inst Electrical.

Ash, Robert, ed. China's Integration in Asia: Economic Security & Strategic Issues. 288p. (C). 1999. text 55.00 (*0-7007-1191-0*, Pub. by Curzon Pr Ltd) UH Pr.

Ash, Robert & Kueh, Y. Y., eds. The Chinese Economy under Deng Ziaoping. (Studies on Contemporary China). (Illus.). 296p. 1996. pap. text 26.00 (*0-19-828822-0*) OUP.

Ash, Robert, jt. auth. see Draguhn, Werner.

Ash, Robert B. & Ash, Carol. The Calculus Tutoring Book. LC 85-23049. 544p. 1985. 49.95 (*0-87942-183-5*, PC01776) Inst Electrical.

***Ash, Robert B. & Doleans-Dade, Catherine A.** Probability & Measure Theory. 2nd ed. 560p. 1999. 59.95 (*0-12-065202-1*) Acad Pr.

Ash, Robert B., jt. auth. see Ash, Carol.

Ash, Robert B., jt. auth. see McEliece, Robert J.

Ash, Robert F., ed. see Walker, Kenneth R.

Ash, Robert M. A Primer of Abstract Mathematics. LC 98-85593. (Classroom Resource Materials Ser.). 191p. 1998. pap. text 27.95 (*0-88385-708-1*) Math Assn.

Ash, Rosalie. Boda Precipitada - Reckless Wedding. (SPA.). 1997. per. 3.50 (*0-373-33413-3*, 1-33413-5) Harlequin Bks.

— Leyendas de la Luna. Orig. Title: Myths of the Moon. (SPA.). 1996. per. 3.50 (*0-373-33352-8*) Harlequin Bks.

— Original Sin. large type ed. (Harlequin Ser.). 1994. lib. bdg. 19.95 (*0-263-13774-0*) Thorndike Pr.

— Original Sin: (Secrets . . .) (Presents Ser.). 1995. per. 3.25 (*0-373-11723-X*, 1-11723-3) Harlequin Bks.

— Un Reve Secret. (Azur Ser.). 1999. mass mkt. 3.50 (*0-373-34763-4*, 1-34763-2) Harlequin Bks.

— El Sabor de la Venganza (Vengeful Bride) (SPA.). 1996. per. 3.50 (*0-373-33380-3*, 1-33380-6) Harlequin Bks.

— Vengeful Bride. large type ed. 288p. 1995. 23.99 (*0-263-14209-4*) Ulverscroft.

— Votos de Matrimonio: Marriage Vows. (Bianca Ser.).Tr. of Marriage Vows. (SPA.). 1997. per. 3.50 (*0-373-33429-X*, 1-33429-1) Harlequin Bks.

Ash, Russell. Dante Gabriel Rossetti. LC 95-12907. (Illus.). 96p. 1995. 29.95 (*0-8109-3784-0*, Pub. by Abrams) Time Warner.

— Discovering Highwaymen. (Illus.). 88p. pap. 8.50 (*0-7478-0260-2*, Pub. by Shire Pubns) Parkwest Pubns.

***Ash, Russell.** Factastic Book of Comparisons. LC 99-47138. 96p. (J). 2000. pap. 9.95 (*0-7894-5400-9*, D K Ink) DK Pub Inc.

Ash, Russell. Factastic Book of 1,000 Lists: Author of the Top Ten of Everything. LC 98-7701. 208p. 1998. 19.95 (*0-7894-3769-4*) DK Pub Inc.

— Factastic Book of 1001 Lists. LC 98-7701. 208p. 1998. pap. 14.95 (*0-7894-3412-1*) DK Pub Inc.

— Factastic Millennium Facts. LC 99-27624. (Millennium Ser.). 128p. (YA). (gr. 3 up). 1999. pap. text 12.95 (*0-7894-4948-X*) DK Pub Inc.

***Ash, Russell.** Fantastic Millennium Facts. LC 99-27624. (Millennium Ser.). 96p. (YA). (gr. 4-10). 1999. 19.95 (*0-7894-4710-X*) DK Pub Inc.

— Great Wonders of the World. (Illus.). 64p. (gr. 4-7). 2000. 19.95 (*0-7894-6505-1*, D K Ink) DK Pub Inc.

Ash, Russell. Impressionist's Seasons. (Illus.). 1999. pap. 16.95 (*1-86205-238-7*, Pub. by Pavilion Bks Ltd) Trafalgar.

— Incredible Comparisons. (Illus.). 64p. (J). 1996. 19.95 (*0-7894-1009-5*) DK Pub Inc.

— James Tissot. (Illus.). 96p. 1992. 29.95 (*0-8109-3864-2*, Pub. by Abrams) Time Warner.

— Lord Leighton. (Illus.). 96p. 1996. 45.00 (*1-85793-732-5*, Pub. by Pavilion Bks Ltd) Trafalgar.

— Lord Leighton. (Illus.). 96p. 1998. pap. 19.95 (*1-86205-150-X*, Pub. by Pavilion Bks Ltd) Trafalgar.

— Sir Edward Burne-Jones. LC 93-3218. (Illus.). 96p. 1993. 29.95 (*0-8109-3126-5*, Pub. by Abrams) Time Warner.

— Sir John Everett Millais. (Illus.). 969p. 1998. pap. 19.95 (*1-86205-155-0*, Pub. by Pavilion Bks Ltd) Trafalgar.

— Sir Lawrence Alma Tadema. (Illus.). 96p. 1990. 29.95 (*0-8109-1898-6*, Pub. by Abrams) Time Warner.

***Ash, Russell.** Top 10 of Everything. (Illus.). 288p. 2000. 24.95 (*0-7894-5960-4*); pap. text 17.95 (*0-7894-6132-3*) DK Pub Inc.

Ash, Russell. The Top Ten of Everything, 1998. LC 97-15018. 256p. 1997. pap. 17.95 (*0-7894-2082-1*) DK Pub Inc.

— The Top 10 of Everything 1999. LC 98-16593. 256p. 1998. pap. 17.95 (*0-7894-3523-3*); pap. 24.95 (*0-7894-3524-1*) DK Pub Inc.

— The Top Ten of Everything, 1996. LC 95-11541. (Illus.). 288p. 1995. 24.95 (*0-7894-0196-7*, 6-70510); pap. 16.95 (*0-7894-0338-2*, 6-70524) DK Pub Inc.

— Top 10 of Everything 2000. LC 99-23292. 288p. 1999. pap. 17.95 (*0-7894-4632-4*) DK Pub Inc.

— Top 10 of Everything 2000. LC 99-23292. (Illus.). 288p. 1999. 24.95 (*0-7894-4892-0*) DK Pub Inc.

— The Top Ten of Everything, 1997. LC 96-14203. 1996. 24.95 (*0-7894-1083-4*) DK Pub Inc.

— Top 10 of Everything 1997. 1996. 24.95 (*0-614-20408-9*); pap. 16.95 (*0-614-20409-7*) DK Pub Inc.

— The World in One Day: Incredible Comparisons. LC 97-16465. (Illus.). 32p. (J). (gr. 3). 1997. 15.95 (*0-7894-2028-7*) DK Pub Inc.

***Ash, Russell & Lake, Brian.** Bizarre Books. (Illus.). 196p. 1998. pap. 13.95 (*1-86205-102-X*, Pub. by Pavilion Bks Ltd) Trafalgar.

Ash, S. R., ed. Bibliography & Index of the New Mexico Geological Society Guidebooks, 1950-63. (Special Publications: No. 1). 31p. 1964. pap. 3.00 (*1-58546-000-1*) NMex Geol Soc.

Ash, S. R. & Davis, L. V., eds. Ruidoso Country: New Mexico. (Guidebook Ser.: No. 15). (Illus.). 195p. 1964. pap. 7.00 (*1-58546-045-1*) NMex Geol Soc.

Ash, Sally. Hedge of Thorns. Goodfellow, Pamela R., ed. LC 93-80294. 288p. (Orig.). 1994. pap. 7.99 (*0-9639882-0-4*) Goodfellow Pr.

— Matutu. Goodfellow, Pamela R., ed. 384p. 1997. pap. 12.99 (*0-9639882-9-8*) Goodfellow Pr.

Ash, Sidney. Petrified Forest: The Story Behind the Scenery. LC 85-81283. (Illus.). 48p. (Orig.). 1986. pap. 7.95 (*0-88714-006-8*) KC Pubns.

Ash, Stephen R. & Thornhill, Jerry A., eds. Handbook of Animal Models of Renal Failure. 232p. 1985. lib. bdg. 203.00 (*0-8493-2975-2*, RC918, CRC Reprint) Franklin.

Ash, Stephen V. Middle Tennessee Society Transformed, 1860-1870: War & Peace in the Upper South. LC 87-3337. (Illus.). 352p. 1988. text 50.00 (*0-8071-1400-6*) La State U Pr.

— When the Yankees Came: Chaos & Conflict in the Occupied South, 1861-1865. LC 94-49525. (Civil War America Ser.). 1995. 37.50 (*0-8078-2223-X*) U of NC Pr.

— When the Yankees Came: Conflict & Chaos in the Occupied South, 1861-1865. LC 94-49525. (Civil War America Ser.). (Illus.). 309p. 1999. pap. 16.95 (*0-8078-4795-X*) U of NC Pr.

Ash, Stephen V., ed. Secessionists & Other Scoundrels: Selections from "Parson Brownlow's Book" LC 98-50888. (Illus.). 144p. 1999. 29.95 (*0-8071-2353-6*); pap. 12.95 (*0-8071-2354-4*) La State U Pr.

***Ash, Timothy Garton.** History of the Present. 448p. 2000. 29.95 (*0-375-50353-6*) Random.

Ash, Timothy Garton. The Magic Lantern. 176p. 1993. pap. 12.00 (*0-679-74048-1*) McKay.

— Witness: The Uses of Adversity: Essays on the Fate of Central Europe. 335p. 1990. 19.95 (*0-685-32964-X*) Random.

Ash, Timothy Garton, ed. Freedom for Publishing, Publishing for Freedom: The Central & East European Publishing Project. LC 96-119392. (Central European University Press Bks.). 202p. (C). 1994. pap. 21.95 (*1-85866-055-6*, Pub. by Ctrl Europ Univ) Bks Intl VA.

***Ash, William.** The Bones of Jesus. 302p. 2000. pap. 7.95 (*1-930575-01-7*, Omni Hse Literary) Omni Pub.

Asha Chaddha. Agricultural Statistics in India. 1990. 40.00 (*81-7169-036-X*, Commonwealth) S Asia.

Asha, Ma P., ed. see Osho.

Ashabranner, Brent. Gavriel & Jemal. (Illus.). 96p. (J). (gr. 3-7). 1984. 11.95 (*0-396-08455-9*, G P Putnam) Peng Put Young Read.

— The New African Americans. LC 99-31388. (Illus.). 120p. (YA). (gr. 6-12). 1999. 21.00 (*0-208-02420-4*, Linnet Bks) Shoe String.

— Their Names to Live: What the Vietnam Veterans Memorial Means to Americans. LC 98-21004. 64p. (YA). (gr. 4-12). 1998. 23.90 (*0-7613-3235-9*) TFC Bks NY.

***Ashabranner, Brent K.** Badge of Valor: The National Law Enforcement Officers Memorial. LC 00-20222. (Illus.). (J). 2000. lib. bdg. write for info. (*0-7613-1522-5*) Millbrook Pr.

Ashabranner, Brent K. Dark Harvest: Migrant Farmworkers in America. LC 93-33170. (Illus.). x, 150p. (YA). (gr. 7 up). 1993. reprint ed. lib. bdg. 18.50 (*0-208-02391-7*, Linnet Bks) Shoe String.

***Ashabranner, Brent K.** Date with Destiny: The Women in Military Service for America Memorial. LC 99-36384. 64p. (J). (gr. 6). 2000. 23.90 (*0-7613-1472-5*) TFC Bks NY.

Ashabranner, Brent K., ed. The Lion's Whiskers & Other Ethiopian Tales. rev. ed. LC 97-3981. (Illus.). xvi, 96p. (J). (gr. 3 up). 1997. lib. bdg. 19.95 (*0-208-02429-8*, Linnet Bks) Shoe String.

Ashabranner, Brent K., jt. auth. see Davis, Russell B.

Ashain, Nashia. Crystal Ally Cards: The Crystal Path to Self Knowledge, 1. 1997. 29.95 (*0-9621910-1-9*) Heaven & Earth.

Ashall, Frank. Remarkable Discoveries! LC 93-46796. (Illus.). 290p. (C). 1994. text 54.95 (*0-521-43317-7*) Cambridge U Pr.

— Remarkable Discoveries! (Illus.). 292p. 1996. pap. 16.95 (*0-521-58953-3*) Cambridge U Pr.

Ashall, Frank, jt. ed. see Goate, Alison.

Ashan, Syed M. Agricultural Insurance: A New Policy for Developing Countries. (C). 1985. 270.00 (*0-7855-4323-6*, Pub. by Witherby & Co) St Mut.

Ashanti, B. J. Nubiana, Vol. I. 48p. 1977. pap. 2.00 (*0-917886-01-1*) Shamal Bks.

Ashanti, Baron J. Nova. 137p. 1991. pap. 9.95 (*0-86316-137-5*) Writers & Readers.

— Nova. 137p. 1991. 19.95 (*0-86316-138-3*) Writers & Readers.

Ashanti, Kwabena F. African Funerals & Burials: A Guide. 65p. (C). 1999. pap. 12.95 (*0-911325-13-1*) Tone Bks Inc.

— African Royal Wedding & Marriage Ceremony: A Guide. 80p. (C). 1999. pap. 14.95 (*0-911325-12-3*) Tone Bks Inc.

— Asaasa Yaa: Black Women Self-Empowerment. 80p. 1995. pap. 14.95 (*0-911325-10-7*) Tone Bks Inc.

— The Ashanti Brainwashing Test Manual: ABT Manual. 80p. (Orig.). (C). 1991. pap. text 12.95 (*0-911325-06-9*) Tone Bks Inc.

— Religion & Spiritual Healing: Africentric. (Illus.). 486p. (C). 1999. pap. 48.50 (*0-911325-07-7*) Tone Bks Inc.

— Rootwork & Voodoo in Mental Health. LC 87-71941. 280p. 1987. lib. bdg. 48.50 (*0-911325-04-2*) Tone Bks Inc.

Ashanti, Kwabena F. Sankofa Tumi: Holy Days for African Americans. 70p. 1999. 9.95 (*0-911325-08-5*) Tone Bks Inc.

***Ashanti, Kwabena F.** Sankofa Tumi: Holy Days for African Americans. 70p. (C). 1999. 9.95 (*0-911325-05-0*) Tone Bks Inc.

***Ashanti, Kwabena Faheem.** Psychotechnology of Brainwashing: Crucifying Willie Lynch. 2nd ed. (Illus.). 230p. 2000. pap. 24.95 (*0-911325-14-X*) Tone Bks Inc.

***Ashar, H.** Assessment of Inservice Conditions of Safety-Related Nuclear Plant Structures. 120p. 1998. per. 33.00 (*0-16-062964-0*) USGPO.

Ashar, Pranav, et al. Sequential Logic Synthesis. (C). 1991. text 106.50 (*0-7923-9187-X*) Kluwer Academic.

Asharina, Nina, et al. Russian Glass of the Seventeenth-Twentieth Centuries. LC 89-81837. (Illus.). 192p. 1990. pap. 9.95 (*0-87290-123-8*) Corning.

Ashbach, Charles & Schermer, Victor L. Object Relations, the Self & the Group. LC 94-9884. (International Library of Group Psychotherapy & Group Process Ser.). 328p. (C). 1994. pap. 27.99 (*0-415-11217-6*, B4262) Routledge.

Ashbach, Dawn & Veal, Janice. Adventures in Greater Puget Sound: An Educational Guide Exploring the Marine Environment of Greater Puget Sound. (Illus.). 56p. (Orig.). (J). (gr. 3-9). 1991. 7.95 (*0-9629778-0-2*) NW Island.

— San Juan Classics Cookbook, No. II. 225p. 1998. pap. 18.95 (*0-9629778-1-0*) NW Island.

Ashbach, Dawn, jt. auth. see Veal, Janice.

Ashbacher, Charles. Collection of Problems on Smarandache Notions. Popescu, Marcela, ed. LC 97-113156. 75p. (Orig.). (C). 1995. pap. text 7.95 (*1-879585-50-2*) Erhus Univ Pr.

— Collection of Problems on Smarandache Notions. LC QA0246.A82. 77p. (Orig.). reprint ed. pap. 30.00 (*0-608-10419-1*, 206992100008) Bks Demand.

— Further Explorations of the Smarandache Notions. 80p. (Orig.). (C). 1996. pap. 8.95 (*1-879585-56-1*) Erhus Univ Pr.

— An Introduction to Smarandache Function. Popescu, Marcela, ed. 70p. (Orig.). (C). 1995. pap. text 7.95 (*1-879585-49-9*) Erhus Univ Pr.

***Ashbacher, Charles.** Plucking from the Tree of the Smarandache Functions & Sequences. LC 99-200248. (Smarandache Notions Ser.). 85 p. (C). 1999. pap. text. write for info. (*1-879585-61-8*) Erhus Univ Pr.

— Sams Teach Yourself XML in 24 Hours. (Teach Yourself... in 24 Hours Ser.). (Illus.). 400p. 2000. pap. 24.99 (*0-672-31950-0*) Sams.

Ashbacher, Charles. The Smarandache Geometries. (Illus.). 100p. (Orig.). (C). 1996. pap. text 13.95 (*1-879585-53-7*) Erhus Univ Pr.

— Study on Some Smarandache Notions. Popescu, Marcela, ed. 75p. (Orig.). (C). 1996. pap. text 7.95 (*1-879585-51-0*) Erhus Univ Pr.

Ashbacher, Charles, ed. see Kashihara, Kenichiro.

Ashbacher, Michael, et al, eds. Olga Taussky Todd, in Memoriam. (Illus.). 357p. 1998. 20.00 (*1-57146-051-9*) Intl Pr Boston.

Ashbaucher, Rozella D. A Rendezvous with You. 1997. pap. write for info. (*1-57553-642-0*) Watermrk Pr.

Ashbaugh, Anne F. Plato's Theory of Explanation: A Study of the Cosmological Account in the Timaeus. LC 87-10256. (SUNY Series in Philosophy). 195p. 1988. text 24.50 (*0-88706-607-0*) State U NY Pr.

Ashbaugh, Annette N. All Hallows Eve. (Illus.). 15p. 1988. 5.95 (*0-943480-66-3*) Friis-Pioneer Pr.

Ashbaugh, Carl R. & Kasten, Katherine L. Educational Leadership. LC 94-20931. 160p. (C). 1991. pap. text 25.95 (*0-8013-0194-7*, 75853) Longman.

— The Licensure of School Administrators: Policy & Practice. 1992. 15.00 (*0-89333-095-7*) AACTE.

Ashbaugh, Carolyn. Lucy Parsons, American Revolutionary. LC 75-23909. (Illus.). 288p. 1976. pap. 30.00 (*0-88286-014-3*) C H Kerr.

***Ashbaugh, David R.** Quantitative-Qualitative Friction Ridge Analysis: An Introduction to Basic & Advanced Ridgeology. LC 99-33096. (Practical Aspects of Criminal & Forensic Investigation Ser.). 248p. 1999. boxed set 69.95 (*0-8493-7007-8*) CRC Pr.

Ashbaugh, Don. Nevada's Turbulent Yesterday. LC 63-16925. (Illus.). 349p. 1981. reprint ed. 26.95 (*0-87026-024-3*) Westernlore.

Ashbaugh, James. The Pacific Northwest: Geographical Perspectives. LC 97-72001. 440p. (C). 1997. per. 50.00 (*0-7872-3606-3*) Kendall-Hunt.

— The Pacific Northwest: Geographical Perspectives, Preliminary Edition. 436p. (C). 1994. per. 40.95 (*0-8403-9347-4*) Kendall-Hunt.

Ashbaugh, Kraid. Studies in Daniel & Revelation. LC 88-50303. 245p. 1988. per. 4.95 (*0-945383-02-9*) Teach Servs.

Ashbaugh, Noel E., jt. ed. see Stinchwomb, Wayne W.

Ashbaugh, Regan C. Downtick. 568p. 1998. mass mkt. 6.99 (*0-671-01889-2*) PB.

***Ashbaugh, Regan C.** In the Red. LC 98-50122. 468p. 1999. 24.00 (*0-671-01890-6*, PB Hardcover) PB.

— In the Red. 608p. 2000. reprint ed. per. 6.99 (*0-671-02774-3*, Pocket Books) PB.

***Ashbe, Jeanne.** That's Me. Orig. Title: La, C'est Moi. (Illus.). 12p. 2000. bds. 15.95 (*1-929132-02-6*) Kane-Miller Bk.

— What's Inside? (Illus.). 13p. (J). 2000. 9.95 (*0-916291-97-9*, Cranky Nell Bks) Kane-Miller Bk.

Ashbee, Andrew, ed. William Lawes (1602-1645) Essays on His Life, Times & Work. LC 97-77628. (Illus.). 380p. 1998. text 78.95 (*1-85928-354-3*, Pub. by Ashgate Pub) Ashgate Pub Co.

Ashbee, Andrew, et al, eds. A Biographical Dictionary of English Court Musicians, 1485-1714, Vols. 1 & 2. LC 98-28955. 9p. 1998. text 152.95 (*1-85928-087-0*, Pub. by Scolar Pr) Ashgate Pub Co.

Ashbee, Andrew & Holman, Peter, eds. John Jenkins & His Time: Studies in English Consort Music. (Illus.). 444p. 1997. text 98.00 (*0-19-816461-0*) OUP.

Ashbee, Andrew, ed. see Jenkins, John.

Ashbee, Charles R., ed. Parish of Bromley-by-Bow. LC 73-138270. (London County Council. Survey of London Ser.: No. 1). 1990. reprint ed. 84.50 (*0-404-51651-3*) AMS Pr.

Ashbee, David. Perpetual Waterfalls. 68p. 1989. reprint ed. pap. 11.95 (*0-905289-84-6*, Pub. by Enitha Pr) Dufour.

***Ashbee, Edward.** US Politics Today. LC 99-42533. 224p. 1999. text 59.95 (*0-7190-5463-X*, Pub. by Manchester Univ Pr) St Martin.

Ashbee, Kenneth H. Fundamental Principles of Fiber Reinforced Composites. 2nd ed. LC 93-60191. 430p. 1993. text 99.95 (*0-87762-923-4*) Technomic.

Ashbee, Paul. Wilsford Shaft: Excavations 1960-2. (Historic Buildings & Monuments Commission for England Archaeological Report Ser.: No. 11). xii, 159p. 1989. 32.00 incl. mic. film (*1-85074-210-3*) Balogh.

Ashberry, John. Flow Chart. 224p. 1998. pap. text 15.00 (*0-374-52549-8*, Noonday) FS&G.

— A Wave: Poems. 96p. 1998. pap. text 12.00 (*0-374-52547-1*, Noonday) FS&G.

Ashbery, John. And the Stars Were Shining. LC 93-14255. 99p. 1994. text 18.00 (*0-374-10500-6*) FS&G.

***Ashbery, John.** April Galleons: Poems. LC 99-18683. 96p. 1999. pap. text 13.00 (*0-374-52588-9*) FS&G.

Ashbery, John. Can You Hear, Bird: Poems. LC 93-14255. 96p. 1995. pap. 11.00 (*0-374-52434-3*, Noonday) FS&G.

— Can You Hear, Bird: Poems. LC 93-14255. 176p. 1995. text 20.00 (*0-374-11831-0*) FS&G.

— Can You Hear, Bird: Poems. 188p. 1997. pap. 12.00 (*0-374-52501-3*, Noonday) FS&G.

***Ashbery, John.** Girls on the Run: A Poem. LC 99-18682. 96p. 1999. text 20.00 (*0-374-16270-0*) FS&G.

— Girls on the Run: A Poem. 96p. 2000. pap. 13.00 (*0-374-52697-4*) FS&G.

— Hotel Lautreamont. 176p. 2000. pap. 15.00 (*0-374-52755-5*) FS&G.

Ashbery, John. Houseboat Days: Poems. LC 99-18681. 88p. 1999. pap. text 13.00 (*0-374-52590-0*) FS&G.

— The Ice Storm. 32p. (Orig.). 1987. pap. 5.95 (*0-937815-07-1*) Hanuman Bks.

— The Mooring Of Starting Out. LC 96-36982. 400p. 1997. 25.00 (*0-88001-527-6*) HarpC.

— The Mooring Of Starting Out. LC 96-36982. 392p. 1998. pap. 18.00 (*0-88001-547-0*) HarpC.

***Ashbery, John.** Other Traditions. LC 00-39648. (Charles Eliot Norton Lectures). 192p. 2000. 22.95 (*0-674-00315-2*) HUP.

Ashbery, John. Reported Sightings: Art Chronicles, 1957-1987. Bergman, David, ed. LC 90-49781. (Illus.). 464p. 1991. reprint ed. pap. text 16.95 (*0-674-76225-8*, ASHREX) HUP.
— Selected Poems. (Penguin Poets Ser.). 386p. 1986. pap. 17.95 (*0-14-058553-2*, Penguin Bks) Viking Penguin.
— Self-Portrait in a Convex Mirror: Poems. 96p. 1990. reprint ed. pap. 14.95 (*0-14-058668-7*, Penguin Bks) Viking Penguin.
— The Tennis Court Oath: A Book of Poems. LC 62-10569. (Wesleyan Poetry Classics Ser.). 94p. 1997. reprint ed. pap. 12.95 (*0-8195-1013-0*, Wesleyan Univ Pr) U Pr of New Eng.
— Three Plays. 1978. 15.00 (*0-915990-12-1*); pap. 7.50 (*0-915990-13-X*) Z Pr.
***Ashbery, John.** Wakefulness: Poems. LC 97-45567. 96p. 1998. 20.00 (*0-374-28598-5*) FS&G.
Ashbery, John. Wakefulness: Poems. 96p. 1999. pap. text 13.00 (*0-374-52593-5*) FS&G.
***Ashbery, John.** Your Name Here. 144p. 2000. 23.00 (*0-374-29598-0*) FS&G.
Ashbery, John & Schuyler, James. A Nest of Ninnies. LC 96-42543. 192p. 1997. 21.00 (*0-88001-523-3*) HarpC.
— A Nest of Ninnies. LC 75-28625. 191p. 1976. reprint ed. pap. 5.00 (*0-915990-02-4*) Z Pr.
Ashbery, John, et al. Apparitions: Poems. deluxe limited ed. 60p. 1981. 75.00 (*0-935716-10-6*) Lord John.
— David Schubert: Works & Days. (QRL Poetry Bks.: Vol. XXIV). (UKR.). 1983. 20.00 (*0-614-06406-6*) Quarterly Rev.
— Poets of the New York School. (Illus.). 1969. 10.00 (*0-910664-14-5*) Gotham.
— Private Seven. Heiniger, D. R. & Saunders, Ken, eds. (Illus.). 175p. (Orig.). 1992. pap. 7.00 (*1-881377-02-4*) Private Lives.
— Zzzzz, Vol. 5. Elmslie, Kenward, ed. (Illus.). 1977. pap. 5.00 (*0-915990-08-3*) Z Pr.
Ashbery, John, ed. see Marcus, Bruce.
Ashbery, John, ed. see Snow, Richard F.
Ashbery, John, tr. see De Chirico, Giorgio.
Ashbery, John, tr. see Martory, Pierre.
Ashbery, John, tr. see Reverdy, Pierre.
Ashbi, Mnata A. The Egyptian Book of the Dead: The Book of Coming Forth by Day. 250p. 1998. pap. 17.95 (*1-884564-28-3*) Cruzian Mystic.
— The Glory of Initiation. (Illus.). 40p. 1997. pap. 3.99 (*1-884564-37-2*) Cruzian Mystic.
— The Mysteries of Shetaut Pautti: Mystical Teachings of the Ancient Egyptian Creation Myth. (Illus.). 64p. 1997. pap. 5.99 (*1-884564-38-0*) Cruzian Mystic.
— The Parent's Guide to the Ausarian Resurrection Myth: How to Teach Yourself & Your Child Principles of Universal Religion. (Illus.). 64p. 1997. pap. 5.99 (*1-884564-30-5*) Cruzian Mystic.
— Sema Yoga Guide: Introduction to Yoga Philosophy & Mystical Religion. 40p. 1997. pap. 2.95 (*1-884564-29-1*) Cruzian Mystic.
— The Story of Asar, Aset & Hero: An Ancient Egyptian Legend, a Storybook & Coloring Book. large type ed. (Illus.). 48p. (J). (gr. 1-2). 1997. pap. 8.99 (*1-884564-31-3*) Cruzian Mystic.
***Ashbless, Janine.** Cruel Enchantment. 2000. mass mkt. 6.95 (*0-352-33483-5*) BLA4.
***Ashbourn, J.** Biometrics - Advanced Identity Verification: The Complete Guide. (Illus.). 350p. 2000. pap. 54.00 incl. cd-rom (*1-85233-243-3*) Spr-Verlag.
Ashbourne, Alexandra. Lithuania: The Rebirth of a Nation, 1991-1994. LC 99-20819. 256p. 1999. 60.00 (*0-7391-0027-0*) Lxngtn Bks.
Ashbrook, A. W., jt. auth. see Ritcey, G. M.
Ashbrook, James B. The Brain & Belief: Faith in Light of Brain Research. LC 88-40340. (Illus.). 250p. (C). 1988. pap. text 28.00 (*1-55605-040-2*) Wyndham Hall.
— The Human Mind & the Mind of God: Theological Promise in Brain Research. (Illus.). 408p. (Orig.). 1985. pap. text 33.00 (*0-8191-4226-3*) U Pr of Amer.
— Minding the Soul: Pastoral Counseling as Remembering. 300p. 1995. pap. 24.00 (*0-8006-2673-7*, 1-2673) Augsburg Fortress.
— Paul Tillich in Conversation: Psychotherapy... Religion... Culture... History... Psychology. LC 88-40118. 156p. (C). 1988. text 40.00 (*1-55605-039-9*); pap. text 20.00 (*1-55605-038-0*) Wyndham Hall.
Ashbrook, James B., ed. Brain, Culture & the Human Spirit: Essays from an Emergent Evolutionary Perspective. (Illus.). 222p. (Orig.). (C). 1992. pap. text 27.00 (*0-8191-8854-9*); lib. bdg. 56.50 (*0-8191-8853-0*) U Pr of Amer.
Ashbrook, James B., intro. Faith & Ministry in Light of the Double Brain. LC 89-40592. 320p. 1990. pap. text 20.00 (*1-55605-112-3*) Wyndham Hall.
Ashbrook, James B. & Albright, Carol R. The Humanizing Brain: Where Religion & Neuroscience Meet. LC 97-25730. 272p. (Orig.). 1997. pap. 20.95 (*0-8298-1200-8*) Pilgrim OH.
Ashbrook, James B. & Hinkle, John E., Jr., eds. At the Point of Need: Living Human Experience: Essays in Honor of Carroll A. Wise. LC 88-5686. (Illus.). 312p. (Orig.). (C). 1988. lib. bdg. 50.50 (*0-8191-6963-3*) U Pr of Amer.
***Ashbrook, John.** Brian DePalma. 2000. pap. 5.95 (*1-903047-12-9*, Pub. by Pocket Essentials) Trafalgar.
— Terry Gilliam. 2000. pap. 5.95 (*1-903047-14-5*, Pub. by Pocket Essentials) Trafalgar.
***Ashbrook, John M. & Cheshire, Ellen.** Joel & Ethan Coen. 2000. pap. 5.95 (*1-903047-03-X*, Pub. by Pocket Essentials) Trafalgar.
Ashbrook, Joseph. Astronomical Scrapbook. (Illus.). 480p. 1984. text 18.95 (*0-933346-24-7*) Sky Pub.
Ashbrook, Karen. Playing the Hammered Dulcimer in the Irish Tradition. (Illus.). 90p. 1987. pap. 17.95 (*0-8256-0310-2*, OK64915, Oak) Music Sales.
Ashbrook, Peter C., jt. ed. see Renfrew, Malcolm M.
Ashbrook, R. L., jt. auth. see American Society for Metals Staff.
Ashbrook, Stella. The PenDelfin Collectors Handbook. (Illus.). 100p. 1998. pap. 19.95 (*1-870703-62-6*, Pub. by Francis Jos Pubns) Krause Pubns.
***Ashbrook, Stella.** Pindelfin Collectors Handbook. (Illus.). 2000. 24.95 (*1-870703-83-9*) Francis Jos Pubns.
***Ashbrook, Tom.** The Leap: A Memoir of Love & Madness in the Internet Gold Rush. 295p. 2000. 26.00 (*0-395-76165-4*) HM.
— The Leap: A Memoir of Love & Madness in the Internet Goldrush. LC 99-59162. 320p. 2000. 26.00 (*0-395-83934-3*) HM.
Ashbrook, William. The Operas of Puccini. LC 84-72674. 288p. (Orig.). 1985. reprint ed. pap. text 17.95 (*0-8014-9309-9*) Cornell U Pr.
Ashburn, Frank D., ed. see Ashburn, Percy M.
Ashburn, Jo. Curse of Monkey Island Vol. 3: The Official Strategy Guide, No. 3. LC 96-71782. 216p. 1998. per. 19.99 (*0-7615-1031-1*) Prima Pub.
— Grim Fandango: Prima's Official Strategy Guide. LC 98-67310. 244p. 1998. per. 19.99 (*0-7615-1797-9*) Prima Pub.
— Star Wars: Episode I: The Phantom Menace. LC 99-61928. (Star Wars). 96p. 1999. pap. 14.99 (*0-7615-2148-8*) Prima Pub.
Ashburn, M. A., jt. ed. see Stanley, Theodore H.
Ashburn, Melba M. Caboose Cobey. 2nd ed. (Illus.). 26p. (J). (gr. 1-6). 1997. reprint ed. pap. 7.95 (*0-9656829-0-0*) Syringa.
— The Little Hobo. (Illus.). 130p. (Orig.). (J). (gr. 3 up). 1997. pap. 15.95 (*0-9656829-4-3*) Syringa.
Ashburn, Michael A., et al, eds. Pain Management & Anesthesiology. LC 98-9867. (Developments in Critical Care Medicine & Anesthesiology Ser.). 324p. 1998. 148.00 (*0-7923-4995-4*) Kluwer Academic.
Ashburn, Michael A. & Rice, Linda J. The Management of Pain. LC 97-36319. (Illus.). 729p. 1997. text 95.00 (*0-443-07679-0*) Church.
Ashburn, Percy M. A History of the Medical Department of the United States Army. LC 75-23675. reprint ed. 49.50 (*0-404-13228-6*) AMS Pr.
— The Ranks of Death: A Medical History of the Conquest of America. Ashburn, Frank D., ed. LC 80-24672. (Perspectives in Latin American History Ser.: No. 2). xix, 298p. 1980. reprint ed. lib. bdg. 45.00 (*0-87991-599-4*) Porcupine Pr.
Ashburn, Shirley S., jt. auth. see Schuster, Clara S.
Ashburne, John F. The Best of Kansai: Kyoto, Osaka, Kobe. 176p. 1998. pap. 12.95 (*0-8048-2069-4*) Tuttle Pubng.
Ashburner, M., et al, eds. The Genetics & Biology of Drosophila, Vol. 3B. 1982. text 99.00 (*0-12-064946-2*) Acad Pr.
Ashburner, Michael. Drosophila, Vol. 2. LC 89-7188. (Illus.). 458p. 1989. reprint ed. pap., lab manual ed. 142.00 (*0-608-04451-2*, 206498200002) Bks Demand.
— Drosophila Vol. 1: A Laboratory Handbook. LC 89-7188. (Illus.). 1375p. 1989. reprint ed. pap. 200.00 (*0-608-04089-4*, 206482100001) Bks Demand.
Ashbury, John W. And All Our Yesterdays: A Chronicle of Frederick County Maryland. (Illus.). 480p. 1997. 39.95 (*0-9661278-0-3*); pap. 32.95 (*0-9661278-1-1*) Diversions Pubns.
Ashby. Dependent, Neglected & Abused Children. LC 96-36013. 1997. 33.00 (*0-8057-4100-3*, G K Hall Lrg Type) Mac Lib Ref.
— Materials Selection Wallchart. ring bd. 40.00 (*0-412-61300-X*) Chapman & Hall.
Ashby. Sea Gift. 1998. 14.95 (*0-395-77603-1*) Ticknor & Fields.
***Ashby.** Voice Notes. 1999. cd-rom 150.00 (*0-205-29964-4*, Longwood Div) Allyn.
Ashby & Jones Staff. Engineering Materials 2. 2nd ed. LC 98-217373. 384p. 1998. pap. text 34.95 (*0-7506-4019-7*) Buttrwrth-Heinemann.
Ashby, Ann F., jt. auth. see Ashby, C.
Ashby, Anna L. The Fox & the Grapes: Aesop Through the Ages: A Checklist of Aesopic Fables in the Pierpont Morgan Library. LC 95-17672. 1995. write for info. (*0-87598-112-7*) Pierpont Morgan.
Ashby, Bonnie, jt. auth. see Turkington, Carol.
Ashby, C., et al, eds. Photons & Low Energy Particles in Surface Processing. (Symposium Proceedings Ser.: Vol. 236). 549p. 1992. text 58.00 (*1-55899-130-1*) Materials Res.
Ashby, C. & Ashby, Ann F. You Be Good Vet, Doc: Venture in Grenada. LC 88-90725. (Illus.). 227p. (Orig.). 1988. pap. 11.95 (*0-9621103-0-2*) A F Ashby.
Ashby, Charles R., Jr., ed. The Modulation of Dopaminergic Neurotransmission by Other Neurotransmitters. LC 95-43990. 240p. 1995. boxed set 159.95 (*0-8493-4780-7*) CRC Pr.
Ashby, Clarin D. A Prophet's Friend. 436p. pap. 14.95 (*1-55517-210-5*) CFI Dist.
Ashby, Clifford. Classical Greek Theatre: New Views of an Old Subject. LC 98-38376. (Illus.). 216p. 1998. text 37.95 (*0-87745-641-0*) U of Iowa Pr.
Ashby, Clifford & May, Suzanne D. Trouping Through Texas: Harley Sadler & His Tent Show. LC 81-82503. 194p. 1982. 15.95 (*0-87972-184-7*) Bowling Green Univ Popular Press.
Ashby, Daphne J. Creative Embroidery Techniques Using Color Through Gold. (Illus.). 176p. 1998. pap. text 19.95 (*1-86108-087-5*, Pub. by Guild Master) Sterling.
— Ribbon Embroidery. (Illus.). 128p. 1998. pap. 16.95 (*0-7153-0827-0*, Pub. by D & C Pub) Sterling.
Ashby, Daphne J. & Woolsey, Jackie. Ribbon Embroidery. LC 97-143653. (Illus.). 128p. 1997. 24.95 (*0-7153-0433-X*, Pub. by D & C Pub) Sterling.
Ashby-Davis, Claire, jt. auth. see Cicchelli, Terry
Ashby, Delbert M. Make Money Trading Mortgages. LC 94-61113. 160p. 1994. pap. 49.95 (*0-9642690-0-7*) Wellington Co.
Ashby, Dianne E. & Krug, Samuel E. Thinking Through the Principalship. LC 97-42924. 220p. 1998. 39.95 (*1-883001-50-1*) Eye On Educ.
Ashby, Dorothy P. Leaves of Love. 1997. pap. write for info. (*1-57553-695-1*) Watermrk Pr.
Ashby, Eric. Adapting Universities to a Technological Society. LC 73-22555. (Jossey-Bass Higher Education Ser.). 176p. reprint ed. pap. 54.60 (*0-8357-5095-7*, 202108300020) Bks Demand.
— Any Person, Any Study: An Essay on Higher Education in the United States. LC 73-144765. 125p. reprint ed. pap. 38.80 (*0-8357-5648-3*, 202087700020) Bks Demand.
— Reconciling Man with the Environment. LC 77-91909. x, 104p. 1978. pap. 10.95 (*0-8047-1041-4*) Stanford U Pr.
Ashby, Eric & Anderson, Mary. Rise of the Student Estate in Britain. 196p. 1970. 25.95 (*0-674-77290-3*) HUP.
Ashby, Eric, et al. On the Meaning of the University. McMurrin, Sterling M., ed. LC 74-22637. 133p. reprint ed. pap. 41.30 (*0-8357-4378-0*, 203720900007) Bks Demand.
Ashby, F. Gregory, ed. Multidimensional Models of Perception & Cognition. (Scientific Psychology Ser.). 538p. 1992. text 125.00 (*0-8058-0577-X*) L Erlbaum Assocs.
Ashby, Franklin C. Revitalize Your Corporate Culture. LC 99-15329. (Improving Human Performance Ser.). 1999. 34.95 (*0-88415-279-0*, 5279, Cashman Dud) Gulf Pub.
Ashby, Franklin C., jt. ed. see Phillips, Jack J.
Ashby, G. W. Go Out & Meet God: A Commentary on the Book of Exodus. LC 97-25268. (International Theological Commentary Ser.). 160p. 1998. pap. 16.00 (*0-8028-4332-8*) Eerdmans.
Ashby, Glenville C. Boot Camp: The Ultimate Fitness Book. 1998. pap. 14.95 (*1-889534-01-3*) Jay St Pubs.
Ashby, Helena. Ramp Creek Rhythms: A Book of Poems. LC 85-90773. 54p. 1985. 8.00 (*0-9614781-0-1*); pap. 4.00 (*0-9614781-1-X*) H Ashby Bks.
Ashby, James, tr. see Addeo, Samuel J.
Ashby, John P., ed. Clinical Laboratory Science in the Changing Scene of Health Care. 1987. text 114.50 (*0-85200-685-3*) Kluwer Academic.
— The Patient & Decentralised Testing. (C). 1987. text 102.50 (*0-7462-0036-6*) Kluwer Academic.
***Ashby, Justine & Higson, Andrew.** British Cinema: Past & Present. LC 99-87266. 2000. pap. write for info (*0-415-22062-9*) Routledge.
Ashby, Le Roy. William Jennings Bryan: Champion of Democracy. (Twayne's 20th Century American Biography Ser.). 256p. 1987. 28.95 (*0-8057-7760-1*) Macmillan.
Ashby, Leroy. The Spearless Leader: Senator Borah & the Progressive Movement in the 1920s. LC 74-170963. 336p. 104.20 (*0-8357-9698-1*, 201173300079) Bks Demand.
Ashby, M. K. Joseph Ashby of Tysoe, 1859-1919: A Study of English Village Life. (C). 1974. text 19.95 (*0-85036-174-5*, Pub. by MRLN) Paul & Co Pubs.
Ashby, Margaret. A Hertfordshire Christmas. (Illus.). 160p. 1998. 15.95 (*0-7509-1709-1*, Pub. by Sutton Pub Ltd) Intl Pubs Mktg.
— Stevenage: History & Guide. (Illus.). 128p. 1994. pap. 14.00 (*0-7509-0426-7*, Pub. by Sutton Pub Ltd) Intl Pubs Mktg.
Ashby, Michael, jt. auth. see Cebon, David.
Ashby, Michael, jt. auth. see Gibson, Lorna J.
Ashby, Michael, ed. see Hornby, A. S.
Ashby, Michael F. Materials Selection in Mechanical Design. (Illus.). 360p. 1992. pap. text 44.95 (*0-7506-2727-1*, Prgamon Press) Buttrwrth-Heinemann.
— Materials Selection in Mechanical Design. 2nd ed. LC 98-55392. 502p. 2000. pap. text 49.95 (*0-7506-4357-9*) Buttrwrth-Heinemann.
Ashby, Michael F., et al, eds. Metal-Ceramic Interfaces: Proceedings of workshop 'Bonding, Structure & Mechanical Properties of Metal-Ceramic Interfaces', University of Metal-Ceramic Interfaces', University of California, USA, 16-18 January 1989. (ACTA-Scripta Metallurgica Conference Ser.: No. 4). (Illus.). 448p. 1990. 173.00 (*0-08-040505-3*, Pergamon Pr) Elsevier.
Ashby, Michael F. & Hirth, J. P., eds. Perspectives on Hydrogen in Metals: Collected Papers on the Effect of Hydrogen on the Properties of Metals & Alloys. 700p. 1986. 339.00 (*0-08-034813-0*) Franklin.
Ashby, Michael F. & Jones, David R. Engineering Materials 1: An Introduction to Their Properties & Applications. 2nd ed. 320p. 2000. pap. text 36.95 (*0-7506-3081-7*) Buttrwrth-Heinemann.
Ashby, Michael F., jt. auth. see Gibson, Lorna J.
Ashby, Mnata A. The Slowness Meditation: How to Discover the Inner Self. (Illus.). 40p. 1997. pap. 3.99 (*1-884564-36-4*) Cruzian Mystic.
Ashby, Muata. Egyptian Yoga: The Philosophy of Enlightenment. 2nd ed. (Illus.). 216p. 1995. reprint ed. pap., per. 18.95 (*1-884564-01-1*) Cruzian Mystic.
Ashby, Muata A. The Ausarian Resurrection: The Ancient Egyptian Bible. (Illus.). 191p. 1996. pap. 18.95 (*1-884564-27-5*) Cruzian Mystic.
— Egyptian Yoga Vol. II: The Supreme Wisdom of Enlightenment. (Illus.). 210p. 1998. pap. 18.95 (*1-884564-39-9*) Cruzian Mystic.
— Healing the Criminal Heart: Introduction to Maat Philosophy & the Path of Redemption. (Illus.). 40p. 1997. pap. 3.99 (*1-884564-17-8*) Cruzian Mystic.
— Healing the Criminal Heart Pt. II: Transforming Your Life from Criminal to Sage Through the Practice of Yoga. 64p. 1998. 5.99 (*1-884564-46-1*) Cruzian Mystic.
— The Hymns of Amun: The Mystical Teachings of Ancient Egyptian Theban Theology. (Illus.). 260p. 1997. pap. 15.99 (*1-884564-08-9*) Cruzian Mystic.
— Meditation: The Ancient Egyptian Path to Enlightenment. (Illus.). 260p. 1997. pap. 14.99 (*1-884564-26-7*) Cruzian Mystic.
Ashby, Mwata A. Growing Beyond Hate: The Mystic Art of Transcending Hate & Discovering Spiritual Enlightenment. (Illus.). 64p. 1997. pap. 5.99 (*1-884564-34-8*) Cruzian Mystic.
Ashby, N., et al, eds. General Relativity & Gravitation 1989: Proceedings of the International Conference on General Relativity & Gravitation. 520p. (C). 1990. text 85.00 (*0-521-38428-1*) Cambridge U Pr.
***Ashby, Neil.** Global Positioning System Receivers & Relativity. 50p. 1999. pap. 4.50 (*0-16-056959-1*) USGPO.
Ashby, Norma B., jt. auth. see Myers, Rex C.
Ashby, Pat. Finishing Touches. 1992. pap. 19.95 (*1-85391-093-7*) Sterling.
Ashby, Pat. Sugarcraft Cake Decorating. (Illus.). 96p. 1991. 22.50 (*0-946429-30-8*, Pub. by M OMara) Trans-Atl Phila.
Ashby, Patricia. Speech Sounds. LC 96-172021. 120p. (C). 1995. pap. 14.99 (*0-415-08571-3*) Routledge.
Ashby, Peter, jt. auth. see Ashby, Tim.
Ashby, Reginald M. Christian Yoga: The Mystical Journey from Jesus to Christ. (Illus.). 350p. (Orig.). 1997. pap. 19.95 (*1-884564-05-4*) Cruzian Mystic.
— How to Self-Publish Your Book & Save over 50of the Cost of a Professional Printer. 1998. pap. 9.95 (*1-884564-40-2*) Cruzian Mystic.
Ashby, Robert L. Ashby & Badger Ancestry. 445p. 1996. reprint ed. pap. 67.50 (*0-8328-5366-6*); reprint ed. lib. bdg. 77.50 (*0-8328-5365-8*) Higginson Bk Co.
— Ashby. Family History of William Hardy Ashby & Nancy Maria Badger Ashby. (Illus.). 226p. 1996. reprint ed. pap. 34.00 (*0-8328-5382-8*); reprint ed. lib. bdg. 44.00 (*0-8328-5381-X*) Higginson Bk Co.
Ashby, Romy. The Cutmouth Lady. LC 97-195773. (Semiotext(e) Native Agents Ser.). 208p. (Orig.). 1995. pap. 7.00 (*1-57027-055-4*) Autonomedia.
Ashby, Rush, ed. see Keene, Carolyn.
Ashby, Ruth. Elizabethan England. LC 96-43868. (Cultures of the Past Ser.). (Illus.). 80p. (J). (gr. 5-12). 1998. lib. bdg. 28.50 (*0-7614-0269-1*, Benchmark NY) Marshall Cavendish.
— Lydia's Scream Date. (Beetlejuice Ser.: No. 2). 96p. (J). 1992. pap. 2.99 (*0-671-75553-6*) PB.
— Orangutan. (Illus.). 60p. (J). (gr. 4-7). 1996. pap. text 5.95 (*0-382-39484-4*) Silver Burdett Pr.
— The Orangutan. LC 93-5754. (Remarkable Animals Ser.). (Illus.). 60p. (YA). (gr. 5 up). 1994. lib. bdg. 13.95 (*0-87518-600-9*) Silver Burdett Pr.
***Ashby, Ruth.** T-Rex: Back to the Cretaceous. LC 98-56134. (Illus.). 56p. (J). (ps up). 2000. 19.95 (*0-439-15341-7*) Scholastic Inc.
Ashby, Ruth, ed. Monster Mix-Up. (Nintendo Bk.: No. III). 128p. (Orig.). (J). 1991. mass mkt. 3.50 (*0-671-74201-9*, Archway) PB.
— Nintendo Book No. 4: Koopa Kapers, No. 4. 128p. (Orig.). (J). 1991. mass mkt. 3.50 (*0-671-74202-7*, Archway) PB.
Ashby, Ruth, ed. see Barber, Antonia.
Ashby, Ruth, ed. see Bosco, Clyde.
Ashby, Ruth, ed. see Cohen, Daniel.
Ashby, Ruth, ed. see Daly, Brian.
Ashby, Ruth, ed. see Dixon, Franklin W.
Ashby, Ruth, ed. see Donnelly, Judy & Kramer, Sydelle A.
Ashby, Ruth, ed. see Dyjak, Elisabeth.
Ashby, Ruth, ed. see Gilden, Mel.
Ashby, Ruth, ed. see Harrell, Janice.
Ashby, Ruth, ed. see Hodgman, Ann.
Ashby, Ruth, ed. see Keene, Carolyn.
Ashby, Ruth, ed. see Kistler, Darci.
Ashby, Ruth, ed. see Nelson, Peter.
Ashby, Ruth, jt. ed. see Ohrn, Deborah G.
Ashby, Ruth, ed. see Rovin, Jeff.
Ashby, Ruth, ed. see Willock, Ruth.
Ashby, Stephen M., jt. ed. see Johnson, Kent.
Ashby, Susan. Granny's Muffin House. 1983. pap. 12.95 (*0-930440-18-8*) Royal Hse.
— The Shadow Hill Book of Mix Easy Cakes. (Illus.). 64p. (Orig.). 1984. pap. 3.95 (*0-912661-05-4*) Woodsong Graph.
— The Shadow Hill Book of Squares, Bars & Brownies. LC 84-52106. (Illus.). 144p. 1984. pap. 7.95 (*0-912661-03-8*) Woodsong Graph.
Ashby, Sylvia. Don Coyote: Folklore, Comedy Style. (Illus.). 40p. 1986. pap. 3.50 (*0-88680-260-1*) I E Clark.
— The King Stag. 42p. (Orig.). (J). (gr. 3-12). 1996. pap. 3.50 (*1-57514-180-9*, 1144) Encore Perform Pub.
— Mrs. Peck's Christmas Puddin' 1998. 3.00 (*1-57514-297-X*, 3098) Encore Perform Pub.
— Once upon a Broomstick: A Halloween Happening in One Act. (Illus.). 28p. (Orig.). (J). (gr. 1-8). 1990. pap. 3.25 (*0-88680-329-2*) I E Clark.
— Professor Zuccini's Traveling Tales: Folk Tales in Commedie Style. 44p. (J). (gr. k up). 1983. pap. 4.00 (*0-88680-208-3*) I E Clark.
— Santa Claus Is Missing! A One-Act Musical. (Illus.). 22p. (J). (ps up). 1989. pap. 3.25 (*0-88680-310-1*) I E Clark.
— Shining Princess of the Slender Bamboo: Dramatization of a Japanese Folk Tale. (Illus.). 44p. (J). (gr. 6 up). 1987. pap. 4.00 (*0-88680-266-0*) I E Clark.
***Ashby, Sylvia.** Tales of Molly Malloy. 54p. 1999. pap. 3.50 (*0-87129-946-1*, TB6) Dramatic Pub.

A

A

Ashby, Sylvia, adapted by. Once upon a Santa Claus: A Musical Play. (Illus.). 44p. (J). (ps up). 1988. pap. 4.00 (*0-88680-296-2*) I E Clark.
— The Secret Garden. 80p. 1997. pap. 5.00 (*0-87440-055-4*) Bakers Plays.
Ashby, Tim & Ashby, Peter. Woodturners Wooden Clock Cases. LC 92-38120. (Illus.). 32p. (Orig.). 1993. pap. 7.95 (*0-941936-23-6*) Linden Pub Fresno.
Ashby, Timothy. Missed Opportunities: The Rise & Fall of Jamaica's Edward Seaga. 40p. 1989. pap. 5.00 (*1-55813-031-4*) Hudson Instit IN.
Ashby, W. Clark & Vogel, Willis G. Tree Planting on Mined Lands in the Midwest: A Handbook. (Illus.). 115p. 1994. lib. bdg. write for info. (*1-885189-01-X*) Coal Res Ctr.
Ashby, W. Ross. Design for a Brain: The Origin of Adaptive Behavior. 2nd ed. 286p. 1966. pap. 13.95 (*0-412-20090-2*, NO.6012) Chapman & Hall.
— Introduction to Cybernetics. 1964. reprint ed. pap. 17.95 (*0-416-68300-2*, NO. 2064) Routledge.
— Mechanisms of Intelligence: Ashby's Writings on Cybernetics. Conant, Roger, ed. (Systems Inquiry Ser.). 394p. (Orig.). (C). 1981. pap. text 17.95 (*0-914105-04-3*) Intersystems Pubns.
Ashby, Wallace L. Fossils of Calvert Cliffs. 3rd ed. (Illus.). 20p. 1995. pap. 4.75 (*0-941647-11-0*) Calvert MM Pr.
Ashby, Warren. Comprehensive History of Western Ethics: What Do We Believe? LC 97-8613. 569p. 1997. 39.95 (*1-57392-152-1*) Prometheus Bks.
Ashby, William J., et al, eds. Linguistic Perspectives on the Romance Languages: Selected Papers from the Linguistic Symposium on Romance Linguistics, Santa Barbara, February 21-24, 1991. LC 93-18384. (Current Issues in Linguistic Theory Ser.: Vol. 103). xxii, 404p. 1993. 100.00 (*1-55619-557-5*) J Benjamins Pubng Co.
Ashby, William J., jt. auth. see Linguistic Symposium on Romance Languages Staff.
Ashby, William M. Redder Blood. LC 73-18570. reprint ed. 34.50 (*0-404-11380-X*) AMS Pr.
Ashcam, Roger & Ford, Horace. Toxophilus: Archery - Theory & Practice, 2 vols. in 1. Manley, Dean V., ed. (Legends of the Longbow Ser.: Vol. 6). (Illus.). 686p. 1992. reprint ed. 45.00 (*1-56416-092-0*) Derrydale Pr.
Ashcoff, Kendall. Las Vegas Cuisine 1998, Vol. 2. rev. ed. 100p. 1998. pap. 5.95 (*0-9632234-3-7*) R Hart Mktg.
***Ashcom, Robert L.** Lost Hound. (Illus.). 161p. 2000. lthr. 150.00 (*1-56416-176-5*) Derrydale Pr.
— Lost Hound: And Other Hunting Stories & Poems. LC 99-46004. (Illus.). 161p. 2000. 45.00 (*1-56416-173-0*) Derrydale Pr.
Ashcraft. Science & Behavior Quickprint. 1998. pap. text 35.00 (*0-536-01781-6*) Pearson Custom.
Ashcraft, Carol-Faye, ed. see Groene, Janet.
Ashcraft, Carol-Faye, ed. see Gurnsey, Frank & Zoerner, Cy.
Ashcraft, Carol-Faye, ed. see Kelley, Clay.
Ashcraft-Eason, Lillian, jt. auth. see Perry, Robert.
Ashcraft, Howard D. As You Were, Vol. 1. Mullenax, Michelle, ed. LC 90-93204. (Illus.). 1990. 14.95 (*0-9626936-0-X*) Ashcraft Enter.
***Ashcraft, Janice.** Lecciones Biblicas Creativas para Jovenes Sobre Juan: Encuentros Con Jesus. (SPA.). 2000. pap. 10.99 (*0-8297-2888-0*) Vida Pubs.
Ashcraft, Jay. Creative Bible Lessons in John: Encounters with Jesus. LC 95-34989. 96p. 1996. pap. 12.99 (*0-310-20769-X*) Zondervan.
Ashcraft, Keith W. Pediatric Surgery. 3rd ed. Lampert, Richard, ed. LC 98-31214. (Illus.). 1055p. 1999. text. write for info. (*0-7216-7312-0*, W B Saunders Co) Harcrt Hlth Sci Grp.
— Pediatric Urology. 544p. 1990. text 156.00 (*0-7216-2746-3*, W B Saunders Co) Harcrt Hlth Sci Grp.
Ashcraft, Keith W. & Holder, Thomas M. Atlas of Pediatric Surgery. LC 93-1848. 336p. 1994. text 153.00 (*0-7216-3720-5*, W B Saunders Co) Harcrt Hlth Sci Grp.
— Pediatric Surgery. 2nd ed. (Illus.). 1080p. 1992. text 209.00 (*0-7216-3737-X*, W B Saunders Co) Harcrt Hlth Sci Grp.
***Ashcraft, Mark.** Human Memory & Cognition. 3rd ed. (C). 2000. text 75.00 (*0-8013-3121-8*) Longman.
Ashcraft, Mark H. Fundamentals of Cognition. LC 97-29458. 412p. (C). 1997. 82.00 (*0-321-01207-0*, Prentice Hall) P-H.
— Human Memory & Cognition. 2nd ed. LC 93-32908. 650p. (C). 1997. 89.00 (*0-673-46789-9*) Addson-Wesley Educ.
Ashcraft, Martha & Malicoat, Myrna. A Place Called Tackett Creek: Home of Good News Grannies & B. R. Beaver & Friends. LC 97-75782. (Illus.). 32p. 1998. pap. 9.95 (*1-57736-070-2*, Hillsboro Pr) Providence Hse.
Ashcraft, Morris. Christian Faith & Beliefs. 1998. pap. text 19.99 (*0-8054-1871-7*) Broadman.
Ashcraft, Morris, ed. see Tull, James E.
Ashcraft, Nancy. At the Scent of Water. 1986. pap. 8.25 (*0-87508-049-9*) Chr Lit.
Ashcraft, Norman. Colonialism & Underdevelopment: Processes of Political Economic Change in British Honduras. LC 72-92055. (Columbia University, Center for Education in Asia, Publications). 192p. reprint ed. pap. 59.60 (*0-608-14895-4*, 202598900048) Bks Demand.
Ashcraft, Richard. John Locke: Critical Assessments, 4 vols., Set. (Critical Assessments of Leading Political Philosophers Ser.). (Illus.). 368p. (C). (gr. 13). 1991. 745.00 (*0-415-00847-6*, A4703) Routledge.
— Locke's Two Treatises on Government. 256p. 1989. pap. text 19.95 (*0-04-445338-8*) Routledge.
Ashcraft, Tami O. & McGearhart, Susea. Red Sky in Mourning: The True Story of a Woman's Courage & Survival at Sea. LC 96-9538. (Illus.). 240p. 1998. pap. 18.95 (*0-9655837-7-5*) Bright Works.
Ashcroft. College Law for Business - Study Report. 10th ed. (SWC-Business Law Ser.). 1986. mass mkt. 17.75 (*0-538-12921-2*) S-W Pub.
— Ion Channels & Disease. LC 98-85618. (Illus.). 472p. (C). 1999. 49.95 (*0-12-065310-9*) Acad Pr.
— Key-Law for Business. 11th ed. (SWC-Business Law Ser.). 1991. mass mkt., student ed. 4.00 (*0-538-81984-7*) S-W Pub.
— Law for Business. 11th ed. (LA - Business Law Ser.). (C). 1991. mass mkt. 22.50 (*0-538-81705-4*) S-W Pub.
— Law For Business. 11th ed. (LA - Business Law Ser.). (C). 1992. mass mkt. 24.25 (*0-538-81708-9*) S-W Pub.
— Solid State Physics. 2nd ed. (C). 1999. text 65.00 (*0-03-058556-2*) Harcourt Coll Pubs.
— Tree of Ecstasy. 1991. pap. 13.95 (*0-85030-899-2*, Pub. by Aqrn Pr) Harper SF.
Ashcroft, A. Ionization Methods in Organic Mass Spectrometry. (RCS Analytical Spectroscopy Monographs). 190p. 1997. 102.00 (*0-85404-570-8*) Am Chemical.
Ashcroft, Bill, et al, eds. The Empire Writes Back: Theory & Practice in Post-Colonial Literatures. 192p. 1989. 39.95 (*0-415-01208-2*, A3548) Routledge.
— The Empire Writes Back: Theory & Practice in Post-Colonial Literatures. 192p. (C). 1989. pap. 18.99 (*0-415-01209-0*, A3552) Routledge.
— The Post-Colonial Studies Reader. LC 94-17829. 384p. (gr. 13). 1995. pap. 25.99 (*0-415-09622-7*, B3134) Routledge.
— The Post-Colonial Studies Reader. LC 94-17829. 384p. (C). (gr. 13). 1995. 90.00 (*0-415-09621-9*, B3130) Routledge.
Ashcroft, Bill & Ahluwalia, D. P. S. Edward Said: Paradox of Identity. LC 99-19707. 1999. pap. write for info. (*0-415-19671-X*) Routledge.
***Ashcroft, Bill & Ahluwalia, D. P. S.** Edward Said: Paradox of Identity. LC 99-19707. 176p. (C). 1999. text. write for info. (*0-415-19670-1*) Routledge.
Ashcroft, Bill, et al. Key Concepts in Post-Colonial Studies. LC 97-28771. 288p. (C). 1998. pap. 17.99 (*0-415-15304-2*) Routledge.
— Key Concepts in Post-Colonial Studies. LC 97-28771. 288p. (C). 1998. 65.00 (*0-415-15303-4*) Routledge.
Ashcroft, Brian & Love, James H. Takeovers, Mergers, & the Regional Economy. (Scottish Industrial Policy Ser.). 256p. 1993. text 65.00 (*0-7486-0400-6*, Pub. by Edinburgh U Pr) Col U Pr.
***Ashcroft, Christine, ed.** Can I Be the Ghost: Teaching Ideas & Activity Sheets. (Illus.). 24p. 1998. pap., teacher ed. 4.95 (*0-8464-4936-6*) Beekman Pubs.
Ashcroft, Cliff. Faithful. LC 97-144728. 80p. 1997. pap. 14.95 (*1-85754-258-4*, Pub. by Carcanet Pr) Paul & Co Pubs.
Ashcroft, E. A., jt. auth. see Orgun, M. A.
Ashcroft, Edward A., et al. Multidimensional Programming. (Illus.). 176p. 1995. text 60.00 (*0-19-507597-8*) OUP.
***Ashcroft, Frances M.** Life at the Extremes: The Science of Survival. LC 00-28672. (Illus.). 320p. 2000. 27.50 (*0-520-22234-2*) U CA Pr.
Ashcroft, Frances M. & Ashcroft, Stephen J., eds. Insulin: Molecular Biology to Pathology. (Illus.). 444p. 1992. pap. text 55.00 (*0-19-963228-6*) OUP.
Ashcroft, G. & Cluff, B. High Efficiency Gear Hobbing. (Nineteen Ninety-One Fall Technical Meeting Ser.: Vol. 91FTM3). (Illus.). 17p. 1991. pap. text 30.00 (*1-55589-600-6*) AGMA.
Ashcroft, G. L., jt. auth. see Hanks, R. J.
Ashcroft, Geoff. A Full Pull: The Sport of Tractor Pulling. (Illus.). 112p. 1993. text 34.95 (*0-85236-261-7*, Pub. by Farming Pr) Diamond Farm Bk.
Ashcroft, Ida, ed. The Book of the Century: St. James: The First 100 Years. LC 90-81588. (Illus.). 176p. 1990. pap. 20.00 (*0-8323-0480-8*) Binford Mort.
Ashcroft, J. R., jt. auth. see Chinn, S. J.
Ashcroft, J. Richard, jt. auth. see Chinn, Stephen J.
Ashcroft, Janet E., jt. auth. see Ashcroft, John D.
Ashcroft, John. Lessons from a Father to His Son. LC 98-10178. 240p. 1998. 14.99 (*0-7852-7540-1*) Nelson.
Ashcroft, John D. It's the Law. 3rd ed. (LA - Business Law Ser.). (C). 1990. mass mkt., wbk. ed. 17.50 (*0-538-70239-7*) S-W Pub.
— Law for Business. 13th ed. LC 98-6014. (LA - Business Law Ser.). (C). 1998. pap. 72.95 (*0-538-88095-3*) S-W Pub.
Ashcroft, John D. & Ashcroft, Janet E. Law for Business. 11th ed. (C). 1991. mass mkt. 40.75 (*0-538-81278-8*, LA92KA) S-W Pub.
— Law for Business. 12th ed. LC 95-13763. (C). 1995. pap. 50.95 (*0-538-84545-7*) S-W Pub.
Ashcroft, John D., et al. Law for Business. 12th ed. (LA - Business Law Ser.). (C). 1996. pap., student ed. 19.50 (*0-538-84576-7*); pap., student ed., wbk. ed. 10.50 (*0-538-84577-5*) S-W Pub.
Ashcroft, Kate. A Practical Guide to the Lecturer's Guide to Quality & Standards in Colleges & Universities. LC 95-3430. 210p. 1995. 85.00 (*0-7507-0338-5*, Falmer Pr); pap. 32.95 (*0-7507-0339-3*, Falmer Pr) Taylor & Francis.
Ashcroft, Kate & Foreman P., Lorraine. Managing Teaching & Learning in Further & Higher Education. LC 94-36524. 212p. 1994. 85.00 (*0-7507-0336-9*, Falmer Pr); pap. 29.95 (*0-7507-0337-7*, Falmer Pr) Taylor & Francis.
***Ashcroft, Kate & Lee, John, eds.** Improving Teaching & Learning in the Core Curriculum. LC 99-28037. (Looking Afresh at the Primary Curriculum Ser.). (Illus.). 144p. 1999. pap. 23.95 (*0-7507-0813-1*, Pub. by Falmer Pr UK) Taylor & Francis.
Ashcroft, Kate & Palacio, David, eds. The New Primary Teacher's Guide to Implementing the National Curriculum. LC 97-202456. 240p. 1996. teacher ed. 79.95 (*0-7507-0592-2*, Falmer Pr); pap., teacher ed. 27.95 (*0-7507-0593-0*, Falmer Pr) Taylor & Francis.
— The Primary Teacher's Guide to the New National Curriculum. LC 95-9165. 1995. 85.00 (*0-7507-0467-5*, Falmer Pr); pap. 27.95 (*0-7507-0468-3*, Falmer Pr) Taylor & Francis.
***Ashcroft, Linda.** Wild Child: Life with Jim Morrison. LC 99-42132. (Illus.). 544p. 2000. pap. 16.95 (*1-56025-249-9*, Thunders Mouth) Avalon NY.
Ashcroft, Mary E. Balancing Act: How Women Can Lose Their Roles & Find Their Calling. LC 96-1659. 180p. (Orig.). 1996. pap. 9.99 (*0-8308-1957-6*, 1957) InterVarsity.
— Temptations Women Face. LC 91-14233. 213p. 1993. reprint ed. pap. 10.99 (*0-8308-1320-9*, 1320, Saltshaker Bk) InterVarsity.
— Tentaciones Que Encantan a las Mujeres. (SPA.). 1994. pap. 7.99 (*0-8297-1845-1*) Vida Pubs.
Ashcroft, Mary E., jt. auth. see Miller, Hildy.
Ashcroft, Mary E., jt. ed. see Becknell, Thomas.
***Ashcroft, Mary Ellen.** Dogspell: A Dogmatic Theology on the Abounding Love of God. (Illus.). 88p. 2000. 10.95 (*0-939516-51-9*) Forest Peace.
— Journey Beckons: Reflections on the Way of the Cross. 2000. 12.99 (*0-8066-4033-2*) Augsburg Fortress.
— Spirited Women: Encountering the First Women Believers. 2000. pap. 11.99 (*0-8066-4027-8*, Augsburg) Augsburg Fortress.
Ashcroft, Neil W. Solid State Physics ISE. 1976. 11.32 (*0-03-049346-3*) Harcourt.
Ashcroft, Neil W. & Mermin, N. David. Solid State Physics. LC 74-9772. 826p. (C). 1976. text 96.50 (*0-03-083993-9*, Pub. by SCP) Harcourt.
Ashcroft-Nowicki, Dolores. Daughters of Eve: The Magical Mysteries of Womanhood. 176p. 1993. 15.00 (*0-85030-977-8*, Pub. by Aqrn Pr) Harper SF.
— Highways of the Mind: The Art & History of Pathworking. (Illus.). 244p. 1987. pap. 12.95 (*0-85030-554-3*, Pub. by Aqrn Pr) HarpC.
— The Ritual Magic Workbook: A Practical Course of Self-Initiation. LC 97-49275. (Illus.). 256p. 1998. reprint ed. pap., wbk. ed. 14.95 (*1-57863-045-2*) Weiser.
— The Servants of the Light Tarot Deck. (Illus.). 112p. 1991. 28.95 (*1-85538-001-3*, Pub. by Aqrn Pr) Harper SF.
— The Shakespearean Tarot. (Illus.). 160p. 1993. 34.00 (*1-85538-054-4*, Pub. by Aqrn Pr) Harper SF.
— The Tree of Ecstasy: An Advanced Manual of Sex Magic. LC 98-37648. (Illus.). 256p. (Orig.). 1999. pap. 12.95 (*1-57863-038-X*) Weiser.
Ashcroft-Nowicki, Dolores & Ashcroft-Nowicki, Tamara. The Initiate's Book of Pathworkings: A Bridge of Dreams. LC 99-13188. 264p. 1999. pap. 14.95 (*1-57863-119-X*) Weiser.
Ashcroft-Nowicki, Tamara, jt. auth. see Ashcroft-Nowicki, Dolores.
Ashcroft, P. G. & Slater, Roger. Quantitative Techniques in a Business Context. (Business in Context Ser.). 416p. 1990. pap. text 34.50 (*0-412-02641-4*, A4433, Chap & Hall NY) Chapman & Hall.
***Ashcroft, Paul, et al.** Human Rights & the Courts: Bringing Justice Home. 142p. 1999. 24.00 (*1-872870-80-5*, Pub. by Waterside Pr) Gaunt.
Ashcroft, Pierrette B. & Haundni, Lindly. Artists at Work. LC 99-19560. 96p. 1998. pap. 19.95 (*1-886388-02-4*) Flower Valley Pr.
Ashcroft, Robin. Britain's Alpine Ridges: Snowdonia & the Lake District. (Illus.). 160p. 1996. pap. 29.95 (*1-85223-929-8*, Pub. by Crolwood) Trafalgar.
— The Long Routes: Mountaineering Rock Climbs in Snowdonia & the Lake District. 224p. 1998. pap. 29.95 (*1-85158-910-4*, Pub. by Mainstream Pubng) Trafalgar.
Ashcroft, Roland. Construction for Interior Designers. 2nd ed. (Illus.). 468p. 1992. pap. 67.50 (*0-582-08125-4*, Pub. by Addison-Wesley) Trans-Atl Phila.
Ashcroft, Samuel C., et al. Instructor's Manual for the New Programmed Instruction in Braille. 2nd ed. 145p. 1994. ring bd. 19.50 (*0-9634229-4-4*) SCALARS Pub.
— New Programmed Instruction in Braille. 2nd ed. 386p. 1994. spiral bd. 49.00 (*0-9634229-3-6*) SCALARS Pub.
Ashcroft, Stephen J., jt. ed. see Ashcroft, Frances M.
Ashcroft, Wendy J. & Smith, Suzanne C. Take Care! A Transdisciplinary Approach to the Development of Health & Safety Programs. 372p. (Orig.). 1993. pap., teacher ed. 40.00 (*0-9634229-2-8*) SCALARS Pub.
Ashdown. The Color Atlas of Veterinary Anatomy Vol. 1: Ruminants. 2nd ed. 1996. pap. 72.00 (*0-7234-2662-7*) Wolfe Pubng AZ.
— The Color Atlas of Veterinary Anatomy Vol. 2: Horse. 2nd ed. 1996. pap. 72.00 (*0-7234-2574-4*) Wolfe Pubng AZ.
Ashdown, Charles H. Armour & Weapons in the Middle Ages. (Illus.). 1971. pap. 25.00 (*0-87556-603-0*) Saifer.
— Armour & Weapons in the Middle Ages. (C). 1988. 240.00 (*0-900470-63-1*) St Mut.
Ashdown, Clifford. From a Surgeon's Diary. 1977. 10.00 (*1-880418-07-X*) D M Grant.
— Queen's Treasure. 1975. 10.00 (*1-880418-12-6*) D M Grant.
Ashdown, Dana. Railway Steamships of Ontario. Hudson, Noel, ed. (Illus.). 288p. 1988. 32.50 (*0-919783-80-5*, Pub. by Boston Mills) Genl Dist Srvs.
***Ashdown, Dana William.** Iron & Steam: A History of the Locomotive & Railway Car Builders of Toronto. (Illus.). 431p. 2000. pap. 18.95 (*1-896941-12-5*, Pub. by RBST) Midpt Trade.
***Ashdown, David.** Hyperstudio Made Very Easy! (Illus.). 64p. (J). 2000. pap. 10.95 (*0-439-13897-3*) Scholastic Inc.
Ashdown, Dulcie M. Royal Murders: Hatred, Revenge & the Seizing of Power. LC 99-193539. 388p. 2000. 32.95 (*0-7509-2053-X*) Sutton Publng.
***Ashdown, Dulcie M.** Royal Murders: Hatred, Revenge & the Seizing of Power. (Illus.). 388p. 2000. pap. 15.95 (*0-7509-2439-X*) Sutton Publng.
Ashdown, Ian. Radiosity: A Programmer's Perspective. 497p. 1994. pap. 44.95 (*0-471-30444-1*) Wiley.
Ashdown, Paddy. Citizen's Britain: A Radical Agenda for the 1990's. LC 90-129818. viii, 159 p. 1989. write for info. (*1-872180-45-0*) Fourth Estate.
Ashdown, Paul, ed. see Agee, James.
Ashdown, Rob, et al, eds. The Curriculum Challenge: Access to the National Curriculum for Pupils with Learning Difficulties. 224p. 1991. pap. 34.95 (*1-85000-881-7*, Falmer Pr) Taylor & Francis.
Ashdown, Sheena. 101 Ways to Improve Your Self-Esteem: A Fast & Easy Guide for Very Busy People. 84p. (Orig.). 1995. pap. text 9.95 (*0-9641975-2-9*) Gibsons Pubng.
— One Hundred One Ways to Promote Yourself: A Fast & Easy Guide for Real Estate Agents. 76p. (Orig.). 1994. pap. 9.95 (*0-9641975-0-2*) Gibsons Pubng.
Ashe, A. W., jt. auth. see Neville, A. G.
Ashe, Aran. Citadel of Servitude. 1999. mass mkt. 6.95 (*0-352-33435-5*) London Brdge.
***Ashe, Aran.** Dungeons of Lidir. 2000. mass mkt. 6.95 (*0-352-33506-8*) Nexus.
— Slave of Lidir. 2000. mass mkt. 6.95 (*0-352-33504-1*) Nexus.
Ashe, Arthur. Arthur Ashe on Tennis: Strokes, Stategies, Traditions, Players, Psychology & Wisdom. 192p. 1996. pap. 10.00 (*0-380-72715-3*, Avon Bks) Morrow Avon.
Ashe, Arthur & Deford, Frank. Arthur Ashe: Portrait in Motion. (Illus.). 304p. 1993. pap. 11.95 (*0-7867-0050-5*) Carroll & Graf.
Ashe, Arthur & Rampersad, Arnold. Days of Grace: A Memoir. large type ed. LC 93-36046. (General Ser.). 500p. 1993. lib. bdg. 25.95 (*0-8161-5883-5*, G K Hall Lrg Type) Mac Lib Ref.
— Days of Grace: A Memoir. (Black History Titles Ser.). 368p. 1994. reprint ed. mass mkt. 6.99 (*0-345-38681-7*) Ballantine Pub Grp.
Ashe, Arthur R., Jr. A Hard Road to Glory, 3 vols., Set. rev. ed. (Illus.). 1993. 89.95 (*1-56743-009-0*, Amistad) HarperTrade.
Ashe, Arthur R., Jr. A Hard Road To Glory: A History Of The African American Athlete: Baseball. LC 93-37950. (Illus.). 288p. 1993. pap. 9.95 (*1-56743-035-X*, Amistad) HarperTrade.
Ashe, Arthur R., Jr. A Hard Road To Glory: A History Of The African American Athlete: Basketball. LC 93-37948. (Illus.). 288p. 1993. pap. 9.95 (*1-56743-037-6*, Amistad) HarperTrade.
Ashe, Arthur R., Jr. A Hard Road To Glory: A History Of The African American Athlete: Boxing. LC 93-37951. (Illus.). 176p. 1993. pap. 9.95 (*1-56743-036-8*, Amistad) HarperTrade.
Ashe, Arthur R., Jr. A Hard Road To Glory: A History Of The African American Athlete: Football. LC 93-37949. (Illus.). 368p. 1993. pap. 9.95 (*1-56743-038-4*, Amistad) HarperTrade.
Ashe, Arthur R., Jr. A Hard Road To Glory: A History Of The African American Athlete: Track And Field. LC 93-37952. (Illus.). 160p. 1993. pap. 9.95 (*1-56743-039-2*, Amistad) HarperTrade.
— A Hard Road To Glory: A History Of The African American Athlete: Vol 2. 1919-1945, 3 vols., Vol. II: 1919-1945. rev. ed. (Illus.). 528p. 1993. reprint ed. 39.95 (*1-56743-007-4*, Amistad) HarperTrade.
— A Hard Road To Glory: A History Of The African American Athlete: Vol 3 1946-Present, 3 vols., Vol. III: 1946-Present. rev. ed. (Illus.). 640p. 1993. reprint ed. 39.95 (*1-56743-008-2*, Amistad) HarperTrade.
— A hard Road To Glory: A History Of The African Athlete: Vol 1:1619-1918, 3 vols., Vol. 1. rev. ed. (Illus.). 224p. 1993. reprint ed. 29.95 (*1-56743-006-6*, Amistad) HarperTrade.
Ashe, Arthur R., Jr. A Hard Road to Glory: The History of the African-American Athlete. abr. ed. (Illus.). 496p. 1993. 24.95 (*1-56743-022-8*, Amistad) HarperTrade.
Ashe, Dora J., compiled by. Four Hundred Years of Virginia, Fifteen Eighty-Four to Nineteen Eighty-Four: An Anthology. 234p. (Orig.). 1985. pap. text 21.50 (*0-8191-4482-7*); lib. bdg. 53.00 (*0-8191-4481-9*) U Pr of Amer.
Ashe, Dora J., ed. A Maryland Anthology, 1608-1986. 262p. (Orig.). (C). 1987. lib. bdg. 47.00 (*0-8191-6572-7*) U Pr of Amer.
Ashe, Dora J., ed. see Beaumont, Francis.
Ashe-Dudley, Suzanne, ed. see Malinchak, James.
Ashe, Geoffrey. Atlantis. LC 91-67306. (Art & Imagination Ser.). (Illus.). 96p. 1992. pap. 15.95 (*0-500-81039-7*, Pub. by Thames Hudson) Norton.
***Ashe, Geoffrey.** The Book of Prophecy: Predictions & Prophets in History & Legend. 288p. 1999. 29.95 (*0-7137-2737-3*) Strlng Pub CA.
— Encyclopedia of Prophecy. 2001. lib. bdg. 70.00 (*1-57607-079-4*) ABC-CLIO.
— Gandhi: A Biography. LC 00-34561. 2000. reprint ed. pap. write for info. (*0-8154-1107-3*, Pub. by Cooper Sq) Natl Bk Netwk.
Ashe, Geoffrey. King Arthur: The Dream of a Golden Age. LC 89-51587. (Art & Imagination Ser.). (Illus.). 96p. 1990. pap. 15.95 (*0-500-81035-4*, Pub. by Thames Hudson) Norton.
— Kings & Queens of Early Britain. 264p. 1998. pap. text 15.00 (*0-89733-469-8*) Academy Chi Pubs.
— Mythology of the British Isles. (Illus.). 304p. 1992. pap. 19.95 (*0-413-66540-2*) Random.

An Asterisk (*) at the beginning of an entry indicates that the title is appearing for the first time.

Ashe, Geoffrey, ed. The Quest for Arthur's Britain. (Illus.). 252p. 1999. reprint ed. pap. 13.95 (0-89733-287-3) Academy Chi Pubs.
Ashe, Geoffrey & Debrett's Peerage. The Discovery of King Arthur. LC 86-9784. (Illus.). 256p. 1995. pap. 10.95 (0-8050-0115-8, Owl) H Holt & Co.
Ashe, Geoffrey, jt. auth. see Lacy, Norris J.
Ashe, Harold, ed. see Busch, Monica J.
Ashe-Jacobs, Gertrud. Mein Wustenbuch. (GER., Illus.). 36p. 1997. ring bd. 9.00 (0-942017-58-7, 04-64653) Amer Assn Teach German.
Ashe, Jeffrey. Assessing Rural Needs: A Manual for Practitioners. 129p. 1978. 7.75 (0-86619-075-9, 11058-BK) Vols Tech Asst.
Ashe, Jenny. Misplaced Loyalty. large type ed. (Magna Large Print Ser.). 300p. 1997. 27.99 (0-7505-1055-2) Ulverscroft.
Ashe, John. Highlights of History. 1981. 30.00 (0-7223-1358-6, Pub. by A H S Ltd) St Mut.
Ashe, Karen. The Pointer: Hunter, Showman, Companion. Anderson, Mark, ed. (Pure Breds Ser.). (Illus.). 320p. Date not set. 28.50 (0-944875-60-2) Doral Pub.
Ashe, Kaye. The Feminization of the Church? LC 97-41160. 192p. 1997. pap. 14.95 (1-58051-028-0, LL2028) Sheed & Ward WI.
Ashe, Martine. Shamanica. (Illus.). (Orig.). 1996. pap. 19.95 (1-898307-76-8, Pub. by Capall Bann Pubng) Holmes Pub.
Ashe, Michael, jt. auth. see Rider, B. A.
Ashe, Penelope. The Naked Chef: An Aphrodisiac Cookbook. LC 70-167722. 1971. 26.95 (0-87949-000-4) Ashley Bks.
Ashe, Rebecca. Masque of the Swan. 320p. 1996. mass mkt. 4.99 (0-7860-0212-3, Pinncle Kensgtn) Kensgtn Pub Corp.
Ashe, Richard. Chinquapins & Chestnuts. LC 98-90575. 191p. 1998. write for info. (1-881851-14-1) Genealogy Pub.
***Ashe, Richard D.** Soulful Poetry. Gordon, Michelle A., ed. 109p. 1998. pap. 9.95 (0-9650422-2-7, Pub. by Marchell Pr) Merging Worlds Publishers.
Ashe, Robert P. Chronicles of Uganda. 480p. 1971. reprint ed. 47.50 (0-7146-1861-6, BHA-01861, Pub. by F Cass Pubs) Intl Spec Bk.
— Two Kings of Uganda: or Life by the Shores of Victoria Nyanza. (Illus.). 354p. 1970. reprint ed. 40.00 (0-7146-1862-4, BHA-01862, Pub. by F Cass Pubs) Intl Spec Bk.
Ashe, Rosalind. The Laying of the Noone Walker. large type ed. 596p. 1988. 27.99 (0-7089-1844-1) Ulverscroft.
***Ashe, Roxi.** Spell Weaver. 368p. (Orig.). 1999. mass mkt. 5.50 (0-8439-4649-0, Leisure Bks) Dorchester Pub Co.
Ashe, Susan, tr. see Bonet, Pilar.
Ashe, Susan, tr. see Deledda, Grazia.
Ashe, Suzanne, ed. see Busch, Monica J.
Ashe, Terrence R. & Wood, Karl V., eds. Novel Techniques in Fossil Fuel Mass Spectrometry. LC 89-352. (Special Technical Publication Ser.: No. STP 1019). (Illus.). 225p. 1989. pap. text 49.00 (0-8031-1198-3, STP1019) ASTM.
Ashear, Linda. The Rowers, the Swimmers & the Drowned. (Illus.). 80p. (Orig.). 1996. pap. 5.95 (1-57502-176-5, P0798) Morris Pubng.
— Toward the Light. 52p. (Orig.). 1989. pap. 8.95 (0-317-93457-0) Croton Review.
Asheghian, Parviz. International Economics. LC 94-38495. 536p. (C). 1995. mass mkt. 95.95 (0-314-04438-8) West Pub.
— The Multinational Corporation: Environments & Operations. LC 98-27526. 432p. 1998. 65.00 (1-56072-555-9) Nova Sci Pubs.
Asheim, ed. Public Library. LC 76-106680. 1970. reprint ed. lib. bdg. 65.00 (0-8371-3351-3, ASPL, Greenwood Pr) Greenwood.
Asheim, Ivar. Christ & Humanity. LC 73-101426. 203p. (Orig.). reprint ed. pap. 63.00 (0-608-16704-5, 202691300053) Bks Demand.
Asheim, Lester. The Humanities & the Library: Problems in the Interpretation, Evaluation, & Use of Library Materials. LC 56-12395. 298p. reprint ed. pap. 92.40 (0-608-14071-6, 202420400035) Bks Demand.
Asheim, Lester, ed. Persistent Issues in American Librarianship. LC 61-15650. (University of Chicago Studies in Library Science). 119p. reprint ed. pap. 36.90 (0-608-09265-7, 205406700002) Bks Demand.
Asheim, Lester, ed. see Conference on Library Manpower (1967: Washington,.
Asheim, Lester, ed. see University of Chicago, Graduate Library School.
Asheim, Olav. Reference in Intentionality. 227p. (C). 1992. text 32.00 (82-560-0811-3, Pub. by Solum Verlag) Intl Spec Bk.
***Ashekenzai, Michael & Clammer, John.** Consumption & Material Culture in Contemporary Japan. 200p. 1998. 110.00 (0-7103-0618-0, Pub. by Kegan Paul Intl) Col U Pr.
Ashelford, Jane. The Art of Dress: Clothes & Society, 1500-1914. LC 95-44103. (Illus.). 320p. 1996. 49.50 (0-8109-6317-5, Pub. by Abrams) Time Warner.
— Care of Clothes. (Household Management Ser.). (Illus.). 48p. 1997. pap. 9.95 (0-7078-0223-7, Pub. by Natl Trust) Trafalgar.
***Ashelman, Martha W.** Stop Smoking Naturally. 160p. 2000. pap. 11.95 (0-658-00384-4) NTC Contemp Pub Co.
Ashelman, Polly, jt. auth. see Martin, Arlene L.
Ashely. English Civil War. 1999. pap. write for info. (0-312-10322-0) St Martin.
Ashely, Bernard. Boat Girl. large type ed. (Illus.). 1993. 13.50 (0-614-09817-3, L-34115-00) Am Printing Hse.
Ashenburg, Katherine. Going to Town: Architectural Walking Tours in Southern Ontario. LC 97-200366. (Illus.). 272p. 1996. pap. 19.95 (0-921912-95-1) MW&R.
Ashenden, Dean. State Aid & the Division of Schooling in Australia. 129p. (C). 1989. 65.00 (0-7300-0672-7, Pub. by Deakin Univ) St Mut.
Ashenden, Peter J. The Designer's Guide to VHDL. 668p. 1998. pap. text 56.00 (1-55860-270-4) Morgan Kaufmann.
— The Student's Guide to VHDL. LC 97-43565. 312p. 1998. pap., student ed. 29.95 (1-55860-520-7) Morgan Kaufmann.
Ashenfelter. Labor Economics. 1998. 23.00 (1-57259-684-8) Worth.
Ashenfelter, John. Choosing a Database for Your Web Site. LC 98-36448. 464p. 1998. pap. 34.99 (0-471-29690-2) Wiley.
***Ashenfelter, O. & Card, D.** Handbook of Labor Economics. (Handbooks in Economics Ser.: Vol. 3-A). 1100p. 1999. 125.00 (0-444-50187-8, North Holland) Elsevier.
— Handbook of Labor Economics. Vol. 3-B. 900p. 1999. 125.00 (0-444-50188-6, North Holland) Elsevier.
— Handbook of Labor Economics. (Handbooks in Economics Ser.: Vol. 3-C). 900p. 1999. 125.00 (0-444-50189-4, North Holland) Elsevier.
Ashenfelter, Orley & Rouse, Cecilia. Cracks in the Bell Curve: Orley Ashenfelter & Cecilia Rouse. 120p. 1998. pap. 10.95 (0-87078-410-2) Century Foundation.
Ashenfelter, Orley C. & Hallock, Kevin F., eds. Labor Economics, 4 vols. LC 94-44341. (International Library of Critical Writings in Economics: Vol. 47). 2032p. 1995. 680.00 (1-85278-207-2) E Elgar.
Ashenfelter, Orley C. & Lalonde, Robert J., eds. The Economics of Training, 2 vols., Set. LC 96-607. (International Library of Critical Writings in Economics: Vol. 65). 864p. 1996. 310.00 (1-85278-917-4) E Elgar.
Ashenfelter, Orley C. & Layard, P., eds. Handbook of Labor Economics, Vol. 1. 510p. 1986. 110.00 (0-444-87857-2) Elsevier.
— Handbook of Labor Economics, Vol. 2. 786p. 1987. 110.00 (0-444-87856-4) Elsevier.
Ashenfelter, Orley C., jt. ed. see Bowen, William G.
Ashenfelter, Orley C., ed. see Princeton University Conference on Discrimination.
Ashenhurst, Robert, ed. ACM Turing Award Lectures. (ACM Press Anthology Ser.). (C). 1987. text 34.95 (0-317-59560-1) Addison-Wesley.
Ashepak, Agnes. Butterfly. large type ed. (Illus.). 8p. (J). (gr. k-3). 1999. pap. text 14.50 (1-58084-058-2) Lower Kuskokwim.
— Caqelngataq (Butterfly) large type ed. (ESK., Illus.). 8p. (J). (gr. k-3). 1999. pap. text 14.50 (1-58084-059-0) Lower Kuskokwim.
— Caqlengtar (Butterfly) large type ed. (ESK., Illus.). 8p. (J). (gr. k-3). 1999. pap. text 14.50 (1-58084-106-6) Lower Kuskokwim.
— Haqalikitaq (Butterfly) large type ed. (ESK., Illus.). 8p. (J). (gr. k-3). 1999. pap. text 14.50 (1-58084-132-5) Lower Kuskokwim.
— Haqalukihaq (Butterfly) large type ed. (ESK., Illus.). 8p. (J). (gr. k-3). 1999. pap. text 14.50 (1-58084-140-6) Lower Kuskokwim.
— Saqaliqitaaq (Butterfly) large type ed. (ESK., Illus.). 8p. (J). (gr. k-3). 1999. pap. text 14.50 (1-58084-125-2) Lower Kuskokwim.
Asher. Love: The Breath of Life. 160p. (Orig.). 1995. pap. 8.50 (0-9636109-1-0) Nuf-Love Pub.
Asher, A. & Webb, W. French for You, Bk. 1. (C). 1982. pap. 45.00 (0-09-146641-5, Pub. by S Thornes Pubs) St Mut.
Asher, Aaron, tr. see Kundera, Milan.
Asher, Alison. Soaring into the Storm: A Book about Those Who Triumph over Adversity. large type ed. (Illus.). 160p. (Orig.). 1996. pap. 17.95 (1-887703-00-4) LifeSkills WA.
Asher, Brad. Beyond the Reservation: Indians, Settlers, & the Law in Washington Territory, 1853-1889. LC 98-42128. 1999. 34.95 (0-8061-3107-1) U of Okla Pr.
Asher, Carol. Especially Herbs: Recipes & Garden Ideas. LC 94-77686. (Illus.). 168p. 1994. pap. 12.95 (0-913383-31-7) McClanahan Pub.
Asher, Catherine B. Architecture of Mughal India. (New Cambridge History of India Ser.: I: 4). (Illus.). 402p. (C). 1992. text 129.00 (0-521-26728-5) Cambridge U Pr.
Asher, Catherine B., ed. Perceptions of South Asia's Visual Past. (C). 1994. 54.00 (0-945921-42-X) South Asia Pubns.
Asher, Don. The Fool-Proof Job Search Workbook. LC 96-145874. 272p. 1995. pap., wbk. ed. 17.95 (0-89815-687-4) Ten Speed Pr.
Asher, Don, jt. auth. see Hawes, Hampton.
Asher, Donald. Asher's Bible of Executive Resumes. 600p. 1996. 29.95 (0-89815-856-7) Ten Speed Pr.
***Asher, Donald.** Cool Colleges: For the Hyper-Intelligent, Self-Directed, Late Blooming & Just Plain Different. 224p. 2000. pap. 14.95 (1-58008-150-9) Ten Speed Pr.
Asher, Donald. Graduate Admissions Essays: What Works, What Doesn't & Why. 2nd rev. ed. 128p. 2000. pap. text 14.95 (1-58008-042-1) Ten Speed Pr.
— The Overnight Resume. 2nd rev. ed. LC 98-54145. 154p. 1999. pap. 14.95 (1-58008-041-3) Ten Speed Pr.
Asher, Elise. The Visionary Gleam: Texts & Transformations. LC 94-19190. (Illus.). 111p. 1994. pap. 30.00 (1-878818-33-3, Pub. by Sheep Meadow) U Pr of New Eng.
Asher, Evelyn W. Urteil ohne Richter: Psychishe Integration oder Charakterentfaltung im Werke Franz Kafkas. LC 83-48884. (Stanford German Studies: Vol. 20). (GER.). 139p. (C). 1984. pap. text 14.75 (0-8204-0062-9) P Lang Pubng.
Asher, Frederick & Gai, G. S., eds. Indian Epigraphy: Its Bearing on the History of Art. 1985. 48.50 (0-8364-1356-3, Pub. by Oxford IBH) S Asia.
***Asher, George M.** The Hell-Fire Clubs: A History of Anti-Morality. 256p. 2000. pap. 17.95 (0-7509-2402-0) Sutton Publng.
***Asher, George Michael.** A Bibliographical & Historical Essay on Dutch Books & Pamphlets Relating to New Netherland, & to the Dutch West India Company. fac. ed. 234p. 2000. 65.00 (1-57898-233-2) Martino Pubng.
Asher, Gerald. Vineyard Tales: Reflections on Wine. LC 95-47429. 208p. 1996. 24.95 (0-8118-1267-7) Chronicle Bks.
***Asher, Gerald.** Vineyard Tales: Reflections on Wine. 2000. pap. 14.95 (0-8118-2952-9) Chronicle Bks.
Asher, Gerald. Wine Journal: A Wine Lover's Album for Cellaring & Tasting. (Illus.). 128p. 1996. 18.95 (0-00-225150-7, Pub. by Harper SF) HarpC.
Asher, Gloria J. Izmirli Proverbs & Songs from the Bronx. 10p. 1976. pap. 1.25 (0-686-74365-2) Adelantre.
Asher-Greve, Julia M. Frauen in Altsumerischer Zeit. LC 85-50720. (Bibliotheca Mesopotamica Ser.: Vol. 18). (GER., Illus.). xxii, 255p. 1985. 60.00 (0-89003-161-4); pap. 50.00 (0-89003-162-2) Undena Pubns.
Asher, Harry. The Alternative Knot Book. (Illus.). 96p. 1989. pap. 12.95 (0-911378-95-2) Sheridan.
Asher, Herbert. Polling & the Public: What Every Citizen Should Know. 3rd ed. LC 95-10464. 199p. (YA). (gr. 11). 1995. pap. text 23.95 (0-87187-755-4) Congr Quarterly.
— Polling & the Public: What Every Citizen Should Know. 4th ed. LC 98-11341. 200p. (C). 1998. pap. text 23.95 (1-56802-400-2) Congr Quarterly.
Asher, Herbert B. Causal Modeling, No. 3. 2nd ed. LC 76-25696. (Quantitative Applications in the Social Sciences Ser.: Vol. 3). 1976. 10.95 (0-8039-0654-4) Sage.
— Presidential Elections & American Politics: Voters, Candidates & Campaigns since 1952. 5th ed. 394p. (C). 1991. pap. text 43.00 (0-534-16926-0) Harcourt.
Asher, Herbert B., et al, eds. Theory Building & Data Analysis in the Social Sciences. LC 83-3458. 464p. 1984. text 45.00 (0-87049-398-1) U of Tenn Pr.
Asher, Ina. Occupational Therapy Assessment Tools: An Annotated Index. 2nd ed. LC 97-147652. 332p. 1996. pap. 40.00 (1-56900-034-4, 1020) Am Occup Therapy.
Asher, J. William, jt. auth. see Lauer, Janice M.
Asher, J. William, jt. auth. see Vockell, Edward L.
Asher, James, ed. see McKay, Todd.
Asher, James J. Brainswitching. 264p. 1988. pap. 14.95 (0-940296-57-8) Sky Oaks Prodns.
— Learning Another Language Through Actions. 6th ed. 278p. 1993. pap. text 15.95 (1-56018-301-2) Sky Oaks Prodns.
— The Super School of the 21st Century. 3rd ed. (Illus.). 195p. (Orig.). (C). 1997. pap. 21.95 (1-56018-003-X) Sky Oaks Prodns.
Asher, James J., ed. see Cabello, Francisco.
Asher, James J., ed. see Garcia, Ramiro.
Asher, James J., ed. see McKay, Todd.
Asher, James J., ed. see Ray, Blaine.
Asher, James J., ed. see Ray, Blaine & Buchan, Greg.
Asher, James J., ed. see Ray, Blaine, et al.
Asher, James J., ed. see Silvers, Stephen M.
Asher, James J., ed. see Silvers, Stephen Mark.
Asher, Jane. The Best of Good Living with Jane Asher: Creative Ideas for Your Family & Home. LC 98-70041. (Illus.). 192p. 1998. pap. 29.95 (0-563-38417-4, BBC-Parkwest) Parkwest Pubns.
***Asher, Jane.** The Question. large type ed. 336p. 1999. 31.99 (0-7089-9069-X, Linford) Ulverscroft.
Asher, Jeremiah. Incidents in the Life of the Rev. J. Asher. LC 74-168506. (Black Heritage Library Collection). 1977. reprint ed. 17.95 (0-8369-8860-4) Ayer.
Asher, Jim. Human Variation: Causes & Consequences. (C). 1993. student ed. 15.00 (1-881592-18-9) Hayden-McNeil.
***Asher, Joey.** Even a Geek Can Speak: Low-Tech Communication Skills for a High-Tech World. LC 00-105150. 224p. 2000. pap. 14.95 (1-56352-628-X) Longstreet.
Asher, John A. Short Descriptive Grammar of Middle High German. 1967. pap. 13.95 (0-19-647410-8) OUP.
Asher, Ken, ed. see Miller, James W.
Asher, Kenneth. T. S. Eliot & Ideology. (Studies in American Literature & Culture Ser.: Vol. 86). 211p. 1998. pap. text 18.95 (0-521-62760-5) Cambridge U Pr.
Asher, Kevin, et al. This Is Me, Answering Your Last Letter. LC 97-104675. (Illus.). 24p. 1995. 17.50 (0-9650548-0-2) K Asher.
Asher, Kinda, ed. see American Volleyball Coaches Association Staff.
Asher, Levi & Crumlish, Christian. Coffeehouse: Writings from the Web. LC 97-19100. (Illus.). 250p. 1997. pap. 24.95 (1-884777-38-4) Manning Pubns.
Asher, Linda, tr. see Cosse, Laurence.
Asher, Linda, tr. see Kundera, Milan.
Asher, Lucille. It Beats Bawling: Some Recollections from a Fading Era. LC 93-79331. (Illus.). 128p. 1993. 19.95 (0-932845-61-4) Lowell Pr.
Asher, M. & Christopher, T. The 20 Minute Gardener. LC 96-29320. 1997. 19.95 (0-679-44814-4) Random.
***Asher, Mark.** Body Language: Easy Ways to Get the Most from Your Relationships, Work & Love Life. 2000. pap. 16.95 (1-85868-774-8, Pub. by Carlton Bks Ltd) Natl Bk Netwk.
— Evolution: The World of Sacred Device. 4th ed. LC 99-67469. (Official Strategy Guides Ser.). (Illus.). 112p. 1999. pap. 14.99 (0-7615-2680-3) Prima Pub.
Asher, Martha, jt. auth. see Lacy, Norris J.
***Asher, Marty.** The Boomer. LC 99-49238. (Illus.). 160p. 2000. pap. 15.00 (0-375-41009-0) Knopf.
Asher, Marty. Fifty-Seven Reasons Not to Have a Nuclear War. (Illus.). 120p. (Orig.). 1984. mass mkt. 4.95 (0-446-38167-5, Pub. by Warner Bks) Little.
Asher, Marty & Christopher, Tom. The 20-Minute Gardener: How to Plant & Maintain the Garden of Your Dreams Without Giving up Your Life, Your Job, or Your Sanity. 1997. 22.00 (0-614-27247-5) Random.
Asher, Marty, jt. ed. see Harr, Jonathan.
Asher, Marty, ed. see Negroponte, Nicholas.
Asher, Maxine. The Waves of Atlantis. LC 97-30017. 1997. pap. 14.95 (0-7734-8525-2) E Mellen.
Asher, Michael. Lawrence: The Uncrowned King of Arabia. LC 99-37255. 400p. 1999. text 37.95 (0-87951-712-3, Pub. by Overlook Pr) Penguin Putnam.
— Michael Asher. (Illus.). 64p. 1991. pap. 15.00 (0-941548-20-1) Ren Soc U Chi.
Asher, Michael, et al. Cahiers 3: L'Oeuvre a-t-Elle Lieu? (Illus.). 172p. pap. 29.95 (3-928762-29-X) Dist Art Pubs.
Asher, Michael J. & Gordon, Steven B. The AD-HD Forms Book: Identification, Measurement & Intervention. LC 99-166150. 128p. 1998. pap. 25.95 (0-87822-378-9) Res Press.
Asher, Michael J., jt. auth. see Gordon, Steven B.
Asher, Mukul G. Social Adequacy & Equity of the Social Security Arrangements in Singapore. (Centre for Advanced Studies Occasional Papers: No. 8). 64p. 1991. 9.50 (981-210-008-3, Pub. by Times Academic) Intl Spec Bk.
Asher, Mukul G. & Public Policy National University of Singapore Sta. Compulsory Savings in Singapore. 19p. 1995. pap. 10.00 (1-56808-063-8, 198) Natl Ctr Pol.
Asher, Mukul G., jt. auth. see Gupta, Avijit.
Asher, Mukul G., jt. auth. see Rajan, Ramkishen S.
Asher, Mukul G., jt. auth. see Ramesh, M.
Asher, Nicholas. Reference to Abstract Objects in Discourse. LC 93-14793. (Studies in Linguistics & Philosophy: Vol. 50). 468p. 1993. lib. bdg. 182.50 (0-7923-2242-8, Pub. by Kluwer Academic) Kluwer Academic.
Asher, Oksana Dray-Khmara. Letters from the Gulag: The Life, Letters & Poetry of Michael Dray-Khmara. (Illus.). 164p. 1983. 15.00 (0-8315-0187-1) Speller.
Asher, R. C. Ultrasonic Sensors for Chemical & Process Plant. LC 97-26111. (Sensors Ser.). (Illus.). 473p. 1997. 158.00 (0-7503-0361-1) IOP Pub.
Asher, R. E. Francus & Samothes: Myth, Legend & History in Renaissance France. (Aberdeen University Press Bks.). 192p. 1991. pap. text 26.91 (0-08-041215-7, Pub. by Aberdeen U Pr) Macmillan.
— Legendary Monarchs & Nationalism in Renaissance France. (Illus.). 269p. 1993. text 76.50 (0-7486-0407-3, Pub. by Edinburgh U Pr) Col U Pr.
— Tamil. (Descriptive Grammars Ser.). 280p. 1986. 72.50 (0-415-03682-8) Routledge.
Asher, R. E. & Kumari, T. C. Malayalam. LC 97-3094. (Descriptive Grammars Ser.). 520p. (C). 1997. 190.00 (0-415-02242-8) Routledge.
Asher, R. E. & Simpson, J. M., eds. Encyclopedia of Language & Linguistics, 10 vols. LC 93-37778. 5782p. 1993. 3062.50 (0-08-035943-4, Pergamon Pr) Elsevier.
Asher, R. E., jt. auth. see Fabbro, F.
Asher, R. E., jt. auth. see Spolsky, Bernard.
Asher, R. E., jt. ed. see Koerner, E. F.
Asher, R. E., jt. ed. see Mosley, Christopher.
Asher, Ramona M. Women with Alcoholic Husbands: Ambivalence & the Trap of Codependency. LC 91-27765. 239p. 1992. reprint ed. pap. 74.10 (0-608-08010-1, 2067975) Bks Demand.
Asher, Raphael, ed. The Jewish Legacy & the German Conscience: Essays. (Illus.). 350p. 1991. 27.95 (0-943376-47-5); pap. 17.95 (0-943376-48-3) Magnes Mus.
Asher, Richard. A Sense of Asher. (Illus.). 112p. 1984. pap. 18.00 (0-7279-0136-2, Pub. by BMJ Pub) Login Brothers Bk Co.
Asher, Robert. Concepts in American History. 242p. (C). 1997. pap. 13.40 (0-06-501483-9) Addson-Wesley Educ.
Asher, Robert & Edsforth, Ronald, eds. Autowork. LC 94-17685. (SUNY Series in American Labor History). 315p. (C). 1995. text 59.50 (0-7914-2409-X); pap. text 19.95 (0-7914-2410-3) State U NY Pr.
Asher, Robert & Stephenson, Charles, eds. Labor Divided: Race & Ethnicity in United States Labor Struggles, 1835-1960. LC 88-26334. (SUNY Series in American Labor History). 378p. (C). 1989. pap. text 24.95 (0-88706-972-X) State U NY Pr.
— Labor Divided: Race & Ethnicity in United States Labor Struggles, 1835-1960. LC 88-26334. (SUNY Series in American Labor History). 378p. (C). 1990. text 74.50 (0-88706-970-3) State U NY Pr.
Asher, Robert, jt. ed. see Stephenson, Charles.
Asher, Robert E., jt. auth. see Mason, Edward S.
Asher, Sandra F. Across the Plains: The Journey of the Palace Wagon Family. 59p. 1997. pap. 5.60 (0-87129-747-7, A70) Dramatic Pub.
— Dancing with Strangers. 1994. 5.50 (0-87129-408-7, D59) Dramatic Pub.
— Once, in the Time of Trolls. 1995. 5.50 (0-87129-594-6, O28) Dramatic Pub.
— Sunday, Sunday. 1994. 3.50 (0-87129-459-1, S14) Dramatic Pub.
— The Wise Men of Chelm. 1992. pap. 3.50 (0-87129-165-7, W73) Dramatic Pub.
— A Woman Called Truth - Full. 1993. pap. 5.50 (0-87129-305-6, W74) Dramatic Pub.

A

An Asterisk (*) at the beginning of an entry indicates that the title is appearing for the first time.

— A Woman Called Truth - One Act. 1981. pap. 3.95 (*0-87129-388-9*, W63) Dramatic Pub.

***Asher, Sandra Fenichel.** I Will Sing Life: Voices from the Hole in the Wall Gang Camp. 58p. 2000. pap. 5.50 (*0-87129-971-2*, I67) Dramatic Pub.

— Little Old Ladies in Tennis Shoes. 80p. 1989. pap. 5.50 (*1-58342-006-1*, L63) Dramatic Pub.

Asher, Sandra Fenichel. The Wolf & Its Shadows. (J). 2000. pap. 7.00 (*0-87602-379-0*) Anchorage.

Asher, Sandy. The Insulting Princess. 23p. (Orig.). (J). (gr. 2-8). 1995. pap. 3.00 (*1-57514-249-X*, 1011) Encore Perform Pub.

— Just Like Jenny. 1982. 9.95 (*0-440-04299-2*) Delacorte.

— Stella's Dancing Days. 2001. write for info. (*0-15-201613-9*) Harcourt.

— Things Are Seldom What They Seem. LC 82-72819. 144p. (J). (gr. 7). 1983. pap. 11.95 (*0-385-29250-3*) Delacorte.

— Where Do You Get Your Ideas? (Illus.). 96p. (J). (gr. 5 up). 1987. 12.95 (*0-8027-6690-0*); lib. bdg. 13.85 (*0-8027-6691-9*) Walker & Co.

— Where Do You Get Your Ideas? LC 86-28258. 96p. (J). (gr. 5 up). 1994. pap. 6.95 (*0-8027-7421-0*) Walker & Co.

Asher, Sandy. Where Do You Get Your Ideas? Favorite Authors Reveal Their Writing Secrets. 1987. 12.05 (*0-606-06870-8*, Pub. by Turtleback) Demco.

Asher, Sandy, ed. But That's Another Story: Favorite Authors Introduce Popular Genres. (Illus.). 176p. (YA). (gr. 5 up). 1996. 16.95 (*0-8027-8424-0*) Walker & Co.

— But That's Another Story: Favorite Authors Introduce Popular Genres. (Illus.). 176p. (YA). (gr. 4 up). 1999. pap. 7.95 (*0-8027-7570-5*) Walker & Co.

Asher, Sandy & Chagall, Marc, eds. With All My Heart, with All My Mind: Thirteen Stories about Growing up Jewish. LC 98-47117. Orig. Title: Today I Am. 176p. (YA). (gr. 6-9). 1999. per. 18.00 (*0-689-82012-7*) S&S Bks Yung.

Asher, Spring & Chambers, Wicke. Wooing & Winning Business: The Foolproof Formula for Making Persuasive Business Presentations. LC 96-39234. (Illus.). 224p. 1996. 24.95 (*0-471-14192-5*) Wiley.

— Wooing & Winning Business: The Foolproof Formula for Making Persuasive Business Presentations, 1. 240p. 1998. pap. 17.95 (*0-471-25370-7*) Wiley.

Asher, Spring, jt. auth. see Chambers, Wicke.

Asher, Steven. The Undercover Single Man. LC 97-90676. 126p. 1998. 14.95 (*0-533-12452-2*) Vantage.

Asher, William L., Jr. Seven Steps to Effective Prayer. 36p. (Orig.). 1978. pap. 2.00 (*0-915235-01-3*) United Res.

— Siete Pasos a las Oracion Efectiva. (SPA.). 44p. (Orig.). 1982. pap. 2.00 (*0-915235-07-2*) United Res.

Asherman. Star Trek Compendium. 1999. pap. write for info. (*0-671-00112-4*) S&S Trade.

Asherman, Allan. The Star Trek Compendium. rev. ed. Ryan, Kevin, ed. 192p. 1993. pap. 14.00 (*0-671-79612-7*) PB.

Asherman, Ira G. & Asherman, Sandra V. 25 Role Plays for Negotiation Skills. 181p. (Orig.). 1996. pap. 39.95 (*0-87425-997-5*) HRD Press.

Asherman, Ira G. & Asherman, Sandra V., eds. The Negotiation Sourcebook. 448p. (Orig.). 1989. pap. 49.95 (*0-87425-116-8*) HRD Press.

***Asherman, Robyn.** I Lived in Texas Before It Was Texas: A Child's Life at Mission Espada, San Antonio, Texas, 1756. Rizopatron, Marina, ed. (Illus.). 32p. (J). (gr. k-5). 1999. per. 20.00 (*0-9700418-0-2*) Mission & Forts.

Asherman, Sandra V., jt. auth. see Asherman, Ira G.

Asherman, Sandra V., jt. ed. see Asherman, Ira G.

Asherson, G. L., jt. ed. see Zembala, M.

Asherson, R. A., et al. Diagnostic & Therapeutic Problems in Connective Tissue Diseases. (C). 1988. text 126.00 (*0-7462-0051-X*) Kluwer Academic.

***Asherson, Ronald A.** Vascular Manifestations of Systematic Autoimmune Diseases. 528p. 1999. 125.00 (*0-8493-1335-X*) CRC Pr.

Asherson, Ronald A., et al, eds. The Antiphospholipid Syndrome. 368p. 1996. boxed set 179.95 (*0-8493-9423-6*) CRC Pr.

***Ashery, Rebecca S.** Drug Abuse Prevention Through Family Interventions. 527p. 1999. per. 26.00 (*0-16-061523-2*) USGPO.

Ashery, Rebecca S., ed. Program Development for Community AIDS Outreach. 70p. (Orig.). (C). 1994. pap. text 20.00 (*0-7881-1488-3*) DIANE Pub.

Asheville Junior League Staff. Mountain Elegance. (Illus.). 320p. 1991. reprint ed. otabind 14.95 (*0-914875-17-5*) Bright Mtn Bks.

Ashey, Michael. Building & Detailing Scale Model Ships. Spohn, Terry, ed. (Illus.). 112p. (Orig.). 1996. per. 18.95 (*0-89024-240-2*, 12152) Kalmbach.

— Detailing Scale Model Aircraft, No. 18. Spohn, Terry, ed. (Illus.). 104p. 1994. per. 16.95 (*0-89024-205-4*, 12137) Kalmbach.

Ashey, Mike. Model Aircraft Tips & Techniques: An Illustrated Guide. LC 97-223551. (Illus.). 112p. (Orig.). 1997. pap. 16.95 (*0-89024-266-6*, 12165, Kalmbach Books) Kalmbach.

Ashe, pseud & Dunleavy, eds. Processing & Testing of Reaction Injection Molding Urethanes - STP 788. 95p. 1982. pap. 13.95 (*0-8031-0779-X*, STP788) ASTM.

Ashe, pseud & Peterson. ASHE Reader Plan & Instructions. 664p. 1999. pap. text 55.00 (*0-536-02368-9*) Pearson Custom.

Ashfar, Haleh, ed. Women & Politics in the Third World. LC 95-34526. (Women in Politics Ser.). 224p. (C). 1996. pap. 24.99 (*0-415-13861-2*) Routledge.

Ashfield. Romantic Women Poets, 1770-88: An Anthology. LC 98-13717. 327p. 1998. pap. 27.95 (*0-7190-5308-0*, Pub. by Manchester Univ Pr) St Martin.

— Romantic Women Poets, 1788-1848. 2nd ed. 256p. 1998. pap. 29.95 (*0-7190-5293-9*, Pub. by Manchester Univ Pr); text 74.95 (*0-7190-5292-0*, Pub. by Manchester Univ Pr) St Martin.

Ashfield, Evan & Stanton, Nicholas. Sale of Goods & Consumer Credit in Practice. 2nd ed. 166p. 1998. pap. 48.00 (*1-85431-715-6*, Pub. by Blackstone Pr) Gaunt.

— Sale of Goods & Consumer Credit in Practice. 3rd ed. 162p. 1999. pap. 50.00 (*1-85431-899-3*, Pub. by Blackstone Pr) Gaunt.

***Ashfield, Evan & Stanton, Nicholas.** Sale of Goods & Consumer Credit in Practice. 4th ed. (Inns of Court School of Law Ser.). 172p. 2000. pap. 46.00 (*1-84174-002-0*, Pub. by Blackstone Pr) Gaunt.

Ashfield, Helen. Sapphire. 174p. 1985. pap. 3.95 (*0-685-43286-6*) St Martin.

Ashfold, M. N. R. & Baggott, J. E. Biomolecular Collisions. 1989. 215.00 (*0-85186-393-0*) CRC Pr.

Ashford, et al. Human Behavior in the Social Environment: A Multidimensional Perspective. 2nd ed. (Social Work Ser.). 2000. pap. text 58.50 (*0-534-35915-9*) Wadsworth Pub.

Ashford, Ann. If I Found a Wistful Unicorn: A Gift of Love. LC 78-59094. (Illus.). 39p. (ps-3). 1978. 18.95 (*0-931948-00-2*) Peachtree Pubs.

— If I Found a Wistful Unicorn: A Gift of Love. (Illus.). 40p. (YA). (ps up). 1992. 6.95 (*1-56145-047-2*) Peachtree Pubs.

Ashford, Bailey K. A Soldier in Science: The Autobiography of Bailey K. Ashford, Colonel M. C., U. S. A. LC 98-26039. xxxiii, 425 p. 1998. write for info. (*0-8477-0351-7*) U of PR Pr.

Ashford, Charlie R., Sr. Ashford. Some of the Ancestors & Descendants of James & George Ashford, Jr., of Fairfield County, SC, (Illus.). 123p. 1997. reprint ed. pap. 21.00 (*0-8328-7297-0*); reprint ed. lib. bdg. 31.00 (*0-8328-7296-2*) Higginson Bk Co.

Ashford, Daisy. The Young Visiters. (Illus.). 105p. 1991. reprint ed. 15.00 (*0-89733-365-9*) Academy Chi Pubs.

Ashford, Deanna. Black Lace Savage Surrender. mass mkt. 5.95 (*0-352-33253-0*, Pub. by BLA4) London Brdge.

— Doctor's Orders. 2000. mass mkt. 6.95 (*0-352-33453-3*) London Brdge.

Ashford, Douglas E. Democracy, Decentralization & Decisions in Subnational Politics LC 75-38314. (Professional Papers in Comparative Politics). 59 p. 1976. 3.00 (*0-8039-0637-4*) Sage.

Ashford, Douglas E. Morocco-Tunisia: Politics & Planning. LC 65-25988. 85p. reprint ed. pap. 30.00 (*0-608-13888-6*, 202039500017) Bks Demand.

— National Development & Local Reform: Political Participation in Morocco, Tunisia, & Pakistan. LC 66-14307. (Princeton Studies on the Near East). 451p. 1967. reprint ed. pap. 139.90 (*0-608-03336-7*, 206404800008) Bks Demand.

— Policy & Politics in Britain: The Limits of Consensus. LC 80-19771. (Policy & Politics in Industrial States Ser.). 330p. 1980. pap. text 19.95 (*0-87722-195-2*) Temple U Pr.

— Policy & Politics in France: Living with Uncertainty. LC 82-5771. (Policy & Politics in Industrial States Ser.). 365p. 1982. pap. text 22.95 (*0-87722-262-2*) Temple U Pr.

Ashford, Douglas E., ed. Comparative Policy Studies. (C). 1977. pap. 15.00 (*0-918592-24-0*) Pol Studies.

— Discretionary Politics: Intergovernmental Social Transfers in Eight Countries. (International Review of Comparative Public Policy Ser.: Vol. 2). 212p. 1990. 73.25 (*1-55938-110-8*) Jai Pr.

Ashford, Douglas E., et al, eds. Comparative Public Policy: A Cross-National Bibliography. LC 77-25371. 276p. reprint ed. pap. 85.60 (*0-608-14223-9*, 202192200026) Bks Demand.

— Nationalizing Social Security in Europe & America. LC 85-23214. (Monographs in Organizational Behavior & Industrial Relations: Vol. 4). 291p. 1986. 78.50 (*0-89232-555-0*) Jai Pr.

Ashford, Gerald. Everyday Publicity. LC 73-132372. 90p. 1970. 6.95 (*0-88238-051-6*) Law Arts.

Ashford, Jane. The Bargain. 352p. 1997. mass mkt. 5.99 (*0-553-57578-3*) Bantam.

— Bride to Be. 368p. 1999. mass mkt. 5.99 (*0-553-57774-3*) Bantam.

— Cachet. large type ed. 464p. (Orig.). 1988. 27.99 (*0-7089-1754-2*) Ulverscroft.

— Charmed & Dangerous. 384p. 1998. mass mkt. 5.99 (*0-553-57773-5*) Bantam.

Ashford, Janet & Odam, John. Start with a Scan: A Guide to Turning Scanned Photos, Drawings & Objects into High-Quality Art. LC 96-167210. (Illus.). 144p. (C). 1996. pap. 34.95 (*0-201-88456-9*, Pub. by Peachpit Pr) Addison-Wesley.

Ashford, Janet I. Mothers & Midwives: A History of Traditional Childbirth. (Illus.). 21p. (Orig.). (C). 1988. pap. 7.95 (*0-9619968-1-1*) J I Ashford.

Ashford, Jeffrey. A Conflict of Interests. large type ed. 336p. 1992. 27.99 (*0-7089-2565-0*) Ulverscroft.

***Ashford, Jeffrey.** The Cost of Innocence. 1999. 25.00 (*0-7278-2211-X*) Severn Hse.

— The Cost of Innocence. large type ed. 320p. 1999. 31.99 (*0-7505-1475-2*, Pub. by Mgna Lrg Print) Ulverscroft.

Ashford, Jeffrey. Forget What You Saw. large type ed. 1991. 27.99 (*0-7089-2438-7*) Ulverscroft.

— The Hands of Innocence. 1996. 19.50 (*0-7451-8692-0*, Black Dagger) Chivers N Amer.

— The Hands of Innocence. large type ed. (Linford Mystery Library). 336p. 1993. pap. 16.99 (*0-7089-7421-X*) Ulverscroft.

— An Honest Betrayal. 224p. 2000. 26.00 (*0-7278-5459-3*, Pub. by Severn Hse) Chivers N Amer.

— Investigations Are Proceeding. large type ed. 1991. 27.99 (*0-7089-2492-1*) Ulverscroft.

— Judgement Deferred. large type ed. LC 94-26181. (Nightingale Ser.). 252p. 1995. pap. 17.95 (*0-8161-7470-9*, G K Hall Lrg Type) Mac Lib Ref.

— The Loss of the Culion. large type ed. (Linford Mystery Library). 1991. pap. 16.99 (*0-7089-7154-7*) Ulverscroft.

— Loyal Disloyalty. LC 99-31889. 1999. 25.95 (*0-7862-2048-1*) Mac Lib Ref.

— Loyal Disloyalty. LC 98-47511. 192p. 1998. text 20.95 (*0-312-19918-X*) St Martin.

— Presumption of Guilt. large type ed. (Dales Mystery Ser.). 1993. pap. 13.95 (*1-85389-345-5*, Dales) Ulverscroft.

— The Price of Failure. LC 97-49345. 195p. 1997. text 20.95 (*0-312-18156-6*) St Martin.

— The Price of Failure. large type ed. LC 97-36721. 278p. 1998. 18.95 (*0-7838-8111-8*, G K Hall Lrg Type) Mac Lib Ref.

— To Protect the Guilty. large type ed. (Linford Mystery Library). 352p. 1992. pap. 16.99 (*0-7089-7223-3*) Ulverscroft.

— Twisted Justice. large type ed. LC 94-18221. 1994. lib. bdg. 17.95 (*0-8161-7409-1*, G K Hall Lrg Type) Mac Lib Ref.

***Ashford, Jeffrey.** A Web of Circumstances. LC 98-36970. 244 p. 1999. write for info. (*0-7540-3546-8*) Mac Lib Ref.

Ashford, Jeffrey. A Web of Circumstances. large type ed. LC 98-36970. 1999. 30.00 (*0-7838-0372-9*, G K Hall Lrg Type) Mac Lib Ref.

— Will Anyone Who Saw the Accident. large type ed. 384p. 1992. pap. 16.99 (*0-7089-7215-2*) Ulverscroft.

Ashford, John. Statistics for Management. 464p. (C). 1980. 78.00 (*0-85292-271-X*) St Mut.

Ashford, John L. The Management of Quality in Construction. 250p. 1989. 59.50 (*0-412-28840-0*) Chapman & Hall.

— The Management of Quality in Construction. (Illus.). 256p. (C). 1989. 95.00 (*0-419-14910-4*, E & FN Spon) Routledge.

Ashford, Jose B., et al. Human Behavior in the Social Enviornment: A Multidimensional Perspective. LC 96-42497. (Social Work Ser.). 700p. (C). 1996. 81.95 (*0-534-14988-X*) Brooks-Cole.

— Human Behavior in the Social Environment: A Multidimensional Perspective. 1997. teacher ed. write for info. incl. VHS (*0-534-34581-6*) Brooks-Cole.

***Ashford, Martin.** Con Tricks. (Illus.). 320p. 1998. 26.00 (*0-7432-0341-0*) S&S Trade.

— Con Tricks: The Shadowy World of Management Consultancy & How to Make It Work for You. (Illus.). 320p. 2000. 25.50 (*0-684-86833-4*) S&S Trade.

Ashford, Nicholas A. Crisis in the Workplace: Occupational Disease & Injury - (A Report to the Ford Foundation) LC 75-28424. 1976. 49.50 (*0-262-01045-3*) MIT Pr.

Ashford, Nicholas A. & Bingham, Eula. Environmental & Occupational Health Training. (Toxicology & Industrial Health Ser.: Vol. 5, No. 4). 145p. 1989. 58.00 (*0-911131-81-7*) Specialist Journals.

Ashford, Nicholas A. & Caldart, Charles C. Technology, Law, & the Working Environment. rev. ed. LC 96-21826. 650p. 1996. pap. text 42.00 (*1-55963-446-4*) Island Pr.

Ashford, Nicholas A. & Miller, Claudia S. Chemical Exposures: Low Levels & High Stakes. 2nd ed. LC 97-19690. (Environmental Health Ser.). 448p. 1997. pap. 29.95 (*0-442-02524-6*, VNR) Wiley.

— Chemical Exposures: Low Levels & High Stakes. 2nd ed. 464p. 1998. 49.95 (*0-471-29240-0*) Wiley.

Ashford, Nigel & Davies, Stephen, eds. A Dictionary of Conservative & Libertarian Thought. 304p. (C). (gr. 13). 1991. 85.00 (*0-415-00302-4*, A5793) Routledge.

Ashford, Nigel, jt. ed. see Jordan, Grant.

Ashford, Norman, et al, eds. Mobility & Transport for Elderly & Handicapped Persons. (Transportation Studies: Vol. 2). xi, 383p. 1982. text 228.00 (*0-677-16380-0*) Gordon & Breach.

Ashford, Norman, et al. Airport Operations. 2nd ed. LC 96-48398. (Illus.). 481p. 1997. 59.95 (*0-07-003077-4*) McGraw.

Ashford, Norman J. & Moore, Clifton A. Airport Finance. (Illus.). 240p. (gr. 13). 1992. text 79.95 (*0-442-00192-4*) Chapman & Hall.

Ashford, Norman J. & Wright, Paul H. Airport Engineering. 3rd ed. LC 91-20384. 536p. 1992. 140.00 (*0-471-52755-6*) Wiley.

Ashford, Norman J., jt. auth. see Wright, Paul H.

Ashford, O. M., ed. see Richardson, Lewis F.

Ashford, Ray. The Quiet Life. LC 98-44292. 1999. pap. 8.00 (*0-687-03489-2*) Dimen for Liv.

— The Surrender & the Singing: Happiness Through Letting Go. 168p. (Orig.). 1984. 7.95 (*0-86683-964-X*, AY8546) Harper SF.

Ashford, Robert & Shakespeare, Rodney. Binary Economics: The New Paradigm. LC 98-51042. 486p. (C). 1999. pap. 24.50 (*0-7618-1321-7*) U Pr of Amer.

***Ashford, Robert & Shakespeare, Rodney.** Binary Economics: The New Paradigm. LC 98-51042. 486p. (C). 1999. 45.00 (*0-7618-1320-9*) U Pr of Amer.

Ashford, Rod. Erotique: Masterpieces of Erotic Photography. LC 98-86012. (Illus.). 224p. 1998. pap. 27.50 (*1-56025-168-9*, Thunders Mouth) Avalon NY.

Ashford, Sheena & Timms, Noel. What Europe Thinks: A Study of Western European Values. 168p. 1992. 78.95 (*1-85521-238-2*, Pub. by Dartmth Pub) Ashgate Pub Co.

***Ashforth, Adam.** Madumo: A Man Bewitched. LC 99-57325. 248p. 1999. 20.00 (*0-226-02971-9*) U Ch Pr.

Ashforth, Adam. The Politics of Official Discourse in Twentieth-Century South Africa. (Oxford Studies in African Affairs). 312p. 1990. 69.00 (*0-19-827702-4*) OUP.

***Ashforth, Blake E.** Role Transitions in Organizational Life: An Identity-Based Perspective. (A Volume in LEA's Organization & Management Series). 2000. write for info. (*0-8058-2892-3*) L Erlbaum Assocs.

— Role Transitions in Organizational Life: An Identity-Based Perspective. LC 00-26457. (Organization & Management Ser.). 300p. 2001. pap. write for info. (*0-8058-2893-1*) L Erlbaum Assocs.

Ashforth, Camila & Alexander, Martha. The Candlewick Book of Bedtime Stories. LC 95-178582. (Illus.). 93p. (J). (ps-3). 1995. 19.99 (*1-56402-652-3*) Candlewick Pr.

Ashforth, Camila, jt. auth. see Albrough, Jez.

Ashforth, Camilla. Calamity. LC 92-54956. (Illus.). 32p. (J). (ps up). 1993. 15.95 (*1-56402-252-8*) Candlewick Pr.

— Horatio's Bed. LC 91-58737. (Illus.). 32p. (J). (ps up). 1994. pap. 4.99 (*1-56402-277-3*) Candlewick Pr.

— Humphrey Thud. LC 94-10449. (Illus.). 32p. (J). (ps up). 1997. reprint ed. pap. 5.99 (*0-7636-0095-4*) Candlewick Pr.

— Monkey Tricks. LC 92-53013. (Illus.). 32p. (J). (ps up). 1993. 15.95 (*1-56402-170-X*) Candlewick Pr.

Ashgriz. Thermodynamics. pap. text 32.00 (*0-471-37822-4*) Wiley.

Ashhauer, David A. Public Investment & Private Sector Growth: The Economic Benefits of Reducing America's "Third Deficit" (Illus.). 36p. (Orig.). 1991. pap. text 12.00 (*0-944826-38-5*) Economic Policy Inst.

Ashi, Manohar. Tribal Arts & Crafts of Madhya Pradesh. (Illus.). 160p. 1996. 39.50 (*0-944142-71-0*, Pub. by Mapin Pubng) Antique Collect.

Ashida, Ichiba. Ikebana with Living Plants. (Illus.). 1998. 25.00 (*0-87040-903-4*) Japan Pubns USA.

Ashihara, Eiryo. The Japanese Dance. LC 79-7749. (Dance Ser.). (Illus.). 1980. reprint ed. lib. bdg. 28.95 (*0-8369-9276-8*) Ayer.

Ashihara, Yoshinobu. The Hidden Order: Tokyo Through the Twentieth Century. Riggs, Lynne E., tr. from JPN. (Illus.). 160p. 1992. pap. 9.00 (*4-7700-1664-6*) Kodansha.

Ashik, Deva, ed. see Osho.

Ashimolowo, Matthew. It's Not Over 'til It's Over. LC 97-216161. 140p. 1997. pap. 9.99 (*1-56043-184-9*) Destiny Image.

Ashish, Sri Madhava. Man, Son of Man: In the Stanzas of Dzyan. LC 79-98267. 1970. 14.95 (*0-8356-0011-4*) Theos Pub Hse.

Ashish, Sri Madhava, jt. auth. see Prem, Sri K.

Ashit, Paul. Woodcut Prints of Nineteenth Century Calcutta. 1984. 34.00 (*0-317-05024-9*, Pub. by Seagull Bks) S Asia.

Ashiurakis, A. M. Spoken Arabic: Self-Taught. 118p. 1985. pap. 55.00 (*1-85077-090-5*, Pub. by Darf Pubs Ltd) St Mut.

***Ashkanasy, Neal M., et al, eds.** Emotions in the Workplace: Research, Theory & Practice. LC 99-462244. 328p. 2000. 75.00 (*1-56720-364-7*, Q364, Quorum Bks) Greenwood.

Ashkanazi-Hankin, Gail. Festivals of Lite Kosher Cookbook. LC 99-18520. (Illus.). 192p. 1999. 23.00 (*1-56554-334-3*) Pelican.

— Passover Lite Kosher Cookbook. LC 95-50597. (Illus.). 192p. 1996. 19.95 (*1-56554-133-2*) Pelican.

Ashkar, Dominic F. Come to the Wedding Feast: An Eight-Session Course for Training Catechists. LC 99-166971. 96p. (Orig.). 1997. pap., teacher ed. 29.95 (*0-89390-400-7*) Resource Pubns.

— Discovering the Joy of Teaching: Seven Formation Sessions for Catechists & Teachers. 1999. pap. text 19.95 (*0-89390-453-8*) Resource Pubns.

— Road to Emmaus: A New Model for Catechesis. LC 93-17566. 208p. (Orig.). (C). 1993. pap. text 14.95 (*0-89390-266-7*) Resource Pubns.

— Transfiguration Catechesis: A New Vision Based on the Liturgy & the "Catechism of the Catholic Church" LC 95-50111. 216p. 1996. pap. 19.95 (*0-89390-342-6*) Resource Pubns.

Ashkar, Fahim, jt. auth. see Bobee, Bernard.

Ashkar, Fuad S. Radiobioassays, 2 vols., I. 1983. 132.00 (*0-8493-6029-3*, RB42) CRC Pr.

— Radiobioassays, 2 vols., II. 240p. 1983. 132.00 (*0-8493-6030-7*, RB42) CRC Pr.

Ashken, M. H., ed. Urinary Diversion. (Clinical Practice in Urology Ser.). (Illus.). 143p. 1982. 114.00 (*0-387-11273-1*) Spr-Verlag.

Ashkenas, Joan. Comics & Conversation: Using Humor to Elicit Conversation & Develop Vocabulary. (Illus.). 30p. pap. 12.95 (*0-943327-00-8*) JAG Pubns.

— Foreign Students' Guide to Pronunciation: Using the Pronunciation Key of the English Dictionary. 1985. pap. text 13.00 (*0-943327-02-4*) JAG Pubns.

— More Comics & Conversation: Using Humor to Elicit Conversation & Develop Vocabulary. (Illus.). 30p. 1991. pap. 12.95 (*0-943327-06-7*) JAG Pubns.

***Ashkenas, Joan, ed.** New Comics & Conversation: Using Humor to Elicit Conversation & Develop Vocabulary. (Illus.). 30p. 1999. pap. 12.95 (*0-943327-24-5*) JAG Pubns.

Ashkenas, Joan, ed. see Bailey, Judith.

Ashkenas, Joan, ed. see Buchring, Michelle.

Ashkenas, Joan, ed. see Buehring, Michelle.

Ashkenas, Joan, ed. see Germer, Lucie C.

Ashkenas, Joan, ed. & intro. see Littauer, Joel.

Ashkenas, Ron, et al. The Boundaryless Organization: Breaking the Chains of Organizational Structure. LC 95-18791. (Management Ser.). 398p. 1995. mass mkt. 30.00 (*0-7879-0113-X*) Jossey-Bass.

— The Boundaryless Organization: Breaking the Chains of Organizational Structure. (Business & Management Ser.). 400p. 1998. reprint ed. pap. 20.00 (*0-7879-4000-3*) Jossey-Bass.

An Asterisk (*) at the beginning of an entry indicates that the title is appearing for the first time.

Ashkenas, Ronald, et al. The Boundaryless Organization Field Guide: Practical Tools for Building the New Organization. LC 98-40099. 416p. 1998. 129.95 (*0-7879-4321-5*) Jossey-Bass.

***Ashkenasi, Abraham, ed.** The Future of Jerusalem. (Ethnien - Regionen - Konflikte. Soziologische und Politologische Untersuchungen. Bd. 11 Ser.). (Illus.). 293p. 1999. 45.95 (*3-631-32216-X*) P Lang Pubng.

— The Future of Jerusalem. LC 99-51348. (Ethnien, Regionen, Konflikte. Soziologische und Politologische Untersuchungen. Bd. 11 Ser.). 293p. (C). 1999. pap. text 45.95 (*0-8204-3505-8*) P Lang Pubng.

Ashkenasi, Avaraham. Palestinian Identities & Preferences: Israel's & Jerusalem's Arabs. LC 91-16682. 208p. 1992. 57.95 (*0-275-93503-5*, C3503, Praeger Pubs) Greenwood.

Ashkenaz. Machzor: Shavuos. 26.99 (*0-89906-876-6*, MAVH) Mesorah Pubns.

Ashkenazi, Avi, jt. ed. see Chamow, Steven M.

Ashkenazi, Elliot, ed. Civil War Diary of Clara Solomon: Growing up in New Orleans, 1861-1862. (Library of Southern Civilization). (Illus.). 504p. 1995. 34.95 (*0-8071-1968-7*) La State U Pr.

Ashkenazi, Elliott. The Business of Jews in Louisiana, 1840-1875. LC 86-7022. (Judaic Studies). (Illus.). 232p. 1988. text 34.95 (*0-8173-0318-9*) U of Ala Pr.

Ashkenazi, J., et al. High-Temperature Superconductivity: Physical Properties, Microscopic Theory & Mechanisms. (Illus.). 680p. (C). 1992. text 174.00 (*0-306-44117-9*, Kluwer Plenum) Kluwer Academic.

Ashkenazi, Michael. Matsuri: Festivals of a Japanese Town. LC 92-31751. 208p. (C). 1993. text 36.00 (*0-8248-1385-5*); pap. text 14.95 (*0-8248-1421-5*) UH Pr.

Ashkenazi, Michael & Jacob, Jeanne. The Essence of Japanese Cuisine: An Anthropological Essay into Food & Culture. 288p. 1998. text 49.00 (*0-7007-1085-X*, Pub. by Curzon Pr Ltd) UH Pr.

***Ashkenazi, Michael & Jacob, Jeanne.** The Essence of Japanese Cuisine: An Essay on Food & Culture. LC 00-23031. (Illus.). 2001. write for info. (*0-8122-3566-5*) U of Pa Pr.

Ashkenazi, Michael & Weingrod, Alex. Ethiopian Jews & Israel. 188p. 1987. text 39.95 (*0-88738-133-2*) Transaction Pubs.

Ashkenazi, Michael, jt. auth. see Markowitz, Fran.

Ashkenazi, Vladimir & Parrot, Jasper. Preodolevaia Grantisy. Efimov, Igor & Yefimov, Marina, trs. (RUS., Illus.). 240p. (Orig.). 1989. pap. 12.50 (*1-55779-008-6*) Hermitage Pubs.

Ashkenazy, Daniella, ed. The Military in the Service of Society & Democracy, 153. LC 93-28030. (Contributions in Military Studies Ser.: No. 153). 256p. 1994. 62.95 (*0-313-29004-0*, GM9004, Greenwood Pr) Greenwood.

Ashkenazy, Vladimir, tr. see Ho, Allan & Feofanov, Dmitry.

Ashker, Helene. Jesus Cares for Women: A Leader's Guide for Hosting an Evangelistic Bible Study for Women. 72p. 1987. pap. 7.00 (*0-89109-190-4*) NavPress.

— Jesus Changes Women. 1998. pap. 7.00 (*1-57683-077-2*) NavPress.

***Ashker, Helene.** Mujer, Jesus Se Interesa Por Ti.Tr. of Jesus Cares for Women. (SPA.). 1999. pap. text 5.99 (*0-311-12110-1*, Edit Mundo) Casa Bautista.

***Ashkin, Arthur.** Optical Trapping & Manipulation of Neutral Particles Using Lasers: A Reprint Volume with Commentaries. 800p. 2000. 98.00 (*981-02-4057-0*); pap. 58.00 (*981-02-4058-9*) World Scientific Pub.

Ashkinaze, Carole, jt. auth. see Orfield, Gary.

Ashlag, Yehuda R. An Entrance to the Tree of Life. Berg, Philip S., ed. 208p. 1977. 12.95 (*0-943688-05-1*); pap. 11.95 (*0-943688-35-3*) Res Ctr Kabbalah.

— An Entrance to the Tree of Life. Berg, Philip S., ed. (SPA.). 212p. 1991. pap. 11.95 (*0-924457-62-7*) Res Ctr Kabbalah.

— An Entrance to the Zohar. Berg, Philip S., ed. 160p. 1974. 11.95 (*0-943688-04-3*); 10.95 (*0-943688-34-5*) Res Ctr Kabbalah.

— Etz Chaim: Hebrew Text, 2 vols. 450p. 1992. 40.00 (*0-943688-18-3*) Res Ctr Kabbalah.

— A Gift of the Bible. 160p. 1984. pap. 10.95 (*0-943688-22-1*) Res Ctr Kabbalah.

— Gift of the Bible. (SPA.). 160p. 1993. pap. 10.95 (*0-924457-72-4*) Res Ctr Kabbalah.

— Gift of the Bible: Hebrew Text. (HEB.). 160p. 1983. pap. 10.95 (*0-943688-30-2*) Res Ctr Kabbalah.

— Ten Luminous Emanations, Vol. 1. rev. ed. 160p. 1991. write for info. (*0-318-70380-7*) Res Ctr Kabbalah.

— Ten Luminous Emanations, Vol. 2. Berg, Philip S., ed. 208p. 1972. 11.95 (*0-943688-09-4*); pap. 10.95 (*0-943688-25-6*) Res Ctr Kabbalah.

— Ten Luminous Emanations, Vol. 3. Berg, Philip S., ed. 256p. 1991. write for info. (*0-943688-90-6*); pap. write for info. (*0-943688-91-4*) Res Ctr Kabbalah.

— Ten Luminous Emanations, Vol. 4. Berg, Philip S., ed. 256p. 1992. write for info. (*0-924457-57-0*); pap. write for info. (*0-924457-58-9*) Res Ctr Kabbalah.

— Ten Luminous Emanations I. Berg, Philip S., ed. (SPA.). 224p. 1994. pap. write for info. (*0-318-70262-2*) Res Ctr Kabbalah.

— Ten Luminous Emanations I. rev. ed. Berg, Philip S., ed. 192p. 1993. pap. 10.95 (*0-924457-91-0*) Res Ctr Kabbalah.

— Ten Luminous Emanations II. Berg, Philip S., ed. (SPA.). 224p. 1994. pap. write for info. (*0-318-70263-0*) Res Ctr Kabbalah.

Ashlee, Laura R., ed. Traveling Through Time: A Guide to Michigan's Historical Markers. (Illus.). 336p. (Orig.). 1992. pap. text 14.95 (*0-935719-18-0*) MI Hist Mag.

Ashleigh, C., tr. see Gladkov, Fyodor V.

Ashley. Working with Behavior Disorder. (C). 1998. pap. text 41.00 (*0-12-784586-0*) Acad Pr.

***Ashley, Amanda.** Captive. 400p. 2000. mass mkt. 5.99 (*0-505-52362-0*, Love Spell) Dorchester Pub Co.

Ashley, Amanda. A Darker Dream. 400p. 1997. mass mkt. 5.90 (*0-505-52208-X*, Love Spell) Dorchester Pub Co.

— Deeper Than the Night. 448p. (Orig.). 1996. mass mkt. 5.99 (*0-505-52113-X*, Love Spell) Dorchester Pub Co.

— Embrace the Night. 448p. (Orig.). 1998. mass mkt. 5.99 (*0-8439-4378-5*, Leisure Bks) Dorchester Pub Co.

— Shades of Gray. 400p. (Orig.). 1998. mass mkt. 5.99 (*0-505-52243-8*, Love Spell) Dorchester Pub Co.

— Sunlight, Moonlight. 400p. (Orig.). 1997. mass mkt. 5.99 (*0-505-52158-X*) Dorchester Pub Co.

Ashley, Anne. The Earl of Rayne's Ward. 1999. mass mkt. 4.99 (*0-373-30318-1*, 1-30318-9, Mira Bks) Harlequin Bks.

— Earl of Rayne's Ward. large type ed. (Mills & Boon Large Print Ser.). 350p. 1997. 23.99 (*0-263-15336-3*, Pub. by Mills & Boon) Ulverscroft.

***Ashley, Anne.** Lady Jane's Physician. large type ed. 320p. 2000. 25.99 (*0-263-16274-5*, Pub. by Mills & Boon) Ulverscroft.

— Lady Knightley's Secret. large type ed. 320p. 1999. 25.99 (*0-263-16019-X*, Pub. by Mgna Lrg Print) Ulverscroft.

Ashley, Anne. Lady Linford's Return. large type ed. (Mills & Boon Large Print Ser.). 350p. 1997. 23.99 (*0-263-15338-X*, Pub. by Mills & Boon) Ulverscroft.

***Ashley, Anne.** The Master of Moor House. 320p. 2000. 26.99 (*0-263-16416-0*, Pub. by Mills & Boon) Ulverscroft.

Ashley, Anne. Miss Harcourt's Dilemma. 1999. per. 4.99 (*0-373-30332-7*, . 1-30332-0) Harlequin Bks.

— The Neglectful Guardian. (Historical Ser.: Bk. 21). 1999. per. 4.99 (*0-373-30330-0*, 1-30330-4) Harlequin Bks.

— The Neglectful Guardian. large type ed. (Mills & Boon Large Print Ser.). 350p. 1998. 24.99 (*0-263-15526-9*, Pub. by Mills & Boon) Ulverscroft.

Ashley, Barbara, intro. Increasing Retailer Productivity: A Guide for Shopping Center Professionals. 124p. (Orig.). 1988. pap. 59.95 (*0-913598-73-9*, 852) Intl Coun Shop.

Ashley, Benedict. Theologies of the Body: Humanist & Christian. LC 84-15031. (Illus.). 770p. (Orig.). 1995. reprint ed. pap. 25.95 (*0-935372-15-6*) NCBC.

Ashley, Benedict & O'Rourke, Kevin D. Ethics of Health Care: A Textbook. 2nd ed. LC 93-36677. 288p. (C). 1994. pap. 24.95 (*0-87840-548-8*) Georgetown U Pr.

***Ashley, Benedict M.** Choosing a World-View & Value-System: An Ecumenical Apologetics. LC 99-33773. x, 326p. (C). 2000. pap. 18.95 (*0-8189-0829-7*) Alba.

Ashley, Benedict M. Justice in the Church: Gender & Participation. LC 96-5379. (McGivney Lectures of the John Paul II Institute for Studies on Marriage & Family, 1992). 234p. 1996. text 39.95 (*0-8132-0857-2*); pap. text 19.95 (*0-8132-0858-0*) Cath U Pr.

— Living the Truth in Love: A Biblical Introduction to Moral Theology. LC 96-10967. 572p. (Orig.). 1996. pap. 24.95 (*0-8189-0756-8*) Alba.

— Spiritual Direction in the Dominican Tradition. LC 94-46496. (Integration Bks.). 176p. (Orig.). 1995. pap. 12.95 (*0-8091-3567-1*) Paulist Pr.

Ashley, Benedict M. & O'Rourke, Kevin D. Health Care Ethics: A Theological Analysis. 4th ed. LC 96-46599. 544p. 1997. pap. 36.00 (*0-87840-644-1*) Georgetown U Pr.

Ashley, Benedict M., ed. see Aquinas, Thomas, Saint.

Ashley, Bernard. All My Men. LC 78-12683. (J). (gr. 6 up). 1978. 26.95 (*0-87599-228-5*) S G Phillips.

— A Break in the Sun. (Illus.). 186p. (J). (gr. 6 up). 1980. 26.95 (*0-87599-230-7*) S G Phillips.

— Cleversticks. (Illus.). 32p. (J). 1995. pap. 6.99 (*0-517-88332-5*) Crown Pub Group.

— Cleversticks. 1995. 12.19 (*0-606-07376-0*, Pub. by Turtleback) Demco.

Ashley, Bernard. Johnnie's Blitz. (Illus.). 176p. (YA). (gr. 6-9). 1996. pap. 9.95 (*0-14-037765-4*, Pub. by Pnguin Bks Ltd) Trafalgar.

— Justin & the Big Fight. (Illus.). 96p. (J). pap. 7.95 (*0-14-038386-7*, Pub. by Pnguin Bks Ltd) Trafalgar.

— Justin & the Demon Drop Kick. (Illus.). 96p. (J). pap. 7.95 (*0-14-038015-9*, Pub. by Pnguin Bks Ltd) Trafalgar.

Ashley, Bernard. A Kind of Wild Justice. LC 78-10899. (Illus.). (J). (gr. 7 up). 1979. 26.95 (*0-87599-229-3*) S G Phillips.

Ashley, Bernard. Puffin Book of School Stories. (Illus.). (J). 1993. pap. 9.95 (*0-14-034675-9*, Pub. by Pnguin Bks Ltd) Trafalgar.

Ashley, Bernard. Seeing off Uncle Jack. large type ed. (J). 1997. 16.95 (*0-7451-6907-4*, Galaxy Child Lrg Print) Chivers N Amer.

— Terry on the Fence. LC 76-39898. (Illus.). (J). (gr. 5-9). 1977. 26.95 (*0-87599-222-6*) S G Phillips.

Ashley, Bernard. Trouble with Donovan Croft. 1984. pap. 9.95 (*0-14-030974-8*, Pub. by Pnguin Bks Ltd) Trafalgar.

Ashley, Bob. Reading Popular Narrative: A Source Book. LC 96-38315. 256p. (C). 1997. pap. 24.95 (*0-7185-0083-0*); text 85.00 (*0-7185-0082-2*) Bks Intl VA.

Ashley, Bob, ed. The Study of Popular Fiction: A Source Book. LC 89-50131. 252p. (C). 1989. pap. text 17.95 (*0-8122-1295-9*) U of Pa Pr.

Ashley, Clara W., et al. Living Latin, Bk. 1. (ENG & LAT., Illus.). 128p. Date not set. pap. 28.20 (*0-8442-8600-1*, E8600-1) NTC Contemp Pub Co.

— Living Latin, Bk. 2. (LAT., Illus.). 128p. (C). Date not set. 28.20 (*0-8442-8602-8*, E8602-8) NTC Contemp Pub Co.

— Living Latin, Includ. Answer Key. (Illus.). Date not set. wbk. ed. 4.25 (*0-8442-8610-9*, E8610-9); pap., wbk. ed. 4.25 (*0-8442-8609-5*, E8609-5) NTC Contemp Pub Co.

Ashley, Clifford W. The Ashley Book of Knots. (Illus.). 640p. 1944. 65.00 (*0-385-04025-3*) Doubleday.

— The Ashley Book of Knots. 1990. 60.00 (*0-07-158384-X*) McGraw.

— The Yankee Whaler. (Illus.). 304p. 1991. reprint ed. pap. 10.95 (*0-486-26854-3*) Dover.

Ashley-Cooper, John. A Ring of Wessex Waters. 224p. (C). 1989. 49.00 (*0-85493-198-8*, Pub. by Witherby & Co) St Mut.

Ashley, David. History without a Subject: The Postmodern Condition. LC 97-14373. (New Perspectives in Sociology Ser.). 288p. (C). 1997. text 79.00 (*0-8133-1732-0*, Pub. by Westview); pap. text 27.00 (*0-8133-1733-9*, Pub. by Westview) HarpC.

Ashley, David & Orenstein, David Michael. Sociological Theory: Classical Statements. 4th ed. LC 97-19764. 554p. (C). 1997. 68.00 (*0-205-27157-X*) P-H.

Ashley, David, jt. ed. see Jiang, Yarong.

Ashley, David B., jt. ed. see Ibbs, C. W.

Ashley, DeeAnn. The Healthiest Dining in America: A Guide for Connoisseurs & Travelers. LC 86-50167. 234p. (Orig.). 1986. pap. 11.95 (*0-9610130-4-4*) Melius Pub.

Ashley, Douglas. Music Beyond Sound: Maria Curcio, a Teacher of Great Pianists. LC 92-44414. (American University Studies: Fine Arts: Ser. XX, Vol. 19). (Illus.). II, 112p. (C). 1993. text 35.95 (*0-8204-2101-4*) P Lang Pubng.

Ashley, Edward & Epperson, Beth. Sybase SQL Server on the World Wide Web. LC 96-19186. (Illus.). 400p. 1996. mass mkt. 36.95 (*1-85032-815-3*) ITCP.

Ashley-Farrand, Thomas. Healing Mantras: Using Sound Affirmations for Personal Power, Creativity & Healing. LC 99-12948. 1999. pap. 12.95 (*0-345-43170-7*) Ballantine Pub Grp.

Ashley, Faye. Lost in My Dreams. 1996. mass mkt. 5.99 (*0-312-95691-6*) Tor Bks.

— September Valentine, Vol. 1. 1997. mass mkt. 5.99 (*0-312-96279-7*) St Martin.

Ashley, Gail M., et al, eds. Glacial Sedimentary Environments. LC QE0471.2.A74. (SEPM Short Course Ser.: No. 16). 254p. reprint ed. pap. 78.80 (*0-8357-6993-3*, 203904300010) Bks Demand.

Ashley, Gail M., jt. ed. see Anderson, J. B.

Ashley, Glenn. Hawker Hunter in Action. (Aircraft in Action Ser.). (Illus.). 50p. 1992. pap. 9.95 (*0-89747-273-X*, 1121) Squad Sig Pubns.

— Meteor in Action. (Aircraft in Action Ser.). (Illus.). 50p. 1995. pap. 9.95 (*0-89747-332-9*) Squad Sig Pubns.

Ashley, Hannah, jt. auth. see Brenner, Claudia.

Ashley, Harry. Dorset Inns. 128p. 1987. pap. 35.00 (*0-905392-83-3*) St Mut.

— The Dorset Village Book. 184p. 1987. pap. 35.00 (*0-905392-35-3*) St Mut.

Ashley, Holt. Engineering Analysis of Flight Vehicles. rev. ed. (Illus.). ix, 386p. 1995. reprint ed. pap. text 13.95 (*0-486-67213-1*) Dover.

Ashley, Holt & Landahl, Marten. Aerodynamics of Wings & Bodies. LC 85-6992. 288p. 1999. reprint ed. pap. 9.95 (*0-486-64899-0*) Dover.

Ashley, Holt, jt. auth. see Bisplinghoff, Raymond L.

Ashley, J. Matthew. Interruptions: Mysticism, Politics & Theology in the Work of Johann Baptist Metz. LC 98-9193. (Studies in Spirituality & Theology). 293p. 1998. 34.00 (*0-268-01185-0*) U of Notre Dame Pr.

Ashley, J. Matthew, ed. & tr. see Metz, Johann B.

Ashley, James. International Purchasing Handbook. LC 98-3195. 408p. (C). 1998. 59.95 (*0-13-251430-3*) P-H.

Ashley, James M. & Arnett, Benjamin H. Duplicate Copy of the Souvenir from the Afro-American League of Tennessee to Hon. James M Ashley, of Ohio. 1977. 45.95 (*0-8369-9218-0*, 9073) Ayer.

Ashley, James M., jt. auth. see Hough, Harry E.

Ashley, James R. The Macedonian Empire: The Era of Warfare under Phillip II & Alexander the Great, 359-323 B. C. LC 97-40332. 496p. 1998. lib. bdg. 62.50 (*0-7864-0407-8*) McFarland & Co.

Ashley, Jane, et al. Breaking the Nation: A Guide to Thatcher's Britain. LC 87-171902. vii, 242 p. 1985. write for info. (*0-7453-0020-0*) LPC InBook.

***Ashley, Jeanne Hall, ed.** The Heritage of Elmore County, Alabama. (Heritage of Alabama Ser.: Vol. 26). 320p. 2001. 50.00 (*1-891647-47-4*) Herit Pub Consult.

Ashley, Jeffrey S., jt. auth. see Smith, Zachary A.

Ashley, Jill. Riddles about Christmas. Brook, Bonnie, ed. (What Can It Be? Ser.). (Illus.). 32p. (J). (ps-3). 1990. pap. 2.95 (*0-382-24383-8*); lib. bdg. 6.95 (*0-671-70552-0*) Silver Burdett Pr.

— Riddles about Easter. (What Can It Be? Ser.). (Illus.). 32p. (J). (ps-3). 1991. pap. 2.95 (*0-382-24380-3*); lib. bdg. 6.95 (*0-671-72726-5*) Silver Burdett Pr.

Ashley, Jo Ann. Hospitals, Paternalism & the Role of the Nurse. LC 76-7908. 158p. 1976. pap. 16.95 (*0-8077-2470-X*) Tchrs Coll.

Ashley, Joann & Wolf, Karen. Joann Ashley: Selected Readings. LC 96-49625. 1996. 25.95 (*0-88737-683-5*) Natl League Nurse.

Ashley, John. Perfect Lives: An Opera. (Illus.). 224p. 1992. 35.00 (*0-9627767-7-7*) Archer Fields.

Ashley, John M., ed. see Aquinas, Thomas, Saint.

Ashley, Joyce. Overcoming Stage Fright in Every Day Life. 176p. 1997. pap. 12.00 (*0-609-80097-3*) Random Hse Value.

***Ashley, Kathleen.** Writing Faith. LC 98-52096. (Illus.). 1p. 1999. 27.50 (*0-226-02966-2*) U Ch Pr.

Ashley, Kathleen, et al, eds. Autobiography & Postmodernism. LC 93-32437. 328p. (C). 1994. pap. 18.95 (*0-87023-900-7*) U of Mass Pr.

Ashley, Kathleen M., ed. Victor Turner & the Construction of Cultural Criticism: Between Literature & Anthropology. LC 89-46338. (Illus.). 206p. 1990. pap. 13.95 (*0-253-20594-8*, MB 594) Ind U Pr.

***Ashley, Kathleen M. & Sheingorn, Pamela.** Writing Faith: Text, Sign & History in the Miracles of Sainte Foy. LC 98-52096. (Illus.). 1998. pap. text 16.00 (*0-226-02967-0*) U Ch Pr.

***Ashley, Kenneth K.** Waterholes in the Wilderness: Encouragement for Dry Thirsty Souls. 246p. 1999. pap. write for info. (*0-7392-0458-0*, PO3765) Morris Pubng.

Ashley, Kevin, jt. ed. see Lenz, Mario.

Ashley, L. R. George Peele. LC 68-17242. 256p. 1970. 34.00 (*0-8290-0175-1*); pap. text 14.95 (*0-8290-2118-3*) Irvington.

***Ashley, Lane J., et al.** California Liability Insurance Practice: Claims & Litigation - 8/98 Update, 2 vols. Waxman, Robert N., ed. LC 90-84639. 361p. 1998. ring bd. 68.00 (*0-7626-0251-1*, CP-39267) Cont Ed Bar-CA.

Ashley, Larry, jt. ed. see Pierce, Bob.

Ashley, Laurence M. Laboratory Anatomy of the Turtle. 100p. (C). 1962. text. write for info. (*0-697-04601-X*, WCB McGr Hill) McGrw-H Hghr Educ.

Ashley, Laurence M. & Chiasson, Robert B. Laboratory Anatomy of the Shark. 5th ed. 98p. (C). 1988. text. write for info. (*0-697-05121-8*, WCB McGr Hill) McGrw-H Hghr Educ.

Ashley, Leonard. Turkey: Names & Naming Practices. 264p. 1998. 74.95 (*1-57309-366-1*); pap. 54.95 (*1-57309-365-3*) Intl Scholars.

Ashley, Leonard R. Colley Cibber. LC 64-8324. (Twayne's English Authors Ser.). 224p. (C). 1965. 20.95 (*0-8290-1730-5*) Irvington.

— Colley Cibber. rev. ed. 200p. 1988. 25.95 (*0-8057-6969-2*, TEAS 17, Twyne) Mac Lib Ref.

— The Complete Book of Devils & Demons. LC 95-26655. (Illus.). 288p. (Orig.). 1996. pap. 12.95 (*1-56980-077-4*) Barricade Bks.

— The Complete Book of Spells, Curses, & Magical Recipes. LC 96-49759. (Illus.). 400p. (Orig.). 1997. pap. 14.95 (*1-56980-110-X*) Barricade Bks.

— The Complete Book of Superstition, Prophecy, & Luck. LC 95-32693. 192p. 1995. pap. 12.95 (*1-56980-050-2*) Barricade Bks.

— The Complete Book of the Devil's Disciples. (Illus.). 368p. (Orig.). 1996. pap. 12.95 (*1-56980-087-1*) Barricade Bks.

— The Complete Book of Vampires, Ghosts, & Poltergeists. LC 98-5151. 1998. write for info. (*1-56980-125-8*) Barricade Bks.

— Elizabethan Popular Culture. LC 88-71063. (Illus.). 340p. (C). 1988. 36.95 (*0-87972-426-9*) Bowling Green Univ Popular Press.

Ashley, Leonard R. N. The Complete Book of Ghosts & Poltergeists. LC 99-55375. 2000. pap. 14.95 (*1-56980-138-X*) Barricade Bks.

***Ashley, Leonard R. N.** George Alfred Henty & the Victorian Mind. LC 98-11947. 290p. 1998. 74.95 (*1-57309-270-3*) Intl Scholars.

Ashley, Liza & Clinton, Bill, intros. Thirty Years at the Mansion. LC 84-73313. (Illus.). 176p. 1985. 24.95 (*0-935304-88-6*) August Hse.

Ashley, Liza & Huber, Carolyn. Thirty Years at the Mansion: The Classic Cookbook Combining Recipes, Recollections & Photographs from the Arkansas Governor's Mansion - Clinton White House Edition. (Illus.). 176p. 1999. pap. text 17.00 (*0-7881-6034-6*) DIANE Pub.

Ashley, Lowell E., ed. Cataloging Musical Moving Image Material: A Guide to the Bibliographic Control of Videorecordings & Films of Musical Performances & Other Music-Related Moving Image Material. LC 95-52543. 108p. 1996. pap. 28.00 (*0-914954-51-2*) Music Library Assn.

Ashley, Mabel E., jt. auth. see Casper, Mary K.

Ashley, Mark J. & Krych, David K., eds. Traumatic Brain Injury Rehabilitation. LC 95-7284. 448p. 1995. boxed set 139.95 (*0-8493-9463-5*, 9463) CRC Pr.

Ashley, Martin. Massage: A Career at Your Fingertips. 3rd ed. (Illus.). 300p. 1998. pap. 22.00 (*0-9644662-6-0*) Enterprse Pub.

Ashley, Martin, ed. Improving Learning & Teaching in the Humanities. (Developing Primary Practice Ser.). 224p. 1999. pap. 26.95 (*0-7507-0801-8*, Falmer Pr) Taylor & Francis.

Ashley, Mary Anne. Fragments I Saved from the Fire. LC 89-16251. 120p. (Orig.). 1989. pap. 9.00 (*0-918949-06-8*) Martz.

Ashley, Mary F., ed. see Berry, Michael A.

Ashley, Maureen. Touring in Wine Country: Northwest Italy. Johnson, Hugh, ed. LC 99-488201. (Touring in Wine Country Ser.). (Illus.). 144p. 1997. pap. 21.95 (*1-85732-864-7*, Pub. by Mitchell Beazley) Antique Collect.

— Touring in Wine Country: Tuscany. Johnson, Hugh, ed. 1996. pap. 21.95 (*1-85732-582-6*, Pub. by Reed Illust Books) Antique Collect.

Ashley, Maureen, jt. auth. see Duijker, Hubrecht.

Ashley, Maureen, jt. auth. see Johnson, Hugh.

Ashley, Maurice. The Battle of Naseby & the Fall of King Charles the First. (Illus.). 189p. 1993. pap. 19.95 (*0-312-10321-2*) St Martin.

— The English Civil War. (Illus.). 224p. 1996. pap. 18.95 (*0-312-16583-8*) St Martin.

— Financial & Commercial Policy under Cromwellian Protectorate. 2nd ed. 190p. 1962. reprint ed. 35.00 (*0-7146-1265-0*, BHA-01265, Pub. by F Cass Pubs) Intl Spec Bk.

— Life & Times of William I, 1. 1999. pap. text 18.95 (*1-56649-009-X*) Welcome Rain.

— The Life & Times of William I. Fraser, Antonia, ed. (Kings & Queens of England Ser.). (Illus.). 224p. 1992. 24.95 (*1-55859-449-3*) Abbeville Pr.

A

— Magna Carta in the Seventeenth Century. LC 65-23456. (Magna Carta Essays Ser.). 76p. (Orig.). reprint ed. pap. 30.00 (*0-8357-3733-0*, 203645900003) Bks Demand.
— The People of England: A Short Social & Economic History. LC 82-84225. 240p. 1982. pap. 74.40 (*0-7837-8533-X*, 204934300011) Bks Demand.
Ashley, Maurice P. Charles I & Cromwell. 256p. 1988. 25.00 (*0-413-51530-3*, A1184) Routledge.
— Louis XIV & the Greatness of France. 1965. pap. 14.95 (*0-02-901080-2*) Free Pr.
— Mr. President: An Introduction to American History. LC 79-38317. (Biography Index Reprint Ser.). 1977. reprint ed. 25.95 (*0-8369-8115-4*) Ayer.
***Ashley, Michael.** Crostics, Vol. 4. 64p. 1999. pap. 9.95 (*0-8129-3211-0*, Times Bks) Crown Pub Group.
Ashley, Michael. Random House Acrostic Puzzles, Vol. 2. 2nd ed. 1997. pap. 10.00 (*0-8129-2670-6*, Times Bks) Crown Pub Group.
— Random House Crostics, Vol. 1. Vol. 1. 80p. 1996. pap. 10.00 (*0-8129-2768-0*, Times Bks) Crown Pub Group.
— Random House Crostics, Vol. 3. 3rd ed. 1998. pap. 9.00 (*0-8129-3071-1*, Times Bks) Crown Pub Group.
— Who's Who in Horror & Fantasy Fiction LC 78-309133. 240 p. 1977. 5.50 (*0-241-89528-6*, H Hamilton) Viking Penguin.
Ashley, Michael, ed. The Mammoth Book of Comic Fantasy. LC 98-6915. (Mammoth Book Ser.). xv, 524 p. 1998. pap. 10.95 (*0-7867-0533-7*) Carroll & Graf.
— The Mammoth Book of Comic Fantasy II. (Mammoth Book Ser.). 544p. 1999. pap. text 10.95 (*0-7867-0694-5*) Carroll & Graf.
Ashley, Michael & Contento, William G. The Supernatural Index: A Listing of Fantasy, Supernatural, Occult, Weird, & Horror Anthologies, 5. LC 95-6290. (Bibliographies & Indexes in Science Fiction, Fantasy & Horror: No. 5). 952p. 1995. lib. bdg. 215.00 (*0-313-24030-2*, Greenwood Pr) Greenwood.
Ashley, Michael, ed. see Styles-Ashley, Kimber.
Ashley, Michael, ed. & intro. see Gaskell, Elizabeth.
Ashley, Mike. Algernon Blackwood: A Bio-Bibliography, 1. LC 87-17808. (Bio-Bibliographies in World Literature Ser.: No. 1). 369p. 1987. lib. bdg. 59.95 (*0-313-25158-4*, AAN/, Greenwood Pr) Greenwood.
— The Random House Book of Fantasy Stories. LC 96-70233. (Illus.). 1997. pap. 9.99 (*0-679-88528-5*) Random.
— The Work of William F. Temple: An Annotated Bibliography & Guide. Clarke, Boden, ed. LC 93-334. (Bibliographies of Modern Authors Ser.: No. 28). 112p. 1994. pap. 17.00 (*0-8095-1507-5*) Millefleurs.
Ashley, Mike, ed. The Camelot Chronicles: Heroic Adventures from the Time of King Arthur. 432p. 1994. pap. 12.95 (*0-7867-0085-8*) Carroll & Graf.
— The Chronicles of the Holy Grail. 448p. 1996. pap. 12.95 (*0-7867-0363-6*) Carroll & Graf.
— The Chronicles of the Round Table. LC 97-29712. 448p. 1997. pap. 12.95 (*0-7867-0464-0*) Carroll & Graf.
— Classical Whodunits. LC 97-15464. 384p. 1997. pap. 9.95 (*0-7867-0418-7*) Carroll & Graf.
— The Mammoth Book of Arthurian Legends. LC 98-16798. (Mammoth Book Ser.). x, 566p. 1998. pap. 10.95 (*0-7867-0532-9*) Carroll & Graf.
***Ashley, Mike, ed.** The Mammoth Book of British Kings & Queens. (Mammoth Book Ser.). (Illus.). 832p. 1999. pap. text 18.95 (*0-7867-0692-9*) Carroll & Graf.
Ashley, Mike, ed. The Mammoth Book of British Kings & Queens of Britain & Ireland. (Mammoth Book Ser.). (Illus.). 544p. 1998. 29.95 (*0-7867-0405-5*) Carroll & Graf.
— The Mammoth Book of Fairy Tales. LC 97-34051. (Mammoth Book Ser.). (Illus.). 544p. 1997. pap. 10.95 (*0-7867-0475-6*) Carroll & Graf.
— The Mammoth Book of Historical Detectives. (Mammoth Book Ser.). 544p. 1995. pap. 9.95 (*0-7867-0214-1*) Carroll & Graf.
— The Mammoth Book of Historical Whodunnits. (Mammoth Book Ser.). 512p. 1993. pap. 9.95 (*0-7867-0024-6*) Carroll & Graf.
***Ashley, Mike, ed.** The Mammoth Book of Locked-Room Mysteries & Impossible Crimes. 512p. 2000. pap. 11.95 (*0-7867-0790-9*, Pub. by Carroll & Graf) Publishers Group.
— The Mammoth Book of Men O'War. (Mammoth Book Ser.). 512p. 1999. pap. text 11.95 (*0-7867-0696-1*) Carroll & Graf.
— The Mammoth Book of Sword & Honor. 512p. 2000. pap. 11.95 (*0-7867-0727-5*, Pub. by Carroll & Graf) Publishers Group.
Ashley, Mike, ed. The Merlin Chronicles. LC 96-154350. 448p. (Orig.). 1995. pap. 12.95 (*0-7867-0275-3*) Carroll & Graf.
— Monthly Terrors: An Index to the Weird Fantasy Magazines Published in the United States & Great Britain, 4. LC 84-19225. (Bibliographies & Indexes in World Literature Ser.: No. 4). 602p. 1985. lib. bdg. 89.50 (*0-313-23989-4*, PMO/) Greenwood.
***Ashley, Mike, ed.** Phantom Perfumes & Other Shades: Memories of Ghost Stories Magazine. xxxvi, 250p. 2000. pap. 42.50 (*1-899562-89-3*) Ash-Tree.
Ashley, Mike, ed. Royal Whodunnits: Tales of Right Royal Murder & Mystery. 448p. 1999. pap. 11.95 (*0-7867-0634-1*) Carroll & Graf.
— Shakespearean Detectives. 1998. pap. 10.95 (*0-7867-0596-5*) Carroll & Graf.
— Shakespearean Whodunnits. LC 97-34046. 416p. 1997. pap. 10.95 (*0-7867-0482-9*) Carroll & Graf.
Ashley, Mike, ed. see Sand, George.
Ashley, Mike, jt. ed. see Tymn, Marshall B.
Ashley, Muata A. The History of Saa: The Ancient Egyptian Origins of Greek Mythology & Philosophy. (Illus.). 64p. 1998. 7.99 (*1-884564-41-0*) Cruzian Mystic.
Ashley, Nicholas. Measurement As a Powerful Software Management Tool. LC 94-27967. (International Software Quality Assurance Ser.). 1994. 29.95 (*0-07-707902-7*) McGraw.
Ashley-Oehm, Dayna & Liddell, Scott. Adult Workers: Retraining the American Workforce. (Investing in People Ser.). 20p. 1994. 15.00 (*1-55516-347-5*, 3124) Natl Conf State Legis.
Ashley, Patricia M. The Other Miss Derwent. large type ed. (Dales Romance Ser.). 286p. 1993. pap. 18.99 (*1-85389-397-8*, Dales) Ulverscroft.
***Ashley, Paul.** Practical Intranet Security: Overview of the State of the Art & Available Technologies. LC 98-49719. 16p. 1999. write for info. (*0-7923-8354-0*) Kluwer Academic.
Ashley, Pauline. The Money Problems of the Poor: A Literature Review. (SSRC-DHSS Studies in Deprivation & Disadvantage: No. 11). xiii, 226p. 1983. text 37.95 (*0-435-82024-9*) Ashgate Pub Co.
Ashley, Perry J. American Newspaper Journalists, 1926-1950. (Dictionary of Literary Biography Ser.: Vol. 29). 424p. 1984. text 155.00 (*0-8103-1707-9*) Gale.
Ashley, Perry J., ed. American Newspaper Journalists, 1873-1900. (Dictionary of Literary Biography Ser.: Vol. 23). 432p. 1983. text 155.00 (*0-8103-1145-3*) Gale.
— American Newspaper Journalists, 1901-1925. (Dictionary of Literary Biography Ser.: Vol. 25). (Illus.). 400p. 1984. text 155.00 (*0-8103-1704-4*) Gale.
— American Newspaper Journalists, Sixteen Ninety to Eighteen Seventy-Two, Vol. 43. (Dictionary of Literary Biography Ser.). 537p. 1985. text 155.00 (*0-8103-1721-4*) Gale.
— Dictionary of Literary Biography, Vol. 4. 456p. 1983. text 146.00 (*0-8103-1113-5*) Gale.
Ashley, Peter, ed. see Deck, John & Tsui, Mary.
Ashley, R. Wilkie Collins. LC 75-30887. (Studies in Fiction: No. 34). 1975. lib. bdg. 75.00 (*0-8383-2095-3*) M S G Haskell Hse.
Ashley, R., ed. Solids in Sewers: Selected Proceedings of the IAWQ International Specialized Conference on Sewer Solids - Characteristics, Movement, Effects & Control, Held in Dundee, Scotland, UK, 6-8 September, 1995. (Water Science & Technology Ser.: 33). 298p. 1996. pap. text 133.00 (*0-08-042901-7*, Pergamon Pr) Elsevier.
Ashley, R. H., ed. Ion Channels: A Practical Approach. No. 160. (Practical Approach Ser.: Vol. 160). (Illus.). 324p. (C). 1996. text 110.00 (*0-19-963475-0*); pap. text 55.00 (*0-19-963474-2*) OUP.
Ashley, Renee. Salt. LC 91-12357. (Brittingham Prize in Poetry Ser.). 70p. (Orig.). (C). 1992. pap. 11.95 (*0-299-13144-0*) U of Wis Pr.
— The Various Reasons of Light. LC 98-84310. 80p. 1998. pap. 12.95 (*0-9661072-1-7*) Avocet Pr.
Ashley, Richard A., jt. auth. see Patterson, Douglas M.
***Ashley, Robert.** Dust: An Opera by Robert Ashley. 160p. 2000. pap. write for info. (*0-9679974-0-2*) Lovely Comns.
Ashley, Robert. Perfect Lives: An Opera. 1991. pap. 35.00 (*0-936050-10-1*) Burning Bks.
— Stolen Train. 160p. (J). (gr. 3-7). 1997. pap. text 3.99 (*0-590-92150-9*) Scholastic Inc.
— Stolen Train. (J). 1997. 9.09 (*0-606-11915-9*, Pub. by Turtleback) Demco.
Ashley, Robert & Miller, George H. Ripon College, a History. (Illus.). 304p. 1992. 18.51 (*0-929331-04-4*) Ripon Coll Pr.
***Ashley, Roderic.** Enhancing Your Employability: How to Improve Your Prospects of Achieving a Fulfilling & Rewarding Career. (Illus.). 144p. (Orig.). 1998. pap. 19.95 (*1-85703-371-X*) How To Bks.
Ashley, Ruth, et al. GW BASIC: A Self-Teaching Guide. LC 91-7390. 331p. 1991. pap. 19.95 (*0-471-53325-4*) Wiley.
Ashley, Ruth, jt. auth. see Fernandez, Judi N.
Ashley, Stephen & Anderson, Sean. Catering for Large Numbers. (Illus.). 304p. 1993. pap. 46.95 (*0-409-30642-8*) Buttrwrth-Heinemann.
Ashley, Stephen S. Bad Faith Actions-Liability & Damages. LC 84-28489. 1984. ring bd. 145.00 (*0-317-17768-0*) West Group.
— Handbook of California Civil Procedure Vol. 1: Starting & Responding to a Lawsuit. LC 98-170257. 500p. 1998. pap. 79.95 (*0-9624813-1-9*) Stratton Pr.
Ashley, Sylvia. A Light Touch. LC 95-90621. (Orig.). 1996. pap. 7.95 (*0-533-11660-0*) Vantage.
Ashley, Timothy R. Numbers. LC 96-28743. (New International Commentary on the Old Testament Ser.). 683p. 1995. 42.00 (*0-8028-2523-0*) Eerdmans.
— Richard Strauss. (20th Century Composers Ser.). 240p. 1999. pap. 24.95 (*0-7148-3794-6*) Phaidon Press.
Ashley, Veronica. Pagan Desires. 352p. 1997. mass mkt. 4.99 (*0-8217-5764-4*, Zebra Kensgtn) Kensgtn Pub Corp.
Ashley, Veronica, et al. A Mother's Heart. 352p. 1998. pap. 5.99 (*0-8217-5896-9*, Zebra Kensgtn) Kensgtn Pub Corp.
***Ashley, Vikki.** Alan's Song of Love: An AIDS Odyssey. 78p. 2000. pap. 17.95 (*0-9669493-2-3*) Atalaria.
Ashley, Vikki. How to Be a Bitch with Style: Being in Total Control of Herself. (Illus.). 480p. 1999. pap. 29.95 (*0-9669493-0-7*) Atalaria.
— How to Be a Bitch with Style Tool Kit. (Illus.). 80p. 1999. pap. 19.95 (*0-9669493-1-5*) Atalaria.
Ashley, William C. & Morrison, James L. Anticipatory Management: 10 Power Tools for Achieving Excellence into the 21st Century. LC 95-80645. 290p. 1995. pap. 29.95 (*0-913869-05-8*) Issue Action Pubns.
Ashley, William E., jt. ed. see Jackson, Roger.
Ashley, William H. British Establishments on the Columbia & the State of the Fur Trade. 60p. 1981. 14.95 (*0-87770-255-1*) Ye Galleon.
Ashley, William J. The Economic Organization of England: An Outline History. LC 83-45574. reprint ed. 47.50 (*0-404-19892-9*) AMS Pr.
— An Introduction to English Economic History & Theory: Pt. 1. The Middle Ages, Pt. 2. The End of the Middle Ages. 4th ed. LC 65-26358. (Reprints of Economic Classics Ser.). 1966. 65.00 (*0-678-00167-7*) Kelley.
— Surveys: Historic & Economic. LC 66-21366. (Reprints of Economic Classics Ser.). xxviii, 476p. 1966. reprint ed. 49.50 (*0-678-00170-7*) Kelley.
— The Tariff Problem. 4th ed. LC 68-30515. (Reprints of Economic Classics Ser.). xxxiv, 269p. 1968. reprint ed. 39.50 (*0-678-00433-1*) Kelley.
Ashley, William J., ed. & intro. see Mill, John Stuart.
Ashley, William J., tr. see Turgot, A. Robert.
Ashley, William L. & Zahniser, Gale L. Helping the Dislocated Worker: Sample Programs. 65p. 1984. 5.75 (*0-318-22114-4*, RD243B) Ctr Educ Trng Employ.
Ashley, William L., et al. Peer Tutoring: A Guide to Program Design. 124p. 1986. 10.50 (*0-318-22165-9*, RD 260) Ctr Educ Trng Employ.
— Preparing for High Technology: Robotics Programs. 57p. 1983. 5.75 (*0-318-22176-4*, RD233) Ctr Educ Trng Employ.
Ashley, William L., jt. auth. see Connell, Janie B.
Ashley, William L., jt. auth. see Zahniser, Gale L.
Ashliman, D. L. A Guide to Folktales in the English Language: Based on the Aarne-Thompson Classification System, 11. LC 87-15017. (Bibliographies & Indexes in World Literature Ser.: No. 11). 384p. 1987. lib. bdg. 85.00 (*0-313-25961-5*, AGF/, Greenwood Pr) Greenwood.
— Voices from the Past: The Cycle of Life in Indo-European Folktale. 2nd ed. 508p. (C). 1996. pap. text, per. 35.95 (*0-7872-1503-1*) Kendall-Hunt.
Ashline, George Lawrence. The Defect Relation of Meromorphic Maps on Parabolic Manifolds. LC 99-19211. (Memoirs of the Society Ser.). 1999. write for info. (*0-8218-1069-3*) Am Math.
Ashlock, Mary Ann. Giant Steps: A Self Esteem Curriculum for 3-7 Years Old: We Are All Special & Wonderful! (J). (ps-2). 1990. spiral bd. 24.95 (*1-930489-03-X*) Act For Kids.
Ashlock, Robert B. Error Patterns in Computation. 7th ed. LC 97-1558. 323p. 1997. pap. text 25.00 (*0-13-573197-6*) P-H.
Ashlock, Robert B., et al. Mathematical Connections: Integrated & Applied. 1996. teacher ed. 56.51 (*0-02-824796-5*); student ed. 46.50 (*0-02-824795-7*); wbk. ed. 8.15 (*0-02-824803-1*) Glencoe.
Ashlund, S., et al, eds. Human Factors in Computing Systems: Interchi '93 Proceedings of the Interchi' 93, Amsterdam, The Netherlands, 24-29 April 1993. LC 93-78478. 547p. (gr. 12). 1993. 98.00 (*90-5199-133-9*, Pub. by IOS Pr) IOS Press.
Ashly, Joice. Spirit of Numerology. Mclellan, Martha, ed. (Illus.). 308p. 1996. pap. text 17.90 (*0-9649077-2-0*) J A Winn.
— Spirit of Numerology. 2nd rev. ed. Mclelland, Martha, ed. LC 96-96226. (Illus.). xxiii, 295p. 1999. reprint ed. pap. 18.98 (*0-9649077-3-9*, Pub. by J A Winn) New Leaf Dist.
***Ashman.** Rub-a-dub. 2002. write for info. (*0-15-202658-4*) Harcourt.
Ashman, Adrian F. & Conway, Robert. An Introduction to Cognitive Education: Theory & Applications. 288p. (C). 1997. 80.00 (*0-415-12839-0*) Routledge.
Ashman, Adrian F. & Conway, Robert N. Cognitive Strategies Special Education. 250p. 1988. pap. text 15.95 (*0-415-00595-7*, A1694) Routledge.
— Cognitive Strategies Special Education. LC 96-27652. 250p. 1997. text 49.95 (*0-415-00594-9*, A1690) Routledge.
— An Introduction to Cognitive Education: Theory & Applications. LC 96-27652. 288p. (C). 1997. pap. 24.99 (*0-415-12840-4*) Routledge.
Ashman, Adrian F., jt. ed. see Laura, Ronald S.
***Ashman, Bernie.** SignMates: Understanding the Games People Play. 2000. pap. 19.95 (*1-56718-046-9*) Llewellyn Pubns.
Ashman, Charles & Wagman, Robert J. The Nazi Hunters: The Shocking True Story of the Continuing Search for Nazi War Criminals. 320p. 1990. mass mkt. 4.95 (*0-446-35831-2*, Pub. by Warner Bks) Little.
***Ashman, I.** Make This Castle. rev. ed. (Cut-Out Models Ser.). (Illus.). 32p. (YA). (gr. 4-7). 2000. pap. 9.95 (*0-7460-3303-6*, Pub. by Usbrne Pbng UK) EDC.
Ashman, I. Make This Medieval Castle. (gr. 2-7). 1998. pap. text 9.95 (*0-7460-3292-7*, Usborne) EDC.
Ashman, I. & Cartwright, Stephen. Nativity Press Out Model. (Illus.). 32p. (J). (gr. 2-7). 1992. text 11.95 (*0-7460-1319-1*, Usborne) EDC.
Ashman, Iain. Dinosaurs Cut-Out Model. (Cut Out Models Ser.). (Illus.). 32p. (J). (gr. 2-7). 1994. pap. 9.95 (*0-7460-1320-5*, Usborne) EDC.
— Make This Egyptian Mummy. (Cut-Out Models Ser.). (Illus.). 32p. (J). (gr. 2-7). 1995. pap. 9.95 (*0-7460-1988-2*, Usborne) EDC.
— Make This Egyptian Temple. (Cut-Out Models Ser.). (Illus.). 32p. (J). (gr. 4 up). 1990. pap. 9.95 (*0-7460-0461-3*) EDC.
— Make This Egyptian Temple. (Usborne Cut-Out Models Ser.). 1999. pap. 9.95 (*0-7460-3781-3*, Usborne) EDC.
— Make This Medieval Town. (Usborne Cut-Out Models Ser.). 1999. pap. 9.95 (*0-7460-3302-8*, Usborne) EDC.
— Make This Model Castle. 32p. (J). (gr. 4 up). 1988. pap. 9.95 (*0-86020-578-9*, Usborne) EDC.
— Make This Model Crusader Castle. (Cut-Out Models Ser.). (Illus.). 32p. (YA). (gr. 4-7). 1996. pap. 9.95 (*0-7460-2435-5*, Usborne) EDC.
— Make This Model Doll's House. (Cut-Out Models Ser.). (Illus.). 32p. (J). (gr. 2-7). 1993. pap. 9.95 (*0-7460-1316-7*, Usborne) EDC.
— Make This Model Haunted House. (Cut-Out Models Ser.). (Illus.). 32p. (J). (gr. 4-7). 1991. pap. 9.95 (*0-7460-0647-0*, Usborne) EDC.
— Make This Model Lost Temple. (Cut-Out Models Ser.). 32p. (YA). (gr. 2-7). 1992. pap. 9.95 (*0-7460-1211-X*, Usborne) EDC.
— Make This Model Medieval Port Cut Out Model. (Cut-Out Models Ser.). (Illus.). 32p. (J). (gr. 2-7). 1994. text 9.95 (*0-7460-1844-4*, Usborne) EDC.
— Make This Model Village. (Cut-Out Models Ser.). (Illus.). 32p. (J). (gr. 4-7). 1988. pap. 9.95 (*0-86020-579-7*) EDC.
— Make This Model Wizards Castle. (Cut-Out Models Ser.). (Illus.). 32p. (J). (gr. 2-7). 1991. pap. 9.95 (*0-7460-0607-1*, Usborne) EDC.
— Make This Roman Fort. (Cut-Out Models Ser.). (Illus.). 32p. (J). (gr. 4 up). 1989. pap. 9.95 (*0-7460-0256-4*) EDC.
— Make This Roman Villa. (Cut-Out Models Ser.). (Illus.). 32p. (J). (gr. 4 up). 1990. pap. 9.95 (*0-7460-0462-1*) EDC.
— Make This Roman Villa. (Usborne Cut-Out Models Ser.). 1999. pap. 9.95 (*0-7460-3690-6*, Usborne) EDC.
— Make This Viking Settlement. (Cut-Out Models Ser.). (Illus.). 32p. (J). (gr. 4 up). 1989. pap. 9.95 (*0-7460-0257-2*) EDC.
— Make This Viking Settlement. 1999. pap. 9.95 (*0-7460-3692-2*, Usborne) EDC.
— Paper Planes Kid Kit. (Usborne Kid Kits Ser.). (Illus.). (J). (gr. 3 up). 1999. 9.95 (*0-88110-882-0*, Usborne) EDC.
Ashman, Iain, ed. Make This Model American Fort. (Cut-Out Models Ser.). (Illus.). 32p. (YA). (gr. 4 up). 1999. pap. text 9.95 (*0-7460-3439-3*, Usborne) EDC.
Ashman, Ian. Make This Model Greek Temple. (Cut-Out Models Ser.). (Illus.). 32p. (J). (gr. 4 up). 1998. pap. 9.95 (*0-7460-3314-1*, Usborne) EDC.
Ashman, Keith M. & Zepf, Stephen E. Globular Cluster Systems. LC 97-17391. (Cambridge Astrophysics Ser.: No. 30). (Illus.). 210p. (C). 1998. text 69.95 (*0-521-55057-2*) Cambridge U Pr.
Ashmand, J. M. Ptolemy's Tetrabiblos or Quadripartite Being Four Books of the Influence of the Stars. 190p. 1993. reprint ed. pap. 13.95 (*1-56459-407-6*) Kessinger Pub.
— Ptolemy's Tetrabiblos, Quadripartite: Being Four Books of the Influence of the Stars. 240p. 1996. reprint ed. pap. 15.50 (*0-7873-0042-X*) Hlth Research.
Ashmand, J. M., tr. see Ptolemy, Claudius.
Ashmawy, Muhammad S., jt. auth. see Fluehr-Lobban, Carolyn.
Ashmead, Ann H. & Phillips, Kyle M., Jr. Catalogue of the Classical Collection: Vases. LC 76-45537. (Illus.). 135p. 1976. pap. 10.00 (*0-911517-11-1*) Mus of Art RI.
Ashmead, Ann Harnwell. Haverford College Collection of Classical Antiquities: The Bequest of Ernest Allen. LC 99-6077. ix, 61p. 1999. write for info. (*0-924171-69-3*) U Museum Pubns.
Ashmead, DeWayne. Chelated Mineral Nutrition in Plants, Animals & Man. (Illus.). 346p. 1982. text 62.95 (*0-398-04603-4*); pap. text 47.95 (*0-398-06624-8*) C C Thomas.
Ashmead, H. DeWayne, ed. The Roles of Amino Acid Chelates in Animal Nutrition. LC 92-25242. (Illus.). 479p. 1993. 96.00 (*0-8155-1312-7*) Noyes.
Ashmead, Henry G. History of Delaware County, Pa. (Illus.). 767p. 1993. reprint ed. lib. bdg. 76.00 (*0-8328-2883-1*) Higginson Bk Co.
Ashmead, Henry G., jt. auth. see Cope, Gilbert.
Ashmole, et al. Lives of Those Eminent Antiquaries Elias Ashmole & Mr. William Lilly. 410p. 1998. reprint ed. pap. 45.00 (*0-7661-0475-3*) Kessinger Pub.
Ashmole, Elias. The History of the Most Noble Order of the Garter & the Several Orders of Knighthood in Europe. 582p. 1997. reprint ed. pap. 75.00 (*0-7661-0058-8*) Kessinger Pub.
— Theatrum Chemicum Britannicum. 1968. reprint ed. 145.00 (*0-318-71886-3*) G Olms Pubs.
— Theatrum Chemicum Britannicum. 494p. 1992. reprint ed. pap. 32.50 (*0-922802-89-0*) Kessinger Pub.
— The Way to Bliss, 1658, 3 bks. 221p. 1993. reprint ed. pap. 24.95 (*1-56459-347-9*) Kessinger Pub.
Ashmole, Elias, tr. see Abraham, Lyndy & Dee, Arthur.
Ashmolean Museum, jt. auth. see Payne, Joan C.
Ashmore. Principles of Reaction Kinetics. 2nd ed. 80p. 1989. 18.00 (*0-85404-024-2*) CRC Pr.
Ashmore, E. F. Osteopathic Mechanics: A Textbook. 1991. lib. bdg. 79.95 (*0-8490-4104-X*) Gordon Pr.
Ashmore, Edward & Grove, Eric. The Battle & the Breeze: Memoirs of an Admiral of the Fleet. LC 97-157017. (Illus.). 224p. 1997. 44.95 (*0-7509-1252-9*, Pub. by Sutton Pub Ltd) Intl Pubs Mktg.
Ashmore, Edythe F. Osteopathic Mechanics. 237p. 1996. reprint ed. pap. 22.00 (*0-7873-0043-8*) Hlth Research.
Ashmore, Ginny & Mickey, Paul A. Clergy Families. 208p. 1991. pap. 12.99 (*0-310-53561-1*) Zondervan.
Ashmore, Ginny W. & Mickey, Paul A. Loneliness. (Lifesearch Ser.). 64p. 1996. pap. 4.95 (*0-687-01500-6*) Abingdon.
Ashmore, Harry S. Civil Rights & Wrongs: A Memoir of Race & Politics, 1944-1996. rev. ed. LC 96-53950. 490p. 1997. pap. 19.95 (*1-57003-187-8*) U of SC Pr.
— Hearts & Minds: A Personal Chronicle of Race in America. LC 88-18470. 516p. 1988. pap. 14.95 (*0-932020-58-5*) Seven Locks Pr.
— Unseasonable Truths: The Life of Robert Maynard Hutchins. 1989. 27.50 (*0-316-05396-1*) Little.

An Asterisk (*) at the beginning of an entry indicates that the title is appearing for the first time.

A

Ashton, Janatha R., ed. ICD-9-CM Workbook for Beginning Coders: In Cooperation with the American Hospital Association's Central Office on ICD-9-CM. 79p. 1997. pap. text 26.25 (*1-55648-204-3*, 148178) AHPI.

Ashton, Jim. Jim Ashton's Serial Poster Price Guide. (Illus.). 110p. 1989. write for info. (*0-318-65767-8*) J Ashton Pubns.

Ashton, Joan. Mother of Nations: Visions of Mary. 228p. 1989. pap. 22.00 (*1-85390-057-5*, Pub. by Veritas Pubns) St Mut.

Ashton, Joanne & Fike, Ruthita, eds. Reengineering for Patient-Focused Care. 198p. 1996. 34.95 (*0-9633819-3-8*) Prescott Pub.

Ashton, John. Eighteenth Century Waifs. LC 71-38741. (Essay Index Reprint Ser.). 1977. reprint ed. 25.95 (*0-8369-2634-X*) Ayer.

— English Caricature & Satire on Napoleon 1st. LC 68-25953. (Illus.). 1972. reprint ed. 31.95 (*0-405-08222-3*, Pub. by Blom Pubns) Ayer.

— History of Gambling in England. LC 69-14910. (Criminology, Law Enforcement, & Social Problems Ser.: No. 73). 1969. reprint ed. 12.00 (*0-87585-073-1*) Patterson Smith.

— The Interpretation of John. 352p. 1997. pap. 29.95 (*0-567-08546-5*, Pub. by T & T Clark) Bks Intl VA.

***Ashton, John.** The Religion of Paul the Apostle. (Illus.). 288p. 2000. 28.50 (*0-300-08441-2*) Yale U Pr.

Ashton, John. A Righte Merrie Christmasse!!! LC 68-56543. (Illus.). 261p. 1972. reprint ed. 18.95 (*0-405-08225-8*, Pub. by Blom Pubns) Ayer.

***Ashton, John.** The Seventh Millenium: The Evidence That We Can Know the Future. 2000. pap. 17.95 (*1-86436-359-2*, Pub. by New Holland) BHB Intl.

Ashton, John. Social Life in the Reign of Queen Anne. (Works of John Ashton). xix, 474p. 1985. reprint ed. 69.00 (*0-685-10447-8*) Rprt Serv.

— Studying John: Approaches to the Fourth Gospel. 240p. 1998. reprint ed. pap. text 19.95 (*0-19-826979-X*) OUP.

— Understanding the Fourth Gospel. 616p. (C). 1993. reprint ed. pap. text 35.00 (*0-19-826353-8*, 14080) OUP.

Ashton, John, ed. Chap-Books of the Eighteenth Century. LC 68-25953. (Illus.). 454p. 1972. 21.95 (*0-405-08221-5*, Pub. by Blom Pubns) Ayer.

— Healthy Cities. 192p. 1991. pap. 37.95 (*0-335-09476-7*) OpUniv Pr.

***Ashton, John, ed.** In 6 Days. 352p. 2000. pap. 14.95 (*1-86436-443-2*, Pub. by New Holland) BHB Intl.

Ashton, John, ed. Modern Street Ballads. LC 68-58949. (Illus.). 1972. reprint ed. 23.95 (*0-405-08223-1*, Pub. by Blom Pubns) Ayer.

— Real Sailor-Songs. LC 78-160612. (Illus.). 1972. reprint ed. 30.95 (*0-405-08224-X*, Pub. by Blom Pubns) Ayer.

Ashton, John & Laura, Ron. Perils of Progress: The Health & Environmental Hazards of Modern Technology & What You Can Do about It. 360p. 1999. text 55.00 (*1-85649-696-1*) St Martin.

— The Perils of Progress: The Health & Environmental Hazards of Modern Technology, & What You Can Do about Them. 350p. 1997. pap. 29.95 (*0-86840-488-8*, Pub. by New South Wales Univ Pr) Intl Spec Bk.

Ashton, John & Seymour, Howard. The New Public Health. 160p. 1988. 110.00 (*0-335-15555-3*); pap. 37.95 (*0-335-15550-2*) OpUniv Pr.

Ashton, John, et al. History of Jack Stock & Mules in Missouri. rev. ed. Dolly, Helen, ed. (Missouri Mule History Project Ser.). (Illus.). 110p. 1987. reprint ed. pap. text 12.50 (*0-933842-07-4*, UED81) Extension Div.

Ashton, John, jt. auth. see Cerexhe, Peter.

Ashton, John, jt. auth. see Wilson, David.

Ashton, John R., ed. The Epidemiological Imagination: A Reader. LC 94-858. 1994. 122.00 (*0-335-19101-0*); pap. 34.95 (*0-335-19100-2*) OpUniv Pr.

Ashton, John W., ed. Types of English Drama. reprint ed. 79.00 (*0-403-07209-3*) Somerset Pub.

Ashton, Joyce M. & Ashton, Dennis. Loss & Grief Recovery: Help Caring for Children with Disabilities, Chronic, or Terminal Illness. LC 95-40492. 193p. 1996. 29.95 (*0-89503-138-8*) Baywood Pub.

Ashton, Kelly & Weinberg, Pamela. City Baby: A Resource for New York Parents from Pregnancy to Preschool. LC 97-2828. 240p. 1997. pap. 15.95 (*1-885492-33-2*) City & Co.

Ashton, Linda, jt. auth. see Lake, Carlton.

Ashton, M., ed. Advances in Reservoir Geology. (Geological Society Special Publications: No. 69). (Illus.). viii, 240p. (C). 1993. 84.00 (*0-903317-84-2*, 282, Pub. by Geol Soc Pub Hse) AAPG.

Ashton, Mark. Absolute Truth? (IVP Booklets Ser.). 32p. (Orig.). 1996. pap. 0.99 (*0-87784-063-6*, 063) InterVarsity.

— That Infernal Triangle. large type ed. 304p. pap. 18.99 (*0-7089-5454-5*) Ulverscroft.

— Try to Find a Dead Man. large type ed. 256p. pap. 18.99 (*0-7089-5443-X*) Ulverscroft.

Ashton, Mark, ed. see Klingensmith, Samuel J.

***Ashton, Mark S., et al, eds.** Protecting Watershed Areas: Case of the Panama Canal. LC QH77.P357P76 1999. (Journal of Sustainable Forestry Ser.: Vol. 8, Nos. 3/4). 214p. (C). 1999. 49.95 (*1-56022-064-3*, Food Products); pap. 29.95 (*1-56022-066-X*, Food Products) Haworth Pr.

***Ashton, Mark S. & Montagnini, Florencia.** The Silvicultural Basis for Agroforestry Systems. LC 99-46106. 278p. 1999. boxed set 79.95 (*0-8493-2206-5*) CRC Pr.

Ashton, Martha B. Yakshagana: A Dance Drama of India. 1977. 35.00 (*0-88386-972-1*) S Asia.

Ashton, Marvin J. Be of Good Cheer. LC 87-22357. vii, 107p. 1994. pap. 6.95 (*0-87579-837-3*) Deseret Bk.

— The Tongue Can Be a Sharp Sword & While They Are Waiting & Be of Good Cheer. LC 98-72593. (Classic Talk Ser.). 53 p. 1998. write for info. (*0-87579-983-3*) Deseret Bk.

Ashton, Mary, jt. auth. see Compton, Ann.

Ashton-Miller, J. A., ed. Proceedings of the 10th International Conference on Mechanics in Medicine & Biology, Honolulu, Hawaii, March 2-5, 1998. 1998. write for info. (*0-9652469-5-7*) Pac Ctr Thermal.

Ashton, Nigel J. Eisenhower, Macmillan, & the Problem of Nasser: Anglo-American Relations & Arab Nationalism, 1955-59. LC 96-10395. (Studies in Military & Strategic History Ser.). 288p. 1997. text 59.95 (*0-312-16108-5*) St Martin.

***Ashton, Owen.** Duty of Discontent: Essays for Dorothy Thompson. 2000. pap. text 28.95 (*0-8264-4758-9*) Continuum.

Ashton, Owen, et al, eds. The Duty of Discontent: Essays for Dorothy Thompson. LC 95-12596. (Illus.). 192p. 1995. 75.00 (*0-7201-2201-5*) Continuum.

Ashton, Owen, et al. The Chartist Movement: A New Annotated Bibliography. annot. ed. LC 94-37219. 192p. 1995. 100.00 (*0-7201-2177-9*) Continuum.

Ashton, Owen R. & Roberts, Stephen. The Victorian Working-Class Writer. LC 98-26706. 1999. write for info. (*0-7201-2324-0*, Pub. by Mansell Pub) Cassell.

Ashton, Owen R., jt. ed. see Munslow, Alun.

Ashton, P. S. Ecological Studies in the Mixed Dipterocarp Forests of Brunei State. 1964. 60.00 (*0-7855-7178-7*) St Mut.

Ashton, Patricia S., jt. auth. see Ashton, Ray E., Jr.

Ashton, Patricia S., jt. auth. see Eashton, Ray, Jr.

Ashton, Paul & Blackmore, Kate. Centennial Park: A History. 1988. 29.95 (*0-86840-346-6*, Pub. by New South Wales Univ Pr) Intl Spec Bk.

Ashton, Paul L. And Somebody Gives a Damn! (Illus.). 439p. 1990. pap. 30.00 (*0-9627164-1-3*); text 35.00 (*0-9627164-2-1*) Ashton Pubns.

— Bataan Diary by Captain Ashton. LC 85-192945. (Illus.). 463p. (Orig.). 1984. pap. 35.00 (*0-9627164-0-5*) Ashton Pubns.

Ashton, Peter M. & Underwood, Richard C., eds. Non-Point Sources of Water Pollution: Proceedings of Southeastern Regional Conference Conducted on May 1, 1975, Blacksburg, Va. LC TD0423.N6. 318p. reprint ed. pap. 98.60 (*0-608-11571-1*, 200512800050) Bks Demand.

Ashton, Peter S., jt. auth. see Panayotou, Theodore.

Ashton, R., ed. Studies in Ancient Coinage from Turkey. (Monographs: Vol. 17). (Illus.). 227p. 1996. lib. bdg. 85.00 (*0-901405-33-7*, Pub. by Brit Inst Arch) David Brown.

Ashton, Ray E., Jr. & Ashton, Patricia S. The Amphibians. Romashko, Sandra D., ed. LC 81-51066. (Handbook of Reptiles & Amphibians of Florida Ser.: Bk. 3). (Illus.). 192p. 1988. pap. 16.95 (*0-89317-037-2*) Windward Pub.

— Handbook of Reptiles & Amphibians of Florida: Lizards, Turtles & Crocodilians, Part 2. 2nd ed. LC 81-51066. (Illus.). 192p. 1991. pap. 18.95 (*0-89317-036-4*) Windward Pub.

Ashton, Ray E., Jr., jt. ed. see Moler, Paul E.

Ashton, Richard & Leppard, Barbara. Diagnosis & Treatment of Dermatology, 2 vols., Set. 2nd ed. 1995. pap. 69.95 (*0-614-07389-8*, Radcliffe Med Pr) Scovill Paterson.

— Differential Diagnosis in Dermatology. 2nd ed. 1993. 115.00 (*1-870905-47-4*, Radcliffe Med Pr); pap. 49.95 (*1-870905-42-3*, Radcliffe Med Pr) Scovill Paterson.

Ashton, Richard, jt. auth. see Leppard, Barbara.

Ashton, Robert. Counter-revolution: The Second Civil War & Its Origins, 1646-48. LC 94-19546. 520p. 1995. 55.00 (*0-300-06114-5*) Yale U Pr.

Ashton, Robert H. Human Information Processing in Accounting, Vol. 17. (Studies in Accounting Research). 215p. 1982. 12.00 (*0-86539-038-X*) Am Accounting.

***Ashton, Romney W.** The Sequential Gospels. 8th ed. (Illus.). xvi, 384p. 2000. pap. 29.95 (*0-9679166-0-7*) R W Ashton.

Ashton, Ronald S., jt. auth. see Derrington, Justice.

Ashton, Rosemary. George Eliot: A Life. LC 97-129626. (Illus.). 496p. 1998. pap. 15.95 (*0-14-024291-0*) Viking Penguin.

— The German Idea: Four English Writers & the Reception of German Thought, 1800-1860. 245p. 1994. reprint ed. 25.95 (*1-870352-28-9*, Pub. by Libris) Paul & Co Pubs.

— The Life of Samuel Taylor Coleridge: A Critical Biography. Rawson, Claude, ed. LC 95-2820. (Critical Biographies Ser.: Vol. 7). (Illus.). 480p. (C). 1996. 60.95 (*0-631-18746-4*) Blackwell Pubs.

— The Life of Samuel Taylor Coleridge: A Critical Biography. Rawson, Claude, ed. LC 95-2820. (Critical Biographies Ser.: Vol. 7). (Illus.). 480p. (C). 1997. pap. 26.95 (*0-631-20754-6*) Blackwell Pubs.

— The Mill on the Floss: A Natural History. (Twayne's Masterwork Studies: No. 54). 144p. (C). 1990. 23.95 (*0-8057-9406-9*, Twyne); per. 13.95 (*0-8057-8134-X*, Twyne) Mac Lib Ref.

Ashton, Rosemary, ed. see Eliot, George, pseud.

Ashton, Rosemary, ed. & intro. see Eliot, George, pseud.

Ashton, Roy S. Fundamental Chiropractic, a Textbook. 100p. 1996. reprint ed. spiral bd. 25.00 (*0-7873-0044-6*) Hlth Research.

— The Fundamental System: Bad Feet - Bad Spine. 2nd ed. 130p. 1996. reprint ed. spiral bd. 15.50 (*0-7873-0045-4*) Hlth Research.

Ashton, Rudy. Todd & Joey: A Teen Adventure. 128p. (J). 1998. pap. 12.00 (*0-8059-4387-0*) Dorrance.

Ashton, S. R. & Killingray, David, eds. The West Indies. (British Documents on the End of Empire, Series B: Vol. 6). 750p. 264.00 (*0-11-290577-3*, Pub. by Statnry Office) Balogh.

Ashton, S. R., jt. auth. see Kent, John.

Ashton, Sheree J. & Maino, Joseph H. Clinical Geriatric Eyecare. (Illus.). 157p. 1993. text 47.50 (*0-7506-9320-7*) Buttrwrth-Heinemann.

Ashton-Sikora, Martha B. & Sikora, Robert P. Krishnattam. (C). 1993. 34.00 (*81-204-0769-5*, Pub. by Oxford IBH) S Asia.

Ashton, Steve. The Hillwalker's Handbook. (Illus.). 160p. 1996. pap. 35.00 (*1-85223-903-4*, Pub. by Crolwood) Trafalgar.

— Rock Climbing Techniques. (Illus.). 127p. 1991. pap. 19.95 (*1-85223-228-5*, Pub. by Crolwood) Trafalgar.

Ashton, Susanna, jt. ed. see Lutz, Tom.

Ashton, Sylvia, ed. see Bassett, Steve.

Ashton, Sylvia, ed. see Brosten, Olga.

Ashton, Sylvia, ed. see Carter, Frank B., Jr.

Ashton, Sylvia, ed. see Curzon, Daniel.

Ashton, Sylvia, ed. see Duncan, John D., Jr.

Ashton, Sylvia, ed. see Fineberg, Robert G.

Ashton, Sylvia, ed. see Gay, Kathlyn & Barnes, Ben E.

Ashton, Sylvia, ed. see Gestwicki, Ronald.

Ashton, Sylvia, ed. see Goodman, Marguerite.

Ashton, Sylvia, ed. see Healy, John.

Ashton, Sylvia, ed. see Kizilos, Tolly.

Ashton, Sylvia, ed. see Miller, Alan C., et al.

Ashton, Sylvia, ed. see Montgomery, Elizabeth.

Ashton, Sylvia, ed. see Peskin, Dean B.

Ashton, Sylvia, ed. see Peterson, Knut D.

***Ashton, T. S.** The Industrial Revolution, 1760-1830. 2nd ed. LC HC254.5.A78 1997. (Illus.). 160p. (C). 1998. pap. text 16.95 (*0-19-289289-4*) OUP.

Ashton, T. S. Iron & Steel in the Industrial Revolution. (Modern Revivals in Economic & Social History Ser.). 288p. (C). 1993. text 63.95 (*0-7512-0242-8*, Pub. by Gregg Revivals) Ashgate Pub Co.

— La Revolucion Industrial. (Breviarios Ser.). (SPA.). pap. 7.99 (*968-16-0323-0*, Pub. by Fondo) Continental Bk.

Ashton-Tate. DBase IV 1.1. (C). 1991. 57.75 incl. 3.5 hd (*0-201-50645-9*) Addison-Wesley.

Ashton-Tate & Krumm. DBase IV 1.1: Programmer's Bundle. 1992. student ed. 86.25 incl. 5.25 hd (*0-201-50684-X*) Addison-Wesley.

— STU DBASE IV 1 1 PROG PK. 1992. 77.50 incl. 3.5 hd (*0-201-50685-8*) Addison-Wesley.

Ashton, Thomas S. Economic & Social Investigations in Manchester, 1833-1933: A Centenary History of the Manchester Statistical Society. LC 77-3570. xi, 179p. 1977. reprint ed. 35.00 (*0-678-08067-4*) Kelley.

— The Industrial Revolution, Seventeen Sixty to Eighteen Thirty. LC 85-27273. 119p. 1986. reprint ed. lib. bdg. 39.75 (*0-313-25041-3*, ASIR, Greenwood Pr) Greenwood.

Ashton, Tia, et al. AutoCAD Release 14, Level II. McGowan, Mark, ed. Adreamine, Ltd. Staff, tr. (FRE., Illus.). Date not set. pap. text, student ed., spiral bd. 100.00 (*1-890484-40-7*, KnowledgeWorks) HTR Inc.

— AutoCAD Release 14 Instructor Guide, Level 1. Moloney, Laurie, ed. (Illus.). 116p. 1997. pap. text, teacher ed. 25.00 (*1-890484-23-7*, KnowledgeWorks) HTR Inc.

— AutoCAD Release 14 Instructor Guide - Italian, Level 1. McGowan, Mark, ed. Adreamine, Ltd. Staff, tr. (Version 1.0 Ser.). (ITA., Illus.). 1997. pap. text, teacher ed., spiral bd. 25.00 (*1-890484-35-0*, KnowledgeWorks) HTR Inc.

— AutoCAD Release 14 Instructor Guide, Level II. McGowan, Mark, ed. Adreamine, Ltd. Staff, tr. (Illus.). 114p. 1997. pap. text, teacher ed., spiral bd. 25.00 (*1-890484-24-5*, KnowledgeWorks) HTR Inc.

— AutoCAD Release 14 Instructor Guide - Italian, Level II. McGowan, Mark, ed. Adreamine, Ltd. Staff, tr. (ITA., Illus.). 1997. pap. text, teacher ed., spiral bd. 25.00 (*1-890484-43-1*, KnowledgeWorks) HTR Inc.

— AutoCAD Release 14 Instructor Guide - French, Level II. McGowan, Mark, ed. Adreamine, Ltd. Staff, tr. (FRE., Illus.). 1997. pap. text, teacher ed., spiral bd. 25.00 (*1-890484-41-5*, KnowledgeWorks) HTR Inc.

— AutoCAD Release 14 Instructor Guide - German, Level II. McGowan, Mark, ed. Adreamine, Ltd. Staff, tr. (GER., Illus.). 1997. pap. text, teacher ed., spiral bd. 25.00 (*1-890484-45-8*, KnowledgeWorks) HTR Inc.

— AutoCAD Release 14 Student Guide, Level 1. (Version 1.0 Ser.). (Illus.). 780p. 1997. pap. text, student ed. 200.00 (*1-890484-02-4*, KnowledgeWorks) HTR Inc.

— AutoCAD Release 14 Student Guide - French, Level 1. Moloney, Laurie & McGowan, Mark, eds. (Version 1.0 Ser.). (FRE., Illus.). 620p. 1997. pap. text, student ed., spiral bd. 200.00 (*1-890484-32-6*, KnowledgeWorks) HTR Inc.

— AutoCAD Release 14 Student Guide, Level II. Adreamine, Ltd. Staff, tr. (Version 1.0 Ser.). (Illus.). 692p. 1997. pap. text, student ed. 100.00 (*1-890484-03-2*, KnowledgeWorks) HTR Inc.

— AutoCAD Release 14 Student Guide - Italian, Level II. Adreamine, Ltd. Staff, tr. (ITA., Illus.). 1997. pap. text, student ed., spiral bd. 100.00 (*1-890484-42-3*, KnowledgeWorks) HTR Inc.

— AutoCAD Release 14 Student Guide - German, Level II. McGowan, Mark, ed. Adreamine, Ltd. Staff, tr. (GER., Illus.). 1997. pap. text, student ed., spiral bd. 100.00 (*1-890484-44-X*, KnowledgeWorks) HTR Inc.

— AutoCAD Release 14 Update Instructor Guide - French Canadian. Moloney, Laurie, ed. (Version 1.0 Ser.). (FRE., Illus.). 1997. pap. text, teacher ed., spiral bd. 25.00 (*1-890484-50-4*, KnowledgeWorks) HTR Inc.

— AutoCAD Release 14 Update Student Guide - French Canadian. Moloney, Laurie & McGowan, Mark, eds. (Version 1.0 Ser.). (FRE., Illus.). 1997. pap. text, student ed., spiral bd. 100.00 (*1-890484-49-0*, KnowledgeWorks) HTR Inc.

— AutoCAD Release 14 Update Training. McGowan, Mark & Jaros, Kate, eds. (Version 1.3 Ser.). (Illus.). 497p. 1997. spiral bd. 100.00 (*1-890484-00-8*, KnowledgeWorks) HTR Inc.

— AutoCAD Release 14 Update Training - French - Student Guide. McGowan, Mark, ed. Adreamine, Ltd. Staff, tr. (FRE., Illus.). 529p. 1997. pap. text, student ed., spiral bd. 100.00 (*1-890484-09-1*, KnowledgeWorks) HTR Inc.

— AutoCAD Release 14 Update Training Student Guide - Italian. McGowan, Mark, ed. Adreamine, Ltd. Staff, tr. (ITA., Illus.). 510p. 1997. pap. text, student ed., spiral bd. 100.00 (*1-890484-11-3*, KnowledgeWorks) HTR Inc.

— AutoCad Release 14 Update Training Instructor Guide - Italian. McGowan, Mark, ed. Adreamine, Ltd. Staff, tr. (ITA., Illus.). 78p. 1997. pap. text, teacher ed., spiral bd. 25.00 (*1-890484-12-1*, KnowledgeWorks) HTR Inc.

— AutoCAD Release 14 Update Training Student Guide - German. McGowan, Marie, ed. Adreamine, Ltd. Staff, tr. (GER., Illus.). 536p. 1997. pap. text, student ed., spiral bd. 100.00 (*1-890484-13-X*, KnowledgeWorks) HTR Inc.

— AutoCAD Release 14 Update Training Instructor Guide - German. McGowan, Mark, ed. Adreamine, Ltd. Staff, tr. (GER., Illus.). 80p. 1997. pap. text, teacher ed., spiral bd. 25.00 (*1-890484-14-8*, KnowledgeWorks) HTR Inc.

— AutoCAD Release 14 Update Training Student Guide - Spanish. McGowan, Mark, ed. (SPA., Illus.). 54p. 1997. pap. text, student ed., spiral bd. 25.00 (*1-890484-15-6*, KnowledgeWorks) HTR Inc.

— AutoCAD Release 14 Update Training Instructor Guide - Spanish. Adreamine, Ltd. Staff, tr. (SPA., Illus.). 1997. pap. text, teacher ed., spiral bd. 25.00 (*1-890484-16-4*, KnowledgeWorks) HTR Inc.

— AutoCAD Release 14 Update Training Student Guide - Taiwan. McGowan, Mark, ed. (Illus.). 1997. pap. text, student ed., spiral bd. 100.00 (*1-890484-17-2*, KnowledgeWorks) HTR Inc.

— AutoCAD Release 14 Update Training Instructor Guide - Taiwan. McGowan, Mark, ed. (Illus.). 1997. pap. text, teacher ed., spiral bd. 25.00 (*1-890484-18-0*, KnowledgeWorks) HTR Inc.

— AutoCAD Release 14 Update Training Student Guide - Japanese. McGowan, Mark, ed. (JPN., Illus.). 1997. pap. text, student ed., spiral bd. 100.00 (*1-890484-19-9*, KnowledgeWorks) HTR Inc.

— AutoCAD Release 14 Update Training Student Guide - Korean. McGowan, Mark, ed. (KOR., Illus.). 1997. pap. text, student ed., spiral bd. 100.00 (*1-890484-21-0*, KnowledgeWorks) HTR Inc.

— AutoCAD Release 14 Update Training Instructor Guide - Korean. McGowan, Mark, ed. (KOR., Illus.). 1997. pap. text, teacher ed., spiral bd. 25.00 (*1-890484-22-9*, KnowledgeWorks) HTR Inc.

— AutoCAD Release Instructor Guide - French, Level 1. Adreamine, Ltd. Staff, tr. (Version 1.0 Ser.). (FRE., Illus.). 1997. pap. text, teacher ed., spiral bd. 25.00 (*1-890484-33-4*, KnowledgeWorks) HTR Inc.

— AutoCAD Release Student Guide - Italian, Level 1. McGowan, Mark, ed. Adreamine, Ltd. Staff, tr. (Version 1.0 Ser.). (ITA., Illus.). 1997. pap. text, student ed., spiral bd. 200.00 (*1-890484-34-2*, KnowledgeWorks) HTR Inc.

Ashton, Tita, et al. AutoCAD Release 14 Student Guide - German, Level 1. McGowan, Mark, ed. Adreamine, Ltd. Staff, tr. (Version 1.0 Ser.). (GER., Illus.). 1997. pap. text, student ed., spiral bd. 200.00 (*1-890484-36-9*, KnowledgeWorks) HTR Inc.

Ashton, W. Bradford & Klavans, Richard S., eds. Keeping Abreast of Science & Technology: Technical Intelligence in Business. LC 96-31063. 565p. 1997. 44.95 (*1-57477-018-7*) Battelle.

Ashton-Warner, Sylvia. Teacher. 224p. 1986. pap. 11.00 (*0-671-61768-0*, Touchstone) S&S Trade Pap.

Ashton, Warren T. Hatchie, the Guardian Slave. LC 72-539. (Black Heritage Library Collection). 1977. reprint ed. 22.95 (*0-8369-8976-7*) Ayer.

Ashtor, Eliyahu. East-West Trade in the Medieval Mediterranean. Kedar, Benjamin Z., ed. (Collected Studies: No. CS245). 344p. (C). 1986. reprint ed. lib. bdg. 107.95 (*0-86078-193-3*, Pub. by Variorum) Ashgate Pub Co.

— The Jews of Moslem Spain, 2 vols., Set. LC 73-14081. 1993. reprint ed. pap. text 38.95 (*0-8276-0432-7*) JPS Phila.

— The Jews of Moslem Spain, 2 vols., Vol. 1. LC 73-14081. 474p. 1993. reprint ed. pap. text 19.95 (*0-8276-0427-0*) JPS Phila.

— The Jews of Moslem Spain, 2 vols., Vol. 2-3. LC 73-14081. 692p. 1993. reprint ed. pap. text 19.95 (*0-8276-0428-9*) JPS Phila.

— Studies on Levantine Trade in the Middle Ages. (Collected Studies: No. CS74). (FRE & ITA.). 372p. (C). 1978. reprint ed. lib. bdg. 128.95 (*0-86078-020-1*, Pub. by Variorum) Ashgate Pub Co.

— Technology, Industry & Trade: The Levant vs. Europe, 1250-1500. Kedar, Benjamin Z., ed. (Collected Studies: No. CS372). 350p. 1992. 115.95 (*0-86078-323-5*, Pub. by Variorum) Ashgate Pub Co.

***Ashtor, Gila.** Silver Lining. 1999. pap. write for info. (*1-57553-885-7*) Watermrk Pr.

Ashtree, Elizabeth. An Officer & a Hero. (Superromance Ser.: No. 828). 1999. mass mkt. 4.25 (*0-373-70828-9*, 1-70828-8) Harlequin Bks.

***Ashu, M. N. F.** Lebialem Story. 135p. 1999. pap. text 20.00 (*0-9663613-1-8*) Nkemnji Global.

Ashuli. Healed & Souled. (C). 1988. 50.00 (*0-85439-270-X*, Pub. by St Paul Pubns) St Mut.

Ashurakis, A. Let's Learn Arabic. 72p. 1984. pap. 45.00 (*1-85077-007-7*, Pub. by Darf Pubs Ltd) St Mut.

Ashurkov, ed. see Alcantara.

An Asterisk (*) at the beginning of an entry indicates that the title is appearing for the first time.

Ashurov, R. R., et al. Commutative Harmonic Analysis, IV: Harmonic Analysis in Rn. Khavin, V. P. & Nikol'skij, N. K., eds. Peetre, J., tr. from RUS. (Encyclopedia of Mathematical Sciences Ser.: Vol. 42). ix, 228p. 1991. 118.95 (*0-387-53379-6*) Spr-Verlag.

Ashurst. Practical Building Conservations, Vol.5. 128p. 1988. 51.95 (*0-291-39776-X*) Ashgate Pub Co.

Ashurst, Doanld, et al. Developmental Scale of Social-Affective Behavior. LC 84-73558. (Southern California Ordinal Scales of Development Ser.). 84p. 1985. student ed. 20.00 (*0-943292-19-0*) Foreworks.

Ashurst, Donald, et al. Developmental Scale of Cognition. LC 84-73556. (Southern California Ordinal Scales of Development Ser.). 146p. 1985. student ed. 25.00 (*0-943292-17-4*) Foreworks.

— Developmental Scale of Communication: Southern California Orginal Scales of Development. LC 85-71210. 184p. 1985. student ed. 25.00 (*0-943292-18-2*) Foreworks.

— Developmental Scale of Fine Motor Abilities. LC 84-73557. (Southern California Ordinal Scales of Development Ser.). 92p. 1985. pap., student ed. 20.00 (*0-943292-21-2*) Foreworks.

— Developmental Scale of Gross Motor Abilities. LC 85-71209. (Southern California Ordinal Scales of Development Ser.). 70p. 1985. student ed. 20.00 (*0-943292-22-0*) Foreworks.

— Developmental Scale of Practical Abilities. LC 85-71211. (Southern California Ordinal Scales of Development Ser.). 62p. 1985. student ed. 20.00 (*0-943292-20-4*) Foreworks.

Ashurst, Henry F. A Many-Colored Toga: Diary. Sparks, George F., ed. LC 62-10625. (Illus.). 435p. reprint ed. pap. 124.30 (*0-608-02354-X*, 2062995) Bks Demand.

Ashurst, J. Conservation of Building & Decorative Stone. 2nd ed. 468p. 1998. pap. text 59.95 (*0-7506-3898-2*) Buttrwrth-Heinemann.

Ashurst, J. & Dimes, F. G. Conservation of Building & Decorative Stone, 2 vols., Set. (Conservation & Museology Ser.: Vols. 1 & 2). (Illus.). 364p. 1991. 210.00 (*0-7506-1277-0*, Butterwrth Archit) Buttrwrth-Heinemann.

Ashurst, John & Malnic, Nicola. Practical Building Conservation, Vol.2. 1988. 51.95 (*0-291-39746-8*) Ashgate Pub Co.

— Practical Building Conservation, Vol.4. 1988. 51.95 (*0-291-39748-4*) Ashgate Pub Co.

Ashurst, P. R. Food Flavorings. 1991. text 105.00 (*0-442-30281-9*) Chapman & Hall.

— Food Flavorings. 3rd rev. ed. 400p. 1999. 89.00 (*0-8342-1318-4*) Aspen Pub.

— Food Flavourings. 3rd ed. LC 99-27422. 1999. 135.00 (*0-8342-1621-3*) Aspen Pub.

Ashurst, Pamela & Hall, Zaida, eds. Understanding Women in Distress. 272p. 1989. 49.95 (*0-415-01832-3*) Routledge.

***Ashurst, Philip R.** Production & Packaging of Non-Carbonated Fruit Juices & Fruit Beverages. 2nd ed. 429p. 1998. 165.00 (*0-8342-1289-7*) Aspen Pub.

Ashwal, Lewis D. Anorthosites. LC 93-9391. (Minerals & Rocks Ser.: Vol. 21). 1993. 135.95 (*0-387-55361-4*) Spr-Verlag.

Ashwal, Lewis D., jt. ed. see De Wit, Maarten J.

Ashwal, Stephen, ed. The Founders of Child Neurology. (Illus.). 952p. 1990. 125.00 (*0-930405-26-9*) Norman SF.

Ashwal, Stephen, jt. ed. see Swaiman, Kenneth F.

Ashwanden & Belcher Staff. Oncology Nursing: Advances, Treatments, & Trends into the Twenty-First Century. LC 90-648. 414p. 1990. 70.00 (*0-8342-0168-2*, 20168) Aspen Pub.

Ashwander, Donald, jt. auth. see Martin, Judith.

Ashwell, D. G., ed. see Conference on Finite Elements Applied to Thin Shells & Curved Members (1974: Univ. College, Cardiff.

Ashwell, Geoffrey J. & Bloor, David, eds. Organic Materials for Non-Linear Optics II. 362p. 1993. 142.00 (*0-85186-625-5*, Q) CRC Pr.

Ashwell, Julia. Beloved Pretender. large type ed. (Linford Romance Library). 272p. 1992. pap. 16.99 (*0-7089-7191-1*, Linford) Ulverscroft.

— The Eighteenth Summer. large type ed. (Linford Romance Library). 272p. 1993. pap. 16.99 (*0-7089-7393-0*) Ulverscroft.

— An Irresistible Force. large type ed. (General Ser.). 512p. 1993. 27.99 (*0-7089-2799-8*) Ulverscroft.

— Never Too Late. large type ed. (Large Print Ser.). 336p. 1997. 27.99 (*0-7089-3660-1*) Ulverscroft.

— The Perfume of Roses. large type ed. (Linford Romance Library). 240p. 1992. pap. 16.99 (*0-7089-7285-3*, Linford) Ulverscroft.

— Summer Storms. large type ed. (Linford Romance Library). 256p. 1994. pap. 16.99 (*0-7089-7550-X*) Ulverscroft.

— A Tangled Web. large type ed. 352p. 1995. 27.99 (*0-7089-3343-2*) Ulverscroft.

— A Touch of Romance. large type ed. 336p. 1996. 27.99 (*0-7089-3623-7*) Ulverscroft.

— Where the Heart Is. large type ed. 336p. 1996. 27.99 (*0-7089-3459-5*) Ulverscroft.

Ashwell, M., ed. Complex Carbohydrates in Food: The Report of the British Nutrition Foundation's Task Force. (Illus.). 176p. 1990. pap. 78.95 (*0-442-31288-1*) Chapman & Hall.

— McCance & Widdowson: A Scientific Partnership of Sixty Years. (Illus.). 264p. 1993. pap. 37.50 (*0-907667-07-4*) ILSI.

Ashwell, Malcolm & Pearson, Sally. Professional Floristry Techniques. (Illus.). 300p. text 49.95 (*0-85236-275-7*, Pub. by Farming Pr) Diamond Farm Bk.

Ashwell, Miranda, jt. auth. see Owen, Andy.

Ashwell, Pauline. Project Farcry. 1996. mass mkt. 5.99 (*0-8125-3446-8*) Tor Bks.

— Unwillingly to Earth. 288p. 1992. mass mkt. 3.99 (*0-8125-1929-9*, Pub. by Tor Bks) St Martin.

Ashwell, Rachel. Rachel Ashwell's Shabby Chic Treasure Hunting & Decorating Guide. LC 98-6994. (Illus.). 224p. 1998. 35.00 (*0-06-039208-8*, ReganBks) HarperTrade.

***Ashwell, Rachel.** The Shabby Chic Home. LC 99-59407. (Illus.). 224p. 2000. 35.00 (*0-06-039319-X*, ReganBks) HarperTrade.

Ashwell, Rachel & Costin, Glynis. Shabby Chic: Simple Living, the Comfort of Age & the Beauty of Imperfection. LC 96-32371. (Illus.). 208p. 1996. 35.00 (*0-06-098204-7*) HarpC.

Ashwell, Reg. Coast Salish. (Illus.). 88p. 1978. pap. 7.95 (*0-88839-009-2*) Hancock House.

— Indian Tribes of the N. W. (Illus.). 64p. 1989. pap. 8.95 (*0-919654-53-3*) Hancock House.

Ashwill, Beverley B. The Blue-Eyed Ninja Warrior. LC 90-83313. (Illus.). 43p. (J). (gr. 3-9). 1990. pap. 5.98 (*0-941381-05-6*) BJO Enterprises.

— Heather & the New Baby. LC 88-63168. (Illus.). 23p. (Orig.). (J). (gr. k-3). 1988. pap. 3.98 (*0-941381-03-X*) BJO Enterprises.

— Marlina & McGee. LC 86-73031. (Illus.). 32p. (J). (ps-3). 1987. pap. 5.95 (*0-941381-00-5*) BJO Enterprises.

— The Runaways. LC 87-72441. (Illus.). 48p. (J). (gr. 4-8). 1988. 12.95 (*0-941381-02-1*); pap. 5.95 (*0-941381-01-3*) BJO Enterprises.

— Too Little, Too Big, Just Right. LC 90-83314. (Illus.). 18p. (J). (ps-3). 1990. pap. 3.98 (*0-941381-04-8*) BJO Enterprises.

Ashwill, Beverly B. Charley the Fearless Zoo Keeper. LC 90-83311. (Illus.). 20p. (J). (ps-3). 1990. pap. 3.98 (*0-941381-07-2*) BJO Enterprises.

— The Invisible Dawn. LC 90-83310. (Illus.). 24p. (J). (ps-5). 1990. pap. 3.98 (*0-941381-08-0*) BJO Enterprises.

— Jeffrey, the Littlest Pig. LC 90-83312. (Illus.). 24p. (J). (ps-3). 1990. pap. 3.98 (*0-941381-06-4*) BJO Enterprises.

Ashwill, Helen. Good Lies for Ladies: Tips, Quips & Quotes Just for Women Golfers. 1994. 6.50 (*1-56245-164-2*) Great Quotations.

Ashwill, Jean W. Nursing Care of Children. 1997. pap. text, student ed. 16.50 (*0-7216-7285-X*, W B Saunders Co) Harcrt Hlth Sci Grp.

Ashwill, Jean W. & Droske, Susan C. Clinical Companion to Nursing Care of Children: Principles & Practice. LC 97-188443. (Illus.). 240p. 1997. pap. text 19.95 (*0-7216-6489-X*, W B Saunders Co) Harcrt Hlth Sci Grp.

— Nursing Care of Children: Principles & Practice. Rader, Ilze, ed. LC 96-16728. (Illus.). 1264p. 1997. pap. text 61.95 (*0-7216-6488-1*, W B Saunders Co) Harcrt Hlth Sci Grp.

Ashwill, Jean W. & Droske, Susan C., eds. Nursing Care of Children: Principles & Practice. 1997. teacher ed. write for info. (*0-7216-6502-0*, W B Saunders Co) Harcrt Hlth Sci Grp.

Ashwill, Jean W., jt. auth. see Thompson, Eleanor D.

Ashwin, Angela, compiled by. The Book of a Thousand Prayers. 461p. 1996. 15.00 (*0-551-02865-3*, Pub. by M Pickering) Harper SF.

Ashwin, E. A., tr. see Guazzo, Francesco M.

Ashwin, Mary, jt. auth. see Compton, Ann.

***Ashwin, Sarah.** Gender, State & Society in Soviet & Post-Soviet Russia. LC 99-88907. 2000. pap. write for info. (*0-415-23883-8*) Routledge.

Ashwin, Sarah. Russian Workers: The Anatomy of Patience. LC 99-491010. 1999. 69.95 (*0-7190-5611-X*, Pub. by Manchester Univ Pr) St Martin.

***Ashwins.** Terratrek, No. 3. 2002. lib. bdg. write for info. (*0-06-028541-9*) HarpC Child Bks.

— Terratrek, No. 3. (J). 2002. pap. write for info. (*0-06-440829-9*, HarpTrophy) HarpC Child Bks.

— Terratrek, No. 4. (J). 2002. pap. write for info. (*0-06-440828-0*, HarpTrophy); lib. bdg. write for info. (*0-06-028540-0*) HarpC Child Bks.

Ashwood-Collins, Anna. Deadly Resolutions. 1995. write for info. (*4-06-184902-6*, Pub. by Kodansha Ltd) Kodansha.

— Deadly Resolutions. 1989. 18.95 (*0-8027-5739-1*) Walker & Co.

Ashwood, Edward R., jt. auth. see Burtis, Carl A.

Ashwood, Neil. Vietnam, a Business Guide. LC 94-29515. 1995. lib. bdg. 110.00 (*1-85966-083-5*) G & T Inc.

Ashworth. Contractual Procedures in Construction Industry. 1991. pap. text. write for info. (*0-582-07617-X*, Pub. by Addison-Wesley) Longman.

— New Perspectives Internal Functionalism. LC 98-16547. 208p. 1998. text 65.00 (*0-312-21575-4*) St Martin.

— Pre-Contract Studies. 1996. pap. text. write for info. (*0-582-24984-8*) Addison-Wesley.

— Tourist Historic City. 1989. 46.25 (*1-85293-022-5*, Belhaven) Halsted Pr.

Ashworth & Clark. Nelson Picture Dictionary English. Date not set. pap. text. write for info. (*0-17-556454-X*) Addison-Wesley.

— Steps to Handwriting. Date not set. pap. text. write for info. (*0-17-556876-6*) Addison-Wesley.

— Where's My Baby? (Footsteps Big Bk.). (J). 1991. pap. text. write for info. (*0-17-556759-X*) Addison-Wesley.

Ashworth & Harvey. Construction Industry of Great Britain. 2nd ed. 1997. pap. 32.50 (*0-7506-3656-4*) Buttrwrth-Heinemann.

Ashworth, A. C., et al. Studies in Quaternary Entomology: An Inordinate Fondness for Insects. LC 97-29223. (Quaternary Proceedings Ser.). 314p. 1998. pap. 75.00 (*0-471-96975-3*) Wiley.

Ashworth, Adele. My Darling Caroline. 352p. 1998. mass mkt. 5.99 (*0-515-12369-2*, Jove) Berkley Pub.

— Stolen Charms, 1 vol. 1999. mass mkt. 5.99 (*0-515-12565-2*, Jove) Berkley Pub.

***Ashworth, Adele.** Winter Garden. 2000. mass mkt. 6.99 (*0-515-12866-X*, Jove) Berkley Pub.

Ashworth, Allan. Civil Engineering Contractural Procedures. (C). 1998. pap. text 54.95 (*0-582-25127-3*) Addison-Wesley.

— Contractual Procedures in the Construction Industry. 3rd ed. (C). 1996. pap. text. write for info. (*0-582-28875-4*, Pub. by Addison-Wesley) Longman.

Ashworth, Andrea. Once in a House on Fire. LC 97-46680. 327p. 1998. 23.00 (*0-8050-5762-5*, Metropol Bks) H Holt & Co.

— Once in a House on Fire: A Memoir. 336p. 1999. pap. 14.00 (*0-8050-5763-3*, Owl) H Holt & Co.

Ashworth, Andrew. Criminal Process: An Evaluative Study. 336p. 1994. 85.00 (*0-19-876262-3*) OUP.

— The Criminal Process: An Evaluative Study. 2nd ed. LC 98-20507. 364p. 1998. pap. text (*0-19-876536-3*) OUP.

— The Criminal Process: An Evaluative Study. 2nd ed. 364p. 1998. text 75.00 (*0-19-876537-1*) OUP.

***Ashworth, Andrew.** Principles of Criminal Law. 3rd ed. LC 99-32728. 568p. 1999. write for info. (*0-19-876557-6*) OUP.

Ashworth, Andrew. Sentencing & Criminal Justice. 2nd ed. 370p. 1995. pap. text 40.00 (*0-406-04538-0*, MICHIE) LEXIS Pub.

***Ashworth, Andrew & Mitchell, Barry, eds.** Rethinking English Homicide Law. (Oxford Monographs on Criminal Law & Justice). 320p. 2000. text 70.00 (*0-19-829904-4*) OUP.

Ashworth, Andrew, et al. Criminal Litigation & Sentencing, 1997/98. 2nd ed. (Inns of Court School of Law Ser.). 375p. 1997. pap. 40.00 (*1-85431-677-X*, Pub. by Blackstone Pr) Gaunt.

— Criminal Litigation & Sentencing, 1998-99. 3rd ed. (Inns of Court School of Law Ser.). 383p. 1998. pap. 42.00 (*1-85431-775-X*) Gaunt.

***Ashworth, Andrew, et al.** Criminal Litigation & Sentencing, 1999-2000. 4th ed. (Inns of Court School of Law Ser.). 401p. 1999. pap. 38.00 (*1-85431-958-2*, Pub. by Blackstone Pr) Gaunt.

Ashworth, Ann-Marie, jt. auth. see Russell, Terence M.

Ashworth, Bessie. Special Special. 53p. (Orig.). 1995. pap. 12.95 (*0-922510-11-3*) Lucky Bks.

***Ashworth, Bessie.** Woman Thou Are Called. 78p. 1999. pap. 10.00 (*0-7392-0242-1*, 3164) Morris Pubng.

Ashworth, Camilla. La Cama De Horacio - Horatio's Bed. 1995. pap. text 11.95 (*1-56014-581-1*) Santillana.

Ashworth, Caroline & Slater, Laurence. An Introduction to SSADM Version 4. LC 92-46102. (International Series in Software Engineering). 1993. 19.95 (*0-07-707725-3*) McGraw.

Ashworth, Clarice, jt. auth. see Jacob, Stanley.

Ashworth, Clark. Steps to Handwriting, Bk. 2. 1991. pap. text. write for info. (*0-00-370422-X*) Addison-Wesley.

Ashworth, Clark & Clark. Nelson Picture Dictionary French. (Illus.). 1993. pap. text. write for info. (*0-17-556452-3*) Addison-Wesley.

Ashworth, Donna. Against This Ground. LC 93-87445. (Illus.). (Orig.). 1994. pap. write for info. (*0-9630364-2-4*) Small Mtn.

Ashworth, E. J. Language & Logic in the Post Medieval Period. LC 74-76478. (Synthese Historical Library: No. 12). 319p. 1974. text 176.50 (*90-277-0464-3*) Kluwer Academic.

— Paul of Venice: Logica Magna, Fascicule 8, Pt. II. (Classical & Medieval Logic Texts Ser.: Vol. V). (Illus.). 426p. 1989. 140.00 (*0-19-726065-9*) OUP.

— Studies in Post-Medieval Semantics. (Collected Studies: No. CS227). 342p. (C). 1985. reprint ed. text 119.95 (*0-86078-175-5*, Pub. by Variorum) Ashgate Pub Co.

Ashworth, E. M. Toronto Hydro Recollections. LC TK1427.O5A8. (Illus.). 246p. reprint ed. pap. 76.30 (*0-608-10248-2*, 201411600096) Bks Demand.

Ashworth, Earline J. The Tradition of Medieval Logic & Speculative Grammar from Anselm to the End of the Seventeenth Century: A Bibliography from 1836 Onwards. x, 111p. pap. 17.14 (*0-88844-358-7*) Brill Academic Pubs.

***Ashworth, Elizabeth.** So I Kissed Her Little Sister. 122p. 2000. pap. 11.95 (*1-902638-02-6*, Pub. by Parthian) Dufour.

Ashworth, Eric. Language Policy in the Primary School: Content & Management. LC 87-30334. 1987. write for info. (*0-7099-5128-0*, Pub. by C Helm); pap. write for info. (*0-7099-5140-X*, Pub. by C Helm) Routldge.

Ashworth-Fielder, Sue. Teach Yourself Beginner's German. (Teach Yourself Beginner's Grammar Ser.). 224p. 1999. pap. 10.95 (*0-8442-2690-4*, Teach Yrslf) NTC Contemp Pub Co.

Ashworth, G. J. & Dietvorst, eds. Tourism & Spatial Transformation: Implications for Policy & Planning. (Illus.). 360p. 1996. text 90.00 (*0-85198-981-0*) OUP.

***Ashworth, G. J. & Tunbridge, J. E.** The Tourist-Historic City: Retrospect & Prospect of Managing the Heritage City. LC 00-29339. 2000. write for info. (*0-08-043675-7*, Pergamon Pr) Elsevier.

Ashworth, G. J. & Voogd, H. Selling the City: Marketing Approaches in Public Sector Urban Planning. 226p. 1993. 130.00 (*0-471-94470-X*) Wiley.

***Ashworth, Gary.** Delivering Shareholder Value Through Integrated Performance Management. (Illus.). 142p. 1999. pap. 167.50 (*0-273-63868-8*, Pub. by F T P-H) Trans-Atl Phila.

***Ashworth, Gregory & Hartmann, Rudi, eds.** Horror & Human Tragedy Revisited: Management of Sites of Atrocities for Tourism. (Unnumbered Ser.). (Illus.). 250p. 2001. text 42.00 (*1-882345-34-7*); pap. text 35.00 (*1-882345-35-5*) Cognizant Comm.

Ashworth, Gregory & Tunbridge, John E. Dissonant Heritage. 1994. text 59.95 (*0-470-22037-6*) Wiley.

— Dissonant Heritage. LC 95-25159. 314p. 1996. 120.00 (*0-471-94887-X*) Wiley.

Ashworth, Gregory, jt. ed. see Howard, Peter.

Ashworth, Gregory J. & Goodall, Brian. Marketing Tourism Places. 304p. (C). (gr. 13). 1990. pap. 74.95 (*0-415-03810-3*, A4064) Thomson Learn.

Ashworth, Gregory J., jt. ed. see Goodall, Brian.

Ashworth, H., jt. auth. see Shacklette, L.

Ashworth, J. R. & Brown, M. High-Temperature Metamorphism & Crustal Anatexis. (Earth & Soil Science: No. 2). (Illus.). 384p. (C). 1990. pap. 149.95 (*0-04-445721-9*) Thomson Learn.

Ashworth, J. S., ed. Product Liability Casebook. (C). 1984. 365.00 (*0-7855-4058-X*, Pub. by Witherby & Co) St Mut.

Ashworth, John. Slavery, Capitalism & Politics in the Antebellum Republic Vol. 1: Commerce & Compromise, 1820-1850. (Illus.). 532p. (C). 1996. pap. text 22.95 (*0-521-47994-0*) Cambridge U Pr.

— Slavery, Capitalism & Politics in the Antebellum Republic Vol. 1: Commerce & Compromise, 1820-1850. (Illus.). 532p. (C). 1996. text 69.95 (*0-521-47487-6*) Cambridge U Pr.

***Ashworth, Julie.** The Longman Picture Dictionary: American English. 1999. pap. text 14.67 (*0-582-29981-0*) Addison-Wesley.

— Longman Picture Dictionary: American-Japanese. 1999. pap. text 16.00 (*0-582-33295-8*) Addison-Wesley.

— Longman Picture Dictionary: American-Korean. 1999. pap. text 16.80 (*0-582-33297-4*) Addison-Wesley.

Ashworth, Karl, jt. auth. see Walker, Robert, Jr.

Ashworth, Kenneth, jt. auth. see Hackerman, Norman.

***Ashworth, Lonny J.** Aerosol Therapy. (CPG Mentor - Patient Cases in Respiratory Care Ser.: Unit 3). 1998. write for info. (*0-8151-2285-3*) Mosby Inc.

— Bronchial Hygiene. (CPG Mentor - Patient Cases in Respiratory Care Ser.: Unit 4). 1998. write for info. (*0-8151-2286-1*) Mosby Inc.

— Hyperinflation Therapy. (CPG Mentor - Patient Cases in Respiratory Care Ser.: Unit 1). 1998. write for info. (*0-8151-2277-2*) Mosby Inc.

— Invasive & Non-Invasive Blood Gas Sampling & Analysis. (CPG Mentor - Patient Cases in Respiratory Care Ser.: Unit 5). 1998. write for info. (*0-8151-2287-X*) Mosby Inc.

— Mechanical Ventilation. (CPG Mentor - Patient Cases in Respiratory Care Ser.: Unit 6). 1998. write for info. (*0-8151-2290-X*) Mosby Inc.

— Mosby's CPG Mentor - Patient Cases in Respiratory Care Series, 8 Units. 1998. write for info. (*0-8151-2276-4*) Mosby Inc.

— Oxygen Therapy. (CPG Mentor - Patient Cases in Respiratory Care Ser.: Unit 2). 1998. write for info. (*0-8151-2278-0*) Mosby Inc.

— Resuscitation. (CPG Mentor - Patient Cases in Respiratory Care Ser.: Unit 7). 1998. write for info. (*0-8151-2300-0*) Mosby Inc.

— Spirometry & Lung Volume Measurement. (CPG Mentor - Patient Cases in Respiratory Care Ser.: Unit 8). 1998. write for info. (*0-8151-2301-9*) Mosby Inc.

Ashworth, Lucian M. Creating International Studies: Angell, Mitrany & the Liberal Tradition. 208p. 1999. text 65.95 (*0-7546-1048-9*, Pub. by Ashgate Pub) Ashgate Pub Co.

Ashworth, Lucille E. Revelation: Signs of the Times. (Illus.). 240p. (Orig.). (YA). (gr. 10). 1990. pap. 5.95 (*0-9627415-0-7*) Advent Times.

Ashworth, M. J. Feedback Design of Systems with Significant Uncertainty. LC 82-1929. No. 1. (Illus.). 262p. reprint ed. pap. 81.30 (*0-8357-6110-X*, 203421200089) Bks Demand.

Ashworth, M. R., tr. see Stahl, E., ed.

Ashworth, Mary. The First Step on the Longer Path: Becoming an ESL Teacher. (Pippin Teacher's Library Ser.). 128p. 1995. pap. text 15.00 (*0-88751-054-X*, 00715) Heinemann.

— Teaching the World's Children: ESL for Ages Three to Seven. LC 95-106828. (Pippin Teacher's Library Ser.). 96p. 1994. pap. text 14.50 (*0-88751-062-0*, 00761) Heinemann.

Ashworth, Mary & Wakefield, Patricia. Teaching the Non-English-Speaking Child: Grades K-2. LC PE1128.A2A75. (Language in Education: Theory & Practice Ser.: No. 45). 60p. reprint ed. pap. 30.00 (*0-8357-3345-9*, 203957800013) Bks Demand.

Ashworth, P., et al, eds. Qualitative Research in Psychology. LC 85-27415. 384p. (C). 1986. text 24.95 (*0-8207-0187-4*) Duquesne.

Ashworth, P. & Bjorn, A. People's Needs for Nursing Care: A European Study. 1987. pap. text 22.00 (*92-890-1041-X*) World Health.

***Ashworth, Peter D.** Psychology & 'Human Nature' LC 00-33761. 2000. write for info. (*0-415-21300-2*) Taylor & Francis.

Ashworth, Peter D. Social Interaction & Consciousness. LC 78-27252. 237p. reprint ed. pap. 73.50 (*0-8357-4608-9*, 203754100008) Bks Demand.

Ashworth, Philip A., jt. auth. see Taswell-Langmead, Thomas P.

Ashworth, Philip A., tr. see Gneist, Rudolph.

Ashworth, Philip J., et al, eds. Coherent Flow Structures in Open Channels. LC 96-17737. 754p. 1996. text 200.00 (*0-471-95723-2*) Wiley.

***Ashworth, Ralph.** Greetings from Pittsburgh: A Picture Postcard History. (Illus.). 2000. pap. 19.95 (*1-879511-45-2*, Vestal Pr) Madison Bks UPA.

Ashworth, Sam & Norberg, Fran, eds. Cincinnati Symphony Orchestra: Centennial Portraits. 160p. 1995. 35.00 (*0-9643686-0-9*); pap. 20.00 (*0-9643686-1-7*) Cincinn Symp.

An Asterisk (*) at the beginning of an entry indicates that the title is appearing for the first time.

Ashworth, Sara, jt. auth. see Mosston, Muska.

Ashworth, Sherry. Money Talks. large type unabridged ed. 416p. 1998. 26.95 (*0-7531-5857-4*, 158574) ISIS Pub.

Ashworth, Sue. Italian Farmhouse Cooking. 1995. 5.98 (*0-7858-0422-6*) Bk Sales Inc.

— James, Jellies & Preserves. 64p. 1995. 5.98 (*0-7858-0424-2*) Bk Sales Inc.

Ashworth, Suzanne. Seed to Seed: Seed Saving Techniques for the Vegetable Gardener. LC 90-62386. (Illus.). 224p. 1995. pap. 20.00 (*0-9613977-7-2*, Pub. by Seed Savers) Chelsea Green Pub.

Ashworth, V. & Booker, C. J. Cathodic Protection: Theory & Practice. LC 85-30537. 357p. 1986. text 87.95 (*0-470-20283-1*) P-H.

Ashworth, William. Encyclopedia of Environmental Studies. (Illus.). 464p. 1991. 65.00 (*0-8160-1531-7*) Facts on File.

***Ashworth, William.** Great Lakes Journey: A New Look at America's Freshwater Coast. (Illus.). 288p. 2000. 29.95 (*0-8143-2836-9*, Great Lks Bks) Wayne St U Pr.

Ashworth, William. History of the British Coal Industry, Vol. 5: 1946-1982 - The Nationalized Industry. (Illus.). 734p. 1986. text 115.00 (*0-19-828295-8*) OUP.

— The Late Great Lakes: An Environmental History. LC 87-6132. (Great Lakes Bks.). 286p. 1987. pap. 19.95 (*0-8143-1887-8*) Wayne St U Pr.

— The Left Hand of Eden: Meditations on Nature & Human Nature. LC 98-54935. 208p. 1999. pap. 19.95 (*0-87071-460-0*) Oreg St U Pr.

— The Wallowas: Coming of Age in the Wilderness. LC 98-37906. (Northwest Reprints Ser.). 192p. 1998. reprint ed. pap. 15.95 (*0-87071-523-2*) Oreg St U Pr.

Ashyralyev, A. & Sobolevskii, P. E. Well-Posedness of Parabolic Difference Operations. Iacob, A., tr. LC 94-4711. (Operator Theory, Advances & Applications Ser.). 1994. 163.00 (*0-8176-5024-5*) Birkhauser.

***Asia & South Pacific Design Automation Conference Staff & Denshi Jeoheo Tseushin Gakkai (Japan) Staff.** Proceedings of the ASP-DAC'98: Asia & South Pacific Design Automation Conference 1998: February 10-13, 1998, Pacifico Yokahama, Yokohama, Japan. LC 97-80907. xxxvii, 506 p. 1998. write for info. (*0-7803-4427-8*) IEEE Standards.

Asia Energy Vision 2020 International Conference Staff, et al. Sustainable Energy Supply in Asia: Proceedings of the International Conference, Asia Energy Vision 2020, Organised by the Indian Member Committee, World Energy Council under the Institution of Engineers (India), During November 15-17, 1996 at New Delhi, 2 vols. LC 97-905335. 1997. write for info. (*81-7022-633-3*) Concept.

Asia House Gallery, New York, ed. see Asia Society Staff, et al.

***Asia Law & Practice Staff.** A-Z of Cutting Risk in the PRC. 1998. pap. text 75.00 (*962-7708-96-8*, Pub. by Asia Law & Practice) Am Educ Systs.

— Asia Law Profiles 2000: The Definitive Guide to Asia's Leading Law Firms. 125p. 1999. pap. text 125.00 (*962-936-071-3*, Pub. by Asia Law & Practice) Am Educ Systs.

— Asia Money Dictionary of Banking & Finance. 424p. 1999. pap. text 88.00 (*962-8307-04-5*, Pub. by Asia Law & Practice) Am Educ Systs.

Asia Law & Practice Staff. Asian Equity Derivatives Handbook. 200p. 1997. pap. 170.00 (*962-360-005-4*) Am Educ Systs.

— Asian Exotics: A Guide to the Currencies of Asia. 183p. 1996. pap. 170.00 (*962-7708-92-5*) Am Educ Systs.

***Asia Law & Practice Staff.** Asian Revival: Risk, Change, & Opportunity. 1999. 125.00 (*962-936-070-5*, Pub. by Asia Law & Practice) Am Educ Systs.

— Asia's Leading Lawyers 2000. 2000. pap. text 95.00 (*962-936-076-4*, Pub. by Asia Law & Practice) Am Educ Systs.

Asia Law & Practice Staff. Avoiding Double Taxation in Hong Kong & China. 220p. 1996. pap. 265.00 (*962-7708-75-5*, Pub. by Asia Law & Practice) Am Educ Systs.

— Bank of America's Guide to Telecommunications in Asia. 204p. 1996. pap. 170.00 (*962-7708-81-X*) Am Educ Systs.

***Asia Law & Practice Staff.** The Barclays' Capital Guide to Private Equity in Asia. 84p. 1999. pap. text 75.00 (*962-936-044-6*, Pub. by Asia Law & Practice) Am Educ Systs.

— China Finance Manual. 2nd ed. 500p. 1998. pap. 265.00 (*962-936-041-1*, Pub. by Asia Law & Practice) Am Educ Systs.

— The China Patient: Managing Risk, Seizing Opportunities. 114p. 1999. pap. text 125.00 (*962-936-065-9*, Pub. by Asia Law & Practice) Am Educ Systs.

— China Solutions. 2000. pap. text 170.00 (*962-936-068-3*, Pub. by Asia Law & Practice) Am Educ Systs.

— China Tax & Accounting Manual. 2nd ed. 400p. 1998. pap. 265.00 (*962-936-035-7*, Pub. by Asia Law & Practice) Am Educ Systs.

— China Troubleshooter. 2000. pap. text 260.00 (*962-936-069-1*, Pub. by Asia Law & Practice) Am Educ Systs.

— China 2000. 1999. pap. text 125.00 (*962-936-073-X*, Pub. by Asia Law & Practice) Am Educ Systs.

Asia Law & Practice Staff. China's New Companies, Vol. 1. 112p. 1993. pap. 260.00 (*962-7708-14-3*, Pub. by Asia Law & Practice) Am Educ Systs.

— China's New Companies, Vol. 2. 216p. 1994. pap. 260.00 (*962-7708-15-1*, Pub. by Asia Law & Practice) Am Educ Systs.

***Asia Law & Practice Staff.** CLP Power China Business Guide: Project Finance Models for Greater China. 148p. 1999. pap. text 125.00 (*962-936-055-1*, Pub. by Asia Law & Practice) Am Educ Systs.

— Competitive Rewarding: The Essential Business Guide to Compensation & Benefits in Hong Kong & the PRC. 81p. 1998. pap. text 95.00 (*962-936-052-7*, Pub. by Asia Law & Practice) Am Educ Systs.

Asia Law & Practice Staff. Complete Guide to Investing in Cambodia, Laos, Myanmar, & Vietnam, Vol. 1. 376p. 1996. pap. 150.00 (*962-7708-76-3*, Pub. by Asia Law & Practice) Am Educ Systs.

— Complete Guide to Investing in Cambodia, Laos, Myanmar, & Vietnam, Vol. 2. 280p. 1996. pap. 150.00 (*962-7708-56-9*, Pub. by Asia Law & Practice) Am Educ Systs.

— Creating & Enforcing Security in Asian Emerging Markets. 225p. 1997. pap. 225.00 (*962-7708-59-3*) Am Educ Systs.

— Creating & Enforcing Security in the PRC-Practical Strategies. 245p. 1997. pap. 260.00 (*962-360-006-2*) Am Educ Systs.

***Asia Law & Practice Staff.** The Definitive Guide to the Regions's Leading HR Service Providers: China's Top 200. 1999. pap. text 95.00 (*962-936-062-4*, Pub. by Asia Law & Practice) Am Educ Systs.

Asia Law & Practice Staff. Developing & Financing Transport Projects in Asia. 212p. 1997. pap. 195.00 (*962-360-014-3*) Am Educ Systs.

— Dispute Resolution in Construction & Infrastructure Projects. 100p. 1997. pap. 95.00 (*962-360-016-X*) Am Educ Systs.

— Dispute Resolution in the PRC: A Practical Guide to Litigation & Arbitration in the PRC. LC 96-153212. 264p. 1995. pap. 260.00 (*962-7708-53-4*, Pub. by Asia Law & Practice) Am Educ Systs.

***Asia Law & Practice Staff.** E-Commerce: Asia. 1999. pap. text 125.00 (*962-936-074-8*, Pub. by Asia Law & Practice) Am Educ Systs.

Asia Law & Practice Staff. Encyclopedia of Chinese Law, Vol. 1. 372p. 1993. pap. 260.00 (*962-7708-13-5*, Pub. by Asia Law & Practice) Am Educ Systs.

— Encyclopedia of Chinese Law, Vol. 2. 248p. 1994. pap. 260.00 (*962-7708-19-4*, Pub. by Asia Law & Practice) Am Educ Systs.

— Establishing Liaison, Branch & Project Offices in India. 200p. 1997. pap. 225.00 (*962-360-008-9*) Am Educ Systs.

— Establishing Representative & Branch Offices: Asian Law. 245p. 1996. pap. 260.00 (*962-7708-85-2*, Pub. by Asia Law & Practice) Am Educ Systs.

— Forex Management for FIEs in the PRC. 150p. 1996. pap. 260.00 (*962-7708-84-4*) Am Educ Systs.

***Asia Law & Practice Staff.** Funding the Future: The Essential Business Guide to the Mandatory Provident Fund. 74p. 1998. pap. text 95.00 (*962-936-039-X*, Pub. by Asia Law & Practice) Am Educ Systs.

Asia Law & Practice Staff. Guide to the Preparation & Evaluation of Boot Project Tenders. 55p. 1996. pap. 70.00 (*962-7708-72-0*) Am Educ Systs.

— India Employment Manual. 284p. 1996. pap. 240.00 (*962-7708-78-X*) Am Educ Systs.

— India Investment Manual. 2nd ed. 381p. 1996. pap. 225.00 (*962-7708-87-9*) Am Educ Systs.

— India Power Projects - Regulation, Policy & Finance, Vol. 1. 330p. 1998. pap. 195.00 (*962-360-003-8*) Am Educ Systs.

— India Power Projects - Regulation, Policy & Finance, Vol. 2. 370p. 1998. pap. 195.00 (*962-360-004-6*) Am Educ Systs.

— India Tax Manual. 250p. 1996. pap. 240.00 (*962-7708-79-8*) Am Educ Systs.

— Indonesia Investment Manual. 211p. 1996. pap. 225.00 (*962-7708-69-0*) Am Educ Systs.

— Infrastructure Development in Sri Lanka: Regulation, Policy & Finance. 200p. 1997. pap. 225.00 (*962-7708-61-5*) Am Educ Systs.

— Intellectual Property Protection in Asia: Practical Strategies. 252p. 1996. pap. 195.00 (*962-7708-77-1*, Pub. by Asia Law & Practice) Am Educ Systs.

— Invest in Indonesia. 255p. 1997. pap. 140.00 (*962-7708-99-2*) Am Educ Systs.

— Investing in Chinese Securities: Strategies for the Foreign Investor. 250p. 1995. pap. 140.00 (*962-7708-30-5*, Pub. by Asia Law & Practice) Am Educ Systs.

***Asia Law & Practice Staff.** IP Profiles 1999. 1999. pap. text 95.00 (*962-936-060-8*, Pub. by Asia Law & Practice) Am Educ Systs.

— Japan: Now Open for Business. 1999. pap. text 95.00 (*962-936-061-6*, Pub. by Asia Law & Practice) Am Educ Systs.

Asia Law & Practice Staff. Life & Death of a Joint Venture in China. 2nd rev. ed. 310p. 1996. pap. 260.00 (*962-7708-86-0*, Pub. by Asia Law & Practice) Am Educ Systs.

— Life & Death of an Infrastructure Project. 2nd ed. 330p. 1997. pap. 225.00 (*962-7708-60-7*, Pub. by Asia Law & Practice) Am Educ Systs.

***Asia Law & Practice Staff.** Localization in China: Best Practice. 1999. 225.00 (*962-936-067-5*, Pub. by Asia Law & Practice) Am Educ Systs.

— Managing for Growth: The Essential Business Guide to Pension Fund Management. 35p. 1999. pap. text 95.00 (*962-936-058-6*, Pub. by Asia Law & Practice) Am Educ Systs.

Asia Law & Practice Staff. Mechanisms for the Award of Competitive Tenders for Works & Supply Contracts. 50p. 1996. pap. 70.00 (*962-7708-91-7*) Am Educ Systs.

— Media Law in the PRC. 250p. 1996. pap. 195.00 (*962-7708-88-7*) Am Educ Systs.

— Natwest Markets' Guide to Power in Asia: Financing, Regulation & Development. 234p. 1997. pap. 140.00 (*962-360-001-1*) Am Educ Systs.

***Asia Law & Practice Staff.** The New India. 1999. pap. text 125.00 (*962-936-072-1*, Pub. by Asia Law & Practice) Am Educ Systs.

— Obtaining PRC Approvals for Foreign investment Enterprises & Infrastructure Projects. 2nd ed. 350p. 1999. pap. text 330.00 (*962-936-066-7*, Pub. by Asia Law & Practice) Am Educ Systs.

Asia Law & Practice Staff. Offshore Finance Handbook, 1998: A Guide to Offshore Centres for Asian Companies. 268p. 1997. pap. 140.00 (*962-360-028-3*, Pub. by Asia Law & Practice) Am Educ Systs.

— The Philippines Investment Manual. 268p. 1997. pap. 225.00 (*962-360-012-7*, Pub. by Asia Law & Practice) Am Educ Systs.

***Asia Law & Practice Staff.** Power Project Documentation. rev. ed. 292p. 1999. pap. text 260.00 (*962-936-057-8*, Pub. by Asia Law & Practice) Am Educ Systs.

Asia Law & Practice Staff. PRC Joint Ventures: Capital Contributions, Asset Valuation & Financing. 2nd ed. 276p. 1997. pap. 330.00 (*962-360-007-0*, Pub. by Asia Law & Practice) Am Educ Systs.

— PRC Joint Ventures: Drafting & Negotiating Contracts. 220p. 1997. pap. 330.00 (*962-7708-89-5*) Am Educ Systs.

— PRC Joint Ventures: Financial Management. 250p. 1997. pap. 330.00 (*962-360-010-0*) Am Educ Systs.

***Asia Law & Practice Staff.** Privatizing Australia: The Deals So Far, the Opportunities Ahead (Victoria) 250p. 1998. pap. 225.00 (*962-936-002-0*, Pub. by Asia Law & Practice) Am Educ Systs.

Asia Law & Practice Staff. Project & Infrastructure Finance in Asia. 2nd ed. 303p. 1996. 240.00 (*962-7708-80-1*) Am Educ Systs.

— Projects Procured by Privately Financed Concession Contracts, Vol. 1. 320p. 1996. pap. 225.00 (*962-7708-73-9*) Am Educ Systs.

— Projects Procured by Privately Financed Concession Contracts, Vol. 2. 280p. 1996. pap. 225.00 (*962-7708-74-7*) Am Educ Systs.

— Securing Loans in the PRC. 196p. 1998. pap. 260.00 (*962-360-026-7*, Pub. by Asia Law & Practice) Am Educ Systs.

— Setting-Up & Financing WFOEs in the PRC. 260p. 1997. pap. 260.00 (*962-360-027-5*, Pub. by Asia Law & Practice) Am Educ Systs.

— Singapore Employment Manual. 350p. 1996. pap. 195.00 (*962-7708-58-5*) Am Educ Systs.

***Asia Law & Practice Staff.** Trade Finance Strategies for the PRC. 240p. 1998. pap. 260.00 (*962-936-025-X*, Pub. by Asia Law & Practice) Am Educ Systs.

Asia Law & Practice Staff. Trade Finance Strategies in the PRC. 300p. 1998. pap. 260.00 (*962-360-025-9*, Pub. by Asia Law & Practice) Am Educ Systs.

Asia Law & Practice Staff. The Treasurer's Handbook: Hong King Futures Exchange. 196p. 1997. pap. text 135.00 (*962-8307-03-7*, Pub. by Asia Law & Practice) Am Educ Systs.

Asia Law & Practice Staff. Vietnam Investment Manual. 286p. 1995. pap. 225.00 (*962-7708-52-6*, Pub. by Asia Law & Practice) Am Educ Systs.

Asia Law & Practice Staff, ed. see Merna & Dubey Staff.

***Asia-Pacific Conference on Computational Mechanics Staff, et al.** Computational Mechanics for the Next Millennium: Proceedings of APCOM '99, 4th Asia-Pacific Conference on Computational Mechanics. LC 99-53081. 1200p. 1999. write for info. (*0-08-043209-3*) Elsevier.

Asia Pacific Economic Cooperation (Organization) Staff, jt. auth. see Maunsell Party, Limited Staff.

Asia Pacific Economic Cooperation (Organization). Task Force on the Human Resource and Social Impacts of the Financial Crisis in Asia, jt. auth. see Haworth, Nigel.

Asia Pacific Economic Cooperation Staff. Foreign Direct Investment & APEC Economic Integration. LC 97-945714. 1995. write for info. (*981-00-6988-X*) Miscell Pubs.

— The Impact of Investment Liberalization in Apec. LC 97-944105. iv, 70 p. 1997. write for info. (*981-00-9645-3*) AgBe Pub.

— The Impact of Subregionalism on APEC. LC 97-944108. iv, 65 p. 1997. write for info. (*981-00-9646-1*) AgBe Pub.

— The Impact of Trade Liberalization in APEC. LC 97-944104. viii, 58p. 1997. write for info. (*981-00-9644-5*) AgBe Pub.

Asia Pacific Economic Cooperation Staff. Selected APEC Documents, 1995. LC 97-940997. ii, 208 p. 1995. write for info. (*981-00-7368-2*) AgBe Pub.

Asia Pacific Economic Cooperation Staff & Taiwan Staff. APEC Directory of Support Organizations for Small & Medium Enterprises. LC 96-942844. 295p. 1996. write for info. (*981-00-8035-2*) Miscell Pubs.

Asia Pacific Press Staff & National Centre for Development Studies Staff, eds. Inflation, Growth & Development. LC 98-233758. (EDAP Joint Policy Studies.). 149p. 1998. write for info. (*0-7315-2376-8*) Aust Nat Univ.

Asia-Pacific Software Engineering Conference Staff, et al. 1998 Asia Pacific Software Engineering Conference: Proceedings, December 2-4, 1998, Taipei, Taiwan. LC 98-87889. xiv, 387 p. 1998. write for info. (*0-8186-9186-7*) IEEE Comp Soc.

Asia Press Co., Ltd. Staff. Who's Who in Japan, 1991-1992. 800p. 1991. 225.00 (*0-685-54324-2*, AP1801, CRC Reprint) Franklin.

Asia Press Staff. Who's Who in Japan. 1991. 236.00 (*4-900618-01-2*) CRC Pr.

Asia Research Centre, jt. auth. see Pinches, Michael.

Asia Society Staff. Asian Art Portfolio. LC 96-9407. 1996. pap. 19.95 (*1-56584-351-7*, Pub. by New Press NY) Norton.

***Asia Society Staff, ed.** Asia in New York City: A Cultural Travel Guide. (Illus.). 280p. 2000. pap. 17.95 (*1-56691-217-2*, Pub. by Avalon Travel) Publishers Group.

Asia Society Staff, et al. Relics of Ancient China, from the Collection of Dr. Paul Singer. Asia House Gallery, New York, ed. 1976. 35.95 (*0-405-06566-3*, 10761) Ayer.

Asia Society Staff, jt. auth. see Hagerty, Devin T.

Asia Watch Staff. The Forgotten War: Human Rights Violations in Afghanistan. LC 91-70184. 150p. 1991. pap. write for info. (*0-929692-81-0*, Asia Watch) Hum Rts Watch.

— Freedom of Expression in the Republic of Korea. 104p. 1988. pap. 8.00 (*0-929692-02-0*, Asia Watch) Hum Rts Watch.

— Human Rights in Burma (Myanmar) LC 90-82957. 48p. 1990. 8.00 (*0-929692-61-6*, Asia Watch) Hum Rts Watch.

— Human Rights in Nepal. 104p. 1989. 8.00 (*0-929692-31-4*, Asia Watch) Hum Rts Watch.

— The Philippines: Violations of the Laws of War by Both Sides. 148p. 1990. pap. 9.00 (*0-929692-52-7*, Asia Watch) Hum Rts Watch.

— Punishment Season: Human Rights in China after Martial Law. 174p. 1990. pap. 10.00 (*0-929692-51-9*, Asia Watch) Hum Rts Watch.

— Rape in Kashmir: A Crime of War. 18p. 1993. pap. 2.50 (*0-614-14423-X*) Phy Human Rights.

— Repression in China since June 4, 1989. LC 90-84977. 120p. 1991. 10.00 (*0-929692-74-8*, Asia Watch) Hum Rts Watch.

— Retreat from Reform: Labor Rights & Freedom of Expression in South Korea. LC 90-85381. 154p. 1990. pap. 10.00 (*0-929692-75-6*, Asia Watch) Hum Rts Watch.

Asia Watch Staff & Women's Rights Project Staff. Double Jeopardy: Police Abuse of Women in Pakistan. Human Rights Watch Staff, ed. LC 92-16361. 160p. (Orig.). 1992. pap. 15.00 (*1-56432-063-4*) Hum Rts Watch.

Asia Watch Staff, jt. auth. see Helsinki Watch Staff.

Asia Watch Staff, jt. auth. see Physicians for Human Rights Staff.

***Asiago, Francisco.** Decorating Awkward Corners. 2000. pap. 24.95 (*84-8185-245-7*) Watsn-Guptill.

Asian & Oceanic Society for Intravenous Anesthesia Staff, jt. auth. see Mori, Kenjiro.

Asian American Coalition Staff. Children of Asian America. LC 94-37405. (J). 1996. 18.95 (*1-879965-15-1*) Polychrome Pub.

Asian American Women. The Politics of Life: Four Plays by Asian American Women. LC 92-13090. (Asian American History & Culture Ser.). 288p. (C). 1993. pap. 22.95 (*1-56639-001-X*) Temple U Pr.

Asian and Pacific Conference of Correctional Administrators Staff. Corrections in Asia & the Pacific: Record of the Eighth Asian & Pacific Conference of Correctional Administrators, Kuala Lumpur, September 1987. LC 88-165779. 41 p. 1987. write for info. (*0-642-12271-7*) Advent Bks Div.

Asian and Pacific Conference of Correctional Administrators Staff & Mugford, Jane. Corrections in Asia & the Pacific: Proceedings of the Sixth Asian & Pacific Conference of Correctional Administrators, Fiji, 13-17 May 1985. LC 86-213210. 264 p. 1986. write for info. (*0-642-09915-4*) Advent Bks Div.

Asian Art Museum Curatorial Staff. Asian Art Museum: Selected Articles from "Orientations" (Illus.). 175p. 1993. reprint ed. pap. text 15.00 (*0-939117-06-1*) Asian Art Mus.

— Looking at Patronage: Recent Acquisitions of Asian Art. LC 89-80817. (Illus.). 112p. (Orig.). 1989. pap. 19.95 (*0-939117-03-7*) Asian Art Mus.

Asian Art Museum of San Francisco Curatorial Staff, et al. The Asian Art Museum of San Francisco: Selected Works. (Illus.). 208p. 1994. 25.00 (*0-614-04697-1*) U of Wash Pr.

Asian Art Museum of San Francisco Staff. Thai Ceramics: The James & Elaine Connell Collection. (Illus.). 188p. 1994. pap. 85.00 (*967-65-3043-3*) OUP.

Asian Art Museum Staff. Living Masters: The Paintings of Zhu Qizhan. (Illus.). 24p. (C). 1995. pap. 5.00 (*0-939117-07-X*) Asian Art Mus.

Asian Coalition of Human Rights Organizations (ACH, ed. Human Rights Activism in Asia: Some Perspectives, Problems & Approaches. 79p. (Orig.). 1984. pap. 8.00 (*0-936876-19-0*) LRIS.

Asian Cultural Center for UNESCO Staff. Folk Tales from Asia for Children Everywhere, Bk. 1. LC 74-82605. (Illus.). 60p. (J). (gr. 1-4). 1975. 6.50 (*0-8348-1032-8*) Weatherhill.

— Folk Tales from Asia for Children Everywhere, Bk. 2. LC 74-82605. (Illus.). 60p. (J). (gr. 3-6). 1975. 6.50 (*0-8348-1033-6*) Weatherhill.

— Folk Tales from Asia for Children Everywhere, Bk. 4. 60p. (J). (gr. 3-6). 1986. pap. 6.50 (*0-8348-1035-2*) Weatherhill.

— Folk Tales from Asia for Children Everywhere, Bk. 5. LC 74-82605. (Illus.). 60p. (J). (gr. 3-6). 1977. 6.50 (*0-8348-1036-0*) Weatherhill.

— Folk Tales from Asia for Children Everywhere, Bk. 6. LC 74-82605. (Illus.). 60p. (J). (gr. 3-6). 1978. 6.50 (*0-8348-1037-9*) Weatherhill.

Asian Cultural Center for UNESCO Staff, ed. Folk Tales from Asia for Children Everywhere, Bk. 3. LC 74-82605. (Illus.). 60p. (J). (gr. 3-6). 1976. 6.50 (*0-8348-1034-4*) Weatherhill.

— Stories from Asia Today: A Collection for Young Readers, Bk. 2. LC 74-82605. (Illus.). 184p. (J). (gr. 4-7). 1980. pap. 8.95 (*0-8348-1040-9*) Weatherhill.

Asian Cultural Centre for UNESCO Staff, ed. Stories from Asia Today: A Collection for Young Readers, Bk. I. LC 74-82605. (Illus.). 144p. (J). (gr. 4-7). 1980. pap. 7.95 (*0-8348-1038-7*) Weatherhill.

***Asian Development Bank.** Asian Development Outlook 1998. (An Asian Development Bank Books). (Illus.). 272p. 1999. pap. 24.95 (*0-19-590938-0*) OUP.

Asian Development Bank. Social Sector Issues in Pakistan: An Overview : Social Sector Profile : Pakistan. LC 97-947322. xiv, 56p. 1997. write for info. (*971-561-119-2*) Asian Devel Bank.

Asian Development Bank Staff. Asian Development Outlook, 1992. (Illus.). 330p. 1992. pap. text 19.95 (*0-19-585742-9*) OUP.
— Asian Development Outlook 1993. (Illus.). 294p. (C). 1993. pap. text 29.95 (*0-19-585941-3*, 11799) OUP.
— Asian Development Outlook 1994. (Illus.). 262p. 1994. pap. text 24.95 (*0-19-586599-5*) OUP.
— Asian Development Outlook 1996 & 1997. (Asian Development Bank Book). (Illus.). 258p. 1996. pap. text 26.00 (*0-19-587745-4*) OUP.
— Asian Development Outlook 1999. (An Asian Development Bank Bks.). (Illus.). 280p. 2000. pap. 24.95 (*0-19-592010-4*) OUP.
— Asian Development Outlook 1995 & 1996: Asian Development Bank. (Illus.). 278p. 1995. pap. text 24.00 (*0-19-587419-6*) OUP.
— Asian Development Outlook 2000. (An Asian Development Bank Books). (Illus.). 280p. 2000. pap. 24.95 (*0-19-592533-5*) OUP.

Asian Development Bank Staff. Asian Energy Problems. LC 81-84610. 304p. 1982. 69.50 (*0-275-90757-0*, C0757, Praeger Pubs) Greenwood.
— Central Asian Environments in Transition. LC 98-474344. xv, 281 p. 1997. write for info. (*971-561-149-4*) Paul & Co Pubs.
— Climate Change in Asia: Regional Study on Global Environmental Issues. LC 96-946592. 1994. write for info. (*971-561-013-7*) Asian Devel Bank.
— A Different Kind of Voyage: Development & Dependence in the Pacific Islands. LC 99-911142. 142p. 1998. pap. 10.00 (*971-561-150-8*, Pub. by Asian Devel Bank) Paul & Co Pubs.
— East Asean Growth Area: Brunei Darussalam, Indonesia, Malaysia, & Philippines, 7 vols. 1998. pap. 100.00 (*971-561-109-5*, Pub. by Asian Devel Bank) Paul & Co Pubs.

***Asian Development Bank Staff.** Education & National Development in Asia: Trends, Issues, Policies & Strategies. 180p. 2000. 15.00 (*971-561-246-6*, Pub. by Asian Devel Bank) Paul & Co Pubs.

Asian Development Bank Staff. Electric Utilities Data Book. LC 97-947313. 1032p. 1998. pap. 70.00 (*971-561-128-1*, Pub. by Asian Devel Bank) Paul & Co Pubs.
— Energy Efficiency Reference for Asian Use. LC 97-947317. 394p. 1998. pap. 25.00 (*971-561-134-6*, Pub. by Asian Devel Bank) Paul & Co Pubs.

***Asian Development Bank Staff.** Environmental Impact Assessment for Developing Countries Vols. 1 & 2: Overview: Selected Case Studies. LC 99-911135. 200.p. 1999. pap. 20.00 (*971-561-110-9*, Pub. by Asian Devel Bank) Paul & Co Pubs.
— Environmental Principles & Concepts: International Law & Public Policy. 180p. 2000. 10.00 (*971-561-213-X*, Pub. by Asian Devel Bank) Paul & Co Pubs.
— Governance, Corruption & Public Financial Management. 120p. 2000. 10.00 (*971-561-248-2*, Pub. by Asian Devel Bank) Paul & Co Pubs.

Asian Development Bank Staff. Guidelines for the Economic Analysis of Projects. LC 97-947315. 204p. 1998. pap. 10.00 (*971-561-127-3*, Pub. by Asian Devel Bank) Paul & Co Pubs.

***Asian Development Bank Staff.** Improving Growth Prospects in the Pacific. LC 99-911128. 130p. 1999. pap. 10.00 (*971-561-165-6*, Pub. by Asian Devel Bank) Paul & Co Pubs.

Asian Development Bank Staff. Key Indicators of Developing Asian & Pacific Countries, Vol. 26. (Illus.). 430p. (C). 1996. pap. text 24.95 (*0-19-587491-9*) OUP.
— Key Indicators of Developing Asian & Pacific Countries, 1992, Vol. XXIII. (Illus.). 434p. (C). 1993. pap. text 24.95 (*0-19-585873-5*) OUP.
— Key Indicators of Developing Asian & Pacific Countries, 1994, Vol. 25. (Illus.). 426p. 1995. pap. text 24.95 (*0-19-586774-2*) OUP.
— Key Indicators of Developing Asian & Pacific Countries, 1996, Vol. XXVII. (Asian Development Bank Bk.). (Illus.). 456p. 1996. pap. text 28.00 (*0-19-587836-1*) OUP.
— Key Indicators of Developing Asian & Pacific Countries 1997, Vol. 28. (Illus.). 446p. 1998. pap. text 42.00 (*0-19-590578-4*) OUP.
— Key Indicators of Developing Asian & Pacific Countries 1998. (Illus.). 436p. 1998. pap. text 29.95 (*0-19-591331-0*) OUP.

***Asian Development Bank Staff.** Key Indicators of Developing Asian & Pacific Countries 1999, Vol. XXX. (An Asian Development Bank Books). (Illus.). 442p. 2000. pap. text 29.95 (*0-19-592082-1*) OUP.

Asian Development Bank Staff. Marshall Islands 1996 Economic Report. 161p. 1998. pap. 10.00 (*971-561-121-4*, Pub. by Asian Devel Bank) Paul & Co Pubs.
— Mongolia: A Centrally Planned Economy in Transition. (Illus.). 266p. 1993. pap. text 24.95 (*0-19-585894-8*) OUP.
— Mongolia: A Centrally Planned Economy in Transition. (Illus.). 266p. (C). 1993. text 49.95 (*0-19-585893-X*) OUP.

***Asian Development Bank Staff.** Pakistan 2010: Realizing Pakistan's Full Potential. 1000p. 2000. 30.00 (*971-561-243-1*, Pub. by Asian Devel Bank) Paul & Co Pubs.
— Proceedings of the Seventh Conference on Subregional Economic Cooperation. 196p. 1999. pap. 35.00 (*971-561-154-0*, Pub. by Asian Devel Bank) Paul & Co Pubs.

Asian Development Bank Staff. Project Planning & Management in the People's Republic of China: Sharing of Development Experience. 98p. 1998. pap. 15.00 (*971-561-135-4*, Pub. by Asian Devel Bank) Paul & Co Pubs.

***Asian Development Bank Staff.** Public Administration & Civil Service in Developing Asia. 350p. 2000. 15.00 (*971-561-244-X*, Pub. by Asian Devel Bank) Paul & Co Pubs.

Asian Development Bank Staff. Regional Economic Cooperation in Central Asia. LC 98-474345. 354p. 1999. pap. 35.00 (*971-561-179-6*, Pub. by Asian Devel Bank) Paul & Co Pubs.
— Roundtable Proceedings on Sociocultural Issues & Economic Development in the Pacific Islands, Vol. II. LC 97-947323. 280p. 1998. pap. 10.00 (*971-561-140-0*, Pub. by Asian Devel Bank) Paul & Co Pubs.
— Second Water Utilities Data Book. LC 97-947316. 210p. 1998. pap. 20.00 (*971-561-125-7*, Pub. by Asian Devel Bank) Paul & Co Pubs.

***Asian Development Bank Staff.** Simplification of Customer Procedures: Reducing Transaction Costs for Efficiency, Integrity & Trade Facilitation. 120p. 2000. 10.00 (*971-561-249-0*, Pub. by Asian Devel Bank) Paul & Co Pubs.

Asian Development Bank Staff. Sri Lanka: Responding to New Social Challenges. LC 99-198131. 64p. 1998. pap. 10.00 (*971-561-133-8*, Pub. by Asian Devel Bank) Paul & Co Pubs.
— Urban Infrastructure Finance. 595p. 1998. pap. 30.00 (*971-561-117-6*, Pub. by Asian Devel Bank) Paul & Co Pubs.
— Vanuatu Economic Performance, Policy & Reform Issues. 368p. 1998. pap. 15.00 (*971-561-116-8*, Pub. by Asian Devel Bank) Paul & Co Pubs.

Asian Development Bank Staff, et al. Health Care Financing: Regional Seminar on Health Care Financing, 27 July-3 August, 1987, Manila, Philippines. x, 457p. 1988. pap. write for info. (*0-318-66605-7*) EW Ctr HI.

Asian Development Bank Staff, jt. auth. see Ganguli, Barin N.

Asian Development Bank Staff, jt. auth. see Illo, Jeanne F.

Asian Development Bank Staff, jt. auth. see Newbrander, William C.

Asian Development Bank Staff, jt. auth. see Regional Seminar on Distance Education Staff.

Asian Educational Services Staff, jt. auth. see Gray, James.

Asian Educational Services Staff, jt. auth. see Martinus, F. F.

Asian Educational Services Staff, jt. auth. see Sandberg, Graham.

Asian Educational Services Staff, jt. auth. see Woodward, F. L.

Asian Pacific Neural Network Assembly Staff, jt. auth. see Amari, Shunichi.

Asian Productivity Organization. APO Productivity Journal Winter, 1997. 229p. 1998. pap. 23.00 (*92-833-4008-6*, AP00086, Pub. by Asian Prod Organ) Bernan Associates.

Asian Productivity Organization Staff. APO Productivity Journal Winter 1996. (Winter 1996 Ser.). 229p. 1996. pap. 23.00 (*92-833-4006-X*, APO006X, Pub. by Asian Prod Organ) Bernan Associates.
— Asian Dynamism Through Human Resource Development. (Illus.). 553p. 1993. pap. text 15.00 (*92-833-2128-6*, 321286) Productivity Inc.
— Consulting Skills in Asian Context. 188p. 1992. pap. text 15.00 (*92-833-2116-2*, 321162) Productivity Inc.
— Cooperation & Productivity for Growth. (Monograph Ser.: No. 14). (Illus.). 112p. 1993. pap. text 7.50 (*92-833-1814-5*, 318145) Productivity Inc.
— Improving Productivity in Civil Service: A Symposium Report. 138p. 1993. pap. text 15.00 (*92-833-2133-2*, 321333) Productivity Inc.
— Intra-Regional Investment & Technology Transfer in Asia: A Symposium Report. LC 96-126003. (Illus.). 205p. 1994. pap. text 15.00 (*92-833-2144-8*, 321448) Productivity Inc.
— Labour Management Cooperation: A Task for Management. LC 96-114705. (Illus.). 130p. 1994. pap. text 7.50 (*92-833-2153-7*) Productivity Inc.
— New Trends in Medical Technologies & Hospital Management: French Experiences. 126p. 1991. pap. text 15.00 (*92-833-2099-9*, 320999) Productivity Inc.
— Top Management Forum: Human-Centered Management. (Illus.). 136p. 1993. pap. text 15.00 (*92-833-2130-8*, 321308) Productivity Inc.
— Top Management Forum: Industrial Organizations in the 90's Management of Linkages. LC 95-130446. (Illus.). 146p. 1994. pap. text 15.00 (*92-833-2143-X*, 32143X) Productivity Inc.
— Top Management Forum: Kyosei with Asia: Corporate Strategy of Japanese Firms Towards the 21st Century. LC 95-155030. (Illus.). 113p. 1994. pap. text 15.00 (*92-833-2156-1*, 321561) Productivity Inc.
— Trade Unions, Productivity & Industrial Relations: A Forum Report. LC 95-154067. 123p. 1994. pap. text 15.00 (*92-833-2142-1*, 321421) Productivity Inc.

Asian Productivity Organization Staff, ed. Productivity Through Consultancy in Small Industrial Enterprises. (Illus.). 504p. 1974. pap. text 17.25 (*92-833-1026-8*, 310268) Productivity Inc.

Asian Productivity Organization Staff, ed. & tr. see Japan Productivity Center Staff.

Asian Theological Conference (3rd, 1989, Korea) Staff. Asian Christian Spirituality: Reclaiming Traditions. Fabella, Virginia et al, eds. LC 91-38771. 165p. reprint ed. pap. 51.20 (*0-608-20202-9*, 207146100012) Bks Demand.

Asian Theological Conference Staff. Asia's Struggle for Full Humanity: Towards a Relevant Theology: Papers from the Asian Theological Conference, January 7-20, 1979, Wennappuwa, Sri Lanka. Fabella, Virginia, ed. LC 80-14923. 208p. reprint ed. pap. 64.50 (*0-8357-4049-8*, 203673900005) Bks Demand.

Asian Women United of California Staff, ed. Making Waves: An Anthology of Writings by & about Asian American Women. LC 88-47661. (Illus.). 480p. (YA). (gr. 9-12). 1989. pap. 22.00 (*0-8070-5905-6*) Beacon Pr.

Asiatic Exclusion League, 1907-1913. Proceedings. Grob, Gerald N., ed. LC 76-46064. (Anti-Movements in America Ser). 1977. reprint ed. lib. bdg. 65.95 (*0-405-09939-8*) Ayer.

Asiaweek Magazine Staff. An Investor's Guide to Asia's Top 1000 Bluechip Companies. LC 98-36849. 296p. 1998. pap. 21.95 (*0-471-82905-6*) Wiley.

Asid, Coblentz A. Coblentz Vigilanc Performance. 1989. lib. bdg. 171.00 (*0-7923-0302-4*) Kluwer Academic

Asiegbu, J. U. Nigeria & Its British Invaders. LC 83-62253. (Illus.). 409p. (C). 1984. 27.95 (*0-88357-101-3*); pap. 12.95 (*0-685-08183-4*) NOK Pubs.

Asif Iqbal Khan. Some Aspects of Iqbal's Thoughts. 100p. 1985. 4.50 (*1-56744-389-3*) Kazi Pubns.

Asifi, Allama M. Children's Guide to Islam. rev. ed. 145p. 1983. reprint ed. pap. 7.00 (*0-941724-11-5*) Islamic Seminary.

Asihene, E. V. Introduction to Traditional Art of Western Africa. LC 72-195063. (Illus.). 96p. reprint ed. pap. 30.00 (*0-608-11307-7*, 201938000011) Bks Demand.

Asihene, Emmanuel V. Traditional Folk-Tales of Ghana. LC 97-48819. (Studies in African Literature: Vol. 5). 432p. 1997. text 109.95 (*0-7734-8466-3*) E Mellen.
— Understanding the Traditional Art of Ghana. (Illus.). 100p. 1978. 29.50 (*0-8386-2130-9*) Fairleigh Dickinson.

Asija, S. Pal. Doing Business with India: A Survey of Problems. unabridged ed. (Illus.). 250p. 1970. 25.00 (*1-891325-01-9*) Our Pal.
— How to Protect Computer Programs: A Case History of the First Pure Software Patent. 2nd rev. ed. (Illus.). xcix, 190p. 1989. 35.00 (*1-891325-00-0*) Our Pal.
— Success Through Speech: A Compilation of Speeches. unabridged ed. 1971. pap. 15.00 (*1-891325-02-7*) Our Pal.

Asikinack, Bill & Scarborough, Kate. Exploration into North America. LC 95-18488. (Exploration Into Ser.). (J). (gr. 4 up). 1996. lib. bdg. 15.95 (*0-02-718086-7*, New Dscvry Bks) Silver Burdett Pr.
— Exploration into North America. LC 95-18488. (Exploration Into Ser.). (Illus.). 48p. (J). (gr. 4 up). 1996. pap. 7.95 (*0-382-39228-0*) Silver Burdett Pr.

***Asikinak, Bill.** North America. (Exploration Into... Ser.). (Illus.). (J). 2000. 17.95 (*0-7910-6025-X*) Chelsea Hse.

Asil, Araber, 4th. Arabiens edle Pferde. (Documenta Hippologica Ser.).Tr. of Noble Arabian Horse. (Illus.). 936p. 1993. 74.00 (*3-487-08339-6*) G Olms Verlag.

Asil, Club. Asil Arabians IV: The Noble Arabian Horses. (Documenta Hippologica Ser.). (Illus.). 923p. 1993. lib. bdg. 100.00 (*3-487-08340-X*) Lubrecht & Cramer.

Asil, Club, ed. Asil Araber IV: Arabiens edle Pferde.Tr. of Noble Arabian Horse. (DUT & ENG., Illus.). 936p. 1993. write for info. (*3-487-08349-3*) G Olms Pubs.

***Asim, Jabari.** The Road to Freedom: A Story of Reconstruction. (Jamestown's American Portraits Ser.). (Illus.). 144p. (J). 2000. pap. 5.95 (*0-8092-0625-0*, 06250E, Jamestwn Pub) NTC Contemp Pub Co.

Asim, Jabari, et al. Young Tongues No. I: A Poetic Exchange. 1992. pap. write for info. (*0-9632456-0-0*) First Civil.

Asimakopulos, Athanasios. Keynes's General Theory & Accumulation. (Modern Cambridge Economics Ser.). 225p. (C). 1991. pap. text 21.95 (*0-521-36815-4*) Cambridge U Pr.

Asimakopulos, Athanasios, ed. Theories of Income Distribution. (C). 1987. lib. bdg. 101.00 (*0-89838-232-7*) Kluwer Academic.

Asimakopulos, Athanasios, et al, eds. Economic Theory, Welfare & the State: Essays in Honour of John C. Weldon. 270p. (C). 1991. text 65.00 (*0-7735-0853-8*, Pub. by McG-Queens Univ Pr) CUP Services.

***Asimakoupoulos, Greg.** Celebrate Jesus! Small Group Leader's Guide. Davis, Brad, ed. (Celebrate Jesus! 2000 50-Day Spiritual Adventure Ser.). 64p. 1999. 8.00 (*1-57849-183-5*) Mainstay Church.
— Jesus: The People's Choice: Adventure Guidebook. Mains, Laurie, ed. (Celebrate Jesus! Ser.). 192p. 1999. 7.00 (*1-57849-172-X*) Mainstay Church.

Asimakoupoulos, Greg. Moses. (Fisherman Bible Studyguide Ser.). 80p. 1998. pap. 4.99 (*0-87788-519-2*, H Shaw Pubs) Waterbrook Pr.

Asimov, Eric. $25 & Under, 1998: A Guide to the Best Inexpensive Restaurants in New York. 4th ed. 288p. 1997. pap. 11.95 (*0-06-273402-4*, Harper Ref) HarpC.

Asimov, Isaac. The Adventures of Science Fiction, Vol. 3. 23.95 (*0-88411-587-9*) Amereon Ltd.
— Asimov Laughs Again: More Than 700 Favorite Jokes, Limericks, & Anecdotes. LC 91-58353. 368p. 1993. reprint ed. pap. 14.00 (*0-06-092448-9*, Perennial) HarperTrade.
— Asimov on Physics. 1979. mass mkt. 4.95 (*0-380-41848-7*, Avon Bks) Morrow Avon.
— Asimov's Chronology of Science & Discovery: Updated & Illustrated. LC 94-2504. (Illus.). 800p. 1994. 39.00 (*0-06-270113-4*, Harper Ref) HarpC.
— Asimov's Chronology of the World. LC 91-55007. 704p. 1991. 40.00 (*0-06-270036-7*, Harper Ref) HarpC.
— Asimov's Guide to the Bible: The New Testament. 640p. 1982. pap. 9.95 (*0-380-01031-3*, Avon Bks) Morrow Avon.
— Asimov's Guide to the Bible: The Old & New Testaments, 2 vols. in 1, Set. (Illus.). 1344p. 1988. 19.99 (*0-517-34582-X*) Random Hse Value.
— Asimov's Guide to the Bible: The Old Testament. 720p. 1976. pap. 10.95 (*0-380-01032-1*, Avon Bks) Morrow Avon.
— Ask Isaac Asimov, 10 bks. Incl. How Do Big Ships Float? Kaplan, Elizabeth. LC 92-32552. (Illus.). 24p. (J). (gr. 1-8). 1992. lib. bdg. 21.27 (*0-8368-0802-9*); How Does a Cut Heal? Dierks, Carrie. LC 93-18271. (Illus.). 24p. (J). (gr. 1-8). 1993. lib. bdg. 21.27 (*0-8368-0805-3*); Why Do We Have Different Seasons? LC 90-26061. (Illus.). 24p. (J). (gr. 2-3). 1991. lib. bdg. 21.27 (*0-8368-0439-2*); Why Do We Need Sleep? Dierks, Carrie. LC 93-20154. (Illus.). 24p. (J). (gr. 2 up). 1993. lib. bdg. 21.27 (*0-8368-0806-1*); Why is the Air Dirty? LC 91-50360. (Illus.). 24p. (J). (gr. 2-3). 1992. lib. bdg. 21.27 (*0-8368-0743-X*); (J). Set lib. bdg. 233.93 (*0-8368-1091-0*) Gareth Stevens Inc.
— Atom: Journey Across the Subatomic Cosmos. (Illus.). 336p. 1992. pap. 15.95 (*0-452-26834-6*, Truman Talley) St Martin.
— Beginnings: The Story of Origins, of Mankind, Life, the Earth, the Universe. 1989. mass mkt. 5.99 (*0-425-11586-0*) Berkley Pub.
— Caves of Steel. 288p. 1991. mass mkt. 6.99 (*0-553-29340-0*) Bantam.
— Chronology of the World. LC 91-55007. 1991. 14.95 (*0-06-270188-6*) HarpC.
— The Edge of Tomorrow. 1986. mass mkt. 5.99 (*0-8125-2132-3*, Pub. by Tor Bks) St Martin.
— Fantastic Voyage. 208p. 1988. mass mkt. 6.50 (*0-553-27572-0*, Bantam Classics) Bantam.
— Fantastic Voyage. 1966. 11.09 (*0-606-00639-7*, Pub. by Turtleback) Demco.
— Far As Human Eye Could See. 1988. mass mkt. 3.95 (*1-55817-107-X*, Pinncle Kensgtn) Kensgtn Pub Corp.
— 50 Short Science Fiction Tales. 1997. per. 6.95 (*0-684-84296-3*) S&S Trade.
— The Final Magic Fantasy Collection. Date not set. write for info. (*0-614-13117-0*, HarperPrism) HarpC.
— Forward the Foundation. 512p. 1994. mass mkt. 6.99 (*0-553-56507-9*) Bantam.

Asimov, Isaac. Forward the Foundation. LC 92-46655. (Foundation Ser.). 1994. 12.09 (*0-606-06388-9*, Pub. by Turtleback) Demco.

Asimov, Isaac. Foundation. (Foundation Series Ser.). 320p. 1991. mass mkt. 6.99 (*0-553-29335-4*) Bantam.
— Foundation & Empire. 320p. 1991. mass mkt. 6.99 (*0-553-29337-0*) Bantam.
— Foundation's Edge. 480p. 1991. mass mkt. 6.99 (*0-553-29338-9*) Bantam.

***Asimov, Isaac.** Fundacion. 5th ed. (Jet de Plaza & Janes Ser.). 1998. pap. text 6.50 (*84-01-49678-0*) Plaza.
— Fundacion E Imperio. 3rd ed. (Jet de Plaza & Janes Ser.). 1998. pap. text 6.95 (*84-01-46332-7*) Plaza.

Asimov, Isaac. The Gods Themselves. 320p. 1990. mass mkt. 6.99 (*0-553-28810-5*, Spectra) Bantam.
— Gold: The Final Science Fiction Collection. 448p. 1996. mass mkt. 6.99 (*0-06-105409-7*); mass mkt. 5.99 (*0-614-15545-2*, HarperPrism) HarpC.
— Great Tales of the Golden Age of Science Fiction. 1991. 9.98 (*0-88365-772-4*) Galahad Bks.

***Asimov, Isaac.** Guia de la Biblia: Nuevo Testamento. (SPA.). 1998. pap. 8.50 (*84-01-45083-7*, Pub. by Plaza) Lectorum Pubns.
— Guia De La Biblia Antiguo Testamento. 1998. pap. text 8.50 (*84-01-45082-9*) Plaza.
— Hacia la Fundacion. (SPA.). 1998. pap. text 6.95 (*84-01-49675-6*) Plaza.

Asimov, Isaac. How Did We Find Out about Comets? LC 74-78115. (How Did We Find Out about...Ser.). (Illus.). 64p. (J). (gr. 5-8). 1975. lib. bdg. 10.85 (*0-8027-6204-2*) Walker & Co.
— How Did We Find Out about Lasers? (How Did We Find Out about...Ser.). (Illus.). (J). (gr. 5 up). 1990. 12.95 (*0-8027-6935-7*); lib. bdg. 13.85 (*0-8027-6936-5*) Walker & Co.
— How Did We Find Out about Microwaves? (How Did We Find Out about...Ser.). (Illus.). 64p. (J). (gr. 1-4). 1989. 11.95 (*0-8027-6837-7*) Walker & Co.
— How Did We Find Out about Neptune? (How Did We Find Out about...Ser.). (Illus.). 64p. (J). (gr. 5 up). 1990. 12.95 (*0-8027-6981-0*) Walker & Co.

Asimov, Isaac. How Did We Find Out about Numbers? (Illus.). 63p. lib. bdg. 19.90 (*0-8027-6136-4*) Walker & Co.

Asimov, Isaac. How Did We Find Out about Solar Power? (How Did We Find Out about...Ser.). (Illus.). 64p. (J). (gr. 4-7). 1983. lib. bdg. 12.85 (*0-8027-6423-1*) Walker & Co.
— How Did We Find Out about Superconductivity? (How Did We Find Out about...Ser.). (Illus.). 64p. 1988. 11.85 (*0-8027-6778-8*) Walker & Co.
— How Did We Find Out about Volcanoes? (Illus.). 64p. (J). (gr. 2-7). 1982. pap. 1.95 (*0-380-59626-1*, 59626-1, Avon Bks) Morrow Avon.
— The Human Brain: Its Capacities & Functions. (Illus.). 384p. 1994. pap. 5.99 (*0-451-61867-X*, Ment) NAL.
— I, Robot. 288p. 1991. mass mkt. 6.99 (*0-553-29438-5*) Bantam.
— Isaac Asimov: The Complete Stories, Vol. I. 624p. 1990. pap. 18.95 (*0-385-41627-X*) Doubleday.

Asimov, Isaac. Isaac Asimov Audio Collection: Asimov,&Isaac, Set. abr. ed. (Foundation Ser.). 1994. audio 19.95 (*1-55994-747-0*, 491995) HarperAudio.

A

Asimov, Isaac. Isaac Asimov's Guide to Earth & Space. (Illus.). 288p. 1993. mass mkt. 5.99 (*0-449-22059-1*) Fawcett.

— Isaac Asimov's New Library of the Universe, 26 bks. Incl. Astronomy in Ancient Times. rev. ed. Walz-Chojnacki, Greg & Reddy, Francis, revs. LC 94-31253. (Illus.). 32p. (J). (gr. 3 up). 1995. lib. bdg. 21.27 (*0-8368-1191-7*); Astronomy Projects. rev. ed. Walz-Chojnacki, Greg & Reddy, Francis, revs. LC 95-40379. (Illus.). 32p. (J). (gr. 3 up). 1996. lib. bdg. 21.27 (*0-8368-1229-8*); Cosmic Debris: The Asteroids. rev. ed. Walz-Chojnacki, Greg & Reddy, Francis, revs. LC 94-15434. (Illus.). (J). (gr. 3 up). 1994. lib. bdg. 21.27 (*0-8368-1130-5*); Death from Space: What Killed the Dinosaurs? rev. ed. Walz-Chojnacki, Greg & Reddy, Francis, revs. LC 94-15432. (Illus.). 32p. (J). (gr. 3 up). 1994. lib. bdg. 21.27 (*0-8368-1129-1*); Discovering Comets & Meteors. rev. ed. Reddy, Francis. LC 95-40404. (Illus.). 32p. (J). (gr. 3 up). 1996. lib. bdg. 21.27 (*0-8368-1230-1*); Double Planet? Pluto & Charon. rev. ed. Walz-Chojnacki, Greg & Reddy, Francis, revs. LC 95-40350. 32p. (J). (gr. 3 up). 1996. lib. bdg. 21.27 (*0-8368-1232-8*); Folklore & Legends of the Universe. rev. ed. Walz-Chojnacki, Greg & Reddy, Francis, revs. LC 95-40363. (Illus.). 32p. (J). (gr. 3 up). 1996. lib. bdg. 21.27 (*0-8368-1234-4*); Global Space Programs. rev. ed. Walz-Chojnacki, Greg & Reddy, Francis, revs. LC 95-40366. (Illus.). 32p. (J). (gr. 3 up). 1996. lib. bdg. 21.27 (*0-8368-1235-2*); Index. Walz-Chojnacki, Greg & Reddy, Francis. LC 95-40364. 32p. (J). (gr. 3 up). 1996. lib. bdg. 21.27 (*0-8368-1237-9*); Modern Astronomy. rev. ed. Walz-Chojnacki, Greg & Reddy, Francis, revs. LC 95-40380. (Illus.). 32p. (J). (gr. 3 up). 1996. lib. bdg. 21.27 (*0-8368-1236-0*); Moon. rev. ed. Walz-Chojnacki, Greg & Reddy, Francis, revs. LC 94-15423. (Illus.). 32p. (J). (gr. 3 up). 1994. lib. bdg. 21.27 (*0-8368-1131-3*); Mysteries of Deep Space: Black Holes, Pulsars & Quasars. rev. ed. Walz-Chojnacki, Greg & Reddy, Francis, revs. LC 94-15429. (Illus.). (J). (gr. 3 up). 1994. lib. bdg. 21.27 (*0-8368-1133-X*); Our Planet Earth. rev. ed. Walz-Chojnacki, Greg & Reddy, Francis, revs. LC 94-32484. (Illus.). 32p. (J). (gr. 3 up). 1995. lib. bdg. 21.27 (*0-8368-1194-1*); Pollution in Space. rev. ed. Walz-Chojnacki, Greg & Reddy, Francis, revs. LC 94-32486. (Illus.). 32p. (J). (gr. 3 up). 1995. lib. bdg. 21.27 (*0-8368-1196-8*); Red Planet: Mars. rev. ed. Walz-Chojnacki, Greg & Reddy, Francis, revs. LC 94-15425. (Illus.). 32p. (J). (gr. 3 up). 1994. lib. bdg. 21.27 (*0-8368-1132-1*); Science Fiction: Visions of Tomorrow? Walz-Chojnacki, Greg, rev. LC 95-7233. (Illus.). 32p. (J). (gr. 3 up). 1995. lib. bdg. 21.27 (*0-8368-1224-7*); Space Colonies. Walz-Chojnacki, Greg, rev. LC 95-7229. (Illus.). 32p. (J). (gr. 3 up). 1995. lib. bdg. 21.27 (*0-8368-1225-5*); Space Explorers. Reddy, Francis, rev. LC 95-7232. Orig. Title: Piloted Space Flights. (Illus.). 32p. (J). (gr. 3 up). 1995. lib. bdg. 21.27 (*0-8368-1226-3*); Star Cycles: The Life & Death of Stars. Reddy, Francis, rev. LC 95-7892. (Illus.). 32p. (J). (gr. 3 up). 1995. lib. bdg. 21.27 (*0-8368-1227-1*); 21st Century in Space. rev. ed. Walz-Chojnacki, Greg & Reddy, Francis, revs. LC 95-40362. (Illus.). 32p. (J). (gr. 3 up). 1996. lib. bdg. 21.27 (*0-8368-1294-8*); UFOs: True Mysteries or Hoaxes? rev. ed. Reddy, Francis & Walz-Chojnacki, Greg. LC 94-34043. (Illus.). 32p. (J). (gr. 3 up). 1995. lib. bdg. 21.27 (*0-8368-1198-4*); (Isaac Asimov's New Library of the Universe Ser.). (Illus.). (J). 1994. Set lib. bdg. 552.93 (*0-8368-1295-6*) Gareth Stevens Inc.

— Isaac Asimov's Treasury of Humor: A Lifetime Collection of Favorite Jokes, Anecdotes, & Limericks with Copious Notes on How to Tell Them & Why. 432p. 1991. pap. 13.95 (*0-395-57226-6*) HM.

— Issac Asimov: A Memoir. 592p. 1995. mass mkt. 7.99 (*0-553-56997-X*) Bantam.

— Lucky Starr & the Rings of Saturn. (Lucky Starr Ser.). 176p. 1984. mass mkt. 1.95 (*0-345-31830-7*, Ballantine) Ballantine Pub Grp.

— Magic: The Final Fantasy Collection. 275p. 1998. text 22.00 (*0-7881-5367-6*) DIANE Pub.

— Magic: The Final Fantasy Collection. 1997. mass mkt. 5.99 (*0-614-27749-3*, HarperPrism) HarpC.

— The Martian Way & Other Stories. LC 81-15009. 224p. 1982. reprint ed. 16.00 (*0-8376-0463-X*) Bentley Pubs.

— Marvels of Science Fiction, Vol. 2. 23.95 (*0-88411-586-0*) Amereon Ltd.

— Masters of Science Fiction, Vol. I. 23.95 (*0-88411-585-2*) Amereon Ltd.

— The Naked Sun. 288p. 1991. mass mkt. 6.99 (*0-553-29339-7*) Bantam.

— Nemesis. 432p. 1990. mass mkt. 6.99 (*0-553-28628-5*) Bantam.

— Past, Present & Future. LC 87-2243. 382p. 1987. 27.95 (*0-87975-393-5*) Prometheus Bks.

— Pebble in the Sky. LC 81-15516. 224p. 1982. reprint ed. 16.00 (*0-8376-0462-1*) Bentley Pubs.

— Prelude to Foundation. 448p. 1989. mass mkt. 6.99 (*0-553-27839-8*) Bantam.

***Asimov, Isaac.** Quinto Jinete. (SPA.). 1998. pap. 6.95 (*84-01-49612-8*, Pub. by Plaza) Lectorum Pubns.

Asimov, Isaac. The Relativity of Wrong. 1989. mass mkt. 3.95 (*1-55817-169-X*, Pinncle Kensgtn) Kensgtn Pub Corp.

— The Relativity of Wrong. 256p. 1996. pap. 12.00 (*1-57566-008-3*) Kensgtn Pub Corp.

— Robot Dreams. (Illus.). 1990. mass mkt. 6.99 (*0-441-73154-6*) Ace Bks.

— The Robot Novels. 656p. 1988. pap. 14.95 (*0-345-33119-2*, Del Rey) Ballantine Pub Grp.

— Robot Visions. (Illus.). 1991. mass mkt. 7.50 (*0-451-45064-7*, ROC) NAL.

— The Robots of Dawn. 448p. 1994. mass mkt. 6.99 (*0-553-29949-2*, Spectra) Bantam.

— The Roving Mind. LC 97-41506. 380p. 1997. pap. text 18.95 (*1-57392-181-5*) Prometheus Bks.

***Asimov, Isaac.** Science Fiction: Great Stories of the Golden Age. 480p. 2000. 9.99 (*1-57866-106-4*) Galahad Bks.

Asimov, Isaac. Second Foundation. 304p. 1991. mass mkt. 6.99 (*0-553-29336-2*) Bantam.

— The Secret of the Universe. 256p. 1992. reprint ed. mass mkt. 4.50 (*1-55817-658-6*, Pinncle Kensgtn) Kensgtn Pub Corp.

***Asimov, Isaac.** Segunda Fundacion. 1998. pap. text 6.95 (*84-01-46333-5*) Plaza.

Asimov, Isaac. A Short History of Biology. LC 80-15464. (American Museum Science Bks.). (Illus.). 189p. 1980. reprint ed. lib. bdg. 45.00 (*0-313-22583-4*, ASSB, Greenwood Pr) Greenwood.

— A Short History of Chemistry. LC 78-25789. (Illus.). 263p. 1979. reprint ed. lib. bdg. 55.00 (*0-313-20769-0*, ASSH, Greenwood Pr) Greenwood.

— Super Hugos. 1992. mass mkt. 5.99 (*0-671-72135-6*) Baen Bks.

— Tales of the Black Widowers. 21.95 (*0-89190-278-3*) Amereon Ltd.

— The Tyrannosaurus Prescription: And One Hundred Other Essays. LC 89-8486. 323p. 1989. 26.95 (*0-87975-540-7*) Prometheus Bks.

— The Universe from Flat Earth to Quasar. (Illus.). 320p. Date not set. 24.95 (*0-8488-2203-X*) Amereon Ltd.

— Worlds Within Worlds: The Story of Nuclear Energy. LC 84-167298. (Illus.). 156p. reprint ed. pap. 48.40 (*0-8357-2922-2*, 203915400011) Bks Demand.

— Yours, Isaac Asimov: A Lifetime of Letters. Asimov, Stanley, ed. & compiled by by. 384p. 1996. pap. 12.95 (*0-385-47624-8*) Doubleday.

Asimov, Isaac, ed. Asimovs Dict Scientific Term. 2000. 16.95 (*0-06-270009-X*, Harper Ref) HarpC.

— Isaac Asimov's Book of Facts. 512p. 1991. 9.99 (*0-517-06503-7*) Random Hse Value.

Asimov, Isaac, et al, eds. Computer Crimes & Capers. 242p. 1983. pap. 10.00 (*0-89733-087-0*) Academy Chi Pubs.

— Isaac Asimov Presents the Best Crime Stories of the 19th Century. LC 95-21685. (Isaac Asimov Presents Ser.). 224p. 1995. pap. 14.95 (*1-56980-051-0*) Barricade Bks.

— The Mammoth Book of Classic Science Fiction: Short Novels of the 1930's. 572p. 1988. pap. 8.95 (*0-88184-410-1*) Carroll & Graf.

— The Mammoth Book of Fantastic Science Fiction: Short Novels of the 1970s. (Mammoth Book Ser.). 512p. 1992. pap. 9.95 (*0-88184-795-X*) Carroll & Graf.

— The Mammoth Book of Golden Age Science Fiction: Short Novels of the 1940s. 512p. 1989. pap. 8.95 (*0-88184-480-2*) Carroll & Graf.

— The Mammoth Book of Modern Science Fiction: Short Novels of the 1980s. (Illus.). 544p. 1993. pap. 9.95 (*0-88184-959-6*) Carroll & Graf.

— The Mammoth Book of New World Science Fiction: Short Novels of the 1960s. 512p. 1991. pap. 9.95 (*0-88184-702-X*) Carroll & Graf.

— The Mammoth Book of Vintage Science Fiction: Short Novels of the 1950s. (Mammoth Book Ser.). 512p. 1990. pap. 8.95 (*0-88184-621-X*) Carroll & Graf.

— 100 Great Fantasy Short Short Stories. 336p. 1985. pap. 3.95 (*0-380-69917-6*, Avon Bks) Morrow Avon.

— Purr-fect Crime. 272p. 1996. 6.98 (*1-56731-084-2*, MJF Bks) Fine Comms.

— The Twelve Frights of Christmas. 272p. 1986. mass mkt. 3.50 (*0-380-75098-8*, Avon Bks) Morrow Avon.

— Young Extraterrestrials. LC 83-49489. 240p. (J). (gr. 6-9). 1984. pap. 7.95 (*0-06-020167-3*) HarpC Child Bks.

— Young Mutants. LC 83-48444. 256p. (J). (gr. 6-9). 1984. pap. 7.95 (*0-06-020156-8*) HarpC Child Bks.

— Young Witches & Warlocks. LC 85-45849. 224p. (YA). (gr. 7 up). 1987. 12.95 (*0-06-020183-5*) HarpC Child Bks.

Asimov, Isaac, intro. Timeline of Discovery & Invention: Tracing the Development of Knowledge from Toolmaking. (J). 1993. 12.98 (*0-88394-973-3*) Promntory Pr.

Asimov, Isaac, et al, selected by. Microcosmic Tales: One Hundred Wondrous Science Fiction Short-Short Stories. 320p. 1992. 4.99 (*0-88677-532-9*, Pub. by DAW Bks) Penguin Putnam.

Asimov, Isaac & Allen, Roger MacBride. Isaac Asimov's Caliban. 320p. 1997. mass mkt. 5.99 (*0-441-00482-2*) Ace Bks.

— Utopia. (Caliban Ser.: No. 3). 320p. (Orig.). 1993. pap. 9.95 (*0-441-09079-6*) Ace Bks.

— Utopia. (Caliban Ser.: No. 3). 320p. (Orig.). 1996. pap. 13.00 (*0-614-17312-4*) Ace Bks.

Asimov, Isaac & Asimov, Janet. Norby & the Lost Princess. 129p. (J). lib. bdg. 20.90 (*0-8027-6593-9*) Walker & Co.

***Asimov, Isaac & Ciardi, John.** Limericks. LC 99-58756. 2000. 6.99 (*0-517-20882-2*) Random Hse Value.

Asimov, Isaac & Ciardi, John. Limericks: Too Gross; or Two Dozen Dirty Stanzas. 101p. 1985. reprint ed. pap. 8.95 (*0-393-04530-7*) Norton.

Asimov, Isaac & Palacios, Rafael. Asimov's Guide to Shakespeare, 2 vols. in 1. (Illus.). 1536p. 1993. 19.99 (*0-517-26825-6*) Random Hse Value.

Asimov, Isaac & Silverberg, Robert. Nightfall. 1991. mass mkt. 5.50 (*0-553-18042-8*) Bantam.

— Nightfall. 352p. 1991. mass mkt. 6.99 (*0-553-29099-1*, Spectra) Bantam.

— The Positronic Man. LC 93-15148. 272p. 1993. 22.50 (*0-385-26342-2*) Doubleday.

— The Ugly Little Boy. 304p. 1992. 22.50 (*0-385-26343-0*) Doubleday.

Asimov, Isaac & Sturgeon, Theodore. The Ugly Little Boy & The Widget, the Wadget, & Boff. Vol. 9. (Double Ser.: No. 9). (J). 1989. 3.50 (*0-8125-5966-5*, Pub. by Tor Bks) St Martin.

Asimov, Isaac & White, Frank. The March of the Millennia: A Key to Looking at History. 224p. 1990. 18.95 (*0-8027-1122-7*) Walker & Co.

— Think about Space: Where Have We Been? Where Are We Going? LC 88-36731. (Think Ser.). (Illus.). 120p. (YA). (gr. 6 up). 1989. pap. 5.95 (*0-8027-6767-2*); lib. bdg. 14.85 (*0-8027-6766-4*) Walker & Co.

Asimov, Isaac, et al. Fantastic Reading: Stories & Activities for Grade 5-8. 168p. (Orig.). 1984. pap. 12.95 (*0-673-15936-1*, GoodYrBooks) Addson-Wesley Educ.

***Asimov, Isaac, et al.** Robot City, Vol. 3. 464p. 2000. per. 14.00 (*0-7434-0007-0*, Pub. by ibooks) S&S Trade.

Asimov, Isaac, jt. auth. see Asimov, Janet.

Asimov, Isaac, jt. auth. see Ellison, Harlan.

Asimov, Isaac, jt. auth. see Fisher, Ken.

Asimov, Isaac, jt. auth. see Fredericks, Anthony D.

Asimov, Isaac, jt. auth. see Pohl, Frederik.

Asimov, Isaac, ed. see Verne, Jules.

Asimov, Janet. Mind Transfer. 1988. 17.95 (*0-8027-6748-6*) Walker & Co.

— Norby & the Terrified Taxi. LC 97-3583. (Norby Ser.). 144p. (J). (gr. 3-7). 1997. 15.95 (*0-8027-8642-1*) Walker & Co.

— The Package in Hyperspace. (Illus.). (J). (gr. 4-7). 1988. 13.95 (*0-8027-6822-9*); lib. bdg. 14.85 (*0-8027-6823-7*) Walker & Co.

Asimov, Janet & Asimov, Isaac. How to Enjoy Writing: A Book of Aid & Comfort. (Illus.). 163p. 1987. 15.95 (*0-8027-0945-1*); pap. 11.00 (*0-8027-7303-6*) Walker & Co.

— Norby & the Court Jester. 1996. mass mkt. 5.50 (*0-441-00341-9*) Ace Bks.

— Norby & the Court Jester. (Norby Ser.). 128p. (J). (gr. 3-7). 1991. 14.95 (*0-8027-8131-4*); lib. bdg. 15.85 (*0-8027-8132-2*) Walker & Co.

— Norby & the Court Jester. large type ed. 158p. 1999. 24.95 (*0-7838-8610-1*, G K Hall & Co) Mac Lib Ref.

— Norby & the Invaders. LC 85-13635. (Norby Ser.). 138p. (J). (gr. 3-5). 1985. 10.95 (*0-8027-6599-8*); lib. bdg. 10.85 (*0-8027-6607-2*) Walker & Co.

— Norby & the Oldest Dragon. (Norby Ser.). (J). (gr. 4-9). 1990. 14.95 (*0-8027-6909-8*); lib. bdg. 15.85 (*0-8027-6910-1*) Walker & Co.

— Norby & the Queen's Necklace. LC 86-11120. (Norby Ser.). 144p. (J). (gr. 4-9). 1986. 11.95 (*0-8027-6659-5*); lib. bdg. 12.85 (*0-8027-6660-9*) Walker & Co.

— Norby & Yobo's Great Adventure. (Norby Ser.). 224p. (J). (gr. 4-9). 1989. 12.95 (*0-8027-6893-8*); lib. bdg. 13.85 (*0-8027-6894-6*) Walker & Co.

— Norby Finds a Villain. 102p. (J). (gr. 4-9). 1987. 12.95 (*0-8027-6710-9*); lib. bdg. 13.85 (*0-8027-6711-7*) Walker & Co.

— Norby, the Mixed up Robot. LC 82-25173. 96p. (J). (gr. 5-7). 1983. lib. bdg. 10.85 (*0-8027-6496-7*) Walker & Co.

Asimov, Janet & Asimov, Isaac. Norby the Mixed-Up Robot. unabridged ed. (J). (gr. 1-5). 1986. audio 10.50 (*0-89845-634-7*, CP 1792, Caedmon) HarperAudio.

Asimov, Janet & Asimov, Isaac. Norby's Other Secret. LC 83-40417. 138p. 1984. 10.95 (*0-8027-6525-4*) Walker & Co.

Asimov, Janet, jt. auth. see Asimov, Isaac.

Asimov, Stanley, ed. & compiled by see Asimov, Isaac.

Asimova, M. S., ed. see Arzumanov, S. D. & Akhrori, K. A.

Asimow. Gilbert Administrative Law. 12th ed. 1992. pap. text 19.95 (*0-15-900000-9*) Harcourt Legal.

— Gilbert Income Tax. 2nd ed. 1997. pap. text 17.95 (*0-15-900384-9*) Harcourt Legal.

— Gilbert Income Tax 1: Individuals. 18th ed. 1994. pap. text 21.95 (*0-15-900266-4*) Harcourt.

— Gilbert Income Tax 2 - Corporate. 11th ed. 1990. pap. text 19.95 (*0-15-900024-6*) Harcourt Legal.

Asimow, L. & Ellis, A. J. Convexity, Theory & Its Application in Functional Analysis. LC 80-40648. (London Mathematical Society Monographs: No. 16). 1981. text 215.00 (*0-12-065340-0*) Acad Pr.

Asimow, Michael, et al. State & Federal Administrative Law. 2nd ed. LC 98-28102. (American Casebook Ser.). 864p. (C). 1998. text, student ed. 40.50 (*0-314-07206-3*) West Pub.

Asimow, Michael R., jt. auth. see Bergman, Paul.

Asimow, Michael R., jt. auth. see Bonfield, Arthur E.

Asin, Arlene, et al. Astro Star Kards. (Illus.). 96p. 1998. 39.95 (*0-9663896-0-3*) Astro Depot.

Asinger, H. Mono-Olefins: Chemistry & Technology. 1968. 513.00 (*0-08-011547-0*, Pub. by Pergamon Repr) Franklin.

Asinof, Eliot. Eight Men Out. large type ed. (Niagara Large Print Ser.). (Illus.). 512p. 1996. 29.50 (*0-7089-5852-4*) Ulverscroft.

— Eight Men Out. (Autographed Sports Classics Ser.). 1981. reprint ed. 24.95 (*0-941372-00-6*) Holtzman Pr.

— Eight Men Out: The Black Sox & the 1919 World Series. LC 77-71358. 336p. 1995. pap. 12.95 (*0-8050-0346-0*, Owl) H Holt & Co.

***Asinof, Eliot.** Eight Men Out: The Black Sox & the 1919 World Series. (Illus.). 302p. 2000. pap. 15.00 (*0-8050-6537-7*, Owl) H Holt & Co.

Asinof, Eliot. Free Agent. 1999. pap. 21.95 (*0-670-85862-5*) Viking Penguin.

— Man on Spikes. LC 97-43204. 1998. 75.00 (*0-8093-2200-5*); pap. 14.95 (*0-8093-2190-4*) S Ill U Pr.

***Asinof, Eliot.** Off-Season. LC 99-32220. (Writing Baseball Ser.). 162p. 2000. 22.50 (*0-8093-2297-8*) S Ill U Pr.

Asinov. Eight Men Out: Black Sox & Nineteen Nineteen Series. 29.95 (*0-8488-1567-X*) Amereon Ltd.

Asinovsky, et al. Cryogenic Discharges. 1990. 125.00 (*0-89116-629-7*) CRC Pr.

Asire, Nancy. To Fall Like Stars. 384p. 1996. per. 5.99 (*0-671-87727-5*) Baen Bks.

Asis, Moises, jt. auth. see Levine, Robert M.

ASIS Staff. Mastering Security Using Management Skills. LC 96-232356. 120p. 1996. pap. text, per. 19.95 (*0-7872-2566-5*, 41256601) Kendall-Hunt.

— Mastering Security Using Technology. LC 96-210067. 122p. 1996. pap. text, per. 19.95 (*0-7872-2565-7*) Kendall-Hunt.

Asiwaju, A. I., jt. ed. see Nugent, Paul.

Ask, K., et al. Health & International Life-Courses. (Bergen Studies in Social Anthropology: No. 37). 120p. 1987. pap. text 13.95 (*0-936508-69-8*, Pub. by Bergen Univ Dept Social Anthro) MBIPubg.

Ask, Karin & Tjomsland, Marit, eds. Women & Islamization. LC 98-233167. 199p. 1998. 60.00 (*1-85973-250-X*, Pub. by Berg Pubs); pap. 19.50 (*1-85973-255-0*, Pub. by Berg Pubs) NYU Pr.

Ask, Robert W. High on a Hill. Jacobson, William C. & Reitz, Robert, eds. (Cedar Rapids Local History Ser.). (Illus.). 182p. (Orig.). 1984. pap. 12.00 (*0-9614227-0-X*) Jefferson High.

Ask, Thomas. The Handbook of Marine Surveying. 1998. 32.95 (*1-84037-034-3*) Waterline.

Aska Knox, Melanie N. & Gucciardi, Joan. Pension Distribution Answer Book. annuals LC 98-171631. 1104p. 1998. boxed set 136.00 (*1-56706-431-0*, 64310) Panel Pubs.

— Pension Distribution Answer Book: Forms & Worksheets. annuals 2nd ed. LC 97-224404. 672p. 1999. pap. 96.00 (*1-56706-445-0*, 64450) Panel Pubs.

Aska, Melanie & Gucciardi, Joan. Pension Distribution Answer Book. annuals 1048p. 1995. 118.00 (*1-56706-118-4*) Panel Pubs.

Aska, Warabe. Who Hides in the Park. (CHI, ENG, FRE & JPN., Illus.). 24p. (J). (gr. k up). 1990. reprint ed. pap. 7.95 (*0-88776-244-1*) Tundra Bks.

Askadskii, A. A. Chemistry Reviews Vol. 16, Pt. 3: Analysis of the Structure & Properties of High-Crosslinked Polymer Networks, Vol. 16. (Soviet Scientific Reviews Ser.: Section B). 137p. 1992. text 173.00 (*3-7186-5220-X*, Harwood Acad Pubs) Gordon & Breach.

— Physical Properties of Polymers: Prediction & Control. (Polymer Science & Engineering Monographs). 208p. 1996. text 51.00 (*2-88449-155-4*); pap. text 27.00 (*2-88449-220-8*) Gordon & Breach.

Askam, Tony, et al. EC Sunday Trading Rules. 200p. 1990. pap. 175.00 (*0-406-04570-4*, UK, MICHIE) LEXIS Pub.

Askanas, Valerie, et al, eds. Inclusion - Body Myositis & Myopathies. (Illus.). 416p. (C). 1998. text 125.00 (*0-521-57105-7*) Cambridge U Pr.

Askanazi, Jeffrey, jt. auth. see Rothkopf, Michael M.

Askar, Ahmed Omar. Quality Assurance in Tropical Fruit Processing. LC 93-9518. (Laboratory Ser.). 1993. 114.95 (*0-387-55766-0*) Spr-Verlag.

— Sharks & Soldiers. LC 93-185034. 113p. 1992. write for info. (*952-90-4484-4*) UN.

Askar, Attila. Lattice Dynamical Foundations of Continuum Theories. 208p. 1986. text 40.00 (*9971-978-89-X*) World Scientific Pub.

Askar, Saoussan, jt. auth. see Munsch, Robert.

Askari. The Tree of Gnosis. 2000. 20.00 (*0-06-060246-5*) HarpC.

Askari, Brent. Not Ready for Prime Time. 272p. 1999. 24.95 (*0-7867-0648-1*) Carroll & Graf.

Askari, F. K. Hepatitis C, the Silent Epidemic: The Authoritative Guide. LC 99-11312. (Illus.). 200p. (C). 1999. 25.95 (*0-306-46012-2*, Kluwer Plenum) Kluwer Academic.

Askari, Hansan, tr. see Hasan, Gul.

Askari, Hasan, tr. see Hasan, Gul.

Askari, Hossein. Saudia Arabia's Economy: Oil & the Search for Economic Development. LC 89-49104. (Contemporary Studies in Economic & Financial Analysis: Vol. 67). 248p. 1990. 78.50 (*1-55938-002-0*) Jai Pr.

Askari, Hossein & Cummings, John T. Agricultural Supply Response: A Survey of the Econometric Evidence. LC 76-23376. 443p. 1984. 64.95 (*0-275-90242-0*, C0242, Praeger Pubs) Greenwood.

Askari, Hossein, et al. Economic Development in the G. C. C. The Blessing & the Curse of Oil. LC 98-5306. (Contemporary Studies in Economic & Financial Analysis: Vol. 81). 1997. 78.50 (*0-7623-0309-3*) Jai Pr.

Askari, Murtaza. A Probe into the History of Hadith. rev. ed. Islamic Seminary Staff & Haq, M. Fazal, trs. from ARA. 181p. (C). reprint ed. pap. 7.00 (*0-941724-16-6*) Islamic Seminary.

***Askari, Nasreen.** Uncut Cloth. 128p. 1999. pap. text 29.95 (*1-85894-083-4*) Merrell Holberton.

Askari, Nasreen & Crill, Rosemary. Colours of the Indus: Costume & Textiles of Pakistan. LC 98-130799. (Illus.). 144p. 1997. 45.00 (*1-85894-044-3*, Pub. by Merrell Holberton) U of Wash Pr.

Askari, Nasreen, et al. Colours of the Indus: Costume & Textiles of Pakistan. LC 98-130799. 144p. 1997. write for info. (*1-85894-045-1*) Merrell Holberton.

Askay, I. A., et al, eds. Hierarchically Structured Materials. (Symposium Proceedings Ser.: Vol. 255). 445p. 1992. text 30.00 (*1-55899-149-2*) Materials Res.

Aske, James. Elizabetha Triumphans: Conteyning the Damned Practizes Used Ever Sithence Her Highnesse First Comming to the Crowne. LC 73-6111. (English Experience Ser.: No. 78). 36p. 1969. reprint ed. 20.00 (*90-221-0078-2*) Walter J Johnson.

Askedal, John O., ed. see Gronvik, Ottar.

Askegren, Pierce. The Avengers & the Thunderbolts. 288p. 1999. pap. 6.50 (*0-425-16675-9*) Blvd Books.

— The Fantastic Four: Countdown to Chaos. (Illus.). 1998. mass mkt. 6.50 (*0-425-16373-3*) Berkley Pub.

— Sabotage. 1997. mass mkt. 6.99 (*0-425-16907-3*) Berkley Pub.

A

— The Professional Cleaner's Personal Handbook. Cartaino, Carol, ed. (Illus.). 197p. (Orig.). 1994. pap. 10.00 (0-937750-11-5) Marsh Creek Pr.

— Speak Up: A Step-by-Step Guide to Presenting Powerful Public Speeches. 2nd rev. ed. Cartaino, Carol, ed. LC 89-5764. Orig. Title: Is There a Speech Inside You?. (Illus.). 160p. (Orig.). 1996. pap. 12.99 (0-937750-15-8) Marsh Creek Pr.

— Who Says It's a Woman's Job to Clean? LC 86-1717. (Illus.). 116p. (Orig.). 1986. pap. 5.95 (0-89879-215-0) Marsh Creek Pr.

Aslett, Grant. The Guide to Easy Wood Floor Care & Maintenance: A Complete Owner's Manual for Hardwood Floors. Cartaino, Carol & Payne, Heidi, eds. (Illus.). 88p. (Orig.). 1994. pap. text 7.95 (1-880759-00-4) Clean Ctr Bks.

Aslin, Richard N., ed. Advances in Neural & Behavioral Development, Vol. 2. 248p. 1986. text 78.50 (0-89391-370-7) Ablx Pub.

Aslund, Anders. Gorbachev's Struggle for Economic Reform. rev. ed. 240p. 1991. pap. 17.95 (0-8014-9943-7) Cornell U Pr.

— How Russia Became a Market Economy. LC 95-786. (Integrating National Economies: Promise & Pitfalls Ser.). 378p. (C). 1995. 42.95 (0-8157-0426-7); pap. 18.95 (0-8157-0425-9) Brookings.

— Post-Communist Economic Revolutions: How Big a Bang? LC 92-37848. (Significant Issues Series - Creating the Post-Communist Order: No. 3). 116p. (C). 1992. pap. text 9.95 (0-89206-203-7) CSIS.

— Russia's Economic Transformation in the 1990s. LC 97-19559. 198p. 1998. 75.00 (1-85567-461-0); pap. 29.95 (1-85567-462-9) Bks Intl VA.

Aslund, Anders, ed. Market Socialism or the Restoration of Capitalism? (International Council for Soviet & East European Studies). (Illus.). 226p. (C). 1991. text 69.95 (0-521-41193-9) Cambridge U Pr.

— The Post-Soviet Economy: Soviet & Western Perspectives. LC 91-37376. 256p. 1992. text 39.95 (0-312-07569-3) St Martin.

— Russian Economic Reform at Risk. 224p. 1995. 99.50 (1-85567-286-3) Bks Intl VA.

***Aslund, Anders & De Menil, Georges, eds.** Economic Reform in Ukraine: The Unfinished Agenda. LC 99-86078. (Illus.). 320p. 2000. text 95.95 (0-7656-0624-0) M E Sharpe.

Aslund, Anders & Olcott, Martha B., eds. Russia after Communism. LC 97-24227. 192p. 1999. pap. text 16.95 (0-87003-151-1) Carnegie Endow.

ASM Conference on Advances in the Production of Tu. Advances in the Production of Tubes, Bars, & Shapes: 10th ASM Conference. LC 87-70151. (Illus.). 106p. reprint ed. pap. 32.90 (0-8357-4086-2, 203685200005) Bks Demand.

ASM International Electronic Materials & Processin. Microelectronic Packaging Technology: Materials & Processes, Proceedings of the 2nd ASM International Electronic Materials & Processing Congress, Philadelphia, Pennsylvania, 24-28 April 1989. Shieh, Wei T., ed. LC 89-80612. 489p. reprint ed. pap. 151.60 (0-7837-2767-4, 204315800006) Bks Demand.

ASM International European Council Tech. Comm. & Bond Voor Materialenkennis Staff. Advanced Aluminum & Magnesium Alloys: Proceedings of the International Conference on Light Metals, Amsterdam, 20-22 June 1990. Khan, T. & Effenberg, G., eds. LC TA0480.A6I58. (Illus.). 862p. 1990. reprint ed. pap. 200.00 (0-608-03979-9, 206470800010) Bks Demand.

ASM International Materials Science Div., Science. Computer Simulation in Materials Science: Papers Presented at the 1986 ASM Materials Science Seminar, 4-5 October, 1986, Lake Buena Vista, Florida. Arsenault, R. J. et al, eds. LC 87-70937. (Illus.). 384p. reprint ed. pap. 119.10 (0-608-03980-2, 206470900010) Bks Demand.

ASM International Staff. Corrosion Vol. 13: ASM Metals Handbook. 9th ed. 1987. 99.20 (0-87201-154-2, 1154) Gulf Pub.

— High Manganese, High Nitrogen Austenitic Steels: Proceedings of Two Conferences on High Manganese Austenitic Steels: The First Conference Held in Conjunction with ASM International's Materials Week '87, Cincinnati, OH, October 10-15, 1987; the Second Conference Held in Conjunction with ASM International's Materials Week '92, Held November 2-4, 1992, in Chicago, IL. Lula, R. A., ed. LC 93-72311. (Illus.). 237p. 1992. reprint ed. pap. 73.50 (0-608-02625-5, 206328300004) Bks Demand.

— High Temperature Superconducting Materials: The Current Situation. LC 89-111211. (Illus.). 194p. reprint ed. pap. 60.20 (0-7837-1870-5, 204207100001) Bks Demand.

— Life Assessment & Repair Technology for Combustion Turbine Hot Section Components: Proceedings of an International Conference, Phoenix, Arizona, U. S. A., 17-19 April 1990. Viswanathan, R. & Allen, J. M., eds. LC 90-83068. (Illus.). 404p. pap. 125.30 (0-7837-1867-5, 204206800001) Bks Demand.

— Processing of Structural Metals by Rapid Solidification: Proceedings of a Seven Session Symposium on Enhanced Properties in Structural Metals Via Rapid Solidification. Froes, F. H. & Savage, S. J., eds. LC 87-81828. (Conference Proceedings Ser.). (Illus.). 483p. 1987. reprint ed. pap. 149.80 (0-608-02612-3, 206327000004) Bks Demand.

— Structural Applications of Mechanical Alloying: Proceedings of an ASM International Conference, Myrtle Beach, South Carolina, March 27-29, 1990. Froes, F. H. et al, eds. LC 90-62191. (Illus.). 302p. 1990. reprint ed. pap. 93.70 (0-608-02615-8, 206327300004) Bks Demand.

— Tribology of Composite Materials: Proceedings of a Conference Held May 1-3, 1990, in Oak Ridge, TN. Rohatgi, P. K. et al, eds. LC 90-83193. (Illus.). 376p. 1990. reprint ed. pap. 116.60 (0-608-02630-1, 206328800004) Bks Demand.

ASM International Staff, et al. Advanced Synthesis of Engineered Structural Materials: Proceedings of the International Conference, 31 August-2 September 1992, San Francisco, California, U. S. A. LC 92-75701. (Illus.). 296p. reprint ed. pap. 91.80 (0-608-03983-7, 206471300010) Bks Demand.

— Failure Analysis - Techniques & Applications: Proceedings of the First International Conference on Failure Analysis, 8-11 July 1991, Montreal, Quebec, Canada. LC 92-81174. (Illus.). 330p. 1992. reprint ed. pap. 102.30 (0-608-03981-0, 206471000010) Bks Demand.

ASM International Staff, jt. auth. see Mackenzie, William C.

ASM Materials Science Seminar Staff. Deformation, Processing & Structure: Papers Presented at the 1982 ASM Materials Science Seminar. Krauss, George, ed. LC 83-48774. (Illus.). 540p. reprint ed. pap. 167.40 (0-8357-6086-3, 203431200089) Bks Demand.

— Flow & Fracture at Elevated Temperatures: Papers Presented at the 1983 ASM Materials Science Seminar. Raj, Rishi, ed. LC 85-71080. (Illus.). 432p. reprint ed. pap. 134.00 (0-8357-6115-0, 203430500089) Bks Demand.

— Fundamentals of Friction & Wear of Materials: Papers Presented at the 1980 ASM Materials Science Seminar. Rigney, David A., ed. LC 81-10789. (Illus.). 480p. reprint ed. pap. 148.80 (0-608-15946-8, 203306100083) Bks Demand.

— Grain-Boundary Structure & Kinetics: Papers Presented at the 1979 ASM Materials Science Seminar, 15-16 September, 1979, Milwaukee, WI. LC 80-22582. 486p. reprint ed. pap. 150.70 (0-608-16475-5, 202703600053) Bks Demand.

ASM Seminar on Interfacial Segregation. Interfacial Segregation: Papers Presented at a Seminar of the Materials Science Division of the American Society for Metals, October 22 & 23, 1977. Johnson, William C. & Blakely, John M., eds. LC 78-17980. 448p. reprint ed. 138.90 (0-608-17153-0, 202698800053) Bks Demand.

ASM Surface Treating & Coating Div. Council Staff. Surface Cleaning, Finishing & Coating. 9th ed. LC 82-13844. (Metals Handbook Ser.: Vol. 5). (Illus.). 736p. 1982. reprint ed. pap. 200.00 (0-608-03984-5, 206471500010) Bks Demand.

Asma, Stephen T. Following Form & Function: A Philosophical Archaeology of Life Science. LC 96-3297. (Northwestern University Studies in Phenomenology & Existential Philosophy). 220p. 1996. 69.95 (0-8101-1397-X); pap. 19.95 (0-8101-1398-8) Northwestern U Pr.

Asma, Steven T. Buddha for Beginners. (for Beginners Ser.). (Illus.). 160p. 11.00 (0-86316-186-3) Writers & Readers.

Asmal. Reconciliation Through Truth: A Reckoning of Apartheid's Criminal Governance. LC 98-139199. 240p. 1998. pap. 17.95 (0-312-21275-5); text 45.00 (0-312-21274-7) St Martin.

Asmann-Finch, Chris, jt. auth. see Kruckman, Laurence.

Asmar, Christine, jt. auth. see Stevens, Kate.

Asmar, Fouzi. To Be an Arab in Israel. LC 76-362116. 1975. write for info. (0-903804-06-9) P P Pubs.

***Asmar, Nakhle H.** Partial Differential Equations & Boundary Value Problems. LC 99-43378. 598p. 1999. 82.67 (0-13-958620-2) P-H.

Asmar, Ramsey. The Birth of a New Tradition. LC 92-35284. (Publish-a-Book Contest Ser.). (Illus.). 32p. (J). (gr. 2-6). 1992. lib. bdg. 22.83 (0-8114-3583-0) Raintree Steck-V.

Asma'u, Nana, et al. Collected Works of Nana Asma'u, Daughter of Usman Dan Fodiyo, (1793-1864) LC 97-15590. 1997. 49.95 (0-87013-475-2) Mich St U Pr.

ASME-ANS International Conference on Advanced Nucl. Advanced Nuclear Energy Systems: Papers Presented at 1976 ASME-ANS International Conference on Advanced Nuclear Energy Systems, Pittsburgh, Pennsylvania, March 14-17, 1976. LC 76-48469. 655p. reprint ed. pap. 200.00 (0-8357-8689-7, 203363700087) Bks Demand.

ASME Applied Mechanics Summer Conference Staff. Mechanics Applied to the Transport of Bulk Materials: Presented at the Joint ASME-CSME Applied Mechanics, Fluids Engineering, & Bioengineering Conference, Niagara Falls, New York, June 18-20, 1979. Cowin, Stephen C., ed. LC 79-50119. (AMD Ser.: Vol. 31). (Illus.). 135p. reprint ed. pap. 41.90 (0-8357-2852-8, 203908700010) Bks Demand.

ASME-ASLE Lubrication Conference Staff. Advances in Computer-Aided Bearing Design: Presented at ASME-ASLE Lubrication Conference, October 5-7, 1982, Washington, D.C. Chang, C. M. & Kennedy, F. E., eds. LC 82-72978. (Illus.). 156p. reprint ed. pap. 48.40 (0-8357-2828-5, 203906400010) Bks Demand.

ASME, CSME Montreal Pressure Vessel. Characterization of Materials for Service at Elevated Temperatures: Presented at 1978 ASME-CSME Montreal Pressure Vessel & Piping Conference, Montreal, Quebec, Canada, June 25-29, 1978. Smith, George V., ed. LC 78-57284. (MPC Ser.: Vol. 7). 542p. reprint ed. pap. 168.10 (0-608-17869-1, 203270000080) Bks Demand.

ASME-CSME Montreal Pressure Vessel & Piping Confer. Coolant Boundary Integrity Considerations in Breeder Reactor Design: Presented at the Pressure Vessels & Piping Conference of the American Society of Mechanical Engineers & the Canadian Society of Mechanical Engineers, Montreal, Quebec, Canada, June 25-29, 1978. Nair, B. R., ed. LC 77-94644. 139p. reprint ed. pap. 43.10 (0-8357-8698-6, 203362700087) Bks Demand.

ASME-CSME Pressure Vessel & Piping Conference Staf. Inelastic Behavior of Pressure Vessel & Piping Components: Presented at the 1978 ASME-CSME Pressure Vessel & Piping Conference, Montreal, Quebec, Canada, June 25-29, 1978. Chang, T. Y. & Krempl, E., eds. LC 78-57283. 181p. reprint ed. pap. 56.20 (0-8357-8729-X, 203362800087) Bks Demand.

ASME DED Vibrations Conference Staff, DED Vibrations Conference Staf. Vibration Testing--Instrumentation & Data Analysis: Presented at ASME - DED Vibrations Conference. Magrab, Edward B. & Shinaishin, Osman A., eds. LC 75-8349. (Illus.). 148p. reprint ed. pap. 42.20 (0-317-09976-0, 2015395) Bks Demand.

ASME Design Engineering Conference, New York, 1967. Designing for High Impact Technology: Papers Presented at the Design Engineering Conference, New York City, May 15-18, 1967. LC 77-20859. (Illus.). 36p. reprint ed. pap. 30.00 (0-608-11835-4, 201132300080) Bks Demand.

ASME International History & Heritage Staff. Landmarks in Mechanical Engineering. LC 96-31573. (Illus.). 400p. 1996. pap. 24.95 (1-55753-094-7) Purdue U Pr.

ASME Pressure Vessels & Piping Conference Staff. Weld Residual Stresses & Plastic Deformation: Presented at the 1989 ASME Pressure Vessels & Piping Conference, JSME Co-Sponsorship, Honolulu, Hawaii, July 23-27, 1989. Rybicki, Edmund F. et al, eds. LC 89-45821. (PVP Ser.: Vol. 173). 77p. 1989. reprint ed. pap. 30.00 (0-608-00286-0, 205931400008) Bks Demand.

ASME Pressure Vessels and Piping Conference, et al. Application of Modal Analysis Techniques to Seismic & Dynamic Loadings: Presented at the 1989 ASME Pressure Vessels & Piping Conference--JSME Co-Sponsorship, Honolulu, Hawaii, July 23-27, 1989 / LC 89-84350. (PVP Ser.). 83 p. 1989. write for info. (0-7918-0311-2) ASME.

— Codes & Standards & Applications for Design & Analysis of Pressure Vessel & Piping Components, 1989: Presented at the 1989 ASME Pressure Vessels & Piping Conference, JSME Co-Sponsorship, Honolulu, Hawaii, July 23-27, 1989. LC 89-84549. (PVP Ser.). 108 p. 1989. write for info. (0-7918-0317-1) ASME.

— Shock & Wave Propagation, Fluid-Structure Interaction, & Structural Responses: Presented at the 1989 ASME Pressure Vessels & Piping Conference, JSME Co-Sponsorship, Honolulu, Hawaii, July 23-27, 1989. LC 89-84547. (PVP Ser.). 123 p. 1989. (0-7918-0315-5) ASME.

ASME Research & Technology Committee on Water & St. A Practical Guide to Avoiding Steam Purity Problems in Industrial Plants Vol. 35: A Practical Guide to Avoiding Steam Purity Problems in Industrial Plants. (CRTD Ser.: Vol. 35). 40p. 1995. pap. 10.00 (0-7918-1220-0, I00383) ASME.

ASME Staff. Dynamic Loads on Gear Teeth. (Technical Papers: Vol. P91). (Illus.). 70p. 1931. pap. text 30.00 (1-55589-266-3) AGMA.

— The Influence of Elasticity & Errors in Tooth Shape on Stresses in Gears. (Technical Papers: Vol. P53). (Illus.). 6p. 1926. pap. text 30.00 (1-55589-261-2) AGMA.

— The Influence of Elasticity on Gear Tooth Loads. (Technical Papers: Vol. P53A). (Illus.). 6p. 1926. pap. text 30.00 (1-55589-262-0) AGMA.

— Multi-Phase Flow Symposium: Proceedings of the Multi-Phase Flow Symposium of ASME, Winter Annual Meeting, Philadelphia, 1963. Lipstein, Norman J., ed. LC TJ0265.M8. 103p. reprint ed. pap. 32.00 (0-608-11706-4, 201331600085) Bks Demand.

— Research on Strength of Gear Teeth. (Technical Papers: Vol. P84). (Illus.). 2p. 1924. pap. text 30.00 (1-55589-265-5) AGMA.

— Spent Nuclear Fuel Heat Transfer: Fuel Casks & Transfer Operations: Proceedings of ASME, Annual Winter Meeting, December 1971. Groetch, D. J. & Todreas, Neil E., eds. LC 79-180673. Vol. 2. 50p. reprint ed. pap. 25.00 (0-317-09924-8, 2016901) Bks Demand.

ASME/ASCE/SES Summer Meeting on Trends in Unstruct. Trends in Unstructured Mesh Generation: Proceedings. Canann, Scott A. & Saigal, Sunil, eds. LC 97-72850. 145p. 1997. pap. text 56.00 (0-7918-1558-7, TA350) ASME.

Asmerom, H. K., et al, eds. Bureaucracies & Developmental Policies in the Third World. 350p. 1992. pap. text 42.50 (90-5383-047-2, Pub. by VU Univ Pr) Paul & Co Pubs.

Asmerom, H. K. & Jain, R. B., eds. Politics, Administration & Public Policy in Developing Countries: Examples from Africa, Asia, & Latin America. 208p. 1993. pap. 40.00 (90-5383-187-8, Pub. by VU Univ Pr) Paul & Co Pubs.

Asmerom, H. K & Reis, Elisa P., eds. Democracy & Bureaucratic Neutrality: Experience from the Developed & Developing Countries. LC 96-19819. 360p. 1996. text 65.00 (0-312-16266-9) St Martin.

Asmis, Elizabeth. Epicurus' Scientific Method. LC 83-45133. (Cornell Studies in Classical Philology). 400p. 1983. 49.50 (0-8014-1465-2) Cornell U Pr.

Asmolov, A. Vygotsky Today: On the Verge of Non-Classical Psychology. LC 98-39083. 1998. 59.00 (1-56072-616-4) Nova Sci Pubs.

Asmontas, Steponas & Dargys, Adolfas, eds. Ultrafast Phenomena in Semiconductors. (Materials Science Forum Ser.: Vols. 297-298). (Illus.). 376p. 1999. text 184.00 (0-87849-824-9, Pub. by Trans T Pub) Enfield Pubs NH.

Asmundson. Health Anxiety. text 65.00 (0-471-99992-X) Wiley.

Asmundson. Health Anxiety. pap. text. write for info. (0-471-49104-7) Wiley.

Asmundson, et al. Tough Guys Don't Give Up: Storytellers. 200p. 1996. pap. 16.95 (0-9644683-3-6) Sunporch Prods.

Asmundsson, Doris R. Georg Brandes: Aristocratic Radical. LC 81-3324. 420p. reprint ed. pap. 130.20 (0-608-11894-X, 202251500030) Bks Demand.

Asmus & Wellington. Diesel Engines & Fuel Systems. 4th ed. 1995. text. write for info. (0-582-90987-2, Pub. by Addison-Wesley) Longman.

Asmus, Barry. Apollo: An Outer-Space Economic Adventure. Orig. Title: The Space Place. (Illus.). 178p. (YA). 1996. pap. 12.95 (0-9640421-6-9) Ameripress.

— ClintonCare: Putting Government in Charge of Your Health. 101p. (Orig.). 1994. pap. 9.95 (0-9640421-0-X) Ameripress.

— When Riding a Dead Horse, for Heavens Sake...Dismount! 243p. 1995. 19.95 (0-9640421-3-4); pap. 12.95 (0-9649421-4-3); pap. text 12.95 (0-9640421-4-2) Ameripress.

Asmus, Barry & Billings, Don. It's Tea Time, Again: The Original American Dream, Vol. I. 225p. 1995. 19.95 (0-9640421-1-8); pap. 12.95 (0-9640421-2-6) Ameripress.

Asmus, Brad. Powder Hound's Guide to Alta. 160p. 1992. pap. write for info. (0-9631113-0-2) Four Mile Pr.

— Powder Hound's Guide to Skiing Snowbird. (Illus.). 160p. (Orig.). 1992. pap. 12.95 (0-9631113-1-0) Four Mile Pr.

Asmus, E. Barry, jt. auth. see Billings, Donald B.

Asmus, Esther C. Moments Between. Squire, Sol, ed. (Illus.). 96p. (C). 1990. text 15.95 (0-9619407-2-7) Country Messenger Inc.

Asmus, Ingrid, jt. auth. see Hoffman, Clare.

Asmus, K. D., jt. ed. see Chryssostomos, C.

***Asmus, Peter.** Reaping the Wind; How Mechanical Wizards, Visionaries, & Profiteers Helped Shape Our Energy Future. 267p. 1999. 27.95 (1-55963-707-2, Shearwater Bks) Island Pr.

Asmus, Peter, jt. auth. see Smeloff, Ed.

Asmus, Ronald D. German Strategy & Opinion after the Wall, 1990-1993. LC 94-16033. 104p. 1994. pap. text 15.00 (0-8330-1543-5, MR-444-FNF/OSD/) Rand Corp.

— Germany's Contribution to Peacekeeping: Issues & Outlook. 64p. 1995. pap. text 15.00 (0-8330-1661-X, MR-602-OSD) Rand Corp.

— Germany's Geopolitical Maturation: Public Opinion & Security Policy in 1994. (Illus.). 60p. 1995. pap. text 15.00 (0-8330-2296-2, MR-608-FNF/OSD) Rand Corp.

— The New U. S. Strategic Debate. 120p. 1994. pap. 15.00 (0-8330-1537-0, MR-240-1-A) Rand Corp.

Asmus, Ronald D., jt. auth. see Szayna, Thomas S.

Asmus, Sigrid, ed. see Begoun, Paula.

Asmus, Sigrid, ed. see Begoun, Paula & Iulsaas, Kris.

Asmuss, Burkhard. Republik Ohne Chance? Akzeplanz und Legitimation der Weimarer Republik in der Deutschen Tagespresse Zwischen 1918 und 1923. (Beitraege zur Kommunikationsgeschichte Ser.: No. 3). (GER.). 639p. (C). 1994. lib. bdg. 215.40 (3-11-014197-3) De Gruyter.

Asmussen, Don. The Effect of Gamma-Rays on Sears' Catalog Underwear Men. (Illus.). 100p. (Orig.). 1986. pap. 6.95 (0-937217-00-X) Fifth Estate.

— The San Francisco Comic Strip Book of Big-Ass Mocha. LC 97-66721. (Illus.). 200p. 1997. 11.95 (0-9653524-6-3) Russn Hill Pr.

Asmussen, E., ed. International Calibration Study of Traffic Conflict Techniques. (NATO ASI Series F: Computer & Systems Sciences, Special Programme AET: Vol. 5). 229p. 1984. 75.95 (0-387-12716-X) Spr-Verlag.

Asmussen, Fleur B. Lao Roots: Fragments of a Nordic-Lao Family Saga. 266p. 1999. pap. 23.00 (974-8299-27-9, Pub. by Weatherhill) Weatherhill.

Asmussen, J., jt. auth. see Reinhard, D.

Asmussen, Jes P., ed. from PER. Manichaean Literature: Representative Texts Chiefly from Middle Persian & Parthian Writings. LC 74-22063. (Persian Heritage Ser.: Vol. 22). 148p. 1975. text 25.00 (0-8201-1141-4) Bibliotheca Persica.

Asmussen, Soren. Ruin Probability. (Advanced Series on Statistical & Applied Probability). 250p. 2000. text 38.00 (981-02-2293-9) World Scientific Pub.

Asmuth, Christoph. Sein, Reflexion, Freiheit: Aspekte der Philosophie Johann Gottlieb Fichtes. LC 97-1982. (Bochumer Studien zur Philosophie: Vol. 25). (GER.). vi, 320p. 1997. lib. bdg. 89.00 (90-6032-349-1) J Benjamins Pubng Co.

Asmuth, Christoph, et al, eds. Die Grenzen der Sprache: Sprachimmanenz-Sprachtranszendenz. LC 98-31621. x, 406p. 1998. 79.00 (90-6032-464-1) J Benjamins Pubng Co.

ASNE (Cronin) Staff. Marine Casuality Response: Salvage Engineering. 800p. text (0-7872-3465-6) Kendall-Hunt.

Asner, Edward, jt. auth. see Burlingame, Jon.

Asner, Fred M. High Field Superconducting Magnets. LC 99-234366. (Illus.). 255p. 1999. text 100.00 (0-19-851764-5) OUP.

Asner, Marie, jt. auth. see Holt, Rochelle L.

Asner, Marie A. Angels. (Spiritual Ser.). 47p. 1997. pap. 10.00 (0-934536-65-1) Rose Shell Pr.

Asner, Michael. The Request for Proposal Handbook. unabridged ed. 300p. 1996. pap. 295.00 (1-890299-00-6) Gov Technology.

***Asner, Michael.** The Request for Proposal Handbook. 2nd ed. LC 99-88270. 450p. 2000. 295.00 (0-07-136027-1, Schaums Outlne) McGraw-Hill Prof.

Asnes & Hamburg. Frommer's Budget Travel Guide New York on $70 a Day, 1996-1997. 1996. per. 15.95 (0-671-51946-8) S&S Trade.

ASNE's Credibility Committee Staff, compiled by. Newspaper Credibility: Two Hundred Six Practical Approaches to Heighten Reader Trust. 63p. 1988. 2.25 (0-317-01534-6) Nwspaper Assn Amer.

Asnes, Fred. These Little Worlds. Taylor, Chuck, ed. (Illus.). 82p. (Orig.). 1985. 10.95 (0-941720-23-3); pap. 4.95 (0-941720-22-5) Slough Pr TX.

***Asnien, Marvin.** Tell-a-Word. LC 98-91130. 100p. 2000. pap. 9.95 (*0-533-13064-6*) Vantage.

Asnis, Gregory M., jt. ed. see Zimmerman, James K.

ASNT Educational Council Staff, ed. see General Dynamics Convair Div. Staff.

ASNT Staff. ASNT Level II Study Guide: Radiographic Testing Method. (Illus.). (C). 1998. pap. 29.95 (*1-57117-062-6*, 6102) Am Soc Nondestructive.
— ASNT Training Program: Magnetic Particle Method (Instructor Package) (Illus.). 91p. (Orig.). 1979. pap. 239.50 (*0-931403-61-8*, 439) Am Soc Nondestructive.
— International Chemical & Petroleum Industry Inspection Technology (ICPIIT) Topical Conference Paper Summaries. (Illus.). 150p. (C). 1997. per. 19.00 (*1-57117-060-X*, 1358) Am Soc Nondestructive.
— 1997 ASNT Fall Conference & Quality Testing Show Paper Summaries. (Illus.). 316p. (C). 1997. per. 31.00 (*1-57117-068-5*, 1360) Am Soc Nondestructive.
— 1997 ASNT Infrared Thermography Topic Conference Paper Summaries. (Illus.). 180p. (C). 1997. per. 19.00 (*1-57117-061-8*, 1359) Am Soc Nondestructive.
— 1997 ASNT Spring Conference & Sixth Annual Research Symposium Paper Summaries. (Illus.). 192p. (C). 1997. per. 31.00 (*1-57117-056-1*, 1356) Am Soc Nondestructive.
— 1997 ASNT Spring Conference/5th Annual Research Symposium Paper Summaries. (Illus.). 252p. 1996. per. 31.00 (*1-57117-017-0*, 1351) Am Soc Nondestructive.
— 1996 ASNT Fall Conference & Quality Testing Show Paper Summaries. (Illus.). 246p. (C). 1996. per. 31.00 (*1-57117-053-7*, 1355) Am Soc Nondestructive.

Aso, T. & Kawagoe, S., eds. New Aspects of Prolactine in Human Reproductive Physiology: Journal: Hormone Research, Vol. 35, Suppl. 1, 1991. (Illus.). iv, 64p. 1991. pap. 29.75 (*3-8055-5470-2*) S Karger.

***Aso, Takeshi & Yanaihara, T.** The Menopause at the Millennium: Proceedings of the 9th World Congress on the Menopause. (Illus.). 550p. 2000. 115.00 (*1-85070-709-X*) Prthnon Pub.

Aso, Y., jt. auth. see Ogura, F.

Asociacion Espanola de Profesores de Derecho Internacional y Relaciones Internacionales Staff, ed. Spanish Yearbook of International Law. (Spanish Yearbook of International Law Ser.: Vol. III). 608p. 1998. 170.00 (*90-411-1007-0*) Kluwer Law Intl.

Asociadas Traductoras, Traductoras, tr. see Huggins, Kenneth & Land, Robert D.

Asociadas Traductoras, Traductoras, tr. see Jones, Harriet E. & Long, Dani L.

Asociaion Espanola de Professores de Derecho Inter, ed. Spanish Yearbook of International Law, 1991, Vol. I. 404p. (C). 1994. lib. bdg. 159.00 (*0-7923-2017-4*) Kluwer Academic.

Asoka, King of Magadha. The Edicts of Asoka. LC 78-72372. reprint ed. 34.50 (*0-404-17219-9*) AMS Pr.

Asokan, Unisa. Non-Prophet. (Poetry Ser.). 1994. pap. 5.00 (*1-880855-03-8*) Fifth Planet.

***Asokan, Unisa.** Pillow in the Kitchen. 50p. 2000. pap. 15.00 (*1-880855-08-9*) Fifth Planet.

Asokanthan, Sam F., intro. National Space Engineering Symposium, 8th, 1993. (National Conference Publication Ser.: No. 93-7). (Illus.). 356p. (Orig.). 1993. pap. 48.00 (*0-85825-577-4*, Pub. by Inst Engrs Aust-EA Bks) Accents Pubns.

Asola, Giammateo. Giammateo Asola: Sixteen Liturgical Works. Fouse, Donald M., ed. (Recent Researches in Music of the Renaissance Ser.: Vol. RR1). (Illus.). xiii, 115p. 1964. pap. 35.00 (*0-89579-000-9*) A-R Eds.

Asolon, Karel B., ed. The Phantom of Devil's Bridge & the Tale of Buffalo Castle. (Moravian Tales, Legends, Myths Ser.). (Illus.). 41p. (Orig.). (J). (gr. 4). 1985. pap. 12.00 (*0-930329-04-X*) Kabel Pubs.

Asongwed, Tah. Born to Rule: Autobiography of a Life President. 228p. (Orig.). (C). 1993. pap. 17.95 (*0-9636439-0-8*) Herit Pub MD.
— Guide to Electoral Fraud: Loser Take All. 130p. (Orig.). (C). 1994. pap. write for info. (*0-9636439-4-0*) Herit Pub MD.

Asopa, Jai N. A Socio-Political & Economic Study of India. 336p. 1990. 120.00 (*81-7158-101-3*, Pub. by Scientific Pubs) St Mut.

Asopa, V. N. & Narayanan, Sampat. Cocoa Production & Marketing in India. 1990. 14.00 (*81-204-0485-8*, Pub. by Oxford IBH) S Asia.

Asopa, V. N. & Shingi, Prakash M. Development & Management of Agriculture. 413p. (C). 1987. 26.00 (*81-204-0221-9*, Pub. by Oxford IBH) S Asia.

Asopa, V. N., et al. Management of Agricultural Research: A Training Manual. LC 98-210567. 10 p. 1997. (*92-5-104098-2*) Bernan Associates.

Asorey, Manuel. Advanced School of Nonperturbative Quantum Field Physics. 1998. 58.00 (*981-02-3474-0*) World Scientific Pub.

ASORN Staff. Core Curriculum for Ophthalmic Nursing. 352p. 1997. 75.00 (*0-7872-2782-X*) Kendall-Hunt.

***Asou, Reiko.** Playful Origami. (Illus.). 98p. 1998. 17.00 (*0-87040-827-5*) Japan Pubns USA.

Asouzu, Innocent. Kritische Betrachtung der Konstruktiven Wissenschaftstheorie. (Philosophische Texte und Studien: Vol. 11). (GER.). viii, 153p. 1984. write for info. (*3-487-07560-1*) G Olms Pubs.

Asp, Gary, et al. Graphic Algebra. (Illus.). 176p. (YA). (gr. 8-11). 1997. pap. text 16.95 (*1-55953-279-3*) Key Curr Pr.

Asp, James W., 2nd, jt. auth. see Worth, Michael J.

Asp, N. G., jt. ed. see Gurr, M. I.

ASP Staff. Basic Skills Curriculum. (Illus.). 728p. 1997. pap. text, student ed. 19.95 (*1-57768-097-9*) MG-Hill OH.
— Basic Skills Curriculum. (Illus.). 728p. 1997. pap., wbk. ed. 19.95 (*1-57768-098-7*) MG-Hill OH.
— Math. (Building Skills Ser.). (Illus.). 48p. (J). (gr. 3). 1997. pap., wbk. ed. 2.49 (*1-57768-053-7*) MG-Hill OH.
— Math. (Building Skills Ser.). (Illus.). 48p. (J). (gr. 4). 1997. pap., wbk. ed. 2.49 (*1-57768-054-5*) MG-Hill OH.
— Math. (Building Skills Ser.). (Illus.). 48p. (J). (gr. 5). 1997. pap., wbk. ed. 2.49 (*1-57768-055-3*) MG-Hill OH.
— Math. (Building Skills Ser.). (Illus.). 48p. (J). (gr. 6). 1997. pap., wbk. ed. 2.49 (*1-57768-056-1*) MG-Hill OH.
— Math. (Building Skills Ser.). (Illus.). 48p. (J). (gr. 7). 1997. pap., wbk. ed. 2.49 (*1-57768-057-X*) MG-Hill OH.
— Math. (Building Skills Ser.). (Illus.). 48p. (J). (gr. 8). 1997. pap., wbk. ed. 2.49 (*1-57768-058-8*) MG-Hill OH.
— Problem Solving. (Building Skills Ser.). (Illus.). 48p. (J). (gr. 3). 1997. pap., wbk. ed. 2.49 (*1-57768-073-1*) MG-Hill OH.
— Problem Solving. (Building Skills Ser.). (Illus.). 48p. (J). (gr. 4). 1997. pap., wbk. ed. 2.49 (*1-57768-074-X*) MG-Hill OH.
— Problem Solving. (Building Skills Ser.). (Illus.). 48p. (J). (gr. 5). 1997. pap., wbk. ed. 2.49 (*1-57768-075-8*) MG-Hill OH.
— Problem Solving. (Building Skills Ser.). (Illus.). 48p. (J). (gr. 6). 1997. pap., wbk. ed. 2.49 (*1-57768-076-6*) MG-Hill OH.
— Problem Solving. (Building Skills Ser.). (Illus.). 48p. (J). (gr. 7). 1997. pap., wbk. ed. 2.49 (*1-57768-077-4*) MG-Hill OH.
— Problem Solving. (Building Skills Ser.). (Illus.). 48p. (J). (gr. 8). 1997. pap., wbk. ed. 2.49 (*1-57768-078-2*) MG-Hill OH.
— Reading. (Building Skills Ser.). (Illus.). 48p. (J). (gr. 3). 1997. pap., wbk. ed. 2.49 (*1-57768-063-4*) MG-Hill OH.
— Reading. (Building Skills Ser.). (Illus.). 48p. (J). (gr. 4). 1997. pap., wbk. ed. 2.49 (*1-57768-064-2*) MG-Hill OH.
— Reading. (Building Skills Ser.). (Illus.). 48p. (J). (gr. 5). 1997. pap., wbk. ed. 2.49 (*1-57768-065-0*) MG-Hill OH.
— Reading. (Building Skills Ser.). (Illus.). 48p. (J). (gr. 6). 1997. pap., wbk. ed. 2.49 (*1-57768-066-9*) MG-Hill OH.
— Reading. (Building Skills Ser.). (Illus.). 48p. (J). (gr. 7). 1997. pap., wbk. ed. 2.49 (*1-57768-067-7*) MG-Hill OH.
— Reading. (Building Skills Ser.). (Illus.). 48p. (J). (gr. 8). 1997. pap., wbk. ed. 2.49 (*1-57768-068-5*) MG-Hill OH.
— Writing. (Spectrum Ser.). (Illus.). 88p. (J). (gr. 1). 1997. pap., wbk. ed. 6.95 (*1-57768-141-X*) MG-Hill OH.
— Writing. (Spectrum Ser.). (Illus.). 136p. (J). (gr. 4). 1997. pap., wbk. ed. 6.95 (*1-57768-144-4*) MG-Hill OH.
— Writing. (Spectrum Ser.). (Illus.). 136p. (J). (gr. 5). 1997. pap., wbk. ed. 6.95 (*1-57768-145-2*) MG-Hill OH.
— Writing. (Spectrum Ser.). (Illus.). 136p. (J). (gr. 6). 1997. pap., wbk. ed. 6.95 (*1-57768-146-0*) MG-Hill OH.
— Writing. (Spectrum Ser.). (Illus.). 136p. (J). (gr. 7). 1997. pap., wbk. ed. 6.95 (*1-57768-147-9*) MG-Hill OH.
— Writing. (Spectrum Ser.). (Illus.). 136p. (J). (gr. 8). 1997. pap., wbk. ed. 6.95 (*1-57768-148-7*) MG-Hill OH.

***Aspatore, Jonathan.** Fire Your Broker & Trade Online: Everything You Need to Start Investing Online. LC 00-35518. (Illus.). 180p. 2000. pap. 22.95 (*0-07-135948-6*) McGraw.

***Aspatore, Jonathan R.** Spinouts: The Key to Market Dominance in the Post Internet Era. 224p. 2000. pap. 27.95 (*1-58762-000-6*) ebrandedbookscom.

Aspatore, Jonathan Reed. College Entrepreneur Handbook: Ideas for a College-Based Business. LC 99-32991. 182p. 1999. pap. text 16.95 (*1-55571-503-6*) PSI Resch.

***Aspatore, Jonathan Reed.** Digital Rush: Nine Internet Start-Ups in the Race for Dot-Com Riches. (Illus.). 2000. 25.00 (*0-8144-0567-3*) AMACOM.
— Electronic Day Trading Elite. 196p. 1999. 24.95 (*0-07-135772-6*) McGraw.

Aspaturian, Vernon V. The Union Republics in Soviet Diplomacy: A Study of Soviet Federalism in the Service of Soviet Foreign Policy. LC 83-22696. 228p. 1984. reprint ed. lib. bdg. 45.00 (*0-313-24368-9*, ASUP, Greenwood Pr) Greenwood.

Aspaturian, Vernon V., et al, eds. Eurocommunism Between East & West. LC 80-7489. 383p. 1980. reprint ed. pap. 118.80 (*0-8357-3943-0*, 205703800004) Bks Demand.

Aspaturian, Vernon V., et al. The Soviet Invasion of Afghanistan: Three Perspectives. (CISA Working Papers: No. 27). 71p. (Orig.). 1980. pap. 15.00 (*0-86682-026-4*) Ctr Intl Relations.

Aspden, P., et al. Shipping Law Faces Europe: European Policy, Competition & Environment. (International Colloquium Ser.). 255p. 1996. pap. 58.00 (*90-6215-476-X*, Pub. by Maklu Uitgev) Gaunt.

Aspden, R. M. & Porter, R. W., eds. Lumbar Spine Disorders: Current Concepts. LC 95-2988. 260p. 1995. text 74.00 (*981-02-2175-4*) World Scientific Pub.

Aspe-Armella, Pedro, et al, eds. Financial Policies & The World Capital Market: The Problem of Latin American Countries. LC 82-24820. (National Bureau of Economic Research Ser.). 304p. 1983. lib. bdg. 46.00 (*0-226-02996-4*) U Ch Pr.

Aspe, Pedro. Economic Transformation the Mexican Way. LC 93-19949. (Lionel Robbins Lectures). (Illus.). 280p. 1993. 35.00 (*0-262-01135-2*) MIT Pr.

Aspe, Pedro, et al. Sea Change in Latin America. (Report Ser.). 41p. 1992. pap. 15.00 (*1-56708-080-4*) Grp of Thirty.

Aspect, A., et al, eds. Coherent & Collective Interactions of Particles & Radiation Bases. LC 96-77456. (International School of Physics Enrico Fermi Ser.: Vol. 131). 620p. 1997. 170.00 (*90-5199-281-5*, 281-5) IOS Press.

Aspell, Dee D., jt. auth. see Aspell, Patrick J.

Aspell, Dee Dee, jt. auth. see Aspell, Patrick J.

Aspell, Denise D., jt. auth. see Aspell, Patrick J.

Aspell, Patrick J. Medieval Western Philosophy: The European Emergence. LC 97-20069. (Cultural Heritage & Contemporary Change Ser.: Vol. 9). 340p. Date not set. pap. text 17.50 (*1-56518-094-1*) Coun Res Values.

Aspell, Patrick J. & Aspell, Dee D. The Enneagram Personality Portraits: Enhancing Professional Relationships. LC 96-45887. (Enneagram Personality Portraits Ser.). 160p. 1997. 24.95 (*0-7879-0883-5*, Pfffr & Co) Jossey-Bass.

Aspell, Patrick J. & Aspell, Dee Dee. The Art of Relating: The 45 Enneagram Relationships. 229p. 1993. 34.95 (*1-881773-03-5*) Lifewings.
— Enneanalysis: Enneagram Psychology. 383p. 1998. spiral bd. 49.95 (*1-881773-01-9*) Lifewings.
— Love for All Seasons: A Do It Yourself Resourcebook to Enhance Marital Relationships. 114p. 1995. spiral bd. 17.95 (*1-881773-02-7*) Lifewings.

Aspell, Patrick J. & Aspell, Denise D. Unlimited Empowerment: Discovering & Enhancing Your Personal Professional Life Via the Enneagram. (Illus.). 1992. student ed., ring bd. 29.95 (*1-881773-00-0*) Lifewings.

Aspell, Patrick J., jt. auth. see McLean, George F.

Aspell, Tom, jt. auth. see Roy, Samuel.

Aspelund, Donald J. & Eriksen, Clarence E. Employee Noncompetition Law. LC 87-11759. (IP Ser.). 1987. ring bd. 140.00 (*0-87632-544-4*) West Group.

Aspen, jt. auth. see Whaley.

Aspen Art Museum Staff, jt. auth. see Standring, Timothy J.

Aspen Books Editors. A Speaker's Sourcebook for Latter-Day Saints: Three Thousand Quotes by LDS Church Leaders. Taylor, Curtis et al, eds. 560p. 1991. pap. 16.95 (*1-56236-201-1*, Pub. by Aspen Bks) Origin Bk Sales.

Aspen Books Staff. Great Thoughts for Latter-Day Saint Sisters from LDS Church Leaders. 80p. 1990. pap. 6.50 (*1-56236-052-3*, Pub. by Aspen Bks) Origin Bk Sales.

***Aspen, E.** Rocky & Bullwinkle in the Box Top Robbery. (Adventures' of Rocky & Bullwinkle & Friends Ser.). 64p. (J). (gr. 2-5). 1998. mass mkt. 3.99 (*0-689-82144-1*, Simon Spot) Litle Simon.

Aspen Editorial Staff. Private School Administration. 1997. 119.00 (*0-8342-0994-2*) Aspen Pub.

Aspen Grants & Nonprofit Development Group Staff, jt. auth. see Mudd, Mollie.

***Aspen Health & Administration Development Group, ed.** Directory of Workers' Compensation Managed Care Organizations 2000 Edition. 307p. 1999. pap. 179.00 (*0-8342-1814-3*) Aspen Pub.
— 1999 National Health Directory. 400p. 1999. pap. 99.00 (*0-8342-1721-X*) Aspen Pub.
— Readings in Him: Clinical Data Applications. 250p. pap. 32.00 (*0-8342-1650-7*) Aspen Pub.
— Stopping School Violence: An Essential Guide. 105p. 1999. pap. 46.00 (*0-8342-1716-3*) Aspen Pub.

Aspen Health & Administration Development Group, ed. see Weidner, David.

***Aspen Health Law & Compliance Center-Aspen Communications & Data Group.** Emergency Department Compliance Manual 1999. 2nd ed. 41-p. 1999. pap. 100.00 (*0-8342-1253-6*) Aspen Pub.

Aspen Health Law & Compliance Center Staff. Health Care Antitrust. LC 98-36285. (Aspen Health Law Center Current Issues Ser.). 144p. 1998. write for info. (*0-8342-1227-7*) Aspen Pub.

Aspen Health Law & Compliance Center Staff, ed. see Zimmerman, L. E., et al.

Aspen Health Law Center Staff. Employment Discrimination in the Health Care Industry. LC 98-3551. (Current Issue Ser.). 128p. 1998. pap. 39.00 (*0-8342-1122-X*, 1122X) Aspen Pub.
— Health Care Fraud & Abuse: Aspen Health Law Center Current Issues. LC 98-9393. 144p. 1998. pap. 39.00 (*0-8342-1123-8*) Aspen Pub.
— Health Care Fraud & Abuse Compliance Manual. LC 96-46731. 388p. 1997. 199.00 (*0-8342-0899-7*, 5451) Aspen Pub.
— Health Maintenance Organizations: State Law Compliance Guide. 1996. 45.00 (*0-8342-0946-2*) Aspen Pub.
— Legal Answer Book for Managed Care. 368p. 1995. 70.00 (*0-8342-0700-1*) Aspen Pub.
— Managed Care Law Manual. Conner, Cynthia, ed. LC 93-44768. 1996. ring bd. 279.00 (*0-8342-0523-8*) Aspen Pub.
— Managed Care Law Manual. 1996. disk 323.00 (*0-8342-0848-2*) Aspen Pub.
— Physician Assistant Legal Handbook. LC 97-16412. 320p. 1997. 59.00 (*0-8342-0925-X*, 20925) Aspen Pub.
— Physician Organizations & Medical Staff: Contracts, Rights & Liabilities, 2 vols. 1996. 249.00 (*0-8342-0792-3*, S287) Aspen Pub.
— Physicians As Employees: Aspen Health Law Center Current Issues. LC 98-9397. 160p. 1998. pap. 39.00 (*0-8342-1121-1*) Aspen Pub.

Aspen Health Law Center Staff & Aspen Reference Group (Aspen Publishers) Staff. Medical Group Practice Legal & Administrative Guide. LC 98-12742. 1998. write for info. (*0-8342-1100-9*) Aspen Pub.

Aspen Health Law Center Staff & Kongstvedt, Peter R. Managed Care Library on CD-ROM. 1997. 199.00 (*0-8342-1063-0*) Aspen Pub.

Aspen Health Law Center Staff, et al. Managed Care Law Manual. 1996. 279.00 (*0-8342-0541-6*) Aspen Pub.

Aspen Health Law Center Staff, jt. auth. see Rosenbloom, Deborah.

Aspen Institute, jt. auth. see Aspen Institute. Nonprofit Sector Research Fund.

Aspen Institute, jt. auth. see Clark, Dick.

Aspen Institute, jt. auth. see Ullman, Richard H.

Aspen Institute. Justice and Society Program, jt. auth. see Henkin, Alice H.

Aspen Institute. Nonprofit Sector Research Fund & Aspen Institute. Competing Visions: The Nonprofit Sector in the Twenty-first Century : Perspectives from a Conference Convened by the Nonprofit Sector Research Fund, July 1995. LC 97-229306. 1997. write for info. (*0-89843-211-1*) The Aspen Inst.

Aspen Institute Roundtable on Information Technology Staff, et al. The Global Advance of Electronic Commerce: Reinventing Markets, Management & National Sovereignty: A Report of the 6th Annual Aspen Institute Roundtable on Information Technology. LC 98-206641. vi, 64 p. 1998. pap. 12.00 (*0-89843-236-7*) The Aspen Inst.

Aspen Institute Staff. International Peace & Security in a New World System. (Aspen Institute Conferences on International Peace & Security Ser.: No. 1). 58p. 1994. pap. 5.00 (*0-89843-157-3*) The Aspen Inst.

Aspen Institute Staff, ed. The Assessment & Alert of Major Hazards. 48p. 1979. pap. text 8.50 (*0-8191-5837-2*) U Pr of Amer.
— Expanding the Choices for Television Viewing. 80p. (Orig.). 1981. pap. text 12.50 (*0-8191-5838-0*) U Pr of Amer.
— In the Public Service: John J. McCloy - on Receipt of the Aspen Institute Statesman-Humanist Award. 48p. 1978. pap. text 11.00 (*0-8191-5897-6*) U Pr of Amer.
— Job Creation: New Ventures for Society. 106p. (Orig.). 1983. pap. text 17.00 (*0-8191-5855-0*) U Pr of Amer.
— Nuclear Power & National & International Security: The Politics & Economic Implications of Closing the Nuclear Fuel Cycle. 28p. (Orig.). 1984. pap. text 8.50 (*0-8191-5854-2*) U Pr of Amer.
— Proliferation, Politics, & the IAEA: The Issue of Nuclear Safeguards. 42p. (Orig.). 1985. pap. text 10.50 (*0-8191-5849-6*) U Pr of Amer.
— Report on a Workshop on Technology Choices, Work & Society's Future. 136p. (Orig.). 1987. pap. text 16.00 (*0-8191-5836-4*) U Pr of Amer.
— The Road to Madrid: Developing a Western Consensus on Human Rights. 104p. 1980. pap. text 13.50 (*0-8191-5900-X*) U Pr of Amer.

Aspen Institute Staff, jt. auth. see Gurwitt, Rob.

Aspen, Jean. Arctic Son: Fulfilling the Dream. 250p. (J). 1995. 19.95 (*0-89732-173-1*) Menasha Ridge.

Aspen, Kristan, jt. compiled by see MacAuslan, Janna.

Aspen, L. Killing Me Softly. mass mkt. 6.95 (*0-7472-5426-5*, Pub. by Headline Bk Pub) Trafalgar.
— Liason: Love Hurts. 1997. mass mkt. 6.95 (*0-7472-5588-1*, Pub. by Headline Bk Pub) Trafalgar.

Aspen L&B Staff. Delaware Corporation Law. LC 97-102066. (Annotated Statute Ser.). 1996. 95.00 (*1-56706-335-7*) Panel Pubs.

***Aspen Law & Business Editorial Staff.** Directory of Corporate Counsel 1999-2000, 2. 2874p. 1999. boxed set 464.00 (*0-7355-0553-5*) Panel Pubs.

Aspen Law & Business Editorial Staff. Directory of Federal Court Guidelines, 2 vols. 1250p. 1996. ring bd. 385.00 (*1-56706-296-2*, 62962) Panel Pubs.
— 1998-99 Directory of Corporate Counsel. boxed set 799.00 incl. cd-rom (*1-56706-658-5*, 66585) Panel Pubs.
— 1997-98 Directory of Corporate Counsel, 2 vols. 2686p. boxed set 449.00 (*1-56706-657-7*) Panel Pubs.
— 1996 the Lawyer's Almanac. annuals 16th ed. 1080p. 1996. 136.00 (*0-614-16676-4*) Aspen Pub.

Aspen Publishers, Inc., Reference Group Staff, et al. Industrial Rehabilitation Services: Forms, Checklists & Guidelines. LC 96-33462. 1997. 159.00 (*0-8342-0873-3*) Aspen Pub.

Aspen Reference Group. Ambulatory Care & Outpatient Services: Forms, Checklist & Guidelines. rev. ed. 1996. ring bd. 189.00 (*0-8342-0804-0*, S285) Aspen Pub.
— Campus Safety & Security Administration: Forms, Checklists & Guidelines. LC 97-18703. 1997. 149.00 (*0-8342-0874-1*, S444) Aspen Pub.
— Chronic Disease Management Manual. LC 97-2652. 1997. ring bd. 169.00 (*0-8342-0872-5*, S315) Aspen Pub.
— Health Care Registration & Admitting Manual: Forms, Checklists & Guidelines. LC 97-11746. 1997. 150.00 (*0-8342-0876-8*, S445) Aspen Pub.
— Home Health Nutrition Patient Education Manual. LC 97-20160. 1997. 129.00 (*0-8342-0871-7*, S441) Aspen Pub.
— National Health Directory, 1997. 250p. 1997. 99.00 (*0-8342-0903-9*, 20903) Aspen Pub.

Aspen Reference Group (Aspen Publishers) Staff, jt. auth. see Aspen Health Law Center Staff.

Aspen Reference Group Staff. Ambulatory Surgery Patient Education Manual. Di Lima, Sara N. & Weavers, Simon B., eds. LC 97-10866. 1997. ring bd. 179.00 (*0-8342-0877-6*, S314) Aspen Pub.
— The Aspen Guide to Effective Health Care Correspondence. Lawrence, Kenneth E., ed. LC 93-12612. 432p. 1993. 65.00 (*0-8342-0305-7*, 20305) Aspen Pub.
— Brain Injury Rehabilitation Patient Education Manual. 1996. 169.00 (*0-8342-0744-3*, S304) Aspen Pub.
— Caregiver Education Guide for Children with Developmental Disabilities. Niemeyer, Suzanne, ed. LC 93-44773. 1994. 189.00 (*0-8342-0560-2*) Aspen Pub.
— Case Manager's Desk Reference: 1999 Edition. 352p. 1999. pap. 69.00 (*0-8342-1053-3*, 10533) Aspen Pub.
— Chiropractic Patient Resource Manual. Lawrence, Kenneth E. & Painter, Sandra J., eds. LC 92-17636. 1992. 179.00 (*0-8342-0267-0*) Aspen Pub.
— Community Health Education & Promotion Manual. LC 96-17242. 428p. 1996. 155.00 (*0-8342-0774-5*, S195) Aspen Pub.
— Dietitian's Patient Education Manual. LC 90-19176. 1048p. 1999. student ed., ring bd. 292.00 (*0-8342-0196-8*) Aspen Pub.
— Geriatric Patient Education Resource Manual, 2 vols. 1996. 247.00 (*0-8342-0225-5*) Aspen Pub.

A

— Health Care Information Management Forms, Checklists, Guidelines, Policies & Procedures. Liebler, Joan, ed. 1998. ring bd. 189.00 (*0-8342-1101-7*, S467) Aspen Pub.
— Health Care Inservice Curriculum Resource Manual. LC 97-16280. 400p. 1997. 159.00 (*0-8342-0879-2*, S446) Aspen Pub.
— Health Care Software Sourcebook & IT Buyer's Guide. expanded rev. ed. Antosz, Lynn & Di Lima, Sara N., eds. 513p. 1999. pap. 129.00 (*0-8342-1328-1*, 13281) Aspen Pub.
— Health Care Software Sourcebook, 1999. 510p. pap. 89.00 (*0-8342-1038-X*, 1038X) Aspen Pub.
— Holistic Health Promotion & Complementary Therapies: A Resource for Integrated Practice. LC 98-29791. 410p. Date not set. ring bd. 139.00 (*0-8342-1005-3*, S488) Aspen Pub.
— Home Health Care Patient Education Manual. LC 94-17353. ring bd. 175.00 (*0-8342-0565-3*, S124) Aspen Pub.
— Hospital Material Management Forms, Checklists, & Guidelines. ring bd. 180.00 (*0-8342-0266-2*) Aspen Pub.
— Hospital Nutrition & Food Service Forms, Checklists & Guidelines. ring bd. 175.00 (*0-8342-0323-5*, S59) Aspen Pub.
— Medical Case Management: Forms, Checklists, & Guidelines. annuals Howe, Rufus, ed. 506p. ring bd., suppl. ed. 175.00 (*0-8342-0624-2*, S173) Aspen Pub.
— Medical Group Practice Legal & Administrative Guide. 1998. 189.00 (*0-8342-1068-1*, S470) Aspen Pub.
— Medical Rehabilitation Services: Forms, Checklists & Guidelines. Di Lima, Sara N. & Painter, Sandra J., eds. LC 94-41112. ring bd. 170.00 (*0-8342-0668-4*, S175) Aspen Pub.
— National Health Directory, 1995. (Illus.). 624p. 1995. text 99.00 (*0-8342-0596-3*) Aspen Pub.
— Oncology Patient Education Manual. Lawrence, Kenneth E. & Di Lima, Sara N., eds. LC 94-1144. ring bd. 210.00 (*0-8342-0543-2*, S125) Aspen Pub.
— Pain Management Patient Education Manuel. annuals Date not set. ring bd., suppl. ed. 179.00 (*0-8342-0634-X*, S168) Aspen Pub.
— Palliative Care Patient & Family Couseling Manual. 1996. 139.00 (*0-8342-0762-1*, S289) Aspen Pub.
— Preventive Care Sourcebook, 1997-1998: 1997 Edition. 288p. 1997. pap. 89.00 (*0-8342-0880-6*, 20880) Aspen Pub.
— Preventive Care Sourcebook, 1998-99. 200p. 1998. pap. 89.00 (*0-8342-1056-8*, 10568) Aspen Pub.
— Primary Care Patient Education Manual. annuals LC 98-45294. 500p. 1999. 149.00 (*0-8342-1015-0*, S498) Aspen Pub.
— Radiology Administration Forms, Checklists & Guidelines. Lawrence, Kenneth E. & Eutsey, Dwayne E., eds. LC 93-35879. ring bd. 200.00 (*0-8342-0546-7*) Aspen Pub.
— Safety & Security Administration in Health Care Facilities: Forms, Checklists & Guidelines. Di Lima, Sara N. & Eutsey, Dwayne E., eds. LC 94-48768. ring bd. 189.00 (*0-8342-0657-9*) Aspen Pub.
— Safety & Security Administration in School Facilities: Forms, Checklists & Guidelines. LC 96-20256. 1996. 129.00 (*0-8342-0821-0*) Aspen Pub.
— Stroke Rehabilitation Patient Education Manual. De Lima, Sara N., ed. LC 95-35240. 454p. 1997. ring bd. 165.00 (*0-8342-0675-7*) Aspen Pub.

Aspen Reference Group Staff, ed. National Health Directory, 1996 Edition. 496p. 1996. 99.00 (*0-8342-0800-8*) Aspen Pub.

Aspen Reference Group Staff & Di Lima, Sara N. Spanish - English Patient Education Collection: Women & Infants. Painter, Sandra J., ed. LC 95-12765. (ENG & SPA.). 672p. 1995. 52.00 (*0-8342-0717-6*) Aspen Pub.

Aspen Reference Group Staff & Eutsey, Dwayne E. Pharmacy Practice Management: Forms, Checklists & Guidelines on CD-ROM. LC 98-30817. 400p. 1999. ring bd. 199.00 (*0-8342-1079-7*, S518) Aspen Pub.

Aspen Reference Group Staff & Lawrence, Kenneth E. Hospital Medical Records Forms, Checklists & Guidelines: A Health Information Management Resource. Di Lima, Sara N., ed. LC 92-49483. 185p. ring bd. 185.00 (*0-8342-0329-4*) Aspen Pub.

Aspen Reference Group Staff, et al. Community Health Education & Promotion: A Guide to Program Design & Evaluation. LC 97-75. 426p. 1997. pap. 49.00 (*0-8342-0953-5*, 20953) Aspen Pub.

Aspen Reference Group Staff, jt. auth. see Weavers, Simon B.

Aspen, Richard. The Professor's Stick Book & Toy. 16p. (J). (gr. 3 up). 1993. pap. text 19.95 (*1-883737-01-X*) Matey Pr.

Aspen Staff. Clinical Pathways for Medical Rehabilitation Supplement, No. 1. LC 98-21821. 1998. 79.00 (*0-8342-1080-0*, S519) Aspen Pub.
— Employee Benefits: A Guide for Health Care Professionals. LC 98-9617. (Current Issue Ser.). 160p. 1998. 39.00 (*0-8342-1158-0*, 11580) Aspen Pub.
— Health Care Fraud & Abuse. LC 98-9393. (Current Issue Ser.). 160p. 1998. 39.00 (*0-8342-1159-9*, 11599) Aspen Pub.
— National Health Directory, 1998. 472p. 1998. 99.00 (*0-8342-1057-6*, 10576) Aspen Pub.
— Oncology Services Administration Forms: Forms, Checklists & Guidelines. LC 97-44161. 1998. 189.00 (*0-8342-0906-3*, S468) Aspen Pub.
— Pediatric Patient Education Manual. LC 98-21790. 1999. ring bd. 59.00 (*0-8342-1000-2*, 489S1) Aspen Pub.
— Physicians As Employees. LC 98-9397. (Current Issue Ser.). 160p. 1998. 39.00 (*0-8342-1157-2*, 11572) Aspen Pub.

***Aspen Staff.** Sports Medicine Patient Education & Practical Resource Manual Supplement, No. 1. LC 98-198010. 138p. 1998. 75.00 (*0-8342-1078-9*, S473) Aspen Pub.

Aspen Staff. State Regulation of Managed Care: State Regulation. LC 98-11538. (Current Issue Ser.). 160p. 1998. 39.00 (*0-8342-1120-3*, 11203) Aspen Pub.

Aspen Staff, et al. Health Information Management Manual. LC 97-43786. 1998. 189.00 (*0-8342-0944-6*, S467) Aspen Pub.

Aspen Strategy Group & European Strategy Group. Chemical Weapons & Western Security Policy. LC 87-1987. 80p. (Orig.). (C). 1987. pap. text 11.00 (*0-8191-6170-5*); lib. bdg. 31.00 (*0-8191-6169-1*) U Pr of Amer.

Aspen Strategy Group Staff. Anti-Satellite Weapons & U. S. Military Space Policy: An Aspen Strategy Group Report. 54p. (Orig.). (C). 1986. lib. bdg. 29.00 (*0-8191-5476-8*) U Pr of Amer.
— Balancing National Security Objectives in an Uncertain World. LC 89-34141. (Aspen Strategy Group Reports). 242p. (Orig.). (C). 1989. pap. text 29.00 (*0-8191-7489-0*); lib. bdg. 48.00 (*0-8191-7488-2*) U Pr of Amer.
— Deep Cuts & the Future of Nuclear Deterrence. LC 88-14744. (Aspen Strategy Group Reports). (Illus.). 92p. (Orig.). (C). 1989. pap. text 11.00 (*0-8191-7005-4*); lib. bdg. 26.50 (*0-8191-7004-6*) U Pr of Amer.
— Facing the Future: American Strategy in the 1990s: An Aspen Strategy Group Report. 364p. (C). 1991. pap. text 32.50 (*0-8191-8160-9*); lib. bdg. 59.00 (*0-8191-8159-5*) U Pr of Amer.

Aspen Strategy Group Staff & European Strategy Group Staff. The Soviet Challenge in the Gorbachev Era: Western Perceptions & Policy Recommendations. LC 89-5537. 170p. (Orig.). (C). 1989. pap. text 19.50 (*0-8191-7400-9*); lib. bdg. 38.00 (*0-8191-7399-1*) U Pr of Amer.

Aspen Strategy Group Staff, et al. After the INF Treaty: Conventional Forces & Arms Control in European Security. LC 88-2463. 84p. (Orig.). (C). 1988. pap. text 10.50 (*0-8191-6919-6*) U Pr of Amer.

Aspengren, Kate. Dear Mrs. Martin: Mother's Day;Two One-act Plays. 1992. pap. text 5.50 (*0-573-60144-5*) French.
— House of Wonders. LC 93-235601. 1993. pap. text 5.50 (*0-573-69386-2*) S French Trade.

***Aspenson, Judy Rea.** For This Child I Prayed. 1999. pap. text 9.99 (*0-9671088-0-2*) Prospect MI.

Aspenson, STeven S. The Philosopher's. LC 97-16070. 144p. (C). (gr. 13). 1998. pap. text 18.95 (*0-7656-0218-0*) M E Sharpe.

Aspenson, Steven Scott. The Philosopher's Tool Kit. LC 97-16070. 144p. (C). (gr. 13). 1998. text 55.95 (*0-7656-0217-2*) M E Sharpe.

Aspenstrom, Werner. Selected Poems. Fulton, Robin, tr. (QRL Poetry Bks.: Vol. XXXIV). 1995. 20.00 (*0-614-06460-0*) Quarterly Rev.
— You & I & the World. Barkan, Stanley H., ed. Cedering, Siv, tr. from ENG. (Cross-Cultural Review Chapbook Ser.: No. 5). 40p. 15.00 (*0-89304-878-X*, CCC130); pap. 5.00 (*0-89304-804-6*) Cross-Cultrl NY.

***Asper, Lynn K.** A Physical Approach to Playing the Trumpet: Using the Body's Reflexes to Enhance Trumpet Performance. Asper, Renee D., ed. LC 98-94064. (Illus.). 104p. 1999. pap. 16.95 (*0-9668847-0-1*) WaveSong.

Asper, Renee D., ed. see Asper, Lynn K.

Asperen de Boer, J. R. J. Van & Rishel, Joseph J. Jan Van Eyck's Two Paintings of Saint Francis Receiving the Stigmata. LC 97-17147. (Illus.). 120p. 1997. 32.00 (*0-87633-115-0*, Pub. by Phila Mus Art) Antique Collect.

Asperheim, Mary K. The Pharmacologic Basis of Patient Care. 5th ed. (Illus.). 620p. 1985. teacher ed. write for info. (*0-7216-2004-3*, W B Saunders Co) Harcrt Hlth Sci Grp.
— The Pharmacologic Basis of Patient Care. 5th ed. (Illus.). 620p. 1985. text 65.00 (*0-7216-1229-6*, W B Saunders Co) Harcrt Hlth Sci Grp.
— Pharmacology: An Introductory Text. 8th ed. (Illus.). 1996. pap., teacher ed. write for info. (*0-7216-6039-8*, W B Saunders Co) Harcrt Hlth Sci Grp.
— Pharmacology: An Introductory Text. 8th ed. Rader, Ilza, ed. LC 95-36451. (Illus.). 275p. 1996. pap. text 24.95 (*0-7216-6038-X*, W B Saunders Co) Harcrt Hlth Sci Grp.

Asperti, Andrea & Guerrini, Stefano. The Optimal Implementation of Functional Programming Languages. (Tracts in Theoretical Computer Science Ser.: Vol. 45). 404p. (C). 1998. text 69.95 (*0-521-62112-7*) Cambridge U Pr.

Aspeslagh, Robert, jt. auth. see Burns, Robin J.

Aspey, Wayne P. & Lustick, Sheldon I., eds. Behavioral Energetics: The Cost of Survival in Vertebrates. LC 82-12512. (Illus.). 312p. reprint ed. pap. 96.80 (*0-608-09653-9*, 206976800006) Bks Demand.

Aspillera, Paraluman S. Basic Tagalog for Foreigners & Non-Tagalogs. (TAG.). 258p. 1993. pap. 13.95 (*0-8048-1910-6*) Tuttle Pubng.

Aspin. Life Management: Individuals, Families & Group. 1995. pap. text. write for info. (*0-582-80547-3*, Pub. by Addison-Wesley) Longman.

Aspin, B. Terry. The Backyard Foundry. (Workshop Practice Ser.: No. 25). (Illus.). 90p. (Orig.). 1997. pap. 21.50 (*1-85486-146-8*) Nexus Special Interests.
— Foundrywork for the Amateur. 2nd ed. (Workshop Practice Ser.: No. 4). (Illus.). 104p. (Orig.). 1998. pap. 18.50 (*1-85486-168-9*, Pub. by Nexus Special Interests) Trans-Atl Phila.
— The Model Locomotive from Scratch. (Illus.). 92p. (Orig.). 1998. pap. 27.50 (*1-85486-165-4*) Nexus Special Interests.

Aspin, Chris. The Cotton Industry. (Album Ser.: No. 63). (Illus.). 32p. 1989. pap. 4.75 (*0-85263-545-1*, Pub. by Shire Pubns) Parkwest Pubns.
— The Woollen Industry. (Album Ser.: No. 81). (Illus.). 32p. pap. 4.75 (*0-85263-598-2*, Pub. by Shire Pubns) Parkwest Pubns.

Aspin, Lee & Dickinson, Bill. Defense for a New Era: Lessons of the Persian Gulf War. (Association of the U. S. Army Book Ser.). 128p. 1992. 18.95 (*0-02-881028-7*, 4109M) Brasseys.

Aspin, Les. The Aspin Papers: Sanctions, Diplomacy, & War in the Persian Gulf. LC 91-7361. (Significant Issues Ser.: Vol. 13, No. 2). 106p. reprint ed. pap. 32.90 (*0-7837-6057-4*, 204587000008) Bks Demand.
— Report of the Secretary of Defense to the President & the Congress: January 1994. (Illus.). 340p. (Orig.). 1996. reprint ed. pap. text 45.00 (*0-7881-2992-9*) DIANE Pub.

Aspin, Roy. Lewis Carroll & His Camera. (C). 1989. text 60.00 (*0-948706-04-X*, Pub. by Brent Pubns) St Mut.
— The Parson on the Hill. 136p. (C). 1990. pap. text 45.00 (*0-948706-05-8*, Pub. by Brent Pubns) St Mut.

Aspinall. Aspinall's Reports of Maritime Cases 1870-1940, 20 vols. boxed set 2600.00 (*0-86205-264-5*, U.K., MICHIE) LEXIS Pub.

Aspinall, A. Formation of Canning's Ministry. (Camden Third Ser.). 35.00 (*0-86193-059-2*) David Brown.

Aspinall, A. & Smith, Anthony, eds. English Historical Documents, 1783-1832, Vol. 8. 1022p. (C). 1996. 265.00 (*0-415-14373-X*) Routledge.

Aspinall, Algernon. Guide to the West Indies. 1978. lib. bdg. 59.95 (*0-8490-1924-9*) Gordon Pr.

***Aspinall, Edward, et al, eds.** The Last Days of President Suharto. 2p. 1999. pap. 24.95 (*0-7326-1175-X*, Pub. by Monash Asia Inst) Intl Spec Bk.

Aspinall, Henry O. Aspinwall & Aspinall Families of Lancashire, 1189-1923. 394p. 1996. reprint ed. pap. 62.00 (*0-8328-5374-7*); reprint ed. lib. bdg. 72.00 (*0-8328-5373-9*) Higginson Bk Co.

Aspinall, James P., et al. Treatise of the Law Relative to Merchant Ships & Seamen. 14th ed. cii, 1356,88p. 1993. reprint ed. 150.00 (*0-8377-1908-9*, Rothman) W S Hein.

Aspinall-Oglander, C. F. Military Opeartions, Gallipoli, 2 vols., Set. (Great War Ser.). (Illus.). 602p. reprint ed. 89.95 (*0-89839-175-X*) Battery Pr.

Aspinallz. Environmental GIS & Data Analysis. text 84.00 (*0-471-98564-3*); pap. text 24.00 (*0-471-98565-1*) Wiley.

Aspinwall. IRQ, DMA & I/O. 2nd ed. 1997. 24.95 (*0-8052-8565-2*, M&T Bks) IDG Bks.

***Aspinwall.** Troubleshooting Your PC. 4th ed. LC TK7887.A87 1999. 912p. 1998. pap. 39.99 (*0-7645-7509-0*) IDG Bks.

Aspinwall, Algernon A. The Aspinwall Genealogy. 262p. 1988. reprint ed. pap. 34.50 (*0-8328-0141-0*); reprint ed. lib. bdg. 44.50 (*0-8328-0140-2*) Higginson Bk Co.
— Aspinwall Genealogy (Peter of Brookline, Mass.) (Illus.). 262p. 1996. reprint ed. pap. 41.00 (*0-8328-5372-0*); reprint ed. lib. bdg. 51.00 (*0-8328-5371-2*) Higginson Bk Co.

***Aspinwall, Jim.** IRQ DMA & I/O: Resolving & Preventing PC System Conflicts. 3rd ed. LC 99-13150. (Illus.). 384p. 1999. pap. 24.99 incl. cd-rom (*0-7645-7519-8*) IDG Bks.

Aspinwall, Jim, et al. Troubleshooting Your PC. 2nd ed. LC 94-35041. 550p. 1994. pap. 32.95 (*1-55828-378-1*, MIS Pr) IDG Bks.

Aspinwall, John. Travels in Britain, 1794-1795: The Diary of John Aspinwall, Great-Grandfather of Franklin Delano Roosevelt, with a Brief History of His Aspinwall Forebears. Collins, Aileen S., ed. LC 94-23232. 1994. 23.95 (*0-9638487-6-3*) Parsons Pr VA.

Aspinwall, Kath, jt. auth. see Pedler, Mike.

Aspinwall, Margaret, jt. auth. see Lipman, Jean.

Aspinwall, Mark. Moveable Feast: Pressure Group Conflict & the European Community Shipping Policy. 208p. 1995. 66.95 (*1-85972-069-2*, Pub. by Avebry) Ashgate Pub Co.

Aspinwall, Richard C. & Eisenbeis, Robert A., eds. Handbook for Banking Strategy. LC 84-19487. 800p. 1985. 175.00 (*0-471-89314-5*) Wiley.

Aspire. Fast Pace, No. 7. (Automotive Technology Ser.). 1989. student ed. 64.95 (*0-8273-5541-6*) Delmar.
— Fast Pace: Auto Tech - Electrical System. (Automotive Technology Ser.). 1989. student ed. 14.00 (*0-8273-5549-1*) Delmar.
— Fast Pace: Auto Tech - Engine Performance. (Automotive Technology Ser.). 1989. student ed. 14.00 (*0-8273-5554-8*) Delmar.
— Fast Pace: Auto Tech - Suspension/Steering. (Automotive Technology Ser.). 1989. student ed. 14.00 (*0-8273-5547-5*) Delmar.
— Fast Pace: Auto Tech-Engine Repair. (Automotive Technology Ser.). 1989. student ed. 14.00 (*0-8273-5545-9*) Delmar.
— Fast Pace: Introduction to Test Taking Skills. (Automotive Technology Ser.). 1989. student ed. 14.00 (*0-8273-5543-2*) Delmar.
— Fast Pase: Auto Tech - Brakes. (Automotive Technology Ser.). 1989. student ed. 14.00 (*0-8273-5556-4*) Delmar.
— Past Pace: Auto Tech - Heating & Air Conditioning. (Automotive Technology Ser.). 1989. student ed. 14.00 (*0-8273-5551-3*) Delmar.

Aspital, A. W., ed. see Latham, Robert.

Aspiz, Harold. Walt Whitman & the Body Beautiful. LC 79-28280. 304p. 1980. 29.95 (*0-252-00799-9*) U of Ill Pr.

Aspland & Lyle. Instant Astrologer. 1999. text 22.95 (*0-312-19427-7*) St Martin.

Aspland, J. R. Textile Dyeing & Coloration. (Illus.). 416p. 1997. 65.00 (*0-9613350-1-7*, 9615) AATCC.

Asplann, Jerry. International Ship Management - 4: Containing Costs for Survival. 96p. 1994. pap. 190.00 (*1-85044-561-3*) LLP.

Aspler, Tony. Blood Is Thicker Than Beaujolais: A Wine Taster's Mystery. 224p. 1994. 19.95 (*1-895629-39-X*) Warwick Publ.
— Blood Is Thicker Than Beaujolais: A Wine Taster's Mystery. large type ed. 416p. 1997. 27.99 (*0-7089-3678-4*) Ulverscroft.
— Titanic. 312p. 1989. 24.95 (*0-385-25213-7*) Doubleday.

Aspley, John. Speculum Nauticum: A Looking Glasse, for Sea-Men. LC 77-6849. (English Experience Ser.: No. 844). 1977. reprint ed. lib. bdg. 20.00 (*90-221-0844-9*) Walter J Johnson.

Aspley, Ketih & France, Peter, eds. Poetry in France: Metamorphosis of a Muse. 288p. 1992. 76.50 (*0-7486-0335-2*, Pub. by Edinburgh U Pr) Col U Pr.

***Asplmary, Franz.** Franz Asplmayr: Six Quatuors Concertantes, Opus 2. Monk, Dennis, ed. (Recent Researches in Music of the Classic Era Ser.: Vol. RRC56). (Illus.). x, 85p. 1999. pap. 40.00 (*0-89579-441-1*) A-R Eds.

Asplund-Campbell, Marni. With Child: Mormon Women on Mothering. LC 98-15271. 200p. 1998. 14.95 (*1-56085-112-0*, Smith Res) Signature Bks.

Asplund, Erik G. Erik Gunnar Asplund: Architect. (Illus.). 132p. 1998. 49.95 (*3-927258-51-2*) Gingko Press.

Asplund, Gisele & Asplund, Goran. An Integrated Development Strategy. LC 81-14822. 141p. reprint ed. pap. 43.80 (*0-7837-6363-8*, 204607500010) Bks Demand.

Asplund, Goran, jt. auth. see Asplund, Gisele.

Asplund, John. The Annual Register of the Baptist Denomination in North America to 1790. 1979. reprint ed. 16.00 (*0-317-01254-1*) Church History.
— The Universal Register of the Baptist Denomiation in North America for the Years 1790, 1791, 1792, 1793, & Part of 1794. Gaustad, Edwin S., ed. LC 79-52581. (Baptist Tradition Ser.). 1980. reprint ed. lib. bdg. 17.95 (*0-405-12448-1*) Ayer.

Asplund, John Malcolm, ed. Principles of Amino Acid Nutrition for Ruminants. 224p. 1994. lib. bdg. 169.00 (*0-8493-4910-9*, SF98) CRC Pr.

Asplund, Karl. Zorn's Engraved Work, Set, Vols. 1 & 2. (Illus.). 666p. 1990. reprint ed. 295.00 (*1-55660-034-8*) A Wofsy Fine Arts.

Asplund, Lars, et al, eds. Reliable Software Technologies - Ada Europe '98: 1998 Ada-Europe International Conference on Reliable Software Technologies, Uppwala, Sweden, June 8-12, 1998, Proceedings, Vol. 141. LC 98-20469. (Lecture Notes in Computer Science Ser.: Vol. 1411). xi, 297p. 1998. pap. 55.00 (*3-540-64536-5*) Spr-Verlag.

Asplund, R., ed. Human Capital Creation in an Economic Perspective. (Illus.). xii, 213p. 1995. 54.00 (*3-7908-0815-6*) Spr-Verlag.

Asplund, Rita, et al, eds. Low Pay & Earnings Mobility in Europe. LC 98-17708. 296p. 1998. 90.00 (*1-85898-854-3*) E Elgar.

Aspo. Journal Perinatal, 1995, Issues 1-4. (Nursing Ser.). pap. 140.00 (*0-614-06985-8*) Jones & Bartlett.

Aspray, William. John Von Neumann & the Origins of Modern Computing. (History of Computing Ser.). 600p. 1990. 48.50 (*0-262-01121-2*) MIT Pr.

Aspray, William, Jr., intro. Technological Competitiveness: Contemporary & Historical Perspectives on the Electrical, Electronics, & Computer Industries. LC 92-30772. (Illus.). 384p. (C). 1993. text 59.95 (*0-7803-0427-6*, PC0324-4) Inst Electrical.

Aspray, William & Cooper, Jill, eds. Engineers As Executives: An International Perspective. LC 94-21224. 328p. 1994. 39.95 (*0-7803-1103-5*, PC4564) Inst Electrical.

Aspray, William & Kitcher, Philip, eds. History & Philosophy of Modern Mathematics. LC 86-30884. (Minnesota Studies in the Philosophy of Science: Vol. 11). 395p. 1988. reprint ed. pap. 122.50 (*0-608-00785-4*, 205933400010) Bks Demand.

Aspray, William, jt. auth. see Goldstein, Andrew.

Aspray, William, jt. auth. see Harvard Computation Laboratory Staff.

***Asprey, Lisa.** Hair Deco for Kids: Fun at Your Fingertips. (Illus.). 48p. (gr. 3-9). 1999. pap. text 14.95 (*1-85868-767-5*, Pub. by Carlton Bks Ltd) Natl Bk Netwk.

Asprey, Michele. Plain Language for Lawyers. 140p. 1991. 48.00 (*1-86287-064-0*, Pub. by Federation Pr); pap. 33.00 (*1-86287-063-2*, Pub. by Federation Pr) Gaunt.
— Plain Language for Lawyers. 2nd ed. LC 96-147371. 250p. 1996. pap. 34.00 (*1-86287-205-8*, Pub. by Federation Pr) Gaunt.

***Asprey, Robert.** The Rise of Napolean Bonaparte. 2000. 37.50 (*0-465-04879-X*) Basic.

Asprey, Robert B. At Belleau Wood. LC 96-25519. (Illus.). 376p. 1996. reprint ed. pap. 19.95 (*1-57441-016-4*) UNTX Pr.

Asprey, Robert B. Frederick the Great: The Magnificent Enigma. (Illus.). 738p. 1988. pap. 12.95 (*0-89919-840-6*, Pub. by Ticknor & Fields) HM.

Asprey, Robert B. War in the Shadows: The Guerrilla in History. rev. ed. (Illus.). 1279p. 1997. reprint ed. text 40.00 (*0-7881-5104-5*) DIANE Pub.

Asprey, Robert B., told to. Once a Marine: The Memoirs of General A. A. Vandegrift, U.S.M.C. 348p. 1982. reprint ed. lib. bdg. 9.95 (*0-940328-03-8*) Marine Corps.

Asprey, Roger. Napolean. 624p. 1998. pap. 18.00 (*0-465-04880-3*) Basic.

Aspril, Elizabeth. As Battles Raged. (Illus.). (Orig.). 1981. 12.95 (*0-9604750-1-X*); pap. 7.95 (*0-9604750-0-1*) E Keys.

***Asprin, Robert & Evans, Linda.** Ripping Time. 480p. 2000. mass mkt. 6.99 (*0-671-57867-7*) PB.

Asprin, Robert L. Another Fine Myth. 208p. 1986. mass mkt. 5.50 (*0-441-02362-2*) Ace Bks.
— The Bug Wars. 224p. 1993. mass mkt. 4.99 (*0-441-07373-5*) Ace Bks.
— Hit or Myth. 176p. 1986. mass mkt. 5.50 (*0-441-33851-8*) Ace Bks.
— Little Myth Marker. (Myth Ser.). 1987. mass mkt. 5.99 (*0-441-48499-9*) Ace Bks.
— M. Y. T. H. Inc. in Action. 1991. mass mkt. 5.99 (*0-441-55282-X*) Ace Bks.
— M. Y. T. H. Inc. Link. (Myth Ser.: No. 7). 176p. (Orig.). 1988. mass mkt. 5.50 (*0-441-55277-3*) Ace Bks.
— Myth Conceptions. 224p. 1986. mass mkt. 5.99 (*0-441-55521-7*) Ace Bks.
— Myth Directions. (Myth Ser.). 1986. mass mkt. 5.99 (*0-441-55529-2*) Ace Bks.
— Myth-ing Persons. 176p. 1986. mass mkt. 5.50 (*0-441-55276-5*) Ace Bks.
— Myth-Nomers & Im-Pervections, No. 8. 1988. mass mkt. 5.99 (*0-441-55279-X*) Ace Bks.
— Phule's Company. (Phule's Company: 1). 1990. mass mkt. 5.50 (*0-441-66251-X*) Ace Bks.
— Phule's Paradise. (Phule's Company: 2). 1992. mass mkt. 5.50 (*0-441-66253-6*) Ace Bks.
— Sweet Myth-tery of Life. 240p. 1995. mass mkt. 5.50 (*0-441-00194-7*) Ace Bks.
Asprin, Robert L. & Evans, Linda. Time Scout. LC 96-176955. 2000. mass mkt. 5.99 (*0-671-87698-8*) PB.
— Wagers of Sin. (Time Scout Ser.: No. 2). 464p. 2000. reprint ed. mass mkt. 5.99 (*0-671-87730-5*) PB.
***Asprin, Robert L. & Heck, Peter J.** A Phule & His Money. (Phule's Company: 3). 1999. mass mkt. 6.99 (*0-441-00658-2*) Ace Bks.
Asprin, Robert L., jt. auth. see Abbey, Lynn.
ASPRS Staff, jt. auth. see ACSM Staff.
***Aspy, Cheryl Blalock & Sandhu, Daya Singh.** Empowering Women for Equity: A Counseling Approach. LC 98-54165. 3p. 1999. pap. 31.95 (*1-55620-214-8*) Am Coun Assn.
Aspy, Cheryl Blalock, jt. auth. see Sandhu, Daya Singh.
Aspy, Cheryl B., jt. auth. see Sandhu, Daya S.
***ASQ-Andersen-Fagerhau, et al.** Root Cause Analysis: Simplified Tools & Techniques. LC 99-42486. 155p. 2000. 27.00 (*0-87389-466-9*) ASQ Qual Pr.
ASQ Chemical & Process Industries Division, Chemic. The Certified Quality Manager Handbook. LC 99-22702. 600p. 1999. 77.00 (*0-87389-387-5*) McGraw.
— ISO 9000 Guidelines for the Chemical & Process Industries. 2nd ed. 150p. 1996. pap. 29.00 (*0-87389-352-2*, H0910) ASQ Qual Pr.
— Quality Assurance for the Chemical & Process Industries: A Manual of Good Practices. 56p. (Orig.). 1987. pap. 22.00 (*0-87389-035-3*, T184) ASQ Qual Pr.
— Specifications for the Chemical & Process Industries: A Manual for Development & Use. LC 95-45500. 183p. 1996. pap. 27.00 (*0-87389-351-4*, H0908) ASQ Qual Pr.
ASQ Design & Construction Division Staff. Interpretive Guidelines for the Application of ANSI/ASQC Q9001-1994 or Q9002-1994 for Owner's, Designer's & Constructor's Quality Management Systems. LC 96-42990. (Illus.). 70p. 1997. 50.00 (*0-87389-420-0*, H0953) ASQ Qual Pr.
ASQ Energy & Environmental Division, International. International Matrix of Nuclear Quality Assurance Program Requirements. LC 95-15645. (Briefing Ser.). 76p. 1995. pap. 19.00 (*0-87389-334-4*, MB112) ASQ Qual Pr.
ASQ Energy & Environmental Division, Nuclear Facil. Inspection Program Handbook. LC 95-14642. 50p. 1995. pap. 13.00 (*0-87389-308-5*, MB116) ASQ Qual Pr.
ASQ Energy & Environmental Division Staff. Definitions of Environmental Quality Assurance Terms. (Briefing Ser.). 34p. 1996. pap. 19.50 (*0-87389-359-X*, MB114) ASQ Qual Pr.
ASQ Energy & Environmental Division Staff, et al. Quality Assurance Guidelines for Research & Development. LC 94-8907. (ASQC Briefing Ser.). 38p. 1994. 13.00 (*0-87389-302-6*, MB104) ASQ Qual Pr.
ASQ Energy Division Staff. Nuclear Quality Systems Auditor Training Handbook. 2nd ed. (Audit Quality Ser.). 194p. 1986. 38.00 (*0-87389-008-6*, H0520) ASQ Qual Pr.
ASQ Food, Drug & Cosmetic Division Staff, ed. Food Processing Industry Quality System Guidelines. LC 97-33087. (Illus.). 176p. (Orig.). 1998. pap. 30.00 (*0-87389-390-5*, H0978) ASQ Qual Pr.
***ASQ Quality Audit Divison Staff.** The Quality Audit Handbook. 2nd ed. LC 99-44972. 320p. 2000. 60.00 (*0-87389-460-X*) ASQ Qual Pr.
ASQ Quality Audit Technical Committee. How to Plan an Audit. Robinson, Charles B., ed. 39p. 1987. pap. 21.00 (*0-87389-032-9*, T801) ASQ Qual Pr.
ASQ Quality Costs Committee. Principles of Quality Costs: Principles, Implementation & Use. 2nd rev. ed. Campanella, Jack, ed. (Quality Ser.). (Illus.). 140p. 1990. pap. 45.00 (*0-87389-084-1*, H0593) ASQ Qual Pr.
— Quality Costs: Ideas & Applications, Vol. I. 2nd ed. Grimm, Andrew F., ed. 592p. 1987. pap. 54.00 (*0-87389-046-9*, H0565) ASQ Qual Pr.
— Quality Costs: Ideas & Applications, Vol. 2. Campanella, Jack, ed. (Illus.). 495p. 1989. 54.00 (*0-87389-047-7*, H0569) ASQ Qual Pr.
ASQ Statistics Division Staff. Glossary & Tables for Statistical Quality Control. 3rd ed. 176p. 1996. pap. 33.00 (*0-87389-354-9*, H0913) ASQ Qual Pr.
***ASQ Statistics Division Staff.** Improving Performance Through Performance Review: A Guide to the Employee. 2000. 23.00 (*0-87389-467-7*) ASQ Qual Pr.
Asquith, A. In the Flesh. mass mkt. 6.95 (*0-7472-5243-2*, Pub. by Headline Bk Pub) Trafalgar.
Asquith, Adam. Revision of the Genus Lopidea in America North of Mexico (Heteroptera: Mridae: Orthotylinae) (Theses Zoologicae Ser.: Vol. 16). (Illus.). 280p. 1991. 135.00 (*3-87429-335-1*, Pub. by Koeltz Sci Bks) Lubrecht & Cramer.
Asquith, Adam, jt. auth. see Polhemus, Dan.
Asquith, Cynthia. Married to Tolstoy. (Illus.). 283p. 1964. 9.95 (*0-251-15039-9*) Dufour.
Asquith, George B. Handbook of Log Evaluation Techniques for Carbonate Reservoirs. LC 85-6212. (Methods in Exploration Ser.: Vol. 5). (Illus.). 53p. reprint ed. pap. 30.00 (*0-608-08734-3*, 206937300004) Bks Demand.
— Log Evaluation of Shaly Sandstones: A Practical Guide. (Continuing Education Course Note Ser.: No. 31). (Illus.). 59p. (Orig.). 1990. pap. 20.00 (*0-89181-179-6*, 900) AAPG.
Asquith, George B. & Gibson, Charles R. Basic Well Log Analysis for Geologists. (Methods in Exploration Ser.: No. 03). (Illus.). 216p. 1983. 29.00 (*0-89181-652-6*, 617) AAPG.
Asquith, Glenn H. Church Officers at Work. rev. ed. 1951. pap. 9.00 (*0-8170-0048-8*) Judson.
Asquith, Herbert H. The Genesis of the War. LC 71-39714. (Select Bibliographies Reprint Ser.). 1977. reprint ed. 22.95 (*0-8369-9926-6*) Ayer.
— Occasional Addresses, 1893 to 1916. LC 76-99715. (Essay Index Reprint Ser.). 1977. reprint ed. 20.95 (*0-8369-1368-X*) Ayer.
Asquith, Herbert H., jt. auth. see Oxford Staff.
Asquith, Julie, jt. auth. see Williams, Carol.
Asquith, L. In the Groove. mass mkt. 6.95 (*0-7472-4527-4*, Pub. by Headline Bk Pub) Trafalgar.
— Sleeping Partners. mass mkt. 6.95 (*0-7472-5107-X*, Pub. by Headline Bk Pub) Trafalgar.
Asquith, Margo. The Autobiography of Margo Asquith. Carter, Mark B., ed. 342p. 1996. pap. 24.95 (*0-297-81602-0*, Pub. by Weidenfeld & Nicolson) Trafalgar.
Asquith, Nancy. WG&L Pension & Benefits Fact Book. 1992nd ed. 1991. per. 88.00 (*0-7913-0440-X*) Warren Gorham & Lamont.
— WGL Human Resources Checklists with Commentary. 2nd ed. 1991. ring bd. 129.00 (*0-685-69676-6*, MPCK) Warren Gorham & Lamont.
Asquith, P. D., jt. ed. see Suppe, F.
Asquith, Pamela J. & Kalland, Arne. Japanese Images of Nature: Cultural Perspectives. 288p. (C). 1997. text 48.00 (*0-7007-0444-2*, Pub. by Curzon Pr Ltd); pap. text 24.95 (*0-7007-0445-0*, Pub. by Curzon Pr Ltd) UH Pr.
Asquith, Pamela J., jt. ed. see Fedigan, Linda M.
Asquith, Peter D. & Giere, Ronald, eds. PSA 1980, 2 Vols., Vol. II. 678p. 1981. 23.75 (*0-917586-16-6*) Philos Sci Assn.
Asquith, Peter D. & Hacking, Ian, eds. PSA 1978, 2 vols., Vol. I. LC 72-624169. 314p. 1978. pap. 6.00 (*0-917586-05-0*) Philos Sci Assn.
— PSA 1978, 2 vols., Vol. II. LC 72-624169. 478p. 1978. 22.50 (*0-917586-10-7*) Philos Sci Assn.
Asquith, Peter D. & Kitcher, Philip, eds. PSA, 1984, Vol. 1. 223p. 1984. 15.50 (*0-917586-21-2*) Philos Sci Assn.
— PSA, 1984, Vol. 2. 903p. 1985. 30.00 (*0-917586-24-7*) Philos Sci Assn.
Asquith, Peter D. & Nickles, Thomas, eds. PSA 1982, 2 Vols., I. 414p. 1982. 21.00 (*0-917586-18-2*) Philos Sci Assn.
— PSA 1982, 2 Vols., Vol. II. 730p. 1983. 25.00 (*0-917586-19-0*) Philos Sci Assn.
Asquith, R. Nora Normal/Great Ghost Adventure. (Illus.). (J). mass mkt. 6.95 (*0-340-68071-7*, Pub. by Hodder & Stought Ltd) Trafalgar.
Asquith, Ros. Ball! LC 98-28829. (Toddlers Playbook Ser.). (Illus.). (J). 1999. 9.95 (*0-7894-3486-5*) DK Pub Inc.
***Asquith, Ros.** Ball! (Toddlers Storybook Ser.). 20p. (J). 2000. pap. text 5.95 (*0-7894-5749-0*, D K Ink) DK Pub Inc.
— I Was a Teenage Worrier. (J). 2000. pap. 8.95 (*0-552-14027-9*, Pub. by Transworld Publishers Ltd) Trafalgar.
— My Do It! LC 00-25737. (Toddlers Storybook Ser.). (Illus.). 24p. (ps-k). 2000. pap. write for info. (*0-7894-5648-6*, Pub. by DK Pub Inc) Pub Resources Inc.
— Teenage Worriers Guide to Life. 2000. pap. 8.95 (*0-552-14534-3*) Transworld Publishers Ltd.
— Teenage Worriers Guide to Life. (J). 2000. pap. 8.95 (*0-552-14339-1*, Pub. by Transworld Publishers Ltd) Trafalgar.
Asquith, Stewart, ed. Children & Young People in Conflict with the Law. LC 96-222631. (Research Highlights in Social Work Ser.: No. 30). 280p. 1996. pap. 31.95 (*1-85302-291-8*, Pub. by Jessica Kingsley) Taylor & Francis.
Asquith, Stewart & Hill, Malcolm, eds. Justice for Children. LC 93-42894. 188p. (C). 1994. lib. bdg. 86.00 (*0-7923-2645-8*) Kluwer Academic.
Asquith, Stuart. The Collector's Guide to New Toy Soldiers: Metal Figures from 1973 to the Present Day. (Illus.). 112p. 1991. 34.50 (*1-85486-051-8*) Nexus Special Interests.
— The New Model Army, 1645-60. (Men-at-Arms Ser.: No. 110). (Illus.). 48p. pap. 11.95 (*0-85045-385-2*, 9043, Pub. by Ospry) Stackpole.
— Wargaming World War II. (Illus.). 192p. (Orig.). 1989. pap. 22.50 (*1-85486-000-3*) Nexus Special Interests.
Asquith, Stuart, ed. see Featherstone, Donald.
Asquith, Stuart, ed. see Herbert, Edwin.
Asra, Ghassem. Theory & Applications of Optical Remote Sensing. LC 88-35182. (Remote Sensing & Image Processing Ser.). 752p. 1989. 250.00 (*0-471-62895-6*) Wiley.
Asrani, U. A. Yoga Unveiled, Pt. 2. (C). 1993. text 22.00 (*81-208-0946-7*, Pub. by Motilal Bnarsidass) S Asia.
Asraoui, Fadi, et al. Current Regional Issues: Florica. 62p. (C). 1994. pap. text 19.00 (*0-03-001953-2*) Dryden Pr.
Asrar, Chassem, jt. auth. see Dozier, Jeff.
Asrar, Ghassem & Dokken, David, eds. The State of Earth Science from Space: Past Progress, Future Prospects. (Illus.). 170p. 1995. 75.00 (*1-56396-492-9*) Am Inst Physics.
Asratian, Armen S., et al. Bipartite Graphs & Their Applications. LC 97-5251. (Tracts in Mathematics Ser.: Vol. 131). (Illus.). 300p. (C). 1998. text 64.95 (*0-521-59345-X*) Cambridge U Pr.
Asregadoo, Edward R. Man from Guyana. LC 89-91456. 1990. 18.95 (*0-87212-231-X*) Libra.
Assad, A. A., jt. ed. see Golden, B. L.
Assad, Arjang A., jt. ed. see Golden, Bruce L.
Assad, Christine L. Love Now! The Secret to Happiness. LC 95-94720. 128p. (Orig.). 1995. pap. 10.00 (*0-9647984-0-9*) Inner Lght Pubs.
Assad, Fawzia, jt. auth. see Zaya, Ocatvio.
Assad, Maria L. Reading with Michel Serres: An Encounter with Time. LC 98-27740. 256p. (C). 1999. text 59.50 (*0-7914-4229-2*); pap. text 19.95 (*0-7914-4230-6*) State U NY Pr.
Assadi, Amir H. Finite Group Actions on Simply-Connected Manifolds & CW Complexes. LC 81-19104. (Memoirs Ser.: No. 35/257). 113p. 1982. pap. 16.00 (*0-8218-2257-8*, MEMO/35/257) Am Math.
Assadi, Barbara. QuarkXPress for Windows Handbook. 600p. 1992. pap. 29.95 (*1-878058-45-2*) IDG Bks.
Assadi, Barbara & Gruman, Galen. MacWorld Quarkxpress 3.2/3.3 Bible. 650p. 1994. pap. 39.95 (*1-878058-85-1*) IDG Bks.
Assadi, John, jt. ed. see Marks, Stephanie.
Assadipour. Learn Autocad. Date not set. pap. text, student ed. write for info. (*0-314-03311-4*) West Pub.
— Microstation. Date not set. teacher ed. write for info. (*0-314-06624-1*) West Pub.
Assadipour, Hossein. Learning AutoCAD in Twenty Projects. Conty, ed. LC 93-39996. 500p. (C). 1994. pap. text 38.25 (*0-314-02837-4*) West Pub.
— Learning MicroStation in 20 Projects. LC 95-31197. 475p. (C). 1996. pap. text 46.95 (*0-314-05539-8*) West Pub.
Assael. Marketing Core Concepts. LC 97-74497. (C). 1997. text 37.00 (*0-03-024811-6*) Harcourt Coll Pubs.
— Marketing Core Concepts. (C). 1997. pap. text, teacher ed. 26.75 (*0-03-024812-4*) Harcourt Coll Pubs.
— Marketing Core Concepts. (C). 1998. pap. text 29.50 (*0-03-024813-2*, Pub. by Harcourt Coll Pubs) Harcourt.
Assael, Alyce. Singular Visions: Long Island Folk Art from the Late 18th Century to the Present. LC 85-70640. (Illus.). 48p. 1985. pap. 5.00 (*0-933793-00-6*) Guild Hall.
Assael, Henry. Consumer Behav & Mktg Action. (SWC-Marketing). 641p. (C). 1981. mass mkt. 27.25 (*0-534-00958-1*) PWS Pubs.
— Consumer Behavior. 3rd ed. (SWC-Marketing). 720p. (C). 1987. mass mkt. 54.75 (*0-534-07530-4*) PWS Pubs.
— Consumer Behavior & Marketing Action. 2nd ed. LC 83-22197. (SWC-Marketing). 720p. (C). 1984. mass mkt. 35.00 (*0-534-02990-6*) S-W Pub.
— Consumer Behavior & Marketing Action. 4th ed. 848p. 1992. text 60.95 (*0-534-92552-9*) S-W Pub.
— Consumer Behavior & Marketing Action. 5th ed. LC 94-30946. (C). 1994. mass mkt. 63.00 (*0-538-84433-7*) S-W Pub.
— Slides from Transparencies to Accompany "Marketing: Principles & Strategy" 2nd ed. 175p. (C). 1993. 133.00 incl. sl. (*0-03-097819-X*) Dryden Pr.
Assael, Henry, ed. A Century of Marketing Series, 33 bks. (Illus.). 1978. lib. bdg. 1157.50 (*0-405-11156-8*) Ayer.
— The Collected Works of C. C. Parlin: An Original Anthology. LC 78-260. (Century of Marketing Ser.). (Illus.). 1979. lib. bdg. 24.95 (*0-405-11159-2*) Ayer.
— Early Development & Conceptualization of the Field of Marketing: An Original Anthology. LC 78-278. (Century of Marketing Ser.). 1979. lib. bdg. 23.95 (*0-405-11188-6*) Ayer.
— A Pioneer in Marketing: L. D. H. Weld: An Original Anthology. LC 78-283. (Century Classic Ser.). 1979. lib. bdg. 58.95 (*0-405-11157-6*) Ayer.
Assael, Henry, ed. see Alderson, Wroe.
Assael, Henry, ed. see Bartels, Robert.
Assael, Henry, ed. see Blankenship, Albert B.
Assael, Henry, ed. see Borden, Neil H.
Assael, Henry, ed. see Breyer, Ralph F.
Assael, Henry, ed. see Clark, Fred E.
Assael, Henry, jt. ed. see Clark, Lincoln H.
Assael, Henry, ed. see Coles, Jessie V.
Assael, Henry, ed. see Collins, Virgil D.
Assael, Henry, ed. see Converse, Paul D.
Assael, Henry, ed. see Copeland, Melvin T.
Assael, Henry, ed. see Frederick, John H.
Assael, Henry, ed. see Frederick, Justus G.
Assael, Henry, ed. see Hower, Ralph M.
Assael, Henry, ed. see Longman, Donald R.
Assael, Henry, ed. see Lyon, Leverett S.
Assael, Henry, ed. see Northwestern University, School of Commerce Staff.
Assael, Henry, ed. see Nystrom, Paul H.
Assael, Henry, ed. see Reilly, William J.
Assael, Henry, ed. see Revzan, David A.
Assael, Henry, jt. ed. see Rosenberg, Larry J.
Assael, Henry, ed. see Scott, Walter D.
Assael, Henry, ed. see Sorenson, Helen.
Assael, Henry, ed. see Starch, Daniel.
Assael, Henry, ed. see Terry, Samuel H.
Assael, Henry, ed. see Tosdal, Harry R.
Assael, Henry, ed. see White, Percival.
Assael, Marc J., et al. Thermophysical Properties of Fluids. LC 96-22987. 372p. 1996. 48.00 (*1-86094-009-9*) World Scientific Pub.
— Thermophysical Properties of Fluids: An Introduction to Their Prediction. LC 96-22987. 372p. 1996. pap. write for info. (*1-86094-019-6*) World Scientific Pub.
Assael, Shaun. Wide Open: Days & Nights on the Nascar Tour. LC 97-37737. 416p. 1998. 25.00 (*0-345-40725-3*) Ballantine Pub Grp.
— Wide Open: Days & Nights on the Nascar Tour. 1999. mass mkt. 5.99 (*0-345-42677-0*) Ballantine Pub Grp.
Assaf, Al & Assaf, Robyn. Managed Care Quality: A Practical Guide. LC 97-35083. 296p. 1997. boxed set 59.95 (*1-57444-073-X*) St Lucie Pr.
Assaf, Robyn, jt. auth. see Assaf, Al.
Assagioli, Robert. Transpersonal Development: The Development Beyond Psychosynthesis. 1991. pap. 18.00 (*1-85274-062-0*, Pub. by Aqrn Pr) Harper SF.
***Assagioli, Roberto.** The Act of Will: A Guide to Self-Actualization & Self-Realization. (Illus.). 278p. 1999. reprint ed. pap. 19.95 (*0-9524004-1-3*, Pub. by Platts Pub Co) Synthesis Dist.
Assagioli, Roberto. Transpersonal Development: The Development Beyond Psychosynthesis. rev. ed. 1993. 19.00 (*1-85538-291-1*) Harper SF.
Assai, T., jt. ed. see Agee, E. M.
Assaiante, Paul, ed. see Braden, Vic, et al.
Assair, Elahe, tr. see Hujjat al-Islan Muhammad Mufatteh.
Assal, J. P. & Liniger, C., eds. Peripheral Neuropathies, 1988: What Is Significantly New? (FIDIA Research Ser.: Vol. 21). 600p. 1990. 139.00 (*0-387-97188-2*) Spr-Verlag.
Assal, Jean-Philippe, et al, eds. New Trends in Patient Education: A Trans-Cultural & Inter-Disease Approach: Proceedings of the Patient Education 2000 Congress, Geneva, 1-4 June 1994. (International Congress Ser.: Vol. 1076). 400p. 1995. 212.50 (*0-444-82234-8*) Elsevier.
Assar, M. M. Guide to Sanitation in Natural Disasters. (Illus.). 135p. 1971. pap. text 16.00 (*92-4-154011-7*, 1150054) World Health.
Assari, Elahe, tr. see Hossein-Ali, Torkamani.
Assassi, Lassassi. Non-Alignment & Algerian Foreign Policy. 249p. 1988. text 77.95 (*0-566-05470-1*, Pub. by Dartmth Pub) Ashgate Pub Co.
Assayas. Beatles & the Sixties. 1996. write for info. (*0-8050-5287-9*) H Holt & Co.
Assayas, Michka. The Beatles & the Sixties. LC 96-26379. (W5 Who, What, Where, When, & Why Ser.). (Illus.). 96p. (YA). (gr. 6 up). 1997. 19.95 (*0-8050-5059-0*) H Holt & Co.
Assche, W. Van, see Van Assche, W.
Asscheman, Marijke & Kuijper, Stephanie. Set It on Paper: Teaching Notes, Vol. 2. 34p. 1994. pap., teacher ed. 27.95 (*90-5356-113-7*, Pub. by Amsterdam U Pr) U of Mich Pr.
Asscher, A. W. & Brumfitt, William, eds. Microbial Diseases in Nephrology. LC 85-91279. (Wiley-Medical Publication). (Illus.). 384p. reprint ed. pap. 119.10 (*0-8357-3095-6*, 203935200012) Bks Demand.
Asscher, A. W., jt. ed. see Walker, S. R.
Asscher-Pinkhof, Clara. Star Children. Edelstein, Terese & Smidt, Inez, trs. LC 86-24543. Orig. Title: Sterrekinderen. (Illus.). 267p. reprint ed. pap. 82.80 (*0-608-10614-3*, 207123600009) Bks Demand.
Asseal, Henry, ed. see Rowell, George P. & Staff.
Assefa, A. Mariam. France. LC 88-3505. (World Education Ser.). (Illus.). 252p. (Orig.). 1988. pap. text 20.00 (*0-910054-90-8*) Am Assn Coll Registrars.
Assefa, A. Miriam. France. (Pelham Guides Ser.). 36p. (C). 1996. 22.00 (*0-929851-93-5*) Am Assn Coll Registrars.
Assefa, Hikias & Wahrhaftig, Paul. Extremist Groups & Conflict Resolution: The MOVE Crisis in Philadelphia. LC 87-25828. 172p. 1988. 55.00 (*0-275-92694-X*, C2694, Praeger Pubs) Greenwood.
Assefa, Hizkias & Wahrhaftig, Paul. The MOVE Crisis in Philadelphia: Extremist Groups & Conflict Resolution. LC 89-39454. (Illus.). 174p. 1990. reprint ed. pap. 12.95 (*0-8229-5430-3*) U of Pittsburgh Pr.
Asselain, B., et al. Stochastic Models of Tumor Latency & Their Applications. 250p. 1996. text 61.00 (*981-02-1831-1*) World Scientific Pub.
Asselin, Claudette, tr. see Risso, Giuseppe.
Asselin, Don. Human Nature & 'Eudaimonia' in Aristotle. (American University Studies: Philosophy: Ser. V, Vol. 64). XVI, 270p. (C). 1989. text 40.50 (*0-8204-0778-X*) P Lang Pubng.
Asselin, John. Trial Handbook for Connecticut Lawyers. LC 86-83060. 1993. 125.00 (*0-317-01510-9*, 68700, MICHIE) LEXIS Pub.
Asselin, John T. The Connecticut Workers' Compensation Practice Manual. 354p. 1989. suppl. ed. 110.00 (*0-910051-03-8*) CT Law Trib.
— Trial Handbook for Connecticut. 1987. im. lthr. write for info. (*0-327-00068-6*) LEXIS Pub.
— Trial Handbook for Connecticut Lawyers. LC 86-83060. 1993. suppl. ed. 55.00 (*0-317-03312-3*) West Group.
***Asselin, John T. & Pope, Daniel C.** Trial Handbook for Connecticut Lawyers, 1999 Supplement: Pocketpart. 2nd ed. 40p. 1999. suppl. ed. write for info. (*0-327-01715-5*, 6870512) LEXIS Pub.
Asselin, John T., jt. auth. see Pope, Daniel.
Asselin, Mario. An Introduction to Aircraft Performance. LC 97-308. (Education Ser.). 320p. 1997. 94.95 (*1-56347-221-X*) AIAA.
Asselin, Marlene, et al. Storyworlds: Linking Minds & Imagination Through Literature. 72p. 1992. pap. text 12.00 (*0-88751-030-2*, 00713) Heinemann.
Asselin, Michelle, tr. see Galloway, Priscilla.

A

Asselin, Susan B., et al. A College Selection Guide Book for Students with Disabilites in Virginia, Their Parents, & High School Staff. (Illus.). 136p. 1998. reprint ed. pap. text 25.00 (*0-7881-7199-2*) DIANE Pub.

Asselineau, Roger. Edgar Allen Poe. LC 72-629875. (University of Minnesota Pamphlets on American Writers Ser.: No. 89). 48p. reprint ed. pap. 30.00 (*0-7837-2901-4*, 205755400006) Bks Demand.

— The Evolution of Walt Whitman. expanded ed. LC 99-33533. 814p. 1999. pap. text 32.95 (*0-87745-682-8*) U of Iowa Pr.

— Evolution of Walt Whitman: The Creation of a Book. LC 60-13297. 400p. reprint ed. pap. 124.00 (*0-8357-9159-9*, 201465100093) Bks Demand.

— The Evolution of Walt Whitman: The Creation of a Personality. LC 60-13297. 390p. reprint ed. pap. 120.90 (*0-608-16217-5*, 201465600093) Bks Demand.

— Literary Reputation of Mark Twain from 1910-1950. LC 73-98744. 240p. 1971. reprint ed. lib. bdg. 65.00 (*0-8371-3069-7*, ASLR, Greenwood Pr) Greenwood.

*__Asselmeyer, Torsten.__ Exotic Structures & Physics: Differential Topology & Spacetime Models. (Illus.). 2000. 53.00 (*981-02-4195-X*) World Scientific Pub.

Asselt, Willem J. van, see van Asselt, Willem J., ed.

Assem, E. S. K., ed. Allergic Reactions to Anaesthetics: Clinical & Basic Aspects. (Monographs in Allergy: Vol. 30). (Illus.). xii, 236p. 1992. 256.75 (*3-8055-5489-3*) S Karger.

Assem, Magdy. On Stability & Endoscopic Transfer of Unipotent Orbital Integrals on P-Adic Symplectic Groups. LC 98-18262. (Memoirs of the American Mathematical Society Ser.: Vol. 134, No. 635). 101p. 1998. pap. 40.00 (*0-8218-0765-X*, MEMO/134/635) Am Math.

Assemani, Giuseppe S. Bibliotheca Orientalis Clementino-Vaticana, 3 vols., Set. mxxxiv, 2002p. 1975. reprint ed. 1185.00 (*3-487-05500-7*) G Olms Pubs.

Assemblee de la Societe Suisse d'Ophthalmologie St, jt. auth. see Colloque du Club Jules Gonin Staff.

Assembly of Behavioral & Social Sciences. Estimating Population & Income of Small Areas. LC 80-26012. 264p. reprint ed. pap. 81.90 (*0-8357-6819-8*, 203550100095) Bks Demand.

— Measurement & Interpretation of Productivity. LC 79-22715. (Illus.). 457p. reprint ed. pap. 141.70 (*0-8357-3184-7*, 203945300012) Bks Demand.

Assembly of Diviness Staff. The Westminster Standards, 1647: An Original Facsimile. unabridged ed. 250p. 1997. 49.95 (*1-889058-05-X*) Old Paths Pubns.

Assembly of Elementary Schools Staff. A Journey Through the Inner School. 61p. 6.50 (*0-318-14819-6*, AES 2) Mid St Coll & Schl.

— Judgement by the Profession. 80p. 6.00 (*0-318-14821-8*, AES 3) Mid St Coll & Schl.

— The Unseen Hand. 87p. 6.50 (*0-318-14824-2*, AES 4); 3.50 (*0-318-14825-0*) Mid St Coll & Schl.

Assembly of Life Sciences (U. S.) Committee on Med. Ozone & Other Photochemical Oxidants. LC 77-1293. (Illus.). 729p. reprint ed. pap. 200.00 (*0-8357-6646-2*, 203531300094) Bks Demand.

Assembly of Life Sciences (U. S.), Committee on Ni. Alternatives to the Current Use of Nitrite in Foods Pt. 2: 2-Part Study. LC 82-81677. 283p. reprint ed. pap. 87.80 (*0-8357-6814-7*, 203549700095) Bks Demand.

— Odors from Stationary & Mobile Sources. LC 79-9068. (Illus.). 509p. reprint ed. pap. 157.80 (*0-8357-6808-2*, 203549100095) Bks Demand.

Assendelft, Marion M. van, see Van Assendelft, Marion M.

Assendelft, O. W. van & England, J. M. Advances in Hematological Methods: The Blood Count. 272p. 1982. 152.00 (*0-8493-6596-1*, RB45, CRC Reprint) Franklin.

Assensoh, A. B. Africa in Retrospect. 76p. 1986. 40.00 (*0-7223-1764-6*, Pub. by A H S Ltd) St Mut.

— Africa in Retrospect. 76p. 1987. pap. 35.00 (*0-7855-1992-0*, Pub. by A H S Ltd) St Mut.

— African Political Leadership: Jomo Kenyatta, Kwame Nkrumah, & Julius K. Nyerere. LC 97-33571. (Anvil Ser.). (Illus.). 220p. (C). 1998. pap. 19.50 (*0-89464-911-6*) Krieger.

— Black Woman, Black Woman. 55p. 1987. 30.00 (*0-7223-1312-8*, Pub. by A H S Ltd) St Mut.

— Kwame Nkrumah, 6 Years in Exile. 68p. 1987. 35.00 (*0-7223-1182-6*, Pub. by A H S Ltd) St Mut.

Asser. Electronics for a Modern Age. (Electronics Technology Ser.). 1995. pap., student ed. 16.95 (*0-8273-4621-2*) Delmar.

Asser, M., ed. Kuwait Political Agency: Arabic Documents, 1899-1949. 13 vols. (ARA.). 8000p. 1994. reprint ed. lib. bdg. 2995.00 (*1-85207-440-X*, Pub. by Archive Editions) N Ross.

Asser, M. & Burdett, A. L., eds. King Abdul-Aziz: Political Correspondence, 1904-1953. (ARA & ENG.). 2000p. 1997. reprint ed. lib. bdg. 795.00 (*1-85207-705-0*, Pub. by Archive Editions) N Ross.

Asser, Stuart & Bahrenburg, Richard. Laboratory Manual to Accompany Mastering Electricity. 254p. 1993. student ed. 28.00 (*0-8273-4603-4*) Delmar.

Asser, Stuart & Stigliano, Vincent. Mastering Electricity. 436p. 1993. mass mkt. 54.25 (*0-8273-4604-2*) Delmar.

— Mastering Electricity: Instructor's Guide. LC 92-26598. 202p. 1993. pap. 28.00 (*0-8273-4605-0*) Delmar.

Asser, Stuart A., et al. Microcomputer Servicing: Practical Systems & Troubleshooting. (C). 1990. pap. text, lab manual ed. 30.60 (*0-675-21109-3*, Merrill Coll) P-H.

Asser, Stuart M., et al. Microcomputer Servicing: Practical Systems & Troubleshooting. 3rd ed. LC 96-3063. 662p. 1996. 105.00 (*0-13-263781-2*) P-H.

*__Asser, Stuart M., et al.__ Microcomputer Theory & Servicing. 4th ed. 896p. 2000. 102.00 (*0-13-010955-X*, Prentice Hall) P-H.

Asser, T. M. C., Instituut Staff, ed. The Influence of the Hague Conference on Private International Law: Selected Essays to Celebrate the 100th Anniversary of the Hague Conference on Private International Law. LC 93-7920. 161p. (C). 1993. lib. bdg. 79.00 (*0-7923-2298-3*) Kluwer Academic.

Assessment Systems Corporation. User's Manual for the MicroCAT Testing System. rev. ed. (Illus.). 1996. ring bd. 30.00 (*0-924724-00-5*) Assmnt Systs.

*__Asset Allocation in a Changing World Staff, et al.__ Asset Allocation in a Changing World: Proceedings of the Aimr Seminar "Asset Allocation in a Changing World", April 1-2, 1998, London, United Kingdom LC 99-208093. (Continuing Education Ser.). vii, 152 p. 1998. write for info. (*0-935015-29-9*) Inst Charter Finan Analysts.

Assetto, Valerie J., jt. ed. see Stevis, Dimitris.

Asseyev, Tamara, jt. auth. see Nickles, Liz.

Assfalg, Julius & Krueger, P. Kleines Woerterbuch des Christlichen Orients. (GER.). 460p. 1975. 12.00 (*0-8288-5907-8*, M7514) Fr & Eur.

Assfy, Zaid H. Islam & Christianity. (C). 1988. 65.00 (*0-900657-38-3*, Pub. by W Sessions) St Mut.

Assheuer, J. & Sager, M. MRI & CT of the Dog. (Illus.). 482p. 1996. 199.95 (*0-86542-825-5*) Blackwell Sci.

Assi, Victorien A. Methods & Techniques of Language Learning: The Secrets of Breaking Through at Any Age & Any Level. LC 97-91366. (Illus.). 206p. 1998. pap. 18.95 (*0-9662402-0-0*) V A Assi.

Assiac. Opening Preparation. 161p. 1982. 19.95 (*0-08-024095-X*, Pergamon Pr); pap. 11.95 (*0-08-024096-8*, Pergamon Pr) Elsevier.

Assicurato, Thomas, see Curato, Guy, pseud.

*__Assimacopoulou, Fotini.__ Gobineau et la Grece. (Studien Zur Geschichte Sudosteuropas Ser.). (Illus.). 299p. 1999. 48.95 (*3-631-34130-X*) P Lang Pubng.

Assimakopoulos, Jane, tr. see Valtinos, Thanases.

Assimakopoulos, Jane, tr. see Valtinos, Thanassis.

Assimil Staff. Allemand des Affaires: German Business for French Speakers. (FRE & GER.). audio 125.00 (*0-8288-9028-5*, F54070) Fr & Eur.

Assimil Staff. Allemand des Affaires: German Business for French Speakers. (FRE & GER.). 28.95 (*0-8288-4479-8*, F46260) Fr & Eur.

— Anglais des Affaires: Business English for French Speakers. (ENG & FRE.). 28.95 (*0-8288-4481-X*, M5808) Fr & Eur.

Assimil Staff. L' Arabe Sans Peine (One) Arabic for French Speakers. (ARA & FRE.). 1990. audio 125.00 (*0-8288-9050-1*, M14740) Fr & Eur.

Assimil Staff. L' Arabe sans Peine (One) Arabic for French Speakers. (ARA & FRE.). 28.95 (*0-8288-4353-8*, M14741) Fr & Eur.

Assimil Staff. L' Arabe Sans Peine (Two) et Livret Phonetique: Arabic for French Speakers. (ARA & FRE.). 1990. 28.95 (*0-7859-0380-1*, M14742); audio 125.00 (*0-8288-9051-X*) Fr & Eur.

— Arabe Sin Esfuerzo: Arabic for Spanish Speakers. (ARA & SPA.). 1990. audio 125.00 (*0-8288-9029-3*, F19960) Fr & Eur.

Assimil Staff. Arabe sin Esfuerzo: Arabic for Spanish Speakers. (ARA & SPA.). 28.95 (*0-8288-4360-0*, S25814) Fr & Eur.

— Arabic with Ease: Arabic for English Speakers. (ARA & ENG.). 28.95 (*0-8288-4359-7*, M14743) Fr & Eur.

— Arabisch Johne Muhe Heute: Arabic for German Speakers. (ARA & GER.). 28.95 (*0-8288-4358-9*, F11959) Fr & Eur.

Assimil Staff. Arabisch Zonder Moeite: Arabic for Dutch Speakers. (ARA & DUT.). 1990. audio 125.00 (*0-8288-9030-7*, M10749) Fr & Eur.

Assimil Staff. Arabisch zonder Moeite: Arabic for Dutch Speakers. (ARA & DUT.). 28.95 (*0-8288-4365-1*, M10749) Fr & Eur.

— Auf Geht's (Allemand) German for French Speakers. (FRE & GER.). 28.95 (*0-8288-4477-1*, F51170) Fr & Eur.

Assimil Staff. Auf Geht's (Allemand) German for French Speakers. (FRE & GER.). 1991. audio 125.00 (*0-8288-9031-5*, M12686) Fr & Eur.

— Bresilien Sans Peine: Portuguese for French Speakers. (FRE & POR.). 1990. audio 125.00 (*0-8288-9032-3*, F48121) Fr & Eur.

Assimil Staff. Bresilien sans Peine: Portuguese for French Speakers. (FRE & POR.). 28.95 (*0-8288-4384-8*, F48125) Fr & Eur.

— Breton sans Peine (One) Breton for French Speakers. (BRE & FRE.). 28.95 (*0-8288-4467-4*, M14495) Fr & Eur.

Assimil Staff. Breton Sans Peine (One) Breton for French Speakers (1) (BRE & FRE.). 1990. audio 125.00 (*0-8288-9033-1*, M14795) Fr & Eur.

Assimil Staff. Breton sans Peine (Two) Breton for French Speakers. (BRE & FRE.). 28.95 (*0-8288-4469-0*, M4624) Fr & Eur.

Assimil Staff. Breton Sans Peine (Two) Breton for French Speakers (2) (BRE & FRE.). 1990. audio 125.00 (*0-8288-9034-X*, M14796) Fr & Eur.

— Business French. 1999. pap. text 29.95 (*2-7005-0211-6*, Pub. by Assimil); pap. text 79.95 (*2-7005-1378-9*, Pub. by Assimil); pap. text 89.95 (*2-7005-2014-9*, Pub. by Assimil) Distribks Inc.

— Catalan Sin Esfuerzo: Catalan for Spanish Speakers. (CAT & SPA.). audio 125.00 (*0-8288-9035-8*, S38601) Fr & Eur.

Assimil Staff. Catalan sin Esfuerzo: Catalan for Spanish Speakers. (CAT & SPA.). 28.95 (*0-8288-4498-4*, S38601) Fr & Eur.

— Chinois sans Peine (One) Chinese for French Speakers. (CHI & FRE.). 28.95 (*0-8288-4379-1*, M12639) Fr & Eur.

Assimil Staff. Chinois Sans Peine (One) Chinese for French Speakers (1) (CHI & FRE.). 1990. pap. 125.00 incl. audio (*0-8288-9036-6*, M12634) Fr & Eur.

Assimil Staff. Chinois sans Peine (Two) Chinese for French Speakers. (CHI & FRE.). 28.95 (*0-8288-4381-3*, M12650) Fr & Eur.

Assimil Staff. Chinois Sans Peine (Two) Chinese for French Speakers (2) (CHI & FRE.). 1990. audio 125.00 (*0-8288-9037-4*, M12651) Fr & Eur.

— Corse Sans Peine: Corsican for French Speakers. (FRE.). 1990. audio 125.00 (*0-8288-9038-2*, M4591) Fr & Eur.

Assimil Staff. Corse sans Peine: Corsican for French Speakers. (FRE.). 28.95 (*0-8288-4463-1*, M10750) Fr & Eur.

— Creole sans Peine: Creole for French Speakers. 28.95 (*0-8288-4461-5*, F25640) Fr & Eur.

Assimil Staff. Danois sans Peine - Danish for French Speakers. (DAN & FRE.). 28.95 (*0-8288-8220-7*); audio 125.00 (*0-8288-8219-3*) Fr & Eur.

— Duits In Het Bedrijfsleven: Business German for Dutch Speakers. (DUT & GER.). audio 125.00 (*0-8288-9039-0*, F55995) Fr & Eur.

Assimil Staff. Duits in Het Bedrijfsleven: Business German for Dutch Speakers. (DUT & GER.). 28.95 (*0-8288-4601-4*) Fr & Eur.

Assimil Staff. Dutch with Ease: Dutch for English Speakers. (DUT & ENG.). audio 125.00 (*0-8288-9040-4*, M12657) Fr & Eur.

Assimil Staff. Dutch with Ease: Dutch for English Speakers. (DUT & ENG.). 28.95 (*0-8288-4352-X*, M12657) Fr & Eur.

Assimil Staff. Ecriture Chinoise: Chinese Writing. (CHI & FRE.). 32.95 (*0-8288-4383-X*, M14581) Fr & Eur.

— Engels in Het Bedrijfsleven: Business English for Dutch Speakers. (DUT & ENG.). audio 125.00 (*0-8288-9041-2*) Fr & Eur.

Assimil Staff. Engels in Het Bedrijfsleven: Business English for Dutch Speakers. (DUT & ENG.). 28.95 (*0-8288-4600-6*, F19980) Fr & Eur.

Assimil Staff. Englisch in der Praxis: Intermediate English for German Speakers. (ENG & GER.). audio 125.00 (*0-8288-9042-0*, F17230) Fr & Eur.

Assimil Staff. Englisch in der Praxis: Intermediate English for German Speakers. (ENG & GER.). 28.95 (*0-8288-4493-3*, F17230) Fr & Eur.

Assimil Staff. Englisch Ohne Muhe Heute. 1999. pap. text 29.95 (*2-7005-0093-8*, Pub. by Assimil) Distribks Inc.

— Englisch Ohne Muhe Heute: English for German Speakers. (ENG & GER.). audio, cd-rom 125.00 (*0-8288-9043-9*, M14921) Fr & Eur.

Assimil Staff. Englisch ohne Muhe Heute: English for German Speakers. (ENG, GER & FRE.). 28.95 (*0-8288-4304-X*, F14921) Fr & Eur.

Assimil Staff. Englisch Ohne Muhe Heute with Cassette(s) (ENG & GER.). 1999. pap. 75.00 incl. audio (*2-7005-1001-1*, Pub. by Assimil) Distribks Inc.

— Englische in Der Praxis. 1999. pap. text 29.95 (*2-7005-0147-0*, Pub. by Assimil); pap. text 75.00 (*2-7005-1017-8*, Pub. by Assimil); pap. text 95.00 (*2-7005-1076-3*, Pub. by Assimil) Distribks Inc.

— Esperanto Sans Peine.Tr. of Esperanto for French Speakers. (ESP & FRE.). audio 125.00 (*0-8288-9044-7*, F48530) Fr & Eur.

Assimil Staff. Esperanto sans Peine: Esperanto for French Speakers. (ESP & FRE.). 28.95 (*0-8288-4388-0*, F48530) Fr & Eur.

Assimil Staff. Frances Perfeccionamiento: Intermediate French for Spanish Speakers. (FRE & SPA.). audio 125.00 (*0-8288-9045-5*, M1823) Fr & Eur.

Assimil Staff. Frances Perfeccionamiento: Intermediate French for Spanish Speakers. (FRE & SPA.). 28.95 (*0-8288-4455-0*, M1823) Fr & Eur.

— Frans in de Praktijk: Intermediate French for Dutch Speakers. (DUT & FRE.). 28.95 (*0-8288-4602-2*) Fr & Eur.

Assimil Staff. Franzosisch In der Praxis: Intermediate French for German Speakers. (FRE & GER.). audio 125.00 (*0-8288-9046-3*, M3032) Fr & Eur.

Assimil Staff. Franzosisch in der Praxis: Intermediate French for German Speakers. (FRE & GER.). 28.95 (*0-8288-4454-2*, M3032) Fr & Eur.

Assimil Staff. Franzosisch Ohne Muhe Heute: French for German Speakers. (FRE & GER.). audio 125.00 (*0-8288-9047-1*, M9909) Fr & Eur.

Assimil Staff. Franzosisch ohne Muhe Heute: French for German Speakers. (FRE & GER.). 28.95 (*0-8288-4329-5*, M9909) Fr & Eur.

Assimil Staff. French for Japanese: French for Japanese Speakers. (FRE & JPN.). 28.95 (*0-685-53008-6*, F54166); audio 125.00 (*0-685-53009-4*) Fr & Eur.

— French with Ease: French for English Speakers. (ENG & FRE.). 28.95 (*0-685-53001-9*, M12670); audio 125.00 (*0-8288-9048-X*, M12672) Fr & Eur.

— German with Ease: German for English Speakers. (ENG & GER.). audio, disk 125.00 (*0-8288-9049-8*, F47140) Fr & Eur.

Assimil Staff. German with Ease: German for English Speakers. (ENG & GER.). 28.95 (*0-8288-4311-2*, F47140) Fr & Eur.

— Le Grec (Moderne) sans Peine: Greek for French Speakers. (FRE & GRE.). 28.95 (*0-8288-4342-2*, F48231) Fr & Eur.

— Grieks zonder Moeite: Greek for Dutch Speakers. (DUT & GRE.). 28.95 (*0-8288-4372-4*, M10748) Fr & Eur.

— Hebreu sans Peine (One) Hebrew for French Speakers. (FRE & HEB.). 28.95 (*0-8288-4373-2*, M12729) Fr & Eur.

— Hebreu sans Peine (Two) Hebrew for French Speakers. (FRE & HEB.). 28.95 (*0-8288-4375-9*, F14170) Fr & Eur.

— Het Nieuwe Duits zonder Moeite: German for Dutch Speakers. (DUT & GER.). 28.95 (*0-8288-4323-6*, F55995) Fr & Eur.

— Het Nieuwe Frans zonder Moeite: French for Dutch Speakers. (DUT & FRE.). 28.95 (*0-8288-4334-1*, F54420) Fr & Eur.

— Het Nieuwe Italiaans zonder Moeite: Italian for Dutch Speakers. (DUT & ITA.). 28.95 (*0-8288-4341-4*, F68913) Fr & Eur.

Assimil Staff. Het Nieuwe Spaans Zonder Moeite: Spanish for Dutch Speakers. (DUT & SPA.). audio 125.00 (*0-685-54622-5*) Fr & Eur.

Assimil Staff. Het Nieuwe Spaans zonder Moeite: Spanish for Dutch Speakers. (DUT & SPA.). 28.95 (*0-8288-4326-0*, S4756) Fr & Eur.

— Hongrois sans Peine: Hungarian for French Speakers. (FRE & HUN.). 28.95 (*0-8288-4397-X*, M4473) Fr & Eur.

Assimil Staff. Hungarian with Ease. (HUN.). 1999. pap. text 29.95 (*2-7005-0205-1*, Pub. by Assimil) Distribks Inc.

Assimil Staff. Ingles de los Negocios: Business English for Spanish Speakers. (ENG & SPA.). 28.95 (*0-8288-4492-5*, S24979) Fr & Eur.

Assimil Staff. Ingles Perfeccionamento. 1999. pap. text 75.00 (*2-7005-1306-1*, Pub. by Assimil) Distribks Inc.

Assimil Staff. Ingles Perfeccionamiento: Intermediate English for Spanish Speakers. (ENG & SPA.). 28.95 (*0-8288-4491-7*) Fr & Eur.

— Initiation au Breton sans Peine: Introduction to Breton for French Speakers. (BRE & FRE.). 28.95 (*0-8288-4465-8*, M14799) Fr & Eur.

— Introduction au Thai: Thai for French Speakers. (FRE & THA.). 28.95 (*0-8288-4451-8*, F14600) Fr & Eur.

— Italian with Ease: Italian for English Speakers. (ENG & ITA.). 28.95 (*0-8288-4340-6*, M2650) Fr & Eur.

— Italienisch in der Praxis: Intermediate Italian for German Speakers. (GER & ITA.). 28.95 (*0-8288-4495-X*) Fr & Eur.

— Italienisch ohne Muhe Heute: Italian for German Speakers. (GER & ITA.). 28.95 (*0-8288-4339-2*, 2700501136) Fr & Eur.

— Japanisch Ohne Muhe (One) Japanese for German Speakers. (GER & JPN.). 28.95 (*0-8288-4458-5*, F25650) Fr & Eur.

Assimil Staff. Japanisch Ohne Muhe (Three) Japanese for German Speakers (3) (GER & JPN.). 28.95 (*0-8288-4460-7*, M4645) Fr & Eur.

Assimil Staff. Japanisch ohne Muhe (Two) Japanese for German Speakers. (GER & JPN.). 28.95 (*0-8288-4459-3*, F11376) Fr & Eur.

— Japonais sans Peine (One) Japanese for French Speakers. (FRE & JPN.). 28.95 (*0-8288-4366-X*, F77670) Fr & Eur.

Assimil Staff. Japonais Sans Peine (Three) L'Ecriture Kanji: Japanese for French Speakers (3): Writing Kanji. (FRE & JPN.). 32.95 (*0-8288-4370-8*, F116130) Fr & Eur.

Assimil Staff. Japonais sans Peine (Two) Japanese for French Speakers. (FRE & JPN.). 28.95 (*0-8288-4368-6*, F99430) Fr & Eur.

Assimil Staff. Jezyk Anglielski. 1999. pap. text 75.00 (*2-7005-1656-7*, Pub. by Assimil) Distribks Inc.

Assimil Staff. Latin sans Peine: Latin for French Speakers. (FRE & LAT.). 28.95 (*0-8288-4390-2*, F14190) Fr & Eur.

— Let's Get Better (Anglais), Bk. 2: English for French Speakers. (ENG & FRE.). 28.95 (*0-8288-4475-5*, M10746) Fr & Eur.

— Let's Start (Anglais), Bk. 1: English for French Speakers. (ENG & FRE.). 28.95 (*0-8288-4473-9*, M10945) Fr & Eur.

Assimil Staff. Livret Phonetique (l'Arabe Sans Peine 2) Seul: Phonetic Pamphlet in Arabic for French Speakers. (ARA & FRE.). 14.95 (*0-8288-4357-0*) Fr & Eur.

Assimil Staff. Neugriechisch ohne Muhe: Greek for German Speakers. (GER & GRE.). 28.95 (*0-8288-4343-0*, F18000) Fr & Eur.

— Niederlandisch ohne Muhe: Dutch for German Speakers. (DUT & GER.). 28.95 (*0-8288-4350-3*, M14896) Fr & Eur.

— Niederlandisch ohne Muhe: Dutch for German Speakers, 3 cass., Set. (DUT & GER.). audio 125.00 (*0-685-53020-5*) Fr & Eur.

— Nieuwe Engels zonder Moeite: English for Dutch Speakers. (DUT & ENG.). 28.95 (*0-8288-4322-8*, M14922) Fr & Eur.

— Le Nouveau Neerlandais sans Peine: Dutch for French Speakers. (DUT & FRE.). 28.95 (*0-8288-4344-9*, M14878) Fr & Eur.

— Nouvel Allemand sans Peine: German for French Speakers. (FRE & GER.). 28.95 (*0-8288-4308-2*, M12664) Fr & Eur.

Assimil Staff. Nouvel Anglais des Affaires. 1999. 95.00 (*2-7005-1088-7*, Pub. by Assimil) Distribks Inc.

— Nouvel Anglais Sans Peine: English for French Speakers. (ENG & FRE.). 1992. 28.95 (*0-685-52979-7*, M14907) Fr & Eur.

Assimil Staff. Nouvel Espagnol sans Peine: Spanish for French Speakers. (FRE & SPA.). 28.95 (*0-8288-4315-5*, S28993) Fr & Eur.

— Le Nouvel Italien sans Peine: Italian for French Speakers. (FRE & ITA.). 28.95 (*0-8288-4346-5*, F63240) Fr & Eur.

— Novi Engleski bez Muke: English for Serbo-Croatian Speakers. (ENG & SER.). 28.95 (*0-8288-4321-X*, M12724) Fr & Eur.

— Novi Francuski Bez Muke: French for Serbo-Croatian Speakers. (FRE & SER.). 28.95 (*0-8288-4333-3*, F62317) Fr & Eur.

— Novi Nemacki Bez Muke: German for Serbo-Croatian Speakers. (GER & SER.). 28.95 (*0-8288-4324-4*, F17130) Fr & Eur.

An Asterisk (*) at the beginning of an entry indicates that the title is appearing for the first time.

— Novi Spanski Bez Muke: Spanish for Serbo-Croatian Speakers. (SER & SPA.). 28.95 (*0-8288-4325-2*, F30860) Fr & Eur.

— Novo Alemao sem Custo: German for Portuguese Speakers. (GER & POR.). 28.95 (*0-8288-4314-7*, F10158) Fr & Eur.

— Novo Ingles sem Custo: English for Portuguese Speakers. (ENG & POR.). 28.95 (*0-8288-4307-4*, M14924) Fr & Eur.

Assimil Staff. Nuevo Aleman Sin Esfuerzo: German for Spanish Speakers. (GER & SPA.). audio 125.00 (*0-685-54621-7*) Fr & Eur.

Assimil Staff. Nuevo Aleman sin Esfuerzo: German for Spanish Speakers. (GER & SPA.). 28.95 (*0-8288-4312-0*, S4667) Fr & Eur.

— El Nuevo Frances sin Esfuerzo: French for Spanish Speakers. (FRE & SPA.). 28.95 (*0-8288-4332-5*, S9342) Fr & Eur.

— Nuevo Ingles sin Esfuerzo: English for Spanish Speakers. (ENG & SPA.). 28.95 (*0-8288-4306-6*, S27285) Fr & Eur.

— El Nuevo Italiano sin Esfuerzo: Italian for Spanish Speakers. (ITA & SPA.). 28.50 (*0-8288-4336-8*, F13320) Fr & Eur.

— Il Nuovo Francese senza Sforzo: French for Italian Speakers. (FRE & ITA.). 28.50 (*0-8288-4330-9*, F9000) Fr & Eur.

— Nuovo Ingles senza Sforzo: English for Italian Speakers. (ENG & ITA.). 28.95 (*0-8288-4305-8*, M14923) Fr & Eur.

Assimil Staff. Il Nuovo Inglese Senza Sforzo. 1999. pap. text 29.95 (*2-7005-0096-2*, Pub. by Assimil) Distribks Inc.

Assimil Staff. Nuovo Spagnolo senza Sforzo: Spanish for Italian Speakers. (ITA & SPA.). 28.95 (*0-8288-4320-1*, S844) Fr & Eur.

— Nuovo Tedesco senza Sforzo: German for Italian Speakers. (GER & ITA.). 28.95 (*0-8288-4313-9*, F10246) Fr & Eur.

— O Novo Frances sem Custo: French for Portuguese Speakers. (FRE & POR.). 28.95 (*0-8288-4331-7*, F10470) Fr & Eur.

Assimil Staff. O Novo Ingles Sem Custo. 1999. pap. text 29.95 (*2-7005-0125-X*, Pub. by Assimil) Distribks Inc.

Assimil Staff. Occitan sans Peine: Occidental for French Speakers. (FRE.). 28.95 (*0-8288-4471-2*, F48570) Fr & Eur.

Assimil Staff. Orthographe Sans Peine: Orthography for French Speakers. (FRE.). 28.95 (*0-8288-4396-1*, M10747) Fr & Eur.

Assimil Staff. Perfectionnement Allemand: Intermediate German for French Speakers. (FRE & GER.). 28.95 (*0-8288-4485-2*, F29170) Fr & Eur.

Assimil Staff. Perfectionnement Anglais. (Assimil). 1999. 29.95 (*2-7005-0133-0*, Pub. by Assimil); 75.00 (*2-7005-1028-3*, Pub. by Assimil); 95.00 (*2-7005-1075-5*, Pub. by Assimil) Distribks Inc.

Assimil Staff. Perfectionnement Anglais: Intermediate English for French Speakers. (ENG & FRE.). 28.95 (*0-8288-4483-6*, M1500) Fr & Eur.

— Perfectionnement Espagnol: Intermediate Spanish for French Speakers. (FRE & SPA.). 28.95 (*0-8288-4487-9*, M1498) Fr & Eur.

— Perfectionnement Italien: Intermediate Italian for French Speakers. (FRE & ITA.). 28.95 (*0-8288-4496-8*, F40322) Fr & Eur.

Assimil Staff. Perfezionamento dell'Inglese. 1999. pap. text 95.00 (*2-7005-1096-8*, Pub. by Assimil); pap. text 75.00 (*2-7005-1359-2*, Pub. by Assimil) Distribks Inc.

Assimil Staff. Polonais sans Peine: Polish for French Speakers. (FRE & POL.). 28.95 (*0-8288-4386-4*, F77660) Fr & Eur.

— Portugiesisch ohne Muhe: Portuguese for German Speakers. (GER & POR.). 28.95 (*0-8288-4349-X*, F49590) Fr & Eur.

— Le Portugues sans Peine: Portuguese for French Speakers. (FRE & POR.). 28.95 (*0-8288-4347-3*, F50560) Fr & Eur.

— Pratique du Neerlandais: Intermediate Dutch for French Speakers. (DUT & FRE.). 28.95 (*0-8288-4489-5*, M11925) Fr & Eur.

— Roumain sans Peine: Roumanian for French Speakers. (FRE & RUM.). 28.95 (*0-8288-4399-6*, M6666) Fr & Eur.

— Russe sans Peine: Russian for French Speakers. (FRE & RUS.). 28.95 (*0-8288-4361-9*, F50690) Fr & Eur.

— Russian Without Toil: Russian for English Speakers. (ENG & RUS.). 28.95 (*0-8288-4364-3*, F38008) Fr & Eur.

— Russisch ohne Muhe: Russian for German Speakers. (GER & RUS.). 28.95 (*0-8288-4363-5*, F49480) Fr & Eur.

— Schwedisch ohne Muhe (One) Swedish for German Speakers. (GER & SWE.). 28.95 (*0-8288-4456-9*, F55570) Fr & Eur.

— Schwedisch ohne Muhe (Two) Intermediate Swedish for German Speakers. (GER & SWE.). 28.95 (*0-8288-4457-7*, F55580) Fr & Eur.

— Serbo-Croate sans Peine: Serbo-Croatian for French Speakers. (FRE & SER.). 28.95 (*0-8288-4377-5*, F40076) Fr & Eur.

— Spanisch in der Praxis: Intermediate Spanish for German Speakers. (GER & SPA.). 28.95 (*0-8288-4494-1*) Fr & Eur.

— Spanisch ohne Muhe Heute: Spanish for German Speakers. (GER & SPA.). 28.95 (*0-8288-4318-X*, M9910) Fr & Eur.

— Spanish with Ease: Spanish for English Speakers. (ENG & SPA.). 28.95 (*0-8288-4319-8*, F70420) Fr & Eur.

— Suedois sans Peine (One) Swedish for French Speakers. (FRE & SWE.). 28.95 (*0-8288-4392-9*, F13090) Fr & Eur.

— Suedois sans Peine (Two) Swedish for French Speakers. (FRE & SWE.). 28.95 (*0-8288-4394-5*) Fr & Eur.

Assimil Staff. Turc sans Peine - Turkish for French Speakers. (FRE & TUR.). 28.95 (*0-8288-8221-5*); audio 125.00 (*0-8288-8222-3*) Fr & Eur.

Assimil Staff. Using French: Intermediate French for English Speakers. (ENG & FRE.). 28.95 (*0-8288-4351-1*, F9010) Fr & Eur.

Assimil Staff. Using Spanish. 1999. pap. text 29.95 (*2-7005-1888-8*, Pub. by Assimil) Distribks Inc.

*__Assing, Ottilie.__ Radical Passion: Ottilie Assing's Reports from America & Letters to Frederick Douglas. Lohmann, Christopher, tr. LC 99-20055. (New Directions in German-American Studies). 416p. 1999. pap. text 32.95 (*0-8204-4526-6*) P Lang Pubng.

Assing, Sigurd & Schmidt, W. Continuous Strong Markov Processes in Dimension One: A Stochastic Calculus Approach, Vol. 168. Dold, A. et al, eds. LC 98-22867. (Lecture Notes in Mathematics Ser.: Vol. 1688). xii, 137p. 1998. pap. 27.00 (*3-540-64465-2*) Spr-Verlag.

Assink. Contaminated Soils. 1985. pap. text. write for info. (*90-247-3268-9*, Pub. by M Nijhoff) Kluwer Academic.

Assink, Egbert. Literacy Acquisition & Social Context. 304p. (C). 1995. pap. text 38.00 (*0-13-342734-X*) P-H.

Assiouly, E. Banking & Financial Dictionary. (ARA, ENG & FRE.). 338p. 1980. pap. 75.00 (*0-8288-0323-4*, M9767) Fr & Eur.

Assire, Jerome. The Book of Bread. (Illus.). 160p. 1996. 45.00 (*2-08-013625-9*, Pub. by Flammarion) Abbeville Pr.

Assis, A. Torres, see Torres Assis, A.

Assis, Andre Koch Torres. Relational Mechanics. LC 99-900382. Orig. Title: Mecanica Relacional. 285p. 1999. pap. (*0-9683689-2-1*) C Roy Keys.

Assis, Joaquim Maria Machado de, see Machado de Assis, Joaquim Maria.

Assis, Yom T. The Golden Age of Aragonese Jewry, 1213-1327. LC 96-27894. (Littman Library of Jewish Civilization). 1997. 95.00 (*1-874774-04-8*) Intl Spec Bk.

— Jewish Economy in the Medieval Crown of Aragon, 1213-1327: Money & Power. LC 96-46469. (Series in Jewish Studies: Vol. 18). (Illus.). 230p. 1997. text 87.50 (*90-04-10615-4*, NLG110) Brill Academic Pubs.

Assis, Yom Tov, see Tov Assis, Yom.

Assistance League of Atlanta Staff. To Serve with Love. (Illus.). 1995. text. write for info. (*0-9648357-0-3*) Assistance League of Corvallis.

Assistance League of Corvallis Staff. Beautiful, Bountiful Oregon: A Collector's Book of Recipes & Travel Ideas. (Illus.). 144p. 1996. 23.95 (*0-9616597-1-8*) Assistance League of Corvallis.

— Oregon Sampler: Resorts & Recipes: Featuring a Sampling of Recipes from the Resorts & People of Oregon. (Illus.). 318p. 1985. 14.95 (*0-9616597-0-X*) Assistance League of Corvallis.

Assistance League of Glendale. From Scratch: A Collection of Recipes from Assistance League of Glendale. (Illus.). 200p. (Orig.). 1987. pap. 14.95 (*0-685-19310-1*) AL Glendale.

Assistance League of Omaha Members. Taste the Good Life. 282p. 1992. 16.95 (*0-9632957-0-5*) Assist Lgue Omaha.

Assistance League of the Bay Area Staff. Settings on the Dock of the Bay. 272p. 1999. 22.95 (*0-9668381-0-6*) Assist Lea Bay.

Assiter. Ponography, Feminism & Individual. 192p. (C). pap. 15.95 (*0-7453-0521-0*) Pluto GBR.

— Pornography, Feminism & Individual. 192p. (C). 44.95 (*0-7453-0319-6*, Pub. by Pluto GBR) Stylus Pub VA.

Assiter, Alison. Enlightened Women: Modernist Feminism in a Postmodern Age. LC 95-16865. 176p. (C). (gr. 13). 1995. 100.00 (*0-415-08338-9*) Routledge.

— Enlightened Women: Modernist Feminism in a Postmodern Age. LC 95-16865. 176p. (C). 1996. pap. 22.99 (*0-415-08339-7*) Routledge.

Assiter, Alison & Carol, Avedon. Bad Girls & Dirty Pictures: The Challenge to Reclaim Feminism. 186p. (C). 1993. 52.50 (*0-7453-0523-7*, Pub. by Pluto GBR); pap. 15.95 (*0-7453-0524-5*, Pub. by Pluto GBR) Stylus Pub VA.

Assman, Jan, et al. Problems & Priorities in Egyptian Archaeology. (Studies in Egyptology). (Illus.). 350p. (C). 1987. text 79.95 (*0-7103-0190-1*, A4606) Routledge.

Assmann. History of Ancient Egypt. 1998. pap. 14.95 (*0-8050-5463-4*) H Holt & Co.

— History of Ancient Egypt. 1999. 29.50 (*0-8050-5462-6*) H Holt & Co.

Assmann, G., ed. HDL Deficiency & Atherosclerosis, No. 174. (Developments in Cardiovascular Medicine Ser.: Vol. 174). 96p. 1996. text 48.00 (*0-7923-8888-7*) Kluwer Academic.

Assmann, G., jt. ed. see Galton, David J.

Assmann, Heinz-Dieter, jt. ed. see Wegen, Gerhard.

*__Assmann, Jan.__ Agyptische Hymnen und Gebete. xvii, 582p. 1999. pap. text 84.00 (*3-7278-1230-3*, Pub. by Ed Univ Fri) Eisenbrauns.

Assmann, Jan. Egyptian Solar Religion in the New Kingdom: Re, Amun & the Crisis of Polytheism. Alcock, Anthony, tr. from GER. LC 94-10620.Tr. of Re und Amun. 256p. 1995. 76.50 (*0-7103-0465-X*) Routledge.

— Moses the Egyptian: The Memory of Egypt in Western Monotheism. LC 96-51600. (Illus.). 288p. 1997. 29.95 (*0-674-58738-3*) HUP.

— Moses the Egyptian: The Memory of Egypt in Western Monotheism. (Illus.). 288p. 1998. pap. 18.95 (*0-674-58739-1*) HUP.

Assmann, Jan & Stroumsa, Gedaliahu A.G. Transformations of the Inner Self in Ancient Religions. LC 99-11362. (Studies in the History of Religions). 1999. write for info. (*90-04-11356-8*) Brill Academic Pubs.

Assmus, E. F., Jr. & Key, J. D. Designs & Their Codes. (Cambridge Tracts in Mathematics Ser.: No. 103). (Illus.). 362p. (C). 1992. text 90.00 (*0-521-41361-3*) Cambridge U Pr.

— Designs & Their Codes. (Cambridge Tracts in Mathematics Ser.: No. 103). (Illus.). 362p. (C). 1994. pap. text 30.95 (*0-521-45839-0*) Cambridge U Pr.

Assn. for Union Democracy Women's Project Staff & NOW Legal Defense & Education Fund Staff. Manual for Survival for Women in Nontraditional Employment. 154p. 1993. pap. 6.00 (*0-614-29600-5*) Assn Union Demo.

Asso, Doreen. The Real Menstrual Cycle. LC 83-5890. (Illus.). 230p. reprint ed. pap. 71.30 (*0-8357-4529-7*, 203746100008) Bks Demand.

Assoc. of Certified Fraud Examiners Staff. The Fraud Trial. 419p. 1998. pap., wbk. ed. 199.00 (*1-889277-10-X*) Assn Certified Fraud.

— Investigating by Computer. 297p. 1997. pap., wbk. ed. 199.00 (*1-889277-09-6*, 97-5401) Assn Certified Fraud.

Associate Inc Training. MCSD Visual Basic Desktop Applications Training Kit. LC 99-13775. 700p. 1999. pap. 69.99 (*0-7356-0620-X*) Microsoft.

*__Associated Designs Inc., Staff.__ Home Plans Collection: Associated Designs, Vol. 5. (Illus.). 304p. 1999. pap. 12.00 (*0-9674077-0-2*) Assoc Dsgns.

Associated Equipment Distributors Staff. Building Powerful People. 10.00 (*0-318-19190-3*) Assn Equip Distrs.

— Construction Equipment Distribution Has the Career You're Looking For. 1.00 (*0-318-19189-X*) Assn Equip Distrs.

— Credit & Collection. 86p. 1985. 25.00 (*0-318-19174-1*) Assn Equip Distrs.

— Financial Management & Strategy. 10.00 (*0-318-19187-3*) Assn Equip Distrs.

— Finding That One-in-a-Million Sales Superstar. 1986. 2.00 (*0-318-19192-X*) Assn Equip Distrs.

— Job Description Manual. 1986. 20.00 (*0-318-19191-1*) Assn Equip Distrs.

— Join the Computer Age. 24p. 1983. 3.50 (*0-318-19181-4*) Assn Equip Distrs.

— The Marketing Imagination. 10.00 (*0-318-19185-7*) Assn Equip Distrs.

— Performance Appraisal Handbook. 20p. 1985. 25.00 (*0-318-19177-6*) Assn Equip Distrs.

— Product Support: Buy Words for the 80's. 48p. 1985. reprint ed. 10.00 (*0-318-19179-2*) Assn Equip Distrs.

— Strategic Marketing. 48p. 1984. 25.00 (*0-318-19175-X*) Assn Equip Distrs.

— We Add Value. 1986. 145.00 incl. VHS (*0-318-19182-2*) Assn Equip Distrs.

Associated General Contractors of America, et al. Equipment Resource Management into the 21st Century: Proceedings of the Conference Sponsored by the Committee on Construction Equipment & Techniques of the Construction Division of the ASCE, the Associated General Conractors of America, & the Equipment Maintenance Council, Nashville, TN, November 13-15, 1994. Weber, Sandra L., ed. LC 95-12012. 216p. 1995. pap. 25.00 (*0-7844-0077-6*) Am Soc Civil Eng.

*__Associated General Contractors Staff.__ Alaska Builders: 50 Years of Construction in the 49th State. LC 99-29198. (Illus.). 240p. 1999. pap. 29.95 (*1-888125-39-X*) Publ Consult.

Associated Grantmakers of Massachusetts, Inc. Staf. Massachusetts Grantmakers. LC 85-52426. 223p. (Orig.). 1993. pap. text 50.00 (*0-912427-05-1*) Assoc Grant.

Associated Ladies for Lipscomb Staff. A Taste for All Seasons: A Collection of Recipes from the Associated Ladies for David Lipscomb University. 272p. 1994. 18.00 (*0-9642809-0-6*) Assoc Ladies.

Associated Press. The Associated Press Stylebook & Libel Manual. 6th ed. 336p. 1996. pap. 14.00 (*0-201-40717-5*) Addison-Wesley.

Associated Press Editors. The Associated Press Crossword Puzzle Book, No. 5. 1989. pap. 5.95 (*0-8092-4429-2*) NTC Contemp Pub Co.

— The Associated Press Sunday Crossword Puzzle, Bk. 3. 96p. (Orig.). 1986. pap. 5.95 (*0-8092-4985-5*) NTC Contemp Pub Co.

Associated Press Staff. AP Stylebook. 7th rev. ed. 336p. 1998. pap. 15.00 (*0-201-33985-4*) Addison-Wesley.

— The Associated Press Library of Disasters. Incl. Associated Press Library of Disasters Vol. 1: Earthquakes & Tsunamis. LC 97-26422. (J). 1997. Not sold separately (*0-7172-9171-5*); Associated Press Library of Disasters Vol. 2: Civil Unrest & Terrorism. (J). 1997. lib. bdg. Not sold separately (*0-7172-9177-4*); Associated Press Library of Disasters Vol. 3: Volcanoes. (J). 1997. lib. bdg. Not sold separately (*0-7172-9172-3*); Associated Press Library of Disasters Vol. 4: Tornadoes & Cyclones. (J). 1997. lib. bdg. Not sold separately (*0-7172-9175-8*); Associated Press Library of Disasters Vol. 7: Fires & Explosions. (J). 1997. lib. bdg. Not sold separately (*0-7172-9173-1*); Associated Press Library of Disasters Vol. 8: Nuclaer & Industrial Disasters. (J). 1997. lib. bdg. Not sold separately (*0-7172-9176-6*); Associated Press of Library Disasters Vol. 6: Air, Sea & Tarin Disasters. LC 97-26422. (J). 1997. lib. bdg. (*0-7172-9174-X*); Vol. 5. Associated Press Library of Disasters: Wild Weather. LC 97-26422. (J). 1997. lib. bdg. Not sold separately (*0-7172-9170-7*); 1997. Set lib. bdg. 295.00 (*0-7172-9169-3*) Grolier Educ.

— Associated Press Pictorial History of the Olympics. 1995. pap. 18.00 (*0-671-89299-1*) S&S Trade.

— The Associated Press Stylebook & Libel Manual. 288p. 1982. pap. 8.95 (*0-201-10091-6*) Addison-Wesley.

— Associated Press Stylebook & Libel Manual. 3rd ed. 1992. pap. 11.95 (*0-201-56760-1*) Addison-Wesley.

— The Associated Press Stylebook & Libel Manual: The Journalist's Bible. rev. ed. LC 87-3572. (Illus.). 336p. 1987. pap. 10.53 (*0-201-10433-4*) Addison-Wesley.

— The Associated Press Sunday Crossword Puzzle, Bk. 6. (Illus.). 96p. 1991. spiral bd. 11.95 (*0-8092-4108-0*, 410800, Contemporary Bks) NTC Contemp Pub Co.

— The Olympics at 100: A Celebration in Pictures. (Illus.). 224p. 1995. 19.95 (*0-02-860346-X*, Arco) Macmillan Gen Ref.

— Random House Sunday Megaomnibus, Vol. 2. 1997. pap. 13.50 (*0-8129-2908-X*, Times Bks) Crown Pub Group.

*__Associated Press Staff, ed.__ Home Run: The Year the Records Fell: Mark McGwire Edition. (Illus.). 144p. 1998. 24.95 (*1-58261-027-4*) Sprts Pubng.

— Home Run: The Year the Records Fell: National Edition. (Illus.). 144p. 1998. 24.95 (*1-58261-023-1*) Sprts Pubng.

— Home Run: The Year the Records Fell: Sammy Sosa Edition. (Illus.). 144p. 1998. 24.95 (*1-58261-026-6*) Sprts Pubng.

— The Sports 100: The 100 Greatest Athletes of the 20th Century & Their Greatest Career Movements. 288p. 2000. 29.95 (*1-58261-206-4*, Pub. by Sprts Pubng) Partners-West.

Associated Press Staff, ed. see Castle, George.

Associated Publishers Group Staff. The Christmas You've Always Longed For: How to Recapture the Wonder of the Season. 1997. pap. 10.99 (*1-57849-037-5*) Chapel of Air.

Associated Students of the University of Californi. Coffee House Cookbook. LC 86-50606. (Illus.). 105p. (Orig.). 1986. pap. 7.95 (*0-934189-02-1*) Unique Pub CA.

Associated Women's Organization, Mars Hill Bible S. Something Special. Simpson, Peggy & Stanley, Linda, eds. 1977. pap. 6.95 (*0-89137-408-6*) Quality Pubns.

— What Are We Doing Here? 1972. pap. 6.95 (*0-89137-404-3*) Quality Pubns.

Associates of Price Pottinger Nutrition Foundation & Connolly, Pat. Candida Albicans Yeast-Free Cookbook. LC 85-9730. 168p. (Orig.). 1985. pap. 12.95 (*0-87983-409-9*, Keats Publng) NTC Contemp Pub Co.

Association, Belle Haleine. Purple Sexe #05. 1999. pap. text 10.00 (*2-912684-13-7*) Assn Belle.

— Purple #04. 1999. pap. text 14.00 (*2-912684-12-9*) Assn Belle.

Association D'Economie Financiere Staff. Money & Morals Worldwide: First Annual Report. annuals 250p. (C). (gr. 13). 1996. text 81.95 (*1-56324-851-4*) M E Sharpe.

*__Association des sbedimentologist es franwcais staff.__ Dynamics & Methods of Study of Sedimentary Basins. LC 98-907099. xiv, 392 p. 1998. write for info. (*81-204-1256-7*) Oxford & IBH Pubng.

Association des Trois Mondes, Paris Staff. Dictionnaire du Cinema Africain, Vol. 1. (FRE.). 398p. 1991. pap. 65.00 (*0-7859-8145-4*, 2865372979) Fr & Eur.

Association Europeene D'etudes Juridiques et Fisca. Product Liability in Europe. Strom, Paul, ed. 160p. 1975. pap. 21.00 (*90-268-0815-1*) Kluwer Academic.

Association for Accounting Marketing Staff & American Institute Of Certified Public Accountants. How to Hire a Marketing Director & Make It Work. LC 96-20214. 1996. 44.00 (*0-87051-179-3*) Am Inst CPA.

Association for Advancement of Medical Instrumenta & Berson, Alan S. Cardiac Monitoring in a Complex Patient Care Environment. 89p. (Orig.). 1982. pap. text 30.00 (*0-910275-09-2*, TAR3-209) Assn Adv Med Instrn.

Association for Asian Studies Staff. Japanese Studies in Canada. LC 95-51991. 1995. 12.00 (*0-924304-35-9*) Assn Asian Studies.

Association for Child Development Staff. Adventures in Learning with the Food Guide Pyramid. (Illus.). 109p. (Orig.). 1993. pap. write for info. (*0-9648135-0-5*) Assn Child Devel.

Association for Childhood Education International Staff. And Everywhere, Children: An International Story Festival. LC 78-25932. 282p. 1979. reprint ed. pap. 87.50 (*0-7837-8942-4*, 204965200002) Bks Demand.

— Learning Centers: Children on Their Own. Rapport, Virginia, ed. LC 71-133244. 84p. reprint ed. pap. 30.00 (*0-608-17255-3*, 202919800059) Bks Demand.

— Learning Opportunities Beyond the School. 2nd rev. ed. Hatcher, Barbara & Beck, Shirley, eds. LC 97-20453. (Illus.). 80p. (C). 1997. pap. text. write for info. (*0-87173-138-X*) ACEI.

— Migrant Children: Their Education. Sunderlin, Sylvia, ed. LC 74-162482. 64p. reprint ed. pap. 30.00 (*0-608-13787-1*, 202063100018) Bks Demand.

— Selecting Educational Equipment & Materials for School & Home. Moyer, Joan, ed. 1995. 15.00 (*0-87173-134-7*) ACEI.

Association for Childhood Education International Staff, compiled by. Activities for the Classroom & Beyond: A Collection of Ideas & Activities to Help Extend Learning & Make It More Relevant to Students' Everyday Lives. LC 98-18630. (Illus.). 64p. 1998. pap. text 15.00 (*0-87173-141-X*) ACEI.

Association for Childhood Education International Staff, jt. auth. see Jalongo, Mary R.

Association for Computational Linguistics Staff, compiled by. ACL Proceedings: Association for Computational Linguistics: The 20th-35th Annual Meetings. 400p. 1997. pap. 60.00 (*1-55860-513-4*) Morgan Kaufmann.

Association for Computational Linguistics Staff, jt. auth. see Viegas, Evelyne.

Association for Computing Machinery Staff & Vedral, Joyce L. Functional Programming Languages & Computer Architecture. 402p. (C). 1989. pap. text 39.95 (*0-201-51389-7*) Addison-Wesley.

A

An Asterisk (*) at the beginning of an entry indicates that the title is appearing for the first time.

Association for Computing Machinery Staff, jt. auth. see ACM SIGUCCS User Services Conference Staff.

Association for Core Texts & Courses Staff. Tradition & Innovation: Selected Plenary & Panel Papers from the 3rd Annual Conference of the Association for Core Texts & Courses, Philadelphia, PA, 10-13 April, 1997. Lee, J. Scott & Speight, Allen, eds. LC 98-49310. 160p. 1999. 46.00 (*0-7618-1308-X*); pap. 24.50 (*0-7618-1309-8*) U Pr of Amer.

Association for Counselor Education & Supervision Staff, ed. see McAuliffe, Garrett & Eriksen, Karen.

Association for Diplomatic Studies & Training Staf. A Brief History of United States Diplomacy. (ADST-DACOR Diplomats & Diplomacy Ser.: Vol. 1). (Illus.). 32p. (Orig.). (C). 1996. pap. 6.00 (*0-9653949-0-5*) Assn Diplomatic Studies.

Association for Educational Communications Governm. Copyright & Educational Media: A Guide to Fair Use & Permissions Procedures. 1977. pap. 4.95 (*0-89240-004-8*) Assn Ed Comm Tech.

— Evaluation of Instructional Materials. 1979. pap. 5.95 (*0-89240-033-1*) Assn Ed Comm Tech.

Association for Educational Communications Governm, jt. auth. see American Association of School Librarians Staff.

Association for Educational Communications Governm, ed. see Frederick, Franz J.

Association for Experiential Education Staff, contrib. by. AEEE International Conference Proceedings, 1997. 308p. (C). 1997. pap. text 20.00 (*0-536-00772-1*) Pearson Custom.

Association for Eye Research, 18th, Bonn, July 197. Gerontological Aspects of Eye Research: Selected Papers. (Interdisciplinary Topics in Gerontology Ser.: Vol. 13). (Illus.). 1978. 112.25 (*3-8055-2877-9*) S Karger.

Association for Finishing Processes of SME Staff. Finishing '85: Conference Proceedings, September 16-19, 1985, Detroit. LC 85-61970. (Illus.). 344p. reprint ed. pap. 106.70 (*0-8357-6504-0*, 203587500097) Bks Demand.

Association for Gerontology Education in Social Work Staff, jt. compiled by see Richardson, Virginia.

Association for Information & Image Management Staff. Alphanumeric COM Quality Test Slide: ANSI-AIIM MS28-1996. 11p. 1996. pap. 33.00 (*0-89258-124-7*, MS28) Assn Inform & Image Mgmt.

Association for Information & Image Management Staff. Application Programming Interface (API) for Scanners in Document Imaging Systems: ANSI/AIIM MS61-1996. 62p. 1996. 52.00 (*0-89258-312-6*, MS61) Assn Inform & Image Mgmt.

Association for Information & Image Management Staff. Bar Coding on Microfiche for Production & Dynamic Distribution Control: AIIM TR12-1988 (R1997) 15p. 1988. pap. 33.00 (*0-89258-146-8*, TR12) Assn Inform & Image Mgmt.

— Color Microforms: AIIM TR9-1989 (R1992) 24p. 1989. pap. 33.00 (*0-89258-188-3*, TR09) Assn Inform & Image Mgmt.

Association for Information & Image Management Staff. Content of Production Specification Sheets for Microform Readers & Reader-Printers: ANSI/AIIM TR16-1996. 10p. 1996. 33.00 (*0-89258-328-2*, TR16) Assn Inform & Image Mgmt.

Association for Information & Image Management Staff. Cores & Spools for Recording Equipment - Dimensions: ANSI AIIM MS29-1992. 9p. 1992. pap. 33.00 (*0-89258-250-2*, MS29) Assn Inform & Image Mgmt.

Association for Information & Image Management Staff. Dimensions & Operational Constraints for Single Core Cartridge for 16mm Processed Microfilm: ANSI/AIIM MS15-1990. 1990. 33.00 (*0-89258-350-9*) Assn Inform & Image Mgmt.

— Dimensions of Unitized Microfilm Carriers & Apertures (Aperture, Camera, Copy & Image Cards) ANSI/AIIM MS41-1996. 12p. 1996. 30.00 (*0-89258-189-1*, MS41) Assn Inform & Image Mgmt.

— Electronic Folder Interchange Datastream: ANSI/AIIM MS60-1996. 37p. 1996. 52.00 (*0-89258-305-3*, MS60) Assn Inform & Image Mgmt.

Association for Information & Image Management Staff. Electronic Imaging Output Displays: ANSI/AIIM TR19-1993. 18p. 1993. pap. 45.00 (*0-89258-254-5*, TR19) Assn Inform & Image Mgmt.

— Electronic Imaging Output Printers: ANSI/AIIM TR29-1993. 18p. 1993. pap. 45.00 (*0-89258-252-9*, TR29) Assn Inform & Image Mgmt.

Association for Information & Image Management Staff. Environmental & Right-to-Know Regulations Affecting Microfilm Processors: ANSI/AIIM TR20-1994. 47p. 1994. 39.00 (*0-89258-284-7*, TR20) Assn Inform & Image Mgmt.

Association for Information & Image Management Staff. Facsimile & Its Role in Electronic Imaging: ANSI/AIIM TR17-1989. (Illus.). 41p. 1989. pap. 39.00 (*0-89258-164-6*, TR17) Assn Inform & Image Mgmt.

— Flow Chart Symbols & Their Use in Micrographics: ANSI-AIIM, MS4-1987. 1987. pap. 33.00 (*0-89258-121-2*, MS04) Assn Inform & Image Mgmt.

— Guidelines for Metrics (A1992) AIIM TR1-1988 with 1992 Addendum. 34p. 1992. pap. 33.00 (*0-89258-135-2*, TR01) Assn Inform & Image Mgmt.

Association for Information & Image Management Staff. Guidelines for the Use of Media Error Monitoring & Reporting Techniques for the Verification of Information Stored on Optical Digital Data Disks: ANSI/AIIM TR39-1996. 44p. 1996. 39.00 (*0-89258-306-1*, TR39) Assn Inform & Image Mgmt.

— Human & Organizational Issues for Successful EIM System Implementation: ANSI/AIIM TR35-1995. 30p. 1995. 46.00 (*0-89258-296-0*, TR35) Assn Inform & Image Mgmt.

— Identification & Indexing of Page Components (Zones) for Automated Processing in an Electronic Image Management (EIM) Environment: ANSI/AIIM MS55-1994. 13p. 1994. 52.00 (*0-89258-282-0*, MS55) Assn Inform & Image Mgmt.

— Identification of Test Images for Document Imaging Applications: ANSI/AIIM TR38-1996. 51p. 1996. 52.00 (*0-89258-302-9*, TR38) Assn Inform & Image Mgmt.

Association for Information & Image Management Staff. Image Mark (Blip) Used in Image Mark Retrieval Systems (R1998) ANSI-AIIM MS8-1988 (R1998) 10p. 1988. pap. 33.00 (*0-89258-126-3*, MS08) Assn Inform & Image Mgmt.

Association for Information & Image Management Staff. Media Error Monitoring & Reporting Techniques for Verification of Stored Data on Optical Digital Data Disks: ANSI/AIIM MS59-1996. 37p. 1996. 52.00 (*0-89258-307-X*, MS59) Assn Inform & Image Mgmt.

— Metadata for Interchange of Files on Sequential Storage Media Between File Storage Management Systems (FSMSs) ANSI/AIIM MS66-1999. 39p. 1999. 39.00 (*0-89258-365-7*, MS66) Assn Inform & Image Mgmt.

Association for Information & Image Management Staff. Method for Determining Adhesion of Protection Sheet to Aperture Adhesive of Unitized Microfilm Carrier (Aperture Card) ANSI-AIIM MS10-1987 (R1993) 8p. 1987. pap. 33.00 (*0-89258-125-5*, MS10) Assn Inform & Image Mgmt.

— Method for Measuring Thickness of Buildup Area on Unitized Microfilm Carriers (Aperture, Camera, Copy & Image Cards) ANSI-AIIM MS9-1987 (A1996) 11p. 1987. pap. 33.00 (*0-89258-122-0*, MS09) Assn Inform & Image Mgmt.

— Microfiche: ANSI-AIIM MS5-1992 (R1998) 24p. 1992. pap. 33.00 (*0-89258-251-0*, MS05) Assn Inform & Image Mgmt.

— Microfilm Computer Assisted Retrieval (CAR) Interface Commands: ANSI-AIIM MS40-1987 (R1999) 8p. 1987. pap. 33.00 (*0-89258-105-0*, MS40) Assn Inform & Image Mgmt.

— Microfilm Jacket Formatting & Loading Techniques: AIIM TR11-1987 (A1993) (R1998) 19p. 1987. pap. 33.00 (*0-89258-111-5*, TR11) Assn Inform & Image Mgmt.

— Microfilm Jackets: ANSI-AIIM MS11-1987 (R1999) 9p. 1987. pap. 33.00 (*0-89258-114-X*, MS11) Assn Inform & Image Mgmt.

Association for Information & Image Management Staff. Microfilm Package Labeling: ANSI/AIIM MS6-1981 (R1999) 7p. 1981. 33.00 (*0-89258-275-8*, MS06) Assn Inform & Image Mgmt.

Association for Information & Image Management Staff. Micrographics - ISO Resolution Test Chart No. 2 Description & Use: ANSI/AIIM MS51-1991. (Illus.). 10p. 1991. pap. 33.00 (*0-89258-225-1*, MS51) Assn Inform & Image Mgmt.

— Microrecording of Engineering Graphics - Computer-Output Microfilm: ANSI-AIIM MS38-1995. 16p. 1995. pap. 33.00 (*0-89258-100-X*, MS38) Assn Inform & Image Mgmt.

— Microrecording of Engineering Source Documents on 35mm Microfilm: ANSI-AIIM MS32-1996. 15p. 1996. pap. 33.00 (*0-89258-085-2*, MS32) Assn Inform & Image Mgmt.

Association for Information & Image Management Staff. Monitoring Image Quality of Aperture Cared Film Image Scanners: ANSI/AIIM MS50-1994. 35p. 1994. 52.00 (*0-89258-285-5*, MS50) Assn Inform & Image Mgmt.

— Operational Procedures/Inspection & Quality Control of Duplicate Microforms of Documents & from COM: ANSI/AIIM MS43-1998. 72p. 1998. 45.00 (*0-89258-348-7*, MS43) Assn Inform & Image Mgmt.

Association for Information & Image Management Staff. Paper Forms Design Optimization for Electronic Image Management (EIM) ANSI/AIIM TR32-1994. 20p. 1993. pap. 45.00 (*0-89258-271-5*, TR32) Assn Inform & Image Mgmt.

Association for Information & Image Management Staff. Performance Guidelines for Legal Acceptance Records Pt. 2: Acceptance by Government Agencies: ANSI/AIIM TR31/2-1993 (R1999) 27p. 1993. pap. 45.00 (*0-89258-276-6*) Assn Inform & Image Mgmt.

Association for Information & Image Management Staff. Performance Guidelines for the Legal Acceptance of Records Pt. 1 Evidence: ANSI/AIIm TR31/1 - 1992 (R1999) 28p. 1992. pap. 39.00 (*0-89258-245-6*, TR31/1) Assn Inform & Image Mgmt.

Association for Information & Image Management Staff. Performance Guidelines for the Legal Acceptance of Records PT. 3 Implementation: ANSI/AIIM TR31/3 - 1994 (R1999) 50p. 1994. 39.00 (*0-89258-290-1*, TR31/3) Assn Inform & Image Mgmt.

— Performance Guidelines for the Legal Acceptance of Records Pt. 4 Model Act & Rule: ANSi/AIIM TR31/4 - 1994 (R1999) 28p. 1994. 39.00 (*0-89258-289-8*, TR31/4) Assn Inform & Image Mgmt.

— Planning Considerations, Addressing Preparation of Documents for Image Capture: ANSI/AIIM TR15-1997. 20p. 1997. 52.00 (*0-89258-336-3*, TR15) Assn Inform & Image Mgmt.

— Practice for Operational Procedures/Inspection & Quality Control of First-Generation Silver-Gelatin Microfilm of Documents: ANSi/AIIM MS23-1998. 108p. 1998. spiral bd. 52.00 (*0-89258-347-9*, MS23) Assn Inform & Image Mgmt.

— Preservation of Microforms in an Active Environment - Guidelines: ANSI/AIIM TR13-1998. 30p. 1998. 33.00 (*0-89258-342-8*, TR13) Assn Inform & Image Mgmt.

— Reader-Printers: ANSI/AIIM MS36-1990. 9p. 1990. 33.00 (*0-89258-205-7*, MS36) Assn Inform & Image Mgmt.

Association for Information & Image Management Staff. Readers for Transparent Microforms - Methods for Measuring Performance Characteristics: ANSI-AIIM MS12-1990. 14p. 1990. pap. 33.00 (*0-89258-206-5*, MS12) Assn Inform & Image Mgmt.

— Readers for Transparent Microforms - Performance Characteristics: ANSI-AIIM MS20-1990. (Illus.). 12p. 1990. pap. 33.00 (*0-89258-204-9*, MS20) Assn Inform & Image Mgmt.

— Recommendations for the Identifying Information to Be Placed on Write-Once-Read-Many (WORM) & Rewritable Optical Disk (OD) Cartridge Label(s) & Optical Disk Cartridge Packaging (Shipping Containers) AIIM TR21-1991. 11p. 1991. 39.00 (*0-89258-232-4*, TR21) Assn Inform & Image Mgmt.

— Recommended Practice for Alphanumeric Computer-Output Microforms - Operational Practices for Inspection & Quality Control: ANSI-AIIM MS1-1996. 26p. 1996. pap. 33.00 (*0-89258-129-8*, MS01) Assn Inform & Image Mgmt.

***Association for Information & Image Management Staff.** Recommended Practice for COM Recording Systems Having an Internal Electronic Forms Generating System - Operational Practices for Inspection & Quality Control: ANSI/AIIM MS62-1999. 18p. 1999. 39.00 (*0-89258-367-3*, MS62) Assn Inform & Image Mgmt.

— Recommended Practice for Identification of Microforms: ANSI/AIIM MS19-1993. 28p. 1993. 33.00 (*0-89258-272-3*, MS19) Assn Inform & Image Mgmt.

Association for Information & Image Management Staff. Recommended Practice for Inspection of Stored Silver Gelatin Microforms for Evidence of Deterioration: ANSI-AIIM MS45-1990. 27p. 1990. pap. 33.00 (*0-89258-203-0*, MS45) Assn Inform & Image Mgmt.

— Recommended Practice for Microfilming Printed Newspapers on 35mm Roll Microfilm: ANSI-AIIM MS111-1994. 16p. 1994. pap. 33.00 (*0-89258-258-8*, MS111) Assn Inform & Image Mgmt.

***Association for Information & Image Management Staff.** Recommended Practice for Microfilming Public Records on Silver-Halide Film: ANSI/AIIM MS48-1999. 10p. 1999. 33.00 (*0-89258-366-5*, MS48) Assn Inform & Image Mgmt.

Association for Information & Image Management Staff. Recommended Practice for Microphotography of Cartographic Materials: ANSI-AIIM MS37-1998 (A1996) 31p. 1988. pap. 33.00 (*0-89258-141-7*, MS37) Assn Inform & Image Mgmt.

— Recommended Practice for Operational Procedures, Quality Control & Inspection of Graphic Computer-Output Microforms: ANSI-AIIM MS39-1987. 28p. 1987. pap. 33.00 (*0-89258-106-9*, MS39) Assn Inform & Image Mgmt.

— Recommended Practice for the Expungement, Deletion, Correction or Amendment of Records on Microforms: ANSI-AIIM MS42-1989. (Illus.). 13p. 1989. pap. 33.00 (*0-89258-173-5*, MS42) Assn Inform & Image Mgmt.

— Recommended Practice for the Requirements & Characteristics of Original Documents Intended for Optical Scanning: ANSI/AIIM MS52-1991. (Illus.). 11p. 1991. pap. 39.00 (*0-89258-234-0*, MS52) Assn Inform & Image Mgmt.

— Recommended Practice for the Requirements & Characteristics of Original Documents That May Be Microfilmed: ANSI-AIIM MS35-1990. 18p. 1990. pap. 33.00 (*0-89258-211-1*, MS35) Assn Inform & Image Mgmt.

— Resolution As It Relates to Photographic & Electronic Imaging: ANSI/AIIM TR26-1993. 23p. 1993. pap. 45.00 (*0-89258-253-7*, TR26) Assn Inform & Image Mgmt.

— Rotary Cameras for 16mm Microfilm - Mechanical & Optical Characteristics: ANSI-AIIM MS47-1990. 10p. 1990. pap. 33.00 (*0-89258-207-3*, MS47) Assn Inform & Image Mgmt.

Association for Information & Image Management Staff. Rotary (Flow) Microfilm Camera Test Chart & Test Target - Descriptions & Use: ANSI/AIIM MS 17-1992. 16p. 1992. 33.00 (*0-89258-247-2*, MS17) Assn Inform & Image Mgmt.

— Sampling Procedures for Inspection by Attributes of Images in Electronic Image Management (EIM) & Micrographics Systems: ANSI/AIIM TR34-1996. 72p. 1996. 52.00 (*0-89258-295-2*, TR34) Assn Inform & Image Mgmt.

— Selecting an Appropriate Image Compression Method to Match User Requirements: ANSI/AIIM TR33-1998. 1998. 39.00 (*0-89258-349-5*) Assn Inform & Image Mgmt.

Association for Information & Image Management Staff. Silver Recovery Techniques: AIIM TR4-1989 (A1993) (Technical Reports). 18p. 1989. pap. 33.00 (*0-89258-191-3*, TR04) Assn Inform & Image Mgmt.

— Specifications for 16- & 35-mm Roll Microfilm: ANSI-AIIM MS14, 1996. (Standards & Recommended Practices Ser.). 24p. 1996. 33.00 (*0-89258-130-1*, MS14) Assn Inform & Image Mgmt.

— Splices for Image Film - Dimensions & Operational Constraints (R1998) ANSI-AIIMI MS18-1992 (R1998) 8p. 1992. pap. 33.00 (*0-89258-248-0*, MS18) Assn Inform & Image Mgmt.

Association for Information & Image Management Staff. Standard Recommended Practice for Implementation of Small Computer Systems Interface (SCSI-2), (X3, 131-1994) for Scanners: ANSI/AIIM MS58-1996. 46p. 1996. 52.00 (*0-89258-291-X*, MS58) Assn Inform & Image Mgmt.

— Suggested Index Fields for Documents in Electronic Image (EIM) Environments: ANSI/AIIM TR40-1995. 14p. 1995. 52.00 (*0-89258-304-5*, TR40) Assn Inform & Image Mgmt.

Association for Information & Image Management Staff. Symbols for Various Functions of Document Handling Equipment (R1999) ANSI/AIIM MS54-1993 (R1999) 13p. 1993. pap. 39.00 (*0-89258-273-1*, MS54) Assn Inform & Image Mgmt.

— Test Target & Test Method for Determining Output of 35mm Microfilm Duplicators (A1996) ANSI-AIIM MS46-1990 (A1996) 10p. 1990. pap. 33.00 (*0-89258-200-6*, MS46) Assn Inform & Image Mgmt.

— Test Target for Use in Microrecording Engineering Graphics on 35mm Microfilm: (ANSI-AIIM MS24-1980 (R1996) (Standards Ser.). 1996. pap. 33.00 (*0-89258-109-3*, MS24) Assn Inform & Image Mgmt.

Association for Information & Image Management Staff. 35mm Planetary Cameras-Procedures for Determining Illumination Uniformity of Microfilming Engineering Drawings: ANSI/AIIM MS26-1990. 1990. 33.00 (*0-89258-195-6*) Assn Inform & Image Mgmt.

Association for Integrative Studies Staff, jt. auth. see Newell, William H.

Association for Investment Management & Research S, jt. auth. see Knutson, Peter H.

Association for Investment Management and Research, jt. auth. see Bernstein, Richard.

Association for Investment Management and Research, jt. auth. see Chance, Don M.

Association for Japanese Language Staff. Japanese for Busy People. 1998. pap. text, teacher ed. 22.00 (*4-7700-2306-5*, Pub. by Kodansha Intl) Kodansha.

***Association for Japanese Language Staff.** Japanese for Busy People: The Video Guide to Volumes I, II & III. (Japanese for Busy People Ser.). (JPN & ENG., Illus.). 288p. 2000. pap. 40.00 (*4-7700-2491-6*) Kodansha Intl.

Association for Japanese Language Staff. Japanese for Young People. 1998. pap. text 22.00 (*4-7700-2178-X*, Pub. by Kodansha Intl) Kodansha.

— Japanese for Young People: Kana Workbook. 1998. pap. text 17.00 (*4-7700-2180-1*, Pub. by Kodansha Intl) Kodansha.

***Association for Japanese Language Staff.** Japanese for Young People III. (Japanese for Young People Ser.). (JPN.). 2000. pap. 55.00 (*4-7700-2495-9*) Kodansha Intl.

— Japanese for Young People III: Kanji Workbook. (Japanese for Young People Ser.). (ENG & JPN., Illus.). 2000. pap., wbk. ed. 55.00 (*4-7700-2496-7*) Kodansha Intl.

Association for Japanese-Language Staff. Reading Japanese Financial Newspapers. 160p. 1991. pap. 35.00 (*0-87011-956-7*) Kodansha.

***Association for Japanese-Language Staff.** Reading Japanese Financial Newspapers. rev. ed. 388p. 1999. pap. 35.00 (*4-7700-2472-X*, Pub. by Kodansha Intl) Kodansha.

Association for Japanese-Language Teaching Staff. Japanese for Busy People, Vol. I. rev. ed. 232p. 1995. pap. text 24.00 (*4-7700-1882-7*) Kodansha.

— Japanese for Busy People: Workbook, Vol. I. rev. ed. 182p. 1995. pap. text, wbk. ed. 19.00 (*4-7700-1907-6*) Kodansha.

— Japanese for Busy People I. rev. ed. 1995. audio 40.00 (*4-7700-1883-5*) Kodansha.

— Japanese for Busy People I, Vol. I. rev. ed. 232p. 1995. audio compact disk 40.00 (*4-7700-1909-2*) Kodansha.

— Japanese for Busy People I: Japanese Teachers' Manual. rev. ed. (JPN.). 232p. 1994. pap. text, teacher ed. 22.00 (*4-7700-1906-8*) Kodansha.

***Association for Japanese Language Teaching Staff.** Japanese for Busy People III. 1999. pap., wbk. ed. 50.00 incl. audio (*4-7700-2358-8*, Pub. by Kodansha Intl) Kodansha.

Association for Japanese-Language Teaching Staff. Japanese for Busy People III, Vol. III. rev. ed. 1995. audio 50.00 (*4-7700-1887-8*) Kodansha.

— Japanese for Busy People III, Vol. III. rev. ed. Vol. 2. 256p. 1995. pap. text 24.00 (*4-7700-1886-X*) Kodansha.

— Japanese for Busy People II, Vol. II. rev. ed. LC 96-122100. 240p. 1995. pap. text 24.00 (*4-7700-1884-3*); audio 50.00 (*4-7700-1885-1*) Kodansha.

— Japanese for Professionals: The Association for Japanese-Language Teaching. LC 98-5341. 1998. pap. text 22.00 (*4-7700-2038-4*, Pub. by Kodansha Intl) Kodansha.

Association for Japanese-Language Teaching Staff, jt. auth. see Hall, Michelle.

Association for Library Collections & Technical Se. Book & Serial Vendors for Africa & the Middle East: Results of a Survey of ARL Libraries. Debus, Karl E., ed. LC 97-24795. (Foreign Book & Serial Vendors Directories Ser.). 1997. 15.00 (*0-8389-7903-3*) ALA.

— Guide to Performance Evaluation of Serial Vendors. LC 97-2134. (ALCTS Acquisitions Guidelines Ser.). 45p. 1997. 15.00 (*0-8389-3469-2*) ALA.

Association for Library Collections & Technical Se, compiled by. Headings for Tomorrow: Public Access Display of Subject Headings. LC 92-14484. 51p. (C). 1992. pap. text 18.00 (*0-8389-3414-5*) ALA.

Association for Library Collections & Technical Services, American Library Association. Outsourcing Library Technical Services Operations: Practices in Academic, Public, & Special Libraries. Wilson, Karen A. & Colver, Marylou, eds. LC 97-22901. 239p. 1997. 38.00 (*0-8389-0703-2*) ALA.

Association for Library Service Staff. The Newbery & Caldecott Awards. 160p. 1998. pap. text 16.00 (*0-8389-3484-6*) ALA.

An Asterisk (*) at the beginning of an entry indicates that the title is appearing for the first time.

Association for Library Service to Children Staff. First Steps to Literacy: Library Programs for Parents, Teachers & Caregivers. 176p. 1989. pap. 25.00 (*0-8389-0521-8*) ALA.

— The Newbery & Caldecott Awards: A Guide to the Medal & Honor Books. LC 91-9909. (Illus.). 143p. 1991. reprint ed. pap. 44.40 (*0-7837-5966-5*, 204576700007) Bks Demand.

— The Newbery & Caldecott Awards: A Guide to the Medal & Honor Books 1995 Edition. LC Z 1037.A2N47. 157p. 1995. reprint ed. pap. 48.70 (*0-608-02967-X*, 206343200006) Bks Demand.

— The Newbery & Caldecott Awards, 1994: A Guide to the Medal & Honor Books. LC Z 1037.A2N47. 151p. 1994. reprint ed. pap. 46.90 (*0-7837-9675-7*, 206040300005) Bks Demand.

— Selecting Materials for Children & Young Adults: A Bibliography of Bibliographies & Review Sources. LC 80-12374. 80p. reprint ed. pap. 30.00 (*0-7837-5957-6*, 204575700007) Bks Demand.

Association for Practitioners in Infection Control. APIC Infection Control & Applied Epidemiology: Principles & Practice. LC 96-14096. (Illus.). 1408p. (C). (gr. 13). 1996. text 165.00 (*0-8151-0243-7*, 24857) Mosby Inc.

Association for Research & Enlightenment, Readings, compiled by. Attitudes & Emotions, Pt. I. (Library: Vol. 13). 445p. 1981. lib. bdg. 22.95 (*0-87604-138-1*, 1113) ARE Pr.

— Attitudes & Emotions, Pt. II. (Library: Vol. 14). 393p. 1982. lib. bdg. 22.95 (*0-87604-140-3*, 1114) ARE Pr.

— Christ Consciousness. (Library: Vol. 11). 277p. 1980. lib. bdg. 19.95 (*0-87604-124-1*, 1111) ARE Pr.

— Daily Living. (Library: Vol. 12). 241p. 1981. lib. bdg. 19.95 (*0-87604-133-0*, 1112) ARE Pr.

— Dreams & Dreaming, 2 parts, Vol. 2. (Library: Vols. 4-5). 587p. 1976. lib. bdg. 24.95 (*0-87604-088-1*, 1105) ARE Pr.

— The Expanded Search for God: Pts. 1 & 2, Pt. 1. (Library: Vol.16 & 17). 499p. 1983. lib. bdg. 24.95 (*0-87604-153-5*, 1116) ARE Pr.

— Jesus the Pattern: Library. (Library: Vol. 10). 336p. 1980. lib. bdg. 22.95 (*0-87604-123-3*, 1110) ARE Pr.

— On Life & Death: The Edgar Cayce Readings. (Library: Vol. 1). 188p. 1973. lib. bdg. 19.95 (*0-87604-065-2*, 1101) ARE Pr.

Association for Research & Enlightenment, Readings, ed. Meditation Pt. 2: Meditation, Endocrine Glands, Prayer, & Affirmations. (Library: Vol. 3). 274p. 1995. lib. bdg. 22.95 (*0-87604-082-2*, 1103) ARE Pr.

Association for Research & Enlightenment, Readings, et al, eds. Search for God, Bk. I. 146p. 1950. 8.95 (*0-87604-000-8*, 279) ARE Pr.

— Search for God, Bk. II. 147p. 1950. 8.95 (*0-87604-001-6*, 280) ARE Pr.

Association for Research in Nervous & Mental Disea, jt. auth. see Folstein, Marshal F.

Association for Social Anthropology in Oceania Sta. Fieldwork & Families: Constructing New Models for Ethnographic Research. Flinn, Juliana et al, eds. LC 97-18075. 240p. 1997. text 45.00 (*0-8248-1928-4*); pap. text 21.95 (*0-8248-1988-8*) UH Pr.

Association for Supervision & Curriculum Developme, jt. auth. see Delisle, Robert.

Association for the Advancement of Medical Instrum. Inhospital Sterility Assurance: Current Perspectives, 1982. (Illus.). 73p. (Orig.). 1982. pap. 30.00 (*0-910275-14-9*, TAR4-209) Assn Adv Med Instrn.

Association for the Advancement of Medical Instrum, jt. auth. see Canadian Healthcare Association Staff.

Association for the Anthropological Study of Play. Meaningful Play, Playful Meaning. Fine, Gary A., ed. LC 86-21513. (Association for the Anthropological Study of Play Ser.: No. 11). 255p. 1987. reprint ed. pap. 79.10 (*0-608-06445-9*, 206728100009) Bks Demand.

— The Paradoxes of Play: Proceedings of the 69th (i. e. 6th) Annual Meeting of the Association for the Anthropological Study of Play. Loy, John W. et al, eds. LC 86-113483. (Illus.). 238p. 1982. reprint ed. pap. 73.80 (*0-608-07061-0*, 206726700009) Bks Demand.

Association for the Anthropological Study of Play, Meeting (7th, Fort Worth, TX) Staff. The World of Play: Proceedings of the 7th Annual Meeting of the Association of the Anthropological Study of Play. Manning, Frank E., ed. LC 83-122436. 229p. reprint ed. pap. 71.00 (*0-608-20842-6*, 207194100003) Bks Demand.

Association for the Anthropological Study of Play, Meeting (9th: 1983: Baton Rouge, LA) Staff. The Many Faces of Play. Blanchard, Kendall et al, eds. LC 85-30602. (Association for the Anthropological Study of Play Ser.: No. 9). (Illus.). 288p. reprint ed. pap. 89.30 (*0-608-06454-8*, 206729200009) Bks Demand.

— The Many Faces of Play. Blanchard, Kendall et al, eds. LC 85-30602. 288p. reprint ed. pap. 89.30 (*0-608-20820-5*, 207191900003) Bks Demand.

Association for the Anthropological Study of Play Staff. The World of Play: Proceedings of the 7th Annual Meeting of the Association of the Anthropological Study of Play, Ft. Worth, TX. Manning, Frank E., ed. LC 83-122436. 332p. 1983. reprint ed. pap. 103.00 (*0-608-07098-X*, 206732500009) Bks Demand.

Association for the Improvement of the Conditions. Housing Conditions in Baltimore: Report of a Special Committee of the Assoc. for the Improvement of the Condition of the Poor & the Charity Organization Society. LC 73-11915. (Metropolitan America Ser.). (Illus.). 104p. 1974. reprint ed. 15.95 (*0-405-05384-3*) Ayer.

Association for the Study of American Indian Liter, jt. ed. see Bruchac, Joseph.

Association for the Study of the Cuban Economy Sta. Cuba in Transition, Vol. 4. 388p. 1994. 30.00 (*0-9649082-4-7*) Assn Study Cuban Econ.

— Cuba in Transition: Papers & Proceedings of Fifth Annual Meeting of ASCE, Aug. 10-12, 1995. 487p. 1996. lib. bdg. 40.00 (*0-9649082-2-0*) Assn Study Cuban Econ.

— Cuba in Transition: Papers & Proceedings of the First Annual Meeting of the Association for the Study of the Cuban Economy. (Study of the Cuban Economy Ser.). 336p. 1992. pap. text 20.00 (*1-879862-03-4*) FL Intl U Latin.

— Cuba in Transition: Third Annual Meeting of the Association for the Study of the Cuban Economy (ASCE) 340p. (Orig.). 1993. 30.00 (*0-9649082-3-9*) Assn Study Cuban Econ.

— Cuba in Transition Vol. II: Papers & Proceedings of the Second Annual Meeting of the Association for the Study of the Cuban Economy. 372p. 1993. pap. text 20.00 (*1-879862-04-2*) FL Intl U Latin.

Association for Women in Science Staff. Grants at a Glance: A Directory of Financial Resources for Women in Science. 2nd rev. ed. LC 92-74376. 120p. 1992. 7.50 (*0-9634590-1-5*) Assn Women Sci.

— Mentoring Means Future Scientists: A Guide for Developing Mentoring Programs Based on the AWIS Mentoring Project. LC 93-72802. 150p. (Orig.). 1993. pap. 15.95 (*0-9634590-3-1*); 6.95 (*0-9634590-5-8*) Assn Women Sci.

Association for Worksite Health Promotion Staff. Economic Impact of Worksite Health Promotion. Opatz, Joseph P., ed. LC 93-19102. (Illus.). 272p. 1993. text 32.00 (*0-87322-436-1*, BOPA0436) Human Kinetics.

— Guidelines for Employee Health Promotion Programs. LC 91-28162. (Illus.). 152p. 1991. pap. text 29.00 (*0-87322-351-9*, BAFB0351) Human Kinetics.

Association Francaise De Normalisation Staff. Dictionnaire Technique des Peintures et des Travaux de Peinturage.Tr. of Technical Dictionary of Painting & the Painting Industry. (FRE.). 156p. 1980. 95.00 (*0-8288-1415-5*, M14358) Fr & Eur.

Association Francaise des Ingenieurs Staff. Dictionary of Project Management: Francais-Anglais. 2nd ed. (ENG & FRE.). 218p. 1992. pap. 95.00 (*0-7859-0974-5*, 2124843214) Fr & Eur.

Association Francaise pour la Defense de la Tradit. Imbroglio, Detraction, Delirium: Remarks on a Report about the TFPs. LC 83-71006. 260p. 1983. pap. 10.00 (*1-877905-25-9*) Am Soc Defense TFP.

Association National For Law Staff. National Directory of Legal Employers: 32,000 Great Job Openings for Law Students & Law School. 1999. pap. text 39.95 (*0-15-900435-7*) Harcourt Legal.

Association National Staff & Paul, Serge. Dictionnaire des Terms Normalises de Sciences et Techniques. (FRE.). 409p. 1993. pap. 55.00 (*0-7859-5609-3*, 2110729139) Fr & Eur.

Association of American Colleges Staff. Liberal Education & the New Scholarship on Women: Issues & Constraints in Institutional Change, a Report of the Wingspread Conference, Racine, Wisconsin, Oct. 22-24, 1981. LC LC1576.L524. 64p. 1982. reprint ed. pap. 30.00 (*0-608-01793-0*, 206244600003) Bks Demand.

Association of American Colleges Staff, et al. Liberal Education & the New Scholarship on Women: Issues & Constraints in Institutional Change. vi, 56p. (Orig.). 1982. pap. 4.00 (*0-911696-12-1*) Assn Am Coll.

Association of American Feed Control Officials, In. Association of American Feed Control Officials Incorporated, Official Publication 1992. rev. ed. Haas, Earl M., ed. 324p. 1992. 20.00 (*1-878341-02-2*) AAFCO.

— Official Publication, 1990: Association of American Feed Control Official Incorporated. rev. ed. Haas, Earl M., ed. 319p. 1990. 20.00 (*1-878341-00-6*) AAFCO.

Association of American Geographers Staff. 1997-1998 Guide to Programs in Geography in the United States & Canada/AAG Handbook & Directory of Geographers. 30th rev. ed. Bradshaw, Linda S., ed. LC 85-641423. (Illus.). 824p. 1997. pap. 50.00 (*0-89291-242-1*) Assn Am Geographers.

— Snapshots of the Carolinas: Landscapes & Cultures. Bennett, D. Gordon, ed. (Illus.). 280p. (Orig.). (C). 1996. pap. 15.00 (*0-89291-225-1*) Assn Am Geographers.

Association of American Geographers Staff & GIS World, Inc. Staff. Business Geographics for Eductors & Researchers: May 1996 Proceedings. (Illus.). 1996. pap. 15.00 (*0-89291-226-X*) Assn Am Geographers.

Association of American Geologists & Naturalists a. Proceedings. Albritton, Claude C., ed. LC 77-6507. (History of Geology Ser.). 1978. reprint ed. lib. bdg. 51.95 (*0-405-10430-8*) Ayer.

Association of American Law Schools Staff. Law Books Recommended for Libraries: Including 1974, 1975 & 1976 Supplements, 10 vols. 1967. reprint ed. ring bd. 475.00 (*0-8377-0201-1*, Rothman) W S Hein.

Association of American Law Schools Staff, ed. see Maitland.

Association of American Universities Research Libraries Project Staff. Reports of the AAU Task Forces. LC 94-226626. 154p. 1994. pap. 12.00 (*0-918006-24-4*) ARL.

Association of American University Presses Staff. The Association of American University Presses Directory, 1989-1990. 200p. 1994. pap. 12.95 (*0-945103-02-6*) U Ch Pr.

***Association of American University Presses Staff.** The Association of American University Presses Directory 1998-1999. 240p. 1998. pap. 16.00 (*0-945103-12-3*, Pub. by Assn Am Univ) U Ch Pr.

— Association of American University Presses Directory 1999-2000. 2000. pap. text 16.00 (*0-945103-13-1*, Pub. by Assn Am Univ) U Ch Pr.

Association of American University Presses Staff, ed. The Association of American University Presses Directory, 1993-94. 1994. pap. 14.95 (*0-945103-07-7*) U Ch Pr.

— One Book - Five Ways: The Publishing Procedures of Five University Presses. (Illus.). xiv, 344p. 1994. pap. text 18.95 (*0-226-03024-5*) U Ch Pr.

Association of American University Staff. Association of American University Presses Directory 1990-1991. LC 54-43046. 1994. pap. 14.95 (*0-945103-03-4*, Pub. by Assn Am Univ) U Ch Pr.

***Association of American Veterinary Medicine Staff, compiled by.** Veterinary Medical School Admission Requirements. 176p. 2000. pap. 16.50 (*1-55753-219-2*) Purdue U Pr.

Association of Asian Social Science Research Counc, ed. Youth in Asia. 350p. 1988. text 40.00 (*0-89891-027-7*, Pub. by New Stateman Pub) Advent Bks Div.

Association of British Chambers of Commerce Staff. Towards National Prosperity: A Policy Statement by Britain's Chambers of Commerce Outlining a Moderate & Practical Approach to Restoring National Prosperity. LC 75-332832. 16 p. 1975. write for info. (*0-901413-07-0*) Assn BCC.

Association of British Disp. Opticians Staff. ABDO Frame Rule. (C). 1989. 50.00 (*0-89771-749-X*, Pub. by Assn Brit Dispen Opticians) St Mut.

Association of Certified Fraud Examiners Staff. Beyond the Numbers: Professional Interview Techniques. LC 94-5401. 213p. 1994. wbk. ed. 199.00 (*1-889277-03-7*) Assn Certified Fraud.

— Cooking the Books: What Every Accountant Should Know about Fraud. LC 91-5401. 184p. 1991. wbk. ed. 199.00 (*1-889277-05-3*) Assn Certified Fraud.

— The Corporate Con: Internal Fraud & the Auditor. LC 92-5401. 217p. 1992. wbk. ed. 199.00 (*1-889277-06-1*) Assn Certified Fraud.

— Crossing the Line: Ethical Lessons for Financial Professionals. LC 98-5404. 110p. 1998. wbk. ed. 65.00 (*1-889277-16-9*) Assn Certified Fraud.

***Association of Certified Fraud Examiners Staff.** Fundamentals of Computer Fraud. 300p. 1999. write for info. (*1-889277-19-3*) Assn Certified Fraud.

— How to Detect & Prevent Financial Statement Fraud. 300p. 1999. pap. 169.00 (*1-889277-17-7*) Assn Certified Fraud.

Association of Certified Fraud Examiners Staff. Introduction to Fraud Examination. LC 95-5404. 521p. 1995. wbk. ed. 249.00 (*1-889277-04-5*) Assn Certified Fraud.

— Making Crime Pay: How to Locate Hidden Assets. LC 98-5403. 315p. 1998. wbk. ed. 199.00 (*1-889277-15-0*) Assn Certified Fraud.

***Association of Certified Fraud Examiners Staff.** Other People's Money: The Basics of Asset Misappropriation. 300p. 1999. 169.00 (*1-889277-18-5*) Assn Certified Fraud.

***Association of Christian Schools International Staff.** ACSI Spelling: Grade Five. (Illus.). 175p. (J). (gr. 5). 1999. reprint ed. student ed. 10.95 (*1-58331-162-9*) Assn Christ Sch.

— ACSI Spelling: Grade Four. (Illus.). 175p. (J). (gr. 4). 1999. reprint ed. student ed. 10.95 (*1-58331-160-2*) Assn Christ Sch.

— ACSI Spelling: Grade One. (Illus.). 175p. (J). (gr. 1). 1999. reprint ed. student ed. 10.95 (*1-58331-154-8*) Assn Christ Sch.

— ACSI Spelling: Grade Six. (Illus.). 175p. (J). (gr. 6). 1999. reprint ed. student ed. 10.95 (*1-58331-164-5*) Assn Christ Sch.

— ACSI Spelling: Grade Three. (Illus.). 175p. (J). (gr. 3). 1999. reprint ed. student ed. 10.95 (*1-58331-158-0*) Assn Christ Sch.

— ACSI Spelling: Grade Two. (Illus.). 175p. (J). (gr. 2). 1999. reprint ed. student ed. 10.95 (*1-58331-156-4*) Assn Christ Sch.

— ACSI Spelling: Grade 6. (Illus.). 223p. (J). (gr. 6). 1999. reprint ed. teacher ed. 35.95 (*1-58331-165-3*) Assn Christ Sch.

Association of Christian Schools International Staff. A Manual for Christian School Secretaries. Damon, Bonnie, ed. 1992. reprint ed. 17.95 (*1-58331-026-6*) Assn Christ Sch.

Association of Christian Schools Int'l Staff. School Accreditation Manual. 2nd rev. ed. (Illus.). 100p. 1997. pap. text 20.00 (*1-58331-030-4*) Assn Christ Sch.

Association of College & Research Libraries. A Copyright Sampler. Johnston, Wanda K. & Roark, Derrie B., eds. LC 96-51467. (CJCLS Guide Ser.: Vol. 2). 224p. (C). 1997. pap. 29.00 (*0-8389-7878-9*) Assn Coll & Res Libs.

— Designs for Active Learning: A Sourcebook of Classroom Strategies for Information Education. Gradowski, Gail et al, eds. LC 98-7100. (Illus.). 248p. 1998. pap. 35.00 (*0-8389-7946-7*) Assn Coll & Res Libs.

— Eighteenth Century English Books: Considered by Librarians & Booksellers, Bibliographers & Collectors. LC Z 2012.E34. 103p. reprint ed. pap. 32.00 (*0-608-12584-9*, 202394500034) Bks Demand.

— Printing & Publishing Evidence: Thesauri for Use in Rare Book & Special Collections Cataloging. 28p. 1986. pap. 9.00 (*0-8389-7108-3*) Assn Coll & Res Libs.

— Reference Training in Academic Libraries. LC 96-20726. (CLIP Note Ser.: No. 24). 180p. 1996. 32.00 (*0-8389-7842-8*) Assn Coll & Res Libs.

Association of College & Research Libraries Staff. Racing Toward Tomorrow: Proceedings of the 9th National Conference of the Association of College & Research Libraries, April 8-11, 1999. LC 99-24804. 433p. 1999. pap. 55.00 (*0-8389-8015-5*) Assn Coll & Res Libs.

Association of College & Research Libraries Staff, jt. auth. see Johnston, Wanda K.

Association of College & Research Libraries Staff, jt. auth. see Traw, Jeri L.

Association of College and Research Libraries, American Library Association. Paper Terms: Thesaurus for Use in Rare Book & Special Collections Cataloging. 52p. 1990. pap. text 9.00 (*0-8389-7427-9*) Assn Coll & Res Libs.

Association of Commonwealth Universities Staff. Awards for First Degree Study, 95-97. 19.95 (*0-85143-138-0*) UBC Pr.

— Awards for Postgraduate Study, 95-97. 49.95 (*0-85143-137-2*) UBC Pr.

— Awards to University Teachers for Research, 94-96. 49.95 (*0-85143-133-X*) UBC Pr.

— Checklist for University Institutions, 94-45. 17.95 (*0-85143-144-5*) UBC Pr.

***Association of Commonwealth Universities Staff, ed.** Commonwealth Universities Yearbook 2000, 2 vols. 75th ed. (Illus.). 2650p. 2000. pap. 265.00 (*1-56159-276-5*) Groves Dictionaries.

Association of Commonwealth Unversities Staff, ed. Commonwealth University Yearbook, 1998-1999, 2 vols. 74th ed. 2650p. 1999. pap. text 265.00 (*1-56159-231-5*) Groves Dictionaries.

Association of Consulting Engineers Staff, et al, eds. Engineering Consultancy in the European Community, 11 vols. 986p. 1991. pap. text 750.00 (*0-7277-1776-6*, Pub. by T Telford) RCH.

Association of Cost Engineers, RICS Staff. Industrial Engineering Projects: Practice & Procedures for Capital Projects in the Engineering, Manufacturing & Process Industries. LC 97-66020. (Illus.). 320p. (C). 1998. 85.00 (*0-419-22510-2*, E & FN Spon) Routledge.

Association of Cost Engineers Staff. Estimating Checklist for Capital Projects. 2nd ed. (Illus.). 133p. (C). 1991. 80.00 (*0-419-15560-0*, E & FN Spon) Routledge.

Association of Desk & Derrick Clubs Staff. D & D Standard Oil Abbreviator. 4th ed. LC 94-17795. 1994. 34.95 (*0-87814-422-6*) PennWell Bks.

***Association of Dutch Design Staff.** Environmental Design: Dutch Design, 2000 - 2001. (Illus.). 104p. 2000. 29.95 (*90-72007-61-1*, Pub. by Bis NLD) Gingko Press.

— Graphic Design: Dutch Design, 2000 - 2001. 512p. 2000. 79.95 (*90-72007-59-X*, Pub. by Bis NLD) Gingko Press.

— Illustration: Dutch Design, 2000 - 2001. (Illus.). 144p. 2000. 29.95 (*90-72007-63-8*, Pub. by Bis NLD) Gingko Press.

— Index plus CD Rom: Dutch Design, 2000 - 2001. (Illus.). 80p. 2000. 29.95 incl. cd-rom (*90-72007-64-6*, Pub. by Bis NLD) Gingko Press.

— Industrial Design: Dutch Design, 2000 - 2001. (Illus.). 112p. 2000. 29.95 (*90-72007-58-1*, Pub. by Bis NLD) Gingko Press.

— New Media: Dutch Design, 2000 - 2001. 152p. 2000. 29.95 (*90-72007-60-3*, Pub. by Bis NLD) Gingko Press.

***Association of Dutch Design Staff, ed.** Packaging Design: Dutch Design, 2000 - 2001. 80p. 2000. 29.95 (*90-72007-62-X*, Pub. by Bis NLD) Gingko Press.

***Association of Energy Engineers Inc., Inc.** Building for the 21st Century: Energy & the Environment. 496p. 1999. pap. text 98.00 (*0-13-017957-4*) P-H.

Association of Energy Engineers Staff. Advances in Energy Cost Savings for Industry & Buildings. Payne, F. William, ed. (Illus.). 500p. 1983. text 54.00 (*0-915586-78-9*); pap. text 38.00 (*0-915586-79-7*) Fairmont Pr.

— Advances in Energy Utilization Technology. 1982. text 54.00 (*0-915586-62-2*); pap. text 38.00 (*0-915586-61-4*) Fairmont Pr.

— AEE Directory of Energy Professionals, 1982-83. rev. ed. 1982. text 28.00 (*0-915586-58-4*) Fairmont Pr.

— Engergy Business & Technology Sourcebook. Ricketts, Jana, ed. & compiled by by. LC 96-61608. (Illus.). 693p. 1998. pap. 98.00 (*0-88173-262-1*, 0388) Fairmont Pr.

— New Directions in Energy Technology. LC 84-81176. 500p. 1984. text 45.00 (*0-915586-87-8*); pap. text 38.00 (*0-915586-88-6*) Fairmont Pr.

— Retrofit Opportunities for Energy Management & Cogeneration. Payne, F. William, ed. LC 88-82219. 600p. 1988. pap. text 62.00 (*0-88173-057-2*) Fairmont Pr.

— Strategic Planning for Cogenteration & Energy Management. Payne, F. William, ed. LC 85-80321. 600p. 1985. text 62.95 (*0-88173-008-4*); pap. text 38.00 (*0-88173-009-2*) Fairmont Pr.

— Strategies for Energy Efficient Plants & Intelligent Buildings. LC 86-82315. 500p. (Orig.). 1986. pap. 38.00 (*0-88173-021-1*); text 62.00 (*0-88173-020-3*) Fairmont Pr.

— Strategies for Reducing Natural Gas, Electric & Oil Costs. Winer, Mary J., ed. LC 89-45581. 540p. 1989. pap. text 75.00 (*0-88173-094-7*) Fairmont Pr.

Association of Energy Engineers Staff & Fairmont Press Staff. Power Generation, Energy Management & Environmental Sourcebook. Jackson, M., ed. 636p. 1991. pap. 75.00 (*0-13-678285-X*) P-H.

***Association of Executive Search Consultants, Inc. Staff.** Association of Executive Search Consultants: 2000 Membership Directory. 150p. 1999. pap. 80.00 (*0-9676756-0-X*) Assn Exec Search.

Association of Facilities Engineers Staff, jt. auth. see RS Means Company, Inc. Staff.

Association of Farmworker Opportunity Programs Sta. Activities for Training Farmworkers on Pesticide Safety: Trainer's Guide. 53p. 1994. pap. text. write for info. (*1-886567-03-4*) Assn Farmwrker.

— Developing a Disaster Guide for Farmworkers: A Guide for Service Providers. 98p. 1994. pap. text. write for info. (*1-886567-02-6*) Assn Farmwrker.

An Asterisk (*) at the beginning of an entry indicates that the title is appearing for the first time.

A

— Farmworker Nutrition Education Resource Guide. 116p. 1993. pap. text. write for info. (*1-886567-01-8*) Assn Farmwrker.
— National Directory of Farmworker Services. 113p. 1991. pap. text. write for info. (*1-886567-00-X*) Assn Farmwrker.
— A Taste of English: Nutrition Workbook for Adult ESL Students - Student Workbook. 126p. 1994. write for info. (*1-886567-04-2*) Assn Farmwrker.
— A Taste of English: Nutrition Workbook for Adult ESL Students - Teacher's Manual. 74p. 1994. write for info. (*1-886567-05-0*) Assn Farmwrker.
Association of Governing Boards & American Council on Education, Higher Education Pa. Composition of Governing Boards, 1985: A Survey of College & University Boards. 43p. 1986. 12.00 (*0-318-21459-8*) Assn Gov Bds.
Association of Governing Boards of Universities & & Cleveland, Harlan. The Costs & Benefits of Openness: Sunshine Laws & Higher Education. LC 85-239957. (AGB Special Reports). ix, 58p. 12.00 (*0-685-13374-5*) Assn Gov Bds.
Association of Higher Education Facilities Officer. Electric Restructuring & Utilities Deregulation: A Facility Manager's Guide. LC 98-28428. 1998. 70.00 (*1-890956-04-X*) APPA VA.
Association of Home B. National Staff. Nahbosha Jobsite Safety Handdbook. 2nd ed. LC 98-42711. 1998. 10.00 (*0-86718-454-X*) Home Builder.
Association of Hospital & Institution Libraries, H. Standards for Library Services in Health Care Institutions. LC 74-124576. 31p. reprint ed. pap. 30.00 (*0-608-13204-7*, 202422000035) Bks Demand.
Association of Junior Leagues International, Inc.,. The Junior League Centennial Cookbook: Over 800 of the Most Treasured Recipes from 200 Junior Leagues. 416p. 1996. 25.00 (*0-385-47731-7*, Main St Bks) Doubleday.
Association of Legal Writing Directors Staff, jt. auth. see Dickerson, Darby.
Association of Licensed Battlefield Guides Staff, jt. auth. see Hawthorne, Fred.
Association of Lloyd's Members. Lloyd's Market Results & Prospects 1998. 467p. 1998. pap. 225.00 (*0-9533282-0-1*, Pub. by Woodhead Pubng) Am Educ Systs.
Association of Management Consulting Firms Staff. ACME Directory of Members, 1994-95. 70p. (C). 1996. 50.00 (*0-614-00303-2*) ACME.
— ACME 1994 Survey of European Key Management Information. (Illus.). 60p. (C). 1994. 295.00 (*0-614-00304-0*) ACME.
— ACME 1994 Survey of European Key Management Information. (Illus.). 60p. (C). 1996. lib. bdg. 75.00 (*0-614-00305-9*) ACME.
— ACME 1994 Survey of United States Key Management Information. (Illus.). 138p. (C). 1994. lib. bdg. 125.00 (*0-614-00307-5*) ACME.
— ACME 1994 Survey of United States Key Management Information. (Illus.). 138p. (C). 1996. 495.00 (*0-614-00306-7*) ACME.
— Careers in Management Consulting: An Overview of Professional Opportunities. rev. ed. 10p. (C). 1996. 50.00 (*0-614-00302-4*) ACME.
— Professional Profile of Management Consultants: A Body of Expertise, Skills & Attributes. rev. ed. 40p. (C). 1992. 15.00 (*0-614-00301-6*) ACME.
Association of Municipal Historian of NY State Staff. New York State Cemeteries Name/Location Inventory, 1995-1997. LC 99-199258. 1248p. 1999. pap. 83.50 (*0-7884-1084-9*, A534) Heritage.
Association of Muslim Scientists & Engineers. The Educational Guide: A Handbook for Foreign Muslim Applicants to U. S. & Canadian Universities. rev. ed. 114p. reprint ed. pap. 7.00 (*0-916581-00-4*) Assn Muslim Sci.
Association of National Advertisers, CASIE Research & Measurement Committee, ed. CASIE Compendium of Interactive Media Research Studies, Vol. VII. 110p. 1998. pap. 20.00 (*1-56318-063-4*) Assn Natl Advertisers.
***Association of National Advertisers, Casie Research & Measurement Committee Staff, ed.** Casie Compendium of Interactive Media Research Studies, Vol. VIII. 147p. 1999. pap. 20.00 (*1-56318-065-0*) Assn Natl Advertisers.
— CASIE Compendium of Interactive Media Research Studies, Vol. IX. 178p. (C). 1999. pap. 20.00 (*1-56318-066-9*) Assn Natl Advertisers.
Association of National Advertisers' New Technologies Committee Staff, jt. auth. see Webster, Robin.
Association of Nepalis in the Americas Staff. The Nepal Cookbook. (Illus.). 168p. 1996. 10.95 (*1-55939-060-3*) Snow Lion Pubns.
Association of News Media Internal Auditors Techni. Internal Auditing & Controls for Newspapers. INFE Internal Reporting Committee & INFE Technical Publications Committee, eds. 76p. (Orig.). (C). 1990. pap. 49.95 (*1-877888-14-1*) Intl Newspaper.
Association of Nigerian Scholars for Dialogue Staff, jt. auth. see Ekeh, Peter P.
Association of Norwegian Chefs Staff. The Norwegian Kitchen: Recipes & Copy Provided by The Association of Norwegian Chefs. Favish, Melody, tr. (Illus.). 1994. 45.00 (*82-90823-23-1*) Skandisk.
Association of Operative Millers Staff. Cereal Miller's Handbook. 1963. 25.00 (*0-686-00364-0*) AG Pr.
— Technical Bulletins, 1944-1974, Vol. 3. 1975. 25.00 (*0-686-00376-4*) AG Pr.
— Technical Bulletins, 1944-1975, Vol. 4. 1977. 25.00 (*0-686-00375-6*) AG Pr.
Association of Oregon Archaeologists Staff. Contributions to the Archaeology of Oregon, 1981-1982. (Occasional Papers: No. 2). (Illus.). 136p. 1983. 8.50 (*0-929553-01-2*) Assn Oregon Arch.
— Contributions to the Archaeology of Oregon, 1983-1986. (Occasional Papers: No. 3). (Illus.). 258p. 1986. 8.50 (*0-929553-02-0*) Assn Oregon Arch.
Association of Pediatric Oncology Nurses Staff. Nursing Care of the Child with Cancer. 2nd ed. Foley, Genevieve V. et al, eds. (Illus.). 548p. 1993. text 70.00 (*0-7216-4006-0*, W B Saunders Co) Harcrt Hlth Sci Grp.
Association of Physicians Staff. The Cholera Bulletin. LC 77-180564. (Medicine & Society in America Ser.). 198p. 1972. reprint ed. 21.95 (*0-405-03942-5*) Ayer.
Association of Rehabilitation Nurses Staff. Standards & Scope of Advanced Rehabilitation Nursing Practice. 25p. (Orig.). (C). 1996. pap. text 7.00 (*1-884278-06-X*) Rehab Nursing.
Association of Research Libraries Staff. Meeting the Preservation Challenge. 70p. 1988. pap. 28.00 (*0-918006-15-5*) ARL.
— Preserving Knowledge: The Case for Alkaline Paper. 130p. 1990. 18.00 (*0-918006-18-X*) ARL.
Association of Research Libraries Task Force on Scholarly Communications Staff. The Changing System of Scholarly Communication. 7p. 1986. pap. 1.00 (*0-918006-12-0*) ARL.
Association of Science-Technology Centers Staff. What Research Says about Learning in Science Museums. 31p. 1990. pap. 14.00 (*0-944040-20-9*) AST Ctrs.
Association of Small Business Staff. Franchising 101: The Complete Guide to Evaluating, Buying & Growing Your Franchised Business. Dugan, Ann, ed. LC 98-14310. 240p. 1998. pap. text 22.95 (*1-57410-097-1*) Dearborn.
Association of Social Anthropologists of the Commo, jt. auth. see Hughes-Freeland, Felicia.
Association of Space Explorers Staff. Greatest Adventure. 1995. 40.00 (*0-929823-43-5*) Mach One.
Association of Specialized & Cooperative Library A. Standards for Cooperative Multitype Library Organizations. 17p. 1990. 10.00 (*0-8389-7399-X*) ASCLA.
Association of Specialized & Cooperative Library A, ed. Revised Standards & Guidelines of Service for the Library of Congress Network of Libraries for the Blind & Physically Handicapped, 1984. LC 84-6356. 55p. 1984. pap. 5.00 (*0-8389-3306-8*) ALA.
Association of Specialized and Cooperative Library Agencies, American Library Asssociation, jt. auth. see American Correctional Association Staff.
Association of Student International Law Societies, ed. see Jessup, Philip C.
Association of Surgical Technologists Staff. Cardiovascular Specialty Manual. (Allied Health Ser.). (C). 2001. pap. 40.00 (*0-7668-1210-3*) Delmar.
— Introduction to Surgical Technology. (Allied Health Ser.). (C). 2000. pap. 69.95 (*0-7668-0662-6*) Delmar.
— Neurosurgery Specialty Manual. (Allied Health Ser.). (C). 2002. pap. 40.00 (*0-7668-1209-X*) Delmar.
— Orthopedic Surgery Manual. (Allied Health Ser.). 2000. pap. 40.00 (*0-7668-1128-X*) Delmar.
***Association of Surgical Technologists Staff.** SWB/Surgical Techncian for Surgery Technologist: A+ Positive Care Approach. (Allied Health Ser.). (C). 2000. pap. 18.00 (*0-7668-0664-2*) Delmar.
Association of Surgical Technologists Staff, ed. Core Curriculum for Surgical First Assisting. 131p. (Orig.). (C). 1993. pap. text 65.00 (*0-926805-03-7*) Assn Surgical.
— Surgical Technologist Certifying Exam Study Guide. 158p. (Orig.). 1995. pap. text 29.95 (*0-926805-07-X*) Assn Surgical.
Association of Symbolic Logic Staff. Logic Colloquium '95: Proceedings of the Annual European Summer Meeting of the Association of Symbolic Logic, Held in Haifa, Israel, August 9-18, 1995. Makowsky, Johanna A. et al, eds. LC 97-51322. (Lecture Notes in Logic: Vol. 11). xvi, 348p. 1998. pap. 84.95 (*3-540-63994-2*) Spr-Verlag.
Association of Teacher Educators Staff. Alternatives, Yes, Lower Standards, No! Minimum Standards for Alternative Teacher Certification Programs. 1989. pap. 3.75 (*0-685-41074-9*) Assn Tchr Ed.
— Educating for Diversity: An Anthology of Multicultural Voices. Grant, Carl A., ed. LC 94-34094. 432p. 1995. pap. text 62.00 (*0-205-16573-7*) Allyn.
Association of the Bar of the City of New York, jt. see Butler, William Allen.
Association of the Bar of the City of New York, Co, et al. National Survey of Corporate Law Compensation & Organization Practices, Set. 11th ed. (Illus.). 1988. 475.00 (*0-317-00876-5*) Assn Bar NYC.
Association of the Bar of the City of New York, Sp. Mental Illness, Due Process & the Criminal Defendant: A Second Report & Additional Recommendations. LC 68-19789. 299p. reprint ed. pap. 92.70 (*0-7837-0481-X*, 204080500018) Bks Demand.
Association of Theatrical Artists & Craftspeople S. The New York Theatrical Sourcebook. Rollins, Leslie E., ed. (Illus.). 550p. 1994. pap. 24.00 (*0-9642679-7-7*) Sourcebk Pr.
Association of Theatrical Artists & Craftspeople Staff. The Entertainment Sourcebook: An Insider's Guide on Where to Find Everything, 2000 Edition. 500p. 2000. pap. 45.00 (*1-55783-423-7*) Applause Theatre Bk Pubs.
Association of University Evening College Conventi. Inter-Association Cooperation Reconsidered. 1964. 2.50 (*0-87060-017-6*, OCP 10) Syracuse U Cont Ed.
Association of Washington Cities Staff, jt. auth. see Municipal Research & Services Center, Washington S.
Association Padmakara Staff, tr. see Rinpoche, Patrul.
Association Staff. Fundamentals of Municipal Bonds: A Basic, Definitive Text on the Municipal Securities Market. 4th rev. ed. LC 89-39361. (Illus.). 236p. 1990. 29.95 (*0-9605198-2-3*) The Bond Market.
Association Technique de l'Industrie du Gaz en Fra, ed. Natural Gas in the World: Outlook to 2000. 200p. (C). 1989. 300.00 (*2-7108-0571-5*, Pub. by Edits Technip) Enfield Pubs NH.
Associations for Research & Enlightenment, Reading, compiled by. Psychic Awareness. (Library: Vol. 9). 400p. 1979. lib. bdg. 22.95 (*0-87604-109-8*, 1109) ARE Pr.
— Psychic Development. (Library: Vol. 8). 327p. 1978. lib. bdg. 22.95 (*0-87604-108-X*, 1108) ARE Pr.
— The Study Group Readings. (Library: Vol. 7). 545p. 1977. lib. bdg. 24.95 (*0-87604-094-6*, 1107) ARE Pr.
Association's Municipal Credit Research Committee & COPS Subcommittee Staff. Certificates of Participation. LC 91-28839. 1991. pap. 49.95 (*0-9605198-3-1*) The Bond Market.
Associazione Geotecnica Italiana Staff. Deformation of Soils, Vol. 2. 1991. 136.00 (*90-5410-003-6*) Ashgate Pub Co.
— Deformation of Soils, Vol. 3. 1991. 136.00 (*90-5410-004-4*) Ashgate Pub Co.
— Deformation of Soils, Vol.1. 1991. 136.00 (*90-5410-002-8*) Ashgate Pub Co.
Associazione Geotecnica Italiana Staff, ed. Deformation of Soils & Displacements of Structures - X ECSMFE: Proceedings of the Tenth European Conference on Soil Mechanics & Foundation Engineering, Florence, 26-30 May 1991, 4 vols., Set. (Illus.). 1500p. (C). 1991. text 300.00 (*90-5410-001-X*) Ashgate Pub Co.
Associazione Italiana Editori, ed. Italian Books in Print, 1997: Catalogo Dei Libri in Commercio. 1997. 635.00 (*3-598-07657-6*) Edit Biblio.
***Associazione Italiana per l'intelligenza Artificiale Staff.** AI*IA 99: Advances in Artificial Intelligence: 6th Congress of the Italian Association for Artificial Intelligence, Bologna, Italy, September 14-17, 1999, Selected Papers. Lamma, E. & Mello, P., eds. LC 00-36577. (Lecture Notes in Artificial Intelligence Ser.: Vol. 1792). xi, 392p. 2000. pap. 69.00 (*3-540-67350-4*) Spr-Verlag.
***Associazone Italiana Editori Staff, ed.** Catalogo dei Libri in Commercio 1999, 6 vol. Incl. 2 Vols.. Soggeti-Bibliografica. 2400p. 1999. 235.00 (*3-598-07675-4*); 4 Vols. Part I. Aurtori, Titoli. 1999. 475.00 (*3-598-07674-6*);Tr. of Italian Books in Print 1999. 6800p. 1999. 650.00 (*3-598-07673-8*) K G Saur Verlag.
Associcio Internacional de Senales Maritimes Staff. Diccionario Internacional de Senales Maritimes, 3 vols. (SPA.). 1990. pap. write for info. (*0-7859-6224-7*, 8474336449) Fr & Eur.
Assoline, Ed. Snapped. 1997. pap. 14.95 (*2-908228-90-4*, Pub. by Assouline) Rizzoli Intl.
Assonyi, Cs. & Richter, R. The Continuum Theory of Rock Mechanics. Balkay, B., tr. from HUN. (Rock & Soil Mechanics Ser.). (Illus.). (C). 1979. 52.00 (*0-87849-027-2*, Pub. by Trans T Pub) Enfield Pubs NH.
Assorted. Making Babies, 3 vols. LC 96-308. 634p. 1995. per. 5.50 (*0-373-20115-X*) Harlequin Bks.
— Missing Memories. 1995. per. 5.50 (*0-373-20110-9*) Harlequin Bks.
Assorted. Over 10 Childrens. (J). 1995. per. 1.25 (*0-671-31438-6*) Simon & Schuster.
— Refurbished Childrens Books. (J). 1996. per. write for info. (*0-689-00291-2*) S&S Childrens.
— Under 10 Childrens. (J). 1995. per. 0.65 (*0-671-31437-8*) Simon & Schuster.
Assouline, Annie. Hotel Sale - The Picasso Museum. (Illus.). 64p. 1998. 19.95 (*3-929078-37-6*, Kehayoff) te Neues.
Assouline, Pierre. Albert Londres. (FRE.). 634p. 1990. pap. 10.95 (*0-7859-2136-2*, 2070382265) Fr & Eur.
— An Artful Life: A Biography of D. H. Kahnweiler, 1884-1979. Ruas, Charles, tr. from FRE. LC 91-16439. (Illus.). 448p. 1991. 14.95 (*0-88064-131-2*) Fromm Intl Pub.
— Une Eminence Grise: Jean Jardin. (FRE.). 491p. 1988. pap. 20.95 (*0-7859-2085-4*, 2070379213) Fr & Eur.
— Gaston Gallimard: A Half Century of French Publishing. Salemson, Harold J., tr. LC 87-202. (Illus.). 448p. 1988. 35.00 (*0-15-134293-8*) Harcourt.
— L' Homme de l'Art. (FRE.). 732p. 1989. pap. 10.95 (*0-7859-2108-7*, 2070381064) Fr & Eur.
— Les Nouveaux Convertis. (FRE.). 316p. 1982. pap. 17.95 (*0-7859-2187-7*, 2226014071) Fr & Eur.
— Simenon: A Biography. Rothschild, John, tr. LC 97-71924. (Illus.). 447p. 1997. 32.50 (*0-679-40285-3*) Knopf.
Assouline, Susan, jt. auth. see Lupowski, Anne.
Assouline, Susan, jt. ed. see Colangelo, Nicholas.
***Assouline, Susan G., et al.** Iowa Accleration Scale: A Guide for Whole-Grade Acceleration. LC 98-45405. 1998. 90.00 (*0-910707-30-8*) Gifted Psych Pr.
***Assoun, Paul-Laurent.** Freud & Nietzsche. LC 00-38946. 2000. write for info. (*0-485-11483-6*, Pub. by Athlone Pr) Humanities.
Assuncao, Celio Santos de & Gajardo, Patricio. Venezuela: Election Technology Assessment, 1995. ii, 106p. 1995. pap. 13.00 (*1-879720-83-3*) Intl Fndt Elect.
Assuncao, Octavio C., et al. The Art of Juan Manuel Blanes. LC 94-61047. 212p. 1997. pap. 29.95 (*1-879128-09-8*) Americas Soc.
Ast, Gabriele, jt. auth. see Volkan, Vamik D.
ASTA Corp Staff, ed. & illus. see Gerken, Louis.
Astadjov, D. N., tr. see Ivanov, I. G., et al.
***Astaire, Fred.** Steps in Time: An Autobiography. (Illus.). 376p. 2000. pap. 17.95 (*0-8154-1058-1*, Pub. by Cooper Sq) Natl Bk Netwk.
Astaire, Lesley & Martine, Roddy. At Home in Scotland. (Illus.). 240p. 1987. 45.00 (*0-89659-767-9*) Abbeville Pr.
— Living in Scotland. LC 96-61190. (Illus.). 240p. 1997. pap. 29.95 (*0-500-27934-9*, Pub. by Thames Hudson) Norton.
***Astaire, Lesley & Martine, Roddy.** Living in the Highlands. LC 99-69291. (Illus.). 168p. 2000. 40.00 (*0-500-01986-X*, Pub. by Thames Hudson) Norton.
Astakhina, L., ed. Dictionary of Eleventh & Seventeenth Century Russian Language, Vol. 14. (ENG & RUS.). 312p. (C). 1988. 100.00 (*0-7855-6675-9*, Pub. by Collets) St Mut.
Astakhov, Viktor. Metal Cutting Mechanics. LC 98-46338. 320p. 1998. boxed set 84.95 (*0-8493-1895-5*) CRC Pr.
Astanin, L. Y. & Kostylev, A. A. Ultrawideband Radar Measurements: Analysis & Processing. (Radar, Sonar, Navigation & Avionics Ser.: No. 7). 244p. 1997. 95.00 (*0-85296-894-9*, RA007) INSPEC Inc.
Astara. Challenge Supreme. (Challenge Trilogy Ser.: Vol. 2). 144p. Date not set. pap. 13.95 (*1-885226-20-9*) StarLineage.
— The Challenge Trilogy, 3 vols. 596p. Date not set. pap. 24.95 (*1-885226-10-1*) StarLineage.
— Challenge Triumphant. (Challenge Trilogy Ser.: Vol. 3). 128p. Date not set. pap. 13.95 (*1-885226-47-0*) StarLineage.
— Challenge Within. LC 96-92176. (Challenge Trilogy Ser.: Vol. 1). 240p. 1996. pap. 13.95 (*1-885226-04-7*) StarLineage.
— Threshold! LC 96-92177. 112p. 1996. pap. 11.95 (*1-885226-11-X*) StarLineage.
Astarita, G. Thermodynamics: An Advanced Textbook for Chemical Engineers. (Illus.). 456p. (C). 1989. 85.00 (*0-306-43048-7*, Plenum Trade) Perseus Pubng.
Astarita, Giovanni, et al, eds. Rheology, 3 vols. Incl. Vol. 1: Principles. LC 80-16929. 438p. 1980. 89.50 (*0-306-40465-6*, Kluwer Plenum); Vol. 2: Fluids. LC 80-16929. 702p. 1980. 115.00 (*0-306-40466-4*, Kluwer Plenum); Vol. 3: Applications. LC 80-16929. 702p. 1980. 125.00 (*0-306-40467-2*, Kluwer Plenum); LC 80-16929. 1980. 275.00 (*0-685-04084-4*, Plenum Trade) Perseus Pubng.
Astarita, Giovanni, et al. Gas Treating with Chemical Solvents. LC 82-11016. 517p. reprint ed. pap. 160.30 (*0-7837-1468-8*, 205716300017) Bks Demand.
Astarita, Robert W. Practical Cytopathology. (Illus.). 472p. 1989. text 160.00 (*0-443-08469-6*) Church.
Astarita, Tommaso. Village Justice: Community, Family, & Popular Culture in Early Modern Italy. LC 99-13654. (Studies in Historical & Political Science: Vol. 117). (Illus.). 336p. 1999. 45.00 (*0-8018-6138-1*) Johns Hopkins.
Astaritta, Tarasa M. & Materna, Gayle. Competency in Home Health Care: A Systematic Approach. LC 98-15036. 288p. 1998. 49.00 (*0-8342-1050-9*, 10509) Aspen Pub.
Astarte. Astrology Made Easy. 1977. pap. 7.00 (*0-87980-009-7*) Wilshire.
Astas, Reider. An Old Norse Biblical Compilation: Studies in Stjorn. LC 91-17596. (American University Studies: Theology & Religion: Ser. VII, Vol. 109). 251p. 1992. 40.95 (*0-8204-1585-5*) P Lang Pubng.
***Astashev, V. K., et al.** Dynamics & Control of Machines. LC 00-26591. (Foundations of Engineering Mechanics Ser.). (Illus.). x, 233p. 2000. 92.00 (*3-540-63722-2*) Spr-Verlag.
***Astashkevich, Alexander & Tabacnikov, Serge, eds.** Differential Topology, Infinite-Dimensional Lie Algebras & Applications: D. B. Fuchs' 60th Anniversary Collection. (American Mathematical Society Translations Ser.). 313p. 1999. 59.00 (*0-8218-2032-X*) Am Math.
Astavakra. Astavakra Samhita. Nityaswarupannda, Swami, tr. (SAN.). 1940. pap. 3.50 (*81-7120-264-0*, Pub. by Advaita Ashrama) Vedanta Pr.
Astbury, ed. Varronis. (LAT.). 1985. 43.50 (*3-322-00420-1*, T1870, Pub. by B G Teubner) U of Mich Pr.
***Astbury, A., et al, eds.** Electroweak Physics. 500p. 2000. 96.00 (*981-02-4068-6*) World Scientific Pub.
— Quantum Chromodynamics: Proceedings of the 13th Lake Louise Winter Institute Lake Louise, Alberta, Canada 15 - 21 February 1998. 600p. 1999. 128.00 (*981-02-3747-2*) World Scientific Pub.
Astbury, A., et al, eds. The Standard Model & Beyond: The Fifth Lake Louise Winter Inst. of Frontiers in Physics. 428p. (C). 1990. text 118.00 (*981-02-0318-7*) World Scientific Pub.
Astbury, A., et al. Collider Physics: Proceedings of the Lake Louise Winter Institute. 560p. 1994. text 121.00 (*981-02-1598-3*) World Scientific Pub.
— Frontiers in Physics: From Colliders to Cosmology: Proceedings of 4th Lake Louise Winter Institute. 500p. 1989. text 151.00 (*981-02-0069-2*, PHI-P977) World Scientific Pub.
Astbury, Alan. Proceedings of the XXIX International Conference on High Energy Physics: Vancouver, Canada 23-29, 2 Vol. 1600p. 1999. 148.00 (*981-02-3772-3*) World Scientific Pub.
Astbury, Anthony. The Emscote Book of Verse. (C). 1990. 55.00 (*0-906887-21-6*, Pub. by Greville Pr) St Mut.
— Particles & the Universe: Proceedings of the Twelfth Lake Louise Winter Institute. 1998. 86.00 (*981-02-3467-8*) World Scientific Pub.
Astbury, Anthony, selected by. Poems for Shakespeare. (C). 1990. 35.00 (*0-906887-48-8*, Pub. by Greville Pr) St Mut.
Astbury, Charmian. Vanishing Point. (C). 1989. pap. 50.00 (*0-7223-2357-3*, Pub. by A H S Ltd) St Mut.
Astbury, Jill. Crazy for You: The Making of Women's Madness. 240p. 1996. pap. 22.95 (*0-19-553768-8*) OUP.

An Asterisk (*) at the beginning of an entry indicates that the title is appearing for the first time.

A

***Astbury, Kate, et al, eds.** Dialogues 2: Endings. 100p. 1999. pap. 17.95 (*1-902454-01-4*, Pub. by Elm Bank Pubns) Intl Spec Bk.

Astbury, Leigh. City Bushmen: The Heidelberg School & Rural Mythology. (Illus.). (C). 1986. 55.00 (*0-19-554501-X*) OUP.

Astbury, R. & Robinson, R. Bibliography & Book Production. LC 66-30623. (Commonwealth & International Library). 1967. 125.00 (*0-08-012328-7*, Pub. by Pergamon Repr) Franklin.

Aste, Mario. Grazia Deledda: Ethnic Novelist. 1990. 38.50 (*0-916379-74-4*) Scripta.

Aste, Mario, et al, eds. Industry, Technology, Labor & The Italian American Communities. (American Italian Historical Association). 1128p. 1995. 19.95 (*0-934675-39-2*); pap. 19.95 (*0-934675-40-6*) Am Italian.

Astedt, B., jt. auth. see Sjoberg, N. O.

Astel, Melvin J., jt. compiled by see Weast, Robert C.

Asteljoki, J. A. & Stephens, R. L., eds. Sulfide Smelting '98: Current & Future Practices. LC 97-75972. (Illus.). 620p. 1998. 78.00 (*0-87339-397-X*, TN10) Minerals Metals.

Astell, Ann W. Chaucer & the Universe of Learning. LC 96-2315. 272p. 1996. text 35.00 (*0-8014-3269-3*) Cornell U Pr.

— Job, Boethius, & Epic Truth. LC 93-27265. 256p. 1994. text 37.50 (*0-8014-2911-0*) Cornell U Pr.

— Political Allegory in Late-Medieval England. LC 98-42272. 1999. 35.00 (*0-8014-3560-9*) Cornell U Pr.

— The Song of Songs in the Middle Ages. LC 89-70831. 208p. 1990. 35.00 (*0-8014-2347-3*) Cornell U Pr.

— The Song of Songs in the Middle Ages. LC 89-70831. 208p. 1995. pap. text 13.95 (*0-8014-8267-4*) Cornell U Pr.

Astell, Ann W., ed. Divine Representations: Postmodernism & Spirituality. LC 94-32753. 176p. 1995. pap. 17.95 (*0-8091-3528-0*) Paulist Pr.

— Lay Sanctity, Medieval & Modern: A Search for Models. LC 99-38114. 256p. 2000. 35.00 (*0-268-01330-6*, Pub. by U of Notre Dame Pr) Chicago Distribution Ctr.

***Astell, Ann W., ed.** Lay Sanctity, Medieval & Modern: A Search for Models. LC 99-38114. 264p. 2000. reprint ed. pap. 25.00 (*0-268-01332-2*, Pub. by U of Notre Dame Pr) Chicago Distribution Ctr.

Astell, Mary. Astell: Political Writings. Springborg, Mary, ed. (Cambridge Texts in the History of Political Thought Ser.). 337p. (C). 1996. text 64.95 (*0-521-41800-3*) Cambridge U Pr.

— Astell: Political Writings. Springborg, Patricia, ed. (Cambridge Texts in the History of Political Thought Ser.). 337p. (C). 1996. pap. text 23.95 (*0-521-42845-9*) Cambridge U Pr.

— A Serious Proposal to the Ladies, Pts. I & II. Springborg, Patricia, ed. LC 95-21345. (Pickering Women's Classics Ser.). 240p. 1997. 55.00 (*1-85196-268-9*, Pub. by Pickering & Chatto) Ashgate Pub Co.

Asten, Dietrich V. America's Way: The Tasks Ahead. LC 99-29553. 64p. 1999. pap. 6.95 (*0-88010-469-4*) Anthroposophic.

— Sacramental & Spiritual Communion. Glas, Werner, ed. 22p. 1984. pap. 2.95 (*0-88010-121-0*) Anthroposophic.

Asten, Maureen A. Lesbian Family Relationships in American Society: The Making of an Ethnographic Film. LC 96-36314. 160p. 1997. 52.95 (*0-275-95642-3*, Praeger Pubs) Greenwood.

Aster, Agnes. Larousse Dictionnaire des Enfants. (FRE.). (J). 1991. 59.95 (*0-7859-7674-4*, 2036521401) Fr & Eur.

Aster, Howard, ed. Challenges for International Broadcasting. 250p. 1991. 24.95 (*0-88962-476-3*) Mosaic.

Aster, Howard, ed. Taking Sides: The Collected Social & Political Writings of Irving Layton, 1935-1977. 244p. 1990. pap. 8.95 (*0-88962-057-1*) Mosaic.

Aster, Howard, et al, eds. The John Calder Festschrift. (Orig.). 1997. pap. 20.00 (*0-88962-625-1*) Mosaic.

Aster, Howard & Potichnyj, Peter J. Jewish-Ukrainian Relations: Two Solitudes. expanded rev. ed. 140p. 1995. reprint ed. pap. 9.95 (*0-88962-367-8*) Mosaic.

Aster, Howard, jt. ed. see Olechowska, Elzbieta.

Aster, Howard, jt. ed. see Potichnyj, Peter J.

Aster, Rick. Professional SAS Programmer's Pocket Reference. 2nd ed. (Illus.). 192p. 1998. pap. 16.00 (*1-891957-02-3*, BR56646, Breakfast) Brkfst Commn Corp.

***Aster, Rick.** Professional SAS Programmers Pocket Reference. 2nd ed. 192p. 1998. pap. 25.00 (*1-58025-148-X*, BR56602) SAS Publ.

— Professional SAS Programmer's Pocket Reference. 3rd ed. 239p. 2000. pap. 18.00 (*1-891957-07-4*, Breakfast) Brkfst Commn Corp.

Aster, Rick. SAS Basics: From Installation to Operation. LC 93-1130. 279p. 1993. pap. 28.95 (*0-8306-4316-8*, BR55093, Windcrest) TAB Bks.

— SAS Foundations: From Installation to Operation. 304p. 1993. pap. 28.95 (*0-07-001543-0*) McGraw.

Aster, Rick. SAS Foundations: From Installation to Operation. 294p. 1996. pap. 71.95 (*1-58025-400-4*, BR57334) SAS Publ.

Aster, Rick & Seidman, Rhena. Professional SAS Program Secrets. 1991. 24.95 (*0-8306-1600-4*) McGraw-Hill Prof.

— Professional SAS Programming Secrets: Updated with New Features of Releases 6.08-6.10. 2nd ed. LC 96-17754. (Illus.). 592p. 1996. pap., pap. text 49.95 incl. cd-rom (*0-07-913095-X*, BR56279) McGraw.

Aster, Samuel. Double Fun Book, Bk. 3. 36p. 1997. pap. text 6.95 (*0-87487-748-2*) Summy-Birchard.

Aster, Samuel, contrib. by. Double Fun, Bk. 1. 24p. 1996. pap. text 5.95 (*0-87487-742-3*) Summy-Birchard.

— Double Fun, Bk. 2. 24p. 1996. pap. text 5.95 (*0-87487-744-X*) Summy-Birchard.

Aster, Sidney. 1939: The Making of the Second World War. (Modern Revivals in History Ser.). 472p. (C). 1993. text 69.95 (*0-7512-0244-4*, Pub. by Gregg Revivals) Ashgate Pub Co.

Aster, Sidney, ed. British Foreign Policy, Nineteen Eighteen to Nineteen Forty-Five: A Guide to Research & Research Materials. rev. ed. LC 90-46466. (European Diplomatic History Ser.). 391p. 1991. 65.00 (*0-8420-2310-0*) Scholarly Res Inc.

Asterion, Oreana. The One Remains: The White Light Classes, Vol. I. 1992. pap. 14.95 (*0-9631502-1-9*) Gray Wolf Pub.

Asteris, Michael. Contemporary Transport Trends. 290p. 1992. 82.95 (*1-85628-284-8*, Pub. by Avebry) Ashgate Pub Co.

Asterita, Mary F. Physical Exercise, Nutrition & Stress. LC 85-12261. 216p. 1985. 67.95 (*0-275-90044-4*, C0044, Praeger Pubs) Greenwood.

— The Physiology of Stress: With Special Reference to the Neuroendocrine System. 240p. (C). 1984. pap. 22.95 (*0-89885-187-4*, Kluwer Acad Hman Sci); text 42.95 (*0-89885-176-9*, Kluwer Acad Hman Sci) Kluwer Academic.

Astesiano, E., ed. Fundamental Approaches to Software Engineering: Proceedings of the 1st International Conference, FASE '98, Held as Part of the Joint European Conferences on Theory & Practice of Software, ETAPS '98, Lisbon, Portugal, March 28-April 4, 1998, Vol. 138. LC 98-14854. (Lecture Notes in Computer Science Ser.: Vol. 1382). xii, 329p. 1998. pap. 55.00 (*3-540-64303-6*) Spr-Verlag.

Astesiano, E., et al, eds. Recent Trends in Data Type Specification: 10th Workshop on Specification of Abstract Data Types Joint with the 5th COMPASS Workshop, S. Margherita, Italy, May 30-June 3, 1994. Proceedings. (Lecture Notes in Computer Science Ser.: Vol. 906). viii, 523p. 1995. 81.00 (*3-540-59132-X*) Spr-Verlag.

Astesiano, E. & Boehm, C., eds. CAAP 1981 Trees in Algebra & Programming: Proceedings. (Lecture Notes in Computer Science Ser.: Vol. 112). 364p. 1981. 25.00 (*0-387-10828-9*) Spr-Verlag.

***Astesiano, Egidio, et al, eds.** Algebraic Foundations of Systems Specification. LC 99-38275. (IFIP State-of-the-Art Reports). xi, 617p. 1999. 90.00 (*3-540-63772-9*) Spr-Verlag.

Astesiano, Egidio, ed. see Workshop on Specification of Abstract Data Types S.

Astfalk, Greg, ed. Applications on Advanced Architecture Computers. (Software, Environments & Tools Ser.: Vol. 3). xviii, 359p. 1996. pap. 37.50 (*0-89871-368-4*, SE03) Soc Indus-Appl Math.

Asthana, A. K. & Srivastava, S. C. Indian Hornworts: A Taxonomic Study. Gradstein, S. R., ed. (Bryophytorum Bibliotheca: Vol. 42). (GER., Illus.). 230p. 1991. pap. 71.00 (*3-443-62014-0*, Pub. by Gebruder Borntraeger) Balogh.

Asthana, R., ed. Solidification Processing of Reinforced Metals. (Key Engineering Materials Ser.: Vols. 151-152). (Illus.). 420p. (C). 1998. text 158.00 (*0-87849-785-4*, Pub. by Trans T Pub) Enfield Pubs NH.

Asthana, Vandana. Politics of Environment: A Profile. (C). 1992. 20.00 (*81-7024-453-6*, Pub. by Ashish Pub Hse) S Asia.

Asthma & Chronic Bronchitis in Children & Their Pr. Proceedings of the Asthma & Chronic Bronchitis in Children & Their Prognosis into Adult Life Symposium, 3rd, Davos, 1969. Suter, F. & Altounyan, R. E., eds. 1970. pap. 73.25 (*3-8055-0754-2*) S Karger.

Asti, G., et al, eds. Magnetic Properties of Matter. 500p. (C). 1991. text 137.00 (*981-02-0530-9*) World Scientific Pub.

Astigarraga, Jose, jt. auth. see Rowat, Malcolm.

Astill, Grenville. Breton Landscape. LC 98-150924. 268p. 1997. 75.00 (*1-85728-452-6*) Taylor & Francis.

Astill, Grenville & Langdon, John, eds. Medieval Farming & Technology: The Impact of Agricultural Change in Northwest Europe. LC 97-7623. (Technology & Change in History Ser.: No. 1). (Illus.). xii, 321p. 1997. 101.00 (*90-04-10582-4*, NLG 172) Brill Academic Pubs.

Astill, Grenville, jt. auth. see Davies, Wendy.

Astin, A. C., et al, eds. Rome & the Mediterranean to 133 B. C. 2nd ed. (Cambridge Ancient History Ser.: Vol. 8). 640p. 1990. text 120.00 (*0-521-23448-4*) Cambridge U Pr.

Astin, A. W., et al. The American Freshman: National Norms for Fall 1993. (Illus.). 169p. (Orig.). 1993. pap. 20.00 (*1-878477-14-5*) UCLA Higher Educ Rsch Inst.

Astin, Alexander W. Academic Gamesmanship: Student-Oriented Change in Higher Education. LC 76-12520. (Illus.). 209p. 1976. 49.95 (*0-275-90243-9*, C0243, Praeger Pubs) Greenwood.

— Assessment for Excellence: The Philosophy & Practice of Assessment & Evaluation in Higher Education. LC 92-44619. 352p. 1991. boxed set 27.95 (*0-89774-805-0*) Oryx Pr.

— Minorities in American Higher Education: Recent Trends, Current Prospects, & Recommendations. LC 81-48663. (Jossey-Bass Series in Higher Education). 285p. reprint ed. pap. 88.40 (*0-7837-2510-8*, 204266900006) Bks Demand.

— Preventing Students from Dropping Out. LC 74-28915. (Jossey-Bass Series in Higher Education). 222p. reprint ed. pap. 68.90 (*0-8357-4803-0*, 203774000009) Bks Demand.

— What Matters in College? Four Critical Years Revisited. LC 92-20581. (Higher & Adult Education Ser.). 512p. 1992. text 39.50 (*1-55542-492-9*) Jossey-Bass.

— What Matters in College? Four Critical Years Revisited. 1997. pap. 25.00 (*0-7879-0838-X*) Jossey-Bass.

Astin, Alexander W. & Korn, William S. The American College Teacher: National Norms for the HERI Faculty Survey, 1989-90. 104p. (Orig.). 1990. pap. 12.00 (*1-878477-04-8*) UCLA Higher Educ Rsch Inst.

Astin, Alexander W. & Scherrei, Rita A. Maximizing Leadership Effectiveness. LC 79-9665. (Jossey-Bass Series in Higher Education). 256p. reprint ed. pap. 79.40 (*0-8357-4930-4*, 203786000009) Bks Demand.

Astin, Alexander W., et al. The American College Student, 1988: National Norms for 1984 & 1986. (American College Student, 1985, 1987 & 1988 Ser.). 210p. (Orig.). 1990. pap. 8.00 (*1-878477-02-1*) UCLA Higher Educ Rsch Inst.

— The American Freshman: National Norms for Fall 1990. 172p. (Orig.). 1990. pap. 19.00 (*1-878477-06-4*) UCLA Higher Educ Rsch Inst.

— The American Freshman: National Norms for Fall 1991. 168p. (Orig.). 1991. pap. 20.00 (*1-878477-10-2*) UCLA Higher Educ Rsch Inst.

— The American Freshman: Twenty-Five Year Trends. rev. ed. 220p. 1991. pap. 27.50 (*1-878477-07-2*) UCLA Higher Educ Rsch Inst.

— Perspectives on Freshman Year: Selected Addresses from the Freshman Year Experience Conferences 1983-89. (Freshman Year Experience Monograph: No. 2). 68p. 1990. pap. 20.00 (*1-889271-01-2*) Nat Res Ctr.

Astin, Helen S. & Leland, Carole A. Women of Influence, Women of Vision: A Cross-Generational Study of Leaders & Social Change. LC 91-10784. (Social & Behavioral Science Ser.). 229p. 1991. 35.95 (*1-55542-357-4*) Jossey-Bass.

Astin, John, jt. auth. see Shapiro, Deane H., Jr.

Astin, M., jt. auth. see Williams, T.

Astin, Mary & Sollors, Werner. The Promised Land. LC 96-26048. 196p. 1997. pap. 10.95 (*0-14-018985-8*) Viking Penguin.

Astington, Janet W. The Child's Discovery of the Mind. LC 93-4784. (Developing Child Ser.). 256p. 1993. pap. text 9.95 (*0-674-11642-9*) HUP.

— The Child's Discovery of the Mind. LC 93-4784. (Developing Child Ser.). 236p. 1994. 32.50 (*0-674-11641-0*) HUP.

***Astington, Janet Wilde, ed.** Minds in the Making: Essays in Honor of David R. Olson. LC 99-58778. (Illus.). 288p. 2000. text 59.95 (*0-631-21805-X*, Pub. by Blackwell Publishers); pap. text 27.95 (*0-631-21806-8*, Pub. by Blackwell Publishers) Blackwell Pubs.

Astington, John H. English Court Theatre, 1558-1642. LC 98-39968. (Illus.). 360p. (C). 1999. text 59.95 (*0-521-64065-2*) Cambridge U Pr.

Astington, John H., ed. The Development of Shakespeare's Theater. LC 87-45810. (Studies in the Renaissance: No. 24). 1992. 34.50 (*0-404-62294-1*) AMS Pr.

Astiz, Carlos A., tr. see Ciria, Alberto.

***Astle, Cynthia B.** Believing Is Seeing. 1999. pap. text 0.00 (*0-9669311-0-6*) High Spend.

Astle, Richard M., jt. auth. see Reinhold, Ronald W.

Astle, Ruth S., et al. California Administrative Hearing Practice. CEB Attorneys Staff, ed. LC 97-68156. 1997. ring bd. 129.00 (*0-7626-0067-5*) Cont Ed Bar-CA.

Astle, Thomas. Origin & Progress of Writing. 2nd ed. LC 76-161701. reprint ed. lib. bdg. 84.50 (*0-404-00413-X*) AMS Pr.

Astles, M. G. Liquid-Phase Epitaxial Growth of III-V Compound Semiconductor Materials & Their Device Applications. (Illus.). 232p. 1990. 122.00 (*0-7503-0044-2*) IOP Pub.

Astley. Muddy Waters. 288p. 1997. mass mkt. 12.95 (*0-552-99630-0*) Bantam.

Astley, Edward, et al. Sex Tips for Modern Girls. 99p. 1989. pap. text 5.95 (*0-685-28071-3*) New Mus Theater Lib.

Astley, Helen. Using Language. (Awareness of Language Ser.). 32p. 1985. pap. text 9.95 (*0-521-28898-3*) Cambridge U Pr.

Astley, Jeff. The Philosophy of Christian Religious Education. LC 93-43675. 322p. (Orig.). 1994. pap. 25.95 (*0-89135-093-4*) Religious Educ.

Astley, Jeff, et al, eds. Theological Perspectives on Christian Formation: A Reader on Theology & Christian Education. 472p. 1997. pap. text 34.00 (*0-8028-3777-1*) Eerdmans.

Astley, Jeff & Day, David. The Contours of Christian Education. 416p. (C). 1988. 59.00 (*0-85597-495-8*, Pub. by McCrimmon Pub) St Mut.

Astley, Jeff & Francis, Leslie. Critical Perspectives for Christian Education. 1995. pap. 22.95 (*0-85244-254-8*, 6328, Pub. by Gracewing) Morehouse Pub.

***Astley, Judy.** Every Good Girl. 240p. (J). 2000. pap. 12.95 (*0-552-99766-8*, Pub. by Transworld Publishers Ltd) Trafalgar.

— Every Good Girl. large type ed. 352p. 1999. 31.99 (*0-7089-4082-X*) Ulverscroft.

— Just for the Summer. 2000. pap. 12.95 (*0-552-20455-2*, Pub. by Transworld Publishers Ltd) Trafalgar.

Astley, Judy. Muddy Waters. large type ed. 1998. 26.95 (*0-7531-5593-1*, Pub. by ISIS Lrg Prnt) T T Beeler.

— Pleasant Vices. 288p. 1998. mass mkt. write for info. (*0-552-99565-7*, Pub. by Corgi Bks Ltd) Doubleday.

***Astley, Judy.** Seven for a Secret. 2000. pap. 10.95 (*0-552-99629-7*, Pub. by Transworld Publishers Ltd) Trafalgar.

— Seven for a Secret. large type unabridged ed. 1999. 25.95 (*0-7531-5153-7*, 151537, Pub. by ISIS Lrg Prnt); pap. 19.95 (*0-7531-5516-8*, 155168, Pub. by ISIS Lrg Prnt) ISIS Pub.

Astley-Kristensen, Ian, tr. The Rishukyo: The Sino-Japanese Tantric Prajnaparamita in 150 Verses. (C). 1991. 57.00 (*0-9515424-2-7*, Pub. by Sch Orient & African Stud) S Asia.

Astley, Neil. Biting My Tongue. 80p. 1996. pap. 16.95 (*1-85224-336-8*, Pub. by Bloodaxe Bks) Dufour.

Astley, Neil, ed. Bossy Parrot. LC 87-73294. (Illus.). 64p. (Orig.). (J). (gr. 1 up). 1988. pap. 10.95 (*1-85224-040-7*, Pub. by Bloodaxe Bks) Dufour.

***Astley, Neil, ed.** New Blood. 240p. 2000. pap. 22.95 (*1-85224-472-0*, Pub. by Bloodaxe Bks) Dufour.

Astley, Neil, ed. Poetry with an Edge. LC 88-51307. 320p. 1993. pap. 22.95 (*1-85224-061-X*, Pub. by Bloodaxe Bks) Dufour.

— Ten North-East Poets. 104p. 1980. pap. 12.95 (*0-906427-13-4*, Pub. by Bloodaxe Bks) Dufour.

— Tony Harrison. 1991. pap. 27.00 (*1-85224-080-6*) Dufour.

— Tony Harrison: Bloodaxe Critical Anthologies, No. 1. 510p. 1991. pap. 27.50 (*0-685-50820-X*, Pub. by Bloodaxe Bks) Dufour.

— Tony Harrison: Bloodaxe Critical Anthologies, No. 1. 510p. 1991. 60.00 (*1-85224-079-2*, Pub. by Bloodaxe Bks) Dufour.

Astley, Neil & Kennelly, Brendan. The Heavy Bear Who Goes with Me. 1997. pap. 22.95 (*1-85224-440-2*, Pub. by Bloodaxe Bks) Dufour.

Astley, Neil & Myers, Alan. North of the Word. 320p. 1996. pap. 18.95 (*1-85224-251-5*, Pub. by Bloodaxe Bks) Dufour.

Astley, S., jt. auth. see Bowyer, K. W.

Astley, Thea. A Descant for Gossips. (Paperbacks Ser.). 259p. 1998. reprint ed. pap. 14.95 (*0-7022-1843-X*, Pub. by Univ Queensland Pr) Intl Spec Bk.

Astley, Thomas. New General Collection of Voyages & Travels, 1745-1747, 4 vols., Set. (Illus.). 1968. reprint ed. 395.00 (*0-7146-1786-5*, Pub. by F Cass Pubs) Intl Spec Bk.

ASTM & ASM International Staff. Friction & Wear Testing: Source of Selected References from ASTM Standards & ASM Handbooks. 185p. 1997. 48.00 (*0-87170-617-2*, 06771GZ) ASM.

ASTM Committee. ASTM Fire Test Standards. 5th ed. LC 98-51417. 14p. 1999. write for info. (*0-8031-2597-6*) ASTM.

***ASTM Committee.** ASTM Standards on Activated Carbon. 2nd ed. LC 00-35564. 2000. write for info. (*0-8031-2736-7*) ASTM.

ASTM Committee. ASTM Standards Related to Fire Hazards in Oxygen Systems: Sponsored by ASTM Committee G-4 on Compatibility & Sensitivity of Materials in Oxygen-Enriched Atmospheres. LC 97-33007. 1997. 68.00 (*0-8031-1844-9*, FIREHAZ) ASTM.

ASTM Committee A-1 on Steel, Stainless Steel, & Re & ASTM Committee E-1 on Analytical Chemistry for Met, contrib. by. ASTM Chemical & Spectrometric Test Methods for Steel. LC 92-15058. 1992. 71.00 (*0-8031-1758-2*, 03-501192-50) ASTM.

ASTM Committee B-10. Refractory Metals & Their Industrial Applications-STP 849. Smallwood, Robert E., ed. LC 84-70136. (Illus.). 115p. 1984. pap. text 19.00 (*0-8031-0203-8*, STP849) ASTM.

ASTM Committee B.01 on Automotive Lubricants & D-2. Multicylinder Test Sequences for Evaluating Automotive Engine Oils. 10th ed. LC 93-14689. (Special Technical Publication Ser.: No. 315I). 1993. 30.00 (*0-8031-1880-5*, STP315I) ASTM.

ASTM Committee C-11 on Gypsum. The Chemistry & Technology of Gypsum - STP 861. Kuntze, Richard A., ed. LC 84-70880. 208p. 1984. text 29.00 (*0-8031-0219-4*, STP861) ASTM.

ASTM Committee D-1 on Paint And Related Coatings,. ASTM Standards for the Health, Performance, & Quality Labeling of Artists' Paints & Related Materials. LC 97-5260. 1997. write for info. (*0-8031-1838-4*, ARTPAINTS) ASTM.

***ASTM Committee D-10 on Packaging Staff.** ASTM Standards & Other Documents Related to Performance Testing of Shipping Containers & Systems 3rd ed. LC 99-40469. 1999. write for info. (*0-8031-2725-1*) ASTM.

ASTM Committee D-10 on Packaging Staff. Selected ASTM Standards on Packaging. 4th ed. LC 94-17264. (Pack Ser.: Vol. 94). 1994. 59.00 (*0-8031-1792-2*, PACK94) ASTM.

ASTM Committee D-10 on Packaging Staff, jt. auth. see American Society for Testing & Materials Staff.

ASTM Committee D-18 on Soil & Rock. ASTM Standards on Determining Subsurface Hydraulic Properties & Ground-Water Modeling 2nd ed. LC 99-34577. 1999. write for info. (*0-8031-2717-0*) ASTM.

— ASTM Standards on Evaluation of Sites for Septic Systems. LC 97-19708. 1997. write for info. (*0-8031-1836-8*, SEPTIC) ASTM.

— ASTM Standards on Ground Water & Vadose Zone Investigations. 2nd ed. LC 93-39811. 1994. 69.00 (*0-8031-1786-8*, GRDWATER) ASTM.

— ASTM Standards on Soil Compaction. LC 91-36474. 1998. write for info. (*0-8031-1750-7*) ASTM.

— ASTM Standards Related to Environmental Site Characterization. LC 97-24292. 1997. 165.00 (*0-8031-1841-4*, ENVSITE) ASTM.

— Laterally Loaded Deep Foundations: Analysis & Performance - STP 835. Langer, J. A. et al, eds. LC 83-72942. 250p. 1984. text 34.00 (*0-8031-0207-0*, STP835) ASTM.

ASTM Committee D-18 on Soil & Rock, contrib. by. ASTM Standards on Ground Water Modeling & Analysis of Hydrologic Parameters. LC 95-49831. 1995. 59.00 (*0-8031-1813-9*, HYDRO) ASTM.

ASTM Committee D-18 on Soil & Rock & Subcommittee D-4 on Road & Paving Materials. Nondestructive Testing of Pavements & Backcalculations of Moduli (STP 1198), Vol. 2. Von Quintus, Harold L. et al, eds. LC 94-24308. 1994. write for info. (*0-8031-1865-1*, STP1198) ASTM.

ASTM Committee D-18 on Soil & Rock, jt. auth. see Johnson, A. Ivan.

A

ASTM Committee D-19 on Water. Ecological Assessment of Macrophyton: Collection, Use, & Meaning of Data - STP 843. Dennis, W. M. & Isom, W. G., eds. LC 83-73513. (Illus.). 120p. 1984. pap. text 20.00 (*0-8031-0204-6*, STP843) ASTM.
— Statistics in the Environmental Sciences - STP 845. Gertz, Steven M. & London, M. D., eds. LC 83-73439. 115p. 1984. pap. 24.00 (*0-8031-0206-2*, STP845) ASTM.
ASTM Committee D-2 on Petroleum Products & Lubrica. ASTM & Other Specifications & Classifications for Petroleum Products & Lubricants: Fuels & Oils, Bituminous Materials, Solvents. 6th ed. LC 93-36967. 516p. 1993. pap. 100.00 (*0-8031-1783-3*, PETR093) ASTM.
***ASTM Committee D-2 on Petroleum Products & Lubrica.** ASTM Standards for Industrial Applications: Including Burners, Diesel Engines, Gas Turbines & Marine Applications. LC 99-45436. 1999. write for info. (*0-8031-2727-8*) ASTM.
Astm Committee D-30 On High Modulus Fibers & Their. Fiber, Matrix & Interface Properties, Vol. 129. Spragg, Christopher J. & Drzal, Lawrence T., eds. LC 96-22167. (Special Technical Publication Ser.). 200p. 1996. pap. 62.00 (*0-8031-2046-X*, STP1290) ASTM.
ASTM Committee D-35 on Geosynthetics Staff, contrib. by. ASTM Standards on Geosynthetics. 4th ed. LC 95-39605. 1995. 59.00 (*0-8031-1811-2*, D35COMP95) ASTM.
ASTM Committee D-4 on Road & Paving Materials. Quality Management of Hot Mix Asphalt. 2nd ed. Decker, Dale S., ed. LC 96-37099. (STP 1299 Ser.). (Illus.). 141p. 1996. pap. text 29.00 (*0-8031-2024-9*) ASTM.
ASTM Committee E-One on Analytical Chemistry for M, contrib. by. Suggested Methods for Analysis of Metals, Ores, & Related Materials. 9th rev. ed. LC 92-13742. Orig. Title: Methods for Analytical Atomic Spectroscopy. 1992. 61.00 (*0-8031-1760-4*, EICOMP92) ASTM.
ASTM Committee E-09. Effects of Defects in Composite Materials - STP 836. Wilkins, D., ed. LC 83-73441. (Illus.). 280p. 1984. 39.00 (*0-8031-0218-6*, STP836) ASTM.
ASTM Committee E-1 on Analytical Chemistry for Met, jt. contrib. by see ASTM Committee A-1 on Steel, Stainless Steel, & Re.
***ASTM Committee E-12 on Appearance Staff, ed.** ASTM Standards on Color & Appearance Measurement. 6th ed. LC 00-26268. (Illus.). 2000. write for info. (*0-8031-2735-9*) ASTM.
ASTM Committee E-18 on Sensory Evaluation of Mater, ed. Guidelines for the Selection & Training of Sensory Panel Members - STP 758. 35p. 1981. pap. 13.00 (*0-8031-0783-8*, STP758) ASTM.
ASTM Committee E-24 on Fracture Testing. Fracture Mechanics: Fifteenth Symposium - STP 833. Sanford, R. J., ed. LC 83-72816. 750p. 1984. text 74.00 (*0-8031-0208-9*, STP833) ASTM.
ASTM Committee E-29 on Particle Size. Liquid Particle Size Measurement Techniques - STP 848. Tichkoff, J. M. et al, eds. LC 83-73515. 200p. 1984. text 37.00 (*0-8031-0227-5*, STP848) ASTM.
ASTM Committee E-31 on Computerized Systems. ASTM Standards on Electronic Data Interchange. LC 95-18101. 101p. 1995. pap. 51.00 (*0-8031-1808-2*, ELECDATA) ASTM.
***ASTM Committee E-31 on Healthcare Informatics.** Standards for Security & Electronic Signatures in Healthcare. LC 99-45437. 1999. write for info. (*0-8031-2729-4*) ASTM.
ASTM Committee E-47 on Biological Effects & Enviro. ASTM Standards on Aquatic Toxicology & Hazard Evaluation. LC 93-5098. 535p. 1993. pap. text 86.00 (*0-8031-1778-7*, AQTOX) ASTM.
***ASTM Committee E-47 on Biological Effects & Enviro.** ASTM Standards on Biological Effects & Environmental Fate 2nd ed. LC 99-34199. 1999. write for info. (*0-8031-2722-7*) ASTM.
ASTM Committee E-50 on Environmental Assessment. Standards on Assessment & Remediation of Petroleum Release Sites. LC 99-20877. 1999. write for info. (*0-8031-2599-2*) ASTM.
ASTM Committee E-6 on Performance of Buildings, compiled by. ASTM Standards on Lead-Based Paint Assessment in Buildings. LC 94-33687. 168p. 1994. 69.00 (*0-8031-1802-3*, PAINT) ASTM.
ASTM Committee E-8 on Fatigue & Fracture. Applications of Continuum Damage Mechanics to Fatigue & Fracture, Vol. 131. McDowell, David L., ed. LC 97-36339. (STP Ser.: Vol. 1315). (Illus.). 245p. 1997. 114.00 (*0-8031-2473-2*, STP1315) ASTM.
ASTM Committee F-18 on Electrical Protective Equip. ASTM Standards for Determining the Ignitability & Arc Thermal Performance of Clothing for Use by Workers Exposed to Thermal Hazards of Momentary Electric Arcs. LC 97-16483. 1997. write for info. (*0-8031-1837-6*, ARCS) ASTM.
ASTM, Committee F-20, Hazardous Substances & Oil S & Furcola, Nicole C., eds. ASTM Standards on Hazardous Substances & Oil Spill Response. 2nd ed. LC 94-36691. (Haz Ser.: Vol. 94). 1994. 54.00 (*0-8031-1798-1*, HAZ94) ASTM.
ASTM Committee F01.18 on Membrane Switches. ASTM Standards Related to Membrane Switches. LC 98-45645. 51p. 1998. 45.00 (*0-8031-2592-5*) ASTM.
ASTM Committee G-1 on Corrosion of Metals. Electrochemical Noise Measurement for Corrosion Applications. Kearns, Jeffery R. et al, eds. LC 92-23890. (STP Ser.: No. 1277). (Illus.). 500p. 1996. text 132.00 (*0-8031-2032-X*, STP1277) ASTM.
— Environmental Sensitive Fracture: Evaluation & Comparison of Test Methods - STP 821. Dean, S. W. et al, eds. LC 83-70260. 554p. 1984. text 59.00 (*0-8031-0264-X*, STP821) ASTM.
ASTM, Committee on Terminology Staff, ed. Compilation of ASTM Standard Definitions. 8th ed. LC 94-36690. (Def Ser.: Vol. 94). 596p. 1994. 99.00 (*0-8031-1804-X*, DEF94) ASTM.
ASTM Committee Staff. ASTM Standards on Electrical Protective Equipment for Workers. 10th ed. LC 96-8859. 1996. pap. 45.00 (*0-8031-1823-6*, ELECPROT96) ASTM.
ASTM Committee Staff, contrib. by. ASTM Standards on Emergency Medical Services. 2nd ed. LC 98-45636. 399p. 1998. 49.00 (*0-8031-2593-3*) ASTM.
— ASTM Standards Related to Materials, Coatings & Testing for Fasteners. 2nd ed. LC 96-54598. 1997. 39.00 (*0-8031-1831-7*, FASTENER97) ASTM.
ASTM Special Technical Publication Staff, Jr., jt. auth. see American Society for Testing & Materials Staff.
ASTM Staff. ASTM Fire Test Standards. 4th ed. LC 93-36985. 1993. 110.00 (*0-8031-1781-7*, FIRE93) ASTM.
— ASTM Standards for Clean Rooms. LC 92-35359. 1993. 65.00 (*0-8031-1768-X*, CLEANRMS) ASTM.
— ASTM Standards on Chromatography. 2nd ed. LC 89-6803. 824p. 1989. pap. 76.00 (*0-8031-1219-X*, CHROM89) ASTM.
***ASTM Staff.** ASTM Standards Related to Trenchless Technology. LC 98-48658. 14p. 1999. write for info. (*0-8031-2594-1*) ASTM.
ASTM Subcommittee E06.25 on Whole Buildings & Facil. ASTM Standards on Whole Building Functionality & Serviceability. LC 96-14910. 233p. 1996. pap. 59.00 (*0-8031-1821-X*, WHOLEBLDG) ASTM.
ASTM Subcommittee D20.96 on Environmentally Degradable Plastics Staff, jt. auth. see American Society for Testing & Materials Staff.
ASTM Subcommittee D26.02 on Vapor Degreasing Staff, ed. Manual on Vapor Degreasing, MNL2. 3rd rev. ed. LC 88-35141. 48p. 1989. pap. text 21.00 (*0-8031-1217-3*, MNL2) ASTM.
***ASTM Subcommittee E06.25 on Whole Buildings & Facilities Staff.** ASTM Standards on Whole Building Functionality & Serviceability. 2nd ed. LC 00-21578. 2000. write for info. (*0-8031-2734-0*) ASTM.
***ASTM Subcommittee F 18.55 on Acoustic Emission Staff.** ASTM Standards on Acoustic Emission Testing LC 99-34579. 1999. write for info. (*0-8031-2715-4*) ASTM.
***ASTM Subcommittee on Building Economics Staff.** ASTM Standards on Building Economics. 4th ed. LC 99-30277. (STP Ser.). 1999. write for info. (*0-8031-2714-6*) ASTM.
ASTM Subcommittees DO5.18 & DO5.23 Joint Task Grou & Stanton, Ronald W., eds. Manual on Drilling, Sampling, & Analysis of Coal. LC 92-5556. (Manual Ser.: Vol. MNL 11). (Illus.). 60p. 1992. text 35.00 (*0-8031-1464-8*, MNL11) ASTM.
Astofi, Alessandro. Modeling & Control of Constrained Mechanical Systems. 1999. 65.00 (*0-8176-4077-0*) Spr-Verlag.
Astola, J., et al, eds. Nonliner Image Processing 3. 1992. 20.00 (*0-8194-0812-3*, 1658) SPIE.
Astola, Jaakko & Kuosmanen, Pauli. Fundamentals of Nonlinear Digital Filtering. LC 97-10385. (Electronic Engineering Systems Ser.). 288p. 1997. boxed set 99.95 (*0-8493-2570-6*) CRC Pr.
Astola, Jaakko, jt. auth. see Dougherty, Edward R.
Astola, Jaakko, jt. ed. see Dougherty, Edward R.
Astola, Jaakko T., jt. ed. see Dougherty, Edward R.
Astolfi, A., et al, eds. Modelling & Control of Mechanical Systems: Proceedings of the Workshop Imperial College, London, U. K., 17-20 June 1997. 340p. 1997. text 84.00 (*1-86094-058-7*) World Scientific Pub.
Astolfi, Douglas M. Foundations of Destiny: A Foreign Policy of the Jacksonians. (Nineteenth Century American Political & Social History Ser.). 265p. 1989. reprint ed. 55.00 (*0-8240-4063-5*) Garland.
Aston, jt. auth. see Griffin.
Aston, R. Lee. The Legal, Environmental & Social Perspectives of Surface Mining Law & Reclamation by Landfilling: Getting Maximum Yield from Surface Mines. LC 98-54446. 410p. 1999. 78.00 (*1-86094-123-0*) World Scientific Pub.
Aston, B. W. & Taylor, Donathan. Along the Texas Forts Trail. rev. ed. LC 97-23491. (Illus.). 168p. 1997. pap. 10.95 (*1-57441-035-0*) UNTX Pr.
Aston, Clive C. A Contemporary Crisis: Political Hostage-Taking & the Experience of Western Europe, 84. LC 82-6165. (Contributions in Political Science Ser.: No. 84). 217p. 1982. 55.00 (*0-313-23289-X*, ASP/, Greenwood Pr) Greenwood.
Aston, David C. Under the Covers. 40p. 1987. 20.00 (*0-7223-2158-9*, Pub. by A H S Ltd) St Mut.
Aston, Dore. Garth Evans: Sculpture & Drawings, 1979-1987. LC 87-51570. (Illus.). 32p. (Orig.). 1988. pap. 7.00 (*0-930606-57-4*) Yale Ctr Brit Art.
Aston, Duane R. Return to Cumorah: Piecing Together the Puzzle Where the Nephites Lived. LC 96-85671. (Illus.). 197p. 19.95 (*0-9655167-0-9*, Pub. by Am River Pubns) Origin Bk Sales.
Aston, E., ed. Getting to Know You. (C). 1989. 60.00 (*0-903534-36-3*, Pub. by Brit Ag for Adopt & Fost) St Mut.
Aston, Elaine. Caryl Churchill. (Writers & Their Work Ser.). (Orig.). 1996. pap. 17.00 (*0-7463-0836-1*, Pub. by Northcote House) U Pr of Miss.
— Handbook of Feminist Theatre Practice. LC 98-37217. 1999. 60.00 (*0-415-13924-4*); pap. 20.00 (*0-415-13925-2*) Routledge.
— An Introduction to Feminism & Theatre. LC 94-12202. 192p. (C). 1994. pap. 20.99 (*0-415-08769-4*, B4774) Routledge.
— Sarah Bernhardt: A French Actress on the British Stage. LC 88-36911. (Women's Ser.). 192p. 1989. 12.50 (*0-85496-019-8*) Berg Pubs.
— Theatre As Sign System. 224p. (C). 1992. pap. 16.95 (*0-415-04932-6*, Pub. by Tavistock) Routldge.
***Aston, Elaine & Reinelt, Janelle, eds.** The Cambridge Companion to Modern British Women Playwrights. (Cambridge Companions to Literature Ser.). (Illus.). 293p. (C). 2000. 54.95 (*0-521-59422-7*); pap. 19.95 (*0-521-59533-9*) Cambridge U Pr.
Aston, Elaine, jt. ed. see Griffin, Gabriele.
Aston, Eliane, jt. ed. see Griffin, Gabriele.
Aston, Graham & Tiffney, John. The Essential Guide to Food Hygiene. 4th ed. 280p. 1991. 60.00 (*0-85314-438-9*, Pub. by Tolley Pubng) St Mut.
Aston, Guy, jt. auth. see Burnard, Lou.
Aston, Judith. Aston Postural Assessment: Skills for Observing & Evaluating Body Patterns. 1999. wbk. ed. 52.00 (*0-12-784593-3*) Acad Pr.
Aston, M. B. Esmeralda County: An Extract from Davis' History of Nevada. fac. ed. (Shorey Historical Ser.). 56p. 1913. reprint ed. pap. 10.00 (*0-8466-0175-3*, S-175) Shoreys Bkstore.
Aston, Margaret. England's Iconoclasts Vol. 1: Laws Against Images. (Illus.). 560p. 1988. text 120.00 (*0-19-822438-9*) OUP.
— Faith & Fire: Popular & Unpopular Religion, 1350-1600. LC 93-4417. 360p. 1993. 60.00 (*1-85285-073-6*) Hambledon Press.
— The King's Bedpost: Reformation & Iconography in a Tudor Group Portrait. (Illus.). 279p. (C). 1995. pap. text 27.95 (*0-521-48457-X*) Cambridge U Pr.
— Lollards & Reformers: Images & Literacy in Late Medieval Religion. 405p. 1984. 60.00 (*0-907628-03-6*); pap. 22.00 (*0-907628-18-4*) Hambledon Press.
— The Panorama of the Renaissance. LC 96-15061. (Illus.). 368p. 1996. 45.00 (*0-8109-3704-2*, Pub. by Abrams) Time Warner.
Aston, Margaret & Richmond, Colin. Lollardy & the Gentry in the Later Middle Ages. LC 96-53219. 290p. 1997. text 65.00 (*0-312-17388-1*) St Martin.
Aston, Martin. Bjork: Bjorkgraphy. (Illus.). 336p. 1999. pap. 12.00 (*0-684-86826-1*) S&S Trade.
Aston, Michael. Interpreting the Landscape: Landscape Archaeology & Local History. LC 97-196478. (Illus.). 194p. (C). 1997. pap. 29.99 (*0-415-15140-6*) Routledge.
Aston, Michael & Lewis, Carenza, eds. The Medieval Landscape of Wessex. (Oxbow Monographs in Archaeology: No. 46). (Illus.). 284p. 1995. 50.00 (*0-946897-78-6*, Pub. by Oxbow Bks) David Brown.
Aston, Michaela K., jt. auth. see Aston, Warren P.
***Aston, Mick.** Mick's Archaeology. (Illus.). 2000. pap. 19.99 (*0-7524-1480-1*, Pub. by Tempus Pubng) Arcadia Publng.
— Monasteries in the Landscape. (Illus.). 176p. 2000. pap. 24.99 (*0-7524-1491-7*, Pub. by Tempus Pubng) Arcadia Publng.
Aston, Mick, jt. auth. see Taylor, Tim.
Aston, Nathan M. Bhabani Bhattacharya: A Stylistic Analysis of His Novels. (C). 1994. write for info. (*81-207-1342-7*) Sterling Pubs.
Aston, Nigel. The End of an Elite: The French Bishops & the Coming of the Revolution, 1786-1790. LC 92-10646. (Oxford Historical Monographs). 352p. (C). 1992. text 80.00 (*0-19-820284-9*, Clarendon Pr) OUP.
— Religion & Revolution in France, 1780-1804. LC 99-49440. 450p. (C). 2000. 44.95 (*0-8132-0976-5*); pap. 24.95 (*0-8132-0977-3*) Cath U Pr.
Aston, Nigel, ed. Religious Change in Europe, 1650-1914: Essays for John McManners. LC 96-22714. (Illus.). 460p. 1997. text 95.00 (*0-19-820596-1*) OUP.
Aston, Paul. Sea. LC 97-24266. (True Stories Ser.). 352p. (J). 1997. pap. text 7.95 (*0-8069-9661-7*) Sterling.
Aston, Philip J., ed. Nonlinear Mathematics & Its Applications: Proceedings of the EPSRC Postgraduate School in Applied Nonlinear Mathematics, University of Surrey, 1995. LC 96-19429. (Illus.). 264p. 1996. pap. text 26.95 (*0-521-57676-8*) Cambridge U Pr.
— Nonlinear Mathematics & Its Applications: Proceedings of the EPSRC Postgraduate School in Applied Nonlinear Mathematics, University of Surrey, 1995. LC 96-19429. (Illus.). 264p. 1996. text 74.95 (*0-521-57190-1*) Cambridge U Pr.
Aston, Richard. Electrical Circuit Analysis Using the Ti85/Ti86. LC 99-27473. (Illus.). 363p. (C). 1999. pap. text 51.00 (*0-13-848698-0*, Macmillan Coll) P-H.
— Principles of Biomedical Instrumentation & Measurement. 576p. (C). 1990. 82.60 (*0-675-20943-9*, Merrill Coll) P-H.
Aston, Richard & Brown, Katherine K. Medical Instrument Nurses - Allied Health. 2nd ed. (Nursing-Health Science Ser.). 336p. (C). 1994. pap. 40.00 (*0-86720-688-8*) Jones & Bartlett.
Aston, Robert H. & Ashton, Alison H., eds. Judgment & Decision-Making Research in Accounting & Auditing. (Series on Judgment & Decision Making). (Illus.). 310p. (C). 1995. text 59.95 (*0-521-41844-5*) Cambridge U Pr.
Aston, S. C. Peirol, Troubadour of Auvergne. LC 80-2185. reprint ed. 35.00 (*0-404-19012-X*) AMS Pr.
Aston, Sherrell J., et al. Grabb & Smith's Plastic Surgery. 5th ed. LC 97-16691. 976p. 1997. cd-rom 135.00 (*0-316-32255-5*) Lppncott W & W.
Aston, T. H. & Philpin, C. H., eds. The Brenner Debate: Agrarian Class Structure & Economic Development in Pre-Industrial Europe. (Past & Present Publications). 350p. 1987. pap. text 24.95 (*0-521-34933-8*) Cambridge U Pr.
Aston, W. G. A History of Japanese Literature: Works of W. G. Aston. (Works of W. G. Aston). vi, 410p. 1985. reprint ed. 59.00 (*0-932051-69-3*) Rprt Serv.
— Shinto, the Way of the Gods. 1973. lib. bdg. 300.00 (*0-87968-076-8*) Krishna Pr.
Aston, Warren P. & Aston, Michaela K. In the Footsteps of Lehi: New Evidence for Lehi's Journey Across Arabic to Bountiful. LC 94-301. vi, 88p. 1994. 15.95 (*0-87579-847-0*) Deseret Bk.
Aston, William G., tr. Nihongi: Chronicles of Japan from the Earliest Times to A.D. 697. LC 70-152110. (Illus.). 852p. 1971. pap. 19.95 (*0-8048-0984-4*) Tuttle Pubng.
Astone, Barbara & Nunez-Wormack, Elsa. Pursuing Diversity: Recruiting College Minority Students. Fife, Jonathan D., ed. LC 91-60268. (ASHE-ERIC Higher Education Reports: No. 90-7). 123p. 1990. pap. 24.00 (*1-878380-04-4*) GWU Grad Schl E&HD.
***Astor.** Understanding Life Insurance. (Cliffs Notes Ser.). 128p. 1999. 8.99 (*0-7645-8515-0*) IDG Bks.
Astor, Bart. Family Guide to Caring for Aging Parents: Key Advice for Planning & Providing. LC 96-78163. 1997. pap. text 15.95 (*0-02-861617-0*, Pub. by Macmillan) S&S Trade.
Astor, Bart, jt. auth. see Allen, Joseph.
Astor, Cynthia. A Song for Cecilia Fantini. LC 96-37539. (Illus.). 32p. (J). (ps-5). 1997. 14.95 (*0-915811-75-8*, Starseed) H J Kramer Inc.
Astor, Gerald. Blood-Dimmed Tide: The Battle of the Bulge by the Men Who Fought It. 544p. 1993. mass mkt. 6.50 (*0-440-21574-9*) Dell.
***Astor, Gerald.** The Bloody Forest: Battle for the Hurtgen: September 1944-January 1945. (Illus.). 480p. 2000. 32.95 (*0-89141-699-4*) Presidio Pr.
Astor, Gerald. The Greatest War: Americans in Combat, 1941-1945. LC 99-43632. (Illus.). 1056p. 1999. 39.95 (*0-89141-695-1*) Presidio Pr.
***Astor, Gerald.** Land, Sea & Air. 1999. write for info. (*1-55611-545-8*, Pub. by D I Fine) Penguin Putnam.
Astor, Gerald. The Mighty Eighth: The Air War in Europe As Told by the Men Who Fought It. 560p. 1998. mass mkt. 6.50 (*0-440-22648-1*) Dell.
— The Mighty Eighth: The Air War in Europe Told by the Men Who Fought It. LC 96-48594. (Illus.). 480p. 1997. pap. 26.95 (*1-55611-510-5*, Pub. by D I Fine) Penguin Putnam.
— Operation Iceberg. 576p. 1996. mass mkt. 6.50 (*0-440-22178-1*) Dell.
— The Right to Fight: A History of African Americans in the Military. LC 98-17063. (Illus.). 576p. 1998. 29.95 (*0-89141-632-3*, Pub. by Presidio Pr) Natl Bk Netwk.
Astor, Gerald & Falls, Joe. The Detroit Tigers: An Illustrated History. (Illus.). 256p. 1989. 24.95 (*0-8027-1082-4*) Walker & Co.
Astor, Hilary. Dispute Resolution in Australia. 388p. 1991. pap. 72.00 (*0-614-05476-1*, Austral, MICHIE) LEXIS Pub.
Astor, Hilary & Chinkin, Christine. Dispute Resolution in Australia. 338p. 1992. pap. 72.00 (*0-409-30316-X*, Austral, MICHIE) LEXIS Pub.
Astor, James. Michael Fordham: Innovations in Analytical Psychology. LC 94-48784. (Makers of Modern Psychotherapy Ser.). 288p. (C). 1995. 75.00 (*0-415-09348-1*); pap. 25.99 (*0-415-09349-X*) Routledge.
Astor, John J. Business Letters. LC 91-77181. 178p. 1991. 35.00 (*1-56541-214-1*) Chalidze.
Astor, Stephen. Empty Your Bucket: Practical Steps to Overcome Allergy & Allergic Asthma. LC 92-80164. (Illus.). 312p. (Orig.). 1993. pap. 14.95 (*0-915001-10-1*) Two As.
— Five Days in May: The Alex Swift Story. LC 96-90201. 352p. 1997. 21.95 (*0-915001-13-6*) Two As.
— Hidden Food Allergies: Finding the Foods That Cause You Problems & Removing Them from Your Diet. 2nd ed. 160p. Date not set. pap. 9.95 (*0-89529-799-X*, Avery) Penguin Putnam.
— Take Charge of Your Health: Professional Secrets You Need to Know to Obtain the Best Medical Care. LC 91-90283. 216p. (Orig.). 1991. pap. 12.95 (*0-915001-07-1*) Two As.
— What's New in Allergy & Asthma: New Developments & How They Help You to Overcome Allergy & Asthma. 4th rev. ed. LC 96-90200. (Illus.). 288p. (Orig.). 1996. pap. 14.95 (*0-915001-12-8*) Two As.
Astor-Stetson, Eileen, jt. auth. see Meehan, Anita M.
Astor, Yaakov, ed. see Rabbi Ezriel Tauber.
Astor, Yaakov, ed. see Tauber, Ezriel.
Astour, Michael C. Hittite History & Absolute Chronology of the Bronze Age. (Studies in Mediterranean Archaeology & Literature: No. 73). 152p. (Orig.). 1989. pap. 46.50 (*91-86098-86-1*, Pub. by P Astroms) Coronet Bks.
***Astrachan.** A Computer Science Tapestry. 2nd ed. LC 99-36139. 1999. 52.25 (*0-07-232203-9*) McGraw.
Astrachan, Joseph H. Mergers, Acquisitions & Employee Anxiety: A Study of Separation Anxiety in a Corporate Context. LC 90-30002. 176p. 1990. 47.95 (*0-275-93568-X*, C3568, Praeger Pubs) Greenwood.
Astrachan, Owen L. A Computer Science Tapestry: Exploring Programming & Computer Science with C++ LC 96-44011. (McGraw-Hill Series in Computer Science). (C). 1996. text 52.25 (*0-07-002036-1*) McGraw.
Astrachan, Samuel. Malaparte in Jassy. LC 89-30755. 156p. (C). 1989. 24.95 (*0-8143-2162-3*) Wayne St U Pr.
— Malaparte in Jassy. LC 89-30755. 155p. reprint ed. pap. 48.10 (*0-608-10587-2*, 2071208) Bks Demand.
Astrain, Luis N. Basque Country: A Modern History. Stephens, Meic, tr. LC 97-175857. 240p. 1997. pap. 19.95 (*1-86057-018-6*, Pub. by Welsh Acad) Intl Spec Bk.

An Asterisk (*) at the beginning of an entry indicates that the title is appearing for the first time.

Astrakhan, Anthony. Brave New World (Huxley) (Barron's Book Notes Ser.). (C). 1984. pap. 3.95 (*0-8120-3405-8*) Barron.

Astrand, Hans, jt. ed. see Larsson, Gunnar.

Astrand, Per-Olof & Grimby, Gunnar. Physical Activity in Health & Disease. (Acta Medica Scandinavica Symposium Ser.: No. 2). (Illus.). 228p. 1986. 87.50 (*91-22-00817-9*) Coronet Bks.

Astrand, Per-Olof & Rodahl, Kaare. Textbook of Work Physiology. 3rd ed. 768p. (C). 1986. text 73.62 (*0-07-002416-2*) McGraw.

Astren, Fred D. The Jewish Printed Book in India: Imprints of the Blumenthal Rare Book & Manuscript Library. (Illus.). 56p. (Orig.). 1992. pap. 14.95 (*0-943376-55-6*) Magnes Mus.

Astrhom, B. T. Manufacturing of Polymer Composites. LC 98-120935. xxi, 469 p. 1997. 57.50 (*0-412-81960-0*) Chapman & Hall.

Astridge, Margaret. Seventh Heaven. (Rainbow Romances Ser.: No. 886). 160p. 1994. 14.95 (*0-7090-4937-4*) Parkwest Pubns.

— Seventh Heaven. large type ed. (Romance Ser.). 288p. 1995. pap. 16.99 (*0-7089-7666-2*, Linford) Ulverscroft.

***Astridge, Margaret.** So Near, So Far. large type ed. 280p. 1999. pap. 18.99 (*0-7089-5580-0*, Linford) Ulverscroft.

Astridge, Margaret. Star of Argence. large type ed. (Linford Romance Library). 288p. 1993. pap. 16.99 (*0-7089-7461-9*) Ulverscroft.

Astro, Alan. Understanding Samuel Beckett. LC 89-70759. (Understanding Modern European & Latin American Literature Ser.). 240p. (C). 1990. text 29.95 (*0-87249-686-4*) U of SC Pr.

— Yale French Studies, 85: Discourses of Jewish Identity in Twentieth-Century France. 1994. pap. 18.00 (*0-300-06015-7*) Yale U Pr.

Astro, Joe. 2002. 408p. 1999. pap. 20.00 (*0-9670852-0-9*, 1551) J Astro Prods.

Astro Numeric Service Staff. Tables of Houses Koch. LC 77-77346. 208p. 1977. 17.00 (*0-86690-251-1*, A2006-054) Am Fed Astrologers.

— Tables of Houses Placidus. LC 77-77344. 208p. 1977. 16.00 (*0-86690-252-X*, A2007-054) Am Fed Astrologers.

Astro, Richard. Edward F. Ricketts. LC 76-46147. (Western Writers Ser.: No. 21). 48p. 1976. pap. 4.95 (*0-88430-020-X*) Boise St U W Writ Ser.

— John Steinbeck & Edward F. Ricketts: The Shaping of a Novelist. LC 73-87252. 273p. reprint ed. pap. 84.70 (*0-608-14668-4*, 205583600039) Bks Demand.

Astro, Richard & Benson, Jackson J., eds. The Fiction of Bernard Malamud. LC 77-23232. 192p. 1977. text 21.95 (*0-87071-446-5*) Oreg St U Pr.

— Hemingway in Our Time: Published Record of a Literary Conference Devoted to a Study of the Work of Ernest Hemingway Held at Oregon State University on April 26-27, 1973. LC 73-18428. 222p. reprint ed. pap. 68.90 (*0-608-13785-5*, 202063400018) Bks Demand.

Astroff, Milton T. & Abbey, James R. Convention Management & Service. 5th ed. LC 98-232809. (Illus.). 664p. (C). 1998. pap. 60.95 (*0-86612-173-0*) Educ Inst Am Hotel.

— Convention Sales & Services. 5th rev. ed. (Illus.). 19p. (C). 1997. pap. text 49.95 (*0-9620710-3-X*) Waterbury Pr.

Astrological Magazine Staff, ed. see Raman, Bangalore V.

Astrology World Staff. Aquarius. (Super Horoscopes Ser.). 1998. pap. 7.99 (*0-425-16334-2*) Berkley Pub.

— Aries. (Super Horoscopes Ser.). 256p. 1998. pap. 7.99 (*0-425-16324-5*) Berkley Pub.

— Cancer. (Super Horoscopes Ser.). 1998. pap. 7.99 (*0-425-16327-X*) Berkley Pub.

— Capricorn. (Super Horoscopes Ser.). 1998. pap. 7.99 (*0-425-16333-4*) Berkley Pub.

— Gemini: 1998. (Berkley Super Horoscopes Ser.). 256p. 1997. pap. 6.99 (*0-425-15888-8*) Berkley Pub.

— Gemini: 1999. (Super Horoscopes Ser.). 1998. pap. 7.99 (*0-425-16326-1*) Berkley Pub.

— Leo '99. (Super Horoscopes Ser.). 256p. 1998. pap. 7.99 (*0-425-16328-8*) Berkley Pub.

— Libra '99. (Super Horoscopes Ser.). 1998. pap. 7.99 (*0-425-16330-X*) Berkley Pub.

— Pisces. (Super Horoscopes Ser.). 1998. pap. 7.99 (*0-425-16335-0*) Berkley Pub.

— Sagittarius: 1998 Edition. (Berkley Super Horoscopes Ser.). 256p. 1997. pap. 6.99 (*0-425-15894-2*) Berkley Pub.

— Sagittarius: 1999 Edition. (Super Horoscopes Ser.). 1998. pap. 7.99 (*0-425-16332-6*) Berkley Pub.

— Scorpio: 1998 Edition. (Berkley Super Horoscopes Ser.). 256p. 1997. pap. 6.99 (*0-425-15893-4*) Berkley Pub.

— Scorpio: 1999 Edition. (Super Horoscopes Ser.). 1998. pap. 7.99 (*0-425-16331-8*) Berkley Pub.

— Taurus. (Super Horoscopes Ser.). (Orig.). 1998. pap. 7.99 (*0-425-16325-3*) Berkley Pub.

— Virgo. (Super Horoscopes Ser.). 1998. pap. 7.99 (*0-425-16329-6*) Berkley Pub.

Astrom. Solutions Manual. 2nd ed. (C). 1996. pap. text. write for info. (*0-201-52689-1*) Addison-Wesley.

Astrom, K. E. & Webster, H. The Early Development of The Neopallial Wall & Area Choroidea in Fetal Rats: A Light & Electron Microscopic Study. (Illus.). vi, 76p. 1991. 75.95 (*0-387-53910-7*) Spr-Verlag.

Astrom, Karl J. & Hagglund, Tore H. PID Controllers: Theory, Design, & Tuning. 2nd ed. LC 88-3010. 343p. 1995. 60.00 (*1-55617-516-7*) ISA.

Astrom, Karl J. & Wittenmark, Bjorn. Adaptive Control. (Illus.). (C). 1988. text 95.00 (*0-201-09720-6*) Addison-Wesley.

— Adaptive Control. 2nd ed. LC 94-12682. 580p. (C). 1994. 105.00 (*0-201-55866-1*) Addison-Wesley.

— Computer-Controlled Systems: Theory & Design. 3rd ed. LC 96-36745. (Illus.). 555p. (C). 1996. 100.00 (*0-13-314899-8*) P-H.

Astrom, Karl J., et al. Adaptive Control, Filtering, & Signal Processing. LC 95-9906. (IMA Volumes in Mathematics & Its Applications Ser.: Vol. 74). (Illus.). 406p. 1995. 79.95 (*0-387-97988-3*) Spr-Verlag.

Astrom, Paul. The Cuirass Tomb & Other Finds at Dendra Pt. 2: Excavations in the Cemetaries, the Lower Town & the Citadel. (Studies in Mediterranean Archaeology: Vol. IV). (Illus.). 94p. (Orig.). 1983. pap. 49.50 (*91-86098-13-6*, Pub. by P Astroms) Coronet Bks.

— Hala Sultan Tekke Pt. 10: The Wells. (Studies in Mediterranean Archaeology: Vol. XLV). (Illus.). 152p. 1997. pap. 67.50 (*91-7081-116-4*, Pub. by P Astroms) Coronet Bks.

— Katydhata: A Bronze Age Site in Cyprus. (Studies in Mediterranean Archaeology: Vol. LXXXVI). (Illus.). 129p. (Orig.). 1989. pap. 95.00 (*91-86098-47-0*, Pub. by P Astroms) Coronet Bks.

Astrom, Paul, ed. Acta Cypria Pt. 1: Acts of an International Congress on Cypriote Archaeology Held in Goteborg on 22-24 August 1991. (Studies in Mediterranean Archaeology & Literature: No. 107). (Illus.). 80p. (Orig.). 1991. pap. 17.50 (*91-7081-048-6*, Pub. by P Astroms) Coronet Bks.

— Acta Cypria Pt. 2: Acts of an International Congress on Cypriote Archaeology Held in Goteborg on 22-24 August 1991. (Studies in Mediterranean Archaeology & Literature: No. 117). (Illus.). 405p. (Orig.). 1992. pap. 57.50 (*91-7081-015-X*, Pub. by P Astroms) Coronet Bks.

— Acta Cypria Pt. 3: Acts of an International Congress on Cypriote Archaeology Held in Goteborg on 22-24 August 1991. (Studies in Mediterranean Archaeology & Literature: No. 120). (Illus.). 429p. (Orig.). 1992. pap. 62.50 (*91-7081-047-8*, Pub. by P Astroms) Coronet Bks.

— High, Middle or Low? Pt. 1: Acts of an International Colloquium on Absolute Chronology Held at the University of Gothenburg 20th-22nd August 1987. (Studies in Mediterranean Archaeology & Literature: No. 56). (Illus.). 137p. (Orig.). 1987. pap. 42.50 (*91-86098-64-0*, Pub. by P Astroms) Coronet Bks.

— High, Middle or Low? Pt. 2: Acts of an International Colloquium on Absolute Chronology Held at the University of Gothenburg 20th-22nd August 1987. (Studies in Mediterranean Archaeology & Literature: No. 57). 86p. (Orig.). 1987. pap. 28.50 (*91-86098-65-9*, Pub. by P Astroms) Coronet Bks.

— High, Middle or Low? Pt. 3: Acts of an International Colloquium on Absolute Chronology Held at the University of Gothenburg 20th-22nd August 1987. (Studies in Mediterranean Archaeology & Literature: No. 80). (Illus.). 207p. (Orig.). 1989. pap. 42.50 (*91-86098-94-2*, Pub. by P Astroms) Coronet Bks.

— Horizons & Styles: Studies in Early Art & Archaeology in Honour of Professor Homer L. Thomas. (Studies in Mediterranean Archaeology: Vol. CI). (Illus.). 291p. (Orig.). 1993. pap. 89.50 (*91-7081-072-9*, Pub. by P Astroms) Coronet Bks.

— Jeno Platthy & Antiquity: An Anthology. (Studies in Mediterranean Archaeology & Literature: No. 92). 84p. (Orig.). 1992. pap. 25.00 (*91-7081-043-5*, Pub. by P Astroms) Coronet Bks.

— Opuscula Atheniensia XIX. (Acta Instituti Atheniensis Regni Sueciae Ser.: Series 4, XLI). (Illus.). 203p. (Orig.). 1992. pap. 78.00 (*91-7916-023-9*, Pub. by P Astroms) Coronet Bks.

— Opuscula Atheniensia XX. (Acta Instituti Atheniensis Regni Sueciae Series in 4: Vol. XLIII). (Illus.). 295p. (Orig.). 1994. pap. 97.50 (*91-7916-030-1*, Pub. by P Astroms) Coronet Bks.

— Opuscula Romana XII. (Acta Instituti Romani Regni Sueciae Ser.: Series 4, XXXVI). (Illus.). 65p. (Orig.). 1978. pap. 22.50 (*91-7042-064-5*, Pub. by P Astroms) Coronet Bks.

— Oscar Montelius 150 Years: Proceedings of a Colloquium Held in the Royal Academy Letters, History & Antiquities, Stockholm, 13 May 1993. (Konferenser: No. 32). (Illus.). 112p. (Orig.). 1995. pap. 32.50 (*91-7402-244-X*) Coronet Bks.

Astrom, Paul, et al, eds. Docto Peregrino: Roman Studies in Honour of Torgil Magnuson. (Illus.). 298p. 1992. 54.50 (*91-7042-145-5*, Pub. by P Astroms) Coronet Bks.

— Hala Sultan Tekke 8: Excavations 1971-79. (Studies in Mediterranean Archaeology: Vol. XLV: 8). (Illus.). 251p. (Orig.). 1983. pap. 87.50 (*91-86098-04-7*, Pub. by P Astroms) Coronet Bks.

— Hala Sultan Tekke 9: Trenches 1972-1987 with an Index for Volumes 1-9. (Studies in Mediterranean Archaeology: Vol. XLV: 9). (Illus.). 142p. (Orig.). 1989. pap. 87.50 (*91-86098-37-3*, Pub. by P Astroms) Coronet Bks.

Astrom, Paul & Eriksson, Sven A. Fingerprints & Archaeology. (Studies in Mediterranean Archaeology: Vol. XXVIII). (Illus.). 88p. (Orig.). 1980. pap. 52.50 (*91-85058-99-8*, Pub. by P Astroms) Coronet Bks.

Astrom, Paul, et al. Corpus of Cypriote Antiquities: The Cypriote Collection of the Museum of Art & Archaeology-University of Missouri-Columbia. (Studies in Mediterranean Archaeology: Vol. XX: 2). (Illus.). 58p. (Orig.). 1979. pap. 32.50 (*91-85058-22-X*, Pub. by P Astroms) Coronet Bks.

— The Cuirass Tomb & Other Finds at Dendra Pt. 1: The Chamber Tombs, Pt. 1. (Studies in Mediterranean Archaeology: Vol. IV). (Illus.). 185p. (Orig.). 1977. pap. 30.50 (*91-85058-03-3*) P Astroms.

— The Fantastic Years on Cyprus: The Swedish Cyprus Expedition & Its Members. (Studies in Mediterranean Archaeology & Literature: No. 79). (Illus.). 53p. (Orig.). 1994. pap. 28.50 (*91-7081-059-1*, Pub. by P Astroms) Coronet Bks.

— Hala Sultan Tekke: Excavations 1897-1971. (Studies in Mediterranean Archaeology: Vol. XLV:1). (Illus.). 217p. (Orig.). 1976. pap. write for info. (*91-85058-72-6*) P Astroms.

— Hala Sultan Tekke 3: Excavations 1972. (Studies in Mediterranean Archaeology: Vol. XLV:3). (Illus.). 203p. (Orig.). 1977. pap. write for info. (*91-85058-77-7*) P Astroms.

— Studies in Aegean Chronology. (Studies in Mediterranean Archaeology & Literature: No. 25). (Illus.). 119p. (Orig.). 1984. pap. 42.50 (*91-86098-15-2*, Pub. by P Astroms) Coronet Bks.

Astrom, Paul, jt. auth. see Sjoquist, Karl-Erik.

Astrom, Paul, jt. auth. see Tengvig, Olaf T.

Astrom, Paul, ed. see Furumark, Arne.

Astrom, Paul, jt. ed. see Piltz, Elisabeth.

Astrom, Paul, ed. see Stewart, James R.

Astrom, Paul, ed. see Stewart, Jimmy.

Astronomical Applications Department, U. S. Naval Observatory Staff. Multiyear Interactive Computer Almanac, 1990-2005: Version 1.5. LC 97-46556. 1997. write for info. (*0-943396-56-5*) Willmann-Bell.

Astronomical Union Symposium Staff. Star Clusters: Proceedings of the International Astronomical Union, 85th Symposium, Victoria, B.C., Canada, Aug. 27-30, 1979. Hesser, James E., ed. (International Astronomical Union Symposia Ser.: No. 85). 540p. 1980. lib. bdg. 158.50 (*90-277-1087-2*) Kluwer Academic.

Astronomisches Rechen-Institut ARI, Heidelberg, Ge, ed. Physics Pt. 1: Literature, 1997. (Astronomy & Astrophysics Abstracts Ser.: Vol. 67). viii, 1904p. 1998. 350.00 (*3-540-63954-3*) Spr-Verlag.

***Astronomisches Rechen-Institut Heidelberg Staff, ed.** Literature, 1998, Pt. 2. (Astronomy & Astrophysics Abstracts Ser.: Vol. 70). xviii, 1931p. 1999. 389.00 (*3-540-66096-8*) Spr-Verlag.

Astronomisches Rechen-Institut Staff, ed. Literature, 1996, Pt. 2. (Astronomy & Astrophysics Abstracts Ser.: Vol. 66). viii, 1904p. 1997. 338.00 (*3-540-63304-9*) Spr-Verlag.

***Astronomisches Rechen-Institut Staff, ed.** Literature, 1999, Pt. 1. (Astronomy & Astrophysics Abstracts Ser.: Vol. 71). x, 1967p. 2000. 375.00 (*3-540-67069-6*) Spr-Verlag.

Astronomy Magazine Staff. The New Cosmos. Emmerich, Michael, ed. LC 92-20538. (Illus.). 160p. (Orig.). 1992. per. 19.95 (*0-913135-15-1*, 18537) Kalmbach.

Astrop, Caroline. Shapes. (Chatterbooks Ser.). (J). 1989. pap. 4.95 (*0-920911-95-1*, Pub. by Breakwater Bks) BookWorld.

Astrop, J. My Little Aquarius. (Little Stars Ser.). (Illus.). 64p. 1994. pap. 5.95 (*1-85230-547-9*, Pub. by Element MA) Penguin Putnam.

— My Little Aries. (Little Stars Ser.). (Illus.). 64p. 1994. text 5.95 (*1-85230-537-1*, Pub. by Element MA) Penguin Putnam.

— My Little Cancer. (Little Stars Ser.). (Illus.). 64p. 1994. pap. 5.95 (*1-85230-540-1*, Pub. by Element MA) Penguin Putnam.

— My Little Capricorn. (Little Stars Ser.). (Illus.). 64p. 1984. pap. 5.95 (*1-85230-546-0*, Pub. by Element MA) Penguin Putnam.

— My Little Gemini. (Little Stars Ser.). (Illus.). 64p. 1994. pap. 5.95 (*1-85230-539-8*, Pub. by Element MA) Penguin Putnam.

— My Little Leo. (Little Stars Ser.). (Illus.). 64p. 1994. pap. 5.95 (*1-85230-541-X*, Pub. by Element MA) Penguin Putnam.

— My Little Libra. (Little Stars Ser.). (Illus.). 64p. 1994. pap. 5.95 (*1-85230-543-6*, Pub. by Element MA) Penguin Putnam.

— My Little Pisces. (Little Stars Ser.). (Illus.). 64p. 1994. pap. 5.95 (*1-85230-548-7*, Pub. by Element MA) Penguin Putnam.

— My Little Sagittarius. (Little Stars Ser.). (Illus.). 64p. 1994. pap. 5.95 (*1-85230-545-2*, Pub. by Element MA) Penguin Putnam.

— My Little Scorpio. (Little Stars Ser.). (Illus.). 64p. 1994. pap. 5.95 (*1-85230-544-4*, Pub. by Element MA) Penguin Putnam.

— My Little Taurus. (Little Stars Ser.). (Illus.). 64p. 1994. pap. 5.95 (*1-85230-538-X*, Pub. by Element MA) Penguin Putnam.

— My Little Virgo. (Little Stars Ser.). (Illus.). 64p. 1994. pap. 5.95 (*1-85230-542-8*, Pub. by Element MA) Penguin Putnam.

Astrop, John, jt. auth. see Smith, Caroline.

Astrophysics & Space Science Staff. The Scientific Satellite Programmed During the International Magnetospheric Study: Proceedings, Vol. 57. Knott, K. & Battrick, Bruce, eds. LC 75-44353. 1975. lib. bdg. 152.00 (*90-277-0688-3*) Kluwer Academic.

Astrophysics School, et al. X-ray Spectroscopy in Astrophysics: Lectures Held at the Astrophysics School X, Organized by the European Astrophysics Doctoral Network (EADN) in Amsterdam, the Netherlands, September 22-October 3, 1997. LC 99-17747. (Lecture Notes in Physics Ser.). xv, 530 p. 1999. 99.00 (*3-540-65548-4*) Spr-Verlag.

Astroth, Joseph H., Jr. Understanding Peasant Agriculture: An Integrated Land-Use Model for the Punjab. (Research Papers). (Illus.). xiii, 173p. 1989. pap. text 14.50 (*0-89065-127-2*) U Ch Pr.

Astrov, Margot, ed. The Winged Serpent: American Indian Prose & Poetry. LC 92-13743. 1992. pap. 16.00 (*0-8070-8105-1*) Beacon Pr.

Astrov, Nicholas J., jt. auth. see Gronsky, Paul P.

Astruc, D. Electron Transfer & Radical Processes in Transition-Metal Chemistry. 652p. 1995. 180.00 (*0-471-18588-4*) Wiley.

Astruc, Didier. Electron Transfer & Radical Processes in Transition-Metal Chemistry. LC 94-25261. (Illus.). 624p. 1995. 140.00 (*1-56081-642-2*, Wiley-VCH) Wiley.

Astrum, Sue. Don't Look Down: Staying Aloft on Damaged Wings. LC 97-32025. (Illus.). 96p. 1998. pap. 9.95 (*1-56474-240-7*) Fithian Pr.

Astrup, Arne, jt. auth. see Kuehn, John.

Asturias, Alvaro, et al, contrib. by. Variations III: Emerging Artists in Southern California. LC 87-80526. (Illus.). 79p. 1987. pap. 15.00 (*0-911291-13-X*, Pub. by Fellows Cont Art) RAM Publications.

Asturias, Miguel Angel. El Arbol de la Cruz. (Coleccion Archivos de Ediciones Criticas). (SPA.). 24.99 (*84-88344-05-8*, Pub. by Fondo) Continental Bk.

— Legendes du Guatemala. (FRE.). 192p. 1985. pap. 10.95 (*0-7859-2007-2*, 2070376249) Fr & Eur.

Asturias, Miguel Angel. Leyendas de Guatemala: Level C Books. text 8.95 (*0-88436-290-6*) EMC-Paradigm.

Asturias, Miguel Angel. Men of Maize. Martin, Gerald, tr. (Latin American Literature Ser.). 504p. (C). 1993. pap. 19.95 (*0-8229-5514-8*) U of Pittsburgh Pr.

— The Mirror of Lida Sal: Tales Based on Mayan Myths & Guatemalan Legends. Alter-Gilbert, Gilbert, tr. from SPA. LC 96-35864. 126p. (C). 1997. pap. 14.95 (*0-935480-83-8*) Lat Am Lit Rev Pr.

— The President. Partridge, Frances, tr. from SPA. Orig. Title: El Senor Presidente. 288p. (C). 1997. reprint ed. pap. text 11.95 (*0-88133-951-2*) Waveland Pr.

— El Senor Presidente, Level 6. (Leer en Espanol Ser.). (SPA.). (C). 1998. pap. 6.95 (*84-294-3590-5*) Santillana.

— Sociologia Guatemalteca: El Problema Social del Indio. Ahern, Maureen, tr. LC 77-8270. 106p. 1977. 20.00 (*0-87918-035-8*); pap. 10.00 (*0-87918-037-4*) ASU Lat Am St.

Astuti, Rita. People of the Sea: Identity & Descent among the Vezo of Madagascar. (Studies in Social & Cultural Anthropology: No. 95). (Illus.). 202p. (C). 1995. text 54.95 (*0-521-43350-9*) Cambridge U Pr.

Astuto, Terry A., et al. Roots of Reform: Challenging the Assumptions That Control Change in Education. 108p. 1994. 9.00 (*0-87367-464-2*) Phi Delta Kappa.

Astwood, Philip & Carpenter, John. Environmental Issues. 3rd ed. 96p. (C). 1999. spiral bd. 23.95 (*0-7872-5679-X*, 41567901) Kendall-Hunt.

Astwood, Philip M. Understanding Earth: Instructor's Resource Manual. 2nd ed. 1997. teacher ed. 24.00 (*0-7167-2765-X*) W H Freeman.

Astwood, William, jt. auth. see Neuhaus, Edmund C.

Asua, Jose M., ed. Polymeric Dispersions: Principles & Applications. LC 97-10630. (NATO ASI Series, Applied Sciences: Series E). 1997. text 301.00 (*0-7923-4549-5*) Kluwer Academic.

Asuagbor, Greg O. Democratization & Modernization in a Multilingual Cameroon. LC 97-47013. 220p. 1997. text 89.95 (*0-7734-2221-8*) E Mellen.

Asuka, Ken, jt. auth. see Barnes, Jill.

Asussen, Don. The Life of Stid. (Illus.). (Orig.). 1986. pap. 5.95 (*0-937217-02-6*) Fifth Estate.

Asvaghosa. The Buddhacarita or Acts of the Buddha, 2 vols. in 1. Johnson, E. H., ed. & tr. by. reprint ed. text 33.50 (*81-215-0710-3*) Coronet Bks.

— The Principle & Practice of Mahayana Buddhism: An Interpretation of Professor Suzuki's Translation of Ashvaghosa's Awakening of Faith. Goodard, Dwight, ed. LC 78-72373. reprint ed. 27.50 (*0-404-17223-7*) AMS Pr.

Asvall, J. E., jt. auth. see Sokolov, D. K.

Asvarishch, B. Friedrich, David Caspar. (C). 1985. 95.00 (*0-7855-4530-1*, Pub. by Collets) St Mut.

Asvarishch, B., ed. David Caspar Friedrich. (Illus.). (C). 1985. text 90.00 (*0-7855-5836-5*, Pub. by Collets) St Mut.

Asvarishch, B., jt. auth. see Nikulin, N.

ASVP Staff. Critical Incident Stress Debriefing - Three-Fourths Inch. (gr. 13). 1991. 159.95 (*1-56200-401-8*) Mosby Inc.

— Critical Incident Stress Debriefing-PAL. (gr. 13). 1991. 159.00 (*1-56200-402-6*) Mosby Inc.

Aswad, Barbara C. Property Control & Social Strategies: Settlers on a Middle Eastern Plain. (Anthropological Papers Ser.: No. 44). 1971. pap. 2.00 (*0-932206-42-5*) U Mich Mus Anthro.

Aswad, Barbara C. & Bilge, Barbara, eds. Family & Gender among American Muslims: Issues Facing Middle Eastern Immigrants & Their Descendants. 304p. (C). 1996. pap. 22.95 (*1-56639-443-0*); lib. bdg. 69.95 (*1-56639-442-2*) Temple U Pr.

Aswad, Dana W., ed. Deamidation & Isoaspartate Formation in Peptides - Proteins. 272p. 1994. boxed set 136.95 (*0-8493-7823-0*, 7823) CRC Pr.

***Aswad, Ed.** Broome County: New York. LC 00-104044. (Postcard History Ser.). (Illus.). 128p. 2000. pap. 18.99 (*0-7385-0447-5*) Arcadia Publing.

Aswal, B. S., ed. Flora of Lahual-Spiti District (North-West Himalaya) 1987. 455.00 (*0-7855-6644-9*, Pub. by Intl Bk Distr) St Mut.

Aswathanarayana, U. Principles of Nuclear Geology. 410p. (C). 1985. text 123.00 (*90-6191-572-4*, Pub. by A A Balkema) Ashgate Pub Co.

***Aswathanarayana, U.** Soil Resources & the Environment. LC 99-39258. (Illus.). 268p. 1999. text 59.50 (*1-57808-067-3*) Science Pubs.

Aswathanarayna, U. Geoenvironment: An Introduction. LC 99-227734. (Illus.). 300p. 1995. 90.00 (*90-5410-608-5*) Ashgate Pub Co.

Aswell, James R., ed. Native American Humor. LC 76-117753. (Essay Index Reprint Ser.). 1977. 28.95 (*0-8369-1862-2*) Ayer.

Aswell, James R., et al. God Bless the Devil: Liars' Bench Tales. LC 84-22054. (Tennesseana Editions Ser.). (Illus.). 299p. reprint ed. pap. 92.70 (*0-608-08620-7*, 206914300003) Bks Demand.

Aswynn, Freya. Northern Mysteries & Magick: Runes, Gods, & Feminine Powers. 2nd rev. ed. LC 98-9832. 288p. 1999. 14.95 (*1-56718-047-7*) Llewellyn Pubns.

***Aswynn, Freya.** Principles of the Runes. 160p. 2000. pap. 11.00 (*0-7225-3883-9*, Pub. by Thorsons PA) HarpC.

Aszalos. The Modern Analysis of Antibiotics. (Drugs & the Pharmaceutical Sciences Ser.: Vol. 27). (Illus.). 568p. 1986. text 230.00 (*0-8247-7358-6*) Dekker.

Aszalos, A., jt. auth. see Berdy, Janos.

Aszalos, Adorjan, ed. Antitumor Compounds of Natural Origin, 2 vols., Vol. 1. 256p. 1981. 148.00 (*0-8493-5520-6*, RC271, CRC Reprint) Franklin.

— Antitumor Compounds of Natural Origin, 2 vols., Vol. 2. 224p. 1981. 125.00 (*0-8493-5521-4*, RC271, CRC Reprint) Franklin.

-Aszodi, L. Fulop, see Fulop-Aszodi, L.

Asztalos, Monika, ed. The Editing of Theological & Philosophical Texts from the Middle Ages. 313p. (Orig.). 1986. pap. text 72.50 (*91-22-00792-X*) Coronet Bks.

***A.T. Kearney, Inc.** Sustaining Corporate Growth: Harnessing Your Critical Competencies. LC 00-36609. 2000. write for info. (*1-57444-289-9*) St Lucie Pr.

At-Tahawi, Imam Abu Jafar. Islamic Belief. Ghazi, A., ed. LC 95-77848. 22p. (YA). (gr. 7-9). 1995. pap. 3.00 (*1-56316-058-7*) Iqra Intl Ed Fdtn.

At-Tayyib, Ibn. Proclus' Commentary on the Pythagorean Golden Verses. Linley, Neil, ed. (Arethusa Monographs: No. 10). xi, 105p. 1984. pap. 10.00 (*0-930881-07-9*) Dept Classics.

AT&T-General Staff. Area Code Handbook, 1994. rev. ed. (Illus.). 66p. 1994. 2.95 (*0-932764-18-5*, 999-600-111) AT&T Customer Info.

AT&T Information Systems, Inc. Staff. AT&T Computer Software Catalog: UNIX R System V Software. 1987. 24.95 (*0-13-050154-9*) P-H.

— AT&T Computer Software Guide PC 6300. write for info. (*0-318-59648-2*) S&S Trade.

— AT&T Computer Software Guide 3B2-3B5-3B20 UNIT PC. write for info. (*0-318-59649-0*) S&S Trade.

AT&T Staff. Design's Impact on Logistics. LC 93-9148. 228p. 1992. 42.00 (*0-07-002562-2*) McGraw.

— System V Interface Definition. 592p. (C). 1991. pap. 58.95 (*0-201-56653-2*) Addison-Wesley.

— System V Interface Definition, Vol. 3. 672p. (C). 1991. pap. 58.95 (*0-201-56654-0*) Addison-Wesley.

— System V Interface Definition, Vol. 4. 3rd ed. 528p. 1991. pap. 58.95 (*0-201-56655-9*) Addison-Wesley.

— UNIX System Administrator's Guide. 1988. pap. 34.95 (*0-13-936139-1*) P-H.

— UNIX System Administrator's Reference Manual. 1988. pap. 24.95 (*0-13-936147-2*) P-H.

— UNIX System V Release 3.2 Streams Programmer's Guide. 256p. 1989. pap. 24.95 (*0-685-27161-7*) P-H.

— UNIX System V-386 System Administrator's Guide. 1988. pap. 34.95 (*0-13-940891-6*) P-H.

AT&T Staff & Vedral, Joyce L. UNIX Rel 3.2 Program Guide. 256p. 1989. pap. 41.00 (*0-13-944810-1*) P-H.

AT&T Staff & Vedral, Joyce L. UNIX System V Release 4 System Administrator's Reference Manual. (C). 1990. pap. text 44.20 (*0-13-947011-5*) P-H.

AT&T Technologies Inc. Staff. The UNIX System V Software Catalog. 1986. 19.95 (*0-8359-8068-5*) S&S Trade.

Ata, Abe. Intermarriage Between Christians & Muslims. 150p. 1999. 76.50 (*0-7103-0655-5*, Pub. by Kegan Paul Intl) Col U Pr.

ATA Foundation Staff. Commercial Driver Rest Area Requirements: No Room at the Inn. 38p. 1996. pap. 25.00 (*0-88711-389-3*) Am Trucking Assns.

— Empty Seats & Musical Chairs: Critical Success Factors in Truck Driver Retention. 29p. 1998. pap. 25.00 (*0-88711-387-7*) Am Trucking Assns.

— From Research to Reality: Alternative Fuels in Commercial Trucking. 1997. pap. 25.00 (*0-88711-386-9*) Am Trucking Assns.

— The Future of Diesel Fuel: The Potential for a National Diesel Fuel Standard. 1998. pap. 25.00 (*0-88711-385-0*) Am Trucking Assns.

— Making the Difference. 29p. 1998. pap. 25.00 (*0-88711-388-5*) Am Trucking Assns.

Ata, Ibrahim W. The West Bank Palestinian Family. 250p. 1987. text 55.00 (*0-7103-0186-3*) Routledge.

ATA National Accounting & Finance Council Staff & Deloitte & Touche Staff. Trucking Industry Valuation Guide. 1995. pap. 40.00 (*0-88711-271-4*) Am Trucking Assns.

Ata, Te. Baby Rattlesnake/Viberita de Cascabel. (J). (ps-3). 1996. pap. 13.00 (*0-89239-143-X*) Childrens Book Pr.

Ata, Te, jt. auth. see Moroney, Lynn.

Ataai, Mohammad M. & Sikdar, Subhas K., eds. New Developments in Bioseparation. LC 92-37375. (AIChE Symposium Ser.: No. 290, Vol. 88). 1992. 35.00 (*0-8169-0577-0*) Am Inst Chem Eng.

Atabai, Badri. A Glimpse at Persian History. Gudarzi, Mahmud, ed. LC 97-25749. (Illus.). 274p. 1998. pap. 16.00 (*0-936347-88-0*) IBEX.

— A Treasury of Iranian Fine Arts. Gudarzi, Mahmud, ed. LC 98-12427. (Illus.). 414p. 1998. lib. bdg. 60.00 (*0-936347-68-6*) IBEX.

Atabai, Badri & Bastani-Parizi, Mohammad E. Collected Articles of Badri Atabai: Sar Gozasht-Ha. Gudarzi, Mahmud, ed. LC 95-39738. (Illus.). 368p. (Orig.). 1996. pap. 16.00 (*0-936347-73-2*) IBEX.

Atabaki. Post-Soviet Central Asia. 342p. 1998. text 59.50 (*1-86064-327-2*, Pub. by I B T) St Martin.

Atabekov, G. Relay Protection of High Voltage Networks. LC 59-13714. 1960. 251.00 (*0-08-013816-0*, Pub. by Pergamon Repr) Franklin.

***Atach, Margaret.** May '68 in French Fiction & Film: Rethinking Society, Rethinking Representation. (Illus.). 192p. 2000. text 60.00 (*0-19-871514-5*); pap. text 24.95 (*0-19-871515-3*) OUP.

Atack, Chris. Project Maldon. 384p. 1997. per. 5.99 (*0-671-87786-0*) Baen Bks.

Atack, Jeremy. New Economic View of American History. 2nd ed. 1994. 35.00 (*0-393-03622-7*) Norton.

Atack, Jeremy & Bateman, Fred. To Their Own Soil: Agriculture in the Antebellum North. LC 86-21349. (Henry A. Wallace Series on Agriculture History & Rural Studies). (Illus.). 334p. 1987. reprint ed. pap. 103.60 (*0-608-06849-7*, 206705500009) Bks Demand.

Atack, M. & Powrie, P., eds. Contemporary French Fiction by Women: Feminist Perspectives. 1991. text 89.95 (*0-7190-3084-6*, Pub. by Manchester Univ Pr) St Martin.

Ataev, S. S. Construction Technology. 462p. 1985. 37.00 (*0-7855-1176-8*) St Mut.

Atai, Tarek & Khalil, Youssef. Pyramid Wisdom: The World's Most Mysterious Monuments Interpreted by Modern-Day Descendants of the Pharaohs. (Illus.). 64p. 1999. mass mkt. 6.99 (*0-9671359-0-7*) Dragonfly Books.

Ataie, Iraj J. & Ritchie, Rob. Night Sun, Our Wounds, Prometheus in Evin, Poems, & Leave to Remain. (Methuen New Theatrescripts Ser.). 179p. (Orig.). (C). 1989. pap. write for info. (*0-413-62250-9*, A0395, Methuen Drama) Methn.

Atak, S., et al, eds. Innovations in Mineral & Coal Processing: Proceedings of the 7th International Mineral Processing Symposium, Istanbul, Turkey, 15-17.09.1998. 922p. (C). 1998. text 114.00 (*90-5809-013-2*, Pub. by A A Balkema) Ashgate Pub Co.

Atal, Bishnu S., et al, eds. Advances in Speech Coding. (International Series in Engineering & Computer Science, VLSI, Computer Architecture, & Digital Screen Processing). 400p. (C). 1990. reprint ed. text 153.50 (*0-7923-9091-1*) Kluwer Academic.

— Papers in Speech Communication: Speech Processing, 3 vols., Vol. 3. 672p. 1991. text 46.00 (*0-88318-960-7*) Acoustical Soc Am.

— Speech & Audio Coding for Wireless & Network Applications. LC 93-13233. (International Series in Engineering & Computer Science, VLSI, Computer Architecture, & Digital Screen Processing). 296p. (C). 1993. text 141.50 (*0-7923-9345-7*) Kluwer Academic.

Atal, C. K. Cultivation & Utilization of Aromatic Plants. (C). 1984. 100.00 (*0-7855-2278-6*, Pub. by Scientific) St Mut.

— Cultivation & Utilization of Medicinal Plants. (C). 1984. 100.00 (*0-7855-2277-8*, Pub. by Scientific) St Mut.

Atal, Yogesh, ed. Culture-Development Interface. 1991. 25.00 (*0-7069-5829-2*) Advent Bks Div.

— Poverty in Transition: Studies in Countries-in-Transition: Hungary, Bulgaria, Romania, Georgia, Russia, Mongolia. LC 98-47226. 272p. 1999. 59.95 (*1-57181-191-5*); pap. 17.50 (*1-57181-192-3*) Berghahn Bks.

Atal, Yogesh, jt. auth. see Narain, Iqbal.

Atala, A., et al, eds. Synthetic Biodegradable Polymer Scaffolds. LC 96-45700. (Tissue Engineering Ser.). 348p. 1997. 99.00 (*0-8176-3919-5*) Birkhauser.

Atalia, Rajai H., ed. The Structures of Cellulose: Characterization of the Solid State. LC 87-11537. (ACS Symposium Ser.: Vol. 340). 328p. 1987. reprint ed. pap. 101.70 (*0-608-03533-5*, 206425200008) Bks Demand.

Atalla, Bill M. & Beitler, Stephen. The Thirteen Months of Pregnancy: A Guide for the Pregnant Father. LC 92-60038. (Illus.). 128p. 1992. 19.95 (*0-9631754-5-9*) Oddly Enough.

Atallah, Mikhail J. Algorithms & Theory of Computation. LC 98-38016. 1312p. 1998. boxed set 94.95 (*0-8493-2649-4*) CRC Pr.

Atallah, Tony. The Techniques of Falsification in Elections. (ARA., Illus.). 104p. 1996. pap. 3.50 (*1-886604-04-5*) Lebanese Ctr.

Atamanov, E. R., jt. auth. see Asanov, A.

Atamian, Sarkis. The Bears of Manley: The Adventures of an Alaskan Trophy Hunter. LC 95-71680. 448p. 1995. 29.95 (*1-888125-01-2*) Publ Consult.

— The Origin of Tarzan: The Mystery of the Creation of Tarzan Solved. LC 97-65127. 128p. (Orig.). 1997. pap. 14.95 (*1-888125-12-8*) Publ Consult.

Atampurge, Nicholas. Behind the Lines of Stone: The Social Impact of a Soil & Water Conservation Project in the Sahel. (Community Development Ser.). (Illus.). 192p. (C). 1993. pap. 17.50 (*0-85598-258-6*, Pub. by Oxfam Pub); text 39.95 (*0-85598-257-8*, Pub. by Oxfam Pub) Stylus Pub VA.

Atamuradov, Khabibulla, jt. ed. see Fet, Victor.

Atanackovic, T. M. Stability Theory of Elastic Rods. LC 97-139952. (Series on Stability Vibration & Control of Systems). 400p. 1997. 68.00 (*981-02-3054-0*) World Scientific Pub.

Atanackovic, Teodor M. & Guran, A. Theory of Elasticity for Scientists & Engineers. LC 98-16929. 472p. 1999. 69.95 (*0-8176-4072-X*); write for info. (*3-7643-4072-X*) Birkhauser.

Atanasijevic, Ksenija. The Metaphysical & Geometrical Doctrine of Bruno. Tomashevich, George V., tr. from FRE. LC 76-155339. 151p. 1972. 12.50 (*0-87527-081-6*) Green.

Atanasiu, P., jt. auth. see Almeida, J.

Atanasov, K., et al. Generalized Nets in Neurology. (Illus.). 359p. 1997. pap. 69.95 (*954-430-522-X*, Pub. by Akadem izdatelstvo) Intl Scholars.

Atanasov, K. T. Generalized Nets & Systems Theory. (Illus.). 158p. 1997. pap. 69.95 (*954-430-521-1*, Pub. by Akadem izdatelstvo) Intl Scholars.

Atanasov, P., ed. Lasers--Physics & Applications. 650p. (C). 1991. text 151.00 (*981-02-0564-3*) World Scientific Pub.

Atanasov, Peter, ed. Quantum Electronics: Lasers - Physics & Applications. LC 96-72057. 426p. 1997. pap. 89.00 (*0-8194-2466-8*) SPIE.

***Atanasov, Peter A. & Stoyanov, Dimitar V., eds.** Quantum Electronics. 420p. 1999. pap. text 92.00 (*0-8194-3034-X*) SPIE.

Atanasson, K., jt. ed. see Perez, M. L.

***Atanasson, Krassimir T.** On Some of the Smarandache's Problems, 1. Perez, M. L., ed. (Illus.). 88p. 2000. pap. text 16.95 (*1-879585-72-3*) American Res Pr.

Atanassov, K. Generalized Nets in Artificial Intelligence Vol. 1. (Illus.). 143p. 1998. pap. 74.95 (*954-430-538-6*, Pub. by Pensoft Pubs) Intl Scholars.

Atanassov, K. T. Generalized Nets. 400p. (C). 1991. text 71.00 (*981-02-0598-8*) World Scientific Pub.

***Atanassov, K. T.** Intuitionistic Fuzzy Sets: Theory & Applications. LC 99-44591. (Studies in Fuzziness & Soft Computing: Vol. 35). xviii, 323p. 1999. 90.00 (*3-7908-1228-5*) Spr-Verlag.

Atanassov, K. T., ed. Applications of Generalized Nets. 300p. (C). 1993. text 98.00 (*981-02-0667-4*) World Scientific Pub.

Atanassova, T. Bulgarian-English Dictionary, 2 vols. 3rd ed. 1050p. 1990. 97.25 (*0-88431-074-4*) IBD Ltd.

— Bulgarian-English Dictionary, 2 vols., Set. 1050p. (C). 1988. 295.00 (*0-89771-904-2*, Pub. by Collets) St Mut.

Atanassova, T., et al. Bulgarian-English Dictionary. 2nd ed. (BUL & ENG.). 1050p. 1990. 85.00 (*0-8288-0447-8*, M9829) Fr & Eur.

Atard, Vincente P. Juan Carlos I y el Advenimiento de la Democracia. (Nueva Austral Ser.: Vol. 87). (SPA.). 1991. pap. text 24.95 (*84-239-1887-4*) Elliots Bks.

— Manual de Historia de Espana Vol. 4: Edad Contemporanea, I (1808-1898) (SPA.). 644p. 1991. 125.00 (*84-239-5094-8*) Elliots Bks.

Atashi, Zeidan. Druze & Jews in Israel - A Shared Destiny? (Illus.). 240p. 1997. 45.00 (*1-898723-17-6*, Pub. by Sussex Acad Pr) Intl Spec Bk.

— Druze & Jews in Israel - A Shared Destiny? A Shared Destiny? (Illus.). 240p. 1997. pap. 24.95 (*1-898723-38-9*, Pub. by Sussex Acad Pr) Intl Spec Bk.

Atasoy, Nurhan. Iznik: The Pottery Ottoman Turkey. 384p. 1999. 125.00 (*1-85669-054-7*, Pub. by L King Pubng) Antique Collect.

Atasoy, Nurhan & Raby, Julian. Iznik: The Pottery of Ottoman Turkey. LC 89-50540. (Illus.). 384p. 1994. reprint ed. 120.00 (*0-500-97374-1*, Pub. by Thames Hudson) Norton.

Atassi, H. M., ed. Air Acoustics: Applications in Engineering. LC 92-43206. 904p. 1993. 129.95 (*0-387-97977-8*); write for info. (*3-540-97977-8*) Spr-Verlag.

Atassi, M. Z., ed. Immunobiology of Proteins & Peptides: Human Immunodeficiency Virus, Antibody Immunoconjugates, Bacterial Vaccines, Immunomodulators, Vol. 6. (Advances in Experimental Medicine & Biology Ser.: Vol. 303). (Illus.). 312p. (C). 1991. text 114.00 (*0-306-44038-5*, Kluwer Plenum) Kluwer Academic.

— Immunobiology of Proteins & Peptides IV: T-Cell Recognition & Antigen Presentation. LC 87-29231. (Advances in Experimental Medicine & Biology Ser.: Vol. 225). (Illus.). 346p. 1987. 85.00 (*0-306-42769-9*, Plenum Trade) Perseus Pubng.

— Immunobiology of Proteins & Peptides, V: Vaccines. (Advances in Experimental Medicine & Biology Ser.: Vol. 251). (Illus.). 368p. 1989. 95.00 (*0-306-43239-0*, Plenum Trade) Perseus Pubng.

— Immunobiology of Proteins & Peptides 7: Unwanted Immune Responses, Vol. 7. (Advances in Experimental Medicine & Biology Ser.: Vol. 347). (Illus.). 244p. (C). 1994. text 95.00 (*0-306-44665-0*, Kluwer Plenum) Kluwer Academic.

— Immunochemistry of Proteins, 3 vols. LC 76-2596. (Illus.). 1977. 79.50 (*0-306-36221-X*, Plenum Trade) Perseus Pubng.

— Immunochemistry of Proteins, 3 vols. LC 76-2596. (Illus.). 1977. 79.50 (*0-306-36222-8*, Plenum Trade) Perseus Pubng.

Atassi, M. Zouhair, et al, eds. Molecular Immunology: A Textbook. (Immunology Ser.: 22). (Illus.). 744p. 1984. text 95.00 (*0-8247-7045-5*, 7045-5) Dekker.

Atassi, M. Zouhair & Appella, Ettore, eds. Methods in Protein Structure Analysis: Proceedings of the 10th International Conference Held in Snowbird, Utah, September 8-13, 1994. LC 95-36854. (Illus.). 552p. (C). 1996. text 135.00 (*0-306-45124-7*, Kluwer Plenum) Kluwer Academic.

Atassi, M. Zouhair & Bixler, Garvin S., Jr., eds. Immunobiology of Proteins & Peptides No. VIII: Manipulation & Modulation of the Immune Response, Proceedings of the Eighth International Symposium Held in Pio Rico, Arizona, November 16-20, 1994, No. 8. LC 95-36866. (Advances in Experimental Medicine & Biology Ser.: Vol. 383). (Illus.). 288p. (C). 1995. text 95.00 (*0-306-45125-5*, Kluwer Plenum) Kluwer Academic.

Atatbaki, Touraj. Azerbaijan: Ethnicity & Autonomy in Iran after the Second World War. 256p. 1993. text 59.50 (*1-85043-640-1*, Pub. by I B T) St Martin.

***Atavavn, E., et al.** First Comes the Night: Mudhalil Iravu Varum. LC 98-908049. 140 p. 1998. write for info. (*81-260-0495-9*) S Asia.

At'ayan, R. A. Armenian Neume System of Notation: Study & Analysis. Nersessian, N. V., tr. (Illus.). 296p. 1997. 79.95 (*0-7007-0636-4*, Pub. by Curzon Pr Ltd) Paul & Co Pubs.

Atazawi, Amir. Active Antennas & Quasi-Optical Arrays. LC 98-7874. 1998. write for info. (*0-7803-3486-8*) IEEE Standards.

ATC Environmental Inc. Staff. Lead-Based Paint Hazards: Assessment & Management. Coluccio, Vincent M., ed. 320p. 1994. 74.95 (*0-471-28601-X*, VNR) Wiley.

— Lead-Based Paint Hazards: Assessment & Management. Coluccio, Vincent M., ed. (Illus.). 320p. 1994. text 60.95 (*0-442-01715-4*, VNR) Wiley.

Atcheson, Daniel. Roofing Construction & Estimating. (Illus.). 432p. (Orig.). 1995. pap. 35.00 (*1-57218-007-2*) Craftsman.

Atcheson, Daniel B. Earthmoving Equipment Rates & Costs: Rates & Costs. LC 93-83233. (Illus.). 489p. 1993. pap. 39.95 (*0-9613202-5-7*) Norseman Pub.

— Estimating Earthwork Quantities. 4th ed. LC 92-64349. (Illus.). 228p. 1992. pap. 39.95 (*0-9613202-1-4*) Norseman Pub.

Atcheson, George G. The Ol' Chef's Favorite Recipes. (Illus.). 130p. (Orig.). 1989. spiral bd. 9.75 (*0-9624683-0-4*) Tillamook Pub.

Atcheson, Wayne. Impact for Christ: How FCA Has Influenced the Sports World. 276p. (Orig.). (YA). (gr. 6 up). 1994. pap. 9.95 (*1-887002-09-X*) Cross Trng.

— In Due Time: The Struggles & Triumphs of Alabama Quarterback Jay Barker. 1995. pap. 10.95 (*0-9635413-7-4*) Birm News.

Atchia, Michael & Tropp, Shawna, eds. Environmental Management: Issues & Solutions. LC 94-35988. 268p. 1995. 180.00 (*0-471-95518-3*) Wiley.

Atchia, Paula. Mansfield Letters: A Sequel to Mansfield Park. 170p. 1996. 36.50 (*1-85776-118-9*, Pub. by Book Guild Ltd) Trans-Atl Phila.

***Atchinson, David & Smith, G.** Optics of the Human Eye. (Illus.). 288p. 2000. pap. 60.00 (*0-7506-3775-7*) Buttrwrth-Heinemann.

Atchinson, Diane P. Long Term Care Facility Policy & Procedure Manual. Johnson, Diana, ed. 427p. 1996. ring bd. 225.00 (*1-929162-01-4*, ltcM006) DPA Assocs.

— Medicare Policy & Procedure Manual. (Illus.). 487p. 1996. 225.00 (*1-929162-00-6*) DPA Assocs.

— Medicare Policy & Procedure Manual: For Long Term Care Facilities. 3rd rev. ed. Johnson, Diana, ed. 495p. 2000. ring bd. 225.00 (*1-929162-05-7*, MedP003) DPA Assocs.

— Medicare Policy & Procedure Manual for Long Term Care Facilities. 2nd ed. Johnson, Diana, ed. 427p. 1998. ring bd. 225.00 (*1-929162-02-2*) DPA Assocs.

— Restorative & Rehabilitation Programs: A Three Phase Approach with Application to Medicare PPS. Turrieta, Dorothy et al, eds. LC 99-90700. (Illus.). 181p. 1999. ring bd. 125.00 (*1-929162-03-0*, ResM005) DPA Assocs.

***Atchinson, Diane P. & Zehr, Debra.** Quality Indicator Resource Manual: Of the Kansas Association of Homes & Services for the Aging. 2nd ed. 441p. 2000. write for info. (*1-929162-04-9*) DPA Assocs.

Atchinson, R. The Botany of the Afghan Delimitation Commission. 139p. (C). 1983. 110.00 (*0-7855-3246-3*, Pub. by Scientific) St Mut.

Atchison, Ben, jt. auth. see Hansen, Ruth.

Atchison, Beth. Our New Baby. Ring, Laura, ed. LC 98-61294. (Happy Day Bks.). (Illus.). 24p. (J). (ps-2). 1999. pap. 1.99 (*0-7847-0894-0*, 04267) Standard Pub.

Atchison County Homemakers Staff, jt. auth. see Hurst, Vera Ellerman.

Atchison, David & Atchison, Elaine. Shaping the Next Generation. 240p. 1999. pap. 12.99 (*0-7852-6968-1*) Nelson.

Atchison, David A., jt. auth. see Smith, George.

Atchison, Elaine, jt. auth. see Atchison, David.

Atchison, James R. A Small Business Innovation Research (SBIR) Program Development Blueprint. LC 97-16574. 1997. lib. bdg. 49.00 (*1-56072-409-9*) Nova Sci Pubs.

Atchison, Jean. Linguistics. (Illus.). 240p. 1995. pap. 10.95 (*0-8442-3929-1*, Teach Yrslf) NTC Contemp Pub Co.

Atchison, Lee & Hewlett-Packard Company Staff. Object-Oriented Test & Measurement Software Development in C++ LC 96-219351. 352p. (C). 1996. pap. 59.00 (*0-13-227950-9*) P-H.

Atchison, Thomas A. Turning Health Care Leadership Around: Cultivating Inspired, Empowered, & Loyal Followers. LC 90-5192. (Health-Management Ser.). 183p. 1990. text 43.95 (*1-55542-295-0*) Jossey-Bass.

Atchity, Kenneth. The Classical Greek Reader: New Encounters with Ancient Greece. LC 96-10180. (Illus.). 416p. 1995. 37.50 (*0-8050-3947-3*) H Holt & Co.

— Classical Roman Reader: New Encounters with Ancient Rome. LC 96-49299. 1995. 37.50 (*0-8050-3950-3*) H Holt & Co.

— A Writer's Time: Making the Time to Write. 2nd rev. expanded ed. LC 94-15014. 260p. 1995. pap. 13.95 (*0-393-31263-1*) Norton.

— Writing Treatments That Sell: How to Create & Market Your Story Ideas to the Motion Picture Industry. LC 97-1534. 1995. pap. 14.95 (*0-8050-4283-0*, Owl) H Holt & Co.

Atchity, Kenneth, et al, eds. Homer. (Critical Essays Ser.). 256p. 1987. 49.00 (*0-8161-8832-7*, Hall Reference) Macmillan.

Atchity, Kenneth J., ed. The Classical Roman Reader: New Encounters with Ancient Rome. LC 98-29785. (Illus.). 480p. 1998. pap. 19.95 (*0-19-512740-4*) OUP.

— The Renaissance Reader. LC 95-26153. (Illus.). 400p. 1996. 35.00 (*0-06-270129-0*, Harper Ref) HarpC.

— The Renaissance Reader: First-Hand Encounters with the Renaissance. (Illus.). 400p. 1997. pap. 20.00 (*0-06-273503-9*, Harper Ref) HarpC.

Atchity, Kenneth J. & McKenna, Rosemary, eds. The Classical Greek Reader. LC 98-12978. (Illus.). 470p. 1998. reprint ed. pap. 19.95 (*0-19-512303-4*) OUP.

Atchity, Kenneth J., jt. ed. see Rimanelli, Giose.

Atchley. Aging: Continuity & Change. (Sociology - Introductory Level Ser.). 1983. pap. 15.00 (*0-534-01417-8*) Wadsworth Pub.

— Social Forces & Aging. 4th ed. (Sociology - Introductory Level Ser.). 1985. pap. write for info. (*0-534-04339-9*) Wadsworth Pub.
— Social Forces & Aging. 6th ed. (Sociology - Intro Level Ser.). 1991. pap., teacher ed. write for info. (*0-534-14671-6*) Wadsworth Pub.
— Social Forces & Aging. 7th ed. (Sociology-Upper Level Ser.). 1994. mass mkt., teacher ed. 22.75 (*0-534-18949-0*) Wadsworth Pub.
— Social Forces in Later Life. (Sociology - Introductory Level Ser.). 1972. pap. 9.75 (*0-534-00186-6*) Wadsworth Pub.
— Social Forces in Later Life. 2nd ed. (Sociology - Introductory Level Ser.). 1977. pap. 13.00 (*0-534-00463-6*) Wadsworth Pub.

***Atchley, Lisa A.** Medical Spanish Made Incredibly Easy. LC 00-33880. 2000. write for info. (*1-58255-040-9*) Springhouse Corp.

Atchley, Rick. Back to the Father: Sermons from Luke 15. 104p. (Orig.). 1994. pap. 6.95 (*1-56794-037-4*, C2299) Star Bible.
— Sinai Summit: Meeting God with Our Character Crisis. (Faith Focus Adult Studies). 1993. pap. 9.95 (*0-8344-0228-9*) Sweet Pub.
— What Men Need to Hear: Becoming God's Spiritual Leader Through Moral Strength. (Small Group Studies). 90p. 1999. pap. 6.99 (*0-89900-826-7*) College Pr Pub.

Atchley, Robert C. Continuity & Adaptation in Aging Creating Positive Experiences. LC 98-51019. 301p. 1999. 38.00 (*0-8018-6122-5*) Johns Hopkins.
— Social Forces & Aging: An Introduction to Social Gerontology 9th ed. LC 99-21215. 1999. 79.95 (*0-534-53343-4*) Wadsworth Pub.
— Social Forces & Aging: An Introduction to Social Gerontology. 4th ed. 510p. (C). 1984. pap. write for info. (*0-534-04338-0*) Wadsworth Pub.
— Social Forces & Aging: An Introduction to Social Gerontology. 5th ed. 527p. (C). 1987. pap. write for info. (*0-534-08790-6*) Wadsworth Pub.
— Social Forces & Aging: An Introduction to Social Gerontology. 6th ed. 578p. (C). 1990. pap. 42.95 (*0-534-14670-8*) Wadsworth Pub.
— Social Forces & Aging: An Introduction to Social Gerontology. 7th ed. 607p. 1993. mass mkt. 44.75 (*0-534-18948-2*) Wadsworth Pub.
— Social Forces & Aging: An Introduction to Social Gerontology. 8th ed. LC 96-9699. (Sociology Ser.). (C). 1996. pap. 50.50 (*0-534-50460-4*) Wadsworth Pub.

***Atchley, Sheila & Halley, Carol.** Fifty Ways to Please Your Lover: An Intimate Ecstasy Guide. 112p. 1999. 17.95 (*0-9677343-0-4*) S Atchley.

Atchley, Virginia G., intro. Japanese Lacquer from Southern California Collections. (Illus.). 34p. 1991. pap. 13.50 (*1-877921-06-8*) Pacific Asia.

Atchley, William R., et al. Bibliography & Keyword-in-Context Index of the Ceratopogonidae (Diptera) from Seventeen Fifty-Eight to Nineteen Seventy-Three. 300p. (Orig.). 1975. pap. 4.00 (*0-89672-052-7*) Tex Tech Univ Pr.

Atchley, William R., jt. auth. see Wirth, Willis W.

ATE Commission Staff. Restructuring the Education of Teachers: Commission on the Education of Teachers into the 21st Century. LC 90-28838. 1991. pap. 6.50 (*0-685-41083-8*) Assn Tchr Ed.

Ateek, Naim S. Justice, & Only Justice: A Palestinian Theology of Liberation. LC 89-30600. 208p. 1989. pap. 15.00 (*0-88344-545-X*, 545-X) Orbis Bks.

Ateek, Naim S., et al, eds. Faith & the Intifada: Palestinian Christian Voices. LC 91-44736. 223p. reprint ed. pap. 69.20 (*0-608-20187-1*, 207144600012) Bks Demand.

Aten, Erhart, jt. auth. see Stewart, William H.

Aten, Jerry. America: From Sea to Shining Sea. 160p. (J). (gr. 4 up). 1988. student ed. 12.99 (*0-86653-434-2*, GA1044) Good Apple.
— Americans, Too! 80p. (J). (gr. 4 up). 1982. 8.99 (*0-86653-099-1*, GA 444) Good Apple.
— Challenge Across America. 96p. (J). (gr. 4-8). 1990. 13.99 (*0-86653-556-X*, GA1157) Good Apple.
— Challenge Around the World. 96p. 1991. 13.99 (*0-86653-587-X*, GA1308) Good Apple.
— Challenge Through American History. (Illus.). 96p. (J). (gr. 4-8). 1992. 13.99 (*0-86653-659-0*, GA1391) Good Apple.
— Democracy for Young Americans. 112p. (J). (gr. 4-8). 1989. 12.99 (*0-86653-483-0*, GA1083) Good Apple.
— Fifty Nifty States. (Illus.). 320p. (J). (gr. 4 up). 1990. 21.99 (*0-86653-532-2*, GA1138) Good Apple.
— Good Apple & Math Fun. 144p. (J). (gr. 3-7). 1981. 13.99 (*0-86653-023-1*, GA 279) Good Apple.
— Maptime . . . U. S. A. 64p. (J). (gr. 4 up). 1982. 8.99 (*0-86653-093-2*, GA 422) Good Apple.
— Our Living Constitution - Then & Now. (Illus.). 168p. (YA). (gr. 5 up). 1986. student ed. 13.99 (*0-86653-386-9*, GA 1000) Good Apple.
— Presidents. (Illus.). 176p. (J). (gr. 4 up). 1985. student ed. 13.95 (*0-86653-281-1*, GA 627) Good Apple.
— Prime Time Life Skills. (Illus.). 64p. (J). (gr. 2-5). 1983. student ed. 8.99 (*0-86653-126-2*, GA 487) Good Apple.
— Prime Time Maps. (Illus.). 64p. (J). (gr. 2-5). 1983. student ed. 8.99 (*0-86653-108-4*, GA 470) Good Apple.
— Prime Time Math Skills. (Illus.). 64p. (J). (gr. 2-5). 1984. student ed. 7.99 (*0-86653-155-6*, GA 524) Good Apple.
— Prime Time Reading Skills. (Illus.). 64p. (J). (gr. 2-5). 1984. student ed. 8.99 (*0-86653-185-8*, GA 525) Good Apple.
— Understanding Our World Through Geography. 208p. (J). (gr. 4-8). 1991. 15.99 (*0-86653-592-6*, GA1309) Good Apple.
— Women in History. (Illus.). 144p. (J). (gr. 4 up). 1986. student ed. 13.99 (*0-86653-344-3*, GA 692) Good Apple.

Aten, Jerry G. Hooray for Columbus! 112p. teacher ed. 7.99 (*0-86653-603-5*, GA1344) Good Apple.
— Presidents. rev. ed. 176p. teacher ed. 14.99 (*0-86653-780-5*, GA1472) Good Apple.

Atencio, Paulette. Cuentos from Long Ago. LC 99-29204. 160p. 1999. pap. 13.95 (*0-8263-2064-3*) U of NM Pr.
— Cuentos from My Childhood: Legends & Folktales of Northern New Mexico. 174p. 1991. pap. 11.95 (*0-89013-226-7*) Museum NM Pr.

Atencio, Rosemarie. Shoulders, Upper Back & Neck: Free Yourself from Pain! LC 94-79485. (Illus.). 128p. (Orig.). 1995. pap. 17.95 (*0-9637360-9-4*) HWD Pub.

Atencio, Rosemarie A. Carpal Tunnel Syndrome: How to Relieve - Prevent Wrist "Burn Out" LC 93-79066. 128p. 1994. pap. 15.95 (*0-9637360-1-9*) HWD Pub.

Ater, Moshe. The Man Freud & Monotheism. 278p. pap. 19.00 (*965-223-808-2*) Gefen Bks.

Ates, Wayne. Loose Livers & Floatin Kidneys. 80p. 1997. pap. 8.00 (*0-8059-4111-8*) Dorrance.

Atget, Eugene, photos by. Paris. (Illus.). 80p. 1998. 19.95 (*3-8238-0363-8*) te Neues.

***Atget, Eugene & J. Paul Getty Museum Staff.** Eugene Atget: Photographs from the J. Paul Getty Museum. LC 00-22119. (In Focus Ser.). (Illus.). 144p. 2000. 17.50 (*0-89236-601-X*, J P Getty Museum) J P Getty Trust.

***Atha, Anthony.** Container Kitchen Garden. (Illus.). 2000. 24.95 (*1-85585-784-7*) Collins & Br.

Athale, Ravindra A., ed. Digital Optical Computing. (Critical Reviews of Optical Science & Technology Ser.: Vol. CR 35). 322p. 1990. 20.00 (*0-8194-0274-5*); pap. 20.00 (*0-8194-0255-9*) SPIE.

***Athan, Mattie S.** African Grey Parrot Handbook. LC 99-48374. (Pet Handbks.). 144p. 2000. pap. 9.95 (*0-7641-0993-6*) Barron.

Athan, Mattie S. Guide to a Well-Behaved Parrot. 144p. 1993. pap. 9.95 (*0-8120-4996-9*) Barron.

***Athan, Mattie S.** Guide to a Well-Behaved Parrot. 2nd ed. LC 99-13751. 176p. 1999. pap. 10.95 (*0-7641-1030-6*) Barron.
— Guide to Companion Parrot Behavior. LC 98-52812. (Illus.). 176p. 1999. pap. 11.95 (*0-7641-0688-0*) Barron.

Athan, Mattie S. Guide to the Quaker Parrot. LC 97-8730. 128p. 1997. pap. text 9.95 (*0-7641-0176-5*) Barron.

Athan, Mattie S. & Deter, Dianalee. Guide to the Senegal Parrot & Its Family. LC 97-48440. (Illus.). 96p. 1998. pap. 9.95 (*0-7641-0332-6*) Barron.

Athan, Polly. Felicity's Cookbook: A Peek at Dining in the Past with Meals You Can Cook Today. (American Girls Collection). (YA). (gr. 2 up). 1994. 11.15 (*0-606-08516-5*, Pub. by Turtleback) Demco.
— Molly's Cookbook: A Peek at Dining in the Past with Meals You Can Cook Today. Evert, Jodi & Thieme, Jeanne, eds. LC 94-17564. (American Girls Collection). (YA). (gr. 2 up). 1994. pap. text 5.95 (*1-56247-117-1*) Pleasant Co.
— Molly's Cookbook: A Peek at Dining in the Past with Meals You Can Cook Today. (American Girls Collection). (YA). (gr. 2 up). 1994. 11.15 (*0-606-08569-6*, Pub. by Turtleback) Demco.

Athan, Polly, et al. Samantha's Cookbook: A Peek at Dining in the Past with Meals You Can Cook Today. Evert, Jodi, ed. LC 94-12059. (American Girls Collection). (Illus.). 44p. (YA). (gr. 2 up). 1994. pap. text 5.95 (*1-56247-114-7*) Pleasant Co.

Athanas, Spiro. The Voice of the Titans: And Other Stories. (Illus.). 84p. (Orig.). 1996. pap. 7.95 (*0-9652078-0-3*) St Spyridon.

Athanas, Verne. Maverick. large type ed. LC 93-25507. 1993. pap. 15.95 (*0-8161-5838-X*, G K Hall Lrg Type) Mac Lib Ref.
— The Proud Ones. large type ed. 316p. 1975. 27.99 (*0-85456-340-7*) Ulverscroft.
— Pursuit: Western Stories. Tuska, Jon, ed. LC 99-41701. 1999. 19.95 (*0-7862-1842-8*) Mac Lib Ref.

***Athanas, Verne & Tuska, Jon.** Pursuit: Western Stories. LC 00-40779. 2000. write for info. (*0-7838-9134-2*, G K Hall & Co) Mac Lib Ref.

Athanasakis, Apostolos, tr. see Pagoulatou, Regina.

Athanasiadou, Angeliki & Dirven, Rene, eds. On Conditionals Again. LC 96-50283. (Current Issues in Linguistic Theory Ser.: Vol. 143). viii, 418p. 1997. lib. bdg. 94.00 (*1-55619-598-2*) J Benjamins Pubng Co.

Athanasiadou, Angeliki & Tabakowska, Elzbieta. Speaking of Emotions: Conceptualisation & Expression. LC 98-9761. (Cognitive Linguistics Research Ser.: No. 10). 444p. 1998. 111.00 (*3-11-015767-5*) De Gruyter.

Athanasiev, D., jt. auth. see Archpriest Michael Kheraskov.

Athanasiou. Orthodontic Cephalometry. 1995. 143.00 (*0-7234-2045-9*) Mosby Inc.

Athanasiou, Maria, ed. Light & Delicious. 66p. 1995. spiral bd. write for info. (*1-57502-020-3*, Cookbks by Morris) Morris Pubng.

Athanasiou, Tom. Divided Planet: The Ecology of Rich & Poor. LC 95-40684. 416p. 1996. 24.95 (*0-316-05635-9*) Little.
— Divided Planet: The Ecology of Rich & Poor. LC 97-30503. 1998. pap. 16.95 (*0-8203-2007-2*) U of Ga Pr.

Athanasius. Contra Gentes & de Incarnatione. Thomas, Robert W., ed. (Oxford Early Christian Texts Ser.). 1971. 59.00 (*0-19-826801-7*) OUP.
— The Life of St. Anthony the Great. 1991. pap. 3.95 (*0-89981-042-X*) Eastern Orthodox.
— On the Incarnation of the Word. 1990. pap. 2.95 (*0-89981-065-9*) Eastern Orthodox.
— Select Treatises of St. Athanasius in Controversy with the Arians, 2 vols., Set. 5th ed. Newman, John Henry, tr. LC 77-84694. (Heresies of the Early Christian & Medieval Era Ser.). reprint ed. 125.00 (*0-404-16100-6*) AMS Pr.

Athanasius, Saint. History of the Arians. 1993. pap. 6.95 (*0-89981-158-2*) Eastern Orthodox.

Athanasius The Great. St. Antony of the Desert. 105p. 1995. pap. 5.00 (*0-89555-525-5*) TAN Bks Pubs.

Athanason, Arthur. Endgame: A Cantation for Two Voices. (Masterwork Studies). 160p. 1993. 23.95 (*0-8057-9416-6*); pap. 13.95 (*0-8057-8576-0*) Macmillan.

Athanasopoulos, C. N. Corporate Productivity Atlas. 2nd ed. LC 82-150492. 220p. (C). 1983. pap. 30.00 (*0-916987-00-0*) Delphi Res.

Athanasopoulos, George. Byzantine Musical Anthology. LC 91-29330. 1989. 35.00 (*0-917651-88-X*, Pub. by Holy Cross Orthodox) BookWorld.

Athanasopoulos, I., et al. Free Boundary Problems: Theory & Applications LC 99-22939. (Chapman & Hall/CRC Research Notes in Mat). 368p. 1999. per. 79.95 (*1-58488-018-X*) CRC Pr.

Athanasopulos, Haralambos. Nuclear Disarmament in International Law. LC 99-53082. (Illus.). 237p. 2000. lib. bdg. 48.50 (*0-7864-0587-2*) McFarland & Co.

Athanasou, Nicholas. Colour Atlas of Bone, Joint & Soft Tissue Pathology. (Illus.). 248p. 1999. text 129.50 (*0-19-262792-9*) OUP.

Athanasoulis, C. A., et al, eds. Therapeutic Angiography. (Illus.). 128p. 1981. 40.95 (*0-387-10526-3*) Spr-Verlag.

Athanassakis, Apostolos N. Hesiod: Theogony, Works & Days. LC 83-6143. 184p. 1983. pap. 10.95 (*0-8018-2999-2*) Johns Hopkins.
— Ranka. LC 78-60634. 64p. 1978. pap. text 4.00 (*0-918618-14-2*) Pella Pub.

Athanassakis, Apostolos N., tr. from GRE. The Homeric Hymns. LC 75-40305. 128p. 1976. pap. 10.95 (*0-8018-1792-7*) Johns Hopkins.
— The Life of Pachomius: Vita Prima Graeca. LC 75-37766. (Society of Biblical Literature. Texts & Translations Ser.: No. 7). 213p. reprint ed. pap. 66.10 (*0-7837-5445-0*, 204521000005) Bks Demand.

Athanassakis, Apostolos N., tr. see Pagoulatou, Regina.

Athanassakis, Apostolos N., tr. see Ritsos, Yannis.

Athanassiadi, Polymnia. Damascius: The Philosophical History. 408p. 1999. pap. 45.00 (*960-85325-2-3*, Pub. by Apameia) David Brown.

***Athanassiadi, Polymnia & Frede, Michael, eds.** Pagan Monotheism in Late Antiquity. LC 98-37019. (Illus.). 220p. 1999. text 70.00 (*0-19-815252-3*) OUP.

Athanassoglou-Kallmyer, Nina M. Eugene Delacroix: Prints, Politics, & Satire. (Illus.). 160p. (C). 1991. 52.50 (*0-300-04931-5*) Yale U Pr.
— Eugene Delacroix: Prints, Politics, & Satire, 1814-1822. LC 90-49494. (Illus.). 167p. 1991. reprint ed. pap. 51.80 (*0-608-07879-4*, 205998600010) Bks Demand.
— French Images from the Greek War of Independence, 1821-1830. LC 88-27782. 188p. (C). 1989. 47.50 (*0-300-04532-8*) Yale U Pr.

Athanassopolou, Ekavi. Turkey: Anglo-American Security Interests, 1945-1952: The First Enlargement of NATO. LC 99-10622. (Illus.). 288p. 1999. 52.50 (*0-7146-4855-8*, Pub. by F Cass Pubs) Intl Spec Bk.

Athanassoula, E. Internal Kinematics & Dynamics of Galaxies. 1983. lib. bdg. 135.00 (*90-277-1546-7*) Kluwer Academic.

Athanassova, Theodora, tr. see Panayotova, Dora.

Athans, Mary C. The Coughlin-Fahey Connection: Father Denis Fahey, C. S. Sp., & Religious Anti-Semitism in the United States, 1938-1954. LC 91-3821. (American University Studies: Theology & Religion: Ser. VII, Vol. 102). 265p. 1992. 43.95 (*0-8204-1534-0*) P Lang Pubng.

Athans, Philip. Baldur's Gate. (Forgotten Realms Ser.). 1999. pap. 5.99 (*0-7869-1525-0*, Pub. by TSR Inc) Random.

***Athans, Philip.** Baldur's Gate II: Shadows of Amn. (Forgotten Realm's Ser.: Vol. II). (Illus.). 256p. 2000. mass mkt. 6.99 (*0-7869-1569-2*) TSR Inc.
— Realms of the Deep. (Forgotten Realms Anthology Ser.). (Illus.). 352p. 2000. mass mkt. 5.99 (*0-7869-1568-4*) TSR Inc.

Athar, Alia N. Hadith & Sira Literature in Western Languages. 470p. 1996. pap. 19.95 (*0-614-21083-5*, 366) Kazi Pubns.
— Muhammad, the Last Messenger, Pt. 1. 1990. 7.50 (*0-934905-05-3*) Kazi Pubns.
— Muhammad, the Last Messenger: Madinah Period, Pt. 2. 110p. 1991. 5.95 (*0-934905-06-1*) Kazi Pubns.
— Muhammad, the Last Prophet, Pt. 1. 1990. pap. 5.50 (*0-934905-03-7*) Kazi Pubns.
— Muhammad, the Last Prophet, Pt. 2. 1992. pap. 5.50 (*0-934905-04-5*) Kazi Pubns.
— Muhammad, the Last Prophet I Workbook. 32p. (J). (gr. 2-4). 1992. pap., student ed. 3.50 (*1-56744-209-9*) Kazi Pubns.
— Muhammad, the Last Prophet II Workbook. 32p. (J). (gr. 3-5). 1992. pap. 3.50 (*1-56744-210-2*) Kazi Pubns.
— Prophets: Models for Humanity. 240p. (YA). 1993. pap. 14.50 (*1-56744-425-3*) Kazi Pubns.

Athar, Alia N., jt. auth. see Anees, Munawar A.

Athar, M. & Vohora, S. B. Heavy Metals & Environment. (Man & Environment Ser.). 1995. write for info. (*81-224-0769-2*, Pub. by Wiley Estrn) Franklin.

Athar, Shahid. Health Concerns of Muslims. 102p. (Orig.). 1995. pap. 9.95 (*0-934905-29-0*) Kazi Pubns.
— Reflections of an American Muslim. 256p. (Orig.). 1994. pap. 14.95 (*0-934905-26-6*) Kazi Pubns.

***Athar, Shahid.** Reflections of Love. 1999. pap. write for info. (*1-58235-309-3*) Watermrk Pr.

Athar, Shahid, ed. Islamic Perspectives in Medicine: A Survey of Islamic Medicine: Achievements & Contemporary Issues. 220p. 1996. pap. 14.95 (*0-614-21551-X*, 643) Kazi Pubns.
— Sex Education: An Islamic Perspective. 102p. (Orig.). 1995. pap. 12.50 (*0-934905-30-4*) Kazi Pubns.

Athas, Daphne. Crumbs for the Bogeyman. 46p. Date not set. pap. 8.95 (*0-932662-97-8*) St Andrews NC.

— Entering Ephesus. LC 89-62517. 440p. 1991. pap. 19.95 (*0-933256-79-5*) Second Chance.
— Entering Ephesus. LC 89-62517. 440p. 1991. reprint ed. 24.95 (*0-933256-73-6*) Second Chance.

Athawale, Sanhita. India's Indian Ocean Islands. (C). 1991. text 14.00 (*81-7123-051-2*) S Asia.

Athawes, Peter D., ed. Yeomanry Wars: History of the Yeomanry - A Civilian Tradition from 1794. 320p. 1990. 35.00 (*1-898218-02-1*) St Mut.

Athay, Lawrence, jt. auth. see Athay, Sherri.

Athay, Lawrence D., jt. auth. see Athay, Sherri L.

Athay, P., et al, eds. Philosopher's Annual, 1986, Vol. IX. vi, 253p. (Orig.). 1988. pap. text 10.00 (*0-917930-71-1*); lib. bdg. 32.00 (*0-917930-91-6*) Ridgeview.
— The Philosopher's Annual, 1983, Vol. VI. xi, 171p. (Orig.). 1985. pap. text 10.00 (*0-917930-68-1*); lib. bdg. 32.00 (*0-917930-82-7*) Ridgeview.

Athay, R. G. Radiation Transport in Spectral Lines. LC 72-188002. (Geophysics & Astrophysics Monographs: No. 1). 266p. 1972. pap. text 73.50 (*90-277-0241-1*); lib. bdg. 104.50 (*90-277-0228-4*) Kluwer Academic.
— The Solar Chromosphere & Corona: Quiet Sun. LC 75-33385. (Astrophysics & Space Science Library: No. 53). 540p. 1975. lib. bdg. 206.50 (*90-277-0244-6*) Kluwer Academic.

Athay, R. G., ed. see International Astronomical Union Staff.

Athay, Sherri & Athay, Lawrence. Present Perfect: Unforgettable Gifts for Every Occasion. 2nd rev. ed. (Illus.). 1998. pap. 15.00 (*0-9650617-4-4*) Mobius UT.

Athay, Sherri L. & Athay, Lawrence D. Present Perfect: The Essential Guide to Gift Giving. Black, Kristen V., ed. (Illus.). (Orig.). 1996. pap. 12.95 (*0-9650617-0-1*) Mobius UT.

Athayde Veiga, Maria Odete, tr. see Veiga, Jose Carlos.

Athearn, Daniel. Scientific Nihilism: On the Loss & Recovery of Physical Explanation. LC 93-12869. (SUNY Series in Philosophy). 387p. (C). 1994. text 64.50 (*0-7914-1807-3*); pap. text 21.95 (*0-7914-1808-1*) State U NY Pr.

Athearn, Edwin B. Chronicle of An Islander. (Illus.). 192p. 1996. pap. 14.95 (*1-883154-01-4*) E B Athearn.
— Origin of the Vineyard Black Dog. (Illus.). 1993. pap. 3.50 (*1-883154-00-6*) E B Athearn.

Athearn, James L. Risk & Insurance. 6th ed. Date not set. text 63.00 (*0-314-64063-0*); pap. text, teacher ed. write for info. (*0-314-65224-8*) West Pub.

Athearn, Robert G. The Denver & Rio Grande Western Railroad: Rebel of the Rockies. LC 76-30296. (Illus.). xv, 395p. 1977. pap. 17.95 (*0-8032-5861-5*, Bison Books) U of Nebr Pr.
— Forts of the Upper Missouri. LC 67-24466. (Bison Bk.). 351p. reprint ed. pap. 108.90 (*0-608-16214-0*, 202714700054) Bks Demand.
— High Country Empire: The High Plains & Rockies. LC 60-8822. (Bison Bk.: No. BB 314). (Illus.). 384p. reprint ed. pap. 119.10 (*0-8357-3180-4*, 203944500012) Bks Demand.
— The Mythic West in Twentieth-Century America. LC 86-11106. (Illus.). xii, 324p. 1986. 35.00 (*0-7006-0304-2*); pap. 14.95 (*0-7006-0377-8*) U Pr of KS.
— Thomas Francis Meagher: An Irish Revolutionary in America. LC 76-6321. (Irish Americans Ser.). (Illus.). 1976. reprint ed. 18.95 (*0-405-09318-7*) Ayer.
— Union Pacific Country. LC 75-11707. (Illus.). 480p. 1976. reprint ed. pap. 148.80 (*0-608-03987-X*, 206471900010) Bks Demand.
— William Tecumseh Sherman & the Settlement of the West. LC 95-11480. (Illus.). 400p. 1995. 17.95 (*0-8061-2769-4*) U of Okla Pr.

Atheling, William, Jr. The Issue at Hand. LC 65-2533. 164p. 1964. 15.00 (*0-911682-09-0*) Advent.
— The Issue at Hand. LC 65-2533. 164p. 1967. pap. 8.00 (*0-911682-17-1*) Advent.
— More Issues at Hand. LC 72-115400. 160p. 1970. 15.00 (*0-911682-10-4*) Advent.
— More Issues at Hand. LC 72-115400. 160p. 1972. pap. 8.00 (*0-911682-18-X*) Advent.

Athelstan, Gary T., jt. auth. see Crewe, Nancy M.

Athena Group, Inc. Staff, jt. auth. see Taylor, Fred.

Athena Nga Chee Liu. Artificial Reproduction & Reproductive Rights. 223p. 1991. text 74.95 (*1-85521-022-3*, Pub. by Dartmth Pub) Ashgate Pub Co.

Athenadorus. Aryan Jehovah: The Indo-European Origin of Hebraeo-Christianism. LC 96-86078. 225p. 1996. pap. 34.95 (*1-890000-05-1*, 001-0710-021404) Danaan Pr.
— The Athenadoran Library. LC 94-69509. 212p. 1996. pap. 24.95 (*1-890000-00-0*, 001-0410-021010) Danaan Pr.
— The Danaa: The Book of the Nicoleos Athenadorus to the People of Athena. LC 96-86089. 54p. 1996. pap. 14.95 (*1-890000-01-9*, 001-0110-021103) Danaan Pr.
— Epistvlae - Phaedranae: The Phaedran Letters of Athenadorus. LC 96-86084. 55p. 1996. pap. 14.95 (*1-890000-02-7*, 001-0210-021111) Danaan Pr.
— The Latogeneia: The Poetry of Athenadorus. LC 96-86551. 75p. 1996. pap. 14.95 (*1-890000-04-3*, 001-0510-021208) Danaan Pr.
— Ta Men Tao: The Tao of Athenadorus. LC 96-86081. 89p. 1996. pap. 14.95 (*1-890000-03-5*, 001-0310-021200) Danaan Pr.

Athenaeum of Philadelphia Staff. Catalog of Architectural Drawings: The Athenaeum of Philadelphia. (G. K. Hall Library Catalogs Ser.). 1430p. (C). 1986. 375.00 (*0-8161-0448-4*, G K Hall & Co) Mac Lib Ref.

Athenaeum Staff. Bibliographic Dictionary of Philadelphia Architects, 1700 to 1930. 1989. 125.00 (*0-8161-1561-3*, G K Hall & Co) Mac Lib Ref.

Athenagoras. Legatio & De Resurrectione. Schoedel, William R., ed. (Oxford Early Christian Texts Ser.). 1972. 45.00 (*0-19-826808-4*) OUP.

A

A

Atheniensis, Apollodorus. Apollodori Atheniensis Bibliothecae Libri Tres et Fragmenta. (Illus.). lvi, 468p. 1972. reprint ed. 120.00 (*3-487-04299-1*) G Olms Pubs.
Athens Avenue Poetry Circle Staff. A Year on the Avenue: A Collection of Poems. (Illus.). 160p. 1997. pap. 8.95 (*1-891090-00-3*) Two Dog Pr.
Athens, Lonnie H. The Creation of Dangerous Violent Criminals. 120p. (C). 1992. text 22.95 (*0-252-01939-3*); pap. text 11.95 (*0-252-06262-0*) U of Ill Pr.
— The Creation of Violent Criminals. 128p. 1989. 29.95 (*0-415-02837-X*) Routledge.
— Violent Criminal Acts & Actors Revisited. LC 96-25235. 192p. 1997. text 24.95 (*0-252-02306-4*); pap. text 14.95 (*0-252-06608-1*) U of Ill Pr.
Athens, Tami & Ulysse, Clark. Everyday Entrepreneurs: Profitable Advice from Genuine Entrepreneurs. LC 98-92906. (Illus.). 136p. (Orig.). 1998. pap. 22.95 (*0-9664352-0-6*) C Ulysse Prodns.
Atheosen, Curt, et al. Teaching about the Last Things. Rinden, David, ed. 9p. 1997. pap. 1.00 (*0-943167-41-8*) Faith & Fellowship Pr.
Atherden, Margaret. Upland Britain: A Natural History. (Illus.). 240p. (C). 1993. pap. text 29.95 (*0-7190-3494-9*, Pub. by Manchester Univ Pr) St Martin.
Atherlay, Sara. Math in a Bath & in Other Fun Places, Too: Everywhere, Everyday Math Concept Book. LC 94-30264. (Illus.). (J). (ps-3). 1995. 15.95 (*0-02-707601-6*) Macmillan.
— Math in the Bath: And Other Fun Places Too! LC 94-30264. (Illus.). 32p. (J). (ps-1). 1995. 12.00 (*0-689-80318-4*) S&S Bks Yung.
Atherly, Alan. The Science of Genetics. LC 98-85629. 800p. (C). 1998. text 93.00 (*0-03-033222-2*, Pub. by SCP) Harcourt.
Atherly, Alan, et al. Instructor's Manual & Test Bank to Accompany The Science of Genetics. 184p. (C). 1999. pap., teacher ed. 31.50 (*0-03-005773-6*) SCP.
Atherly, Alan G., et al. Student Solutions Manual to Accompany the Science of Genetics. 288p. (C). 1999. student ed. 11.25 (*0-03-097649-9*, Pub. by SCP) Harcourt.
Atherly, Mary E. The Farm House: College Farm to University Museum. (Illus.). 192p. 1995. 24.95 (*0-8138-2111-8*) Iowa St U Pr.
Atherosclerosis Reviews Staff. Atherosclerosis Reviews, Vol. 4. fac. ed. Paoletti, Rudolfo & Gotto, Antonio M., Jr., eds. LC 76-640124. (Illus.). 277p. pap. 85.90 (*0-7837-7173-8*, 204712500004) Bks Demand.
— Atherosclerosis Reviews: Measurement & Control of Cardiovascular Risk Factors, Vol. 7. fac. ed. LC 76-640124. (Illus.). 352p. pap. 102.20 (*0-7837-7172-X*, 2047125) Bks Demand.
— Atherosclerosis Reviews Vol. 3. Paoletti, Rodolfo & Gotto, Antonio M., Jr., eds. LC 76-640124. (Illus.). 279p. pap. 86.50 (*0-7837-7174-6*, 204712500003) Bks Demand.
— Atherosclerosis Reviews Vol. 14: 1987. LC 76-640124. 233p. reprint ed. pap. 72.30 (*0-7837-7118-5*, 204694700004) Bks Demand.
Atherton. Science Around You, Bk. 3. 1992. pap. text. write for info. (*0-582-87554-4*, Pub. by Addison-Wesley) Longman.
Atherton, Catherine. The Stoics on Ambiguity. LC 92-2469. (Cambridge Classical Studies). 583p. (C). 1993. text 95.00 (*0-521-44139-0*) Cambridge U Pr.
Atherton, Celia, jt. auth. see Manthorpe, Jill.
Atherton, Cynthia P. The Sculpture of Early Medieval Rajasthan. LC 97-5133. (Studies in South Asian Culture: No. 21). (Illus.). xiv, 238p. 1997. 88.50 (*90-04-10789-4*, NLG 143) Brill Academic Pubs.
Atherton, D. P., jt. auth. see Linkens, Derek A.
Atherton, David J. Eczema in Childhood: The Facts. (Facts Ser.). (Illus.). 274p. 1994. pap. text 19.95 (*0-19-262398-2*) OUP.
Atherton, Derek P. Stability of Nonlinear Systems. LC 80-40947. (Control Theory & Applications Studies: No. 1). (Illus.). 243p. reprint ed. pap. 75.40 (*0-8357-4552-X*, 203745100008) Bks Demand.
Atherton, Derek P. & Borne, Pierre, eds. Concise Encyclopedia of Modelling & Simulation. (Advances in Systems Control & Information Engineering Ser.: No. 5). 554p. 1991. 263.75 (*0-08-036201-X*, Pergamon Pr) Elsevier.
Atherton, Gertrude. Adventures of a Novelist. 1992. reprint ed. lib. bdg. 75.00 (*0-7812-5001-3*) Rprt Serv.
— California, an Intimate History. 1992. reprint ed. lib. bdg. 75.00 (*0-7812-5002-1*) Rprt Serv.
Atherton, Gertrude F. Adventures of a Novelist. Baxter, Annette K., ed. LC 79-8769. (Signal Lives Ser.). 1980. reprint ed. lib. bdg. 68.95 (*0-405-12819-3*) Ayer.
— The Aristocrats. LC 68-20003. (Americans in Fiction Ser.). reprint ed. pap. text 4.95 (*0-89197-661-2*); reprint ed. lib. bdg. 17.00 (*0-8398-0062-2*) Irvington.
— The Bell in the Fog & Other Stories. 1972. reprint ed. 31.00 (*0-8422-8003-0*) Irvington.
— Black Oxen. (BCL1-PS American Literature Ser.). 346p. 1992. reprint ed. lib. bdg. 89.00 (*0-7812-6670-X*) Rprt Serv.
— California: An Intimate History. rev. ed. LC 74-152969. (Select Bibliographies Reprint Ser.). 1977. reprint ed. 31.95 (*0-8369-5721-0*) Ayer.
— The Californians. LC 68-23712. (Americans in Fiction Ser.). reprint ed. pap. text 9.95 (*0-89197-689-2*); reprint ed. lib. bdg. 19.00 (*0-8398-0063-0*) Irvington.
— Can Women Be Gentlemen? LC 70-117754. (Essay Index Reprint Ser.). 1977. reprint ed. 20.95 (*0-8369-1692-1*) Ayer.
— Los Cerritos. LC 68-23711. (Americans in Fiction Ser.). 1977. reprint ed. pap. text 8.50 (*0-89197-695-7*); reprint ed. lib. bdg. 20.50 (*0-8398-0065-7*) Irvington.
— The Conqueror. 32.95 (*0-88411-588-7*) Amereon Ltd.
— Conqueror: Dramatized Biography of Alexander Hamilton. (BCL1-PS American Literature Ser.). 536p. 1993. reprint ed. lib. bdg. 129.00 (*0-7812-6946-6*) Rprt Serv.
— The Doomswoman. 375p. 1977. reprint ed. lib. bdg. 15.50 (*0-89966-281-1*) Buccaneer Bks.
— The Doomswoman: An Historical Romance of Old California. LC 71-104406. reprint ed. lib. bdg. 17.00 (*0-8398-0064-9*) Irvington.
— The Doomswoman: An Historical Romance of Old California. 1987. reprint ed. pap. text 7.95 (*0-8290-2103-5*) Irvington.
— Foghorn. LC 78-116928. (Short Story Index Reprint Ser.). 1977. 20.95 (*0-8369-3430-X*) Ayer.
— Patience Sparhawk & Her Times. LC 75-104407. 488p. reprint ed. lib. bdg. 32.50 (*0-8398-0066-5*) Irvington.
— Patience Sparhawk & Her Times. (C). 1986. reprint ed. pap. text 8.95 (*0-8290-1867-0*) Irvington.
— Rezanov. LC 78-96873. (Illus.). 320p. reprint ed. lib. bdg. 32.00 (*0-8398-0067-3*) Irvington.
— Rezanov. (Illus.). 320p. 1986. reprint ed. pap. text 6.95 (*0-8290-1924-3*) Irvington.
— Senator North. LC 67-29258. (Americans in Fiction Ser.). 367p. reprint ed. lib. bdg. 32.00 (*0-8398-0068-1*) Irvington.
— Senator North. (Americans in Fiction Ser.). 367p. 1986. reprint ed. pap. text 7.95 (*0-8290-2021-7*) Irvington.
— The Splendid Idle Forties. LC 68-20004. (Americans in Fiction Ser.). (Illus.). reprint ed. pap. text 7.95 (*0-89197-947-6*); reprint ed. lib. bdg. 22.50 (*0-8398-0069-X*) Irvington.
***Atherton, Gertrude Franklin.** The Californians. 252p. 2000. pap. 9.95 (*0-594-03820-0*) Eightn Hundrd.
— The Conqueror. 252p. 2000. pap. 9.95 (*0-594-00468-3*) Eightn Hundrd.
— Dormant Fires. 252p. 2000. pap. 9.95 (*0-594-00045-9*) Eightn Hundrd.
— Rezanov. 252p. 2000. pap. 9.95 (*0-594-03580-5*) Eightn Hundrd.
— Senator North. 252p. 2000. pap. 9.95 (*0-594-00123-4*) Eightn Hundrd.
— The Valiant Runaways. 252p. 2000. pap. 9.95 (*0-594-00420-9*) Eightn Hundrd.
***Atherton, Ian, contrib. by.** Ambition & Failure in Stuart England: The Career of John, 1st Viscount Scudamore. LC 99-41573. (Politics, Culture & Society in Early Modern Britain Ser.). 1999. 79.95 (*0-7190-5091-X*, Pub. by Manchester Univ Pr) St Martin.
Atherton, Ian, et al, eds. Norwich Cathedral: Church, City, & Diocese, 1096-1996. LC 95-49426. 1996. 60.00 (*1-85285-134-1*) Hambledon Press.
Atherton, J. G., et al. ICTV Code for the Description of Virus Characters. (Monographs in Virology: Vol. 14). vi, 154p. 1983. 85.25 (*3-8055-3769-7*) S Karger.
Atherton, J. P., ed. see Aristotle.
Atherton, James S. The Books at the Wake: A Study of Literary Allusions in James Joyce's "Finnegans Wake" rev. ed. LC 74-5407. 314p. 20.00 (*0-911858-26-1*) Appel.
— Interpreting Residential Life: Values to Practise. 208p. 1989. 39.50 (*0-415-00814-X*, A3496) Routledge.
Atherton, Jeffrey. Black-Letter: An Interpretation of Events Relating to the Time & Presence of Johann Gutenberg. (Illus.). 45p. 2000. 1500.00 (*0-931460-29-8*) Bieler.
Atherton, John. Faith in the Nation: A Christian Vision for Britain LC 88-189357. vii, 150p. 1988. write for info. (*0-281-04320-5*) Society Prom Christ Know.
***Atherton, John.** Imperial Steel: The History of the Isthmian Steamship Company: 1910-1956. LC 00-190401. 2000. 25.00 (*0-7388-1641-8*); pap. 18.00 (*0-7388-1642-6*) Xlibris Corp.
Atherton, John, ed. Christian Social Ethics: A Reader. LC 94-6913. 424p. (Orig.). 1994. pap. 24.95 (*0-8298-0999-6*) Pilgrim OH.
Atherton, Larry. DeskTop Dynos: Using Computers to Build & Test Engines. (Illus.). 112p. (Orig.). 1996. pap. 39.95 incl. disk (*1-884089-23-2*, S-A Design) CarTech.
Atherton, Lewis. The Cattle Kings. LC 61-13722. (Illus.). xii, 342p. 1972. reprint ed. pap. text 9.95 (*0-8032-5759-7*, Bison Books) U of Nebr Pr.
Atherton, Linda F. & Atherton, Robert W. Wafer Fabrication: Performance & Analysis. LC 95-40381. (Kluwer International Series in Engineering & Computer Science: SECS 339). 488p. (C). 1995. text 159.50 (*0-7923-9619-7*) Kluwer Academic.
***Atherton, Louise.** Never Complain, Never Explain. 1999. 16.00 (*1-873162-13-8*, Pub. by PRO Pubns) Midpt Trade.
Atherton, M. A. & Lawrence, James K. An Experimental Introduction to Reaction Kinetics. LC 72-575245. (Longman Concepts in Chemistry Ser.). 176p. reprint ed. pap. 54.60 (*0-608-18551-5*, 200455600043) Bks Demand.
Atherton, M. A., jt. ed. see Collins, M. W.
Atherton, Margaret. Berkeley's Revolution in Vision. LC 89-49632. (Illus.). 264p. 1990. text 39.95 (*0-8014-2358-9*) Cornell U Pr.
— Women Philosophers of the Early Modern Period. LC 94-27004. 176p. (C). 1994. pap. text 7.95 (*0-87220-259-3*); lib. bdg. 29.95 (*0-87220-260-7*) Hackett Pub.
Atherton, Margaret, ed. The Empiricists: Critical Essays on Locke, Berkeley, & Hume. LC 98-39077. (Critical Essays on the Classics Ser.). 240p. 1998. 45.00 (*0-8476-8912-3*); pap. 17.95 (*0-8476-8913-1*) Rowman.
Atherton, Mary K., et al. Touch with Your Eyes! (Illus.). 48p. (Orig.). (J). (gr. k-8). 1982. pap. 4.50 (*0-9613069-0-4*) Orinda Art Coun.
Atherton, Michael. Australian Made...Australian Played. 1990. 48.95 (*0-86840-323-7*, Pub. by New South Wales Univ Pr) Intl Spec Bk.
Atherton, Mike. A Test of Cricket: Know the Game. (Illus.). 144p. 1995. text 40.00 (*0-340-63775-7*, Pub. by Hodder & Stought Ltd) Trafalgar.
Atherton, N. M., et al. Electron Spin Resonance, Vol. 14. (Specialist Periodical Reports). 320p. 1994. 263.00 (*0-85186-921-1*, R6921) CRC Pr.
Atherton, Nancy. Aunt Dimity & the Duke. 304p. 1995. pap. 6.99 (*0-14-017841-4*, Penguin Bks) Viking Penguin.
***Atherton, Nancy.** Aunt Dimity Beats the Devil. (Illus.). 224p. (J). 2000. 22.95 (*0-670-89179-7*, Viking) Viking Penguin.
Atherton, Nancy. Aunt Dimity Digs In. LC 97-34633. 288p. 1998. 21.95 (*0-670-87061-7*) Viking Penguin.
— Aunt Dimity Digs In. 288p. 1999. pap. 5.99 (*0-14-027569-X*) Viking Penguin.
***Atherton, Nancy.** Aunt Dimity's Christmas. (Illus.). 2000. pap. 5.99 (*0-14-029630-1*) Penguin Putnam.
— Aunt Dimity's Christmas. LC 99-36750. 224p. 1999. 22.95 (*0-670-88453-7*, Viking) Viking Penguin.
— Aunt Dimity's Christmas. large type ed. LC 99-58606. (Mystery Ser.). 2000. 24.95 (*1-57490-260-1*, Beeler LP Bks) T T Beeler.
Atherton, Nancy. Aunt Dimity's Death. 256p. 1993. reprint ed. pap. 5.99 (*0-14-017840-6*, Penguin Bks) Viking Penguin.
— Aunt Dimity's Good Deed. 1998. pap. 5.99 (*0-14-025881-7*) Viking Penguin.
***Atherton, Philip, et al, eds.** International Commission for Uniform Methods of Sugar Analysis (ICUMSA) Report of the Proceedings of the 22nd Session Held in Berlin 25-29 May 1998. 396p. 2000. write for info. (*0-905003-17-9*, Pub. by ICUMSA) Intl Media Grp.
Atherton, R. F. & Vines, P. Australian Succession Law: Commentary & Materials. 1000p. 1996. write for info. (*0-409-30306-2*, MICHIE) LEXIS Pub.
Atherton, Robert W., jt. auth. see Atherton, Linda F.
Atherton, Stan. Martha Ostenso & Her Works. (Canadian Author Studies). 43p. (C). 1990. pap. 9.95 (*1-55022-053-5*, Pub. by ECW) Genl Dist Srvs.
Atherton, W. A. From Compass to Computer: A History of Electrical & Electronics Engineering. (Illus.). 1983. 20.00 (*0-911302-48-4*) San Francisco Pr.
Athey, C. E. Athey. Genealogy of the Athey Family in America, 1642-1932. (Illus.). 95p. 1997. reprint ed. pap. 17.50 (*0-8328-7301-2*); reprint ed. lib. bdg. 27.50 (*0-8328-7300-4*) Higginson Bk Co.
***Athey, David.** Hunting & Gathering Heaven. 84p. 2000. pap. 12.00 (*0-944920-37-3*) Bellowing Ark Pr.
Athey, Jackie, jt. auth. see Meintjes, Ria.
Athey, Jackie, ed. see Smuts, Margie.
***Athey, Jean L., et al.** Building the Future: The Maternal & Child Health Training Program. LC 00-131028. (Illus.). 88p. 2000. pap. write for info. (*1-57285-062-0*) Nat Ctr Educ.
Athey, Jean L., jt. auth. see Freely, Herta B.
Athey, Jean L., jt. ed. see Ahearn, Frederick L., Jr.
Athey, Julie. Defusing the Overtime Bomb: How to Comply with the FLSA. LC 99-18926. 80p. 1999. spiral bd. 47.00 (*0-925773-48-4*) M Lee Smith.
Athey, Julie, ed. see Adkerson, Michelle.
Athey, Kathleen, jt. auth. see Ewen, Ann J.
Athey, Linda S. Southland Firestorms: October, 1993 Fires. Guyette, Ronda, ed. 150p. (Orig.). 1994. pap. write for info. (*1-885612-00-1*) Significant Events.
Athey, Lois, tr. see Partnoy, Alicia.
Athey, Margaret & Hotchkiss, Gwen. A Galaxy of Games for the Music Class. LC 75-4889. 216p. (C). 1975. text 24.95 (*0-13-346064-9*, Parker Publishing Co) P-H.
Athey, Miles. The Great Cause. 190p. 1991. pap. 9.95 (*1-880144-44-1*) Arrowmist.
Athey, Raymond, jt. auth. see Browne, Edward T., Jr.
Athey, Robert D., Jr. Emulsion Polymer Technology. 2nd ed. (Plastics Engineering Ser.: Vol. 22). (Illus.). 296p. 1991. text 170.00 (*0-8247-7850-2*) Dekker.
***Athey, Robert Leland.** The Retreads. LC 00-190196. 355p. 2000. pap. 18.00 (*0-7388-1582-9*) Xlibris Corp.
— The Retreads: June 25, 1950 - The Korean War - July 27, 1953. LC 00-190196. 355p. 2000. 25.00 (*0-7388-1581-0*) Xlibris Corp.
Athey, Thomas H. Systematic Systems Approach: An Integrated Method for Solving Systems Problems. (Illus.). 416p. (C). 1982. text 47.00 (*0-13-880914-3*) P-H.
Athey, Virginia. Zonkey, the Donkey. (Illus.). 20p. (J). (ps-2). 1993. pap. 6.50 (*0-922510-10-5*) Lucky Bks.
Athey, Virginia, jt. auth. see Kaster, Bonnie.
Athickal, Joseph. Maram Nagas: A Socio-Cultural Study. (C). 1992. 28.00 (*81-7099-354-7*, Pub. by Mittal Pubs Dist) S Asia.
***Athie, Mohamed Nacir.** Second Guess. v, 120p. 2000. pap. write for info. (*0-9702335-0-7*) Athie Friend.
Athill, Diana. After a Funeral. 176p. 1986. 15.45 (*0-89919-454-0*, Pub. by Ticknor & Fields) HM.
Athill, Diana. Make Believe: A True Story. LC 93-47421. 130p. 1994. 18.00 (*1-883642-21-3*) Steerforth Pr.
Athkins, D. E. The Ripper. 176p. (YA). (gr. 7-9). 1992. 3.25 (*0-590-45349-1*, Point) Scholastic Inc.
Athnassakis, Apostolos N., tr. see Antony of Choziba.
Athnassakis, Apostolos N., jt. tr. see Vivian, Tim.
Atholl, Katherine. Conscription of a People. LC 73-161703. reprint ed. 20.00 (*0-404-00414-8*) AMS Pr.
Athology Reprints Staff. Deadly Waters: The Great Flood of '94. Elgison, Howard & Reeves, Betsy, eds. (Illus.). 100p. 1994. pap. 12.95 (*1-882526-03-1*) BD Pub.
Athos, Petrou, jt. auth. see Gasparini, Francisco.
Athreya, K. B. & Ney, P. E. Branching Processes. LC 72-75819. (Grundlehren der Mathematischen Wissenschaften Ser.: Vol. 196). 300p. 1972. 59.00 (*0-387-05790-0*) Spr-Verlag.
Athreya, Krishna B. & Jagers, Peter, eds. Classical & Modern Branching Processes. LC 96-38165. (IMA Volumes in Mathematics & Its Applications). 356p. 1996. 59.95 (*0-387-94872-4*) Spr-Verlag.
Athreya, Venkatesh B. & Chunkath, Sheela R. Literacy & Empowerment. LC 96-28843. 1996. 38.00 (*0-8039-9337-4*) Sage.
Athreya, Venkatesh B., et al. Barriers Broken: Production Relations & Agrarian Change in Tamil Nadu. (Illus.). 336p. (C). 1990. 32.50 (*0-8039-9639-X*) Sage.
— Literacy & Empowerment. LC 96-28843. 290p. (C). 1997. 38.00 (*0-8039-9336-6*, 93366) Sage.
ATHS Members Staff. Bible Records. 150p. 1987. pap. 16.00 (*1-889221-00-7*) Ancestral Trails.
— Kentucky Ancestor Charts. 550p. 1987. 43.00 (*1-889221-23-6*) Ancestral Trails.
Athukorala, Karunatissa, jt. auth. see Silva, Kalinga T.
Athukorala, Prema-Chandra & Manning, Chris. Structural Change & International Labour Migration in East Asia. 272p. 2000. text 65.00 (*0-19-554173-1*) OUP.
***Athukorala, Prema-Chandra & Rajapatirana, Sarath.** Liberalization & Industrial Transformation: Sri Lanka in International Perspective. 280p. 2000. text 26.95 (*0-19-565179-0*) OUP.
Athukorala, Premachandra & Jayasuriya, Sisira. Macroeconomics Policies, Crises & Growth in Sri Lanka, 1969-90. LC 94-31612. (Comparative Macroeconomic Studies). 192p. 1994. pap. 22.00 (*0-8213-2297-4*, 12297) World Bank.
Athukoralge, Premachandra. Trade Policy Issues in Asian Development. LC 98-6012. (Studies in the Growth Economies of Asia Ser.). (Illus.). 352p. (C). 1998. 90.00 (*0-415-16927-5*) Routledge.
***Athukoralge, Premachandra, et al.** Growth Employment & Migration in Southeast Asia: Structural Change in the Greater Mekong Countries. LC 99-51515. 160p. 1999. 70.00 (*1-84064-271-8*) E Elgar.
Ati. The Book of Hope: Testament of a Master Guide. Murray, Bob & Fortinberry, Alicia, eds. 256p. (Orig.). 1995. pap. 11.95 (*1-885610-09-2*) European Amer.
— Healing. Murray, Bob & Fortinberry, Alicia, eds. 256p. (Orig.). 1995. pap. 11.95 (*1-885610-00-9*) European Amer.
— Seven Steps to Home: Coming to Internal Harmony. Murray, Bob & Fortinberry, Alicia, eds. 32p. 1995. pap. 5.00 (*1-885610-05-X*) European Amer.
Ati, H. A. Islam in Focus. 1987. pap. 10.50 (*1-56744-081-9*) Kazi Pubns.
Ati, Hammoudah A. Islam in Focus. 3rd rev. ed. Hasayin, Shaykh S. & Sway, Mustafa A., eds. LC 97-35871. (Illus.). 224p. 1998. pap. 7.95 (*0-915957-74-4*) amana pubns.
Atias, Christian. The French Civil Law: An Insider's View. Levasseur, Alain A. & Mihoubi, Bachir, trs. from FRE. 161p. (Orig.). 1987. pap. text 13.00 (*0-940448-16-5*) LSU Law Pubns.
Atieh, Sam. How to Get a College Degree Via the Internet: Complete Guide to Getting an Undergraduate Degree. LC 98-18722. 216p. 1998. per. 16.00 (*0-7615-1370-1*) Prima Pub.
Atieno Odhiambo, E. S., jt. auth. see Cohen, David W.
Atienza, F. Beigbeder. New Polytechnic Dictionary of the Spanish & English Languages Vol. 1: English-Spanish. (ENG & SPA.). 1733p. 1988. 395.00 (*0-7859-7141-6*) Fr & Eur.
— New Polytechnic Dictionary of the Spanish & English Languages Vol. 2: Spanish-English. (ENG & SPA.). 1662p. 1988. 395.00 (*0-7859-7142-4*) Fr & Eur.
— Polytechnical Dictionary of the English & Spanish Languages, English-Spanish, Vol. 1. (ENG & SPA.). Date not set. 395.00 (*0-7859-9589-7*) Fr & Eur.
Atienza, F. Beigbeder, see Beigbeder Atienza, F.
Atienza, Federico B. New Polytechnic Dictionary of the Spanish & English Languages Vol. 1: Nuevo Diccionario Politecnico de las Lenguas English-Spanish. (ENG & SPA.). 3420p. 1988. 295.00 (*0-7859-0399-2*, M6238) Fr & Eur.
— New Polytechnic Dictionary of the Spanish & English Languages Vol. 2: Nuevo Diccionario Politecnico de las Lenguas Espanola - Inglesa. (ENG & SPA.). 3420p. 1988. 300.00 (*0-8288-0664-0*, M6237) Fr & Eur.
Atienza, Manuel & Manero, Juan R. A Theory of Legal Sentences. LC 97-44705. (Law & Philosophy Library: No. 34). 208p. 1997. 117.50 (*0-7923-4856-7*) Kluwer Academic.
Atik, Anne. Offshore. 80p. (Orig.). 1991. pap. 16.95 (*1-870612-02-7*, Pub. by Enitha Pr) Dufour.
Atil, Esin. Brush of the Masters: Drawings from Iran & India. LC 78-70427. (Illus.). 1978. pap. 20.00 (*0-934686-29-7*) Freer.
***Atil, Esin.** Levni & the Surname: The Story of an Eighteenth-Century Ottoman Festival. (Illus.). 252p. 2000. 75.00 (*975-6845-03-1*) U of Wash Pr.
Atil, Esin. Suleymanname: The Illustrated History of Suleyman the Magnificent. 270p. 1996. 75.00 (*0-614-21591-9*, 1199) Kazi Pubns.
Atil, Esin, et al. Islamic Metalwork in the Freer Gallery of Art. LC 85-40502. (Illus.). 280p. (Orig.). 1985. pap. text 17.50 (*0-934686-54-8*) Freer.
Atil, Yesim. On Freedom Street. 1991. 18.95 (*0-89924-076-3*); pap. 10.95 (*0-89924-075-5*) Lynx Hse.
Atilla. Finnish/Turkish/Finnish Dictionary. (FIN & TUR.). 549p. 1995. 69.95 (*0-320-00099-0*) Fr & Eur.
Atimtay, A. T. & Harrison, D. P., eds. Desulfurization of Hot Coal Gas. (NATO ASI Ser.: Vol. 42). (Illus.). viii, 408p. 1998. 179.00 (*3-540-64726-0*) Spr-Verlag.
Atingdui, Lawrence. Defining the Nonprofit Sector: Ghana. Salamon, Lester M. & Anheier, Helmut K., eds. (Working Papers of the Johns Hopkins Comparative Nonprofit Sector Project: No. 14). (Illus.). 27p. 1995. pap. text 6.00 (*1-886333-07-6*) JH Univ Inst Pol Studies.
Atiquzzaman, Mohammed, jt. auth. see Hassan, Mahbub.

An Asterisk (*) at the beginning of an entry indicates that the title is appearing for the first time.

A

Atiya, Aziz S. The Coptic Encyclopedia, 8 vols. Incl. Vol. 5. 1991. 125.00 (*0-02-897034-9*); Vol. 3. 1991. 125.00 (*0-02-897026-8*); Vol. 4. 1991. 125.00 (*0-02-897027-6*); Vol. 7. 1991. 125.00 (*0-02-897035-7*); Vol. 7. 1991. 125.00 (*0-02-897036-5*); 1991. 1000.00 (*0-02-897025-X*) Macmillan.
— The Crusade of Nicopolis. LC 76-29829. (Illus.). reprint ed. 42.50 (*0-404-15410-7*) AMS Pr.
— History of Eastern Christianity. LC 67-31393. 500p. reprint ed. pap. 155.00 (*0-608-15043-6*, 202594400047) Bks Demand.
— History of Eastern Christianity. LC 80-232. 1980. reprint ed. lib. bdg. 65.00 (*0-527-03703-6*) Periodicals Srv.
Atiya, Aziz S., ed. Coptic Encyclopedia, Vol. 1. 1991. 125.00 (*0-02-897023-3*) Mac Lib Ref.
— Coptic Encyclopedia, Vol. 2. 1991. 125.00 (*0-02-897024-1*) Mac Lib Ref.
— Coptic Encyclopedia, Vol. 8. 1991. 125.00 (*0-02-897037-3*) Mac Lib Ref.
Atiya, Nayra. Khul-Khaal. Five Egyptian Women Tell Their Stories. LC 82-5773. (Contemporary Issues in the Middle East Ser.). (Illus.). 216p. 1982. pap. 17.95 (*0-8156-0181-6*) Syracuse U Pr.
— Khul-Khaal, Five Egyptian Women Tell Their Stories. LC 82-5773. (Contemporary Issues in the Middle East Ser.). (Illus.). 211p. 1982. reprint ed. pap. 65.50 (*0-608-06963-9*, 206717100009) Bks Demand.
Atiya, Nayra, tr. see El Kouloub, Out.
Atiya, Nayra, tr. see Out el Kouloub.
Atiya, Nayra, tr. & intro. see Out el Kouloub.
Atiyah. K-Theory. 1989. pap. 26.46 (*0-201-40792-2*) Addison-Wesley.
Atiyah, M. Introduction to Commutative Algebra. (C). 1993. pap. 49.00 (*0-201-40751-5*) Addison-Wesley.
Atiyah, Michael & Iagolnitzer, Daniel, eds. Fields Medallists Lectures. LC 99-912472. (20th Century Mathematics Ser.: No. 5). x, 632p. 1997. text 33.00 (*981-02-3117-2*) World Scientific Pub.
— Fields Medallists Lectures, 5. LC 99-912472. 800p. 1997. text 60.00 (*981-02-3102-4*) World Scientific Pub.
Atiyah, Michael F. Elliptic Operators & Compact Groups. (Lecture Notes in Mathematics Ser.: Vol. 401). v, 93p. 1974. pap. 18.00 (*3-540-06855-4*) Spr-Verlag.
— The Geometry & Physics of Knots. (Lezioni Lincee Lectures). (Illus.). 88p. (C). 1990. pap. text 19.95 (*0-521-39554-2*) Cambridge U Pr.
— Michael Atiyah Vol. 1: Collected Works: Early Papers: General Papers. (Illus.). 388p. 1988. 85.00 (*0-19-853275-X*) OUP.
— Michael Atiyah Vol. 2: Collected Works: K-Theory. 854p. 1988. 125.00 (*0-19-853276-8*) OUP.
— Michael Atiyah Vol. 3: Collected Works: Index Theory: 1. (Illus.). 618p. 1988. 95.00 (*0-19-853277-6*) OUP.
— Michael Atiyah Vol. 4: Collected Works: Index Theory: 2. (Illus.). 642p. 1988. 115.00 (*0-19-853278-4*) OUP.
— Michael Atiyah Vol. 5: Collected Works: Gauge Theories. (Illus.). 720p. 1988. 130.00 (*0-19-853279-2*) OUP.
Atiyah, Michael F. & Hitchin, Nigel. The Geometry & Dynamics of Magnetic Monopoles. (Illus.). 228p. 1988. text 42.50 (*0-691-08480-7*, Pub. by Princeton U Pr) Cal Prin Full Svc.
Atiyah, Michael F., et al. Vector Bundles on Algebraic Varieties: Papers Presented at the Bombay Colloquium 1984. (Illus.). 562p. 1987. pap. text 38.00 (*0-19-562014-3*) OUP.
Atiyah, Muhiyialdin. Al Kashshaf al Iqtisadi li Ayat al Qur'an al Karim: Economic Index to the Verses of the Noble Qur'an. LC 91-28510. (Silsilat al Ma'ajim wa al Adillah wa al Kashshafat Ser.: No. 1). (ARA.). 598p. (Orig.). 1991. 25.00 (*0-912463-98-8*) IIIT VA.
— Al Kashshaf al Mawdu'i li Ahadith Sahih al Bukhari: Subject Index to the Hadiths of Sahih al Bukhari. LC 91-31964. (Silsilat al Ma'jim wa al Adillah wa al Kashshafat: No. 2). (ARA.). 766p. (Orig.). 1992. 25.00 (*0-685-70434-3*) IIIT VA.
Atiyah, Muhyialdin. Al Kashshaf al Iqtisadi li Ayat al Qur'an al Karim: Economic Index to the Verses of the Noble Qur'an. LC 91-28510. (Silsilat al Ma'ajim wa al Adillah wa al Kashshafat Ser.: No. 1). (ARA.). 598p. (Orig.). 1991. pap. 15.00 (*0-912463-97-X*) IIIT VA.
— Al Kashshaf al Mawdu'i li Ahadith Sahih al Bukhari: Subject Index to the Hadiths of Sahih al Bukhari. LC 91-31964. (Silsilat al Ma'ajim wa al Adillah wa al Kashshafat Ser.: No. 2). (ARA.). 766p. (Orig.). 1992. pap. 20.00 (*1-56564-100-0*) IIIT VA.
— Fikr al Tarbawi al Islami: Qa'imah Bibliyugrafiyah: (Islamic Educational Thought: A Bibliography) 2nd rev. ed. LC 91-44551. (Silsilat al Ma'ajim wa al Adillah wa al Kashshafat Ser.: No. 5). (ARA.). 136p. 1992. pap. 5.00 (*1-56564-211-2*) IIIT VA.
— Qa'imah Mukhtarah Hawla al Ma'rifah wa al Fikr wa al Manhaj wa al Thaqafah wa al Hadarah: (A Select Bibliography on Knowledge, Thought, Method, Culture, & Civilization) LC 92-20080. (Silsilat al Maraji' wa al Adillah Wa'l Kashshafat Ser.: No. 4). (ARA.). 111p. (Orig.). 1992. pap. 6.00 (*1-56564-038-1*) IIIT VA.
Atiyah, P. S. Accidents, Compensation & the Law. (C). 1987. 190.00 (*0-7855-4330-9*, Pub. by Witherby & Co) St Mut.
— The Damages Lottery. LC 98-164503. 206p. 1997. 50.00 (*1-901362-05-1*, Pub. by Hart Pub); pap. 18.00 (*1-901362-06-X*, Pub. by Hart Pub) Northwestern U Pr.
— Law & Modern Society. 2nd ed. 238p. 1995. pap. text 17.95 (*0-19-289267-3*) OUP.
Atiyah, P. S. & Adams, J. N. The Sale of Goods. 9th ed. 506p. 1995. pap. 64.50 (*0-273-60301-9*, Pub. by F T P-H) Trans-Atl Phila.
Atiyah, Patrick S. Essays on Contract. 2nd rev. ed. 404p. 1990. pap. text 35.00 (*0-19-825444-X*) OUP.
— An Introduction to the Law of Contract. 5th ed. (Clarendon Law Ser.). 504p. 1995. text 80.00 (*0-19-825952-2*, Clarendon Pr); pap. text 39.95 (*0-19-825953-0*, Clarendon Pr) OUP.
— Promises, Morals, & Law. 214p. 1983. pap. text 24.95 (*0-19-825479-2*) OUP.
— The Rise & Fall of Freedom of Contract. LC 85-10515. 804p. 1985. pap. text 60.00 (*0-19-825527-6*) OUP.
Atiyah, Patrick S. & Summers, Robert S. Form & Substance in Anglo-American Law: A Comparative Study in Legal Reasoning, Legal Theory, & Legal Institutions. 448p. 1987. text 79.00 (*0-19-825577-2*) OUP.
Atiyah, Patrick S. & Summers, Robert S. Form & Substance in Anglo-American Law: A Comparative Study in Legal Reasoning, Legal Theory, & Legal Institutions. 458p. 1991. reprint ed. pap. text 35.00 (*0-19-825734-1*) OUP.
Atiyeh, George Nicholas, ed. The Book in the Islamic World. 205p. 1996. pap. 19.95 (*0-614-21571-4*, 1437) Kazi Pubns.
— The Book in the Islamic World: The Written Word & Communication in the Middle East. LC 94-29487. 305p. (C). 1995. text 59.50 (*0-7914-2473-1*); pap. text 19.95 (*0-7914-2474-X*) State U NY Pr.
Atiyeh, George Nicholas & Oweiss, Ibrahim M., eds. Arab Civilization: Challenges & Responses: Studies in Honor of Dr. Constantine Zurayk. LC 87-18452. 365p. (C). 1988. text 74.50 (*0-88706-698-4*); pap. text 24.95 (*0-88706-699-2*) State U NY Pr.
Atiyeh, George Nicholas, ed. see Al-Furqan Islamic Heritage Foundation (London, England), et al.
Atiyeh, Wadeeha. Fourth Wise Man. (Illus.). (J). (gr. 4 up). 1959. pap. 5.00 (*0-8315-0038-7*) Speller.
Atiyyah, Hamid. How to Live & Work in the Gulf: Planning Your Stay in the Gulf Arab States. 128p. 1995. pap. 19.95 (*1-85703-142-3*, Pub. by How To Bks) Trans-Atl Phila.
Atiyyah, Hani M. Na Hwa Manhaj Li-Tan Zim Al-Mus Talah Al Shari: Dir Asah Fial-Mak Aniz Wa-Istikhd Am Atiha. LC 97-45666. (Silsilat Al-Manhaj Iyah Al-Islam Iyah Ser.). 1997. write for info. (*1-56564-263-5*) IIIT VA.
— Quranic Text: Toward A Retrieval System. LC 94-24729. 1994. write for info. (*1-56564-212-0*); pap. write for info. (*1-56564-213-9*) IIIT VA.
ATK Staff. ATK Dataprocessing Dictionary, Finnish, English, French, Russian, Swedish, German: ATK Sanakirja Suomi-Englanti-Franska-Ruotsi-Saksa-Venaja. (ENG, FIN, FRE, GER & RUS.). 233p. 1986. 125.00 (*0-8288-0262-9*, F23900) Fr & Eur.
Atkeson, Edward B. The Final Argument of Kings: Reflections on the Art of War. 260p. (C). 1988. 23.95 (*0-915979-21-7*) NOVA Pubns.
— The Powder Keg: An Intelligence Officer's Guide to Military Forces in the Middle East, 1996-2000. 300p. (Orig.). (C). 1996. pap. 15.00 (*0-9638692-5-6*) NOVA Pubns.
— A Tale of Three Wars. 400p. 1997. 27.95 (*1-889927-00-7*) US Army War Coll Found Pr.
Atkeson, Mary. A Study of the Local Literature of the Upper Ohio Valley: With Especial Reference to the Early Pioneer & Indian Tales, 1820-1840. LC 74-7917. (Ohio State University, Columbus Contributions to English Ser.: No. 2). reprint ed. 31.50 (*0-404-11800-3*) AMS Pr.
Atkeson, Ray. Washington & Oregon in Color. (Illus.). 24p. 1954. pap. 1.00 (*0-8323-0077-2*) Binford Mort.
Atkeson, Ray, photos by. Oregon III. LC 86-83247. (Illus.). 160p. 1987. 39.95 (*0-932575-28-5*) Gr Arts Ctr Pub.
***Atkeson, Ray, photos by.** Ski & Snow Country. 2000. 23.95 (*1-55868-538-3*) Gr Arts Ctr Pub.
Atkeson, Ray & Glass, Catherine. Oregon My Oregon. LC 98-19322. (Illus.). 128p. 1998. 29.50 (*1-55868-321-6*) Gr Arts Ctr Pub.
Atkeson, Ray & Schafer, Rick, photos by. Wind on the Waves. (Illus.). 144p. 1992. 29.50 (*1-55868-090-X*) Gr Arts Ctr Pub.
Atkey, Ronald G., jt. ed. see Lyon, J. Noel.
Atkin. Evaluating Change in Community. LC 98-36989. (C). 1999. pap. text. write for info. (*0-7020-2324-8*) W B Saunders.
— Right in France, 1789-1996. 250p. 1997. text 59.50 (*1-86064-197-0*, Pub. by I B T) St Martin.
Atkin, Abraham. Chelkeinu. (Illus.). 200p. (J). 1984. text 7.75 (*0-914131-09-5*, A120) Torah Umesorah.
— Darkeinu Aleph & Bais: In One Volume. (J). 1996. pap. text 4.75 (*0-914131-12-5*, A100) Torah Umesorah.
— Darkeinu Daled. (HEB., Illus.). (YA). (gr. 7-12). 1997. pap., wbk. ed. 4.95 (*0-914131-13-3*, A102) Torah Umesorah.
— Darkeinu Gimel. (J). (gr. 4 up). 1996. text 4.95 (*0-914131-14-1*, A101) Torah Umesorah.
Atkin, Adam. Alarms & Mirrors. LC 91-67356. 188p. (Orig.). 1991. pap. 7.95 (*0-9631360-3-8*) Sea Tree Pr.
Atkin, Bill, jt. ed. see Henaghan, Mark.
Atkin, Brian, ed. Intelligent Buildings: Applications of IT & Building Automation to High Technology Construction Projects. (UNICOM Applied Information Technology Ser.). 275p. 1993. 93.95 (*1-85742-172-8*, Pub. by Avebury Technical) Ashgate Pub Co.
Atkin, Charles K. & Wallack, Lawrence, eds. Mass Communication & Public Health. (Focus Editions Ser.: Vol. 121). (Illus.). 250p. (C). 1990. 59.95 (*0-8039-3924-8*); pap. 26.00 (*0-8039-3925-6*) Sage.
Atkin, Charles K., jt. ed. see Rice, Ronald E.
Atkin, Don. Like Father, Like Son. LC 96-113698. 154p. (Orig.). 1995. pap. 9.99 (*1-56043-252-7*, Treasure Hse) Destiny Image.
Atkin, E. K., jt. ed. see Brent, E. J.
Atkin, Edmond. The Appalachian Indian Frontier: The Edmond Atkin Report & Plan of 1755. Jacobs, Wilbur R., ed. LC 68-2064. 154p. 1967. reprint ed. pap. 47.80 (*0-608-02777-4*, 206384400007) Bks Demand.
Atkin-Etienne, Ruth, tr. see Fischer, Gustave-Nicolas.
Atkin, Graham, jt. auth. see Armstrong, Katherine.
Atkin, J. Myron, et al. Changing the Subject. Black, Paul, ed. 240p. (C). 1996. 80.00 (*0-415-14622-4*) Routledge.
— Changing the Subject: Innovations in Science, Mathematics, & Technology Education. Black, Paul, ed. 240p. (C). 1996. pap. 25.99 (*0-415-14623-2*) Routledge.
Atkin, Janet, et al. Listening to Parents: An Approach to the Improvement of Home-School Relations. 208p. 1988. lib. bdg. 47.50 (*0-7099-5039-X*, Pub. by C Helm) Routldge.
Atkin, John M. British Overseas Investment: 1918-1931. Bruchey, Stuart, ed. LC 77-81821. (Dissertations in European Economic History Ser.). (Illus.). 1978. lib. bdg. 41.95 (*0-405-10774-9*) Ayer.
Atkin, K. Le Francais Sans Souci. (Canadian French Ser.). 304p. (J). (gr. 4-6). 1987. pap. text 50.12 (*0-201-17624-6*) Addison-Wesley.
Atkin, Karl, jt. auth. see Twigg, Julia.
Atkin, Karl, jt. ed. see Ahmad, Waqar I.
Atkin, Malcolm. Civil War in Worcestershire. LC 96-203556. 1997. pap. text 22.95 (*0-7509-1050-X*, Pub. by Sutton Pub Ltd) Intl Pubs Mktg.
— Cromwell's Crowning Mercy: The Battle of Worcester, 1651. LC 98-204452. 1998. 35.95 (*0-7509-1888-8*, Pub. by Sutton Pub Ltd) Intl Pubs Mktg.
Atkin, Michael. International Grain Trade. 2nd ed. (International Trade Ser.). (Illus.). 192p. 1995. 170.00 (*1-85573-202-5*, Pub. by Woodhead Pubng) Am Educ Systs.
— Snouts in the Trough: European Farmers, The Common Agricultural Policy & the Public Purse. 192p. 1993. 69.95 (*1-85573-114-2*, Pub. by Woodhead Pubng) Am Educ Systs.
Atkin, N. B. Cytogenetic Aspects of Malignant Transformation. Wolsky, A, ed. (Experimental Biology & Medicine Ser.: Vol. 6). (Illus.). 200p. 1976. 64.50 (*3-8055-2330-0*) S Karger.
Atkin, Nicholas. Church & Schools in Vichy France, 1940-1944. LC 91-32628. (Modern European History Ser.). 279p. 1991. text 20.00 (*0-8153-0664-4*) Garland.
Atkin, Nicholas. Petain. LC 97-14220. (Profiles in Power Ser.). 256p. (C). 1997. pap. 23.53 (*0-582-07037-6*) Longman.
Atkin, Nicholas. Petain Profiles in Power Series. LC 97-14220. (Profiles in Power Ser.). (C). 1997. text 62.81 (*0-582-07036-8*) Longman.
Atkin, Nicholas, jt. ed. see Tallett, Frank.
Atkin, Pip. A Tender Hand. 1999. pap. 21.00 (*1-85072-114-9*, Pub. by W Sessions) St Mut.
Atkin, R., et al. New Directions in Small Business Research. (Avebury Business School Library). 214p. 1993. 67.95 (*1-85628-378-X*, Pub. by Avebury) Ashgate Pub Co.
Atkin, R. K., jt. ed. see Day, W.
Atkin, S. Beth. Voices from the Fields: Children of Migrant Farmworkers Tell Their Stories. LC 92-32248. 96p. (J). (gr. 4-6). 1993. 17.95 (*0-316-05633-2*) Little.
***Atkin, S. Beth.** Voices from the Fields: Children of Migrant Farmworkers Tell Their Stories. 96p. (YA). (gr. 5 up). 2000. pap. 12.95 (*0-316-05620-0*) Little.
Atkin, S. Beth, photos by. Voices from the Street: Young Former Gang Members Tell Their Stories. LC 95-26757. (Illus.). 144p. (J). (gr. 4-6). 1996. 19.95 (*0-316-05634-0*) Little.
Atkin, W. R. Living Together Without Marriage: The Law in New Zealand. 240p. 1991. pap. 81.00 (*0-409-70221-8*, NZ, MICHIE) LEXIS Pub.
Atkin, William. Of Yachts & Men. (Illus.). 160p. 1997. pap. 22.95 (*1-888671-07-6*) Tiller.
Atkins. Chem: Mole, Matter, Change, Vol. 1. 3rd ed. 1997. pap. text, wbk. ed. 20.95 (*0-7167-3064-2*) St Martin.
— Chem: Mole, Matter, Change, Vol. 1. 3rd ed. (C). 1997. pap. 48.00 (*0-7167-2794-3*) W H Freeman.
— Chemical Principles. 1998. 47.90 (*0-7167-3362-5*); 47.90 (*0-7167-3363-3*) W H Freeman.
— Chemistry. 3rd ed. 1997. teacher ed. write for info. (*0-7167-3154-1*) W H Freeman.
— Chemistry. 4th ed. (C). 2000. pap. text 64.00 (*0-7167-2349-2*) W H Freeman.
— Chemistry: Mole 4E/Teaching Assist Manual. 1998. teacher ed. write for info. (*0-7167-3456-7*) W H Freeman.
— Chemistry: Molecules. 1997. lab manual ed. 95.00 (*0-7167-3157-6*) W H Freeman.
***Atkins.** Comparative Analysis of Latin Amer. 2000. pap. 25.95 (*0-8133-3381-4*, Pub. by Westview) HarpC.
— Crossroad Blues. 256p. 1999. mass mkt. 5.99 (*0-312-97192-3*) St Martin.
Atkins. Elements of Physical Chemistry & Concepts in Physical Chemistry. (C). Date not set. text 62.00 (*0-7167-2981-4*) W H Freeman.
— Elements of Physical Chemistry. 2nd ed. 1997. write for info. (*0-7167-3105-3*) W H Freeman.
— General Chemistry. 2nd ed. student ed. 61.60 (*0-7167-2734-X*); student ed. 56.00 (*0-7167-2735-8*) W H Freeman.
— General Chemistry. 2nd ed. (C). student ed. 75.00 (*0-7167-2921-0*); text, student ed. 64.00 (*0-7167-2549-5*) W H Freeman.
— General Chemistry. 3rd ed. 1997. 90.00 (*0-7167-3308-0*) W H Freeman.
— General Chemistry & Molecules. 2nd ed. (C). 2000. pap. text 60.80 (*0-7167-2348-4*) W H Freeman.
— General Chemistry Updated Version/Student Solutions Manual. (C). 1993. student ed. 60.00 (*0-7167-2507-X*) W H Freeman.
***Atkins.** Handbook of Research on Latin America. 320p. 2000. pap. 43.50 (*0-8133-3379-2*, Pub. by Westview) HarpC.
Atkins. Honors Chemistry. 1998. write for info. incl. cd-rom (*0-7167-3359-5*) W H Freeman.
— Honors Chemistry. 1999. teacher ed. 160.00 (*0-7167-3425-7*) W H Freeman.
— Honors Chemistry. 1999. pap. text, student ed. 29.95 (*0-7167-3357-9*) W H Freeman.
— Honors Chemistry. 3rd ed. 1998. teacher ed. 23.90 (*0-7167-3361-7*); pap. text, student ed. 25.95 (*0-7167-3360-9*) W H Freeman.
— Organic Chemistry. 2nd ed. 1996. 26.88 (*0-07-011339-4*) McGraw.
— Organic Chemistry. 3rd ed. 2001. student ed. 18.00 (*0-07-231945-3*) McGraw.
— Physical Chemistry. 1998. write for info. incl. cd-rom (*0-7167-3166-5*) W H Freeman.
***Atkins.** Physical Chemistry. 6th ed. 1998. pap. text, student ed. 25.95 (*0-7167-3167-3*) W H Freeman.
Atkins. Total Area Networking. 2nd ed. LC 98-30921. 326p. (C). 1998. 84.95 (*0-471-98464-7*) Wiley.
Atkins, jt. auth. see Jones Staff.
Atkins, jt. auth. see Montgomery, William H.
Atkins, A. G., jt. ed. see Alsmeyer, D.
***Atkins, A. V.** Ishmael: or The Origin of the Red Man. (LC History-America-E). 42p. 1999. reprint ed. lib. bdg. 69.00 (*0-7812-4303-3*) Rprt Serv.
Atkins, Ace. Crossroad Blues. LC 98-19416. (Nick Travers Mysteries Ser.). 226p. 1998. 21.95 (*0-312-19254-1*, Thomas Dunne) St Martin.
***Atkins, Ace.** Leavin Trunk Blues: A Nick Travers Mystery. LC 00-29691. 256p. 2000. text 22.95 (*0-312-24212-3*) St Martin.
Atkins, Alex, jt. auth. see Schlomer, Elizabeth.
Atkins, Anne. Split Image: Male & Female after God's Likeness. 1998. pap. text 12.99 (*0-340-70986-3*, Pub. by Hodder & Stought Ltd) Trafalgar.
Atkins, Annette. Harvest of Grief: Grasshopper Plagues & Public Assistance in Minnesota, 1873-78. LC 84-10855. 147p. 1984. 12.95 (*0-87351-171-9*) Minn Hist.
***Atkins, Annette.** We Grew Up Together: Brothers & Sisters in Nineteenth-Century America. 208p. 2001. 29.95 (*0-252-02605-5*) U of Ill Pr.
Atkins, Anselm. The Notebooks of Lana Skimnest. 240p. 1992. pap. 11.95 (*0-916288-33-1*) Micah Pubns.
Atkins, Anthony G. & Mai, Y. W. Elastic & Plastic Fracture. (Mechanical Engineering Ser.). 817p. 1989. pap. text 57.95 (*0-470-21241-1*) P-H.
Atkins, Anthony G., jt. auth. see Felbeck, David K.
Atkins, Antony, ed. see Lawrence, D. H.
Atkins, Barbara F., jt. auth. see Hassanein, Ashraf M.
Atkins, Bernard O. Hawaii Now Color/Sticker Book. 2nd rev. ed. (Illus.). 20p. (J). (ps-6). 1995. pap. 4.95 (*0-9642050-3-3*) Great Creations.
— Hawaiian Dancers Paper Doll Book. (Illus.). 12p. (Orig.). (J). (ps-6). 1995. pap. 4.95 (*0-9642050-1-7*) Great Creations.
— The Hawaiiana Color/Sticker Book. (Illus.). 20p. (Orig.). (J). (ps-6). 1995. pap. 4.95 (*0-9642050-6-8*) Great Creations.
— Sights of Hawaii Color - Sticker Book. (Illus.). 20p. (Orig.). (J). (ps-6). 1995. pap. 4.95 (*0-9642050-4-1*) Great Creations.
— This Is Hawaii Color/Sticker Book. 4th ed. (Illus.). 20p. (J). (ps-6). 1995. pap. 4.95 (*0-9642050-2-5*) Great Creations.
Atkins, Beryl. Collins Robert French/English-English/French Unabridged Dictionary. (ENG & FRE.). 1998. 69.95 (*0-7859-9405-X*) Fr & Eur.
Atkins, Beryl T. Collins-Robert French & English Dictionary. 2nd ed. (ENG & FRE.). 929p. 1987. 35.00 (*0-8288-0059-6*, M6898) Fr & Eur.
— HarperCollins Robert French Dictionary Unabridged 5th Edition: Fifth edition. 5th unabridged rev. ed. LC 97-46140. (ENG & FRE.). 2016p. 1998. 55.00 (*0-06-270816-3*) HarpC.
— Robert & Collins Senior: Dictionnaire Francais-Anglais, Anglais-Francais. 5th ed. LC 97-46140. xl, 2081 p. 1998. write for info. (*2-85036-528-9*) Robert.
Atkins, Beryl T., et al, eds. Collins-Robert French-English, English-French Dictionary. 3rd ed. (ENG & FRE.). 1848p. 1993. 50.00 (*0-7859-7396-6*, 0062755099) Fr & Eur.
Atkins-Burnett, Sally, jt. auth. see Meisels, Samuel J.
Atkins, C. & Wickers, D. Nueva York Guiarama. 128p. 1991. pap. 15.95 (*0-7859-9031-3*) Fr & Eur.
Atkins, Caroline. Decorating Your First Home. (Illus.). 144p. 1996. pap. 19.95 (*0-304-34746-9*, Pub. by Cassell) Sterling.
— Instant Impact: Over 200 Ideas for the Weekend Decorator. 1999. pap. text 19.95 (*0-7063-7786-9*) WrLock.
Atkins, Caroline. Instant Impact: Over 200 Ideas for the Weekend Decorator. (Quick & Easy Ser.). 1999. pap. text 19.95 (*0-7063-7806-7*) WrLock.
Atkins, Cary C. & Owens, Sally L. Compact Dish: The Home on the Range Cookbook. LC 93-71980. (Compact Dish Cookbooks Ser.). 60p. (Orig.). 1993. spiral bd. write for info. (*1-883810-05-1*) Compact Ckbk.
***Atkins, Catherine.** When Jeff Comes Home. LC 98-44016. 224p. (YA). (gr. 7-12). 1999. 17.99 (*0-399-23366-0*) Putnam Pub Group.
Atkins, Charlotte, jt. auth. see Wickers, David.
Atkins, Chet, jt. auth. see Flint, Tommy.
Atkins, Chloe. Atkins Girls Night Out. LC 97-35349. 1998. text 13.00 (*0-312-18044-6*) St Martin.
Atkins, D. J. & Meier, R. H., III, eds. Comprehensive Management of the Upper Limb Amputee. (Illus.). 280p. 1988. 119.00 (*0-387-96779-6*) Spr-Verlag.

A

Atkins, Dale & Powell, Meris, eds. From the Heart: Men & Women Write Their Private Thoughts about Their Married Lives. LC 94-22152. 1995. 14.95 (*0-8050-3498-6*) H Holt & Co.

***Atkins, Dale & Powell, Meris, eds.** From the Heart: Men & Women Write Their Private Thoughts about Their Married Lives. 239p. 2000. reprint ed. text 15.00 (*0-7881-6877-0*) DIANE Pub.

***Atkins, Darrin.** The End of Me: And 11 Other Sinful Stories. 389p. 2000. 25.00 (*0-7388-0848-2*); pap. 18.00 (*0-7388-0849-0*) Xlibris Corp.

— The Quitter. LC 00-100815. 198p. 1999. pap. 18.00 (*0-7388-1231-5*) Xlibris Corp.

— The Quitter: And Other Tables of Employment. LC 00-100815. 198p. 1999. 25.00 (*0-7388-1230-7*) Xlibris Corp.

Atkins, David. The Cuckoo in June. large type ed. 400p. 1996. 27.99 (*0-7089-3624-5*) Ulverscroft.

Atkins, Dawn, ed. Lesbian Sex Scandals: Sexual Practices, Identities, & Politics. 145p. 1998. 39.95 (*0-7890-0547-6*, Harrington Park) Haworth Pr.

— Lesbian Sex Scandals: Sexual Practices, Identities & Politics. LC 98-34517. 150p. 1998. 49.95 (*0-7890-0548-4*, Harrington Park); pap. 19.95 (*1-56023-118-1*, Harrington Park) Haworth Pr.

— Looking Queer: Body Image & Identity in Lesbian, Bisexual, Gay, & Transgender Communities. LC 98-14678. 467p. (C). 1998. 69.95 (*0-7890-0463-1*, Harrington Park); pap. 32.95 (*1-56023-931-X*, Harrington Park) Haworth Pr.

Atkins, Dixie. Resurgam. 240p. (C). 1989. text 60.00 (*1-872795-89-7*, Pub. by Pentland Pr) St Mut.

Atkins, Don. Correlation Analysis. LC 92-2341. (Six Sigma Research Institute Ser.). 1992. pap. text 19.95 (*0-201-63421-X*) Addison-Wesley.

Atkins, Donny D. Alamo Letters. unabridged ed. 18p. (Orig.). 1995. pap. 12.95 (*0-9653880-0-X*) Bear Paw.

— Caleb's Bridge. (Orig.). Date not set. pap. write for info. (*0-9653880-2-6*) Bear Paw.

— Shadows of Alamo Plaza. 216p. (Orig.). 1995. pap. 14.95 (*0-9653880-1-8*) Bear Paw.

Atkins, Douglas G., jt. auth. see Bergeron, David M.

Atkins, Edwin F. Sixty Years in Cuba: Reminiscences of Edwin F. Atkins. Bruchey, Stuart, ed. LC 80-555. (Multinational Corporations Ser.). (Illus.). 1981. reprint ed. lib. bdg. 48.95 (*0-405-13352-9*) Ayer.

Atkins, Elaine, jt. auth. see Kesson, Monica.

Atkins, F. H. Atkins, Joseph Atkins: The Story of a Family. 158p. 1992. reprint ed. pap. 25.00 (*0-8328-2622-7*); reprint ed. lib. bdg. 35.00 (*0-8328-2621-9*) Higginson Bk Co.

Atkins, Frank. The Devil-Tree of el Dorado: A Novel. Reginald, R. & Melville, Douglas, eds. LC 77-84196. (Lost Race & Adult Fantasy Ser.). (Illus.). 1978. reprint ed. lib. bdg. 36.95 (*0-405-10955-5*) Ayer.

— King of the Dead: A Weird Romance. Reginald, R. & Melville, Douglas, eds. LC 77-84197. (Lost Race & Adult Fantasy Ser.). 1978. reprint ed. lib. bdg. 29.95 (*0-405-10956-3*) Ayer.

Atkins, G. Douglas. Quests of Difference: Reading Pope's Poems. LC 85-20228. 208p. 1986. 25.00 (*0-8131-1565-5*) U Pr of Ky.

— Reading Deconstruction Deconstructive Reading. LC 83-10308. 168p. 1985. pap. 12.50 (*0-8131-0165-4*) U Pr of Ky.

Atkins, G. Douglas & Johnson, Michael L., eds. Writing & Reading Differently: Deconstruction & the Teaching of Composition & Literature. LC 85-13464. x, 222p. (C). 1985. pap. 14.95 (*0-7006-0283-6*) U Pr of KS.

Atkins, G. Douglas & Morrow, Laura, eds. Contemporary Literary Theory. LC 88-14692. 272p. (Orig.). 1989. pap. 18.95 (*0-87023-642-3*) U of Mass Pr.

— Contemporary Literary Theory. LC 88-14692. 272p. (Orig.). (C). 1989. lib. bdg. 40.00 (*0-87023-641-5*) U of Mass Pr.

Atkins, G. Douglas, ed. see Gundy, Jeff.

Atkins, G. Lawrence. Spend It or Save It? Pension Lump-Sum Distributions & Tax Reform. LC 86-6413. 85p. 1986. pap. 14.95 (*0-86643-046-6*) Empl Benefit Res Inst.

Atkins, G. Pope. Encyclopedia of the Inter-American System. LC 96-9035. 592p. 1997. lib. bdg. 115.00 (*0-313-28600-0*, Greenwood Pr) Greenwood.

***Atkins, G. Pope.** Handbook of Research on Latin American International Relations. 320p. 2000. 116.00 (*0-8133-3378-4*) Westview.

Atkins, G. Pope. Latin America & the Caribbean in the International System. 4th ed. LC 98-42262. 472p. 1998. pap. text 35.00 (*0-8133-3383-0*, Pub. by Westview) HarpC.

— Latin America & the Caribbean in the International System. 4th ed. LC 98-42262. 472p. 1998. text 85.00 (*0-8133-3382-2*, Pub. by Westview) HarpC.

— The United States & Latin America: Redefining U. S. Purposes in the Post-Cold War Era. (Tom Slick World Peace Ser.). 176p. 1992. pap. 12.50 (*0-89940-426-X*) LBJ Sch Pub Aff.

Atkins, G. Pope & Wilson, Larman C. The Dominican Republic & the United States: From Imperialism to Transnationalism. LC 97-30046. (United States & the Americas Ser.). 288p. (C). 1998. text 50.00 (*0-8203-1930-9*); pap. text 20.00 (*0-8203-1931-7*) U of Ga Pr.

Atkins, Gaius. Modern Religious Cults & Movements. LC 74-126684. reprint ed. 47.50 (*0-404-00415-6*) AMS Pr.

Atkins, Gaius G. Pilgrims of the Lonely Road. LC 67-28741. (Essay Index Reprint Ser.). 1977. 20.95 (*0-8369-0162-2*) Ayer.

— Resources for Living. LC 77-117756. (Essay Index Reprint Ser.). 1977. 21.95 (*0-8369-1741-3*) Ayer.

Atkins, Gaius G., ed. see Maclaren, Alexander.

Atkins, Gary, jt. auth. see Rivers, William L.

Atkins, George. Baseball Heaven. LC 94-75314. (Illus.). 128p. (Orig.). 1994. pap. 14.95 (*0-9640266-0-0*) Lux Fiat.

Atkins, George D. The Faith of John Dryden: Change & Continuity. LC 80-12890. 208p. reprint ed. pap. 64.50 (*0-7837-5796-4*, 204546200006) Bks Demand.

Atkins, Greg. The Emperor's New Clothes (The Musical) 1998. pap. 5.00 (*0-87440-072-4*) Bakers Plays.

— Improv! A Handbook for the Actor. LC 93-27091. 142p. (C). 1993. pap. 13.95 (*0-435-08627-8*, 08627) Heinemann.

— Puberty: The Game Show. 31p. 1998. pap. 4.00 (*0-87440-064-3*) Bakers Plays.

— Through the Storybook: A Musical for Children's Theatre. (Illus.). 24p. (J). (ps-4). 1988. pap. 3.25 (*0-88680-306-3*) I E Clark.

Atkins, Harold. Highway Materials Soils & Concrete. 3rd ed. LC 96-13198. 386p. (C). 1996. 85.00 (*0-13-212862-4*) P-H.

Atkins, Harold L. Pulmonary Nuclear Medicine: Techniques in Diagnosis of Lung Disease. (Lung Biology in Health & Disease Ser.: Vol. 23). (Illus.). 386p. 1984. text 175.00 (*0-8247-7233-4*) Dekker.

Atkins, Helen, tr. see Frank, Manfred.

Atkins, Helen, tr. see Guthke, Karl S.

Atkins, Helen, tr. see Kreisky, Bruno.

Atkins, Irene K. Arthur Jacobson: Interviewed by Irene Kahn Atkins. LC 91-27516. (Directors Guild of American Oral History Ser.). (Illus.). 270p. 1991. 31.00 (*0-8108-2468-X*) Scarecrow.

— Source Music in Motion Pictures. LC 81-65338. (Illus.). 192p. 1983. 32.50 (*0-8386-3076-6*) Fairleigh Dickinson.

Atkins, Ivor A. The Early Occupants of the Office of Organist & Master of the Choristers of the Cathedral Church of Christ & the Blessed Virgin Mary, Worcester. LC 74-27329. reprint ed. 39.50 (*0-404-12855-6*) AMS Pr.

Atkins, J. Walter De La Mare: An Exploration. LC 75-22359. (Studies in Poetry: No. 38). 1975. lib. bdg. 75.00 (*0-8383-2105-4*) M S G Haskell Hse.

Atkins, Jacqueline M., jt. auth. see Bishop, Robert.

Atkins, James & Taylor. Automated Defibrillation. 80p. 1991. pap. text 27.00 (*0-13-051459-4*) P-H.

— Automated Defibrillation. 1991. pap. 15.25 (*0-13-514594-5*) P-H.

Atkins, James, et al. Automated Defibrillation. 2nd ed. (C). 2001. 16.00 (*0-89303-068-6*) P-H.

Atkins, Jeannine. Aani & the Tree Huggers. LC 95-2036. (Illus.). 32p. (J). (ps-5). 2000. 14.95 (*1-880000-24-5*) Lee & Low Bks.

***Atkins, Jeannine.** Aani & the Tree Huggers. (Illus.). 32p. (J). (ps-5). 2000. pap. 6.95 (*1-58430-004-3*, Pub. by Lee & Low Bks) Publishers Group.

— Aani & the Tree Huggers. (Illus.). (J). 2000. 12.40 (*0-606-18245-4*) Turtleback.

Atkins, Jeannine. Dessert First. LC 95-43884. (Illus.). (J). 1997. 16.00 (*0-689-80345-1*) S&S Bks Yung.

— Get Set! Swim! LC 97-31410. (Illus.). 32p. (YA). (ps up). 1998. 15.95 (*1-880000-66-0*) Lee & Low Bks.

— Mary Anning & the Sea Dragon. LC 97-47547. (Illus.). 32p. (YA). (gr. k-3). 1999. 16.00 (*0-374-34840-5*) FS&G.

***Atkins, Jeannine.** A Name on the Quilt: A Story of Remembrance. LC 97-42303. (Illus.). 32p. (J). 1999. 16.00 (*0-689-81592-1*) S&S Trade.

Atkins, Jeannine. Preparadas... Listas... Ya! Sarfatti, Esther, tr. LC 98-7777. (SPA., Illus.). 32p. (YA). (ps up). 1998. 15.95 (*1-880000-77-6*); pap. 6.95 (*1-880000-78-4*) Lee & Low Bks.

***Atkins, Jill.** Chateau of Love. 280p. 2000. 18.99 (*0-7089-5694-7*) Ulverscroft.

— An Honest Rogue. large type ed. 192p. 2000. pap. 18.99 (*0-7089-5640-8*, Linford) Ulverscroft.

— Passionate Concerto. large type ed. 264p. 1999. pap. 18.99 (*0-7089-5544-4*, Linford) Ulverscroft.

— Spanish Rhapsody. large type ed. 208p. 1999. pap. 18.99 (*0-7089-5610-6*, Linford) Ulverscroft.

Atkins, John. Atkins Enterprise Networks: Designing for Total Area Networks. (C). 2000. pap. text 35.95 (*0-201-87751-1*) Addison-Wesley.

— The British Spy Novel. 288p. 1989. pap. 14.95 (*0-7145-4056-0*) Riverrun NY.

— J. B. Priestley. 1983. pap. 12.95 (*0-7145-3950-3*) Riverrun NY.

— Sex in Literature. 400p. 1982. 24.95 (*0-7145-3756-X*) Riverrun NY.

— Sex in Literature, Vol. 1. 1981. pap. 12.95 (*0-7145-0523-4*) Riverrun NY.

— Sex in Literature, Vol. 2. 1980. pap. 12.95 (*0-7145-1138-2*) Riverrun NY.

— Sex in Literature, Vol. 3. 1981. pap. 12.95 (*0-7145-3861-2*) Riverrun NY.

— Sex in Literature, Vol. 4: The Eighteenth Century. 400p. 1982. pap. 12.95 (*0-7145-3977-5*) Riverrun NY.

— Six Novelists Look at Society. 288p. (Orig.). 1983. pap. 11.95 (*0-7145-3863-9*) Riverrun NY.

— The Who on Record: A Critical History, 1963-1998. LC 99-87872. 352p. 2000. lib. bdg. 55.00 (*0-7864-0609-7*) McFarland & Co.

Atkins, John W. English Literary Criticism: The Medieval Phase. 1990. 16.50 (*0-8446-1032-1*) Peter Smith.

— Literary Criticism in Antiquity Vol. 2: Graeco-Roman. (Orig.). 1961. 16.50 (*0-8446-1033-X*) Peter Smith.

Atkins, Jonathan M. Parties, Politics, & the Sectional Conflict in Tennessee, 1832-1861. LC 96-1002. 1997. 38.00 (*0-87049-950-5*) U of Tenn Pr.

Atkins, Josiah. The Diary of Josiah Atkins. 1976. 17.95 (*0-405-10472-3*, 12625) Ayer.

Atkins, Juliet. The Essential Elements of Intimacy: Uncover the Power in You...to Enhance Your Relationship. 124p. 1997. pap. write for info. (*1-57502-534-5*, PO1572) Morris Pubng.

— Exploring the Elements: For Men. 76p. 1997. write for info. (*1-57579-076-9*) Pine Hill Pr.

— Exploring the Elements: For Women. 76p. 1997. pap. write for info. (*1-57579-075-0*) Pine Hill Pr.

Atkins, K. & Rainey, R. Winning Basketball Drills. 288p. (C). 1985. text 27.95 (*0-13-960618-1*) P-H.

Atkins, Kathleen. A Physics Problem. 32p. 1984. pap. 12.00 (*0-930513-00-2*) Blackwells Pr.

Atkins, Kathryn A. Masters of the Italic Letter: Twenty-Two Exemplars from the Sixteenth Century. LC 85-45968. (Illus.). 192p. 1988. 45.00 (*0-87923-594-2*) Godine.

Atkins, Keletso E. The Moon Is Dead! Give Us Our Money! The Cultural Origins of an African Work Ethic, Natal, South Africa, 1843-1900. LC 92-41611. 190p. (C). 1994. pap. 22.95 (*0-435-08078-4*, 08078) Heinemann.

Atkins, Kenneth R., et al. Oracle Designer Generation. (Illus.). 1154p. 2000. pap. 64.99 incl. cd-rom (*0-07-882475-3*) Osborne-McGraw.

Atkins, Kirsten. How Long Is a Piece of String? LC 93-18062. (Voyages Ser.). (Illus.). (J). 1994. write for info. (*0-383-03672-0*) SRA McGraw.

Atkins, Leah, et al. An Alabama Legacy: Images of a State. LC 95-36487. 1995. write for info. (*0-89865-950-7*) Donning Co.

Atkins, Leah R. Birmingham & Jefferson County: An Illustrated History: The Valley & the Hills. 2nd rev. ed. (Illus.). 192p. 1996. 34.95 (*0-89781-482-7*) Am Historical Pr.

Atkins, Leo. Deadbeat. 320p. 1999. 5.99 (*0-425-16781-X*, Prime Crime) Berkley Pub.

***Atkins, Leo.** Play Dead. (P. I. Mysteries Ser.). 2000. mass mkt. 5.99 (*0-425-17362-3*, Prime Crime) Berkley Pub.

***Atkins, Linda.** Absence of Reason. 272p. 2000. mass mkt. 6.99 (*1-58374-017-1*) Chicago Spectrum.

Atkins, Luther. Drinking Water: Information on the Quality of Water Found at Community Water Systems & Private Wells. (Illus.). 47p. 1998. pap. text 20.00 (*0-7881-7202-6*) DIANE Pub.

Atkins, M. E. The Gemini. 178p. 1964. 17.00 (*0-8464-0445-1*) Beekman Pubs.

Atkins, Madeleine, jt. auth. see Brown, George.

***Atkins, Marc & Sinclair, Iain.** Liquid City: Houston Writers on Houston. (Illus.). 223p. 1999. pap. 29.95 (*1-86189-037-0*, Pub. by RBL) Consort Bk Sales.

Atkins, Martyn. Informal Empire in Crisis: British Diplomacy & the Chinese Customs Succession, 1927-1929. LC 95-170991. (Cornell East Asia Ser.: Vol. 74). 142p. (C). 1995. 18.70 (*0-939657-79-1*, 74); pap. 11.90 (*0-939657-74-0*) Cornell East Asia Pgm.

Atkins, Meg E. By the North Door. large type ed. (Dales Large Print Ser.). 320p. 1998. pap. 19.99 (*1-85389-838-4*, Dales) Ulverscroft.

Atkins, Michael B. & Mier, James W. Therapeutic Applications of Interleukin-2. (Basic & Clinical Oncology Ser.: Vol. 2). (Illus.). 520p. 1993. text 230.00 (*0-8247-8809-5*) Dekker.

Atkins, P. W. Creation Revisited. LC 92-24848. 1993. text 20.00 (*0-7167-4500-3*) W H Freeman.

— The Elements of Physical Chemistry. LC 92-10429. (C). 1992. 52.50 (*0-19-855724-8*); pap. 22.50 (*0-19-855723-X*) OUP.

— The Elements of Physical Chemistry. 2nd ed. LC 96-27901. 550p. 1996. text 73.95 (*0-7167-3077-4*) W H Freeman.

— Molecular Quantum Mechanics: Solutions Manual. (Illus.). 212p. 1983. pap. 25.95 (*0-19-855180-0*) OUP.

— The Periodic Kingdom: A Journey into the Land of the Chemical Elements. (Science Masters Ser.). 1997. pap. 12.00 (*0-465-07266-6*, Pub. by Basic) HarpC.

— The Periodic Kingdom: A Journey into the Land of the Chemical Elements. (Illus.). 163p. (C). 1998. pap. text 15.00 (*0-7881-5518-0*) DIANE Pub.

— Physical Chemistry. 6th ed. LC 97-34485. (Illus.). 1140p. 1997. text 89.95 (*0-7167-2871-0*) W H Freeman.

— Quanta: A Handbook of Concepts. 2nd ed. (Illus.). 440p. 1991. pap. text 55.00 (*0-19-855573-3*) OUP.

Atkins, P. W. & Friedman, R. S. Molecular Quantum Mechanics. 3rd ed. (Illus.). 562p. 1999. pap. text 55.00 (*0-19-855947-X*) OUP.

Atkins, P. W., jt. see Shriver, D. F.

Atkins, P. W., jt. ed. see Muus, L. T.

***Atkins, Peter.** Ascension Now: Implications of Christ's Ascension for Today's Church. LC 00-38461. 2001. write for info. (*0-8146-2725-0*) Liturgical Pr.

Atkins, Peter. General Chemistry. 3rd ed. LC 96-21771. 1024p. 1996. pap. text 90.95 (*0-7167-2832-X*) W H Freeman.

— Physical Chemistry. 6th ed. 1998. 23.90 incl. cd-rom (*0-7167-3168-1*) W H Freeman.

— Second Law: Energy, Chaos & Form. rev. ed. (Illus.). 230p. (C). 1994. pap. text 19.95 (*0-7167-6006-1*) W H Freeman.

***Atkins, Peter.** Soul Care: Facing Life with God. 2001. pap. 18.99 (*0-8272-3449-X*) Chalice Pr.

— Soul Time: Building a Relationship with God. LC 99-50440. 184p. 2000. pap. 16.99 (*0-8272-3445-7*) Chalice Pr.

Atkins, Peter. Vocabulaire Anglais et Americain Robert & Collins. 394p. 1994. 59.95 (*0-7859-9198-0*) Fr & Eur.

***Atkins, Peter.** The Wishmaster. (Illus.). 255p. 1999. 28.00 (*1-901914-18-6*, Pub. by Pumpkin Bks) Firebird Dist.

— Worship 2000. LC 99-488465. 1999. pap. 19.95 (*0-00-599377-6*, Pub. by HarpC) Trafalgar.

***Atkins, Peter & Bowler, Ian.** Food & Society: Economy, Culture, Geography. (An Arnold Publication). (Illus.). 320p. 2000. pap. 29.95 (*0-340-72004-2*, Pub. by E A); text 74.00 (*0-340-72003-4*) E A.

Atkins, Peter, et al. People, Land & Time: An Historical Introduction to the Relations Between Landscape, Culture & Environment. LC 98-175518. (Arnold Publications). (Illus.). 304p. 1998. pap. text 29.95 (*0-340-67714-7*) OUP.

Atkins, Peter A. & Sharp, Stephen A. Mergers & Acquisitions in the Communications Industry. iv, 232p. write for info. (*0-318-61624-6*) Harcourt.

Atkins, Peter W. Concepts in Physical Chemistry. LC 95-22701. 380p. (C). 1995. text 20.95 (*0-7167-2928-8*) W H Freeman.

— Physical Chemistry. LC 85-7048. (C). text, teacher ed. write for info. (*0-7167-2562-2*) W H Freeman.

— Physical Chemistry. 4th ed. LC 85-7048. (C). 1990. text 45.60 (*0-7167-2073-6*) W H Freeman.

Atkins, Peter W. & Friedman, Ron S. Solutions Manual for Molecular Quantum Mechanics. 3rd ed. LC 97-34523. (Illus.). 264p. 1997. pap. text, teacher ed. 31.95 (*0-19-855968-2*) OUP.

***Atkins, R.** Dr. Atkins New Diet. 2000. 14.00 (*0-380-20948-9*) Morrow Avon.

Atkins, Rachel. It All Began with a Doormat. (Illus.). 32p. (J). 1994. 15.95 (*1-56062-236-9*) CIS Comm.

Atkins, Richard D., ed. see International Criminal Law Seminar Staff.

Atkins, Rick. Let's Scare 'Em! Grand Interviews & a Filmography of Horrific Proportions, 1930-1961. LC 97-12580. (Illus.). 260p. 1997. boxed set 48.50 (*0-7864-0373-X*) McFarland & Co.

Atkins, Robert. After Church, after Cole: Stephen Hannock's Oxbow. (Illus.). 24p. (Orig.). 1995. pap. 10.00 (*1-879067-00-5*) Putnam Found.

— Artspeak: A Guide to Contemporary Ideas, Movements, & Buzzwords. (Illus.). 176p. 1990. pap. 18.95 (*1-55859-010-2*) Abbeville Pr.

— Artspeak: A Guide to Contemporary Ideas, Movements & Buzzwords, 1945 to the Present. 2nd ed. (Illus.). 208p. 1997. 28.95 (*0-7892-0415-0*) Abbeville Pr.

— ArtSpeak: A Guide to the Contemporary Ideas, Movements, & Buzzwords, 1945 to the Present. 2nd rev. ed. LC 97-10858. (Illus.). 208p. 1997. pap. 18.95 (*0-7892-0365-0*) Abbeville Pr.

— Artspoke: A Guide to Modern Ideas, Movements, & Buzzwords, 1848-1944. LC 92-25982. (Illus.). 224p. 1993. 28.95 (*1-55859-389-6*); pap. 18.95 (*1-55859-388-8*) Abbeville Pr.

Atkins, Robert & Sokolowski, Thomas. From Media to Metaphor: Art about AIDS. (Illus.). 96p. 1992. pap. 20.00 (*0-685-57557-8*) Ind Curators.

Atkins, Robert A. Egalitarian Community: Ethnography & Exegesis. LC 90-38665. (Illus.). 278p. 1991. pap. 86.20 (*0-608-05182-9*, 206569000006) Bks Demand.

Atkins, Robert A., jt. auth. see Tapson, Frank.

Atkins, Robert A., jt. auth. see Williams, Edward.

***Atkins, Robert C.** Dr. Atkins' Age-Defying Diet Revolution. LC 99-55690. 308p. 2000. text 24.95 (*0-312-25189-0*) St Martin.

Atkins, Robert C. Dr. Atkins' Diet Revolution. 336p. 1981. mass mkt. 6.99 (*0-553-27157-1*) Bantam.

— Dr. Atkins' Health Revolution: How Complementary Medicine Can Extend Your Life. 448p. 1990. mass mkt. 6.99 (*0-553-28360-X*) Bantam.

— Dr. Atkins' New Carbohydrate Gram Counter. LC 96-61523. 96p. 1997. pap. 2.95 (*0-87131-815-6*) M Evans.

***Atkins, Robert C.** Dr. Atkins' New Diet Cookbook. (Illus.). 2000. 22.95 (*0-87131-925-X*) M Evans.

Atkins, Robert C. Dr. Atkins' New Diet Revolution, 1. 1999. 21.95 (*0-87131-886-5*) M Evans.

***Atkins, Robert C.** Dr. Atkins' New Diet Revolution. 1999. pap. 180.00 (*0-380-81458-7*, Avon Bks); pap. 90.00 (*0-380-81457-9*, Avon Bks) Morrow Avon.

— Dr. Atkins' New Diet Revolution: Conger,&Eric. abr. ed. 1998. audio 18.00 (*0-694-52001-2*) HarperAudio.

— Dr. Atkins' New Diet Revolution: Revised & Updated. 464p. 1999. pap. 14.00 (*0-380-80368-2*, Avon Bks); mass mkt. 7.50 (*0-380-72729-3*, Avon Bks) Morrow Avon.

Atkins, Robert C. Dr. Atkins' Quick & Easy New Diet Cookbook. LC 96-37403. 224p. 1997. per. 12.95 (*0-684-83701-3*) S&S Trade.

— Dr. Atkins' Vita-Nutrient Solution: Nature's Answer to Drugs. LC 97-42790. 407p. 1998. 23.50 (*0-684-81849-3*) S&S Trade.

— Dr. Atkins' Vita-Nutrient Solution: Nature's Answers to Drugs. 448p. 1999. per. 15.00 (*0-684-84488-5*) S&S Trade.

***Atkins, Robert C.** Los Vita Nutrientes. 1999. pap. 23.95 (*970-05-1083-2*) Distribks Inc.

Atkins, Robert C. El Nuevo Libro de Cocina Diete. (SPA.). 224p. 1997. per. 12.95 (*0-684-84195-9*, Libros) S&S Trade Pap.

— Organic Chemistry: A Brief Course. 3rd ed. 2001. 48.74 (*0-07-231944-5*) McGraw.

— Revolucion Dietetica Del Dr. Atkins. 1997. pap. text 18.98 (*970-05-0302-X*) Grijalbo Edit.

***Atkins, Robert C. & Buff, Sheila.** Dr. Atkins' Age-Defying Diet Revolution. 2001. reprint ed. pap. 7.50 (*0-312-97701-8*, St Martins Paperbacks) St Martin.

Atkins, Robert C. & Carey, Frank A. A Brief Introduction to Organic Chemistry. 142p. (C). 1989. text 67.50 (*0-07-009919-7*) McGraw.

— Organic Chemistry: A Brief Course. (C). 1989. text, student ed. 23.75 (*0-07-009921-9*) McGraw.

— Organic Chemistry: A Brief Course. (C). 1989. trans. 240.00 (*0-07-074455-6*) McGraw.

— Organic Chemistry: A Brief Course. 2nd ed. LC 96-79060. 524p. (C). 1996. 81.56 (*0-07-011337-8*) McGraw.

Atkins, Robert C. & Gare, Fran. Dr. Atkins' New Diet Cookbook. LC 94-1273. 264p. 2000. 22.95 (*0-87131-794-X*) M Evans.

*Atkins, Robert C. & Gare, Fran. Dr. Atkins' New Diet Value Pack. 256p. 2000. pap. 22.95 (0-87131-937-3) Natl Bk Netwk.

Atkins, Robert C., jt. auth. see Carey, Francis A.

Atkins, Ronald. Beer. (Collins Gem Ser.). 1997. pap. 8.00 (0-00-470882-2) Collins.

*Atkins, Ronald. Beer. (Collins Gem Ser.). (Illus.). 256p. 2000. pap. 7.95 (0-00-472261-2, Pub. by HarpC) Trafalgar.

*Atkins, Ronald, ed. Jazz: The Ultimate Guide. (Illus.). 224p. 2000. pap. 19.95 (1-85868-592-3, Pub. by Carlton Bks Ltd) Natl Bk Netwk.

Atkins, Ruth E. The Measurement of the Intelligence of Young Children by an Object-Fitting Test, Vol. 5. LC 75-12673. (University of Minnesota Institute of Child Welfare Monographs: No. 5). (Illus.). 89p. 1970. reprint ed. lib. bdg. 45.00 (0-8371-8083-X, CWAI) Greenwood.

Atkins, S. & Wagner, A. S., eds. Transputer Research & Applications 6: Proceedings of the Sixth North American Transputer Users Group (NATUG-6) (Transputer & Ocean Engineering Ser.: Vol. 34). 363p. (gr. 12). 1993. pap. 117.00 (90-5199-120-7, Pub. by IOS Pr) IOS Press.

Atkins, Simon, jt. auth. see McIntyre, Chris.

Atkins, Sinclair. England & Wales under the Tudors. (Illus.). 277p. 1975. pap. 30.00 (0-7131-1982-9, Pub. by Hodder & Stought Ltd) Lubrecht & Cramer.

— From Stone Age to Conquest. LC 85-73167. (Illus.). 96p. (J). (gr. 5-8). 1984. pap. 14.95 (0-7175-1305-X) Dufour.

Atkins, Stephen E. Arms Control, Disarmament, International Security & Peace: An Annotated Guide to Sources, 1980-1987. LC 88-21822. 411p. 1988. lib. bdg. 79.00 (0-87436-488-4) ABC-CLIO.

— Critical Paths: Designing for Secure Travels. (Issues in Design Ser.). (Illus.). 96p. (C). 1989. pap. 22.95 (0-85072-279-9, Pub. by Gower) Ashgate Pub Co.

— Historical Encyclopedia of Atomic Energy. LC 99-29618. 504p. 2000. 65.00 (0-313-30400-9, Greenwood Pr) Greenwood.

— Terrorism: A Reference Handbook. LC 92-28530. (Contemporary World Issues Ser.). 199p. 1992. lib. bdg. 39.50 (0-87436-670-4) ABC-CLIO.

Atkins, Stuart. Essays on Goethe. Brown, Jane K. & Saine, Thomas P., eds. (GERM Ser.). viii, 334p. (C). 1996. 75.00 (1-57113-027-6) Camden Hse.

— The Name of Your Game: Four Game Plans for Success at Home & at Work. (Illus.). (C). 1982. 17.95 (0-942532-00-7); pap. 6.95 (0-942532-01-5) Ellis & Stewart Pub.

Atkins, Stuart, ed. & tr. see Goethe, Johann Wolfgang Von.

Atkins, Thomas. History of Middlefield & Long Hill, Connecticut. 175p. 1997. reprint ed. lib. bdg. 26.50 (0-8328-5666-5) Higginson Bk Co.

*Atkinson. Advances in Remote Sensing & GIS Analysis. LC 99-10017. 288p. 1999. 99.00 (0-471-98577-5) Wiley.

— Behind the Scenes at the Museum. 2000. pap. 10.95 (0-552-99618-1, Pub. by Transworld Publishers Ltd) Trafalgar.

— Business Accounting in Hospitality & Tourism. 1995. pap. 21.99 (1-86152-470-6, Pub. by ITBP) Thomson Learn.

Atkinson. Business & Computer Careers. 1991. mass mkt. 42.50 (0-314-77272-3) West Pub.

Atkinson. Climbing out of Depression. 1993. pap. 14.95 (0-7459-2248-1, Pub. by Lion Pubng) Trafalgar.

Atkinson. Exploring Business & Computer Careers. (Career Development Ser.). 1992. pap. text, student ed. 20.75 (0-314-90418-2) West Pub.

— Introduction to Psychology. 12th ed. (C). 1995. student ed. 87.00 (0-15-503912-1) Harcourt.

— Introduction to Psychology. 12th ed. (C). 1996. pap. text, teacher ed. 35.00 (0-15-503073-6) Harcourt Coll Pubs.

— Introduction to Psychology. 13th ed. (C). 1999. text Price not set. (0-15-508044-X) Harcourt Coll Pubs.

— Introduction to Psychology: Test Bank. 12th ed. (C). 1996. pap. text, teacher ed., suppl. ed. 41.50 (0-15-503075-2, Pub. by Harcourt Coll Pubs) Harcourt.

*Atkinson. Jonah's Whale of a Time Book. (J). 1999. pap. 7.50 (0-7459-3682-2, Pub. by Lion Pubng) Trafalgar.

Atkinson. Laboratory Testing of Soils & Soft Rocks. (Illus.). 448p. 1998. pap. 164.95 (0-7514-0388-1) Thomson Learn.

— Legal Research via the Internet. (Paralegal Ser.). 1996. teacher ed. 12.95 (0-8273-7451-8) Delmar.

— Medical Office Practice. 6th ed. (Allied Health Ser.). 128p. (C). 1998. text 52.95 (0-7668-0605-7) Delmar.

— Medical Office Practice - IML. 6th ed. 1998. teacher ed. 25.95 (0-7668-0855-6) Delmar.

— Power Notes for Management Accounting. 1996. text 19.75 (0-13-266651-0) P-H.

— Psychologie. 2nd ed. (C). 1991. pap. write for info. (0-03-998273-4) Harcourt Coll Pubs.

— Regulatory Proteins of the Complement System. 1992. write for info. (0-8493-6710-7, CRC Reprint) Franklin.

— Salt Water Intrusion. 1986. 223.00 (0-87371-054-1, GB1197, CRC Reprint) Franklin.

Atkinson. Sexual Morality. 208p. 1993. 61.95 (0-7512-0158-8) Ashgate Pub Co.

Atkinson. Understanding Nursing. 6th ed. 2000. write for info. (0-07-135079-9) McGraw.

— Understanding Nursing (set 3) 6th ed. 243p. 2000. pap. 25.00 (0-07-135078-0) McGraw.

Atkinson & Banker. Management Accounting & Cases. 2nd ed. 1996. pap. text, student ed. 33.40 (0-13-262965-8) P-H.

Atkinson & Hackett. Counseling Diverse Po. 2nd ed. LC 97-8388. 416p. 1997. pap. 43.13 (0-697-25280-9) McGraw.

*Atkinson & Longman. Go: Getting Oriented. 2nd ed. 2000. pap. 30.00 (0-534-55387-7) Thomson Learn.

Atkinson & Mechem, Floyd R. Wills & Administration. 5th ed. 1961. text 29.00 (0-88277-392-5) Foundation Pr.

Atkinson & Reilly, T., eds. Sports, Leisure & Ergonomics. (Illus.). 336p. (C). 1995. 110.00 (0-419-20600-0, E & FN Spon) Routledge.

Atkinson, jt. auth. see Hilgard.

Atkinson, jt. auth. see Hilgard, Atkinson.

Atkinson, jt. auth. see Longman.

Atkinson, A. The Himalayan Gazetter: Historical, Ethnological, Geographical & Scientific, 6 pts. in 3 vols., Set. (C). 1988. 590.00 (0-7855-0055-3, Pub. by Print Hse) St Mut.

— Modern Organic Chemistry. 3rd ed. 272p. (C). 1994. pap. 25.00 (0-85950-656-8, Pub. by S Thornes Pubs) Trans-Atl Phila.

*Atkinson, A. & Riani, M. Robust Diagnostic Regression Analysis. (Springer Series in Statistics). 344p. 2000. 79.95 (0-387-95017-6) Spr-Verlag.

Atkinson, A. B. The Economic Consequences of Rolling Back the Welfare State. LC 99-11116. (Munich Lectures). (Illus.). 216p. 1999. 22.50 (0-262-01171-9) MIT Pr.

— Empirical Studies of Earnings Mobility, Vol. 52. (Fundamentals of Pure & Applied Economics Ser.). xi, 149p. 1992. pap. text 41.00 (3-7186-5214-5, Harwood Acad Pubs) Gordon & Breach.

— Incomes & the Welfare State: Essays on Britain & Europe. 380p. (C). 1996. text 74.95 (0-521-46250-9) Cambridge U Pr.

— Incomes & the Welfare State: Essays on Britain & Europe. 380p. (C). 1996. pap. text 25.95 (0-521-55796-8) Cambridge U Pr.

— Poverty in Europe. LC 98-11439. 192p. 1998. 44.95 (0-631-20909-3); pap. 22.95 (0-631-21029-6) Blackwell Pubs.

Atkinson, A. B., ed. Wealth, Income, & Inequality. 2nd ed. (Illus.). 1981. pap. 29.95 (0-19-877144-4) OUP.

Atkinson, A. B. & Bourguignon, F., eds. Handbook of Income Distribution. (Handbooks in Economics Ser.). 1996. write for info. (0-444-81631-3, North Holland) Elsevier.

Atkinson, A. B. & Micklewright, M. Economic Transformation in Eastern Europe & the Distribution of Income. 464p. (C). 1992. text 69.95 (0-521-43329-0); pap. text 22.95 (0-521-43882-9) Cambridge U Pr.

Atkinson, A. B. & Morgensen, Gunnar V., eds. Welfare & Work Incentives. (Illus.). 344p. 1994. text 65.00 (0-19-828860-3) OUP.

Atkinson, A. B., et al. Parents & Children: Incomes in Two Generations. (DHSS Studies in Deprivation & Disadvantage: No. 10). 224p. 1983. text 78.95 (0-435-82097-4) Ashgate Pub Co.

— Wealth & Personal Incomes. LC 77-30556. 1978. 74.00 (0-08-022450-4, Pub. by Pergamon Repr) Franklin.

Atkinson, A. C. Plots, Transformations & Regression: An Introduction to Graphical Methods of Diagnostic Regression Analysis. (Oxford Statistical Science Ser.). (Illus.). 296p. 1987. pap. text 45.00 (0-19-853371-3) OUP.

Atkinson, A. C., et al, eds. MODA 5 - Advances in Model-Oriented Data Analysis & Experimental Design: Proceedings of the 5th International Workshop in Marseilles, France, June 22-26, 1998. LC 98-21609. (Contributions to Statistics Ser.). (Illus.). xvi, 300p. 1998. pap. 73.00 (3-7908-1111-4) Spr-Verlag.

Atkinson, A. C. & Donev, A. N. Optimum Experimental Designs. LC 92-8342. (Oxford Statistical Science Ser.: Vol. 7). (Illus.). 344p. (C). 1992. text 75.00 (0-19-852254-1, Clarendon Pr) OUP.

Atkinson, A. C. & Fienberg, Stephen E., eds. A Celebration of Statistics. (Illus.). 608p. 1985. 79.95 (0-387-96111-9) Spr-Verlag.

Atkinson, Adrian, et al, eds. The Challenge of Environmental Management in Urban Areas. LC 99-72605. (Studies in Environmental Policy & Practice). 302p. 1999. text 61.95 (1-84014-525-0, Pub. by Ashgate Pub) Ashgate Pub Co.

Atkinson, Alan. The Europeans in Australia: The Beginning, Vol. 1. (Illus.). 448p. 1997. text 60.00 (0-19-553641-X) OUP.

— The Muddle-Headed Republic. 160p. 1994. pap. 24.95 (0-19-553638-X) OUP.

Atkinson, Alexander. Social Order & the General Theory of Strategy. LC 81-17906. 305p. (Orig.). 1982. pap. 18.95 (0-7100-0907-0, Routledge Thoemms) Routledge.

Atkinson, Ann, et al. The Dictionary of Performing Arts in Australia Vol. I: Theatre, Film, Television, Radio. LC 96-207111. 360p. 1996. pap. 29.95 (1-86373-660-3, Pub. by Allen & Unwin Pty) Paul & Co Pubs.

— The Dictionary of Performing Arts in Australia Vol. II: Opera, Music, Dance. (Illus.). 284p. 1997. pap. 29.95 (1-86373-898-3, Pub. by Allen & Unwin Pty) Paul & Co Pubs.

Atkinson, Anne, compiled by. Dictionary of Western Australians Vol. V: Asian Immigrants to Western Australia 1829-1901. 1989. 29.95 (0-85564-287-4, Pub. by Univ of West Aust Pr) Intl Spec Bk.

*Atkinson, Anne J. The Successful School Resource Officer Program: Building Effective School & Law Enforcement Partnerships. LC 00-130999. 210p. 2000. pap. 33.95 (0-9679562-0-X) Greystone VA.

Atkinson, Anthony A., jt. auth. see Kaplan, Robert S.

Atkinson, Anthony A., ed. see Banker, Rajiv D.

Atkinson, Anthony B. Poverty in Britain & the Reform of Social Security. LC 76-85711. (University of Cambridge, Dept. of Applied Economics, Occasional Papers: 18). 224p. reprint ed. pap. 63.90 (0-608-12313-7, 2024402) Bks Demand.

— Public Economics in Action: The Basic Income - Flat Tax Proposal. (Lindahl Lectures on Monetary & Fiscal Policy). (Illus.). 184p. 1997. reprint ed. pap. text 17.95 (0-19-829216-3) OUP.

Atkinson, Anthony B., ed. Modern Public Finance, 2 vols. (International Library of Critical Writings in Economics: No. 15). 880p. 1991. text 360.00 (1-85278-153-X) E Elgar.

Atkinson, Anthony B. & Harrison, A. J. Distribution of Personal Wealth in Britain. LC 77-2715. 344p. reprint ed. pap. 98.10 (0-608-15690-6, 2031617) Bks Demand.

Atkinson, Anthony B., ed. see International Economic Association Staff.

Atkinson, Arthur. The Cosmic Fairy: The New Challenge of a Darwinian Approach to Humanism. 160p. 1997. pap. 14.95 (0-86140-403-3, Pub. by Smyth) Dufour.

*Atkinson, Austen. Impact Earth: Asteroids, Comets & Meteoroids, the Growing Threat. (Illus.). 352p. 2000. mass mkt. 7.95 (0-7535-0401-4) Virgin Pubng.

Atkinson, Austen. Impact Earth: Asteroids, Comets & Meteors--The Growing Threat. 1999. 24.95 (1-85227-789-0) Virgin Bks.

Atkinson, B. W., et al. Weather & Water. LC 85-6594. (Reviews of U. K. Statistical Sources Ser.: Vol. 7). 240p. 1985. 122.00 (0-08-031844-4, Pergamon Pr) Elsevier.

Atkinson, Barbara, jt. auth. see Hernandez, Enrique.

Atkinson, Barbara F. Atlas of Diagnostic Cytopathology. (Illus.). 706p. 1992. text 240.00 (0-7216-3528-8, W B Saunders Co) Harcrt Hlth Sci Grp.

Atkinson, Barbara F. & Silverman, Jan F. Atlas of Difficult Diagnoses in Cytopathology. Ross, Alan, ed. LC 97-31213. 432p. (C). 1998. text 245.00 (0-7216-4076-1, W B Saunders Co) Harcrt Hlth Sci Grp.

Atkinson, Barry. Mining Sites in Cornwall & South-West Devon. 96p. (C). 1989. text 50.00 (1-85022-044-1, Pub. by Dyllansow Truran) St Mut.

Atkinson, Barry K., ed. Fracture Mechanics of Rocks. (Geology Ser.: Academic Press). 544p. 1989. reprint ed. pap. text 65.00 (0-12-066266-3) Acad Pr.

Atkinson, Basil F. Ezekiel (Eleven Chapters for Soul Winners) pap. 1.99 (1-56632-004-6) Revival Lit.

— Judges & Ruth. 1969. pap. 3.99 (1-56632-003-8) Revival Lit.

Atkinson, Belinda. Tarot of the Soul: How to Explore Your Soul & Intuition. 80p. 1995. pap. 8.95 (1-893183-21-1, Swan Raven) Granite Pub.

Atkinson, Benjamin P., jt. ed. see Waite, Harlow O.

Atkinson, Bernard, jt. ed. see Cooper, P. F.

*Atkinson, Bill. Electrical Installation Designs 2nd ed. LC 99-38064. 1999. write for info. (0-632-05398-4) Blackwell Sci.

Atkinson, Brian. Atkinson's Updates in Economics, Vol. 5, 1. 5th ed. (C). 1997. pap. text. write for info. (0-201-17788-9) Addison-Wesley.

— Updates in Economics, vol. 7. 7th ed. (C). 1999. pap. text. write for info. (0-201-64855-5) Addison-Wesley.

Atkinson, Brooks & Hirschfeld, Al. The Lively Years, 1920-1973. (Quality Paperbacks Ser.). (Illus.). 312p. 1985. reprint ed. pap. 9.95 (0-306-80234-1) Da Capo.

Atkinson, Brooks, ed. see Emerson, Ralph Waldo.

Atkinson, Brooks, ed. see Thoreau, Henry David.

Atkinson, C. T., jt. auth. see Johnson, Arthur H.

Atkinson, Camille, jt. auth. see Fredrick, Candice.

*Atkinson, Catherine. From Borshch To Blinis. 96p. 2000. 14.95 (1-84215-158-4) Anness Pub.

— 7-Day Fat Burning Diet Plan: Change Your Eating Habits for Life. 160p. 2000. pap. 13.95 (0-572-02565-3) Foulsham UK.

Atkinson, Cecil & Tilley, Kathy. Camp Claiborne. (Illus.). 164p. (Orig.). 1990. pap. 16.95 (0-9626853-0-5) Ack Hill Pub.

Atkinson, Charles. The Best of Us on Fire. (Chapbook Ser.: Series 8). 32p. 1992. 13.95 (0-933573-16-2) Wayland Pr.

— The Only Cure I Know. Iddings, Kathleen, ed. LC 91-90048. (American Bk.). 71p. 1991. pap. text, per. 10.00 (0-931289-06-8) San Diego Poet Pr.

— The Portrait. LC 98-11357. 272p. 1998. text 23.95 (0-312-18652-5) St Martin.

*Atkinson, Charles. Risk Factor. LC 99-33505. 256p. 1999. text 23.95 (0-312-20920-7) St Martin.

Atkinson, Charles F. Portrait, Vol. 1. Date not set. write for info. (0-312-96698-9) Tor Bks.

Atkinson, Charles F., tr. see Spengler, Oswald.

Atkinson, Charles M. Jeremy Bentham: His Life & Work. LC 78-98208. 247p. 1970. reprint ed. lib. bdg. 35.00 (0-8371-3243-6, ATJB, Greenwood Pr) Greenwood.

— Jeremy Bentham, His Life & Work. (BCL Ser.: No. 1). reprint ed. 29.50 (0-404-00416-4) AMS Pr.

Atkinson, Christopher T. A History of Germany, Seventeen Fifteen to Eighteen Fifteen. LC 70-114456. (Illus.). 732p. 1971. reprint ed. lib. bdg. 85.00 (0-8371-4807-3, ATHG, Greenwood Pr) Greenwood.

Atkinson, Chuck. Automation Pays! How to Automate Your Retail Business - Success Stories. Record, Sandra H., ed. 215p. (Orig.). 1995. pap. text 19.95 (0-917081-33-1) Aces Four Pr.

— Quick Check: Bookkeeping with Personal Computers. 2nd ed. 1994. pap. text 10.00 (0-917081-04-8) CAP Automation.

— Sell Wise: Automate Your Retail, Repair or Mail Order Business. 2nd ed. 148p. 1994. pap. text 14.95 (0-917081-29-3) CAP Automation.

Atkinson, Clarissa. The Oldest Vocation: Christian Motherhood in the Middle Ages. (Illus.). 288p. 1994. pap. text 16.95 (0-8014-8204-6) Cornell U Pr.

Atkinson, Clarissa W. Mystic & Pilgrim: The "Book" & the World of Margery Kempe. LC 82-22219. 242p. (C). 1983. pap. text 16.95 (0-8014-9895-3) Cornell U Pr.

— Mystic & Pilgrim: The Book & the World of Margery Kempe. LC 82-22219. (Illus.). 245p. reprint ed. pap. 76.00 (0-608-20087-5, 207135900011) Bks Demand.

Atkinson, Clarissa W., et al, eds. Shaping New Vision: Gender & Values in American Culture. LC 87-13854. (Studies in Religion: No. 5). 236p. reprint ed. pap. 73.20 (0-8357-1803-4, 207062500009) Bks Demand.

Atkinson, Clifford W. A Lay Minister's Guide to the Book of Common Prayer. rev. ed. LC 88-5147. 96p. 1988. reprint ed. pap. 8.95 (0-8192-1454-X) Morehouse Pub.

Atkinson, Colin. Object-Oriented Reuse, Concurrency, & Distribution: An Ada-Based Approach. 288p. (C). 1991. 39.95 (0-201-56527-7) Addison-Wesley.

Atkinson, D. Scott, et al. An American Pulse: The Lithographs of George Wesley Bellows. LC 98-55490. 1999. write for info. (0-937108-22-7) San Diego Museum of Art.

Atkinson, Dale R., et al. Low Speed Automobile Accidents: Accident Reconstruction & Occupant Kinematics, Dynamics & Biomechanics. 2nd ed. LC 96-23978. 688p. 1999. 115.00 (0-913875-23-6, 5236-N) Lawyers & Judges.

Atkinson, Daniel E. Cellular Energy Metabolism & Its Regulation. 1977. text 79.00 (0-12-066150-0) Acad Pr.

Atkinson, Daniel E., et al. Dynamic Models in Chemistry: A Workbook of Computer Simulations Using Electronic Spreadsheets. Barkley, David S., ed. (Illus.). 320p. (C). 1990. pap. text 19.95 (0-9622556-2-9) Simonson & Co.

Atkinson, Daniel E., jt. auth. see Elliott, Larry.

Atkinson, David. Jesus, Lamb of God: Biblical Meditations. 120p. 1995. pap. 9.95 (0-687-06626-3) Abingdon.

Atkinson, David. Probation in a Cold Climate: Assessing Suitability for Community Sentences & Putting Supervision into Effect for a Sceptical Audience. LC 98-101707. (Illus.). 1997. write for info. (0-901382-19-1) Cambs Criminology.

Atkinson, David. Teaching Monolingual Classes: Longman Keys to Language Teaching. LC 92-26630. (Keys to Language Teaching Ser.). 1993. pap. text 17.95 (0-582-06110-5, 79900) Longman.

Atkinson, David, jt. auth. see Dodds, Klaus J.

Atkinson, David, jt. ed. see Dodds, Klaus.

Atkinson, David A., jt. ed. see Hill, Herbert H., Jr.

*Atkinson, David B. & Dallas, James W. Life Insurance Products & Finance: Charting a Clear Course. (Illus.). 800p. (C). 2000. text. write for info. (0-938959-67-0) Soc Actuaries.

Atkinson, David E., et al. Dynamic Models in Biochemistry: A Workbook of Computer Simulations Using Electronic Spreadsheets. Barkley, David S., ed. (Illus.). 347p. (C). 1989. reprint ed. pap. text 19.95 (0-9622556-0-2) Simonson & Co.

Atkinson, David J., et al, eds. New Dictionary of Christian Ethics & Pastoral Theology. LC 94-40802. 944p. 1994. 39.99 (0-8308-1408-6, 1408) InterVarsity.

Atkinson, David N. Leaving the Bench: Supreme Court Justices at the End. LC 98-54752. (Illus.). 264p. 1999. 29.95 (0-7006-0946-6) U Pr of KS.

*Atkinson, David N. Leaving the Bench: Supreme Court Justices at the End. 2000. pap. 16.95 (0-7006-1058-8) U Pr of KS.

Atkinson, David W. The English Ars Moriendi. LC 92-13185. (Renaissance & Baroque Studies & Texts: Vol. 5). 387p. (C). 1992. text 52.95 (0-8204-1903-6) P Lang Pubng.

— An Introduction to the World's Major Religions. LC 87-28461. (Illus.). 312p. (C). 1988. lib. bdg. 99.95 (0-88946-015-9) E Mellen.

Atkinson, David W., ed. Selected Sermons of Zachary Boyd. (STS Ser.). 335p. 1989. text 45.00 (0-08-037000-4, Pub. by Aberdeen U Pr) Macmillan.

Atkinson, Diana. Highways & Dancehalls. LC 96-45531. (Illus.). 235p. 1997. text 21.95 (0-312-15139-X) St Martin.

Atkinson, Diane. Votes for Women: Women & the Suffrage Movement. (Women in History Ser.). (Illus.). 48p. (C). 1989. pap. 13.95 (0-521-31044-X) Cambridge U Pr.

Atkinson, Dick. Radical Urban Solutions: Urban Renaissance for City Schools & Communities. (Education Ser.). (Illus.). 192p. 1994. pap. 37.95 (0-304-32830-8) Continuum.

Atkinson, Dick, ed. Cities of Pride: Rebuilding Community, Refocusing Government. (Cassell Social Science Ser.). (Illus.). 176p. 1995. 100.00 (0-304-33403-0); pap. 27.95 (0-304-33404-9) Continuum.

Atkinson, Donald, et al. Counseling American Minorities. 5th ed. LC 97-12937. (C). 52.95 (0-697-20171-6, WCB McGr Hill) McGrw-H Hghr Educ.

— Counseling American Minorities. 6th ed. 2000. pap. 25.50 (0-697-36185-3) McGraw.

Atkinson, Donald A. & Roesel, Charles L. Meeting Needs, Sharing Christ: Ministry Evangelism in Today's New Testament Church. 176p. 1995. pap. text 12.95 (0-8054-9842-7, LifeWay Press) LifeWay Christian.

Atkinson, Donald R. & Hackett, Gail. Counseling Diverse Populations. LC 94-70182. 400p. (C). 1994. text. write for info. (0-697-21129-0) Brown & Benchmark.

Atkinson, Donald R., et al. Counseling American Minorities: A Cross-Cultural Perspective. 4th ed. 400p. (C). 1992. text. write for info. (0-697-10444-3) Brown & Benchmark.

Atkinson, Donald T. Magic, Myth & Medicine. LC 72-8510. (Essay Index Reprint Ser.). 1977. reprint ed. 21.95 (0-8369-7316-X) Ayer.

Atkinson, Doreen, jt. ed. see Friedman, Steven.

Atkinson, Dorothy. An Auto-Biographical Approach to Learning Disability Research. LC 97-72080. (Illus.). 160p. 1997. text 59.95 (1-85628-645-2, Pub. by Avebry) Ashgate Pub Co.

Atkinson, Dorothy. The Children's Book Room. 190p. 1989. pap. 16.00 (0-948080-24-8, Trentham Bks) Stylus Pub VA.

Atkinson, Dorothy, et al, eds. Women in Russia. LC 75-39333. xiv, 410p. 1977. reprint ed. pap. 16.95 (0-8047-0920-3) Stanford U Pr.

Atkinson, Dorothy F. Edmund Spenser: Bibliographical Supplement. LC 67-30806. (Studies in Spenser: No. 26). 1969. reprint ed. lib. bdg. 75.00 (0-8383-0705-1) M S G Haskell Hse.

A

Atkinson, Doug & Zippan, Fiona. Videos for Kids: The Essential, Indispensable Parent's Guide to Children's Movies on Video. LC 94-27680. 432p. 1994. pap. 9.95 (*1-55958-635-4*) Prima Pub.

Atkinson, Dwight. Scientific Discourse in Sociohistorical Context: The Philosophical Transactions of the Royal Society of London, 1675-1975. LC 98-25130. (Rhetoric, Society & Knowledge Ser.). 240p. 1998. 49.95 (*0-8058-2085-X*); pap. 22.50 (*0-8058-2086-8*) L Erlbaum Assocs.

Atkinson, E. T. Economic Botany of the Himalayan Regions. (C). 1988. 60.00 (*0-7855-2279-4*, Pub. by Scientific) St Mut.

— Himalayan Gazetteer, Historical, Ethnological, Geographical & Scientific, 3 vols., Set. 1445p. 1974. text 110.00 (*0-685-14031-8*) Coronet Bks.

Atkinson, Earl. Advanced Hustle. (Ballroom Dance Ser.). 1986. lib. bdg. 250.00 (*0-8490-3623-2*) Gordon Pr.

— American Swing. (Ballroom Dance Ser.). 1986. lib. bdg. 250.00 (*0-8490-3633-X*) Gordon Pr.

— American Waltz. (Ballroom Dance Ser.). 1986. lib. bdg. 250.00 (*0-8490-3635-6*) Gordon Pr.

— Ballroom Polka. (Ballroom Dance Ser.). 1983. lib. bdg. 250.00 (*0-87700-476-5*) Revisionist Pr.

— Ballroom Terminology. (Ballroom Dance Ser.). 1986. lib. bdg. 79.95 (*0-8490-3624-0*) Gordon Pr.

— Ballroom Terminology. (Ballroom Dance Ser.). 1983. lib. bdg. 250.00 (*0-87700-480-3*) Revisionist Pr.

— Bolero-Rumba. (Ballroom Dance Ser.). 1986. lib. bdg. 250.00 (*0-8490-3620-8*) Gordon Pr.

— Bolero-Rumba. (Ballroom Dance Ser.). 1983. lib. bdg. 250.00 (*0-87700-488-9*) Revisionist Pr.

— Bossa Nova. (Ballroom Dance Ser.). 1983. lib. bdg. 250.00 (*0-87700-487-0*) Revisionist Pr.

— Bossa Nova: Ballroom Dance Ser. 1986. lib. bdg. 250.00 (*0-8490-3621-6*) Gordon Pr.

— Cha Cha Cha. (Ballroom Dance Ser.). 1986. lib. bdg. 250.00 (*0-8490-3622-4*) Gordon Pr.

— Cha Cha Cha. (Ballroom Dance Ser.). 1983. lib. bdg. 250.00 (*0-87700-478-1*) Revisionist Pr.

— Eighteen Steps in the Basic Fox-Trot. (Ballroom Dance Ser.). 1986. lib. bdg. 250.00 (*0-8490-3638-0*) Gordon Pr.

— Fox Trot. (Ballroom Dance Ser.). 1983. lib. bdg. 250.00 (*0-87700-471-4*) Revisionist Pr.

— Fox Trot (Advaneed Routine) (Ballroom Dance Ser.). 1986. lib. bdg. 250.00 (*0-8490-3641-0*) Gordon Pr.

— Hustle, Advanced. (Ballroom Dance Ser.). 1983. lib. bdg. 250.00 (*0-87700-485-4*) Revisionist Pr.

— Hustle & Disco. (Ballroom Dance Ser.). 1986. lib. bdg. 250.00 (*0-8490-3625-9*) Gordon Pr.

— Hustle & Disco. (Ballroom Dance Ser.). 1983. lib. bdg. 250.00 (*0-87700-482-X*) Revisionist Pr.

— Latin Ballroom Dancing. (Ballroom Dance Ser.). 1983. lib. bdg. 79.95 (*0-87700-481-1*) Revisionist Pr.

— Latin Ballroom Dancing: Including Rumba, Cha Cha Cha, Tango, Samba, Mambo, Merengue & Paso Doble. (Ballroom Dance Ser.). 1986. lib. bdg. 250.00 (*0-8490-3626-7*) Gordon Pr.

— Line Dancing Including Line, Circle, Novelty, & Mixers. (Ballroom Dance Ser.). 1986. lib. bdg. 250.00 (*0-8490-3640-2*) Gordon Pr.

— Mambo. (Ballroom Dance Ser.). 1986. lib. bdg. 250.00 (*0-8490-3627-5*) Gordon Pr.

— Mambo Combinations. (Ballroom Dance Ser.). 1983. lib. bdg. 250.00 (*0-87700-475-7*) Revisionist Pr.

— Merengue. (Ballroom Dance Ser.). 1986. lib. bdg. 250.00 (*0-8490-3628-3*) Gordon Pr.

— Merengue. (Ballroom Dance Ser.). 1983. lib. bdg. 250.00 (*0-87700-472-2*) Revisionist Pr.

— Modern American Waltz. (Ballroom Dance Ser.). 1986. lib. bdg. 250.00 (*0-8490-3643-7*) Gordon Pr.

— Modern Triple Swing. (Ballroom Dance Ser.). 1986. lib. bdg. 250.00 (*0-8490-3645-3*) Gordon Pr.

— Paso Doble. (Ballroom Dance Ser.). 1986. lib. bdg. 250.00 (*0-8490-3629-1*) Gordon Pr.

— Paso Doble. (Ballroom Dance Ser.). 1983. lib. bdg. 250.00 (*0-87700-489-7*) Revisionist Pr.

— Peabody. (Ballroom Dance Ser.). 1986. lib. bdg. 250.00 (*0-8490-3630-5*) Gordon Pr.

— Peabody Steps. 1983. lib. bdg. 250.00 (*0-87700-484-6*) Revisionist Pr.

— Polka. (Ballroom Dance Ser.). 1986. lib. bdg. 250.00 (*0-8490-3637-2*) Gordon Pr.

— Quickstep. (Ballroom Dance Ser.). 1986. lib. bdg. 250.00 (*0-8490-3644-5*) Gordon Pr.

— Rumba. (Ballroom Dance Ser.). 1986. lib. bdg. 250.00 (*0-8490-3631-3*) Gordon Pr.

— Rumba Combinations. (Ballroom Dance Ser.). 1983. lib. bdg. 250.00 (*0-87700-477-3*) Revisionist Pr.

— Salsa. (Ballroom Dance Ser.). 1986. lib. bdg. 250.00 (*0-8490-3639-9*) Gordon Pr.

— Samba. (Ballroom Dance Ser.). 1986. lib. bdg. 250.00 (*0-8490-3632-1*) Gordon Pr.

— Samba. (Ballroom Dance Ser.). 1983. lib. bdg. 250.00 (*0-87700-473-0*) Revisionist Pr.

— Swing. (Ballroom Dance Ser.). 1983. lib. bdg. 250.00 (*0-87700-470-6*) Revisionist Pr.

— Tango. (Ballroom Dance Ser.). 1986. lib. bdg. 250.00 (*0-8490-3634-8*) Gordon Pr.

— Tango. (Ballroom Dance Ser.). 1983. lib. bdg. 250.00 (*0-87700-490-0*) Revisionist Pr.

— Three Count Hustle. (Ballroom Dance Ser.). 1986. lib. bdg. 250.00 (*0-8490-3642-9*) Gordon Pr.

— Viennese Waltz. (Ballroom Dance Ser.). 1986. lib. bdg. 250.00 (*0-8490-3636-4*) Gordon Pr.

— The Waltz (American) (Ballroom Dance Ser.). 1983. lib. bdg. 250.00 (*0-87700-479-X*) Revisionist Pr.

— Waltz (Viennese) 1983. lib. bdg. 250.00 (*0-87700-486-2*) Revisionist Pr.

Atkinson, Edward. The Industrial Progress of the Nation. LC 73-1989. (Big Business; Economic Power in a Free Society Ser.). 1973. reprint ed. 26.95 (*0-405-05073-9*) Ayer.

Atkinson, Edwin F. Notes on the History of Religion in the Himalaya of the N. W. P., India. LC 78-72374. reprint ed. 37.50 (*0-404-17224-5*) AMS Pr.

Atkinson, Eleanor. Greyfriars Bobby. 20.95 (*0-8488-1243-3*) Amereon Ltd.

— Greyfriars Bobby. 192p. 1991. reprint ed. lib. bdg. 25.95 (*0-89966-819-4*) Buccaneer Bks.

Atkinson, Eunice & Atkinson, Grant. The Perfect Idiot. 1949. 5.25 (*0-87129-558-X*, P21) Dramatic Pub.

Atkinson, F. V. Multiparameter Spectral Theory for Sturm-Liouville Operators. LC 92-26872. (Pitman Monographs & Surveys in Pure & Applied Mathematics). 1996. write for info. (*0-582-08175-0*) Longman.

Atkinson, Frank. Fiction Librarianship. LC 81-193139. (Outlines of Modern Librarianship Ser.). (Illus.). 115p. reprint ed. pap. 35.70 (*0-7837-5297-0*, 204505100005) Bks Demand.

— Training Workshop for Supervisors: Building the Essential Skills. LC 94-22347. 1995. 96.95 (*0-566-07610-1*, Pub. by Gower) Ashgate Pub Co.

Atkinson, Frank B. Dynamic Dominion: Realignment & the Rise of Virginia's Republican Party since 1945. 1992. 29.95 (*0-913969-39-7*) Univ Pub Assocs.

Atkinson, G., jt. auth. see Scott, K. J.

Atkinson, G. B., et al. Studying Society: An Introduction to Social Science. (Illus.). 182p. 1987. text 49.95 (*0-19-878013-3*); pap. text 14.95 (*0-19-878012-5*) OUP.

Atkinson, G. B., jt. auth. see Bouma, Gary D.

Atkinson, Gary & Kennedy, Robert G. The Ethical Profession of Business. 152p. (Orig.). (C). 1989. pap. text 12.00 (*0-9624229-0-8*) St Thomas Tech.

Atkinson, Gary M. & Moraczewski, Albert S. Genetic Counseling, the Church & the Law. LC 79-92084. xvii, 259p. (Orig.). 1980. pap. 9.95 (*0-935372-06-7*) NCBC.

— A Moral Evaluation of Contraception & Sterilization: A Dialogical Study. LC 79-90971. viii, 115p. (Orig.). 1979. pap. 4.95 (*0-935372-05-9*) NCBC.

Atkinson, George. Construction Quality & Quality Standards: The European Perspective. (Illus.). 352p. (C). 1995. 115.00 (*0-419-18490-2*, E & FN Spon) Routledge.

— Construction Quality Standards. 1986. 79.50 (*0-442-31777-8*) Thomson Learn.

Atkinson, George F. Curry & Rice on Forty Plates: or The Ingredients of Social Life at Our Station in India. LC 99-938099. (C). 1995. reprint ed. 44.00 (*81-206-0531-4*, Pub. by Asian Educ Servs) S Asia.

Atkinson, George H., ed. Time-Resolved Vibrational Spectroscopy: Proceedings of the JSPS-NSF Symposium Held in Honolulu, Hawaii, November 18-22, 1985. 432p. 1987. text 198.00 (*2-88124-191-3*) Gordon & Breach.

Atkinson, George H., jt. ed. see Phillips, David.

Atkinson, George W. History of Kanawha County: From Its Organization in 1789 until the Present Time (1876), Embracing Accounts of Early Settlements & Thrilling Adventures with the Indians; Also, Biographical Sketches of a Large Number of the Early Settlers of the Great Kanawha Valley. (Illus.). 338p. 1997. reprint ed. lib. bdg. 39.00 (*0-8328-6946-5*) Higginson Bk Co.

Atkinson, Gerald L. From Trust to Terror: Radical Feminism Is Destroying the U. S. Navy. (Illus.). 114p. 1997. pap. 17.50 (*0-9653277-2-8*) Atkinson Assocs.

Atkinson, Giles, et al. Measuring Sustainable Development: Macroeconomics & the Environment. LC 96-39592. 272p. 1997. 95.00 (*1-85898-572-2*) E Elgar.

— Measuring Sustainable Development: Macroeconomics & the Environment. LC 96-39592. 272p. 1999. pap. 30.00 (*1-84064-198-3*) E Elgar.

Atkinson, Grant, jt. auth. see Atkinson, Eunice.

Atkinson, Greg. In Season: Culinary Adventures of a San Juan Island Chef. LC 97-22011. (Illus.). 256p. (Orig.). 1997. pap. 16.95 (*1-57061-119-X*) Sasquatch Bks.

***Atkinson, Greg.** The Northwest Essentials Cookbook: Cooking with the Ingredients That Define a Regional Cuisine. LC 99-15346. 272p. 1999. pap. 19.95 (*1-57061-179-3*) Sasquatch Bks.

Atkinson, Greg. Recipes from the San Juan Islands. (Illus.). 28p. 1992. text 5.95 (*0-912365-70-6*) Sasquatch Bks.

Atkinson, Hal F., III. Mantramotion: The Next Step in Mind-Body Fitness. 13p. 1997. pap. 14.95 incl. audio (*0-9667003-0-9*) Mantramotion Inc.

Atkinson, Harley. Ministry with Youth in Crisis. LC 96-45209. 270p. (Orig.). 1997. pap. 24.95 (*0-89135-099-3*) Religious Educ.

Atkinson, Harley, ed. Handbook of Young Adult Religious Education. 416p. (Orig.). 1995. pap. text 24.95 (*0-89135-098-5*) Religious Educ.

Atkinson, Harold W. Atkinson: Families of Atkinson of Roxby & Dearman of Braithwaite. (Illus.). 516p. 1995. reprint ed. pap. 77.00 (*0-8328-4896-4*); reprint ed. lib. bdg. 87.00 (*0-8328-4895-6*) Higginson Bk Co.

Atkinson, Hawley, et al. Linking Quality to Profits: Quality Based Cost Management. LC 94-17503. 405p. 1994. 43.00 (*0-87389-189-9*, H0725) ASQ Qual Pr.

Atkinson, Helen, et al. Business Accounting for Hospitality & Tourism. (Illus.). 432p. 1996. mass mkt. 34.95 (*0-412-48080-8*) Chapman & Hall.

Atkinson, Henry. Mechanics of Small Engines. 192p. (C). 1989. text 23.96 (*0-07-002537-1*) McGraw.

***Atkinson, Henry, et al.** Wheel Boats on the Missouri: The Journals & Documents of the Atkinson-O'Fallon Expedition, 1824-1826. LC 99-86485. (Illus.). 2000. write for info. (*0-917298-69-1*) MT Hist Soc.

Atkinson, Hilary & Deane, Andree. The Dyna-Band Challenge: A Fabulous Figure in Only Ten Minutes a Day. LC 94-8865. (Illus.). 160p. 1994. 19.95 (*0-87951-562-7*, Pub. by Overlook Pr) Penguin Putnam.

Atkinson, Holly. Women & Fatigue. 1989. mass mkt. 6.50 (*0-671-69216-X*) PB.

Atkinson, Holly & Novotny, Pamela P. The Best Medical Treatments for Women. LC 97-26409. 640p. 2000. 27.95 (*0-316-05636-7*) Little.

Atkinson, J. Baines. Beauty of Holiness. 1980. pap. 5.99 (*0-88019-053-1*) Schmul Pub Co.

Atkinson, J. Brooks. Broadway Scrapbook. LC 71-104221. 312p. 1970. reprint ed. lib. bdg. 65.00 (*0-8371-3331-9*, ATBS, Greenwood Pr) Greenwood.

Atkinson, J. E. A Commentary on Q. Curtius Rufus' Historiae Alexandri Magni Books 3 & 4. (London Studies in Classical Philology: Vol. 4). (Illus.). vi, 495p. (Orig.). 1980. pap. 94.00 (*90-70265-61-3*, Pub. by Gieben) J Benjamins Pubng Co.

Atkinson, J. Maxwell & Heritage, John, eds. Structures of Social Action: Studies in Conversation Analysis. 480p. 1985. pap. text 35.95 (*0-521-31862-9*) Cambridge U Pr.

Atkinson, J. T., jt. auth. see Droffelaar, H. Van.

Atkinson, Jack H. Export Marketing Manual: A Results-Oriented Guide for the Eighties. (Illus.). 267p. 1981. ring bd. 49.95 (*0-931094-00-3*) MacKenzie-Koch.

Atkinson, Jacqueline M. & Coia, Denise A. Families Coping with Schizophrenia: A Practitioner's Guide to Family Groups. LC 94-33593. 294p. 1995. pap. 59.95 (*0-471-94181-6*) Wiley.

Atkinson, James. Chow-Chows. (Complete Pet Owner's Manual Ser.). (Illus.). 80p. 1988. pap. 6.95 (*0-8120-3952-1*) Barron.

— Martin Luther: Prophet to the Church Catholic. LC 83-16462. 232p. reprint ed. 72.00 (*0-608-16650-2*, 202753500055) Bks Demand.

Atkinson, James, ed. Customs & Manners of the Women of Persia. xvi, 93p. 1985. reprint ed. lib. bdg. 39.00 (*0-7812-0851-3*) Rprt Serv.

Atkinson, James, jt. ed. see Lehmann, Helmut T.

Atkinson, James, ed. see Luther, Martin.

Atkinson, James, ed. see Machiavelli, Niccolo.

Atkinson, James, tr. see Firdawsi.

Atkinson, James B., et al. Machiavelli & His Friends: Their Personal Correspondence. Sices, David, tr. LC 96-31069. 600p. 1996. lib. bdg. 48.00 (*0-87580-210-9*) N Ill U Pr.

Atkinson, James W. The Soldier's Chronology. LC 92-16454. 624p. 1993. text 30.00 (*0-8153-0813-2*, H1577) Garland.

***Atkinson, Jane.** The Developing Visual Brain. LC 99-56762. (Oxford Psychology Series). (Illus.). 240p. 2000. text 75.00 (*0-19-852297-5*) OUP.

Atkinson, Jane M. The Art & Politics of Wana Shamanship. (Illus.). 365p. (C). 1989. pap. 18.95 (*0-520-07877-2*, Pub. by U CA Pr) Cal Prin Full Svc.

Atkinson, Jane M. & Errington, Shelly, eds. Power & Difference: Gender in Island Southeast Asia. LC 89-78330. 520p. 1990. 57.50 (*0-8047-1781-8*); pap. 18.95 (*0-8047-1779-6*) Stanford U Pr.

Atkinson, Jay. Caveman Politics. 304p. 1997. 22.00 (*1-55821-565-4*, Pub. by Breakaway Bks) Consort Bk Sales.

Atkinson, Jeff. APEC Winners & Losers. (C). 1995. pap. 11.95 (*1-875870-15-6*, Pub. by Oxfam Pub) Stylus Pub VA.

— GATT: What Do the Poor Get? (Books from Community Aid Abroad). 44p. (C). 1994. pap. 11.95 (*1-875870-03-2*, Pub. by Oxfam Pub) Stylus Pub VA.

— Modern Child Custody: 1989 Supplement. 1989. write for info. (*0-930273-62-1*, 60214-10, MICHIE) LEXIS Pub.

— Modern Child Custody Practice, 1998 Cumulative Supplement, 2 vols. 475p. 1998. suppl. ed. write for info. (*0-327-00352-9*, 6021715) LEXIS Pub.

— Modern Child Custody Practice, 1998 Cumulative Supplement, Vol. 1. 475p. 1998. suppl. ed. write for info. (*0-327-00353-7*, 6021715) LEXIS Pub.

— Modern Child Custody Practice, 1998 Cumulative Supplement, Vol. 2. 475p. 1998. suppl. ed. write for info. (*0-327-00354-5*, 6021715) LEXIS Pub.

— Modern Child Custody Practices with 1991 Cumulative Supplements, 2 vols., Set. 1986. 170.00 (*0-930273-34-6*, 60210-10, MICHIE) LEXIS Pub.

Atkinson, Jennifer. Collage Art: The Step-By-Step Guide & Showcase. (Illus.). 144p. 1996. 29.99 (*1-56496-215-6*, Quarry Bks) Rockport Pubs.

***Atkinson, Jennifer.** Collage Art: The Step-by-Step Guide & Showcase. (Illus.). 144p. 1999. pap. 24.99 (*1-56496-640-2*) Rockport Pubs.

— The Drowned City. 104p. 2000. pap. 11.95 (*1-55553-454-6*) NE U Pr.

Atkinson, Jennifer. Java Studio Blue Book. LC 98-46083. (Illus.). 1999. pap. 30.00 incl. cd-rom (*1-57610-322-6*) Coriolis Grp.

Atkinson, Jennifer, ed. see O'Neill, Eugene.

Atkinson, Jennifer M. Eugene O'Neill: A Descriptive Bibliography. LC 73-13312. (Series in Bibliography). (Illus.). 440p. 1974. 100.00 (*0-8229-3279-2*) U of Pittsburgh Pr.

Atkinson, John. Bamboo & Friends. LC 88-50844. (Illus.). 104p. (J). (gr. 1-12). 1988. 13.95 (*0-929155-05-X*) Windward Bks.

— The Enchanted Forest. large type ed. (Illus.). 46p. (Orig.). (J). (gr. k-5). 1995. pap. 5.99 (*0-929155-40-8*) Windward Bks.

— An Introduction to the Mechanics of Soils & Foundations. LC 92-37323. (McGraw-Hill International Series in Civil Engineering). 416p. (C). 1993. 60.00 (*0-07-707713-X*) McGraw.

— Welcome to Paradise. large type ed. (Illus.). 58p. (Orig.). (J). (gr. k-5). 1995. pap. 5.99 (*0-929155-06-8*) Windward Bks.

Atkinson, John & Storey, David J. The Small Firm & Labour Market. LC 93-13080. 240p. (C). (gr. 13). 1993. pap. 81.95 (*0-415-10035-6*) Thomson Learn.

Atkinson, John, tr. see Vuorela, Toivo.

Atkinson, John H. Linsey-Woolsey & Pongees: John Hampton Atkinson: A Retrospective 1868-1953. Tisdale, Marian, ed. LC 86-50281. (Illus.). 176p. 1986. write for info. (*0-9616672-0-6*) Tisdale Pub.

Excerpts from articles & books of a native of rural, southern Ohio, reflecting the life, ideals & values of early settlers of the 19th Century, plus a complete collection of the poems of this dedicated professor of English. *Publisher Paid Annotation.*

Atkinson, John H., et al. Current Trends in Cost of Quality: Linking the Cost of Quality & Continuous Improvement. Barth, Claire, ed. (Bold Step Ser.). (Illus.). 136p. (Orig.). 1991. pap. 40.00 (*0-86641-197-6*, 91259) Inst Mgmt Account.

Atkinson, John N. Atkinson. The Atkinsons of N. J. from the Record of Friends Meetings & from the Offices of Record in the State. (Illus.). 40p. 1997. reprint ed. pap. 8.00 (*0-8328-7303-9*); reprint ed. lib. bdg. 18.00 (*0-8328-7302-0*) Higginson Bk Co.

Atkinson, John W. Personality, Motivation & Action: Selected Papers. Spielberger, Charles D., ed. LC 83-4261. (Centennial Psychology Ser.). 432p. 1983. 38.95 (*0-275-90937-9*, C0937, Praeger Pubs) Greenwood.

Atkinson, John W., et al. Motivation & Achievement. LC 73-21754. (Illus.). 491p. reprint ed. pap. 152.30 (*0-608-11144-9*, 205070700082) Bks Demand.

Atkinson, John W., jt. auth. see Kuhl, Julius.

Atkinson, Joseph D., Jr. & Shafritz, Jay M. The Real Stuff: A History of NASA's Astronaut Recruitment Policy. LC 85-9460. 240p. 1985. 55.00 (*0-275-90195-5*, C0195, Praeger Pubs); pap. 17.95 (*0-275-91808-4*, B1808, Praeger Pubs) Greenwood.

***Atkinson, Joseph F., et al.** Development of Particle Image Technology for Water Treatment Studies. LC 99-47823. 1999. write for info. (*1-58321-007-5*) Am Water Wks Assn.

Atkinson, Judith, jt. auth. see Protherough, Robert.

Atkinson, Justin B. Henry Thoreau, the Cosmic Yankee. (BCL1-PS American Literature Ser.). 158p. 1992. reprint ed. lib. bdg. 69.00 (*0-7812-6881-8*) Rprt Serv.

Atkinson, Karen & Liss, Andrea. Remapping Tales of Desire: Writing Across the Abyss. (Illus.). 36p. 1992. pap. 9.95 (*0-9666963-0-1*) Side Street Pr.

Atkinson, Kate. Behind the Scenes at the Museum: A Novel. LC 95-39787. 333p. 1999. pap. 14.00 (*0-312-15060-1*, Picador USA) St Martin.

— Behind the Scenes at the Museum: A Novel. 2000. pap. write for info. (*0-312-25174-2*) St Martin.

— Behind the Scenes at the Museum: A Novel. large type ed. LC 96-3427. 1996. pap. 22.95 (*1-56895-373-9*, Compass) Wheeler Pub.

***Atkinson, Kate.** Emotionally Weird. 346p. 2000. text 25.00 (*0-312-20324-1*, Picador USA) St Martin.

Atkinson, Kate. Human Croquet. 352p. 1998. mass mkt. write for info. (*0-552-99619-X*, Pub. by Corgi Bks Ltd) Doubleday.

— Human Croquet. 1997. pap. 19.95 (*0-385-40935-4*) Doubleday.

— Human Croquet. LC 97-802. 352p. 1997. text 24.00 (*0-312-15550-6*, Picador USA) St Martin.

Atkinson, Kathey. Grief of a Nation: Kathey's Story. LC 97-90448. 1998. 16.95 (*0-533-12405-0*) Vantage.

Atkinson, Kathie. Birds. (Illus.). 24p. (J). (ps-2). 1995. pap. 3.95 (*1-86373-675-1*) IPG Chicago.

— The Blue Layer. LC 93-28993. (J). 1994. 4.25 (*0-383-03747-6*) SRA McGraw.

— Creepy Crawlies. LC 92-31908. (Voyages Ser.). (J). 1993. 3.75 (*0-383-03562-7*) SRA McGraw.

— In the Backyard. 24p. (J). (ps-2). 1994. pap. 3.95 (*1-86373-588-7*) IPG Chicago.

— Worms, Wonderful Worms. LC 93-28968. (J). 1994. 4.25 (*0-383-03788-3*) SRA McGraw.

Atkinson, Kathleen M. Ancient Sparta, a Re-Examination of the Evidence. LC 73-114457. (Illus.). 527p. 1971. reprint ed. lib. bdg. 35.00 (*0-8371-4709-3*, ATAS, Greenwood Pr) Greenwood.

Atkinson, Ken. Geography of Renewable Resources. 1994. pap. text 25.00 (*0-340-52861-3*, Pub. by E A) Routldge.

— Highway Maintenance Handbook. 2nd ed. 574p. 1997. 143.00 (*0-7277-2531-9*) Am Soc Civil Eng.

Atkinson, Ken, ed. Highway Maintenance Handbook. 460p. 1990. text 136.80 (*0-7277-1577-1*, Pub. by T Telford) RCH.

Atkinson, Kendall E. Elementary Numerical Analysis. 2nd ed. 448p. (C). 1993. text 89.95 (*0-471-50999-X*) Wiley.

— An Introduction to Numerical Analysis. 2nd ed. LC 88-718. 712p. 1989. text 105.95 (*0-471-62489-6*) Wiley.

— The Numerical Solution of Integral Equations of the Second Kind. (Cambridge Monographs on Applied & Computational Mathematics: No. 4). 568p. 1997. text 74.95 (*0-521-58391-8*) Cambridge U Pr.

Atkinson, Kerry. The BMT Data Book: A Manual for Bone Marrow & Blood Stem Cell Transplantation. LC 96-27079. (Illus.). 606p. (C). 1997. text 125.00 (*0-521-55615-5*) Cambridge U Pr.

Atkinson, Kerry, ed. Clinical Bone Marrow & Blood Stem Cell Transplantation: A Reference Textbook. 2nd ed. (Illus.). 1440p. (C). 1999. 295.00 (*0-521-62288-3*) Cambridge U Pr.

***Atkinson, Kim & Wells, Catherine.** Creative Therapies: A Psychodynamic Approach with Occupational Therapy. (Illus.). 256p. 2000. pap. 34.95 (*0-7487-3310-8*, Pub. by S Thornes Pubs) Intl Spec Bk.

Atkinson, L. & Gerull, Sally-Anne, eds. National Conference on Juvenile Justice. (Australian Institute Conference Proceedings Ser.: Vol. 22). 477p. 1993. pap. 45.00 (0-642-19620-6, Pub. by Aust Inst Criminology) Advent Bks Div.

Atkinson, L. E., jt. ed. see Sairam, M. R.

Atkinson, L. P., et al, eds. Oceanography of the Southeastern U. S. Continental Shelf. (Coastal & Estuarine Sciences Ser.: Vol. 2). 200p. 1985. 20.00 (0-87590-251-0) Am Geophysical.

Atkinson, L. V. & Harley, Peter J. Microbial Ecology: Fundamentals & Applications. (Life Sciences Ser.). 500p. 1981. write for info. (0-201-00051-2) Addison-Wesley.

*Atkinson, Lee. One Woman's Thoughts: She is You & Me. 240p. 2000. pap. 14.95 (0-88347-454-9, Pub. by T More) BookWorld.

Atkinson, Lee. Using Borland C++ LC 93-86865. 938p. (Orig.). 1994. 40.00 (1-56529-304-5) Que.

Atkinson, Leland. Cocina! A Hands-On Guide to the Techniques of Southwestern Cooking. LC 96-12995. (Illus.). 144p. (Orig.). 1996. pap. 19.95 (0-89815-841-9) Ten Speed Pr.

*Atkinson, Leon. Core Php. 2nd ed. 650p. 2000. pap. 39.99 (0-13-089398-6) P-H.

Atkinson, Leon. Using PHP to Build Dynamic Web Sites. LC 99-27884. 450p. (C). 1999. pap. text 39.99 (0-13-020787-X) P-H.

Atkinson, Leroy & Lake, Austen. Famous American Athletes of Today, Third Series. LC 70-93348. (Essay Index Reprint Ser.). 1977. reprint ed. 26.95 (0-8369-2580-7) Ayer.

Atkinson, Leroy, et al. Famous American Athletes of Today, Fifth Series. LC 70-93348. (Essay Index Reprints - Famous Leaders Ser). 1977. reprint ed. 26.95 (0-8369-2480-0) Ayer.

Atkinson, Leslie & Zucker, Kenneth J., eds. Attachment & Psychopathology. LC 96-49001. 328p. 1997. lib. bdg. 40.00 (1-57230-191-0) Guilford Pubns.

Atkinson, Leslie D. & Murray, Mary E. Clinical Guide to Care Planning: Data - Diagnosis. LC 94-34820. (Illus.). 336p. 1995. pap. text 18.95 (0-07-105466-9) McGraw-Hill HPD.

— Understanding the Nursing Process: Fundamentals of Care Planning. 4th ed. (Illus.). 319p. 1990. pap. text 21.95 (0-08-040299-2, Pub. by PPI) McGraw.

Atkinson, Leslie D., jt. auth. see Murray, Mary E.

Atkinson, Linda M. & Soper, Katharine B., eds. Torts: Michigan Law & Practice. 1300p. 1991. ring bd., suppl. ed. 155.00 (0-685-51912-0, 91-024) U MI Law CLE.

— Torts: Michigan Law & Practice. 1300p. 1993. suppl. ed. 50.00 (0-685-59117-4, 93-001) U MI Law CLE.

*Atkinson, Louisa. Gertrude the Emigrant: A Tale of Colonial Life. Lawson, Elizabeth, ed. 440p. 1999. pap. 39.50 (0-7317-0363-4, Pub. by ADFA) Intl Spec Bk.

Atkinson, Lucy. Recollections of Tartar Steppes & Their Inhabitants. 351p. 1972. reprint ed. 49.50 (0-7146-1531-5, Pub. by F Cass Pubs) Intl Spec Bk.

Atkinson, Lucy J. Berry & Kohn's Operating Room Techniques: Text & Resource Manual Package. 8th ed. (Illus.). 1996. write for info. (0-8151-0828-1) Mosby Inc.

Atkinson, Lucy J. & Fortunato, Nancymarie H. Berry & Kohn's Operating Room Technique. 8th ed. (Illus.). teacher ed. write for info. (0-8151-0826-5) Mosby Inc.

— Berry & Kohn's Operating Room Technique. 8th ed. (Illus.). 1008p. (C). (gr. 13). 1995. text 53.00 (0-8151-0103-1, 24556); pap. text, student ed. 17.95 (0-8151-0827-3, 27886) Mosby Inc.

Atkinson, Lynn, ed. State & Federal EEO Compliance Encyclopedia, 3 vols., Set. 1989. ring bd. 200.00 (0-685-53350-6, P998) Busn Legal Reports.

Atkinson, Lynn & Gerull, Sally-Anne. National Conference on Juvenile Detention. LC 96-172314. (Australian Institute Conference Proceedings Ser.: Vol. 25). 220p. 1994. pap. 35.00 (0-642-21301-1, Pub. by Aust Inst Criminology) Advent Bks Div.

Atkinson, Lynn P. Power & Empowerment: The Power Principle. LC 88-80073. 128p. 1988. pap. 9.95 (0-941404-77-3) New Falcon Pubns.

Atkinson, M. Our Masters' Voices: The Language & Body-Language of Politics. 224p. (C). 1984. pap. 17.99 (0-415-01875-7) Routledge.

Atkinson, M., jt. auth. see Tyrrall, D.

Atkinson, M. C. An African Life: Tales of a Colonial Officer. (Illus.). 136p. 1992. text 45.00 (1-85043-523-5) I B T.

*Atkinson, M. E. & Dickson, D. C. M. An Introduction to Actuarial Studies. LC 00-37643. 192p. 2000. 65.00 (1-84064-446-X) E Elgar.

Atkinson, M. F. Structural Foundations Manual for Low-Rise Buildings. LC 93-3334. 1993. mass mkt. 84.95 (0-419-17940-2, E & FN Spon) Routledge.

Atkinson, M. P., et al, eds. Data Types & Persistence. (Topics in Information Systems Ser.). (Illus.). 320p. 1988. 69.95 (0-387-18785-5) Spr-Verlag.

Atkinson, Malcolm P., et al, eds. Persistent Object Systems: Proceedings of the 6th International Workshop on Persistent Object Systems, Tarascon, Provence, France, 5-9 September 1994. LC 94-42659. (Workshops in Computing Ser.). xi, 546p. 1995. 69.00 (3-540-19912-8) Spr-Verlag.

*Atkinson, Malcolm P. & Welland, R., eds. Fully Integrated Data Enviroments: Persistent Programming Languages, Object Stores & Programming Environments. LC 99-49677. (ESPRIT Basic Research Ser.). 660p. 1999. 74.00 (3-540-65772-X) Spr-Verlag.

Atkinson, Malcolm P., jt. auth. see Jordan, Mickey.

Atkinson, Margaret E. August Wilhelm Schlegel As a Translator of Shakespeare. LC 76-51367. (Studies in Shakespeare: No. 24). 1977. lib. bdg. 55.00 (0-8383-2135-6) M S G Haskell Hse.

Atkinson, Mark, jt. auth. see Leiter, Edward.

Atkinson, Mark J. & Zibin, Sharon. Quality of Life Measurement among Persons with Chronic Mental Illness: A Critique of Measures & Methods. iv, 65p. 1996. write for info. (0-662-25002-8) Intl Spec Bk.

Atkinson, Martin, et al. Foundations of General Linguistics. 2nd ed. (Illus.). 384p. 1987. pap. text 24.95 (0-04-410005-1) Routledge.

*Atkinson, Mary. Art of Indian Head Massage: Learn the Art of Indian Head Massage. (Illus.). 2000. pap. 18.95 (1-85868-864-7, Pub. by Carlton Bks Ltd) Natl Bk Netwk.

Atkinson, Mary. Maria Teresa. 2nd ed. LC 79-90393. (ENG & SPA., Illus.). 39p. (J). 1979. 5.95 (0-914996-21-5) Lollipop Power.

Atkinson, Mary, jt. auth. see Hornby, Garry.

Atkinson, Max. Our Masters' Voices: The Language & Body-Language of Politics. (Illus.). 176p. 1984. 25.00 (0-416-37690-8, NO. 9265); pap. 14.95 (0-416-37700-9, NO. 9085) Routledge.

*Atkinson, Michael. Ask Dr. Mike: Frequently Asked Questions about Psychology. 208p. 2000. pap. 22.00 (0-205-33109-2) Allyn.

Atkinson, Michael. Blue Velvet. (Modern Classics Ser.). (Illus.). 96p. 1998. pap. 10.95 (0-85170-559-6, Pub. by British Film Inst) Ind U Pr.

*Atkinson, Michael. Ghosts in the Machine: Speculating on the Dark Heart of Pop Cinema. LC 99-39871. 228p. 1999. pap. 14.95 (0-87910-285-3) Limelight Edns.

Atkinson, Michael. The Secret Marriage of Sherlock Holmes & Other Eccentric Readings. LC 96-10299. 208p. (C). 1996. text 34.50 (0-472-10710-0, 10710) U of Mich Pr.

— The Secret Marriage of Sherlock Holmes & Other Eccentric Readings. (Illus.). 208p. 1998. pap. 16.95 (0-472-08566-2, 08566) U of Mich Pr.

*Atkinson, Michael, et al, eds. Computational & Geometric Aspects of Modern Algebra. (London Mathematical Society Lecture Note Ser.: Vol. 275). (Illus.). 288p. (C). 2000. pap. 44.95 (0-521-78889-7) Cambridge U Pr.

*Atkinson, Michael F. Structural Defects Reference Manual for Low-Rise Buildings. 400p. 2000. 65.00 (0-419-25790-X) Routledge.

Atkinson, Michael M. & Chandler, Marsha A., eds. The Politics of Canadian Public Policy. 296p. 1983. pap. text 18.95 (0-8020-6517-1) U of Toronto Pr.

Atkinson, Minnie. Hinckley Township, or Grand Lake Stream Plantation. (Illus.). 122p. 1997. reprint ed. pap. 18.00 (0-8328-5857-9) Higginson Bk Co.

*Atkinson, Nancy A. Forever Thin: The Revolutionary Mind/Body Solution to Permanent Weight Loss. LC 00-100484. xiv, 250p. 2000. pap. 24.95 (1-892805-17-0) LifeQuest Pubg.

Atkinson, Nigel. Richard Hooker & the Authority of Scripture, Tradition & Reason: Reformed Theologian of the Church of England? xxii, 138p. 1997. reprint ed. pap. 20.00 (0-85364-801-8, Pub. by Paternoster Pub) OM Literature.

Atkinson, Norman. Sir Joseph Whitworth: The World's Best Mechanician. (Illus.). 352p. (Orig.). 1997. pap. 26.95 (0-7509-1648-6, Pub. by Sutton Pub Ltd) Intl Pubs Mktg.

Atkinson, Oriana. Big Eyes: A Story of the Catskill Mountains. 1980. reprint ed. pap. 7.95 (0-910746-34-6, BE01) Hope Farm.

Atkinson, P. Feedback Control Theory for Engineers. LC 68-31674. (Illus.). 448p. 1968. reprint ed. pap. 138.90 (0-608-05456-9, 206592500006) Bks Demand.

Atkinson, Pansye. Brown vs. Topeka: Desegregation & Miseducation (An African American's View) (Illus.). 127p. (Orig.). 1993. pap. 10.95 (0-913543-33-0) African Am Imag.

Atkinson, Paul. Medical Talk & Medical Work: The Liturgy of the Clinic. 192p. 1995. 69.95 (0-8039-7730-1); pap. 26.95 (0-8039-7731-X) Sage.

— Sociological Readings & Re-Readings. (Cardiff Papers in Qualitative Research: Vol. 4). 160p. 1996. 66.95 (1-85628-578-2, Pub. by Avebry) Ashgate Pub Co.

— Understanding Ethnographic Texts. (Qualitative Research Methods Ser.: Vol. 25). 88p. (C). 1992. text 24.00 (0-8039-3936-1); pap. text 10.50 (0-8039-3937-X) Sage.

Atkinson, Paul & Hammersley, Martyn. Ethnography: Principles in Practice. 2nd ed. LC 94-30136. 304p. (C). 1995. pap. 24.99 (0-415-08664-7, B4787) Routledge.

Atkinson, Paul, jt. auth. see Coffey, Amanda.

Atkinson, Paul, jt. auth. see Delamont, Sara.

Atkinson, Paul, jt. auth. see Hammersley, Martyn.

Atkinson, Paul, jt. auth. see Weaver, Anna.

Atkinson, Paul, ed. see Davies, Brian & Delamont, Sara.

Atkinson, Paul A. The Clinical Experience: The Construction & Reconstruction of Medical Reality. 2nd ed. LC 97-73874. (Cardiff Papers in Qualitative Research). 224p. 1997. text 69.95 (1-85628-577-4, Pub. by Ashgate Pub) Ashgate Pub Co.

*Atkinson, Peter M. & Martin, David. GIS & Geocomputation. LC 00-23886. 2000. write for info. (0-7484-0928-9) Taylor & Francis.

Atkinson, Phiip, ed. see Heighton, Hugh.

Atkinson, Philip. The Iceberg Agenda: Mastering Corporate Potential. LC 97-151174. 224p. 1998. pap. text 29.95 (0-7134-8348-2, Pub. by B T B) Branford.

Atkinson, Phillip S. Medical Office Practice Set. 5th ed. (Medical Assisting Ser.). (C). 1994. 36.00 (0-538-71204-X) S-W Pub.

Atkinson, Phillip S. & Begg, Deborah. Medical Office Practice Set. 4th ed. (C). 1990. pap. 29.95 (0-538-70010-6, RL40DC) S-W Pub.

Atkinson, Phillips. Exploring Business & Computer Careers. 2nd ed. (CA - Career Development Ser.). 1997. mass mkt. 57.95 (0-314-20416-4) S-W Pub.

— Exploring Business & Computer Careers. 2nd ed. (CA - Career Development Ser.). (C). 1998. mass mkt., wbk. ed. 23.95 (0-314-20833-X) S-W Pub.

Atkinson, R. C., ed. see National Research Council Staff.

Atkinson, R. L. Copper & Copper Mining. (Album Ser.: No. 201). (Illus.). 32p. 1989. pap. 6.25 (0-85263-895-7, Pub. by Shire Pubns) Parkwest Pubns.

— Tin & Tin Mining. 1989. pap. 25.00 (0-85263-733-0, Pub. by Shire Pubns) St Mut.

Atkinson, R. S. & Boulton, T. B., eds. The History of Anaesthesia. (History of Medicine Ser.). (Illus.). 649p. 1989. 118.00 (1-85070-276-4) Prthnon Pub.

Atkinson, R. Valentine, photos by. Trout & Salmon: The Greatest Fly Fishing for Trout & Salmon Worldwide. LC 98-37525. (Illus.). 176p. 1999. 39.95 (1-55821-804-1) Lyons Pr.

Atkinson, Raymond C. The Federal Role in Unemployment Compensation Administration: A Report Prepared for the Committee on Social Security. LC 77-74927. (American Federalism-the Urban Dimension Ser.). 1978. reprint ed. lib. bdg. 19.95 (0-405-10476-6) Ayer.

Atkinson, Raymond C., et al. Public Employment Service in the United States. LC 72-69. (Select Bibliographies Reprint Ser.). 1977. reprint ed. 24.95 (0-8369-9950-9) Ayer.

Atkinson, Rebecca, ed. see Dull, Ralph & Dull, Christine.

Atkinson, Rebecca, ed. see Wagner, Frank.

Atkinson, Rhonda H. & Longman, Debbie G. C. L. A. S. S. College Learning & Study Skills. 3rd ed. LC 92-30204. 450p. (C). 1993. pap. text 32.75 (0-314-01231-1) West Pub.

— C. L. A. S. S. College Learning & Study Skills. 4th ed. LC 95-24005. 550p. (C). 1995. 28.25 (0-314-06808-2) West Pub.

— C. L. A. S. S. College Learning & Study Skills. 5th ed. (Freshman Orientation/College Success Ser.). 1998. pap. 44.95 (0-534-54972-1) Wadsworth Pub.

— Getting Oriented. Date not set. pap. text, teacher ed. write for info. (0-314-04783-2) West Pub.

— Getting Oriented. LC 94-3566. 336p. (C). 1995. 40.95 (0-314-04439-6) West Pub.

— R. E. A. D. Reading Enhancement & Development. 4th ed. Baxter, ed. 525p. (C). 1992. pap. text 31.50 (0-314-93357-3) West Pub.

— R. E. A. D. Reading Enhancement & Development. 5th ed. LC 94-31084. 622p. (C). 1995. 29.50 (0-314-04440-X) West Pub.

— R. E. A. D. Reading Enhancement & Development. 6th ed. LC 98-49348. 624p. 1998. pap. 39.95 (0-534-54756-7) Wadsworth Pub.

— S. M. A. R. T. Study Methods & Reading Techniques. LC 93-23612. 400p. (C). 1994. 29.50 (0-314-02804-8) West Pub.

— S. M. A. R. T. Study Methods & Reading Techniques. 2nd ed. LC 98-52847. (Freshman Orientation/College Success Ser.). 1999. 46.95 (0-534-54981-0) Wadsworth Pub.

— V. O. C. A. B. Vocabulary for College & Beyond. Date not set. pap. text, teacher ed. write for info. (0-314-70531-7) West Pub.

— V. O. C. A. B. Vocabulary for College & Beyond, Vol. 1. 294p. (C). 1989. pap. text 27.25 (0-314-56885-9) West Pub.

Atkinson, Rhonda H., et al. S. T. A. R. Strategic Thinking & Reading. LC 96-21078. 500p. (J). 1996. mass mkt. 50.95 (0-314-20181-5) West Pub.

Atkinson, Richard C., et al, eds. Stevens' Handbook of Experimental Psychology, 2 vols. 2nd ed. 1078p. 1988. 600.00 (0-471-61625-7) Wiley.

— Stevens' Handbook of Experimental Psychology Vol. 1: Perception & Motivation, Vol. 1, Perception and Motivation. 2nd ed. LC 87-31637. 905p. 1988. 275.00 (0-471-04203-X) Wiley.

— Stevens' Handbook of Experimental Psychology Vol. 2: Learning & Cognition, Vol. 2. 2nd ed. 1027p. 1988. 275.00 (0-471-04207-2) Wiley.

*Atkinson, Rick. All the Trumpets Sounded. 1999. text. write for info. (0-8050-6290-4) St Martin.

Atkinson, Rick. Crusade: The Untold Story of the Persian Gulf War. (Illus.). 512p. 1994. pap. 17.00 (0-395-71083-9) HM.

— Crusade: The Untold Story of the Persian Gulf War. (Illus.). 575p. 1997. reprint ed. text 25.00 (0-7881-5133-9) DIANE Pub.

Atkinson, Rick. In the Shadow of the Wall. Date not set. text. write for info. (0-8050-6289-0) H Holt & Co.

— The Long Gray Line: The American Journey of West Point's Class of 1966. LC 99-15023. (Illus.). 608p. 1999. pap. text 15.00 (0-8050-6291-2) H Holt & Co.

— Seize A Hostile Shore. 2002. text. write for info. (0-8050-6288-2) St Martin.

Atkinson, Rita L., jt. auth. see Hilgard, Richard C.

Atkinson, Rob & Moon, Graham. Urban Policy in Britain: The City, the State & the Market. LC 93-27202. 1994. text 59.95 (0-312-10627-0) St Martin.

Atkinson, Robert. The Gift of Stories: Practical & Spiritual Applications of Autobiography, Life Stories, & Personal Mythmaking. LC 94-39208. 168p. 1995. 55.00 (0-89789-430-8, Bergin & Garvey); pap. 17.95 (0-89789-443-X, Bergin & Garvey) Greenwood.

— Irish Metrics. 1998. pap. 10.00 (0-89979-099-2) British Am Bks.

— Island Going. (Illus.). 384p. pap. 19.95 (1-874744-31-9, Pub. by Birlinn Ltd) Dufour.

— The Life Story Interview. LC 97-33761. (Qualitative Research Methods Ser.). 1998. write for info. (0-7619-0427-1); pap. write for info. (0-7619-0428-X) Sage.

Atkinson, Robert, ed. The Book of Ballymote. LC 78-72618. (Celtic Language & Literature Ser.: Goidelic & Brythonic). reprint ed. 130.00 (0-404-17535-X) AMS Pr.

— The Book of Leinster. LC 78-72619. (Celtic Language & Literature Ser.: Goidelic & Brythonic). reprint ed. 135.00 (0-404-17536-8) AMS Pr.

Atkinson, Robert, intro. The Yellow Book of Lecan. LC 78-72657. (Celtic Language & Literature Ser.: Goidelic & Brythonic). reprint ed. 125.00 (0-404-17616-X) AMS Pr.

Atkinson, Robert, tr. The Passions & the Homilies from Leabhar Breac. LC 78-72680. (Royal Irish Academy. Todd Lecture Ser.: Vol. 2). reprint ed. 72.50 (0-404-60562-1) AMS Pr.

Atkinson, Robert & Nelson, Kelly, eds. Celebrating the Lives of Students. 1990. write for info. (0-939561-08-5) Univ South ME.

Atkinson, Robert S. Stereoselective Synthesis. LC 94-20918. 542p. 1995. 275.00 (0-471-95250-8); pap. 95.00 (0-471-95419-5) Wiley.

Atkinson, Rodney. The Emancipated Society: State Authority & Individual Freedom. (C). 1990. text 59.00 (0-9509353-2-8, Pub. by Compuprint) St Mut.

— The Failure of the State: The Democratic Costs of Government. (C). 1990. text 60.00 (0-9509353-3-6, Pub. by Compuprint) St Mut.

— Government Against the People. 158p. 1988. 25.00 (0-9509353-1-X, Pub. by Compuprint) St Mut.

Atkinson, Roland M., ed. Alcohol & Drug Abuse in Old Age. LC 84-6271. (Clinical Insights Ser.). 82p. reprint ed. pap. 30.00 (0-8357-7810-X, 203618200002) Bks Demand.

Atkinson, Ron. A Fire in the Rain. 1991. pap. 9.95 (0-88982-106-2, Pub. by Oolichan Bks) Genl Dist Srvs.

— Looking for My Name. 1973. pap. 10.00 (0-912846-06-2) Bookstore Pr.

Atkinson, Ronald R. The Roots of Ethnicity: The Origins of the Acholi of Uganda Before 1800. LC 94-12548. (Ethnohistory Ser.). (Illus.). 344p. (C). 1994. text 37.50 (0-8122-3248-8) U of Pa Pr.

Atkinson, Rose, jt. auth. see Sam, Sarah.

Atkinson Rose, Lucy. Songs in the Night: A Witness to God's Love in Life & in Death. 132p. 1998. pap. 9.95 (1-885121-22-9) CTS Press.

Atkinson, Ross W., jt. ed. see Osburn, Charles B.

Atkinson, S., et al, eds. Urban Health Research in Developing Countries: Implications for Policy. LC 97-121189. 208p. 1996. text 70.00 (0-85199-135-1) OUP.

Atkinson, Sally. The Tales of Tango Bk. II: The Sticky Situation. LC 98-60370. (Illus.). 32p. (J). (gr. k-4). 1998. 14.95 (0-9653034-1-1) Tangos Grove.

*Atkinson, Sally. The Tales of Tango Bk. III: The Fair of the Pharaohs. LC 99-71425. (Illus.). 32p. 1999. 14.95 (0-9653034-2-X) Tangos Grove.

Atkinson, Sally. The Tales of Tango Vol. 1: The Brave Lesson. LC 96-90338. (Illus.). 32p. (J). (gr. k-5). 1996. 14.95 (0-9653034-0-3) Tangos Grove.

Atkinson, Sandra. Jezebel Then & Now. LC 96-60630. 96p. 1996. per. 6.95 (1-57258-117-4) Teach Servs.

Atkinson, Sarah D. & Gabbard, Glen O. Study Guide to Treatments of Psychiatric Disorders. 2nd ed. 525p. 1996. pap. text, student ed. 39.95 (0-88048-858-1, 8858) Am Psychiatric.

Atkinson, Scott & Sharpe, Fred. Wild Plants of the San Juan Islands. 2nd ed. LC 93-10809. 192p. (Orig.). 1994. pap. 12.95 (0-89886-356-2) Mountaineers.

Atkinson, Stephanie A., ed. Proteins & Non-Protein Nitrogen in Human Milk. 256p. 1989. lib. bdg. 210.00 (0-8493-6795-6, QP246) CRC Pr.

Atkinson, Stephen. Discoverie & Historie of the Gold Mynes in Scotland. LC 77-38492. (Bannatyne Club, Edinburgh. Publications: No. 14). reprint ed. 42.50 (0-404-52714-0) AMS Pr.

Atkinson, Steven D., ed. Hypertext - Hypermedia: An Annotated Bibliography, 5. LC 90-31736. (Bibliographies & Indexes in Science & Technology Ser.: No. 5). 224p. 1990. lib. bdg. 59.95 (0-313-27221-2, KHE, Greenwood Pr) Greenwood.

Atkinson, Steven D. & Hudson, Judith, eds. Women Online: Research in Women's Studies Using Online Databases. LC 90-4430. (Series in Library & Information Sciences). (Illus.). 420p. 1990. text 49.95 (1-56024-037-7); pap. text 29.95 (1-56024-053-9) Haworth Pr.

Atkinson, Stuart. Astronomy. (Understanding Science Ser.). (Illus.). 48p. (YA). (gr. 7-13). 1995. pap. 7.95 (0-7460-1361-2, Usborne) EDC.

— Astronomy. (Understanding Science Ser.). (Illus.). 48p. (YA). (gr. 7-13). 1999. lib. bdg. 15.95 (0-88110-741-7, Usborne) EDC.

— Storms & Hurricanes. (Understanding Geography Ser.). (Illus.). 32p. (J). (gr. 6-11). 1996. pap. 7.95 (0-7460-2012-0, Usborne) EDC.

— Storms & Hurricanes. (Understanding Geography Ser.). (Illus.). 32p. (YA). (gr. 6-11). 1999. lib. bdg. 15.95 (0-88110-827-8, Usborne) EDC.

Atkinson, Sue. Making & Dressing Dolls' House Dolls in One Twelfth Scale. (Illus.). 192p. 1993. 29.95 (0-7153-9909-8, Pub. by D & C Pub) Sterling.

— Making & Dressing Dolls' House Dolls in 1/12 Scale. (Illus.). 192p. pap. 19.95 (0-7153-0788-6, Pub. by D & C Pub) Sterling.

Atkinson, Sue, ed. Mathematics with Reason: The Emergent Approach to Primary Maths. LC 92-35837. 176p. (C). (gr. k). 1992. pap. text 21.50 (0-435-08333-3, 08333) Heinemann.

Atkinson, Sue & Fleer, Marilyn, eds. Science with Reason: A Developmental Approach. LC 95-24700. 179p. 1995. pap. text 21.00 (0-435-08381-3, 08381) Heinemann.

*Atkinson, Terry & Claxton, Guy. The Intuitive Practitioner: On the Value of Not Always Knowing What One Is Doing/ LC 99-16162. 192p. 2000. 29.95 (0-335-20362-0) OpUniv Pr.

A

Atkinson, Terry, et al. A Guide to Teaching Languages: A Methodology. (Handbooks for Language Teachers Ser.: No. 10). 40p. (Orig.). 1997. pap. 23.50 (*0-7487-3151-2*, Pub. by S Thornes Pubs) Trans-Atl Phila.

Atkinson, Thomas E. Hornbook on Wills. 2nd ed. (Hornbook Ser.). 975p. (C). 1953. reprint ed. 36.50 (*0-314-28333-1*) West Pub.

Atkinson, Thomas R. The Pattern of Financial Asset Ownership, Wisconsin Individuals, 1949: A Study by the National Bureau of Economic Research, New York. LC 56-8387. 196p. 1956. reprint ed. pap. 60.80 (*0-608-02881-9*, 206394500007) Bks Demand.

Atkinson, Thomas R. & Simpson, Elizabeth T. Trends in Corporate Bond Quality. (Financial Research Program V: Studies in Corporate Bond Financing: No. 4). 122p. 1967. reprint ed. 31.80 (*0-87014-148-1*) Natl Bur Econ Res.

Atkinson, Thomas W. Oriental & Western Siberia: A Narrative of Seven Years' Explorations & Adventures in Siberia, Mongolia, the Kirghissteppes, Chinese Tartary & Part of Central Asia. LC 75-115504. (Russia Observed Ser., No. 1). 1978. reprint ed. 33.95 (*0-405-03002-9*) Ayer.

— Recollections of Tartar Steppes & Their Inhabitants. LC 71-115503. (Russia Observed, Ser. 1). 1970. reprint ed. 23.95 (*0-405-03003-7*) Ayer.

Atkinson, Tom. The Empty Lands: A Guidebook to the North-West of Scotland, from Fort William to Cape Wrath, & from Bettyhill to Lairg. 170p. 1989. pap. 9.95 (*0-946487-13-8*) Luath Pr Ltd.

— The Lonely Lands: A Guidebook to Inveraray, Kintyre, Glen Coe, Loch Awe, Loch Lomond, Cowal, The Kyles of Bute, & All of Central Argyll. LC 99-185008. 171p. 1989. pap. text 9.95 (*0-946487-10-3*) Luath Pr Ltd.

***Atkinson, Tom.** The North West Highlands: Roads to the Isles, the Obvious Beauty & Hidden Delights of the Mountainous Lands from Fort William to Ullapool. (Illus.). 160p. 1999. pap. 4.95 (*0-946487-54-5*, Pub. by Luath Pr Ltd) Midpt Trade.

— The Northern Highlands: The Empty Lands, Lands of Endless Natural Beauty, Including Wester Ross, Caithness & Sutherland. (Guides to Scotland Ser.). (Illus.). 160p. 1999. pap. 9.95 (*0-946487-55-3*, Pub. by Luath Pr Ltd) Midpt Trade.

Atkinson, Tom. Poems to Be Read Aloud: A Victorian Drawing Room Entertainment. (Illus.). 113p. 1999. pap. 9.95 (*0-946487-00-6*, Pub. by Luath Pr Ltd) Midpt Trade.

— Roads to the Isles: A Guidebook to Scotland's Far West: Morar, Moidart, Morvern Ardnamurchan. LC 99-185023. 128p. 1989. pap. text 9.95 (*0-946487-01-4*) Luath Pr Ltd.

— South West Scotland: A Guidebook to the Best Of: Kyle, Carrick, Galloway, Dumfries-Shire, Kircudbright-Shire, Wigtownshire. (Illus.). 180p. 1989. pap. 9.95 (*0-946487-04-9*) Luath Pr Ltd.

***Atkinson, Tom.** The West Highlands: The Lonely Lands, Including All the Glories of That Land Known as Argyll. (Illus.). 160p. 1999. pap. 9.95 (*0-946487-56-1*, Pub. by Luath Pr Ltd) Midpt Trade.

Atkinson, Valentine. Distant Waters: The Greatest Fly-Fishing World. LC 98-150450. 192p. 1997. 35.00 (*0-679-45761-5*) Random.

Atkinson, Valerie J. The Law of Real Property Texas Student Pocket Part. 42p. 1993. 9.95 (*0-8273-6026-6*) Delmar.

— Paralegal Guide to Intellectual Property. 1. (Paralegal Law Library). 392p. 1994. boxed set 82.00 (*0-471-04303-6*) Wiley.

Atkinson, W. Patrick, compiled by. Theatrical Design in the Twentieth Century: An Index to Photographic Reproductions of Scenic Designs, 21. LC 96-4975. (Bibliographies & Indexes in the Performing Arts Ser.). 488p. 1996. lib. bdg. 105.00 (*0-313-29701-0*, Greenwood Pr) Greenwood.

Atkinson, W. W. Memory Culture: The Science of Observing, Remembering & Recalling. 1991. lib. bdg. 75.00 (*0-8490-4967-9*) Gordon Pr.

Atkinson, Wade. Two Feet from the Third Rail: Being a Compendium of Thoughts, Ideas, Advice, Castigations, & Memoirs on 50 Years in Public Relations. 305p. 1994. per. write for info. (*0-9640851-1-9*) W Atkinson.

Atkinson, Walter B. It's a Long Way from Scooba. LC 86-71591. (Illus.). 320p. 1986. 14.95 (*0-938991-01-9*) Colonial Pr AL.

Atkinson, William. The Consumer's Guide to Coin Collecting: Buying, Selling, Grading: Satisfaction Guaranteed. 150p. 1999. pap. 9.99 (*0-944945-30-9*) Amos Ohio.

— The Next New Madrid Earthquake: A Survival Guide for the Midwest. LC 86-31637. (Shawnee Bks.). (Illus.). 192p. 1989. pap. 14.95 (*0-8093-1320-0*) S Ill U Pr.

Atkinson, William, ed. see Conrad, Joseph.

Atkinson, William, ed. see Humiston, Sharon & Good, Cynthia.

Atkinson, William W. Dynamic Thought: The Law of Vibrant Energy. 281p. 1996. spiral bd. 18.00 (*0-7873-0047-0*) Hlth Research.

— Dynamic Thought or the Law of Vibrant Energy (1906) 231p. 1996. reprint ed. pap. 17.95 (*1-56459-768-7*) Kessinger Pub.

— How to Read Human Nature: Its Inner States & Outer Forms. 202p. 1996. reprint ed. spiral bd. 16.00 (*0-7873-0054-3*) Hlth Research.

— The Law of the New Thought. 93p. 1993. pap. 8.00 (*0-89540-270-X*, SB-270) Sun Pub.

— The Law of the New Thought. 93p. 1996. reprint ed. spiral bd. 10.00 (*0-7873-0057-8*) Hlth Research.

— The Law of the New Thought: A Study of Fundamental Principles & Their Application (1902) 94p. 1996. reprint ed. pap. 7.95 (*1-56459-846-2*) Kessinger Pub.

— The Mastery of Being. 196p. 1996. reprint ed. spiral bd. 15.00 (*0-7873-0052-7*) Hlth Research.

— The Mastery of Being: A Study of the Ultimate Principle of Reality, & the Practical Application Thereof (1911) 198p. 1996. reprint ed. pap. 14.25 (*1-56459-656-7*) Kessinger Pub.

— Memory Culture. 92p. 1996. reprint ed. spiral bd. 11.00 (*0-7873-0051-9*) Hlth Research.

— Memory Culture. 92p. 1976. reprint ed. 11.00 (*0-911662-61-8*) Yoga.

— Memory Culture: The Science of Observing, Remembering & Recalling (1903) 92p. 1996. reprint ed. pap. 9.95 (*1-56459-769-5*) Kessinger Pub.

— Mental Fascination No. 1: Side Light Manual. 253p. 1993. reprint ed. spiral bd. 17.00 (*0-7873-0056-X*) Hlth Research.

— Mental Fascination, 1907. 253p. 1996. reprint ed. pap. 16.50 (*1-56459-767-9*) Kessinger Pub.

— Mental Influence. reprint ed. pap. 3.00 (*0-911662-42-1*) Yoga.

— Mind & Body or Mental States & Physical Conditions. 208p. 1998. reprint ed. pap. 19.95 (*0-7661-0274-2*) Kessinger Pub.

— Mind Power: The Secret of Mental Magic. limited ed. reprint ed. 15.00 (*0-911662-27-8*) Yoga.

— Mind Power: The Secret of Mental Magic. 444p. 1997. reprint ed. pap. 29.95 (*0-7661-0091-X*) Kessinger Pub.

— The New Psychology: Its Message, Principles & Practice (1909) 200p. 1998. reprint ed. pap. 18.95 (*0-7661-0265-3*) Kessinger Pub.

— Practical Mental Influence (1908) 96p. 1998. reprint ed. pap. 16.95 (*0-7661-0197-5*) Kessinger Pub.

— Practical Mind Reading. reprint ed. pap. 3.00 (*0-911662-43-X*) Yoga.

— Practical New Thought: Several Things That Have Helped People. 96p. 1997. reprint ed. pap. 16.95 (*0-7661-0049-9*) Kessinger Pub.

— Practical Psychomancy & Crystal Gazing (1907) 100p. 1998. reprint ed. pap. 6.95 (*0-7661-0247-5*) Kessinger Pub.

— Psychomancy & Crystal Gazing. reprint ed. pap. 3.00 (*0-911662-41-3*) Yoga.

— Reincarnation & Law of Karma. reprint ed. 15.00 (*0-911662-26-X*) Yoga.

— Reincarnation & the Law of Karma. 249p. 1996. reprint ed. spiral bd. 16.50 (*0-7873-0059-4*) Hlth Research.

— Reincarnation & the Law of Karma. 250p. 1997. reprint ed. 15.95 (*0-7661-0079-0*) Kessinger Pub.

— The Secret of Success. 92p. 1996. spiral bd. 10.00 (*0-7873-0049-7*) Hlth Research.

— The Secret of Success: A Course of Nine Lessons on the Subject of the Application of the Latent Powers of the Individual Toward Attainment of Success in Life. 92p. 1996. reprint ed. pap. 9.95 (*1-56459-647-8*) Kessinger Pub.

— Self Healing by Thought Force. 92p. 1997. pap. 8.00 (*0-89540-286-6*, SB-286) Sun Pub.

— Self Healing by Thought Force. 91p. 1996. reprint ed. spiral bd. 10.00 (*0-7873-0048-9*) Hlth Research.

— Self-Healing by Thought Force. 91p. 1996. reprint ed. pap. 7.95 (*1-56459-646-X*) Kessinger Pub.

— The Subconscious & the Superconscious Planes of Mind. 200p. 1996. reprint ed. spiral bd. 12.50 (*0-7873-0055-1*) Hlth Research.

— The Subconscious & the Superconscious Planes of Mind (1909) 200p. 1996. reprint ed. pap. 11.95 (*1-56459-731-8*) Kessinger Pub.

— Suggestion & Auto-Suggestion. 218p. 1997. reprint ed. pap. 16.95 (*0-7661-0097-9*) Kessinger Pub.

— Suggestion & Autosuggestion. 217p. 1996. reprint ed. spiral bd. 18.00 (*0-7873-0058-6*) Hlth Research.

— Telepathy: Its Theory, Facts, & Proof (1910) 94p. 1996. reprint ed. pap. 9.95 (*1-56459-732-6*) Kessinger Pub.

— Telepathy, Its Theory, Facts & Proof. 94p. 1993. reprint ed. spiral bd. 11.50 (*0-7873-0053-5*) Hlth Research.

— Thought Force in Business & Everyday Life. 91p. 1996. reprint ed. spiral bd. 11.50 (*0-7873-0061-6*) Hlth Research.

— Thought-Force in Business & Everyday Life. 92p. 1996. reprint ed. pap. 9.95 (*1-56459-933-7*) Kessinger Pub.

— Thought Vibration: The Law of Attraction in the Thought Word. 112p. 1996. reprint ed. spiral bd. 12.00 (*0-7873-0060-8*) Hlth Research.

— Thought Vibration of the Law of Attraction in the Thought World (1906) 142p. 1996. reprint ed. pap. 10.95 (*1-56459-660-5*) Kessinger Pub.

— Your Greater Self: The Inner Consciousness. 94p. 1996. reprint ed. spiral bd. 9.00 (*0-7873-0062-4*) Hlth Research.

— Your Mind & How to Use It. 224p. 1996. reprint ed. spiral bd. 15.00 (*0-7873-0050-0*) Hlth Research.

— Your Mind & How to Use It (1911) A Manual of Practical Psychology. 224p. 1996. reprint ed. pap. 14.50 (*1-56459-749-0*) Kessinger Pub.

Atkinson, Wilmer. Wilmer Atkinson: An Autobiography. (American Newspapermen 1790-1933 Ser.). (Illus.). 375p. 1974. reprint ed. text 29.95 (*0-8464-0032-4*) Beekman Pubs.

Atkinston, Diane. The Suffragettes in Pictures. LC 96-9083. (Illus.). 224p. 1996. 26.95 (*0-7509-1017-8*, Pub. by Sutton Pub Ltd) Intl Pubs Mktg.

Atkisson, A. A. & Petak, William J. Natural Hazard Risk Assessment & Public Policy: Anticipating the Unexpected. (Environmental Management Ser.). (Illus.). 489p. 1982. 108.00 (*0-387-90645-2*) Spr-Verlag.

***Atkisson, Alan.** Believing Cassandra: An Optimist Looks at a Pessimists' World. LC 99-37784. (Illus.). 236p. 1999. pap. 16.95 (*1-890132-16-0*) Chelsea Green Pub.

— Believing Cassandra CD. 2000. pap. 12.95 (*1-890132-70-5*) Chelsea Green Pub.

Atkisson, Alan. The Community Indicators Handbook: Measuring Progress Toward Healthy & Sustainable Communities. 155p. (C). 1998. pap. text 35.00 (*0-7881-7356-1*) DIANE Pub.

Atknson, Norman. Sir Joseph Whitworth. (Illus.). 320p. 1996. 44.95 (*0-7509-1211-1*, Pub. by Sutton Pub Ltd) Intl Pubs Mktg.

ATKOL Staff. ATKOL Comprehensive Guide to Adult Male Video. Satkin, Jeff, ed. LC 90-83641. 184p. 1990. pap. text. write for info. (*1-878176-00-5*) ATKOL.

Atkov, Oleg & Bednenko, V. S. Hypokinesia & Weightlessness: Clinical & Physiological Aspects. 561p. (C). 1992. 85.00 (*0-8236-2415-3*) Intl Univs Pr.

ATL Staff. ATL-Sanasto Suomi-Englanti-Suomi. (ENG & FIN.). 171p. 1985. 75.00 (*0-8288-0261-0*, F24011) Fr & Eur.

ATLA Press Staff, ed. Crashworthiness. 242p. 1989. pap. 32.00 (*0-941916-49-9*) West Group.

ATLA Press Staff, ed. see Hare, Francis H., Jr., et al.

ATLA Press Staff, ed. see Perlman, Peter.

ATLA Staff, ed. Best of Trial: Products Liability. LC 91-35815. 376p. 1991. 85.00 (*0-941916-63-4*) West Group.

Atlan, H. & Cohen, I. R., eds. Theories of Immune Networks. (Synergetics Ser.: Vol. 46). (Illus.). 160p. 1989. 67.95 (*0-387-51678-6*) Spr-Verlag.

Atlan, Henri. Enlightenment to Enlightenment: Intercritique of Science & Myth. Schramm, Lenn J., tr. from FRE. LC 92-19023. 416p. (C). 1993. text 64.50 (*0-7914-1451-5*); pap. text 21.95 (*0-7914-1452-3*) State U NY Pr.

Atlan, Liliane. Theatre Pieces, an Anthology. Knapp, Bettina L., ed. Feitlowitz, Marguerite, tr. from FRE. (Modern Literatures Annual Ser.: Vol. I). 225p. 1985. lib. bdg. 15.00 (*0-913283-03-7*) Penkevill.

Atlanasio, Salvator, jt. auth. see Gilson, Etienne.

Atlanta Athletic Club Staff & Neill, Nancy. More Than Bricks & Mortar: A History of the Atlanta Athletic Club. LC 87-51024. (Illus.). 200p. (C). 1988. text. write for info. (*0-9613474-2-2*) Wolfe Pubng.

Atlanta Braves Staff. From Home Plate to Home Cooking. (Illus.). 110p. (Orig.). 1993. 9.95 (*0-9614832-5-3*) Atlanta Braves.

Atlanta Committee for the Olympic Games. The Official Report of the Centennial Olympic Games. LC 97-23578. 1997. 325.00 (*1-56145-150-9*) Peachtree Pubs.

— The Official Report of the Centennial Olympic Games, Vol. 2. LC 97-23578. 1997. pap. 150.00 (*1-56145-151-7*) Peachtree Pubs.

Atlanta Falcons Staff. Atlanta Falcons. CWC Sports Inc., ed. (NFL Team Yearbooks Ser.). (J). 1998. pap. 9.99 (*1-891613-02-2*) Everett Sports.

Atlanta Historical Society. Atlanta in Eighteen Ninety: The Gate City. LC 86-12463. (Illus.). xxx, 98p. 1986. text 19.95 (*0-86554-241-4*, H-211) Mercer Univ Pr.

***Atlanta History Center Staff & Rose, Michael.** Atlanta: A Portrait of the Civil War. (Images of America Ser.). (Illus.). 128p. 1999. pap. 18.99 (*0-7385-0138-7*) Arcadia Publng.

Atlanta History Center Staff, jt. auth. see Doster, Gary L.

***Atlanta International School Staff.** Cooking Without Borders. 276p. 1999. 19.95 (*0-9663732-0-0*, Pub. by Atlanta Intl Schl) Wimmer Bks.

Atlanta Journal & Constitution Staff. The Ultimate Atlanta Guidebook. LC 93-81140. (Illus.). 144p. 1994. pap. 8.95 (*1-56352-135-0*) Longstreet.

Atlanta Journal and Constitution Staff. Appalachian Adventure: From Georgia to Maine: A Spectacular Journey on the Great American Trail. LC 95-77253. (Illus.). 208p. 1995. 25.00 (*1-56352-234-9*) Longstreet.

Atlanta University Staff. Atlanta University Publications: Nos. 1, 2, 4, 8, 9, 11, & 13-18, Set. LC 68-28965. (American Negro: His History & Literature. Series 1). 1969. reprint ed. 32.95 (*0-405-01804-5*) Ayer.

— Atlanta University Publications: Nos. 3, 5-7, 10, 12, 19 & 20, Set. LC 68-28985. (American Negro: His History & Literature. Series 3). 1970. reprint ed. 27.95 (*0-405-01914-9*) Ayer.

Atlantic Coast Conference Schools' (Clemson, Duke, Florida State, VA, Wake Forest, GA Tech, Maryland, NC, NC State) Staff, jt. auth. see Atlantic Coast Conference Staff.

Atlantic Coast Conference Staff & Atlantic Coast Conference Schools' (Clemson, Duke, Florida State, VA, Wake Forest, GA Tech, Maryland, NC, NC State) Staff. 1998 Official ACC Basketball Handbook. abr. ed. (Illus.). 176p. 1998. pap. 6.95 (*0-9642611-5-4*) BellSouth Advert.

Atlantic Council of the United States Staff. Reversing Relations with Former Adversaries: U. S. Foreign Policy after the Cold War. Nelson, C. Richard & Weisbrode, Kenneth, eds. LC 97-34113. 216p. 1998. 39.95 (*0-8130-1545-6*) U Press Fla.

— The United States & Japan: Cooperative Leadership for Peace & Global Prosperity. 125p. (C). 1990. pap. text 11.75 (*0-8191-7693-1*) Atl Coun US.

— The United States & Japan: Cooperative Leadership for Peace & Global Prosperity. 138p. 1990. text 32.50 (*0-8191-7712-1*) U Pr of Amer.

Atlantic Council of the United States Staff, et al. The United States & Japan: Cooperative Leadership for Peace & Global Prosperity. 125p. (C). 1990. pap. text 11.75 (*0-8191-7713-X*) Atl Coun US.

Atlantic Monthly Staff, jt. auth. see Jolis, Alan.

Atlantic Provinces Economic Council Staff, ed. Atlantic Canada Today. 206p. 1987. pap. 19.95 (*0-88780-059-9*, Pub. by Formac Publ Co) Formac Dist Ltd.

Atlantic-Richfield Company Staff, jt. auth. see ALMACA Staff.

Atlantis Rising Editors. The Search for Lost Origins. (Paradigm Busters Ser.: Vol. 1). (Illus.). 181p. (Orig.). 1996. pap. 14.95 (*0-9653310-0-8*) Atlan Rising.

AtlantiSoft Staff. How to Keep MS-DOS 3.1 Running. Stern, Lisa & Estler, Cora, eds. (DOS for You & Me Ser.: Vol. 1). (Illus.). 136p. 1995. write for info. (*0-9657152-3-X*) AtlantiSoft.

Atlas. Principles of Microbiology. 1995. 30.62 (*0-8151-0319-0*) McGraw.

Atlas, Alan. The Cappella Giulia Chansonnier, Pt. 1. (Wissenschaftliche Abhandlungen-Musicological Studies: Vol. 27). 220p. 1976. lib. bdg. 74.00 (*0-912024-23-2*) Inst Mediaeval Mus.

— The Cappella Giulia Chansonnier, Pt. 2. (Wissenschaftliche Abhandlungen-Musicological Studies: Vol. 27). 220p. 1976. lib. bdg. 60.00 (*0-912024-24-0*) Inst Mediaeval Mus.

Atlas, Allan. The Salve Reginas of G. B. Pergolesi: Pergo Edition. (Complete Works of G. B. Pergolesi: No. 4, Vol. XV). 1994. 110.00 (*0-945193-58-0*) Pendragon NY.

Atlas, Allan, ed. see Morton, Robert.

Atlas, Allan A., ed. Music in the Classic Period: Essays in Honor of Barry S. Brook. LC 84-27391. (Festschrift Ser.: No. 5). 400p. 1985. lib. bdg. 48.00 (*0-918728-37-1*) Pendragon NY.

Atlas, Allan W. Renaissance Music. LC 97-19816. (Norton Introduction to Music History Ser.). (Illus.). 600p. (C). 1998. text 50.00 (*0-393-97169-4*) Norton.

— The Wheatstone English Concertina in Victorian England. LC 96-13333. (Illus.). 168p. 1996. text 68.00 (*0-19-816580-3*, Clarendon Pr) OUP.

Atlas, Allan W., ed. Anthology of Renaissance Music. 550p. (C). 1998. pap. text 44.50 (*0-393-97170-8*) Norton.

Atlas, David, ed. Atmospheric Science & Public Policy. 105p. 1976. pap. 11.00 (*0-933876-43-2*) Am Meteorological.

— Radar in Meteorology: Battan Memorial & 40th Aniversary Radar Meteorology Conference. (Illus.). 824p. 1990. 101.00 (*0-933876-86-6*) Am Meteorological.

Atlas, David, et al. Severe Local Storms. (Meteorological Monograph: Vol. 5, No. 27). (Illus.). 247p. 1963. pap. 20.00 (*0-933876-17-3*) Am Meteorological.

Atlas, James. Bellow: A Biography. (Illus.). 688p. 2000. 35.00 (*0-394-58501-1*) Random.

— Delmore Schwartz: The Life of an American Poet. LC 85-5501. (Illus.). 432p. 1985. reprint ed. pap. 10.95 (*0-15-625272-4*, Harvest Bks) Harcourt.

— Delmore Schwartz: The Life of an American Poet. (Illus.). 434p. 2000. reprint ed. pap. 14.00 (*1-56649-120-7*) Welcome Rain.

Atlas, James, ed. see Schwartz, Delmore.

Atlas, Jay D. Philosophy Without Ambiguity: A Logico-Linguistic Essay. (Clarendon Library of Logic & Philosophy). (Illus.). 198p. 1989. text 55.00 (*0-19-824454-1*) OUP.

***Atlas, Jay David.** Logic, Meaning & Conversation: Semantical Underdeterminacy, Implicature & Their Interface. (Illus.). 400p. 2000. text 55.00 (*0-19-513300-5*) OUP.

Atlas, Michel C. Author's Handbook of Styles for Life Science Journals. LC 95-38010. 704p. 1995. boxed set 104.95 (*0-8493-2503-X*, 2503) CRC Pr.

***Atlas, Nancy F., et al.** Alternative Dispute Resolution. LC 00-23849. 2000. write for info. (*1-57073-812-2*) Amer Bar Assn.

Atlas, Nava. Great American Vegetarian Cookbook: Traditional & Regional Recipes for the Enlightened Cook. 3rd ed. LC 98-4717. 288p. 1998. 24.95 (*0-87131-853-9*) M Evans.

— Pasta East & West. LC 98-37970. 1999. pap. text 14.95 (*1-57067-066-8*) Book Pub Co.

— Vegetarian Celebrations: Festive Menus for Holidays & Other Special Occasions. rev. ed. (Illus.). 288p. 1996. pap. 15.95 (*0-316-05739-8*) Little.

— Vegetarian Soups for All Seasons: A Treasury of Bountiful Low-fat Soups & Stews. rev. ed. LC 95-49915. (Illus.). 176p. 1996. pap. 14.95 (*0-316-05733-9*) Little.

— Vegetariana: A Rich Harvest of Wit, Lore, & Recipes. LC 92-13452. (Illus.). 234p. 1993. pap. 15.95 (*0-316-05743-6*) Little.

***Atlas, Nava.** Vegetariana: A Rich Harvest of Wit, Love & Recipe. (Illus.). 236p. 1999. pap. 16.00 (*0-9630243-5-3*, Pub. by Amberwood Pr) Book Pub Co.

Atlas, Nava & Kayte, Lillian. Vegetarian Express: Easy, Tasty & Healthy Menus in 28 Minutes or Less. (Illus.), 224p. 1995. pap. 15.95 (*0-316-05740-1*) Little.

Atlas, Nava & Tabak, Harry C., eds. The Idea Book: A Journal for Creative Thinkers. (Illus.). 112p. 9.95 (*0-9630243-2-9*) Amberwood Pr.

Atlas, Rafael & Cherlin, Michael, eds. Musical Transformation & Musical Intuition: Eleven Essays in Honor of David Lewin. (Illus.). 241p. (Orig.). (C). 1994. pap. 40.00 (*1-886464-00-6*) Ovenbird Pr.

***Atlas, Ronald, ed.** Many Faces, Many Microbes: Personal Reflections in Microbiology. (Illus.). 340p. 2000. pap. 39.95 (*1-55581-190-6*) ASM Pr.

Atlas, Ronald M. Handbook of Media for Environmental Microbiology. LC 95-32261. 544p. 1995. boxed set 149.95 (*0-8493-0603-5*, 603) CRC Pr.

— Handbook of Microbiological Media. 2nd ed. LC 96-41382. 1712p. 1996. boxed set 154.95 (*0-8493-2638-9*) CRC Pr.

— Handbook of Microbiological Media & Reagents. 1088p. 1993. boxed set 125.00 (*0-8493-2944-2*, QR) CRC Pr.

— The Handbook of Microbiological Media for the Examination of Food. LC 94-44498. 320p. 1995. boxed set 149.95 (*0-8493-2704-0*, 2704) CRC Pr.

— Handbook of Microbiological Procedures. 2001. 94.95 (*0-8493-2948-5*) CRC Pr.

— Handbook of Microbiological Reagents. 2000. 94.95 (*0-8493-2947-7*) CRC Pr.

— Microbial Ecology. 4th ed. LC 97-31965. (Illus.). 640p. (C). 1997. 94.00 (*0-8053-0655-2*) Addison-Wesley.

Atlas, Ronald M. & Browm, Alfred E. Experimental Microbiology. 2nd ed. 624p. (C). 1988. teacher ed. write for info. (0-318-63274-8) Macmillan.

— Experimental Microbiology. 2nd ed. 624p. (C). 1988. pap. text 38.20 (0-02-304280-X, Macmillan Coll) P-H.

Atlas, Ronald M. & Parks, Lawrence C. Microorganisms in Our World. 400p. (C). 1995. text, lab manual ed. write for info. (0-8151-0337-9, WCB McGr Hill) McGrw-H Hghr Educ.

— Principles of Microbiology. 576p. (C). 1995. text, lab manual ed. write for info. (0-8151-0324-7, WCB McGr Hill) McGrw-H Hghr Educ.

Atlas, Ronald M. & Renk. Principles of Microbiology. 144p. (C). 1995. text, student ed. 30.00 (0-8151-0323-9, WCB McGr Hill) McGrw-H Hghr Educ.

Atlas, Ronald M. & Wellnitz, William R. Microorganisms in Our World. 216p. (C). 1995. text, student ed. 20.62 (0-8151-0336-0, WCB McGr Hill) McGrw-H Hghr Educ.

Atlas, Ronald M., et al. Basic Experimental Microbiology. 316p. (C). 1986. 21.30 (0-02-304390-3, Macmillan Coll) P-H.

Atlas, Ronald M., jt. auth. see Snyder, James W.

Atlas, Scott W., ed. Magnetic Resonance Imaging of the Brain & Spine. 2nd ed. LC 95-6253. (Illus.). 1675p. 1995. text 270.00 (0-7817-0282-8) Lppncott W & W.

Atlas Staff. Dictionnaire Archaeologique de la France, 2 vols. (FRE.). 1990. 295.00 (0-7859-7981-6, 2731205008) Fr & Eur.

— Micro World. 1995. teacher ed., lab manual ed. (0-8151-0329-8) Mosby Inc.

— Princ. Microbiology. 2nd ed. 416p. 1997. pap. 30.63 (0-8151-8451-4) McGraw.

— Princ. Microbiology. 2nd ed. 1997. 290.31 (0-8151-1306-4) Mosby Inc.

— Principle Microbiology. 1995. (0-8151-0315-8) Mosby Inc.

Atlas, Susan. Passover Passage. (YA). (gr. 4-7). 1991. pap. 5.95 (0-933873-46-8) Torah Aura.

Atlas, Susan, jt. auth. see Crown, Bonnie.

Atlass, Kathleen, tr. see Borgeaud, Philippe.

Atlay, J. B., ed. Trial of the Staunstons. (Notable British Trials Ser.). 332p. 1995. reprint ed. 103.00 (1-56169-141-0, 15110) Gaunt.

***Atlee, Gwyneth.** Night Winds. 2000. mass mkt. 5.99 (0-8217-6642-2, Zebra Kensgtn) Kensgtn Pub Corp.

Atlee, Gwyneth. Touched by Fire. (Zebra Splendor Historical Romances Ser.). 352p. 1999. mass mkt. 4.99 (0-8217-6227-3) Kensgtn Pub Corp.

Atlee, Helena, jt. auth. see Ramsey, Alex.

Atlee, J. L., III, et al, eds. Perioperative Management of Pacemaker Patients. LC 92-49912. (Illus.). xi, 155p. 1992. write for info. (3-540-53874-7); pap. 59.00 (0-387-53874-7) Spr-Verlag.

Atlee, John L. Arrhythmias & Pacemakers. (Illus.). 469p. 1995. text 66.00 (0-7216-5880-6, W B Saunders Co) Harcrt Hlth Sci Grp.

— Complications in Anesthesia. Ross, Allan, ed. LC 98-5821. 928p. (C). 1998. text 95.00 (0-7216-7161-6, W B Saunders Co) Harcrt Hlth Sci Grp.

Atleson, James B. Labor & The Wartime State: Labor Relations & Law During World War II. LC 97-21069. 312p. 1998. text 49.95 (0-252-02370-6) U of Ill Pr.

— Labor & the Wartime State: Labor Relations & Law During World War II. LC 97-21069. 312p. 1998. text 21.95 (0-252-06674-X) U of Ill Pr.

Atleson, James B. Values & Assumptions in American Labor Law. LC 82-21993. 256p. 1983. pap. 18.95 (0-87023-390-4) U of Mass Pr.

***Atley, Steve.** Dungeons & Dragons: The Movie. 2000. pap. 5.99 (0-7869-1785-7) Wizards Coast.

Atlmann, J. & Rotblat, Joseph, eds. Verification of Arms Reduction. (Illus.). xiv, 228p. 1989. 52.00 (0-387-51596-8) Spr-Verlag.

Atlschul, Aaron M., ed. Weight Control: A Guide for Counselors & Therapists. LC 87-11725. 305p. 1987. 69.50 (0-275-92697-4, C2697, Praeger Pubs) Greenwood.

Atluri, S. N., et al, eds. Computational Mechanics '95, Vol. I. 1600p. (C). 1995. text. write for info. (1-883793-10-6) Wolfe Pubng.

— Computational Mechanics '95, Vol. II. 1600p. (C). 1995. text. write for info. (1-883793-11-4) Wolfe Pubng.

— Computational Mechanics '95: Theory & Applications, 2 vols., Set. 3200p. 1996. 771.00 (3-540-59114-1) Spr-Verlag.

— Durability of Metal Aircraft Structures. 520p. (C). 1992. text. write for info. (0-9613474-6-5) Wolfe Pubng.

— Structural Integrity of Aging Airplanes. (Computational Mechanics Ser.). (Illus.). 512p. 1991. 139.95 (0-387-53461-X) Spr-Verlag.

Atluri, S. N. & Amos, A. K., eds. Large Space Structures: Dynamics & Control. (Computational Mechanics Ser.). (Illus.). viii, 356p. 1988. 139.95 (0-387-18900-9) Spr-Verlag.

Atluri, S. N. & Yagawa, Genki, eds. Computational Mechanics '88, 2 vols., Set. 1900p. 1988. 343.95 (0-387-19015-5) Spr-Verlag.

Atluri, S. N., jt. ed. see Beskos, D. E.

Atluri, S. N., jt. ed. see Yagawa, Genki.

Atluri, Satya N. Structural Integrity & Durability. (Illus.). 888p. (C). 1997. text 250.00 (0-9657001-1-9) Tech Sci Pr.

Atluri, Satya N., ed. Computational Nonlinear Mechanics in Aerospace Engineering. (Progress in Astronautics & Aeronautics Ser.: Vol. 147). 541p. 1992. 99.95 (1-56347-044-6, V-146) AIAA.

Atluri, Satya N., et al, eds. Hybrid & Mixed Finite Element Methods. LC 82-8615. (Wiley Series in Numerical Methods in Engineering). 598p. reprint ed. pap. 185.40 (0-608-15416-4, 202926700059) Bks Demand.

***Atluri, Satya N. & Brust, Frederick W., eds.** Advances in Computational Engineering & Sciences, 2 vols., Set. (Illus.). 2100p. 2000. 600.00 (0-9657001-3-5) Tech Sci Pr.

***Atluri, Satya N. & O'Donoghue, P. E., eds.** Modeling & Simulation Based Engineering, 2 vols. (Illus.). 2209p. (C). 1998. 625.00 (0-9657001-2-7) Tech Sci Pr.

Atluri, Satya N. & Yagawa, Genki, eds. Advances in Computational Engineering Science. (Illus.). 1334p. (C). 1997. 325.00 (0-9657001-0-0) Tech Sci Pr.

Atluri, Satya N., ed. see Applied Mechanics, Bioengineering & Fluids Enginee.

***Atluri, Vijay & Hale, John.** Research Advances in Database & Information Systems Security. 360p. 2000. 99.50 (0-7923-7848-2) Kluwer Academic.

***Atluri, Vijay & Samarati, Pierangela.** Security of Data & Transaction Processing. LC 99-89328. 152p. 2000. 99.95 (0-7923-7761-3) Kluwer Academic.

ATM Forum Technical Committee Staff. ATM User-Network Interface. LC 95-18452. 1995. pap. text 42.00 (0-13-393828-X) Prntice Hall Bks.

Atman, Kim. Forbidden Questions about Abortion. 192p. 1992. pap. 12.95 (0-9632564-6-7) More to Life.

***Atman, Sally.** One Hour from "Always Broke" Easy Money Solutions for the Perpetually Overdrawn. abr. ed. 1999. 10.95 incl. audio (1-928843-07-7) Ad Lib Res.

Atmanspacher, H. & Dalenoort, G. J., eds. Inside vs Outside: Endo- & Exo-Concepts of Observation & Knowledge in Physics, Philosophy, & Cognitive Science. LC 93-44940. (Synergetics Ser.: Vol. 63). (Illus.). 427p. 1994. 73.95 (0-387-57088-8) Spr-Verlag.

Atmanspacher, H. & Scheingraber, H. Information Dynamics. (NATO ASI Ser.: Vol. 256). (Illus.). 376p. (C). 1991. text 120.00 (0-306-43912-3, Kluwer Plenum) Kluwer Academic.

Atmanspacher, Harald & Ruhnau, Eva. Time, Temporality, Now: Experiencing Time & Concepts of Time in an Interdisciplinary Perspective. LC 97-7812. 381p. 1997. 54.95 (3-540-62486-4) Spr-Verlag.

Atmore, Anthony, jt. auth. see Oliver, Roland Anthony.

Atmore, Barbara, ed. see Kindler, Herbert S.

Atmore, Barbara, ed. see Rigsbee, Edwin Richard.

Atmospheric & Space Environments Committee on Standards, jt. auth. see American Institute of Aeronautics & Astronautics Staff.

Atmosumarto, Sutanto. Colloquial Indonesian. 336p. 1994. pap., pap. text 45.00 incl. audio (0-415-09201-9) Routledge.

— Colloquial Indonesian. LC 93-44403. 19p. (C). (gr. 13). 1994. audio 27.99 (0-415-09200-0) Routledge.

— Colloquial Indonesian. LC 93-44403. (Illus.). 336p. (C). (gr. 13). 1994. pap. 20.99 (0-415-09199-3) Routledge.

Atmosumarto, Sutanto, jt. auth. see Othman, Zaharah.

Atnip, Carol & Benner, Richard. Beginning Algebra: A Process Education Approach. (Illus.). 266p. (C). 1997. pap. text 24.00 (1-878437-61-5) Pac Crest Soft.

— Prealgebra: A Process Education Approach. (Illus.). 316p. (C). 1997. pap. text 24.00 (1-878437-60-7) Pac Crest Soft.

Atnip, Linda. Miranda's Magic Garden. LC 97-9928. (Illus.). 32p. (J). (ps-7). 1997. 19.95 (1-885394-21-7) Bluestar Communs.

Atoda, Takashi. The Square Persimmon & Other Stories. Horton, Millicent, tr. LC 89-51723. 180p. (Orig.). 1991. 12.95 (0-8048-1678-6) Tuttle Pubng.

Atomic Energy of Canada Limited Staff. Eddy Current Testing, 2 Vols., Vol. 1. (Illus.). 196p. 1987. spiral bd. 55.00 (0-87683-890-5, A890-5) GP Courseware.

— Eddy Current Testing, 2 Vols., Vol. 2. (Illus.). 125p. 1987. pap. text 55.00 (0-87683-891-3, A891-3) GP Courseware.

— Eddy Current Testing, 2 Vols., Vols. 1 & 2. (Illus.). 1987. pap. text 99.00 (0-87683-889-1, A889-1) GP Courseware.

Aton, Bert B., jt. auth. see Thorndale, William.

Ator, Joe T. The Return of Credibility. LC 97-90582. 105p. 1998. pap. 9.95 (0-533-12425-5) Vantage.

Ator, Nancy, jt. auth. see Henningfield, Jack E.

Atran, Scott, jt. ed. see Medin, Douglas L.

Atre, S. Data Base: Structured Techniques for Designs, Performance & Management. 442p. 1980. 31.95 (0-318-17046-9); 33.95 (0-318-17047-7) AITP.

Atre, Shaka. Atre's Road Map for Data Warehouse/Dart Mart Implementation. Wilderman, Jack, ed. (Illus.). 210p. (C). 1997. pap. 395.00 (1-891234-01-3, 9530) InfoEdge.

Atre, Shaku. Data Base Management Systems for the Eighties. LC 83-60769. 609p. reprint ed. pap. 188.80 (0-608-15619-1, 203174800076) Bks Demand.

Atrens, D. M. & Curthoys, J. S., eds. Neuroscience & Behavior: An Introduction. 2nd ed. 214p. 1982. text 55.00 (0-12-066850-5) Acad Pr.

***Atrey, Mukta & Kirpal, Viney.** Shashi Deshpande: A Feminist Study of Her Fiction. LC 98-904231. (Indian Writers Ser.). 134 p. 1998. write for info. (81-7018-973-X, Pub. by BR Pub) S Asia.

Atreya. Ayurvedic Healing for Women: Herbal Gynecology. LC 99-11474. (Illus.). 304p. 1999. pap. 14.95 (1-57863-116-5) Weiser.

— Practical Ayurveda: Secrets to Physical, Sexual & Spiritual Health. LC 97-48967. (Illus.). 256p. 1998. pap. 14.95 (1-57863-029-0) Weiser.

— Prana: The Secret of Yogic Healing. LC 96-15586. (Illus.). 176p. (Orig.). 1996. pap. 12.95 (0-87728-885-2) Weiser.

Atreya, A., et al, eds. ASME Heat Transfer Division: Proceedings of the ASME International Mechanical Engineering Congress & Exposition, 1995, San Francisco, CA. LC 95-81065. (HTD Ser.: Vol. 317). 1995. pap. 150.00 (0-685-55714-6) ASME.

— 1995 International Mechanical Engineering Congress & Exposition - Proceedings of the ASME Heat Transfer Division, Vol. 2. 592p. 150.00 (0-614-97064-4, H1032B) ASME.

Atreya, B. L. Deification of Man: Its Methods & Stages According to the Yoga Vasistha Including a Translation of the Essence of Vasistha's Teachings. 116p. 1980. reprint ed. pap. 4.50 (0-935548-02-5) Codex Pr.

Atreya, S. K., et al, eds. Origin & Evolution of Planetary & Satellite Atmospheres. LC 89-4651. (Space Science Ser.). 881p. 1989. 67.50 (0-8165-1105-5) U of Ariz Pr.

Atreya, S. K. & Caldwell, J. J., eds. Planetary Aeronomy & Astronomy. (Advances in Space Research Ser.: Vol. 1, No. 9). (Illus.). 216p. 1981. pap. 34.00 (0-08-028385-3, Pergamon Pr) Elsevier.

Atreya, S. K., jt. ed. see Johnson, T. V.

Atri, F. R. Arsen, Elemente in der Awuatischen Umwelt II Vol. 75: Biotische Un Abiotische Systeme. (Schriftenreihe des Vereins Fuer Wassrt-Boden Und Lufthygiene). 198p. 1987. pap. text 30.00 (3-437-30576-X) Lubrecht & Cramer.

Atria, Fernando, jt. auth. see MacCormick, Neil.

Atrill, Peter. Financial Management for Non-Specialists. 380p. 1996. pap. 52.00 (0-13-376740-X, Prentice Hall) P-H.

Atrill, Peter & Lindley, Lindsey, eds. Issues in Accounting & Finance. LC 96-79843. 336p. 1997. 78.95 (1-85972-465-5, Pub. by Avebry) Ashgate Pub Co.

***Atrill, Peter & McLaney, E. J.** Accounting & Finance for Non-Specialists. 3rd ed. LC 00-39350. 2000. write for info. (0-273-64632-X, Finc Times) F T P-H.

Atrill, Peter & McLaney, E. J. Management Accounting for Non-Specialists 2nd ed. LC 98-50053. 1998. write for info. (0-13-982927-X) P-H.

Atrill, Peter & McLaney, Eddie. Accounting & Finance for Non-Specialists. LC 94-13289. 1994. 37.90 (0-13-309865-6) P-H Intl.

Atrill, Peter & McLaney, Eddie. Accounting & Finance for Non-Specialists. 2nd ed. 410p. 1996. pap. 42.00 (0-13-571746-9) P-H.

Atrill, Peter & McLaney, Eddie. Management Accounting. (Illus.). 512p. (C). 1994. pap. 47.95 (0-631-19538-6) Blackwell Pubs.

— Management Accounting for Non-Specialists. LC 95-17923. 1995. write for info. (0-13-376724-8, Prntice Hall Bks.

Atrill, Peter, jt. auth. see McLaney, E. J.

Atrium. Charming Hotels. 2000. 37.50 (0-688-16833-7, Wm Morrow) Morrow Avon.

— City Squares & Plaza. 1998. pap. 35.00 (0-688-15778-5, Wm Morrow) Morrow Avon.

***Atrium.** Extraordinary Office. 1998. pap. 35.00 (0-688-16438-2, Wm Morrow) Morrow Avon.

Atrium. Lofts. 1999. 37.50 (0-688-16831-0, Wm Morrow) Morrow Avon.

— Masters, Vol 2. 1997. pap. 42.00 (84-8185-109-4, St Martin.

— Minimalism. 1999. pap. 35.00 (0-688-16222-3, Wm Morrow) Morrow Avon.

— Redesigning City Squares & Plazas. (Illus.). 168p. 1997. pap. text 39.95 (0-8230-4514-5) Watsn-Guptill.

— Spectacular Pools. 1924. pap. 35.00 (0-688-17240-7, Wm Morrow) Morrow Avon.

— Spectacular Pools. 1999. 37.50 (0-688-16832-9, Wm Morrow) Morrow Avon.

Atrium Press Staff. Multiresidential-Archways. 1999. pap. 35.00 (0-688-16223-1, Wm Morrow) Morrow Avon.

— A Remarkable Restaurant. 1998. pap. 35.00 (0-688-16439-0, Wm Morrow) Morrow Avon.

Atrium Staff. Architecture of Glass. 1999. pap. 35.00 (0-688-16221-5, Wm Morrow) Morrow Avon.

— Architecture of Light & Shapes. 1998. 42.50 (0-688-15712-2, Wm Morrow) Morrow Avon.

— Architecture of Minimalism. 1998. 42.50 (0-688-15723-8, Wm Morrow) Morrow Avon.

— Architecture of Museums. 1998. 42.50 (0-688-15713-0, Wm Morrow) Morrow Avon.

— Museum of Architecture. 1999. pap. 35.00 (0-688-16224-X, Wm Morrow) Morrow Avon.

— Theme & Amusement Parks. (Illus.). 168p. 1997. pap. text 39.95 (0-8230-5350-4) Watsn-Guptill.

Atroshenko, V. I. & Collins, Judith. The Origins of the Romanesque: Near Eastern Influences on European Art Fourth to Twelfth Centuries. LC 85-21635. (Illus.). 176p. 1986. 60.00 (0-87951-247-4, Pub. by Overlook Pr) Penguin Putnam.

ATS (Hansen) Staff. Lung Disease: State of the Art 1995-1996. 356p. 1997. per. 65.00 (0-7872-3709-4) Kendall-Hunt.

Atsarkina, E. N. & Volodarskii, V. M. The State Tretyakov Gallery. (RUS., Illus.). 720p. 1984. 63.00 (0-7855-1669-7) St Mut.

Atsberger, Deborah B. & Zichuhr, Monica T., eds. Pre- & Post-Anesthesia Nursing Knowledge Base & Clinical Competiencies. (Illus.). 158p. 1994. pap. text 47.00 (0-7216-5645-5, W B Saunders Co) Harcrt Hlth Sci Grp.

Atse, David. Commodity Futures Trading & International Market Stabilization. (Studia Oeconomica Upsaliensia: No. 10). 151p. (Orig.). 1986. pap. text 33.00 (0-317-57980-0, Pub. by Uppsala Univ Acta Univ Uppsaliensis) Coronet Bks.

Atseriak, Elizabeth & Sparck, Amy. How I Helped During the Week. 11.00 (1-55036-499-5) Todd Commns.

Atseriak, Liz. Ciumek Tungliakun.Tr. of Making Yo Yos. (ESK., Illus.). 16p. (J). (gr. k-3). 1998. pap. text 6.00 (1-58084-033-7) Lower Kuskokwim.

Atseriak, Liz, et al. At the Beach. large type ed. (Illus.). 8p. (J). (gr. k-3). 1999. pap. text 6.00 (1-58084-050-7) Lower Kuskokwim.

— Cenami (At the Beach) large type ed. (ESK., Illus.). 8p. (J). (gr. k-3). 1999. pap. text 6.00 (1-58084-116-3) Lower Kuskokwim.

— Higyami (At the Beach) large type ed. (ESK., Illus.). 8p. (J). (gr. k-3). 1999. pap. text 6.00 (1-58084-134-1) Lower Kuskokwim.

— Imarpiim Ceniini (At the Beach) large type ed. (ESK., Illus.). 8p. (J). (gr. k-3). 1999. pap. text 6.00 (1-58084-051-5) Lower Kuskokwim.

***Atseriak, Liz, et al.** Sigyami (At the Beach) large type ed. (ESK., Illus.). 8p. (J). (gr. k-3). 1999. pap. text 6.00 (1-58084-127-9) Lower Kuskokwim.

— Sirrami (At the Beach) large type ed. (ESK., Illus.). 8p. (J). (gr. k-3). 1999. pap. text 6.00 (1-58084-141-4) Lower Kuskokwim.

— Tagium Sinaani (At the Beach) large type ed. (ESK., Illus.). 8p. (J). (gr. k-3). 1999. pap. text 6.00 (1-58084-121-X) Lower Kuskokwim.

Atsma, Bert. Essentials of Anatomy & Physiology. 3rd ed. LC 98-46568. 170p. (C). 1998. spiral bd., lab manual ed. 28.60 (0-8053-5092-6) Benjamin-Cummings.

Atsumi, Ikuko, jt. tr. see Rexroth, Kenneth.

Atsumi, K. & Kajiya, F., eds. Medical Engineering in Japan: Research & Development. (C). 1987. pap. text 278.50 (0-89838-973-9) Kluwer Academic.

Atta, Dale Van, see Van Atta, Dale.

Atta, Robert E. Van, see Van Atta, Robert E.

Atta-ur-Rahman. Nuclear Magnetic Resonance: Basic Principles. (Illus.). 260p. 1986. 89.00 (0-387-96243-3) Spr-Verlag.

Atta-ur-Rahman, ed. Studies in Natural Products Chemistry Vol. 20, Pt. F: Structure & Chemistry. 1364p. 1998. 773.00 (0-444-50105-3) Elsevier.

Atta-Ur-Rahman & Basha, Anwer, eds. Indole Alkaloids. (Frontiers in Natural Product Research Ser.: Vol. 2). 336p. 1998. text 55.00 (90-5702-268-0, ECU71, Harwood Acad Pubs) Gordon & Breach.

Atta-ur-Rahman & Choudhary, Muhammad I. Solving Problems with NMR Spectroscopy. LC 95-15392. (Illus.). 430p. 1995. pap. text 39.95 (0-12-066320-1) Acad Pr.

Atta-Ur-Rahman & Kaman, K. Stereoselective Synthetic Reductions in Organic Chemistry. Date not set. write for info. (0-8247-9533-4) Dekker.

Atta-Ur-Rahman & Shah, Zahir. Stereoselective Synthesis in Organic Chemistry. LC 93-284. 1994. 105.00 (0-387-94029-4) Spr-Verlag.

Attah-Poku, Agyemang. African Ethnicity: History, Conflict Management, Resolution & Prevention. LC 97-40194. 168p. (C). 1997. 49.00 (0-7618-0959-7); pap. 27.50 (0-7618-0960-0) U Pr of Amer.

— I'm Mother Africa: Poetic Reflections on History & Culture. LC 98-46265. 84p. 1999. pap. 14.95 (0-7734-3102-0, Mellen Poetry Pr) E Mellen.

— The Socio-Cultural Adjustment Question: The Role of Ghanaian Immigrant Ethnic Associations in America. 185p. 1996. text 63.95 (1-85972-392-6, Pub. by Avebry) Ashgate Pub Co.

Attainment Co. Inc. Staff. Community Success: An Illustrated Guide to Community Access. 177p. 1998. 49.00 (1-57861-023-0) Attainment.

Attal, Jean-Pierre. Grammaire et Usage de L'Anglais. (ENG & FRE.). 991p. 1987. 115.00 (0-8288-3356-7, F84360) Fr & Eur.

Attal, Pierre & Muller, Claude, eds. De la Syntaxe a la Pragmatique: Actes du Colloque de Rennes, Universite de Haute-Bretagne. LC 84-9329. (Lingvisticae Investigationes Supplementa Ser.: 8). (FRE.). 389p. 1984. 78.00 (90-272-3118-4) J Benjamins Pubng Co.

Attali, J. Dictionnaire du 21e Siecle. (FRE.). 1998. 59.95 (0-320-00281-0) Fr & Eur.

Attali, Jacques. Histoire du Temps. (FRE.). 318p. 1983. pap. 16.95 (0-7859-3115-5) Fr & Eur.

— Noise. Massumi, Brian, tr. LC 84-28069. (Theory & History of Literature Ser.: Vol. 16). 180p. 1985. pap. 14.95 (0-8166-1287-0) U of Minn Pr.

— Les Trois Mondes. (FRE.). 415p. 1983. pap. 17.95 (0-7859-3116-3) Fr & Eur.

Attali, Jacques & Rowe, Joseph H. The Labyrinth in Culture & Society: Pathways to Wisdom. LC 97-49276. (Illus.). 250p. 1999. pap. 16.95 (1-55643-265-8) North Atlantic.

Attalia, Joseph, jt. auth. see Byrd, William.

Attalla, Kathryn. Baby Bargain, 1, 3. (Zebra Bouquet Ser.). 1999. mass mkt. 3.99 (0-8217-6280-X) Kensgtn Pub Corp.

Attalla, Kathy. Silent Heart. 192p. 1997. 18.95 (0-8034-9243-X, Avalon Bks) Bouregy.

***Attallah, Fahmy.** Beauty of Being: Psychological Tips for Holistic Wellness of the Person as a Whole - Mind, Body, Spirit & Soul. LC 99-14240. 264p. 1999. 18.95 (0-929765-64-8, Chapman Univ) Seven Locks Pr.

Attallah, Naim. Women. 1167p. 1993. pap. 14.95 (0-7043-0080-X, Pub. by Quartet) Interlink Pub.

***Attanasi, O. A. & Spinelli, D.** Targets in Heterocyclic Systems Vol. 2: Chemistry & Properties. 496p. 1999. 65.00 (88-86208-11-1) Spr-Verlag.

Attanasio, A., ed. Eighth International Symposium on Endocrinology & Development, Telfs, Austria, October 1991. (Hormone Research Ser.: Vol. 38, Suppl. 2, 1992). (Illus.). iv, 88p. 1992. pap. 40.00 (3-8055-5740-X) S Karger.

— International Symposium on Endocrinology & Development: 15th Symposium, Paris, November 1997. (Hormone Research Ser.: Vol. 48, Suppl. 4, 1997). (Illus.). iv, 76p. 1997. pap. 35.00 (3-8055-6582-8) S Karger.

— Tenth International Symposium on Endocrinology & Development, Venice, Italy, October 1992: Growth &

Metabolism: Obesity, Insulin Action & Use of Anthropometry. (Journal: Hormone Research Ser.: Vol. 39, Suppl. 3, 1993). (Illus.). vi, 118p. 1993. pap. 54.00 (3-8055-5884-8) S Karger.

Attanasio, A. & Henderson, Robert S. Silent. 312p. 1996. 30.00 (0-939767-24-4) D McMillan.

Attanasio, A., jt. ed. see Argente, J.

Attanasio, A. A. Beastmarks. LC 84-52083. (Illus.). 120p. 1984. 13.95 (0-9612970-2-6) Mark Ziesing.

— The Dragon & The Unicorn. 560p. 1999. mass mkt. 6.99 (0-06-105779-7, HarperPrism) HarpC.

— The Eagle & the Sword: An Arthurian Epic. 448p. 1999. mass mkt. 6.50 (0-06-105839-4, HarperPrism) HarpC.

— The Serpent & the Grail. LC 99-12611. 368p. 1999. pap. 16.00 (0-06-107340-7) HarpC.

***Attanasio, A. A.** The Serpent & the Grail. 400p. 2000. mass mkt. 6.99 (0-06-105973-0) Morrow Avon.

Attanasio, A. A. The Wolf & the Crown. LC 98-153679. 352p. 1998. pap. 14.00 (0-06-105370-8, HarperPrism) HarpC.

— The Wolf & the Crown. 432p. 1999. mass mkt. 5.99 (0-06-105776-2) HarpC.

— Wyvern. 480p. 1988. 19.95 (0-89919-409-5, Pub. by Ticknor & Fields) HM.

Attanasio, Salvator, tr. see Danielou, Jean.

Attanasio, Salvator, tr. see Gabrieli, Francesco.

Attanasio, Salvator, tr. see Kolakowski, Leszek.

Attanasio, Salvator, tr. see Ratzinger, Joseph C. & Messori, Vittorio.

Attansio, A. & Bernasconi, S., eds. Present & Future Aspects in Endocrinology: Thirteenth International Symposium on Endocrinology & Development, Rome, October 1994. (Journal Ser.: Vol. 43, No. 4, 1995). (Illus.). 60p. 1995. pap. 47.00 (3-8055-6139-3) S Karger.

Attar, Cynthia. The Mule Companion: A Guide to Understanding the Mule. 3rd rev. ed. LC 93-92659. Orig. Title: Mule Companion: Essential Mule Wisdom. (Illus.). 188p. 1998. pap. 19.95 (0-9651776-1-0) Prtnr Communs.

Attar, Dena. A Bibliography of Household Books Published in Britain, 1800-1914 LC 87-208494. 438p. 1987. write for info. (0-907325-35-1) Prospect.

***Attar, Farid Al-Din.** Attar Stories for Young Adults. (Illus.). 2000. pap. text 12.95 (1-930637-06-3) ABC Intl Grp.

Attar, Farid Al-Din. The Conference of Birds. Darbandi, Afkham & Davis, Dick, trs. (Classics Ser.). 240p. 1984. pap. 12.95 (0-14-044434-3) Viking Penguin.

— The Conference of the Birds. Darbandi, Afkham, tr. 235p. 1996. pap. 8.95 (0-614-21638-9, 165) Kazi Pubns.

— The Conference of the Birds. Nott, C. S., tr. (Illus.). 148p. 1998. pap. 12.00 (1-879708-13-2) Pir Pubns.

— Tadhkaratul Auliya. Behari, Bankey, tr. 1987. 12.95 (1-56744-446-6) Kazi Pubns.

— Tadhkaratul Auliya. Behari, Bankey, tr. 213p. 1996. 12.95 (0-614-21367-3, 1209) Kazi Pubns.

Attar, Farid Al-Din, et al, contrib. by. The Conference of the Birds. 79p. 1982. pap. 5.95 (0-87129-106-1, C55) Dramatic Pub.

***Attar, Farid Ud-Din.** The Conference of the Birds. 160p. 2000. 14.95 (0-8264-5000-8) Continuum.

Attar, Safuh, ed. Hemostasis in Cardiac Surgery. LC 98-31869. (Illus.). 13p. 1999. 59.00 (0-87993-410-7) Futura Pub.

— New Developments in Cardiac Assist Devices, Vol. 6. LC 85-6585. (Surgical Science Ser.: No. 6). 222p. 1985. 69.50 (0-275-91330-9, C13306, Praeger Pubs) Greenwood.

Attar, Samar. House at Arnus Square. (C). 1998. pap. 14.00 (1-57889-086-1) Passeggiata.

— Lina: Portrait of a Damascene Girl. 217p. (Orig.). 1994. pap. 16.00 (0-89410-780-1, Three Contnts) L Rienner.

— Modern Arabic. (ARA.). 1988. pap., teacher ed. 5.95 (0-86685-703-6, Pub. by Librairie du Liban) Intl Bk Ctr.

— Modern Arabic, Wkbk. I. (ARA.). 1988. pap., student ed. 10.95 (0-86685-701-X, LDL439B, Pub. by Librairie du Liban) Intl Bk Ctr.

— Modern Arabic, Wkbk. II. (ARA.). pap., student ed. 10.95 (0-86685-702-8, LKL440B, Pub. by Librairie du Liban) Intl Bk Ctr.

— Modern Arabic: An Introductory Course for Foreign Students, Bk. I. (ARA., Illus.). 88p. 1988. pap. 11.95 (0-86685-439-8, Pub. by Librairie du Liban) Intl Bk Ctr.

Attar, Samar. Modern Arabic: Grammar in Context. 24.95 (0-86685-736-2) Intl Bk Ctr.

— Modern Arabic: The Arab-European Encounter. 939p. 1998. pap. 35.00 (0-86685-745-1) Intl Bk Ctr.

Attar, Samar. Modern Arabic Bk. 2: An Introductory Course for Foreign Students. (ARA., Illus.). 263p. 1988. audio 179.95 (0-86685-544-0) Intl Bk Ctr.

— Modern Arabic Bk. 2: An Introductory Course for Foreign Students, Bk. 2. (ARA., Illus.). 263p. 1988. teacher ed. 6.95 (0-86685-441-X) Intl Bk Ctr.

— Modern Arabic Bk. 2: An Introductory Course for Foreign Students, Bk. II. (ARA., Illus.). 364p. 1988. pap. 19.95 (0-86685-440-1, Pub. by Librairie du Liban) Intl Bk Ctr.

Attaran, Mohsen. Management Science Information Systems: Text & Software. LC 92-6614. 288p. (C). 1992. pap. text 62.95 incl. disk (0-471-52998-2) Wiley.

— Operations Management Information Systems. LC 91-44229. 320p. (C). 1992. pap. 62.95 incl. disk (0-471-52999-0) Wiley.

— Operations Management Information Systems: Text & Software. 320p. (C). 1992. pap. 62.95 incl. disk (0-471-57647-6) Wiley.

Attard, Gary & Barnes, Colin. Surfaces. (Oxford Chemistry Primers Ser.: No. 59). (Illus.). 96p. (C). 1998. pap. text 12.95 (0-19-855686-1) OUP.

Attard, Janet. Business Know-How. LC 99-28883. 352p. 1999. pap. 17.95 (1-58062-206-2) Adams Media.

***Attard, Janet.** The Home Office & Small Business Answer Book. LC 00-20819. 2000. pap., wbk. ed. 22.00 (0-8050-6450-8) St Martin.

Attard, Janet. The Home Office & Small Business Answer Book: Solutions to the Most Frequently Asked Questions about Starting & Running Home Offices & Small Businesses. LC 92-35504. (Henry Holt Reference Bks.). 560p. 1995. 40.00 (0-8050-2078-0); pap. 19.95 (0-8050-2565-0) H Holt & Co.

— The Home Office & Small Business Success Book: How to Run Your Business More Profitably with Less Effort. 1996. 45.00 (0-8050-3942-2); pap. 19.95 (0-8050-3943-0, Owl) H Holt & Co.

***Attard-Montalto, S. & Saha, V.** Paediatrics. LC 99-36782. (Illus.). 200p. 1998. pap. write for info. (0-443-05516-5) Church.

Attard-Montalto, Simon, et al. Paediatric MCQs for Postgraduate Exams, Vol. 2. LC 96-197400. 112p. 1996. pap. text 37.50 (0-7506-2845-6, Focal) Buttrwrth-Heinemann.

Attard, Simon, et al. Paediatric MCQs for Postgraduate Exams, Vol. 1. 848p. 1996. pap. text 37.50 (0-7506-2769-7) Buttrwrth-Heinemann.

Attardi, Giuseppe M., et al, eds. Mitochondrial Biogenesis & Genetics, Pt. A. (Methods in Enzymology Ser.: Vol. 260). (Illus.). 540p. 1995. text 95.00 (0-12-182161-7) Acad Pr.

— Mitochondrial Biogenesis & Genetics, Pt. B. (Methods in Enzymology Ser.: Vol. 264). (Illus.). 621p. 1996. text 95.00 (0-12-182165-X) Acad Pr.

Attardo, Salvatore. Linguistic Theories of Humor. LC 93-43697. (Humor Research Ser.: No. 1). 426p. 1994. lib. bdg. 144.65 (3-11-014255-4) Mouton.

Attardo, Salvatore, jt. auth. see Brown, Steven.

Attari, A. & Klass, D. L., eds. Natural Gas Energy Measurement. 482p. 1987. 75.00 (0-910091-61-7) Inst Gas Tech.

Attari, A. A. Odorization III. Wilson, G. G., ed. x, 676p. 1993. 80.00 (0-910091-89-7) Inst Gas Tech.

Attari, Amir A., jt. ed. see Wilson, Gerald G.

Attaway, D. H. & Zaborsky, O. R. Marine Biotechnology Vol. 1: Pharmaceutical & Bioactive Natural Products. (Illus.). 520p. (C). 1993. text 110.00 (0-306-44174-8, Kluwer Plenum) Kluwer Academic.

Attaway, Fances S. The Entrance of Thy Word Gives Light. 25p. 1996. pap. 2.99 (0-9651338-0-X) Attaway SonRise.

Attaway, John A. A History of Florida Citrus Freezes. LC 97-649. (Illus.). xvi, 364p. 1997. 48.00 (0-944961-03-7) FL Sci Source.

***Attaway, John A.** Hurricanes & Florida Agriculture. LC 99-40086. xii, 435p. 1999. 60.00 (0-944961-05-3) FL Sci Source.

Attaway, John A., jt. ed. see Nagy, Steven.

Attaway, Michele. Rosie's Recipes: Delicious Dog Biscuit Recipes Taste-Tested by Our Best Friends. (Illus.). 16p. 1997. pap. 6.99 (0-9661756-0-3) Rosies Recipes.

Attaway, Roy. A Home in the Tall Marsh Grass. 160p. 1993. 18.95 (1-55821-254-X) Lyons Pr.

Atte, O. David. Connaissance Endogene Local Comme Cle du Developpement au Niveau Local: Possibilities, Constraintes & Problemes de Planification dans le Contexte Africain. Nigerian Resource Centre for Indigenous Knowledge, tr. (Studies in Technology & Social Change: No. 20). (FRE.). 64p. (C). 1995. pap. text 8.00 (0-945271-38-7) ISU-CIKARD.

Atte, Oluwayomi D. Indigenous Local Knowledge As a Key to Local Level Development: Possibilities, Constraints, & Planning Issues. (Studies in Technology & Social Change: No. 20). 60p. (Orig.). (C). 1992. pap. 8.00 (0-945271-29-8) ISU-CIKARD.

Atteberry, Mark, ed. see Cann, John.

Atteberry-Rogers, Mary. Leisure & Family Fun. LC 92-62934. (Illus.). 95p. 1993. pap. 19.95 (0-910251-59-2) Venture Pub PA.

Attebery, Brian. The Fantasy Tradition in American Literature: From Irving to Le Guin. LC 80-7670. 222p. 1980. pap. 68.90 (0-608-05009-1, 205967000004) Bks Demand.

— Strategies of Fantasy. LC 91-15884. 180p. 1992. text 10.00 (0-253-31070-9) Ind U Pr.

— Strategies of Fantasy. LC 91-15884. 167p. Date not set. reprint ed. pap. 51.80 (0-608-20578-8, 205449300002) Bks Demand.

Attebery, Brian, jt. ed. see Le Guin, Ursula K.

Attebery, Jennifer E. Building with Logs: Western Log Construction in Context. LC 97-29660. (Illus.). 166p. 1997. 39.95 (0-89301-208-4) U of Idaho Pr.

— Surveying Historic Buildings. (Local History Technical Leaflets Ser.). (Illus.). 16p. (Orig.). 1985. pap. 1.50 (0-931406-11-0) Idaho State Soc.

Attebery, Louie W. Albertson College of Idaho: The Second Hundred Years. LC 99-94424. (Illus.). 100p. 1999. write for info. (0-9630028-1-3) Albertson Col ID.

— The College of Idaho, 1891-1991: A Centennial History. 410p. 1991. write for info. (0-9630028-0-5) Albertson Col ID.

Attebery, Louie W., ed. Idaho Folklife: Homesteads to Headstones. LC 84-17341. 253p. (Orig.). reprint ed. pap. 78.50 (0-7837-6873-7, 204670300003) Bks Demand.

Attebery, Philip & Honeycutt, Dean. Galilean Leadership & Recreation Guide. 48p. 1996. pap. 3.95 (0-89114-234-7) Baptist Pub Hse.

Atteia, Marc. Hilbertian Kernels & Spline Functions. LC 92-21537. (Studies in Computational Mathematics: Vol. 4). 386p. 1992. 181.00 (0-444-89718-6, North Holland) Elsevier.

Attell, Barbara. The Insiders Pocket Guide to Disneyland. unabridged ed. (Illus.). 130p. 1999. pap. 9.95 (0-9668214-0-8) Wasserman Enter.

Attema, Martha. A Light in the Dunes. LC 97-65300. 176p. (YA). (gr. 6-9). 1997. pap. 6.95 (1-55143-085-1) Orca Bk Pubs.

Attenborough, David. The Life of Birds. LC 98-30705. (Illus.). 320p. 1998. 29.95 (0-691-01633-X, Pub. by Princeton U Pr) Cal Prin Full Svc.

— The Private Life of Plants: A Natural History of Plant Behavior. LC 95-17514. 320p. 1995. 29.95 (0-691-00639-3, Pub. by Princeton U Pr) Cal Prin Full Svc.

— The Private Life of Plants: A Natural History of Plant Behavior. large type ed. LC 95-47822. 22.95 (1-56895-291-0, Compass) Wheeler Pub.

— Zoo Quest: A Trek to British Guiana to Round up Zoo Animals. large type ed. 23.95 (1-85695-203-7, Pub. by ISIS Lrg Prnt) Transaction Pubs.

Attenborough, David, jt. auth. see Reader's Digest Editors.

Attenborough, David, ed. see Chinery, Michael.

Attenborough, John. The Day of Small Things. large type ed. 1995. 27.99 (0-7089-3405-6) Ulverscroft.

— Destiny Our Choice. large type ed. 496p. 1988. 27.99 (0-7089-8450-9) Ulverscroft.

— The Priest's Story. large type ed. 288p. 1986. 27.99 (0-7089-1398-9) Ulverscroft.

Attenborough, Liz. When All The World's Asleep: A Children's Book of Poems, Prayers & Meditations. 128p. 1999. pap. 10.95 (1-902618-73-4, Pub. by Onewrld Pubns) Penguin Putnam.

Attenborough, Liz, compiled by. The Children's Book of Poems, Prayers & Meditations. (Illus.). 128p. (YA). (gr. 5 up). 1998. 19.95 (1-901881-85-7, Pub. by Element MA) Penguin Putnam.

Attenborough, Mary. Engineering Mathematics Exposed. LC 94-802. (C). 1994. text 75.00 (0-07-707975-2) McGraw.

Attenborough, Robert D. & Alpers, Michael P., eds. Human Biology in Papua New Guinea: The Small Cosmos. (Research Monographs on Human Population Biology: No. 10). (Illus.). 440p. 1993. text 105.00 (0-19-857514-9) OUP.

Attenhofer, Andrea. Privatisierung des Basler Kunstmuseums: Eine Okonomische Analyse der Alternativen In Zusammenarbeit mit dem Wirtschaftswissenschaftlichen Zentrum (WWZ) der Universitat Basel. (GER., Illus.). 181p. 1997. 31.95 (3-906757-45-5, Pub. by P Lang) P Lang Pubng.

***Atter, Sheila.** All about Your Jack Russell Terrier. 32p. 1999. pap. text 3.50 (0-7641-1190-6) Barron.

Atteraas. Underwater Technology. 1980. pap. write for info. (0-08-026142-6, Pergamon Pr) Elsevier.

Atterbury, A. Islam in Africa. 240p. 1987. 230.00 (1-85077-152-9, Pub. by Darf Pubs Ltd) St Mut.

Atterbury, Anson P. Islam in Africa. LC 73-91254. 208p. 1969. reprint ed. lib. bdg. 35.00 (0-8371-2064-0, ATI&) Greenwood.

Atterbury, Betty W., ed. Elementary General Music: The Best of M. E. J. (Best of M. E. J. Ser.). 136p. 1992. pap. 20.00 (1-56545-013-2, 1613) MENC.

Atterbury, Betty W. & Richardson, Carol P. The Experience of Teaching General Music. LC 94-33946. 352p. (C). 1994. pap. 50.63 (0-07-002859-1) McGraw.

Atterbury, Paul. Bulfinch Anatomy of Antique Furniture: An Illustrated Guide to Identifying Period, Detail &..., Vol. I. LC 96-76459. (Illus.). 160p. 1996. 35.00 (0-8212-2325-9, Pub. by Bulfinch Pr) Little.

— Bulfinch Illustrated Encyclopedia of Antiques. (Illus.). 332p. 1998. pap. 29.95 (0-8212-2506-5, Pub. by Bulfinch Pr) Little.

— Country Railways. (Country Ser.). (Illus.). 160p. 1997. 24.95 (0-297-83565-3, Pub. by Orion Pubng Grp) Trafalgar.

— Moorcroft: A Guide to Moorcroft Pottery, 1897-1993. 1996. 85.00 (0-903685-33-7, Pub. by R Dennis) Antique Collect.

— The Parian Phenomenon: A Survey of Victorian Parian Porcelain Statuary & Busts. (Illus.). 268p. 1989. 95.00 (0-903685-22-1, Pub. by R Dennis) Antique Collect.

— Pugin: A Gothic Passion. Wainwright, Clive, ed. LC 94-15209. 310p. 1995. pap. 35.00 (0-300-06014-9) Yale U Pr.

— Ruskin Pottery: The Pottery of Edward Richard Taylor & William Howson Taylor 1898-1935. (Illus.). 160p. 1993. 95.00 (0-9520933-0-8, Pub. by R Dennis) Antique Collect.

***Atterbury, Paul.** The Thames. 2000. pap. 16.95 (0-7538-0694-0) Phoenix Hse.

Atterbury, Paul & Batkin, Maureen. The Dictionary of Minton. (Illus.). 368p. 1999. reprint ed. 89.50 (1-85149-272-0) Antique Collect.

Atterbury, Paul & Burgum, Ian. Country Railways. (Country Ser.). (Illus.). 160p. 1997. pap. 16.95 (1-85799-919-3) Phoenix Hse.

Atterbury, Paul & Denker, Ellen P. Miller's 20th Century Ceramics. (Illus.). 256p. 1999. 40.00 (1-84000-034-1) Antique Collect.

Atterbury, Paul & Haines, Anthony. The Thames: From the Source to the Sea. (Country Ser.). (Illus.). 160p. 1998. 27.50 (0-297-82414-7, Pub. by Weidenfeld & Nicolson) Trafalgar.

Atterbury, Paul, et al. A. W. N. Pugin: Master of Gothic Revival. LC 95-78296. (Illus.). 415p. 1996. 70.00 (0-300-06656-2); pap. 40.00 (0-300-06657-0) Yale U Pr.

Atterbury, Paul, ed. see Anderson, Anne.

Atterbury, Paul, jt. ed. see Hayward, Leslie.

Atterbury, Peter. Cornish Ware: Kitchen & Domestic Pottery. 1997. pap. text 17.95 (0-903685-48-5, Pub. by R Dennis) Antique Collect.

Atterbury, T. J., et al. Measurements of Secondary Stresses in Pipeline: Report 1, Additional Data. 80p. 1959. pap. 3.00 (0-318-12653-2, L00220) Am Gas Assn.

Attermeier, Susan M., ed. Augmentative Communication: Clinical Issues. 137p. 1987. 39.95 (0-86656-657-0) Haworth Pr.

***Atterwill, C. K.** Approaches to High Throughput Toxicity Screening. LC 99-35680. (Illus.). 256p. 1999. 125.00 (0-7484-0752-9) Tay Francis Ltd.

Atterwill, Christopher K. & Flack, J. D., eds. Endocrine Toxicology. (Illus.). 489p. (C). 1992. text 125.00 (0-521-40225-5) Cambridge U Pr.

Atterwill, Christopher K., jt. ed. see O'Hare, Sheila.

***Atteslander, Peter, et al, eds.** Comparative Anomie Research: Hidden Barriers--Hidden Potential for Social Development. LC 99-72610. 266p. 1999. text 69.95 (1-84014-887-X, Pub. by Ashgate Pub) Ashgate Pub Co.

Attewell, Peter B. Ground Pollution: Environment, Geology, Engineering, & Law. LC 92-41796. 1993. pap. write for info. (0-419-18320-5, E & FN Spon) Routledge.

Attfield. God & the Secular. 232p. 1993. 56.95 (0-7512-0243-6) Ashgate Pub Co.

Attfield, Harlan H. D. A Beekeeping Guide. rev. ed. (Illus.). 45p. 1989. 7.25 (0-86619-154-2); 7.25 (0-86619-140-2) Vols Tech Asst.

— How to Make Fertilizer. 9p. 1990. 5.25 (0-86619-088-0); 5.25 (0-86619-193-3); 5.25 (0-86619-194-1) Vols Tech Asst.

— Raising Chickens & Ducks. (Illus.). 140p. 1990. 12.95 (0-86619-309-X) Vols Tech Asst.

— Raising Rabbits. (FRE.). 81p. 1977. pap. 9.50 (0-86619-061-9, 19040-BK); per. 9.50 (0-86619-060-0, 11040-BK) Vols Tech Asst.

***Attfield, Harlan H. D.** Raising Rabbits: A Field Guide. 120p. 2000. pap. 18.00 (1-85339-508-0, Pub. by Intermed Tech) Stylus Pub VA.

Attfield, Jane, jt. auth. see Wood, Elizabeth.

***Attfield, Judy.** Wild Things: The Material Culture of Everyday Life. 224p. 2000. 65.00 (1-85973-364-6, Pub. by Berg Pubs); pap. 19.50 (1-85973-369-7, Pub. by Berg Pubs) NYU Pr.

Attfield, Judy & Kirkham, Pat, eds. A View from the Interior: Women & Design-NE. pap. 29.95 (0-7043-4451-3, Pub. by Womens Press) Trafalgar.

Attfield, Robin. Environmental Philosophy: Principles & Prospects. (Avebury Series in Philosophy). 272p. 1994. 72.95 (1-85628-566-9, Pub. by Avebury) Ashgate Pub Co.

— Ethics of Environmental Concern. 2nd ed. LC 91-7954. 280p. 1991. reprint ed. pap. 18.00 (0-8203-1344-0) U of Ga Pr.

***Attfield, Robin.** Ethics of the Global Environment. 1999. pap. 24.95 (1-55753-189-7) Purdue U Pr.

Attfield, Robin. A Theory of Value & Obligation. 272p. 1987. lib. bdg. 45.00 (0-7099-0572-6, Pub. by C Helm) Routldge.

Attfield, Robin & Dell, Katharine, eds. Values, Conflict & the Environment. (Avebury Series in Philosophy). 180p. 1996. text 70.95 (1-85972-491-4, Pub. by Avebury) Ashgate Pub Co.

Attfield, Robin, jt. ed. see Wilkins, Barry.

Atthill, William L., ed. Documents Relating to the Foundation & Antiquities of the Collegiate Church of Middleham in the County of York. LC 70-161702. (Camden Society, London. Publications, First Ser.: No. 38). reprint ed. 35.00 (0-404-50138-9) AMS Pr.

Atthreya, N. H. The You & I in Business & Life: What Makes People Give Their Best. 4th rev. ed. 154p. 1987. pap. 9.95 (0-942207-05-X) Starsong CA.

Atti, C. Ciofi Degli, see Degli Atti, C. Ciofi.

Atti, Claudio Ciofi Degli, see Boffi, Sigfrido.

***Attia, John Okyere.** Electronics & Circuit Analysis Using MATLAB. LC 98-46071. 400p. 1999. boxed set 59.95 (0-8493-1176-4) CRC Pr.

Attia, M. H. & Komanduri, R., eds. Contact Problems & Surface Interactions in Manufacturing & Tribological Systems. LC 93-74185. 353p. 1993. pap. 75.00 (0-7918-1263-4) ASME.

Attia, M. Helmi & Waterhouse, R. B., eds. Standardization of Fretting Fatigue Test Methods & Equipment. LC 92-17237. (Special Technical Publication Ser.: No. 1159). (Illus.). 275p. 1992. text 82.00 (0-8031-1448-6, STP1159) ASTM.

Attia, Y. A. Sol-Gel Processing & Applications. (Illus.). 406p. (C). 1995. text 150.00 (0-306-44837-8, Kluwer Plenum) Kluwer Academic.

Attianese, David J., et al. Earned Income Credit: Claimants' Credit Participation & Income Patterns, Tax Years 1990 Through 1994. (Illus.). 68p. (C). 1998. pap. text 20.00 (0-7881-4877-X) DIANE Pub.

— Tax Administration: Lessons Learned from IRS' Initial Experience in Redeploying Employees. (Illus.). 61p. (C). 1999. reprint ed. pap. text 20.00 (0-7881-4381-6) DIANE Pub.

Attias, Dolores R. Maite. (SPA.). 280p. 1994. pap. 12.95 (0-9628328-5-5) Starlite Inc.

Attias-Donfut, Claudine, jt. auth. see Arber, Sara.

Attias, William. Caveat Emptor. LC 85-90958. 1987. 15.00 (0-87212-193-3) Libra.

Attic Pr. Staff. Irish Women's Guidebook & Diary, 1991. 192p. (C). 1990. pap. text 65.00 (1-85594-009-4) St Mut.

— Mad & Bad Fairies. 1991. 34.95 (0-946211-40-X) St Mut.

Atticista, Moeris. Lexicon Atticum, 2 vols. in 1. (Illus.). cvii, 494p. 1969. reprint ed. write for info. (0-318-70977-5) G Olms Pubs.

***Atticks, Kevin.** Discovering Lake Erie Wineries: A Travel Guide to Lake Erie's Wine Country. (Illus.). 200p. 1999. pap. 11.95 (0-9668716-3-4) Resonant Pubg.

— Discovering New Jersey Wineries: A Travel Guide to New Jersey's Wine Country. Dobler, Judith, ed. (Illus.). 2000. pap. 9.95 (0-9668716-6-9) Resonant Pubg.

Atticks, Kevin M. Discovering Maryland Wineries: A Travel Guide to Maryland's Wine Country. LC 98-98112. (Illus.). x,102p. 1998. pap. 9.95 (0-9668716-0-X, 01) Resonant Pubg.

An Asterisk (*) at the beginning of an entry indicates that the title is appearing for the first time.

Attie, Jeanie. Patriotic Toil: Northern Women & the American Civil War. LC 98-25717. (Illus.). 256p. 1998. 35.00 (*0-8014-2224-8*) Cornell U Pr.

Attie, Shimon, tr. Sites Unseen: European Projects. (Illus.). 120p. 1998. 39.95 (*0-9660352-1-6*) Verve Edtns.

Attig, D., et al, eds. European Society for Surgical Research, 25th Congress, Berlin GDR, May 1990 Abstracts. (Illus.). x, 110p. 1990. pap. 52.25 (*3-8055-5221-1*) S Karger.

Attig, John C. The Works of John Locke: A Comprehensive Bibliography from the Seventeenth Century to the Present, 1. LC 85-14670. (Bibliographies & Indexes in Philosophy Ser.: No. 1). 185p. 1985. lib. bdg. 62.95 (*0-313-24359-X*, AJL/, Greenwood Pr) Greenwood.

***Attig, Thomas.** The Heart of Grief: The Desire for Lasting Love. LC 99-49842. 256p. 2000. 25.00 (*0-19-511873-1*) OUP.

Attig, Thomas A. How We Grieve: Relearning the World. 224p. 1996. pap. 19.95 (*0-19-507456-4*) OUP.

Attila, J. & Demir, G. Finnish-Turkish, Turkish-Finnish Pocket Dictionary: Suomi-Turkki-Suomi Taskusanakirja. (FIN & TUR.). 320p. 1984. 95.00 (*0-8288-1643-3*, F13471) Fr & Eur.

Attila the Stockbroker. Scornflakes. (Illus.). 63p. 1994. pap. 13.95 (*1-85224-231-0*, Pub. by Bloodaxe Bks) Dufour.

Attinasi, John, et al. Intergenerational Perspectives on Bilingualism: From Community to Classroom. 2nd ed. 446p. 1988. pap. 10.00 (*1-878483-11-0*) Hunter Coll CEP.

Attinasi, Pietro. Bella Europa. 71p. 1989. 20.00 (*0-89304-517-9*); pap. 10.00 (*0-89304-516-0*) Cross-Cultrl NY.

Attinello, Lauren. Peek-a-Boo, Lizzy Lou! A Daytime Book & Muppet Puppet. (Illus.). 16p. (J). 1997. 16.95 (*0-7611-0948-X*) Workman Pub.

Attinger, E. O., ed. Global System Dynamics: Proceedings of the International Symposium, Charlottesville, Virginia, 1969. 1970. 81.75 (*3-8055-0866-2*) S Karger.

Attinger, Markus, ed. see Sallaberger, Walther & Westenholz, Aage.

Attinger, P. Elements de Linguistique Sumerienne: La Construction de du11/e/di "dire" (Orbis Biblicus et Orientalis Ser.). (FRE.). 1993. text 112.00 (*3-7278-0869-1*, Pub. by Presses Univ Fribourg) Eisenbrauns.

Attinger, Pascal, ed. see Sallaberger, Walther & Westenholz, Aage.

Attisani, Antonio, jt. ed. see House, Jane.

Attitude Research Conference Staff. Attitude Research Enters the '80s: Proceedings of the Attitude Research Conference, 11th, Carlsbad, CA, 1980. Olshavsky, Richard W., ed. LC 80-20621. (American Marketing Association, Proceedings Ser.). 206p. reprint ed. pap. 63.90 (*0-8357-5865-6*, 202335500032) Bks Demand.

— Attitude Research Plays for High Stakes: Proceedings of the Attitude Research Conference, 8th, Las Vegas, NV, 1977. Maloney, John C. & Silverman, Bernard, eds. LC 78-14033. (American Marketing Association, Proceedings Ser.). 287p. reprint ed. pap. 89.00 (*0-8357-5866-4*, 202334900032) Bks Demand.

— Attitude Research under the Sun: Proceedings of the Attitude Research Conference, 9th, Tarpon Springs, FL, 1978. Eighmey, John, ed. LC 78-13992. (American Marketing Association, Proceedings Ser.). 225p. reprint ed. pap. 69.80 (*0-8357-5867-2*, 202334800032) Bks Demand.

— A Look Back, a Look Ahead: Proceedings of the Attitude Research Conference, 10th, Hilton Head Island, SC, 1979. Hafer, George B., ed. LC 80-10370. (American Marketing Association, Proceedings Ser.). 217p. reprint ed. pap. 67.30 (*0-608-14655-2*, 202335600032) Bks Demand.

Attiwill, P. M. & Adams, M. A., eds. Nutrition of Eucalypts. (Illus.). 448p. 1996. 150.00 (*0-643-05757-9*, Pub. by CSIRO) Accents Pubns.

Attiwill, P. M. & Leeper, G. W. Forest Soils & Nutrient Cycles. 212p. 1987. 29.95 (*0-522-84315-8*, Pub. by Melbourne Univ Pr) Paul & Co Pubs.

Attix, Frank H. Introduction to Radiological Physics & Radiation Dosimetry. LC 86-13222. 640p. 1986. 140.00 (*0-471-01146-0*) Wiley.

Attix, Frank H., ed. Luminescence Dosimetry: Proceedings. LC 67-60038. (AEC Symposium Ser.). 527p. 1967. pap. 21.25 (*0-87079-263-6*, CONF-650637); fiche 9.00 (*0-87079-264-4*, CONF-650637) DOE.

***Attiya, Hagit & Welch, Jennifer.** Distributed Computing: Fundamentals, Simulations & Advanced Topics. 451p. (C). 1998. 69.69 (*0-07-709352-6*) McGrw-H Hghr Educ.

Attiyah, George M. Al-Kindi: The Philosopher of the Arabs. 1990. pap. 16.50 (*0-935782-30-3*) Kazi Pubns.

Attiyate. Woerterbuch Mikroelecktronik: English-German-English. 2nd ed. (ENG & GER.). 594p. 1992. 150.00 (*0-7859-7246-3*, 3184011097) Fr & Eur.

Attiyate, Yvonne H. Lexicon CAD, CAM, FMS, CIM: Numerical Control Lexicon. (ENG, FRE & GER.). 939p. 1989. 95.00 (*0-8288-7594-4*, M6013) Fr & Eur.

Attla, Catherine. K'etetaalkkaanee: The One Who Paddled among the People & Animals. Jones, Eliza, tr. (Illus.). xiii, 149p. 1990. pap. 16.00 (*1-55500-038-X*) Alaska Native.

— Sitsiy Yugh Noholnik Ts'in: As My Grandfather Told It. (Illus.). 258p. (Orig.). 1983. pap. 18.00 (*0-933769-07-5*) Alaska Native.

Attlee, Rupert. The Trail to Titicaca. (Illus.). 288p. 1999. pap. 12.95 (*1-84024-095-4*, Pub. by Summers) Seven Hills Bk.

Attles, Henrietta S. The Effects of Homelessness on the Academic Achievement of Children. Bruchey, Stuart, ed. LC 97-40780. (Children of Poverty Ser.). (Illus.). 107p. 1997. text 37.00 (*0-8153-3014-6*) Garland.

Attmore, Marie, compiled by. Career Perspectives: Interviews with Blind & Visually Impaired Professionals. large type ed. LC 90-430. 96p. 1990. pap. 19.95 (*0-89128-170-3*) Am Foun Blind.

Attmore, Stephen. Children's Atlas of the World. rev. ed. (Illus.). 32p. (J). (gr. 1-3). 1994. reprint ed. pap. 5.95 (*0-8249-8662-8*, Ideals Child) Hambleton-Hill.

Attneave, Carolyn L., jt. compiled by see Kelso, Dianne R.

Attner & Allen. Management: Meeting & Exceeding Customer Expectations. 7th ed. 2001. pap. text 65.25 (*0-324-02725-7*) Thomson Learn.

— Study Guide for Management. 7th ed. (Management Ser.). 2001. pap. text, student ed. 20.25 (*0-324-02727-3*) Thomson Learn.

Attner, jt. auth. see Plunkett.

Attner, Paul, jt. auth. see Wolf, Ron.

Attner, Raymond F. & Straub, Joseph T. Introduction To Business. 2nd ed. LC 84-20115. (SWC-General Business). 635p. (C). 1985. pap. 27.75 (*0-534-04173-6*) PWS Pubs.

Attner, Raymond F., jt. auth. see Plunkett, Warren R.

Attner, Raymond F., jt. auth. see Straub, Joseph T.

Attoe, David. Lion at the Door: A Novel. 240p. 1989. 17.95 (*0-316-05800-9*) Little.

Attoe, Wayne. Architecture & Critical Imagination. LC NA2599.5.A88. 208p. reprint ed. pap. 64.50 (*0-8357-5722-6*, 202668500051) Bks Demand.

Attoe, Wayne & Logan, Donn. American Urban Architecture: Catalysts in the Design of Cities. (Illus.). 1992. pap. 24.95 (*0-520-08105-6*, Pub. by U CA Pr) Cal Prin Full Svc.

Attoe, Wayne, jt. auth. see Young, Mary E.

Attoe, Wayne, jt. ed. see Moore, Charles W.

Attoe, Wayne, jt. ed. see Speck, Lawrence W.

Attoe, Wayne O. Transit, Land Use & Urban Form. (Illus.). 200p. 1988. text 20.00 (*0-934951-01-2*) Ctr for Amer Archit.

***Attoh-Okine, N. O.** Artificial Intelligence & Mathematical Methods. 204p. 1998. 79.00 (*90-5809-028-0*) Ashgate Pub Co.

Atton, Chris. Alternative Literature: A Practical Guide for Librarians. LC 95-37319. 224p. 1996. 74.95 (*0-566-07665-9*, Pub. by Gower) Ashgate Pub Co.

Atton, Henry & Holland, Henry H. King's Customs: An Account of Maritime Revenue & Contraband Traffic, 2 vols. (Illus.). 1968. reprint ed. 75.00 (*0-7146-1266-9*, Pub. by F Cass Pubs) Intl Spec Bk.

Atton, Henry & Holland, Henry H. The King's Customs, 2 Vols, Set. LC 67-21884. 1967. reprint ed. 70.00 (*0-678-00272-X*) Kelley.

Atton, Tessa & Fidler, Brian. Poorly Performing Staff & How to Manage them: Capability, Competence, & Motivation. LC 98-37420. 1999. pap. write for info. (*0-415-19817-8*) Routledge.

Attorney General's Committee Report. 1956. write for info. Fed Legal Pubn.

Attorney-General's Department - Australia Staff. Workplace Relations Act, 1996. 3rd ed. 555p. 1997. reprint ed. pap. 51.95 (*0-644-47548-X*) Aust Gov Pub.

Attorney General's Department, Australia Staff. Asian Pacific Regional Trade Law Seminar Vols. 1-10: 1975-1983, 6 bks., Set. LC 85-80508. 1985. reprint ed. 295.00 (*0-89941-454-0*, 303620) W S Hein.

Attorney General's Dept. Staff, contrib. by. Copyright Act 1968. 248p. (Orig.). 1995. pap. 19.95 (*0-644-45462-8*, Pub. by AGPS Pr) Intl Spec Bk.

— Crimes Act 1914. 266p. (Orig.). 1995. pap. 19.95 (*0-644-36035-6*, Pub. by AGPS Pr) Intl Spec Bk.

***Attoui, Ammar.** Concurrent & Real-Time Systems. (Illus.). 2000. pap. 54.95 (*1-85233-252-2*) Spr-Verlag.

Attr. Handbook of Natural Pesticides, Vol. VI: Microbial Insecticides. 264p. 1990. lib. bdg. 169.00 (*0-8493-3662-7*, SB951) CRC Pr.

Attreed, Lorraine C. York House Books, 1461-1490, 2 vols., Set. (Illus.). (C). 1991. text 135.00 (*0-86299-936-7*, Pub. by Sutton Pub Ltd) Intl Pubs Mktg.

Attride, Hilda. Lure & Lore of Language. 302p. (C). 1994. text 69.00 (*0-536-58651-9*) Pearson Custom.

***Attridge, Derek.** Joyce Effects: On Language, Theory & History. LC 99-30727. 226p. (C). 2000. 59.95 (*0-521-66112-9*) Cambridge U Pr.

— Joyce Effects: On Language, Theory & History. 226p. (C). 2000. pap. 19.95 (*0-521-77788-7*) Cambridge U Pr.

Attridge, Derek. Peculiar Language: Literature as Difference from the Renaissance to James Joyce. LC 87-19060. 288p. 1988. pap. text 18.95 (*0-8014-9407-9*) Cornell U Pr.

— Poetic Rhythm: An Introduction. 294p. (C). 1995. text 59.95 (*0-521-41302-8*) Cambridge U Pr.

— Poetic Rhythm: An Introduction. 294p. (C). 1996. pap. text 18.95 (*0-521-42369-4*) Cambridge U Pr.

— Rhthyms English Poetry. 395p. (C). 1995. pap. text 36.69 (*0-582-55105-6*) Longman.

Attridge, Derek, ed. The Cambridge Companion to James Joyce. (Cambridge Companions to Literature Ser.). 321p. (C). 1990. pap. text 17.95 (*0-521-37673-4*) Cambridge U Pr.

***Attridge, Derek & Howes, Marjorie Elizabeth, eds.** Semicolonial Joyce. LC 99-51422. (Illus.). 260p. 2000. write for info. (*0-521-66179-X*); write for info. (*0-521-66628-7*) Cambridge U Pr.

Attridge, Derek & Jolly, Rosemary, eds. Writing South Africa: Literature, Apartheid, & Democracy, 1970-1995. LC 97-17217. (Illus.). 308p. (C). 1998. text 64.95 (*0-521-59218-6*); pap. text 19.95 (*0-521-59768-4*) Cambridge U Pr.

Attridge, Derek, ed. see Derrida, Jacques.

Attridge, Harold W. Hebrews. LC 87-46084. (Hermeneia: A Critical & Historical Commentary on the Bible Ser.). 440p. 1988. 50.00 (*0-8006-6021-8*, 1-6021, Fortress Pr) Augsburg Fortress.

Attridge, Harold W., et al, eds. Of Scribes & Scrolls: Studies on the Hebrew Bible, Intertestamental Judaism, & Christian Origins. 298p. (C). 1990. pap. text 31.50 (*0-8191-7903-5*); lib. bdg. 50.00 (*0-8191-7902-7*) U Pr of Amer.

Attridge, Harold W. & Hata, Gohei, eds. Eusebius, Christianity, & Judaism. LC 92-24048. (Studia Post-Biblica Ser.: Vol. 42). 1992. 123.00 (*90-04-09688-4*) Brill Academic Pubs.

— Eusebius, Christianity, & Judaism. LC 92-5954. 802p. 1992. 54.95 (*0-8143-2361-8*) Wayne St U Pr.

Attridge, Harold W. & Oden, Robert A., Jr. Philo of Byblos: The Phoenician History. Vawter, Bruce, ed. LC 80-25781. (Catholic Biblical Quarterly Monographs: No. 9). x, 110p. 1981. pap. 3.50 (*0-915170-08-6*) Catholic Bibl Assn.

— The Syrian Goddess (De Dea Syria) Attributed to Lucian. LC 76-135. (Texts & Translations Ser.: No. 9). 69p. reprint ed. pap. 30.00 (*0-7837-5459-0*, 204522400005) Bks Demand.

Attridge, Harold W., ed. see Strecker, Georg.

Attridge, T. H. Light & Plant Responses: A Study of Plant Photophysiology & the Natural Environment. 160p. (C). 1992. pap. text 22.95 (*0-521-42748-7*) Cambridge U Pr.

Attwater, Charles H. Atwater History & Genealogy Vol. V: The Great Adventure, 1456 to 1956. (Illus.). 316p. 1996. reprint ed. pap. 48.00 (*0-8328-5368-2*); reprint ed. lib. bdg. 58.00 (*0-8328-5367-4*) Higginson Bk Co.

Attwater, David, ed. Names & Name-Days. LC 89-43340. xii, 124p. 1991. reprint ed. lib. bdg. 44.00 (*1-55888-877-2*) Omnigraphics Inc.

Attwater, Donald. Golden Book of Eastern Saints. LC 72-156607. (Essay Index Reprint Ser.). 1977. reprint ed. 20.95 (*0-8369-2267-0*) Ayer.

— A New Dictionary of Saints. Cumming, John, ed. 336p. 1994. pap. 27.00 (*0-86012-207-7*, Pub. by Srch Pr) St Mut.

Attwater, Donald, ed. A Catholic Dictionary. LC 97-60871. 552p. 1997. reprint ed. pap. 24.00 (*0-89555-549-2*, 1521) TAN Bks Pubs.

— Modern Christian Revolutionaries. LC 76-156608. (Essay Index Reprint Ser.). 1977. reprint ed. 25.95 (*0-8369-2304-9*) Ayer.

Attwater, Donald & John, Catherine R. The Penguin Dictionary of Saints. 3rd ed. 400p. 1996. pap. 15.95 (*0-14-051312-4*, Penguin Bks) Viking Penguin.

Attwater, Donald, jt. auth. see Thurston.

Attwater, Donald, tr. see Delehaye, Hippolyte.

Attwater, Donald, tr. see Lawrence, Brother.

***Attwater, Helen.** My Gorilla Journey. (Illus.). 384p. 2000. 31.99 (*0-7089-9155-6*) Ulverscroft.

Attwell, Al & Attwell, Betty. No Room in the Play. 1986. pap. 3.50 (*0-687-28039-7*) Abingdon.

Attwell, Art. Expanding Your Child's Horizons: A Whole Learning Activities Book for Parents & Teachers. LC 94-8040. (Illus.). 160p. 1994. pap. 12.95 (*0-933025-28-9*) Blue Bird Pub.

Attwell, Betty, jt. auth. see Attwell, Al.

Attwell, David. J. M. Coetzee: South Africa & the Politics of Writing. 147p. (C). 1998. pap. text 15.00 (*0-7881-5434-6*) DIANE Pub.

— J. M. Coetzee: South Africa & the Politics of Writing. LC 92-13468. (Perspectives on Southern Africa Ser.: Vol. 48). 1993. 45.00 (*0-520-07810-1*, Pub. by U CA Pr); pap. 18.95 (*0-520-07812-8*, Pub. by U CA Pr) Cal Prin Full Svc.

Attwell, Graham, jt. ed. see Van Wieringen, Fons.

Attwell, Mabel L. Mabel Lucie Attwell's Going to Bed Tales. (Illus.). 128p. (J). 1996. 14.95 (*1-85479-938-X*, Pub. by M OMara) Assoc Pubs Grp.

Attwood, Bain. The Making of the Aborogines. 240p. (C). 1990. pap. text 19.95 (*0-04-370185-X*) Routledge.

Attwood, Bain & Arnold, John, eds. Power, Knowledge, & Aborigines. (Orig.). (C). 1993. pap. 19.95 (*1-86324-013-6*, Pub. by LaTrobe Univ) Intl Spec Bk.

Attwood, Bain, et al. A Life Together, a Life Apart: A History of Relations Between Europeans & Aborigines. 232p. 1994. pap. 24.95 (*0-522-84536-3*, Pub. by Melbourne Univ Pr) Paul & Co Pubs.

Attwood, Brian. Introduction to Boardmaking. 2nd ed. 89p. 1996. pap. 95.00 (*1-85802-119-7*, Pub. by Pira Internatl) Bks Intl VA.

Attwood, Brian & Moore, Graham. An Introduction to the Theory & Practice of Multiply Forming. 179p. 1996. pap. 70.00 (*1-85802-037-9*, Pub. by Pira Internatl) Bks Intl VA.

Attwood, Charles. A Vegetarian Doctor Speaks Out. LC 98-29999. 176p. 1998. pap. 14.95 (*0-934252-85-8*, Pub. by Hohm Pr) SCB Distributors.

Attwood, Charles R. Dr. Attwood's Low-Fat Prescription for Kids. 320p. 1996. pap. 11.95 (*0-14-023644-9*, Viking) Viking Penguin.

Attwood, D. & Florence, Alexander T. Surfactant Systems: Their Chemistry, Pharmacy & Biology. 736p. (C). (gr. 13). 1983. text 132.50 (*0-412-14840-4*, 6714) Chapman & Hall.

Attwood, D., jt. auth. see Florence, Alexander T.

Attwood, D. T. & Bokor, J., eds. Short Wavelength Coherent Radiation: Generation & Applications. LC 86-71674. (AIP Conference Proceedings Ser.: No. 147). 480p. 1986. lib. bdg. 70.00 (*0-88318-346-3*) Am Inst Physics.

Attwood, D. T. & Henke, B. L., eds. Low Energy X-Ray Diagnostics: Monterey, 1981. (AIP Conference Proceedings Ser.: No. 75). 394p. 1981. lib. bdg. 44.00 (*0-88318-174-6*) Am Inst Physics.

***Attwood, David.** Changing Values: How to Find Moral Truth in Modern Times. 204p. 1998. reprint ed. pap. 16.99 (*0-85364-806-9*, Pub. by Paternoster Pub) OM Literature.

Attwood, David. Paul Ramsey's Political Ethics. 244p. (C). 1991. pap. 24.50 (*0-8476-7686-2*); text 62.50 (*0-8476-7685-4*) B&N Imports.

— Soft X-Rays & Extreme Ultraviolet Radiation: Principles & Applications. LC 99-21078. (Illus.). 600p. (C). 1999. write for info. (*0-521-65214-6*) Cambridge U Pr.

Attwood, David & Ryecart, Guy. The Pen. (Illus.). 1999. pap. 9.95 (*1-85410-595-7*, Pub. by Aurum Press Ltd) London Brdge.

Attwood, Dennis A. The Complete Office Relocation Sourcebook. LC 96-13424. 288p. 1996. 75.00 (*0-471-13016-8*) Wiley.

Attwood, Donald W. & Baviskar, B. S., eds. Who Shares? Co0peratives & Rural Development. (Oxford India Paperbacks Ser.). (Illus.). 444p. 1993. pap. text 15.95 (*0-19-563200-1*) OUP.

Attwood, F. A. Auditing Principles & Practices. 16th ed. (Illus.). 1977. pap. 25.00 (*0-8464-0162-2*) Beekman Pubs.

Attwood, John. Dick Whittington: Fact & Fable. 112p. (C). 1988. 40.00 (*0-7212-0739-1*, Pub. by Regency Pr GBR) St Mut.

Attwood, Lynne. Creating the New Soviet Woman: Women's Magazines as Engineers of Female Identity, 1922-53. LC 99-25942. 256p. 1999. text 65.00 (*0-312-22544-X*) St Martin.

Attwood, Nigel, jt. auth. see Attwood, Peter.

Attwood, Peter & Attwood, Nigel. Logistics of a Distribution System. 279p. 1992. 74.95 (*0-566-09098-8*, Pub. by Gower) Ashgate Pub Co.

Attwood, Tony. Asperger's Syndrome: A Guide for Parents & Professionals. (Illus.). 223p. 1997. pap. 16.95 (*1-85302-577-1*, Pub. by Jessica Kingsley) Taylor & Francis.

— Blake's 7: The Programme Guide. (Illus.). 300p. 1996. mass mkt. 5.95 (*0-426-19449-7*, Pub. by Virgin Bks) London Brdge.

Attwooll, Elspeth. The Tapestry of the Law: Scotland, Legal Culture & Legal Theory. LC 96-48834. (Law & Philosophy Library). 270p. (C). 1996. text 124.00 (*0-7923-4310-7*) Kluwer Academic.

Attwooll, Elspeth, ed. Shaping Revolution. (Enlightenment Rights & Revolution Ser.). 160p. 1991. pap. 37.90 (*0-08-040925-3*, Pub. by Aberdeen U Pr) Macmillan.

Atuk-Derrick, Caroline, jt. ed. see Steinbright, Jan.

Atuk-Derrick, Caroline, ed. see Wallen, Lynn A. & Senungetuk, Ronald W.

Atul Pandya, Meenal. Vivah: Design a Perfect Hindu Wedding. (Illus.). 112p. 2000. 24.95 (*0-9635539-2-5*) Meera Pubns.

Atulananda, Swami. With the Swamis in America & India. Brahmaprana, Pravrajika, ed. (Illus.). 347p. (Orig.). 1989. pap. 9.95 (*0-87481-233-X*, Pub. by Advaita Ashrama) Vedanta Pr.

Atungaye, Monifa. Provisions. LC 88-83009. 60p. (YA). (gr. 9-12). 1989. pap. 5.00 (*0-916418-68-5*) Lotus.

Aturpat-i, Emetan. The Wisdom of the Sasanian Sages. Shaked, Shaul, tr. from PER. (Persian Heritage Ser.: Vol. 34). lv, 384p. 1979. text 19.50 (*0-89158-376-9*) Bibliotheca Persica.

Aturupane, Chonira, jt. auth. see Krueger, Anne O.

Atwal, Jasbir, jt. auth. see Balawanta, Aisa.

Atwan. America Now. 2nd ed. 89p. 1997. pap. text 5.00 (*0-312-15343-0*) St Martin.

— America Now. 2nd ed. 241p. 1997. pap. text, wbk. ed. 6.95 (*0-312-15250-7*) St Martin.

— America Now. 3rd ed. Date not set. pap. text. write for info. (*0-312-19170-7*); pap. text, teacher ed. write for info. (*0-312-19172-3*) St Martin.

— America Now. 3rd ed. 1999. pap. text 10.00 (*0-312-19186-3*) St Martin.

***Atwan.** America Now. 3rd ed. LC 98-87519. 1999. pap. text 30.95 (*0-312-19182-0*) St Martin.

Atwan. America Now: Answer Key. 2nd ed. 1998. pap. text 0.01 (*0-312-15342-2*) St Martin.

— America Now: Exploratory Basic Writing. 2000. pap. text 35.55 (*0-312-11619-5*) St Martin.

— America Now: Pocket Style Manual. 2000. pap. text 24.30 (*0-312-11635-7*) St Martin.

***Atwan.** Essayists in Depth. 2001. pap. text. write for info. (*0-312-25854-2*) St Martin.

Atwan. History of America. 1999. pap. write for info. (*0-14-009445-8*, Viking) Viking Penguin.

— Left, Right, & Center. 620p. 1996. pap. text 38.95 (*0-312-10200-3*) St Martin.

— Left Right Center. 2nd ed. 1995. pap. text. write for info. (*0-312-17152-8*) St Martin.

— Our Times Pocket Style. 4th ed. 1996. pap. text 27.45 (*0-312-14968-9*) St Martin.

— Ten on Ten, Vol. 1. 2000. pap. text. write for info. (*0-312-10337-9*) St Martin.

Atwan & Een. Exploring America Now. 1999. pap. text 6.95 (*0-312-19184-7*) St Martin.

Atwan, jt. auth. see Mcquade.

Atwan, Helene, ed. see Jones, Gayl.

Atwan, Robert. Our Times. 4th ed. 1995. pap. text, teacher ed. 22.00 (*0-312-11701-9*); pap. text, teacher ed. 5.00 (*0-312-11705-1*) St Martin.

— Our Times. 5th ed. LC 97-74955. 544p. 1998. pap. text 35.95 (*0-312-14931-X*); pap. text 5.00 (*0-312-15262-0*); pap. text 23.00 (*0-312-15263-9*) St Martin.

— Ten on Ten: Major Essayists on Recurring Themes. LC 91-61137. 526p. (Orig.). (C). 1992. pap. 38.95 (*0-312-06236-2*) St Martin.

Atwan, Robert, ed. Best American Essays: College Edition. 480p. (C). 1995. pap. text 25.16 (*0-395-69467-1*); pap. text, teacher ed. 11.96 (*0-395-71622-5*) HM.

An Asterisk (*) at the beginning of an entry indicates that the title is appearing for the first time.

— Some Suggestions for Using Popular Writing in America: The Interaction of Style & Audience. 5th ed. LC 92-22724. (Illus.). 784p. (C). 1993. pap. text 34.95 (*0-19-507308-8*) OUP.

***Atwan, Robert & Ozick, Cynthia, eds.** The Best American Essays: 1998 Edition. (Best American Essays Ser.). 260p. 1998. pap. 13.00 (*0-395-86052-0*) HM.

Atwan, Robert & Ozick, Cynthia, eds. The Best American Essays, 1998. LC 87-640062. 320p. 1998. 27.50 (*0-395-86051-2*) HM.

Atwan, Robert & Vesterman, William, eds. One Hundred Major Modern Writers: Essays for Composition. 704p. (C). 1984. pap. text. write for info. (*0-672-61602-5*) Macmillan.

***Atwan, Robert & Wieder, Laurance.** Chapters into Verse: A Selection of Poetry in English Inspired by the Bible from Genesis Through Revelation. LC 99-56691. 528p. 2000. 21.95 (*0-19-513676-4*) OUP.

Atwan, Robert, jt. auth. see McQuade, Donald.

Atwan, Robert, jt. ed. see Dillard, Annie.

Atwan, Robert, jt. ed. see Frazier, Ian.

Atwan, Robert, jt. ed. see Kaplan, Justin E.

Atwan, Robert, jt. ed. see Lightman, Alan P.

Atwan, Robert, jt. ed. see McQuade, Donald.

Atwan, Robert, jt. ed. see Oates, Joyce Carol.

Atwan, Robert, jt. ed. see Talese, Gay.

Atwan, Robert, jt. ed. see Wolff, Geoffrey.

Atwater. Microstructural Evolution in Thin Films. 450p. 1998. write for info. (*0-12-067010-0*) Acad Pr.

Atwater, Caleb. Description of the Antiquities Discovered in the State of Ohio & Other Western States. LC 72-4997. (Harvard University. Peabody Museum of Archaeology & Ethnology. Antiquities of the New World Ser.: No. 1). (Illus.). reprint ed. 55.00 (*0-404-57301-0*) AMS Pr.

— History of the State of Ohio. 1993. reprint ed. lib. bdg. 89.00 (*0-7812-5338-1*) Rprt Serv.

— Remarks Made on a Tour to Prairie du Chien: Thence to Washington City in 1829. LC 75-82. (Mid-American Frontier Ser.). 1975. reprint ed. 28.95 (*0-405-06851-4*) Ayer.

Atwater, Eastwood. Adolescence. 4th ed. LC 95-8960. 607p. (C). 1995. pap. text 73.00 (*0-13-366964-5*) P-H.

Atwater, Eastwood. I Hear You. rev. ed. 144p. (Orig.). 1992. pap. 12.95 (*0-8027-7362-1*) Walker & Co.

Atwater, Eastwood & Duffy, Karen G. Psychology for Living: Adjustment, Growth, & Behavior Today. 6th ed. LC 98-15321. 507p. (C). 1998. pap. text 63.00 (*0-13-958778-0*) P-H.

Atwater, Edw. E., et al. History of the Colony of New Haven to Its Absorption into Conn., with Supplementary History & Personnel of the Towns of Branford, Guilford, Milford, Stratford, Norwalk, Southold, Etc., 2 vols. in 1. (Illus.). 767p. 1995. reprint ed. lib. bdg. 75.00 (*0-8328-4458-6*) Higginson Bk Co.

***Atwater, Elton & Carnegie Endowment for International Peace Staff.** American Regulation of Arms Exports. LC 99-48876. (Carnegie Endowment for International Peace Monograph Ser.: No. 4). x, 287p. 2000. reprint ed. 47.50 (*1-57588-561-1*, 323930) W S Hein.

Atwater, F. The History of the Town of Plymouth, Connecticut. (Illus.). 447p. 1988. reprint ed. lib. bdg. 47.00 (*0-8328-6543-5*, CT0032) Higginson Bk Co.

Atwater, Florence, jt. auth. see Atwater, Richard.

Atwater, Frances. Atwater, Vol. IV. (Illus.). 364p. 1996. reprint ed. pap. 56.00 (*0-8328-5354-2*); reprint ed. lib. bdg. 66.00 (*0-8328-5353-4*) Higginson Bk Co.

Atwater, Francis. History of Southington. (Illus.). 549p. 1995. reprint ed. lib. bdg. 55.00 (*0-8328-4603-1*) Higginson Bk Co.

Atwater, George P. The Episcopal Church: Its Message for Today. rev. ed. 128p. 1984. pap. 7.95 (*0-8192-1244-X*) Morehouse Pub.

Atwater, H., et al, eds. Surface Chemistry & Beam-Solid Interactions Vol. 201: Materials Research Society Symposium Proceedings. 637p. 1991. text 55.00 (*1-55899-093-3*) Materials Res.

Atwater, H. A. Introduction to General Relativity. LC 73-16251. (C). 1979. 105.00 (*0-08-017692-5*, Pub. by Pergamon Repr) Franklin.

Atwater, H. A., et al, eds. Evolution of Surface & Thin Film Microstructure. (Materials Research Society Symposium Proceedings Ser.: Vol. 280). 749p. 1993. text 30.00 (*1-55899-175-1*) Materials Res.

Atwater, Harry A. Introduction to Microwave Theory. rev. ed. LC 80-28677. 272p. (C). 1981. lib. bdg. 29.50 (*0-89874-192-0*) Krieger.

Atwater, Illani, et al, eds. Biophysics of the Pancreatic B-Cell. LC 87-7713. (Advances in Experimental Medicine & Biology Ser.: Vol. 211). 506p. 1987. 125.00 (*0-306-42555-6*, Plenum Trade) Perseus Pubng.

Atwater, Isaac. History of the City of Minneapolis, 2 vols. (Illus.). 1010p. 1994. reprint ed. lib. bdg. 105.00 (*0-8328-3846-2*) Higginson Bk Co.

Atwater, Kevin G. American Legislative Leaders In the Northeast 1911-1994. Sharp, James Roger & Sharp, Nancy Weatherly, eds. LC 99-16144. 352p. 2000. lib. bdg. 89.50 (*0-313-30215-4*) Greenwood.

Atwater, Leanne E., jt. auth. see Waldman, David A.

Atwater, Lynn. The Extramarital Connection: Sex, Intimacy & Identity. LC 82-6561. 272p. 1982. 30.50 (*0-8290-0460-2*); pap. 12.95 (*0-8290-0549-8*) Irvington.

Atwater, Mary M. Byways in Handweaving. LC 88-18432. (Illus.). 128p. 1988. pap. 14.95 (*0-916658-47-3*) Shuttle Craft.

— Crime in Corn Weather. 2nd ed. Ligon, Linda C., ed. 160p. 1992. reprint ed. pap. 6.95 (*0-934026-84-X*) Interweave.

— Design & the Handweaver. LC 61-4138. (Guild Monographs: No. 3). (Illus.). 26p. 1961. pap. 9.95 (*0-916658-03-1*) Shuttle Craft.

— Handwoven Rugs. LC 76-24018. (Guild Monographs: No. 29). (Illus.). 28p. 1948. pap. 9.95 (*0-916658-29-5*) Shuttle Craft.

Atwater, Maxine H. Washington Revealed: The Only Guide to Washington, D. C. That Allows You to Focus on Your Individual Interest. LC 91-28555. 240p. 1992. pap. 14.95 (*0-471-54673-9*) Wiley.

Atwater, P. M. Beyond the Light: What Isn't Being Said about the Near-Death Experience. LC 93-42169. 1994. 16.95 (*1-55972-229-0*) Carol Pub Group.

— Beyond the Light: What Isn't Being Said about the Near-Death Experience. 352p. 1995. mass mkt. 6.50 (*0-380-72540-1*, Avon Bks) Morrow Avon.

— Future Memory. LC 99-71621. 344p. 1999. pap. 14.95 (*1-57174-135-6*) Hampton Roads Pub Co.

Atwater, P. M., abr. Goddess Runes: A Comprehensive Guide to Casting & Divination with a Unique Set of Ancient Nordic Runes. LC 95-50286. 224p. 1996. pap. 12.00 (*0-380-78292-8*, Avon Bks) Morrow Avon.

Atwater, P. M. H. Children of the New Millenium: Children's Near Death Experiences & the Evolution of Humankind. LC 99-25229. 288p. 1999. pap. 14.00 (*0-609-80309-3*) Crown.

— Future Memory: How Those Who "See the Future" Shed New Light on the Workings of the Human Mind. 224p. 1995. 17.95 (*1-55972-320-3*, Birch Ln Pr) Carol Pub Group.

Atwater, R. Scott, ed. see Lustig & Brown Staff.

***Atwater-Rhodes, Amelia.** Demon in My View. LC 99-51782. 224p. (YA). (gr. 7-12). 2000. 9.95 (*0-385-32720-X*, Delacorte Pr Bks) BDD Bks Young Read.

— In the Forests of the Night. LC 98-46692. 160p. (YA). 1999. 8.95 (*0-385-32674-2*) BDD Bks Young Read.

***Atwater-Rhodes, Amelia.** In the Forests of the Night. (Illus.). 176p. (YA). (gr. 7 up). 2000. mass mkt. 4.99 (*0-440-22816-6*, LLL BDD) BDD Bks Young Read.

— In the Forests of the Night. (Illus.). (J). 2000. 10.34 (*0-606-17999-2*) Turtleback.

Atwater, Richard. Mr. Popper's Penguins. 139p. (J). (gr. 4-7). 1992. pap. 4.95 (*0-316-05843-2*) Little.

Atwater, Richard. Mr. Popper's Penguins. (J). 1988. 10.05 (*0-606-02218-X*, Pub. by Turtleback) Demco.

Atwater, Richard & Atwater, Florence. Mr. Popper's Penguins. (Illus.). 139p. (J). (gr. 4-6). 1988. 16.95 (*0-316-05842-4*) Little.

Atwater, Richard, tr. see Procopius.

Atwater, Richard-Merlin. The Three Degrees of Christmas: An Inspirational Christmas Classic. Atwater, Yekaterina A., tr. from RUS. (Illus.). 254p. 1997. 24.95 (*0-9661380-0-7*, 006-1001); 24.95 (*0-9661380-2-3*, 006-1001); pap. 11.95 (*0-9661380-1-5*, 006-1001) Three Swans.

Atwater, Sally, ed. see Nelson, John A.

Atwater, Steve. To Know God: Understanding the Nature of God. 1997. pap. text 4.97 (*1-55748-977-7*) Barbour Pub.

Atwater, W. Eastwood. Adolescence. 2nd ed. (Illus.). 432p. (C). 1988. pap. text 52.50 (*0-13-008699-1*) P-H.

— I Hear You: Listening Skills to Make You a Better Manager. 127p. 1981. 12.95 (*0-13-450684-7*) P-H.

Atwater, Wilbur O., jt. auth. see Billings, John S.

Atwater, Yekaterina A., tr. see Atwater, Richard-Merlin.

***Atweh, Bill, et al, eds.** Socio-Cultural Aspects on Mathematics Education: An International Research Perspective. 640p. 2001. write for info. (*0-8058-3725-6*) L Erlbaum Assocs.

— Socio-Cultural Aspects on Mathematics Education: An International Research Perspectives. 640p. 2001. pap. write for info. (*0-8058-3726-4*) L Erlbaum Assocs.

Atweh, Bill, et al. Action Research in Practice: Partnership for Social Justice. LC 97-25558. 384p. (C). 1998. pap. 25.99 (*0-415-17152-0*) Routledge.

— Action Research in Practice: Partnership for Social Justice. LC 97-25558. (Illus.). 384p. (C). 1998. 85.00 (*0-415-17151-2*) Routledge.

***Atwell, Brian.** Plants in Action. (Illus.). (YA). 1999. 74.95 (*0-7329-4439-2*) Macmill Educ.

Atwell, Cheryl & Clarida, Vincent. Daytona Beach & the Halifax River Area. LC 98-87772. (Images of America Ser.). (Illus.). 128p. 1998. pap. 18.99 (*0-7524-1342-2*) Arcadia Publng.

Atwell, David, ed. see Coetzee, J. M.

Atwell, Debby. Barn. LC 96-11044. (Illus.). 32p. (J). (ps-3). 1996. 15.95 (*0-395-78568-5*) HM.

***Atwell, Debby.** Pearl. LC 00-35110. (Illus.). (J). 2001. write for info. (*0-395-88416-0*) HM.

— River. LC 99-10327. (Illus.). 31p. (J). (gr. k-3). 1999. 16.00 (*0-395-93546-6*) HM.

Atwell, Freda C., jt. auth. see Douglas, Jack D.

Atwell, H. W., jt. compiled by see Sprague, C. P.

Atwell, John D. Paediatric Surgery. LC 98-12130. (An Arnold Publication). (Illus.). 864p. 1998. text 250.00 (*0-340-58608-7*) OUP.

Atwell, John E. Ends & Principles in Kant's Moral Thought. 240p. 1986. lib. bdg. 132.50 (*90-247-3167-4*, Pub. by M Nijhoff) Kluwer Academic.

— Schopenhauer: The Human Character. 240p. 1990. 49.95 (*0-87722-748-9*) Temple U Pr.

— Schopenhauer on the Character of the World: The Metaphysics of Will. LC 94-18811. 1995. 45.00 (*0-520-08770-4*, Pub. by U CA Pr) Cal Prin Full Svc.

Atwell, Karen A. & Conner, Michael D., eds. The Kuhlman Mound Group & Late Woodland Mortuary Behavior in the Mississippi River Valley of West-Central Illinois. LC 91-42655. (Kampsville Archeological Center Research Ser.: No. 9). (Illus.). 335p. (Orig.). 1992. pap. 15.95 (*0-942118-32-4*) Ctr Amer Arche.

Atwell, Lester. Private. 500p. 1997. reprint ed. 39.95 (*0-9678035-0-0*) A & A Pubng.

***Atwell, Mark.** Falcon's Nest. 1999. pap. 8.95 (*0-9670583-1-7*) Lindsay Publng.

— Mother of Inventions. 242p. 1999. pap. 8.95 (*0-9670583-0-9*) Lindsay Pr.

Atwell, Nancie. In the Middle: New Understandings about Writing, Reading, & Learning. 2nd ed. LC 97-51627. 546p. 1998. pap. 32.50 (*0-86709-374-9*, Pub. by Boynton Cook Pubs) Heinemann.

— In the Middle: Writing, Reading & Learning with Adolescents. LC 86-24408. 295p. (Orig.). (C). 1986. 29.95 (*0-86709-164-9*, 0164, Pub. by Boynton Cook Pubs) Heinemann.

— In the Middle: Writing, Reading & Learning with Adolescents. LC 86-24408. 295p. (Orig.). (C). 1987. pap. text 25.00 (*0-86709-163-0*, 0163, Pub. by Boynton Cook Pubs) Heinemann.

— Side by Side: Essays on Teaching to Learn. LC 91-6670. 164p. (C). 1991. pap. 19.50 (*0-435-08586-7*, 08586) Heinemann.

Atwell, Nancie, ed. Coming to Know: Writing to Learn in the Intermediate Grades. LC 89-31483. (Illus.). 233p. (Orig.). (C). 1989. pap. text 23.00 (*0-435-08500-X*, 08500) Heinemann.

— Workshop 1: Writing & Literature. (Workshops by & for Teachers Ser.). 133p. (Orig.). (C). (gr. k). 1989. pap. text 18.50 (*0-435-08492-5*, 08492) Heinemann.

— Workshop 3: The Politics of Process. (Workshops by & for Teachers Ser.). 149p. (Orig.). (C). (gr. k). 1991. pap. text 18.50 (*0-435-08576-X*) Heinemann.

— Workshop 2: Beyond the Basal. (Workshops by & for Teachers Ser.). 135p. (Orig.). (C). (gr. k). 1990. pap. text 18.50 (*0-435-08523-9*, 08523) Heinemann.

Atwell, Nancie, jt. ed. see Newkirk, Thomas.

Atwell, Pamela. British Mandarins & Chinese Reformers: The British Administration of Weihaiwei (1898-1930) & the Territory's Return to Chinese Rule. (East Asian Historical Monographs). 276p. 1985. 34.50 (*0-19-583798-3*) OUP.

Atwell, Richard B., jt. ed. see Boreham, Peter L.

***Atwell, Robert.** Celebrating the Saints: Daily Spiritual Readings for the Calendar of the Church in England. 532p. 1999. 19.95 (*1-85311-218-6*, 6114, Pub. by Canterbury Press Norwich) Morehouse Pub.

***Atwell, Robert, ed.** Celebrating the Seasons: Daily Spiritual Readings for the Christian Year. 592p. 2000. 32.95 (*0-8192-1847-2*, 6296) Morehouse Pub.

Atwell, Robert & Pierce, David, eds. American Community Colleges: A Guide. 10th rev. ed. (Illus.). 920p. 1995. boxed set 135.00 (*0-89774-874-3*) Oryx Pr.

Atwell-Vasey, Wendy. Nourishing Words: Bridging Private Reading & Public Teaching. LC 97-45757. (SUNY Series in Feminist Theory in Education). 246p. (C). 1998. text 59.50 (*0-7914-3631-4*); pap. text 19.95 (*0-7914-3632-2*) State U NY Pr.

Atwell, William A., jt. auth. see Thomas, David J.

Atwell, William D. Development of a Modular Design Methodology to Facilitate Design Reuse: The Six Sigma Research Institute Series. LC 92-25879. (Six Sigma Research Institute Ser.). 1992. pap. text 10.95 (*0-201-63422-8*) Addison-Wesley.

Atwill, Janet M. Rhetoric Reclaimed: Aristotle & the Liberal Arts Tradition. LC 97-35244. 248p. 1998. text 35.00 (*0-8014-3263-4*) Cornell U Pr.

Atwill, Tom. Earn Fame & Fortune with Your Home Videos. (Illus.). 198p. (Orig.). 1997. pap. text 29.95 (*0-9659034-0-0*) Atwood Pub.

***Atwood, Aileen H.** Husbands Who Love Men: Deceit, Disease & Despair, Vol. 1. LC 99-197336. 1998. pap. 19.95 (*0-9665942-0-7*) AMI Pubg.

Atwood, Alice C., jt. auth. see Blake, S. F.

Atwood, Arvilla. Atwood Family, Dating from 1741. (Illus.). 52p. 1997. reprint ed. pap. 11.00 (*0-8328-7305-5*); reprint ed. lib. bdg. 21.00 (*0-8328-7304-7*) Higginson Bk Co.

Atwood, Barbara Ann. A Courtroom of Her Own: The Life & Work of Judge Mary Anne Richey. LC 96-39329. 376p. 1998. 40.00 (*0-89089-654-2*) Carolina Acad Pr.

Atwood, Brian. In the Age of Mabo: History, Aborigines & Australia. LC 96-118225. 232p. pap. 24.95 (*1-86373-841-X*, Pub. by Allen & Unwin Pty) Paul & Co Pubs.

***Atwood, C. L.** Evaluation of Loss of Offsite Power Events at Nuclear Power Plants: 1980-1996. 129p. 1998. per. 10.00 (*0-16-062971-3*) USGPO.

***Atwood, Craig D.** Always Reforming: A History of Christianity Since 1300. 400p. 2000. pap. 25.00 (*0-86554-679-7*) Mercer Univ Pr.

***Atwood, Debbie A.** Jasper's Magic Blanket. (Illus.). 32p. (J). (ps-4). 2000. 14.95 (*0-9701013-0-9*) Novel Approach.

— No More Diapers. (Illus.). 10p. (J). (ps-k). 2000. 6.95 (*0-9701013-1-7*) Novel Approach.

Atwood, E. Barrett, Sr., et al. Guide to Preparing Governmental Financial Statements, 2 vols. Incl. Vol. 1. 1997. ring bd. (*0-7646-0185-7*); Set pap. 150.00 (*1-56433-872-X*); Set pap. 156.00 (*0-7646-0184-9*) Prctnrs Pub Co.

***Atwood, E. Barrett, Sr., et al.** Guide to Preparing Governmental Financial Statements, 2 vols. Incl. Vol. 1. Guide to Preparing Governmental Financial Statements. 1999. ring bd. (*0-7646-0901-7*); Vol. 2. Guide to Preparing Governmental Financial Statements. 1999. ring bd. (*0-7646-0902-5*); 1999. Set ring bd. 164.00i (*0-7646-0900-9*) Prctnrs Pub Co.

Atwood, E. Barrett, Sr., et al. Guide to Preparing Governmental Financial Statements, Vol. 2. 1997. ring bd. write for info. (*0-7646-0186-5*) Prctnrs Pub Co.

Atwood, E. F. Atwood. Philip Atwood, 1619/20-1700, of Malden & Bradford, & Descendants of Early Generations. 48p. 1996. reprint ed. pap. 10.00 (*0-8328-5360-7*); reprint ed. lib. bdg. 20.00 (*0-8328-5359-3*) Higginson Bk Co.

Atwood, Evangeline. We Shall Be Remembered. (ENG.). 191p. 1966. text 20.00 (*1-57833-079-3*) Todd Commns.

Atwood, Evangeline & De Armond, Robert N., compiled by. Who's Who in Alaskan Politics: A Biographical Dictionary of Alaskan Political Personalities, 1884-1974. LC 77-76025. 1977. 10.00 (*0-8323-0287-2*) Binford Mort.

***Atwood, Frederick D.** Rocks & Minerals, 1. 1998. pap. text 10.95 (*1-57717-027-X*) Todtri Prods.

Atwood, George E., et al, eds. Faces in a Cloud: Intersubjectivity in Personality Theory. LC 93-14932. 224p. 1994. 45.00 (*1-56821-050-7*) Aronson.

Atwood, George E. & Stolorow, Robert D. Structures of Subjectivity: Explorations in Psychoanalytic Phenomenology. (Psychoanalytic Inquiry Bk.: Vol. 4). 144p. (C). 1993. reprint ed. pap. 22.50 (*0-88163-166-3*) Analytic Pr.

Atwood, George E., jt. auth. see Stolorow, Robert D.

Atwood, Glenna W. Living Well with Parkinsons. LC 90-42200. 208p. 1991. pap. 15.95 (*0-471-52539-1*) Wiley.

Atwood, Harold L., jt. ed. see Bliss, Dorothy E.

Atwood, Harry. Constitution Explained. 5.00 (*0-685-08800-6*) Destiny.

Atwood, Harry F. Back to the Republic: The Golden Mean: the Standard Form of Government. (Illus.). 103p. 1996. reprint ed. pap. 9.00 (*1-883228-14-X*) Invictus MI.

Atwood, Illa. Law Office Procedures. 1993. teacher ed. 12.25 (*0-02-800067-6*) Glencoe.

Atwood, Illa W. Law Office Procedures. LC 92-35871. 1993. 33.00 (*0-02-800066-8*) Glencoe.

Atwood, J. L. Speciation & Geographic Variation in Black-Tailed Gnatcatchers. (Ornithological Monographs: Vol. 42). (Illus.). 74p. 1988. pap. 10.00 (*0-943610-53-2*) Am Ornithologists.

Atwood, James, jt. auth. see Brewster, Kingman Staff.

Atwood, James R., jt. auth. see Waller, Spencer W.

***Atwood, Jane E.** Too Much Time: Women in Prison. (Illus.). 196p. 2000. 49.95 (*0-7148-3973-6*) Phaidon Pr.

Atwood, Jerry L., ed. Inclusion Phenomena & Molecular Recognition. (Illus.). 422p. (C). 1990. text 150.00 (*0-306-43508-X*, Kluwer Plenum) Kluwer Academic.

Atwood, Jerry L., et al, eds. Inclusion Compounds: Key Organic Host Systems, Vol. 4. (Illus.). 528p. 1991. 110.00 (*0-19-855292-0*) OUP.

Atwood, Jerry L. & Davies, J. Eric, eds. Inclusion Phenomena in Inorganic, Organic & Organometallic Hosts. (C). 1988. text 211.50 (*90-277-2601-9*) Kluwer Academic.

Atwood, Jerry L. & Osa, Tetsuo, eds. Inclusion Aspects of Membrane Chemistry. (C). 1991. text 166.50 (*0-7923-1123-X*) Kluwer Academic.

Atwood, Jerry L., et al. Inclusion Compounds, Vol. 2. 1984. text 215.00 (*0-12-067102-6*) Acad Pr.

— Inclusion Compounds, Vol. 3. 1985. text 215.00 (*0-12-067103-4*) Acad Pr.

Atwood, Jesse H., et al. Thus Be Their Destiny: The Personality Development of Negro Youth in Three Communities. LC 71-155631. reprint ed. 24.50 (*0-404-00135-1*) AMS Pr.

Atwood, Jim D. Inorganic & Organometallic Reaction Mechanisms. 2nd ed. LC 96-12525. (Illus.). 350p. 1996. 59.95 (*1-56081-955-3*, Wiley-VCH) Wiley.

Atwood, Jim D. Inorganic & Organometallic Reaction Mechanisms. 2nd ed. 328p. 1997. 79.95 (*0-471-18897-2*, Wiley-VCH) Wiley.

Atwood, Jim D., jt. auth. see Zuckerman, J. J.

Atwood, Joan. Making Contact with Human Sexuality. (Illus.). 96p. (Orig.). pap. 6.95 (*0-942494-66-0*) Coleman Pub.

Atwood, Joan, ed. Family Therapy: A Behavioral-Systemic Approach. (Social Welfare Ser.). 400p. (C). 1999. pap. text 45.95 (*0-8304-1300-6*) Thomson Learn.

Atwood, Joan & Chester, Robert. Treatment Techniques for Common Mental Disorders. LC 87-17471. 352p. 1993. pap. 40.00 (*1-56821-136-8*) Aronson.

Atwood, Joan D. Family Scripts. 384p. 1996. pap. text 34.95 (*1-56032-401-5*) Taylor & Francis.

Atwood, Joan D., ed. Challenging Family Therapy Situations: Perspectives in Social Constructionism. LC 97-23148. (Illus.). 296p. 1997. 43.95 (*0-8261-9820-1*) Springer Pub.

— Family Scripts. 384p. 1996. 69.95 (*1-56032-411-2*) Taylor & Francis.

Atwood, Joan D. & Levine, Laurie B. Combining Sex & Couples Therapy. (C). 1995. 34.95 (*0-205-15408-5*, Macmillan Coll) P-H.

Atwood, Kay. Blossoms & Branches: A Gathering of Rogue Valley Orchard Memories. (Illus.). 231p. 1980. pap. 15.95 (*0-685-24086-X*) K Atwood.

— Illahe: The Story of Settlement in the Rogue River Canyon. (Illus.). 251p. 1978. pap. 15.95 (*0-9621592-1-2*) K Atwood.

— Mill Creek Journal: Ashland, Oregon, 1850-1860. (Illus.). 216p. 1987. pap. 15.95 (*0-685-24088-6*) K Atwood.

Atwood, L. E., jt. auth. see McKerns, Joseph P.

Atwood, L. Erwin, et al, eds. International Perspectives on News. LC 82-3273. 215p. 1982. 26.95 (*0-8093-1069-4*) S Ill U Pr.

Atwood, L. Erwin & Major, Ann M. Good-Bye, Gweilo: Public Opinion & the 1997 Problem in Hong Kong. LC 95-47151. (Communication Ser.). 320p. 1996. pap. 27.50 (*1-57273-011-0*) Hampton Pr NJ.

— Good-Bye, Gweilo: Public Opinion & the 1997 Problem in Hong Kong. LC 95-47151. (Communication Ser.). 320p. 1996. 65.00 (*1-57273-010-2*) Hampton Pr NJ.

Atwood, Lyman, jt. auth. see Marshall, S. L.

Atwood, Margaret. Alias Grace. 1997. mass mkt. 7.99 (*0-7704-2759-6*) Bantam.

— The Blind Assassin. LC 99-462109. 400p. 2000. 26.00 (*0-385-47572-1*, N A Talese) Doubleday.

— Blind Assassin. large type ed. 2000. 26.00 (*0-375-43085-7*) Random Hse Lrg Prnt.

Atwood, Margaret. Bluebeard's Egg. 272p. 1984. mass mkt. 7.99 (*0-7704-2134-2*) Bantam.
— Bluebeard's Egg. LC 96-1861. 304p. 1996. pap. 10.95 (*0-553-37860-0*) Bantam.
— Bluebeard's Egg. LC 97-32459. 256p. 1998. pap. 12.00 (*0-385-49104-2*, Anchor NY) Doubleday.
— Bluebeard's Egg. large type ed. LC 97-37113. (Basic Ser.). 421p. 1997. lib. bdg. 24.95 (*0-7862-1252-7*) Thorndike Pr.
— Bodily Harm. LC 95-36189. 304p. 1995. pap. 10.95 (*0-553-37789-2*) Bantam.
— Bodily Harm. LC 97-48289. 304p. 1998. pap. 12.95 (*0-385-49107-7*, Anchor NY) Doubleday.
— Bodily Harm. 1982. 45.00 (*0-671-44153-1*) Ultramarine Pub.
— Cat's Eye. 464p. 1989. pap. 8.99 (*0-7704-2334-5*) Bantam.
— Cat's Eye. 480p. 1995. pap. 10.95 (*0-553-37790-6*) Bantam.
— Cat's Eye. 496p. 1998. pap. 12.95 (*0-385-49102-6*, Anchor NY) Doubleday.
Atwood, Margaret. Cat's Eye. 1996. 17.10 (*0-606-00533-1*, Pub. by Turtleback) Demco.
Atwood, Margaret. The Circle Game. 95p. 1978. pap. 4.95 (*0-88784-070-1*, Pub. by Hse of Anansi Pr) Genl Dist Srvs.
— Dancing Girls: And Other Stories. 256p. 1982. mass mkt. 6.99 (*0-7704-2332-9*) Bantam.
— Dancing Girls: And Other Stories. LC 97-48290. 256p. 1998. pap. 12.00 (*0-385-49109-3*, Anchor NY) Doubleday.
— The Edible Woman. 1984. pap. 3.95 (*0-7704-1811-2*) Bantam.
— The Edible Woman. 304p. 1984. mass mkt. 7.99 (*0-7704-2301-9*) Bantam.
— The Edible Woman. LC 95-31304. 320p. 1995. pap. 10.95 (*0-553-37792-2*) Bantam.
— The Edible Woman. LC 97-47184. 336p. 1998. pap. 12.95 (*0-385-49106-9*, Anchor NY) Doubleday.
— The Edible Woman. 288p. 1989. mass mkt. 4.95 (*0-446-31498-6*) Warner Bks.
— Good Bones & Simple Murders. large type ed. LC 95-3695. (Large Print Bks.). 1995. 22.95 (*1-56895-172-8*) Wheeler Pub.
— The Handmaid's Tale. 304p. 1986. pap. 8.99 (*0-7704-2263-2*) Bantam.
— The Handmaid's Tale. 408p. 1987. mass mkt. 6.99 (*0-449-21260-2*, Crest) Fawcett.
— The Handmaid's Tale. LC 86-129018. 1985. 12.09 (*0-606-03797-7*, Pub. by Turtleback) Demco.
— Interlunar. 1984. pap. (*0-19-540451-3*) OUP.
— The Journals of Susanna Moodie: Poems. 64p. 1970. pap. text 16.95 (*0-19-540169-7*) OUP.
— Lady Oracle. 1984. pap. 4.50 (*0-7704-2179-2*) Bantam.
— Lady Oracle. 352p. 1984. mass mkt. 8.99 (*0-7704-2299-3*) Bantam.
— Lady Oracle. LC 95-36576. 352p. 1995. pap. 10.95 (*0-553-37781-7*) Bantam.
***Atwood, Margaret.** Lady Oracle. LC 97-48403. 368p. 1998. pap. 12.95 (*0-385-49108-5*) Doubleday.
Atwood, Margaret. Life Before Man. 304p. 1984. mass mkt. 5.95 (*0-7704-2029-X*) Bantam.
— Life Before Man. 368p. 1995. pap. 10.95 (*0-553-37782-5*) Bantam.
— Life Before Man. LC 97-48288. 384p. 1998. pap. 12.00 (*0-385-49110-7*, Anchor NY) Doubleday.
Atwood, Margaret. Margaret Atwood Reads: Atwood,&Margaret. abr. ed. 1993. audio 12.00 (*1-55994-838-8*, DCN 1537) HarperAudio.
Atwood, Margaret. Morning in the Burned House. 127p. 1996. pap. 14.00 (*0-395-82521-0*) HM.
— Selected Poems II: Poems Selected & New, 1976-1986. 160p. 1987. pap. 16.00 (*0-395-45406-9*) HM.
— Power Politics. 58p. 1971. pap. 4.95 (*0-88784-020-5*, Pub. by Hse of Anansi Pr) Genl Dist Srvs.
— Power Politics: Poems. 2nd rev. ed. LC 96-930636. 76p. 1996. pap. 9.95 (*0-88784-579-7*, Pub. by Hse of Anansi Pr) Genl Dist Srvs.
— Princess Prunella & the Purple Peanut. LC 95-21059. (Illus.). 32p. (J). (ps-3). 1995. 13.95 (*0-7611-0166-7*, 10166) Workman Pub.
— The Robber Bride. 544p. 1994. mass mkt. 6.99 (*0-7704-2616-6*) Bantam.
— The Robber Bride. 544p. 1995. mass mkt. 6.50 (*0-553-56905-8*) Bantam.
— The Robber Bride. 480p. 1993. 23.50 (*0-385-26008-3*, N A Talese) Doubleday.
— The Robber Bride. 544p. 1998. pap. 14.00 (*0-385-49103-4*, Anchor NY) Doubleday.
Atwood, Margaret. Second Words: Selected Critical Prose. LC 83-132787. 444p. 1982. write for info. (*0-88784-095-7*) Anansi Prodns.
Atwood, Margaret. Selected Poems, 1965-1975, 001. 1987. pap. 14.00 (*0-395-40422-3*) HM.
— Strange Things: The Malevolent North In Canadian Literature. (Clarendon Lectures in English Literature). 134p. 1996. 25.00 (*0-19-811976-3*) OUP.
— Surfacing. LC 95-36575. 208p. 1995. pap. 10.95 (*0-553-37780-9*) Bantam.
— Surfacing. LC 97-43807. 224p. 1998. pap. 12.95 (*0-385-49105-0*, Anchor NY) Doubleday.
— Surfacing. 1997. pap. 6.95 (*0-7710-9899-5*) McCland & Stewart.
— Survival: A Thematic Guide to Canadian Literature. LC 72-91501. 287 p. 1972. write for info. (*0-88784-713-7*) Anansi.
— Wilderness Tips. 256p. 1992. mass mkt. 5.99 (*0-7704-2524-0*) Bantam.
— Wilderness Tips. 320p. 1993. mass mkt. 6.99 (*0-553-56046-8*) Bantam.
***Atwood, Margaret.** Wilderness Tips. 240p. 1998. pap. 12.00 (*0-385-49111-5*) Doubleday.
— York Notes: The Handmaid's Tale. 1997. pap. write for info. (*0-582-21538-2*) Addison-Wesley.
Atwood, Margaret & Barkhouse, Joyce. Anna's Pet. (Kids of Canada Ser.). 32p. (J). 1980. bds. 12.95 (*0-88862-249-X*, Pub. by J Lorimer) Formac Dist Ltd.
Atwood, Margaret & Beaulieu, Victor-Levy. Two Solicitudes: Conversations. Aronoff, Phyllis & Scott, Howard, trs. from FRE. Orig. Title: Deux Sollicitudes: Entretiens. 240p. 1998. pap. 15.95 (*0-7710-0836-8*) McCland & Stewart.
***Atwood, Margaret & White, Robin.** A Practitioner's Guide to Professional Development. 224p. 2000. pap. 39.95 (*0-632-05629-0*) Blackwell Sci.
Atwood, Margaret Eleanor. Alias Grace. 468p. 1997. pap. 14.00 (*0-385-49044-5*, Anchor NY) Doubleday.
— The Handmaid's Tale. LC 97-42966. 325p. 1998. pap. 12.95 (*0-385-49081-X*, Anchor NY) Doubleday.
***Atwood, Margaret Eleanor.** Handmaid's Tale. (Illus.). (J). 1998. 18.30 (*0-606-18124-5*) Turtleback.
Atwood, Marjorie, Jr. Galisteo Legend: A Story. Smith, James C., ed. LC 91-41394. (Illus.). 48p. (Orig.). (J). 1992. pap. 6.95 (*0-86534-154-0*) Sunstone Pr.
Atwood, Mary. Adventures in Indian Cooking. 256p. 1978. 9.95 (*0-318-36281-3*) Asia Bk Corp.
***Atwood, Mary.** Spirit Herbs: Native American Healing. LC 99-165089. 160p. 1998. pap. 12.95 (*0-8069-3862-5*) Sterling.
Atwood, Mary A. Suggestive Inquiry into the Hermetic Mystery: With a Dissertation on the More Celebrated of the Alchemical Philosophers Being an Attempt Towards the Recovery of the Ancient Experiment of Nature (1918) 692p. 1999. reprint ed. pap. 29.95 (*0-7661-0811-2*) Kessinger Pub.
Atwood, Mary A. & Wilmshurst, Walter L. Hermetic Philosophy & Alchemy. LC 79-8592. reprint ed. 74.50 (*0-404-18446-4*) AMS Pr.
Atwood, Mary Anne. A Suggestive Inquiry into the Hermetic Mystery. LC 75-36825. (Occult Ser.). 1976. reprint ed. 56.95 (*0-405-07938-9*) Ayer.
— A Suggestive Inquiry into the Hermetic Mystery. 597p. 1976. reprint ed. 24.00 (*0-911662-64-2*) Yoga.
Atwood, Mary D. Spirit Healing: Native American Magic & Medicine. LC 91-21220. (Illus.). 160p. 1991. pap. 12.95 (*0-8069-8266-7*) Sterling.
***Atwood, Melinda.** Jambo Mama. (Illus.). 240p. 2000. write for info. (*1-879384-38-8*) Cypress Hse.
Atwood, Nettie B. Berries on the Hill: Cookbook. LC 87-91506. 448p. 1987. 12.50 (*0-9618721-0-1*) Nettie B Atwood.
Atwood, Nina. Be Your Own Dating Service: A Step-by-Step Guide to Finding & Maintaining Healthy Relationships. LC 95-22964. 304p. 1995. pap. 9.95 (*0-8050-4097-8*, Owl) H Holt & Co.
— Conversations with a Date. LC 97-28247. 1998. pap. 9.95 (*0-8050-5537-1*) H Holt & Co.
Atwood, Rita & McAnany, Emile G., eds. Communication & Latin America Society: Trends in Critical Research, 1960-1985. LC 86-40044. (Studies in Communication & Society). 231p. reprint ed. pap. 71.70 (*0-608-09842-6*, 206923000003) Bks Demand.
— Communication & Society in Latin America: Trends in Critical Research 196-1985. LC 86-40044. (Studies in Communication & Society). 288p. 1986. text 36.00 (*0-299-10720-5*) U of Wis Pr.
Atwood, Rodney. The Hessians: Mercenaries from Hessen-Kassel in the American Revolution. LC 79-20150. 304p. reprint ed. pap. 86.70 (*0-608-15691-4*, 2031618) Bks Demand.
Atwood, Roy A. Mass Communication Law in Idaho. (State Law Ser.). 112p. (C). 1992. pap. text 12.95 (*0-913507-35-0*) New Forums.
Atwood, Russell. East of A. LC 98-19610. 1999. 22.00 (*0-345-42776-9*) Ballantine Pub Grp.
***Atwood, Russell.** East of A. 2000. mass mkt. 6.50 (*0-345-42778-5*) Fawcett.
Atwood, Sandra & Stanton, Cheryl. Introduction to Basic Cardiac Dysrhythmias. 2nd ed. (Illus.). 288p. (C). (gr. 13). 1996. pap. text 26.00 (*0-8151-0123-6*, 24407) Mosby Inc.
Atwood, Susan J. & Kimber, Clive. Georgia: On-Site Technical Election Assistance Project. ii, 276p. 1992. pap. 9.00 (*1-879720-84-1*) Intl Fndt Elect.
Atwood, Susan J., et al. Georgia: IFES Technical Election Assistance Project, July 27-August 3. ii, 90p. 1992. pap. 11.00 (*1-879720-85-X*) Intl Fndt Elect.
Atwood, Thomas C. 1997-98 Guide to Public Policy Experts. 695p. 1995. pap. 16.95 (*0-89195-068-0*) Heritage Found.
Atwood, Tom, intro. Radio Control Airplane How-To's: Tips from the Experts. (Illus.). 138p. (Orig.). 1992. pap. 14.95 (*0-911295-24-0*) Air Age.
Atwood, Tom, ed. see Gierke, C. David.
Atwood, Tom, ed. see Patrick, Dave.
Atwood, Tom, ed. see Stilley, Faye.
Atwood, Virginia A., ed. Elementary School Social Studies: Research As a Guide to Practice. LC 86-63064. (Bulletin Ser.: No. 79). 176p. 1991. reprint ed. pap. text 14.95 (*0-87986-054-5*) Nat Coun Soc Studies.
Atwood, Wes, ed. see Palm, Gordon F.
Atwood, William G. Fryderyk Chopin: Pianist from Warsaw. LC 86-12986. 317p. reprint ed. pap. 98.30 (*0-7837-0423-2*, 204074600018) Bks Demand.
***Atwood, William G.** The Parisian Worlds of Frederic Chopin. LC 99-27886. (Illus.). 447p. 1999. 35.00 (*0-300-07773-4*) Yale U Pr.
Atwood, William L. The Lottery Solution. LC 92-560. 110p. 1992. 9.95 (*0-944957-13-7*) Rivercross Pub.
— The Lottery Solution: With Accompanying Software. rev. ed. LC 96-24427. (Illus.). 176p. (Orig.). 1996. pap. 19.95 (*0-944957-96-X*) Rivercross Pub.
Atxaga, Bernardo. The Lone Man. 336p. 1998. mass mkt. 11.00 (*1-86046-340-1*) Harvill Press.
***Atxaga, Bernardo.** The Lone Woman. Costa, Margaret J., tr. from BAQ. 160p. 1998. 22.00 (*1-86046-421-1*, Pub. by Harvill Press) FS&G.
Atyeo, Marilyn, jt. auth. see Udhe, Anna.
Atzberger, Leonhard. Die Logos lehre des Heiligen Athanasius. vii, 246p. 1975. reprint ed. 50.00 (*3-487-05618-6*) G Olms Pubs.
Atzel-Bethlen, Szabolcs & Mimieux, Yvette. Aerobic Yoga: The Cosmic Fountain of Youth Yoga Workout. LC 97-4178. 1997. pap. 24.95 (*1-885203-40-3*) Jrny Editions.
Atzeni, P., et al, eds. The World Wide Web & Databases: Selected Papers of the EDBT Workshop WebDB'98, Valencia, Spain, March 27-28, 1998. LC 99-26572. (Lecture Notes in Computer Science Ser.: Vol. 1590). viii, 213p. 1999. pap. 45.00 (*3-540-65890-4*) Spr-Verlag.
Atzeni, Paolo. Database Systems. 1999. pap., student ed. 83.75 (*0-07-235387-2*) McGraw.
Atzeni, Paolo, ed. LOGIDATA: Deductive Databases with Complex Objects. LC 93-11824. (Lecture Notes in Computer Science Ser.: Vol. 701). 1993. 44.95 (*0-387-56974-X*) Spr-Verlag.
— LOGITDATA Plus: Deductive Databases with Complex Objects. (Lecture Notes in Computer Science Ser.: Vol. 701). vii, 273p. 1993. pap. write for info. (*3-540-56974-X*) Spr-Verlag.
Atzeni, Paolo, et al. Relational Database Theory. Elliott, Sally, ed. 350p. (C). 1992. 50.33 (*0-8053-0249-2*) Addison-Wesley.
Atzeni, Paolo, jt. ed. see Austello, G.
Atzeni, Paolo, ed. see British Computer Society Staff, et al.
Atzeni, Sergio. Bakunin's Son. Rugman, John H., tr. from ITA. LC 96-16576. 100p. (Orig.). 1996. pap. 11.00 (*0-934977-44-5*) Italica Pr.
Atzmon, M., et al, eds. Phase Transformations in Thin Films: Thermodynamics & Kinetics. (Symposium Proceedings Ser.: Vol. 311). 399p. 1993. text 72.00 (*1-55899-207-3*) Materials Res.
Au, Joseph J., jt. ed. see Masters, John E.
Au, Joy. What If Elephants Wore Hula Skirts at the Honolulu Zoo. (Illus.). 28p. (J). 1997. 9.95 (*1-56647-150-8*) Mutual Pub HI.
Au, Joy S. A Bug Hunt in Hawaii nei. (Illus.). 32p. 1993. 12.95 (*1-56647-046-3*) Mutual Pub HI.
Au, Joy S. Going to the Tide Pools in Hawaii Nei. (Illus.). 32p. (J). 1995. 12.95 (*1-56647-082-X*) Mutual Pub HI.
— Hawai'i Sings. (Illus.). 24p. (J). (gr. k-4). 1995. 14.95 (*1-56647-083-8*) Mutual Pub HI.
Au, Kathryn H. Literacy Instruction In Multicultural Settings. 224p. (C). 1993. pap. text 34.00 (*0-03-076847-0*, Pub. by Harcourt Coll Pubs) Harcourt.
Au, Kathryn H., et al. Balanced Literacy Instruction: A Teachers Resource Book. 350p. 1997. pap., teacher ed. 38.95 (*0-926842-66-8*) CG Pubs Inc.
Au, Kathryn H., jt. ed. see Raphael, Taffy E.
Au, L. B., jt. auth. see Solymar, L.
Au, Margaret, jt. auth. see Corrigan, Mike.
***Au, Steven T.** Beijing Odyssey: The Life & Times of Liang Shiyi. LC 99-74554. (Illus.). 456p. 1999. pap. 14.95 (*1-878044-68-0*, Wld Rose) Mayhaven Pub.
Au, Susan. Ballet & Modern Dance: A Concise History. LC 87-50193. (World of Art Ser.). (Illus.). 200p. (Orig.). (C). 1988. pap. 14.95 (*0-500-20219-2*, Pub. by Thames Hudson) Norton.
Au, Tung. Engineering Economics for Capital Investment Analysis. 600p. (C). 1983. text 55.00 (*0-205-07911-3*, H79114); teacher ed. write for info. (*0-318-57285-0*, H79122) P-H.
Au, Whitlow W. The Sonar of Dolphins. LC 92-22696. (Illus.). 344p. 1997. 89.95 (*0-387-97835-6*) Spr-Verlag.
***Au, Whitlow W., et al, eds.** Hearing by Whales & Dolphins. LC 99-40947. (Handbook of Auditory Research Ser.: Vol. 12). (Illus.). 384p. 2000. 94.95 (*0-387-94906-2*) Spr-Verlag.
Au, Wilkie. By Way of the Heart: Toward a Holistic Christian Spirituality. LC 89-39731. 240p. 1990. pap. 14.95 (*0-8091-3118-8*) Paulist Pr.
***Au, Wilkie.** The Enduring Heart: Spirituality for the Long Haul. 176p. 2000. 16.95 (*0-8091-0524-1*) Paulist Pr.
Au, Wilkie & Cannon, Noreen. Urgings of the Heart: A Spirituality of Integration. LC 95-35391. 192p. (Orig.). 1996. pap. 14.95 (*0-8091-3604-X*) Paulist Pr.
Au, William A. The Cross, the Flag, & the Bomb: American Catholics Debate War & Peace, 1960-1983. LC 87-11593. 304p. 1987. pap. 12.95 (*0-275-92777-6*, B2777, Praeger Pubs) Greenwood.
— The Cross, the Flag, & the Bomb: American Catholics Debate War & Peace, 1960-1983, 12. LC 84-25290. (Contributions to the Study of Religion Ser.: No. 12). 278p. 1985. 59.95 (*0-313-24754-4*, AUC/, Greenwood Pr) Greenwood.
Au-Yang, M. K., ed. Flow-Induced Vibration & Transient Thermal-Hydraulics, 1998: Proceedings, ASME/JSME Joint Pressure Vessels & Piping Conference (1998, San Diego, CA) LC 98-73172. 363. 191p. 1998. pap. 96.00 (*0-7918-1859-4*) ASME.
— Flow-Induced Vibration 1994: Proceedings of the Pressure Vessels & Piping Conference, Minneapolis, MN, 1994. LC 87-72467. (PVP Ser.: Vol. 273). 315p. 1994. pap. 65.00 (*0-7918-1196-4*) ASME.
— Technology for the '90s. LC 93-70159. 1131p. 1993. pap. 200.00 (*0-7918-0684-7*) ASME.
Au-Yang, M. K. & Ma, D. C., eds. Flow-Induced Vibration & Fluid-Structure Interaction - 1993. (PVP Ser.: Vol. 258). 232p. 1993. 55.00 (*0-7918-0985-4*, H00817) ASME.
Au-Yang, M. K., ed. see American Society of Mechanical Engineers Staff.
Au-Yang, M. K., jt. ed. see Lin, C.
Au-Yang, M. K., ed. see National Congress on Pressure Vessels & Piping Sta.
Au-Yang, M. K., jt. ed. see Paidoussis, M. P.
Au-Yang, M. K., jt. ed. see Shin, Y. S.
Auakian, Monique. The Meiji Restoration & the Rise of Modern Japan. (Turning Points in World History Ser.). (Illus.). 64p. (YA). (gr. 7 up). 1991. pap. 7.95 (*0-382-24139-8*); lib. bdg. 14.95 (*0-382-24132-0*) Silver Burdett Pr.
Aub, Joseph C. & Hapgood, Ruth K. Pioneer in Modern Medicine: David Linn Edsall of Harvard. LC 78-145896. (Illus.). 384p. 1970. 22.50 (*0-674-66875-8*) HUP.
Aub, Kathleen A. Children Are Survivors Too: A Guide Book for Young Homicide Survivors. LC 95-77389. (Illus.). 70p. (J). (gr. k-12). 1995. spiral bd. 11.95 (*0-9645989-0-6*) Grief Educ Res.
Aubart, et al. L' Art Monumental roman en France: Coll. Art et Geoge. 21.95 (*0-685-38374-1*) Fr & Eur.
Aube, jt. auth. see Gawley, R. E.
Aube, J., jt. auth. see Gawley, R. E.
Aube, John R. Appraisal of Unique Properties. 38p. (Orig.). 1996. pap. 25.00 (*0-614-23694-0*) Todd Pub.
Aubeelack, Amarjeet K. The Scientific Laws of Hinduism. LC 97-90187. 1998. pap. 11.95 (*0-533-12319-4*) Vantage.
Auberg, R., jt. auth. see Setzer, M. J.
Auberleitner, Waltruad. In Ihm Leben Wir: Eine Beziehungstheologische und Beziehungsdynamische Sicht Religioser Entwicklung. (Europaische Hochschulschriften Ser.: Reihe 23, Bd. 517). (GER.). 487p. 1994. 62.95 (*3-906752-67-4*, Pub. by P Lang) P Lang Pubng.
Aubert, A. E., et al, eds. Cardiac Pacing & Electrophysiology: A Bridge to the 21st Century. LC 93-38818. 1994. text 148.50 (*0-7923-2627-X*) Kluwer Academic.
Aubert, Alvin. Against the Blues. 1972. pap. 4.00 (*0-910296-73-1*) Broadside Pr.
— Harlem Wrestler & Other Poems. LC 95-2624. 1995. pap. 10.00 (*0-87013-369-1*) Mich St U Pr.
— If Winter Come: Collected Poems, 1967-1992. LC 93-73471. (Poetry Ser.). 150p. (Orig.). 1994. pap. 12.95 (*0-88748-165-5*) Carnegie-Mellon.
Aubert, Brigitte. Death from the Woods. Koral, David L., tr. from FRE. 256p. 2000. 24.95 (*1-56649-109-6*) Welcome Rain.
Aubert, Charles. The Art of Pantomime. LC 68-56484. (Illus.). 1972. reprint ed. 23.95 (*0-405-08226-6*, Pub. by Blom Pubns) Ayer.
Aubert de la Chenaye-Desbois, Francais. Dictionnaire de la Noblesse, 10 vols., Set. (FRE.). 9800p. 1978. 1695.00 (*0-8288-5178-6*, M6015) Fr & Eur.
Aubert, Eugene J. & Stephens, Matthew. Personal Financial Planning Made Easy. (Illus.). (Orig.). (C). 1988. pap. 59.95 (*0-929416-00-7*) AFPG Inc.
— Personal Financial Planning Made Easy. (Illus.). 170p. (Orig.). (C). 1988. pap. text 79.00 (*0-317-90583-X*) Advan Finan Plan.
Aubert, G., jt. auth. see Moreau, R.
Aubert, Henri. Diccionario de Mitologia. (SPA.). 238p. 1961. 19.95 (*0-8288-6816-6*, S33055) Fr & Eur.
Aubert, Jean-Paul, et al, eds. Biochemistry & Genetics of Cellulose Degradation. (Fems Symposia Ser.). 428p. 1988. text 104.00 (*0-12-067575-7*) Acad Pr.
Aubert, M., et al, eds. Malignant Hyperthermias. 1993. 38.00 (*0-926592-11-4*) Normed Verlag.
Aubert, Marcel. Cathedrale de Chartre. (FRE., Illus.). 84p. 1961. lib. bdg. 14.95 (*0-8288-3983-2*) Fr & Eur.
— Scultures du Moyen Age. (ENG & FRE., Illus.). 1948. lib. bdg. 24.95 (*0-8288-3991-3*) Fr & Eur.
Aubert, Marcel & Goubet. Cathedrales Abbatiales, Collegiales et Prieures Romans en France. 153.25 (*0-685-34010-4*) Fr & Eur.
— Cathedrales et Tresors Gothiques en France. 153.25 (*0-7859-0344-5*, F22241) Fr & Eur.
Aubert, Roger. Dictionnaire Histoire, Geographie Ecclesiastiques, Fascicle 1-155. (FRE.). 1998. 8000.00 (*0-320-00378-7*) Fr & Eur.
Aubert, Roger & Van Cauwenberg. Dictionnaire d'Histoire et du Geographie Ecclesiastiques, 16 vols., Set. (FRE.). pap. 2795.00 (*0-7859-0389-5*, M6014) Fr & Eur.
Aubert, Ronald E., et al. Diabetes in America. 2nd ed. (Illus.). 782p. (C). 1996. pap. text 75.00 (*0-7881-2662-8*) DIANE Pub.
Aubert, Rosemary. The Feast of Stephen: An Ellis Portal Mystery. LC 98-44000. (Ellis Portal Mystery Ser.). 257p. 1999. 22.95 (*1-882593-27-8*) Bridge Wrks.
— Free Reign. 1998. mass mkt. 6.99 (*0-425-16427-6*) Berkley Pub.
— Free Reign. LC 96-43479. 321p. 1997. 21.95 (*1-882593-18-9*) Bridge Wrks.
— A Thousand to One. LC 96-96136. 192p. 1996. 18.95 (*0-8034-9173-5*, Avalon Bks) Bouregy.
Aubert, Timothy J., jt. auth. see Bernstein, Richard K.
Aubert, Vilhelm. The Hidden Society. LC 80-18939. (Social Science Classics Ser.). 359p. 1982. reprint ed. pap. 24.95 (*0-87855-730-X*) Transaction Pubs.
Aubertin, M., et al, eds. Rock Mechanics: Tools & Techniques: Proceedings of the 2nd North American Rock Mechanics Symposium, NARMS '96, Montreal, Quebec, 19-21 June 1996, Vol. 2. (Illus.). 2050p. (C). 1996. text 194.00 (*90-5410-838-X*, Pub. by A A Balkema) Ashgate Pub Co.

A

Aubet, Maria E. The Phoenicians & the West: Politics, Colonies & Trade. (Illus.). 366p. 1996. pap. text 23.95 (*0-521-56598-7*) Cambridge U Pr.

***Aubetaem, Gabriele.** Thematisierung von Frauenerwerbstatigkeit im Spanischen Kommerziellen Theater: Gregorio Martinez Sierra, 1881-1947. (Europaische Hochschulschriften Theater-, Film- und Fernsehwissenschaften Ser.). X, 305p. 1999. 51.95 (*3-631-34892-4*) P Lang Pubng.

Aubier, Catherine & Ravignant, Patrick. Dictionnaire Pratique D'Astrologie. (FRE.). 1989. 69.95 (*0-7859-8154-3*, 2-86676-476-5) Fr & Eur.

Aubignac, Francois H. The Whole Art of the Stage. LC 68-21218. 1972. 36.95 (*0-405-08227-4*, Pub. by Blom Pubns) Ayer.

Aubin de Teran, Lisa St., see St. Aubin de Teran, Lisa.

Aubin, E. Morocco of Today. 1977. lib. bdg. 59.95 (*0-8490-2283-5*) Gordon Pr.

Aubin, Ed de St., see McAdams, Dan P. & de St. Aubin, Ed, eds.

Aubin, Francoise, ed. see Serruys, Henry.

Aubin, Jean P. Dynamic Economic Theory: A Viability Approach. LC 97-13000. (Studies in Economic Theory). 1997. write for info. (*3-540-62687-5*) Spr-Verlag.

— Mathematical Methods of Game & Economic Theory. 2nd ed. (Studies in Mathematics & Its Applications: Vol. 7). 616p. 1980. 257.50 (*0-444-85184-4*, North Holland) Elsevier.

— Optima & Equilibria: An Introduction to Nonlinear Analysis. Wilson, Stephen, tr. from FRE. LC 92-45828. (Graduate Texts in Mathematics Ser.: Vol. 130). (Illus.). 417p. 1993. 65.95 (*0-387-52121-6*) Spr-Verlag.

— Optima & Equilibria: An Introduction to Nonlinear Analysis. 2nd ed. LC 98-39225. (Graduate Texts in Mathematics Ser.: Vol. 140). 1998. 69.95 (*3-540-64983-2*) Spr-Verlag.

— Viability Theory. (Systems & Control: Foundations & Applications Ser.). (Illus.). xxv, 543p. 1991. 99.50 (*0-8176-3571-8*) Birkhauser.

Aubin, Jean P., ed. Mutational & Morphological Analysis: Tools for Shape Evolution & Morphogenesis. LC 98-2857. 400p. 1998. 74.50 (*0-8176-3935-7*) Birkhauser.

Aubin, Jean P. & Cellina, A. Differential Inclusions: Set-Valued Maps & Viability Theory. LC 84-1327. (Grundlehren der Mathematischen Wissenschaften Ser.: Vol. 264). (Illus.). 350p. 1984. 135.95 (*0-387-13105-1*) Spr-Verlag.

Aubin, Jean P. & Frankowska, H. Set-Valued Analysis. (Systems & Control: Foundations & Applications Ser.: No. 2). 450p. 1990. 78.50 (*0-8176-3478-9*) Birkhauser.

Aubin, Jean P., et al. Dynamics of Macrosystems. (Lecture Notes in Economics & Mathematical Systems Ser.: Vol. 257). vi, 280p. 1985. 38.50 (*0-387-15987-8*) Spr-Verlag.

Aubin, Jean Pierre. Applied Functional Analysis. 2nd ed. LC 99-15355. 498p. 2000. 99.95 (*0-471-17976-0*) Wiley.

Aubin, Jean-Pierre. Mutational & Morphological Analysis. LC 98-2857. (Systems & Control Ser.). xxxvii, 425 p. 1998. write for info. (*3-7643-3935-7*) Birkhauser.

— Neural Networks & Qualitative Physics: A Viability Approach. (Illus.). 298p. (C). 1996. text 54.95 (*0-521-44532-9*) Cambridge U Pr.

Aubin, L. X., jt. auth. see Miller, D. F.

Aubin, Michael. City for Sale: International Financiers Take a Major North American City by Storm. Orig. Title: Vrais Proprietais de Montreal. (Illus.). 389p. 1977. 19.95 (*0-88515-094-5*, Pub. by J Lorimer) Formac Dist Ltd.

— A Day at Home. (Child's World Library). (Illus.). 32p. (J). (gr. k-5). 1992. lib. bdg. 18.50 (*0-89565-762-7*) Childs World.

Aubin, Michel & Picard, Phillipe. Homeopathy & Your Health: A Different Way of Treating Common Everyday Ailments. 2nd ed. 176p. 1996. mass mkt. 5.95 (*0-89529-741-8*, Avery) Penguin Putnam.

Aubin, Penelope, tr. see Challes, Robert, et al.

Aubin, Pierre & Cotter, George. Agencies for Development Assistance: Sources of Support for Community-Based Socio-Economic & Religious Projects in Developing Countries. 5th rev. ed. Orig. Title: Agencies for Project Assistance. (ENG, FRE & SPA.). 355p. (Orig.). Date not set. reprint ed. pap. 60.00 (*0-913671-07-X*) Mission Proj Serv.

Aubin, Remy A. Mammalian Cell Transformation Protocols. (Methods in Molecular Biology Ser.). (Illus.). 1999. 74.50 (*0-89603-442-9*) Humana.

Aubin, Stephen P. Distorting Defense: Network News & National Security. LC 98-25228. 280p. 1998. 59.95 (*0-275-96303-9*, Praeger Pubs) Greenwood.

Aubin, T. Nonlinear Analysis on Manifolds: Monge-Ampere Equations. (Grundlehren der Mathematischen Wissenschaften Ser.: Vol. 252). 204p. 1982. 107.95 (*0-387-90704-1*) Spr-Verlag.

***Aubin, T.** Some Nonlinear Problems in Riemannian Geometry. LC 98-4150. (Springer Monographs in Mathematics). (Illus.). xvii, 395p. 1998. 109.00 (*3-540-60752-8*) Spr-Verlag.

Aubinais, Marie. Birds. (Big, Bigger, Biggest Ser.). (Illus.). 32p. (J). 1998. 16.95 (*0-7892-0387-1*, Abbeville Kids) Abbeville Pr.

— The Farm. (Big, Bigger, Biggest Ser.). (Illus.). 32p. (J). 1996. 14.95 (*0-7892-0152-6*, Abbeville Kids) Abbeville Pr.

— The Jungle. (Big, Bigger, Biggest Ser.). (Illus.). 32p. (J). 1996. 14.95 (*0-7892-0175-5*, Abbeville Kids) Abbeville Pr.

— Sea Animals. (Big, Bigger, Biggest Ser.). (Illus.). 32p. (J). 1998. 16.95 (*0-7892-0386-3*, Abbeville Kids) Abbeville Pr.

Aubineau, Michel. Chrysostome, Severien, Proclus, Hesychius et Alii Patrisique et Hagiographie Grecques. (Collected Studies: No. CS276). 380p. (C). 1988. reprint ed. lib. bdg. 135.95 (*0-86078-224-7*, Pub. by Variorum) Ashgate Pub Co.

Aubineau, Michel, ed. Hesychius - Index Verborum Homiliarum Festalium Hesychii Hierosolymitani. (Alpha-Omega, Reihe A Ser.: Vol. LII). (GER.). 404p. 1983. 105.00 (*3-487-07341-2*) G Olms Pubs.

Aublet, J. B. Histoire des Plantes de la Guiane Francaise, 4 vols. bd. in one. (Historia Naturalis Classica Ser.: No. 100). 1977. reprint ed. lib. bdg. 400.00 (*3-7682-1105-3*) Lubrecht & Cramer.

***Aubley, Curt.** HTML 4.0 with JavaScript. LC 99-213412. 496p. (C). 1998. pap. text 49.99 (*0-13-095783-6*) P-H.

— Sizing & Tuning of Windows Two Thousand. 300p. 2000. pap. 49.99 (*0-13-089105-3*) Pearson Pubns.

Aubley, Curt. Tuning & Sizing of NT Server. LC 98-4226. 432p. (C). 1998. pap. 49.95 (*0-13-095388-1*) P-H.

Aubol, Petrina. Drive Time. LC 98-85303. 192p. 1999. pap. 11.95 (*1-56315-191-X*, Pub. by SterlingHse) Natl Bk Netwk.

Abouin, Jean & Bourgois, Jacques, eds. Tectonics of Circum-Pacific Continental Margins: Proceedings of the 28th International Geology Congress, July 1989. (Illus.). 243p. 1990. 115.00 (*90-6764-132-4*, Pub. by VSP) Coronet Bks.

Auboyer, Jeannine. Daily Life in Ancient India from Approximately 200 B. C. to A. D. 700: From c. 200 BC to AD 700. Taylor, Simon W., tr. (Illus.). 360p. (C). 1994. 37.50 (*81-215-0632-8*, Pub. by M Manoharial) Coronet Bks.

Aubrac, Lucie. Outwitting the Gestapo. Wing, Betsy & Bieber, Konrad, trs. LC 92-26861. (Illus.). xxiii, 241p. 1993. pap. 12.00 (*0-8032-5923-9*, Bison Books) U of Nebr Pr.

— Outwitting the Gestapo. large type ed. Bieber, Konrad & Wing, Betsy, trs. from GER. LC 93-30906. 408p. 1993. lib. bdg. 17.95 (*0-7862-0039-1*) Thorndike Pr.

Aubrac, Lucie, jt. auth. see Aubrac, Raymond.

Aubrac, Raymond & Aubrac, Lucie. The French Resistance. (Illus.). 200p. 1997. pap. 12.95 (*2-85025-567-X*) Dist Art Pubs.

***Aubrecht.** Physics for Scientists & Engineers: Doing Physics with Spreadsheets. 3rd ed. 304p. 2000. pap. 26.00 incl. disk (*0-13-021474-4*) P-H.

Aubrecht, Gordon, ed. Quarks, Quasars, & Quandaries. (Occasional Publications). 358p. (C). 1987. per. 22.00 (*0-917853-26-1*, OP-56) Am Assn Physics.

Aubrecht, Gordon J. Energy. 2nd ed. (Illus.). 700p. (C). 1995. pap. 56.00 (*0-02-304601-5*, Macmillan Coll) P-H.

Aubrey. Meltdown: Collapse of the Nuclear Dream. pap. 15.95 (*1-85585-017-6*, Pub. by Jonathan Cape) Trafalgar.

— Thorp: The Whitehall Nightmare. 1993. pap. 11.95 (*1-897766-07-6*, Pub. by Jon Carpenter) Paul & Co Pubs.

Aubrey, Brian. English Romantic Poetry. (Magill Bibliographies Ser.). 296p. 1991. 45.00 (*0-8108-2812-X*) Scarecrow.

Aubrey, Bryan, ed. see Goddard, Larry.

Aubrey, Carol. Mathematics Teaching in the Early Years: An Investigation of Teachers' Subject Knowledge. LC 97-144803. 192p. 1996. pap. 27.95 (*0-7507-0597-3*, Falmer Pr) Taylor & Francis.

Aubrey, Carol, ed. The Role of Subject Knowledge in the Early Years. LC 93-32628. 1994. pap. 34.95 (*0-7507-0195-1*, Falmer Pr) Taylor & Francis.

Aubrey, Charles A., II & Felkins, Patricia K. Teamwork: Involving People in Quality & Productivity Improvement. 180p. 1988. pap. text 21.50 (*0-527-91626-9*, 916269) Productivity Inc.

Aubrey, Crispin. Nukespeak, the Media & the Bomb. LC 83-101127. (Comedia/Minority Press Group Ser.). vii, 135p. 1982. write for info. (*0-906890-26-8*) Routledge.

Aubrey, D. G., jt. auth. see Emery, K. O.

Aubrey, David G. & Friedrichs, C. T., eds. Buoyancy Effects on Coastal & Estuarine Dynamics. LC 96-38037. (Coastal & Estuarine Studies: Vol. 53). 359p. 1996. 60.00 (*0-87590-267-7*) Am Geophysical.

Aubrey, David G. & Giese, Graham S., eds. Formation & Evolution of Multiple Tidal Inlets. LC 93-38051. (Coastal & Estuarine Ser.: Vol. 44). 1993. 35.00 (*0-87590-258-8*) Am Geophysical.

Aubrey, Elizabeth. The Music of the Troubadours. LC 96-10358. (Music: Scholarship & Performance Ser.). (Illus.). 352p. 1996. lib. bdg. 49.95 (*0-253-33207-9*) Ind U Pr.

***Aubrey, Elizabeth.** The Music of the Troubadours. (Illus.). 352p. 2000. pap. 24.95 (*0-253-21389-4*) Ind U Pr.

Aubrey-Fletcher, John. Sir John Aubrey, Sixth Baronet of Llantrithyd (1739-1826) 376p. 1988. 18.00 (*0-904920-15-1*, Pub. by Leopards Head Pr) David Brown.

Aubrey, Frank. A Queen of Atlantis: Romance of the Caribbean Sea. LC 74-15949. (Science Fiction Ser.). 394p. 1975. reprint ed. 33.95 (*0-405-06275-3*) Ayer.

Aubrey, Henry G. Coexistence: Economic Challenge & Response. LC 75-28675. 323p. 1976. reprint ed. lib. bdg. 69.50 (*0-8371-8471-1*, AUCO, Greenwood Pr) Greenwood.

— The Dollar in World Affairs: An Essay in International Financial Policy. LC 82-6086. 295p. 1982. reprint ed. lib. bdg. 65.00 (*0-313-23577-5*, AUDW, Greenwood Pr) Greenwood.

Aubrey, James R. John Fowles: A Reference Companion. LC 91-9553. 344p. 1991. lib. bdg. 59.95 (*0-313-26399-X*, AJW, Greenwood Pr) Greenwood.

— John Fowles & Nature: Fourteen Perspectives on Landscape. LC 98-47658. 1999. write for info. (*0-8386-3796-5*) Fairleigh Dickinson.

Aubrey, John. Aubrey's Brief Lives. Dick, Oliver L., ed. LC 95-35331. (Nonpareil Bks.: Vol. 77). (Illus.). 514p. 1999. 20.95 (*1-56792-063-2*) Godine.

***Aubrey, John.** Brief Lives. (Penguin Classics Ser.). 608p. 2000. pap. 15.00 (*0-14-043589-1*, Penguin Bks) Viking Penguin.

Aubrey, John. Brief Lives. Barber, Richard, ed. 336p. 1998. reprint ed. pap. 24.95 (*0-85115-206-6*) Boydell & Brewer.

— Monumenta Britannica. Fowles, John, ed. 1982. 125.00 (*0-316-05908-0*); 250.00 (*0-316-05907-2*) Little.

— Remaines of Gentilisme & Judaisme, Sixteen Hundred Eighty-Six to Eighty-Seven. Britten, James, ed. (Folk-Lore Society, London Monographs: Vol. 4). 1974. reprint ed. pap. 35.00 (*0-8115-0501-4*) Periodicals Srv.

— Three Prose Works. Buchanan-Brown, John, ed. Incl. Miscelanies. LC 77-183306. 1972. Observations. LC 77-183306. 1972. Remaines of Gentilisme & Judaisme. LC 77-183306. 1972. LC 77-183306. (Centaur Classics Ser.). 624p. 1972. 35.00 (*0-8093-0567-4*) S Ill U Pr.

Aubrey, K., ed. see Schulenberg, T. S.

Aubrey, Karen, ed. see Frey, Joseph, III.

Aubrey, Lisa M. The Politics of Development Co-Operation: Ngos, Gender & Partnership in Kenya. LC 97-14343. (Routledge Studies in Development & Society). (Illus.). 256p. (C). 1997. 75.00 (*0-415-15185-6*) Routledge.

Aubrey, Philip. Mr. Secretary Thurloe: Cromwell's Secretary of State, 1652-1660. LC 89-45379. 272p. 1990. 38.50 (*0-8386-3388-9*) Fairleigh Dickinson.

Aubrey, Pierre. Trouveres et Troubadours. 2nd ed. 223p. 1981. reprint ed. 50.00 (*3-487-07119-3*) G Olms Pubs.

Aubry, Arthur S., Jr. & Caputo, Rudolph R. Criminal Interrogation. 3rd ed. 464p. 1980. 73.95 (*0-398-03978-X*); pap. 56.95 (*0-398-06010-X*) C C Thomas.

Aubry Costello, Mary C., contrib. by. Climbing the Mississippi River Bridge by Bridge. LC 94-96856. (Illus.). 216p. (Orig.). 1995. 39.95 (*0-9644518-1-6*) Aubry Costello.

— Climbing the Mississippi River Bridge by Bridge, Vol. I. LC 94-96856. (Illus.). 200p. (Orig.). 1995. pap. text 24.95 (*0-9644518-0-8*) Aubry Costello.

Aubry, Francoise & Vandenbreeden, Jos, eds. Horta: Art Nouveau to Modernism. LC 97-150453. (Illus.). 232p. 1997. 60.00 (*0-8109-6333-7*, Pub. by Abrams) Time Warner.

Aubry, Joseph. Savio: A Study Guide for Parents, Priests & Educators. Boenzi, Joe, tr. from ITA. LC 79-50460. 69p. (Orig.). 1979. pap. 2.50 (*0-89944-038-X*) Salesiana Pubs.

Aubry, Lloyd W., Jr. California Wage & Hour Guide. 375p. 1990. ring bd. 87.50 (*1-881024-01-6*) Employers Grp.

Aubry, M. Homotopy Theory & Models. (DMV Seminar Ser.: Vol. 24). 117p. 1995. pap. 33.00 (*3-7643-5185-3*) Birkhauser.

Aubry, M. P. Handbook of Cenozoic Calcareous Nannoplankton, 9 vols., Set. 1985. 550.00 (*0-685-73533-8*) Am Mus Natl Hist.

Aubry, Marc, ed. see Baues, Hans J., et al.

***Aubry, Marie-Pierre.** Late Paleocene - Early Eocene Biotic & Climatic Events in the Marine & Terrestrial Records. LC 98-20969. (Illus.). 528p. 1998. 100.00 (*0-231-10238-0*) Col U Pr.

Aubry, Pam. Youth for Youth Staying Free. 20p. (J). (gr. 1-2). 1990. pap. 2.22 (*0-914127-50-0*) Univ Class.

Aubry, Pierre. Cent Motets du XIIIe Siecle, 3 vols. (FRE., Illus.). 540p. 1964. reprint ed. pap. 150.00 (*0-8450-0001-2*) Broude.

***Aubry-Westergaard.** Collegiate Communication. 166p. (C). 2000. 35.95 (*0-7872-7151-9*) Kendall-Hunt.

Aubuchon, James P. & Issitt, Linda A., eds. Limiting Donor Exposure in Hemotherapy. LC 94-32345. (Illus.). 99p. (C). 1994. 40.00 (*1-56395-030-8*) Am Assn Blood.

AuBuchon, James P., jt. ed. see Allen, Robert W.

Aubuchon, Norbert. The Anatomy of Persuasion: How to Persuade Others to Act on Your Ideas... LC 96-51050. 208p. (Orig.). 1997. pap. 17.95 (*0-8144-7952-9*) AMACOM.

Auburger, Leopold. Sprachvarianten und Ihr Status in Den Sprachsystemen. (Philosophische Texte und Studien: Vol. 36). (GER.). iv, 382p. 1993. write for info. (*3-487-09768-0*) G Olms Pubs.

Auburn, David. Skyscraper. 1998. pap. 5.25 (*0-8222-1652-3*) Dramatists Play.

Auburn, Jill S., ed. see Campidonica, Mark.

***Auburn, Jonathan.** Legal Professional Privilege: Law & Theory. 288p. 2000. 54.00 (*1-84113-101-6*, Pub. by Hart Pub) Intl Spec Bk.

Auburn, Mark S. Sheridan's Comedies: Their Contexts & Achievements. LC 77-7205. 231p. reprint ed. pap. 71.70 (*0-7837-6459-6*, 204646300001) Bks Demand.

Auburn, Mark S., ed. see Dryden, John.

Auburn University, Department of Architecture Staf, jt. ed. see Birmingham Historical Society Staff.

Auburn University English Department Staff. Guidelines & Suggested Syllabus for EH 110, 1999-00. 65p. (C). pap. text 4.95 (*0-89892-201-1*) Contemp Pub Co of Raleigh.

Auburn University Staff. Winter. (Nursing Texts Ser.). (C). (gr. 13). 1996. text 165.95 (*0-8151-4499-7*, 30629) Mosby Inc.

Aubu, pseud. Gita Runnin' Da Sweetman Iz Comin' 'n' Da Rappers Be Rhymein' A Fool's Guide for Livin' LC 98-70603. 133 p. 1998. write for info. (*0-9663227-0-3*) J L Clark.

Aubyn, Lorna St. Everyday Rituals & Ceremonies: Special Ways to Mark Important Events in Your Life. 1999. pap. 14.95 (*0-7499-1927-2*, Pub. by Piatkus Bks) London Brdge.

Aucamp, A. J. Bilingual Education & Nationalism with Special Reference to South Africa. Cordasco, Francesco, ed. LC 77-90405. (Bilingual-Bicultural Education in the U. S. Ser.). 1978. reprint ed. lib. bdg. 26.95 (*0-405-11074-X*) Ayer.

Auch, Mary J. Angel & Me. (J). 1989. 9.95 (*0-316-05914-5*) Little.

— Angel & Me & the Bayside Bombers. (Illus.). (J). (gr. 2-4). 1991. pap. 2.95 (*0-316-05915-3*) Little.

— Bantam of the Opera. LC 96-40169. (Illus.). 32p. (J). (gr. k-3). 1997. lib. bdg. 16.95 (*0-8234-1312-8*) Holiday.

— Bird Dogs Can't Fly. LC 93-2746. (Illus.). (J). (gr. k-3). 1993. lib. bdg. 15.95 (*0-8234-1050-1*) Holiday.

— The Easter Egg Farm. LC 91-15681. (Illus.). 32p. (J). (gr. k-3). 1992. lib. bdg. 16.95 (*0-8234-0917-1*) Holiday.

— The Easter Egg Farm. LC 91-15681. (Illus.). (J). (gr. 4-7). 1992. pap. 6.95 (*0-8234-1076-5*) Holiday.

— The Easter Egg Farm. (Egg Ser.). (Illus.). (J). (gr. k-3). 24.95 incl. audio (*0-87499-344-X*); pap. 15.95 incl. audio (*0-87499-343-1*) Live Oak Media.

— The Easter Egg Farm, Set. (Egg Ser.). (Illus.). (J). (gr. k-3). pap. 37.95 incl. audio (*0-87499-345-8*) Live Oak Media.

— Eggs Mark the Spot. LC 95-44930. (Illus.). 32p. (J). (gr. k-3). 1996. 16.95 (*0-8234-1242-3*) Holiday.

— Eggs Mark the Spot. (Egg Ser.). (J). (gr. k-3). 1997. pap., teacher ed. 37.95 incl. audio (*0-87499-389-X*) Live Oak Media.

— Eggs Mark the Spot. unabridged ed. (Egg Ser.). (J). (gr. k-3). 1997. 24.95 incl. audio (*0-87499-388-1*) Live Oak Media.

— Frozen Summer. LC 98-23485. (J). (gr. 3-7). 1998. 15.95 (*0-8050-4923-1*, Bks Young Read) H Holt & Co.

— Hen Lake. (Illus.). 32p. (J). (gr. k-3). 1995. pap. 6.95 (*0-8234-1270-9*); lib. bdg. 16.95 (*0-8234-1188-5*) Holiday.

— I Was a Third Grade Science Project. LC 97-41996. (Illus.). 96p. (J). (gr. 2-5). 1980. 15.95 (*0-8234-1357-8*) Holiday.

— Journey to Nowhere. 208p. (J). 1998. pap. 4.50 (*0-440-41491-1*) BDD Bks Young Read.

— Journey to Nowhere. LC 96-42249. (J). (gr. 4-7). 1997. 15.95 (*0-8050-4922-3*) H Holt & Co.

— Monster Brother. LC 93-41746. (Illus.). 32p. (J). (gr. k-3). 1994. lib. bdg. 15.95 (*0-8234-1095-1*) Holiday.

— Moving On. 190p. 1996. 14.95 (*0-8050-4921-5*) H Holt & Co.

— Peeping Beauty. (Illus.). 32p. (J). (gr. k-3). 1993. pap. 6.95 (*0-8234-1170-2*) Holiday.

— Peeping Beauty. LC 92-16374. (Illus.). 32p. (J). (gr. k-3). 1993. lib. bdg. 16.95 (*0-8234-1001-3*) Holiday.

— Peeping Beauty. (Illus.). (J). (gr. k-4). 24.95 incl. audio (*0-87499-327-X*) Live Oak Media.

— Peeping Beauty, 4 bks., Set. (Illus.). (J). (gr. k-4). pap. 37.95 incl. audio (*0-87499-328-8*) Live Oak Media.

— Seven Long Years until College. LC 91-2094. 176p. (J). (gr. 4-6). 1991. 13.95 (*0-8234-0901-5*) Holiday.

— Seven Long Years until College. Clancy, Lisa, ed. 176p. (YA). (gr. 3-6). 1994. reprint ed. pap. 2.99 (*0-671-78140-5*, Minstrel Bks) PB.

— A Sudden Change of Family. MacDonald, Patricia, ed. 160p. (J). (gr. 3-6). 1993. reprint ed. pap. 2.99 (*0-671-74892-0*, Minstrel Bks) PB.

Auch, Mary J. & Live Oak Media Staff. Eggs Mark the Spot. unabridged ed. (Egg Ser.). (J). (gr. k-3). 1997. pap. 15.95 incl. audio (*0-87499-387-3*) Live Oak Media.

Auch, Mary Jane. Eggs Mark the Spot. (Illus.). (J). (gr. k-3). 1996. reprint ed. pap. text 6.95 (*0-8234-1305-5*) Holiday.

***Auch, Mary Jane.** Frozen Summer. (Illus.). 208p. (J). (gr. 5-9). 2000. pap. 4.50 (*0-440-41624-8*, Yearling) BDD Bks Young Read.

— Frozen Summer. (Illus.). (J). 2000. 9.85 (*0-606-18783-9*) Turtleback.

Auch, Mary Jane. I Was a Third Grade Science Project. 112p. (J). (gr. 2-5). 1999. pap. 4.50 (*0-440-41606-X*) Bantam.

— Noah's Aardvark. 32p. 1999. 9.95 (*0-307-10229-7*) Golden Bks Pub.

— The Nutquacker. LC 99-18347. (Illus.). 32p. (J). (gr. k-3). 1999. 16.95 (*0-8234-1524-4*) Holiday.

— Peeping Beauty. (Illus.). (J). (gr. k-4). pap. 15.95 incl. audio (*0-87499-326-1*) Live Oak Media.

Auch, Ron. He Hears Your Prayers: Simple Steps to God. LC 98-66302. 144p. 1998. pap. 9.99 (*0-89221-423-6*) New Leaf.

— The Heart of the King. LC 94-68844. 192p. (Orig.). 1995. 12.95 (*0-89221-278-0*) New Leaf.

— Prayer Can Change Your Marriage. rev. ed. LC 90-63496. 176p. 1990. pap. 8.95 (*0-89221-118-0*) New Leaf.

Auch, Ron. Secret Place: Untying the Love Letters from the Song of Songs. LC 99-69240. Date not set. pap. 10.99 (*0-89221-490-2*) New Leaf.

Auch, Ron. The Seven Spirits of God. LC 93-84462. 192p. 1993. pap. 9.95 (*0-89221-238-1*) New Leaf.

— Swept Away: Refreshing the Church with the Power of Prayer. LC 97-75891. 160p. 1998. pap. 11.99 (*0-89221-377-9*) New Leaf.

— Taught by the Spirit. LC 90-64184. 232p. (Orig.). 1991. pap. 9.95 (*0-89221-191-1*) New Leaf.

— Unshakable Man: A Stable Spiritual Force in the Home. LC 95-73134. 160p. 1996. pap. 9.95 (*0-89221-323-X*) New Leaf.

***Auch, Ron.** When He Appears. 2000. pap. 9.99 (*0-89221-498-8*) New Leaf.

Auch, Ron & Crone, John. Church in Crisis. LC 90-61176. 176p. 1990. pap. 6.95 (*0-89221-181-4*) New Leaf.

Auchard, John. Silence in Henry James: The Heritage of Symbolism & Decadence. LC 85-21750. 192p. 1986. 28.50 (*0-271-00420-7*) Pa St U Pr.

Auchard, John, ed. see James, Henry.

Auchard, John, ed. & intro. see James, Henry.

Auchincloss, Hugh, jt. ed. see Bach, Fritz H.

Auchincloss, Louis. The Anniversary & Other Stories. LC 99-18697. 208p. 1999. 25.00 (*0-395-97074-1*) HM.

— Collected Stories of Louis Auchincloss. 482p. 1998. reprint ed. 34.95 (*0-7351-0051-9*) Replica Bks.

An Asterisk (*) at the beginning of an entry indicates that the title is appearing for the first time.

— Ellen Glasgow. LC 64-63338. (University of Minnesota Pamphlets on American Writers Ser.: No. 33). 48p. reprint ed. pap. 30.00 (*0-608-14140-2*, 205592900039) Bks Demand.

***Auchincloss, Louis.** The Embezzler. LC 00-25567. 325p. 2000. 32.95 (*0-7658-0778-5*) Transaction Pubs.

Auchincloss, Louis. The Embezzler. 1993. reprint ed. lib. bdg. 21.95 (*1-56849-151-4*) Buccaneer Bks.

— La Gloire: The Roman Empire of Corneille & Racine. LC 96-33634. 110p. 1996. 19.95 (*1-57003-122-3*) U of SC Pr.

— Henry Adams. LC 70-633322. (University of Minnesota Pamphlets on American Writers Ser.: No. 93). 48p. (Orig.). reprint ed. pap. 30.00 (*0-7837-2900-6*, 205755500006) Bks Demand.

***Auchincloss, Louis.** Her Infinite Variety. LC 99-47302. 224p. 2000. 25.00 (*0-618-02191-4*) HM.

Auchincloss, Louis. The House of the Prophet. 343p. 1990. pap. 21.95 (*0-88738-857-4*) Transaction Pubs.

— J. P. Morgan: The Financier As Collector. (Illus.). 144p. 1990. 45.00 (*0-8109-3610-0*, Pub. by Abrams) Time Warner.

— Louis Auchincloss: Family Fortunes Three Collected Novels. 1993. 11.98 (*0-88365-825-9*) Galahad Bks.

— Love Without Wings: Some Friendships in Literature & Politics. 187p. 1999. reprint ed. pap. text 19.00 (*0-7881-6266-7*) DIANE Pub.

— Pioneers & Caretakers: A Study of Nine American Women Novelists. LC 65-17016. 208p. reprint ed. pap. 64.50 (*0-608-16700-2*, 205619700055) Bks Demand.

— Reading Henry James. LC 74-25934. (Illus.). 189p. reprint ed. pap. 58.60 (*0-8357-7001-X*, 203320000085) Bks Demand.

— The Rector of Justin. 1999. pap. write for info. (*0-375-75323-0*) Modern Lib NY.

— Sybil. LC 75-108840. 284p. 1972. reprint ed. lib. bdg. 35.00 (*0-8371-3728-4*, AUSY, Greenwood Pr) Greenwood.

— Tales of Yesteryear. large type ed. LC 94-4250. 320p. 1994. lib. bdg. 22.95 (*0-7862-0235-1*) Thorndike Pr.

— Three "Perfect Novels" - & What They Have in Common. limited ed. 1981. 20.00 (*0-89723-025-6*) Bruccoli.

***Auchincloss, Louis.** Woodrow Wilson: A Penguin Life. LC 99-46890. (Penguin Lives Ser.). 128p. 2000. 19.95 (*0-670-88904-0*, Viking) Viking Penguin.

Auchly, William J., et al. A Pictorial History of Montgomery County: One Hundred & Seventy-Five Years, 1818-1993. LC 93-29511. (Illus.). 1993. write for info. (*0-89865-878-0*) Donning Co.

Auchmutey, Jim, et al, eds. True South: Travels Through a Land of White Columns, Black-eyed Peas & Redneck Bars. LC 93-81148. (Illus.). 192p. 1994. pap. 12.95 (*1-56352-136-9*) Longstreet.

Auchmutey, Jim & Puckett, Susan. The Ultimate Barbecue Sauce Cookbook: Your Guide to the Best Sauce, Rubs, Sops, Mops, & Marinades. 1995. 14.95 (*1-56352-201-2*) Longstreet.

Auchmuty, Rosemary. Women & the Family Home. 63.95 (*1-85521-744-9*) Ashgate Pub Co.

Auchmuty, Rosemary. A World of Girls: The Appeal of the Girls' School Story. pap. 17.95 (*0-7043-4310-X*, Pub. by Womens Press) Trafalgar.

***Auchmuty, Rosemary.** A World of Woman: Growing Up in the Girls' School Story. (J). 2000. pap. 17.95 (*0-7043-4538-2*, Pub. by Womens Press) Trafalgar.

***Auchmuty, Rosemary & Wotton, Joy.** The Encyclopaedia of School Stories. LC 99-42635. 2000. write for info. (*0-7546-0082-3*, Pub. by Ashgate Pub); write for info. (*0-7546-0083-1*, Pub. by Ashgate Pub) Ashgate Pub Co.

Auchter, Dorothy. Dictionary of Historical Allusions & Eponyms. LC 98-19641. ix, 295 p. 1998. pap. write for info. (*1-57607-099-9*) ABC-CLIO.

— Dictionary of Historical Allusions & Eponyms. LC 98-19641. 295p. 1998. lib. bdg. 65.00 (*0-87436-950-9*) ABC-CLIO.

Auchter, Norma, jt. auth. see Albarez, Paul.

Auchter, Norma, jt. auth. see Alvarez, Paul.

Auchter, Terri. Almost Coping. LC 83-61876. (Illus.). 160p. 1983. pap. 2.95 (*0-931762-20-0*) Phunn Pubs.

Auchterlonie, Paul, ed. Yemen. 2nd rev. ed. LC 98-137613. (World Bibliographical Ser.: Vol. 50). 372p. 1998. lib. bdg. 91.00 (*1-85109-255-2*) ABC-CLIO.

Auciello, Orlando, et al, eds. In Situ Process Diagnostics & Modelling Vol. 569: Materials Research Society Symposium Proceedings. LC 99-41788. 199p. 1999. text 70.00 (*1-55899-476-9*) Materials Res.

Auciello, Orlando, et al, eds. Plasma-Surface Interactions & Processing of Materials. (Proceedings of the NATO Advanced Study Institute on Carbon Fibers & Filamets Held in Alvor, Portugal, May 15-27, 1989 Ser.). (C). 1990. text 285.00 (*0-7923-0584-1*) Kluwer Academic.

Auciello, Orlando & Engemann, Jurgen, eds. Multicomponent & Multilayered Thin Films for Advanced Microtechnologies: Techniques, Fundamentals, & Devices. LC 93-20488. (NATO Advanced Study Institutes Series E, Applied Sciences: Vol. 234). 1993. text 339.00 (*0-7923-2265-7*) Kluwer Academic.

Auciello, Orlando & Flamm, Daniel L., eds. Plasma Diagnostics, Vol. 2. (Plasma Materials Interactions Ser.). 337p. 1989. text 146.00 (*0-12-067636-2*) Acad Pr.

Auckenthaler, Karlheinz F. Numinoses und Heiliges in der Osterreichischen Literatur. (GER.). 1995. 62.95 (*3-906753-88-3*) P Lang Pubng.

— Sympaian: Jahrbuch der Internationalen Franz Werfel-Gesellschaft, I/96. (Schriften der Internationalen Franz Werfel-Gesellschaft Ser.: Bd. 1). (GER., Illus.). 270p. 1997. 34.95 (*3-906759-02-4*, Pub. by P Lang) P Lang Pubng.

Aucker, Robert S., jt. auth. see Lilley, Linda L.

Auckett, Amelia. Baby Massage: Parent-Child Bonding Through Touch. rev. ed. LC 82-2172. (Illus.). 128p. 1994. pap. 11.95 (*1-55704-022-2*, Pub. by Newmarket) Norton.

Auckland City Art Gallery Staff. Advance Australian Painting. (Illus.). 106p. 1991. pap. 24.95 (*0-86463-164-2*) U of Wash Pr.

Auckland, Jim. Pirates Ahoy! (Doodle Art Mini Tubes Ser.). (J). (gr. k up). 1997. pap. 6.95 (*0-8431-6563-4*, Price Stern) Peng Put Young Read.

Auckland, Martha. Pinball Pandemonium. (Doodle Art Medium Tubes Ser.). (J). (gr. k up). 1997. pap. 8.95 (*0-8431-6569-3*, Price Stern) Peng Put Young Read.

Auclair, jt. auth. see Ellis.

Auclair, jt. auth. see Ellis, Albert.

Auclair, D. & Dupraz, Christian. Agroforestry for Sustainable Land-Use: Fundamental Research & Modelling with Emphasis on Temperate & Mediterrean Applications: Selected Papers from a Workshop Held in Montpellier, France, 23-29 June 1997 LC 99-29490. 1999. write for info. (*0-7923-5799-X*) Kluwer Academic.

Auclair, Marcelle. St. Teresa of Avila. Pond, Kathleen, tr. from FRE. LC 53-6126. (Illus.). 454p. 1988. reprint ed. pap. 18.95 (*0-932506-67-4*) St Bedes Pubns.

AuClaire, Philip, jt. ed. see Schwartz, Ira M.

Aucoin, David. Target: The Antimicrobial Reference Guide to Effective Treatment. (Illus.). 161p. (Orig.). 1994. pap. 85.00 (*1-889750-04-2*); disk 35.00 (*1-889750-05-0*) Nrth Amer Compendiums.

Aucoin, James. Water in Nebraska: Use, Politics, Policies. LC 83-12512. (Illus.). 183p. 1984. reprint ed. pap. 56.80 (*0-608-02667-0*, 206332000004) Bks Demand.

Aucoin, Kevin. The Art of Makeup. 176p. 1996. pap. 35.00 (*0-06-273042-8*) HarpC.

***Aucoin, Kevyn.** Face Forward. (Illus.). 176p. 2000. 32.95 (*0-316-28644-3*) Little.

Aucoin, Kevyn. Making Faces. LC 97-12658. (Illus.). 160p. (gr. 8). 1997. 29.95 (*0-316-28686-9*) Little.

— Making Faces. 1998. write for info. (*0-316-28641-9*) Little.

***Aucoin, Kevyn.** Making Faces. 160p. 1999. pap. 20.00 (*0-316-28685-0*) Little.

Aucoin, Kevyn, jt. auth. see Oldham, Todd.

AuCoin, Michelle, et al, eds. Papers from the 32nd Regional Meeting of the Chicago Linguistic Society Vol. 2: The Parasession on Theory & Data in Linguistics. 1996. write for info. (*0-914203-51-7*) Chicago Ling.

Aucoin, Peter. The New Public Management Canada in Comparative. 280p. 1996. pap. 19.95 (*0-88645-180-9*, Pub. by Inst Res Pub) Ashgate Pub Co.

Aucot-Yee, Eisa. A Victorian Wedding Planner. 2nd rev. ed. (Illus.). 1979. pap. write for info. (*0-9634211-9-0*) Lheure Victorian.

Aucsmith, D., et al, eds. Information Hiding II: 2nd International Workshop, IH '98, Portland, Oregon, U. S. A., April 14-17, 1998, Proceedings, Vol. # 152. LC 98-52803. (Lecture Notes in Computer Science Ser.: Vol. 1525). 369p. 1998. 59.00 (*3-540-65386-4*) Spr-Verlag.

Aucutt, Janet, jt. ed. see Finn, Marie T.

Aucutt, Ronald D. & Zaritsky, Howard M. Structuring Estate Freezes: Analysis with Forms. 2nd ed. LC 96-61587. 1997. pap. 155.00 incl. disk (*0-7913-2955-0*, SEF) Warren Gorham & Lamont.

Auda, Antoine. Les Modes et les Tons de la Musique et Specialement de la Musique Medievale. (Academie Royale De Belgique. Classe Des Beaux-Arts Collection: Vol. 3, Fasc. 1). 203p. 1979. reprint ed. lib. bdg. 40.00 (*3-487-06852-4*) G Olms Pubs.

Audah, Abdul Q. Islam Between Ignorant Followers & Incapable Scholars. 1990. pap. 5.50 (*1-56744-078-9*) Kazi Pubns.

Audah, Abdul Q. Islam Between Ignorant Followers & Incapable Scholars. 115p. pap. 3.50 (*0-939830-01-9*, Pub. by IIFSO KW) New Era Publns MI.

***Audain, Anne.** Uncommon Heart: One Woman's Triumph. 272p. 2000. 23.00 (*0-915297-27-2*, Pub. by Cedarwinds) Midpt Trade.

Audax & Adams, Vyvyon. Men in Our Time. LC 70-99680. (Essay Index Reprint Ser.). 1977. 23.95 (*0-8369-1389-2*) Ayer.

Aude, Karen. Sophisticated Surfaces: Ideas & Inspirations from Fifteen Professional Surface Painters. (Illus.). 160p. 1998. 35.00 (*1-56496-483-3*) Rockport Pubs.

Aude, Olga. Cocina Para Diabeticos. 1997. pap. text 8.98 (*970-643-124-1*) Selector.

Audebert, A., jt. ed. see Emperaire, J. C.

Audeh, Ida, jt. auth. see Lariviere, Katherine.

Audeh, Ida, jt. ed. see Lariviere, Katherine.

Auden, Amy. Wow! 324p. 1996. pap. 19.95 (*1-85158-694-6*, Pub. by Mainstream Pubng) Trafalgar.

Auden, Garrett, jt. auth. see Auden, W. H.

Auden, H. W. Greek Phrase Book. 128p. 1990. reprint ed. pap. text 14.95 (*0-89341-624-X*, Longwood Academic) Hollowbrook.

Auden, H. W., tr. see Meissner, C.

Auden, H. W., tr. see Messiner, C.

Auden, W. H. As I Walked Out One Evening: Songs, Ballads, Lullabies, Limericks, & Other Light Verse. LC 95-5428. 256p. 1995. pap. 12.00 (*0-679-76170-5*) Random.

— Collected Poems. LC 90-50192. (Vintage International Ser.). 960p. 1991. pap. 22.50 (*0-679-73197-0*) Vin Bks.

— Complete Works Auden Series. (C). write for info. (*0-691-06772-4*) Princeton U Pr.

— Complete Works of W. H. Auden, Vols. VII-VIII: Complete Poetry. 1988. 39.50 (*0-691-06804-6*, Pub. by Princeton U Pr) Cal Prin Full Svc.

— Dyer's Hand & Other Essays. LC 90-50192. 1990. pap. 18.00 (*0-679-72484-2*) Vin Bks.

— The Enchafed Flood: or The Romantic Iconography of the Sea. LC PN0056.S4A8. 160p. reprint ed. pap. 49.60 (*0-608-08558-8*, 206908100002) Bks Demand.

— Forewords & Afterwords. 1990. pap. 15.00 (*0-679-72485-0*) Vin Bks.

— In Solitude, for Company: W. H. Auden after 1940: Unpublished Prose & Recent Criticism. Bucknell, Katherine & Jenkins, Nicholas, eds. (Auden Studies: Vol. 3). 352p. 1996. text 75.00 (*0-19-818294-5*) OUP.

Auden, W. H. Juvenilia: Poems, 1922-1928. Bucknell, Katherine, ed. LC 93-35485. 336p. (C). 1994. text 35.00 (*0-691-03415-X*, Pub. by Princeton U Pr) Cal Prin Full Svc.

Auden, W. H. The Language of Learning & the Language of Love: Uncollected Writings, New Interpretations. Jenkins, Nicholas & Bucknell, Katherine, eds. (Illus.). 302p. 1995. text 32.00 (*0-19-812257-8*) OUP.

***Auden, W. H.** Lectures on Shakespeare. Kirsch, Arthur, ed. LC 00-28479. (W. H. Auden--Critical Editions Ser.). 452p. 2001. 29.95 (*0-691-05730-3*) Princeton U Pr.

Auden, W. H. The Map of All My Youth: Early Works, Friends, & Influences. Bucknell, Katherine & Jenkins, Nicholas, eds. (Auden Studies Ser.). 256p. (C). 1990. text 65.00 (*0-19-812964-5*) OUP.

— The Orators: An English Study. reprint ed. lib. bdg. 39.00 (*0-7812-0289-2*) Rprt Serv.

— The Orators: An English Study. LC 77-131613. 116p. 1932. reprint ed. 39.00 (*0-403-00500-0*) Scholarly.

— The Platonic Blow & My Epitaph. LC 85-339. 8p. 1985. pap. 5.00 (*0-914061-04-6*) Orchises Pr.

Auden, W. H. Poems: Auden. 1995. 12.50 (*0-679-44367-3*) Knopf.

Auden, W. H. Prolific & the Devourer. LC 93-2409. 1993. 18.00 (*0-88001-345-1*) HarpC.

— The Prolific And The Devourer. (Illus.). 101p. 1996. reprint ed. pap. 11.00 (*0-88001-465-2*) HarpC.

— Prose & Travel Books in Prose & Verse. Mendelson, Edward, ed. LC 95-38162. (Complete Works of W. H. Auden: Vol. 1). (Illus.). 952p. 1997. text 59.50 (*0-691-06803-8*, Pub. by Princeton U Pr) Cal Prin Full Svc.

— Tell Me the Truth about Love: Ten Poems. 1994. pap. 6.00 (*0-679-75782-1*) Vin Bks.

— W. H. Auden, Poems, 1927-1929: A Photographic & Typographic Facsimile of the Original Notebook in the Berg Collection of English & American Literature. limited ed. Jenkins, Nicholas, ed. (Harcourt Brace Jovanovich Fund Ser.: No. 3). (Illus.). 142p. 1989. 95.00 (*0-87104-415-3*) NY Pub Lib.

Auden, W. H., ed. Portable Greek Reader. (Portable Library: No. 39). 726p. 1977. pap. 15.95 (*0-14-015039-0*, P39, Penguin Bks) Viking Penguin.

— Van Gogh: A Self-Portrait. (Illus.). 302p. 1994. pap. 12.00 (*1-56924-862-1*) Marlowe & Co.

Auden, W. H. & Auden, Garrett. The Poets Tongue. 1988. reprint ed. lib. bdg. 49.00 (*0-7812-0243-4*) Rprt Serv.

Auden, W. H. & Garrett, John, eds. The Poet's Tongue. LC 75-161942. 222p. 1935. reprint ed. 49.00 (*0-403-01326-7*) Scholarly.

Auden, W. H. & Isherwood, Christopher. On the Frontier: A Melodrama in Three Acts. LC 75-41011. (BCL Ser.: No. 2). reprint ed. 27.50 (*0-404-14638-4*) AMS Pr.

— Plays & Other Dramatic Writings by W. H. Auden, 1928-1938, Vol. I. Mendelson, Edward, ed. 544p. 1989. text 69.50 (*0-691-06740-6*, Pub. by Princeton U Pr) Cal Prin Full Svc.

Auden, W. H. & Kallman, Chester. W. H. Auden & Chester Kallman: Libretti & Other Dramatic Writings by W. H. Auden, 1939-1973, Set. Mendelson, Edward, ed. LC 92-18681. 823p. 1993. text 65.00 (*0-691-03301-3*, Pub. by Princeton U Pr) Cal Prin Full Svc.

Auden, W. H. & Pearson, Norman H., eds. Poets of the English Language Vol. 4: Romantic Poets. (Portable Library: No. 52). 576p. 1977. pap. 15.95 (*0-14-015052-8*, P52, Penguin Bks) Viking Penguin.

Auden, W. H., et al. Authors Take Sides on the Spanish Civil War. 1971. 59.95 (*0-87968-680-4*) Gordon Pr.

Auden, W. H., jt. auth. see Jung, C. G.

Auden, W. H., jt. ed. see Greenberg, Noah.

Auden, W. H., ed. see Kierkegaard, Soren.

Auden, W. H., ed. see Wilde, Oscar, et al.

Auden, W. H., tr. see Brecht, Bertolt.

Auden, W. H., tr. see Goethe, Johann Wolfgang Von.

Auden, W. H., tr. see Goldoni, Carlo.

Auden, W. H., tr. see Lagerkvist, Par.

Auden, W. H., tr. & frwd. see Goethe, Johann Wolfgang Von.

Auderieth, Steven. Limited Liability Companies: Complete Planning & Practice Guide. 1994. 195.00 (*0-614-00560-4*); ring bd. 195.00 (*1-55645-021-4*, 500004) Busn Legal Reports.

Audesirk. Biology. 4th ed. 1996. text. write for info. (*0-13-377987-4*) Allyn.

Audesirk. Biology: Life on Earth & Audesirk Interactive. 5th ed. 1999. 72.00 (*0-13-083268-5*) P-H.

***Audesirk.** Life on Earth. 2nd ed. 1999. suppl. ed. write for info. (*0-13-018815-8*) P-H.

Audesirk. Print & Media Resources. 5th ed. 280p. (C). 1998. text, teacher ed. write for info. (*0-13-081036-3*) P-H.

Audesirk, Gerald, jt. auth. see Audesirk, Teresa.

Audesirk, Gerald, jt. auth. see Audesirk, Teresa E.

Audesirk, S. Life on Earth. 2nd ed. LC 99-30751. 728p. 1999. pap. text 68.00 incl. audio compact disk (*0-13-915687-9*, Pub. by P-H) S&S Trade.

Audesirk, Teresa E. & Audesirk, Gerald. Biology: Life on Earth. 5th ed. LC 98-23688. 947p. 1998. 90.67 incl. cd-rom (*0-13-792615-4*) P-H.

Audesirk, Teresa E. & Audesirk, Gerald. Biology: Life on Earth. 4th ed. LC 95-34325. 947p. 1995. text 88.00 (*0-13-368150-5*) P-H.

Audet, et al. Wrongful Dismissal in Quebec. 496p. 1990. pap. 83.00 (*0-89073-730-4*, MICHIE) LEXIS Pub.

Audet, Denis, ed. Market Access Issues in the Automobile Sector. LC 98-136145. 264p. 1997. pap. 32.00 (*92-64-15680-1*, 22-97-01-1, Pub. by Org for Econ) OECD.

Audett, Florentine, tr. see Doze, Andrew.

Audette. Neanderthin: Eat Like a Caveman to Achieve a Lean, Strong, Healthy Body. LC 99-36356. 256p. 1999. text 23.95 (*0-312-24338-3*) St Martin.

Audette, Anna H. The Blank Canvas: Inviting the Muse. LC 93-9524. (Illus.). 120p. (Orig.). 1993. pap. 14.00 (*0-87773-938-2*, Pub. by Shambhala Pubns) Random.

***Audette, Raymond V. & Gilchrist, Tony.** Neanderthin: Eat Like a Caveman to Achieve a Lean, Strong, Healthy Body. 2000. mass mkt. 6.99 (*0-312-97591-0*) St Martin.

Audette, Raymond V. & Gilchrist, Troy. Neander-Thin: A Caveman's Guide to Nutrition. 2nd ed. (Illus.). 112p. (Orig.). 1995. pap. 12.00 (*0-9646345-1-1*) Paleolithic Pr.

Audette, Susan T. & Baker, David E. The Old Town Canoe Company: Our First Hundred Years. LC 98-41658. (Illus.). 1998. 50.00 (*0-88448-202-2*); pap. 30.00 (*0-88448-203-0*) Tilbury House.

***Audette, Vicki & Graham, J. Tom.** Hal & Charlie: The Texas Peterson Brothers Who Risked a Fortune for a Hill Country Foundation. LC 00-28014. 2000. write for info. (*1-57168-387-9*, Eakin Pr) Sunbelt Media.

Audi. Belief, Justification & Knowledge. 2nd ed. (Philosophy Ser.). 2001. pap. 19.50 (*0-534-55116-5*) Wadsworth Pub.

Audi AG Staff. Audi a History of Progress: Chronicle of the Audi AG. (Illus.). 276p. 1997. 29.95 (*0-8376-0384-6*) Bentley Pubs.

Audi, Michael. The Interpretation of Quantum Mechanics. 2000. lib. bdg. 14.00 (*0-226-03177-2*) U Ch Pr.

— The Interpretation of Quantum Mechanics. LC 73-78663. 214p. reprint ed. pap. 66.40 (*0-608-30615-0*, 201995300015) Bks Demand.

Audi of America. Audi 4000S, 4000CS & Coupe GT Official Factory Repair Manual: 1984-1987, Including Quattro & Quattro Turbo. (Illus.). 1600p. 1989. 94.95 (*0-8376-0373-0*) Bentley Pubs.

— Audi 5000S, 5000CS Official Factory Repair Manual: 1984-1988 Gasoline, Turbo, & Turbo Diesel, Including Wagon & Quattro, 2 vols. (Illus.). 2240p. 1988. 139.95 (*0-8376-0370-6*) Bentley Pubs.

Audi of America, Inc. Staff. Audi 5000, 5000S Official Factory Repair Manual, Gasoline & Turbo Gasoline, Diesel & Turbo Diesel, 1977-1983. LC 83-71486. (Illus.). 992p. (Orig.). 1983. pap. 59.95 (*0-8376-0352-8*) Bentley Pubs.

— Audi 100, 200 Official Factory Repair Manual: 1989-1991 Including Quattro & 20-Valve, 3 vols. (Illus.). 1759p. 1992. 169.95 (*0-8376-0372-2*) Bentley Pubs.

— Audi 4000 Coupe Official Factory Repair Manual 1980 to 1983. LC 83-70221. (Illus.). 880p. (Orig.). 1983. pap. 59.95 (*0-8376-0349-8*) Bentley Pubs.

Audi of America, Inc. Staff, jt. auth. see Bentley, Robert, Inc. Staff.

Audi, Robert. Action, Intention, & Reason. 362p. 1994. text 49.95 (*0-8014-2866-1*); pap. text 19.95 (*0-8014-8105-8*) Cornell U Pr.

***Audi, Robert.** The Architecture of Reason: The Structure & Substance of Rationality. 304p. 2000. 35.00 (*0-19-514112-1*) OUP.

Audi, Robert. Epistemology: A Contemporary Introduction to the Theory of Knowledge. LC 97-11598. (Routledge Contemporary Introduction to Philosophy Ser.). 352p. (C). 1997. 70.00 (*0-415-13042-5*); pap. 20.99 (*0-415-13043-3*) Routledge.

— Moral Knowledge & Ethical Character. LC 96-36703. 320p. 1997. pap. 19.95 (*0-19-511469-8*); text 60.00 (*0-19-511468-X*) OUP.

***Audi, Robert.** Religious Commitment & Secular Reason. LC BL65.P7A84 2000. 272p. (C). 2000. text 54.95 (*0-521-77260-5*); pap. text 18.95 (*0-521-77570-1*) Cambridge U Pr.

Audi, Robert. The Structure of Justification. LC 92-37498. 493p. (C). 1993. pap. text 28.95 (*0-521-44612-0*) Cambridge U Pr.

— The Structure of Justification. LC 92-37498. 493p. (C). 1993. text 69.95 (*0-521-44064-5*) Cambridge U Pr.

Audi, Robert, ed. Action, Decision, & Intention. 134p. 1986. text 72.50 (*90-277-2274-9*, D Reidel) Kluwer Academic.

— The Cambridge Dictionary of Philosophy. 912p. 1995. text 89.95 (*0-521-40224-7*) Cambridge U Pr.

— The Cambridge Dictionary of Philosophy. 2nd ed. LC 99-12920. 1001p. 1999. 74.95 (*0-521-63136-X*); pap. 29.95 (*0-521-63722-8*) Cambridge U Pr.

Audi, Robert & Wolterstorff, Nicholas. Religion in the Public Square: Convictions in Political Debate. LC 96-44646. (Point/Counterpoint: Philosophers Debate Contemporary Issues Ser.: No. 94). 190p. 1997. 55.50 (*0-8476-8341-9*); pap. 17.95 (*0-8476-8342-7*) Rowman.

Audiard, Michel. La Nuit, le Jour et Toutes les Autres Nuits. (FRE.). 1980. pap. 10.95 (*0-7859-1917-1*, 2070372014) Fr & Eur.

Audibert, M. E., jt. ed. see Briaud, Jean-Louis.

Audiberti, Jacques. Abraxas. (FRE.). 289p. 1977. pap. 16.95 (*0-7859-2751-4*, 2070297756) Fr & Eur.

— Le Cavalier Seul. (FRE.). 256p. 1974. pap. 11.95 (*0-7859-1147-2*, 2070321304) Fr & Eur.

— Cent Jours. (FRE.). 288p. 1950. pap. 14.95 (*0-8288-9052-8*) Fr & Eur.

— Cosette, Set. (FRE.). 296p. 1965. pap. 39.95 (*0-7859-0358-5*, F83710) Fr & Eur.

— L' Empire et la Trappe. (FRE.). 192p. 1969. pap. 9.95 (*0-7859-0359-3*, F83730) Fr & Eur.

— Les Enfants Naturels. (FRE.). 126p. 1956. pap. 20.95 (*0-7859-0360-7*, F83740) Fr & Eur.

— Entretiens avec Georges Charbonnier. 176p. 1965. 11.95 (*0-7859-0361-5*, F83750) Fr & Eur.

A

An Asterisk (*) at the beginning of an entry indicates that the title is appearing for the first time.

A

— La Fin du Monde, Actes Sud, Labor, Aire. (FRE.). 112p. 1989. pap. 13.95 (*0-7859-3306-9*, 2868693628) Fr & Eur.
— Infanticide Preconise. (FRE.). 288p. 1958. pap. 32.95 (*0-7859-5371-X*) Fr & Eur.
— Les Jardins et les Fleuves. (FRE.). 400p. 1954. pap. 17.95 (*0-7859-1100-6*, 2070203417) Fr & Eur.
— La Logeuse. 14.95 (*0-686-54491-9*) Fr & Eur.
— Le Maitre de Milan. 264p. 1950. 9.95 (*0-7859-0362-3*, F83780) Fr & Eur.
— Marie Dubois. (FRE.). 288p. 1952. pap. 22.95 (*0-7859-0363-1*, F83800) Fr & Eur.
— Les Medecins de Sont pas des Plombiers. (FRE.). 200p. 1949. pap. 16.95 (*0-7859-0364-X*, F83810) Fr & Eur.
— Moliere. (FRE.). 144p. 1973. pap. 22.95 (*0-7859-0381-X*, M1621) Fr & Eur.
— Poesies, 1934-1943: La Pluie sur les Boulevards, Des Tonnes de Semences, Toujours. (FRE.). 266p. 1976. pap. 26.95 (*0-7859-1144-8*, 2070294765) Fr & Eur.
— La Poupee. (FRE.). 112p. 1969. pap. 9.95 (*0-7859-0365-8*, F83872) Fr & Eur.
— Quoat-Quoat. 9.95 (*0-686-54501-X*, FA790) Fr & Eur.
— Race des Hommes, l'Empire et la Trappe. (FRE.). 224p. 1968. pap. 12.95 (*0-7859-0366-6*, F83890) Fr & Eur.
— Rempart. (FRE.). 144p. 1953. pap. 28.95 (*0-7859-0367-4*, F83900) Fr & Eur.
— Le Retour du Divin. (FRE.). 1983. pap. 16.95 (*0-7859-2740-9*) Fr & Eur.
— Theatre, Vol. 4. (FRE.). 1970. pap. 39.95 (*0-7859-3957-1*, 2070203492) Fr & Eur.
— Theatre, Vol. 4. 1970. pap. 29.95 (*0-686-54507-9*) Fr & Eur.
— Theatre Vol. 1: Quoat-Quoat, l'Ampelour, les Femmes de Boeuf, la Mal Court. (FRE.). 200p. 1970. pap. 39.95 (*0-7859-0355-0*, F83650) Fr & Eur.
— Theatre Vol. 2: Pucelle, La Fete Noire, Les Naturels du Borelais. (FRE.). 312p. 1970. pap. 39.95 (*0-7859-0356-9*, F83651) Fr & Eur.
— Theatre Vol. 3: La Logeuse, Opera Parle, le Oullou, Aetanima. (FRE.). 264p. 1956. pap. 24.95 (*0-7859-0357-7*, F83652) Fr & Eur.
— Theatre Vol. 5: Pomme, Pomme, Pomme; Baton et Ruban; Boutique Fermee; La Brigitta. (FRE.). 264p. 1962. pap. 45.00 (*0-7859-3958-X*, 2070203506) Fr & Eur.
— Les Tombeaux Ferment Mal. (FRE.). 240p. 1963. pap. 24.95 (*0-7859-1101-4*, 2070203522) Fr & Eur.

Audiello, Massimo, text. David Salle. (Illus.). 80p. 1998. pap. 19.95 (*88-8158-145-0*, 810953, Pub. by Charta) Dist Art Pubs.

Audigier, Jean Y. Connections. 172p. (C). 1991. lib. bdg. 41.00 (*0-8191-8099-8*) U Pr of Amer.

Audin, M. The Topology of Torus Actions on Symplectic Manifolds. 181p. 1991. 73.00 (*0-8176-2602-6*) Birkhauser.

Audin, Michele. Spinning Tops: A Course on Integrable Systems. LC 96-11648. (Studies in Advanced Mathematics: No. 51). (Illus.). 145p. (C). 1996. text 39.95 (*0-521-56129-9*) Cambridge U Pr.
— Spinning Tops: A Course on Integrable Systems. (Cambridge Studies in Advanced Mathematics: No. 51). (Illus.). 147p. 1999. pap. 24.95 (*0-521-77919-7*) Cambridge U Pr.

Audin, Michele & Lafontaine, Jacques, eds. Holomorphic Curves in Symplectic Geometry. LC 93-48724. 328p. 1994. 74.50 (*0-8176-2997-1*) Birkhauser.

Audinarayan, N. Socio-Cultural Dimension of Marriage in Rural India. 1990. 32.50 (*81-7099-188-9*, Pub. by Mittal Pubs Dist) S Asia.

***Audinet, Pierre, ed.** India's Energy: Essays on Sustainable Development. 2000. 36.00 (*81-7304-351-5*, Pub. by Manohar) S Asia.

Audio. Audio Fall'98 Sampler. 1998. 20.00 (*0-676-57865-9*) Random.

Audio Amateur Magazine Staff, ed. Audio Amateur Loudspeaker Projects. LC 85-81547. (Illus.). 135p. 1985. pap. text 20.00 (*0-8338-0193-7*) Audio Amateur.

Audio-Forum Staff, et al. Brush up Your Shorthand. unabridged ed. 48p. 1989. 24.95 incl. audio (*0-88432-263-7*, S17070) Audio-Forum.

Audio Preservation Task Force Staff, jt. auth. see Dale, Robin.

Audio Vision Staff, ed. see Spence, Nancy.

Audirac, Ivonne, ed. Rural Sustainable Development in America. LC 96-34519. 448p. 1997. 99.00 (*0-471-15233-1*) Wiley.

Audirac, Ivonne & Zifou, Maria. Urban Development Issues: What Is Controversial in Urban Sprawl? (Bureau of Economic & Business Research Monographs). 52p. (Orig.). 1989. pap. text 12.00 (*0-930885-02-3*) Bur Econ & Bus Res.

Audiral, Ivonne, et al. Concurrency Management Systems in Florida: A Catalog & Analysis. (BEBR Monographs: Issue No. 7). 164p. (Orig.). 1992. pap. 15.00 (*0-930885-09-0*) Bur Econ & Bus Res.

Audisio, Gabriel. The Waldensian Dissent: Persecution & Survival, c. 1170-c. 1570. Davison, Claire, tr. from FRE. LC 98-49526. (Medieval Textbks.). (Illus.). 280p. 1999. 59.95 (*0-521-55029-7*); pap. 21.95 (*0-521-55984-7*) Cambridge U Pr.

Audisio, Silvia. Hassan II Trophy of Golf. 1980. 39.95 (*0-905743-79-2*, Pub. by Stacey Intl) Intl Bk Ctr.

Audit Bureau of Circulations Staff. Scientific Space Selection. LC 75-22798. (America in Two Centuries Ser.). 1976. reprint ed. 18.95 (*0-405-07669-X*) Ayer.

Audley-Charles, M. G. & Hallam, A., eds. Gondwana & Tethys. (Geological Society Special Publications). (Illus.). 326p. 1988. 120.00 (*0-19-854448-0*) OUP.

Audley, John J. Green Politics & Global Trade: NAFTA & the Future of Environmental Politics. Rabe, Barry et al, eds. LC 97-7907. (American Governance & Public Policy Ser.). 288p. 1997. 55.00 (*0-87840-650-6*); pap. 21.95 (*0-87840-651-4*) Georgetown U Pr.

Audley, L. Michael. The Hazards of 12 Step Programs & Religious Fanaticism. (Orig.). 1989. 9.95 (*0-685-30054-4*) Carpe Diem Pubs.

Audley, Paul. Culture of Commerce: Canadian Culture after Free Trade. (Illus.). 256p. 1997. pap. 17.95 (*0-7737-5887-9*) Stoddart Publ.

Audley, R. J. & BBC Staff. Decision Making. LC 68-99816. 95 p. 1967. write for info. (*0-563-07382-9*) BBC.

Audoin, C., jt. auth. see Vanier, Jacques.

Audoin, C., jt. ed. see Vanier, Jacques.

Audoin-Rouzeau, Stephane. Men at War, 1914-1918: National Sentiment & Trench Journalism in France During the First World War. (Reports from the French Trenches). (Illus.). 207p. 1992. pap. 17.00 (*0-85496-333-2*, Pub. by Berg Pubs) NYU Pr.

Audouin, Raoul, ed. & tr. see Bastiat, Frederic.

Audoux, Marguerite. Valserine & Other Stories. LC 73-110178. (Short Story Index Reprint Ser.). 1977. 20.95 (*0-8369-3329-X*) Ayer.

Audouze, Francoise & Buchsenschutz, Olivier. Towns, Villages, & Countryside of Celtic Europe. Cleere, Henry, tr. LC 91-37593. (Illus.). 258p. 1992. text 49.95 (*0-253-31082-2*) Ind U Pr.

Audouze, Jean, ed. CNO Isotopes in Astrophysics. (Astrophysics & Space Science Library: No. 67). 1977. lib. bdg. 82.50 (*90-277-0807-X*) Kluwer Academic.

Audouze, Jean, et al, eds. Diffuse Matter in Galaxies. 1983. text 126.50 (*90-277-1626-9*) Kluwer Academic.

Audouze, Jean & Mathieu, Nicole, eds. Nucleosynthesis & Its Implications on Nuclear & Particle Physics. 1986. text 220.00 (*90-277-2173-4*) Kluwer Academic.

Audouze, Jean & Tran Thanh Van, Jean. Formation & Evolution of Galaxies & Large Structures in the Universe. 1983. text 220.00 (*90-277-1685-4*) Kluwer Academic.

Audouze, Jean & Vauclair, Sylvie. An Introduction to Nuclear Astrophysics: The Formation & Evolution of Matter in the Universe. (Geophysics & Astrophysics Monographs: No. 18). 1979. pap. text 73.50 (*90-277-1053-8*); lib. bdg. 104.50 (*90-277-1012-0*) Kluwer Academic.

Audouze, Jean, jt. ed. see Sato, Kazuo.

Audra, R. Ashley, tr. see Bergson, Henri.

Audretsch, David B. The Effectiveness of Antitrust Policy Towards Horizontal Mergers. LC 83-6985. (Research in Business Economics & Public Policy Ser.: No. 1). (Illus.). 164p. 1983. reprint ed. pap. 50.90 (*0-8357-1434-9*, 207035700088) Bks Demand.
— Innovation & Industry Evolution. LC 94-33655. (Illus.). 280p. 1995. 37.50 (*0-262-01146-8*) MIT Pr.
— Market & the State. (C). 1991. text 57.50 (*0-8147-1432-3*) NYU Pr.

Audretsch, David B., ed. Industrial Policy & Competitive Advantage, 3 vols. LC 97-37980. (International Library of Critical Writings in Economics Ser.). 1848p. 1998. 655.00 (*1-85898-470-X*) E Elgar.

***Audretsch, David B. & Klepper, Steven, eds.** Innovation, Evolution of Industry & Economic Growth, 3 vols. LC 00-28822. (International Library of Critical Writings in Economics Ser.). 1576p. 2000. 560.00 (*1-84064-175-4*) E Elgar.

Audretsch, David B. & Siegfried, John J., eds. Empirical Studies in Industrial Organization: Essays in Honor of Leonard W. Weiss. LC 92-14813. (Studies in Industrial Organization: Vol. 16). 296p. (C). 1992. lib. bdg. 168.50 (*0-7923-1806-4*) Kluwer Academic.

Audretsch, David B. & Thurik, Roy, eds. Innovation, Industry Evolution & Employment. LC 98-35101. (Illus.). 320p. (C). 1999. text 69.95 (*0-521-64166-7*) Cambridge U Pr.

Audretsch, David B., jt. auth. see Acs, Zoltan J.

Audretsch, David B., jt. ed. see Acs, Zoltan J.

Audretsch, David B., jt. ed. see Kindleberger, Charles P.

Audretsch, David B., jt. ed. see Stephan, Paula E.

Audretsch, David B., ed. see Weiss, Leonard W.

Audretsch, J. & De Sabbata, Venzo, eds. Quantum Mechanics in Curved Space-Time. LC 90-14188. (NATO ASI Ser.: Vol. 230). (Illus.). 566p. (C). 1990. text 168.00 (*0-306-43661-2*, Kluwer Plenum) Kluwer Academic.

Audry, Collette. Derriere la Baignoire. (FRE.). 256p. 1983. pap. 12.95 (*0-7859-1979-1*, 2070375048) Fr & Eur.

Audry, W. New Tracks for Thomas. LC 93-85588. (Pictureback Shapes Ser.). (Illus.). 24p. (J). (ps-2). 1994. pap. 3.25 (*0-679-85699-4*, Pub. by Random Bks Yng Read) Random.

Audsley, G., jt. auth. see Audsley, W.

Audsley, George A. The Art of Organ Building, 2 vols. Incl. Vol. 1. Proem. (Illus.). x, 600p. 1988. 17.95 (*0-486-21314-5*); Vol. 2. Specifications of Organs. (Illus.). iv, 750p. 1988. 17.95 (*0-486-21315-3*); write for info. (*0-318-51748-5*) Dover.
— Color Harmony in Dress (1928) 134p. 1998. reprint ed. pap. 16.95 (*0-7661-0199-1*) Kessinger Pub.

Audsley, George A. Cut & Use Stencils: Victorian Floral. (Illus.). 1989. pap. 5.95 (*0-486-26072-0*) Dover.

Audsley, George A. Duo-Art Aeolian Pipe-Organ. (Illus.). 1921. pap. 10.00 (*0-913746-15-0*) Organ Lit.
— The Temple of Tone. LC 79-108119. (BCL Ser.: No. 1). (Illus.). 1970. reprint ed. lib. bdg. 37.50 (*0-404-00417-2*) AMS Pr.
— The Temple of Tone: A Disquisition on the Scientific & Artistic Tonal Appointment & Control of Concert-Room, Church, & Theater Organs. 1990. reprint ed. lib. bdg. 75.00 (*0-7812-9109-7*) Rprt Serv.

Audsley, George A. & Audsley, Maurice A. Victorian Patterns & Designs in Full Color. 112p. 1988. pap. 14.95 (*0-486-25756-8*) Dover.

Audsley, Maurice A., jt. auth. see Audsley, George A.

Audsley, W. & Audsley, G. Designs & Patterns from Historic Ornament. Orig. Title: Outlines of Ornament in the Leading Styles. 200p. 1968. pap. 7.95 (*0-486-21931-3*) Dover.
— Victorian Sourcebook of Medieval Decoration: With 166 Full-Color Designs. (Pictorial Archive Ser.). Orig. Title: Polychromatic Decoration As Applied to Buildings in the Medieval Styles. (Illus.). 64p. 1991. reprint ed. pap. 9.95 (*0-486-26834-9*) Dover.

Audubon, John James. Audubon & His Journals, 2 vols, Set. Audubon, Maria R., ed. LC 75-38340. (Select Bibliographies Reprint Ser.). 1977. 62.95 (*0-8369-6660-0*) Ayer.

Audubon, John James. Audubon Bird Seals: Twenty-Four Pressure-Sensitive Designs. (Illus.). 1993. pap. 1.00 (*0-486-27611-2*) Dover.

Audubon, John James. Audubon Birds of America Postcards. 81st ed. 1987. pap. 4.95 (*0-486-25457-7*) Dover.
— Audubon Reader: The Best Writings of John James Audubon. Sanders, Scott R., ed. LC 85-45773. 256p. reprint ed. pap. 79.40 (*0-7837-9666-8*, 205930000005) Bks Demand.
— The Birds of America, Vols. 1, 5, 6, 7. (Illus.). 1967. reprint ed. 15.00 (*0-8446-1567-6*) Peter Smith.
— Delineations of American Scenery & Character. LC 70-125730. (American Environmental Studies). 1974. reprint ed. 26.95 (*0-405-02655-2*) Ayer.
— John James Audubon: Selected Journals & Other Writings. Forkner, Ben, ed. & intro. by. LC 95-40325. (Penguin Nature Classics Ser.). (Illus.). 718p. 1996. pap. 15.95 (*0-14-024126-4*, Penguin Bks) Viking Penguin.
— Life of John James Audubon, the Naturalist. 1993. reprint ed. lib. bdg. 89.00 (*0-7812-5422-1*) Rprt Serv.
— Treasury of Audubon Birds in Full Color: Two Hundred Twenty-Four Plates from The Birds of America. LC 93-9698. Orig. Title: Birds of America - Selections. (Illus.). 112p. 1993. reprint ed. pap. 15.95 (*0-486-27604-X*) Dover.

Audubon, John James. Writings & Drawings. Irmscher, Christoph, ed. LC 99-18337. 928p. 1999. 40.00 (*1-883011-68-X*, Pub. by Library of America) Penguin Putnam.

***Audubon, John James.** Writings & Drawings. Irmscher, Christoph, ed. (Illus.). 942p. 1999. 40.00 (*1-883011-81-7*, Pub. by Library of America) Penguin Putnam.

Audubon, John James & Bachman, John. The Quadrupeds of North America, 3 vols., Set. LC 73-17796. (Natural Sciences of America Ser.). (Illus.). 1406p. 1975. reprint ed. 108.95 (*0-405-05706-7*) Ayer.
— The Quadrupeds of North America, 3 vols., Vol. 1. LC 73-17796. (Natural Sciences of America Ser.). (Illus.). 1406p. 1974. reprint ed. 36.95 (*0-405-05707-5*) Ayer.
— The Quadrupeds of North America, 3 vols., Vol. 2. LC 73-17796. (Natural Sciences of America Ser.). (Illus.). 1406p. 1974. reprint ed. 36.95 (*0-405-05708-3*) Ayer.
— The Quadrupeds of North America, 3 vols., Vol. 3. LC 73-17796. (Natural Sciences of America Ser.). (Illus.). 1406p. 1974. reprint ed. 36.95 (*0-405-05709-1*) Ayer.

Audubon, John W. Audubon's Western Journal: 1849-1850. 1992. reprint ed. lib. bdg. 90.00 (*0-7812-5003-X*) Rprt Serv.
— Audubon's Western Journal, 1849-1850: Record of a Trip from New York to Texas, & an Overland Jouney Through Mexico & Arizona to the Gold-Fields of California. LC 83-17860. 252p. 1905. pap. 78.20 (*0-608-05624-3*, 206608000006) Bks Demand.

Audubon, Maria R. Audubon & His Journals, Vol. I. unabridged ed. (Illus.). 1994. pap. text 12.95 (*0-486-28391-7*) Dover.
— Audubon & His Journals, Vol. II. unabridged ed. (Illus.). 1994. pap. text 12.95 (*0-486-28392-5*) Dover.

Audubon, Maria R., ed. see Audubon, John James.

Audubon Society Staff. The Birds of America. (Illus.). 29.95 (*0-02-504440-0*) Macmillan.
— Clouds & Storms. (National Audubon Society Pocket Guides Ser.). 1995. pap. 7.99 (*0-679-77999-X*) Knopf.
— Earth from Space. (National Audubon Society Pocket Guides Ser.). 1995. pap. 7.99 (*0-679-76057-1*) Knopf.
— Familiar Birds: North American East. 1987. pap. 9.00 (*0-394-74839-5*) Knopf.
— Familiar Birds, Tress & Wildflowers: Eastern & Western, 3 vols., Set. (Audubon Society Pocket Guides Ser.). 1988. pap. 27.00 (*0-394-75790-4*) Knopf.
— Familiar Birds, Western Region. 1987. pap. 9.00 (*0-394-74842-5*) Knopf.
— Familiar Trees, Eastern Region. 192p. 1987. pap. 9.00 (*0-394-74851-4*) Knopf.
— Familiar Trees of North America, Western Region. 192p. 1987. pap. 9.00 (*0-394-74852-2*) Knopf.
— Field Guide to the Bald Eagle: With Maps & Directions to Eagle-Watching Sites in Alaska, British Columbia, Washington, Oregon, Idaho & Montana. (Sasquatch Field Guide Ser.). (Illus.). 48p. (Orig.). 1991. pap. 5.95 (*0-912365-46-3*) Sasquatch Bks.

***Audubon Society Staff.** Master Guide to Birds. 2001. 29.95 (*0-679-45123-4*) Knopf.

Audubon Society Staff. Planets & Their Moons. (National Audubon Society Pocket Guides Ser.). 1995. pap. 7.99 (*0-679-77997-3*) Knopf.

Audubon Society Staff & Chesterman, Charles W. Rocks & Minerals. LC 78-54893. (Illus.). 1979. 19.00 (*0-394-50269-8*) Knopf.

Audubon Society Staff & Lincoff, Gary H. Mushrooms. LC 81-80827. (Illus.). 864p. 1981. 19.00 (*0-394-51992-2*) Knopf.

Audubon Society Staff & Little, Elbert L., Jr. Trees: Eastern Edition. 1980. 19.00 (*0-394-50760-6*) Knopf.
— Trees: Western Area. (Audubon Society Nature Guides Ser.). 1980. 19.00 (*0-394-50761-4*) Knopf.

Audubon Society Staff & Meinkoth, Norman A. Seashore Creatures. LC 81-80828. (Illus.). 799p. 1981. 19.00 (*0-394-51993-0*) Knopf.

Audubon Society Staff & Pyle, Robert M. Butterflies. LC 80-84240. (Illus.). 864p. 1981. 19.00 (*0-394-51914-0*) Knopf.

Audubon Society Staff & Rehder, Harold A. Seashells. LC 80-84239. 1981. 19.00 (*0-394-51913-2*) Knopf.

Audubon Society Staff & Thompson, Ida. Fossils. LC 81-84772. (Illus.). 1982. 19.00 (*0-394-52412-8*) Knopf.

Audubon Society Staff, et al. Familiar Flowers, Eastern Region: Eastern Region. 192p. 1987. pap. 9.00 (*0-394-74843-3*) Knopf.
— Familiar Wildflowers of North America: Western Region. 192p. 1987. pap. 9.00 (*0-394-74844-1*) Knopf.
— Fishes, Whales & Dolphins. LC 83-47962. (Illus.). 864p. 1983. 19.00 (*0-394-53405-0*) Knopf.
— Insects. LC 80-7620. (Illus.). 1008p. 1980. 19.00 (*0-394-50763-0*) Knopf.
— Reptiles & Amphibians. LC 79-2217. (Illus.). 1979. 19.00 (*0-394-50824-6*) Knopf.

***Audubon Staff.** Backroads America, 1999. 1998. pap. 10.95 (*1-57965-100-3*) Artisan.

Audubon Staff & Mitchell, Carolyn B. The National Audobon Society Pocket Guide: Galaxies & Other Deep-Sky Objects. LC 94-41623. (National Audubon Society Pocket Guides). 1995. pap. 7.99 (*0-679-77996-5*) Knopf.

Audus, K. L. & Raub, T. L. Biological Barriers to Protein Delivery. (Pharmaceutical Biotechnology Ser.: Vol. 4). (Illus.). 522p. (C). 1993. text 110.00 (*0-306-44368-6*, Kluwer Plenum) Kluwer Academic.

Aue, A., et al. SSADM & Grapes: A Comparison of Two Major European Methodologies for Information Systems Engineering. Duschl, Richard A. & Hopkins, N. C., eds. LC 92-11653. 324p. 1992. 82.95 (*0-387-55380-0*) Spr-Verlag.

Aue, A. E., tr. see Wittgenstein, Ludwig Josef Johann.

Aue, M. A., tr. see Wittgenstein, Ludwig Josef Johann.

Aue, Pamela Willwerth. What Inspirational Literature Do I Read Next? 479p. 1999. 99.00 (*0-7876-3942-7*, GML00299-113740, Gale Res Intl) Gale.

Auel, Jean M. The Clan of the Cave Bear. (Earth's Children Ser.). 528p. 1997. mass mkt. 7.99 (*0-553-25042-6*) Bantam.
— The Clan of the Cave Bear. LC 97-48397. 480p. 1998. 9.99 (*0-517-18918-6*) Random Hse Value.
— Clan of the Cave Bear. (Earth's Children Ser.). (J). 1980. 13.09 (*0-606-00288-X*, Pub. by Turtleback) Demco.
— The Clan of the Cave Bear. large type ed. LC 83-445. 946p. 1991. pap. 17.95 (*1-56054-983-1*) Thorndike Pr.
— Earth's Children: Collector's Edition, 3 vols., Set. deluxe ed. 1986. 75.00 (*0-517-56486-6*) Crown Pub Group.
— Jean Auel, 2 vols., Set. 1984. boxed set 9.00 (*0-553-30852-1*) Bantam.
— The Mammoth Hunters. (Earth's Children Ser.: No. 3). 752p. 1986. mass mkt. 7.99 (*0-553-28094-5*, Bantam Classics) Bantam.
— The Mammoth Hunters. LC 85-17503. (Earth's Children Ser.). 656p. 1985. 19.95 (*0-517-55627-8*, Crown) Crown Pub Group.

Auel, Jean M. The Mammoth Hunters. (Earth's Children Ser.). (J). 1985. 12.60 (*0-606-03115-4*, Pub. by Turtleback) Demco.

Auel, Jean M. The Mammoth Hunters. large type ed. LC 86-4284. 1211p. 1991. pap. 17.95 (*1-56054-981-5*) Thorndike Pr.
— The Plains of Passage. (Earth's Children Ser.). 880p. 1991. mass mkt. 7.99 (*0-553-28941-1*) Bantam.
— The Plains of Passage. large type ed. 1465p. 1992. pap. 17.95 (*1-56054-985-8*) Thorndike Pr.
— The Valley of Horses. (Earth's Children Ser.). 544p. 1984. mass mkt. 7.99 (*0-553-25053-1*) Bantam.
— The Valley of Horses. (Earth's Children Ser.). 512p. 1982. 19.95 (*0-517-54489-X*, Crown) Crown Pub Group.
— The Valley of Horses. large type ed. 1039p. 1991. lib. bdg. 17.95 (*1-56054-982-3*) Thorndike Pr.

Auel, Lisa B. Tokens & Treasures: Gifts to Twelve Presidents. LC 96-871. (Illus.). 144p. 1996. pap. 24.95 (*1-880875-10-1*, 200052) National Archives & Recs.

Auer, Anna, jt. contrib. by see Coleman, A. D.

Auer, Arthur I., jt. ed. see Neumyer, Marsha M.

Auer, Carolin, jt. ed. see Kraus, Elisabeth.

Auer, David, et al. Quattro Pro 5 for Windows - New Perspectives Introductory, Incl. instr. resource kit, test bank, transparency. (New Perspectives Ser.). (Illus.). 304p. 1994. text. write for info. (*1-56527-162-9*) Course Tech.
— Quattro Pro 6 for Windows - New Perspectives Introductory, Incl. instr. resource kit, test bank, transparency. (New Perspectives Ser.). (Illus.). 320p. 1995. pap. 29.95 (*0-7600-3280-7*) Course Tech.

Auer, Frank. Combined Electromagnetic Suspension & Propulsion for Positioning with Sub-Micrometer Accuracy. (Illus.). 190p. 1995. pap. 67.50 (*90-407-1193-3*, Pub. by Delft U Pr) Coronet Bks.

Auer, J. C. P. Bilingual Conversation. LC 85-7404. (Pragmatics & Beyond Ser.: Vol. V-8). ix, 116p. 1985. pap. 46.00 (*0-915027-49-6*) J Benjamins Pubng Co.

Auer, J. E. Candle Magick: A Guide for the Novice. (Illus.). 96p. (Orig.). 1996. pap. 7.50 (*1-57353-110-3*) Eschaton Prods.

Auer, J. Jeffery, ed. Antislavery & Disunion, Eighteen Fifty-Eight to Eighteen Sixty-One: Studies in the Rhetoric of Compromise & Conflict. 1990. 16.50 (*0-8446-0464-X*) Peter Smith.

Auer, J. Jeffery & Jenkinson, Edward B., eds. On Teaching Speech in Elementary & Junior High Schools. LC 73-138412. (Indiana University English Curriculum Studies). 192p. reprint ed. 59.60 (*0-8357-9228-5*, 201546400094) Bks Demand.

Auer, J. T. Joy of Selling. 1991. pap. 7.95 (*1-55850-011-1*) Adams Media.

***Auer, James E.** Elf-Help for Raising a Teen. LC 00-100729. (Illus.). 88p. 2000. pap. 4.95 (*0-87029-336-2*) Abbey.

Auer, James E. The Postwar Rearmament of Japanese Maritime Forces, 1945-1971. LC 72-83564. (Special Studies in International Politics & Government). 1973. 40.50 (*0-275-28633-9*) Irvington.

Auer, Jim. Don't Read This Book! LC 96-75300. 112p. (YA). 1996. pap. 5.95 (*0-89243-908-4*) Liguori Pubns.

— Real Life Takes Guts: Go for It! LC 97-74318. 64p. 1998. pap. 3.95 (*0-7648-0186-4*) Liguori Pubns.

— Sex & the Christian Teen. LC 94-75179. 64p. (Orig.). 1994. pap. 3.95 (*0-89243-632-8*) Liguori Pubns.

— Ten Good Reasons to Be a Catholic: A Teenager's Guide to the Church. LC 87-80988. (YA). (gr. 7-12). 1987. pap. 4.95 (*0-89243-271-3*) Liguori Pubns.

— 10 More Good Reasons to Be Catholic: A Teenager's Guide. LC 98-67381. 64p. 1999. pap. 4.95 (*0-7648-0322-0*) Liguori Pubns.

— Ten Ways to Get into the New Testament: A Teenager's Guide. LC 90-64270. 80p. (YA). (gr. 9-12). 1991. pap. text 4.95 (*0-89243-342-6*) Liguori Pubns.

— Ten Ways to Meet God: Spirituality for Teens. LC 88-83574. 64p. (YA). (gr. 7-12). 1989. pap. 4.95 (*0-89243-299-3*) Liguori Pubns.

Auer, Johann. The Church: The Universal Sacrament of Salvation. Riley, Hugh M., ed. Waldstein, Michael, tr. LC 91-44734. (Dogmatic Theology Ser.: Vol. 8). 541p. 1993. text 39.95 (*0-8132-0684-7*); pap. text 24.95 (*0-8132-0685-5*) Cath U Pr.

— A General Doctrine of the Sacraments & the Mystery of the Eucharist. Riley, Hugh M., ed. Leiva-Merikakis, Erasmo, tr. from GER. LC 94-35606. (Dogmatic Theology Ser.: Vol. 6). 425p. 1996. 39.95 (*0-8132-0824-6*); pap. 24.95 (*0-8132-0825-4*) Cath U Pr.

Auer, Jorg A. Equine Surgery. 2nd ed. 1992. text 240.00 (*0-7216-2860-5*, W B Saunders Co) Harcrt Hlth Sci Grp.

Auer, Jorg A. & Stick, John A. Equine Surgery. 2nd ed. Donley, Stephanie, ed. (Illus.). 955p. 1999. text. write for info. (*0-7216-7733-9*, W B Saunders Co) Harcrt Hlth Sci Grp.

Auer, L. M., et al, eds. Prolactinomas: An Interdiciplinary Approach. (Illus.). x, 439p. 1985. 134.65 (*3-11-010153-X*) De Gruyter.

Auer, L. M. & Kassel, N., eds. Timing of Aneurysm Surgery. (Illus.). xiv, 685p. 1985. 176.95 (*3-11-010156-4*) De Gruyter.

Auer, L. M. & Loew, F., eds. The Cerebral Veins. (Illus.). 380p. 1984. 148.00 (*0-387-81767-0*) Spr-Verlag.

Auer, Leopold. Graded Course of Violin, Bk. 1. (Illus.). 64p. 1926. pap. 11.50 (*0-8258-0251-2*, 0-1416) Fischer Inc NY.

— Violin Playing As I Teach It. 111p. 1980. reprint ed. pap. 4.95 (*0-486-23917-9*) Dover.

— Violin Playing As I Teach It. LC 75-35022. (Illus.). 99p. 1976. reprint ed. lib. bdg. 42.50 (*0-8371-8573-4*, AUVP, Greenwood Pr) Greenwood.

Auer, Leopold, ed. see Bach, Johann Sebastian.

Auer, Leopold, ed. see Handel, George Frideric.

Auer, P. L., ed. see Kirkwood, John G.

Auer, Peter. Phonologie der Alltagssprache: Eine Untersuchung zur Standard-Dialekt-Variation am Beispiel der Konstanzer Stadtsprache. (Studia Linguistica Germanica: Band 28). (Illus.). x, 358p. (C). 1990. lib. bdg. 126.15 (*3-11-011954-4*) De Gruyter.

***Auer, Peter, ed.** Changing Labour Markets in Europe: The Role of Institutions & Policies. 300p. 2000. pap. 22.95 (*92-2-111385-X*, Pub. by ILO) ILO Pubns Ctr.

— Code-Switching in Conversation. 368p. (Orig.). (C). 1999. pap. 32.99 (*0-415-21609-5*) Routledge.

Auer, Peter, ed. Code Switching in Conversation: Linguistic Perspectives on Bilingualism. LC 97-22664. 368p. (C). 1998. 90.00 (*0-415-15831-1*) Routledge.

— Energy & the Developing Nations: Proceedings of the Electric Power Research Institute (EPRI) Workshop on Energy & the Developing Nations, Hoover Institution, Stanford University, March 18-20, 1980. LC 80-29586. (Policy Studies on Energy). (Illus.). 528p. 1981. 145.00 (*0-08-027527-3*, Pergamon Pr) Elsevier.

Auer, Peter & Di Luzio, Aldo, eds. Variation & Convergence: Studies in Social Dialectology. (Sociolinguistics & Language Contact Ser.: Vol. 4). 320p. (C). 1988. lib. bdg. 142.35 (*3-11-011045-8*) De Gruyter.

Auer, Peter, et al. Language in Time: The Rhythm & Tempo of Spoken Interaction. LC 98-20722. (Oxford Studies in Sociolinguistics). (Illus.). 256p. 1999. text 65.00 (*0-19-510928-7*) OUP.

***Auer, Peter L.** Employment Revival in Europe: Labor Market Success in Austria, Denmark, Ireland & the Netherland. 148p. 2000. pap. text 17.95 (*92-2-110841-4*, Pub. by ILO) ILO Pubns Ctr.

Auer, Varvara, jt. auth. see Linnell, Andrew.

***Auerbach.** Bankers Hegemony or State Autonomy. 280p. 2000. 70.00 (*0-8133-6764-6*, Pub. by Westview) HarpC.

Auerbach. Dr. Toys Smart Play, Vol. 1. 1997. mass mkt. write for info. (*0-312-96342-4*) St Martin.

— The World of Work: An Introduction to Industrial/ Organizational Psychology. 1995. pap. 44.06 (*1-56134-185-1*, Dshkn McG-Hill) McGrw-H Hghr Educ.

Auerbach & Donner. Field Guide Wilderness Medicine. LC 98-29514. (Illus.). 576p. (C). (gr. 13). 1998. pap. text 34.95 (*0-8151-0926-1*, 28913) Mosby Inc.

Auerbach, A. J. & Feldstein, M. Handbook of Public Economics, Vol. III. (Handbooks in Economics Ser.: III). 1998. write for info. (*0-444-82314-X*) Elsevier.

— Handbook of Public Economics, Vol. IV. 1999. write for info. (*0-444-82315-8*) Elsevier.

Auerbach, Alan, jt. ed. see Corsini, Raymond J.

Auerbach, Alan J. Corporate Takeovers: Causes & Consequences. (National Bureau of Economic Research Project Report Ser.). (Illus.). x, 344p. 1988. lib. bdg. 45.00 (*0-226-03211-6*) U Ch Pr.

***Auerbach, Alan J.** Generational Accounting Around the World. LC 98-45329. 1999. 72.00 (*0-226-03213-2*) U Ch Pr.

— Public Finance. LC 99-45658. (Series in Outstanding Contributions). 1999. write for info. (*1-57259-927-8*) Worth.

Auerbach, Alan J. The Taxation of Capital Income. (Economic Studies: No. 153). 136p. 1983. 20.00 (*0-674-86845-5*) HUP.

Auerbach, Alan J., ed. Corporate Takeovers: Causes & Consequences. LC 87-37497. (National Bureau of Economic Research Ser.). 353p. reprint ed. pap. 109.50 (*0-7837-4093-X*, 205791400011) Bks Demand.

— Corporate Takeovers: Causes & Consequences. LC 87-37497. (National Bureau of Economic Research Ser.). 354p. 1988. reprint ed. pap. text 19.95 (*0-226-03212-4*) U Ch Pr.

— Fiscal Policy: Lessons from Economic Research. LC 96-53456. (Illus.). 488p. 1997. 55.00 (*0-262-01160-3*) MIT Pr.

— Mergers & Acquisitions. (National Bureau of Economic Research Project Report Ser.). (Illus.). 120p. 1988. 17.95 (*0-226-03209-4*) U Ch Pr.

— Mergers & Acquisitions. (National Bureau of Economic Research Project Report Ser.). (Illus.). 120p. 1991. pap. text 11.95 (*0-226-03210-8*) U Ch Pr.

Auerbach, Alan J. & Feldstein, Martin, eds. Handbook of Public Economics, Vol. 2. (Handbooks in Economics Ser.: II). 640p. 1987. 110.00 (*0-444-87908-0*) Elsevier.

Auerbach, Alan J. & Kotlikoff, Laurence J. Macroeconomics: An Integrated Approach. 2nd ed. LC 98-6765. (Illus.). 500p. 1998. 65.00 (*0-262-01170-0*) MIT Pr.

— Macroeconomics: An Integrated Approach. 2nd ed. 1998. pap. text 35.00 (*0-262-51103-7*) MIT Pr.

***Auerbach, Alan J. & Lee, Ronald D., eds.** Demographic Change & Fiscal Policy. (Illus.). 416p. (C). 2000. Price not set. (*0-521-66244-3*) Cambridge U Pr.

Auerbach, Alan J., jt. auth. see Corsini, Raymond J.

Auerbach, Aliza. Aliya. (Illus.). 220p. 1993. 38.00 (*965-05-0644-6*, Pub. by Israel Ministry Def) Gefen Bks.

Auerbach, Ann. Wild Ride. 1995. write for info. (*0-8050-2003-9*) H Holt & Co.

— Wild Ride. 1995. pap. 14.95 (*0-8050-4242-3*) H Holt & Co.

Auerbach, Ann Hagedorn. Ransom: The Untold Story of International Kidnapping. 496p. 1999. pap. 14.95 (*0-8050-6126-6*, Pub. by H Holt & Co) VHPS.

— Ransom: The Untold Story of International Kidnapping. LC 97-51625. 352p. 1998. text 25.00 (*0-8050-4078-1*) St Martin.

***Auerbach, Annie.** Catdog Trivia Book. (Cat Dog Ser.). 48p. 1999. pap. 2.99 (*0-689-83002-5*) S&S Childrens.

— Cookin with Catdog. (Catdog Chapter Bks.: Vol. 7). (Illus.). 64p. (J). (gr. 2-5). 2000. mass mkt. 3.99 (*0-689-83395-4*, Simon Spot) Litle Simon.

— The Most World Records. Vol. 8. (Illus.). 64p. (gr. 2-5). 2000. 3.99 (*0-689-83465-9*) S&S Trade.

Auerbach, Assa. Strongly Interacting Electrons & Quantum Magnetism. LC 94-6510. (Graduate Texts in Contemporary Physics Ser.). (Illus.). 256p. 1994. 39.95 (*0-387-94286-6*) Spr-Verlag.

Auerbach, Barbara & Snyder, Beth. Paragraph Patterns. 147p. (C). 1983. pap. text 20.50 (*0-15-567983-X*) Harcourt Coll Pubs.

Auerbach, Barbara J. & Castellano, Thomas C., eds. Successful Community Sanctions & Services for Special Offenders: Proceedings of the 1994 Conference of the International Community Corrections Association (ICCA) LC 98-16876. 270p. 1998. pap. 24.95 (*1-56991-092-8*, 241) Am Correctional.

Auerbach, Bernard, tr. see Elon, Menachem.

Auerbach, Berthold. Black Forest Village Stories. Goepp, Charles, tr. LC 70-101791. (Short Story Index Reprint Ser.). 1979. 23.95 (*0-8369-3179-3*) Ayer.

Auerbach, Bruce E. Unto the Thousandth Generation: Conceptualizing Intergenerational Justice, Vol. 43. LC 93-2300. (American University Studies, Political Science Ser.: Ser. X, Vol. 42). XIV, 270p. (C). 1995. 46.95 (*0-8204-2228-2*) P Lang Pubng.

Auerbach, Debbie, jt. ed. see Satterlee, Sarah.

Auerbach, E., ed. Experimental & Clinical Amblyopia. (Documenta Ophthalmologica Proceedings Ser.: Vol. 11). 1977. pap. text 107.50 (*90-6193-151-7*) Kluwer Academic.

Auerbach, Ellen, jt. auth. see Porter, Eliot.

Auerbach, Elsa. ESL for Action Teacher's Guide. 64p. 1987. pap. text, teacher ed. 8.16 (*0-201-00102-0*) Addison-Wesley.

Auerbach, Elsa, et al. Adult E. S. L./Literacy from the Community to the Community: A Guidebook for Participatory Literacy Training. 240p. 1996. pap. text 18.50 (*0-8058-2267-4*) L Erlbaum Assocs.

Auerbach, Elsa R. & Wallerstein, Nina. ESL for Action: Problem Posing at Work. (Illus.). 192p. 1987. pap. text 14.91 (*0-201-00101-2*) Addison-Wesley.

Auerbach, Emily. Maestros, Dilettantes, & Philistines: The Musician in the Victorian Novel. (American University Studies: English Language & Literature: Ser. IV, Vol. 103). 213p. (C). 1989. text 38.95 (*0-8204-0926-X*) P Lang Pubng.

Auerbach, Erich. Dante: Poet of the Secular World. Silverstein, Theodore, ed. Manheim, Ralph, tr. 204p. 1992. pap. text 13.95 (*0-226-03205-1*, Midway Reprint) U Ch Pr.

— Mimesis. (SPA.). pap. 16.99 (*968-16-0282-X*, Pub. by Fondo) Continental Bk.

— Mimesis: The Representation of Reality in Western Literature. Trask, Willard R., tr. 576p. 1953. pap. text 17.95 (*0-691-01269-5*, 124, Pub. by Princeton U Pr) Cal Prin Full Svc.

Auerbach, J. H., tr. see Hartling, Peter.

***Auerbach, James A. & National Policy Association (U.S.).** Through a Glass Darkly: Building the New Workplace for the 21st Century. LC 98-65502. (Illus.). 1998. write for info. (*0-89068-144-9*) Natl Planning.

Auerbach, James A. & Welsh, Joyce C., eds. U. S. Competitiveness & the Aging American Workforce. 257p. (Orig.). 1994. pap. text 17.50 (*0-89068-128-7*) Natl Planning.

Auerbach, James A., et al. The Inequality Paradox: Growth of Income Disparity. LC 98-65107. (Npa Report Ser.). xii, 264p. 1998. write for info. (*0-89068-143-0*) Natl Planning.

***Auerbach, Jeffrey.** The Great Exhibition of 1851. LC 99-32177. (Illus.). 288p. 1999. 40.00 (*0-300-08007-7*) Yale U Pr.

Auerbach, Jerold S. Jacob's Voices: Reflections of a Wandering American Jew. LC 95-39568. 208p. (C). 1996. 29.95 (*0-8093-2055-X*) S Ill U Pr.

— Labor & Liberty: The La Follette Committee & the New Deal. LC 66-28233. 1966. 29.50 (*0-672-51153-3*); pap. text 12.95 (*0-685-02670-1*) Irvington.

— Unequal Justice: Lawyers & Social Change in Modern America. LC 75-7364. 412p. 1977. reprint ed. pap. text 13.95 (*0-19-502170-3*) OUP.

Auerbach, Jerold S., ed. American Labor: The Twentieth Century. LC 69-14822. (American Heritage Ser.). 1969. pap. 9.95 (*0-672-60128-1*, 78, Bobbs) Macmillan.

Auerbach, Jerome M., tr. & intro. see Simonnet, Jean.

Auerbach, Jessica. Sleep, Baby, Sleep. Date not set. mass mkt. 5.99 (*0-449-14952-8*, GM) Fawcett.

Auerbach, Joel. Dive Miami: The Complete Divers Guide of Shipwrecks & Reefs off Miami, Florida. LC 91-71064. (Illus.). 80p. (Orig.). 1991. pap. 19.95 (*0-9629330-0-7*) Scuba Pubns.

Auerbach, Jonathan. Male Call: Becoming Jack London. LC 96-14682. (New Americanists Ser.). (Illus.). 296p. 1996. text 49.95 (*0-8223-1827-X*); pap. text 17.95 (*0-8223-1820-2*) Duke.

Auerbach, Jonathan, ed. see London, Jack.

Auerbach, Judith D. In the Business of Child Care: Employer Initiatives & Working Women. LC 87-27393. 183p. 1988. 52.95 (*0-275-92858-6*, C2858, Praeger Pubs) Greenwood.

Auerbach, Judith D., ed. see Institute of Medicine, Committee on Substance Abuse Staff.

Auerbach, Judith G., jt. ed. see Greenbaum, Charles W.

***Auerbach, Kathleen.** Clinical Lactation: A Visual Guide. (Illus.). 96p. (C). 1999. pap. text 37.50 (*0-7637-0919-0*) Jones & Bartlett.

— Current Issues in Clinical Lactation. (Illus.). 64p. (C). 1999. pap. text 32.50 (*0-7637-1024-5*) Jones & Bartlett.

Auerbach, Kathleen & Riordan, Janice. Breastfeeding & Human Lactation. (Nursing Ser.). 168p. (C). 1993. pap., student ed. 21.25 (*0-86720-632-2*) Jones & Bartlett.

Auerbach, Kathleen, jt. auth. see Riordan, Jan.

Auerbach, Kathleen G. & Riordan, Janice. Breastfeeding & Human Lactation. (Nursing-Health Science Ser.). 720p. (C). 1993. 88.75 (*0-86720-343-9*) Jones & Bartlett.

Auerbach, Kathleen G. & Riordan, nice. Pocket Guide to Breastfeeding & Human Lactation. LC 96-25990. 1996. pap. 18.75 (*0-7637-0258-7*) Jones & Bartlett.

Auerbach, Kathleen G., jt. auth. see Riordan, Jan.

Auerbach, Leslia A., tr. see Kagarlitsky, Boris.

Auerbach, Loyd. Mind over Matter: A Comprehensive Guide to Discovering Your Psychic Powers. LC 96-165065. 1996. pap. 14.00 (*1-57566-047-4*) Kensgtn Pub Corp.

Auerbach, Michael. Conversations about Cancer. 139p. 1997. pap. 14.95 (*0-683-30432-1*) Lppncott W & W.

— Conversations about Cancer: A Patient's Guide to Informed Decision Making. LC 96-16212. 121p. 1996. pap. 24.95 (*0-683-30072-5*) Lppncott W & W.

Auerbach, Nina. Communities of Women: An Idea in Fiction. LC 77-21213. 224p. 1978. 25.50 (*0-674-15168-2*) HUP.

— Communities of Women: An Idea in Fiction. LC 77-21213. 224p. 1986. pap. 12.95 (*0-674-15169-0*) HUP.

***Auerbach, Nina.** Daphne Du Maurier, Haunted Heiress. LC 99-34174. 192p. 1999. 24.95 (*0-8122-3530-4*) U of Pa Pr.

Auerbach, Nina. Ellen Terry, Player in Her Time. LC 96-36437. (Illus.). 528p. 1997. pap. 22.50 (*0-8122-1613-X*) U of Pa Pr.

***Auerbach, Nina.** Lost Lives. 1998. 25.00 (*0-226-03199-3*) U Ch Pr.

Auerbach, Nina. Our Vampires, Ourselves. LC 95-1044. 216p. 1995. pap. text 22.00 (*0-226-03201-9*) U Ch Pr.

— Our Vampires, Ourselves. 1997. pap. 12.95 (*0-226-03202-7*); pap. 12.95 (*0-614-27423-0*) U Ch Pr.

— Private Theatricals: The Lives of the Victorians. (Illus.). 144p. 1990. text 25.95 (*0-674-70755-9*) HUP.

— Woman & the Demon: The Life of a Victorian Myth. (Illus.). 270p. 1982. 37.95 (*0-674-95406-8*) HUP.

— Woman & the Demon: The Life of a Victorian Myth. (Illus.). 270p. 1984. pap. text 17.50 (*0-674-95407-6*) HUP.

Auerbach, Nina & Knoepflmacher, U. C., eds. Forbidden Journeys: Fairy Tales & Fantasies by Victorian Women Writers. LC 91-31824. (Illus.). vi, 380p. 1993. pap. 11.95 (*0-226-03204-3*) U Ch Pr.

— Forbidden Journeys: Fairy Tales & Fantasies by Victorian Women Writers. LC 91-31824. (Illus.). 380p. 1996. 31.95 (*0-226-03203-5*) U Ch Pr.

Auerbach, Nina, ed. see Stoker, Bram, et al.

Auerbach, Paul S. Bad Medicine. 355p. 1998. pap. 16.95 (*0-9639960-7-X*) Spec Pubns MO.

— Diving the Rainbow Reefs: Adventures of an Underwater Photographer. LC 90-40340. (Illus.). 236p. 1991. 45.00 (*0-87850-072-3*) Darwin Pr.

— Diving the Rainbow Reefs: Adventures of an Underwater Photographer. 236p. (gr. 13). 1991. 24.95 (*0-8016-0321-8*, 00321) Mosby Inc.

— A Medical Guide to Hazardous Marine Life. 3rd rev. ed. LC 96-79063. (Illus.). 72p. 1997. pap. 19.95 (*0-941332-55-1*, D267) Best Pub Co.

— Medicine for the Outdoors: A Guide to Emergency Medical Procedures & First Aid for Wilderness Travelers. (Illus.). 1986. 24.95 (*0-316-05928-5*, Little Brwn Med Div); pap. 12.95 (*0-316-05929-3*, Little Brwn Med Div) Lppncott W & W.

***Auerbach, Paul S.** Medicine for the Outdoors: The Essential Guide to Emergency Medical Procedures & First Aid. 3rd rev. ed. LC 98-12402. (Illus.). 512p. 1999. pap. 22.50 (*1-55821-723-1*) Lyons Pr.

Auerbach, Paul S. An Ocean of Colors. (Illus.). 144p. (Orig.). 1996. pap. 24.95 (*0-87850-114-2*) Darwin Pr.

Auerbach, Paul S., ed. Wilderness Medicine: Management of Wilderness & Environment Emergencies. 3rd ed. (Illus.). 1536p. (C). (gr. 13). 1994. text 179.00 (*0-8016-7044-6*, 07044) Mosby Inc.

Auerbach, Phillip. Try It Again. 121p. 1992. pap. 20.00 (*0-685-14676-6*) NJ Inst CLE.

***Auerbach Publishers Staff.** Technology Management. 1999. 79.95 (*0-8493-9827-4*) CRC Pr.

Auerbach, Red & Dooley, Ken. MBA - Management by Auerbach: Management Tips from the Leader of One of America's Most Successful Organizations. 256p. 1991. text 19.95 (*0-02-504481-8*) Macmillan.

Auerbach, Rena R., ed. see Vidal Sassoon International Center for Study of An.

Auerbach, Robert, jt. auth. see Fan, Tai-Ping.

Auerbach, Ronald D. Segwagwanyana: Ein Beitung zur Afrikanischen Ethnoherpetologie. (GER.). 248p. (Orig.). 1995. pap. 32.95 (*3-930612-00-3*, Pub. by Edition Chimaira) Bibliomania.

Auerbach, Simon. Legislating for Conflict. (Oxford Monographs on Labour Law). (Illus.). 288p. 1991. 75.00 (*0-19-825275-7*) OUP.

Auerbach, Simon, jt. auth. see Bowers, John.

Auerbach, Stephen M. & Gramling, Sandy E. Stress Management. LC 97-5294. 272p. 1997. pap. text 48.00 (*0-13-722281-5*) P-H.

Auerbach, Stephen M., jt. auth. see Gramling, Sandy E.

Auerbach, Stevanne. Dr. Toy's Smart Play: How to Raise a Child with a High PQ (Play Quotient) LC 97-41485. 288p. 1998. pap. 13.95 (*0-312-18089-6*, St Martin Griffin) St Martin.

— Keys to Choosing Child Care. 160p. 1991. pap. 6.95 (*0-8120-4527-0*) Barron.

— The Toy Chest. (Illus.). 256p. 1986. pap. 12.95 (*0-8184-0405-1*) Carol Pub Group.

Auerbach, Susan. Queen Elizabeth II. LC 92-46478. (World Leaders Ser.). 112p. (YA). 1993. lib. bdg. 25.27 (*0-86625-481-1*) Rourke Pubns.

— Vietnamese Americans. LC 91-15806. (American Voices Ser.). 112p. (J). (gr. 5-9). 1991. lib. bdg. 18.95 (*0-86593-136-4*) Rourke Corp.

Auerbach, Susan, ed. Encyclopedia of Multiculturalism, 6 vols. LC 93-23405. 1993. 657.07 (*1-85435-670-4*) Marshall Cavendish.

***Auerbach, Susan, ed.** Encyclopedia of Multiculturalism, 2 vols. LC 93-23405. 596p. 1999. 214.21 (*0-7614-7096-4*) Marshall Cavendish.

Auerbach, Sylvia. How to Be Smart Parents Now That Your Kids Are Adults. 192p. (Orig.). 1995. pap. 14.95 (*0-9624945-8-5*) Silvercat Pubns.

Auerbacher, Inge. Beyond the Yellow Star to America. (Illus.). 224p. (YA). 1995. pap. 9.99 (*0-88092-252-4*) Royal Fireworks.

— I Am a Star: Child of the Holocaust. LC 88-2018. (Illus.). (J). 1989. pap. 4.95 (*0-671-66644-4*) PB.

— I Am a Star: Child of the Holocaust. LC 92-31444. (Illus.). 80p. (J). (gr. 3-7). 1993. pap. 5.99 (*0-14-036401-3*, PuffinBks) Peng Put Young Read.

Auerbacher, Inge. I Am a Star: Child of the Holocaust. 1993. 11.09 (*0-606-02680-0*, Pub. by Turtleback) Demco.

***Auerbacher, Inge & Shanteau, Pamela.** Running Against the Wind. (Illus.). 117p. (YA). (gr. 4-9). 2000. pap. 9.99 (*0-88092-437-3*, 4373) Royal Fireworks.

***Auerback, Annie, et al.** Romancing the Shriek. (Cat Dog Ser.). 64p. 1999. pap. 3.99 (*0-689-83000-9*) S&S Childrens.

Auerback, Elsa R. Making Meaning, Making Change: Participatory Curriculum Development for Adult ESL Literacy. Keenan, Fran, ed. (Language in Education Ser.). (Illus.). 140p. (Orig.). 1992. pap. text 16.50 (*0-937354-79-1*) Delta Systems.

Auerback, Ray, et al, eds. Environmental Liability for Banks. 250p. 1995. 110.00 (*1-85044-582-6*) LLP.

Auerback, Stevanne. FAO Schwarz: Toys for a Lifetime: Enhancing Childhood Through Play. LC 99-23711. (Illus.). 144p. 1999. 25.00 (*0-7893-0355-8*, Pub. by Universe) St Martin.

A

Auernheimer, Leonardo. Trading with the Future & Futures Trading. Pejovich, Steve & Dethloff, Henry, eds. (Series on Public Issues: No. 14). 23p. 1985. pap. 2.00 (*0-86599-050-6*) PERC.

Auernheimer, Roy. Memories of a Farm Boy. LC 97-62076. (Illus.). viii, 172p. 1997. pap. 14.95 (*0-945530-18-8*) Wordsworth KS.

Auerswald, David, ed. see Wagner, Richard, et al.

***Auerswald, David P.** Disarmed Democracies: Domestic Institutions & the Use of Force. LC 99-50474. (Illus.). 216p. (C). 2000. text 39.50 (*0-472-11120-5*, 11120) U of Mich Pr.

Auerswald, Karl. Bodeneigenschaften und Bodenerosion. (Relief, Boden, Palaeoklima Ser.: Band 8). (GER., Illus.). viii, 208p. 1993. pap. 40.00 (*3-443-09008-7*, Pub. by Gebruder Borntraeger) Balogh.

Auerswald, Philip E., jt. auth. see Branscomb, Lewis M.

Auerswald, W., ed. see International Atherosclerosis Conference Staff.

Auf der Heide, F. Meyer, et al, eds. Parallel Architectures & Their Efficient Use: First Heinz Nixdorf Symposium, Paderborn, Germany, November 11-13, 1992 Proceedings. LC 93-29041. (Lecture Notes in Computer Science Ser.: Vol. 678). xii, 227p. 1993. 39.95 (*0-387-56731-3*) Spr-Verlag.

Auf der Heide, Lisl. Morning Glories Out of Stone. LC 90-42896. 64p. (Orig.). 1990. pap. 7.50 (*0-931832-55-1*) Fithian Pr.

Auf Der Maur, Fritz, jt. auth. see Imber, Walter.

Auf der Maur, Nick, ed. see Chodos, Robert.

Aufdemberge, C. T. Christian Worship: Handbook. LC 95-73085. 997p. 1997. 49.99 (*0-8100-0584-0*, 03N3016) Northwest Pub.

Aufderheide, Anne, ed. see Narada Media Staff.

Aufderheide, Arthur C. & Rodriguez-Martin, Conrado. The Cambridge Encyclopedia of Human Paleopathology. LC 97-16223. (Illus.). 496p. (C). 1998. text 100.00 (*0-521-55203-6*) Cambridge U Pr.

Aufderheide, Charles. Garden of Games: The Collected Poems of Charles Aufderheide. LC 92-72710. 96p. (Orig.). 1993. pap. 9.95 (*1-878580-14-0*) Asylum Arts.

Aufderheide, K. J., jt. ed. see Grimes, G. W.

Aufderheide, Patricia. Communications Policy & the Public Interest: The Telecommunications Act of 1996. LC 98-54130. 323p. 1999. pap. text 24.00 (*1-57230-425-1*); lib. bdg. 45.00 (*1-57230-418-9*) Guilford Pubns.

***Aufderheide, Patricia.** The Daily Planet: A Critic on the Capitalist Culture Beat. LC 99-44814. 2000. pap. 19.95 (*0-8166-3342-8*) U of Minn Pr.

Aufderheide, Tom P., et al, eds. Heartsave AED for the Lay Rescuer & First Responder, Vol. 70-2006. (Illus.). 104p. 1998. pap. text 10.00 (*0-87493-690-X*) Am Heart.

— Instructor's Manual Heartsaver AED, Vol. 70-2007. (Illus.). 63p. 1998. pap. text, teacher ed. 15.00 (*0-87493-691-8*) Am Heart.

Aufderstrasse, H., jt. auth. see Lupson, Peter.

Aufermann, B. Zur Chemotaxonomie Mariner Rhodophyceen am Beispiel einer Leucin-Decarboxylase. (Bibliotheca Phycologica Ser.: No. 43). (Illus.). 1978. pap. text 30.00 (*3-7682-1206-8*) Lubrecht & Cramer.

Auffarth, Christoph. Der Drohende Untergang: "Schopfung" In Mythos und Ritual Im Alten Orient und In Griechenland Am Beispiel der Odysee und Des Ezechielbuches. (Religionsgeschichtliche Versuche und Vorarbeiten Ser.: Vol. 39). (GER.). xviii, 655p. 1991. lib. bdg. 175.40 (*3-11-012640-0*) De Gruyter.

Auffenberg, Walter. Behavioral Ecology of the Komodo Monitor. LC 80-26683. (Illus.). x, 406p. 1981. 59.95 (*0-8130-0621-X*) U Press Fla.

— The Bengal Monitor. LC 94-3869. (Illus.). 592p. 1994. 79.95 (*0-8130-1295-3*) U Press Fla.

— Gray's Monitor Lizard. LC 86-15894. (Illus.). 432p. 1988. 49.95 (*0-8130-0841-7*) U Press Fla.

Aufferman, W., jt. ed. see Higgins, C. B.

Auffhammer, C. W., tr. see Hapgood, Marilyn O.

Auffhammer, W., tr. see Duncan, Alastair, et al.

Auffray, C. Dictionnaire de la Biologie. (ENG & FRE.). 1998. 69.95 (*0-320-00182-2*) Fr & Eur.

Auffret, P. Voyez de Vos Yeux: Etude Structurelle de Vingt Psaumes, dont le Psaume 119. LC 92-34557. (Supplements to Vetus Testamentum Ser.: Vol. 48). xii, 414p. 1993. 181.50 (*90-04-09707-4*) Brill Academic Pubs.

Aufhammer, Bruce. Singing with Coyote. 96p. 1990. pap. 7.50 (*1-879025-02-7*) Christopher-Burghardt.

Aufhammer, Bruce, intro. Portrait in Memory. 60p. 1990. pap. 6.00 (*1-879025-03-5*) Christopher-Burghardt.

Aufiero, Larry J. Manna for a Modern Age: Essential Nourishment for Total Well-Being & Life-Long Personal Success. 250p. Date not set. pap. 14.95 (*0-9679839-2-4*) Hilton NY.

Aufiero, Lawrence J., jt. auth. see Fuori, William M.

Aufmann. Algebra for College Students. (C). Date not set. text, teacher ed., suppl. ed. 61.96 (*0-395-69283-0*) HM.

— Algebra for College Students. (C). 1994. pap. text, student ed. 21.96 (*0-395-69284-9*) HM.

— Algebra For College Students. (C). 1994. pap., teacher ed. 5.96 (*0-395-69286-5*) HM.

— Algebra with Trigonometry. (C). 1990. pap., student ed. 9.84 (*0-395-53132-2*) HM.

— Algebra with Trigonometry. (C). 1991. pap., teacher ed. 2.76 (*0-395-57057-3*) HM.

— Algebra With Trigonometry. (C). 1990. pap., student ed. 11.96 (*0-395-57058-1*) HM.

— Aufmann Algebra: Intrduction to Intermediate Algebra. 2nd ed. 1999. pap. text 53.07 (*0-395-97603-0*) HM.

— Aufmann Algebra: Introduction to Imtermediate. 2nd ed. Date not set. pap. text 17.97 (*0-395-97606-5*) HM.

— Aufmann Beginner Algebra. 5th ed. 1999. text 55.47 (*0-395-96979-4*) HM.

— Aufmann Beginner Algebra. 5th ed. 1999. pap. text, student ed. 18.87 (*0-395-96985-9*) HM.

— Aufmann Intermediate Algebra. 5th ed. 1999. pap. text, student ed. 18.87 (*0-395-96965-4*) HM.

— Aufmann Precalculus W/limits S. Date not set. text 60.87 (*0-395-97592-1*) HM.

— Basic College Math. 4th ed. (C). 1995. pap. text 32.36 (*0-395-73851-2*) HM.

— Beginner Algebra, 4 vols. (C). 1995. pap., teacher ed., suppl. ed. 11.96 (*0-395-74614-0*) HM.

— Beginner Algebra, 4 vols. (C). 1995. pap., teacher ed., suppl. ed. 17.56 (*0-395-74613-2*) HM.

— Beginner Algebra, 4 vols. 4th ed. (C). 1995. pap. text, student ed. 21.56 (*0-395-74612-4*) HM.

— Beginner's Algebra, 3 vols. (C). 1991. text, teacher ed. 64.76 (*0-395-58884-7*) HM.

***Aufmann.** Beginner's Algebra. 5th ed. 1999. pap. text 8.97 (*0-395-96991-3*) HM.

Aufmann. Beginning Algebra, 3 vols. (C). 1991. pap., student ed. 21.56 (*0-395-58887-1*) HM.

— Beginning Algebra, 3 vols. (C). 1991. pap., teacher ed., suppl. ed. 9.16 (*0-395-58888-X*) HM.

— Beginning Algebra, 3 vols. 3rd ed. (C). 1991. pap. text, student ed. 15.96 (*0-395-58886-3*) HM.

— Business Math, 2 vols. (C). 1994. pap., teacher ed., suppl. ed. 7.96 (*0-395-67535-9*) HM.

— Business Mathematics, 2 vols. (C). 1993. pap. 48.36 (*0-395-69112-5*) HM.

— Business Mathematics, 2 vols. (C). 1993. pap., teacher ed. 5.96 (*0-395-67533-2*) HM.

— Business Mathematics, 2 vols. 2nd ed. (C). 1993. pap. text 33.16 (*0-395-67532-4*); pap. text 47.16 (*0-395-67531-6*) HM.

— College Algebra. (C). Date not set. text 67.16 (*0-395-71705-1*) HM.

— College Algebra, 2 vols. (C). 1992. text, teacher ed. 68.36 (*0-395-63808-9*) HM.

— College Algebra, 2 vols. 2nd ed. (C). 1992. text 67.16 (*0-395-63807-0*) HM.

— College Algebra, 3 vols. 3rd ed. LC 96-76856. (C). 1996. text 67.16 (*0-395-78644-4*) HM.

— College Algebra: Graphing. (C). 1995. text 67.16 (*0-395-70821-4*) HM.

— College Algebra & Trigonometry, 2 vols. (C). 1993. pap., student ed. 21.96 (*0-395-63821-6*) HM.

— College Algebra & Trigonometry. (C). 1995. text 72.36 (*0-395-70822-2*) HM.

— College Algebra & Trigonometry. (C). 1995. pap., teacher ed., suppl. ed. 11.96 (*0-395-72542-9*) HM.

— College Algebra & Trigonometry. (C). 1995. pap., teacher ed. 9.96 (*0-395-72540-2*); pap. text 31.16 (*0-395-77168-4*); pap. text, student ed. 21.96 (*0-395-72541-0*) HM.

— College Algebra & Trigonometry, 2 vols. 2nd ed. (C). 1992. text 72.36 (*0-395-63818-6*) HM.

— College Trigonometry, 2 vols. 2nd ed. (C). 1993. text 67.16 (*0-395-63813-5*) HM.

— College Trigonometry, 3 vols. 3rd ed. LC 96-76858. (C). 1996. text 67.16 (*0-395-78645-2*) HM.

— Elementary Algebra. (C). 1989. pap., teacher ed., suppl. ed. 9.96 (*0-395-50725-1*) HM.

— Elementary Algebra with Basic Mathematics. (C). 1989. pap., student ed. 11.16 (*0-395-48635-1*); pap. text 48.76 (*0-395-48634-3*) HM.

— Elementary Algebra with Basic Mathematics. (C). 1989. pap., teacher ed. 4.76 (*0-395-48636-X*) HM.

— Intermediate Algebra, 3 vols. (C). 1991. pap., student ed. 21.56 (*0-395-58893-6*) HM.

— Intermediate Algebra, 3 vols. (C). 1992. pap., teacher ed. 9.16 (*0-395-58891-X*) HM.

— Intermediate Algebra, 4 vols. (C). 1994. pap., teacher ed., suppl. ed. 11.96 (*0-395-71905-4*) HM.

— Intermediate Algebra, 4 vols. (C). 1994. pap. 63.16 (*0-395-71222-X*) HM.

— Intermediate Algebra, 4 vols. (C). 1995. pap., suppl. ed. 19.96 (*0-395-71224-6*) HM.

— Intermediate Algebra. (C). 1995. pap. 64.36 (*0-395-76847-0*) HM.

— Intermediate Algebra, 3 vols. 3rd ed. (C). 1990. pap. text 46.36 (*0-395-57073-5*) HM.

— Intermediate Algebra, 3 vols. 3rd ed. (C). 1991. pap. text, student ed. 11.96 (*0-395-57074-3*) HM.

— Intermediate Algebra, 4 vols. 4th ed. LC 94-76469. (C). 1994. pap. text 61.96 (*0-395-70832-X*) HM.

— Intermediate Algebra, 4 vols. 4th ed. (C). 1995. pap. text, student ed. 21.56 (*0-395-71225-4*) HM.

— Intermediate Algebra, 4 vols. 4th ed. (C). 1995. pap. text, teacher ed. 11.96 (*0-395-71223-8*) HM.

***Aufmann.** Intermediate Algebra. 5th ed. 1999. pap. text 8.97 (*0-395-96964-6*) HM.

Aufmann. Introduction to Algebra, 2 vols. (C). Date not set. pap., teacher ed., suppl. ed. 63.56 (*0-395-76485-8*) HM.

— Introduction to Algebra, 4 vols. (C). 1994. pap., student ed. 19.96 (*0-395-71220-3*) HM.

— Introduction to Algebra. (C). 1995. pap. text 59.56 (*0-395-76563-3*) HM.

— Introduction to Algebra, 4 vols. (C). 1995. pap., teacher ed. 11.96 (*0-395-71219-X*) HM.

— Introduction to Algebra, 3 vols. 3rd ed. (C). 1990. pap. text, student ed. 11.96 (*0-395-57068-9*) HM.

— Introduction to Algebra, 4 vols. 4th ed. LC 94-76470. (C). 1994. pap. text 61.16 (*0-395-70831-1*) HM.

— Introduction to Algebra. 5th ed. 1998. pap. text 50.37 (*0-395-92321-2*) HM.

— Introduction to Algebra with Basic Math, 2 vols. (C). 1996. pap., teacher ed., suppl. ed. 9.96 (*0-395-74624-8*) HM.

— Introduction to Algebra with Basic Math, 2 vols. (C). 1996. pap., teacher ed., suppl. ed. 17.16 (*0-395-74623-X*) HM.

— Introduction to Algebra with Basic Math, 2 vols. 2nd ed. LC 96-114994. (C). 1995. pap. text 63.56 (*0-395-74621-3*) HM.

— Introduction to Algebra with Basic Math, 2 vols. 2nd ed. (C). 1996. pap. text, student ed. 20.36 (*0-395-74622-1*) HM.

— Introductory Algebra. (C). 1995. pap. text 39.16 (*0-395-72359-0*) HM.

— Prealgebra. (C). 1993. pap. text 58.76 (*0-395-66524-8*) HM.

— Prealgebra. (C). 1993. pap., teacher ed., suppl. ed. 7.96 (*0-395-66526-4*) HM.

— Prealgebra. (C). 1994. pap. text, student ed. 22.36 (*0-395-69291-1*) HM.

— Precalculus, 2 vols. (C). Date not set. text, teacher ed., suppl. ed. 72.36 (*0-395-63826-7*) HM.

— Precalculus, 2 vols. (C). 1993. pap., student ed. 13.16 (*0-395-63829-1*) HM.

— Precalculus, 2 vols. (C). 1993. pap. 9.16 (*0-395-63830-5*) HM.

— Precalculus, 2 vols. 2nd ed. (C). 1993. text 72.36 (*0-395-63825-9*) HM.

— Precalculus, 2 vols. 2nd ed. (C). 1993. pap. text, student ed. 21.96 (*0-395-63828-3*) HM.

Aufmann & Lee. College Algebra with Trigonometry. (C). 1995. pap. text 47.96 (*0-395-74773-2*) HM.

Aufmann, Richard N. Basic College Math. 6th ed. LC 98-71979. 1998. pap. text 51.87 (*0-395-90704-7*) HM.

Aufmann, Richard N. & Barker, Vernon C. Basic College Mathematics: An Applied Approach, 3 vols. 3rd ed. (C). 1986. pap. text 35.96 (*0-395-42782-7*) HM.

— Basic College Mathematics: An Applied Approach, 5 vols. 5th ed. 576p. (C). 1994. pap. text 61.96 (*0-395-70830-3*); pap. text, student ed. 21.56 (*0-395-71217-3*) HM.

— Basic College Mathematics: An Applied Approach, 5 vols. 5th ed. (C). 1994. text, teacher ed. 19.96 (*0-395-71216-5*) HM.

— Basic College Mathematics: An Applied Approach, 5 vols. 5th ed. (C). 1995. pap. text, teacher ed. 11.96 (*0-395-71215-7*) HM.

— Basic College Mathematics: An Applied Approach, 5 vols. 5th annot. ed. (C). 1995. text, teacher ed. 63.16 (*0-395-71214-9*) HM.

— Beginning Algebra with Applications. (C). 1986. 3.50 (*0-685-43437-0*) HM.

— Beginning Algebra with Applications, 3 vols. 3rd ed. (C). 1992. text 63.56 (*0-395-58883-9*) HM.

— Intermediate Algebra: An Applied Approach. 2nd ed. 1987. teacher ed. 11.96 (*0-318-36883-8*) HM.

— Intermediate Algebra: An Applied Approach. 2nd annot. ed. 1987. teacher ed. 35.56 (*0-318-36882-X*) HM.

— Introductory Algebra: An Applied Approach, 4 vols. 4th ed. (C). 1994. pap. text, student ed. 21.56 (*0-395-71221-1*) HM.

— Introductory Algebra: An Applied Approach, 4 vols. 4th annot. ed. (C). 1994. text, teacher ed. 62.36 (*0-395-71218-1*) HM.

Aufmann, Richard N. & Lockwood, Joanne S. Algebra for College Students: A Functions Approach. 768p. (C). 1994. text 61.96 (*0-395-67530-8*) HM.

— Algebra for College Students: A Functions Approach. (C). 1994. text, teacher ed. 7.96 (*0-395-69285-7*) HM.

Aufmann, Richard N. & Nation, Richard D. College Algebra, 3 vols. 3rd annot. ed. (C). 1996. text, teacher ed. 68.36 (*0-395-81530-4*) HM.

— College Algebra: Instructor's Resource Manual with Chapter Tests, 3 vols. (C). 1997. text 11.96 (*0-395-83446-5*) HM.

— College Algebra & Trigonometry, 3 vols. 3rd ed. 768p. (C). 1996. text 72.36 (*0-395-78643-6*) HM.

— College Algebra & Trigonometry, 3 vols. 3rd annot. ed. (C). 1996. text, teacher ed. 73.56 (*0-395-81529-0*) HM.

Aufmann, Richard N., et al. Algebra: Introductory & Intermediate. 704p. (C). 1996. pap. text 60.36 (*0-395-75579-4*) HM.

— Algebra: Introductory & Intermediate. (C). 1996. text, teacher ed. 15.96 (*0-395-75581-6*) HM.

— Algebra: Introductory & Intermediate. (C). 1996. pap. text, student ed. 20.36 (*0-395-75580-8*) HM.

— Algebra with Trigonometry. (C). 1990. text. write for info. (*0-395-54437-8*) HM Soft Schl Col Div.

— Basic College Mathematics: An Applied Approach. 6th ed. LC 98-71979. 1999. write for info. (*0-395-92320-4*) HM.

— Beginning Algebra with Applications. 2nd ed. LC 88-81319. 480p. 1988. teacher ed. 38.36 (*0-318-36878-1*) HM.

— Beginning Algebra with Applications. 2nd annot. ed. LC 88-81319. 480p. 1988. teacher ed., student ed. 15.16 (*0-318-36877-3*) HM.

— Beginning Algebra with Applications, 4 vols. 4th ed. 624p. (C). 1995. text 63.56 (*0-395-74610-8*) HM.

— Beginning Algebra with Applications, 4 vols. 4th annot. ed. (C). 1995. text, teacher ed. 64.76 (*0-395-74611-6*) HM.

— Business Mathematics: Brief Version, 2 vols. 2nd ed. (C). 1993. pap. text, student ed. 21.96 (*0-395-67534-0*) HM.

— College Algebra. (C). 1990. text, teacher ed. 2.76 (*0-395-43012-7*) HM.

— College Algebra & Trigonometry. (C). 1990. pap. text 11.96 (*0-395-43009-7*) HM.

— College Algebra & Trigonometry. (C). 1990. text 2.76 (*0-395-43008-9*); pap. text 3.16 (*0-395-43011-9*) HM.

— College Trigonometry. (C). 1990. text, teacher ed. 2.76 (*0-395-43016-X*); pap. text, teacher ed. 11.96 (*0-395-43017-8*) HM.

— Elementary Algebra with Basic Math Review. 1989. teacher ed. 11.16 (*0-318-36880-3*); 4.76 (*0-318-36881-1*) HM.

— Elementary Algebra with Basic Math Review. annot. ed. 1989. teacher ed. 37.16 (*0-318-36879-X*) HM.

— Intermediate Algebra with Applications. 2nd ed. 1988. teacher ed. write for info. (*0-318-63305-1*) HM.

— Intermediate Algebra with Applications, 4 vols. 4th ed. 768p. (C). 1995. text 63.56 (*0-395-74616-7*) HM.

— Intermediate Algebra with Applications, 4 vols. 4th ed. (C). 1996. pap. text, student ed. 21.56 (*0-395-74618-3*) HM.

— Intermediate Algebra with Applications, 4 vols. 4th annot. ed. (C). 1995. text, teacher ed. 64.76 (*0-395-74617-5*) HM.

— Introductory Algebra: An Applied Approach 5th ed. LC 98-71981. 1999. pap. text 52.17 (*0-395-90706-3*) HM.

— Precalculus: The Graphing Workbook, 2 vols. 2nd ed. (C). 1993. pap. text 13.16 (*0-395-65941-8*) HM.

Aufmann, Richard N., jt. auth. see Barker, Vernon C.

Aufort, Jean, ed. see Mauriac, Francois.

Aufray, Fred. Nu. 96p. 2000. 19.95 (*1-893263-07-X*) Ipso Facto.

Aufrecht, Walter E. A Corpus of Ammonite Inscriptions. LC 88-1535. (Ancient Near Eastern Texts & Studies: Vol. 4). (Illus.). 516p. 1989. lib. bdg. 119.95 (*0-88946-089-2*) E Mellen.

Aufrecht, Walter E., et al, eds. Urbanism in Antiquity: From Mesopotamia to Crete. (JSOT Supplement Ser.: No. 244). 296p. 1997. 85.00 (*1-85075-666-X*, Pub. by Sheffield Acad) CUP Services.

Aufrecht, Walter E. & Hurd, John. A Synoptic Concordance of Aramaic Inscriptions. (International Concordance Library: Vol. I). 1975. pap. 20.00 (*0-935106-24-3*) E Mellen.

Aufricht, Hans. Guide to League of Nations Publications. LC 73-161711. (BCL Ser.: No. 1). reprint ed. 45.00 (*0-404-00418-0*) AMS Pr.

Auftrag des Institutes fur Zeitgeschichte Bearbeit, ed. Inventar Archivalischer Quellen des NS Staates: Die Laberlieferung von Behrden & Einrichtungen des Reiches der Lunder & der NSDAP. (GER.). 717p. 1991. lib. bdg. 120.00 (*3-598-10861-3*) K G Saur Verlag.

***Aug, Bobbie.** Charm Quilts with Style. (Illus.). 96p. 2000. pap. 19.95 (*1-57432-751-8*, Am Quilters Soc) Collector Bks.

***Aug, Bobbie & Newman, Sharon.** Vertical Quilts with Style. Jonsson, Lee, ed. LC 00-29283. (Illus.). 112p. 2000. pap. 18.95 (*1-57432-732-1*, Am Quilters Soc) Collector Bks.

Aug, Bobby & Newman, Sharon. String Quilts with Style. LC 99-14407. 112p. 1999. per. 18.95 (*1-57432-720-8*, Am Quilters Soc) Collector Bks.

Aug, Lisa. Beyond the Falls: A Modern History of the Lower Niagara River. 220p. 1992. pap. 14.95 (*0-9632815-8-5*) Niagara Bks.

Aug, Marc. An Anthropology for Contemporaneous Worlds. LC 98-30986. (Mestizo Spaces Ser.). 1999. write for info. (*0-8047-3474-7*); pap. 16.95 (*0-8047-3475-5*) Stanford U Pr.

Augarde, A. J. The English-Kannada Dictionary. 1985. write for info. (*0-8288-1765-0*, M6835) Fr & Eur.

Augarde, A. J., ed. The Oxford Dictionary of Modern Quotations. 384p. 1991. 45.00 (*0-19-866141-X*, 12288) OUP.

Augarde, Steve. Fire Engine to the Rescue. LC 98-230496. (Illus.). 10p. (J). 1998. pap. 14.95 (*0-688-16328-9*, Wm Morrow) Morrow Avon.

— The Hokey Pokey & Other Party Rhymes. (Playtime Pop-Ups Ser.). (Illus.). 12p. (J). (ps-k). 1997. 6.95 (*0-590-88021-7*, Cartwheel) Scholastic Inc.

— The Itsy Bitsy Spider & Other Hand Rhymes. (Playtime Pop-Ups Ser.). (Illus.). 12p. (J). (ps-k). 1997. 6.95 (*0-590-88022-5*, Cartwheel) Scholastic Inc.

***Augarde, Steve.** Vroom! Vroom! A Pop-Up Race To The Finish. (J). 2001. 13.95 (*0-316-07111-0*) Little.

— When I Grow Up. (Illus.). (J). (ps-3). 2000. 12.99 (*0-448-42179-8*, Planet Dexter) Peng Put Young Read.

Augarde, Steve. Five Speckled Frogs: And Other Counting Rhymes. (Playtime Pop-Ups Ser.). 12p. (J). (ps). 1997. bds. 6.95 (*0-590-88024-1*) Scholastic Inc.

— Row, Row, Row Your Boat: And Other Play Ryhmes. (Playtime Pop-Ups Ser.). 12p. (J). (ps-k). 1997. bds. 6.95 (*0-590-88023-3*, Cartwheel) Scholastic Inc.

Augarde, Steve, jt. auth. see Price, Mathew.

Augarde, Tony. The Oxford A to Z of Word Games. (Illus.). 270p. 1996. pap. 9.95 (*0-19-866231-9*) OUP.

— The Oxford Guide to Word Games. LC 76-352512. (Illus.). 256p. 1986. pap. 7.95 (*0-19-282005-2*) OUP.

— Oxford Word Challenge. LC 98-3224. 160p. 1999. pap. 8.95 (*0-19-860113-1*) OUP.

Augarde, Tony, ed. The Oxford Dictionary of Modern Quotations. 542p. 1993. pap. 14.95 (*0-19-283086-4*) OUP.

***Auge, Christian & Dentzer, Jean-Marie.** Petra: Lost City of the Ancient World. LC 99-53256. 128p. 2000. pap. 12.95 (*0-8109-2896-5*, Pub. by Abrams) Time Warner.

Auge-Laribe, Michel & Pinot, Pierre. Agriculture & Food Supply in France During the War. (Economic & Social History of the World War Ser.). 1927. 100.00 (*0-686-83458-5*) Elliots Bks.

Auge, M. The Meaning of Illness: Anthropology, History & Sociology of Illness, No. 5. 270p. 1995. text 53.00 (*3-7186-5207-2*) Gordon & Breach.

Auge, M. & Herzlich, C. Le Sens du Mal. 4th ed. (FRE.). 278p. 1984. pap. text 31.00 (*2-903928-06-1*) Gordon & Breach.

Auge, Marc. Non-Places: Introduction to an Anthropology of Supermodernity. Howe, John, tr. LC 94-46299.Tr. of Non-Lieux. (ENG & FRE.). 128p. (C). 1995. 55.00 (*1-85984-956-3*, C0517, Pub. by Verso); pap. 18.00 (*1-85984-051-5*, C0518, Pub. by Verso) Norton.

— A Sense for the Other: The Timeliness & Relevance of

An Asterisk (*) at the beginning of an entry indicates that the title is appearing for the first time.

Anthropology. Jacobs, Amy, tr. from FRE. LC 97-26448. (Mestizo Spaces Ser.). 176p. 1997. 39.50 (*0-8047-3034-2*); pap. 14.95 (*0-8047-3035-0*) Stanford U Pr.

***Auge, Marc.** The War of Dreams: Exercises in Ethno-Fiction. LC 99-14273. 1999. write for info. (*0-7453-1389-2*) Pluto GBR.

— The War of Dreams: Studies in Ethno Fiction. 128p. 1999. pap. text 18.95 (*0-7453-1384-1*) Pluto GBR.

Auge, Marc, ed. Interpreting Illness, Vol. 2, No. 1. (History & Anthropology Ser.: Vol. 2, Pt. 1). ii, 206p. 1986. 168.00 (*3-7186-0295-4*) Gordon & Breach.

Augee, Goodman. Echidnas of Australia & New Guinea. (Illus.). 120p. 1993. pap. text 21.95 (*0-86840-046-7*, Pub. by New South Wales Univ Pr) Intl Spec Bk.

Augee, M. L., ed. Marine Mammals of Australasia: Field Biology & Captive Management. 140p. (C). 1988. text 55.00 (*0-7855-0032-4*, Pub. by Surrey Beatty & Sons) St Mut.

Augelli, Enrico & Murphy, Craig N. America's Quest for Supremacy in the Third World: An Essay in Gramscian Analysis. 200p. 1989. text 49.00 (*0-86187-930-9*) St Martin.

Augello, M. M. Josef Alois Schumpeter: A Reference Guide. xiii, 353p. 1990. 100.95 (*0-387-53040-1*) Spr-Verlag.

***Augen, D. R.** Guitar Toons Coloring Book & CD. Kirlin, Jim, ed. (Illus.). 25p. (J). (ps-7). 1999. pap. 14.00 incl. audio compact disk (*0-9669881-3-2*) D R Auten.

Augenblick, John, ed. Public Schools: Issues in Budgeting & Financial Management. 204p. (Orig.). 1985. pap. text 21.95 (*0-88738-626-1*) Transaction Pubs.

Augenbraum, Harold & Fernandez-Olmos, Margarite, eds. The Latino Reader: An American Literary Tradition, 1542 to the Present Day. 400p. 1997. pap. 16.00 (*0-395-76528-5*) HM.

Augenbraum, Harold & Stavans, Ilan. Growing up Latino: Memoirs & Stories. 416p. 1993. pap. 13.95 (*0-395-66124-2*) HM.

***Augenbraum, Harold Fernandez & Olmos, Margarite Fernandez, eds.** U. S. Latino Literature: A Critical Guide for Students & Teachers. LC 99-462065. 270p. 2000. 50.00 (*0-313-31137-4*, GR1137, Greenwood Pr) Greenwood.

***Augendre, Jacque.** Fausto Coppi. Bromley, David, ed. (Illus.). 158p. 1999. 39.95 (*0-9531729-6-1*, Pub. by Bromley Bks) Buonpane.

Augenfeld, Rivka, tr. see Ravitch, Melech.

Augenlicht, Leonard H., ed. Cell & Molecular Biology of Colon Cancer. LC 88-7589. 224p. 1989. 125.00 (*0-8493-4710-6*, RC280, CRC Reprint) Franklin.

Augensen, Harry J., tr. see Roth, Gunter D., ed.

Augenstein, B. W. & Bonner, B. E. Antiproton Science & Technology: Proceedings of the Rand Workshop. 772p. 1988. text 141.00 (*9971-5-0587-8*) World Scientific Pub.

Augenstein, Bruno W., et al. Improving the Means for Intergovernmental Communications in Crisis. LC 84-13302. 1984. pap. text 4.00 (*0-8330-0580-4*, R-3157-FF) Rand Corp.

Augenstein, David M. The EnviroMotivator: An Environmental Awareness & Training Tool. 40p. (Orig.). 1995. pap. 49.00 (*0-9644663-2-5*) Environ Develop.

— Environmental, Health & Safety Compliance Audit System for Motor Vehicle Maintenance & Refueling: Facilities & Operations. 46p. 1994. student ed. 79.00 (*0-9644663-1-7*) Environ Develop.

— The Shop Environmental Awareness Training Guide for Mechanics & Technicians: A Self-Study Guide of Environmental Rules & Practices for Vehicle/Equipment Maintenance & Refueling Operations. 45p. (C). Date not set. pap. 17.80 (*0-9644663-3-3*) Environ Develop.

Augenstein, David M. & Swartz, George, eds. Shop Safety/OSHA Compliance Guide for Managers of Motor Vehicle/Equipment Maintenance & Refueling Operations: A Standard Industry Reference on OSHA Compliance & Recommended Safety Practices. (Illus.). 358p. (C). Date not set. pap. 239.00 (*0-9644663-4-1*) Environ Develop.

Augenstein, Jeffrey S., jt. ed. see Maull, Kimball I.

Augenstein, John J. Lighting the Way, 1908-1935: The Early Years of Catholic School Superintendency. 149p. (Orig.). 1996. pap. 13.00 (*1-55833-168-9*) Natl Cath Educ.

Augenstein, John J., jt. auth. see Konnert, M. William.

Augenstine, Moshe J., jt. auth. see Tenenbaum, Aaron M.

Augenstine, David M. The Environmental Guidebook for Managers of Motor Vehicle Maintenance & Refueling Operations. 2nd ed. 210p. 1994. pap. 189.00 (*0-9644663-0-9*) Environ Develop.

Auger, Charles P. Information Sources in Grey Literature. 4th ed. LC 97-33378. (Guides to Information Sources Ser.). 177p. 1998. write for info. (*1-85739-194-2*) Bowker-Saur.

Auger, Giselle, jt. auth. see Meadow.

Auger, Peter. Information Sources in Patents. Foskett, D. J. & Hill, M. W., eds. (Guides to Information Sources Ser.). 200p. 1992. 75.00 (*0-86291-906-1*) Bowker-Saur.

***Auger, Philip.** Native Sons in "No Man's Land" Rewriting Afro-American Manhood in Novels of James Baldwin, Alice Walker, John Edgar Wideman, & Ernest Gaines. (Studies in African American History & Culture). 250p. 1999. 50.00 (*0-8153-3060-X*) Garland.

Auger, Pierre & Rousseau, Louis-Jean. English-French Lexicon of the Mining Industry Vol. 1: Mining. (ENG & FRE.). 89p. 1981. pap. 49.95 (*0-8288-6310-5*, M6016) Fr & Eur.

Auger, Roland. French Canadian & Acadian Genealogical Review, Vol. 1, No. 2. 68p. 1997. pap. 7.50 (*1-886560-51-X*) Quintin Pub RI.

— French Canadian & Acadian Genealogical Review, Vol. 1, No. 3. 68p. 1997. pap. 7.50 (*1-886560-50-1*) Quintin Pub RI.

— French Canadian & Acadian Genealogical Review: Winter 1972. 64p. 1997. pap. 7.50 (*1-886560-29-3*) Quintin Pub RI.

— French Canadian & Acadian Genealogical Review Vol. 3, No. 1: Spring 1971. 64p. 1997. pap. 7.50 (*1-886560-31-5*) Quintin Pub RI.

— French Canadian & Acadian Genealogical Review Vol. 3, No. 2: Summer 1971. 64p. 1997. pap. 7.50 (*1-886560-33-1*) Quintin Pub RI.

— French Canadian & Acadian Genealogical Review Vol. 4, No. 1: Spring 1972. 64p. 1997. pap. 7.50 (*1-886560-53-6*) Quintin Pub RI.

— French Canadian & Acadian Genealogical Review Vol. 4, No. 2: Summer 1972. 64p. 1997. pap. 7.50 (*1-886560-26-9*) Quintin Pub RI.

— French Canadian & Acadian Genealogical Review Vol. 4, No. 3: Fall 1972. 64p. 1997. pap. 7.50 (*1-886560-28-5*) Quintin Pub RI.

— French Canadian & Acadian Genealogical Review, 1978, Vol. 7, No. 1. 64p. 1997. pap. 7.50 (*1-886560-24-2*) Quintin Pub RI.

— French Canadian & Acadian Genealogical Review, 1978, Vol. 7, No. 2. 76p. 1997. pap. 8.00 (*1-886560-25-0*) Quintin Pub RI.

— French Canadian & Acadian Genealogical Review, 1980, Vol. 8, Nos. 1-2. 128p. 1997. pap. 15.00 (*1-886560-32-3*) Quintin Pub RI.

Auger, Roland, ed. French Canadian & Acadian Genealogical Review Vol. 1, No. 1: Spring 1968. 96p. 1997. 10.00 (*1-886560-54-4*) Quintin Pub RI.

— French Canadian & Acadian Genealogical Review Vol. 2, No. 1: Spring 1969. 64p. 1997. 7.50 (*1-886560-55-2*) Quintin Pub RI.

— French Canadian & Acadian Genealogical Review Vol. 3, No. 4: Winter 1971. 64p. 1997. 7.50 (*1-886560-20-X*) Quintin Pub RI.

— French Canadian & Acadian Genealogical Review Vol. 4, No. 1: Spring 1972. 64p. 1997. pap. 7.50 (*1-886560-06-4*) Quintin Pub RI.

— French Canadian & Acadian Genealogical Review Vol. 8, Nos. 3 & 4: Winter 1980. 143p. 1997. 15.00 (*1-886560-05-6*) Quintin Pub RI.

— French Canadian & Acadian Genealogical Review, 1975, Vol. 5, Nos. 3-4. 160p. 1997. 15.00 (*1-886560-07-2*) Quintin Pub RI.

Auger, Roland. French Canadian & Acadian Genealogical Review Vol. 1, No. 4: Winter 1968. 64p. 1997. 10.00 (*1-886560-58-7*) Quintin Pub RI.

— French Canadian & Acadian Genealogical Review Vol. 2, No. 2: Spring 1969. 80p. 1997. 8.50 (*1-886560-56-0*) Quintin Pub RI.

— French Canadian & Acadian Genealogical Review Vol. 2, No. 3: Spring 1969. 64p. 1997. 7.50 (*1-886560-57-9*) Quintin Pub RI.

— French Canadian & Acadian Genealogical Review Vol. 3, No. 3: Fall 1971. 64p. 1997. 7.50 (*1-886560-21-8*) Quintin Pub RI.

— French Canadian & Acadian Genealogical Review, 1981, Vol. 9, Nos. 1-4. 260p. 1997. 25.00 (*1-886560-23-4*) Quintin Pub RI.

Auger, Susan J., jt. ed. see Niemeyer, Louis V.

Auger, Vincent. Human Rights & Trade: The Clinton Administration & China. (Pew Case Studies in International Affairs). 50p. (C). 1995. pap. text 3.50 (*1-56927-168-2*, GU Schl Foreign) Geo U Inst Dplmcy.

Auger, Vincent A. The Dynamics of Foreign Policy Analysis: The Carter Administration & the Neutron Bomb. LC 96-32891. 160p. 1996. 55.50 (*0-8476-8339-7*); pap. 23.95 (*0-8476-8340-0*) Rowman.

— The War Powers Resolution & U. S. Policy in Lebanon, 1982-1984. (Pew Case Studies in International Affairs). 50p. (C). 1993. pap. text 3.50 (*1-56927-358-8*) Geo U Inst Dplmcy.

Augerhofer, Paul J., et al. In Aedibus Aldi: The Legacy of Aldus Manutius & His Press. LC 95-12312. (Illus.). ix, 173p. 1995. pap. 30.00 (*0-8425-2329-4*, Friends of the Library) Brigham.

Augerinos, Mary. Alternative Dispute Resolution No. 26: GAP Reports. 48p. 1997. pap. 17.50 (*0-944715-54-0*) CAI.

Augerot, James E. Romanian/Limba Romana: A Course in Modern Romanian. (RUM & ENG., Illus.). 360p. 1999. 48.00 (*973-98392-0-7*, Pub. by Ctr Romanian Studies) Intl Spec Bk.

***Augerson, William S.** A Review of the Scientific Literature As It Pertains to Gulf War Illnesses: Chemical & Biological Warfare Agents. 2000. pap. 30.00 (*0-8330-2680-1*) Rand Corp.

Aughanbaugh, John. An Ecological Study of Crall Woods. (Biological Notes Ser.: No. 2). 1964. pap. text 2.00 (*0-86727-053-5*) Ohio Bio Survey.

Aughenbaugh, Anna. Easy Recipes for One, Two or a Few. LC 94-2045. 292p. (Orig.). 1994. pap., spiral bd. 12.95 (*0-9625869-1-9*) Starlite CO.

— More Than Soup - Bean Bookbook. LC 90-91471. 128p. 1995. spiral bd. 7.95 (*0-9625869-2-7*) Starlite CO.

Aughey, Arthur & Morrow, Duncan. Northern Ireland Politics. LC 95-45047. 224p. (C). 1996. pap. text 23.44 (*0-582-25346-2*, Pub. by Addison-Wesley) Longman.

Aughey, Arthur, et al. The Conservative Political Tradition in Britain & the United States. LC 91-42201. 180p. 1992. 39.50 (*0-8386-3500-8*) Fairleigh Dickinson.

***Aughey, Elizabeth & Frye, Fredric.** A Color Handbook of Veterinary Histology & Correlates. (Illus.). 320p. 2000. 99.95 (*0-8138-2874-0*) Iowa St U Pr.

Aughey, John H. Tupelo. LC 75-37300. (Black Heritage Library Collection). 1977. reprint ed. 37.95 (*0-8369-8937-6*) Ayer.

***Aughinbaugh, J.** Unfinished Business. 182p. 2000. pap. 13.95 (*0-7414-0346-3*) Buy Books.

Aughterson, Kate, ed. English Renaissance: Anthology of Sources & Documents. LC 97-49601. 624p. (C). (gr. 13). 1998. 150.00 (*0-415-18554-8*) Routledge.

— Renaissance Woman - a Sourcebook: Constructions of Femininity in England. LC 95-9518. 344p. (C). 1995. pap. 25.99 (*0-415-12046-2*) Routledge.

Aughterson, Ned. Extradition Law in Australia. 300p. 1995. 95.00 (*0-455-21330-5*, Pub. by LawBk Co); pap. 70.00 (*0-455-21329-1*, Pub. by LawBk Co) Gaunt.

Augier, Emile. Four Plays: Olympe's Marriage, the House of Fourchambault, Monsieur Poirier's Son-In-Law, The Post-Script. Clark, B. H., tr. from FRE. LC 87-7396. 260p. 1989. reprint ed. lib. bdg. 39.50 (*0-86527-367-7*) Fertig.

Augoisti, A. T., ed. Sensors & Their Applications VII: Proceedings of the Seventh Conference, Held in Dublin, Ireland, 10-13 September 1995. LC 95-33264. (Sensors Ser.). (Illus.). 447p. 1995. 210.00 (*0-7503-0331-X*) IOP Pub.

Augoustatos, Rosemarie, tr. see Kontomerkou, Vana.

Augousti & Grattan. Introduction to Fiber Optic Sensors. (Sensor Physics & Technology Ser.). (Illus.). 208p. (C). 1997. text. write for info. (*0-412-63090-7*, Chap & Hall NY) Kluwer Academic.

Augousti, A. T., jt. ed. see Grattan, K. T.

Augousti, A. T., Sensors & Their Applications Staf & White, Neil. Sensors & Their Applications VIII: Proceedings of the Eighth Conference on Sensors & Their Applications, Held in Glasgow, Scotland, 7-10 September 1997. LC 97-28598. (Sensors Ser.). 1997. write for info. (*0-7503-0421-9*) IOP Pub.

Augoustinos, Martha & Walker, Lain. Social Cognition: An Integrated Perspective. 304p. (C). 1995. 69.95 (*0-8039-8989-X*); pap. 26.95 (*0-8039-8990-3*) Sage.

Augros, Robert M. & Stanciu, George N. The New Biology: Discovering the Wisdom in Nature. LC 86-28058. (Illus.). 274p. 1995. reprint ed. 29.95 (*1-889792-00-4*) Principle Source.

Augsburg, Cray & Willoughby, Lauren, eds. The Fourth Rainbow Book of Adventures. (Illus.). 174p. (Orig.). 1988. pap. 10.95 (*0-932471-11-0*) Falsoft.

Augsburg Fortress Staff. Active Christian Parenting Parents Guide. 1995. pap. 14.99 (*0-8066-0386-0*, 23-2323) Augsburg Fortress.

— Augsburg Sermons for Children: Gospels, Ser. C. 128p. 1994. pap. 10.99 (*0-8066-2623-2*, 9-2623, Augsburg) Augsburg Fortress.

— Gospel Sermons for Children. (Gospel Series B). 128p. 1996. pap. 10.99 (*0-8066-2781-6*, 9-2781) Augsburg Fortress.

— Intersections Caring & Community: Perspectives from Ephesians. 1995. pap. text 5.49 (*0-8066-0129-9*, 15-164) Augsburg Fortress.

— Lifelong Learning: A Guide to Adult Education in the Church. Grothe, R., ed. LC 97-13011. 1997. pap. 16.99 (*0-8066-2999-1*, 9-2999) Augsburg Fortress.

— Ten Key People from the Bible. (Bible Basics for Adults Ser.). 64p. 1996. pap., teacher ed. 6.99 (*0-8066-2324-1*, 15-7391, Augsburg); pap., student ed. 4.99 (*0-8066-2323-3*, 15-7390) Augsburg Fortress.

***Augsburg Fortress Staff.** What Happens in The End Leaders Guide. 1999. pap. text 6.99 (*0-8066-3818-4*, Augsburg) Augsburg Fortress.

— What Happens in The End Learner Book. 1999. pap. text 4.99 (*0-8066-3817-6*, Augsburg) Augsburg Fortress.

— What Next? Connecting Your Ministry to Generation X. 176p. 1999. pap. text 29.99 (*0-8066-3970-9*, Augsburg) Augsburg Fortress.

— Who Is God Leaders Guide. 1999. pap. text 6.99 (*0-8066-3824-9*, Augsburg) Augsburg Fortress.

— Who Is God Learner Book. 1999. pap. text 4.99 (*0-8066-3823-0*, Augsburg) Augsburg Fortress.

— Who Is Jesus Leaders Guide. 1999. pap. text 6.99 (*0-8066-3822-2*, Augsburg) Augsburg Fortress.

— Who Is Jesus Learner Book. 1999. pap. text 4.99 (*0-8066-3821-4*, Augsburg) Augsburg Fortress.

— Who Is The Holy Spirit Leaders Guide. 1999. pap. text 6.99 (*0-8066-3820-6*, Augsburg) Augsburg Fortress.

— Who Is The Holy Spirit Learner Book. 1999. pap. text 4.99 (*0-8066-3819-2*, Augsburg) Augsburg Fortress.

— Why Bother Leaders Guide. 1999. pap. text 6.99 (*0-8066-3816-8*, Augsburg) Augsburg Fortress.

— Why Bother Learner Book. 1999. pap. text 4.99 (*0-8066-3815-X*, Augsburg) Augsburg Fortress.

Augsburg Fortress Staff, contrib. by. Venture Bible 2.0. 1996. mac hd 69.95 (*0-8066-0146-9*, Augsburg) Augsburg Fortress.

Augsburg Fortress Staff, prod. Ten Key Events from the Bible. (Bible Basics for Adults Ser.). 1996. pap., student ed. 4.99 (*0-8066-2325-X*, 15-7392, Augsburg) Augsburg Fortress.

— Ten Key Events in Jesus' Life. (Bible Basics for Adults Ser.). 1996. pap., student ed. 4.99 (*0-8066-2327-6*, 15-7394, Augsburg) Augsburg Fortress.

— Ten Key Passages from the Bible. (Bible Basics for Adults Ser.). 1996. pap., student ed. 4.99 (*0-8066-2329-2*, 15-7396, Augsburg) Augsburg Fortress.

Augsburger, A. Don. Reshaping Your Marriage. 149p. 1997. pap. 9.95 (*1-883294-41-X*) Masthof Pr.

Augsburger, David. El Amor Que Nos Sostiene.Tr. of Sustaining Love. (SPA.). 208p. 1992. 8.99 (*0-88113-115-6*, B012-1156) Caribe Betania.

— Caring Enough to Confront: How to Understand & Express your Deepest Feelings Toward Others. rev. ed. LC 80-65268. 142p. 1980. pap. 9.99 (*0-8361-1928-2*) Herald Pr.

— Freedom of Forgiveness. pap. 9.99 (*0-8024-2884-3*, 145) Moody.

— The Freedom of Forgiveness - Chinese Edition. Huang, Caroline, tr. (CHI.). 167p. 1998. pap. 5.50 (*1-56582-013-4*) Christ Renew Min.

***Augsburger, David.** New Freedom of Forgiveness. LC 99-86117. 2000. pap. 12.99 (*0-8024-3292-1*) Moody.

Augsburger, David. Perdonar para Ser Libre. Orig. Title: Freedom of Forgiveness. (SPA.). 160p. 1977. mass mkt. 5.99 (*0-8254-1046-0*, Edit Portavoz) Kregel.

— When Enough Is Enough. LC 84-81255. 192p. 1984. pap. 9.99 (*0-8361-3375-7*) Herald Pr.

Augsburger, David W. Conflict Mediation Across Cultures: Pathways & Patterns. 1995. pap. 28.95 (*0-664-25609-0*) Westminster John Knox.

— Helping People Forgive. LC 96-21400. 192p. (Orig.). 1996. pap. 19.95 (*0-664-25686-4*) Westminster John Knox.

— Pastoral Counseling Across Cultures. 1995. pap. 26.95 (*0-664-25616-3*) Westminster John Knox.

Augsburger, Esther, jt. auth. see Augsburger, Myron.

Augsburger, Jeff, et al. The Beatles Memorabilia Price Guide. LC 88-70713. (Illus.). 256p. 1988. pap. 19.95 (*0-929207-00-9*) Branyan Pr.

— The Beatles Memorabilia Price Guide. 3rd rev. ed. LC 97-72622. (Illus.). 240p. 1997. pap. 24.95 (*0-930625-68-4*) Krause Pubns.

Augsburger, L. L. & Jones, B. Capsule Technology. (Drugs & the Pharmaceutical Sciences Ser.: Vol. 88). Date not set. write for info. (*0-8247-8090-6*) Dekker.

Augsburger, M. Matthew. (Mastering the Old & New Testament Ser.: Vol. 1). pap. 14.99 (*0-8499-3317-X*) Word Pub.

Augsburger, Myron & Augsburger, Esther. How to Be a Christ-Shaped Family. LC 93-39543. 180p. (Orig.). 1994. pap. 9.99 (*1-56476-073-1*, 6-3073, Victor Bks) Chariot Victor.

Augsburger, Myron & Kincanon, Marcia A. The Deacon. (Illus.). 120p. (Orig.). 1990. pap. 3.95 (*0-919797-94-6*) Kindred Prods.

***Augsburger, Myron S.** The Robe of God: Reconciliation, the Believers' Church Essential. LC 00-33453. 2000. write for info. (*0-8361-9136-6*) Herald Pr.

Augsdorter, Peter. Forbidden Fruit: An Analysis of Bootlegging, Uncertainty, & Learning in Corporate R & D. 240p. 1996. 68.95 (*1-85972-333-0*, Pub. by Avebry) Ashgate Pub Co.

***Augspurger, Eric K.** 3D Studio Max & Its Applications: Release 3.1. LC 00-42995. 2000. write for info. (*1-56637-600-9*) Goodheart.

Augst, Gerhard, ed. New Trends in Graphemics & Orthography: Kolloquium Siegen 22-24 August, 1985. xii, 464p. 1986. 119.25 (*3-11-010804-6*) De Gruyter.

Augst, Gerhard, ed. see Beier, Rudolf.

Augst, Nancy, ed. see Baums, Roosevelt.

Augstein, Hannah, ed. Race: The Origins of an Idea, 1760-1850. (Key Issues Ser.: No. 14). 240p. 1996. 72.00 (*1-85506-455-3*) Bks Intl VA.

— Race: The Origins of an Idea, 1760-1850. (Key Issues Ser.: No. 14). (Illus.). 240p. 1996. pap. 23.00 (*1-85506-454-5*) Bks Intl VA.

Augur. The Hickey Multi-Sensory Language Course. 2nd ed. 300p. 1992. pap. 143.75 (*1-56593-556-X*, 0240) Singular Publishing.

Augur, Edwin P. Family History & Genealogy of the Descendants of Robert Augur of New Haven Colony. (Illus.). 260p. 1988. reprint ed. pap. 39.00 (*0-8328-0139-9*); reprint ed. lib. bdg. 49.00 (*0-8328-0138-0*) Higginson Bk Co.

Augur, Helen. The Book of Fairs. LC 89-29244. (Illus.). 308p. 1994. reprint ed. lib. bdg. 42.00 (*1-55888-892-6*) Omnigraphics Inc.

— The Secret War of Independence. LC 75-25250. 381p. 1976. reprint ed. lib. bdg. 45.00 (*0-8371-8380-4*, AUSW, Greenwood Pr) Greenwood.

Augur, Jean. This Book Doesn't Make Sense: Living & Learning with Dyslexia. 130p. 1995. pap. 34.95 (*1-56593-605-1*, 1256) Singular Publishing.

— This Book Doesn't Make Sense: Living & Learning with Dyslexia. rev. ed. 1995. 34.95 (*1-897635-13-3*, Pub. by Whurr Pub) Singular Publishing.

August, ed. see Haffty.

August, Andrew. Poor Women's Lives: Gender, Work & Poverty in Late-Victorian London. LC 98-54806. 1999. write for info. (*0-8386-3807-4*) Fairleigh Dickinson.

August, Angel T. Postcard from Graceland. Carr, Martha R., ed. 267p. (Orig.). 1994. pap. 14.95 (*0-9638639-1-6*) Nimrod Hse.

***August, Arnold.** Democracy in Cuba & the 1997-98 Elections. deluxe ed. Taria, Fernando Napoles, ed. (Illus.). 416p. (Orig.). (C). 1999. pap. 24.95 (*0-9685084-0-5*) Can Cuba Dist.

August, B. Alan. Advanced Training for Microsoft Excel 7 for Windows 95. unabridged ed. 85p. 1996. pap. 225.00 incl. audio (*1-56562-073-9*, 294) OneOnOne Comp Trng.

— How to Use Microsoft Excel, '97. Menges, Patricia A., ed. (Illus.). 78p. 1997. pap. 225.00 (*1-56562-089-5*) OneOnOne Comp Trng.

— How to Use Microsoft Excel '97 - CD. Menges, Patricia A., ed. 1998. pap. 225.00 incl. cd-rom (*1-56562-087-9*) OneOnOne Comp Trng.

— How to Use Microsoft Excel 7. unabridged ed. Young, Nataile B., ed. 185p. 1996. pap. 225.00 incl. disk (*1-56562-069-0*, 292) OneOnOne Comp Trng.

***August, Byron D.** Are You Profitable to Your Pastor. Hansen, Cynthia, ed. (Illus.). 39p. 2000. pap. 3.95 (*0-9673727-1-2*) Ready for World.

— How to Be the Greatest in God's Kingdom: Understanding the Value of Servanthood. Glover, Marissa, ed. (Illus.). 70p. 1999. 5.95 (*0-9673727-0-4*) Ready for World.

August, David, jt. auth. see Lutz, John.

A

An Asterisk (*) at the beginning of an entry indicates that the title is appearing for the first time.

August, Diane. Conference on Inclusion Guidelines & Accommodations for Limited English Proficient Students in the National Assessment of Educational Progress, December 5-6, 1994. 53p. 1996. pap. 3.75 (0-16-063581-0) USGPO.

August, Diane & McArthur, Edith. Proceedings of the Conference on Inclusion Guidelines & Accommodations for Limited English Proficient Students in the National Assessment of Educational Progress. 51p. (C). 1998. pap. text 20.00 (0-7881-7050-3) DIANE Pub.

August, Diane, ed. see Institute of Medicine, National Research Council.

August, Elizabeth. Author's Choice. (Men Made in America Ser.). 1993. per. 3.59 (0-373-45158-X, 1-45158-2) Silhouette.

— Un Avenir Plein de Promesse. (Horizon Ser.: No. 488). (FRE.). 1998. mass mkt. 3.50 (0-373-39488-8, 1-39488-1) Harlequin Bks.

— The Bridal Shower. (Romance Ser.). 1995. per. 2.99 (0-373-19091-3, 1-19091-7) Silhouette.

— The Bride's Second Thought. 1998. per. 3.50 (0-373-19288-6, 1-19288-9) Silhouette.

— Cinderella Story. 1997. per. 4.50 (0-373-65010-8) Harlequin Bks.

— The Cowboy & the Chauffeur. (Here Come the Grooms Ser.: No. 10). 1996. per. 3.99 (0-373-30110-3, 1-30110-0) Harlequin Bks.

— The Cowboy & the Chauffeur. (Romance Ser.: No. 833). 1991. per. 2.59 (0-373-08833-7, 5-08833-1) Silhouette.

— The Determined Virgin. (Romance Ser.: No. 1229). 1997. per. 3.25 (0-373-19229-0, 1-19229-3) Silhouette.

— A Father's Vow. (Romance Ser.). 1996. per. 2.99 (0-373-19126-X, 1-19126-1) Silhouette.

— The Forgotten Husband. (Romance Ser.). 1994. per. 2.75 (0-373-19019-0, 1-19019-8) Harlequin Bks.

— Girls' Night Out. (Intimate Moments Ser.). 1998. per. 4.25 (0-373-07880-3, 1-07880-7) Silhouette.

— A Handy Man to Have Around. (Romance Ser.). 1996. per. 3.25 (0-373-19157-X, 1-19157-6) Silhouette.

— Haunted Husband. 1993. pap. 2.69 (0-373-08922-8, 5-08922-2) Silhouette.

— Haunted Husband. large type ed. LC 93-13222. 1993. pap. 13.95 (1-56054-759-6) Thorndike Pr.

— The Husband. 1996. per. 3.99 (0-373-24059-7, 1-24059-7) Silhouette.

— A Husband for Sarah: (Where the Heart Is) (Romance Ser.). 1995. per. 2.99 (0-373-19067-0, 1-19067-7) Silhouette.

— Ideal Dad. (Romance Ser.). 1995. per. 2.75 (0-373-19054-9, 1-19054-5) Silhouette.

— Joey's Father. (Family Continuity Program Ser.: No. 18). 1999. per. 4.50 (0-373-82166-2, 1-82166-9) Harlequin Bks.

— Like Father Like Son. 1992. per. 2.69 (0-373-08857-4) Harlequin Bks.

— Logan's Bride. (Intimate Moments Ser.: No. 950). 1999. per. 4.25 (0-373-07950-8, 1-07950-8) Silhouette.

— Lucky Penny. (Romance Ser.). 1993. per. 2.75 (0-373-08945-7, 5-08945-3) Silhouette.

— The Man from Natchez. (Romance Ser.: No. 790). 1991. per. 2.50 (0-373-08790-X) Silhouette.

— Marrying O'Malley. (Romance Ser.: No. 1386). 1999. per. 3.50 (0-373-19386-6, 1-19386-1) Silhouette.

— One Last Fling! 1994. per. 3.50 (0-373-09871-5, 5-09871-0) Silhouette.

***August, Elizabeth.** Un Passe Trouble. (Rouge Passion Ser.: No. 526). (FRE.). 1999. mass mkt. 3.99 (0-373-37526-3, 1-37526-0) Harlequin Bks.

August, Elizabeth. Paternal Instincts: Men! (Romance Ser.: No. 1265). 1997. per. 3.25 (0-373-19265-7, 1-19265-7) Harlequin Bks.

— Pirate Bride. (Historical Ser.: No. 730). 1992. mass mkt. 3.99 (0-373-28730-5, 1-28730-9) Harlequin Bks.

— The Rancher & the Baby. 1996. per. 3.25 (0-373-19187-1, 1-19187-3) Silhouette.

— Un Reve D'Enfance. (Horizon Ser.: Vol. 465). (FRE.). 1998. mass mkt. 3.50 (0-373-39465-9, 1-39465-9) Harlequin Bks.

— The Seeker. (Romance Ser.). 1994. per. 2.75 (0-373-08989-9, 5-08989-1) Silhouette.

— A Small Favor. (Romance Ser.: No. 809). 1991. per. 2.50 (0-373-08809-4) Silhouette.

— Truly, Madly, Deeply. (Romance Ser.: No. 1404). 1999. mass mkt. 3.50 (0-373-19404-8, 1-19404-2) Silhouette.

— The Virgin Wife. (Romance Ser.). 1993. per. 2.69 (0-373-08921-X, 5-08921-4) Silhouette.

— A Wedding for Emily. large type ed. LC 93-21000. 1993. pap. 13.95 (0-7862-0057-X) Thorndike Pr.

— A Wedding for Emily Smytheshire. (Romance Ser.). 1993. per. 2.75 (0-373-08953-8, 5-08953-7) Silhouette.

— The Wife He Wanted. (Romance Ser.: No. 881). 1992. per. 2.69 (0-373-08881-7) Silhouette.

August, Eugene R. The New Men's Studies: A Selected & Annotated Interdisciplinary Bibliography. 2nd ed. xx, 440p. 1995. lib. bdg. 65.00 (1-56308-084-2) Libs Unl.

August, H., et al, eds. Advanced Landfill Liner Systems. LC 98-177155. 389p. 1997. 145.00 (0-7277-2590-4, 2590, Pub. by T Telford) RCH.

August, Herzog, jt. ed. see Raabe, Paul.

August, J. Thomas. Advances in Pharmacology, Vol. 3. 426p. 1996. text 89.00 (0-12-032938-7) Acad Pr.

— Advances in Pharmacology, Vol. 4. (C). 1998. text 99.95 (0-12-032945-X) Acad Pr.

August, J. Thomas, ed. Monoclonal Antibodies in Drug Development. (Illus.). 237p. (Orig.). 1982. 24.00 (0-9609094-0-0) Am Phar & Ex.

August, J. Thomas, et al, eds. Advances in Pharmacology, Vol. 4. (Illus.). 614p. (C). 1997. text 99.95 (0-12-032942-5) Morgan Kaufmann.

— Advances in Pharmacology, Vol. 28. (Illus.). 361p. 1994. text 104.00 (0-12-032928-X) Acad Pr.

— Advances in Pharmacology, Vol. 30. (Illus.). 399p. 1994. text. write for info. (0-12-032931-X) Acad Pr.

— Advances in Pharmacology, Vol. 32. (Illus.). 583p. 1995. text 104.00 (0-12-032933-6) Acad Pr.

— Advances in Pharmacology, Vol. 33. (Illus.). 461p. 1995. text 90.00 (0-12-032934-4) Acad Pr.

— Advances in Pharmacology, Vol. 35. (Illus.). 409p. 1996. text 95.00 (0-12-032936-0) Acad Pr.

— Advances in Pharmacology, Vol. 39. (Illus.). 505p. 1997. text 99.00 (0-12-032940-9) Morgan Kaufmann.

August, J. Thomas, et al, eds. Advances in Pharmacology: Conjugation-Dependent Carcinogenicity & Toxicity of Foreign Compounds, Vol. 27. (Illus.). 519p. 1994. text 104.00 (0-12-032927-1) Acad Pr.

— Advances in Pharmacology: Cyclic GMP: Synthesis, Metabolism, & Function, Vol. 26. (Illus.). 335p. 1994. text 104.00 (0-12-032926-3) Acad Pr.

August, J. Thomas, et al, eds. Advances in Pharmacology Vol. 40: Gene Therapy. (Illus.). 508p. 1997. text 95.00 (0-12-032941-7) Morgan Kaufmann.

— Advances in Pharmacology Vol. 45: Cumulative Subject Index, Vol. 4. (Illus.). 198p. (C). 1998. boxed set 99.95 (0-12-032946-8) Acad Pr.

August, Jack. We Call It "Preskit" A Guide to Prescott & Central Arizona High Country. 64p. 1998. pap. 12.95 (0-916179-57-5) Ariz Hwy.

August, Jack L., Jr. Vision in the Desert: Carl Hayden & Hydropolitics in the American Southwest. LC 98-16386. (Illus.). 290p. 1999. 29.95 (0-87565-191-7) Tex Christian.

August, Jerald D., ed. Journal of S Corporation Taxation. 175.00 (0-685-69540-9, JSCT) Warren Gorham & Lamont.

August, Jerald D., ed. see Institutional Staff.

August, John R. Consultations in Feline Internal Medicine. (Illus.). 635p. text. write for info. (0-7216-8003-8) Harcrt Hlth Sci Grp.

August, John R. Consultations in Feline Internal Medicine, Vol. 1. (Illus.). 672p. 1990. text 105.00 (0-7216-2226-7, W B Saunders Co) Harcrt Hlth Sci Grp.

— Consultations in Feline Internal Medicine No. 3, Vol. III. 3rd ed. Kersey, Ray, ed. LC 96-18814. 1996. text 90.00 (0-7216-5814-8, W B Saunders Co) Harcrt Hlth Sci Grp.

August, John R., ed. Consultations in Feline Internal Medicine, Vol. 2. 2nd ed. LC 93-1499. (Illus.). 608p. 1993. text 90.00 (0-7216-4674-3, W B Saunders Co) Harcrt Hlth Sci Grp.

August, J.Thomas, et al, eds. Advances in Pharmacology, Vol. 46. (Illus.). 344p. 1999. 99.95 (0-12-032947-6) Acad Pr.

August, Mark, et al. Black Voices in Commentary: The Trotter Group. 50p. pap. 7.50 (0-9639460-0-5) News Jrnl.

August, Paul N. Drugs & Women. (Encyclopedia of Psychoactive Drugs Ser.: No. 2). (Illus.). 128p. (YA). (gr. 7 up). 1987. lib. bdg. 19.95 (1-55546-227-8) Chelsea Hse.

***August, Ray.** International Business Law: Text, Cases & Readings. 3rd ed. LC 99-37727. (Illus.). 760p. 1999. 94.00 (0-13-014377-4) P-H.

August, Ray. Public International Law. LC 94-40810. 624p. 1995. 69.80 (0-13-299892-0) P-H.

August, Roland. Cruelty & Civilization: The Roman Games. LC 94-191303. (Illus.). 224p. (C). 1994. pap. 24.99 (0-415-10453-X) Routledge.

***August, Sandra.** Chasing Alfie, 1. 320p. 1999. mass mkt. 4.99 (0-8439-4566-4, Pub. by Dorchester Pub Co) CMG.

August, Thomas G. The Selling of the Empire: British & French Imperialist Propaganda, 1890-1940, 19. LC 84-25233. (Contributions in Comparative Colonial Studies: No. 19). (Illus.). 234p. 1985. 62.95 (0-313-24722-6, AUA/, Greenwood Pr) Greenwood.

August, William J. Bridge: Light Up Your Understanding of Bidding. 256p. 1995. 19.95 (0-9643937-0-0) Rutledge Bks.

Augusta, Cal. Budgeting Essentials: Personal Financing to Save Money Time & Effort. Sliwiak, Thomas, ed. LC 94-76684. 64p. 1994. pap. 5.95 (0-9638761-1-2) Graphic Thought.

— Employment Essentials: A Confidential Maybe Even Top Secret Journal for Work Related Data & Job Search Resources. LC 93-73513. 160p. (Orig.). 1993. pap. 9.95 (0-9638761-0-4) Graphic Thought.

Augustan Translators. Augustan Translators: Restoration & Eighteenth Century English Translations of the Classics, 23 vols. in 26. 1666. reprint ed. 1582.00 (0-404-54100-3) AMS Pr.

Augustauskas, J., ed. In the World of Insects. 216p. (C). 1989. 240.00 (0-89771-831-3, Pub. by Collets) St Mut.

Auguste, Byron G. The Economics of International Payments Unions & Clearing Houses: Theory, Measurement & Two Case-Studies. LC 96-27851. (St. Antony's Ser.). 224p. 1997. text 69.95 (0-312-16427-0) St Martin.

Auguste de Villiers de L'Isle, Adam. Contes Cruels. (FRE.). 302p. 1980. pap. 10.95 (0-7859-1437-4, 2080703404) Fr & Eur.

Auguste de Villiers de l'Isle, Adam. Les Contes Cruels. unabridged ed. (FRE.). pap. 5.95 (2-87714-225-6, Pub. by Bookking Intl) Distribks Inc.

Auguste de Villiers de L'Isle, Adam. Correspondance Generale, 2 vols. (FRE.). 620p. 1962. pap. 59.95 (0-7859-5502-X) Fr & Eur.

Auguste de Villiers de l'Isle, Adam. Oeuvres Completes, 2 tomes. deluxe ed. (Pleiade Ser.). (FRE.). 179.95 (2-07-011103-2) Schoenhof.

Auguste de Villiers de l'Isle, Adam & Castex, Pierre-Georges. Oeuvres Completes, Vol. 1. (FRE.). 1986. lib. bdg. 140.00 (0-7859-3866-4) Fr & Eur.

Augusteijn, Joost. From Public Defiance to Guerilla Warfare: The Experience of Ordinary Volunteers in the Irish War of Independence. 240p. 1996. 54.50 (0-7165-2589-5, Pub. by Irish Acad Pr); pap. 24.95 (0-7165-2607-7, Pub. by Irish Acad Pr) Intl Spec Bk.

Augusteijn, Joost, ed. Ireland in the 1930's: New Perspectives. 240p. 1999. 65.00 (1-85182-399-9, Pub. by Four Cts Pr); pap. 29.95 (1-85182-405-7, Pub. by Four Cts Pr) Intl Spec Bk.

Augusti, G., et al, eds. Structural Dynamics: Proceedings of the 3rd European Conference on Structural Dynamics, EURODYN '96, Florence, Italy, 5-8 June 1996, 2 vols., Set. (Illus.). 1178p. (C). 1996. text 220.00 (90-5410-813-4, Pub. by A A Balkema) Ashgate Pub Co.

Augusti, G., et al. Probabilistic Methods in Structural Engineering. (Illus.). 636p. (gr. 13). 1984. mass mkt. 193.50 (0-412-22230-2, NO. 6823) Chapman & Hall.

Augustihis, S. S. Atlas of Metamorphic-Metasomatic Textures & Processes. 238p. 1990. 254.00 (0-444-88600-1) Elsevier.

Augustijn, C. Erasmi Opera Omnia, Vol. IX-1. xiii, 506p. 1982. 485.50 (0-444-86269-2) Elsevier.

Augustijn, Cornelis. Erasmus: Der Humanist Als Theologe Und Kirchenreformer. Vol. 59. (Illus.). X, 376p. 1996. text 126.00 (90-04-10496-8) Brill Academic Pubs.

Augustijn, Cornelis. Erasmus: His Life, Works, & Influence. Grayson, J. C., tr. from DUT. (Erasmus Studies: No. 10). (Illus.). 260p. 1991. text 39.95 (0-8020-5864-7) U of Toronto Pr.

— Erasmus: His Life, Works & Influence. 272p. 1996. pap. text 19.95 (0-8020-7177-5) U of Toronto Pr.

Augustin, Jose. Dos Horas de Sol. 1997. 22.95 (84-08-02116-8) Planeta Edit.

Augustin, Ebba, ed. Palestinian Women: Identity & Experience. LC 93-5394. 256p. (C). 1993. text 22.50 (1-85649-234-6, Pub. by Zed Books) St Martin.

Augustin, J. Glossaire Nautique - Dictionary Multilingue Marine a Voiles. (FRE.). 1998. 95.00 (0-320-00224-1) Fr & Eur.

Augustin, Jorg, et al, eds. Methods of Vitamin Assay. 4th ed. LC 84-7335. (Wiley-Interscience Publications). 608p. reprint ed. pap. 188.50 (0-7837-2382-2, 204006800006) Bks Demand.

Augustin, Larry M., et al. Hardware Design & Simulation in VAL-VHDL. (C). 1990. text 120.50 (0-7923-9087-3) Kluwer Academic.

Augustin, Matthias & Schunck, Klaus-Dietrich, eds. Dort Ziehen Schiffe Dahin . . . Collected Communications to the XIVth Congress of the International Organization for the Study of the Old Testament, Paris, 1992. (Beitrage zur Erforschung des Alten Testaments & Antiken Judentums Ser.: Bd. 28). (GER.). 229p. 1996. 57.95 (3-631-48673-1) P Lang Pubng.

Augustin, Matthias, jt. ed. see Kegler, Jurgen.

Augustin, Matthias, jt. ed. see Schunck, Klaus-Dietrich.

Augustin, R., ed. Peritonitis in CAPS. (Contributions to Nephrology Ser.: Vol. 57). (Illus.). viii, 256p. 1987. 29.75 (3-8055-4519-3) S Karger.

Augustin, Ursula. Star Trek Collectibles: Classic Series, Next Generation, Deep Space Nine, Voyager. (Classic Ser.). (Illus.). 240p. 1997. pap. 19.95 (0-7643-0378-3) Schiffer.

Augustine, Abby, jt. auth. see Tunuchuk, Mary.

Augustine, Aurelius, jt. auth. see Clark, Gordon H.

Augustine, Benny B. Orphanages: Index of New Information. 150p. 1998. 47.50 (0-7883-2026-2); pap. 44.50 (0-7883-2027-0) ABBE Pubs Assn.

Augustine, D. Smith, jt. ed. see Beauboeuf-Lafontant, Tamara.

Augustine, Denis F., jt. auth. see Walker, Morton.

Augustine, Dennis F. The Foot Care Revolution: How to Walk Away from a Foot Operation on Your Own Two Feet. 2nd ed. (Illus.). 213p. 1993. reprint ed. pap. 15.00 (0-9636736-1-0) Gldn Gate Pub.

— How to Market Your Professional Services: A Professional's Guide to Advertising & Public Relations. 2nd ed. (Illus.). 1993. reprint ed. pap. 15.00 (0-9636736-2-9) Gldn Gate Pub.

— Invisible Means of Support: A Transformational Journey. LC 93-78398. 384p. 1994. boxed set 24.95 (0-9636736-0-2) Gldn Gate Pub.

Augustine, Dolores L. Patricians & Parvenues: Wealth & High Society in Wilhelmine Germany. LC 93-29862. 350p. 1994. 47.50 (0-85496-397-9) Berg Pubs.

Augustine, Don, jt. auth. see Bender's Editors.

Augustine Fellowship Staff. Sex & Love Addicts Anonymous. 280p. 1986. text 23.50 (0-9615701-0-5); pap. text 13.50 (0-9615701-1-3) Augustine Fellow.

Augustine, Jane. French Windows. (Poetry New York Pamphlet Ser.: Vol. 6). 16p. 1998. pap. 5.00 (0-923389-18-0) Meet Eyes Bind.

Augustine, Jane, ed. & anno. see H. D., pseud.

Augustine, John L. & Leonard, Joseph M. Pocket Power No. 5: Veterinary. 48p. (Orig.). 1988. pap. 2.95 (0-945893-04-3) Pocket Power.

Augustine, John S., ed. Strategies for Third World Development. 156p. (C). 1989. text 24.00 (0-8039-9612-8) Sage.

Augustine, Judith D. A Christmas Carol: A Literature Unit. (Literature Units Ser.). (Illus.). 48p. (Orig.). 1993. pap., student ed. 7.95 (1-55734-434-5) Tchr Create Mat.

Augustine, L., ed. see Melody, A.

Augustine, Laodeciae, ed. see Melody.

Augustine, Morris J., tr. see Numata Center for Buddhist Translation & Research.

Augustine, Nicholas & Augustine, Victoria C. Conny the Clown. (Illus.). 32p. (J). 1991. pap. write for info. (1-879783-00-2) Staccato Prodns.

— Little Lady Star. (Illus.). 32p. (J). 1991. pap. write for info. (1-879783-01-0) Staccato Prodns.

Augustine, Norman & Adelman, Kenneth L. Shakespeare in Charge: How to Lead & Succeed on the Business Stage. LC 99-42888. 219p. 1999. text 22.95 (0-7868-6601-2, Pub. by Hyperion) Time Warner.

Augustine, Norman R. Augustine's Laws. LC 83-22409. (Illus.). 241p. 1984. 29.95 (0-915928-81-7, 81-7) AIAA.

— Augustine's Laws. 6th ed. LC 97-22200. (Illus.). 395p. 1997. 34.95 (1-56347-239-2) AIAA.

— Augustine's Travels: A World Class Leader Looks at Life, Business, & What It Takes to Succeed at Both. LC 97-28985. 320p. 1997. 24.95 (0-8144-0397-2) AMACOM.

Augustine, Norman R., ed. The United States in Antarctica: Report of the U. S. Antartic Program External Panel. (Illus.). 94p. (C). 1999. reprint ed. pap. text 25.00 (0-7881-7811-3) DIANE Pub.

Augustine, Norman R., jt. auth. see Adelman, Kenneth L.

***Augustine of Hippo Staff.** Soliloquies: Augustine's Interior Dialogue. Rotelle, John, ed. 104p. 2000. pap. 9.95 (1-56548-142-9) New City.

Augustine, P. A. Social Equality in Indian Society. (C). 1991. text 21.50 (81-7022-303-2, Pub. by Concept) S Asia.

Augustine, Patricia C., et al, eds. Biotechnology for Solving Agricultural Problems. (Beltsville Symposia in Agricultural Research Ser.). 1986. text 252.50 (90-247-3311-1) Kluwer Academic.

Augustine, Peg. A Child's Garden of Virtues. (Illus.). 96p. 1996. 10.00 (0-687-01610-X) Dimen for Liv.

— The Little Book of Virtues. 48p. 1996. 5.00 (0-687-01600-2) Dimen for Liv.

Augustine, Peg, ed. Best Regards: Recovering the Art of Soulful Letter Writing. 72p. 1997. 14.95 (0-687-02292-4) Abingdon.

Augustine, Peggy, ed. see Gaither, Gloria.

Augustine, Peggy, ed. see Perry, Alan & Perry, Linda.

Augustine, Robert L. Catalysis of Organic Reactions. LC 85-10242. (Chemical Industries Ser.: Vol. 22). (Illus.). 416p. (C). 1985. text 215.00 (0-8247-7263-6) Dekker.

— Catalytic Hydrogenation: Techniques & Applications in Organic Synthesis. LC 65-27430. 200p. reprint ed. pap. 62.00 (0-608-16743-6, 202631200049) Bks Demand.

— Heterogeneous Catalysis for the Synthetic Chemist. (Illus.). 672p. 1995. text 150.00 (0-8247-9021-9) Dekker.

Augustine, Robert L., ed. Oxidation. LC 69-18430. (Techniques & Applications in Organic Synthesis Ser.: Vol. 1). 378p. 1969. reprint ed. pap. 117.20 (0-608-02233-0, 204107200001) Bks Demand.

— Reduction: Techniques & Applications in Organic Synthesis. LC 68-12550. (Techniques & Applications in Organic Synthesis Ser.). (Illus.). 252p. reprint ed. pap. 78.20 (0-7837-3385-2, 204334300008) Bks Demand.

Augustine, Robert L. & Trecker, David J. Oxidation, Vol. 2. LC 69-18430. (Techniques & Applications in Organic Synthesis Ser.). (Illus.). 216p. reprint ed. pap. 67.00 (0-7837-0758-4, 204107200002) Bks Demand.

Augustine, Rosemary. Facing Changes in Employment: A Guide to Creating Employment for Today's Workforce. LC 95-94593. 136p. (Orig.). 1995. pap. 12.95 (0-9644711-9-1) Blue Sprce Pub.

— How to Live & Work with Passion & Still Earn an Income. 1999. pap. write for info. (0-9644711-7-5) Blue Sprce Pub.

— Job Seekers Beware: How to Recognize Scams Shams & Pitfalls. 1999. pap. write for info. (0-9644711-8-3) Blue Sprce Pub.

Augustine, Saint. Against Julian. Schumacher, Matthew A., tr. LC 77-81347. (Fathers of the Church Ser.: Vol. 35). 407p. 1957. 23.95 (0-8132-0035-0) Cath U Pr.

— Against the Academicians. Garvey, M. Patricia, tr. (Medieval Philosophical Texts in Translation Ser.: No. 1). 1957. pap. 10.00 (0-87462-202-6) Marquette.

— Against the Academicians & the Teacher. King, Peter, tr. & intro. by. LC 95-32851. 208p. (C). 1995. pap. text 12.95 (0-87220-212-7); lib. bdg. 29.95 (0-87220-213-5) Hackett Pub.

— The Augustine Catechism: The Enchiridon on Faith, Hope, & Love. Harbert, Bruce, tr. from LAT. LC 99-18777. 144p. 1999. pap. text 9.95 (1-56548-124-0) New City.

— Augustine De Doctrina Christiana. Green, R. P. H., ed. (Oxford Early Christian Texts Ser.).Tr. of On Christian Doctrine. 320p. 1996. text 89.00 (0-19-826334-1) OUP.

— Augustine of Hippo: Selected Writings. Clark, Mary T., tr. (Classics of Western Spirituality Ser.). 544p. 1984. pap. 19.95 (0-8091-2573-0) Paulist Pr.

— Augustine on the Sunday Gospel. Rotelle, John E., ed. LC 98-19221. 545p. 1998. pap. 12.95 (1-889542-04-0, AP-4030) Augustinian Pr.

— Carbon-Carbon Bond Formation. (Techniques & Applications in Organic Synthesis Ser.: Vol. 6). (Illus.). 464p. 1979. text 215.00 (0-8247-6787-X) Dekker.

— Christian Instruction, Admonition & Grace, The Christian Combat, Faith, Hope & Charity. Gavigan, John J. et al, trs. LC 66-20314. (Fathers of the Church Ser.: Vol. 2). 494p. 1950. 36.95 (0-8132-0002-4) Cath U Pr.

— City of God. Knowles, David, ed. Bettenson, Henry, tr. (Classics Ser.). 1150p. 1984. pap. 15.95 (0-14-044426-2, Penguin Classics) Viking Penguin.

— The City of God. LC 58-5717. 560p. 1958. pap. 12.95 (0-385-02910-1, Image Bks) Doubleday.

***Augustine, Saint.** City of God. (Library Classics). 2000. pap. 14.95 (0-679-78319-9) Modern Lib NY.

Augustine, Saint. The City of God. abr. ed. Dods, Marcus & Merton, Thomas, trs. LC 93-27971. 912p. 1994. 21.00 (0-679-60087-6) Modern Lib NY.

— City of God, Bks. 1-7. Zema, Demetrius B. & Walsh, Gerald G., trs. LC 63-19613. (Fathers of the Church Ser.: Vol. 8). 401p. 1950. 36.95 (0-8132-0008-3) Cath U Pr.

An Asterisk (*) at the beginning of an entry indicates that the title is appearing for the first time.

— City of God, Bks. 17-22. Walsh, Gerald G. & Honan, Daniel J., trs. LC 63-19613. (Fathers of the Church Ser.: Vol. 24). 561p. 1954. 29.95 (*0-8132-0024-5*) Cath U Pr.

— The City of God Against the Pagans. Dyson, R. W., ed. & tr. by. LC 97-38751. (Cambridge Texts in the History of Political Thought Ser.). 1280p. (C). 1998. text 64.95 (*0-521-46475-7*); pap. text 24.95 (*0-521-46843-4*) Cambridge U Pr.

— Confessions. Pine-Coffin, R. S., tr. & intro. by. (Classics Ser.). 352p. 1961. pap. 8.95 (*0-14-044114-X*, Penguin Classics) Viking Penguin.

— Confessions. Chadwick, Henry, tr. 350p. 1991. 32.50 (*0-19-281779-5*) OUP.

— The Confessions. Rotelle, John E., ed. Boulding, Maria, tr. (Works of St. Augustine Ser.: Vol. I/1). 416p. 1996. 29.95 (*1-56548-083-X*); pap. 19.95 (*1-56548-084-8*) New City.

— Confessions. Bourke, Vernon J., tr. LC 66-20310. (Fathers of the Church Ser.: Vol. 21). 513p. 1966. reprint ed. pap. 159.10 (*0-7837-9143-7*, 204994300004) Bks Demand.

— Confessions. 376p. 1999. reprint ed. pap. 17.95 (*0-7661-0813-9*) Kessinger Pub.

— Confessions. Chadwick, Henry, tr. & intro. by. (Oxford World's Classics Ser.). 340p. 1998. reprint ed. pap. 7.95 (*0-19-283372-3*) OUP.

— Confessions. Sheed, Francis J., tr. from LAT. LC 93-4931. (Hackett Classics Ser.). 320p. (C). 1993. reprint ed. pap. text 7.95 (*0-87220-186-4*); reprint ed. lib. bdg. 29.95 (*0-87220-187-2*) Hackett Pub.

— Confessions, Bks. I-IV. Clark, Gillian, ed. (Cambridge Greek & Latin Classics - Imperial Library). 208p. (C). 1996. text 59.95 (*0-521-49734-5*) Cambridge U Pr.

— Confessions, Bks. I-IV. Clarke, Gillian, ed. (Cambridge Greek & Latin Classics - Imperial Library). 208p. (Orig.). (C). 1995. pap. text 22.95 (*0-521-49763-9*) Cambridge U Pr.

— Confessions, No. 5. Boulding, Maria, tr. LC 98-35481. 400p. 1998. pap. 10.95 (*0-375-70021-8*) Vin Bks.

— Confessions, 2 vols., Vol. 1. (Loeb Classical Library: No. 26-27). 480p. 1912. 19.95 (*0-674-99029-3*) HUP.

— Confessions, 2 vols., Vol. 2. Watts, W., tr. (Loeb Classical Library: No. 26-27). 488p. 1912. 19.95 (*0-674-99030-7*) HUP.

— The Confessions of Augustine. Gibb, John et al, eds. LC 78-67139. (Latin Texts & Commentaries Ser.). (ENG & LAT.). 1979. reprint ed. lib. bdg. 40.95 (*0-405-11604-7*) Ayer.

— The Confessions of Augustine in Modern English. Wirt, Sherwood E., tr. 144p. 1986. pap. 7.95 (*0-310-34641-X*, 10807P) Zondervan.

— Confessions of Saint Augustine. Leleu, Joseph Mary, tr. from LAT. LC 97-202994. 462p. (Orig.). 1997. pap. 7.95 (*0-89942-169-5*, 173/09) Catholic Bk Pub.

— The Confessions of Saint Augustine. LC 60-13725. 432p. 1960. pap. 8.95 (*0-385-02955-1*, Image Bks) Doubleday.

— The Confessions of Saint Augustine. Warner, Rex, tr. 1963. mass mkt. 6.99 (*0-451-62474-2*, Ment) NAL.

— The Confessions of Saint Augustine. LC 99-18903. (Nelson's Royal Classic Ser.: Vol. 4). 320p. 1999. 18.99 (*0-7852-4225-2*) Nelson.

— The Confessions of Saint Augustine. 302p. 1996. mass mkt. 6.99 (*0-88368-382-2*) Whitaker Hse.

— The Confessions of St. Augustine: A Modern English Version. Helms, Hal M., ed. LC 86-216797. 326p. 1986. pap. 12.95 (*0-941478-55-6*, 930-016, Pub. by Paraclete MA) BookWorld.

— Confessions of St. Augustine. Pusey, Edward Bouverie, tr. LC 99-30895. 1999. 19.95 (*0-679-60326-3*) Modern Lib NY.

— Daily Readings with St. Augustine. Llewelyn, Robert, ed. (Daily Readings Ser.). 96p. 1986. pap. 4.95 (*0-87243-152-5*) Templegate.

— Early Will I Seek You. rev. ed. (Rekindling the Inner Fire Ser.). 144p. 1991. pap. 8.99 (*1-55661-204-4*) Bethany Hse.

— Eighty-Three Different Questions. Mosher, David L., tr. LC 81-2546. (Fathers of the Church Ser.: Vol. 70). 271p. 1982. 31.95 (*0-8132-0070-9*) Cath U Pr.

— The Enchiridion on Faith, Hope & Love. 173p. 1996. pap. text 10.95 (*0-89526-703-9*, Gateway Editions) Regnery Pub.

— The Essential Augustine. (HPC Classics Ser.). 274p. (C). 1974. reprint ed. 29.95 (*0-915144-08-5*); reprint ed. pap. text 8.95 (*0-915144-07-7*) Hackett Pub.

— Expositions of the Psalms, 1-50, Vol. 3. 1999. pap. text 7.95 (*1-56548-126-7*) New City.

— Four Anti-Pelagian Writings: On Nature & Grace, on the Proceedings of Pelagius, on the Predestination of the Saints, & on the Gift of Perseverence. Mourant, John A. & Collinge, William J., trs. from LAT. LC 91-2972. (Fathers of the Church Ser.: Vol. 86). 351p. 1992. text 36.95 (*0-8132-0086-5*) Cath U Pr.

— Immortality of the Soul & Other Works. Schopp, Ludwig et al, trs. LC 77-81336. (Fathers of the Church Ser.: Vol. 4). 489p. 1947. 36.95 (*0-8132-0004-0*) Cath U Pr.

— King Alfred's Version of St. Augustine's Soliloquies. Carnicelli, Thomas A., ed. LC 69-12719. 136p. 1969. 19.95 (*0-674-50360-0*) HUP.

— Letters, Vol. 1, Nos. 1-82. Parsons, Wilfrid, tr. LC 64-19948. (Fathers of the Church Ser.: Vol. 12). 420p. 1951. 34.95 (*0-8132-0012-1*) Cath U Pr.

— Letters, Vol. 3, Nos. 131-164. Parsons, Wilfrid, tr. LC 64-19948. (Fathers of the Church Ser.: Vol. 20). 402p. 1953. 36.95 (*0-8132-0020-2*) Cath U Pr.

— Letters, Vol. 4, Nos. 165-203. Parsons, Wilfrid, tr. LC 64-19948. (Fathers of the Church Ser.: Vol. 30). 421p. 1955. 36.95 (*0-8132-0030-X*) Cath U Pr.

— Letters, Vol. 5, Nos. 204-270. Parsons, Wilfrid, tr. LC 64-19948. (Fathers of the Church Ser.: Vol. 32). 317p. 1956. 31.95 (*0-8132-0032-6*) Cath U Pr.

— Letters, Vol. 6, Nos. 1-29. Eno, Robert B., tr. LC 64-19948. (Fathers of the Church Ser.: Vol. 81). 208p. 1989. 31.95 (*0-8132-0081-4*) Cath U Pr.

— The Literal Meaning of Genesis. Taylor, John H., tr. & anno. by. (Ancient Christian Writers Ser.: No. 41, Vol. 1). 292p. 1983. 29.95 (*0-8091-0326-5*) Paulist Pr.

— The Literal Meaning of Genesis. Taylor, John H., tr. & anno. by. (Ancient Christian Writers Ser.: No. 42, Vol. 2). 358p. 1983. 22.95 (*0-8091-0327-3*) Paulist Pr.

— Managing Projects & Programs. 299p. 1989. 34.95 (*0-07-103204-5*) McGraw.

— Meditations of Saint Augustine. Rotelle, John E., ed. O'Connell, Matthew J., tr. 1995. 14.95 (*0-941491-80-3*); pap. 9.95 (*0-941491-79-X*) Augustinian Pr.

— My Mother. Rotelle, John E., ed. O'Connell, Matthew J., tr. from ITA. LC 87-70277. 144p. (Orig.). 1987. pap. 4.00 (*0-941491-01-3*) Augustinian Pr.

— On Christian Teaching. Green, ed. LC 96-40146. 194p. 1999. pap. 9.95 (*0-19-283928-4*) OUP.

— On Faith & Works. Lombardo, Gregory J., tr. (Ancient Christian Writers Ser.: No. 48). 128p. 1988. 14.95 (*0-8091-0406-7*) Paulist Pr.

— On Free Choice of the Will. Williams, Thomas, tr. from LAT. & intro. by. LC 93-22170. (Hackett Classics Ser.).Tr. of De Libero Arbitrio. (ENG.). 192p. (C). 1993. pap. text 6.95 (*0-87220-188-0*); lib. bdg. 27.95 (*0-87220-189-9*) Hackett Pub.

— On Genesis: Two Books on Genesis Against the Manichees & on the Literal Interpretation of Genesis: An Unfinished Book. Teske, Roland J., tr. from LAT. LC 90-39711. (Fathers of the Church Ser.: Vol. 84). 198p. 1991. text 29.95 (*0-8132-0084-9*) Cath U Pr.

— On the Inner Life of the Mind. Meagher, Robert E., ed. LC 98-34867. 340p. 1998. pap. 12.95 (*0-87220-444-8*); lib. bdg. 37.95 (*0-87220-445-6*) Hackett Pub.

— Political Writings. Fortin, E. L., ed. Kries, Douglas & Tkacz, Michael W., trs. from LAT. 256p. (Orig.). (C). 1994. pap. text 9.95 (*0-87220-210-0*); lib. bdg. 34.95 (*0-87220-211-9*) Hackett Pub.

— The Political Writings. Paolucci, Henry, ed. LC 96-23273. 358p. (Orig.). 1996. pap. 12.95 (*0-89526-704-7*, Gateway Editions) Regnery Pub.

— Prayers of St. Augustine: A Contemporary Anthology. Ulanov, Barry, ed. 160p. 1985. pap. 7.95 (*0-86683-881-3*, 7460) Harper SF.

— Restless till We Rest in You. LC 98-5142. (Saints Speak Today Ser.). 1998. pap. text 9.99 (*1-56955-034-4*) Servant.

— The Retractations. Bogan, Mary I., tr. LC 67-30513. (Fathers of the Church Ser.: Vol. 60). 321p. 1968. 19.95 (*0-8132-0060-1*) Cath U Pr.

***Augustine, Saint.** The Retractations. Bogan, Mary Inez, tr. LC 67-30513. (Fathers of the Church Ser.: Vol. 60). xxvi, 321p. 2000. pap. 30.95 (*0-8132-0970-6*) Cath U Pr.

Augustine, Saint. The Rule of Saint Augustine. Rotelle, John, ed. (Mini-Augustine Ser.). 2000. pap. 8.95 (*1-56548-130-5*) New City.

— St. Augustine: The Greatness of the Soul. Quasten, J. & Plumpe, J., eds. Colleran, Joseph M., tr. LC 78-62455. (Ancient Christian Writers Ser.: No. 9). 255p. 1950. 16.95 (*0-8091-0060-6*) Paulist Pr.

— St. Augustine, Against the Academics. Burghardt, Walter J. et al, eds. LC 78-62461. (Ancient Christian Writers Ser.: No. 12). 220p. 1950. 16.95 (*0-8091-0252-8*) Paulist Pr.

— St. Augustine on the Psalms. Quasten, J. & Burghardt, Walter J., eds. Hebgin, D. Scholastica & Corrigan, D. Felicitas, trs. LC 60-10722. (Ancient Christian Writers Ser.: No. 30, Vol. 2). 425p. 1961. 26.95 (*0-8091-0105-X*) Paulist Pr.

— St. Augustine on the Psalms, Vol. 1. Quasten, J. & Burghardt, Walter J., eds. Hebgin, Scholastica & Corrigan, Felicitas, trs. LC 60-10722. (Ancient Christian Writers Ser.: No. 29). 360p. 1960. 34.95 (*0-8091-0104-1*) Paulist Pr.

— St. Augustine, Sermons for Christmas & Epiphany. Quasten, J. & Plumpe, J., eds. Lawler, Thomas C., tr. LC 78-62464. (Ancient Christian Writers Ser.: No. 15). 250p. 1952. 16.95 (*0-8091-0137-8*) Paulist Pr.

— St. Augustine, the First Catechetical Instruction. Quasten, J. & Plumpe, J., eds. Christopher, Joseph P., tr. LC 78-62449. (Ancient Christian Writers Ser.: No. 2). 170p. 1946. 14.95 (*0-8091-0047-9*) Paulist Pr.

— St. Augustine, the Lord's Sermon on the Mount. Burghardt, Walter J. et al, eds. LC 78-62451. (Ancient Christian Writers Ser.: No. 5). 227p. 1948. 22.95 (*0-8091-0246-3*) Paulist Pr.

— St. Augustine, the Problem of Free Choice. Burghardt, Walter J. et al, eds. LC 78-62469. (Ancient Christian Writers Ser.: No. 22). 298p. 1955. 19.95 (*0-8091-0259-5*) Paulist Pr.

— Select Letters. (Loeb Classical Library: No. 239). 590p. 1930. 19.95 (*0-674-99264-4*) HUP.

— Selected Letters. LC 75-41014. (BCL Ser. II). reprint ed. 34.50 (*0-404-14503-5*) AMS Pr.

— Sermons 51-94 (on the New Testament), Vol. III/3. Rotelle, John E., ed. Hill, Edmund, tr. 520p. 1991. 39.00 (*0-911782-85-0*) New City.

— Sermons 94A-147A (on the New Testament), Vol. III/4. Rotelle, John E., ed. Hill, Edmund, tr. 480p. 1992. 39.00 (*1-56548-000-7*) New City.

— Sermons on the Liturgical Seasons, Saint Augustine. Muldowney, Mary S., tr. LC BR0060.F3A82. (Fathers of the Church Ser.: Vol. 38). 471p. 1984. reprint ed. pap. 146.10 (*0-7837-9200-X*, 204995000004) Bks Demand.

— Sermons 184-229Z (on the Litergical Seasons), Vol. III/6. Rotelle, John E., ed. Hill, Edmund, tr. from LAT. (Works of St. Augustine). 300p. 1993. 39.00 (*1-56548-050-3*) New City.

— Sermons 148-183 (on the New Testament), Vol. III/5. Rotelle, John E., ed. Hill, Edmund, tr. from LAT. (Works of St. Augustine). 400p. 1992. 39.00 (*1-56548-007-4*) New City.

— Sermons 1-19 (on the Old Testament), Vol. III/1. Rotelle, John E., ed. Hill, Edmund & O'Connell, Matthew, trs. from LAT. 400p. 1990. 39.00 (*0-911782-75-3*) New City.

— Sermons 341-400 (on Various Themes), Vol. III/10. Rotelle, John E., ed. Hill, Edmund, tr. from LAT. (Works of St. Augustine). 528p. 1995. lib. bdg. 39.00 (*1-56548-028-7*) New City.

— Sermons 306-340A (on the Saints), Vol. III/9. Rotelle, John E., ed. Hill, Edmund, tr. from LAT. (Works of St. Augustine). 368p. 1994. lib. bdg. 39.00 (*1-56548-068-6*) New City.

— Sermons 20-50 (on the Old Testament), Vol. III/2. Rotelle, John E., ed. Hill, Edmund, tr. 400p. 1990. 39.00 (*0-911782-78-8*) New City.

— Sermons 273-305A (on the Saints), Vol. III/8. Rotelle, John E., ed. Hill, Edmund, tr. from LAT. (Works of St. Augustine). 368p. 1994. lib. bdg. 39.00 (*1-56548-060-0*) New City.

— Sermons 230-272 B (on the Liturgical Seasons), Vol. III/7. Rotelle, John E., ed. Hill, Edmund, tr. from LAT. (Works of St. Augustine). 344p. 1993. 39.00 (*1-56548-059-7*) New City.

— Soliloquies & Immortality of the Soul. Watson, Gerard, ed. (Classical Texts Ser.). 1980. 59.99 (*0-85668-505-4*, Pub. by Aris & Phillips); pap. 28.00 (*0-85668-505-2*, Pub. by Aris & Phillips) David Brown.

— St. Augustine on Marriage & Sexuality. Clark, Elizabeth Ann, ed. LC 96-8089. (Fathers of the Church Ser.: Vol. 1). 112p. 1996. text 29.95 (*0-8132-0866-1*); pap. text 13.95 (*0-8132-0867-X*) Cath U Pr.

— The Teacher & the Soliloquies of Saint Augustine. Rotelle, John, ed. (Mini-Augustine Ser.). 2000. pap. 8.95 (*1-56548-134-8*) New City.

— The Teacher, the Free Choice of the Will, Grace & Free Will. Russell, Robert P., tr. LC 67-30350. (Fathers of the Church Ser.: Vol. 59). 323p. 1968. 36.95 (*0-8132-0059-8*) Cath U Pr.

— Teaching Christianity, Vol. I/11. Rotelle, John E., ed. Hill, Edmund, tr. from LAT. (Works of St. Augustine). 248p. 1996. 29.95 (*1-56548-048-1*) New City.

— Tractates on the Gospel of John, 11-27. Rettig, John W., tr. LC 87-18387. (Fathers of the Church Ser.: Vol. 79). 306p. 1988. 31.95 (*0-8132-0079-2*) Cath U Pr.

— Tractates on the Gospel of John, 55-111. Rettig, John W., tr. from LAT. LC 87-18387. (Fathers of the Church Ser.: Vol. 90). 328p. 1994. 36.95 (*0-8132-0090-3*) Cath U Pr.

— Tractates on the Gospel of John, 112-124. Rettig, John W., tr. LC 87-18387. (Fathers of the Church Ser.). 30 p. 1995. 36.95 (*0-8132-0092-X*) Cath U Pr.

— Tractates on the Gospel of John, 1-10. Rettig, John W., tr. LC 87-18387. (Fathers of the Church Ser.: Vol. 78). 236p. 1988. 31.95 (*0-8132-0078-4*) Cath U Pr.

— Tractates on the Gospel of John, 28-54. Rettig, John W., tr. from LAT. LC 87-18387. (Fathers of the Church Ser.: Vol. 88). 326p. 1993. 36.95 (*0-8132-0088-1*) Cath U Pr.

***Augustine, Saint.** Treatises on Marriage & Other Subjects. Wilcox, Charles T., tr. LC 73-75002. (Fathers of the Church Ser.: Vol. 27). 2000. pap. 41.95 (*0-8132-0967-6*) Cath U Pr.

Augustine, Saint. Treatises on Various Subjects. Muldowney, Mary S. et al, trs. LC 65-18319. (Fathers of the Church Ser.: Vol. 16). 479p. 1952. 26.95 (*0-8132-0016-4*) Cath U Pr.

— The Trinity. McKenna, Stephen, tr. LC 63-12482. (Fathers of the Church Ser.: Vol. 45). 557p. 1963. reprint ed. pap. 172.70 (*0-7837-9202-6*, 204995200004) Bks Demand.

— We Are Your Servants: Augustine's Homilies on Ministry. Rotelle, John E., ed. Fellowes, Audrey, tr. from LAT. LC 86-71645. 156p. 1986. pap. 4.50 (*0-941491-10-2*) Augustinian Pr.

— Writings of Saint Augustine Vol. 1: Saint Augustine: the Happy Life by Ludwig Schopp. LC 66-20314. (Fathers of the Church Ser.: Vol. 5). 454p. 1948. reprint ed. pap. 140.80 (*0-7837-9147-X*, 204994700001) Bks Demand.

Augustine, Saint & Kwikscan, Inc. Staff. St. Augustine's Confessions in Kwikscan. LC 90-35315. 1990. write for info. (*0-941485-29-3*); write for info. (*0-941485-30-7*) KWIKSCAN.

Augustine, Saint, et al. Spiritual Journey: Augustine's Reflections on the Christian Life. LC 96-24008. 1996. pap. 13.95 (*0-941491-97-8*) Augustinian Pr.

Augustine, Saint, jt. auth. see Groeschel, Benedict J

Augustine, Saint, jt. auth. see Saint Jerome.

Augustine, Saint, jt. auth. see Starnes, Colin.

Augustine, Saint, ed. see Jeffs, Stephanie.

Augustine, Saint, ed. see Stickler, LeeDell.

Augustine, Sister Mary, jt. auth. see Crouch, Howard E.

Augustine, Sue. With Wings, There Are No Barriers: A Woman's Guide to a Life of Magnificent Possibilities. LC 96-30364. 280p. 1996. 18.95 (*1-56554-195-2*) Pelican.

Augustine, Timothy J. & Curcio, Rana C. How Hard Are You Knocking? The College Student's Guide to Opening Corporate Doors. LC 96-15403. 132p. 1996. pap. 12.95 (*1-886939-08-X*, Pub. by OakHill Pr VA) ACCESS Pubs Network.

Augustine, Victoria C., jt. auth. see Augustine, Nicholas.

Augustini, Gina, et al, eds. Raiding the Southwest Conference: The Collective History of Red Raider Sports in the Southwest Conference. (Illus.). 176p. 1996. 39.95 (*0-9653513-0-0*) Tex Tech Univ Pr.

Augustini, S. Aurelii. Concordantia in Libros XIII Confessionum, 2 vols., Set. (Alpha-Omega, Reihe A Ser.: Bd. CXXIV). (GER.). 1191p. 1991. write for info. incl. 3.5 hd (*3-487-09402-9*) G Olms Pubs.

Augustinian Educational Conferences Staff. Augustinian Studies: Papers Read at Recent Augustinian Educational Conferences. LC 67-22052. (Essay Index Reprint Ser.). 1977. 20.95 (*0-8369-0163-0*) Ayer.

Augustinius, Aurelius. De Haeresibus. Muller, Liguori G., tr. LC 78-63165. (Heresies of the Early Christian & Medieval Era Ser.: Second Ser.). reprint ed. write for info. (*0-404-16178-2*) AMS Pr.

Augustino, Diane K., jt. compiled by see Barnes, Grace M.

Augustinos, Gerasimos. Consciousness & History: Nationalist Critics of Greek Society, 1897-1914. (East European Monographs: No. 32). 182p. 1977. text 58.00 (*0-914710-25-7*, Pub. by East Eur Monographs) Col U Pr.

— The Greeks of Asia Minor: Confession, Community, & Ethnicity in the Nineteenth Century. LC 92-1308. 280p. 1992. reprint ed. pap. 86.80 (*0-608-07343-1*, 206757100009) Bks Demand.

Augustinos, Gerasimos, ed. Diverse Paths to Modernity in Southeastern Europe: Essays in National Development, 20. LC 90-38424. (Contributions to the Study of World History Ser.: No. 20). 192p. 1990. 52.95 (*0-313-26670-0*, ANF, Greenwood Pr) Greenwood.

— The National Idea in Eastern Europe: The Politics of Ethnic & Civic Community. 211p. (C). 1996. pap. text 18.76 (*0-669-39626-5*) HM Trade Div.

Augustinos, Olga. French Odysseys: Greece in French Travel Literature from the Renaissance to the Romantic Era. LC 93-8705. 1994. text 44.00 (*0-8018-4616-1*) Johns Hopkins.

Augustinos, Theodore P. & Emmanuel, John N. Bank Insurance Sales Methods: All 50 States & the District of Columbia. Smith, Carole, ed. 592p. pap. 1395.00 (*0-8080-0394-1*) CCH INC.

— Bank Insurance Sales Methods: Central Region. Smith, Carole, ed. 144p. pap. 389.00 (*0-8080-0397-6*) CCH INC.

— Bank Insurance Sales Methods: Northeast Region. Smith, Carole, ed. 152p. pap. 389.00 (*0-8080-0395-X*) CCH INC.

— Bank Insurance Sales Methods: Southern Region. Smith, Carole, ed. 176p. pap. 389.00 (*0-8080-0396-8*) CCH INC.

— Bank Insurance Sales Methods: Western Region. Smith, Carole, ed. 152p. pap. 389.00 (*0-8080-0398-4*) CCH INC.

Augustithis, S. S. Atlas of the Textural Patterns of Basic & Ultrabasic Rocks & Their Genetic Significance. (C). 1979. 207.70 (*3-11-006571-1*) De Gruyter.

***Augustithis, S. S.** Maverick. LC 99-76193. 2000. pap. 13.95 (*1-57197-197-1*, Pub. by Pentland Pr) Assoc Pubs Grp.

Augustithis, Stylianos-Sarvas P. Atlas of the Textural Patterns of Ore Minerals & Metallogenic Processes. LC 94-41197. x, 664p. (C). 1995. lib. bdg. 346.45 (*3-11-013639-2*) De Gruyter.

Augustodunensis, Honorius. The Seal of Blessed Mary. Carr, Amelia, tr. (Translation Ser.). 103p. 1991. pap. 15.00 (*0-920669-18-2*, Pub. by Peregrina Pubng) Cistercian Pubns.

Augustus, John. John Augustus, First Probation Officer: With Intro. & Index Added. LC 79-129308. (Criminology, Law Enforcement, & Social Problems Ser.: No. 130). (Illus.). 16.00 (*0-87585-130-4*) Patterson Smith.

Augustus, Justinianus. Digesta, Vol. I. Kreuger, Paulus & Mommsen, Theodorus, eds. 960p. 1962. write for info. (*3-296-13801-3*) G Olms Pubs.

— Digesta, Vol. II. Kreuger, Paulus & Mommsen, Theodorus, eds. iv, 1044p. 1963. write for info. (*3-296-13802-1*) G Olms Pubs.

Augustus, Patrick. Baby Father. 1997. pap. 9.95 (*1-874509-05-0*, Pub. by X Pr) LPC InBook.

— Baby Father 2. 192p. 1996. 9.95 (*1-874509-15-8*, Pub. by X Pr) LPC InBook.

— When a Man Loves a Woman. 192p. 1996. pap. 9.95 (*1-874509-24-7*) LPC InBook.

Augustyn, Brian. Batman: Master of the Future. O'Neil, Dennis, ed. 64p. 1991. pap. 5.95 (*1-56389-015-1*) DC Comics.

***Augustyn, Brian.** Crimson: Heaven & Earth. (Crimson Ser.). (Illus.). 160p. (YA). 2000. pap. 14.95 (*1-56389-647-8*, Pub. by DC Comics) Time Warner.

Augustyn, Brian & Ramos, Humerto. Crimson: Loyalty & Loss. (Illus.). 160p. 1999. pap. text 12.95 (*1-56389-532-3*, Pub. by DC Comics) Time Warner.

Augustyn, Brian, jt. auth. see Waid, Mark.

Augustyn, Michael. Vlad Dracula Vol. 1: The Dragon Prince. unabridged ed. (Illus.). 310p. 1995. pap. 14.99 (*0-9660865-0-3*, MA0001) Vasso Studios.

Augustyn, Robert T., jt. auth. see Cohen, Paul E.

Augustyn, Wolfgang. Der Lateinische Hamilton-Psalter im Berliner Kupferstichkabinett. (Spolia Berolinensia Ser.: Bd. 9). (GER.). x, 450p. 1996. 158.00 (*3-615-00179-6*, Pub. by Weidmann) Lubrecht & Cramer.

Augustynek, Zdzislaw. Time: Past, Present & Future. (Nijhoff International Philosophy Ser.). 146p. 1991. lib. bdg. 131.50 (*0-7923-0270-2*, Pub. by Kluwer Academic) Kluwer Academic.

Augustyniak, J. Michael. The Barbie Doll Boom: Identification & Values. LC 96-139870. 160p. 1996. pap. 18.95 (*0-89145-686-4*, 4631) Collector Bks.

— Thirty Years Fashion Dolls, 1967-1997: Identification & Value Guide. 1998. pap. text 19.95 (*1-57432-052-1*, 5049) Collector Bks.

Augustyniak, Michael. Collector's Encyclopedia of Barbie Doll Exclusives & More: Identification & Values. 2nd ed. 464p. 1999. 24.95 (*1-57432-134-X*) Collector Bks.

Auh, Yong, jt. auth. see Firebaugh, Morris W.

A

Auh, Yoon-Il. Auh Etudes: Fifth Etude. (Auh School of Violin Ser.). 35p. (J). (gr. 1-12). 1986. student ed. 10.00 (*1-882858-26-3*) Yoon-il Auh.
— Auh Etudes: First Etude. (Auh School of Violin Ser.). 15p. (YA). (gr. 5-12). 1992. student ed. 10.00 (*1-882858-13-1*) Yoon-il Auh.
— Auh Etudes: Fourth Etude. (Auh School of Violin Ser.). 30p. (J). (gr. 1-12). 1985. student ed. 10.00 (*1-882858-16-6*) Yoon-il Auh.
— Auh Etudes: Second Etude. (Auh School of Violin Ser.). 17p. (YA). (gr. 5-12). 1992. student ed. 10.00 (*1-882858-14-X*) Yoon-il Auh.
— Auh Etudes: The Art of Bowing. (Auh School of Violin Ser.). 20p. (J). (gr. 1-12). 1993. student ed. 10.00 (*1-882858-07-7*) Yoon-il Auh.
— Auh Etudes: The Art of Double Stop, Bk. I. (Auh School of Violin Ser.). 20p. (J). (gr. 1-12). 1993. student ed. 10.00 (*1-882858-08-5*) Yoon-il Auh.
— Auh Etudes: The Art of Double Stop, Bk. II. (Auh School of Violin Ser.). 20p. (J). (gr. 1-12). 1993. student ed. 10.00 (*1-882858-09-3*) Yoon-il Auh.
— Auh Etudes: Third Etude. (Auh School of Violin Ser.). 19p. (YA). (gr. 5-12). 1992. student ed. 10.00 (*1-882858-15-8*) Yoon-il Auh.
— Concert Books for the Young: EZ Duet I. (Auh School of Violin Ser.). 30p. (J). (gr. 1-12). 1993. student ed. 10.00 (*1-882858-22-0*) Yoon-il Auh.
— Concert Books for the Young: EZ Duet II. (Auh School of Violin Ser.). 30p. (J). (gr. 1-12). 1993. student ed. 10.00 (*1-882858-23-9*) Yoon-il Auh.
— Concert Books for the Young: Moto Perpetuo I. (Auh School of Violin Ser.). 8p. (J). (gr. 1-8). 1990. student ed. 10.00 (*1-882858-37-9*) Yoon-il Auh.
— Concert Books for the Young: Moto Perpetuo II. (Auh School of Violin Ser.). 8p. (J). (gr. 1-8). 1990. student ed. 10.00 (*1-882858-38-7*) Yoon-il Auh.
— Concert Books for the Young: Moto Perpetuo III. (Auh School of Violin Ser.). 9p. (J). (gr. 1-8). 1983. student ed. 10.00 (*1-882858-39-5*) Yoon-il Auh.
— Concert Books for the Young: My First Concert Book. (Auh School of Violin Ser.). 35p. (J). (gr. k-5). 1988. student ed. 10.00 (*1-882858-19-0*) Yoon-il Auh.
— Concert Books for the Young: My Second Concert Book. (Auh School of Violin Ser.). 35p. (J). (gr. k-5). 1988. student ed. 10.00 (*1-882858-18-2*) Yoon-il Auh.
— Concert Books for the Young: My Third Concert Book. (Auh School of Violin Ser.). 35p. (J). (gr. k-7). 1988. student ed. 10.00 (*1-882858-21-2*) Yoon-il Auh.
— Concert Books for the Young: Pizzicato Wonder Land. (Auh School of Violin Ser.). 22p. (J). (gr. k-8). 1988. student ed. 10.00 (*1-882858-27-1*) Yoon-il Auh.
— Concert Books for the Young: Theme & Variations I. (Auh School of Violin Ser.). 12p. (J). (gr. 1-6). 1987. student ed. 10.00 (*1-882858-24-7*) Yoon-il Auh.
— Concert Books for the Young: Theme & Variations II. (Auh School of Violin Ser.). 12p. (J). (gr. 1-6). 1987. student ed. 10.00 (*1-882858-25-5*) Yoon-il Auh.
— Concert Books for the Young: Twenty-Four Contemporary Easy Duets, Bk. I. (Auh School of Violin Ser.). 25p. (YA). 1987. student ed. 10.00 (*1-882858-41-7*) Yoon-il Auh.
— Concert Books for the Young: Twenty-Four Contemporary Easy Duets, Bk. II. (Auh School of Violin Ser.). (YA). 1987. student ed. 10.00 (*1-882858-42-5*) Yoon-il Auh.
— Contemporary Rhythm & Dynamics: Ten Contemporary EZ Duets. (Auh School of Violin Ser.). 20p. (J). (gr. 4-12). 1986. student ed. 10.00 (*1-882858-40-9*) Yoon-il Auh.
— Contemporary Rhythm & Dynamics Bk. I. (Auh School of Violin Ser.). 20p. (J). (gr. 1-12). 1986. student ed. 10.00 (*1-882858-43-3*) Yoon-il Auh.
— Contemporary Rhythm & Dynamics Bk. II. (Auh School of Violin Ser.). 20p. (J). (gr. 1-12). 1986. student ed. 10.00 (*1-882858-44-1*) Yoon-il Auh.
— Position Studies: Advance Position Study. (Auh School of Violin Ser.). 35p. (J). (gr. 1-12). 1985. student ed. 10.00 (*1-882858-46-8*) Yoon-il Auh.
— Position Studies: Scales & Shifting 1. (Auh School of Violin Ser.). 30p. (YA). (gr. 5-12). 1990. student ed. 10.00 (*1-882858-11-5*) Yoon-il Auh.
— Position Studies: Scales & Shifting 2. (Auh School of Violin Ser.). 30p. (YA). (gr. 5-12). 1990. student ed. 10.00 (*1-882858-12-3*) Yoon-il Auh.
— Position Studies: Third Position. (Auh School of Violin Ser.). 35p. (YA). (gr. 5-12). 1986. student ed. 10.00 (*1-882858-45-X*) Yoon-il Auh.
— Pre-School Virtuoso, Bk. I. (Auh School of Violin Ser.). 40p. (J). (gr. k-5). 1988. student ed. 10.00 (*1-882858-03-4*) Yoon-il Auh.
— Pre-School Virtuoso, Bk. II. (Auh School of Violin Ser.). 40p. (J). (gr. k-5). 1988. student ed. 10.00 (*1-882858-04-2*) Yoon-il Auh.
— Pre-School Virtuoso, Bk. III. (Auh School of Violin Ser.). 40p. (J). (gr. k-5). 1988. student ed. 10.00 (*1-882858-05-0*) Yoon-il Auh.
— Pre-School Virtuoso, Bk. IV. (Auh School of Violin Ser.). 40p. (J). (gr. k-5). student ed. 10.00 (*1-882858-06-9*) Yoon-il Auh.
— Preliminary, Bk. 1. (Auh School of Violin Ser.). 60p. (J). (gr. 1-8). 1983. student ed. 14.00 (*1-882858-00-X*) Yoon-il Auh.
— Preliminary, Bk. 2. (Auh School of Violin Ser.). 60p. (J). (gr. 1-8). 1983. student ed. 14.00 (*1-882858-01-8*) Yoon-il Auh.
— Preliminary, Bk. 3. (Auh School of Violin Ser.). 45p. (J). (gr. 1-8). 1983. student ed. 14.00 (*1-882858-02-6*) Yoon-il Auh.
— Preliminary Advance, Bk. 1. (Auh School of Violin Ser.). 50p. (J). (gr. 1-8). 1983. student ed. 14.00 (*1-882858-17-4*) Yoon-il Auh.
— Scale System for Young: EZ Scales. (Auh School of Violin Ser.). 45p. (J). (gr. 1-12). 1993. student ed. 10.00 (*1-882858-10-7*) Yoon-il Auh.
— Tricks for the Wild Fiddler, Bk. I. (Auh School of Violin Ser.). 35p. (J). (gr. 1-12). 1985. student ed. 10.00 (*1-882858-28-X*) Yoon-il Auh.
— Tricks for the Wild Fiddler, Bk. II. (Auh School of Violin Ser.). 35p. (J). (gr. 1-12). 1985. student ed. 10.00 (*1-882858-29-8*) Yoon-il Auh.

Auh, Yoon-il & Lawrence, Fred. A Guide to the Programming Process: A Complement to a Multi-Sensory Approach for Learning Programming Construct & Problem Solving. 500p. Date not set. text 85.00 (*1-882858-47-6*); disk. write for info. (*1-882858-48-4*) Yoon-il Auh.

Auh, Yoonil, jt. auth. see Lawrence, Frederick.

Auhagen, Ann E., et al, eds. The Diversity of Human Relationships. (Illus.). 356p. (C). 1996. text 64.95 (*0-521-47463-9*); pap. text 24.95 (*0-521-47983-5*) Cambridge U Pr.

Auhagen, Wolfgang, jt. ed. see Kopiez, Reinhard.

***Auiler, Dan.** Hitchcock's Notebooks. 2001. pap. write for info. (*0-380-79945-6*, HarpEntertain) Morrow Avon.

Auiler, Dan. Hitchcock's Notebooks: An Authorized & Illustrated Look Inside the Creative Mind of Alfred Hitchcock. LC 98-31904. (Illus.). 576p. 1999. 30.00 (*0-380-97783-4*, Avon Bks) Morrow Avon.

Auiler, Dan. Vertigo: The Making of a Hitchcock Classic. LC 97-31654. 240p. 1998. text 27.95 (*0-312-16915-9*) St Martin.

***Auiler, Dan.** Vertigo: The Making of a Hitchcock Classic. (Illus.). 240p. 2000. pap. 17.95 (*0-312-26409-7*) St Martin.

Auiler, Rebello. North by Northwest. 2000. text 27.95 (*0-312-24413-4*) St Martin.

Auilles, Edwin. Architectural Drafting. LC 79-730976. 1980. student ed. 7.00 (*0-8064-0289-X*, 725) Bergwall.
— Architectural Drafting II. LC 80-730728. 1981. student ed. 7.00 (*0-8064-0291-1*, 726) Bergwall.

Auinasha, Bodhi, jt. auth. see Saraswati, Sunyata.

Auinn, John P. Law Firm Accounting. 340p. 1986. boxed set 90.00 (*0-318-23680-X*) NY Law Pub.

Aujard, Richard, photos by. Boxing. (Illus.). 290p. 1997. pap. 29.95 (*0-7893-0106-7*, Pub. by Universe) St Martin.

Aujoulat, Noel. Le Neo-Platonisme Alexandrin: Hierocles d'Alexandrie: Filiations Intellectuelles et Spirituelles d'un Neo-Plantonicien du Ve Siecle. (Philosophia Antiqua Ser.). x, 461p. 1986. pap. 123.00 (*90-04-07510-0*) Brill Academic Pubs.

Aukema, C. Asylum. (Chapbook Ser.). 20p. (Orig.). 1996. pap. 2.50 (*0-9636959-4-0*) Coe Review Pr.
— Climbing Jacob's Ladder. (Chapbook Ser.). 12p. (Orig.). 1996. pap. 2.00 (*0-9636959-3-2*) Coe Review Pr.
— Jack & the Beanstalk Revisited. (Chapbook Ser.). 10p. (Orig.). 1996. pap. 2.50 (*1-889678-01-5*) Coe Review Pr.
— The Mechanics of Deformable Bodies. (Chapbook Ser.). 20p. (Orig.). 1996. pap. 2.50 (*0-9636959-2-4*) Coe Review Pr.

Aukeman, Anastasia. Doris Kloster. (GER, FRE & ENG., Illus.). 340p. 1995. 29.99 (*3-8228-8875-3*) Taschen Amer.

Auken, Candace L. Van, see Van Auken, Candace L.

Auken, John Van, see Van Auken, John.

Auken, Z. Van, see Van Auken, Z.

Aukerman, Dale. Darkening Valley. 1986. 8.95 (*0-8164-2295-8*) Harper SF.

***Aukerman, Dale.** Hope Beyond Healing: A Cancer Journal. LC 99-59737. 2000. 14.95 (*0-87178-023-2*) Brethren.

Aukerman, Dale. Reckoning with Apocalypse: Terminal Politics & Christian Hope. 264p. 1993. 24.95 (*0-8245-1243-X*) Crossroad NY.

Aukerman, Robert C., ed. Some Persistent Questions on Beginning Reading. LC 73-190454. 183p. reprint ed. pap. 56.80 (*0-608-15280-3*, 202959500061) Bks Demand.

Aukerman, Ruth. Move over, Picasso! A Young Painter's Primer. (Illus.). 44p. (Orig.). (J). (gr. 1-6). 1994. pap. 12.95 (*1-884555-01-2*) P Depke Bks.

Auklandus, Joellyn. Wild Hunt. Pini, Wendy, ed. (Elfquest Reader's Collection: Vol. 11B). (Illus.). 240p. (YA). 2000. pap. 13.95 (*0-936861-70-3*, Pub. by Warp Graphics) Midpt Trade.

Aukshunas, Jane, jt. auth. see Samson, Karl.

Auksi, Peter. Christian Plain Style: The Evolution of a Spiritual Ideal. 384p. 1995. 65.00 (*0-7735-1220-9*, Pub. by McG-Queens Univ Pr) CUP Services.

Aul, C. & Schneider, W. Interferons: Biological Activities & Clinical Efficacy. LC 96-36491. (Illus.). 310p. 1997. pap. 59.00 (*3-540-61051-0*) Spr-Verlag.

Aul, E. T. As You Desire Me: The Psychology of a Multiple Personality. (Illus.). 232p. (Orig.). 1996. pap. 19.95 (*1-889206-25-3*) J H White.

Aul, K. Martin. Beyond the Wall of Tears. (Illus.). 1984. 7.95 (*0-940244-18-7*) Flying Buffalo.

Aulakh. Rethinking Globalizations. LC 99-37670. 2000. text 65.00 (*0-312-22600-4*) St Martin.

Aulard, Francois V. Paris Pendant la Reaction Thermidorienne et sous le Directoire, 5 vols., Set. LC 70-161713. (Collection de documents relatifs a l'histoire de Paris pendant la Revolution francaise). reprint ed. 675.00 (*0-404-52570-9*) AMS Pr.
— Paris sous le Consulat, 4 vols., Set. LC 74-161714. (Collection de documents relatifs a l'histoire de Paris pendant la Revolution francaise). reprint ed. 540.00 (*0-404-52580-6*) AMS Pr.
— Paris sous le Premier Empire, 3 vols., Set. LC 74-161706. (Collection de documents relatifs a l'histoire de Paris pendant la Revolution francaise). reprint ed. 405.00 (*0-404-52576-8*) AMS Pr.

Aulard, Francois V., tr. La Societe des Jacobins, 6 vols. LC 78-161707. (Collection de documents relatifs a l'histoire de Paris pendant la Revolution francaise). reprint ed. 810.00 (*0-404-52560-1*) AMS Pr.

Aulard, Francois V., et al. Collection de Documents Relatifs a l'Histoire de Paris Pendant la Revolution Francaise, 16 titles in 54 vols., Set. reprint ed. 7335.00 (*0-404-52550-4*) AMS Pr.

Aulbach, B. Continuous & Discrete Dynamics near Manifolds of Equilibria. (Lecture Notes in Mathematics Ser.: Vol. 1058). ix, 142p. 1984. 32.95 (*0-387-13329-1*) Spr-Verlag.

Aulbach, Robert E. Energy & Water Resource Management. 2nd ed. LC 88-11213. (Illus.). 262p. 1988. pap. text. write for info. (*0-86612-039-4*) Educ Inst Am Hotel.

Aulbach-Smith, Cynthia A., et al. Aquatic & Wetland Plants of South Carolina. 2nd rev. ed. LC 96-622144. (Illus.). 127p. (Orig.). 1996. pap. 15.00 (*0-9632821-1-5*); spiral bd. 16.00 (*0-9632821-2-3*) SC Dept Nat Res.

Aulbach, Stefan. Spiritualitat Schafft Befreiung: Der Entwurf Christlicher Existenz Bei Juan Luis Segundo. (Wurzburger Studien Zur Fundamentaltheologie Ser.: Bd. 10). (GER.). IX, 152p. 1992. 33.80 (*3-631-45078-8*) P Lang Pubng.

Aulby, Mike, et al. Bowling 200+ (Illus.). 192p. 1989. pap. 11.95 (*0-8092-4338-5*, 433850, Contemporary Bks) NTC Contemp Pub Co.

Auld, A. G. Amos. (Old Testament Guides Ser.: No. 26). 93p. 1987. pap. 12.50 (*1-85075-005-X*, Pub. by Sheffield Acad) CUP Services.

Auld, A. Graeme. Joshua, Judges & Ruth. 292p. 1993. pap. 22.00 (*0-7152-0535-8*, Pub. by St Andrew) St Mut.

Auld, A. Graeme. Joshua Retold: Synoptic Perspectives. 192p. 44.95 (*0-567-08603-8*) T&T Clark Pubs.

Auld, A. Graeme. Kings. 272p. 1993. pap. 22.00 (*0-7152-0523-4*, Pub. by St Andrew) St Mut.
— Kings Without Privilege: David & Moses in the Story of the Bible's Kings. 224p. 1994. text 44.95 (*0-567-09639-4*, Pub. by T & T Clark) Bks Intl VA.
— Understanding Poets & Prophets: Essays in Honour of George Wishart Anderson. (JSOTS Ser.: Vol. 152). 445p. 1993. 90.00 (*1-85075-427-6*, Pub. by Sheffield Acad) CUP Services.

Auld, A. Graeme, ed. Society for Old Testament Study Book List 1991. 170p. 1991. pap. 16.00 (*0-905495-10-1*, Pub. by Sheffield Acad) CUP Services.

Auld, A. Graeme, ed. Society for Old Testament Study Book List 1992. 154p. 1992. pap. 16.00 (*0-905495-11-X*, Pub. by Sheffield Acad) CUP Services.

Auld, Alan G. & Steiner, Margreet. Jerusalem Vol. 1: From the Bronze Age to the Maccabees. 112p. (Orig.). 1996. 16.95 (*0-86554-520-0*, MUP/P145) Mercer Univ Pr.

Auld, B. A., jt. ed. see Sastroutomo, S. S.

Auld, Bertram A. Acoustic Fields & Waves in Solids, 2 vols. 2nd rev. ed. 878p. 1990. 120.00 (*0-89464-490-4*) Krieger.
— Acoustic Fields & Waves in Solids, 2 vols., Vol. II. rev. ed. 432p. 1990. 60.50 (*0-89874-783-X*) Krieger.

Auld, Dennis. Periodical Abstracts Ondisc User Guide. 1989. write for info. incl. cd-rom (*0-914604-33-3*) UMI Louisville.
— Resource - One Ondisc User Guide. 1989. write for info. incl. cd-rom (*0-914604-34-1*) UMI Louisville.

Auld, Frank & Hyman, Marvin. Resolution of Inner Conflict: An Introduction to Psychoanalytic Therapy. 267p. 1991. text 29.95 (*1-55798-116-7*) Am Psychol.

Auld, J. W., jt. auth. see Courtney, W.

Auld, Janice L. Cut & Paste Phonics: Extra Help for Troublesome Letter Combinations. (J). (gr. 1-3). 1985. pap. 8.99 (*0-8224-5540-4*) Fearon Teacher Aids.
— Shape-a-Poem. (J). (gr. 1-3). 1986. pap. 6.99 (*0-8224-6393-8*) Fearon Teacher Aids.
— Shape-a-Story. (J). (gr. 1-3). 1986. pap. 6.99 (*0-8224-6392-X*) Fearon Teacher Aids.

Auld, L. Lyric Art of Pierre Perrin Vol. 60/3B, Pt. 1: Birth of French Opera. (Wissenschaftliche Abhandlungen - Musicological Studies). 1996. 75.00 (*0-931902-28-2*) Inst Mediaeval Mus.
— Lyric Art of Pierre Perrin Vol. 62, Pt.4: Recueil de Paroles. (Wissenschaftliche Abhandlungen - Musicological Studies). 1996. 75.00 (*0-931902-34-7*) Inst Mediaeval Mus.

Auld, Lawrence W. Computer Spreadsheets for Library Applications. 2nd ed. LC 92-26884. (Illus.). 168p. 1993. pap. 47.50 (*0-89774-724-0*) Oryx Pr.

Auld, Louis E., jt. auth. see Lewin, Frank.

Auld, Mary. Daniel in the Lions' Den. LC 98-25250. (Bible Stories Ser.). (Illus.). 31p. (J). (gr. k-3). 1999. 20.25 (*0-531-14514-X*) Watts.

***Auld, Mary.** Daniel in the Lions' Den. (Bible Stories Ser.). (Illus.). (J). 2000. pap. 7.95 (*0-531-15385-1*) Watts.
— David & Goliath LC 99-29723. (Bible Stories Ser.). (Illus.). (J). 2000. 7.95 (*0-531-15393-2*) Watts.
— Exodus from Egypt. LC 99-53304. (Bible Stories Ser.). 2000. 20.50 (*0-531-14585-9*) Watts.
— Exodus from Egypt. (Bible Stories Ser.). (Illus.). (J). 2000. pap. 7.95 (*0-531-15437-8*) Watts.
— Jacob & Esau. (Bible Stories Ser.). (Illus.). (J). 2000. pap. 7.95 (*0-531-15436-X*) Watts.

Auld, Mary. Joseph & His Brothers. LC 98-33204. (ps-3). 1999. 20.25 (*0-531-14515-8*) Watts.

***Auld, Mary.** Joseph & His Brothers. (Bible Stories Ser.). (Illus.). (J). 2000. pap. 7.95 (*0-531-15386-X*) Watts.

Auld, Mary. Moses in the Bulrushes. LC 98-33203. 31p. (J). (ps-3). 1999. 20.25 (*0-531-14516-6*) Watts.
— The Story of Jonah. LC 98-25254. (Bible Stories Ser.). (Illus.). 31p. (J). (gr. k-3). 1999. 20.25 (*0-531-14517-4*) Watts.

***Auld, Mary.** Story of Jonah. (Bible Stories Ser.). (Illus.). (J). 2000. pap. 7.95 (*0-531-15388-6*) Watts.

Auld, Mary & Mayo, Diana. Moses in the Bulrushes. LC 98-33203. (Bible Stories Ser.). 31 p. (ps-3). 1999. lib. bdg. 7.95 (*0-531-15387-8*) Watts.

***Auld, Mary & Mayo, Diana.** Noah's Ark LC 99-15335. (Bible Stories Ser.). 2000. 7.95 (*0-531-15394-0*) Watts.

Auld, Peter A., jt. ed. see Scarpelli, Emile M.

Auld, William D., ed. Sing & Rejoice: Favorite Hymns in Large Print. large type ed. 264p. (Orig.). 1997. pap. 17.95 (*0-664-25712-7*) Westminster John Knox.

Auld, William M. Christmas Tidings. LC 89-29237. 185p. 1990. reprint ed. lib. bdg. 38.00 (*1-55888-862-4*) Omnigraphics Inc.

***Aulds, Charles.** Linux Apache Web Server Administration. (Illus.). 2000. pap. 39.99 (*0-7821-2734-7*) Sybex.

Auleb, Ann W. Laboratory Exercises for Human Biology. 4th ed. 112p. (C). 1990. text 22.00 (*0-536-57719-6*) Pearson Custom.

Aulen, Gustaf. Dag Hammarskjold's White Book: An Analysis of Markings. LC 75-84608. 162p. reprint ed. pap. 50.30 (*0-608-16991-9*, 202697400053) Bks Demand.
— In Scandinavia. (Where to Watch Birds Ser.). (Illus.). 216p. 1997. pap. 25.00 (*0-8117-3115-4*) Stackpole.

Aulen, Gustaf E. Reformation & Catholicity. Wahlstrom, Eric H., tr. from SWE. LC 78-25981. 1979. reprint ed. lib. bdg. 65.00 (*0-313-20809-3*, AURC, Greenwood Pr) Greenwood.

Aulenbach, William H. How to Get to Heaven, Without Going to Church. (Illus.). 154p. 1997. pap. 10.00 (*0-9656572-0-5*) Creative Vntres.

Aulenbacher, Wolfgang. Seventy-Two Hours to Success: The Definitive Workbook for Personal Fulfillment. 384p. (Orig.). 1992. pap. 24.95 (*1-881845-11-7*) Blue Phoenix Bks.

Auler, Virginia. Break Down Every Idol. (Illus.). 168p. 1995. pap. 12.00 (*1-885857-02-0*) Four Wnds Pubng.

Aulestia, Gorka. Basque-English Dictionary. LC 88-32992. (Basque Ser.). (Illus.). 672p. 1989. 50.00 (*0-87417-126-1*) U of Nev Pr.
— The Basque Poetic Tradition. White, Linda, tr. (Basque Ser.). (Illus.). 248p. 2000. text 44.95 (*0-87417-283-7*) U of Nev Pr.
— Improvisational Poetry from the Basque Country. Corcostegui, Lisa & White, Linda, trs. from SPA. LC 93-22447. (Basque Ser.). 272p. (C). 1995. text 44.95 (*0-87417-201-2*) U of Nev Pr.

Aulestia, Gorka & White, Linda. Basque English - English Basque Dictionary. LC 91-44306. (Basque Ser.). (BAQ & ENG.). 688p. (C). 1992. pap. 20.00 (*0-87417-178-4*) U of Nev Pr.
— English-Basque Dictionary. LC 90-33787. (Basque Ser.). 416p. (C). 1990. 45.00 (*0-87417-156-3*) U of Nev Pr.

***Auletta, Gennaro.** Foundations & Interpretation of Quantum Mechanics. 1000p. 1999. 86.00 (*981-02-4039-2*) World Scientific Pub.

Auletta, Ken. The Highwaymen: Warriors on the Information Superhighway. rev. expanded ed. LC 97-45175. 368p. 1998. pap. 13.00 (*0-15-600573-5*) Harcourt.
— Three Blind Mice: How the TV Networks Lost Their Way. LC 92-50105. 1992. pap. 18.00 (*0-679-74135-6*) Vin Bks.
— Underclass. LC 98-47781. 352p. 1999. pap. 16.95 (*0-87951-929-0*, Pub. by Overlook Pr) Penguin Putnam.

***Auletta, Ken.** World War 3.0. 2001. 27.95 (*0-375-50366-8*) Random.

Auletta, Ken, et al, contrib. by. 1-800-President: The Report of the Twentieth Century Fund Task Force on Television Coverage of Presidential Elections. LC 93-9722. (Orig.). 1993. pap. 9.95 (*0-87078-349-1*) Century Foundation.

Auletta, Michael J. & Grekin, Roy C. Local Anesthesia for Dermatologic Surgery. (Practical Manuals in Dermatologic Surgery Ser.). (Illus.). 99p. 1990. pap. text 41.00 (*0-443-08704-0*) Church.

Auletta, R. Walk the Dog Willie. 1985. pap. 5.95 (*0-88145-032-4*) Broadway Play.

Auletta, Richard. 201 Swedish Verbs. LC 74-9748. (SWE & ENG.). 1977. pap. 13.95 (*0-8120-0528-7*) Barron.

Auletta, Robert. The Persians. (American Theater in Literature - A Mark Taper Forum Play Ser.). (Illus.). 104p. (Orig.). 1993. pap. 9.95 (*1-55713-135-X*) Sun & Moon CA.

Aulette. Changing Families. 2nd ed. (Sociology-Upper Level Ser.). 2000. pap. 45.75 (*0-534-51420-0*) Wadsworth Pub.

Aulette, Judy R. Changing Families. 506p. 1993. 47.50 (*0-534-21306-5*) Wadsworth Pub.

Aulger, Addison. Adrift in New York. 1971. pap. 5.60 (*0-87129-313-7*, A11) Dramatic Pub.

***Aulich, James.** Political Posters Central & East Europe 1945-95: Signs of the Times. (Illus.). 300p. 2000. pap. 29.95 (*0-7190-5419-2*, Pub. by Manchester Univ Pr) St Martin.
— Political Posters Central East. 2000. text 69.95 (*0-7190-5418-4*, Pub. by Manchester Univ Pr) St Martin.

Aulich, James, ed. Framing the Falklands War: Nationhood, Culture & Identity. 160p. 1991. 113.00 (*0-335-09684-0*); pap. 36.95 (*0-335-09683-2*) OpUniv Pr.

***Aulich, James & Lynch, John, eds.** Critical Kitaj. LC 00-34206. (Illus.). 256p. (C). 2000. 55.00 (*0-8135-2899-2*); pap. text 26.00 (*0-8135-2900-X*) Rutgers U Pr.

Aulich, Johanna J. Orphische Weltanschauung der Antike und Ihr Erbe Bei Den Dichtern Nietzsche, Holderlin, Novalis und Rilke, Vol. 10. . (Illus.). 204p. 1997. 37.95 (*3-631-32568-1*) P Lang Pubng.

Auliciems, A. & Stanhill, G., eds. Human Bioclimatology. (Advances in Bioclimatology Ser.: Vol. 5). (Illus.). 192p. 1997. 159.00 (*3-540-63057-0*) Spr-Verlag.

Auliciems, Andris. The Atmospheric Environment: A Study of Comfort & Performance. LC 72-80647. (University of Toronto, Department of Geography Research Publications: No. 8). 182p. reprint ed. pap. 56.50 (*0-8357-5847-8*, 202648200049) Bks Demand.

An Asterisk (*) at the beginning of an entry indicates that the title is appearing for the first time.

***Aulicino, Christine & Deak, JoAnn, eds.** The Book of Hopes & Dreams for Girls & Young Women: Notable Women Share Their Experiences & Wisdom. LC 99-73709. (Illus.). 136p. 1999. pap. 19.95 (*0-9664066-1-3*) Laurel Schl.

Aulick, June L., ed. see Seligman, Edith.

***Aulier, Dan.** Alfred Hitchcock in the Vertigo Murders. 2000. 24.00 (*0-7434-0017-8*, Pub. by ibooks); per. 14.00 (*0-7434-0728-8*, Pub. by ibooks) S&S Trade.

Auliff, Lillian A. The Evolution of the Yoruba Video Industry & Its Potential for Development Communication. (Studies in Technology & Social Change: Vol. 27). 135p. (Orig.). 1997. pap. text 14.00 (*0-945271-43-3*) ISU-CIKARD.

Aulik, John J. Highway Mile Marker Guide to the Rocky Mountains. (Central Idaho Ser.: Bk. 1). (Illus.). 293p. (Orig.). 1988. pap. 14.95 (*0-9621574-0-6*) Hwy Mile Mark.

Aulin, A. Foundations of Mathematical System Dynamics: The Fundamental Theory of Causal Recursion & Its Application to Social Science & Economics. (IFSR International Series on Systems Science: 2). (Illus.). 337p. 1989. 112.00 (*0-08-036964-2*, Pergamon Pr) Elsevier.

— The Impact of Science on Economic Growth & Its Cycles: The Mathematical Dynamics Determined by the Basic Macroeconomic Facts. Fandel, G. & Trockel, W., eds. LC 98-29077. (Lecture Notes in Economics & Mathematical Systems Ser.: Vol. 464). (Illus.). x, 204p. 1998. pap. 61.00 (*3-540-64727-9*) Spr-Verlag.

Aulin, Arvid. Casual & Stochastic Elements in Business Cycles: An Essential Extension of Macroeconomics Leading to Improved Predictions of Data. LC 95-45634. (Lecture Notes in Economics & Mathematical Systems Ser.: No. 431). (Illus.). 116p. 1996. pap. 46.00 (*3-540-60593-2*) Spr-Verlag.

— Foundations of Economic Development. LC 92-23942. (Illus.). xvi, 370p. 1992. 148.95 (*0-387-55604-4*) Spr-Verlag.

— The Origins of Economic Growth: The Fundamental Interaction Between Material & Nonmaterial Values. LC 97-1231. 1997. write for info. (*3-540-62517-8*) Spr-Verlag.

Aulin, Lisen. Establishing Joint Ventures in the USSR. 160p. 1990. pap. 52.00 (*90-6544-515-3*) Kluwer Law Intl.

Aull. Rings of Continuous Function. (Lecture Notes in Pure & Applied Mathematics Ser.: Vol. 95). (Illus.). 344p. 1985. pap. text 155.00 (*0-8247-7144-3*) Dekker.

Aull, Charles E. & Lowen, R., eds. Handbook of the History of General Topology, Vol. 1. LC 97-7258. 408p. 1997. text 183.00 (*0-7923-4479-0*) Kluwer Academic.

Aull, Felice, ed. On-Line Database of Literature, Arts, & Medicine: An Annotated Bibliography. annot. ed. 445p. (Orig.). (C). 1996. pap. 35.00 (*0-9651593-1-0*) NY Univ Med Ctr.

Aulls, Mark. Active Composing & Thinking: Teacher's Manual (Act II) 7th ed. 192p. 1988. ring bd. 34.90 (*0-8403-4312-4*) Kendall-Hunt.

— Active Composing & Thinking: Teacher's Manual (Act III) 7th ed. 160p. 1988. ring bd. 34.90 (*0-8403-4315-9*) Kendall-Hunt.

Aulniers, Guy Des, see Des Aulniers, Guy.

Aulombard, R. L., et al. Semiconductors & Organic Materials for Optoelectronic Applications: Proceedings of Symposium C on UV, Blue & Green Light Emission of the 1996 E-MRS Spring Conference, Strasbourg, France, June 4-7, 1996. (European Materials Research Society Symposia Proceedings Ser.: 60). 460p. 1997. 273.00 (*0-444-20501-2*) Elsevier.

Aulombard, R. L., jt. ed. see Gil, B.

Aulson, Nan & Aulson, Pam. Fun 'n Festive Holiday Trimmers. (Illus.). 1983. pap. 3.00 (*0-9601896-6-1*) Patch As Patch.

Aulson, Pam. Crafty Ideas with Placemats. (Illus.). 24p. (J). (gr. 6 up). 1979. pap. 3.00 (*0-9601896-3-7*) Patch As Patch.

— No-Sew Patchwork. (Illus.). 1984. pap. 3.00 (*0-9601896-7-X*) Patch As Patch.

— Placemat Pets 'n Playmates. (Illus.). 24p. (J). (gr. 6 up). 1980. pap. 3.00 (*0-9601896-2-9*) Patch As Patch.

— Placement Plus & Plenty More. (Illus.). 64p. 1982. pap. 3.50 (*0-9601896-5-3*) Patch As Patch.

— Pretty As a Picture: Fabric Frames. (Illus.). 24p. 1981. pap. 3.00 (*0-9601896-4-5*) Patch As Patch.

Aulson, Pam, ed. Timeless Fashions. (Illus.). 72p. (Orig.). 1981. pap. 2.00 (*0-918178-25-8*) Simplicity.

Aulson, Pam, jt. auth. see Aulson, Nan.

Aulsoos, Pierre & Lias, Sharon G., eds. Structure Reactivity & Thermochemistry of Ions. 1987. text 279.50 (*90-277-2422-9*) Kluwer Academic.

Ault. Race & Ethnicity. 2000. pap. text 11.97 (*0-395-97304-X*) HM.

Ault, Addison. Techniques & Experiments for Organic Chemistry. 5th ed. (Illus.). 541p. (C). 1994. reprint ed. text 57.95 (*0-88133-803-6*) Waveland Pr.

— Techniques & Experiments for Organic Chemistry. 6th ed. LC 97-1814. 1998. text 65.00 (*0-935702-76-8*) Univ Sci Bks.

— Techniques & Experiments in Organic Chemistry. 5th ed. 1986. teacher ed. write for info. (*0-318-61511-8*, H87539) P-H.

Ault, Addison & Ault, Margaret R. A Handy & Systematic Catalog of NMR Spectra: Instruction Through Examples. LC 79-57227. 425p. 1980. text 32.00 (*0-935702-00-8*) Univ Sci Bks.

Ault, Addison & Dudek, Gerald. An Introduction to Proton NMR Spectroscopy. LC 75-26286. 141p. 1976. pap. text 15.95 (*0-8162-0331-8*) Holden-Day.

Ault, C. Thomas, tr. & intro. see Fabris, Jacopo & Boullet, Cityoen.

Ault, Donald. Narrative Unbound. (Illus.). 544p. Date not set. pap. 43.00 (*1-886449-75-9*, C9795, Pub. by Barrytown Ltd) Consort Bk Sales.

— Narrative Unbound: Re-Visioning Blake's "The Four Zoas" LC 85-3037. 520p. 1987. 43.00 (*0-88268-011-0*) Station Hill Pr.

Ault, Donald D. Visionary Physics: Blake's Response to Newton. LC 73-77128. 229 p. 1974. write for info. (*0-226-03225-6*) U Ch Pr.

— Visionary Physics: Blake's Response to Newton. LC 73-77128. (Midway Reprint Ser.). 245p. reprint ed. pap. 76.00 (*0-608-16504-2*, 202676200052) Bks Demand.

Ault, Frank M. Claiborne & Beyond. LC 98-22109. 256p. 1998. 24.95 (*1-877633-41-0*) Luthers.

Ault, Frank W., jt. auth. see Thole, Marsha L.

Ault, G. M., et al, eds. High Temperature Materials II: Proceedings of a Technical Conference, Cleveland, Ohio, April 26-27, 1961. LC 62-18703. (Metallurgical Society Conference Ser.: Vol. 18). 860p. reprint ed. pap. 200.00 (*0-608-11185-6*, 200150600079) Bks Demand.

Ault, G. M., jt. ed. see Hehemann, R. F.

Ault, Hugh J. Comparative Income Taxation, a Structural Analysis. LC 97-781. 1997. 110.00 (*90-411-0601-4*) Kluwer Law Intl.

Ault, Hugh J. & Radler, Albert J., trs. from GER. German Corporation Tax Reform Law 1977. 117p. 1976. pap. text 15.00 (*0-8377-0223-2*, Rothman) W S Hein.

— German Corporation Tax Reform Law 1977 (Korperschaftsteuerreformgesetz 1977) 117p. 1976. pap. 25.00 (*3-7875-5261-8*) W S Hein.

Ault, Hugh J., jt. auth. see McDaniel, Paul R.

Ault, Karuna K., ed. see Baba Hari Dass.

Ault, Ken A., jt. auth. see Hillman, Robert S.

Ault, Leonard, jt. ed. see Smith, W. Novis.

Ault, Leonard A. & Smith, W. Novis, eds. Federal R & D & Scientific Innovation. LC 79-13114. (ACS Symposium Ser.: Vol. 105). 184p. 1979. reprint ed. pap. 57.10 (*0-608-03090-2*, 206354200007) Bks Demand.

Ault, Margaret R., jt. auth. see Ault, Addison.

Ault, Michael. Oracle 8 Administration & Management. LC 97-36223. 880p. 1997. pap., pap. text 54.99 incl. cd-rom (*0-471-19234-1*) Wiley.

Ault, Michael R. Oracle DBA: Proven Techniques to Pass the Oracle Certified Professional Exam. LC 98-16072. (Exam Cram Ser.). 1998. pap. text 29.99 (*1-57610-262-9*) Coriolis Grp.

— Oracle DBA Exam Cram: Test 3 & Test 4. LC 98-29351. (Exam Cram Ser.). xxiii, 385 p. 1999. pap. 29.99 (*1-57610-331-5*) Coriolis Grp.

— Oracle 8 Black Book. LC 97-37926. (C). 1998. mass mkt. 49.99 (*1-57610-187-8*) Coriolis Grp.

***Ault, Michael R.** Oracle8 DBA: SQL & PL/SQL Exam Cram. (Exam Cram Ser.). 2000. pap. 29.99 (*1-57610-577-6*) Coriolis Grp.

— Oracle8i Administration & Management. LC 99-53657. 1024p. 1999. pap. 59.99 incl. cd-rom (*0-471-35453-8*) Wiley.

Ault, Michael R. UNIX System Administrator's Companion. LC 95-37073. 356p. 1995. pap. 39.95 (*0-471-11144-9*) Wiley.

Ault, Norman. Life in Ancient Britain. LC 70-39667. (Select Bibliographies Reprint Ser.). 1977. reprint ed. 18.95 (*0-8369-9927-4*) Ayer.

— Poets' Life of Christ. LC 72-2513. (Select Bibliographies Reprint Ser.). 1977. reprint ed. 24.95 (*0-8369-6847-6*) Ayer.

Ault, Norman, ed. Elizabethan Lyrics from the Original Texts. 3rd ed. reprint ed. 69.00 (*0-686-02251-3*) Somerset Pub.

Ault, Norman, ed. see Pope, Alexander.

Ault, Richard, et al. What Works: A Decade of Change at Champion International. LC 98-19730. (Business & Management Ser.). 224p. 1998. 32.95 (*0-7879-4181-6*) Jossey-Bass.

Ault, Richard, jt. auth. see Ekelund, Robert B., Jr.

Ault, Rosalie S. BASIC Programming for Kids. LC 83-12773. (Illus.). 192p. (J). (gr. 5 up). 1983. 10.95 (*0-685-06975-3*) HM.

Ault, Roy E. The Best of Roy's Rhetoric. LC 98-68376. 400 p. 1999. write for info. (*0-9640539-9-3*) Natures Pubng.

Ault, Stephen K., tr. see Bartra, Roger.

Ault, Stephen K., tr. see Hoetink, Harry.

Ault, Steve, ed. see Dahl, Bonnie.

Aultman, Dick & Bowden, Ken. The Methods of Golf's Masters. rev. ed. (Classics of Golf Ser.). (Illus.). 190p. 1985. 28.00 (*0-940889-11-0*) Classics Golf.

Aultman, Donald S. Contemporary Christian Education. 122p. 1981. pap. 3.95 (*0-87148-160-X*) Pathway Pr.

— Learning Christian Leadership. 1981. 4.95 (*0-87148-501-X*) Pathway Pr.

— The Ministry of Christian Teaching. 111p. 1981. pap. 3.95 (*0-87148-555-9*) Pathway Pr.

Aulton, Michael E. Pharmaceutics: The Science of Dosage Form Design. (Illus.). 774p. 1988. text 59.95 (*0-443-03643-8*) Church.

Auluo, Z. & Sugong, W., eds. Floristic Characteristics & Diversity of East Asian Plants. 550p. 1998. 99.00 (*3-540-64532-2*) Spr-Verlag.

Aumack, Sheryl. Second Generation. (Illus.). 70p. (Orig.). (C). 1990. pap. 5.00 (*0-9625180-2-6*) Sea-Maid Pr.

— Song & Dance: An Encyclopedia of Musicals. LC 89-92707. 462p. (C). 1990. spiral bd. 29.95 (*0-9625180-1-8*) Sea-Maid Pr.

Aumack, Sheryl, ed. "Coming Soon..." A Collection of Original Studio Film Pressbook Advertisements. (Illus.). 361p. (Orig.). (C). 1995. pap. 24.95 (*0-9625180-3-4*) Sea-Maid Pr.

Auman, Jordan, jt. tr. see Lodi, Enzo.

Auman, Kenneth & Herring, Basil, eds. The Prenuptial Agreement: Halakhic & Pastoral Considerations. LC 95-48948. 94p. 1996. pap. 20.00 (*1-56821-917-2*) Aronson.

***Auman, Maureen.** Step up to Writing: Basic, Practical & Helpful Instruction for Writing Assignments, Assessments & Everyday Writing Tasks. (Illus.). 476p. 1999. ring bd. 49.00 (*1-57035-208-9*) Sopris.

— Step up to Writing Handy Pages: Level 1, Accordian Paragraphs, 10 bks. 14p. 1999. pap. 15.00 (*1-57035-257-7*, 126HAND1) Sopris.

— Step up to Writing Handy Pages: Level 2, The 5 Elements of Expository Writing, 10 bks. 14p. 1999. 15.00 (*1-57035-217-8*, 126HAND2) Sopris.

— Step up to Writing 101 Reproducibles for Beginning Writers: Basic, Practical & Helpful Instructions for Writing Assignments & Everyday Writing Tasks. 105p. 1999. ring bd. 12.50 (*1-57035-240-2*) Sopris.

Auman, Orrin W. By the Help of the Infinite: A Spiritual Interpretation of Life. 2nd ed. 80p. 1996. reprint ed. pap. 7.95 (*0-944851-08-8*) Earth Star.

Aumann, Jordan. Christian Spirituality in the Catholic Tradition. 336p. 1985. pap. 16.95 (*0-89870-068-X*) Ignatius Pr.

— The Unquiet Heart: Reflections on Love & Sexuality. Baars, Conrad, ed. LC 91-27910. 1991. pap. 9.95 (*0-8189-0619-7*) Alba.

Aumann, Jordan, tr. from ITA. Compendium of Spirituality, 2 vols., Set. Incl. Doctrinal & Pastoral Teaching. LC 95-10473. 204p. (Orig.). 1995. pap. 12.95 (*0-8189-0724-X*); Schools of Spirituality. 216p. 1996. pap. 12.95 (*0-8189-0725-8*); 1996. Set pap. 22.50 (*0-8189-0723-1*) Alba.

Aumann, Jordan, tr. see Accattoli, Luigi.

Aumann, Jordan, tr. see Arintero, John G.

Aumann, Jordan, tr. see Borriello, Luigi.

Aumann, Jordan, tr. see Conconi, Giorgio.

Aumann, Jordan, tr. see Gjergji, Lush.

Aumann, Jordan, tr. see Louis of Granada.

Aumann, Jordan, tr. see Preziuso, Gennaro.

Aumann, Jordan, tr. see Zambonini, Franca.

Aumann, Jordan, tr. & adapted by see Louis of Granada.

Aumann, R. J. Advances in Game Theory. Dresher, M. et al, eds. LC 63-9985. (Annals of Mathematics Studies: Vol. 52). 691p. 1964. reprint ed. pap. 200.00 (*0-608-07366-3*, 201403500089) Bks Demand.

Aumann, R. J. & Hart, S. Handbook of Game Theory with Economic Applications, Vol. III. (Handbooks in Economics Ser.). 1998. write for info. (*0-444-89428-4*) Elsevier.

Aumann, R. J. & Hart, S. R., eds. Handbook of Game Theory: With Economic Applications, Vol. 1. LC 91-38429. (Handbooks in Economics Ser.: Vol. 11) 760p. 1992. 110.00 (*0-444-88098-4*) Elsevier.

— Handbook of Game Theory: With Economic Applications, Vol. II. (Handbooks in Economics Ser.: Vol. 11). 814p. 1994. 110.00 (*0-444-89427-6*, North Holland) Elsevier.

Aumann, R. J. & Shapley, L. S. Values of Non-Atomic Games. LC 72-4038. (Rand Corporation Research Study). 347p. 1974. reprint ed. pap. 107.60 (*0-608-02884-3*, 206394800007) Bks Demand.

Aumann, Robert J. Robert J. Aumann: Collected Papers, Vol. 1. LC 96-6332. (Illus.). 720p. 1999. 65.00 (*0-262-01154-9*) MIT Pr.

— Robert J. Aumann Vol. 2: Collected Papers. LC 96-6332. (Illus.). 672p. 1999. 65.00 (*0-262-01155-7*) MIT Pr.

Aumann, Robert J. & Maschler, Michael B. Repeated Games with Incomplete Information. 368p. 1995. 45.00 (*0-262-01147-6*) MIT Pr.

Aumann, W. Earl, jt. auth. see Youngberg, George E., Sr.

Aumayr, Friedrich & Winter, Hannspeter, eds. Photonic, Electronic & Atomic Collisions: Invited Papers of the 20th International Conference on the Physics of Electronic & Atomic Collisions, Vienna, Austria, 23-29 July 1997. LC 98-215271. 800p. 1998. 132.00 (*981-02-3425-2*) World Scientific Pub.

Aumen, Nicholas G. & Wetzel, Robert G., eds. Ecological Studies on the Littoral & Pelagic Systems of Lake Okeechobee, Florida (U. S. A.) (Advances in Limnology Ser.: Vol. 45). (GER., Illus.). vi, 356p. 1995. pap. text 82.00 (*0-614-97987-0*, Pub. by E Schweizerbartsche) Balogh.

Aumente, Jerome. New Electronic Pathways: Videotex, Teletex, & Online Databases. LC 87-3354. (Sage Commtext Ser.: No. 17). 159p. 1987. reprint ed. pap. 49.30 (*0-608-01185-1*, 205948300001) Bks Demand.

***Aumente, Jerome, et al.** Eastern European Journalism: Before, During & after Communism. LC 99-27158. (Communication Ser.). 224p. (C). 1999. 49.50 (*1-57273-177-X*); pap. 21.95 (*1-57273-178-8*) Hampton Pr NJ.

Aumiaux, Michel. Microprocessor Systems. LC 81-1625. (Wiley Series in Computing). (Illus.). 228p. reprint ed. pap. 70.70 (*0-8357-4565-1*, 203746700008) Bks Demand.

— The Use of Microprocessors. LC 79-42904. (Wiley Series in Computing). 208p. reprint ed. pap. 64.50 (*0-608-15824-0*, 203129500074) Bks Demand.

Aumiller, Dr. Jochen. You Don't Have to Be Next. 1980. pap. 5.95 (*0-8065-0683-0*, Citadel Pr) Carol Pub Group.

Aumiller, Gary S. Keeping It Simple: Sorting Out What Really Matters in Your Life. 216p. (Orig.). 1995. reprint ed. pap. 9.95 (*0-9667454-0-X*) Probity Press.

***Aumiller, Gary S. & Goldfarb, Daniel A.** Red Flags! How to Know When You're Dating a Loser. LC 99-13699. 288p. 1999. pap. 12.95 (*0-452-28117-2*, Plume) Dutton Plume.

Aumonier, Stacy. Overheard. LC 72-3289. (Short Story Index Reprint Ser.). 1977. reprint ed. 20.95 (*0-8369-4142-X*) Ayer.

Aumonier, Stacy & Belcher, George F. Odd Fish. LC 71-116929. (Short Story Index Reprint Ser.). 1977. 16.95 (*0-8369-3431-8*) Ayer.

Aumont, Jacques. The Image. Pajackowska, Claire, tr. from FRE. LC 96-146245. (Illus.). 256p. 1997. 60.00 (*0-85170-409-3*, Pub. by British Film Inst); pap. 24.95 (*0-85170-410-7*, Pub. by British Film Inst) Ind U Pr.

— Montage Eisenstein. Hildreth, Lee et al, trs. from FRE. LC 85-45074. (Theories of Representation & Difference Ser.). (Illus.). 256p. (C). 1987. 41.95 (*0-253-33874-3*) Ind U Pr.

— Montage Eisenstein. Hildreth, Lee et al, trs. LC 85-45074. (Theories of Representation & Difference Ser.). (Illus.). 253p. Date not set. reprint ed. pap. 78.50 (*0-608-20579-6*, 205449400002) Bks Demand.

Aumont, Jacques, et al. Aesthetics of Film. Neupert, Richard, tr. LC 91-33706. (Film Studies). (Illus.). 279p. (Orig.). 1992. text 40.00 (*0-292-70428-3*) U of Tex Pr.

Aumra. As of a Trumpet. 85p. 1968. 5.95 (*0-932869-03-3*) Emissaries.

Aumueller, G. Prostate Gland & Seminal Vesicle. (Handbuch der Mikroskopischen Anatomie Des Menschen Ser.: Vol. 7, Pt. 6). (Illus.). 1979. 191.00 (*0-387-09191-2*) Spr-Verlag.

Aumuller, G., et al, eds. New Aspects in the Regulation of Prostatic Function. (Clinical & Experimental Urology Ser.). (Illus.). 186p. 1989. text 61.00 (*3-88603-318-X*, Pub. by W Zuckschwerdt) Scholium Intl.

Aun, Frederico, jt. auth. see Cohen, Ricardo V.

Aun, Wu M., jt. auth. see Hickling, R. H.

Aune. Revelation 6-16. (Word Biblical Commentary Ser.: Vol. 52B). 29.99 (*0-8499-0786-1*) Word Pub.

Aune, Al. Arcade Toys. (Illus.). 314p. (Orig.). 1993. pap. 29.95 (*0-614-09354-6*) R F Manella.

Aune, B. A. Knowledge, Mind & Nature. xvi, 296p. (C). 1977. reprint ed. pap. text 13.00 (*0-917930-07-X*); reprint ed. lib. bdg. 27.00 (*0-917930-27-4*) Ridgeview.

Aune, Bruce. Metaphysics: The Elements. LC 85-2540. xiv, 235p. 1985. pap. 18.95 (*0-8166-1414-8*) U of Minn Pr.

Aune, Bruce A. Rationalism, Empiricism & Pragmaticism: An Introduction. LC 94-48523. (C). 1970. pap. text 18.74 (*0-07-553543-2*) McGraw.

— Reason & Action. (Studies in Philosophy & Religion: No. 9). 217p. 1977. pap. text 51.50 (*90-277-0851-7*, D Reidel); lib. bdg. 88.00 (*90-277-0805-3*, D Reidel) Kluwer Academic.

Aune, Carolyn, ed. see Cory, Pepper.

Aune, Carolyn, ed. see Moran, Freddy.

Aune, Carolyn, ed. see Pam Bono Designs Staff.

Aune, Carolyn, ed. see Wolfrom, Joen.

Aune, David. Revelation 1-12. (Biblical Commentary Ser.: Vol. 52). 600p. 29.99 (*0-8499-0251-7*) Word Pub.

— Revelation 17-22. (Biblical Commentary Ser.: Vol. 52C). 592p. 1998. 29.99 (*0-8499-1545-7*) Word Pub.

Aune, David E. The New Testament in Its Literary Environment. LC 86-18949. (Library of Early Christianity: Vol. 8). 262p. 1985. pap. 24.95 (*0-664-25018-1*) Westminster John Knox.

— Prophecy in Early Christianity. 522p. 1991. pap. 25.00 (*0-8028-0635-X*) Eerdmans.

Aune, Elizabeth & Ness, Jean. Tools for Transition: Complete Program. 1991. 129.95 (*0-88671-413-3*, 8250) Am Guidance.

— Tools for Transition Manual. (Tools for Transition Ser.). (Orig.). 1991. pap. 27.95 (*0-88671-412-5*, 8251) Am Guidance.

— Tools for Transition Script Book. (Tools for Transition Ser.). (Orig.). 1991. pap. 9.95 (*0-88671-415-X*, 8254) Am Guidance.

— Tools for Transition Student Book. (Tools for Transition Ser.). (Orig.). 1991. pap. 8.95 (*0-88671-414-1*, 8252) Am Guidance.

***Aune, James Arnt.** Selling the Free Marker: The Rhetorici of Economic Correctness. (Revisioning Rhetoric Ser.). 210p. 2000. lib. bdg. 23.95 (*1-57230-598-3*) Guilford Pubns.

Aune, Michael B. Rhetoric & Ritual in the Theology of Philip Melanchthon: To Move the Heart. 136p. 1995. 54.95 (*1-883255-35-X*); pap. 34.95 (*1-883255-34-1*) Intl Scholars.

Aune, Michael B. & DeMarinis, Valerie, eds. Religious & Social Ritual: Interdisciplinary Explorations. LC 95-17022. 323p. (C). 1996. text 59.50 (*0-7914-2825-7*); pap. text 19.95 (*0-7914-2826-5*) State U NY Pr.

Aune, Philip S., ed. Proceedings of the Symposium on Giant Sequoias: Their Place in the Ecosystem & Society. (Illus.). 170p. (C). 1997. reprint ed. pap. text 40.00 (*0-7881-4165-1*) DIANE Pub.

***Auner, Joseph.** Postmodern Music/Postmodern Thought. (Studies in Contemporary Music & Culture Ser.). 2000. 75.00 (*0-8153-3819-8*); pap. 24.95 (*0-8153-3820-1*) Garland.

Auner, Joseph, jt. ed. see Bruhn, Siglind.

***Auner, Morbert & Weis, Johann, eds.** Organosilicon Chemistry Four: From Molecules to Materials. 4th ed. 852p. 2000. 155.00 (*3-527-29854-1*) Wiley.

Auner, Norbert & Weis, Johann, eds. Organosilicon Chemistry III: From Molecules to Materials. 742p. 1998. 195.00 (*3-527-29450-3*, Wiley-VCH) Wiley.

Aung, Chin. O Burma! rev. ed. Aung, Win, ed. LC 00-91503. 200p. 2000. pap. 20.00 (*0-9652612-6-3*) Yoma Pubng.

Aung Chin Win Aung. Burma: From Monarchy to Dictatorship. rev. ed. Lee, Don Y., ed. LC 94-71659. 180p. 1999. pap. 20.00 (*0-939758-28-8*) Yoma Pubng.

— Burma & the Last Days of General Ne Win. LC 95-90603. 200p. (Orig.). 1996. pap. 25.00 (*0-9652612-0-4*) Yoma Pubng.

— The Burma Cry. LC 96-90428. 114p. (Orig.). 1997. pap. 15.00 (*0-9652612-9-8*) Yoma Pubng.

A

— Southeast Asia/Escape from Socialist Burma & Capitalist Thailand. 220p. (Orig.). 1997. pap. 30.00 (0-9652612-7-1) Yoma Pubng.

Aung, S. Z. & Davids, C. A. F. Rhys, trs. from PLI. Compendium of Philosophy. (C). 1910. 39.00 (0-86013-000-2, Pub. by Pali Text) Elsevier.

Aung, S. Z. & Davids, Mrs. C. A., trs. from PLI. Points of Controversy. (C). 1915. 37.00 (0-86013-002-9, Pub. by Pali Text) Elsevier.

Aung San Suu Kyi. Burma & India: Some Aspects of Intellectual Life under Colonialism. LC 91-904835. 84p. 1990. write for info. (81-7023-134-5) Allied Pubs of Amer.

Aung San Suu Kyi. The Political Legacy of Aung San. LC 73-174143. (Cornell University, Southeast Asia Program, Data Paper Ser.: No. 86). 121p. reprint ed. pap. 37.60 (0-8357-6270-X, 201048300068) Bks Demand.

Aung-Thwin, Margaret, tr. see Lay, Ma M.

Aung-Thwin, Michael. Irrigation in the Heartland of Burma: Foundations of the Pre-Colonial Burmese State. (Occasional Papers: No. 15). 76p. 1990. pap. 9.95 (1-877979-15-5) SE Asia.

Aung-Thwin, Michael A. Myth & History in the Historiography of Early Burma: Paradigms, Primary Sources, & Prejudices. LC 97-49191. (Monographs in International Studies, Southeast Asia Ser.: Vol. 102). 220p. (C). 1998. pap. text 25.00 (0-89680-201-9) Ohio U Pr.

Aung, Win, ed. Cooling Techniques for Computers. 600p. 1991. 160.00 (0-89116-756-0) Hemisp Pub.

Aung, Win, ed. see Aung, Chin.

Aung, Win, jt. ed. see Carmi, Shlomo.

Aunger, Edmund A. In Search of Political Stability: A Comparative Study of New Brunswick & Northern Ireland. LC 81-174075. (Illus.). 238p. reprint ed. pap. 73.80 (0-7837-1153-0, 204168200022) Bks Demand.

Aungier, George J., ed. The French Chronicle of London. LC 77-161712. (Camden Society First Ser.: No. 28). (ENG & FRE.). 1977. reprint ed. 42.50 (0-404-50128-1) AMS Pr.

***Aungier, Ronald H.** Centrifugal Compressors: A Strategy for Aerodynamic Design & Analysis LC 99-39156. 1999. write for info. (0-7918-0093-8) ASME Pr.

Aungles, Ann. The Prison & the Home: A Study of the Relationship Between Domesticity & Penality. (Institute of Criminology Monographs: No. 5). vii, 302p. 1994. pap. 33.95 (0-86758-903-5) Gaunt.

Aungles, Stan, ed. Information Technology in Australia: The Transformation of Organizational Structure & Culture. 1992. pap. 31.95 (0-86840-037-8, Pub. by New South Wales Univ Pr) Intl Spec Bk.

Aungles, Stan & Parker, Stan. Work, Organizations & Change. 2nd ed. 240p. 1993. pap. text 22.95 (1-86373-338-8, Pub. by Allen & Unwin Pty) Paul & Co Pubs.

Aunon, Jorge I. Introduction to Probability & Random Variables. LC 96-44042. 608p. (C). 1997. 85.00 (0-07-001563-5) McGraw.

Aunt Darla. There's a Monster under the Captain's Bed!!! Erik's Monster. (Illus.). 32p. Date not set. 16.00 (0-9658926-1-1) Poet Tree.

Aunt Eeebs. The Baby Buddy. (Dino-Buddies Ser.). (Illus.). 160p. (Orig.). (J). (ps-2). 1993. pap. 3.95 (1-878908-04-9) Rivercrest Indus.

— The Dinosaur Debut. rev. ed. (Dino-Buddies Ser.). (Illus.). 160p. (J). (ps-2). 1996. reprint ed. pap. 3.95 (1-878908-00-6) Rivercrest Indus.

— The Happy Campers. (Dino-Buddies Ser.). (Illus.). 160p. (Orig.). (J). (ps-2). 1991. pap. 3.95 (1-878908-02-2) Rivercrest Indus.

— Hit the Beach. LC 94-67657. (Dino-Buddies Ser.). (Illus.). 160p. (Orig.). (J). (ps-2). 1994. pap. 3.95 (1-878908-08-1) Rivercrest Indus.

— Let's Go to Grammy's. LC 94-67656. (Dino-Buddies Ser.). (Illus.). 160p. (Orig.). (J). (ps-2). 1994. pap. 3.95 (1-878908-06-5) Rivercrest Indus.

Aunt Mary Jane, jt. auth. see High Times Editors.

Aunt Naomi, pseud & Landa, Gertrude. Jewish Fairy Tales & Legends. 23.95 (0-89190-314-3) Amereon Ltd.

Aunt Peggy. Caterpillar. (Illus.). 24p. (J). 1995. 12.95 (0-9636185-3-9); pap. 6.95 (0-9636185-0-4) Aunt Peggys Pub.

— Caterpillar. 2nd ed. (Illus.). 24p. (J). (ps). 1994. 13.95 (0-9636185-2-0) Aunt Peggys Pub.

— Caterpillar: Fun Pack. (Illus.). 24p. (J). (ps). 1994. 8.95 (0-9636185-4-7) Aunt Peggys Pub.

— How Did You Come to School Today. LC 93-90173. (Illus.). 42p. (J). 1993. pap. 6.95 (0-9636185-1-2) Aunt Peggys Pub.

Aupetit, B. A Primer on Spectral Theory. Ewing, J. H. et al, eds. (Universitext Ser.). (Illus.). 208p. 1990. 48.95 (0-387-97390-7) Spr-Verlag.

Aupetit, Bernard. Complex Approximation, Proceedings, Quebec, Canada. (Progress in Mathematics Ser.: No. 4). 128p. 1980. 34.50 (0-8176-3004-X) Birkhauser.

Aupetitallot, Yves. Wide White Space, 1966-1976. (Illus.). 400p. 85.00 (3-928762-31-1) Dist Art Pubs.

Auping, Michael. Agnes Martin, Richard Tuttle. LC 97-76172. (Illus.). 75p. 1998. 29.00 (0-929865-17-0) Mod Art Mus Ft Worth.

— Clyfford Still. pap. 35.00 (0-914782-86-X) Buffalo Fine-Albrght-Knox.

— Georg Baselitz: Portraits of Elke. LC 97-73804. (Illus.). 126p. 1997. 35.00 (0-929865-16-2) Mod Art Mus Ft Worth.

— Jenny Holzer. (Women Artists Ser.). (Illus.). 128p. (Orig.). 1992. pap. 13.95 (0-87663-615-6, Pub. by Universe) St Martin.

— Jess: Pasteups, 1951 to 1983. LC 83-82281. (Illus.). 157p. 1983. 24.95 (0-916758-14-1) Ringling Mus Art.

— John Chamberlain: Reliefs, 1960-1983. LC 82-83513. (Illus.). 85p. (Orig.). 1983. pap. 15.95 (0-916758-10-9) Ringling Mus Art.

— Judy Pfaff: Installation, Collages & Drawings. LC 81-82511. (Illus.). 16p. (Orig.). 1981. pap. 4.95 (0-916758-06-0) Ringling Mus Art.

— Marcel Duchamp: Works from the John & Mable Ringling Museum of Art Collection. LC 83-81504. (Illus.). 50p. (Orig.). 1983. pap. 4.95 (0-916758-13-3) Ringling Mus Art.

— Philip Pearlstein: Paintings & Watercolors. LC 81-51324. (Illus.). 16p. 1981. pap. 4.95 (0-916758-05-2) Ringling Mus Art.

— Stephen Shore Photographs. LC 81-83669. (Illus.). 20p. 1981. pap. 4.95 (0-916758-07-9) Ringling Mus Art.

— Tatsuo Miyajima: Big Time. LC 96-77588. (Illus.). 70p. 1996. pap. 24.95 (0-929865-15-4) Mod Art Mus Ft Worth.

Auping, Michael, et al. Arshile Gorky: The Breakthrough Years. LC 94-22795. (Illus.). 1995. 29.95 (0-914782-92-4) Buffalo Fine-Albrght-Knox.

— Howard Hodgkin: Paintings. LC 95-22591. (Illus.). 216p. 1995. 49.50 (0-8109-3433-7, Pub. by Abrams) Time Warner.

— Howard Hodgkin: Paintings. (Illus.). 220p. 1995. pap. write for info. (0-929865-12-X) Mod Art Mus Ft Worth.

— Jess, a Grand Collage, 1951-1993. LC 92-41674. (Illus.). 264p. 1993. 75.00 (0-914782-89-4); pap. 45.00 (0-914782-85-1) Buffalo Fine-Albrght-Knox.

Auping, Michael, jt. auth. see Fulton, Hamish.

Auping, Michael, jt. auth. see Hickey, David.

Auping, Michael G., jt. auth. see Anderson, Maxwell L.

Aura, Alejandro. L' Autre Cote - The Other Side. (FRE., Illus.). 32p. (J). (gr. k up). 1995. lib. bdg. 16.95 (1-55037-404-4, Pub. by Annick) Firefly Bks Ltd.

— The Other Side. (Illus.). 32p. (YA). (gr. k up). 1995. lib. bdg. 16.95 (1-55037-405-2, Pub. by Annick) Firefly Bks Ltd.

— El Otro Lado. (Illus.). 44p. 1995. 12.99 (968-16-3672-4) Fondo.

Aurand, A. Monroe, Jr., ed. see Church, Jeremiah.

***Aurand, Henry.** Geology Terms in English & Spanish: Terminologia Geologica en Ingles y Espanol. LC 99-19537. (Sunbelt Pocket Guide Ser.). 128p. (Orig.). 1999. pap. 7.95 (0-932653-29-4) Sunbelt Pubns.

Aurand, Layne, ed. see Jacobs, Sheldon.

Aurand, Martin. The Progressive Architecture of Frederick G. Scheibler, Jr. LC 93-40788. (Illus.). 184p. 1994. text 37.50 (0-8229-3781-6) U of Pittsburgh Pr.

Aurandt. Professional Medical Secretary. 1984. teacher ed. 30.95 (0-87350-336-8) Milady Pub.

— Professional Medical Secretary. 1989. text 29.95 (0-87350-333-3) Milady Pub.

— Professional Medical Secretary Student Transcripts. (General Business & Business Education Ser.). 1986. pap. 28.00 (0-87350-608-1, VNR) Wiley.

***Aurandt, Althea.** Secrets Your Church Never Told You: An Expose of the Injustice of Christian Doctrine. (Illus.). x, 172p. 1999. pap. 19.95 (0-9673774-0-4) Paraclsus Pr.

Aurandt, Paul. More of Paul Harvey's the Rest of the Story. 208p. 1984. mass mkt. 6.50 (0-553-26074-X) Bantam.

— Paul Harvey's the Rest of the Story. 192p. 1984. mass mkt. 6.50 (0-553-25962-8) Bantam.

Aurasian, Peter W. Classroom Assessment. 3rd ed. LC 96-33530. 416p. (C). 1996. pap. 60.00 (0-07-000774-8) McGraw.

***Auray, Dea P.** Easy Art Activities That Spark Super Writing: Mini-Lessons, Quick How-To's & Perfect Poems. (Illus.). (J). 2000. pap. 10.95 (0-439-16518-0) Scholastic Inc.

Aurbach, Gerald D. & McCormick, Donald B., eds. Vitamins & Hormones, Vol. 45. 375p. 1989. text 136.00 (0-12-709845-3) Acad Pr.

Aurbach, Gerald D. & McCormick, Donald M., eds. Vitamins & Hormones: Advances in Research & Applications, Vol. 43. 316p. 1986. text 136.00 (0-12-709843-7) Acad Pr.

***Aureli, Filippo & De Waal, Frans B. M., eds.** Natural Conflict Resolution. LC 99-43046. (Illus.). 424p. 2000. 65.00 (0-520-21671-7, Pub. by U CA Pr) Cal Prin Full Svc.

***Aureli, Filippo & Waal, F. B. M.** Natural Conflict Resolution. LC 99-43046. (Illus.). 424p. 2000. pap. 24.95 (0-520-22346-2, Pub. by U CA Pr) Cal Prin Full Svc.

Aurelian, Laure, ed. Herpesviruses, the Immune System & AIDS. (Developments in Medical Virology Ser.). (C). 1990. text 199.00 (0-7923-0803-4) Kluwer Academic.

Aurelianensis, Aegidius. Aegidius Aurelianensis Quaestones Super de Generatione et Corruptione. Kuksewicz, Zdzislaw, ed. LC 92-36084. (Bochumer Studien zur Philosophie Ser.: No. 18). xxviii, 237p. 1993. 76.00 (90-6032-323-8, Pub. by B R Gruner) Humanities.

Aurelio, John. Earth Stories: Signs of God's Love & Mystery. LC 96-48455. 132p. 1997. 15.95 (0-8264-0949-0) Continuum.

— Returnings: Life-after-Death Experiences: A Christian View. 112p. (C). 1997. pap. 10.95 (0-8264-0877-X) Continuum.

Aurelio, John R. Myth Man: A Storyteller's Jesus. 240p. 1993. reprint ed. pap. 11.95 (0-8245-1210-3) Crossroad NY.

Aurelius, Augustinus. Select Letters. Baxter, James H., tr. LC 75-41012. reprint ed. 37.50 (0-404-14502-7) AMS Pr.

Aurelius, Marcus. The Commentaries of the Emperor Marcus Antoninus: Containing His Maxims of Science & Rules of Life, Wrote for His Own Use & Address'd to Himself. LC 77-158297. (Augustan Translators Ser.). reprint ed. 49.50 (0-404-54103-8) AMS Pr.

— The Meditations. Long, George, tr. from LAT. LC 97-18832. (Dover Thrift Editions Ser.). (Illus.). 128p. 1997. pap. 1.50 (0-486-29823-X) Dover.

— The Meditations. Goold, G. P., ed. (Loeb Classical Library: No. 58). 448p. 1930. 19.95 (0-674-99064-1) HUP.

— The Meditations. Staniforth, Maxwell, tr. & intro. by. (Classics Ser.). 192p. (YA). (gr. 9 up). 1964. pap. 13.99 (0-14-044140-9, Penguin Classics) Viking Penguin.

— Meditations. Long, George, tr. LC 91-61906. (Great Books in Philosophy). 122p. 1991. pap. 5.95 (0-87975-702-7) Prometheus Bks.

— The Meditations. Grube, G. M. A., ed. & tr. by. from GRE. LC 83-22722. (HPC Classics Ser.). 170p. (C). 1984. reprint ed. pap. text 6.95 (0-915145-79-0); reprint ed. lib. bdg. 24.95 (0-915145-78-2) Hackett Pub.

— The Meditations of Marcus Aurelius. 1992. 17.00 (0-679-41271-9) Everymns Lib.

— The Meditations of Marcus Aurelius Antoninus & a Selection from the Letters of Marcus & Fronto. Rutherford, R. B. & Farquharson, A. S., trs. 224p. 1990. 55.00 (0-19-814761-9) OUP.

Aurell, Mattias & Ulfendahl, Hans, eds. Rerin-Angiotensur. (Wenner Gren International Ser.: No. 74). (Illus.). 250p. 1998. text 127.50 (1-85578-128-X, Pub. by Portland Pr Ltd) Ashgate Pub Co.

Aurell, Tage. Rose of Jericho & Other Stories. Allwood, Martin S. et al, trs. from SWE. LC 68-14036. (Nordic Translation Ser.). Orig. Title: Smarre besattelser & Nya bersattelser. 151p. 1968. reprint ed. pap. 46.90 (0-608-01928-3, 206258300003) Bks Demand.

Aurenche, Olivier. Dictionnaire Illustre Multilingue de l'Architecture du Proche-Orient Ancien. (FRE.). 391p. 1977. 150.00 (0-8288-9536-8) Fr & Eur.

— Dictionnaire Illustre Multilinque de l'Architecture du Proche-Orient Ancien: Multilingual Illustrated Dictionary of the Architecture of the Ancient Near-East. (FRE.). 392p. 1978. 125.00 (0-8288-5199-9, M6017) Fr & Eur.

Aurenz, Heiko. Controlling Verteilter Informationssysteme: Client - Server-Architekturen. Krcmar, Helmut, ed. (Beitrage zur Wirtschaftsinformatik Ser.: Bd. 4). (GER., Illus.). 433p. 1997. 63.95 (3-631-31021-8) P Lang Pubng.

Aureon, pseud. Anybody's Instant Power Formula. LC 84-70874. 75p. (Orig.). 1984. pap. 6.95 (0-9613386-0-1) Aureon Pub.

Auricchio, S., et al, eds. Musocal Immunity & the Gut Epithelium: Interactions in Health & Disease. (Dynamic Nutrition Research Ser.: Vol. 4). (Illus.). viii, 188p. 1995. 186.25 (3-8055-6063-X) S Karger.

Auricchio, S. & Troncone, R., eds. Common Food Intolerances Two: Milk in Human Nutrition & Adult-Type Hypolactasia. (Dynamic Nutrition Research Ser.: Vol. 3). (Illus.). x, 212p. 1993. 170.50 (3-8055-5741-8) S Karger.

Auricchio, S. & Visakorpi, J., eds. Common Food Intolerances One: Epidemiology of Coeliac Disease. (Dynamic Nutrition Research Ser.: Vol. 2). (Illus.). x, 192p. 1993. 161.75 (3-8055-5616-0) S Karger.

Aurich, Charles. How Do I Decide? The Young Adult's Guide to Career Planning. LC 94-92034. (Illus.). 165p. (Orig.). (YA). (gr. 7-12). 1994. pap. write for info. (0-9640083-8-6) Natl Career.

Aurich, Jurgen. Computer Englisch fur Einsteiger. 2nd ed. (ENG & GER.). 108p. 1993. 29.95 (0-7859-6878-4, 3349010334) Fr & Eur.

Aurich, Lynn W. Overcoming Sexual Performance Problems: A Self-Help Guide for Men. (Illus.). 173p. 1997. pap. 39.95 incl. audio (0-9659482-0-X) New Hope Publns.

Auriemma, Frank V., et al. Graying Teachers: A Report on State Pension Systems & School District Early Retirement Incentives. LC 92-71618. (C). 1992. pap. 12.50 (0-86552-118-2) U of Oreg ERIC.

Auriemma, Michael J. & Coley, Robert S. The Bankcard Business. Dehmlow, Veida, ed. (Illus.). 350p. (C). 1992. pap. text 46.00 (0-89982-335-1) Am Bankers.

Aurifeille, Jacques-Marie & Deissenberg, Christoph. Bio-Mimetic Approaches in Management Science. LC 98-9705. (Advances in Computational Management Science Ser.). 1998. 110.00 (0-7923-4993-8) Kluwer Academic.

Auriga. Enciclopedia Juvenil Auriga: Inventos Que Conmovieron el Mundo, Descubrimientos e Inventos, Armas Que Conmovieron el Mundo, Historia Ilustrada de los Barcos, Artistas Que Conmovieron el Mundo. (SPA.). 360p. (J). 1977. 42.00 (84-201-0202-4) Fr & Eur.

***Aurisch, Helga, et al.** Romantics, Realists, Revolutionaries: Masterpieces of 19th-Century German Painting from the Museum of Fine Arts, Leipzig. (Illus.). 224p. 2000. 65.00 (3-7913-2380-6) Prestel Pub NY.

Aurner, C. Ray, ed. Topical History of Cedar County Vol. II: Biographies. (Illus.). 919p. 1997. reprint ed. lib. bdg. 92.00 (0-8328-6674-1) Higginson Bk Co.

Aurnet, C. Ray, ed. Topical History of Cedar County. (Illus.). 1435p. 1998. lib. bdg. 139.00 (0-8328-9598-9) Higginson Bk Co.

Aurnhammer, Achim, ed. Torquato Tasso in Deutschland: Seine Wirkung in Literatur, Kunst und Musik Seit der Mitte des 18.Jahrhunderts. (Quellen und Forschungen zur Literatur und Kulturgeschichte: Bd. 3(237)). (GER.). xii, 742p. (C). 1995. lib. bdg. 223.10 (3-11-014546-4) De Gruyter.

Aurobindo. Glossary of Terms in Sri Aurobindo's Writings. 1979. 10.95 (0-89744-980-0, Pub. by Sri Aurob Ashram Trust); pap. 8.95 (0-89744-981-9, Pub. by Sri Aurob Ashram Trust) Acrpls Bks CO.

Aurobindo, tr. from FRE. Prayers & Meditations. rev. ed. 380p. (Orig.). (C). 1979. pap. 13.00 (0-89744-998-3, Pub. by Sri Aurob Ashram Trust); text 16.00 (0-89744-219-9, Pub. by Sri Aurob Ashram Trust) Acrpls Bks CO.

Aurobindo, Sri. Baji Prabhou. 4th ed. 16p. 1990. pap. 0.75 (81-7058-213-X, Pub. by SAA) E-W Cultural Ctr.

Aurobindo, Sri. Bande Mataram: Early Political Writings. 1979. 18.00 (0-686-85667-8); pap. 10.00 (0-89744-900-2) Auromere.

— Bankim - Tilak - Dayananda. 49p. 0.50 (0-317-17425-8) Auromere.

Aurobindo, Sri. Bankim - Tilak - Dayananda. 5th ed. 67p. 1995. pap. 0.50 (81-7058-242-3, Pub. by SAA) E-W Cultural Ctr.

Aurobindo, Sri. Bases of Yoga. LC 93-79795. 108p. 1993. pap. 6.95 (0-941524-77-9) Lotus Pr.

— Bases of Yoga. 9th ed. 108p. 1998. pap. 2.00 (81-7058-021-8, Pub. by SAA) E-W Cultural Ctr.

— Bhagavad Gita & Its Message: With Text, Translation & Sri Aurobindo's Commentary. Roy, Anilbaran, ed. LC 94-75589. 325p. (Orig.). 1994. pap. 15.95 (0-941524-78-7) Lotus Pr.

— Bhagavad Gita in Light of Sri Aurobindo. Maheshwar, ed. 1979. 12.50 (0-89744-902-9); pap. 8.25 (0-89744-903-7) Auromere.

***Aurobindo, Sri.** The Century of Life: The Nitishataka of Bhartrihari Freely Rendered into English Verse. 4th ed. 60p. 1999. pap. 1.00 (81-7058-243-1, Pub. by SAA) E-W Cultural Ctr.

Aurobindo, Sri. Collected Plays & Short Stories, 2 vols. 1090p. 1997. 48.00 (81-7058-089-7, Pub. by SAA) E-W Cultural Ctr.

— Collected Poems. 631p. 1986. pap. 16.95 (81-7058-016-1, Pub. by SAA) E-W Cultural Ctr.

Aurobindo, Sri. Collected Poems. 631p. 1994. 17.50 (81-7058-333-0, Pub. by SAA) E-W Cultural Ctr.

— Conversations of the Dead. 22p. 1993. pap. 1.25 (81-7058-158-3, Pub. by SAA) E-W Cultural Ctr.

Aurobindo, Sri. Dictionary of Sri Aurobindo's Yoga. Pandit, M. P., ed. LC 92-74994. 320p. 1992. pap. 11.95 (0-941524-74-4) Lotus Pr.

— The Durga Stotra. 31p. (Orig.). (C). 1982. pap. 2.50 (0-89744-235-0) Auromere.

— Essays Divine & Human. 580p. 1999. 21.95 (81-7058-365-9, Pub. by SAA); pap. 15.95 (81-7058-364-0, Pub. by SAA) E-W Cultural Ctr.

— Essays on the Gita. (Life Companion Library). 1983. 14.95 (0-89744-907-X); pap. 14.95 (0-89744-908-8); lib. bdg. 20.00 (0-89744-906-1) Auromere.

— Essays on the Gita. LC 95-78152. 588p. 1997. pap. 19.95 (0-914955-18-7) Lotus Pr.

— Essays on the Gita. 588p. 1987. 16.95 (81-7058-000-5, Pub. by SAA); pap. 14.95 (0-685-30670-4, Pub. by SAA) Acrpls Bks CO.

— Essays on the Gita. 9th ed. 595p. 1997. 18.95 (81-7058-306-3, Pub. by SAA) Lotus Pr.

— The Essential Writings of Sri Aurobindo. Heehs, Peter, ed. LC 98-902992. 418p. 1998. text 35.00 (0-19-564284-8) OUP.

Aurobindo, Sri. The Eternal Wisdom: Central Sayings of Great Sages of all Times. 595p. 1995. pap. 14.95 (81-7058-319-5, Pub. by SAA) E-W Cultural Ctr.

— Ever to the New & the Unknown: 50th Anniversary of the Sri Aurobindo International Centre of Education (1943-1993) 330p. 1993. pap. 19.95 (81-7058-354-3, Pub. by SAA) E-W Cultural Ctr.

Aurobindo, Sri. Evolution. 28p. 1.25 (0-317-17430-4) Auromere.

Aurobindo, Sri. Evolution. 8th ed. 32p. 1994. pap. 1.25 (81-7058-164-8, Pub. by SAA) E-W Cultural Ctr.

— Food. 4th ed. Vijay, ed. 27p. 1997. pap. 1.00 (81-7060-088-X, Pub. by SAA) E-W Cultural Ctr.

Aurobindo, Sri. Foundations of Indian Culture. 1979. reprint ed. pap. 11.00 (0-89744-909-6) Auromere.

Aurobindo, Sri. The Foundations of Indian Culture. 3rd ed. 404p. 1995. pap. 12.50 (81-7058-013-7, Pub. by SAA) E-W Cultural Ctr.

Aurobindo, Sri. The Future Evolution of Man. Saint-Hilaire, P. B., ed. 157p. 1982. pap. 4.50 (0-89071-323-5, Pub. by SAA) Acrpls Bks CO.

Aurobindo, Sri. The Future Evolution of Man. 3rd ed. Saint-Hilaire, P. B., ed. 148p. 1996. pap. 6.95 (81-7058-219-9, Pub. by SAA) E-W Cultural Ctr.

Aurobindo, Sri. The Future Poetry. 307p. 1991. 16.95 (0-318-37154-5) Asia Bk Corp.

— The Future Poetry. 2nd ed. 307p. 1985. 9.95 (81-7058-253-9, Pub. by SAA); pap. 7.95 (81-7058-252-0, Pub. by SAA) E-W Cultural Ctr.

— The Future Poetry & Letters on Poetry, Literature, Art. 1979. pap. 14.95 (0-89744-919-3) Auromere.

— Gems from Sri Aurobindo. Pandit, M. P., ed. LC 94-76013. (Second Ser.). 288p. (Orig.). 1994. pap. 12.95 (0-941524-73-6) Lotus Pr.

— Gems from Sri Aurobindo. Pandit, M. P., ed. LC 95-78154. (Third Ser.). 143p. (Orig.). 1995. pap. 10.95 (0-914955-16-0) Lotus Pr.

— Gems from Sri Aurobindo, Series 4. Pandit, M. P., ed. LC 95-78151. (Fourth Ser.). 69p. (Orig.). 1995. pap. 8.95 (0-914955-17-9) Lotus Pr.

— The Gita for the Youth. Pershad, Guru, ed. 126p. 1998. pap. 3.95 (81-7060-039-1, Pub. by SAA) E-W Cultural Ctr.

Aurobindo, Sri. Glossary of Terms in Sri Aurobindo's Writings. 300p. 1994. pap. 8.95 (81-7058-032-3, Pub. by SAA) E-W Cultural Ctr.

Aurobindo, Sri. Growing Within: The Psychology of Inner Development. Dalal, A. S., ed. 192p. 1997. pap. 8.95 (81-7058-315-2, Pub. by SAA) E-W Cultural Ctr.

***Aurobindo, Sri.** Heraclitus. 4th ed. 46p. 1998. pap. 2.00 (81-7058-163-X, Pub. by SAA) E-W Cultural Ctr.

— Hidden Forces of Life. Dalal, A. S., ed. 203p. 1998. pap. 8.95 (*81-7058-177-X*, Pub. by SAA) E-W Cultural Ctr.
— The Hour of God. 4th ed. 124p. 1998. pap. 3.95 (*81-7058-217-2*, Pub. by SAA) E-W Cultural Ctr.
— How to Bring up a Child. Vijay, ed. 64p. 1998. pap. 4.50 (*81-7060-009-X*, Pub. by SAA) E-W Cultural Ctr.
Aurobindo, Sri. The Human Cycle: The Ideal of Human Unity. 690p. 1985. 16.95 (*0-318-36389-5*) Asia Bk Corp.
Aurobindo, Sri. The Human Cycle: The Ideal of Human Unity; War & Self-Determination. 2nd ed. 689p. 1997. 22.00 (*81-7058-281-4*, Pub. by SAA) E-W Cultural Ctr.
— The Human Cycle, Psychology of Social Development. 2nd ed. 280p. 1999. pap. 14.95 (*0-914955-44-6*) Lotus Pr.
— The Human Cycle, The Ideal of Human Unity, War & Self-Determination. 2nd ed. 689p. 1997. pap. text 17.50 (*81-7058-014-5*, Pub. by SAA) E-W Cultural Ctr.
Aurobindo, Sri. Hymns to the Mystic Fire. pap. 19.95 (*0-89744-918-5*) Auromere.
— Hymns to the Mystic Fire. 506p. 1985. pap. 19.95 (*0-89071-298-0*, Pub. by SAA) Acrpls Bks CO.
— Hymns to the Mystic Fire. 3rd ed. 507p. 1991. pap. 14.95 (*81-7058-220-2*, Pub. by SAA) E-W Cultural Ctr.
Aurobindo, Sri. Hymns to the Mystic Fire. 3rd ed. 507p. 1995. 19.95 (*81-7058-415-9*, Pub. by SAA) E-W Cultural Ctr.
Aurobindo, Sri. Hymns to the Mystic Fire: With Sanskrit Text, Translation & Sri Aurobindo's Commentary. unabridged ed. LC 96-75800. 502p. 1997. pap. 17.95 (*0-914955-22-5*) Lotus Pr.
***Aurobindo, Sri.** The Ideal of Human Unity. 2nd ed. 460p. 1999. pap. 17.95 (*0-914955-43-8*) Lotus Pr.
Aurobindo, Sri. Ilion: An Epic in Quantitative Hexameters. 2nd ed. 148p. 1989. 24.00 (*81-7058-169-9*, Pub. by SAA) E-W Cultural Ctr.
Aurobindo, Sri. Infinite Adventure & Other Poems. 24p. 1993. pap. 3.50 (*81-7058-313-6*, Pub. by SAA) E-W Cultural Ctr.
Aurobindo, Sri. The Integral Yoga: Sri Aurobindo's Teaching & Method of Practice. Sri Aurobindo Ashram Archives & Research Library S, ed. LC 93-78233. 416p. (Orig.). 1993. pap. 14.95 (*0-941524-76-0*) Lotus Pr.
Aurobindo, Sri. The Integral Yoga: Sri Aurobindo's Teaching & Method of Practice. Sri Aurobindo Archives & Research Library Staff, ed. 401p. (Orig.). 1997. pap. 14.95 (*81-7058-308-X*, Pub. by SAA) E-W Cultural Ctr.
— Invitation & Other Poems. 35p. 1993. pap. 3.95 (*81-7058-314-4*, Pub. by SAA) E-W Cultural Ctr.
— Isha Upanishad. 7th ed. 79p. 1998. pap. 3.95 (*81-7058-041-2*, Pub. by SAA) E-W Cultural Ctr.
— Letters on Poetry, Literature & Art. 271p. 1994. 6.95 (*81-7058-351-9*, Pub. by SAA); pap. 5.95 (*81-7058-098-6*, Pub. by SAA) E-W Cultural Ctr.
Aurobindo, Sri. Letters on Yoga, 2 vols. (Life Companion Library). 1984p. 29.90 (*0-89744-014-5*) Auromere.
Aurobindo, Sri. Letters on Yoga. 3rd ed. 502p. 1996. 18.95 (*81-7058-438-8*, Pub. by SAA) E-W Cultural Ctr.
Aurobindo, Sri. Letters on Yoga, Vol. I. 502p. 1979. 16.00 (*0-89744-984-3*, Pub. by Sri Aurob Ashram Trust); pap. 14.00 (*0-89744-985-1*, Pub. by Sri Aurob Ashram Trust) Acrpls Bks CO.
— Letters on Yoga, Vol. 1. 3rd ed. 502p. 1988. pap. 13.00 (*81-7058-007-2*, Pub. by SAA) E-W Cultural Ctr.
— Letters on Yoga, Vol. II. 587p. 1979. 16.50 (*0-89744-986-X*); pap. 15.00 (*0-89744-987-8*) Auromere.
— Letters on Yoga, Vol. 2. 3rd ed. 587p. 1988. pap. 14.50 (*81-7058-008-0*, Pub. by SAA) E-W Cultural Ctr.
Aurobindo, Sri. Letters on Yoga, Vol. 2. 3rd ed. 587p. 1996. 21.95 (*81-7058-439-6*, Pub. by SAA) E-W Cultural Ctr.
Aurobindo, Sri. Letters on Yoga, Vol. III. 720p. 1979. 20.00 (*0-89744-988-6*, Pub. by Sri Aurob Ashram Trust); pap. 18.50 (*0-89744-989-4*, Pub. by Sri Aurob Ashram Trust) Acrpls Bks CO.
— Letters on Yoga, Vol. 3. 3rd ed. 719p. 1988. pap. 16.50 (*81-7058-009-9*, Pub. by SAA) E-W Cultural Ctr.
Aurobindo, Sri. Letters on Yoga, Vol. 3. 3rd ed. 719p. 1996. 24.95 (*81-7058-440-X*, Pub. by SAA) E-W Cultural Ctr.
Aurobindo, Sri. The Life Divine. 2nd ed. LC 89-63859. 1113p. 1990. 39.95 (*0-941524-62-0*); pap. 29.95 (*0-941524-61-2*) Lotus Pr.
Aurobindo, Sri. The Life Divine. 5th ed. 1113p. 1996. 34.95 (*81-7058-188-5*, Pub. by SAA) E-W Cultural Ctr.
— The Life Divine. 5th ed. 1113p. 1998. pap. 29.95 (*81-7058-187-7*, Pub. by SAA) E-W Cultural Ctr.
Aurobindo, Sri. The Life Divine: A Commentary on Isha Upanished. 108p. (Orig.). 1981. pap. 5.00 (*0-89744-230-X*, Pub. by Sri Aurob Ashram Trust) Acrpls Bks CO.
Aurobindo, Sri. Light Endless Light. 96p. 1991. pap. 0.75 (*81-7060-004-9*, Pub. by SAA) E-W Cultural Ctr.
Aurobindo, Sri. Lights on Yoga. 9th ed. 63p. 1996. pap. 2.95 (*81-7058-057-9*, Pub. by SAA) E-W Cultural Ctr.
***Aurobindo, Sri.** Living Within: The Yoga Approach to Psychological Health & Growth. Dalal, A. S., ed. 179p. 1998. pap. 7.95 (*81-7058-051-X*, Pub. by SAA) E-W Cultural Ctr.
— Looking from Within: A Seeker's Guide to Attitudes for Mastery & Inner Growth. Dalal, A. S., ed. 185p. 1997. pap. 7.95 (*81-7058-406-X*, Pub. by SAA) E-W Cultural Ctr.
— Love & Death. 5th ed. 27p. 1990. pap. 1.50 (*81-7058-162-1*, Pub. by SAA) E-W Cultural Ctr.
Aurobindo, Sri. Love Treasures: "The Mother", Book One. (Illus.). 98p. 1985. 36.00 (*0-89071-333-2*, Pub. by SAA) Acrpls Bks CO.
— Major Works of Sri Aurobindo, 20 vols. 12500p. 1989. 250.00 (*0-89071-336-7*, Pub. by SAA) Acrpls Bks CO.
Aurobindo, Sri. Major Works of Sri Aurobindo. 13200p. 1996. 300.00 (*81-7058-469-8*, Pub. by SAA) E-W Cultural Ctr.
Aurobindo, Sri. Major Works of Sri Aurobindo, 10 vols., Set. (Life Companion Library). 1983. 125.00 (*0-685-59363-0*, Pub. by Madanlal Himatsinghka) MMC.
— Major Works of Sri Aurobindo, 22 vols., Set. 1990. 300.00 (*0-685-59362-2*, Pub. by Sri Aurob Ashram Trust) Acrpls Bks CO.
Aurobindo, Sri. The Meeting of East & West in Sri Aurobindo's Philosophy. 2nd ed. 470p. 1988. pap. 0.50 (*81-7058-488-4*, Pub. by SAA) E-W Cultural Ctr.
Aurobindo, Sri. The Message of the Gita: With Text, Translation & Notes. Roy, Anilbaran, ed. (ENG & SAN.). 1979. pap. 12.95 (*0-89744-977-0*, Pub. by Sri Aurob Ashram Trust) Acrpls Bks CO.
— More Lights on Yoga. 1979. pap. 2.95 (*0-89744-950-9*) Auromere.
Aurobindo, Sri. More Lights on Yoga. 4th ed. 86p. 1995. pap. 2.50 (*81-7058-277-6*, Pub. by SAA) E-W Cultural Ctr.
Aurobindo, Sri. The Mother. LC 94-72971. 62p. (Orig.). 1995. pap. 2.95 (*0-941524-79-5*) Lotus Pr.
Aurobindo, Sri. The Mother. 14th ed. 63p. (Orig.). 1996. pap. 1.25 (*81-7058-484-1*, Pub. by SAA) E-W Cultural Ctr.
— The Mother: With Letters on the Mother. 496p. 1997. pap. 10.95 (*81-7058-010-2*, Pub. by SAA) E-W Cultural Ctr.
— The Mother: With Letters on the Mother. 496p. 1997. 16.50 (*81-7058-373-X*, Pub. by SAA) E-W Cultural Ctr.
Aurobindo, Sri. The Mother, with Letters on the Mother & Translations of Prayers & Meditations. 500p. 1982. 16.00 (*0-89071-311-1*, Pub. by SAA); pap. 13.00 (*0-89071-310-3*, Pub. by SAA) Acrpls Bks CO.
Aurobindo, Sri. The National Value of Art. 6th ed. 27p. 1994. pap. 1.50 (*81-7058-228-8*, Pub. by SAA) E-W Cultural Ctr.
— A New Education for a New Consciousness: Sri Aurobindo & the Mother on Education. 2nd ed. 246p. 1995. pap. 15.95 (*81-7058-426-4*, Pub. by SAA) Auromere.
Aurobindo, Sri. Nirodbaran's Correspondence with Sri Aurobindo, 2nd ed. Nirodbaran, ed. 1221p. 1995. pap. 39.50 (*81-7058-020-X*, Pub. by SAA) E-W Cultural Ctr.
— On the Mahabharata. 187p. 1997. pap. 4.95 (*81-7058-256-3*, Pub. by SAA) Lotus Pr.
Aurobindo, Sri. Perseus the Deliverer. 175p. 1991. pap. 4.00 (*81-7058-040-4*, Pub. by SAA) E-W Cultural Ctr.
— The Phantom Hour & Other Stories. 44p. 1995. pap. 0.50 (*81-7058-434-5*, Pub. by SAA) E-W Cultural Ctr.
— The Philosophy of the Upanishads. 73p. 1998. pap. 2.95 (*81-7058-362-4*, Pub. by SAA) E-W Cultural Ctr.
— Powers Within. 196p. 1999. pap. text 5.95 (*0-941524-96-5*) Lotus Pr.
Aurobindo, Sri. A Practical Guide to Integral Yoga. 7th ed. Manibhai, ed. 1979. pap. 7.95 (*0-89744-942-8*) Auromere.
Aurobindo, Sri. The Problem of Rebirth. 3rd ed. 186p. 1994. pap. 4.95 (*81-7058-215-6*, Pub. by SAA) E-W Cultural Ctr.
— The Problem of Rebirth. 3rd ed. 186p. 1995. 6.95 (*81-7058-216-4*, Pub. by SAA) E-W Cultural Ctr.
Aurobindo, Sri. Rebirth & Karma. LC 90-63095. 190p. (Orig.). 1991. pap. 9.95 (*0-941524-63-9*) Lotus Pr.
— The Riddle of This World. 98p. 1984. pap. 2.75 (*0-89071-306-5*, Pub. by SAA) Acrpls Bks CO.
***Aurobindo, Sri.** The Riddle of This World. 6th ed. 72p. 1998. pap. 2.75 (*81-7058-160-5*, Pub. by SAA) E-W Cultural Ctr.
Aurobindo, Sri. Santan Dharma Ka Mahatva: (Uttarpara Speech) 14p. 1.00 (*0-317-17480-0*) Auromere.
— Savitri: A Legend & a Symbol. LC 94-72970. 816p. 1995. pap. 24.95 (*0-941524-80-9*) Lotus Pr.
— Savitri: A Legend & a Symbol. 725p. 1998. 12.50 (*81-7058-018-8*, Pub. by SAA) E-W Cultural Ctr.
Aurobindo, Sri. Savitri: A Legend & a Symbol. 4th ed. 827p. 1997. 26.95 (*81-7058-341-1*, Pub. by SAA) E-W Cultural Ctr.
Aurobindo, Sri. The Secret of the Veda. 581p. 1982. 16.50 (*0-89071-303-0*, Pub. by SAA); pap. 12.50 (*0-89071-302-2*, Pub. by SAA) Acrpls Bks CO.
— The Secret of the Veda. (ENG & SAN.). 1979. 19.00 (*0-89744-975-4*, Pub. by Sri Aurob Ashram Trust); pap. 17.95 (*0-685-00596-8*, Pub. by Sri Aurob Ashram Trust) Acrpls Bks CO.
— Secret of the Veda. LC 95-78153. 581p. 1997. pap. 19.95 (*0-914955-19-5*) Lotus Pr.
Aurobindo, Sri. The Secret of the Veda. 3rd ed. (Guidance from Sri Aurobindo Ser.). 582p. 1997. 21.95 (*81-7058-192-3*, Pub. by SAA) E-W Cultural Ctr.
— Sonnets. 109p. 1999. pap. 6.00 (*81-7058-264-4*, Pub. by SAA) E-W Cultural Ctr.
— Sri Aurobindo & His Ashram. 6th ed. (Illus.). 50p. 1997. pap. 1.50 (*81-7058-221-0*, Pub. by SAA) E-W Cultural Ctr.
— Sri Aurobindo & His Ashram. 7th ed. 48p. 1999. pap. 7.00 (*81-7058-526-0*, Pub. by SAA) E-W Cultural Ctr.
Aurobindo, Sri. Sri Aurobindo on Himself. 512p. 1985. 15.95 (*0-89071-317-0*, Pub. by SAA); pap. 12.00 (*0-89071-316-2*, Pub. by SAA) Acrpls Bks CO.
Aurobindo, Sri. Sri Aurobindo on Himself. 515p. 1995. pap. 12.95 (*81-7058-019-6*, Pub. by SAA) E-W Cultural Ctr.
Aurobindo, Sri. Sri Aurobindo on Indian Art Selection from His Writings, 1. LC 98-68332. 1999. 60.00 (*1-890206-14-8*) Grantha.
Aurobindo, Sri. Sri Aurobindo on the Veda. 20p. 1997. pap. 1.00 (*81-7058-303-9*, Pub. by SAA) E-W Cultural Ctr.
Aurobindo, Sri. Sri Aurobindo's "Primary Works" Set: U. S. Edition, 12 vols., Set. 5731p. 1998. pap. 180.00 (*0-941524-93-0*) Lotus Pr.
***Aurobindo, Sri.** The Superman. 6th ed. 20p. 1998. pap. 0.75 (*81-7058-270-9*, Pub. by SAA) E-W Cultural Ctr.
— The Supramental Manifestation & Other Writings. 2nd ed. 530p. 1994. 18.95 (*81-7058-352-7*, Pub. by SAA) E-W Cultural Ctr.
— The Supramental Manifestation & Other Writings. 2nd ed. 530p. 1997. pap. 17.95 (*81-7058-109-5*, Pub. by SAA) E-W Cultural Ctr.
Aurobindo, Sri. The Supramental Manifestation upon Earth. 2nd ed. 108p. 1995. pap. 3.50 (*81-7058-311-X*, Pub. by SAA) E-W Cultural Ctr.
— The Synthesis of Yoga. LC 91-76706. 899p. 1992. 34.95 (*0-941524-66-3*); pap. 29.95 (*0-941524-65-5*) Lotus Pr.
— Synthesis of Yoga. (Life Companion Library). 1984p. 15.95 (*0-89744-017-X*) Auromere.
— The Synthesis of Yoga. 4th ed. 899p. 1996. pap. 19.00 (*81-7058-011-0*, Pub. by SAA) E-W Cultural Ctr.
— The Synthesis of Yoga. 4th ed. 899p. 1996. 16.00 (*81-7058-257-1*, Pub. by SAA) E-W Cultural Ctr.
— Synthesis of Yoga. 6th ed. 1979p. 26.00 (*0-89744-931-2*) Auromere.
Aurobindo, Sri. Thoughts & Aphorisms. 5th ed. 96p. 1996. pap. 2.95 (*81-7058-108-7*, Pub. by SAA) E-W Cultural Ctr.
Aurobindo, Sri. Thoughts & Glimpses. 8th ed. 30p. 1996. pap. 1.50 (*81-7058-150-8*, Pub. by SAA) E-W Cultural Ctr.
— The Upanishads. (ENG & SAN.). 466p. 1981. reprint ed. 17.95 (*0-89744-026-9*, Pub. by Sri Aurob Ashram Trust); reprint ed. pap. 14.95 (*0-89744-025-0*, Pub. by Sri Aurob Ashram Trust) Acrpls Bks CO.
Aurobindo, Sri. The Upanishads. 2nd ed. 466p. 1997. pap. 14.95 (*81-7058-003-X*, Pub. by SAA) E-W Cultural Ctr.
— The Upanishads. 2nd ed. 466p. 1997. 17.95 (*81-7058-280-6*, Pub. by SAA) E-W Cultural Ctr.
Aurobindo, Sri. The Upanishads: Texts, Translations & Commentaries, Pt. 1. 466p. 1986. 17.95 (*0-89071-295-6*, Pub. by SAA); pap. 14.95 (*0-89071-294-8*, Pub. by SAA) Acrpls Bks CO.
— The Upanishads: With Sanskrit Text, Translation & Sri Aurobindo's Commentary. unabridged ed. LC 96-75803. 466p. 1997. pap. 17.95 (*0-914955-23-3*) Lotus Pr.
Aurobindo, Sri. Uttarpara Speech. 8th ed. 13p. 1996. pap. 1.00 (*81-7058-288-1*, Pub. by SAA) E-W Cultural Ctr.
Aurobindo, Sri. Vedic Symbolism. Pandit, M. P., ed. LC 88-80999. 122p. (Orig.). (C). 1988. pap. 6.95 (*0-941524-30-2*) Lotus Pr.
Aurobindo, Sri. Whispers of Nature. Vijay, ed. 87p. 1993. pap. 6.95 (*81-7060-023-5*, Pub. by SAA) E-W Cultural Ctr.
Aurobindo, Sri. Wisdom of the Gita: Second Series. 208p. 1992. pap. 10.95 (*0-941524-75-2*) Lotus Pr.
— Wisdom of the Upanishads. LC 88-83078. 134p. (Orig.). 1988. pap. 7.95 (*0-941524-43-4*) Lotus Pr.
— The Yoga & Its Objects. 33p. 1984. pap. 1.50 (*0-89071-314-6*, Pub. by SAA) Acrpls Bks CO.
Aurobindo, Sri. The Yoga & Its Objects. 10th ed. 39p. 1994. pap. 1.50 (*81-7058-151-6*, Pub. by SAA) E-W Cultural Ctr.
Aurobindo, Sri & Mother. Aspiration. Vijay, ed. 28p. 1993. pap. 1.00 (*81-7060-018-9*, Pub. by SAA) E-W Cultural Ctr.
— Death. 4th ed. Vijay, ed. 28p. 1997. pap. 1.00 (*81-7060-107-X*, Pub. by SAA) E-W Cultural Ctr.
— Helping Humanity. 4th ed. Vijay, ed. 28p. 1996. pap. 1.00 (*81-7060-114-2*, Pub. by SAA) E-W Cultural Ctr.
Aurobindo, Sri & Mother. The Hierarchy of Minds. Sobel, Prem & Sobel, Jyoti, eds. 174p. 1984. pap. 5.95 (*0-89071-324-3*, Pub. by SAA) Acrpls Bks CO.
***Aurobindo, Sri & Mother.** Illness - Causes & Cure. 4th ed. Vijay, ed. 28p. 1998. pap. 1.00 (*81-7060-111-8*, Pub. by SAA) E-W Cultural Ctr.
— Illness & Perfect Health. 4th ed. Vijay, ed. 36p. 1998. pap. 1.00 (*81-7060-112-6*, Pub. by SAA) E-W Cultural Ctr.
Aurobindo, Sri & Mother. Looking from Within: A Seeker's Guide to Attitudes for Mastery & Inner Growth. LC 94-73075. 185p. 1995. pap. 6.95 (*0-941524-81-7*) Lotus Pr.
Aurobindo, Sri & Mother. Meditation. Vijay, ed. 27p. 1996. pap. 1.00 (*81-7060-026-X*, Pub. by SAA) E-W Cultural Ctr.
— Money. 4th ed. Vijay, ed. 28p. 1997. pap. 1.00 (*81-7060-090-1*, Pub. by SAA) E-W Cultural Ctr.
— Occultism. 4th ed. Vijay, ed. 28p. 1997. pap. 1.00 (*81-7060-108-8*, Pub. by SAA) E-W Cultural Ctr.
Aurobindo, Sri & Mother. On Education. 168p. 1986. pap. 4.95 (*81-7058-028-5*, Pub. by SAA) E-W Cultural Ctr.
— On Love. 3rd ed. Pavitra, ed. 49p. 1988. pap. 2.95 (*81-7058-104-4*, Pub. by SAA) E-W Cultural Ctr.
Aurobindo, Sri & Mother. On Physical Education. 2nd ed. 248p. 1996. pap. 15.95 (*81-7058-441-8*, Pub. by SAA) E-W Cultural Ctr.
Aurobindo, Sri & Mother. On Women. Vijay, ed. 126p. 1985. pap. 5.95 (*81-7060-014-6*, Pub. by SAA) E-W Cultural Ctr.
— A Practical Guide to Integral Yoga. 7th ed. Manibhai, ed. (Illus.). 338p. 1995. pap. 7.95 (*81-7058-034-X*, Pub. by SAA) E-W Cultural Ctr.
***Aurobindo, Sri & Mother.** Prayer & Japa. 4th ed. Vijay, ed. 28p. 1998. pap. 1.00 (*81-7060-027-8*, Pub. by SAA) E-W Cultural Ctr.
— Prayers & Mantras. Vijay, ed. 120p. 1996. 4.95 (*81-7060-022-7*, Pub. by SAA) E-W Cultural Ctr.
— The Psychic Being: Soul: Its Nature, Mission & Evolution. Dalal, A. S., ed. 223p. 1997. pap. 8.95 (*81-7058-138-9*, Pub. by SAA) E-W Cultural Ctr.
— Rebirth. Vijay, ed. 32p. 1997. pap. 1.00 (*81-7060-117-7*, Pub. by SAA) E-W Cultural Ctr.
— Sleep & Dreams. 4th ed. Vijay, ed. 27p. 1997. pap. 1.00 (*81-7060-097-9*, Pub. by SAA) E-W Cultural Ctr.
— Surrender & Grace. 4th ed. Vijay, ed. 28p. 1993. pap. 1.00 (*81-7060-019-7*, Pub. by SAA) E-W Cultural Ctr.
— Truth. 4th ed. Vijay, ed. 28p. 1998. pap. 1.00 (*81-7060-109-6*, Pub. by SAA) E-W Cultural Ctr.
— Work. 4th ed. Vijay, ed. 27p. 1997. pap. 1.00 (*81-7060-089-8*, Pub. by SAA) E-W Cultural Ctr.
— Yoga. 4th ed. Vijay, ed. 28p. 1993. pap. 1.00 (*81-7060-070-7*, Pub. by SAA) E-W Cultural Ctr.
Aurobindo, Sri & Mother, The. Growing Within: The Psychology of Inner Development. Dalal, A. S., ed. LC 92-73676. 192p. (Orig.). 1992. pap. 9.95 (*0-941524-71-X*) Lotus Pr.
— The Hidden Forces of Life: The Psychology of Inner Development. Dalal, A. S., ed. LC 89-51865. 203p. (Orig.). 1990. pap. 9.95 (*0-941524-60-4*) Lotus Pr.
— Living Within (Yoga Approach to Psychological Health & Growth) Dalal, A. S., ed. LC 85-82639. 179p. (Orig.). (C). 1987. pap. 8.95 (*0-941524-22-1*) Lotus Pr.
— The Psychic Being: The Soul in Evolution. LC 89-85198. 223p. (Orig.). 1990. pap. 8.95 (*0-941524-56-6*) Lotus Pr.
Aurobindo, Sri, et al. The Hierarchy of Minds: The Mind Levels. 174p. 1996. pap. 6.95 (*81-7058-033-1*, Pub. by SAA) E-W Cultural Ctr.
Aurobindo, Sri, jt. auth. see Sri Aurobindo Ashram Publications Department Staff.
Aurobindo, Sri, tr. see Sri Aurobindo.
Auroi, Claude. Latin American & East European Economies in Transition: A Comparative View. LC 97-26196. (EADI Book Ser.: No. 21). 180p. (C). 1998. pap. 29.50 (*0-7146-4403-X*, Pub. by F Cass Pubs) Intl Spec Bk.
Auroi, Claude, ed. The Role of the State in Development Processes. LC 92-26250. (EADI Book Ser.: Vol. 15). 1992. 37.50 (*0-7146-3493-X*, Pub. by F Cass Pubs) Intl Spec Bk.
Auron, Yair. The Banality of Indifference: Zionism & the Armenian Genocide. 332p. 1999. 39.95 (*1-56000-412-6*) Transaction Pubs.
Aurora. Lesbian Love Signs: An Astrological Guide to Women Loving Women. (Illus.). 130p. 1991. pap. 8.95 (*0-89594-467-7*) Crossing Pr.
Aurora Echevarria. Aliens. 1998. pap. 4.50 (*84-01-54048-8*) Lectorum Pubns.
— Death & Beyond. 1998. pap. 4.50 (*84-01-54047-X*) Lectorum Pubns.
— Fantasmas y Poltegeists. 1998. pap. 4.50 (*84-01-54044-5*) Lectorum Pubns.
— El Mundo Psiquico. 1998. pap. 4.50 (*84-01-54043-7*) Lectorum Pubns.
— Ovnis. 1998. pap. 4.50 (*84-01-54045-3*) Lectorum Pubns.
Auroux, Sylvain. Dictionnaire des Auteurs et des Themes de la Philosophie. (FRE.). 526p. 1991. pap. 36.95 (*0-7859-7607-8*, 2010159705) Fr & Eur.
— Les Notions Philosophiques Dictionnaire, 2 vols. (FRE.). 3344p. 1992. 995.00 (*0-7859-9268-5*) Fr & Eur.
Aurthur, Robert & Cohlmia, Kenneth. The Third Marine Division. 15th ed. (Elite Unit Ser.). (Illus.). 399p. 1989. reprint ed. 49.95 (*0-89839-110-5*) Battery Pr.
***Aurum Press Staff.** Golf World's 1000 Best Golf Courses of Britain & Ireland. (Illus.). 1999. text 16.95 (*1-85410-623-6*, Pub. by Aurum Press Ltd) London Brdge.
***Aurum Press Staff, ed.** Best Courses of Ireland: Every one rated & reviewed. (Golf World Guides Bks.). (Illus.). 128p. 2000. pap. 9.95 (*1-85410-684-8*, Pub. by Aurum Pr) London Brdge.
— Best Courses of Scotland: Every one rated & reviewed. (Golf World Guides Bks.). (Illus.). 128p. 2000. pap. 9.95 (*1-85410-683-X*, Pub. by Aurum Pr) London Brdge.
AuRutick, Frances R. Kosher Cookery. 420p. (Orig.). 1991. pap. 14.00 (*0-8246-0352-4*) Jonathan David.
Aus, Roger, jt. auth. see Hultgren, Arland J.
Ausband, Stephen C. Myth & Meaning, Myth & Order. LC 83-5478. xiv, 126p. 1983. 10.45 (*0-86554-089-6*, MUP-H079) Mercer Univ Pr.
Ausberger, Carolyn & Mullica, Karyn. How to Use Reproducible Illustrations in Language Remediation. 224p. (Orig.). 1983. pap. text 21.95 (*0-685-09162-7*) Syndactics.
Ausburn, Marshall. Days of Glory, a Gentleman's Chronicle. (Illus.). 112p. 1992. pap. 14.95 (*0-9613287-4-6*) Strawberry GA.
AUSC International Staff. Family Planning Counseling: A Curriculum Prototype, Trainer's Package. LC 94-48622. 1995. ring bd. 75.00 (*1-885063-10-5*) AVSC Int.
— Talking with Clients about Family Planning: A Guide for Health Care Providers. 102p. 1995. pap. text 10.00 (*1-885063-11-3*) AVSC Int.
Ause, Wayne. How to Use the World Wide Web. LC 97-102977. 240p. 1996. pap. 24.99 (*1-56276-392-X*, Ziff-Davis Pr) Que.
— Instant HTML Web Pages. LC 96-124492. 144p. 1995. pap. text 24.95 incl. cd-rom (*1-56276-363-6*, Ziff-Davis Pr) Que.
Ausebel, J. & Biswas, Asit K. Climatic Constraints & Human Activities. LC 80-41073. (IITASA Proceedings Ser.: Vol. 10). (Illus.). 215p. 1980. 102.00 (*0-08-026721-1*, Pub. by Pergamon Repr) Franklin.
Ausejo, Ana M. Algunos Muchachos. 3rd ed. (SPA.). 170p. 1990. pap. 11.95 (*0-7859-4993-3*) Fr & Eur.
— Fiesta Al Noroeste. 5th ed. (SPA.). 128p. 1991. pap. 13.95 (*0-7859-4989-5*) Fr & Eur.
— Historias de Artamila. 5th ed. (SPA.). 168p. 1990. pap. 24.95 (*0-7859-4991-7*) Fr & Eur.
— El Rio. 2nd ed. (SPA.). 198p. 1973. pap. 19.95 (*0-7859-4992-5*) Fr & Eur.
— El Tiempo. 2nd ed. (SPA.). 264p. 1991. pap. 17.95 (*0-7859-4994-1*) Fr & Eur.
Ausejo, Ana Matute. Primera Memoria. 8th ed. (SPA.). 248p. 1991. pap. 12.95 (*0-7859-4990-9*) Fr & Eur.
Ausenda, Giorgio, ed. After Empire: Towards an Ethnology of Europe's Barbarians. (Studies in Historical Archaeoethnology: No. 1). 326p. (C). 1995. 90.00 (*0-85115-634-7*) Boydell & Brewer.

A

A

Ausfeld-Hafter, Brigitte. Intuition in der Medizin, Bd. 2. (Komplementare Medizin Im Interdisziplinaren Diskurs Ser.). 204p. 1999. 32.00 (*3-906760-47-2*) P Lang Pubng.

Ausfeld-Hafter, Brigitte, et al, eds. "Energestische" Medizin: Gibt es Nur Physikalische Wirkprinzipien? (Komplementare Medizin Im Interdisziplinaren Diskurs Ser.: Vol. 1). (Illus.). 225p. 1998. pap. 32.95 (*3-906759-84-9*) P Lang Pubng.

Ausfeld, Margaret L., jt. auth. see Mecklenburg, Virginia M.

Ausfeld, Margaret L., ed. see Montgomery Museum of Fine Arts Staff.

Ausfeld, Margaret L., ed. see Willett, E. Henry & Brackner, Joey.

Ausfelder, Richard. Die Einfuhrung von Telefonbanking als Vertriebswege-Entscheidung von Kreditinstituten, Vol. XX. (GER., Illus.). XX, 190p. 1996. pap. 38.95 (*3-631-30319-X*) P Lang Pubng.

Ausgabe, Kritische. Johann Heinrich Pestalozzi Samtliche Werke. 592p. 1997. 63.00 (*3-11-015540-0*) De Gruyter.

Aushenker, Michael. Get That Goat! Thatch, Nancy R., ed. LC 90-5930. (Books for Students by Students). (Illus.). 26p. (J). (gr. k-4). 1990. lib. bdg. 15.95 (*0-933849-28-1*) Landmark Edns.

Ausich, William I. & Lane, N. Gary. Life of the Past. 4th ed. LC 98-18770. 321p. 1998. pap. text 48.00 (*0-13-896069-0*) P-H.

Ausiello, G., et al, eds. Algorithm Design for Computer System Design. (CISM International Centre for Mechanical Sciences Ser.: No. 284). (Illus.). vii, 236p. 1984. 59.95 (*0-387-81816-2*) Spr-Verlag.

— Automata, Languages & Programming. (Lecture Notes in Computer Science Ser.: Vol. 372). xi, 788p. 1989. 87.00 (*0-387-51371-X*, 3248) Spr-Verlag.

Ausiello, G. & Boehm, C., eds. Automata, Languages & Programming '78. (Lecture Notes in Computer Science Ser.: Vol. 62). 1978. 31.95 (*0-387-08860-1*) Spr-Verlag.

Ausiello, G. & Protasi, M., eds. CAAP, 1983. (Lecture Notes in Computer Science Ser.: Vol. 159). (ENG & FRE.). 416p. 1983. 40.00 (*0-387-12727-5*) Spr-Verlag.

Ausiello, G., ed. see Bovet, D. P. & Petreschi, R.

***Ausiello, Giorgio, et al.** Complexity & Approximation: Combinatorial Optimization Problems & Their Approximability Properties. LC 99-40936. 550p. 1999. 59.95 incl. cd-rom (*3-540-65431-3*) Spr-Verlag.

***AusIndustry Enterprise Improvement Staff.** Key Performance Indicators Manual: A Practical Guide for the Best Practice Development, Implementation & Use of KPIs. 169p. 1999. 99.99 (*0-7299-0326-5*) Pitman Pubng.

Ausink, John A. Watershed in Rwanda: The Evolution of President Clinton's Humanitarian Intervention Policy. (Pew Case Studies in International Affairs). 50p. (C). 1997. text 3.50 (*1-56927-374-X*) Geo U Inst Dplmcy.

Auskalnis, Richard J., et al. Purchasing from Minority Business Enterprises: Best Practices. 79p. (C). 1995. pap. text 20.00 (*0-945968-23-X*) Ctr Advanced Purchasing.

Auslaender, Rose. The Forbidden Tree: Englische Gedichte. Helmut, Braun, ed. (GER.). 288p. 1995. pap. 15.25 (*3-596-11153-6*, Pub. by Fischer Tasch) Intl Bk Import.

Ausland, John C. Kennedy, Khrushchev, & the Berlin-Cuba Crisis, 1961-1964: The 1961-64 Wall. (Illus.). 256p. 1996. 31.00 (*82-00-22635-2*) Scandnvan Univ Pr.

Auslander, D. M., ed. see American Society of Mechanical Engineers Staff.

Auslander, David M. & Kempf, Carl J. Mechatronics: Mechanical System Interfacing. LC 95-21844. 243p. (C). 1995. 97.00 (*0-13-120338-X*) P-H.

Auslander, Gail K., ed. International Perspectives on Social Work in Health Care: Past, Present, & Future. LC 97-10583. 272p. 1997. 39.95 (*0-7890-0325-2*) Haworth Pr.

Auslander, J. & Hill, F. E. Winged Horse: The Story of the Poets & Their Poetry. LC 68-24959. (Studies in Poetry: No. 38). (C). 1968. reprint ed. lib. bdg. 75.00 (*0-8383-0328-5*) M S G Haskell Hse.

Auslander, L. Lecture Notes on Nil-Theta Functions. LC 77-16471. (CBMS Regional Conference Series in Mathematics: No. 34). 96p. 1978. reprint ed. pap. 19.00 (*0-8218-1684-5*, CBMS/34) Am Math.

Auslander, L., et al, eds. Signal Processing Pt. I. (IMA Volumes in Mathematics & Its Applications Ser.: Vol. 22). (Illus.). xiii, 251p. 1990. 42.95 (*0-387-97215-3*) Spr-Verlag.

— Signal Processing Pt. II: Control Theory & Applications. (IMA Volumes in Mathematics & Its Applications Ser.: Vol. 23). (Illus.). xiii, 411p. 1990. 62.95 (*0-387-97230-7*) Spr-Verlag.

Auslander, Leora. Taste & Power: Furnishing Modern France. LC 95-715. (Studies on the History of Society & Culture: Vol. 24). (Illus.). 526p. (C). 1996. 45.00 (*0-520-08894-8*, Pub. by U CA Pr) Cal Prin Full Svc.

— Taste & Power: Furnishing Modern France. (Studies on the History of Society & Culture). 526p. 1998. pap. text 19.95 (*0-520-21365-3*, Pub. by U CA Pr) Cal Prin Full Svc.

Auslander, Louis & Mackenzie, Robert E. Introduction to Differentiable Manifolds. 218p. (C). 1977. pap. 8.95 (*0-486-63455-8*) Dover.

Auslander, Louis & Markus, L. Flat Lorentz 3-Manifolds. LC 52-42839. (American Mathematical Society Ser.: Vol. 30). (Illus.). 62p. reprint ed. pap. 30.00 (*0-608-09602-4*, 205276000007) Bks Demand.

Auslander, Louis & Markus, Lawrence. Flat Lorentz Three Manifolds. LC 52-42839. (Memoirs Ser.: No. 1/30). 60p. 1987. reprint ed. pap. 18.00 (*0-8218-1230-0*, MEMO/1/30) Am Math.

Auslander, Louis & Moore, C. C. Unitary Representations of Solvable Lie Groups. LC 52-42839. (Memoirs Ser.: No. 1/62). 199p. 1990. reprint ed. pap. 19.00 (*0-8218-1262-9*, MEMO/1/62) Am Math.

Auslander, Louis & Moore, Calvin C. Unitary Representations of Solvable Lie Groups. LC 52-42839. (American Mathematical Society Ser.: Vol. 62). 206p. reprint ed. pap. 63.90 (*0-608-09603-2*, 205276100007) Bks Demand.

Auslander, Louis, et al. Flows on Homogeneous Spaces. LC 62-19959. (Annals of Mathematics Studies: No. 53). 117p. 1963. reprint ed. pap. 36.30 (*0-608-06619-2*, 206681600009) Bks Demand.

Auslander, M. & Bridger, M. Stable Module Theory. LC 52-42839. (Memoirs Ser.: No. 1/94). 146p. 1969. pap. 17.00 (*0-8218-1294-7*, MEMO/1/94) Am Math.

Auslander, Maurice. Selected Works of Maurice Auslander, 2 pts. Reiten, Idun et al, eds. Incl. Selected Works of Maurice Auslander. LC 98-2926. 743p. 1998. 155.00 (*0-8218-1000-6*, CWORKS/10.2); LC 98-2926. 895p. 1998. 165.00 (*0-8218-0998-9*, CWORKS/10.1); 299.00 (*0-8218-0679-3*) Am Math.

Auslander, Maurice, et al. Representation Theory of Artin Algebras. LC 93-43326. (Studies in Advanced Mathematics: No. 36). (Illus.). 437p. (C). 1995. text 85.00 (*0-521-41134-3*) Cambridge U Pr.

— Representation Theory of Artin Algebras. LC 98-115558. (Cambridge Studies in Advanced Mathematics: No. 36). 440p. 1997. pap. text 36.95 (*0-521-59923-7*) Cambridge U Pr.

Auslander Munich, Adrienne, jt. ed. see Maynard, John.

Auslander, Philip. From Acting to Performance: Essays in Modernism & Postmodernism. LC 97-170095. 184p. (C). 1997. 65.00 (*0-415-15786-2*); pap. 18.99 (*0-415-15787-0*) Routledge.

— Liveness: Performance in a Mediatized Culture. LC 98-43440. 1999. 65.00 (*0-415-19689-2*); pap. 19.99 (*0-415-19690-6*) Routledge.

— The New York School Poets As Playwrights: O'Hara, Ashberry, Koch, Schuyler & the Visual Arts. (Literature & the Visual Arts Ser.: Vol. 3). 187p. (C). 1989. text 37.50 (*0-8204-1094-2*) P Lang Pubng.

— Presence & Resistance: Postmodernism & Cultural Politics in Contemporary American Performance. (Theater: Theory-Text-Performance Ser.). 216p. 1994. pap. text 17.95 (*0-472-08278-7*, 08278) U of Mich Pr.

Auslander, Rachel, ed. see Institute of Electrical & Electronics Engineers, I.

Auslander, Zachary. First Publisher 3.0 Quick Reference Guide. (DDC Quick Reference Guides Ser.). (Orig.). 1990. spiral bd. 12.00 (*0-936862-96-3*, F-17) DDC Pub.

Ausley, Lisa, ed. see Tarvin, Al.

***Ausloos, M., et al, eds.** When Materials Matter -- Analyzing, Predicting & Preventing Disasters: Materials Research Society Symposium Proceedings, Vol. 630. 2000. text 66.00 (*1-55899-538-2*) Materials Res.

Ausloos, M & Elliot, R. J., eds. Magnetic Phase Transitions. (Solid-State Sciences Ser.: Vol. 48). (Illus.). 269p. 1984. 73.95 (*0-387-12842-5*) Spr-Verlag.

Ausloos, M. & Kruchinin, Sergei. Symmetry & Pairing in Superconductors: Proceedings of a Nato Advanced Research Workshop Held At Oreanda Hotel, Yalta, Ukraine On April 29-may 2, 1998 / LC 98-43888. (NATO ASI Ser.). 14p. 1999. write for info. (*0-7923-5520-2*) Kluwer Academic.

Ausloos, Marcel & Varlamov, Andrei A., eds. Fluctuation Phenomena in High Temperature Superconductors. LC 97-16611. 456p. 1997. text 234.00 (*0-7923-4575-4*) Kluwer Academic.

Ausmus, Bob. East Mojave Diary. (Illus.). 176p. 1989. 17.50 (*0-914224-18-2*) Tales Mojave Rd.

Ausmus, Harry J. The Pragmatic God: On the Nihilism of Reinhold Niebuhr. LC 90-34440. (American University Studies: Theology & Religion: Ser. VII, Vol. 80). XIV, 308p. (C). 1990. text 57.95 (*0-8204-1379-8*) P Lang Pubng.

— A Schopenhauerian Critique of Nietzsche's Thought: Toward a Restoration of Metaphysics. LC 95-19349. (Studies in the History of Philosophy: Vol. 38). 440p. 1996. text 109.95 (*0-7734-8891-X*) E Mellen.

Ausmus, Harry J. Will Herberg: A Bio-Bibliography, 2. LC 85-21955. (Bio-Bibliographies in Law & Political Science Ser.: No. 2). 120p. 1986. lib. bdg. 47.95 (*0-313-25067-7*, AWH/, Greenwood Pr) Greenwood.

Ausnit, C. N., et al. ADA in Practice: Books on Professional Computing Series. (Illus.). xv, 195p. 1985. 65.95 (*0-387-96182-8*) Spr-Verlag.

Ausnit-Hood, Christine, et al, eds. Ada 95, Quality & Style: Guidelines for Professional Programmers, Vol. 134. LC 97-43253. (Lecture Notes in Computer Science Ser.: Vol. 1344). xv, 292p. 1998. pap. 43.00 (*3-540-63823-7*) Spr-Verlag.

Ausonius. Opera. Green, Roger P. H., ed. LC 98-33801. (Oxford Classical Texts Ser.). 354p. 1999. text 55.00 (*0-19-815039-3*) OUP.

— Poems, 2 vols. No. 96, 115. write for info. (*0-318-53140-2*) HUP.

— Poems, 2 Vols, 1. (Loeb Classical Library: No. 96, 115). 442p. 1919. 19.95 (*0-674-99107-9*) HUP.

— Poems, 2 Vols, 2. (Loeb Classical Library: No. 96, 115). 374p. 1921. 19.95 (*0-674-99127-3*) HUP.

Ausonius, Decimus M. The Works of Ausonius. 836p. 1991. text 200.00 (*0-19-814463-6*) OUP.

Ausonius, Decimus M. & Fortunatus, Venantus. Die Moselgedichte. (GER.). 126p. 1981. reprint ed. 20.00 (*0-318-70578-8*) G Olms Pubs.

Ausperk, Michael D. Teenagers Come & Pray! Celebrating Milestones, Memorials, & Holy Days. LC 94-61851. 110p. (Orig.). 1995. pap. 12.95 (*0-89622-642-5*) Twenty-Third.

Auspicessm Staff. How to Prevent Child Abduction. LC 96-90919. (Orig.). 1997. pap. 10.00 (*0-533-12214-7*) Vantage.

***Auspitz, Robb.** Bad Timing. 174p. 1999. pap. 13.95 (*0-7414-0146-0*) Buy Books.

Aussenac, N., et al. Knowledge Acquisition for Knowledge-Based Systems: 7th European Workshop, EKAW '93, Toulouse & Caylus, France, September 6-10, 1993: Proceedings. LC 93-23378. 1993. 65.00 (*0-387-57253-8*) Spr-Verlag.

Aussenegg, F. R., et al, eds. Surface Studies with Lasers. (Chemical Physics Ser.: Vol. 33). (Illus.). 270p. 1983. 55.95 (*0-387-12598-1*) Spr-Verlag.

***Aust, Anthony I.** Modern Treaty Law & Practice. 384p. (C). 2000. 90.00 (*0-521-59153-8*); pap. 39.95 (*0-521-59846-X*) Cambridge U Pr.

Aust, Derek & Zello, Mike. Nuova Grammatica Communicativa: Answer Key, Answer Key. (ITA.). pap. 4.95 (*0-8442-8090-9*, X8090-9) NTC Contemp Pub Co.

Aust, Derek, et al. Nuova Grammatica Comunicativa: A Communicative Grammar Worktext with Written & Oral Practice. LC 97-69975. (ITA.). 416p. (C). 1998. pap., student ed. 14.95 (*0-8442-8089-5*, 80895) NTC Contemp Pub Co.

Aust, Eberhard. Simultane Conjointanalyse, Benefitsegmentierung, Produktlinien- & Preisgestaltung. (GER., Illus.). 264p. 1996. 51.95 (*3-631-49057-7*) P Lang Pubng.

Aust, J. Bradley, jt. auth. see Peltier, Leonard F.

Aust, Louise B., ed. Cosmetic Claims Substantion. LC 97-35933. (Cosmetic Science & Technology Ser.: Vol. 18). (Illus.). 280p. 1997. text 135.00 (*0-8247-9855-4*) Dekker.

Aust, Manfred & Jacobs, Rainer. Die Enteignungsentschadigung. rev. ed. 520p. 1996. write for info. (*3-11-014735-1*) De Gruyter.

Aust, Marilee, ed. see Reed, Ken.

Aust, Patricia H. Benni & Victoria: Friends Through Time. (Illus.). 117p. (J). (gr. 3-9). 1996. pap. 5.95 (*0-87868-629-0*, Child-Family Pr) Child Welfare.

Aust, Siegfried. Lenses! Take a Closer Look. (Illus.). 32p. (J). 1996. pap. text 7.95 (*0-8225-9732-2*) Lerner Pub.

Aust, W. The Conservative Management of Squint. Bedwell, C. H. & Obstfeld, H., trs. (Illus.). 152p. 1970. 24.50 (*3-8055-0752-6*) S Karger.

Austad. Why We Grow Old. (C). 1998. write for info. (*0-201-40968-2*) Addison-Wesley.

Austad & Rosenzweig. Biology 100 Laboratory Manual. 174p. (C). 1997. spiral bd., lab manual ed. 19.95 (*0-7872-3956-9*, 41395601) Kendall-Hunt.

Austad, Carol S. & Berman, William H., eds. Psychotherapy in Managed Health Care: The Optimal Use of Time & Resources. 285p. 1991. pap. text 19.95 (*1-55798-314-3*) Am Psychol.

***Austad, Steven.** Why We Age: What Science Is Discovering about the Body's Journey Through Life. 256p. 1999. pap. 16.95 (*0-471-29646-5*) Wiley.

Austad, Steven N. Why We Age: What Science Is Discovering about the Bodies' Journey Through Life. LC 97-5542. 256p. 1997. 24.95 (*0-471-14803-2*) Wiley.

Austcare. Refugee Children Around the World. 1991. pap. text. write for info. (*0-582-87486-6*, Pub. by Addison-Wesley) Longman.

Austello, G. & Atzeni, Paolo, eds. ICDT Eighty-Six. (Lecture Notes in Computer Science Ser.: Vol. 243). vi, 444p. 1986. 45.00 (*0-387-17187-8*) Spr-Verlag.

Austen, Ben. Computers & Three-Dimensional Product Design Education. 64p. 1987. 75.00 (*0-85072-163-6*) St Mut.

Austen, Brian M. & Westwood, Olwyn M. Protein Targeting & Secretion. (Illus.). 96p. (C). 1991. pap. text 18.95 (*0-19-963217-0*, 126) OUP.

Austen, Charlotte. Love Everlasting. 352p. (Orig.). 1988. mass mkt. 3.95 (*0-446-34966-6*, Pub. by Warner Bks) Little.

Austen, Hallie. The Heart of the Goddess: Art, Myth & Meditations of the World's Sacred Feminine. (Illus.). 202p. (Orig.). 1990. pap. 24.95 (*0-914728-69-5*) Wingbow Pr.

Austen, Jane. Catharine: And Other Writings. Doody, Margaret Anne & Murray, Douglas, eds. (Oxford World's Classics Ser.). 418p. 1998. pap. 9.95 (*0-19-283521-1*) OUP.

— Collected Poems & Verse of the Austen Family. Selwyn, David, ed. 1996. 0.00 (*1-85754-313-0*); pap. 0.00 (*1-85754-263-0*) Carcanet Pr.

— The Complete Novels of Jane Austen. 1344p. (C). 1989. pap. 17.95 (*0-14-010649-9*, Penguin Bks) Viking Penguin.

— The Complete Novels of Jane Austen, Vol. 1. LC 92-50209. 912p. 1992. 21.00 (*0-679-60026-4*) Modern Lib NY.

— The Complete Novels of Jane Austen, Vol. 2. LC 92-50209. 728p. 1992. 22.00 (*0-679-60025-6*) Modern Lib NY.

— David Alden's Daughter, & Other Stories of Colonial Times. LC 71-98556. (Short Story Index Reprint Ser.). 1977. 21.95 (*0-8369-3130-0*) Ayer.

— Emma. 232p. Date not set. 21.95 (*0-8488-2522-5*) Amereon Ltd.

— Emma. (Bantam Classics Ser.). 448p. 1984. mass mkt. 4.95 (*0-553-21273-7*) Bantam.

— Emma. 1986. lib. bdg. 19.95 (*0-89966-242-0*) Buccaneer Bks.

— Emma. Berry, Mary, ed. (Literature Ser.). 384p. 1999. pap. 10.95 (*0-521-63498-9*) Cambridge U Pr.

— Emma. 96p. 1997. pap. 5.50 (*0-87129-812-0*, E36) Dramatic Pub.

— Emma. (Everyman's Library). 484p. 1991. write for info. (*1-85715-036-8*) Everymns Lib.

— Emma. 464p. 1991. 20.00 (*0-679-40581-X*) Everymns Lib.

Austen, Jane. Emma, 001. Trilling, Lionel, ed. (C). 1972. pap. 13.96 (*0-395-05115-0*) HM.

Austen, Jane. Emma. (Cloth Bound Pocket Ser.). 7.95 (*3-8290-0827-9*) Konemann.

— Emma. Cheetham, Paul, ed. (Study Texts Ser.). 1984. pap. text 4.29 (*0-582-33153-6*, 72058) Longman.

— Emma. 400p. 1996. mass mkt. 4.95 (*0-451-52627-9*, Sig Classics) NAL.

— Emma. Kinsley, James, ed. LC 98-218541. (Oxford World's Classics Ser.). 484p. 1998. pap. 6.95 (*0-19-283357-X*) OUP.

— Emma. LC 99-461942. (Oxford World's Classics Hardcovers Ser.). 460p. 1999. 13.00 (*0-19-210030-0*) OUP.

— Emma. 1998. pap. 11.95 (*84-320-3877-6*) Planeta.

— Emma. (World's Best Reading Ser.). 391p. 1994. write for info. (*0-89577-582-4*) RD Assn.

— Emma. 1995. 14.95 (*0-679-60193-7*) Random.

— Emma. (Signet Classics). 1980. 10.05 (*0-606-03147-2*, Pub. by Turtleback) Demco.

— Emma. 464p. 1994. 3.95 (*0-460-87467-5*, Everyman's Classic Lib) Tuttle Pubng.

— Emma. LC 97-157767. 1997. pap. 7.95 (*0-14-043415-1*) Viking Penguin.

— Emma. (Classics Library). 360p. 1997. pap. 3.95 (*1-85326-028-2*, 0282WW, Pub. by Wrdsworth Edits) NTC Contemp Pub Co.

***Austen, Jane.** Emma. large type ed. 624p. 2000. pap. 22.00 (*0-06-095693-3*, HarpCollins) HarpeTrade.

Austen, Jane. Emma. large type ed. 547p. 1985. 27.99 (*0-7089-8258-1*, Charnwood) Ulverscroft.

— Emma. large type ed. 610p. 1997. reprint ed. lib. bdg. 25.00 (*0-939495-08-2*) North Bks.

— Emma. (Illus.). 464p. (J). 1996. reprint ed. pap. 9.70 (*0-7868-8183-6*, Pub. by Hyperion) Time Warner.

— Emma. 478p. 1998. reprint ed. lib. bdg. 24.00 (*1-58287-025-X*) North Bks.

***Austen, Jane.** Emma. unabridged ed. LC 98-50939. 384p. 1999. pap. text 2.50 (*0-486-40648-2*) Dover.

Austen, Jane. Emma. 2nd ed. Parrish, Stephen M., ed. LC 92-28638. (Critical Editions Ser.). 430p. (C). 1993. pap. text 15.50 (*0-393-96014-5*) Norton.

***Austen, Jane.** Emma. 3rd ed. LC 99-48830. (Illus.). 432p. 2000. pap. 15.50 (*0-393-97284-4*) Norton.

Austen, Jane. Favorite Jane Austen Novels: Pride & Prejudice, Sense & Sensibility, 3 vols. unabridged ed. 800p. pap., boxed set 6.00 (*0-486-29748-9*) Dover.

— Jane Austen. (Great Writers Ser.). (Illus.). 64p. 1993. 9.95 (*1-85410-260-5*, Pub. by Aurum Pr) London Brdge.

Austen, Jane. Jane Austen. abr. ed. 1983. mass mkt. 19.95 incl. audio (*1-85998-275-1*) Trafalgar.

Austen, Jane. Jane Austen. deluxe ed. 1136p. 1995. 19.99 (*0-517-14768-8*) Random Hse Value.

— Jane Austen: The Complete Novels. 1136p. 1994. 15.99 (*0-517-11829-7*) Random Hse Value.

— A Jane Austen Miscellany: Sisters, Suitors, Families & friends. Sommmer, Robin L. & Cleary, Kristen M., eds. 64p. 1996. 4.98 (*0-614-29845-8*) DoveTail Bks.

— A Jane Austen Miscellany: Sisters, Suitors, Families & friends. Cleary, Kristen Maree & Sommer, Robin Langley, eds. 1996. pap. write for info. (*0-9636673-8-6*) DoveTail Bks.

— Jane Austen Poems & Favourite Poems. (Everyman's Library). 1998. mass mkt. 3.50 (*0-460-87959-6*, Everyman's Classic Lib) Tuttle Pubng.

— Jane Austen's Christmas: The Festive Season in Georgian England. (Illus.). 128p. 1996. pap. 19.95 (*0-7509-1307-X*, Pub. by Sutton Pub Ltd) Intl Pubs Mktg.

— Jane Austen's Lady Susan: A Facsimile of the Manuscript in the Pierpont Morgan Library. 368p. 1989. reprint ed. text 30.00 (*0-8240-3435-X*) Garland.

— Jane Austen's Letters. 3rd ed. Le Faye, Deirdre, ed. 672p. 1995. text 55.00 (*0-19-811764-7*) OUP.

— Jane Austen's Letters. 3rd ed. Le Faye, Deirdre, ed. LC 96-38253. 672p. 1997. pap. 19.95 (*0-19-283297-2*) OUP.

— Jane Austen's Manuscript Letters in Facsimile: Reproductions of Every Known Extant Letter, Fragment, & Autograph Copy, with an Annotated List of All Known Letters. Modert, Jo, ed. LC 88-39599. (Illus.). 572p. (C). 1989. 60.00 (*0-8093-1403-7*) S Ill U Pr.

— Jane Austen's Sir Charles Grandison. Southam, Brian, ed. (Illus.). 164p. 1981. text 28.00 (*0-19-812637-9*) OUP.

— Jane Austen's the History of England: From the Reign of Henry the Fourth to the Death of Charles the First. LC 93-17637. (Illus.). 60p. 1993. 14.95 (*1-56512-055-8*) Algonquin Bks.

— Lady Susan. (The Jane Austen Library). (C). 1984. text 37.50 (*0-485-10500-4*, Pub. by Athlone Pr) Humanities.

— Lady Susan, the Watsons, Sanditon. Drabble, Margaret, ed. (English Library). 224p. 1975. pap. 7.95 (*0-14-043102-0*, Penguin Classics) Viking Penguin.

— Mansfield Park. 227p. Date not set. 21.95 (*0-8488-2533-0*) Amereon Ltd.

— Mansfield Park. 400p. 1983. mass mkt. 4.95 (*0-553-21276-1*, Bantam Classics) Bantam.

— Mansfield Park. 1987. lib. bdg. 20.95 (*0-89966-244-7*) Buccaneer Bks.

***Austen, Jane.** Mansfield Park. 419p. 1999. pap. 10.95 (*0-7868-8524-6*, Pub. by Disney Pr) Time Warner.

Austen, Jane. Mansfield Park. LC 97-24777. 496p. 1997. 18.50 (*0-385-48726-6*) Doubleday.

— Mansfield Park. 1992. 20.00 (*0-679-41269-7*) Everymns Lib.

— Mansfield Park. (Cloth Bound Pocket Ser.). 240p. 1998. 7.95 (*3-89508-459-X*) Konemann.

— Mansfield Park. 1995. 15.50 (*0-679-60194-5*) Modern Lib NY.

— Mansfield Park. 1996. mass mkt. 4.95 (*0-451-52629-5*, Sig Classics) NAL.

— Mansfield Park. Johnson, Claudia L., ed. LC 96-49462. (Critical Editions Ser.). (C). 1998. pap. text 11.25 (*0-393-96791-3*, Norton Paperbks) Norton.

An Asterisk (*) at the beginning of an entry indicates that the title is appearing for the first time.

— Mansfield Park. Kinsley, James, ed. (Oxford World's Classics Ser.). 474p. 1998. pap. 5.95 (*0-19-283363-4*) OUP.
— Mansfield Park. (Signet Classics). 1996. 10.05 (*0-606-03852-3*, Pub. by Turtleback) Demco.
— Mansfield Park. Norris, Pamela, ed. 512p. 1993. pap. 3.95 (*0-460-87294-X*, Everyman's Classic Lib) Tuttle Pubng.
— Mansfield Park. Sutherland, Kathryn, ed. LC 95-72351. 464p. 1996. pap. 6.95 (*0-14-043414-3*, Viking) Viking Penguin.
— Mansfield Park. (Classics Library). 345p. 1998. pap. 3.95 (*1-85326-032-0*, 0320WW, Pub. by Wrdsworth Edits) NTC Contemp Pub Co.
— Mansfield Park. large type ed. 547p. 1988. 27.99 (*0-7089-8504-1*, Charnwood) Ulverscroft.
— Manuscript Chapters of Persuasion: Jane Austen Library. Chapman, R. W., ed. LC 85-6174. (C). 1985. text 37.50 (*0-485-10502-0*, Pub. by Athlone Pr) Humanities.
— Northanger Abbey. Date not set. lib. bdg. 20.95 (*0-8488-1244-1*) Amereon Ltd.
— Northanger Abbey. LC 99-215581. (Classics Ser.). 224p. 1985. mass mkt. 4.95 (*0-553-21197-8*) Bantam.
— Northanger Abbey. 320p. 1999. pap. 4.95 (*0-553-21494-2*, Bantam Classics) Bantam.
— Northanger Abbey. Grogan, Claire, ed. 276p. (C). 1996. pap. text 7.95 (*1-55111-078-4*) Broadview Pr.
***Austen, Jane.** Northanger Abbey. 2000. pap. 2.00 (*0-486-41412-4*) Dover.
Austen, Jane. Northanger Abbey. LC 92-52895. 1992. 15.00 (*0-679-41715-X*) Everymns Lib.
***Austen, Jane.** Northanger Abbey. 290p. 2000. pap. 11.95 (*1-892295-92-X*) Green Integer.
— Northanger Abbey. (Cloth Bound Pocket Ser.). 1999. 7.95 (*3-8290-3001-0*) Konemann.
Austen, Jane. Northanger Abbey. 1995. 13.50 (*0-679-60192-9*) Modern Lib NY.
— Northanger Abbey. 1996. mass mkt. 4.95 (*0-451-52636-8*) NAL.
— Northanger Abbey. 304p. 1994. 3.95 (*0-460-87434-9*, Everyman's Classic Lib) Tuttle Pubng.
— Northanger Abbey. Butler, Marilyn, ed. 288p. 1996. pap. 6.95 (*0-14-043413-5*) Viking Penguin.
— Northanger Abbey. (Classics Library). 167p. 1998. pap. 3.95 (*1-85326-043-6*, 0436WW, Pub. by Wrdsworth Edits) NTC Contemp Pub Co.
— Northanger Abbey. large type ed. (Isis Clear Type Classic Ser.). 234p. 1991. 24.95 (*1-85089-434-5*, Pub. by ISIS Lrg Prnt) Transaction Pubs.
— Northanger Abbey. large type ed. (Large Print Heritage Ser.). 357p. 1998. lib. bdg. 33.95 (*1-58118-030-6*, 22022) LRS.
— Northanger Abbey. large type ed. 359p. 1995. 27.99 (*0-7089-8876-8*, Charnwood) Ulverscroft.
— Northanger Abbey. large type ed. 370p. 2000. reprint ed. lib. bdg. 24.00 (*0-939495-48-1*) North Bks.
— Northanger Abbey. 220p. 1986. reprint ed. lib. bdg. 18.95 (*0-89966-534-9*) Buccaneer Bks.
***Austen, Jane.** Northanger Abbey. (Twelve-Point Ser.). 230p. 2000. reprint ed. lib. bdg. 24.00 (*1-58287-121-3*) North Bks.
Austen, Jane. Northanger Abbey, Lady Susan, the Watsons & Sandition. Davie, John, ed. & notes by. (Oxford World's Classics Ser.). 432p. 1998. pap. 5.95 (*0-19-283368-5*) OUP.
— The Oxford Illustrated Jane Austen, 6 vols. 3rd ed. Chapman, R. W., ed. Incl. Vol. I. Sense & Sensibility. 3rd ed. (Illus.). 446p. 1988. reprint ed. 20.00 (*0-19-254701-1*); Vol. III. Mansfield Park. 3rd ed. (Illus.). 580p. 1988. reprint ed. 20.00 (*0-19-254703-8*); Vol. IV. Emma. 3rd ed. (Illus.). 536p. 1988. reprint ed. 20.00 (*0-19-254704-6*); Vol. V. Northanger Abbey. 3rd ed. (Illus.). 624p. 1988. reprint ed. 20.00 (*0-19-254705-4*); Vol. VI. Minor Works. (Illus.). 504p. 1988. reprint ed. 20.00 (*0-19-254706-2*); (Illus.). 3,184p. 1988. 120.00 (*0-19-254707-0*) OUP.
— Oxford Progressive English Readers: Emma. 2nd ed. (Illus.). 62p. 1993. pap. text 5.95 (*0-19-585270-2*) OUP.
— Penguin Readers Level 3: Sense Sensibility. 48p. 1998. pap. 7.00 (*0-14-081634-8*) Viking Penguin.
— Persuasion. Harding, D. W., ed. (English Library). 400p. (C). 1998. pap. 5.95 (*0-14-043005-9*) Addson-Wesley Educ.
— Persuasion. 122p. Date not set. 17.95 (*0-8488-2542-X*) Amereon Ltd.
— Persuasion. 240p. 1984. mass mkt. 3.95 (*0-553-21137-4*, Bantam Classics) Bantam.
— Persuasion. Bree, Linda, ed. LC 98-231555. (Literary Texts Ser.). (Illus.). 306p. 1998. pap. text 7.95 (*1-55111-131-4*) Broadview Pr.
— Persuasion. (Cloth Bound Pocket Ser.). 350p. 1998. 7.95 (*3-8290-0901-1*, 520664) Konemann.
— Persuasion. 1992. 15.00 (*0-679-40986-6*) McKay.
— Persuasion. 1995. 13.50 (*0-679-60191-0*) Modern Lib NY.
— Persuasion. 1996. mass mkt. 4.95 (*0-451-52638-4*) NAL.
— Persuasion. Spacks, Patricia M., ed. LC 94-4510. (Critical Editions Ser.). 316p. (C). 1994. pap. text 9.75 (*0-393-96018-8*) Norton.
— Persuasion. Davie, John, ed. (Oxford World's Classics Ser.). 302p. 1998. pap. 4.95 (*0-19-283361-8*) OUP.
***Austen, Jane.** Persuasion. 256p. 1999. mass mkt. 2.99 (*0-8125-6588-6*, Pub. by Tor Bks) St Martin.
Austen, Jane. Persuasion. 1984. 9.05 (*0-606-02200-7*, Pub. by Turtleback) Demco.
— Persuasion. Beer, Gillian, ed. & intro. by. LC 99-228376. 236p. (C). 1999. pap. write for info. (*0-14-043467-4*) Viking Penguin.
— Persuasion. (Classics Library). 224p. 1998. pap. 3.95 (*1-85326-056-8*, 0568WW, Pub. by Wrdsworth Edits) NTC Contemp Pub Co.
— Persuasion. large type ed. (Large Print Heritage Ser.). 371p. 1998. lib. bdg. 34.95 (*1-58118-027-6*, 22023) LRS.
— Persuasion. large type ed. 389p. 1990. 27.99 (*0-7089-8534-3*, Charnwood) Ulverscroft.
— Persuasion. large type ed. 405p. 1996. reprint ed. lib. bdg. 24.00 (*0-939495-04-X*) North Bks.
— Persuasion. 240p. 1986. reprint ed. lib. bdg. 18.95 (*0-89966-538-1*) Buccaneer Bks.
— Persuasion. LC 97-10948. 224p. 1997. reprint ed. pap. text 2.00 (*0-486-29555-9*) Dover.
— Persuasion. 243p. 1998. reprint ed. lib. bdg. 24.00 (*1-58287-055-1*) North Bks.
— Persuasion, Set. abr. ed. 1996. pap. 23.95 incl. audio (*0-14-086058-4*, 693419, Png AudioBks) Viking Penguin.
— Persuasion: Penguin Reader Level 2. 1998. pap. 7.00 (*0-14-081527-9*) Viking Penguin.
— The Poetry of Jane Austen & the Austen Family. Selwyn, David, ed. LC 96-61382. 124p. (Orig.). 1997. pap. 12.95 (*0-87745-580-5*) U of Iowa Pr.
— Pride & Prejudice. LC 95-69125. 352p. 1998. mass mkt. 4.95 (*0-451-52588-4*) Addson-Wesley Educ.
— Pride & Prejudice. (YA). Date not set. lib. bdg. 25.95 (*0-8488-0420-1*) Amereon Ltd.
— Pride & Prejudice. 304p. (YA). (gr. 9-12). 1983. mass mkt. 4.95 (*0-553-21310-5*, Bantam Classics) Bantam.
— Pride & Prejudice. 1991. mass mkt. 4.95 (*0-553-54088-2*) Bantam.
***Austen, Jane.** Pride & Prejudice. LC 99-25620. (Classic Novels). 392p. 1999. pap. text 8.95 (*0-7641-1147-7*) Barron.
Austen, Jane. Pride & Prejudice. Kendrick, Walter, ed. (Mcdonald Classics Ser.). 410p. (YA). 1980. 19.95 (*0-8464-1071-0*) Beekman Pubs.
— Pride & Prejudice. (YA). 1988. lib. bdg. 19.95 (*0-89966-243-9*) Buccaneer Bks.
— Pride & Prejudice. Bain, Richard, ed. LC 97-190825. (Literature Ser.). 384p. (C). 1996. pap. 11.95 (*0-521-57654-7*) Cambridge U Pr.
— Pride & Prejudice. 107p. 1942. pap. 5.50 (*0-87129-686-1*, P36) Dramatic Pub.
Austen, Jane. Pride & Prejudice. 327p. 1991. write for info. (*1-85715-001-5*) Everymns Lib.
— Pride & Prejudice, 001. Schorer, Mark, ed. LC 56-13877. (YA). (gr. 9 up). 1956. pap. 13.96 (*0-395-05101-0*, RivEd) HM.
Austen, Jane. Pride & Prejudice. (YA). 1997. pap. 8.25 (*0-03-051487-8*) Holt R&W.
— Pride & Prejudice. (Cloth Bound Pocket Ser.). 240p. 1998. 7.95 (*3-89508-207-4*) Konemann.
— Pride & Prejudice. Adams, Richard, ed. (Study Texts Ser.). (YA). 1983. pap. text 5.95 (*0-582-33086-6*, 72039) Longman.
— Pride & Prejudice. 368p. 1991. 17.00 (*0-679-40542-9*) Modern Lib NY.
***Austen, Jane.** Pride & Prejudice. (Classics Ser.). 2000. pap. 7.95 (*0-679-78326-1*) Modern Lib NY.
— Pride & Prejudice. (C). pap. text. write for info. (*0-393-99771-5*) Norton.
— Pride & Prejudice. Hedge, Tricia, ed. (Illus.). 112p. 1995. pap. text 5.95 (*0-19-422710-3*) OUP.
Austen, Jane. Pride & Prejudice. Kinsley, James, ed. (Oxford World's Classics Ser.). 390p. 1998. pap. 6.95 (*0-19-283355-3*) OUP.
— Pride & Prejudice. LC 99-462506. (Oxford World's Classics Hardcovers Ser.). 366p. 1999. 12.50 (*0-19-210026-2*) OUP.
Austen, Jane. Pride & Prejudice. 144p. 1996. pap. 20.00 (*81-209-0025-1*, Pub. by Pitambar Pub) St Mut.
Austen, Jane. Pride & Prejudice. (Short Classics Learning Files Ser.). (J). (gr. 4 up). 1988. 22.00 (*0-8172-2188-3*) Raintree Steck-V.
— Pride & Prejudice. (J). 1998. pap. 6.95 (*0-8114-6836-4*) Raintree Steck-V.
— Pride & Prejudice. (Illus.). 304p. 1995. 13.00 (*0-679-60168-6*) Random.
***Austen, Jane.** Pride & Prejudice. LC 92-50183. (Literary Classics Ser.). 368p. 1999. 8.98 (*0-7624-0550-3*) Running Pr.
Austen, Jane. Pride & Prejudice. Worrall, Andrew, ed. (Thornes Classic Novels Ser.). (Illus.). 376p. 1997. pap. 19.95 (*0-7487-2977-1*, Pub. by S Thornes Pubs) Trans-Atl Phila.
— Pride & Prejudice. (J). 1996. pap. 2.25 (*0-590-08576-X*) Scholastic Inc.
***Austen, Jane.** Pride & Prejudice. 416p. (YA). (gr. 7-12). 2000. pap. 4.99 (*0-439-10135-2*) Scholastic Inc.
Austen, Jane. Pride & Prejudice. 384p. 1994. pap. 2.50 (*0-8125-2336-9*, Pub. by Tor Bks) St Martin.
***Austen, Jane.** Pride & Prejudice. (Signature Classics Ser.). (Illus.). 352p. 1999. 24.95 (*1-58279-032-9*) Trident Pr Intl.
Austen, Jane. Pride & Prejudice. (J). 1997. pap. 2.95 (*0-89375-611-3*) Troll Communs.
Austen, Jane. Pride & Prejudice. 1950. 10.05 (*0-606-01933-2*, Pub. by Turtleback) Demco.
Austen, Jane. Pride & Prejudice. Norris, Pamela, ed. 384p. 1993. pap. 3.95 (*0-460-87212-5*, Everyman's Classic Lib) Tuttle Pubng.
— Pride & Prejudice. LC 97-140981. (Penguin Classics Ser.). 336p. 1996. pap. 7.95 (*0-14-043426-7*, Penguin Classics) Viking Penguin.
— Pride & Prejudice. (Classics Library). 265p. 1997. pap. 3.95 (*1-85326-000-2*, 0002WW, Pub. by Wrdsworth Edits) NTC Contemp Pub Co.
— Pride & Prejudice. abr. ed. (Puffin Classics Ser.). (Illus.). 384p. (YA). (gr. 5 up). 1995. pap. 4.99 (*0-14-037337-3*, PuffinBks) Peng Put Young Read.
Austen, Jane. Pride & Prejudice. abr. large type ed. (Great Illustrated Classics Ser.: Vol. 52). (Illus.). 240p. (gr. 3-7). 1996. 9.95 (*0-86611-871-3*) Playmore Inc.
— Pride & Prejudice. deluxe ed. (Signature Classics Ser.). (Illus.). 352p. 1999. 29.95 (*1-58279-044-2*) Trident Pr Intl.
Austen, Jane. Pride & Prejudice. large type ed. (Large Print Heritage Ser.). 560p. 1997. lib. bdg. 36.95 (*1-58118-009-8*, 21967) LRS.
— Pride & Prejudice. large type ed. 480p. 1998. lib. bdg. 24.00 (*0-939495-50-3*) North Bks.
— Pride & Prejudice. large type ed. 532p. (YA). 1984. 27.99 (*0-7089-8228-X*, Charnwood) Ulverscroft.
***Austen, Jane.** Pride And Prejudice. large type ed. 480p. 1999. pap. 20.00 (*0-06-093325-9*) HarpC.
Austen, Jane. Pride & Prejudice. 355p. 1998. reprint ed. lib. bdg. 24.00 (*1-58287-058-6*) North Bks.
— Pride & Prejudice. unabridged ed. (Classics Ser.). (YA). (gr. 10 up). 1962. mass mkt. 4.95 (*0-8049-0001-5*, CL-1) Airmont.
— Pride & Prejudice. unabridged ed. (Thrift Editions Ser.). 272p. 1995. pap. 2.00 (*0-486-28473-5*) Dover.
— Pride & Prejudice. 2nd ed. (Illus.). 126p. 1993. pap. text 5.95 (*0-19-585472-1*) OUP.
Austen, Jane. Pride & Prejudice. 3rd ed. (Norton Critical Editions Ser.). (C). pap. text. write for info. (*0-393-97604-1*) Norton.
Austen, Jane. Pride & Prejudice, Vol. II. 3rd ed. Chapman, R. W., ed. (Illus.). 430p. (YA). 1988. reprint ed. 20.00 (*0-19-254702-X*) OUP.
— Pride & Prejudice: An Authoritative Text, Backgrounds, Reviews, & Essays in Criticism. 2nd ed. Gray, Donald J., ed. LC 92-32426. (Critical Editions Ser.). (C). 1993. pap. text 12.50 (*0-393-96294-6*) Norton.
— Pride & Prejudice: Penguin Readers Level 5. 80p. 1998. pap. 7.00 (*0-14-081507-4*) Viking Penguin.
— Pride & Prejudice Readalong. (Illustrated Classics Collection 5). 64p. 1994. pap. 14.95 incl. audio (*0-7854-0801-0*, 40573) Am Guidance.
***Austen, Jane.** Sanditon. LC 98-34790. 320p. 1998. per. 12.00 (*0-684-84342-0*) S&S Trade Pap.
Austen, Jane. Sanditon. large type ed. 1998. 26.95 (*0-7838-0391-5*, G K Hall Lrg Type) Mac Lib Ref.
— Sanditon & Other Stories. LC 96-223593. 528p. 1996. 20.00 (*0-679-44719-9*) Everymns Lib.
— Selected Letters, 1796-1817. Chapman, R. W., ed. 254p. 1985. pap. 13.95 (*0-19-281485-0*) OUP.
— Sense & Sensibility. Ballaster, Ros, ed. & intro. by. 368p. (C). 1999. pap. text 4.00 (*0-14-043425-9*) Addison-Wesley.
— Sense & Sensibility. 181p. Date not set. 19.95 (*0-8488-2549-7*) Amereon Ltd.
— Sense & Sensibility. 352p. (YA). (gr. 9-12). 1982. mass mkt. 4.95 (*0-553-21334-2*, Bantam Classics) Bantam.
— Sense & Sensibility. 356p. 1996. (*0-7607-0043-5*); pap. (*0-7607-0045-1*) Barnes & Noble Inc.
— Sense & Sensibility. (Cloth Bound Pocket Ser.). 240p. 1998. 7.95 (*3-89508-233-3*) Konemann.
— Sense & Sensibility. 1992. 15.95 (*0-679-40987-4*) McKay.
— Sense & Sensibility. 1995. 14.50 (*0-679-60195-3*) Modern Lib NY.
— Sense & Sensibility. 320p. 1997. mass mkt. 4.95 (*0-451-52589-2*, Sig Classics) NAL.
— Sense & Sensibility. Kinsley, James, ed. (Oxford World's Classics Ser.). 398p. 1998. pap. 5.95 (*0-19-283352-8*) OUP.
— Sense & Sensibility. 380p. 1996. 17.00 (*0-676-50868-1*) Random.
— Sense & Sensibility. 1999. 8.98 (*0-7624-0566-X*) Running Pr.
— Sense & Sensibility. 1995. mass mkt. 2.99 (*0-8125-4312-2*, Pub. by Tor Bks) St Martin.
— Sense & Sensibility. 1961. 10.05 (*0-606-00959-0*, Pub. by Turtleback) Demco.
— Sense & Sensibility. 1983. 9.05 (*0-606-13771-8*, Pub. by Turtleback) Demco.
— Sense & Sensibility. Todd, Janet, ed. (Everyman Paperback Classics). 416p. 1997. pap. 4.95 (*0-460-87914-6*, Everyman's Classic Lib) Tuttle Pubng.
— Sense & Sensibility. (Classics Library). 336p. 1998. pap. 3.95 (*1-85326-016-9*, 0169WW, Pub. by Wrdsworth Edits) NTC Contemp Pub Co.
— Sense & Sensibility. large type ed. 501p. 1985. 27.99 (*0-7089-8246-8*, Charnwood) Ulverscroft.
— Sense & Sensibility. large type ed. 465p. 1997. reprint ed. lib. bdg. 24.00 (*0-939495-09-0*) North Bks.
— Sense & Sensibility. 544p. (YA). 1981. reprint ed. lib. bdg. 18.95 (*0-89966-287-0*) Buccaneer Bks.
— Sense & Sensibility. 363p. 1998. reprint ed. lib. bdg. 24.00 (*1-58287-070-5*) North Bks.
— Sense & Sensibility. unabridged ed. LC 95-49594. (Thrift Editions Ser.). 272p. 1996. reprint ed. pap. text 2.00 (*0-486-29049-2*) Dover.
***Austen, Jane.** Sentido & Sensibilidad. (SPA.). 1998. pap. 6.95 (*84-01-46292-4*, Pub. by Plaza) Lectorum Pubns.
Austen, Jane. A Transcription & Analysis of Jane Austen's Last Work, Sanditon. Sacco, Teran Lee, ed. LC 94-46935. 200p. 1995. text 79.95 (*0-7734-8995-9*) E Mellen.
— The Watsons. Chapman, R. W., ed. LC 85-7352. (Jane Austen Library: vol. 4). 164p. (C). 1985. reprint ed. text 25.00 (*0-485-10503-9*, Pub. by Athlone Pr) Humanities.
— The Watsons. LC 72-9808. 318p. 1973. reprint ed. lib. bdg. 65.00 (*0-8371-6598-9*, AUTW, Greenwood Pr) Greenwood.
— The Works of Jane Austen. 882p. 1995. pap. write for info. (*1-57215-131-5*) World Pubns.
— York Notes: Mansfield Park. 1992. pap. text. write for info. (*0-582-03967-3*, Pub. by Addison-Wesley) Longman.
Austen, Jane & Bronte, Charlotte. The Juvenilia of Jane Austen & Charlotte Bronte. Beer, Frances, ed. 400p. 1986. pap. 9.95 (*0-14-043267-1*, Penguin Classics) Viking Penguin.
***Austen, Jane & Kerrigan, Michael.** Pride & Prejudice. (Literature Made Easy Ser.). (Illus.). 96p. (YA). 1999. pap. 4.95 (*0-7641-0834-4*) Barron.
Austen, Jane, et al. Bite-Size Jane Austen: Sense & Sensibility from one of England's Greatest Writers. LC 99-17699. 112p. 1999. text 13.95 (*0-312-20501-5*) St Martin.
— Jane Austen's Little Advice Book. LC 96-8432. 144p. 1996. 15.00 (*0-06-018707-7*) HarpC.
Austen, Jane, jt. auth. see Aiken, Joan.
Austen, Jane, jt. auth. see Barrett, Julia, pseud.
Austen, Jane, jt. auth. see Billington, Rachel.
Austen, Jane, jt. auth. see Tennant, Emma.
Austen, Jane, jt. auth. see Thompson, Emma.
Austen, Jayne, tr. see Bataille, Georges.
***Austen, K. F., et al.** Therapeutic Immunology. 2nd rev. ed. (Illus.). 720p. 2000. 199.95 (*0-632-04359-8*) Blackwell Sci.
Austen, K. Frank, et al, eds. Therapeutic Immunology. (Illus.). 650p. 1996. 215.00 (*0-86542-375-X*) Blackwell Sci.
Austen, K. Frank, jt. ed. see Galli, Stephen J.
***Austen, Kay & Caulfield, Myra, eds.** Rocky Horrors. (Illus.). 160p. 2000. pap. 12.95 (*0-9686661-0-8*) PA Prodns.
Austen-Leigh, James E. Memoir of Jane Austen, by Her Nephew. (BCL1-PR English Literature Ser.). 235p. 1992. reprint ed. lib. bdg. 79.00 (*0-7812-7428-1*) Rprt Serv.
Austen-Leigh, William. Jane Austen: Her Life & Letters, a Family Record. (BCL1-PR English Literature Ser.). 437p. 1992. reprint ed. lib. bdg. 99.00 (*0-7812-7427-3*) Rprt Serv.
***Austen, Mark & Richards, Tamara, eds.** Basic Legal Documents on International Animal Welfare & Wildlife Conservation. 720p. 2000. text 240.00 (*90-411-9780-X*) Kluwer Law Intl.
Austen, Ralph A. African Economic History: Internal Development & External Dependency. LC 86-25639. 294p. (Orig.). (C). 1987. pap. text 25.00 (*0-435-08017-2*, 08017) Heinemann.
— The Elusive Epic: Text & History in the Oral Narrative of Jeki la Njambe (Cameroon Coast) LC 95-37299. (African Historical Sources Ser.: Vol. 13). 1996. pap. 20.00 (*0-918456-75-4*) African Studies Assn.
Austen, Ralph A., ed. In Search of Sunjata: The Mande Oral Epic As History, Literature, & Performance. 1998. pap. 18.95 (*0-253-21248-0*); lib. bdg. 49.95 (*0-253-33452-7*) Ind U Pr.
Austen, Ralph A. & Derrick, Jonathan M. Middlemen of the Cameroon Rivers: The Duala & Their Hinterland, c.1600 - c.1960. (African Studies: No. 96). (Illus.). 270p. (C). 1999. text 64.95 (*0-521-56228-7*); pap. text 24.95 (*0-521-56664-9*) Cambridge U Pr.
Austen, Roger. Genteel Pagan: The Double Life of Charles Warren Stoddard. Crowley, John W., ed. LC 91-8502. (Illus.). 256p. 1995. pap. 17.95 (*0-87023-980-5*) U of Mass Pr.
Austen, Rolf. Personal Financial Planning: The Advisor's Guide. 3rd ed. Norris, Lawrence, ed. LC 98-173139. xxvi, 476p. 1998. 65.00 (*0-8080-0264-3*) CCH INC.
Austen, Ruth. Riverside: The Heritage, the People, the Vision. (Illus.). 152p. 1996. 39.00 (*1-885352-24-7*) Community Comm.
— Riverside City Business Profiles: Riverside, CA. 1996. pap. text 19.95 (*1-885352-26-3*) Community Comm.
Austen, S. Desires Unlimited. 1997. mass mkt. 6.95 (*0-7472-5630-6*, Pub. by Headline Bk Pub) Trafalgar.
— Maids in Heaven. mass mkt. 6.95 (*0-7472-4663-7*, Pub. by Headline Bk Pub) Trafalgar.
Austen-Smith, David & Banks, Jeffrey S. Positive Political Theory I: Collective Preference. (Illus.). 224p. (C). pap. text 19.95 (*0-472-08721-5*, 08721) U of Mich Pr.
Austen-Smith, David & Banks, Jeffrey S. Positive Political Theory I: Collective Preference. (Studies in Political Analysis). 224p. 1998. text 39.50 (*0-472-10480-2*, 10480) U of Mich Pr.
Austenat, E. & Stahl, T. Insulin Pump Therapy: Indication-Method-Technology. (Illus.). xii, 187p. (C). 1990. pap. 98.50 (*3-11-012265-0*) De Gruyter.
Auster, Albert. Actresses & Suffragists: Women in the American Theatre, 1890-1920. LC 83-19253. 177p. 1984. 52.95 (*0-275-91731-2*, C1731, Praeger Pubs) Greenwood.
Auster, Albert & Quart, Leonard. American Film & Society since 1945. rev. ed. LC 90-24128. 208p. 1991. pap. 19.95 (*0-275-93327-X*, B3327, Praeger Pubs) Greenwood.
— American Film & Society since 1945. 2nd rev. ed. LC 90-24128. 200p. 1991. 55.00 (*0-275-93326-1*, C3326, Praeger Pubs) Greenwood.
Auster, Albert & Quart, Leonard. How the War Was Remembered: Hollywood & Vietnam. LC 87-36125. 186p. 1988. 45.00 (*0-275-92383-5*, C2383, Praeger Pubs); pap. 16.95 (*0-275-92479-3*, B2479, Praeger Pubs) Greenwood.
Auster, Benjamin. I Like It When... 32p. (J). (ps-3). 1995. pap. text 4.95 (*0-8114-6742-2*) Raintree Steck-V.
— I Like It When . . . (Ready-Set-Read Ser.). (Illus.). 32p. (J). (ps-3). 1990. lib. bdg. 21.40 (*0-8172-3578-7*) Raintree Steck-V.
Auster, Carol J. The Sociology of Work: Concepts & Cases. LC 95-20396. 1996. pap. 36.95 (*0-8039-9033-2*) Pine Forge.
Auster, Ethel, ed. Managing Online Reference Services. LC 85-21542. 408p. 1986. pap. text 45.00 (*0-918212-93-6*) Neal-Schuman.

A

A

Auster, Ethel & Chun Wei Choo, eds. Managing Information for the Competitive Edge. 554p. 1996. pap. 82.50 (*1-55570-215-5*) Neal-Schuman.

Auster, Henry. Local Habitations: Regionalism in the Early Novels of George Eliot. LC 74-116734. 244p. 1970. reprint ed. pap. 75.70 (*0-7837-2218-4*, 205730800004) Bks Demand.

Auster, Lawrence. The Path to National Suicide: An Essay on Immigration & Multiculturalism. 96p. (Orig.). 1990. pap. text 3.00 (*0-936247-12-6*) Amer Immigration.

Auster, Paul. The Art of Hunger. 312p. 1991. 24.95 (*1-55713-056-6*) Sun & Moon CA.

— Art of Hunger. LC 97-200892. 400p. 1997. pap. 13.95 (*0-14-026750-6*) Viking Penguin.

— City of Glass. 208p. 1987. pap. 12.95 (*0-14-009731-7*, Penguin Bks) Viking Penguin.

— Disappearances. 96p. 1989. pap. 12.95 (*0-87951-341-1*, Pub. by Overlook Pr) Penguin Putnam.

— Disappearances: Selected Poems. 96p. 1988. 16.95 (*0-87951-328-4*, Pub. by Overlook Pr) Penguin Putnam.

— Dream Days in Hotel. 1999. pap. 20.95 (*0-670-85210-4*) Viking Penguin.

— Facing the Music. 1980. pap. 20.00 (*0-930794-29-X*) Station Hill Pr.

— Ghosts. (New American Fiction Ser.: No. 5). 102p. 1986. 12.95 (*0-940650-70-3*) Sun & Moon CA.

— Hand to Mouth: A Chronicle of Early Failure. LC 97-7. 449p. 1997. 25.00 (*0-8050-5406-5*) H Holt & Co.

— Hand to Mouth: A Chronicle of Early Failure. (Illus.). 464p. 1998. pap. 14.95 (*0-8050-5489-8*) H Holt & Co.

— In the Country of Last Things. 208p. 1988. pap. 12.95 (*0-14-009705-8*, Penguin Bks) Viking Penguin.

— The Invention of Solitude. 176p. (Orig.). 1988. pap. 12.95 (*0-14-010628-6*, Penguin Bks) Viking Penguin.

— Leviathan. 272p. 1993. pap. 12.95 (*0-14-017813-9*, Penguin Bks); pap. 11.00 (*0-14-017958-5*) Viking Penguin.

— Lulu on the Bridge. LC 98-17750. (Illus.). 304p. 1998. pap. 15.00 (*0-8050-5978-4*, Owl) H Holt & Co.

— Mr. Vertigo. 256p. 1995. pap. 12.95 (*0-14-023190-0*, Penguin Bks) Viking Penguin.

— Moon Palace. 320p. 1990. pap. 12.95 (*0-14-011585-4*, Penguin Bks) Viking Penguin.

— The Music of Chance. (Contemporay American Fiction Ser.). 224p. 1991. reprint ed. pap. 12.95 (*0-14-015407-8*, Penguin Bks) Viking Penguin.

— The New York Trilogy: City of Glass; Ghosts; The Locked Room. LC 89-70997. (Illus.). 448p. 1990. pap. 20.99 (*0-14-013155-8*, Penguin Bks) Viking Penguin.

— The New York Trilogy: City of Glass; Ghosts; The Locked Room. rev. ed. (New American Fiction Ser.: No. 4-6). 472p. 1995. 21.95 (*1-55713-166-X*) Sun & Moon CA.

— Smoke & Blue in the Face: Two Films. (Illus.). 304p. (J). 1995. pap. 12.45 (*0-7868-8098-8*, Pub. by Hyperion) Time Warner.

***Auster, Paul.** Timbuktu. LC 98-46742. 192p. 1999. 23.00 (*0-8050-5407-3*) H Holt & Co.

— Timbuktu. 2000. mass mkt. 7.99 (*0-312-97528-7*) St Martin.

— Timbuktu. LC 00-25190. 192p. 2000. pap. 11.00 (*0-312-26399-6*, Picador USA) St Martin.

Auster, Paul. Translations. 300p. 1996. 28.00 (*1-56886-032-3*); pap. 14.95 (*1-56886-033-1*) Marsilio Pubs.

— Why Write? Personal Essays. LC 96-5350. (Illus.). 64p. 1996. 20.00 (*1-886224-15-3*) Burning Deck.

Auster, Paul, ed. The Random House Book of Twentieth-Century French Poetry: With Translations by American & British Poets. LC 82-17342. 688p. 1984. pap. 26.00 (*0-394-71748-1*) Vin Bks.

Auster, Paul & Blickle, Frieder. Paul Auster's New York. LC 97-11756. 1997. 0.01 (*0-8050-5667-X*) H Holt & Co.

Auster, Paul & Spiegelman, Art. City of Glass. Callahan, Bob, ed. (Neon Lit Ser.). (Illus.). 144p. 1994. reprint ed. pap. 12.50 (*0-380-77108-X*, Avon Bks) Morrow Avon.

Auster, Paul, et al. The Poetry of Anthony Barnett. Barnett, Anthony, tr. (FRE, ITA & RUS.). 192p. (Orig.). 1993. pap. write for info. (*0-907954-21-9*, Pub. by Allardyce Barnett) SPD-Small Pr Dist.

Auster, Paul, tr. see Blanchot, Maurice.

Auster, Paul, tr. see Clastres, Pierre.

Auster, Paul, tr. see Dupin, Jacques.

Auster, Paul, tr. see Friedlander, Saul & Hussein, Mahmoud.

Auster, Paul, tr. see Miro, Joan.

Auster, Paul, tr. & frwd. see Clastres, Pierre.

Auster, Rolf. Personal Financial Planning: The Adviser's Guide. 2nd ed. 576p. 1993. pap. 49.50 (*0-8080-0003-9*, BLS-3256) CCH INC.

Austerlitz, Howard. Data Acquisition Techniques Using Personal Computers. (Illus.). 316p. (C). 1991. text 67.00 (*0-12-068370-9*) Acad Pr.

Austerlitz, Paul. Merengue: Dominican Music & Dominican Identity. LC 96-24778. (Illus.). 224p. (Orig.). 1997. 69.95 (*1-56639-483-X*); pap. 22.95 (*1-56639-484-8*) Temple U Pr.

Austerlitz, Robert, ed. The Scope of American Linguistics: The First Golden Anniversary Symposium of the Linguistic Society of America. v, 209p. (Orig.). (C). 1975. pap. text 46.15 (*3-11-013343-1*) Mouton.

Austerman, Wayne R. Sharps Rifles & Spanish Mules: The San Antonio-El Paso Mail, 1851-1881. LC 84-40557. (Illus.). 336p. 1985. 34.95 (*0-89096-220-0*) Tex A&M Univ Pr.

Austern, David T., jt. auth. see Steinberg, Sheldon S.

Austern, Esther. Silence Is Thy Praise. 15.99 (*0-89906-568-6*, SILH); pap. 12.99 (*0-89906-569-4*, SILP) Mesorah Pubns.

Austern, Linda P. Music in English Children's Drama, 1597-1613. LC 92-14000. 374p. 1992. text 30.00 (*2-88124-558-7*) Gordon & Breach.

— Music in English Children's Drama of the Later Renaissance. (Musicology: A Book Ser.). 374p. 1992. pap. text 14.00 (*2-88124-564-1*) Gordon & Breach.

Austern, Matthew H. Generic Programming & the STL: Using & Extending the C++ Standard Template Library. LC 98-29950. (Addison-Wesley Professional Computing). 576p. (C). 1998. 49.95 (*0-201-30956-4*) Addison-Wesley.

Austern, Norman. Direct Nuclear Reaction Theories. LC 78-100327. (Interscience Monographs & Texts in Physics & Astronomy: Vol. 25). 400p. reprint ed. pap. 124.00 (*0-608-30484-0*, 200634300058) Bks Demand.

Austic, Richard E. & Nesheim, Malden C. Poultry Production. 13th ed. LC 89-35186. (Illus.). 325p. 1990. pap. text 47.50 (*0-8121-1241-5*) Lppncott W & W.

***Austin.** Audio in Media. 6th ed. 2001. text 57.00 (*0-534-54804-0*) Thomson Learn.

Austin. Math of Money. 2nd ed. Date not set. pap. text, teacher ed. write for info. (*0-314-09464-4*) West Pub.

— Math of Money. 2nd ed. 1994. mass mkt., wbk. ed. 26.75 (*0-314-04648-8*) West Pub.

— My Favorite American Quick Print. 328p. (C). 1998. pap. text 18.50 (*0-536-00649-0*) Pearson Custom.

— My Favorite American Stories. 328p. (C). 1998. pap. text 26.50 (*0-536-01165-6*) Pearson Custom.

***Austin.** PKI Essentials: Implementing & Planning Digital Certificate Systems. 384p. 2000. pap. 44.99 (*0-471-35380-9*) Wiley.

Austin. Technical Math. 4th ed. (C). 1988. pap. text, teacher ed. 34.00 (*0-03-013232-0*) Harcourt Coll Pubs.

— To Greet the Dawn. 2000. text 22.95 (*0-312-86436-1*) St Martin.

Austin & Howard. Mathematics of Money. 21st ed. (Um - International Math Ser.). 1994. pap. 56.25 (*0-314-02948-6*) West Pub.

Austin & Lett. How to Write the Perfect Ballot: A Handbook for Judging High School Speech & Debate Tournaments. LC 99-181760. 98p. (C). 1998. spiral bd. 16.95 (*0-7872-5274-3*, 41527401) Kendall-Hunt.

Austin & Nelson. Beginner's Guide Microsoft Office 97. 1997. pap. text 19.99 (*1-57671-012-2*) INST Publishing.

Austin, et al. Born to Sing Deluxe Voice Training Course. unabridged ed. (YA). 1985. pap. 39.95 incl. audio (*0-934419-03-5*, SO1985) Audio-Forum.

— Quarterly Review of Literature: The 1940s, Poetry. (Poetry Ser.: Vol. III, No. 2). 1940. pap. 15.00 (*1-888545-18-6*) Quarterly Rev.

Austin, jt. auth. see Cheney.

Austin, jt. auth. see Davies.

Austin, jt. auth. see Irwin.

***Austin & Company Inc. Staff.** Courage of Sarah Noble Literature. 2000. pap. 7.95 (*1-57690-642-6*) Tchr Create Mat.

***Austin & Company Inc. Staff, contrib. by.** Meeting Writing Standards: Descriptive Writing Intermediate. 144p. 2000. pap. 14.95 (*1-57690-991-3*) Tchr Create Mat.

— Meeting Writing Standards: Enhancing Writing with Visuals. 144p. 2000. pap. 14.95 (*1-57690-993-X*) Tchr Create Mat.

Austin, A. J., jt. auth. see Bova, Ben.

Austin, Alan, jt. auth. see Cruickshank, Gordon.

Austin, Alfred. Autobiography of Alfred Austin, Poet Laureate, 1835-1910, 2 vols. in 1. LC 79-148744. (Illus.). reprint ed. 46.50 (*0-404-08717-5*) AMS Pr.

— Bridling of Pegasus: Prose Papers on Poetry. LC 67-22053. (Essay Index Reprint Ser.). 1977. 20.95 (*0-8369-0164-9*) Ayer.

Austin, Alfred L. The Rabbit on the Face of the Moon: Mythology in the Mesoamerican Tradition. Ortiz De Montellano, Bernard R. & Ortiz De Montellano, Thelma, trs. (Illus.). 144p. 1996. pap. 14.95 (*0-87480-527-9*) U of Utah Pr.

Austin, Alfredo L. The Rabbit on the Face of the Moon: Mythology in the Mesoamerican Tradition. Ortiz De Montellano, Bernard R. & Ortiz De Montellano, Thelma, trs. (Illus.). 144p. 1996. text 35.00 (*0-87480-521-X*) U of Utah Pr.

— Tamoanchan, Tlalocan: Places of Mist. Ortiz De Montellano, Thelma & Ortiz De Montellano, Bernard R., trs. LC 96-53289. (Mesoamerican Worlds Ser.). (Illus.). 440p. 1997. 34.95 (*0-87081-445-1*) Univ Pr Colo.

— Tamoanchan y Tlalocan. (SPA.). 261p. 1994. 24.99 (*968-16-4574-X*, Pub. by Fondo) Continental Bk.

Austin, Alfredo Lopez, see Lopez Austin, Alfredo.

Austin, Alin. 100 Hundred Things to Always Remember. . . And One Thing to Never Forget. LC 93-25766. (Illus.). 64p. 1993. pap. 8.95 (*0-88396-373-6*) Blue Mtn Art.

Austin, Allan D., ed. African Muslims in Antebellum America: Proud Exiles. (Illus.). 205p. 1997. pap. 18.99 (*0-415-91270-9*) Routledge.

— African Muslims in Antebellum America: Proud Exiles. (Illus.). 207p. (C). 1997. 75.00 (*0-415-91269-5*) Routledge.

Austin, Allan D., ed. see Kaplan, Sidney.

Austin, Allan E. Elizabeth Bowen. rev. ed. (English Authors Ser.: No. 123). 120p. (C). 1989. 32.00 (*0-8057-6972-2*, TEAS 123) Macmillan.

Austin, Allan L. Strategies for Managing Change: Practical Tools to Help You Make the Right Decisions. (Financial Times Management Ser.). 256p. 1995. 72.50 (*0-273-60194-6*, Pub. by Pitman Pub) Trans-Atl Phila.

Austin, Alvyn J. Saving China: Canadian Missionaries in the Middle Kingdom, 1888-1959. LC BV3415.2.A87. 413p. reprint ed. pap. 128.10 (*0-7837-0604-9*, 204095200019) Bks Demand.

Austin, Ann E. & Baldwin, Roger G. Faculty Collaboration: Enhancing the Quality of Scholarship & Teaching. Fife, Jonathan D., ed. LC 92-81699. (ASHE-ERIC Higher Education Reports: No. 91-7). 108p. (Orig.). 1992. pap. text 24.00 (*1-878380-12-5*) GWU Grad Schl E&HD.

Austin, Ann E., jt. ed. see Sorcinelli, Mary D.

***Austin, Annemarie.** Door upon Door. 64p. 2000. pap. 16.95 (*1-85224-459-3*, Pub. by Bloodaxe Bks) Dufour.

Austin, Annemarie. The Flaying of Marsyas. 64p. 1996. pap. 16.95 (*1-85224-328-7*, Pub. by Bloodaxe Bks) Dufour.

— On the Border. 64p. 1994. pap. 12.95 (*1-85224-214-0*, Pub. by Bloodaxe Bks) Dufour.

***Austin, Anthony & Crowley, Brian.** The Dragon's Tail: Rediscovering the Tenth Planet. (Illus.). 248p. 2000. pap. 18.95 (*1-881532-22-4*) IllumiNet Pr.

Austin, Arthur. The Empire Strikes Back: Outsiders & the Struggle over Legal Education. LC 98-9046. (Critical America Ser.). 1998. pap. 30.00 (*0-8147-0651-7*); text 30.00 (*0-8147-0650-9*) NYU Pr.

Austin, Arthur D. Complex Litigation Confronts the Jury System: A Case Study. LC 84-19500. 111p. 1984. lib. bdg. 59.95 (*0-313-27099-6*, U7099, Greenwood Pr) Greenwood.

— In Stalin's Secret Service. LC 84-27122. (Foreign Intelligence Book Ser.). 273p. 1985. reprint ed. lib. bdg. 55.00 (*0-313-27026-0*, U7026, Greenwood Pr) Greenwood.

Austin, Aurelia. Georgia Boys with "Stonewall" Jackson: James Thomas Thompson & the Walton Infantry. LC 67-31515. 115p. reprint ed. pap. 35.70 (*0-608-15798-8*, 203104700073) Bks Demand.

Austin, B., et al, eds. The Genus Aeromonas. LC 96-5722. 364p. 1997. 176.95 (*0-471-96741-6*) Wiley.

Austin, B. & Austin, D. Bacterial Fish Pathogens: Diseases of Farmed & Wild Fish. 3rd rev. ed. LC 98-52790. 500p. 1999. 189.00 (*1-85233-120-8*) Spr-Verlag.

Austin, B. & Austin, D. A. Bacterial Fish Pathogens: Disease in Farmed & Wild Fish. LC 86-21375. (Aquaculture & Fisheries Support Ser.). 364p. 1987. text 68.95 (*0-470-20765-5*) P-H.

Austin, B. & Austin, D. A., eds. Methods for the Microbial Examination of Shellfish. 1989. text 89.95 (*0-470-21486-4*) P-H.

***Austin, B., et al.** Pathological Diagnosis of Vascular Diseases. 400p. 1999. 165.00 (*2-287-59660-7*) Spr-Verlag.

Austin, B., jt. auth. see Mothersill, C.

Austin, Bertram, Jr. & Lloyd, W. Francis. The Secret of High Wages. Chandler, Alfred D., ed. LC 79-7529. (History of Management Thought & Practice Ser.). 1980. reprint ed. lib. bdg. 15.95 (*0-405-12314-0*) Ayer.

Austin, Betty. J. William Fulbright: A Bibliography, 22. LC 94-38435. (Bibliographies & Indexes in Law & Political Science Ser.: Vol. 22). 216p. 1995. lib. bdg. 69.50 (*0-313-26336-1*, Greenwood Pr) Greenwood.

Austin, Bliss. Bibliomania. LC 97-5013. 50p. 1996. pap. 8.00 (*1-896648-74-6*) Battered Silicon.

Austin, Bobby. Los Fundamentos De la Gracia. 182p. 1993. pap. write for info. (*0-9639640-0-3*) Grace Vision.

Austin, Bobby, ed. see Moody, et al.

Austin, Bobby W. The Principles of Grace. rev. ed. 175p. 1995. pap. write for info. (*0-9639640-3-8*) Grace Vision.

— Repairing the Breach: A Report from the National Task Force on African American Men & Boys. 272p. 1996. pap. text 13.95 (*1-879360-45-4*) Noble Pr.

Austin, Bobby W., ed. Repairing the Breach. LC 96-17532. 288p. 1996. 34.95 (*0-931712-21-1*) Alpine Guild.

Austin, Bobby W., ed. see Mackay, W. P.

Austin, Bobby W., ed. & intro. see Moody, Spurgeon, Whitefield, MacKay Staff.

Austin, Brendan, ed. Proceedings of the 31st Meeting of the European High Pressure Research Group. 368p. 1995. pap. text 653.00 (*2-88449-024-8*) Gordon & Breach.

Austin, Brett. Arizona Saddles. large type ed. (Linford Western Library). 1991. pap. 16.99 (*0-7089-7017-6*) Ulverscroft.

— Two Sons of Satan. large type ed. (Linford Western Library). 304p. 1994. pap. 16.99 (*0-7089-7572-0*, Linford) Ulverscroft.

Austin, Brian. Bacterial Fish Pathogens. 301p. 1990. 130.00 (*0-13-065756-5*, Prentice Hall) P-H.

Austin-Broos, Daine J. Jamaica Genesis: Religion & the Politics of Moral Orders. LC 96-39540. 1997. pap. text 19.95 (*0-226-03286-8*) U Ch Pr.

Austin, Bruce, ed. Current Research in Film: Audiences, Economics, & Law, Vol. 1. 232p. (C). 1985. text 73.25 (*0-89391-269-7*) Ablx Pub.

— Current Research in Film: Audiences, Economics, & Law, Vol. 2. 268p. 1986. text 73.25 (*0-89391-315-4*) Ablx Pub.

— Current Research in Film: Audiences, Economics, & Law, Vol. 3. 240p. (C). 1987. text 73.25 (*0-89391-319-7*) Ablx Pub.

Austin, Bruce A. The Film Audience: An International Bibliography of Research. LC 83-3316. (Illus.). 224p. 1983. 23.50 (*0-8108-1622-9*) Scarecrow.

Austin, Bruce A., ed. Current Research in Film: Audiences, Economics, & Law, Vol. 4. 240p. 1988. text 73.25 (*0-89391-414-2*) Ablx Pub.

— Current Research in Film: Audiences, Economics, & Law, Vol. 5. 224p. 1991. text 73.25 (*0-89391-552-1*) Ablx Pub.

Austin, Bunny. Frank Buchman As I Knew Him. 1975. 2.65 (*0-901269-15-8*) Grosvenor USA.

Austin, C., jt. ed. see Kassel, Rudolfo.

Austin, C., jt. ed. see Kassel, R.

Austin, C. R. & Short, R. V., eds. Hormonal Control of Reproduction. 2nd ed. LC 81-18060. (Reproduction of Mammals Ser.: Bk. 3). 252p. 1984. pap. text 29.95 (*0-521-27594-6*) Cambridge U Pr.

— Human Sexuality. LC 78-18959. (Reproduction in Mammals Ser.: Bk. 8). (Illus.). 192p. 1980. text 54.95 (*0-521-22361-X*); pap. text 19.95 (*0-521-29461-4*) Cambridge U Pr.

— Reproductive Fitness. 2nd ed. (Reproduction in Mammals Ser.: Bk. 4). (Illus.). 256p. 1985. pap. text 26.95 (*0-521-31984-6*) Cambridge U Pr.

Austin, Carol, jt. auth. see Applebaum, Robert.

Austin, Carol D. & McClelland, Robert W., eds. Perspectives on Case Management Practice. LC 96-619. 278p. 1996. reprint ed. pap. 25.95 (*1-896918-12-3*, Manticore Europe) Manticore Pubs.

Austin, Carole, ed. see Schwendinger, Robert.

Austin, Caroline A., jt. ed. see Cowell, Ian G.

Austin, Cassandra. Cally & the Sheriff. 1997. per. 4.99 (*0-373-28981-2*, 1-28981-8) Harlequin Bks.

— Flint Hills Bride. (Historical Ser.: Vol. 430). 1998. per. 4.99 (*0-373-29030-6*, 1-29030-3) Harlequin Bks.

***Austin, Cassandra.** Heart & Home. (Harlequin Historical Ser.). 1999. mass mkt. 4.99 (*0-373-29090-X*, Harlequin) Harlequin Bks.

Austin, Cassandra. Hero of the Flint Hills. (Historical Ser.: No. 397). 1998. per. 4.99 (*0-373-28997-9*, 1-28997-4) Harlequin Bks.

— Trusting Sarah. LC 96-491. (Historical Ser.). 353p. 1995. per. 4.50 (*0-373-28879-4*, 1-28879-4) Harlequin Bks.

— The Unlikely Wife. (Historical Ser.: No. 462). 1999. per. 4.99 (*0-373-29062-4*, 1-29062-6) Harlequin Bks.

— Wait for the Sunrise. (Historical Ser.). 1993. mass mkt. 3.99 (*0-373-28790-9*, 1-28790-3) Harlequin Bks.

Austin, Catherine. Christmas Past & Christmas Presents. LC 93-7456. (Illus.). 144p. 1993. 27.95 (*0-8069-0404-6*, Chapelle) Sterling.

— Christmas Past & Christmas Presents. (Illus.). 144p. 1994. pap. 14.95 (*0-8069-0405-4*, Chapelle) Sterling.

— Fill the House with Cross Stitch. (Illus.). 128p. 1995. pap. 14.95 (*0-8069-0621-9*, Chapelle) Sterling.

— A New Twist on Tatting: More Than One Hundred Glorious Designs. (Illus.). 144p. 1994. pap. 14.95 (*0-8069-0290-6*, Chapelle) Sterling.

Austin, Charles J. & Boxerman, Stuart B. Information Systems for Health Services Administration. 5th ed. LC 97-29106. 1997. 60.00 (*1-56793-070-0*) Health Admin Pr.

— Quantitative Analysis for Health Services Administration. 333p. 1995. 60.00 (*1-56793-032-8*, 0964) Health Admin Pr.

Austin, Charles M. Paul Laurence Dunbar's Roots & Much More: A Scrapbook of His Life & Legacy. (Illus.). 90p. (Orig.). 1989. pap. 20.00 (*0-9625461-0-0*) Sense Roots Pubns.

Austin, Clyde N. Cross-Cultural Reentry: A Book of Readings. LC 85-73568. 320p. 1986. pap. 14.95 (*0-915547-74-0*) Abilene Christ U.

Austin, Clyde N., ed. Cross-Cultural Reentry: An Annotated Bibliography. annot. ed. 1986. 13.95 (*0-915547-00-7*) Abilene Christ U.

Austin, Colinus, ed. Comicorum Graecorum Fragmenta in Papyris Reperta (1838-1971) (C). 1973. 415.40 (*3-11-004046-8*) De Gruyter.

Austin, Cyril K. Formwork to Concrete. 3rd ed. LC 78-315629. 327p. reprint ed. pap. 101.40 (*0-608-13214-4*, 202525500043) Bks Demand.

Austin, D., jt. auth. see Austin, B.

Austin, D. A., jt. auth. see Austin, B.

Austin, D. A., jt. ed. see Austin, B.

***Austin, D. Brian.** The End of Certainty & the Beginning of Faith: Religion & Science for the 21st Century. LC 99-56444. 192p. 2000. pap. 20.00 (*1-57312-262-9*) Smyth & Helwys.

Austin, D. F. Flora of Ecuador No. 165: Convolvulaceae. 98p. 1982. pap. 28.00 (*91-86344-02-1*, Pub. by Coun Nordic Pubs) Balogh.

Austin, D. F., et al. The Florida of John Kunkel Small: His Species & Types, Collecting Localities, Bibliography, & Selected Reprinted Works. LC 87-12414. (Contributions from the New York Botanical Garden Ser.: Vol. 18). 350p. 1987. pap. 15.00 (*0-89327-318-X*) NY Botanical.

Austin, Danford. My God & My Dogs. 100p. 1998. pap. write for info. (*1-57502-878-6*, PO2392) Morris Pubng.

Austin, Daniel F. Finland As a Gateway to Russia: Issues in European Security. (Illus.). 248p. 1996. text 72.95 (*1-85972-494-9*, Pub. by Avebry) Ashgate Pub Co.

***Austin, Dave.** Unfinished Cross: Listen to the Voice Within. 2000. 18.95 (*1-57174-232-8*) Hampton Roads Pub Co.

Austin, David. David Austin's English Roses: Glorious New Roses for American Gardens. rev. ed. LC 96-75873. (Illus.). 160p. (gr. 8). 1997. 45.00 (*0-316-05973-0*) Little.

— Decouvrir les Roses Anciennes et Anglaises. (FRE., Illus.). 220p. 1993. lib. bdg. 59.95 (*0-7859-3643-2*, 2706617330) Fr & Eur.

***Austin, David.** English Rose. 2000. 14.95 (*0-670-88880-X*, Viking) Viking Penguin.

Austin, David. The Heritage of the Rose. (Illus.). 456p. 1988. 79.50 (*1-85149-020-5*) Antique Collect.

— Migrating from Oracle7.X to Oracle8i. 500p. 1999. pap. text 39.99 (*0-672-31577-7*) Sams.

— Old Roses & English Roses. (Illus.). 224p. (Orig.). 1993. 25.00 (*1-85149-150-3*) Antique Collect.

— Outlaw with a Star. 256p. 1999. 5.99 (*0-425-16817-4*) Berkley Pub.

— Shrub Roses & Climbing Roses: With Hybrid Tea & Floribunda Roses. (Illus.). 288p. (Orig.). 1993. 25.00 (*1-85149-166-X*) Antique Collect.

An Asterisk (*) at the beginning of an entry indicates that the title is appearing for the first time.

— Therapeutic Recreation: Processes & Techniques. 4th rev. ed. (Illus.). 500p. (C). 1999. text 44.95 (*1-57167-032-7*) Sagamore Pub.

Austin, David, frwd. Botanica's Roses: The Encyclopedia of Roses. (Illus.). 704p. 1999. 59.95 (*1-56649-176-2*) Welcome Rain.

Austin, David & Alcock, Leslie, eds. From the Baltic to the Black Sea: Studies in Medieval Archaeology. LC 97-8286. (One World Archaeology Ser.: Vol. 18). (Illus.). 352p. (C). 1997. pap. 32.99 (*0-415-15225-9*) Routledge.

***Austin, David & Crawford, Michael.** Therapeutic Recreation: An Introduction. 3rd ed. 350p. 2000. 45.33 (*0-205-32829-6*) Allyn.

Austin, David F. What Is the Meaning of "This"? A Puzzle about Demonstrative Belief. LC 89-22110. 192p. 1990. text 32.50 (*0-8014-2409-7*) Cornell U Pr.

Austin, David F., ed. Philosophical Analysis: A Defense by Example. 365p. (C). 1988. lib. bdg. 173.50 (*90-277-2674-4*, Pub. by Kluwer Academic) Kluwer Academic.

Austin, David H., jt. auth. see Williams, Lovett E., Jr.

Austin, David L. Henri Sauguet: A Bio-Bibliography, 39. LC 90-29278. (Bio-Bibliographies in Music Ser.: No. 39). 288p. 1991. lib. bdg. 62.95 (*0-313-26564-X*, Greenwood Pr) Greenwood.

Austin, David M. The Political Economy of Human Service Programs. Levy, Judith A., ed. LC 88-9043. (Contemporary Studies in Applied Behavioral Science: Vol. 5). 257p. 1988. 73.25 (*0-89232-958-0*) Jai Pr.

Austin, David R. Comprehensive Glossary of Recreational Therapy. 54p. (Orig.). 1994. pap. text 12.50 (*1-889435-05-8*) Am Therapeutic.

Austin, David R. & Crawford, Michael E. Therapeutic Recreation: An Introduction. 2nd ed. LC 95-50756. 576p. (C). 1996. 64.00 (*0-13-110736-4*) Allyn.

Austin, Denise. Denise Austin's Healthy Pregnancy Book: How to Stay Fit & Healthy Through the Nine Months--and Beyond! LC 99-13378. 240p. 1999. pap. 12.00 (*0-684-80219-8*, Fireside) S&S Trade Pap.

— Getting Fit with Denise Austin. 1997. write for info. (*0-614-25224-5*, Fireside) S&S Trade Pap.

— Hit the Spot! LC 96-45162. 192p. 1997. per. 11.00 (*0-684-80218-X*) S&S Trade.

— Jumpstart: The 21 Day Plan to Lose Weight, Get Fit & Increase Your Energy & Enthusiasm. 400p. 1998. per. 14.00 (*0-684-82698-4*, Fireside) S&S Trade Pap.

***Austin, Denise.** Lose Those Last 10 Pounds: The 28-Day Fool-Proof Plan to a Healthy Body. LC 99-49879. (Illus.). 288p. 2000. 21.95 (*0-7679-0469-9*) Broadway BDD.

Austin, Dennis. Britain & South Africa. LC 81-4550. (Illus.). 191p. 1981. reprint ed. lib. bdg. 59.50 (*0-313-22994-5*, AUBS, Greenwood Pr) Greenwood.

— Ghana Observed: Essays on the Politics of a West African Republic. LC 76-15398. 200p. 1976. 32.50 (*0-8419-0278-X*, Africana) Holmes & Meier.

Austin, Dennis, ed. Liberal Democracy in Non-Western States. LC 92-3014. 1995. pap. text 14.95 (*0-943852-99-4*) Prof World Peace.

— Liberal Democracy in Non-Western States. LC 92-3014. 256p. (C). 1995. text 24.95 (*0-943852-98-6*) Prof World Peace.

Austin, Dennis & Lucuham, Robin, eds. Politicians & Soldiers in Ghana, 1966-1972. (Studies in Commonwealth Politics & History: No. 3). 332p. 1975. 40.00 (*0-7146-3049-7*, Pub. by F Cass Pubs); pap. 19.50 (*0-7146-4019-0*, Pub. by F Cass Pubs) Intl Spec Bk.

***Austin, Dennis & O'Neill, Michael, eds.** Democracy & Cultural Diversity. 210p. 2000. pap. 24.95 (*0-19-929000-8*) OUP.

Austin, Diane J. Urban Life in Kingston, Jamaica. (Caribbean Studies: Vol. 3). xxvi, 282p. 1984. text 117.00 (*2-88124-006-2*) Gordon & Breach.

Austin, Donald F. & Werner, S. Benson. Epidemiology for the Health Sciences: A Primer on Epidemiologic Concepts & Their Uses. (Illus.). 88p. 1982. pap. 17.95 (*0-398-02949-0*) C C Thomas.

Austin, Dorothea. The Name Book: More Than 2000 Names, Their Meanings, Origin & Significance. LC 97-21023. 34p. 1997. pap. 9.99 (*1-55661-982-0*) Bethany Hse.

Austin, Douglas. Commercial Bank Directory Liabilities. 1993. per. 18.95 (*0-7602-0049-1*, Irwn Prfssnl) McGraw-Hill Prof.

— Financial Institution Director Liabilities & Responsibility. 4th ed. 1996. text 19.95 (*0-7863-1062-6*, Irwn Prfssnl) McGraw-Hill Prof.

— Strategic Planning for Banks. 1990. text 50.00 (*1-55520-171-7*, Irwn Prfssnl) McGraw-Hill Prof.

Austin, Douglas, jt. auth. see Graves, Judy Reid.

Austin, Douglas V. The Community Bank Survival Guide: Overcoming the Challenges of an Increasingly Competitive Marketplace. 144p. 1996. pap. 19.95 (*0-7863-1107-X*, Irwn Prfssnl) McGraw-Hill Prof.

— Financial Institution Director's Handbook: Essential Readings to Minimize Liabilities & Increase Profitability for You & Your Institution. Bond, Kris, ed. 375p. Date not set. pap. text 70.00 (*0-8080-0369-0*) CCH INC.

Austin, Douglas V. How to Charter a Commercial Bank. Bond, Kris, ed. 260p. pap. text 350.00 (*0-8080-0431-X*) CCH INC.

Austin, Douglas V. & Bernard, Craig D. Strategic Planning Guide for Community Banks & Thrifts. rev. ed. LC 97-32836. 1998. 55.00 (*0-7863-1183-5*, Irwn Prfssnl) McGraw-Hill Prof.

Austin, Douglas V. & Fishman, Jay A. Corporations in Conflict ... the Tender Offer. LC 75-94688. 1970. 21.50 (*0-912164-08-5*) Masterco Pr.

Austin, Duncan. Climate Protection Policies: Can We Afford to Delay? 56p. 1997. pap. 20.00 (*1-56973-231-0*) World Resources Inst.

***Austin, Duncan & Faeth, Paul.** How Much Sustainable Development Can We Expect from the Clear Development Mechanism? 1999. 5.00 (*1-56973-434-8*) World Resources Inst.

Austin, Duncan, jt. auth. see Repetto, Robert.

Austin, E. L. & Hauser, Odell. The Sesqui-Centennial International Exposition. LC 75-24109. (America in Two Centuries Ser.). 1976. reprint ed. 58.95 (*0-405-07670-3*) Ayer.

Austin, E. V. A House by the Side of the Road. Wilcox, Patricia, ed. LC 75-31566. (Illus.). 105p. (Orig.). 1975. pap. 7.95 (*0-916078-01-9*) Iris Pr.

Austin, Ed. Spokane Portland & Seattle Color Guide to Freight & Passenger Equipment. (Illus.). 128p. 1998. 49.95 (*1-878887-93-9*) Morning NJ.

Austin, Ed & Dill, Tom. Southern Pacific in Oregon. 2nd ed. Pacific Fast Mail Staff et al, eds. (Illus.). 320p. 1994. 54.50 (*0-915713-14-4*) Pac Fast Mail.

Austin, Ed, jt. auth. see Dill, Tom.

Austin, Elizabeth. Our Journey with God: With Passport Instructions. 80p. (Orig.). 1997. pap. 4.99 (*0-9655514-1-5*, Inspir Wrd Pub) Inspiring Word.

Austin, Elizabeth, jt. auth. see Whitaker, Leslie.

Austin, Emily. Mormonism: Or Life Among the Mormons. LC 74-134388. 1972. reprint ed. 44.50 (*0-404-08480-X*) AMS Pr.

***Austin, Erica Weintraub & Pinkleton, Bruce E.** Strategic Public Relations Management: Planning & Managing Effective Communication Programs. LC 00-34758. 2000. pap. write for info. (*0-8058-3160-6*) L Erlbaum Assocs.

Austin, Erik W. & Clubb, Jerome M. Political Facts of the United States since 1789. LC 86-2605. 450p. 1986. text 104.00 (*0-231-06094-7*) Col U Pr.

Austin, Erik W., et al. The Process of Historical Inquiry: Everyday Lives of Working Americans. (Illus.). 248p. 1989. pap. text 21.00 (*0-231-06967-7*) Col U Pr.

Austin, Florence, jt. auth. see Austin, Marshie.

Austin, Frances. The Language of the Metaphysical Poets. LC 91-26389. (Language of Literature Ser.). 180p. 1992. text 39.95 (*0-312-06885-9*) St Martin.

Austin, Frederick B. Red Flag. LC 72-37258. (Short Story Index Reprint Ser.). 1977. reprint ed. 23.95 (*0-8369-4069-5*) Ayer.

— Saga of the Sea. LC 76-116930. (Short Story Index Reprint Ser.). 1977. reprint ed. 21.95 (*0-8369-3432-6*) Ayer.

— Saga of the Sword. LC 75-106243. (Short Story Index Reprint Ser.). 1977. 21.95 (*0-8369-3279-X*) Ayer.

— When Mankind Was Young. LC 71-125201. (Short Story Index Reprint Ser.). 1977. 19.95 (*0-8369-3568-3*) Ayer.

Austin, Gareth, jt. ed. see Sugihara, Kaoru.

Austin, Gary. Layout Techniques for Landscape Architecture. (Illus.). 184p. (C). 1995. ring bd. 19.80 (*0-87563-524-5*) Stipes.

Austin, Gary R. The Systems Auditing Capability Framework. Campbell, Lee A., ed. LC 97-215970. 102p. 1997. pap. 200.00 (*0-89413-380-2*) Inst Inter Aud.

Austin, Gayle. Feminist Theories for Dramatic Criticism. 146p. 1990. pap. text 14.95 (*0-472-06429-0*, 06429) U of Mich Pr.

Austin, George & Noble, Jim. Swimming for Fitness. 2nd ed. pap. write for info. (*0-7136-4040-5*, 93299, Pub. by A & C Blk) Midpt Trade.

Austin, George L. The Life of Franz Schubert. LC 74-27330. reprint ed. 32.50 (*0-404-12856-4*) AMS Pr.

Austin, George S. Albuquerque Downtown from a Geologic Point of View: A Walking Tour of the City Center. (Scenic Trips to the Geologic Past Ser.). 58p. 1998. pap. 8.50 (*1-883905-02-8*) NM Bureau Mines.

Austin, Gerard. Anointing with the Spirit: The Rite of Confirmation: The Use of Oil & Chrism. 178p. 1992. pap. 12.95 (*0-8146-6070-3*, Pueblo Bks) Liturgical Pr.

Austin, Gerard, ed. Fountain of Life. (NPM Studies in Church Music & Liturgy). (Orig.). 1991. pap. text 24.95 (*0-912405-85-6*, Pastoral Press) OR Catholic.

Austin, Glenda. More Christmas Classics. 16p. (J). 1996. pap. 3.95 (*0-87718-101-2*, 12070E) Willis Music Co.

Austin, Glenn. Love & Power: How to Raise Competent, Confident Children. 244p. 1994. reprint ed. pap. 12.95 (*0-471-02498-8*) Wiley.

Austin, Glenn, et al. The Parents' Guide to Child Raising. 384p. pap. 7.95 (*0-318-43151-3*) P-H.

— The Parents' Medical Manual. 426p. 11.95 (*0-13-650317-9*) P-H.

Austin, Gordon. Production of Specific United States Gemstones. 45p. 1995. pap. 6.50 (*0-16-061630-1*) USGPO.

Austin, Graeme W., jt. ed. see Rickett, Charles E. F.

***Austin, Granville.** The Indian Constitution: Cornerstone of a Nation. 2nd ed. (Law in India Ser.). 416p. 2000. pap. 15.95 (*0-19-564959-1*) OUP.

— Working a Democratic Constitution: The Indian Experience. (Law in India Ser.). 800p. 1999. text 49.95 (*0-19-564888-9*) OUP.

***Austin, Greg.** Armed Forces of Russia in Asia. 2000. pap. 19.95 (*1-86064-485-6*); text 55.00 (*1-86064-505-4*, Pub. by I B T) St Martin.

Austin, Greg. China's Ocean Frontier: International Law, Military Force & National Development. LC 98-200610. 200p. 1998. pap. 29.95 (*1-86373-982-3*, Pub. by Allen & Unwin Pty) Paul & Co Pubs.

Austin, Gregory N. The 7 Myths Promoted by Conservatives, No. 7001. 136p. (Orig.). 1996. pap. 10.95 (*0-9653296-0-7*) GLS Publng.

***Austin, Guy.** Claude Chabrol. (Illus.). 240p. 1999. pap. 19.95 (*0-7190-5272-6*, Pub. by Manchester Univ Pr) St Martin.

— Claude Chabrol, Autoportrait. 240p. 1999. text 59.95 (*0-7190-5271-8*, Pub. by Manchester Univ Pr) St Martin.

Austin, Howard & Howard, Elisabeth. ABC's of Vocal Harmony - Also Known As Music Reading & Hearing, Singing Harmony. unabridged ed. (Illus.). 88p. (J. (gr. 7 up). 1989. pap. 29.95 incl. audio (*0-934419-24-8*, BTS-HD) Vocal Power.

Austin, Howard & Howard, Elisabeth. Born to Sing: Sing Like a Pro. unabridged ed. pap. 19.95 incl. audio compact disk (*0-934419-37-X*, BTS-S-CD) Vocal Power.

— Born to Sing: Vocal Technique. unabridged ed. pap. 19.95 incl. audio compact disk (*0-934419-36-1*, BTS-T-CD) Vocal Power.

Austin, Howard, jt. auth. see Howard, Elisabeth.

Austin, J. L. How to Do Things with Words. 2nd ed. Urmsson, J. O. & Sbisa, Marina, eds. 176p. 1975. pap. 12.95 (*0-674-41152-8*) HUP.

— Philosophical Papers. 3rd ed. Urmson, J. O. & Warnock, Geoffrey J., eds. 316p. 1990. pap. text 24.95 (*0-19-283021-X*) OUP.

Austin, J. L., tr. see Frege, Gottlob.

Austin, J. O. Genealogical Dictionary of Rhode Island, Comprising Three Generations of Settlers Who Came Before 1690. With Many Families Carried to the 4th Generation. 446p. 1998. reprint ed. lib. bdg. 49.00 (*0-8328-7035-8*) Higginson Bk Co.

Austin, Jacqueline, et al. Technical Mathematics. 4th ed. 728p. (C). 1988. pap. text 82.50 (*0-03-013233-9*) SCP.

***Austin, James.** The Collaboration Challenge: How Nonprofits & Businesses Succeed Through Strategic Alliances. LC 99-88237. 2000. 25.00 (*0-7879-5220-6*) Jossey-Bass.

Austin, James. From Within the Negro Problem: The Way It Was. LC 98-170593. 112p. 1997. pap. 10.00 (*0-8059-4204-1*) Dorrance.

— Ram-Based Neural Networks. LC 97-47134. (Progress in Neural Processing Ser.). 200p. 1997. 38.00 (*981-02-3253-5*) World Scientific Pub.

Austin, James, et al. National Assessment of Structured Sentencing. (Illus.). 138p. (Orig.). (C). 1996. pap. text 40.00 (*0-7881-3734-4*) DIANE Pub.

Austin, James, jt. auth. see Irwin, John.

Austin, James C. Bill Arp. LC 68-24308. (Twayne's United States Authors Ser.). 1969. pap. text 4.95 (*0-8290-0081-X*); lib. bdg. 11.95 (*0-89197-678-7*) Irvington.

— Fields of the Atlantic Monthly: Letters to an Editor. 1861-1870. LC 53-12551. (Huntington Library Publications). 457p. 1953. reprint ed. pap. 141.70 (*0-608-03163-1*, 206361600007) Bks Demand.

Austin, James C., jt. auth. see Shafroth, Stephen M

Austin, James E. Agroindustrial Project Analysis: Critical Design Factors. 2nd ed. 272p. 1992. pap. 30.00 (*0-8018-4530-0*, 44530) World Bank.

— Confronting Urban Malnutrition: The Design of Nutrition Programs. LC 79-3705. (World Bank Staff Occasional Papers: No. 28). 132p. reprint ed. pap. 41.00 (*0-7837-4253-3*, 204394300012) Bks Demand.

— Managing in Developing Countries: Strategic Analysis & Operating Techniques. 1990. 40.00 (*0-02-901102-7*) Free Pr.

Austin, James E. & Esteva, Gustavo, eds. Food Policy in Mexico: The Search for Self-Sufficiency. LC 86-19815. (Illus.). 400p. 1987. pap. text 21.95 (*0-8014-9453-2*) Cornell U Pr.

Austin, James E. & Kohn, Thomas O. Strategic Management in Developing Countries: Case Studies. 624p. 1990. 45.00 (*0-02-901105-1*) Free Pr.

Austin, James F., jt. auth. see Krisberg, Barry.

Austin, James H. Chase, Chance, & Creativity. LC 77-23011. 236p. 1985. pap. text 23.00 (*0-231-04295-7*) Col U Pr.

— Zen & the Brain: Toward an Understand of Meditation & Consciousness. (Illus.). 1999. pap. 24.95 (*0-262-51109-6*) MIT Pr.

Austin, James T. The Life of Elbridge Gerry, 2 vols. LC 77-99470. (American Public Figures Ser.). 1970. reprint ed. lib. bdg. 89.50 (*0-306-71841-3*) Da Capo.

Austin, James T., jt. ed. see Leong, Frederick T.

Austin, Jane. The Works of Jane (Goodwin) Austin, 1831-1894, Set. 1987. reprint ed. lib. bdg. 800.00 (*0-685-18608-3*) Rprt Serv.

Austin, Jane, ed. see Cory, Kim D.

Austin, Jane, ed. see Fontenay, Charles L.

Austin, Jane G. Betty Alden. (Works of Jane (Goodin Austin). 1989. reprint ed. lib. bdg. 79.00 (*0-7812-1833-0*) Rprt Serv.

— Cipher: A Romance. (Works of Jane (Goodin) Austin). 1989. reprint ed. lib. bdg. 79.00 (*0-7812-1824-1*) Rprt Serv.

— David Aldens Daughter & Other Stories. (Works of Jane (Goodin) Austin). 1989. reprint ed. lib. bdg. 79.00 (*0-7812-1836-5*) Rprt Serv.

— The Desmond Hundred. (Works of Jane (Goodin) Austin). 1989. reprint ed. lib. bdg. 79.00 (*0-7812-1829-2*) Rprt Serv.

— Dr. LeBaron & His Daughters. (Works of Jane (Goodin) Austin). 1989. reprint ed. lib. bdg. 79.00 (*0-7812-1832-2*) Rprt Serv.

— Dora Darling. (Works of Jane (Goodin) Austin). 1989. reprint ed. lib. bdg. 79.00 (*0-7812-1838-1*) Rprt Serv.

— Fairy Dreams. (Works of Jane (Goodin) Austin). 1989. reprint ed. lib. bdg. 79.00 (*0-7812-1820-9*) Rprt Serv.

— It Never Did Run Smooth. (Works of Jane (Goodin) Austin). 1989. reprint ed. lib. bdg. 79.00 (*0-7812-1834-9*) Rprt Serv.

— Moonfolk. (Works of Jane (Goodin) Austin). 1989. reprint ed. lib. bdg. 79.00 (*0-7812-1826-8*) Rprt Serv.

— Mrs. Beauchamp Brown. (Works of Jane (Goodin) Austin). 1989. reprint ed. lib. bdg. 79.00 (*0-7812-1827-6*) Rprt Serv.

— A Nameless Nobleman. (Works of Jane (Goodin) Austin). 1989. reprint ed. lib. bdg. 79.00 (*0-7812-1828-4*) Rprt Serv.

— Nantucket Scraps. (Works of Jane (Goodin) Austin). 1989. reprint ed. lib. bdg. 79.00 (*0-7812-1830-6*) Rprt Serv.

— Outpost. (Works of Jane (Goodin) Austin). 1989. reprint ed. lib. bdg. 79.00 (*0-7812-1823-3*) Rprt Serv.

— Queen Tempest. (Works of Jane (Goodin) Austin). 1989. reprint ed. lib. bdg. 79.00 (*0-7812-1835-7*) Rprt Serv.

— The Shadow of Moloch Mountain. (Works of Jane (Goodin) Austin). 1989. reprint ed. lib. bdg. 79.00 (*0-7812-1825-X*) Rprt Serv.

— Standish of Standish. (Works of Jane (Goodin) Austin). 1989. reprint ed. lib. bdg. 79.00 (*0-7812-1831-4*) Rprt Serv.

— The Tailor Boy. (Works of Jane (Goodin) Austin). 1989. reprint ed. lib. bdg. 79.00 (*0-685-44732-4*) Rprt Serv.

— The Twelve Great Diamonds. (Works of Jane (Goodin) Austin). 1989. reprint ed. lib. bdg. 79.00 (*0-7812-1837-3*) Rprt Serv.

Austin, Jane H., et al. Calabash. LC 97-65372. 126p. (Orig.). 1997. pap. 12.95 (*0-9656052-0-5*) Pot Shard.

Austin, Jaqueline. Angel Child. 1996. mass mkt. 6.99 (*0-671-70917-8*) PB.

***Austin, Jay & Bruch, Carl, eds.** The Environmental Consequences of War: Legal, Economic & Scientific Perspectives. LC 99-87919. (Illus.). 600p. (C). 2000. text Price not set. (*0-521-78020-9*) Cambridge U Pr.

Austin, Jean S., jt. auth. see Austin, Norman A.

Austin, Jeanette H. Georgia Bible Records. LC 84-70998. 538p. 2000. reprint ed. pap. 42.50 (*0-8063-1125-8*, Pub. by Clearfield Co) ACCESS Pubs Network.

— The Georgians: Genealogies of Pioneer Families. LC 84-80783. 479p. 1998. reprint ed. pap. 36.50 (*0-8063-1081-2*, Pub. by Clearfield Co) ACCESS Pubs Network.

— Index to Georgia Wills. LC 84-73074. 169p. 1998. reprint ed. pap. 17.50 (*0-8063-1112-6*, Pub. by Clearfield Co) ACCESS Pubs Network.

Austin, Jeanne, ed. see Jasinski, Juli.

Austin, Jeannette H. Georgia Interstate Records. 433p. 1995. reprint ed. 22.50 (*0-8063-1146-0*) Genealog Pub.

Austin, Jill. Treasures from the Throne of God. 128p. 1999. pap. 7.99 (*1-884369-63-4*) McDougal Pubng.

Austin, Jim. Fury Book No. 5: Nevada Guns. (Fury Ser.: No. 5). 192p. (Orig.). 1995. mass mkt. 4.50 (*0-515-11473-1*, Jove) Berkley Pub.

Austin, Jim, jt. auth. see Krisberg, Barry.

Austin, Jim, jt. ed. see Hodge, Victoria.

Austin, Joan K., jt. ed. see McBride, Angela B.

Austin, Joe D., ed. Applications of Secondary School Mathematics: Readings from the "Mathematics Teacher" LC 91-5044. (Illus.). 339p. 1991. pap. 24.95 (*0-87353-336-4*) NCTM.

Austin, Joe D., et al. Mathematics of Finance. 2nd ed. LC 93-42967. 1994. mass mkt. 44.95 (*0-314-02947-8*) West Pub.

Austin, Joel, ed. Generations of Youth. LC 97-45397. 1998. pap. 22.95 (*0-8147-0646-0*); text 65.00 (*0-8147-0645-2*) NYU Pr.

Austin, John. British Delft at Williamsburg. (Illus.). 299p. 1997. 135.00 (*0-9512140-6-3*, Pub. by J Horne) Antique Collect.

— John Austin: The Province of Jurisprudence Determined. Rumble, Wilfrid E., ed. (Cambridge Texts in the History of Political Thought Ser.). 340p. (C). 1995. pap. text 21.95 (*0-521-44756-9*) Cambridge U Pr.

— Lectures on Jurisprudence. 1988. reprint ed. lib. bdg. 75.00 (*0-7812-0393-7*) Rprt Serv.

— Lectures on Jurisprudence: or the Philosophy of Positive Law. 1976. 79.00 (*0-403-06116-4*, Regency) Scholarly.

— Lectures on Jurisprudence: or The Philosophy of Positive Law, 2 vols. 4th rev. ed. Campbell, Robert, ed. xxiii, 1169p. 1998. reprint ed. 298.00 (*1-56169-360-X*) Gaunt.

— The Providence of Jurisprudence Determined, 1832. LC 99-33457. 2000. reprint ed. 75.00 (*1-58477-023-6*) Lawbk Exchange.

— The Province of Jurisprudence - Determined & the Uses of the Study of Jurisprudence. LC 98-30371. 432p. (C). 1998. reprint ed. pap. 16.95 (*0-87220-432-4*); reprint ed. lib. bdg. 37.95 (*0-87220-433-2*) Hackett Pub.

— The Province of Jurisprudence Determined. LC 96-6122. (Classical Jurisprudence Ser.). (Illus.). 280p. 1996. text 68.95 (*1-85521-649-3*, Pub. by Dartmth Pub) Ashgate Pub Co.

***Austin, John.** Province of Jurisprudence Determined. 410p. 2000. pap. 14.95 (*1-57392-845-3*) Prometheus Bks.

Austin, John. Why Stripe a Lighthouse? LC 98-102294. (Illus.). 80p. (Orig.). 1997. pap. 22.00 (*1-884824-09-9*, Timonier Bks) Tryon Pubng.

Austin, John, jt. auth. see Blake, Andrew.

Austin, John, tr. see Moore, Shirley, ed.

Austin, John Langshaw. Sense & Sensibilia. Warnock, Geoffrey J., ed. 156p. 1964. text 17.95 (*0-19-500307-1*) OUP.

Austin, John O. Genealogical Dictionary of Rhode Island: Comprising Three Generations of Settlers Who Came Before 1690. With Additions & Corrections by G. Andrews Moriarty, 1943-1863, & a New Foreword. LC 68-56072. 496p. 1995. reprint ed. 50.00 (*0-8063-0006-X*) Genealog Pub.

Austin, Jon W. The Heart Lung Machine & Related Technologies of Open Heart Surgery. Harner, David L., ed. (Illus.). 235p. (C). 1985. text. write for info. (*0-938633-00-7*) Phoenix Medical.

Austin, Judith, jt. ed. see Rikoon, J. Sanford.

Austin, Judith M. The Chinese New Year Dragon. (GlobalFriends Adventures Ser.). (Illus.). 64p. (J). (gr. 2-6). 1997. pap. 5.95 (*1-58056-005-9*, GlobalFr Pr) GlobalFriends.

— Discovery in a French Garden. (GlobalFriends Adventures Ser.). (Illus.). 64p. (J). (gr. 2-6). 1997. pap. 5.95 (1-58056-007-5, GlobalFr Pr) GlobalFriends.

— The Ghostly German Castle. (GlobalFriends Adventures Ser.). (Illus.). 64p. (J). (gr. 2-6). 1997. pap. 5.95 (1-58056-008-3, GlobalFr Pr) GlobalFriends.

— The Haunted English Riding Stable. (GlobalFriends Adventures Ser.). (Illus.). 64p. (J). (gr. 2-6). 1996. pap. 5.95 (1-58056-001-6, GlobalFr Pr) GlobalFriends.

— The Lost Treasure of the Rainforest. (GlobalFriends Adventures Ser.). (Illus.). 64p. (J). (gr. 2-6). 1996. pap. 5.95 (1-58056-002-4, GlobalFr Pr) GlobalFriends.

— The Missing Japanese Festival Dolls. (GlobalFriends Adventures Ser.). (Illus.). 64p. (J). (gr. 2-6). 1997. pap. 5.95 (1-58056-004-0, GlobalFr Pr) GlobalFriends.

— The Mystery of the Russian Circus School. (GlobalFriends Adventures Ser.). (Illus.). 64p. (J). (gr. 2-6). 1996. pap. 5.95 (1-58056-003-2, GlobalFr Pr) GlobalFriends.

— Rescue in Kenya. (GlobalFriends Adventures Ser.). (Illus.). 64p. (J). (gr. 2-6). 1997. pap. 5.95 (1-58056-006-7, GlobalFr Pr) GlobalFriends.

— The Secret Egyptian Code. (GlobalFriends Adventures Ser.). (Illus.). 64p. (J). (gr. 2-6). 1996. pap. 5.95 (1-58056-000-8, GlobalFr Pr) GlobalFriends.

Austin Junior Forum, Inc. Staff. Lone Star Legacy: A Texas Cookbook. LC 81-69340. (Illus.). 368p. 1981. spiral bd. 17.95 (0-9607152-0-7) Austin Junior.

— Lone Star Legacy II: A Texas Cookbook. LC 85-72515. (Illus.). 368p. 1985. spiral bd. 17.95 (0-9607152-1-5) Austin Junior.

Austin, Karen. Blind Trust: A Child's Legacy. LC 98-90422. vi, 217p. 1999. pap. 13.95 (0-9665191-0-8) Snowbird Bks.

Austin, Karen, tr. see Galdos, Benito Perez.

Austin, Karen O., tr. see Galdos, Benito P.

Austin, Karin, et al. An Illustrated Guide to Taping & Bandaging. (Illus.). 120p. 1993. 24.95 (0-8151-0347-6) Mosby Inc.

Austin, Kathi. Invisible Crimes: U. S. Private Intervention in the War in Mozambique. Minter, William, ed. (Illus.). 64p. (Orig.). 1994. pap. 7.95 (0-9634238-2-7) Africa Policy Info.

Austin, Kathi, jt. auth. see Lund, Michael.

Austin, Ken, jt. auth. see Boroson, Warren.

Austin, Kenneth, Jr., jt. auth. see Taylor, Jeffrey.

Austin, Kenneth M. Confronting Malpractice: Legal & Ethical Dilemmas in Psychotherapy. 368p. (C). 1990. text 55.00 (0-8039-3081-X); pap. text 25.00 (0-8039-3978-7) Sage.

Austin, Kenneth M., et al. Confronting Malpractice: Legal & Ethical Dilemmas in Psychotherapy. LC 90-8742. (Illus.). 368p. reprint ed. pap. 114.10 (0-608-09774-8, 206994800007) Bks Demand.

Austin, L. Allan & Cheek, Logan M. Zero-Base Budgeting: A Decision Package Manual. LC 79-12657. 217p. reprint ed. pap. 67.30 (0-608-11960-1, 202350500033) Bks Demand.

Austin-LaFrance, Robert J., ed. see Bronzino, Joseph D. & Roosa, Vernon.

Austin, Lambert D., ed. 344th Bomb Group (M) "Silver Streaks" History & Remembrances World War II. 358p. 1996. 39.95 (0-941072-20-7) Southern Herit.

Austin, Leah, ed. see Barratt, Iris K.

Austin, Leonard A. Counseling Primer. LC 98-31563. 356p. 1998. 24.95 (1-56032-697-2) Hemisp Pub.

Austin, Lewis, ed. Japan: The Paradox of Progress. LC 75-18163. (Illus.). 344p. reprint ed. pap. 106.70 (0-608-10756-5, 202197500024) Bks Demand.

Austin, Linda. Inconvenient Ambition. Date not set. write for info. (0-465-03263-X) Basic.

— What's Holding You Back? 8 Critical Choices for Women's Success. 214p. 2000. 25.00 (0-465-03262-1, Pub. by Basic) HarpC.

Austin, Linda G. Mountain Bike! Northern California. (Illus.). 416p. 1999. pap. 15.95 (0-89732-288-6) Menasha Ridge.

Austin, Linda M. The Practical Ruskin: Economics & Audience in the Late Work. LC 90-23911. 264p. 1991. text 42.00 (0-8018-4162-3) Johns Hopkins.

Austin, Linda S., ed. Responding to Disaster: A Guide for Mental Health Professionals. LC 91-44366. (Clinical Practice Ser.: No. 24). 256p. 1992. 12.95 (0-88048-464-0, 8464) Am Psychiatric.

Austin, Linda T. Babies for Sale: The Tennessee Children's Home Adoption Scandal. LC 92-46165. 192p. 1993. 49.95 (0-275-94585-5, C4585, Praeger Pubs) Greenwood.

Austin, Lloyd H., ed. see American Water Resources Association, Spring Symposium Staff.

Austin, Lloyd J., et al, eds. Stephane Mallarme: Correspondance: Complements et Supplements. (Legenda Ser.: 2). 275p. (Orig.). 1998. pap. 49.50 (1-900755-07-6, Pub. by E H R C) David Brown.

Austin, Lou. Little Me - Great Me: Parents & Teachers Manual, Vol. 1. (J). (ps-5). 1985. pap., teacher ed. 1.25 (0-934538-06-9) Partnership Foundation.

— The Little Me & the Great Me, Vol. 1. (J). (ps-5). 1985. 6.95 (0-934538-26-3) Partnership Foundation.

— A Lou Austin Anthology. 1983. 8.50 (0-685-06307-0) Partnership Foundation.

— My Secret Power, Vol. 2. (J). (gr. 1-6). 1960. 4.95 (0-934538-22-0) Partnership Foundation.

— Why & How Was I Born, Vol. 3. (J). (gr. 1-6). 1963. 4.95 (0-934538-28-X) Partnership Foundation.

— You Are Greater Than You Know. 1955. 8.50 (0-934538-16-6) Partnership Foundation.

Austin, Louis. The Living Trust Alternative: End Probate Worries for Your Family. pap. 18.95 incl. audio (0-9625528-3-6) Hudspeth Pub.

Austin, Louise. Ferris Ancestry. 85p. 1997. reprint ed. pap. 16.00 (0-8328-8550-9); reprint ed. lib. bdg. 26.00 (0-8328-8549-5) Higginson Bk Co.

***Austin, Lynn.** Wings of Refuge. LC 99-51018. 400p. 2000. pap. 11.99 (0-7642-2196-5) Bethany Hse.

Austin, Lynn N. Among the Gods. LC 98-14813. 320p. 1998. 12.99 (0-8341-1733-9) Nazarene.

***Austin, Lynn N.** Eve's Daughters. LC 99-6517. 448p. 1999. 10.99 (0-7642-2195-7) Bethany Hse.

Austin, Lynn N. Fly Away. LC 96-47373. 208p. (Orig.). 1996. pap. 10.99 (0-8341-1595-6) Beacon Hill.

— The Lord Is My Salvation. (Chronicles of the King Ser.: Bk. 3). 272p. (Orig.). 1996. pap. 12.99 (0-8341-1603-0) Beacon Hill.

— The Lord Is My Song. LC 96-227552. (Chronicles of the King Ser.: Bk. 2). 304p. (Orig.). 1996. pap. 12.99 (0-8341-1602-2) Beacon Hill.

— The Lord Is My Strength. (Chronicles of the King Ser.: Bk. 1). 304p. 1995. pap. 12.99 (0-8341-1538-7) Beacon Hill.

— My Father's God: A Novel. LC 97-13729. (Chronicles of the Kings Ser.). 284p. 1997. pap. 12.99 (0-8341-1675-8) Beacon Hill.

Austin, M. M. The Hellenistic World from Alexander to the Roman Conquest: A Selection of Ancient Sources in Translation. LC 81-6136. (Illus.). 506p. 1981. pap. text 36.95 (0-521-29666-8) Cambridge U Pr.

Austin, M. M. & Vidal-Naquet, P. Economic & Social History of Ancient Greece. 1978. pap. 19.95 (0-520-04267-0, Pub. by U CA Pr) Cal Prin Full Svc.

Austin, Margot. A Friend for Growl Bear. LC 97-34347. (Illus.). 32p. (J). (ps-1). 1999. 14.95 (0-06-027802-1) HarpC Child Bks.

***Austin, Margot.** A Friend for Growl Bear. (J). 2001. pap. write for info. (0-06-443745-0, HarpTrophy) HarpC Child Bks.

Austin, Margot. Gabriel Churchkitten. (Illus.). 42p. 1992. reprint ed. lib. bdg. 14.95 (0-89968-308-8, Lghtyr Pr) Buccaneer Bks.

— Peter Churchmouse. (Illus.). 42p. 1992. reprint ed. lib. bdg. 14.95 (0-89968-307-X, Lghtyr Pr) Buccaneer Bks.

Austin, Margot & McPhail, David. A Friend for Growl Bear Board Book. (Illus.). 32p. (J). (ps-k). 1999. 6.95 (0-694-01257-2) HarpC.

Austin, Marilyn. Love More Precious. (Serenade Serenata Ser.: No. 40). 1986. pap. 1.49 (0-310-47482-5, 15594P) Zondervan.

***Austin, Mark & Chancogne, David.** Engineering Programming: C, Matlab & Java. LC 98-8481. 672p. 1999. pap. 73.95 (0-471-00116-3) Wiley.

Austin, Marshie & Austin, Florence. Austin. History of Rev. William Austin & His Wife Elizabeth with the Names & Addresses of Their Living Descendants (1940), Vols. I & II. (Illus.). 104p. 1997. reprint ed. pap. 17.00 (0-8328-7307-1); reprint ed. lib. bdg. 27.00 (0-8328-7306-3) Higginson Bk Co.

Austin, Martha R. & Pfeiffer, Mil R. Flowers in My Soup! Conversations about Incredible Edibles. (Illus.). vi, 22p. 1997. spiral bd. 9.95 (0-9660380-0-2) Greyhavens.

Austin, Mary. Earth Horizon. LC 91-17149. 403p. 1991. reprint ed. pap. 11.95 (0-8263-1316-7) U of NM Pr.

— Experiences Facing Death. Kastenbaum, Robert J., ed. LC 76-19557. (Death & Dying Ser.). 1977. reprint ed. lib. bdg. 25.95 (0-405-09553-8) Ayer.

— The Ford. LC 96-14396. (California Fiction Ser.). 440p. 1997. pap. 14.95 (0-520-20757-2, Pub. by U CA Pr) Cal Prin Full Svc.

— Isidro. LC 79-104408. (Illus.). 439p. reprint ed. pap. text 12.95 (0-8290-2129-9); reprint ed. lib. bdg. 37.00 (0-8398-0070-3) Irvington.

— The Land of Little Rain. LC 97-178695. 1997. pap. 10.95 (0-14-024919-2) Penguin Putnam.

***Austin, Mary.** Land of Little Rain. 116p. 2000. pap. 9.95 (1-55709-507-8) Applewood.

Austin, Mary. The Land of Little Rain. unabridged ed. LC 95-49113. (Thrift Editions Ser.). 96p. 1996. reprint ed. pap. text 1.50 (0-486-29037-9) Dover.

— Philip Freneau: The Poet of the Revolution. 285p. 1993. reprint ed. lib. bdg. 79.00 (0-7812-5266-0) Rprt Serv.

— Stories from the Country of Lost Borders. Pryse, Marjorie, ed. (American Women Writers Ser.). 267p. 1987. text 40.00 (0-8135-1217-4); pap. text 16.00 (0-8135-1218-2) Rutgers U Pr.

Austin, Mary & Muir, John. Writing the Western Landscape. LC 94-9139. (Concord Library). (Illus.). 182p. 1994. 17.50 (0-8070-8526-X) Beacon Pr.

— Writing the Western Landscape. Zwinger, Ann, ed. & illus. by. 208p. 1999. reprint ed. pap. 14.00 (0-8070-8527-8) Beacon Pr.

Austin, Mary C. & Jenkins, Esther C. Literature for Children & Young Adults about Oceania: Analysis & Annotated Bibliography with Additional Readings for Adults, 49. LC 95-24515. 352p. 1996. lib. bdg. 75.00 (0-313-26643-3, Greenwood Pr) Greenwood.

Austin, Mary C., et al. The First R: The Harvard Report on Reading in Elementary Schools. LC 77-13883. (Illus.). 263p. 1978. reprint ed. lib. bdg. 59.75 (0-8371-9877-1, AUFR, Greenwood Pr) Greenwood.

Austin, Mary C., jt. auth. see Jenkins, Esther C.

Austin, Mary H. The American Rhythm. (Collected Works of Mary Hunter Austin). 155p. 1998. reprint ed. lib. bdg. 88.00 (1-58201-510-4) Classic Bks.

— The Arrow-Maker. (Collected Works of Mary Hunter Austin). 128p. 1998. reprint ed. lib. bdg. 88.00 (1-58201-511-2) Classic Bks.

— Arrow-Maker. rev. ed. LC 70-90082. (BCL Ser.: No. 2). reprint ed. 37.50 (0-404-00419-9) AMS Pr.

— The Basket Woman. 1969. reprint ed. 37.50 (0-404-00429-6) AMS Pr.

— The Basket Woman. (Collected Works of Mary Hunter Austin). 222p. 1998. reprint ed. lib. bdg. 88.00 (1-58201-512-0) Classic Bks.

— The Basket Woman: A Book of Indian Tales. LC 98-27733. 136p. (gr. 3-7). 1999. reprint ed. pap. 17.00 (0-87417-336-1) U of Nev Pr.

— Beyond Borders: The Essays of Mary Austin. Ellis, Reubin J., ed. LC 94-47456. 192p. (C). 1996. 24.95 (0-8093-1997-7) S Ill U Pr.

— California, the Land of the Sun. (Collected Works of Mary Hunter Austin). 178p. 1998. reprint ed. lib. bdg. 88.00 (1-58201-513-9) Classic Bks.

— Christ in Italy. (Collected Works of Mary Hunter Austin). 162p. 1998. reprint ed. lib. bdg. 88.00 (1-58201-514-7) Classic Bks.

— Fire; a Drama in Three Acts. (Collected Works of Mary Hunter Austin). 52p. 1998. reprint ed. lib. bdg. 88.00 (1-58201-515-5) Classic Bks.

— The Flock. (Collected Works of Mary Hunter Austin). 166p. 1998. reprint ed. lib. bdg. 88.00 (1-58201-516-3) Classic Bks.

— The Ford. (Collected Works of Mary Hunter Austin). 440p. 1998. reprint ed. lib. bdg. 108.00 (1-58201-517-1) Classic Bks.

— The Green Bough. (Collected Works of Mary Hunter Austin). 40p. 1998. reprint ed. lib. bdg. 88.00 (1-58201-518-X) Classic Bks.

— Isidro. (Collected Works of Mary Hunter Austin). 424p. 1998. reprint ed. lib. bdg. 108.00 (1-58201-519-8) Classic Bks.

— The Land of Journeys' Ending. LC 70-86831. (BCL Ser.: No. I). (Illus.). 1969. reprint ed. 84.50 (0-404-00435-0) AMS Pr.

— The Land of Journeys' Ending. LC 83-1217. (Illus.). 489p. reprint ed. pap. 151.60 (0-8357-3179-0, 203944400012) Bks Demand.

— The Land of Journeys' Ending. (BCL1 - United States Local History Ser.). 459p. 1991. reprint ed. lib. bdg. 99.00 (0-7812-6330-1) Rprt Serv.

— The Land of Journey's Ending. (Collected Works of Mary Hunter Austin). 459p. 1998. reprint ed. lib. bdg. 108.00 (1-58201-520-1) Classic Bks.

— The Land of Little Rain. 1973. lib. bdg. 250.00 (0-87968-182-9) Gordon Pr.

— The Land of Little Rain. (Collected Works of Mary Hunter Austin). 280p. 1998. reprint ed. lib. bdg. 98.00 (1-58201-521-X) Classic Bks.

— The Land of Little Rain. (BCL1 - United States Local History Ser.). 280p. 1991. reprint ed. lib. bdg. 79.00 (0-7812-6331-X) Rprt Serv.

— The Land of Little Rain. LC 74-84233. (Zia Bks.). (Illus.). 171p. 1974. reprint ed. pap. 11.95 (0-8263-0358-7) U of NM Pr.

— Lost Borders. (Collected Works of Mary Hunter Austin). 208p. 1998. reprint ed. lib. bdg. 88.00 (1-58201-523-6); reprint ed. lib. bdg. 88.00 (1-58201-522-8) Classic Bks.

— Love & the Soul Maker. (Collected Works of Mary Hunter Austin). 286p. 1998. reprint ed. lib. bdg. 88.00 (1-58201-524-4) Classic Bks.

— The Lovely Lady. (Collected Works of Mary Hunter Austin). 272p. 1998. reprint ed. lib. bdg. 88.00 (1-58201-525-2) Classic Bks.

— The Man Jesus. (Collected Works of Mary Hunter Austin). 214p. 1998. reprint ed. lib. bdg. 88.00 (1-58201-526-0) Classic Bks.

— No. 26 Jayne Street. (Collected Works of Mary Hunter Austin). 353p. 1998. reprint ed. lib. bdg. 98.00 (1-58201-527-9) Classic Bks.

— Outland. (Collected Works of Mary Hunter Austin). 306p. 1998. reprint ed. lib. bdg. 98.00 (1-58201-528-7) Classic Bks.

— Philip Freneau, the Poet of the Revolution. (Collected Works of Mary Hunter Austin). 285p. 1998. reprint ed. lib. bdg. 88.00 (1-58201-529-5) Classic Bks.

— Western Trails: A Collection of Short Stories. Graulich, Melody, ed. LC 87-16501. (Western Literature Ser.). 317p. 1987. reprint ed. pap. 98.30 (0-608-04564-0, 206530300001) Bks Demand.

— A Woman of Genius. LC 85-7069. 336p. 1985. pap. 9.95 (0-935312-44-7) Feminist Pr.

— A Woman of Genius. LC 76-51663. (Rediscovered Fiction by American Women Ser.). 1977. reprint ed. lib. bdg. 33.95 (0-405-10043-4) Ayer.

Austin, Mary Hunter. A Woman of Genius. (Collected Works of Mary Hunter Austin). 510p. 1998. reprint ed. lib. bdg. 118.00 (1-58201-530-9) Classic Bks.

— The Young Woman Citizen. (Collected Works of Mary Hunter Austin). 183p. 1998. reprint ed. lib. bdg. 88.00 (1-58201-531-7) Classic Bks.

Austin, Maureen. Crafting with Dried Rosebuds: 12 Terrific Projects. (Craft Collection). (Illus.). 79p. (Orig.). (YA). (gr. 7-12). 1996. pap. 9.95 (1-889044-25-3) Ladybug Bks.

Austin, Max E. Rabbiteye Blueberries: Development, Production, & Marketing. LC 94-10048. (Illus.). 160p. (C). 1994. 39.00 (0-9631397-2-X) AgScience.

Austin-McRae, Edward. Lilies: A Guide for Growers & Collectors. LC 97-22341. (Illus.). 392p. 1998. 34.95 (0-88192-410-5) Timber.

Austin, Michael. Cry of the Drummer. LC 94-62207. 1996. pap. 6.99 (0-9645131-0-2) Wrldrock Pub.

Austin, Michael. Chill Out! And Control Stress, It's up to You. large type ed. 24p. 1998. pap. 4.75 (0-939838-48-6) Pritchett & Hull.

Austin, Michael E., ed. Austins of America Vol. 1: Genealogical Society Serving Austin Family Researchers. LC 95-80763. 310p. 1995. 75.00 (0-9648804-0-7) Austin Print.

Austin, Michael J. Management Simulations for Mental Health & Human Services Administration. LC 78-12172. 436p. 1995. pap., student ed. 24.95 (0-917724-07-0) Haworth Pr.

— Professionals & Paraprofessionals. LC 77-26273. 295p. 1978. text 41.95 (0-87705-305-7, Kluwer Acad Hman Sci) Kluwer Academic.

Austin, Michael J., ed. Human Services Integration. LC 97-37551. 178p. 1997. 49.95 (0-7890-0353-8) Haworth Pr.

Austin, Michael J. & Hershey, William E., eds. Handbook on Mental Health Administration. LC 82-48058. (Jossey-Bass Social & Behavioral Science Ser.). 661p. reprint ed. pap. 200.00 (0-7837-6502-9, 204561400007) Bks Demand.

Austin, Michael J., et al. Delivering Human Services: An Introductory Programmed Text. (C). 1977. pap. text 16.50 (0-06-040396-9) HarpC.

Austin, Michael J., et al. Evaluating Your Agency's Programs. (Human Services Guides Ser.: Vol. 29). 192p. 1982. pap. 18.95 (0-8039-0989-6) Sage.

Austin, Michael J., jt. auth. see Betten, Neil.

Austin, Michael J., jt. auth. see Pecora, Peter J.

Austin, Milli. The Healing Bath: Using Essential Oil Therapy to Balance Body Energy. LC 96-21033. (Illus.). 176p. 1997. pap. 12.95 (0-89281-632-5, Heal Arts VT) Inner Tradit.

***Austin, Miriam.** Yoga for Wimps: Poses for the Flexibly Impaired. LC 99-44617. 128p. 2000. pap. 17.95 (0-8069-4339-4) Sterling.

Austin, Murray & Honey, Rex. Human Geography. Baxter, Clark, ed. 540p. (C). 1987. pap. text 57.00 (0-314-85216-6); pap. text, teacher ed. write for info. (0-314-34710-0) West Pub.

Austin, N., jt. auth. see Bryson, C.

Austin, N. J. & Rankov, N. B. Exploration: Military & Political Intelligence in the Roman World from the Second Punic War to the Battle of Adrianople. LC 94-46647. (Illus.). 320p. (C). (gr. 13). 1995. 90.00 (0-415-04945-8) Routledge.

Austin, N. J. E. Exploration: Military & Political Intelligence in the Roman World. (Illus.). 320p. (C). 1998. pap. 29.99 (0-415-18301-4) Routledge.

Austin, Nancy, jt. auth. see Phelps, Stanlee.

Austin, Nancy K., jt. auth. see Peters, Tom.

Austin, Neal F. Biography of Thomas Wolfe. (Illus.). 1968. 35.00 (0-911796-00-2) Beacham.

Austin, Neffetiti. Abandon. 256p. 1996. mass mkt. 4.99 (0-7860-0326-X, Pinncle Kensgtn) Kensgtn Pub Corp.

— Eternity. 224p. 1995. mass mkt. 4.99 (0-7860-0180-1, Pinncle Kensgtn) Kensgtn Pub Corp.

Austin-Niell, Leola. To Dance with a Dream Catcher. LC 98-68267. 320p. 1999. pap. 14.95 (1-57197-148-3) Pentland Pr.

Austin, Noel & Dopson, Sue. The Clinical Directorate. LC 96-37037. 1996. write for info. (1-85775-037-3, Radcliffe Med Pr) Scovill Paterson.

Austin, Norman. Archery at the Dark of the Moon: Poetic Problems in Homer's Odyssey. LC 73-94442. 311p. reprint ed. pap. 96.50 (0-7837-4762-4, 204450900003) Bks Demand.

— Helen of Troy & Her Shameless Phantom. (Myth & Poetics Ser.). (Illus.). 240p. 1994. text 35.00 (0-8014-2955-2) Cornell U Pr.

— Meaning & Being in Myth. LC 89-34186. 256p. 1990. lib. bdg. 35.00 (0-271-00681-1) Pa St U Pr.

Austin, Norman A. & Austin, Jean S. The Complete American Cocker Spaniel. (Illus.). 256p. 1993. 27.95 (0-87605-129-8) Howell Bks.

Austin, O. L., ed. Antarctic Bird Studies. LC 68-61438. (Antarctic Research Ser.: Vol. 12). (Illus.). 262p. 1968. 21.00 (0-87590-112-3) Am Geophysical.

Austin, Paul. The Exotic Prisoner in Russian Romanticism. LC 96-18972. (Middlebury Studies in Russian Languages & Literature: Vol. 9). XIV, 214p. (C). 1997. text 46.95 (0-8204-3346-2) P Lang Pubng.

Austin, Paul, jt. ed. see Lindfors, Viveca.

Austin, Paul B. 1812: The Great Retreat. LC 96-29074. 300p. 1996. 50.00 (1-85367-246-7, Pub. by Greenhill Bks) Stackpole.

— 1812: Napoleon in Moscow. LC 94-40996. (Illus.). 272p. 1995. 40.00 (1-85367-195-9, Pub. by Greenhill Bks) Stackpole.

Austin, Paul B., tr. see Bjorkman, Stig, et al.

Austin, Paul B., tr. see Friis, Erik J., et al, eds.

Austin, Paul B., tr. see Sjowall, Maj & Wahloo, Per.

***Austin, Paul Britten.** 1812 - Napoleon's Invasion of Russia. LC 00-38075. 2000. write for info. (1-85367-415-X) Stackpole.

Austin, Paul Britten, tr. see Olsson, Nils-Olof.

Austin, Penelope. Waiting for a Hero: Poems. LC 87-26354. 80p. (Orig.). 1988. pap. 12.95 (0-8262-0673-5) U of Mo Pr.

Austin, Peter, ed. Complex Sentence Constructions in Australian Languages. LC 87-29971. (Typological Studies in Language: Vol. 15). vii, 289p. 1988. 71.00 (1-55619-016-6); pap. 38.00 (1-55619-017-4) J Benjamins Pubng Co.

Austin, Phil. On Bethel Ridge: A Christmas Fable. LC 98-34797. 128p. 1998. 15.00 (1-890932-03-5) Sherman Asher Pub.

Austin, Phylis, et al. Fatigue: Causes, Treatment & Prevention. 61p. 1989. pap. 4.95 (1-878726-22-6) Fam Hlth Pubns.

— Food Allergies Made Simple: The Complete Manual for Diagnosis, Treatment, & Prevention of Food Allergies. 85p. 1985. reprint ed. pap. 4.95 (1-878726-05-6) Fam Hlth Pubns.

— More Natural Remedies: What to Do to Prevent & Treat Disease...Naturally. 123p. 1985. pap. 6.95 (1-878726-18-8) Fam Hlth Pubns.

An Asterisk (*) at the beginning of an entry indicates that the title is appearing for the first time.

— Natural Healthcare for Your Child: Trustworthy Information on the Prevention, Causes & Treatment of the Diseases & Ailments Which are Common from Birth Through the Teenage Years. (Illus.). 268p. (Orig.). 1990. pap. 9.95 (*1-878726-01-3*) Fam Hlth Pubns.

— Natural Remedies: A Manual. 171p. (Orig.). 1983. reprint ed. pap. 6.95 (*1-878726-14-5*) Fam Hlth Pubns.

Austin, R., Jr., et al, eds. Protein Structure. (Illus.). 1987. 124.00 (*0-387-96567-X*) Spr-Verlag.

Austin, R. C., et al. Legal Protection of Civil Liberties: The Legal Protection of Civil Liberties. 500p. 1994. pap. text 60.00 (*0-406-55511-7*, UK, MICHIE) LEXIS Pub.

Austin, R. G., ed. see Cicero, Marcus Tullius.

Austin, R. H. & Chan, S. Biophysics for Physicists. 400p. (C). 1997. text 78.00 (*981-02-0500-7*); pap. text 37.00 (*981-02-0501-5*) World Scientific Pub.

Austin, R. L., jt. ed. see Higgins, A. C.

Austin, R. P., jt. auth. see Ford, H. A.

Austin, R. W., ed. Ibn-Al-Arabi: The Bezels of Wisdom. LC 80-83892. (Classics of Western Spirituality Ser.). 320p. 1980. pap. 26.95 (*0-8091-2331-2*) Paulist Pr.

Austin, R. W., tr. see Al-Arabi, Ibn.

Austin, R. W., tr. see Ibn al-Arabi.

Austin, Raymond, intro. Stanford Environmental Law Journal, Vol. 14, Issue 2. 250p. (Orig.). 1998. pap. text 15.00 (*0-942007-40-9*) Stanford Enviro.

Austin, Rebecca & Nelson, Jennifer. Traverse City: And the Beautiful Surrounding Area. (Illus.). ix, 80p. (Orig.). 1997. pap. 16.95 (*0-9657153-0-2*) Austin & Nelson.

Austin, Reginald P. The Stoichedon Style in Greek Inscriptions. LC 72-7884. (Greek History Ser.). 1979. reprint ed. 18.95 (*0-405-04778-9*) Ayer.

Austin, Reid S. Petty Classic Pin-Up Art. 1997. 40.00 (*0-517-18840-6*) Random Hse Value.

Austin, Richard. The Official Price Guide to Military Collectibles. 6th ed. 1998. pap. 20.00 (*0-676-60052-2*) Random.

Austin, Richard B., Jr. Who Says Men Don't Talk or Listen? Safe-Talk Guidelines. Schmidt, Connie L., ed. 46p. (Orig.). (C). 1993. pap. text 9.95 (*0-614-11344-X*) Brockton Pubng.

Austin, Richard C. Baptized into Wilderness: A Christian Perspective on John Muir. 2nd ed. LC 91-75857. (Environmental Theology Ser.: Vol. 1). (Illus.). 104p. (Orig.). 1991. reprint ed. pap. 9.75 (*0-9625831-2-X*) Creekside VA.

— Beauty of the Lord: Awakening the Senses. LC 87-46292. (Environmental Theology Ser.). (Illus.). 225p. (Orig.). 1988. pap. 13.00 (*0-8042-0859-X*, 0-9625831) Creekside VA.

— Environmental Theology, 4 vols., Set. 830p. (Orig.). 1990. pap. 38.00 (*0-9625831-1-1*) Creekside VA.

— Hope for the Land: Nature in the Bible. LC 88-45550. (Environmental Theology Ser.: Vol. 3). (Illus.). 262p. (Orig.). 1988. pap. 14.00 (*0-8042-0861-1*, 0-9625831) Creekside VA.

— Reclaiming America: Restoring Nature to Culture. LC 87-45550. (Environmental Theology Ser.: Bk. 4). (Illus.). 240p. (Orig.). 1990. pap. 14.00 (*0-9625831-0-3*) Creekside VA.

Austin, Richard Cartwright, ed. & intro. see Stroup, Russell Cartwright.

Austin, Richard L. Lawn Sprinklers: One-Weekend Design & Installation. (Illus.). 208p. (Orig.). 1989. 23.95 (*0-8306-2093-1*); pap. 12.95 (*0-8306-3193-3*) McGraw-Hill Prof.

Austin, Rick. Homespun Poems by a Plumber. 128p. Date not set. pap. 8.95 (*0-89896-053-3*) Larksdale.

Austin, Robert B. Early American Medical Imprints: A Guide to Works Printed in the United States, 1668-1880. 240p. 1999. reprint ed. 50.00 (*1-57898-139-5*) Martino Pubng.

— Early American Medical Imprints 1668-1820. 240p. 1987. reprint ed. pap. text 15.00 (*0-915497-01-8*) Printers Devil.

— Early American Medical Imprints, 1668-1820: A Guide to Works Printed in the U. S. LC 81-12077. 240p. 1981. 175.00 (*0-89235-078-4*) Primary Srce Media.

Austin, Robert D. Measuring & Managing Performance in Organizations. LC 96-9146. 216p. 1996. pap. 24.95 (*0-932633-36-6*) Dorset Hse Pub Co.

Austin, Robert F. A Historical Gazetteer of Southeast Asia. (Monographs: No. 4). 118p. (Orig.). (C). 1986. pap. 15.95 (*1-877751-08-1*); pap. text 15.95 (*1-877751-09-X*) Inst Math Geo.

***Austin, Robert J.** A Manual of Fingerweaving. Fenner, Earl C., ed. (Illus.). 56p. 2000. pap. text 17.95 (*1-929572-00-X*) C C T P Reddick.

Austin, Roland G., ed. see Virgil.

Austin, Ronald L., ed. Conodonts: Investigative Techniques & Applications. (Geology Ser.). 1987. text 97.95 (*0-470-20697-7*) P-H.

Austin, Ruth, ed. The Grants Register, 1997. 15th ed. 1300p. 1996. text 110.00 (*0-312-15898-X*) St Martin.

Austin, Sandra. Color in Garden Design. LC 97-13127. (Illus.). 160p. 1998. 34.95 (*1-56158-187-9*, 070314) Taunton.

Austin, Sandra B., jt. auth. see Coleman, Michael G.

***Austin, Sandy.** Focus on Your Future: High School Planning for Career - College Choices. LC 00-190046. x, 54p. (YA). (gr. 9 up). 2000. 14.99 (*0-9678027-0-9*) Focus on Future.

Austin, Sarat, ed. see Steinbeck, John.

***Austin, Seth.** Bottlenecking Blues & Beyond. 66p. 1999. pap. 19.95 incl. audio compact disk (*0-7866-4355-2*, 97823BCD) Mel Bay.

Austin, Simon A., ed. Sprayed Concrete Technology. 312p. (C). (gr. 13). 1996. 120.00 (*0-419-22270-7*) Routledge.

Austin-Sparks, T. The Centrality of Jesus Christ, Vol. I. unabridged ed. Orig. Title: Anthology of 5 Books. 608p. 1997. reprint ed. pap. 19.95 (*0-940232-60-X*) Seedsowers.

— The House of God. (Works of T. Austin-Sparks: Vol. 2). 680p. 1998. reprint ed. pap. 29.95 (*0-940232-63-4*) Seedsowers.

— Ministry. 1999. pap. 29.95 (*0-940232-66-9*) Seedsowers.

Austin, Stephen F., jt. auth. see Hartman, Bernard-Thomas.

Austin, Steve & Hitchcock, Cathy. Breast Cancer: What You Should Know (But May Not Be Told) about Prevention, Diagnosis, & Treatment. LC 93-49716. (Illus.). 336p. 1994. pap. 14.95 (*1-55958-362-2*) Prima Pub.

— Breast Cancer: What You Should Know (but May Not Have Been Told) about Prevention, Diagnosis & Treatment. 2nd rev. ed. LC 98-33466. 336p. 2000. pap. 16.00 (*0-7615-1258-6*) Prima Pub.

Austin, Steve, see Austin, Stone Cold Steve, pseud.

***Austin, Stone Cold Steve, pseud.** Cause Stone Said So! 224p. 2000. 22.95 (*0-06-039328-9*) HarpC.

Austin, Susan & Meister, Gail. Responding to Children at Risk: A Guide to Recent Reports. 95p. 1990. pap. 21.95 (*1-56602-031-X*) Research Better.

Austin, T., ed. Two Fifteenth-Century Cookery-Books. (EETS, OS Ser.: Vol. 91). 1974. reprint ed. 45.00 (*0-8115-0148-5*) Periodicals Srv.

Austin, T. Al, ed. National Water Conference. 606p. 1989. pap. text 8.00 (*0-87262-714-4*, 714) Am Soc Civil Eng.

Austin, Terri. Changing the View: Student Led Parent Conferences. LC 94-21497. (Teacher-to-Teacher Ser.). 106p. 1994. pap. text 17.50 (*0-435-08818-1*, 08818) Heinemann.

Austin, Terry. Splinter of the Mind's Eye. (Star Wars Ser.). (Illus.). (YA). (gr. 5 up). 1997. pap. text 14.95 (*1-56971-223-9*) Dark Horse Comics.

Austin, Tex, jt. auth. see American Water Works Association. Computer Conference.

Austin, Thomas, jt. auth. see Barker, Martin.

***Austin, Thomas David.** A Faith Journey of a Pilgrim: The Wisdom of Thomas Austin. LC 99-45015. (Illus.). 160p. 1999. 15.00 (*1-57312-297-1*) Smyth & Helwys.

***Austin, Thomas E.** New Retail Power & Muscle: Remarkable Weapon to Win the War at the Point of Sale. LC 00-131367. 64p. 2000. mass mkt. 12.95 (*0-9661144-5-0*, Pub. by BRG Pub) Baker & Taylor.

Austin, Thomas J. A Practical Account of General Paralysis, Its Mental & Physical Symptoms, Statistics, Causes, Seat, & Treatment. LC 75-16681. (Classics in Psychiatry Ser.). 1976. reprint ed. 20.95 (*0-405-07413-1*) Ayer.

Austin, Timothy R. Poetic Voices: Discourse Linguistics & the Poetic Text. LC 93-41329. 240p. (Orig.). 1994. pap. text 24.95 (*0-8173-0726-5*) U of Ala Pr.

Austin, Tom. The O'Malley Saga Bk. 2: Thunder Mountain. LC 98-96233. 192p. 1998. 18.95 (*0-8034-9311-8*, Avalon Bks) Bouregy.

— Uniform Consumer Disclosure Standards for New England: Report & Recommedations to the New England Utility Regulatory Commissions. LC 99-181781. (Consumer Information Disclosure Ser.). 63 p. 1998. write for info. (*1-55516-566-4*) Natl Conf State Legis.

Austin, Tony. I Can Picture the Old Home so Clearly: The Commonwealth & 'Half-Caste' Youth in the Northern Territory 1911-1939. LC 93-205289. xi, 280p. 1993. write for info. (*0-85575-239-4*) AIB & TSIS.

Austin, Trina K. All Aboard the S. S. Nutrient. (Illus.). 26p. (Orig.). (J). (gr. k-4). 1986. pap. 6.50 (*0-9615840-0-9*) Trinas Pr.

Austin, Trudy K. Sydney Mouse Coloring Book. (Illus.). 12p. (Orig.). 1995. pap. 2.00 (*0-9640210-5-6*) Jackson Harbor.

***Austin, Valerie.** Free Yourself from Fear: Self-Hypnosis for Anxiety, Panic Attacks & Phobias. 1998. pap. 11.00 (*0-7225-3553-8*, Thorsons PA) HarpCollins.

Austin, Valerie. Hypnosex: Self-Hypnosis for Greater Sexual Fulfillment. LC 97-17001. 144p. 1997. pap. write for info. (*0-8065-1914-2*) Carol Pub Group.

Austin, Virginia. Say Please. LC 94-10576. (Illus.). (J). (ps). 1996. pap. 4.99 (*1-56402-833-X*) Candlewick Pr.

Austin, W. Timothy. Banana Justice: Field Notes on Philippine Crime & Customs. LC 98-41347. 192p. 1999. 59.95 (*0-275-96204-0*, Praeger Pubs) Greenwood.

Austin, Walter F., jt. ed. see Horne, Charles F.

Austin, William. Peter Rugg: The Missing Man. LC 72-104409. reprint ed. lib. bdg. 22.00 (*0-8398-0071-1*) Irvington.

— Peter Rugg: The Missing Man. (C). 1988. reprint ed. pap. text 6.95 (*0-317-66458-1*) Irvington.

— The Works of William Austin, 1778-1841. reprint ed. lib. bdg. 500.00 (*0-685-18609-1*) Rprt Serv.

Austin, William J. A Deconstruction of T. S. Eliot: The Fire & the Rose. LC 96-31235. 306p. 1996. text 99.95 (*0-7734-4222-7*) E Mellen.

— Underworld 1 & 2. LC 94-65417. 64p. (C). 1994. pap. 10.00 (*1-884970-00-1*) S Press.

— Underworld 3 & 4. Mindock, Gloria & Satan, Igor, eds. LC 97-62060. 72p. 1998. pap. 10.00 (*1-884970-01-X*) S Press.

Austin, William M., ed. Papers in Linguistics in Honor of Leon Dostert. (Janua Linguarum, Ser. Major: No. 25). 1967. text 83.85 (*90-279-0616-5*) Mouton.

***Austin, William R.** The Bunnell/Bonnell Family in America. 207p. 1999. pap. 32.00 (*0-7884-1330-9*, A878) Heritage Bk.

Austin, William W. Susanna, "Jeanie," & "The Old Folks at Home" The Songs of Stephen C. Foster from His Time to Ours. 2nd ed. LC 87-13931. (Music in American Life Ser.). 456p. 1989. text 34.95 (*0-252-01476-6*); pap. text 15.95 (*0-252-06069-5*) U of Ill Pr.

Austin, William W., ed. New Looks at Italian Opera: Essays in Honor of Donald J. Grout. LC 76-1010. (Illus.). 290p. 1976. reprint ed. lib. bdg. 35.00 (*0-8371-8761-3*, AUNL, Greenwood Pr) Greenwood.

Austin, William W., ed. see Debussy, Claude.

Austin-Garrison, Martha, tr. see Brugge, Doug, et al.

Austoker, Joan. A History of the Imperial Cancer Research Fund 1902-1986. (Illus.). 398p. 1988. 84.00 (*0-19-723075-X*) OUP.

Austoker, Joan, ed. Cancer Prevention in Primary Care. 150p. (Orig.). 1995. pap. text 27.00 (*0-7279-0825-1*, Pub. by BMJ Pub) Login Brothers Bk Co.

Austoker, Joan & Bryder, Linda, eds. Historical Perspectives on the Role of the MRC: Essays in the History of the Medical Research Council of the United Kingdom & Its Predecessor, the Medical Research Committee, 1913-1953. (Illus.). 272p. 1989. 58.00 (*0-19-261651-X*) OUP.

Austoker, Joan & McPherson, Ann. Cervical Screening. 2nd ed. (Practical Guides for General Practice Ser.: No. 14). (Illus.). 80p. 1992. pap. 12.95 (*0-19-262170-X*) OUP.

Auston, D. H. & Eisenthal, Kenneth B., eds. Ultrafast Phenomena IV. (Chemical Physics Ser.: Vol. 38). (Illus.). xvi, 509p. 1984. 71.00 (*0-387-13834-X*) Spr-Verlag.

Austone, Lionel. Liberty Enlightening the World. (Illus.). 1986. 55.00 (*0-938237-04-7*) Gold Stein Pr.

Austral Staff. Diccionario Austral de la Lengua Espanol. (SPA.). 350p. 1991. pap. 12.95 (*0-7859-5748-0*) Fr & Eur.

***Australasian Computer Human Interaction Conference Staff, et al.** 1998 Australasian Computer Human Interaction Conference, Ozchi '98: Proceedings, November 30 December 4, 1998, Adelaide, South Australia. LC 98-88396. xii, 350 p. 1998. write for info. (*0-8186-9207-3*) IEEE Comp Soc.

Australasian Congress on Genealogy & Heraldry Staff, et al. Landfall in Southern Seas: Proceedings of the 8th Australasian Congress on Genealogy & Heraldry Held at Lincoln University, Christchurch, New Zealand, February, 1997 by the New Zealand Society of Genealogists Inc. under the Auspices of the Australasian Federation of Family History Organizations, 2 vols. LC 97-198440. 1997. write for info. (*0-473-04140-5*) New Leaf Dist.

Australia, jt. auth. see Richards, Chris.

Australia Bureau of Census & Statistics Staff. The Mathematical Theory of Population, of Its Character & Fluctuations, & of the Factors Which Influence Them. LC 75-38132. (Demography Ser.). (Illus.). 1976. reprint ed. 44.95 (*0-405-07985-0*) Ayer.

Australia-Japan Research Centre Staff, jt. auth. see Sheard, P.

Australia Parliament Senate Committee on Foreign Affairs & Defense. Indochinese Refugee Resettlement: Australia's Involvements. LC 83-144638. xiv, 61p. 1982. write for info. (*0-642-07096-2*) Aust Inst Criminology.

Australia Staff. Report of the Human Rights Commissioner on Certain Provisions of the Tasmanian Criminal Code. LC 96-145566. (Parliamentary Paper of the Parliament of the Commonwealth of Australia). 21p. 1994. write for info. (*0-642-20407-1*, Pub. by Aust Inst Criminology) Advent Bks Div.

— Report of the Interim Committee on the National Estate: Report to the Minister for Urban & Regional Development & the Minister for Environment, May 1975. LC 79-305031. 48p. 1975. write for info. (*0-642-01179-6*, Pub. by Aust Inst Criminology) Lib Res.

— Travel & Tourism LC 90-204258. (Report Ser.). 1989. write for info. (*0-644-10848-7*) Intl Spec Bk.

Australian Administrative Review Council Staff, jt. auth. see Australian Law Reform Commission.

Australian Army Staff. The Australian Army at War: An Official Record of Service in Two Hemispheres, 1939-1944. 3rd rev. ed. (World War II Monograph: Vol. 304). (Illus.). 66p. 1997. reprint ed. 17.95 (*1-57638-077-7*, M304H); reprint ed. pap. 7.95 (*1-57638-019-X*, M304S) Merriam Pr.

Australian Attorney-General's Department Staff, ed. Commonwealth Evidence Law. 1997. pap. 35.95 (*0-644-39601-6*, Pub. by Aust Gov Pub) Accents Pubns.

Australian Aviation Editors. Zero, Hurricane & P-38: Legends of the Air 4. (Legends of the Air Ser.: No. 4). (Illus.). 200p. 1996. pap. 22.95 (*1-875671-24-2*, Pub. by Aerospace Pubns) Motorbooks Intl.

Australian Aviation Staff, jt. auth. see Wilson, Stewart.

Australian Baha'i Children Education Task Force St, ed. Ridvan (1993) Message for Children. 13p. 1992. pap. 2.00 (*0-909991-59-6*) Bahai.

Australian Biological Resources Study Staff. Fungi of Australia Vol. 1B: Introduction - Fungi in the Environment. (Illus.). 405p. 1996. 69.95 (*0-643-05935-0*, Pub. by CSIRO); pap. 54.95 (*0-643-05936-9*, Pub. by CSIRO) Accents Pubns.

Australian Biological Resources Study Staff, ed. Fauna of Australia No. 5, Pts. A & B: Mollusca. (Illus.). 1250p. 1998. 295.00 (*0-643-05756-0*, Pub. by CSIRO) Accents Pubns.

***Australian Bookseller & Publisher Staff, ed.** Directory of Australian Publishers 1999-2000. 350p. 1999. 50.00 (*1-86452-030-2*, Pub. by D W Thorpe) Bowker.

Australian Bureau of Statistics Staff. Implications of the UN/WTO Tourism Definitions: The Canadian Case Study Australia: Comparison of Concepts, Definitions & Classifications Used in Australia. LC 98-137103. 60p. 1997. pap. 15.00 (*92-844-0199-2*, WTO0199, Pub. by Wrld Tourism Org) Bernan Associates.

Australian Bureau of Statistics Staff & Rogers, R. J. Adelaide... A Social Atlas: Census of Population & Housing, 30 June, 1986. LC 93-676209. iv, 48 p. 1988. write for info. (*0-642-14129-0*) Aust Inst Criminology.

Australian Bureau of Statistics Staff, jt. auth. see Madden, Richard.

Australian Bureau of Statistics Staff, jt. auth. see McLennan, W.

***Australian Cricket Board Staff.** Coaching Youth Cricket. (Coaching Youth Ser.). (Illus.). 200p. 2000. pap. 14.95 (*0-7360-3330-0*) Human Kinetics.

Australian Department of Immigration & Multicultur & Foster, William, eds. Immigration & Australian Economy. (Illus.). 192p. 1996. pap. 28.00 (*0-644-47422-X*, Pub. by Aust Gov Pub) Accents Pubns.

Australian Drilling Industry Training Committee St. Drilling: The Manual of Methods, Applications & Management. 624p. 1997. boxed set 94.95 (*1-56670-242-9*, L1242) Lewis Pubs.

Australian Government Publishing Service Staff. Review of the National Capital Plan: Report of the Joint Parliamentary Committee on the Australian Capital Territory. LC 92-187312. (Parliamentary Paper Ser.). ix, 74 p. 1990. write for info. (*0-644-12662-0*, Pub. by AGPS Pr) Intl Spec Bk.

Australian Government Publishing Service Staff, ed. Commonwealth Government Directory, June 1997. 1997. pap. 64.95 (*0-644-50189-8*, Pub. by Aust Gov Pub) Accents Pubns.

Australian Health Ministers' Advisory Council Staf, ed. The Final Report of the Task Force on Quality in Australian Health Care. (Illus.). 1996. pap. 32.95 (*0-644-39703-9*, Pub. by Aust Gov Pub) Accents Pubns.

Australian Heritage Commission. Conserving the National Estate: A Bibliography of National Estate Studies. LC 93-144088. (Bibliography Ser.). vii, 217 p. 1991. write for info. (*0-644-24024-5*, Pub. by Aust Gov Pub) Accents Pubns.

Australian Heritage Commission Staff, jt. auth. see Yencken, David.

Australian Industry Commission, ed. The Pharmaceutical Industry. 912p. 1996. pap. 45.50 (*0-644-36257-X*, Pub. by Aust Gov Pub) Accents Pubns.

— Tourism Accommodation & Training. (Illus.). 611p. 1996. pap. 32.95 (*0-644-36254-5*) Aust Gov Pub.

Australian Institute of Aboriginal & Torres Strait Islander Studies Staff, jt. auth. see Briscoe, Gordon.

Australian Institute Of International Affairs Staf. Australia & the Pacific. LC 70-106405. (Essay Index Reprint Ser.). 1977. 21.95 (*0-8369-1443-0*) Ayer.

Australian Institute of International Affairs Staf. Looking North to South-East Asia: The View from Australia. Wolfers, Edward P., ed. LC 76-50495. 288p. reprint ed. pap. 89.30 (*0-7837-0996-X*, 204130200020) Bks Demand.

Australian Journalists' Association Staff. Ethics in Journalism: Report to the Ethics Review Committee. LC 99-179979. 128p. 1998. pap. 19.95 (*0-522-84814-1*, Pub. by Melbourne Univ Pr) Paul & Co Pubs.

Australian Koala Foundation Staff, jt. auth. see Sharp, Ann.

Australian Law Reform Commission & Australian Administrative Review Council Staff. Open Government: A Review of the Federal Freedom of Information Act 1982. LC 98-114580. (Parliamentary Paper/Parliament of the Commonwealth of Australia Ser.). 270p. 1995. write for info. (*0-642-24477-4*) Aust Inst Criminology.

Australian Legislature Staff, ed. Workplace Relations Regulations. 4th ed. 1997. reprint ed. pap. 27.95 (*0-644-39788-8*) Aust Gov Pub.

Australian Military Forces Staff. Ambush & Counter Ambush. (Illus.). 80p. 1965. reprint ed. pap. 12.00 (*0-87364-098-5*) Paladin Pr.

Australian National Health & Medical Research Coun, ed. Depression in Young People. 176p. 1997. pap. 24.95 (*0-644-39771-3*, Pub. by Aust Gov Pub) Accents Pubns.

Australian National Office of Overseas Skills Reco, ed. Skills Recognition Directory for Professional Occupations in ASEAN & Australia. 681p. 1996. pap. 49.50 (*0-644-36065-8*, Pub. by Aust Gov Pub) Accents Pubns.

Australian National University Press Staff. Kwork Kwork the Green Frog. (Australian National University Press Ser.). (J). 1978. text 18.00 (*0-08-032866-0*, Pergamon Pr) Elsevier.

Australian National University Press Staff, jt. auth. see Di, Hua.

Australian National University Press Staff, jt. auth. see Franpcois, E. Bernard.

Australian National University Press Staff, jt. auth. see Harris, Stuart.

Australian National University Press Staff, jt. auth. see Larmour, Peter J.

Australian National University Press Staff, jt. auth. see Saffu, Yaw.

Australian National University Staff & Ovington, J. D. A Study of the Impact of Tourism at Ayers Rock-MT. Olga National Park. LC 75-309019. viii, 143 p. 1973. write for info. (*0-642-94966-2*) Advent Bks Div.

Australian National University Staff, jt. auth. see Cotton, James.

Australian National University Staff, jt. auth. see Fox, James J.

Australian National University Staff, jt. auth. see Gilding, Simeon.

Australian National University Staff, jt. auth. see Lea, John P.

Australian National University Staff, jt. auth. see Leifer, Michael.

Australian National University Staff, jt. auth. see McGavin, P. A.

Australian National University Staff, jt. auth. see Parkin, Andrew.

A

An Asterisk (*) at the beginning of an entry indicates that the title is appearing for the first time.

Australian Society of Animal Production Staff. Animal Production in Australia: Proceedings of the Australian Society of Animal Production, 14th Biennial Conference, Brisbane, Queensland, May 1982. (Illus.). 708p. 1982. pap. 40.00 (*0-08-024837-3*, Pergamon Pr) Elsevier.
— Animal Production in Australia: Proceedings of the Australian Society of Animal Production, 14th Biennial Conference, Brisbane, Queensland, May 1982. (Illus.). 708p. 1982. 72.00 (*0-08-024836-5*, Pergamon Pr) Elsevier.
— Animal Production in Australia: Proceedings of the Australian Society of Animal Production, 14th Biennial Conference, Brisbane, Queensland, May 1982. 521p. 1988. pap. 40.00 (*0-08-034439-9*) Elsevier.
Australian Society of Ultrasound in Medicine Staff, ed. Proceedings of the Fourth Meeting of the World Federation for Ultrasound in Medicine & Biology. 500p. 1986. pap. 155.00 (*0-08-032792-3*) Elsevier.
Australian Society Staff. Animal Production in Australia. Date not set. pap. write for info. (*0-08-024811-X*, Pergamon Pr) Elsevier.
***Australian Sports Commission.** Physiological Tests for Elite Athletes. LC 99-88959. (Illus.). 480p. 2000. 69.00 (*0-7360-0326-6*) Human Kinetics.
Australian Tourist Commission. Survey of International Visitors: Travel Within Australia. LC 74-167368. 110 p. 1972. write for info. (*0-642-95013-X*) Advent Bks Div.
Austrian, Geoffrey. Ben Austrian, Artist. LC 96-41948. 1997. write for info. (*0-9620844-8-4*) Garrigues Hse.
Austrian, Geoffrey D. Herman Hollerith: Forgotten Giant of Information Processing. LC 81-7752. (Illus.). 242p. 1984. pap. text 23.00 (*0-231-05147-6*) Col U Pr.
***Austrian, Guy, et al.** Ancient Times: A Watts Guide for Children. LC 99-57816. (Guides Ser.). (Illus.). (J). 2000. 32.50 (*0-531-11731-6*) Watts.
Austrian Institute for Economic Research Staff & Vienna Institute for Comparative Economic Studies. Competitiveness of Transition Economies. (OECD Proceedings Ser.). 236p. 1998. pap. 44.00 (*92-64-16121-X*, 14 98 11 1 P, Pub. by European Conference Ministers Transp) OECD.
Austrian Institute Staff. Humanizing Prisons: Experiences from the Austrian Model. 1982. 6.45 (*0-318-02053-X*) Natl Coun Crime.
Austrian, Robert. Life with the Pneumococcus: Notes from the Bedside, Laboratory & Library. LC 85-1001. (Illus.). 160p. 1985. 49.95 (*0-8122-7977-8*) U of Pa Pr.
Austrian Society for Aerospace Medicine Staff, ed. Health from Space Research: Austrian Accomplishments. LC 92-31166. 1992. 40.95 (*0-387-82413-8*) Spr-Verlag.
Austrian, Sonia G. Mental Disorders, Medications, & Clinical Social Work. LC 95-14322. 1995. 44.00 (*0-231-08124-3*) Col U Pr.
***Austrian, Sonia G.** Mental Disorders, Medications & Clinical Social Work. 2nd ed. LC 00-24069. (Illus.). 2000. 45.00 (*0-231-11296-3*) Col U Pr.
Austridan, Yeshayahu. Diccionario Castellano-Hebreo-Castellano. 4th ed. (HEB & SPA.). 400p. 1988. pap. 29.95 (*0-8288-0463-X*, S37819) Fr & Eur.
***Austrin.** Managed Health Care Simplified: A Glossary of Terms. 176p. (C). 2000. text 17.95 (*0-7668-2050-5*) Delmar.
Austrin, Harvey R., jt. auth. see Austrin, Miriam G.
***Austrin, Michael S.** Managed Health Care Simplified: A Glossary of Terms. LC 99-56122. (Illus.). 1999. write for info. (*0-7668-2078-5*) Delmar.
***Austrin, Miriam G.** Learning Medical Terminology: A Worktext, 9th Ed. 9th ed. LC R123.Y6 1999. 1999. 32.00 (*0-323-00279-X*) Mosby Consmer Hlth.
***Austrin, Miriam G. & Austrin, Harvey R.** Learning Medical Terminology. 9th ed. 1998. teacher ed. write for info. (*0-323-00282-X*) Mosby Inc.
— Learning Medical Terminology: A Work Text. 1998. text. write for info. incl. audio (*0-8151-0340-9*) Mosby Inc.
— Learning Medical Terminology: A Work Text. 8th ed. 1998. teacher ed. write for info. (*0-8151-7898-0*) Mosby Inc.
***Austswim Inc. Staff.** Teaching Infant & Preschool Aquatics: Water Experiences the Australian Way. (Illus.). 240p. 2000. pap. 18.95 (*0-7360-3250-9*) Human Kinetics.
— Teaching Swimming & Water Safety: The Australian Way. (Illus.). 280p. 2000. pap. 18.95 (*0-7360-3251-7*) Human Kinetics.
Austyn, C. Gun Engraving. 1998. 50.00 (*1-57157-124-8*) Safari Pr.
— Modern Sporting Guns. (Illus.). 128p. 1994. 40.00 (*1-57157-025-X*) Safari Pr.
Austyn, Christopher. Classic Sporting Rifles. (Illus.). 128p. 1997. 50.00 (*1-57157-100-0*) Safari Pr.
— Gun Engraving. (Illus.). 128p. 1999. 50.00 (*1-57157-119-1*, Pub. by Safari Pr) Natl Bk Netwk.
Austyn, Jonathan M. & Wood, Kathryn J. Principles of Cellular & Molecular Immunology. (Illus.). 746p. 1994. pap. text 59.50 (*0-19-854195-3*) OUP.
Ausubel. Short Protocols in Molecular Biology. 4th ed. LC 00-265552. 1104p. 1999. pap. 120.00 (*0-471-32938-X*) Wiley.
Ausubel, David. Ego Development & Psychopathology. 313p. 1996. text 49.95 (*1-56000-266-2*) Transaction Pubs.
Ausubel, Frederick M., ed. see Brent, Roger, et al.
Ausubel, Herman. In Hard Times: Reformers among the Late Victorians. LC 72-9826. 403p. 1973. reprint ed. lib. bdg. 69.50 (*0-8371-6600-4*, AUHT, Greenwood Pr) Greenwood.
Ausubel, Jesse H. & Herman, Robert, eds. Cities & Their Vital Systems: Infrastructure Past, Present, & Future. LC 88-12517. (Series on Technology & Social Priorities). 363p. 1988. reprint ed. pap. 112.60 (*0-608-02343-4*, 206298400004) Bks Demand.
Ausubel, Jesse H., ed. see National Academy of Engineering Staff.
Ausubel, Jessee H., ed. see Rockefeller University Staff, et al.
Ausubel, Kenny. Restoring the Earth: Visionary Solutions from the Bioneers. LC 97-16958. 288p. 2000. pap. 14.95 (*0-915811-76-6*) Chelsea Green Pub.
***Ausubel, Kenny.** When Healing Becomes a Crime: The Amazing Story of the Hoxsey Cancer Clinics & the Return of Alternative Therapies. LC 99-461975. (Illus.). 480p. 2000. pap. 19.95 (*0-89281-925-1*) Inner Tradit.
Ausubel, Nathan. A Treasury of Jewish Humor. 768p. 1993. 16.99 (*0-88365-842-9*) Galahad Bks.
— A Treasury of Jewish Humor. 1998. 35.00 (*0-87131-862-8*) M Evans.
Ausubel, Nathan, ed. Treasury of Jewish Folklore. 768p. 1989. 22.00 (*0-517-50293-3*, Crown) Crown Pub Group.
Ausubel, Nathan, tr. see Asch, Sholem.
Ausubel, Nathen. A Treasury of Jewish Poetry. 471p. 1977. 30.95 (*0-8369-6178-1*) Ayer.
Auswaks, Alex, tr. see Aron, Paul.
Autauga Quality Cotton Association Staff & Gibbons, Faye. Breaking New Ground: The History of the Autauga Quality Cotton Association. LC 93-17238. 140p. 1993. 30.00 (*1-881320-08-1*, Black Belt) Black Belt Communs.
Auten, Arthur. Critical Thinking Exercises for Western Civilization Courses. 352p. (C). 1993. per. 27.95 (*0-8403-8404-1*, 40840401) Kendall-Hunt.
Auten, D. R. Guitar Toons: Coloring Book. Kirlin, Jim, ed. (Illus.). 25p. (J). (ps-10). 1999. pap. 6.00 (*0-9669881-1-6*) D R Auten.
***Auten, D. R.** Guitar Toons: Music Book, No. 1. Kirlin, Jim, ed. 61p. 1999. Price not set. incl. audio (*0-9669881-0-8*) D R Auten.
— Guitar Toons Music Book & CD. Kirlin, Jim, ed. (Illus.). 61p. 1999. 18.00 incl. audio compact disk (*0-9669881-4-0*) D R Auten.
Auten, D. R. The Gutiar Toons: Music Book, Coloring Book & CD. Kirlin, Jim, ed. (Illus.). 86p. 1999. pap. 22.95 incl. cd-rom (*0-9669881-2-4*) D R Auten.
Auten, Robert C., ed. Le Mans 1950 Photo Archive: The Briggs Cunningham Campaign. LC 94-77251. (Photo Archive Ser.). (Illus.). 144p. 1994. pap. 29.95 (*1-882256-21-2*) Iconografix.
— Sebring 12-Hour Race 1970 Photo Archive. LC 94-77482. (Illus.). 144p. 1994. pap. 29.95 (*1-882256-20-4*) Iconografix.
Autenrieth, Georg. A Homeric Dictionary for Schools & Colleges. Flagg, Isaac, ed. Keep, Robert P., tr. (Illus.). 318p. 1976. reprint ed. pap. 19.95 (*0-8061-1289-1*) U of Okla Pr.
Autenrieth, Hans P., jt. auth. see Hoffmann, Volker.
Auterhoff, H. Dictionary of the Pharmach Vol. 1: Woerterbuch der Pharmazie: Biologie, Chemie, Technologie. (ENG & GER.). 532p. 1981. 95.00 (*0-8288-1835-5*, M15388) Fr & Eur.
Auterhoff, Harry Von, see Von Auterhoff, Harry.
Auteroche, B., et al. Acupuncture & Moxibustion: A Guide to Clinical Practice. (Illus.). 164p. 1992. text. write for info. (*0-443-04556-9*) Church.
Autery & Holl. Help I Need a Bulletin Board. 1979. pap. 7.75 (*0-89137-621-6*) Quality Pubns.
Autexier, Philippe A. Beethoven: The Composer as Hero. (Discoveries Ser.). (Illus.). 144p. 1992. pap. 12.95 (*0-8109-2832-9*, Pub. by Abrams) Time Warner.
Auth, Betty. The Weekend Crafter: Woodburning; 20 Great-Looking Projects to Decorate in a Weekend. Duncan, Katherine, ed. LC 99-31343. (Weekend Crafter Ser.). (Illus.). 80p. 1999. pap. 14.95 (*1-57990-135-2*, Pub. by Lark Books) Sterling.
***Auth, Charles R., et al.** A Dominican Bibliography & Book of Reference, 1216-1992: A List of Works in English by & about Members of the Order of Friars Preachers, Founded by St. Dominic De Guzman (c. 1171-1221) & Confirmed by Pope Honorius III, December 22, 1216. LC 99-35071. 1224p. (C). 2000. text 99.95 (*0-8204-4445-6*) P Lang Pubng.
Auth, Janice, ed. To Beijing & Back: Pittsburgh & the United Nation's Fourth World Conference on Women. LC 97-45366. (Illus.). 225p. 1998. pap. 14.95 (*0-8229-5653-5*) U of Pittsburgh Pr.
Auth, Patrick & Kerstein, Morris. Review for Physician Assistants. 320p. pap. text 45.00 (*0-7817-1927-5*) Lppncott W & W.
Auth, Susan H. Ancient Glass at the Newark Museum. LC 76-47222. 1977. 15.95 (*0-932828-02-7*); pap. 9.95 (*0-932828-08-6*) Newark Mus.
Authelet, Jack. Foxborough. (Images of America Ser.). 128p. 1996. pap. 16.99 (*0-7524-0266-8*) Arcadia Publng.
Authement, Eural & McCabe, James D. Building Resilient & Scalable IP Networks Using OPF. 350p. 1999. pap. 44.95 (*1-55860-565-7*, Pub. by Morgan Kaufmann) Harcourt.
Authi, K. S., et al. Mechanisms of Platelet Activation & Control. LC 93-32065. (Advances in Experimental Medicine & Biology Ser.: Vol. 334). (Illus.). 286p. (C). 1994. text 89.50 (*0-306-44631-6*, Kluwer Plenum) Kluwer Academic.
Authi, Kalwant, jt. ed. see Watson, Stephen.
Authi, Kalwant S., et al. Platelets & Their Factors. LC 96-39635. (Handbook of Experimental Pharmacology Ser.). 1997. write for info. (*3-540-61997-6*) Spr-Verlag.
Authier, Andre, et al, eds. X-Ray & Neutron Dynamical Diffraction, Theory & Applications: Proceedings of a NATO ASI Held in Erice, Italy, April 9-21, 1996. (NATO ASI Series B: Vol. 357). 430p. (C). 1997. text 125.00 (*0-306-45501-3*) Plenum.
Authier, J. Marc, ed. see Linguistic Symposium on Romance Languages Staff.
Authier, Jerry, jt. auth. see Ivey, Allen E.
Author Aid-Research Associates International Staff, ed. Freelancers of North America, 1984-1985 Marketplace: Editors, Ghostwriters-Collaborators, Speechwriters, Business-Technical-Medical-Writers. 316p. 1984. pap. 32.95 (*0-911085-01-7*) Author Aid.
— Literary Agents of North America: 1984-85 Marketplace. 144p. (Orig.). 1984. pap. 16.95 (*0-911085-00-9*, 0082-1) Author Aid.
Authors, Mandy & Riders, Leigh. Chupacabra, You Don't Scare Me! (Illus.). 32p. (J). (gr. 3-6). 1999. pap. 7.00 (*0-8059-4490-7*) Dorrance.
Author22 Publishing Staff. Mama Was a Preacher. deluxe ed. LC 98-96141. 460p. 1999. pap. 19.95 (*1-892183-02-1*) DTTN.
— My Father the Czar. deluxe ed. LC 98-96138. 510p. 1999. pap. 22.95 (*1-892183-00-5*) DTTN.
— My Teenage Heart. deluxe ed. LC 98-96140. 440p. 1999. pap. 19.95 (*1-892183-01-3*) DTTN.
— The Pirate Affair. deluxe ed. LC 98-96142. 300p. 1999. pap. 19.95 (*1-892183-03-X*) DTTN.
Autin, Amelia. Gideon's Bride. 1995. per. 3.75 (*0-373-07666-5*) Harlequin Bks.
— Reilly's Return. 1997. per. 3.99 (*0-373-07820-X*, 1-07820-3) Silhouette.
***Autin, Marie-Christine, et al.** Jewels in Painting. (Illus.). 200p. 1999. 60.00 (*88-8118-527-X*, Pub. by Skira IT) Abbeville Pr.
Autin, Whitney J., et al. Two Caddoan Farmsteads in the Red River Valley: The Archeology of the McLelland & Joe Clark Sites. LC 97-16922. (Research Ser.: No. 51). (Illus.). 1997. 15.00 (*1-56349-082-X*) AR Archaeol.
***Autio, Clyde F.** Full Bellies & Empty Hearts. 118p. 1999. pap. 11.99 (*1-928965-03-2*) New Convenant.
Autio, James. The Digital Mantrap: A Training Program for Business Professionals. 55.00 (*0-9678487-0-9*) eBola Comms.
Auto Bingo Staff. Augo Bingo 1. Date not set. 2.95 (*1-879424-82-7*) Nickel Pr.
Auto Body News Staff, ed. see Franklin, Thomas B.
***Auto Club, South California Editors.** Sequoia & Kings Canyon Guide. 1998. pap. 3.95 (*1-56413-391-5*) Auto Club.
Auto Club, Southern California Editors. Colorado River Guide Map AAA. (Illus.). 1998. 3.95 (*1-56413-348-6*) Auto Club.
— Death Valley Guide Map AAA. (Illus.). 1997. 3.95 (*1-56413-393-1*) Auto Club.
— Downtown Los Angeles Guide Map AAA. (Illus.). 1999. 3.95 (*1-56413-476-8*) Auto Club.
— Golf Courses - Central & Southern California Guide Map AAA. rev. ed. 91p. 1997. pap. 3.95 (*1-56413-333-8*) Auto Club.
— Indian Country Guide Map AAA. 1998. 3.95 (*1-56413-441-5*) Auto Club.
— Los Angeles County Mountain & Desert Explore Map AAA. (Illus.). 1997. 3.95 (*1-56413-354-0*) Auto Club.
— Los Angeles International Airport Map AAA. (Illus.). 1998. 1.95 (*1-56413-347-8*) Auto Club.
— Los Angeles/Long Beach Harbors Map AAA. (Illus.). 1999. 1.95 (*1-56413-402-4*) Auto Club.
— Mother Lode Guide Map AAA. (Illus.). 1997. 3.95 (*1-56413-367-2*) Auto Club.
— Riverside County Explore Map AAA. 1998. 3.95 (*1-56413-433-4*) Auto Club.
— San Bernardino Mountains Guide Map AAA. (Illus.). 1998. 3.95 (*1-56413-409-1*) Auto Club.
— San Diego County Explore Map. 1998. 3.95 (*1-56413-398-2*) Auto Club.
— San Diego Guide Map AAA. (Illus.). 1997. 3.95 (*1-56413-376-1*) Auto Club.
— Southern & Central California Camping Map AAA. (Illus.). 1998. 3.95 (*1-56413-416-4*) Auto Club.
— Southern & Central California Golf Courses - Map AAA. (Illus.). 1997. 3.95 (*1-56413-385-0*) Auto Club.
— Wineries - Central & Southern California Guide Map AAA. (Illus.). 1998. 3.95 (*1-56413-425-3*) Auto Club.
— Yosemite National Park Guide Map AAA. (Illus.). 1998. 3.95 (*1-56413-430-X*) Auto Club.
***Auto Club, Southern California Editors Staff.** Eastern Sierra Map AAA. (Illus.). 1998. pap. 3.95 (*1-56413-428-8*) Auto Club.
— Orange County Explore Map AAA. (Illus.). 1997. pap. 3.95 (*1-56413-397-4*) Auto Club.
— Santa Barbara Explore Map AAA. (Illus.). 1997. pap. 3.95 (*1-56413-356-7*) Auto Club.
— Wineries - Northern California Map AAA. (Illus.). 1998. pap. 3.95 (*1-56413-426-1*) Auto Club.
Auto Desk Press Staff. A Visitor's Guide, Whitehouse Is Our House. (Cord Communications Ser.). 1997. pap. 7.95 (*0-538-67180-7*) S-W Pub.
Auto Sport Int'l. Inc. Staff. Indy Car, 93-94: The Men & Machines of Indy Car Racing. (Illus.). 192p. 1994. 29.90 (*0-929323-11-4*) Autosport Intl.
Autodesk, Inc. Staff. Autosketch R2 Windows. (CAD/CAM Ser.). 1995. 132.00 (*0-8273-7532-8*) Delmar.
— 3D Studio. (General Engineering Ser.). 1996. pap. 5.95 (*0-534-95376-X*) PWS Pubs.
— 3D Studio. (General Engineering Ser.). 1996. cd-rom 79.50 (*0-534-95382-4*) PWS Pubs.
— 3D Studio - Educational Version: Reference Manual. (General Engineering Ser.). 1996. pap., suppl. ed. 31.75 (*0-534-95370-0*) PWS Pubs.
— 3D Studio - Educational Version: Tutorial Guide. (General Engineering Ser.). 1996. pap., suppl. ed. 31.75 (*0-534-95364-6*) PWS Pubs.
Autodesk, Inc. Staff, et al. Personal Computer-Based CAD-CAM, CAE Markets & Opportunities. (Illus.). 225p. 1987. ring bd. 1395.00 (*0-938484-21-4*) Daratech.
Autodesk Press Staff. Inside Track for Mechanical Design & Drafting. 32p. (C). 1997. pap. text, teacher ed. 15.00 (*0-8273-8489-0*) Delmar.
Autodesk Press Staff. Learning Autocad LT for Windows 95: A CADD Desktop Tutor Interactive CD-Rom. 21.95 (*0-7668-0269-8*, Pub. by Delmar) Thomson Learn.
— Making Models in 3D Studio R4: Interactive CD-Rom for Windows 3.1 & 95. (Illus.). 56.95 incl. cd-rom (*0-7668-0085-7*, Pub. by Delmar) Thomson Learn.
Autodesk Press Staff. Mechanical Desktop Training Material. 752p. 1997. pap. text, teacher ed. write for info. (*0-7668-0056-3*) Delmar.
— Mechanical Desktop Training Material. 752p. 1997. text, student ed. 75.00 (*0-7668-0054-7*) Delmar.
AutoDesk Press Staff. Using AutoCAD R14 for DOS: Text & Quick Reference Package, Release 12. 1000p. 1998. pap. write for info. (*0-8273-7021-0*, AutoDesk Pr) Delmar.
— Using AutoCAD R14 for DOS: Text & Quick Reference Package, Release 13. 1000p. 1998. pap. write for info. (*0-8273-7018-0*, AutoDesk Pr) Delmar.
Autodesk Press Staff. Using AutoCAD R14 Windows. 1152p. 1998. pap. 19.95 (*0-7668-0128-4*, AutoDesk Pr) Delmar.
***AutoDesk Press Staff.** Using AutoCAD 2000. Grabowski, Ralph, ed. LC 99-32667. 1152p. 1999. 64.95 (*0-7668-1236-7*) Delmar.
AutoDesk Press Staff & Grabowski, Ralph. Using AutoCAD R14 for Windows: Release 14. abr. rev. ed. LC 97-25349. 1152p. 1997. pap. 69.95 (*0-7668-0127-6*, AutoDesk Pr) Delmar.
Autodeskpress Staff. Inside Track For Architectural Draft & Design. (Onword - CAD Titles Ser.). 1997. 149.95 (*0-8273-7708-8*) Delmar.
— Inside Track For Mechanical Drafting & Design. (Onword - CAD Titles Ser.). 1995. 20.95 (*0-8273-7694-4*) Delmar.
— Links to Architecture: AutoCAD & 3D Studio. (Onword - CAD Titles Ser.). 1996. 249.95 (*0-8273-7729-0*) Delmar.
— Links to Mechanical Design & Drafting: CAD Design 3D. (Onword - CAD Titles Ser.). 1996. 250.00 (*0-8273-7730-4*) Delmar.
Autofact '85 (1985: Detroit, MI) Staff. Autofact, '85: Conference Proceedings, November 4-7, 1985, Detroit, MI. LC 85-62651. (Illus.). 919p. reprint ed. pap. 200.00 (*0-8357-6502-4*, 203587300097) Bks Demand.
Automata Publishing Staff. Programming the I386-I486. 1994. text. write for info. (*0-442-01427-9*, VNR) Wiley.
Automated Design & Engineering for Electronics Sta. Automated Design & Engineering for Electronics: Proceedings of the Technical Sessions, February 26-28, 1985, Anaheim, CA. LC TK7835.. 389p. reprint ed. pap. 120.60 (*0-8357-5910-5*, 202519100042) Bks Demand.
— Automated Design & Engineering for Electronics: Proceedings of the Technical Sessions, Moscone Convention Center, San Francisco, CA, March 11-13, 1986. LC TK7835.. 320p. reprint ed. pap. 99.20 (*0-8357-5911-3*, 202768800056) Bks Demand.
— Automated Design & Engineering for Electronics: Proceedings of the Technical Sessions, October, 15-17, 1985 Boston, MA. LC TK7835.. 415p. reprint ed. pap. 128.70 (*0-8357-5912-1*, 202768900056) Bks Demand.
— Automated Design & Engineering for Electronics--East: Proceedings of the Technical Sessions, World Trade Center, Boston, MA., Sept. 30 - Oct. 2, 1986. LC TK7835.. 449p. reprint ed. pap. 139.20 (*0-8357-5909-1*, 202936400060) Bks Demand.
— Automated Design & Engineering for Electronics-West: Proceedings of the Technical Sessions, March 31-April 2, 1987. LC TK7835.. (Illus.). 387p. pap. 120.00 (*0-8357-5913-X*, 203023600067) Bks Demand.
Automatic Control in Electricity Supply Staff. Symposium on Automatic Control in Electricity Supply, 29-31 March, 1966 in Manchester, England. LC TJ0212.S96. (IEE Conference Publication: No. 16, Pt. 1). (Illus.). 392p. reprint ed. pap. 121.60 (*0-608-10874-X*, 205158800092) Bks Demand.
Automobile Association of Great Britain Staff. AA Walks & Tours in France. 256p. 1996. pap. 25.00 (*0-393-31512-6*) Norton.
— Automobile Association Illustrated Guide to France. 1992. 45.00 (*0-393-03456-9*) Norton.
***Automobile Association of Great Britain Staff.** Frommer's Road Atlas Europe. 2nd ed. (Frommer's Road Atlas Ser.). (Illus.). 240p. 2000. pap. 22.99 (*0-7645-6175-8*) IDG Bks.
Automobile Association of Great Britain Staff. The Illustrated Guide to Britain. (Illus.). 256p. 1997. pap. 25.95 (*0-393-31643-2*) Norton.
— Village France. (Illus.). 224p. 2000. pap. 25.95 (*0-393-31666-1*) Norton.
— Where to Go in Britain. (Illus.). 192p. 1993. 35.00 (*0-393-03459-3*) Norton.
Automobile Association Staff. AAA Britain Road Atlas. 92p. 1997. pap. text 19.95 (*1-56251-237-4*) AAA.
— AAA Britain TravelBook. 1997. pap. 14.95 (*1-56251-243-9*) AAA.
***Automobile Association Staff.** AAA Europe Road Atlas. 128p. 2000. pap. 19.95 (*1-56251-303-6*, Pub. by AAA) S&S Trade.
Automobile Association Staff. AAA France TravelBook. 1997. pap. 14.95 (*1-56251-242-0*) AAA.
— The AAA Guide to North America's Theme Parks. 3rd ed. 270p. 1997. pap. 16.00 (*1-56251-244-7*) AAA.
— AAA Pocket Atlas: Germany, Austria & Switzerland. (Illus.). 1994. pap. 9.95 (*1-56251-223-4*) AAA.
— AAA Pocket Atlas: Italy, Austria, & Switzerland. (Illus.). 1996. pap. 9.95 (*1-56251-218-8*) AAA.
— AAA Pocket Atlas: Spain & Portugal. (Illus.). 1996. pap. 9.95 (*1-56251-222-6*) AAA.
— AAA Pocket Atlas, 1992: Britain. (Illus.). 96p. 1996. pap. 9.95 (*1-56251-219-6*) AAA.
— AAA Pocket Atlas, 1992: France & Benelux. (Illus.). 96p. 1996. pap. 9.95 (*1-56251-221-8*) AAA.

An Asterisk (*) at the beginning of an entry indicates that the title is appearing for the first time.

— AAA Pocket Atlas, 1992: Ireland. (Illus.). 96p. 1996. pap. 9.95 (*1-56251-220-X*) AAA.

— Best Pubs & Inns. (Illus.). 368p. 1999. pap. 16.95 (*0-8442-9566-3*, 95663, Passprt Bks) NTC Contemp Pub Co.

***Automobile Association Staff.** Britain Guide. 464p. 2000. pap. 18.95 (*0-658-00626-6*, 006266) NTC Contemp Pub Co.

Automobile Association Staff. France Bed & Breakfast. (Illus.). 1997. pap. 16.95 (*1-56251-240-4*) AAA.

Automobile Association Staff. Ireland. (AA Guides Ser.). 49.95 (*0-393-05025-4*) Norton.

Automobile Association Staff. A Ordnance Survey Leisure Guide: Lake District. Date not set. pap. text 15.95 (*0-7495-1195-8*, Pub. by Auto Assn Guides) Hunter NJ.

— Scotland Highlands & Islands. (AA - Ordnance Survey Leisure Guides). 1996. pap. text 15.95 (*0-7495-1199-0*, Pub. by Auto Assn Guides) Hunter NJ.

— Village Walks in Britain. 264p. 1996. pap. 25.00 (*0-393-31502-9*) Norton.

— Walks & Tours in Britain: AA Weekend Walks in Britain. 320p. 1996. pap. 25.00 (*0-393-31501-0*) Norton.

Automobile Quarterly Staff. Corvette: A Piece of the Action. 2nd ed. LC 84-61085. (Illus.). 224p. 1985. 39.95 (*0-915038-44-7*, 3-AQ-1086) Auto Quarterly.

Automobile Quarterly Staff, jt. auth. see Query, Roy D.

Automotive Consulting Group, Inc. Staff. Supplier Opportunities into the 21st Century: A Look to the Future for Suppliers. Date not set. 495.00 (*0-614-95832-6*) Wards Comm.

Automotive Materials Symposium Staff. Numerical Simulation of Casting Solidification in Automotive Applications: Proceedings of the 18th Annual Automotive Materials Symposium Sponsored by the Detroit Section of TMS, Held on May 1-2, Kellogg Center, Michigan State University. Kim, Chongmin & Kim, Chung-Whee, eds. LC 91-51008. (Illus.). 364p. 1991. reprint ed. pap. 112.90 (*0-608-05692-8*, 206620700007) Bks Demand.

Auton, Graeme P., ed. Arms Control & European Security. LC 89-3663. 211p. 1989. 57.95 (*0-275-93153-6*, C3153, Praeger Pubs) Greenwood.

Autonomedia Collective Staff & Felshin, Nina. No Laughing Matter, 1991. (Illus.). 48p. 1991. 8.00 (*0-916365-33-6*) Ind Curators.

Autorentaem Staff. Management Enzyklopaedie, 7 vols., Set. (GER.). 1973. 1750.00 (*0-8288-6317-2*, M7091) Fr & Eur.

— Management Enzyklopaedie, 10 vols., Set, Vols. 1-10. (GER.). 3200p. 1975. pap. 395.00 (*0-8288-5934-5*, M7092) Fr & Eur.

Autosport Editors. CART 87-88, the Men & Machines of Indy Car Racing. (Yearbook Ser.). (Illus.). 168p. 1987. 29.00 (*0-929323-00-9*) Autosport Intl.

— Daytona 500: The Men & Machines of Speed Week 1993. (Yearbook Ser.). (Illus.). 160p. 1993. 29.90 (*0-929323-10-6*) Autosport Intl.

— Daytona Five Hundred: The Men & Machines of Speed Week '94. (Racing Annual Ser.). (Illus.). 160p. 1994. 29.90 (*0-929323-12-2*) Autosport Intl.

Autosport International Editorial Staff. Motorsports America: The Men & Machines of American Motorsport, 1998-1999. (Illus.). 196p. 1999. 29.90 (*0-929323-17-3*, Pub. by Autosport Intl) Motorbooks Intl.

Autosport International, Inc. Staff. Motorsports America: The Men & Machines of Motorsports, 1994-95. (Illus.). 192p. 1995. 29.90 (*0-929323-13-0*) Autosport Intl.

Autosport International Staff. Motorsport America: The Men & Machines of American Motorsports, 1997-98. 1998. 29.90 (*0-929323-16-5*) Autosport Intl.

***Autosport International Staff.** Motorsports America: The Men & Machines of American Motorsport. (Illus.). 196p. 2000. 29.90 (*0-929323-18-1*, 130140AE, Pub. by Autosport Intl) Motorbooks Intl.

Autosport International Staff. Motorsports America: The Men & Machines of American Motorsport, 1995-96. (Illus.). 192p. 1996. 29.90 (*0-929323-14-9*) Autosport Intl.

AutoTek Staff, ed. see Boynton, Thomas J.

Autrey, Stephanie L. Jackson, the Flying Laptop Computer. LC 95-79387. (Illus.). 40p. (J). (gr. 1-5). 1996. 14.95 (*0-9648144-0-4*) Monarch Grp.

Autrum, H., et al, eds. Handbook of Sensory Physiology, 8 vols. Incl. Pt. 1: Olfaction. Chemical Sense. Beidler, L. M., ed. 1972. 138.00 (*0-387-05291-7*); Vol. 7, Pt. 4. Visual Psychophysics. Jameson, D. & Hurvich, L. M., eds. 1972. 182.00 (*0-387-05146-5*); write for info. (*0-318-55786-X*) Spr-Verlag.

— Progress in Sensory Physiology, Vol. 12. (Illus.). 260p. 1991. 136.00 (*0-387-52985-3*) Spr-Verlag.

— Progress in Sensory Physiology: Ionic & Volume Changes in the Microenvironment of Nerve & Receptor Cells, Vol. 13. (Illus.). 176p. 1992. 123.00 (*0-387-54553-0*) Spr-Verlag.

Autrum, H., ed. see Wilson, P. & Snow, P. J.

Autrup, Herman & Williams, Gary M., eds. Experimental Colon Carcinogenesis. 320p. 1983. 180.00 (*0-8493-5543-5*, RC280, CRC Reprint) Franklin.

Autry, Ewart A. & Autry, Lola M. Don't Look Back Mama. 171p. 1990. reprint ed. 14.97 (*0-9602806-0-X*) Whippoorwill.

— The Turtle & the Oak. 104p. 1992. pap. 7.95 (*0-9602806-2-6*) Whippoorwill.

***Autry, George B., et al.** The Carolinas: Yesterday, Today, Tomorrow: An Exploration of Social & Economic Trends, 1924-1999. LC 99-47147. 1999. write for info. (*0-9651907-2-2*) MDC.

Autry, George B., et al. The State of the South. LC 96-94245. (Illus.). xiv, 80p. (Orig.). 1996. pap. 20.00 (*0-9651907-0-6*) MDC.

— The State of the South, 1998. (Illus.). 1998. pap. 20.00 (*0-9651907-1-4*) MDC.

Autry, Gloria D. & Allen, T. Diener. The Color-Coded Allergy Cookbook. LC 82-17826. 400p. 1983. 19.95 (*0-672-52746-4*) Macmillan.

Autry, James A. Confessions of an Accidental Businessman: It Takes a Lifetime to Find Wisdom. LC 96-28186. 250p. 1996. 24.95 (*1-57675-003-5*) Berrett-Koehler.

— Life & Work: A Manager's Search for Meaning. 304p. 1995. pap. 11.00 (*0-380-72564-9*, Avon Bks) Morrow Avon.

— Love & Profit: The Art of Caring Leadership. 224p. 1992. pap. 12.50 (*0-380-71749-2*, Avon Bks) Morrow Avon.

— Nights under a Tin Roof. 1983. 15.95 (*0-916242-26-9*) Yoknapatawpha.

Autry, James A. & Mitchell, Stephen. Real Power: Business Lessons from the Tao Te Ching. 219p. 1999. reprint ed. pap. 14.00 (*1-57322-720-X*, Riverhd Trade) Berkley Pub.

Autry, Lola M., jt. auth. see Autry, Ewart A.

Autry Museum of Western Heritage Staff, jt. auth. see Dippie, Brian W.

Autry, Peyton. Warrick County. (Illus.). 144p. 1986. 21.95 (*0-9617663-1-X*); pap. 14.95 (*0-9617663-0-1*) McDowell Pubns.

Autry, Raz. The Adventures of Bad Sam. LC 85-15748. (Illus.). 100p. (J). (gr. 7-10). 1985. 7.95 (*0-934145-00-8*) Airborne Pr.

— Nothing but the Truth. (Illus.). 250p. 1988. pap. 7.95 (*0-934145-61-X*) Airborne Pr.

— Sam in Flight: Further Adventures of Bad Sam. LC 92-496. (Illus.). 64p. (Orig.). (J). (gr. 1-6). 1992. pap. 5.95 (*1-56474-029-3*) Fithian Pr.

— With Whom Do You Walk? LC 89-35148. 144p. (Orig.). 1990. pap. 8.95 (*0-931832-36-5*) Fithian Pr.

Auty, B., jt. auth. see Obolensky, J.

Auty, Islay, ed. see British Horse Society Staff.

Auty, Nadira, et al. Just Listen 'n Learn Arabic: Beginning Through Intermediate. (ARA & ENG.). 240p. (C). 1998. pap. 17.95 (*0-8442-8468-8*, X8468-8) NTC Contemp Pub Co.

Auty, R., et al, eds. Oxford Slavonic Papers, Vol.11. (New Ser.). (Illus.). 1979. 32.00 (*0-19-815653-7*) OUP.

Auty, R. & Obolensky, D., eds. Companion to Russian Studies: An Introduction to Russian History, Vol. 1. LC 75-10688. 420p. 1981. pap. text 29.95 (*0-521-28038-9*) Cambridge U Pr.

Auty, R. M. & Brown, Katrina. Approaches to Sustainable Development. LC 96-20532. (Global Development & the Environment Ser.). (Illus.). 256p. 1997. 89.95 (*1-85567-439-4*) Bks Intl VA.

Auty, Richard. Patterns of Development: Resources, Policy & Economic Growth. LC 95-176209. (Arnold Publications). (Illus.). 320p. 1994. pap. text 35.00 (*0-340-59502-7*) OUP.

Auty, Richard M. Economic Development & Industrial Policy: Korea, Brazil, Mexico, India & China. LC 93-42671. (Global Development & the Environment Ser.). 272p. 1995. 110.00 (*0-7201-2175-2*) Continuum.

— Resource-Based Industrialization: Sowing the Oil in Eight Developing Countries. (Illus.). 304p. 1990. 75.00 (*0-19-823299-3*) OUP.

Auty, Richard M. & Mikesell, Raymond F. Sustainable Development in Mineral Economies. LC 98-8568. (Illus.). 297p. 1999. text 65.00 (*0-19-829487-5*) OUP.

Auty, Richard M. & Toye, John, eds. Challenging the Orthodoxies. 272p. 1996. text 85.00 (*0-312-16017-8*) St Martin.

Auty, Robert. Handbook of Old Church Slavonic, Pt. 2: Texts & Glossary. 2nd ed. (London East European Ser.). 148p. (C). 1968. pap. 48.50 (*0-485-17518-5*, Pub. by Athlone Pr) Humanities.

Auvenshine, Martha & Enriquez, Martha. Comprehensive Maternity Nursing. 2nd ed. 1000p. 1989. 58.75 (*0-86720-421-4*) Jones & Bartlett.

Auvenshine, Martha A. & Enriquez, Martha G. Maternal & Newborn Nursing. 3rd ed. (Illus.). 656p. 1997. pap. text. write for info. (*0-316-06293-6*) Lppncott W & W.

Auvergne, Daniel & Hartenstein, Reiner, eds. Power & Timing Modeling for Performance of Integrated Circuits. (Microsystems Engineering Ser.: No. 204). (Illus.). 248p. (Orig.). 1993. pap. 42.80 (*0-9639887-4-3*) IT Press.

Auvergne, William. De Trinitate. Switalski, Bruno, ed. (LAT.). xiv, 269p. pap. 36.57 (*0-88844-034-0*) Brill Academic Pubs.

Auvil. Applications of Desktop Publishing: Simulation. (DF - Computer Applications Ser.). (C). 1996. pap. 26.95 (*0-538-70742-9*) S-W Pub.

— Fundamentals of Building Automations Systems & Pneumatic Systems. (C). 1998. pap. text, teacher ed. 10.00 (*0-8273-7928-5*) Delmar.

— Hvac Control Systems. (C). 2002. pap. text 45.75 (*0-7668-1629-X*) Delmar.

Auvil, jt. auth. see Boyce.

Auvil, Daniel. Elementary Algebra. 4th ed. (C). 1992. pap. text, student ed. 21.00 (*0-201-14987-7*) Addison-Wesley.

— Elementary Algebra: Kent State Student's Solutions Manual. 4th ed. (C). 1992. pap. text, student ed. 17.00 (*0-201-65037-1*) Addison-Wesley.

Auvil, Daniel L. Algebra for College Students. LC 95-24774. 736p. (C). 1995. 66.56 (*0-07-003106-1*) McGraw.

— Algebra for College Students: Student Solutions Manual. (C). 1996. pap. text, student ed. 37.19 (*0-07-003182-7*) McGraw.

— Calculus with Applications. LC 81-14914. 1982. student ed. write for info. (*0-201-10064-9*) Addison-Wesley.

— Intermediate Algebra. 2nd ed. 505p. (C). 1987. text. write for info. (*0-318-61725-0*); disk 120.00 (*0-201-11048-2*) Addison-Wesley.

— S/S/M Intermediate Alg. 2nd ed. LC 85-18515. 505p. (C). 1987. pap. text, student ed. 19.50 (*0-201-11047-4*) Addison-Wesley.

Auvil, Kenneth W. Introduction to Business Graphics: Concepts & Applications. (C). 1991. mass mkt. 27.95 (*0-538-70320-2*) S-W Pub.

— MACtivities: Learning to Use the Macintosh Computer. 1990. mass mkt. 22.95 (*0-538-60704-1*) S-W Pub.

— Perspective Drawing. 2nd rev. ed. LC 96-9382. (Illus.). 87p. (C). 1996. pap. text 14.95 (*1-55934-697-3*, 1697) Mayfield Pub.

Auvil, Mary S., et al. MS-PC DOS Lab Manual. 2nd ed. 304p. (C). 1991. mass mkt. 17.95 (*0-534-92559-6*) Course Tech.

Auvil, Peggy A. We Bought a Bird That Said Dirty Words. (Illus.). 24p. (J). (gr. k-6). 1999. pap. 8.00 (*0-8059-4656-X*) Dorrance.

Auvine, Brian, et al. A Manual for Group Facilitators (Illus.). 89p. 1999. pap. 16.00 (*0-9602714-7-3*) Fllwshp Intent.

Auw, Andre. Gentle Roads to Survival: Making Self-Healing Choices in Difficult Circumstances. LC 90-48311. 160p. (Orig.). 1991. pap. 10.95 (*0-944031-18-8*) Aslan Pub.

— The Gift of Wounding: Making Self-Healing Choices in Difficult Circumstances. LC 98-30152. 160p. 1999. pap. 13.95 (*0-944031-79-X*) Aslan Pub.

— The Gift of Wounding: Making Self-Healing Choices in Difficult Circumstances. 160p. 15.95 (*0-944031-77-3*) Aslan Pub.

Auwarter, Raymond G., ed. see Tolhurst, Desmond.

Auwera, Johan Van Der, see Van Der Auwera, Johan.

Auwera, Johan Van Der, see Kefer, Michael & Van Der Auwera, Johan, eds.

Auwera, Johan Van der, see Van der Auwera, Johan.

Auwera, Johan Van Der, see Van Der Auwera, Johan, ed.

Auwerda, Robert. Fatherhood: Life in a Three-Ring Circus. LC 97-157272. 1997. pap. text 5.99 (*0-87788-235-5*, H Shaw Pubs) Waterbrook Pr.

Auxaneer, Nancy. Here Will I Dwell: The Story of Caldwell County, North Carolina. (Illus.). 230p. 1993. reprint ed. lib. bdg. 29.50 (*0-8328-3537-4*) Higginson Bk Co

Auxentios, Hieromonk. The Paschal Fire in Jerusalem: A Study of the Rite of the Holy Fire in the Church of the Holy Sepulchre. 225p. (Orig.). 1993. pap. 8.95 (*0-9634692-0-7*) St John Chrysostom.

Auxier, George R. Discovering Your Hidden Wealth: Coopers & Lybrand's Guide to Finding & Growing Your Personal Assets. 320p. 1999. pap. 12.95 (*0-452-27342-0*, Plume) Dutton Plume.

Auxier, George R., et al. Discovering Your Hidden Wealth: Coopers & Lybrand's Guide to Finding & Growing Your Personal Assets. 300p. 1999. pap. 24.95 (*0-525-93923-7*, Dutt) Dutton Plume.

Auxier, John A. Ichiban: Radiation Dosimetry for the Survivors of the Bombings of Hiroshima & Nagasaki. LC 76-30780. (ERDA Critical Review Ser.). 131p. 1977. pap. 11.25 (*0-685-01476-2*, TID-27080); fiche 9.00 (*0-87079-244-X*, TID-27080) DOE.

***Auxier, Randall E. & Davies, Mark Y. A., eds.** Hartshorne & Brightman on God, Process & Persons: The Correspondence, 1922-1945. 2000. 39.95 (*0-8265-1376-X*) Vanderbilt U Pr.

Auxiliary of University Hospitals of Cleveland Sta. Five Star Sensations. 208p. 1991. 21.95 (*0-9630749-0-3*) Aux Univ Hosp.

Auxiliary of Women & Infants Hospital of Rhode Isl. The Melting Pot Cookbook. LC 92-31743. 1992. 11.95 (*0-87197-353-7*) Favorite Recipes.

Auxiliary to the American Osteopathic Association. Still Gathering: A Centennial Celebration. (Illus.). 250p. 1992. text 19.95 (*0-9633542-0-5*) Aux Am Osteopathic.

***Auxter, David, et al.** Principles & Methods of Adapted Physical Education & Recreation. 9th ed. LC 00-37990. 2000. write for info. (*0-07-232926-2*) McGraw.

Auyang, Sunny A. Foundations of Complex-System Theories: In Economics, Evolutionary Biology, & Statistical Physics. LC 97-27006. (Illus.). 408p. (C). 1998. text 64.95 (*0-521-62167-4*) Cambridge U Pr.

***Auyang, Sunny A.** Foundations of Complex-System Theories: In Economics, Evolutionary Biology & Statistical Physics. (Illus.). 416p. (C). 1999. pap. 29.95 (*0-521-77826-3*) Cambridge U Pr.

Auyang, Sunny Y. How Is Quantum Field Theory Possible? (Illus.). 288p. 1995. text 75.00 (*0-19-509344-5*); pap. text 40.00 (*0-19-509345-3*) OUP.

***Auyero, Javier.** Poor Peoples Politics: Peronist Survival Networks & the Legacy of Evita. (Illus.). 296p. 2000. lib. bdg. 54.95 (*0-8223-2627-2*) Duke.

— Poor Peoples Politics: Peronist Survival Networks & the Legacy of Evita. (Illus.). 296p. 2000. pap. 18.95 (*0-8223-2621-3*) Duke.

Auyong, Jan, jt. ed. see Miller, Marc L.

Auzary-Luton, Sylvie. 1, 2, 3, Music! LC 99-10200. (Illus.). 40p. (J). (ps-2). 1999. 15.95 (*0-531-30188-5*) Orchard Bks Watts.

Auzas, Pierre M., jt. auth. see Merimee, Prosper.

Auzenne, Valliere R. The Visualization Quest: A History of Computer Animation. LC 90-56229. 1994. 32.50 (*0-8386-3440-0*) Fairleigh Dickinson.

***Auzepy, Marie-France.** Hagiographie et Iconoclasme: Le Cas de la "Vie d'Etienne Le Jeune" (Birmingham Byzantine & Ottoman Monographs: Vol. 5). 370p. 1999. text 83.95 (*0-86078-812-1*, Pub. by Ashgate Pub) Ashgate Pub Co.

Auzepy, Marie-France. La Vie d'Etienne le Jeune par Etienne le Diacre. LC 96-29713. (FRE.). 368p. 1997. text 78.95 (*0-86078-637-4*, Pub. by Ashgate Pub) Ashgate Pub Co.

Auzias, D. & Labourdette, J. P. Le Petit Fute: Country Guide New York, in French. (FRE.). 302p. 1994. pap. 33.95 (*0-7859-9034-8*) Fr & Eur.

Auzinsh, Marcis & Ferber, Ruvin. Optical Polarization of Molecules, 4 vols. (Monographs on Atomic, Molecular, & Chemical Physics: No. 4). (Illus.). 322p. (C). 1995. text 90.00 (*0-521-44346-6*) Cambridge U Pr.

Auzou. Encyclopedie Medecines Douces (Natural Medicine) (FRE.). 228p. 1998. 69.95 (*0-320-00669-7*) Fr & Eur.

Avaanesov, R. I. Orthopedic Dictionary. (RUS.). 704p. 1983. 35.00 (*0-8288-2002-3*, M15155) Fr & Eur.

Avabhasa, Da. Dawn Horse Testament: The Testament of Secrets of the Divine World-Teacher & True Heart-Master, Da Avabhasa. rev. ed. LC 90-25915. (Illus.). 822p. 1991. pap. 24.95 (*0-918801-03-6*) Dawn Horse Pr.

— Dawn Horse Testament: The Testament of Secrets of the Divine World-Teacher & True Heart-Master, Da Avabhasa (The "Bright") rev. ed. LC 90-25915. (Illus.). 820p. 1991. 48.00 (*0-918801-33-8*) Dawn Horse Pr.

— Incarnation of Love: Radical Spiritual Wisdom & Practical Instruction on Self-Transcending. LC 93-74170. (Illus.). 314p. 1994. reprint ed. pap. 13.95 (*0-918801-86-9*) Dawn Horse Pr.

Avabhasa, Sri Da. Darshan of the Divine World-Teacher. (Illus.). 64p. (Orig.). 1992. 19.95 (*0-918801-55-9*) Dawn Horse Pr.

Avadhuta, Acarya M., tr. see Prabhat Rainjan Sarkar.

Avadhuta, Acarya T. & Kumar, Jayanta. The New Wave. 150p. (Orig.). (C). 1985. pap. text 3.95 (*0-317-93884-3*) Proutist Universal.

Avadhuta, Acarya V., tr. see Prabhat Rainjan Sarkar.

Avadhutika Anamda Mitra Acarya, tr. see Prabhat Rainjan Sarkar.

Avadhutika Ananda Mitra Acarya, ed. see Prabhat Rainjan Sarkar.

Avadian, Brenda. Drive North in Your Career. 166p. 1992. pap. 14.95 (*0-9632752-0-8*) N Star Bks.

***Avadian, Brenda.** Where's My Shoes? My Father's Walk Through Alzheimer's. LC 98-87480. 217p. 1999. 21.95 (*0-9632752-1-6*, Pub. by N Star Bks) Partners Pubs Grp.

Avakian, Anne M. Armenian Folklore Bibliography. LC 94-13033. (Catalogs & Bibliographies Ser.: No. 11). 1995. 45.00 (*0-520-09794-7*, Pub. by U CA Pr) Cal Prin Full Svc.

Avakian, Arlene V., ed. Through the Kitchen Window: Women Writers Explore the Intimate Meanings of Food & Cooking. 336p. 1998. pap. text 14.00 (*0-8070-6509-9*) Beacon Pr.

Avakian, Arra, ed. see Sheohmelian, O.

Avakian, Arra S. Armenia: J A Journey Through History. LC 98-88113. (Illus.). 306p. 1998. 24.95 (*0-916919-20-X*) Electric Pr.

Avakian, Bob. Charting the Uncharted Course: Questions of Revolutionary Strategy for the 1980s: Leadership, No. 2. 306p. 1983. 5.00 (*0-685-06713-0*) RCP Pubns.

— Charting the Uncharted Course: Questions of Revolutionary Strategy for the 1980s: Strategic Outlook & Alliances, No. 1. 279p. 1983. 5.00 (*0-685-06712-2*) RCP Pubns.

— Democracy: Can't We Do Better Than That? LC 86-3650. 277p. 1986. 29.95 (*0-916650-30-8*); pap. 10.95 (*0-916650-29-4*) Banner Pr Intl.

— For a Harvest of Dragons: On the "Crisis of Marxism" & the Power of Marxism, Now More Than Ever. LC 83-13715. 160p. (Orig.). 1983. 13.95 (*0-89851-066-X*); pap. 6.95 (*0-89851-065-1*) RCP Pubns.

— A Horrible End, or an End to the Horror. LC 84-18215. 216p. (Orig.). 1984. pap. 6.95 (*0-89851-070-8*) RCP Pubns.

— Leadership. Incl. Anarchism. 1982. 2.25 (*0-89851-068-6*); Bob Avakian Speaks on the Mao Defendants' Railroad & the Historic Battles Ahead. 69p. 1981. 1.50 (*0-89851-047-3*); Communists Are Rebels. 1980. 0.50 If There Is to be Revolution, There Must be a Revolutionary Party. 74p. 1982. 2.00 (*0-89851-056-2*); Important Struggles in Building the RCP. 55p. 1978. 1.00 (*0-89851-018-X*); New Constitution of the RCP, U. S. A. 1981. 0.75 (*0-89851-064-3*); Summing Up the Black Panther Party. 1980. 0.60 (*0-89851-042-2*); 5.00 (*0-89851-059-7*) RCP Pubns.

— The Loss in China & the Revolutionary Legacy of Mao Tsetung. (Illus.). 1978. pap. 2.00 (*0-89851-017-1*) RCP Pubns.

— Mao Tse-Tung's Immortal Contributions. 1978. 12.95 (*0-89851-020-1*); pap. 4.95 (*0-89851-021-X*) RCP Pubns.

— Phony Communism Is Dead . . . Long Live Real Communism! 123p. (Orig.). 1992. pap. 5.00 (*0-89851-112-7*) RCP Pubns.

***Avakian, Bob.** Preaching from a Pulpit of Bones: We Need Morality but Not Traditional Morality. LC 83-22294. 90p. 1999. pap. 8.00 (*0-916650-49-9*, Pub. by Banner Pr Intl) Liberation Distributors.

Avakian, Bob. Reflections, Sketches, & Provocations: Essays & Commentary, 1981-1987. 225p. 1989. 15.00 (*0-89851-102-X*); pap. 5.95 (*0-89851-101-1*) RCP Pubns.

Avakian, Linda L. Armenian Immigrants. LC 96-70167. (Illus.). 248p. 1996. 25.00 (*0-89725-275-6*, 1741) Picton Pr.

Avakian, Lindy, jt. auth. see Watanabe, Jilchi.

Avakian, Lindy V. The Cross & the Crescent. LC 89-4759. (Illus.). 256p. 1989. 18.95 (*0-943247-06-3*) UCS Press.

— The Cross & the Crescent. 3rd ed. LC 98-92620. (Illus.). 256p. 1998. pap. 12.95 (*0-9662836-0-0*) Golden West.

Avakian, Monique. A Historical Album of Massachusetts. LC 93-39014. (Historical Albums Ser.). (Illus.). 64p. (J). (gr. 4-8). 1994. pap. 6.95 (*1-56294-762-1*); lib. bdg. 23.40 (*1-56294-481-9*) Millbrook Pr.

— Reformers: Activists, Educators, Religious Leaders. LC 98-54841. (Women of Achievement Ser.). (Illus.). 80p. (gr. 4-7). 2000. lib. bdg. 28.55 (*0-8172-5733-0*) Raintree Steck-V.

A

A

Avakian, Monique & Smith, Carter, III. A Historical Album of New York. LC 92-41135. (Historical Albums Ser.). (Illus.). 64p. (J). (gr. 4-8). 1993. pap. 6.95 (*1-56294-758-3*); lib. bdg. 23.40 (*1-56294-005-8*) Millbrook Pr.

Avakumovic, Ivan, jt. auth. see Woodcock, George.

Avakyan, S. V. Collision Processes & Excitation of UV Emission from Planetary Atmospheric Gases: A Handbook of Cross Sections. 390p. 1998. text 120.00 (*90-5699-147-7*) Gordon & Breach.

Avalione, E. A. & Baumeister, Theodore, III, eds. Marks Standard Handbook for Mechanical Engineers. 9th ed. 2048p. 98.00 (*0-685-70908-6*, E00028) ASME Pr.

Avalle-Arce, J. B. & Riley, E. C., eds. Suma Cervantina. (Monografias A Ser.: No. 14). (SPA.). 452p. (C). 1973. pap. 51.00 (*0-900411-66-X*, Pub. by Tamesis Bks Ltd) Boydell & Brewer.

Avalle-Arce, Juan B. La Galatea de Cervantes: Cuatrocientos Anos Despues (Cervantes y lo Pastoril) LC 84-80095. (Documentacion Cervantina Ser.: No. 5). 109p. 1985. 12.50 (*0-936388-11-0*) Juan de la Cuesta.

— Lecturas (Del Temprano Renacimiento a Valle Inclan) 139p. 1990. 28.50 (*0-916379-43-4*) Scripta.

Avalle-Arce, Juan B., ed. see Rodriquez de Montalvo, Garci.

Avallone, E. A. & Baumeister, Theodore, eds. Mark's Standard Handbook for Mechanical Engineers. 10th ed. (Illus.). 1792p. 1996. 150.00 (*0-07-004997-1*) McGraw.

Avallone, Fran, ed. see Draper, Paul.

***Avallone, Francesco, et al, eds.** Innovative Theories, Tools & Practices in Work & Organizational Psychology. (Illus.). 332p. 2000. 39.00 (*0-88937-237-3*) Hogrefe & Huber Pubs.

Avallone, Michael. Gryphon Double: Open Season on Cops; The Arabella Nude, No. 4. 1993. per. 12.00 (*0-936071-24-9*) Gryphon Pubns.

Avallone, Susan, ed. Film Writers Directory 1999. 8th ed. 700p. 1999. pap. 80.00 (*1-58065-018-X*, Pub. by Lone Eagle Pub) Natl Bk Netwk.

— 1998 Film Writers Guide. 7th ed. 675p. 1998. pap. 70.00 (*0-943728-98-3*) Lone Eagle Pub.

Avalon, Arthur, pseud. Mahanirvana Tantra with the Commentary of Hariharananda Bharati. (C). 1989. 27.00 (*81-208-0541-0*, Pub. by Motilal Bnarsidass) S Asia.

— The Serpent Power: The Secrets of Tantric & Shaktic Yoga. LC 74-75259. (Illus.). 541p. 1974. pap. 12.95 (*0-486-23058-9*) Dover.

— Tantraraja Tantra. (C). 1981. 22.00 (*0-8364-2356-9*, Pub. by Motilal Bnarsidass) S Asia.

Avalon, Arthur, pseud, ed. Sarada-Tilaka Tantram. (C). 1996. 44.00 (*81-208-1337-5*, Pub. by Motilal Bnarsidass); pap. 34.00 (*81-208-1338-3*, Pub. by Motilal Bnarsidass) S Asia.

Avalon, Janna P., ed. see Ellington, Cleta S.

Avalon, Moses. Confessions of a Record Producer: How to Survive the Scams & Shams of the Music Business. LC 98-30581. (Illus.). 241p. 1998. pap. 17.95 (*0-87930-532-0*) Miller Freeman.

Avalos, Cecilia. The Sombrero of Luis Lucero. (Illus.). (J). (gr. k-2). 1993. pap. 8.95 incl. audio (*0-7608-0497-4*); pap. 4.95 (*1-56801-059-1*); pap. 8.95 incl. audio (*0-7608-0498-2*); pap. 4.95 (*1-56801-061-3*) Sundance Pub.

— The Sombrero of Luis Lucero, Big bk. (Illus.). (J). (gr. k-2). 1993. pap. 17.95 (*1-56801-058-3*); pap. 17.95 (*1-56801-060-5*) Sundance Pub.

— Your Wonderful Heart. (Illus.). 20p. (Orig.). (J). 1995. pap. 3.95 (*1-887578-06-4*) SpanPr.

Avalos, Cecilia O. Asi Soy Yo! (SPA., Illus.). 24p. (J). (gr. k-3). 1997. 15.95 (*1-887578-42-0*) SpanPr.

Avalos, Decilia. La Fiesta del Abecedario. (Illus.). (J). (gr. k-2). 1993. pap. 8.95 incl. audio (*0-7608-0485-0*); pap. 4.95 (*1-56801-051-6*); pap. 17.95 (*1-56801-171-7*) Sundance Pub.

Avalos, Francisco. Mexican Legal System. 2nd ed. 1999. write for info. (*1-57588-410-0*, 311550) W S Hein.

***Avalos, Francisco.** The Mexican Legal System. 2nd ed. LC 99-57329. 2000. write for info. (*0-8377-0226-7*) W S Hein.

Avalos, Francisco A. The Mexican Legal System No. 1: Reference Guides to National Legal Systems, I. LC 91-39512. 272p. 1992. lib. bdg. 59.95 (*0-313-27565-3*, AMN/, Greenwood Pr) Greenwood.

Avalos, Francisco A., ed. Latin American Legal Abbreviations: A Comprehensive Spanish-Portuguese Dictionary with English Translations. LC 89-17169. 615p. 1989. lib. bdg. 115.00 (*0-313-26200-4*, TLN/, Greenwood Pr) Greenwood.

Avalos, Hector. Health Care & the Rise of Christianity. LC 99-11023. (Illus.). 176p. 1999. 12.95 (*1-56563-337-7*) Hendrickson MA.

Avalos, Javier & Maibach, Howard I. Dermatologic Botany. (Dermatology: Clinical & Basic Science Ser.). 464p. 1999. boxed set 79.95 (*0-8493-7361-1*) CRC Pr.

Avandele, E. A. African Historical Studies. 314p. 1979. 47.50 (*0-7146-2942-1*, Pub. by F Cass Pubs) Intl Spec Bk.

— Holy Johnson, Pioneer of African Nationalism: 1836-1917. (Illus.). 417p. 1970. 42.50 (*0-7146-1743-1*, Pub. by F Cass Pubs) Intl Spec Bk.

Avanesova, R. I., ed. see Borunova, S. N., et al.

Avanessian, Aida B. Iran-United States Claims Tribunal in Action. (International Arbitration Law Library). 400p. (C). 1993. lib. bdg. 127.00 (*1-85333-902-4*, Pub. by Graham & Trotman) Kluwer Academic.

Avani, Nathan. Mentoring Works! Facilitator's Guide. 70p. 1998. pap. text, teacher ed. 24.95 (*1-56688-439-X*, 3861) Bur For At-Risk.

— Mentoring Works! Program: A Peer Helping Program for Middle & High School Students. (Illus.). 94p. (YA). (gr. 5-12). 1998. pap. text, teacher ed., wbk. ed. 189.95 (*1-56688-442-X*, 3860A) Bur For At-Risk.

— Mentoring Works! Student Workbook. (Illus.). 24p. (YA). (gr. 5-12). 1998. pap. text 5.95 (*1-56688-440-3*, 3862) Bur For At-Risk.

Avant, Arthur M. The Art of Love: A Collection of Romantic & Love Poems. (Illus.). 79p. 1998. pap. 10.00 (*0-9666148-0-1*) AVANT.

Avant, D. A. Like a Straight Pine Tree: Stories of Reconstruction Days in Alabama & Florida 1855-1971. (Illus.). 124p. 1971. 7.95 (*0-914570-03-X*) LAvant Studios.

Avant, David A., Jr. Illustrated Index, J. Randall Stanley's History of Gadsden County. LC 85-81686. (Illus.). 248p. 1948. 30.00 (*0-914570-07-2*) LAvant Studios.

Avant, David A., III. Plantation Management on a Sharecropper's Budget. LC 91-84670. (Illus.). 120p. pap. 15.00 (*0-914570-12-9*) LAvant Studios.

— Professional Raccoon Trapping. 3rd rev. ed. LC 78-57404. (Illus.). 61p. pap. 4.95 (*0-317-03287-9*) LAvant Studios.

Avant, David A., Jr. Some Southern Colonial Families, Vol. 1. LC 81-84670. 528p. 1983. 35.00 (*0-914570-04-8*) LAvant Studios.

— Some Southern Colonial Families, Vol. 2. LC 81-84670. 467p. 1982. 35.00 (*0-914570-06-4*) LAvant Studios.

— Some Southern Colonial Families, Vol. 3. LC 81-84670. (Illus.). 1260p. 1989. 45.00 (*0-914570-08-0*) LAvant Studios.

— Some Southern Colonial Families, Vol. 4. LC 81-84670. (Illus.). 860p. 1991. 45.00 (*0-914570-10-2*) LAvant Studios.

— Some Southern Colonial Families, Vol. 5. 1132p. 1996. 65.00 (*0-914570-11-0*) LAvant Studios.

Avant, Deborah D. Political Institutions & Military Change: Lessons from Peripheral Wars. (Studies in Security Affairs). 176p. 1994. text 35.00 (*0-8014-3034-8*) Cornell U Pr.

Avant, Eugenia T. A Town Called Longnose & Other Writings. LC 90-84670. (Illus.). 56p. 1990. 15.00 (*0-914570-09-9*) LAvant Studios.

Avant, Fenton G. The Davis-Wood Family of Gadsden County, Florida & Their Forebears. LC 79-189245. (Illus.). 535p. 1979. 35.00 (*0-685-57876-3*) LAvant Studios.

Avant, Gayle R., ed. Great Documents Test: Foundations of Citizenship. 2nd ed. 117p. 1994. pap. text 17.00 (*0-9621712-0-4*) CES Pr.

Avant, John, et al, eds. Revival! The Current Spiritual Awakening in Brownwood, Fort Worth, Wheaton & Beyond. LC 95-22937. 176p. 1996. pap. 10.99 (*0-8054-6191-4*, 4261-91) Broadman.

Avant, Kay C., jt. auth. see Walker, Lorraine W.

Avant, Marie. Passage to Peru: A Novel of Love & Intrigue. LC 97-62091. 192p. 1998. pap. 12.99 (*1-57921-072-4*) WinePress Pub.

***Avant, Richard, Jr.** The Essentials of Christian Living. LC 99-96617. 2000. pap. 12.95 (*0-533-13331-9*) Vantage.

Avanti, Benito. El Manual Practico de las Ventas. (SPA., Illus.). 98p. (Orig.). 1997. pap. 8.99 (*1-890701-01-7*) La Mancha.

Avanzini. Epileptogenic & Excitotoxic Mechanisms. 168p. 56.00 (*0-86196-386-5*, Pub. by J Libbey Med) Bks Intl VA.

— Molecular & Cellular Targets for Anti Epileptic Drugs. 272p. 114.00 (*0-86196-554-X*, Pub. by J Libbey Med) Bks Intl VA.

***Avanzini, G., et al.** Limbic Seizures in Children. 256p. 2000. 68.00 (*0-86196-595-7*, Pub. by John Libby) Buttrwrth-Heinemann.

Avanzini, G., jt. auth. see Fariello, R.

Avanzini, Guy. La Pedagogia Desde el Siglo XVII. (SPA.). pap. 13.99 (*968-16-3360-1*, Pub. by Fondo) Continental Bk.

Avanzini, John. Always Abounding. 128p. pap. 6.95 (*0-89274-581-9*, HH581) Harrison Hse.

— The Basics of Abundance. LC 99-163715. 1998. pap. 6.99 (*1-57794-068-7*) Harrison Hse.

Avanzini, John. Rich God, Poor God. 192p. pap. 10.99 (*1-930027-14-1*, 921-030, Pub. by Insght Pub) BookWorld.

Avanzini, John. Stolen Property Returned. rev. ed. LC 94-159866. 116p. 1989. pap. 5.95 (*0-89274-598-3*) Harrison Hse.

— What Jesus Taught about Manifesting Abundance. LC 96-163200. 130p. 1996. pap. 5.95 (*0-89274-941-5*, HH-941) Harrison Hse.

Avanzini, John F. Birds, Roots, Weeds, & the Good Ground. (Illus.). 32p. 1980. pap. 3.00 (*0-941117-06-5*) HIS Publish.

— Breakthrough for Unanswered Prayer. 92p. 1993. pap. 5.95 (*1-878605-11-9*) HIS Pub Co.

— The Debt Term-O-Nator. abr. ed. (Financial Freedom Ser.). 84p. 1993. pap. 5.95 (*1-878605-13-5*) HIS Pub Co.

— Faith Extenders: Everyday Ways to Increase Your Faith. 172p. 1988. pap. 8.95 (*1-878605-05-4*) HIS Pub Co.

— Financial Excellence. LC 94-143832. 216p. (Orig.). 1993. pap. 9.95 (*0-89274-918-0*, HH-918) Harrison Hse.

— God's Debt Free Guarantee. (Financial Freedom Ser.). 91p. (Orig.). 1994. pap. 5.95 (*0-89274-919-9*, HH-919) Harrison Hse.

— It's Not Working Brother John. 217p. (Orig.). 1992. pap. 9.99 (*0-89274-898-2*, HH-898) Harrison Hse.

— John Avanzini Answers Your Questions about Biblical Economics. 123p. 1992. pap. 6.99 (*0-89274-906-7*, HH-906) Harrison Hse.

— Paul's Thorn. Balcombe, Dennis, tr. from CHI. (Illus.). 32p. 1980. pap. 3.00 (*0-941117-01-4*) HIS Publish.

— Powerful Principles of Increase. LC 93-206075. (POR.). 230p. (Orig.). 1990. pap. 7.95 (*0-89274-579-7*, HH579) Harrison Hse.

— Rapid Debt-Reduction Strategies. (Financial Freedom Ser.). 306p. 1990. pap. 12.95 (*1-878605-01-1*) HIS Pub Co.

— Things That Are Better Than Money. LC 96-123532. 98p. 1995. pap. 5.99 (*0-89274-781-1*, HH-781) Harrison Hse.

— Thirty, Sixty, Hundredfold: The Laws of the Financial Harvest. 192p. (Orig.). 1989. pap. 8.95 (*0-89274-596-7*) Harrison Hse.

— War on Debt: Breaking the Power of Debt. (Financial Freedom Ser.). 190p. 1990. pap. 7.95 (*1-878605-00-3*) HIS Pub Co.

— The Wealth of the World: The Proven Wealth Transfer System. 162p. (Orig.). 1989. pap. 7.99 (*0-89274-580-0*, HH580) Harrison Hse.

Avanzini, John F. & McNaughton, Deborah. Have a Good Report: Christian Credit Repair. (Financial Freedom Ser.). 183p. (Orig.). 1991. pap. 8.95 (*1-878605-08-9*) HIS Pub Co.

Avanzini, John F. & Ondrey, Patrick. Master Plan. (Financial Freedom Ser.). 62p. 1993. pap. 5.95 (*1-878605-12-7*) HIS Pub Co.

— The Victory Book: The Workbook That Will Take You Rapidly Out of Debt. (Financial Freedom Ser.). 1851p. 1991. pap., student ed. 14.95 (*1-878605-07-0*) HIS Pub Co.

Avarisch, Boris, compiled by. Caspar David Friedrich. 36p. 1985. 95.00 (*0-7855-0952-6*) St Mut.

Avary, Myrta L. Dixie after the War. LC 76-124224. (Select Bibliographies Reprint Ser.). 1977. 36.95 (*0-8369-5412-2*) Ayer.

Avary, Myrta L., ed. see Chesnut, Mary Boykin Miller.

Avary, Myrta L., ed. see Stephens, Alexander H.

Avasthi, Abha. Hindu Marriage in Continuity & Change. 244p. 1979. 19.95 (*0-318-36835-8*) Asia Bk Corp.

Avatar, Ram. Theory of Indian Music. (Illus.). 160p. 1980. 19.95 (*0-940500-13-2*) Asia Bk Corp.

Avault, James W., Jr. Fundamentals of Aquaculture Vol. I: A Step-by-Step Guide to Commercial Aquaculture. (Illus.). 889p. 1996. pap. text 69.95 (*0-9649549-0-7*) AVA Pubng.

***Avav, Rami & Freund, Richard A., eds.** Bethsaida: A City by the North Shore of the Sea of Galilee. (Bethsaida Excavations Project: Vol. 2). (Illus.). 483p. 1999. 45.00 (*0-943549-49-3*); pap. 30.00 (*0-943549-48-5*) Truman St Univ.

Avdevich, Boris S. The Inside Scoop on the Lottery. LC 89-91468. (Illus.). 176p. (Orig.). 1990. pap. 9.95 (*0-9624586-0-0*) Lot Co Amer.

Avdeyeva, Irina, tr. see Usov, Vladimir.

Avdohin, V. M., jt. auth. see Abramov, A.

Avdonin, Sergei A. & Ivanov, Sergei A. Families of Exponentials: The Method of Moments in Controllability Problems for Distributed Parameter Systems. 320p. (C). 1995. text 59.95 (*0-521-45243-0*) Cambridge U Pr.

Avduevsky, V. S., et al, eds. Mathematical Modeling of Convective Heat & Mass Transfer on the Basis of Navier Stokes Equations. 200p. 1991. 115.00 (*1-56032-005-2*) CRC Pr.

Ave, Gastone, ed. Urban Land & Property Markets in Italy. LC 96-225563. (European Land & Property Markets Ser.: No. 5). 256p. 1996. 90.00 (*1-85728-053-9*, Pub. by UCL Pr Ltd) Taylor & Francis.

Ave, Jeanne, jt. auth. see Jeanne, Ave.

Ave-Lallemant, E., jt. auth. see Spiegelberg, Herbert.

Ave-Lallemant, Friedrich C. Das Deutsche Gaunerthum. (GER.). lxiv, 1854p. 1980. reprint ed. write for info. (*3-487-06698-X*) G Olms Pubs.

Ave Marie Ed. Staff, contrib. by. The Bride's Bible: Catholic Edition. (Illus.). 96p. 1999. 16.95 (*0-87793-686-2*) Ave Maria.

Ave, Mary Shannon. The Christian's Cuss Book. 200p. mass mkt. 4.99 (*1-55197-036-8*) Picasso Publ.

Avebury, John L. Essays & Addresses, 1900-1903. LC 67-22069. (Essay Index Reprint Ser.). 1977. 23.95 (*0-8369-0165-7*) Ayer.

— Origin of Civilisation & the Primitive Condition of Man. LC 72-1280. (Select Bibliographies Reprint Ser.). 1977. reprint ed. 31.95 (*0-8369-6819-0*) Ayer.

Avedesian, M., et al. 1996 Proceedings Magnesium - A Material Advancing to the 21st Century. (Illus.). 1996. 80.00 (*0-910233-03-9*) Intl Magnesium.

Avedesian, M. M., et al. Light Metals 1996. 1996. 110.00 (*0-919086-69-1*) CIM.

***Avedesian, Michael & Baker, Hugh, eds.** ASM Specialty Handbook: Magnesium & Magnesium Alloys. LC 99-20208. 314p. 1999. 198.00 (*0-87170-657-1*) ASM.

Avedisian, C. T. & Arpaci, V. A., eds. Heat Transfer in Microgravity. LC 93-73613. (HTD Ser.: Vol. 269). 179p. 1994. pap. 55.00 (*0-7918-1257-X*) ASME.

***Avedon, Don M.** Film-Based Imaging: New Views & Applications. 295p. 1998. per. 79.00 (*0-89258-346-0*, C143) Assn Inform & Image Mgmt.

— Glossary of Document Technologies: ANSI/AIIM TR2-1998. 106p. 1998. spiral bd. 52.00 (*0-89258-343-6*, TR02) Assn Inform & Image Mgmt.

Avedon, Don M. Introduction to Electronic Imaging. 3rd ed. 214p. 1994. per. 77.00 (*0-89258-279-0*, C125) Assn Inform & Image Mgmt.

Avedon, Don M. Quality Control of Electronic Images. 70p. 1997. per. 79.00 (*0-89258-309-6*, C137) Assn Inform & Image Mgmt.

— Telecommunications in Document Management. 150p. 1997. per. 79.00 (*0-89258-334-7*, C138) Assn Inform & Image Mgmt.

Avedon, Don M., ed. New Federal Procedures & Regulations for Document Management. 47p. 1997. 100.00 (*0-89258-333-9*, D067) Assn Inform & Image Mgmt.

Avedon, Don M. & Exelbert, Rodd. All about Micrographics. (Illus.). 20p. 1990. pap. text 15.00 (*1-879391-00-7*) Avedon Assocs.

Avedon, Elliott M. & Sutton-Smith, Brian. The Study of Games. LC 79-21194. 544p. 1979. reprint ed. lib. bdg. 59.50 (*0-89874-045-2*) Krieger.

Avedon, John. Divine Realm. 384p. 1997. 25.00 (*0-06-016894-3*) HarperTrade.

Avedon, John F. In Exile from the Land of Snows: The Dalai Lama & Tibet Since the Chinese Conquest. LC 94-9866. (Illus.). 448p. 1994. pap. 16.00 (*0-06-097574-1*) HarpC.

— In Exile from the Land of Snows RI. LC 98-145511. 512p. 1997. pap. 16.00 (*0-06-097741-8*) HarpC.

Avedon, Phyllis, ed. see Pooser, Doris.

Avedon, Richard. An Autobiography. LC 93-440. 1993. 100.00 (*0-679-40921-1*) Random.

— An Autobiography. limited ed. 1993. 500.00 (*0-679-42964-6*) Random.

— Evidence: 1944-1994. LC 93-43906. 184p. 1994. 65.00 (*0-679-40922-X*) Random.

***Avedon, Richard, ed.** Hiro. LC 98-68373. (Illus.). 144p. 1999. 65.00 (*0-8212-2592-8*, Pub. by Bulfinch Pr) Little.

Avedon, Richard, et al, photos by. Rock & Royalty. (Tiny Folio Ser.). (Illus.). 288p. 1998. bds. 11.95 (*0-7892-0489-4*) Abbeville Pr.

— Rock & Royalty. (Illus.). 272p. 1997. 75.00 (*0-7892-0177-1*) Abbeville Pr.

***Avedon, Richard & Arbus, Doon.** The Sixties. LC 99-24954. 256p. 1999. 75.00 (*0-679-40923-8*) Random House.

Avedon, Richard & Wilson, Laura. In the American West: Richard Avedon-Photographs, 1979-1984. (Illus.). 184p. 1996. 75.00 (*0-8109-1105-1*, Pub. by Abrams) Time Warner.

Avedyan, Eduard. Learning Systems. 136p. 1995. 49.00 (*3-540-19996-9*) Spr-Verlag.

Avelar, Idelber. The Untimely Present: Postdictatorial Latin American Fiction & the Task of Mourning. LC 99-14157. 272p. 1999. pap. 17.95 (*0-8223-2415-6*) Duke.

***Avelar, Idelber.** The Untimely Present: Postdictatorial Latin American Fiction & the Task of Mourning. LC 99-14157. 272p. 1999. 49.95 (*0-8223-2381-8*) Duke.

Avelichev, Alexander, ed. Putsch: The Diary: Three Days That Collapsed the Empire. (Illus.). 155p. 1998. pap. text 22.00 (*0-7881-5833-3*) DIANE Pub.

Aveline, Claude. L' Abonne de la Ligne U. (FRE.). 1973. pap. 10.95 (*0-7859-1727-6*, 2070363120) Fr & Eur.

***Aveline, Jean.** Giselle. (Orig.). 1999. mass mkt. 6.95 (*0-352-33440-1*) London Bridge.

Aveline, Mark & Dryden, Wendy. Group Therapy in Britain. (Psychotherapy in Britain Ser.). 320p. 1988. pap. 41.95 (*0-335-09829-0*) OpUniv Pr.

Aveline, Mark & Shapiro, David A., eds. Research Foundations for Psychotherapy Practice. 346p. 1995. 215.00 (*0-471-95219-2*) Wiley.

Aveline, Mark O. From Medicine to Psychotherapy. 278p. 1992. pap. 49.95 (*1-56593-557-8*, 0311) Singular Publishing.

Aveling, Edward, jt. auth. see Aveling, Eleanor M.

Aveling, Edward, jt. auth. see Marx, Eleanor.

Aveling, Edward B. & Aveling, Eleanor M. Working Class Movement in America. LC 78-89716. (American Labor, from Conspiracy to Collective Bargaining Ser., No. 1). 239p. 1971. reprint ed. 17.95 (*0-405-02102-X*) Ayer.

Aveling, Edward B., tr. see Engels, Friedrich.

Aveling, Eleanor, tr. see Bernstein, Edward.

Aveling, Eleanor M. & Aveling, Edward. Thoughts on Women & Society. LC 86-27203. Orig. Title: The Woman Question. (Illus.). 100p. (Orig.). 1987. 4.95 (*0-7178-0648-0*) Intl Pubs Co.

Aveling, Eleanor M., jt. auth. see Aveling, Edward B.

Aveling, Harry. Osho Rajaneesh & His Disciples: Some Western Perceptions. LC 99-931099. xl, 441 p. 1999. pap. 160.00 (*81-208-1599-8*, Pub. by Motilal Bnarsidass) St Mut.

***Aveling, Harry.** Osho Rajneesh & His Disciples: Some Western Perceptions. LC 99-931099. 442p. 1999. 265.00 (*81-208-1598-X*, Pub. by Motilal Bnarsidass) St Mut.

Aveling, J. C., et al. Rome & the Anglicans: Historical & Doctrinal Aspects of Anglican-Roman Catholic Relations. Haase, Wolfgang, ed. 301p. 1982. 126.95 (*3-11-008267-5*) De Gruyter.

Aveling, James H. The Chamberlens & the Midwifery Forceps. LC 75-23677. reprint ed. 41.50 (*0-404-13230-8*) AMS Pr.

— English Midwives: Their History & Prospects. LC 75-23678. reprint ed. 42.50 (*0-404-13231-6*) AMS Pr.

Avella, Anna S. A Springtime's Dream: An Italian Girl's Story. LC 97-75666. 190p. 1997. pap. 12.95 (*0-9643374-8-7*) Pubng Connect.

Avella, Steven M. & McKeown, Elizabeth, eds. Public Voices: Catholics in the American Context. LC 99-48732. (American Catholic Identities Ser.). 256p. 1999. 50.00 (*1-57075-267-2*); pap. 25.00 (*1-57075-266-4*) Orbis Bks.

Avellana, Jancie. White Knob Wind up Collectible Toys. LC 98-87584. (Illus.). 80p. (Orig.). 1999. pap. 19.95 (*0-7643-0711-8*) Schiffer.

— Who Will House Farmworkers? An Examination of State Programs. 44p. (Orig.). 1986. pap. text 4.50 (*1-58064-072-9*) Housing Assist.

Avellana, Janice, ed. see Hilderbrand, Kelly M.

Avellaneda, Alonso F. Don Quixote de la Mancha Pt. II: Being the Spurious Continuation of Miguel de Cervantes's part I. Server, Alberta & Keller, J. E., trs. (Documentacion Cervantina Ser.: No. 2). (Illus.). 350p. 1980. 16.00 (*0-936388-01-3*) Juan de la Cuesta.

***Avellaneda, Marco & Laurence, P.** Quantitative Modeling of Derivative Securities: From Theory to Practice. LC 99-47242. 336p. 1999. boxed set 59.95 (*1-58488-031-7*, Chap & Hall CRC) CRC Pr.

***Avellaneda, Marlo.** Pricing Options & Derivative Securities: An Engineering Approach. 268p. 1999. 59.95 (*0-8493-0383-4*, Chap & Hall CRC) CRC Pr.

An Asterisk (*) at the beginning of an entry indicates that the title is appearing for the first time.

Avellaneda y Arteaga, Gertrudis G. De, see De Avellaneda y Arteaga, Gertrudis G.

Avellar-Fleming, Cyda. Core Values for the Third Millenium. LC 98-93079. 160p. 1998. pap. 10.00 (*1-57502-844-1*, PO2315) Morris Pubng.

Avellino, Anita, jt. auth. see Knudsen, Richard.

Avellino-Cantwell, Anita, ed. see Sevaly, Karen.

Avellone, Chris. Dystopia. (Champions Ser.). 48p. 1994. pap. 9.00 (*1-887801-31-6*, Atlas Games) Trident MN.

— Planescape: Torment Official Strategies & Secrets. 4th ed. (Strategies & Secrets Ser.). 240p. 1999. pap. 19.99 (*0-7821-2585-9*, Strategies & Secrets) Sybex.

Aven. Developing Management Skills. 3rd ed. (C). 1997. pap. text, teacher ed., suppl. ed. 18.00 (*0-673-55831-2*) Addson-Wesley Educ.

Aven, O. I., et al. Stochastic Analysis of Computer Storage. (C). 1987. text 206.50 (*90-277-2515-2*) Kluwer Academic.

Aven, T. & Jensen, U. Stochastic Models in Reliability. LC 98-31039. (Applications of Mathematics Ser.: Vol. 41). 288p. 1999. 64.95 (*0-387-98633-2*) Spr-Verlag.

Avena, M. R. The Libel Suitors & Other Stories. v, 82p. (Orig.). (C). 1990. pap. 8.75 (*971-10-0392-9*, Pub. by New Day Pub) Cellar.

Avena, Nancy. Effective Electrotherapy Application, a Physical Therapist's Manual. 163p. (C). 1999. pap. 24.95 (*0-9670978-0-0*) Avena Pubg.

Avena, Thomas. Dream of Order. LC 96-40348. 128p. (Orig.). 1997. pap. 14.00 (*1-56279-102-8*) Mercury Hse Inc.

Avena, Thomas, ed. Life Sentences: Writers, Artists, & AIDS. LC 93-38922. (Illus.). 304p. 1994. pap. 14.95 (*1-56279-051-X*) Mercury Hse Inc.

Avenarius, Richard, jt. auth. see Gazali, Abu H.

Avendano, Fausto. Los Terricolas. 120p. 1992. pap. 7.25 (*1-881781-01-1*) Spanish Press.

Avendano, Norma K. Wait for Me: A True Life Story. 394p. 1994. pap. text 18.99 (*1-57336-900-4*) Interactn Pubs.

***Avendano, Norma Kipp.** The Crossing. 157p. 1999. spiral bd. write for info. (*1-889553-14-X*) WhitMar Elect.

Avendano y Loyola, Fray A. De, see De Avendano y Loyola, Fray A.

Avenell, Donne & Romero, Enrique. AXA 8. (First American Edition Ser.). (Illus.). 64p. 1987. reprint ed. pap. 5.95 (*0-912277-35-1*) K Pierce Bks.

— AXA 5. (First American Edition Ser.). (Illus.). 64p. 1984. pap. 5.95 (*0-912277-21-1*) K Pierce Bks.

— AXA 9: The Last AXA. (First American Edition Ser.). (Illus.). 80p. 1988. reprint ed. pap. 7.95 (*0-912277-36-X*) K Pierce Bks.

— AXA 7. (First American Edition Ser.). (Illus.). 64p. 1985. pap. 5.95 (*0-912277-29-7*) K Pierce Bks.

— AXA 6. (First American Edition Ser.). (Illus.). 64p. 1984. pap. 5.95 (*0-912277-22-X*) K Pierce Bks.

— AXA 2. (First American Edition Ser.). (Illus.). 64p. 1982. pap. 5.95 (*0-912277-05-X*) K Pierce Bks.

Avenell, Donne, et al. AXA 4. (First American Edition Ser.). (Illus.). 64p. 1983. pap. 5.95 (*0-912277-01-7*) K Pierce Bks.

— AXA 3. (First American Edition Ser.). (Illus.). 64p. 1983. pap. 5.95 (*0-912277-06-8*) K Pierce Bks.

Avenhaus, Rudolf. Safeguards Systems Analysis: With Applications to Nuclear Material Safeguards & Other Inspection Problems. (Illus.). 380p. (C). 1986. 132.00 (*0-306-42169-0*, Plenum Trade) Perseus Pubng.

Avenhaus, Rudolf, et al, eds. Defense Decision Making: Analytical Support & Crisis Management. (Illus.). xii, 342p. 1991. 109.00 (*0-387-54022-9*) Spr-Verlag.

Avenhaus, Rudolf & Canty, Morton J. Compliance Quantified: An Introduction to Data Verification. (Illus.). 269p. (C). 1996. text 64.95 (*0-521-55366-0*) Cambridge U Pr.

***Aveni.** Stairways. 230p. 1999. pap. 15.95 (*0-471-32976-2*) Wiley.

Aveni, Anthony. Conversing with the Planets: How Science & Myth Invented the Cosmos. (Illus.). 272p. 1994. pap. 14.00 (*1-56836-021-5*) Kodansha.

— Observadores en el Cielo. (SPA.). 20.99 (*968-16-2702-4*, Pub. by Fondo) Continental Bk.

Aveni, Anthony, jt. auth. see McKenzie, V. Michael.

Aveni, Anthony F. The Ancient Astronomers. LC 93-38463. (Exploring the Ancient World Ser.). (Illus.). 176p. 1996. text 24.95 (*0-89599-037-7*) Smithsonian.

***Aveni, Anthony F.** Between the Lines: The Mystery of the Giant Ground Drawings of Ancient Nasca, Peru. LC 99-50535. (Illus.). 320p. 2000. 39.95 (*0-292-70496-8*) U of Tex Pr.

Aveni, Anthony F. Skywatchers of Ancient Mexico. (Texas Pan American Ser.). (Illus.). 369p. 1980. pap. 27.50 (*0-292-77578-4*) U of Tex Pr.

— Stairways to the Stars: Skywatching in Three Great Ancient Cultures. LC 96-36517. 240p. 1997. 24.95 (*0-471-15942-5*) Wiley.

Aveni, Anthony F., ed. Archaeoastronomy in Pre-Columbian America. LC 74-17622. (Illus.). 452p. reprint ed. pap. 140.20 (*0-8357-6659-4*, 203532800094) Bks Demand.

— The Lines of Nazca. LC 89-84667. (Memoirs Ser.: Vol. 183). (Illus.). 230p. (C). 1990. 30.00 (*0-87169-183-3*, M183-AVA) Am Philos.

— Native American Astronomy. LC 78-53569. 302p. reprint ed. pap. 93.70 (*0-608-17843-8*, 203260500080) Bks Demand.

***Aveni, Louise Rose.** Can I Ride My Bike to Heaven? LC 99-96320. (Illus.). 16p. (J). (ps-6). 1999. 14.95 (*0-9675124-0-9*) Angel House Pubng.

Avenick, Joseph, ed. see Scialli, Anita.

Avenoso, Ellen, jt. ed. see McCrudden, John.

***Avens, Roberts.** Imagination Is Reality. 152p. 2000. pap. 15.00 (*0-88214-382-4*, Pub. by Spring Pubns) Continuum.

Avent, Barbara P. The Leopard Speaks about Changes in Life. Alston, Nelson G., ed. LC 93-72214. (Illus.). 64p. (Orig.). (YA). 1993. pap. 9.95 (*0-9632202-1-7*) Alpha Bk N Pr.

Avent, Barbara P., ed. see Alston, Nelson G.

Avent, Jan R. Manual of Cooperative Group Therapy for Aphasia. LC 97-21508. 174p. 1997. pap. text 32.50 (*0-7506-9921-3*) Buttrwrth-Heinemann.

Aventin, Christine. Le Coeur En Poche. (FRE.). 1989. pap. 10.95 (*0-7859-2132-X*, 2070382079) Fr & Eur.

Aventura. La Profecia. 1996. mass mkt. 9.99 (*0-446-67300-5*, Pub. by Warner Bks) Little.

Averbach, Albert. Handling Accident Cases, 8 vols., Set. LC 58-4149. 1973. 840.00 (*0-685-59873-X*) West Group.

— Handling Accident Cases - Auto Cases, 2 vols., Set. LC 58-4149. 1973. 225.00 (*0-685-59877-2*) West Group.

— Handling Accident Cases - Crt Prj Trauma, 2 vols., Set. LC 58-4149. 1963. 225.00 (*0-685-59878-0*) West Group.

— Handling Accident Cases - General, 2 vols., Set. LC 58-4149. 1972. 225.00 (*0-685-59874-8*) West Group.

— Handling Accident Cases - Malpractice Cases. LC 58-4149. 1970. 125.00 (*0-685-59875-6*) West Group.

— Handling Accident Cases - Product Liability. LC 58-4149. 1971. 125.00 (*0-685-59876-4*) West Group.

Averbach, Bonnie. Problem Solving Through Recreational Mathematics. LC 99-52198. 480p. 2000. pap. text 14.95 (*0-486-40917-1*) Dover.

Averbach, Jerold S., jt. auth. see Schroeder, Theodore A.

Averbach, Lera. The Steps to the Eternity. Malisova, Nataliya, ed. (RUS., Illus.). 92p. 1998. pap. 5.00 (*0-9658114-6-8*) Mir Collection.

Averback. Old Girls' Network. pap. 11.00 (*0-06-251057-6*) HarperTrade.

Averbakh, Yuri. Bishop V. Knight Endings, Rook V. Minor Pierce Endings, Vol. 2. Neat, Kenneth P., tr. (Illus.). 320p. 1985. 39.90 (*0-08-026902-8*, Pergamon Pr) Elsevier.

— Chess Endings: Essential Knowledge. 2nd ed. Clarke, P. H., tr. from RUS. (Chess Ser.: No. 5). (Illus.). 150p. 1987. 19.95 (*0-08-032050-3*, Pergamon Pr); pap. 13.90 (*0-08-032045-7*, Pergamon Pr) Elsevier.

— Chess Middle Games: Essential Knowledge. 128p. 1996. pap. 14.95 (*1-85744-125-7*, Pub. by Cadgn Bks) Macmillan.

Averbakh, Yuri & Checkover, V. Comprehensive Chess Endings: Bishop Endings & Knight Endings, Vol. 1. Neat, Kenneth P., tr. from RUS. (Russian Chess Ser.). 232p. 1983. 37.95 (*0-08-026900-1*, Pergamon Pr) Elsevier.

Averbakh, Yuri & Kopayev, N. Comprehensive Chess Endings: Rook Endings. LC 81-23428. (Russian Chess Ser.). 310p. 1987. 49.95 (*0-08-026908-7*, Pergamon Pr); pap. 29.95 (*0-08-032048-1*, Pergamon Pr) Elsevier.

Averbakh, Yuri & Maizelis, I. Comprehensive Chess Endings: Pawn Endings. (Russian Chess Ser.: Vol. 4). (Illus.). 304p. 1987. 47.90 (*0-08-026906-0*, Pergamon Pr) Elsevier.

Averbakh, Yuri, et al. Comprehensive Chess Endings: Queen & Pawn Endings, Queen Against Rook Endings, Queen Against Minor Piece Endings, Vol. 3. (Russian Chess Ser.). (Illus.). 330p. 1986. 43.90 (*0-08-026904-4*, P115, Pub. by PPL) Elsevier.

Averbeck, Mary S. & Stinnett, Beth M. Creative Kids: Fun Art Activities from A to Z. 236p. 1996. pap. 12.95 (*0-9648566-1-1*) CK Pr.

***Averbuch, Gloria & Hammond, Ashley M.** Goal! A Soccer Mom & an Award Winning Coach Reveal How to Make Youth Soccer Healthy, Exhilarating, & Rewarding for Both Parents & Children. LC 99-24197. 240p. 1999. pap. 15.95 (*1-57954-080-5*) Rodale Pr Inc.

Averbuch, Gloria & Samuelson, Joan B. Joan Benoit Samuelson's Running for Women. 256p. (Orig.). 1995. pap. 16.95 (*0-87596-239-4*) Rodale Pr Inc.

Averbuch, Gloria, jt. auth. see Waitz, Grete.

Averbuch, Irit. The Gods Come Dancing: A Study of the Ritual Dance of Yamabushi Kagura. LC 96-142609. (Cornell East Asia Ser.: Vol. 79). 346p. (C). 1995. 23.80 (*1-885445-67-9*, 79); pap. 14.45 (*1-885445-79-2*, 79) Cornell East Asia Pgm.

Averbuch-Pouchot, M. & Durif, A. Topics in Phosphate Chemistry. LC 96-28448. 420p. 1996. write for info. (*981-02-2634-9*) World Scientific Pub.

Averch, Harvey A. A Strategic Analysis of Science & Technology Policy. LC 84-47961. 232p. 1985. text 37.50 (*0-8018-2467-2*) Johns Hopkins.

Averch, Harvey A., et al. How Effective Is Schooling? A Critical Review of Research. LC 74-2165. 280p. 1974. 39.95 (*0-87778-071-4*) Educ Tech Pubns.

Averchenko, Arkadii. Salat Iz Bulavok. LC 82-60958. 230p. (C). 1982. pap. 9.95 (*0-89830-064-9*) Russica Pubs.

Averett, Robert C. & McKnight, Diane M., eds. Chemical Quality of Water & the Hydrologic Cycle. (Illus.). 382p. 1987. lib. bdg. 97.50 (*0-87371-081-9*, L081) Lewis Pubs.

Averett, Walter. Through the Rainbow Canyon: A Personal Narrative of the People, Places & Events, from Caliente to Carp, Nevada. (Illus.). 192p. 1995. 20.00 (*0-87062-237-4*) A H Clark.

Averett, Walter R. Beyond the Ranges. LC 97-93561. (Illus.). 133p. 1997. 25.00 (*0-87062-279-X*) A H Clark.

Averill. Day for Hunter Day for Prey. LC 96-34209. 1997. lib. bdg. 45.00 (*0-226-03291-4*) U Ch Pr.

Averill, Andrea D., ed. Venango County, Pennsylvania Declarations of Intention & Petitions for Naturalization: 1806-1868. LC 98-70197. 1998. per. 10.95 (*1-55856-263-X*, 263) Closson Pr.

Averill, C. F. Sprinkler Systems Design: Past, Present & Future. 1979. 2.50 (*0-685-04683-4*, TR 79-3) Society Fire Protect.

Averill, Deborah M. The Irish Short Story from George Moore to Frank O'Connor. LC 81-40188. 338p. (Orig.). 1982. pap. text 26.50 (*0-8191-2134-7*); lib. bdg. 59.00 (*0-8191-2133-9*) U Pr of Amer.

Averill, Diane. Branches Doubled over with Fruit. 80p. 1991. 19.95 (*0-8130-1033-0*); pap. 10.95 (*0-8130-1034-9*) U Press Fla.

— Turtle Sky. 26p. 1995. 5.00 (*0-614-30117-3*) Skydog OR.

***Averill, Diane & Bajema, Edith.** Intimo y Personal. Pimentel, Alejandro, ed. Lumpuy, Luis Bernal, tr.Tr. of Up Close & Personal. (SPA.). 56p. 1999. 8.95 (*1-55883-115-0*) Libros Desafio.

Averill, Diane, jt. auth. see Bajema, Edith.

Averill, Esther H. Fire Cat. (I Can Read Bks.). (Illus.). (J). (ps-1). 2000. 6.93 (*0-06-020195-9*, 076859) HarpC.

— Fire Cat. LC 60-10234. (I Can Read Bks.). (Illus.). 64p. (J). (ps-3). 1960. lib. bdg. 15.89 (*0-06-020196-7*) HarpC Child Bks.

— Fire Cat. LC 60-10234. (I Can Read Bks.). (Illus.). 64p. (J). (ps-3). 1983. pap. 3.95 (*0-06-444038-9*, HarpTrophy) HarpC Child Bks.

Averill, Esther H. Fire Cat. (I Can Read Bks.). (J). (ps-1). 1960. 8.95 (*0-606-03202-9*, Pub. by Turtleback) Demco.

Averill, Esther H. Hotel Cat. LC 74-77941. (Trophy Bk.). (Illus.). (J). (gr. k-3). 1974. pap. 2.95 (*0-06-440057-3*, HarpTrophy) HarpC Child Bks.

— Jenny's Adopted Brothers. (J). (gr. 1-3). 1988. 19.25 (*0-8446-6286-0*) Peter Smith.

— King Philip, the Indian Chief. LC 92-32156. (Illus.). v, 147p. (YA). (gr. 6-12). 1993. reprint ed. lib. bdg. 18.50 (*0-208-02357-7*, Linnet Bks) Shoe String.

Averill, Gage. Day for Hunter Day for Prey. LC 96-34209. 1997. pap. text 17.95 (*0-226-03292-2*) U Ch Pr.

Averill, Gerald. Ridge Runner: The Story of a Maine Woodsman. LC 79-14339. (Illus.). 224p. 1979. reprint ed. pap. 8.95 (*0-945980-28-0*) Nrth Country Pr.

***Averill, Harry.** SSI Enriched Air Nitrox Diving Manual. Christini, Ed, ed. (Illus.). 80p. 1999. reprint ed. pap. text 16.95 (*1-880229-39-0*, 2501 EAN) Concept Sys.

Averill, Harry. Underwater Photography. (Specialty Diver Ser.). 128p. 1995. pap. text. write for info. (*1-880229-26-9*) Concept Sys.

— Underwater Photography: Instructor Manual. (Specialty Diver Ser.). 52p. 1995. pap. text, teacher ed. write for info. (*1-880229-27-7*) Concept Sys.

Averill, Harry, jt. auth. see Stewart, Gloria.

Averill, James, ed. see Wordsworth, William.

Averill, James H. Wordsworth & the Poetry of Human Suffering. LC 79-21783. 318p. 1980. 45.00 (*0-8014-1249-8*) Cornell U Pr.

Averill, James R. Anger & Aggression: An Essay on Emotion. (Social Psychology Ser.). (Illus.). 402p. 1982. 66.00 (*0-387-90719-X*) Spr-Verlag.

Averill, James R. & Nunley, Elma P. Voyages of the Heart: Living an Emotionally Creative Life. 1992. 27.95 (*0-02-901108-6*) Free Pr.

Averill, James R., et al. Rules of Hope. (Recent Research in Psychology Ser.). vii, 134p. 1990. 44.95 (*0-387-97219-6*) Spr-Verlag.

Averill, Lawrence H. UNIFORM PROBATE CODE IN A NUTSHELL 4E. 4th ed. LC 93-31236. (Paralegal). 566p. (C). 1998. pap. text 19.50 (*0-314-07083-4*) West Pub.

Averill, Lloyd J. Illiberal Education: A Novel. LC 98-66797. 188p. 1998. pap. text 19.95 (*1-881908-20-8*) PanPress.

— Reconsider Love. LC 95-71169. (Illus.). 104p. 1995. pap. 12.95 (*1-881908-13-5*) PanPress.

Averill, Lloyd J. & Morris, Daphne K. Northwest Coast Native & Native-Style Art: A Guidebook for Western Washington. LC 95-21962. (Illus.). xxxix, 215p. (C). 1995. pap. 17.95 (*0-295-97468-0*) U of Wash Pr.

Averill, Lloyd J., jt. auth. see Brown, Steven C.

Averill, M. & Corkin, B. How to Succeed As a Network Marketeer. (Marketing & Sales Ser.). 1995. pap. 14.95 (*0-7494-1615-7*) Kogan Page Ltd.

Averill, Mary, jt. auth. see Corkin, Bud.

Averill, Ric. Alex & the Shrink World. 72p. 1998. pap. 5.50 (*0-87129-835-X*, A75) Dramatic Pub.

***Averill, Ric.** The Princess & the Pea, No TV & Other Plays. 75p. 1999. pap. 5.60 (*0-87129-926-7*, P90) Dramatic Pub.

Averill, Ric, jt. auth. see Willmott, Kevin.

Averill, Robert W. The Moosilaukee Reader, Vol. I. Noon, Jack, ed. LC 98-44413. (Illus.). 300p. 1999. pap. 20.00 (*0-9642213-7-3*) Moose Cntry.

— The Moosilaukee Reader, Vol. II. Noon, Jack, ed. LC 98-44413. (Illus.). 300p. 1999. pap. 20.00 (*0-9642213-8-1*) Moose Cntry.

Averill, Thomas F. Oleander's Guide to Kansas: Guide to Kansas. (Illus.). 160p. 1996. pap. 12.95 (*1-880652-88-9*) Wichita Eagle.

— Seeing Mona Naked. 172p. 1989. pap. 9.75 (*0-922820-01-5*) Watermark Pr.

Averill, Thomas F., ed. What Kansas Means to Me: Twentieth-Century Writers on the Sunflower State. LC 90-41688. (Illus.). 256p. 1995. pap. 12.95 (*0-7006-0710-2*) U Pr of KS.

Averill, Thomas F., ed. see Elliott, Harley.

Averill, Tom, ed. see Cutler, Bruce.

Averina, T. A., jt. auth. see Artemiev, S. S.

Averintsev, Sergey, et al, eds. Christianity: Encyclopedic Dictionary, 3 vols. Incl. Vol. I: A to K. (Illus.). 864p. Date not set. 70.00 (*5-85270-050-9*); Vol. III: T to Z. (Illus.). 784p. Date not set. 70.00 (*5-85270-100-9*); Vol. II: L to S. (Illus.). 672p. Date not set. 70.00 (*5-85270-153-X*); 1995. 150.00 (*5-85270-023-1*) Intl Scholars.

Averitt, Joy & Smith, Donna B. Bible Handwork Ideas for Twos & Threes. 1983. pap. 4.35 (*0-89137-613-5*) Quality Pubns.

Averitt, Max W., ed. Boatwatch: Armchair Shopping Three Hundred Forty Sailboats 17'-28' LC 94-156217. 192p. 1994. pap. 24.00 (*0-9627152-2-0*) Boatwatch.

— Boatwatch: Armchair Shopping Three Hundred Forty Sailboats 29'-35' LC 94-163858. 192p. 1994. pap. 24.00 (*0-9627152-3-9*) Boatwatch.

— Boatwatch: Master Guide to Powerboats. LC 96-83462. 396p. (Orig.). 1996. pap. 78.00 (*0-9627152-4-7*) Boatwatch.

Averitt, Max W. Boatwatch: Master Guide to Sailboats of the World. LC 92-93088. (ENG, FRE & GER.). 592p. 1992. pap. 75.00 (*0-9627152-1-2*) Boatwatch.

— Boatwatch: On-the-Water Guide to Pleasure Boat Identification. 2nd ed. LC 90-91833. 384p. 1990. pap. 22.00 (*0-9627152-0-4*) Boatwatch.

***Averitt, Richard C.** Scriptural Music Indexed. 64p. 2001. 16.95 (*0-8158-0543-8*) Chris Mass.

Averitt, Richard C. Singular-Meaning Lexicon of the New Testament. 205p. 1996. pap. 7.00 (*1-887612-00-9*) Script Semantics.

Averitt, Robert T. Dual Economy. (C). 1968. pap. text 11.25 (*0-393-09781-1*) Norton.

Averkiev, V. P. Shipboard Fish Scouting & Electronavigational Equipment. Kane, S. K., tr. from RUS. 485p. (C). 1985. text 181.00 (*90-6191-436-1*, Pub. by A A Balkema) Ashgate Pub Co.

Averkieva, Julia P. & Sherman, Mark A. Kwakiutl String Figures. LC 92-2728. (Anthropological Papers of the American Museum of Natural History: Vol. 71). (Illus.). 232p. 1992. 40.00 (*0-295-97172-X*) U of Wash Pr.

Averley, Gwen, ed. Title Index to the Nineteenth Century Short Title Catalogue, 1801-1815, Series I. 850p. 1984. lib. bdg. write for info. (*0-907977-82-0*) Chadwyck-Healey.

Averoff-Tossizza, Evangelos. By Fire & Axe: The Communist Party & the Civil War in Greece, 1944-49. Rigos, Sarah A., tr. LC 77-91603. (Modern Greek History Ser.: No. 1). (Illus.). 438p. 1978. 20.00 (*0-89241-078-7*) Caratzas.

— The Call of the Earth. Michalopoulos, Andre, tr. from GRE. 300p. 1988. 20.00 (*0-89241-134-1*) Caratzas.

— Lost Opportunities: The Cyprus Question, 1950-1963. Cullen, Timothy & Kyriakides, Susan, trs. from GRE. viii, 440p. 1986. 30.00 (*0-89241-389-1*) Caratzas.

Averous, M. & Balkanski, M., eds. Semimagnetic Semiconductors & Diluted Magnetic Semiconductors. (Ettore Majorana International Science Ser., Life Sciences: Vol. 55). (Illus.). 288p. (C). 1991. text 114.00 (*0-306-43931-X*, Kluwer Plenum) Kluwer Academic.

Averre, Charles W., III, jt. auth. see Shurtleff, Malcolm C.

Averroes. Averroes: Epitome of Parva Naturalia. Blumberg, Harry, tr. LC 58-3296. (Medieval Academy Bks.: No. 71). 1961. 30.00 (*0-910956-45-6*) Medieval Acad.

— Averroes Commentarium Medium et Epitome in Aristotelis De Generatione et Corruptione Libros, Heb Ed. Kurland, Samuel, ed. LC 50-1421. (Medieval Academy Bks.: No. 66). 1958. 30.00 (*0-910956-40-5*) Medieval Acad.

— Averroes Commentarium Medium in Aristotelis De Generatione et Corruptione Libros, Lat. Ed. Fobes, F. H. & Kurland, Samuel, eds. LC 50-1421. (Medieval Academy Bks.: No. 65). 1956. 30.00 (*0-910956-39-1*) Medieval Acad.

— Averroes Commentarium Medium in Porphyrii Isagogen et Aristotelis Categorias, Heb. Ed. Davidson, Herbert A., ed. LC 68-24426. (Medieval Academy Bks.: No. 78). 1969. 30.00 (*0-910956-52-9*) Medieval Acad.

— Averroes Compendia Librorum Aristotelis Qui Parva Naturalia Vocantur, Heb. Ed. Blumberg, Harry, ed. LC 50-1421. (Medieval Academy Bks.: No. 62). (HEB.). 1954. 30.00 (*0-910956-36-7*) Medieval Acad.

— Averroes Compendia Librorum Aristotelis Qui Parva Naturalia Vocantur, Lat. Ed. Shields, E. L. & Blumberg, Harry, eds. (Medieval Academy Bks.: No. 54). (LAT.). 1949. 30.00 (*0-910956-28-6*) Medieval Acad.

— Averroes' "De Substantia Orbis" Vol. 96: Critical Edition of the Hebrew Text, with English Translation & Commentary. Hyman, Arthur, ed. (ENG & HEB.). 1986. 30.00 (*965-208-071-3*) Medieval Acad.

***Averroes.** Averroes' Middle Commentary on Aristotle's Poetics. unabridged ed. LC 99-47256. 184p. 1999. reprint ed. 35.00 (*1-890318-03-5*, Pub. by St Augustines Pr) Chicago Distribution Ctr.

Averroes. Averroes' Middle Commentary on Aristotle's Posterior Analytics. Kassem, Mahmoud M. et al, eds. (American Research Center in Egypt, Publications Ser.: No. 7). (ARA & ENG.). 232p. 1982. pap. 16.50 (*0-936770-07-4*, Pub. by Amer Res Ctr Egypt) Eisenbrauns.

— Averroes on Aristotle's De Generatione et Corruptione: Middle Commentary & Epitome. Kurland, Samuel, tr. LC 50-1421. (Medieval Academy Bks.: No. 67). 1958. 30.00 (*0-910956-41-3*) Medieval Acad.

— Commetorum Omnium Aueroys: Super Librum Aristotelis De Physico Auditu Expositor Clarissimus. ix, 558p. reprint ed. write for info. incl. 3.5 hd (*0-318-71484-1*) G Olms Pubs.

— Destructio Destructionum Philosophiae Algazelis in the Latin Version of Calo Calonymos. Zedler, Beatric H., ed. & intro. by. LC 60-10262. 491p. reprint ed. pap. 152.30 (*0-608-04189-0*, 206492400011) Bks Demand.

Averrohes, et al. Jihad in Mediaeval & Modern Islam: The Chapter on Jihad from Averroes' Legal Handbook 'Bideayat Al-mudjtahid' & the Treatise 'Koran & Fighting' By the Late Shaykh-al-azhar, Mahmeud Shaltout. annot. ed. LC 77-471514. (Nisaba Ser.). 90p. 1977. write for info. (*90-04-04854-5*) Brill Academic Pubs.

Averrois. Averroes: Middle Commentary on Porphyry's Isagoge. Davidson, Herbert A., ed. LC 68-24427. (Medieval Academy Bks.: No. 79). 1969. 30.00 (*0-910956-53-7*) Medieval Acad.

A

A

Avers. Genetics. (Biology Ser.). 1980. pap. 19.75 (*0-534-26233-3*) Wadsworth Pub.

Avers, Charlotte J. Biology of Sex. (Illus.). 293p. (C). 1991. reprint ed. text 82.00 (*1-878907-45-X*) TechBooks.

— Process & Pattern in Evolution. (Illus.). 608p. (C). 1989. text 57.00 (*0-19-505275-7*) OUP.

Avers, Paul, ed. see Palmer, Joe, et al.

Aversa, Elizabeth S., et al. Online Information Services for Secondary School Students. 2nd ed. 1989. 10.00 (*0-8389-0524-2*) ALA.

Aversa, Elizabeth S., jt. auth. see Blazek, Ronald.

Aversa, Nicholas. The Little Prince: A Study Guide. Friedland, J. & Kessler, R., eds. (Novel-Ties Ser.). (J). (gr. 6-8). 1987. pap. text, student ed. 15.95 (*0-88122-118-X*) Lrn Links.

Aversano, Vince. NBA Superstars: A Live Action Look at the Heroes of the NBA. (Illus.). 32p. 1994. pap. 6.99 (*1-55958-701-6*) Prima Pub.

Avery. Women of Mongolia. LC 96-22277. (Illus.). 160p. 1996. pap. 19.95 (*0-937321-05-2*) Avery Pr CO.

Avery & Smith. Basic Botany. 440p. (C). 1994. pap. text 74.00 (*0-536-58692-6*) Pearson Custom.

Avery, jt. auth. see Dimitroulis.

Avery, Dorene G. The Way of Change: A Manual for the Millennium. 86p. 1997. 11.95 (*1-890500-00-3*) Angel Works Pub.

Avery, Amos G. & Connecticut Historical Society Staff. Clockmakers & Craftsmen of the Avery Family in Connecticut. 165p. 1988. 25.00 (*0-940748-94-0*) Conn Hist Soc.

Avery, Anika. The Vegetarian Female. LC 98-28316. (Illus.). 128p. 1999. pap. 12.95 (*0-89529-840-6*, Avery) Penguin Putnam.

Avery, Anne. All's Fair. 400p. (Orig.). 1994. mass mkt. 4.99 (*0-505-51937-2*, Love Spell) Dorchester Pub Co.

— All's Fair. 400p. (Orig.). 1998. mass mkt. 5.50 (*0-505-52257-8*, Love Spell) Dorchester Pub Co.

***Avery, Anne.** A Distant Star. 400p. (Orig.). 1999. mass mkt. 5.50 (*0-505-52335-3*, Pub. by Dorchester Pub Co) CMG.

Avery, Anne. Fortune's Fancy. 1998. mass mkt. 5.99 (*0-451-40740-7*, Onyx) NAL.

— Hidden Heart. 448p. (Orig.). 1996. mass mkt. 5.99 (*0-505-52109-1*, Love Spell) Dorchester Pub Co.

— The Highwayman's Daughter. 400p. 1998. mass mkt. 5.99 (*0-505-52259-4*, Love Spell) Dorchester Pub Co.

— The Snow Queen. Orig. Title: Snedronningen. 400p. (Orig.). 1996. mass mkt. 5.99 (*0-505-52151-2*) Dorchester Pub Co.

Avery Architectural & Fine Arts Library Staff. Avery Index to Architectural Periodicals, 1992, Vol. 1. 2nd large type ed. 1993. suppl. ed. 125.00 (*0-7838-2053-4*, G K Hall Lrg Type) Mac Lib Ref.

— Avery Index to Architectural Periodicals, 1992, Vol. 3. 2nd large type ed. 1993. suppl. ed. 125.00 (*0-7838-2055-0*, G K Hall Lrg Type) Mac Lib Ref.

— Avery Index to Architectural Periodicals, 1994, Vol. 1, No. 15. 2nd ed. 1996. 120.00 (*0-7838-2143-3*, Hall Reference) Macmillan.

— Avery Index to Architectural Periodicals, 1994, Vol. 2, No. 15. 2nd ed. 1996. 120.00 (*0-7838-2144-1*, Hall Reference) Macmillan.

— Avery Index to Architectural Periodicals, 1994, Vol. 3, No. 15. 2nd ed. 1996. 120.00 (*0-7838-2145-X*, Hall Reference) Macmillan.

— Avery Index to Architectural Periodicals, 1994, Vol. 4, No. 15. 2nd ed. 1996. 120.00 (*0-7838-2146-8*, Hall Reference) Macmillan.

Avery, Benedict R., tr. see Gregorius I.

Avery, Benjamin A. The Works of Benjamin Parke Avery, 1828-1875. 1987. reprint ed. 79.00 (*0-685-18610-5*) Rprt Serv.

Avery, Bill. Federation Track: From Circular Quay to Stanwell Park. 160p. (Orig.). 1997. pap. 11.95 (*0-86417-813-1*, Pub. by Kangaroo Pr) Seven Hills Bk.

Avery, Brian. Soils of the British Isles. 480p. 1990. text 150.00 (*0-85198-649-8*) OUP.

***Avery, Bryce D.** Correspondence Chess in America. LC 99-48418. (Illus.). 287p. 1999. lib. bdg. 45.00 (*0-7864-0733-6*) McFarland & Co.

Avery, Burniece. Walk Quietly Through the Night & Cry Softly. LC 77-2891. (Illus.). 1977. 7.00 (*0-913642-08-8*) Balamp Pub.

Avery, Byllye. An Altar of Words: Wisdom, Comfort & Inspiration. LC 98-39533. 192p. 1999. reprint ed. pap. 9.00 (*0-7679-0080-4*) Broadway BDD.

Avery, C. Louise. An Exhibition of Early New York Silver. LC 77-168417. (Metropolitan Museum of Art Publications in Reprint). (Illus.). 92p. 1974. reprint ed. 12.95 (*0-405-02255-7*) Ayer.

Avery, Carol. And with a Light Touch: Learning About Reading, Writing, & Teaching with First Graders. LC 92-42680. 480p. 1993. pap. text 34.00 (*0-435-08787-8*, 08787) Heinemann.

***Avery, Carol.** And with a Light Touch: Learning about Reading, Writing & Teaching with Young Children. 2nd ed. 2002. pap. text. write for info. (*0-325-00286-X*) Heinemann.

Avery, Charles. Bernini: Genius of the Baroque. LC NB623.B5A94 1997. (Illus.). 288p. 1997. 85.00 (*0-8212-2465-4*, Pub. by Bulfinch Pr) Little.

— David Le Marchand 1674-1726: An Ingenious Man for Carving in Ivory. (Illus.). 96p. 1996. pap. 29.95 (*0-85331-686-4*, Pub. by Lund Humphries) Antique Collect.

— Florentine Renaissance Sculpture. (Illus.). 274p. 1989. pap. 19.95 (*0-7195-1932-2*, Pub. by John Murray) Trafalgar.

— Giambologna: The Complete Sculpture. (Illus.). 288p. (C). 1993. reprint ed. pap. 35.00 (*0-7148-2953-6*, Pub. by Phaidon Press) Phaidon Pr.

— Lissa Stratton Strikes: Musical Comedy Suggested by Aritophanes' Lysistrata. (Illus.). 60p. 1986. pap. 4.50 (*0-88680-277-6*) I E Clark.

— The Seven Ages of Dan: All the World's a Stage, A Two Act Comedy. (Illus.). 57p. 1993. pap. 4.00 (*0-88680-387-X*) I E Clark.

***Avery, Charles & Hall, Michael, texts.** Giambologna: An Exhibition of Sculpture by the Master & His Followers. (Illus.). 173p. 1998. 75.00 (*1-58821-022-7*) Salander OReilly.

Avery, Charles, et al. Effigies & Ecstasies: Roman Baroque Sculpture & Design in the Age of Bernini. (Illus.). 176p. 1998. pap. 50.00 (*0-903598-83-3*) Natl Galleries.

Avery, Charles E. Everybody Has Feelings: Todos Tenemos Sentimientos: The Moods of Children. LC 97-47454. (ENG & SPA.). 50p. (J). 1998. 8.95 (*0-87659-197-7*) Gryphon Hse.

***Avery, Chris.** Cut Loose. 432p. 2000. mass mkt. 5.99 (*0-7860-1115-7*, Pinncle Kensgtn) Kensgtn Pub Corp.

***Avery, Christine & Zabel, Diane.** The Flexible Workplace: A Sourcebook of Information & Research. LC 00-25461. 200p. 2000. 60.00 (*1-56720-189-X*, Q189) Greenwood.

Avery, Christine & Zable, Diane. The Quality Management Sourcebook. LC 96-8911. 336p. (C). 1996. 125.00 (*0-415-10831-4*) Routledge.

Avery, Christopher M. The Technology Transfer Grid. 1999. write for info. (*0-201-56307-X*) Addison-Wesley.

Avery, Chuck. A Committee of One. 168p. 1998. pap. 7.95 (*0-932970-88-5*) Prinit Pr.

— Just Browsing. 136p. 1994. pap. 6.95 (*0-932970-94-X*) Prinit Pr.

Avery, Clara A. The Averell-Avery Family: A Record of the Descendants of William & Abigail Averell of Ipswich, Mass., 2 vols., Set. (Illus.). 1094p. 1993. reprint ed. pap. 149.00 (*0-8328-3008-9*); reprint ed. lib. bdg. 159.00 (*0-8328-3007-0*) Higginson Bk Co.

Avery, Constance & Cimbuna, Al. Bischoff Kord & Kamotsuru Bottles. 1969. pap. 10.00 (*0-87505-276-2*) Borden.

Avery, Craig, ed. see Portland Cement Association Staff.

Avery, Dale. Oil Prices & the Manufacturing Sector in Asia-Pacific Net Oil-Importing Developing Countries (with Special Reference to the Philippines) LC HD9576.A689. (Working Papers: No. 81-18). 70p. reprint ed. pap. 30.00 (*0-608-14940-3*, 202597400047) Bks Demand.

Avery, David, jt. auth. see Avery, Maryjean W.

Avery, David R., jt. ed. see McDonald, Ralph E.

***Avery, Dennis T.** Saving the Planet Through Pesticides & Plastics. 2nd ed. 2000. pap. 20.00 (*1-55813-069-1*) Hudson Instit IN.

Avery, Dennis T. Saving the Planet with Pesticides & Plastic: The Environmental Triumph of High-Yield Farming. (Illus.). 432p. (Orig.). 1995. pap. text 19.95 (*1-55813-051-9*) Hudson Instit IN.

Avery, Dianne, jt. auth. see Belton, Robert.

Avery, Donald H. The Science of War: Canadian Scientists & Allied Military Technology During the Second World War. LC 98-229694. (Illus.). 304p. 1998. text 40.00 (*0-8020-5996-1*) U of Toronto Pr.

Avery, Doug. Fundamentals of Practical Lighting Efficiency: A Lighting Handbook. (C). 2000. text 74.00 (*0-13-577917-0*) P-H.

Avery, E. M. Avery Notes & Queries: A Quarterly Magazine Devoted to the History of the Groton Averys, No. 1-18. (Illus.). 1988. reprint ed. pap. 37.00 (*0-8328-0145-3*); reprint ed. lib. bdg. 47.00 (*0-8328-0144-5*) Higginson Bk Co.

Avery, Emmett L. London Stage, 1700-1729: A Critical Introduction, Pt. 2. LC 60-6539. (Arcturus Books Paperbacks). (Illus.). 199p. 1968. pap. 9.95 (*0-8093-0337-X*) S Ill U Pr.

Avery, Emmett L., ed. see Congreve, William.

Avery, G. S., ed. see Milner, G.

Avery, Giles. Sketches of Shakers & Shakerism. 50p. 1993. reprint ed. lib. bdg. 69.00 (*0-7812-5306-3*) Rprt Serv.

Avery, Gillian. Behold the Child: American Children & Their Books, 1621-1922. LC 94-29832. (Illus.). 239p. 1995. text 29.95 (*0-8018-5066-5*) Johns Hopkins.

— Maria Escapes. LC 91-36730. (Illus.). 272p. (J). (gr. 4-8). 1992. pap. 15.00 (*0-671-77074-8*) S&S Bks Yung.

— Origins & English Predecessors of the New England Primer. (Illus.). 28p. 1999. pap. write for info. (*0-944026-95-8*) Am Antiquarian.

***Avery, Gillian.** Representations of Childhood Death. LC 99-37672. 2000. text 49.95 (*0-312-22408-7*) St Martin.

Avery, Gillian, ed. Holiday Romance & Other Writings for Children. 368p. (Orig.). 1995. pap. 8.95 (*0-460-87601-5*, Everyman's Classic Lib) Tuttle Pubng.

Avery, Gillian & Ransome, Arthur. Russian Fairy Tales. LC 95-15334. 1995. 14.95 (*0-679-43641-3*) Knopf.

Avery, Glenn R. Washington State Advanced Technology, 1993 Directory. (Illus.). 324p. 1993. pap. 34.00 (*0-9634596-0-0*) CCH INC.

— Washington State Advanced Technology, 1994 Directory. (Illus.). 296p. (Orig.). 1994. pap. text 34.00 (*0-9634596-1-9*) CCH INC.

— Washington State Advanced Technology, 1995 Directory. (Illus.). 296p. (Orig.). 1995. pap. 34.00 (*0-9634596-2-7*) CCH INC.

Avery, Glenn R., ed. Washington State Advanced Technology, 1996 Directory. 232p. (Orig.). 1996. pap. 34.00 (*0-9634596-3-5*) CCH INC.

Avery, Gordon B., et al, eds. Neonatology: Pathophysiology & Management of the Newborn. 5th ed. 1999. 145.00 (*0-7817-1210-6*) Lppncott W & W.

Avery, Gordon B., et al. Neonatology: Pathophysiology & Management of the Newborn. 4th ed. 1,552p. 1993. text 153.00 (*0-397-51101-9*) Lppncott W & W.

Avery, Graham & Phillips, Maberly. Sherlock Holmes & the Strange Events at the Bank of England; The Bank of England, Its History & Development, 2 vol. set. unabridged ed. Wilkes, Ian, ed. LC 97-24023. (Illus.). 144p. 1997. pap. 20.00 (*0-86025-288-4*) Players Pr.

Avery, Helen P. The Ghost of Canterville Hall. (J). 1977. 6.00 (*0-87602-112-7*) Anchorage.

— The Secret Garden: Playscript. (J). (gr. k-3). 1987. pap. 6.50 (*0-87602-271-9*) Anchorage.

Avery, Isaac T. & Easley, Mary. Legal Aspects of Police Supervision. LC 97-65224. 150p. (C). 1997. pap. 24.95 (*0-942728-80-7*) Copperhouse.

— Legal Aspects of Police Supervision: Legal Resource Book. LC 97-65244. 206p. (C). 1997. pap. 24.95 (*0-942728-81-5*) Copperhouse.

Avery, Isaac W. History of the State of Georgia from 1850-1881. LC 75-161709. reprint ed. 67.50 (*0-404-04571-5*) AMS Pr.

Avery, Jack. Injection Molding Alternatives: A Guide for Designers & Product Engineers. LC 98-34480. 1998. 98.00 (*1-56990-251-8*) Hanser-Gardner.

Avery, James K. Essentials of Oral Histology & Embryology: A Clinical Approacch. 224p. (C). (gr. 13). 1991. pap. text 38.95 (*1-55664-188-5*) Mosby Inc.

— Oral Development & Histology. 2nd ed. LC 94-30332. (Illus.). 416p. 1994. 59.00 (*0-86577-553-2*) Thieme Med Pubs.

***Avery, James K. & Steele, Pauline F.** Essentials of Oral Histology & Embryology. 2nd ed. LC 99-25601. (Illus.). 256p. (C). 1999. text. write for info. (*0-323-00460-1*) Mosby Inc.

Avery, Jeanne. Past Lives, Present Loves. 1999. mass mkt. 6.50 (*0-451-19680-5*) NAL.

— Rising Sign: Your Astrological Mask. LC 77-16894. (Illus.). 416p. 1991. pap. 14.95 (*0-385-13278-6*) Doubleday.

— A Soul's Journey: Empowering the Present Through Past Life Regression. Gatewood, Nann, ed. LC 96-85199. 175p. (Orig.). 1996. pap. 13.95 (*1-887161-12-0*) Boru Pubng.

***Avery, Jim.** Advertising Campaign Planning. 3rd rev. ed. Bendinger, Bruce H., ed. 264p. (C). 2000. pap. text 24.95 (*1-887229-06-X*) Copy Wrkshp.

Avery, John. History of the Town of Ledyard, Connecticut, 1650-1900. (Illus.). 334p. 1992. reprint ed. lib. bdg. 35.00 (*0-8328-2348-1*) Higginson Bk Co.

— Hyperspherical Harmonics: Applications in Quantum Theory. (C). 1989. text 175.00 (*0-7923-0165-X*) Kluwer Academic.

***Avery, John.** Hyperspherical Harmonics & Generalized Sturmians. LC 99-57526. (Progress in Theoretical Chemistry & Physics Ser.). (C). 1999. write for info. (*0-7923-6087-7*) Kluwer Academic.

Avery, John. Progress, Poverty & Population: Re-Reading Condorcet, Godwin & Malthus. 168p. (C). 1997. pap. text 19.50 (*0-7146-4404-8*, Pub. by F Cass Pubs) Intl Spec Bk.

Avery, John, et al, eds. Understanding Molecular Properties. 1987. text 251.50 (*90-277-2419-9*) Kluwer Academic.

— Understanding Molecular Properties. 1987. pap. text 105.00 (*90-277-2439-3*) Kluwer Academic.

Avery, John, et al. Progress, Poverty & Population: Re-Reading Condorcet, Godwin & Malthus. LC 97-30117. 168p. (C). 1997. text 47.50 (*0-7146-4750-0*, Pub. by F Cass Pubs) Intl Spec Bk.

Avery Jones, J. F., ed. Tax Havens & Measures Against Tax Evasion & Avoidance in the EEC. xiv, 144p. 1974. reprint ed. text 25.00 (*0-85227-027-5*) W S Hein.

Avery, Jordon. City of the Dreamers. 274p. (Orig.). 1993. pap. 9.95 (*0-9636355-0-6*) StarStream Pr.

Avery, Keith. Ridden Hard & Put up Wet. LC 90-92078. (Illus.). vi, 62p. (Orig.). 1990. pap. 10.95 (*0-9624489-2-3*) G Logsdon Bks.

Avery, Keith, et al. Coolin' Down: An Anthology of Contemporary Cowboy Poetry. xii, 90p. 1992. 24.95 (*0-9624489-4-X*); pap. 14.95 (*0-9624489-5-8*) G Logsdon Bks.

Avery, Kevin J. Church's Great Picture: The Heart of the Andes. (Illus.). 64p. 1993. 10.95 (*0-685-71013-0*) Metro Mus Art.

Avery, Kevin J. & Fodera, Peter L. John Vanderlyn's Panoramic View of the Gardens of Versailles. (Illus.). 56p. 1988. pap. 1.00 (*0-87099-536-7*) Metro Mus Art.

Avery, Kevin Q. & King, George. The Age of Aetherius. 2nd rev. ed. LC 86-198666. 96p. 1982. pap. 3.95 (*0-937249-08-4*) Aetherius Soc.

Avery, Kim. The World of Raggedy Ann Collectibles: Identification & Values. LC 97-203012. (Illus.). 240p. 1997. pap. 24.95 (*0-89145-792-5*, 4880) Collector Bks.

Avery, Kristin. La Colcha de Retazos. Ada, Alma F., tr. (Dejame Leer Ser.).Tr. of Crazy Quilt. (SPA., Illus.). 16p. (J). (ps-2). 1995. 2.95 (*0-673-36303-1*, GoodYrBooks) Addson-Wesley Educ.

— The Crazy Quilt. 2nd ed. (Let Me Read Ser.). (Illus.). 16p. (J). (ps-2). 1994. text 2.95 (*0-673-36199-3*, GoodYrBooks) Addson-Wesley Educ.

Avery, L. The Basic Writing Handbook. (C). 1990. pap. text 24.00 (*0-03-026587-8*, Pub. by Harcourt Coll Pubs) Harcourt.

Avery, Laurence G., ed. A Southern Life: Letters of Paul Green, 1916-1981. LC 93-24738. (Fred W. Morrison Series in Southern Studies). (Illus.). 737p. (C). 1994. 55.00 (*0-8078-2105-5*) U of NC Pr.

Avery, Laurence G., et al. The Writing Tutor, with Disk. 98p. (C). 1989. pap. text 16.00 (*0-685-45455-X*); pap. text 16.00 (*0-685-45456-8*) Harcourt.

Avery, Laurence G., ed. see Anderson, Maxwell.

Avery, Laurence G., ed. see Green, Paul.

Avery Library. Avery Index to Architectural Periodicals: 1994, 15th Supplement. 2nd ed. 1995. 470.00 (*0-7838-2142-5*) Mac Lib Ref.

Avery Library Staff. Avery Index to Architectural Periodicals: 1996, Vol. 1. 2nd ed. 1997. 120.00 (*0-7838-2035-6*) Mac Lib Ref.

— Avery Index to Architectural Periodicals: 1996, 14th Supplement, Set, vols. 4. 2nd ed. 1995. 480.00 (*0-8161-0629-0*) Mac Lib Ref.

— Avery Index to Architectural Periodicals: 1996, 17th Supplement. 2nd ed. 1997. 470.00 (*0-7838-2039-9*) Mac Lib Ref.

— Avery Index To Architectural Periodicals: 1996, 17th Supplement, Vol. 14. 2nd ed. 1997. 120.00 (*0-7838-2038-0*) Mac Lib Ref.

— Avery Obituary Index of Architects. 2nd ed. LC 81-110302. iii, 530 p. 1980. write for info. (*0-8161-1068-9*, G K Hall & Co) Mac Lib Ref.

Avery, Lillian D. Drake Genealogy, in the Line of Samuel Drake of Lower Smithfield Township, Northampton (Now Monroe) Co., Penna. 130p. 1996. reprint ed. pap. 21.00 (*0-8328-5258-9*); reprint ed. lib. bdg. 31.00 (*0-8328-5257-0*) Higginson Bk Co.

Avery, Louisia. The Risks of RO - Episode 4: Child's Play. Wimberly, Potice & Andrews, Dianne, eds. (Illus.). 110p. (Orig.). (J). 1988. pap. text 5.95 (*0-945779-03-8*) Ethnic Role Model.

***Avery, Luther J., et al.** California Attorney's Damages Guide: April 2000 Update. Piatt, Norma, ed. LC 74-620090. 504p. 2000. write for info. (*0-7626-0425-5*) Cont Ed Bar-CA.

— California Attorney's Damages Guide - 6/99 Update. LC 74-620090. 496p. 1999. ring bd. 78.00 (*0-7626-0336-4*, CP-31437) Cont Ed Bar-CA.

Avery, Lynn F. Activity Programming in Long Term Care. LC 97-12476. 200p. 1997. 31.95 (*0-8261-9750-7*) Springer Pub.

Avery, M. Biophysical Research for Asian Agroforestry. (C). 1992. text 18.00 (*81-204-0569-2*, Pub. by Oxford IBH) S Asia.

Avery, M. L., ed. National Wildlife Research Center Highlights Report, Fiscal Year 1996. (Illus.). 45p. (C). 1997. pap. text 15.00 (*0-7881-3948-7*) DIANE Pub.

Avery, Marilyn. Set the Table: Recipes from Teens to Grandma. (Illus.). 160p. (Orig.). 1986. pap. 8.95 (*0-9620775-0-X*, TX1-994-127) M Avery.

Avery, Mark & Leslie, Roderick. Birds & Forestry. (Illus.). 320p. 1990. text (*0-85661-058-5*, 784658) Poyser.

Avery, Martha, tr. see Xianliang, Zhang.

Avery, Martha, tr. see Ying, Hong.

Avery, Mary E. & First, Lewis R. Pediatric Medicine. 2nd ed. (Illus.). 1632p. 1994. 99.00 (*0-683-00293-7*) Lppncott W & W.

Avery, Mary W. Government of Washington State. rev. ed. (Illus.). 288p. 1973. pap. 25.00 (*0-295-95256-3*) U of Wash Pr.

— Washington: A History of the Evergreen State. LC 61-8211. (Illus.). 374p. 1965. 25.00 (*0-295-95126-5*) U of Wash Pr.

Avery, Maryjean W. & Avery, David. What Is Beautiful? LC 95-1203. (Illus.). 20p. (J). (ps-2). 1995. 12.95 (*1-883672-27-9*) Tricycle Pr.

Avery, Max & Shores, Christopher. Spitfire Leader: The Flying Career of Wing Cdr. Evan "Rosie" Mackie, DSO, DFC & BAR, DFC (U. S.), New Zealand Ace. 240p. 1997. 29.95 (*1-898697-58-2*, Pub. by Grub St) Seven Hills Bk.

Avery, Michael & Rudovsky, David. Police Misconduct: Law & Litigation. 2nd ed. LC 80-23165. (Civil Rights Ser.). 1980. ring bd. 135.00 (*0-87632-112-0*) West Group.

Avery, Michael, et al. Do Your Own Divorce in Connecticut. rev. ed. 1991. pap. 30.00 (*0-89166-014-3*) Cobblesmith.

— Police Misconduct: Law & Litigation. 3rd ed. LC 96-37113. 1996. write for info. (*0-8366-1099-7*) West Group.

Avery, Michel, et al. Building United Judgment: A Handbook for Consensus Decision Making. (Illus.). 124p. (Orig.). 1999. pap. 16.00 (*0-9602714-6-5*) Fllwshp Intent.

Avery, Mike. The Secret Language of Waking Dreams. 137p. 1992. pap. 12.00 (*1-57043-060-8*) Eckankar.

Avery, Najiyyah. My Grandmother's House Plant. 16p. (J). (gr. k-6). 1999. 7.00 (*0-8059-4539-3*) Dorrance.

Avery, Norman. North American Aircraft, 1934-1998, Vol. 1. LC 98-60468. (American Aircraft Manufacturers Ser.: No. 4). (Illus.). 200p. 1998. pap. 35.95 (*0-913322-05-9*) Jonathan T Pub.

***Avery, Norman L.** B-25 Mitchell: The Magnificent Medium. rev. ed. (Illus.). 200p. 2000. pap. 26.95 (*1-58007-008-6*) Specialty Pr.

Avery, Orabell, et al. Stories of the Seasons. Niebergall, Jane S., ed. (Illus.). 30p. (J). (gr. k-3). 1990. pap. 6.95 (*1-878051-02-4*) Circumpolar Pr.

Avery, Pat McGrath, see McGrath Avery, Pat.

Avery, Patricia, et al. Tolerance for Diversity of Beliefs: A Secondary Curriculum Unit. (Illus.). 113p. (Orig.). 1993. pap. 18.50 (*0-89994-374-8*) Soc Sci Ed.

***Avery-Peck, Alan & Neusner, Jacob.** Judaism in Late Antiquity, 4. Death, Life-after-death, Resurrection & the World-to-Come in the Judaisms of Antiquity. (Handbook of Oriental Studies). 320p. 1999. text 112.00 (*90-04-11262-6*) Brill Academic Pubs.

Avery-Peck, Alan, jt. ed. see Neusner, Jacob.

***Avery-Peck, Alan J.** The Encyclopaedia of Judaism. Neusner, Jacob & Green, William Scott, eds. 1750p. 1999. text 495.00 (*90-04-10583-2*) Brill Academic Pubs.

***Avery-Peck, Alan J., ed.** The Annual of Rabbinic Judaism Vol. 3: Ancient, Medieval & Modern. 213p. 2000. 79.00 (*90-04-11893-4*) Brill Academic Pubs.

Avery-Peck, Alan J., jt. ed. see Neusner, Jacob.

Avery-Peck, Alan J., tr. see Neusner, Jacob, ed.

An Asterisk (*) at the beginning of an entry indicates that the title is appearing for the first time.

Avery, Peter, tr. from PER. The Speech of the Birds: The Mantiqu't-Tair of Faridu'd-Din Attar. LC 98-215534. 560p. 1998. 70.00 (*0-946621-69-1*, Pub. by Islamic Texts); pap. 32.95 (*0-946621-70-5*, Pub. by Islamic Texts) Intl Spec Bk.

Avery, Peter & Ehrlich, Susan. Teaching American English Pronounciations. (Illus.). 270p. 1992. pap. text 15.95 (*0-19-432815-5*) OUP.

Avery, Peter & Grossman, Stanley I., eds. Cambridge History of Iran, Vol. 7: From Nadir Shah to the Islamic Republic. LC 67-12845. (Illus.). 1096p. 1991. text 155.00 (*0-521-20095-4*) Cambridge U Pr.

Avery, Peter, tr. see Khayyam, Omar.

Avery, Phyllis. The Garden of Eden Raw Fruit & Vegetable Recipes. (Illus.). 144p. (Orig.). 1992. pap. 11.95 (*1-880598-24-8*) P Avery.

— Stop Your Indigestion: Causes, Remedies, Recipes. (Illus.). 228p. (Orig.). 1993. pap. 14.95 (*1-880598-36-1*) P Avery.

— Stop Your Tinnitus: Causes, Preventatives, & Alternatives. (Illus.). 192p. (Orig.). 1991. pap. 14.95 (*1-880598-22-1*) P Avery.

— The Ten-Minute Vegetarian Cook Book. (Illus.). 144p. (Orig.). 1992. pap. 11.95 (*1-880598-74-4*) P Avery.

Avery, R. America's Triumph at Panama. 1976. lib. bdg. 59.95 (*0-8490-1420-4*) Gordon Pr.

Avery, R. Milet Redhouse Mini Dictionary, Mini Ed. 1997. pap. text 8.50 (*975-8176-09-9*) MLE Inc.

Avery, Ralph A. Enlightenment: A Solution to Some Problems. 187p. 1993. pap. text. write for info. (*0-9641064-2-6*); lib. bdg. 15.00 (*0-9641064-4-2*) Averys Philosop.

— Enlightenment: A Solution to Some Problems. 187p. 1993. text 15.00 (*0-9641064-1-8*) Averys Philosop.

Avery, Robert. Installation, Operation & Maintenance of Air Filtration Systems: IOM Manual. Johnson, Jacqueline S., ed. (Illus.). 120p. 1997. 35.00 (*0-614-26954-7*) Nat Air Filtra.

— The Redhouse Portable Turkish-English, English-Turkish Dictionary. 11th ed. (ENG & TUR.). 503p. 1988. 29.95 (*0-8288-9053-6*, F65420) Fr & Eur.

Avery, Robert H. I. O. M. Manual of Air Filter Systems. Mckenna, Sean, ed. (Illus.). 50p. 1996. write for info. (*0-614-13545-1*) Nat Air Filtra.

— NAFA Guide to Air Filtration. (Illus.). 180p. 1993. 80.00 (*1-884152-00-7*) Nat Air Filtra.

— NAFA Guide to Air Filtration. (Illus.). 180p. 1996. 80.00 (*1-884152-01-5*) Nat Air Filtra.

Avery, Robert K. & Eason, David, eds. Critical Perspectives on Media & Society. LC 91-22126. (Communication Ser.). 417p. 1991. pap. text 27.00 (*0-89862-289-1*); lib. bdg. 49.95 (*0-89862-315-4*) Guilford Pubns.

Avery, Robert S. Experiment in Management: Personnel Decentralization in the Tennessee Valley Authority. LC 54-11202. 224p. reprint ed. pap. 69.50 (*0-608-10190-7*, 202221100025) Bks Demand.

Avery, Ron. City of Brotherly Mayhem: Philadelphia Crimes & Criminals. LC 97-91942. (Illus.). 144p. 1997. 12.95 (*0-9658825-0-0*) Otis Bks.

— A Concise History of Philadelphia. (Illus.). 96p. 1999. pap. 9.95 (*0-9658825-1-9*) Otis Bks.

Avery, Rosemary J., ed. Adoption Policy & Special Needs Children. LC 96-43930. 240p. 1997. 57.95 (*0-86569-212-2*, Auburn Hse) Greenwood.

Avery, Samuel. The Dimensional Structure of Consciousness: A Physical Basis for Immaterialism. (Illus.). 108p. 1995. pap. 8.00 (*0-9646291-0-0*) Compari.

Avery, Samuel P. The Diaries, 1871-1882, of Samuel P. Avery, Art Dealer. Fidell-Beaufort, Madeleine et al, eds. 1979. 72.95 (*0-405-11517-2*) Ayer.

Avery, Sharon G. History of Saint John's Episcopal Church, Winnsboro, South Carolina, 1839-1989. LC 94-39492. 1995. write for info. (*0-87152-487-2*) Reprint.

Avery, Sheldon. Up from Washington: William Pickens & the Negro Struggle for Equality, 1900-1954. 1989. 39.50 (*0-87413-361-0*) U Delaware Pr.

Avery Staff. Avery Index to Architectural Periodicals, Set, 4 vols. 2nd ed. 1996. 470.00 (*0-7838-1525-5*) Mac Lib Ref.

— Avery Index to Architectural Periodicals, 1995 Vol. 1: 16th Supplement. 2nd ed. 1997. 115.00 (*0-7838-1526-3*, G K Hall & Co) Mac Lib Ref.

— Avery Index to Architectural Periodicals, 1995 Vol. 2: 16th Supplement. 2nd ed. 1997. suppl. ed. 115.00 (*0-7838-1527-1*, G K Hall & Co) Mac Lib Ref.

— Avery Index to Architectural Periodicals, 1995 Vol. 3: 16th Supplement. 2nd ed. 1997. suppl. ed. 115.00 (*0-7838-1528-X*, G K Hall & Co) Mac Lib Ref.

— Avery Index to Architectural Periodicals, 1995 Vol. 4: 16th Supplement. 2nd ed. 1997. 115.00 (*0-7838-1529-8*, G K Hall & Co) Mac Lib Ref.

Avery, Susan. Extraordinary American Indians. LC 92-11358. (Extraordinary People Ser.). (Illus.). 260p. (YA). (gr. 6-12). 1992. pap. 16.95 (*0-516-40583-7*) Childrens.

***Avery, Thomas E.** A Student's Guide to Thesis Research. 2000. pap. 7.95 (*0-8087-0148-7*) Pearson Custom.

Avery, Thomas E. & Berlin, Graydon L. Fundamentals of Remote Sensing & Airphoto Interpretation. 5th ed. LC 91-18241. (Illus.). 472p. (C). 1992. 91.00 (*0-02-305035-7*, Macmillan Coll) P-H.

Avery, Thomas E. & Burkhart, Harold E. Forest Measurements. 4th ed. LC 93-3783. (Series in Forest Resources). 416p. (C). 1993. 80.94 (*0-07-002556-8*) McGraw.

Avery, Valeen T. From Mission to Madness: Last Son of the Mormon Prophet. LC 97-45251. 368p. 1998. text 49.95 (*0-252-02399-4*) U of Ill Pr.

— From Mission to Madness: Last Son of the Mormon Prophet. LC 97-45251. 368p. 1998. pap. 19.95 (*0-252-06701-0*) U of Ill Pr.

Avery, Valeen T., jt. auth. see Newell, Linda K.

Avery, Virginia. Hats: A Heady Affair. Kuhn, Barbara K. & Lanzarotti, Sally, eds. LC 94-18483. (Illus.). 32p. 1995. pap. 11.95 (*0-914881-83-3*, 10104) C & T Pub.

— Nifty Neckwear. Kuhn, Barbara K. & Lanzarotti, Sally, eds. LC 94-20797. (Illus.). 32p. 1995. pap. 11.95 (*0-914881-84-1*, 10105) C & T Pub.

— Quilts to Wear. (Illus.). 168p. 1990. pap. 9.95 (*0-486-26336-3*) Dover.

— Wonderful Wearables, a Celebration of Creative Clothing. 1991. pap. 24.95 (*0-89145-980-4*) Collector Bks.

Avery, William H. & Wu, Chih. Ocean Thermal Energy Conversion. (Johns Hopkins Applied Physics Laboratory Series in Science & Engineering). (Illus.). 480p. (C). 1994. text 90.00 (*0-19-507199-9*, 6185) OUP.

Avery, William O. Empowered Laity: The Story of the Lutheran Laity Movement for Stewardship. LC 97-21564. 1997. 12.00 (*0-8066-3593-2*, 10-35932) Augsburg Fortress.

Avery, William P. Beyond Dependency. 1996. text 30.00 (*0-8133-0099-1*) Westview.

— Beyond Dependency. (C). 1996. pap. text 12.95 (*0-8133-0100-9*) Westview.

Avery, William P. & Rapkin, David P., eds. Markets, Politics, & Change in the Global Political Economy. LC 89-3626. (International Political Economy Yearbook Ser.: No. 4). 225p. 1989. lib. bdg. 40.00 (*1-55587-148-8*) L Rienner.

Avery, William P., jt. ed. see Rapkin, David P.

Averyt, Anne C., jt. ed. see Averyt, William F.

Averyt, William F., Jr. Agropolitics in the European Community: Interest Groups & the Common Agricultural Policy. LC 77-10619. 144p. 1977. 31.95 (*0-03-039666-2*, Praeger Pubs) Greenwood.

Averyt, William F., ed. Canadian - U. S. Telecommunications in a Global Context. 159p. (Orig.). 1986. pap. text 18.00 (*0-944799-00-0*) U VT Schl Busn Admin.

Averyt, William F. & Averyt, Anne C., eds. Managing Global Telecommunications: North American Perspectives. 212p. (Orig.). 1988. pap. text 25.00 (*0-944799-01-9*) U VT Schl Busn Admin.

Aves, Alison. Bedrooms. (Interior Design Library). (Illus.). 80p. 1996. pap. 16.99 (*1-56496-252-0*) Rockport Pubs.

— Commercial. (Interior Design Library). (Illus.). 80p. (Orig.). 1996. pap. 16.99 (*1-56496-237-7*) Rockport Pubs.

— Dining Rooms. (Interior Design Library). (Illus.). 80p. 1996. pap. 16.99 (*1-56496-240-7*) Rockport Pubs.

— Kitchens. (Interior Design Library). (Illus.). 80p. 1996. pap. 16.99 (*1-56496-238-5*) Rockport Pubs.

— Living Rooms: Interior Design Library. 80p. 1996. pap. text 14.95 (*1-56496-239-3*) Rockport Pubs.

Aves, Alison, ed. Dictionary of World Biography, 10 vols. (Illus.). 1000p. 1999. lib. bdg. 975.00 (*1-57958-050-5*) Fitzroy Dearborn.

Aves, John C. Kitchen & Bathroom Showcase. LC 94-38067. 235p. 1995. 39.00 (*1-883065-03-8*) Rockport Pubs.

Aves, John C., ed. Showcase of Interior Design: Eastern II. LC 94-2454. 232p. 1994. 39.00 (*1-883065-01-1*) Rockport Pubs.

Aves, John C. & Aves, Melanie. Interior Designer's Showcase of Color. 160p. 1993. pap. 29.99 (*1-56496-056-0*) Rockport Pubs.

Aves, John C., jt. auth. see Aves, Melanie.

Aves, Jonathan. Politics in Contmeporary Georgia: From Instability to Statehood. 62p. 1996. pap. text 12.95 (*1-899658-17-3*, Pub. by Royal Inst Intl Affairs) Brookings.

Aves, Melanie & Aves, John C. Comfort Colors: Palettes for Liveable Rooms. (Illus.). 160p. 1998. pap. 29.99 (*1-56496-464-7*, Pub. by Rockport Pubs) F & W Pubns Inc.

— The Kitchen & Bath Color. (Illus.). 160p. 1998. pap. 29.99 (*1-56496-470-1*) Rockport Pubs.

Aves, Melanie, jt. auth. see Aves, John C.

A'vese. Fifty Pennies & a Dream. 110p. 1995. 19.95 (*1-886871-01-9*); pap. 10.95 (*1-886871-00-0*) Avese.

— In Sheep's Clothing. 200p. 19.95 (*1-886871-11-6*); pap. 10.95 (*1-886871-12-4*) Avese.

Aveuris, Phaedon, ed. Atomic & Nanometer-Scale Modification of Materials: Fundamentals & Applications. LC 93-1725. (NATO Advanced Study Institutes Series E, Applied Sciences: Vol. 239). 356p. (C). 1993. text 205.50 (*0-7923-2334-3*) Kluwer Academic.

***Avey, F. M.** Legacy Workbook: Teacher's Edition. (Illus.). 50p. 2000. pap., teacher ed., wbk. ed. 34.95 (*1-930758-61-8*, Legacy Kids) Yeva Corp.

— My Legacy Book: Student Workbook. (Illus.). 50p. (YA). (gr. 5-10). 2000. pap., student ed., wbk. ed. 12.95 (*1-930758-60-X*, Legacy Kids) Yeva Corp.

***Avey, Mechelle.** A Lifetime Loving You. 272p. 2000. pap. 6.99 (*1-930758-40-5*) Yeva Corp.

Avey, Michael J. The Demobilization of American Voters: A Comprehensive Theory of Voter Turnout, 244. LC 89-11881. (Contributions in Political Science Ser.: No. 244). 162p. 1989. 49.95 (*0-313-26600-X*, ADV/, Greenwood Pr) Greenwood.

Avey, Renny J. Real Property Basics. 1986. per. 12.00 (*0-88252-132-2*) Paladin Hse.

***Avey, Tedd, et al.** The CPA's Handbook of Fraud & Commercial Crime Prevention. LC 00-22946. 2000. write for info. (*0-87051-292-7*) Am Inst CPA.

***Aveyard, Tony.** Lotus Notes/Domino 5 System Administration. (CLP Fast Track Ser.). 600p. 2000. pap. 39.99 (*0-7357-0878-9*) New Riders Pub.

Avezaat, C. J., et al, eds. Intracranial Pressure VIII. 1993. 336.00 (*0-387-55946-9*) Spr-Verlag.

Avgar, Amy, jt. auth. see Mayer, Egon.

Avgerou, Chrisanthi & Cornford, Tony. Developing Information Systems. (Macmillan Information Systems Ser.). (Illus.). 237p. (C). 1993. pap. text 35.00 (*0-333-57726-4*) Scholium Intl.

Avgikos, Jan, text. Lucas Samaras: Cubes, Pragmata & Trapezoids. (Illus.). 48p. (Orig.). 1994. pap. write for info. (*1-878283-48-0*) PaceWildenstein.

Avgikos, Jan, et al. Renee Green: World Tour. (Focus Ser.). (Illus.). 61p. (Orig.). 1993. pap. 14.95 (*0-914357-31-X*) Los Angeles Mus Contemp.

***Avi.** Abigail Takes the Wheel. LC 98-36887. (I Can Read Chapter Bks.). (Illus.). 64p. (J). (gr. 3-5). 1999. 14.95 (*0-06-027662-2*); lib. bdg. 14.89 (*0-06-027663-0*) HarpC Child Bks.

— Abigail Takes the Wheel. LC 98-36887. (I Can Read Chapter Bks.). (Illus.). 64p. (J). (gr. 3-5). 2000. mass mkt. 3.95 (*0-06-444281-0*, HarpTrophy) HarpC Child Bks.

— Abigail Takes the Wheel. (Illus.). (J). 2000. 9.40 (*0-606-18672-7*) Turtleback.

— The Barn. 128p. (J). 1996. mass mkt. 4.99 (*0-380-72562-2*, Avon Bks) Morrow Avon.

— The Barn. LC 94-6920. 112p. (J). (gr. 4-6). 1994. 14.95 (*0-531-06861-7*); lib. bdg. 15.99 (*0-531-08711-5*) Orchard Bks Watts.

— The Barn. (J). 1996. 9.60 (*0-606-09056-8*, Pub. by Turtleback) Demco.

Avi. Beyond the Western Sea, 2 vol. 1996. boxed set 34.95 (*0-531-09547-9*) Orchard Bks Watts.

***Avi.** Beyond the Western Sea: Lord Kirkle's Money, Bk. 2. 432p. (J). (gr. 5 up). 1998. reprint ed. mass mkt. 4.99 (*0-380-72876-1*, Avon Bks) Morrow Avon.

— Beyond the Western Sea: The Escape from Home, Bk. 1. (Beyond the Western Sea Ser.: Bk. 1). 320p. (J). 1997. mass mkt. 4.99 (*0-380-72875-3*, Avon Bks) Morrow Avon.

— Beyond the Western Sea Bk. 1: The Escape from Home. LC 95-36058. 304p. (J). (gr. 6-9). 1996. 18.95 (*0-531-09513-4*); lib. bdg. 19.99 (*0-531-08863-4*) Orchard Bks Watts.

— Beyond the Western Sea Bk. 2: Lord Kirkle's Money. LC 95-36058. 400p. (J). (gr. 6-9). 1996. 18.95 (*0-531-09520-7*); lib. bdg. 19.99 (*0-531-08870-7*) Orchard Bks Watts.

Avi. Blue Heron. LC 91-4308. 192p. (YA). (gr. 4-7). 1993. mass mkt. 4.50 (*0-380-72043-4*, Avon Bks) Morrow Avon.

Avi. Blue Heron. LC 91-4308. 192p. (J). (gr. 5-9). 1992. lib. bdg. 15.00 (*0-02-707751-9*, Bradbury S&S) S&S Childrens.

— Blue Heron. 1992. 9.60 (*0-606-05163-5*, Pub. by Turtleback) Demco.

Avi. Bright Shadow. 2nd ed. LC 93-20918. 1994. 9.05 (*0-606-06250-5*, Pub. by Turtleback) Demco.

— Bright Shadow. 2nd ed. LC 93-20918. 176p. (J). (gr. 3-7). 1994. reprint ed. mass mkt. 3.95 (*0-689-71783-0*) Aladdin.

Avi. Captain Grey. LC 92-37643. 144p. (J). 1993. mass mkt. 4.95 (*0-380-73244-0*) Morrow Avon.

Avi. Captain Grey. LC 92-37643. 160p. (YA). (gr. 5 up). 1993. pap. 4.95 (*0-688-12234-5*, Wm Morrow) Morrow Avon.

Avi. Captain Grey. (J). 1993. 10.05 (*0-606-05780-3*, Pub. by Turtleback) Demco.

— Captain Grey. LC 92-37643. (Illus.). 160p. (J). (ps-3). 1993. 16.00 (*0-688-12233-7*, Wm Morrow) Morrow Avon.

— The Christmas Rat. LC 99-87429. (Illus.). (J). 2000. per. 16.00 (*0-689-83842-5*) S&S Childrens.

Avi. Devil's Race. LC 84-47636. (Chiller Ser.). 160p. (YA). (gr. 7 up). 1995. pap. 4.95 (*0-06-440586-9*, HarpTrophy) HarpC Child Bks.

— Devil's Race. 128p. 1987. pap. 3.50 (*0-380-70406-4*, Avon Bks) Morrow Avon.

— Devil's Race. 1995. 9.60 (*0-606-07431-7*, Pub. by Turtleback) Demco.

***Avi.** Encounter at Easton. LC 94-81. 144p. (J). (gr. 3-7). 2000. mass mkt. 4.99 (*0-380-73241-6*) Morrow Avon.

Avi. Encounter at Easton. LC 94-81. 1994. 10.05 (*0-606-06362-5*, Pub. by Turtleback) Demco.

***Avi.** Encounter at Easton. (Illus.). (J). 2000. 10.34 (*0-606-17969-0*) Turtleback.

— Ereth's Birthday. LC 99-46481. (Illus.). 192p. (J). (gr. 4-7). 2000. 15.95 (*0-380-97734-6*, Avon Bks) Morrow Avon.

Avi. Escape from Home. (Beyond the Western Sea Ser.). (J). 1997. 10.34 (*0-606-12633-3*) Turtleback.

— The Fighting Ground. LC 82-47719. (Illus.). 160p. (YA). (gr. 5 up). 1984. 12.95 (*0-397-32073-6*); lib. bdg. 15.89 (*0-397-32074-4*) HarpC Child Bks.

Avi. The Fighting Ground. 152p. pap. 4.95 (*0-8072-1378-0*) Listening Lib.

Avi. The Fighting Ground. (J). 1987. 10.05 (*0-606-01662-7*, Pub. by Turtleback) Demco.

Avi. The Fighting Ground. LC 82-47719. (Trophy Bk.). 160p. (YA). (gr. 3-7). 1987. reprint ed. pap. 4.95 (*0-06-440185-5*, HarpTrophy) HarpC Child Bks.

Avi. Finding Providence: The Story of Roger Williams. (I Can Read Chapter Bks.). (J). (gr. 3-5). 1997. 8.95 (*0-606-11325-8*, Pub. by Turtleback) Demco.

— Lord Kirkle's Money, 2. (Beyond the Western Sea Ser.). (J). 1998. 10.34 (*0-606-13200-7*) Turtleback.

Avi. Man from the Sky. ALC Staff, ed. LC 92-389. (Illus.). 96p. (YA). (gr. 5 up). 1992. mass mkt. 4.95 (*0-688-11897-6*, Wm Morrow) Morrow Avon.

Avi. Man from the Sky. (J). 1992. 9.05 (*0-606-01381-4*, Pub. by Turtleback) Demco.

— Man from the Sky. large type ed. (Illus.). (J). 1993. 33.50 (*0-614-09840-8*, L-34110-00) Am Printing Hse.

— The Man Who Was Poe. LC 89-42537. 224p. (YA). (gr. 7 up). 1991. mass mkt. 4.99 (*0-380-71192-3*, Avon Bks) Morrow Avon.

— The Man Who Was Poe. 1997. mass mkt. 4.99 (*0-380-73022-7*, Avon Bks) Morrow Avon.

— The Man Who Was Poe. (J). 1989. 9.60 (*0-606-04970-3*, Pub. by Turtleback) Demco.

Avi. The Man Who Was Poe: A Spine-Chilling Tale of Mystery & Murder. (J). 1997. 9.60 (*0-606-11595-1*, Pub. by Turtleback) Demco.

— Midnight Magic. LC 98-50192. (Illus.). 192p. (YA). (gr. 5-9). 1999. 15.95 (*0-590-36035-3*, Pub. by Scholastic Inc) Penguin Putnam.

— Night Journeys. LC 93-50233. 160p. (J). (gr. 3-7). 2000. mass mkt. 4.99 (*0-380-73242-4*, Avon Bks) Morrow Avon.

— Night Journeys. LC 93-50233. 1994. 10.05 (*0-606-06621-7*, Pub. by Turtleback) Demco.

Avi. Night Journeys. LC 93-50233. 160p. (J). (gr. 5 up). 1994. reprint ed. mass mkt. 4.95 (*0-688-13628-1*, Wm Morrow) Morrow Avon.

Avi. Night Journeys, Homework Set. unabridged ed. (YA). 1997. 40.20 incl. audio (*0-7887-1838-X*, 40618) Recorded Bks.

Avi. No More Magic. 1997. 10.09 (*0-606-11687-7*, Pub. by Turtleback) Demco.

— Nothing but the Truth: A Documentary Novel. 224p. (YA). (gr. 5 up). 1993. mass mkt. 4.99 (*0-380-71907-X*, Avon Bks) Morrow Avon.

Avi. Nothing but the Truth: A Documentary Novel. LC 91-9200. 192p. (YA). (gr. 6 up). 1991. 16.95 (*0-531-05959-6*) Orchard Bks Watts.

— Nothing but the Truth: A Documentary Novel. (J). 1991. 9.60 (*0-606-05518-5*, Pub. by Turtleback) Demco.

Avi. Nothing but the Truth: A Documentary Novel. large type ed. LC 93-42497. (J). 1994. pap. 16.95 (*0-7862-0131-2*) Thorndike Pr.

— Perloo the Bold. LC 97-10681. (Illus.). 240p. (J). (gr. 3-7). 1998. 16.95 (*0-590-11002-0*, Pub. by Scholastic) Scholastic Inc.

***Avi.** Perloo the Bold. (Illus.). 256p. (J). (gr. 3-7). 1999. pap. 4.99 (*0-590-11003-9*, Pub. by Scholastic Inc) Penguin Putnam.

Avi. A Place Called Ugly. (J). 1995. 10.34 (*0-606-08018-X*) Turtleback.

Avi. Place Called Ugly. 144p. (YA). (gr. 7 up). 1995. mass mkt. 4.99 (*0-380-72423-5*, Avon Bks) Morrow Avon.

Avi. Poppy. (Illus.). 176p. (J). 1997. mass mkt. 4.99 (*0-380-72769-2*, Avon Bks) Morrow Avon.

Avi. Poppy. LC 95-6040. (Illus.). 160p. (J). (gr. 4-6). 1995. 15.95 (*0-531-09483-9*) Orchard Bks Watts.

— Poppy & Rye. LC 97-31000. (Illus.). 182p. (J). (gr. 4-7). 1998. 14.95 (*0-380-97638-2*, Avon Bks) Morrow Avon.

— Poppy & Rye. (Illus.). 208p. (J). (gr. 3-7). 1999. mass mkt. 4.95 (*0-380-79717-8*, Avon Bks) Morrow Avon.

Avi. Poppy & Rye. (J). 1997. 9.60 (*0-606-10906-4*, Pub. by Turtleback) Demco.

— Punch with Judy. 1997. mass mkt. 4.50 (*0-380-72980-6*, Avon Bks) Morrow Avon.

Avi. Punch with Judy. LC 92-27157. 1993. 9.09 (*0-606-06684-5*, Pub. by Turtleback) Demco.

Avi. Punch with Judy. 1997. 9.60 (*0-606-11771-7*, Pub. by Turtleback) Demco.

***Avi.** Ragweed: A Tale from Dimwood Forest. LC 98-55160. (Tales from Dimwood Forest Ser.). (Illus.). 192p. (J). (gr. 3-7). 1999. 15.00 (*0-380-97690-0*, Avon Bks) Morrow Avon.

— Ragweed: A Tale from Dimwood Forest. Howard, E., ed. LC 98-55160. 208p. (J). (gr. 3-7). 2000. pap. 4.95 (*0-380-80167-1*, Avon Bks) Morrow Avon.

Avi. Romeo & Juliet - Together (& Alive!) at Last. LC 87-7680. 128p. (J). (gr. 6-8). 1987. lib. bdg. 16.99 (*0-531-08321-7*) Orchard Bks Watts.

Avi. Romeo & Juliet - Together (& Alive!) at Last. LC 87-7680. 128p. (J). (gr. 6-8). 1987. 15.95 (*0-531-05721-6*) Orchard Bks Watts.

Avi. Romeo & Juliet - Together (& Alive!) at Last. LC 87-7680. 1988. 9.60 (*0-606-11808-X*, Pub. by Turtleback) Demco.

Avi. Romeo & Juliet--Together (And Alive!) at Last. 128p. (J). 1988. pap. 4.50 (*0-380-70525-7*, Avon Bks) Morrow Avon.

Avi. S. O. R. Losers. LC 84-11022. 112p. (J). (gr. 5-7). 1984. text 15.00 (*0-02-793410-1*, Bradbury S&S) S&S Childrens.

— S. O. R. Losers. (J). 1984. 9.60 (*0-606-03074-3*, Pub. by Turtleback) Demco.

***Avi.** S O R Losers. (Illus.). (J). 2000. per. 15.00 (*0-689-84157-4*) S&S Childrens.

Avi. S. O. R. Losers. 93rd ed. 1993. pap. text 14.40 (*0-15-300351-0*, Harcourt Child Bks) Harcourt.

— Smuggler's Island. LC 93-35964. Orig. Title: Shadrach's Crossing. 192p. (J). (gr. 4-7). 1994. mass mkt. 4.95 (*0-688-12797-5*, Wm Morrow) Morrow Avon.

Avi. Smugglers' Island. pap. 4.95 (*0-380-73243-2*) Morrow Avon.

Avi. Smugglers' Island. 1994. 10.05 (*0-606-06745-0*, Pub. by Turtleback) Demco.

— Something Upstairs. 128p. (J). 1997. mass mkt. 4.99 (*0-380-79086-6*, Avon Bks) Morrow Avon.

— Something Upstairs. 1997. 9.60 (*0-606-11860-8*, Pub. by Turtleback) Demco.

— Something Upstairs. 116p. (J). (gr. 4-7). 1990. reprint ed. mass mkt. 4.99 (*0-380-70853-1*, Avon Bks) Morrow Avon.

Avi. Something Upstairs: A Tale of Ghosts. LC 88-60094. 128p. (J). (gr. 5-7). 1988. 15.95 (*0-531-05782-8*) Orchard Bks Watts.

Avi. Something Upstairs: A Tale of Ghosts. LC 88-60094. 128p. (J). (gr. 5-7). 1988. lib. bdg. 16.99 (*0-531-08382-9*) Orchard Bks Watts.

A

— Something Upstairs: A Tale of Ghosts. 1990. 9.60 (*0-606-04803-0*, Pub. by Turtleback) Demco.

— Sometimes I Think I Hear My Name. (J). 1995. 9.60 (*0-606-08180-1*) Turtleback.

— Sometimes I Think I Hear My Name. 160p. (YA). (gr. 7 up). 1995. reprint ed. mass mkt. 4.50 (*0-380-72424-3*, Avon Bks) Morrow Avon.

Avi. S.O.R. Losers. 96p. (J). (gr. 3-7). 1986. reprint ed. mass mkt. 4.99 (*0-380-69993-1*, Avon Bks) Morrow Avon.

— Tom, Babette, & Simon: Three Tales of Transformation. LC 94-35195. (Illus.). 43p. (J). (gr. 4-7). 1995. pap. 15.00 (*0-02-707765-9*, Mac Bks Young Read) S&S Childrens.

— Tom, Babette, & Simon: Three Tales of Transformation. LC 94-35195. (J). 1997. 9.60 (*0-606-12138-2*, Pub. by Turtleback) Demco.

Avi. The True Confessions of Charlotte Doyle. 240p. (J). 1997. mass mkt. 4.99 (*0-380-72885-0*, Avon Bks) Morrow Avon.

***Avi.** The True Confessions of Charlotte Doyle. LC 99-33702. (Masterpiece Series Access Editions). (J). 1999. write for info. (*0-8219-1983-0*) Paradigm MN.

Avi. The True Confessions of Charlotte Doyle. (J). 1990. 9.60 (*0-606-00273-1*, Pub. by Turtleback) Demco.

— True Confessions of Charlotte Doyle. LC 90-30624. (J). 1997. 9.60 (*0-606-12013-0*, Pub. by Turtleback) Demco.

— The True Confessions of Charlotte Doyle. large type ed. (J). 1995. 64.50 (*0-614-09613-8*, L-81879-00) Am Printing Hse.

— The True Confessions of Charlotte Doyle. large type ed. LC 92-37075. 288p. (YA). 1993. reprint ed. lib. bdg. 15.95 (*1-56054-592-5*) Thorndike Pr.

Avi. What Do Fish Have to Do with Anything? And Other Stories. 1997. 10.09 (*0-606-13896-X*, Pub. by Turtleback) Demco.

— Who Stole the Wizard of Oz? LC 81-884. (J). 1997. 10.09 (*0-606-12090-4*, Pub. by Turtleback) Demco.

Avi. Who Was That Masked Man, Anyway? 176p. (J). 1994. pap. 3.99 (*0-380-72113-9*, Avon Bks) Morrow Avon.

— Who Was That Masked Man, Anyway? LC 92-7942. 176p. (YA). (gr. 4-7). 1992. 16.95 (*0-531-05457-8*); lib. bdg. 17.99 (*0-531-08607-0*) Orchard Bks Watts.

— Who Was That Masked Man, Anyway? (J). 1992. 9.09 (*0-606-06097-9*, Pub. by Turtleback) Demco.

— Who Was That Masked Man, Anyway? large type ed. (J). 1995. 45.50 (*0-614-09615-4*, L-81864-00) Am Printing Hse.

***Avi.** Windcatcher. (gr. 4-7). 1999. pap. 12.25 (*0-8335-9328-5*) Econo-Clad Bks.

— Windcatcher. 128p. (J). (gr. 4-7). 1992. mass mkt. 4.99 (*0-380-71805-7*, Avon Bks) Morrow Avon.

Avi. Windcatcher. LC 90-40574. 128p. (J). (gr. 3-7). 1991. mass mkt. 15.00 (*0-02-707761-6*, Bradbury S&S) S&S Childrens.

— Wolf Rider: A Tale of Terror. LC 86-13607. 224p. (YA). (gr. 7 up). 1986. mass mkt. 17.00 (*0-02-707760-8*, Bradbury S&S) S&S Childrens.

— Wolf Rider: A Tale of Terror. LC 86-13607. (J). 1988. 9.05 (*0-606-03680-6*, Pub. by Turtleback) Demco.

— Wolf Rider: A Tale of Terror. 2nd ed. LC 86-13607. 224p. (YA). (gr. 7 up). 1993. reprint ed. mass mkt. 4.50 (*0-02-041513-3*) Aladdin.

Avi-Hai, Avraham. Ben Gurion: State Builder. 365p. 1974. boxed set 39.95 (*0-87855-156-5*) Transaction Pubs.

Avi-Itzhak, Benjamin. Developments in Operations Research, 2 vols., Vol. 1. LC 78-141897. (Illus.). xvi, 292p. 1971. text 288.00 (*0-677-30830-2*) Gordon & Breach.

Avi-Itzhak, Benjamin, jt. auth. see Vardi, Joseph.

Avi-Yonah, Avi. Piece by Piece! Mosaics of the Ancient World. LC 93-10746. (Buried Worlds Ser.). (YA). (gr. 6 up). 1993. lib. bdg. 23.93 (*0-8225-3204-2*, Lerner Publctns) Lerner Pub.

Avi-Yonah, Michael. Art in Ancient Palestine: Selected Studies Published in the Years 1930-1976. (Illus.). 404p. 1981. text 20.00 (*965-223-369-2*, Pub. by Magnes Pr) Eisenbrauns.

Avi-Yonah, Michael & Shatzman, Israel. The Illustrated Encyclopedia of the Classical World. LC 95-43723. (Illustrated Encyclopedia Series). (Illus.). 544p. 1996. 50.00 (*0-8050-4654-2*) H Holt & Co.

Avi-Yonah, Reuven S., et al. Taxation of Financial Instruments. (Tax Law Ser.). ring bd. write for info. (*0-614-96289-7*) West Group.

Aviad, Janet, jt. auth. see Elazar, Daniel J.

Aviad, Janet O. Return to Judaism: Religious Renewal in Israel. LC 82-17663. 204p. (C). 1985. pap. text 11.00 (*0-226-03235-3*) U Ch Pr.

— Return to Judaism: Religious Renewal in Israel. LC 82-17663. 207p. reprint ed. pap. 64.20 (*0-608-09266-5*, 205406800002) Bks Demand.

Aviad, Janet O., jt. auth. see O'Dea, Thomas F.

Aviado, D. M. Lung Circulation, 2 vols., Set, Vols. 1 & 2. LC 64-24302. 1965. 633.00 (*0-08-010988-8*, Pub. by Pergamon Repr) Franklin.

Aviado, Domingo, et al. Non-Fluorinated Propellants & Solvents for Aerosols. (Solvents in the Environment Ser.). 1977. 36.50 (*0-8493-5199-5*, RA1270, CRC Reprint) Franklin.

Aviado, Domingo M., et al. Methyl Chloroform & in the Environment. Golberg, Leon, ed. (Solvents in the Environment Ser.). 1976. 70.00 (*0-87819-098-8*, RA1242, CRC Reprint) Franklin.

Aviation Daily & Aerospace Daily Editors & Aviation Week Group Staff. The Aviation & Aerospace Almanac, 1999: Aviation Week Group. 812p. 1998. pap. 138.95 (*0-07-007096-2*) McGraw-Hill Prof.

Aviation Language School, Inc. Staff. Air Traffic Control Communications for I. F. R. Pilots. 132p. 1981. pap. text. write for info. (*0-941456-07-2*) Aviation Lang Sch.

— Air Traffic Control Communications for V. F. R. Pilots. 138p. 1997. pap. text. write for info. (*0-941456-02-1*) Aviation Lang Sch.

— Primary Aeronautical Language Manual. 201p. 1994. pap. text. write for info. (*0-941456-00-5*) Aviation Lang Sch.

Aviation Language Schools, Inc. Staff. Intermediate Aeronautical Language for Maintenance Personnel. 166p. 1998. pap. text 60.00 (*0-941456-22-6*) Aviation Lang Sch.

Aviation Publications Staff. Comprehensive Reference Guide to Airfoil Sections for Light Aircraft. (Illus.). 168p. 1982. pap. 21.95 (*0-87994-038-7*) Aviat Pub.

Aviation Staff. Business & General Aviation Aircraft Pilot Reports. LC 95-36611. 277p. 1995. pap. 21.95 (*0-07-003092-8*) McGraw-Hill Prof.

Aviation Week Group Staff. Aviat & Aero Alman '99 Drop Bk. 1998. 95.00 (*0-07-134960-X*) McGraw.

***Aviation Week Group Staff.** Aviation & Aerospace Almanac 2001. (AIM/FAR Ser.). (Illus.). 2000. pap. 95.00 (*0-07-136264-9*) McGraw.

Aviation Week Group Staff, jt. auth. see Aviation Daily & Aerospace Daily Editors.

***Aviation Week Staff.** Aviation & Aerospace Almanac, 2000. 800p. 1999. pap. 15.95 (*0-07-134684-8*) McGraw.

Avicenna. Codices: Descripsit M.-T. d'Alverny. Addenda Collegerunt S. van Riet et P. Jodogne. (Avicenna Latinus Ser.). 475p. 1995. 92.00 (*2-8031-0124-6*) Brill Academic Pubs.

— The Propositional Logic of Avicenne. LC 73-75642. (Synthese Historical Library: No. 7). 309p. 1973. text 191.50 (*90-277-0360-4*, D Reidel) Kluwer Academic.

— A Treatise on the Canon of Medicine of Avicenna. LC 73-12409. reprint ed. 145.00 (*0-404-11231-5*) AMS Pr.

Avicenna, Ibn S. Canon of Medicine. 500p. (C). 1997. 59.95 (*1-871031-67-2*) Kazi Pubns.

— Liber Canonis (Al-Qanun Fi't-Tibb, Lateinisch) Avicenne Revisus et ab Omni Errore Mendaque Purgatus Summaque Cum Diligentia Impressus. (GER.). 573p. 1998. write for info. (*3-487-00594-8*) G Olms Pubs.

Avicennae. Avicennae de Congelatione et Conglutinatione Lapidum, Being Sections of the Kitab Al-Shifa the Latin & Arabic Texts Edited with English Translation & Critical Notes. Holmyard, E. J. & Mandeville, D. C., trs. (ARA.). 1986. text 85.00 (*0-935548-08-4*) Codex Pr.

Avidon, Sarajane, jt. auth. see Sussman, Susan.

Avienus, Lucius F. Ora Maritima. 2nd ed. Murphy & Miller, eds. (Ancient Greek & Roman Writers Ser.). xii, 180p. 1977. pap. 15.00 (*0-89005-175-5*) Ares.

Avienus, Rufus F. Carmina. lxv, 294p. 1965. reprint ed. 70.00 (*0-318-71074-9*) G Olms Pubs.

Avieson, John. Applied Journalism in Australia. 159p. (C). 1995. pap. 20.00 (*0-86828-393-2*, Pub. by Deakin Univ) St Mut.

— Desktop Publishing a Newspaper. 129p. 1995. pap. 56.00 (*0-7300-1681-1*, HUJ307, Pub. by Deakin Univ) St Mut.

— Editing Australian Newspapers. 212p. (C). 1985. 84.00 (*0-7300-0349-3*, Pub. by Deakin Univ) St Mut.

Aviezer, Nathan. Fossils & Faith. 2000. 23.00 (*0-88125-607-2*) Ktav.

— In the Beginning...Biblical Creation & Science. 1990. 22.95 (*0-685-33255-1*) Ktav.

***Aviezer, Patricia K.** Peterson's Game Plan for Getting into College. LC 99-88974. 200p. 2000. pap. 14.95 (*0-7689-0390-4*) Petersons.

Avignon, Jim. Busy. 144p. 1998. pap. 38.99 (*3-931126-17-X*, Pub. by Die Gestalten) Consort Bk Sales.

Avignone, F. T., 3rd & Gabriel, T. A., eds. The Savannah River Accelerator Project & Complementary Spallation Neutron Sources: University of South Carolina, Columbia 14-15 May, 1996. LC 98-170897. 200p. 1997. 48.00 (*981-02-3287-X*) World Scientific Pub.

Avignone, June. Cianci Street: A Neighborhood in Transition. (Illus.). 44p. 1996. pap. 7.00 (*0-9654628-0-3*) Mill St.

***Avignone, June.** Paterson. (Images of America Ser.). 1999. pap. 16.99 (*0-7524-0937-9*) Arcadia Publng.

Avila. English for Managment: Reading Skills in Business. (C). 1995. pap., student ed. 17.81 (*0-07-001869-3*) McGrw-H Hghr Educ.

Avila. Professional Selling Skills. (C). 1995. pap. text, wbk. ed. 37.00 (*0-03-016332-3*) Harcourt Coll Pubs.

— A Professional Selling Workbook. (C). 1995. pap. text, teacher ed. 28.00 (*0-03-017482-1*) Harcourt Coll Pubs.

Avila A., Mariano, jt. auth. see Lenters, William R.

Avila, Alexander. Lovetypes: Discover Your Romantic Style & Find Your Soul Mate. LC 98-46457. 304p. 1999. pap. 13.50 (*0-380-80014-4*, Avon Bks) Morrow Avon.

Avila, Alfred. Mexican Ghost Tale of the Southwest. Avila, Kat, ed. LC 94-6919. 172p. (YA). (gr. 6-12). 1994. pap. 9.95 (*1-55885-107-0*, Pinata Bks) Arte Publico.

Avila, Carl, ed. see Gural, Macit.

Avila, Carolina, jt. auth. see Root, Marilyn.

Avila, Charles. Ownership: Early Christian Teaching. LC 83-8330. 240p. (Orig.). reprint ed. pap. 74.40 (*0-7837-5525-2*, 204529500005) Bks Demand.

Avila, Donald L., et al. The Helping Relationship. 2nd ed. 1977. pap. text 42.00 (*0-205-05843-4*, H58431) Allyn.

Avila, Elena & Parker, Joy. Woman Who Glows in the Dark: A Curandera Reveals Traditional Aztec Secrets of Physical & Spiritual Health. LC 98-36475. 337p. 1999. 24.95 (*0-87477-958-8*, Tarcher Putnam) Putnam Pub Group.

***Avila, Elena & Parker, Joy.** Woman Who Glows in the Dark: A Curandera Reveals Traditional Aztec Secrets of Physical & Spiritual Health. 352p. 2000. reprint ed. pap. 14.95 (*1-58542-022-0*, Tarcher Putnam) Putnam Pub Group.

Avila, Emily N., jt. auth. see Sherwin, Gregory R.

Avila, Ernesto A., jt. auth. see Eidinger, John M.

Avila, Javier. Mas Alla de la Herrumbre I. (Ciencia para Todos Ser.). (SPA.). pap. 6.99 (*968-16-2396-7*, Pub. by Fondo) Continental Bk.

— Mas Alla de la Herrumbre II. (Ciencia para Todos Ser.). (SPA.). pap. 6.99 (*968-16-3153-6*, Pub. by Fondo) Continental Bk.

Avila, Jesus, et al, eds. Brain Microtubule Associated Proteins: Modifications in Disease. 376p. 1997. text 64.00 (*90-5702-173-0*, Harwood Acad Pubs) Gordon & Breach.

Avila, John. HTML for WWW Developers. 300p. (C). 1999. pap. text 23.10 (*1-57676-028-6*) Scott Jones Pubng.

***Avila, John.** Server Side Programming for WWW Developers. 2000. pap. text 23.10 (*1-57676-042-1*) Scott Jones Pubng.

Avila, Jose-Luis, jt. auth. see Galli, Uri.

Avila, Juan R., jt. auth. see Fetrow, Charles W.

Avila, Kat, ed. see Avila, Alfred.

Avila, Kay, et al. Harian Creative Awards - I: Featuring the Gospel According to Everyman by Baron Mikan. Barba, Harry, ed. 220p. 1981. pap. 9.95 (*0-911906-16-9*) Harian Creative Bks.

Avila-Lupe, Therese. Let's Eat Spanish at Home! (Let's Eat...at Home! Ser.). 160p. 1995. pap. 5.95 (*0-572-01835-5*, Pub. by Foulsham UK) Assoc Pubs Grp.

Avila, Micki. Mirrors of Your Castle. (Illus.). 38p. 1993. pap. 5.95 (*1-891634-02-X*) Azure Pr.

— Mirrors of Your Castle, Vol. II. (Illus.). 95p. 1997. pap. 9.95 (*1-891634-03-8*) Azure Pr.

Avila, Mitchell, jt. auth. see Furman, Todd M.

Avila, Patricia G. Fitness for Health & Sports: Published in Association with the U. S. Olympic Training Centers. LC 99-10291. (Illus.). 224p. 1999. 29.95 (*1-883955-09-2*) Penmarin Bks.

Avila, Rafael. Worship & Politics. LC 81-38356. 144p. (Orig.). reprint ed. pap. 44.70 (*0-8357-2664-9*, 204020000015) Bks Demand.

Avila, Raul. Chinampas de Iztapalapa, D. F. 183p. 1991. pap. 11.00 (*968-6487-14-X*, IN043) UPLAAP.

Avila, Rosemary, jt. auth. see Avila, Thomas.

Avila, Thomas & Avila, Rosemary. Sure Signs That You're Addicted to Beanie Babies. (Illus.). 85p. 1999. pap. 4.95 (*0-9672796-0-7*) Drake Pubg Co.

Avila, Vernon L. Biology: A Human Endeavor. 270p. (C). 1992. student ed. 15.00 (*1-880161-02-8*); text 50.00 (*1-880161-00-1*) Bookmark Pubs.

— Biology: Life on Earth. 2nd ed. LC 94-39326. (Life Science Ser.). 1008p. 1995. 71.25 (*0-86720-942-9*) Jones & Bartlett.

— Biology: Student Study Guide. 2nd ed. (Life Science Ser.). 320p. 1995. pap. 23.75 (*0-86720-908-9*) Jones & Bartlett.

— Biology: Test Bank. 2nd ed. (Life Science Ser.). 256p. 1995. pap., teacher ed. 10.00 (*0-86720-909-7*) Jones & Bartlett.

***Avila, Vernon L.** Smokescreen: A Novel of Medical Intrigue. LC 99-52462. 336p. 2000. 23.95 (*1-883955-29-7*, Pub. by Penmarin Bks) Midpt Trade.

Avila-Weil, Donna & Glaccum, Mary. The Independent Medical Transcriptionist: The Comprehensive Guidebook for Career Success in a Medical Transcription Business. 3rd ed. LC 97-31753. 480p. 1997. pap. 34.95 (*1-877810-23-1*) Rayve Prodns.

Avila-Weil, Donna & Regan, Rhonda. Independent Medical Coding: The Comprehensive Guidebook for Career Success As a Medical Coder. LC 98-48122. (Illus.). 288p. 1999. pap. 34.95 (*1-877810-17-7*, IMC) Rayve Prodns.

Avila, Yiye. El Anticristo.Tr. of Antichrist. (SPA.). 108p. 1995. pap. 4.99 (*1-56063-592-4*, 550038) Editorial Unilit.

— El Ayuno del Senor.Tr. of Lord's Fast. (SPA.). 1995. pap. 4.99 (*1-56063-591-6*, 550037) Editorial Unilit.

— La Ciencia de la Oracion.Tr. of Science of Prayer. (SPA.). 145p. 1995. 5.99 (*1-56063-633-5*, 550049) Editorial Unilit.

— El Cristo de los Milagros.Tr. of Miracle Christ. (SPA.). 56p. 3.99 (*0-7899-0073-4*, 550041) Editorial Unilit.

— El Cuerpo Glorificado.Tr. of Glorified Body. (SPA.). 3.99 (*0-7899-0071-8*, 550047) Editorial Unilit.

— Los Dones del Espiritu.Tr. of Gift of the Holy Spirit. (SPA.). 81p. 1994. pap. 3.99 (*1-56063-434-0*, 550036) Editorial Unilit.

— Pasara la Iglesia por la Gran Tribulacion?Tr. of Will the Church Go Through the Tribulation?. (SPA.). 82p. 1995. 4.99 (*1-56063-743-9*, 550046) Editorial Unilit.

— Perfecto Amor.Tr. of Perfect Love. (SPA.). 52p. pap. 3.50 (*0-7899-0070-X*, 550045) Editorial Unilit.

— El Profeta Elias.Tr. of Prophet Elijah. (SPA.). 50p. 3.50 (*0-7899-0074-2*, 550042) Editorial Unilit.

— Quienes Se Iran? Arrebatamiento.Tr. of Who Shall Go?: Rapture of the Church. (SPA.). 49p. 1995. 3.50 (*1-56063-996-2*, 550039) Editorial Unilit.

— El Sacrificio de la Cruz.Tr. of Sacrifice of the Cross. (SPA.). 44p. 1996. 3.50 (*0-7899-0075-0*, 550044) Editorial Unilit.

— Sanidad Divina.Tr. of Divine Healing. (SPA.). 170p. 1995. 3.50 (*1-56063-634-3*, 550050) Editorial Unilit.

— Senales de Su Venida.Tr. of Signs of His Coming. (SPA.). 110p. 1995. pap. 5.99 (*1-56063-433-2*, 550035) Editorial Unilit.

— Sin Santidad Nadie le Vera.Tr. of Without Holiness He Will Not Be Seen. (SPA.). 42p. 1995. 3.50 (*1-56063-742-0*, 550043) Editorial Unilit.

— El Valle de los Heusos Secos.Tr. of Valley of Dry Bones. (SPA.). 48p. 1996. 3.50 (*0-7899-0072-6*, 550040) Editorial Unilit.

Aviles, Frances X., ed. Innovations in Proteases & Their Inhibitors. LC 93-37074. x, 534p. (C). 1993. lib. bdg. 152.35 (*3-11-013635-X*, 6-94) De Gruyter.

Aviles, J. J. Ecuador. 1977. lib. bdg. 59.95 (*0-8490-1749-1*) Gordon Pr.

Aviles, Martin, jt. auth. see Turrentine, John E.

Aviles, Rene. Tantadel. (SPA.). pap. 6.99 (*968-16-3121-8*, Pub. by Fondo) Continental Bk.

Aviles, Roberto A. & Velazquez, Gloria. Ultraje, un Crimen Que No Cometi. (SPA.). 137p. (Orig.). 1991. pap. 6.99 (*0-9630423-0-0*) R A Aviles.

Avillez, Martin, ed. Lusitania: Kultura Control. (Illus.). 128p. (Orig.). (C). 1990. pap. text 8.00 (*0-936756-65-9*) Autonomedia.

Avillion, Adrianne E. & Mirgon, Barbara B. Quality Assurance in Rehabilitation Nursing: A Practical Guide. 206p. (C). 1989. 59.00 (*0-8342-0053-8*, 20053) Aspen Pub.

Avina, Rose H. Spanish & Mexican Land Grants in California. Cortes, Carlos E., ed. LC 76-1231. (Chicano Heritage Ser.). (Illus.). 1977. 18.95 (*0-405-09483-3*) Ayer.

Avina, Rubena. Aline, la Gloria per el Infierno. 1997. pap. 11.98 (*970-05-0935-4*) Grijalbo Edit.

— Como Se Hace una Estralla. 1997. pap. text 14.98 (*970-05-0518-9*) Grijalbo Edit.

***Avinasha, Bodhi & Sanaswati, Sunyata.** Jewel in the Lotus: The Tantric Path to Higher Consciousness. rev. ed. (Illus.). 250p. 2000. pap. 18.95 (*1-887472-67-3*, Pub. by Sunstar Pubng) Quality Bks IL.

Avineri, Shlomo. Hegel's Theory of the Modern State. LC 70-186254. (Cambridge Studies in the History & Theory of Politics). 263p. 1974. pap. text 28.95 (*0-521-09832-7*) Cambridge U Pr.

— Social & Political Thought of Karl Marx. LC 68-12055. (Studies in the History & Theory of Politics). 278p. 1970. pap. text 29.95 (*0-521-09619-7*) Cambridge U Pr.

— Varieties of Marxism. (Van Leer Jerusalem Foundation Ser.). 414p. 1977. lib. bdg. 112.50 (*90-247-2024-9*, Pub. by M Nijhoff) Kluwer Academic.

Avineri, Shlomo & De-Shalit, Avner, eds. Communitarianism & Individualism. (Oxford Readings in Politics & Government Ser.). 244p. 1992. pap. text 22.00 (*0-19-878028-1*) OUP.

Avineri, Shlomo, jt. auth. see Sajo, Andras.

***Avinger, Judith.** The Empty Bowl (Le Bol Vide) Mizouni, Hedi, tr. (FRE & ENG.). 67p. 1999. 22.95 (*0-88887-837-0*); pap. 11.95 (*0-88887-835-4*) Borealis.

Avins, Carol, tr. see Ratushinskaya, Irina.

Avins, Carol J., ed. see Babel, Isaac.

Avins, Carol J., ed. & intro. see Babel, Isaac.

Avins, Styra, ed. & tr. see Brahms, Johannes.

***Avioli, Louis V.** Osteoporotic Syndrome: Detection, Prevention & Treatment. 2000. pap. text 59.95 (*0-12-068705-4*) Acad Pr.

Avioli, Louis V. & Krane, Stephen M. Metabolic Bone Disease & Clinically Related Disorders. 2nd ed. (Illus.). 912p. 1990. text 270.00 (*0-7216-2766-8*, W B Saunders Co) Harcrt Hlth Sci Grp.

Avioli, Louis V. & Krane, Stephen M., eds. Metabolic Bone Disease. 3rd ed. (Illus.). 811p. 1997. text 179.95 (*0-12-068700-3*) Morgan Kaufmann.

Avioli, R.C. Truth Nuggets. unabridged ed. 105p. 1998. pap. 11.95 (*1-892896-65-6*) Buy Books.

Avionics Communications Inc. Staff, ed. Principles of Avionics Databusses. 260p. 1993. pap. 89.00 (*1-885544-00-6*) Avionics Comm.

Avionics Communications Staff, ed. Avionics Acronyms & Abbreviations. 204p. (C). 1994. pap. 49.00 (*1-885544-01-4*) Avionics Comm.

— Guide to Avionics Standards & Regulations. 260p. 1994. pap. 89.00 (*1-885544-03-0*) Avionics Comm.

— Validating Digital Systems in Avionics Flight Control. 530p. 1994. 95.00 (*1-885544-02-2*) Avionics Comm.

Aviram, A. Molecular Electronics - Science & Technology. (Conference Proceeding Ser.: No. 262). 344p. 1992. 95.00 (*1-56396-041-9*) Am Inst Physics.

Aviram, Amittai F. Telling Rhythm: Body & Meaning in Poetry. 320p. 1994. text 44.50 (*0-472-10513-2*, 10513) U of Mich Pr.

Aviram, Ari. Molecular Electronics: Science & Technology. 372p. 1999. pap. text 22.50 (*0-8018-6302-3*) Johns Hopkins.

Aviram, Ari & Ratner, Mark, eds. Molecular Electronics: Science & Technology. LC 98-9927. (Annals of the New York Academy of Sciences Ser.: Vol. 852). 372p. 1998. 140.00 (*1-57331-155-3*); pap. 140.00 (*1-57331-156-1*) NY Acad Sci.

Aviram, J. & Shanks, Hershel. Archaeology's Publication Problem. LC 96-20852. 1996. pap. 4.95 (*1-880317-46-X*, 7H87) Biblical Arch Soc.

Aviram, Mariva H. Palm Computing for Dummies. (For Dummies). 224p. 2000. spiral bd. 12.99 (*0-7645-0580-7*) IDG Bks.

— Quick Reference/XML for Dummies. LC 98-85374. (For Dummies). 224p. 1998. spiral bd. 14.99 (*0-7645-0383-9*) IDG Bks.

Aviram, Uri, ed. Social Work in Mental Health: Trends & Issues. LC 97-37786. (The Social Work In Health Care Ser.). 134p. 1997. 29.95 (*0-7890-0383-X*) Haworth Pr.

Avirett, James B. The Memoirs of General Turner Ashby & His Campaigns. 428p. 1987. reprint ed. 28.50 (*0-942211-31-6*) Olde Soldier Bks.

— The Memoirs of General Turner Ashby & His Compeers. 428p. 1984. reprint ed. 35.50 (*0-913419-04-4*, J M C & Co) Amereon Ltd.

Aviron-Violet, R. Bareis. Lord, Help Me: I'm Grieving. (Illus.). 24p. 1993. pap. 1.25 (*0-915531-15-1*) OR Catholic.

— Lord, Help Me: I'm Sick. (Illus.). 24p. 1993. pap. 1.25 (*0-915531-14-3*) OR Catholic.

Avis. Drugs & Life. 2nd ed. 1992. teacher ed. 13.75 (*0-697-12599-8*, WCB McGr Hill) McGraw-H Hghr Educ.

An Asterisk (*) at the beginning of an entry indicates that the title is appearing for the first time.

— Drugs & Life. 3rd ed. 1995. teacher ed. 14.68 (*0-697-22291-8*, WCB McGr Hill) McGrw-H Hghr Educ.

— Drugs & Life. 5th ed. 1999. 33.72 (*0-07-231975-5*) McGraw.

Avis, Anthony, ed. Brewers Tale: A History of Ale in Yorkshire. (Illus.). 192p. 1995. text 45.00 (*1-86064-018-4*) St Martin.

Avis, Harry. Drugs & Life. 4th ed. LC 99-206398. 272p. 1998. pap. 43.13 (*0-697-29424-2*) McGraw.

Avis, Harry H. Drugs & Life. 2nd ed. 528p. (C). 1992. text. write for info. (*0-697-12598-X*) Brown & Benchmark.

— Drugs & Life. 3rd ed. 480p. (C). 1995. text. write for info. (*0-697-22290-X*) Brown & Benchmark.

Avis, James, et al. Knowledge & Nationhood: Education, Politics & Work. (Education Ser.). 160p. 1996. pap. 33.95 (*0-304-33581-9*); text 80.00 (*0-304-33580-0*) Continuum.

Avis, Jen & Ward, Kathy F. Gone with the Fat. (Illus.). 288p. 1994. spiral bd. 16.95 (*0-9628683-6-1*) Avis & Ward.

— Just for Kids. (Illus.). 166p. (J). 1990. spiral bd. 12.95 (*0-9628683-1-0*) Avis & Ward.

Avis, Jen B. & Ward, Kathy F. Southern But Lite. (Illus.). 278p. 1989. 15.95 (*0-9628683-0-2*) Avis & Ward.

Avis, Joan, jt. auth. see Evans, Susan.

Avis, Judith M. Group Treatment for Sexually-Abused Adolescents. 1992. pap. 22.95 (*1-55691-079-7*, 797) Learning Pubns.

Avis, Kenneth, ed. Sterile Pharmaceutical Products: Process Engineering Applications I. LC 95-24999. (Drug Manufacturing Technology Ser.). (Illus.). 415p. 1995. 189.00 (*0-935184-81-3*) Interpharm.

Avis, Kenneth, et al, eds. Biotechnology: Quality Assurance & Validation. LC 98-40953. (Drug Manufacturing Technology Ser.). 268p. 1998. 179.00 (*1-57491-089-2*) Interpharm.

Avis, Kenneth E., et al, eds. Pharmaceutical Dosage Forms Vol. 1: Parental Medications, Vol. 1. 2nd expanded rev. ed. (Illus.). 689p. 1991. text 199.00 (*0-8247-8576-2*) Dekker.

— Pharmaceutical Unit Operations: Coating. LC 98-27219. (Drug Manufacturing Technology Ser.: Vol. 3). 1998. 189.00 (*1-57491-082-5*) Interpharm.

Avis, Kenneth E. & Wagner, Carmen M., eds. Cryopreservation: Applications in Pharmaceuticals & Biotechnology. LC 99-21101. (Drug Manufacturing Technology Ser.). 300p. 1998. 179.00 (*1-57491-090-6*) Interpharm.

Avis, Kenneth E. & Wu, Vincent, eds. Biotechnology & Biopharmaceutical Manufacturing, Processing, & Preservation. (Drug Manufacturing Technology Ser.). (Illus.). 386p. 1996. 179.00 (*1-57491-016-7*) Interpharm.

Avis, Kenneth E., et al. Pharmaceutical Dosage Forms: Parenteral Medication, Vol. 3. 2nd expanded rev. ed. Lieberman, Leon, ed. (Illus.). 592p. 1993. text 199.00 (*0-8247-9020-0*) Dekker.

— Pharmaceutical Dosage Forms: Parenteral Medications, Vol. 2. 2nd ed. Liberman, Leon, ed. (Illus.). 616p. 1992. text 199.00 (*0-8247-8771-4*) Dekker.

Avis, Paul. Anglicanism & the Christian Church: Theological Resources in Historical Perspective. 336p. 1997. text 49.95 (*0-567-09512-6*, Pub. by T & T Clark) Bks Intl VA.

— Divine Revelation. LC 97-33600. (Theology Ser.). 1997. pap. 20.00 (*0-8028-4219-4*) Eerdmans.

— Eros & the Sacred. LC 89-48238. 176p. (Orig.). 1989. pap. 7.95 (*0-8192-1528-7*) Morehouse Pub.

Avis, Paul, ed. see Evans, Gillian R., et al.

Avis, Paul, ed. see Rogerson, John.

Avis, Paul D. God & the Creative Imagination: Metaphor, Symbol, & Myth in Religion & Theology. LC 99-19282. 176p. 1999. pap. 24.99 (*0-415-21503-X*) Routledge.

***Avis, Paul D. L.** God & Creative Imagination: Metaphor Symbol & Myth in Religion & Theology. LC 99-19282. 176p. (C). 1999. text 75.00 (*0-415-21502-1*) Routledge.

***Avis, Robert.** Using Radar: A Practical Guide for Small Craft. LC 99-56900. (Illus.). 112p. 1999. pap. 17.95 (*1-57409-105-0*) Sheridan.

Avis, Warren. Take a Chance to Be First. 1986. 16.95 (*0-02-504410-9*) Macmillan.

Avisar, Ilan. Screening the Holocaust: Cinema's Images of the Unimaginable. LC 87-45400. (Jewish Literature & Culture Ser.). (Illus.). 240p. 1988. reprint ed. pap. 74.40 (*0-7837-9644-7*, 205927700005) Bks Demand.

Avise, John C. The Genetic Gods: Evolution & Belief in Human Affairs. LC 98-3255. 288p. 1998. 29.95 (*0-674-34625-4*) HUP.

— Phylogeography: The History & Formation of Species. LC 99-19648. (Illus.). 447p. 1999. 49.95 (*0-674-66638-0*) HUP.

Avise, John C. & Hamrick, James L. Conservation Genetics. 536p. 1996. pap. write for info. (*0-412-14581-2*) Kluwer Academic.

Avise, John C., jt. ed. see Hamrick, James L.

Avishai, Y., ed. Recent Progress in Many-Body Theories, Vol. 2. (Illus.). 372p. (C). 1990. text 138.00 (*0-306-43705-8*, Kluwer Plenum) Kluwer Academic.

***Avishur, Yitzhak.** Studies in Biblical Narrative: Style, Structure & the Ancient Near Eastern Literary Background. 375p. 1999. text 58.50 (*965-90240-0-2*, Pub. by Archaeol Ctr) Eisenbrauns.

Avishur, Yitzhak. Studies in Hebrew & Ugaritic Psalms. 388p. 1994. text 35.00 (*965-223-864-3*, Pub. by Magnes Pr) Eisenbrauns.

***Avishur, Yitzhak & Deutsch, Robert, eds.** Michael: Historical, Epigraphical & Biblical Studies in Honor of Professor Michael Heltzer. 301p. 1999. text 80.00 (*965-222-939-3*, Pub. by Archaeol Ctr) Eisenbrauns.

***Avison.** Information Systems Development. 3rd ed. 1999. pap. text 43.44 (*0-07-709375-5*) McGrw-H Hghr Educ.

Avison, Brigid. Essential Ireland. (Essential Travel Guides Ser.). (Illus.). 128p. (Orig.). 1995. pap. 7.95 (*0-8442-8945-0*, Passprt Bks) NTC Contemp Pub Co.

— I Wonder Why I Blink: And Other Questions about My Body. LC 92-45599. (I Wonder Why Ser.). (Illus.). 32p. (J). (ps-3). 1993. 11.95 (*1-85697-875-3*, Kingfisher) LKC.

— I Wonder Why I Blink: And Other Questions about My Body. (I Wonder Why Ser.). (Illus.). 32p. (J). (gr. k-3). 1997. pap. 7.95 (*1-85697-662-9*) LKC.

Avison, Charles. An Essay on Musical Expression: London, 1753. 2nd enl. ed. (Monuments of Music & Music Literature in Facsimile Ser., Series II: Vol. 55). 1967. lib. bdg. 45.00 (*0-8450-2255-5*) Broude.

Avison, D., et al, eds. Human, Organizational & Social Dimensions of Information Systems Development. (IFIP Transactions A: Computer Science & Technology Ser.: vol. A-24). 508p. 1993. pap. 160.00 (*0-444-89983-9*, North Holland) Elsevier.

Avison, D. E. & Fitzgerald, G. Information Systems Development: Methodologies, Techniques, & Tools. 2nd ed. LC 95-39760. (Information Systems Ser.). 1998. pap., student ed. 45.31 (*0-07-709233-3*) McGraw.

Avison, Jo. Decorative Effects: Short Cuts to Designer Style. (Illus.). 128p. 1998. pap. text 14.95 (*0-7063-7739-7*, Pub. by WrLock) Sterling.

— Short Cuts to Designer Style: Decorative Effects. (Illus.). 128p. 1997. 24.95 (*0-7063-7516-5*, Pub. by WrLock) Sterling.

— Short Cuts to Designer Style: Soft Furnishings. (Illus.). 128p. 1997. 19.95 (*0-7063-7515-7*, Pub. by WrLock) Sterling.

— Short Cuts to Designer Style: Soft Furnishings. (Illus.). 128p. 1998. pap. 14.95 (*0-7063-7738-9*, Pub. by WrLock) Sterling.

Avison, W. R. & Gotlib, I., eds. Stress & Mental Health: Contemporary Issues & Prospects for the Future. (Stress & Coping Ser.). (Illus.). 358p. (C). 1994. 52.50 (*0-306-44687-1*, Plenum Trade) Perseus Pubng.

Avitabile, Alphonse, jt. auth. see Sammataro, Diana.

Avitabile, Gunhild. From the Dragons Treasure. (Illus.). 168p. 1987. 85.00 (*1-870076-05-2*, Pub. by Bamboo Pub) Antique Collect.

Avitabile, Gunhild, et al. The Early Masters: Ukioy-e Prints & Paintings from 1680-1750. rev. ed. Brown, Celia, tr. (Illus.). 139p. 1995. pap. 28.00 (*0-913304-33-6*, 336) Japan Soc.

Avitabile, Teresio, ed. Societa' Italiana di Eco-Oftalmologia (SIEO) 20th Century, Ferrara, November 1995: Proceedings, Vol.212. (Opthalmologica Ser.: Vol. 212, Suppl. 1 (1998)). (Illus.). v, 120p. 1998. pap., suppl. ed. 55.00 (*3-8055-6740-5*) S Karger.

Avital, Samuel. Mime & Beyond: The Silent Outcry. (Illus.). 173p. (Orig.). 1990. pap. 17.00 (*0-934252-10-6*) Players Pr.

— Mime Workbook. (Illus.). 158p. Date not set. pap., wbk. ed. write for info. (*0-88734-638-3*) Players Pr.

Avital, Samuel, jt. auth. see Olsen, Mark.

Avitus. The Fall of Man: De Spiritalis Historiae Gestis, Libri I-III. Nodes, Daniel J., ed. (LAT.). viii, 71p. pap. text 7.43 (*0-88844-466-4*) Brill Academic Pubs.

Avitus & Shea, George W. The Poems of Alcimus Ecdicius Avitus: Translation & Introduction. LC 96-52898. (Medieval & Renaissance Texts & Studies: No. 172). 168p. 1997. 24.00 (*0-86698-214-0*, MR172) MRTS.

Avitus, Alcimus E. Avitus: Concordantiae in Alcimi Ecdicii Aviti Carmina. Ramminger, Johann, ed. (Alpha-Omega, Reihe A Ser.: Bd. CIV). (GER.). 396p. 1990. 120.00 (*3-487-09179-8*) G Olms Pubs.

Avitzur, B., ed. see American Society for Metals Staff.

Avitzur, Betzalel. Metal Forming: The Application of Limit Analysis. LC 79-25348. (Manufacturing Engineering & Materials Processing Ser.: Vol. 4). (Illus.). 220p. reprint ed. pap. 68.20 (*0-608-08910-9*, 206954500005) Bks Demand.

Avitzur, Betzalel, jt. auth. see Talbert, Samuel H.

Aviv International Fine Art Gallery Staff. Reflection: An Exhibition of Original Paintings by Shlomo Schwartz. (Illus.). 40p. (Orig.). 1989. pap. 15.00 (*0-940429-07-1*) M B Glass Assocs.

Aviv, Jonathan E. & Blitzer, Andrew. Fundamentals of Head & Neck Reconstruction Vol. I: The Angiosome Concept & Pedicled Myocutaneous Flaps. LC 97-42867. (Self-Instructional Package Ser.). (Illus.). 47p. 1998. pap. text 25.00 (*1-56772-058-7*, 5506315) AAO-HNS.

***Avivi, Baruch.** I Have Waited for You So: Love Stories. Karev, Iris, tr. from HEB. 1999. pap. 10.95 (*0-533-13123-5*) Vantage.

Avivi, Yosef. Rabbinic Manuscripts; Mendel Gottesman Library, Yeshiva University. Hirschler, Gertrude & Berger, Pearl, trs. (ENG & HEB., Illus.). 408p. 1998. 49.95 (*0-9620856-1-8*) Yeshiva U Lib.

Aviza, Edward A. Thinking Tarot. LC 97-10329. 1997. pap. 19.95 (*0-684-82274-1*) S&S Trade.

Avizienis, A., et al, eds. The Evolution of Fault-Tolerant Computing. (Dependable Computing & Fault-Tolerant Systems Ser.: Vol. 1). (Illus.). 480p. 1987. 98.00 (*0-387-81941-X*) Spr-Verlag.

Avizienis, A. & Laprie, J. C., eds. Dynamic Computing for Critical Applications. (Dependable Computing & Fault-Tolerant Systems Ser.: Vol. 4). xiii, 431p. 1991. 117.95 (*0-387-82249-6*) Spr-Verlag.

Avizienis, A., ed. see Lee, P. A. & Anderson, T.

Avizius. AutoCAD. Date not set. pap. text, teacher ed. write for info. (*0-314-04781-6*) West Pub.

Avizius, A. Rudy. AutoCAD: A Tutorial with Drafting Principles. LC 95-8832. 500p. (C). 1995. pap. 46.95 (*0-314-04441-8*) West Pub.

AVMA Staff. Medical Accidents & the Law: A Practical Guide to the Legal Rights of the Patient. 448p. 1999. pap. 51.95 (*0-471-96642-8*) Wiley.

Avner, Ellis, jt. auth. see Spitzer, Adrian.

Avner, Judith I. Sexual Harassment: Building a Concensus for Change. (Illus.). 300p. (Orig.). (C). 1995. pap. text 50.00 (*0-7881-2262-2*) DIANE Pub.

Avneri, Arieh L. The Claim of Dispossession: Jewish Land Settlement & the Arabs, 1878-1948. 303p. 1982. pap. 24.95 (*0-87855-964-7*) Transaction Pubs.

Avnet, I. Duke. How to Prove Damages in Wrongful Personal Injury & Death Cases. 2nd ed. (Illus.). 1978. 34.95 (*0-13-429415-7*, Busn) P-H.

Avnet, Stephanie. Wonderful Weekends from Los Angeles: Great Escapes Within 250 Miles of L. A. (Wonderful Weekends Ser.). 320p. 1998. pap. text 15.95 (*0-02-861776-2*, Frommer) Macmillan Gen Ref.

***Avnet, Stephanie Yates.** Frommer's Los Angeles 2001. (Illus.). 320p. 2000. pap. 14.99 (*0-7645-6093-X*) IDG Bks.

— Frommer's San Diego 2001. (Illus.). 304p. 2000. pap. 14.99 (*0-7645-6091-3*) IDG Bks.

Avni, Amatzia. Creative Chess. 1997. pap. text 19.95 (*1-85744-149-4*) Macmillan.

Avni, Baruch, tr. see Nachman of Breslov.

Avni, E., jt. auth. see Kandel, Abraham.

Avni, Eitan, jt. ed. see Kandel, Abraham.

***Avni, Haim.** The Six-Day War & World Jewry. LC 00-36675. (Studies & Texts in Jewish History & Culture). 2000. write for info. (*1-883053-59-5*) Univ Pr MD.

Avni, Haim, jt. auth. see Steindling, Dolly.

Avni, Ora. The Resistance of Reference: Linguistics, Philosophy, & the Literary Text. LC 90-30585. 352p. 1990. text 48.50 (*0-8018-3993-9*) Johns Hopkins.

— Tics, Tics & Tics: Figures, Syllogismes, Recit Dans les Chants de Maldoror. LC 84-81849. (French Forum Monographs: No. 54). 186p. (Orig.). 1984. pap. 13.45 (*0-917058-54-2*) French Forum.

Avnimelech, Y., jt. ed. see Chen, Y.

Avnir, D. & Braun, Sergei. Biochemical Aspects of Sol-Gel Science & Technology: A Special Issue of the Journal of Sol-Gel Science & Technology. LC 96-28462. 143p. 1996. text 139.00 (*0-7923-9763-0*) Kluwer Academic.

Avnir, David, ed. Biochemical Aspects of Sol-Gel Science & Technology. LC 96-31104. 148p. (C). 1996. text 187.50 (*0-7923-9764-9*) Kluwer Academic.

Avnon, Dan. Martin Buber: The Hidden Dialogue. LC 97-41158. (Twentieth Century Political Thinkers Ser.). 256p. 1998. pap. 21.95 (*0-8476-8688-4*) Rowman.

— Martin Buber: The Hidden Dialogue. LC 97-41158. (Twentieth Century Political Thinkers Ser.). 256p. 1998. 58.00 (*0-8476-8687-6*) Rowman.

Avnon, Dan & De Shalit, Avner. Liberalism & Its Practice. LC 98-27628. 13p. 1999. write for info. (*0-415-19354-0*); pap. 27.99 (*0-415-19355-9*) Routledge.

AVO International Staff, jt. auth. see Cadick, John.

AVO Multi-Amp Institute Staff. Test Equipment: Instructor's Guide. 86p. 1992. 15.50 (*0-8273-4924-5*) Delmar.

Avogadro, A., ed. Technologies for Environmental Cleanup - Soil & Groundwater: Based on the Lectures Given During the Eurocourse on Technologies for Environmental Cleanup: Soil & Groundwater Held at the Joint Research Centre, Ispra, Italy, 21-25 September 1992. (Eurocourses: Environmental Management Ser.). 480p. (C). 1993. text 233.00 (*0-7923-2145-6*) Kluwer Academic.

Avogadro, A. & Ragaini, R. C., eds. Technologies for Environmental Cleanup Toxic & Hazardous Waste Management: Based on the Lectures Given During the Eurocourse on Technologies for Environmental Cleanup - Toxic & Hazardous Waste Management, Held at the Joint Research Centre, Ispra, Italy, September 13-17, 1993. LC 94-7724. (Eurocourses: Environmental Management Ser.: Vol. 2). 268p. (C). 1994. text 166.50 (*0-7923-2776-4*) Kluwer Academic.

Avogaro, P., jt. ed. see Galli, Corraldo L.

Avogaro, Pietro, et al, eds. Phospholipids & Atherosclerosis. LC 83-9678. (Illus.). 292p. 1983. reprint ed. pap. 90.60 (*0-608-00633-5*, 206122100007) Bks Demand.

***Avoli, Diane.** A Chef for All Seasons: A Practical 2-Week Microbiotic Menu Plan. 96p. 1999. pap. 10.95 (*1-882984-36-6*) One Peaceful World.

Avoli, M., et al, eds. Neurotransmitters & Cortical Function: From Molecules to Mind. LC 87-37401. 632p. 1988. 130.00 (*0-306-42729-X*, Plenum Trade) Perseus Pubng.

Avoli, M., et al. Generalized Epilepsy. 500p. 1990. 127.50 (*0-8176-3445-2*) Birkhauser.

***Avolio, Bruce J.** Full Leadership Development: Building the Vital Forces in Organizations. LC 98-51235. (Advanced Topics in Organizational Behavior Ser.). 234p. 1999. 48.00 (*0-7619-0602-9*) Sage.

Avolio, Bruce J. Leadership Development: Enhancing the Vital Forces in Organizations LC 98-51235. (Advanced Topics in Organizational Behavior Ser.). 1999. write for info. (*0-7619-0603-7*) Sage.

Avolio, Bruce J., jt. ed. see Bass, Bernard M.

Avolio, Frederick M. & Vixie, Paul. Sendmail: Theory & Practice. 262p. (C). 1995. pap. text 34.95 (*1-55558-127-7*, Digital DEC) Buttrwrth-Heinemann.

— Sendmail: Theory & Practice. 2nd ed. 304p. 1999. pap. 29.95 (*1-55558-229-X*) Buttrwrth-Heinemann.

Avon, Patrick & Karinch, Maryann. Boot Camp: Be All You Used to Be, the Sergeant's Fitness & Nutritional Program. LC 98-37013. (Illus.). 240p. 1999. per. 12.00 (*0-684-84899-6*, Fireside) S&S Trade Pap.

Avon Staff. Nothing But The Truth. 1993. mass mkt. 4.99 (*0-380-26539-7*, Avon Bks) Morrow Avon.

Avondo-Bodino, Giuseppe. Economic Applications of the Theory of Graphs. (Illus.). 126p. 1963. text 178.00 (*0-677-00030-8*) Gordon & Breach.

Avotins, Ivars. On the Greek of the Code of Justinian: A Supplement of Liddell-Scott-James Together with Observations on the Influence of Latin on Legal Greek. (Altertumswissenschaftliche Texte und Studien: Vol. 17). (GER.). x, 178p. 1989. pap. 30.00 (*3-487-09196-8*) G Olms Pubs.

Avotins, Ivars & Avotins, Miriam M. Philostratus: An Index to the Lives of the Sophists of Philostratus. (Alpha-Omega, Reihe A Ser.: No. XXV). xi, 308p. 1978. 70.00 (*3-487-06540-1*) G Olms Pubs.

Avotins, Ivars & Avotins, Miriam M., eds. Eunapius - Index in Eunapii Vitas Sophistarum. (Alpha-Omega, Reihe A Ser.: Bd. LXIII). x, 258p. 1983. 80.00 (*3-487-07339-0*) G Olms Pubs.

Avotins, Miriam M., jt. auth. see Avotins, Ivars.

Avotins, Miriam M., jt. ed. see Avotins, Ivars.

Avouris, Nicholas M., ed. Environmental Informatics Methodology & Applications of Environmental Information Processing: Based on the Lectures Given During the Eurocourse on "Environmental Informatics Applications" Held at Athens, June 21-25, 1993. (EUROCOURSES Ser.). 468p. (C). 1995. text 242.50 (*0-7923-3445-0*) Kluwer Academic.

Avouris, Nicholas M. & Gasser, Les, eds. Distributed Artificial Intelligence: Theory & Praxis. (C). 1992. text 157.50 (*0-7923-1585-5*) Kluwer Academic.

Avraamov, Yu S., jt. auth. see Dubinin, G. N.

Avraham, Eliyahu Ben, see Ben Avraham, Eliyahu.

***Avraham, Regina.** Circulatory System. LC 99-47870. (Illus.). 128p. 1999. 24.95 (*0-7910-5519-1*) Chelsea Hse.

— Digestive System. LC 99-47869. (Twenty-First Century Health & Wellness Ser.). (Illus.). 128p. 1999. 24.95 (*0-7910-5526-4*) Chelsea Hse.

Avraham, Regina. The Downside of Drugs. (Encyclopedia of Psychoactive Drugs Ser.: No. 2). (Illus.). 128p. (YA). (gr. 7 up). 1987. lib. bdg. 19.95 (*1-55546-232-4*) Chelsea Hse.

— The Reproductive System. (Encyclopedia of Health Ser.). (Illus.). 116p. (YA). (gr. 7 up). 1991. lib. bdg. 19.95 (*0-7910-0025-7*) Chelsea Hse.

— Substance Abuse: Prevention & Treatment. (Encyclopedia of Psychoactive Drugs Ser.: No. 2). (Illus.). 128p. (YA). (gr. 7 up). 1988. lib. bdg. 19.95 (*1-55546-219-7*) Chelsea Hse.

— Substance Abuse: Prevention & Treatment. (Encyclopedia of Psychoactive Drugs Ser.: No. 2). 128p. (YA). (gr. 7 up). 1989. pap. 8.95 (*0-7910-0807-X*) Chelsea Hse.

— Substance Abuse Prevention & Treatment. (Encyclopedia of Psychoactive Drugs Ser.). 1988. 13.05 (*0-606-04336-5*, Pub. by Turtleback) Demco.

Avraham, Yad, comment. Seder Kodashim: Arachin. (Mishnah Ser.). pap. 15.99 (*0-89906-311-X*) Mesorah Pubns.

— Seder Kodashim: Bechoros. (Mishnah Ser.). 22.99 (*0-89906-307-1*, K2BH) Mesorah Pubns.

— Seder Kodashim: Kereisos. (Mishnah Ser.). 19.99 (*0-89906-309-8*, K3CH); pap. 13.99 (*0-89906-310-1*) Mesorah Pubns.

— Seder Tohoros: Mikvaos. (Mishnah Ser.). 22.99 (*0-89906-330-6*, T4BH) Mesorah Pubns.

— Seder Zeraim: Kilayim. (Mishnah Ser.). 22.99 (*0-89906-332-2*, R3AH) Mesorah Pubns.

— Seder Zeraim: Peah. (Mishnah Ser.). 22.99 (*0-89906-328-4*) Mesorah Pubns.

Avram, A., jt. auth. see Wilmarth, S. S.

Avram, C. C. Protegee. LC 93-83905. 1993. 22.00 (*1-883545-00-5*) Shields Pub.

Avram, Constantin, et al. Numerical Analysis of Reinforced Concrete Structures. LC 92-46460. (Developments in Civil Engineering Ser.: Vol. 41). (Illus.). 510p. 1993. 238.00 (*0-444-98842-4*) Elsevier.

Avram, M. M., ed. Proteinuria. LC 85-9305. (Illus.). 248p. 1985. 90.00 (*0-306-41956-4*, Kluwer Plenum) Kluwer Academic.

Avram, M. M. & Giordano, C. Ambulatory Peritoneal Dialysis. (Illus.). 356p. (C). 1990. text 95.00 (*0-306-43351-6*, Kluwer Plenum) Kluwer Academic.

Avram, Morrell M. & Klahr, Saulo, eds. Renal Disease Progression & Management: Role of Vasoactive Agents, Cytokines, Lipids & Nutrition. (Illus.). 372p. 1996. text 99.00 (*0-7216-3833-3*, W B Saunders Co) Harcrt Hlth Sci Grp.

Avram, Percy. Life's Detours. Avram, Vicky, ed. 352p. 1996. pap. 8.95 (*0-9651737-0-4*) Marva Ent.

Avram, Vicky, ed. see Avram, Percy.

Avrami, Malkah L., jt. auth. see Rossel, Seymour.

***Avramidi, Ivan G.** Heat Kernel & Quantum Gravity. LC 00-27496. (Lecture Notes in Physics Ser.). ix, 143p. 2000. 45.00 (*3-540-67155-2*) Spr-Verlag.

Avramis, Tom. Preparing to Receive Holy Communion. 1986. pap. 2.95 (*0-937032-43-3*) Light&Life Pub Co MN.

***Avramov, dragana, ed.** Coping with Homelessness: Issues to Be Tackled & the Best Practices in Europe. LC 98-46597. 580p. 1999. text 86.95 (*1-84014-909-4*, Pub. by Ashgate Pub) Ashgate Pub Co.

Avramov, L. L. & Tchakerian, K. B., eds. Algebra Some Current Trends. (Lecture Notes in Mathematics Ser.: Vol. 1352). ix, 240p. 1988. 31.95 (*0-387-50371-4*) Spr-Verlag.

Avran, M. M., ed. see International Symposium on Parathyroid in Uremia Staff.

Avrashov, Lee, tr. see Kilov, Haim, et al.

Avrashov, Regina, jt. auth. see Piatak, Jean.

Avresky, Dimiter R. & Kaeli, David R., eds. Fault-Tolerant Parallel & Distributed Systems. LC 97-39030. 416p. 1998. lib. bdg. 145.00 (*0-7923-8069-X*) Kluwer Academic.

A

Avresky, Dimitri R. Hardware & Software Fault Tolerance in Parallel Computing Systems. LC 92-18184. (Ellis Horwood Workshop Ser.). 250p. 1993. text 62.00 (*0-13-381021-6*, Pub. by Tavistock-E Horwood) Routldge.

Avrett, Eugene, ed. Frontiers of Astrophysics. (Illus.). 551p. 1976. 57.00 (*0-674-32659-8*) HUP.

Avrich, Barry & Gill, Len. Event & Entertainment Marketing: A Must Guide for Corporate Event Sponsors & Entertainment Entrepreneurs. 300p. 1994. text 32.50 (*1-55738-573-4*, Irwn Prfssnl) McGraw-Hill Prof.

Avrich, Paul. An American Anarchist: The Life of Voltairine de Cleyre. LC 78-51153. 313p. 1978. reprint ed. pap. 97.10 (*0-608-03320-0*, 206403320008) Bks Demand.

— Anarchist Portraits. (Illus.). 344p. (Orig.). 1988. pap. text 18.95 (*0-691-00609-1*, Pub. by Princeton U Pr) Cal Prin Full Svc.

— Anarchist Voices: An Oral History of Anarchism in America. LC 94-16620. 536p. 1995. text 75.00 (*0-691-03412-5*, Pub. by Princeton U Pr) Cal Prin Full Svc.

— Bakunin & Nechaev. 2nd ed. 32p. 1987. pap. 2.50 (*0-900384-09-3*) Left Bank.

— Sacco & Vanzetti: The Anarchist Background. 278p. 1991. pap. text 15.95 (*0-691-02604-1*, Pub. by Princeton U Pr) Cal Prin Full Svc.

Avrich, Paul, intro. Proudhon & His Bank of the People. (Young America Ser.: No. 1). 80p. reprint ed. pap. 7.00 (*0-88286-066-6*) C H Kerr.

Avriel, M., et al. Generalized Concavity. LC 87-25799. (Mathematical Concepts & Methods in Science & Engineering Ser.: Vol. 36). (Illus.). 342p. (C). 1987. text 95.00 (*0-306-42656-0*, Kluwer Plenum) Kluwer Academic.

Avriel, Mordecai & Golany, Boaz, eds. Mathematical Programming for Industrial Engineers. (Industrial Engineering Ser.: Vol. 20). (Illus.). 656p. 1996. text 190.00 (*0-8247-9620-9*) Dekker.

Avriette, Michael, jt. auth. see Evosevich, J. M.

Avril, Ellen. East Meets West: Chinese Export Art & Design. LC 98-60843. (Illus.). 20p. 1998. pap. 6.95 (*0-915577-29-1*) Taft Museum.

Avril, Ellen & Ling-Yun, Nora. Chinese Art in the Cincinnati Art Museum. LC 97-38647. (Illus.). 226p. 1997. pap. 31.95 (*0-295-97663-2*) U of Wash Pr.

Avril, Francois. Manuscript Painting at the Court of France: The Fourteenth Century (1310-1380) LC 77-78721. (Illus.). 120p. 1978. pap. 11.95 (*0-8076-0879-3*, Pub. by Braziller) Norton.

Avril, Francois, jt. intro. see Thomas, Marcel.

Avril, J. T. Provencal-French Dictionary with French-Provencal Vocabulary. fac. ed. (FRE & PRO.). 656p. 1990. pap. 95.00 (*0-7859-5214-4*, M14179) Fr & Eur.

Avril, Jane. Munch. 1995. pap. 8.99 (*3-8228-9758-2*) Taschen Amer.

Avril, Jean - Loup. Dictionnaire Pratique de Bacteriologie Clinique. 1988. write for info. (*0-7859-8644-8*, 272988842x) Fr & Eur.

Avrin, Leila. Scribes, Script & Books: The Book Arts from Antiquity to the Rennaissance. LC 89-18024. (Illus.). 350p. 1991. 80.00 (*0-8389-0522-6*) ALA.

Avron, M., jt. ed. see Trebst, A.

Avruch, Kevin. American Immigrants in Israel: Social Identities & Change. LC 81-1291. (Illus.). (C). 1981. 30.00 (*0-226-03241-8*) U Ch Pr.

— Culture & Conflict Resolution. LC 98-30951. 172p. 1998. 29.95 (*1-878379-83-6*); pap. 14.95 (*1-878379-82-8*) US Inst Peace.

Avruch, Kevin & Zenner, Walter P., eds. Critical Essays on Israeli Society, Religion, & Government: Books on Israel, Vol. IV. LC 96-17788. (SUNY Series in Israeli Studies). 224p. (C). 1996. text 49.50 (*0-7914-3253-X*); pap. text 17.95 (*0-7914-3254-8*) State U NY Pr.

Avruch, Kevin, et al. Conflict Resolution: Cross-Cultural Perspectives, 28. LC 91-15991. (Contributions in Ethnic Studies: No. 28). 256p. 1991. 59.95 (*0-313-25796-5*, AVC, Greenwood Pr) Greenwood.

***Avruch, Kevin, et al.** Information Campaigns for Peace Operations LC 99-35566. 1999. write for info. (*1-893723-01-1*) CCRP.

Avruch, Kevin W., ed. see Black, Peter A. & Scimecca, Joseph.

Avruch, Sheryl, ed. see Roerden, Laura P.

Avrunin, George S., jt. auth. see Coombs, Clyde H.

AvRutick, Frances R. The Complete Passover Cookbook. LC 80-39633. 432p. 1981. 19.95 (*0-8246-0262-5*) Jonathan David.

Avrutin, Sergey, et al, eds. Formal Approaches to Slavic Linguistics: The MIT Meeting, 1993. LC 94-10451. (Michigan Slavic Materials Ser.: Vol. 36). 1994. pap. 26.00 (*0-930042-74-3*) Mich Slavic Pubns.

AVS Staff. Life of a Karma Yogi. (Illus.). 32p. 1973. pap. 4.50 (*0-942401-04-2*) Am Vegan Soc.

AVSC International Staff. Client-Oriented, Provider-Efficient Services (COPE) Tzanis, Joanne, ed. 1995. pap. text 15.00 (*1-885063-01-6*) AVSC Int.

— Consentimiento Informado y Esterilizacion Voluntaria: Guia Practica para Administradores de Programas. (SPA.). 26p. 1995. reprint ed. pap. text 5.00 (*1-885063-14-8*) AVSC Int.

***AVSC International Staff.** Emergency Management for the Operating & Recovery Rooms: Reference Manual. (Illus.). 32p. 2000. pap. Price not set. (*1-885063-25-3*) AVSC Int.

AVSC International Staff. Facilitative Supervision Handbook. (Quality Improvement Ser.). (Illus.). 161p. 1999. pap. text 6.50 (*1-885063-22-9*) AVSC Int.

— Family Planning Counseling: A Curriculum Prototype, Participant's Handbook. LC 94-48622. 79p. (Orig.). 1995. pap., student ed. 8.00 (*1-885063-09-1*) AVSC Int.

— Family Planning Counseling: The International Experience. 54p. 1993. pap. 8.00 (*1-885063-02-4*) AVSC Int.

***AVSC International Staff.** Infection Prevention: A Reference Booklet for Health Care Providers. LC 99-32711. 2000. pap. write for info. (*1-885063-23-7*) AVSC Int.

— Infection Prevention: Multimedia Package, Training CD-ROM & Reference Booklet. (Illus.). 81p. 2000. pap. text 40.00 (*1-885063-24-5*) AVSC Int.

— Infection Prevention Curriculum: A Training Course for Health Care Providers & other Staff of Hospitals & Clinics: Participant's Handbook. LC 99-10152. 1999. 10.00 (*1-885063-20-2*) AVSC Int.

AVSC International Staff. Medical & Service Delivery Guidelines for Family Planning: Russian Edition. 2nd ed. Sacci, Inna & Grigorieva, Vera, eds. (RUS.). 250p. 1999. pap. write for info. (*1-885063-21-0*) AVSC Int.

— Minilaparotomy under Local Anaesthesia: A Curriculum for Doctors & Nurses, Participant's Handbook. Mullen, Ruth, ed. (Illus.). 72p. 1995. student ed. 8.00 (*1-885063-08-3*) AVSC Int.

— Minilaparotomy under Local Anaesthesia: A Curriculum for Doctors & Nurses, Trainer's Package. Mullen, Ruth, ed. (Illus.). 140p. 1993. pap. text 75.00 (*1-885063-07-5*) AVSC Int.

— Safe & Voluntary Surgical Contraception: Guidelines for Service Programs. 104p. 1995. reprint ed. pap. text 8.00 (*1-885063-06-7*) AVSC Int.

AVSC Staff & Moss, William M. Contraceptive Surgery for Men & Women. 2nd ed. 182p. 1991. 12.95 (*0-929240-26-X*) EMIS.

Avsey, Ignat, tr. see Dostoyevsky, Fyodor.

Avsey, Ignat, tr. & intro. see Dostoyevsky, Fyodor.

Avtar, Ram. Learn to Play on Harmonium. (Illus.). 42p. 1980. 12.95 (*0-318-36327-5*) Asia Bk Corp.

— Learn to Play on Tabla No. 2: Advance Course. 52p. 1985. 12.95 (*0-318-36328-3*) Asia Bk Corp.

AVTRW Working Party UFAW Staff. Guidelines for the Recognition & Assessment of Pain in Animals. (C). 1989. 75.00 (*0-7855-3761-9*) St Mut.

Avula, Xavier J., jt. auth. see Rodin, Ervin Y.

Avunduk, Canan, jt. auth. see Eastwood, Gregory L.

***Avvakumov, A.** Analysis of Pin-by-Pin Effects for LWR Rod Ejection Accident. 89p. 2000. pap. 8.50 (*0-16-059122-8*) USGPO.

Avyle, M. J. Van Den, see Hall, G. E. & Van Den Avyle, M. J., eds.

Aw, T. C., jt. auth. see Low, Linda.

Awabdy, Tanya, ed. see Vanbuskirk, Robert.

Awabi. Ventilation of Buildings. 328p. (C). 1995. pap. 49.99 (*0-419-21080-6*, E & FN Spon) Routledge.

Awad, A. G., jt. ed. see Gaebel, W.

Awad, Elias, et al, contrib. by. New Generation Knowledge Engineering: I. A. K. E. '92 Proceedings. 832p. (Orig.). 1992. pap. 35.00 (*0-938801-06-6*) Systemsware.

Awad, Elias M. Building Expert Systems: Principles, Procedures, & Applications. 600p. (C). 1996. 58.00 (*0-314-09514-4*) West Pub.

— Building Expert Systems: Principles, Procedures, & Applications. 10th ed. LC 97-151617. 600p. (C). 1996. mass mkt. 18.00 (*0-314-08982-9*) West Pub.

Awad, Elias M. & Gotterer, Malcolm. Database Management. 800p. (C). 1992. mass mkt. 62.95 (*0-87835-713-0*) Course Tech.

Awad, Elias M., jt. auth. see Tremaine, M. David.

Awad, Issam A., jt. auth. see Little, John R.

Awad, Joseph. Leaning to Hear the Music. Adams, Joseph D., ed. LC 96-70863. (Illus.). 96p. (Orig.). (C). 1997. pap. 12.00 (*1-880016-24-9*) Road Pubs.

Awad, Joseph F. The Power of Public Relations. LC 85-6258. 176p. 1985. 42.95 (*0-275-90054-1*, C0054, Praeger Pubs) Greenwood.

Awad, Maher. Object-Oriented Technology for Real-Time Systems. 320p. (C). 1996. 59.00 (*0-13-227943-6*) P-H.

Awad, Maher, et al. Optics: An Introduction for Technicians & Technologists. LC 99-17279. (Illus.). 229p. (C). 1999. 87.00 (*0-13-227794-8*) P-H.

***Awadu, Keidi Obi.** The Road to Power: Seven Steps to an African Global Order. 250p. 1999. pap. 12.00 (*1-56411-199-7*) Untd Bros & Sis.

Awalt, Barbe & Rhetts, Paul. Charlie Carrillo: Tradition & Soul - Tradicion y Alma. LC 94-77890. (Illus.). 128p. (Orig.). 1995. pap. 39.95 (*0-9641542-0-X*) LPD Pr.

— Our Saints among Us: 400 Years of New Mexican Devotional Art. LC 97-71662.Tr. of Nuestros Santos entre Nosotros. (Illus.). 120p. 1997. 59.95 (*0-9641542-2-6*); pap. 44.95 (*0-9641542-8-5*) LPD Pr.

Awalt, Barbe, ed. see Steele, Thomas J.

***Awan.** Voice Diagnostic Handbook. 2000. pap. 55.00 incl. disk (*0-8342-1717-1*) Aspen Pub.

Awan, Shaila. The Burrow Book: Tunnel into a World of Wildlife. LC 97-18891. (Illus.). 24p. (J). (gr. 2). 1997. 14.95 (*0-7894-2025-2*) DK Pub Inc.

Awana, Rita H. Radiation: The Hidden Enemy. 1994. pap. text 12.95 (*1-881116-22-0*) Black Forest Pr.

***Awane, Azzouz & Goze, Michel.** Pfaffian Systems, K-Symplectic Systems. LC 00-33049. 2000. write for info. (*0-7923-6373-6*) Kluwer Academic.

Awang, Amir, jt. ed. see Othman, Abdul H.

Awang, Kamis B. & Taylor, David A. Tropical Acacias in East Asia & the Pacific. (Report on COGREDA Ser.). 106p. (Orig.). 1992. pap. 12.50 (*0-933595-71-9*) Winrock Intl.

Awani, Alfred O. Project Management Techniques. (Illus.). 192p. 1983. text 24.95 (*0-89433-197-3*) Petrocelli.

Award Gift Inc. Staff. Gift & Award Bible. 1999. 7.99 (*0-8423-3589-7*) Tyndale Hse.

Awasthi, A. & Bagga, B., eds. Yearly All India Criminal Digest, 1988. (C). 1990. 210.00 (*0-89771-191-2*) St Mut.

Awasthi, A. B. Purana Index. (C). 1992. 42.00 (*81-7013-074-3*, Pub. by Navarang) S Asia.

Awasthi, Abl. Studies in Skanda Purana Pt. 1: Thesis Accepted for the Ph.D. Degree of the Lucknow University. (C). 1965. 28.00 (*0-8364-2867-6*, Pub. by Manohar) S Asia.

Awasthi, Anandeshwari. Indian Climatology. LC 95-902562. (Illus.). xxxi, 283p. 1995. 29.00 (*81-7024-690-3*, Pub. by Ashish Pub Hse) Nataraj Bks.

Awasthi, D. D. A Monograph of the Lichen Genus Dirinaria. 1975. 32.00 (*3-7682-0957-1*) Lubrecht & Cramer.

Awasthi, D. S. Gandhian Economic Theory. 190p. 1987. 10.00 (*0-8364-2016-0*, Pub. by Usha) S Asia.

Awasthi, Dhar D. A Key to the Microlichens of India, Nepal & Sri Lanka. Wirth, Volkmar et al, eds. (Bibliotheca Lichenologica: Vol. 40). (GER., Illus.). 337p. 1991. pap. 77.00 (*3-443-58019-X*, Pub. by Gebruder Borntraeger) Balogh.

Awasthi, Dinesh N. & Sebastian, Jose. Evaluation of Entrepreneurship Development Programmes. 280p. 1995. 29.95 (*0-8039-9254-8*) Sage.

Awasthi, I. Rural Women in India: A Socio-Economic Profile. 482p. 1982. 39.95 (*0-318-37073-5*) Asia Bk Corp.

Awasthi, K. N. Contemporary Indian English Fiction: An Anthology of Essays. (C). 1992. 22.50 (*81-7022-051-3*, Pub. by Asian Educ Servs) S Asia.

Awasthi, R., ed. Hindi Short Stories. 184p. 1981. 19.95 (*0-318-36955-9*) Asia Bk Corp.

Awasthi, S. K., ed. Energy Conservation in the Chemical & Allied Industries: Proceedings of National Seminar Held at HBTI, Kanpur, India. (C). 1989. 35.00 (*81-7003-103-6*, Pub. by S Asia Pubs) S Asia.

Awasthi, Suresh, ed. Chambers English-Hindi Dictionary. 1985. 18.00 (*0-8364-1474-8*, Pub. by Allied Pubs) S Asia.

Awasthi, V. B. Introduction to General & Applied Entomology. 1997. pap. 135.00 (*81-7233-149-5*, Pub. by Scientific Pubs) St Mut.

Awasthy, G. S. Broadcasting in India. 270p. 1965. 7.95 (*0-318-37276-2*) Asia Bk Corp.

Awasum, Toby. Ministering to Your Pastor. LC 97-174159. 168p. 1997. pap. 10.99 (*1-56043-288-8*, Treasure Hse) Destiny Image.

Awater, Geert A. Broadband Communication: Modeling, Analysis & Synthesis of an ATM Switching Element. (Illus.). 221p. (Orig.). 1994. pap. 62.50 (*90-407-1029-5*, Pub. by Delft U Pr) Coronet Bks.

Away, Clip. Direct Marketing Coupon Designs: 300 Creative, Copyright Free Camera-Ready Professional Layouts. 1990. pap. 19.95 (*0-8306-3482-7*) McGraw-Hill Prof.

***Awbi, H. B.** Air Distribution in Rooms: Ventilation for Health & Sustainable Environment: Proceedings of the 7th International Conference on Air Distribution in Rooms, 9-12 July 2000, Reading, UK, 2 vols. LC 00-42979. 2000. write for info. (*0-08-043017-1*) Elsevier.

Awbi, H. B. Ventilation of Buildings. 384p. 1991. pap. 107.95 (*0-419-15690-9*) Thomson Learn.

Awbrey, Brian J., jt. auth. see Tarpinian, Steve.

***Awbrey, David S.** Finding Hope in the Age of Melancholy. LC 98-6267. 272p. (gr. 8). 1999. 25.00 (*0-316-03811-3*) Little.

Awbrey, K., ed. see Schulenberg, T.

Awde, Nicholas. Chechen Dictionary & Phrasebook. (CHE.). 160p. (Orig.). 1996. pap. 11.95 (*0-7818-0446-9*) Hippocrene Bks.

— Georgian-English - English-Georgian Dictionary & Phrasebook. LC 97-19318. (Dictionary & Phrasebook Ser.). 150p. 1997. pap. 11.95 (*0-7818-0542-2*) Hippocrene Bks.

— Hausa-English - English-Hausa Practical Dictionary. LC 96-6827. (ENG & HAU.). 431p. 1995. 16.95 (*0-7818-0426-4*) Hippocrene Bks.

— Serbo-Croatian-English, English-Serbo-Croatian Dictionary. (CRO, ENG & SER.). 400p. (Orig.). 1996. pap. 16.95 (*0-7818-0445-0*) Hippocrene Bks.

***Awde, Nicholas.** Swahili-English, English-Swahili Practical Dictionary. (ENG & SWA.). 465p. 2000. pap. 16.95 (*0-7818-0480-9*) Hippocrene Bks.

Awde, Nicholas, ed. Armenian Perspectives. 320p. 1997. 65.00 (*0-7007-0610-0*, Pub. by Curzon Pr Ltd) Paul & Co Pubs.

— Treasury of African Love Poems & Proverbs. LC 97-19296. 128p. 1997. 11.95 (*0-7818-0483-3*) Hippocrene Bks.

— Women in Islam: An Anthology from the Qur'an & Hadith. LC 98-4312. 220p. 1999. text 55.00 (*0-312-21523-1*) St Martin.

Awde, Nicholas & Samano, Putros. The Arabic Alphabet: How to Read & Write It. 95p. 1987. pap. 7.95 (*0-8184-0430-2*) Carol Pub Group.

***Awde, Nicolas.** Armenian First Names. 2000. 11.95 (*0-7818-0750-6*) Hippocrene Bks.

Awdeley, J. The Fraternitye of Vacabondes. Viles, Edward, ed. (EETS, ES Ser.: No. 9). 1969. reprint ed. 35.00 (*0-527-00223-2*) Periodicals Srv.

Awdry, C. Thomas the Tank Engine's Big Blue Treasury. (Thomas the Tank Engine & Friends Ser.). (J). 1998. 6.99 (*0-679-89478-0*, Pub. by Random Bks Yng Read) Random.

***Awdry, C.** Thomas the Tank Engine's Big Yellow Treasury. LC 98-66282. (Thomas the Tank Engine & Friends Ser.). (Illus.). 96p. (J). (gr. k-3). 1998. 6.99 (*0-679-89479-9*, Pub. by Random Bks Yng Read) Random.

Awdry, Christopher. Electronic Mail. (Illus.). 16p. 1996. 2750.00 (*0-614-03466-3*, G049U) BCC.

— Learn with Thomas. LC 95-74747. (Illus.). (J). (ps-3). 1996. 12.99 (*0-679-87951-X*) McKay.

— Learn with Thomas. (Illus.). (J). (ps-2). 1996. 12.99 (*0-614-15712-9*) Random.

Awdry, Christopher. Tell the Time with Thomas Clock Book. LC 91-67877. (Illus.). 32p. (J). (ps-3). 1993. 8.99 (*0-679-83461-3*, Pub. by Random Bks Yng Read) Random.

Awdry, Christopher. Thomas & the Helicopter Rescue: A Revolving Picture Book with Flaps. LC 95-67485. (Illus.). 24p. (J). (ps-3). 1995. 15.00 (*0-679-87690-1*) Random.

***Awdry, Christopher.** Thomas & the Missing Christmas Tree. (Jellybean Bks.). (Illus.). 24p. (J). (ps-k). 1999. 1.99 (*0-375-80078-6*, Pub. by Random Bks Yng Read); lib. bdg. 7.99 (*0-375-90078-0*, Pub. by Random Bks Yng Read) Random.

***Awdry, Christopher, ed.** Thomas: The Really Useful Engine. LC 98-53769. 48p. (ps-3). 1999. 11.99 (*0-375-80242-8*, Pub. by Random Bks Yng Read) Random.

Awdry, Christopher & Awdry, Reverend Wilbert V. Tell Time with Thomas. (J). (gr. 2 up). 1993. 107.88 (*0-679-86107-6*) Random Bks Yng Read.

***Awdry, Rev W.** Tank Engine Thomas Again. (Thomas the Tank Engine & Friends Ser.). (Illus.). 64p. (J). 2000. 6.99 (*0-375-80532-X*, Pub. by Random Bks Yng Read) Random.

Awdry, Reverend Wilbert V. Breakfast-Time for Thomas. (Thomas the Tank Engine & Friends Ser.). (Illus.). (J). (ps-3). 1998. lib. bdg. 7.99 (*0-679-99237-5*, Pub. by Random Bks Yng Read) Random.

— Breakfast Time for Thomas: A Thomas the Tank Engine Storybook. LC 98-65583. (Illus.). 24p. (J). (ps-3). 1998. 1.99 (*0-679-89237-0*, Pub. by Random Bks Yng Read) Random.

— Catch Me, Catch Me! A Thomas the Tank Engine Story. LC 89-37547. (Pictureback Ser.). (Illus.). 24p. (J). (ps-3). 1990. pap. 3.25 (*0-679-80485-4*, Pub. by Random Bks Yng Read) Random.

Awdry, Reverend Wilbert V. Catch Me, Catch Me! A Thomas the Tank Engine Story. (Pictureback Reader Ser.). (Illus.). (J). 1990. 8.45 (*0-606-12215-X*) Turtleback.

Awdry, Reverend Wilbert V. Choo-Choo, Peek-a-Boo. LC 91-61250. (Peek-a-Boo Board Bks.). (Illus.). 14p. (J). (ps). 1992. 4.99 (*0-679-82262-3*, Pub. by Random Bks Yng Read) Random.

Awdry, Reverend Wilbert V. A Cow on the Line: And Other Thomas the Tank Engine Stories. Starr, Ringo, ed. (Thomas the Tank Engine & Friends Ser.). (Illus.). 32p. (J). (ps-3). 1992. 7.95 incl. audio (*0-679-83476-1*, Pub. by Random Bks Yng Read) Random.

Awdry, Reverend Wilbert V. A Cow on the Line & Other Thomas the Tank Engine Stories. LC 91-21706. (Thomas the Tank Engine Picturebacks Ser.). (Illus.). 32p. (J). (ps-3). 1992. pap. 3.25 (*0-679-81977-0*, Pub. by Random Bks Yng Read) Random.

Awdry, Reverend Wilbert V. Diesel's Devious Deed. Starr, Ringo, ed. (Thomas the Tank Engine & Friends Ser.). (Illus.). 32p. (J). (ps-3). 1992. pap. 7.95 incl. audio (*0-679-83474-5*, Pub. by Random Bks Yng Read) Random.

Awdry, Reverend Wilbert V. Diesel's Devious Deed & Other Thomas the Tank Engine Stories. LC 91-21133. (Thomas the Tank Engine Picturebacks Ser.). (Illus.). 32p. (J). (ps-3). 1992. pap. 3.25 (*0-679-81976-2*, Pub. by Random Bks Yng Read) Random.

— Happy Birthday, Thomas. LC 89-49649. (Step into Reading Ser.: A Step 1 Book). (Illus.). 32p. (J). (ps-1). 1990. lib. bdg. 11.99 (*0-679-90809-9*, Pub. by Random Bks Yng Read) Random.

— Happy Birthday, Thomas. LC 89-49649. (Step into Reading Ser.: A Step 1 Book). (Illus.). 32p. (J). (ps-3). 1990. pap. 3.99 (*0-679-80809-4*, Pub. by Random Bks Yng Read) Random.

Awdry, Reverend Wilbert V. Happy Birthday, Thomas. (Step into Reading Ser.: A Step 1 Book). (J). (ps-1). 1990. 9.19 (*0-606-04689-5*, Pub. by Turtleback) Demco.

Awdry, Reverend Wilbert V. Henry & the Elephant. LC 98-65936. (Thomas the Tank Engine & Friends Ser.). (Illus.). 24p. (J). (ps-3). 1999. lib. bdg. 7.99 (*0-679-99414-9*, Pub. by Random Bks Yng Read) Random.

— Henry & the Elephant: A Thomas the Tank Engine Storybook. (Thomas the Tank Engine & Friends Ser.). (Illus.). 24p. (J). (ps-3). 1999. 1.99 (*0-679-89414-4*, Pub. by Random Bks Yng Read) Random.

— Henry & the Tunnel. (Illus.). 16p. (ps-k). 1997. 5.99 (*0-679-88679-6*, Pub. by Random Bks Yng Read) Random.

Awdry, Reverend Wilbert V. James & the Trucks. (Illus.). 16p. (ps-k). 1997. 5.99 (*0-679-88680-X*, Pub. by Random Bks Yng Read) Random.

Awdry, Reverend Wilbert V. James the Red Engine. LC 99-228513. (Thomas the Tank Engine & Friends Ser.). (J). 1999. 6.99 (*0-679-89389-X*, Pub. by Random Bks Yng Read) Random.

— Meet Thomas & His Friends. (J). 1998. 4.99 (*0-679-89003-3*, Pub. by Random Bks Yng Read) Random.

— The Midnight Ride of Thomas the Tank Engine. LC 93-26587. (Illus.). 16p. (J). (ps-3). 1994. pap. 5.99 (*0-679-85643-9*, Pub. by Random Bks Yng Read) Random.

Awdry, Reverend Wilbert V. Percy & Harold. (Illus.). (J). 1997. 5.99 (*0-679-88681-8*, Pub. by Random Bks Yng Read) Random.

Awdry, Reverend Wilbert V. Stop, Train, Stop! A Thomas the Tank Engine Story. (Thomas the Tank Engine Picturebacks Ser.). (Illus.). 12p. (J). (ps). 1998. 4.99 (*0-679-89273-7*, Pub. by Random Bks Yng Read) Random.

An Asterisk (*) at the beginning of an entry indicates that the title is appearing for the first time.

— Surprise, Thomas! A Thomas the Tank Engine Book. (Chunky Flap Bks. Ser.). (Illus.). 22p. (J). (ps). 1994. 3.99 (*0-679-85446-0*, Pub. by Random Bks Yng Read) Random.

Awdry, Reverend Wilbert V. Thomas & Bertie. (Illus.). 16p. 1997. 5.99 (*0-679-88682-6*, Pub. by Random Bks Yng Read) Random.

— Thomas & the Freight Train. LC 90-62371. (Chunky Shape Bks.). (Illus.). 22p. (J). (ps). 1991. 3.99 (*0-679-81599-6*, Pub. by Random Bks Yng Read) Random.

— Thomas & the Hide-&-Seek Animals: A Thomas the Tank Engine Flap Book. LC 90-62114. (Flap Bks.). (Illus.). 24p. (J). (ps-1). 1991. 10.95 (*0-679-81316-0*, Pub. by Random Bks Yng Read) Random.

— Thomas & the Naughty Diesel. LC 98-45211. (Pictureback Ser.). (Illus.). 24p. (J). (gr. k-3). 1999. pap. 3.25 (*0-375-80079-4*, Pub. by Random Bks Yng Read) Random.

— Thomas & the Weather. LC 98-137452. (J). 1998. 4.99 (*0-679-89004-1*, Pub. by Random Bks Yng Read) Random.

— Thomas Gets Tricked & Other Stories. (Thomas the Tank Engine & Friends Book & Cassette Ser.). (Illus.). 32p. (J). (ps-2). 1991. 7.95 incl. audio (*0-679-80108-1*, Pub. by Random Bks Yng Read) Random.

— Thomas Gets Tricked & Other Stories: Based on the Railway Series. LC 89-8502. (Thomas the Tank Engine Picturebacks Ser.). (Illus.). 32p. (J). (ps-3). 1989. pap. 3.25 (*0-679-80100-6*, Pub. by Random Bks Yng Read) Random.

— Thomas Tank Engine's ABC Fun Book. 64p. (J). 1998. pap. 1.99 (*0-679-89158-7*, Pub. by Random Bks Yng Read) Random.

Awdry, Reverend Wilbert V. Thomas Tank Engine's Read & Color Me Book. 64p. (J). 1998. pap. 1.99 (*0-679-89157-9*, Pub. by Random Bks Yng Read) Random.

— Thomas the Tank Engine. LC 99-228514. (Illus.). 10p. (J). (ps). 1999. 6.99 (*0-679-89388-1*) Random.

***Awdry, Reverend Wilbert V.** Thomas the Tank Engine. 64p. 2000. 6.99 (*0-375-80533-8*) Random.

— Thomas the Tank Engine: Cranky Bug. LC 99-35492. (Illus.). 24p. (J). (gr. k-3). 2000. pap. 3.25 (*0-375-80246-0*) Random.

Awdry, Reverend Wilbert V. Thomas the Tank Engine: The Complete Collection. (Illus.). 416p. (J). 1997. 19.99 (*0-517-18786-8*) Random Hse Value.

— Thomas the Tank Engine & the School Trip. LC 92-33711. (Step into Reading Ser.: A Step 1 Book). (Illus.). 32p. (J). (ps-3). 1993. pap. 3.99 (*0-679-84365-5*, Pub. by Random Bks Yng Read) Random.

***Awdry, Reverend Wilbert V.** Thomas the Tank Engine Springtime Adventure Coloring Book. (J). 2000. pap. 1.99 (*0-375-80057-3*) Random.

Awdry, Reverend Wilbert V. Thomas the Tank Engine's Big Lift-&-Look Book. LC 95-70943. (Great Big Flap Bks.). 1996. 11.99 (*0-679-88072-0*, Pub. by Random Bks Yng Read) Random.

— Thomas the Tank Engine's Hidden Surprises. LC 98-67783. (Let's Go Lift & Peek Bks.). (Illus.). 7p. (J). (ps). 1999. 4.99 (*0-679-89482-9*, Pub. by Random Bks Yng Read) Random.

— Thomas the Tank Engine's Noisy Trip. LC 89-60089. (Chunky Bks. Ser.). (Illus.). 28p. (J). 1989. 3.99 (*0-679-80083-2*, Pub. by Random Bks Yng Read) Random.

Awdry, Reverend Wilbert V. Thomas Visits a Farm. (Bathtime Bks.). (Illus.). 10p. (J). (ps). 1991. 4.99 (*0-679-81580-5*, Pub. by Random Bks Yng Read) Random.

Awdry, Reverend Wilbert V. Thomas's ABC Book. LC 98-6233. (Please Read to Me Ser.). (Illus.). 24p. (J). (ps-3). 1998. pap. 3.25 (*0-679-89357-1*, Pub. by Random Bks Yng Read) Random.

— Tracking Thomas the Tank Engine & His Friends: A Book with Finger Tabs. LC 91-67876. (Illus.). 16p. (J). (ps-1). 1992. 8.99 (*0-679-83458-3*, Pub. by Random Bks Yng Read) Random.

— Trouble for Thomas & Other Stories. abr. ed. (Thomas the Tank Engine & Friends Book & Cassette Ser.). (Illus.). 32p. (J). (ps-2). 1991. 7.95 incl. audio (*0-679-80106-5*, Pub. by Random Bks Yng Read) Random.

— Trouble for Thomas & Other Stories: Based on the Railway Series. LC 89-8503. (Thomas the Tank Engine Picturebacks Ser.). (Illus.). 32p. (J). (ps-3). 1989. pap. 3.25 (*0-679-80101-4*, Pub. by Random Bks Yng Read) Random.

Awdry, Reverend Wilbert V., jt. auth. see Awdry, Christopher.

Awdry, Reverend Wilbert V., jt. auth. see Davies, Robin.

Awdry, Reverend Wilbert V., jt. auth. see Stubbs, Tommy.

***Awdry, Wilbert V.** Christmastime with Thomas! (Painting Time Ser.). (Illus.). 32p. (J). (ps-3). 2000. pap. 3.99 (*0-375-80642-3*, Pub. by Random Bks Yng Read) Random.

Awe, Susan C., ed. Arba Guide to Subject Encyclopedias & Dictionaries. 2nd ed. LC 96-44571. 475p. 1997. lib. bdg. 65.00 (*1-56308-467-8*) Libs Unl.

***Awedoba, A. K.** An Introduction to Kasena Society & Culture Through Their Proverbs. LC 99-52244. 296p. 2000. 47.00 (*0-7618-1542-2*) U Pr of Amer.

Awege, Gayna. Kelim Canvaswork. (Craft Library). 48p. pap. 5.50 (*0-85532-617-4*, 617-4, Pub. by Srch Pr) A Schwartz & Co.

Awerbuch, Shimon & Preston, Alistair, eds. The Virtual Utility: Accounting, Technology & Competitive Aspects of the Emerging Industry. LC 97-6293. (Topics in Regulatory Economics & Policy Ser.). 1997. lib. bdg. 110.00 (*0-7923-9902-1*) Kluwer Academic.

Awerbuch, Shimon, et al. Advances in Solar Energy: An Annual Review of Research & Development, Vol. 10. Boer, Karl W., ed. (Illus.). 530p. 1995. text 125.00 (*0-89553-253-0*) Am Solar Energy.

***Awerbuch, Shimon, et al.** Unlocking the Benefits of Restructuring: A Blueprint for Transmission. LC 99-48072. (Illus.). 300p. 1999. pap. 98.00 (*0-910325-79-0*) Public Util.

***Awerbuck, Louis.** Tactical Reality: An Uncommon Look at Common-Sense Firearms Training & Tactics. (Illus.). 272p. 1999. pap. 30.00 (*1-58160-051-8*) Paladin Pr.

Awerkamp, Don. Ethics & Politics: The Philosophy of Emanuel Lavinas. 1974. lib. bdg. 250.00 (*0-87700-235-5*) Revisionist Pr.

Awford, Ian. Developments in Aviation Products Liability. (C). 1985. 550.00 (*0-7855-4184-5*, Pub. by Witherby & Co) St Mut.

Awhonn. Core Curr for Material-Newborn. 2nd ed. LC 98-52111. (C). 1999. pap. text 59.95 (*0-7216-7424-0*, W B Saunders Co) Harcrt Hlth Sci Grp.

AWHONN Staff. Fetal Heart Monitoring Principles & Practices. 288p. 1997. per. 29.95 (*0-7872-3412-5*) Kendall-Hunt.

Awiakta, Marilou. Abiding Appalachia: Where Mountain & Atom Meet. LC 94-35462. 1994. write for info. (*0-916078-38-8*) Iris Pr.

— Rising Fawn & the Fire Mystery. Easson, Roger R., ed. LC 83-13824. (Child's Christmas in Memphis Ser.: Vol. 1). (Illus.). 48p. (Orig.). (J). (gr. 5 up). 1984. pap. 11.95 (*0-918518-29-6*) Iris Pr.

— Selu: Seeking the Corn-Mother's Wisdom. (Illus.). 352p. 1994. pap. 14.95 (*1-55591-206-0*) Fulcrum Pub.

Awiakta, Marilou B. Abiding Appalachia: Where Mountain & Atom Meet. LC 78-12970. (Illus.). 94p. 1978. pap. 8.95 (*0-918518-15-6*) Iris Pr.

Awiakta, Marylou, et al. Telling Tales Teacher's Guide. 2nd ed. (Telling Tales TV Ser.). 84p. 1991. pap. 3.50 (*0-910475-53-9*) KET.

AWIC Staff & UFAW Staff. Environmental Enrichment Information Resources for Laboratory Animals, 1965-1995: Birds, Cats, Dogs, Farm Animals, Ferrets, Rabbits & Rodents. 294p. 1995. pap. 60.00 (*0-900767-91-X*, Pub. by Univs Fed Animal Welfare) St Mut.

Awinger, Ann. Yosemite: Valley of Thunder. (Genesis Ser.). 1996. 37.50 (*0-614-96864-X*) Harper SF.

Awkward, Michael. Inspiriting Influences: Tradition, Revision, & Afro-American Women's Novels. Heilbrun, Carolyn G. & Miller, Nancy K., eds. (Gender & Culture Ser.). 208p. 1989. text 57.50 (*0-231-06806-9*) Col U Pr.

— Inspiriting Influences: Tradition, Revision, & Afro-American Women's Novels. Heilbrun, Carolyn G. & Miller, Nancy K., eds. (Gender & Culture Ser.). 208p. 1991. pap. text 17.50 (*0-231-06807-7*) Col U Pr.

— Negotiating Difference: Race, Gender & the Politics of Positionality. (Illus.). 240p. 1995. pap. text 14.95 (*0-226-03301-5*); lib. bdg. 42.50 (*0-226-03300-7*) U Ch Pr.

— Scenes of Instruction: A Memoir. LC 99-25938. 240p. 1999. 24.95 (*0-8223-2402-4*) Duke.

Awlinson, Richard. Shadowdale. LC 88-51723. (Forgotten Realms Avatar Trilogy Ser.: Bk. 1). 352p. 1989. pap. 5.99 (*0-88038-730-0*, Pub. by TSR Inc) Random.

— Tantras. LC 88-51724. (Forgotten Realms Avatar Trilogy Ser.: Bk. 2). 352p. (Orig.). 1989. pap. 5.99 (*0-88038-748-3*, Pub. by TSR Inc) Random.

— Waterdeep. LC 88-51725. (Forgotten Realms Avatar Trilogy Ser.: Bk. 3). 352p. 1989. pap. 5.99 (*0-88038-759-9*, Pub. by TSR Inc) Random.

Awliya, Nizam A. Morals for the Heart. Lawrence, Bruce B., tr. 404p. 1996. 19.95 (*0-614-21314-2*, 804) Kazi Pubns.

Awmiller, Craig. This House on Fire: The Story of the Blues. (African-American Experience Ser.). (Illus.). 176p. (YA). (gr. 9-12). 1996. pap. 8.00 (*0-531-15797-0*) Watts.

— Wynton Marsalis: Gifted Trumpet Player. (Picture-Story Biographies Ser.). (Illus.). 32p. (J). (gr. 3-4). 1996. pap. 3.95 (*0-516-20070-4*) Childrens.

Awn, P. J. Satan's Tragedy & Redemption: Iblis in Sufi Psychology. 246p. 1996. 59.50 (*0-614-21558-7*, 1105) Kazi Pubns.

***Awodey, Marc.** Telegrams from the Psych Ward: And Other Poems. 1999. pap. write for info. (*0-9658903-4-1*) Writers Pubg Coop.

Awolalu, J. Omosade. Yoruba Beliefs & Sacrificial Rites. unabridged ed. (Illus.). 207p. 1996. reprint ed. pap. 19.95 (*0-9638787-3-5*, Pub. by Athelia-Henrietta) BookWorld.

Awoonor, Kofi. The Breast of the Earth: A Survey of the History, Culture & Literature of Africa South of the Sahara. 1983. reprint ed. 19.95 (*0-685-03583-2*); reprint ed. pap. text 7.95 (*0-88357-103-X*) NOK Pubs.

— Comes the Voyager at Last: A Tale of Return to Africa. LC 91-75602. 148p. 1992. 24.95 (*0-86543-262-7*); pap. 7.95 (*0-86543-263-5*) Africa World.

— Fire in the Valley: Ewe Folktales. LC 73-88805. 10.00 (*0-88357-079-3*); pap. text 3.95 (*0-88357-080-7*) NOK Pubs.

— Guardians of the Sacred Word: Ewe Poetry. LC 73-85559. 104p. 1974. text 11.95 (*0-88357-007-6*) NOK Pubs.

— The Latin American & Caribbean Notebook, Vol. 1. LC 92-70644. 94p. 1993. 24.95 (*0-86543-314-3*); pap. 7.95 (*0-86543-315-1*) Africa World.

— This Earth, My Brother... (African Writers Ser.). 183p. (C). 1972. pap. 8.95 (*0-435-90108-7*, 90108) Heinemann.

— Until the Morning After: Selected Poems, 1963-1985. LC 87-80177. 212p. (Orig.). 1987. pap. 10.95 (*0-912678-69-0*, Greenfld Rev Pr) Greenfld Rev Lit.

Awoonor, Kofi, tr. see Akpalu, Vinoko.

***Awosika-Fapetu, Abiola.** Business Made Easy. 2nd ed. 140p. (C). 2000. per. 33.95 (*0-7872-7265-5*) Kendall-Hunt.

Awosika-Faputu, Abiola. Business Made Easy. 112p. (C). 1997. per. 30.95 (*0-7872-3603-9*, 41360301) Kendall-Hunt.

Awosika, Larry F., et al, eds. Coastlines of Western Africa. LC 93-14143. (Coastlines of the World Ser.). 408p. 1993. 38.00 (*0-87262-966-X*) Am Soc Civil Eng.

Awotokun, Kunle. Governance & Legislative Control in Nigeria: Lessons from the Second & Third Republics. LC 98-5518. 320p. 1998. 74.95 (*1-57309-273-8*) Intl Scholars.

Awotona, Adenrele. Reconstruction after Disaster: Issues & Practices. 208p. 1997. text 64.95 (*1-85972-551-1*, Pub. by Avebry) Ashgate Pub Co.

Awotona, Adenrele, ed. Housing Provision & Bottom-Up Approaches: Family Case Studies from Africa, Asia & South America. LC 98-73753. 9p. 1999. text 74.95 (*1-84014-303-7*, Pub. by Ashgate Pub) Ashgate Pub Co.

Awotona, Adenrele & Teymur, Mecdet, eds. Tradition, Location & Community: Place-Making & Development. (Ethnoscapes Ser.). 352p. 1997. 83.95 (*1-85972-320-9*, Pub. by Avebry) Ashgate Pub Co.

Awouters, Frans M. Proceedings - KSO XIVth International Symposium on Medicinal Chem: Maastricht, 8-12 September 1996. LC 97-22116. (Pharmacochemistry Library). 1997. write for info. (*0-444-82798-6*) Elsevier.

Awramik, S. M., jt. ed. see Ridinger, Robert B.

Awrejcewicz, J. Bifurcation & Chaos in Coupled Oscillators. 256p. (C). 1991. text 61.00 (*981-02-0579-1*) World Scientific Pub.

Awrejcewicz, J., ed. Bifurcation & Chaos: Theory & Applications. LC 94-39751. (Nonlinear Dynamics Ser.). 1994. 92.95 (*3-540-58531-1*) Spr-Verlag.

— Bifurcation & Chaos in Simple Dynamical Systems. 136p. (C). 1989. text 33.00 (*981-02-0038-2*) World Scientific Pub.

Awuku, Emmanual, jt. compiled by see Hatchard, John.

AWWA Research Foundation, jt. auth. see Reiber, Steve Harold.

AWWA Research Foundation Staff. Factors Affecting Disinfection By-Prodcut Formation During Chloramination. Symons, James, ed. LC 97-17672. 1997. pap. write for info. (*0-89867-906-0*, 90728) Am Water Wks Assn.

— Future of Water Reuse: Proceedings, Vols. 1, 2, 3. (Illus.). 1810p. (Orig.). 1985. pap. 50.00 (*0-915295-02-4*, 90506) AWWA Research.

AWWA Research Foundation Staff & International Water Supply Assn. Staff. Treatment Process Selection for Particle Removal. LC 97-39620. 1997. write for info. (*0-89867-887-0*, 90701) Am Water Wks Assn.

AWWA Research Foundation Staff & Japan Water Works Association Staff. Instrumentation & Computer Integration of Water Utility Operations. (Illus.). 483p. 1993. 125.00 (*0-89867-630-4*, 90588) Am Water Wks Assn.

AWWA Research Foundation Staff, jt. auth. see Abbaszadegan, Morteza.

AWWA Research Foundation Staff, jt. auth. see Amy, Gary L.

AWWA Research Foundation Staff, jt. auth. see Belosevic, Miodrag.

AWWA Research Foundation Staff, jt. auth. see Camper, Anne K.

AWWA Research Foundation Staff, jt. auth. see Clancy, Jennifer L.

AWWA Research Foundation Staff, jt. auth. see Daniel, Phillippe A.

AWWA Research Foundation Staff, jt. auth. see EMA Services, Inc. Staff.

AWWA Research Foundation Staff, jt. auth. see Graham, Mark.

AWWA Research Foundation Staff, jt. auth. see Hoffman, Rebecca.

AWWA Research Foundation Staff, jt. auth. see Kirmeyer, Gregory J.

AWWA Research Foundation Staff, jt. auth. see Lechevallier, Mark W.

AWWA Research Foundation Staff, jt. auth. see Peyton, Gary R.

AWWA Research Foundation Staff, jt. auth. see Rajani, Balvant.

AWWA Research Foundation Staff, jt. auth. see Sattar, S. A.

AWWA Research Foundation Staff, jt. auth. see Shannon, Larry D.

AWWA Research Foundation Staff, jt. auth. see Smith, Allan H.

AWWA Research Foundation Staff, jt. auth. see Summers, R. Scott.

AWWA Water Rights & Allocation Committee, jt. auth. see Wright, Kenneth R.

Awwad, Hassan K. Radiation Oncology - Radiobiological & Physiological Perspectives: The Boundary-Zone Between Clinical Radiotherapy & Fundamental Radiobiology & Physiology. (Developments in Oncology Ser.). (C). 1990. text 309.50 (*0-7923-0783-6*) Kluwer Academic.

Awwad, Mike A. The Personal Computer: Operating, Troubleshooting & Upgrading. LC 97-15811. 88p. (C). 1997. pap. 47.00 (*0-13-674417-6*) P-H.

***Awwad, Mike Mutasem.** IntranetWare/NetWare 4.11: Administration, Troubleshooting & TCP/IP. LC 99-17221. (Illus.). 414p. 1999. 83.00 (*0-13-927138-4*) P-H.

***Awwad, Mike Mutasen.** The Personal Computer: Operating, Troubleshooting & Upgrading. 2nd ed. 208p. 2000. pap. 48.00 (*0-13-020039-5*, Prentice Hall) P-H.

Awwad, Toufik. Collection of Toufik Awwad, Vol. 1. (ARA.). 900p. 1987. 35.00 (*0-86685-602-1*) Intl Bk Ctr.

Awwad, Toufik. Collection of Toufik Awwad, Vol. 1. (ARA.). 900p. 1987. 30.00 (*0-86685-286-7*, LDL726X, Pub. by Librairie du Liban) Intl Bk Ctr.

Awwad, Toufik. Collection of Toufik Awwad, Vol. 2. 900p. 1987. 35.00 (*0-86685-760-5*) Intl Bk Ctr.

Awwal, Abdul A., jt. auth. see Karim, Mohammad A.

Ax, ed. Ciceronis, M. Tulli Fascicule 46: De Divinatione, De Fato, Timaeus. (LAT.). 1987. reprint ed. pap. 24.95 (*3-519-01222-7*, T1222, Pub. by B G Teubner) U of Mich Pr.

Ax, Peter. Microfauna Marina, Band 10. (Illus.). 332p. 1995. 60.00 (*3-437-30828-9*) Gustav Fischer.

— Microfauna Marina: Metahuntemarria, Vol. 7. (Illus.). 342p. 1992. 59.00 (*1-56081-359-8*) Balogh.

— Microfauna Marina Vol. 5: Kalyptorhynchia. (Illus.). 1989. 57.00 (*0-89574-305-1*) Balogh.

— Multicellular Animals: A New Approach to the Phylogenetic Order in Nature, Vol. 1. LC 96-15839. 224p. 1996. 89.50 (*3-540-60803-6*) Spr-Verlag.

— The Phylogenetic System: The Systematization of Organisms on the Basis of Their Phylogenesis. Jeffries, R. P., tr. LC 86-16002. (Wiley-Interscience Publications). (Illus.). 354p. reprint ed. pap. 109.80 (*0-7837-3412-3*, 204337900008) Bks Demand.

Ax, Peter, ed. Microfauna Marina, Band 2. (Illus.). 410p. 1985. lib. bdg. 60.00 (*3-437-30490-9*, Pub. by Gustav Fischer) Balogh.

— Microfauna Marina, Band 1. (Illus.). 277p. 1984. lib. bdg. 54.00 (*3-437-30460-7*, Pub. by Gustav Fischer) Balogh.

— Microfauna Marina, Band 3. (Illus.). 438p. 1987. lib. bdg. 60.00 (*3-437-30558-1*, Pub. by Gustav Fischer) Balogh.

— Microfauna Marina, Band 5. (Illus.). 329p. 1989. pap. 57.00 (*3-437-30608-1*, Pub. by Gustav Fischer) Balogh.

— Microfauna Marina, Band 9. (ENG & GER.). 350p. 1994. 60.00 (*3-437-30779-7*, Pub. by Gustav Fischer) Balogh.

— Microfauna Marina, Vol. 6. 272p. 1991. lib. bdg. 70.00 (*1-56081-318-0*, Pub. by Gustav Fischer) Balogh.

— Microfauna Marina Band 4: The Ultrasound of Polychaeta. (Illus.). 494p. 1988. 72.00 (*3-437-30581-6*, Pub. by Gustav Fischer) Balogh.

— Microfauna Marina Band 6: Brackish Water, Playhelminthes of Alaska etc. etc. (Illus.). 272p. 1990. lib. bdg. 54.00 (*3-437-30663-4*, Pub. by Gustav Fischer) Balogh.

Ax, Peter, et al, eds. Free-Living & Symbiotic Plathelminthes. LC 88-38630. (Progress in Zoology Ser.: Vol. 36). 529p. 1989. lib. bdg. 235.00 (*0-89574-275-6*, Pub. by Gustav Fischer) Balogh.

Ax, Wolfram. Probleme des Sprachstils Als Gegenstand der Lateinischen Philologie. (Beitrage Zur Altertumswissenschaft Ser.: Band 1). (GER.). x, 304p. 1976. 50.00 (*3-487-06004-3*) G Olms Pubs.

***Axboe, Jens, et al.** Professional Linux Programming. 750p. 2000. pap. 49.99 (*1-86100-301-3*) Wrox Pr Inc.

Axcell, Claudia, et al. Simple Foods for the Pack: The Sierra Club Guide to Delicious Natural Foods for the Trail. rev. ed. LC 85-22076. (Outdoor Activities Guides Ser.). (Illus.). 224p. 1986. pap. 9.00 (*0-87156-757-1*, Pub. by Sierra) Random.

Axe, John. The Best of John Axe: Collectible & Modern Dolls. (Illus.). 192p. 1991. pap. 14.95 (*0-87588-373-7*) Hobby Hse.

***Axe, John.** Country Music Singers Paper Dolls. (Illus.). 24p. 1999. 5.95 (*0-87588-453-9*) Hobby Hse.

Axe, John. Effanbee: A Collector's Encyclopedia 1949-Present. rev. ed. (Illus.). 312p. 1998. 24.95 (*0-87588-470-9*, H5236) Hobby Hse.

— Effanbee's Candy Kid & Honey Paper Dolls. (Illus.). 24p. (gr. 1-4). 1997. pap. text 6.95 (*0-87588-481-4*, 5302) Hobby Hse.

— Effanbee's Patsy Paper Doll Family. (Illus.). 24p. (gr. 1-4). 1997. pap. text 6.95 (*0-87588-484-9*, 5305) Hobby Hse.

— Effanbee's Patsyette Paper Doll Family. (Illus.). 24p. (gr. 1-4). 1997. pap. text 6.95 (*0-87588-482-2*, 5303) Hobby Hse.

***Axe, John.** Effanbee's Wee Patsy Paper Dolls & Playhouse: Wee Edition. (Illus.). (gr. 4-7). 2000. pap. 5.95 (*0-87588-461-X*) Hobby Hse.

Axe, John. Effanbee's Wee Patsy Paperdolls & Playhouse. (Illus.). 24p. (gr. 4-7). 1995. pap. text 5.95 (*0-87588-439-3*) Hobby Hse.

Axe, John. Figure Skating Champions Paper Dolls. (Illus.). 24p. 1996. pap. 5.95 (*0-87588-451-2*) Hobby Hse.

— Kewpies Dolls & Collectibles Identification & Price Guide. 2nd rev. ed. (Illus.). 2000. 29.95 (*0-87588-589-6*) Hobby Hse.

— The Secret of Collecting Girls' Series Books. 2000. pap. 19.95 (*0-87588-577-2*) Hobby Hse.

Axe, John. Tammy & Her Family of Dolls. LC 95-195322. (Illus.). 128p. 1996. pap. 14.95 (*0-87588-433-4*, H4857) Hobby Hse.

Axe, Ruth F., ed. see Oak, Henry L.

Axel, Alison A. My Commute. LC 98-68529. 76p. 1998. pap. 14.00 (*1-892379-09-0*) Five & Ten.

***Axel, Brian Keith.** The Nation's Tortured Body: Violence, Representation & the Formation of a Sikh "Diaspora" LC 00-29399. (Illus.). 376p. 2000. pap. write for info. (*0-8223-2615-9*) Duke.

— The Nation's Tortured Body: Violence, Representation, & the Formation of a Sikh "Diaspora" LC 00-29399. (Illus.). 376p. 2000. lib. bdg. 64.95 (*0-8223-2607-8*) Duke.

Axel, F. & Gratias, D., eds. Beyond Quasicrystals. xvi, 619p. 1995. pap. 137.95 (*3-540-59251-2*) Spr-Verlag.

Axel, Helen & Nollen, Stanley D. Managing Contingent Workers: How to Reap the Benefits & Reduce the Risks. 256p. 1995. 55.00 (*0-8144-0242-9*) AMACOM.

Axel, Larry E., jt. ed. see Peden, Creighton.

Axel, Larry E., jt. ed. see Peden, W. Creighton.

A

***Axel-Lute, Melanie.** Quotation Index to Children's Literature. 300p. 2001. 40.00 (1-56308-809-6) Libs Unl.
Axel-Lute, Paul. New Jersey Legal Research Handbook 1984. 395p. 1984. 45.00 (0-318-02062-9) NJ Inst CLE.
Axelgard, Fred. U. S. - Arab Relations: The Iraq Dimension, No. 5. 45p. (Orig.). 1985. pap. 4.00 (0-916729-05-2) Natl Coun Arab.
Axelgard, Frederick W. A New Iraq: The Gulf War & the Implications for U. S. Policy, 133. LC 88-2403. (Washington Papers: No. 133). 139p. 1988. 49.95 (0-275-93013-0, C3013); pap. 18.95 (0-275-93014-9, B3014) Greenwood.
Axelgard, Frederick W. & Georgetown University Staff. Iraq in Transition: A Political, Economic & Strategic Perspective LC 85-31525. (Special Studies on the Middle East). x, 111 p. 1986. pap. 19.50 (0-7201-1821-2) Continuum.
Axell, Albert. Stalin's War Through the Eyes of His Commanders. LC 97-180025. (Illus.). 224p. 1997. 29.95 (1-85409-402-5, Pub. by Arms & Armour) Sterling.
Axelos, Christos. Die Ontologischen Grundlagen der Freiheitstheorie von Leibniz. LC 72-81544. 385p. (C). 1973. 76.15 (3-11-002221-4) De Gruyter.
Axelrad, Albert S. Call to Conscience: Jews, Judaism, & Conscientious Objection. LC 85-24010. 207p. 1986. pap. 16.95 (0-88125-081-3); text 25.00 (0-88125-092-9) Ktav.
Axelrad, D. R. Stochastic Mechanics of Discrete Media. LC 93-36464. 1993. 174.95 (0-387-57070-5) Spr-Verlag.
Axelrad, D. R. & Muschik, W., eds. Constitutive Laws & Microstructure. (Illus.). ix, 206p. 1988. 62.95 (0-387-18654-9) Spr-Verlag.
— Recent Developments in Micromechanics: Proceedings of the Mini-Symposium on Micromechanics at the CSME Mechanical Engineering Forum 1990, University of Toronto, June 3-9, 1990. viii, 204p. 1991. 59.00 (0-387-53362-1) Spr-Verlag.
Axelrad, E. L. & Emmerling, F. A., eds. Flexible Shells: Theory & Applications. (Illus.). 290p. 1984. 54.95 (0-387-13526-X) Spr-Verlag.
***Axelrad, Lee & Kagan, Robert Allen.** Regulatory Encounters: Multinational Corporations & American Adversarial Legalism. LC 99-57669. Vol. 1. (Illus.). 440p. 2000. 60.00 (0-520-22287-3, Pub. by U CA Pr); pap. 24.95 (0-520-22288-1, Pub. by U CA Pr) Cal Prin Full Svc.
Axelrad, S., jt. ed. see Muensterberger, Werner L.
Axelrad, Sidney, jt. auth. see Brody, Sylvia.
Axelrod. Ace Your Midterms & Final: Introduction to Pysics. (Midterms & Finals Ser.). (Illus.). 318p. 1999. pap. 16.95 (0-07-007010-5) McGraw.
— Ace Your Midterms & Finals: Introduction to Psychology. (Midterms & Finals Ser.). (Illus.). 336p. 1999. pap. 16.95 (0-07-007007-5) McGraw.
— Concise Guide. 2nd ed. 1997. pap. text 20.70 (0-312-18782-3); pap. text 24.85 (0-312-18858-7) St Martin.
— Concise Guide, Chapter 3. 1996. pap. 24.95 (0-312-14936-0) St Martin.
— Concise Guide, Chapter 3. 2nd ed. 1996. pap. text 33.75 (0-312-14944-1) St Martin.
— Concise Guide: Outlooks. 4th ed. 2000. pap. text 38.70 (0-312-13371-5) St Martin.
— Concise Guide: Writer's Reference. 3rd ed. 2000. pap. text 35.65 (0-312-13351-0) St Martin.
— Concise Guide to Writing. 2nd ed. 1995. pap. text 22.70 (0-312-11703-5) St Martin.
Axelrod. Concise Guide to Writing. 2nd ed. LC 95-67053. 286p. 1995. pap. text 32.95 (0-312-11604-7) St Martin.
Axelrod. Foundations of Mathematics: The Big 10 Way. (Midterms & Finals Ser.). (Illus.). 298p. 1999. pap. 16.95 (0-07-007008-3) McGraw.
***Axelrod.** Freefalling & Other Student Essays. 2nd ed. 2000. pap. text 12.95 (0-312-20983-5) St Martin.
Axelrod. Introduction to Biology: The Big 10 Way. (Midterms & Finals Ser.). (Illus.). 340p. 1999. pap. 16.95 (0-07-007009-1) McGraw.
— Pigs Will Be Pigs. (J). 1998. pap. 5.99 (0-87628-989-8) S&S Trade.
— Principles of Economics: The Big 10 Way. LC 99-17542. (Midterms & Finals Ser.). (Illus.). 340p. 1999. pap. 16.95 (0-07-007006-7) McGraw.
— Reading Critically & Writing Well. 4th ed. 1996. pap. text, teacher ed. 22.50 (0-312-11527-X) St Martin.
— Reading Critically & Writing Well: Pocket Style Manual. 1996. pap. text 27.90 (0-312-11709-4) St Martin.
Axelrod. Reading into Writing. 1995. pap. write for info. (0-312-07522-7) St Martin.
Axelrod. Smoking Fine Cigars. 1997. 5.95 (0-7938-0300-4, XY203) TFH Pubns.
— St Martin's Guide to Writing. 4th ed. 1994. pap. text, teacher ed. 2.44 (0-312-11164-9) St Martin.
— Writer Guidebook. 1997. pap. text 24.00 (0-312-19096-4) St Martin.
— Writers Guidebook. 432p. 1998. pap. text 32.95 (0-312-16755-5) St Martin.
***Axelrod & Cooper.** Reading Critically Writing Well: 1999 Mla Update. 5th ed. 1999. pap. text 35.95 (0-312-25029-0) St Martin.
— St Martins Guide Exercises. 1997. pap. text 6.95 (0-312-15360-0) St Martin.
— St Martin's Guide to Writing. 6th ed. 2000. pap. text 46.95 (0-312-20106-0) St Martin.
— St Martin's Guide to Writing Grammar Exercises. 6th ed. pap. text. write for info. (0-312-24807-5) St Martin.
— St Martins Guide to Writing Short. 6th ed. 2000. pap. text 42.95 (0-312-24059-7) St Martin.
— Who Are We? rev. ed. pap. text. write for info. (0-312-25038-X) St Martin.
Axelrod, et al. Management. 4th ed. (C). 1986. student ed. write for info. (0-318-60299-7) Addison-Wesley.
Axelrod, jt. auth. see Phillips.
Axelrod, Herbert R., et al. Dr. Axelrod's Mini Atlas of Freshwater Aquarium Fishes. (Illus.). 992p. 1987. 35.95 (0-86622-385-1, H-1090) TFH Pubns.
Axelrod, Alan. Art of the Golden West. (Illus.). 500p. 1990. 95.00 (1-55859-103-6) Abbeville Pr.
— The Complete Idiot's Guide to American History. LC 96-84620. 352p. 1996. 16.95 (0-02-861275-2) Macmillan Gen Ref.
***Axelrod, Alan.** The Complete Idiot's Guide to the American Revolution. 432p. 1999. pap. text 16.95 (0-02-863379-2) Macmillan.
Axelrod, Alan. Complete Idiot's Guide to the Civil War. LC 97-80981. 407p. 1998. 17.95 (0-02-862122-0) Macmillan Gen Ref.
***Axelrod, Alan.** The Complete Idiot's Guide to 20th Century History. LC 99-62049. (Illus.). 512p. 1999. pap. text 16.95 (0-02-863385-7, Pub. by Macmillan Gen Ref) S&S Trade.
— Elizabeth I CEO: Strategic Lessons from the Leader Who Built an Empire. 288p. 2000. 23.00 (0-7352-0189-7) PH Pr.
— Encyclopedia of Historical Treaties & Alliances. (Illus.). 544p. 2001. 75.00 (0-8160-3090-1) Facts on File.
— Guide to American Treaties & Alliances. LC 00-37902. 450p. 2000. 125.00 (1-56802-440-1) CQ Pr.
Axelrod, Alan. The International Encyclopedia of Secret Societies & Fraternal Orders. 304p. 1998. pap. 18.95 (0-8160-3871-6, Checkmark) Facts on File.
— Jazz. LC 98-87600. (Complete Idiot's Guides (Lifestyle) Ser.). (Illus.). 347p. 1999. pap. 17.95 (0-02-862731-8) Macmillan Gen Ref.
— The Macmillan Dictionary of Military Biography. LC 97-31779. 463p. 1997. 39.95 (0-02-861994-3) Macmillan.
— Miss Nomer's Guide to Painfully Incorrect English. LC 98-217135. 1998. mass mkt. 6.99 (0-425-16422-5) Berkley Pub.
— Patton on Leadership: Strategic Lessons for Corporate Warfare. LC 99-28533. (Illus.). 271p. 1999. text 23.00 (0-7352-0091-2) PH Pr.
— Quick Tips Survival Guide, Vol. S3. 160p. 1997. pap. 32.85 (0-07-913220-0) McGraw.
— 201 Ways to Deal with Difficult People. (Quick-Tip Survival Guides Ser.). 150p. 1997. pap. 10.95 (0-07-006218-8) McGraw.
— 201 Ways to Manage Your Time Better. LC 97-178476. (Quick Tip Survival Guides Ser.). 150p. 1997. pap. 10.95 (0-07-006217-X) McGraw.
— 201 Ways to Say No Effectively & Gracefully. LC 97-178477. (Quick-Tip Survival Guides Ser.). 150p. 1997. pap. 10.95 (0-07-006219-6) McGraw.
— U. S. History: The Big 10 Way. LC 99-24816. (Midterms & Finals Ser.). (Illus.). 336p. 1999. pap. 16.95 (0-07-007005-9) McGraw.
— What Everyone Should Know about the 20th Century: 200 Events That Shaped the World. LC 98-8707. 352p. 1998. pap. text 12.00 (1-58062-066-3) Adams Media.
Axelrod, Alan, comment. Songs of the Wild West. (Illus.). 128p. (YA). (gr. 4 up). 1991. pap. 19.95 (0-671-74775-4) S&S Bks Yung.
Axelrod, Alan & Hicks, Roger. Encyclopedia of Fraternal Orders & Secret Societies. 304p. 1997. lib. bdg. 40.00 (0-8160-2307-7) Facts on File.
Axelrod, Alan & Phillips, Charles. Dictators & Tyrants: Absolute Rulers & Would-Be Rulers in World History. LC 94-6200. (Illus.). 352p. 1994. 45.00 (0-8160-2866-4) Facts on File.
— The Environmentalists: Who's Who in Conservation. LC 92-38773. (Illus.). 272p. 1993. 45.00 (0-8160-2715-3) Facts on File.
— What Every American Should Know about American History: Two Hundred Events That Shaped the Nation. 384p. 1993. pap. 10.95 (1-55850-309-9) Adams Media.
— What Everyone Should Know about the 20th Century: 200 Events That Shaped the World. 300p. 1995. 16.00 (1-55850-506-7) Adams Media.
Axelrod, Alan, et al. Cops, Crooks & Criminologists: An International Biographical Dictionary of Law Enforcement. LC 95-30564. (Illus.). 336p. 1996. 45.00 (0-8160-3016-2) Facts on File.
***Axelrod, Alan, et al.** Cops, Crooks & Criminologists: An International Biographical Dictionary of Law Enforcement. LC 99-462070. 2000. pap. write for info. (0-8160-4145-8) Facts on File.
Axelrod, Alan, et al. The Penguin Dictionary of American Folklore. LC 99-14073. 527p. 2000. 45.00 (0-670-88752-8) Viking Penguin.
***Axelrod, Alan, et al.** Recent Advances & Issues in Astronomy. (Frontiers of Science Ser.). (Illus.). 256p. 2000. 44.95 (1-57356-348-X) Oryx Pr.
Axelrod, Alan, jt. auth. see Phillips, Charles.
Axelrod, Alan, jt. auth. see Player's Club Staff.
Axelrod, Alex, ed. The Quotable Historian. 224p. 2000. 14.95 (0-07-135733-5) McGraw.
***Axelrod, Amy.** The News Hounds Catch a Wave: A Geography Adventure. LC 99-47056. (Illus.). (J). 2001. write for info. (0-689-82410-6) S&S Childrens.
— The News Hounds in the Great Balloon Race: A Geography Adventure. LC 98-47638. (Illus.). 40p. (J). (gr. 1-4). 2000. pap. 13.00 (0-689-82409-2) S&S Childrens.
Axelrod, Amy. Pigs Go to Market: Fun with Math & Shopping. LC 96-25566. (Illus.). 40p. (J). (ps-4). 1999. per. 5.99 (0-689-82553-6, 076714005990) Aladdin.
— Pigs Go to Market: Fun with Math & Shopping. LC 96-25566. (Illus.). 40p. (J). (ps-4). 1997. per. 13.00 (0-689-81069-5) S&S Childrens.
— Pigs in the Pantry: Fun with Math & Cooking. LC 95-30021. (Illus.). 40p. (J). (ps-4). 1999. per. 5.99 (0-689-82555-2, 076714005990) Aladdin.
— Pigs in the Pantry: Fun with Math & Cooking. LC 95-30021. (Illus.). 40p. (J). (ps-4). 1997. 14.00 (0-689-80665-5) S&S Bks Yung.
— Pigs on a Blanket. LC 95-3677. (Illus.). (J). 1996. 15.95 (0-02-707766-7) S&S Bks Yung.
— Pigs on a Blanket. LC 95-3677. (Illus.). 40p. (J). (ps-4). 1996. per. 13.00 (0-689-80505-5) S&S Childrens.
— Pigs on a Blanket: Fun with Math & Time. LC 95-3677. (Illus.). 40p. (J). (ps-3). 1998. per. 5.99 (0-689-82252-9) Aladdin.
— Pigs on the Ball. LC 97-39776. (Illus.). 40p. (J). (gr. 1-3). 1998. mass mkt. 14.00 (0-689-81565-4) S&S Trade.
***Axelrod, Amy.** Pigs on the Ball: Fun with Math & Sports. (Illus.). 40p. (J). (gr. k-3). 2000. per. 5.99 (0-689-83537-X) Aladdin.
Axelrod, Amy. Pigs on the Move. LC 98-19566. (Illus.). 40p. (J). 1999. 14.00 (0-689-81070-9) S&S Bks Yung.
Axelrod, Amy. Pigs Will Be Pigs. LC 93-7640. (Illus.). 40p. (J). (ps-4). 1994. mass mkt. 14.00 (0-02-765415-X, Four Winds Pr) S&S Childrens.
Axelrod, Amy. Pigs Will Be Pigs. (Fun with Math & Money Ser.). 1997. 11.19 (0-606-13706-8, Pub. by Turtleback) Demco.
— Pigs Will be Pigs: Fun with Math & Money. (Illus.). 1997. per. 5.99 (0-689-81219-1) S&S Childrens.
***Axelrod-Contrada, Joan.** The Lizzie Borden "Axe Murder" Trial: A Headline Court Case. (Headline Court Cases Ser.). (Illus.). 104p. (YA). (gr. 6 up). 2000. lib. bdg. 20.95 (0-7660-1422-3) Enslow Pubs.
Axelrod-Contrada, Joan. Women Who Led Nations. LC 98-10958. (Profiles Ser.: Vol. XXVIII). (Illus.). 160p. (YA). (gr. 5-12). 1999. lib. bdg. 18.95 (1-881508-48-X) Oliver Pr MN.
Axelrod, Cooper. St. Martin Guide Writing, Vol. 1. 5th ed. LC 95-73177. 816p. 1997. pap. text 46.95 (0-312-11634-9) St Martin.
Axelrod, Daniel, jt. auth. see Kaku, Michio.
Axelrod, Daniel E. Dreams. (Illus.). 24p. (J). (gr. 1-4). 1991. pap. 6.00 (0-925062-05-7) Writers Ink Pr.
— Staircase Wisdom: New Poems. (Illus.). 54p. 1997. pap. 10.00 (0-925062-12-X) Writers Ink Pr.
Axelrod, Daniel I. Contributions to the Neogene Paleobotany of Central California. LC 80-15355. (University of California Publications in Geological Sciences: No. 121). 224p. 1980. pap. 69.50 (0-7837-7465-6, 204918700010) Bks Demand.
— The Early Miocene Buffalo Canyon Flora of Western Nevada. (Publications in Geological Sciences: Vol. 135). (C). 1991. 35.00 (0-520-09766-1, Pub. by U CA Pr) Cal Prin Full Svc.
***Axelrod, Daniel I.** The Eocene Thunder Mountain Flora of Central Idaho. LC 97-34727. (University of California Publications in Geological Sciences). 1998. pap. 15.00 (0-520-09823-4, Pub. by U CA Pr) Cal Prin Full Svc.
Axelrod, Daniel I. History of the Maritime Closed-Cone Pines, Alta & Baja, California. LC 80-51200. (University of California Publications in Social Welfare: No. 120). (Illus.). 153p. reprint ed. pap. 47.50 (0-608-17444-0, 202987500066) Bks Demand.
— The Late Oligocene Creede Flora, Colorado. LC 87-14300. (University of California Publications in Entomology: No. 130). 247p. (Orig.). 1987. pap. 76.60 (0-7837-7468-0, 204919000010) Bks Demand.
— The Middle Miocene Pyramid Flora of Western Nevada. (Publications in Geological Sciences: Vol. 137). (C). 1993. pap. 19.95 (0-520-09776-9, Pub. by U CA Pr) Cal Prin Full Svc.
— Miocene Floras from the Middlegate Basin, West-Central Nevada. LC 84-2414. (University of California Publications in Entomology: No. 129). 311p. 1985. pap. 96.50 (0-7837-7467-2, 204918900010) Bks Demand.
— The Miocene Purple Mountain Flora of Western Nevada. LC 94-32291. (University of California Publications in Geological Sciences Ser.: No. 139). 1995. 16.95 (0-520-09797-1, Pub. by U CA Pr) Cal Prin Full Svc.
***Axelrod, Daniel I.** A Miocene (10-12 MA) Evergreen Laurel-Oak Forest from Carmel Valley, California. LC 00-21952. (Publications in Geological Sciences: Vol. 145). (Illus.). 36p. 2000. pap. 13.00 (0-520-09839-0, Pub. by U CA Pr) Cal Prin Full Svc.
Axelrod, Daniel I. New Pleistocene Conifer Records, Coastal California. 2nd ed. LC 83-6874. (University of California Publications in Geological Sciences: No. 127). 122p. 1983. pap. 37.90 (0-7837-7466-4, 204918800010) Bks Demand.
— The Oligocene Haynes Creek Flora of Eastern Idaho. LC 98-6394. (Publications in Geological Sciences). 160p. 1998. pap. 22.00 (0-520-09824-2, Pub. by U CA Pr) Cal Prin Full Svc.
— Role of Volcanism in Climate & Evolution. fac. ed. LC 81-80345. (Geological Society of America, Special Paper: No. 185). (Illus.). 62p. 1981. reprint ed. pap. 30.00 (0-7837-7940-2, 204769600008) Bks Demand.
Axelrod, David. Jerusalem of Grass. Burmaster, Orvis C., ed. LC 92-72095. (Ahsahta Press Modern & Contemporary Poets of the West Ser.). 60p. (Orig.). 1992. pap. 6.95 (0-916272-53-2) Ahsahta Pr.
— White Lies. Iddings, Kathleen, ed. LC 87-83063. (Illus.). 48p. (Orig.). 1988. per. write for info. (0-931721-08-3) La Jolla Poets.
Axelrod, David, et al. Risings: An Anthology. Voege, Jeanne, ed. (Illus.). 48p. 1991. pap. text 6.00 (0-9616160-5-9) Bench Pr NY.
Axelrod, David B. The Chi of Poetry: New & Selected Poems, 1960-1995. Kennedy, X. J., ed. & pref. by. (Illus.). 248p. 1995. pap. 20.00 (1-878173-08-1) Writers Ink Pr.
— A Dream of Feet. LC 76-21123. (Poetry Ser.). (Illus.). (J). 1976. pap. 7.50 (0-89304-007-X) Cross-Cultrl NY.
— A Dream of Feet. deluxe limited ed. LC 76-21123. (Poetry Ser.). (Illus.). 1976. 15.00 (0-89304-042-8) Cross-Cultrl NY.
— Home Remedies: New & Selected Poems, 1961-1981. 2nd ed. Barkan, Stanley H., ed. LC 81-69433. (Illus.). 174p. 1982. 20.00 (0-89304-051-7, CCC-145); pap. 10.00 (0-89304-052-5, CCC-145) Cross-Cultrl NY.
— Love in the Keys. 3rd ed. 28p. 1991. pap. 6.00 (0-925062-17-0) Writers Ink Pr.
— The Man Who Fell in Love with a Chicken. Barkan, Stanley H., ed. (Cross-Cultural Review Chapbook Ser.: No. 2). 16p. 1980. 15.00 (0-89304-825-9, CCC127); pap. 5.00 (0-89304-801-1); audio 10.00 (0-89304-826-7) Cross-Cultrl NY.
— Meeting with David B. Axelrod & Gnazino Russo. Scammacca, Nat, ed. & tr. by. LC 79-90012. (Sicilian Antigruppo Ser.: No. 3). (Illus.). 1979. 15.00 (0-89304-505-5); pap. 5.00 (0-89304-507-1) Cross-Cultrl NY.
— Meeting with David B. Axelrod & Gnazino Russo. deluxe limited ed. Scammacca, Nat, ed. & tr. by. LC 79-90012. (Sicilian Antigruppo Ser.: No. 3). (Illus.). 1979. 20.00 (0-89304-506-3) Cross-Cultrl NY.
— Myths, Dreams & Dances: Poems, 1968-1973. (Illus.). 110p. 1974. pap. 12.00 (0-925062-31-6); pap. 8.00 (0-925062-33-2) Writers Ink Pr.
— Perpetual Calendar of Poems: With Twelve Signed Prints. deluxe limited ed. Scammacca, Nina et al, trs. (Illus.). 31p. 1989. 100.00 (0-89304-533-0) Cross-Cultrl NY.
— Resurrections. 118p. 1989. 20.00 (0-685-49063-7); pap. 10.00 (0-685-49064-5) Cross-Cultrl NY.
— The Universal Language. 30p. (Orig.). (C). 1993. pap. text 6.00 (1-878173-30-8) Birnham Wood.
Axelrod, David B. & Pero, Robert. Stills from a Cinema: Poems, 1964-1968. 2nd ed. (Illus.). 62p. 1971. 30.00 (0-925062-36-7); pap. 25.00 (0-925062-37-5) Writers Ink Pr.
Axelrod, David B., et al. Starting from Paumanok: Five Long Island Poets. 118p. 1971. 30.00 (0-925062-34-0); pap. 20.00 (0-925062-35-9) Writers Ink Pr.
Axelrod, David B., ed. see Norton, Anthony R.
Axelrod, David B., ed. see Wallace, George.
Axelrod, David B., ed. & pref. see Levine, Marvin.
Axelrod, David B., ed. & pref. see Opyr, Linda.
Axelrod, Donald. The Shadow Government: The Hidden World of Public Authorities. LC 91-44086. 352p. 1992. 24.95 (0-471-52767-X) Wiley.
Axelrod, H., et al. Exotic Tropical Fishes. rev. ed. (Illus.). 1302p. 1980. 49.95 (0-87666-537-7, H-1028L) TFH Pubns.
Axelrod, H. R. Designing Your Garden Pond. 64p. 1997. 12.95 (0-7938-0219-9) TFH Pubns.
Axelrod, H. R., et al. The Completely Illustrated Guide to Koi for Your Pond. (Illus.). 320p. 1996. 59.95 (0-7938-0597-X, TS268) TFH Pubns.
Axelrod, Herbert. Adopting a Dog. (Cats & Dogs). (Illus.). 84p. (YA). (gr. 3 up). 1999. 19.95 (0-7910-4813-6) Chelsea Hse.
— Aquariums for Those Who Care. (Illus.). 32p. 1994. pap. 4.95 (0-7938-1375-1, B101) TFH Pubns.
— Feline Behavior. (Cats & Dogs). (Illus.). 84p. (YA). (gr. 3 up). 1999. 19.95 (0-7910-4810-1) Chelsea Hse.
— Housebreaking & Other Puppy Problems. LC 97-29340. (Cats & Dogs). (Illus.). 84p. (YA). (gr. 3 up). 1999. 19.95 (0-7910-4818-7) Chelsea Hse.
— The Myth & Magic of Cats. (Cats & Dogs). (Illus.). 84p. (YA). (gr. 3 up). 1999. 19.95 (0-7910-4808-X) Chelsea Hse.
— The Perfect Retriever. (Cats & Dogs). (Illus.). 84p. (YA). (gr. 3 up). 1999. 19.95 (0-7910-4814-4) Chelsea Hse.
— Persians. (Cats & Dogs). (Illus.). 84p. (YA). (gr. 3 up). 1999. 19.95 (0-7910-4809-8) Chelsea Hse.
— Skin & Coat Care for Dogs. LC 98-198520. (Cats & Dogs). (Illus.). 84p. (YA). (gr. 3 up). 1999. 19.95 (0-7910-4815-2) Chelsea Hse.
— Skin Care for Cats. (Cats & Dogs). (Illus.). 84p. (YA). (gr. 3 up). 1999. lib. bdg. 19.95 (0-7910-4807-1) Chelsea Hse.
— Training Older Dogs. (Cats & Dogs). (Illus.). 84p. (YA). (gr. 3 up). 1999. 19.95 (0-7910-4817-9) Chelsea Hse.
— Traveling with Dogs. (Cats & Dogs). (Illus.). 84p. (YA). (gr. 3 up). 1999. 19.95 (0-7910-4816-0) Chelsea Hse.
— You & Your Puppy. (Cats & Dogs). (Illus.). 84p. (YA). (gr. 3 up). 1999. lib. bdg. 19.95 (0-7910-4823-3) Chelsea Hse.
— Your First Tropical Fish. (Illus.). 32p. 1992. pap. 2.29 (0-86622-104-2, YF116) TFH Pubns.
— Your Healthy Puppy. (Cats & Dogs). (Illus.). 84p. (YA). (gr. 3 up). 1999. lib. bdg. 19.95 (0-7910-4820-9) Chelsea Hse.
Axelrod, Herbert & Vorderwinkler, William. Goldfish & Koi in Your Home. rev. ed. (Illus.). 208p. 1985. 17.95 (0-86622-636-2, H-909) TFH Pubns.
Axelrod, Herbert R. African Cichlids of Lakes Malawi & Tanganyika. (Illus.). 384p. 1988. 29.95 (0-86622-856-X, PS-703) TFH Pubns.
— Aquarium Setting Up. (Illus.). 64p. (YA). (gr. 3 up). 1999. lib. bdg. 17.95 (0-7910-5087-4) Chelsea Hse.
— Breeding Aquarium Fishes: A Complete Introduction. (Complete Introduction to...Ser.). (Illus.). 128p. (Orig.). 1987. pap. 8.95 (0-86622-294-4, CO007S) TFH Pubns.
— Cichlid Lexicon. (TS Ser.). (Illus.). 1888p. 1993. 100.00 (0-86622-422-X, TS-190) TFH Pubns.
— A Complete Introduction to Community Aquariums. (Illus.). 128p. 1987. pap. 8.95 (0-86622-283-9, CO013S) TFH Pubns.
— A Complete Introduction to Koi & Garden Ponds. rev. ed. (Complete Introduction to...Ser.). (Illus.). 96p. (Orig.). 1998. pap. 8.95 (0-86622-399-1, CO-040S) TFH Pubns.
— Designing Your Garden Pond. (Illus.). 64p. 1998. pap. text 12.95 (0-7938-0220-2, WW-054) TFH Pubns.
— Dr. Axelrod's Atlas of Tropical Freshwater Aquarium Fishes. 9th ed. LC 99-172616. (Illus.). 1168p. 1997. 99.95 (0-7938-0033-1, H1077) TFH Pubns.

Axelrod, Herbert R. Dr. Axelrod's Atlas of Freshwater Aquarium Fishes LC 85-184618. 780p. 1985. write for info. (*0-86622-052-6*) TFH Pubns.

— Dr. Axelrod's Atlas of Freshwater Aquarium Fishes 2nd ed. LC 89-133461. 782p. 1986. write for info. (*0-86622-139-5*) TFH Pubns.

Axelrod, Herbert R. Exotic Marine Fish. 608p. 1989. 29.95 (*0-86622-744-X*, H938) TFH Pubns.

— Fishes for Community Tank. 32p. pap. 1.79 (*0-87666-072-3*) TFH Pubns.

— A Guide to Corals for the Mini Reef Aquarium. (Illus.). 96p. 1997. pap. 19.95 (*0-7938-0505-8*, TS-301) TFH Pubns.

— A Guide to the Selection, Care & Breeding of Corals for the Mini-Reef Aquarium. (Illus.). 288p. 1997. 39.95 (*0-7938-0500-7*, TS294) TFH Pubns.

— Healthy Pond Fish: A Complete Authoritative Guide. 64p. 1998. 12.95 (*0-7938-0343-8*) TFH Pubns.

— Jumbo Fishes for the Large Aquarium. (TS Ser.). (Illus.). 352p. 1992. text 47.95 (*0-86622-348-7*, TS-177) TFH Pubns.

— KOI Varieties. (Illus.). 144p. 1998. 23.95 (*0-86622-162-X*, PS-875) TFH Pubns.

— Lexicon of Cichlids. 2nd ed. (TS Ser.). (Illus.). 864p. 1993. 100.00 (*0-7938-0026-9*, TS-190) TFH Pubns.

— Salamanders & Newts. (Illus.). 32p. pap. 1.79 (*0-87666-222-X*, A-315) TFH Pubns.

— Setting up Your First Aquarium. (Setting up your first Aquarium). 32p. pap. 1.79 (*0-87666-011-1*) TFH Pubns.

— Starting Your Tropical Aquarium. (Illus.). 288p. 1986. 11.95 (*0-86622-697-4*, PS-840) TFH Pubns.

— Stocking Your Garden Pond. (Illus.). 64p. 1997. 12.95 (*0-7938-0221-0*, WW-055) TFH Pubns.

— Tropical Fish. (Illus.). 96p. 1988. 9.95 (*0-87666-510-5*, KW-020) TFH Pubns.

— Tropical Fish As a New Pet. (Illus.). 64p. 1991. pap. 6.95 (*0-86622-532-3*, TU-020) TFH Pubns.

— Tropical Fish for Those Who Care. (Illus.). 32p. 1994. pap. 4.95 (*0-7938-1379-4*, B102) TFH Pubns.

Axelrod, Herbert R. & Burgess, Warren E. Freshwater Angelfish. (Illus.). 96p. 1979. 9.95 (*0-86622-765-2*, KW-048) TFH Pubns.

— Marine Fishes. (Illus.). 96p. 1979. 9.95 (*0-87666-513-X*, KW-031) TFH Pubns.

— Saltwater Aquarium Fishes. (Illus.). 288p. 1992. 23.95 (*0-86622-499-8*, H-914) TFH Pubns.

Axelrod, Herbert R. & Gordon, Myron. Swordtails: Keeping & Breeding Them in Captivity. (Illus.). 64p. 1997. pap. 6.95 (*0-7938-0365-9*, RE-616) TFH Pubns.

Axelrod, Herbert R. & Schultz, Leonard P. Handbook of Tropical Aquarium Fishes. rev. ed. (Illus.). 718p. 1989. 11.95 (*0-86622-138-7*, PS-663) TFH Pubns.

Axelrod, Herbert R. & Vorderwinkler, William. Encyclopedia of Tropical Fish. 631p. 1995. 19.95 (*0-7938-1288-7*, H-905) TFH Pubns.

Axelrod, Herbert R. & Wischnath, Lothar. Swordtails & Platies. (Illus.). 192p. 1991. text 79.95 (*0-86622-090-9*, TS-131) TFH Pubns.

Axelrod, Herbert R., et al. Aquarium Fishes of the World. (Illus.). 1019p. 1998. 29.95 (*0-7938-0493-0*, TS292) TFH Pubns.

— The Atlas of Discus of the World. (TS Ser.). (Illus.). 368p. 1991. text 100.00 (*0-86622-543-9*, TS-164) TFH Pubns.

— The Atlas of Garden Ponds. (Illus.). 272p. 1992. text 59.95 (*0-86622-343-6*, TS178) TFH Pubns.

— Exotic Marine Fish. ring bd. 35.95 (*0-87666-103-7*, H938L) TFH Pubns.

— Exotic Tropical Fishes. expanded ed. (Illus.). 1312p. 1996. 39.95 (*0-7938-0027-7*, H1028) TFH Pubns.

Axelrod, Herbert R., jt. auth. see Vriends, Matthew M.

Axelrod, Herbert R., jt. auth. see Walker, Braz.

Axelrod, Herbert R., ed. see Untergasser, Dieter.

Axelrod, Herman, jt. auth. see Bachrach, Kalman.

Axelrod, Herman C. Bilingual Background & Its Relation to Certain Aspects of Character & Responsibility of Elementary School Children. Cordasco, Francesco, ed. LC 77-90406. (Bilingual-Bicultural Education in the U. S. Ser.). 1979. lib. bdg. 23.95 (*0-405-11075-8*) Ayer.

Axelrod, Jerold L. Architectural Plans for Adding on or Remodeling. 336p. 1992. pap. 19.95 (*0-07-157844-7*) McGraw.

— Architectural Plans for Adding on or Remodeling. 336p. 1992. 26.95 (*0-8306-3930-6*, 2803); pap. 19.95 (*0-8306-3929-2*, 2803) McGraw-Hill Prof.

— Dream Homes: Sixty-Six Plans to Make Your Dreams Come True. 1987. 29.95 (*0-8306-2129-6*, 2829) McGraw-Hill Prof.

***Axelrod, Jerold L.** Time-Saver Standards Concise Plans for Adding on & Remodeling. (Time-Saver Concise Ser.). (Illus.). 400p. 2000. pap. 54.95 (*0-07-135236-8*) McGraw-Hill Prof.

Axelrod, Joeseph. College & Character. Sanford, R. Nevitt, ed. 1979. pap. 11.95 (*0-917430-01-8*) Montaigne.

Axelrod, Joseph. The University Teacher As Artist. LC 73-3773. (Jossey-Bass Higher Education Ser.). 262p. reprint ed. pap. 81.30 (*0-608-15027-4*, 205215900045) Bks Demand.

Axelrod, Joseph, et al. Search for Relevance: The Campus in Crisis. LC 72-75941. (Jossey-Bass Higher Education Ser.). 256p. reprint ed. 79.40 (*0-8357-9346-X*, 201394600087) Bks Demand.

Axelrod, Karen, jt. auth. see Brumberg, Bruce.

Axelrod, Lauryn. TV-Proof Your Kids: A Parent's Guide to Safe & Healthy Viewing. LC 97-12069. 256p. 1997. 12.00 (*1-55972-408-0*, Birch Ln Pr) Carol Pub Group.

Axelrod, Lawrence. Saudi Oil Policy. (C). 1996. pap. text 39.95 (*0-8133-8423-0*) Westview.

Axelrod, M. Creative Timed Writings. 1975. text 13.56 (*0-07-002610-6*) McGraw.

Axelrod, Mark. Bombay California: Hollywood, Somewhere West of Vine. (Illus.). 382p. (Orig.). 1994. pap. 14.95 (*0-944870-06-6*) Pacific Writers Pr.

— Cardboard Castles. 232p. 1996. pap. 15.95 (*0-944870-08-2*) Pacific Writers Pr.

Axelrod, Melissa. The Semantics of Time: Aspectual Categorization in Koyukon Athabaskan. LC 92-42719. (Studies in the Anthropology of North American Indians). xii, 200p. 1993. text 55.00 (*0-8032-1032-9*) U of Nebr Pr.

Axelrod, Michelle, ed. see Dobkin, Jeffrey.

***Axelrod, Mitch.** Beatletoons: The Real Story Behind the Cartoon Beatles. Wincentsen, Edward, ed. LC 99-73872. (Illus.). 206p. 1999. pap. 22.95 (*0-9642808-7-6*) Wynn Pubng.

Axelrod, Mitch. Beatletoons: The Story Behind the Cartoon Beatles. (Illus.). 160p. (Orig.). 1996. pap. 18.95 (*0-9642808-2-5*) Wynn Pubng.

Axelrod, Nancy R. The Chief Executive's Role in Developing the Nonprofit Board. (Nonprofit Governance Ser.: No. 2). 16p. 1992. reprint ed. pap. text 12.00 (*0-925299-01-4*) Natl Ctr Nonprofit.

— Creating & Renewing Advisory Boards: Strategies for Success. rev. ed. (Committee Ser.: No. 09 a). 1998. reprint ed. pap. text 12.00 (*0-925299-13-8*) Natl Ctr Nonprofit.

— O Papel do Director Executivo no Desenvoluimento do Conselho Director.Tr. of Chief Executive's Role in Developing the Nonprofit Board. (POR.). 16p. (Orig.). 1996. pap. write for info. (*0-925299-66-9*) Natl Ctr Nonprofit.

Axelrod, Nathan. Executive Leadership. 1969. teacher ed. 6.67 (*0-672-96055-9*, Bobbs); pap. text 10.95 (*0-672-96054-0*, Bobbs) Macmillan.

— Selected Cases in Fashion Marketing, 2 vols. 3rd ed. 1968. pap. write for info. (*0-318-51118-5*) Macmillan.

— Selected Cases in Fashion Marketing, 2 vols., 2. 3rd ed. 1968. pap. write for info. (*0-672-96038-9*) Macmillan.

Axelrod, Paul. Making a Middle Class: Student Life in English Canada during the Thirties. 304p. (C). 1990. text 55.00 (*0-7735-0753-1*, Pub. by McG-Queens Univ Pr) CUP Services.

— The Promise of Schooling: Education in Canada, 1800-1914. LC 97-159155. (Themes in Canadian Social History Ser.). 155p. 1997. text 45.00 (*0-8020-0825-9*, LA411) U of Toronto Pr.

— Scholars & Dollars: Politics, Economics, & the Universities of Ontario 1945-1980. (State & Economic Life Ser.). 388p. 1982. pap. text 17.95 (*0-8020-6492-2*) U of Toronto Pr.

Axelrod, Paul & Reid, John G., eds. Youth, University, & Canadian Society: Essays in the Social History of Higher Education. 416p. (C). 1989. text 65.00 (*0-7735-0685-3*, Pub. by McG-Queens Univ Pr) CUP Services.

— Youth, University & Canadian Society: Essays in the Social History of Higher Education. 416p. (C). 1989. pap. text 24.95 (*0-7735-0709-4*, Pub. by McG-Queens Univ Pr) CUP Services.

Axelrod, Regina S., jt. ed. see Vig, Norman J.

***Axelrod, Richard H.** Terms of Engagement: Changing the Way We Change Our Organizations. LC 99-44009. 220p. 2000. text 29.95 (*1-57675-084-1*, Pub. by Berrett-Koehler) Publishers Group.

Axelrod, Rise B. The Concise Guide to Writing. 2nd ed. 1995. pap. text 5.00 (*0-312-11704-3*) St Martin.

— Who Are We? Readings on identity, community, work & career. LC 97-65638. 1997. pap. text 13.95 (*0-312-15717-7*) St Martin.

Axelrod, Rise B. & Cooper, Charles R. The St. Martin's Guide to Writing. LC 95-73176. 704p. 1997. pap. text 42.95 (*0-312-13326-X*) St Martin.

— The St. Martin's Guide to Writing: Shorter Version. 3rd ed. 611p. (C). 1991. teacher ed. write for info. (*0-318-68120-X*) St Martin.

Axelrod, Robert. The Evolution of Cooperation. LC 83-45255. 252p. 1985. pap. 18.00 (*0-465-02121-2*, Pub. by Basic) HarpC.

***Axelrod, Robert & Cohen, Michael D.** Harnessing Complexity: Organizational Implications of a Scientific Frontier. LC 99-58063. 208p. 2000. 25.50 (*0-684-86717-6*) Free Pr.

Axelrod, Robert M. The Complexity of Cooperation: Agent-Based Models of Competition & Collaboration. LC 97-1107. (Princeton Studies in Complexity). 248p. 1997. text 49.50 (*0-691-01568-6*, Pub. by Princeton U Pr); pap. text 18.95 (*0-691-01567-8*, Pub. by Princeton U Pr) Cal Prin Full Svc.

Axelrod, Robert M., ed. The Structure of Decision: The Cognitive Maps of Political Elites; Written under the Auspices of the Institute of International Studies, University of California (Berkeley) & the Institute of Public Policy Studies, the University of Michigan. LC 76-3242. (Illus.). 421p. reprint ed. pap. 130.60 (*0-8357-3852-3*, 203658500004) Bks Demand.

Axelrod, Saul. Behavior Modification for the Classroom Teacher. 2nd ed. (Illus.). 272p. (C). 1983. 57.19 (*0-07-002572-X*) McGraw.

— How to Use Group Contingencies. 2nd ed. LC 97-43042. (How to Manage Behavior Ser.). 1998. pap. text 8.00 (*0-89079-760-9*, 8672) PRO-ED.

***Axelrod, Saul & Hall, R. Vance.** Behavior Modification: Basic Principles. 2nd ed. LC 98-30834. (Managing Behavior Ser.). ix, 83 p. 1999. write for info. (*0-89079-804-4*) PRO-ED.

Axelrod, Saul, jt. auth. see Rolider, Amos.

Axelrod, Saul, jt. ed. see Van Houten, R.

Axelrod, Stephen Gould. The Critical Response to Robert Lowell, 33. LC 99-11307. (Critical Responses in Arts & Letters Ser.: Vol. 33). 344p. 1999. lib. bdg. 75.00 (*0-313-29037-7*) Greenwood.

Axelrod, Steven D. Work & the Evolving Self: Theoretical & Clinical Considerations. LC 98-48420. 176p. 1999. 29.95 (*0-88163-207-4*) Analytic Pr.

Axelrod, Steven G., et al, eds. Robert Lowell: Essays on the Poetry. (Cambridge Studies in American Literature & Culture: No. 29). (Illus.). 296p. 1989. pap. text 24.95 (*0-521-37803-6*) Cambridge U Pr.

Axelrod, Steven G. & Deese, Helen, eds. Critical Essays on Wallace Stevens. (Critical Essays Ser.). 272p. 1988. 47.00 (*0-8161-8886-6*, G K Hall & Co) Mac Lib Ref.

Axelrod, Steven G., jt. auth. see Deese, Helen.

Axelrod, Terry S. Fractures of the Wrist & Hand. 112p. 1997. 69.00 (*3-540-61811-2*) Spr-Verlag.

***Axelrod, Terry S.** Raising More Money: A Step by Step Guide to Building Lifelong Donors. LC 00-131777. 205p. 2000. 36.95 (*0-9700455-4-9*) Boylston Bks.

***Axelrod, Toby.** Hans & Sophie Scholl: German Resisters of the White Rose. LC 00-8780. (Holocaust Biographies Ser.). 2000. lib. bdg. write for info. (*0-8239-3316-4*) Rosen Group.

Axelrod, Toby. Working Together Against Teen Suicide. LC 95-6960. (Library of Social Activism). (Illus.). 64p. (YA). (gr. 7-12). 1996. lib. bdg. 16.95 (*0-8239-2261-8*) Rosen Group.

***Axelrod, Victoria G., ed.** American Management Association Handbook of Best Practices in Management. 544p. 2000. 75.00 (*0-8144-0575-4*) AMACOM.

Axelrod, Warren C. Computer Productivity: A Planning Guide for Cost-Effective Management. 255p. 1982. 24.95 (*0-318-17049-3*) AITP.

Axelsen, Jenny, jt. auth. see Axelsen, Stephen.

Axelsen, Jens. Danish-English Dictionary, Dansk-Engelsk Ordbog. (DAN & ENG.). Date not set. 67.95 (*0-7859-9595-1*) Fr & Eur.

— Dansk - Engelsk Rode Ordboger. 9th ed. (DAN & ENG.). 656p. 1984. 49.95 (*0-7859-6515-7*) Fr & Eur.

— Dansk-Engelsk, Engelsk-Dansk Rode Ordboger. 11th ed. (DAN & ENG.). 631p. 1988. 49.95 (*0-7859-6517-3*); disk 225.00 (*0-7859-6516-5*) Fr & Eur.

— Dansk-Engelsk Ordbog - Danish-English Dictionary. (DAN & ENG.). 1040p. 1995. 50.00 (*87-01-42494-7*) IBD Ltd.

Axelsen, Stephen & Axelsen, Jenny. Little Sisters. LC 92-34261. (Voyages Ser.). (Illus.). (J). 1993. 4.25 (*0-383-03637-2*) SRA McGraw.

Axelson. Counseling & Development in a Multicultural Society. 3rd ed. LC 98-4779. (Counseling Ser.). 1998. pap. 67.95 (*0-534-34490-9*) Brooks-Cole.

Axelson-Berry, Kitty, ed. see Bernstein, Steve.

Axelson-Berry, Kitty, ed. see Bynum, Edward Bruce, et al.

Axelson, Donna. Multimedia Projects. 80p. (J). (gr. 3-5). 1997. pap. 9.95 (*1-55734-513-9*) Tchr Create Mat.

Axelson, Edith F. A Guide to Episcopal Church Records in Virginia. LC 89-7310. 170p. 1988. pap. 15.95 (*0-935931-45-7*) Iberian Pub.

Axelson, J. Danish-English Dictionary: Rode Ordbog - Gyldendals. 9th ed.Tr. of Rode Ordbog-Gyldendals. (DAN & ENG.). 1991. 47.00 (*0-7859-8928-5*) Fr & Eur.

— English-Danish. 11th ed. 580p. 1990. reprint ed. 49.50 (*87-00-09312-2*) IBD Ltd.

— English-Danish Dictionary. 11th ed. (DAN & ENG.). 1990. 47.00 (*0-7859-8951-X*) Fr & Eur.

Axelson, Jan. The Microcontroller Idea Book: Circuits, Programs & Applications Featuring the 8052-Basic Single-Chip Computer. (Illus.). 277p. (Orig.). 1997. pap. 31.95 (*0-9650819-0-7*) Lakeview Res.

— Parallel Port Complete: Programming, Interfacing & Using the PC's Parallel Printer Port. LC 97-150463. (Illus.). 343p. (Orig.). 1997. pap. 39.95 (*0-9650819-1-5*) Lakeview Res.

— Serial Port Complete: Programming & Circuits for RS-232 & RS-485 Links & Networks. LC 98-216433. (Illus.). 304p. 1998. pap. 39.95 (*0-9650819-2-3*) Lakeview Res.

— USB Complete: Everything You Need to Develop Custom USB Peripherals. (Illus.). 396p. 1999. pap. 49.95 (*0-9650819-3-1*, Pub. by Lakeview Res) IPG Chicago.

Axelson, Janet L. Making Printed Circuit Boards. 352p. 1993. pap. 22.95 (*0-07-002799-4*) McGraw.

— Making Printed Circuit Boards. LC 93-9149. 1993. text 29.95 (*0-8306-3950-0*); pap. text 19.95 (*0-8306-3951-9*) McGraw-Hill Prof.

Axelson, John A. Counseling & Development in a Multicultural Society. LC 85-5920. (Counseling-Psychology Ser.). 462p. (C). 1985. pap. 37.75 (*0-534-04974-5*) Brooks-Cole.

— Counseling & Development in a Multicultural Society. 2nd ed. LC 92-26095. 498p. 1993. 46.50 (*0-534-19902-X*) Brooks-Cole.

Axelson, John A., jt. auth. see McGrath, Patrick.

Axelson, M. L. & Brinberg, D. A Social-Psychological Perspective on Food-Related Behavior. (Recent Research in Psychology Ser.). (Illus.). viii, 190p. 1989. 78.95 (*0-387-97095-9*) Spr-Verlag.

Axelson, Peter, et al. A Guide to Wheelchair Selection: How to Use the ANSI-RESNA Wheelchair Standards to Buy a Wheelchair. (Illus.). (Orig.). 1994. pap. write for info. (*0-929819-06-3*) Paralyzed Vets.

Axelsson, Alf, et al, eds. Scientific Basis of Noise-Induced Hearing Loss. LC 95-45011. 472p. 1995. 87.00 (*0-86577-596-6*) Thieme Med Pubs.

Axelsson, Arne. The Links in the Chain: Isolation & Interdependence in Nathaniel Hawthorne's Fictional Characters. (Studia Anglistica Upsaliensia Ser.: No. 17). 190p. (Orig.). 1974. pap. 27.50 (*91-554-0124-4*, Pub. by Uppsala Univ Acta Univ Uppsaliensis) Coronet Bks.

— Restrained Response: American Novels of the Cold War & Korea, 1945-1962, 97. LC 89-11907. (Contributions in American Studies: No. 97). 239p. 1990. 62.95 (*0-313-26291-8*, AXR/, Greenwood Pr) Greenwood.

Axelsson, Lars E. The Lord Rose up from Seir: Studies in the History & Tradition of the Negev & Southern Judah. (Coniectanea Biblica. Old Testament Ser.: No. 25). 210p. (Orig.). 1987. pap. text 48.00 (*91-22-00876-4*) Coronet Bks.

Axelsson, Margareta W. Contraction in British Newspapers in the Late 20th Century. LC 98-171198. (Studia Anglistica Upsaliensia Ser.: Vol. 102). 270p. 1998. pap. 53.50 (*91-554-4176-9*) Coronet Bks.

Axelsson, O. Iterative Solution Methods. (Illus.). 667p. 1996. pap. text 31.95 (*0-521-55569-8*) Cambridge U Pr.

Axelsson, O. & Kolotilina, L. Y., eds. Preconditioned Conjugate Gradient Methods: Proceedings of a Conference Held in Nijmegen, The Netherlands, June 19-21, 1989. (Lecture Notes in Mathematics Ser.: Vol. 1457). v, 196p. 1991. 41.95 (*0-387-53515-2*) Spr-Verlag.

***Axelsson, Per.** Diagnosis & Risk Prediction of Dental Caries. LC 99-55485. (Series on Preventive Dentistry). (Illus.). 2000. write for info. (*0-86715-362-8*) Quint Pub Co.

— An Introduction to Risk Prediction & Preventive Dentistry. LC 99-16511. (Axelsson Series on Preventive Dentistry : Vol. 1). 159p. 2000. pap. 58.00 (*0-86715-361-X*) Quint Pub Co.

Axelsson, Rune. Upper Secondary School in Retrospect: The View of Former Students. (Uppsala Studies in Education: No. 30). 223p. (Orig.). 1989. pap. 46.50 (*91-554-2400-7*) Coronet Bks.

Axen, D., et al, eds. The Vancouver Meeting: Particles & Fields '91, 2 vols. 1000p. (C). 1991. text 164.00 (*981-02-0768-9*) World Scientific Pub.

Axen, Kathleen, jt. auth. see Axen, Kenneth.

Axen, Kenneth & Axen, Kathleen. Physiology Coloring Book. 1997. pap. 18.00 (*0-679-77850-0*) Random.

Axen, Kenneth, jt. auth. see Haas, Francois.

Axenrod, T. & Ceccarelli, G., eds. NMR in Living Systems. 1986. text 186.00 (*90-277-2174-2*) Kluwer Academic.

Axford, Barrie. The Global System: Politics, Economics & Culture. LC 95-34537. 265p. 1995. pap. 19.95 (*0-312-15829-7*); text 65.00 (*0-312-15828-9*) St Martin.

Axford, Barry & Browning, Gary. Politics: An Introduction. LC 97-180623. 512p. (C). 1997. 90.00 (*0-415-11074-2*) Routledge.

Axford, Barry, et al. Politics: An Introduction. LC 97-180623. 512p. (C). 1997. pap. 24.99 (*0-415-11075-0*) Routledge.

***Axford, Elizabeth C.** Merry Christmas Happy Hanukkah: A Multilingual Songbook & CD, Vol. 1. LC 99-93461. (ENG, HEB & SPA.). 112p. 1999. pap. 24.95 incl. audio compact disk (*0-9673325-0-8*, PP1001) Piano Pr.

Axford, Elizabeth C. Traditional World Music Influences in Contemporary Solo Piano Literature: A Selected Bibliographic Survey & Review. LC 97-19901. 1997. 55.00 (*0-8108-3380-8*) Scarecrow.

Axford, J., jt. auth. see Spector, T. D.

Axford, J. S. & Rees, D. H. Lyme Borreliosis. (NATO ASI Ser.: Vol. 260). (Illus.). 344p. (C). 1994. text 115.00 (*0-306-44664-2*, Kluwer Plenum) Kluwer Academic.

Axford, J. S., jt. auth. see Alavi, A.

Axford, John S., ed. Glycoimmunology 2: Proceedings of the Fourth Jenner International Glycoimmunology Meeting Held in Loutraki, Greece, November 12-15, 1996. LC 97-50383. (Advances in Experimental Medicine & Biology Ser.: Vol. 435). (Illus.). 280p. 1998. 95.00 (*0-306-45777-6*, Kluwer Plenum) Kluwer Academic.

— Medicine. (Essentials Ser.). (Illus.). 800p. 1996. 69.95 (*0-632-02707-X*) Blackwell Sci.

Axford, R. F. E., et al, eds. Breeding for Disease Resistance in Farm Animals. 2nd ed. LC 99-27340. (CABI Publishing Ser.). 550p. 2000. text 140.00 (*0-85199-325-7*) OUP.

Axford, Ray. Archery Anatomy: An Introduction to Techniques for Improved Performance. (Illus.). 164p. 1996. pap. text 16.95 (*0-285-63265-5*, Pub. by Souvenir Pr Ltd) IPG Chicago.

***Axford, Roger W.** Mirror for Marriage LC 99-194509. 85p. 1999. write for info. (*1-893453-05-7*) Media Prods.

Axford, Roger W. Native Americans: Twenty-three Indian Biographies. (Illus.). 128p. 1981. pap. 5.00 (*0-935648-02-X*) Halldin Pub.

Axford, Wendy A. & McMurtrie, Douglas C. Handicapped Children in Britain: Their Problems & Education & Index Catalogue of a Library of Rehabilitation of the Disabled, 2 vols. Phillips, William R. & Rosenberg, Janet, eds. LC 79-6894. (Physically Handicapped in Society Ser.). 1980. reprint ed. lib. bdg. 19.95 (*0-405-13105-4*) Ayer.

Axi, Nanhua. Representations of Affine Hecke Algebras. LC 09-22893. (Lecture Notes in Mathematics Ser.: 1587). 1994. 23.00 (*0-387-58389-0*) Spr-Verlag.

Axilrod, Stephen. Interdependence of Capital Markets & Policy Implications. (Occasional Paper Ser.: No. 32). 25p. 1991. pap. 10.00 (*1-56708-031-6*) Grp of Thirty.

Axinn, Catherine N. Social Welfare: A History of the American Response to Need. 5th ed. 416p. (C). 2000. pap. 38.67 (*0-8013-3040-8*) Longman.

Axinn, Donald E. The Colors of Infinity. 51p. 1990. pap. 8.95 (*0-929654-92-7*) FoxRock.

— The Colors of Infinity. 51p. 1990. 16.95 (*0-929654-96-X*) FoxRock.

— Dawn Patrol. Scammacca, Nat, tr. (ENG & ITA., Illus.). 64p. 1991. 15.00 (*0-89304-696-5*) Cross-Cultrl NY.

— Dawn Patrol. Scammacca, Nat et al, trs. (ENG & ITA., Illus.). 64p. 1991. pap. 7.50 (*0-89304-697-3*) Cross-Cultrl NY.

— The Ego Makers: A Novel. LC 95-53073. 320p. 1998. 23.45 (*1-55970-336-9*, Pub. by Arcade Pub Inc) Time Warner.

— The Latest Illusion. LC 94-43028. 96p. 1995. pap. 12.45 (*1-55970-298-2*, Pub. by Arcade Pub Inc) Time Warner.

— Spin. 256p. 1991. 19.95 (*0-88268-125-7*) Station Hill Pr.

— Spin. LC 93-50945. 328p. 1994. reprint ed. pap. 11.45 (1-55970-250-8, Pub. by Arcade Pub Inc) Time Warner.

Axinn, George H. & Axinn, Nancy W. Collaboration in International Rural Development: A Practitioner's Handbook. LC 97-27342. 334 p. 1997. write for info. (81-7036-653-4) Sage.

— Collaboration in International Rural Development: A Practitioner's Handbook. LC 97-27342. 1997. 39.95 (0-7619-9200-6); pap. 18.95 (0-7619-9201-4) Sage.

Axinn, June. Social Welfare: A History of the American Response to Need. 4th ed. LC 96-9085. 384p. (C). 1996. pap. 50.00 (0-8013-1700-2) Addison-Wesley.

Axinn, Nancy W., jt. auth. see Axinn, George H.

Axinn, Sidney. A Moral Military. LC 88-29294. 264p. (C). 1989. 37.95 (0-87722-615-6) Temple U Pr.

— A Moral Military. 264p. 1990. pap. 22.95 (0-87722-780-2) Temple U Pr.

Axinn, Sidney, jt. ed. see Kneller, Jane.

Axinn, Stephen M., et al. Acquisitions under the Hart-Scott-Rodino Antitrust Improvements Act, 2 vols. rev. ed. 1100p. 1988. ring bd. 140.00 (0-317-05392-2, 00550) NY Law Pub.

Axiom, A. A. Outrageous! Education Practices: Truth about Our Education System. LC 89-91065. 96p. (Orig.). 1989. pap. 15.95 (0-922958-09-2) H W Parker.

Axiom Information Resources Staff. Celebrity Birthday Directory: Name & Birthdays of Thousands Celebrities Alphabetical Arranged. 4th rev. ed. Robinson, Terry, ed. 80p. 1997. pap. 10.95 (0-943213-26-6) Axiom Info Res.

— Celebrity Birthday Guide. 4th ed. Robinson, Terry, ed. 88p. 1997. pap. text 10.95 (0-943213-25-8) Axiom Info Res.

— Celebrity Directory: Where to Reach over 9,000 Movie & TV Stars & Other Famous People. 9th rev. ed. Robinson, Terry, ed. 258p. 1999. pap. 39.95 (0-943213-31-2) Axiom Info Res.

— Celebrity Directory 2000-2001: Where to Reach Over 9000 Movie/tv Stars & Other Famous People. 1999. pap. text 39.95 (0-943213-35-5) Axiom Info Res.

— Celebrity Web Site & E-mail Directory 2000-2001. 1999. pap. text 9.95 (0-943213-33-9) Axiom Info Res.

— Star Guide 2000-2001: Where To Reach Over 3200 Movie/tv Stars & Other Famous People. 1999. pap. text 14.95 (0-943213-34-7) Axiom Info Res.

Axler, Bruce A. Foodservice: A Managerial Approach. LC 78-70714. 1979. teacher ed., student ed. 32.50 (0-669-02722-7); text 17.95 (0-697-00079-6) Educ Found.

Axler, Bruce H. Adding Eye Appeal to Foods. 1974. pap. 3.70 (0-672-96115-6, Bobbs) Macmillan.

— Breakfast Cookery. 1974. pap. 3.95 (0-672-96120-2, Bobbs) Macmillan.

— Building Care for Hospitality Operations. 1974. pap. 3.95 (0-672-96124-5, Bobbs) Macmillan.

— Increasing Lodging Revenues & Restaurant Checks. 1974. pap. 3.95 (0-672-96121-0, Bobbs) Macmillan.

— Kitchen Sanitation & Food Hygiene. 1974. pap. 3.50 (0-672-96409-0, Bobbs) Macmillan.

— Practical Wine Knowledge. 1974. pap. 3.95 (0-672-96119-9, Bobbs) Macmillan.

— Profitable Catering. 1974. pap. 3.95 (0-672-96118-0, Bobbs) Macmillan.

— Room Care for Hotels & Motels. 1974. pap. 3.95 (0-672-96125-3, Bobbs) Macmillan.

— Sanitation, Safety, & Maintenance Management. 1974. 13.25 (0-672-96106-7, Bobbs); teacher ed. 5.00 (0-672-96108-3, Bobbs); student ed. 6.45 (0-672-96107-5, Bobbs) Macmillan.

— Security for Hotels, Motels, & Restaurants. 1974. pap. 3.95 (0-672-96123-7, Bobbs) Macmillan.

— Showmanship in the Dining Room. 1974. pap. 5.01 (0-672-96117-2, Bobbs) Macmillan.

— Tableservice Techniques. 1974. pap. 3.95 (0-672-96116-4, Bobbs) Macmillan.

Axler, Bruce H. & Litrides, Carol A. Food & Beverage Service. LC 89-28391. 240p. 1990. 44.95 (0-471-62176-5) Wiley.

Axler, Bruce H., jt. auth. see Litrides, Carol A.

Axler, James. Aurora Quest. (Earthblood Ser.). 1994. per. 4.99 (0-373-63809-4, 1-63809-7) Harlequin Bks.

— Bitter Fruit. (Deathlands Ser.: No. 35). 1997. per. 5.50 (0-373-62535-9) Harlequin Bks.

— Bloodlines. LC 95-22303. (Deathlands Ser.: No. 29). 348p. 1995. per. 4.99 (0-373-62529-4, Wrldwide Lib) Harlequin Bks.

— Chill Factor. (Deathlands Ser.: Bk. 15). 1999. per. 5.99 (0-373-62553-7, 1-62553-2, Wrldwide Lib) Harlequin Bks.

— Circle Thrice. (Deathlands Ser.: No. 32). 1996. per. 5.50 (0-373-62532-4, 1-62532-6, Wrldwide Lib) Harlequin Bks.

— Cold Asylum. (Deathlands Ser.: 20). 1994. mass mkt. 4.99 (0-373-62520-0, 1-62520-1) Harlequin Bks.

— Cold Asylum. (Deathlands Ser.: Bk. 20). 1999. per. 5.99 (0-373-62558-8, 1-62558-1, Wrldwide Lib) Harlequin Bks.

— Crater Lake. (Deathlands Ser.: No. 4). 256p. 1987. mass mkt. 4.99 (0-373-63060-3) Harlequin Bks.

— Crater Lake. Vol. 4. 1997. per. 5.99 (0-373-48598-0, 1-48598-6) Harlequin Bks.

— Crucible of Time. (Deathlands Ser.: No. 44). 1998. per. 5.99 (0-373-62544-8, 1-62544-1, Mira Bks) Harlequin Bks.

— Dark Carnival. (Deathlands Ser.: No. 14). 1992. mass mkt. 4.99 (0-373-62514-6) Harlequin Bks.

— Dark Carnival. (Deathlands Ser.: Bk. 14). 1999. per. 5.99 (0-373-62552-9, 1-62552-4, Wrldwide Lib) Harlequin Bks.

***Axler, James.** Dark Reckoning. (Deathlands Ser.: No. 48). 1999. per. 5.99 (0-373-62548-0) Harlequin Bks.

Axler, James. Dectra Chain. 1997. per. 5.99 (0-373-89005-2, 1-89005-2) Harlequin Bks.

— Deep Empire. (Deathlands Ser.: No. 19). 1999. per. 5.99 (0-373-62557-X, 1-62557-3, Wrldwide Lib) Harlequin Bks.

— Deep Trek. (Earthblood Ser.). 1994. mass mkt. 4.99 (0-373-63808-6, 1-63808-9) Harlequin Bks.

— Demons of Eden. (Deathlands Ser.: No. 37). 1997. per. 5.50 (0-373-62537-5, 1-62537-5, Wrldwide Lib) Harlequin Bks.

— Destiny Run. 1997. per. 5.50 (0-373-63815-9, 1-63815-4, Wrldwide Lib) Harlequin Bks.

— Doomstar Relic. (Outlanders Ser.). 1998. per. 5.99 (0-373-63819-1, 1-63819-6, Wrldwide Lib) Harlequin Bks.

— Earthblood. 1993. per. 4.99 (0-373-63807-8, 1-63807-1) Harlequin Bks.

— Eclipse at Noon. (Deathlands Ser.: No. 33). 1996. per. 5.50 (0-373-62533-2, Wrldwide Lib) Harlequin Bks.

— Emerald Fire. LC 95-22304. 347p. 1995. per. 4.99 (0-373-62528-6, 1-62528-4) Harlequin Bks.

***Axler, James.** Encounter. (Deathlands Ser.). 384p. 1999. per. 5.99 (0-373-81197-7, Gold Eagle) Harlequin Bks.

Axler, James. Exile to Hell. (Outlanders Ser.: No. 1). 1997. per. 5.50 (0-373-63814-0, 1-63814-7, Wrldwide Lib) Harlequin Bks.

— Freedom Lost. (Deathlands Ser.: No. 41). 1998. per. 5.99 (0-373-62541-3, 1-62541-7, Wrldwide Lib) Harlequin Bks.

— Fury's Pilgrims. (Deathlands Ser.: Bk. 17). 1999. per. 5.99 (0-373-62555-3, 1-62555-7, Wrldwide Lib) Harlequin Bks.

— Gaia's Demise. (Deathlands Ser.: No. 47). 346p. 1999. mass mkt. 5.99 (0-373-62547-2, Wrldwide Lib) Harlequin Bks.

— Gemini Rising. (Deathlands Ser.: Bk. 46). 1999. per. 5.99 (0-373-62546-4, 1-62546-6, Wrldwide Lib) Harlequin Bks.

— Homeward Bound. (Deathlands Ser.: No. 5). 320p. 1988. mass mkt. 4.99 (0-373-63061-1) Harlequin Bks.

— Homeward Bound. Vol. 5. 1997. per. 5.99 (0-373-48599-9, 1-48599-4) Harlequin Bks.

— Ice & Fire. 1997. per. 5.99 (0-373-89006-0, 1-89006-0) Harlequin Bks.

— Iceblood. (Outlanders Ser.: No. 7). 352p. 1999. mass mkt. 5.99 (0-373-63820-5, 0-63820-5, Wrldwide Lib) Harlequin Bks.

— Keepers of the Sun. (Deathlands Ser.: Vol. 31). 1996. per. 4.99 (0-373-62531-6, 1-62531-8, Wrldwide Lib) Harlequin Bks.

— Latitude Zero. (Deathlands Ser.: No. 12). 1991. mass mkt. 4.50 (0-373-62512-X) Harlequin Bks.

— Latitude Zero. (Deathlands Ser.: Bk. 12). 1999. per. 5.99 (0-373-62550-2, 1-62550-8, Wrldwide Lib) Harlequin Bks.

— The Mars Arena. 1997. per. 5.50 (0-373-62538-3, 1-62538-3, Wrldwide Lib) Harlequin Bks.

— Moon Fate. (Deathlands Ser.: No. 16). 1992. per. 4.99 (0-373-62516-2, 1-62516-9) Harlequin Bks.

— Moon Fate. (Deathlands Ser.: Bk. 16). 1999. per. 5.99 (0-373-62554-5, 1-62554-0, Wrldwide Lib) Harlequin Bks.

— Neutron Solstice. (Deathlands Ser.: No. 3). 256p. 1987. mass mkt. 4.99 (0-373-63059-X) Harlequin Bks.

— Neutron Solstice. 1997. per. 5.99 (0-373-48597-2, 1-48597-8) Harlequin Bks.

— Night Eternal: The Lost Earth. (Outlanders Ser.: No. 9). 1999. per. 5.99 (0-373-63822-1, 1-63822-0, Wrldwide Lib) Harlequin Bks.

— Nightmare Passage. (Deathlands Ser.: No. 40). 1998. per. 5.50 (0-373-62540-5, 1-62540-9, Wrldwide Lib) Harlequin Bks.

— Northstar Rising. 1997. per. 5.99 (0-373-89008-7, 1-89008-6) Harlequin Bks.

— Omega Path. (Outlanders Ser.: No. 4). 1998. per. 5.99 (0-373-63817-5, 1-63817-0, Wrldwide Lib) Harlequin Bks.

— Outer Darkness: The Lost Earth. (Outlanders Ser.: No. 10). 1999. mass mkt. 5.99 (0-373-63823-X, 1-63823-8, Wrldwide Lib) Harlequin Bks.

— Outlanders: Hellbound Fury. (Outlanders Ser.: No. 8). 1999. mass mkt. 5.99 (0-373-63821-3, 1-63821-2, Wrldwide Lib) Harlequin Bks.

***Axler, James.** Pandora's Redoubt. (Deathlands Ser.: Bk. 50). 352p. 2000. per. 5.99 (0-373-62560-X, 1-62560-7, Wrldwide Lib) Harlequin Bks.

Axler, James. Parallax Red. (Outlanders Ser.). 1998. per. 5.99 (0-373-63818-3, 1-63818-8, Wrldwide Lib) Harlequin Bks.

— Pilgrimage to Hell. 1997. per. 5.99 (0-373-48595-6, 1-48595-2) Harlequin Bks.

— Pony Soldiers. (Christmas Slipcase Ser.: No. 4). 1997. per. 5.99 (0-373-89004-4, 1-89004-5) Harlequin Bks.

***Axler, James.** Rat King. (Deathlands Ser.: Vol. 51). 352p. 2000. mass mkt. 5.99 (0-373-62561-8, 1-62561-5, Wrldwide Lib) Harlequin Bks.

Axler, James. Red Equinox. (Deathlands Ser.: No. 9). 1997. per. 5.99 (0-373-89007-9, 1-89007-8) Harlequin Bks.

— Red Holocaust. (Deathlands Ser.: No. 2). 1997. per. 5.99 (0-373-48596-4, 1-48596-0) Harlequin Bks.

— Road Wars. (Deathlands Ser.: No. 23). 1994. per. 4.99 (0-373-62523-5, 1-62523-5) Harlequin Bks.

— Savage Sun. (Outlanders Ser.: No. 3). 1997. per. 5.50 (0-373-63816-7, 1-63816-2, Wrldwide Lib) Harlequin Bks.

— Seedling. (Deathlands Ser.: No. 13). 1991. mass mkt. 4.95 (0-373-62513-8) Harlequin Bks.

— Seedling. (Deathlands Ser.: Bk. 13). 1999. per. 5.99 (0-373-62551-0, 1-62551-6, Wrldwide Lib) Harlequin Bks.

***Axler, James.** Shadow Scourge. 352p. 2000. per. 5.99 (0-373-63826-4, Gold Eagle) Harlequin Bks.

— Shadow World. (Deathlands Ser.: 49). 352p. 2000. per. 5.99 (0-373-62559-6, Wrldwide Lib) Harlequin Bks.

Axler, James. Shadowfall. (Deathlands Ser.). 1995. mass mkt. 4.99 (0-373-62526-X, 1-62526-8) Harlequin Bks.

— Shockscape. (Deathlands Ser.: Bk. 18). 1999. per. 5.99 (0-373-62556-1, 1-62556-5, Wrldwide Lib) Harlequin Bks.

— Skydark. 352p. 1997. per. 5.50 (0-373-62536-7, 1-62536-7, Wrldwide Lib) Harlequin Bks.

— Starfall. (Deathlands Ser.: No. 45). 1999. per. 5.99 (0-373-62545-6, 1-62545-8, Wrldwide Lib) Harlequin Bks.

— Time Nomads. (Deathlands Ser.: Bk. 11). 1999. per. 5.99 (0-373-62549-9, 1-62549-0, Wrldwide Lib) Harlequin Bks.

— Trader Redux. (Deathlands Ser.: No. 24). 1994. mass mkt. 4.99 (0-373-62524-3, 1-62524-3) Harlequin Bks.

— Twilight Children. (Deathlands Ser.: No. 21). 1994. mass mkt. 4.99 (0-373-62521-9, 1-62521-9) Harlequin Bks.

— Watersleep. (Deathlands Ser.: No. 39). 1997. per. 5.50 (0-373-62539-1, 1-62539-1, Wrldwide Lib) Harlequin Bks.

— Way of the Wolf. (Deathlands Ser.: No. 42). 1998. per. 5.99 (0-373-62542-1, 1-62542-5, Wrldwide Lib) Harlequin Bks.

***Axler, James.** Wreath of Fire. (Outlanders Ser.: Vol. 12). 2000. per. 5.99 (0-373-63825-6) Harlequin Bks.

***Axler, James, creator.** Trigger Point. (Executioner Ser.: Vol. 262). 2000. mass mkt. 4.50 (0-373-64262-8, 1-64262-8, Wrldwide Lib) Harlequin Bks.

Axler, Leo. Final Viewing: A Bill Hawley Undertaking. 256p. (Orig.). 1994. pap. 4.50 (0-425-14244-2, Prime Crime) Berkley Pub.

— Grave Matters: A Bill Hawley Undertaking. 256p. (Orig.). 1995. mass mkt. 4.99 (0-425-14581-6, Prime Crime) Berkley Pub.

— Separated at Death. 272p. 1996. mass mkt. 5.99 (0-425-15257-X) Berkley Pub.

Axler, S., et al, eds. An Introduction to Coding & Information Theory. LC 96-11738. (Undergraduate Texts in Mathematics Ser.). 323p. 1996. 39.95 (0-387-94704-3) Spr-Verlag.

— Modern Graph Theory. LC 98-11960. (Graduate Texts in Mathematics Ser.: Vol. 184). 408p. 1998. 59.95 (0-387-98491-7); pap. 34.95 (0-387-98488-7) Spr-Verlag.

Axler, S., ed. see Browder, Andrew.

Axler, S., ed. see Cox, D. A., et al.

Axler, S., ed. see Dixon, John D. & Mortimer, Brian.

Axler, S., ed. see Douglas, Ronald G.

Axler, S., ed. see Elaydi, S. N.

Axler, S., ed. see Exner, George R.

Axler, S., ed. see Frazier, Michael W.

Axler, S., ed. see Hirsch, Francis & Lacombe, G.

Axler, S., ed. see Jhanich, Klaus.

Axler, S., ed. see Kress, R.

Axler, S., ed. see Lee, John M.

Axler, S., ed. see MacLane, Saunders.

Axler, S., ed. see Megginson, Robert E.

Axler, S., ed. see Nathanson, Melvyn B.

Axler, S., ed. see Robinson, Derek J.

Axler, S., ed. see Schaefer, Helmut H. & Wolff, Manfred.

Axler, S., ed. see Srivastava, S. M.

Axler, S., ed. see Troutman, John L.

Axler, S., ed. see Walter, W. & Thompson, R.

Axler, S., ed. see Zhang, Fuzhen.

Axler, Sheldon. Linear Algebra Done Right. Gehring, F. W. & Halmos, P. R., eds. LC 95-44889. (Undergraduate Texts in Mathematics Ser.). 248p. (C). 1995. 53.95 (0-387-94595-4); pap. 31.95 (0-387-94596-2) Spr-Verlag.

Axler, Sheldon, et al, eds. Holomorphic Spaces. LC 98-4656. (Mathematical Sciences Research Institute Publications: No. 33). 450p. (C). 1998. text 54.95 (0-521-63193-9) Cambridge U Pr.

Axler, Sheldon, et al. Harmonic Function Theory. Ewing, J. H. et al, eds. LC 92-16950. (Graduate Texts in Mathematics Ser.: Vol. 137). (Illus.). 248p. 1992. 42.95 (0-387-97875-5) Spr-Verlag.

Axler, Sheldon J. Linear Algebra Done Right. 2nd ed. LC 97-16664. (Undergraduate Texts in Mathematics Ser.). 1997. 59.95 (0-387-98259-0) Spr-Verlag.

— Linear Algebra Done Right. 2nd ed. LC 97-16664. (Undergraduate Texts in Mathematics Ser.). 251p. 1997. pap. 29.00 (0-387-98258-2) Spr-Verlag.

Axlerod, David, et al. Money. 1964. pap. 7.00 (0-8222-0771-0) Dramatists Play.

Axley, Stephen R. Communication at Work: Management & the Communication-Intensive Organization. LC 95-34540. 232p. 1996. 59.95 (0-89930-913-5, Quorum Bks) Greenwood.

Axline, Andrew, ed. The Political Economy of Regional Co-Operation: Comparative Case Studies. 256p. 1994. 90.00 (1-85567-190-5) Bks Intl VA.

Axline, John, ed. see Fletcher, Robert H.

***Axline, Jon.** Speaking Ill of the Dead: Jerks in Montana History. LC 00-44310. 2000. write for info. (1-58592-032-0) Falcon Pub Inc.

Axline, Michael D. Environmental Citizen Suits. 390p. 1991. suppl. ed. 52.00 (0-685-74339-X, MICHIE) LEXIS Pub.

Axline, Virginia M. Dibs: In Search of Self. 1967. 11.09 (0-606-00561-7, Pub. by Turtleback) Demco.

— Dibs in Search of Self. 220p. 1976. mass mkt. 5.99 (0-345-33925-8) Ballantine Pub Grp.

— Play Therapy. rev. ed. (Illus.). 374p. (C). 1981. mass mkt. 6.99 (0-345-30335-0) Ballantine Pub Grp.

Axline, Virginia M. Terapia de Juego. (SPA., Illus.). 383p. 1997. pap. text 24.98 (968-13-0265-6) Edit Diana.

Axline, W. Andrew. The Political Economy of Regional Corporation: Comparative Case Studies. LC 94-20226. 256p. 1994. 39.50 (0-8386-3608-X) Fairleigh Dickinson.

Axmacher, Elke & Schwarzwaller, Klaus, eds. Belehrter Glaube: Festschrift Fur Johannes Wirsching. (GER., Illus.). 405p. 1994. 62.95 (3-631-46957-8) P Lang Pubng.

Axman, Andi. Work at Home Wisdom: A Collection of Quips, Tips & Inspirations to Balance Work, Family & Home. LC 98-28294. 176p. 1998. pap. 9.95 (1-57410-100-5, 56145601) Dearborn.

Axman, Andi, jt. auth. see Bangs, David H., Jr.

Axman, Andi, jt. auth. see Bangs, David H.

Axman, Steve. Coaching Offensive Backs. 2nd ed. LC 97-65520. (Art & Science of Coaching Ser.). (Illus.). 216p. 1997. pap. 19.95 (1-57167-088-2) Coaches Choice.

— Coaching Quarterback Passing Mechanics. LC 97-69613. (Illus.). 77p. 1998. pap. 16.95 (1-57167-194-3) Coaches Choice.

— 101 Quarterback Drills. LC 97-69612. (Art & Science of Coaching Ser.). (Illus.). 128p. 1998. pap. 16.95 (1-57167-195-1) Coaches Choice.

Axon, Ernest. Grenville. Pedigree of the Family of Grenville, with the Descent of High R. C. Birley & Bevil L. Birley from Sir Bevil Grenville. (Illus.). 24p. 1997. reprint ed. pap. 5.50 (0-8328-8836-2) Higginson Bk Co.

***Axon, Jo.** Sidecars. (Album Ser.: No. 332). (Illus.). 32p. 1999. pap. 5.25 (0-7478-0344-7, Pub. by Shire Pubns) Parkwest Pubns.

Axon, Savell Bird, jt. auth. see Hillier Parker, C. B.

Axon, William, ed. English Dialect Words of the Eighteenth Century: As Shown in the "Universal Etymological Dictionary" of Nathaniel Bailey. (English Dialect Society Publications: No. 41). 1972. reprint ed. pap. 30.00 (0-8115-0466-2) Periodicals Srv.

Axon, William E. Shelley's Vegetarianism. LC 79-116789. (Studies in Shelley: No. 25). 1971. reprint ed. lib. bdg. 49.00 (0-8383-1031-1) M S G Haskell Hse.

Axsater, S., et al, eds. Multi-Stage Production: Planning & Inventory Control. (Lecture Notes in Economics & Mathematical Systems Ser.: Vol. 266). v, 264p. 1986. 37.70 (0-387-16436-7) Spr-Verlag.

Axsom, Dora & Pelham, Erra. Mountain Mama: Courageous Backwoods Mistress. (Illus.). 210p. (Orig.). 1988. reprint ed. pap. 7.00 (0-317-92291-2) Lil Red Hen OK.

— Mountain Mama: Courageous Backwoods Mistress. 3rd rev. ed. (Orig.). (YA). 1990. pap. 10.00 (0-9621669-1-X) Lil Red Hen OK.

— No Lace for Cricket: Sequel to Mountain Mama. 216p. (Orig.). (YA). (gr. 10 up). 1991. pap. 5.50 (0-9621669-2-8) Lil Red Hen OK.

— No Lace for Cricket: Sequel to Mountain Mama. 2nd ed. 207p. (Orig.). (YA). 1997. reprint ed. pap. 10.00 (0-9621669-3-6) Lil Red Hen OK.

Axsom, Richard, intro. Frank Stella Prints: Nineteen Sixty-Seven to Nineteen Eighty-Two. (Illus.). 8p. 1982. 1.00 (0-318-18405-2) Michigan Mus.

Axsom, Richard H. Frank Stella's Prints, 1967-1982: Catalogue Raisonne. (Illus.). 192p. 1983. pap. 60.00 (1-55660-201-4) A Wofsy Fine Arts.

Axsom, Richard H. & Platzker, David. Printed Stuff: Prints, Posters, & Ephemera by Claes Oldenburg: A Catalogue Raisonne 1958-1996. LC 96-39970. (Illus.). 454p. 1997. 125.00 (1-55595-123-6) Hudson Hills.

Axsom, Richard H., et al. Ellsworth Kelly: Recent Prints. (Illus.). 64p. (C). 1998. pap. 20.00 (1-881450-10-4) Boston U Art.

Axson, Stockton. Brother Woodrow: A Memoir of Woodrow Wilson by Stockton Axson. Link, Arthur S. et al, eds. LC 92-45168. (Supplementary Volumes to the Papers of Woodrow Wilson). (Illus.). 256p. (C). 1993. text 37.50 (0-691-03255-6, Pub. by Princeton U Pr) Cal Prin Full Svc.

Axtell, Carson A. Axtell Genealogy. (Illus.). 380p. 1997. reprint ed. pap. 62.00 (0-8328-7309-8); reprint ed. lib. bdg. 72.00 (0-8328-7308-X) Higginson Bk Co.

***Axtell, David.** We're Going on a Lion Hunt. LC 98-47507. (Illus.). 32p. (J). 2000. 15.95 (0-8050-6159-2) H Holt & Co.

***Axtell, Guy.** Knowledge, Belief & Character: Readings in Virtue Epistemology. LC 99-59826. (Studies in Epistemology & Cognitive Theory). 256p. 2000. pap. 21.95 (0-8476-9653-7) Rowman.

Axtell, Harold L. The Deification of Abstract Ideas in Roman Literature & Inscriptions. 100p. (C). 1987. reprint ed. lib. bdg. 30.00 (0-89241-159-7) Caratzas.

Axtell, Horace & Aragon, Margo. A Little Bit of Wisdom: Conversations with a Nez Perce Elder. LC 96-85612. 1997. 25.00 (1-881090-23-X) Confluence Pr.

***Axtell, Horace & Aragon, Margo.** A Little Bit of Wisdom: Conversations with a Nez Perce Elder. (Illus.). 232p. 2000. pap. 11.95 (0-8061-3269-8) U of Okla Pr.

Axtell, James. After Columbus: Essays in the Ethnohistory of Colonial North America. (Illus.). 320p. 1990. reprint ed. pap. text 21.00 (0-19-505376-1) OUP.

Axtell, James. Beyond 1492: Encounters in Colonial North America. (Illus.). 400p. 1992. pap. text 19.95 (0-19-508033-5) OUP.

Axtell, James. The European & the Indian: Essays in the Ethnohistory of Colonial North America. (Illus.). 402p. 1982. pap. text 14.95 (0-19-502904-6) OUP.

— Imagining the Other: First Encounters in North America. Phillips, Carla R. & Weber, David J., eds. LC 91-77202. (Essays on the Columbian Encounter Ser.). 64p. 1991. pap. 7.00 (0-87229-064-6) Am Hist Assn.

— Indians' New South: Cultural Change in the Colonial

Southeast. LC 96-39945. (Walter Lynwood Fleming Lectures in Southern History Ser.). (Illus.). 120p. 1997. pap. 11.95 (*0-8071-2172-X*); text 22.95 (*0-8071-2171-1*) La State U Pr.

— The Invasion Within: The Contest of Cultures in Colonial North America. (Cultural Origins of North America Ser.). (Illus.). 405p. 1986. pap. text 24.95 (*0-19-504154-2*) OUP.

***Axtell, James.** Natives & Newcomers: The Cultural Origins of North America. LC 99-56089. (Illus.). 416p. 2000. text 59.95 (*0-19-513770-1*); pap. text. write for info. (*0-19-513771-X*) OUP.

Axtell, James. The Pleasures of Academe: A Celebration & Defense of Higher Education. LC 97-51865. xix, 293p. 1998. text 40.00 (*0-8032-1049-3*) U of Nebr Pr.

— The Pleasures of Academe: A Celebration & Defense of Higher Education. 1999. pap. 15.00 (*0-8032-5938-7*) U of Nebr Pr.

— The Rise & Fall of the Powhatan Empire: Indians in Seventeenth-Century Virginia. (Foundations of America Ser.). (Illus.). 42p. 1995. pap. 9.95 (*0-87935-153-5*) Colonial Williamsburg.

— White Indians of Colonial America. 38p. 1991. reprint ed. pap. 6.95 (*0-87770-210-1*) Ye Galleon.

Axtell, James, ed. The Indian Peoples of Eastern America: A Documentary History of the Sexes. (Illus.). 256p. (C). 1981. pap. text 21.95 (*0-19-502741-8*) OUP.

Axtell, John L. Ashes of War. unabridged ed. Wegeng, Lana, ed. 51p. 1998. pap. 8.95 (*0-9659454-7-2*) Columbia Pubns.

Axtell, Mike, et al. The Great American Art Auction & Free Give Away. Uphoff, Joseph A., Jr., ed. 110p. 1991. pap. 6.00 (*0-943123-17-8*) Arjuna Lib Pr.

Axtell, Robert L., jt. auth. see Epstein, Joshua M.

Axtell, Roger E. Do's & Taboos Around the World. 3rd ed. (Illus.). 208p. 1993. pap. 15.95 (*0-471-59528-4*) Wiley.

— The Do's & Taboos of Hosting International Visitors. 236p. 1990. 34.95 (*0-471-51572-8*); pap. 17.95 (*0-471-51570-1*) Wiley.

***Axtell, Roger E.** Do's & Taboos of Humor Around the World: Stories & Tips from Business & Life. LC 98-20912. 227p. 1998. pap. 15.95 (*0-471-25403-7*) Wiley.

Axtell, Roger E. The Do's & Taboos of International Trade: A Small Business Primer. 2nd rev. ed. LC 94-8586. 336p. 1994. pap. 17.95 (*0-471-00760-9*) Wiley.

— The Do's & Taboos of Public Speaking: How to Get Those Butterflies Flying in Formation. LC 91-42526. 224p. 1992. pap. 15.95 (*0-471-53670-9*) Wiley.

— Do's & Taboos of Using English Around the World. LC 94-25738. (Illus.). 224p. 1995. pap. 14.95 (*0-471-30841-2*) Wiley.

— Gestures: The Do's & Taboos of Body Language Around the World. rev. ed. LC 97-29043. (Illus.). 238p. 1997. pap. 15.95 (*0-471-18342-3*) Wiley.

Axtell, Roger E. & Healy, John P. The Do's & Taboos of Preparing for Your Trip Abroad. 160p. 1994. pap. 12.95 (*0-471-02567-4*) Wiley.

Axtell, Roger E., et al. Do's & Taboos Around the World for Women in Business. 1997. pap. 16.95 (*0-614-28128-8*) Wiley.

Axtell, Roger E., ed. see Briggs, Tami, et al.

Axtell, Susan, jt. auth. see Bethell, Jean.

Axthelm, Pete. The City Game: Basketball from the Garden to the Playgrounds. LC 98-51369. (Illus.). 232p. 1999. pap. 12.00 (*0-8032-5934-4*, Bison Books) U of Nebr Pr.

— The City Game: Basketball from the Garden to the Playgrounds. 224p. 1999. reprint ed. 29.95 (*1-56849-719-9*) Buccaneer Bks.

Axthelm, Peter M. The Modern Confessional Novel. LC 67-13428. (Yale College Ser.: No. 6). 201p. reprint ed. pap. 62.40 (*0-608-30112-4*, 202197600024) Bks Demand.

Axtman, William H., ed. see American Boiler Manufacturers Association Staff.

Axtmann. Liberal Democracy into 21st Century: Globalization, Integration & the Nation-State. LC 97-181935. (Political Analyses Ser.). 1997. pap. 24.95 (*0-7190-4305-0*, Pub. by Manchester Univ Pr) St Martin.

Axtmann, Margaret M., jt. ed. see Price, Mary K.

Axtmann, Marilyn, et al. Show What You Know on Ohio's Fourth Grade Proficiency Test. 288p. 1996. pap., teacher ed. 14.95 (*1-884183-08-5*) Englfld & Arnold.

Axtmann, Roland. Globalization & Europe: Theoretical & Empirical Investigations. LC 97-27667. Date not set. pap. 24.95 (*1-85567-437-8*) Bks Intl VA.

Axtmayer, Alfred, tr. see Etala, Emilio.

Axton, Marie, ed. Three Tudor Classical Interludes: Thersites, Jacke Jugeler, Horestes. (Tudor Interludes Ser.: No. III). (Illus.). 247p. 1977. 60.00 (*0-85991-096-2*) Boydell & Brewer.

Axton, Richard & Happe, Peter, eds. The Plays of John Heywood. (Tudor Interludes Ser.: No. VI). 368p. (C). 1991. 90.00 (*0-85991-319-8*) Boydell & Brewer.

Axton, W. F. & Martin, Wendy Lee. Field Hockey. (Illus.). 128p. (Orig.). 1993. pap. 12.95 (*0-940279-81-9*, 79819H, Mstrs Pr) NTC Contemp Pub Co.

Axton, W. F., jt. auth. see Hewett, Edward W.

Axworthy, Anni. Along Came Toto. LC 92-52992. (Illus.). 32p. (J). (ps-3). 1993. 12.95 (*1-56402-172-6*) Candlewick Pr.

— Along Came Toto. LC 95-52992. (Illus.). (J). (ps up). 1995. pap. 4.99 (*1-56402-501-2*) Candlewick Pr.

— Anni's Diary of France. LC 93-27278. (Illus.). 32p. (J). (gr. 4-7). 1994. 16.95 (*1-879085-58-5*, Whispering Coyote) Charlesbridge Pub.

***Axworthy, Anni.** Anni's Diary of France. 32p. (J). (gr. 2-5). 2000. pap. 6.95 (*1-58089-024-5*, Whispering Coyote) Charlesbridge Pub.

— Anni's Diary of France. (Illus.). (J). 2000. 12.40 (*0-606-18746-4*) Turtleback.

Axworthy, Anni. Anni's India Diary. LC 92-17524. (Illus.). 32p. (J). (gr. 2-5). 1992. 16.95 (*1-879085-59-3*, Whispering Coyote) Charlesbridge Pub.

***Axworthy, Anni.** Anni's India Diary. (Illus.). 32p. (J). (gr. 2-5). 2000. 96p. pap. 6.95 (*1-58089-050-4*, Whispering Coyote) Charlesbridge Pub.

— Anni's India Diary. 2000. 12.40 (*0-606-18747-2*, Pub. by Turtleback) Demco.

Axworthy, Anni. Guess What I Am: A Peephole Book. LC 98-70336. (Illus.). 28p. (J). (ps). 1998. 7.99 (*0-7636-0625-1*) Candlewick Pr.

— Guess What I'll Be: A Peephole Book. LC 98-70536. (Illus.). 28p. (J). (ps). 1998. 7.99 (*0-7636-0626-X*) Candlewick Pr.

***Axworthy, Anni.** Guess Where I Live. LC 98-73379. (Peephole Book Ser.). (Illus.). 28p. (J). (ps). 1999. text 7.99 (*0-7636-0733-9*, Pub. by Candlewick Pr) Penguin Putnam.

— Guess Who My Mommy Is. LC 98-73077. (Illus.). 28p. (J). (ps). 1999. text 7.99 (*0-7636-0734-7*, Pub. by Candlewick Pr) Penguin Putnam.

Axworthy, Anni. Count Me In. 64p. (J). (ps-3). write for info. (*0-7136-2622-4*, Pub. by A & C Blk) Midpt Trade.

Axworthy, Anni, jt. auth. see Nilsen, Anna.

Axworthy, M. The Romanian Army of World War II. (Men-at-Arms Ser.: No. 246). (Illus.). 48p. pap. 11.95 (*1-85532-169-6*, 9209, Pub. by Ospry) Stackpole.

Axworthy, Mark. Balkan Battleground, 1939-1945. 1999. text 34.95 (*1-85410-628-7*) Aurum Pr.

Axworthy, S. Thomas, jt. auth. see Goldfarb, Martin.

Ay-Ming Wang, jt. auth. see Bisese, John H.

***Aya (Raven Woman).** The Way of the Warrior Priestess: A Handbook for the Woman of the 21st Century. LC 99-90699. 275p. 1999. 25.00 (*0-7388-0460-6*); pap. 18.00 (*0-7388-0461-4*) Xlibris Corp.

Ayache, Georges. Petroleum Dictionary: Dictionnaire du Petrole. (FRE.). 256p. 1981. 35.00 (*0-8288-2291-3*, M14189) Fr & Eur.

Ayache, Georges & Gallissot, Rene. Dictionnaire Biographique du Mouvement Ouvrier au Maghreb. (FRE.). 1998. 125.00 (*0-320-00400-7*) Fr & Eur.

Ayache, N., et al, eds. Computer Vision, Virtual Reality & Robotics in Medicine: First International Conference, CVRMed '95, Nice, France, April 3-6, 1995. Proceedings. (Lecture Notes in Computer Science Ser.: Vol. 905). (Illus.). xiv, 567p. 1995. 99.00 (*3-540-59120-6*) Spr-Verlag.

Ayache, Nicholas. Artificial Vision for Mobile Robots: Stereo Vision & Multisensory Perception. (Artificial Intelligence - Bobrow, Brady & Davis Ser.). (Illus.). 360p. 1991. 55.00 (*0-262-01124-7*) MIT Pr.

Ayache, Nicholas, ed. Computer Vision, Virtual Reality, & Robotics in Medicine: First International Conference, CVRMed '95, Nice, France, April 3-6, 1995, Proceedings. LC 95-7442. (Lecture Notes in Computer Sciences Ser.: Vol. 905). 1995. write for info. (*0-387-59120-6*) Spr-Verlag.

Ayad, Grace & Panzer, Richard. Mommy, Daddy, Where Do Babies Come From? LC 96-72331. (Wonderful World of True Love Ser.). (Illus.). (J). 1997. 12.95 (*1-888933-04-6*) Ctr Educ Media.

Ayad, Graciela & Panzer, Richard. Mami, Papi, de Donde Vienen los Bebes? Makowski, Nancy, ed. LC 96-72340. (Maravilloso Mundo del Amor Verdadero Ser.). (ENG & SPA., Illus.). 24p. (Orig.). (J). (gr. k-3). 1997. pap. 12.95 (*1-888933-08-9*) Ctr Educ Media.

Ayad, Shirley, et al, eds. The Extracellular Matrix Factsbook. (Facts Book Ser.). (Illus.). 163p. 1994. pap. text 45.00 (*0-12-068910-3*) Acad Pr.

— The Extracellular Matrix Factsbook. 2nd ed. LC 98-14439. (Factsbooks Ser.). (Illus.). 320p. (C). 1998. pap. 49.95 (*0-12-068911-1*) Acad Pr.

Ayadurai. Insurance Law in Malaysia. 260p. 1992. boxed set 121.00 (*0-409-99615-7*, MICHIE) LEXIS Pub.

Ayadurai, D. The Employer, the Employee & the Law in Malaysia. 359p. 1985. 60.00 (*0-409-99504-5*, MICHIE) LEXIS Pub.

Ayala. Microprocessor 8086. Date not set. pap. text, student ed. write for info. (*0-314-06387-0*) West Pub.

Ayala, Anguiano. Juarez. 1997. pap. text 12.98 (*968-6694-00-5*) Edit Diana.

Ayala, Antonio C. Alternative Progression. 40p. 1998. pap. 19.95 (*0-9663101-0-1*) Carre Corp.

Ayala, Balthazar. De Jure & Officiis Bellicis & Disciplina Militari Libri Iii. LC 95-77189. (Classics in International Law Reprint Ser.: No.2, Vol.1). 7, 227p. 1995. reprint ed. 95.00 (*1-57588-506-9*) W S Hein.

***Ayala, Carlos & Spellberg, Brad.** Pathophysiology for the Boards & Wards: A Review of the USMLE Step 1. 3rd ed. (Boards & Wards Ser.). (Illus.). 305p. 2000. pap. 27.95 (*0-632-04485-3*) Blackwell Sci.

— A Review for USMLE, Steps 2 & 3. LC 99-49379. (Boards & Wards Ser.). (Illus.). 352p. 2000. pap. 27.95 (*0-632-04493-4*) Blackwell Sci.

Ayala, Cesar J. American Sugar Kingdom: The Plantation Economy of the Spanish Caribbean, 1898-1934. LC 99-17349. (Illus.). 384p. 1999. pap. 19.95 (*0-8078-4788-7*) U of NC Pr.

Ayala, Cisar. American Sugar Kingdom: The Plantation Economy of the Spanish Caribbean, 1898-1934. LC 99-17349. (Illus.). 384p. 1999. lib. bdg. 49.95 (*0-8078-2506-9*) U of NC Pr.

Ayala, Cristobal D. Discografia de la Musica Cubana I, 1898-1925. (SPA., Illus.). 365p. (Orig.). 1994. pap. 29.95 (*0-89729-721-0*) Ediciones.

— Musica Cubana del Areyto a la Neuva Trova. 3rd ed. LC 81-23127. (Coleccion Arte). (Illus.). 416p. 1993. pap. 29.00 (*0-89729-703-2*) Ediciones.

— Si Te Quieres por el Pico Divertir: Historia del Pregon Musical Latinoamericano. LC 88-92157. (SPA., Illus.). 371p. (Orig.). 1988. pap. 25.00 (*0-89729-525-0*) Ediciones.

Ayala, Cristobal Diaz, see Diaz Ayala, Cristobal.

***Ayala, E. L.** Will You Be Made Whole. 195p. 2000. 15.00 (*1-55630-954-6*) Brentwood Comm.

Ayala, Emma. Styling Competition: A Guide to Winning Technique. (Illus.). 96p. 1990. pap. 30.95 (*0-87350-359-7*) Milady Pub.

Ayala, Felipe, jt. ed. see Sanchez-Camara, Florencio.

Ayala, Fernando. Diccionario Bolsillo Cuyas Italiano-Espanol, Spagnuelo-Italiano. 4th ed. (ITA & SPA.). 639p. 1958. 24.95 (*0-7859-6192-5*, 8471830604) Fr & Eur.

Ayala, Francisco. Muertes de Perro. 1995. pap. 14.95 (*0-679-76656-1*) Random.

— Muertes de Perro: El Jondo De Vaso. (Nueva Austral Ser.: No. 212). (SPA.). 1991. pap. text 24.95 (*84-239-7212-7*) Elliots Bks.

— El Problema de Liberalismo. 2nd ed. 285p. 1963. pap. 3.50 (*0-8477-2402-6*) U of PR Pr.

— Usurpers. 1999. pap. write for info. (*0-14-025419-5*) Viking Penguin.

Ayala, Francisco J. & Kiger, J. A., Jr. Modern Genetics: Solutions Manual. 2nd ed. 1984. pap. text, teacher ed. 10.75 (*0-8053-0317-0*) Benjamin-Cummings.

Ayala, Francisco J., ed. see National Academy of Sciences Staff.

Ayala, Jennifer, et al. Caution Speed Bumps Ahead: Reflections on the Politics & Methods of Qualitative Work. Weis, Lois & Fine, Michelle, eds. 75p. (C). 1998. pap. 15.00 (*0-924197-19-6*) SUNYB Coun Intl Studies.

Ayala, Josep de. Diccionario de Gobierno y Legislacion. (SPA.). 5040p. 1988. write for info. (*0-7859-3365-8*, 8472324494) Fr & Eur.

Ayala, Julio R. Problemas de Interpretacion y Conocimiento en la Filosofia Europea. Marrero, Rafael A., ed. (SPA.). 200p. (Orig.). (C). pap. 10.00 (*0-924418-01-X*) Ecitorial El Coqui.

Ayala, Kenneth J. The 8086 Microprocessor: Programming & Interfacing the PC. LC 94-31196. 704p. (C). 1995. mass mkt. 98.95 (*0-314-01242-7*) West Pub.

— The Eighty Fifty-One Microcontroller: Architecture, Programming, & Applications. Tucker, ed. 241p. (C). 1991. mass mkt. 38.25 (*0-314-77278-2*) West Pub

— The 8051 Microcontroller: Architecture, Programming & Applications. 2nd ed. LC 96-29308. 350p. (C). 1996. mass mkt. 65.95 (*0-314-20188-2*) West Pub.

— The Microcontroller 80251. LC 99-20362. (Illus.). 374p. (Orig.). 1999. pap. 97.00 incl. audio compact disk (*0-13-907551-8*) P-H.

Ayala, Laura J., jt. auth. see Woodruff-Wieding, Margaret S.

Ayala, Leticia M., ed. see Papa Jim, pseud.

Ayala, Leticia M., ed. see Sickafus, James E.

Ayala, Lourdes. Los Ninos Alfabeticos. (SPA.). 1995. 12.15 (*0-606-09574-8*, Pub. by Turtleback) Demco.

Ayala, Lourdes & Isona-Rodriguez, Margarita. Los Ninos Alfabeticos. LC 95-6187. (Illus.). 32p. (J). 1995. pap. 6.95 (*0-88106-815-2*) Charlesbridge Pub.

Ayala, Marta, tr. see Grant, Joe.

Ayala, Marta Stiefel, et al, eds. Technical Dictionary of Library & Information Science. LC 92-43348. (Reference Library of Social Science: Vol. 815).Tr. of Diccionario Tecnico do Biblioteconologia y Ciencias de la Informacion. (ENG & SPA.). 680p. 1993. text 121.00 (*0-8153-0655-5*, SS815) Garland.

Ayala, Mary F. Traduccion e Interpretacion: Cuaderno de Ejercicios. 98p. (C). 1994. 20.00 (*1-881604-14-4*) Scopcraeft.

Ayala, Naomi. Wild Animals on the Moon: And Other Poems. LC 96-45140. 70p. (Orig.). 1997. pap. 10.95 (*1-880684-44-6*) Curbstone.

Ayala, Pero L. De, see De Ayala, Pero L.

Ayala, Pero Lopez de, see de Ayala, Pero Lopez.

Ayala, Ramon Perez De, see Perez De Ayala, Ramon.

Ayala, Reynaldo, tr. see Grant, Joe.

***Ayala, Roselyne de & Gueno, Jean-Pierre, eds.** Brilliant Beginnings: The Youthful Works of Great Artists, Writers & Composers. LC 00-31316. 232p. 2000. 55.00 (*0-8109-4117-1*, Pub. by Abrams) Time Warner.

— Illustrated Letters: Artists & Writers Correspond. Goodman, John, tr. from FRE. LC 99-22310. (Illus.). 240p. 1999. 60.00 (*0-8109-0653-8*, Pub. by Abrams) Time Warner.

Ayala, Victor. Falling Through the Cracks: AIDS & the Urban Poor. LC 95-70518. 125p. (Orig.). 1996. pap. 17.95 (*0-9644437-0-8*) Social Change Pr.

Ayalon, David. Gunpowder & Firearms in the Mamluk Kingdom: A Challenge to Mediaeval Society. 2nd ed. 154p. 1978. 47.50 (*0-7146-3090-X*, Pub. by F Cass Pubs) Intl Spec Bk.

— Islam & the Abode of War: Military Slaves & the Adversaries of Islam. LC 94-6793. (Collected Studies: Vol. 456). 1994. 108.95 (*0-86078-430-4*, Pub. by Variorum) Ashgate Pub Co.

— The Mamleuk Military Society. LC 81-464204. (Collected Studies). 364 p. 1979. 22.00 (*0-86078-049-X*) Variorum.

— Outsiders in the Lands of Islam: Mamluks, Mongols & Eunuchs. (Collected Studies: No. CS269). 328p. (C). 1988. reprint ed. lib. bdg. 109.95 (*0-86078-217-4*, Pub. by Variorum) Ashgate Pub Co.

Ayalon, Hanna, et al. Community in Transition: Mobility, Integration, & Conflict, 104. LC 92-20063. (Contributions in Sociology Ser.: No. 104). 208p. 1993. 55.00 (*0-313-28699-X*, GM8699, Greenwood Pr) Greenwood.

Ayalon, Judith, jt. auth. see Simkin, Ariel.

Ayalon, Ofra & Flasher, Adina. Chain Reaction: Children & Divorce. 200p. 1993. pap. 25.95 (*1-85302-136-9*) Taylor & Francis.

Ayalti, Hanan. The Presence Is in Exile, Too: Collected Stories. LC 96-52864. (Illus.). 256p. 1998. 25.00 (*1-881320-22-7*, Black Belt) Black Belt Communs.

Ayan, Jordan. Aha! 10 Ways to Free Your Creative Spirit & Find Your Great Ideas. LC 96-49431. 1996. pap. 15.00 (*0-517-88400-3*) Crown Pub Group.

Ayanabe, A. & Dart, P. J., eds. Biological Nitrogen Fixation in Farming Systems of the Tropics. LC 77-1304. 391p. reprint ed. pap. 121.30 (*0-7837-6364-6*, 204607600010) Bks Demand.

Ayandele, E. A. Nigerian Historical Studies. 305p. 1979. 47.50 (*0-7146-3113-2*, Pub. by F Cass Pubs) Intl Spec Bk.

Ayani, Jessie E. Kintui, Vision of the Incas: The Shaman's Journey to Enlightenment. (Illus.). 222p. (Orig.). 1995. pap. 15.95 (*0-9648763-0-2*) Hrt of the Sun.

— The Lineage of the Codes of Light. 304p. 1998. pap. 18.00 (*0-9648763-1-0*) Hrt of the Sun.

***Ayanoglu, Byron.** Montreal's Best Restaurants. (Illus.). 172p. 2000. pap. 14.95 (*1-55065-130-7*) Vehicule Pr.

Ayanoglu, Byron. The New Vegetarian Gourmet. (Illus.). 192p. (Orig.). 1996. pap. 17.95 (*1-896503-26-8*, Pub. by R Rose Inc) Firefly Bks Ltd.

— Simply Mediterranean Cooking. (Illus.). 192p. 1998. pap. 17.95 (*1-896503-68-3*, Pub. by R Rose Inc) Firefly Bks Ltd.

Ayanoglu, Byron, jt. auth. see Young, Wandee.

Ayapetian, jt. ed. see Apkarian, A. V.

Ayars, Albert L. Home-Crafted Verses - A Sampler. 1998. pap. write for info. (*1-57553-994-2*) Watermrk Pr.

Ayars, Mimi, jt. auth. see Campbell, Patricia B.

Ayarslan, Solmaz D. A Dynamic Stochastic Model for Current Asset & Liability Management of a Multinational Corporation. Bruchey, Stuart, ed. LC 80-565. (Multinational Corporations Ser.). (Illus.). 1981. lib. bdg. 31.95 (*0-405-13362-6*) Ayer.

Ayatey, Siegfried B. Elementary FORTRAN IV Microeconomics Programs. LC 84-5155. 238p. (Orig.). (C). 1984. pap. text 22.00 (*0-8191-3950-5*) U Pr of Amer.

Ayati, Ibrahim. A Probe into the History of Ashura.Tr. of Barasi Tarkh-i-Ashura. 234p. 1985. pap. 8.00 (*0-941724-41-7*) Islamic Seminary.

Ayatullah Al-Khu'i. Islamic Practical Law. Shaikh Muhammad Sarwar, tr. from ARA. 1981. pap. 8.00 (*0-941724-01-8*) Islamic Seminary.

— Islamic Practical Law, Pts. 1 & 2. Shaikh Muhammad Sarwar, tr. from ARA. 1981. 10.00 (*0-941724-08-5*) Islamic Seminary.

— Rules of HAJJ. Shaikh Muhammad Sarwar, tr. from ARA. 50p. 1981. pap. 2.00 (*0-941724-02-6*) Islamic Seminary.

Ayatullah Mirza Mahdi Pooya. Essence of the Holy Qur'an. 1990. pap. write for info. (*0-944880-03-7*, 17); pap. 20.00 (*0-685-66729-4*, 17A) Tahrike Tarsile Quran.

Ayatullah Ruhullah Khomeini. Clarification of Questions on Worship & Self-Development: In Islamic Jurisprudence. Bakhtiar, Laleh, tr. from PER. 192p. (Orig.). (C). 1989. pap. 10.00 (*1-871031-02-8*) Abjad Bk.

Ayaz, Sandi & Ayers, Kenya F. Hitching a Ride to Success. 288p. (C). 1996. text 28.80 (*0-536-59457-0*) Pearson Custom.

Ayaz, Shaikh. A Storm's Call for Prayer: Selections from Shaikh Ayaz. (Illus.). 100p. 2000. text 9.95 (*0-19-579007-3*) OUP.

Aybet, Gulnur. The Dynamics of European Security Cooperation, 1945-91. LC 97-9175. 160p. 1997. text 69.95 (*0-312-17525-6*) St Martin.

***Aybet, Gulnur.** A European Security Architecture after the Cold War: Questions of Legitimacy. LC 99-53379. 336p. 2000. text 69.95 (*0-312-23057-5*) St Martin.

Ayckbourn, Alan. Absurd Person: Singul. 1997. pap. write for info. (*0-582-06020-6*) Addison-Wesley.

Ayckbourn, Alan. Alan Ayckbourn: Plays One: A Chorus of Disapproval, a Small Family Business, Henceforward... 1995. pap. 13.95 (*0-571-17680-1*) Faber & Faber.

— Alan Ayckbourn: Plays 2, Invisible Friends, My Very Own Story, This Is Where We Came in, Ernie's. 1998. pap. 16.95 (*0-571-19457-5*) Faber & Faber.

— Comic Potential. 96p. 2000. pap. 13.00 (*0-571-19787-6*) Faber & Faber.

— Communicating Doors. 96p. (Orig.). 1995. pap. 10.95 (*0-571-17682-8*) Faber & Faber.

— Confusions. (Methuen Student Editions Ser.). (Illus.). 63p. (J). 1988. pap. write for info. (*0-413-53270-4*, A0063, Methuen Drama) Methn.

Ayckbourn, Alan. Family Circles LC 98-165652. 81 p. 1997. write for info. (*0-573-01764-6*) S French Trade.

Ayckbourn, Alan. Invisible Friends. 125p. (Orig.). 1991. pap. 11.95 (*0-571-14476-4*) Faber & Faber.

— The Norman Conquests: Table Manners, Living Together, Round & Round the Garden. LC 78-73501. 224p. 1988. pap. 13.00 (*0-8021-3134-4*, Grove) Grove-Atltic.

— The Revengers' Comedies. 128p. 1992. pap. 13.95 (*0-571-14358-X*) Faber & Faber.

— Things We Do for Love. 1998. pap. 11.95 (*0-571-19445-1*) Faber & Faber.

— Three Plays: Absurd Person Singular, Absent Friends, Bedroom Farce. LC 78-20339. 320p. 1989. pap. 9.95 (*0-8021-3157-3*, Grove) Grove-Atltic.

— Woman in Mind. 96p. (Orig.). 1986. pap. 9.95 (*0-571-14520-5*) Faber & Faber.

***Ayckbourn, Alan, et al.** Gizmo/Don't Eat Little Charlie. (Connections Ser.). (Illus.). 112p. (YA). 2000. pap. 17.95 (*0-7487-4289-1*, Pub. by S Thornes Pubs) Trans-Atl Phila.

Aycliffe, Jonathan. A Shadow on the Wall. 224p. 26.00 (*0-7278-5505-0*) Severn Hse.

— The Talisman. vii, 216p. 1999. 40.00 (*1-899562-85-0*) Ash-Tree.

Aycoberry, Pierre. The Social History of the Third Reich, 1933-1945. Lloyd, Janet, tr. from FRE. LC 99-14059. 400p. 2000. 30.00 (*1-56584-549-8*, Pub. by New Press NY) Norton.

A

A

*__Aycoberry, Pierre.__ The Social History of the Third Reich, 1933-1945. Lloyd, Janet, tr. from FRE. (Illus.). 2000. pap. 15.95 (*1-56584-635-4*, Pub. by New Press NY) Norton.

Aycock, Barrie C. Glen-Ella Springs: Recipes & Remembrances. Kollock, John, ed. LC 97-74770. (Illus.). Date not set. 19.95 (*0-9659404-0-3*) Glen-Ella Sprngs.

*__Aycock, Don.__ Be Still & Know: How to Have a Conversation with God. 128p. 1999. 10.99 (*0-8054-1847-4*) Broadman.

Aycock, Don. Living by the Fruit of the Spirit. LC 99-19009. 1999. pap. 9.99 (*0-8254-2003-2*) Kregel.

Aycock, Don M. Apathy in the Pew. LC 87-71394. 130p. (Orig.). 1988. pap. 7.99 (*0-88270-636-5*) Bridge-Logos.

— Eight Days That Changed the World: A Devotional Study from Palm Sunday to Easter. LC 96-46394. 128p. 1997. pap. 8.99 (*0-8254-2142-X*) Kregel.

— God's Most Unmistakable Message: Sermons for Lent. LC 93-47176. 76p. 1993. pap. 9.25 (*1-55673-514-6*, 9401) CSS OH.

*__Aycock, Don M.__ Prayer 101: What It Is. What It Isn't. How to Do It. LC 98-11175. 144p. 1998. 9.99 (*0-8054-1500-9*) Broadman.

— The Word Is Near You: Sermons for the Church. LC 00-34302. 2000. write for info. (*0-7880-1766-7*) CSS OH.

Aycock, Don M., ed. God's Man: A 366-Day Devotional for Developing Christlike Character. LC 98-44656. 304p. 1998. pap. 13.99 (*0-8254-2000-8*) Kregel.

Aycock, Don M. & Goss, Leonard G. The Christian Writer's Book: A Practical Guide to Writing. LC 96-84820. Orig. Title: Writing Religiously: A Guide to Writing Nonfiction Religious Books. (Orig.). 1996. pap. 15.99 (*0-88270-695-0*) Bridge-Logos.

Aycock, Don M., jt. ed. see Goss, Leonard G.

Aycock, Johnnie R., jt. auth. see O'Donnell, Joseph D.

Aycock, Wendell M., ed. Shakespeare's Art from a Comparative Perspective. LC 80-54322. (Proceedings of the Comparative Literature Symposium Ser.: Vol.12). (Illus.). 197p. (Orig.). 1981. pap. 12.00 (*0-89672-081-0*) Tex Tech Univ Pr.

— The Teller & the Tale: Aspects of the Short Story. LC 81-52254. (Proceedings of the Comparative Literature Symposium Ser.: Vol. 13). 156p. (C). 1982. pap. 12.00 (*0-89672-100-0*) Tex Tech Univ Pr.

— Twentieth-Century Short Story Explication, New Series, 1991-1993. LC 92-22790. (Short Story Explication Ser.: Vol. II). viii, 295p. (C). 1995. lib. bdg. 49.50 (*0-208-02370-4*) Shoe String.

— Twentieth-Century Short Story Explication, New Series, 1993-1994. LC 92-22790. (Short Story Explication Ser.: Vol. III). viii, 347p. (C). 1997. lib. bdg. 49.50 (*0-208-02419-0*) Shoe String.

Aycock, Wendell M. & Cravens, Sydney P., eds. Calderon de la Barca at the Tercentenary: Comparative Views. LC 82-80309. (Proceedings of the Comparative Literature Symposium Ser.: Vol. 14). 195p. 1982. pap. 12.00 (*0-89672-101-9*) Tex Tech Univ Pr.

Aycock, Wendell M. & Klein, Theodore M., eds. Classical Mythology in Twentieth-Century Thought & Literature. (Proceedings of the Comparative Literature Symposium Ser.: Vol. XI). (Illus.). 221p. (Orig.). 1980. pap. 12.00 (*0-89672-079-9*) Tex Tech Univ Pr.

Aycock, Wendell M. & Schoenecke, Michael, eds. Film & Literature: A Comparative Approach to Adaptation. LC 88-24965. (Comparative Literature Ser.: No. 19). 202p. (C). 1998. reprint ed. pap. 12.95 (*0-89672-169-8*) Tex Tech Univ Pr.

Aycock, Wendell M., jt. auth. see Whitlark, James.

Aycock, Wendell M., jt. ed. see Clarke, Bruce.

Aycock, Wendell M., jt. ed. see Dennis, Philip A.

Aycock, Wendell M., jt. ed. see Dennis, Phillip A.

Aycock, Wendell M., jt. ed. see Hopkins, Patricia M.

Aycock, Wendell M., jt. ed. see Perez, Janet.

Aycock, Wendell M., jt. ed. see Zyla, Wolodymyr T.

Aycock, Wendell M., tr. see Zilyns'Kyj, Ivan.

Aycox, Frank. Games We Should Play in School: A Revealing Analysis of the Social Forces in the Classroom & a Practical Approach to Understanding & Shaping Them Including over 55 Dynamic & Fun Social Games. Alexander, Frank, ed. LC 97-225376. (Illus.). 103p. (Orig.). (gr. 1-12). 1985. pap. 16.00 (*0-915256-16-9*) Front Row.

Ayd, Frank, et al, eds. Affective Disorders Reassessed, 1983. 250p. (Orig.). 1983. text 35.00 (*0-931858-05-4*) Ayd Medical Comm.

Ayd, Frank & Blackwell, Barry, eds. Discoveries in Biological Psychiatry, 1984. LC 78-124542. 254p. text 28.50 (*0-685-19220-2*) Ayd Medical Comm.

Ayd, Frank J., Jr. Lexicon of Psychiatry, Neurology, & Neurosciences. 2nd ed. 1120p. pap. text 69.95 (*0-7817-2468-6*) Lppncott W & W.

Ayd, Frank J., Jr. Lexicon of Psychiatry, Neurology, & the Neurosciences. LC 94-38956. 720p. 1995. pap. text 50.00 (*0-683-00298-8*) Lppncott W & W.

Aydelott, George C. Aydelott. History of the Aydelott Family in the U. S. Matteson, H. P., ed. (Illus.). 101p. 1996. reprint ed. pap. 18.00 (*0-8328-5274-0*); reprint ed. lib. bdg. 28.00 (*0-8328-5273-2*) Higginson Bk Co.

Aydelotte, Frank. Elizabethan Rogues & Vagabonds. (Illus.). 187p. 1967. 25.00 (*0-7146-1099-2*, Pub. by F Cass Pubs) Intl Spec Bk.

— Oxford Stamp, & Other Essays. LC 67-26712. (Essay Index Reprint Ser.). 1977. 19.95 (*0-8369-0166-5*) Ayer.

Aydelotte, William O., ed. The History of Parliamentary Behavior. LC 78-24290. (Quantitative Studies in History). 336p. 1977. reprint ed. pap. 104.20 (*0-7837-9294-8*, 206003300004) Bks Demand.

Ayden, Erje. The Crazy Green of Second Avenue. 160p. 1992. pap. 9.95 (*0-8065-1292-X*, Citadel Pr) Carol Pub Group.

— The Crazy Green of Second Avenue & from Hauptbahnhof I Took a Train: Two Novels. 307p. 1971. pap. 15.00 (*0-89366-002-7*) Ultramarine Pub.

— Sadness at Leaving. 250p. 1989. pap. 6.00 (*0-936756-57-8*) Autonomedia.

— Sadness at Leaving: A Novel of Espionage. 110p. (Orig.). 1972. pap. 15.00 (*0-89366-005-1*) Ultramarine Pub.

Aydette, Vicki, ed. see Simon, Jerry.

Aydi, Mohammed E., jt. auth. see Doughty, Dick.

Aydin, Ahmet H. Police Organisation & Legitimacy: Case Studies in England, Wales, & Turkey. 216p. 1997. text 64.95 (*1-85972-644-5*, Pub. by Avebry) Ashgate Pub Co.

*__Aydin, Kamil.__ Images of Turkey in Western Literature. 199p. 2000. pap. 19.95 (*0-906719-29-1*, Pub. by Eothen) Paul & Co Pubs.

Aydin, Mustafa. Turkish Foreign Policy During the Gulf War of 1990-91. (Cairo Papers in Social Science: Vol. 21, No. 1). 92p. 1999. pap. 10.00 (*977-424-506-7*, Pub. by Am Univ Cairo Pr) Col U Pr.

Aydt, Deborah. Love Games. (J). 1984. pap. 2.25 (*0-590-32431-4*) Scholastic Inc.

Aye, Nila. Orchard's Little Blue Book of Nursery Rhymes. LC 97-12370. (Illus.). 32p. (J). (ps-1). 1998. 5.95 (*0-531-30063-3*) Orchard Bks Watts.

— Orchard's Little Green Book of Nursery Rhymes. LC 97-12371. (Illus.). 32p. (J). (ps-1). 1998. 5.95 (*0-531-30060-9*) Orchard Bks Watts.

— Orchard's Little Red Book of Nursery Rhymes. LC 97-12372. (Illus.). 32p. (J). (ps-1). 1998. 5.95 (*0-531-30061-7*) Orchard Bks Watts.

Aye, Nila. Orchard's Little Yellow Book of Nursery Rhymes. LC 97-12369. 32p. (J). (ps-1). 1998. 5.95 (*0-531-30062-5*) Orchard Bks Watts.

Ayee, Joseph R. An Anatomy of Public Policy Implementation: The Case of Decentralization Policies in Ghana. (Making of Modern Africa Ser.). 256p. 1994. 77.95 (*1-85628-957-5*, Pub. by Avebry) Ashgate Pub Co.

Ayela, Nega, jt. auth. see Markakis, John.

Ayele, Tizita. Ethiopian Cooking in the American Kitchen. LC 98-91435. 1998. pap. 10.95 (*0-533-12671-1*) Vantage.

Ayella, Marybeth F. Insane Therapy: Portrait of a Psychotherapy Cult. LC 97-38146. 224p. (C). 1998. text 54.95 (*1-56639-600-X*); pap. text 19.95 (*1-56639-601-8*) Temple U Pr.

Ayensu, Edward S. Medicinal Plants of West Africa. Irvine, Keith, ed. LC 78-3110. (Medicinal Plants of the World Ser.: No. 1). (Illus.). 1978. 45.00 (*0-917256-07-7*) Ref Pubns.

Ayensu, Edward S. & DeFilipps, Robert A. Endangered & Threatened Plants of the United States. LC 77-25138. (Illus.). 404p. 1978. text 46.00 (*0-87474-222-6*, AYEP) Smithsonian.

Ayensu, Edward S., jt. auth. see Duke, James A.

Ayensu, Edward S., ed. see Boulos, Loutfy.

Ayer, A. J. Logical Positivism. 1966. pap. 18.95 (*0-02-901130-2*) Free Pr.

Ayer, Adelaide M. Some Difficulties in Elementary School History. LC 72-176527. (Columbia University. Teachers College. Contributions to Education Ser.: No. 212). reprint ed. 37.50 (*0-404-55212-9*) AMS Pr.

Ayer, Alfred Jules. Bertrand Russell. 176p. 1988. pap. text 19.00 (*0-226-03343-0*) U Ch Pr.

— Language, Truth & Logic. 1990. 21.25 (*0-8446-1571-4*) Peter Smith.

— Language, Truth & Logic. 2nd ed. 160p. 1952. pap. 5.95 (*0-486-20010-8*) Dover.

— Logical Positivism. LC 78-6321. 455p. 1978. reprint ed. lib. bdg. 89.50 (*0-313-20462-4*, AYLP, Greenwood Pr) Greenwood.

— Memorial Essays. Griffiths, A. Phillips, ed. (Royal Institute of Philosophy Supplements Ser.: No. 30). 239p. (C). 1992. pap. text 22.95 (*0-521-42246-9*) Cambridge U Pr.

— Philosophical Essays. LC 79-24852. 289p. 1980. reprint ed. lib. bdg. 35.00 (*0-313-20902-2*, AYPE, Greenwood Pr) Greenwood.

— Probability & Evidence. 1972. text 44.00 (*0-231-03650-7*) Col U Pr.

— Probability & Evidence. 1979. pap. text 20.00 (*0-231-04767-3*) Col U Pr.

— Thomas Paine. LC 88-16622. 206p. 1990. pap. 15.95 (*0-226-03339-2*) U Ch Pr.

— Wittgenstein. LC 86-11278. 168p. (C). 1986. pap. 13.95 (*0-226-03337-6*) U Ch Pr.

Ayer, Edward E., compiled by. Narratives of Indian Captivity among the Indians of North America. 169p. 1991. reprint ed. 65.00 (*1-888262-37-0*) Martino Pubng.

Ayer, Eleanor. Colorado Traveler: Birds - A Guide to Colorado's Unique Varieties. (American Traveler Ser.: Vol. 40). (Illus.). 48p. 1987. pap. 6.95 (*1-55838-075-2*) R H Pub.

— Colorado Traveler: Parks & Monuments - A Scenic Guide to Colorado. (American Traveler Ser.: Vol. 34). (Illus.). 48p. 1987. pap. 3.95 (*1-55838-066-3*) R H Pub.

— Colorado Traveler: Skiing - A Guide to the Colorado High Country. (American Traveler Ser.: Vol. 39). (Illus.). 48p. 1987. pap. 3.95 (*1-55838-073-6*) R H Pub.

— Colorado Traveler: Wildlife - A Guide to Colorado's Unique Animals. (American Traveler Ser.: Vol. 37). (Illus.). 48p. 1987. pap. 3.95 (*1-55838-071-X*) R H Pub.

Ayer, Eleanor. Our Flag. LC 91-38892. (I Know America Ser.). (Illus.). 48p. (J). (gr. 2-4). 1992. pap. 8.95 (*1-878841-86-6*) Millbrook Pr.

— Our National Monuments. LC 91-43230. (I Know America Ser.). (Illus.). 48p. (J). (gr. 2-4). 1992. pap. 8.95 (*1-56294-816-4*); lib. bdg. 20.90 (*1-56294-078-3*) Millbrook Pr.

Ayer, Eleanor H. Adolf Hitler. LC 95-1277. (Importance Of Ser.). (Illus.). 112p. (YA). (gr. 7 up). 1996. lib. bdg. 22.45 (*1-56006-072-7*) Lucent Bks.

— The Anasazi. LC 92-14701. 112p. (J). 1993. 14.95 (*0-8027-8184-5*); lib. bdg. 15.85 (*0-8027-8185-3*) Walker & Co.

— Arizona Traveler: Arizona Wildflowers - A Guide to Common Varieties. (American Traveler Ser.: Vol. 10). (Illus.). 48p. 1989. pap. 4.95 (*1-55838-109-0*) R H Pub.

*__Ayer, Eleanor H.__ Arizona Traveler: Birds of Arizona--A Guide to Unique Varieties. (American Traveler Ser.: Vol. 6). (Illus.). 48p. 1999. pap. 6.95 (*1-55838-093-0*) R H Pub.

— Arizona Traveler: Discover Arizona--The Grand Canyon State. (American Traveler Ser.: Vol. 9). (Illus.). 48p. 1988. pap. 4.95 (*1-55838-096-5*) R H Pub.

Ayer, Eleanor H. Arizona Traveler: Indians of Arizona - A Guide to Arizona's Heritage. (American Traveler Ser.: Vol. 11). (Illus.). 48p. 1999. pap. 6.95 (*1-55838-112-0*) R H Pub.

— Berlin. LC 91-29721. (Cities at War Ser.). (Illus.). 96p. (YA). (gr. 6 up). 1992. lib. bdg. 18.00 (*0-02-707800-0*, Mac Bks Young Read) S&S Childrens.

— California Traveler: Earthquake Country - Traveling California's Fault Lines. LC 92-200647. (American Traveler Ser.: Vol. 15). (Illus.). 48p. 1992. pap. 4.95 (*1-55838-120-1*) R H Pub.

— California Traveler: Parks & Monuments of California - A Scenic Guide. LC 92-200563. (American Traveler Ser.: Vol. 46). (Illus.). 48p. 1992. pap. 6.95 (*1-55838-119-8*) R H Pub.

— Charles Dickens. LC 97-34957. (Importance of Ser.). (Illus.). (YA). (gr. 5 up). 1997. lib. bdg. 22.45 (*1-56006-525-7*) Lucent Bks.

— Colorado Traveler: Colorado Wildflowers - A Guide to Unique Varieties. (American Traveler Ser.: Vol. 36). (Illus.). 48p. 1987. pap. 3.95 (*1-55838-070-1*) R H Pub.

— Colorado Traveler: Discover Colorado - The Centennial State. (American Traveler Ser.: Vol. 42). (Illus.). 48p. 1987. pap. 3.95 (*1-55838-087-6*) R H Pub.

— Colorado Traveler: Hall of Fame - A Gallery of the Rich & Famous. (American Traveler Ser.: Vol. 2). (Illus.). 48p. 1987. pap. 4.95 (*0-939650-64-9*) R H Pub.

— Everything You Need to Know about Stress. rev. ed. LC 94-434. (Need to Know Library). (Illus.). 64p. (YA). (gr. 7-12). 1998. lib. bdg. 17.95 (*0-8239-2628-1*) Rosen Group.

— Everything You Need to Know about Teen Fatherhood. Rosen, Ruth C., ed. (Need to Know Library). (Illus.). 64p. (YA). (gr. 7-12). 1995. lib. bdg. 16.95 (*0-8239-2100-X*) Rosen Group.

— Everything You Need to Know about Teen Fatherhood. rev. ed. (Illus.). 64p. (gr. 8-12). 1998. lib. bdg. 17.95 (*0-8239-2842-X*) Rosen Group.

— A Firestorm Unleashed: January 1942 to June 1943. Shulman, William, ed. LC 96-44430. (Holocaust Ser.). (Illus.). 80p. (YA). (gr. 7 up). 1997. lib. bdg. 19.45 (*1-56711-204-8*) Blackbirch.

— Germany. LC 98-15471. (Modern Nations of the World Ser.). 144p. (J). 1999. lib. bdg. 23.70 (*1-56006-355-6*) Lucent Bks.

— Germany. (World Partners Ser.). (Illus.). 64p. (YA). (gr. 7 up). 1990. lib. bdg. 18.95 (*0-86593-093-7*) Rourke Corp.

— Hispanic Colorado. (Colorado Chronicles Ser.: Vol. 4). (Illus.). 48p. (J). (gr. 4-7). 1982. 11.95 (*0-939650-11-8*); pap. 6.95 (*0-939650-10-X*) R H Pub.

— Homeless Children. LC 96-17343. (Overview Ser.). (Illus.). (YA). (gr. 4-12). 1996. lib. bdg. 22.45 (*1-56006-177-4*) Lucent Bks.

— Inferno: July 1943 to April 1945. Shulman, William, ed. LC 96-48528. (Holocaust Ser.). (Illus.). 80p. (YA). (gr. 7 up). 1997. lib. bdg. 19.45 (*1-56711-205-6*) Blackbirch.

— Lewis Latimer: Creating Bright Ideas. LC 96-18930. (Innovative Minds Ser.). 112p. (J). 1997. lib. bdg. 27.11 (*0-8172-4407-7*) Raintree Steck-V.

— Life As a Nazi Soldier. (Way People Live Ser.). (Illus.). (YA). (gr. 4-12). 1998. lib. bdg. 22.45 (*1-56006-484-6*) Lucent Bks.

— Margaret Bourke-White: Photographing the World. LC 91-39800. (People in Focus Ser.). (Illus.). 112p. (YA). (gr. 5 up). 1992. lib. bdg. 13.95 (*0-87518-513-4*, Dillon Silver Burdett) Silver Burdett Pr.

— Our Flag. LC 91-38892. (I Know America Ser.). 1992. 14.15 (*0-606-06644-6*, Pub. by Turtleback) Demco.

— Our National Monuments. LC 91-43230. (I Know America Ser.). 1992. 14.15 (*0-606-06648-9*, Pub. by Turtleback) Demco.

*__Ayer, Eleanor H.__ Parallel Journeys. (Illus.). 256p. (YA). (gr. 7). 2000. per. 5.99 (*0-689-83236-2*) Aladdin.

Ayer, Eleanor H. Ruth Bader Ginsburg. (People in Focus Ser.). 112p. (J). (gr. 5). 1994. pap. 7.95 (*0-382-24721-3*) Silver Burdett Pr.

— Ruth Bader Ginsburg. LC 94-17854. (People in Focus Ser.). (J). (gr. 5). 1994. lib. bdg. 22.00 (*0-87518-651-3*, Dillon Silver Burdett) Silver Burdett Pr.

— Southwest Traveler: A Guide to the Anasazi & Other Ancient Southwest Indians. LC 92-171064. (American Traveler Ser.: Vol. 20). (Illus.). 48p. 1991. pap. 4.95 (*1-55838-126-0*) R H Pub.

— The Survivors. LC 97-27260. (Holocaust Library). (Illus.). (YA). (gr. 5 up). 1997. lib. bdg. 22.45 (*1-56006-096-4*) Lucent Bks.

— Teen Smoking. LC 98-25983. (Overview Ser.). (Illus.). (YA). (gr. 4-12). 1998. lib. bdg. 23.70 (*1-56006-442-0*) Lucent Bks.

— U. S. Holocaust Memorial Museum. 72p. (J). (gr. 4). 1995. pap. 7.95 (*0-382-24728-0*) Silver Burdett Pr.

Ayer, Eleanor H. & Chicoine, Stephen D. From the Ashes: May 1945 & After. Shulman, William, ed. LC 96-47707. (Holocaust Ser.). (Illus.). 80p. (YA). (gr. 7 up). 1997. lib. bdg. 19.45 (*1-56711-206-4*) Blackbirch.

Ayer, Eleanor H., et al. Parallel Journeys. LC 94-23277. (Illus.). 256p. (J). (gr. 7 up). 1995. 16.00 (*0-689-31830-8*) Atheneum Yung Read.

Ayer, Harriet H. Harriet Hubbard Ayer's Book: A Complete & Authentic, Treatise on the Laws of Health & Beauty. LC 74-3927. (Women in America Ser.). (Illus.). 546p. 1974. reprint ed. 45.95 (*0-405-06074-2*) Ayer.

Ayer, Hilary. Battle Technology: The Lost Issues. 144p. 1992. pap. 12.95 (*0-9633268-0-5*) Pac Rim CA.

— Variations on the Hermit. 64p. 1973. pap. 30.00 (*0-87924-025-3*) Membrane Pr.

Ayer, Hilary, ed. see Kidd, Paul.

Ayer, Hilary, ed. see Kidd, Paul & Gallaci, S. A.

Ayer, Jane. Guided Meditations for Advent, Christmas, New Year, & Epiphany. (Quiet Place Apart Ser.). 52p. (YA). (gr. 6-12). 1997. pap., teacher ed. 9.95 (*0-88489-517-3*) St Marys.

— Guided Meditations for Lent, Holy Week, Easter & Pentecost. (Quiet Place Apart Ser.). 52p. 1997. pap. 9.95 (*0-88489-520-3*) St Marys.

— Guided Meditations for Ordinary Time: Courage, Loss, Gratitude & Needs. Koch, Carl, ed. LC 98-219577. (Quiet Place Apart Ser.). (Illus.). 52p. 1998. pap. 9.95 (*0-88489-586-6*) St Marys.

*__Ayer, Jane.__ Guided Meditations on Discipleship: Readiness, Faithfulness, Conviction, Transformation. (Quiet Place Apart Ser.). 52p. 2000. pap. 11.95 (*0-88489-653-6*) St Marys.

— Guided Meditations on Discipleship: Readiness, Faithfulness, Conviction. Transformation. (Quiet Place Apart Ser.). 2000. audio compact disk 17.95 (*0-88489-655-2*) St Marys.

Ayer, Jane E. Guided Meditations for Adults Vol. 3: Salvation, Joy, Faith, Healing. (Quiet Place Apart Ser.). 48p. 1996. pap. 9.95 (*0-88489-393-6*) St Marys.

— Guided Meditations for Junior High: Good Judgment, Gifts, Obedience, Inner Blindness. (Quiet Place Apart Ser.). 48p. 1997. pap., teacher ed. 9.95 (*0-88489-500-9*) St Marys.

*__Ayer, Jane E.__ Guided Meditations on God's Justice & Compassion: Accountability, Judgment, Acknowledgment, Selfishness. (Quiet Place Apart Ser.). 52p. (C). 2001. pap. 11.95 (*0-88489-650-1*) St Marys.

Ayer, Jane E. Guided Meditations on Images of God: Mother, Potter, Compassion & Love. 48p. 1999. pap. 11.95 (*0-88489-609-9*) St Marys.

— Guided Meditations on the Paschal Mystery: Consequences, Idolatry, Revelation & Reconciliation. 1999. pap. 11.95 (*0-88489-612-9*) St Marys.

Ayer, John D., et al. Secured Transactions in California Commercial Law Practice. 363p. 1986. text 100.00 (*0-88124-142-3*, BU-32310) Cont Ed Bar-CA.

Ayer, Joseph C. Sourcebook of Ancient Church History. LC 70-113536. reprint ed. lib. bdg. 64.50 (*0-404-00436-9*) AMS Pr.

Ayer, Jules A. Part of My Life. (Illus.). 1978. pap. 7.95 (*0-19-281245-9*) OUP.

Ayer, Steve. Object-Oriented Client-Server Application Development: Using ObjectPal & C. 1995. text 40.00 (*0-07-002861-3*) McGraw.

Ayer, W. R., ed. Some Social Aspects of Dentistry. 100p. 1981. pap. 18.00 (*0-08-028132-X*, Pergamon Pr) Elsevier.

Ayerbe-Chaux, Reinaldo. Yo, Don Juan Manuel: Apologia de una Vida. (Spanish Ser.: No. 91). xxii, 241p. 1993. 25.00 (*1-56954-003-9*) Hispanic Seminary.

Ayerbe-Chaux, Reinaldo, ed. Textos y Concordancia de la Obra Completa de Juan Manuel. (Spanish Ser.: No. 28). 12p. 1986. 15.00 incl. fiche (*0-942260-70-8*) Hispanic Seminary.

Ayerbe-Chaux, Reinaldo, ed. see Manuel, Juan.

Ayerbe, J. M., et al. Measures of Noncompactness in Metric Fixed Point Theory. LC 97-38052. (Operator Theory, Advances & Applications Ser.: Vol. 99). vii, 211p. 1997. text 90.00 (*3-7643-5794-0*) Birkhauser.

Ayerbe Toledano, J. M., et al. Measures of Noncompactness in Metric Fixed Point Theory. LC 97-38052. (Operator Theory, Advances & Applications Ser.). 1997. write for info. (*0-8176-5794-0*) Birkhauser.

Ayeroff, Stan. Benny Goodman for Bb Clarinet, MFM201. (Illus.). 64p. 1980. pap. 14.95 (*0-8256-4201-9*, AM29307) Music Sales.

— Charlie Christian. 72p. pap. 14.95 (*0-8256-4084-9*, AM24316) Music Sales.

— Jazz Masters: Benny Goodman. 1980. pap. 14.95 (*0-8256-4092-X*, AM41831) Music Sales.

— Jazz Masters: Django Reinhardt. 72p. 1997. pap. 14.95 (*0-8256-4083-0*, AM23235) Music Sales.

Ayers. American History. (C). 1999. text 53.50 (*0-03-072479-1*, Pub. by Harcourt Coll Pubs) Harcourt.

— American History, Vol. 2. (C). 1999. pap. text 39.00 (*0-03-072574-7*, Pub. by Harcourt Coll Pubs) Harcourt.

— American Passages, Vol. 1. (C). 1999. pap. text 39.00 (*0-03-072573-9*, Pub. by Harcourt Coll Pubs) Harcourt.

— American Passages: A History of the U. S. (C). 1999. pap. text 44.50 (*0-03-021249-9*) Harcourt Coll Pubs.

— American Passages: A History of the U. S., Vol. 1. (C). 1999. pap., student ed. 18.50 (*0-03-072577-1*, Pub. by Harcourt Coll Pubs) Harcourt.

— American Passages: A History of the U. S., Vol. 2. (C). 1999. pap. text, student ed. 18.50 (*0-03-072576-3*, Pub. by Harcourt Coll Pubs) Harcourt.

— Metaphysics & Common Sense. (Philosophy Ser.). (C). 1997. mass mkt. 29.50 (*0-534-54243-3*) Wadsworth Pub.

Ayers, Alex, ed. see King, Martin Luther, Jr.

*__Ayers, Alfred.__ Hume. (Very Short Introductions Ser.). (Illus.). 112p. 2000. pap. 8.95 (*0-19-285406-2*) OUP.

*__Ayers, Andrew.__ The Architecture of Paris. (Illus.). 300p. 2001. 42.00 (*3-930698-96-X*) Edition A Menges.

Ayers, Becky, jt. auth. see Crist, Caroline.

Ayers, Camilla, ed. see Scott, Gini G.

An Asterisk (*) at the beginning of an entry indicates that the title is appearing for the first time.

A

Ayers, Camilla, ed. see Thornhill, Annette.
Ayers, Camilla, ed. see Whitney, Charlotte.
Ayers, Catherine. Maximizing Your Impact in Contract Education: A Handbook for Community Colleges. 256p. (Orig.). 1995. pap. 59.95 (*0-938075-59-4*) Ocean View Bks.
Ayers, Charles. Memories Are Made of This: An Anecdotal Autobiography. Messinger Press Staff, ed. LC 89-91192. (Illus.). 428p. (Orig.). 1989. write for info. (*0-9623170-0-4*) Limelight Celina.
Ayers, Chuck, jt. auth. see Batiuk, Tom.
***Ayers, Danny, et al.** Professional Java Server Programming. (Illus.). 1121p. 1999. pap. 59.99 (*1-86100-277-7*) Wrox Pr Inc.
***Ayers, David.** English Literature of the 1920s. LC 99-487767. 256p. 1999. 72.00 (*0-7486-0985-7*, Pub. by Edinburgh U Pr) Col U Pr.
***Ayers, David M.** Anatomy of a Crisis: Education, Development & the State in Cambodia, 1953-1998. LC 99-42870. 2000. 45.00 (*0-8248-2238-2*) UH Pr.
Ayers, Donald M. Bioscientific Terminology. LC 74-163010. 325p. (C). 1972. pap. 15.95 (*0-8165-0305-2*) U of Ariz Pr.
***Ayers, Dottie & Harrison, Donna, eds.** Advertising Art of Steiff: Teddy Bears & Playthings. Pauli, Lydia, tr. (Illus.). 127p. 1999. reprint ed. text 20.00 (*0-7881-6829-0*) DIANE Pub.
Ayers, Edward. The Valley of the Shadow: Two Communities in the American Civil War. LC 97-33061. (Illus.). 128p. 2000. 49.95 incl. cd-rom (*0-393-04604-4*) Norton.
Ayers, Edward, ed. see Chearney, Lee A.
Ayers, Edward L. The Promise of the New South: Life after Reconstruction. (Illus.). 592p. (C). 1993. reprint ed. pap. text 18.95 (*0-19-508548-5*) OUP.
— Southern Crossing: A History of the American South, 1877-1906. LC 94-9755. (Illus.). 304p. 1995. pap. 14.95 (*0-19-508689-9*) OUP.
— Vengeance & Justice: Crime & Punishment in the 19th Century American South. 362p. 1985. pap. text 23.95 (*0-19-503988-2*) OUP.
Ayers, Edward L. & Mittendorf, Bradley C., eds. The Oxford Book of the American South: Testimony, Memory & Fiction. LC 96-45135. 608p. 1997. 30.00 (*0-19-508522-1*) OUP.
— The Oxford Book of the American South: Testimony, Memory, & Fiction. 608p. 1998. reprint ed. pap. 19.95 (*0-19-512493-6*) OUP.
Ayers, Edward L. & Willis, John C., eds. The Edge of the South: Life in Nineteenth-Century Virginia. (Illus.). (C). 1991. text 35.00 (*0-8139-1298-9*) U Pr of Va.
Ayers, Edward L., et al. All over the Map: Rethinking American Regions. LC 95-21455. 144p. 1996. pap. text 13.95 (*0-8018-5392-3*) Johns Hopkins.
Ayers, Esther R., jt. auth. see Oberlin, Sarah B.
Ayers, Glenn. La Gramatica Ixil. LC 91-71410. (Lingustic Ser.: Vol. 2). (SPA.). 220p. 1991. pap. text 12.00 (*0-910443-09-2*) Plumsock Meso Studies.
***Ayers, Harry.** Classroom Management A Practical Approach for Primary & Secondary Teachers. LC 98-203720. 1998. pap. text 24.95 (*1-85346-510-0*) Taylor & Francis.
Ayers, Harry, et al. Assessing Individual Needs: A Practical Approach. 64p. 1993. pap. 19.00 (*1-85346-285-3*, Pub. by David Fulton) Taylor & Francis.
— Assessing Individual Needs: A Practical Approach. 2nd ed. LC 96-229242. 96p. 1996. pap. text 24.95 (*1-85346-440-6*, Pub. by David Fulton) Taylor & Francis.
— Perspectives on Behaviour: A Practical Guide to Effective Interventions for Teachers (Resource Materials for Teachers) 64p. 1995. pap. 17.95 (*1-85346-364-7*, Pub. by David Fulton) Taylor & Francis.
Ayers, Harry, jt. auth. see Nicolson, Doula.
Ayers, Helge, tr. see Redeker, Hans.
Ayers, Herlinde N. Selbstverwirklichung/Selbstverneinung Vol. 15: Rollenkonflikte im Werk von Hebbel, Ibsen und Strindberg. (Studies on Themes & Motifs in Literature). (GER.). 184p. (C). 1995. text 45.95 (*0-8204-2668-7*) P Lang Pubng.
***Ayers, Hugh.** Spanglish: A Course of Communication Celebrating Similarity (Un Curso de Communicacion Celebrando Similaridad) (SPA., Illus.). 101p. 1999. wbk. ed. write for info. (*0-9674526-0-0*) Spanglish NC.
Ayers, James A., ed. see Board, Sherri.
***Ayers, James B.** Handbook of Supply Chain Management. LC 00-39021. 2000. write for info. (*1-57444-273-2*) St Lucie Pr.
Ayers, James C. Pepsi: Cola Bottles: Collectors Guide. (Illus.). 148p. 1995. ring bd. 29.50 (*0-9645443-0-X*) RJM Enter.
Ayers, Jerry B. & Berney, Mary F., eds. A Practical Guide to Teacher Education Evaluation. (C). 1989. lib. bdg. 86.00 (*0-7923-9042-3*) Kluwer Academic.
Ayers, Jerry B., jt. ed. see Berney, Mary F.
Ayers, Jerry B., jt. ed. see Gephart, William J.
Ayers, Jim, ed. see Paulson, Roland.
Ayers, Jim, ed. see Whelchel, Sandy.
Ayers, John. Chinese Ceramics: The Koger Collection. 180p. 1994. pap. 22.95 (*1-57003-010-3*) U of SC Pr.
— Japanese Ceramics. (Baur Collection Catalogues). (Illus.). 184p. 1994. 255.00 (*0-7103-0408-0*) Routledge.
Ayers, John, et al. Porcelain for Palaces: The Fashion for Japan in Europe, 1650-1750. (Illus.). 328p. 1990. 70.00 (*0-903421-24-0*, Pub. by P Wilson) Scala Books.
Ayers, John, ed. see Krahl, Regina & Erbahar, Nurdan.
Ayers, Joseph W., ed. see Buckley, James.
Ayers, Joseph W., ed. see Rice, Phil.
Ayers, Kenneth W., et al. Environmental Science & Technology Handbook. LC 93-27558. 389p. 1994. text 79.00 (*0-86587-362-3*) Gov Insts.
Ayers, Kenya F., jt. auth. see Ayaz, Sandi.
Ayers, M. R., ed. see Berkeley, George.
Ayers, Martha, et al. Community-Based Nursing Care: Making the Transition. LC 98-50554. (Illus.). 431p. (C). (gr. 13). 1999. pap. text 29.00 (*0-8151-1339-0*, 29954) Mosby Inc.
***Ayers, Martha, et al.** Community-Based Nursing Care: Making the Transition, Includes Testbank. 1999. teacher ed. write for info. (*0-323-00747-3*) Mosby Inc.
Ayers, Michael. Locke. LC 93-15180. (Arguments of the Philosophers Ser.). 704p. (C). 1993. pap. 29.99 (*0-415-10030-5*, B2455) Routledge.
***Ayers, Michael.** Locke: Great Philosophers, 8. LC 99-22647. Vol. 8. 64p. 1999. pap. 6.00 (*0-415-92383-2*) Routledge.
Ayers, Michael, jt. ed. see Garber, Daniel.
Ayers, Mimi, jt. auth. see Campbell, Patricia B.
Ayers, Patricia. A Kids Guide to How Flowers Grow. LC 98-51630. (Digging in the Dirt Ser.). 24p. (J). 2000. lib. bdg. 18.60 (*0-8239-5462-5*, PowerKids) Rosen Group.
— A Kids Guide to How Fruits Grow. LC 98-51631. (Digging in the Dirt Ser.). 24p. (J). 1999. lib. bdg. 18.60 (*0-8239-5466-8*, PowerKids) Rosen Group.
***Ayers, Patricia.** A Kids Guide to How Herbs Grow. LC 99-28911. (Digging in the Dirt Ser.). 24p. (J). 1999. lib. bdg. 18.60 (*0-8239-5464-1*, PowerKids) Rosen Group.
— A Kid's Guide to How Plants Grow. LC 99-28910. (Digging in the Dirt Ser.). 24p. (J). 1999. lib. bdg. 18.60 (*0-8239-5465-X*, PowerKids) Rosen Group.
Ayers, Patricia. A Kid's Guide to How Trees Grow. LC 99-23319. (Digging in the Dirt Ser.). 24p. (J). 1999. lib. bdg. 18.60 (*0-8239-5463-3*, PowerKids) Rosen Group.
***Ayers, Patricia.** A Kid's Guide to How Vegetables Grow. LC 99-23632. (Digging in the Dirt Ser.). 24p. (J). 1999. 18.60 (*0-8239-5461-7*) Rosen Group.
Ayers, Peter K., ed. see Ogali, Ogali A.
Ayers, Rachel. Nursing Service in Transition: A Description of Organization for Classification & Utilization of Nurse Practitioners. 124p. 1972. pap. 5.00 (*0-940876-03-5*) City Hope.
Ayers, Ralph. Teaching on TV & Video. LC 94-44166. (Engineer's Guide to Business Ser.: Vol. 6). 1994. 19.95 (*0-7803-2246-0*, EG106) Inst Electrical.
Ayers, Rebecca W., ed. see Bowman, Warren D.
Ayers, Rick, ed. see Terkel, Studs.
Ayers, Robert H. Christian Theology in a Contemporary World. LC 96-51513. (Studies in Religion & Society: Vol. 38). 228p. 1997. text 89.95 (*0-7734-8739-5*) E Mellen.
— Judaism & Christianity: Origins, Developments & Recent Trends. LC 83-3548. (Illus.). 478p. (Orig.). (C). 1983. lib. bdg. 67.00 (*0-8191-3156-3*) U Pr of Amer.
— Language, Logic & Reason in the Church Fathers: A Study of Tertullian, Augustine, & Aquinas. (Altertumswissenschaftliche Texte und Studien: Bd. 6). viii, 146p. 1979. 25.00 (*3-487-06629-7*) G Olms Pubs.
Ayers, Ronald M. & Collinge. Economics By Design: Principles & Issues. 2nd ed. LC 99-28277. (Illus.). 509p. 1999. pap. text 70.60 (*0-13-013298-5*) P-H.
Ayers, Ronald M., jt. auth. see Collinge, Robert A.
***Ayers, Samuel J.** Buddy Holly: A Legacy of Music. large type ed. (Illus.). 32p. (J). (gr. 3-8). 1999. pap. 8.00 (*0-9667681-1-6*) Hermosa Creats.
— Ella Iles: Early Texas Teacher. large type ed. (Illus.). 32p. (J). (gr. 2-6). 1999. 13.00 (*0-9667681-0-8*) Hermosa Creats.
— Roscoe Wilson: Champion of the Law, Education & Community Service. large type ed. (Illus.). 32p. (J). (gr. 3-8). 2000. 14.00 (*0-9667681-2-4*) Hermosa Creats.
***Ayers, Shirley.** Bomb Threat: Model Procedures Guide. 28p. 1999. pap. 20.00 (*0-945790-14-7*) Detrick Lawrence.
Ayers, Shirley. Breathing Apparatus Guide: Leader's Guide. 60p. (Orig.). 1992. pap. 20.00 (*0-945790-03-1*) Detrick Lawrence.
— Chemical Protective Clothing: Leader's Guide. 58p. (Orig.). 1992. pap. 20.00 (*0-945790-02-3*) Detrick Lawrence.
— Confined Space Emergency: Leader's Guide. 56p. 1995. pap. 20.00 (*0-945790-10-4*) Detrick Lawrence.
— Decon Team Guide. 51p. (Orig.). 1992. pap. 20.00 (*0-945790-01-5*) Detrick Lawrence.
— First Responder Awareness: Leader's Guide. 56p. 1993. pap. 20.00 (*0-945790-05-8*) Detrick Lawrence.
— Oil Spill Response: Leader's Guide. 64p. 1994. pap., teacher ed. 20.00 (*0-945790-08-2*) Detrick Lawrence.
— Trucking Hazardous Materials: Leader's Guide. 52p. 1993. pap. 20.00 (*0-945790-06-6*) Detrick Lawrence.
— Understanding MSDS: Material Safety Data Sheets. 48p. 1995. pap. 20.00 (*0-945790-09-0*) Detrick Lawrence.
Ayers, Shirley, ed. Model Procedures Guide: Industrial Incident Management. 20p. 1993. pap. 20.00 (*0-945790-07-4*) Detrick Lawrence.
Ayers, Shirley & Miller, Bill. Introduction to Hazardous Chemicals: Leaders Guide. (HazChem Ser.). 64p. 1998. pap. 20.00 (*0-945790-13-9*) Detrick Lawrence.
Ayers, Shirley, jt. auth. see Ronan, John.
Ayers, Stephen M. The Selection Process for the National Endowment for the Arts Theatre Program: An Historical - Critical Study. LC 91-4343. (American University Studies: General Literature: Ser. XIX, Vol. 26). (Illus.). 208p. (C). 1992. text 38.95 (*0-8204-1510-3*) P Lang Pubng.
Ayers, Steven D. The Discovery. 64p. 1994. pap. 5.95 (*0-9642319-0-5*) S D Ayers.
Ayers, Tess & Brown, Paul. The Essential Guide to Lesbian & Gay Weddings. (Illus.). 286p. 1999. pap. 17.95 (*1-55583-484-1*, Pub. by Alyson Pubns) Consort Bk Sales.
Ayers, Timothy W. Living Parables: Illustrated the Message with Drama. LC 97-29589. 106p. 1998. pap. 10.25 (*0-7880-1171-5*) CSS OH.
Ayers, Tom. The Illustrated Rules of Ice Hockey. (Illustrated Rules of the Game Ser.). (Illus.). 32p. (J). (gr. 1-4). 1996. lib. bdg. 21.27 (*1-884756-12-3*) Davidson Titles.
— The Illustrated Rules of Ice Hockey. LC 95-8068. (Illustrated Sports Ser.). (Illus.). 32p. (J). (gr. 1-4). 1995. per. 6.95 (*1-57102-048-9*, Ideals Child) Hambleton-Hill.
Ayers, W. B., Jr. & Kaiser, W. R., eds. Coalbed Methane in the Upper Cretaceous Fruitland Formation, San Juan Basin, New Mexico & Colorado. (Reports of Investigations: Vol. RI 218). (Illus.). 216p. 1994. pap. 15.00 (*0-614-01867-6*) Bur Econ Geology.
Ayers, W. B., Jr., jt. auth. see Morton, R. A.
Ayers, William. Chang Chih-Tung & Educational Reform in China. LC 71-129121. (Harvard East Asian Ser.: No. 54). 304p. 1971. reprint ed. pap. 94.30 (*0-7837-2219-2*, 205730900004) Bks Demand.
— The Good Preschool Teacher: Six Teachers Reflect on Their Lives. (Early Childhood Education Ser.: No. 21). 176p. (C). 1989. pap. text 16.95 (*0-8077-2946-9*) Tchrs Coll.
— A Kind & Just Parent: The Children of the Juvenile Court. 224p. 1998. pap. text 12.00 (*0-8070-4403-2*) Beacon Pr.
***Ayers, William.** Simple Justice: The Challenge for Small Schools. (Teaching for Social Justice Ser.). 2000. pap. 21.95 (*0-8077-3962-6*) Tchrs Coll.
Ayers, William. To Become a Teacher: Making a Difference in Children's Lives. 264p. (C). 1995. text 42.00 (*0-8077-3456-X*); pap. text 17.95 (*0-8077-3455-1*) Tchrs Coll.
— To Teach: The Journey of a Teacher. LC 92-43749. 160p. (C). 1993. 14.95 (*0-8077-3262-1*) Tchrs Coll.
Ayers, William, et al, eds. Teaching for Social Justice: A Democracy & Education Reader. LC 97-49382. (Illus.). 320p. 1998. pap. 18.95 (*1-56584-420-3*, Pub. by New Press NY) Norton.
Ayers, William & Ford, Patricia, eds. City Kids, City Teachers: Reports from the Front Row. LC 95-40353. 400p. 1996. 25.00 (*1-56584-328-2*, Pub. by New Press NY); pap. 16.00 (*1-56584-051-8*, Pub. by New Press NY) Norton.
Ayers, William, jt. ed. see Schubert, William H.
Ayers, William M., ed. Catalytic Activation of Carbon Dioxide. LC 87-30832. (Symposium Ser.: No. 363). (Illus.). 214p. 1988. 54.95 (*0-8412-1447-6*) Am Chemical.
— Catalytic Activation of Carbon Dioxide. LC 87-30832. (ACS Symposium Ser.: Vol. 363). 224p. 1988. reprint ed. pap. 69.50 (*0-608-03885-7*, 206433200008) Bks Demand.
Ayes, Sabine L., tr. see Du Bois-Reymond, Emil H.
***Ayesh, Aladdin.** Essential Dynamic HTML Fast. (Essential Ser.). x, 168p. 2000. 28.00 (*1-85233-626-9*, Pub. by Spr-Verlag) Spr-Verlag.
Ayesh, Raid & Hubbard, Anthony, eds. Volunteers in Research & Testing. LC 97-147630. 208p. 1996. 99.95 (*0-7484-0397-3*) Taylor & Francis.
Aygi, Gennady, ed. An Anthology of Chuvash Poetry. France, P., tr. from TUR. LC 90-86404. (UNESCO Library of World Poetry). 220p. (Orig.). 1991. pap. 27.00 (*1-85610-003-0*, Pub. by Forest Bks) Dufour.
Aygi, Gennady I. Selected Poems, 1954-1994. France, Peter, tr. LC 96-40076. 1997. pap. 14.95 (*0-8101-1540-9*) Northwestern U Pr.
Ayham, Ece. The Blind Cat Black & Orthodoxies. Nemet-Nejat, Murat, tr. from TUR. (Classics Ser.: No. 125). 110p. (Orig.). 1997. pap. 10.95 (*1-55713-102-3*) Sun & Moon CA.
Ayhan, Teoman, jt. ed. see Dincer, Ibrahim.
Ayianoglou, Pantelis. Money, Inflation & Recession in the U. K. & U. S. A. The Fallacies of Monetarism - A Marxist View. LC 93-23578. 280p. 1993. text 89.95 (*0-7734-9373-5*) E Mellen.
Ayim, Martin A. A Comparison of Health Education Perceptions Between the Chamba & Widikum Ethnic Groups in the Northwest Province of Cameroon: A Dissertation. Hurley, Robert S. et al, eds. 210p. 1998. pap. text 35.00 (*0-9659474-2-4*) Vita Pr.
— Comprehensive Official Handbook of the Northwest Provincial Academy of Cameroon. unabridged ed. NWPA Executive Staff, ed. 40p. 1998. pap. 50.00 (*0-9659474-3-2*) Vita Pr.
— Empowerment Through Health Education: Organization, Administration, & the Practice of Comprehensive Health Education in Developing Countries & Multicultural Settings. 2nd ed. 385p. 1998. pap. text 35.00 (*0-9659474-0-8*) Vita Pr.
— Infectious Disease Epidemiology: An Introduction to Communicable Diseases for Health Professionals. 290p. 1998. pap. text 30.00 (*0-9659474-1-6*) Vita Pr.
Ayim, Maryann N. The Moral Parameters of Good Talk: A Feminist Analysis. 265p. 1997. 45.00 (*0-88920-282-6*) W Laurier U Pr.
Ayisi, Eric O. St. Eustatius: The Treasure Island of the Caribbean. LC 92-14520. (Illus.). 250p. 1992. 45.00 (*0-86543-347-X*); pap. 12.95 (*0-86543-348-8*) Africa World.
Ayittey, George B. Africa in Chaos. LC 97-11236. 416p. 1997. text 35.00 (*0-312-16400-9*) St Martin.
— Africa in Chaos. 416p. 1999. pap. 18.95 (*0-312-21787-0*) St Martin.
— Indigenous African Institutions. 548p. (C). 1992. lib. bdg. 45.00 (*0-941320-65-0*) Transnatl Pubs.
Aykroyd, Juliet, et al, eds. Female Voices. 104p. 1989. pap. text 12.95 (*0-948553-10-3*) Routledge.
Aykroyd, Lucas. 1984: The Ultimate Van Halen Trivia Book. 155p. 1997. spiral bd. 18.00 (*1-55212-089-9*, No. 97-0007) Trafford Pub.
Aykroyd, Stephanie, jt. auth. see Wilson, Hap.
Aykroyd, W. R. Conquest of Deficiency Diseases: Achievements & Prospects. (Freedom from Hunger Campaign Basic Study Ser: No. 24). 98p. 1970. pap. text 9.00 (*92-4-156018-5*, 1150024) World Health.
Aykroyd, Wallace R. Three Philosophers: Lavoisier, Priestley & Cavendish. LC 77-98808. 227p. 1970. reprint ed. lib. bdg. 65.00 (*0-8371-2890-0*, AYTB, Greenwood Pr) Greenwood.
Aylen, J., jt. ed. see Ranieri, R.
***Aylen, John.** Commonsense Guide to Running Your Own Business. LC 99-39957. 150p. 1999. pap. 12.95 (*1-57112-100-5*, P1005) Park Ave.
Aylen, Leo. Dancing the Impossible: New & Selected Poems. 1997. pap. 14.95 (*3-7052-0051-8*, Pub. by Poetry Salzburg) Intl Spec Bk.
— The Greek Theater. LC 82-49313. (Illus.). 384p. 1985. 50.00 (*0-8386-3184-3*) Fairleigh Dickinson.
Aylesworth. Bedtime Stories. LC 97-77744. (Illus.). 144p. (J). (gr. 4-6). 1998. 19.95 (*0-689-82077-1*) S&S Childrens.
***Aylesworth.** Folks in the Valley Big Book. 32p. (J). (ps-3). 1999. pap. 19.95 (*0-06-443394-3*) HarpC Child Bks.
Aylesworth. Splash. LC 98-36620. (J). 2000. 16.00 (*0-689-82079-8*) S&S Childrens.
Aylesworth, Gary E., jt. ed. see Silverman, Hugh J.
Aylesworth, Gary E., tr. see Heidegger, Martin.
Aylesworth, Gary E., tr. see Rotzer, Florian.
***Aylesworth, Jim.** Aunt Pitty Patty's Piggy. LC 98-46263. (Illus.). 32p. (J). (ps-2). 1999. 15.95 (*0-590-89987-2*, Pub. by Scholastic Inc) Penguin Putnam.
Aylesworth, Jim. The Completed Hickory Dickory Dock. LC 94-1226. (Illus.). 32p. (J). (ps-2). 1994. per. 5.99 (*0-689-71862-4*) Aladdin.
— Country Crossing. (J). 1995. mass mkt. 4.95 (*0-689-71895-0*) Aladdin.
— Country Crossing. 1995. 10.15 (*0-606-07391-4*, Pub. by Turtleback) Demco.
— The Folks in the Valley: A Pennsylvania Dutch ABC. LC 91-12451. (Illus.). 32p. (J). (ps-3). 1994. pap. 5.95 (*0-06-443363-3*, HarpTrophy) HarpC Child Bks.
— Folks in the Valley: A Pennsylvania Dutch ABC. 32p. (J). 1998. 6.95 (*0-694-00981-4*) HarpC Child Bks.
— Folks in the Valley: A Pennsylvania Dutch ABC. LC 91-12451. (Trophy Picture Bks.). (Illus.). 1992. 11.15 (*0-606-06381-1*, Pub. by Turtleback) Demco.
— The Full Belly Bowl. LC 98-14052. (Illus.). 40p. (J). (gr. k-3). 1999. 15.00 (*0-689-81033-4*) Atheneum Yung Read.
— The Gingerbread Man. LC 96-52781. (Illus.). 21.99p. (J). (ps-1). 1998. 15.95 (*0-590-97219-7*) Scholastic Inc.
— The Good-Night Kiss. LC 91-40952. (Illus.). 32p. (J). (ps-1). 1993. text 14.95 (*0-689-31515-5*) Atheneum Yung Read.
— McGraw's Emporium. (Illus.). 88p. (J). 1995. 15.95 (*0-8050-3192-8*) H Holt & Co.
— McGraw's Emporium. (Illus.). (J). (ps-2). 1998. pap. 5.95 (*0-8050-5797-8*) H Holt & Co.
— Mr. McGill Goes to Town. LC 89-31111. (Illus.). 32p. (J). (gr. k-2). 1995. pap. 4.95 (*0-8050-2096-9*, Owlet BYR) H Holt & Co.
— My Sister's Rusty Bike. LC 94-20117. (Illus.). 32p. (J). (gr. k-3). 1996. 16.00 (*0-689-31798-0*) Atheneum Yung Read.
— My Son John. 1997. 11.15 (*0-606-13637-1*, Pub. by Turtleback) Demco.
— My Son John. (Illus.). 32p. (J). (ps-2). 1997. reprint ed. pap. 5.95 (*0-8050-5517-7*) H Holt & Co.
— Old Black Fly. LC 91-26825. (Illus.). 32p. (J). (ps-2). 1995. 15.95 (*0-8050-1401-2*, Bks Young Read); pap. 5.95 (*0-8050-3924-4*) H Holt & Co.
— Old Black Fly. 1995. 11.15 (*0-606-12458-6*, Pub. by Turtleback) Demco.
***Aylesworth, Jim.** Old Fox's Sack. LC 00-35773. (Illus.). (J). 2001. pap. write for info. (*0-439-09544-1*) Scholastic Inc.
— 1 CROW. LC 85-45856. (Trophy Picture Bk.). (Illus.). 32p. (J). (ps-1). 1990. pap. 5.95 (*0-06-443242-4*, HarpTrophy) HarpC Child Bks.
— Teddy Bear Tears. (Illus.). 32p. (J). (gr. k). 2000. per. 5.99 (*0-689-83525-6*) Aladdin.
Aylesworth, Jim. Teddy Bear Tears. LC 95-44858. (Illus.). 32p. (J). (ps-k). 1997. 16.00 (*0-689-31776-X*) Atheneum Yung Read.
— Through the Night. LC 97-7281. (Illus.). 32p. (J). (ps-2). 1998. 16.00 (*0-689-80642-6*) S&S Childrens.
— Wake up, Little Children: A Rise-&-Shine Rhyme. (Illus.). 32p. (J). (ps-2). 1996. 16.00 (*0-689-31857-X*) Atheneum Yung Read.
Aylesworth, Jim & Gammell, Stephen. Old Black Fly. LC 91-26825. (Illus.). 32p. (J). (ps-2). 1995. pap. 19.95 (*0-8050-3925-2*) H Holt & Co.
Aylesworth, Owen R. Caleb Sheldon Butts Aylesworth, His Descendants. LC 82-90493. (Illus.). 287p. 1982. text 25.00 (*0-9609312-0-1*) O R Aylesworth.
***Aylesworth, Thomas G.** The Best of Warner Bros. rev. ed. (Illus.). 192p. 2000. reprint ed. 25.00 (*0-7881-9262-0*) DIANE Pub.
Aylesworth, Thomas G. Best of Warner Brothers. 1993. 15.98 (*1-55521-952-7*) Bk Sales Inc.
— Eastern Great Lakes. (Discovering America Ser.). 88p. (J). (gr. 4 up). 1995. 19.95 (*0-7910-3409-7*) Chelsea Hse.
— Eastern Great Lakes: Indiana, Michigan, Ohio. (Let's Discover the States Ser.). (J). 1996. 14.15 (*0-606-04218-0*, Pub. by Turtleback) Demco.
— The Kid's World Almanac of Baseball. rev. ed. LC 95-62358. 288p. 1996. text 8.95 (*0-88687-787-3*) Wrld Almnc.
— Monsters from the Movies. LC 72-1995. (Illus.). 160p. (J). (gr. 5-9). 1972. 12.95 (*0-397-31590-2*) HarpC Child Bks.

A

— Movie Monsters. LC 75-12997. (Illus.). 80p. (J). (gr. 4-7). 1975. 12.95 (*0-397-31639-9*) HarpC Child Bks.

— Movie Monsters. LC 75-12997. (Eerie Ser.). (Illus.). 80p. (J). (gr. 4-8). 1990. lib. bdg. 12.89 (*0-397-32467-7*) HarpC Child Bks.

— Southern New England: Connecticut, Massachusetts, Rhode Island. (Let's Discover the States Ser.). (J). 1988. 12.15 (*0-606-04331-4*, Pub. by Turtleback) Demco.

— Territories & Possessions: Puerto Rico, U. S. Virgin Islands, Guam, American Samoa, Wake, Midway. (Let's Discover the States Ser.). (J). 1988. 12.15 (*0-606-04356-X*, Pub. by Turtleback) Demco.

— West: Arizona, Nevada, Utah. (Let's Discover the States Ser.). (J). 1988. 12.15 (*0-606-04361-6*, Pub. by Turtleback) Demco.

— Western Great Lakes. 88p. (J). (gr. 4 up). 1995. 18.95 (*0-7910-3405-4*) Chelsea Hse.

Aylesworth, Thomas G. & Aylesworth, Virginia L. Eastern Great Lakes: Ohio, Indiana, Michigan. (Let's Discover the States Ser.). (Illus.). 64p. (J). (gr. 4 up). 1990. lib. bdg. 16.95 (*1-55546-559-5*) Chelsea Hse.

— The Great Plains: Montana, Nebraska, North Dakota, South Dakota, Wyoming. LC 94-45823. (Discovering America Ser.). 88p. (J). (gr. 4 up). 1995. pap. 8.95 (*0-7910-3422-4*); lib. bdg. 19.95 (*0-7910-3404-6*) Chelsea Hse.

— Lower Atlantic: North Carolina, South Carolina. LC 94-40429. (State Studies). 88p. (J). (gr. 4 up). 1995. pap. 8.95 (*0-7910-3419-4*); lib. bdg. 18.95 (*0-7910-3401-1*) Chelsea Hse.

— Northern New England: Maine, New Hampshire, Vermont. LC 94-42012. (State Studies). 88p. (J). (gr. 4 up). 1995. lib. bdg. 18.95 (*0-7910-3397-X*) Chelsea Hse.

— Northern New England: Maine, New Hampshire, Vermont. LC 94-42012. (State Studies). 88p. (J). (gr. 7 up). 1995. pap. 8.95 (*0-7910-3415-1*) Chelsea Hse.

— The Northwest: Alaska, Idaho, Oregon, Washington. LC 94-45824. (Discovering America Ser.). 88p. (J). (gr. 4 up). 1995. lib. bdg. 19.95 (*0-7910-3406-2*) Chelsea Hse.

Aylesworth, Thomas G. & Aylesworth, Virginia L. The Northwest: Alaska, Idaho, Oregon, Washington. LC 94-45824. (Discovering America Ser.). 88p. (J). (gr. 4 up). 1995. pap. 8.95 (*0-7910-3424-0*) Chelsea Hse.

— The Pacific: California, Hawaii. LC 94-45822. (Discovering America Ser.). 88p. (J). (gr. 4 up). 1995. pap. 8.95 (*0-7910-3425-9*) Chelsea Hse.

Aylesworth, Thomas G. & Aylesworth, Virginia L. The Pacific: California, Hawaii. LC 94-45822. (Discovering America Ser.). (Illus.). 88p. (J). (gr. 4 up). 1995. lib. bdg. 19.95 (*0-7910-3407-0*) Chelsea Hse.

— The Southeast: Georgia, Kentucky, Tennessee. LC 94-42017. 88p. (J). (gr. 4 up). 1995. pap. 8.95 (*0-7910-3429-1*); lib. bdg. 18.95 (*0-7910-3411-9*) Chelsea Hse.

— Southern New England: Connecticut, Massachusetts, Rhode Island. LC 94-45825. (Discovering America Ser.). 88p. (J). (gr. 4 up). 1995. lib. bdg. 19.95 (*0-7910-3398-8*) Chelsea Hse.

— The Southwest: Colorado, New Mexico, Texas. LC 94-45786. (Discovering America Ser.). 88p. (J). (gr. 4 up). 1995. lib. bdg. 19.95 (*0-7910-3412-7*) Chelsea Hse.

Aylesworth, Thomas G. & Aylesworth, Virginia L. The Southwest: Colorado, New Mexico, Texas. LC 94-45786. (Discovering America Ser.). 88p. (J). (gr. 4 up). 1995. pap. 8.95 (*0-7910-3430-5*) Chelsea Hse.

Aylesworth, Thomas G. & Aylesworth, Virginia L. Upper Atlantic: New Jersey, New York. LC 94-45826. (Discovering America Ser.). 88p. (J). (gr. 4 up). 1995. pap. 8.95 (*0-7910-3417-8*); lib. bdg. 19.95 (*0-7910-3399-6*) Chelsea Hse.

— Western Great Lakes: Illinois, Iowa, Minnesota, Wisconsin. LC 94-40425. (State Studies). 88p. (J). (gr. 4 up). 1995. pap. 8.95 (*0-7910-3423-2*) Chelsea Hse.

Aylesworth, Virginia L., jt. auth. see Aylesworth, Thomas G.

Aylesworth, Jim. Old Black Fly. (Illus.). 32p. (J). 1998. bds. 6.95 (*0-8050-5840-0*) H Holt & Co.

Aylett, B. J. Fundamentals of Inorganic Chemistry: A Programmed Introduction. Billing, D. E., ed. LC QD0151.5.A95. 108p. reprint ed. pap. 33.50 (*0-608-14067-8*, 202400600035) Bks Demand.

Aylett, B. J. & Smith, B. C. Problems in Inorganic Chemistry. LC 66-18189. 160p. reprint ed. pap. 49.60 (*0-608-10192-3*, 200764300065) Bks Demand.

Aylett, J. F. Medieval Realms, 1066-1500. (Illus.). 64p. 1992. pap. 15.75 (*0-340-54823-1*, Pub. by Hodder & Stought Ltd) Lubrecht & Cramer.

Aylett, Robert & Gregory, Kenneth, eds. Evaluating Teacher Quality in Higher Education. 148p. 1996. 69.95 (*0-7507-0577-9*, Falmer Pr); pap. 24.95 (*0-7507-0578-7*, Falmer Pr) Taylor & Francis.

Aylett, Robert & Skrine, Peter, eds. Hans Sachs & Folk Theatre in the Late Middle Ages: Studies in the History of Popular Culture. LC 94-48871. (Illus.). 240p. 1995. text 89.95 (*0-7734-1344-8*) E Mellen.

***Aylett, Steve.** Atom: A Novel. 176p. 2000. pap. 14.95 (*1-56858-175-0*, Pub. by FWEW) Publishers Group.

Aylett, Steve. Bigot Hall. LC 96-143354. 160p. Date not set. pap. 13.99 (*1-897959-20-6*, Pub. by Serif) IPG Chicago.

— The Crime Studio. LC 96-143596. 160p. 1998. pap. 11.95 (*1-897959-12-5*, Pub. by Serif) IPG Chicago.

— Slaughtermatic. LC 97-41132. 181p. 1998. pap. 13.95 (*1-56858-103-3*) FWEW.

— Toxicology: Stories. LC 99-33899. 141p. 1999. pap. 12.95 (*1-56858-131-9*) FWEW.

***Ayliffe, Alex.** Who's on Noah's Ark? (Baby Blessings Ser.). 6p. (J). 2000. 10.99 (*0-7847-1134-8*, 04314) Standard Pub.

Ayliffe, Alex, jt. auth. see French, Vivian.

Ayliffe, G. A. J., et al. Hospital-Acquired Infection. 2nd ed. (Illus.). 152p. 1990. pap. 50.00 (*0-7506-1560-5*) Buttrwrth-Heinemann.

***Ayliffe, Graham A. J., et al, eds.** Control of Hospital Infection. 4th ed. 2000. text 79.50 (*0-340-75911-9*, Pub. by E A) OUP.

Ayliffe, Jerry. American Premium Guide to Jukeboxes & Slot Machines: Identification & Value Guide. 3rd ed. 352p. 1991. pap. 14.95 (*0-89689-082-1*, Bks Amrcana) Krause Pubns.

Ayliffe, Rosie. Rough Turkey, No. 3. 3rd ed. (Illus.). 832p. 1997. pap. 19.95 (*1-85828-242-X*) Viking Penguin.

Aylin, Elizabeth & Bounds, Marjorie. Windows to God: Worship with Young Children. (J). (ps-3). 1986. 23.00 (*1-881678-34-2*) CSEE.

Ayling, Augustus D., ed. Civil War, Revised Register of the Soldiers & Sailors of New Hampshire in the War of the Rebellion, 1861-1866. (Illus.). 1347p. 1995. reprint ed. lib. bdg. 135.00 (*0-8328-4625-2*) Higginson Bk Co.

— Revised Register of the Soldiers & Sailors of New Hampshire in the War of the Rebellion, 1861-1866. rev. ed. 1347p. 1994. reprint ed. lib. bdg. 129.50 (*0-8328-3966-3*) Higginson Bk Co.

Ayling, David E. Underwriting Decisions under Uncertainty: The Catastrophe Market. (C). 1984. 275.00 (*0-7855-4049-0*, Pub. by Witherby & Co) St Mut.

Ayling, Geoff. Rapid Response Advertising. (Illus.). 267p. 1999. pap. 34.95 (*1-875680-57-8*) Woodslane.

Ayling, J. E., et al. Chemistry & Biology of Pteridines & Folates. (Advances in Experimental Medicine & Biology Ser.: Vol. 338). (Illus.). 852p. (C). 1993. text 179.50 (*0-306-44581-6*, Kluwer Plenum) Kluwer Academic.

***Ayling, Robert I.** Reverend John Ayling: Australian Pioneer: The Life of Reverend John Ayling - Clergyman, Educator, Beekeeper: 1825-1897. Barrett, Peter, ed. LC 99-97188. (Illus.). 260p. 1999. 55.00 (*0-9675675-0-5*); pap. 30.00 (*0-9675675-1-3*) R I Ayling.

Ayling, Rodney. The Downsizing of America. LC 97-190860. 205p. 1997. 60.00 (*1-56072-431-5*, Nova Kroshka Bks) Nova Sci Pubs.

Ayling, Ronald. Practical Computer Engineering Skills. LC 96-26970. (Illus.). 149p. (Orig.). 2000. pap. 18.95 (*1-56072-366-1*, Nova Kroshka Bks) Nova Sci Pubs.

Ayling, Ronald, ed. see O'Casey, Sean.

Ayling, Rose. Flight from Love. large type ed. (Linford Romance Library). 1991. pap. 16.99 (*0-7089-7041-9*) Ulverscroft.

Ayllon, Candido, et al. Spanish Composition through Literature. 3rd ed. 356p. (C). 1995. pap. text 52.67 (*0-13-186586-2*) P-H.

Ayllon, Teodoro. How to Use Token Economy & Point Systems. 2nd ed. LC 98-35124. 1999. pap. write for info. (*0-89079-794-3*) PRO-ED.

Ayllon, Teodoro & McKittrick, Sandra M. How to Set up a Token Economy. (How to Teach Ser.). 39p. 1982. pap. 8.00 (*0-89079-069-8*, 1015) PRO-ED.

Ayllon, Teodoro & Milan, Michael A. Correctional Rehabilitation & Management: A Psychological Approach. LC 78-21703. (Wiley Series in Behavior). 296p. reprint ed. pap. 91.80 (*0-7837-3424-7*, 205774500008) Bks Demand.

Aylmer, G. E. Rebellion or Revolution? England, 1640-1660. (Opus Ser.). 288p. 1987. pap. text 16.95 (*0-19-289212-6*) OUP.

Aylmer, G. E. & Cant, R. C., eds. A History of York Minster. (Illus.). 1977. 32.50 (*0-19-817199-4*) OUP.

***Aylmer, G. E. & Tiller, J. E.** Hereford Cathedral: A History. LC 99-87615. 2000. write for info. (*1-85285-194-5*) Hambledon Press.

Aylmer, John. An Harborowe for Faithfull & Trewe Subjects Agaynst the Late Blowne Blaste, Concerning the Government of Wemen. LC 76-38142. (English Experience Ser.: No. 423). 134p. 1972. reprint ed. 30.00 (*90-221-0423-0*) Walter J Johnson.

Aylmer, Maude, tr. see Tolstoy, Leo.

Aylmer, Ursula & McCrum, Carolyn. Oxford Food: An Anthology. (Illus.). 218p. 1996. 37.50 (*1-85444-063-2*, 0632, Pub. by Ashmolean Mus); pap. 25.00 (*1-85444-058-6*, 0586, Pub. by Ashmolean Mus) A Schwartz & Co.

Aylott, Jane. The Soft Secret Word. (Illus.). 32p. (J). 1993. 12.95 (*0-9631440-0-6*) Winged Peoples.

***Aylott, Nicholas.** Swedish Social Democracy & European Integration: The People's Home on the Market. LC 99-73319. 232p. 1999. text 74.95 (*0-7546-1028-4*, Pub. by Ashgate Pub) Ashgate Pub Co.

***Aylward.** Chemical Data. 4th ed. 1999. pap. text 33.95 (*0-471-34021-9*) Wiley.

Aylward, Anthony. Trends in Venture Capital Finance in Developing Countries. LC 98-8730. (IFC Discussion Paper Ser.: No. 36). 46p. 1998. pap. 22.00 (*0-8213-4303-3*, 14303) World Bank.

***Aylward, Anthony & Glen, Jack.** Primary Securities Markets: Cross Country Findings. LC 99-23806. (IFC Discussion Paper Ser.: No. 39). 48p. 1999. pap. 22.00 (*0-8213-4522-2*, 14522) World Bank.

Aylward, David, tr. see Ibuse, Masuji.

Aylward, E. T. Cervantes: Pioneer & Plagiarist. (Monagrafias A Ser.: Vol. XCIII). 96p. (Orig.). (C). 1982. pap. 41.00 (*0-7293-0136-2*, Pub. by Tamesis Bks Ltd) Boydell & Brewer.

— The Crucible Concept: Thematic & Narrative Patterns in Cervantes's Novelas ejemplares. LC 98-7694. 328p. 1999. 46.50 (*0-8386-3777-9*) Fairleigh Dickinson.

— Towards a Revaluation of Avellaneda's False Quixote. (Documentacion Cervantina Ser.: No. 9). 92p. pap. 8.50 (*0-936388-43-9*) Juan de la Cuesta.

Aylward, G. P. Practitioner's Guide to Developmental & Psychological Testing. (Critical Issues in Developmental & Behavioral Pediatrics Ser.). (Illus.). 276p. (C). 1994. spiral bd. 39.50 (*0-306-44689-8*, Kluwer Plenum) Kluwer Academic.

Aylward, Gladys. La Pequena Gran Mujer en la China. Orig. Title: Little Woman in China. (SPA.). 160p. 1974. pap. 4.99 (*0-8254-1048-7*, Edit Portavoz) Kregel.

Aylward, Gladys & Hunter, Christine. Gladys Aylward. mass mkt. 4.99 (*0-8024-2986-6*, 150) Moody.

Aylward, Glen P. Infant & Early Childhood Neuropsychology. LC 97-30571. (Clinical Child Psychology Library). (Illus.). 140p. (C). 1997. 45.00 (*0-306-45672-9*, Kluwer Plenum) Kluwer Academic.

— Infant & Early Childhood Neuropsychology. LC 97-30571. (Clinical Child Psychology Library). 120p. 1997. pap. 21.50 (*0-306-45673-7*, Kluwer Plenum) Kluwer Academic.

Aylworth, Susan. At the Rainbow's End. LC 96-96149. (Rainbow Rock Ser.: Bk. 2). 192p. 1996. 18.95 (*0-8034-9172-7*, Avalon Bks) Bouregy.

— Don't Promise Me Rainbows. LC 96-96381. 192p. 1996. 18.95 (*0-8034-9208-1*, Avalon Bks) Bouregy.

***Aylworth, Susan.** A Little Night Rainbow. LC 98-96844. 192p. 1999. lib. bdg. 18.95 (*0-8034-9333-9*, Avalon Bks) Bouregy.

Aylworth, Susan. A Rainbow in Paradise. LC 99-90144. 192p. 1997. lib. bdg. 18.95 (*0-8034-9354-1*, Avalon Bks) Bouregy.

— Ride the Rainbow Home. LC 95-94894. (Rainbow Rock Ser.: Bk. 1). 192p. 1995. 18.95 (*0-8034-9143-3*, Avalon Bks) Bouregy.

***Aylworth, Susan.** The Trouble with Rainbows. LC 99-66127. 192p. 1999. 18.95 (*0-8034-9382-7*, Avalon Bks) Bouregy.

Ayman, Iraj, ed. Transition to a Global Society. 176p. 1994. pap. 12.95 (*1-85168-039-X*, Pub. by Onewrld Pubns) Penguin Putnam.

Ayman, Lily. A Persian Reader: Farsi Biyamuzim: Ravesh-E Tadris. 2nd rev. ed. LC 93-61059. (PER.). 96p. (J). (gr. 1). 1994. pap., teacher ed. 18.00 (*0-936347-36-8*) IBEX.

— A Persian Reader Bk. 1: Farsi Biyamuzim: Ketab-E Aval. 2nd rev. ed. LC 93-61060. (PER., Illus.). 104p. (Orig.). 1994. pap. text 9.95 (*0-936347-34-1*) IBEX.

Ayman, Roya, jt. ed. see Chemers, Martin M.

Aymann, Jordan, tr. see Balducci, Corrado.

Aymans, Winfried. Beitraege Zum Verfassungsrecht der Kirche. (Kanonistische Studien und Texte: Vol. 39). (GER.). vi, 300p. 1992. lib. bdg. 97.00 (*90-6032-324-6*) J Benjamins Pubng Co.

Aymar, Brandt & Sagarin, Edward, eds. Personality of the Dog. 368p. 1995. 9.99 (*0-517-14665-7*) Random Hse Value.

Aymar, Brant, ed. The Personality of the Cat. (Illus.). 352p. (J). 1993. 9.99 (*0-517-00016-4*) Random Hse Value.

Ayme. La Jument Verte. (FRE.). (C). 1933. pap. 9.95 (*0-8442-1824-3*, VF1824-3) NTC Contemp Pub Co.

— Le Passe-Muraille. (FRE.). (C). 1958. pap. 9.95 (*0-8442-1974-6*, VF1974-6) NTC Contemp Pub Co.

Ayme, Marcel. Aller Retour. 1927. pap. 10.95 (*0-7859-0373-9*, 2070374459) Fr & Eur.

— Aller Retour. (FRE.). 1983. pap. 10.95 (*0-7859-1970-8*, 2070374459) Fr & Eur.

— Le Boeuf Clandestin. (FRE.). 72p. 1991. pap. 10.95 (*0-7859-1671-7*, 2070310760) Fr & Eur.

— Boites de Peinture. (Folio - Cadet Bleu Ser.: No. 199). (FRE., Illus.). 72p. (J). (gr. 1-5). 1990. pap. 9.95 (*2-07-031199-6*) Schoenhof.

— Brulebois. (FRE.). 1988. pap. 24.95 (*0-7859-1669-5*, 2070203859) Fr & Eur.

— Canard et la Panthere. (Folio - Cadet Bleu Ser.: No. 128). (FRE., Illus.). 63p. (J). (gr. 1-5). 1991. pap. 9.95 (*2-07-031128-7*) Schoenhof.

— Le Chemin des Ecoliers. (FRE.). 1990. pap. 10.95 (*0-7859-1703-9*, 2070361438) Fr & Eur.

— Chemin des Ecoliers. (Folio Ser.: No. 143). (FRE.). pap. 8.95 (*2-07-036143-8*) Schoenhof.

— Chien. (Folio - Cadet Bleu Ser.: No. 201). (FRE., Illus.). 72p. (J). (gr. 1-5). 1990. pap. 10.95 (*2-07-031201-1*) Schoenhof.

— Clerambard. (FRE.). 1984. pap. 18.95 (*0-7859-3043-4*) Fr & Eur.

— Le Confort Intellectual. (FRE.). 156p. 1988. pap. 9.95 (*0-7859-4709-4*, F84140) Fr & Eur.

— Les Contes Bleues du Chat Perche. (FRE.). 222p. 1987. pap. 12.95 (*0-7859-0345-3*, F24580) Fr & Eur.

— Les Contes du Chat Perche. (Folio Ser.: No. 343). (FRE.). 1964. 9.95 (*2-07-036343-0*) Schoenhof.

— Les Contes Du Chat Perche. (FRE.). 1973. pap. 11.95 (*0-7859-1737-3*, 2070363430) Fr & Eur.

— Les Contes Rouge du Chat Perche. (FRE.). 221p. 1987. pap. 12.95 (*0-7859-0383-6*, M3013) Fr & Eur.

— Cygnes. (Folio - Cadet Bleu Ser.: No. 235). (FRE., Illus.). 72p. (J). (gr. 1-5). 1990. pap. 9.95 (*2-07-031235-6*) Schoenhof.

— Derriere Chez Martin. 1973. pap. 7.95 (*0-7859-0384-4*, M3016) Fr & Eur.

— En Arriere. (FRE.). 272p. 1950. pap. 12.95 (*0-7859-0375-5*, F84190) Fr & Eur.

— Gustalin. (FRE.). 236p. 1938. pap. 9.95 (*0-7859-0376-3*, F84210) Fr & Eur.

— La Jument Verte. 1960. 11.95 (*0-7859-0386-0*, M5998) Fr & Eur.

— La Jument Verte. (FRE.). 249p. 1976. pap. 10.95 (*0-7859-1830-2*, 2070368173) Fr & Eur.

— La Jument Verte. (Folio Ser.: No. 817). (FRE.). 1976. pap. 8.95 (*2-07-036817-3*) Schoenhof.

— Louisiane. (FRE.). 248p. 1961. pap. 22.95 (*0-7859-0415-8*, M83980) Fr & Eur.

— Lucienne et le Boucher. (FRE.). 348p. 1959. pap. 16.95 (*0-7859-4881-3*) Fr & Eur.

— Maison Basse. (FRE.). 248p. 1978. pap. 10.95 (*0-7859-1870-1*, 2070370194) Fr & Eur.

— Mauvais Jars. (Folio - Cadet Bleu Ser.: No. 236). (FRE., Illus.). 72p. (J). (gr. 1-5). 1990. pap. 10.95 (*2-07-031236-4*) Schoenhof.

— Les Maxibules. (FRE.). 224p. 1962. pap. 19.95 (*0-7859-0369-0*, F8400) Fr & Eur.

— Le Moulin de la Sourdine. (FRE.). 1973. pap. 10.95 (*0-7859-2200-8*, 207036321X) Fr & Eur.

— Le Nain. (FRE.). 273p. 1977. pap. 10.95 (*0-7859-1844-2*, 2070369129) Fr & Eur.

— Oeuvres Romanesques. 1977. 150.00 (*0-686-51920-5*, F23830) Fr & Eur.

— Oeuvres Romanesques Completes. deluxe ed. (Pleiade Ser.). (FRE.). 1648p. 1989. 150.00 (*0-8288-3419-9*, F23830) Fr & Eur.

— Paon. (Folio - Cadet Ser.: No. 87). (FRE., Illus.). (J). 1985. pap. 8.95 (*2-07-031087-6*) Schoenhof.

— Passe-Muraille. 1943. 12.95 (*0-7859-0377-1*, F84280) Fr & Eur.

— Passe-Muraille. (Folio Ser.: No. 961). (FRE.). 1943. pap. 9.25 (*2-07-036961-7*) Schoenhof.

— Le Passe-Muraille. (FRE.). 1982. pap. 10.95 (*0-8288-3620-5*, F84282); pap. 10.95 (*0-7859-1856-6*, F84282) Fr & Eur.

— Patte du Chat. (Folio - Cadet Bleu Ser.: No. 200). (FRE., Illus.). 72p. (J). (gr. 1-5). 1990. pap. 9.95 (*2-07-031200-3*) Schoenhof.

— Probleme. (Folio - Cadet Bleu Ser.: No. 198). (FRE., Illus.). 71p. (J). (ps-1). 1989. pap. 9.95 (*2-07-031198-8*) Schoenhof.

— Le Puits aux Images. (FRE.). 254p. 1932. pap. 13.95 (*0-7859-1102-2*, 2070203883) Fr & Eur.

— Les Quatres Verites. 1954. pap. 14.95 (*0-7859-0370-4*, F84040) Fr & Eur.

— La Rue Sans Nom. (FRE.). 1979. pap. 10.95 (*0-7859-1898-1*, 2070371255) Fr & Eur.

— Shihouette du Scandale. (FRE.). 208p. 1973. pap. 14.95 (*0-7859-0385-2*, M3019) Fr & Eur.

— La Table aux Creves. 1929. pap. 29.95 (*0-8288-9054-4*) Fr & Eur.

— La Table aux Creves. (FRE.). 1990. reprint ed. pap. 12.95 (*0-7859-1699-7*, 2070361160) Fr & Eur.

— La Tete des Autres. (FRE.). 192p. 1956. pap. 10.95 (*0-7859-0371-2*, F84050) Fr & Eur.

— Tiroirs de L'Inconnu. (FRE.). 1960. pap. 19.95 (*0-8288-9056-0*) Fr & Eur.

— Les Tiroirs de L'Inconnu. (FRE.). 279p. 1986. pap. 12.95 (*0-7859-2030-7*, 2070377245) Fr & Eur.

— Travelingue. (FRE.). 288p. 1973. pap. 12.95 (*0-7859-3565-7*, F84350) Fr & Eur.

— Uranus. (FRE.). 384p. 1990. pap. 11.95 (*0-7859-1712-8*, 2070362248) Fr & Eur.

— Uranus. (Folio Ser.: No. 224). (FRE.). 376p. 1948. pap. 9.95 (*2-07-036224-8*) Schoenhof.

— Vaches. (Folio - Cadet Bleu Ser.: No. 215). (FRE., Illus.). 72p. (J). (gr. 1-5). 1990. pap. 9.95 (*2-07-031215-1*) Schoenhof.

— Le Vin de Paris. (FRE.). 1984. pap. 12.95 (*0-7859-1981-3*, 2070375153) Fr & Eur.

— Le Vin de Paris. (Folio Ser.: No. 1515). (FRE.). 1947. pap. 9.95 (*2-07-037515-3*) Schoenhof.

— Vogue la Galere. 176p. 1944. pap. 11.95 (*0-7859-0372-0*, F84060) Fr & Eur.

— La Vouivre. (FRE.). 256p. 1972. pap. 10.95 (*0-7859-3467-7*, 2070361675) Fr & Eur.

— La Vouivre. (Folio Ser.: No. 167). (FRE.). pap. 8.95 (*2-07-036167-5*) Schoenhof.

Aymer, Paula L. Uprooted Women: Migrant Domestics in the Caribbean. LC 96-53939. 184p. 1997. 55.00 (*0-275-95883-3*, Praeger Pubs) Greenwood.

Aymerich, Angela F. The Three Pups. (ESL Theme Links Ser.). (Illus.). (Orig.). 1993. teacher ed., ring bd. 99.50 incl. audio (*1-56334-292-8*); 35.00 (*1-56334-291-X*); audio 10.50 (*1-56334-290-1*) Hampton-Brown.

— The Three Pups: Big Book, Big bk. (ESL Theme Links Ser.). (Illus.). 16p. (Orig.). (J). (gr. 1-3). 1991. pap. text 29.95 (*1-56334-049-6*) Hampton-Brown.

— The Three Pups: Small Book, Small bk. (ESL Theme Links Ser.). (Illus.). 16p. (Orig.). (J). (gr. 1-3). 1991. pap. text 6.00 (*1-56334-055-0*) Hampton-Brown.

— Los Tres Perritos: Big Book. (Que Maravilla! Ser.). (SPA., Illus.). 16p. (Orig.). (J). (gr. 1-3). 1991. pap. text 29.95 (*1-56334-021-6*) Hampton-Brown.

— Los Tres Perritos: Small Book. (Que Maravilla! Ser.). (SPA., Illus.). 16p. (Orig.). (J). (gr. 1-3). 1991. pap. text 6.00 (*1-56334-035-6*) Hampton-Brown.

Aymond, Laura, ed. see Wagner, Harold E.

Aynesmith, Lawrence, ed. see Friedman, Robert Lawrence.

Aynesmith, Lawrence, ed. see Gerard, Charley & Sheller, Marty.

Aynesmith, Lawrence, ed. see Locke, David.

Aynesworth, Hugh, jt. auth. see Michaud, Stephen G.

Aynsley-Green, A. Paediatric Endocrinology in Clinical Practice. 1984. text 147.50 (*0-85200-864-3*) Kluwer Academic.

Aynsley-Green, A. & Kelnar, Christopher J., eds. European Society for Pediatric Endocrinology (ESPE), 34th Annual Meeting, Edinburgh, June 1995 Abstracts. (Journal Ser.: Vol. 44, Suppl. 1, 1995). viii, 110p. 1995. pap. 52.25 (*3-8055-6174-1*) S Karger.

***Aynsley, Jeremy.** Graphic Design in Germany 1890-1945. (Weimar & Now Ser.). (Illus.). 240p. 2000. 60.00 (*0-520-22796-4*) U CA Pr.

Aynsley, Jeremy. Nationalism & Internationalism: Design in the Twentieth Century. (Illus.). 72p. 1993. pap. 14.95 (*1-85177-121-2*, Pub. by V&A Ent) Antique Collect.

Ayo, Nicholas. The Creed as Symbol. LC 88-40321. 196p. (C). 1990. reprint ed. pap. text 14.00 (*0-268-00771-3*) U of Notre Dame Pr.

— The Hail Mary: A Verbal Icon of Mary. LC 93-24743. (C). 1994. text 38.00 (*0-268-01101-X*) U of Notre Dame Pr.

An Asterisk (*) at the beginning of an entry indicates that the title is appearing for the first time.

— The Hail Mary: A Verbal Icon of Mary. LC 93-24743. (C). 1994. reprint ed. pap. text 18.95 (0-268-01102-8) U of Notre Dame Pr.

— The Lord's Prayer: A Survey Theological & Literary. LC 90-50929. (C). 1993. pap. text 17.50 (0-268-01292-X) U of Notre Dame Pr.

— Sacred Marriage: The Wisdom of the Song of Songs. LC 82-40253. (Illus.). 240p. 1997. 29.95 (0-8264-1030-8) Continuum.

Ayo, Nicholas, et al. Where Joy & Sorrow Meet: A Way of the Cross. LC 98-37489. 184p. 1999. pap. 12.95 (0-87793-668-4) Ave Maria.

Ayo, Nicholas, ed. & intro. see Aquinas, Thomas, Saint.

***Ayo, Yvonne.** Africa. (Eyewitness Books). (Illus.). (J). (gr. 4-7). 2000. 19.99 (0-7894-6610-4) DK Pub Inc.

— Ancient Africa. (Illus.). 64p. (J). (gr. 5). 1995. 19.00 (0-679-87334-1); lib. bdg. 20.99 (0-679-97334-6) Random.

Ayoade, J. O. Introduction to Climatology for the Tropics. LC 82-2648. (Illus.). 274p. reprint ed. pap. 85.00 (0-7837-1886-1, 204208700001) Bks Demand.

Ayodele, Benjamin. Rape: You Can Beat It. 1994. pap. 8.95 (0-533-11006-8) Vantage.

Ayodo, Awor & Odhiambo, Atieno. The Luo, 14 vols. Boud, George, ed. (Heritage Library of African Peoples). (Illus.). 64p. (YA). (gr. 7-12). 1995. lib. bdg. 16.95 (0-8239-1758-4) Rosen Group.

Ayoob, Massad F. Advanced Combat Shotgun: The Stressfire Concept. 1982. 11.95 (0-936279-11-7) Police Bkshelf.

— Ayoob Files: The Book. (Illus.). 214p. 1995. pap. text 14.95 (0-936279-16-8) Police Bkshelf.

— Fundamentals of Modern Police Impact Weapons. (Illus.). 158p. 1986. reprint ed. text 15.95 (0-936279-02-8) Police Bkshelf.

— Gunproof Your Children - Handgun Primer. 19p. (Orig.). 1986. pap. 4.95 (0-936279-05-2) Police Bkshelf.

— Hit the White Part. (Illus.). 107p. 1986. reprint ed. pap. 11.95 (0-936279-01-X) Police Bkshelf.

— In the Gravest Extreme: The Role of the Firearm in Personal Protection. (Illus.). 130p. 1980. reprint ed. pap. 11.95 (0-936279-00-1) Police Bkshelf.

— The Semi-Automatic Pistol in Police Service & Self Defense. 1987. pap. 11.95 (0-936279-07-9) Police Bkshelf.

— Stressfire. (Gunfighting for Police: Advanced Tactics & Techniques Ser.: Vol. 1). (Illus.). 149p. 1986. pap. 11.95 (0-936279-03-6) Police Bkshelf.

Ayoob, Mohammed. The Third World Security Predicament: State Making, Regional Conflict, & the International System. LC 94-27603. (Emerging Global Issues Ser.). 1995. pap. text 18.95 (1-55587-576-9) L Rienner.

Ayoob, Mohammed, ed. The Middle East in World Politics. LC 81-169898. 217p. reprint ed. pap. 67.30 (0-608-11744-7, 201935900011) Bks Demand.

Ayoub, Ali T., jt. ed. see Squires, Victor R.

Ayoub, M. Great Tiding: Thirtieth Part of Holy Quran. 1989. pap. 9.95 (1-56744-028-2) Kazi Pubns.

Ayoub, M. M. & Mital, Anil. Manual Materials Handling: Design & Injury Control Through Ergonomics. 350p. 1989. 126.00 (0-85066-383-0) Taylor & Francis.

Ayoub, Mahmoud. The Great Dominion & the Awesome News: An Introduction to Parts 29 & 30 of the Holy Qur'an. 288p. 1992. 66.95 (0-7103-0442-0, A6985) Routledge.

— Redemptive Suffering in Islam. (Religion & Society Ser.: No. 10). 1978. 70.00 (90-279-7948-0) Mouton.

Ayoub, Mahmoud M. Islam & the Third Universal Theory: The Religious Thought of Mu'ammar al Qadhdhafi. 200p. 1987. 60.00 (0-7103-0260-6, A0088) Routledge.

— Islam & the Third Universal Theory: The Religious Thought of Mu'ammar al-Qadhdhafi. 155p. 1991. pap. 15.95 (0-7103-0404-8, A7002) Routledge.

— The Qur'an & Its Interpreters: Surah Baqarah, Vol. 1. LC 82-21713. 450p. 1984. text 29.50 (0-87395-727-X) State U NY Pr.

— The Qur'an & Its Interpreters, Vol. II: The House of 'Imran. LC 82-21713. 444p. (C). 1992. text 64.50 (0-7914-0993-7); pap. text 21.95 (0-7914-0994-5) State U NY Pr.

Ayoub, Raymond G. An Introduction to the Analytic Theory of Numbers. LC 63-11989. (American Mathematical Society Mathematical Surveys Ser.: Vol. 10). 393p. reprint ed. 121.90 (0-608-11627-0, 202224900026) Bks Demand.

***Ayoub, Susan.** Hockey Pups, 1. (Illus.). (J). 1999. pap. 6.50 (0-9665637-1-9) Smirk Prods.

Ayrai, Sia. Baby Bright Board Books: 123's. (Illus.). 20p. (J). 1993. 5.95 (1-56565-048-4) Lowell Hse.

Ayrapetyan, Sinerik, jt. ed. see Carpenter, David O.

Ayre, D. A. Chemical Process Safety at Fuel Cycle Facilities. 26p. 1997. pap. 2.75 (0-16-054687-7) USGPO.

Ayre, Florence. Recycled High Fashion. (Illus.). 108p. (Orig.). 1997. pap. 12.95 (0-9658064-0-5) F Ayre.

Ayre, Iain. Sports Car Classics: A Marque-By-Marque Guide to over 35 Dream Cars. 1998. 12.95 (1-85967-656-1, Lorenz Bks) Anness Pub.

Ayre, Iain, jt. auth. see Sparrow, David.

Ayre, J. Randolph. Corporate Legal Departments: Strategies for the 1990s. 519p. 1990. 115.00 (0-614-17136-9, B1-1325) PLI.

Ayre, Jim, jt. auth. see Hoffos, Signe.

***Ayre, Theodore P.** Win Your Race, Gain the Prize: Rewards & Inheritance after Jesus Returns. LC 99-76278. (Illus.). 224p. 2000. pap. 15.00 (0-9661750-2-6) Olive Pr Pubs.

Ayre, Theodore P. Your Royal Destiny: How to Achieve It. (Illus.). ix, 210p. 1998. pap. 15.00 (0-9661750-1-8) Olive Pr Pubs.

Ayres. Eye of Gator, Vol. 1. 1998. write for info. (0-312-95888-9) Tor Bks.

— Other Girls. 1999. pap. 16.95 (0-9666750-3-7, Pub. by Nocturnum Pr) Consort Bk Sales.

— Sorting Out Darkness. 1992. pap. 10.95 (0-944870-05-8) Pacific Writers Pr.

— Turning Point: An End to the Growth Paradigm. LC 98-191574. 1998. text 59.95 (0-312-21453-7) St Martin.

Ayres & Miller. Effective Public Speaking. 4th ed. 1993. teacher ed. 13.43 (0-697-12912-8) McGraw.

Ayres, A. Jean. Developmental Dyspraxia & Adult-Onset Apraxia: A Lecture Prepared for Sensory Integration International. LC 88-151167. 85p. (Orig.). 1985. pap. 15.00 (1-882068-00-9) Sensory Integration.

— Sensory Integration & Learning Disorders. LC 72-91446. 294p. (C). 1973. 69.50 (0-87424-303-3, W-303) Western Psych.

— Sensory Integration & the Child. LC 79-66987. 191p. 1979. pap. text 23.50 (0-87424-158-8, W-158) Western Psych.

Ayres, Alex, ed. The Wit & Wisdom of Abraham Lincoln. 240p. (Orig.). 1992. pap. 11.95 (0-452-01089-6, Mer) NAL.

— The Wit & Wisdom of Will Rogers. LC 93-424. 256p. 1993. pap. 13.95 (0-452-01115-9, Mer) NAL.

Ayres, Alex, ed. see Kennedy, John F.

Ayres, Alex, ed. see Truman, Harry S.

Ayres, Alex, ed. see Twain, Mark, pseud.

Ayres, Anne, et al. L. A. Pop in the '60s. LC 89-3256. (Illus.). 144p. 1989. pap. 27.50 (0-917493-14-1) Orange Cnty Mus.

Ayres, Becky. Salt Lake City. LC 90-2968. (Downtown America Ser.). (Illus.). 60p. (J). (gr. 3 up). 1990. lib. bdg. 17.95 (0-87518-436-7, Dillon Silver Burdett) Silver Burdett Pr.

Ayres-Bennett, Wendy. A History of French Through Texts. LC 95-31812. 320p. (C). 1995. pap. 25.99 (0-415-10000-3) Routledge.

Ayres, Bill, jt. auth. see Fornatale, Pete.

Ayres, Brenda. Dissenting Women in Dickens' Novels: The Subversion of Domestic Ideology, 168. LC 98-12151. (Contributions in Women's Studies: Vol. 168). 200p. 1998. 55.00 (0-313-30763-6, Greenwood Pr) Greenwood.

Ayres, Carter M. Pilots & Aviation. (Space & Aviation Ser.). (Illus.). 72p. (J). (gr. 5 up). 1990. lib. bdg. 9.50 (0-8225-1590-3, Lerner Publctns) Lerner Pub.

Ayres, Carter M., jt. auth. see Mortensen, C. David.

Ayres, D. R. Double Track. 2nd ed. (Railroad Fiction Ser.). (Illus.). 288p. 1992. reprint ed. pap. 8.95 (0-943857-07-4) D R Ayres.

— We Find the Jury Guilty. (Railway Fiction Ser.: Vol. 4). (Illus.). 324p. (Orig.). 1997. pap. 8.95 (0-943857-10-4) D R Ayres.

— Who Stole the 2134. (Railroad Fiction Ser.: Vol. 2). (Illus.). 266p. 1997. pap. 8.95 (0-943857-09-0) D R Ayres.

Ayres, D. R., ed. see Rodell, Mark.

***Ayres, David C. & Hellier, Desmond.** Dictionary of Environmentally Important Chemicals. 332p. 1999. 55.00 (1-57958-206-0) Fitzroy Dearborn.

Ayres, David C. & Loike, John D. Lignans. (Chemistry & Pharmacology of Natural Products Ser.). 422p. (C). 1990. text 125.00 (0-521-30421-0) Cambridge U Pr.

Ayres, Don R. Double Track. deluxe ed. (Illus.). 288p. (Orig.). 1992. pap. 12.95 (0-943857-06-6) D R Ayres.

Ayres, E. C. Hour of the Manatee Vol. 1. 1995. mass mkt. 4.99 (0-312-95406-9) St Martin.

— Lair of the Lizard. LC 98-19405. 288p. 1998. text 22.95 (0-312-19295-9) St Martin.

***Ayres, Ed.** God's Last Offer: Negotiating for a Sustainable Future. (Illus.). 336p. 1999. 22.00 (1-56858-125-4) FWEW.

— God's Last Offer: Negotiating for a Sustainable Future. 358p. 2000. reprint ed. pap. 14.95 (1-56858-174-2, Pub. by FWEW) Publishers Group.

Ayres, Ed, jt. ed. see Brown, Lester R.

***Ayres, Elizabeth.** Writing the Wave: Inspired Rides for Aspiring Writers. LC 99-56264. (Illus.). 288p. 2000. pap. 13.00 (0-399-52577-7, Perigee Bks) Berkley Pub.

Ayres, Frank, Jr. Calculus. 1999. pap. text 8.95 (0-07-052710-5) McGraw-Hill Pubng.

— First-Year College Mathematics. 2nd ed. 459p. (Orig.). (C). 1992. pap. 14.95 (0-07-002664-5) McGraw.

— Modern Algebra. (Schaum's Outline Ser.). 256p. (Orig.). (C). 1965. pap. 14.95 (0-07-002655-6) McGraw.

Ayres, Frank, Jr. & Mendelson, Elliot. Schaum's Outline of Calculus. 3rd ed. 484p. (C). 1990. pap. 14.95 (0-07-002662-9) McGraw.

Ayres, Frank, Jr. & Moyer, Robert E. Schaum's Outline of Trigonometry. 2nd rev. ed. 240p. (C). 1990. pap. 11.95 (0-07-002659-9) McGraw.

Ayres, Frank, Jr., jt. auth. see Moyer, Robert E.

Ayres, Gabriella S., tr. see Geiseler, Wilhelm.

Ayres, H. Joseph & Miller, Janice M. Effective Public Speaking. 3rd ed. 368p. (C). 1989. text. write for info. (0-697-04420-3) Brown & Benchmark.

— Effective Public Speaking. 4th ed. 368p. (C). 1993. text. write for info. (0-697-12911-X) Brown & Benchmark.

Ayres, Harry M. Mary of Nimmegen: A Facsimile Reproduction of the Copy of the English Version in the Huntington Library. LC 32-31585. (Huntington Library Publications). 80p. reprint ed. pap. 30.00 (0-608-14000-7, 205554000028) Bks Demand.

Ayres, Harry M., intro. Medieval Song & Story, Vol. 4. Date not set. 30.95 (0-8369-4795-9) Ayer.

Ayres, Harry M., tr. see Dante Alighieri.

Ayres, Ian. Pervasive Prejudice. 1997. 39.95 (0-226-03351-1); pap. text 24.95 (0-226-03353-8) U Ch Pr.

Ayres, Ian. Revised Teaching Notes to Accompany Studies in Contract Law. 4th ed. (University Casebook Ser.). 437p. 1995. pap. text. write for info. (1-56662-268-9) Foundation Pr.

Ayres, Ian & Braithwaite, John. Responsive Regulation: Transcending the Deregulation Debate. (Oxford Socio-Legal Studies). (Illus.). 216p. 1992. text 70.00 (0-19-507070-4) OUP.

— Responsive Regulation: Transcending the Deregulation Debate. (Oxford Socio-Legal Studies). (Illus.). 216p. 1995. reprint ed. pap. text 22.00 (0-19-509376-3) OUP.

Ayres, Ian, jt. auth. see Speidel, Richard E.

Ayres, J. G., et al. Peak Flow Measurement: An Illustrated Guide. LC 96-83632. (Illus.). 144p. 1996. pap. text 22.95 (0-412-73620-9, Pub. by E A) OUP.

Ayres, Jack, ed. see Holland, William.

Ayres, Jak, jt. auth. see McLachlan, Dan H.

Ayres, James. British Folk Art. LC 76-57876. (Illus.). 144p. 1977. 37.95 (0-87951-060-9, Pub. by Overlook Pr) Penguin Putnam.

— Building the Georgian City. LC 98-7174. (Illus.). 288p. 1998. 65.00 (0-300-07548-0) Yale U Pr.

— Two Hundred Years of English Naive Art, 1700-1900. LC 96-18681. 1996. pap. 24.95 (0-88397-120-8) Art Srvc Intl.

Ayres, James E. Historic Archaeology at the Tucson Community Center. (Archaeological Ser.: No. 181). (Illus.). 110p. 1990. pap. 9.95 (1-889747-46-7) Ariz St Mus.

Ayres, James E., compiled by. The Archaeology of Spanish & Mexican Colonialism in the American Southwest No. 3: Guides to the Archaeological Literature of the Immigrant Experience in America. (Columbian Quincentenary Ser.). 133p. (Orig.). 1995. pap. 15.00 (1-886818-01-0) Society Hist Arch.

Ayres, Janet, et al. Leadership: Sustaining Action on Community & Organizational Issues. Stewart, Julie, ed. 250p. 1993. student ed., ring bd. 20.00 (0-936913-08-8, RRD 164) NCRCRD.

Ayres, Janet, jt. auth. see Borich, Timothy O.

Ayres, Janet S., et al. Revitalizing the Retail Trade Sector in Rural Communities: Lessons from Three Midwestern States. Stewart, Julie, ed. 50p. (C). 1992. pap. text 3.50 (0-936913-05-3, RRD 162) NCRCRD.

Ayres, Jeffrey M. Defying Conventional Wisdom: Political Movements & Popular Contention Against North American Free Trade. LC 99-218292. (Studies in Comparative Political Economy). (Illus.). 232p. 1998. text 55.00 (0-8020-4246-5); pap. text 19.95 (0-8020-8089-8) U of Toronto Pr.

Ayres, Joe. A Component Theory of Communication Apprehension. LC 98-92492. 1997. lib. bdg. write for info. (0-9651646-4-0) Commun Vntures.

— Speech Sampler: Speeches & Analyses. (Illus.). 11 p. (Orig.). (C). 1997. pap. text 22.00 (0-9651646-2-4) Commun Vntures.

— Successful Speaking: The Basics of Public Speaking. 2nd rev. ed. (Illus.). 265p. 1998. pap. text 22.00 (0-9651646-5-9) Commun Vntures.

— Successful Speaking: The Basics of Public Speaking, Vol. 1. (Illus.). 200p. (C). 1996. pap. text 22.00 (0-9651646-0-8) Commun Vntures.

Ayres, Joe & Hopf, Tim. Coping with Speech Anxiety. LC 92-30164. (Communication & Information Science Ser.). 152p. 1993. pap. 39.50 (0-89391-986-1); text 73.25 (0-89391-882-2) Ablx Pub.

Ayres, John. Delphi Graphics & Game Programming Exposed! LC 99-50392. 1999. pap. 59.95 (1-55622-637-3) Wordware Pub.

***Ayres, John.** Tomes of Delphi: Win 32 Core API Windows 2000 Edition. (Illus.). 700p. 2000. pap. 59.95 (1-55622-750-7) Wordware Pub.

— Tomes of Delphi: Win 32 Shell API Windows 2000 Edition. (Illus.). 700p. 2000. pap. 59.95 (1-55622-749-3) Wordware Pub.

Ayres, John. Tomes of Delphi 3. LC 97-49186. 1997. pap. text 49.95 (1-55622-610-1) Wordware Pub.

Ayres, John C., et al. Microbiology of Foods. LC 79-16335. (Food & Nutrition Ser.). (Illus.). 708p. (C). 1980. text 32.00 (0-7167-1049-8) W H Freeman.

***Ayres, Jon.** Air Pollution & Health, Vol. 3. (Air Pollution Reviews Ser.). 250p. 1999. 54.00 (1-86094-191-5) World Scientific Pub.

Ayres, Jon. American College of Physicians Home Medical Guide: Asthma. LC 98-44067. (ACP Home Medical Guides). (Illus.). 96p. 2000. pap. 6.95 (0-7894-4152-4, D K Ink) DK Pub Inc.

Ayres, Joy. Speech Sampler: Speeches & Analyses. 2nd rev. ed. (Illus.). 125p. (C). 1999. pap. text 25.00 (0-9651646-7-5) Commun Vntures.

Ayres, Julia. Monotype: Mediums & Methods for Painterly Printmaking. (Illus.). 144p. 1991. 29.95 (0-8230-3129-2) Watsn-Guptill.

***Ayres, Julia.** Monotype: Mediums & Methods for Painterly Printmaking. (Illus.). 144p. 2000. pap. 19.95 (0-8230-3128-4) Watsn-Guptill.

Ayres, Kate, jt. auth. see McConnell, Pam.

Ayres, Katherine. Family Tree. 176p. (J). (gr. 3-7). 1997. pap. 3.99 (0-440-41193-9) BDD Bks Young Read.

— Family Tree. (J). 1997. 9.09 (0-606-13074-8, Pub. by Turtleback) Demco.

***Ayres, Katherine.** North by Night: A Story of the Underground Railroad. (Illus.). 192p. (YA). 2000. pap. 4.50 (0-440-22747-X, YB BDD) BDD Bks Young Read.

Ayres, Katherine. North by Night: A Story of the Underground Railroad. LC 98-10039. 192p. (J). (gr. 5-9). 1998. 15.95 (0-385-32564-9) Delacorte.

***Ayres, Katherine.** Silver Dollar Girl. LC 99-86903. (Illus.). (J). 2000. 14.95 (0-385-32763-3) Delacorte.

— Under Copp's Hill. LC 00-27883. (History Mysteries Ser.). (Illus.). (J). 2000. write for info. (1-58485-089-2) Pleasant Co.

— Voices at Whisper Bend. LC 99-24456. (American Girl History Mysteries Ser.). 162p. (J). (gr. 5-9). 1999. 9.95 (1-56247-817-6) Pleasant Co.

Ayres, Katherine. Voices at Whisper Bend. LC 99-24456. 162p. (J). (gr. 4-7). 1999. pap. 5.95 (1-56247-761-7) Pleasant Co.

Ayres, Katherine S. Charcoal Sketches. LC 72-6512. (Black Heritage Library Collection). 1977. reprint ed. 16.95 (0-8369-9156-7) Ayer.

Ayres, L. D., ed. Pyroclastic Volcanism & Deposits of Cenozoic Intermediate to Felsic Volcanic Islands with Implications for Precambrian Greenstone-Belt Volcanoes. LC QE0522.P97. (Geological Association of Canada. Short Course Notes Ser.: Vol. 2). 369p. reprint ed. pap. 114.40 (0-608-17194-8, 202784700056) Bks Demand.

Ayres, Larry, et al. Howard Warshaw: A Continuing Tradition. (Illus.). 35p. 1977. pap. 5.00 (0-942006-61-5) U of CA Art.

Ayres, Larry M. A Medieval Miscellany: Romanesque & Early Gothic Metalwork. (Illus.). 39p. 1974. pap. 5.00 (0-942006-49-6) U of CA Art.

Ayres, Leonard P. Cleveland School Survey: Summary Volume. LC 72-112539. (Rise of Urban America Ser.). (Illus.). 1970. reprint ed. 23.95 (0-405-02433-9) Ayer.

— A Measuring Scale for Ability in Spelling. 1986. pap. 5.99 (0-88062-039-0) Mott Media.

— Turning Points in Business Cycles. LC 68-20527. (Reprints of Economic Classics Ser.). xii, 170p. 1969. reprint ed. 35.00 (0-678-00453-6) Kelley.

— The War with Germany. Kohn, Richard H., ed. LC 78-22374. (American Military Experience Ser.). (Illus.). 1980. reprint ed. lib. bdg. 15.95 (0-405-11852-X) Ayer.

Ayres, Leslie W., jt. auth. see Ayres, Robert U.

Ayres, Lewis. The Trinity: Classic & Contemporary Readings. (Blackwell Readings in Modern Theology Ser.). Date not set. 59.95 (0-631-19954-3) Blackwell Pubs.

— The Trinity: Classic & Contemporary Readings. (Blackwell Readings in Modern Theology Ser.). 1997. pap. 22.95 (0-631-19955-1) Blackwell Pubs.

Ayres, Lewis, ed. The Passionate Intellect: The Transformation of Classical Traditions. LC 95-9847. (Rutgers University Studies in Classical Humanities: Vol. 7). 376p. 1995. 49.95 (1-56000-210-7) Transaction Pubs.

Ayres, Lewis & Jones, Gareth. Christian Origins: Theology, Rhetoric & Community. LC 97-26997. 232p. (C). 1998. 75.00 (0-415-10750-4); pap. 24.99 (0-415-10751-2) Routledge.

Ayres, Linda. Harvard Divided. (Illus.). 176p. 1976. pap. 4.95 (0-916724-05-0) Harvard Art Mus.

Ayres, Linda R., jt. auth. see Paris, Scott G.

Ayres, Lorne D., et al, eds. Evolution of Archean Supracrustal Sequences. LC 86-107080. (Geological Association of Canada. Special Paper: No. 28). 423p. reprint ed. pap. 131.20 (0-608-17733-4, 203200600077) Bks Demand.

Ayres, Maria E. Let My People Learn: The Biography of Wil Lou Gray. 228p. 1988. 16.95 (0-87921-078-8) Attic Pr.

Ayres, Mary Jo. Natural Learning from A-Z: Thematic Activities & Phonemic Awareness for Letters & Letter Sounds. Allen-Bradley, Janie, ed. LC 97-75610. (Illus.). 160p. (Orig.). 1997. pap. 19.95 (0-9661298-0-6) Natural Lrning.

Ayres, Noreen. A World the Color of Salt. 304p. 1993. mass mkt. 4.99 (0-380-71571-6, Avon Bks) Morrow Avon.

Ayres, P. G., ed. Pests & Pathogens: Plant Responses to Foliar Attack. (Environmental Plant Biology Ser.). 216p. 1992. 152.50 (1-872748-01-5, Pub. by Bios Sci) Coronet Bks.

Ayres, Pam. Guess What. 2nd ed. LC 93-22356. (Illus.). 32p. (J). (ps up). 1994. 3.99 (1-56402-346-X) Candlewick Pr.

— Guess Where. LC 93-24336. (Illus.). 32p. (J). (ps up). 1994. 3.99 (1-56402-314-1) Candlewick Pr.

— Guess Who. 2nd ed. LC 93-22357. (Illus.). 32p. (J). (ps up). 1994. 3.99 (1-56402-345-1) Candlewick Pr.

— Piggo & the Nosebag. (Illus.). 32p. (J). (gr. k-3). 1991. 7.95 (0-563-20922-4, BBC-Parkwest) Parkwest Pubns.

Ayres, Pat, ed. see Klapthor, Margaret & Lucas, Dione.

Ayres, Patricia. Thanks, But No Banks! Great Ways to Finance Your Business. 100p. (Orig.). 1994. pap. text 14.95 (0-9643237-0-2) Am Womans Econ.

Ayres, Philip. Classical Culture & the Idea of Rome in Eighteenth-Century England. (Illus.). 266p. (C). 1997. text 59.95 (0-521-58490-6) Cambridge U Pr.

***Ayres, Philip.** Sejanus, His Fall: Ben Jonson. 1999. pap. text 19.95 (0-7190-5702-7, Pub. by Manchester Univ Pr) St Martin.

Ayres, Philip, ed. see Cooper, Anthony A.

Ayres, Phillip J., ed. see Munday, Anthony.

Ayres, Quincy C. Soil Erosion & Its Control. LC 72-2832. (Use & Abuse of America's Natural Resources Ser.). (Illus.). 382p. 1980. reprint ed. 33.95 (0-405-04501-8) Ayer.

Ayres, R. U., et al. Computer-Integrated Manufacturing Vol. 4: Economic & Social Impacts. 388p. 1991. 79.95 (0-442-31367-5) Chapman & Hall.

Ayres, Robert. The Essence of Professional Issues in Computing. LC 98-34137. (Essence of Computing Ser.). 1998. pap. write for info. (0-13-908740-0) P-H.

— Turning Point: The End of the Growth Paradigm. 224p. 1997. 32.00 (1-85383-444-0, Pub. by Escan Pubns) Island Pr.

Ayres, Robert L. Crime & Violence As Development Issues in Latin America. LC 97-50017. (Latin American & Caribbean Studies). 32p. 1998. pap. 22.00 (0-8213-4163-4, 14163) World Bank.

Ayres, Robert U. Computer Integrated Manufacturing, 4 vols. (IIASA Computer Integrated Manufacturing Ser.). (Illus.). 536p. (C). (gr. 13). 1991. text 338.95 (0-412-40480-X, Chap & Hall NY) Chapman & Hall.

— Information Entropy & Progress. LC 93-43472. 301p. 1994. 60.00 (*0-88318-911-9*) Am Inst Physics.

Ayres, Robert U., et al, eds. Eco-Restructuring: Implications for Sustainable Development. LC 98-8938. 328p. 1998. pap. 29.95 (*92-808-0984-9*) UN Univ Pr.

— Global Aspects of the Environment, 2. LC 99-29678. 1200p. 1999. 435.00 (*1-85898-741-5*) E Elgar.

Ayres, Robert U. & Ayres, Leslie W. Accounting for Resources No. 1: Economy-Wide Applications of Mass-Balance Principles to Materials & Waste. LC 98-17085. 264p. 1999. 95.00 (*1-85898-640-0*) E Elgar.

— Accounting for Resources No. 2: The Life Cycle of Materials. LC 97-37980. 380p. 1999. 120.00 (*1-85898-923-X*) E Elgar.

— Industrial Ecology: Towards Closing the Materials Cycle. LC 96-923. 416p. (C). 1996. 100.00 (*1-85898-397-5*) E Elgar.

Ayres, Robert U. & McKenna, Richard P. Alternatives to the Internal Combustion Engine: Impacts on Environmental Quality. LC 74-181555. (Resources for the Future Ser.). 340p. 1972. 27.50 (*0-8018-1369-7*) Johns Hopkins.

Ayres, Robert U. & McKenna, Robert P. Alternatives to the Internal Combustion Engine: Impacts on Environmental Quality. LC 74-181555. (Illus.). 340p. reprint ed. pap. 105.40 (*0-8357-5334-4*, 203019000067) Bks Demand.

Ayres, Robert U. & Miller, Steven M. Robotics: Applications & Social Implications. LC 82-13881. 368p. 1983. text 34.95 (*0-88410-891-0*, HarpBusn) HarpInfo.

Ayres, Robert U. & Simonis, Udo E., eds. Industrial Metabolism: Restructuring for Sustainable Development. LC 95-178450. 376p. 1995. pap. 35.00 (*92-808-0841-9*) UN.

***Ayres, Ron.** Against the Clock: The Incredible Story of the 7/49: 49 States in 7 Days by Motorcycle. (Incredible Journeys Ser.). (Illus.). 256p. 1999. pap. 19.95 (*1-884313-19-1*, CLOCK) Whitehorse NH.

Ayres, Ron. Against the Wind: A Rider's Account of the Incredible Iron Butt Rally. LC 98-100205. (Incredible Journeys Ser.). (Illus.). 239p. (Orig.). 1997. pap. 19.95 (*1-884313-09-4*) Whitehorse NH.

Ayres, Ron, ed. Development Studies: An Introduction Through Selected Readings. 712p. (C). 1996. pap. 45.00 (*1-874529-32-9*, Pub. by Greenwich Univ Pr) NYU Pr.

— Exploring Macroeconomics: An Introduction to Theory & Policy Through Selected Readings. 439p. (C). 1996. pap. text 28.00 (*1-874529-58-2*, Pub. by Greenwich Univ Pr) NYU Pr.

Ayres, Ruby M. The Master Man. large type ed. 184p. 1989. 19.95 (*0-7451-0941-1*, G K Hall Lrg Type) Mac Lib Ref.

— The Road That Bends. 1975. lib. bdg. 15.80 (*0-89966-004-5*) Buccaneer Bks.

Ayres, Stephen M. Health Care in America: The Facts & the Choices. (The Last Quarter Century: A Guide to the Isues & the Literature: 4). 280p. 1996. pap. 38.00 (*0-8389-0663-X*, 0663-X-2045) ALA.

Ayres, Stephen M., jt. ed. see Bryan-Brown, Christopher W.

***Ayres, Thomas.** Dark & Bloody Ground: The Battle of Mansfield & the Forgotten Civil War in Louisana. 2001. 24.95 (*0-87833-180-8*) Taylor Pub.

— That's Not in My American History Book: A Compilation of Little-Known Events & Forgotton Heroes. 2000. 19.95 (*0-87833-185-9*) Taylor Pub.

Ayres, Tony. Hard: Stories about Gay Men & Sex. 1997. pap. text 12.95 (*1-875243-24-0*, Pub. by Blackwattle) LPC InBook.

Ayres, Wendy, et al. Integrated Lake & Reservoir Management: World Bank Approach & Experience. LC 96-52606. (Technical Paper Ser.: No. 358). 48p. 1997. pap. 22.00 (*0-8213-3867-6*) World Bank.

Ayres, Wendy S., et al. Setting Priorities for Environment Management: An Application to the Mining Sector in Bolivia. LC 97-46571. (Technical Paper Ser.: No. 398). 120p. 1998. pap. 22.00 (*0-8213-4166-9*, 14166) World Bank.

Ayres, William, et al. George Washington: American Symbol. Mitnick, Barbara J., ed. LC 98-40429. (Illus.). 160p. 1999. 35.00 (*1-55595-148-1*, Pub. by Hudson Hills) Natl Bk Netwk.

Ayres, William S., tr. see Geiseler, Wilhelm.

Ayrey, Craig & Everist, Mark, eds. Analytical Strategies & Musical Interpretation: Essays on Nineteenth- & Twentieth-Century Music. (Illus.). 333p. (C). 1996. text 69.95 (*0-521-46249-5*) Cambridge U Pr.

Ayrey, G., jt. auth. see Chapman, J. M.

***Ayris, Arthur A. Atlantis, 1. 368p. 2000. 22.95 (*0-9676738-0-1*) Kingstone.**

A freighter carrying a secretive load of silica destined for a U. S. Defence cyberductor program disappears in a typhoon after leaving Australia. Public controversy erupts after the American Science Foundation denies funding to a highly recommended project. The president of the ASF carries the dark secret of a decades old crime. These events intersect as graduate student Brian Haugabrook's study of oxygen isotopes in oceanic sediments leads to an outcry that he has found irrefutable evidence of Noah's Great Flood. He joins the intrepid inventor of the Atlantis, the world's largest deep sea salvage submarine, along with international scientific teams on a quest to the bottom of the Pacific. While the crew of the Atlantis struggles to recover the sunken silica, the research teams make a discovery that will rock the world. Brian & his companions soon find themselves thrust into a web of intrigue & betrayal as an unholy trinity seeks to keep their discovery buried forever. *Publisher Paid Annotation.*

Ayris, Paul & Selwyn, David, eds. Thomas Cranmer: Churchman & Scholar. (Illus.). 372p. 1999. pap. 35.00 (*0-85115-740-8*) Boydell & Brewer.

Ayriss, Linda. Literary Paris. (Literary Maps Ser.). (Orig.). (J). (gr. 6-12). 1988. pap. 4.95 (*0-937609-09-9*) Aaron Blake Pubs.

Ayrom. Linear/Non Linear Circuits. 1987. student ed. 27.50 (*0-07-010899-4*) McGraw.

Ayrout, Henry H. Moeurs et Coutumes des Fellahs. 5th ed. LC 74-15009. (Illus.). reprint ed. 47.50 (*0-404-12004-0*) AMS Pr.

Aysan, Yasemin, et al. Developing Building for Safety Programmes: Guidelines for Organizing Safe Building Programmes in Disaster-Prone Areas. LC 94-129138. (Building for Safety Ser.). 120p. 1995. pap. 17.50 (*1-85339-184-0*, Pub. by Intermed Tech) Stylus Pub VA.

Ayscough, Florence. Chinese Women: Yesterday & Today. LC 74-32095. (China in the 20th Century Ser.). (Illus.). xiv, 324p. 1975. reprint ed. lib. bdg. 42.50 (*0-306-70700-4*) Da Capo.

— Florence Ayscough & Amy Lowell. (American Autobiography Ser.). 288p. 1995. reprint ed. lib. bdg. 79.00 (*0-7812-8444-9*) Rprt Serv.

Ayscough, P. B., ed. Electron Spin Resonance, Vols. 1-5. Incl. 1971-72 Literature. LC 72-95099. 1973. 36.00 (*0-85186-751-0*); 1972-73 Literature. LC 72-95099. 1974. 38.00 (*0-85186-761-8*); 1973-75 Literature. LC 72-95099. 1976. 45.00 (*0-85186-771-5*); Vol. 4. 1975-76 Literature. LC 72-95099. 1977. 61.00: 1977-79 Literature. LC 72-95099. 1979. 77.00 (*0-85186-791-X*); LC 72-95099. write for info. (*0-318-50467-7*) Am Chemical.

Ayscough, S. Index to the Remarkable Passages & Words Made Use of by Shakespeare. LC 74-135728. reprint ed. 55.00 (*0-404-00437-7*) AMS Pr.

Aysha, Noor, jt. auth. see Khan, Mumtaz A.

Aysto, Juha, ed. see Kantele, Juhani.

Ayto. Hutchinson Dictionary of Difficult Words. 1993. pap. write for info. (*0-09-177079-3*, Pub. by Hutchnson) Random House.

Ayto, Eric. Clay Tobacco Pipes. (Album Ser.: No. 37). (Illus.). 32p. pap. 6.25 (*0-7478-0248-3*, Pub. by Shire Pubns) Parkwest Pubns.

***Ayto, John.** Dictionary of Word Origins. 590p. 2000. pap. 24.95 (*0-7475-4570-7*, Pub. by Blmsbury Pub) Trafalgar.

Ayto, John. Dictionary of Word Origins. 592p. (C). 1993. reprint ed. pap. 18.45 (*1-55970-214-1*, Pub. by Arcade Pub Inc) Time Warner.

— The Oxford Dictionary of Slang. LC 99-201836. 480p. 1999. 35.00 (*0-19-863157-X*) OUP.

— The Oxford School A-Z of English. 320p. (J). Date not set. write for info. (*0-19-910308-9*) OUP.

— Twentieth Century Words. LC 98-47417. 640p. 1999. 25.00 (*0-19-860230-8*) OUP.

***Ayto, John, ed.** The Oxford Dictionary of Slang. 2000. pap. 13.95 (*0-19-280104-X*) OUP.

Ayto, John & Barratt, Alexander, eds. Aelred of Rievaulx's de Institutione Inclusarum: Two Middle English Translations. (EETS Original Ser.: Vol. 287). 1985. 14.95 (*0-19-722289-7*) OUP.

Ayto, John, jt. ed. see Simpson, John.

Ayto, Russell, jt. auth. see Jungman, Ann.

Ayton, Andrew. Knights & Warhorses: Military Service & the English Aristocracy under Edward III. LC 94-20623. 311p. (C). 1994. 75.00 (*0-85115-568-5*, Boydell Pr) Boydell & Brewer.

***Ayton, Andrew.** Knights & Warhorses: Military Service & the English Aristocracy under Edward III. 311p. 1999. pap. 35.00 (*0-85115-739-4*) Boydell & Brewer.

Ayton, Andrew. Medieval Military Revolution, Vol. 1. 1995. text 65.00 (*1-85043-830-7*, Pub. by I B T) St Martin.

Ayton, Andrew & Price, Leslie, eds. Medieval Military Revolution: State, Society & Military Change in Medieval & Early Modern Europe. 216p. 1998. pap. 24.50 (*1-86064-353-1*, Pub. by I B T) St Martin.

Ayton, Peter, jt. ed. see Wright, George.

Ayton, W. A. Alchemist of the Golden Dawn: The Letters of the Reverend W.A. Ayton to F.L. Gardner & Others, 1880. LC 85-172556. pap. write for info. (*0-85030-288-9*, Pub. by Aqrn Pr) HarpC.

Ayton, Will. Four Song Settings for Voice & Three Viols. (Contemporary Vocal Ser.: Vol. 7). 32p. (Orig.). 1997. pap. 15.00 (*1-56571-150-5*) PRB Prods.

***Ayton, Will.** Music for Three Viols: (Or String Trio) (Contemporary Consort Ser.: Vol. 35). 23p. 1999. pap. 8.00 (*1-56571-176-9*, CC035) PRB Prods.

Ayture-Scheele, Z. The Great Origami Book. LC 87-10062. (Illus.). 80p. 1987. 24.95 (*0-8069-6600-9*); pap. 12.95 (*0-8069-6640-8*) Sterling.

Ayture-Scheele, Zubal. Beautiful Origami. LC 90-9735. (Illus.). 80p. 1990. pap. 12.95 (*0-8069-7382-X*) Sterling.

Ayubi, Nazih. Political Islam: Religion & Politics in the Arab World. 304p. (C). 1993. pap. 27.99 (*0-415-10385-1*) Routledge.

Ayubi, Shaheen. Nasser & Sadat: Decision Making & Foreign Policy, 1970-1972. LC 94-18550. 276p. (C). 1994. reprint ed. pap. text 34.50 (*0-8191-9604-5*); reprint ed. lib. bdg. 57.50 (*0-8191-9603-7*) U Pr of Amer.

Ayubi, Shaheen, et al. Economic Sanctions in U. S. Foreign Policy. LC 82-13589. (Philadelphia Policy Papers). 1982. pap. 3.95 (*0-910191-01-8*) For Policy Res.

Ayum, Evelyn & Council-George, Marian. Braid Styles for Your Lifestyle: How to Find the Right Braid Styles for You. 60p. 1997. pap. 24.95 (*0-9665901-0-4*) Essent NJ.

Ayume, Francis J. Criminal Procedure & Law in Uganda. LC 90-981997. xxx, 257p. 1986. write for info. (*0-582-64487-9*) Longman.

Ayuninjam, Funwi F. A Reference Grammar of Mbili. LC 98-15152. 480p. (C). 1998. 69.00 (*0-7618-1119-2*); pap. 48.50 (*0-7618-1120-6*) U Pr of Amer.

Ayupov, Shavkat, et al. Jordan, Real & Lie Structures in Operator Algebras. LC 97-23872. (MAIA Mathematics & Its Applications Ser.: Vol. 418). 225p. 1997. text 130.50 (*0-7923-4684-X*) Kluwer Academic.

Ayusawa, Iwao. A History of Labor in Modern Japan. LC 76-20683. 406p. 1976. reprint ed. lib. bdg. 65.00 (*0-8371-8991-8*, AYHL, Greenwood Pr) Greenwood.

Ayusawa, Iwao F. International Labor Legislation. LC 75-82244. (Columbia University. Studies in the Social Sciences: No. 208). reprint ed. 20.00 (*0-404-51208-9*) AMS Pr.

Ayuso, Agnes & Pederson, Judith. Directory of Marine Monitoring Programs in Massachusetts. 6.00 (*1-56172-009-7*) MIT Sea Grant.

Ayuso, Antonio J. & Soler, Juan M., eds. Speech Recognition & Coding: New Advances & Trends, Vol. XI. (NATO ASI Series F: Computer & Systems Science: Vol. 147). 505p. 1995. 150.00 (*3-540-60098-1*) Spr-Verlag.

Ayvasian, Leslie. Nine Armenians. 1998. pap. 5.25 (*0-8222-1602-7*) Dramatists Play.

Ayvazian, Argam. The Historical Monuments of Nakhichevan. Maksoudian, Krikor H., tr. LC 88-38939. (Illus.). 152p. reprint ed. pap. 47.20 (*0-608-10560-0*, 207118000009) Bks Demand.

Ayvazian, Arthur A. Armenian Victories at Khznavous & Sardarabad on May 23, 1918 & Program for Re-establishment of Independent & Neutral State of Armenia. (Illus.). 120p. 1983. 10.00 (*0-934728-15-1*) D O A C.

Ayyangar, P. T. The Stone Age in India. 1988. reprint ed. 10.00 (*81-206-0148-3*, Pub. by Asian Educ Servs) S Asia.

Ayyangar, S. Krishnaswamy, ed. Sources of Vijayanagar History. 414p. 1986. 22.00 (*81-212-0038-5*, Pub. by Gian Publng Hse) S Asia.

Ayyangar, T. R. Srinivasa, see Subrahmanya Sastri, Pandit S. & Srinivasa Ayyangar, T. R.

Ayyappapanicker, K. & Sahitya Akademi Staff. Medieval Indian Literature: An Anthology LC 98-901293. 1997. write for info. (*81-260-0365-0*, Pub. by Rabindra Bhawn) S Asia.

Ayyar, C. P. Town Planning in Ancient Dekkan. (C). 1994. text 17.50 (*81-206-0972-7*, Pub. by Asian Educ Servs) S Asia.

— Town Planning in Early South India. 197p. 1987. 17.50 (*0-8364-2083-7*, Pub. by Mittal Pubs Dist) S Asia.

Ayyar, P. V. South Indian Customs. 182p. 1986. reprint ed. 18.00 (*0-8364-1723-2*, Pub. by Usha) S Asia.

***Ayyar, P. V.** South Indian Festivities. 1998. pap. 9.00 (*81-7167-373-2*, Pub. by Rupa) S Asia.

Ayyar, P. V. South Indian Festivities. (Illus.). 212p. 1986. 32.00 (*0-8364-1722-4*, Pub. by Usha) S Asia.

— South Indian Shrines. 648p. 1986. reprint ed. 14.00 (*0-8364-1721-6*, Pub. by Usha) S Asia.

Ayyar, R. S., ed. see Ivovich, V. A. & Pokrovskii, L. N.

Ayyildiz, Judy L. Mud River. (Illus.). 80p. (Orig.). 1988. 10.00 (*0-931642-20-5*) Lintel.

— Mud River: Poems by Judy Light Ayyildiz. (Illus.). 80p. (Orig.). 1988. pap. 8.95 (*0-931642-19-1*) Lintel.

Ayyub, Bilal M. Uncertainty Modeling & Analysis in Civil Engineering. LC 97-31074. 528p. 1997. boxed set 79.95 (*0-8493-3108-0*) CRC Pr.

Ayyub, Bilal M. & Gupta, Madan M., eds. Uncertainty Analysis in Engineering & Sciences: Fuzzy Logic, Statistics, & Neural Network Approach. LC 97-39812. (The Kluwer International Series in Intelligent Technologies: No. 11). 400p. 1997. text 181.50 (*0-7923-8030-4*) Kluwer Academic.

— Uncertainty Modelling & Analysis: Theory & Applications. LC 94-36567. (Machine Intelligence & Pattern Recognition Ser.: 17). (Illus.). 558p. 1994. 187.50 (*0-444-81954-1*) Elsevier.

Ayyub, Bilal M. & McCuen, Richard H. Numerical Methods for Engineers. LC 95-20132. 362p. 1995. 97.00 (*0-13-337361-4*, Pub. by P-H) S&S Trade.

— Solutions Manual for Probability, Statistics, & Reliability for Engineers. LC 97-22210. 1997. lib. bdg. write for info. (*0-8493-2699-0*) CRC Pr.

Ayzenberg, Olga, jt. auth. see Kuznetsova, Irina.

Azad, A. K. Tarjaman-ul-Quran, 3 vols. 1992. 60.00 (*0-933511-73-6*) Kazi Pubns.

— Tarjaman-ul-Quran, 3 vols., 1. 1991. 16.50 (*1-56744-205-6*) Kazi Pubns.

— Tarjaman-ul-Quran, 3 vols., 2. 1992. 20.00 (*1-56744-207-2*) Kazi Pubns.

— Tarjaman-ul-Quran, 3 vols., 3. 1989. 20.00 (*1-56744-208-0*) Kazi Pubns.

***Azad, Bahman.** Heroic Struggle!--Bitter Defeat: Factors Contributing to the Dismantling of the Socialist State in the Soviet Union. LC 00-40729. 2000. write for info. (*0-7178-0726-6*) Intl Pubs Co.

Azad, G. M. Judicial System of Islam. 1988. pap. 12.95 (*1-56744-111-4*) Kazi Pubns.

Azad, K. C., et al. Horticultural Development in Hill Areas: A Study of Himachal Pradesh. 1988. 30.00 (*81-7099-052-1*, Pub. by Mittal Pubs Dist) S Asia.

Azad, Rams S. The Atmospheric Boundary Layer for Engineers. (Fluid Mechanics & Its Applications Ser.). 584p. (C). 1993. text 245.00 (*0-7923-2187-1*) Kluwer Academic.

Azadeh, Carol. The Marriage at Antibes. 224p. 2000. 22.95 (*0-7867-0708-9*) Carroll & Graf.

***Azadian, Edmond Y.** History on the Move: Views, Interviews & Essays on Armenian Issues. Hacikyan, Agop J. & Franchuk, Edward S., eds. 296p. 2000. pap. 24.95 (*0-8143-2916-0*) Wayne St U Pr.

Azaglo, August C. Photographs of the Ivory Coast. (Soleil Ser.). (Illus.). 1997. pap. 18.00 (*0-614-25351-9*) Dist Art Pubs.

***Azam-ALi, S. N. & Squire, G. R.** Principles of Tropical Agronomy. (CABI Publishing Ser.). (Illus.). 304p. 2001. pap. text. write for info. (*0-85199-136-X*) OUP.

Azam-Ali, Sue, et al. More Traditional Foods Vol. 2: Processing for Profit. (Illus.). 224p. 1998. pap. 47.50 (*1-85339-429-7*, Pub. by Intermed Tech) Stylus Pub VA.

Azam, Hina, ed. see Ghazi, Abidullah.

Azam, Hina, ed. see Ghazi, Abidullah & Ghazi, Tasneema K.

Azam, Jean-Paul & Daubree, Cecile. Bypassing the State: Economic Growth in Kenya 1964-1990. LC 97-180033. (Development Centre Studies, Long Term Growth Ser.). 80p. (Orig.). 1997. pap. 16.00 (*92-64-15474-4*, 41-97-07-1, Pub. by Org for Econ) OECD.

***Azam, Jean-Paul, et al.** Conflict & Growth in Africa: The Sahel. (Development Centre Studies). 184p. 1999. pap. 34.00 (*92-64-17101-0*, 41 1999 09 1 P, Pub. by Org for Econ) OECD.

Azam, Kousar J. India's Defence Policy for the 1990s. 128p. (C). 1992. 18.95 (*81-207-1408-3*) Apt Bks.

Azam, M. UNIX in Easy Steps. 1993. write for info. (*81-224-0552-5*, Pub. by Wiley Estrn) Franklin.

Azama, Michael. Crossfire. (Oberon Bks.). 104p. 1997. pap. 12.95 (*1-870259-34-3*) Theatre Comm.

Azami, Habib-Urrahman. The Sunnah in Islam: The Eternal Relevance of the Teachings & Example of the Prophet, Muhammad. 2nd rev. ed. Ul-Hassan, Khwaja M. & Hassan, Labiba, eds. LC 95-77847. (Quranic Studies). 55p. 1995. mass mkt. 3.00 (*1-56316-112-5*) Iqra Intl Ed Fdtn.

Azami, M. Studies in Early Hadith. 510p. 1996. pap. 15.50 (*0-614-21096-8*, 1175) Kazi Pubns.

— Studies in Hadith: Methodology & Literature. 124p. 1996. pap. 7.95 (*0-614-21072-0*, 1177) Kazi Pubns.

Azami, M. M. Studies in Early Hadith Literature. LC 77-90341. 1978. pap. 12.75 (*0-89259-125-0*) Am Trust Pubns.

Azami, Mustafa. Studies in Hadith Methodology & Literature. Beg, Anwer, ed. LC 77-90335. 1978. pap. 5.25 (*0-89259-011-4*) Am Trust Pubns.

Azana, Manuel. Vigil in Benicarlo. Stewart, Josephine & Stewart, Paul, eds. LC 81-65339. (Illus.). 136p. 1982. 24.50 (*0-8386-3093-6*) Fairleigh Dickinson.

Azania, Zolo A. Money & Power: Hook or Crook. 56p. (Orig.). reprint ed. pap. write for info. (*1-56411-144-X*) Untd Bros & Sis.

— Who Is the New Afrikan? (Illus.). 13p. (Orig.). 1991. pap. 2.00 (*1-56411-007-9*) Untd Bros & Sis.

Azaola, Miguel, tr. La Escuela de Magia y Otros Cuentos.Tr. of Magic School & Other Stories. (GER., Illus.). 151p. 1998. pap. 6.50 (*84-348-4733-7*, Pub. by SM Ediciones) IBD Ltd.

Azaola, Miguel, tr. see Ungerer, Tomi.

Azar. The Basic Fundamentals of English Grammar. 2nd ed. 1994. pap. text, teacher ed. 18.00 (*0-13-347121-7*) P-H.

— Chartbook Understanding & Using. 3rd ed. 1999. pap. text 23.60 (*0-13-958703-9*) P-H.

— Understanding & Using. 3rd ed. 1999. pap. text, student ed. 16.46 (*0-13-958679-2*) P-H.

— Understanding & Using. 3rd ed. 1999. pap., wbk. ed. 21.80 (*0-13-958687-3*) P-H.

***Azar, Betty & Schrampfer.** Understanding & Using English Grammar. 3rd ed. 224p. (C). 1998. pap. text 18.00 (*0-13-958752-7*) P-H.

Azar, Betty S. Basic English Grammar, Bk. A. 2nd ed. 256p. 1995. pap. text 17.53 (*0-13-368424-5*) P-H.

— Basic English Grammar, Vol. B. 2nd ed. 224p. (C). 1995. pap. text 17.53 (*0-13-368358-3*) P-H.

— Basic English Grammar Combined Volume. 2nd ed. 480p. (C). 1996. pap. text 32.93 (*0-13-368317-6*) P-H.

— Fundamentals of English Grammar. 2nd ed. 448p. (C). 1992. pap. 32.93 (*0-13-338278-8*) P-H.

— Fundamentals of English Grammar, Vol. A. 2nd ed. 256p. 1992. 17.53 (*0-13-327552-3*) P-H.

— Fundamentals of English Grammar, Vol. B. 2nd ed. 208p. (C). 1992. pap. text 17.53 (*0-13-347139-X*) P-H.

— Fundamentals of English Grammar: Chartbook - a Reference Grammar. 2nd ed. LC 94-37181. (C). 1994. pap. text 23.60 (*0-13-340704-7*) P-H.

— Understanding & Using English Grammar, Bk. B. 2nd ed. 208p. (C). 1989. pap. text 18.93 (*0-13-943671-5*) P-H.

— Understanding & Using English Grammar Chart Book. 2nd ed. LC 92-22548. 140p. (C). 1992. pap. text 24.80 (*0-13-948233-4*) P-H.

Azar, Betty Schrampfer. Understanding & Using English Grammar. 3rd ed. 256p. 1998. pap. text 18.00 (*0-13-958729-2*) P-H.

Azar, Betty Schrampfer. Understanding & Using English Grammer. 2nd ed. 1992. pap. 22.75 (*0-13-952839-3*) P-H.

Azar, Diana. Looking for the Worm. 128p. 1989. 19.95 (*0-89754-057-3*); pap. 8.95 (*0-89754-056-5*) Dan River Pr.

Azar, Dimitri. Refractive Surgery. LC 97-126370. 691p. (C). 1997. pap. text 175.00 (*0-8385-8276-1*, A8276-6, Apple Lange Med) McGraw.

Azar, Dimitri M.D., jt. auth. see Jakobiec, Frederick A., M.D.

Azar, Dimitri T., et al, eds. Excimer Laser Therapy Phototherapeutic Keratectomy. (Illus.). 225p. 1997. write for info. (*0-89640-332-7*) Igaku-Shoin.

***Azar, Dimitri T. & Melki, Samir A.** 101 Pearls in Refractive, Cataract & Corneal Surgery. 150p. (C). 2001. pap. text 45.00 (*1-55642-489-2*) SLACK Inc.

An Asterisk (*) at the beginning of an entry indicates that the title is appearing for the first time.

Azar, Dimitri T., et al. Excimer Laser Phototherapeutic Keratectomy. LC 96-40065. 1997. write for info. (*4-260-14332-8*) Igaku-Shoin.
— Excimer Laser Phototherapeutic Keratectomy: Management of Scars, Dystrophies, & PRK Complications. LC 96-40065. 214p. 1997. 79.00 (*0-683-30346-5*) Lppncott W & W.
Azar, Edward E. The Management of Protracted Social Conflict: Theory & Cases. 168p. 1990. text 72.95 (*1-85521-063-0*, Pub. by Dartmth Pub) Ashgate Pub Co.
Azar, Edward E. & Ben-Dak, Joseph. Theory & Practice of Events Research: Studies in Inter-Nation Actions & Interactions. xxii, 304p. 1975. text 292.00 (*0-677-15550-6*) Gordon & Breach.
Azar, Edward E., et al. The Emergence of a New Lebanon: Fantasy or Reality? LC 84-15974. 302p. 1984. 49.95 (*0-275-91121-7*, C1121, Praeger Pubs) Greenwood.
Azar, Henry A. & Potter, Michael. Multiple Myeloma & Related Disorders, Vol. 1. LC 72-13525. (Illus.). 440p. reprint ed. 136.40 (*0-8357-9426-1*, 201334900086) Bks Demand.
Azar, Ines. Discurso Retorico y Mundo Pastoral en la 'Egloga Segunda' de Garcilaso. (Purdue University Monographs in Romance Languages: Vol. 5). (SPA.). x, 172p. 1981. 46.00 (*90-272-1715-7*) J Benjamins Pubng Co.
Azar, J. J. Matrix Structural Analysis. 1972. 109.00 (*0-08-016781-0*, Pub. by Pergamon Repr) Franklin.
Azar, J. J., jt. auth. see Lummus, James L.
Azar, J. J., jt. auth. see Peery, David J.
Azar, Kaveh. Heat Sink Design Analysis & Manufacturing. (Thermal Management of Electronic Systems Ser.). 2000. 89.95 (*0-8493-9541-0*) CRC Pr.
— Thermal Interface Materials in Electronics. (Thermal Management of Electronic Systems Ser.). 2000. 79.95 (*0-8493-9542-9*) CRC Pr.
— Thermal Measurements in Electronics Cooling. LC 97-10722. 496p. 1997. boxed set 99.95 (*0-8493-3279-6*) CRC Pr.
Azar, Larry. Man: Computer, Ape or Angel? LC 88-71528. 1989. 19.95 (*0-8158-0452-0*) Chris Mass.
Azar, Rutler, ed. see Chesterton, G. K.
Azar, Valerie M. The Florida Jobline Directory. 58p. 1992. pap. text 32.95 (*0-9633473-0-6*) Careers FLA.
Azara, Don Felix De, see De Azara, Don Felix.
Azariadis, Costas. Intertemporal Macroeconomics. LC 92-16498. (Illus.). 504p. 1993. 54.95 (*1-55786-366-0*) Blackwell Pubs.
Azarian, Mary. A Farmer's Alphabet. LC 80-84938. (Illus.). 64p. (J). (ps-2). 1981. 19.95 (*0-87923-394-X*); pap. 14.95 (*0-87923-397-4*) Godine.
***Azarian, Mary.** A Gardener's Alphabet. LC 99-42242. (Illus.). 32p. (YA). 2000. 16.00 (*0-618-03380-7*) HM.
Azarin, V. S., et al. Thirteen Papers on Functions of Real & Complex Variables. (Translations Ser.: Series 2, Vol. 80). 278p. 1969. 50.00 (*0-8218-1780-9*, TRANS2/80) Am Math.
Azarkh, Z. A., jt. auth. see Tsukerman, V. A.
Azarm, Shapour, et al, eds. Advances in Design Automation, DE-Vol. 82. LC 84-45945. (Proceedings of the 1995 ASME Design Technical Engineering Conferences Ser.: Vol. 1). 1008p. 1995. 320.00 (*0-7918-1716-4*, H00998) ASME.
Azarmas, Reza. Powerful Multimedia Presentations: Interactive Video Production. 352p. (C). 1995. pap. 50.95 (*0-534-25416-0*) Wadsworth Pub.
Azarmi, Nadar, jt. auth. see Nwana, Hyacinth S.
Azarmsa, Reza. Educational Computing: Principles & Applications. LC 90-48989. (Illus.). 230p. 1991. pap. 24.95 (*0-87778-222-9*) Educ Tech Pubns.
— Educators Guide to Desktop Publishing: Using Adobe PageMaker. 288p. (C). 1997. pap. text 40.00 (*0-205-26626-6*, T6626-0) Allyn.
***Azarmsa, Reza.** Educator's Guide to Desktop Publishing Using QuarkXPress: Windows & Macintosh. (Illus.). 258p. (C). 1999. pap., teacher ed. 28.00 incl. disk (*0-205-26403-4*, Longwood Div) Allyn.
Azarmsa, Reza. Telecommunications: A Handbook for Educators. LC 92-28454. (Source Books on Education: Vol. 30). 320p. 1993. text 57.00 (*0-8153-0743-8*, SS849) Garland.
Azarnoff, Pat, ed. Medically-Oriented Play for Children in Health Care: The Issues. (Issues in Pediatric Mental Health Ser.: No. 3). (Illus.). 100p. 1986. spiral bd. 18.95 (*0-912599-05-7*) Pediatric Projects.
Azarnoff, Pat & Lindquist, Patricia, eds. Psychological Abuse of Children in Health Care: The Issues. 2nd rev. ed. (Issues in Pediatric Mental Health Ser.: No. 2). 130p. (C). 1997. spiral bd. 28.00 (*0-912599-06-5*) Pediatric Projects.
Azaroff, Leonid V. Elements of X-Ray Crystallography. (Illus.). 628p. (C). 1990. reprint ed. text 93.00 (*1-878907-11-5*) TechBooks.
— Physics over Easy. LC 96-200777. 250p. 1996. text 48.00 (*981-02-2357-9*); pap. text 26.00 (*981-02-2367-6*) World Scientific Pub.
Azaroff, Leonid V. & Brophy, James J. Electronic Processes in Materials. (Illus.). 478p. (C). 1990. reprint ed. 115.00 (*1-878907-41-7*) TechBooks.
Azarya, Victor. Aristocrats Facing Change: The Fulbe in Guinea, Nigeria & Cameroon. LC 77-15025. 307p. reprint ed. pap. 95.20 (*0-608-09267-3*, 205406900002) Bks Demand.
— Nomads & the State in Africa: The Political Roots of Marginality. (African Studies Centre Leiden). 108p. 1996. pap. 43.95 (*1-85972-576-7*, Pub. by Avebry) Ashgate Pub Co.
Azarya, Victor, ed. Pastoralists under Pressure? Fulbe Societies Confronting Change in West Africa. LC 99-27461. (Social, Economic & Political Studies of the Middle East & Asia). 454p. 1999. 80.00 (*90-04-11364-9*) Brill Academic Pubs.
Azbel, David S., jt. auth. see Cheremisinoff, Nicholas P.
Azbel, Vladimir D., tr. see Sychev, V. V., et al, eds.
Azbelev, N., et al. Introduction to the Theory of Linear Functional Differential Equations, Vol. 3. LC 95-34177. (Advanced Series in Mathematical Science & Engineering). 1995. write for info. (*1-885978-02-2*) Wrld Fed Pubs.
Azbelev, N. V., et al. Fifteen Papers on Differential Equations. LC 51-5559. (Translations Ser.: Series 2, Vol. 42). 288p. 1964. 36.00 (*0-8218-1742-6*, TRANS2/42) Am Math.
Azcar. How to Talk Directly with God. 51p. 1977. pap. 4.95 (*0-931865-13-1*) Proj Renaissance.
Azcarate, Leonor, et al. Contemporary Mexican Drama in Translation: Azcarate, Rascon, Urtusastegui, Vol. I. Gann, Myra S., ed. & tr. by. from SPA. LC 94-69405. (Illus.). 144p. (Orig.). 1994. pap. text, per. 15.00 (*0-9643288-0-1*) Danzon Pr.
Azcarate, Pablo De, see De Azcarate, Pablo.
Azcarate, Patricio D., tr. see Aristotle.
Azcarraga, Jose A. De, see De Azcarraga, Jose A.
Azcue, Jose, jt. auth. see Mudroch, Alena.
Azcue, Jose M. Environmental Impacts of Mining Activities: Emphasis on Mitigation & Remedial Measures. LC 98-38385. (Environmental Science Ser.). 220p. 1999. 119.00 (*3-540-64344-3*) Spr-Verlag.
Azcue, Jose M., jt. auth. see Mudroch, Alena.
Azcuy, Lucila E. Poesias de Lucila E. Azcuy: Poesias de Ayer y de Hoy. Para Siempre... LC 81-69540. (Coleccion Espejo de Paciencia). (SPA., Illus.). 67p. (Orig.). 1982. pap. 5.95 (*0-89729-267-7*) Ediciones.
Azean, Evon, Sr. Aataq Maktuq (Father Gets Up) large type ed. (ESK., Illus.). 12p. (J). (gr. k-3). 1999. pap. text 6.00 (*1-58084-145-7*) Lower Kuskokwim.
— At'a Maktur (Father Gets Up) large type ed. (ESK., Illus.). 12p. (J). (gr. k-3). 1999. pap. text 6.00 (*1-58084-146-5*) Lower Kuskokwim.
— Father Gets Up. large type ed. (Illus.). 12p. (J). (gr. k-3). 1999. pap. text 6.00 (*1-58084-144-9*) Lower Kuskokwim.
Azed, Jagan N., tr. see Ali, Agha S.
Azeez, Ghietas. Dictionary of Archaeological & Artistic Terms English-French-Arabic. (ARA & FRE.). 1994. 35.00 (*0-86685-611-0*) Intl Bk Ctr.
***Azel, Anne.** Seasons: Autumn Winds & Winter Snows, 2 vols. x, 322p. 2000. pap. 18.99 (*1-930928-00-9*, Yellow Rose) Renaissance Alliance.
Azem, Alireza. Software Reliability Determination for Conventional & Logic Programming. (Programming Complex Systems Ser.: No. 7). xvi, 175p. (C). 1995. lib. bdg. 64.95 (*3-11-014807-2*) De Gruyter.
Azema, J., et al, eds. Seminaire de Probabilites, Vol. 1583. 334p. 1994. 59.95 (*0-387-58331-9*) Spr-Verlag.
— Seminaire de Probabilites, 1988-1989, No. XXIV. (Lecture Notes in Mathematics Ser.: Vol. 1426). (Illus.). v, 490p. 1990. 79.95 (*0-387-52694-3*) Spr-Verlag.
— Seminaire de Probabilites XXX. viii, 382p. 1996. pap. 68.00 (*3-540-61336-6*) Spr-Verlag.
— Seminaire de Probabilites XXV. (Lecture Notes in Mathematics Ser.: Vol. 1485). viii, 440p. 1991. 75.95 (*0-387-54616-2*) Spr-Verlag.
— Seminaire de Probabilites XXIX, Vol. VI. (Lecture Notes in Mathematics Ser.: Vol. 1613). 326p. 1995. pap. 62.95 (*3-540-60219-4*) Spr-Verlag.
— Seminaire de Probabilites XXVI. (Lecture Notes in Mathematics Ser.: Vol. 1526). x, 633p. 1992. 114.95 (*0-387-56021-1*) Spr-Verlag.
***Azema, J., et al, eds.** Seminaire de Probabilites XXXIV. (Lecture Notes in Mathematics Ser.: Vol. 1729). vi, 431p. 2000. pap. 76.80 (*3-540-67314-8*) Spr-Verlag.
— Seminaire de Probabilites XXXIII. (Lecture Notes in Mathematics Ser.: Vol. 1709). vii, 418p. 1999. pap. 73.00 (*3-540-66342-8*) Spr-Verlag.
Azema, J., et al, eds. Seminaire de Probabilities XXXII. (Lecture Notes in Mathematics Ser.). vi, 430p. 1998. pap. 73.00 (*3-540-64376-1*) Spr-Verlag.
— Seminaire de Probabilities XXXI. (Lecture Notes in Mathematics Ser.: Vol. 1655). 329p. 1997. pap. 51.00 (*3-540-62634-4*) Spr-Verlag.
— Siminare des Probabilites XXI. (Lecture Notes in Mathematics Ser.: Vol. 1247). iv, 579p. 1987. 79.95 (*0-387-17768-X*) Spr-Verlag.
Azema, J. & Meyer, P. A., eds. Seminaire de Probabilites, XXVII: Lecture Notes in Mathematics Ser. (Vol. 1557). vi, 327p. 1993. 60.95 (*0-387-57282-1*) Spr-Verlag.
Azema, J. & Yor, M., eds. Seminaire de Probabilites XIX, 1983-84. (Lecture Notes in Mathematics Ser.: Vol. 1123). (ENG & FRE.). iv, 504p. 1985. 64.95 (*0-387-15230-X*) Spr-Verlag.
— Seminaire de Probabilites XX, 1984-85. (Lecture Notes in Mathematics Ser.: Vol. 1204). v, 639p. 1986. 85.95 (*0-387-16779-X*) Spr-Verlag.
Azema, P. & Balbo, G., eds. Application & Theory of Petri Nets 1997: Proceedings 18th International Conference, ICATPN'97, Toulouse, France, June 23-27, 1997. (Lecture Notes in Computer Science Ser.: Vol. 1248). viii, 467p. 1997. pap. 73.00 (*3-540-63139-9*) Spr-Verlag.
Azemove, H. Jean. Writing Time: Writing Strategies That Achieve Results. (Illus.). vi, 140p. 1998. pap., teacher ed. 25.00 (*0-9662830-0-7*) H J Azemove.
Azen, Margot, jt. auth. see Grant, Jim.
Azen, Stanley P., jt. auth. see Afifi, Abdelmonem A.
Azencott, R. & Dacunha-Castelle, D. Series of Irregular Observations. McHale, D., tr. from FRE. (Applied Probability Ser.). 250p. 1986. 72.95 (*0-387-96263-8*) Spr-Verlag.
Azencott, R. & Wilson, E. N. Homogeneous Manifolds with Negative Curvature II. LC 76-44403. (Memoirs Ser.: No. 8/178). 102p. 1976. pap. 21.00 (*0-8218-2178-4*, MEMO/8/178) Am Math.
Azencott, Robert. Boltzmann Machines, Gibbs Fields & Artificial Vision. (C). 1999. write for info. (*0-201-52738-3*) Addison-Wesley.
— Simulated Annealing: Parallelization Techniques. LC 91-4198. (Interscience Series in Discrete Mathematics). 256p. 1992. 115.00 (*0-471-53231-2*) Wiley.
Azerad, R. & Sih, C., eds. Enantioselective Synthesis Using Biological Systems, Vol. 7, No. 1. (Biocatalysis Ser.). 180p. 1990. pap. text 293.00 (*3-7186-5025-8*) Gordon & Breach.
Azeredo, Ruth. Oklahoma Elementary School Injury Prevention Eduation: The Subject-Integrated Safety Curriculum for Teachers - Grade Four. Mallonee, Sue & Stidham, Shelli S., eds. (Illus.). 130p. (Orig.). 1995. pap. 7.50 (*1-889728-05-5*) OK St Dept Hlth Injury.
— Oklahoma Elementary School Injury Prevention Education: The Subject-Integrated Safety Curriculum for Teachers - Grade Five. Mallonee, Sue & Stidham, Shelli S., eds. (Illus.). 130p. (Orig.). 1995. pap. 7.50 (*1-889728-06-3*) OK St Dept Hlth Injury.
— Oklahoma Elementary School Injury Prevention Education: The Subject-Integrated Safety Curriculum for Teachers - Grade One. Mallonee, Sue & Stidham, Shelli S., eds. (Illus.). 130p. (Orig.). 1995. pap. 7.50 (*1-889728-02-0*) OK St Dept Hlth Injury.
— Oklahoma Elementary School Injury Prevention Education: The Subject-Integrated Safety Curriculum for Teachers - Grade Three. Mallonee, Sue & Stidham, Shelli S., eds. (Illus.). 130p. (Orig.). 1995. pap. 7.50 (*1-889728-04-7*) OK St Dept Hlth Injury.
— Oklahoma Elementary School Injury Prevention Education: The Subject-Integrated Safety Curriculum for Teachers - Grade Two. Mallonee, Sue & Stidham, Shelli S., eds. (Illus.). 130p. (Orig.). 1995. pap. 7.50 (*1-889728-03-9*) OK St Dept Hlth Injury.
— Oklahoma Elementary School Injury Prevention Education: The Subject-Integrated Safety Curriculum for Teachers - Kindergarten. Mallonee, Sue & Stidham, Shelli S., eds. (Illus.). 130p. (Orig.). 1995. pap. 7.50 (*1-889728-01-2*) OK St Dept Hlth Injury.
— Oklahoma Elementary School Injury Prevention Education: The Subject-Integrated Safety Curriculum for Teachers - Kindergarten Through Grade Five. Mallonee, Sue & Stidham, Shelli S., eds. (Illus.). 130p. (Orig.). 1995. pap. 40.50 (*1-889728-00-4*) OK St Dept Hlth Injury.
Azerrad, Jacob. Anyone Can Have a Happy Child: The Simple Secret of Positive Parenting. 2nd rev. ed. LC 97-4935. 192p. 1997. pap. 12.00 (*0-87131-810-5*) M Evans.
Azerrad, Michael. Come As You Are: The Story of Nirvana. LC 93-19821. 336p. 1993. pap. 18.95 (*0-385-47199-8*) Doubleday.
— Gimmie Indie Rock! The American Indie Rock Movement 1976-1991. 2000. write for info. (*0-316-06379-7*) Little.
Azevedo, Aluisio. Mulatto. MacNicoll, Murray G., ed. & tr. by. from POR. LC 89-45755. 304p. 1990. 39.50 (*0-8386-3380-3*) Fairleigh Dickinson.
***Azevedo, Aluisio.** The Slum. Rosenthal, David H. et al, eds. LC 98-48748. (Library of Latin America). 240p. 2000. 30.00 (*0-19-512186-4*); pap. 15.95 (*0-19-512187-2*) OUP.
Azevedo, Aluizio. A Brazilian Tenement. Brown, Harry W., tr. 1977. lib. bdg. 59.95 (*0-8490-1552-9*) Gordon Pr.
Azevedo, Celia M. Abolitionism in the United States & Brazil: A Comparative Perspective. LC 95-37819. (Studies in African American History & Culture). 200p. 1995. text 61.00 (*0-8153-2332-8*) Garland.
Azevedo de Menezes, Carlos. Flora Do Archipelago Da Madeira: Phanerogamicazs E Cryptogamicas Vasculares. (SPA.). 282p. 1984. pap. 130.00 (*3-87429-213-4*, Pub. by Koeltz Sci Bks) Lubrecht & Cramer.
Azevedo Howard, Theresa M. Shanghai to Semper Fi: Vignettes of My Life. large type ed. Cary, Anna Marie, ed. LC 98-74058. (Illus.). 102p. 1998. pap. 14.95 (*0-9664126-1-3*) AMC Pubns.
Azevedo, Jane. Mapping Reality: An Evolutionary Realist Methodology for the Natural & Social Sciences. LC 96-2367. (SUNY Series in the Philosophy of the Social Sciences). (Illus.). 322p. (C). 1997. pap. text 22.95 (*0-7914-3208-4*) State U NY Pr.
— Mapping Reality: An Evolutionary Realist Methodology for the Natural & Social Sciences. LC 96-2367. (SUNY Series in the Philosophy of the Social Sciences). (Illus.). 322p. (C). 1997. text 68.50 (*0-7914-3207-6*) State U NY Pr.
Azevedo, Jose Lacerda de, see Lacerda de Azevedo, Jose.
Azevedo, Luiz Gabriel T. Brazil, Management of Water Resources: Bulk Water Pricing. LC 99-21712. (Technical Paper Ser.). 112p. 1999. pap. 22.00 (*0-8213-4437-4*) World Bank.
Azevedo, M. T., jt. auth. see Bicudo, Carlos E.
Azevedo Mafra, Clara de, tr. see Pessoa, Fernando.
Azevedo, Mario. Historical Dictionary of Mozambique. LC 91-15423. (African Historical Dictionaries Ser.: No. 47). (Illus.). 282p. 1991. 40.00 (*0-8108-2413-2*) Scarecrow.
Azevedo, Mario, ed. Africana Studies: A Survey of Africa & the African Diaspora. LC 92-75339. 546p. 1993. pap. 29.95 (*0-89089-528-7*) Carolina Acad Pr.
— Africana Studies: A Survey of Africa & the African Diaspora. 2nd ed. LC 98-86462. 546p. 1998. pap. write for info. (*0-89089-655-0*) Carolina Acad Pr.
— Cameroon & Chad in Historical & Contemporary Settings. LC 88-27652. (African Studies: Vol. 10). (Illus.). 212p. 1989. lib. bdg. 89.95 (*0-88946-191-0*) E Mellen.
— Cameroon & Its National Character. LC 84-80033. (Illus.). 105p. (Orig.). 1984. pap. text 8.50 (*0-317-04155-X*) Educ Awareness.
— Kenya: The Land, the People, & the Nation. LC 93-73053. 230p. (Orig.). (C). 1993. pap. 16.95 (*0-89089-525-2*) Carolina Acad Pr.
Azevedo, Mario & Nnadozie, Emmanuel. Chad: A Nation in Search of Its Future. LC 97-15097. (Profiles of Africa Ser.). 1997. pap. 79.00 (*0-8133-8677-2*, Pub. by Westview) HarpC.
Azevedo, Mario J. Roots of Violence: A History of War in Chad. (War & Society Ser.). 191p. 1998. text 47.00 (*90-5699-582-0*); pap. text 24.00 (*90-5699-583-9*) Gordon & Breach.
Azevedo, Milton M. Introduccion a la Linguistica Espanola. 432p. (C). 1991. 66.00 (*0-13-484031-3*) P-H.
— Lecturas Periodisticas. 4th ed. LC 89-80718. (SPA.). 290p. (C). 1990. pap. text 30.76 (*0-669-17401-7*) HM Trade Div.
— Lecturas Periodisticas. 5th ed. (SPA.). 285p. (C). 1996. pap. text 30.76 (*0-669-35494-5*) HM Trade Div.
— Passive Sentences in English & Portuguese. LC 79-24987. 128p. reprint ed. pap. 39.70 (*0-7837-6305-0*, 204602000010) Bks Demand.
Azevedo, Milton M., ed. Contemporary Catalonia in Spain & Europe. LC 91-38880. (Research Ser.: No. 81). xii, 140p. (Orig.). 1991. pap. text 13.50 (*0-87725-181-9*) U of Cal IAS.
Azevedo, Milton M., jt. ed. see Dougherty, Dru.
Azevedo, R. F., et al, eds. Applications of Computational Mechanics in Geotechnical Engineering: Proceedings of the 2nd International Workshop, Rio de Janeiro, Brazil, 3-5 November, 1994. LC 99-496403. (Illus.). 419p. (C). 1998. text 126.00 (*90-5410-864-9*, Pub. by A A Balkema) Ashgate Pub Co.
Azevedo, Ross E., jt. auth. see Mitchell, Daniel J.
Azevedo, Warren, ed. Washo Indians of California & Nevada. (Utah Anthropological Papers: No. 67). reprint ed. 22.50 (*0-404-60667-9*) AMS Pr.
AZH Staff, jt. auth. see AABGA Staff.
Azhar, A. Christianity in History. 1991. 14.50 (*0-935782-56-7*) Kazi Pubns.
Azhighitov. English-Russian Medical Dictionary. (ENG & RUS.). 604p. 1993. reprint ed. 24.95 (*0-8288-7580-4*, F33450) Fr & Eur.
Azibo, Daudi A. Ya, see Ya Azibo, Daudi A., ed.
Azibo, Daudi Ajani Ya, ed. African Psychology in Historical Perspective. 288p. 1995. pap. text 18.95 (*0-86543-293-7*) Africa World.
***Azicat, Wilhelm.** Abandon Every Hope. 2000. pap. 11.95 (*0-9700492-8-5*) Steel Pr Pubng.
Azicri, Max. Cuba: Politics, Economics & Society. 220p. 1988. text 49.00 (*0-86187-406-4*, Pub. by P P Pubs) Cassell & Continuum.
— Cuba: Politics, Economics & Society. (Marxist Regimes Ser.). 220p. 1988. text 17.50 (*0-86187-407-2*) St Martin.
Azif, Herbert B. China Trade: A Guide to Doing Business with the People's Republic of China. LC 80-84105. (Illus.). 131p. (Orig.). 1981. pap. 17.50 (*0-9605190-0-9*) China Res.
Azikiwe, Uche, compiled by. Women in Nigeria: An Annotated Bibliography, 20. LC 95-47167. (African Special Bibliogrpahic Ser.: No. 20). 160p. 1996. lib. bdg. 62.95 (*0-313-29960-9*, Greenwood Pr) Greenwood.
Azim, Firdous. The Colonial Rise of the Novel: From Aphra Behn to Charlotte Bronte. LC 92-40810. 264p. (C). 1993. pap. 25.99 (*0-415-09569-7*, B0374) Routledge.
Azima, Fern J. & Richmond, Lewis H., eds. Adolescent Group Psychotherapy, No. 4. LC 89-1972. xiv, 246p. 37.50 (*0-8236-0082-3*, BN 00082) Intl Univs Pr.
Azimabadi, Badr, tr. see Ul-Hind, Sehban.
Azimi, Nassrine, ed. Humanitarian Action & Peace-Keeping Operations: Debriefing & Lessons. 340p. 1997. 119.50 (*90-411-0724-X*) Kluwer Law Intl.
Azimi, Nassrine, ed. The United Nations Transitional Authority in Cambodia: Debriefing & Lessons. LC 96-29. 304p. 1996. 123.00 (*90-411-0886-6*) Kluwer Law Intl.
Azimi, Sharene L., jt. auth. see Winter, John P.
***Azimuth Interactive Staff.** Inter@ctiveLearning: Complete Microsoft Office 97. (Illus.). 2000. 74.95 (*1-930581-18-1*) Azimuth.
— Inter@ctiveLearning: Complete Microsoft Office 97 Bundle. (Illus.). 2000. 199.95 (*1-930581-16-5*) Azimuth.
— Inter@ctiveLearning: HTML. (Illus.). 2000. 19.95 (*1-930581-40-8*) Azimuth.
— Inter@ctiveLearning: Microsoft Access 2000. (Illus.). 2000. 19.95 (*1-930581-35-1*) Azimuth.
— Inter@ctiveLearning: Microsoft Access 2000 Bundle. (Illus.). 2000. 39.95 (*1-930581-33-5*) Azimuth.
— Inter@ctiveLearning: Microsoft Excel 2000. (Illus.). 2000. 19.95 (*1-930581-29-7*) Azimuth.
— Inter@ctiveLearning: Microsoft Excel 2000 Bundle. (Illus.). 2000. 39.95 (*1-930581-27-0*) Azimuth.
— Inter@ctiveLearning: Microsoft FrontPage. (Illus.). 2000. 19.95 (*1-930581-42-4*) Azimuth.
— Inter@ctiveLearning: Microsoft Internet Explorer 5.0. (Illus.). 2000. 19.95 (*1-930581-43-2*) Azimuth.
— Inter@ctiveLearning: Microsoft Office 2000. (Illus.). 2000. 89.95 (*1-930581-38-6*) Azimuth.
— Inter@ctiveLearning: Microsoft Office 2000 Bundle (Promotional) (Illus.). 2000. 179.95 (*1-930581-37-8*) Azimuth.
— Inter@ctiveLearning: Microsoft Outlook 2000. (Illus.). 2000. 19.95 (*1-930581-41-6*) Azimuth.
— Inter@ctiveLearning: Microsoft PowerPoint 2000. (Illus.). 2000. 19.95 (*1-930581-32-7*) Azimuth.
— Inter@ctiveLearning: Microsoft PowerPoint 2000 Bundle. (Illus.). 2000. 39.95 (*1-930581-30-0*) Azimuth.
— Inter@ctiveLearning: Microsoft Windows 98. (Illus.). 2000. 19.95 (*1-930581-21-1*) Azimuth.
— Inter@ctiveLearning: Microsoft Windows 98 Bundle. (Illus.). 2000. 39.95 (*1-930581-19-X*) Azimuth.
— Inter@ctiveLearning: Microsoft Word 2000. (Illus.). 2000. 19.95 (*1-930581-26-2*) Azimuth.
— Inter@ctiveLearning: Microsoft Word 2000 Bundle. (Illus.). 2000. 39.95 (*1-930581-25-4*) Azimuth.

— Inter@ctiveLearning: Netscape 4.0. (Illus.). 2000. 14.95 (*1-930581-24-6*) Azimuth.
— Inter@ctiveLearning: Microsoft Office 2000 Bundle. (Illus.). 2000. 239.95 (*1-930581-39-4*) Azimuth.
— Inter@ctiveLearning: Netscape 4.0 Bundle. (Illus.). 2000. 29.95 (*1-930581-22-X*) Azimuth.
— Microsoft Access 97. (Inter@ctiveLearning Ser.). (Illus.). 108p. 2000. pap. 14.95 (*1-930581-00-9*) Azimuth.
— Microsoft Access 97. deluxe ed. (Inter@ctiveLearning Ser.). 2000. pap. 39.95 incl. cd-rom (*1-930581-01-7*) Azimuth.
— Microsoft Excel 97. (Inter@ctiveLearning Ser.). (Illus.). 148p. 2000. pap. 19.95 (*1-930581-08-4*) Azimuth.
— Microsoft Excel 97. deluxe ed. (Inter@ctiveLearning Ser.). (Illus.). 148p. 2000. pap. 39.95 incl. cd-rom (*1-930581-09-2*) Azimuth.
— Microsoft PowerPoint 97. (Inter@ctiveLearning Ser.). (Illus.). 148p. 2000. pap. 19.95 (*1-930581-02-5*) Azimuth.
— Microsoft PowerPoint 97. deluxe ed. (Inter@ctiveLearning Ser.). 148p. 2000. pap. 39.95 incl. cd-rom (*1-930581-03-3*) Azimuth.
— Microsoft Windows 95. (Inter@ctiveLearning Ser.). (Illus.). 116p. 2000. pap. 19.95 (*1-930581-06-8*) Azimuth.
— Microsoft Windows 95. deluxe ed. (Inter@ctiveLearning Ser.). (Illus.). 116p. 2000. pap. 39.95 incl. cd-rom (*1-930581-07-6*) Azimuth.
— Microsoft Word 97. (Inter@ctiveLearning Ser.). (Illus.). 164p. 2000. pap. 19.95 (*1-930581-04-1*) Azimuth.
— Microsoft Word 97. deluxe ed. (Inter@ctiveLearning Ser.). (Illus.). 164p. 2000. pap. 39.95 incl. cd-rom (*1-930581-05-X*) Azimuth.

Azis, Iwan J. Modelling Policy Analysis. 55.95 (*1-84014-587-0*) Ashgate Pub Co.

Aziz. Computer Graphics & Computational Geometry for Engineers. (C). 1998. text. write for info. (*0-321-01059-0*) Addson-Wesley Educ.

Aziz, A. & Na, Tsung. Perturbation Methods in Heat Transfer. LC 84-6624. (Computational Methods in Mechanics & Thermal Sciences Ser.). (Illus.). 225p. 1984. text 85.00 (*0-89116-376-X*) Hemisp Pub.

Aziz, Abdul. Decentralised Planning: The Karnataka Experiment. LC 93-6861. 146p. (C). 1993. 26.00 (*0-8039-9113-4*) Sage.
— Poverty Alleviation in India: Policies & Programmes. (Illus.). viii, 173p. 1994. 20.00 (*81-7024-626-1*, Pub. by Ashish Pub Hse) Nataraj Bks.

Aziz, Abdul & Arnold, David D., eds. Decentralized Governance in Asian Countries. 280p. (C). 1996. 32.00 (*0-8039-9292-0*) Sage.

Aziz, Abdul & Hanumappa, H. G. Silk Industry: Problems & Prospects. 1985. 18.50 (*0-8364-1511-6*, Pub. by Ashish Pub Hse) S Asia.

Aziz, Abdul & Institute for Social & Economic Change Staff. Industrialisation, Socio-Economic Externalities & State Policy. LC 97-905189. 241p. 1997. write for info. (*81-7022-629-5*) Concept.

Aziz, Abdul & Krishna, Sudhir, eds. Land Reforms in India Vol. 4: Karnataka: Promises Kept & Missed. 292p. 1997. 38.00 (*0-8039-9384-6*) Sage.

Aziz, Abdul, et al. Miniature Political Economies: The Survival Strategies of the Poor. LC 97-903882. 129p. 1997. pap. 100.00 (*81-7533-040-6*, Pub. by Print Hse) St Mut.

Aziz, Abdul, jt. auth. see Rao, V. M.

Aziz, Abdul, jt. ed. see Bamberger, Michael.

Aziz, Abdul, jt. ed. see Shafi, Mohammad.

Aziz, Barbara N. & Kapstein, Matthew. Soundings in Tibetan Civilization. 1986. 32.00 (*0-8364-1587-6*, Pub. by Manohar) S Asia.

***Aziz, Jadeed.** No Rhyme or Meter. 2000. write for info. (*1-58235-613-0*) Watermrk Pr.

***Aziz, K. K.** All India Muslim Conference: 1928-1935 - A Documentary Record. 2000. 38.00 (*81-85199-72-8*, Pub. by Gyan Publishing Hse) S Asia.

***Aziz, Khalid.** Presenting to Win: A Guide for Finance & Business Professionals. 270p. 2001. pap. 19.95 (*1-86076-167-4*, Pub. by Oak Tr) Midpt Trade.

Aziz, Laurel. Decoys: A Celebration of Contemporary Wildfowl Carving. (Illus.). 122p. 1994. 34.95 (*0-921820-83-6*) Firefly Bks Ltd.

Aziz, Laurel & Edwards, Frank B. Ottawa: A Kid's Eye View. (Illus.). 72p. (YA). (gr. 5 up). 1993. pap. 9.95 (*0-921285-26-4*, Pub. by Bungalo Books) Firefly Bks Ltd.

Aziz, Maqbool, ed. see James, Henry.

Aziz, Michael, et al, eds. Fundamentals of Beam-Solid Interactions & Transient Thermal Processing. (Materials Research Society Symposium Proceedings Ser.: Vol. 100). 1988. text 17.50 (*0-931837-68-5*) Materials Res.

***Aziz, Nurjehan, ed.** Floating the Borders: New Contexts in Canadian Criticism. 279p. 1999. pap. 24.95 (*0-920661-80-7*, Pub. by TSAR Pubns) SPD-Small Pr Dist.

Aziz, Nurjehan, ed. Her Mother's Ashes. 1995. pap. 14.95 (*0-920661-40-8*) LPC InBook.
— Her Mother'S Ashes 2: More Stories By South Asian Women In The Canada & The United States. 2nd ed. 176p. 1998. pap. 14.95 (*0-920661-63-7*, Pub. by TSAR Pubns) LPC InBook.

Aziz, Robert. C. G. Jung's Psychology of Religion & Synchronicity. LC 89-30039. (SUNY Series in Transpersonal & Humanistic Psychology). 269p. (C). 1990. text 64.50 (*0-7914-0166-9*); pap. text 23.95 (*0-7914-0167-7*) State U NY Pr.

Aziz, Sartaj. Privatisation in Pakistan: An Evaluation. LC 95-930676. 76p. (Orig.). 1996. pap. 14.00 (*92-64-15310-1*, 41-96-13-1) OECD.
— Rural Development: Learning from China. LC 78-489. 201p. (C). 1978. 39.95 (*0-8419-0371-9*); pap. 19.00 (*0-8419-0372-7*) Holmes & Meier.

Aziz, Sartaz, jt. auth. see Cleary, Thomas.

Aziz, Sina. On the Nature of the Bilirubin Pigments in the Newborn Infant. (Acta Biomedica Lovaniensia Ser.). 194p. (Orig.). 1995. pap. 36.50 (*90-6186-696-0*, Pub. by Leuven Univ) Coronet Bks.

Aziz, Tariq, tr. see Iqbal, Muhammad.

Aziz, Ungku A., ed. Strategies for Structural Adjustment: The Experience of Southeast Asia. LC 90-5296. x, 202p. 1990. pap. 18.50 (*1-55775-147-1*) Intl Monetary.

Aziz-us-Samad, U. Islam & Christianity. 150p. 1985. write for info. (*0-318-61458-8*, Pub. by IIFSO KW) New Era Publns MI.

Aziz, Zahid. Intro to Islam. 66p. 1989. pap. 4.95 (*0-913321-08-7*) Ahmadiyya Anjuman.

Aziz, Zahid, tr. & intro. see Sahib, Hazrat M.

Aziza, C., et al. Dictionnaire des Figures et des Personnages. (FRE.). 464p. 1981. 39.95 (*0-8288-1218-7*, M14213) Fr & Eur.

Azize-Vargas, Yamila, ed. La Mujer en Puerto Rico: Ensayos de Investigacion. LC 87-82377. (Huracan Academia Ser.). (SPA.). 238p. 1987. pap. 9.25 (*0-940238-91-8*) Ediciones Huracan.

***Azizi, Fethi.** Applied Analyses in Geotechnics LC 99-35126. 1999. pap. text. write for info. (*0-419-25350-5*, E & FN Spon) Routledge.
— Applied Analyses in Geotechnics. LC 99-35126. 736p. (C). 1999. text. write for info. (*0-419-25340-8*, E & FN Spon) Routledge.

Azizian, Rouben, jt. ed. see Zhang, Yongjin.

Azizkhan, Richard G., jt. auth. see Seeds, John W.

Azizollahoff, J. R. The Illustrated Buyer's Guide to Oriental Carpets. LC 97-44388. (Illus.). 196p. 1998. 39.95 (*0-7643-0436-4*) Schiffer.

Azizullah. Glimpses of Hadith, 3. 164p. (J). 1991. pap. 7.95 (*1-56744-021-5*) Kazi Pubns.
— Glimpses of the Holy Quran. 1993. pap. 7.95 (*1-56744-023-1*) Kazi Pubns.

Azkenazy, Ludwig. Eres Unico (You Are Unique) (SPA.). 64p. (J). (gr. 5-6). 1991. pap. 5.99 (*968-16-3671-6*, Pub. by Fondo) Continental Bk.

Azkoul, Michael. Augustine of Hippo. 48p. 1995. pap. 5.00 (*1-879038-73-0*, 9043) Synaxis Pr.
— The Influence of Augustine of Hippo on the Orthodox Church. (Texts & Studies in Religion: Vol. 56). 312p. 1991. lib. bdg. 99.95 (*0-88946-733-1*) E Mellen.
— St. Gregory of Nyssa & the Tradition of the Fathers. LC 94-45748. (Texts & Studies in Religion: Vol. 63). 238p. 1995. text 89.95 (*0-7734-8993-2*) E Mellen.
— The Teachings of the Holy Orthodox Church. George, Gregory, ed. 1986. text 18.00 (*0-935889-01-9*) Dormition Pubns.
— The Toll House Myth: Neognosticism. 85p. Date not set. pap. 5.00 (*1-879038-74-9*, 9044) Synaxis Pr.
— Why Christianity? LC 93-85955. 54p. (Orig.). 1994. pap. 2.50 (*0-913026-41-7*) St Nectarios.

Azkue, Resurreccion M. Diccionario Vasco-Espanol-Frances, 2 vols., Set. deluxe ed. (FRE & SPA.). 195.00 (*0-7859-0952-4*, S12384) Fr & Eur.

Azlarov, R. A. & Volodin, N. A. Characterization Problems Associated with the Exponential Distribution. Stein, M., tr. from RUS. 140p. 1986. 65.95 (*0-387-96316-2*) Spr-Verlag.

Azmitia, Efrain C., et al. Cell & Tissue Transplantation into the Adult Brain. LC 87-15408. (Annals of the New York Academy of Science Ser.). xvi, 813p. 1987. write for info. (*0-89766-386-1*) NY Acad Sci.

Azmon, Yael & Izraeli, Dafna N., eds. Women in Israel. (Studies of Israeli Society: Vol. VI). 480p. (C). 1993. text 49.95 (*1-56000-024-4*) Transaction Pubs.

Azmoodeh, Manoochehr. Abstract Data Types & Algorithms. 2nd ed. Sumner, F. H., ed. (Computer Science Ser.). (Illus.). 400p. (C). 1990. text 80.00 (*0-333-51209-X*, Pub. by Macmillan Ed); pap. text 42.50 (*0-333-51210-3*, Pub. by Macmillan Ed) Scholium Intl.

Aznares, Alexander. Donde Nace la Corriente. LC 88-81473. (Coleccion Caniqui). (SPA.). 80p. (Orig.). 1989. pap. 7.95 (*0-89729-486-6*) Ediciones.

Azodi, Azizeh, tr. see Boyer-Xambeu, Marie-Therese, et al.

Azodi, Azizeh, tr. see Deleplace, Ghislain, et al.

Azodmanesh, Sam, jt. auth. see Morandi, Larry.

Azodo, Ada U. L' Imaginaire dans les Romans de Camara Laye. LC 92-31986. (Studies in African & African-American Culture: Vol. 4). XXIII, 165p. (C). 1993. text 39.95 (*0-8204-2039-5*) P Lang Pubng.

Azodo, Ada U. & Wilentz, Gay, eds. Emerging Perspectives on Ama Ata Aidoo. LC 98-7823. 500p. 1998. 79.95 (*0-86543-580-4*) Africa World.

Azodo, Ada U., ed. see Africa World Press Staff.

Azoff, Edward A. On Finite Rank Operators & Preannihilators. LC 86-22274. (Memoirs of the American Mathematical Society Ser.: No. 64/357). 85p. 1986. pap. 18.00 (*0-8218-2419-8*, MEMO/64/357) Am Math.

Azoff, Eitan M. Neural Network Time Series of. LC 93-42336. (Finance Editions Ser.). 212p. 1994. 125.00 (*0-471-94356-8*) Wiley.

Azoff, Elliot S. Guide to Wage & Hour Regulation. LC 98-134159. (Corporate Practice Ser.). 1997. 95.00 (*1-55871-360-3*) BNAC.

Azoff, Elliot S., jt. auth. see Murphy, Betty S.

***Azonwu, Charles A.** Christ's Deliverence for the Depths of Satan LC 98-92988. 242p. 1998. write for info. (*0-9664274-2-4*) Full Dlvrnce Wrld.
— Spiritual Mandellah: Freedom at Last LC 98-92990. 238p. 1998. write for info. (*0-9664274-0-8*) Full Dlvrnce Wrld.

Azordegan, Kambiz. The Ant & the Honey: Andy the Ant. abr. large type ed. (Tootee's Magical Stories Ser.: Vol. 2). (Illus.). 40p. (J). 1998. 9.95 (*1-890571-26-1*) Parrot Prod.
— The Bear's Den: Bear's Family. abr. large type ed. (Tootee's Magical Stories Ser.: Vol. 5). (Illus.). 40p. (J). 1998. 9.95 (*1-890571-29-6*) Parrot Prod.
— The Brave Donkey & the Cowardly Lion: Donkey, Lion & Fox. abr. large type ed. (Tootee's Magical Stories Ser.: Vol. 6). (Illus.). 40p. (J). 1998. 9.95 (*1-890571-30-X*) Parrot Prod.
— Dukunoo Island: Anancy the Spider. abr. large type ed. (Tootee's Magical Stories Ser.: Vol. 3). (Illus.). 34p. (J). 1998. 9.95 (*1-890571-27-X*) Parrot Prod.
— Mr. Rain: The Grate Rain. abr. large type ed. (Tootee's Magical Stories Ser.: Vol. 4). (Illus.). 40p. (J). 1998. 9.95 (*1-890571-28-8*) Parrot Prod.
— Precarious Pond. (Tootee's Magical Stories Ser.: Vol. 1). (Illus.). 40p. (J). 1998. 9.95 (*1-890571-25-3*) Parrot Prod.

Azorin, pseud. Castilla. Vande Berg, Michael, tr. from SPA. LC 92-35991. XIII, 81p. (C). 1996. reprint ed. text 35.95 (*0-8204-1793-9*) P Lang Pubng.
— Las Confesiones De un Pequeno Filosofo. Martinez Cachero, Jose M., ed. (Nueva Austral Ser.: No. 136). (SPA.). 1991. pap. text 11.95 (*84-239-1936-6*) Elliots Bks.
— Confesiones Pequeno Filosofo. 6th ed. (SPA.). 144p. 1990. pap. 12.95 (*0-7859-5177-6*, S362) Fr & Eur.
— Lecturas Espanolas, No. 36. (SPA.). 146p. 1976. write for info. (*0-8288-8554-0*) Fr & Eur.

Azoulay, Avagail & Vicenete, Arie. Spanish Grammar for Independent Learners: SGIL. (ENG & SPA., Illus.). 380p. 1996. pap. text. write for info. (*1-888762-00-4*) VIC Lang.

Azoulay, Dan. Keeping the Dream Alive: The Survival of the Ontario CCF/NDP, 1950-1963. (Illus.). 328p. 1997. text 49.95 (*0-7735-1634-4*, Pub. by McG-Queens Univ Pr) CUP Services.

***Azoulay, Itamar.** Light as an Eagle: Relaxation Exercises for a Healthy Spirit. LC 00-39328. 2000. spiral bd. write for info. (*1-58330-418-5*) Feldheim.

Azoulay, Katya G. Black, Jewish, & Interracial: It's Not the Color of Your Skin, but the "Race" of Your Kin & Other Myths of Identity. LC 97-6297. 224p. 1997. pap. 15.95 (*0-8223-1971-3*); lib. bdg. 45.95 (*0-8223-1975-6*) Duke.

Azoury, Pierre. Chopin Through His Contemporaries: Friends, Lovers, & Rivals, 54. LC 98-48900. (Contributions to the Study of Music & Dance Ser.: No. 54). 256p. 1999. 59.95 (*0-313-30971-X*, GM097, Greenwood Pr) Greenwood.

***Azous, Amanda & Horner, Richard R.** Wetlands & Urbanization: Implications for the Future. 352p. 1999. 69.95 (*1-56670-386-7*) Lewis Pubs.

***Azpiri.** Sensations. 2000. pap. 18.95 (*1-56163-269-4*) NBM.

Azpiri, Alfonso. Lorna Mouse Club. (J). 1996. 14.95 (*1-882931-22-X*) Heavy Metal Magazine.

Azrael, J. Apple Tree Poems. LC 83-72019. 1983. pap. 4.00 (*0-917652-33-9*) Confluence Pr.

Azrael, Jeremy R. Managerial Power & Soviet Politics. LC 66-21330. (Russian Research Center Studies: No. 52). 272p. reprint ed. pap. 84.40 (*0-7837-2220-6*, 205731000004) Bks Demand.

Azrael, Jeremy R., ed. Soviet Nationality Policies & Practices. LC 77-83478. 393p. 1978. 75.00 (*0-275-90283-8*, C0283, Praeger Pubs) Greenwood.

Azrael, Jeremy R. & Payin, Emil A. Cooperation & Conflict in the Former Soviet Union: Implications for Migration. (Illus.). 194p. 1996. pap. text 15.00 (*0-8330-2466-3*, CF-130-CRES) Rand Corp.

Azrael, Jeremy R. & Payin, Emil A., eds. Conflict & Consensus in Ethno-Political & Center-Periphery Relations in Russia. LC 98-145124. 60p. 1998. pap. text 10.00 (*0-8330-2593-7*, CF-139-CRES) Rand Corp.
— U. S. & Russian Policymaking with Respect to the Use of Force. 225p. (Orig.). 1996. pap. 15.00 (*0-8330-2468-X*, CF-129-CRES) Rand Corp.

Azrael, Jeremy R. & Rahr, Alexander G. The Formation & Development of the Russian KGB, 1991-1994. LC 93-42934. 1993. pap. text 15.00 (*0-8330-1491-9*, MR-355-USDP) Rand Corp.

Azrael, Mary. Riddles for a Naked Sailor. LC 91-66988. (Illus.). 48p. (Orig.). 1991. pap. 10.00 (*0-9631385-2-9*) Stonevale Pr.

Azrak, Michel G., tr. from ARA. Modern Syrian Short Stories. LC 86-51002. 131p. (Orig.). 1988. pap. 10.95 (*0-89410-441-1*, Three Contnts) L Rienner.
— Modern Syrian Short Stories. rev. ed. LC 86-51002. 131p. (Orig.). 1988. 25.00 (*0-89410-440-3*, Three Contnts) L Rienner.

Azria, M. Le Calcitonine: Fisiologia e Farmacologia. (Illus.). x, 152p. 1990. 85.25 (*3-8055-5088-X*) S Karger.
— Calcitonins: Physiology & Pharmacology. (Illus.). x, 152p. 1989. 85.25 (*3-8055-4851-6*) S Karger.

Azrieli, Avraham. Your Lawyer on a Short Leash: A Survivor's Guide to Dealing with Lawyers. LC 96-42170. 1997. 16.95 (*1-57105-036-1*) Transnatl Pubs.

Azrin, Nathan H. & Besalel, Victoria A. How to Use Overcorrection. (How to Teach Ser.). 37p. (C). 1980. 8.00 (*0-89079-047-7*, 1011) PRO-ED.
— How to Use Positive Practice. (How to Teach Ser.). 44p. 1981. 8.00 (*0-89079-060-4*, 1012) PRO-ED.
— Job Club Counselor's Manual: A Behavioral Approach to Vocational Counseling. LC 79-20865. (Illus.). 212p. 1980. pap. text 34.00 (*0-936104-98-8*, 1167) PRO-ED.

Azrin, Nathan H. & Foxx, Richard M. Toilet Training in Less Than a Day. (Illus.). 189p. 1989. per. 5.99 (*0-671-69380-8*) PB.

Azrin, Nathan H., jt. auth. see Besalel-Azrin, Victoria A.

Azua, Raul Valadez, see Valadez Azua, Raul.

***Azuela, Antonio, et al.** Evictions & the Right to Housing. 350p. 1999. pap. 25.00 (*0-88936-861-9*, Pub. by IDRC Bks) Stylus Pub VA.

Azuela, Arturo. Estuche para Dos Violines (A Case for Two Violins) (SPA.). 243p. 1994. 15.99 (*968-16-4421-2*, Pub. by Fondo) Continental Bk.

Azuela, Mariano. Los De Abajo. (SPA.). 128p. 1997. pap. 10.95 (*0-14-026621-6*) Viking Penguin.
— Los De Abajo: Novela De la Revolucion Mexicana. Englekirk, John E. & Kiddle, Lawrence, eds. (SPA.). 175p. (C). 1992. reprint ed. pap. text 12.50 (*0-88133-662-9*) Waveland Pr.
— Los de Abajo (The Underdogs) (SPA.). 143p. 1960. pap. 8.99 (*968-16-4777-7*, Pub. by Fondo) Continental Bk.
— Los de Abajo. (SPA.). pap. 12.95 (*968-16-0320-6*, Pub. by Fondo) Continental Bk.
— Mala Yerba y Esa Sangre (Bad Weed & This Blood) (SPA.). 226p. 1958. pap. 8.99 (*968-16-0910-7*, Pub. by Fondo) Continental Bk.
— Nueva Burguesia (The New Bourgeoisie) 2nd ed. (SPA.). 140p. 1985. pap. 7.99 (*968-16-1853-X*, Pub. by Fondo) Continental Bk.
— Obras Completas (Complete Works), 3 vols., Vol. 1. (SPA.). 1132p. 34.99 (*968-16-4093-4*, Pub. by Fondo) Continental Bk.
— Obras Completas (Complete Works), 3 vols., Vol. 2. (SPA.). 1132p. 34.99 (*968-16-4095-0*, Pub. by Fondo) Continental Bk.
— Obras Completas (Complete Works), 3 vols., Vol. 3. (SPA.). 1134p. 34.99 (*968-16-4284-8*, Pub. by Fondo) Continental Bk.
— Tres Novelas. (SPA.). pap. 8.95 (*968-16-0426-1*, Pub. by Fondo) Continental Bk.
— Two Novels of Mexico: The Flies & The Bosses. Simpson, Lesley B., tr. 1956. pap. 14.95 (*0-520-00053-6*, Pub. by U CA Pr) Cal Prin Full Svc.
— Underdogs. 1998. mass mkt. 5.95 (*0-451-52625-2*) Addson-Wesley Educ.
— Underdogs. 149p. Date not set. 18.95 (*0-8488-2559-4*) Amereon Ltd.
— The Underdogs. Fornoff, Frederick H., tr. LC 92-10582. (Latin American Ser.). (ENG & SPA., Illus.). 184p. (C). 1992. pap. 14.95 (*0-8229-5484-2*) U of Pittsburgh Pr.
— The Underdogs. 160p. 1986. reprint ed. lib. bdg. 21.95 (*0-89966-515-2*) Buccaneer Bks.

Azuh, Dominic E. Child Survival under Threat. (C). 1994. 21.00 (*81-7018-821-0*, Pub. by BR Pub) S Asia.

Azuki. Zen Graffiti. 97p. 1995. pap. 9.95 (*0-946672-24-5*, Pub. by Buddhist Pub) Assoc Pubs Grp.

Azul, Piaf. Xoloitzcuintle: Selected Poems, October '86-April '91. LC 94-60978. (SFX Poets Ser.: Vol. 1). (Illus.). 40p. (Orig.). 1996. 25.00 (*0-935865-06-3*); pap. 13.00 (*0-935865-05-5*); pap. 7.00 (*0-935865-07-1*) SFX Pr.

Azulay, Allegra, jt. auth. see Azulay, Erik.

Azulay, Erik & Azulay, Allegra. The Russian Far East. (Companion Guides Ser.). (Illus.). 311p. (Orig.). 1995. pap. 18.95 (*0-7818-0325-X*) Hippocrene Bks.

Azuma, Akira. The Biokinetics of Flying & Swimming. LC 92-590. 1993. 223.95 (*0-387-70106-0*) Spr-Verlag.

Azuma, Eiichiro, jt. auth. see Inada, Lawson F.

Azuma, Eiichiro, ed. see Ichioka, Yuji.

Azuonye, Chukwuma. Dogon. Bond, George & Wyck, Gary V., eds. LC 94-45814. (Heritage Library of African Peoples). (Illus.). 64p. (YA). (gr. 7-12). 1995. lib. bdg. 16.95 (*0-8239-1976-5*) Rosen Group.
— Edo: The Bini People of the Benin Kingdom. LC 94-138414. (Heritage Library of African Peoples). (Illus.). 64p. (YA). (gr. 7-12). 1996. lib. bdg. 16.95 (*0-8239-1985-4*) Rosen Group.

***Azurdia, Arturo.** Spirit Empowered Preaching: Involving the Holy Spirit in Your Ministry. 192p. 2000. pap. text 15.99 (*1-85792-413-4*) Christian Focus.

Azurin, Arnold M. Reinventing the Filipino Sense of Being & Becoming. (Illus.). 240p. 1996. pap. text 24.00 (*971-542-073-7*, Pub. by U of Philippines Pr) UH Pr.

Azwell, Tara, jt. auth. see Schmar, Elizabeth.

Azzahir, Ahmad. The Three Books of Khepra, Bks. I & II. 180p. 1992. write for info. (*1-881421-00-7*) Intl Khepran Inst.

***Azzahir, Ahmad.** Utezat N Maat Pt. II: The Council of Truth. iv, 64p. 2000. write for info. (*1-881421-03-1*) Intl Khepran Inst.

Azzalini, A. Statistical Inference Based on the Likelihood. (Monographs on Statistics & Applied Probability). 352p. 1996. ring bd. 65.95 (*0-412-60650-X*) CRC Pr.

Azzalini, Adelchi, jt. auth. see Bowman, Adrian W.

Azzam, Abdul R. The Eternal Message of Muhammad. 2nd ed. Farah, Caesar E., tr. 136p. 1993. pap. 13.95 (*0-946621-48-9*, Pub. by Islamic Texts) Intl Spec Bk.

Azzam, Albert. High Speed Cable Modems: Including IEEE 802.14 Standards. LC 97-14635. (Computer Communications Ser.). (Illus.). 570p. 1997. pap. 69.95 (*0-07-006417-2*) McGraw.

Azzam, Albert A. Broadband Access Technologies. 1999. 60.00 (*0-07-135060-8*) McGraw.

Azzam, Fouad. Civilized Hiking. Anderson, Connie & Adams, Milton E., eds. (Illus.). 144p. 1998. pap. 12.95 (*1-890676-21-7*) Beavers Pond.

Azzam, Henry T. The Emerging Arab Capital Markets: Investment Opportunities & Constraints in a Relatively Unplayed Market. LC 96-13833. 1996. 110.00 (*0-7103-0549-4*, Pub. by Kegan Paul Intl) Col U Pr.

Azzam, Leila & Gouverneur, Aisha. The Life of the Prophet Muhammad. (Illus.). 137p. (Orig.). (YA). (gr. 10 up). 1995. pap. 19.95 (*0-946621-02-0*, Pub. by Islamic Texts) Intl Spec Bk.

Azzam, R. M. & Bashara, N. M. Ellipsometry & Polarized Light. (North-Holland Personal Library). 558p. 1992. reprint ed. pap. 74.50 (*0-444-87016-4*, North Holland) Elsevier.

An Asterisk (*) at the beginning of an entry indicates that the title is appearing for the first time.

Azzan, R. M., ed. Selected Papers on Ellipsometry. 736p. 1991. pap. 50.00 (*0-8194-0571-X*, VOL. MS27) SPIE.

***Azzara, Alan J.** Prehospital Providers' Guide to Medication. LC 99-21429. (Illus.). 255p. 1998. pap. write for info. (*0-7216-1136-2*, W B Saunders Co) Harcrt Hlth Sci Grp.

Azzara, Alan J., jt. auth. see Cohn, Bruce M.

Azzara, Mike, jt. auth. see Hassan, Rich.

Azzara, Thomas P. Tax Havens of the World. 6th ed. 350p. 1999. write for info. (*1-893522-00-8*) New Providence.

Azzara, Thomas P. & Christensen, Max L. Tax Havens of the World. 7th ed. (Illus.). 340p. 1999. pap. 75.00 (*1-893522-01-6*) New Providence.

***Azzarello, Brian.** 100 Bullets: First Shot, Last Call. (Illus.). 128p. 2000. pap. text 9.95 (*1-56389-645-1*, Pub. by DC Comics) Time Warner.

Azzaretti. Dictionnaire International d'Abbreviations Scientifiques et Techniques. (FRE.). 300p. 1978. lib. bdg. 95.00 (*0-7859-3905-9*, 2856080030) Fr & Eur.

Azzaretti, M. International Dictionary of Scientific & Technical Abbreviations. (ENG, FRE, GER, ITA & RUS.). 300p. 1978. pap. 52.50 (*2-85608-003-0*) IBD Ltd.

Azzi, A., et al, eds. Adenine Nucleotides in Cellular Energy Transfer & Signal Transduction. LC 92-17729. (Molecular & Cell Biology Updates Ser.). ix, 476p. 1992. 137.00 (*0-8176-2673-5*, Pub. by Birkhauser) Princeton Arch.

— Anion Carries of Mitochondrial Membranes. (Illus.). xii, 381p. 1989. 103.95 (*0-387-50853-8*) Spr-Verlag.

Azzi, A. & Zahler, P., eds. Enzymes, Receptors & Carriers of Biological Membranes: A Laboratory Manual. (Illus.). 135p. 1986. lab manual ed. 42.95 (*0-387-13751-3*) Spr-Verlag.

***Azzi, Maria Susana & Collier, Simon.** Le Grand Tango: The Life & Music of Astor Piazzolla. LC 99-30795. (Illus.). 308p. 2000. 30.00 (*0-19-512777-3*) OUP.

Azzi, Stephen. Walter Gordon & the Rise of Canadian Nationalism. 34.95 (*0-7735-1840-1*) McG-Queens Univ Pr.

Azziz, Ricardo, et al, eds. Androgen Excess Disorders in Women. LC 97-5984. (Illus.). 512p. 1997. text 160.00 (*0-397-51721-1*) Lppncott W & W.

Azziz, Ricardo & Murphy, Ana A. Practical Manual of Operative Laparoscopy & Hysteroscopy. 2nd ed. LC 96-21229. 347p. 1997. 85.00 (*0-387-94696-9*) Spr-Verlag.

Azzolina, L. S., ed. Comparative Immunology: Proceedings of the Verona Workshop, 16-17 July 1980, Verona, Italy. (Illus.). 180p. 1982. pap. 45.00 (*0-08-028019-6*, Pergamon Pr) Elsevier.

Azzolino, Agnes. Exploring Functions Through the Use of Manipulatives. LC 94-96503. (Illus.). 100p. (C). 1994. spiral bd. 45.00 (*0-9623593-3-5*) Mathematical.

— Math Games for Adult & Child: Math Games for 2 Through 7-Year-Olds. rev. ed. LC 93-7994. (Illus.). 90p. (Orig.). (J). (ps-2). 1993. spiral bd. 20.00 (*0-9623593-4-3*) Mathematical.

— Math Shown Here! Illustrations from Math Spoken Here. LC 96-94236. (Illus.). 200p. 1996. pap. 20.00 (*0-9623593-6-X*, MSHH) Mathematical.

— Math Spoken Here! Math Dictionary for Arithmetic & Algebra. LC 95-94794. (Illus.). 140p. (Orig.). 1995. pap., spiral bd. 10.00 (*0-9623593-5-1*) Mathematical.

Azzone, Giovanni Felice. Medicine from Art to Science: The Role of Complexity & Evolution. (Veneto Institute of Sciences, Letters & Arts Ser.: Vol. 1). 197p. 1998. 60.00 (*90-5199-390-0*, Pub. by IOS Pr) IOS Press.

Azzopardi-Alexander, Marie, jt. auth. see Borg, Albert.

Azzopardi, Gilles. The Complete Book to Develop Your IQ. 320p. (Orig.). 1993. pap. 19.95 (*0-572-01934-3*, Pub. by W Foulsham) Trans-Atl Phila.

— Measure Your IQ. 160p. (Orig.). 1993. pap. 12.95 (*0-572-01935-1*, Pub. by W Foulsham) Trans-Atl Phila.

— Succeed at I. Q. Tests. 160p. 1994. pap. 13.95 (*0-572-01948-3*, Pub. by W Foulsham) Trans-Atl Phila.

***Azzopardi, Lilian M., ed.** Validation Instruments for Community Pharmacy: Pharmaceutical Care for the Third Millennium. LC 00-20476. (Illus.). 366p. 2000. pap. text 39.95 (*0-7890-1109-3*, Pharmctl Prods) Haworth Pr.

— Validation Instruments for Community Pharmacy: Pharmaceutical Care for the Third Millennium. LC 00-20476. (Illus.). 366p. 2000. 89.95 (*0-7890-0900-5*, Pharmctl Prods) Haworth Pr.

Azzopardi, Mario. Naked As Water: Poems by Mario Azzopardi. Falzon, Grazio, tr. from MLT. (Illus.). xiii, 178p. 1996. pap. 13.00 (*1-879378-11-6*) Xenos Riverside.

***Azzouni, Jody.** Knowledge & Reference in Empirical Science. LC 99-88208. (International Library of Philosophy). 288p. 2000. 85.00 (*0-415-22383-0*) Routledge.

— The Lust for Blueprints. (Illus.). 88p. 1999. pap. 14.95 (*0-922558-07-8*) Poets Pr.

Azzouni, Jody. Metaphysical Myths, Mathematical Practice. 261p. (C). 1994. text 80.00 (*0-521-44223-0*) Cambridge U Pr.

Azzouz, Elsayed & Nandi, Asoke K. Automatic Modulation Recognition of Communication Signals. LC 96-36615. 217p. (C). 1996. text 119.00 (*0-7923-9796-7*) Kluwer Academic.

B

B., Ray Michael. Poker Farce & Poker Truth: The Actual & Real World Of Poker. LC 99-229011. (Illus.). 246p. 1999. pap. 19.95 (*1-880685-20-5*) Two Plus NV.

B & A Neilbauer Staff. Your Total Body Health. 1998. 24.95 (*0-7897-0769-1*) Macmillan USA.

B & P Publishing Co. Staff. New Big Book of Games. 1992. 13.00 (*0-394-23520-7*) Random.

— W. Shortz Brain Busters. 1992. 11.00 (*0-394-23519-3*) Random.

B. A. S. S. Inc. Staff. 100+ B. A. S. S. Tips: Tricks, Techniques & Tactics to Better Bassin. (Illus.). 162p. (Orig.). 1992. pap. 4.95 (*1-890280-02-X*) B A S S.

— 100+ Ways to Better Deer Hunting. 2nd ed. (Illus.). 128p. 1990. pap. 4.95 (*1-890280-03-8*) B A S S.

— Southern Hunter's Guide. (Illus.). 130p. (Orig.). 1994. pap. 4.95 (*1-890280-01-1*) B A S S.

— Southern Outdoors Guide to Deer Hunting: A How-To Treasury - The Best of 25 Years. (Illus.). 304p. (Orig.). 1991. pap. 19.95 (*1-890280-05-4*) B A S S.

— Spinnerbait Bassin' 100 Tips for Using Spinner Baits. 2nd ed. (Illus.). 160p. 1994. pap. 4.95 (*1-890280-04-6*) B A S S.

B. Altman & Co. Staff. Altman's Spring & Summer Fashions Catalog: 1915, Vol. 915. LC 94-44617. (Illus.). 96p. pap. 9.95 (*0-486-28527-8*) Dover.

— 1920s Fashions from B. Altman & Company. Cirker, Blanche, ed. (Illus.). 128p. 1999. pap. 12.95 (*0-486-40293-2*) Dover.

B. B. C. Staff. Current Central Legislation, 1990. (C). 1991. ring bd. 180.00 (*0-89771-464-4*) St Mut.

B. B. P. Staff. Bringing Out the Best in Your People. 300p. (C). 1992. 11.95 (*0-13-085655-X*, Macmillan Coll) P-H.

— How Supervisors Should Appraise Employee Performance. 2p. (C). 1992. pap. 11.95 (*0-13-396789-1*, Macmillan Coll) P-H.

B., Bill. Compulsive Overeater. LC 80-70095. 320p. 18.95 (*1-56838-062-3*) Hazelden.

B. Cahill, Robert & J. Hrebic, Herbert. Stack the Deck. (Writing Program Ser.). (YA). (gr. 9-12). 1973. pap. 15.95 (*0-933282-26-5*) Stack the Deck.

B. D. & L. Staff, ed. Webster's New Encyclopedic Dictionary. rev. ed. LC 95-13165. (Illus.). 1696p. 24.98 (*1-884822-20-7*) Blck Dog & Leventhal.

B., David, jt. auth. see B., Sally.

B., Dick. The Akron Genesis of Alcoholics Anonymous. 2nd rev. ed. LC 92-97026. (History of Early A. A.'s Spiritual Roots & Successes Ser.: Vol. 3). 400p. 1998. per. 17.95 (*1-885803-17-6*, 944) Paradise Res Inc.

***B., Dick.** Anne Smith's Journal, 1933-1939: A. A.'s Principles of Success. 3rd rev. ed. LC 98-92158. (History of Early A.A.'s Spiritual Roots & Successes Ser.: Vol. 2). Orig. Title: Anne Smith's Spiritual Workbook. 180p. 1998. per. 16.95 (*1-885803-24-9*, 992) Paradise Res Inc.

B., Dick. The Books Early AAs Read for Spiritual Growth. 7th rev. ed. LC 98-92159. (History of Early A. A.'s Spiritual Roots & Successes Ser.: Vol. 7). 126p. 1998. per. 15.95 (*1-885803-26-5*, 995) Paradise Res Inc.

***B., Dick.** By the Power of God: A Guide to Early A. A. Groups & Forming Similar Groups Today. LC 99-76227. (Why It Worked: Vol. 3). 260p. 2000. per. 16.95 (*1-885803-30-3*, Pub. by Paradise Res Inc) Good Bk Pub.

B., Dick. Dr. Bob & His Library: A Major A. A. Spiritual Source. 3rd rev. ed. LC 98-92130. (History of Early A. A.'s Spiritual Roots Ser.: Vol. 1). 156p. 1998. per. 15.95 (*1-885803-25-7*, 991) Paradise Res Inc.

— The Golden Text of A. A. Early A. A., God & Real Spirituality. LC 99-93045. (Early A. A. History Ser.: Vol. 2). 76p. 1999. per. 14.95 (*1-885803-29-X*) Paradise Res Inc.

— The Good Book & the Big Book: A. A.'s Roots in the Bible. 2nd rev. ed. LC 95-69696. (History of Early A. A.'s Spiritual Roots & Successes Ser.: Vol. 5). 264p. 1997. per. 17.95 (*1-885803-16-8*, 946) Paradise Res Inc.

— Good Morning! Quiet Time, Morning Watch, Meditation & Early A. A. 2nd rev. ed. LC 96-68529. (History of Early A. A.'s Spiritual Roots & Successes Ser.: Vol. 8). 154p. 1998. per. 16.95 (*1-885803-22-2*) Paradise Res Inc.

— Hope! The Story of Geraldine D., Alina Lodge & Recovery. LC 97-91207. 142p. 1999. per. 15.95 (*1-885803-15-X*, TOT 1) Paradise Res Inc.

***B., Dick.** New Light on Alcoholism: God, Sam Shoemaker & A. A. 2nd rev. ed. LC 98-92124. (History of Early A.A.'s Spiritual Roots Ser.: Vol. 9). Orig. Title: New Light on Alcoholism: The A. A. Legacy from Sam Shoemaker. 638p. 1999. pap. 24.95 (*1-885803-27-3*, 996) Paradise Res Inc.

B., Dick. The Oxford Group & Alcoholics Anonymous: A Design for Living That Works. 2nd rev. ed. LC 98-91226. (History of Early A. A.'s Spiritual Roots & Successes Ser.: Vol. 4). Orig. Title: Design for Living: The Oxford Group's Contribution to Early A. A.. 432p. 1998. per. 17.95 (*1-885803-19-2*, 951) Paradise Res Inc.

— That Amazing Grace: The Role of Clarence & Grace S. in Alcoholics Anonymous. LC 95-92858. (History of Early A. A.'s Spiritual Roots & Successes Ser.: Vol. 6). 160p. 1996. per. 16.95 (*1-885803-06-0*, 947) Paradise Res Inc.

— Turning Point: A History of Early A. A.'s Spiritual Roots & Successes. LC 96-92645. (History of Early A. A.'s Spiritual Roots & Successes Ser.: Vol. 10). 776p. 1997. per. 29.95 (*1-885803-07-9*, 950) Paradise Res Inc.

— Utilizing Early A. A.'s Spiritual Roots for Recovery Today. LC 99-93032. (Early A. A. History Ser.: Vol. 1). 106p. 1999. per. 14.95 (*1-885803-28-1*) Paradise Res Inc.

B., Hamilton. Getting Started in AA. LC 95-24001. 211p. pap. 8.95 (*1-56838-091-7*) Hazelden.

— Twelve Step Sponsorship: How It Works. 260p. pap. 11.95 (*1-56838-122-0*) Hazelden.

B., Howard. Leary: A Portrait of an Alcoholic. LC 95-35824. 144p. (Orig.). 1996. pap. 10.95 (*1-56474-152-4*) Fithian Pr.

B., Iris. Workers Compensation & Disability Insurance: All American Holocaust. unabridged ed. Kotke, William & Reed, Scott, eds. LC 95-60763. 204p. (Orig.). 1995. pap. 14.50 (*0-9645353-5-1*) Windigo Pr.

B. K. Co., Staff, jt. auth. see Camino, E. E.

B. M. R. Staff & Wright, Deborah K. Rapid Nursing Interventions: Neurologic. LC 95-20814. (Rapid Nursing Interventions Ser.). 224p. (C). 1996. pap. 31.95 (*0-8273-7093-8*) Delmar.

***B., Mel.** Bill W. An Autobiography. LC 99-87571. 240p. 2000. 21.95 (*1-56838-373-8*) Hazelden.

B., Mel. Ebby: The Man Who Sponsored Bill W. LC 99-232074. 96p. 1998. pap. 9.95 (*1-56838-162-X*, 5699 A) Hazelden.

***B., Mel.** My Search for Bill W. 160p. 2000. pap. 14.00 (*1-56838-374-6*) Hazelden.

B, Mel. Pride. 24p. (Orig.). 1985. pap. 2.00 (*0-89486-267-7*, 1397B) Hazelden.

— Step Ten: A Good Tenth Step. 20p. (Orig.). 1982. pap. 2.00 (*0-89486-153-0*) Hazelden.

B., Mel. Walk in Dry Places. 400p. pap. 11.00 (*1-56838-127-1*) Hazelden.

***B., Mel & P., Bill.** The Seven Key Principles of Successful Recovery: The Basic Tools for Progress, Growth, & Happiness. LC 99-38956. 160p. 1999. pap. text 12.00 (*1-56838-344-4*) Hazelden.

B., Philip. Blended Beauty. (Illus.). 160p. 1996. pap. 19.95 (*0-89815-865-6*) Ten Speed Pr.

B. Phillips, Ruth. Representing Woman: Sande Masquerades of the Mende of Sierra Leone. (Illus.). 200p. 1995. pap. 29.00 (*0-930741-45-5*) UCLA Fowler Mus.

B. R. E. S. Staff. To God with Love: Children & Communion. (C). 1996. pap. 39.95 (*0-85439-112-5*, Pub. by St Paul Pubns) St Mut.

— To God with Love & Sorrow: Children & Confession. (C). 1996. pap. 39.95 (*0-85439-117-7*, Pub. by St Paul Pubns) St Mut.

B, Rick E. Soulmarkers Vol. 2: RickE. B. O, Ron, tr. & photos by by. LC 98-96970. (Illus.). 80p. (C). 1999. 100.00 (*1-893764-02-8*) Soulmarkers Inc.

— Soulmarkers Vol. 3: RickE. B. O, Ron, tr. & photos by by. LC 98-96970. Vol. 3. (Illus.). 80p. (C). 1999. 100.00 (*1-893764-03-6*) Soulmarkers Inc.

B., Ron, compiled by. My Mind Is Out to Get Me: Humor & Wisdom in Recovery. 180p. pap. 6.95 (*1-56838-040-0*) Hazelden.

B. S. I. Staff. Records of the Botanical Survey of India. (C). 1991. text 2750.00 (*0-89771-575-6*, Pub. by Intl Bk Distr) St Mut.

B., Sally & B., David. Our Children Are Alcoholics: Coping with Children Who Have Addictions. Graham, Mary J., ed. LC 97-70959. xiv, 174p. 1997. per. 14.95 (*1-888461-02-0*) Islewest Pub.

B Small Publishing Staff. Best Friends Activity Book: Great Things to Do & Make with Your Friends. (Illus.). 16p. 1999. pap. 5.95 (*1-874735-54-9*, Pub. by B Small Publishing) BHB Intl.

— Crafty Christmas Stars. 16p. (J). (gr. 1-4). 1999. pap. 4.95 (*1-874735-59-X*) B Small Publishing.

— Crafty Halloween Pumpkins. 16p. (J). (gr. 4-7). 1999. pap. 4.95 (*1-874735-58-1*) B Small Publishing.

— My Friends. 1999. pap. 5.95 (*1-874735-50-6*) B Small Publishing.

B Small Staff. Three Billy Goats Gruff. 1999. pap. text 5.95 (*1-874735-29-8*) B Small Publishing.

B. Y. U. Religious Studies Center Staff. The Book of Mormon Vol. 9: Fourth Nephi Through Moroni from Zion to Destruction. Nyman, Monte S. & Tate, Charles D., Jr., eds. 1995. 12.95 (*0-88494-974-5*) Bookcraft Inc.

— Church History in Black & White. Cottle, T. Jeffery et al, eds. LC 95-79001. 1995. 29.95 (*0-88494-998-2*) Bookcraft Inc.

B&J Publications Staff. Campus Lodging Guide. 19th ed. 1999. pap. write for info. (*0-945499-10-8*) B&J Pubns.

Ba, Amadou H. Amkoullel, L'Enfant Peul, Memoires. (FRE.). 534p. 1992. pap. 24.95 (*0-7859-3307-7*, 2868699065) Fr & Eur.

— L' Etrnage Destin de Wangrin. (FRE.). 320p. 1973. pap. 18.95 (*0-7859-3182-1*, 2264003863) Fr & Eur.

— Kaidara. Whitman, Daniel, tr. from FRE. LC 84-51200. (Illus.). 159p. 1988. 12.50 (*0-89410-448-9*, Three Contnts) L Rienner.

Ba, Amadou Hampate. The Fortunes of Wangrin. Taylor, Aina Pavolini, tr. from FRE. LC 98-17131. 376p. 2000. pap. 17.95 (*0-253-21226-X*); lib. bdg. 39.95 (*0-253-33429-2*) Ind U Pr.

Ba Chung, Nguyen, tr. see Bowen, Kevin, et al, eds.

Ba, Jean-Claude & Wilson, David E. Mechanics Laboratory Manual. Mayer, Laurence, ed. (Illus.). 52p. 1996. pap. text, lab manual ed. 16.25 (*1-889766-02-X*) Columbus State Bks.

Ba, Jin. The Family. Shapiro, Sidney, tr. from CHI. LC 87-73398. (C & T Asian Literature Ser.). 351p. 1992. reprint ed. pap. 5.95 (*0-917056-40-X*) Cheng & Tsui.

Ba, Mariama. Scarlet Song. (Longman African Writers Ser.). 171p. (C). 1995. pap. 14.87 (*0-582-26455-3*) Addison-Wesley.

Ba, Ro. Lyfe of Syr Thomas More. Hitchcock, E. V. & Hallett, P. E., eds. (EETS Original Ser.: Vol. 222). 1996. reprint ed. 30.00 (*0-19-722222-6*, Pub. by EETS) Boydell & Brewer.

Ba, Sylvia W. The Concept of Negritude in the Poetry of Leopold Sedar Senghor. LC 72-7797. 316p. reprint ed. pap. 98.00 (*0-8357-4039-0*, 203673000005) Bks Demand.

***Ba-Yunus, Ilyas & Siddiqui, M. Moin.** A Report on Muslim Population in the U. S. A. 40p. 1998. pap. 9.95 (*1-884394-03-5*) CAMRI.

Baa, Enid M., ed. Theses on Caribbean Topics, Seventeen Seventy-Eight to Nineteen Sixty-Eight. 146p. 1970. pap. 2.50 (*0-8477-2000-4*) U of PR Pr.

***Baab, James.** Crosscurrents: A Fly Fisher's Progress. LC 99-29607. 224p. 1999. 24.95 (*1-55821-946-3*) Lyons Pr.

Baab, Lynne M. Personality Type in Congregations: How to Work with Others More Effectively. LC 97-78129. xvi, 155p. 1998. pap. 15.25 (*1-56699-199-4*, AL190) Alban Inst.

Baack. Organizational Behavior. LC 97-67106. 1998. 78.95 (*0-87393-636-1*) Dame Pubns.

— Organizational Behavior: Study Guide. LC \\. 1998. student ed. 24.95 (*0-87393-664-7*) Dame Pubns.

Baack, Clemens, ed. Optical Wideband Transmission Systems. 288p. 1986. 128.00 (*0-8493-6152-4*, TK5103, CRC Reprint) Franklin.

Baack, Donald. How to Survive Your Child's College Education: From Application to Graduation. LC 97-19659. (Illus.). 176p. 1997. pap. 10.95 (*0-8065-1908-8*) Carol Pub Group.

Baacke, Dieter, et al. Meyers Enzyklopaedisches Lexikon Vol. 17: Nau-Os. 9th ed. (GER.). 848p. 1976. 275.00 (*0-7859-6907-1*, 3411012676) Fr & Eur.

Baacke, Don, jt. auth. see Dolnick, Barrie.

Baackmann, Susanne, jt. ed. see Sy-Quia, Hilary Collier.

Baade, Anne A. Melchior Goldast von Heiminsfeld: Collector, Commentator, & Editor. LC 91-43013. (Studies in Old Germanic Languages & Literatures: Vol. 2). X, 206p. (C). 1993. text 39.95 (*0-8204-1835-8*) P Lang Pubng.

Baade, Hans W., et al. Comparative Law, Cases - Text - Materials. 6th ed. LC 98-11441. (University Casebook Ser.). 1007p. 1998. text. write for info. (*1-56662-458-4*) Foundation Pr.

Baader, Clemens A. Lexikon Verstorbener Baierischer Schriftsteller des 18 und 19 Jahrhunderts, 2 vols., Set. (Schriftsteller- und Gelehrtenlexika des 17, 18 und 19 Jahrhunderts Ser.). 1971. reprint ed. 225.00 (*3-487-04048-4*) G Olms Pubs.

Baader, Franz & Nipkow, Tobias. Term Rewriting & All That. LC 97-28286. (Illus.). 314p. (C). 1998. text 49.95 (*0-521-45520-0*) Cambridge U Pr.

— Term Rewriting & All That. (Illus.). 313p. 1999. pap. 19.95 (*0-521-77920-0*) Cambridge U Pr.

Baader, Franz, ed. see Schulz, K. U.

Baadhio, Randy A., jt. auth. see Kauffman, Louis H.

Baadsgaard, Janene Wolsey. Families Who Laugh ... Last. LC 92-16178. 167p. (Orig.). 1992. pap. 8.95 (*0-87579-606-0*) Deseret Bk.

— Family Finances for the Flabbergasted. LC 95-2011. 180p. (Orig.). 1995. pap. 11.95 (*0-87579-895-0*) Deseret Bk.

— Grin & Share It: Raising a Family with a Sense of Humor. LC 98-51030. 1999. write for info. (*1-57345-472-9*) Deseret Bk.

BAAF Staff. Adoption Services: Safe in Our Hands? 1997. pap. 35.00 (*1-873868-50-2*, Pub. by BAAF) St Mut.

— Belonging Doesn't Mean Forgetting: Nathan's Story. 1997. pap. 33.00 (*1-873868-45-6*, Pub. by BAAF) St Mut.

BAAF Staff. Career Held Health Record. 1998. pap. 25.00 (*1-873868-52-9*, Pub. by BAAF) St Mut.

— Hoping for the Best: Jack's Story. 1997. pap. 33.00 (*1-873868-46-4*, Pub. by BAAF) St Mut.

BAAF Staff. Living with a New Family: Nadia & Rashid's Story. 1997. pap. 33.00 (*1-873868-44-8*, Pub. by BAAF) St Mut.

BAAF Staff. Securing the Future: A Five Year Strategic Plan 1997-2002. 1997. pap. 22.00 (*1-873868-42-1*, Pub. by BAAF) St Mut.

Baafi, E. Y. & Schofield, N. A., eds. Geostatistics Wollongong '96. LC 97-7519. (Quantitative Geology & Geostatistics Ser.). 1997. text 735.50 (*0-7923-4496-0*) Kluwer Academic.

Baagh, Beck, jt. auth. see Lang, Annie J.

Baagi, E. Y. Geostatistics Wollongong. (Quantitative Geology & Geostatistics Ser.). 1997. lib. bdg. write for info. (*0-7923-4494-4*) Kluwer Academic.

Baagil, H. M. Christian Muslim Dialogue. 47p. 1984. pap. write for info. (*1-882837-14-2*) W A M Y Intl.

***Baah, Richard A.** Human Rights in Africa: The Conflict of Implementation. LC 00-41176. 136p. 2000. 32.50 (*0-7618-1754-9*) U Pr of Amer.

Baaijens, F. P., jt. ed. see Huetink, J.

Baaijens, J. M., et al. Changing Functions of Lower & Middle Management in the Netherlands. (Illus.). 46p. (Orig.). (C). 1993. pap. text 30.00 (*0-7881-0140-4*) DIANE Pub.

Baak, J. P. Manual of Quantitative Pathology in Cancer Diagnosis & Prognosis. 2nd ed. (Illus.). 696p. 1991. 250.00 (*0-387-51275-6*) Spr-Verlag.

Baak, J. P. & Oort, J. A Manual of Morphometry in Diagnostic Pathology. (Illus.). 230p. 1983. 78.95 (*0-387-11431-9*) Spr-Verlag.

Baak, Paul E. Plantation Production & Political Power: Plantation Development in South-West India in a Long-Term Historical Perspective, 1743-1963. LC 97-900358. (Illus.). 392p. (C). 1998. 29.95 (*0-19-564103-5*) OUP.

Baake, M., jt. auth. see Grimm, U.

Baake, Tom. Out Our Back Door: 24 Driving Tours from Coos Bay Area. LC 97-90390. (Illus.). 144p. (Orig.). 1997. pap. 9.95 (*0-9658012-0-9*) Westways Pr.

B

***Baake, Uwe & Zobel, Richard, eds.** Concurrent Engineering: The Way Forward. 317p. 1998. 33.00 (*1-56555-147-8*) Soc Computer Sim.

***Baaklini, Abdo, et al.** Legislative Politics in the Arab World: The Resurgence of Democratic Institutions. LC 98-46654. 278p. 1999. pap. 22.50 (*1-55587-840-7*); lib. bdg. 59.95 (*1-55587-839-3*) L Rienner.

Baaklini, Abdo I. The Brazilian Legislature & Political System: Contributions in Political Science, No. 298, 298A. LC 91-44633. 256p. 1992. 65.00 (*0-313-28450-4*, BZG/, Greenwood Pr) Greenwood.

Baaklini, Abdo I. & Desfosses, Helen, eds. Designs for Democratic Stability: Studies in Viable Constitutionalism. LC 96-36920. (Comparative Politics Ser.). 350p. (C). (gr. 13). 1997. text 78.95 (*0-7656-0051-X*); pap. text 35.95 (*0-7656-0052-8*) M E Sharpe.

***Baaklini, G., et al, eds.** Nondestructive Methods for Materials Characterization Vol. 591: Materials Research Society Symposium Proceedings. LC 00-23037. 322p. 2000. text 90.00 (*1-55899-499-8*) Materials Res.

***Baaklini, George Y., et al, eds.** Nondestructive Evaluation of Aging Materials & Composites III. LC 99-229031. 416p. 1999. pap. text 92.00 (*0-8194-3055-2*) SPIE.

Baal, Pierre Van, see Van Baal, Pierre, ed.

Baal-Teshuva, Jacob. Alexander Calder. 1998. pap. 9.99 (*3-8228-7642-9*) Taschen Amer.

***Baal-Teshuva, Jacob.** Chagall. (Illus.). 1998. 49.99 (*3-8228-7375-6*) Benedikt Taschen.

— Chagall: Tapestries Tapisserien Tapisseries. 1999. 9.99 (*3-8228-6609-1*) Taschen Amer.

Baal-Teshuva, Jacob. Christo & Jeanne-Claude. LC 97-121821. (Basic Ser.). 1995. pap. text 9.99 (*3-8228-8884-2*) Taschen Amer.

— Marc Chagall, 1887-1985. (Illus.). 280p. 1998. 39.99 (*3-8228-8271-2*) Taschen Amer.

— Mission of Israel. 1963. 10.95 (*0-8315-0046-8*) Speller.

Baal-Teshuva, Jacob, et al, eds. Andy Warhol, 1928-1987: Paintings from the Collection of Jose Mugrabi. (Illus.). 144p. 1993. 24.95 (*3-7913-1277-4*, Pub. by Prestel) te Neues.

Ba'Albaki, M. English-Arabic Pocket Dictionary. (ARA & ENG.). 484p. 1980. pap. 9.95 (*0-8288-1583-6*, M9973) Fr & Eur.

Ba'Albaki, Munir. English-Arabic & Arabic-English Dictionary: Al-Mawrid Al-Waset. (ARA & ENG.). 1985. 55.00 (*0-86685-060-0*) Intl Bk Ctr.

— English-Arabic Small Pocket Dictionary: Al Mawrid. 1978. 4.00 (*0-86685-325-1*) Intl Bk Ctr.

— Modern English-Arabic Dictionary (Al-Mawrid) (ARA., Illus.). 1118p. 1997. 55.00 (*0-86685-059-7*, DAR0597, Pub. by Librairie du Liban) Intl Bk Ctr.

— Modern English-Arabic Dictionary (Al-Mawrid al-Qareb) (ARA.). 484p. 1995. pap. 6.95 (*0-86685-062-7*, DAR3251, Pub. by Librairie du Liban) Intl Bk Ctr.

— Modern English-Arabic Dictionary (Mawrid al Mayassar) (ARA., Illus.). 575p. 1995. 17.95 (*0-86685-061-9*, DAR0619, Pub. by Librairie du Liban) Intl Bk Ctr.

Ba'Albaki, Munir. Modern Pocket Dictionaries: Arabic-English. 464p. 1996. pap. 6.95 (*0-86685-752-4*) Intl Bk Ctr.

Ba'Albaki, Munir, tr. Jane Eyre. (ARA.). 200p. pap. 14.95 (*0-86685-755-9*) Intl Bk Ctr.

— Les Miserables. (ARA.). 200p. pap. 14.95 (*0-86685-758-3*) Intl Bk Ctr.

Ba'Albaki, Munir & Ba'Albaki, Rohi. Concise Dictionary Al-Mawrid. (Illus.). 1400p. 1997. 55.00 (*0-86685-726-5*) Intl Bk Ctr.

Baalbaki, Rohi. Al-Mawrid: A Modern English-Arabic Dictionary. (ARA & ENG.). 1254p. 1996. 55.00 (*0-614-21718-0*, 22) Kazi Pubns.

Ba'Albaki, Rohi. Modern Arabic-English Dictionary: Al-Mawrid. 1994. 55.00 (*0-86685-553-X*) Intl Bk Ctr.

Ba'Albaki, Rohi, jt. auth. see Ba'Albaki, Munir.

Baalen, J. Van. Caos de las Sectas. (SPA.). 375p. 1990. pap. 8.50 (*0-939125-45-5*) CRC Wrld Lit.

Baali, F. Ibn Khaldun's Science of Human Culture. 1981. 16.50 (*1-56744-050-9*) Kazi Pubns.

Baali, Fuad. Relation of the People to the Land in Southern Iraq. LC 66-64914. (University of Florida Monographs: Social Sciences: No. 31). 74p. reprint ed. pap. 30.00 (*0-7837-5033-1*, 204470600004) Bks Demand.

— Social Institutions: Ibn Khaldun's Social Thought. LC 92-14020. 1992. 36.50 (*0-8191-8726-7*) U Pr of Amer.

— Society, State, & Urbanism: Ibn Khaldun's Sociological Thought. LC 87-9925. 175p. (C). 1988. pap. text 24.95 (*0-88706-610-0*) State U NY Pr.

BAAN Institute Staff. Implementing Baan IV. LC 97-65016. 608p. 1998. 59.99 (*0-7897-1114-1*) Que.

Baan, Jan, et al, eds. Cardiac Dynamics: A Selection of Papers Presented at the Third International Conference on Cardiovascular System Dynamics Held at the University of Leiden, the Netherlands, August 1978. (Developments in Cardiovascular Medicine Ser.: No. 2). 545p. 1980. text 239.50 (*90-247-2212-8*) Kluwer Academic.

Baan, Jan, ed. see Ballistocardiograph Research Society Staff.

Baanante, Carlos, jt. auth. see Henao, Julio.

Baanante, Carlos A., jt. ed. see Tshibaka, Tshikala B.

Baantjer, Albert C. Dekok & Murder in Ecstacy. Smittenaar, H. G., tr. from DUT. LC 97-42994. (Dekok Ser.: Vol. 16).Tr. of Decock en de Moord in Extase. 196p. 1998. pap. 9.95 (*1-881164-16-0*, Pub. by Intercont VA) ACCESS Pubs Network.

— Dekok & Murder in Seance. Smittenaar, H. G., tr. from DUT. LC 96-48758. 205p. (Orig.). 1996. pap. 8.95 (*1-881164-15-2*, Pub. by Intercont VA) ACCESS Pubs Network.

— DeKok & Murder on the Menu. Smittenaar, H. G., tr. from DUT. 180p. 1992. pap. 7.95 (*1-881164-31-4*, Pub. by Intercont VA) ACCESS Pubs Network.

— Dekok & the Begging Death. Smittenaar, H. G., tr. from DUT. LC 98-45858. 200p. (Orig.). 1999. pap. 9.95 (*1-881164-17-9*, Pub. by Intercont VA) ACCESS Pubs Network.

— DeKok & the Brothers of the Easy Death. Smittenaar, H. G., tr. from DUT. 196p. 1995. pap. 7.95 (*1-881164-13-6*, Pub. by Intercont VA) ACCESS Pubs Network.

— DeKok & the Careful Killer. Smittenaar, H. G., tr. from DUT. 245p. 1993. pap. 7.95 (*1-881164-07-1*) Intercont VA.

— DeKok & the Corpse at the Church Wall. Smittenaar, H. G., tr. from DUT. 202p. 1994. pap. 7.95 (*1-881164-10-1*, Pub. by Intercont VA) ACCESS Pubs Network.

— DeKok & the Dancing Death. Smittenaar, H. G., tr. from DUT. LC 94-184728. 217p. (Orig.). 1994. pap. 7.95 (*1-881164-11-X*) Intercont VA.

— DeKok & the Dead Harlequin. Smittenaar, H. G., tr. from DUT. 226p. (Orig.). 1993. pap. 7.95 (*1-881164-04-7*) Intercont VA.

— Dekok & the Deadly Accord. Smittenaar, H. G., tr. from DUT. LC 96-36721. 205p. 1996. pap. 8.95 (*1-881164-14-4*, Pub. by Intercont VA) ACCESS Pubs Network.

— DeKok & the Disillusioned Corpse. Smittenaar, H. G., tr. from DUT. 246p. (Orig.). 1993. pap. 7.95 (*1-881164-06-3*) Intercont VA.

— DeKok & the Dying Stroller. Smittenaar, H. G., tr. from DUT. LC 94-173350. 199p. (Orig.). 1994. pap. 7.95 (*1-881164-09-8*, Pub. by Intercont VA) ACCESS Pubs Network.

— Dekok & the Geese of Death. Smittenaar, H. G., tr. from DUT. 200p. pap. 9.95 (*1-881164-18-7*) Intercont VA.

— DeKok & the Naked Lady. Smittenaar, H. G., tr. from DUT. LC 94-181120. 205p. 1994. pap. 7.95 (*1-881164-12-8*, Pub. by Intercont VA) ACCESS Pubs Network.

— DeKok & the Romantic Murder. Smittenaar, H. G., tr. from DUT. LC 94-173351. 199p. (Orig.). 1994. pap. 7.95 (*1-881164-08-X*) Intercont VA.

— DeKok & the Somber Nude. Smittenaar, H. G., tr. from DUT. 232p. (Orig.). 1992. pap. 7.95 (*1-881164-01-2*) Intercont VA.

— DeKok & the Sorrowing Tomcat. Smittenaar, H. G., tr. from DUT. 240p. 1993. pap. 13.95 (*1-881164-61-6*); pap. 7.95 (*1-881164-05-5*) Intercont VA.

***Baantjer, Albert C.** DeKok & the Sorrowing Tomcat: Mystery. 256p. 2000. text 22.95 (*0-312-24191-7*) St Martin.

Baantjer, Albert C. Murder in Amsterdam: Two "Dekok" Adventures: "Dekok & the Sunday Strangler" & "Dekok & the Corpse on Christmas Eve" Smittenaar, H. G., tr. from DUT. LC 96-36722. 215p. (Orig.). 1996. reprint ed. pap. 9.95 (*1-881164-00-4*, Pub. by Intercont VA) ACCESS Pubs Network.

Baaquie, B. E., et al, eds. Conformal Field Theory Anomalies & Superstrings: Proceedings. 576p. (C). 1988. pap. 52.00 (*9971-5-0446-4*); text 125.00 (*9971-5-0445-6*) World Scientific Pub.

Baar, Carl, jt. auth. see Millar, Perry S.

Baar, Karen, jt. auth. see Baker, Sidney M.

Baar, Karen, jt. auth. see Kavasch, E. Barrie.

Baard, J. H., et al. Nuclear Data Guide for Reactor: Neutron Metrology. (C). 1989. text 266.50 (*0-7923-0486-1*) Kluwer Academic.

Baard, Ronald W. Talking with Your Child about Fantasy & Dreams. LC 96-30144. (Growing Together Ser.). 32p. 1996. pap. 2.25 (*0-8298-1135-4*) Pilgrim OH.

Baark, Erik. Lightning Wires: The Telegraph & China's Technological Modernization, 1860-1890, 6. LC 96-24217. (Contributions in Asian Studies: No. 6). 240p. 1997. 69.50 (*0-313-30011-9*, Greenwood Pr) Greenwood.

Baark, Erik & Sigurdson, Jon. India-China Comparative Research: Science, Technology & Development. 160p. (C). 1996. pap. text 18.00 (*0-7007-0138-9*, Pub. by Curzon Pr Ltd) UH Pr.

Baarman, Jenifer H., ed. see Hinton, William & Rahming, D'Arcy.

Baarman, Jenifer H., ed. see Rahming, D'Arcy.

Baarman, Jenifer H., ed. see Sullivan, Edward F.

Baarr, Vilma & Broudy, Charles E. Time-Saver Details for Retail Planning & Design. 272p. 1994. 45.50 (*0-07-004386-8*) McGraw.

Baars, B. J. Experimental Slips & Human Error: Exploring the Architecture of Volition. (Cognition & Language). (Illus.). 366p. (C). 1992. 65.00 (*0-306-43866-6*, Plenum Trade) Perseus Pubng.

Baars, Bernard J. The Cognitive Revolution in Psychology. LC 84-25311. 443p. 1986. pap. text 30.00 (*0-89862-912-8*) Guilford Pubns.

— In the Theater of Consciousness: The Workspace of the Mind. LC 96-10379. (Illus.). 210p. 1997. 27.50 (*0-19-510265-7*) OUP.

Baars, Conrad, ed. see Aumann, Jordan.

Baars, Conrad W. Born Only Once: The Miracle of Affirmation. 124p. 1984. pap. 5.00 (*0-8199-0671-9*, Frncscn Herld) Franciscan Pr.

— Doctor of the Heart: An Autobiography. LC 95-25824. 254p. (Orig.). 1996. pap. 12.50 (*0-8189-0717-7*) Alba.

— Feeling & Healing Your Emotions: A Christian Psychiatrist Shows How to Grow in Wholeness. 275p. 1979. pap. 8.99 (*0-88270-510-5*) Bridge-Logos.

— How to Treat & Prevent the Crisis in the Priesthood. 1972. pap. 1.00 (*0-8199-0399-X*, Frncscn Herld) Franciscan Pr.

— A Priest for All Seasons: Masculine & Celibate. LC 72-87091. (Synthesis Ser.). 1972. pap. 1.00 (*0-8199-0375-2*, Frncscn Herld) Franciscan Pr.

Baars, Conrad W. & Terruwe, Anna A. Healing the Unaffirmed: Recognizing the Deprivation Neurosis. LC 76-7897. 214p. 1979. reprint ed. pap. 6.95 (*0-8189-0393-7*) Alba.

— Psychic Wholeness & Healing: Using All the Powers of the Human Psyche. LC 81-4964. 278p. (Orig.). 1981. pap. 12.95 (*0-8189-0410-0*) Alba.

Baars, D. L., jt. ed. see Riad, S.

Baars, Don. Cataract Canyon & Approaches: A River Runner's Guide. LC 87-70045. (Waterproof River Runners Guides Ser.). (Illus.). 80p. 1987. pap. 15.95 (*0-9616591-1-4*) Canon Pubs.

— The River Rattler: Guidebook to the San Juan River. (River Runner's Guides Ser.: Vol. 4). (Illus.). 96p. (J). (gr. 4-9). 1995. pap. 9.95 (*0-9616591-4-9*) Canon Pubs.

Baars, Don, ed. see Gernant, Bob, et al.

Baars, Donald L. The American Alps: The San Juan Mountains of Southwest Colorado. LC 92-8859. (Illus.). 194p. 1992. pap. 13.95 (*0-8263-1352-3*) U of NM Pr.

— Arches National Park. (Geology of National Parks & Monuments Ser.: Vol. 2). (Illus.). 16p. 1998. pap. 4.50 (*0-9616591-7-3*) Canon Pubs.

— Canyon de Chelly, NM. (Geology of National Parks & Monuments Ser.: Vol. 3). (Illus.). 16p. 1998. pap. 3.25 (*0-9616591-8-1*) Canon Pubs.

— Canyonlands Country: Geology of Canyonlands & Arches National Park. rev. ed. LC 93-23140. (Illus.). 156p. 1993. pap. 12.95 (*0-87480-432-9*) U of Utah Pr.

— Colorado National Monument. (Geology of National Parks & Monuments Ser.: Vol. 1). (Illus.). 16p. 1998. pap. 3.25 (*0-9616591-6-5*) Canon Pubs.

— The Colorado Plateau: A Geologic History. rev. ed. LC 83-1349. (Illus.). 279p. 1983. pap. 14.95 (*0-8263-0599-7*) U of NM Pr.

***Baars, Donald L.** The Colorado Plateau: A Geologic History. rev. ed. LC 00-9291. (Illus.). 2000. pap. write for info. (*0-8263-2301-4*) U of NM Pr.

Baars, Donald L. Death on the Colorado Express: The Glen & Bessie Hyde Mystery. (Illus.). 200p. (Orig.). 1997. pap. 10.95 (*0-9616591-5-7*) Canon Pubs.

— Monument Valley Park. (Geology of National Parks & Monuments Ser.: Vol. 4). (Illus.). 16p. 1998. pap. 3.25 (*0-9616591-9-X*) Canon Pubs.

— Navajo Country: A Geology & Natural History of the Four Corners Region. LC 95-4344. (Illus.). 255p. 1995. pap. 19.95 (*0-8263-1587-9*) U of NM Pr.

Baars, Donald L. & Buchanan, Rex C. The Canyon Revisited: A Rephotography of the Grand Canyon, 1923-1991. (Illus.). 160p. 1994. pap. 19.95 (*0-87480-458-2*) U of Utah Pr.

Baars, Jan W., jt. ed. see Longshore, Randolph E.

Baarschers, William H. Eco-Facts & Eco-Fiction: Understanding the Environmental Debate. LC 95-25369. (Illus.). 280p. (C). 1996. pap. 24.99 (*0-415-13021-2*) Routledge.

Baart, M. Louisa, jt. auth. see McLeod, Robin J.

Baartmans, Frans. Apah - The Sacred Waters: An Analysis of a Primordial Symbol in Hindu Myths. 1990. 54.00 (*81-7018-582-3*, Pub. by BR Pub) S Asia.

Baartz, A. P., tr. see Hahn, W.

Baas Becking, L. G., jt. auth. see Veendorp, H.

Baas, P. New Perspectives in Wood Anatomy. 1982. text 184.00 (*90-247-2526-7*) Kluwer Academic.

Baas, P., et al, eds. The Plant Diversity of Malesia: Proceedings of the Flora Malesiana Symposium Commemorating Prof. Dr. C. G. G. J. van Steenis. (C). 1990. text 129.50 (*0-7923-0883-2*) Kluwer Academic.

Baase, Sara. Computer Algorithms: Introduction to Design & Analysis. LC 77-81197. 1978. text. write for info. (*0-201-00327-9*) Addison-Wesley.

— Computer Algorithms: Introduction to Design & Analysis. 2nd ed. LC 87-9205. (Illus.). 600p. (C). 1988. 69.00 (*0-201-06035-3*) Addison-Wesley.

***Baase, Sara.** Computer Algorithms: Introduction to Design & Analysis. 3rd ed. LC 99-14185. 688p. (C). 1999. 68.00 (*0-201-61244-5*) Addison-Wesley.

Baase, Sara. A Gift of Fire: Social, Legal & Ethical Issues in Computing. LC 96-45254. 382p. (C). 1996. pap. 48.00 (*0-13-458779-0*) P-H.

— VAX Assembly Language. 2nd ed. 528p. 1992. 74.00 (*0-13-942152-1*) P-H.

Baasel, William D. Economic Methods for Multipollutant Analysis & Evaluation. LC 85-16307. (Pollution Engineering & Technology Ser.: No. 25). (Illus.). 357p. reprint ed. pap. 110.70 (*0-7837-0867-X*, 204117500019) Bks Demand.

Baasher, T. A., ed. see WHO Staff.

Baaske, Edwin. Volkswagen Beetle: Portrait of a Legend. LC 97-42149. (Illus.). 1998. 29.95 (*0-8376-0162-2*) Bentley Pubs.

Baaske, Kevin T., jt. auth. see Hollihan, Thomas A.

Baasten, Matthew. Pride According to Gregory the Great: A Study of the Moralia. LC 86-18057. (Studies in the Bible & Early Christianity: Vol. 7). 216p. 1986. lib. bdg. 89.95 (*0-88946-606-8*) E Mellen.

Baatz, Simon. Venerate the Plough: A History of the Philadelphia Society for Promoting Agriculture, 1785-1985. LC 84-26453. (Illus.). 124p. 1985. 25.00 (*0-9614267-0-5*) Phila Soc Prom.

Baatz, W. Photography. Schreiber, Sally, tr. LC 97-71965. (Crash Course Ser.). (Illus.). 192p. 1997. pap. 13.95 (*0-7641-0243-5*) Barron.

Baatz, Wilmer H., jt. ed. see Klotman, Phyllis R.

Baau, Alokesh. Global Order: Recent Changes & Responses. (C). 1992. 36.00 (*81-7095-029-5*, Pub. by Lancer India) S Asia.

Baay, Dirk. Blowing the Whistle: A Referee's View of Soccer. Maas, Georgia S., ed. (Illus.). 164p. 1997. pap. 12.95 (*0-9656463-0-0*) Halftime Pr.

Baayens. WP Works in Theorie en Praktyk. (C). 1993. pap. text. write for info. (*0-201-54527-6*) Addison-Wesley.

Bab. Selections from the Writings of the Bab. LC 79-670141. 223p. 1977. 12.95 (*0-85398-066-7*, 105-050) Bahai.

Bab, et al. Inspiring the Heart: Selected Writings of the Bab, Baha'u'llah & Abdu'l-Baha Chosen by the Universal House of Justice. 200p. 1984. pap. 5.95 (*0-900125-45-4*) Bahai.

— Trustworthiness. 32p. 1987. pap. 4.95 (*0-900125-85-3*) Bahai.

***Bab-Hadiashar, Alireza & Suter, D., eds.** Data Segmentation & Model Selection for Computer Vision. LC 99-36220. (Illus.). 240p. 1999. 52.95 (*0-387-98815-7*) Spr-Verlag.

Baba, Bangali. The Yogasutra of Patanjali: With Commentary of Vyasa. 115p. 1996. reprint ed. pap. 18.00 (*81-208-0155-5*, Pub. by Motilal Bnarsidass) S Asia.

Baba, Bangali, tr. from SAN. The Yogasutra of Patanjali: With Commentary of Vyasa. 115p. (C). 1997. reprint ed. 18.00 (*81-208-0154-7*, Pub. by Motilal Bnarsidass) S Asia.

Baba Hari Dass. Ashtanga Yoga Primer. Ault, Karuna K., ed. LC 81-51052. (Illus.). 72p. (Orig.). 1981. pap. 10.95 (*0-918100-04-6*) Sri Rama.

— Binding Thoughts & Liberation. (Essays on the Search for Peace in Daily Life Ser.: Vol. 1). 16p. (Orig.). 1992. pap. 3.00 (*0-918100-14-3*) Sri Rama.

— Cat & Sparrow. LC 81-51915. (Illus.). 32p. (J). (gr. k-3). 1982. pap. 4.95 (*0-918100-06-2*) Sri Rama.

— A Child's Garden of Yoga. Ault, Karuna K., ed. LC 80-80299. (Illus.). 108p. (J). (ps-7). 1980. pap. 9.95 (*0-918100-02-X*) Sri Rama.

— Fire Without Fuel. Renu, Ma & Tabachnick, A. Dass, eds. LC 86-60051. (Illus.). 200p. 1986. 25.00 (*0-918100-09-7*) Sri Rama.

— Fire Without Fuel: The Aphorisms of Baba Hari Dass. Ma Renu & Tabachnick, A. Dass, eds. LC 86-60051. (Illus.). 200p. (Orig.). (C). 1986. pap. 15.95 (*0-918100-08-9*) Sri Rama.

— Jai Shiva! - Kirtan for Shivaratri. Ault, Karuna K., ed. (Illus.). 32p. (Orig.). 1988. pap. 2.50 (*0-918100-10-0*) Sri Rama.

— The Magic Gem: A Story Coloring Book. LC 76-10032. (Illus.). 32p. (Orig.). (J). (ps-2). 1976. pap. 3.50 (*0-918100-07-0*) Sri Rama.

— Mind Is Our World. (Essays on the Search for Peace in Daily Life Ser.: Vol. 2). 16p. (Orig.). 1992. pap. 3.00 (*0-918100-15-1*) Sri Rama.

— Mystic Monkey. LC 81-51051. (Illus.). 64p. (Orig.). (J). (gr. 4-8). 1984. pap. 9.95 (*0-918100-05-4*) Sri Rama.

— The Path to Enlightenment Is Not a Highway. Renu, Ma, ed. & frwd. by. LC 96-67104. (Illus.). 332p. (Orig.). 1996. pap. 12.95 (*0-918100-18-6*) Sri Rama.

— Silence Speaks: From the Chalkboard of Baba Hari Dass. 2nd rev. ed. Ault, Karuna K., ed. LC 96-92500. (Illus.). 280p. (Orig.). 1997. pap. 16.95 (*0-918100-19-4*) Sri Rama.

— Sweeper to Saint: Stories of Holy India. Renu, Ma, ed. LC 80-52021. (Illus.). 208p. (Orig.). 1980. pap. 6.95 (*0-918100-03-8*) Sri Rama.

— Vinaya Chalisa: Forty Prayers. LC 97-127377. (Illus.). 92p. (Orig.). 1994. pap. 10.95 (*0-918100-16-X*) Sri Rama.

Baba, K. & Jurkovic, D., eds. Three-Dimensional Ultrasound in Obstetrics & Gynecology. LC 96-51892. (Progress in Obstetric & Gynecological Sonography Ser.). (Illus.). 120p. 1997. 78.00 (*1-85070-619-0*) Prthnon Pub.

Baba, Marietta L., jt. auth. see Hill, Carole E.

Baba, Meher. Beams from Meher Baba on the Spiritual Panorama. LC 58-59805. 88p. 1996. reprint ed. 12.50 (*0-915828-03-0*) Sufism Reoriented.

— Darshan Hours. Jessawala, Eruch & Chapman, Rick, eds. 80p. 1973. 8.95 (*0-940700-06-9*); pap. 4.95 (*0-940700-05-0*) Meher Baba Info.

— Discourses. 7th rev. ed. Natu, Bal et al, eds. LC 94-36972. (Illus.). 452p. 1995. 25.00 (*1-880619-08-3*); pap. 15.00 (*1-880619-09-1*) Sheriar Found.

Baba, Meher. The Everything & the Nothing. 2nd ed. 115p. 1996. reprint ed. pap. 7.95 (*1-880619-13-X*) Sheriar Found.

Baba, Meher. God Speaks. (PER., Illus.). 330p. 1998. 25.00 (*0-9661241-0-3*) Love St Pr.

— God Speaks: The Theme of Creation & Its Purpose. LC 72-13984. 313p. 1997. reprint ed. 27.00 (*0-915828-02-2*) Sufism Reoriented.

— Life at Its Best. LC 57-14432. 73p. 1995. reprint ed. 2.00 (*0-915828-04-9*) Sufism Reoriented.

— Listen, Humanity. 5th rev. ed. Stevens, Don E., ed. & narrated by. LC 97-32417. 288p. 1998. 24.95 (*0-8245-1731-8*, Crsrd) Crossroad NY.

— Sparks of the Truth: From the Dissertations of Meher Baba. Deshmukh, C. D., ed. (Illus.). 96p. (Orig.). 1971. pap. 5.95 (*0-913078-02-6*) Sheriar Pr.

***Baba, Meher.** Universal Prayer. large type ed. (Illus.). 80p. 1999. pap. 18.50 (*0-913078-71-9*) Sheriar Pr.

Baba, Meher, et al. Treasures from the Meher Baba Journals: 1938-1942. Haynes, Jane B., ed. LC 79-92169. (Illus.). 246p. 1980. pap. 8.95 (*0-913078-37-9*) Sheriar Pr.

Baba, N. New Topics in Learning Automata Theory & Applications. (Lecture Notes in Control & Information Sciences: Vol. 71). 150p. 1985. pap. 22.00 (*0-387-15613-5*) Spr-Verlag.

Baba, Noor A. Organization of Islamic Conference: Theory & Practice of Pan-Islamic Cooperation. (C). 1995. write for info. (*81-207-1617-5*) Sterling Pubs.

Baba, Prem R. The God Book. large type ed. 64p. 1999. pap. 10.00 (*0-9645010-3-1*, Pub. by Prem Raja Baba) Bookpeople.

An Asterisk (*) at the beginning of an entry indicates that the title is appearing for the first time.

Baba, Sathya Sai. Dharma Vahini (Writings on Morality) rev. ed. 1996. pap. 1.50 (*1-57836-060-9*, BA-302) Sathya Sai Bk Ctr.

Baba, Shigeaki & Kaneko, Toshio, eds. Diabetes 1994: Proceedings of the 15th International Diabetes Federation Congress, Kobe, 6-11, November 1994. LC 95-14961. (International Congress Ser.: 1100). 1302p. 1995. 364.50 (*0-444-81725-5*) Elsevier.

***Baba, Steve.** Poetic Wanderings. LC 99-61939. 140p. 1999. 25.00 (*0-7388-0374-X*); pap. 18.00 (*0-7388-0375-8*) Xlibris Corp.

Baba, Yoshikazu, jt. auth. see Nagashima, Hiroyuki.

Babad, Elisha Y., et al. The Social Self: Group Influences on Personal Identity. LC 82-21553. (Sage Library of Social Reserach: Vol. 144). 267p. 1983. reprint ed. pap. 82.80 (*0-608-02798-7*, 206386500007) Bks Demand.

Babad, Harry, ed. Roll Me Over. (Illus.). 144p. 1972. pap. 16.95 (*0-8256-0067-7*, OK62455, Oak) Music Sales.

Babad, Michael & Mulroney, Catherine. Pillars: The Coming Crisis in Canada's Finance Industry. 240p. 1993. 24.95 (*0-7737-2743-4*) Genl Dist Srvs.

Babad, Shifra. Shipur Halashon. rev. ed. (HEB.). 109p. (Orig.). wbk. ed. write for info. (*0-9645822-1-X*) S Babad.

Babaev, Agadzhan Gel'dyevich, ed. see Choller instituty (Turkmenistan SSR ylymlar akademiiasy) Staff.

Babaevskii, P. G., et al. English - Russian Dictionary of Chemistry & Technology of Polymers. (ENG & RUS.). 536p. (C). 1977. 30.95 (*0-8285-0589-6*) Firebird NY.

Babaie, Sussan & Swietochowski, Marie L. Persian Drawings in the Metropolitan Museum of Art. (Illus.). 96p. 1989. pap. 7.95 (*0-87099-564-2*, 0-8109-6468-6) Metro Mus Art.

Babain, Sharon A. & National Museum of Science and Technology (Canada) Staff. Radio Communication in Canada: A Historical & Technological Survey. LC 92-223308. (Transformation Ser.). (FRE.). 112p. 1992. write for info. (*0-660-12017-8*) Natl Mus S&T.

Babaja, Thomas. Take Jesus for Example. (Illus.). 66p. (Orig.). 1985. pap. text 3.50 (*0-942345-20-7*) Dovehaven Pr Ltd.

Babaji, Ramananda, jt. auth. see Narasimha, N. S.

Babakhanian, Ararat. Cohomological Methods in Group Theory. LC 70-182212. (Pure & Applied Mathematics Ser.: No. 11). 253p. reprint ed. pap. 78.50 (*0-608-16790-8*, 202708300054) Bks Demand.

Babal, Ken, jt. auth. see Lieberman, Shari.

Babalawo, Francis R., jt. auth. see Babalawo, Ifagbemi R.

Babalawo, Ifagbemi R. & Babalawo, Francis R. Ancestors: Hidden Hands, Healing Spirits for Your Use & Empowerment. Roger, Francis, ed. LC 98-70254. (Illus.). 48p. 1999. pap. 9.95 (*1-890157-11-2*, Pub. by Athelia-Henrietta) BookWorld.

Babalawo, Min Ra Ifagbemi. Ifa's Obi Abata: Little Oracle That Goes a Long Way. LC 98-70255. 73p. 1999. pap. text 12.95 (*1-890157-12-0*, Pub. by Athelia-Henrietta) BookWorld.

Babale, Chaibou, jt. ed. see Glew, Robert S.

Baban, Rozgar. Design of Diversion Weirs: Small Scale Irrigation in Hot Climates. 242p. 1995. pap. 80.00 (*0-471-95211-7*) Wiley.

Babaoglu, O., et al, eds. Distributed Algorithms: 10th International Workshop, WDAG '96, Bologna, Italy, October 9-11, 1996 - Proceedings. (Lecture Notes in Computer Science Ser.: Vol. 1151). viii, 381p. 1996. pap. 62.00 (*3-540-61769-8*) Spr-Verlag.

Babar Emperor of Hindustan. Babur-Nama in English: Memoirs of Babur, 2 vols. Beveridge, Annette S., tr. LC 72-161719. (BCL Ser.: No. I). reprint ed. 137.50 (*0-404-00510-1*) AMS Pr.

***Babar, Syed M.** Neck Injuries. LC 99-33583. xii, 148p. 1999. pap. 89.00 (*1-85233-637-4*) Spr-Verlag.

Babary, J. P., jt. auth. see IFAC Symposium Staff.

Babatumji, Ayotunde A. Vision of Apartheid's Death. LC 94-75278. (Illus.). 176p. (Orig.). 1994. pap. 16.95 (*0-9640639-0-5*) GTNN Pr.

Babatunde, Emmanuel. Women's Rites Versus Women's Rights: A Study of Circumcision among the Ketu Yoruba of South Western Nigeria. LC 97-32516. 330p. 1997. 79.95 (*0-86543-625-8*); pap. 21.95 (*0-86543-626-6*) Africa World.

Babatunde, Emmanuel D. A Critical Study of Bini & Yoruba Value Systems of Nigeria in Change: Culture, Religion, & the Self. LC 92-12477. (Illus.). 308p. 1992. lib. bdg. 99.95 (*0-7734-9501-0*) E Mellen.

Babawale, B., ed. see Toyin, Falola & Ajayi, A.

Babayan, Aramashot. Be Nice, I'm Dead. Parlakian, Nishan, tr. & intro. by. LC 89-77564. (Illus.). 130p. (Orig.). 1990. pap. 8.00 (*0-934728-22-4*) D O A C.

Babayan, Edward A. The Structure of Psychiatry in the U. S. S. R. LC 85-18100. 350p. 1986. 55.00 (*0-8236-6169-5*) Intl Univs Pr.

Babayan, Edward A., et al, eds. Modern Approaches to the Treatment of Hypertension. 1976. 21.75 (*3-8055-2400-5*) S Karger.

Babayan, Edward A. & Gonopolsky, M. W. Textbook on Alcoholism & Drug Abuse in the Soviet Union. Bobrov, V., tr. from RUS. LC 85-18086. (Illus.). vii, 353p. 1985. 52.50 (*0-8236-6470-8*) Intl Univs Pr.

Babb, Arthur. My Sketchbook. Cameron, Neill, ed. LC 96-69675. (Illus.). 122p. (Orig.). 1996. pap. 14.95 (*0-917898-19-2*) NSU Pr LA.

Babb, Florence E. Between Field & Cooking Pot: The Political Economy of Market Women in Peru. rev. ed. LC 99-174946. (Illus.). 264p. 1998. 17.95 (*0-292-70870-X*) U of Tex Pr.

— Between Field & Cooking Pot: The Political Economy of Marketwomen in Peru. LC 89-4800. (Texas Press Sourcebooks in Anthropology Ser.: No. 15). 260p. 1989. pap. 74.10 (*0-608-05104-7*, 2065665) Bks Demand.

Babb, Fred. Go to Your Studio & Make Stuff: The Fred Babb Poster Book: Paintings & Essays. LC 98-18891. (Illus.). 1999. pap. 15.95 (*0-7611-1392-4*) Workman Pub.

Babb, H. A., jt. auth. see Taylor, V. J.

***Babb, Janet L.** Hawaii Volcanoes: The Story Behind the Scenery. 2nd rev. ed. LC 98-66948. (Illus.). 48p. 1999. pap. 7.95 (*0-88714-143-9*) KC Pubns.

Babb, Jerry D., Sr. The Crimson Thread. (Illus.). 168p. 2000. 19.95 (*0-9649513-2-0*); pap. 9.95 (*0-9649513-3-9*) White Buck.

Babb, Jerry D. A Love Eternal: A Heart Cries, Yet Love E'er Abides. LC 95-62094. (Illus.). 128p. (Orig.). 1996. 19.95 (*0-9649513-1-2*); pap. 9.95 (*0-9649513-0-4*) White Buck.

Babb, John. Our Most Requested Recipes from Richmond Hill. 48p. 1995. pap. write for info. (*1-887756-05-1*) Richmnd Hill.

Babb, L. The Physiological Concept of Love in the Elizabethan & Early Stuart Drama. 1972. 59.95 (*0-8490-0833-6*) Gordon Pr.

Babb, L. Anne. Ethics in American Adoption. LC 98-30988. 264p. 1999. 35.00 (*0-89789-538-X*, Bergin & Garvey) Greenwood.

Babb, L. Anne & Laws, Rita. Adopting & Advocating for the Special Needs Child: A Guide for Parents & Professionals. LC 96-50474. 280p. 1997. 35.00 (*0-89789-489-8*, Bergin & Garvey) Greenwood.

Babb, Lawrence A. Absent Lord: Ascetics & Kings in a Jain Ritual Culture. LC 95-35643. (Comparative Studies in Religion & Society: Vol. 8). (Illus.). 256p. 1996. 55.00 (*0-520-20323-2*, Pub. by U CA Pr); pap. 17.95 (*0-520-20324-0*, Pub. by U CA Pr) Cal Prin Full Svc.

***Babb, Lawrence A.** Ascetics & Kings in a Jain Ritual Culture. 244p. 1998. 113.00 (*81-208-1538-6*, Pub. by Motilal Bnarsidass); pap. 63.00 (*81-208-1539-4*, Pub. by Motilal Bnarsidass) St Mut.

Babb, Lawrence A. The Divine Hierarchy: Popular Hinduism in Central India. LC 75-61693. (Illus.). 266p. 1989. pap. text 19.00 (*0-231-08387-4*) Col U Pr.

— Redemptive Encounters: Three Modern Styles in the Hindu Tradition. (Comparative Studies in Religion & Society: No. 1). 268p. 1991. reprint ed. pap. 16.95 (*0-520-07636-2*, Pub. by U CA Pr) Cal Prin Full Svc.

— Sanity in Bedlam: A Study of Robert Burton's "Anatomy of Melancholy" LC 77-13309. 116p. 1977. lib. bdg. 35.00 (*0-8371-9856-9*, BBSB, Greenwood Pr) Greenwood.

Babb, Lawrence A. & Wadley, Susan S., eds. Media & the Transformation of Religion in South Asia. LC 95-13168. (Illus.). 352p. 1995. text 39.95 (*0-8122-3304-2*); pap. text 17.50 (*0-8122-1547-8*) U of Pa Pr.

Babb, Mark R., jt. auth. see Crouch, Timothy J.

Babb, Paul & Owen, Gay. Bonzo, the Life & Work of George Studdy. (Illus.). 128p. 1988. 45.00 (*0-903685-23-X*, Pub. by R Dennis) Antique Collect.

Babb, Sanora. Cry of the Tinamou: Stories. LC 97-2073. xvi, 170p. 1997. pap. 16.95 (*0-8032-6138-1*) U of Nebr Pr.

Babb, Sanora. The Lost Traveler. LC 95-7569. 314p. 1995. pap. 10.95 (*0-8263-1568-2*) U of NM Pr.

Babb, Sanora. Owl on Every Post. LC 94-15110. 240p. 1994. pap. 10.95 (*0-8263-1531-3*) U of NM Pr.

— Told in the Seed: Poems. 56p. 1998. pap. 8.95 (*0-931122-90-2*) West End.

Babb, Valerie. Whiteness Visible. LC 98-9055. 227p. 1998. pap. 17.95 (*0-8147-1312-2*); text 50.00 (*0-8147-1302-5*) NYU Pr.

Babb, Victor. A Golden Eagle Story: How I Soared to Millions of Dollars in Sales. LC 98-70335. 130p. 1998. 21.95 (*1-878647-51-2*, WriteMore) APU Pub Grp.

Babb, Warren. Hucbald, Guido, & John on Music: Three Medieval Treatises. LC 77-1331. (Music Theory Translation Ser.: No. 3). (Illus.). 223p. reprint ed. pap. 69.20 (*0-8357-8172-0*, 203385100087) Bks Demand.

Babbage, Charles. A Comparative View of the Various Institutions for the Assurance of Lives. LC 67-18568. (Reprints of Economic Classics Ser.). 1967. reprint ed. 35.00 (*0-678-00335-1*) Kelley.

— Ninth Bridgewater Treatise Fragment. 270p. 1967. reprint ed. 22.50 (*0-7146-1106-9*, Pub. by F Cass Pubs) Intl Spec Bk.

— On the Economy of Machinery & Manufactures. 4th ed. LC 86-10645. (Reprints of Economic Classics Ser.). xxiv, 408p. 1986. reprint ed. 49.50 (*0-678-00001-8*) Kelley.

— Reflections on the Decline of Science in England: And on Some of the Causes. LC 77-115928. xv, 228p. 1970. reprint ed. 39.50 (*0-678-00645-8*) Kelley.

— Science & Reform: Selected Works of Charles Babbage. Hyman, Anthony, ed. (Illus.). 364p. (C). 1989. text 74.95 (*0-521-34311-9*) Cambridge U Pr.

— The Works of Charles Babbage, 11 vols., Set. Campbell-Kelly, Martin, ed. 2160p. (C). 1989. lib. bdg. 675.00 (*0-8147-1113-8*) NYU Pr.

— The Works of Charles Babbage, Vol. 1. (C). 1989. lib. bdg. 150.00 (*0-8147-1114-6*) NYU Pr.

— The Works of Charles Babbage, Vol. 2. (C). 1989. lib. bdg. 125.00 (*0-8147-1115-4*) NYU Pr.

— The Works of Charles Babbage, Vol. 3. (C). 1989. lib. bdg. 150.00 (*0-8147-1116-2*) NYU Pr.

— The Works of Charles Babbage, Vol. 4. (C). 1989. lib. bdg. 150.00 (*0-8147-1117-0*) NYU Pr.

— The Works of Charles Babbage, Vol. 5. (C). 1989. lib. bdg. 150.00 (*0-8147-1118-9*) NYU Pr.

— The Works of Charles Babbage, Vol. 6. (C). 1989. lib. bdg. 125.00 (*0-8147-1119-7*) NYU Pr.

— The Works of Charles Babbage, Vol. 7. (C). 1989. lib. bdg. 125.00 (*0-8147-1120-0*) NYU Pr.

— The Works of Charles Babbage, Vol. 8. (C). 1989. lib. bdg. 150.00 (*0-8147-1121-9*) NYU Pr.

— The Works of Charles Babbage, Vol. 9. (C). 1989. lib. bdg. 125.00 (*0-8147-1122-7*) NYU Pr.

— The Works of Charles Babbage, Vol. 10. (C). 1989. lib. bdg. 125.00 (*0-8147-1123-5*) NYU Pr.

— The Works of Charles Babbage, Vol. 11. (C). 1989. lib. bdg. 150.00 (*0-8147-1124-3*) NYU Pr.

Babbage, Charles, et al. Charles Babbage: On the Principle & Development of the Calculator & Other Seminal Writings. 438p. 1984. reprint ed. pap. 9.95 (*0-486-24691-4*) Dover.

Babbage, Charles, jt. auth. see Champion, Neil.

Babbage, Frances, ed. Working Without Boal: Digressions & Development in the Theatre of the Oppressed, Vol. 3, Part 1. (Comtemporary Theatre Review Ser). 128p. 1995. pap. text 15.00 (*3-7186-5600-0*, Harwood Acad Pubs) Gordon & Breach.

Babbage, Keen. High-Impact Teaching. LC 98-60210. 192p. 1998. pap. text 34.95 (*1-56676-637-0*) Scarecrow.

Babbage, Keen J. Meetings for School-Based Decision Making. LC 96-60908. 123p. 1996. pap. text 24.95 (*1-56676-450-5*) Scarecrow.

— 911: The School Administrator's Guide to Crisis Management. LC 96-60906. 180p. 1996. pap. text 29.95 (*1-56676-454-8*) Scarecrow.

***Babbage, Ron.** Approaches to Teaching & Learning: Including Pupils with Learnin Diffculties. (Illus.). 1999. pap. 29.95 (*1-85346-575-5*) David Fulton.

Babbage, Ross. The Soviets in the Pacific in the 1990s. 130p. 1989. 33.95 (*0-08-037159-0*, Pergamon Pr) Elsevier.

Babbage, Ross, jt. auth. see Ball, Desmond J.

Babbel, David & Bertozzi, Stefano. Insuring Sovereign Debt Against Default. LC 96-8670. (Discussion Paper Ser.: No. 328). 58p. 1996. pap. 22.00 (*0-8213-3657-6*) World Bank.

Babbel, David, jt. auth. see Santomero, Anthony.

Babbel, David F. & Fabozzi, Frank J., eds. Investment Management for Insurers. (Illus.). 1999. 125.00 (*1-883249-47-3*) F J Fabozzi.

Babbel, David F., jt. auth. see Santomero, Anthony M.

Babbel, Frederick. On Wings of Faith. pap. 13.98 (*1-55517-354-3*) CFI Dist.

Babbel, Frederick & Babbel, June. Bring Forth Your Light. pap. 12.95 (*1-55517-355-1*) CFI Dist.

— To Him That Believeth. pap. 13.95 (*1-55517-336-5*) CFI Dist.

Babbel, June, jt. auth. see Babbel, Frederick.

Babbibi, Lorenza & Bressan, Guido. Recensement de Corallinacees de la Mer Mediterranee et Considerations Phytogeographiques. (Bibliotheca Phycologica Ser.: Vol. 103). (FRE., Illus.). 422p. 1997. 100.00 (*3-443-60030-1*, Pub. by Gebruder Borntraeger) Balogh.

Babbidge, Homer D., jt. auth. see Watney, Bernard M.

Babbidge, Mike. Catch Fish Now! in the Florida Panhandle. (Illus.). 134p. (Orig.). 1996. pap. 12.95 (*0-9655529-1-8*) Babbidge & Co.

— Catch Fish Now! on Florida's East Coast. LC 99-474307. (Illus.). 220p. 1998. mass mkt. 16.95 (*0-9655529-3-4*) Babbidge & Co.

— Catch Fish Now! on Florida's West Coast. (Illus.). 177p. 1997. mass mkt. 14.95 (*0-9655529-2-6*) Babbidge & Co.

Babbie. The Basics of Social Research. (Sociology - Introductory Level Ser.). 1998. pap., student ed. 14.00 (*0-534-55955-7*) Wadsworth Pub.

***Babbie.** The Basics of Social Research. 2nd ed. (Sociology - Introductory Level Ser.). 2002. 40.50 (*0-534-51904-0*) Wadsworth Pub.

Babbie. Practice of Social Research. (Sociology - Introductory Level Ser.). 1975. pap. 13.00 (*0-534-00381-8*) Wadsworth Pub.

— Practice of Social Research. 2nd ed. (Sociology - Introductory Level Ser.). 1979. pap. 20.00 (*0-534-00630-2*) Wadsworth Pub.

— The Practice of Social Research. 8th ed. (Sociology Ser.). 1997. 50.25 (*0-534-50507-4*) Wadsworth Pub.

***Babbie.** The Practice of Social Research. 9th ed. (Sociology - Intro Level Ser.). 2001. 50.25 (*0-534-57474-2*) Wadsworth Pub.

Babbie. Practice of Sociology. 5th ed. (Sociology - Introductory Level Ser.). 1988. pap., teacher ed. write for info. (*0-534-09728-6*) Wadsworth Pub.

— Practice of Sociology. 6th ed. (Sociology Ser.). 1992. teacher ed. write for info. (*0-534-15578-2*) Wadsworth Pub.

— Practicing Social. 5th ed. (Sociology - Introductory Level Ser.). 1988. pap. 12.00 (*0-534-09727-8*) Wadsworth Pub.

— Practicing Social Research. 3rd ed. (Sociology - Introductory Level Ser.). 1983. pap., student ed. 8.75 (*0-534-01256-6*) Wadsworth Pub.

— Practicing Social Research. 4th ed. (Sociology - Introductory Level Ser.). 1985. pap., student ed. 9.50 (*0-534-05659-8*) Wadsworth Pub.

— Practicing Social Research. 6th ed. (Sociology-Introduction Level Ser.). 1991. pap., student ed. 12.75 (*0-534-15577-4*) Wadsworth Pub.

***Babbie.** Practicing Social Research: Guided Activities. 9th ed. 2000. pap. 18.75 (*0-534-57480-7*) Wadsworth Pub.

Babbie. Solving Social Problems. (Sociology-Introduction Level Ser.). 2001. pap. 41.00 (*0-534-53676-X*) Wadsworth Pub.

Babbie, jt. auth. see Baxter.

Babbie, jt. auth. see Maxfield.

Babbie, jt. auth. see Rubin, Allen.

Babbie, Earl. Observing Ourselves: Essays in Social Research. (Illus.). 189p. (C). 1998. reprint ed. pap. text 12.95 (*1-57766-019-6*) Waveland Pr.

— The Practice of Social Research. 4th ed. 577p. (C). 1985. pap. write for info. (*0-534-05658-X*) Wadsworth Pub.

— The Practice of Social Research. 5th ed. 501p. (C). 1988. pap. write for info. (*0-534-09726-X*) Wadsworth Pub.

— The Practice of Social Research. 6th ed. 493p. (C). 1991. pap. 48.95 (*0-534-15576-6*) Wadsworth Pub.

— The Practice of Social Research. 7th ed. LC 94-25048. 476p. 1994. mass mkt. 60.95 (*0-534-18744-7*) Wadsworth Pub.

— The Practice of Social Research. 8th ed. LC 97-25892. (Sociology Ser.). 672p. (C). 1997. pap. 50.25 (*0-534-50468-X*) Brooks-Cole.

— The Sociological Spirit. 2nd ed. 241p. 1993. 12.50 (*0-534-20202-0*) Wadsworth Pub.

— The Sociological Spirit: Critical Essays in a Critical Science. 186p. (C). 1987. pap. 10.95 (*0-534-08982-8*) Wadsworth Pub.

— Survey Research Methods. 384p. (C). 1973. mass mkt. write for info. (*0-534-00224-2*) Wadsworth Pub.

Babbie, Earl. Survey Research Methods. 2nd ed. 395p. (C). 1990. 36.25 (*0-534-12672-3*) Wadsworth Pub.

Babbie, Earl & Halley, Fred. Adventures in Socia Research: Data Analysis Using SPSS for Windows 95. 2nd rev. ed. LC 98-140153. (Illus.). 335p. (C). 1998. pap. text 37.95 (*0-7619-8524-7*) Pine Forge.

— Adventures in Social Research: Data Analysis Using SPSS. 300p. 1993. pap. 35.95 incl. disk (*0-8039-9007-3*) Pine Forge.

— Adventures in Social Research: Data Analysis Using SPSS for Windows. LC 94-48281. 1995. pap. 35.95 (*0-8039-9055-3*) Pine Forge.

Babbie, Earl & Wagenaar. The Practice of Social Research: Study Guide. 8th ed. 1997. student ed. 16.50 (*0-534-50469-8*) Brooks-Cole.

Babbie, Earl, jt. auth. see Maxfield, Michael G.

Babbie, Earl, jt. auth. see Rubin, Allen.

Babbie, Earl R. The Basics of Social Research. (Sociology - Intro Level). 1998. pap. 37.50 (*0-534-55959-X*); pap. 50.95 (*0-534-55953-0*) Wadsworth Pub.

— Practicing Social Research. 7th ed. (Sociology Ser.). 1994. pap., student ed. 18.95 (*0-534-18746-3*) Wadsworth Pub.

— What Is Society? Reflections on Freedom, Order, & Change. LC 93-15178. 172p. 1993. pap. 16.95 (*0-8039-9015-4*) Pine Forge.

Babbie, Earl R., jt. auth. see Rubin, Allen.

***Babbin, Jed L.** Legacy of Valor. LC 99-80018. 320p. 2000. write for info. (*1-57197-213-7*, Pub. by Pentland Pr) Assoc Pubs Grp.

Babbington, S. The Back-to-the-Supper-Table Cookbook. (Illus.). 222p. 1997. spiral bd. 11.95 (*1-57166-095-X*) Hearts N Tummies.

Babbini, Barbara E. Manual Communication Vol. 1: Fingerspelling & the Langauge of Signs. fac. ed. LC 72-94999. (Illus.). 391p. 1974. pap. 121.30 (*0-7837-7607-1*, 204736000001) Bks Demand.

— Manual Communication Vol. 2: Fingerspelling & the Langauge of Signs, Vol. 2. fac. ed. LC 72-94999. (Illus.). 203p. 1974. pap. 63.00 (*0-7837-7608-X*, 204736000002) Bks Demand.

Babbit, Harold W., jt. auth. see Gotherman, John E.

***Babbit, Nikki.** Adolescent Drug & Alcohol Abuse: How to Spot It, Stop It & Get Help for Your Family. Lamb, Linda, ed. LC 99-87517. (Illus.). 260p. 2000. pap. 17.95 (*1-56592-755-9*, Patient-Centered) OReilly & Assocs.

Babbit, Nikki. Is My Child Chemically Dependent? A Professional's Personal Experience. 36p. (Orig.). 1988. pap. 3.95 (*0-945485-04-2*) Comm Intervention.

Babbit, Roy & King, Lawrence P. Collier Bankruptcy Cases: Second Series, 6 vols. 1979. ring bd. write for info. (*0-8205-1222-2*) Bender.

Babbitt. Shelf Talker. (J). 1998. write for info. (*0-06-205178-4*) HarpC Child Bks.

Babbitt, Bob, jt. auth. see Allen, Mark.

Babbitt, Bruce, jt. frwd. see Kuralt, Charles.

Babbitt, D. & Varadarajan, V. Deformations of Nilpotent Matrices Over Rings & Reduction of Analytic Families of Meromorphic Differential Equations. LC 85-5997. (Memoirs Ser.: No. 55/325). 147p. 1985. pap. 26.00 (*0-8218-2326-4*, MEMO/55/325) Am Math.

***Babbitt, Donald G. & Kister, Jane E., eds.** Featured Reviews in Mathematical Reviews Set, 1995-1999, Set. (FREV Ser.). 2000. 86.00 (*0-8218-2631-X*) Am Math.

Babbitt, Donald G. & Kister, Jane E., eds. Featured Reviews in Mathematical Reviews, 1995-1996. (Featured Reviews from Mathematical Reviews Ser.: Vol. BABBITT). 380p. 1997. pap. 39.00 (*0-8218-0771-4*) Am Math.

***Babbitt, Donald G. & Kister, Jane E., eds.** Featured Reviews in Mathematical Reviews, 1997-1999: With Selected Reviews of Classic Books & Papers. (FREV Ser.: Vol. 2). 754p. 2000. 69.00 (*0-8218-2166-0*) Am Math.

Babbitt, Edwin B. The Principles of Light & Color. 1980. pap. text 9.95 (*0-8065-0748-9*, Citadel Pr) Carol Pub Group.

Babbitt, Edwin D. The Principles of Light & Color. (Illus.). 576p. 1992. pap. 55.00 (*0-89540-060-X*, SB-060) Sun Pub.

— Principles of Light & Color (1878) 290p. 1998. reprint ed. pap. 24.95 (*0-7661-0537-7*) Kessinger Pub.

Babbitt, Elwood. Perfect Health: Accept No Substitutes. 300p. 1993. pap. 15.95 (*1-881343-01-4*) Channel One.

Babbitt, Irving. Character & Culture: Essays on East & West. LC 94-41611. (Library of Conservative Thought). 1995. pap. 24.95 (*1-56000-806-7*) Transaction Pubs.

— Democracy & Leadership. LC 78-11418. 1979. reprint ed. 14.00 (*0-913966-54-1*); reprint ed. pap. 7.00 (*0-913966-55-X*) Liberty Fund.

— Irving Babbitt, Representative Writings. Panichas, George A., ed. LC 81-2968. 356p. 1981. reprint ed. pap. 110.40 (*0-608-02690-5*, 206334300004) Bks Demand.

— Literature & the American College: Essays in Defense of the Humanities. LC 86-62218. 228p. 1986. text 12.00 (*0-932783-01-5*) Natl Human Inst.

B

— Literature & the American College: Essays in Defense of the Humanities. LC 74-138537. viii, 263p. 1972. reprint ed. lib. bdg. 37.50 (*0-678-03561-X*) Kelley.
— The Master of Modern French Criticism. LC 76-56408. 427p. 1977. reprint ed. lib. bdg. 75.00 (*0-8371-9415-6*, BAMF, Greenwood Pr) Greenwood.
— Rousseau & Romanticism. 426p. (C). 1991. pap. 24.95 (*0-88738-888-4*) Transaction Pubs.
— Rousseau & Romanticism. LC 75-28989. (BCL Ser.: No. II). 1976. reprint ed. 49.50 (*0-404-14000-9*) AMS Pr.
— Spanish Character & Other Essays: With a Bibliography of His Publications & an Index to His Collected Works. Manchester, Frederick et al, eds. LC 83-45695. reprint ed. 34.50 (*0-404-20013-3*) AMS Pr.
Babbitt, Irving, tr. see Buddha, Guatama.
Babbitt, James & Thybony, Scott. Guide to So. & No. Bass Trails. Houk, Rose & Frazier, Pam, eds. (Trail Guide Ser.). (Illus.). 1991. pap. 2.95 (*0-938216-40-6*) GCA.
Babbitt, James E., ed. Rainbow Trails: Adventures in Rainbow Bridge Country. 120p. (Orig.). (YA). 1989. pap. 5.95 (*0-317-93359-0*) Glen Canyon Nat Hist Assn.
Babbitt, John, et al, eds. Sarajevo: An Anthology for Bosnian Relief. 360p. 1993. pap. 14.95 (*0-9638516-0-8*) Elgin Comm Coll.
Babbitt, Katharine M. Janet Montgomery: Hudson River Squire. rev. ed. LC 75-9600. 80p. 1992. pap. 9.95 (*0-912526-18-1*) Lib Res.
Babbitt, Lucy C. Children of the Maker. LC 88-45482. 208p. (YA). (gr. 6 up). 1988. 15.00 (*0-374-31245-1*) FS&G.
Babbitt, Natalie. Bub or the Very Best Thing. LC 93-78758. (Michael di Capua Bks.). (Illus.). 32p. (J). (gr. k up). 1994. lib. bdg. 15.89 (*0-06-205045-1*) HarpC Child Bks.
— Bub or the Very Best Thing. LC 93-78758. (Michael di Capua Bks.). (Illus.). 32p. (J). (gr. k up). 1994. 15.95 (*0-06-205044-3*) HarpC Child Bks.
Babbitt, Natalie. Bub, or, the Very Best Thing. LC 93-78758. 1994. 11.15 (*0-606-09113-0*, Pub. by Turtleback) Demco.
Babbitt, Natalie. Bub or The Very Best Thing. LC 93-78758. (Trophy Picture Bk.). (Illus.). 32p. (J). (gr. k up). 1996. pap. 6.95 (*0-06-205912-2*, HarpTrophy) HarpC Child Bks.
***Babbitt, Natalie.** BUB, or the Very Best Thing. unabridged ed. (Illus.). (J). (ps-3). 1998. pap. 15.95 incl. audio (*0-87499-465-9*) Live Oak Media.
— BUB, or the Very Best Thing, 4 bks., Set. (Illus.). (J). (ps-3). 1998. pap., teacher ed. 37.95 incl. audio (*0-87499-467-5*) Live Oak Media.
Babbitt, Natalie. Cuentos del Pobre Diablo. (SPA.). 112p. (J). (gr. 4-7). 1994. pap. 4.95 (*0-374-41624-9*) FS&G.
— The Devil's Other Storybook. 96p. (J). (gr. 4-7). 1987. pap. 4.95 (*0-374-41704-0*) FS&G.
— The Devil's Storybook. LC 74-5488. (Illus.). 102p. (J). (ps-3). 1974. 13.00 (*0-374-31770-4*) FS&G.
— The Devil's Storybook. LC 74-5488. (Sunburst Ser.). (Illus.). 102p. (J). (ps-3). 1984. pap. 3.95 (*0-374-41708-3*) FS&G.
— The Eyes of the Amaryllis. LC 77-11862. 160p. (J). (gr. 4-7). 1977. 15.00 (*0-374-32241-4*) FS&G.
— The Eyes of the Amaryllis. LC 77-11862. 128p. (J). (gr. 4-7). 1986. pap. 3.95 (*0-374-42238-9*) FS&G.
Babbitt, Natalie. The Eyes of the Amaryllis. 1977. 9.05 (*0-606-02823-4*, Pub. by Turtleback) Demco.
Babbitt, Natalie. Goody Hall. LC 73-149221. (Sunburst Ser.). (Illus.). 176p. (J). (ps-3). 1986. pap. 4.95 (*0-374-42767-4*) FS&G.
— Knee-Knock Rise. (J). 1984. 9.05 (*0-606-04375-6*, Pub. by Turtleback) Demco.
Babbitt, Natalie. Kneeknock Rise. LC 79-105622. (Illus.). 96p. (J). (gr. 4-7). 1984. pap. 3.95 (*0-374-44260-6*) FS&G.
Babbitt, Natalie. Nellie: A Cat on Her Own. (Illus.). 32p. (J). (ps up). 1989. 14.00 (*0-374-35506-1*) FS&G.
— Nellie: A Cat on Her Own. 1992. 10.15 (*0-606-07165-2*, Pub. by Turtleback) Demco.
— Nellie: A Cat on Her Own. (Illus.). 32p. (J). (ps-3). 1992. reprint ed. pap. 4.95 (*0-374-45496-5*, Sunburst Bks) FS&G.
Babbitt, Natalie. Los Ojos del Amarilis. (Via Libre Ser.). (SPA.). (J). 1988. 10.05 (*0-606-05915-6*, Pub. by Turtleback) Demco.
— Ouch! LC 97-78382. (Illus.). 32p. (J). 1998. lib. bdg. 15.89 (*0-06-205067-2*) HarpC Child Bks.
Babbitt, Natalie. Phoebe's Revolt. LC 68-13679. (Illus.). 40p. (J). (ps-3). 1988. pap. 3.95 (*0-374-45792-1*) FS&G.
— The Search for Delicious. LC 69-20374. (Illus.). 176p. (J). (gr. 3 up). 1969. 16.00 (*0-374-36534-2*) FS&G.
Babbitt, Natalie. The Search for Delicious. 167p. pap. 3.95 (*0-8072-1481-7*) Listening Lib.
— The Search for Delicious. (J). 1985. 9.05 (*0-606-02822-6*, Pub. by Turtleback) Demco.
Babbitt, Natalie. The Search for Delicious. large type ed. 1995. 45.50 (*0-614-09608-1*, L-34852-00) Am Printing Hse.
Babbitt, Natalie. The Something. 40p. (J). (gr. k-2). pap. 2.95 (*0-8072-1333-0*) Listening Lib.
Babbitt, Natalie. Tuck Everlasting. LC 75-33306. (Sunburst Ser.). 160p. (J). (gr. 3 up). 1975. 15.00 (*0-374-37848-7*) FS&G.
— Tuck Everlasting. LC 75-33306. (Sunburst Ser.). 160p. (J). (gr. 4-7). 1985. pap. 4.95 (*0-374-48009-5*) FS&G.
***Babbitt, Natalie.** Tuck Everlasting. (Illus.). 160p. (YA). 2000. pap. 4.95 (*0-374-48012-5*, Sunburst Bks) FS&G.
Babbitt, Natalie. Tuck Everlasting. (J). (gr. 6). 1995. 9.28 (*0-395-73267-0*) HM.
Babbitt, Natalie. Tuck Everlasting. 139p. (J). (gr. 4-6). pap. 4.95 (*0-8072-1385-3*) Listening Lib.
— Tuck Everlasting. 1985. 10.05 (*0-606-00767-9*, Pub. by Turtleback) Demco.
Babbitt, Natalie. Tuck Everlasting. large type ed. 160p. (J). (gr. 6). 41.00 (*0-614-20624-3*, L-38208-00 APHB) Am Printing Hse.
Babbitt, Natalie. Tuck Everlasting. unabridged ed. (J). (gr. 4-6). 1988. pap. 21.98 incl. audio (*0-8072-8534-X*, LB4SP) Listening Lib.
Babbitt, Natalie. Tuck Para Siempre. (Mirasol/Libros Juveniles Ser.).Tr. of Tuck Everlasting. (SPA.). 1993. 10.30 (*0-606-06067-7*) Turtleback.
— Tuck Para Siempre: Tuck Everlasting. Fradera, Narcis, tr. (Mirasol Ser.). (SPA.). 158p. (YA). (gr. 5 up). 1991. 15.00 (*0-374-37849-5*) FS&G.
— Tuck Para Siempre: Tuck Everlasting. 144p. (J). (gr. 3-7). 1993. pap. 4.95 (*0-374-48011-7*) FS&G.
Babbitt, Natalie, et al. Ouch! LC 97-78382. (Illus.). 32p. (J). 1998. 14.95 (*0-06-205066-4*) HarpC Child Bks.
Babbitt, Susan. Oresme's Livre de Politiques & the France of Charles V. LC 84-71076. (Transactions Ser.: Vol. 75, Pt. 1). 156p. 1985. pap. 15.00 (*0-87169-751-3*, T751-BAS) Am Philos.
***Babbitt, Susan & Campbell, Sue.** Racism & Philosophy. LC 99-13358. 295p. 1999. pap. 17.95 (*0-8014-8504-5*) Cornell U Pr.
Babbs, John. The Divine Hotine. LC 87-71555. 1987. pap. 7.95 (*0-9619039-0-2*) Cloud River Pub.
— The Idyllic Angler. (Illus.). 96p. (Orig.). 1997. pap. 9.95 (*0-941695-04-2*) Angle Productions.
Babbs, Ken, jt. auth. see Kesey, Ken.
Babbs, Ken, jt. auth. see Perry, Paul.
Babbush, Charles A. Dental Implants: Principles & Practice. (Illus.). 320p. 1991. text 165.00 (*0-7216-2227-5*, W B Saunders Co) Harcrt Hlth Sci Grp.
Babbush, H. Edward, et al. College Relations & Recruiting: A Guide for Developing an Effective Program. LC 82-71184. 1982. 11.95 (*0-913936-18-9*) Coll Placement.
Babby, Ellen R. The Play Language & Spectacle: A Structural Reading of Selected Texts by Gabrielle Roy. 140p. (C). 1985. text 25.00 (*0-920763-02-2*, Pub. by ECW); pap. text 15.00 (*0-920802-97-4*, Pub. by ECW) Genl Dist Srvs.
Babby, Ellen R., jt. ed. see Doran, Charles F.
Babby, Leonard H. A Transformational Grammar of Russian Adjectives. LC 73-83929. (Janua Linguarum, Ser. Practica: No. 235). 242p. (C). 1975. pap. text 75.40 (*90-279-3022-8*) Mouton.
Babchick, Barbara, jt. auth. see Haber, Margie.
Babchinitser, T. M. & Kazaryan, L. G. Chemistry Reviews Vol. 19, No. 1: Effect of Chemical Structure of Aromatic Heterochain Polymers of Certain Classes on their Crystallizability, Vol. 19. (Soviet Scientific Reviews Ser.: Section B). 50p. 1995. pap. text 76.00 (*3-7186-5547-0*, Harwood Acad Pubs) Gordon & Breach.
Babcock. The French New Novel. 1997. 33.00 (*0-8057-7858-6*, Twyne) Mac Lib Ref.
Babcock, jt. auth. see Whitford.
Babcock, Sandy, ed. see Mitchell, Randy.
Babcock, Agnes, jt. auth. see Eberhart, Hal.
Babcock, Alice K. & Wilkins, George A., eds. The Earth's Rotation & Reference Frames for Geodesy & Geodynamics. (C). 1988. lib. bdg. 171.00 (*90-277-2657-4*) Kluwer Academic.
***Babcock, Ann.** Eating Well for a Healthy Heart. 2000. 14.45 (*0-9627121-6-7*) A&G Babcock.
— Everyday Recipes for the Diabetic. 2000. 14.95 (*0-9627121-5-9*) A&G Babcock.
Babcock, Ann. Super Breads, Plain & Fancy. LC 99-180976. 111p. 1989. write for info. (*0-933992-45-9*) Coffee Break.
— Yuletide Breads. 26p. (Orig.). 1995. pap. 6.95 (*0-9627121-1-6*) A&G Babcock.
Babcock, Barbara, ed. see Parsons, Elsie C.
Babcock, Barbara A., et al. The Pueblo Storyteller: Development of a Figurative Ceramic Tradition. LC 86-4279. (Illus.). 201p. 1990. reprint ed. pap. 25.95 (*0-8165-1193-4*) U of Ariz Pr.
Babcock, Barbara A., jt. auth. see Carrington, Paul.
Babcock, Barbara A., jt. ed. see Weigle, Marta.
Babcock, Barbara Allen. Sex Discrimination. LC 96-75593. 1514p. 1996. 60.00 (*0-316-07488-8*) Little.
Babcock, Barbara Allen & Massaro, Toni M. Civil Procedure: Cases & Problems - With Teacher's Manual. 1200p. 1997. teacher ed., boxed set 60.00 (*0-316-07459-4*, 74594) Aspen Law.
Babcock, Betty L., ed. First Ladies' Cookbook. 3rd rev. ed. (Illus.). 336p. 1996. pap. 16.95 (*0-9654302-0-0*) Shodair Chldrs.
Babcock, Bruce. Christmas with the Little People. unabridged ed. (Illus.). 46p. (J). (ps-6). 1998. pap. 7.95 (*1-892161-04-4*) Babcock Publ.
— The Four Cardinal Principles of Trading: How the World's Top Traders Identify Trends, Cut Losses, Maximize Profits, & Manage Risk. LC 96-2062. (Illus.). 224p. 1996. 40.00 (*0-7863-1010-3*, Irwn Prfssnl) McGraw-Hill Prof.
— I Wished upon a Falling Star. unabridged ed. (Illus.). 54p. (J). (ps-6). 1998. pap. 7.95 (*1-892161-03-6*) Babcock Publ.
— The Life of Jesus. unabridged ed. (Illus.). 15p. (J). (ps-6). 1998. pap. 5.95 (*1-892161-01-X*) Babcock Publ.
— The Year Santa Got Sick. unabridged ed. (Illus.). 32p. (J). (ps-6). 1998. pap. 7.95 (*1-892161-02-8*) Babcock Publ.
Babcock, Bruce A., et al, contrib. by. RAPS 1997: Agricultural & Environmental Outlook : RAPS Resource & Agricultural Policy Systems. LC 97-77920. 1997. write for info. (*0-936911-10-7*) Ctr Agri & Rural Dev.
Babcock, C. Merton & Maurer, David W. Some Expressions from Herman Melville; A Word-Finder List for Whiz Mob; Louise Pound - In Memoriam. (Publications of the American Dialect Society: No. 31). 41p. 1959. pap. 4.20 (*0-8173-0631-5*) U of Ala Pr.
Babcock, C. Merton, et al. A Word-List from Zora Neale Hurston; To As a Preposition of Location in Linguistic Atlas Materials; The 1961 Conference on Dialectology. (Publications of the American Dialect Society: No. 40). 38p. 1963. pap. 3.95 (*0-8173-0640-4*) U of Ala Pr.
Babcock, Carl, ed. see Barber, Jacqueline & Willard, Carolyn.
Babcock, Carl, ed. see Barber, Jacqueline, et al.
Babcock, Carl, ed. see Echols, Jean C.
Babcock, Carl, ed. see Goodman, Jan M.
Babcock, Carl, ed. see Kopp, Jaine & Bergman, Lincoln.
Babcock, Charles A. Venango County, Pennsylvania & Her Pioneers & People, 2 vols., Set. (Illus.). 1087p. 1994. reprint ed. lib. bdg. 110.00 (*0-8328-4006-8*) Higginson Bk Co.
***Babcock, Charlotte.** Shot Down! Capital Crimes of Casper, Wyoming. LC 99-25763. 1999. 29.95 (*0-931271-51-7*) Hi Plains Pr.
Babcock, Charlotte M. Shot Down! Capital Crimes of Casper, Wyoming. LC 99-25763. 2000. 13.95 (*0-931271-52-5*) Hi Plains Pr.
Babcock, Charlotte M., et al, eds. Windsingers. 125p. (Orig.). 1984. pap. text. write for info. (*0-917557-01-8*) Wyo Writers.
Babcock, Chris. No Moon, No Milk! (Illus.). 32p. (J). (ps-3). 1995. pap. 6.99 (*0-517-88540-9*) Random Hse Value.
Babcock, Chris. No Moon, No Milk! 1995. 12.19 (*0-606-07955-6*, Pub. by Turtleback) Demco.
Babcock, Clarence L. Silicate Glass Technology Methods. LC 76-30716. (Wiley Series in Pure & Applied Optics). 336p. reprint ed. pap. 104.20 (*0-608-13359-0*, 205576800037) Bks Demand.
Babcock, Dale A., jt. auth. see Branson, Kellie.
Babcock, Daniel L. Managing Engineering & Technology: An Introduction to Management for Engineers. 2nd ed. LC 95-12378. (International Series in Industrial & Systems Engineering). 422p. 1995. 95.00 (*0-13-141392-9*) P-H.
Babcock, David, jt. auth. see Gruenberger, Fred.
Babcock, Diane S., ed. Neonatal & Pediatric Ultrasonography. (Clinics in Diagnostic Ultrasound Ser.: Vol. 24). (Illus.). 251p. 1992. text 83.00 (*0-443-08606-0*) Church.
Babcock, Diane S. & Han, Bokyung K. Cranial Ultrasonography of Infants. LC 81-10340. 263p. reprint ed. pap. 81.60 (*0-608-15173-4*, 205607300046) Bks Demand.
Babcock, Dorothy E. Client Education: Theory & Practice. LC 93-12114. (Illus.). 344p. (C). (gr. 13). 1993. pap. text 35.00 (*0-8016-6942-1*, 06942) Mosby Inc.
Babcock, Dorothy E., jt. auth. see Miller, Mary A.
Babcock, Eileen, jt. auth. see Brown, Marilyn.
Babcock, Elise N. When Life Becomes Precious: A Guide for Loved Ones & Friends of Cancer Patients. LC 96-30256. 304p. 1997. pap. 14.95 (*0-553-37869-4*) Bantam.
***Babcock, Elizabeth.** Sidewinder - Invention & Early Years. unabridged ed. (Illus.). 28p. 1999. pap. 6.95 (*0-9676977-0-0*) China Lake.
Babcock, Havilah. The Best of Babcock. LC 70-117281. 275p. 1985. reprint ed. 19.95 (*0-936075-10-4*) Gunnerman Pr.
— The Education of Pretty Boy. LC 60-7334. 149p. 1985. reprint ed. 19.95 (*0-936075-08-2*) Gunnerman Pr.
— I Don't Want to Shoot an Elephant & Other Stories. LC 58-7636. 184p. 1985. 19.95 (*0-936075-04-X*) Gunnerman Pr.
— Jaybirds Go to Hell on Friday & Other Stories. LC 64-21917. 149p. 1985. reprint ed. 19.95 (*0-936075-06-6*) Gunnerman Pr.
— My Health Is Better in November: Thirty-Five Stories of Hunting & Fishing in the South. LC 85-225748. (Illus.). 298p. 1985. 24.95 (*0-87249-440-3*) U of SC Pr.
— Tales of Quails n' Such. LC 85-231378. (Illus.). 248p. 1985. reprint ed. 24.95 (*0-87249-441-1*) U of SC Pr.
Babcock, Henry. Appraisal Principles & Procedures. 289p. 1989. reprint ed. pap. text 29.95 (*0-937828-19-X*) Am Soc Appraisers.
Babcock, Jerry. Children's Keepsake Educational Coloring Book, Bk. 1. large type unabridged ed. (Illus.). 44p. (J). (gr. k-4). 1998. pap. 4.99 (*1-892161-05-2*) Babcock Publ.
Babcock, Jim. International Atlanta 1999, Vol. 8. 8th rev. ed. (FRE., Illus.). 184p. 1998. text 10.00 (*1-886760-02-0*) Atl Chamber Publ.
Babcock, John. LAPD Chiefs: The Famous, the Infamous & the Forgettable. 29.95 (*0-9636381-8-1*) Whyte Rose Pr.
***Babcock, John B.** Farmboy: Hard Work & Good Times on a Farm That Helped Change Northeast Agriculture of Tompkins County. Marcham, John, ed. LC 99-27296. (Illus.). 240p. 1999. pap. 21.95 (*0-942690-43-5*) DeWitt Hist.
Babcock, K. W. Rise of American Nationality, 1811-1819. LC 68-24970. (American History & Americana Ser.: No. 47). 1969. reprint ed. lib. bdg. 75.00 (*0-8383-0910-0*) M S G Haskell Hse.
Babcock, Kendric C. The Scandinavian Element in the United States. LC 69-18757. (American Immigration Collection. Series 1). 1969. reprint ed. 12.95 (*0-405-00505-9*) Ayer.
Babcock, Lucia M. Advances in Gas Phase Ion Chemistry, Vol. 1. Adams, Nigel, ed. 329p. 1992. 109.50 (*1-55938-331-3*) Jai Pr.
— Advances in Gas Phase Ion Chemistry, Vol. 2. Adams, Nigel, ed. 1996. 109.50 (*1-55938-703-3*) Jai Pr.
Babcock, Lucia M., jt. ed. see Adams, Nigel G.
Babcock, Lucia M., jt. ed. see Adams, Nigel.
Babcock, Maltbie D. Letters from Egypt & Palestine. Davis, Moshe, ed. LC 77-70662. (America & the Holy Land Ser.). (Illus.). 1977. reprint ed. lib. bdg. 21.95 (*0-405-10223-2*) Ayer.
Babcock, Marguerite & McKay, Christine, eds. Challenging Codependency: Feminist Critiques. 240p. 1995. text 60.00 (*0-8020-0440-7*); pap. text 19.95 (*0-8020-7230-5*) U of Toronto Pr.
Babcock, Michael. Go Big Red: The Ultimate Fan's Guide to Nebraska Cornhusker Football. LC 98-23499. 256p. 1998. pap. 15.95 (*0-312-19457-9*) St Martin.
— The Power of the Bear: Paintings by Susan Seddon Boulet. LC 97-50126. (Illus.). 96p. 1998. 25.00 (*0-7649-0612-7*) Pomegranate Calif.
***Babcock, Michael.** Susan Seddon Boulet: A Retrospective. LC 99-51878. (Illus.). 272p. 2000. 65.00 (*0-7649-1030-2*) Pomegranate Calif.
Babcock, Michael W. & German, H. Wade. Freight Transportation Market Shares. LC 90-63526. (Illus.). 318p. 1990. 295.00 (*0-911382-10-0*) Simmons-Boardman.
Babcock, Monroe C. The Millionaire's Bible: How to Start Your Own Business. rev. ed. LC 87-81480. 171p. (Orig.). 1987. pap. 12.95 (*0-87208-201-6*) Shoeless Pub.
Babcock, Richard & Sorensen, Peter. Strategies & Tactics in Management by Objectives. (Illus.). 273p. (C). 1980. pap. text 8.40 (*0-87563-119-3*) Stipes.
Babcock, Richard F. & Larsen, Wendy U. Special Districts: The Ultimate in Neighborhood Zoning. 187p. 1990. pap. 15.00 (*1-55844-112-3*) Lincoln Inst Land.
Babcock, Richard F. & Siemon, Charles L. The Zoning Game Revisited. LC 90-13471. 304p. 1985. pap. 14.50 (*1-55844-116-6*) Lincoln Inst Land.
Babcock, Richard F., jt. auth. see Weaver, Clifford L.
Babcock, Richard W. & Stevens, Lauren R. Old Barns in the New World: Reconstructing History. LC 96-21932. (Illus.). 256p. 1996. reprint ed. pap. 21.95 (*0-936399-79-1*, Pub. by Berkshire Hse) Natl Bk Netwk.
Babcock, Robert G., et al, eds. Catalogue of Medieval & Renaissance Manuscripts in the Beinecke Rare Book & Manuscript Library Yale University Vol. IV: MSS 481-485. (Medieval & Renaissance Texts & Studies: Vol. 176). (Illus.). 450p. 2000. 50.00 (*0-86698-218-3*, MR176) MRTS.
Babcock, Robert G. & Sosower, Mark L. Learning from the Greeks: An Exhibition Commemorating the Five-Hundredth Anniversary of the Founding of the Aldine Press. LC 94-12098. (Illus.). 85p. (Orig.). 1994. pap. 15.00 (*0-8457-3128-9*) Yale U Lib.
Babcock, Robert H. Gompers in Canada: A Study in American Continentalism Before the First World War. LC 74-78507. 306p. reprint ed. pap. 94.90 (*0-608-13158-X*, 205595800041) Bks Demand.
Babcock, Robert W. The Genesis of Shakespeare Idolatry, 1766-1799. LC 75-28990. reprint ed. 49.50 (*0-404-14001-7*) AMS Pr.
Babcock, Rufus. Lessons for the Young. unabridged ed. (Children's Heritage Ser.). 135p. (J). (gr. 4-6). 1996. pap. 6.98 (*1-58339-107-X*, D7) Triangle Press.
Babcock, Sandra S. Syntax of Spanish Reflexive Verbs: The Parameters of the Middle Verb. LC 74-106468. (Janua Linguarum, Ser. Practica: No. 105). (Orig.). 1970. pap. text 33.85 (*90-279-0742-0*) Mouton.
***Babcock, Scott & Carson, Robert.** Hiking Washington's Geology. LC 99-50693. (Hiking Geology Ser.). (Illus.). 224p. 2000. pap. 16.95 (*0-89886-548-4*) Mountaineers.
Babcock, Stephen. The Babcock Genealogy. (Illus.). 640p. 1988. reprint ed. pap. 81.00 (*0-8328-0151-8*); reprint ed. lib. bdg. 91.00 (*0-8328-0150-X*) Higginson Bk Co.
***Babcock, Stephen.** The Babcock Genealogy, 2 vols., Set. 2000. reprint ed. pap. 90.00 (*0-8063-4992-1*, Pub. by Clearfield Co) ACCESS Pubs Network.
Babcock, William E. Hess-Higbee Genealogy (of New York & Pennsylvania) 175p. 1997. reprint ed. pap. 26.00 (*0-8328-9108-8*); reprint ed. lib. bdg. 36.00 (*0-8328-9107-X*) Higginson Bk Co.
Babcock, William H. Early Norse Visits to North America. 1976. lib. bdg. 59.95 (*0-8490-1742-4*) Gordon Pr.
— Legendary Islands of the Atlantic: Study in Medieval Geography. LC 72-8459. (Select Bibliographies Reprint Ser.). 1977. reprint ed. 20.95 (*0-8369-6963-4*) Ayer.
Babcock, William S., ed. Paul & the Legacies of Paul. LC 89-78490. (Illus.). 460p. 1990. text 32.50 (*0-87074-305-8*); pap. text 16.95 (*0-87074-306-6*) SMU Press.
Babe, Robert. Telecommunications in Canada. 392p. 1989. text 55.00 (*0-8020-5831-0*); pap. text 25.95 (*0-8020-6738-7*) U of Toronto Pr.
Babe, Robert E. Cable Television & Telecommunications in Canada: An Economic Analysis. LC 75-620061. (International Business & Economic Studies). 311p. reprint ed. pap. 96.50 (*0-608-20489-7*, 207174100002) Bks Demand.
Babe, Robert E., ed. Information & Communication in Economics. LC 93-13259. (Recent Economic Thought Ser.). 1993. lib. bdg. 150.00 (*0-7923-9358-9*) Kluwer Academic.
Babe, Thomas. Billy Irish. 1982. pap. 5.25 (*0-8222-0120-8*) Dramatists Play.
— Buried Inside Extra. 1985. pap. 5.25 (*0-8222-0163-1*) Dramatists Play.
— Demon Wine. 1989. pap. 5.25 (*0-8222-0300-6*) Dramatists Play.
— Fathers & Sons. 1980. pap. 5.25 (*0-8222-0392-8*) Dramatists Play.
— Great Solo Town. 1981. pap. 5.25 (*0-8222-0485-1*) Dramatists Play.
— Kid Champion. 1979. pap. 5.25 (*0-8222-0610-2*) Dramatists Play.
— Planet Fires. 1987. pap. 5.25 (*0-8222-0896-2*) Dramatists Play.

An Asterisk (*) at the beginning of an entry indicates that the title is appearing for the first time.

— Rebel Women. 1976. pap. 5.25 (*0-8222-0935-7*) Dramatists Play.

— Salt Lake City Skyline. 1980. pap. 5.25 (*0-8222-0982-9*) Dramatists Play.

— Taken in Marriage. 1979. pap. 5.25 (*0-8222-1108-4*) Dramatists Play.

Babeau, Albert A. La Province sous l'Ancien Regime, 2 vols., Vols. 1 - 2. LC 77-161720. 87.50 (*0-404-07506-1*) AMS Pr.

— Ville sous l'Ancien Regime, 2 vols. 2nd ed. reprint ed. 115.00 (*0-404-07516-9*) AMS Pr.

Babeckis, James & Chapman, Benita. One True Doctrine. 148p. 1994. pap. 9.95 (*1-57353-104-9*, Eschaton Bks) Eschaton Prods.

Babel, B. L. Chikitsa Nyaya Shastra: (Medical Jurisprudence) (HIN.). (C). 1988. 40.00 (*0-7855-5116-6*) St Mut.

— Forensic Science: (Being a Study of Scientific Aids to Investigation in Hindi) (HIN.). (C). 1987. 95.00 (*0-7855-5606-0*) St Mut.

— Handwriting & Fingerprint Science. (HIN.). (C). 1989. 60.00 (*0-7855-5115-8*) St Mut.

— Handwriting & Fingerprints Science. (HIN.). (C). 1989. 65.00 (*0-7855-5544-7*) St Mut.

— Hindu Vidhi Par Pramukh Nirnaya.Tr. of Cases on Hindu Law. (HIN.). 132p. 1983. 60.00 (*0-7855-1419-8*) St Mut.

— Hindu Vidhi Par Pramukh Nirnaya: (Cases on Hindu Law in Hindi) (HIN.). (C). 1983. 30.00 (*0-7855-5542-0*) St Mut.

— Law Relating to Forest & Wild Life Protection. (HIN.). (C). 1990. text 80.00 (*0-89771-461-X*) St Mut.

Babel, B. L. Law Relating to Forest & Wild Life Protection. (C). 1990. 75.00 (*0-7855-7550-2*) St Mut.

Babel, B. L. Policy Anveshan: Police Investigation in Hindi. (C). 1984. 50.00 (*0-89771-790-2*, Pub. by Eastern Book) St Mut.

— Sansad Evam Sansadiya Prakriya: (Parliament & Parliamentary Procedure in Hindi) (HIN.). (C). 1990. 50.00 (*0-7855-5459-9*) St Mut.

Babel, B. L., ed. Apradh Shastra: (Criminology in Hindi) (HIN.). (C). 1988. 45.00 (*0-7855-5597-8*) St Mut.

Babel Communications Staff, tr. see Buck, Marcia L. & Hendrick, Anne.

***Babel, D. E.** An Atlas of Fungal Diseases. (Encyclopedia of Visual Medicine Ser.). (Illus.). 100p. 2000. 85.00 (*1-85070-600-X*) Prthnon Pub.

Babel, I. Red Cavalry: A Critical Companion. Rougle, Charles, ed. LC 96-8498. (Northwestern/Aatseel Critical Companions To Russian Literature Ser.). 180p. (C). 1996. pap. text 14.95 (*0-8101-1213-2*) Northwestern U Pr.

Babel, Isaac. Cavalerie Rouge. (FRE.). 1983. pap. 10.95 (*0-7859-1968-6*, 2070374408) Fr & Eur.

— Collected Stories. McDuff, David, ed. & intro. by. 400p. 1995. pap. 12.95 (*0-14-018462-7*, Penguin Classics) Viking Penguin.

— Collected Stories of Isaac Babel. LC 60-6743. 199p. 1955. 38.95 (*0-87599-009-6*) S G Phillips.

Babel, Isaac. The Complete Works of Isaac Babel. 45.00 (*0-393-04846-2*) Norton.

Babel, Isaac. Contes d'Odessa Suivi de Nouvelles. (FRE.). 320p. 1980. pap. 12.95 (*0-7859-1899-X*, 2070371263) Fr & Eur.

— Istoriia Moei Golubiatni. (RUS.). 1978. reprint ed. pap. 4.00 (*0-933884-03-6*) Berkeley Slavic.

— The Lonely Years, 1925-1939: The Unpublished Stories & Correspondence. Hayward, Max & MacAndrew, A. R., trs. from RUS. (Verba Mundi Ser.). 432p. 1995. pap. 15.95 (*0-87923-978-6*) Godine.

— 1920 Diary. Avins, Carol J., ed. Willetts, H. T., tr. from RUS. LC 94-24535. (Illus.). 192p. 1995. 27.50 (*0-300-05966-3*) Yale U Pr.

— 1920 Diary. Avins, Carol J., ed. & intro. by. 192p. 1997. pap. 14.00 (*0-300-07054-3*) Yale U Pr.

Babel, W. Elsevier's Dictionary of Biotechnology: English-German. (ENG & GER.). 116p. 1988. lib. bdg. 150.00 (*0-8288-3594-2*, M1721) Fr & Eur.

Babel, W., et al. Dictionary of Biotechnology: English - German. (ENG & GER.). 116p. 1989. 150.00 (*0-8288-9308-X*, M1721) Fr & Eur.

Babelon, Ernest. Introduction Generale a l'Etude des Monnaies de l'Antiquite. Finley, Moses, ed. LC 79-4960. (Ancient Economic History Ser.). (FRE.). 1979. reprint ed. lib. bdg. 37.95 (*0-405-12348-5*) Ayer.

— Les Origines de la Monnaie a Athenes. (FRE., Illus.). 92p. 1979. reprint ed. 20.00 (*0-916710-59-9*) Obol Intl.

Babelon, Jean. Histoire de l'Art: L'Europe Medievale, Vol. 2. (Historique Ser.). 1760p. 99.50 (*0-686-56451-0*) Fr & Eur.

— Histoire de l'Art: Renaissance, Baroque , Romantisme, Vol. 3. (Historique Ser.). 1712p. 99.50 (*0-686-56452-9*) Fr & Eur.

— Histoire de l'Art, Vol. 2: L'Europe Medievale. (FRE.). 1748p. write for info. (*0-8288-7601-0*) Fr & Eur.

— Histoire de l'Art, Vol. 3: Renaissance, Baroque, Romantisme. (FRE.). 1704p. write for info. (*0-8288-7602-9*) Fr & Eur.

***Babelon, Jean P.** Chantilly. 2000. 45.00 (*2-86656-204-6*) Scala Edit.

***Babelon, Jean-Pierre & Chamblas-Ploton, Mic.** The French Garden. LC 00-38144. (Illus.). 300p. 2000. 75.00 (*0-86565-216-3*) Vendome.

Babelon, O., et al. Lectures on Integrable Systems: Proceedings of the Cimpa School in Memory of Jean-Louis Verdier. 368p. 1994. text 68.00 (*981-02-1757-9*) World Scientific Pub.

— Lectures on Integrable Systems - In Memory of Jean-Louis Verdier: Proceedings of the Cimpa School. 1994. text 86.00 (*981-02-1713-7*) World Scientific Pub.

Babelon, Olivier, ed. see Cartier, Pierre & Kosmann-Schwarzbach, Yvette.

Babener, Jeffrey A. & Stewart, David. The Network Marketer's Guide to Success. (Illus.). 240p. 1990. text 24.95 (*0-9628055-0-5*) Forum Network Mktg.

Babenko, K. I. The Theory of Extremal Problems for Univalent Functions of Class S, No. 101. LC 74-23425. (Proceedings of the Steklov Institute of Mathematics Ser.). 327p. 1975. pap. 123.00 (*0-8218-3001-5*, STEKLO/101) Am Math.

Babenko, K. I., et al. Twelve Papers on Approximations & Integrals. (Translations Ser.: Series 2, Vol. 44). 268p. 1965. reprint ed. 35.00 (*0-8218-1744-2*, TRANS2/44) Am Math.

Baber. The Co-Operative Republic of Guyana. (C). 1992. text 49.00 (*0-86187-418-8*) St Martin.

Baber & Waymon. Smart Networking: How to Turn Contacts into Cash, Clients, & Career Success. LC 97-72175. 208p. 1997. per. 18.00 (*0-7872-3612-8*, 41361201) Kendall-Hunt.

Baber, et al. Practical Problems in Financial Management. 160p. (C). 1997. spiral bd. 17.95 (*0-7872-4279-9*, 41427901) Kendall-Hunt.

Baber, Alfred W. Handbook of Hi-Fi Audio Systems & Projects. 235p. 1981. 18.95 (*0-13-378307-3*, Parker Publishing Co) P-H.

Baber, Asa. The Land of a Million Elephants. 2nd ed. (Vietnam Generation Ser.). (Illus.). 142p. (Orig.). (C). 1992. reprint ed. pap. 15.00 (*0-9628524-2-2*) Burning Cities Pr.

— Naked at Gender Gap: A Man's View of the War Between the Sexes. 224p. 1992. 18.95 (*1-55972-114-6*, Birch Ln Pr) Carol Pub Group.

— Tranquillity Base & Other Stories. LC 79-89138. 141p. 1979. pap. 6.00 (*0-931362-01-6*) Fiction Intl.

Baber, Bob H., et al, eds. Old Wounds, New Words: An Anthology of Recent Appalachian Poetry. LC 94-7994. 224p. 1994. pap. 9.95 (*0-945084-44-7*) J Stuart Found.

Baber, Brendan & Spitznagel, Eric. A Guy's Guide to Dating: Everything You Need to Know about Love, Sex, Relationships & Other Things Too Terrible to Contemplate. LC 97-24259. (Illus.). 224p. 1998. pap. 11.95 (*0-385-48553-0*) Doubleday.

Baber, Brendan, et al. From Beyond: A Cthulhu Mythos Play in Two Acts. (Illus.). 76p. (Orig.). 1996. pap. 8.00 (*1-887797-04-1*) Tynes Cowan.

Baber, C., jt. auth. see Noyes, J. M.

Baber, Carolyn S. Little Billy. (Illus.). 200p. (J). (gr. 5-9). 1995. lib. bdg. 14.95 (*0-944727-29-8*) Jason & Nordic Pubs.

— Pony. (Illus.). 22p. (J). 1990. pap. 9.95 (*0-9628937-0-6*, TX2910777) Richmond Saddlery.

Baber, Christopher & Noyes, Janet M., eds. Interactive Speech Technology: Human Factors Issues in the Application of Speech Input-Output to Computers. LC 93-34425. 224p. 1993. 79.95 (*0-7484-0127-X*, Pub. by Tay Francis Ltd) Taylor & Francis.

Baber, Colin & Williams, L. J., eds. Modern South Wales: Essays in Economic History. xii, 324p. 1986. 70.00 (*0-7083-0943-7*, Pub. by Univ Wales Pr) Paul & Co Pubs.

Baber, Elizabeth A., jt. auth. see Adler, Anne G.

Baber, Kristine M. & Allen, Katherine R. Women & Families: Feminist Reconstructions. LC 92-20561. (Perspectives on Marriage & the Family Ser.). 276p. 1992. pap. text 24.00 (*0-89862-083-X*) Guilford Pubns.

Baber, Lawrence, ed. see Black, Eugene R.

Baber, Lucy H. & Williamson, Hazel L. Marriages of Campbell County, Virginia, 1782-1810. LC 79-56412. (Illus.). 185p. 2000. reprint ed. pap. 22.50 (*0-8063-0879-6*, Pub. by Clearfield Co) ACCESS Pubs Network.

Baber, M. Yvette, jt. auth. see Borman, Kathryn.

Baber, M. Yvette, jt. auth. see Borman, Kathryn M.

Baber, Ralph. It Happened This Way . . . (It Really Did!) 160p. 1998. pap. 8.95 (*0-9634733-3-6*) Ogden Pr TX.

— The Last of Rose Sommer. 250p. 1998. pap. 6.95 (*0-9634733-2-8*) Ogden Pr TX.

Baber, Ralph, ed. see Harbison, Fay & Surber, Ellen M.

Baber, Ralph K., ed. see Fry, Dale.

Baber, Ralph K., ed. see Harbison, Fay & Surber, Ellen M.

Baber, Robert, jt. auth. see Meyer, Marilyn.

Baber, Robert L. Error-Free Software: Know-How & Know-Why of Program Correctness. LC 91-12380. (Wiley Series in Software Engineering Practice). 168p. reprint ed. pap. 52.10 (*0-608-20170-7*, 205280300012) Bks Demand.

— The Spine of Software: Designing Provably Correct Software: Theory & Practice, Or a Mathematical Introduction to the Semantics of Computer Programs. LC 86-32483. (Illus.). 329p. 1987. pap. 102.00 (*0-608-05254-X*, 206579200001) Bks Demand.

Baber, Roberta, jt. auth. see Meyer, Marilyn.

Baber, Walter F. Organizing the Future: Matrix Models for the Postindustrial Polity. LC 82-7009. 146p. 1983. pap. 45.30 (*0-608-05181-0*, 206568900006) Bks Demand.

Baber, Willie L., jt. ed. see Gay, Geneva.

Baber, Zaheer. The Science of Empire: Scientific Knowledge, Civilization, & Colonial Rule in India. LC 95-30116. (SUNY Series in Science, Technology, & Society). 299p. (C). 1996. text 71.50 (*0-7914-2919-9*); pap. text 23.95 (*0-7914-2920-2*) State U NY Pr.

Babet, Bruneau. Borland C Plus Plus 5.0 Programming. 1995. pap. 34.95 incl. disk (*1-55851-452-X*, M&T Bks) IDG Bks.

Babeva. Geographic Aspects of Yeast Ecology, Vol. 9, No. 3. 54p. 1997. pap. text 27.00 (*3-7186-5825-9*, Harwood Acad Pubs) Gordon & Breach.

Babevsky. English Russian Dictionary of Chemistry & Technology of Polymers. (ENG & RUS.). 1977. 75.00 (*0-8288-3969-7*, F29090) Fr & Eur.

Babiarz, Frank. Jesus: His Messages on Life Here & the Hereafter. LC 98-219099. 29 p. 1998. write for info. (*1-55630-860-4*) Brentwood Comm.

Babiarz, Michael. Asset Protection Planning for Seniors: A Guide for Seniors & Their Families. LC 98-92894. 241p. 1998. pap. 19.95 (*1-57502-809-3*, PO2237) Morris Pubng.

Babias, Marius, ed. In Zentrum der Peripherie. (GER.). 352p. 1995. text 11.00 (*3-364-00315-7*) Gordon & Breach.

Babiasz, Thomas, jt. auth. see Harris, Monte.

Babic, jt. auth. see Pirkl.

Babic, S. Serbo-Croatian for Foreigners, Bk. 1. 233p. (C). 1988. 125.00 (*0-569-20342-2*, Pub. by Collets) St Mut.

Babic, V. M., ed. Mathematical Questions in the Theory of Wave Diffraction I: Proceedings. LC 74-2362. (Proceedings of the Steklov Institute of Mathematics Ser.: No. 115). 167p. 1974. pap. 82.00 (*0-8218-3015-5*, STEKLO/115) Am Math.

Babic, V. M. & Buldyrev, V. S. Asymptotic Methods in Short-Wave Diffraction Theory. Brekhovskikh, L. M. et al, eds. Kuester, E. F., tr. from RUS. (Wave Phenomena Ser.: Vol. 4). (Illus.). 464p. 1991. 109.95 (*0-387-19189-5*) Spr-Verlag.

Babic, V. M. & Kirpichnikova, N. Y. The Boundary-Layer Method in Diffraction Problems. (Electrophysics Ser.: Vol. 3). (Illus.). 1980. 28.95 (*0-387-09605-1*) Spr-Verlag.

Babicev, N. T. Dictionary of Latin Standard Quotations. (LAT & RUS.). 958p. 1982. 45.00 (*0-8288-2286-7*, M15185) Fr & Eur.

Babich. Ray Methods. 1996. write for info. (*0-582-20902-1*, Pub. by Addison-Wesley) Longman.

Babich, Babette, ed. Continental & Postmodern Perspectives in the Philosophy of Science. 272p. 1995. 82.95 (*1-85972-192-3*, Pub. by Avebry) Ashgate Pub Co.

Babich, Babette E. Nietzsche's Philosophy of Science: Reflecting Science on the Ground of Art & Life. LC 93-17271. (SUNY Series, The Margins of Literature). 350p. (C). 1994. text 64.50 (*0-7914-1865-0*); pap. text 21.95 (*0-7914-1866-9*) State U NY Pr.

Babich, Babette E., ed. From Phenomenology to Thought, Errancy, & Desire: Essays in Honor of William J. Richardson, S. J. (Phaenomenologica Ser.: Vol. 133). 1995. pap. text. write for info. (*0-7923-3568-6*, Pub. by Kluwer Academic) Kluwer Academic.

— From Phenomenology to Thought, Errancy, & Desire: Essays in Honor of William J. Richardson, S.J. (Phaenomenologica Ser.: No. 133). 1995. lib. bdg. 250.00 (*0-7923-3567-8*, Pub. by Kluwer Academic) Kluwer Academic.

***Babich, Babette E., ed.** Nietzsche, Epistemology & the Philosophy of Science: Nietzsche & the Sciences II. LC 99-15081. (Boston Studies in the Philosophy of Science). 368p. 1999. 171.00 (*0-7923-5743-4*) Kluwer Academic.

Babich, Jo C. Journey to Welcome. LC 95-90365. 292p. (YA). (gr. 6-12). 1995. pap., per. 9.95 (*0-9647171-0-7*) Zinka Pr.

Babich, Pete. Hoshin Handbook en Espanol. 2nd ed. Ragazzo, Ernesto, tr. (SPA., Illus.). 1998. pap. 23.00 (*0-9651861-1-3*) Totl Qual Eng.

Babich, Peter. Hoshin Handbook. 2nd ed. 150p. 1996. pap. 23.00 (*0-9651861-0-5*) Totl Qual Eng.

Babich, Vasili M., et al. The Space-Time Ray Method: Linear & Nonlinear Waves. Tew, R., ed. Rozenblum, G. V., tr. LC 97-17394. (Texts in Applied Mathematics Ser.: No. 20). (Illus.). 300p. (C). 1998. text 74.95 (*0-521-62201-8*); pap. text 34.95 (*0-521-62735-4*) Cambridge U Pr.

Babieri, Alexander F., et al. Pennsylvania Workmen's Compensation & Occupational Disease, 3 vols. with case finder. LC 96-79930. 1999. per. 275.00 (*1-887024-17-4*) Bisel Co.

Babighian, G., ed. Otology Today. (Advances in OtoRhinoLaryngology Ser.: Vol. 37). (Illus.). viii, 200p. 1987. 152.25 (*3-8055-4498-7*) S Karger.

Babighian, G., et al, eds. Transplants & Implants in Otology. LC 88-12784. (Illus.). 402p. 1988. text 143.00 (*90-6299-047-9*, Pub. by Kugler) Kugler Pubns.

Babiiha, Thaddeo K. The James-Hawthorne Relation: Biographical Essays. 1980. 45.00 (*0-8161-8431-3*, Hall Reference) Macmillan.

Babikian, Viken L. & Wechsler, Lawrence R. Transcranial Doppler Ultrasonography. 2nd ed. LC 99-12513. 512p. 1999. text 145.00 (*0-7506-9969-8*) Buttrwrth-Heinemann.

Babikian, Yeghia E. Declare the Glory of God. 164p. 1991. pap. 9.99 (*0-8341-1377-5*) Beacon Hill.

Babilon, Timothy, ed. see EDI User Requirements Task Force Staff.

Babin, A. V. Iterations of Differential Operators. Zahavi, H., tr. from RUS. xiv, 470p. 1989. text 383.00 (*2-88124-707-5*) Gordon & Breach.

Babin, A. V. & Vishik, M. I. Attractors of Evolution Equations. (Studies in Mathematics & Its Applications: Vol. 25). 532p. 1992. 181.00 (*0-444-89004-1*, North Holland) Elsevier.

Babin, A. V. & Vishik, M. I., eds. Properties of Global Attractors of Partial Differential Equations. LC 91-640741. (Advances in Soviet Mathematics Ser.: Vol. 10). 172p. 1992. text 106.00 (*0-8218-4109-2*, ADVSOV/10C) Am Math.

***Babin, Charles & Donovan, William J.** Investing Secrets of the Masters: Applying Classical Investment Ideas to Today's Turbulent Markets. LC 99-15633. 216p. 1999. 29.95 (*0-07-134100-5*) McGraw.

Babin, Claude, ed. Elements of Palaeontology. Orriss, N., tr. LC 79-1323. (Illus.). 471p. reprint ed. pap. 146.10 (*0-608-17666-4*, 203038000069) Bks Demand.

Babin, Edith & Harrison, Kimberly. Contemporary Composition Studies: A Guide to Theorists & Terms. LC 99-27183. 344p. 1999. lib. bdg. 79.50 (*0-313-30087-9*, Greenwood Pr) Greenwood.

Babin, Edith H., et al. Toefl: Test of English As a Foreign Language. 1992. pap. 32.00 incl. audio (*0-13-923368-7*, Arco) Macmillan Gen Ref.

Babin, Holly, ed. see Lessard, Betty.

Babin, Maria T. Estudios Lorquianos. LC 76-1827. (Coleccion Mente y Palabra). (SPA.). 503p. 1976. 6.00 (*0-8477-0528-5*); pap. 5.00 (*0-8477-0529-3*) U of PR Pr.

Babin, Michael. T'ai Chi Ch'uan: The Martial Side. (Illus.). 152p. 1992. pap. 16.00 (*0-87364-679-7*) Paladin Pr.

Babin, Michael, jt. auth. see Montaigue, Erle.

Babin, Michael, ed. see Santiago, Julio & Mulroy, Darrell.

Babin, Ronald. The Nuclear Power Game. Richmond, Ted, tr. from FRE. Orig. Title: L'Option Nucleaire. 236p. 1985. 43.99 (*0-920057-30-6*, Pub. by Black Rose); pap. 14.99 (*0-920057-31-4*, Pub. by Black Rose) Consort Bk Sales.

Babin, Thomas S. Designing a New Factory with Manufacturing Simulation & Planned Experimentation. LC 92-25878. (Six Sigma Research Institute Ser.). 1992. pap. text 10.95 (*0-201-63419-8*) Addison-Wesley.

Babin, Veronique. Enciclopedia Mega-Chiquitin. (SPA., Illus.). 116p. (J). (ps-2). 1994. reprint ed. 9.95 (*970-607-181-4*, Larousse LKC) LKC.

Babinat, Sally K. Letters of a Lifetime. iii, 235p. 1999. 38.50 (*0-9672966-0-9*) Babblins.

Babineau, Edmour J. Love of God & Social Duty in the Ramcaritmanas. 1979. 13.95 (*0-89684-050-6*, Pub. by Motilal Bnarsidass) S Asia.

Babineau, Steve, ed. see Booth, Clark.

Babineaux, Floyd. Simple Creole Cajun. 165p. 1986. 12.00 (*0-317-69245-3*) F Babineaux.

Babinger, Franz. Mehmed the Conquerer & His Time. Hickman, William C., ed. (Bollingen Ser.: No. XCVI). (Illus.). 569p. 1978. pap. text 21.95 (*0-691-01078-1*, Pub. by Princeton U Pr) Cal Prin Full Svc.

— Mehmed the Conqueror & His Time. Manheim, Ralph, tr. from GER. LC 77-71972. (Bollingen Ser.: No. 96). (Illus.). 604p. reprint ed. pap. 187.30 (*0-8357-3696-2*, 203642000003) Bks Demand.

Babington, Anthony. For the Sake of Example: Capital Courts Martial, 1914-1920. 238p. 1993. 24.95 (*0-85052-384-2*, Pub. by Leo Cooper) Trans-Atl Phila.

Babington, B. G., ed. see Von Feuchtersleben, Ernst F.

Babington, B. G., tr. see Hecker, J. F.

Babington, Churchill & Lumby, Joseph R., eds. Polychronicon Ranulphi Higden, Monachi Cestrenis, Together with the English Translation of John of Trevisa & of an Unknown Writer in the 15th Century, 9 vols. (Rolls Ser.: No. 41). 1974. reprint ed. 630.00 (*0-8115-1100-6*) Periodicals Srv.

Babington, Churchill, ed. see Peacock, Reginald.

Babington, Doug & LePan, Don. The Broadview Guide to Writing. 260p. 1991. pap. 9.95 (*0-921149-76-X*) Broadview Pr.

Babington, John. A Short Treatise of Geometrie. LC 76-25837. (English Experience Ser.: No. 296). 200p. 1971. reprint ed. 50.00 (*90-221-0296-3*) Walter J Johnson.

Babington, Mima, et al. Lexical Usage in Southern Louisiana; Word List of Construction Terms. (Publications of the American Dialect Society: No. 36). (Illus.). 31p. 1961. pap. 3.20 (*0-8173-0636-6*) U of Ala Pr.

Babini, Gian N., et al, eds. Engineering Ceramics, 1996: Higher Reliability Through Processing. LC 97-3652. 1997. text 234.00 (*0-7923-4458-8*) Kluwer Academic.

Babini, Luca. Francesco Clemente: Art & Life. 1999. text 45.00 (*0-89381-872-0*) Aperture.

Babinski, Edward T. Leaving the Fold: Testimonies of Former Fundamentalists. LC 94-26945. (Illus.). 462p. (C). 1995. 33.95 (*0-87975-907-0*) Prometheus Bks.

***Babinski, Mark.** Addendum to Henry Popple's 1733 Map of the British Empire in America. (Illus.). 34p. 2000. write for info. (*0-9656301-2-9*) Krinder Peak.

— Henry Popple's 1733 Map of the British Empire in America. deluxe ed. LC 97-74608. (Illus.). 229p. 1998. write for info. (*0-9656301-1-0*) Krinder Peak.

Babinski, Mark, et al. Notes on C. J. Sauthier & Lord Percy. LC 98-183871. 50p. 1997. write for info. (*0-9656301-0-2*) Krinder Peak.

— Notes on C. J. Sauthier & Lord Percy: With Listing of Maps of the State of New York Drawn by Simeon De Witt & David H. Burr. expanded ed. LC 97-76636. 65p. 1997. write for info. (*0-9656301-3-7*) Krinder Peak.

Babinski, Michael. Gemstones: Beauty, Lore & Fascination. (Illus.). 96p. 1995. pap. 7.95 (*0-9644079-0-6*) Intarsia Pr.

Babinsky, Kate, tr. see Joy, Janet L.

Babior, Bernard M., ed. Cobalamin: Biochemistry & Pathophysiology. LC 74-32499. 489p. reprint ed. pap. 151.60 (*0-608-30216-3*, 201739800007) Bks Demand.

Babior, Bernard M. & Stossel, Thomas P. Hematology: A Pathophysiological Approach. 3rd ed. (Illus.). 1994. pap. text 49.95 (*0-443-08939-6*) Church.

Babior, Shirley & Goldman, Carol. Overcoming Panic, Anxiety, & Phobias: New Strategies to Free Yourself from Worry & Fear. LC 95-42389. 176p. (Orig.). 1995. pap. 12.95 (*1-57025-072-3*) Whole Person.

— Working with Groups to Overcome Panic, Anxiety & Phobias. LC 95-62472. 192p. (Orig.). 1996. otabind 24.95 (*1-57025-117-7*) Whole Person.

Babister, A. W. Aircraft Dynamic Stability & Response. (Illus.). 230p. 1980. 106.00 (*0-08-024769-5*, Pub. by Pergamon Repr) Franklin.

***Babits, L. E. & Van Tilburg, H.** Maritime Archaeology: A Reader of Substantive & Theoretical Contributions. LC 97-49977. (Series in Underwater Archaeology). (Illus.). 425p. (C). 1998. 95.00 (*0-306-45330-4*, Plenum Trade); pap. 49.50 (*0-306-45331-2*, Plenum Trade) Perseus Pubng.

Babits, Lawrence E. Cowpens Battlefield: A Walking Guide. (Illus.). 80p. (Orig.). 1993. pap. 4.95 (*0-932807-79-8*) Overmountain Pr.

— A Devil of a Whipping: The Battle of Cowpens. LC 98-13059. (Illus.). 231p. 1998. 34.95 (*0-8078-2434-8*) U of NC Pr.

Babitsky Esq., Steven. Understanding the Ama Guides in Workers' Compensation, 1. 408p. 1997. boxed set 145.00 (*0-7355-1256-6*) Panel Pubs.

Babitsky, Steven J. & Mangraviti, James J., Jr. How to Excel During Cross-Examination: Techniques for Experts That Work. 197p. 1997. pap. 59.95 (*0-9652197-2-0*) SEAK.

Babitsky, Steven J., jt. auth. see Mangraviti, James J., Jr.

Babitsky, Timlynn, jt. ed. see Salmons, Jim.

Babitsky, V. I. Theory of Vibro-Impact Systems & Applications. Birkett, N., tr. from RUS. LC 98-40043. (Foundations of Engineering Mechanics Ser.). (Illus.). xvi, 319p. 1998. 109.00 (*3-540-63723-0*) Spr-Verlag.

Babitsky, V. I., ed. Dynamics of Vibro-Impact Systems: Proceedings of the Euromech Colloquium 15-18 September, 1998. LC 99-25665. (Illus.). xvi, 346p. 1999. 189.00 (*3-540-65600-6*) Spr-Verlag.

Babitsky, V. I., ed. see Kovaleva, A. S.

Babitsky, V. I., ed. see Skrzypek, J. & Ganczarski, A.

Babitt, Roy, jt. auth. see King, Lawrence P.

***Babitz, Eve.** Two by Two. LC 99-38228. 208p. 1999. 21.50 (*0-684-83392-1*) S&S Trade.

Babiuk, L. A., et al, eds. Animal Biotechnology: Comprehensive Biotechnology. (Comprehensive Biotechnology Supplement Ser.: No. 1). (Illus.). 250p. 1989. 118.75 (*0-08-034730-4*, Pergamon Pr) Elsevier.

Babkin, Boris P. Pavlov: A Biography. LC 49-11887. xiv, 366p. 1975. pap. text 4.25 (*0-226-03373-2*, P621) U Ch Pr.

Babkin, V. A., et al. Quantum Aspects of Catoinic Polymerization of Olffins. LC 98-106172. (Illus.). 247p. 1997. lib. bdg. 115.00 (*1-56072-501-X*) Nova Sci Pubs.

***Babkina, A. M.** Nuclear Proliferation: An Annotated Biography. 239p. 1999. 49.00 (*1-56072-646-6*) Nova Sci Pubs.

Babkina, A. M. Terrorism: An Annotated Bibliography. 327p. 1998. 49.00 (*1-56072-623-7*) Nova Sci Pubs.

Babkina, A. M., ed. Affirmative Action: An Annotated Bibliography. 183p. 1998. 49.00 (*1-56072-553-2*, HF5549) Nova Sci Pubs.

— Domestic Economic Modernization in China. 237p. (C). 1997. lib. bdg. 85.00 (*1-56072-415-3*) Nova Sci Pubs.

***Babkina, A. M., ed.** Grants: A Selective Bibliography with Indexes. (Finance & Business Bibliography Series I). 217p. 1999. lib. bdg. 49.00 (*1-56072-712-8*) Nova Sci Pubs.

— NATO's Role, Missions & Futures. 147p. 1999. lib. bdg. 59.00 (*1-56072-667-9*) Nova Sci Pubs.

Babkina, A. M., ed. New Political Parties & Movements in the Soviet Union. 160p. (C). 1991. pap. text 125.00 (*1-56072-041-7*) Nova Sci Pubs.

***Babkina, A. M., ed.** Politics of Immigration: Current Issues & Future Directions. 187p. 2000. text 59.00 (*1-56072-733-0*) Nova Sci Pubs.

Babkina, A. M., ed. Trade in the Asian Pacific Region. (Illus.). 237p. (C). 1996. lib. bdg. 95.00 (*1-56072-358-0*) Nova Sci Pubs.

***Babkina, A. M., ed.** World Trade Organization: Issues & Bibliography. 237p. 2000. lib. bdg. 59.00 (*1-56072-780-2*) Nova Sci Pubs.

Babler-Schipperges, Judith. Gebet Aus Dem Schweigen: Eine Religionsphilosophische Untersuchung Zur Gebetssprache. (GER.). 216p. 1997. 42.95 (*3-631-31329-2*) P Lang Pubng.

Babler, Susan. Communication Station. Bittinger, Gayle, ed. LC 97-62224. (Kinderstation Ser.). (Illus.). 160p. (J). (ps). 1998. pap. 14.95 (*1-57029-159-4*, 4502) Totline Pubns.

Bablet, Denis. The Theatre of Edward Gordon Craig. Woodward, D., tr. LC 66-23134. Orig. Title: Edward Gordon Craig. (Illus.). 1966. pap. 8.95 (*0-87830-581-5*, Thtre Arts Bks) Routledge.

— The Theatre of Edward Gordon Craig. Woodward, D., tr. LC 66-23134. Orig. Title: Edward Gordon Craig. (Illus.). 160p. (gr. 13). 1993. pap. 18.99 (*0-87830-042-2*, Thtre Arts Bks) Routledge.

Babloyantz, A. Molecules, Dynamics & Life: An Introduction to Self-Organization of Matter. LC 85-26413. (Nonequilibrium Problems in the Physical Sciences & Biology Ser.). 345p. 1986. 150.00 (*0-471-82380-5*) Wiley.

Babloyantz, A., ed. Self-Organization, Emerging Properties & Learning. (NATO ASI Ser.: Vol. 260). (Illus.). 320p. (C). 1991. text 102.00 (*0-306-43930-1*, Kluwer Plenum) Kluwer Academic.

Babock, jt. auth. see Whitford.

Babock, Bruce, Jr. The Irwin Guide to Commodity Futures Trading Systems. 240p. 1989. text 70.00 (*1-55623-126-1*, Irwn Prfssnl) McGraw-Hill Prof.

Baboian, R., ed. Automotive Corrosion & Protection. (Illus.). 570p. 1992. pap. 10.00 (*1-877914-39-8*) NACE Intl.

— Electrochemical Techniques for Corrosion, 1976: 1976 Symposium. LC 77-71054. (Illus.). 117p. 1977. 48.00 (*0-915567-88-1*) NACE Intl.

Baboian, R., et al, eds. The Statue of Liberty Restoration. LC 90-61053. (Illus.). 149p. 1990. 25.00 (*1-877914-12-6*) NACE Intl.

Baboian, Robert, ed. Corrosion Tests & Standards: Application & Interpretation. LC 95-6879. (Manual Ser.: Vol. 20). 764p. 1995. 143.00 (*0-8031-2058-3*, MNL2) ASTM.

— Materials Degradation Caused by Acid Rain. LC 86-20560. (ACS Symposium Ser.: No. 318). (Illus.). ix, 438p. 1986. 87.95 (*0-8412-0988-X*) Am Chemical.

— Materials Degradation Caused by Acid Rain. LC 86-20560. (ACS Symposium Ser.: Vol. 318). 466p. 1986. reprint ed. pap. 144.50 (*0-608-03522-X*, 206424100008) Bks Demand.

Baboian, Robert, jt. ed. see Haynes, G. S.

Babones, Pete. Warning This Is Not a Book. (New Shoes Ser.). 83p. (Orig.). 1995. pap. 7.00 (*0-9641196-3-3*) Champion Bks.

Babor, Thomas F., et al, eds. Types of Alcoholics: Evidence from Clinical, Experimental & Genetic Research. LC 94-3082. (Annals Ser.: Vol. 708). 1994. pap. 75.00 (*0-89766-800-6*) NY Acad Sci.

Babovic, V. & Larsen, L. C., eds. Hydroinformatics '98: Proceedings of an International Conference, Copenhagen, 24-26 August, 1998, 2 vols. (Illus.). 1532p. (C). 1998. 146.00 incl. cd-rom (*90-5410-983-1*) Ashgate Pub Co.

Babovic, Vladan. Hydroinformatics: Emergence, Evolution, Intelligence. (Illus.). 344p. (Orig.). (C). 1996. text 65.00 (*90-5410-404-X*, Pub. by A A Balkema) Ashgate Pub Co.

Babraa. Sikhism. 1990. pap. text. write for info. (*0-582-31787-8*, Drumbeat) Longman.

Babrauskas, V. & Grayson, S. J., eds. Heat Release in Fires. (Illus.). 295p. (C). 1992. 170.00 (*0-419-16100-7*, E & FN Spon) Routledge.

Babrius. Babrius & Phaedrus. Perry, B. E., tr. (Loeb Classical Library: No. 436). 1965. 19.95 (*0-674-99480-9*) HUP.

Babskii, V. G., et al. Mathematical Theory of Electrophoresis. (Illus.). 250p. (C). 1988. 110.00 (*0-306-11018-0*, Kluwer Plenum) Kluwer Academic.

Babson, David W. When Chester Lost Maybelle. LC 96-60274. (Illus.). 14p. (Orig.). (J). (gr. k-5). 1996. pap. 2.95 (*0-940787-09-1*) Winstead Pr.

Babson, Harold. Management. (C). 1993. pap. text, student ed. 25.00 (*0-07-006836-4*) McGraw.

Babson, Jane F. Babson's Bestiary. LC 90-71155. (Illus.). 32p. (J). (ps-4). 1991. boxed set 10.95 (*0-940787-02-4*) Winstead Pr.

— The Epsteins: A Family Album. LC 85-156674. (Illus.). 160p. 1984. lib. bdg. 30.00 (*0-907807-01-1*) Winstead Pr.

— The Nest on the Porch. LC 88-51084. (Illus.). 32p. (Orig.). (J). (ps up). 1989. pap. 4.95 (*0-940787-01-6*) Winstead Pr.

Babson, John J. History of the Town of Gloucester, (Mass.) Cape Ann: Including the Town of Rockport. (Illus.). 1972. 45.50 (*0-8446-0014-8*) Peter Smith.

Babson, Marian. Break a Leg, Darlings. LC 96-48767. 1997. 20.95 (*0-312-15285-X*, Thomas Dunne) St Martin.

— Canapes for the Kitties. LC 97-16232. 272p. 1997. 21.95 (*0-312-16929-9*, Thomas Dunne) St Martin.

— Canapes for the Kitties. 1999. mass mkt. 5.99 (*0-312-96897-3*, Thomas Dunne) St Martin.

— Canapes for the Kitties. large type ed. LC 97-47193. (Large Print Bks.). 1998. pap. 22.95 (*1-56895-522-7*) Wheeler Pub.

— The Company of Cats. LC 98-52967. 224p. 1999. text 20.95 (*0-312-19924-4*) St Martin.

***Babson, Marian.** The Company of Cats. 192p. 2000. pap. 5.99 (*0-312-97501-5*, St Martins Paperbacks) St Martin.

— The Company of Cats. large type ed. LC 99-25055. (Mystery Ser.). 1999. 24.95 (*1-57490-209-1*, Beeler LP Bks) T T Beeler.

Babson, Marian. Cover-up Story. large type ed. (Nightingale Ser.). 264p. 1991. pap. 14.95 (*0-8161-4926-7*, G K Hall Lrg Type) Mac Lib Ref.

— Death Warmed Up. 192p. 1994. mass mkt. 4.99 (*0-446-36493-2*, Pub. by Warner Bks) Little.

— The Diamond Cat. 1996. mass mkt. 5.50 (*0-312-95660-6*) St Martin.

— Encore Murder. large type ed. LC 91-16523. (Nightingale Ser.). 275p. 1991. pap. 14.95 (*0-8161-5139-3*, G K Hall Lrg Type) Mac Lib Ref.

***Babson, Marian.** Murder Sails at Midnight. 168p. 2000. 21.95 (*0-7540-8555-4*, Black Dagger) Chivers N Amer.

Babson, Marian. Nine Lives to Murder. 1995. mass mkt. 4.99 (*0-312-95580-4*) St Martin.

— Past Regret. 208p. 1993. mass mkt. 4.99 (*0-446-36437-1*, Pub. by Warner Bks) Little.

— Paws for Alarm, Vol. 1. 1998. 5.99 (*0-312-96513-3*, Pub. by Tor Bks) St Martin.

— Pretty Lady. 128p. 1992. mass mkt. 4.50 (*0-446-36212-3*, Pub. by Warner Bks) Little.

— Pretty Lady. large type ed. LC 92-35899. (General Ser.). 221p. 1993. lib. bdg. 15.95 (*0-8161-5256-X*, G K Hall Lrg Type) Mac Lib Ref.

— Shadows in Their Blood. large type ed. LC 93-46829. 322p. 1994. lib. bdg. 16.95 (*0-8161-5952-1*, G K Hall Lrg Type) Mac Lib Ref.

— There Must Be Some Mistake. 192p. 1993. mass mkt. 4.99 (*0-446-36385-5*, Pub. by Warner Bks) Little.

— Tightrope for Three. 192p. 1990. 16.95 (*0-8027-5750-2*) Walker & Co.

— Tightrope for Three. large type ed. LC 93-8879. (Nightingale Ser.). 251p. 1993. lib. bdg. 16.95 (*0-8161-5255-1*, G K Hall Lrg Type) Mac Lib Ref.

***Babson, Marian.** To Catch a Cat. 192p. 2000. 21.95 (*0-312-20918-5*, Minotaur) St Martin.

Babson, Marian. The Twelve Deaths of Christmas. 1996. mass mkt. 4.99 (*0-614-20526-3*) St Martin.

— 12 Deaths of Christmas, Vol. 1. 1996. mass mkt. 4.99 (*0-312-96039-5*) St Martin.

— Whiskers & Smoke. 1997. mass mkt. 5.99 (*0-312-96181-2*) St Martin.

Babson, Roger W. The Folly of Installment Buying. LC 75-39241. (Getting & Spending: The Consumer's Dilemma Ser.). 1976. reprint ed. 23.95 (*0-405-08006-9*) Ayer.

— Washington & the Revolutionists: A Characterization of Recovery Policies & of the People Who Are Giving Them Effect. LC 76-111812. (Essay Index Reprint Ser.). 1977. reprint ed. 23.95 (*0-8369-1642-5*) Ayer.

Babson, Stanley M., Jr. Fringe Benefits: The Depreciation, Obsolescence & Transience of Man: Cost, Strategies & Trends for Financial Managers, Personnel Directors & General Management. LC 74-13767. (Systems & Controls for Financial Management Ser.). 182p. reprint ed. 56.50 (*0-8357-9894-1*, 201259600083) Bks Demand.

Babson, Steve. Building the Union: Skilled Workers & Anglo-Gaelic Immigrants in the Rise of the UAW. LC 90-45947. (Class & Culture Ser.). 250p. (C). 1991. text 52.00 (*0-8135-1657-9*) Rutgers U Pr.

— Working Detroit. LC 86-5510. (Illus.). 264p. 1986. reprint ed. pap. 21.95 (*0-8143-1819-3*) Wayne St U Pr.

Babson, Steve, ed. Lean Work: Empowerment & Exploitation in the Global Auto Industry. 382p. (Orig.). 1995. pap. text 27.95 (*0-8143-2535-1*) Wayne St U Pr.

Babson, Steve & Nunez, Huberto. Confronting Change: Autoworkers & Lean Production in North America. 1998. pap. text 15.95 (*0-8143-2819-9*) Wayne St U Pr.

***Babson, Steven.** The Unfinished Struggle: Turning Points in American Labor: 1877 to Present. LC 99-35062. 224p. 1999. pap. 12.95 (*0-8476-8829-1*) Rowman.

— Unfinished Struggle: Turning Points in American Labor, 1877 to Present. LC 99-35062. 224p. 1999. 22.95 (*0-8476-8828-3*) Rowman.

Babson, Thomas W. The Actor's Choice: The Transition from Stage to Screen. LC 96-4350. 138p. (Orig.). 1996. pap. 15.95 (*0-435-07009-6*, 07009) Heinemann.

Babson-United Investment Staff, contrib. by. Successful Investing. 5th ed. 1991. 29.95 (*0-671-72835-0*) S&S Trade.

Babson, W. Warren, jt. auth. see Brooks, Laurence F.

Babst, Earl D. & Vander Velde, Lewis G., eds. Michigan & the Cleveland Era: Sketches of University of Michigan Staff Members & Alumni Who Served the Cleveland Administrations, 1885-89,1893-97. LC 70-179724. (Biography Index Reprint Ser.). 1977. reprint ed. 30.95 (*0-8369-8092-1*) Ayer.

Babstock, Ken. Mean. LC 99-235421. 96p. 1999. pap. text 14.95 (*0-88784-634-3*, Pub. by Hse1 of Anansi) Genl Dist Srvs.

***Babu.** Memoirs of a Whenwe: Colonial Life in Tanzania. (Illus.). 128p. 2000. 23.50 (*1-85776-483-8*, Pub. by Book Guild Ltd) Trans-Atl Phila.

Babu, A. Satish. Tourism Development in India. 1998. 58.00 (*81-7024-971-6*) Ashish Pub Hse.

***Babu, Abdul Rahman Mohamed, et al.** The Future That Works: Selected Writings of A. M. Babu. LC 00-33218, 2000. pap. write for info. (*0-86543-834-X*) Africa World.

Babu, Arvind, jt. auth. see Verma, Ram S.

Babu, Avadhanula V. Bhavanarayana Temples. xxiv, 192 p. (C). 1991. 94.00 (*81-85067-68-6*, Pub. by Sundeep Prak) S Asia.

Babu, B. Niranjan. Handbook of Vastu. (C). 1997. reprint ed. pap. 11.00 (*81-7476-175-6*, Pub. by UBS Pubs Dist) S Asia.

***Babu, B. R.** Globalization & the South Asian State. 1998. pap. 94.00 (*0-7855-7587-1*) St Mut.

***Babu, B. Ramesh, ed.** Globalization & the South Asian State. LC 98-907557. 1998. 28.00 (*81-7003-232-6*, Pub. by South Asian Pubs) S Asia.

Babu, B. Ramesh, ed. Minorities & the American Political System. (C). 1989. 21.00 (*81-7003-108-7*, Pub. by S Asia Pubs) S Asia.

Babu, D. Shyam. Nuclear Non-Proliferation: Towards a Universal NPT Regime. 1993. 27.50 (*81-220-0292-7*, Pub. by Konark Pubs Pvt Ltd) Advent Bks Div.

Babu, Gutti J. & Feigelson, Eric. Astrostatistics. (Illus.). 224p. 1996. ring bd. 72.95 (*0-412-98391-5*, Chap & Hall CRC) CRC Pr.

Babu, Gutti J. & Feigelson, Eric D. Statistical Challenges in Modern Astronomy II. LC 97-5785. 1997. 64.95 (*0-387-98203-5*) Spr-Verlag.

Babu, Gutti J., jt. auth. see Feigelson, Eric D.

Babu, M. Devendra, ed. see Rao, Hemlata.

Babu, S. V., et al, eds. Chemical-Mechanical Polishing--Fundamentals & Challenges Vol. 566: Materials Research Society Symposium Proceedings. LC 99-58801. 281p. 1999. text 70.00 (*1-55899-473-4*) Materials Res.

***Babu, Salma & Wilson, Amrit, eds.** The Future that Works: Selected Writings of A. M Babu. 280p. 2000. 84.95 (*0-86543-833-1*) Africa World.

Babu, Suresh C., et al. The Economics of Biotechnology: The Case of Biofertilizers in South Indian Agriculture. (Studies in Technology & Social Change: No. 7). 60p. (Orig.). (C). 1988. pap. 6.00 (*0-945271-10-7*) ISU-CIKARD.

Babu, Suresh P., ed. Trace Elements in Fuel: A Symposium Sponsored by the Division of Fuel Chemistry at the 166th Meeting of the American Chemical Society, Chicago, IL, August 30, 1973. LC 75-15522. (Advances in Chemistry Ser.: No. 141). (Illus.). 227p. 1975. reprint ed. pap. 70.40 (*0-608-06738-5*, 206693500009) Bks Demand.

Babula, William. St. John & the Seven Veils. 1991. 15.95 (*1-55972-071-9*, Birch Ln Pr) Carol Pub Group.

— St. John's Baptism. 256p. 1988. 14.95 (*0-8184-0461-2*) Carol Pub Group.

— St. John's Bestiary. 264p. 1994. 19.95 (*1-885173-01-6*) Write Way.

Babunakis, Michael. Budget Reform for Government: A Comprehensive Allocation & Management System (CAMS) LC 82-354. 231p. 1982. 55.00 (*0-89930-016-2*, BBG/, Quorum Bks) Greenwood.

— Budgets: An Analytical & Procedural Handbook for Government & Non-Profit Organizations. LC 76-5323. (Illus.). 257p. 1976. lib. bdg. 69.50 (*0-8371-8900-4*, BBP/, Greenwood Pr) Greenwood.

Baburin, Alexander. Winning Pawn Structures. 1998. pap. text 24.95 (*0-7134-8009-2*, Pub. by B T B) Branford.

Babuscio, Jack. We Speak for Ourselves. 224p. 1988. pap. 13.95 (*0-687-86470-4*) Abingdon.

— We Speak for Ourselves: Experiences in Homosexual Counselling. LC 77-78623. 160p. reprint ed. pap. 49.60 (*0-608-16823-8*, 202683700052) Bks Demand.

Babushkin, V. I., et al. Thermodynamics of Silicates. Frenkel, B. N. & Terentyev, V. A., trs. from RUS. (Illus.). 470p. 1984. 287.95 (*0-387-12750-X*) Spr-Verlag.

Babuska, Ivo, et al, eds. Adaptive Computational Methods for Partial Differential Equations. LC 83-51382. (Proceedings in Applied Mathematics Ser.: No. 16). xii, 251p. 1984. 35.50 (*0-89871-191-6*) Soc Indus-Appl Math.

— Modeling, Mesh Generation & Adaptive Numerical Methods for Partial Differential Equations. LC 95-17342. (IMA Volumes in Mathematics & Its Applications Ser.: Vol. 75). (Illus.). 502p. 1995. 79.95 (*0-387-94542-3*) Spr-Verlag.

Babuska, Ivo, jt. auth. see Szabo, Barna.

Babuska, Robert. Fuzzy Modeling for Control. LC 98-14966. 1998. 125.00 (*0-7923-8154-8*) Kluwer Academic.

Babuska, V. & Cara, M. Seismic Anisotropy in the Earth. (C). 1991. lib. bdg. 88.50 (*0-7923-1321-6*) Kluwer Academic.

Babuts, Nicolae. Baudelaire: At the Limits & Beyond. LC 97-20434. (Illus.). 184p. 1997. 34.50 (*0-87413-644-X*) U Delaware Pr.

— The Dynamics of the Metaphoric Field: A Cognitive View of Literature. LC 90-50931. 184p. 1992. 35.00 (*0-87413-424-2*) U Delaware Pr.

Baby, Raymond. Unique Hopewellian Mask-Headdress. (Illus.). 2p. 1956. reprint ed. pap. 0.50 (*0-318-00853-X*) Ohio Hist Soc.

Baby, Raymond & Potter, Martha. Exploration of the O.C. Voss Mound. (Illus.). 34p. 1966. pap. 3.50 (*0-318-00844-0*) Ohio Hist Soc.

Babyak, Brain. Test Title. 1979. mass mkt. 6.95 (*0-394-49279-X*) Random Bks Yng Read.

Babyak, Jolene. Birdman: The Many Faces of Robert Stroud. LC 94-94179. (Illus.). 352p. (Orig.). 1994. pap. 12.95 (*0-9618752-2-4*) Ariel Vamp Pr.

— Eyewitness on Alcatraz: Life on the Rock As Told by the Guards, Families & Prisoners. LC 88-70100. 1988. 11.95 (*0-9618752-0-8*) Ariel Vamp Pr.

— Reportage Uber Alcatraz: Die Geschichte der Gefangnisinsel erzaht von Fruheren Bewohnern. Chestnut, Renate, tr. from ENG. (GER., Illus.). 130p. (YA). 1991. pap. 11.95 (*0-9618752-1-6*) Ariel Vamp Pr.

Babylon, Donna. How to Dress a Naked Window. LC 96-51018. 96p. 1997. pap. 19.95 (*0-8019-8743-1*) Krause Pubns.

— More Splash Than Cash Decorating Ideas. (Illus.). 222p. 1999. pap. 15.95 (*0-9668227-0-6*) Windsor Oak Pubg.

Babylon, Donna, ed. see Singleton, Suzanne.

Babyn, Paul S., jt. auth. see Stringer, David A.

Babyonishev, Alexander, ed. see Pavlenkov, Victor.

Bac Vacher, Eugene De, see Vacher, Josephine A.

Baca & Harpring. Categories for the Description of Works of Art. 255p. 1995. pap. text 11.00 (*2-88449-237-2*) Gordon & Breach.

Baca, Albert R. Napoleon, Russia, & the Olympian Gods: The Olympic Service of the Armory Museum in the Kremlin - an Illustrated Guide to Greek Mythology. (Illus.). 80p. (Orig.). (C). 1996. pap. text 12.95 (*0-930437-01-2*) NewTEK Indust.

Baca, Albert R., ed. Epistola ad Mahomatem Two: Epistle to Mohammed Two. LC 89-12299. (American University Studies: Romance Languages & Literature: Ser. II, Vol. 127). 233p. (C). 1990. text 43.95 (*0-8204-1123-X*) P Lang Pubng.

Baca, Ana. Benito's Bizcochitos: Los Bizcochitos de Benito. Castilla, Julia M., tr. LC 99-24809. (Illus.). 32p. (J). (gr. k-4). 1999. 14.95 (*1-55885-264-6*, Pinata Bks) Arte Publico.

Baca, Elmo. Mabel's Santa Fe & Taos: Bohemian Legends (1900-1950) LC 99-16868. (Illus.). 184p. 1999. 29.95 (*0-87905-913-3*) Gibbs Smith Pub.

***Baca, Elmo.** Rio Grande High Style: High Style Furniture Craftsmen. (Illus.). 160p. 2000. reprint ed. pap. 24.95 (*0-87905-990-7*) Gibbs Smith Pub.

Baca, Elmo. Romance of the Mission. LC 95-45343. (Illus.). 128p. 1996. 37.95 (*0-87905-740-8*) Gibbs Smith Pub.

— Santa Fe Fantasy. LC 92-53959. (Illus.). 109p. 1993. 34.95 (*0-940666-14-6*) Clear Light.

Baca, Elmo & Van Deventer, M. J. Native American Style. LC 97-7802. (Illus.). 144p. 1998. 39.95 (*0-87905-789-0*) Gibbs Smith Pub.

Baca Fabiola, Cabeza De, see Cabeza de Baca, Fabiola.

Baca Gilbert, Fabiola C. De, see De Baca Gilbert, Fabiola C.

Baca, H. Rene, et al. Local Area Networks with Novell. 304p. 1994. mass mkt. 34.95 (*0-534-21516-5*) Course Tech.

— Local Area Networks with Novell. 273p. 1995. 30.00 (*0-534-21510-6*) Course Tech.

Baca, J. A. Fernandez, see Fernandez Baca, J. A.

Baca, Jimmy S. Black Mesa Poems. LC 89-31605. Vol. 676. 128p. 1989. pap. 9.95 (*0-8112-1102-9*, NDP676, Pub. by New Directions) Norton.

An Asterisk (*) at the beginning of an entry indicates that the title is appearing for the first time.

— Immigrants in Our Own Land: Poems. LC 79-9812. 64p. 1979. pap. 30.00 (*0-7837-8461-9*, 204926600010) Bks Demand.

— Immigrants in Our Own Land & Selected Early Poems. enl. ed. LC 90-6444. Vol. 701. 96p. 1990. reprint ed. pap. 8.95 (*0-8112-1145-2*, NDP701, Pub. by New Directions) Norton.

— Martin & Meditations on the South Valley. LC 87-10983. 128p. 1987. pap. 8.95 (*0-8112-1032-4*, NDP648, Pub. by New Directions) Norton.

— A Place to Stand. 2001. 23.00 (*0-8021-1602-7*, Grove) Grove-Atltic.

— What's Happening. LC 82-5089. 36p. (Orig.). 1999. pap. 5.95 (*0-915306-27-1*) Curbstone.

— Working in the Dark: Reflections of a Poet of the Barrio. LC 91-60328. (Illus.). 182p. (Orig.). 1993. 19.95 (*1-878610-08-2*) Red Crane Bks.

— Working in the Dark: Reflections of a Poet of the Barrio. LC 91-60328. (Illus.). 182p. (Orig.). 1994. pap. 11.95 (*1-878610-47-3*) Red Crane Bks.

***Baca, Jimmy Santiago.** Set This Book on Fire! Closing the Circle Trilogy. xiv, 70p. 1999. pap. 15.00 (*1-891812-23-8*, Pub. by Cedar Hill Pubns) Endeavor Bks.

Baca, Leonard & Cervantes, Hermes T. The Bilingual Special Education Interface. 3rd ed. LC 97-39969. 448p. (C). 1997. pap. 56.00 (*0-13-769373-7*) P-H.

Baca, Leonard M. & Almanza, Estella. Language Minority Students with Disabilities. (Exceptional Children at Risk Ser.). 56p. 1991. pap. text 9.00 (*0-86586-214-1*, P357) Coun Exc Child.

Baca, Murtha, tr. see Martines, Lauro.

Baca, Phil, ed. see Martinez, Elizabeth.

***Baca, Thomas E. & Florkowski, Tadeusz.** The Environmental Challenges of Nuclear Disarmament. 368p. 2000. pap. 80.00 (*0-7923-6203-9*) Kluwer Academic.

Baca, Zinn, jt. auth. see Eitzen.

***Baca-Zinn, Maxine, et al, eds.** Gender Through the Prism of Difference. 2nd ed. LC 99-25085. 526p. 1999. pap. 48.00 (*0-205-30225-4*) Allyn.

Baca-Zinn, Maxine & Eitzen, D. Stanley. Diversity in Families. 4th ed. 457p. (C). 1997. 75.00 (*0-673-99080-X*) Addson-Wesley Educ.

***Baca-Zinn, Maxine, et al.** Diversity in Families. 5th ed. LC 98-17565. 590p. (C). 1998. text 69.00 (*0-321-02279-3*) Allyn.

Baca-Zinn, Maxine, jt. auth. see Eitzen, D. Stanley.

Bacal, et al, trs. The Human Side of Human Beings: Spanish Translation. 2nd ed.Tr. of Lado Humano de los Seres Humanos. 4.00 (*1-885357-08-7*) Rational Isl.

Bacal, Azril, tr. see Jackins, Harvey.

Bacal, Glenn S., et al. Trademark Administration. 334p. 1990. ring bd. 71.95 (*0-939190-04-4*) Intl Trademark.

Bacal, Howard. Optimal Responsiveness: How Therapists Heal Their Patients. LC 97-24483. 416p. 1998. 55.00 (*0-7657-0114-6*) Aronson.

Bacal, Howard A. & Newman, Kenneth. Theories of Object Relations: Bridges to Self Psychology. (Personality, Psychopathology & Psychotherapy: Theoretical & Clinical Perspectives Ser.). 312p. 1990. text 47.50 (*0-231-06102-1*) Col U Pr.

Bacal, Robert. Performance Management. LC 98-41555. (Briefcase Books Ser.). (Illus.). xiv, 208 p. 1998. pap. 14.95 (*0-07-071866-0*) McGraw.

Bacall, Lauren. Lauren Bacall. 1985. mass mkt. 6.99 (*0-345-33321-7*) Ballantine Pub Grp.

— Now. 1996. mass mkt. 6.99 (*0-345-40232-4*) Ballantine Pub Grp.

— Now. LC 94-9819. (Illus.). 224p. 1994. 25.50 (*0-394-57412-5*) Knopf.

***Bacall-Zwirn, Alina & Stark, Jared.** No Common Place: The Holocaust Testimony of Alina Bacall-Zwirn. LC 99-12593. (Illus.). 124p. 1999. text 30.00 (*0-8032-1296-8*) U of Nebr Pr.

— No Common Place: The Holocaust Testimony of Alina Bacall-Zwirn. LC 99-12593. (Illus.). 124p. 2000. pap. 15.00 (*0-8032-6178-0*, Bison Books) U of Nebr Pr.

Bacalski, Robert, tr. see Daurella, Paco.

Bacaracco, Joseph L., Jr. & Ellsworth, Richard R. Leadership & the Quest for Integrity. 1989. text 24.95 (*0-07-103207-X*) McGraw.

Bacarella, Michael. Lincoln's Foreign Legion: The 39th New York Infantry, the Garibaldi Guard. LC 96-33042. (Illus.). 330p. 1996. 34.95 (*1-57249-016-0*) White Mane Pub.

Bacarisse, Pamela. The Necessary Dream: A Study of the Novels of Manuel Puig. LC 88-23243. 320p. (C). 1988. lib. bdg. 56.00 (*0-389-20809-4*, N8367) B&N Imports.

Bacarr, Jina. How to Succeed in a Japanese Company: Strategies for Bridging the Business & Culture Gap. LC 93-45559. 1994. pap. 10.95 (*0-8065-1509-0*, Citadel Pr) Carol Pub Group.

— How to Work for a Japanese Boss. 224p. 1992. 18.95 (*1-55972-119-7*, Birch Ln Pr) Carol Pub Group.

Bacarrere-Becane, Catherine. The Soviet Army in Search of a New Identity. Grant, Robert P., tr. from FRE. (European Viewpoint Ser.). 51p. (Orig.). 1991. pap. 9.00 (*0-9629930-1-8*) US CREST.

Bacarro, Joseph P., Sr. Getting Started in Human Resource Management: The Basics. (Illus.). 1996. pap. 30.00 (*0-939900-69-6*) Soc Human Resc Mgmt.

Bacarro, Joseph P. Worker's Compensation Insurance: The Survival Guide for Business. LC 92-19915. 450p. 1994. ring bd., suppl. ed. 45.00 (*0-685-74450-7*, MICHIE) LEXIS Pub.

— Worker's Compensation Insurance: The Survival Guide for Business, Issue 6. LC 92-19915. 88p. 1997. ring bd. 85.00 (*0-409-25676-5*, 82842-16, MICHIE) LEXIS Pub.

Bacay. Financial Service: You & Your Industry. 360p. 1998. pap. text 76.00 (*0-536-01986-X*) Pearson Custom.

Baccelli, Francois L., et al, eds. Quantitative Models in Parallel Systems, Vol. XVIII. LC 95-37495. (ESPRIT Basic Research Ser.). 298p. 1995. 62.00 (*3-540-60125-2*) Spr-Verlag.

***Baccelli, Francois L. & Bremaud, P.** Elements of Queueing Theory: Palm Martingale Calculus & Stochastic Recurrences. 2nd ed. (Applications of Mathematics Ser.: Vol. 26). (Illus.). x, 306p. 2000. 59.95 (*3-540-66088-7*) Spr-Verlag.

Baccelli, Francois L. & Bremaud, P. Palm Probabilities & Stationary Queues. (Lecture Notes in Statistics Ser.: Vol. 41). vii, 106p. 1987. 41.95 (*0-387-96514-9*) Spr-Verlag.

Baccelli, Francois L. & Bremaud, Pierre. Elements of Queueing Theory: Palm-Martingale Calculus & Stochastic Recurrences. LC 93-41286. 1994. 79.95 (*0-387-53347-8*) Spr-Verlag.

Baccelli, Francois L. & Fayolle, G., eds. Modelling & Performance Evaluation Methodology: Proceedings of the International Seminar, Paris, France, January 24-26, 1983. (Lecture Notes in Control & Information Sciences: Vol. 60). (ENG & FRE., Illus.). vii, 653p. 1984. 73.95 (*0-387-13288-0*) Spr-Verlag.

Baccetti, Baccio. Evolutionary Biology of Orthopteroid Insects. LC 87-3653. (Entomology & Acarlogy Ser.). 612p. 1987. text 132.95 (*0-470-20882-1*) P-H.

Baccetti, Gerald, jt. auth. see Hoffman, Michael K.

Bacchelli, Gabriella, et al, contrib. by. HarperCollins Italian-English, English-Italian Dictionary. LC 94-42350. (ENG & ITA.). 1440p. 1995. 25.00 (*0-06-275517-X*) HarpC.

Bacchetta. Economic Policy in Switzerland. LC 97-8644. 1997. text 79.95 (*0-312-17619-8*) St Martin.

Bacchi, Carol. Same Difference: Feminism & Sexual Difference. 1991. pap. text 19.95 (*0-04-442152-4*, Pub. by Allen & Unwin Pty) Paul & Co Pubs.

— Same Difference: Feminism & Sexual Difference. pap. 19.95 (*0-04-370189-2*) Paul & Co Pubs.

Bacchi, Carol L. Liberation Deferred? The Ideas of the English-Canadian Suffragists, 1877-1918. (Social History of Canada Ser.). 222p. 1983. pap. text 17.95 (*0-8020-6466-3*) U of Toronto Pr.

— The Politics of Affirmative Action: Women, Equality & Category Politics. 224p. 1996. 75.00 (*0-8039-8792-7*); pap. 24.95 (*0-8039-8793-5*) Sage.

Bacchi, Lee F. The Theology of Ordained Ministry in the Letters of Augustine of Hippo. (Catholic Scholars Press Ser.). 320p. 1998. pap. 54.95 (*1-57309-046-8*, Cath Scholar Pr) Intl Scholars.

Bacchi, Lee Francis. The Theology of Ordained Ministry in the Letters of Augustine of Hippo. (Catholic Scholars Press Ser.). 320p. 1997. 69.95 (*1-57309-047-6*, Cath Scholar Pr) Intl Scholars.

Bacchielli, Lidiano, jt. auth. see Di Vita, Antonino.

Bacchilega, Cristina. Postmodern Fairy Tales: Gender & Narrative Strategies. LC 96-49318. 218p. 1997. text 32.50 (*0-8122-3392-1*) U of Pa Pr.

— Postmodern Fairy Tales: Gender & Narrative Strategies. 1999. pap. text 14.95 (*0-8122-1683-0*) U of Pa Pr.

Bacchilega, Cristina, ed. see East-West Center Staff, et al.

Bacchilega, Cristina, jt. ed. see Roemer, Danielle M.

Bacchina, Anthony J. & Sonenshein, David A. A Practical Guide to Federal Evidence: Objections, Responses, Rules, & Practice Commentary. 3rd ed. LC 98-106575. 298p. 1997. 32.95 (*1-55681-557-3*) Natl Inst Trial Ad.

Bacchiocchi, Samuele. The Advent Hope for Human Hopelessness: A Theological Study of the Meaning of the Second Advent. 4th deluxe ed. (Biblical Perspectives Ser.: Vol. 6). 384p. (YA). 1994. pap. 20.00 (*1-930987-05-6*) Biblical.

— The Christian & Rock Music: A Study of Biblical Principles of Music. deluxe ed. (Biblical Perspectives Ser.: Vol. 15). (YA). 2000. pap. 20.00 (*1-930987-14-5*) Biblical.

— Christian Dress & Adornment. 2nd deluxe ed. (Biblical Perspectives Ser.: Vol. 10). 206p. (YA). 1995. pap. 20.00 (*1-930987-09-9*) Biblical.

— Divine Rest for Human Restlessness: A Theological Investigation of the Good News of the Sabbath. 9th rev. ed. (Biblical Perspectives Ser.: Vol. 2). 319p. (C). 1997. pap. 20.00 (*1-930987-01-3*) Biblical.

— From Sabbath to Sunday: A Historical Investigation of the Rise of Sunday Observance in Early Christianity. 17th ed. (Biblical Perspectives Ser.: Vol. 1). 372p. 2000. pap. 20.00 (*1-930987-00-5*) Biblical.

— God's Festivals in Scripture & History Pt. 1: The Spring Festivals. 2nd deluxe ed. (Biblical Perspectives Ser.: Vol. 11). (YA). 1995. pap. 20.00 (*1-930987-10-2*) Biblical.

— God's Festivals in Scripture & History Pt. 2: The Fall Festivals. deluxe ed. (Biblical Perspectives Ser.: Vol. 12). (YA). 1996. pap. 20.00 (*1-930987-11-0*) Biblical.

— Hal Lindsey's Prophetic Jigsaw Puzzle: Five Predictions That Failed! 6th deluxe ed. (Biblical Perspectives Ser.: Vol. 3). 150p. (YA). 1998. pap. 20.00 (*1-930987-02-1*) Biblical.

— Immortality or Resurrection? A Biblical Study on Human Nature & Destiny. deluxe ed. (Biblical Perspectives Ser.: Vol. 13). 304p. (YA). 1997. pap. 20.00 (*1-930987-12-9*) Biblical.

— Lord's Day Seminar in Four Audio Cassettes: A Biblical Study of the Validity & Value of the Sabbath. unabridged ed. (Biblical Perspectives Ser.: Vol. 1). 1995. audio 20.00 (*1-930987-25-0*, LDSA4) Biblical.

— The Sabbath in the New Testament: Answers to Questions. 3rd deluxe ed. (Biblical Perspectives Ser.: Vol. 5). 296p. (YA). 1995. pap. 20.00 (*1-930987-04-8*) Biblical.

— The Sabbath under Crossfire: A Biblical Analysis of Recent Sabbath/Sunday Developments. 2nd deluxe ed. (Biblical Perspectives Ser.: Vol. 14). 304p. (YA). 1998. pap. 20.00 (*1-930987-13-7*) Biblical.

— The Time of the Crucifixion & the Resurrection. 3rd deluxe ed. (Biblical Perspectives Ser.: Vol. 4). 195p. (YA). 1994. pap. 20.00 (*1-930987-03-X*) Biblical.

— Wine in the Bible: A Biblical Study on the Use of Alcoholic Beverages. abr. deluxe ed. (Biblical Perspectives Ser.: Vol. 16). 64p. (YA). 1989. pap. 5.00 (*1-930987-15-3*) Biblical.

— Wine in the Bible: A Biblical Study on the Use of Alcoholic Beverages. 3rd deluxe ed. (Biblical Perspectives Ser.: Vol. 8). (YA). 1989. pap. 20.00 (*1-930987-07-2*) Biblical.

— Women in the Church: A Biblical Study on the Role of Women in the Church. 4th deluxe ed. (Biblical Perspectives Ser.: Vol. 7). 295p. (YA). 1995. pap. 20.00 (*1-930987-06-4*) Biblical.

Bacchiocchi, Samuele, ed. The Marriage Covenant: A Biblical Study on Marriage, Divorce & Remarriage. 4th deluxe ed. (Biblical Perspectives Ser.: Vol. 9). 223p. (YA). 1991. pap. 20.00 (*1-930987-08-0*) Biblical.

***Bacchus, Alban & Bacchus, Carol.** Personal Wellness: How to Go the Distance. Savage, Margaret, ed. (Illus.). 336p. 1999. pap. 24.95 (*0-9674834-0-9*, Medawellcom) Engin Systms Sol.

Bacchus, Carol, jt. auth. see Bacchus, Alban.

Bacchus, Fahiem. Representing & Reasoning with Probabilistic Knowledge: A Logical Approach to Probabilities. 256p. 1990. 37.00 (*0-262-02317-2*, MIT Pr.

Bacchus, M. Kazim. Education As & for Legitimacy: Developments in West Indian Education Between 1846 & 1895. 384p. (C). 1995. pap. 29.95 (*0-88920-231-1*) W Laurier U Pr.

— Utilization, Misuse & Development of Human Resources in the Early West Indian Colonies. 480p. (C). 1990. pap. 19.95 (*0-88920-982-0*) W Laurier U Pr.

Bacchus, Noel C. Guyana Farewell. Rogalin, Elizabeth, ed. LC 96-102460. (Illus.). 214p. 1995. 22.50 (*0-9624192-1-4*) N Bacchus.

***Bacchus, Patricia Jones.** Passing. LC 99-94869. 384p. 1999. pap. 12.50 (*0-380-80585-5*, Avon Bks) Morrow Avon.

Bacchus, Tom. Rahm. (Orig.). 1995. mass mkt. 5.95 (*1-56333-315-5*, Badboy) Masquerade.

Bacchus, Wilfred A. Mission in Mufti: Brazil's Military Regimes, 1964-1985, 255. LC 89-26069. (Contributions in Political Science Ser.: No. 255). (Illus.). 184p. 1990. 52.95 (*0-313-25535-0*, BMM/, Greenwood Pr) Greenwood.

Bacchus, William I. The Price of American Foreign Policy: Congress, the Executive & Foreign Affairs Funding. LC 96-49106. 1997. 55.00 (*0-271-01692-2*); pap. 18.95 (*0-271-01693-0*) Pa St U Pr.

Bacchus, William L. Foreign Policy & the Bureaucratic Process: The State Department's Country Director System. LC 73-16759. 367p. reprint ed. pap. 113.80 (*0-7837-6778-1*, 204660800003) Bks Demand.

Bacchylides. The Poems & Fragments. Claverhouse, Richard, tr. & intro. by. xviii, 524p. 1967. reprint ed. 130.00 (*3-487-09858-X*) G Olms Pubs.

Bacci, Andrea, ed. see Nagel, Molli E.

Bacci, Antonio C., jt. auth. see Ottaviani, Alfredo C.

Bacci, Eros. Ecotoxicology of Organic Contaminants. LC 93-8849. 176p. 1993. lib. bdg. 95.00 (*1-56670-022-1*, L1022) Lewis Pubs.

Bacci, G. & Kerkut, G. A. Sex Determination. LC 65-17948. (International Series of Monographs on Pure & Applied Mathematics: Vol. 26). 1965. 138.00 (*0-08-011291-9*, Pub. by Pergamon Repr) Franklin.

***Bacci, Ingrid.** The Art of Effortless Living: Simple Techniques for Healing Mind, Body & Spirit. 2000. pap. write for info. (*0-9678507-0-3*) Vision Wrks NY.

Bacci, Massimo Livi, see Livi Bacci, Massimo.

***Bacciagaluppi, Guido.** The Modal Interpretation of Quantum Mechanics. 220p. (C). 2000. 64.95 (*0-521-62200-X*) Cambridge U Pr.

Baccini, P., ed. The Landfill. (Lecture Notes in Earth Sciences Ser.: Vol. 20). (Illus.). 439p. 1989. 72.95 (*0-387-50694-2*) Spr-Verlag.

Baccini, P. & Brunner, P. H. Metabolism of the Anthroposphere. (Illus.). xii, 157p. 1991. 94.95 (*0-387-53778-3*) Spr-Verlag.

Bacciotti, A. Local Stabilizability of Nonlinear Control System. 200p. (C). 1991. text 39.00 (*981-02-0713-1*) World Scientific Pub.

Bacco, Enrico, et al. Naples: An Early Guide. Gardinar, Eileen, ed. & tr. by. from ITA. LC 89-46222. (Historical Travel Ser.). (Illus.). 272p. (Orig.). 1991. pap. 17.50 (*0-934977-20-8*) Italica Pr.

Bacco, M. Di, see Di Bacco, M.

Baccus, Florence. It's Fun to Be Smart: A Parent's Guide to Stress-Free Early Learning from Birth Through Age Five. 281p. 1991. pap. 17.95 (*0-9649059-1-4*) LilliBooks.

— The Magic Flower. 30p. (J). (ps-8). 1991. 12.95 (*0-9649059-0-6*) LilliBooks.

Baccus, Janet N., compiled by. Roy Area, Pierce County Washington: An Historical Overview. (Illus.). 425p. 1995. pap. text 46.40 (*0-9629578-5-2*) Intl Long WA.

Baccus, Jim. I'm Thinking It Over: Spectator Columns, 1974-1984. LC 85-61953. 213p. (Orig.). 1985. pap. 8.95 (*0-911042-31-8*) NDSU Inst Reg.

Bace, Jill. Miller's Collecting Silver: The Facts at Your Fingertips. (Illus.). 176p. 1999. 19.95 (*1-84000-143-7*, Pub. by Millers Pubns) Antique Collect.

***Bace, Jill.** Miller's Collecting Silver: The Facts at Your Fingertips. (Illus.). 1999. 19.95 (*1-84000-231-X*) Mitchell Beazley.

***Bace, Rebecca Gurley.** Intrusion Detection. (Technology Ser.). 400p. 1999. pap. 50.00 (*1-57870-185-6*) New Riders Pub.

Bacescu, Mihai. Crustaceorum Catalogus, Pt. 7, Cumacea I. Gruner, H. E. & Holthuis, L. B., eds. 173p. 1988. pap. 94.00 (*90-5103-014-2*, Pub. by SPB Acad Pub) Balogh.

— Crustaceorum Catalogus, Pt. 8, Cumacea II. Gruner, H. E. & Holthuis, L. B., eds. 293p. 1992. pap. 141.00 (*90-5103-078-9*, Pub. by SPB Acad Pub) Balogh.

Bacetti, B. & Afzelius, B. The Biology of the Sperm Cell. (Monographs in Developmental Biology: Vol. 10). (Illus.). 250p. 1975. 110.50 (*3-8055-2204-5*) S Karger.

Bacevich, A. J. Diplomat in Khaki: Major General Frank Ross McCoy & American Foreign Policy, 1898-1949. LC 89-5749. (Modern War Studies). (Illus.). xii, 276p. 1989. 29.95 (*0-7006-0401-4*) U Pr of KS.

— The Pentomic Era: The U. S. Army Between Korea & Vietnam. 197p. (Orig.). (C). 1995. pap. text 30.00 (*0-7881-2150-2*) DIANE Pub.

Bacevich, A. J., et al. Supporting Peace: America's Role in an Israel-Syria Peace Agreement. LC 94-24119. 88p. 1994. pap. 14.95 (*0-944029-59-0*) Wash Inst NEP.

Bach. Distributed UNIX Systems. 1999. 48.00 (*0-13-216730-1*) P-H.

— Prealgebra, 2 vols. (C). Date not set. pap., teacher ed., suppl. ed. 58.76 (*0-395-71707-8*) HM.

— Prealgebra. (C). 1991. pap. text, student ed. 11.96 (*0-395-57080-8*) HM.

— Prealgebra, 2 vols. (C). 1994. pap., teacher ed., suppl. ed. 11.96 (*0-395-72391-4*) HM.

— Prealgebra, 2 vols. 2nd ed. (C). 1995. pap. text, student ed. 22.36 (*0-395-72389-2*) HM.

— The Twelve Healers. 111p. 1941. pap. 3.00 (*0-85207-041-1*, Pub. by C W Daniel) Natl Bk Netwk.

Bach & Dolkas. Product Evolution Mad World. 1997. text 29.95 (*0-07-002039-6*) McGraw.

Bach & McGinty. Little Fugue. 1990. 10.00 (*0-685-32109-6*, 77-189) Hansen Ed Mus.

Bach, Alexander. Indistinguishable Classical Particles, Vol. VIII. LC 96-37586. (Lecture Notes in Physics: No. M44). 157p. 1996. 46.00 (*3-540-62027-3*) Spr-Verlag.

Bach, Alice. The Most Delicious Camping Trip Ever. LC 76-2956. (Illus.). 48p. (J). (gr. k-3). 1976. 10.95 (*0-06-020338-2*) HarpC Child Bks.

— Women, Seduction, & Betrayal in Biblical Narrative. (Illus.). 310p. (C). 1997. text 69.95 (*0-521-47532-5*); pap. text 22.95 (*0-521-47560-0*) Cambridge U Pr.

Bach, Alice, ed. Ad Feminam. xiv, 242p. (Orig.). 1989. pap. 15.00 (*0-9624564-0-3*) Union Seminary.

— Women in the Hebrew Bible: A Reader. LC 98-3774. 566p. (C). 1999. 80.00 (*0-415-91560-0*); pap. 29.99 (*0-415-91561-9*) Routledge.

Bach, Alice, ed. see Buchan, Morag.

Bach, Barbara, jt. auth. see Krasemann, Stephen J.

Bach, Bob. Our Huckleberry Friend. 1987. pap. 14.95 (*0-8184-0450-7*, L Stuart) Carol Pub Group.

Bach, Bob & Mercer, Ginger. Our Huckleberry Friend: The Life, Times & Lyrics of Johnny Mercer. 256p. 1982. 24.95 (*0-8184-0331-4*) Carol Pub Group.

Bach, C., jt. auth. see Pilcox Cons Svc Staff.

Bach, C. P. Magnificat: Vocal Score Chorus. (ENG & LAT.). 128p. 1986. per. 7.95 (*0-7935-1129-1*, 50324490) H Leonard.

***Bach, Caleb Ives, text.** Elena Climent: Windows from Here to Then, 2000 Edition. (Illus.). 24p. 2000. pap. 15.00 (*1-930191-11-1*) M Martin Fine Art.

Bach, Caleb Ives, jt. text see Damian, Carol.

Bach, Carl P. Carl Philipp Emanuel Bach Edition Ser. I, Vol. 18: Seven Keyboard Sonatas (1714-1788): H.40, 43, 46-49, 51. Schulenberg, David et al, eds. 164p. 1995. text 125.00 (*0-19-324018-1*) OUP.

— Carl Philipp Emanuel Bach Edition Vol. 15: Series II: Keyboard Concerto No. 38 in C minor, H 448, Keyboard Concerto No. 39 in F major, H 454. Kulukundis, Elias N. et al, eds. (Illus.). 112p. 1989. 125.00 (*0-19-324001-7*) OUP.

— Carl Philipp Emanuel Bach Edition, Series I, Vol. 24: (Eight) Keyboard Sonatas (1763-6): H. 176-8, 189, 92, 211-13. Wiggery, Claudia et al, eds. 127p. 1990. 125.00 (*0-19-324008-4*) OUP.

— Carl Philipp Emanuel Bach Edition: Series II Vol. 23: Concertos & Sonatinas. Wiley, Paul G., II & Widgery, Claudia, eds. 92p. 1992. 105.00 (*0-19-324011-4*) OUP.

— Essay on the True Art of Playing Keyboard Instruments. Mitchell, William J., ed. (Illus.). (C). 1948. text 37.50 (*0-393-09716-1*) Norton.

— Great Keyboard Sonatas, 2 vols., 1. 384p. 1985. pap. 9.95 (*0-486-24853-4*) Dover.

— Great Keyboard Sonatas, 2 vols., 2. 384p. 1985. pap. 10.95 (*0-486-24854-2*) Dover.

— The Letters of C. P. E. Bach. Clark, Stephen L., ed. & tr. by. LC 97-5414. (Illus.). 370p. (C). 1997. text 98.00 (*0-19-816238-3*) OUP.

Bach, Cile M. & Tonelli, Edith A. Frank Mechau: Artist of Colorado. Yenawine, Philip, ed. (Illus.). 100p. 1981. 10.00 (*0-934324-02-6*) Aspen Art Mus.

***Bach, Daniel.** Regionalization in Africa: Integration & Disintegration. LC 99-15416. 1999. write for info. (*0-253-21340-1*) Ind U Pr.

Bach, Daniel J. & Leitner, Patricia J. Prealgebra: Mathematics for a Variable World, 2 vols. 2nd ed. 620p. (C). 1995. pap. text 58.76 (*0-395-71106-1*) HM.

***Bach, David.** Smart Couple Finish Rich: 9 Steps for a Rich Future for You & Your Partner. 2000. 25.00 (*0-7679-0483-4*) Broadway BDD.

Bach, David. Smart Women Finish Rich: Seven Steps to Achieving Financial Security & Funding Your Dreams. 256p. 1999. pap. 13.00 (*0-7679-0243-2*) Bantam.

— Smart Women Finish Rich: Seven Steps to Achieving Financial Security & Funding Your Dreams. LC 98-26769. (Illus.). 242p. 1998. 25.00 (*0-7679-0242-4*) Broadway BDD.

Bach, David, ed. Give What You Didn't Get: Steps Toward a Karmic Psychology. 96p. Date not set. pap. 13.95 (*1-57087-423-9*) Prof Pr NC.

B

Bach, Debi. Leveraging Design: Finance & the Kitchen & Bathroom Specialist. (Illus.). 106p. (Orig.). 1996. pap. text 30.00 (*1-887127-31-3*, 5301) Natl Kit Bath.

Bach, Edward. Collected Writings of Edward Bach: The Man Who Discovered the Bach Flower Remedies. Barnard, Julian, ed. 236p. (Orig.). 1997. pap. 12.50 (*1-85398-073-0*, Pub. by Ashgrove Pr) Words Distrib.

— Heal Thyself. 106p. 1931. pap. 5.00 (*0-85207-040-3*, Pub. by C W Daniel); pap. 5.00 (*0-85207-301-1*, Pub. by C W Daniel) Natl Bk Netwk.

— Heal Thyself. 25th ed. 56p. pap. 7.95 (*0-8464-4224-8*) Beekman Pubs.

— Heal Thyself: An Explanation of the Real Cause & Cure of Disease. 52p. 1985. pap. 4.50 (*0-89540-152-5*, SB-152) Sun Pub.

— The Twelve Healers. 23rd ed. 32p. pap. 5.95 (*0-8464-4306-6*) Beekman Pubs.

— The Twelve Healers & Other Remedies. 50p. 1988. pap. 3.50 (*0-89540-174-6*, SB-174) Sun Pub.

Bach, Edward & Wheeler, F. J. The Bach Flower Remedies. 2nd rev. ed. LC 97-29689. 248p. 1997. pap. 12.95 (*0-87983-869-8*, 38698K, Keats Publng) NTC Contemp Pub Co.

Bach, Egon W. UFOs from the Volcanoes. LC 93-1903. (Illus.). 400p. (Orig.). 1994. pap. 21.95 (*1-55779-062-0*) Hermitage Pubs.

Bach, Eleanor. Astrology from A to Z: An Illustrated Source Book. LC 91-17601. (Illus.). 224p. 1992. pap. 14.95 (*0-87131-674-9*) M Evans.

Bach, Emma, et al, eds. Quantification in Natural Languages, Vol. I. (Studies in Linguistics & Philosophy: No. 54). 1994. lib. bdg. write for info. (*0-7923-3128-1*, Pub. by Kluwer Academic) Kluwer Academic.

Bach, Emmon. Informal Lectures on Formal Semantics. LC 87-26719. (SUNY Series in Linguistics). 150p. (C). 1989. text 59.50 (*0-88706-771-9*); pap. text 19.95 (*0-88706-772-7*) State U NY Pr.

Bach, Emmon, et al, eds. Quantification in Natural Languages, Vol. II. (Studies in Linguistics & Philosophy: No. 54). 1995. lib. bdg. write for info. (*0-7923-3351-9*, Pub. by Kluwer Academic) Kluwer Academic.

— Quantification in Natural Languages, Vols. I & II. (Studies in Linguistics & Philosophy: Vol. 54). 740p. 1995. lib. bdg. 261.00 (*0-7923-3352-7*, Pub. by Kluwer Academic) Kluwer Academic.

Bach, Eric. Analytic Methods in the Analysis & Design of Number Theoretic Algorithms. (ACM Distinguished Dissontation Award Ser.). 50p. 1985. 17.50 (*0-262-02219-2*) MIT Pr.

Bach, Eric & Shallit, Jeffrey. Algorithmic Number Theory Vol. 1: Efficient Algorithms, Vol. 1. LC 95-25458. (Foundations of Computing Ser.). (Illus.). 496p. 1996. 57.50 (*0-262-02405-5*) MIT Pr.

Bach, Friedrich T., et al. Constantin Brancusi, 1876-1957. LC 95-33184. (Illus.). 412p. 1995. 60.00 (*0-262-02395-4*) Phila Mus Art.

Bach, Fritz H. & Auchincloss, Hugh, eds. Transplantation Immunology. LC 94-49601. 424p. 1995. 149.95 (*0-471-30448-4*) Wiley.

Bach, George L., jt. ed. see Anshen, Melvin.

Bach, George R. & Deutsch, Ronald M. Pairing. 1976. mass mkt. 4.95 (*0-380-00394-5*, Avon Bks) Morrow Avon.

Bach, George R. & Wyden, Peter. The Intimate Enemy: How to Fight Fair in Love & Marriage. 384p. 1976. mass mkt. 5.99 (*0-380-00392-9*, Avon Bks) Morrow Avon.

Bach, Gerhard. The Critical Response to Saul Bellow, 20. LC 95-22756. (Critical Responses in Arts & Letters Ser.: Vol. 20). 392p. 1995. lib. bdg. 65.00 (*0-313-28370-2*, Greenwood Pr) Greenwood.

Bach, Gerhard, ed. see Moogk, Peter.

Bach, H., et al, eds. The Properties of Optical Glass. 330p. 1995. 168.00 (*0-387-58357-2*) Spr-Verlag.

Bach, H. & Florant, J. Luftartsteknisk Ordbog Engelsk-Dansk. (DAN & ENG.). 255p. 1968. 49.95 (*0-7859-0801-3*, M1280) Fr & Eur.

Bach, Hans, ed. Low Thermal Expansion Glass Ceramics. (Schott Series on Glass & Glass Ceramics). (Illus.). 304p. 1996. 149.00 (*3-540-58598-2*) Spr-Verlag.

***Bach, Hans & Krause, Dieter, eds.** Analysis of the Composition & Structure of Glass & Glass Ceramics. LC 99-44342. (Schott Series on Glass & Glass Ceramics). (Illus.). xvi, 528p. 1999. 205.00 (*3-540-58610-5*) Spr-Verlag.

Bach, Hans & Krause, Dieter, eds. Thin Films on Glass. LC 97-29134. (Schott Series on Glass & Glass Ceramics). (Illus.). 420p. 1997. 169.00 (*3-540-58597-4*) Spr-Verlag.

Bach, Heidi. Eternal Medicine: The Spirit of True Mothering. large type ed. (Illus.). vii, 75p. 1996. write for info. (*0-9655548-8-0*) Studio Eight.

Bach, I. W., et al, eds. Carbon Dioxide: Current Views & Developments in Energy-Climate Research. 1983. text 248.50 (*90-277-1485-1*) Kluwer Academic.

Bach, Ira J. Chicago's Famous Buildings: A Photographic Guide to the City's Architectural Landmarks & Other Notable Buildings. enl. rev. ed. LC 79-23365. (Illus.). 1980. pap. 9.95 (*0-226-03396-1*) U Ch Pr.

Bach, Ira J. & Gray, Mary L. A Guide to Chicago's Public Sculpture. LC 82-20214. (Illus.). 404p. (C). 1983. 24.00 (*0-226-03398-8*); pap. 9.95 (*0-226-03399-6*) U Ch Pr.

Bach, Ira J. & Wolfson, Susan. Chicago on Foot: Walking Tours of Chicago's Architecture. 5th rev. ed. LC 93-39802. (Illus.). 360p. 1994. pap. 14.95 (*1-55652-209-6*) Chicago Review.

Bach, Ira J. & Wolfson, Susan. A Guide to Chicago's Historic Suburbs on Wheels & on Foot. LC 81-9516. (Illus.). xvi, 726p. 1981. 24.95 (*0-8040-0374-2*); pap. 14.95 (*0-8040-0384-X*) Swallow.

Bach, J. Sheep & Lambs May Safely Graze. 12p. 1997. per. 4.95 (*0-7935-8324-1*) H Leonard.

Bach, J. C. Music for Wind Band. LC 83-48727. (Collected Works of Johann Christian Bach). 225p. 1990. reprint ed. text 94.00 (*0-8240-6086-5*) Garland.

Bach, J. S. Two Part Inventions, 2 bks., Bk. I. (Quality Edition Classics Ser.). 32p. 1983. pap. text 2.95 (*0-935474-12-9*) Carousel Pubns Ltd.

— Two Part Inventions, 3 bks., Bk. II. (Quality Edition Classics Ser.). 32p. 1983. pap. 2.95 (*0-935474-13-7*) Carousel Pubns Ltd.

Bach, Jackie A. Brain Storms. LC 97-95287. (Illus.). 120p. 1998. pap. 10.95 (*0-9662403-1-6*) Bach Pub Co.

— Through the Bach Door. LC 96-94861. (Illus.). 99p. 1996. pap. 9.95 (*0-9662403-0-8*) Bach Pub Co.

Bach, Jean-Francois, ed. T-Cell-Directed Immunointervention. LC 92-49921. (Frontiers in Pharmacology & Therapeutics Ser.). (Illus.). 336p. 1993. 145.00 (*0-632-03105-0*) Blackwell Sci.

Bach, Jeff, jt. auth. see Mummert, John R.

Bach, Jenipher, ed. see Clayton, K. Marshall.

Bach, Johann Sebastian. Album of Various Works Transcribed for Guitar. Stang, Aaron, ed. 12p. (Orig.). (C). 1985. pap. text 6.95 (*0-7692-1303-0*, K04239) Wrner Bros.

— The Art of the Fugue & a Musical Offering. 192p. 1992. pap. 11.95 (*0-486-27006-8*) Dover.

***Bach, Johann Sebastian.** Bach: English & French Suites. (Illus.). 1999. 7.95 (*963-9155-61-6*) Kone Music.

— Bach: Individaul Piano Pieces II. 1999. pap. 7.95 (*963-9155-03-9*) Kone Music.

— Bach: Inventions & Little Preludes. (Illus.). 1999. 7.95 (*963-9155-62-4*) Kone Music.

— Bach: Piano Exercises I-IV. (Illus.). 1999. 7.95 (*963-9155-60-8*) Kone Music.

Bach, Johann Sebastian. Bach: Piano Solo, 4 Vols. (Urtext Editions for Piano). 1999. boxed set 59.95 (*963-9059-47-1*) Konemann.

— Bach: Spiritual Songs. 1999. pap. 7.95 (*963-9155-32-2*) Kone Music.

***Bach, Johann Sebastian.** Bach: Wohltemperiertes Klavier I-II. (Illus.). 1999. 7.95 (*963-9155-59-4*) Kone Music.

Bach, Johann Sebastian. Bach Cantata No. 192: Nun Danket Alle Gott. (Kalmus Vocal Ser.). (GER.). 28p. 1985. reprint ed. pap. 5.50 (*0-7692-1699-4*, K06632) Wrner Bros.

***Bach, Johann Sebastian.** Bach Composer: Concert Excercises. 1999. pap. 7.95 (*963-9155-00-4*) Kone Music.

— Bach Composer: Individaul Piano Pieces I. 1999. pap. 7.95 (*963-9155-02-0*) Kone Music.

— Bach Composer: The Art of the Fugue. 1999. pap. 7.95 (*963-9155-04-7*) Kone Music.

Bach, Johann Sebastian. Bach Masterpieces for Solo Piano. 1999. pap. text 9.95 (*0-486-40847-7*) Dover.

— Bach/Inventions & Sinfonias. rev. ed. Palmer, Willard A., ed. (Masterwork Editions). 116p. 1968. pap. text 11.95 (*0-88284-524-1*, 606) Alfred Pub.

— Bach/Inventions & Sinfonias. rev. ed. Palmer, Willard A., ed. (Masterwork Editions). 116p. 1992. text 50.00 (*0-88284-525-X*, 4867) Alfred Pub.

— The Calov Bible of J. S. Bach. Cox, Howard H., ed. LC 85-24557. (Studies in Musicology: No. 92). 470p. reprint ed. pap. 145.70 (*0-8357-1706-2*, 207054000001) Bks Demand.

— Cantata. Herz, Gerhard, ed. (Critical Scores Ser.: No. 4). (Illus.). (C). 1967. pap. text 15.50 (*0-393-09761-7*) Norton.

— Cantata. Herz, Gerhard, ed. (Critical Scores Ser.: No. 140). (Illus.). (C). 1972. pap. text 15.50 (*0-393-09555-X*) Norton.

— Christ Jesus Lay Enchained by Death. Bower, Alan, tr. 48p. 1994. pap. 7.00 (*0-9643394-0-4*) Stonehill MI.

— Christmas Oratorio in Full Score. 272p. 1992. pap. 14.95 (*0-486-27230-3*) Dover.

— Classic Bach. 32p. 1997. pap. 8.95 (*0-7935-8329-2*) H Leonard.

— Clavier-Buchlein Vor Wilhelm Friedemann Bach. (Music Reprint Ser.). 1979. reprint ed. 29.50 (*0-306-79558-2*) Da Capo.

— Complete Concertos for Two or More Harpsichords in Full Score. 240p. 1992. pap. 12.95 (*0-486-27136-6*) Dover.

— Complete Keyboard Transcription of Concertos by Baroque Composers. 128p. 1988. pap. text 9.95 (*0-486-25529-8*) Dover.

— Complete Preludes & Fugues for Organ. (Music Scores to Play & Study Ser.). 168p. 1985. reprint ed. pap. 10.95 (*0-486-24816-X*) Dover.

— Complete Suites for Unaccompanied Cello & Sonatas for Viola da Gamba. 112p. 1988. pap. 8.95 (*0-486-25641-3*) Dover.

— Domine Ad Adjuvandum: For Soprano, SATB Chorus & Orchestra. Charteris, Richard, ed. (Classical Music Ser.: Vol. 3). (LAT., Illus.). iii, 56p. 1998. pap. 24.00 (*1-56571-164-5*, CL003) PRB Prods.

***Bach, Johann Sebastian.** Domine Ad Adjuvandum: Vocal Score. Charteris, Richard, ed. (Classical Music Ser.: Vol. 3). (LAT.). 12p. 1999. pap. 3.00 (*1-56571-171-8*, CL003V) PRB Prods.

Bach, Johann Sebastian. Eleven Great Cantatas. 350p. 1976. pap. 16.95 (*0-486-23268-9*) Dover.

***Bach, Johann Sebastian.** English Suites. (Music Scores Ser.). 1998. pap. 7.98 (*963-8303-24-7*) Kone Music.

— Fifteen Two-Part Inventions for Piano. Czerny, Carl, ed. (Carl Fischer Music Library: No. L254). (Illus.). 1903. pap. 7.50 (*0-8258-0098-6*) Fischer Inc NY.

Bach, Johann Sebastian. The Four-Part Chorals of J. S. Bach. Terry, Charles S., ed. LC 74-27331. reprint ed. 49.50 (*0-404-12857-2*) AMS Pr.

***Bach, Johann Sebastian.** French Suites, 1 Vol. 1998. pap. text 7.98 (*963-8303-70-0*) Kone Music.

— Inventions, Little Preludes & Fughetta 1998. pap. text 7.98 (*963-8303-23-9*) Konemann.

Bach, Johann Sebastian. Italian Concerto, Chromatic Fantasia & Fugue & Other Works. 112p. 1987. pap. 8.95 (*0-486-25387-2*) Dover.

— J. S. Bach's Precepts & Principles for Playing the Thorough Bass or Accompanying in Four Parts. Poulin, Pamela L., tr. & comment by. (Early Music Ser.: Vol. 16). (Illus.). 140p. 1995. text 55.00 (*0-19-816225-1*) OUP.

— Johann Christoph Friedrich Bach: Four Early Sinfonias. Nolte, Ewald V., ed. (Recent Researches in Music of the Classic Era Ser.: Vol. RRC15). (Illus.). xv, 95p. 1982. pap. 40.00 (*0-89579-170-6*) A-R Eds.

— Johann Christoph Friedrich Bach: Four Late Sinfonias. Nolte, Ewald V., ed. (Recent Researches in Music of the Classic Era Ser.: Vol. RRC28). (Illus.). xxi, 112p. 1988. pap. 45.00 (*0-89579-226-5*) A-R Eds.

— Johann Sebastian Bach: Flute Solos with Guitar. 1990. 5.95 (*0-685-32142-8*, T510) Hansen Ed Mus.

— Keyboard Music. 312p. 1970. pap. 11.95 (*0-486-22360-4*) Dover.

— Laudate Pueri (E Major) For Soprano Solo & Orchestra. Charteris, Richard, ed. (Classical Music Ser.: Vol. 4). iv, 163p. 1998. pap. 54.00 (*1-56571-165-3*, CL004) PRB Prods.

***Bach, Johann Sebastian.** Laudate Pueri (G Major) For Soprano, Tenor & Orchestra. Charteris, Richard, ed. (Classical Music Ser.: Vol. 5). (Illus.). viii, 217p. 1999. pap. 58.00 (*1-56571-170-X*, CL005) PRB Prods.

— Magnifica. (Music Scores Ser.). (Illus.). 1998. pap. text 7.98 (*963-9059-21-8*) Kone Music.

Bach, Johann Sebastian. Magnificat in D the Six Motets in Full Score. 208p. 1995. text 13.95 (*0-486-28804-8*) Dover.

— Mass in B Minor in Full Score. 320p. pap. 13.95 (*0-486-25992-7*) Dover.

— Miscellaneous Keyboard Works: Toccatas, Fugues & Other Pieces. 304p. 1991. pap. 15.95 (*0-486-26681-8*) Dover.

— Organ Music. 357p. 1970. pap. 13.95 (*0-486-22359-0*) Dover.

***Bach, Johann Sebastian.** Piano Exercises I - Partita. 1998. pap. text 7.98 (*963-8303-91-3*) Kone Music.

Bach, Johann Sebastian. Prelude & Three Fugues for Five Viols. Ballinger, Peter, ed. (Viol Consort Ser.: No. 7). i, 50p. 1991. pap. text 12.00 (*1-56571-027-4*) PRB Prods.

— Prelude No. 24 & Fugue No. 8 for Three Viols. Ballinder, Peter, ed. (Viol Consort Ser.: No. 3). i, 17p. 1990. pap. text 8.00 (*1-56571-024-X*) PRB Prods.

— Ricercar & Aus Tiefer Noth for Six Viols. Ballinger, Peter, ed. (Viol Consort Ser.: No. 1). 39p. 1991. pap. text 12.00 (*1-56571-022-3*) PRB Prods.

— Ricercar for Two Harpsichords. Loring, Tamara, ed. (Early Keyboard Ser.: No. 1). ii, 28p. 1991. pap. text 12.00 (*1-56571-018-5*) PRB Prods.

— St. John Passion in Full Score. 60p. 1993. pap. 10.95 (*0-486-27755-0*) Dover.

***Bach, Johann Sebastian.** St. Matthew Passion, BWV 232, in Full Score. unabridged ed. 304p. 1999. pap. 6.95 (*0-486-40635-0*) Dover.

Bach, Johann Sebastian. St. Matthew Passion in Full Score. 304p. 1990. pap. 14.95 (*0-486-26257-X*) Dover.

Bach, Johann Sebastian. Selections from the Notebook for Anna Maqdalena Bach: For Piano. 4.95 (*0-7692-9015-9*) Wrner Bros.

Bach, Johann Sebastian. Seven Great Sacred Cantatas. 256p. 1985. pap. 14.95 (*0-486-24950-6*) Dover.

— Short Preludes & Fugues for Piano. (Carl Fischer Music Library: No. 516). 1914. pap. 6.95 (*0-8258-0132-X*, L516) Fischer Inc NY.

— The Six Brandenburg Concertos & the Four Orchestral Suites in Full Score. 273p. 1976. reprint ed. pap. 11.95 (*0-486-23376-6*) Dover.

— Six Brandenburg Concertos BWV 1046-1051. (Miniature Scores Ser.). pap. 4.95 (*0-486-29795-0*) Dover.

— Six Great Secular Cantatas in Full Score. 286p. (Orig.). 1980. pap. 13.95 (*0-486-23934-9*) Dover.

— Six Sonatas for Unaccompanied Violin. Auer, Leopold, ed. (Carl Fischer Music Library: No. 788). 1917. pap. 9.95 (*0-8258-0088-9*, L788) Fischer Inc NY.

***Bach, Johann Sebastian.** Step By Step, Twenty Piano Pieces. (Illus.). 1999. 7.95 (*963-9155-38-1*) Kone Music.

Bach, Johann Sebastian. Symphonies IV. Warburton, Ernest, ed. (Johann Christian Bach Ser.). 400p. 1989. text 94.00 (*0-8240-6078-4*) Garland.

Bach, Johann Sebastian, et al. 36 Hymn Preludes for Two Manuals & Pedal: Organ Preludes on Hymn Tunes by Bach, Goode, Held, Hodgson, Lovelace, Powell, Tindal. 116p. (Orig.). 1996. pap., student ed. 25.00 (*1-889079-09-X*) Darcey Pr.

Bach, Johann Sebastian. The Three Violin Concerti in Full Score. 64p. 1986. pap. 6.95 (*0-486-25124-1*) Dover.

— Toccatas, Fantasias, Passacaglia & Other Works for Organ. 176p. 1987. pap. 9.95 (*0-486-25403-8*) Dover.

***Bach, Johann Sebastian.** Toccaten, 1. 1998. pap. text 7.95 (*963-8303-94-8*) Kone Music.

Bach, Johann Sebastian. Two & Three Part Inventions (Fifteen Inventions & Fifteen Symphonies) Simon, Eric, ed. LC 68-11918. (Facsimile Series of Musical Manuscripts). (Orig.). 1969. pap. 8.95 (*0-486-21982-8*) Dover.

— Two & Three-Part Inventions for Piano. Czerny, Carl, ed. (Carl Fischer Music Library: No. 304). (ENG & GER.). 63p. 1903. pap. 7.95 (*0-8258-0102-8*, L 304) Fischer Inc NY.

Bach, Johann Sebastian. Two-Part Inventions (Zweistimmige Inventionen) 10.95 (*88-8291-558-1*) Warner Bros.

Bach, Johann Sebastian. The Well-Tempered Clavier: Books I & II Complete. (Music Ser.). 208p. (Orig.). 1984. pap. 9.95 (*0-486-24532-2*) Dover.

Bach, Johann Sebastian. Wohltemperiertes Klavier I. (GER.). 128p. pap. text 7.95 (*963-8303-02-6*) Konemann.

Bach, Johann Sebastian. Wohltemperiertes Klavier II. (GER.). 160p. pap. 7.95 (*963-8303-03-4*) Konemann.

— Works for Violin: The Complete Sonatas & Partitas for Unaccompanied Violin & the Six Sonatas for Violin & Clavier. 158p. 1978. pap. 9.95 (*0-486-23683-8*) Dover.

Bach, Johann Sebastian & Gounod, Charles F. Ave Maria. 4p. 1997. per. 4.95 (*0-7935-8323-3*) H Leonard.

Bach, Johann Sebastian, et al. Keyboard Transcriptions from the Bach Circle. Stinson, Russell, ed. (Recent Researches in Music of the Baroque Era Ser.: Vol. RRB69). xviii, 131p. 1992. pap. 50.00 (*0-89579-269-9*) A-R Eds.

Bach, John R. Guide to the Evaluation & Management of Neuromuscular Disease. LC 98-86791. (Illus.). 200p. 1998. pap. text 29.00 (*1-56053-301-3*) Hanley & Belfus.

Bach, John R., ed. Pulmonary Rehabilitation. 450p. 1995. text 71.95 (*1-56053-109-6*) Hanley & Belfus.

Bach, Johnathan P. Between Sovereignty & Integration: German Foreign Policy & National Identity. LC 98-29183. 1p. 1999. text 59.95 (*0-312-21922-9*) St Martin.

Bach, Jonathan, tr. see Gantzel, Klaus J. & Schwinghammer, Torsten.

Bach, Julie. Bicycling. LC 98-33682. (World of Sports Ser.). (Illus.). 32p. (YA). (gr. 4 up). 2000. lib. bdg. 22.60 (*1-887068-53-8*) Smart Apple.

— Kayaking. LC 98-33681. (World of Sports Ser.). (Illus.). 32p. (YA). (gr. 4 up). 2000. lib. bdg. 22.60 (*1-887068-56-2*) Smart Apple.

— Sailing. LC 98-36406. (World of Sports Ser.). (Illus.). 32p. (YA). (gr. 4 up). 2000. lib. bdg. 22.60 (*1-887068-58-9*) Smart Apple.

Bach, Julie S. Hillary Clinton. LC 93-15325. (Leading Ladies Ser.). (Illus.). (J). 1993. lib. bdg. 13.98 (*1-56239-221-2*) ABDO Pub Co.

— Imagine You Are a Pro Football Player. LC 98-26330. (Professional Sports Library). (J). 2002. lib. bdg. 21.35 (*1-57765-194-4*) ABDO Pub Co.

— Tipper Gore. LC 93-15326. (Leading Ladies Ser.). (Illus.). (J). 1993. lib. bdg. 13.98 (*1-56239-220-4*) ABDO Pub Co.

— Tom Cruise. LC 93-1981. (Reaching for the Stars Ser.). (Illus.). 32p. (J). (gr. 4 up). 1993. lib. bdg. 13.98 (*1-56239-228-X*) ABDO Pub Co.

Bach, Julie S. & Wallner, Rosemary. Imagine You Are a Pro Hockey Player. LC 98-26331. (Professional Sports Library). (J). 2002. lib. bdg. 21.35 (*1-57765-195-2*) ABDO Pub Co.

Bach, Julie S., ed. see Kincher, Jonni.

Bach, Kathleen K. Research Guide: Surrogate Motherhood. LC 87-37863. (Legal Research Guides Ser.: Vol. 6). vii, 43p. 1987. lib. bdg. 35.00 (*0-89941-588-1*, 305420) W S Hein.

Bach, Kent. Thought & Reference. 314p. 1988. text 75.00 (*0-19-824983-7*) OUP.

— Thought & Reference. 332p. 1994. reprint ed. pap. text 21.00 (*0-19-824077-5*) OUP.

Bach, Lana E. Single Again - Not by Choice, Vol. 1. 75p. 1997. pap. 9.95 (*0-9654209-1-4*, Bach Comm) S Bach.

Bach-Lareaux, Mary. Of Things Once Shared. Juaseaux, Xavier O., ed. 32p. (Orig.). 1990. pap. text 4.50 (*0-9623666-1-7*) Green Rvr Writers.

Bach, Lester. Called to Rebuild the Church: A Spiritual Commentary on the General Constitutions of the Secular Franciscan Order. LC 97-6550. (SFO Resource Library). 1997. pap. 16.95 (*0-8199-0976-9*) Franciscan Pr.

— Catch Me a Rainbow. rev. ed. (Illus.). 412p. 1991. pap. 10.00 (*0-944996-08-6*) Carlsons.

— Where Bible & Life Connect: Reflections of a Spiritual Director. 256p. (Orig.). 1995. pap. 17.95 (*0-8146-2247-X*) Liturgical Pr.

Bach, M. Analysis, Numerics & Applications of Differential & Integral Equations. 1997. lib. bdg. 79.95 (*0-582-31710-X*, Pub. by Addison-Wesley) Longman.

Bach, Marcus. I, Monty. LC 77-82232. 94p. 1992. reprint ed. pap. 12.95 (*0-87516-648-2*) DeVorss.

— Let Life Be Like This! 2nd ed. LC 63-22126. 199p. 1997. reprint ed. pap. 12.95 (*0-87516-707-1*) DeVorss.

— Major Religions of the World. 128p. 1984. reprint ed. pap. 5.95 (*0-87516-543-5*) DeVorss.

Bach, Marcus. The Power of Perception. LC 73-5535. 156p. 1983. pap. 8.95 (*0-87516-523-0*) DeVorss.

Bach, Marcus. Whispers from Wildlife. LC 90-61424. (Illus.). 108p. 1990. pap. 12.95 (*0-87516-628-8*) DeVorss.

— The World of Serendipity. 167p. 1980. reprint ed. pap. 8.95 (*0-87516-398-X*) DeVorss.

Bach, Marcus L. They Have Found a Faith. LC 74-134049. (Essay Index Reprint Ser.). 1977. reprint ed. 20.95 (*0-8369-2481-9*) Ayer.

***Bach, Marilyn L.** ShapeWalking: Six Easy Steps to a Healthier Life. LC 98-65831. (Illus.). 164p. 1998. pap. 14.95 (*0-9662975-0-4*) Heel to Toe.

— ShapeWalking: Six Easy Steps to a Healthier Life. Esser, Anna I., tr. LC 98-65831. 164p. 1998. 14.95 (*0-9662975-1-2*) Heel to Toe.

Bach, Mary. Termitas. Romo, Alberto, tr. (Books for Young Learners).Tr. of Termites. (SPA., Illus.). 16p. (J). (gr. k-2). 1999. pap. text 5.00 (*1-57274-291-7*) R Owen Pubs.

— Termites. (Books for Young Learners). (Illus.). 16p. (J). (gr. k-2). 1998. pap. text 5.00 (*1-57274-150-3*, A2520) R Owen Pubs.

Bach, Maurice J. The Design of the UNIX Operating System. 512p. (C). 1987. 70.00 (*0-13-201799-7*) P-H.

An Asterisk (*) at the beginning of an entry indicates that the title is appearing for the first time.

Bach, Michael K., ed. Immediate Hypersensitivity: Modern Concepts & Developments. LC 77-16503. (Immunology Ser.: No. 7). (Illus.). 872p. reprint ed. pap. 200.00 (*0-7837-0626-X*, 204097000019) Bks Demand.

Bach, Morcus. Because of Christmas. (Illus.). 192p. 1986. pap. 8.00 (*0-940581-00-0*) Fellowship Spirit.

***Bach, Nelson.** A History of Lewis Crittenden Back & His Children. LC 99-94831. 248p. 1999. write for info. (*1-57579-155-2*) Pine Hill Pr.

Bach Ngo & Zimmerman, Gloria. The Classic Cuisine of Vietnam. 256p. 1986. pap. 9.95 (*0-425-25833-5*, Plume) Dutton Plume.

Bach, Orville. Exploring the Yellowstone Back. 3rd ed. 1988. pap. 16.00 (*1-57805-002-2*, Pub. by Sierra) Random.

Bach, Orville, Jr. Exploring the Yellowstone Backcountry. rev. ed. LC 91-35111. (Totebook Ser.). (Illus.). 256p. 1992. reprint ed. pap. 16.00 (*0-87156-628-1*, Pub. by Sierra) Random.

Bach, Othello. The Biggest Sneeze LC 85-7790. (Funny Bone Poems Ser.). (Illus.). 31 p. 1986. write for info. (*0-89845-379-8*, Caedmon) HarperAudio.

***Bach, Othello.** How to Write a Great Story: A Fiction Writer's Handbook. LC 99-46823. 96p. 2000. pap. 12.95 (*0-929765-73-7*) Seven Locks Pr.

Bach, P. H., et al. Biotechnology Applications of Microinjection, Microscopic Imaging & Fluorescence. LC 93-10726. (Illus.). 266p. (C). 1993. text 89.50 (*0-306-44497-6*, Kluwer Plenum) Kluwer Academic.

Bach, P. H., ed. see International Symposium on Nephrotoxicity (1981: U.

Bach, Penny B. Public Art in Philadelphia. LC 92-11735. (Illus.). 288p. (C). 1992. 29.95 (*0-87722-822-1*) Temple U Pr.

Bach, Penny B., et al. Art for the Public: New Collaborations. Carr, Eileen, ed. (Illus.). 56p. (Orig.). 1988. pap. text 12.95 (*0-937809-03-9*) Dayton Art.

Bach, Peter. Collector's Treasury of Antique Slot Machines: A Primary Source Book. Post, Dan, ed. (Illus.). 480p. 1980. 22.95 (*0-934422-26-5*, BKS-100261) Mead Pub Corp.

Bach, Peter, ed. Collector's Treasury of Antique Slot Machines from Contemporary Advertising 1925-1950. LC 80-82463. (Illus.). 480p. 1980. 28.95 (*0-911160-61-2*) Post Group.

Bach, Peter H., et al, eds. Nephrotoxicity: Mechanisms, Early Diagnosis & Therapeutic Management. 600p. 1991. text 215.00 (*0-8247-8366-2*) Dekker.

Bach, Peter H. & Baker, John R. Histochemical & Immunohistochemical Techniques: Applications to Pharmacology & Toxicology. (Illus.). 256p. (C). (gr. 13). 1991. text 104.00 (*0-412-35100-5*, A5576) Chapman & Hall.

Bach, Peter H. & Lock, E. A., eds. Nephrotoxicity: In Vitro & in Vivo, Animals to Man. (Illus.). 788p. 1989. 145.00 (*0-306-43153-X*, Plenum Trade) Perseus Pubng.

— Nephrotoxicity in the Experimental & Clinical Situation, Pt. 1. (Developments in Nephrology Ser.). (C). 1987. lib. bdg. 179.50 (*0-89838-977-1*) Kluwer Academic.

— Nephrotoxicity in the Experimental & Clinical Situation, Pt. 2. (Developments in Nephrology Ser.). (C). 1987. text 195.50 (*0-89838-980-1*) Kluwer Academic.

Bach, Pieter, jt. ed. see Shep, R. L.

Bach, Quintin V. Soviet Economic Assistance to the Less Developed Countries: A Statistical Analysis. (Illus.). 200p. 1988. 65.00 (*0-19-828572-8*) OUP.

Bach, R. O. & Gallicchio, V. S., eds. Lithium & Cell Physiology. (Illus.). 200p. 1990. 125.00 (*0-387-97128-9*) Spr-Verlag.

Bach, Rebecca Ann. Colonial Transformations: The Cultural Production of the New Atl. text. write for info. (*0-312-23099-0*) St Martin.

Bach, Ricardo, ed. Lithium: Current Applications in Science, Medicine & Technology. LC 84-22210. 442p. 1985. text 100.00 (*0-471-80073-2*) Krieger.

***Bach, Ricardo O.** Buddy. 194p. 1999. pap. 13.95 (*0-7414-0122-3*) Buy Books.

Bach, Richard. Biplane. 176p. 1990. mass mkt. 7.50 (*0-440-20657-X*) Dell.

— The Bridge Across Forever: A True Love Story. 400p. 1989. mass mkt. 7.50 (*0-440-10826-8*) Dell.

— A Gift of Wings. 304p. 1989. mass mkt. 6.99 (*0-440-20432-1*) Dell.

— Illusions: The Adventures of a Reluctant Messiah. 128p. 1977. 22.95 (*0-385-28501-9*) Delacorte.

— Illusions: The Adventures of a Reluctant Messiah. 128p. 1998. pap. 11.95 (*0-385-31925-8*) Delacorte.

Bach, Richard. Illusions: The Adventures of a Reluctant Messiah. 192p. 1989. mass mkt. 6.99 (*0-440-20488-7*) Dell.

Bach, Richard. Jonathan L Seagull. LC 75-119617. (Illus.). 128p. (YA). (gr. 7 up). 1976. mass mkt. 5.99 (*0-380-01286-3*, Avon Bks) Morrow Avon.

Bach, Richard. Jonathan le Goeland. (French Audiobks.).Tr. of Jonathan Livingston Seagull. (FRE.). pap., boxed set 14.95 incl. audio (*2-921997-92-4*, Pub. by Coffragants) Penton Overseas.

Bach, Richard. Jonathan Livingston Seagull. LC 75-119617. (Illus.). 93p. (J). 1970. 20.00 (*0-02-504540-7*) Macmillan.

— Jonathan Livingston Seagull. (Illus.). 1970. 20.00 (*0-684-84684-5*) S&S Trade.

— Jonathan Livingston Seagull. (Illus.). 94p. 1991. reprint ed. lib. bdg. 21.95 (*0-89966-803-8*) Buccaneer Bks.

— Jonathan Livingston Seagull: A Story. (J). 1973. 11.09 (*0-606-03682-2*, Pub. by Turtleback) Demco.

— Jonathan Livingston Seagull: 20th Anniversary Edition. rev. ed. (Illus.). 96p. 1990. 25.00 (*0-02-504541-5*) Macmillan.

— Juan Salvador Gaviota: Bolsillo. 1997. pap. text 8.98 (*950-15-0579-0*) Vergara.

— Nothing by Chance. 240p. 1990. mass mkt. 7.50 (*0-440-20656-1*) Dell.

— Nothing by Chance: A Gypsy Pilot's Adventures in Modern America. (Illus.). 194p. 1983. text 18.95 (*0-02-504690-X*) Macmillan.

— One. 400p. 1989. mass mkt. 7.50 (*0-440-20562-X*) Dell.

***Bach, Richard.** Out of My Mind: The Discovery of Saunders-Vixen. 112p. 2000. pap. 12.95 (*0-385-33490-7*, Delta Trade) Dell.

Bach, Richard. Out of My Mind: The Discovery of Saunders-Vixen. LC 99-22728. (Illus.). 112p. 1999. 18.00 (*0-688-17296-2*, Wm Morrow) Morrow Avon.

— Running from Safety. 368p. 1995. reprint ed. pap. 12.95 (*0-385-31528-7*, Delta Trade) Dell.

— Running from Safety: An Adventure of the Spirit. large type ed. LC 95-2008. (Large Print Bks.). 1995. 23.95 (*1-56895-174-4*) Wheeler Pub.

— Running from Safety: International Edition. 288p. 1995. mass mkt. 6.99 (*0-440-29543-2*) Dell.

— Stranger to the Ground. 192p. 1990. mass mkt. 7.99 (*0-440-20658-8*) Dell.

— Stranger to the Ground. (Illus.). 192p. 1983. 17.95 (*0-02-504520-2*) Macmillan.

— There's No Such Place As Far Away. (Illus.). 48p. 1990. 19.95 (*0-385-30211-8*) Delacorte.

— There's No Such Place As Far Away. 48p. 1998. pap. 9.95 (*0-385-31927-4*) Delacorte.

— Three Books by Richard Bach. 1990. boxed set 12.40 (*0-440-36006-4*) Dell.

Bach, Robert, tr. Object-Oriented Programming in Oberon-2. 2nd ed. 1995. write for info. (*0-387-60062-0*) Spr-Verlag.

Bach, Robert, tr. see Mossenbock, Hanspeter.

Bach, Robert, tr. see Strobel, S.

Bach, Robert, tr. see Strobel, Stefan & Uhl, Thomas.

Bach, Robert L., jt. auth. see National Board of the Changing Relations Project S.

Bach, Robert L., jt. auth. see Portes, Alejandro.

Bach, Ruth. Easy German Exercises: Practice for Beginners. LC 98-18308. (Easy Exercises Ser.). (GER., Illus.). 96p. 1996. pap. 7.95 (*0-8442-2531-2*, Passprt Bks) NTC Contemp Pub Co.

***Bach, Sheldon.** The Language of Perversion & the Language of Love. LC 94-7906. 224p. 1999. pap. 40.00 (*0-7657-0230-4*) Aronson.

Bach, Sheldon. Narcissistic States & the Therapeutic Process. LC 85-1440. 250p. 1985. 45.00 (*0-87668-893-8*) Aronson.

Bach, Shirley J., jt. auth. see Binkin, Martin.

Bach, Stanley J. & Smith, Steven S. Managing Uncertainty in the House of Representatives: Adaptation & Innovation in Special Rules. 154p. 1988. 28.95 (*0-8157-0742-8*); pap. 10.95 (*0-8157-0741-X*) Brookings.

***Bach, Stephen, et al, eds.** Public Service Employment Relations in Europe: Transformation, Modernization or Inertia? LC 99-10532. 288p. (C). 1999. text. write for info. (*0-415-20342-2*) Routledge.

Bach, Stephen E. Cumulative Subject & Author Indexes of Dr. Dobb's Journal, 1982-1994. 160p. (Orig.). 1994. pap. 23.95 (*1-882850-07-6*) Springtree Partners.

— Public Service Employment Relations in Europe: Transformation, Modernization or Inertia? LC 99-10532. (Routledge in Employment Relations Studies). 1999. pap. write for info. (*0-415-20343-0*) Routledge.

Bach, Stephen E., jt. auth. see Sisson, Keith.

Bach, Steve & O'Reilly, John. Strictly Strings Pop-Style Solos, Violin. 1997. pap. 14.95 incl. audio compact disk (*0-88284-803-8*) Alfred Pub.

— Strictly Strings Pop-Style Solos/Cello. 16p. 1997. pap. 4.95 (*0-7390-0006-3*, 17452); pap. 14.95 incl. audio compact disk (*0-7390-0007-1*, 17450) Alfred Pub.

— Strictly Strings Pop-Style Solos/Violin. 16p. 1997. pap. 4.95 (*0-7390-0005-5*, 17446) Alfred Pub.

— Yamaha Pop-Style Solos, E-Flat Alto Saxophone/Baritone Saxophone, Bk. 1. (Yamaha Pop-Style Solos Ser.). 1995. pap. 14.95 incl. audio compact disk (*0-88284-801-1*) Alfred Pub.

Bach, Steve, et al. Yamaha Pop-Style Solos/Alto Saxophone/Baritone Saxophone. (Yamaha Pop-Style Solos Ser.). 1994. pap. 4.50 (*0-7390-0152-3*, 14603) Alfred Pub.

— Yamaha Pop-Style Solos/Clarinet/Bass Clarinet. (Yamaha Pop-Style Solos Ser.). 1994. pap. 4.50 (*0-7390-0151-5*, 14602) Alfred Pub.

— Yamaha Pop-Style Solos/Clarinet/Bass Clarinet. (Yamaha Pop-Style Solos Ser.). 1995. 14.95 incl. audio compact disk (*0-7390-0143-4*, 14611) Alfred Pub.

— Yamaha Pop-Style Solos/Flute/Oboe/Mallet Percussion. (Yamaha Pop-Style Solos Ser.). 1994. pap. 4.50 (*0-7390-0150-7*, 14601) Alfred Pub.

— Yamaha Pop-Style Solos/Flute/Oboe/Mallett. (Yamaha Pop-Style Solos Ser.). 1995. 14.95 incl. audio compact disk (*0-7390-0142-6*, 14610) Alfred Pub.

— Yamaha Pop-Style Solos/French Horn. (Yamaha Pop-Style Solos Ser.). 1995. pap. 14.95 incl. audio compact disk (*0-7390-0147-7*, 14615) Alfred Pub.

— Yamaha Pop-Style Solos/Horn in F. (Yamaha Pop-Style Solos Ser.). 1994. pap. 4.50 (*0-7390-0155-8*, 14606) Alfred Pub.

— Yamaha Pop-Style Solos/Teacher Piano Accompaniment. (Yamaha Pop-Style Solos Ser.). 1994. pap. 5.95 (*0-7390-0141-8*, 14609) Alfred Pub.

— Yamaha Pop-Style Solos/Tenor Sax. (Yamaha Pop-Style Solos Ser.). 1995. pap. 14.95 incl. audio compact disk (*0-7390-0145-0*, 14613) Alfred Pub.

— Yamaha Pop-Style Solos/Tenor Saxophone. (Yamaha Pop-Style Solos Ser.). 1994. pap. 4.50 (*0-7390-0153-1*, 14604) Alfred Pub.

— Yamaha Pop-Style Solos/Trombone/Baritone B. C./Bassoon. (Yamaha Pop-Style Solos Ser.). 1994. pap. 4.50 (*0-7390-0156-6*, 14607) Alfred Pub.

— Yamaha Pop-Style Solos/Trombone/Baritone B. C./Bassoon. (Yamaha Pop-Style Solos Ser.). 1995. pap. 14.95 incl. audio compact disk (*0-7390-0148-5*, 14616) Alfred Pub.

— Yamaha Pop-Style Solos/Trumpet/Baritone T. C. (Yamaha Pop-Style Solos Ser.). 1994. pap. 4.50 (*0-7390-0154-X*, 14605) Alfred Pub.

— Yamaha Pop-Style Solos/Trumpet/Baritone T. C. (Yamaha Pop-Style Solos Ser.). 1995. pap. 14.95 incl. audio compact disk (*0-7390-0146-9*, 14614) Alfred Pub.

— Yamaha Pop-Style Solos/Tuba. (Yamaha Pop-Style Solos Ser.). 1994. pap. 4.50 (*0-7390-0157-4*, 14608) Alfred Pub.

— Yamaha Pop-Style Solos/Tuba. (Yamaha Pop-Style Solos Ser.). 1995. pap. 14.95 incl. audio compact disk (*0-7390-0149-3*, 14617) Alfred Pub.

Bach, Steven. Final Cut: Art, Money & Ego in the Making of the Film That Sank United Artists. LC 99-34001. 432p. 1999. reprint ed. pap. 14.95 (*1-55704-374-4*, Pub. by Newmarket) Norton.

— Final Cut: Dreams & Disasters in the Making of Heaven's Gate. 1986. 8.95 (*0-425-25845-9*, Plume) Dutton Plume.

— Final Cut: Dreams & Disasters in the Making of Heaven's Gate. 1994. pap. 13.00 (*0-688-13307-X*, Quil) HarperTrade.

— Final Cut: Dreams & Disasters in the Making of Heaven's Gate. LC 85-4983. (Illus.). 420p. 1985. 19.95 (*0-688-04382-8*, Wm Morrow) Morrow Avon.

***Bach, Steven.** Marlene Dietrich: Life & Legend. (Illus.). 672p. 2000. pap. text 18.00 (*0-306-80934-6*) Da Capo.

— See No Evil. write for info. (*0-375-40400-7*) Knopf.

Bach, Steven A. I Found Life Through Suicide. LC 96-97019. (Illus.). 130p. 1996. pap. 9.95 (*0-9654209-0-6*) S Bach.

Bach, Susan. Life Paints Its Own Span: On the Significance of Spontaneous Paintings by Severly Ill Children. 213p. 1995. pap. 35.95 (*3-85630-516-5*) Continuum.

Bach, Suzanne. Assuming the Guise: African Masks Considered & Reconsidered. LC 91-50617. (Illus.). 80p. (Orig.). 1991. pap. text 14.95 (*0-913697-13-3*) Williams Art.

Bach, Victor. Housing at Risk: Expiring Federal Subsidies: Summary Characteristics of the At-Risk Inventory of HUD-Subsidized, Private Rental Projects in New York City. 37p. 1988. pap. text 5.00 (*0-88156-068-5*) Comm Serv Soc NY.

Bach, Victor & Steinhagen, Renee. Alternatives to the Welfare Hotel: Using Emergency Assistance to Provide Decent Transitional Shelter for Homeless Families. LC 87-402526. (Illus.). 54p. (Orig.). 1987. pap. text 7.00 (*0-88156-047-2*) Comm Serv Soc NY.

Bach, Victor & West, Sherece Y. Housing on the Block: Disinvestment & Abandonment Risks in New York City Neighborhoods. 125p. 1993. 12.00 (*0-88156-154-1*) Comm Serv Soc NY.

Bach, Wilfrid. Our Threatened Climate. 1983. text 135.00 (*90-277-1680-3*) Kluwer Academic.

Bach, Wilfrid, ed. Interactions of Food & Climate. 1981. pap. text 85.50 (*90-277-1354-5*); lib. bdg. 158.50 (*90-277-1353-7*) Kluwer Academic.

Bach, Wilfrid, et al, eds. Interactions of Energy & Climate. 568p. 1980. pap. text 81.00 (*90-277-1177-1*); lib. bdg. 146.00 (*90-277-1179-8*) Kluwer Academic.

— Renewable Energy Prospects: Proceedings of the Conference on Non-Fossil Fuel & Non-Nuclear Fuel Energy Strategies, Honolulu, USS, January 1979. 340p. 1980. 29.00 (*0-08-024252-9*, Pergamon Pr) Elsevier.

Bach-y-Rita, Paul. Nonsynaptic Diffusion Neurotransmission & Late Brain Reorganization. LC 95-2187. 232p. 1995. pap. 69.95 (*0-939957-77-9*) Demos Medical.

Bach-Y-Rita, Paul, jt. auth. see Levy, Joseph V.

Bacha. Social Change in Brazil: The Incomplete Transition. LC 88-19895. 355p. (Orig.). 1989. pap. 12.95 (*0-8263-1111-3*) U of NM Pr.

Bacha, Andy, ed. & contrib. by see Myers, Walter Dean.

Bacha, Edmar L., ed. Economics in a Changing World Vol. 4: Development Trade & the Environment. 310p. 1994. text 79.95 (*0-312-10738-2*) St Martin.

— Savings & Investment Requirements for the Resumption of Growth in Latin America. 222p. (C). 1993. pap. text 18.50 (*0-940602-61-X*) IADB.

Bacha, Edmar L. & Diaz Alejandro, Carlos F. International Financial Intermediation: A Long & Topical View. LC 82-3096. (Essays in International Finance Ser.: No. 147). 142p. 1982. pap. text 10.00 (*0-88165-054-4*) Princeton U Int Finan Econ.

Bacha, John D., et al, eds. Petroleum-Derived Carbons. LC 86-7894. (ACS Symposium Ser.: No. 303). (Illus.). x, 416p. 1986. 82.95 (*0-8412-0964-2*, PA 410) Am Chemical.

— Petroleum-Derived Carbons. LC 86-7894. (ACS Symposium Ser.: Vol. 303). 416p. 1986. reprint ed. pap. 129.00 (*0-608-03849-0*, 206429600008) Bks Demand.

Bacha, William J., Jr. & Wood, Linda M. Color Atlas of Veterinary Histology. LC 89-14516. (Illus.). 269p. 1990. text 46.00 (*0-8121-1303-9*) Lppncott W & W.

Bachan, Lisa. Ultrasound Scanning Guide. (Orig.). 1996. pap. write for info. (*0-9651644-0-3*) Chrlston Ultrasnd.

Bachand, Danyelle. What Time Is It? It's My Time to Reach Success! 136p. 1996. pap. text, per. 19.95 (*0-7872-3018-9*) Kendall-Hunt.

Bachand, Robert G. Coastal Atlantic Sea Creatures: A Natural History. O'Connor, Michelle, ed. (Illus.). 194p. (Orig.). 1994. pap. 16.95 (*0-9616399-5-4*) Sea Sports Pubns.

Bachand, Stephen. Christmas for Kristi. (Booktime Buddies Ser.). (Illus.). (J). (ps-2). 1999. pap. 5.00 (*1-928972-02-0*) Critter Pubns.

***Bachand, Stephen.** Floater the Frog. (Booktime Buddies Ser.). (Illus.). (J). (ps-2). 1999. pap. 5.00 (*1-928972-04-7*) Critter Pubns.

Bachand, Stephen. My Friend Penguin. (Booktime Buddies Ser.). (Illus.). (J). (ps-2). 1999. 4.25 (*1-928972-01-2*) Critter Pubns.

— Patch in I Want to Be a Pilot. (Booktime Buddies Ser.). (Illus.). (J). (ps-2). 1999. 4.25 (*1-928972-00-4*) Critter Pubns.

***Bachand, Stephen.** Velma the Lost Calf. (Booktime Buddies Ser.: Vol. 4). (Illus.). (J). (ps-2). 1999. pap. 5.00 (*1-928972-03-9*) Critter Pubns.

— Where's Floater? (Booktime Buddies Ser.). (Illus.). (J). (ps-2). 2000. pap. 5.00 (*1-928972-05-5*) Critter Pubns.

Bachann. Intelligent Systems. (C). 1995. pap. text 33.56 (*0-395-69404-3*) HM.

Bachant, Janet Lee, jt. auth. see Adler, Elliot.

Bachar, Jacqueline L. Life on the Ohio Frontier: A Collection of Letters from Mary Lott to Deacon John Phillips, 1826-1846. LC 94-77122. (Illus.). 146p. 1994. 30.00 (*1-886934-00-2*) Intl Forum.

Bachar, Jacqueline M., ed. Poetry in the Garden. LC 96-75021. (Illus.). 128p. 1996. 19.95 (*1-886934-07-X*) Intl Forum.

Bachar, John & Boga, Steven. Free Climbing with John Bachar. (Illus.). 96p. 1996. pap. 10.95 (*0-8117-2517-0*) Stackpole.

Bachar, Miriam, jt. auth. see Arena, Jay M.

***Bacharach & David.** Bacharach & David: American Classics. 72p. 1999. otabind 10.95 (*0-634-01148-0*) H Leonard.

Bacharach, Alfred L. British Music of Our Time: Music Book Index. 256p. 1993. reprint ed. lib. bdg. 79.00 (*0-7812-9565-3*) Rprt Serv.

— The Music Masters: Music Book Index, 4 vols., Set. 1993. reprint ed. lib. bdg. 300.00 (*0-7812-9579-3*) Rprt Serv.

Bacharach, Alfred L., ed. The Lives of the Great Composers. LC 72-276. (Essay Index Reprint Ser.). 1977. reprint ed. 33.95 (*0-8369-2783-4*) Ayer.

Bacharach, Jere L., ed. The Early Economy of al-Fustat: Evidence from the Henri Amin Awad Collection. (Illus.). 224p. 1996. 29.50 (*977-424-393-5*, Pub. by Am Univ Cairo Pr) Col U Pr.

— The Restoration & Conservation of Islamic Monuments in Egypt. (World XEgypt Ser.). (Illus.). 240p. 1995. 35.00 (*977-424-356-0*, Pub. by Am Univ Cairo Pr) Col U Pr.

Bacharach, Jere L. & Kouymjian, Dickran K., eds. Near Eastern Numismatics, Iconography, Epigraphy & History: Studies in Honor of George C. Miles. 1974. 55.00 (*0-8156-6041-3*, Pub. by Am U Beirut) Syracuse U Pr.

Bacharach, Jere L., ed. see Ehrenkreutz, Andrew S.

Bacharach, Jere L., ed. see Hinds, Martin.

Bacharach, M. O., et al, eds. Epistemic Logic & the Theory of Games & Decisions. LC 97-38203. (Theory & Decision Library). 400p. 1997. 154.00 (*0-7923-4804-4*, D Reidel) Kluwer Academic.

Bacharach, M. O. L., et al, eds. Mathematical Models in Economics: Oxford University Mathematical Economic Seminar 25th Anniversary. anniversary ed. (Illus.). 476p. 2000. text 55.00 (*0-19-823296-9*) OUP.

Bacharach, Nancy, et al. Learning Together: A Manual for Multiage Grouping. (Illus.). 96p. 1995. pap. 16.95 (*0-8039-6267-3*) Corwin Pr.

— Learning Together: A Manual for Multiage Grouping. (Illus.). 96p. 1995. 39.95 (*0-8039-6266-5*) Corwin Pr.

Bacharach, Samuel, et al. Research in the Sociology of Organizations Vol. 16: Networks in & Around Organizations. 1999. 78.50 (*0-7623-0473-1*) Jai Pr.

Bacharach, Samuel B. Education Reform: Making Sense of It All. 412p. 1989. pap. 39.95 (*0-685-29831-0*, H19573) Allyn.

— Organizational Behavior in Schools & School Districts. LC 81-5138. 532p. 1981. 45.50 (*0-275-90579-9*, C0579, Praeger Pubs) Greenwood.

— Research in the Sociology of Organizations, Vol. 15. 1998. 78.50 (*0-7623-0180-5*) Jai Pr.

Bacharach, Samuel B., et al, eds. Advances in Research & Theories of School Management & Educational Policy, Vol. 1. 352p. 1990. 78.50 (*0-89232-767-7*) Jai Pr.

— Advances in Research & Theories of School Management & Educational Policy, Vol. 2. 288p. 1993. 78.50 (*1-55938-253-8*) Jai Pr.

— Advances in Research & Theories of School Management & Educational Policy, Vol. 3. 288p. 1995. 78.50 (*1-55938-725-4*) Jai Pr.

— Advances in Research & Theories of School Management & Educational Policy, Vol. 4. Date not set. 78.50 (*0-7623-0024-8*) Jai Pr.

— Research in the Sociology of Organizations, Vol. 1. 352p. 1982. 78.50 (*0-89232-170-9*) Jai Pr.

— Research in the Sociology of Organizations, Vol. 2. 276p. 1983. 78.50 (*0-89232-203-9*) Jai Pr.

— Research in the Sociology of Organizations, Vol. 3: The Social Psychological Processes. 256p. 1984. 78.50 (*0-89232-340-X*) Jai Pr.

— Research in the Sociology of Organizations, Vol. 4. 377p. 1986. 78.50 (*0-89232-451-1*) Jai Pr.

— Research in the Sociology of Organizations, Vol. 5. 340p. 1987. 78.50 (*0-89232-637-9*) Jai Pr.

— Research in the Sociology of Organizations, Vol. 6. 344p. 1989. 78.50 (*0-89232-881-9*) Jai Pr.

— Research in the Sociology of Organizations, Vol. 8: Organizations & Professions. 297p. 1991. 78.50 (*1-55938-206-6*) Jai Pr.

— Research in the Sociology of Organizations, Vol. 9. 358p. 1991. 78.50 (*1-55938-398-4*) Jai Pr.

— Research in the Sociology of Organizations, Vol. 10: Organizational Demography. 220p. 1992. 78.50 (*1-55938-423-9*) Jai Pr.

B

— Research in the Sociology of Organizations, Vol. 11. 297p. 1993. 78.50 (*1-55938-462-X*) Jai Pr.
— Research in the Sociology of Organizations, Vol. 14. 1996. 78.50 (*0-7623-0019-1*) Jai Pr.
— Research in the Sociology of Organizations: Structuring Participation in Organizations, Vol. 7. 269p. 1991. 78.50 (*1-55938-009-8*) Jai Pr.
— Research in the Sociology of Organizations: Studies of Organization in the Eur Tradit, Vol. 13. 325p. 1995. 78.50 (*1-55938-895-1*) Jai Pr.
— Research in the Sociology of Organizations Vol. 12: Special Issue on Labor Relations & Unions. 309p. 1994. 78.50 (*1-55938-736-X*) Jai Pr.
Bacharach, Samuel B. & Lawler, Edward J. Bargaining, Power, Tactics, & Outcomes. LC 81-8197. (Jossey-Bass Social & Behavioral Science Ser.). (Illus.). 254p. reprint ed. pap. 78.80 (*0-7837-6506-1*, 204561800007) Bks Demand.
— Power & Politics in Organizations. LC 79-92460. (Jossey-Bass Social & Behavioral Science Ser.). 269p. reprint ed. pap. 83.40 (*0-8357-4849-9*, 203778000009) Bks Demand.
Bacharach, Samuel B. & Mundell, Bryan, eds. Images of Schools: Structures & Roles in Organizational Behavior. LC 95-2533. (Illus.). 424p. 1995. pap. 45.95 (*0-8039-6251-7*) Corwin Pr.
Bacharach, Samuel B., et al. Member Assistance Programs in the Workplace: The Role of Labor in the Prevention & Treatment of Substance Abuse. LC 94-31790. (Bulletin Ser.: 69). 104p. 1994. pap. text 12.95 (*0-87546-336-3*, ILR Press) Cornell U Pr.
Bacharach, Samuel B., ed. see Bidwell, Charles E., et al.
Bacharach, Samuel B., ed. see Carroll, Glenn R.
Bacharach, Samuel B., jt. ed. see Grant, John H.
Bacharach, Samuel B., ed. see Jones, L. R. & Baldwin, John H.
Bacharach, Samuel B., ed. see Price, James L. & Mueller, Charles W.
Bacharach, Samuel B., ed. see Yunker, Gary W.
Bacharach, Stephen L., ed. Information Processing in Medical Imaging. 1986. text 273.50 (*0-89838-787-6*) Kluwer Academic.
Bacharach, Walter Z. Anti-Jewish Prejudices in German-Catholic Sermons. Galai, Chaya, tr. from HEB. LC 92-37137. 204p. 1993. reprint ed. text 89.95 (*0-7734-9181-3*) E Mellen.
***Bachardy, Don.** Stars in My Eyes. LC 99-6741. 2000. 34.95 (*0-299-16730-5*) U of Wis Pr.
Bachardy, Don. Drawings of the Male Nude. 96p. 1985. 50.00 (*0-942642-18-X*) Twelvetrees Pr.
Bachardy, Don, ed. see Isherwood, Christopher.
Bacharova, Ljuba. Atlas of Clinical Vectorcardiography. 119p. (Orig.). (C). 1994. pap. 19.50 (*0-685-71258-3*) Kabel Pubs.
— Atlas of Clinical Vectorcardiography. (Illus.). 121p. (Orig.). (C). 1994. pap. text 29.50 (*0-930329-59-7*) Kabel Pubs.
Bacharova, Ljuba & Macfarlane, Peter W., eds. Electrocardiology, '97: Proceedings of the 29th International Congress Bratislava, Slovak Republic 24-28 June, 1997. LC 98-213028. 310p. 1998. 84.00 (*981-02-3380-9*) World Scientific Pub.
Bachay, Judith. Creating Peace, Building Community. Burke, James A., II et al, eds. (Illus.). (J). (gr. 6). 1997. pap. text, teacher ed. 23.95 (*1-878227-42-4*) Peace Educ.
— Creating Peace, Building Community: Grade 7. Burke, James A., II et al, eds. (Illus.). 134p. (J). (gr. 7). 1997. pap. text, teacher ed. 23.95 (*1-878227-46-7*) Peace Educ.
— Creating Peace, Building Community: Student Activity Book. Burke, James A., II et al, eds. (Illus.). 60p. (Orig.). (J). (gr. 7). 1996. pap. text 2.79 (*1-878227-47-5*) Peace Educ.
— Creating Peace, Building Community: Student Activity Book. Brice, Nancy et al, eds. (Illus.). 48p. (Orig.). (J). (gr. 6). 1997. pap. text 2.79 (*1-878227-43-2*) Peace Educ.
Bachchan, Harivansh Rai. In the Afternoon of Time: An Autobiography. Snell, Rupert, tr. from HIN. LC 98-901300. xi, 498p. 1998. 44.00 (*0-670-88158-9*) Viking Penguin.
Bache, Carl. The Study of Aspect, Tense & Action: Towards a Theory of the Semantics of Grammatical Categories. (Illus.). 350p. 1995. 63.95 (*3-631-49510-2*) P Lang Pubng.
— The Study of Aspect, Tense & Action: Towards a Theory of the Semantics of Grammatical Categories. 2nd ed. LC 97-40224. (Illus.). 348p. 1997. pap. 63.95 (*0-8204-3509-0*) P Lang Pubng.
Bache, Carl, et al, eds. Tense, Aspect, & Action: Empirical & Theoretical Contributions to Language Typology. LC 94-25766. (Empirical Approaches to Language Typology Ser.: No. 12). viii, 428p. (C). 1994. lib. bdg. 175.40 (*3-11-012713-X*) Mouton.
Bache, Carl & Davidsen-Nielsen, Niels. Mastering English: An Advanced Grammar for Non-Native & Native Speakers. LC 97-23493. 538p. 1997. text 112.00 (*3-11-015535-4*); pap. text 24.00 (*3-11-015536-2*) Mouton.
Bache, Carl & Klinge, Alex, eds. Sounds, Structures, & Senses: Essays Presented to Niels Davidsen-Nielsen on the Occasion of His Sixtieth Birthday. LC 98-173986. 286p. 1997. 32.00 (*87-7838-307-2*, Pub. by Odense Univ) Intl Spec Bk.
***Bache, Christopher M.** Dark Night, Early Dawn: Steps to a Deep Ecology of Mind. LC 99-49013. (C). 2000. text 71.50 (*0-7914-4605-0*) State U NY Pr.
— Dark Night, Early Dawn: Steps to a Deep Ecology of Mind. LC 99-49013. 2000. pap. 23.95 (*0-7914-4606-9*) State U NY Pr.
Bache, Christopher M. Lifecycles: Reincarnation & the Web of Life. 237p. 1991. 18.95 (*1-55778-350-0*) Paragon Hse.
— Lifecycles: Reincarnation & the Web of Life. 256p. 1993. pap. 14.95 (*1-55778-645-3*) Paragon Hse.
Bache, Constance, tr. see Liszt, Franz & La Mara.
Bache, David H. & Johnstone, Donald R. Microclimate & Spray Dispersion. LC 92-30471. (Ellis Horwood Series in Environmental Management, Science & Technology). 1992. 76.95 (*0-13-217910-5*, Pub. by Tavistock-E Horwood) Routldge.
Bache, Ellyn. The Activist's Daughter. LC 97-1159. 264p. (Orig.). 1997. pap. 10.95 (*1-883523-18-4*) Spinsters Ink.
— Festival in Fire Season. LC 95-83806. 240p. 1996. reprint ed. pap. 11.95 (*0-9635967-6-4*) Banks Channel.
— Safe Passage. LC 93-90159. 234p. 1993. reprint ed. pap. 10.95 (*0-9635967-7-2*) Banks Channel.
Bache, Ian. The Politics of European Union Regional Policy: Multi-Level Governance or Flexable Gatekeeping? (Contemporary European Studies: Vol. 3). 172p. 1998. pap. 15.00 (*1-85075-863-8*, Pub. by Sheffield Acad) CUP Services.
***Bache, John, et al.** Practical Procedures in the Emergency Department. (Illus.). 184p. 1998. pap. write for info. (*0-7234-3013-6*) Mosby Inc.
Bache, John, jt. ed. see Hardy, R. H.
Bache, Richard & Bazanna, Gualtiero. Software Metrics for Product Assessment. LC 93-29406. (International Series in Software Assurance). 1993. write for info. (*0-07-707923-X*) McGraw.
Bache, Soren. A Chronicle of Old Muskego, the Diary of Soren Bache, 1839-1847. Clausen, Clarence A. & Elviken, Andreas, eds. LC 52-433. (Publications of the Norwegian-American Historical Association). 263p. reprint ed. pap. 81.60 (*0-8357-3437-4*, 203969400013) Bks Demand.
Bache-Wiig, Barbara. Lessons. (Illus.). ii, 51p. 1997. pap. 5.00 (*1-890644-00-5*) Union Cnty.
Bache, William B. Design & Closure in Shakespeare's Major Plays: The Nature of Recapitulation. LC 90-42673. (American University Studies: English Language & Literature: Ser. IV, Vol. 123). XIII, 398p. (C). 1991. pap. 56.95 (*0-8204-1382-8*) P Lang Pubng.
Bache, William B. & Loggins, Vernon P. Shakespeare's Deliberate Art. LC 96-10396. 276p. 1996. pap. text 36.50 (*0-7618-0301-7*); lib. bdg. 57.50 (*0-7618-0300-9*) U Pr of Amer.
***Bachel, Beverly K.** What Do You Really Want? How to Set a Goal & Go for It! A Guide for Teens. (Illus.). 152p. (YA). (gr. 6 up). 2000. pap. 12.95 (*1-57542-085-6*) Free Spirit Pub.
Bachelard, Gaston. Air & Dreams: An Essay on the Imagination of Movement. Farrell, Edith & Farrell, Frederick, trs. LC 88-25704. (Bachelard Translation Ser.). 298p. 1988. pap. 18.00 (*0-911005-13-7*) Dallas Inst Pubns.
— L' Air et les Songes: Essai sur L'Imagination du Mouvement. (FRE.). 350p. 1992. pap. 18.95 (*0-7859-3424-3*) Fr & Eur.
***Bachelard, Gaston.** Dialectic of Duration. McAllester-Jones, Mary, tr. 218p. 2000. pap. 29.95 (*1-903083-07-9*, Pub. by Clinamen Pr) Paul & Co Pubs.
Bachelard, Gaston. La Dialectique de la Duree. 2nd ed. (FRE.). 168p. 1993. pap. 22.95 (*0-7859-3009-4*) Fr & Eur.
— The Flame of a Candle. Caldwell, Joni, tr. from FRE. LC 89-7870. (Bachelard Translation Ser.). 89p. 1989. 18.00 (*0-911005-14-5*); pap. 16.00 (*0-911005-15-3*) Dallas Inst Pubns.
— La Flamme d'une Chandelle. 8th ed. (FRE.). 1986. pap. 16.95 (*0-7859-3006-X*, 2130394868) Fr & Eur.
— Fragments of a Poetics of Fire. Haltman, Kenneth, tr. from FRE. LC 90-39813. (Bachelard Translation Ser.). (Illus.). 196p. (C). 1991. 25.00 (*0-911005-17-X*); pap. 18.00 (*0-911005-18-8*) Dallas Inst Pubns.
— Intuition de l'Instant. (FRE.). 160p. 1993. reprint ed. pap. 38.95 (*0-7859-2188-5*, 2234024161) Fr & Eur.
— Lautreamont. Dupree, Robert S., tr. from FRE. & contrib. by by. Hillman, James, contrib. by. LC 86-16866. (Bachelard Translation Ser.). 150p. 1986. 20.00 (*0-911005-08-0*); pap. 16.00 (*0-911005-09-9*) Dallas Inst Pubns.
— On Poetic Imagination & Reverie: Selections from Gaston Bachelard. rev. ed. Gaudin, Colette, tr. from FRE. & intro. by. LC 87-23314. lviii, 112p. 1987. pap. 14.00 (*0-88214-331-X*) Spring Pubns.
— La Philosophie du Non. 3rd ed. (FRE.). 160p. 1988. pap. 20.95 (*0-7859-3010-8*) Fr & Eur.
— The Poetics of Reverie: Childhood, Language & the Cosmos. 1971. reprint ed. pap. 16.50 (*0-8070-6413-0*) Beacon Pr.
— The Poetics of Space. LC 93-27874. 288p. 1994. reprint ed. pap. 15.00 (*0-8070-6473-4*) Beacon Pr.
— La Poetique de la Reverie. 3rd ed. (FRE.). 192p. 1990. pap. 19.95 (*0-7859-3012-4*) Fr & Eur.
— La Poetique de L'Espace. 5th ed. (FRE.). 214p. 1992. pap. 19.95 (*0-7859-3019-1*) Fr & Eur.
— La Psychanalyse du Feu. (FRE.). 1985. pap. 12.95 (*0-7859-2799-9*) Fr & Eur.
— La Psychanalyse du Feu. (Folio Essais Ser.: No. 25). (FRE.). 184p. 1985. pap. 9.95 (*2-07-032325-0*) Schoenhof.
— Psychoanalysis of Fire. Ross, A. C., tr. 1964. pap. 15.50 (*0-8070-6461-0*) Beacon Pr.
— Le Rationalisme Applique. (FRE.). 224p. 1986. pap. 20.95 (*0-7859-3007-8*) Fr & Eur.
— The Right to Dream. Underwood, J. A., tr. LC 89-1302. (Bachelard Translation Ser.). 190p. 1989. pap. 17.00 (*0-911005-16-1*) Dallas Inst Pubns.
— Water & Dreams: An Essay on the Imagination of Matter. Farrell, Edith R., tr. from FRE. LC 83-23641. (Bachelard Translation Ser.). 213p. 1999. reprint ed. pap. 21.00 (*0-911005-25-0*) Dallas Inst Pubns.
Bachelard, Herman, ed. Magnetic Resonance Spectroscopy & Imaging in Neurochemistry. LC 97-15443. (Advances in Neurochemistry Ser.: Vol. 8). (Illus.). 436p. (C). 1997. text 115.00 (*0-306-45520-X*, Kluwer Plenum) Kluwer Academic.
Bachelard, Herman S., jt. ed. see Turner, A. J.
Bachelard, Suzanne. A Study of Husserl's Formal & Transcendental Logic. Embree, Lester, tr. from FRE. (Studies in Phenomenology & Existential Philosophy). 227p. 1990. reprint ed. pap. 19.95 (*0-8101-0859-3*) Northwestern U Pr.
Bachelder, B., et al, eds. Hallowell Memories. (Illus.). 65p. 1991. pap. text 7.00 (*0-9626823-2-2*) Perry ME.
Bachelder, Dan, jt. auth. see Hunt, Norman J.
***Bachelder, Frances H.** The Iron Gate. (Illus.). 166p. 2000. pap. write for info. (*0-7541-1058-3*, Pub. by Minerva Pr) Unity Dist.
Bachelder, Frances H. Mary Roberts Rinehart: Mistress of Mystery. LC 93-342. (Brownstone Mystery Guides Ser.: No. 15). 120p. 1993. pap. 17.00 (*0-8095-5175-6*) Millefleurs.
Bachelder, John. History of the Battle of Gettysburg. (Illus.). 842p. 1997. 60.00 (*0-89029-330-9*) Morningside Bkshop.
Bachelder, Louise, ed. Abraham Lincoln Wisdom & Wit. LC 98-219854. (Pocket Gift Editions Ser.). 1998. 4.95 (*0-88088-066-X*) Peter Pauper.
— The Little Flowers of Saint Francis of Assisi. large type ed. (Large Print Inspirational Ser.). (Illus.). 112p. 1986. pap. 7.95 (*0-8027-2526-0*) Walker & Co.
Bachelder, Marvin. Snow Treasure: A Study Guide. Friedland, Joyce & Kessler, Rikki, eds. (Novel-Ties Ser.). (J). (gr. 5-7). 1991. pap. text 15.95 (*0-88122-582-7*) Lrn Links.
Bachelder, Patti L. A Stitcher's Christmas Album. LC 92-33334. (Illus.). 66p. (Orig.). 1992. pap. 9.95 (*0-9622565-3-6*) Chitra Pubns.
Bachelder, Patti L., ed. see Voudrie, Sylvia T.
Bachelder, Peter D. The Great Steel Pier: An Illustrated History of the Old Orchard Ocean Pier. LC 99-213411. (Illus.). viii, 136p. 1998. pap. 19.95 (*0-9664831-0-3*) Breakwater ME.
— The Lighthouses & Lightships of Casco Bay. rev. ed. LC 95-12006. Orig. Title: Lighthouses of Casco Bay. 1995. write for info. (*0-931675-01-4*) Prov Pr Maine.
— Shipwrecks & Maritime Disasters of the Maine Coast. LC 97-13640. 1997. write for info. (*0-931675-03-0*) Prov Pr Maine.
Bachelder, Peter D. & Smith, Mason P. Four Short Blasts: The Gale of 1898 & the Loss of the Steamer Portland. LC 98-34545. 138p. 1998. 17.50 (*0-931675-06-5*) Prov Pr Maine.
Bachelder, Robert S. Between Dying & Birth. 1983. 6.25 (*0-89536-623-1*, 0236) CSS OH.
Bachelet, E., et al, eds. High Temperature Materials for Power Engineering, 1990: Proceedings of a Conference Held in Liege, Belgium, 24-27 September 1990, 2 vols., Set. (C). 1990. text 567.00 (*0-7923-0927-8*) Kluwer Academic.
Bachelis, Faren, ed. see Ramsay, Linda M.
Bacheller, Franklin I. Listening & Recall. (Illus.). 192p. (C). 1986. pap. text 30.00 (*0-13-537481-2*) P-H.
— Start Reading: A Basic Reader in English. 192p. (C). 1990. pap. text 18.40 (*0-13-753724-7*) P-H.
— Start Writing. (Illus.). 128p. (C). 1988. pap. text 26.20 (*0-13-843012-8*) P-H.
Bacheller, Irving. Eben Holden. (Classics Library). 1998. pap. 3.95 (*1-85326-573-X*, 573XWW, Pub. by Wrdsworth Edits) NTC Contemp Pub Co.
— Eben Holden: A Tale of the North Country. (BCL1-PS American Literature Ser.). 432p. 1992. reprint ed. lib. bdg. 99.00 (*0-7812-6671-8*) Rprt Serv.
— Eben Holden: A Tale of the North Country. LC 03-32793. 1969. reprint ed. 16.00 (*0-403-00142-0*) Scholarly.
— Eben Holden, a Tale of the North Country. LC 74-128934. (BCL Ser.: No. I). 1974. 27.50 (*0-404-00439-3*) AMS Pr.
— Lost in the Fog. LC 88-25923. (Illus.). (J). (gr. k-3). 1990. 14.95 (*0-316-07462-4*) Little.
Bacheller, John. A Native American Sourcebook. (C). 1997. pap. 28.13 (*0-07-289901-8*) McGrw-H Hghr Educ.
***Bacheller, Milton H., Jr.** American Marking Gages: Patented & Manufactured. (Illus.). 448p. 2000. 75.00 (*0-9678928-0-5*) M H Bacheller.
Bachelor, A. & Haley, J. Practice of English Fundamentals: V. Form. 1945. pap. text 12.95 (*0-685-03901-3*) P-H.
Bachelor, Evelyn, et al, eds. Teen Conflicts. (Illus.). 240p. (Orig.). (YA). (gr. 8 up). 1972. pap. 7.95 (*0-87297-007-8*) Diablo.
Bachelor, Lynn W., jt. auth. see Jones, Bryan D.
Bachem, A. & Derigs, U. Operations Research '93. 555p. 1996. pap. 159.00 (*3-7908-0794-X*) Spr-Verlag.
Bachem, Achim, et al, eds. Mathematical Programming - Bonn, 1982: The State of the Art. (Illus.). 660p. 1983. 180.00 (*0-387-12082-3*) Spr-Verlag.
Bachem, Achim & Kern, Walter. Linear Programming Duality: An Introduction to Oriented Matroids. LC 92-14021. 1992. 62.95 (*0-387-55417-3*) Spr-Verlag.
***Bacher, Bruce R.** Four Hymn Intonations for Organ/Organ Music. 12p. 1998. pap. 7.00 (*0-8100-0956-0*) Northwest Pub.
Bacher, Elman. Astrology, 9 vols., Set. 3rd ed. 907p. 1990. reprint ed. pap. text 45.00 (*0-911274-99-5*) Rosicrucian.
Bacher, Jean-Luc. L' Escroquerie a l'Assurance Privee: Etude Penale et Criminologique. (Publications Universitaires Europeennes Ser.: Series 2, Vol. 1801). (FRE.). xxiv, 406p. 1995. 55.95 (*3-906754-09-X*, Pub. by P Lang) P Lang Pubng.
Bacher, John C. Keeping to the Marketplace: The Evolution of Canadian Housing Policy. 344p. 1993. 65.00 (*0-7735-0984-4*, Pub. by McG-Queens Univ Pr) CUP Services.
Bacher, June M. Diary of a Loving Heart. large type ed. LC 87-34061. 1988. pap. 8.95 (*0-8027-2623-2*) Walker & Co.
— Homeward Bound: Love is a Gentle Stranger. 1998. pap. 12.99 (*0-88486-193-7*, Inspirational Pr) Arrowood Pr.
— Journey West: Love Is a Gentle Stranger, 3 vols. in 1. 560p. 1996. 12.99 (*0-88486-154-6*) Arrowood Pr.
— Love Follows the Heart. large type ed. 352p. (Orig.). 1991. pap. 8.95 (*0-8027-2662-3*) Walker & Co.
— Love Is a Gentle Stranger. large type ed. 1987. pap. 8.95 (*0-8027-2611-9*) Walker & Co.
— Love Leads Home. large type ed. 1988. pap. 8.95 (*0-8027-2624-0*) Walker & Co.
— Love's Enduring Hope: A Pioneer Romance. large type ed. 296p. 1992. reprint ed. pap. 9.95 (*0-8027-2670-4*) Walker & Co.
— Love's Silent Song. large type ed. (Orig.). 1987. pap. 8.95 (*0-8027-2610-0*) Walker & Co.
— The Quiet Heart: Daily Devotionals for Women. LC 87-82261. 368p. (Orig.). 1988. pap. 11.99 (*0-89081-624-7*) Harvest Hse.
— Quiet Moments for Women: A Daily Devotional. LC 79-84722. 1979. pap. 11.99 (*0-89081-187-3*) Harvest Hse.
***Bacher, June Masters.** Devotions for Morning & Evening with June Masters Bacher. 2000. 14.99 (*0-88486-284-4*, Inspirational Pr) Arrowood Pr.
Bacher, L. The Mobile Mise En Scene: A Critical Analysis of the Theory & Practice of Long Take Camera Movement in the Narrative Film. LC 77-22904. (Dissertations on Film Ser.). 1978. lib. bdg. 26.95 (*0-405-10750-1*) Ayer.
Bacher, Lutz. Max Ophuls in the Hollywood Studios. LC 95-52726. (Illus.). 400p. (C). 1996. text 72.00 (*0-8135-2291-9*) Rutgers U Pr.
Bacher, Robert F. Robert Oppenheimer. Gursky, Judy, ed. & intro. by. LC 99-26500. (Los Alamos Story Ser.: No. 2). (Illus.). 64p. 1999. pap. 10.00 (*0-941232-22-0*) Los Alamos Hist Soc.
Bacher, Wilhelm. Abraham Ibn Esra Als Grammatiker: Ein Beitrag zur Geschichte der Hebraischen Sprachwissenschaft. Katz, Steven, ed. LC 79-7125. (Jewish Philosophy, Mysticism & History of Ideas Ser.). 1980. reprint ed. lib. bdg. 18.95 (*0-405-12239-X*) Ayer.
— Die Anfange der Hebraischen Grammatik (1895) Together with Die Hebraisch Sprachwissenschaft Vom 10. Bis Zum 16. Jahrhundert (1892) (Studies in the History of Linguistics Sciences : 4). xix, 235p. 1974. pap. 68.00 (*90-272-0895-6*) J Benjamins Pubng Co.
Bachhofer, Ludwig. Early Indian Sculpture, 2 vols. in 1. (Illus.). 1974. text 57.50 (*0-685-13843-7*) Coronet Bks.
— A Short History of Chinese Art. LC 83-45695. reprint ed. 47.50 (*0-404-20014-1*) AMS Pr.
Bachhuber, Thomas. Best Graduate Business Schools. 3rd ed. LC 97-81104. 352p. 1998. 18.95 (*0-02-862503-X*, Arc) IDG Bks.
Bachhuber, Thomas D. Best Graduate Business Schools. 336p. 1994. pap. 17.00 (*0-671-88541-3*) P-H.
Bachhuber, Thomas D., ed. The Best Graduate Business Schools. 2nd ed. LC 96-213059. 1996. 16.95 (*0-02-861164-0*) Macmillan.
Bachhuber, Thomas D., jt. auth. see Van Roden, Albert C.
Bachi, R. New Methods of Geostatistical Analysis & Graphical Presentation: Distributions of Populations over Territories. LC 99-17060. (Illus.). 578p. (C). 1998. text. write for info. (*0-306-45544-7*, Kluwer Plenum) Kluwer Academic.
Bachi, Roberto. Graphical Rational Patterns: A New Approach to Graphical Presentation of Statistics. 264p. 1968. boxed set 44.95 (*0-87855-201-4*) Transaction Pubs.
Bachica, Martin R. Kingdom of the Bride: A Book on the Last Days. 1997. pap. 9.99 (*0-9676215-0-X*) KBRIDE.
Bachicha, Gayle. The Master Book of Astrology. 250p. (Orig.). 1997. pap. 29.95 (*1-885084-22-6*) Tickerwick.
— Pocket Dictionary of Astrological Terms. LC 94-11441. 64p. (Orig.). 1994. pap. 6.95 (*1-885084-11-0*) Tickerwick.
— What Is an Astrology Chart? Spiritual View. LC 95-21961. 1995. pap. text. write for info. (*1-885084-12-9*) Tickerwick.
Bachicha, Gayle, ed. see St. John, Sandra.
Bachin, Peter & Beck, Ernest. The Anatomical Chart Series: Classic Library Edition. 4th ed. LC 86-71078. (Illus.). 48p. 1985. 42.95 (*0-9603730-3-9*); 64.95 (*0-9603730-4-7*) Anatomical Chart.
Bachinger, Katrina. Edgar Allan Poe's Biographies of Byron: Byrons Differed - Byrons Deferred in the Tales of the Folio Club. LC 94-38899. (Salzburg University Studies). 204p. 1995. text 89.95 (*0-7734-1272-7*) E Mellen.
— Male Pretense: A Gender Study of Sir Philip Sidney's Life & Texts. LC 94-39589. (Salzburger Studien Ser.). 164p. 1995. text 79.95 (*0-7734-1270-0*) E Mellen.
Bachkheti, N. D. Social Forestry in India: Problems & Prospects. 115p. 1987. text 22.50 (*81-7027-103-7*, Pub. by Radiant Pubs) S Asia.
Bachl, N., et al, eds. Advances in Ergometry. (Illus.). 544p. 1991. pap. 65.00 (*0-387-53684-1*) Spr-Verlag.
***Bachleda, F. Lynne, ed.** Blue Mountain: A Spiritual Anthology Celebrating the Earth. 2000. pap. 15.95 (*0-89732-311-4*, Pub. by Menasha Ridge) Globe Pequot.
Bachmaier, Helmut, ed. Paradigmen der Moderne. LC 88-35224. (Viennese Heritage - Wiener Erbe Ser.: Vol. 3). (GER.). xxiii, 287p. (C). 1990. 89.00 (*90-272-3885-5*) J Benjamins Pubng Co.
Bachmair, A. Dictionary of Steam Generator Engineering. 2nd ed. (ENG, FRE, POR & SPA.). 768p. 1983. 115.00 (*0-8288-4023-7*, M9010) Fr & Eur.

B

An Asterisk (*) at the beginning of an entry indicates that the title is appearing for the first time.

Bachmair, Leo. Canonical Equational Proofs: Progress in Theoretical Computer Science. (Illus.). 140p. 1991. 43.50 (*0-8176-3555-6*) Birkhauser.

Bachman. Between Worlds: MLA Update. 2nd ed. 586p. (C). 1998. pap. 38.00 (*0-321-04963-2*) Addison-Wesley.

— Julius Caesar. (Shakespeare Ser.). 1994. pap., teacher ed. 6.99 (*0-8442-5740-0*) NTC Contemp Pub Co.

— A Midsummer Night's Dream. (Shakespeare Ser.). 1995. pap., teacher ed. 6.99 (*0-8442-5742-7*) NTC Contemp Pub Co.

— Romeo & Juliet. (Shakespeare Ser.). 1994. pap., teacher ed. 6.99 (*0-8442-5748-6*) NTC Contemp Pub Co.

Bachman & Sigband, Norman B. English & Vocabulary for Careers. (PS - Communication/English Ser.). (C). 1995. pap. 37.25 (*0-538-70938-3*) S-W Pub.

Bachman, ed. see Shakespeare, William.

***Bachman, A.** Between Worlds: A Reader, Rhetoric & Handbook. 1998. text. write for info. (*0-321-01194-5*) Addison-Wesley.

Bachman, Barbara. Frisky Phonics Fun I. (Illus.). 152p. (J). (gr. 1-3). 1984. student ed. 13.99 (*0-86653-195-5*, GA 548) Good Apple.

— Frisky Phonics Fun II. (Illus.). 152p. (J). (gr. 1-3). 1984. student ed. 13.99 (*0-86653-212-9*, GA 549) Good Apple.

Bachman, Bill & Winton, Tim. Australian Colors: Images of the Outback. (Illus.). 256p. 1998. 35.00 (*0-8174-4234-0*) Watsn-Guptill.

Bachman-Carter, Karen, et al. Navajo Food Practices, Customs, & Holidays. 2nd ed. LC 98-30899. (Ethnic & Regional Food Practices Ser.). 1998. 10.00 (*0-88091-170-0*) Am Dietetic Assn.

Bachman-Carter, Karen, jt. auth. see Pelican, Suzanne.

Bachman, Christian G. Laser Radar Systems & Techniques. LC 78-31528. 207p. reprint ed. pap. 64.20 (*0-608-15016-9*, 205608300047) Bks Demand.

Bachman, David. Bureaucracy, Economy, & Leadership in China: The Institutional Origins of the Great Leap Forward. 284p. 1991. text 57.95 (*0-521-40275-1*) Cambridge U Pr.

— Bureaucracy, Economy, & Leadership in China: The Institutional Origins of the Great Leap Forward. 242p. (C). 1991. write for info. (*0-521-40269-7*) Cambridge U Pr.

Bachman, David & Yang, Dali L., eds. Yin Jiaqi & China's Struggle for Democracy. LC 90-9051. (Chinese Studies on China). 240p. (C). (gr. 13). 1991. text 79.95 (*0-87332-780-2*); pap. text 42.95 (*0-87332-781-0*) M E Sharpe.

Bachman, David M. Chen Yun & the Chinese Political System. LC 85-80729. (China Research Monographs: No. 29). 177p. 1985. pap. 15.00 (*0-912966-80-7*) IEAS.

Bachman, Debra H., jt. ed. see Lind, Regina F.

Bachman, Frank P., jt. auth. see McHugh, Michael J.

***Bachman, G., et al.** Fourier & Wavelet Analysis. LC 99-36217. (Universitext Ser.). (Illus.). 510p. 1999. 59.95 (*0-387-98899-8*) Spr-Verlag.

Bachman, Gennady. On the Coefficients of Cyclotomic Polynomials. LC 93-31295. (Memoirs of the American Mathematical Society Ser.: No. 510). 80p. 1993. pap. 28.00 (*0-8218-2572-0*, MEMO/106/510) Am Math.

Bachman, George & Narici, Lawrence. Functional Analysis. 2nd unabridged ed. 544p. 1998. pap. 17.95 (*0-486-40251-7*) Dover.

Bachman, George W. & Meriam, Lewis. The Issue of Compulsory Health Insurance. LC 75-17203. (Social Problems & Social Policy Ser.). (Illus.). 1976. reprint ed. 23.95 (*0-405-07475-1*) Ayer.

Bachman, Henry F., see Somos, pseud.

Bachman, James, jt. auth. see Hintikka, Jaakko.

Bachman, James E. & Cummins, J. David, intros. Capitalization Requirements for Multiple Line Property Liability Insurance Companies. LC 78-57297. (S. S. Huebner Foundation Monographs: No. 6). (Illus.). 94p. (C). 1978. pap. 14.50 (*0-918930-06-5*) Huebner Foun Insur.

Bachman, Jane, ed. see Shakespeare, William.

Bachman, Jerald C., jt. auth. see Johnston, Jerome.

Bachman, Jerald G. Adolescence to Adulthood: Change & Stability in the Lives of Young Men. LC 78-109016. (Youth in Transition Ser.: No. 6). 350p. reprint ed. pap. 108.50 (*0-7837-5241-5*, 204497500005) Bks Demand.

— The Impact of Family Background & Intelligence on Tenth-Grade Boys. LC 79-630045. (Michigan University Survey Research Center Youth in Transition Ser.: Vol. 2). 307p. reprint ed. pap. 95.20 (*0-608-30837-4*, 200542400053) Bks Demand.

Bachman, Jerald G., et al. The All-Volunteer Force: A Study of Ideology in the Military. LC 77-5631. 220p. 1977. reprint ed. pap. 68.20 (*0-7837-4710-1*, 205906200003) Bks Demand.

— Blueprint for a Longitudinal Study of Adolescent Boys. LC 72-610663. (Michigan University Survey Research Center Youth in Transition Ser.: Vol. 1). 285p. reprint ed. pap. 88.40 (*0-8357-7332-9*, 200541300053) Bks Demand.

— Dropping Out: Problem or Symptom? LC 72-179807. (Youth in Transition Ser.: No. 3). (Illus.). 264p. reprint ed. pap. 81.90 (*0-608-18272-9*, 203149200075) Bks Demand.

— Smoking, Drinking, & Drug Use in Young Adulthood: The Impact of New Freedoms & New Responsibilities. LC 96-45203. (Research Monographs in Adolescence Ser.). 256p. 1997. 59.95 (*0-8058-2547-9*) L Erlbaum Assocs.

— Smoking, Drinking, & Drug Use in Young Adulthood: The Impacts of New Freedoms & New Responsibilities. 1997. pap. 29.95 (*0-8058-2732-3*) L Erlbaum Assocs.

Bachman, Jerald G., jt. auth. see Johnston, Jerome.

Bachman, Joan. Policies & Procedures Guidebook for Assisted Living Centers. 194p. 77.00 (*0-929442-56-3*) Prof Prnting & Pub.

Bachman, John, jt. auth. see Audubon, John James.

Bachman, John W. Together in Hope: Fifty Years of Lutheran World Relief. LC 95-3114. 192p. 1995. pap. 11.95 (*1-886513-01-5*) Kirk Hse Pubs.

Bachman, Jonathan, et al, eds. Bureau of Reclamation: An Assessment of the Environmental Impact Statement on the Operations of the Glen Canyon Dam. (Illus.). 213p. (Orig.). (C). 1997. text 40.00 (*0-7881-4057-4*) DIANE Pub.

Bachman, Jonathan T. Air Pollution: Estimated Benefits & Costs of the Navajo Generating Station's Emissions Limit. (Illus.). 54p. 1999. text 20.00 (*0-7881-7944-6*) DIANE Pub.

Bachman, Judith. A History of Indian Policy: Syllabus. 1978. pap. text 8.95 (*0-89420-038-0*, 333020); audio 146.10 (*0-89420-149-2*, 333000) Natl Book.

Bachman, Judy L. Keys to Dealing with Childhood Allergies. (Parenting Keys Ser.). 160p. 1992. pap. 5.95 (*0-8120-4836-9*) Barron.

Bachman, Lee. Evolution of Motion: The Bladed Weapon. LC 96-96961. (Illus.). 110p. (Orig.). (C). 1997. pap. 12.95 (*0-9652672-2-9*) Bachman Pub.

***Bachman, Lee.** Kenpo Foundations. (Illus.). 75p. 2000. pap. 14.95 (*0-9652672-8-8*) Bachman Pub.

Bachman, Lee. Kenpo Physics: The Science of Motion. LC 99-94750. (Illus.). 110p. 1999. pap. 12.95 (*0-9652672-6-1*) Bachman Pub.

— Quantum Kenpo: Pulling the Pieces Together. 92p. (C). 1997. pap. 10.95 (*0-9652672-3-7*) Bachman Pub.

***Bachman, Lee.** Universals of Kenpo. (Illus.). 110p. 2000. pap. 14.95 (*0-9652672-7-X*) Bachman Pub.

Bachman, Lee A. The Edge: How Not to Become a Victim. LC 96-96389. 75p. (C). 1996. pap. 12.95 (*0-9652672-0-2*) Bachman Pub.

— Kenpo Logic: "Overcoming Multiple Attackers" (Illus.). iv, 100p. 1999. pap. 12.95 (*0-9652672-5-3*) Bachman Pub.

— Kenpo Theory: "The Why" (Illus.). 90p. (Orig.). 1997. pap. 12.95 (*0-9652672-4-5*) Bachman Pub.

Bachman, Leonard R. & Thaddeus, David J. Spreadsheets for Architects. (Architecture Ser.). 123p. 1995. pap. 69.95 (*0-471-28674-5*, VNR) Wiley.

Bachman, Leonard R. & Thaddeus, David J. Spreadsheets for Architects: Swiss Army Knife Software. LC 94-23795. 1995. pap. 54.95 (*0-442-01950-5*, VNR) Wiley.

Bachman, Lyle & Palmer, Adrian. Language Testing in Practice: Designing & Developing Useful Language Tests. (Illus.). 384p. 1996. pap. text 23.95 (*0-19-437148-4*) OUP.

Bachman, Lyle F. Fundamental Considerations in Language Testing. (Illus.). 420p. 1990. pap. text 23.95 (*0-19-437003-8*) OUP.

Bachman, Lyle F. & Cohen, Andrew D., eds. Interfaces Between Second Language Acquisition & Language Testing Research. LC 98-24269. (Cambridge Applied Linguistics Ser.). (Illus.). 272p. (C). 1998. text 54.95 (*0-521-64023-7*); pap. text 20.95 (*0-521-64963-3*) Cambridge U Pr.

Bachman, M., jt. auth. see Hynes, M.

Bachman, Manfred. Holzspielzeug aus dem Erzgebirge. 2nd rev. ed. (GER., Illus.). 260p. 1994. text 37.00 (*3-364-00080-8*) Gordon & Breach.

Bachman, Mary. God Gets First Place. 1987. pap. 3.00 (*0-89137-052-8*) Quality Pubns.

— Hair Combs: Identification & Values. LC 98-152997. (Collector's Guide to Ser.). 1998. pap. text 16.95 (*1-57432-048-3*, 5045) Collector Bks.

— I Believe in God Because... 1989. pap. 4.15 (*0-89137-059-5*) Quality Pubns.

— Is It in the Bible? 1987. pap. 2.40 (*0-89137-051-X*) Quality Pubns.

Bachman, Mary. True to the Bible: Stories about Jesus. unabridged ed. 123p. 1997. pap. 6.95 (*0-89137-832-4*, 78324) Quality Pubns.

Bachman, Mary, jt. auth. see Bachman, Susan.

Bachman, Paul M., ed. 1995 AAFCO Official Publication. rev. ed. 357p. 1995. 25.00 (*1-878341-06-5*) AAFCO.

Bachman, Paul W. Research for Profit: The Problem, the Solution, a Case History. LC 78-75633. (Illus.). 202p. reprint ed. pap. 62.70 (*0-608-10741-7*, 201240300081) Bks Demand.

Bachman, Richard, jt. auth. see King, Stephen.

Bachman, Richard, pseud. The Regulators. (Illus.). 489p. 1997. mass mkt. 7.99 (*0-451-19101-3*, Sig) NAL.

— The Regulators. 1997. mass mkt. 383.52 (*0-451-98396-3*) Signet.

— The Regulators. (Illus.). 466p. 1996. text 24.95 (*0-670-87281-4*) Viking Penguin.

— The Regulators. large type ed. LC 96-31831. 584p. 1996. 26.95 (*0-7862-0844-9*) Thorndike Pr.

— The Regulators. large type ed. LC 96-31831. 584p. 1997. pap. 24.95 (*0-7862-0845-7*) Thorndike Pr.

— The Running Man, 1 vol. 304p. 1999. mass mkt. 7.99 (*0-451-19796-8*) NAL.

— The Running Man. 1982. 11.09 (*0-606-03907-4*, Pub. by Turtleback) Demco.

— Thinner. 1984. 12.09 (*0-606-00776-8*, Pub. by Turtleback) Demco.

— Thinner. 320p. 1985. reprint ed. mass mkt. 7.99 (*0-451-16134-3*, Sig) NAL.

Bachman, Robert A., jt. auth. see Stahl, Ralph G.

Bachman, Ronald D., jt. ed. see Koenker, Diane P.

Bachman, Ronald D., ed. see Library of Congress.

Bachman, Ronet. Death & Violence on the Reservation: Homicide, Family Violence, & Suicide in American Indian Populations. LC 91-37158. 192p. 1992. 52.95 (*0-86569-015-4*, T015, Auburn Hse) Greenwood.

Bachman, Ronet & Pasternoster, Raymond. Statistical Methods for Criminology & Criminal Justice. LC 96-22514. 704p. (C). 1996. 63.44 (*0-07-003000-6*) McGraw.

Bachman, Ronet, jt. ed. see Paternoster, Raymond.

Bachman, Scott, ed. see Knievel, Evel.

Bachman, Steven B., jt. ed. see Crouch, James K.

Bachman, Susan. Because God Loves Us. 1988. pap. 3.00 (*0-89137-056-0*) Quality Pubns.

Bachman, Susan & Bachman, Mary. Julie's Special Day. 1988. pap. 2.75 (*0-89137-054-4*) Quality Pubns.

Bachman, V. John. Camus's Rebellious Thought: Legacy of Lucidity. LC 98-90608. x, 140p. 1998. pap. 12.95 (*0-9666421-0-4*) Talus Titles.

Drawing on Albert Camus's early journalism & the wide range of his later works, this book shows rebellion to be central. He rebelled against propositional thinking & posed alternatives to established thought in his many literary genres. All his work is derivative of his personal habit of attending to desirable & undesirable features of human life, eyes wide open to both. French by birth & upbringing, he graphically described the contradictions between the joyous land of his native Algeria & the deprivations imposed by his French compatriots. A man of leftist sensibilities, he nevertheless condemned atrocities & wrongness wherever found, despite the objections of associates. Aggressive Fascism & assertive Communism, the massive killings of a world war, continuous internecine stress & ongoing ethnic antagonisms & exterminations stimulated Camus to depict the highs & lows of human realities--in essays, fiction & drama. His writings won attention in France & of many in the United States. Camus became a European voice for what has been called "America's greatest generation." Camus's philosophic essay, The Rebel, advances rebellion as a corrective, not a replacer, of orders & systems of thought & politics. And that, says Bachman, could be the needed antidote for today's prevalent, often virulent politics.
Publisher Paid Annotation.

Bachman, Van Cleaf. Peltries or Plantations: The Economic Policies of the Dutch West India Company in New Netherland, 1623-1639. LC 74-91336. (Johns Hopkins University Studies in Historical & Political Science: Ser. 87, No. 2). 193p. reprint ed. pap. 59.90 (*0-8357-8263-8*, 203414100088) Bks Demand.

Bachman, W. Bryant, Jr. Forty Old Icelandic Tales. 322p. (Orig.). (C). 1992. pap. text 37.50 (*0-8191-8500-0*); lib. bdg. 64.00 (*0-8191-8499-3*) U Pr of Amer.

Bachman, W. Bryant, Jr., tr. from ICE. Four Old Icelandic Sagas & Other Tales. 252p. (Orig.). 1985. pap. text 25.00 (*0-8191-4704-4*); lib. bdg. 46.00 (*0-8191-4703-6*) U Pr of Amer.

Bachman, W. Bryant, Jr. & Erlingsson, Gudmundur, trs. The Saga of Finnbogi the Strong. LC 89-22527. (Illus.). 130p. (C). 1990. pap. text 15.00 (*0-8191-7595-1*); lib. bdg. 44.00 (*0-8191-7594-3*) U Pr of Amer.

— The Sagas of King Half & King Hrolf. (Illus.). 144p. (Orig.). (C). 1991. pap. text 24.50 (*0-8191-8123-4*); lib. bdg. 47.50 (*0-8191-8122-6*) U Pr of Amer.

— Six Old Icelandic Sagas. 134p. (Orig.). (C). 1993. pap. text 26.50 (*0-8191-9157-4*); lib. bdg. 49.50 (*0-8191-9156-6*) U Pr of Amer.

Bachman, W. Bryant, Jr & Erlingsson, Guomundur, trs. from ICE. Heidarviga Saga. 118p. (C). 1995. lib. bdg. 35.00 (*0-7618-0091-3*) U Pr of Amer.

— Svarfdale Saga: And Other Tales. LC 94-4900. 142p. (Orig.). 1994. lib. bdg. 29.00 (*0-8191-9513-8*) U Pr of Amer.

Bachman, Walt. Law vs. Life: What Lawyers Are Afraid to Say about the Legal Profession. LC 95-60315. 140p. 1995. 17.95 (*0-9627659-8-8*) Four Directions.

Bachmanj, H. & Slaby, W. A., eds. Concordance to the Novum Testamentum Graece of Nestle-Aland, 26th Edition, & to the Greek N. T. 3rd ed. 1016p. (C). 1987. lib. bdg. 127.15 (*3-11-011570-0*) De Gruyter.

Bachmann, Alberto. An Encyclopedia of the Violin. Weir, Albert E., ed. Martens, Frederick H., tr. from GER. LC 65-23406. (Music Ser.). 1975. reprint ed. lib. bdg. 47.50 (*0-306-70912-0*) Da Capo.

— An Encyclopedia of the Violin. Weir, Albert E., ed. Martens, Frederick H., tr. from GER. LC 65-23406. (Music Ser.). (Illus.). 470p. 1975. reprint ed. pap. 16.95 (*0-306-80004-7*) Da Capo.

Bachmann, Barbara & Strickland, Walter N. Neurospore Bibliography & Index. LC 65-12538. 234p. reprint ed. pap. 72.60 (*0-608-11118-X*, 202197700024) Bks Demand.

Bachmann, Bernhard. Grosses Lexikon der Computerfachbegriffe. 2nd ed. (GER.). 632p. 1992. 125.00 (*0-7859-8535-2*, 3883222577) Fr & Eur.

— Neue Computer-Lexikon Von A-Z. (GER.). 280p. 1993. 29.95 (*0-7859-8438-0*, 3572006333) Fr & Eur.

Bachmann, Bill. Clicking the Shutter Is the Easy Part: An Inside Look into the Exciting World of Advertising Photography. (Illus.). 224p. 1989. 21.95 (*1-877659-00-2*) Ernest & Conrad Pub.

— Introspective World. LC 95-61327. (Illus.). 144p. 1989. 59.95 (*1-877659-02-9*) Ernest & Conrad Pub.

Bachmann, Cornelia. Public Relations: Ghostwriting fur Medien? Eine Linguistische Analyse der Journalistischen Leistung Bei Der Adaption Von Pressemitteilungen. (Zurcher Germanistische Studien Ser.: No. 49). 252p. 1997. 40.95 (*3-906757-87-0*, Pub. by P Lang) P Lang Pubng.

Bachmann, Diana. An Elusive Freedom. 288p. 24.00 (*0-7278-4969-7*) Severn Hse.

— Sound Like Thunder. 288p. 24.00 (*0-7278-4887-9*) Severn Hse.

— Tides of the Heart. large type ed. Orig. Title: Janthina. 560p. 1987. 27.99 (*0-7089-8444-4*, Charnwood) Ulverscroft.

— Winds of Change. (Sarnia Saga Ser.: Vol. 3). 224p. 1998. 25.00 (*0-7278-5351-1*) Severn Hse.

Bachmann, E. Theodore & Bachmann, Mercia B. Lutheran Churches in the World: A Handbook. LC 89-31064. 640p. 1989. text 54.99 (*0-8066-2371-3*, 10-4157, Augsburg) Augsburg Fortress.

Bachmann, E. Theodore, et al. The United Lutheran Church in America, 1918-1962. LC 97-20819. 384p. 1997. pap. 25.00 (*0-8006-2925-6*, 1-2925, Fortress Pr) Augsburg Fortress.

Bachmann, F., et al, eds. International Congress on Fibrinolysis, 6th, Lausanne, July 1982: Abstracts. (Journal: Haemostasis: Vol. 11, Suppl. 1, 1982). iv, 108p. 1982. pap. 30.50 (*3-8055-3590-2*) S Karger.

***Bachmann, G. H. & Lerche, I., eds.** Epicontinental Triassic. (Zentralblatt fur Geologie & Palaontologie Ser.: Vol. 1). 402p. 2000. pap. 106.00 (*3-510-66011-0*, Pub. by E Schweizerbartsche) Balogh.

— Epicontinental Triassic. (Zentralblatt fur Geologie & Palaontologie Ser.: Vol. 2). 408p. 2000. pap. 106.00 (*3-510-66012-9*, Pub. by E Schweizerbartsche) Balogh.

— Epicontinental Triassic. (Zentralblatt fur Geologie & Palaontologie Ser.: Vol. 3). 2000. pap. 91.00 (*3-510-66013-7*, Pub. by E Schweizerbartsche) Balogh.

***Bachmann, Glenn.** Palm Programming. (Illus.). 363p. 1999. pap. 29.99 incl. cd-rom (*0-672-31493-2*) Sams.

Bachmann, H. Vibration Problems in Structures: Practical Guidelines. xvii, 234p. 1995. reprint ed. 58.00 (*3-7643-5148-9*) Birkhauser.

Bachmann, Heinz. Implementing Deregulation & Promoting Foreign Direct Investment in Africa - Les Politiques de Dereglementation et de Promotion des Investissements Directs Estrangers en Afrique: A Report on Six Workshops - Un Compte Rendu de Six Ateliers. LC 96-16978. (IMS Research Papers). (ENG & FRE.). 136p. 1996. pap. 22.00 (*0-8213-3626-6*) World Bank.

— Der Weg der mathematischen Grundlagenforschung. (GER.). 240p. 1985. 31.00 (*3-261-05089-6*) P Lang Pubng.

***Bachmann, Hermann.** Through the German Colonies of the Beresan District & Colonist Tales. Wagner, Roland, tr. from GER. Orig. Title: Durch die Deutshen Koloien des Beresaner Gebietes. 180p. 2000. write for info. (*1-891193-12-0*) ND State Univ.

Bachmann, Holger, jt. ed. see Minden, Michael.

Bachmann, Hugo. Partial Prestressing of Concrete Structures. (IBA Ser.: No. 95). 20p. 1980. 14.50 (*0-8176-1150-9*) Birkhauser.

Bachmann, Hugo, et al. Vibration Problems in Structures: Practical Guidelines. LC 94-41548. 234p. 1997. 58.00 (*0-8176-5148-9*) Birkhauser.

***Bachmann, Ingeborg.** The Book of Franza & Requiem for Fanny Goldman. Filkins, Peter, tr. from GER. LC 99-35468. 256p. 1999. 26.95 (*0-8101-1204-3*, Hydra Bks) Northwestern U Pr.

Bachmann, Ingeborg. Complete Poems by Ingeborg Bachmann: Bilingual Edition. Filkins, Peter, tr. from GER. 368p. 1994. 40.00 (*1-56886-009-9*) Marsilio Pubs.

— Complete Poems by Ingeborg Bachmann: Bilingual Edition. Filkins, Peter, tr. from GER. 368p. 1994. pap. 19.95 (*1-56886-010-2*) Marsilio Pubs.

Bachmann, Ingeborg. Franza Case & Requiem for Fan. pap. 26.00 (*0-09-414198-3*) Arrow Bks.

Bachmann, Ingeborg. Malina. Boehm, Philip, tr. from GER. LC 90-4953. (Modern German Voices Ser.). 256p. 1991. 27.50 (*0-8419-1192-4*) Holmes & Meier.

— Malina. Boehm, Philip, tr. (Portico Paperbacks Ser.). 1999. pap. 15.95 (*0-8419-1189-4*) Holmes & Meier.

— The Thirtieth Year. Bullock, Michael, tr. from GER. LC 87-14846. (Modern German Voices Ser.). 200p. 1987. 19.95 (*0-8419-1068-5*) Holmes & Meier.

— The Thirtieth Year. Bullock, Michael, tr. from GER. LC 87-14846. (Portico Paperbacks Ser.). 200p. 1995. pap. 12.95 (*0-8419-1069-3*) Holmes & Meier.

— Three Paths to the Lake. Gilbert, Mary F. & Anderson, Mark, trs. from GER. LC 88-21243. (Modern German Voices Ser.). Orig. Title: Simultan. 212p. (C). 1989. 29.95 (*0-8419-1070-7*) Holmes & Meier.

— Three Paths to the Lake. Gilbert, Mary F., tr. from GER. LC 96-53686. (Portico Paperbacks Ser.). Orig. Title: Simultan. 212p. (C). 1997. reprint ed. pap. 14.00 (*0-8419-1071-5*) Holmes & Meier.

— Three Radio Plays: A Deal in Dreams; The Cicadas; The Good God of Manhattan. Friedberg, Lilian, tr. from GER. (Studies in Austrian Literature, Culture & Thought).Tr. of Drei Horspiele. 223p. 1999. pap. 21.50 (*1-57241-079-5*) Ariadne CA.

Bachmann, Ingeborg & Wolf, Christa. Selected Prose & Drama. Herminghouse, Patricia A., ed. LC 79-107032. (The German Library). 324p. 1997. 39.50 (*0-8264-0956-3*); pap. 19.95 (*0-8264-0957-1*) Continuum.

Bachmann, Jutta, jt. auth. see Rammensee, Hans-Georg.

Bachmann, K. J. The Materials Science of Microelectronics. 541p. 1994. 110.00 (*0-471-18544-2*) Wiley.

Bachmann, Klaus J. The Materials Science of Microelectronics. LC 93-7878. (Illus.). xiv, 530p. 1994. 79.95 (*0-89573-280-7*, Wiley-VCH) Wiley.

B

An Asterisk (*) at the beginning of an entry indicates that the title is appearing for the first time.

Bachmann, Konstanze, ed. Conservation Concerns: A Guide for Collectors & Curators. LC 91-39500. (Illus.). 149p. (Orig.). (C). 1992. pap. text 14.95 (1-56098-174-1) Cooper-Hewitt Museum.

Bachmann, Ludwig. Anecdota Graeca e Codicibus Manuscriptis Bibliothecae Regiae Parisiensis, 2 vols., Set. xii, 978p. 1965. reprint ed. 240.00 (0-318-70871-X) G Olms Pubs.

Bachmann, Manuel. Die Strukturalistische Artefakt - und Kunstanalyse: Exposition der Grundlagen Anhand der Vorderoientalischen, Agyptischen und Griechischen Kunst. (Orbis Biblicus et Orientalis Ser.: Vol. 148). (GER.). 80p. 1996. pap. text 19.75 (3-7278-1077-7, Pub. by Presses Univ Fribourg) Eisenbrauns.

Bachmann, Marie L. Delcroz Today: An Education Through & into Music. Parlett, David, tr. (Illus.). 388p. 1993. pap. text 29.95 (0-19-816400-9) OUP.

Bachmann, Mark. Sandy River, OR. (Steelhead River Journal Ser.: Vol. 3, No. 1). (Illus.). 48p. 1997. pap. 15.95 (1-57188-081-X) F Amato Pubns.

Bachmann, Mercia B., jt. auth. see Bachmann, E. Theodore.

***Bachmann, Michael.** Antijudaismus im Galaterbrief: Exegetische Studien zu Einem Polemischen Schreiben und Zur Theologie des Apostels Paulus. (Novum Testamentum et Orbis Antiquus Ser.: No. 40). (GER.). vii, 220p. 1999. text 48.00 (3-7278-1256-7, Pub. by Ed Univ Fri) Eisenbrauns.

Bachmann, Paul. Niedere Zahlentheorie, 2 Vols. in 1. LC 66-20395. 902p. 1968. reprint ed. text 39.50 (0-8284-0217-5) Chelsea Pub.

Bachmann, Peter, et al, eds. Assessment of Biodiversity for Improved Forest Planning. LC 97-44795. (Forestry Sciences Ser.). 421p. 1998. lib. bdg. 169.00 (0-7923-4872-9) Kluwer Academic.

Bachmann, Ramona. Simply Kosher: Exotic Food from Around the World. (Illus.). 218p. 1994. 19.95 (965-229-104-8, Pub. by Gefen Pub Hse) Gefen Bks.

Bachmann, Reinhard, jt. ed. see Lane, Christel.

Bachmann, Robert. Hand of a Thousand Rings: And Other Chinese Stories. LC 76-178435. (Short Story Index Reprint Ser.). 1977. reprint ed. 18.95 (0-8369-4035-0) Ayer.

Bachmann, S., et al. Sichtwechsel NEU Level 1: Text- und Arbeitsbuch. (GER.). 176p. (Orig.). (C). 1995. pap. text 27.00 (3-12-675020-6, Pub. by Klett Edition); audio 34.25 (3-12-675023-0, Pub. by Klett Edition) Intl Bk Import.

Bachmann, Steve, ed. Preach Liberty: Selections from the Bible for Progressives. LC 89-35507. (Illus.). 120p. (Orig.). 1989. pap. 10.95 (0-941423-29-8) FWEW.

Bachmann, Sybille. Kirchliche Basisgemeinden in Zentralamerika: Entstehung, Entwicklung, Gedankengut. (Wurzburger Studien Zur Fundamentaltheologie Ser.: Bd. 15). (GER.). 263p. 1993. 44.95 (3-631-45189-X) P Lang Pubng.

Bachmann, T. Psychophysiology of Visual Masking: The Fine Structure of Conscious Experience, Horizons in Psychology. LC 93-19895. 191p. (C). 1994. pap. text 125.00 (1-56072-066-2) Nova Sci Pubs.

Bachmann, Theodore & Lehmann, Helmut T., eds. Luther's Works: Word & Sacrament I, Vol. 35. LC 55-9893. 426p. 1960. 30.00 (0-8006-0335-4, 1-335, Fortress Pr) Augsburg Fortress.

Bachmann, Troy. Frontier Flies: Patterns on the Cutting Edge. (Illus.). 128p. 1998. pap. 29.95 (1-57188-129-8); spiral bd. 39.95 (1-57188-130-1) F Amato Pubns.

Bachmann, W., et al, eds. Insulin Sulfonylharnstoff: Kombinationstherapie Bei Typ II-Diabetes. (Illus.). viii, 168p. 1988. 43.50 (3-8055-4601-7) S Karger.

— Insulin-Sulphonylurea: Combination Therapy in Type-II Diabetes. (Illus.). viii, 160p. 1988. 36.75 (3-8055-4862-1) S Karger.

Bachmann, W. & Mehnert, H., eds. Kombinationtherapie Insulin-Sulfonylharnstoff. (Illus.). viii, 208p. 1984. 56.75 (3-8055-3850-2) S Karger.

Bachmann, W., ed. see Honnold, Dierdre W.

Bachmanova, G. I., jt. auth. see Archakov, I. A.

Bachmat, Yehuda. Management of Groundwater Observation Programmes. (WMO, No. 705 & Operational Hydrology Reports: No. 31). 96p. 1989. pap. 22.00 (92-63-10705-X, Pub. by Wrld Meteorological) St Mut.

Bachmayer, H., jt. ed. see Laver, W. G.

Bachmeyer, Tim & Snyder, William A. Preserving the Legacy of a Small Business Family: Estate Planning & Business Succession. 225p. 1998. pap. 24.95 (0-9660538-0-X) Est Busn Comns.

Bachner, Bryan S. & Fu, H. L. Commercial Laws in the People's Republic of China - Regulation & Reform Affecting the Market. (CHI & ENG.). xix, 247p. 1995. pap. write for info. (0-409-99796-X, MICHIE) LEXIS Pub.

Bachner, Jane, jt. auth. see Stone, Janet.

Bachner, John P. Alternative Dispute Resolution for the Construction Industry. 124p. (Orig.). Date not set. pap. 65.00 (1-58074-058-8) ASFE.

— ASFE Contract Reference Guide. 180p. (Orig.). 1997. pap. 95.00 (1-58074-056-1) ASFE.

— Case Histories of Professional Liability Losses. (Orig.). 1996. pap. write for info. (1-58074-055-3) ASFE.

— Expert: A Guide to Services As a Forensic Professional & Expert Witness. 56p. 1995. pap. 65.00 (1-58074-051-0) ASFE.

— Practice Management for Design Professionals: A Practical Guide to Avoiding Liability & Enhancing Profitability. LC 90-47916. 400p. 1991. 110.00 (0-471-52205-8) Wiley.

Bachner, John P. & Khosla, Naresh K. Marketing & Promotion for Design Professionals. LC 76-57975. (Illus.). 368p. reprint ed. pap. 114.10 (0-608-11328-X, 201490200094) Bks Demand.

Bachner, Susan. Picture This: An Illustrated Guide to Complete Dinners. (Illus.). 72p. 1984. 27.50 (0-9613439-0-7) Spec Addns.

Bachner, Susan, jt. ed. see Ross, Mildred.

Bachnik, Jane M. & Quinn, Charles J., Jr., eds. Situated Meaning: Inside & Outside in Japanese Self, Society, & Language. 368p. 1994. text 57.50 (0-691-06965-4, Pub. by Princeton U Pr); pap. text 17.95 (0-691-01538-4, Pub. by Princeton U Pr) Cal Prin Full Svc.

Bacho. Dark Blue Suit. LC 97-24806. 192p. 1997. 30.00 (0-295-97664-0); pap. 16.95 (0-295-97637-3) U of Wash Pr.

Bacho. The Boxing Book. Date not set. pap. 6.95 (0-8050-5780-3) H Holt & Co.

Bacho, Peter. Boxing in Black & White. LC 99-14086. 122p. (YA). (gr. 7 up). 1999. 18.95 (0-8050-5779-X) H Holt & Co.

— Cebu. LC 91-323. 212p. (Orig.). 1991. pap. 16.95 (0-295-97132-0); text 25.00 (0-295-97113-4) U of Wash Pr.

Bachofen, R. & Mislin, H., eds. New Trends in Research & Utilization of Solar Energy Through Biological Systems. (Experientia Supplementa Ser.: Vol. 43). 156p. 1982. 46.50 (0-8176-1335-8) Birkhauser.

Bachom, Sandi. Denial Is Not a River in Egypt. LC 97-49917. (Illus.). 96p. 1998. pap. 9.95 (1-56838-188-3) Hazelden.

— Denial is Not a River in Egypt: 365 Wise & Humorous Recovery Sayings. 366p. 1999. 9.95 (1-56838-324-X) Hazelden.

***Bachom, Sandi.** The Wrath of Grapes: Packed with - Recovery, Insight & Humor. (Illus.). 96p. 2000. pap. 10.00 (1-56838-552-8) Hazelden.

***Bachor, H.** A Guide to Experiments in Quantum Optics. LC QC446.2.B32 1998. 378p. 1998. pap. 95.00 (3-527-29298-5, Wiley-VCH) Wiley.

Bachor, H. A., et al. Atomic & Molecular Physics & Quantum Optics: Proceedings of the 5th Summer School. 560p. 1993. text 116.00 (981-02-1124-4) World Scientific Pub.

Bachrach. Pathways Child. (JRA Ser.: Vol. 3, No. 4). 1993. 20.00 (0-8058-9983-9) L Erlbaum Assocs.

Bachrach, A. G., ed. & tr. see Huygens, L., et al.

Bachrach, A. L. & Pearce, J. R., eds. The Musical Companion. 800p. 1984. pap. 13.95 (0-15-662321-8, Harvest Bks) Harcourt.

Bachrach, Ann W., et al. Developmental Therapy for Young Children with Autistic Characteristics. LC 77-16370. (Illus.). 185p. 1978. pap. text 34.00 (0-936104-61-9, 1123) PRO-ED.

Bachrach, Ann W., jt. auth. see Slough, Rebecca.

Bachrach, Arthur J. & Egstrom, Glen H. Stress & Performance in Diving. 183p. (C). 1987. text 38.50 (0-941332-06-3, D235) Best Pub Co.

Bachrach, Bernard S. Armies & Politics in the Early Medieval West. (Collected Studies: No. CS 405). 751p. 1993. 109.95 (0-86078-374-X, Pub. by Variorum) Ashgate Pub Co.

***Bachrach, Bernard S.** Early Carolingian Warfare: Prelude to Empire. LC 99-87239. 2000. 55.00 (0-8122-3533-9) U of Pa Pr.

Bachrach, Bernard S. Early Medieval Jewish Policy in Western Europe. LC 77-152159. 227p. reprint ed. pap. 70.40 (0-8357-8864-4, 203320200085) Bks Demand.

— Fulk Nerra, The Neo-Roman Consul, 987-1040: A Political Biography of the Angevin Count. LC 93-13891. 1993. 65.00 (0-520-07996-5, Pub. by U CA Pr) Cal Prin Full Svc.

— A History of the Alans in the West: From Their First Appearance in the Sources of Classical Antiquity Through the Early Middle Ages. LC 73-77710. (Minnesota Monographs in the Humanities: No. 7). (Illus.). 185p. reprint ed. pap. 57.40 (0-8357-8909-8, 203320100085) Bks Demand.

— Jews in Barbarian Europe. 1977. 10.00 (0-87291-088-1) Coronado Pr.

— Merovingian Military Organization, 481-751. LC 70-187164. 169p. reprint ed. pap. 52.40 (0-608-14648-X, 205583700039) Bks Demand.

— State-Building in Medieval France: Studies in Early Angevin History. LC 94-42647. (Variorum Collected Studies: No. CS486). 336p. 1995. 109.95 (0-86078-468-1, Pub. by Variorum) Ashgate Pub Co.

Bachrach, Bernard S., ed. Liber Historae Francorum. 123p. 1973. pap. 7.50 (0-87291-058-X) Coronado Pr.

Bachrach, Bernard S. & Nicholas, David, eds. Law, Custom, & the Social Fabric in Medieval Europe. LC 89-13759. (Studies in Medieval Culture: No. 28). 1990. pap. 15.95 (0-918720-31-1); boxed set 34.95 (0-918720-30-3) Medieval Inst.

Bachrach, David J. & Nicholas, William R., eds. One Revolution: Managing the Academic Medical Practice in an Era of Rapid Change. 360p. 1997. pap. 75.00 (1-56829-083-7) Med Group Mgmt.

Bachrach, Deborah. The Charge of the Light Brigade. LC 96-21505. (Great Battles Ser.: Battles of the Nineteenth Century). (Illus.). 112p. (J). (gr. 5-12). 1996. lib. bdg. 26.20 (1-56006-455-2) Lucent Bks.

— The Crimean War. LC 97-34045. (World History Ser.). (Illus.). 112p. (YA). (gr. 8 up). 1997. lib. bdg. 22.45 (1-56006-315-7) Lucent Bks.

— Custer's Last Stand: Opposing Viewpoints. LC 90-36967. (Great Mysteries Ser.). (Illus.). 112p. (J). (gr. 5-8). 1990. lib. bdg. 22.45 (0-89908-077-4) Greenhaven.

— Espionage. LC 92-37438. (Overview Ser.). (Illus.). 112p. (YA). (gr. 5-8). 1992. lib. bdg. 22.45 (1-56006-134-0) Lucent Bks.

— The Inquisition. (World History Ser.). (Illus.). 128p. (J). (gr. 6-9). 1995. lib. bdg. 22.45 (1-56006-247-9) Lucent Bks.

— Margaret Sanger. LC 92-46878. (Importance of Ser.). (Illus.). 112p. (J). (gr. 5-8). 1993. lib. bdg. 22.45 (1-56006-032-8) Lucent Bks.

Bachrach, Deborah. The Resistance. LC 97-26844. (Holocaust Library). (Illus.). (YA). (gr. 5 up). 1997. lib. bdg. 22.45 (1-56006-092-1) Lucent Bks.

— Victorian England. (World History Ser.). (Illus.). (YA). (gr. 4-12). 2001. lib. bdg. 22.45 (1-56006-323-8) Lucent Bks.

Bachrach, Fred G. Turner's Holland. (Illus.). 72p. 1995. pap. 30.00 (1-85437-140-1, Pub. by Tate Gallery) U of Wash Pr.

Bachrach, George J. Salvage by the Surety. LC 98-28314. 1998. 74.95 (1-57073-593-X) Amer Bar Assn.

Bachrach, Kalman. Hasefer Alef-Beis Hametzuyar (In Color) (HEB., Illus.). 67p. (J). (gr. 1). 1960. pap. text 2.50 (1-878530-01-1) K Bachrach Co.

— Hasefer Chelek Rishon, Pt. 1: Alef-Beis. (HEB., Illus.). 68p. (J). (gr. 1). 1941. pap. text 2.25 (1-878530-00-3) K Bachrach Co.

— Hasefer Chelek Sheini, Pt. 2. (HEB., Illus.). 91p. (J). (gr. 2). 1942. pap. text 2.25 (1-878530-09-7) K Bachrach Co.

— Hasefer Chelek Shlishi, Pt. 3. (HEB., Illus.). 74p. (J). (gr. 3). 1947. pap. text 2.25 (1-878530-10-0) K Bachrach Co.

— Me Ah P'Amin V'Echad - Asid (1,000 Times & 1 Future Tense) Dikduk L'Talmidim (Grammar for Students) (HEB.). 46p. (J). (gr. 1-3). 1937. pap. text 1.00 (1-878530-21-6) K Bachrach Co.

— Meyah P'Amin V'Echad - Haveh (One Thousand Times & One - Present Tense) Dikduk L'Talmidim (Grammar for Students) (HEB.). 32p. (J). (gr. 1-3). 1937. pap. text 1.00 (1-878530-22-4) K Bachrach Co.

— Meyah P'Amin V'Echad - Ovar (One Thousand Times & One - Past Tense) Dikduk L'Talmidim (Grammar for Students) (HEB.). 48p. (J). (gr. 1-3). 1937. pap. text 1.00 (1-878530-20-8) K Bachrach Co.

— Olami Sefer Rishon, Bk. 1. rev. ed. (HEB., Illus.). 59p. (J). (gr. 2). 1943. pap. text 2.00 (1-878530-14-3) K Bachrach Co.

— Olami Sefer Sheini, Bk. 2. rev. ed. (HEB., Illus.). 71p. (J). (gr. 3-4). 1950. pap. text 2.00 (1-878530-15-1) K Bachrach Co.

— Olami Sefer Shlishi, Bk. 3. (HEB., Illus.). 92p. (J). (gr. 4-6). 1936. pap. text 2.00 (1-878530-16-X) K Bachrach Co.

— Targilon Hasefer Chelek Rishon, Pt. 1. (HEB.). 42p. (J). (gr. 1). 1950. student ed. 2.25 (1-878530-11-9) K Bachrach Co.

— Targilon Hasefer Chelek Sheini, Pt. 2. (HEB.). 76p. (J). (gr. 1). 1949. student ed. 2.25 (1-878530-12-7) K Bachrach Co.

— Targilon Hasefer Chelek Shlishi, Pt. 3. (HEB.). 60p. (J). (gr. 3). 1953. student ed. 2.25 (1-878530-13-5) K Bachrach Co.

— Targilon Olami Sefer Rishon, Bk. 1. (HEB.). 54p. (J). (gr. 2). 1936. student ed. 2.00 (1-878530-17-8) K Bachrach Co.

— Targilon Olami Sefer Sheini, Bk. 2. (HEB.). 54p. (J). (gr. 3-4). 1936. student ed. 2.00 (1-878530-18-6) K Bachrach Co.

— Targilon Olami Sefer Shlishi, Bk. 3. (HEB.). 60p. (J). (gr. 4-6). 1939. student ed. 2.00 (1-878530-19-4) K Bachrach Co.

Bachrach, Kalman & Axelrod, Herman. Ketivoni Chelek Chamishi, Pt. 5. (HEB., Illus.). 64p. (J). (gr. 6). 1972. pap. text 3.50 (1-878530-06-2) K Bachrach Co.

— Ketivoni Chelek Rishon, Pt. 1. (HEB., Illus.). 72p. (J). (gr. 2). 1957. pap. text 3.50 (1-878530-02-X) K Bachrach Co.

— Ketivoni Chelek R'Viyi, Pt. 4. (HEB., Illus.). 55p. (J). (gr. 5). 1972. pap. text 3.50 (1-878530-05-4) K Bachrach Co.

— Ketivoni Chelek Sheni, Pt. 2. (HEB., Illus.). 62p. (J). (gr. 3). 1958. pap. text 3.50 (1-878530-03-8) K Bachrach Co.

— Ketivoni Chelek Shishi, Pt. 6. (HEB., Illus.). 62p. (J). (gr. 7). 1974. pap. text 3.50 (1-878530-07-0) K Bachrach Co.

— Ketivoni Chelek Shlishi, Pt. 3. (HEB., Illus.). 64p. (J). (gr. 4). 1959. pap. text 3.50 (1-878530-04-6) K Bachrach Co.

— Ketivoni Chelek Sh'Viyi, Pt. 7. (HEB., Illus.). 64p. (J). (gr. 8). 1974. pap. text 3.50 (1-878530-08-9) K Bachrach Co.

Bachrach, Leona L., et al, eds. Mental Health Care in Canada. LC 87-646993. (New Directions for Mental Health Services Ser.: No. MHS 61). 105p. (Orig.). 1994. pap. 25.00 (0-7879-9965-2) Jossey-Bass.

Bachrach, Leona L., jt. ed. see Harris, Maxine.

Bachrach, Peter. The Theory of Democratic Elitism: A Critique. LC 80-5747. 125p. 1980. pap. text 14.00 (0-8191-1185-6) U Pr of Amer.

Bachrach, Peter & Botwinick, Aryeh. Power & Empowerment: A Radical Theory of Participatory Democracy. 250p. (C). 1992. 59.95 (0-87722-930-9); pap. 22.95 (0-87722-939-2) Temple U Pr.

Bachrach, R. Z. Advances in Surface & Interface Science Vol. 1: Techniques, Vol. 1. (Synchrotron Radiation Research Ser.). (Illus.). 552p. (C). 1992. text 130.00 (0-306-43872-0, Kluwer Plenum) Kluwer Academic.

— Issues & Technology, Vol. 2. (Synchrotron Radiation Research Ser.). (Illus.). 419p. (C). 1992. text 120.00 (0-306-43873-9, Kluwer Plenum) Kluwer Academic.

Bachrach, Steven J., jt. auth. see Miller, Freeman.

Bachrach, Steven M., ed. The Internet: A Guide for Chemists. LC 95-41967. (ACS Professional Reference Bks.). 360p. 1996. text 34.95 (0-8412-3223-7, Pub. by Am Chemical); pap. text 27.00 (0-8412-3224-5, Pub. by Am Chemical) OUP.

Bachrach, Susan. Dames Employees: The Feminization of Postal Workers in Nineteenth-Century France. LC 83-22879. (Women & History Ser.: No. 8). 134p. 1984. text 39.95 (0-86656-205-2) Haworth Pr.

Bachrach, Susan D. The Nazi Olympics: Berlin 1936. LC 99-31423. 132p. (YA). 2000. 21.95 (0-316-07086-6); pap. 14.95 (0-316-07087-4) Little.

— Tell Them We Remember: The Story of the Holocaust. (J). 1994. 18.15 (0-606-06799-X, Pub. by Turtleback) Demco.

Bachrach, Uriel & Heimer, Yair M., eds. The Physiology of Polyamines, 2 vols., Vol. I. 384p. 1989. lib. bdg. 259.00 (0-8493-6808-1, QP801) CRC Pr.

— The Physiology of Polyamines, 2 vols., Vol. II. 336p. 1989. lib. bdg. 249.00 (0-8493-6809-X) CRC Pr.

Bachrach, Yehoshua. Mother of Royalty. Oschry, Leonard, tr. 1995. 9.95 (0-87306-727-4) Feldheim.

Bachs, Oriol, jt. auth. see Agell, Neus.

Bachstein, Harry, ed. see Academy of Marine Sciences & Underwater Research Staff.

Bachstein, Harry S. Guerrilla Divorce for Men, Vol. 1. 200p. 1995. pap. text 19.95 (1-887529-00-4) Polaris Pub Grp.

Bachtell, Donald S. Always a Winner: An Experiment under Grace. LC 92-17390. 96p. (Orig.). 1993. pap. 8.95 (1-56474-028-5) Fithian Pr.

Bachtin, Michail. Fomalny Metod v Literaturovedenu: The Formal Method in Literary. 2nd ed. Kurtanovich, Konstantin, ed. (RUS., Illus.). 236p. (Orig.). pap. 12.50 (0-940294-14-1) Silver Age Pub.

Bachtler, John & Turok, Ivan, eds. The Coherence of EU Policy: Contrasting Perspectives on the Structural Funds. (Regional Policy & Development Ser.: No. 17). 405p. 1996. pap. 39.95 (1-85302-396-5, Pub. by Jessica Kingsley) Taylor & Francis.

Bachtler, Joseph R. Fire Instructor's Training Guide. 2nd ed. (Illus.). 1989. 36.00 (0-87814-912-0) Fire Eng.

Bachtler, Joseph R. & Brennan, Thomas F., eds. The Fire Chief's Handbook. 5th ed. LC 95-5748. 1100p. 1995. 74.95 (0-912212-40-3) Fire Eng.

Bachus, Nancy. The Baroque Spirit, Bk. 1. 64p. 1999. pap. 8.95 (0-7390-0094-2, 16718) Alfred Pub.

— The Romantic Spirit, Bk. 1. 64p. 1998. pap. 8.50 (0-88284-861-5, 4638) Alfred Pub.

— The Romantic Spirit, Bk. 2. 64p. 1998. pap. 8.50 (0-88284-862-3, 4639) Alfred Pub.

Bachus, Nancy, ed. The Baroque Spirit, Bk. 2. write for info. (0-7390-0502-2, 16719) Alfred Pub.

Bachus, Nancy & Agay, Denes. The Technic Companion. (Illus.). 80p. 1990. pap. 9.95 (0-8256-8081-6, YK20600, Yorktown Mus) Music Sales.

Bachus, Robert C., jt. ed. see Esrig, Melvin I.

Bachus, Spencer, ed. Counterfeiting of U. S. Currency Abroad: Hearing Before the Subcommittee on General Oversight & Investigations. 180p. 1999. reprint ed. text 30.00 (0-7881-4540-1) DIANE Pub.

Bachus, Walter O. Retirement . . . The Time for Real Happiness. LC 96-94855. 160p. (Orig.). 1996. pap. 9.95 (0-9655395-0-4) W O Bachus.

Bacia, Jennifer. Chapter One: Everything You Want to Know about Starting Your Novel! 1999. pap. text 11.95 (1-86448-331-8) Allen & Unwn AT.

Bacic, Jacques. Red Sea - Black Russia: Prolegomena to the History of North-Central Eurasia in Antiquity & the Middle Ages. LC 95-60873. 396p. 1995. 59.00 (0-88033-318-9, 421, Pub. by East Eur Monographs) Col U Pr.

Bacigal. Criminal Law & Procedure Study Guide. (Paralegal). (C). 1995. pap. text, student ed. 13.00 (0-314-06965-8) West Pub.

— Criminal Law & Processes. Date not set. pap. text, teacher ed. write for info. (0-314-06964-X) West Pub.

Bacigal, Ronald J. Criminal Law & Procedure: An Introduction. LC 95-24153. 425p. (C). 1995. mass mkt. 66.95 (0-314-06736-1) West Pub.

— The Limits of Litigation: The Dalkon Shield Controversy. LC 90-81011. 160p. 1990. 25.00 (0-89089-391-8); pap. 12.75 (0-89089-392-6) Carolina Acad Pr.

— May It Please the Court: A Biography of Judge Robert R. Merhige, Jr. LC 92-16325. 332p. (Orig.). (C). 1992. lib. bdg. 49.50 (0-8191-8757-7) U Pr of Amer.

Bacigalupi, Barbara. By the Grace of Your Gifts. (Truly Human Ser.). Date not set. pap. write for info. (1-893470-03-2) Umano.

— The Daily Practice. (Truly Human Ser.). Date not set. pap. write for info. (1-893470-05-9) Umano.

— Plan for It All. (Truly Human Ser.). Date not set. pap. write for info. (1-893470-04-0) Umano.

— Success Without Sacrificing Yourself. (Truly Human Ser.). Date not set. pap. write for info. (1-893470-02-4) Umano.

— Truly Human: An Invitation to Think about Yourself in New & Powerful Ways. LC 94-12045. (Illus.). 16p. 1999. pap. 14.95 (1-893470-00-8) Umano.

Bacigalupi, Don. Continental Discourse: Art of Mexico & the United States Today. LC 95-71572. (Illus.). 36p. (Orig.). 1995. pap. 12.95 (1-883502-05-5) San Ant Mus Art.

— Synesthesia: Sound & Vision in Contemporary Art. LC 94-67647. (Illus.). 41p. (Orig.). 1994. pap. 5.00 (1-883502-02-0) San Ant Mus Art.

Bacigalupi, Don & Hixon, Nancy. 1996 Houston Area Exhibition. (Illus.). 36p. 1996. pap. 10.00 (0-941193-11-X) U Houst Sarah.

Bacigalupi, Don & Kern-Foxworth, Marilyn. Michael Ray Charles, 1989-1997: An American Artist's Work. LC 96-78844. (Illus.). 52p. 1997. pap. 24.95 (0-941193-12-8) U of Tex Pr.

Bacigalupo, Andrea, jt. ed. see Schrezenmeier, Hubert.

An Asterisk (*) at the beginning of an entry indicates that the title is appearing for the first time.

Bacigalupo, Marvyn H. A Changing Perspective: Attitudes Toward Creole Society in New Spain (1521-1610) (Monagrafias A Ser.: Vol. LXXVI). 159p. (C). 1981. 51.00 (*0-7293-0072-2*, Pub. by Tamesis Bks Ltd) Boydell & Brewer.

Bacik, James. Spirituality in Action. LC 97-25338. 240p. 1997. pap. 15.95 (*1-55612-958-0*, LL1958) Sheed & Ward WI.

Bacik, James J. Contemporary Theologians: An Overview of Influential 20th Century Thinkers Who Have Helped Shape Christian Dialogue. LC 90-47876. 304p. 1991. reprint ed. 14.95 (*0-89243-492-9*, Liguori Triumph) Liguori Pubns.

— Spirituality in Transition. 226p. (Orig.). 1996. pap. 15.95 (*1-55612-857-6*, LL1857) Sheed & Ward WI.

— Tensions in the Church: Facing the Challenges, Seizing the Opportunities. 192p. (Orig.). 1993. pap. 9.95 (*1-55612-624-7*) Sheed & Ward WI.

Bacik, Michael G. Assignment in Augsburg: A Tanker in Europe. (Illus.). 240p. 2000. 19.95 (*0-9651173-1-6*) Basic Hse.

Bacilious, et al. Reform in Empowerment, Choice & Adult Learning. (Orig.). (C). 1992. pap. text 7.00 (*1-55996-154-6*) Univ Council Educ Admin.

***Bacino, Leo J.** Reconstructing Russia: U. S. Policy in Revolutionary Russia, 1917-1922. LC 99-21764. 368p. 1999. text 39.00 (*0-87338-635-3*) Kent St U Pr.

***Baciulis, Donna & Roerden, Chris, contrib. by.** Seven Days in Florence: A Parable of Timeless Spiritual Lessons. 80p. 1999. 12.95 (*0-9674459-0-6*) J Shanle.

***Back, Allan T.** Aristotle's Theory of Predication. 320p. 2000. 105.00 (*90-04-11719-9*) Brill Academic Pubs.

Back, Allan T. On Reduplication: Logical Theories of Qualification. LC 95-53247. (Studien und Texte zur Geistesgeschichte des Mittelalters Ser.: Bd. 49). 1996. 185.50 (*90-04-10539-5*) Brill Academic Pubs.

— On Reduplication: Logical Theories of Qualification. (Analytica Ser.). 768p. (C). 1991. 188.50 (*3-88405-045-1*) Philosophia Pr.

Back, B. B., et al. Advances in Nuclear Dynamics: Proceedings of the 9th Winter Workshop Nuclear Dynamics. 328p. 1993. text 114.00 (*981-02-1565-7*) World Scientific Pub.

Back, B. B., jt. auth. see Bauer, Wolfgang.

Back, Betsy W., jt. auth. see Albrecht, Terrance L.

***Back, C. S.** Perambulations: The Search for a Self. 260p. 1999. 25.00 (*0-7388-0768-0*); pap. 18.00 (*0-7388-0769-9*) Xlibris Corp.

Back, Christine. Bean & Plant. LC 86-9634. (Stopwatch Ser.). (Illus.). 25p. (J). (gr. 2-5). 1986. pap. 3.95 (*0-382-24014-6*); lib. bdg. 9.95 (*0-382-09286-4*, Silver Pr NJ) Silver Burdett Pr.

— Chicken & Egg. LC 86-10019. (Stopwatch Ser.). (Illus.). 25p. (J). (gr. k-4). 1991. pap. 3.95 (*0-382-09959-1*); lib. bdg. 9.95 (*0-382-09284-8*, Silver Pr NJ) Silver Burdett Pr.

Back, Christine & Watts, Barrie. Spider's Web. LC 86-10017. (Stopwatch Ser.). (Illus.). 25p. (J). (gr. k-4). 1986. pap. 3.95 (*0-382-24020-0*, Silver Pr NJ) Silver Burdett Pr.

— Tadpole & Frog. LC 86-10049. (Stopwatch Ser.). (Illus.). 25p. (J). (gr. k-4). 1986. pap. 3.95 (*0-382-24021-9*); lib. bdg. 9.95 (*0-382-09285-6*, Silver Pr NJ) Silver Burdett Pr.

Back, Douglas. American Pioneers Classic. 1994. audio 10.98 (*0-7866-0052-7*, 95203C) Mel Bay.

Back, Ernst L. Developments in Drying Technologies: A Literature Review. (Pira Reviews of Pulp & Paper Technology Ser.). 117p. 1991. pap. 95.00 (*0-902799-87-8*, TS1120, Pub. by Pira Internatl) Bks Intl VA.

Back, H. The Synonyms for "Child", "Boys", "Girl" in Old English: An Etymological-Semiasiological Investigation. (Lund Studies in English: Vol. 2). 1974. reprint ed. pap. 45.00 (*0-8115-0545-6*) Periodicals Srv.

Back, Harry. Multilingual Dictionary of Politics & Economics: English, French, German. 2nd ed. (ENG, FRE & GER.). 1037p. 1967. 175.00 (*0-7859-9990-6*) Fr & Eur.

— Polec Dictionary of Politics & Economics German-English-French. 2nd ed. (ENG, FRE & GER.). 1037p. 1967. 150.00 (*0-7859-6857-1*, 3110008920) Fr & Eur.

Back, Harry, et al, eds. Polec: Dictionary of Politics & Economics. 2nd enl. rev. ed. (ENG, FRE & GER.). (C). 1967. 76.15 (*3-11-000892-0*) De Gruyter.

***Back, Howard.** Waters of Yellowstone with Rod & Fly. (Illus.). 2000. 24.95 (*1-58574-040-3*) Lyons Pr.

***Back, Jerry.** Can We Talk?... About Matters of This Life. LC 99-65340. 272p. 2000. pap. 17.95 (*1-57921-247-6*, Pub. by WinePress Pub) BookWorld.

Back, Kurt W. Beyond Words: The Story of Sensitivity Training & the Encounter Movement. LC 73-182935. 266p. (Orig.). 1972. 45.00 (*0-87154-077-0*) Russell Sage.

— Family Planning & Population Control: The Challenges of a Successful Movement. (Social Movements Past & Present Ser.). (C). 1989. 33.00 (*0-8057-9711-4*) Macmillan.

— Slums, Projects & People. LC 73-19572. 123p. (C). 1974. reprint ed. lib. bdg. 57.50 (*0-8371-7289-6*, BASL, Greenwood Pr) Greenwood.

Back, Kurt W., ed. Social Psychology. LC 76-30835. 512p. reprint ed. pap. 158.80 (*0-608-30164-7*, 205518800011) Bks Demand.

***Back, Les & Solomos, John.** Theories of Race & Racism: Reader. LC 99-16826. 1999. pap. 29.95 (*0-415-15672-6*) Routledge.

***Back, Les & Solomos, John, eds.** Theories of Race & Racism: Reader. LC 99-16826. 672p. (C). 2000. text. write for info. (*0-415-15671-8*) Routledge.

Back, Les, jt. auth. see Solomos, John.

Back, Lillian & Wolk, Merla. Arenas Mind. LC 92-18244. 480p. (C). 1997. pap. text 43.00 (*0-673-46312-5*) Addson-Wesley Educ.

Back, Peg. Crickets & Corn. 1985. 3.50 (*0-377-00152-X*) Friendship Pr.

Back, Philippa F. Corporate Cash Management: Strategy & Practice. (Association of Corporate Treasurers Ser.). 208p. 1997. boxed set 135.00 (*1-85573-344-7*, Pub. by Woodhead Pubng) Am Educ Systs.

Back, R. P. The Runes Are Cast. 1981. 30.00 (*0-7223-1368-3*, Pub. by A H S Ltd) St Mut.

Back, Ralph J., et al. Refinement Calculus: A Systematic Introduction. Gries, D. & Schneider, F. B., eds. LC 97-47336. (Graduate Texts in Computer Science Ser.). 520p. 1998. 59.95 (*0-387-98417-8*) Spr-Verlag.

Back, Siegfried. The Pelican. Rotelle, John E., ed. O'Connell, Matthew J., tr. from GER. LC 87-72253. 88p. 1987. pap. 7.95 (*0-941491-07-2*) Augustinian Pr.

Back, T. Bradley & Gallion, Timothy J. Wehrmacht: Diceless Science-Fiction Wargaming. (Illus.). 120p. (Orig.). 1996. pap. 24.95 (*0-9653173-0-7*) Tyrant Games.

Back, Thomas. Evolutionary Algorithms in Theory & Practice: Evolution Strategies, Evolutionary Programming, Genetic Algorithms. (Illus.). 328p. 1996. text 60.00 (*0-19-509971-0*) OUP.

Back, Thomas G., ed. Organoselenium Chemistry: A Practical Approach. LC 99-28970. (The Practical Approach in Chemistry Ser.). (Illus.). 310p. 1999. text 140.00 (*0-19-850141-2*) OUP.

Back to Bible Staff. Giants of the Faith. 1999. 34.99 (*0-8474-1570-8*) Back to Bible.

Back, William R., et al, eds. Hydrogeology. (DNAG, Geology of North America Ser.: Vol. 02). (Illus.). 534p. 1989. 27.50 (*0-8137-5206-X*) Geol Soc.

Backa, Bruce, jt. auth. see Mann, William.

Backaitis, Stanley H., ed. Biomechanics of Impact Injury & Injury Tolerances of the Abdomen, Lumbar Spine & Pelvic Complex. 60p. 1995. pap. 149.00 (*1-56091-592-7*, PT47) Soc Auto Engineers.

— Biomechanics of Impact Injury & Injury Tolerances of the Extremities. LC 96-67656. (Progress in Technology Ser.). 896p. 1996. 149.00 (*1-56091-749-0*, PT-56) Soc Auto Engineers.

— Biomechanics of Impact Injury & Injury Tolerances of the Head-Neck Complex. 69p. 1993. 149.00 (*1-56091-363-0*, PT-43) Soc Auto Engineers.

— Biomechanics of Impact Injury & Injury Tolerances of the Thorax-Shoulder Complex. LC 93-87697. (Progress in Technology Ser.). 1320p. 1994. 149.00 (*1-56091-501-3*, PT-45) Soc Auto Engineers.

Backaitis, Stanley H. & Mertz, Harold J., eds. Hybrid III: The First Human Like Crash Test Dummy. LC 93-87030. 830p. 1994. 29.00 (*1-56091-449-1*, PT-44) Soc Auto Engineers.

Backalenick, Irene. East Side Story: Ten Years with the Jewish Repertory Theatre. (Illus.). 212p. (Orig.). (C). 1988. lib. bdg. 49.00 (*0-8191-6495-X*) U Pr of Amer.

Backaus, Balbir. The Arboretum at Arizona State University: A Guide. Namio, Jody, ed. LC 95-83897. (Illus.). 100p. 1996. pap. 9.95 (*0-9650847-1-X*) Arbrtm AZ St U.

Backauskas, Anne L. Computer Capers. (Illus.). 32p. (Orig.). 1983. pap. 1.95 (*0-913405-00-0*) ALB Assocs.

***Backauskas, Staci.** The Fifth Goddess. LC 99-91249. 352p. 1999. pap. 14.95 (*0-9675259-0-X*) Jai Creat.

Backels, Shirley. Experiencing Self-Esteem Through the Wonders of Science. 172p. 1993. pap. text 19.99 (*1-57156-019-X*) Wild Goose UT.

— Feel It! Feel It! Leg Go. (Feelings & Communication Unit Ser.). 22p. 1992. pap. text 4.99 (*1-57156-021-1*) Wild Goose UT.

— The Flip Machine. (Self-Talk Unit Ser.). 22p. 1992. pap. text 4.99 (*1-57156-026-1*) Wild Goose UT.

— The Friendship Adventure. (Friendship Unit Ser.). 22p. 1992. pap. text 4.99 (*1-57156-024-6*) Wild Goose UT.

— The Garbage Collector. (Self-Talk Unit Ser.). 22p. 1992. pap. text 4.99 (*1-57156-028-9*) Wild Goose UT.

— Hunt for Special Talents. (Friendship Unit Ser.). 22p. 1992. pap. text 4.99 (*1-57156-025-4*) Wild Goose UT.

— It's Real to Feel. (Feelings & Communication Unit Ser.). 22p. 1992. pap. text 4.99 (*1-57156-020-3*) Wild Goose UT.

— Make New Friends. (Friendship Unit Ser.). 22p. 1992. pap. text 4.99 (*1-57156-023-8*) Wild Goose UT.

— The Stinkin' Thinkin' Tape. (Self-Talk Unit Ser.). 22p. 1992. pap. text 4.99 (*1-57156-027-0*) Wild Goose UT.

— Twinkle, Twinkle, Little SK. (Feelings & Communication Unit Ser.). 22p. 1992. pap. text 4.99 (*1-57156-022-X*) Wild Goose UT.

Backemayer, Sylvia. Eric Fraser: Artist & Illustrator. (Illus.). 1998. 60.00 (*0-85331-753-4*, Pub. by Lund Humphries) Antique Collect.

Backemeyer, Sylvia, ed. Object Lessons: Central Saint Martins Art & Design Archive. 1996. pap. 29.95 (*0-85331-712-7*, Pub. by Lund Humphries) Antique Collect.

Backenstoss Family, compiled by. Backenstoss Family Association of America: Genealogy. 188p. 1993. reprint ed. pap. 29.50 (*0-8328-3255-3*); reprint ed. lib. bdg. 39.50 (*0-8328-3254-5*) Higginson Bk Co.

***Backer, A. P.** Politische und Okonomische Landerrisiken. (GER.). 240p. 1998. text 49.00 (*90-5708-031-1*, Harwood Acad Pubs); pap. text 23.00 (*90-5708-032-X*, Harwood Acad Pubs) Gordon & Breach.

Backer, A. P., et al. A Plant Ecological Bibliography & Thesaurus for Southern Africa up to 1975. (Memoirs of the Botanical Survey of South Africa Ser.: No. 52). (Illus.). 216p. 1986. 15.00 (*0-621-08871-4*, Pub. by Natl Botanical Inst) Balogh.

Backer, Aloys De, see De Backer, Aloys.

Backer, Barbara. 101 Tips for Preschool Teachers - Encouraging Creativity. Hodges, Susan, ed. (Illus.). 24p. (Orig.). 1996. mass mkt. 3.95 (*1-57029-093-8*, 4008) Totline Pubns.

— 101 Tips for Preschool Teachers - Developing Language Skills. Hodges, Susan, ed. (Illus.). 24p. (Orig.). 1996. mass mkt. 3.95 (*1-57029-097-0*, 4010) Totline Pubns.

— 101 Tips for Preschool Teachers - Developing Motor Skills. Hodges, Susan, ed. (Illus.). 24p. (Orig.). 1996. mass mkt. 3.95 (*1-57029-096-2*, 4009) Totline Pubns.

— 101 Tips for Preschool Teachers - Creating Theme Environments. Hodges, Susan, ed. (Illus.). 24p. (Orig.). 1996. mass mkt. 3.95 (*1-57029-092-X*, 4007) Totline Pubns.

— 101 Tips for Preschool Teachers - Spicing up Learning Centers. Hodges, Susan, ed. (Illus.). 24p. (Orig.). 1996. 3.95 (*1-57029-099-7*, 4012) Totline Pubns.

— 101 Tips for PS Teachers - Teaching Basic Concepts. Hodges, Susan, ed. (Illus.). 24p. (Orig.). 1996. mass mkt. 3.95 (*1-57029-098-9*, 4011) Totline Pubns.

Backer, Barbara, jt. auth. see Goren, Ada H.

Backer, Barbara, jt. auth. see Larkin, Patricia.

Backer, Barbara A., et al. Psychiatric Mental Health Readings. LC 84-29937. (Contemporary Readings Ser.). 300p. (C). 1985. pap. text 36.25 (*0-534-04644-4*) Jones & Bartlett.

Backer, Barbara F. Blocks. (Play & Learn Ser.). (Illus.). 48p. (J). (ps-k). 1998. pap. 3.95 (*1-57029-223-X*, W02306) Totline Pubns.

— Introducing Concepts at Circle Time. Hodges, Susan, ed. LC 98-61457. (Circle Time Book Ser.). (Illus.). 96p. (J). (ps-k). 1999. pap. 9.95 (*1-57029-239-6*, 04901) Totline Pubns.

— Kitchen Gadgets. (Play & Learn Ser.). (Illus.). 48p. (J). (ps-k). 1998. pap. 3.95 (*1-57029-227-2*, W02303) Totline Pubns.

— Paper. (Play & Learn Ser.). (Illus.). 48p. (J). (ps-k). 1998. pap. 3.95 (*1-57029-229-9*, W02309) Totline Pubns.

— Problem Solving Safari - Art. McKinnon, Elizabeth S., ed. (Problem Solving Safari Ser.). (Illus.). 32p. (Orig.). (J). (ps). 1997. pap. 4.95 (*1-57029-118-7*) Totline Pubns.

— Problem Solving Safari - Manipulatives. Bittinger, Gayle, ed. (Problem Solving Safari Ser.). (Illus.). 32p. (Orig.). 1997. pap. 4.95 (*1-57029-121-7*, 4304) Totline Pubns.

— Problem Solving Safari - Science. Bittinger, Gayle, ed. (Problem Solving Safari Ser.). (Illus.). 32p. (Orig.). 1997. pap. 4.95 (*1-57029-123-3*, 4306) Totline Pubns.

— Terrific Tips for Preschool Teachers. rev. ed. Cubley, Kathleen, ed. LC 98-60800. (Terrific Tips Ser.). (Illus.). 128p. 1998. pap. 3.95 (*1-57029-236-1*, W04020) Totline Pubns.

Backer, Bradden C., et al. Hiring & Firing in Wisconsin. 1998th ed. LC 98-34448. 190p. 1998. pap. 29.00 (*1-57862-015-5*) State Bar WI.

— Wisconsin Employment Law, 3 vols. 2nd ed. LC 98-23087. 1630p. 1998. ring bd. 195.00 (*1-57862-013-9*) State Bar WI.

Backer, Donald C., ed. The Galactic Center. LC 86-73186. (Conference Proceeding Ser.: No. 155). 222p. 1987. lib. bdg. 55.00 (*0-88318-355-2*) Am Inst Physics.

Backer, E., jt. auth. see Kandel, Abraham.

Backer, John H. Priming the German Economy: American Occupational Policies, 1945-1948. LC 70-142289. 222p. reprint ed. pap. 68.90 (*0-608-13867-3*, 202375800033) Bks Demand.

Backer, Karen. Immigration: Then & Now. 80p. (J) 1997. pap. 15.95 (*0-590-93097-4*) Scholastic Inc.

Backer, Lori. Presenter's Survival Kit: It's a Jungle Out There. LC 95-171568. 432p. (C). (gr. 13). 1994. spiral bd. 28.95 (*0-8151-0373-5*, 26258) Mosby Inc.

Backer, Lori & Deck, Michele. The Presenter's EZ Graphics Kit: A Guide for the Artistically Challenged. (Illus.). 240p. (gr. 13). 1996. spiral bd. 37.95 (*0-8151-1378-1*, 29944) Mosby Inc.

***Backer, Lynn.** Sequencing: Reading Strategies: Grades K-2. (Illus.). 64p. 1998. pap., teacher ed. 6.95 (*1-889369-29-2*, TI0200) Teaching Ink.

— Winter Olympics: Grades K-3. (Illus.). 64p. 1997. pap., teacher ed. 6.95 (*1-889369-22-5*, TI0090) Teaching Ink.

***Backer, Lynn & Cline, Debbie.** Map Reading: Grades K-2. (Illus.). 64p. 1998. pap., teacher ed. 6.95 (*1-889369-25-X*, TI0100) Teaching Ink.

— Phonics Activities: Long Vowel Sounds: Grades K-2. (Illus.). 64p. 1999. pap., teacher ed. 6.95 (*1-889369-37-3*, TI0063) Teaching Ink.

— Phonics Activities: Short Vowel Sounds: Grades K-2. (Illus.). 64p. 1999. pap., teacher ed. 6.95 (*1-889369-36-5*, TI0062) Teaching Ink.

— Phonics Mini-Books: Long Vowel Sounds: Grades K-2. (Illus.). 64p. 1997. pap., teacher ed. 6.95 (*1-889369-19-5*, TI0061) Teaching Ink.

— Phonics Mini-Books: Short Vowel Sounds: Grades K-2. (Illus.). 64p. 1997. pap., teacher ed. 6.95 (*1-889369-18-7*, TI0060) Teaching Ink.

Backer, Lynne. Surprise Stories. unabridged ed. Muffoletto, Mary L., ed. (Illus.). 64p. 1996. pap. 6.95 (*1-889369-13-6*, TI0050) Teaching Ink.

Backer, Lynne & Cline, Debbie. Elections. (Illus.). 64p. (J). (gr. k-3). 1996. pap., teacher ed. 6.95 (*1-889369-10-1*, TI0030) Teaching Ink.

— Step by Step Math: K-2. Muffoletto, Mary L., ed. (Illus.). 64p. 1996. pap., teacher ed. 6.95 (*1-889369-05-5*, TI0010) Teaching Ink.

Backer, Mireille. Handbook of Baroque Dance Steps in Labanotation. LC 85-73577. 55p. (Orig.). (C). 1987. pap. text 9.95 (*0-932582-54-0*, Pub. by Dance Notation) Princeton Bk Co.

Backer, Morton, et al. Financial Accounting: Concepts & Practices. 5th ed. 704p. (C). 1988. teacher ed. 6.50 (*0-15-527372-8*) Dryden Pr.

Backer, Thomas E. Designing Health Communication Campaigns: What Works? 200p. (C). 1992. text 44.00 (*0-8039-4331-8*); pap. text 21.95 (*0-8039-4332-6*) Sage.

Backer, Thomas E. Reviewing the Behavioral Science Knowledge Base on Technology Transfer. 293p. 1995. pap. text 13.00 (*0-16-048352-2*) USGPO.

Backer, Thomas E., et al, eds. Psychology & AIDS. (Special Issue, American Psychologist Ser.: Vol. 43, No. 11). 156p. 1988. pap. 16.00 (*1-55798-053-5*) Am Psychol.

Backer, Thomas E. & O'Hara, Kirk B. Organizational Change & Drug-Free Workplaces: Templates for Success. LC 90-23117. 208p. 1991. 59.95 (*0-89930-434-6*, BDU, Quorum Bks) Greenwood.

Backer, Thomas E. & Rogers, Everett M., eds. Organizational Aspects of Health Communication Campaigns. (Illus.). 280p. (C). 1993. text 49.95 (*0-8039-4997-9*); pap. text 24.00 (*0-8039-4998-7*) Sage.

Backer, W. & Helsing, E., eds. Food & Health Data: Their Use in Nutrition Policy-Making. (WHO Regional Publications: No. 34). (ENG, FRE & GER.). xii, 171p. 1991. pap. text 26.00 (*92-890-1125-4*, 1310034) World Health.

Backes, C. & Betlem, G. Integrated Pollution Prevention & Control: The EC Directive from a Comparative Legal & Economic Perspective. LC 99-17426. 1999. 57.00 (*90-411-9718-4*) Kluwer Law Intl.

Backes, David. A Wilderness Companion. Linder, Greg, ed. LC 92-24535. 96p. (Orig.). 1992. pap. 6.95 (*1-55971-185-X*, NorthWord Pr) Creat Pub Intl.

— A Wilderness Within: The Life of Sigurd F. Olson. LC 97-10891. 387p. 1997. 24.95 (*0-8166-2842-4*) U of Minn Pr.

— A Wilderness Within: The Life of Sigurd F. Olson. 424p. 1999. pap. 19.95 (*0-8166-2843-2*, Pub. by U of Minn Pr) Chicago Distribution Ctr.

Backes, Nick, jt. illus. see Tripp, Valerie.

Backes, Otto, jt. auth. see Albrecht, Peter A.

Backett, E. M., et al. The Risk Approach in Health Care with Special Reference to Maternal & Child Health, including Family Planning. (Public Health Papers: No. 76). 121p. 1984. pap. text 11.00 (*92-4-130076-0*, 1110076) World Health.

Backett, E. Maurice. Domestic Accidents. (Public Health Papers: No. 26). (ENG, FRE, RUS & SPA.). 137p. 1965. pap. text 6.00 (*92-4-130026-4*, 1110026) World Health.

Backhaus, J., jt. ed. see Nutzinger, H. G.

Backhaus, Jurgen, ed. Health Policy: International & Historical Dimensions. (International Review of Comparative Public Policy Ser.: Vol. 6). 347p. 1995. 78.50 (*1-55938-878-1*) Jai Pr.

Backhaus, Jurgen G. The Elgar Companion to Law & Economics. LC 98-38241. 544p. 1999. 200.00 (*1-85898-516-1*) E Elgar.

Backhaus, Jurgen G., ed. Christian Wolff & Law & Economics: The Heilbronn Symposium. LC 98-227126. 304 p. 1998. write for info. (*3-487-10701-5*) G Olms Pubs.

Backhaus, K. & Wilson, D. T., eds. Industrial Marketing. (Illus.). 373p. 1985. 106.95 (*0-387-16114-7*) Spr-Verlag.

Backhaus, Karl-Otto. Dictionary of Crystallography. (ENG, FRE, GER & RUS.). 1983. 39.95 (*3-87144-744-7*) Adlers Foreign Bks.

— Dictionary of Crystallography. (ENG, FRE, GER & RUS.). 132p. 1983. pap. write for info. (*0-8288-1474-0*, M15709) Fr & Eur.

Backhaus, Phyllis Barker. Tempered by Fire: The True Story of Phyllis Barker Dilley Backhaus. O'Bryan, Elsie M., ed. LC 98-73875. (Illus.). 200p. 1998. pap. 19.95 (*0-9661665-1-5*, 02) Bear Paw AK.

***Backhaus, Phyllis Barker.** Tempered by Fire: An Alaskan's True Story of Survival Against All Odds. LC 99-67084. (Illus.). 192p. 1999. pap. 19.95 (*1-888125-55-1*) Publ Consult.

***Backhaus, Werner G.** Neuronal Coding of Perceptual Systems. (Biophysics & Biocybernetics Ser.: Vol. 9). (Illus.). 2000. 86.00 (*981-02-4164-X*) World Scientific Pub.

Backhaus, Werner G., et al, eds. Color Vision: Perspectives from Different Disciplines. LC 97-46863. 430p. 1998. 89.95 (*3-11-016100-1*); pap. 49.95 (*3-11-015431-5*) De Gruyter.

Backhou. Color Atlas of Surface Anatomy. 2nd ed. 1997. mass mkt. 26.00 (*0-7234-2495-0*) Wolfe Pubng AZ.

Backhouse. Surface Anatomy. 1991. write for info. (*0-8151-0372-7*) Mosby Inc.

Backhouse, A. E. The Lexical Field of Taste: A Semantic Study of Japanese Taste Terms. (Cambridge Studies in Linguistics: Supplementary Volumes). 210p. (C). 1994. text 52.95 (*0-521-44535-3*) Cambridge U Pr.

Backhouse, A. F. The Japanese Language: An Introduction. (Illus.). 204p. 1994. pap. 14.95 (*0-19-553509-X*) OUP.

Backhouse, Christopher J. & Brookes, Naomi J. Concurrent Engineering. 250p. 1996. 72.95 (*0-566-07666-7*, Pub. by Gower) Ashgate Pub Co.

Backhouse, Christopher J. & Brookes, Naomi J., eds. Concurrent Engineering: What's Working Where. LC 96-4825. 248p. 1997. 90.00 (*0-470-23728-7*) Wiley.

Backhouse, Constance. Petticoats & Prejudice: Women & Law in 19th Century Canada. 470p. pap. 20.95 (*0-88961-161-0*, Pub. by Womens Pr) LPC InBook.

Backhouse, Constance & Flaherty, David H., eds. Challenging Times: The Women's Movement in Canada & the United States. 352p. 1992. pap. 24.95 (*0-7735-0919-4*, Pub. by McG-Queens Univ Pr) CUP Services.

— Challenging Times: The Women's Movement in Canada & the United States. 352p. 1992. 65.00 (*0-7735-0910-0*, Pub. by McG-Queens Univ Pr) CUP Services.

Backhouse, Frances. Women of the Klondike. (Illus.). 224p. 1995. pap. text 14.95 (*1-55110-375-3*) Whitecap Bks.

B

B

***Backhouse, Frances & Dorst, Adrian.** Hiking with Ghosts: The Chilkoot Trail, Then & Now. (Journeys Ser.). (Illus.). 2000. pap. 18.95 (*1-55192-276-2*) Raincoast Bk.

Backhouse, Gary & Jeans, Jeffrey. The Orchids of Victoria. (Miegunyah Press Ser.: 2:4). (Illus.). 412p. 1995. text 59.95 (*0-522-84393-X*, Pub. by Melbourne Univ Pr) Paul & Co Pubs.

Backhouse, Jane, jt. auth. see Martin, Janet.

Backhouse, Janet. Becket Leaves. (Illus.). 32p. 1988. pap. 14.75 (*0-7123-0141-0*, Pub. by B23tish Library) U of Toronto Pr.

— The Bedford Hours. (Medieval Manuscripts from the British Library). (Illus.). 64p. (Orig.). 1991. pap. 18.95 (*1-56131-021-2*, NAB) I R Dee.

— Books of Hours. 2nd ed. 1985. pap. text 13.95 (*0-7123-0052-X*, Pub. by B23tish Library) U of Toronto Pr.

— The Illuminated Manuscript. (Illus.). 80p. (C). 1990. reprint ed. pap. 14.95 (*0-7148-2468-2*, Pub. by Phaidon Pr) Phaidon Pr.

— Illuminated Page: Ten Centuries of Manuscript Painting in the British Library. LC 98-108144. (Illus.). 244p. 1998. text 39.95 (*0-8020-4346-1*) U of Toronto Pr.

— The Isabella Breviary. (Illus.). 64p. 1993. pap. 21.95 (*0-7123-0269-7*, Pub. by B23tish Library) U of Toronto Pr.

— The Lindisfarne Gospels. (Illus.). 96p. 1990. pap. 14.95 (*0-7148-2461-5*, Pub. by Phaidon Pr) Phaidon Pr.

Backhouse, Janet, jt. ed. see Webster, Leslie.

Backhouse, John, et al. Improving the Learning of Mathematics. 173p. (C). (gr. 6). 1992. pap. text 25.00 (*0-435-08330-9*, 08330) Heinemann.

Backhouse, Kenneth M. & Hutchings, Ralph T. A Color Atlas of Surface Anatomy: Clinical & Applied. (Illus.). 350p. (C). 1986. pap. text 35.00 (*0-683-00307-0*) Lppncott W & W.

Backhouse, Robert. The Big Book of Bible Facts. LC 92-32366. (J). 1993. 9.99 (*0-8407-7743-4*) Nelson.

***Backhouse, Robert.** A Feast of Anglican Spirituality. 288p. 1999. 15.95 (*1-85311-195-3*, 6113, Pub. by Canterbury Press Norwich) Morehouse Pub.

Backhouse, Robert. The Kregel Pictorial Guide to the Temple. LC 96-10725. (Illus.). 32p. 1996. pap. 8.99 (*0-8254-3039-9*) Kregel.

— Manual Portavoz del Templo Judio.Tr. of Kregel Pictorial Guide to the Temple. (SPA.). 32p. 1996. pap. 8.99 (*0-8254-1047-9*, Edit Portavoz) Kregel.

***Backhouse, Robert.** The Oral History of Christianity: Eye Witness Accounts of the Dramatic Turning Points in the Story of the Church. Collins, Owen, ed. 474p. 1998. pap. 14.95 (*0-00-628098-6*, Pub. by HarpC) Trafalgar.

Backhouse, Robert. Personajes Biblicos Portavoz. (SPA., Illus.). 32p. 1996. pap. 8.99 (*0-8254-1049-5*, Edit Portavoz) Kregel.

— The Student Bible Guide to Jerusalem. LC 97-1657. (J). 1997. 6.99 (*0-8066-3340-9*) Augsburg Fortress.

— The Student Guide to Bible People. LC 95-47645. (Illus.). 32p. (J). 1996. pap. 6.99 (*0-8066-2039-0*, 9-2039, Augsburg) Augsburg Fortress.

Backhouse, Roger. Economists & the Economy: The Evolution of Economic Ideas. 2nd ed. LC 93-6875. 260p. (C). 1993. pap. text 24.95 (*1-56000-715-X*) Transaction Pubs.

— Explorations in Economic Methodology: From Lakatos to Empirical Philosophy of Science. LC 97-27160. 288p. (C). 1998. 75.00 (*0-415-17470-8*) Routledge.

— Interpreting Macroeconomics: Explorations in the History of Economic Thought. 256p. (C). 1996. pap. 29.99 (*0-415-15360-3*) Routledge.

***Backhouse, Roger.** Keynes. LC 99-39475. (Key Issues Ser.). 1999. 25.00 (*1-890318-28-0*) St Augustines Pr.

Backhouse, Roger, ed. Keynes: Contemporary Responses to the General Theory, 1 Vol. 250p. 1999. 75.00 (*1-85506-610-6*); pap. 24.95 (*1-85506-611-4*) Thoemmes Pr.

— New Directions in Economic Methodology. LC 93-37623. (Economics as Social Theory Ser.). 400p. (C). 1994. pap. 29.99 (*0-415-09637-5*, B3179) Routledge.

Backhouse, Roger, intro. The Methodology of Economics, 7 vols. 1900p. (C). (gr. 13). 1997. 950.00 (*0-415-15380-8*) Routledge.

***Backhouse, Roger & Middleton, Roger, eds.** Exemplary Economists Vol. 1: North America. LC 00-23771. 480p. 2000. 100.00 (*1-85898-959-0*) E Elgar.

Backhouse, Roger E. Truth & Progress in Economic Knowledge. LC 97-12142. (Advances in Economic Methodology Ser.). 256p. 1997. 85.00 (*1-85278-691-4*) E Elgar.

***Backhouse, Roger E. & Middleton, Roger, eds.** Exemplary Economists Vol. 2: Europe, Asia & Australasia. 480p. 2000. 100.00 (*1-85898-960-4*) E Elgar.

***Backhouse, Roger E. & Salanti, Andrea, eds.** Macroeconomics & the Real World: Econometric Techniques & Macroeconomic, Vol. 1. 384p. 2000. text 90.00 (*0-19-829795-5*) OUP.

— Macroeconomics & the Real World: Keynesian Economics, Unemployment, Vol. 2. 432p. 2000. text 90.00 (*0-19-829796-3*) OUP.

Backhouse, Roger E., jt. ed. see Biddle, Jeff E.

Backhurst, J., jt. auth. see Harker, J. H.

Backhurst, J. R. & Harker, J. H. Coulson & Richardsons Chemical Engineering, Vol. 4. 2nd ed. (Chemical Engineering Technical Ser.). 2000. pap. text 49.95 (*0-08-042083-4*, Prgamon Press) Buttrwrth-Heinemann.

— Coulson & Richardson's Chemical Engineering Vol. 5: Solutions to the Problems in Chemical Engineering. 2nd ed. 264p. 1997. pap. text 39.95 (*0-7506-2612-7*) Buttrwrth-Heinemann.

***Backhus, Stephen P., ed.** VA Hospitals: Issues & Challenges for the Future. (Illus.). 324p. (C). 2000. pap. text 45.00 (*0-7881-8205-6*) DIANE Pub.

Backhuys, W. Edouard Fischer-Piete, 1899-1988: Biography, Bibliography, New Taxa. 48p. 1990. pap. 10.00 (*90-73348-10-2*, Pub. by Backhuys Pubs) Balogh.

Backinowski, L. V., tr. see Tarchevsky, I. A. & Marchenko, G. N.

Backinowsky, L. V., tr. see Bessonov, M. I., et al.

Backler, Alan L. & Hanvey, Robert. Global Geography. LC 85-12558. (Illus.). 408p. reprint ed. pap. 126.50 (*0-7837-3890-0*, 204373800010) Bks Demand.

Backler, Martin H., jt. ed. see Angers, Trent.

Backley, Steve & Stafford, Ian. Winning Mind: Steve Backley's Guide to Achieving Success & Overcoming Failure. LC 97-108907. (Illus.). 256p. 1996. text 19.95 (*1-85410-404-7*, Pub. by Aurum Pr) London Brdge.

Backlund, Barbara A., jt. auth. see Huber, Charles H.

Backlund, Ingegerd, jt. ed. see Tottie, Gunnel.

Backlund, Karin & Sandstrom, Madelene. The Integration of Acquired Companies into the Defence Industry: Experiences from Western Europe. 150p. (C). 1998. pap. text 35.00 (*0-7881-4859-1*) DIANE Pub.

Backlund, Phil, jt. auth. see Ivy, Diana K.

Backman, A. Pesach - One, Two, Three. 1992. 10.99 (*0-89906-988-6*); pap. 7.99 (*0-89906-989-4*) Mesorah Pubns.

Backman, Aidel. One Night, One Hanukkah Night. (Illus.). 32p. (J). (ps-2). 1990. 9.95 (*0-8276-0368-1*) JPS Phila.

Backman, C. A. The Forest Industrial Sector of Russia: Opportunity Awaiting. LC 98-30442. (Illus.). 308p. 1999. 72.00 (*1-85070-602-1*) Prthnon Pub.

Backman, Carl A., jt. ed. see Smith, Seaton E., Jr.

Backman, Clifford R. The Decline & Fall of Medieval Sicily: Politics, Religion & Economy in the Reign of Frederick III, 1296-1337. 374p. (C). 1995. text 64.95 (*0-521-49664-0*) Cambridge U Pr.

Backman, Eugene L. Religious Dances in the Christian & in Popular Medicine. Classen, E., ed. LC 77-8069. 364p. 1977. reprint ed. lib. bdg. 65.00 (*0-8371-9678-7*, BARD, Greenwood Pr) Greenwood.

Backman, Gregory. My Prayer Journal Book. 150p. 1997. pap. 6.95 (*1-57502-611-2*, PO1755) Morris Pubng.

Backman, Gunnar. Learning by Metaphor: A Metaphoric Reading of Two Short Stories by Stephen Crane. (Studia Anglistica Upsaliensia Ser.: No. 75). 203p. (Orig.). 1991. pap. 42.50 (*91-554-2741-3*) Coronet Bks.

Backman, James & Thomas, David. Practical Guide to Disputes Between Adjoining Landowners Easements, 2 vols. 1989. ring bd. 165.00 (*0-8205-1060-2*) Bender.

Backman, James H. Questions & Answers: Property. (Winning in Law School Ser.: Bk. 8). 175p. (Orig.). 1987. pap. text 12.95 (*0-915667-15-0*) Spectra Pub Co.

Backman, Jules. Business Problems of the Eighties. (ITT Key Issues Lecture). 1980. pap. write for info. (*0-672-97499-1*) Macmillan.

— Regulation & Deregulation. (ITT Key Issues Lecture). 188p. (Orig.). 1981. pap. text. write for info. (*0-672-97879-2*) Macmillan.

Backman, Jules, ed. Economic Growth or Stagnation. LC 78-10874. (ITT Key Issues Lecture). (C). 1979. text. write for info. (*0-672-97323-5*); pap. text. write for info. (*0-672-97322-7*) Macmillan.

Backman, Jules, jt. auth. see Czepiel, John.

Backman, Lars, jt. ed. see Dixon, Roger A.

Backman, M. E. The Psychology of the Physically Ill Patient: A Clinician's Guide. LC 88-39667. (Illus.). 252p. (C). 1989. 49.50 (*0-306-43051-7*, Plenum Trade) Perseus Pubng.

Backman, Margaret E. Coping with Choosing a Therapist: A Young Person's Guide to Counseling & Psychotherapy. LC 93-29661. (YA). (gr. 7-12). 1994. lib. bdg. 17.95 (*0-8239-1699-5*) Rosen Group.

Backman, Mark. Sophistication: Rhetoric & the Rise of Self-Consciousness. LC 91-31004. 1992. 24.95 (*0-918024-91-9*) Ox Bow.

Backman, Mary. Bible Count & Color. 1992. pap. 3.00 (*0-89137-065-X*) Quality Pubns.

Backman, Michael. Asian Eclipse: Exposing the Dark Side of Business in Asia. LC 99-12262. 412p. (C). 1999. 29.95 (*0-471-83530-7*) Wiley.

Backman, Milton V., Jr. & Cowan, Richard O. Joseph Smith & the Doctrine & Covenants. LC 92-33120. x, 165p. 1992. 12.95 (*0-87579-653-2*) Deseret Bk.

Backman, Milton V., Jr., jt. auth. see Cook, Lyndon.

Backman, Stephanie, jt. ed. see Wheeler, Gordon.

Backman, U., et al. Renal Stones: Etiology, Management, & Treatment. 206p. (Orig.). 1985. 65.00 (*91-22-00764-4*) Coronet Bks.

***Backmeyer, Sylvia.** Making Their Mark: Central School of Art Staff & Students 1896-1966. 160p. 2000. pap. 29.95 (*0-7136-5261-6*, Pub. by A & C Blk) Midpt Trade.

Backofen, Walter A. Deformation Processing. LC 71-132054. (Engineering Science Ser.). (C). 1972. text. write for info. (*0-201-00388-0*) Addison-Wesley.

Backoff, Robert W., jt. auth. see Nutt, Paul C.

Backonja, Misha. Introduction to Neurological Examinations, 001. 1998. lib. bdg. 195.00 (*0-8493-1199-3*) CRC Pr.

— Introduction to Neuropathic Pain. 1998. lib. bdg. 195.00 (*0-8493-1645-6*) CRC Pr.

Backous, Timothy, jt. auth. see Graham, William C.

Backouse, Robert. Panorama Portavoz de Jerussalem. 32p. 1997. pap. text 8.99 (*0-8254-1052-5*) Kregel.

Backpacker Magazine Editors. Trailside's Hints & Tips for Outdoor Living. (Illus.). 128p. (Orig.). 1993. pap. 9.95 (*0-87596-170-3*) Rodale Pr Inc.

— Trailside's Trail Food. (Illus.). 128p. (Orig.). 1993. pap. 9.95 (*0-87596-169-X*) Rodale Pr Inc.

Backrach, Susan D. Tell Them We Remember: Produced in Association with the United States Memorial Holocaust Museum. LC 93-40090. 128p. (J). (gr. 4-6). 1994. 21.95 (*0-316-69264-6*) Little.

— Tell Them We Remember: The Story of the Holocaust Produced in Association with the United States Memorial Holocaust Museum. LC 93-40090. 128p. (J). (gr. 4-6). 1994. pap. 14.95 (*0-316-07484-5*) Little.

Backris, Victor, jt. auth. see Cale, John.

Backs, Richard W. & Boucsein, Wolf, eds. Engineering Psychophysiology: Issues & Applications. LC 99-14047. 300p. 1999. write for info. (*0-8058-2452-9*); pap. write for info. (*0-8058-2453-7*) L Erlbaum Assocs.

Backscheider, Paula. Daniel Defoe: His Life. LC 88-26752. (Illus.). 688p. 1989. 60.00 (*0-8018-3785-5*) Johns Hopkins.

— Daniel Defoe: His Life. (Illus.). 688p. 1992. reprint ed. pap. 24.95 (*0-8018-4512-2*) Johns Hopkins.

Backscheider, Paula R. A Being More Intense: A Study of the Prose Works of Bunyan, Swift, & Defoe. LC 83-45274. (Studies in the Eighteenth Century: No. 7). 1984. 45.00 (*0-404-61473-6*) AMS Pr.

— Daniel Defoe: Ambition & Innovation. LC 86-12076. 312p. 1986. 34.95 (*0-8131-1596-5*) U Pr of Ky.

— Reflections on Biography. LC 99-34521. (Illus.). 312p. 2000. text 45.00 (*0-19-818641-X*) OUP.

— Spectacular Politics: Theatrical Power & Mass Culture in Early Modern England. LC 92-40746. (Illus.). 296p. (C). 1993. text 44.00 (*0-8018-4568-8*) Johns Hopkins.

Backscheider, Paula R., ed. Probability, Time & Space in Eighteenth-Century Literature. LC 78-20850. (Studies in the Eighteenth Century: No. 3). 1979. 39.50 (*0-404-16046-8*) AMS Pr.

***Backscheider, Paula R., ed.** Revising Women: Eighteenth-Century "Women's Fiction" & Social Engagement. LC 99-32386. (Illus.). 288p. 1999. 39.95 (*0-8018-6236-1*) Johns Hopkins.

Backscheider, Paula R. & Dykstal, Timothy, eds. The Intersections of the Public & Private Spheres. 284p. (C). 1996. pap. 29.00 (*0-7146-4275-4*, Pub. by F Cass Pubs) Intl Spec Bk.

Backscheider, Paula R., ed. see Brooke, Frances.

Backscheider, Paula R., ed. see Haywood, Eliza.

Backsheider, Paula. Moll Flanders: The Making of a Criminal Mind. (Twayne's Masterwork Studies: No. 48). 144p. (C). 1990. 25.95 (*0-8057-9429-8*, Twyne); pap. 13.95 (*0-8057-8130-7*, Twyne) Mac Lib Ref.

Backsheider, Paula, ed. see Defoe, Daniel.

Backsheider, Paula R. & Richetti, John J., eds. Popular Fiction by Women 1660-1730: An Anthology. LC 96-31093. (Illus.). 368p. 1997. text 90.00 (*0-19-871136-0*); pap. text 19.95 (*0-19-871137-9*) OUP.

Backstein, Karen. Blind Men & the Elephant. (Hello, Reader! Ser.). (J). 1992. 8.70 (*0-606-02528-6*, Pub. by Turtleback) Demco.

— The Blind Men & the Elephant, Level 3. (Hello Reader! Ser.). 48p. (J). (gr. 1-2). 1992. pap. 3.50 (*0-590-45813-2*) Scholastic Inc.

— Los Seis Ciegos y el Elefante. (Hello Reader! Ser.). 1999. pap. 3.99 (*0-439-06338-8*) Scholastic Inc.

— Saturday Is Ballet Day. (My Pretty Ballerina Ser.: No. 1). (Illus.). 32p. (J). (ps-3). 1991. pap. 2.99 (*0-590-45143-X*) Scholastic Inc.

Backstrom, C. & Sandewall. Current Trends in AI Planning. LC 93-81159. (Frontiers in Artifical Intelligence & Applications Ser.: Vol. 20). 316p. (YA). (gr. 12). 1994. pap. 79.00 (*90-5199-153-3*, Pub. by IOS Pr) IOS Press.

Backstrom, Charles H. & Hursh-Cesar, Gerald D. Survey Research. 2nd ed. LC 81-1738. 436p. (C). 1986. text 66.00 (*0-02-305080-2*, Macmillan Coll) P-H.

Backstrom, Gayle. When Muscle Pain Won't Go Away: The Relief Handbook for Fibromyalgia & Chronic Muscle Pain. LC 92-3289. 168p. 1992. pap. 12.95 (*0-87833-794-6*) Taylor Pub.

Backstrom, Gayle & Rubin, Bernard. When Muscle Pain Won't Go Away: The Relief Handbook for Fibromyalgia & Chronic Muscle Pain. 3rd rev. ed. LC 98-7860. (Illus.). 224p. 1998. pap. 12.95 (*0-87833-998-1*) Taylor Pub.

Backstrom, Lars-Ake, et al. Organizing Your Youth Soccer Team: Swedish Soccer Federation. 2nd ed. LC 87-22535. (Illus.). 216p. reprint ed. pap. 67.00 (*0-608-20836-1*, 207193500003) Bks Demand.

Backstrom, T. E. & Reid, Lydia J., eds. Controlling Toxic Substances in Agricultural Drainage: Emerging Technologies & Research Needs. 149p. (Orig.). 1990. pap. 36.00 (*0-9618257-6-6*) US Comm Irrigation.

Backus. Asian Americans Information Directory. 2nd ed. 577p. 1993. 75.00 (*0-8103-8501-5*) Gale.

***Backus & Chapian, Marie.** Telling Yourself Truth. 224p. 1999. pap. 9.99 (*0-7642-2325-9*) Bethany Hse.

***Backus, Ad & Aarssen, Jeroen.** Colloquial Turkish: The Complete Course for Beginners. LC 99-56874. 2000. pap. 0.00 incl. audio (*0-415-15748-X*) Routledge.

Backus, Anna J. Mountain Meadows Witness: The Life & Times of Bishop Philip Klingensmith. LC 95-37173. (Western Frontiersmen Ser.: Vol. XXV). (Illus.). 315p. 1995. 32.50 (*0-87062-229-3*) A H Clark.

Backus, Candace, jt. auth. see Backus, William.

Backus, George, et al. Foundations of Geomagnetism. (Illus.). 383p. (C). 1996. text 69.95 (*0-521-41006-1*) Cambridge U Pr.

Backus, Harriet F. Tomboy Bride: A Woman's Personal Account of Life in Mining Camps of the West. 2nd rev. ed. LC 79-80764. (Illus.). 273p. 2000. reprint ed. pap. 16.95 (*0-87108-512-7*) Pruett.

Backus, Henny. Care for the Caretaker: How Jim Backus' Wife Did It: An Upbeat Guide for Those Who Care for Others. 120p. 2000. pap. 11.95 (*0-9663465-2-1*) Jasper Pubns.

***Backus, Irena.** Reformation Readings of the Apocalypse: Geneva, Zurich, & Wittenberg. (Oxford Studies in Historical Theology). 208p. 2000. text 45.00 (*0-19-513885-6*) OUP.

Backus, Irena. The Reformed Roots of the English New Testament: The Influence of Theodore Beza on the English New Testament. LC 80-17915. (Pittsburgh Theological Monographs: No. 28). 1980. pap. 10.00 (*0-915138-36-0*) Pickwick.

Backus, Irena D., ed. see Bevan, Antoinina.

Backus, Isaac. The Diary of Isaac Backus, Vol. 1, 1741-1764. McLoughlin, William G., ed. LC 76-12018. 624p. 1979. reprint ed. pap. 193.50 (*0-7837-0368-6*, 204069000001) Bks Demand.

— The Diary of Isaac Backus, Vol. 2, 1765-1785. McLoughlin, William G., ed. LC 76-12018. 598p. 1979. reprint ed. pap. 185.40 (*0-7837-0369-4*, 204069000002) Bks Demand.

— The Diary of Isaac Backus, Vol. 3, 1786-1806. McLoughlin, William G., ed. LC 76-12018. 609p. 1979. reprint ed. pap. 188.80 (*0-7837-0370-8*, 204069000003) Bks Demand.

— History of New England. LC 76-83410. (Religion in America, Ser. 1). 1975. reprint ed. 82.95 (*0-405-00231-9*) Ayer.

Backus, John. Acoustical Foundations of Music. 2nd ed. LC 68-54957. (Illus.). (C). 1977. text 39.00 (*0-393-09096-5*) Norton.

Backus, Julie, jt. ed. see Haberman, Martin.

***Backus, Margot Gayle.** The Gothic Family Romance: Heterosexuality, Child Sacrifice & the Anglo-Irish Colonial Order. LC 99-20689. 1999. write for info. (*0-8223-2380-X*) Duke.

— The Gothic Family Romance: Heterosexuality, Child Sacrifice & the Anglo-Irish Colonial Order. LC 99-20689. (Post-Contemporary Interventions Ser.). 291p. 1999. pap. 17.95 (*0-8223-2414-8*) Duke.

Backus, Megan, tr. see Yoshimoto, Banana.

Backus, Milo M., jt. ed. see Castagna, John P.

Backus, Reno W. Backus Families of Early New England. 199p. 1994. reprint ed. pap. 32.50 (*0-8328-4399-7*); reprint ed. lib. bdg. 42.50 (*0-8328-4398-9*) Higginson Bk Co.

— Backus Families of Early New England. (Illus.). 199p. 1994. reprint ed. pap. 32.00 (*0-8328-4274-5*); reprint ed. lib. bdg. 42.00 (*0-8328-4273-7*) Higginson Bk Co.

Backus, Richard H., ed. Georges Bank. (Illus.). 632p. 1987. 245.00 (*0-262-02223-0*) MIT Pr.

Backus, Richard H., jt. auth. see Lineaweaver, Thomas H., III.

Backus, Robert L., tr. from JPN. The Riverside Counselor's Stories: Vernacular Fiction of Late Heian Japan. LC 84-40446. 272p. 1985. 39.50 (*0-8047-1260-3*) Stanford U Pr.

Backus, Truman. The Outlines of Literature, English & American. 1972. 250.00 (*0-8490-0791-7*) Gordon Pr.

Backus, W. A Genealogical Memorial of the Backus Family, with the Private Journal of James Backus Bearing on the First Settlement of Ohio at Marietta. 392p. 1988. reprint ed. pap. 60.00 (*0-8328-0155-0*); reprint ed. lib. bdg. 70.00 (*0-8328-0154-2*) Higginson Bk Co.

Backus, William. Adios a la Ansiedad.Tr. of Good News about Worry. (SPA.). pap. 10.99 (*0-88113-138-5*) Caribe Betania.

— La Brecha Entre Tu y Dios.Tr. of Hidden Rift with God. (SPA.). 192p. 1993. 9.99 (*0-88113-104-0*, B052-1040) Caribe Betania.

— Finding the Freedom of Self-Control. LC 87-1792. 176p. (Orig.). 1987. pap. 8.99 (*0-87123-676-1*) Bethany Hse.

— The Good News about Worry. 224p. (Orig.). 1991. pap. 9.99 (*1-55661-187-0*) Bethany Hse.

— The Healing Power of the Christian Mind. 192p. 1998. pap. 8.99 (*0-7642-2101-9*, 212101) Bethany Hse.

— The Hidden Rift with God. 192p. (Orig.). 1990. pap. 8.99 (*1-55661-097-1*) Bethany Hse.

— Learning to Tell Myself the Truth: A 12-Week Guide to Freedom from Anger, Anxiety, Depression. LC 93-43432. 224p. 1994. pap. 13.99 (*1-55661-290-7*) Bethany Hse.

— Telling Each Other the Truth. LC 85-20003. 192p. (Orig.). 1985. pap. 9.99 (*0-87123-852-7*) Bethany Hse.

— Telling the Truth to Troubled People. LC 84-28413. 256p. (Orig.). 1985. pap. 10.99 (*0-87123-811-X*) Bethany Hse.

— Truth Talk, 2 vols. in 1. 368p. 1995. 9.98 (*0-88486-117-1*) Arrowood Pr.

***Backus, William.** What Your Counselor Never Told You: Seven Secrets Revealed. 240p. 2000. pap. 10.99 (*0-7642-2392-5*) Bethany Hse.

Backus, William & Backus, Candace. Autoridad y Sabiduria.Tr. of Empowering Parents. (SPA.). 176p. 1993. 8.99 (*0-88113-124-5*, B052-1245) Caribe Betania.

— Teaching Your Children to Tell Themselves the Truth: Helping Children Before Misbeliefs Become Deeply Entrenched. LC 92-30635. 176p. (Orig.). 1992. pap. 8.99 (*1-55661-279-6*) Bethany Hse.

Backus, William & Chapian, Marie. Telling Yourself the Truth. LC 80-10136. 192p. (Orig.). 1980. pap. 8.99 (*0-87123-562-5*) Bethany Hse.

— Telling Yourself the Truth. LC 80-10136. 48p. (Orig.). 1981. pap., student ed. 4.99 (*0-87123-567-6*) Bethany Hse.

Backwell, C., jt. ed. see Grimble, G.

Backwords, Ace. Twisted Image. LC 90-63506. 120p. (Orig.). 1990. pap. 12.95 (*1-55950-056-5*, 85120) Loompanics.

Baclawski, Karen. The Guide to Historic Costume. (Illus.). 256p. (C). 1995. pap. 35.00 (*0-89676-213-0*, Costume & Fashion Pr) QSMG Ltd.

Baclic, Branislav S., jt. auth. see Dragutinovic, Gordan D.

Bacmeister, Arnold. Das Grosse Lexikon der Fischwaid. (GER.). 1969. 95.00 (*0-8288-6600-7*, M7324) Fr & Eur.

Bacon. Essays. (Classics of World Literature Ser.). 1998. pap. 5.95 (*1-85326-472-5*, 4725WW, Pub. by Wrdsworth Edits) NTC Contemp Pub Co.

— Geography of Texas. 1989. pap. text 7.00 (*0-15-373550-3*); pap. text, teacher ed. 14.50 (*0-15-373551-1*) Holt R&W.

— Intermediate Wordperfect for Window. (DF - Computer Applications Ser.). (C). 1993. mass mkt. 13.25 (*0-314-00370-3*) West Pub.

— West's DOS 6.X & System. (C). 1994. mass mkt. 7.50 (*0-314-02864-1*) West Pub.

— West's Essentials of Wordperfect 6.1 for Windows. LC 95-196616. 1995. mass mkt. 9.50 (*0-314-04639-9*) West Pub.

— West's Intermediate Wordperfect 6.1 for Windows. LC 95-193109. 1995. mass mkt. 17.95 (*0-314-04667-4*) West Pub.

— Wind. (J). 1989. pap. 19.95 (*0-590-72703-6*) Scholastic Inc.

— World Geography: Activity Worksheets. 1989. pap. text 21.50 (*0-15-373532-5*); pap. text, teacher ed. 25.50 (*0-15-373533-3*) Holt R&W.

Bacon & Moorho. The Bass Book. 1995. 22.95 (*0-7935-5000-9*, 00330034) H Leonard.

Bacon, jt. auth. see Allyn.

Bacon & Allyn Staff. Joining Together. 1996. 30.99 (*0-205-26755-6*) Allyn.

Bacon, A. Japanese Girls & Women. 1975. 250.00 (*0-87968-253-1*) Gordon Pr.

Bacon, Alan. The Nineteenth-Century History of English Studies. LC 98-8700. (Nineteenth Century Ser.). 330p. 1998. text 78.95 (*1-84014-278-2*, Pub. by Ashgate Pub) Ashgate Pub Co.

Bacon, Albion F. Beauty for Ashes. Baxter, Annette K., ed. LC 79-8770. (Signal Lives Ser.). (Illus.). 1980. reprint ed. lib. bdg. 49.95 (*0-405-12820-7*) Ayer.

***Bacon, Alice M.** Japanese Girls & Women. 348p. 2000. text 110.00 (*0-7103-0691-1*) Col U Pr.

Bacon, Ann, tr. see Jewel, John.

Bacon, B. R. & Di Bisceglie, A. M., eds. Diseases of the Liver. (Illus.). 512p. 1998. text. write for info. (*0-443-05712-5*) Church.

Bacon, Barbara S., ed. see Korza, Pam & Magie, Dian.

Bacon, Benjamin W. Sinews of War: How Technology, Industry, & Transportation Won the Civil War. LC 97-531. (Illus.). 208p. 1997. 24.95 (*0-89141-626-9*) Presidio Pr.

Bacon, Betty, ed. How Much Truth Do We Tell the Children? The Politics of Children's Literature. LC 87-22663. (Marxist Dimensions Ser.: Vol. 1). 257p. 1988. 29.95 (*0-930656-55-5*); pap. 10.95 (*0-930656-56-3*) MEP Pubns.

Bacon, Betty W. Halstead Family History, 1827-1990. (Illus.). 168p. 1998. reprint ed. pap. 25.00 (*0-8328-9661-6*); reprint ed. lib. bdg. 35.00 (*0-8328-9660-8*) Higginson Bk Co.

Bacon, Bill. How to Buy a Used Car & Never Get a Lemon. (Illus.). 94p. (Orig.). (C). 1992. pap. write for info. (*1-882330-15-3*) Magni Co.

— How to Buy a Used Car Successfully. (Illus.). 144p. (Orig.). 1992. pap. 8.95 (*0-9632723-0-6*) Auto Merit.

***Bacon, Billie.** One Deluxe Order of Healthy Self-Esteem to Go: An Easy to Follow Recipe for Positive Self-Esteem. (Illus.). 99p. 1999. pap. 11.95 (*0-9672971-0-9*) P Result SC.

Bacon, Cassius F., jt. auth. see Taylor, Arthur L.

Bacon, Charles F. National Profile of Local Boards of Health. (Illus.). 54p. (C). 1998. pap. text 20.00 (*0-7881-7316-2*) DIANE Pub.

Bacon, Charles S., jt. auth. see Thayer-Bacon, Barbara J.

Bacon, Charles W. & Hill, Nicholas S., eds. Neotyphodium & Grass Interactions: Proceedings of the Third International Symposium on Acremonium/Grass Interactions Held in Athens, Georgia, May 28-31, 1997. LC 97-17157. 472p. 1997. 129.50 (*0-306-45688-5*, Kluwer Plenum) Kluwer Academic.

Bacon, Charles W. & White, James F., Jr., eds. Biotechnology of Endophytic Fungi of Grasses. 226p. 1994. boxed set 171.95 (*0-8493-6276-8*, 6276) CRC Pr.

***Bacon, Charles W. & White, James F., Jr., eds.** Microbial Endophytes. (Books in Soils, Plants & the Environment: Vol. 75). 487p. 2000. 175.00 (*0-8247-8831-1*) Dekker.

***Bacon, Charlotte.** Lost Geography. LC 99-43958. 288p. 2000. 24.00 (*0-374-19160-3*) FS&G.

Bacon, Charlotte. A Private State: Stories. LC 97-14672. 200p. 1997. 24.95 (*1-55849-114-7*) U of Mass Pr.

Bacon, Corinne. Prison Reform: Together with a Discussion of the Prison of the Future by Thomas M. Osborne. LC 70-38659. reprint ed. 37.50 (*0-404-09147-4*) AMS Pr.

Bacon, D. H. & Stephens, R. C. Mechanical Technology. 2nd ed. (Illus.). 552p. 1990. 29.95 (*0-8311-3003-2*) Indus Pr.

— Mechanical Technology. 3rd ed. LC 98-10453. 544p. 1998. pap. text 44.95 (*0-7506-3886-9*) Buttrwrth-Heinemann.

Bacon, Dan. Moroccan Arabic Phrasebook. (ARA., Illus.). 176p. 1991. pap. 3.95 (*0-86442-071-4*) Lonely Planet.

— Moroccan Arabic Phrasebook. 2nd ed. (Lonely Planet Phrasebooks). 180p. 1999. pap. text 5.95 (*0-86442-586-4*) Lonely Planet.

Bacon, Daniel. Barbary Coast Trail Official Guide. (Illus.). 32p. 1998. pap. 8.95 (*0-9646804-2-4*) Quicksilvr CA.

— Walking San Francisco on the Barbary Coast Trail. 2nd rev. ed. (Illus.). (Orig.). 1997. pap. 13.95 (*0-9646804-1-6*) Quicksilvr CA.

Bacon, Daniel W. From Faith to Faith: The Influence of Hudson Taylor on the Faith Missions Movement. 1984. pap. 9.95 (*9971-972-03-4*) OMF Bks.

Bacon, David & Maslov, Norman. The Beatles' England: There Are Places I'll Remember. LC 81-82555. (Illus.). 144p. 1982. pap. 12.95 (*0-9606736-1-X*) N Maslov.

Bacon, Deborah. The Man God Loved. LC 87-60005. (Illus.). 315p. (Orig.). 1987. pap. 13.95 (*0-9606498-2-4*) Candlebeam Pr.

Bacon, Delia S. Philosophy of the Plays of Shakspere Unfolded. LC 73-113547. reprint ed. 44.50 (*0-404-00443-1*) AMS Pr.

Bacon, Denise. Hold Fast to Dreams: Writings Inspired by Zoltan Kodaly. (Illus.). 249p. (Orig.). 1993. lib. bdg. 19.95 (*0-935432-03-5*) Kodaly Ctr Am.

Bacon, Derek. Culture Shock! Jakarta at Your Door. LC 98-87496. (Culture Shock! Ser.). 283p. 1999. pap. text 12.95 (*1-55868-419-0*) Gr Arts Ctr Pub.

Bacon, Dolores. Operas Every Child Should Know. 29.95 (*0-8488-0909-2*) Amereon Ltd.

— Operas That Every Child Should Know. 1911. pap. 25.00 (*0-8196-1385-1*) Biblo.

Bacon, Donald C., jt. auth. see Hardeman, D. B.

Bacon, E. M., ed. Acts & Laws, of the Commonwealth of Massachusetts, 1780-1797: With Supplements 1780-1784, 13 vols., Set. LC 74-19617. reprint ed. 950.00 (*0-404-12439-9*) AMS Pr.

Bacon, Edgar M. Chronicles of Tarrytown & Sleepy Hollow. (Illus.). 163p. 1997. reprint ed. lib. bdg. 26.50 (*0-8328-9951-8*) Higginson Bk Co.

— Hudson River from Ocean to Source. 590p. 1993. reprint ed. lib. bdg. 99.00 (*0-7812-5116-8*) Rprt Serv.

Bacon, Edgar M., ed. First English Record Book of the Reformed Dutch Church in Sleepy Hollow, Formerly the Manor Church of Philipsburgh, Now the First Reformed Church of Tarrytown. 122p. 1997. reprint ed. pap. 15.50 (*0-8328-6242-8*) Higginson Bk Co.

***Bacon, Edgar Mayhew.** Chronicles of Tarrytown & Sleepy Hollow. (Illus.). 211p. 1999. pap. 19.00 (*0-7884-1335-X*, B015) Heritage Bk.

— Narragansett Bay: Its History & Romantic Associations & Picturesque Setting. (Illus.). 391p. 1999. reprint ed. pap. 30.00 (*0-7884-1392-9*, B016) Heritage Bk.

Bacon, Edmund N., et al. Henry Mitchell: Philadelphia Sculptor. Longhauser, Elsa, ed. LC 90-71062. (Illus.). 30p. 1990. pap. 15.00 (*1-58442-035-9*) Galleries at Moore.

Bacon, Edward. Among the Cotton Thieves. 3rd ed. LC 89-83689. 300p. 1989. reprint ed. pap. text 11.95 (*0-944419-26-7*) Everett Inc.

Bacon, Edward D. Catalogue of the Crawford Library of Philatelic Literature: At the British Museum. rev. ed. 550p. 1991. reprint ed. 225.00 (*0-941480-10-0*, Postilion Pubns) Subway Stamp.

Bacon, Edwin. The Gulag at War: Stalin's Forced Labour System in the Light of the Archives. LC 94-29449. (C). 1994. text 40.00 (*0-8147-1243-6*) NYU Pr.

Bacon, Edwin M., jt. ed. see Weeks, Lyman H.

Bacon, Elizabeth E. Central Asians under Russian Rule: A Study in Culture Change. (Illus.). 291p. 1980. pap. text 17.95 (*0-8014-9211-4*) Cornell U Pr.

Bacon, Erdix N. Bacon. Genealogy of Asa Bacon, Native of Wrentham, Ma., also a Condensed Report of His English Ancestry. (Illus.). 32p. 1997. reprint ed. pap. 6.50 (*0-8328-7319-5*); reprint ed. lib. bdg. 16.50 (*0-8328-7318-7*) Higginson Bk Co.

Bacon, Ernst. Fifty Songs. (Living Composers' Library). pap. 5.00 (*0-686-05636-1*) Dragons Teeth.

— The Hootnanny. 56p. 1954. pap. text 8.95 (*0-87487-668-0*) Summy-Birchard.

— It's a Kid's World. 17p. 1992. pap. text 5.95 (*0-87487-667-2*) Summy-Birchard.

— Notes on the Piano. LC 63-13887. (Illus.). 175p. 1963. reprint ed. pap. 54.30 (*0-608-06969-8*, 206717700009) Bks Demand.

— Words on Music. LC 73-427. 183p. 1973. reprint ed. lib. bdg. 55.00 (*0-8371-6768-X*, BAWM, Greenwood Pr) Greenwood.

Bacon, Ethel. To See the Moon. LC 95-8070. (Illus.). 32p. (J). (ps-3). 1996. 14.95 (*0-8167-3822-X*) BrdgeWater.

Bacon, Eugene H., jt. auth. see Bernardo, C. Joseph.

Bacon, Eugenia J. Lyddy. LC 77-37582. (Black Heritage Library Collection). 1977. reprint ed. 22.95 (*0-8369-8958-9*) Ayer.

Bacon, Eugenia J. & MacKethan, Lucinda H. Lyddy: A Tale of the Old South. LC 97-31436. iix, 287p. 1998. pap. 17.00 (*0-8203-1967-8*) U of Ga Pr.

Bacon, F. Petit Lexique de la Manutentio Anglais-Francais (Small English-French Lexicon of Storage) Chartrand, P., ed. (ENG & FRE.). 37p. 1974. pap. 9.95 (*0-8288-6205-2*, M9226) Fr & Eur.

***Bacon, Francis.** The Advancement of Learning. Kiernan, Michael, ed. (The Oxford Francis Bacon Ser.: Vol. 4). (Illus.). 800p. 2000. text 160.00 (*0-19-812348-5*) OUP.

Bacon, Francis. The Advancement of Learning. (Books of the Monarchs of England). 624p. 1998. reprint ed. pap. 405.00 (*1-85297-012-X*, Pub. by Archival Facs) St Mut.

***Bacon, Francis.** The Advancement of Learning. 235p. 2000. reprint ed. pap. 14.95 (*0-9664913-6-X*, Pub. by Paul Dry Bks) IPG Chicago.

Bacon, Francis. The Advancement of Learning: With a Brief Memoir of the Author. 170p. 1994. reprint ed. pap. 16.95 (*1-56459-436-X*) Kessinger Pub.

***Bacon, Francis.** An Advertisement Touching a Holy War. Lampert, Laurence, ed. 93p. (C). 2000. pap. 8.95 (*1-57766-128-1*) Waveland Pr.

Bacon, Francis. Apophthegmes New & Old. LC 73-38144. (English Experience Ser.: No. 424). 310p. 1972. reprint ed. 45.00 (*90-221-0424-9*) Walter J Johnson.

— Bacon's Essays. 5th rev. ed. LC 73-1147. (Essay Index Reprint Ser.). 1977. reprint ed. 32.95 (*0-518-10035-9*) Ayer.

— Certaine Miscellany Works. LC 79-25440. (English Experience Ser.: No. 222). 166p. 1970. reprint ed. 35.00 (*90-221-0222-X*) Walter J Johnson.

— The Charge of Sir F. Bacon Touching Duells. LC 68-27475. (English Experience Ser.: No. 7). 62p. 1968. reprint ed. 15.00 (*90-221-0007-3*) Walter J Johnson.

— A Collection of Apophthegms: New & Old. 50p. 1995. reprint ed. pap. 9.95 (*1-56459-476-9*) Kessinger Pub.

— De Sapientia Veterum, Repr. Of 1609 Ed. LC 75-27863. (Renaissance & the Gods Ser.: Vol. 20). (Illus.). 1976. lib. bdg. 34.00 (*0-8240-2068-5*) Garland.

— The Essayes or Counsels, Civill & Morall. Kiernan, Michael, ed. (Illus.). 544p. 1986. 45.00 (*0-674-31740-8*) HUP.

— Essays. LC 95-35312. (Great Books in Philosophy). 157p. 1995. pap. 6.95 (*1-57392-032-0*) Prometheus Bks.

— Essays. 260p. 1994. 7.50 (*0-460-87433-0*, Everyman's Classic Lib) Tuttle Pubng.

— The Essays. (Classics Ser.). 288p. 1986. pap. 12.95 (*0-14-043216-7*, Penguin Classics) Viking Penguin.

— Essays: Religious Meditations; Places of Perswasion & Disswasion. LC 68-54612. (English Experience Ser.: No. 17). 1968. reprint ed. 20.00 (*90-221-0017-0*) Walter J Johnson.

— Essays & Colours of Good & Evil. LC 72-56. (Select Bibliographies Reprint Ser.). 1977. reprint ed. 22.95 (*0-8369-9951-7*) Ayer.

— The Essayes or Counsels Civil & Moral. Vickers, Brian, ed. LC 98-31241. (Oxford World's Classics Ser.). 272p. 1999. pap. 11.95 (*0-19-283802-4*) OUP.

— Essays or Counsels, Civil & Moral. 182p. 1992. reprint ed. pap. 17.95 (*1-56459-228-6*) Kessinger Pub.

***Bacon, Francis.** The Essays or Counsels, Civill & Morall. Kiernan, Michael, ed. (Illus.). 450p. 2000. text 110.00 (*0-19-818673-8*) OUP.

Bacon, Francis. Francis Bacon. 1998. pap. text 19.95 (*87-90029-24-0*, Pub. by Louisana) Dist Art Pubs.

— Francis Bacon. Vickers, Brian, ed. (The Oxford Authors Ser.). 864p. (C). 1996. pap. 24.95 (*0-19-282025-7*) OUP.

— Francis Bacon: Important Paintings from the Estate. 1999. 60.00 (*1-891475-16-9*) T Shafrazi.

***Bacon, Francis.** Francis Bacon: The New Organon. Jardine, Lisa & Silverthorne, Michael, eds. (Cambridge Texts in the History of Philosophy Ser.). 296p. (C). 2000. pap. 18.95 (*0-521-56483-2*) Cambridge U Pr.

— Francis Bacon: The New Organon. Jardine, Lisa & Silverthorne, Michael, eds. (Cambridge Texts in the History of Philosophy Ser.). 296p. (C). 2000. 59.95 (*0-521-56399-2*) Cambridge U Pr.

Bacon, Francis. The Great Instauration & the Novum Organum. 257p. 1996. reprint ed. pap. 19.95 (*1-56459-638-9*) Kessinger Pub.

— The Historie of Life & Death: Observations Naturall & Experimentall for the Prolonging of Life. Kastenbaum, Robert J., ed. LC 76-19558. (Death & Dying Ser.). 1977. reprint ed. lib. bdg. 33.95 (*0-405-09554-5*) Ayer.

— The Historie of Life & Death: With Observations Naturall & Experimentall. LC 68-54613. (English Experience Ser.: No. 20). 324p. 1968. reprint ed. 35.00 (*90-221-0020-0*) Walter J Johnson.

— History of the Reign of King Henry the Seventh. Levy, Fritz J., ed. LC 70-177471. (European Historiography Ser). (C). 1972. pap. write for info. (*0-672-61420-0*, Bobbs) Macmillan.

— The History of the Reign of King Henry the Seventh: A New Edition with Introduction, Annotation, & Interpretive Essay by Jerry Weinberger. LC 95-25862. 264p. 1996. text 32.50 (*0-8014-3067-4*) Cornell U Pr.

***Bacon, Francis.** The Instauratio Magna: Last Writings, 13 vols. Rees, Graham, ed. (The Oxford Francis Bacon Ser.: Vol. 13). (Illus.). 624p. 2000. text 140.00 (*0-19-818470-0*) OUP.

Bacon, Francis. The Life & Correspondence of Francis Bacon, 2 vols. 1985. reprint ed. lib. bdg. 69.00 (*0-932051-83-9*) Rprt Serv.

— Meditations Sacrae & Human Philosophy. 50p. 1996. reprint ed. pap. 9.95 (*1-56459-641-9*) Kessinger Pub.

— New Atlantis. 51p. 1992. reprint ed. pap. 12.00 (*1-56459-230-8*) Kessinger Pub.

— The Novum Organum. Gibson, John & Urbach, Peter, eds. & trs. by. LC 93-39277. 362p. 1994. pap. 16.00 (*0-8126-9245-4*) Open Court.

— On the Interpretation of Nature. 50p. 1996. reprint ed. pap. 9.95 (*1-56459-645-1*) Kessinger Pub.

Bacon, Francis. Philosophical Studies c.1611-c.1619: Phaenomena universi; De fluxu et refluxu maris; Descriptio globi intellectualis; Thema coeli; De principis atque originibus; De vijs mortis, Vol. 6. Rees, Graham, ed. (Oxford Francis Bacon Ser.: Vol. 5). (Illus.). 620p. (C). 1996. text 140.00 (*0-19-812290-X*) OUP.

Bacon, Francis. Philosophical Works of Francis Bacon. LC 70-119952. (Select Bibliographies Reprint Ser.). 1977. 41.95 (*0-8369-5395-9*) Ayer.

— The Physical & Metaphysical Works of Lord Bacon, Including the Advancement of Learning & Novum Organum. 1976. reprint ed. 95.00 (*0-403-06142-1*, Regency) Scholarly.

— Selected Philosophical Works of Francis Bacon. Sargent, Rose-Mary, ed. LC 99-28713. 328p. (C). 1999. pap. text 12.95 (*0-87220-470-7*); lib. bdg. 34.95 (*0-87220-471-5*) Hackett Pub.

— Sylva Sylvarum: or A Natural History in Ten Centuries & Miscellaneous Philosophical Tracts. 190p. 1996. reprint ed. pap. 17.95 (*1-56459-639-7*) Kessinger Pub.

— Thoughts on the Holy Scripture. 410p. 1997. reprint ed. pap. 24.95 (*0-7661-0042-1*) Kessinger Pub.

— Thoughts on the Nature of Things. 50p. 1996. reprint ed. pap. 9.95 (*1-56459-642-7*) Kessinger Pub.

— Two Books... Of the Proficience & Advancement of Learning. LC 70-25525. (English Experience Ser.: No. 218). 236p. 1970. reprint ed. 45.00 (*90-221-0218-1*) Walter J Johnson.

— Wisdom of the Ancients. 96p. 1992. reprint ed. pap. 14.00 (*1-56459-229-4*) Kessinger Pub.

— Wisedome of the Ancients. Gorges, A., tr. LC 68-54614. (English Experience Ser.: No. 1). 176p. 1968. reprint ed. 25.00 (*90-221-0001-4*) Walter J Johnson.

— Works, 14 Vols. Spedding, J. et al, eds. 3750.00 (*3-7728-0023-8*) Adlers Foreign Bks.

— Works of Francis Bacon, 15 vols., Set. 1995. reprint ed. lib. bdg. 1200.00 (*0-403-00003-3*) Scholarly.

— The Works of Sir Francis Bacon, 15 vols., Set. 1987. reprint ed. lib. bdg. 1074.00 (*0-7812-0731-2*) Rprt Serv.

Bacon, Francis & Grigson, Geoffrey, intros. Essays. LC 83-45408. reprint ed. 31.50 (*0-404-20015-X*) AMS Pr.

Bacon, Frank. Barnstorming. (Illus.). 224p. 1987. 7.95 (*0-914139-04-5*) Hist San Jose.

***Bacon, Frank R., Jr. & Butler, Thomas W., Jr.** Achieving Planned Innovation: A Proven System for Creating Successful New Products & Services. 160p. 2000. reprint ed. text 30.00 (*0-7881-9168-3*) DIANE Pub.

Bacon, Frank R. & Butler, Thomas W. Achieving Planned Innovation: A Proven System for Success with New Products & Services. LC 97-25141. 176p. 1998. 29.50 (*0-684-83990-3*) Free Pr.

Bacon, G. E. Architecture of Solids. LC 81-9762. (Wykeham Science Ser.: No. 58). 138p. 1981. pap. 18.00 (*0-8448-1397-4*, Crane Russak) Taylor & Francis.

Bacon, G. E., ed. Fifty Years of Neutron Diffraction: The Advent of Neutron Scattering. (Illus.). 296p. 1987. 118.00 (*0-85274-587-7*) IOP Pub.

Bacon, Gary. Essential Education: Drawing Forth the Golden Child. (Illus.). 286p. (Orig.). 1982. pap. 7.95 (*0-9615210-0-7*) Rainbow Bdg.

Bacon, Gaspar G. The Constitution of the U. S. A. In Some of Its Fundamental Aspects. LC 79-37328. (Select Bibliographies Reprint Ser.). 1977. reprint ed. 22.95 (*0-8369-6673-2*) Ayer.

Bacon, George B. Siam: The Land of the White Elephant, As It Was & Is. LC 77-87064. reprint ed. 35.00 (*0-404-16792-6*) AMS Pr.

Bacon, Gershon C., jt. auth. see Hundert, Gershon D.

Bacon, Henry. Visconti: His Life, His Films. LC 97-19635. 304p. (C). 1998. text 54.95 (*0-521-59057-4*); pap. text 19.95 (*0-521-59960-1*) Cambridge U Pr.

Bacon, Herbert M. Bacon: "Bacon's Adventure" with Bacon & Wood Genealogies. (Illus.). 197p. 1992. reprint ed. pap. 29.50 (*0-8328-2385-6*); reprint ed. lib. bdg. 39.50 (*0-8328-2384-8*) Higginson Bk Co.

Bacon, Isabelle W. Walking Beside Jesus in the Holy Land. 100p. (Orig.). 1990. pap. 6.95 (*0-915597-53-5*) Amana Bks.

Bacon, J. Maths & Statistics for the Built Environment. 1997. pap. write for info. (*0-582-23188-4*) Longman.

Bacon, Jason W. The C/UNIX Programmer's Guide. LC 99-72453. (Illus.). 635p. (C). 1999. pap. text 70.00 (*0-9670596-0-7*) Acadix Sftware.

Bacon, Jean. Bacon Concurrent Systems 2. 2nd ed. LC 97-40612. (Illus.). 720p. (C). 1997. pap. text 63.00 (*0-201-17767-6*) Addison-Wesley.

— Life Lines: Community, Family & Assimilation among Chicago's Asian Indians. 320p. 1997. text 70.00 (*0-19-509972-9*); pap. text 22.00 (*0-19-509973-7*) OUP.

Bacon, Jeff. The Best of Broadside: A Humorous Look at Life in the Navy. LC 92-72180. (Illus.). 96p. (Orig.). 1992. pap. 9.95 (*1-881651-11-8*) Deep Water VA.

— The Rest of Broadside Vol. 1. LC 98-73182. (Broadside Cartoons Ser.: Vol. 2). (Illus.). 96p. 1998. pap. 9.95 (*1-881651-12-6*) Deep Water VA.

Bacon, Jeremy. The Audit Committee: A Broader Mandate. (Report: No. 914). (Illus.). viii, 53p. (Orig.). 1988. pap. text 60.00 (*0-8237-0358-4*) Conference Bd.

— Board Committees in European Companies. (Report: No. 886). (Illus.). vii, 16p. 1986. pap. text 60.00 (*0-8237-0325-8*) Conference Bd.

Bacon, Jeremy & Brown, James K. Corporate Directorship Practices: Role, Selection & Legal Status of the Board. (Report: No. 646). 161p. (Orig.). 1975. pap. text 40.00 (*0-8237-0065-8*) Conference Bd.

Bacon, John. Forging Metal Made Easy. (Illus.). 279p. 1991. reprint ed. pap. 13.00 (*1-877767-21-2*) Univ Publng Hse.

— Universals & Property Instances. LC 94-28779. (Aristotelian Society Ser.: 15). Orig. Title: Relations Particularized. 200p. 1995. 64.95 (*0-631-19629-3*) Blackwell Pubs.

Bacon, John, et al, eds. Ontology, Causality, & Mind: Essays in Honor of D.M. Armstrong. LC 92-469. (Illus.). 313p. (C). 1993. text 80.00 (*0-521-41562-4*) Cambridge U Pr.

***Bacon, John B.** Logic From A to Z: The Routledge Encyclopedia of Philosophy Glossary of Logical & Mathematical. 1999. pap. 16.99 (*0-415-21375-4*) Routledge.

Bacon, Jon L. Flannery O'Connor & Cold War Culture. (Cambridge Studies in American Literature & Culture: No. 72). 188p. (C). 1994. text 59.95 (*0-521-44529-9*) Cambridge U Pr.

Bacon, Jonathan & Sindt, Robert G. West's Intermediate Wordperfect 6.0. (C). 1995. pap. text 14.50 (*0-314-02866-8*) West Pub.

***Bacon, Jonathan P.** Director 7 & Lingo Bible. LC 99-30310. (Bible Ser.). 1000p. 1999. pap. 49.99 (*0-7645-3348-7*) IDG Bks.

Bacon, Jonathan P. DOS 5 & System. (DF - Computer Applications Ser.). (C). 1991. mass mkt. 7.50 (*0-314-00031-3*) West Pub.

— Essentials of WordPerfect 5.1. (DF - Computer Applications Ser.). 1991. mass mkt. 9.75 (*0-314-84888-6*) West Pub.

— Understanding & Using Microsoft Word. 200p. (C). 1988. pap. text 28.75 (*0-314-72625-X*) West Pub.

— Understanding & Using Microsoft Word 5.0. Leyh, ed. 350p. (C). 1991. pap. write for info. (*0-318-68307-5*) West Pub.

B

An Asterisk (*) at the beginning of an entry indicates that the title is appearing for the first time.

— Understanding & Using MS-DOS - PC-DOS 5.0. Leyh, ed. LC 92-26261. (Microcomputer Ser.). 450p. (C). 1992. mass mkt. 27.25 (*0-314-01110-2*) West Pub.
— Understanding & Using MS-DOS 6.0. Leyh, ed. LC 93-41645. 450p. (C). 1994. mass mkt. 26.00 (*0-314-02863-3*) West Pub.
— Understanding & Using WordPerfect 6.0 for Windows. LC 94-13254. (Microcomputing Ser.). 672p. (C). 1995. mass mkt. 25.75 (*0-314-03974-0*) West Pub.
— Understanding & Using WordPerfect 6.1. 400p. (C). 1995. pap. text. write for info. (*0-314-04660-7*) West Pub.
— Understanding & Using WordPerfect 6.1 for Windows. 2nd ed. LC 95-8112. (Microcomputing Ser.). 600p. (C). 1995. mass mkt. 36.95 (*0-314-06016-2*) West Pub.
Bacon, Jonathan P. & Sindt, Robert G. Understanding & Using Netscape Navigator. 10th ed. LC 96-41388. (Microcomputing Ser.). 1996. mass mkt. 37.95 (*0-314-20606-X*) West Pub.
— Understanding & Using WordPerfect 6.0. Leyh, ed. LC 94-13253. (Microcomputing Ser.). 450p. (C). 1994. spiral bd. write for info. (*0-314-02868-4*) West Pub.
Bacon, Jonathan P., jt. auth. see Copeland, Cody C.
Bacon, Jonathan P., jt. auth. see Copeland, Cody T.
Bacon, Josephine. Cooking the Israeli Way. LC 85-18059. (Easy Menu Ethnic Cookbooks Ser.). (Illus.). 48p. (J). (gr. 5 up). 1986. lib. bdg. 19.93 (*0-8225-0912-1*, Lerner Publctns) Lerner Pub.
— Exotic Vegetables A-Z. (Illus.). 1989. 14.95 (*0-88162-356-3*) McGraw.
— Little Book of Baking. 1994. 4.98 (*1-55521-979-9*) Bk Sales Inc.
— Little Book of Bread. 1995. 4.98 (*0-7858-0346-7*) Bk Sales Inc.
— Little Book of Cake Making. 1995. 4.98 (*0-7858-0230-4*) Bk Sales Inc.
— Little Book of Chicken. 1994. 4.98 (*1-55521-980-2*) Bk Sales Inc.
— Little Book of Chinese Cooking. 1994. 4.98 (*1-55521-983-7*) Bk Sales Inc.
— Little Book of Cookery for Diabetics. 1995. 4.98 (*0-7858-0289-4*) Bk Sales Inc.
— Little Book of Cookies. 1995. 4.98 (*0-7858-0233-9*) Bk Sales Inc.
— Little Book of Cooking for 1. 1995. 4.98 (*0-7858-0292-4*) Bk Sales Inc.
— Little Book of Cooking for 2. 1995. 4.98 (*0-7858-0291-6*) Bk Sales Inc.
— Little Book of Fish & Seafood. 1995. 4.98 (*0-7858-0229-0*) Bk Sales Inc.
— Little Book of Indian Cooking. 1994. 4.98 (*1-55521-984-5*) Bk Sales Inc.
— Little Book of Irish Recipes. 1995. 4.98 (*0-7858-0293-2*) Bk Sales Inc.
— Little Book of Italian Cooking. 1995. 4.98 (*0-7858-0234-7*) Bk Sales Inc.
— Little Book of Low Calorie Cooking. 1994. 4.98 (*1-55521-978-0*) Bk Sales Inc.
— Little Book of Mexican Cooking. 1995. 4.98 (*0-7858-0236-3*) Bk Sales Inc.
— Little Book of Pasta Cooking. 1994. 4.98 (*1-55521-982-9*) Bk Sales Inc.
— Little Book of Potatoes. 1995. 4.98 (*0-7858-0347-5*) Bk Sales Inc.
— Little Book of Soups. 1995. 4.98 (*0-7858-0232-0*) Bk Sales Inc.
— Little Book of Thai Cooking. 1995. 4.98 (*0-7858-0231-2*) Bk Sales Inc.
— Little Book of Vegetarian Cooking. 1994. 4.98 (*1-55521-977-2*) Bk Sales Inc.
— Little Book of Wok & Stir Fry. 1995. 4.98 (*0-7858-0235-5*) Bk Sales Inc.
Bacon, Josephine, tr. see Rosenzweig, Luc & Cohen, Bernard.
Bacon, Josephine D. Her Fiance. LC 73-121520. (Short Story Index Reprint Ser.). (Illus.). 1977. 17.95 (*0-8369-3476-8*) Ayer.
— Imp & the Angel. LC 74-81260. (Short Story Index Reprint Ser.). (Illus.). 1977. 18.95 (*0-8369-3012-6*) Ayer.
— In the Border Country. LC 79-106244. (Short Story Index Reprint Ser.). 1977. 17.95 (*0-8369-3280-3*) Ayer.
— Madness of Philip & Other Tales of Childhood. LC 75-98557. (Short Story Index Reprint Ser.). 1977. 19.95 (*0-8369-3131-9*) Ayer.
— Middle Aged Love Stories. LC 74-169538. (Short Story Index Reprint Ser.). 1977. reprint ed. 20.95 (*0-8369-3285-4*) Ayer.
— Smith College Stories. LC 70-94701. (Short Story Index Reprint Ser.). 1977. 21.95 (*0-8369-3079-7*) Ayer.
— Whom the Gods Destroyed. LC 70-116931. (Short Story Index Reprint Ser.). 1977. 19.95 (*0-8369-3433-4*) Ayer.
Bacon, Joy. Oliver Bean Can't Get Clean. LC 93-60480. (Illus.). 48p. (Orig.). (J). (ps-3). 1996. pap. 8.95 (*1-883650-31-3*) Windswept Hse.
— Oliver Bean Visits the Queen. LC 97-62543. (Illus.). 48p. (J). (gr. k-5). 1998. pap. 8.95 (*1-883650-45-3*) Windswept Hse.
— Oliver Bean's Halloween. Weinberger, Jane, ed. LC 90-70907. (Illus.). 68p. (J). (ps-3). 1991. pap. 8.95 (*0-932433-73-1*) Windswept Hse.
— Oliver Bean's Thanksgiving. Weinberger, Jane, ed. LC 93-61630. (Illus.). 40p. (Orig.). (J). (ps-3). 1994. pap. 8.95 (*1-883650-13-5*) Windswept Hse.
Bacon, Karen. Tasting Paradise: Restaurants & Recipes of the Hawaiian Islands. LC 94-73936. 201p. 1995. pap. 14.95 (*0-9644327-0-6*) Coastal Impressions.
***Bacon, Karen.** Tasting Paradise: Restaurants & Recipes of the Hawaiian Islands. 2nd ed. (Illus.). 200p. 2000. pap. 18.95 (*0-9644327-1-4*) Coastal Impressions.
***Bacon, Katharine J.** Finn. LC 98-10778. 171p. (J). (gr. 5-9). 1998. pap. 16.00 (*0-689-82216-2*) S&S Childrens.
Bacon, Kenneth D. Red River Prosecutor: True Cases of Oklahoma Crime. LC 95-38693. (Illus.). 320p. (Orig.). 1995. pap. 19.95 (*1-880090-14-7*) Galde Pr.
***Bacon, Kevin, et al.** E-Government: The Blueprint. 2000. pap. 27.95 (*0-471-39336-3*) Wiley.
Bacon, Leonard. A Discourse Preached in the Center Church. LC 78-168507. (Black Heritage Library Collection). 1977. reprint ed. 14.95 (*0-8369-8861-2*) Ayer.
— The Genesis of the New England Churches. LC 74-38435. (Religion in America, Ser. 2). 510p. 1972. reprint ed. 35.95 (*0-405-04056-3*) Ayer.
— Slavery Discussed in Occasional Essays from 1833-1846. LC 72-82167. (Anti-Slavery Crusade in America Ser.). 1970. reprint ed. 22.95 (*0-405-00607-1*) Ayer.
Bacon, Leonard, tr. from POR. The Lusiads of Luis de Camoes. (Illus.). 435p. 1980. reprint ed. pap. text 10.00 (*0-87535-128-X*) Hispanic Soc.
Bacon, Lynn Marie, jt. auth. see Wiley Publication Staff.
Bacon, M. E. Automotive Steering, Suspension & Wheel Alignment. 128p. 1987. 60.88 (*0-07-079577-0*) McGraw.
***Bacon, Mardges.** Le Corbusier in America: Travels in the Land of the Timid. LC 00-32900. (Illus.). 2001. write for info. (*0-262-02479-9*) MIT Pr.
Bacon, Mardges. Ernest Flagg: Beaux-Arts Architect & Urban Reformer. (Architectural History Foundation American Monographs: No. 6). (Illus.). 400p. 1986. 52.50 (*0-262-02222-2*) MIT Pr.
***Bacon, Margaret.** The Ewe Lamb. 284p. 2000. 26.00 (*0-7278-5435-6*, Pub. by Severn Hse) Chivers N Amer.
Bacon, Margaret. Journey to Guyana. large type ed. (Ulverscroft Large Print Ser.). (Illus.). 480p. 1997. 27.99 (*0-7089-3714-4*) Ulverscroft.
— Kitty. large type ed. (Magna Large Print Ser.). 480p. 1996. 27.99 (*0-7505-0972-4*, Pub. by Mgna Lrg Print) Ulverscroft.
Bacon, Margaret. Other Women. 320p. 1994. mass mkt. 11.95 (*0-7472-4532-0*, Pub. by Headline Bk Pub) Trafalgar.
Bacon, Margaret. The Serpent's Tooth. large type ed. (Magna Large Print Ser.). 545p. 1996. 27.99 (*0-7505-0971-6*, Pub. by Mgna Lrg Print) Ulverscroft.
Bacon, Margaret H. I Speak for My Slave Sister: The Life of Abby Kelley Foster. LC 74-4042. (J). (gr. 5-12). 1974. 12.95 (*0-690-00515-6*) HarpC Child Bks.
— Let This Life Speak: The Legacy of Henry Joel Cadbury. LC 86-14669. (Illus.). 272p. 1987. text 43.95 (*0-8122-8045-8*) U of Pa Pr.
— Lucretia Mott Speaking: Excerpts from the Sermons & Speeches of a Famous 19th Century Quaker Minister & Reformer. LC 80-84980. 31p. (Orig.). 1980. pap. 4.00 (*0-87574-234-3*) Pendle Hill.
— Mothers of Feminism: The Story of Quaker Women in America. 2nd ed. (Illus.). 273p. 1995. reprint ed. pap. 12.95 (*0-9620912-9-4*) Friends Genl Conf.
— One Woman's Passion for Peace & Freedom: The Life of Mildred Scott Olmsted. LC 92-13755. (Syracuse Studies on Peace & Conflict Resolution). (Illus.). 413p. 1993. reprint ed. pap. 128.10 (*0-608-07590-6*, 205990500010) Bks Demand.
— Valiant Friend: The Life of Lucretia Mott. 265p. 1989. reprint ed. pap. 12.95 (*0-8027-7190-4*) Walker & Co.
***Bacon, Margaret Hope.** Abby Hopper Gibbons: Prison Reformer & Social Activist. LC 99-39701. 256p. (C). 2000. text 59.50 (*0-7914-4497-X*); pap. text 19.95 (*0-7914-4498-8*) State U NY Pr.
— Love Is the Hardest Lesson: A Memoir. LC 99-45314. 1999. 10.00 (*0-87574-936-4*) Pendle Hill.
— The Quiet Rebels: The Story of the Quakers in America. LC 99-45119. 1999. 12.00 (*0-87574-935-6*) Pendle Hill.
— Valiant Friend: The Life of Lucretia Mott. rev. ed. (Illus.). 304p. 1999. 14.95 (*1-888305-11-8*) Friends Genl Conf.
Bacon, Margaret Hope, ed. Wilt Thou Go on My Errand? Three 18th Century Journals of Quaker Women Ministers. LC 94-21187. (Illus.). 406p. 1995. pap. 16.00 (*0-87574-921-6*, 1072) Pendle Hill.
— Wilt Thou Go on My Errand? Three 18th Century Journals of Quaker Women Ministers. (Illus.). 406p. 1995. 26.00 (*0-87574-956-9*, 1071) Pendle Hill.
Bacon, Marie L., jt. auth. see Russakoff, Sylvia.
Bacon, Mark. Do-It-Yourself Direct Marketing: Secrets for Small Business. 2nd ed. LC 98-115260. 290p. 1997. pap. 16.95 (*0-471-16384-8*) Wiley.
Bacon, Mark S. The California Escape Manual: Your Guide to Finding a New Hometown. LC 97-74889. xvi, 267p. 1998. pap. 19.95 (*0-9660000-2-1*) Archer & Clark.
Bacon, Martha S. Puritan Promenade. LC 81-1913. (Illus.). 160p. 1981. reprint ed. lib. bdg. 55.00 (*0-313-22954-6*, BAPUP, Greenwood Pr) Greenwood.
Bacon, Matt. No Strings Attached: The Inside Story of Jim Henson's Creature Factory. LC 97-23622. 192p. 1997. 35.00 (*0-02-862008-9*) Macmillan.
Bacon, Michael & Bacon, Nicholas. Taxation & Assessment of Civil Costs. LC 98-186545. 112p. 1998. pap. 41.00 (*1-85811-141-2*, Pub. by CLT Prof) Gaunt.
Bacon, Michael, jt. ed. see Rogers, Peter.
Bacon, Midge, ed. see Browning, Judith H.
Bacon, Nancy, jt. auth. see Ammons, Kevin.
Bacon, Nicholas, jt. auth. see Bacon, Michael.
Bacon, Oliver N. History of Natick, MA, from It's First Settlement in 1651, with Notices of the First White Families. (Illus.). 261p. 1990. reprint ed. lib. bdg. 32.50 (*0-8328-1631-0*) Higginson Bk Co.
Bacon, P. World Geography: Earth People. 1989. text 73.20 (*0-15-373530-9*) Harcourt.
— World Geography: Earth People, '89. 1989. 102.25 (*0-15-373531-7*) Holt R&W.
Bacon, Pamela S. The Beach Club Begins & the Big Dance. LC 96-54582. (Beach Club Ser.). (J). 1997. write for info. (*1-56763-302-1*); pap. write for info. (*1-56763-303-X*) Ozark Pub.
— The Beach Club Begins & the Big Dance. (Beach Club Ser.). 70p. (YA). (gr. 4-10). 1999. mass mkt. 3.99 (*0-9669201-0-4*) Pams Pages.
***Bacon, Pamela S.** 100 Library Lifesavers: A Survival Guide for School Library Media Specialists. LC 99-38136. 270p. 1999. pap. 37.50 (*1-56308-750-2*) Libs Unl.
Bacon, Peter E., ed. Nitrogen Fertilization in the Environment. LC 94-42809. (Books in Soils, Plants & the Environment: Vol. 42). (Illus.). 624p. 1995. text 215.00 (*0-8247-8994-6*) Dekker.
Bacon, R. For Better Relations with Our Latin American Neighbors. 1976. lib. bdg. 59.95 (*0-8490-1855-2*) Gordon Pr.
— Norton Twin Restoration. (Illus.). 256p. 1996. pap. 39.95 (*0-85045-708-4*, Pub. by Ospry) Motorbooks Intl.
Bacon, Richard. Forgotten Arts, Bk. 3. LC 75-10770. (Illus.). 64p. reprint ed. pap. 6.95 (*0-911658-71-8*, 80-250-4) Yankee Bks.
— Horses & Money: Equine Business Management Made Easy. LC 96-17684. 192p. (Orig.). 1996. pap. 36.95 (*0-632-04021-1*, Pub. by Blckwll Scitfc UK) Blackwell Sci.
— Revealed to Babes: Children in the Worship of God. 75p. (Orig.). pap. text 7.95 (*0-9632557-3-8*) Old Paths Pubns.
Bacon, Richard M. The Elements of Vocal Science. Foreman, Edward V., ed. (Masterworks on Singing Ser.: Vol. I). (Orig.). 1996. reprint ed. pap. 15.00 (*1-887117-06-7*) Pro musica pr.
— The Forgotten Arts, Bk. 1. LC 75-10770. (Forgotten Arts Ser.). (Illus.). 64p. (Orig.). 1975. pap. 6.95 (*0-911658-65-3*, 80-250-2) Yankee Bks.
— The Forgotten Arts, Bk. 2. LC 75-10770. (Forgotten Arts Ser.). (Illus.). 64p. (Orig.). 1975. pap. 6.95 (*0-911658-66-1*, 80-250-3) Yankee Bks.
— The Forgotten Arts: Growing, Gardening & Cooking with Herbs. LC 72-91864. (Forgotten Arts Ser.). (Illus.). 128p. (Orig.). 1972. pap. 8.95 (*0-911658-51-3*, 80-251-2) Yankee Bks.
Bacon, Robert. Measurement of Welfare Changes Caused by Large Price Shifts: An Issue in the Power Sector. LC 94-45701. (Discussion Paper Ser.: No. 273). 40p. 1995. pap. 22.00 (*0-8213-3155-8*, 13155) World Bank.
Bacon, Robert, jt. auth. see Rubenstein, James M.
Bacon, Robert, ed. see Root, Elihu.
Bacon, Robert W. & Eltis, Walter. Britain's Economic Problem: Too Few Producers LC 76-362917. xiii, 194p. 1976. write for info. (*0-333-19728-3*) Macmillan.
— Britain's Economic Problem: Too Few Producers. 2nd ed. LC 78-308036. xv, 255p. 1978. write for info. (*0-333-23346-8*) Macmillan.
Bacon, Robert W., et al. Estimating Construction Costs & Schedules: Experience with Power Generation Projects in Developing Countries. LC 96-22845. (Technical Papers: No. 325). 144p. 1996. pap. 22.00 (*0-8213-3670-3*, 13670) World Bank.
Bacon, Roger. An Excellent Discourse on the Admirable Force & Efficacy of Art & Nature. Smith, Patrick, ed. (Alchemical Studies Ser.: Vol. 24). 1999. pap. 7.95 (*1-55818-451-1*, Alchemical) Holmes Pub.
— Magical Letter of Roger Bacon. 1988. pap. 6.95 (*1-55818-102-4*, Sure Fire) Holmes Pub.
— The Mirror of Alchemy. Charles, Michael, ed. 1992. reprint ed. pap. 6.95 (*1-55818-146-6*) Holmes Pub.
— Roger Bacon & the Origins of Perspectiva in the Middle Ages: A Critical Edition & English Translation of Bacon's Perspectiva with Introduction & Notes. Lindberg, David C., tr. & intro. by. (Illus.). 522p. 1996. text 115.00 (*0-19-823992-0*) OUP.
— Roger Bacon's Letter: Concerning the Marvelous Power of Art & Nature & Concerning the Nullity of Magic Together with Notes & an Account of Bacon's Life & Work. Davis, Tenney L., tr. 77p. 1992. reprint ed. pap. 5.95 (*1-56459-278-2*) Kessinger Pub.
— Roger Bacon's Letter Concerning the Marvelous Power of Art & of Nature & Concerning the Nullity of Magic. Davis, Tenney L., tr. from LAT. LC 79-8594. 80p. reprint ed. 42.50 (*0-404-18495-2*) AMS Pr.
— Roger Bacon's Philosophy of Nature: A Critical Edition, with English Translation, Introduction & Notes of De Multiplicatione Specierum & De Speculis Comburentibus. Lindberg, David C., ed. & tr. by. LC 97-37653. 502p. 1997. reprint ed. 75.00 (*1-890318-75-2*) St Augustines Pr.
— Root of the World. 1998. reprint ed. pap. 3.95 (*0-916411-42-7*) Holmes Pub.
Bacon, Roger, tr. see Khalid.
Bacon, Ron. The Bone Tree. LC 93-20806. (Illus.). (J). 1994. 4.25 (*0-383-03738-7*) SRA McGraw.
— Fish of Our Fathers. (Illus.). 36p. (J). 1989. 11.99 (*0-85953-301-8*) Childs Play.
— Home of the Winds. LC 90-45701. (Illus.). 36p. (J). 1989. 11.99 (*0-85953-302-6*) Childs Play.
— House of the People. LC 90-46408. (Illus.). 36p. (J). 1989. 11.99 (*0-85953-300-X*) Childs Play.
— Wash Day. LC 92-34270. (Voyages Ser.). (Illus.). (J). 1993. 2.50 (*0-383-03665-8*) SRA McGraw.
Bacon, Roy. BMW. 1994. 10.98 (*0-7858-0006-9*) Bk Sales Inc.
Bacon, Roy. BMW Motorcycles. 208p. 1997. 24.95 (*1-85579-027-0*) Motorbooks Intl.
Bacon, Roy. BSA, Illustrated Motorcycle Legends. (Illus.). 96p. 1995. 10.98 (*0-7858-0254-1*) Bk Sales Inc.
***Bacon, Roy.** Ford Thunderbird. (Illus.). 128p. 2000. 12.99 (*0-517-16173-7*) Random Hse Value.
Bacon, Roy. Honda, Illustrated Motorcycle Legends. (Illus.). 96p. 1995. 10.98 (*0-7858-0256-8*) Bk Sales Inc.
— Illustrated BSA Buyer's Guide. (Illustrated Buyer's Guide Ser.). (Illus.). 160p. 1990. pap. 17.95 (*0-9514204-1-0*) MBI Pubg.
— Illustrated Triumph Motorcycle Buyers Guide. 2nd ed. (Illustrated Buyer's Guide Ser.). (Illus.). 176p. 1997. pap. 17.95 (*1-85579-033-5*) MBI Pubg.
— Illustrator Motorcycle Legends: Norton. 96p. 1996. 10.98 (*0-7858-0638-5*) Bk Sales Inc.
— Illustrator Motorcycle Legends: Suzuki. 96p. 1996. 10.98 (*0-7858-0637-7*) Bk Sales Inc.
— Illustrator Motorcycle Legends: Yamaha. 96p. 1996. 10.98 (*0-7858-0636-9*) Bk Sales Inc.
— Kawasaki. 96p. 1994. 10.98 (*0-7858-0004-2*) Bk Sales Inc.
— Motorcycle Legends: Harley Davidson. (Illus.). 1995. 19.95 (*0-7858-0253-3*) Bk Sales Inc.
— Triumph. 1994. 10.98 (*0-7858-0005-0*) Bk Sales Inc.
— World of Cars. (Illus.). 192p. 1996. 24.99 (*1-57215-134-X*, PRC003) World Pubns.
Bacon, Samuel. Memoir of the Life & Character of the Rev. Samuel Bacon. Ashmun, Jehudi, ed. (Black Heritage Library Collection). 1977. 22.95 (*0-8369-8781-0*) Ayer.
Bacon-Smith, Camille. Enterprising Women: Television Fandom & the Creation of Popular Myth. LC 91-29875. (Publications of the American Folklore Society, Bibliographical & Special Ser.). (Illus.). 352p. (C). 1991. pap. text 18.95 (*0-8122-1379-3*) U of Pa Pr.
— Eye of the Daemon. 336p. 1996. mass mkt. 5.50 (*0-88677-673-2*, Pub. by DAW Bks) Penguin Putnam.
***Bacon-Smith, Camille.** Eyes of the Empress. 304p. 1998. mass mkt. 5.99 (*0-88677-796-8*, Pub. by DAW Bks) Penguin Putnam.
Bacon-Smith, Camille. Face of Time. 1996. pap. 5.99 (*0-88677-707-0*, Pub. by DAW Bks) Penguin Putnam.
***Bacon-Smith, Camille.** Science Fiction Culture. LC 99-44730. 336p. 1999. pap. 24.95 (*0-8122-1530-3*) U of Pa Pr.
***Bacon-Smith, Camillle.** Science Fiction Culture. LC 99-44730. 336p. 1999. 49.95 (*0-8122-3223-2*) U of Pa Pr.
Bacon, Susan & Mejias. Arriba! Communicacion y Cultura.Tr. of Up! with Communication & Culture. 1993. pap. text 29.20 (*0-13-106584-X*) P-H.
***Bacon, Susan M., et al.** Leyendas del Mundo Hispano. LC 99-58934. (SPA.). 120p. 1999. pap. text 29.33 (*0-13-010010-2*) P-H.
Bacon, Susan M., jt. auth. see Zayas-Bazan, Eduardo.
Bacon, Sydney, tr. see Brown, Katie.
Bacon, Terry R. Effective People Skills. Singer, Barbara, ed. (Illus.). viii, 128p. (Orig.). 1996. pap. write for info. (*1-57740-050-X*, ILW011) Intl LrningWrk.
— Facilitative Selling: Helping Customers Buy. (Illus.). 86p. 1996. ring bd. write for info. (*1-57740-002-X*, ILW020) Intl LrningWrk.
— High Impact Facilitation. (Illus.). 205p. (Orig.). 1996. pap. write for info. (*1-57740-051-8*, ILW016) Intl LrningWrk.
— Leadership Through Influence. (Illus.). 148p. 1994. write for info. (*1-57740-001-1*, ILW002) Intl LrningWrk.
— Leading for Empowerment. (Illus.). 110p. 1994. write for info. (*1-57740-003-8*, ILW001) Intl LrningWrk.
— Program Development. (Illus.). 114p. 1994. write for info. (*1-57740-004-6*, ILW004) Intl LrningWrk.
— Selling to Major Accounts: Tools, Techniques & Practical Solutions for the Sales Manager. LC 99-24260. (Illus.). 322p. 1999. 59.95 (*0-8144-0462-6*) AMACOM.
Bacon, Terry R. & Doggett, Thomas. Achieving Individual & Team Goals: Self Study. (Illus.). x, 72p. (Orig.). 1996. ring bd. write for info. (*1-57740-013-5*, ILW015) Intl LrningWrk.
— Achieving Individual & Team Goals: Trainer Package. (Illus.). xvi, 93p. 1996. ring bd. write for info. (*1-57740-014-3*, ILW021) Intl LrningWrk.
Bacon, Terry R. & Doggett, Thomas B. Forest Fire Simulation: Facilitator Guide. Kolb, David & Singer, Barbara, eds. LC 97-180500. (Illus.). 1056p. 1996. ring bd. write for info. (*1-57740-029-1*, ILW043) Intl LrningWrk.
Bacon, Terry R. & Freeman, Lawrence H. Business Writer's Quick Reference Guide. LC 85-29533. 336p. 1986. pap. 64.95 (*0-471-84541-8*) Wiley.
Bacon, Terry R., et al. Facilitative Selling: Helping Customers Buy Workbook. (Illus.). 180p. 1996. ring bd., wbk. ed. write for info. (*1-57740-000-3*) Intl LrningWrk.
— High Impact Facilitation: Trainer Package. (Illus.). 98p. 1996. ring bd. write for info. (*1-57740-009-7*, ILW029) Intl LrningWrk.
— High Impact Facilitation Workbook. (Illus.). vi, 104p. 1996. ring bd., wbk. ed. write for info. (*1-57740-010-0*, ILW030) Intl LrningWrk.
— Marketing the Value of Excellence. (Illus.). 94p. 1994. write for info. (*1-57740-005-4*, ILW003) Intl LrningWrk.
— Personal Influence: Training Package. (Illus.). 91p. 1996. ring bd. write for info. (*1-57740-025-9*, ILW025) Intl LrningWrk.
— Personal Influence Workbook. (Illus.). 57p. 1996. ring bd., wbk. ed. write for info. (*1-57740-026-7*, ILW026) Intl LrningWrk.
— Proposing to Win - Workbook. (Illus.). 180p. 1994. wbk. ed. write for info. (*1-57740-023-2*, ILW057) Intl LrningWrk.
— Target Planet Earth! (Illus.). 1998. spiral bd. 149.00 (*1-57740-074-7*, ILW178) Intl LrningWrk.
— Who Killed Boris Blunt? Team Learning on Influence. (Mystery Simulation Ser.: No. 1). (Illus.). 80p. 1998. spiral bd. 149.00 (*1-57740-073-9*, ILW179) Intl LrningWrk.
Bacon, Terry R., jt. auth. see Best, Larry.
Bacon, Thomas, jt. auth. see Taylor, Meadows.
Bacon, Thorn. Flowers, Friends & Lovers. (Illus.). 124p. 2000. pap. 12.95 (*1-885221-41-X*) BookPartners.

An Asterisk (*) at the beginning of an entry indicates that the title is appearing for the first time.

— A Letter to Mother - With Love: From the Boy with the Bean in His Ear. (Illus.). 48p. 2000. pap. 9.95 (1-58151-052-7) BookPartners.

— Remme's Ride for the Gold. (Illus.). 120p. (J). 1994. 12.95 (1-885221-07-X); pap. 8.95 (1-885221-11-8) BookPartners.

Bacon, Thorn, ed. Why I Believe in God: Stories to Uplift Your Heart & Confirm the Presence of the Spirit. LC 98-73740. 208p. Date not set. 24.95 (1-58151-017-9) BookPartners.

Bacon, Thorn, ed. see Hopfinger, David R.

Bacon, Thorn, ed. see O'Hearn, Bill.

Bacon, Tony. Classic Guitars of the '50s: The Electric Guitar & the Musical Revolution of the '50s. (Illus.). 88p. 1996. 29.95 (0-87930-427-8) Miller Freeman.

*Bacon, Tony. Electric Guitars: The Illustrated Encyclopedia. (Illus.). 2000. 29.98 (1-57145-281-8, Thunder Bay) Advantage Pubs.

— 50 Years of Fender. (Illus.). 128p. 2000. pap. 19.95 (0-87930-621-1, M Freeman Bks) Miller Freeman.

Bacon, Tony. London Live: From the Yardbirds to Pink Floyd to the Sex Pistols. (Illus.). 192p. 1999. pap. 19.95 (0-87930-572-X) Miller Freeman.

— The Ultimate Guitar Book. 1997. pap. 25.00 (0-375-70090-0) Vin Bks.

Bacon, Tony, ed. The Sax & Brass Book: Saxophones, Trumpets & Trombones in Jazz, Rock & Pop. (Illus.). 112p. 1998. 24.95 (0-87930-531-2) Miller Freeman.

Bacon, Tony & Canty, Laurence. What Bass. 2nd ed. (Orig.). 1991. pap. 12.95 (0-933224-54-0, T029) Bold Strummer Ltd.

Bacon, Tony & Day, Paul. The Fender Book: A Complete History of Fender Electric Guitars. 2nd ed. (Illus.). 120p. 1999. 24.95 (0-87930-554-1) Miller Freeman.

— The Gibson Les Paul Book: A Complete History of Les Paul Guitars. (Illus.). 96p. 1993. 22.95 (0-87930-289-5) Miller Freeman.

— The Gretsch Book: A Complete History of Gretsch Electric Guitars. 108p. 1996. 24.95 (0-87930-408-1) Miller Freeman.

— The Guru's Guitar Guide: A Comprehensive, Easy to Use Reference Book Identifying & Valuing over 270 Brands of Electric Guitars from the Past 30 Years. 3rd ed. (Illus.). 96p. 1990. pap. 12.95 (0-933224-55-9, T030) Bold Strummer Ltd.

— The Rickenbacker Book: A Complete History of Rickenbacker Electric Guitars. (Illus.). 96p. (Orig.). 1994. text 19.95 (0-87930-329-8) Miller Freeman.

Bacon, Tony & Moorhouse, Barry. The Bass Book: A Complete Illustrated History of Bass Guitars. (Illus.). 108p. 1995. 22.95 (0-87930-368-9) Miller Freeman.

Bacon, Tony & Stowell, Robin, eds. The Violin Book. limited deluxe ed. (Illus.). 126p. 1999. boxed set 75.00 (0-87930-553-3) Miller Freeman.

Bacon, Tony, jt. auth. see Howe, Steve.

Bacon, Ursula. The Nervous Hostess Cookbook: A Comforting Guide to Worry-Free Entertaining. LC 96-75459. 272p. 1998. 15.95 (1-885221-09-6, Pub. by BookPartners) Midpt Trade.

Bacon, Virginia, ed. see Rudy, Diane & Rudy, Dale.

*Bacon, W. Stevenson, ed. Bringing the Excitement of Science to the Classroom: Using Summer Research Programs to Invigorate High School Science. 112p. 2000. pap. 4.00 (0-9633504-4-7) Res Corp.

Bacon, Wallace A., ed. see Warner, W.

Bacon, Warren & Chicklas, Claudia. Ware. LC 97-149516. (Images of America Ser.). 1996. pap. 16.99 (0-7524-0453-9) Arcadia Publng.

Bacon, William P. Gallatin-Nicholson. Ancestry of Albert Gallatin, b. Geneva, Switzerland, 1761 - d. New York, 1849, & Hannah Nicholson, b. New York, 1766 - d. New York, 1849, with a List of Their Descendants to the 2nd & 3rd Generation. (Illus.). 57p. 1997. reprint ed. lib. bdg. 21.00 (0-8328-8689-0) Higginson Bk Co.

Bacot, et al. State & Local Government. Date not set. 49.95 (0-534-54909-8) Wadsworth Pub.

Bacot, Barbara S., jt. ed. see Poesch, Jessie.

Bacot, H. Parrott. Nineteenth-Century Lighting. LC 87-61704. (Illus.). 240p. 1987. 59.95 (0-88740-098-1) Schiffer.

*Bacot, H. Parrott, et al, eds. Marie Adrien Persac: Louisiana Artist. (Illus.). 144p. 2000. 39.95 (0-8071-2641-1); pap. 24.95 (0-8071-2642-X) La State U Pr.

Bacot, J. Three Tibetan Mysteries: Tchrimekundan, Nansal, Djroazanmo. (C). 1990. reprint ed. 21.00 (81-85326-42-8, Pub. by Vintage) S Asia.

Bacot, Jacques. Three Tibetan Mysteries: Tchrimekundan, Nansal, Djroazanmo, As Performed in the Tibetan Monasteries. Woolf, H. I., tr. from FRE. LC 78-72375. (Illus.). reprint ed. 49.50 (0-404-17225-3) AMS Pr.

Bacote, Samuel W. Who's Who among the Colored Baptists of the United States. Gaustad, Edwin S., ed. LC 79-52588. (Baptist Tradition Ser.). (Illus.). 1980. reprint ed. lib. bdg. 25.95 (0-405-12455-4) Ayer.

Bacotti. Opportunities in Opticianry Today. LC 75-32613. (Illus.). 1993. pap. text 10.95 (0-8442-6326-5, VGM Career) NTC Contemp Pub Co.

— Opportunities in Opticianry Today. LC 75-32613. (Illus.). 1995. lib. bdg. 13.95 (0-8442-6325-7, VGM Career) NTC Contemp Pub Co.

Bacovcin, Helen. The Way of a Pilgrim: And the Pilgrim Continues His Way. 208p. 1985. pap. 9.95 (0-385-46814-8) Doubleday.

Bacow, Adele F. Designing the City: A Guide for Advocates & Public Officials. LC 94-30144. (Illus.). 304p. (C). 1995. text 50.00 (1-55963-290-9); pap. text 29.95 (1-55963-291-7) Island Pr.

Bacow, Adele F. & Kruckemeyer, Kenneth, eds. Bridge Design: Aesthetics & Developing Technologies. LC 86-61840. 186p. 1986. 5.00 (0-9617326-0-1, BD01) Am Soc Civil Eng.

Bacow, L. S. & Wheeler, M. Environmental Dispute Resolution. LC 84-16066. (Environment, Development, & Public Policy: Public Policy & Social Services Ser.). (Illus.). 388p. (C). 1984. 59.00 (0-306-41594-1, Plenum Trade) Perseus Pubng.

Bacq, Z. M. Chemical Transmission of Nerve Impulses: A Historical Sketch. 1975. 59.00 (0-08-020512-7, Pub. by Pergamon Repr) Franklin.

Bacquart, Jean-Baptiste. The Tribal Arts of Africa. LC 98-60234. (Illus.). 240p. 1998. 50.00 (0-500-01870-7, Pub. by Thames Hudson) Norton.

Bacque, James. Big Lonely. (New Canadian Library). 1978. pap. text 4.95 (0-7710-9258-X) McCland & Stewart.

Bacque, James. Crimes & Mercies: The Fate of German Civilians under Allied Occupation, 1944-1950. LC 98-104230. 288p. 1997. 22.95 (0-316-64070-0) Little.

Bacri, Clotilde. Daum. LC 92-41536. (Illus.). 272p. 1993. 85.00 (0-8478-1668-0, Pub. by Rizzoli Intl) St Martin.

Bacry, Henri. Lectures on Group Theory & Particle Theory. LC 72-78879. (Documents on Modern Physics Ser.). (Illus.). xviii, 580p. (C). 1977. text 531.00 (0-677-30190-1) Gordon & Breach.

*Bacs, Zoltban J. Regional Innovation, Knowledge, & Global Change. LC 99-34140. (Science, Technology & the International Political Economy Ser.). 2000. 24.95 (1-85567-443-2) P P Pubs.

Bacsich, P. D., jt. ed. see Mason, R.

Bacskai, Erika, jt. auth. see Gerevich, Jozsef.

Bacskai, V. Towns & Urban Society in Early Nineteenth-Century Hungary. 151p. (C). 1989. pap. 60.00 (963-05-5259-0, Pub. by Akade Kiado) St Mut.

Bacso, Bela. Georg Lukacs: Heidelberger Notizen, 1910-1913. (GER.). 232p. pap. 123.00 (963-05-7336-9, Pub. by Akade Kiado) St Mut.

Bacso, Harriet. Thanks. LC 95-61812. 224p. 1996. pap. 11.95 (0-9649008-0-7) TreeTop Books.

Bacstrom, Sigismund, ed. Bacstrom's Alchemical Anthology: or A Selection of Rare Alchemical Fragments. 1994. pap. 9.95 (1-55818-283-7) Holmes Pub.

Bacus, Elisabeth A., et al, eds. A Gendered Past: A Critical Bibliography of Gender in Archaeology. (Technical Reports Ser.: No. 25). xx, 172p. (Orig.). (C). 1993. pap. text 19.00 (0-915703-31-9) U Mich Mus Anthro.

Bacuya-Robbins, Ann, et al. Yefief 4 Vol. 1: Prescience: The Constitution of Mercy. (Illus.). 150p. 2000. pap. 24.95 (1-884434-06-1) Images For Media.

Baczewski, Paul C. Just for Kicks. LC 90-30528. 192p. (J). (gr. 6 up). 1990. 13.95 (0-397-32465-0) HarpC Child Bks.

— Just for Kicks. LC 90-30528. (Trophy Keypoint Bk.). 192p. (YA). (gr. 7 up). 1992. mass mkt. 3.95 (0-06-447074-1, HarpTrophy) HarpC Child Bks.

Baczko, Bronislaw. Ending the Terror: The French Revolution after Robespierre. Petheram, Michel, tr. LC 93-30389. 281p. (C). 1994. text 59.95 (0-521-44105-6) Cambridge U Pr.

Baczynski. Bathrooms. LC 98-9652. 176p. 2000. 34.95 (0-86636-676-8) PBC Intl Inc.

Baczynski, Bernadette L. Bathrooms. LC 98-9652. 1998. pap. 34.95 (0-86636-677-6) PBC Intl Inc.

Baczynski, Bernadette L., jt. auth. see Krengel, Jim.

Baczynsky, Mark. Camera Repair, Restoration & Adaptation. (Illus.). 52p. 1982. pap. 29.95 (0-89816-009-X) Embee Pr.

— Creative Photographic Processes. (Illus.). 54p. 1982. pap. 24.95 (0-89816-007-3) Embee Pr.

— How I Make a Comfortable Living Writing & Publishing Short Mini-Guides. (Illus.). 1981. pap. 9.95 (0-89816-003-0) Embee Pr.

— How to Make Custom Cameras & Equipment. unabridged ed. (Illus.). 28p. 1982. spiral bd. 22.95 (0-89816-008-1) Embee Pr.

— How to Select a Site for Your Photo Business. 1988. 4.95 (0-89816-117-7) Embee Pr.

— Photocrafts Book of Guides, Vol. 2. LC 78-70581. (Illus.). 104p. 1980. pap. 21.95 (0-89816-002-2) Embee Pr.

— Profitable Photographic Ventures. unabridged ed. (Illus.). 44p. 1990. spiral bd. 24.95 (0-89816-006-5) Embee Pr.

Bad Dog Press Editors. Rubber Chickens for the Soul: 50 1/2 Tales to Rekindle Your Heartburn. LC 95-83150. (Illus.). 96p. (Orig.). 1995. pap. 7.00 (1-887317-03-1) Bad Dog Pr.

Bad Object-Choices Staff, ed. How Do I Look? Queer Film & Video. LC 91-17052. 296p. (Orig.). 1991. pap. 16.95 (0-941920-20-8) Bay Pr.

Bad Otis Link. The Alphabet of Murder. 32p. 1994. 4.95 (1-885730-03-9) Verotik.

Bad Subjects Production Team Staff. Bad Subjects: Political Education for Everyday Life. LC 97-21143. (Cultural Front Ser.). 288p. 1997. text 52.00 (0-8147-5792-8); pap. text 18.50 (0-8147-5793-6) NYU Pr.

Bada, Jeffrey, jt. auth. see Wills, Christopher.

Badajoz, Diego Sanchez De, see Sanchez de Badajoz, Diego.

*Badakhchani, Seyyed H. Contemplation & Action: The Spiritual Autobiography of a Muslim. 1999. pap. 24.50 (1-86064-523-2, Pub. by I B T) St Martin.

Badakhchani, Seyyed H., tr. & intro. see Al-Din Tusi, Nasir.

Badal, James. Recording the Classics: Maestros, Music, & Technology. LC 95-35978. (Illus.). 225p. 1996. 24.00 (0-87338-542-X) Kent St U Pr.

Badal, Jindriska, tr. see Pavel, Ota.

Badalamenti. Grammar Dimensions, Vol. 1. 2nd ed. (Miscellaneous/Catalogs Ser.). (J). 1997. mass mkt., teacher ed. 7.95 (0-8384-7363-6) Heinle & Heinle.

*Badalamenti. Grammar Dimensions Platinum Book. 3rd ed. (C). 2000. pap. 30.95 incl. cd-rom (0-8384-0260-7) Heinle & Heinle.

Badalamenti & Stanchina. Grammar Dimensions, Bk. 1. 2nd ed. 1997. text 26.00 incl. audio (0-8384-7399-7) Heinle & Heinle.

Badalamenti, Anthony F. How to Have Your Way with Men. 147p. (Orig.). 1996. pap. 12.50 (0-9648590-0-9) Scientific Support.

— How to Succeed with Women. 132p. (Orig.). 1993. pap. 12.00 (1-880365-90-1) Scientific Support.

*Badalamenti, Anthony F. How to Succeed with Women. 2nd ed. 300p. (Orig.). 2000. pap. 19.00 (0-9648590-1-7) Scientific Support.

Badalamenti, Victoria & Stanchina, Carolyn. Grammar Dimensions: Form, Meaning & Use, Bk. 1. (J). 1993. pap., teacher ed. 8.25 (0-8384-4127-0) Heinle & Heinle.

— Grammar Dimensions: Form, Meaning, & Use, Bk. 1A. 2nd ed. 1997. 19.95 (0-8384-7154-4) Heinle & Heinle.

— Grammar Dimensions: Form, Meaning, & Use, Bk. 1B. 2nd ed. 1997. 19.95 (0-8384-7163-3) Heinle & Heinle.

— Grammar Dimensions 1, Bk. 1. (College ESL). (J). 1993. mass mkt. 25.00 (0-8384-3968-3) Heinle & Heinle.

Badalian, H. N., ed. see Thales, Norman.

*Badalucco, Laura. Kirigami: The Art of 3-Dimensional Paper Cutting. LC 99-87163. 2000. 24.95 (0-8069-4490-0) Sterling.

Badaracco. Loading the Dice. 1985. 24.95 (0-07-103206-1) McGraw.

Badaracco, Claire. American Culture & the Marketplace: R.R. Donnelley's Four American Books Campaign, 1926-1930. LC 91-45120. 67p. 1992. 15.00 (0-8444-0724-0) Lib Congress.

Badaracco, Claire H. Trading Words: Poetry, Typography, & Illustrated Books in the Modern Literary Economy. LC 94-45323. (Illus.). 232p. 1995. text 37.00 (0-8018-4859-8) Johns Hopkins.

Badaracco, Joseph. Business Ethics: Roles & Responsibilities. LC 94-27615. 588p. (C). 1994. text 63.50 (0-256-14946-1, Irwn McGrw-H) McGrw-H Hghr Educ.

Badaracco, Joseph L., Jr. Defining Moments: When Managers Must Choose Between Right & Right. LC 97-17613. 160p. 1997. 19.95 (0-87584-803-6, HBS Pr) Harvard Busn.

Badaracco, Joseph L., Jr. & Ellsworth, Richard R. Leadership & the Quest for Integrity. 240p. 1993. pap. 17.50 (0-87584-408-1) Harvard Busn.

Badarayana. Brahma Sutra: The Philosophy of Spiritual Life. Radhakrishnan, Sarvepalli, tr. LC 68-21330. 606p. 1968. reprint ed. lib. bdg. 85.00 (0-8371-0291-X, BABS, Greenwood Pr) Greenwood.

— Brahma-Sutra Bhasya of Sankaracarya. Gambhirananda, Swami, tr. 942p. 1965. 20.00 (81-7505-105-1, Pub. by Advaita Ashrama) Vedanta Pr.

— Brahma Sutras (Sri Ramanuja) 1979. 7.95 (81-7505-006-3, Pub. by Advaita Ashrama) Vedanta Pr.

— Brahma-Sutras (Vedanta-Sutras) Vireswarananda, Swami, tr. 7.95 (81-85301-95-6, Pub. by Advaita Ashrama) Vedanta Pr.

Badarinathi, Ravija. Introduction to SAS. 95p. (C). 1993. pap. 11.95 (0-534-51008-6) Wadsworth Pub.

— Introduction to SPSS. 87p. (C). 1993. pap. 11.95 (0-534-51007-8) Wadsworth Pub.

Badasch. Essential Nursing Assistant in Long Term Care. 2nd ed. 280p. 1994. pap. text 41.95 (0-8273-5633-1) Delmar.

— Essential/Nursing Assistant Long Term Care CT3. 2nd ed. (Home Care Aide Ser.). 1994. 41.95 (0-8273-6393-1) Delmar.

Badasch & Chesebro, Doreen S. An Introduction to Health Occupations. 144p. 1994. pap., student ed. 17.40 (0-89303-174-7) P-H.

— An Introduction to Health Occupations. 3rd ed. 1993. pap., student ed. 20.20 (0-89303-850-4) P-H.

Badasch, jt. auth. see Chapman.

Badasch, Shirely A. Essentials for Nursing Assisted Long-Term Care. (Home Care Aide Ser.). 1990. pap. 27.95 (0-8273-3989-5) Delmar.

*Badasch, Shirley A. Introduction to Health Occupations. 5th ed. LC 99-38341. (Illus.). 724p. 1999. 59.00 (0-13-013147-4) P-H.

Badasch, Shirley A. & Chesebro, Doreen. Comprehensive Medical Assisting. (C). 1995. write for info. (0-89303-154-2) Appleton & Lange.

Badasch, Shirley A. & Chesebro, Doreen S. Brief Introduction to Health Occupations. LC 93-24410. 304p. 1993. 41.00 (0-89303-170-4) P-H.

— Essentials for the Nursing Assistant in Long Term Care. 512p. 1994. pap. 40.40 (0-8273-8786-5) Delmar.

— Essentials for the Nursing Assistant in Long-Term Care. 2nd ed. 512p. (C). 1994. pap. 41.95 (0-8273-5531-5) Delmar.

— Essentials for the Nursing Assistant in Long-Term Care - Student Workbook. 334p. (C). 1994. wbk. ed. 18.00 (0-8273-5632-3) Delmar.

— The Health Care Worker: An Introduction to Health Occupations. (Illus.). 288p. 1984. teacher ed. 11.95 (0-89303-502-5); text 23.95 (0-89303-514-9) P-H.

— Introduction to Health Occupations. 4th ed. LC 96-20448. 720p. 1996. 59.00 (0-8359-5010-7) P-H.

Badash, Lawrence. Kapitza, Rutherford, & the Kremlin. fac. ed. LC 84-11822. (Illus.). 141p. 1994. pap. 43.80 (0-7837-7721-3, 208020500003) Bks Demand.

— Scientists & the Development of Nuclear Weapons: From Fission to the Limited Test Ban Treaty, 1939-1963. LC 94-17471. (Control of Nature Ser.). 144p. (C). 1995. pap. 12.50 (0-391-03874-5) Humanities.

— Scientists & the Development of Nuclear Weapons: From Fission to the Limited Test Ban Treaty, 1939-1963. LC 98-52948. (Control of Nature Ser.). 1998. write for info. (1-57392-538-1) Prometheus Bks.

*Badash, Lawrence. Scientists & the Development of Nuclear Weapons: From Fission to the Limited Test Ban Treaty, 1939-1963. LC 98-52948. (Control of Nature Ser.). 1998. write for info. (1-57392-715-5) Prometheus Bks.

Badash, Lawrence & Broida, H. P., eds. Reminiscences of Los Alamos: 1943-1945. (Studies in the History of Modern Science: No. 5). 209p. 1980. pap. text 55.50 (90-277-1098-8, D Reidel); lib. bdg. 70.50 (90-277-1097-X, D Reidel) Kluwer Academic.

Badash, Lawrence, et al. Nuclear Fission: Reaction to the Discovery in 1939. (IGCC Research Papers Ser.: No. 1). 58p. (Orig.). 1985. pap. text 3.50 (0-934637-01-6) U of CA Inst Global.

Badash, Lawrence, ed. see Rutherford, Ernest & Boltwood, Bertram B.

Badash, Semyon. Kolyma Ty, Moiya Kolyma . . . LC 85-81009. (RUS., Illus.). 120p. 1986. 10.00 (0-911971-14-9) Effect Pub.

Badasu, Cosmas K. Le Meme et l'Autre: Espace et Rapports de Pouvoir dans le Roman Francais (1871-1914), Vol. 62. (Currents in Comparative Romance Languages & Literatures Ser.). XIV, 207p. (C). 1998. text 45.95 (0-8204-3836-7) P Lang Pubng.

Badauni, M. T. Seerat-un-Nabi: Shibli Numani, 2 vols. 1993. 29.95 (0-933511-51-5) Kazi Pubns.

Badavas, Paul C. Real-Time Statistical Process Control. 320p. (C). 1992. text 52.60 (0-13-763574-5) P-H.

Badaway, Michael K. Developing Managerial Skills in Engineers & Scientists: Succeeding As a Technical Manager. 2nd ed. (Industrial Engineering Ser.). 456p. 1995. 69.95 (0-471-28634-6, VNR) Wiley.

Badawi, jt. auth. see Hinds.

Badawi, Jamal. Polygamy in Islamic Law. 20p. 1994. pap. 3.00 (1-56744-191-2) Kazi Pubns.

Badawi, Jamal A. Gender Equity in Islam: Some Preliminary Thoughts. 1995. write for info. (0-89259-159-5) Am Trust Pubns.

— Islamic Teachings. LC 95-19625. 1995. write for info. (0-89259-143-9) Am Trust Pubns.

— Muhammad's Prophthood: An Analytical View. 26p. 1990. pap. write for info. (1-882837-19-3) W A M Y Intl.

— Selected Prayers. 78p. (Orig.). 1979. pap. 2.50 (0-89259-092-0) Am Trust Pubns.

— The Status of Woman in Islam. Al-Jarrahi, Abdussamad, ed. Bekkari, Muhammad, tr. from ENG. (Illus.). 28p. (Orig.). 1982. pap. 1.50 (0-89259-036-X) Am Trust Pubns.

— The Status of Woman in Islam. 28p. (Orig.). 1980. pap. write for info. (1-882837-13-4) W A M Y Intl.

Badawi, Jamal A., jt. auth. see Beekun, Rafik I.

Badawi, M. M. A Short History of Modern Arabic Literature. LC 92-23257. 326p. (C). 1993. text 58.00 (0-19-826542-5) OUP.

Badawi, M. M., ed. Modern Arabic Literature. (History of Arabic Literature Ser.). (Illus.). 585p. (C). 1993. text 129.95 (0-521-33197-8) Cambridge U Pr.

Badawi, Mohamed. Probleme des Fachwortschatzes im Arabischen. (Arabistische Texte und Studien: Bd. 11). (GER.). viii, 177p. 1997. write for info. (3-487-10564-0) G Olms Pubs.

Badawi, Muhammad M. Coleridge: Critic of Shakespeare. LC 72-86417. 230p. reprint ed. pap. 65.60 (0-608-13322-1, 2025575) Bks Demand.

Badawi, S. Basic Course in Arabic: Kitabal Assasi. (Kitab al Assasi Ser.). (ARA.). 1994. audio 160.00 (0-86685-641-2) Intl Bk Ctr.

— Basic Course in Arabic: Kitabal Assasi, Bk. 1. (Kitab al Assasi Ser.). (ARA.). 1994. 34.95 (0-86685-638-2) Intl Bk Ctr.

— Basic Course in Arabic: Kitabal Assasi, Bk. 2. (ARA.). 1994. 34.95 (0-86685-639-0) Intl Bk Ctr.

— Basic Course in Arabic: Kitabal Assasi, Bk. 3. (ARA.). 1994. 36.95 (0-86685-640-4) Intl Bk Ctr.

Badawi, Zaki. Dictionary of Social Sciences: English-French-Arabic. (ARA, ENG & FRE.). 591p. 1985. 35.00 (0-86685-115-1, LDL1151, Pub. by Librairie du Liban) Intl Bk Ctr.

Badawy, A. A., ed. Biomedical Aspects of Drug Dependence: International Biomedical Research Symposium on Drug Dependence, Tangier, Morocco, 11-15 October 1982. (Illus.). 120p. 1984. pap. 22.00 (0-08-030785-X, Pergamon Pr) Elsevier.

Badawy, A. A., jt. ed. see Taberner, P. V.

Badawy, Alexander. A Monumental Gateway for a Temple of King Sety I. (Wilbur Monographs). (Illus.). 26p. 1985. reprint ed. pap. 2.50 (0-913696-20-X) Bklyn Mus.

— The Tomb of Nyhetep-Ptah at Giza & the Tomb of Ankhmahor at Saqqara. LC 77-7350. (University of California Publications: No. 11, Archaeology). 208p. 1978. pap. 64.50 (0-7837-7469-9, 204919100010) Bks Demand.

— Tombs of Iteti, Sekhem ankh-Ptah, & Kaemnofert at Giza. LC 75-620057. (University of California Publications, Occasional Papers: No. 9). 105p. pap. 32.60 (0-608-13945-9, 202138600021) Bks Demand.

Badawy, Michael K. Developing Managerial Skills in Engineers & Scientists: Succeeding As a Technical Manager. 2nd ed. (Industrial Engineering Ser.). 456p. 1995. 55.95 (0-442-01861-4, VNR) Wiley.

*Badawy, Shawky ZA, ed. Clinical Management of the Perimenopause. (An Arnold Publication). 208p. 1999. text 49.95 (0-340-74150-3) OUP.

Badayum, T. B. A Short Handbook of Fiqh. 1992. pap. 3.50 (0-933511-54-X) Kazi Pubns.

Badcock, Colin & Frank, Ernest. Winchester. (C). 1987. text 50.00 (0-907115-51-9, Pub. by Pevensey) St Mut.

B

An Asterisk (*) at the beginning of an entry indicates that the title is appearing for the first time.

Badcock, Gary, ed. & intro. see McIntyre, John.

Badcock, Gary D. Light of Truth & Fire of Love: A Theology of the Holy Spirit. LC 96-53941. 296p. 1997. pap. 25.00 (*0-8028-4288-7*) Eerdmans.

— The Way of Life: A Theology of Christian Vocation. LC 98-28329. 128p. 1998. pap. 12.00 (*0-8028-4490-1*) Eerdmans.

Badcock, Gary D., jt. ed. see Wright, David F.

Badcock, John, Jr. Slaves to Duty. LC 72-77199. (Libertarian Broadsides Ser.: No. 2). 36p. 1972. reprint ed. pap. 0.85 (*0-87926-013-0*) R Myles.

Badcock, John & Tingay, Graham I. The Romans & Their Empire. (History Matters Ser.). (Illus.). 75p. (Orig.). (J). (gr. 6-8). 1991. pap. 17.95 (*0-7487-1186-4*) Dufour.

Badcock, John, et al. The World of Greece & Rome. (C). 1989. 42.00 (*0-7487-0030-7*, Pub. by S Thornes Pubs) Trans-Atl Phila.

Badcock, John, jt. auth. see Tingay, Graham I.

Baddaloo, E. G., jt. auth. see Ramamoorthy, Sub.

Baddeley, Adrian, ed. see Ambartzumian, R. V.

Baddeley, Alan D. Essentials of Human Memory. 368p. 1999. 59.95 (*0-86377-544-6*) L Erlbaum Assocs.

— Essentials of Human Memory. 368p. 1998. pap. text 29.95 (*0-86377-545-4*) Taylor & Francis.

— Handbook of Memory Disorders. LC 99-204415. 1999. pap. text 65.00 (*0-471-96704-1*) Wiley.

— The Human Memory. 2nd rev. ed. LC 97-25817. 423p. 1997. pap. 58.00 (*0-205-27948-1*) P-H.

— Working Memory. (Oxford Psychology Ser.: No. 11). (Illus.). 304p. 1987. pap. text 45.00 (*0-19-852133-2*) OUP.

— Your Memory: A User's Guide. 390p. 1996. pap. 14.95 (*1-85375-213-4*, Pub. by Prion) Trafalgar.

Baddeley, Alan D., et al, eds. Handbook of Memory Disorders. LC 94-28317. 668p. 1995. 315.00 (*0-471-95078-5*) Wiley.

Baddeley, Alan D. & Weiskrantz, Lawrence, eds. Attention - Selection, Awareness, & Control: A Tribute to Donald Broadbent. (Illus.). 454p. 1995. pap. text 50.00 (*0-19-852374-2*) OUP.

Baddeley, Alan D., jt. ed. see Long, John.

Baddeley, Gavin. Dissecting Marilyn Manson. (Illus.). 160p. 1999. pap. text 16.95 (*0-85965-283-1*) Plexus.

***Baddeley, Gavin.** Lucifer Rising: A Book of Sin, Devil-Worship & Rock-'N'-Roll. 1999. pap. 16.95 (*0-85965-280-7*, Pub. by Plexus) Publishers Group.

Baddeley, J. St. John, tr. see Baudrillard, Jean.

Baddeley, John F. The Rugged Flanks of Caucasus, 2 vols. LC 73-6267. (Middle East Ser.). 1973. reprint ed. 60.95 (*0-405-05321-5*) Ayer.

— Russia, Mongolia & China, 2 vols. 1976. lib. bdg. 500.00 (*0-8490-2549-4*) Gordon Pr.

— The Russian Conquest of the Caucasus. (Illus.). 660p. 1997. reprint ed. 120.00 (*0-7007-0634-8*, Pub. by Curzon Pr Ltd) Paul & Co Pubs.

Baddeley, Jon. Nautical Antiques & Collectables. (Illus.). 192p. 1993. 70.00 (*0-85667-394-3*, Pub. by P Wilson) Scala Books.

***Baddeley, Oriana.** Sanai, Byzantium, Russia: Orthodox Christian Art from the Sixth to the Twentieth Century. (Illus.). 456p. 2000. 100.00 (*0-295-98027-3*) U of Wash Pr.

Baddeley, Roland, et al, eds. Information Theory & the Brain. LC 98-32172. (Illus.). 365p. (C). 2000. text 85.00 (*0-521-63197-1*) Cambridge U Pr.

Baddeley, St. Clair & Gordon, L. D. Rome & Its Story. 1977. lib. bdg. 59.95 (*0-8490-2543-5*) Gordon Pr.

Badden, Diane, ed. The Mailbox, 1995-1996 Primary Yearbook. (Illus.). 320p. 1996. 29.95 (*1-56234-137-5*) Educ Ctr.

— The Mailbox, 1996-1997 Primary Yearbook. 320p. 1997. 29.95 (*1-56234-166-9*) Educ Ctr.

Badders, Veldon. Collector's Guide to Inkwells. LC 95-157645. 176p. 1995. pap. 18.95 (*0-89145-639-2*, 3966) Collector Bks.

— Collector's Guide to Inkwells, Vol. II. LC 95-157645. (Illus.). 256p. 1997. pap. 19.95 (*1-57432-020-3*, 4947) Collector Bks.

***Baddiel, Ivor.** Fantastic Creatures. 32p. 1999. pap. text 6.95 (*0-7641-1153-1*) Barron.

Baddiel, Ivor. The Future. (Mysterious World Ser.). 32p. (gr. 5-9). 1999. pap. text 6.95 (*0-7641-1155-8*) Barron.

— The Ultimate Soccer Book. LC 97-36602. (Illus.). 96p. (J). (gr. 3 up). 1998. 16.95 (*0-7894-2795-8*) DK Pub Inc.

Baddiel, Ivor & Blezard, Tracey. Extraterrestrials: Investigations into the Unexplained. (Mysterious World Bks.). (Illus.). 32p. (YA). (gr. 5 up). 1999. pap. 6.95 (*0-7641-0907-3*) Barron.

— The Supernatural. (Mysterious World Bks.). (Illus.). 32p. (YA). (gr. 5 up). 1999. pap. 6.95 (*0-7641-0906-5*) Barron.

Baddiel, Sarah. Golf: The Golden Years. 1989. 15.98 (*1-55521-503-3*) Bk Sales Inc.

— World of Golf Collectibles. 1992. 17.98 (*1-55521-746-X*) Bk Sales Inc.

Baddock, James. Piccolo. 252p. 1992. 19.95 (*0-8027-1201-0*) Walker & Co.

— Piccolo. large type ed. LC 92-33397. 402p. 1993. reprint ed. lib. bdg. 18.95 (*1-56054-589-5*) Thorndike Pr.

Baddour, Margaret B. Easy Magic. 78p. Date not set. pap. 8.95 (*0-932662-93-5*) St Andrews NC.

Baddour, R. & Timmins, R. Application of Plasmas to Chemical Processing. LC 67-17494. 1967. 99.00 (*0-08-012735-5*, Pub. by Pergamon Repr) Franklin.

Bade, jt. auth. see Parkin, Michael.

Bade, David H., jt. auth. see Blakely, James.

Bade, James N., ed. The German Connection: New Zealand & German-Speaking Europe in the Nineteenth Century. (Illus.). 272p. 1994. text 45.00 (*0-19-558283-7*) OUP.

Bade, Klaus J., ed. Population, Labour & Migration in 19th & 20th-Century Germany. LC 86-24470. (German Historical Perspectives Ser.: Vol. 1). 212p. 1987. 37.50 (*0-85496-503-3*) Berg Pubs.

Bade, Klaus J. & Weiner, Myron, eds. Migration Past, Migration Future: Germany & the United States. LC 97-7505. (Migration & Refugees: Vol. 1). 176p. 1997. 29.95 (*1-57181-125-7*) Berghahn Bks.

Bade, Klaus J., jt. auth. see Caestecker, Frank.

Bade, Nichola E. Marketing Without Money! 175, Cheap & Offbeat Ways for Small Businesses to Increase Sales! LC 97-50528. (Illus.). 160p. 1994. pap. 12.95 (*0-8442-3343-9*) NTC Contemp Pub Co.

Bade, Nicholas E. Marketing Without Money! 175 Free, Cheap & Offbeat Ways for Small Businesses to Increase Sales! LC 92-76216. 148p. 1993. pap. 12.95 (*1-882923-12-X*) Halle Hse Pub.

— Marketing Without Money! 175 Free Cheap & Offbeat Ways for Small Businesses to Increase Sales! LC 93-44562. (Illus.). 160p. 1994. 19.95 (*0-8442-3335-8*, NTC Business Bks) NTC Contemp Pub Co.

***Bade, Nicholas E.** Marketing Without Money for Small & Midsize Businesses! 300 FREE & Cheap Ways to Increase Your Sales! LC 99-73072. 164p. 1999. pap. 16.95 (*1-882923-20-0*) Halle Hse Pub.

Bade, Nicholas E. More Marketing Without Money for Small Businesses! 246 Free & Cheap Ways to Increase Your Sales! LC 94-79474. 164p. (Orig.). 1995. pap. text 16.95 (*1-882923-15-4*) Halle Hse Pub.

***Bade, Patrick.** Degas. (Reveries Ser.). (Illus.). 120p. 2000. 14.95 (*1-85995-715-3*) Parkstone Pr.

— The Erotic Museum of Berlin. (Illus.). 224p. 2000. 55.00 (*1-85995-775-7*) Parkstone Pr.

Bade, Patrick. Gustave Courbet: French Painter. (Reveries Ser.). 120p. 1999. 14.95 (*1-85995-461-8*) Parkstone Pr.

— Ingres: French Painter. (Reveries Ser.). 120p. 1999. 14.95 (*1-85995-471-5*) Parkstone Pr.

Bade, Robin, jt. auth. see Parkin, Michael.

Bade, Ted. Help Wanted. LC 97-61039. (Aesop's Fables Running Start Ser.). (Illus.). 32p. (J). (gr. 2-4). 1997. pap. 4.95 (*1-890570-39-7*) Huckleberry CT.

Bade, Tom, jt. auth. see Stevenson, Robin.

Bade, W. G. Algebraic & Strong Splittings of Extensions of Banach Algebras. LC 98-46541. (Memoirs of the American Mathematical Society Ser.). 1999. 41.00 (*0-8218-1058-8*) Am Math.

Bade, W. G., et al. Multipliers of Radical Banach Algebras of Power Series. LC 84-3070. (Memoirs Ser.: No. 49/303). 84p. 1984. pap. 17.00 (*0-8218-2304-3*, MEMO/49/303) Am Math.

Bade, William F. Life & Letters of John Muir, 2 vols. LC 77-153302. (BCL Ser.: No. I). reprint ed. 92.50 (*0-404-00444-X*) AMS Pr.

Badea, F. Reaction Mechanisms in Organic Chemistry. (Abacus Bks.). 702p. 1977. text 85.00 (*0-85626-002-9*) Gordon & Breach.

Badeau, Adam. Grant in Peace: From Appomattox to Mount McGregor. LC 72-152971. (Select Bibliographies Reprint Ser.). 1977. reprint ed. 42.95 (*0-8369-5723-7*) Ayer.

— Military History of Ulysses S. Grant, from April, 1861 to April, 1865. 1977. 79.95 (*0-8369-7150-7*, 7982) Ayer.

Badeau, John S. The American Approach to the Arab World. LC 67-22494. (Policy Books of the Council on Foreign Relations). 223p. reprint ed. pap. 69.20 (*0-8357-5353-0*, 200294100016) Bks Demand.

— The Middle East Remembered. LC 83-61202. 271p. 1983. 5.00 (*0-916808-21-1*) Mid East Inst.

Badeer, H. S. Cardiovascular Physiology. (Continuing Education Ser.: Vol. 6). (Illus.). xvi, 276p. 1984. 50.50 (*3-8055-3796-4*) S Karger.

Badejo, Diedre. Osun Seegesi: The Elegant Deity of Wealth, Power, & Femininity. LC 95-51678. 248p. 1996. text 59.95 (*0-86543-354-2*) Africa World.

— Osun Seegesi: The Elegant Deity of Wealth, Power & Femininity. LC 95-51678. 248p. 1996. pap. 18.95 (*0-86543-355-0*) Africa World.

Badeker, Karl. Baedeker's Hong Kong. 3rd ed. 192p. 1993. pap. 23.00 (*0-671-87131-5*, P-H Travel) Prntice Hall Bks.

***Bademis, Nikolaos.** Gymnastik-Verstandnis in der Antike und das Ihm Zugrunde Liegende Bild des Menschen: Zur Entwicklung des Gymnastik-Verstandnisses von Homer Bis in die Hellenistische Zeit. (Europaische Hochschulschriften Ser.: Vol. 11). (GER.). xiii, 405p. 1999. 52.95 (*3-631-34742-1*) P Lang Pubng.

Baden. The Greatest Gift Is Love. LC 59-1314. (Arch Bks.). 24p. (J). (gr. k-4). 1985. pap. 1.99 (*0-570-06196-2*, 59-1314) Concordia.

— Rejuvenating the Mature Business. 272p. 1994. 29.95 (*0-07-103585-0*) McGraw.

Baden, Clifford. Adult Learning in Associations: Models for Good Practice. LC 98-167574. (Foundation Ser.). (Illus.). 80p. 1998. pap. 35.95 (*0-88034-138-6*) Am Soc Assn Execs.

Baden-Fuller, A. J. Engineering Field Theory: Text & Examples, 2 vols. 1982. pap. 267.00 (*0-08-029320-4*, Pub. by Pergamon Repr) Franklin.

— Ferrites at Microwave Frequencies. (Electromagnetic Waves Ser.: No. 23). 1987. 99.00 (*0-86341-064-2*, EW023) INSPEC Inc.

Baden-Fuller, Charles. Rejuvenating The Mature Business 2nd ed. 1996. pap. text 24.95 (*1-86152-513-3*) Thomson Learn.

Baden-Fuller, Charles & Pitt, Martyn. Strategic Innovation: Casebook. (Illus.). 480p. (C). 1996. mass mkt. 31.95 (*0-415-12870-6*) Routledge.

— Strategic Innovation: Casebook. (Illus.). 480p. (C). 1996. pap. 78.95 (*0-415-12869-2*) Thomson Learn.

Baden-Fuller, Charles & Pitt, Martyn, eds. Strategic Innovation: An International Casebook on Strategic Management. 480p. 1996. pap. 20.99 (*1-86152-202-9*) Thomson Learn.

Baden-Fuller, Charles & Stopford, John. Rejuvenating the Mature Business: The Competitive Challenge. LC 95-30382. 304p. 1996. pap. 19.95 (*0-415-13520-6*) Routledge.

Baden-Fuller, Charles & Stopford, John M. Rejuvenating the Mature Business: The Competitive Challenge. LC 93-36706. 1994. 29.95 (*0-87584-476-6*) Harvard Busn.

— Rejuvenating the Mature Business: The Competitive Challenge. LC 92-26237. 224p. 1992. pap. 42.95 (*0-415-08987-5*) Thomson Learn.

Baden, H. Danish/English-English/Danish Medical Dictionary. 913p. 1994. 140.00 (*0-7859-9559-5*) Fr & Eur.

Baden, H. P. The Chemotherapy of Psoriasis. (International Encyclopedia of Pharmacology & Therapeutics Ser.: 110). 325p. 1984. 122.50 (*0-08-029823-0*, Pergamon Pr) Elsevier.

Baden, Jacqueline H. Bits & Pieces: Maryland's Eastern Shore Counties, Talbot & Kent. LC 92-62221. 1993. pap. text 7.95 (*0-9624619-5-4*) Travel Tape.

***Baden, John.** Applying Science & Risk Analysis to Endangered Species. 272p. 2000. 79.95 (*1-84014-915-9*) Ashgate Pub Co.

Baden, John, ed. The Vanishing Farmland Crisis: Critical Views of the Movement to Preserve Agricultural Land. LC 84-7472. (Studies in Government & Public Policy). x, 174p. 1984. 25.00 (*0-7006-0253-4*) U Pr of KS.

Baden, John & Noonan, Douglas S. Managing the Commons. 2nd ed. LC 97-20390. 1998. pap. write for info. (*0-02-532115-3*) Macmillan.

Baden, John, jt. ed. see Hardin, Garrett.

Baden, John A. Environmental Gore: A Constructive Response to Earth in the Balance. LC 94-6362. 1994. 21.95 (*0-936488-76-6*) PRIPP.

Baden, John A., ed. Federal Judge's Desk Reference to Environmental Economics. LC 98-9206. (Illus.). 324p. 1998. pap. text 19.95 (*0-936488-84-0*) PRIPP.

Baden, John A. & Leal, Donald E., eds. The Yellowstone Primer: Land & Resource Management in the Greater Yellowstone Ecosystem. LC 88-64201. (Illus.). 226p. (Orig.). 1990. 29.95 (*0-936488-23-9*); pap. 12.95 (*0-936488-24-7*) PRIPP.

Baden, John A. & Noonan, Douglas S., eds. Managing the Commons. 2nd ed. LC 97-20390. (Illus.). 264p. 1998. 39.95 (*0-253-33361-X*); pap. 16.95 (*0-253-21153-0*) Ind U Pr.

Baden, John A. & Snow, Donald, eds. The Next West: Public Lands, Community & Economy in the American West. LC 96-52664. 272p. 1997. pap. 22.95 (*1-55963-460-X*, Shearwater Bks); text 45.00 (*1-55963-459-6*, Shearwater Bks) Island Pr.

Baden, John A., jt. ed. see Hess, Karl, Jr.

***Baden, Karl.** Contact Sheet 106 Volume 106: Karl Baden - How Did I Get Here? Hoone, Jeffrey, ed. (Contact Sheet Ser.). (Illus.). 32p. 2000. pap. 10.00 (*0-935445-15-3*) Light Work.

Baden, Marian, et al. Servants of the Lord. 1995. pap. text 3.99 (*0-570-09531-X*, 20-2601) Concordia.

Baden, Michael M. & Hennesee, Judith A. Unnatural Death: Confessions of a Medical Examiner. 240p. 1990. mass mkt. 5.99 (*0-8041-0599-5*) Ivy Books.

Baden, Nancy T. Muffled Cries: The Writer & Literature in Authoritarian Brazil, 1964-1985. LC 99-15142. 272p. 1999. 55.00 (*0-7618-1420-5*); pap. 34.50 (*0-7618-1421-3*) U Pr of Amer.

Baden-Powell, Baden H. Land Systems of British India: Being a Manual of the Land-Tenures & of the Systems of Land-Revenue Administration Prevalent in the Several Provinces, 3 vols., Set. (C). 1990. reprint ed. 48.00 (*81-85418-30-6*, Pub. by Low Price) S Asia.

— The Origin & Growth of Village Communities in India. 155p. 1985. reprint ed. 125.00 (*81-85046-14-X*, Pub. by Scientific) St Mut.

Baden-Powell, Charlotte. Architect's Pocket Book. LC 97-23819. 192p. 1997. text 28.95 (*0-7506-2592-9*) Buttrwrth-Heinemann.

***Baden-Powell, Charlotte.** Architect's Pocket Book. 320p. 2001. 28.95 (*0-7506-4764-7*, Architectural Pr) Buttrwrth-Heinemann.

Baden-Powell, Francis. Building Overseas: Butterworth Architecture Management Guide. LC 97-21710. 209p. 1996. reprint ed. pap. 59.95 (*0-7506-2889-8*) Buttrwrth-Heinemann.

Baden-Powell, Robert. Adventures & Accidents. (Illus.). 184p. 1995. pap. 16.95 (*1-885529-18-X*) Stevens Pub.

— Aids to Scoutmastership: A Handbook for Scoutmasters on the Theory of Scout Training. 127p. (Orig.). 1992. pap. 14.95 (*0-9632054-2-0*) Stevens Pub.

— Boy Scouts Beyond the Seas: My World Tour. (Illus.). 250p. 1992. pap. 17.95 (*0-9632054-4-7*) Stevens Pub.

— My Adventures As a Spy. (Illus.). 132p. (Orig.). (YA). 1993. pap. 16.95 (*0-9632054-8-X*) Stevens Pub.

— Scouting for Boys: A Handbook for Instruction in Good Citizenship. (Illus.). 273p. (Orig.). (YA). 1992. pap. 17.95 (*0-9632054-1-2*) Stevens Pub.

— What Scouts Can Do: More Yarns. (Illus.). 173p. 1992. pap. 14.95 (*0-9632054-5-5*) Stevens Pub.

Baden-Powell, Robert S. The Downfall of the Prempeh: A Diary of Life with the Native Levy in Ashanti, 1895-96. LC 72-6481. (Black Heritage Library Collection). 1977. reprint ed. 26.95 (*0-8369-9157-5*) Ayer.

Baden, R. Tim. Housing & Urban Development: Potential Implications of Legislation Proposing to Dismantle HUD. (Illus.). 128p. (C). 1999. pap. text 30.00 (*0-7881-4359-X*) DIANE Pub.

Baden, Robert. Caleb, God's Special Spy: Numbers 13-14. (Arch Bks.). (Illus.). 24p. (Orig.). (J). (ps-4). 1993. pap. 1.99 (*0-570-09031-8*, 59-1454) Concordia.

— The Coming of the Holy Spirit: Acts 2:1-41. (Arch Bks.). (Illus.). 24p. (Orig.). (J). (ps-4). 1992. pap. 1.99 (*0-570-09029-6*, 59-1452) Concordia.

— My Book about Life in Jesus' Time. LC 97-27909. (Illus.). 96p. (J). (ps-3). 1998. 9.99 (*0-570-05036-7*, 56-1860) Concordia.

— Thomas, the Doubting Disciple. LC 97-136043. 1997. pap. text 1.99 (*0-570-07531-9*, 59-1504) Concordia.

— Y Domingo, Siete. Mathews, Judith, ed. Ada, Alma F., tr. LC 89-37823. (SPA., Illus.). 40p. (J). (ps-3). 1990. lib. bdg. 14.95 (*0-8075-9355-9*) A Whitman.

***Baden, S. B., et al, eds.** Structured Adaptive Mesh Refinement (SAMR) Grid Methods. LC 99-43388. (IMA Volumes in Mathematics & Its Applications Ser.: Vol. 117). (Illus.). 184p. 1999. 59.95 (*0-387-98921-8*) Spr-Verlag.

Badenhorst, D. C., jt. auth. see Lemmer, E. M.

Badenhorst, Phillip N., et al, eds. Platelet Kinetics & Imaging. Incl. Vol. I. Techniques & Normal Platelet Kinetics. 184p. 1985. 134.00 (*0-8493-5441-2*, RC670); Vol. II. Clinical Applications. Badenhorst, Philip N., ed. 128p. 1985. 79.00 (*0-8493-5442-0*, CRC Reprint); 1985. 134.00 (*0-318-60653-4*) CRC Pr.

Badeni, June. The Slender Tree: A Life of Alice Meynell. 30.00 (*0-907018-01-7*, Pub. by Tabb Hse) Seven Hills Bk.

Badenoch, Lindsay. Crosscurrents. LC 88-4265. 1989. 20.00 (*1-85063-114-X*, Arkana) Viking Penguin.

Bader & Burt. MAT: Miller Analogies Test. 6th ed. 1995. pap. 11.95 (*0-671-52112-8*) PB.

Bader, Alfred. Alfred Bader: Adventures of a Chemist Collector. (Illus.). 288p. 1995. 25.00 (*0-297-83461-4*, Pub. by Weidenfeld & Nicolson) Trafalgar.

Bader, Barry S. Five Keys to Building An Excellent Governing Board. Veatch, Reggi, ed. (Keys to Better Governance Through Better Information Ser.: Vol. 1). (Illus.). (Orig.). 1991. pap. text 9.00 (*0-915963-06-X*, FKGB) Capitol Publns.

— Informing the Board about Medical Staff Credentialing & Development. Veatch, Reggi, ed. (Keys to Better Governance Through Better Information Ser.: Vol. 3). (Illus.). (Orig.). 1991. pap. text 9.00 (*0-915963-08-6*, MSC) Capitol Publns.

— Informing the Board about Quality. Veatch, Reggi, ed. (Keys to Better Governance Through Better Information Ser.: Vol. 2). (Illus.). 96p. (Orig.). 1991. pap. text 9.00 (*0-915963-07-8*, QUAL) Capitol Publns.

— Keys to Better Governance Through Better Information, 3 vols. Veatch, Reggi, ed. (Orig.). 1991. pap. text 42.95 (*0-915963-05-1*) Bader Assoc Inc.

— Planning Successful Board Retreats: A Guide for Board Members & Chief Executives. (Nonprofit Governance Ser.: No. 10). 28p. 1992. reprint ed. pap. text 12.00 (*0-925299-14-6*) Natl Ctr Nonprofit.

— Rediscovering Quality: What Healthcare Leaders & Managers Need to Know about the Total Quality Transformation. (Illus.). 121p. (Orig.). 1992. pap. text 9.50 (*0-915963-11-6*, RDQ) Capitol Publns.

Bader, Barry S. & Umbdenstock, Richard J. Improving & Evaluating Board Performance. Candage, Mellen, ed. (Illus.). 84p. (Orig.). 1986. pap. text 12.00 (*0-915963-01-9*) Bader Assoc Inc.

Bader, Barry S., et al. Board Self-Evaluation Manual. 2nd ed. 141p. (Orig.). 1988. student ed. 59.00 (*0-915963-04-3*) Bader Assoc Inc.

Bader, Beth D., jt. auth. see Firestone, William A.

Bader, Bonnie. East Side Story. LC 93-1919. (Stories of the States Ser.). (Illus.). 80p. (J). (gr. 4-7). 1993. lib. bdg. 14.95 (*1-881889-22-X*) Silver Moon.

— East Side Story. (Stories of the States Ser.). (Illus.). 108p. (J). (gr. 4-7). 1995. pap. 5.95 (*1-881889-71-8*) Silver Moon.

— Golden Quest. LC 93-16461. (Stories of the States Ser.). (Illus.). 64p. (J). (gr. 4-7). 1993. lib. bdg. 14.95 (*1-881889-30-0*) Silver Moon.

— Golden Quest. (Stories of the States Ser.). (Illus.). 96p. (J). (gr. 4-7). 1995. pap. 5.95 (*1-881889-74-2*) Silver Moon.

— Highway Robbery. (Carmen Sandiego Mystery Ser.). (J). (gr. 4-6). 1997. 9.60 (*0-606-11193-X*, Pub. by Turtleback) Demco.

— One T. Rex over Easy. (Carmen Sandiego Mystery Ser.). (J). (gr. 4-6). 1997. 9.60 (*0-606-11190-5*, Pub. by Turtleback) Demco.

Bader, Bonnie & West, Tracey. Highway Robbery. LC 97-18054. (Carmen Sandiego Mystery Ser.). (Illus.). 144p. (J). (gr. 3-7). 1997. pap. 4.50 (*0-06-440685-7*, HarpTrophy) HarpC Child Bks.

Bader, Carol & Anton, Harley. Keys to Better College Reading. 550p. 1994. pap. text 16.00 (*0-944210-65-1*) Townsend NJ.

Bader, Chris. Strange Northwest: Weird Encounters in Alaska, British Columbia, Idaho, Oregon, & Washington. 144p. 1995. pap. 11.95 (*0-88839-359-8*) Hancock House.

Bader, Clarisse. Women in Ancient India: Moral & Literary Studies. LC 72-9617. (Human Sexual Behavior Ser.). reprint ed. 45.00 (*0-404-57408-4*) AMS Pr.

Bader, David M. Haikus For Jews. LC 99-31954. 96p. 1999. 11.00 (*0-609-60502-X*, Crown) Crown.

***Bader, Elizabeth E.** California Administrative Mandamus: March 2000 Update. Piatt, Norma, ed. LC 72-619669. 252p. 2000. 53.00 (*0-7626-0410-7*, CP-38811) Cont Ed Bar-CA.

***Bader, Ellyn.** Tell Me No Lies. LC 00-29684. 288p. 2000. text 24.95 (*0-312-26238-8*) St Martin.

Bader, Ellyn & Pearson, Peter T. In Quest of the Mythical Mate: A Developmental Approach to Diagnosis & Treatment in Couples Therapy. LC 88-14556. 285p. 1988. text 30.95 (*0-87630-516-8*) Brunner-Mazel.

An Asterisk (*) at the beginning of an entry indicates that the title is appearing for the first time.

Bader, Emily, et al, eds. Pegasus Presents: A Culinary & Equine Guide to Germantown, Tennessee. (Illus.). 240p. (Orig.). (C). 1989. 14.95 (*0-9622844-0-8*) Pegasus Germantown.

Bader, F., et al. Studies in Honor of Jaan Puhvel Pt. 2: Mythology & Religion. Greppin, John & Polome, Edgar C., eds. LC 97-204933. (Journal of Indo-European Studies Monograph Ser.: No. 21). (Illus.). 280p. (Orig.). (C). 1997. pap. 48.00 (*0-941694-55-0*) Inst Study Man.

Bader, Gershom. Encyclopedia of Talmudic Sages. LC 87-33465. 800p. 1988. 50.00 (*0-87668-903-9*) Aronson.

Bader, Gloria E. Make Your Training Results Last: A Practical Guide to Tracking Training Follow-Through. 1995. pap. 14.95 (*1-883553-39-3*) R Chang Assocs.

Bader, Gloria E. & Bloom, Audrey E. Make Your Training Results Last: A Practical Guide to Tracking Training Follow-Through. (High Impact Training Ser.). (Illus.). 120p. 1994. pap. 14.95 (*0-7879-5093-9*) R Chang Assocs.

Bader, Gloria E., et al. Measuring Team Performance: A Practical Guide to Tracking Team Success. LC 94-94045. (High Performance Team Ser.). (Illus.). 120p. 1994. pap. 12.95 (*1-883553-29-6*) R Chang Assocs.

Bader, Harry. Who Has the Legal Right to Fish? Constitutional & Common Law in Alaska Fisheries Management. LC 98-172433. (Marine Advisory Bulletin Ser.). 24p. 1998. 4.00 (*1-56612-053-5*) AK Sea Grant CP.

Bader, Hilary. Batman Adventures: The Lost Years. (Illus.). 128p. (Orig.). 1999. pap. text 9.95 (*1-56389-483-1*, Pub. by DC Comics) Time Warner.

Bader, Hilary. Borg: Experience the Collective. abr. ed. (Star Trek Original Ser.). 1996. audio 12.00 (*0-671-57491-4*) S&S Audio.

***Bader, Hilary J.** Batman Beyond. (Illus.). 136p. (J). 2000. pap. text 9.95 (*1-56389-604-4*, Pub. by DC Comics) Time Warner.

Bader, Jenny L. He Meant/She Meant: The Definitive Male/Female Dictionary. 1997. mass mkt. 35.94 (*0-446-16535-2*) Warner Bks.

Bader, Jenny L. & Brazell, Bill. He Meant/She Meant: The Definitive Male/Female Dictionary. LC 98-106186. 224p. 1997. mass mkt. 5.99 (*0-446-60502-6*, Pub. by Warner Bks) Little.

— The Male-Female - Female-Male Dictionary. (Orig.). 1996. pap. write for info. (*0-446-67187-8*) Warner Bks.

Bader, John B. Taking the Initiative: Leadership Agendas in Congress & the "Contract with America" LC 96-12025. (American Governance & Public Policy Ser.). 288p. (C). 1996. pap. 19.95 (*0-87840-629-8*); lib. bdg. 49.95 (*0-87840-628-X*) Georgetown U Pr.

Bader, Jonathan. Meditation in Sankaras Vedanta. (C). 1990. 22.50 (*81-85179-51-4*, Pub. by Aditya Prakashan) S Asia.

Bader, Lois A. Bader Reading & Language Inventory. 3rd ed. LC 97-15646. 167p. 1997. pap. text 49.00 (*0-13-755000-6*) P-H.

— Read to Succeed: Tutor's Guide. LC 97-23364. 128p. (C). 1997. teacher ed., spiral bd. 24.00 (*0-13-690561-7*, Merrill Coll) P-H.

Bader, Lou. The Great Kachina. 64p. (Orig.). 1996. pap. 11.95 (*0-929385-60-8*, Strchld Pr) Light Tech Pubng.

— In the Shadow of the San Francisco Peaks. 152p. (Orig.). 1988. pap. 9.95 (*0-929385-52-7*) Light Tech Pubng.

Bader, M. J., et al, eds. Images in Weather Forecasting: A Practical Guide for Interpreting Satellite & Radar Imagery. (Illus.). 523p. 1997. pap. text 59.95 (*0-521-62915-2*) Cambridge U Pr.

Bader, Michael G., et al. Delaware Composites Design Encyclopedia Vol. 3: Processing & Fabrication Technology. LC 89-51098. 256p. 1990. lib. bdg. 116.95 (*0-87762-701-0*) Technomic.

Bader, Morton E. Practical Quality Management in the Chemical Process Industry. (Industrial Engineering Ser.: Vol. 7). (Illus.). 160p. 1983. text 75.00 (*0-8247-1903-4*) Dekker.

Bader, Myles. Grandma's Home Remedies. 1999. 14.95 (*0-688-16217-7*, Hearst) Hearst Commns.

***Bader, Myles.** 1,001 Secret Money Saving Formulas. LC 00-27510. 2000. write for info. (*1-58663-000-8*, Friedman-Fairfax) M Friedman Pub Grp Inc.

Bader, Myles. The Wizard of Food Presents 10,001 Food Facts, Chef's Secrets & Household Hints: More Usable Food Facts & Household Hints Than Any Single Book Ever Published. LC 98-222580. 629 p. 1998. 24.95 (*0-9646741-7-3*) Northstar NV.

Bader, Myles H. Cherry Creations: The Ultimate Cherry Cookbook. LC 94-77704. 224p. 1995. pap. 15.95 (*0-9646741-1-4*) Northstar NV.

***Bader, Myles H.** 5001 Mysteries of Liquids & Cooking Secrets: Plus 100 World-Class Recipes. (Illus.). 384p. 2000. pap. 16.95 (*1-56799-945-X*, Friedman-Fairfax) M Friedman Pub Grp Inc.

Bader, Myles H. Four Thousand One Food Facts & Chefs' Secrets. 292p. (Orig.). 1992. pap. 12.95 (*0-9632899-0-X*) Mylin Pub.

— Four Thousand One Food Facts & Chef's Secrets. rev. ed. 292p. 1993. pap. 14.95 (*0-9632899-1-8*) Mylin Pub.

— Grandmother's Kitchen Wisdom: Over 6,001 Solutions to Common Kitchen Problems. Glikman, Naomi, ed. LC 98-22442. 304p. 1999. 19.95 (*0-688-16216-9*, Wm Morrow) Morrow Avon.

— 6001 Food Facts & Chef's Secrets. (Illus.). 504p. 1995. pap. 18.95 (*0-9646741-0-6*) Northstar NV.

— 10,001 Food Facts: Chef's Secrets & Hints. LC 99-38517. 1999. pap. text 24.95 (*1-56799-865-8*, Friedman-Fairfax) M Friedman Pub Grp Inc.

— To Supplement or Not to Supplement. 1995. pap. 17.95 (*0-9632899-5-0*) Mylin Pub.

Bader, Oliver & Theret, Michel. Diccionario Enciclopedico de Metalurgia. (ENG, FRE & SPA.). 960p. 1975. 75.00 (*0-8288-5817-9*, S50132) Fr & Eur.

Bader, Paul, jt. auth. see Hart-Davis, Adam.

***Bader, Philip.** France. LC 00-23924. (Dropping in On Ser.). (Illus.). 2000. write for info. (*1-55916-280-5*) Rourke Bk Co.

— Iran. LC 00-38722. (Dropping In On Ser.). (Illus.). 2000. write for info. (*1-55916-285-6*) Rourke Bk Co.

— Spain. LC 00-29073. (Dropping in on Ser.). (Illus.). 2000. pap. write for info. (*1-55916-282-1*) Rourke Bk Co.

Bader, Richard F. Atoms in Molecules: A Quantum Theory. LC 93-46241. (International Series of Monographs on Chemistry: No. 22). (Illus.). 456p. (C). 1994. pap. text 50.00 (*0-19-855865-1*, Clarendon Pr) OUP.

Bader, Robert S. The Great Kansas Bond Scandal. LC 82-9056. (Illus.). xiv, 398p. 1982. pap. 12.95 (*0-7006-0248-8*) U Pr of KS.

— Hayseeds, Moralizers, & Methodists: The Twentieth Century Image of Kansas. LC 88-97. x, 214p. 1988. 19.95 (*0-7006-0360-3*); pap. 12.95 (*0-7006-0361-1*) U Pr of KS.

— Prohibition in Kansas: A History. LC 86-231. (Illus.). xiv, 322p. 1986. 15.95 (*0-7006-0298-4*) U Pr of KS.

— A Second Look: Reading the Bible Again for the First Time. LC 97-91401. (Illus.). 1998. pap. 14.95 (*0-533-12664-9*) Vantage.

Bader, Robert S., ed. see Marx, Groucho.

Bader, S. D., jt. ed. see Freeman, A. J.

***Bader-Saye, Scott.** Church & Israel after Christendom: The Politics of Election. LC 98-50481. (Radical Traditions Ser.). 208p. 1999. text 65.00 (*0-8133-6706-9*, Pub. by Westview) HarpC.

Bader, Shellie R. Accent Reduction International. 160p. (Orig.). 1995. pap. text 79.95 (*0-9646666-0-X*) Clear Speech.

Bader, Ted, et al. Desire & Duty: A Sequel to Jane Austen's Pride & Prejudice. LC 96-92575. (Illus.). 286p. 1997. 19.95 (*0-9654299-0-3*, 97-1) Revive.

Bader, Ted, ed. see Brinton, Sybil G.

***Bader, Teddy F.** Viral Hepatitis: Practical Evaluation & Treatment. 3rd rev. ed. (Illus.). 284p. 2000. 39.00 (*0-88937-232-2*) Hogrefe & Huber Pubs.

Bader, William B. & Bergner, Jeffrey T., eds. The Taiwan Relations Act: A Decade of Implementation. 210p. (C). 1989. 14.95 (*1-55813-028-4*) Hudson Instit IN.

Bader, William C. An American Village: The Light at the North End of the Tunnel. Redmer, Pamela M., ed. (Illus.). 232p. 1998. 40.00 (*0-9653431-3-8*) Design to Prnt.

Baderschneider, Earl R. & Stone, Morris, eds. Arbitration of Discrimination Grievances: A Case Book. 335p. 1974. pap. 10.00 (*0-318-43194-7*) Am Arbitration.

Badertscher, Amos. Badertscher. (Illus.). 64p. 1998. text 13.00 (*0-312-18047-0*, 842475, Stonewall Inn) St Martin.

***Badertscher, Amos.** Baltimore Portraits. LC 98-43770. (Illus.). 112p. 1999. 69.95 (*0-8223-2334-6*); pap. 24.95 (*0-8223-2368-0*) Duke.

Badertscher, Kerrie & Hughes, Harrison. Growing Small Fruit: For the High Plains & Rocky Mountain West. Weitzel, Debby, ed. (Illus.). 64p. (Orig.). 1996. pap. 12.00 (*1-889143-02-2*, 561A) CO St U Coop.

Badescu, L. & Popescu, D., eds. Algebraic Geometry, Bucharest 1982: Proceedings of the International Conference, Held in Bucharest, Romania, August 2-7, 1982. (Lecture Notes in Mathematics Ser.: Vol. 1056). vii, 380p. 1984. 46.95 (*0-387-12930-8*) Spr-Verlag.

***Badessi, Laurent Elie, photos by.** Skin. (Illus.). 132p. 2000. 75.00 (*3-908163-14-5*, Pub. by Edit Stemmle) Abbeville Pr.

Badgaiyan, S. D. Industrialization & Peasant Social Formation. 1992. 28.00 (*81-7033-150-1*, Pub. by Rawat Pubns) S Asia.

Badge, G. M., ed. see Churchill, Gardner A. & Churchill, Nathaniel W.

Badger. Boy in the Stone. 150p. (Orig.). 1995. pap. 4.99 (*0-9647120-0-8*) Badger Publng.

Badger, Anthony J. The New Deal: The Depression Years, 1933-1940. 360p. 1989. pap. 10.95 (*0-374-52174-3*) FS&G.

— North Carolina & the New Deal. (Illus.). xiii, 102p. 1981. pap. 5.00 (*0-86526-186-5*) NC Archives.

Badger, Beryl & Chaston, Ian. Activities for Problem Solving. 248p. 1992. ring bd. 253.95 (*1-85904-042-X*, Pub. by Gower) Ashgate Pub Co.

Badger, Curtis, jt. auth. see Sprankle, Jim.

Badger, Curtis J. Bellevue Farm: Exploring Virginia's Coastal Countryside. LC 96-23308. 128p. 1997. 19.95 (*0-8117-0226-X*) Stackpole.

— Bird Carving Basics: Bills & Beaks. LC 90-9491. (Illus.). 96p. (Orig.). 1991. pap. 12.95 (*0-8117-2340-2*) Stackpole.

— Bird Carving Basics: Eyes. LC 90-9491. (Illus.). 96p. (Orig.). 1990. pap. 12.95 (*0-8117-2334-8*) Stackpole.

— Bird Carving Basics: Feet. LC 90-9491. (Illus.). 96p. (Orig.). 1990. pap. 12.95 (*0-8117-2338-0*) Stackpole.

— Bird Carving Basics: Habitat. LC 90-9491. (Illus.). 96p. 1992. pap. 12.95 (*0-8117-3053-0*) Stackpole.

— Bird Carving Basics: Heads. LC 90-9491. (Illus.). 96p. (Orig.). 1991. pap. 12.95 (*0-8117-2339-9*) Stackpole.

— Bird Carving Basics: How to Compete. (Illus.). 96p. 1994. pap. 17.95 (*0-8117-3056-5*) Stackpole.

— Bird Carving Basics: Painting. LC 90-9491. (Illus.). 96p. 1991. pap. 19.95 (*0-8117-3051-4*) Stackpole.

— Bird Carving Basics: Songbird Painting. (Illus.). 96p. (Orig.). 1993. pap. 17.95 (*0-8117-3055-7*) Stackpole.

— Bird Carving Basics: Special Painting Techniques. LC 90-9491. (Illus.). 96p. 1992. pap. 17.95 (*0-8117-3052-2*) Stackpole.

— Bird Carving Basics: Texturing. LC 90-9491. (Illus.). 112p. 1991. pap. 12.95 (*0-8117-3050-6*) Stackpole.

— Bird Carving Basics: Tools. (Illus.). 96p. (Orig.). 1993. pap. 12.95 (*0-8117-3054-9*) Stackpole.

— Carving & Painting a Black-Capped Chickadee with Ernest Muehlmatt. LC 96-41798. 96p. 1997. pap. 19.95 (*0-8117-2423-9*) Stackpole.

— Carving & Painting a Red-Tailed Hawk with Floyd Scholz. LC 97-2486. (Illus.). 96p. 1997. pap. 19.95 (*0-8117-2704-1*) Stackpole.

— Fish Carving Basics: How to Carve. LC 93-30588. (Illus.). 96p. 1994. pap. 12.95 (*0-8117-2524-3*) Stackpole.

— Fish Carving Basics: How to Paint. (Illus.). 96p. 1994. pap. 17.95 (*0-8117-2440-9*) Stackpole.

— How to Paint Tropicals. 96p. 1996. write for info. (*0-8117-2760-2*) Stackpole.

— How to Paint Trout. (Fish Carving Basics Ser.). (Illus.). 96p. 1996. pap. 17.95 (*0-8117-2458-1*) Stackpole.

— A Naturalist's Guide to the Virginia Coast. LC 96-8192. (Illus.). 96p. 1996. pap., spiral bd. 16.95 (*0-8117-2562-6*) Stackpole.

— Painting Waterfowl with J. D. Sprankle. (Illus.). 256p. 1998. pap. 34.95 (*0-8117-2893-5*) Stackpole.

— Salt Tide: Cycles & Currents of Life along the Coast. LC 92-28804. (Illus.). 160p. 1993. 16.95 (*0-8117-1632-5*) Stackpole.

***Badger, Curtis J.** Salt Tide: Cycles & Currents of Life along the Mid-Atlantic Coast. LC 98-53509. (Illus.). 134p. 1999. pap. 12.95 (*0-88150-463-7*, Pub. by Countryman) Norton.

Badger, Curtis J. & Guge, Bob. Carving & Painting a Northern Cardinal with Bob Guge. LC 98-2729. (Illus.). 96p. 1998. pap. 19.95 (*0-8117-2753-X*) Stackpole.

Badger, Curtis J. & Kellam, Rick. The Barrier Islands: A Photographic History of Life on Hog, Cobb, Smith, Cedar, Parramore, Metompkin, & Assateaque. LC 88-24826. (Illus.). 160p. 1989. 24.95 (*0-8117-0213-8*) Stackpole.

Badger, Curtis J. & Vizier, Jimmie. Carving & Painting a Pintail Drake. LC 98-8288. iii, 92 p. 1999. 19.95 (*0-8117-2701-7*) Stackpole.

Badger, Curtis J., jt. auth. see Chesser, Grayson.

Badger, Curtis J., jt. auth. see Sprankle, J. D.

Badger, Curtis J., jt. auth. see Tancredi, John T.

Badger, D. & Whitehead, G. Elements of Cargo Insurance. (C). 1982. 125.00 (*0-7855-4179-9*, Pub. by Witherby & Co) St Mut.

Badger, D., jt. auth. see Vaughan, P.

Badger, Daniel D. Badger's Illustrated Catalogue of Cast-Iron Architecture. (Illus.). 144p. 1982. pap. 12.95 (*0-486-24223-4*) Dover.

Badger, David. Frogs Postcards Book. (Illus.). 22p. (Orig.). 1996. pap. 8.95 (*0-89658-307-4*) Voyageur Pr.

— Snakes. LC 98-52379. (Illus.). 144p. 1999. 35.00 (*0-89658-408-9*) Voyageur Pr.

Badger, David, ed. see Netherton, John.

Badger, David, ed. see Netherton, John & Duhl, David.

***Badger, David P.** Frogs: WorldLife Library. LC 99-44854. (WorldLife Library). (Illus.). 72p. (YA). 2000. pap. 16.95 (*0-89658-456-9*) Voyageur Pr.

Badger-Dole, Carol, jt. auth. see Denslow, David A.

Badger-Dole, Carol, jt. auth. see Rush, Mark.

Badger, G. P. Nestorian & Their Rituals, Vol. 1. 464p. 1987. 350.00 (*1-85077-166-9*, Pub. by Darf Pubs Ltd) St Mut.

— Nestorian & Their Rituals, Vol. 2. 1987. 350.00 (*1-85077-167-7*, Pub. by Darf Pubs Ltd) St Mut.

Badger, G. R. & Winters, Sidney D. Celebrations: A Resource Guide for Utah's Most Important Occasions. 208p. (Orig.). 1997. pap. 7.95 (*0-9656380-0-6*) Keystone Pub UT.

Badger, G. R., jt. contrib. by see Winters, Sidney D.

Badger, Geoffrey. Explorers of the Pacific. 2nd ed. 1997. pap. text 24.95 (*0-86417-794-1*, Pub. by Kangaroo Pr) Seven Hills Bk.

Badger, Geoffrey M. The Structures & Reactions of the Aromatic Compounds. LC 54-3317. 470p. reprint ed. pap. 134.00 (*0-608-10111-7*, 2051390) Bks Demand.

Badger, George P. An English-Arabic Lexicon. (ARA & ENG.). 1250p. 1979. 115.00 (*0-86685-064-3*, LDL0643, Pub. by Librairie du Liban) Intl Bk Ctr.

Badger, Joseph E. Trailer Underride: Conspicuity, Human Factors, & Rear Bumpers. (Illus.). 22p. (C). 1993. pap. text 12.95 (*1-884566-14-6*) Inst Police Tech.

Badger, Lee W., et al. Child Abuse in the Deep South: Geographical Modifiers of Abuse Characteristics. LC 86-30891. (Institute for Social Science Research Monograph Ser.). (Illus.). 178p. (Orig.). 1988. pap. 55.20 (*0-608-05129-2*, 206568800005) Bks Demand.

Badger, Peter. Outdoor Projects for the Country Home. LC 92-45742. 1993. pap. 14.95 (*0-8306-4399-0*) McGraw-Hill Prof.

Badger, Phillip C. Bioenergy in the Southeast: Status, Opportunities & Challenges: Recommendations of the Southeast Bioenergy Roundtable. (Illus.). 83p. (C). 1998. pap. text 25.00 (*0-7881-4773-0*) DIANE Pub.

Badger, R. Reid & Clayton, Lawrence A., eds. Alabama & the Borderlands: From Prehistory to Statehood. fac. ed. LC 83-17957. (Illus.). 266p. 1985. pap. 82.50 (*0-7837-8362-0*, 205917100009) Bks Demand.

Badger, Reid. The Great American Fair: The World's Columbian Exposition & American Culture. LC 79-11774. (Illus.). 1979. text 51.95 (*0-88229-448-2*) Burnham Inc.

Badger, Robert. Geology along Skyline Drive: Virginia's Shenandoah National Park. LC 98-55548. (Illus.). 76p. 1999. pap. 10.95 (*1-56044-691-9*) Falcon Pub Inc.

***Badger, Rosemary & Scott, Elaine.** Little Badger Knitwear: Knitted Projects for Babies & Toddlers. LC 99-86090. (Illus.). 2000. pap. 19.95 (*1-56158-414-2*) Taunton.

Badger, Terry E. A Full Deck of Double-Dummy Problems: A Book of Bridge Puzzles. (Illus.). 136p. (Orig.). 1996. pap. 11.95 (*0-932529-58-5*) Oldcastle.

Badger, Terry M. Puzzles & Games in Logic & Reasoning. LC 94-36774. 1995. pap. 4.95 (*0-486-28583-9*) Dover.

Badger, Tim. Killer Love Poems. 1988. pap. 3.00 (*0-938979-10-8*) EG Bksellers.

Badger, Tony, jt. ed. see Ward, Brian.

Badger, William. History of Gilmanton, Embracing Its Civil, Ecclesiastical, Literary & Biographical History to 1875: Including the History of Belmont. Zea, Philip M., ed. (Illus.). 116p. 1998. reprint ed. pap. 19.00 (*0-8328-9717-5*); reprint ed. lib. bdg. 27.00 (*0-8328-9716-7*) Higginson Bk Co.

Badgett. Badgett el Genio de Wordperfect 6 para Windows: Todos Sus Deseos Serancumplidos. (SPA.). 400p. (C). 1995. pap. text 18.66 (*0-201-63116-4*) Addison-Wesley.

***Badgett, Lee.** Economic Lives Lesbians & Gay Men. 1998. 25.95 (*0-226-03400-3*) U Ch Pr.

Badgett, M. V. Lee. Economic Lives Lesbians & Gay Men. 1996. pap. text 14.95 (*0-226-03401-1*) U Ch Pr.

Badgett, Tom. Teach Yourself . . . PowerPoint for Windows 95. 89p. 1995. pap. 24.95 (*1-55828-442-7*, MIS Pr) IDG Bks.

Badgett, Tom & Sandler, Corey. Creating Multimedia Presentations on Your PC. 469p. 1993. pap. 29.95 incl. cd-rom (*0-471-58928-4*) Wiley.

— Teach Yourself PowerPoint 4.0 for Windows. LC 94-20874. 462p. 1994. pap. 21.95 (*1-55828-367-6*, MIS Pr) IDG Bks.

— Welcome to . . . Internet: From Mystery to Mastery. 2nd ed. 89p. 1995. pap. 19.95 (*1-55828-424-9*, MIS Pr) IDG Bks.

Badgett, Tom, jt. auth. see IDG Books Staff.

***Badgett, Wally.** Cowboyin with Earl 9. LC 99-61703. (Book of Earl Ser.). (Illus.). 96p. 2000. pap. 10.00 (*1-892661-10-1*, CWE9) Holmlund Dist.

Badgett, Wally. The Fifth Book of Earl. (Book of Earl Ser.). (Illus.). ii, 86p. (Orig.). 1996. pap. 9.95 (*1-892661-04-7*, 5BOE) Holmlund Dist.

— The Fourth Book of Earl. (Book of Earl Ser.). (Illus.). iii, 85p. (Orig.). 1996. pap. 9.95 (*1-892661-03-9*) Holmlund Dist.

— Ranchin' with Earl. LC 99-60543. (Book of Earl Ser.). (Illus.). 96p. (Orig.). 1999. pap. 9.95 (*1-892661-07-1*) Holmlund Dist.

— The Second Book of Earl. (Book of Earl Ser.). (Illus.). iii, 85p. (Orig.). 1994. pap. 14.95 (*1-892661-01-2*, 2BOE) Holmlund Dist.

— The Seventh Book of Earl. (Book of Earl Ser.). (Illus.). iii, 85p. (Orig.). 1998. pap. 9.95 (*1-892661-06-3*) Holmlund Dist.

— The Sixth Book of Earl. (Book of Earl Ser.). (Illus.). iii, 85p. (Orig.). 1997. pap. 9.95 (*1-892661-05-5*, 6BOE) Holmlund Dist.

— The Third Book of Earl. (Book of Earl Ser.). (Illus.). iii, 85p. (Orig.). 1997. pap. 9.95 (*1-892661-02-0*, 3BOE) Holmlund Dist.

***Badgley, Franklin I.** No Bed of Roses. 164p. 1999. pap. 10.00 (*1-57579-163-3*, Pub. by Pine Hill Pr) Penmarch Pub.

Badgley, Franklin I., et al. Profiles of Wind, Temperature, & Humidity over the Arabian Sea. LC 70-129539. (International Indian Ocean Expedition. Meteorological Monographs: No. 6). 68p. reprint ed. pap. 30.00 (*0-7837-3987-7*, 204381700011) Bks Demand.

***Badgley, Kerry.** Ringing in the Common Love of Good: The United Farmers of Ontario, 1914-1916. 360p. 2000. text 55.00 (*0-7735-1895-9*) McG-Queens Univ Pr.

Badgley, Laurence E. Choose to Live: An AIDS Healing Companion. LC 87-81624. 70p. 1993. pap. 13.95 (*0-941523-01-2*) Human Energy Pr.

— Energy Medicine. (Illus.). 173p. 1985. 40.00 (*0-941523-02-0*) Human Energy Pr.

— Healing AIDS Naturally: Natural Therapies for the Immune System. LC 86-83290. (Illus.). 410p. 1990. pap. 14.95 (*0-941523-00-4*) Human Energy Pr.

Badgley, Peter C., ed. Scientific Experiments for Manned Orbital Flight, 3rd Godard Memorial Symposium, Mar. 18-19, 1965, Washington, D.C. 3rd Goddard Memorial Symposium, Washington, D. C., Mar. 18-19, 1965. (Science & Technology Ser.: Vol. 4). 372p. 1965. 30.00 (*0-87703-032-4*, Am Astronaut Soc) Univelt Inc.

Badgley, Richard. Real Estate Buying-Selling Guide for Florida. (Legal Ser.). 176p. 1992. pap. 9.95 (*0-88908-778-4*) Self-Counsel Pr.

Badgwell, J. Michael & Hall, Steven C. Clinical Pediatric Anesthesia. LC 97-18627. (Illus.). 650p. 1997. text 85.00 (*0-397-51476-X*) Lppncott W & W.

Badham, Michael, et al. Tiller & the Pen: A Collection of Sailors' Stories. Ellsworth, John, ed. LC 94-90405. (Illus.). 192p. (Orig.). 1994. pap. 12.00 (*0-9642853-0-4*) Eighth Moon.

Badham, Mike & Robinson, Robby, eds. Sailors' Secrets: Advice from the Masters. LC 96-47681. (Illus.). 288p. 1996. 29.95 (*0-07-039088-6*) Intl Marine.

— Sailor's Secrets: Advice from the Masters. LC 99-29314. 320p. (Orig.). 1999. pap. 19.95 (*0-07-134869-7*) McGraw.

***Badham, Paul.** The Contemporary Challenge of Modernist Theology. 196p. 1999. (*0-7083-1501-1*, Pub. by Univ Wales Pr); pap. (*0-7083-1503-8*, Pub. by Univ Wales Pr) Paul & Co Pubs.

Badham, Paul. Near-Death Experience, Beliefs about Life after Death, & the Tibetan Book of the Dead. (ENG & JPN.). 40p. 1990. pap. 3.50 (*0-914910-95-7*) Buddhist Bks.

Badham, Paul, ed. A John Hick Reader. LC 89-38417. 224p. (Orig.). 1990. pap. 15.00 (*0-334-00599-X*) TPI PA.

— Religion, State & Society in Modern Britain. LC 89-36710. (Texts & Studies in Religion). 416p. 1989. lib. bdg. 109.95 (*0-88946-832-X*) E Mellen.

Badham, Roger A., ed. Introduction to Christian Theology: Contemporary North American Perspectives. LC 97-22794. 1998. pap. 25.00 (*0-664-25674-0*) Westminster John Knox.

***Badham, Sally & Norris, Malcolm.** Early Incised Slabs & Brasses from the London Marblers. (Reports of the Research Comm: No. 60). (Illus.). 182p. 1999. 49.50 (*0-85431-272-2*, Pub. by Aris & Phillips) David Brown.

Badham, W. A. Ablaut in the Modern Dialects of the South of England. (English Dialect Society Publications: No. 63).Tr. of Geschichte des Ablautes der Starken Zeitworter Innerhalb des Sudenglischen. Von K. D. Buelbring. 1972. reprint ed. pap. 25.00 (*0-8115-0483-2*) Periodicals Srv.

Badham, William T. Memoirs & Art of William Terry Badham: A World War I Ace, Flying with the Ninety-First Squadron U. S. Army. (FRE & SPA., Illus.). 91p. (Orig.). 1987. 39.95 (*0-9618093-0-2*); pap. 25.00 (*0-9618093-1-0*) Menton Repro.

Badhwar, Nandini, jt. auth. see Charles, Rodney.

Badhwar, Neera K., ed. Friendship: A Philosophical Reader. LC 92-56786. 352p. 1993. 49.95 (*0-8014-2854-8*); pap. text 17.95 (*0-8014-8097-3*) Cornell U Pr.

Badia, Leonard F. Basic Catholic Beliefs for Today: The Creed Explained. LC 84-14632. 170p. (Orig.). 1984. pap. 8.95 (*0-8189-0469-0*) Alba.

***Badian, Nathlie A., ed.** Prediction & Prevention of Reading Failure. (C). 2000. Price not set. (*0-912752-57-2*) York Pr.

Badian, E. From Plataea to Potidaea: Studies in the History & Historiography of the Pentecontaetia. LC 92-17327. 216p. 1993. text 39.95 (*0-8018-4431-2*) Johns Hopkins.

— Publicans & Sinners: Private Enterprise in the Service of the Roman Republic, with a Critical Bibliography. 176p. (Orig.). 1983. pap. text 12.95 (*0-8014-9241-6*) Cornell U Pr.

Badian, E., et al. Transitions to Empire: Essays in Greco-Roman History, 360-146 B. C., in Honor of E. Badian. Wallace, Robert W. & Harris, Edward M., eds. LC 96-18192. (Oklahoma Series in Classical Culture: Vol. 21). 512p. 1996. text 49.95 (*0-8061-2863-1*) U of Okla Pr.

Badian, E., ed. see Polybius.

Badian, Seydou. Caught in the Storm. Noiset, Marie-Therese, tr. from FRE. LC 95-51197. 124p. 1998. lib. bdg. 25.00 (*0-89410-793-3*, Three Contnts) L Rienner.

— Caught in the Storm: A Novel. Noiset, Marie-Therese, tr. from FRE. LC 95-51197. 124p. 1998. pap. 12.50 (*0-89410-794-1*, Three Contnts) L Rienner.

Badiani, Aldo, tr. see Mazzarello, Paolo.

***Badie, Bertrand.** Imported State: The Westernization of Political Order. (Mestizo Spaces/Espaces Metisses Ser.). 2000. 49.50 (*0-8047-3766-5*); pap. 18.95 (*0-8047-3767-3*) Stanford U Pr.

Badie, Bertrand & Birnbaum, Pierre. The Sociology of the State. Goldhammer, Arthur, tr. from FRE. LC 82-20249. 182p. (C). 1983. pap. text 16.50 (*0-226-03549-2*) U Ch Pr.

Badiee, Julie. An Earthly Paradise: Baha'i Houses of Worship Around the World. (Illus.). 144p. 1993. 31.95 (*0-85398-316-X*) G Ronald Pub.

Badii, Remo & Politi, Antonio. Complexity: Hierarchical Structures & Scaling in Physics. LC 96-18903. (Cambridge Nonlinear Science Ser.: No. 6). (Illus.). 332p. (C). 1997. text 74.95 (*0-521-41890-9*) Cambridge U Pr.

***Badii, Remo & Politi, Antonio.** Complexity: Hierarchical Structures & Scaling in Physics. (Nonlinear Science Ser.: Vol. 6). (Illus.). 318p. (C). 1999. pap. write for info. (*0-521-66385-7*) Cambridge U Pr.

Badikian, Beatriz. Mapmaker: Poems. 84p. (Orig.). 1994. pap. 8.95 (*0-9641825-0-5*) Gladsome Bks.

Badillo Gerena, Pedro. Ciceron y el Imperio. LC 76-10131. (UPREX, Humanidades Ser.: Serie Humanidades No. 50). 199p. (Orig.). 1976. pap. 1.50 (*0-8477-0050-X*) U of PR Pr.

Badillo Gerena, Pedro A. Antologia de la Filosofia Griega. 2nd rev. ed. (SPA.). 254p. 1995. pap. 9.50 (*0-8477-0246-4*) U of PR Pr.

Badillo, Jose L., ed. see Badillo, Tony.

Badillo, Pedro A., compiled by. Antologia de Filosofia Griega. 6th rev. ed. (Illus.). 253p. (C). 1995. pap. 9.50 (*0-8477-2800-5*) U of PR Pr.

Badillo, Robert. The Emancipative Theory of Jurgen Habermas & Metaphysics. (Cultural Heritage & Contemporary Change Series I: Vol. I, No. 13). 222p. 1991. 45.00 (*1-56518-043-7*, B3258.H234B33); pap. 17.50 (*1-56518-042-9*) Coun Res Values.

Badillo, Tony. Mastering Craps. Badillo, Jose L. & Chew, Earl, eds. (Illus.). 192p. 1996. pap. 21.95 (*0-9700571-0-5*) L L David.

Badin, Alexander. Dacia Din Vestul Europei in Istoriografia Europeana.Tr. of Dacia from Western Europe in European Historiography. (Illus.). 50p. 1998. pap. 6.00 (*0-9665574-0-9*) A Badin.

Badin, Donatella A. Thomas Kinsella. 1996. 32.00 (*0-8057-7047-X*, Twyne) Mac Lib Ref.

Badinter, Elisabeth. XY: On Masculine Identity. LC 94-41016. (European Perspectives Ser.).Tr. of X Y, de l'Identite Masculine. 224p. 1995. 42.00 (*0-231-08434-X*) Col U Pr.

— XY: On Masculine Identity.Tr. of X Y, de l'Identite Masculine. 1997. pap. 16.50 (*0-614-27591-1*); pap. text 17.50 (*0-231-08435-8*) Col U Pr.

Badinter, Elizabeth. Mother Love. 1981. 13.95 (*0-02-504610-1*) Macmillan.

Badiou, Alain. Deleuze: The Clamor of Being. Churchill, Louise, tr. from FRE. LC 99-41281. (Theory Out of Bounds Ser.). 160p. 1999. pap. 18.95 (*0-8166-3140-9*, Pub. by U of Minn Pr) Chicago Distribution Ctr.

— Deleuze: The Clamor of Being. Churchill, Louise, tr. from FRE. LC 99-41281. (Theory Out of Bounds Ser.: Vol. 16). 160p. 1999. lib. bdg. 47.95 (*0-8166-3139-5*, Pub. by U of Minn Pr) Chicago Distribution Ctr.

***Badiou, Alain.** Ethics: An Essay on the Understanding of Evil. (Wo Es War Ser.). 224p. 2001. 27.00 (*1-85984-297-6*, Pub. by Verso) Norton.

Badiou, Alian. Manifesto for Philosophy. Madarasz, Norman, tr. from FRE. LC 98-43903. (SUNY Series, Intersections). 128p. (C). 1999. text 44.50 (*0-7914-4219-5*, Suny Pr) State U NY Pr.

— Manifesto for Philosophy: Followed by Two Essays: "The (Re)Turn of Philosophy Itself" & "Definition of Philosophy" Madarasz, Norman, ed. & intro. by. LC 98-43903. (Suny Series, Intersections: Philosophy & Critical Theory). 181p. (C). 1999. pap. text 14.95 (*0-7914-4220-9*, Suny Pr) State U NY Pr.

Badiru, Adedeji B. Expert Systems Applications in Engineering. 456p. 1991. text 50.20 (*0-13-278219-7*) P-H.

— Industry's Guide to ISO 9000. LC 94-48504. (Engineering & Technology Management Ser.). 232p. 1995. 99.00 (*0-471-04598-5*) Wiley.

— Managing Industrial Development Projects: A Project Management Approach. LC 93-68. 386p. 1993. text 69.95 (*0-442-01087-7*, VNR) Wiley.

Badiru, Adedeji B. Managing Industrial Development Projects: A Project Management Approach. (VNR Project Management Ser.). 386p. 1993. 99.00 (*0-471-28475-0*, VNR) Wiley.

Badiru, Adedeji B. Project Management in Manufacturing & High Technology Operations. 2nd ed. LC 95-46164. (Wiley Series in Engineering & Technology). 600p. 1996. 110.00 (*0-471-12721-3*) Wiley.

— Quantitative Models for Project Planning. LC 92-34377. 376p. 1993. 69.50 (*0-89930-730-2*, BQT, Quorum Bks) Greenwood.

Badiru, Adedeji B. & Nnaji, Bartholomew O. Modern Manufacturing Planning & Control. (C). 2000. 48.99 (*0-13-095761-5*, Macmillan Coll) P-H.

Badiru, Adedeji B. & Pulat, P. Simin. Comprehensive Project Management: Integrating Optimization Models, Management Practices & Computers. LC 94-8035. 576p. 1994. text 50.20 (*0-13-030925-7*) P-H.

Badiru, Adedeji Bodunde. Fuzzy Engineering Expert Systems with Neural Network Applications. 400p. 89.95 (*0-471-29331-8*) Wiley.

Badiyan Productions Staff, jt. auth. see Paradigm Publishing Incorporated.

***Badizadegan, Mort.** Texas Hold'em Flop Types. (Illus.). 149p. 2000. spiral bd. 24.95i (*0-615-11732-5*) Goldstar Bks.

Badke, William. Avenger, Vol. 3. LC 96-48707. (Ben Sylvester Mystery Ser.: Vol. 3). 250p. 1997. pap. 9.99 (*1-57673-031-X*, Multnomah Bks) Multnomah Pubs.

***Badke, William.** Saluso's Game. large type ed. LC 00-24262. (Christian Mystery Ser.). 317p. 2000. 23.95 (*0-7862-2524-6*) Thorndike Pr.

***Badke, William B.** Avenger. LC 99-58238. (Christian Mystery Ser.). 2000. 23.95 (*0-7862-2382-0*) Thorndike Pr.

Badke, William B. Search. LC 99-21868. 1999. 21.95 (*0-7862-1967-X*, G K Hall & Co) Mac Lib Ref.

Badla. Fundamentals of Behavioral Research. 1998. 36.25 (*0-07-229965-7*) McGraw.

Badler. Making Them Move. 1998. 88.95 incl. VHS (*1-55860-951-2*) Morgan Kaufmann.

Badler, Norman, et al, eds. Making Them Move: Mechanics, Control & Animation of Articulated Figures. (Computer Graphics & Geometric Modeling Ser.). (Illus.). 348p. 1998. pap. text 57.95 (*1-55860-106-6*) Morgan Kaufmann.

— Making Them Move: Mechanics, Control & Animation of Articulated Figures. (Computer Graphics & Geometric Modeling Ser.). (Illus.). 1998. VHS 36.95 (*1-55860-154-6*) Morgan Kaufmann.

Badler, Norman, et al. Virtual Humans. 300p. 1999. pap. 44.95 incl. cd-rom (*1-55860-553-3*) Morgan Kaufmann.

Badler, Norman I., et al, eds. Making Them Move: Mechanics, Control & Animation of Articulated Figures. (Computer Graphics & Geometric Modeling Ser.). (Illus.). 348p. 1990. text 85.95 incl. VHS (*1-55860-155-4*) Morgan Kaufmann.

Badler, Norman I., et al. Virtual Humans & Simulated Agents. LC 93-12061. (Illus.). 288p. (C). 1993. text 70.00 (*0-19-507359-2*) OUP.

Badley, Linda. Film, Horror & the Body Fantastic, 48. LC 95-16006. (Contributions to the Study of Popular Culture Ser.: No. 48). 208p. 1995. 59.95 (*0-313-27523-8*, Greenwood Pr) Greenwood.

— Writing Horror & the Body: The Fiction of Stephen King, Clive Barker, & Anne Rice, 51. LC 95-38665. (Contributions to the Study of Popular Culture Ser.: No. 51). 200p. 1996. 59.95 (*0-313-29716-9*, Greenwood Pr) Greenwood.

***Badman, David G., et al.** Iron Chelators: New Development Strategies. LC 00-24097. (Illus.). 2000. write for info. (*1-879894-20-3*) Saratoga Pub.

Badman, J. Legal Frameworks for the Built Environment. 200p. (C). (gr. 13). 1996. pap. 29.99 (*0-419-21270-1*) Routledge.

***Badman, Keith.** Beatles: Separate Ways after the Break-Up. (Illus.). 631p. 1999. 34.95 (*0-7119-7520-5*) Music Sales.

***Badman, Rick.** The Belt: The Kuiper Belt Incident. LC 99-91766. 140p. 2000. 25.00 (*0-7388-1244-7*); pap. 18.00 (*0-7388-1245-5*) Xlibris Corp.

Badmin. Leisure Operations Management: People, Vol. 2. 1988. pap. text. write for info. (*0-582-02326-2*, Pub. by Addison-Wesley) Longman.

***Badmington, Neil.** Posthumanism. LC 00-33320. 2000. pap. write for info. (*0-312-23794-4*) St Martin.

Badness, Ray F. Drum Programming: A Complete Guide That Teaches You How to Think & Program Like a Drummer. Graham, Roger, ed. 62p. (Orig.). 1991. pap. text 9.95 (*0-931759-54-4*) Centerstream Pub.

***Badnuelos, Rodrigo & Moore, Charles N.** Probabilistic Behavior of Harmonic Functions LC 99-32643. (Progress in Mathematics Ser.). 1999. write for info. (*0-8176-6062-3*) Birkhauser.

Bado, Jim, jt. auth. see Ivancic, Catherine.

Badoe, Adwoa. Crabs for Dinner. (Illus.). (J). 1996. pap. write for info. (*0-920813-27-5*) Sister Vis Pr.

***Badoe, Adwoa A.** The Queen's New Shoes. (Illus.). 24p. (J). (gr. 3-7). 1998. pap. 6.95 (*0-88961-232-3*, Pub. by Womens Pr) LPC InBook.

Badoglio, Pietro. Italy in the Second World War: Memories & Documents. Currey, Muriel, tr. LC 75-28658. 234p. 1976. reprint ed. lib. bdg. 59.50 (*0-8371-8485-1*, BAIT, Greenwood Pr) Greenwood.

Badone, Donalda. Dundurn Castle. (Illus.). 48p. (Orig.). 1990. pap. 4.95 (*1-55046-001-3*, Pub. by Boston Mills) Genl Dist Srvs.

Bador, Bernard. Sea Urchin Harakiri. Eshleman, Clayton, tr. (Illus.). 120p. 1986. 16.95 (*0-915572-77-X*); pap. 6.95 (*0-915572-76-1*) Panjandrum.

Bador, Bernard, ed. & tr. see Artaud, Antonin.

Badoux, R., jt. ed. see Sander, P.

Badovinac, Zdenka. Body & the East: From the 1960's to the Present. LC 99-13156. (Illus.). 350p. 1999. pap. text 25.00 (*0-262-52264-0*) MIT Pr.

***Badowich, D. M.** Mine. (Illus.). 16p. (J). (ps-3). 1999. pap. 5.95 (*1-894303-19-9*) RRP.

Badr, Ahmed M. Education of the Palestinians: An Annotated Bibliography. (Bibliography Ser.: No. 3). 29p. (Orig.). 1977. pap. text 2.00 (*0-937694-16-9*) Assn Arab-Amer U Grads.

Badr, Gamal, jt. auth. see Keesee, Allen P.

Badr, Gamal M. State Immunity. 1984. lib. bdg. 110.00 (*90-247-2880-0*) Kluwer Academic.

***Badr, Ibrahim H.** Giono et la Guerre: Ideologie et Imaginaire. (Currents in Comparative Romance Languages & Literatures Ser.: Vol. 77). (FRE.). 256p. (C). 2000. text 51.95 (*0-8204-4073-6*) P Lang Pubng.

Badr, Ibrahim H. Jean Giono: L'Esthetique de la Violence, Vol. 60. LC 97-13069. (Currents in Comparative Romance Languages & Literatures Ser.). XIX, 214p. (C). 1998. text 46.95 (*0-8204-3809-X*) P Lang Pubng.

Badr, Liyana. A Balcony over the Fakihani. Clark, P. & Tingley, Christopher, trs. from ARA. LC 92-23387. (Emerging Voices: New International Fiction Ser.). 128p. 1993. 19.95 (*1-56656-104-3*); pap. 9.95 (*1-56656-107-8*) Interlink Pub.

Badra, Robert. Meditations for Spiritual Misfits. (Illus.). 93p. (Orig.). 1982. pap. 7.95 (*0-9610274-0-1*) JCL Hse.

Badran, Adnan. At the Crossroads: Education in the Middle East. 335p. 1989. 29.95 (*0-943852-46-3*) Prof World Peace.

Badran, Adnan & Khader, Bichara. The Economic Development of Jordan. 320p. 1986. 59.95 (*0-7099-3110-7*, Pub. by C Helm) Routldge.

Badran, Margot. Feminists, Islam & Nation: Gender & the Making of Modern Egypt. LC 94-19055. 360p. 1995. text 55.00 (*0-691-03706-X*, Pub. by Princeton U Pr); pap. text 18.95 (*0-691-02605-X*, Pub. by Princeton U Pr) Cal Prin Full Svc.

Badran, Margot & Cooke, Miriam, eds. Opening the Gates: A Century of Arab Feminist Writing. LC 89-46345. 448p. 1990. 41.95 (*0-253-31121-7*); pap. 19.95 (*0-253-20577-8*, MB 577) Ind U Pr.

Badran, Margot, ed. see Shaarawi, Huda.

Badrawi, Malak. Isma'il Sidqi, 1875-1950. LC 97-124107. (Illus.). 288p. 1996. 60.00 (*0-7007-0408-6*, Pub. by Curzon Pr Ltd) Paul & Co Pubs.

Badre, Paul. Classic Convertibles. 1989. 9.98 (*0-671-09604-4*) S&S Trade.

Badrena, Ana Rita & Wood, Maria R. Dictation Manual, 2 vols., Set. 2nd ed. 171p. 1977. pap. 6.00 (*0-8477-2630-4*) U of PR Pr.

Badri, et al. The Ramadan War: The Egyptian View. 1979. pap. 6.95 (*0-88294-600-5*) NOVA Pubns.

Badri, M. B. Islam & Alcoholism. LC 76-42173. 1976. pap. 3.00 (*0-89259-005-X*) Am Trust Pubns.

— Islam & Alcoholism. 130p. 1996. pap. 5.95 (*0-614-21512-9*, 540) Kazi Pubns.

Badri, Malik. Al Tafakhur min al Mushahadah ila al Shuhud: Dirasah Nafsiyah Islamiyah - (Contemplation, from Witnessing to Testifying: An Islamic Psychological Perspective) 3rd rev. ed. LC 91-38924. (Silsilat Abhath 'Ilmiyah Ser.: No. 3). (ARA.). 1993. pap. text 5.00 (*1-56564-007-1*) IIIT VA.

— Hikmat Al-Islam Fi Tahrim Al-Khamr. LC 96-6449. (Silsilat Islamiyat Al-Marifah Ser.: No. 16). 1996. write for info. (*0-614-13026-3*) IIIT VA.

Badrinath, Chaturvedi. Insights Dharma, India & the World Order. 272p. 1993. pap. 40.00 (*0-86153-172-8*, Pub. by St Andrew) St Mut.

Badrkhan, Kamiran S. Video Systems: Television Principles & Servicing. 2nd ed. LC 85-20348. 630p. 1986. text 39.95 (*0-471-81694-9*) P-H.

Badrocke, Mike & Bunston, Bill. Lockheed Aircraft Cutaways. (Illus.). 144p. 1998. 29.95 (*1-85532-775-9*, 126595AE, Pub. by Ospry) Motorbooks Intl.

***Badrocke, Mike & Gunston, Bill.** Mcdonnell Douglas Aircraft Cutaways. (Illus.). 144p. 1999. 34.95 (*1-85532-924-7*, Pub. by Osprey) Motorbooks Intl.

Badru, Pade. Imperialism & Ethnic Politics in Nigeria, 1960-1996. LC 97-35162. 178p. 1997. 69.95 (*0-86543-603-7*); pap. 19.95 (*0-86543-604-5*) Africa World.

— International Banking & Rural Development: The World Bank & Rural Poverty in Nigeria. LC 97-76937. (Making of Modern Africa Ser.). (Illus.). 160p. 1998. text 63.95 (*1-84014-305-3*, Pub. by Ashgate Pub) Ashgate Pub Co.

Badrud-Din. The Bank of Lebanon. (C). 1992. text 59.00 (*0-86187-461-7*, Pub. by P P Pubs) Cassell & Continuum.

Badruddin. Land Revenue Law: Cases & Comment. (C). 1991. 30.00 (*81-7024-396-3*, Pub. by Ashish Pub Hse) S Asia.

Badruddin, Shaikh. Inspirations: On the Path of Blame. Bayrak, Tosun, tr. 200p. 1993. pap. 13.00 (*0-939660-47-4*) Threshold CA.

Badsey, Stephen. Arnhem 1944. (Campaign Ser.: No. 24). (Illus.). 96p. pap. 14.95 (*1-85532-302-8*, 9523, Pub. by Osprey) Stackpole.

— Normandy, 1944. (Campaign Ser.: No. 1). (Illus.). 96p. 1990. pap. 14.95 (*0-85045-921-4*, 9500, Pub. by Osprey) Stackpole.

***Badsey, Stephen, ed.** The Hutchinson Atlas of World War II Battle Plans: Before & After. 275p. 2000. 55.00 (*1-57958-265-6*) Fitzroy Dearborn.

— The Media & International Security. LC 99-49658. 296p. 2000. 64.50 (*0-7146-4848-5*, Pub. by F Cass Pubs); pap. 26.50 (*0-7146-4406-4*, Pub. by F Cass Pubs) Intl Spec Bk.

Badsey, Stephen & Lambert, Andrew D. The Crimean War from the Times War Correspondents. (Illus.). 352p. 1994. 31.95 (*0-7509-0043-1*, Pub. by Sutton Pub Ltd) Intl Pubs Mktg.

Badsey, Stephen, jt. ed. see Sheffield, Gary D.

Badshah, Akhtar A. Our Urban Future: New Paradigms for Equity & Sustainability. (Illus.). 256p. 1996. pap. 22.50 (*1-85649-406-3*, Pub. by Zed Books) St Martin.

***Badt, Evan M.** Unlocking the Mystery of Foreclosures. (Illus.). vi, 86p. 2000. pap. 15.95 (*0-9676092-0-8*) E B Investments.

Badt, Karin L. Good Morning, Let's Eat. LC 94-12645. (World of Difference Ser.). (Illus.). 32p. (J). (gr. 4-6). 1994. pap. 6.95 (*0-516-48190-8*); lib. bdg. 21.00 (*0-516-08190-X*) Childrens.

— Greetings. LC 94-18777. (World of Difference Ser.). (Illus.). 32p. (J). (gr. 4-6). 1994. pap. 6.95 (*0-516-48188-6*); lib. bdg. 21.00 (*0-516-08188-8*) Childrens.

— Hair There & Everywhere. LC 94-11652. (World of Difference Ser.). (Illus.). 32p. (J). (gr. 4-6). 1994. pap. 6.95 (*0-516-48187-8*); lib. bdg. 21.00 (*0-516-08187-X*) Childrens.

— Let's Go! LC 94-36911. (World of Difference Ser.). (Illus.). 32p. (J). (gr. 3-7). 1995. lib. bdg. 21.00 (*0-516-08195-0*) Childrens.

— Let's Go! (World of Difference Ser.). (Illus.). 32p. (J). (gr. 3-7). 1995. pap. 6.95 (*0-516-48195-9*) Childrens.

— The Mississippi Flood of 1993. LC 94-9493. (Cornerstones to Freedom Ser.). (Illus.). 32p. (J). (gr. 3-6). 1994. lib. bdg. 19.50 (*0-516-06680-3*) Childrens.

— On Your Feet! LC 94-11651. (World of Difference Ser.). (Illus.). 32p. (J). (gr. 4-6). 1994. pap. 6.95 (*0-516-48189-4*); lib. bdg. 21.00 (*0-516-08189-6*) Childrens.

— Pass the Bread! LC 94-38003. (World of Difference Ser.). (Illus.). 32p. (J). (gr. 2-5). 1995. lib. bdg. 20.30 (*0-516-08191-8*) Childrens.

— Pass the Bread! (World of Difference Ser.). (Illus.). 32p. (J). (gr. 3-7). 1995. pap. 6.95 (*0-516-48191-6*) Childrens.

— The Underground Railroad: A Play in Three Acts. 20p. (Orig.). (J). (gr. 5-9). 1995. pap., wbk. ed. 10.00 (*1-878668-58-7*) Disc Enter Ltd.

Badt, Karin L., ed. Indians of the Northeast. LC 97-67538. (Perspectives on History Ser.: Pt. II). (Illus.). 60p. 1997. pap. 6.95 (*1-878668-80-3*) Disc Enter Ltd.

— Indians of the Southwest. LC 96-84758. (Perspectives on History Ser.: Pt. I). (Illus.). 64p. 1996. pap. 6.95 (*1-878668-71-4*) Disc Enter Ltd.

Badt, Kurt. John Constable's Clouds. Godman, Stanley, tr. from GER. (Illus.). 1971. reprint ed. pap. 25.00 (*0-87556-017-2*) Saifer.

Badt-Strauss, Bertha. White Fire: The Life & Works of Jessie Sampter. Davis, Moshe, ed. LC 77-70663. (America & the Holy Land Ser.). (Illus.). 1977. reprint ed. lib. bdg. 23.95 (*0-405-10224-0*) Ayer.

Badten, L. Atightuusim Aallghi (Another Reader) (ESK.). 67p. 1974. pap. 3.50 (*0-933769-66-0*) Alaska Native.

Baduh, Nana P. Reflections of Inner Mind's Eye. 32p. 1998. pap. 7.00 (*0-8059-4291-2*) Dorrance.

Badura, B. & Kickbusch, Ilona, eds. Health Promotion Research: Towards a New Social Epidemiology. (WHO Regional Publications, European Ser.: No. 37). x, 496p. 1991. pap. text 78.00 (*92-890-1128-9*, 1310037) World Health.

Badura, James M. The Land of Wilno: or My First Journey to Poland, Lithuania & Byelorussia. 250p. 1995. 32.00 (*0-614-02654-7*); pap. 16.00 (*0-614-02655-5*) Szwede Slavic.

Badura-Skoda, Eva. Interpreting Mozart on the Keyboard. 1985. 32.50 (*0-306-76265-X*) Da Capo.

Badura-Skoda, Paul. Interpreting Bach at the Keyboard. Clayton, Alfred, tr. from GER. (Illus.). 592p. 1995. reprint ed. pap. text 32.00 (*0-19-816576-5*) OUP.

Badura-Triska, Eva, et al. Helmut Federle Five Plus One. limited ed. Kalthoff, Brigitte, tr. (ENG & GER., Illus.). 67p. 1990. 35.00 (*0-935875-08-5*) P Blum Edit.

Badwal, S., et al, eds. Fifth International Conference on the Science & Technology of Zirconia. LC 93-60723. 875p. 1993. text 110.95 (*1-56676-073-9*) Technomic.

Bady, Richard. Lab Manual for Physical Science 109L & Extra Materials. 4th ed. 156p. (C). 1998. spiral bd. 26.95 (*0-7872-4903-3*, 41490301) Kendall-Hunt.

— Physical Science 110. 4th ed. 160p. (C). 1998. spiral bd., lab manual ed. 26.95 (*0-7872-1152-4*, 41115201) Kendall-Hunt.

Bady, Richard J. Laboratory Manual for Physical Science 109L: And Extra Materials for Physical Science 109 Lecture. 156p. (C). 1996. pap. text, per. 16.95 (*0-7872-2188-0*) Kendall-Hunt.

— Physical Science 110L Lab Manual. 3rd ed. 164p. (C). 1996. pap. text 16.95 (*0-7872-2379-4*) Kendall-Hunt.

Badzinski, Stanley, Jr. Stair Layout. LC 96-203046. (Illus.). 172p. 1995. pap. 18.96 (*0-8269-0701-6*) Am Technical.

Badzyo, Yuriy. State of Siege: Ukraine's National Predicament. Senkus, Roman, ed. LC 81-67209. (Illus.). 130p. (Orig.). 1981. 9.95 (*0-86725-001-1*); pap. 3.75 (*0-86725-000-3*) ERUHG.

Bae, Johngseok, jt. ed. see Rowley, Chris.

Bae, Sung H. Living Well with a Thorn in the Flesh: Brain Priming for Healthy Life. LC 97-90297. (Illus.). 141p. (Orig.). 1997. pap. 12.95 (*0-533-12348-8*) Vantage.

Bae, Yupin, et al. Women in Mathematics & Science. Pratt, Rebecca, ed. LC 98-179031. (Findings from the Condition of Edication Ser.). 30p. 1997. write for info. (*0-16-049220-3*) USGPO.

Baechle, Thomas R. & Earle, Roger W. Fitness Weight Training. LC 94-28361. (Fitness Spectrum Ser.). (Illus.). 176p. (Orig.). 1994. pap. 15.95 (*0-87322-445-0*, PBAE0445) Human Kinetics.

Baechle, Thomas R. & Groves, Barney R. Weight Training: Steps to Success. LC 93-38005. (Steps to Success Activity Ser.). (Illus.). 192p. 1994. pap. text 15.95 (*0-87322-618-6*, PBAE0618) Human Kinetics.

***Baechle, Thomas R. & Groves, Barney R.** Weight Training: Steps to Success. 2nd ed. 192p. 1998. 39.95 incl. VHS (*0-88011-946-2*) Human Kinetics.

Baechle, Thomas R. & Groves, Barney R. Weight Training: Steps to Success. 2nd rev. ed. LC 97-44075. (Steps to Success Activity Ser.). (Illus.). 192p. 1998. pap. 15.95 (*0-88011-718-4*, PBAE0718) Human Kinetics.

Baechle, Thomas R., jt. auth. see Westcott, Wayne L.

Baechle, Thomas R., ed. see National Strength & Conditioning Staff.

Baechler, Christian & Fink, Carole, eds. L' Etablissement des Frontieres en Europe apres les Deux Guerres Mondiales (The Establishment of European Frontiers after the Two World Wars: Actes des Colloques de Strasbourg et de Montreal, Juin et Septembre 1995 (Proceedings of the International Conferences Strasbourg & Montreal, June & September 1995) (FRE.). xi, 453p. 1996. 43.95 (*3-906754-62-6*, Pub. by P Lang) P Lang Pubng.

Baechler, Ghunther. Violence Through Environmental Discrimination: Cause, Rwanda Arena & Conflict Model. LC 98-49923. (Social Indicators Research Ser.). 4p. 1999. 112.00 (*0-7923-5495-8*) Kluwer Academic.

Baechler, Lea, et al, eds. Ezra Pound's Poetry & Prose, 1918-1919: 1918-1919, Vol. 3. LC 91-32724. 392p. 1991. reprint ed. text 55.00 (*0-8240-5388-5*) Garland.

— Ezra Pound's Poetry & Prose, 1920-1927, Vol. 4. LC 91-32724. 408p. 1992. reprint ed. text 60.00 (*0-8240-5389-3*) Garland.

— Ezra Pound's Poetry & Prose, 1928-1932, Vol. 5. LC 91-32724. 400p. 1992. reprint ed. text 60.00 (*0-8240-5390-7*) Garland.

— Ezra Pound's Poetry & Prose, 1933-1935, Vol. 6. LC 91-32724. 368p. 1992. reprint ed. text 55.00 (*0-8240-5391-5*) Garland.

— Ezra Pound's Poetry & Prose, 1956-1965, Vol. 9. LC 91-32724. 568p. 1992. reprint ed. text 80.00 (*0-8240-5394-X*) Garland.

Baechler, Lea & Litz, A. Walton, eds. American Writers: A Collection of Literary Biographies, 2 vols., Suppl. III. 800p. 1991. 100.00 (*0-684-19356-6*, Scribners Ref); 100.00 (*0-684-19357-4*, Scribners Ref) Mac Lib Ref.

— American Writers: A Collection of Literary Biographies, 2 vols., Vol. 2. 800p. 1991. 225.00 (*0-684-19196-2*, Scribners Ref) Mac Lib Ref.

Baechler, M. C., et al. Sick Building Syndrome: Sources, Health Effects, Mitigation. LC 91-20423. (Pollution Technology Review Ser.: No. 205). (Illus.). 328p. 1992. 98.00 (*0-8155-1289-9*) Noyes.

Baechtel, John. Chevy TPI Fuel Injection Swapper's Guide: How to Interchange & Modify Tuned Port Injection Systems. LC 99-218298. (Illus.). 128p. (Orig.). 1997. pap. 18.95 (*1-884089-12-7*, S-A Design) CarTech.

— High Performance Crate Motor Buyer's Guide: How to Select & Install High Performance Crate Motors. LC 99-219514. (Illus.). 128p. (Orig.). 1996. pap. 18.95 (*1-884089-13-5*, S-A Design) CarTech.

Baeck, Leo, Institute Staff, ed. see Wassermann, Henry.

Baeck, Louis. The Mediterranean Tradition in Economic Thought. LC 94-16498. 272p. (C). (gr. 13). 1994. 85.00 (*0-415-09301-5*, B4238) Routledge.

Baeck, Thomas, ed. Proceedings of the Seventh International Conference on Genetic Algorithms: Michigan State University, East Lansing, MI, July 19-23, 1997. LC 97-25149. 800p. (C). 1997. pap. text 49.95 (*1-55860-487-1*) Morgan Kaufmann.

***Baecker, Dirk.** Problems of Form. LC 99-21522. 248p. 1999. 55.00 (*0-8047-3423-2*) Stanford U Pr.

Baecker, Dirk. Problems of Form. LC 99-21522. (Writing Science Ser.). 1999. pap. text 22.95 (*0-8047-3424-0*) Stanford U Pr.

Baecker, Dirk, tr. see Luhmann, Niklas.

Baecker, Ronald. A Graphic Design Manual for the C Programming Language. (Illus.). 368p. (C). 1990. pap. text 31.95 (*0-201-10745-7*) Addison-Wesley.

Baecker, Ronald & Buxton, William, eds. Readings in Human-Computer Interaction: A Multidisciplinary Approach. LC 87-12512. (Illus.). 738p. (Orig.). 1998. pap. text 46.95 (*0-934613-24-9*) Morgan Kaufmann.

Baecker, Ronald M., ed. Readings in Groupware & Computer-Supported Cooperative Work: Assisting Human-Human Collaboration. LC 92-43986. 882p. 1993. pap. text 62.95 (*1-55860-241-0*) Morgan Kaufmann.

Baecker, Ronald M., et al. Readings in Human-Computer Interaction: Toward the Year 2000. 2nd ed. 900p. 1995. pap. text 64.95 (*1-55860-246-1*) Morgan Kaufmann.

Baecker, Ronald M., jt. auth. see Marcus, Aaron R.

Baeckler, Virginia. Sparkle: PR for Library Staff. LC 80-50566. (Illus.). 80p. (Orig.). 1980. pap. 5.00 (*0-9603232-1-X*) Sources.

Baeckler, Virginia & Larson, Linda. Go, Pep & Pop! Two Hundred & Fifty Tested Ideas for Lively Libraries. LC 75-20328. 1976. pap. 4.50 (*0-916444-01-5*) UNABASHED Lib.

— Go, Pep & Pop! Two Hundred Fifty Tested Ideas for Lively Libraries. LC 87-91262. 72p. 1987. reprint ed. pap. 6.00 (*0-9603232-3-6*) Sources.

Baeckler, Virginia V. Storytime Science: Have You Clanged Your Hanger Banger Today? Van Wynen, Kenneth G., ed. LC 86-61013. (Illus.). 100p. 1986. pap. text 10.00 (*0-9603232-2-8*) Sources.

Baecque, Antoine de, ed. A History of Democracy in Europe. (Social Science Monographs). 302p. 1995. 47.50 (*0-88033-971-3*, Pub. by East Eur Monographs) Col U Pr.

Baecque, Antoine De, see Toubiana, Serge & De Baecque, Antoine.

Baecque, Antoine De, see De Baecque, Antoine.

Baeda, Eamon. Venetian Woods. LC 88-81109. ix, 66p. 1988. 10.95 (*0-9620529-0-6*); pap. 5.95 (*0-9620529-1-4*) Aldine Pr Ltd.

Baedeker, Jarrold. Baedeker Amsterdam. 3rd ed. 136p. 1995. 17.00 (*0-02-860680-9*) Macmillan.

— Baedeker Athens. 2nd rev. ed. 224p. 1995. 17.00 (*0-02-860480-6*) Macmillan.

— Baedeker Austria. 3rd rev. ed. 640p. 1995. 24.00 (*0-02-860481-4*) Macmillan.

— Baedeker Bali. 2nd rev. ed. 208p. 1995. 17.00 (*0-02-860671-X*) Macmillan.

— Baedeker Budapest. 3rd rev. ed. 184p. 1995. 17.00 (*0-02-860672-8*) Macmillan.

— Baedeker California. 2nd ed. 448p. 1995. 24.00 (*0-02-860678-7*) Macmillan.

— Baedeker Copenhagen. 3rd ed. 192p. 1995. 17.00 (*0-02-860668-X*) Macmillan.

— Baedeker Florence. 3rd ed. 208p. 1995. 17.00 (*0-02-860679-5*) Macmillan.

— Baedeker Florida. 2nd ed. 400p. 1995. 24.00 (*0-02-860681-7*) Macmillan.

— Baedeker Greece: Updated. 608p. 1995. 24.00 (*0-02-860119-X*) Macmillan.

— Baedeker Greek Islands: Updated. 288p. 1995. 17.00 (*0-02-860117-3*) Macmillan.

— Baedeker Hawaii. 2nd ed. 256p. 1995. 24.00 (*0-02-860483-0*) Macmillan.

— Baedeker Hong Kong. 3rd rev. ed. 136p. 1995. 17.00 (*0-02-860669-8*) Macmillan.

— Baedeker Israel. 3rd rev. ed. 452p. 1995. 24.00 (*0-02-860484-9*) Macmillan.

— Baedeker Prague. 2nd ed. 224p. 1995. 17.00 (*0-02-860488-1*) Macmillan.

— Baedeker Singapore. 2nd rev. ed. 160p. 1995. 17.00 (*0-02-860489-X*) Macmillan.

— Baedeker Spain. 3rd ed. 608p. 1995. 24.00 (*0-02-860683-3*) Macmillan.

— Baedeker Switzerland. 3rd ed. 584p. 1995. 24.00 (*0-02-860684-1*) Macmillan.

— Baedeker Tokyo. 2nd rev. ed. 192p. 1995. 17.00 (*0-02-860490-3*) Macmillan.

— Baedeker Vienna. 3rd rev. ed. 284p. 1995. 17.00 (*0-02-860492-X*) Macmillan.

— Baedeker's Australia. 640p. 1995. 24.00 (*0-02-860456-3*) Macmillan.

— Baedeker's Caribbean. 3rd ed. (Baedeker's Travel Guides Ser.). 832p. 1997. 24.00 (*0-02-861366-X*) Macmillan USA.

— Baedeker's China. (Baedeker's Travel Guides Ser.). 1997. 24.00 (*0-02-861365-1*) Macmillan USA.

— Baedeker's Crete. (Baedeker's Travel Guides Ser.). 1996. 15.95 (*0-02-861364-3*) Macmillan USA.

— Baedeker's France. (Baedeker's Travel Guides Ser.). 1997. 24.00 (*0-02-861363-5*) Macmillan USA.

— Baedeker's Germany. 3rd ed. (Baedeker's Travel Guides Ser.). 1996. 24.00 (*0-02-861362-7*) Macmillan USA.

— Baedeker's Great Britain. (Baedeker's Travel Guides Ser.). 1997. 24.00 (*0-02-861361-9*) Macmillan USA.

— Baedeker's Ireland. 4th ed. (Baedeker's Travel Guides Ser.). 1997. 24.00 (*0-02-861360-0*) Macmillan USA.

— Baedeker's Mexico. 3rd ed. (Baedeker's Travel Guides Ser.). 1996. 24.00 (*0-02-861359-7*) Macmillan USA.

— Baedeker's Nepal. 320p. 1995. 24.00 (*0-02-860458-X*) Macmillan.

— Baedeker's Portugal. (Baedeker's Travel Guides Ser.). 1997. 23.00 (*0-02-861358-9*) Macmillan USA.

— Baedeker's Scandinavia. 3rd ed. (Baedeker's Travel Guides Ser.). 1996. 23.00 (*0-02-861356-2*) Macmillan USA.

— Baedeker's South Africa. (Baedeker's Travel Guides Ser.). 1996. 23.95 (*0-02-861355-4*) Macmillan USA.

— Baedeker's St. Petersburg. 2nd ed. (Baedeker's Travel Guides Ser.). 1997. 15.95 (*0-02-861357-0*) Macmillan USA.

— U. S. A. (Baedeker's Travel Guides Ser.). 608p. 1995. 24.00 (*0-02-860069-X*) Macmillan.

Baedeker, Karl. Baedeker Handbook for Travellers: Russia. xiv, 590 p. 1973. 12.95 (*0-405-03004-5*) Arno Press.

— Baedeker New York. 2nd rev. ed. 192p. 1995. 17.00 (*0-02-860673-6*) Macmillan.

— Baedeker Provence. 2nd rev. ed. 296p. 1995. 17.00 (*0-02-860675-2*) Macmillan.

— Baedeker San Francisco. 3rd rev. ed. 176p. 1995. 17.00 (*0-02-860667-1*) Macmillan.

***Baedeker, Karl.** Baedeker's Amsterdam. Fodors Travel Publications, Inc. Staff, ed. 1999. pap. 18.00 (*0-7495-2183-X*) Fodors Travel.

— Baedeker's Austria. 416p. 2000. pap. 25.00 (*0-7495-2203-8*) Random.

Baedeker, Karl. Baedeker's Belgium. 460p. 1993. pap. 23.00 (*0-671-87155-2*, P-H Travel) Prntice Hall Bks.

— Baedeker's Israel. 2nd ed. 460p. 1993. pap. 23.00 (*0-671-87132-3*, P-H Travel) Prntice Hall Bks.

— Baedeker's Lisbon. 224p. 1993. pap. 17.00 (*0-671-87130-7*, P-H Travel) Prntice Hall Bks.

***Baedeker, Karl.** Baedeker's Mexico. 2000. pap. 25.00 (*0-7495-2201-1*) Random.

Baedeker, Karl. Baedeker's Scandinavia. 2nd ed. 600p. 1993. pap. 23.00 (*0-671-87153-6*, P-H Travel) Prntice Hall Bks.

— Baedeker's Sicily. 424p. 1993. pap. 20.00 (*0-67.-84938-7*, P-H Travel) Prntice Hall Bks.

— Baedeker's Thailand. 400p. 1993. pap. 23.00 (*0-671-87154-4*, P-H Travel) Prntice Hall Bks.

***Baedeker, Karl.** Baedeker's Thailand. 2000. pap. 25.00 (*0-7495-2199-6*) Random.

Baedeker, Karl. Baedeker's Tuscany. (Illus.). 256p. 1985. pap. 12.95 (*0-13-056482-6*) P-H.

— Copenhagen. (Baedeker's City Guides Ser.). (Illus.). 1986. pap. 10.95 (*0-685-17130-2*) P-H.

— Jerusalem. (Baedeker's City Guides Ser.). 192p. 1989. pap. 12.95 (*0-13-058017-1*) P-H.

— Singapore. (Baedeker's City Guides Ser.). 1986. pap. 12.95 (*0-13-058090-2*) P-H.

— Tokyo. (Baedeker's City Guides Ser.). 1987. pap. 10.95 (*0-317-51985-9*) P-H.

Baedeker, Karl, ed. Baedeker's U. S. A. LC 76-77703. (American Scene Ser.). Orig. Title: The United States with an Excursion into Mexico. (Illus.). 520p. 1971. reprint ed. lib. bdg. 25.00 (*0-306-71341-1*) Da Capo.

Baedeker Staff. Baedeker's Brazil. 480p. 1995. 24.00 (*0-02-860457-1*) Macmillan.

— Baedeker's Greek Islands. 1988. pap. 12.95 (*0-13-058132-1*) P-H.

— Baedeker's Guide to Florence. 2nd ed. 208p. 1994. pap. 17.00 (*0-671-89013-1*) P-H.

***Baedeker Staff.** Baedeker's Vienna. (Illus.). 2000. pap. 18.00 (*0-7495-2240-2*) Auto Assn Guides.

Baedeker Staff. Netherlands. (Baedeker's Travel Guide Ser.). 543p. 1995. 24.00 (*0-02-860083-5*, P-H Travel) Prntice Hall Bks.

— Venice. (Baedeker's Travel Guides Ser.). 304p. 1995. 17.00 (*0-02-860085-1*) Macmillan.

Baedeker Staff, ed. Baedeker Italy. 3rd ed. 624p. 1995. 24.00 (*0-02-860485-7*) Macmillan.

— Baedeker Rome. 3rd ed. 256p. 1995. 17.00 (*0-02-860118-1*) Macmillan.

— Baedeker's Istanbul. 2nd ed. 192p. 1997. 17.00 (*0-02-860677-9*) Macmillan.

— Baedeker's London. 4th ed. 224p. 1995. 17.00 (*0-02-860682-5*) Macmillan.

***Baedekers Guides Staff, ed.** Baedeker's Athens. 2000. pap. 18.00 (*0-7495-2406-5*) Auto Assn Guides.

— Baedeker's Belgium. (Illus.). 2000. pap. 25.00 (*0-7495-2407-3*) Auto Assn Guides.

— Baedeker's Brussels. (Illus.). 2000. pap. 18.00 (*0-7495-2422-7*) Auto Assn Guides.

— Baedeker's China. (Illus.). 2000. pap. 25.00 (*0-7495-2409-X*) Auto Assn Guides.

— Baedeker's Great Britain. (Illus.). 2000. pap. 25.00 (*0-7495-2408-1*) Auto Assn Guides.

— Baedeker's Malta. (Illus.). 2000. pap. 18.00 (*0-7495-2411-1*) Auto Assn Guides.

— Baedeker's Tenerife. (Illus.). 2000. pap. 18.00 (*0-7495-2412-X*) Auto Assn Guides.

***Baedekers, Jarrold.** Baedeker's California. (Illus.) 2000. pap. text 25.00 (*0-7495-2258-5*) Auto Assn Guides.

Baeder, Claire, ed. La Domme: A Dominatrix Anthology. 2nd ed. (Orig.). 1998. reprint ed. mass mkt. 6.95 (*1-56333-649-9*) Masquerade.

Baeder, John. Diners. rev. ed. LC 94-21218. (Illus.). 144p. 1995. pap. 19.95 (*0-8109-2611-3*, Pub. by Abrams) Time Warner.

— Gas, Food & Lodging: A Postcard Odyssey Through the Great American Roadside. (Illus.). 132p. 1986. pap. 24.95 (*0-89659-322-3*) Abbeville Pr.

Baefour, Bernice, jt. auth. see Ronen, Ela.

Baegert, Johann J. Observations in Lower California. Brandenburg, M. M. & Baumann, Carl L., trs. from GER. 1979. reprint ed. 48.00 (*0-520-03873-8*, Pub. by U CA Pr) Cal Prin Full Svc.

Baeher, Helen, ed. Women & Media. LC 80-41424. (Illus.). 142p. 1980. 21.50 (*0-08-026061-6*, Pergamon Pr) Elsevier.

Baehler, James R. The New Manager's Guide to Success. LC 80-19509. 147p. 1980. 52.95 (*0-275-91684-7*, C1684, Praeger Pubs) Greenwood.

Baehler, Karen J., jt. auth. see Galston, William A.

Baehr. Human Rights. LC 98-55203. 1999. text 65.00 (*0-312-22180-0*) St Martin.

— New Horizons. 2nd ed. 276p. 1998. pap. text 36.00 (*0-536-02000-0*) Pearson Custom.

— The United Nations at the End of the 1990's. 3rd ed. xviii, 203 p. 1999. pap. 21.95 (*0-312-22017-0*) St Martin.

— The United Nations, 1990s. 2nd ed. 1994. pap. 25.95 (*0-312-12071-0*) St Martin.

Baehr, Anna R. Moonflowers at Dusk. (Illus.). 1996. pap. 10.00 (*1-878173-15-4*) Birnham Wood.

Baehr, B. & Baehr, M. Welche Spinne Ist Das? (Which Spider Is That?) (Kosmos Naturfuehrer (Nature Guides) Ser.). (GER., Illus.). 128p. 1987. pap. 30.00 (*3-440-05798-4*, Pub. by Franckh-Kosmos) Balogh.

Baehr, Carl. Milwaukee Streets: The Stories Behind Their Names. LC 94-94149. 1994. pap. 19.95 (*0-9640204-4-0*) Cream City Pr.

Baehr, H. D. & Stephan, K. Heat & Mass-Transfer. Park, N. J., tr. from GER. (Illus.). 670p. 1998. 79.95 (*3-540-63695-1*) Spr-Verlag.

Baehr, Helen & Gray, Ann, eds. Turning It On: A Reader in Women & the Media. LC 95-37773. (Illus.). 240p. 1995. pap. text 16.95 (*0-340-61396-3*) OUP.

— Turning It On: A Reader in Women & the Media. LC 95-37773. 1995. text 59.95 (*0-340-63220-8*) St Martin.

Baehr, M., jt. auth. see Baehr, B.

Baehr, Marie, jt. auth. see Krumsieg, Karl.

Baehr, Melany E. Predicting Success in Higher-Level Positions: A Guide to the System for Testing & Evaluation of Potential. LC 91-22017. 296p. 1992. 65.00 (*0-89930-626-8*, BTS, Quorum Bks) Greenwood.

Baehr, Ninia. Abortion Without Apology: A Radical History for the 1990s. 68p. (C). 1990. pap. 6.00 (*0-89608-384-5*) South End Pr.

Baehr, P. R., et al. The Role of the Nation-State in the 21st Century: Human Rights, International Organizations & Foreign Policy Essays In Honour Of Peter Baehr / LC 98-43826. 1999. 150.00 (*90-411-1141-7*) Kluwer Law Intl.

Baehr, P. R., jt. auth. see Arendt, Hannah.

Baehr, Patricia. Mouse in the House. LC 93-4068. (Illus.). 32p. (J). (ps-3). 1994. lib. bdg. 15.95 (*0-8234-1102-8*) Holiday.

— School Isn't Fair! LC 88-21461. (Illus.). 32p. (J). (ps-k). 1989. lib. bdg. 13.95 (*0-02-708130-3*, Four Winds Pr) S&S Childrens.

— School Isn't Fair! LC 91-38485. (Illus.). 32p. (J). (ps). 1992. reprint ed. pap. 4.95 (*0-689-71544-7*) Aladdin.

Baehr, Peter. Caesar & the Fading of the Roman World: A Study in Republicanism & Caesarism. LC 97-16701. 382p. 1997. text 39.95 (*1-56000-304-9*) Transaction Pubs.

Baehr, Peter, ed. see Weber, Max.

Baehr, Peter R. The Role of Human Rights in Foreign Policy. LC 94-5975. 1994. text 49.95 (*0-312-12173-3*) St Martin.

Baehr, Peter R., et al, eds. Human Rights: Chinese & Dutch Perspectives. LC 96-6732. 1996. lib. bdg. 74.50 (*90-411-0210-8*, Pub. by M Nijhoff) Kluwer Academic.

Baehr, Peter R. & Wittrock, Bjorn, eds. Policy Analysis & Policy Innovation: Patterns, Problems & Potentials. LC 80-41079. (Sage Modern Politics Ser.: No. 5). 244p. reprint ed. pap. 75.70 (*0-8357-4721-2*, 203763500009) Bks Demand.

Baehr, Richard. Architectural Rendering in Tempera. (Illus.). 160p. 1995. text 52.95 (*0-442-01261-6*, VNR) Wiley.

Baehr, Richard A., ed. Engineering a Hospital Turnaround: Proven Strategies for Reinvigorating Financial & Operating Performance. LC 93-9622. (Illus.). 228p. 1993. pap. 45.00 (*1-55648-102-0*, 001120) AHPI.

Baehr, Richard C. Architectural Rendering in Tempera. (Architecture Ser.). 136p. 1995. pap. 59.95 (*0-471-28512-9*, VNR) Wiley.

Baehr, Russell. Oregon's Outback. Reaves, Verne, ed. (Illus.). 250p. (Orig.). 1985. pap. 15.95 (*0-89288-108-9*) Maverick.

Baehr, Stephen L. The Paradise Myth in Eighteenth-Century Russia: Utopian Patterns in Early Secular Russian Literature & Culture. (Illus.). 330p. 1991. 42.50 (*0-8047-1533-5*) Stanford U Pr.

Baehr, Ted. The Media-Wise Family. LC 97-29005. 350p. 1998. 10.99 (*0-7814-0301-4*, Victor Bks) Chariot Victor.

Baehr, Timothy J. Handbook for Writing Educational Materials. 168p. (Orig.). 1989. pap. 19.95 (*0-9621503-0-4*) Brown Pub Network.

***Baehre, Rainer K., ed.** Outrageous Seas: Shipwreck & Survival in the Waters off Newfoundland, 1583-1893. (Illus.). 152p. 1999. pap. 22.95 (*0-88629-319-7*) McG-Queens Univ Pr.

Baehre, Rainer K., ed. see Rainer, Kathleen.

***Baekeland, Frederick.** Images of America: The Painter's Eye, 1833-1925. (Illus.). 160p. 2000. reprint ed. pap. text 22.00 (*0-7881-9098-9*) DIANE Pub.

Baelz, Peter. Does God Answer Prayer? (Illus.). 122p. (Orig.). 1983. pap. 12.95 (*0-87243-117-7*) Templegate.

***Baen Bks. Staff & Brown, Mary.** The Unlikely Ones. 1999. per. 6.99 (*0-671-57844-8*) Baen Bks.

Baen, Jim. New Destinies. 288p. (Orig.). 1992. per. 4.99 (*0-671-72086-4*) Baen Bks.

Baen, Jim, jt. auth. see Pournelle, Jerry.

***Baena, Cesar E.** The Policy Process in a Petro-State. (Political Economy of Latin America Ser.). 274p. 1999. text 69.95 (*0-7546-1070-5*, Pub. by Ashgate Pub) Ashgate Pub Co.

Baena, Julio. El Circulo y la Flecha: Principio y Fin, Triunfo y Fracasa del Persiles. LC 95-34850. (University of North Carolina Studies in the Romance Languages & Literature). (SPA.). 210p. (C). 1996. text 24.95 (*0-8078-9256-4*) U of NC Pr.

— El Poemario de Fray Luis de Leon. (American University Studies: Romance Languages & Literature: Ser. II, Vol. 107). X, 232p. (C). 1989. text 35.95 (*0-8204-1015-2*) P Lang Pubng.

Baena, Julio, jt. ed. see Gonzalez-del-Valle, Luis T.

Baender, Margaret W. Tail Waggings of Maggie. (Illus.). 64p. (J). (gr. 8-10). 1982. pap. 6.00 (*0-88100-012-4*) Philmar Pub.

Baender, Paul, ed. A Hero Perished: The Diary & Selected Letters of Nile Kinnick. LC 91-10195. (Illus.). 334p. 1991. pap. 16.95 (*0-87745-390-X*); text 29.95 (*0-87745-336-5*) U of Iowa Pr.

Baender, Paul, intro. The Adventures of Tom Sawyer: A Facsimile Edition of Mark Twain's Complete Manuscript. 920p. 1982. lib. bdg. 155.00 (*0-313-27062-7*, U7062, Greenwood Pr) Greenwood.

Baender, Paul, ed. & intro. see Twain, Mark, pseud.

Baenen, Judith. H. E. L. P. How to Enjoy Living with a Preadolescent - Get Ready for Changes. 20p. 1991. 3.00 (*1-56090-061-X*) Natl Middle Schl.

Baenkler, H. W., ed. Rheumatic Diseases & Sports. (Rheumatology Ser.: Vol. 16). (Illus.). vii, 232p. 1992. 191.50 (*3-8055-5425-7*) S Karger.

Baens, Mathijs. Isolation & Regional Assignment of New Genes on the Short Arm of Human Chromosome 12. (Acta Biomedica Lovaniensia Ser.: Vol. 111). (Illus.). vi, 89p. (Orig.). 1995. pap. 32.50 (*90-6186-684-7*, Pub. by Leuven Univ) Coronet Bks.

Baensch, Hans & Loiselle, Paul V. Marine Aquarist Manual: Comprehensive Edition. (Illus.). 286p. 26.95 (*3-89356-130-7*, 16031) Tetra Pr.

Baensch, Hans, jt. auth. see Riehl, Rudiger.

Baensch, Hans A. Marine Aquarist's Manual. (Illus.). 1991. 10.95 (*3-923880-15-4*, 16030) Tetra Pr.

Baensch, Hans A. & Debelius, Helmut. Baensch Marine Atlas, Vol. 1. rev. ed. (Illus.). 1216p. 1997. 54.95 (*1-890087-09-2*); pap. 29.95 (*1-890087-08-4*) Microcosm Ltd.

***Baensch, Hans A. & Fischer, Gero W.** Baensch Aquarium Atlas: Photo Index: 1-5. (Illus.). 1215p. 1999. pap. 39.95 (*1-890087-25-4*) Microcosm Ltd.

— Baensch Aquarium Atlas: Photo Index: 1-5. rev. ed. (Illus.). 1215p. 1999. 54.95 (*1-890087-24-6*) Microcosm Ltd.

Baensch, Hans A., et al. Marine Atlas: The Joint Aquarium Care of Invertebrates & Tropical Marine Fishes. rev. ed. Fischer, Gero W., tr. & rev. by. LC 93-46617. 1994. 59.95 (*1-56465-113-4*, 16820) Tetra Pr.

Baensch, Hans A., jt. auth. see Riehl, Rudiger.

Baensch, Ulrich. Digest for the Successful Aquarium. rev. ed. 1994. pap. 1.95 (*1-56465-165-7*, 16080) Tetra Pr.

Baensch, Ulrich, et al. Bromeliaceas en Flor.Tr. of Blooming Bromeliads. (SPA., Illus.). 272p. 1996. 119.00 (*0-9641056-1-6*) Tropic Beauty.

Baensch, Ulrich, jt. auth. see Andrews, Chris.

Baenziger, P. Stephen, et al, eds. Intellectual Property Rights: Protection of Plant Materials. LC 93-5949. (CSSA Special Publication Ser.: Vol. 21). 187p. 1993. pap. 20.00 (*0-89118-537-2*) Crop Sci Soc Am.

Baenziger, R. Stephen, jt. ed. see Buxton, D. R.

Baepler, Paul, ed. White Slaves, African Masters: An Anthology of American Barbary Captivity Narratives. LC 98-40368. (Illus.). 376p. 1999. pap. 19.00 (*0-226-03404-6*) U Ch Pr.

Baepler, Paul Michel, ed. White Slaves, African Masters: An Anthology of American Barbary Captivity Narratives. LC 98-40368. (Illus.). 376p. 1999. lib. bdg. 46.00 (*0-226-03403-8*) U Ch Pr.

Baer. Book Review Index 1995 Cumulation. 95th ed. 1410p. 1996. 260.00 (*0-8103-0597-6*) Gale.

— Children's Book Review Index: Cumulative Index, 4 vols., Set. 94th ed. 1995. 400.00 (*0-8103-5457-8*) Gale.

***Baer.** DIY Car Care. 2001. pap. 14.95 (*0-7668-2061-0*) Delmar.

Baer. Electronics & Elonics Drawing. 5th ed. 1985. teacher ed. 11.55 (*0-07-003029-4*) McGraw.

— The Structure, Energetics & Dynamics of Organic Ions. LC 95-54157. (Series in Ion Chemistry & Physics: Vol. 5). 380p. 1996. 280.00 (*0-471-96241-4*) Wiley.

Baer, jt. auth. see Lemaster.

Baer, A. Health, Disease & Survival: A Biomedical & Genetic Analysis of the Orang Asli of Malaysia. LC 98-945286. (Illus.). 1999. pap. text 30.00 (*983-40042-0-6*, Pub. by Ctr Orang Asli) OR St Zoology.

Baer, Andrea. Quit Smoking for Good: A Supportive Program for Permanent Smoking Cessation. LC 98-24697. (Personal Power Ser.). 96p. 1998. pap. 10.95 (*0-89594-943-1*) Crossing Pr.

Baer, Ann. Down the Common: A Year in the Life of a Medieval Woman. 240p. 1998. pap. text 14.95 (*0-87131-874-1*) M Evans.

— Down the Common: The Charmed Life of Marion Carpenter. LC 97-5842. (Illus.). 240p. 1997. 19.95 (*0-87131-818-0*) M Evans.

***Baer, Avi & Neumark, Alexander.** The Zippo Companion. (Connoisseur's Guides Ser.). (Illus.). 2000. 24.95 (*0-7624-0700-X*) Running Pr.

Baer, Barbara L., et al. Cartwheels on the Faultline: Works by Twenty-Seven Sonoma County Women. unabridged ed. Jennings, Maureen, ed. LC 95-61967. (Illus.). 294p. (Orig.). 1996. pap. 12.50 (*0-9649497-0-9*) Floreant Pr.

— Saltwater, Sweetwater: Women Write from California North Coast. unabridged ed. LC 97-61562. (Illus.). 350p. (Orig.). 1998. pap. 13.50 (*0-9649497-1-7*) Floreant Pr.

Baer, Beverly. Book Review Index 1994 Cumulation. 94th ed. 1550p. 1995. 260.00 (*0-8103-0596-8*) Gale.

— Children's Book Review 1995: Cumulative Index. 95th ed. 1996. 138.00 (*0-8103-0610-7*) Gale.

Baer, Beverly, ed. Children's Book Review, 1994. 94th ed. 1050p. 1995. 138.00 (*0-8103-0598-4*) Gale.

Baer, Beverly, jt. auth. see Walker, Barbara G.

Baer, Beverly, jt. ed. see Walker, Neil E.

Baer, Brigitte. Picasso the Engraver, 1900-1942. LC 97-60543. (Illus.). 112p. 1997. 34.95 (*0-500-09269-9*, Pub. by Thames Hudson) Norton.

Baer-Brown, Leslie & Rhein, Bob. Earth Keepers: A Sourcebook for Environmental Issues & Action. LC 94-17541. 304p. (Orig.). 1995. pap. 14.95 (*1-56279-070-6*) Mercury Hse Inc.

Baer, Carol A. Elders' Views on the Right to Die: Facilitating Decisions about Life Sustaining Treatment. rev. ed. LC 97-487. (Studies on the Elderly in America). (Illus.). 144p. 1997. text 33.00 (*0-8153-2675-0*) Garland.

Baer, Charles J. & Ottaway, John R. Electrical & Electronic Drawing. 5th ed. 560p. 1985. text 54.95 (*0-07-003028-6*) McGraw.

Baer, Charold L., jt. auth. see Williams, Bradley R.

Baer, Christopher T. Canals & Railroads of the Mid-Atlantic States 1800-1860. (Illus.). 64p. 1981. pap. 15.00 (*0-914650-19-X*) Hagley Museum.

Baer, Christopher T., jt. auth. see Kane, Martin W.

Baer, D. R., jt. ed. see Jones, R. H.

Baer, D. Richard, ed. Harrison's Reports & Film Reviews, 1919-1962, 15 vols., Set. LC 91-16207. 1995. lib. bdg. 1985.00 (*0-913616-10-9*) Hollywd Film Arch.

— Harrison's Reports Film Review Index, 1919-1962, Vol. 15. 364p. (C). 1995. lib. bdg. 145.00 (*0-913616-25-7*) Hollywd Film Arch.

— Movie World Almanac, 2001-2002. (Illus.). 360p. 2000. lib. bdg. 75.00 (*0-913616-06-0*) Hollywd Film Arch.

Baer, Denise L. & Bositis, David A. Elite Cadres & Party Coalitions: Representing the Public in Party Politics, 218. LC 88-5703. (Contributions in Political Science Ser.: No. 218). 255p. 1988. 59.95 (*0-313-26153-9*, BED/, Greenwood Pr) Greenwood.

Baer, Donald M. Environment & Behavior. LC 96-6594. (C). 1997. pap. text 26.00 (*0-8133-3159-5*, Pub. by Westview) HarpC.

— How to Plan for Generalization. (How to Teach Ser.). 36p. 1981. 8.00 (*0-89079-061-2*, 1009) PRO-ED.

— How to Plan for Generalization. LC 98-38350. (How to Manage Behavior Ser.). 1999. pap. write for info. (*0-89079-793-5*) PRO-ED.

Baer, Donald M., jt. auth. see Geller, E. Scott.

Baer, E. Kristina & Shenholm, Daisy E. Leo Spitzer on Language & Literature: A Descriptive Bibliography. LC 91-9845. vi, 172p. 1991. lib. bdg. 50.00 (*0-87352-195-1*, T124C) Modern Lang.

Baer, Edith. Asi Vamos a la Escuela Un Libro Acerca de Ninos En Diferentes Paises del Mundo. (Mariposa Scholastica en Espanol Ser.). 1993. 10.15 (*0-606-06189-4*, Pub. by Turtleback) Demco.

— A Frost in the Night. 224p. (YA). (gr. 4-7). 1997. pap. 5.95 (*0-374-42482-9*) FS&G.

***Baer, Edith.** A Frost in the Night. (YA). 2000. 19.75 (*0-8446-7137-1*) Peter Smith.

Baer, Edith. Signposts French. 104p. 1983. pap. 13.95 (*0-521-28192-X*) Cambridge U Pr.

— Signposts German. 104p. 1982. pap. 13.95 (*0-521-28186-5*) Cambridge U Pr.

— This Is the Way We Eat Our Lunch: A Book about Children Around the World. LC 94-9753. (Illus.). 40p. (J). (gr. 2-5). 1995. 14.95 (*0-590-46887-1*, Scholastic Hardcover) Scholastic Inc.

— This Is the Way We Go to School. LC 89-48511. (Illus.). 40p. (J). (ps-3). 1992. reprint ed. pap. 4.99 (*0-590-43162-5*, Blue Ribbon Bks) Scholastic Inc.

— This Is the Way We Go to School: A Book about Children Around the World. (Blue Ribbon Bks.). (J). 1990. 10.19 (*0-606-01961-8*, Pub. by Turtleback) Demco.

— This Is the Way We Go to School (Asi Vamos a la Escuala) (ENG & SPA., Illus.). 40p. (J). (ps-3). 1994. pap. 4.99 (*0-590-49443-0*) Scholastic Inc.

— Walk the Dark Streets. LC 97-36572. 279p. (J). (gr. 4-7). 1998. 18.00 (*0-374-38229-8*, Frances Foster) FS&G.

Baer, Edith & Weber, Celia. French for Starters. 160p. 1986. pap. text 16.95 (*0-521-27043-X*) Cambridge U Pr.

Baer, Edith & Wightman, Margaret. Signposts: Spanish. (Illus.). 104p. (C). 1990. pap. 13.95 (*0-521-28193-8*) Cambridge U Pr.

Baer, Edith, et al. French for Starters. 160p. pap. 30.95 incl. audio (*0-521-24883-3*) Cambridge U Pr.

***Baer, Elizabeth, compiled by.** Seventeenth Century Maryland. 219p. 2000. reprint ed. 85.00 (*1-57898-209-X*) Martino Pubng.

Baer, Elizabeth, jt. auth. see Fowler, Laurence H.

Baer, Elizabeth, ed. see Herbermann, Nanda.

Baer, Elizabeth H. The History of the Miami University Libraries. Dubinsky, James, ed. LC 97-215027. (Illus.). 333p. 1997. 25.00 (*0-918761-05-0*); per. 18.00 (*0-918761-06-9*) Miami U Pubns.

Baer, Elizabeth R., ed. Shadows on My Heart: The Civil War Diary of Lucy Rebecca Buck of Virginia. LC 96-766. (Southern Voices from the Past Ser.). 1997. 50.00 (*0-8203-1852-3*) U of Ga Pr.

Baer, Ellen D., et al, eds. Abandonment of the Patient: The Impact of Profit-Driven Health Care on the Public. LC 96-271. 132p. 1996. text 31.95 (*0-8261-9470-2*) Springer Pub.

Baer, Emo. The Transcendental Rose: Childhood in Germany, Growing up with Israel, Meditating in Iowa. Baer Lerman, Naomi & Bright, Martha, eds. LC 40-472452. (Illus.). xvi, 280p. 1998. pap. 20.00 (*0-9670107-0-5*) E E Baer.

Baer, Eric & Moet, Abdelsamie. High Performance Polymers: Structure, Properties, Composites, Fibers. 335p. (C). 1991. 98.50 (*1-56990-002-7*) Hanser-Gardner.

***Baer, Eric, et al.** Laboratory Manual for Physical Geology. 166p. (C). 1999. spiral bd., lab manual ed. 20.95 (*0-7872-6416-4*) Kendall-Hunt.

Baer, Eugen. Medical Semiotics. Deely, John & Williams, Brooke, eds. (Sources in Semiotics Ser.: Vol. VII). (Illus.). 434p. (Orig.). (C). 1988. lib. bdg. 62.50 (*0-8191-6705-3*) U Pr of Amer.

Baer, Eva. Islamic Ornament. LC 97-44816. 288p. 1998. 49.95 (*0-8147-1329-7*) NYU Pr.

Baer, F., et al, eds. Climate in Human Perspective: A Tribute to Helmut A. Landsberg. (Atmospheric Sciences Library). 156p. 1991. lib. bdg. 76.50 (*0-7923-1072-1*) Kluwer Academic.

Baer, Franklin. Creative Quotations from Creative Women for 1997. 58p. 1996. spiral bd. 4.95 (*1-888990-07-4*) Baertracks.

— Creative Quotations from Creative Women for 1998. (Illus.). 58p. 1997. spiral bd. 3.95 (*1-888990-08-2*) Baertracks.

Baer, Franklin C. Creative Quotations from Famous Dramatists & Poets. (Illus.). 102p. 1996. spiral bd. 4.99 (*1-888990-03-1*) Baertracks.

— Creative Quotations from Famous Governmental, Political & Military Leaders. (Illus.). 78p. 1996. spiral bd. 3.99 (*1-888990-05-8*) Baertracks.

— Creative Quotations from Famous Nonfiction Writers. (Illus.). 102p. 1996. spiral bd. 4.99 (*1-888990-04-X*) Baertracks.

— Creative Quotations from Famous Novelists & Short-Story Writers. (Illus.). 102p. 1996. spiral bd. 4.99 (*1-888990-01-5*) Baertracks.

— Creative Quotations from Famous Philosophers, Reformers & Religious Leaders. (Illus.). 78p. 1996. spiral bd. 3.99 (*1-888990-02-3*) Baertracks.

Baer, G. & Heimann, A., eds. Physics & Chemistry of Dykes: Proceedings: International Dyke Conference (3d: 1995: Jerusalem, Israel) (Illus.). 350p. (C). 1995. text 162.00 (*90-5410-551-8*, QE511, Pub. by A A Balkema) Ashgate Pub Co.

Baer, G. Thomas. Self-Paced Phonics: A Text for Education. 2nd ed. LC 97-45705. 122p. (C). 1998. pap. 21.00 (*0-13-956889-1*, Merrill Coll) P-H.

Baer, Gabriel. Fellah & Townsman in the Middle East: Studies in Social History. 350p. 1982. 52.50 (*0-7146-3126-4*, Pub. by F Cass Pubs) Intl Spec Bk.

— Population & Society in the Arab East. Szoke, Hanna, tr. LC 76-16835. (Illus.). 275p. 1976. reprint ed. lib. bdg. 35.00 (*0-8371-8963-2*, BAPSA, Greenwood Pr) Greenwood.

— Studies in the Social History of Modern Egypt. Polk, William R., ed. LC 69-17537. (Publications of the Center for Middle Eastern Studies: No. 4). 1969. lib. bdg. 20.00 (*0-226-03405-4*) U Ch Pr.

Baer, Gene. Thump, Thump, Rat-a-Tat-Tat. LC 88-28469. (Charlotte Zolotow Bk.). (Illus.). 32p. (J). (ps-3). 1991. pap. 5.95 (*0-06-443265-3*, HarpTrophy) HarpC Child Bks.

— Thump, Thump, Rat-a-Tat-Tat. (J). 1991. 10.15 (*0-606-01091-2*, Pub. by Turtleback) Demco.

— Thump, Thump, Rat-a-Tat-Tat: Big Book. LC 88-28469. (Illus.). 32p. (J). (ps-1). 1992. 21.95 (*0-694-00386-7*) HarpC Child Bks.

Baer, George M., ed. The Natural History of Rabies. 2nd ed. 640p. 1991. lib. bdg. 375.00 (*0-8493-6760-3*, QR201) CRC Pr.

Baer, George W. One Hundred Years of Sea Power: The U. S. Navy, 1890-1990. LC 94-2595. xii, 553p. 1994. 65.00 (*0-8047-2273-0*) Stanford U Pr.

— One Hundred Years of Sea Power: The U. S. Navy, 1890-1990. 566p. 1996. pap. 24.95 (*0-8047-2794-5*) Stanford U Pr.

Baer, George W., ed. International Organizations, 1918 to 1945: A Guide to Research & Research Materials. LC 90-34842. (European Diplomatic History Ser.). 212p. 1991. 65.00 (*0-8420-2309-7*) Scholarly Res Inc.

— A Question of Trust: The Origins of U. S.-Soviet Diplomatic Relations; The Memoirs of Loy W. Henderson. (Publication Series: Archival Documentaries: No. 333). 579p. (C). 1987. text 17.98 (*0-8179-8331-7*) Hoover Inst Pr.

Baer, Gerhard, jt. ed. see Langdon, E. Jean.

Baer, Greg. The Truth about Parenting: A Simple & Powerfully Effective Way to Raise Happy & Responsible Children. 1999. spiral bd. 29.95 (*1-892319-03-9*) Blue Rdge GA.

— The Truth about Relationships. unabridged ed. LC 98-92971. x, 310p. 1998. 22.95 (*1-892319-00-4*) Blue Rdge GA.

— The Wart King: The Truth about Love & Lies. LC 97-71674. xiv, 274p. 1997. 22.95 (*0-9653714-0-9*) LA Press.

— Wart King: The Truth about Love & Lies, Vol. I. LC 97-71674. 270p. (YA). (gr. 9-12). 1997. write for info. (*1-892319-02-0*) Blue Rdge GA.

— The Wise Man Vol. I: Telling the Truth & Finding Love. unabridged ed. iv, 259p. (YA). (gr. 9-12). 1997. spiral bd. 29.95 (*1-892319-01-2*) Blue Rdge GA.

Baer, H. A., jt. ed. see Singer, M.

Baer, H. U., jt. ed. see Buchler, M. W.

Baer, Hans, jt. auth. see Singer, Merrill.

Baer, Hans A. The Black Spiritual Movement: A Religious Response to Racism. LC 83-14559. 232p. 1984. pap. 17.00 (*0-87049-515-1*) U of Tenn Pr.

— Crumbling Walls & Tarnished Ideals: An Ethnography of East Germany Before & after Unification. LC 97-49283. 1998. 37.00 (*0-7618-1020-X*) U Pr of Amer.

— Recreating Utopia in the Desert: A Sectarian Challenge to Modern Mormonism. LC 87-10133. 225p. (C). 1988. text 24.50 (*0-88706-681-X*) State U NY Pr.

Baer, Hans A., ed. Encounters with Biomedicine: Case Studies in Medical Anthropology. (Health, Society & Culture Ser.: Vol. 1). xxvi, 350p. 1987. text 158.00 (*2-88124-195-6*) Gordon & Breach.

Baer, Hans A. & Jones, Yvonne, eds. African Americans in the South: Issues of Race, Class, & Gender. LC 91-17728. 192p. 1992. 15.00 (*0-8203-1376-9*) U of Ga Pr.

Baer, Hans A. & Singer, Merrill. African-American Religion in the Twentieth Century: Varieties of Protest & Accommodation. LC 91-40209. 296p. 1992. 34.00 (*0-87049-746-4*); pap. text 17.00 (*0-87049-747-2*) U of Tenn Pr.

Baer, Hans A., et al. Medical Anthropology & the World System: A Critical Perspective. LC 97-16134. 288p. 1997. 72.95 (*0-89789-424-3*, Bergin & Garvey); pap. 24.95 (*0-89789-539-8*, Bergin & Garvey) Greenwood.

Baer, Harold & Broder, Aaron J. How to Prepare & Negotiate Cases for Settlement. rev. ed. LC 72-80204. 240p. 1973. 17.50 (*0-88238-031-1*) Law Arts.

Baer, Harold L. & Williams, Bradley R. Clinical Pharmacology & Nursing. 3rd ed. (Illus.). 1408p. 1995. 54.95 incl. disk (*0-87434-772-6*) Springhouse Corp.

Baer, Hester, ed. & tr. see Herbermann, Nanda.

Baer, James A. Cities of Hope: People, Protests & Progress in Urbanizing Latin America, 1870-1930. Pineo, Ronn, ed. LC 97-45103. 304p. (C). 1998. 79.00 (*0-8133-2443-2*, Pub. by Westview) HarpC.

— Cities of Hope: People, Protests & Progress in Urbanizing Latin America, 1870-1930. Pineo, Ronn, ed. (C). 1999. pap. 25.00 (*0-8133-2444-0*) Westview.

Baer, Jean. How to Be an Assertive (Not Aggressive) Woman in Life, in Love, & on the Job: The Classic Guide to Becoming a Self-Assured Person. 1976. mass mkt. 6.99 (*0-451-16522-5*, Sig) NAL.

Baer, Jean, jt. auth. see Fensterheim, Herbert.

Baer, Jeanne. You Can't Do It All: Effective Delegation for Supervisors. Miller, Karen M., ed. LC 98-74673. (How-To Book Ser.). 111p. 1999. pap. 12.95 (*1-884926-99-1*, EMPW2) Amer Media.

Baer, Joachim T. Vladimir Ivanovicdal As a Belletrist. LC 72-88190. (Slavistic Printings & Reprintings Ser.: No. 276). 204p. 1972. text 46.15 (*90-279-2334-5*) Mouton.

Baer, Joachim T., tr. see Hubscher, Arthur.

Baer, John. Creativity & Divergent Thinking: A Task-Specific Approach. 144p. 1993. text 36.00 (*0-8058-1295-4*) L Erlbaum Assocs.

Baer, John, jt. auth. see Lemaster, A. James.

Baer, John J. Witness for a Generation. LC 97-10810. (Illus.). 144p. (Orig.). 1997. pap. 10.95 (*1-56474-219-9*) Fithian Pr.

Baer, John S., et al. Addictive Behaviors Across the Life Span: Prevention, Treatment, & Policy Issues. (Illus.). 330p. (C). 1993. text 52.00 (*0-8039-5078-0*); pap. text 26.00 (*0-8039-5079-9*) Sage.

Baer, Joshua. Collecting the Navajo Child's Blanket. (Illus.). 60p. (Orig.). 1986. pap. 21.00 (*0-9617085-0-6*) Morning Star Gal.

— The Moki Serape. (Illus.). 1990. write for info. (*0-318-66829-7*) J Baer & Co.

— Twelve Classics. (Illus.). 32p. 1989. 12.95 (*0-685-28861-7*) J Baer & Co.

Baer, Judith A. The Chains of Protection: The Judicial Response to Women's Labor Legislation, 1. LC 77-82695. (Contributions in Women's Studies: No. 1). 238p. 1978. 57.95 (*0-8371-9785-6*, BCP/, Greenwood Pr) Greenwood.

— Equality under the Constitution: Reclaiming the Fourteenth Amendment. LC 83-6220. 304p. 1983. 49.95 (*0-8014-1555-1*) Cornell U Pr.

— Equality under the Constitution: Reclaiming the Fourteenth Amendment. LC 83-6220. 309p. 1983. reprint ed. pap. 95.80 (*0-608-01695-0*, 206235000002) Bks Demand.

— Our Lives Before the Law: Constructing a Feminist Jurisprudence LC 98-55309. 1999. 55.00 (*0-691-03316-1*, Pub. by Princeton U Pr) Cal Prin Full Svc.

***Baer, Judith A.** Our Lives Before the Law: Constructing a Feminist Jurisprudence. LC 98-55309. 272p. 1999. 18.95 (*0-691-01945-2*, Pub. by Princeton U Pr) Cal Prin Full Svc.

Baer, Judith A. Women in American Law Vol. 2: The Struggle Toward Equality from the New Deal to the Present. 2nd rev. ed. LC 96-24654. 380p. (C). 1996. pap. text 19.95 (*0-8419-1366-8*) Holmes & Meier.

Baer, Judy. Broken Promises. (Cedar River Daydreams Ser.: No. 5). 128p. (Orig.). (YA). (gr. 7-10). 1989. mass mkt. 4.99 (*1-55661-087-4*) Bethany Hse.

— Dear Judy, Did You Ever Like a Boy Who Didn't Like You? 192p. (YA). (gr. 7-10). 1993. pap. 7.99 (*1-55661-341-5*) Bethany Hse.

— Dear Judy, What's It Like at Your House? 16p. (Orig.). (J). (gr. 7-10). 1992. pap. 7.99 (*1-55661-291-5*) Bethany Hse.

Baer, Judy. The Discovery. LC 92-75598. (Cedar River Daydreams Ser.: No. 20). 128p. (Orig.). (YA). (gr. 7-10). 1993. mass mkt. 4.99 (*1-55661-330-X*) Bethany Hse.

Baer, Judy. Double Danger. (Live From Brentwood High Ser.: Bk. 3). 144p. (YA). (gr. 7-10). 1994. mass mkt. 4.99 (*1-55661-388-1*) Bethany Hse.

— Faded Dreams. (Live from Brentwood High Ser.: No. 6). 16p. (YA). (gr. 7-10). 1996. mass mkt. 4.99 (*1-55661-391-1*) Bethany Hse.

— Fill My Empty Heart. (Cedar River Daydreams Ser.: No. 8). 128p. (Orig.). (J). (gr. 7-10). 1990. mass mkt. 4.99 (*1-55661-128-5*) Bethany Hse.

— Forever Friends. (Cedar River Daydreams Ser.: No. 28). 144p. (YA). (gr. 7-10). 1999. mass mkt. 4.99 (*1-55661-838-7*) Bethany Hse.

— Heartless Hero. LC 96-45908. (Cedar River Daydreams Ser.: No. 25). 144p. (YA). (gr. 7-10). 1997. mass mkt. 4.99 (*1-55661-835-2*) Bethany Hse.

— The Intruder. (Cedar River Daydreams Ser.: No. 6). 16p. (Orig.). (J). (gr. 7-12). 1989. mass mkt. 4.99 (*1-55661-088-2*) Bethany Hse.

— Jennifer's Secret. LC 88-63463. (Cedar River Daydreams Ser.: No. 3). 128p. (Orig.). (YA). (gr. 7-10). 1989. mass mkt. 4.99 (*1-55661-058-0*) Bethany Hse.

***Baer, Judy.** Jenny's Story. 2000. pap. 9.99 (*0-8423-1922-0*) Tyndale Hse.

Baer, Judy. Journey to Nowhere. LC 88-63462. (Cedar River Daydreams Ser.: No. 4). 128p. (Orig.). (YA). (gr. 7-10). 1989. mass mkt. 4.99 (*1-55661-067-X*) Bethany Hse.

— Lonely Girl. (Cedar River Daydreams Ser.: No. 17). 16p. (Orig.). (J). (gr. 7-10). 1992. mass mkt. 4.99 (*1-55661-280-X*) Bethany Hse.

— Lost & Found. (Cedar River Daydreams Ser.: No. 15). 144p. (Orig.). (J). (gr. 7-10). 1992. mass mkt. 4.99 (*1-55661-243-5*) Bethany Hse.

An Asterisk (*) at the beginning of an entry indicates that the title is appearing for the first time.

— Love's Perfect Image, No. 9. (Serenade Serenata Ser.). 1984. pap. 1.49 (*0-310-46522-2*, 15512P) Zondervan.

— Moonglow. 224p. (Orig.). 1986. pap. 5.70 (*0-310-47681-X*) Zondervan.

— More Than Friends. (Cedar River Daydreams Ser.: No. 18). 128p. (J). (gr. 7-10). 1992. mass mkt. 4.99 (*1-55661-298-2*) Bethany Hse.

— Never Look Back. LC 97-33842. (Cedar River Daydreams Ser.: No. 27). 144p. (YA). (gr. 7-10). 1997. mass mkt. 4.99 (*1-55661-837-9*) Bethany Hse.

— Never Too Late. (Cedar River Daydreams Ser.: No. 19). 128p. (Orig.). (YA). (gr. 7-10). 1993. mass mkt. 4.99 (*1-55661-329-6*) Bethany Hse.

— New Girl in Town. LC 88-71504. (Cedar River Daydreams Ser.: No. 1). 144p. (Orig.). (YA). (gr. 7-10). 1988. mass mkt. 4.99 (*1-55661-022-X*) Bethany Hse.

***Baer, Judy.** No Me Digas Mentiras. (SPA.). (J). (gr. 4-7). 1999. mass mkt. 3.99 (*0-7899-0644-9*) Spanish Hse Distributors.

Baer, Judy. No Turning Back. (Cedar River Daydreams Ser.: No. 13). 144p. (Orig.). (YA). (gr. 7-10). 1991. mass mkt. 4.99 (*1-55661-216-8*) Bethany Hse.

— Paige. (Springsong Bks.). 16p. (YA). (gr. 7-10). 1995. mass mkt. 4.99 (*1-55661-585-X*) Bethany Hse.

— Pamela. (Springsong Ser.). 176p. (YA). (gr. 7-10). 1996. mass mkt. 4.99 (*1-55661-749-6*) Bethany Hse.

— Price of Silence. LC 93-74538. (Live from Brentwood High Ser.: No. 2). 16p. (YA). (gr. 7-10). 1994. mass mkt. 4.99 (*1-55661-387-3*) Bethany Hse.

— Risky Assignment. LC 93-74537. (Live from Brentwood High Ser.: No. 1). 16p. (YA). (gr. 7-10). 1994. mass mkt. 4.99 (*1-55661-386-5*) Bethany Hse.

— Sarah's Dilemma. (Live From Brentwood High Ser.: No. 4). 144p. (J). 1995. mass mkt. 4.99 (*1-55661-389-X*) Bethany Hse.

— Second Chance. (Cedar River Daydreams Ser.: No.14). 144p. (Orig.). (YA). (gr. 7-10). 1991. mass mkt. 4.99 (*1-55661-217-6*) Bethany Hse.

— Shadows along the Ice, No. 28. (Serenade Serenata Ser.). 1985. pap. 2.50 (*0-310-46962-7*, 15553P) Zondervan.

— Silent Tears No More. LC 89-82689. (Cedar River Daydreams Ser.: No. 7). 144p. (Orig.). (YA). (gr. 7-10). 1990. mass mkt. 4.99 (*1-55661-119-6*) Bethany Hse.

— Silent Thief. (Cedar River Daydreams Ser.: No. 23). 16p. (YA). (gr. 7-10). 1995. mass mkt. 4.99 (*1-55661-588-4*) Bethany Hse.

— Something Old, Something New. (Cedar River Daydreams Ser.: No. 11). 144p. (Orig.). (YA). (gr. 7-10). 1991. mass mkt. 4.99 (*1-55661-183-8*) Bethany Hse.

— A Special Kind of Love. (Cedar River Daydreams Ser.: No. 21). 128p. (YA). (gr. 7-10). 1993. mass mkt. 4.99 (*1-55661-367-9*) Bethany Hse.

— The Suspect. (Cedar River Daydreams Ser.: No. 24). 144p. (J). (gr. 7-10). 1996. mass mkt. 4.99 (*1-55661-834-4*) Bethany Hse.

— Tender Adversary. (Serenade Serenata Ser.: No. 18). 192p. (Orig.). 1985. pap. 2.50 (*0-310-46772-1*, 15536P) Zondervan.

— Three's a Crowd. (Cedar River Daydreams Ser.: No. 22). 144p. (YA). (gr. 7-10). 1994. mass mkt. 4.99 (*1-55661-526-4*) Bethany Hse.

— Tomorrow's Promise. (Cedar River Daydreams Ser.: No. 10). 128p. (Orig.). (YA). (gr. 7-10). 1990. mass mkt. 4.99 (*1-55661-143-9*) Bethany Hse.

— Trouble with a Capital "T" LC 88-71503. (Cedar River Daydreams Ser.: No. 2). 144p. (Orig.). (YA). (gr. 7-10). 1988. mass mkt. 4.99 (*1-55661-021-1*) Bethany Hse.

— Undercover Artists. (Live from Brentwood High Ser.: Vol. 5). 144p. (J). (gr. 7-10). 1996. mass mkt. 4.99 (*1-55661-390-3*) Bethany Hse.

— Unheard Voices. (Cedar River Daydreams Ser.: No. 16). 144p. (Orig.). (J). (gr. 7-10). 1992. mass mkt. 4.99 (*1-55661-257-5*) Bethany Hse.

Baer, Judy. Vanishing Star. LC 90-56209. (Cedar River Daydreams Ser.: No. 12). 16p. (Orig.). (YA). (gr. 7-10). 1991. mass mkt. 4.99 (*1-55661-197-8*) Bethany Hse.

Baer, Judy. Worlds Apart. LC 97-33841. (Cedar River Daydreams Ser.: No. 26). 144p. (YA). (gr. 7-10). 1997. mass mkt. 4.99 (*1-55661-836-0*) Bethany Hse.

Baer, Judy, et al. Reunited. LC 98-21890. 300p. 1998. pap. 9.99 (*0-8423-0868-7*) Tyndale Hse.

***Baer, Kenneth S.** Reinventing Democrats: The Politics of Liberalism from Reagan to Clinton. LC 99-43434. (Illus.). 376p. 2000. text 29.95 (*0-7006-1009-X*) U Pr of KS.

Baer, Larry L. The Parker Gun. 35.00 (*0-88227-047-8*) Gun Room.

Baer, Lee. Getting Control: Overcoming Your Obsessions & Compulsions. 256p. 1992. pap. 12.95 (*0-452-26889-3*, Plume) Dutton Plume.

***Baer, Lee.** Getting Control: Overcoming Your Obsessions & Compulsions. rev. ed. 2000. pap. 13.95 (*0-452-28177-6*, Plume) Dutton Plume.

— Imp of the Mind: Exploring the Silent Epidemic of Obsessive Bad Thoughts. 240p. 2001. 23.95 (*0-525-94562-8*, Dutt) Dutton Plume.

Baer, Lee & Ahern, David K. StatChoice: The Statistical Consulting Program. 50p. 1988. student ed., ring bd. 189.00 incl. disk (*0-88416-590-6*); student ed., ring bd. 189.00 incl. disk (*0-88416-589-2*) Mosby Inc.

Baer Lerman, Naomi, ed. see Baer, Emo.

Baer, Lois B., jt. ed. see Sheinin, David.

Baer, M. Delal, et al, eds. NAFTA & Sovereignty: Trade-Offs for Canada, Mexico, & the United States. (Significant Issues Ser.). 176p. (C). 1997. pap. text 20.00 (*0-89206-322-X*) CSIS.

Baer, M. Delal & Weintraub, Sidney, eds. The NAFTA Debate: Grappling with Unconventional Trade Issues. LC 93-38663. 211p. 1994. lib. bdg. 49.95 (*1-55587-464-9*) L Rienner.

Baer, Marjorie, ed. see Cohen, Sandee.

Baer, Martha. As Francesca. 288p. 1998. pap. 13.00 (*0-7679-0127-4*) Broadway BDD.

Baer, Mervin J., jt. auth. see Mantle, Gregory.

Baer, Michael, ed. Theory of Chemical Reaction Dynamics, Vol. 1. 248p. 1985. 140.00 (*0-8493-6114-1*, CRC Reprint) Franklin.

— Theory of Chemical Reaction Dynamics, Vol. IV. 264p. 1985. 216.00 (*0-8493-6117-6*) CRC Pr.

— Theory of Chemical Reaction Dynamics, Vols. II, III, & IV. 1985. 719.80 (*0-8493-6113-3*, QD501) CRC Pr.

Baer, Michael & Ng, Cheuk-Yiu, eds. State-Selected & State-to-State Ion-Molecule Reaction Dynamics: Theoretical Aspects, Vol. 82, Pt. 2, Theory. (Advances in Chemical Physics Ser.: Vol. 82, Pt. 2). 576p. 1992. 249.00 (*0-471-53263-0*) Wiley.

Baer, Michael, jt. ed. see Ng, Cheuk-Yiu.

Baer, Nancy & Dino, Steven. Choosing a Dog: Your Guide to Picking the Perfect Breed. (Illus.). 256p. (Orig.). 1995. pap. 14.00 (*0-425-14958-7*) Berkley Pub.

Baer, Nancy & Duno, Steve. Leader of the Pack: How to Take Control of Your Relationship with Your Dog. LC 96-19490. 160p. 1996. mass mkt. 9.99 (*0-06-101019-7*, Harp PBks) HarpC.

Baer, Nancy V. Paris Modern: The Swedish Ballet, 1920-1925. LC 95-61830. (Illus.). 168p. 1996. pap. 24.95 (*0-88401-081-3*) Fine Arts Mus.

Baer, Norbert S., intro. Training in Conservation: A Symposium on the Occasion of the Dedication of the Stephen Chan House. (Illus.). iv, 92p. (Orig.). (C). 1989. pap. text. write for info. (*0-9623175-0-0*) NYU Inst Fine.

Baer, Norbert S. & Snethlage, Rolf. Saving Our Architectural Heritage: The Conservation of Historic Stone Structures. LC 96-49091. (Dahlem Workshop Reports - Life Sciences). 448p. 1997. 160.00 (*0-471-96526-X*) Wiley.

Baer, Randall. Inside the New Age Nightmare. LC 80-83851. 204p. 1989. pap. 12.99 (*0-910311-58-7*, Pub. by Huntington Hse) BookWorld.

— Inside the New Age Nightmare. LC 91-78413. (Salt Ser.). 48p. 1992. pap. 3.49 (*1-56384-022-7*) Huntington Hse.

Baer, Richard. Mixed Emotions. LC 95-230940. 1994. pap. 5.25 (*0-8222-1395-8*) Dramatists Play.

Baer, Roberta D. Cooking & Coping among the Cacti: Diet, Nutrition & Available Income in Northwestern Mexico. (Food & Nutrition in History & Anthropology Ser.). 130p. 1998. text 33.00 (*90-5699-575-8*); pap. text 16.00 (*90-5699-576-6*) Gordon & Breach.

Baer, Rodney L., et al. The Beauty of Perfume No. VI: Monsen & Baer Perfume Bottle Auction. (Illus.). 112p. 1996. 35.00 (*0-9636102-4-4*) Monsen & Baer.

Baer, Rodney L., ed. see Monsen, Randall B. & Lefkowith, Christie M.

Baer, Ronni. So Many Brilliant Talents: Art & Craft in the Age of Rubens. (Illus.). 216p. 1999. pap. 29.95 (*1-928917-00-3*) M C Carlos Mus.

***Baer, Shirley S. & Gearin, M. Jeanne, eds.** Decorative Arts - 18th & 19th Century: Research & Writings of Shirley Spaulding DeVoe. (Illus.). 182p. 1999. 20.00 (*1-928855-00-8*) HSEAD.

Baer, Steve. Dome Cookbook. 4th ed. (Illus.). iv, 48p. 1996. reprint ed. pap. 12.00 (*0-9655388-0-X*) Trial & Error.

— Sunspots. LC 75-20779. 1977. pap. 6.95 (*0-686-21779-9*) Zomeworks Corp.

Baer, Ted. Communicating with Your Dog: A Humane Approach to Dog Training. (Illus.). 1989. pap. 10.95 (*0-8120-4203-4*) Barron.

— Communicating with Your Dog: A Humane Approach to Dog Training. 2nd enl. ed. LC 98-43583. (Illus.). 176p. 1999. pap. 10.95 (*0-7641-0758-5*) Barron.

— How to Teach Your Old Dog New Tricks. 144p. 1991. pap. 9.95 (*0-8120-4544-0*) Barron.

Baer, Tom. Roller Rink. 24p. (Orig.). 1994. pap. 3.00 (*1-57141-001-5*) Runaway Spoon.

***Baer, Tom.** Visual Quickstart Guide. 304p. 2000. pap. 19.99 (*0-201-70365-3*) Addison-Wesley.

Baer, Tomas, et al, eds. Large Ions: Their Vaporization, Detection & Structural Analysis. LC 96-6758. (Series in Ion Chemistry & Physics). 198p. 1997. 195.00 (*0-471-96239-2*) Wiley.

Baer, Tomas & Hase, William. Unimolecular Reaction Dynamics: Theory & Experiments, (International Series of Monographs on Chemistry: Vol. 31). (Illus.). 448p. (C). 1996. text 85.00 (*0-19-507494-7*) OUP.

***Baer, Ulrich.** Remnants of Song: Trauma & the Experience of Modernity in Charles Baudelaire & Paul Celan. 2000. 55.00 (*0-8047-3826-2*); pap. 24.95 (*0-8047-3927-7*) Stanford U Pr.

Baer, Walter S. & Farnsworth, Gwendolyn. Computer Donations to Schools: A Review of Selected Private-Sector, Nonprofit & State Programs. (Documented Briefing Ser.). 34p. 1997. pap. 6.00 (*0-8330-2540-6*, DB-222-OSTP) Rand Corp.

***Baer, Walter S., et al.** Facing Deregulation: Alternative Governance Structures for the Los Angeles Department of Water & Power (DWP) xvii, 60p. 2000. pap. 12.00 (*0-8330-2841-3*, MR-1189-LADWP) Rand Corp.

Baer, Werner. The Brazilian Economy: Growth & Development. 4th ed. LC 94-15878. 440p. 1995. 79.50 (*0-275-94509-X*, Praeger Pubs); pap. 22.95 (*0-275-94510-3*, Praeger Pubs) Greenwood.

— Industrialization & Economic Development in Brazil. LC 65-22410. (Publication of the Economic Growth Center, Yale University Ser.). 329p. reprint ed. pap. 102.00 (*0-8357-8727-3*, 203366400087) Bks Demand.

Baer, Werner, et al, eds. Brazil & the Ivory Coast: The Impact of International Lending, Investment & Aid. LC 87-3667. (Contemporary Studies in Economic & Financial Analysis: Vol. 58). 225p. 1987. 78.50 (*0-89232-819-3*) Jai Pr.

Baer, Werner & Birch, Melissa H., eds. Privatization in Latin America: New Roles for the Public & Private Sectors. LC 93-45487. 232p. 1994. 55.00 (*0-275-94664-9*, Praeger Pubs) Greenwood.

Baer, Werner & Coes, Donald V., eds. United States Policies & the Latin American Economies. LC 90-31182. 208p. 1990. 57.95 (*0-275-93502-7*, C3502, Praeger Pubs) Greenwood.

***Baer, Werner & Love, Joseph LeRoy.** Liberalization & Its Consequences: A Comparative Perspective on Latin America & Eastern Europe. LC 00-37622. 2001. write for info. (*1-84064-436-2*) E Elgar.

Baer, Werner & Samuelson, Larry A. Latin America in the Post-Import Substitution Era. 1977. pap. 25.00 (*0-08-021822-9*, Pergamon Pr) Elsevier.

Baer, Werner & Tulchin, Joseph S., eds. Brazil & the Challenge of Economic Reform. LC 93-30786. (Special Studies). 160p. (C). 1993. pap. text 13.95 (*0-943875-53-6*) W Wilson Ctr Pr.

Baer, Will Christopher. Kiss Me, Judas. LC 98-22883. 256p. 1998. 21.95 (*0-670-88175-9*) Viking Penguin.

***Baer, Will Christopher.** Kiss Me, Judas. 320p. 2000. pap. 12.95 (*0-14-028901-1*, Penguin Bks) Viking Penguin.

— Penny Dreadful. LC 99-39592. 224p. 2000. 22.95 (*0-670-88920-2*) Viking Penguin.

Baer, William. The Unfortunates. LC 97-11544. 65p. 1997. 22.00 (*0-943549-46-9*); pap. 15.00 (*0-943549-47-7*) Truman St Univ.

***Baer, William, ed.** Elia Kazan: Interviews. 268p. 2000. text 45.00 (*1-57806-223-3*) U Pr of Miss.

Baer, William, jt. auth. see Banerjee, Tridib.

Baer, William, ed. see Kazan, Elia.

Baer, William, ed. see Walcott, Derek.

Baer, William K., ed. see Society for Applied Spectroscopy Staff, et al.

Baer, Willis N. Baer. Genealogy of Henry Baer of Leacock, Pa. (Baer-Bear-Bare) (Illus.). 290p. 1997. reprint ed. pap. 45.00 (*0-8328-7321-7*); reprint ed. lib. bdg. 55.00 (*0-8328-7320-9*) Higginson Bk Co.

Baer, Yitzhak. A History of the Jews in Christian Spain, 2 vols., Set. Schoffman, Louis, tr. LC 61-16852. 1993. reprint ed. pap. text 38.95 (*0-8276-0431-9*) JPS Phila.

— A History of the Jews in Christian Spain, 2 vols., Vol. I. Schoffman, Louis, tr. LC 61-16852. 470p. 1993. reprint ed. pap. text 19.95 (*0-8276-0425-4*) JPS Phila.

— A History of the Jews in Christian Spain, 2 vols., Vol. II. Schoffman, Louis, tr. LC 61-16852. 520p. 1993. reprint ed. pap. text 19.95 (*0-8276-0426-2*) JPS Phila.

Baer, Yitzhak F. Galut. (Brown Classics in Judaica Ser.). 132p. (C). 1988. reprint ed. pap. text 17.00 (*0-8191-5783-X*) U Pr of Amer.

Baerends, G. P., jt. auth. see Baerends-Van Roon, J. M.

Baerends-Van Roon, J. M. & Baerends, G. P. The Morphogenesis of the Behaviour of the Domestic Cat. (Verhandelingen der Koninklijke Nederlandse Akademie van Wetenschappen, Afd. Natuurkunde Ser.: No. 72). 116p. 1979. pap. text 43.75 (*0-7204-8480-4*) Elsevier.

Baerentzen, Lars, et al, eds. Studies in the History of the Greek Civil War, 1945-1949. (Modern Greek & Balkin Studies: Suppl. Vol. 2). 324p. (Orig.). 1987. pap. 99.50 (*87-7289-004-5*) Coronet Bks.

Baerentzen, Per, ed. see Danielsen, Niels & Maher, Peter J.

Baerg, Harry. Bible Plants & Animals, 3 vols. 1989. 29.99 (*0-8280-0560-5*) Review & Herald.

— Bible Plants & Animals, 3. 1998. 29.99 (*0-8280-1380-2*) Review & Herald.

— Bible Plants & Animals, 3 vols., Vol. 1. 144p. 1989. 11.99 (*0-8280-0498-6*) Review & Herald.

— Bible Plants & Animals, 3 vols., Vol. 2. 138p. 1989. 11.99 (*0-8280-0499-4*) Review & Herald.

— Bible Plants & Animals, 3 vols., Vol. 3. 138p. 1989. 11.99 (*0-8280-0500-1*) Review & Herald.

Baerg, Harry J. Common American Birds. (Illus.). 64p. (C). 1994. pap. 8.95 (*0-87961-235-5*) Naturegraph.

Baerga, Maria Del Carmen, see Del Carmen Baerga, Maria.

Baergen. Contemporary Epistemology. LC 94-240058. (C). 1994. pap. text 37.00 (*0-15-501372-6*, Pub. by Harcourt Coll Pubs) Harcourt.

— Ethics at the End of Life. (Philosophy Ser.). 2000. pap. 29.00 (*0-534-55845-3*) Wadsworth Pub.

Baergen, Rudy. The Mennonite Story. 62p. 1981. reprint ed. pap. 4.95 (*0-87303-066-4*) Faith & Life.

Baeriswyl, D., et al, eds. Applications of Statistical & Field Theory Methods to Condensed Matter. LC 90-7153. (NATO ASI Ser.: Vol. 218). (Illus.). 418p. (C). 1990. text 155.00 (*0-306-43526-8*, Kluwer Plenum) Kluwer Academic.

— Physics in Living Matter. (Lecture Notes in Physics Ser.: Vol. 284). v, 180p. 1987. 34.95 (*0-387-18192-X*) Spr-Verlag.

Baeriswyl, D. & Bishop, A. R. Solitons & Polarons in Solid State Physics. 300p. (C). 1999. text 79.00 (*9971-5-0407-3*); pap. text 45.00 (*9971-5-0408-1*) World Scientific Pub.

Baeriswyl, D. & Campbell, David K. Interacting Electrons in Reduced Dimensions. (NATO ASI Ser.: Vol. 213). (Illus.). 414p. (C). 1989. text 156.00 (*0-306-43415-6*, Kluwer Plenum) Kluwer Academic.

Baeriswyl, D., et al. The Hubbard Model: Its Physics & Mathematical Physics, No. 343. LC 95-16420. (NATO ASI Series B: Vol. 344). (Illus.). 420p. (C). 1995. text 130.00 (*0-306-45003-8*) Plenum.

Baerlein, Henry. Diwan of Abu'l-Ala (1915) 70p. 1998. reprint ed. pap. 8.95 (*0-7661-0607-1*) Kessinger Pub.

— March of the Seventy Thousand. LC 72-115506. (Russia Observed Ser.). (Illus.). 1971. reprint ed. 23.95 (*0-405-03076-2*) Ayer.

Baerman, Noah. Beginning Jazz Keyboard. (National Guitar Workshop Arts Ser.). 1998. pap. 20.90 incl. audio compact disk (*0-88284-910-7*, 17855) Alfred Pub.

— Intermediate Jazz Keyboard. (National Guitar Workshop Arts Ser.). 1998. pap. 20.90 incl. audio compact disk (*0-88284-912-3*, 17858) Alfred Pub.

***Baerman, Noah.** Mastering Jazz Keyboard. (National Guitar Workshop Arts Ser.). 1998. pap. 20.90 incl. audio compact disk (*0-88284-914-X*, 17861) Alfred Pub.

Baerman, Colin. Thought, Vol. 36. 100p. (Orig.). 1994. pap. write for info. (*1-880764-01-6*) Northwind NJ.

Baermann, Carl. Complete Method for Clarinet: First & Second Division. Langenus, Gustave, ed. (Illus.). 92p. 1918. pap. 10.95 (*0-8258-0170-2*, 0-32) Fischer Inc NY.

— Complete Method for Clarinet: Third Division. (Illus.). 55p. 1917. pap. 11.95 (*0-8258-0215-6*, 0-33) Fischer Inc NY.

Baermann, Michael. Herr Goeli: Neidhart-Rezeption in Basel. (Quellen und Forschungen zur Literatur und Kulturgeschichte: Bd. 4(238)). (GER.). x, 343p. (C). 1995. lib. bdg. 133.85 (*3-11-014670-3*) De Gruyter.

Baernstein, A., II & Sawyer, E. T. Embedding & Multiplier Theorems for Hp(Rn) LC 84-24294. (Memoirs of the AMS Ser.: No. 53/318). 82p. 1990. reprint ed. pap. 18.00 (*0-8218-2318-3*, MEMO/53/318) Am Math.

Baerresen, Donald W., et al. Latin American Trade Patterns. LC 80-479. (Illus.). 329p. 1980. reprint ed. lib. bdg. 79.50 (*0-313-22288-6*, BALT, Greenwood Pr) Greenwood.

Baers, David, et al. WISC 2 - The History of Wisconsin Through Integrated Student Creations. 96p. (J). (gr. 3-10). 1996. pap. text 29.95 incl. audio (*1-886790-02-7*) WISC Publ.

Baert & Theunisse, Luc. Digital Audio & Compact Disc Technology. 1988. 55.00 (*0-434-91868-7*) CRC Pr.

Baert, A. Biomedical & Health Research at European Level: The EU Biomed 1 Program. LC 94-77313. (Biomedical & Health Research Ser.: Vol. 9). 1000p. (gr. 12). 1995. 130.00 (*90-5199-173-8*) IOS Press.

Baert, A. E. & Razquin, M. C. AIDS Research at E. C. Level: Results of the 4th E. C. Biomedical & Health Research Program. LC 94-75420. (Biomedical & Health Research Ser.). 400p. (gr. 12). 1995. 99.00 (*90-5199-159-2*) IOS Press.

Baert, A. L., et al, eds. Emergency Pediatric Radiology. LC 98-40967. (Medical Radiology Ser.). (Illus.). 450p. 1999. 249.00 (*3-540-63882-2*) Spr-Verlag.

— Frontiers in European Radiology, Vol. 6. (Illus.). 110p. 1989. 94.95 (*0-387-50466-4*) Spr-Verlag.

— Functional MRI. LC 98-45190. (Illus.). 450p. 1999. 225.00 (*3-540-64263-3*) Spr-Verlag.

— Radiology of the Pancreas. 2nd rev. ed. LC 98-50337. (Illus.). 320p. 1999. 249.00 (*3-540-63479-7*) Spr-Verlag.

Baert, A. L. & Delorme, G., eds. Radiology of the Pancreas. LC 94-6222. (Medical Radiology, Diagnostic Imaging & Radiation Oncology Ser.). (Illus.). 296p. 1994. 249.00 (*0-387-56514-0*) Spr-Verlag.

Baert, A. L. & Heuck, F. H., eds. Frontiers in European Radiology, Book 9. (Illus.). 250p. 1993. 137.00 (*0-387-55280-4*) Spr-Verlag.

— Frontiers in European Radiology, Vol. 8. (Illus.). 144p. 1991. 118.00 (*0-387-53189-0*) Spr-Verlag.

Baert, A. L., et al. Modern Head & Neck Imaging. Mukherji, S. K. et al, eds. LC 98-17985. (Medical Radiology Ser.). (Illus.). 300p. 1999. 189.00 (*3-540-62549-6*) Spr-Verlag.

Baert, A. L., ed. see Schnyder, P. & Wintermark, M.

Baert, A. L., ed. see Van Gils, A. P., et al.

Baert, L., jt. ed. see Petrovich, Z.

Baert, Luc, et al, eds. Digital Audio & Compact Disc Technology. 3rd ed. LC 94-36853. 320p. 1995. pap. text 57.95 (*0-240-51397-5*, Focal) Buttrwrth-Heinemann.

Baert, Mary L., tr. see Harper, Steve.

Baert, Patrick. Social Theory in the Twentieth Century. LC 98-18650. 1998. text 55.00 (*0-8147-1340-8*); pap. text 17.50 (*0-8147-1339-4*) NYU Pr.

— Time in Contemporary Intellectual Thought LC 99-23944. (Azimuth Ser.). 1999. write for info. (*0-444-82903-2*) Elsevier.

— Time, Self & Social Being: Temporality Within a Sociological Context. (Avebury Series in Philosophy). 172p. 1992. 77.95 (*1-85628-286-4*, Pub. by Avebry) Ashgate Pub Co.

Baerthlein, Karl. Transzendentalienlehre der alten Ontologie Pt. 1: Transzendentalienlehre im Corpus Aristotelicum. 415p. (C). 1972. 108.50 (*3-11-004021-2*) De Gruyter.

Baertschi, Hans-Peter. Industrialisierung, Eisenbahnschlachten und Staedtebau in Zuerich, Aussersihl. (Geschichte und Theorie der Architektur Ser.: Vol. 25). 528p. 1980. 85.00 (*0-8176-1312-9*) Birkhauser.

Baerwald, Hans H. Party Politics in Japan. 160p. (C). 1986. text 49.95 (*0-04-320183-0*); pap. text 16.95 (*0-04-320184-9*) Routledge.

— The Purge of Japanese Leaders under the Occupation, Vol. 8--8. LC 77-22428. (University of California Publications in Social Welfare: No. 8). 111p. 1977. reprint ed. lib. bdg. 35.00 (*0-8371-9088-6*, BAPJ, Greenwood Pr) Greenwood.

***Baerwaldt, Wayne, et al.** Beck & Al Hansen: Playing with Matches. (Illus.). 144p. 1998. pap. 24.95 (*0-921381-13-1*, Pub. by Plug In Editions) RAM Publications.

Baes, Charles F., Jr. & Mesmer, Robert E. The Hydrolysis of Cations. LC 85-18094. 512p. 1986. reprint ed. lib. bdg. 74.50 (*0-89874-892-5*) Krieger.

Baese, Geary L. Classic Italian Violin Varnish. limited ed. (Illus.). 99p. 1985. 180.00 (*0-9615510-0-3*) Geary L Baese.

Baeseler, Frank & Bovill, Bruce. Scanning & Image Processing for the PC. LC 93-31120. 1993. write for info. (*0-07-707819-5*) McGraw.

B

Baessler, Manfred, ed. Flora de la Republica de Cuba: Mimosaceae. (Plantas Vasculares Ser.: Serie A, Fasciculo 2). (SPA., Illus.). 206p. Date not set. pap. text 60.00 (*3-87429-408-0*, Pub. by Koeltz Sci Bks) Lubrecht & Cramer.

Baeten, Angela M. Documenting Physical Therapy: The Reviewer Perspective. LC 99-23379. 249p. 1999. pap. text 45.00 (*0-7506-9950-7*) Buttrwrth-Heinemann.

Baeten, Elizabeth M. The Magic Mirror: Myth's Abiding Power. LC 96-27863. (SUNY Series in the Philosophy of the Social Sciences). 245p. (C). 1996. text 65.50 (*0-7914-3091-X*); pap. text 21.95 (*0-7914-3092-8*) State U NY Pr.

Baeten, G. & Ziolkowski, Anton. The Vibroseis Source. (Advances in Exploration Geophysics Ser.: No. 3). 300p. 1990. 147.00 (*0-444-88879-9*) Elsevier.

Baeten, J. C., ed. Applications of Process Algebra. (Cambridge Tracts in Theoretical Computer Science Ser.: No. 16). (Illus.). 326p. (C). 1990. text 54.95 (*0-521-40028-7*) Cambridge U Pr.

Baeten, J. C., et al, eds. Concur '90: Theories of Concurrency: Unification & Extension, Amsterdam, the Netherlands, August 27-30, 1990 Proceedings. (Lecture Notes in Computer Science Ser.: Vol. 458). vii, 537p. 1990. 50.95 (*0-387-53048-7*) Spr-Verlag.

— CONCUR '91: 2nd International Conference on Concurrency Theory Amsterdam, The Netherlands, August 26-29, 1991 Proceedings. (Lecture Notes in Computer Science Ser.: Vol. 527). viii, 541p. 1991. 53.95 (*0-387-54430-5*) Spr-Verlag.

Baeten, J. C. & Weijland, W. P. Process Algebra. (Cambridge Tracts in Theoretical Computer Science Ser.: No. 17). (Illus.). 256p. (C). 1990. text 44.95 (*0-521-40043-0*) Cambridge U Pr.

***Baeten, J. C. M., et al, eds.** CONCUR'99: Concurrency Theory: 10th International Conference, Eindhoven, The Netherlands, August 24-27, 1999, Proceedings. (Lecture Notes in Computer Science Ser.: Vol. 1664). xi, 573p. 1999. pap. 85.00 (*3-540-66425-4*) Spr-Verlag.

Baeten, Lieve. Is Tom Ready for Bed? LC 96-86491. (Tom & Maggie Ser.). (Illus.). 8p. 1997. 3.95 (*0-7641-5023-5*) Barron.

— Nicky at the Magic House. (Illus.). 32p. (J). (ps-2). 1993. pap. 6.95 (*1-55037-271-8*, Pub. by Annick); lib. bdg. 14.95 (*1-55037-273-4*, Pub. by Annick) Firefly Bks Ltd.

— Nicky's Birthday. (Illus.). 32p. (J). (ps-2). 1993. pap. 9.95 (*1-55037-464-8*, Pub. by Annick); text 16.95 (*1-55037-465-6*, Pub. by Annick) Firefly Bks Ltd.

— What Is Maggie Eating? LC 96-86496. (Tom & Maggie Ser.). (Illus.). 8p. (J). 1997. 3.95 (*0-7641-5021-9*) Barron.

— What Is Maggie Wearing? LC 96-86497. (Tom & Maggie Ser.). (Illus.). 8p. 1997. 3.95 (*0-7641-5022-7*) Barron.

— Where Is Tom? LC 96-86499. (Tom & Maggie Ser.). (Illus.). 8p. 1998. 3.95 (*0-7641-5024-3*) Barron.

Baethmann, A., et al, eds. Current Progress in the Understanding of Secondary Brain Damage from Trauma & Ischemia. LC 99-23445. (Acta Neurochirurgica Ser.: Suppl. 73). 200p. 1999. 50.00 (*3-211-83313-7*) Spr-Verlag.

— Mechanisms of Secondary Brain Damage. LC 86-22671. (NATO ASI Series A, Life Sciences: Vol. 115). 416p. 1986. 95.00 (*0-306-42397-9*, Plenum Trade) Perseus Pubng.

— Mechanisms of Secondary Brain Damage: Current State. LC 92-49078. (Acta Neurochirugica - Supplementum Ser.: No. 57). 1993. write for info. (*3-211-82421-9*); 140.00 (*0-387-82421-9*) Spr-Verlag.

— Mechanisms of Secondary Brain Damage in Cerebral Ischemia & Trauma, Vol. 66. LC 96-3928. (Acta Neurochirugica - Supplementum Ser.: No. 66). (Illus.). 150p. 1996. suppl. ed. 139.50 (*3-211-82817-6*) Spr-Verlag.

Baetjer, Anna M. Women in Industry: Their Health & Efficiency. Stein, Leon, ed. LC 77-70480. (Work Ser.). (Illus.). 1977. reprint ed. lib. bdg. 35.95 (*0-405-10154-6*) Ayer.

Baetjer, Howard. Software As Captial: An Economic Perspective on Software Engineering. LC 97-38111. 175p. 1997. 25.00 (*0-8186-7779-1*, BP07779) IEEE Comp Soc.

Baetjer, Katharine. European Paintings in the Metropolitan Museum of Art by Artists Born Before 1865: A Summary Catalogue. LC 94-39136. 554p. 1996. 65.00 (*0-87099-734-3*) Metro Mus Art.

***Baetjer, Katharine, et al.** Only the Best: Masterpieces of the Calouste Gulbenkian Museum, Lisbon. LC 99-44794. (Illus.). 176p. 1999. pap. 45.00 (*0-8109-6546-1*, Pub. by Abrams) Time Warner.

Baetjer, Katharine, jt. auth. see Reynolds, Graham.

Baetjer, Katharine, jt. auth. see Links, J. G.

Baets, M. De, see De Baets, M.

Baets, Marc H. De, see De Baets, Marc H., ed.

Baets, W. R. Organization Learning & Knowledge Technologies in a Dynamic Environment. LC 98-21025. xiv, 275 p. 1998. 89.95 (*0-7923-8170-X*) Kluwer Academic.

Baets, Walter. Complexity & Management Proceedings of the Summer School on Managerial Complexity, Granada, S. (Collection of Essays Ser.). 1999. 112.00 (*981-02-3714-6*) World Scientific Pub.

Baets, Walter, jt. auth. see Galliers, Robert.

Baetsle, L. H., ed. The Belgian R & D Programme, Vol.3. (Special Issue of Radioactive Waste Management & the Nuclear Fuel Cycle Ser.). 230p. 1985. pap. text 184.00 (*3-7186-0320-9*) Gordon & Breach.

Baettig, K., ed. Behavioral Effects of Nicotine: Proceedings of the International Workshop, Zurich, September 15-17, 1976. (Illus.). 1978. 42.75 (*3-8055-2763-2*) S Karger.

Baetz, Mark C. & Beamis, Paul W. Strategic Management: Canadian Cases. 2nd ed. (C). 1990. 54.95 (*0-256-08340-1*, Irwn McGrw-H) McGrw-H Hghr Educ.

Baetz, Ruth. Wild Communion: Experiencing Peace in Nature. LC 97-27080. 175p. pap. 14.00 (*1-56838-187-5*, 1092 A) Hazelden.

Baetzhold, Howard G., ed. see Twain, Mark, pseud.

Baetzold, Roger C., ed. Physical Methods of Chemistry: Supplement & Cumulative Index, Vol. 10. 2nd ed. LC 92-24512. 416p. 1993. 299.00 (*0-471-57086-9*) Wiley.

Baetzold, Roger C., jt. auth. see Rossiter, Bryant W.

Baetzold, Roger C., jt. ed. see Rossiter, Bryant W.

Baeuerle, Erich & Gaedke, Ursula, contrib. by. Advances in Limnology, Heft 53. (Illus.). 610p. 1999. 123.00 (*3-510-47055-9*) E Schweizerbartsche.

Baeuerle, Patrick & Landa, Norbert. How The Y Makes the Guy. (Microexplorers Ser.). (Illus.). 42p. (J). (gr. 3-7). 1997. 11.95 (*0-7641-5064-2*) Barron.

— Ingenious Genes. (Microexplorers Ser.). (Illus.). 42p. (J). (gr. 3-7). 1997. 11.95 (*0-7641-5063-4*) Barron.

Baeuerle, Patrick A. & Landa, Norbert. The Cell Works Vol. 4: Microexplorers. (Microexplorers Ser.: No. 4). (Illus.). 42p. 1999. lib. bdg. 18.95 (*1-56674-235-8*) Forest Hse.

— How the Y Makes the Guy Vol. 2: Microexplorers. (Microexplorers Ser.: No. 4). (Illus.). 42p. (J). (gr. k up). 1999. lib. bdg. 18.95 (*1-56674-236-6*) Forest Hse.

— Ingenious Genes Vol. 3: Microexplorers. (Microexplorers Ser.). (Illus.). 42p. (J). (gr. k up). 1999. lib. bdg. 18.95 (*1-56674-237-4*) Forest Hse.

— Microexplorers Series: Physical Science, 4 vols., Set. (Illus.). 168p. 1999. lib. bdg. 75.80 (*1-56674-946-8*) Forest Hse.

— Your Body's Heroes & Villains Vol. 4: Microexplorers. (Microexplorers Ser.). (Illus.). 42p. (J). (gr. k up). 1999. lib. bdg. 18.95 (*1-56674-238-2*) Forest Hse.

Baev, K. V. Biological Neural Networks: Hierarchical Concept of Brain Function. LC 97-30734. 273p. 1997. write for info. (*0-8176-3859-8*) Birkhauser.

Baev, Pavel. Russia's Policies in the Caucasus. LC 97-157222. (Former Soviet South Ser.). 61p. 1997. pap. 12.95 (*1-86203-055-3*, Pub. by Royal Inst Intl Affairs) Brookings.

Baev, Pavel K. The Russian Army in a Time of Troubles. LC 96-68423. (Peace Research Institute, Oslo Ser.). 224p. 1996. 75.00 (*0-7619-5186-5*); pap. 29.95 (*0-7619-5187-3*) Sage.

Baeyens, Willy, ed. Global & Regional Mercury Cycles - Sources, Fluxes & Mass Balances: Proceedings of the NATO Advanced Research Workshop, Novosibirsk, Russia, July 10-14, 1995. LC 96-45570. (NATO ASI Series: Partnership Sub-Series 2). 588p. (C). 1996. text 331.50 (*0-7923-4314-X*) Kluwer Academic.

Baeyens, Willy R., et al, eds. Luminescence Techniques in Chemical & Biochemical Analysis. (Practical Spectroscopy Ser.: Vol. 12). (Illus.). 664p. 1990. text 235.00 (*0-8247-8369-7*) Dekker.

Baeyer, Hans C. Von, see Von Baeyer, Hans C.

Baeyers, Willy F. Trace Metals in the Westerschelde Estuary: A Case-study of a Polluted, Partially Anoxic Estuary. LC 98-24601. (Developments in Hydrobiology Ser.). 21p. 1998. write for info. (*0-7923-5158-4*) Kluwer Academic.

Baez, A. V., et al, eds. The Environment & Science & Technology Education. LC 86-252390. (Science & Technology Education & Future Human Needs Ser.: Vol. 8). (Illus.). 446p. 1987. 200.00 (*0-08-033952-2*, Pub. by Pergamon Repr) Franklin.

Baez, Benjamin & Centra, John A. Tenure, Promotion, & Reappointment: Legal & Administrative Implications. Fife, Jonathan D., ed. LC 96-76556. (ASHE-ERIC Higher Education Reports: No. 95-1). (Illus.). 203p. (Orig.). 1996. pap. 24.00 (*1-878380-65-6*) GWU Grad Schl E&HD.

Baez, Constanza, tr. see Powell, Clark.

Baez, Daisy. Families LC 99-188405. 16 p. 1995. write for info. (*0-8136-7991-5*) Modern Curr.

Baez, Fabian, ed. see Varela-Cid, Eduardo.

Baez, J. & Muniain, J. Gauge Fields, Knots & Gravity. (Series on Knots & Everything). 396p. 1994. text 81.00 (*981-02-1729-3*); pap. text 43.00 (*981-02-2034-0*) World Scientific Pub.

Baez, Joan C., Sr. My Childhood: As I Remember It. (Illus.). 124p. (Orig.). 1996. pap. 12.00 (*0-945131-04-6*) Terrace Pr.

Baez, John C., et al. Introduction to Algebraic & Constructive Quantum Field Theory. 368p. 1992. text 75.00 (*0-691-08546-3*, Pub. by Princeton U Pr) Cal Prin Full Svc.

Baez, Josefina. Por Que Mi Nombre Es Marisol? Un Cuento De la Republica Dominicana. (Marisol Ser.: Vol. 1). (SPA., Illus.). 24p. (Orig.). (J). (gr. k-3). 1993. pap. 12.95 (*1-882161-01-7*) Latinarte.

— Why Is My Name Marisol? A Dominican Children's Story. (Marisol Ser.: Vol. 1). (Illus.). 24p. (Orig.). (J). (gr. k-3). 1993. pap. 12.95 (*1-882161-02-5*) Latinarte.

Baez, Kjersti H. Corrie Ten Boom. (Young Reader's Christian Library). (Illus.). 224p. (J). (gr. 3 up). 1989. pap. 1.39 (*1-55748-102-4*) Barbour Pub.

— Samuel Morris. (Young Reader's Christian Library). (Illus.). 224p. (J). (gr. 3-7). 1995. pap. text 1.39 (*1-55748-603-4*) Barbour Pub.

Baez, Kjersti H., et al. Inspirational Romance Reader No. 3: Contemporary Collection. 400p. 1999. pap. 4.97 (*1-57748-606-4*) Barbour Pub.

Baez, Manuel M. Vida de Pasteur. (Fondo 2000 Ser.). (SPA.). pap. 2.99 (*968-16-5053-0*, Pub. by Fondo) Continental Bk.

Baez, Pedro F. Insomnia. LC 88-80221. (Coleccion Espejo de Paciencia). (SPA.). 80p. (Orig.). 1989. pap. 7.95 (*0-89729-477-7*) Ediciones.

Baez, Ramon R. Microscopio: Los Muertos Tambien Hablan. (SPA.). 240p. 1997. pap. 14.95 (*0-9658743-0-3*) Edit Sitel.

Baez-Yates, Ricardo, et al, eds. Latin '95: Theoretical Informatics: Proceedings of the Second Latin American Symposium, Valpariso, Chile, April 17-21, 1995. LC 95-10547. (Lecture Notes in Computer Science Ser.: Vol. 911). 1995. write for info. (*0-387-59175-3*) Spr-Verlag.

Baeza, Aberlarda & Anaya, Rudolfo A. Keep Blessing Us, Ultima: A Teacher's Guide for Bless Me, Ultima by Rudolfo Anaya. LC 97-163113. 88p. 1997. pap., teacher ed. 9.95 (*1-57168-158-2*, 158-2, Eakin Pr) Sunbelt Media.

Baeza, Silvia P. Music & Dance. LC 95-3718. (Latino Life Ser.). 48p. (J). (gr. 4-8). 1996. lib. bdg. 23.93 (*0-86625-545-1*) Rourke Pubns.

— Musica y Baile. (Vida Latina Ser.).Tr. of Music & Dance. (SPA.). 48p. (J). (gr. 4-8). 1995. lib. bdg. 23.93 (*0-86625-565-6*) Rourke Pubns.

Baeza, Veronica, ed. Directions 1998: People Helping People: Directory of Health & Human Services in San Diego County. rev. ed. 500p. 1998. per. 35.00 (*0-9629793-6-8*) United Way SD.

***Baeza, Veronica, et al, eds.** Directions... People Helping People: Directory of Health & Human Services, San Diego County. 26th ed. 420p. 1999. reprint ed. pap. 30.00 (*0-9629793-7-6*) United Way SD.

Baeza-Yates, R. Computer Science 2: Research & Applications. (Illus.). 608p. (C). 1994. 145.00 (*0-306-44730-4*, Plenum Trade) Perseus Pubng.

Baeza-Yates, Ricardo. Baeza-yates Modern Imformation Retrieval. LC 99-10033. 464p. 1999. pap. text 50.00 (*0-201-39829-X*) Addison-Wesley.

Baeza-Yates, Ricardo A., jt. ed. see Manber, Udi.

Bafaro, Johanna, ed. see Freedman, Melvin H. & Silver, Samuel M.

Bafas, G. V., ed. Telecommunication & Control - TELECON, '84: Proceedings, IASTED Symposium, Halkidiki, Greece, August 27-30, 1984. 498p. 1984. 120.00 (*0-88986-072-6*, 075) Acta Pr.

Baffa, Lou. If You Own a Car Or a Van, You Must Own This Book: The Collision Resource Book: LC 96-69280. 208p. (Orig.). 1996. pap. 19.95 (*1-884570-50-X*) Research Triangle.

***Baffert, Bob & Haskin, Steve.** Baffert: Dirt Road to the Derby. (Illus.). 224p. 1999. 24.95 (*1-58150-025-4*, Pub. by Blood-Horse) IPG Chicago.

***Baffler Staff.** Backlash Retrospective, Part 1, 13. 1999. pap. text 7.50 (*1-888984-02-3*) Baffler.

Baffny, Milklos. They Were Counted... 1999. pap. text 15.99 (*1-900850-15-X*) Arcadia Bks.

Bag, A. K. Science & Civilization in India Vol. 1: Harappan Period, c. 3000-1500 B. C. 175p. 1986. 32.50 (*0-8364-1549-3*, Pub. by Navarang) S Asia.

Bagaasen, L. M. Discontinuous - Fiber - Reinforced Composites. 22p. 1991. reprint ed. pap. 35.00 (*0-938648-28-4*) T-C Pr CA.

Bagachwa, Mboya S., et al. Small Scale Urban Enterprises in Tanzania: Results from a 1991 Survey. (Working Papers: No. 44). 48p. 1993. pap. 7.00 (*1-56401-144-5*) Cornell Food.

Bagachwa, Mboya S., jt. auth. see Maliyamkono, T. L.

Bagader, Abubaker, et al, eds. Voices of Change: Short Stories by Saudi Arabian Women Writers. Heinrichsdorff, Ava M. et al, trs. LC 97-26942. (Three Continents Ser.). 171p. 1997. 35.00 (*1-55587-750-8*); pap. 15.95 (*1-55587-775-3*) L Rienner.

Bagader, Abubaker, jt. ed. see Heinrichsdorf, Ava M.

Bagader, Abubakr Ahmed. Environmental Protection in Islam. LC 96-177626. 1997. 16.00 (*2-88032-088-7*, Pub. by IUCN) Island Pr.

Bagai, Eric. Simple Knots for a Lifetime. (Illus.). 20p. (J). (gr. 4-12). 1998. 5.00 (*0-943292-25-5*, 602) Foreworks.

— What I Did with My Trash: Adventures with a TRS-80 Microcomputer. (Illus.). 80p. (Orig.). 1990. pap. text 5.95 (*0-943292-24-7*, Flaming Sparrow) Foreworks.

Bagai, Eric & Bagai, Judith. System FORE Handbook. (System FORE Ser.: Vol. 1). 96p. (Orig.). (C). 1979. pap. text 7.00 (*0-943292-01-8*) Foreworks.

Bagai, Eric & Bagai, Judith, eds. System FORE, 5 Vols. (Illus.). 1328p. (C). 1979. student ed. 90.00 (*0-943292-00-X*) Foreworks.

Bagai, Eric, ed. see Los Angeles Unified School District Staff, et al.

Bagai, Eric, ed. see West Linn Unified School District Staff.

Bagai, Judith, jt. auth. see Bagai, Eric.

Bagai, Judith, jt. ed. see Bagai, Eric.

Bagai, Judith, ed. see Los Angeles Unified School District Staff, et al.

Bagai, Judith, ed. see West Linn Unified School District Staff.

Bagajewa-Urbanek, Irina, tr. see Usakov, Valeriy I.

Bagan, Joe. Lukas at Auction. 300p. (Orig.). 1989. pap. 25.00 (*0-9622850-0-5*) Sachs Lawlor.

Baganha, Maria I. Portuguese Emigration to the U. S. 1820-1930. LC 90-46975. (European Immigrants & American Society Ser.). 440p. 1990. reprint ed. text 30.00 (*0-8240-7421-1*) Garland.

Bagaraj, D. Joseph, jt. auth. see Powell, Conway L.

Bagarov, Vladimir. English Openings Symmetrical. 1995. pap. 24.95 (*1-85744-032-3*) S&S Trade.

Bagarozzi, Dennis, jt. auth. see Wodarski, John S.

Bagarozzi, Dennis A. The Couple & Family in Managed Care: Assessment, Evaluation & Treatment. LC 96-16041. (Mental Health Practice under Managed Care Ser.: No. 4). 176p. 1996. pap. text 21.95 (*0-87630-810-8*) Brunner-Mazel.

Bagarozzi, Dennis A., jt. auth. see Anderson, Stephen A.

Bagarozzi, Dennis A., jt. auth. see L'Abate, Luciano.

Bagasra, Omar. HIV & Molecular Immunity: Prospects for the AIDS Vaccine. LC 99-10473. (Illus.). 216p. 1999. text 42.95 (*1-881299-10-4*, BioTechniques) Eaton Pub Co.

Bagasra, Omar & Hansen, John A. In-Situ PCR Amplification & Hybridization. LC 96-47734. 160p. 1997. pap. 54.95 (*0-471-15946-8*) Wiley.

Bagby, Albert I., Jr., tr. see Machado de Assis, Joaquim Maria.

Bagby, Albert M. Mammy Rosie. LC 71-38638. (Black Heritage Library Collection). 1977. reprint ed. 20.95 (*0-8369-8996-1*) Ayer.

***Bagby, Alfred.** King & Queen County, Virginia. LC 73-17399. (Illus.). 402p. 1999. reprint ed. pap. 32.50 (*0-8063-7993-6*) Clearfield Co.

Bagby, Daniel G. El Poder de la Iglesia Para Ayudar O Danar: The Church, the Power to Help & to Hurt. De Gherman, Mabel G., tr. (SPA.). 112p. 1990. pap. 6.99 (*0-311-17034-X*) Casa Bautista.

— Seeing Through Our Tears: Why We Cry, How We Heal. LC 98-50114. 160p. 1999. pap. 11.99 (*0-8066-3731-5*, 9-3731, Augsburg) Augsburg Fortress.

Bagby, George F. Frost & the Book of Nature. LC 93-18330. 232p. (C). 1993. 29.95 (*0-87049-805-3*) U of Tenn Pr.

Bagby, Grover C., ed. The Preleukemic Syndrome: Hemopoietic Dysplasia. LC 84-14975. 256p. 1985. 147.00 (*0-8493-5084-0*, RC642, CRC Reprint) Franklin.

Bagby, John W., jt. auth. see McCarty, F. William.

Bagby, Julie, jt. ed. see Eriksen, Arne.

Bagby, Lewis. Alexander Bestuzhev-Marlinsky & Russian Byronism. LC 93-47591. (Illus.). 376p. 1995. 48.50 (*0-271-01336-2*) Pa St U Pr.

***Bagby, Lewis, ed.** Lermontov's "A Hero of Our Time" A Critical Companion. 2001. pap. 18.95 (*0-8101-1680-4*) Northwestern U Pr.

Bagby, Martha C. Consumer Economics & Personal Finance: Syllabus. 1974. pap. text 9.95 (*0-89420-063-1*, 100030); audio 224.55 (*0-89420-136-0*, 100000) Natl Book.

Bagby, Meredith. Annual Report of the United States of America: What Every Citizen Needs to Know about the Real State of the Nation, 1998 Edition. annuals rev. ed. (Illus.). 144p. 1998. pap. 15.95 (*0-07-006708-2*, BusinessWeek Bks) McGraw.

— Rational Exuberance: The Influence of Generation X on the New American Economy. LC 98-7453. 288p. 1998. 24.95 (*0-525-94408-7*) NAL.

***Bagby, Meredith.** We've Got Issues. LC 99-86008. 224p. 2000. pap. 12.00 (*1-891620-79-7*, Pub. by PublicAffairs NY) HarpC.

Bagby, Meredith E. The Annual Report of the United States of America, 1996: What Every Citizen Should Know About... (Illus.). 140p. 1995. pap. 12.50 (*0-88730-780-9*, HarpBusn) HarpInfo.

Bagby, Michael. Just Another Lump of Clay. Elento, Wendell et al, eds. 248p. 1996. pap. write for info. (*0-9628127-4-9*) Straight St.

***Bagby, Milton.** Private Soldiers & Public Heroes: An American Album of the Common Man's Civil War. LC 98-27465. 1998. 29.95 (*1-55853-688-4*) Rutledge Hill Pr.

Bagby, Rachel. Divine Daughters: Liberating the Power & Passion of Women's Souls. pap. 14.00 (*0-06-251427-X*) HarpC.

— Divine Daughters: Liberating the Power & Passion of Women's Souls. LC 98-45046. 288p. 1999. 22.00 (*0-06-251426-1*, Pub. by Harper SF) HarpC.

***Bagby, Richard J.** Second Look at Calculus. (Illus.). 220p. (C). 2000. 69.95 (*0-12-072550-9*) Acad Pr.

Bagby, Wesley M. America's International Relations Since World War I. LC 98-16039. (Illus.). 448p. (C). 1999. text 49.95 (*0-19-512388-3*); pap. text 24.95 (*0-19-512389-1*) OUP.

— Contemporary International Problems. LC 82-12615. 248p. 1983. pap. text 19.95 (*0-88229-775-9*) Burnham Inc.

— The Eagle-Dragon Alliance: America's Relations with China in World War II. LC 90-50932. (Illus.). 312p. 1992. 50.00 (*0-87413-418-8*) U Delaware Pr.

— Introduction to Social Science & Contemporary Issues. 2nd ed. (Sociology - Intro Level). 1995. pap. text 46.95 (*0-8304-1391-X*) Thomson Learn.

— The Road to Normalcy: The Presidential Campaign & Election of 1920. LC 78-64237. (Johns Hopkins University. Studies in the Social Sciences. Thirtieth Ser. 1912: 1). reprint ed. 45.00 (*0-404-61342-X*) AMS Pr.

— The Road to Normalcy: The Presidential Campaign & the Election of 1920. LC JK0526.B2. (Johns Hopkins University Studies in Historical & Political Science: Ser. 80, No. 1). 208p. reprint ed. pap. 64.50 (*0-608-14607-2*, 202310700032) Bks Demand.

Bagchee, Aruna. Agricultural Extension in Africa. LC 93-45658. (Discussion Paper, Africa Technical Department Ser.: Vol. 231). 104p. 1994. pap. 22.00 (*0-8213-2756-9*, 12756) World Bank.

— Agricultural Extension in Africa. (FRE.). 112p. 1995. pap. 22.00 (*0-8213-3126-4*, 13126) World Bank.

***Bagchee, Sandeep.** Nad: Understanding the Raga Music. LC 98-903071. (Illus.). 1998. 498.00 (*81-86982-08-6*, Pub. by Business Pubns); pap. 198.00 (*81-86982-07-8*, Pub. by Business Pubns) St Mut.

Bagchi, A. K. Methods in Neurology. (C). 1989. 70.00 (*0-89771-377-X*, Pub. by Current Dist) St Mut.

Bagchi, Amalendu. Design, Construction, & Monitoring of Landfills. 2nd ed. 376p. 1994. 110.00 (*0-471-30681-9*) Wiley.

Bagchi, Amaresh & Stern, Nicholas, eds. Tax Policy & Planning in Developing Countries. (Illus.). 492p. (C). 1994. text 29.95 (*0-19-562957-4*) OUP.

Bagchi, Amiya K. Evolution of the State Bank of India, Vol. 1, Pts 1 & 2. 1090p. 1987. 49.95 (*0-19-562042-9*) OUP.

— The Evolution of the State Bank of India: The Era of the Presidency Banks, 1876-1920. LC 96-46555. 200p. (C). 1997. 45.00 (*0-8039-9359-5*, 93595) Sage.

— The Presidency Banks & the Indian Economy, 1876-1914. 312p. 1990. 12.95 (*0-19-562412-2*) OUP.

An Asterisk (*) at the beginning of an entry indicates that the title is appearing for the first time.

— Stackelberg Differential Games in Economic Models. (Lecture Notes in Control & Information Sciences: Vol. 64). viii, 203p. 1984. pap. 27.00 (0-387-13587-1) Spr-Verlag.

Bagchi, Amiya K., ed. Economy, Polity & Society: Essays in the Political Economy of Indian Planning. In Honour of Professor Bhabatosh Datta. (Perspectives in Social Sciences Ser.: No. 3). (Illus.). 284p. 1988. text 18.95 (0-19-562059-3) OUP.

— New Technology & the Workers' Response: Microelectronics, Labour & Society. LC 94-19449. 348p. 1995. 39.95 (0-8039-9198-3) Sage.

Bagchi, Amiya Kumar, ed. Democracy & Development: States, Markets, & Societies in Their Context: Proceedings of the IEA Conference Held in Barcelona, Spain. LC 94-44767. (IEA Conference Ser.: Vol. 113). 1995. text 90.00 (0-312-12465-1) St Martin.

Bagchi, Asoke K. Great Women of Sciences. (C). 1994. text 22.50 (81-220-0344-3, Pub. by Konark Pubs) S Asia.

— Tales from a Small Town. 1993. text 15.95 (81-220-0295-1, Pub. by Konark Pubs) Advent Bks Div.

Bagchi, Asoke K., ed. The Hinduja Foundation Encyclopaedia of Nobel Laureates, 1901-1987: The Encyclopaedia of Excellence. (Illus.). 660p. 1989. text 75.00 (81-220-0099-1, Pub. by Konark Pubs Pvt Ltd) Advent Bks Div.

Bagchi, B., ed. Solvation Dynamics & Charge Transfer Reactions. 250p. (C). 1991. text 67.00 (981-02-0338-1) World Scientific Pub.

Bagchi, Debasis. Green Tea: Antioxidant Power to Fight Disease. (Good Health Guides Ser.). 48p. 1999. pap. 3.95 (0-87983-934-1, 39341K, Keats Publng) NTC Contemp Pub Co.

— Resveratrol & Human Health. (Good Health Guides Ser.). 48p. Date not set. pap. 3.95 (0-87983-955-4, 39554K, Keats Publng) NTC Contemp Pub Co.

Bagchi, Debasis & Barilla, Jean. Huperzine A: Boost Your Brain Power. (Good Health Guides Ser.). 48p. 1998. pap. 3.95 (0-87983-959-7, 39597K, Keats Publng) NTC Contemp Pub Co.

Bagchi, Jhunu. History & Culture of the Palas of Bengal & Bihar: (Cir. 750 A. D.-Cir. 1200 A. D.) (C). 1993. 28.00 (81-7017-301-9, Pub. by Abhinav) S Asia.

Bagchi, K. Guidelines for the Management of Nutrition Programmes: A Manual for Nutrition Officers. (WHO EMRO Technical Publications: No. 15). xi, 165p. 1990. pap. text 20.00 (92-9021-099-0, 1450015) World Health.

Bagchi, K., ed. Towards a National Nutrition Policy: Guidelines for Countries of the Eastern Mediterranean Region. 65p. 1990. pap. text 2.00 (92-9021-118-0, 1450017) World Health.

Bagchi, K., jt. ed. see Hafez, G.

Bagchi, Kallol, et al, eds. Advanced Computer Performance Modeling & Simulation. 356p. 1998. text 42.00 (90-5699-569-3) Gordon & Breach.

Bagchi, Kallol, jt. ed. see Walrand, Jean.

Bagchi, Santosh, tr. see Vishwashrayananda, Swami.

Bagchi, T. P. & Chaudhri, V. K. Interactive Relational Database Design. (Lecture Notes in Computer Science Ser.: Vol. 402). xi, 186p. 1989. 31.00 (0-387-51881-9) Spr-Verlag.

*Bagchi, Tapan P. Multiobjective Scheduling by Genetic Algorithms. LC 99-37211. 1999. write for info. (0-7923-8561-6) Kluwer Academic.

Bagchi, Tilak. Profile of Some Indian Tribes: An Anthropo-Nutritional Micro Study. LC 94-902403. (C). 1995. 44.00 (81-85094-73-X, Pub. by Punthi Pus) S Asia.

Bagci, C. A New Theory for the Design of Helical Gears for Surface Fatigue Using Hertzian Point Contact Stresses. (Nineteen Eighty-Seven Fall Technical Meeting Ser.: Vol. 87FTM1). (Illus.). 11p. 1985. pap. text 30.00 (1-55589-477-1) AGMA.

Bagdade, Al, jt. auth. see Bagdade, Sue.

Bagdade, Al, jt. ed. see Bagdade, Susan.

Bagdade, John D. 1998 Year Book of Endocrinology. 2nd ed. (Illus.). 432p. (C). (gr. 13). 1998. text 79.00 (0-8151-9626-1, 24963) Mosby Inc.

— 1997 Year Book of Endocrinology. (Illus.). 512p. (C). (gr. 13). 1997. text 79.00 (0-8151-9625-3, 24962) Mosby Inc.

Bagdade, Sue & Bagdade, Al. Collector's Guide to American Toy Trains. LC 89-51556. (Illus.). 244p. 1990. pap. 19.95 (0-87069-532-0, Wllce-Homestd) Krause Pubns.

— Warman's American Pottery & Porcelain. LC 94-3191. (Encyclopedia of Antiques & Collectibles Ser.). (Illus.). 320p. 1994. pap. 19.95 (0-87069-693-9, Wllce-Homestd) Krause Pubns.

Bagdade, Susan & Bagdade, Al, eds. Warman's English & Continental Pottery & Porcelain. 3rd ed. LC 91-50430. (Illus.). 320p. 1998. pap. 27.95 (0-87341-641-4, ECPP3, Warmans) Krause Pubns.

*Bagdade, Susan D. Warman's American Pottery & Porcelain. 2nd rev. ed. LC 94-3191. (Illus.). 224p. 2000. pap. 24.95 (0-87341-822-0, WAPP2) Krause Pubns.

Bagdasari. A Chipmunk Easter. 1995. 7.98 (1-57042-241-9) Warner Bks.

*Bagdasarian, Adam. Forgotten Fire. LC 99-46465. 2000. 17.95 (0-7894-2627-7) DK Pub Inc.

Bagdasarian, Nicholas Der, see Der Bagdasarian, Nicholas.

Bagdasarov, Kh S. & Lube, E. L. Growth of Crystals, Vol. 16. (Illus.). 286p. (C). 1990. text 125.00 (0-306-18116-9, Kluwer Plenum) Kluwer Academic.

Bagdasarov, S. Chebyshev Splines & Kolmogorov Inequalities. LC 98-37006. (Operator Theory: Advances & Applications Ser.: Vol. 105). 224p. 1999. 109.00 (3-7643-5984-6) Birkhauser.

Bagdasarov, Sergey. Chebyshev Splines & Kolmogorov Inequalities. LC 98-37006. (Operator Theory, Advances & Applications Ser.). 1998. 109.00 (0-8176-5984-6) Birkhauser.

Bagdikian, Ben H. Double Vision: Reflections on My Heritage, Life & Profession. 256p. 1997. pap. 14.00 (0-8070-7067-X) Beacon Pr.

*Bagdikian, Ben H. The Media Monopoly. 6th ed. LC 00-21035. 2000. pap. 17.50 (0-8070-6179-4) Beacon Pr.

Bagdon, Phillip V. & Farrel, John W. Essential Cass: An Overview of Cass Scenic Railroad State Park, Cass, West Virginia. LC 99-158485. 23 p. 1997. write for info. (0-9658475-0-0) Dog & Pony.

Bagdon, Paul. Scrapper John: Rendezvous at Skull Mountain. 128p. (Orig.). (J). 1992. pap. 3.50 (0-380-76418-0, Avon Bks) Morrow Avon.

— Scrapper John: Showdown at Burnt Rock. 128p. (Orig.). (J). (gr. 6). 1992. pap. 3.50 (0-380-76417-2, Avon Bks) Morrow Avon.

— Scrapper John: Valley of the Spotted Horse. (J). (gr. 4-7). 1992. pap. 3.50 (0-380-76416-4, Avon Bks) Morrow Avon.

*Bagdonas, Richard. Advanced Internet Sales Skills. Lane, Susan M., ed. (Illus.). 1999. pap. write for info. (1-58143-010-8, PSG1GDIS) Prosoft I-net.

— Advanced Internet Sales Skills: A4. Lane, Susan M., ed. 1999. write for info. (1-58143-064-7) Prosoft I-net.

— Advanced Internet Sales Skills: Version 2.07. Lane, Susan M., ed. (CIW Foundations Track Ser.). (Illus.). 1999. pap. write for info. (1-58143-067-1) Prosoft I-net.

— Basic Internet Sales Skills. Lane, Susan M., ed. (Illus.). 1999. pap. write for info. (1-58143-008-6, PSG1BISS) Prosoft I-net.

— Intermediate Internet Sales Skills. Lane, Susan M., ed. (Illus.). 1999. write for info. (1-58143-009-4, PSG1IISS) Prosoft I-net.

*Bagdonavicius, V., et al. Additive & Multiplicative Semiparametric Models in Accelerated Life Testing & Survival Analysis. LC 98-231608. (Illus.). 1998. write for info. (0-88911-802-7) Queens U Inst Intergov.

Bage, B., jt. auth. see Hawkins, H.

Bagehot, Richard. Music Business Agreements. (Waterlow Practitioner's Library). 416p. 1989. 90.00 (0-08-036905-7, Pergamon Pr) Elsevier.

— Sales Promotion, Advertising & PR. (Waterlow Publications). 256p. 1991. pap. 40.01 (0-08-040856-7) Macmillan.

— Sponsorship. (Waterlow Practitioner's Library). 192p. 1990. pap. 50.00 (0-08-040116-3) Macmillan.

Bagehot, Walter. Biographical Studies. Hutton, Richard H., ed. LC 75-111469. (BCL Ser.: No. I). reprint ed. 21.50 (0-404-00445-8) AMS Pr.

— Bioraphical Studies. Hutton, Richard H., ed. LC 70-144862. vii, 368p. 1972. reprint ed. 12.00 (0-403-00850-6) Scholarly.

Bagehot, Walter. The Collected Works of Walter Bagehot, 15 vols. John-Stevas, Norman S., ed. 1986. 850.00 (0-85058-039-0) OUP.

Bagehot, Walter. Collected Works of Walter Bagehot, Set, Vols 3 & 4. St. John-Stevas, Norman, ed. LC 66-1165. 1097p. 1968. 104.00 (0-674-14002-8) HUP.

— The Collected Works of Walter Bagehot Vols. I & II: Literary Essays. John-Stevas, Norman S., ed. 1986. 175.00 (0-85058-077-3) OUP.

— The Collected Works of Walter Bagehot Vols. III & IV: Historical Essays. John-Stevas, Norman S., ed. 1986. 155.00 (0-85058-078-1) OUP.

— The Collected Works of Walter Bagehot Vols. V & VI: Political Essays. John-Stevas, Norman S., ed. 1986. 155.00 (0-85058-079-X) OUP.

— The Collected Works of Walter Bagehot Vols. VII & VIII: Political Essays. John-Stevas, Norman S., ed. 1986. 155.00 (0-85058-080-3) OUP.

— The Collected Works of Walter Bagehot Vols. IX, X & XI: Economic Essays. John-Stevas, Norman S., ed. 1986. 165.00 (0-85058-081-1) OUP.

— The Collected Works of Walter Bagehot Vols. XII & XIII: Letters. John-Stevas, Norman S., ed. 1986. 135.00 (0-85058-082-X) OUP.

— The Collected Works of Walter Bagehot Vols. XIV & XV: Miscellany. John-Stevas, Norman S., ed. 1986. 135.00 (0-85058-083-8) OUP.

— Economic Studies. Hutton, Richard H., ed. 1976. reprint ed. 59.00 (0-403-06161-X) Scholarly.

— Economic Studies: The Works of Walter Bagehot. 280p. 1986. reprint ed. lib. bdg. 79.00 (0-932051-97-9) Rprt Serv.

— The English Constitution. 320p. 1966. pap. text 13.95 (0-8014-9023-5) Cornell U Pr.

— The English Constitution. LC 97-20740. 224p. 1997. pap. 16.95 (1-898723-71-0, Pub. by Sussex Acad Pr) Intl Spec Bk.

— The English Constitution. (World's Classics Ser.). xxvi, 312p. 1998. reprint ed. 85.00 (1-56169-403-7) Gaunt.

— Literary Studies (Miscellaneous Essays) Hutton, Richard H., ed. (Works of Walter Bagehot, 1826-1877). 357p. reprint ed. lib. bdg. 49.00 (0-7812-0893-9) Rprt Serv.

— Literary Studies with a Prefatory Memoir, 2 vols. Hutton, Richard H., ed. LC 72-148745. (BCL Ser.: No. I). reprint ed. 115.00 (0-404-07235-6) AMS Pr.

— Lombard Street. Wilkins, Mira, ed. LC 78-3895. (International Finance Ser.). 1979. reprint ed. lib. bdg. 33.95 (0-405-11201-7) Ayer.

*Bagehot, Walter. Lombard Street: A Description of the Money Market. LC 98-51463. (Investment Classics Ser.). 359p. 1999. 34.95 (0-471-34499-0) Wiley.

Bagehot, Walter. Lombard Street: A Description of the Money Market; with "The Currency Monopoly" 218p. 1991. reprint ed. pap. 14.95 (0-87991-252-9) Porcupine Pr.

*Bagehot, Walter. Lombard Street P. LC 98-51463. (Investment Classics Ser.). 359p. 1999. pap. 19.95 (0-471-34536-9) Wiley.

Bagehot, Walter. Physics & Politics. LC 99-19271. 256p. 1999. pap. 14.95 (1-56663-221-8, Elephant Paperbacks) I R Dee.

— Shakespeare, the Man. LC 71-126678. reprint ed. 31.50 (0-404-00446-6) AMS Pr.

Bagel, Marilyn. The Bagel Bible: For Bagel Lovers, the Complete Guide to Great Toppings. 3rd ed. LC 98-28795. (Illus.). 200p. 1998. pap. 10.95 (0-7627-0321-0) Globe Pequot.

*Bagella, M. & Becchetti, L., eds. The Competitive Advantage of Industrial Districts: Theoretical & Empirical Analysis. LC 99-58512. (Contributions to Economics Ser.). (Illus.). xii, 231p. 2000. pap. 63.00 (3-7908-1254-4) Spr-Verlag.

Bagella, Michele. Finance, Investment & Innovation: Theory & Empirical Evidence. LC 96-80378. 432p. 1997. text 91.95 (1-85972-568-6, Pub. by Avebry) Ashgate Pub Co.

Bagely, Bruce M. & Tokatlian, Juan G. Contadora: The Limits of Negotiations. (Pew Case Studies in International Affairs). 69p. (C). 1989. pap. text 3.50 (1-56927-309-X) Geo U Inst Dplmcy.

Bagemihl, Bruce. Biological Exuberance: Animal Homosexuality & Natural Diversity. LC 98-28528. (Illus.). 768p. 1999. text 40.00 (0-312-19239-8) St Martin.

*Bagemihl, Bruce. Biological Exuberance: Animal Homosexuality & Natural Diversity. 768p. 2000. pap. 21.95 (0-312-25377-X) St Martin.

Bagemihl, F., tr. see Khinchin, Aleksandra & Akovlevich, I.

Bagemihl, Frederick, tr. see Kamke, E.

Bagemihl, Frederick, tr. see Knopp, Konrad.

*Bagent, Brad. Rainbows, Head Lice & Pea-Green Tile: Poems in the Voice of the Classroom Teacher. LC 99-20003. (Illus.). 64p. (J). 1999. 15.95 (0-929895-28-2) Maupin Hse.

Bager, Gustav, jt. ed. see Szabo-Pelsci, Miklos.

Bager, Torben. Marketing Cooperatives & Peasants in Kenya. (Centre for Development Research Publications: No. 5). 116p. 1980. write for info. (91-7106-174-6, Pub. by Nordic Africa) Transaction Pubs.

Bagert, Brad, jt. auth. see Cullinan, Bernice.

Bagert, Brod. A Bullfrog at Cafe du Monde: Poems from the Heart, Funnybone & Soul of New Orleans. (Illus.). 53p. 1986. pap. 10.00 (0-9614228-1-5) Juliahouse Pubs.

*Bagert, Brod. Chicken Socks: An Other Contagious Poems. (Illus.). (J). 2000. 14.40 (0-606-18012-5) Turtleback.

Bagert, Brod. Chicken Socks: And Other Contagious Poems. LC 93-60474. (Illus.). 32p. (J). (gr. 3-7). 1994. 15.95 (1-56397-292-1, Wordsong) Boyds Mills Pr.

*Bagert, Brod. Chicken Socks: And Other Contagious Poems. LC 93-60474. (Illus.). 32p. (YA). (gr. 3 up). 2000. pap. 8.95 (1-56397-861-X) Boyds Mills Pr.

Bagert, Brod. Elephant Games: And Other Playful Poems. LC 94-73319. (Illus.). 32p. (J). (gr. 3-7). 1995. 15.95 (1-56397-293-X, Wordsong) Boyds Mills Pr.

*Bagert, Brod. Elephant Games: And Other Playful Poems to Perform. LC 94-73319. (Illus.). 32p. (YA). (gr. 3 up). 2000. pap. 8.95 (1-56397-862-8, Wordsong) Boyds Mills Pr.

Bagert, Brod. The Gooch Machine: A Collection of Humorous Poems to Perform. LC 96-84680. (Illus.). 32p. (J). (gr. 3-7). 1997. 15.95 (1-56397-294-8, Wordsong) Boyds Mills Pr.

— Let Me Be the Boss. LC 91-91408. (Illus.). 48p. (J). (gr. 3-7). 1992. 14.95 (1-56397-099-6, Wordsong) Boyds Mills Pr.

— Let Me Be... The Boss: Poems for Kids to Perform. LC 91-91408. (Illus.). 48p. (J). (gr. 3-7). 1995. pap. 6.95 (1-56397-524-6, Wordsong) Boyds Mills Pr.

— Let Me Be... The Boss: Poems for Kids to Perform. 1996. pap. 9.95 incl. audio (1-56397-540-8, Wordsong) Boyds Mills Pr.

— Steel Cables: Love Poems from Adam Rib. (Illus.). 49p. (Orig.). 1991. pap. 12.00 (0-9614228-8-2) Juliahouse Pubs.

— Throw Me Somethin' Mistuh! The Mardi Gras Book. (Illus.). (Orig.). 1996. pap. 14.95 (1-887746-02-1) Juliahouse Pubs.

Bagert, Brod, ed. see Poe, Edgar Allan.

Bagetskaya, Irina. The Moscow Kremlin in Watercolour: A Tribute to Eternal Russia. (Illus.). 200p. 1994. 85.00 (2-909838-05-6) Antique Collect.

Bagford, Ballads. Bagford Ballads, 2 vols. Ebsworth, J. W., ed. (Ballad Society, London Publications: Nos. 14-17 & 20). (Illus.). reprint ed. 187.50 (0-404-50830-8) AMS Pr.

Bagg, Elma W., et al. Cooking Without a Grain of Salt. LC 99-185333. 352p. 1998. mass mkt. 5.99 (0-553-57951-7) Bantam.

Bagg, Leona. South New Berlin, Chenango Co., New York: Records & Recollections of Leona Bagg. Goerlich, Shirley B., ed. & intro. by. 112p. 1994. 38.00 (0-9614858-7-6) RSG Pub.

Bagg, Lyman H., see Kron, Karl, pseud.

Bagg, M. M. The Pioneers of Utica, New York. (Illus.). 665p. 1993. reprint ed. lib. bdg. 67.50 (0-8328-2872-6) Higginson Bk Co.

— The Pioneers of Utica, New York. (Illus.). 665p. 1993. reprint ed. lib. bdg. 67.50 (0-8328-2912-9) Higginson Bk Co.

Bagg, Robert. Body Blows: Poems New & Selected. LC 87-35720. 128p. (C). 1988. 20.00 (0-87023-630-X); pap. 12.95 (0-87023-631-8) U of Mass Pr.

Bagg, Robert, tr. see Euripides.

Bagg, Robert, tr. see Sophocles.

Bagga, B., jt. ed. see Awasthi, A.

Bagga, Jaswant S. Laugh or Cry It's Your Choice: A Book about Reclaiming Your Lost Self Esteem. (Illus.). 202p. 1989. 10.00 (0-9624832-0-6) J S Bagga.

Bagga, P. C., jt. auth. see Aggarwal, V. B.

Bagga, P. C., jt. auth. see Arora, P. N.

Bagga, Raj K., tr. see Kabir.

Bagga, Raj K., tr. see Singh, Ajaib.

Baggage, Bea U., tr. see Johnson, Alice, ed.

Baggaley, Andrew R. Mathematics for Introductory Statistics: A Programmed Review. LC 69-19103. 185p. reprint ed. pap. 57.40 (0-608-30001-2, 205527100011) Bks Demand.

*Baggarly, Stephen, et al. Disciples & Dissidents: The Prison Writings of the Prince of Peace Plowshares. Wilcox, Fred, ed. (Illus.). 200p. 2000. pap. 16.95 (1-884540-42-2) Haleys.

Bagge, Dominique. Les Idees Politiques en France sous la Restauration. Mayer, J. P., ed. LC 78-67327. (European Political Thought Ser.). 1979. lib. bdg. 37.95 (0-405-11674-8) Ayer.

Bagge, Peter. Buddy Go Home. 1997. pap. text 16.95 (1-56097-276-9) Fantagraph Bks.

— Buddy the Dreamer. 120p. 1994. 35.00 (1-56097-155-X) Fantagraph Bks.

— Buddy the Dreamer. LC 95-192731. (Illus.). 120p. 1994. pap. 12.95 (1-56097-154-1) Fantagraph Bks.

— Buddy's Got Three Moms. 1999. pap. 16.95 (1-56097-335-8) Fantagraph Bks.

— Fun with Buddy & Lisa. (Illus.). 120p. 1995. pap. 12.95 (1-56097-175-4) Fantagraph Bks.

— Fun with Buddy & Lisa. 120p. 1995. 35.00 (1-56097-176-2) Fantagraph Bks.

— Hey, Buddy! 120p. 1993. 34.95 (1-56097-114-2); pap. 12.95 (1-56097-113-4) Fantagraph Bks.

— Studs Kirby: The Voice of America. (Illus.). 112p. 1989. pap. 13.95 (1-56097-010-3) Fantagraph Bks.

— Stupid Comics. 100p. 1991. pap. 10.95 (1-56097-069-3, Pub. by Fantagraph Bks) Seven Hills Bk.

Bagge, Sverre. Society & Politics in Snorri Sturluson's "Heimskringla" LC 91-2038. 434p. 1991. 55.00 (0-520-06887-4, Pub. by U CA Pr) Cal Prin Full Svc.

Bagge, U. & Born, G. V. White Blood Cells. 1982. text 112.50 (90-247-2681-6) Kluwer Academic.

Bagger, Donald, ed. see Cushman, Helen B.

Bagger, Eugene S. Eminent Europeans. LC 71-121446. (Essay Index Reprint Ser.). 1977. 26.95 (0-8369-1693-X) Ayer.

Bagger, Jonathan. Particles, Strings & Cosmology: Proceedings of the Johns Hopkins Workshop on Current Problems in Particle Theory 19 & the Pascos Interdisciplinary Symposium 5, Baltimore, 1995, March 22-25. LC 96-16481. 496p. 1996. write for info. (981-02-2512-1) World Scientific Pub.

Bagger, Jonathan, et al. Particle Physics - Perspectives & Opportunities: Report of the DPF Committee on Long-Term Planning. Peccei, Roberto, ed. LC 95-24956. 400p. 1995. text 82.00 (981-02-2271-8) World Scientific Pub.

Bagger, Jonathan, jt. auth. see Wess, Julius.

*Bagger, Jonathan A. Supersymmetry, Supergravity & Supercolliders; Proceedings of the 1997 Theoretical Advanced Stu. 600p. 1999. 96.00 (981-02-3816-9) World Scientific Pub.

*Bagger, Matthew C. Religious Experience, Justification & History. LC 98-33302. 271p. (C). 1999. 59.95 (0-521-62255-7) Cambridge U Pr.

*Baggerman, Lisa. Design for Interaction: User-Friendly Graphics. 2000. 45.00 (1-56496-652-6) Rockport Pubs.

Baggett, jt. auth. see Baron.

Baggett, A. S. America in the China Relief Expedition. (Wars of America Ser.: Vol. 1). (Illus.). 279p. 1997. reprint ed. 39.95 (0-89839-266-7) Battery Pr.

*Baggett, Bart A. The Grapho-Deck Handwriting Flash Cards Set: A Set of 50 Handwriting Analysis Flash Cards with Instructional Booklet/Manual. (Illus.). 60p. 2000. pap. 19.95 (1-882929-00-4) Empresse.

Baggett, Bart A. The Secrets to Making Love Happen: Using Handwriting Analysis to Improve Relationships, Vol. 4. 2nd ed. (Illus.). 304p. (Orig.). 1999. reprint ed. pap. 15.95 (1-882929-24-1) Empresse.

*Baggett, Bart A. Success Secrets of the Rich & Happy: Discover the Belief Systems, Habits & Personality Characteristics. Beattie, Honlee, ed. 304p. 2001. pap. 17.95 (1-882929-01-2) Empresse.

Baggett, Byrd. The Book of Excellence. LC 92-5897. 128p. 1992. 12.95 (1-55853-167-X) Rutledge Hill Pr.

— The Pocket Power Book of Integrity. LC 99-17237. 1999. 4.95 (1-55853-739-2) Rutledge Hill Pr.

— The Pocket Power Book of Leadership. LC 97-191698. 96p. 1997. 4.95 (1-55853-461-X) Rutledge Hill Pr.

— Pocket Power Book of Motivation. LC 99-17238. 96p. 1999. 4.95 (1-55853-740-6) Rutledge Hill Pr.

— The Pocket Power Book of Performance. LC 97-191705. 96p. 1997. 4.95 (1-55853-462-8) Rutledge Hill Pr.

— Power Serve: 236 Inspiring Ideas on Servant Leadership. (Illus.). 128p. 1998. 12.95 (1-890651-00-1, Saltillo Press); pap. 6.95 (1-890651-03-6, Saltillo Press) Williford Communs.

— Satisfaction Guaranteed: Two-Hundred & Thirty-Six Ideas to Make Your Customers Feel Like. LC 94-2500. 1994. 12.95 (1-55853-286-2) Rutledge Hill Pr.

*Baggett, Holly. I Know a Way: The Letters of Jane Heap & Florence Reynolds. LC 99-50760. 208p. 1999. 55.00 (0-8147-1246-0) NYU Pr.

Baggett, Holly. I Know a Way: The Letters of Jane Heap & Florence Reynolds. LC 99-50760. 1999. pap. text 20.00 (0-8147-9856-X) NYU Pr.

An Asterisk (*) at the beginning of an entry indicates that the title is appearing for the first time.

Baggett, Irv. Primer on Success in the Private Investigative Profession: A Business & Investigative Manual for Establishing a Successful Investigative Agency & Working the Most In-Demand Types of Cases! (Illus.). 65p. (C). 1996. pap. text 25.00 (*0-918487-89-7*) Thomas Investigative.

***Baggett, Jerome P.** Habitat for Humanity: Building Private Homes, Building Public Religion. (Illus.). 360p. 2000. 74.50 (*1-56639-802-9*); pap. 24.95 (*1-56639-803-7*) Temple U Pr.

Baggett, Lawrence W. Functional Analysis: A Primer. (Pure & Applied Mathematics Ser.: Vol. 153). (Illus.). 288p. 1991. text 69.75 (*0-8247-8598-3*) Dekker.

Baggett, Lawrence Wasson, ed. see AMS Special Session on the Functional & Harmonic Analysis of Wavelets Staff, et al.

Baggett, Leland. So Where's the Dawn? A Journey of Emotional Healing. LC 88-32154. 100p. (Orig.). 1989. pap. 8.95 (*0-929153-01-4*) Royal Pub NC.

Baggett, Margaret, jt. auth. see L'Abate, Luciano.

Baggett, Margaret S., jt. auth. see L'Abate, Luciano.

Baggett, Nancy. Dream Desserts: Low-Fat, Calorie-Wise Recipes. LC 92-37781. (Illus.). 160p. 1993. 12.50 (*1-55670-273-6*) Stewart Tabori & Chang.

— The International Chocolate Cookbook. LC 91-3124. (Illus.). 288p. 1991. 40.00 (*1-55670-178-0*); pap. 24.95 (*1-55670-363-5*) Stewart Tabori & Chang.

— The International Cookie Cookbook. LC 88-15310. (Illus.). 240p. 1988. 30.00 (*1-55670-041-5*) Stewart Tabori & Chang.

— The International Cookie Cookbook. (Illus.). 240p. 1998. pap. 19.95 (*1-55670-328-7*) Stewart Tabori & Chang.

Baggett, Nancy & Glick, Ruth. 100Pleasure: From Appetizers to Desserts, the Low-Fat Cookbook for People Who Love to Eat. 384p. 1996. pap. 15.95 (*0-87596-368-4*) Rodale Pr Inc.

Baggett, Nancy, jt. auth. see Glick, Ruth, pseud.

Baggett, Patricia & Ehrenfeucht, Andrezj. Breaking Away from the Math Book II. LC 97-61634. 288p. 1997. pap. text 29.95 (*1-56676-571-4*) Scarecrow.

Baggett, Patricia & Ehrenfeucht, Andrzej. Breaking Away from the Math Book: Creative Projects. LC 95-61207. 195p. 1995. spiral bd. 29.95 (*1-56676-299-5*) Scarecrow.

Baggett, Rebecca. Still Life with Children. 26p. 1995. pap. 7.95 (*0-944754-28-7*) Pudding Hse Pubns.

Baggett, Sharon A. Residential Care for the Elderly: Critical Issues in Public Policy, 13. LC 89-2152. (Contributions to the Study of Aging Ser.: No. 13). 185p. 1989. 59.95 (*0-313-26759-6*, BRZ/, Greenwood Pr) Greenwood.

Baggett, Shirley & Bussey, Melody. Getting It All Together: A Program on Feelings for Pre-School Through 2nd Grade Students. LC 93-79225. (Illus.). 76p. 1993. pap. text 12.95 (*1-884063-00-4*) Mar Co Prods.

Baggett, Vicki G. Picky Vicki & the Magical Squirrel. (Illus.). 16p. (Orig.). (J). (gr. 3-6). 1995. pap. text 4.50 (*0-9644795-0-8*) Baggett Bks.

Baggett, W. Michael. Texas Foreclosure: Law & Practice. LC 84-5376. 562p. 1984. text 120.00 (*0-07-003027-8*) Shepards.

Baggette, Susan K. Jonathan & Papa. LC 99-72439. (Jonathan Adventures Ser.). (Illus.). 24p. (J). (gr. 2-5). 1999. bds. 7.95 (*0-9660172-7-7*, Pub. by Brookfield Read) Brodart.

— Jonathan Goes to the Airport. LC 98-72532. (Jonathan Adventures Ser.). (Illus.). 16p. (J). (ps-k). 1998. bds. 5.95 (*0-9660172-6-9*) Brookfield Read.

— Jonathan Goes to the Doctor. LC 97-75092. (Jonathan Adventures Ser.). (Illus.). 16p. (J). (ps). 1998. bds. 5.95 (*0-9660172-1-8*) Brookfield Read.

— Jonathan Goes to the Fire Station. LC 98-72533. (Jonathan Adventures Ser.). (Illus.). 16p. (J). (ps). 1998. bds. 5.95 (*0-9660172-4-2*) Brookfield Read.

— Jonathan Goes to the Grocery Store. LC 97-75091. (Jonathan Adventures Ser.). (Illus.). 16p. (J). (ps). 1998. bds. 5.95 (*0-9660172-2-6*) Brookfield Read.

— Jonathan Goes to the Library. LC 97-75090. (Jonathan Adventures Ser.). (Illus.). 16p. (J). (ps). 1998. bds. 5.95 (*0-9660172-3-4*) Brookfield Read.

— Jonathan Goes to the Post Office. LC 98-72534. (Jonathan Adventures Ser.). (Illus.). 16p. (J). (ps-k). 1998. bds. 5.95 (*0-9660172-5-0*) Brookfield Read.

***Baggette, Susan K.** The Night the Moon Slept. LC 99-76580. (Illus.). 32p. (J). (ps-3). 2000. 16.95 (*0-9660172-8-5*, Pub. by Brookfield Read) Book Wholesalers.

Baggi, Denis. Readings in Computer-Generated Music. LC 92-15303. 232p. 1992. 45.00 (*0-8186-2747-6*, 2747) IEEE Comp Soc.

Baggiani, J. M. & Tewell, V. M. The Chess Set & Other Stories. (Illus.). 21p. (J). (gr. 2-3). 1966. pap. 3.50 (*0-934329-07-9*) Baggiani-Tewell.

— In the Country. (Illus.). 26p. (J). (gr. 2-4). 1966. pap. 3.50 (*0-934329-08-7*) Baggiani-Tewell.

— Phonics: A Tool for Better Reading & Spelling, Bk. I. (Illus.). (J). (gr. 1-2). 1982. reprint ed. teacher ed. 10.75 (*0-934329-01-X*); reprint ed. pap., student ed. 9.50 (*0-934329-00-1*) Baggiani-Tewell.

— Phonics: A Tool for Better Reading & Spelling, Bk. II. (Illus.). (J). (gr. 3-6). 1967. student ed. 2.00 (*0-934329-03-6*); pap. 3.50 (*0-934329-02-8*) Baggiani-Tewell.

— Phonics: A Tool for Better Reading & Spelling, Bk. III. (Illus.). (J). (gr. 5-12). 1984. reprint ed. student ed. 4.00 (*0-934329-05-2*); reprint ed. pap. 5.75 (*0-934329-04-4*) Baggiani-Tewell.

— Read & Draw. (Illus.). 12p. (J). (gr. 1-3). 1966. pap. 2.00 (*0-934329-06-0*) Baggiani-Tewell.

Baggins, David S. Drug Hate & the Corruption of American Justice. LC 97-32946. 200p. 1998. 49.95 (*0-275-95956-2*, Praeger Pubs) Greenwood.

Baggiolini, M., ed. Immunopathology & Immunopharmacology of the Lung. (Journal: International Archives of Allergy & Applied Immunology: Vol. 76, Suppl. 1). (Illus.). iv, 128p. 1985. pap. 39.25 (*3-8055-4057-4*) S Karger.

Baggiolini, M. & Sorg, C. Muenster, eds. Interleukin-8(NAP-1) & Related Chemotactic Cytokines. (Cytokines Ser.: Vol. 4). (Illus.). viii, 164p. 1991. 156.75 (*3-8055-5426-5*) S Karger.

Baggioni, Daniel. Dictionnaire Reunionnais-Francais. (FRE.). 376p. 1990. 75.00 (*0-8288-9462-0*) Fr & Eur.

Baggish, Jeff. Making the Prostate Therapy Decision. 208p. 1995. 22.95 (*1-56565-207-X*) Lowell Hse.

— Making the Prostate Therapy Decision. (Illus.). 208p. 1996. pap. 16.00 (*1-56565-433-1*) Lowell Hse.

***Baggish, Jeff.** Making the Prostate Therapy Decision. 2nd rev. ed. 240p. 1998. pap. 16.00 (*1-56565-869-8*, 08698W, Pub. by Lowell Hse) NTC Contemp Pub Co.

Baggish, Michael S. Basic & Advanced Laser Surgery in Gynecology. 2nd ed. 398p. (C). 1999. pap. text 85.00 (*0-8385-0521-X*, A0521-3) Appleton & Lange.

Baggish, Michael S. & Barbot, Jacques. Diagnostic & Operative Hysteroscopy: A Text Atlas. 2nd ed. LC 99-190767. (Illus.). 432p. (C). (gr. 13). 1998. text 169.00 (*0-8151-0457-X*, 26931) Mosby Inc.

***Baggley, John.** Festival Icons for the Christian Year. LC 99-57259. (Illus.). 2000. write for info. (*0-88141-201-5*) St Vladimirs.

Baggley, John & Temple, Richard. Doors of Perception: Icons & Their Spiritual Significance. (Illus.). 160p. (Orig.). 1988. pap. 15.95 (*0-88141-071-3*) St Vladimirs.

Baggot, J. Desmond, jt. auth. see Hardee, Gregory E.

***Baggot, Julianna.** Girl Talk. 2001. 22.95 (*0-7434-0082-8*, PB Hardcover) PB.

Baggot, Thomas. Cultivating Effective Lawyer-Juror Relationships: Understanding the Process. LC 99-28200. 170p. 1999. per. 55.00 (*0-913875-60-0*) Lawyers & Judges.

Baggott, Andy. Celtic Wisdom. (Piatkus Guides Ser.). (Illus.). 144p. 1999. pap. text 6.95 (*0-7499-1866-7*) London Brdge.

— Crystal Wisdom. (Piatkus Guides Ser.). 1999. pap. text 6.95 (*0-7499-1873-X*) London Brdge.

***Baggott, Andy.** Dreams: Transform Your Life Through the Power of Your Dreams. (Illus.). 128p. 2000. pap. 16.95 (*0-8069-3625-8*) Sterling.

— Health & Well-being: Runes. 64p. 2000. pap. 6.95 (*1-84215-112-6*) Anness Pub.

— Teach Yourself I Ching. (Teach Yourself Ser.). 192p. 1999. pap. 11.95 (*0-8442-1585-6*, 15856') NTC Contemp Pub Co.

Baggott, Andy, jt. auth. see Wolf, Grey.

Baggott, J. E., jt. auth. see Ashfold, M. N. R.

Baggott, Jim. The Meaning of Quantum Chemistry: A Guide for Students of Chemistry & Physics. (Illus.). 244p. 1992. pap. text 29.95 (*0-19-855575-X*) OUP.

— Perfect Symmetry: The Accidental Discovery of a New Form of Carbon. (Illus.). 328p. 1995. 45.00 (*0-19-855790-6*) OUP.

— Perfect Symmetry: The Accidental Discovery of a New Form of Carbon. (Illus.). 328p. (C). 1996. pap. 19.95 (*0-19-855789-2*) OUP.

***Baggott, John.** Mini: The Racing Story. (Illus.). 232p. 2000. 44.95 (*1-86126-254-X*, 129771AE, Pub. by Cro1wood) Motorbooks Intl.

Baggott, Joseph. Cost & Management Accounting Made Simple. 395p. (C). 1988. 45.00 (*0-7855-3777-5*, Pub. by Inst Pur & Supply) St Mut.

— Cost & Management Accounting Made Simple. 395p. (C). 1989. 85.00 (*0-7855-5669-9*, Pub. by Inst Pur & Supply) St Mut.

Baggott, Karen A. Within Arm's Reach: A Contemplation of Nature in Words & Photographs. 32p. 1991. pap. 8.95 (*0-9627087-5-5*) Mt Olive Coll Pr.

Baggott, Rob. Alcohol, Politics & Social Policy. 192p. 1990. 67.95 (*0-566-07075-8*, Pub. by Avebry) Ashgate Pub Co.

— Health & Health Care in Britain. LC 93-43781. 1994. text 49.95 (*0-312-12109-1*) St Martin.

***Baggott, Rob.** Public Health: Policy & Politics. LC 00-33319. 2000. write for info. (*0-312-23814-2*) St Martin.

Baggs, Jeremy, et al. Essentials of Microbiology for Dental Students. LC 99-10433. (Illus.). 344p. 1999. pap. text 69.95 (*0-19-263076-8*) OUP.

Baggs, S., et al. Australian Earth-Covered Building. (Illus.). 184p. 1991. pap. 29.95 (*0-86840-060-2*, Pub. by New South Wales Univ Pr) Intl Spec Bk.

Baggs, S., et al. Australian EarthCovered Building. 184p. pap. 35.00 (*0-86840-363-6*, Pub. by NSW U Pr) Intl Spec Bk.

***Bagguley.** Transforming Politics. LC HM131.T673 1999. 1999. text 65.00 (*0-312-22231-9*) St Martin.

Bagguley, D. M., ed. Pulsed Magnetic Resonance: NMR, ESR, & Optics. (Illus.). 566p. 1992. text 140.00 (*0-19-853962-2*) OUP.

Bagguley, Paula. Restructuring: Place, Class & Gender. 248p. (C). 1990. text 45.00 (*0-8039-8214-3*) Sage.

Bagguley, Paula, jt. ed. see Seymour, Juliet.

Bagguley, William H. Andrew Marvell, 1621-1678: Tercentenary Tributes, by Augustine Birrell & Others. (BCL1-PR English Literature Ser.). 131p. 1992. reprint ed. lib. bdg. 69.00 (*0-7812-7373-0*) Rprt Serv.

Baghai, Mehrdad, et al. The Alchemy of Growth: Practical Insights for Building the Enduring Enterprise. LC 99-60938. 272p. 1999. text 27.50 (*0-7382-0100-6*, Pub. by Perseus Pubng) HarpC.

***Baghai, Mehrdad, et al.** The Alchemy of Growth: Practical Insights for Building the Enduring Enterprise. 272p. 2000. pap. text 17.00 (*0-7382-0309-2*) Perseus Pubng.

Baghban, Marcia. Our Daughter Learns to Read & Write: A Case Study from Birth to 3. LC 84-10868. 170p. reprint ed. pap. 52.70 (*0-8357-2637-1*, 204012500014) Bks Demand.

Baghdachi, J. Paint & Coatings for Corrosion Protection. (Materials Engineering Ser.). (Illus.). Date not set. text. write for info. (*0-8247-0065-1*) Dekker.

Baghdachi, Jamil A. Adhesion Aspects of Polymeric Coatings. (Illus.). 34p. 1996. pap. 30.00 (*0-934010-06-4*) Fed Soc Coat Tech.

Baghdadi, Rafique & Rao, Rajiv. Talking Films. (C). 1995. 34.00 (*81-7223-197-0*, Pub. by Indus Pub) S Asia.

Baghdady, Nabil H. German-English - English-German Environmental Dictionary. 519p. 1994. 65.00 (*3-464-49425-X*) IBD Ltd.

— German-English/English-German Environmental Dictionary. (ENG & GER.). 519p. 1994. 59.95 (*0-7859-9562-5*) Fr & Eur.

Baghdasarian, Louisa & Zorc, R. David. Armenian (Eastern)-English Dictionary. LC 95-67162. 1995. 89.00 (*1-881265-07-2*) Dunwoody Pr.

Baghdasarian, Louisa, jt. auth. see Zorc, R. David.

Baghdoyan, Helen A., jt. auth. see Lydic, Ralph.

***Baghramian, Maria.** Modern Philosophy of Language. LC 99-31592. 432p. 1999. text 30.00 (*1-58243-042-X*, Pub. by Counterpt DC) HarpC.

Bagiackas, Joseph. Mighty in Spirit. LC 82-72094. 54p. 1982. pap. 3.95 (*0-943780-00-4*, 8004) Greenlawn Pr.

Bagilhole, Barbara. Equal Opportunities & Social Policy: Issues of Gender, Race, & Disability. LC 97-3427. (Social Policy in Britain Ser.). 1997. write for info. (*0-582-27951-8*) Longman.

— Women, Work & Equal Opportunity: A Study of Underachievement in the Civil Service. 223p. 1994. 72.95 (*1-85628-525-1*, Pub. by Avebry) Ashgate Pub Co.

Bagin, Don, jt. auth. see Gallagher, Donald R.

Baginda, Abdul R., et al. Malaysia's Defence & Foreign Policies. LC 95-940736. 137 p. 1995. write for info. (*967-978-512-2*, Pub. by Pelanduk) Weatherhill.

***Baginski.** Management Decision & Financial Acount Reports, Vol. 2. (C). 2000. pap. 11.25 (*0-324-05584-6*) Sth-Wstrn College.

Baginski. Management Decisions & Financial Accounting. (AB - Accounting Principles Ser.). (C). 2000. 87.95 (*0-538-84086-2*) S-W Pub.

Baginski, Bodo & Sharamon, Shalila. Reiki - Universal Life Energy: Heals Body, Mind & Spirit - A Holistic Method Suitable for Self-Treatment & the Home, Professional Practice, Teleotherapeutics-Spiritual Healing. Baker, Chris & Harrison, Judith, trs. from GER. (Illus.). 211p. (Orig.). 1988. pap. 12.95 (*0-940795-02-7*) LifeRhythm.

Baginski, Bodo, jt. auth. see Sharamon, Shalila.

Baginski, Thomas & Liontas, John. Gesichtspunkte: Aktuelle Lesetexte von Gestern, Heute, und Morgen. (Bridging the Gap Ser.). (C). 1994. text 36.95 (*0-8384-4647-7*) Heinle & Heinle.

Baginsky, Bodo J., jt. auth. see Sharamon, Shalila.

Baginsky, Mary, jt. auth. see Stanley, Stephen.

Bagish, Stephen, ed. see Ben Meir, Dov B.

Baglan & Clark. Effective Communication Skills. 2nd ed. (C). 1993. pap. text 17.25 (*0-07-003054-5*) McGraw.

Baglee, Christopher & Morley, Andrew. Street Jewelery. (Illus.). 104p. 1996. 35.00 (*0-904568-16-4*, Pub. by New Cavendish) Pincushion Pr.

— Street Jewelery: A History of Enamel Advertising Signs. (Illus.). 104p. 1996. pap. 16.95 (*0-904568-21-0*, Pub. by New Cavendish) Pincushion Pr.

***Baglery, Archie L., Jr.** More Than Conquerors: The Ultimate Christian Lifestyle. 185p. 2000. pap. 13.95 (*0-7414-0373-0*) Buy Books.

***Bagley.** The Entrepeneur' Guide to Business Law. 2nd ed. (SWC-Business Law Ser.). (C). 2000. text 18.75 (*0-324-04291-4*) Thomson Learn.

Bagley, Ayers, ed. The Black Education Professoriate. (SPE Monographs). 1984. 10.00 (*0-933669-23-2*) Soc Profs Ed.

— The Continuing Education of College Professors. (Occasional Papers: No. 2). 1974. pap. 10.00 (*0-933669-05-4*) Soc Profs Ed.

— Continuing Education of College Professors, Pts. I & II. (Occasional Papers: No. 6). 1974. pap. 10.00 (*0-933669-09-7*) Soc Profs Ed.

— An Invitation to Wisdom & Schooling. (SPE Monographs). 1985. 10.00 (*0-933669-35-6*) Soc Profs Ed.

— Making Teacher Education More Relevant. (NSCTE Monographs). 1970. 10.00 (*0-933669-03-8*) Soc Profs Ed.

— Professional Ethics & the Education Professoriate. (SPE Monographs). 1984. 10.00 (*0-933669-24-0*) Soc Profs Ed.

— The Professor of Education: An Assessment of Conditions. (SPE Monographs). 125p. 1975. 10.00 (*0-933669-15-1*) Soc Profs Ed.

— Professors of Education & Education Librarians. (SPE Monographs). 1985. 10.00 (*0-933669-34-8*) Soc Profs Ed.

— The Right Questions? (SPE Monographs). 1983. 10.00 (*0-933669-20-8*) Soc Profs Ed.

— The School of Education As a Workplace. 1986. 10.00 (*0-933669-36-4*) Soc Profs Ed.

— Study & Love: Aristotle's Fall. (SPE Monographs). 1986. 10.00 (*0-933669-39-9*) Soc Profs Ed.

— Teacher Education: Role-Playing & Analogies to Art. (Occasional Papers: No. 7). 1975. pap. 10.00 (*0-933669-10-0*) Soc Profs Ed.

— Teacher Education As Actor Training. (Occasional Papers: No. 3). 1974. pap. 10.00 (*0-933669-06-2*) Soc Profs Ed.

— Three Schools of Education: Approaches to Institutional History. (SPE Monographs). 1984. 10.00 (*0-933669-25-9*) Soc Profs Ed.

Bagley, Ayers, et al, eds. The Telling Image: Explorations in the Emblem. LC 92-16981. (Studies in the Emblem: No. 12). 1993. 76.50 (*0-404-63712-4*) AMS Pr.

Bagley, Bill & Challis, Bob. Inside Open Learning. 1986. 85.00 (*0-907659-37-3*) St Mut.

Bagley, Bruce M., ed. Drug Trafficking Research in the Americas: An Annotated Bibliography. annot. ed. LC 96-2431. 472p. 1997. pap. 35.00 (*1-57454-001-7*, Pub. by U Miami N-S Ctr) L Rienner.

Bagley, Bruce M. & Quezada, Sergio A., eds. Mexico: In Search of Security. LC 93-527. (University of Miami North-South Center Ser.). 384p. (C). 1993. pap. 24.95 (*1-56000-686-2*, Pub. by U Miami N-S Ctr) L Rienner.

Bagley, Bruce M. & Walker, William O., III, eds. Drug Trafficking in the Americas. LC 94-24418. 572p. (C). 1994. pap. 36.00 (*1-56000-752-4*, Pub. by U Miami N-S Ctr) L Rienner.

Bagley, Christopher. Child Sexual Abuse & Mental Health in Adolescents & Adults: British & Canadian Perspectives. LC 95-23052. 240p. 1995. 66.95 (*1-85628-943-5*) Ashgate Pub Co.

Bagley, Christopher. Children, Sex & Social Policy: Humanistic Solutions for Problems of Child Sexual Abuse. 360p. 1997. text 76.95 (*1-85972-324-1*, Pub. by Avebry) Ashgate Pub Co.

— International & Transracial Adoptions: A Mental Health Perspective. 376p. 1993. 76.95 (*1-85628-082-9*, Pub. by Avebry) Ashgate Pub Co.

Bagley, Christopher & King, Kathleen. Child Sexual Abuse: The Search for Healing. LC 88-36431. 286p. reprint ed. pap. 88.70 (*0-608-20310-6*, 207156300002) Bks Demand.

Bagley, Christopher & Mallick, Kanka, eds. Child Sexual Abuse & Adult Offenders: New Theory & Research. LC 98-73858. (Centre for Evaluative Developmental Research (In Association With) Ser.). 7p. 1999. text 78.95 (*1-84014-839-X*) Ashgate Pub Co.

Bagley, Christopher & Ramsay, Richard. Suicidal Behaviour in Adolescents & Adults: Research, Taxonomy & Prevention. LC 97-71719. 288p. 1997. text 73.95 (*1-85972-540-6*, Pub. by Ashgate Pub) Ashgate Pub Co.

Bagley, Christopher & Thurston, Wilfreda, eds. Understanding & Preventing Child Sexual Abuse, 2 vols., Set. 800p. 1996. text 182.95 (*1-85742-322-4*, Pub. by Arena) Ashgate Pub Co.

Bagley, Clarence. The Acquisition & Pioneering of Old Oregon & in the Beginning. 181p. 1983. reprint ed. 16.95 (*0-87770-280-2*) Ye Galleon.

Bagley, Clarence B. In the Beginning. Meeker, Ezra, ed. (Northwest Historical Classics Ser.). (Illus.). 88p. 1980. reprint ed. pap. 7.95 (*0-939806-00-2*) Hist Soc Seattle.

— Indian Myths of the Northwest. (Illus.). 145p. 1991. reprint ed. pap. 15.00 (*1-878592-35-1*); reprint ed. lib. bdg. 29.00 (*1-878592-38-6*) Native Amer Bk Pubs.

Bagley, Constance E. Entrepreneur's Guide to Business Law. LC 97-10421. 1997. pap. 29.95 (*0-314-22316-9*) West Pub.

Bagley, Constance E. Managers & Legal Environment 3. 3rd ed. LC 98-18789. (Business Law Ser.). 1998. pap. 98.95 (*0-538-88485-1*) S-W Pub.

— Managers & the Legal Environment of Business: Strategies for the 21st Century. Perlee, Clyde, ed. 667p. (C). 1991. text 64.25 (*0-314-79790-4*) West Pub.

— Mgr & The Legal Environment 2e. 2nd ed. LC 94-45225. (SWC-Business Law). 974p. (C). 1995. mass mkt. 68.50 (*0-314-04391-8*) West Pub.

Bagley, Constance E. & Berger, David J. Proxy Contests & Corporate Control: Conducting the Proxy Campaign. (Corporate Practice Ser.: No. 70). (Illus.). 1997. ring bd. 95.00 (*1-55871-351-4*) BNA.

— Proxy Contests & Corporate Control: Strategic Considerations. (Corporate Practice Ser.: No. 69). (Illus.). 1997. ring bd. 95.00 (*1-55871-349-2*) BNA.

Bagley, Constance E. & Khanna, Rakesh R. Cutting Edge Cases in the Legal Environment of Business. 2nd ed. LC 98-205412. (SWC-Business Law Ser.). vii, 109p. 1998. pap. 23.95 (*0-324-00209-2*) Thomson Learn.

Bagley, Demetirus H., et al. Urologic Endoscopy: A Manual & Atlas. 336p. 1985. 165.00 (*0-316-07518-3*, Little Brwn Med Div) Lppncott W & W.

Bagley, Ed. Inside a Job Interview: Answers to the 15 Most Frequently Asked Questions. 4th rev. ed. Orig. Title: Answers to the 15 Most Frequently Asked Questions During a Job Interview. 16p. (Orig.). 1997. pap. 5.00 (*0-9658094-0-4*) NW Mktg.

— Personal Marketing & Quality Resumes. LC 97-91974. 184p. (Orig.). 1997. pap. 18.52 (*0-9658094-1-2*) NW Mktg.

Bagley, Emmet. The Secret Ambition of Mayer A. Rothschild. Date not set. pap. write for info. (*0-915315-01-7*) Patterson Pr.

Bagley, F. R., ed. Sadeq Chubak: An Anthology. (Modern Persian Literature Ser.: Vol. 3). vii, 286p. 1982. text 25.00 (*0-88206-048-1*) Bibliotheca Persica.

Bagley, F. R., et al. The Last Great Muslim Empires: History of the Muslim World, III. 2nd ed. Bagley, R. C., tr. from GER. 333p. 1996. reprint ed. pap. text 19.95 (*1-55876-112-8*) Wiener Pubs Inc.

Bagley, F. R., tr. see Dashti, Ali.

Bagley, F. R., tr. see Spuler, Bertold.

Bagley, F. R.C., tr. see Spuler, Bertold.

Bagley, Garland C. History of Forsyth County, Georgia 1832-1932. 2nd ed. (Illus.). 921p. 1997. reprint ed. 50.00 (*0-9644858-8-5*) Boyd Pub Co.

Bagley, George E. My Four Decades with Alabama Baptists: An Oral History Memoir. LC 89-85560. (Illus.). 272p. 1990. 15.95 (*0-9624149-0-5*) AL Baptist.

Bagley, Harry C. Listening to the Grass Grow. Bagley, Richard H., ed. (Illus.). 162p. 1987. 10.00 (0-9619190-0-0) R H Bagley.

Bagley, Helen G. Sand in My Shoe: Homestead Day's in Twenty-Nine Palms. 3rd ed. Weight, Harold & Weight, Lucile, eds. LC 77-949990. (Illus.). 269p. 1978. reprint ed. pap. 17.95 (0-912714-08-5) Adobe Road.

Bagley, J. A. & Finley, P. J., eds. Progress in Aerospace Sciences, Vol. 18, No. 1. LC 74-618347. 1977. pap. 35.00 (0-08-022133-5, Pergamon Pr) Elsevier.

Bagley, Julian. Candle-Lighting Time in Bodidalee. LC 70-144772. 128 P.p. (J). 1971. write for info. (0-07-003018-9) McGraw.

***Bagley, Katie.** Coaches. LC 00-9700. (Community Helpers Ser.). 2001. write for info. (0-7368-0807-8) Capstone Pr.

Bagley, Merle. Sidestepping the Barbarians. (American Autobiography Ser.). 45p. 1995. reprint ed. lib. bdg. 69.00 (0-7812-8445-7) Rprt Serv.

Bagley, Michael. Image Acceleration: Innovative Thinking Through Imagery. 1990. pap. 14.99 (0-89824-518-4) Trillium Pr.

Bagley, Michael & Kemnitz, Myrna. Suppose the Wolf were an Octopus: A Guide to Creative Questioning - Grades 3-4. 2nd rev. ed. 148p. (J). (gr. 3-4). 1995. pap. 14.99 (0-88092-248-6, 2486, Kav Bks) Royal Fireworks.

— Suppose the Wolf were an Octopus: A Guide to Creative Questioning - Grades 5-6. 2nd rev. ed. 169p. (J). (gr. 5-6). 1995. pap. 14.99 (0-88092-249-4, 2494) Royal Fireworks.

Bagley, Michael & Lavin, Claire. Consultant As Communicator. 1990. pap. 9.99 (0-89824-202-9) Trillium Pr.

Bagley, Michael T. Using Imagery in Creative Problem Solving. 1986. pap. 9.99 (0-89824-104-9) Trillium Pr.

— Using Imagery to Develop Memory. 118p. 1987. pap. 9.99 (0-89824-040-9) Trillium Pr.

Bagley, Michael T., et al. Two Hundred Ways of Using Imagery in the Classroom: A Guide for Developing Imagination & Creativity in Elementary Students. (gr. 1-8). 1987. pap. 15.00 (0-89824-084-0) Trillium Pr.

Bagley, Micheal. Suppose the Wolf Were an Octopus: Guide to Creative Questioning for Elementary Grade Literature: K-2. 1996. pap. 14.99 (0-88092-247-8) Royal Fireworks.

Bagley, Mischa Kk. The Rose of Ashes. 252p. 1999. 26.00 (0-9531490-0-5) Honest to Goodness.

Bagley, Nancy F. Reunions for Fun-Loving Families. LC 94-11405. 128p. (Orig.). 1994. pap. 9.95 (0-918420-21-0) Brighton Pubns.

Bagley, Pat. Hana, the No-Cow Wife. LC 93-412. (Illus.). 1993. 12.95 (0-87579-714-8) Deseret Bk.

— Peek-a-Boo Magic. LC 95-15050. (Illus.). 32p. (J). 1995. 12.95 (1-885628-00-5, Pub. by Buckaroo Bks) Origin Bk Sales.

— Showdown at Slickrock. (Illus.). 32p. (J). (gr. k-5). 1996. 15.95 (1-885628-02-1, Pub. by Buckaroo Bks) Origin Bk Sales.

***Bagley, Paul J., ed.** Piety, Peace & the Freedom to Philosophize. LC 99-47089. (New Synthese Historical Library). 304p. 1999. text 128.00 (0-7923-5984-4) Kluwer Academic.

Bagley, R. C., tr. see Bagley, F. R., et al.

Bagley, Richard H., ed. see Bagley, Harry C.

Bagley, Ron, ed. Sharing God's Work Through the Year: A Small Group Guide for Young Adults. 200p. 1997. pap. 19.95 (1-890516-03-1) Ctr Minist Dev.

— Waiting with Hope: Reflections by Young Adults for Everyday of Advent. 40p. (Orig.). 1997. pap. 6.95 (1-890516-00-7) Ctr Minist Dev.

Bagley, Ted D. The Complete Fundraising Guide to Successful Campaigns: What Your Board Needs to Know. 200p. 1999. 32.95 (1-887617-66-3); pap. 19.95 (1-887617-67-1) St Bart Pr Ltd.

Bagley, Toni. Know What to Do & How to Do It: Parliamentary Procedure Simplified. 3rd rev. ed. 116p. 12.00 (0-9608794-0-4) Bagley Pubn.

Bagley, Val. Choose the Right. (Illus.). (J). 1996. pap. 2.95 (1-57734-032-9, 01112546) Covenant Comms.

***Bagley, Val.** I Will Make & Keep My Baptismal Covenant. (J). 1999. pap. 3.95 (1-57734-516-9, 01114166) Covenant Comms.

Bagley, Val. Jesus Visits the Americas. (Illus.). (J). 1995. pap. 2.49 (1-55503-829-8, 01111981) Covenant Comms.

Bagley, Val. Mormon Mailables: Peculiar Postcards for a Peculiar People. pap. 5.95 (1-57734-187-2, 01113259) Covenant Comms.

— Mormon Mailables for Sister Missionaries: Peculiar Postcards for a Peculiar People. pap. 5.95 (1-57734-291-7, 01113453) Covenant Comms.

— My Book about Me. (J). pap. 4.95 (1-57734-341-7, 01113682) Covenant Comms.

— My Book of Mormon ABC's. (J). 1999. 8.95 (1-57734-517-7, 01114174) Covenant Comms.

— My Missionary Book. 1999. pap. 3.95 (1-57734-518-5, 01114182) Covenant Comms.

Bagley, Val. Preparing for My Baptism. (J). 1996. pap. 2.95 (1-55503-564-7, 01111299) Covenant Comms.

Bagley, Val C. Elder's Epistles: Cartoons for Missionaries. 64p. 1980. pap. 6.98 (0-88290-539-2, 2034) Horizon Utah.

— Mission Mania: A Cartoonist's View of the Best 2 Years of Life. (Illus.). 98p. (Orig.). 1980. pap. 6.98 (0-88290-140-0) Horizon Utah.

— Missionary Grams: Cartoons for Missionaries. 64p. 1980. pap. 6.98 (0-88290-538-4, 2032) Horizon Utah.

Bagley, Will. Scoundrel's Tale: The Samuel Brannan Papers. LC 99-12606. 477p. 1999. pap. 21.95 (0-87421-273-1) Utah St U Pr.

Bagley, Will. This Is the Place. LC 95-40502. (Illus.). 32p. (J). (gr. 2-8). 1996. pap. 9.95 (1-885628-25-0, Pub. by Buckaroo Bks) Origin Bk Sales.

Bagley, Will. This Is the Place. (Illus.). 32p. (J). (gr. 2-8). 1996. 16.95 (1-885628-26-9, 8269, Pub. by Buckaroo Bks) Origin Bk Sales.

Bagley, Will, ed. Kingdom in the West: The Mormons & the American Frontier, 15 vols. (Illus.). 400p. 1997. 39.50 (0-87062-266-8) A H Clark.

— The Pioneer Camp of the Saints: The 1846 & 1847 Mormon Trail Journals of Thomas Bullock. LC 96-51745. (Kingdom in the West Ser.: Vol. I). (Illus.). 400p. 1997. 39.50 (0-87062-276-5) A H Clark.

— Scoundrel's Tale: The Samuel Brannan Papers. LC 98-51070. (Kingdom in the West Ser.: Vol. 3). (Illus.). 464p. 1999. 39.50 (0-87062-287-0) A H Clark.

Bagley, Will, jt. auth. see Bigler, David L.

Bagley, William C. Determinism in Education. LC 70-89146. (American Education: Its Men, Institutions, & Ideas. Series 1). 1977. reprint ed. 18.95 (0-405-01383-3) Ayer.

Bagley, William C., jt. auth. see Keith, J. A.

Bagley, William D. & Whynott, Philip P. The Limited Liability Company. 2nd ed. 525p. 1994. ring bd. 199.00 (0-938065-64-5) James Pub Santa Ana.

Bagli, Vince & Macht, Norman L. Sundays at 2:00 with the Baltimore Colts. LC 95-359805. (Illus.). 264p. 1995. pap. 17.95 (0-87033-476-X, Tidewtr Pubs) Cornell Maritime.

Baglin, A., jt. ed. see Weiss, W. W.

Baglin, Carol A. & Bender, Michael, eds. Handbook on Quality Child Care for Young Children: Setting Standards & Resources. LC 93-21684. (Illus.). 300p. (C). 1993. pap. text 37.95 (1-56593-093-2, 0397) Thomson Learn.

Baglin, Carol A., jt. ed. see Bender, Michael.

Baglin, David, jt. auth. see Robinson, Roy.

Baglin, John E., ed. see Electrochemical Society, Thin Film Phenomena-Inter.

Baglin, John E., ed. see Symposium on Thin Film Interfaces & Interactions.

Baglin Jones, Eileen & Jones, Neville, eds. Education for Citizenship: A Cross-Curricular Approach. 178p. 1992. pap. 25.00 (0-7494-0820-0, Kogan Pg Educ) Stylus Pub VA.

Baglini, Norman A. Global Risk Management: How U. S. International Corporations Manage Foreign Risks. (Illus.). 134p. 1983. pap. 15.00 (0-937802-04-2) RMSP.

Bagliniaere, Jean-Luc & Maisse, G. Biology & Ecology of the Brown Sea Trout. LC 98-51613. (Series in Acquaculture & Fisheries). 305p. 1999. 95.00 (1-85233-117-8) Spr-Verlag.

***Baglio, Ben.** Owl in the Office, Vol. 11. (Animal Ark Ser.: No. 11). (Illus.). 192p. (J). (gr. 3-6). 1999. pap. text 3.99 (0-439-08416-4) Scholastic Inc.

Baglio, Ben M. Animal Ark Pony on the Porch. (Animal Ark Ser.: Vol. 2). (Illus.). (J). (gr. 4-7). 1997. pap. text 3.99 (0-590-18750-3) Scholastic Inc.

— Badger in the Basement. (Animal Ark Ser.: No. 6). (J). (gr. 4-7). 1998. pap. 3.99 (0-590-18754-6, Apple Paperbacks) Scholastic Inc.

***Baglio, Ben M.** Bunnies in the Bathroom. 15. (Animal Ark Ser.: No. 15). (Illus.). 160p. (J). (gr. 4-7). 2000. pap. 3.99 (0-439-09700-2) Scholastic Inc.

Baglio, Ben M. Cub in the Cupboard. (Animal Ark Ser.: No. 8). 160p. (J). (gr. 3-6). 1999. pap. 3.99 (0-590-18755-4, Little Apple) Scholastic Inc.

***Baglio, Ben M.** Goat in the Garden. (Animal Ark Ser.: No. 4). (J). (gr. 3-5). 1998. 9.09 (0-606-13132-9, Pub. by Turtleback) Demco.

— Goose on the Loose. (Animal Ark Ser.: No. 14). 160p. (J). (gr. 3-6). 2000. pap. 3.99 (0-439-09699-5) Scholastic.

— Hamster in a Handbasket. (Animal Ark Ser.: No. 16). (Illus.). 160p. (J). (gr. 3-5). 2000. pap. 3.99 (0-439-09701-0) Scholastic Inc.

Baglio, Ben M. Hedgehogs in the Hall. (Animal Ark Ser.: No. 5). (J). (gr. 4-7). 1998. pap. text 3.99 (0-590-37684-5, Little Apple) Scholastic Inc.

***Baglio, Ben M.** Kitten in the Cold, 1 vol., Vol. 13. (Animal Ark Ser.: No. 13). (J). (gr. 3-5). 1999. pap. text 3.99 (0-439-09698-7) Scholastic Inc.

— The Kitten That Won First Prize. (Animorphs Ser.: No. 31). 160p. (J). (gr. 4-7). 2000. pap. 3.99 (0-439-09703-7) Scholastic Inc.

Baglio, Ben M. Kittens in the Kitchen. (Animal Ark Ser.: No. 1). (Illus.). 147p. (J). (gr. 3-6). 1998. pap. 3.99 (0-590-18749-X) Scholastic Inc.

***Baglio, Ben M.** Kittens in the Kitchen. (Animal Ark Ser.: No. 1). (J). (gr. 3-5). 1998. 9.09 (0-606-13129-9, Pub. by Turtleback) Demco.

— Lamb in the Laundry, 1 vol., Vol. 12. (Animal Ark Ser.: No. 12). 160p. (J). (gr. 3-6). 1999. pap. text 3.99 (0-439-08642-6) Scholastic Inc.

— Piglet in a Playpen, Vol. 9. (Animal Ark Ser.: No. 9). (J). (gr. 3-5). 1999. pap. 3.99 (0-590-18756-2) Scholastic Inc.

Baglio, Ben M. Ponies at the Point, Vol. 10. (Animal Ark Ser.: No. 10). 144p. (J). (gr. 3-6). 1999. pap. 3.99 (0-590-66231-7) Scholastic Inc.

***Baglio, Ben M.** Pony on the Porch. (Animal Ark Ser.: No. 2). (J). (gr. 3-5). 1998. 9.09 (0-606-13130-2, Pub. by Turtleback) Demco.

Baglio, Ben M. Puppies in the Pantry. (Animal Ark Ser.: No. 3). (Illus.). 133p. (J). (gr. 3-5). 1998. pap. 3.99 (0-590-18751-1) Scholastic Inc.

— Sheepdog in the Snow. (Animal Ark Ser.: No. 6). (Illus.). 160p. (J). (gr. 3-6). 1998. pap. text 3.99 (0-590-18757-0) Scholastic Inc.

***Baglio, Ben M.** Squirrels in the School. (Animal Ark Ser.: No. 17). (Illus.). 160p. (J). (gr. 4-7). 2000. pap. 3.99 (0-439-09702-9, Little Apple) Scholastic Inc.

Baglione, Lisa A. To Agree or Not to Agree: Leadership, Bargaining, & Arms Control. LC 98-25388. (Illus.). 248p. 1999. text 49.50 (0-472-10930-8, 10930) U of Mich Pr.

Baglioni, Guido. Impossible Democracy? The Progress & Problems of Participation in the Firm. 208p. 1996. text 68.95 (1-85972-537-6, Pub. by Avebry) Ashgate Pub Co.

Baglioni, Guido & Crouch, Colin, eds. European Industrial Relations: The Challenge of Flexibility. 384p. (C). 1990. text 49.95 (0-8039-8242-9); pap. text 22.50 (0-8039-8544-4) Sage.

Baglivi, Christina. Northern Italy: A Taste of Trattoria. rev. ed. LC 95-7028. (Illus.). 240p. (Orig.). 1995. pap. 12.95 (0-914457-72-1) Mustang Pub.

Baglole, Harry, et al. The Chappell Diary. LC 78-300856. 60p. 1977. write for info. (0-920304-02-8) Ragweed Pr.

Baglow, John. Hugh MacDiarmid: The Poetry of Self. 272p. 1987. 60.00 (0-7735-0571-7, Pub. by McG-Queens Univ Pr) CUP Services.

Baglow, Len. Contemporary Christian Counseling. 115p. (Orig.). 1997. pap. 9.95 (0-85574-302-6, Pub. by E J Dwyer) Morehouse Pub.

Bagma, L. T., jt. auth. see Bljach, I. S.

Bagnal, K., et al. The Packing of Particles. (Handbook of Powder Technology Ser.: 6). 150p. 1979. pap. 116.50 (0-444-41041-4) Elsevier.

Bagnal, Tom. Let Us Pray: A Book of Uncommon Prayers. LC 98-66926. 64p. 1998. pap. 11.95 (1-57736-115-6) Providence Hse.

Bagnall, Gary. Law As Art. (Applied Legal Philosophy Ser.). (Illus.). 232p. 1996. text 81.95 (1-85521-758-9, Pub. by Dartmth Pub) Ashgate Pub Co.

Bagnall, Gellisse. Educating Young Drinkers. 176p. (C). (gr. 13). 1991. text 74.95 (0-415-01718-1, A5223) Routledge.

Bagnall, Jim, jt. auth. see Koberg, Don.

Bagnall, Joseph A. The Politics of Survival: Resolving the Seven Deadly Trends. 2nd ed. (C). 1997. pap. 22.19 (0-07-289259-5) McGrw-H Hghr Educ.

Bagnall, Joseph A., ed. see Kennedy, John F.

Bagnall, Nicholas. Newspaper Language. 280p. 1993. pap. 39.95 (0-7506-0399-2) Buttrwrth-Heinemann.

Bagnall, Norma H. On Shaky Ground: The New Madrid Earthquakes of 1811-1812. Schroeder, Rebecca B., ed. (Missouri Heritage Readers Ser.). (Illus.). 128p. (C). 1996. pap. 9.95 (0-8262-1054-6) U of Mo Pr.

Bagnall, Philip M. Meteorite & Tektite Collectors Handbook. 1991. 24.95 (0-943396-31-X) Willmann-Bell.

Bagnall, R. S. The Administration of the Ptolemaic Possessions Outside Egypt. 1976. 31.00 (90-04-04490-6, CSCT, 4) Brill Academic Pubs.

Bagnall, R. S. & Harris, W. V., eds. Studies in Roman Law. xviii, 168p. 1986. 54.50 (90-04-07568-2, CSCT, 13) Brill Academic Pubs.

Bagnall, Roger S. Digital Imaging of Papyri: A Report to the Commission on Preservation & Access. 8p. 1995. pap. 10.00 (1-887334-44-0) Coun Lib & Info.

— Egypt in Late Antiquity. 388p. (C). 1993. pap. text 17.95 (0-691-01096-X, Pub. by Princeton U Pr) Cal Prin Full Svc.

— Egypt in Late Antiquity. LC 92-40332. (Illus.). 352p. 1993. text 49.50 (0-691-06986-7, Pub. by Princeton U Pr) Cal Prin Full Svc.

— Reading Papyri, Writing Ancient History. LC 95-4136. (Approaching the Ancient World Ser.). (Illus.). 168p. (C). 1995. pap. 19.99 (0-415-09377-5) Routledge.

Bagnall, Roger S., ed. Columbia Papyri VII: Fourth Century Documents from Karanis. LC 78-31952. (American Studies in Papyrology: No. 20). (Illus.). 289p. reprint ed. pap. 89.60 (0-7837-5492-2, 20452570005) Bks Demand.

Bagnall, Roger S. & Frier, Bruce W. The Demography of Roman Egypt. LC 93-32406. (Studies in Population, Economy & Society in Past Time: No. 23). (Illus.). 376p. (C). 1994. text 57.95 (0-521-46123-5) Cambridge U Pr.

Bagnall, Roger S. & Worp, K. A. Regnal Formulas in Byzantine Egypt. LC 79-1316. (Bulletin of the American Society of Papyrologists Supplements Ser.: No. 2). 102p. reprint ed. pap. 31.70 (0-7837-5419-1, 204518300005) Bks Demand.

Bagnall, Roger S., et al. Consuls of the Later Roman Empire. LC 86-31452. (American Philological Association Philological Monographs). 769p. 1987. 53.00 (1-55540-099-X, 40-00-36) OUP.

Bagnall, William R. The Textile Industries of the United States, 1639-1810, Vol. 1. LC 68-22370. (Library of Early American Business & Industry: No. 15). xxii, 660p. 1971. reprint ed. 65.00 (0-678-00735-7) Kelley.

Bagnara, J., ed. see International Pigment Cell Conference Staff.

***Bagnasco, Arnaldo & Le Gales, Patrick, eds.** Cities in Contemporary Europe. 216p. 2000. 59.95 (0-521-66248-6) Cambridge U Pr.

— Cities in Contemporary Europe. (Illus.). 216p. 2000. pap. 22.95 (0-521-66488-8) Cambridge U Pr.

Bagnasco, Arnaldo & Sabel, Charles F., eds. Small- & Medium-Size Enterprises. LC 95-8062. (Social Change in Western Europe Ser.). 1995. 19.95 (1-85567-308-8); pap. 45.95 (1-85567-309-6) St Martin.

Bagnasco, Erminio & Grossman, Mark. Regina Marina, Italian Battleships of WW II: A Pictorial History. LC 86-60436. (Illus.). 76p. 1986. pap. 7.95 (0-933126-75-1) Pictorial Hist.

Bagnasco, John J. Plants for the Home, Vol. 1. 1975. 15.00 (0-918134-01-3) Nature Life.

Bagnato, Hilary Richardson, jt. auth. see Kellman, Jerold L.

Bagnato, Stephen J. & Neisworth, John T. Assessment for Early Intervention: Best Practices for Professionals. LC 91-6540. 260p. 1991. pap. text 24.00 (0-89862-238-7) Guilford Pubns.

Bagnato, Stephen J., et al. Linking Assessment & Early Intervention: An Authentic Curriculum-Based Approach. 3rd ed. LC 96-43160. 1996. 44.95 (1-55766-263-0) P H Brookes.

Bagne, Gwen. Embracing Life Again: Finding Your Way in the Midst of Loss. LC 99-60726. 144p. 1999. pap. 10.95 (1-57921-215-8, Pub. by WinePress Pub) BookWorld.

Bagne, Paul. River of Fire. 1999. mass mkt. write for info. (0-449-15047-X, GM) Fawcett.

Bagnell, Prisca V. & Soper, Patricia S., eds. Perceptions of Aging in Literature: A Cross-Cultural Study, 11. LC 88-34723. (Contributions to the Study of Aging Ser.: No. 11). 200p. 1989. 52.95 (0-313-26292-6, BAJ, Greenwood Pr) Greenwood.

Bagness, Carmel. Genetics, the Fetus & Our Future. 112p. 1998. pap. text 25.00 (1-898507-65-1, RJ131) Buttrwrth-Heinemann.

Bagni, Paolo, et al. Seminario sul Racconto. Rustichelli, Luigi, ed. LC 98-26942. (VIA Folios Ser.: No. 16). (ITA.). 96p. (C). 1998. pap. 10.00 (1-884419-21-6, VIA Folios) Bordighera.

Bagnimski. Bridging the Gap: Advanced German Reader. (College German Ser.). (GER.). (C). 1994. mass mkt., teacher ed. 13.95 (0-8384-4634-5) Heinle & Heinle.

Bagno, Daniel Del, see Adamson, Mark & Del Bagno, Daniel.

Bagno, Daniel M. Del, see Del Bagno, Daniel M.

Bagno, Daniel R. Del, see Adamson, Mark & Del Bagno, Daniel R.

Bagnold. Sand, Wind & War: Memoirs of a Desert Explorer. LC 90-46430. (Illus.). 209p. 1991. 37.50 (0-8165-1211-6) U of Ariz Pr.

Bagnold, Enid. Enid Bagnold's Autobiography (from 1889) LC 75-457120. 293 p. 1969. write for info. (0-434-04303-6) Buttrwrth-Heinemann.

— The Loved & the Envied. LC 75-110820. 276p. 1970. reprint ed. lib. bdg. 38.50 (0-8371-2700-9, BALE, Greenwood Pr) Greenwood.

— National Velvet. 272p. (J). 1991. mass mkt. 4.99 (0-380-71235-0, Avon Bks) Morrow Avon.

***Bagnold, Enid.** National Velvet. 272p. (J). 1999. mass mkt. 4.99 (0-380-81056-5, Avon Bks) Morrow Avon.

Bagnold, Enid. National Velvet. 1991. 9.60 (0-606-12446-2, Pub. by Turtleback) Demco.

— National Velvet. 320p. (J). 1981. reprint ed. lib. bdg. 35.95 (0-89966-359-1); reprint ed. lib. bdg. 18.95 (0-89967-033-4, Harmony Rain) Buccaneer Bks.

— The Squire. 1988. 23.95 (0-8488-0421-X) Amereon Ltd.

Bagnold, Ralph A. Libyan Sands: Travel in a Dead World. 228p. (C). 1995. pap. 24.00 (0-907151-90-6, Pub. by IMMEL Pubng) St Mut.

— The Physics of Sediment Transport by Wind & Water: A Collection of Hallmark Papers. Thorne, Colin R. et al, eds. 376p. 1988. 49.00 (0-87262-665-2) Am Soc Civil Eng.

Bagnoli, Alessandra, jt. auth. see Albertini, Bianca.

Bagnoli, Franco. Dynamical Modelling in Biotechnology. 1998. 78.00 (981-02-3604-2) World Scientific Pub.

Bagnoli, Giorgio. The La Scala Encyclopedia of the Opera. LC 93-10024. 1993. 50.00 (0-671-87042-4) S&S Trade.

Bagnoli, P. & Hodos, William, eds. The Changing Visual System: From Early to Late Stages of Life. (NATO ASI Ser.: Vol. 222). (Illus.). 432p. (C). 1992. text 156.00 (0-306-44090-3, Kluwer Plenum) Kluwer Academic.

***Bagnoli, Paolo.** The Liberal Socialism: Four Essays on the Political Thought of Carlo Rosselli. 124p. 1999. pap. 7.00 (0-913298-98-0) S F Vanni.

Bagnoli, Paolo. Il Liberalsocialismo. (ITA.). 151p. 1997. pap. 22.00 (0-913298-40-9) S F Vanni.

— La Politica delle Idee: Giovan Pietro Vieusseux e Giuseppe Montanelli Nella Toscana Preunitaria. (ITA.). 269p. 1996. pap. 30.00 (0-913298-04-2) S F Vanni.

— La Politica e il Tempo: Idee e Problemi Della Transizione Italiana. (ITA.). 114p. 1998. pap. 18.00 (0-913298-16-6) S F Vanni.

— The Ulysses Complex: Italy & Europe in the Political Transition/Two Lectures. 60p. 1997. pap. 5.00 (0-913298-96-4) S F Vanni.

Bagnull, Marlene. God, I Need to Talk to You: Prayer Diary for Girls. LC 97-6307. 1997. 5.99 (0-570-04982-2, 12-3332) Concordia.

— Write His Answer: A Bible Study for Christian Writers. 2nd rev. ed. 176p. 1999. pap. 12.00 (1-892525-12-7, Pub. by ACW Press) Spring Arbor Dist.

— Write His Answer: Encouragement for Christian Writers. 96p. (Orig.). 1990. pap. 6.95 (0-939513-41-2) Joy Pub SJC.

Bagnull, Marlene, ed. see Ludy, Eric & Ludy, Leslie.

Bagnull, Marlene, ed. see Runkles, Richard & Runkles, Janet.

Bagot, Brian N. Aikido: Traditional Art & Modern Sport. (Illus.). 224p. 1993. pap. 29.95 (1-85223-715-5, Pub. by Cro1wood) Trafalgar.

Bagot, Jean P. Petit Dictionnaire de la Catechese. (FRE.). 96p. 1990. pap. 15.95 (0-7859-7794-5, 222031306) Fr & Eur.

Bagot, Jean-Pierre. How to Understand Marriage. (Adult Christian Formation Program Ser.). (Illus.). 144p. (Orig.). 1987. pap. 14.95 (0-8245-0810-6) Crossroad NY.

Bagot, Joyce T., ed. 1998 Source Book on Collective Bargaining: Wages, Benefits, & Other Contract Issues. 1998. 75.00 (1-55871-366-2, XCMP 45) BNA PLUS.

***Bagot, Joyce T., ed.** 1999 Source Book on Collective Bargaining: Wages, Benefits & Other Contract Issues. 1999. ring bd. 80.00 (1-55871-397-2) BNA PLUS.

Bagot, Richard. The Italian Lakes. 1977. lib. bdg. 59.95 (0-8490-2086-7) Gordon Pr.

Bagotzky, V. S. Fundamentals of Electrochemistry. (Illus.). 608p. (C). 1993. text 125.00 (0-306-44338-4, Kluwer Plenum) Kluwer Academic.

B

Bagozzi, Richard P., ed. Advanced of Marketing Research. LC 93-40009. 384p. (Orig.). (C). 1994. pap. 50.95 (*1-55786-549-3*) Blackwell Pubs.

Bagozzi, Richard P., et al. Marketing Management. LC 97-36484. 718p. 1998. 96.00 (*0-02-305162-0*) P-H.

Bagraev, Nickolay T., ed. Defects in Semiconductors I: NCDS-1. (Defect & Diffusion Forum Ser.: Vol. 103-105). (Illus.). 691p. (C). 1993. text 283.00 (*0-87849-666-1*, Pub. by Trans T Pub) Enfield Pubs NH.

Bagratashvili, V. N., et al. Multiple Photon Infrared Laser Photophysics & Photochemistry. xii, 512p. 1985. text 237.00 (*3-7186-0269-5*) Gordon & Breach.

Bagrodia, Rajive & Jefferson, David, eds. 7th Workshop on Parallel & Distributed Simulation (PADS '93) 168p. 1993. pap. 24.00 (*1-56555-055-2*, PADS-93) Soc Computer Sim.

***Bagrov, Igor A.** In the Battle. LC 99-90819. 1999. 25.00 (*0-7388-0524-6*); pap. 18.00 (*0-7388-0525-4*) Xlibris Corp.

Bagrov, V. G. & Gitman, D. M. Exact Solutions of Relativistic Wave Equations. (C). 1990. text 226.50 (*0-7923-0215-X*) Kluwer Academic.

Bagryana, Elisaveta. Penelope of the Twentieth Century: Selected Poems. Dimitrova, Blaga, ed. Walker, B. et al, trs. from BUL. LC 93-70419. 138p. 1994. pap. 19.95 (*1-85610-026-X*, Pub. by Forest Bks) Dufour.

Bagschik, Thorsten. Utopias in the English-Speaking World & the Perception of Economic Reality. (Freiberger Beitraege zum Einflub der Angloamerikanischen Sprache und Kultur auf Europa Ser.: Bd. 2). 248p. 1996. pap. 44.95 (*3-631-49970-1*) P Lang Pubng.

Bagsgall, M. E., et al. Journal of California & Great Basin Anthropology. fac. ed. (Malki Museum, Journal of California & Great Basin Anthropology Ser.: Vol. 4:1). (Illus.). 164p. (C). 1982. reprint ed. pap. text 17.50 (*1-55567-769-X*) Coyote Press.

Bagshaw, I. W. Worked Examples in Relative Radar Plotting. (C). 1987. 65.00 (*0-85174-330-7*) St Mut.

Bagshaw, M., jt. auth. see Campbell, R.

Bagshaw, M., jt. auth. see Campbell, R. D.

Bagshaw, Malcolm A. Cancer of the Prostate, 18. (Oncologic Ser.: Vol. 18). (Illus.). 260p. 1984. pap. 120.00 (*0-08-027471-4*, Pergamon Pr) Elsevier.

Bagshaw, Norman E. Batteries on Ships. LC 82-10954. (Electronic & Electrical Engineering Research Ser.: No. 1). (Illus.). 215p. reprint ed. pap. 66.70 (*0-8357-6035-9*, 203421300089) Bks Demand.

Bagshaw, Samuel. History, Gazetteer, & Directory of Shropshire. 721p. 1995. reprint ed. pap. 43.00 (*0-7884-0272-2*) Heritage Bk.

Bagshawe, L. E., tr. The Maniyadanabon of Shin Sandalinka. 132p. 1981. pap. 7.00 (*0-87727-115-1*, DP 115) Cornell SE Asia.

Bagshawe, Loiuse. Triple Feature. LC 96-44059. 1997. 22.50 (*0-684-83069-8*) S&S Trade.

Bagshawe, Louise. Burns Indiana Statutes. annot. ed. 384p. write for info. (*0-614-05786-8*, MICHIE) LEXIS Pub.

Bagshawe, Richard W. Roman Roads. (Shire Archaeology Ser.: Vol. 10). (Illus.). 64p. 10.50 (*0-85263-458-7*, Pub. by Shire Pubns) Lubrecht & Cramer.

***Bagster, Jonathan.** Daily Light on the Daily Path. LC 99-34809. 384p. 1999. pap. 11.99 (*0-88368-556-6*) Whitaker Hse.

***Bagster, Samuel.** Daily Light. (Essential Christian Library Ser.). 400p. 1999. 9.97 (*1-57748-524-6*) Barbour Pub.

— Daily Light. (Christian Classics). 376p. 2000. 4.97 (*1-57748-791-5*) Barbour Pub.

— Daily Lightt: King James Text. 1999. 14.99 (*1-889893-43-9*) Emerald House Group Inc.

— Historical Account of the English Translations. 1999. pap. text 33.00 (*1-58329-009-5*) Lazarus Minist.

***Bagster, Samuel, compiled by.** Daily Light. 96p. 2000. mass mkt. 0.99 (*1-57748-669-2*) Barbour Pub.

Bagster, Samuel & Lotz, Anne G. Daily Light Devotional. 800p. 1998. lthr. 24.99 (*0-8499-5406-1*) Word Pub.

Baguant, J. & Teferra, M. Transport Energy in Africa. Bhagavan, M. R., ed. LC 96-23126. (African Energy Policy Research Network Ser.). (Illus.). 144p. (C). 1996. text 25.00 (*1-85649-462-4*, Pub. by Zed Books) St Martin.

Baguelin, F., et al. The Pressuremeter & Foundation Engineering. (Rock & Soil Mechanics Ser.). (Illus.). (C). 1978. 60.00 (*0-87849-019-1*, Pub. by Trans T Pub) Enfield Pubs NH.

Bagui, Subhash C. Handbook of Percentiles of Non-Central Distributions. 400p. 1993. lib. bdg. 169.00 (*0-8493-8669-1*, QA273) CRC Pr.

Baguio, Mary E. My Statement to the World. 1997. 6.95 (*0-533-08440-7*) Vantage.

Baguley, David. Bibliographie de la Critique sur Emile Zola, 1971-1980. (FRE.). 242p. 1982. text 40.00 (*0-8020-2456-4*) U of Toronto Pr.

***Baguley, David.** Napoleon III & His Regime: An Extravaganza. (Modernist Studies). (Illus.). 392p. 2000. 49.95 (*0-8071-2624-1*) La State U Pr.

Baguley, David. Naturalist Fiction: The Entropic Vision. (Cambridge Studies in French: No. 28). 295p. (C). 1990. text 69.95 (*0-521-37380-8*) Cambridge U Pr.

— Zola: "L'Assommoir" (Landmarks of World Literature Ser.). (Illus.). 128p. (C). 1992. text 36.95 (*0-521-38426-5*) Cambridge U Pr.

— Zola et les Genres. 208p. 1993. 60.00 (*0-85261-278-8*, Pub. by Univ of Glasgow) St Mut.

Baguley, David, ed. A Critical Bibliography of French Literature Vol. 5: The 19th Century, 2 vols., Set. 1600p. 1992. lib. bdg. 235.00 (*0-8156-2566-9*) Syracuse U Pr.

Baguley, David, ed. see Zola, Emile.

***Baguley, Kitt & Chambers, Kevin.** Culture Shock! Venezuela. 1999. pap. 12.95 (*1-55868-501-4*) Gr Arts Ctr Pub.

Baguley, Phil. Effective Communication for Modern Business. LC 93-37967. 1994. write for info. (*0-07-707827-6*) McGraw.

— Improving Organizational Performance: Handbook for Managers. LC 94-30158. 1994. write for info. (*0-07-709006-3*) McGraw.

***Baguley, Philip.** The Communicating Manager: Build Teams & Make It Happen with the Number One Management Skill. (Pathways Ser.: No. 10). (Illus.). 204p. (Orig.). 1999. pap. 24.50 (*1-85703-481-3*, Pub. by How To Bks) Trans-Atl Phila.

— Teach Yourself Project Management. (Teach Yourself Ser.). (Illus.). 192p. 2000. pap. 12.95 (*0-658-00078-0*) NTC Contemp Pub Co.

Baguley, Roy B., jt. auth. see Woods, Glynn E.

Bagus, P. S., et al. Core Level Spectroscopies for Magnetic Phenomena: Theory & Experiment. (NATO ASI Ser.: Series B, Vol. 345). (Illus.). 284p. (C). 1995. text 95.00 (*0-306-45006-2*) Plenum.

Bagust, H. London Through the Ages. (C). 1988. 39.00 (*0-904110-99-0*, Pub. by Thornhill Pr) St Mut.

***Bagust, Harold.** Breadmaking at Home. 384p. 1999. pap. 16.95 (*0-7090-6252-4*, Pub. by R Hale Ltd) Seven Hills Bk.

Bagwe, Anjani. Of Woman Caste: The Experience of Gender in Rural India. LC 95-31267. 192p. (C). 1995. text 65.00 (*1-85649-321-0*, Pub. by Zed Books); text 25.00 (*1-85649-322-9*, Pub. by Zed Books) St Martin.

Bagwell, Beth. Oakland, the Story of a City. (Illus.). 292p. Date not set. reprint ed. 22.50 (*0-9640087-1-8*); reprint ed. pap. 11.95 (*0-9640087-0-X*) Oakland Herit.

***Bagwell, James.** Rice Gold: James Hamilton Couper & Plantation Life on the Georgia Coast. LC 99-54193. 320p. 1999. 27.95 (*0-86554-651-7*) Mercer Univ Pr.

Bagwell, Joyce B. Low Country Quake Tales. 88p. (YA). 1986. pap. 7.50 (*0-89308-593-6*, SC 84) Southern Hist Pr.

Bagwell, Mark T. Empowered for the Call: Understanding the Dynamics of the Anointing. 192p. (Orig.). 1996. pap. 11.95 (*0-9654268-0-7*) His Pen Minist.

Bagwell, Philip S. & Lawley, Joan L., eds. From Prison Cell to Council Chamber: The Life of Philip William Bagwell 1885-1958. LC 95-151135. 1995. pap. 45.00 (*1-85072-150-5*, Pub. by W Sessions) St Mut.

Bagwell, Philip S. & Mingay, G. E. Britain & America: A Study of Economic Change 1850-1939. 2nd ed. 328p. 1987. pap. 17.95 (*0-7102-1297-6*, Routledge Thoemms) Routledge.

Bagwell, Stella. The Bridal Bargain. (Romance Ser.). 2000. per. 3.50 (*0-373-19414-5*, 1-19414-1) Silhouette.

— Corporate Cowgirl. (Romance Ser.). 1994. per. 2.75 (*0-373-08991-0*, 5-08991-7) Silhouette.

— The Cowboy & the Debutante: Twins on the Doorstep. (Romance Ser.: No. 1334). 1998. per. 3.50 (*0-373-19334-3*, 0-19334-2) Silhouette.

— A Cowboy for Christmas: (Under the Mistletoe) (Romance Ser.). 1994. per. 2.75 (*0-373-19052-2*, 1-19052-9) Silhouette.

— Daddy Lessons. (Romance Ser.). 1995. per. 2.99 (*0-373-19085-9*, 1-19085-9) Silhouette.

— Done to Perfection. (Family Continuity Program Ser.: No. 34). 1999. per. 4.50 (*0-373-82182-4*, 1-82182-6) Harlequin Bks.

***Bagwell, Stella.** Falling for Grace. (Romance Ser.: Bk. 1456). 2000. mass mkt. 3.50 (*0-373-19456-0*, 1-19456-2) Silhouette.

Bagwell, Stella. Found: One Runaway Bride. (Special Edition Ser.). 1996. per. 3.99 (*0-373-24049-X*, 1-24049-8) Silhouette.

***Bagwell, Stella.** The Heiress & the Sheriff. (Fortunes of Texas Ser.). 256p. 2000. per. 4.50 (*0-373-65037-X*) Silhouette.

— L' Heritier Amoureux. (FRE.). 2000. mass mkt. 3.99 (*0-373-39543-4*) Harlequin Bks.

Bagwell, Stella. Hero in Disguise. (Romance Ser.). 1993. per. 2.75 (*0-373-08954-6*, 5-08954-5) Silhouette.

— Millionaire on Her Doorstep: Twins on the Doorstep. (Romance Ser.: No. 1368). 1999. per. 3.50 (*0-373-19368-8*, 1-19368-9) Silhouette.

— Penny Parker's Pregnant! Twins on the Doorstep. (Special Edition Ser.: Bk. 1258). 1999. per. 4.25 (*0-373-24258-1*, 1-24258-5) Silhouette.

— The Rancher's Blessed Event. 1998. per. 3.50 (*0-373-19296-7*, 1-19296-2) Silhouette.

— Rancher's Bride. (Twins on the Doorstep Ser.). 1997. per. 3.25 (*0-373-19224-X*, 1-19224-4) Silhouette.

— The Ranger & the Widow Woman. (Romance Ser.). 1998. per. 3.50 (*0-373-19314-9*, 1-19314-3) Silhouette.

— The Sheriff's Son. (Twins on the Doorstep Ser.). 1997. per. 3.25 (*0-373-19218-5*, 1-19218-6) Silhouette.

— The Tycoon's Tots. (Romance Ser.: No. 1228). 1997. per. 3.25 (*0-373-19228-2*, 1-19228-5) Silhouette.

— Wanted: Wife. LC 96-7283. (Romance Ser.). 186p. 1996. per. 3.25 (*0-373-19140-5*, 1-19140-2) Silhouette.

Bagwell, Tim. Possessing Your Prophetic Promise. 160p. (Orig.). 1995. pap. 9.99 (*1-884369-12-X*) McDougal Pubng.

Bagwell, Timothy J. Empowered for the Call: Understanding the Dynamics of the Anointing. 2nd rev. ed. 168p. 1998. pap. 9.99 (*1-884369-73-1*) McDougal Pubng.

— When I See the Blood. 182p. 1998. pap. 9.99 (*1-884369-74-X*) McDougal Pubng.

Bagwell, Tyler. The Jekyll Island Club. LC 98-87323. (Images of America Ser.). (Illus.). 128p. 1998. pap. 16.99 (*0-7524-0935-2*) Arcadia Publng.

Bagwell, Weldon M., jt. ed. see Trimble, Joseph E.

Bagybakay, P. Summoning Tablets of Guilds in Hungary. 1981. 45.00 (*0-7855-1623-9*) St Mut.

Bah, Alpha M. Fulbe Presence in Sierra Leone: A Case History of Twentieth-Century Migration & Settlement Among the Kissi of Koindu. Vol. 140. LC 93-22958. (American University Studies IX: Ser. IX, Vol. 140). (Illus.). X, 191p. (C). 1998. text 40.95 (*0-8204-2180-4*) P Lang Pubng.

Bah-Lalya, Ibrahima & O'Toole, Thomas E. Historical Dictionary of Guinea, Vol. 16. 3rd ed. LC 95-34783. (African Historical Dictionaries Ser.). 1995. 60.00 (*0-8108-3065-5*) Scarecrow.

Baha, Akiko. Heavenly Maiden Tanka. Kawamura, Hatsue & Reichhold, Jane, trs. from JPN. 128p. 1999. pap. 10.00 (*0-944676-42-1*) AHA Bks.

Bahadori, Mehdi. The University of Life. LC 93-41303. (Illus.). 96p. (Orig.). 1993. pap. 7.95 (*0-931892-70-8*) B Dolphin Pub.

Bahadori, Mehdi N. Love to Be Happy: The Secrets of Sustainable Joy. LC 93-64110. 176p. (Orig.). 1993. pap. 10.95 (*0-931892-71-6*) B Dolphin Pub.

— The University of Life. (Illus.). 83p. (Orig.). 1988. pap. 6.75 (*0-9620384-0-7*) M N Bahadori.

Bahadur, B. Liquid Crystals: Applications & Uses, Vol. 2. 448p. 1991. text 101.00 (*981-02-0111-7*) World Scientific Pub.

— Liquid Crystals: Applications & Uses, Vol. 3. 325p. 1992. text 102.00 (*981-02-0403-5*) World Scientific Pub.

Bahadur, B., ed. Liquid Crystals: Applications & Uses, Vol. 1. 604p. (C). 1990. text 138.00 (*981-02-0110-9*) World Scientific Pub.

Bahadur, Birendra. Liquid Crystal Displays. (Molecular Crystals & Liquid Crystals Ser.). 100p. 1984. pap. text 142.00 (*0-677-06675-9*) Gordon & Breach.

***Bahadur, Gavin G. & Sinskey, Robert M.** Manual of Cataract Surgery. 2nd ed. LC 99-29627. 128p. 1999. pap. text 45.00 (*0-7506-7082-7*) Buttrwrth-Heinemann.

Bahadur, K., et al. Inside Afghanistan. 147p. 1986. 16.00 (*0-8364-1908-1*, Pub. by Patriot Pubs) S Asia.

Bahadur, K. P. Caste, Tribes & Culture of India, 7 vols., Set. 1981. 149.95 (*0-318-36807-2*) Asia Bk Corp.

— The Gita. 88p. 1980. 11.95 (*0-318-37168-5*) Asia Bk Corp.

— A History of Indian Civilization, 3 vols., Set. 1983. 275.00 (*0-318-36873-0*) Asia Bk Corp.

— Love Poems of Ghanand. (C). 1991. reprint ed. 12.50 (*81-208-0836-3*, Pub. by Motilal Bnarsidass) S Asia.

— Population Crisis in India. 180p. 1977. 15.95 (*0-318-36855-2*) Asia Bk Corp.

Bahadur, Kaisher. The Judicial Customs of Nepal, Pt. 1. 432p. (C). 1971. 35.00 (*0-89771-060-6*, Pub. by Ratna Pustak Bhandar) St Mut.

Bahadur, Kaisher, tr. see Bharavi.

Bahadur, Kalim & Singh, Uma, eds. Pakistan Transition to Democracy: Joint Study of Indian & Pakistani Scholars. (C). 1989. 32.50 (*81-7050-100-8*, Pub. by Patriot Pubs) S Asia.

***Bahadur, Krishna.** Poems of Suradasa. LC 99-931369. 364p. 1999. 32.00 (*81-7017-369-8*, Pub. by Abhinav Pubns) S Asia.

Bahadur, Krishna P., jt. auth. see Bai, Bahini.

Bahadur, Krishna Prakash. Sufi Mysticism. LC 98-917114. 265 p. 1999. write for info. (*81-7000-250-8*) Asia Bk Corp.

Bahadur, Laksman. Recent Nepal: An Analysis of Recent Democratic Upsurge & Its Aftermath. xxiiii, 217p. 1993. 25.00 (*81-85693-24-2*, Pub. by Nirala Pubns) Nataraj Bks.

Bahadur, Om L. The Book of Hindu Festivals & Ceremonies. (C). 1995. 8.50 (*81-86112-23-5*, Pub. by UBS Pubs Dist) S Asia.

Bahadur, Om Lata, see Lata Bahadur, Om.

Bahadur, R. R. Some Limit Theorems in Statistics. (CBMS-NSF Regional Conference Ser.: No. 4). vi, 42p. 1971. pap. text 17.00 (*0-89871-175-4*) Soc Indus-Appl Math.

Bahadur, Rai P. Garhwal Ancient & Modern. (C). 1992. reprint ed. 25.00 (*81-85326-59-2*, Pub. by Vintage) S Asia.

Bahadur, S. P., tr. Complete Works of Goswami Tulsidas Vol. 3: Gitavali. (C). 1996. 32.00 (*81-215-0669-7*, Pub. by M Manoharial) Coronet Bks.

— Complete Works of Goswami Tulsidas Vol. 2: Vinaya Patrika (A Letter of Plaint) (C). 1995. reprint ed. 29.00 (*81-215-0650-6*, Pub. by M Manoharial) Coronet Bks.

— Complete Works of Goswami Tulsidas Vol. V: Kavitavali. (C). 1997. 30.00 (*81-215-0702-2*, Pub. by M Manoharial) Coronet Bks.

Bahadur Shakya, Nanda, see Shakya, Nanda Bahadur.

Bahadur, Shyam, ed. Effect of Surface Coatings & Treatments On Wear. LC 96-14900. (Special Technical Publication Ser.: No. 1278). (Illus.). 160p. 1996. pap. 99.00 (*0-8031-2036-2*, STP1278) ASTM.

***Bahadur, Shyam & Mogel, John, eds.** Wear Process in Manufacturing. LC 99-11819. (STP Ser.: Vol. 1362). (Illus.). 14p. 1999. pap. text 58.00 (*0-8031-2603-4*, STP1362) ASTM.

Bahadur Singh, I., ed. Indians in Southeast Asia. 232p. 1982. 24.95 (*0-940500-53-1*, Pub. by Sterling) Asia Bk Corp.

Baha'i International Community-Office of Public In. Baha'u'llah - General Edition. 88p. 1992. 7.50 (*0-909991-53-7*) Bahai.

— Baha'u'llah - Presentation Edition. 56p. 1991. pap. 5.95 (*0-87743-232-5*) Bahai.

Baha'i Publishing Trust (Australia) Staff. Social & Economic Development. 48p. 1989. pap. 4.95 (*0-909991-31-6*) Bahai.

Bahamonde, Ramon. International Policy Institutions Around the Pacific Rim: A Directory of Resources in East Asia & the Americas. LC 97-40585. 317p. 1998. pap. 35.00 (*1-55587-795-8*) L Rienner.

Bahan, Ben & Dannis, Joe. My ABC Signs of Animal Friends. (Illus.). 32p. (J). 1994. pap. 8.95 (*0-915035-31-6*, 4201) Dawn Sign.

Bahan, Ben, et al. Sign Language Clowns. 16p. (J). 1983. pap. 4.50 (*0-915035-00-6*, 4160) Dawn Sign.

Bahan, Ben, jt. auth. see Paul, Frank A.

Bahan, Ben, jt. auth. see Supalla, Samuel J.

Bahan, Benjamin, et al. Signs for Me: Basic Sign Vocabulary for Children, Parents & Teachers. (Illus.). 128p. 1987. pap. 12.95 (*0-915035-27-8*, 4166) Dawn Sign.

Bahan, Deanie C. Sugarfree Holidays. LC 98-87565. (Illus.). 24p. 1998. pap. 4.95 (*0-9660804-2-4*) AFM LLC.

— Sugarfree New Orleans: A Cookbook Based on the Glycemic Index. (Illus.). 175p. 1997. 15.95 (*0-9660804-0-8*) AFM LLC.

— Sugarfree Quick & Easy. (Illus.). 150p. 1998. 15.95 (*0-9660804-1-6*) AFM LLC.

Bahan, Lee H. Migration Solo. (Indiana Poetry Chapbook Contest Ser.: No. 1). 43p. 1989. pap. 3.95 (*1-880649-23-3*) Writ Ctr Pr.

Bahanon, Claire, ed. see Miller, Janice.

Bahar, Ann. Santa Dolls: Historical to Contemporary. LC 93-118598. 176p. 1992. 29.95 (*0-87588-397-4*) Hobby Hse.

Bahar, Ann & Riesser, Ingeborg. Contemporary Artist Dolls from Germany. LC 95-143886. (Illus.). 192p. 1994. 39.95 (*0-87588-430-X*, 4812) Hobby Hse.

Bahar, Ighal. How to Stay Alive. LC 97-90853. (Illus.). 58p. 1998. pap. 9.95 (*0-533-12497-2*) Vantage.

— Saving Society. LC 98-90023. 1998. pap. 8.95 (*0-533-12687-8*) Vantage.

Bahar, Mory. Object Technology Made Simple. unabridged ed. Waterman, Ann, ed. (Illus.). x, 78p. (Orig.). 1996. pap. 14.95 (*0-9652457-0-5*) Smple Sftwre.

Baharami. Rapid Software Deployment. (DC - Introduction to Computing Ser.). 1996. pap. 43.95 (*0-7895-0583-5*) Course Tech.

Baharan, Avraham. Two Way Channel. 484p. 1994. 18.95 (*1-56871-068-2*, Pub. by Targum Pr) Feldheim.

Baharanyi, Ntam, et al, eds. Natural Resources & the Environment: Community Development Issues. LC 97-60977. 336p. 1997. pap. write for info. (*1-891196-00-6*) Tuskegee U CAENS.

— Outreach to the Rural Disadvantaged: Issues & Strategies for the 21st Century. LC 90-71907. 267p. (Orig.). (C). 1990. pap. text. write for info. (*0-9625021-1-1*) Tuskegee U CAENS.

Baharav, Gene, tr. see Noy, Dov, ed.

Baharav, Gene, tr. see Noy, Dov & Ben-Amos, Dan, eds.

Baharav, I. D. Winds of April. LC 65-17184. 1965. 10.00 (*0-911184-04-X*) Primary.

Bahari, Ebadollah. Bihzad, Master of Persian Painting. LC 95-61522. (Illus.). 288p. 1996. 95.00 (*1-85043-966-4*, Pub. by I B T) St Martin.

Baharna, H. M. Al, see Al Baharna, H. M.

Bahash, Stan, ed. see Brown, Dee.

Bahat, D. Tectonofractography. (Illus.). xviii, 354p. 1991. 260.95 (*0-387-53281-1*) Spr-Verlag.

***Bahat, Dan & Ben-Shalom, Ram.** Israel 2000 Years: A History of People & Places. (Illus.). 158p. 2000. 60.00 (*0-88391-058-6*) F Fell Pubs Inc.

Bahat, Dan & Sabar, Shalom. Jerusalem Stone & Spirit: 3000 Years of History & Art. LC 98-65752. (Illus.). 147p. 1998. 60.00 (*0-8478-2124-2*, Pub. by Rizzoli Intl) St Martin.

Bahat, Dan, jt. auth. see Cole, Dan P.

Baha'u'llah. Epistle to the Son of the Wolf. 3rd ed. 194p. 1988. pap. 3.95 (*0-87743-235-X*) Bahai.

— Epistle to the Son of the Wolf, pocket-sized. rev. ed. Effendi, Shoghi, tr. from PER. LC 53-18798. 194p. 1979. 15.95 (*0-87743-048-9*, 103-001) Bahai.

— Gleanings from the Writings of Baha'u'llah. 2nd rev. ed. Shoghi Effendi, tr. from PER. LC 76-45364. (Illus.). 346p. 1977. 15.95 (*0-87743-111-6*, 103-003) Bahai.

— Gleanings from the Writings of Baha'u'llah, pocket-sized. 2nd rev. ed. Effendi, Shoghi, tr. from PER. LC 76-45364. (Illus.). 346p. 1984. pap. 3.95 (*0-87743-112-4*, 103-004) Bahai.

— Gleanings from the Writings of Baha'u'llah: British Edition. 350p. 1986. 17.50 (*0-900125-38-1*) Bahai.

Baha'u'llah. The Hidden Words: And Selected Writings. St. Rain, Justice, ed. Effendi, Shoghi, tr. (Pocket Inspirations Ser.: Vol. 1). 64p. 1994. pap. 2.75 (*1-888547-00-6*, HW) Special Ideas.

Baha'u'llah. The Hidden Words: British Edition. Effendi, Shoghi, tr. (Illus.). 91p. 1984. pap. 10.95 (*0-900125-93-4*) Bahai.

— The Hidden Words of Baha'u'llah. 112p. 1995. pap. 13.95 (*1-85168-001-2*, Pub. by Onewrld Pubns) Penguin Putnam.

— The Hidden Words of Bahaullah. 112p. 1994. pap. 6.95 (*1-85168-007-1*, Pub. by Onewrld Pubns) Penguin Putnam.

— The Hidden Words of Baha'u'llah. rev. ed. Effendi, Shoghi, tr. LC 54-7328. 52p. 1975. reprint ed. 7.95 (*0-87743-007-1*, 103-005) Bahai.

— The Hidden Words of Baha'u'llah, pocket-sized. rev. ed. Effendi, Shoghi, tr. LC 54-7328. 52p. 1975. reprint ed. pap. 3.00 (*0-87743-002-0*, 103-006) Bahai.

— Kitab-i-Aqdas. 315p. 1993. pap. 9.95 (*0-909991-97-9*) Bahai.

— The Kitab-i-Aqdas. deluxe ed. 315p. 1993. 39.95 (*0-909991-99-5*) Bahai.

— The Kitab-i-Aqdas: The Most Holy Book. LC 93-2030.Tr. of Kitab Al-Aqdas. 315p. 1993. pap. 3.95 (*0-87743-240-6*) Bahai.

— Kitab-i-Iqan: The Book of Certitude. 274p. 1955. 15.95 (*0-87743-022-5*) Bahai.

— Kitab-i-Iqan: The Book of Certitude. 274p. 1983. pap. 3.95 (*0-87743-189-2*) Bahai.

B

An Asterisk (*) at the beginning of an entry indicates that the title is appearing for the first time.

— Kitab-i-Iqan: The Book of Certitude. Effendi, Shoghi, tr. 168p. 1986. 17.50 (*0-900125-47-0*) Bahai.

— Meditations of the Blessed Beauty. 90p. 1992. 29.95 (*1-870989-17-1*); pap. 18.95 (*1-870989-18-X*) Bahai.

— The Most Holy Tablet. Effendi, Shoghi & Taherzadeh, Habib, trs. (Illus.). 72p. 1995. 19.95 (*1-870989-39-2*); pap. 13.95 (*1-870989-40-6*) Bahai.

— Prayers & Meditations. Effendi, Shoghi, tr. LC 53-10767. 347p. 1955. 15.95 (*0-87743-024-1*, 103-010) Bahai.

— Prayers & Meditations. Effendi, Shoghi, tr. 262p. 1984. 17.50 (*0-900125-39-X*) Bahai.

— Prayers & Meditations. 347p. 1987. pap. 3.95 (*0-87743-181-7*) Bahai.

— The Proclamation of Baha'u'llah. LC 72-237435. 127p. 1967. pap. 4.95 (*0-87743-065-9*, 103-013) Bahai.

— The Seven Valleys & the Four Valleys. Gail, Marzieh, tr. (Illus.). 120p. 1992. pap. 13.25 (*1-870989-16-3*) Bahai.

— The Seven Valleys & the Four Valleys. 4th ed. Gail, Marzieh, tr. from PER. 65p. 1955. 7.95 (*0-87743-226-0*); pap. 3.00 (*0-87743-227-9*) Bahai.

— The Seven Valleys of Baha'u'llah. 96p. 1994. pap. 8.95 (*1-85168-031-4*, Pub. by Onewrld Pubns) Penguin Putnam.

— Tablet of Carmel. 55p. 1992. 21.95 (*1-870989-13-9*); pap. 13.25 (*1-870989-14-7*) Bahai.

— Tablet of Visitation. deluxe limited ed. Effendi, Shoghi, tr. from ARA. LC 94-96884. (Illus.). 32p. 1995. 1000.00 (*0-9645136-0-9*) Taraz Pubng.

— Tablets of Baha'u'llah Revealed after the Kitab-i-Agdas. Taherzadeh, Habib, tr. from PER. LC 88-6250. 299p. 1988. 3.95 (*0-87743-216-3*) Bahai.

Baha'u'llah & Abdul-Baha. O Thou Kind Lord: Prayers & Roadings for Children from the Baha'i Writings. (Illus.). 57p. (J). (gr. 1-6). Date not set. 5.50 (*1-870989-38-4*) Bahai.

Baha'u'llah & Abdu'l-Baha. Reality of Man. 93p. 1990. pap. 5.95 (*0-909991-39-1*) Bahai.

Bahaullah & Abdu'l-Baha. Waging Peace: Selections from the Baha'i Writings on Universal Peace. 106p. 1985. pap. 14.95 (*0-933770-34-0*) Kalimat.

Baha'u'llah & Abdu'l-Baha. Words of God: Australian Edition. large type ed. 32p. 1989. pap. 1.50 (*0-909991-44-8*) Bahai.

Baha'u'llah, et al. Baha'i Prayers: A Selection of Prayers Revealed by Baha'u'llah, the Bab, & 'Abdu'l-Baha. 277p. 1982. 7.95 (*0-87743-230-9*); pap. 4.95 (*0-87743-229-5*) Bahai.

***Baha'u'llah, et al.** Bahai Teachings for a New Millennium. St. Rain, Karen, ed. (Pocket Inspirations Ser.: Vol. 4). 58p. 1999. pap. 2.95 (*1-888547-06-5*, BK-NM) Special Ideas.

Baha'u'llah, et al. Divorce: Writings Discouraging: Compilation of Extracts from the Baha'i Teachings Discouraging Divorce. 16p. 1986. pap. 3.95 (*0-909991-17-0*) Bahai.

Baha'u'llah, et al. A Gift of Prayers: And Selected Baha'i Writings. St. Rain, Karen, ed. (Pocket Inspirations Ser.: Vol. 2). 64p. 1995. pap. 2.75 (*1-888547-01-4*) Special Ideas.

Baha'u'llah, et al. The Pattern of Baha'i Life. 3rd ed. 64p. 1984. pap. 4.50 (*0-900125-15-2*, 315-030-10) Bahai.

— Peace (Compilation) 46p. 1986. pap. 3.95 (*0-909991-32-4*) Bahai.

***Baha'u'llah, et al.** Wings of Prayer: Baha'i Prayers for Women. St. Rain, Karen, ed. (Pocket Inspirations Ser.: Vol. 3). 45p. 1999. pap. 2.75 (*1-888547-04-9*, BK-WP) Special Ideas.

Baha'u'llah, Bab & Abdu'l-Baha. O God, Guide Me! A Selection of Prayers Revealed. (Illus.). 41p. (J). (gr. k-6). 1985. pap. 5.95 (*0-87743-202-3*) Bahai.

Bahaun, Claire, ed. see Miller, Janice, et al.

Bahbah, Bishara. Israel & Latin America: The Military Connection. LC 86-1904. 228p. 1986. 29.95 (*0-685-13559-4*) St Martin.

***Bahba.u.llbah.** Bahba.bi Prayers for Women: Selections from the Writings of Bahba.u.llbah, The Bbab, 0abdu.l-bahba & the Greatest Holy Leaf. LC 00-30960. (Illus.). 16p. 2000. 14.95 (*1-890688-09-6*, 09-6) Kalimat.

Bahcall, John N. Solar Neutrinos: The First Thirty Years. 464p. (C). 1995. 65.00 (*0-201-40791-4*) Addison-Wesley.

Bahcall, John N., et al, eds. Dark Matter in the Universe: Proceedings of the 4th Jerusalem Winter School for Theoretical Physics, Vol. 4. 264p. (Orig.). (C). 1988. text 61.00 (*9971-5-0535-5*); pap. text 37.00 (*9971-5-0536-3*) World Scientific Pub.

Bahcall, John N. & Ostriker, Jeremiah P. Unsolved Problems in Astrophysics. LC 96-45581. (Princeton Series in Astrophysics). 382p. 1997. pap. text 24.95 (*0-691-01606-2*, Pub. by Princeton U Pr) Cal Prin Full Svc.

Bahcall, John N., et al. Neutrino Astrophysics: Proceedings of 10th Jerusalem Winter School for Theoretical Physics. 1994. text 72.00 (*981-02-1367-0*) World Scientific Pub.

Bahchu, Parminder, jt. ed. see Light, Ivan H.

Bahder, Thomas B. Mathematica for Scientists & Engineers. (Illus.). 359p. 1993. pap. write for info. (*0-318-70293-2*) Addison-Wesley.

— Mathematica for Scientists & Engineers. 864p. (C). 1994. pap. text 51.95 (*0-201-54090-8*) Addison-Wesley.

Bahei-El-Din, Y. A., et al. IUTAM Symposium on Transformation Problems in Composite & Active Materials: Proceedings of the IUTAM Symposium Held in Cairo, Egypt, 9-12 March, 1997. LC 98-22283. 1998. 143.00 (*0-7923-5122-3*) Kluwer Academic.

Baher, H. Microelectronic Switched Capacitor Filters with ISICAP: A Computer-Aided-Design Package. LC 95-38186. 384p. 1996. 215.00 (*0-471-95404-7*) Wiley.

— Synthesis of Electrical Networks. LC 83-21905. (Illus.). 299p. reprint ed. pap. 92.70 (*0-8357-4609-7*, 203754200008) Bks Demand.

Baher, Hussein. Analog & Digital Signal Processing. LC 89-24766. 492p. 1990. pap. 84.95 (*0-471-92342-7*) Wiley.

***Baher, Hussein.** Analog & Digital Signal Processing. 2nd ed. 504p. 2000. pap. 64.95 (*0-471-62354-7*) Wiley.

Baher, Hussein. Selective Linear-Phase Switched-Capacitor & Digital Filters. LC 92-34564. (Kluwer International Series in Engineering & Computer Science). 160p. (C). 1993. text 100.50 (*0-7923-9298-1*) Kluwer Academic.

Bahgat, Gawdat. The Future of the Gulf. (Journal of Social Political & Economic Studies Monographs: No. 26). 106p. 1997. pap. 16.00 (*0-930690-55-9*) Coun Soc Econ.

— The Persian Gulf at the Dawn of the New Millenium. LC 99-25142. 219p. 1999. 49.00 (*1-56072-678-4*) Nova Sci Pubs.

Bahgat, Reem. Non-Deterministic Concurrent Logic Programming in Pandora. LC 92-33357. 220p. 1993. text 61.00 (*981-02-1251-8*) World Scientific Pub.

Bahia Translators Staff, tr. see McKenzie, Michelle.

Bahill, A. Terry. Bioengineering: Biomedical, Medical, & Clinical Engineering. (Illus.). 336p. 1981. text 67.00 (*0-13-076380-2*) P-H.

Bahill, A. Terry & Watts, Robert G. Keep Your Eye on the Ball: The Science & Folklore of Baseball. LC 89-49293. (Illus.). 224p. 1991. pap. 14.95 (*0-7167-2248-8*) W H Freeman.

Bahill, A. Terry, jt. auth. see Watts, Robert G.

Bahill, Terry, jt. auth. see Szidarovszky, Ferenc.

Bahirat, B. P. Philosophy of Jnanadeva. (C). 1993. 9.00 (*81-7154-737-0*, Pub. by Popular Prakashan) S Asia.

***Bahjat, Andrew H. & Wedertz, Bill.** Dictionary of Naval Abbreviations. 4th ed. LC 99-52593. 320p. 2000. 29.95 (*1-55750-166-1*) Naval Inst Pr.

Bahk, Whangbai. El Surrealism Poetico en el Mundo Europeo y el Extremo Oriente: La Propagacion del Surrealismo Europeo al Japon y a Corea, y un Comparativo de la Poesia Vanguardista. LC 91-23030. (American University Studies: Romance Languages & Literature: Ser. II, Vol. 167). (SPA.). 224p. (C). 1992. text 41.95 (*0-8204-1531-6*) P Lang Pubng.

Bahk, Y. W. Combined Scintigraphic & Radiographic Diagnosis of Bone & Joint Diseases. 250p. 1996. 206.00 (*0-387-56857-3*) Spr-Verlag.

***Bahk, Y. W.** Combined Scintigraphic & Radiographic Diagnosis of Bone & Joint Diseases. 2nd rev. enl. ed. xviii, 280p. 2000. 189.00 (*3-540-66424-6*) Spr-Verlag.

Bahk, Yong W., et al. Nuclear Imaging of the Chest. LC 97-29699. (Illus.). 320p. 1997. write for info. (*3-540-62766-9*) Spr-Verlag.

Bahkvalov, N. S., et al. Nonlinear Theory of Sound Beams. Beyer, Robert T., tr. from RUS. LC 87-1850. (Translation Ser.). (Illus.). 184p. 1987. text 60.00 (*0-88318-520-2*) Am Inst Physics.

Bahl, O. P. Recent Trends in Carbon. LC 97-913714. xvi, 470p. 1997. write for info. (*81-85402-92-2*) Shipra Pubns.

Bahl, Inder J. & Bhartia, Prakash. Microwave Solid State Circuit design. LC 87-31652. 944p. 1988. 240.00 (*0-471-83189-1*) Wiley.

Bahl, Inder J., jt. auth. see Bhartia, Prakash.

Bahl, Kali C. Studies in the Semantic Structure of Hindi, Two. 1979. 17.50 (*0-8364-0513-7*) S Asia.

Bahl, Om P., jt. ed. see Dhindsa, Dharam S.

Bahl, P. N. Indira Gandhi: The Crucial Years 1973-1984. (C). 1994. 16.00 (*81-241-0183-3*, Pub. by Har-Anand Pubns) S Asia.

Bahl, P. N., ed. Genetic, Cytogenetics & Breeding of Crop Plants, Vol. 1. 1996. lib. bdg. 70.00 (*1-886106-59-2*) Science Pubs.

— Genetics, Cytogenetics & Breeding of Crop Plants: Cereals & Cash Crops, Vol. 2. (Illus.). 360p. (C). 1997. 78.00 (*1-886106-94-0*) Science Pubs.

Bahl, Roy, ed. Taxation & Economic Development: A Blueprint for Tax Reform in Ohio. 1995. 44.95 (*1-57477-015-2*) Battelle.

Bahl, Roy & Duncombe, William. Economic Growth & Fiscal Planning: New York in the 1990s. LC 91-7516. 352p. (C). 1991. text 1.00 (*0-88285-134-9*) Ctr Urban Pol Res.

Bahl, Roy, et al. The Guatemalan Tax Reform. LC 96-9319. 176p. (C). 1996. pap. 69.00 (*0-8133-8928-3*, Pub. by Westview) HarpC.

Bahl, Roy, ed. see Jamaica Tax Structure Examination Project Staff.

Bahl, Roy W. Local Government Finance in the Third World. 1983. 52.95 (*0-275-90939-5*, C0939, Praeger Pubs) Greenwood.

Bahl, Roy W., Jr. Taxation Reform in China. LC 98-68001. 224p. 1999. text 39.50 (*0-472-59003-0*, 59003) U of Mich Pr.

Bahl, Roy W., ed. The Taxation of Urban Property in Less Developed Countries. LC 78-65018. (Publications of the Committee on Taxation, Resources & Economic Development: Vol. 10). 299p. 1979. reprint ed. pap. 92.70 (*0-608-01973-9*, 206262800003) Bks Demand.

— Urban Government Finance: Emerging Trends. LC 80-39559. (Urban Affairs Annual Reviews Ser.: No. 20). 287p. reprint ed. pap. 89.00 (*0-8357-8468-1*, 203473600091) Bks Demand.

Bahl, Roy W., et al. Public Finance During the Korean Modernization Process. (East Asian Monographs: No. 107). 1986. 30.00 (*0-674-72233-7*) HUP.

Bahl, Sonia, ed. Dear Parents: Letters by Teens Who Dare to Tell All, Vol. 1. LC 95-83089. (Letters Ser.).Tr. of Chers Parents. (FRE., Illus.). 104p. (J). 1996. pap. text 12.95 (*1-896650-00-7*) Betwn Us Pubng.

Bahl, Sushil. Business Communication Today. LC 96-16090. 1996. 29.95 (*0-8039-9320-X*) Sage.

Bahl, Vinay. The Making of the Indian Working Class: The Case of the Tata Iron & Steel Company, 1880-1946. LC 94-32846. 432p. (C). 1995. text 49.95 (*0-8039-9187-8*) Sage.

Bahlburg, Heinrich. The Ordovician Basin in the Puna of NW-Argentina & N-Chile Geodynamic Evolution from Back-Arc to Foreland Basin. (Geotektonische Forschungen Ser.: Vol. 75). (GER.). 107p. 1990. pap. 52.00 (*3-510-50041-5*, Pub. by E Schweizerbartsche) Balogh.

Bahleda, Suellen J. Fingerspelling: The Real World. (Illus.). (C). 1996. pap. text 24.95 (*0-9651898-7-2*) Real Wrld.

Bahler, Bradley. 24 Favorite Stories. (SPA.). 97p. (J). 1985. pap. 3.80 (*0-7399-0291-1*, 2464.1) Rod & Staff.

Bahler, Ingrid & Gatto, Katherine G. Of Kings & Poets: Cancionero Poetry of the Trastamara Courts. LC 92-13266. (American University Studies: Romance Languages & Literature: Ser. II, Vol. 194). 130p. (C). 1994. text 35.95 (*0-8204-1974-5*) P Lang Pubng.

Bahler, Ingrid, tr. see Kilpatrick, Kathryn & Jones, Cynthia L.

Bahlke, George W. Critical Essays on W. H. Auden. (Critical Essays on British Literature Ser.). 200p. (C). 1991. 49.00 (*0-8161-8855-6*, Hall Reference) Macmillan.

— The Later Auden: From New Year Letter to about the House. LC 74-98179. 208p. 1970. 20.00 (*0-8135-0663-8*) Lib Soc Sci.

Bahlman, Dudley W., ed. The Diary of Sir Edward Hamilton: 1885-1906. 475p. 1994. 39.95 (*0-85958-612-X*, Pub. by Univ of Hull Pr) Paul & Co Pubs.

Bahlmann, C., et al. Unterwegs: Lehrwerk fur die Mittelstufe Deutsch als Fremdsprache, Materialienbuch. (GER., Illus.). 168p. (C). 1998. 24.00 (*3-468-47640-X*) Langenscheidt.

Bahlmann, J. & Brod, J., eds. Disturbances of Water & Electrolyte Metabolism. (Contributions to Nephrology Ser.: Vol. 21). (Illus.). 1980. pap. 29.75 (*3-8055-0215-X*) S Karger.

Bahlmann, J. & Liebau, H., eds. Stress & Hypertension. (Contributions to Nephrology Ser.: Vol. 30). (Illus.). xiv, 206p. 1982. pap. 29.75 (*3-8055-3450-7*) S Karger.

Bahloul, Joelle. The Architecture of Memory: A Jewish-Muslim Household in Colonial Algeria, 1937-1962. (Studies in Social & Cultural Anthropology: No. 99). 172p. (C). 1996. pap. text 17.95 (*0-521-56892-7*) Cambridge U Pr.

— The Architecture of Memory: A Jewish-Muslim Household in Colonial Algeria, 1937-1962. (Studies in Social & Cultural Anthropology: Vol. 99). 172p. (C). 1996. text 54.95 (*0-521-41891-7*) Cambridge U Pr.

***Bahm, Archie.** Directory of American Philosophers 2000-2001. 20th ed. 550p. (C). 2000. write for info. (*1-889680-17-6*) Philos Document.

Bahm, Archie J. Comparative Philosophy: Western, Indian, & Chinese Philosophies Compared. rev. ed. LC 95-61792. 117p. 1995. pap. 11.00 (*0-911714-22-7*) World Bks.

— Computocracy (Government by Computer Users) LC 85-70209. 83p. 1985. pap. text 6.00 (*0-911714-16-2*) World Bks.

— Epistemology: Theory of Knowledge. LC 94-90614. 268p. (Orig.). 1995. pap. 15.00 (*0-911714-21-9*) World Bks.

— The Heart of Confucius: Interpretations of "Genuine Living" & "Great Wisdom" 2nd ed. LC 92-20720. (Illus.). 160p. 1993. reprint ed. pap. 12.95 (*0-87573-021-3*) Jain Pub Co.

— Metaphysics: An Introduction. LC 73-7469. 266p. 1974. pap. 15.00 (*0-911714-17-0*) World Bks.

— Organicism: Origin & Development, Life & Publications of the Author. LC 96-90092. 569p. 1996. pap. 25.00 (*0-911714-23-5*) World Bks.

— The Philosopher's World Model, 12. LC 78-67569. (Contributions in Philosophy Ser.: No. 12). (Illus.). 295p. 1979. 59.95 (*0-313-21198-1*, BPW/, Greenwood Pr) Greenwood.

— Philosophy of the Buddha. 2nd rev. ed. LC 92-33904. 176p. 1993. pap. 12.95 (*0-87573-025-6*) Jain Pub Co.

— Polarity, Dialectic, & Organicity. LC 77-81834. 293p. 1976. reprint ed. pap. 10.00 (*0-911714-18-9*) World Bks.

— The Specialist: His Philosophy, His Disease, His Cure. LC 76-16883. 126p. 1977. 8.00 (*0-911714-08-1*) World Bks.

— Tao-Teh-King by Lao Tzu. 2nd ed. LC 58-9331. 130p. 1992. pap. 9.00 (*0-911714-20-0*) World Bks.

— Why Be Moral? 2nd ed. LC 92-90090. 447p. 1992. pap. 20.00 (*0-911714-19-7*) World Bks.

— The World's Living Religions. 2nd ed. LC 92-20681. 384p. (C). 1993. reprint ed. pap. 14.95 (*0-87573-000-0*) Jain Pub Co.

— Yoga Sutras of Patanjali. 2nd ed. LC 92-39859. 160p. 1993. reprint ed. pap. 12.95 (*0-87573-024-8*) Jain Pub Co.

Bahm, Archie J., ed. Directory of American Philosophers, 1998-1999. 19th ed. 545p. (C). 1998. 129.00 (*0-912632-74-7*) Philos Document.

Bahm, Archie J. & Tzu, Lao. Tao Teh King: Interpreted As Nature & Intelligence. 2nd rev. ed. LC 96-13670. (CHI.). 128p. (Orig.). 1997. reprint ed. pap. 12.95 (*0-87573-040-X*) Jain Pub Co.

***Bahm, Carolyn, ed.** Eat, Drink & Profit: Moneymaking Ideas for Food & Beverage Operators. 129p. 1999. pap. 59.00 (*0-9701262-1-2*) Oxford Pubng.

— Successful Club Operations: Tips from Savvy Operators. 145p. 1999. pap. 59.00 (*0-9701262-2-0*) Oxford Pubng.

— Top Bar Promotions from Successful Operators. Date not set. pap. 89.00 (*0-9701262-3-9*) Oxford Pubng.

Bahm, Raymond E., ed. see Aronson, E. A., et al.

Bahme, Charles W., jt. auth. see Kramer, William M.

Bahmer, F. A., ed. see Schaller, K. F.

Bahmer, Lonni. Antike Rhetorik und Kommunikative Aufsatzdidaktik. (Germanistische Texte und Studien: Bd. 37). 299p. 1991. 40.00 (*3-487-09454-1*) G Olms Pubs.

Bahmer, William J. Centennial History of Coshocton, Co. Ohio, Vol. 2: Biography. (Illus.). 488p. 1993. reprint ed. lib. bdg. 52.00 (*0-8328-3003-8*) Higginson Bk Co.

— Centennial History of Coshocton County, Ohio Vol. 1: History. (Illus.). 531p. 1993. reprint ed. lib. bdg. 52.00 (*0-8328-3002-X*) Higginson Bk Co.

***Bahmueller, Charles F., ed.** World Conflicts & Confrontations, 4 vols. LC 99-33574. (Illus.). 1450p. (C). (gr. 7 up). 1999. lib. bdg. 320.00 (*0-89356-219-X*) Salem Pr.

Bahn, Charles. The Psychosocial Costs of Police Corruption. (Criminal Justice Center Monographs). 1979. pap. text 3.00 (*0-318-37483-8*) John Jay Pr.

***Bahn, Charles Edward.** Bird Without Feathers. 1999. pap. 23.00 (*1-85072-193-9*, Pub. by W Sessions) St Mut.

Bahn, Gilbert S. Infestation of Yankees: Reference Guide to Union Troops in Confederate Territory. LC 98-194104. 332p. pap. 45.00 (*0-8063-4756-2*, 9305) Clearfield Co.

— Kinetics, Equilibria, & Performance of High Temperature Systems. xii, 404p. 1963. text 477.00 (*0-677-10030-2*) Gordon & Breach.

***Bahn, Gilbert S.** Slaves & Nonwhite Free Persons in the 1790 Federal Census of New York. 192p. 2000. pap. 25.00 (*0-8063-4979-4*, Pub. by Clearfield Co) ACCESS Pubs Network.

Bahn, Gilbert S., intro. American Place Names of Long Ago: A Republication of the Index to Cram's Unrivaled Atlas of the World, as Based on the Census of 1890. LC 97-78458. 347p. 1999. reprint ed. 35.00 (*0-8063-1557-1*) Genealog Pub.

Bahn, Kenneth D., ed. see Academy of Marketing Science Staff.

Bahn, P. Pyrenean Prehistory. pap. 85.00 (*0-85668-260-8*, Pub. by Aris & Phillips) David Brown.

Bahn, Paul. Archaeology: A Very Short Introduction. (Very Short Introductions Ser.). (Illus.). 112p. 1997. pap. 8.95 (*0-19-285325-2*) OUP.

***Bahn, Paul.** Archaeology: A Very Short Introduction. (Very Short Introductions Ser.). 112p. 2000. 8.95 (*0-19-285379-1*) OUP.

— The Bluffer's Guide to Archaeology: Bluff Your Way in Archaeology. (Bluffer's Guides Ser.). 64p. 1999. pap. 5.95 (*1-902825-47-0*) Oval Bks.

Bahn, Paul. Collins Dictionary of Archaeology. LC 93-37784. 654p. 1993. lib. bdg. 65.00 (*0-87436-744-1*) ABC-CLIO.

Bahn, Paul, ed. Lost Cities: 50 Discoveries in World Archaeology. (Illus.). 216p. 1999. pap. 24.95 (*1-56649-002-2*) Welcome Rain.

Bahn, Paul & Rosenfeld, Andree, eds. Rock Art & Prehistory. (Illus.). 144p. 1991. pap. 27.00 (*0-946897-32-8*, Pub. by Oxbow Bks) David Brown.

Bahn, Paul, jt. auth. see Lister, Adrian.

Bahn, Paul, jt. auth. see Martell, Hazel M.

Bahn, Paul, jt. auth. see Renfrew, Colin.

Bahn, Paul, ed. see Gvozdover, Mariana.

Bahn, Paul, jt. ed. see Lorblanchet, Michel.

Bahn, Paul, tr. see Courbin, Paul.

Bahn, Paul G. The Cambridge Illustrated History of Prehistoric Art. LC 96-51099. (Illustrated Histories Ser.). (Illus.). 352p. (C). 1998. 39.95 (*0-521-45473-5*) Cambridge U Pr.

— Journey Through the Ice Age. LC 97-14680. (Illus.). 240p. 1997. 39.95 (*0-520-21306-8*, Pub. by U CA Pr) Cal Prin Full Svc.

Bahn, Paul G., ed. The Cambridge Illustrated History of Archaeology. (Illustrated Histories Ser.). (Illus.). 400p. (C). 1996. 39.95 (*0-521-45498-0*) Cambridge U Pr.

***Bahn, Paul G., ed.** The Cambridge Illustrated History of Archaeology. (History Ser.). (Illus.). 400p. 1999. pap. 27.95 (*0-521-66946-4*) Cambridge U Pr.

***Bahn, Paul G. & Cunliffe, Barry, eds.** The Atlas of World Archaeology. (Illus.). 208p. 2000. 39.95 (*0-8160-4051-6*, Checkmark) Facts on File.

Bahn, Paul G. & Fossati, Angelo, eds. Rock Art Studies: News of the World I. (Oxbow Monographs in Archaeology: No. 72). (Illus.). 229p. 1996. pap. 45.00 (*1-900188-21-X*, Pub. by Oxbow Bks) David Brown.

Bahn, Paul G., tr. see Chauvet, Jean-Marie, et al.

Bahn, Paul G., tr. see Gruzinski, Serge.

Bahn, Paul G., tr. see Lavallee, Daniele.

Bahn, Paul G., tr. see Orliac, Catherine & Orliac, Michel.

Bahn, Paul G., tr. see Thomas, Herbert.

Bahnasawi, A. A. & Mahmoud, Magdi S. Control of Partially-Known Dynamical Systems. (Lecture Notes in Control & Information Sciences: Vol. 124). (Illus.). xi, 228p. 1989. 46.95 (*0-387-51144-X*, 2950) Spr-Verlag.

Bahnassi, Afif. Dictionary d'Architecture & Des Arts. (FRE., Illus.). 180p. 1994. 39.95 (*0-86685-647-1*) Intl Bk Ctr.

— Dictionary of Architecture & Arts: Arabic-English & English-Arabic with an English-French Glossary. (ARA & FRE.). 180p. 1995. 39.95 (*0-86685-656-0*) Intl Bk Ctr.

Bahne, Charles. The Complete Guide to Boston's Freedom Trail. 2nd ed. (Illus.). 80p. (Orig.). 1993. pap. 5.95 (*0-9615705-1-2*) Newtowne Pub.

Bahne, Siegfried. Archives de Jules Humbert-Droz: Nineteen Twenty-Three to Nineteen Twenty-Seven, Vol. II. 1982. lib. bdg. 403.00 (*90-277-1241-7*) Kluwer Academic.

Bahne, Siegfried, ed. see Humbert-Droz, J.

Bahner-Duncan, Linda, ed. Summer Folks 'n Year-Round Neighbors Vol. 2: The Bayshore's History, Settlement to 1962. LC 92-61252. (Illus.). 350p. 1995. lib. bdg. write for info. (*0-9633751-2-1*) TX Marquee Pub.

B

Bahner, Othmar. Intersubjektivitat, Kommunikation und Natur: Theoretische und Ethische Aspekte der Sprachuntersuchungen Mit Groben Menschenaffen. (Europaische Hochschulschriften Ser.: Reihe 20, Bd. 543). (GER., Illus.). 339p. 1997. 57.95 (*3-631-32375-1*) P Lang Pubng.

Bahner, Rita C., et al, eds. Aquatic Toxicology & Hazard Assessment: Eighth Symposium STP 891. LC 85-23014. (Illus.). 485p. 1985. text 52.00 (*0-8031-0437-5*, STP891) ASTM.

Bahner, Werner, et al, eds. Proceedings of the International Congress of Linguistics, 14th: Berlin, GDR, Aug. 10-15, 1987, Vols. 1-3. 2818p. 1991. 400.00 (*3-05-000654-4*, Pub. by Akademie Verlag) Wiley.

Bahnick, Karen R. The Determination of Stages in the Historical Development of the Germanic Languages by Morphological Criteria: An Evaluation. (Janua Linguarum, Series Practica: No. 139). 1973. pap. text 65.40 (*90-279-2389-2*) Mouton.

Bahnimptewa, Cliff. Hopi Kachinas: A Postcard Collection. 20p. (Orig.). 1993. pap. 7.95 (*0-87358-555-0*) Northland AZ.

Bahniuk, Margaret H., jt. auth. see Mansfield, Carmella E.

Bahnsen, Greg L. By This Standard. 372p. 1985. pap. 6.95 (*0-930464-06-0*) Inst Christian.

— Five Views on Law & Gospel. LC 96-21888. (Counterpoints Ser.). 1996. pap. 19.99 (*0-310-21271-5*) Zondervan.

— Five Views on Sanctification. LC 96-9067. (Counterpoints Ser.). 256p. 1996. pap. 14.99 (*0-310-21269-3*) Zondervan.

— He Aqui el Estandar. Howden, Paul, tr. from ENG. (SPA.). 298p. 1990. pap. 6.95 (*0-930464-35-4*) Inst Christian.

— No Other Standard: Theonomy & Its Critics. LC 91-18274. 345p. 1991. 25.00 (*0-930464-55-9*); pap. 9.95 (*0-930464-56-7*) Inst Christian.

— Van Til's Apologetic: Readings & Analysis. LC 98-23866. 1998. 39.99 (*0-87552-098-7*) P & R Pubng.

Bahnsen, Greg L. & Gentry, Kenneth L., Jr. House Divided: The Break-up of Dispensional Theology. LC 97-5054. 411p. 1997. reprint ed. 25.00 (*0-930464-27-3*) Inst Christian.

Bahntge, Mary A., jt. auth. see Baumann, Mary A.

***Baholydin, Ou.** Living with Zen. 2000. 40.00 (*0-8048-3266-8*) Tuttle Pubng.

Bahorik, Elizabeth S. Frost on the Rose. 72p. 1990. 10.95 (*1-884768-00-8*) Charming Forge.

Bahorik, J. Wesley, jt. auth. see Duddy, Patrick J.

Bahorsky, Russ, ed. Official Internet Dictionary: A Comprehensive Reference for Professionals. LC 98-10585. 227p. 1998. pap. text 49.00 (*0-86587-606-1*, 606) Gov Insts.

Bahous, Sally. Sitti & the Cats: A Tale of Friendship. (Illus.). 32p. (J). (gr. 1-5). 1997. pap. 7.95 (*1-57098-171-X*) Roberts Rinehart.

Bahouth, Candace. Flowers, Birds, & Unicorns: Medieval Needlepoint. LC 93-3043. (Illus.). 128p. 1993. 39.95 (*0-8109-3316-0*, Pub. by Abrams) Time Warner.

Bahouth, Candace, jt. auth. see Fassett, Kaffe.

Bahr, A. J. Microwave Nondestructive Testing Methods. xvi, 86p. 1982. pap. 75.00 (*0-685-47156-X*) Gordon & Breach.

***Bahr, Alice H., ed.** Future Teaching Roles for Academic Librarians. LC 00-21101. 113p. 2000. 19.95 (*0-7890-0974-9*) Haworth Pr.

— Future Teaching Roles for Academic Librarians. LC 00-21101. 113p. 2000. pap. text 19.95 (*0-7890-0992-7*) Haworth Pr.

Bahr, Amy C., jt. auth. see Golant, Mitch.

Bahr, Arthur W. Certifiably Insane: A Novel. LC 98-43660. 272p. 1999. 20.50 (*0-684-80232-5*) S&S Trade.

Bahr, Christian, jt. ed. see Kitzerow, Heinz S.

***Bahr, Damon.** Teaching Math the Way Children Think. (Illus.). 300p. (C). 1999. pap. 59.95 (*1-56861-062-9*) Swift Lrn Res.

Bahr, Diana M. From Mission to Metropolis: Cupeno Indian Women in Los Angeles. LC 93-13176. 208p. 1993. 24.95 (*0-8061-2549-7*) U of Okla Pr.

Bahr, Donald. Piman & Papago Ritual Oratory. 1975. pap. 7.00 (*0-685-64956-3*) Indian Hist Pr.

Bahr, Donald, et al. Ants & Orioles: Showing the Art of Pima Poetry. LC 97-29657. 1997. 29.95 (*0-87480-549-X*) U of Utah Pr.

— The Short, Swift Time of Gods on Earth: The Hohokam Chronicles. LC 93-41131. 1994. pap. 18.95 (*0-520-08468-3*, Pub. by U CA Pr) Cal Prin Full Svc.

Bahr, Donald M. Piman Shamanism & Staying Sickness. Alvarez, Albert, ed. LC 72-92103. (Illus.). 144p. 1974. pap. 44.70 (*0-7837-8349-3*, 204913800010) Bks Demand.

Bahr, Ehrhard. The Novel As Archive: Or the Genesis, Reception & Criticism of Goethe's Wilhelm Meister's Wanderjahre. LC 98-35703. (Studies in German Literature & Culture). 224p. 1998. 55.00 (*1-57113-096-9*) Camden Hse.

Bahr, Ehrhard, et al, eds. Humanitat und Dialog: Supplement to the Lessing Yearbook. LC 81-16027. 374p. 1982. 20.00 (*0-8143-1693-X*) Lessing Soc.

Bahr, Ehrhard & Saine, Thomas P., eds. The Internalized Revolution: German Reactions to the French Revolution, 1789-1989. LC 92-25174. 280p. 1992. text 15.00 (*0-8153-1144-3*, H1661) Garland.

***Bahr, Hans-Peter & Vogtle, Thomas, eds.** GIS for Environmental Monitoring. (Illus.). 360p. 1999. 56.00 (*3-510-65191-X*, Pub. by E Schweizerbartsche) Balogh.

Bahr, Howard. The Black Flower: A Novel of the Civil War. LC 97-47287. 266p. 1998. pap. 12.00 (*0-8050-5445-6*, Owl) H Holt & Co.

— The Black Flower: A Novel of the Civil War. LC 97-1029. 230p. 1997. 24.95 (*1-877853-50-X*) Nautical & Aviation.

***Bahr, Howard.** The Black Flower: A Novel of the Civil War. LC 00-28478. 272p. 2000. pap. 13.00 (*0-312-26507-7*) St Martin.

Bahr, Howard. The Black Flower: A Novel of the Civil War. large type ed. (Niagara Large Print Ser.). 464p. 1997. 29.50 (*0-7089-5882-6*) Ulverscroft.

— Home for Christmas. LC 97-30877. (J). 1997. write for info. (*1-877853-51-8*) Nautical & Aviation.

***Bahr, Howard.** The Year of Jubilo: A Novel of the Civil War. LC 99-88634. 376p. 2000. 25.00 (*0-8050-5972-5*) H Holt & Co.

***Bahr, Howard M.** Dine Bibliography to the 1990s: A Companion to the Navajo Bibliography of 1969. LC 99-10061. (Native American Bibliography Ser.: No. 23). 736p. 1999. 95.00 (*0-8108-3651-3*) Scarecrow.

Bahr, Howard M., jt. auth. see Caplow, Theodore.

Bahr, Jerome. Five Novellas. LC 76-53357. 220p. 1977. 13.95 (*0-685-59469-6*) Trempealeau.

— The Lonely Scoundrel: A Supplement to the Perishing Republic. LC 73-80240. 89p. 1974. 12.95 (*0-686-63592-2*) Trempealeau.

— The Perishing Republic. LC 79-129182. 148p. 1971. 10.95 (*0-686-63593-0*) Trempealeau.

Bahr, Joseph M. Dietary Fiber, Calories & Cancer: Index of Modern Authors & Subjects with Guide for Rapid Research. LC 92-36369. 1992. 47.50 (*1-55914-958-2*); pap. 44.50 (*1-55914-959-0*) ABBE Pubs Assn.

Bahr, Kathleen, et al. Family Science 371. 240p. (C). 1996. pap. text, per. 39.95 (*0-7872-2651-3*) Kendall-Hunt.

Bahr, Lauren S. & Johnston, Bernard, eds. Collier's Encyclopedia, 24 vols. (Illus.). 19844p. 1993. 699.00 (*0-02-942548-4*) Free Pr.

Bahr, Mary. The Memory Box. Tucker, Kathleen, ed. LC 91-21628. (Illus.). 32p. (J). (gr. 1-4). 1992. pap. 5.95 (*0-8075-5053-1*) A Whitman.

Bahr, Morton. From the Telegraph to the Internet, 1. 1999. 24.95 (*1-56649-949-6*) Welcome Rain.

Bahr, Nicholas J. System Safety Engineering & Risk Assessment: A Practical Approach. LC 97-10526. 1997. boxed set. write for info. (*1-56032-416-3*) Hemisp Pub.

Bahr, Peggy, et al. I Love Teamwork: Math Activities. Collection I. 40p. 1994. pap., teacher ed. 9.95 (*1-885775-00-8*) BBY Pubns.

— I Love Teamwork: Math Activities; Collection Primary. 46p. Date not set. pap. 16.95 (*1-885775-08-3*) BBY Pubns.

Bahr, Robert. Dramatic Technique in Fiction. 158p. 1998. pap. 12.95 (*1-887650-08-3*, Pub. by Factor Pr) BookWorld.

— Indecent Exposures: Short Fiction. (Illus.). 165p. 1993. pap. 9.50 (*0-9626531-2-8*, Pub. by Factor Pr) BookWorld.

— Indecent Exposures: Short Fiction. (Illus.). 1993. 17.95 (*0-9626531-3-6*) Factor Pr.

— Sex Show. (Orig.). 1994. mass mkt. 4.95 (*1-56333-225-6*, Badboy) Masquerade.

— The Virility Factor: Masculinity Through Testosterone, the Male Sex Hormone. rev. ed. 213p. 1993. pap. 12.95 (*0-9626531-1-X*) Factor Pr.

Bahr, Robert, ed. Home Again, Home Again: New Voices in the Southern Tradition. 160p. (Orig.). 1994. pap. 9.95 (*0-9626531-5-2*) Factor Pr.

Bahr, Robert, jt. auth. see Whybrow, Peter.

Bahr, Rosemary S. Outside Looking In: The Near-Death Experience. (Illus.). 180p. (Orig.). (C). 1992. pap. text 35.00 (*1-881604-00-4*) Scopcraeft.

Bahr, Walter, jt. auth. see Ditchfield, Michael.

Bahra, N. 306 Degree Appraisal: A Best Practical Guide. 1996. pap. 145.00 (*1-85953-052-4*, Pub. by Tech Comm) St Mut.

Bahra, N. 360 Degree Appraisal. (Financial Times Management Briefings Ser.). 1997. pap. 94.50 (*0-273-63170-5*, Pub. by F T P-H) Trans-Atl Phila.

Bahrami. Object-Oriented Systems Development. 1997. pap. 13.50 (*0-256-25382-X*) McGraw.

— Rapid Software Deployment. (DC - Introduction to Computing Ser.). 1996. pap. 47.95 (*0-534-24186-7*) S-W Pub.

***Bahrami, Ali.** Object Oriented Systems Development. LC 98-43126. 432p. 1999. 52.74 (*0-256-25348-X*) Dorsey.

Bahrami, Homa, jt. auth. see Leavitt, Harold J.

Bahrami, Mehdi. Gurgan Faiences. (Islamic Art Reprint Ser.: No. 1). (Illus.). 134p. 1987. reprint ed. lib. bdg. 25.00 (*0-939214-54-7*) Mazda Pubs.

***Bahrampour, Tara.** To See & See Again: A Life in Iran & America. LC 98-27360. 356p. 1999. 24.00 (*0-374-28767-8*) FS&G.

— To See & See Again: A Life in Iran & America. LC 00-20627. 361p. 2000. pap. text 17.95 (*0-520-22354-3*, Pub. by U CA Pr) Cal Prin Full Svc.

Bahrani, Zainab, tr. see Bottero, Jean.

***Bahrdt, Carl Friedrich.** The Edict of Religion: A Comedy & the Story & Diary of My Imprisonment. Laursen, John Christian & Van der Zande, Johan, trs. 144p. 1999. 70.00 (*0-7391-0089-0*); pap. 23.95 (*0-7391-0090-4*) Lexington Bks.

Bahre, Conrad J. Destruction of the Natural Vegetation of North-Central Chile. LC 78-50836. (University of California Publications in Geography: No. 23). 138p. pap. 42.80 (*0-7837-7470-2*, 204919200010) Bks Demand.

— A Legacy of Change: Historic Human Impact on Vegetation in the Arizona Borderlands. LC 90-39777. (Illus.). 231p. 1991. 36.00 (*0-8165-1204-3*) U of Ariz Pr.

Bahre, Rolf, jt. ed. see Yu, Wei-Wen.

Bahreininejad, A., jt. auth. see Topping, B. H. V.

Bahrenberg, Gerhard, et al, eds. Recent Developments in Spatial Data Analysis: Methodology, Measurement, Models. 426p. 1984. text 103.95 (*0-566-00685-5*) Ashgate Pub Co.

Bahrenburg, Richard, jt. auth. see Asser, Stuart.

Bahrey, et al. History of the Galla (Oromo) of Ethiopia: With Ethnology & History of SW Ethiopia. xiii, 93p. (Orig.). 1993. reprint ed. pap. 8.00 (*1-883701-00-7*) African Sun.

Bahri, Abbas. Classical Quantic Periodic Motions. 1997. pap. 79.95 (*0-582-32749-0*, Pub. by Addison-Wesley) Longman.

Bahri, Abbas. Critical Points at Infinity in Some Variational Problems. LC 88-12264. (Pitman Research Notes in Mathematics Ser.). 307p. 1989. write for info. (*0-582-02164-2*) Longman.

Bahri, Deepika & Vasudeva, Mary, eds. Between the Lines: South Asians & Postcoloniality. LC 95-52972. (Asian American History & Culture Ser.). 400p. 1996. pap. 27.95 (*1-56639-468-6*); lib. bdg. 69.95 (*1-56639-467-8*) Temple U Pr.

Bahri, H. Illustrated Essential Dictionary: English into English & Hindi. (ENG & HIN.). 1989. 12.50 (*0-8364-2556-1*, Pub. by Usha) S Asia.

— Learner's Hindi-English Dictionary. (ENG & HIN.). 758p. 1987. 49.95 (*0-8288-1130-X*, M14384) Fr & Eur.

— Learners' Hindi-English Dictionary. xix, 758p. 1994. 14.95 (*1-881338-42-8*) Nataraj Bks.

Bahruth, Robert E. & Venditti, Phillip, eds. Profiles in Success: Reflections on the Community College Experience. 1990. pap. 10.00 (*0-87117-220-8*, 1313) Comm Coll Pr Am Assn Comm Coll.

Bahruth, Robert E. & Venditti, Phillip N., eds. Profiles in Success. LC 90-84156. (Illus.). 320p. reprint ed. pap. 99.20 (*0-608-20517-6*, 207176900002) Bks Demand.

Bahry, Donna L. Outside Moscow: Power, Politics & Budgetary Policy in the Soviet Republics. LC 87-8020. (Illus.). 224p. 1987. text 50.00 (*0-231-06290-7*) Col U Pr.

Bahti, Mark. Pueblo Stories & Storytellers. 2nd rev. ed. LC 96-61115. (Illus.). 56p. 1996. pap. 12.95 (*1-887896-01-5*, Rio Nuevo) Treas Chest Bks.

— Southwest Indian Designs: With Some Explanations. (Illus.). 32p. 1995. pap. 4.95 (*0-918080-51-7*, Rio Nuevo) Treas Chest Bks.

— Spirit in the Stone: A Handbook of Southwestern Indian Animal Carvings & Beliefs. (Illus.). 192p. (Orig.). 1999. pap. 15.95 (*1-887896-09-0*, Rio Nuevo) Treas Chest Bks.

Bahti, Mark & Joe, Eugene Baatsos Lanii. A Guide to Navajo Sandpaintings. rev. ed. (Illus.). 56p. 2000. pap. 9.95 (*1-887896-05-8*, Rio Nuevo) Treas Chest Bks.

Bahti, Mark, jt. auth. see Bahti, Tom.

Bahti, Timothy. Allegories of History: Literary Historiography after Hegel. LC 91-41130. 352p. 1992. text 47.00 (*0-8018-4342-1*) Johns Hopkins.

— Ends of the Lyric: Direction & Consequence in Western Poetry. LC 95-22341. 288p. (C). 1996. text 47.00 (*0-8018-5192-0*); pap. text 16.95 (*0-8018-5193-9*) Johns Hopkins.

Bahti, Timothy & Fries, Marilyn S., eds. Jewish Writers, German Literature: The Uneasy Examples of Nelly Sachs & Walter Benjamin. 232p. (C). 1996. text 49.50 (*0-472-10621-X*, 10621) U of Mich Pr.

Bahti, Timothy, tr. see Jauss, Hans R.

Bahti, Tom & Bahti, Mark. Southwestern Indian Arts & Crafts. 3rd rev. ed. LC 97-70255. (Illus.). 64p. 1997. pap. 7.95 (*0-88714-095-5*) KC Pubns.

— Southwestern Indian Ceremonials. 3rd rev. ed. LC 97-70256. (Illus.). 64p. 1997. pap. 7.95 (*0-88714-096-3*) KC Pubns.

— Southwestern Indian Tribes. 2nd rev. ed. LC 97-70257. (Illus.). 80p. 1997. pap. 7.95 (*0-88714-097-1*) KC Pubns.

— Southwestern Indians: Arts & Crafts - Tribes - Ceremonials. LC 97-70258. (Illus.). 228p. 1997. 34.50 (*0-88714-110-2*) KC Pubns.

Bahtin, I. A., et al. Eleven Papers on Differential Equations, Functional Analysis & Measure Theory. LC 51-5559. (Translations Ser.: No. 2, Vol. 51). 332p. 1966. 55.00 (*0-8218-1751-5*, TRANS2/51) Am Math.

Bahto, George. The National School of Golf Design. (Illus.). 288p. Date not set. 85.00 (*1-886947-20-1*) Sleepng Bear.

Bahturin, Yuri A. Basic Structures of Modern Algebra. LC 93-11839. (Mathematics & Its Applications Ser.). 434p. (C). 1993. text 285.50 (*0-7923-2459-5*) Kluwer Academic.

— Identical Relations in Lie Algebras. 324p. 1986. lib. bdg. 187.50 (*90-6764-052-2*) Coronet Bks.

Bahturin, Yuri A., et al. Infinite Dimensional Lie Superalgebras. LC 92-29650. (Expositions in Mathematics Ser.: Vol. 7). x, 250p. (C). 1992. lib. bdg. 99.95 (*3-11-012974-4*) De Gruyter.

Bahu, Richard & Crittenden, Barry, eds. Management of Process Industry Waste. LC 94-229322. 1997. pap. 70.00 (*0-85295-324-0*, 53240) Gulf Pub.

Bahuchet, Serge, jt. auth. see Thomas, Jacqueline.

***Bahugna, B. N.** The Golden Treasury of Wisdom: Great Thoughts of Great Minds. xii, 331p. 1998. 30.00 (*81-7099-699-6*, Pub. by Mittal Pubns) Nataraj Bks.

Bahuguna, Anjali, ed. Science & Technology in Relation to Rural Women. (C). 1995. 28.00 (*81-241-0359-3*, Pub. by Har-Anand Pubns) S Asia.

Bahuguna, V. K. Management of Forestry Research in India. 150p. (C). 1991. text 160.00 (*0-89771-542-X*, Pub. by Intl Bk Distr) St Mut.

— Management of Forestry Research in India. 96p. 1992. pap. 125.00 (*81-7089-178-7*, Pub. by Intl Bk Distr) St Mut.

— Tropical Forest Ecosystem Soil Fauna in Sub-Tropics. (C). 1991. text 175.00 (*0-89771-543-8*, Pub. by Intl Bk Distr) St Mut.

— Tropical Forest Ecosystem Soil Fauna in Sub-Tropics. 110p. 1991. pap. 225.00 (*81-7089-138-8*, Pub. by Intl Bk Distr) St Mut.

Bai. Reporting Systems for Bank Man. 1990. text 40.00 (*0-07-413137-0*) McGraw.

Bai & Powis, Robert E. Bank Secrecy Act Compliance & Flipchart. 4th ed. 1993. text 100.00 (*0-7602-0063-7*, Irwn Prfssnl) McGraw-Hill Prof.

Bai, jt. auth. see Salam, F. M.

Bai, tr. see Seth, Vikram.

Bai, Bahini & Bahadur, Krishna P. Bahirnea Beaei & Her Abhangas. LC 98-902494. xi, 94 p. 1998. 22.50 (*81-215-0787-1*, Pub. by M Manoharial) Coronet Bks.

Bai, C. Scanning Tunneling Microscopy & Its Application. Ertl, G. et al, eds. LC 95-34587. (Springer Series in Surface Sciences: Vol. 32). (Illus.). 320p. 1995. 99.50 (*3-540-59346-2*) Spr-Verlag.

***Bai, Chunli.** Scanning Tunneling Microscopy & Its Application. 2nd rev. ed. LC 99-34035. (Series in Surface Sciences: Vol. 32). (Illus.). 365p. 2000. 85.00 (*3-540-65715-0*) Spr-Verlag.

Bai, Hua. The Remote Country of Women: A Novel by Bai Hua. Wu, Qingyun & Beebee, Thomas O., trs. from CHI. LC 94-9956. (Fiction from Modern China Ser.). (Illus.). 344p. 1994. pap. 16.95 (*0-8248-1611-0*); text 38.00 (*0-8248-1591-2*) UH Pr.

Bai, J., jt. ed. see Ma, X.

Bai, Jianhua & Sung, Juyu. Beyond the Basics: Communicative Chinese for Intermediate - Advanced Learners. rev. ed. Xing, Janet Z., ed. LC 96-84640. (C & T Language Ser.). (Illus.). 240p. (C). 1996. pap. text 22.95 (*0-88727-226-6*) Cheng & Tsui.

Bai-Lin, Hao. Chaos. 592p. 1984. text 89.00 (*9971-966-50-6*); pap. text 41.00 (*9971-966-51-4*) World Scientific Pub.

Bai-lin, Hao. Elementary Symbolic Dynamics & Chaos in Dissipative Systems. 476p. 1989. text 99.00 (*9971-5-0682-3*); pap. text 48.00 (*9971-5-0698-X*) World Scientific Pub.

Bai, X. Heparan Sulfate Proteoglycans in Embryonic Development. No. 60. 125p. (Orig.). 1993. pap. 52.50 (*90-6186-535-2*, Pub. by Leuven Univ) Coronet Bks.

Bai, Xinghua & Baron, R. B. Acupuncture in Clinical Practice: A Practical Guide to the Use of Acupuncture & Related Therapies. LC 96-21659. 288p. 1996. pap. text 62.50 (*0-7506-2670-4*) Buttrwrth-Heinemann.

Bai, Y. & Dodd, B. Adiabatic Shear Localization: Occurrence, Theories & Applications. (Illus.). 388p. 1992. 151.00 (*0-08-041266-1*, Pergamon Pr) Elsevier.

Baiamonte, Edward. Understanding the Difference Between Democrats & Republicans. 262p. 1992. 21.95 (*0-9631799-0-X*) Am Polit Pr.

Baiamonte, John. Immigrants in Rural Society: A Study of Italians of Tangiipahoa Parish, Louisiana. LC 90-3514. (European Immigrants & American Society Ser.). 260p. 1990. reprint ed. text 20.00 (*0-8240-0211-3*) Garland.

Baiamonte, Ted. The 91Factor: Why Women Initiate 91of Divorce, End Most Relationships, & What Can Be Done about It. 251p. 1998. 21.95 (*0-9631799-2-6*) Am Polit Pr.

Baibi, S. Y. At the Threshold of Premonition. 1984. pap. 3.50 (*0-913054-38-0*) Poet Gal Pr.

Baibi, Soy. In Kafka Castle. 1973. pap. 3.50 (*0-913054-07-0*) Poet Gal Pr.

— The Secretary. 1971. pap. 3.50 (*0-913054-04-6*) Poet Gal Pr.

Baican, R., jt. auth. see Necsulescu, Dan-Sorin.

Baichelor. Existence et Imagination: Essai sur le Theatre de Montherlant. Laredu, tr. (FRE.). 14.50 (*0-8288-9057-9*, F115870) Fr & Eur.

Baichtal, James F. & Swanston, Douglas N. Karst Landscapes & Associated Resources: A Resource Assessment. (Illus.). 20p. 1997. reprint ed. 8.00 (*0-89904-567-7*, Bear Meadows Resrch Grp); reprint ed. pap. 2.50 (*0-89904-568-5*, Ecosytems Resrch) Crumb Elbow Pub.

Baicich, Paul J., ed. A Birder's Guide to Virginia. LC 97-71776. (ABA/Lane Birdfinding Guides Ser.). (Illus.). 288p. (Orig.). 1997. pap. 18.95 (*1-878788-12-4*, 233) Amer Birding Assn.

Baicich, Paul J. & Harrison, Colin J. A Guide to the Nests, Eggs & Nestlings of North American Birds. 2nd ed. LC 96-47959. (Illus.). 350p. (C). 1997. pap. text 22.95 (*0-12-072831-1*) Morgan Kaufmann.

Baicich, Paul J., jt. auth. see Holt, Harold R.

Baicich, Paul J., ed. see Bird Observer Staff & Van Dusen, Barry W.

Baicich, Paul J., ed. see Chartier, Bonnie.

Baicich, Paul J., ed. see Cooper, Jerry A.

Baicich, Paul J., ed. see Delorey, Alan.

Baicich, Paul J., ed. see Holt, Harold R.

Baicich, Paul J., ed. see Pranty, Bill.

Baicich, Paul J., ed. see Scott, Oliver K.

Baicich, Paul J., ed. see Svingen, Daniel N. & Dumroese, Kas.

Baicich, Paul J., ed. see Taylor, Richard C.

Baicich, Paul J., ed. see White, Mel.

***Baicker-McKee.** Federal Rules of Civil Procedure 2nd ed. (C). 1999. pap., student ed. 17.50 (*0-314-23805-0*) Sth-Wstrn College.

Baicker-McKee, Carol. Mapped Out! The Search for Snookums. LC 96-27680. (Illus.). 32p. (YA). (gr. 3 up). 1997. 19.95 (*0-87905-788-2*) Gibbs Smith Pub.

Baicker-McKee, Steven, et al. Federal Civil Rules Handbook, 1993. 94th ed. 1150p. 1993. pap. text 39.00 (*0-314-02731-9*) West Pub.

— Federal Civil Rules Handbook 1997 Edition. 1250p. 1996. pap. text. write for info. (*0-314-20269-2*) West Pub.

Baider, Lea, et al, eds. Cancer & the Family. LC 95-30724. 452p. 1996. 195.00 (*0-471-95890-5*) Wiley.

***Baider, Lea, et al.** Cancer & the Family. 2nd ed. LC 99-56524. 572p. 2000. 185.00 (*0-471-80300-6*) Wiley.

Baidin, Kerry J. Sea Dream. LC 96-96000. (Illus.). iv, 125p. (Orig.). 1996. pap. 15.95 (*0-9651110-0-8*) K J Baidin.

Baidya, Karunakar. Teach Yourself Nepali. 105p. (C). 1986. 40.00 (*0-89771-083-5*, Pub. by Ratna Pustak Bhandar) St Mut.
— Teach Yourself Nepali. 1991. 30.00 (*0-7855-0288-2*, Pub. by Ratna Pustak Bhandar) St Mut.

Baier, Annette C. The Commons of the Mind. LC 97-113. 110p. 1997. 26.95 (*0-8126-9349-3*); pap. 16.95 (*0-8126-9350-7*) Open Court.
— Moral Prejudices: Essays on Ethics. LC 93-2442. 368p. 1994. text 49.95 (*0-674-58715-4*) HUP.
— Moral Prejudices: Essays on Ethics. 384p. 1995. pap. text 19.50 (*0-674-58716-2*, BAIMOX) HUP.
— A Progress of Sentiments: Reflections on Hume's Treatise. LC 90-5124. (Illus.). 352p. 1991. 53.50 (*0-674-71385-0*, BAIPRO) HUP.
— A Progress of Sentiments: Reflections on Hume's Treatise. 352p. 1994. pap. 22.95 (*0-674-71386-9*) HUP.

Baier, G. & Klein, M., eds. A Chaotic Hierarchy. 412p. (C). 1991. text 104.00 (*981-02-0023-4*) World Scientific Pub.

Baier, Jiri. Mushroom & Toadstools. 184p. 1995. write for info. (*1-57215-133-1*) World Pubns.

Baier, John L. & Strong, Thomas S., eds. Technology in Student Affairs: Issues, Applications, & Trends. LC 93-23439. 296p. (Orig.). 1994. pap. text 32.50 (*1-883485-03-7*); lib. bdg. 57.50 (*1-883485-02-9*) Am Coll Personnel.

Baier, Kurt. Problems of Life & Death: A Humanist Perspective. LC 97-12834. (Prometheus Lecture). 239p. 1997. 29.95 (*1-57392-153-X*) Prometheus Bks.
— The Rational & the Moral Order: The Social Roots of Reason & Morality. (Paul Carus Lectures: Ser. 18). 465p. 1995. 44.95 (*0-8126-9263-2*); pap. 21.95 (*0-8126-9264-0*) Open Court.

Baier, Lesley K. & Shestack, Alan. The Katharine Ordway Collection, Yale University Art Gallery. (Illus.). 128p. 1983. pap. 13.00 (*0-89467-025-5*) Yale Art Gallery.

Baier, Lesley K., ed. see Weber, Nicholas F.

Baier, Lesley K., ed. see Yale University Art Gallery Staff.

Baier, Martin. How to Find & Cultivate Customers Through Direct Marketing. (Illus.). 272p. 1996. 47.95 (*0-8442-3666-7*, NTC Business Bks) NTC Contemp Pub Co.

Baier, R., jt. ed. see Wegener, D.

Baier, Robert E., ed. Applied Chemistry at Protein Interfaces: A Symposium. LC 75-25969. (Advances in Chemistry Ser.: No. 145). (Illus.). 408p. reprint ed. pap. 126.50 (*0-608-04355-9*, 206513600001) Bks Demand.

Baier, Stephen. An Economic History of Central Niger. (OSAA Ser.). (Illus.). 340p. 1980. text 59.00 (*0-19-822717-5*) OUP.

Baier, Sue & Schomaker, Mary Z. Bed Number Ten. 304p. 1989. per. 29.95 (*0-8493-4270-8*, RC416) CRC Pr.

Baier, V. N., et al. Electromagnetic Processes at High Energies in Oriented Single Crystals. LC 98-216119. 500p. 1997. text 106.00 (*981-02-1603-3*) World Scientific Pub.

Baierlain, E. R. In the Wilderness with the Red Indians: German Missionary to the Michigan Indians, 1847-1853. rev. ed. Moll, Harold W., ed. Boldt, Anita Z., tr. from GER. LC 96-28165. (Great Lakes Bks.). (Illus.). 136p. (C). 1996. pap. 13.95 (*0-8143-2581-5*) Wayne St U Pr.

Baierle, Heinz U. Vegetation und Flora Im Suedwestlichen Jordanien. (Dissertationes Botanicae Ser.: Band 200). (Illus.). 256p. 1993. pap. 106.00 (*3-443-64112-1*, Pub. by Gebruder Borntraeger) Balogh.

Baierlein. Newtonian Dynamics. 1983. student ed. 20.62 (*0-07-003017-0*) McGraw.

Baierlein, E. R. Land of the Tamilians & Its Missions. Gribble, J. D., tr. (C). 1995. reprint ed. 24.00 (*81-206-1006-7*, Pub. by Asian Educ Servs) S Asia.

Baierlein, Ralph. Newton to Einstein: The Trail of Light: An Excursion to the Wave-Particle Duality & the Special Theory of Relativity. (Illus.). 345p. (C). 1992. text 42.95 (*0-521-41171-8*) Cambridge U Pr.
— Newtonian Dynamics. (Illus.). 336p. (C). 1983. 88.44 (*0-07-003016-2*) McGraw.
— Thermal Physics. (Illus.). 560p. (C). 1999. pap. 42.95 (*0-521-65838-1*) Cambridge U Pr.
— Thermal Physics. LC 98-38617. (Illus.). 560p. (C). 1999. text 95.00 (*0-521-59082-5*) Cambridge U Pr.

Baifang. Chinese Brain Twisters: Fifty-Six Fast, Fun Puzzles That Help Children Develop Quick, Logical Minds. 128p. 1994. pap. 14.95 (*0-471-59505-5*) Wiley.
— More Chinese Brain Twisters: 57 Fast, Fun Puzzles That Help Children Develop Quick Minds. LC 99-12224. 118p. 1999. pap. 14.95 (*0-471-24613-1*) Wiley.

Baifus, Y. Y. Longing for Dawn: The Jewish Guide to Consolation. LC 95-18057. 1995. 20.95 (*0-87306-719-3*) Feldheim.

Baig, M. A. Educational Philosophy of the Quran. 220p. (Orig.). 1993. pap. 22.50 (*1-56744-467-9*) Kazi Pubns.

Baig, Reshma. The Memory of Hands. 216p. (YA). (gr. 9-12). 1998. pap. write for info. (*1-889720-27-5*, Pub. by Amirah Pubng) Intl Bks & Tapes.

Baig, S. S. Cancer Research at the European Level. LC 95-75273. (Biomedical & Health Research Ser.). (gr. 12). 1995. 60.00 (*90-5199-215-7*) IOS Press.

Baig, Samina, jt. auth. see Najar, Qasim M.

Baig, Shari. Women in Islam: Role of Women in Modern Islam. 320p. 1992. pap. 9.95 (*1-881893-01-4*) Universal Unity.

***Baigell, Matthew.** Artist & Identity in Twentieth-Century America. (Contemporary Artists & Their Critics Ser.). (Illus.). 192p. (C). 2001. Price not set. (*0-521-77239-7*); pap. text Price not set. (*0-521-77601-5*) Cambridge U Pr.

Baigell, Matthew. Concise History of American Painting & Sculpture. rev. ed. LC 96-220575. 464p. (C). 1996. pap. 35.00 (*0-06-430986-X*, Pub. by Westview) HarpC.
— Jewish-American Artists & the Holocaust. LC 96-39806. (Illus.). xi, 138p. (C). 1997. text 35.00 (*0-8135-2404-0*) Rutgers U Pr.
— Thomas Cole. (Great Artists Ser.). (Illus.). 88p. 1999. pap. 16.95 (*0-8230-0648-4*) Watsn-Guptill.

Baigell, Matthew, comment. Nineteenth Century Painters of the Delaware Valley. (Illus.). 60p. (Orig.). 1983. pap. 7.00 (*0-938766-01-5*) NJ State Mus.

***Baigell, Matthew & Heyd, Milly, eds.** Complex Identities: Jewish Consciousness & Modern Art. LC 00-40289. (Illus.). 288p. 2001. pap. 28.00 (*0-8135-2869-0*); text 55.00 (*0-8135-2868-2*) Rutgers U Pr.

Baigell, Matthew & Williams, Julia, eds. Artists Against War & Fascism: Papers of the First American Artists' Congress. (Illus.). 200p. (C). 1986. 40.00 (*0-8135-1125-9*) Rutgers U Pr.

Baigell, Matthew, et al. The American Scene & the South: Paintings & Works on Paper, 1930-1946. Phagan, Patricia Elaine, ed. LC 95-52395. (Illus.). 263p. 1996. pap. 43.00 (*0-915977-24-9*) Georgia Museum of Art.

Baigell, Matthew, jt. auth. see Baigell, Renee.

Baigell, Renee & Baigell, Matthew. Soviet Dissident Artists: Interviews after Perestroika. LC 95-12435. (Illus.). 375p. (C). 1995. text 39.95 (*0-8135-2223-4*) Rutgers U Pr.

Baigent, Elizabeth, jt. auth. see Kain, Roger J.

Baigent, Michael. The Temple & the Lodge. 1990. mass mkt. 8.99 (*0-552-13596-8*) Bantam.

Baigent, Michael & Leigh, Richard. The Dead Sea Scrolls Deception. (Illus.). 288p. 1993. per. 13.00 (*0-671-79797-2*, Touchstone) S&S Trade Pap.
— The Temple & the Lodge. (Illus.). 324p. 1991. pap. 13.45 (*1-55970-126-9*, Pub. by Arcade Pub Inc) Time Warner.

Baigent, Michael, et al. The Dead Sea Scrolls Deception. 320p. 1992. mass mkt. 8.99 (*0-552-13878-9*) Bantam.
— Holy Blood, Holy Grail. 496p. 1983. mass mkt. 7.99 (*0-440-13648-2*) Dell.
— The Messianic Legacy. 512p. 1988. pap. 8.99 (*0-552-13182-2*) Bantam.
— The Messianic Legacy. 448p. 1989. mass mkt. 7.50 (*0-440-20319-8*) Dell.
— Mundane Astrology: An Introduction to the Astrology of Nations & Groups. 496p. 1988. pap. 12.95 (*0-85030-302-8*, Pub. by Aqrn Pr) Harper SF.
— Mundane Astrology: An Introduction to the Astrology of Nations & Groups. rev. ed. 544p. pap. 19.95 (*1-85538-140-0*, Pub. by Aqrn Pr) HarpC.

Baiggeman, Paula, jt. ed. see Burns, Joseph.

Baigrie, Brian S., ed. Picturing Knowledge: Historical & Philosophical Problems Concerning the Use of Art in Science. (Toronto Studies in Philosophy). (Illus.). 400p. 1996. text 80.00 (*0-8020-2985-X*); pap. text 24.95 (*0-8020-7439-1*) U of Toronto Pr.

Baij, Maria Cecilia. The Life of Saint Joseph. 416p. 1997. pap. 10.00 (*1-890137-01-4*) One Hund-One Fnd.

Baijal, Mahendra D., ed. Plastics Polymer Science & Technology. LC 81-13066. (SPE Monographs). 959p. reprint ed. pap. 200.00 (*0-7837-2383-0*, 204006900006) Bks Demand.

Baijinnyam, I., et al. Ruptures of Major Earthquakes & Active Deformation in Mongolia. (Memoir Ser.: No. 181). 1993. 18.75 (*0-8137-1181-9*) Geol Soc.

Baik, Sang-Ho, jt. auth. see Sadler, Thomas W.

Baikie, James. Egyptian Papyri & Papyrus-Hunting. LC 76-152972. (Select Bibliographies Reprint Ser.). (Illus.). 1977. reprint ed. 29.95 (*0-8369-5724-5*) Ayer.
— A History of Egypt: From the Earliest Times to the End of the Eighteenth Dynasty, 2 Vols., Set. LC 79-157323. (Select Bibliographies Reprint Ser.). (C). 1977. reprint ed. 72.95 (*0-8369-5782-2*) Ayer.
— The Life of the Ancient East - Being Some Chapters of Romance of Modern Excavation. (African Studies). 464p. reprint ed. 60.00 (*0-685-56711-7*) ECA Assoc.

Baikie, W. B. Narrative of an Exploring Voyage up to the Rivers Kuora & Binue Commonly Known As the Niger & Tsadda in 1854. 456p. 1966. 57.50 (*0-7146-1788-1*, Pub. by F Cass Pubs) Intl Spec Bk.

Baikov, V. E. & Sigalov, E. E. Reinforced Concrete Structures, 2 vols., Vols. 1 & 2. (C). 1983. 120.00 (*0-685-46651-5*, Pub. by Collets) St Mut.

Baikow, V. E. Manufacture & Refining of Raw Cane Sugar. 2nd ed. (Sugar Ser.: Vol. 2). xx,588p. 1982. 362.00 (*0-444-41896-2*) Elsevier.

Bail, Christopher. The Future of North-South Relations. 1998. pap. text 25.00 (*0-7494-2708-6*) Kogan Page Ltd.
— Future of North South Relations: Towards Sustainable Economic & Social Development. (Forward Studies Ser.). 1998. 25.00 (*0-7494-2783-3*) Kogan Page Ltd.
— The Future of North-South Relations: Towards Sustainable Economic & Social Development. LC 98-17450. 118p. 1998. text 39.95 (*0-312-21601-7*) St Martin.

Bail, Eli. From Railway to Freeway: Pacific Electric & the Motor Coach. LC 84-705. (Illus.). 196p. 1990. 19.95 (*0-916374-61-0*, SPECIAL 90) Pentrex Media.

Bail, Murray. The Drover's Wife & Other Stories. (Paperbacks Ser.). Orig. Title: Contemporary Portraits. 183p. 1985. pap. 14.95 (*0-7022-1818-9*, Pub. by Univ Queensland Pr) Intl Spec Bk.
— Eucalyptus: A Novel. LC 98-5880. 272p. 1998. 23.00 (*0-374-14857-0*) FS&G.
— Eucalyptus: A Novel. LC 99-15148. 264p. 1999. pap. 13.00 (*0-15-600781-9*, Harvest Bks) Harcourt.

***Bail, Murray.** Homesickness. LC 99-34981. 432p. (Orig.). 1999. pap. 14.00 (*0-374-17247-1*) FS&G.

Bail, Paul. Anne Tyler: A Critical Companion. LC 98-12152. (Critical Companions to Popular Contemporary Writers Ser.). 232p. 1998. 29.95 (*0-313-30249-9*, Greenwood Pr) Greenwood.

Bail, Paul. John Saul: A Critical Companion. LC 95-39492. (Critical Companions to Popular Contemporary Writers Ser.). 224p. 1995. 29.95 (*0-313-29575-1*, Greenwood Pr) Greenwood.

Bailache, Laura M., tr. see Jannella, Cecilia.

Bailar, J. C., et al, eds. Comprehensive Inorganic Chemistry, 5 vols., Set. Incl. Actinides, Master Index, Vol. 4. 1973. 316.00 (*0-08-016990-2*); Vol. 1. H, Noble Gases, Group 1A, Group 11A, Group 111B, C, & Si. 1973. 733.00 (*0-08-016987-2*); Vol. 2. Ge, Sn, Pb, Group VE, Group VIB, Group VIIB. 1973. 606.00 (*0-08-016988-0*); Vol. 3. Lanthanides, Transition Metal Compounds. 1973. 448.00 (*0-08-016989-9*); (C). 1973. 2724.00 (*0-08-017275-X*, Pub. by Pergamon Repr) Franklin.

Bailar, J. C. & Emeleus, H. J. Comprehensive Inorganic Chemistry Vol. 1: H - Noble Gases Group IA, IIA, IIIB, C & Si, 5 Vols. LC 77-189736. 1973. 653.00 (*0-08-015655-X*, Pub. by Pergamon Repr) Franklin.

Bailar, John C. Inorganic Syntheses, 4. 230p. 1978. 35.00 (*0-88275-868-3*) Krieger.

Bailar, John C., III, et al, eds. Assessing Risks to Health: Methodologic Approaches. LC 88-6203. 344p. 1993. 59.95 (*0-86569-167-3*, T167, Auburn Hse) Greenwood.

Bailar, John C., III & Mosteller, Frederick, eds. Medical Uses of Statistics. 2nd ed. (Illus.). 449p. 1992. pap. text 39.95 (*0-910133-36-0*) Mass Med Pub Div.

Bailard, Biehl & Kaiser, Inc. Staff. How to Be Successful Investor. 1989. pap. 54.75 (*1-55623-201-2*, Irwn Prfssnl) McGraw-Hill Prof.

Bailbe. Agrippa d'Aubigne, Poete des Tragiques. (Publ. Fac. des Lettres et Sc. Hum. Universite de Caen). 38.95 (*0-8288-6088-2*, F28350) Fr & Eur.

***Baildam, John D.** Paradisal Love: Johann Gottfried Herder & the Song of Songs. (Journal for the Study of the Old Testament Supplement Ser.: No. 298). 368p. 1999. 90.00 (*1-84127-022-9*, Pub. by Sheffield Acad) CUP Services.

Baildon, John, jt. auth. see De Beau Chesne, John.

Baildon, W. Paley. Keighley Family (Reprinted from "Yorkshire Archaelogical Journal") (Illus.). 109p. 1997. reprint ed. pap. 16.50 (*0-8328-9385-4*); reprint ed. lib. bdg. 26.50 (*0-8328-9384-6*) Higginson Bk Co.

Bailer, Darice. Humpback Goes North. LC 97-47615. (Smithsonian Oceanic Collection). (Illus.). 32p. (J). (ps-2). 1998. 15.95 (*1-56899-525-3*); 19.95 incl. audio (*1-56899-527-X*, BC4015) Soundprints.
— Humpback Goes North, Incl. large toy. (Smithsonian Oceanic Collection). (Illus.). 32p. (J). (ps-2). 1998. 29.95 (*1-56569-529-6*) Soundprints.
— Humpback Goes North, Incl. micro bk. LC 97-47515. (Smithsonian Oceanic Collection). (Illus.). 32p. (J). (ps-2). 1998. 4.95 (*1-56899-526-1*) Soundprints.
— Humpback Goes North, Incl. Sm. & Lg. Plush Toy. (Smithsonian Oceanic Collection). (Illus.). 32p. (J). (ps-2). 1998. 38.95 incl. audio (*1-56899-631-4*) Soundprints.
— Humpback Goes North, Micro bk., incl. small toy (Smithsonian Oceanic Collection). (Illus.). 32p. (J). (ps-2). 1998. pap. 9.95 (*1-56899-530-X*) Soundprints.
— The Last Rail: The Building of the First Transcontinental Railroad. LC 96-15036. (Smithsonian Odyssey Ser.). (Illus.). 32p. (J). (gr. 2-5). 1996. 14.95 (*1-56899-362-5*); pap. 5.95 (*1-56899-363-3*) Soundprints.
— The Last Rail: The Building of the First Transcontinental Railroad, Incl. toy. (Smithsonian Odyssey Ser.). (Illus.). 32p. (J). (gr. 2-5). 1996. 29.95 (*1-56899-364-1*); pap. 17.95 (*1-56899-365-X*) Soundprints.

Bailer, Darice. The Last Rail: The Building of the Transcontinental Railroad. (Odyssey Ser.). 32p. (J). (gr. 2-5). 1996. 7.95 incl. audio (*1-56899-369-2*, C6003) Soundprints.

Bailer, Darice. The Last Rail: The Building of the Transcontinental Railroad. (Odyssey Ser.). (Illus.). 32p. (J). (gr. 2-5). 1996. 19.95 incl. audio (*1-56899-356-8*, B5009) Soundprints.
— The Last Rail, the Building of the First Transcontinental Railroad. LC 96-15036. (Smithsonian Institution Odyssey Ser.). 1996. 11.15 (*0-606-10248-5*, Pub. by Turtleback) Demco.

***Bailer, Darice.** The Official Milky Book & Pen Kit. (Illus.). 48p. (J). (gr. k-3). 2000. pap. 9.99 (*0-689-83806 9*) Litle Simon.

Bailer, Darice. Puffin's Homecoming: The Story of an Atlantic Puffin. (Smithsonian Wild Heritage Collection). (Illus.). 32p. (J). (gr. k-3). 1995. pap. 4.95 (*1-56899-141-X*) Soundprints.
— Puffin's Homecoming: The Story of an Atlantic Puffin, Incl. 8" toy. (Smithsonian Wild Heritage Collection). (Illus.). 32p. (J). (gr. k-3). 1995. pap. 15.95 (*1-56899-147-9*) Soundprints.
— Puffin's Homecoming: The Story of an Atlantic Puffin, Incl. Sm. & Lg. Plush Toy. (Smithsonian Wild Heritage Collection). (Illus.). 32p. (J). (gr. k-3). 1993. 43.95 incl. audio (*1-56899-647-0*) Soundprints.
— Puffin's Homecoming, the Story of an Atlantic Puffin. (Smithsonian Wild Heritage Collection). 1993. 10.15 (*0-606-08046-5*, Pub. by Turtleback) Demco.

***Bailer, Darice.** Solid Gold: Gymnastic Stars. (Illus.) 48p. (ps-3). 2000. 11.99 (*0-375-90694-0*); pap. 3.99 (*0-375-80694-6*) Random.

Bailer, Darice. Touchdown! Great Quarterbacks in Football History. LC 98-51537. (Step into Reading Ser.: A Step 4 Book). 48p. (J). (gr. 3-5). 1999. pap. 3.99 (*0-679-88621-4*) Random.
— Touchdown! Great Quarterbacks in Football History. LC 98-51537. (Step into Reading Ser.: A Step 4 Book). (Illus.). 48p. (J). (gr. 2-4). 1999. lib. bdg. 11.99 (*0-679-98621-9*) Random.
— Wanted - A Few Bold Riders: A Story of the Pony Express. LC 97-7206. (Smithsonian Odyssey Ser). (Illus.). 32p. (J). (gr. 2-5). 1997. 14.95 (*1-56899-464-8*); 19.95 incl. audio (*1-56899-472-9*, BC6008); pap. 5.95 (*1-56899-465-6*) Soundprints.
— Wanted - A Few Bold Riders: A Story of the Pony Express, Incl. toy. (Smithsonian Odyssey Ser.). (Illus.). 32p. (J). (gr. 2-5). 1997. 29.95 (*1-56899-466-4*); 35.95 incl. audio (*1-56899-471-0*); pap. 17.95 (*1-56899-467-2*); pap. 25.95 incl. audio (*1-56899-468-0*) Soundprints.

Bailer, Darice, jt. auth. see Levine, David.

Bailer, Josef, jt. auth. see Rey, Eibe-Rudolf.

Bailer, Peggy. Seedtime & Harvest. 80p. (Orig.). 1993. pap. 7.50 (*1-879260-08-5*) Evanston Pub.

Bailes, Edith G. An Album of Fragrance: With Complete Instructions for Making Your Own Perfume, Potpourri, Sachet, Herbal Moth Repellant & Incense. (Illus.). 100p. (Orig.). 1983. pap. 9.95 (*0-9611118-0-1*) Cardamom.
— But Will It Bite Me? A Reference Book of Insects for Children & Their Grownups. LC 85-71440. (Illus.). 112p. (Orig.). (J). (gr. 1-6). 1985. pap. 9.95 (*0-9611118-1-X*) Cardamom.

Bailes, Edith G., ed. Brunswick Farmers Market Cookbook. (Illus.). 160p. 1987. spiral bd. 9.95 (*0-9611118-2-8*) Cardamom.

Bailes, Frederick W. Basic Principles of the Science of Mind. 5th ed. 182p. 1987. reprint ed. pap. 17.95 (*0-87516-404-8*) DeVorss.
— Healing Power of Balanced Emotions. 1972. pap. 7.95 (*0-87516-124-3*) DeVorss.
— Hidden Power for Human Problems. LC 57-13274. 240p. 1994. pap. 11.95 (*0-87516-678-4*) DeVorss.
— Your Mind Can Heal You. LC 78-128864. 206p. 1975. reprint ed. pap. 10.95 (*0-87516-201-0*) DeVorss.

Bailes, Fredrick W. Collected Essays of Frederick W. Bailes. LC 86-71938. (Mentors of New Thought Ser.). 141p. 1986. pap. 9.95 (*0-87516-581-8*) DeVorss.

Bailes, Gordon L. & Riser, Robert R. The IBM-370: Computer Organization & Assembly Language. (Illus.). 628p. (Orig.). (C). 1986. mass mkt. 62.50 (*0-314-93148-1*) West Pub.

Bailes, Jack C., jt. auth. see Gudger, Charles M.

Bailes, Julian E. & Spetzler, Robert F., eds. Microsurgical Carotid Endarterectomy. (Illus.). 208p. 1995. text 155.00 (*0-7817-0149-X*) Lppncott W & W.

Bailes, Julian E., et al. Sports Related Concussion. LC 98-30556. 261p. 1998. 30.00 (*1-57626-050-X*) Quality Med Pub.

Bailes, Kendall E. Science & Russian Culture in an Age of Revolutions: V. I. Vernadsky & His Scientific School, 1863-1945. LC 89-45358. (Indiana-Michigan Series in Russian & East European Studies). (Illus.). 252p. 1990. 12.95 (*0-253-31123-3*) Ind U Pr.

Bailes, Lenny. Byte Guide to Optimizing Windows 95. LC 96-148004. (Byte Ser.). 416p. 1996. pap. text 29.95 (*0-07-882120-7*) McGraw.
— Maximizing Windows 98. LC 98-235191. 912p. 1998. pap. text 34.99 (*0-07-882539-3*) Osborne-McGraw.
— Windows Revealed. (Illus.). 912p. (Orig.). 1998. pap. 34.99 (*0-07-882400-1*, Oracle Press) Osborne-McGraw.

Bailes, Michael. The Healing Garden. (Illus.). 96p. (Orig.). 1995. pap. 10.95 (*0-86417-636-8*) Seven Hills Bk.

Bailess, Natalie, et al, eds. Vintage Vicksburg. 464p. 1985. 16.95 (*0-9614988-0-3*) Jr Aux Vicksburg.

Bailet, Laura L. & Moats, Louisa C. Written Language Disorders: Theory into Practice. Bain, Ann M. et al, eds. LC 89-13839. (Illus.). 209p. 1991. pap. text 27.00 (*0-89079-417-0*, 1580) PRO-ED.

Bailey. American Pageant, 11 Vols. (C). 1997. pap. 11.96 (*0-669-45174-3*) HM.
— Caribbean Lands. Date not set. pap. text. write for info. (*0-582-03987-8*, Pub. by Addison-Wesley) Longman.
— Compilation & Review, 1995. 1995. 79.00 (*0-15-602530-2*) Harcourt Legal.
— Congress & Air Pollution. LC 98-222092. 224p. 1998. text 79.95 (*0-7190-3661-5*, Pub. by Manchester Univ Pr) St Martin.

***Bailey.** Creating a Budget. LC 99-64201. (Cliffs Notes Ser.). 128p. 1999. 8.99 (*0-7645-8512-6*) IDG Bks.
— Earth Report 2000. 400p. 1999. 19.95 (*0-07-134260-5*) McGraw.
— Echoes of Paradise: A Poet's Workbook. 1999. pap., wbk. ed. write for info. (*1-57553-664-1*) Watermrk Pr.
— Environmental Accounting: Integrating Business & Environmental Performance. 304p. 2000. text 69.95 (*0-471-24470-8*) Wiley.

Bailey. GAAS Guide: College Edition. (C). 1999. pap. text 57.50 (*0-03-021024-0*, Pub. by Harcourt Coll Pubs) Harcourt.
— GaAs Guide, 1996. 96th ed. 1995. pap. 55.00 (*0-15-601916-7*) Harcourt Legal.
— GaAS Guide 1998: College Edition. (C). 1997. pap. text 60.00 (*0-03-027094-4*) Harcourt Coll Pubs.
— GAAS GUIDE 1999 COLLEGE EDITIO. (C). 1998. pap. text 41.00 (*0-03-021117-4*) Harcourt Coll Pubs.

***Bailey.** Getting Out of Debt. (Cliffs Notes Ser.). 128p. 1999. 8.99 (*0-7645-8513-4*) IDG Bks.
— Investing in the Stock Market. (Cliffs Consumer Extension Ser.). 128p. 1999. 8.99 (*0-7645-8518-5*) IDG Bks.
— Managing Your Money. (Cliffs Consumer Extension Ser.). 128p. 1999. 8.99 (*0-7645-8516-9*) IDG Bks.
— Miller 2000 Compilations & Reviews: Electronic Workpapers & Reference Guide. 903p. (C). 1999. pap. 131.00 incl. cd-rom (*0-15-606873-7*, Pub. by Harcourt Coll Pubs) Harcourt.

Bailey. Multiple Choice Questions, Vol. 4. 1984. text 8.00 (*0-7216-0951-1*) Harcourt.
— 1999 GAAS Guide. 99th ed. (C). 1998. pap. text 69.00 (*0-15-606314-X*, Pub. by Harcourt Coll Pubs) Harcourt.
— Oregon Uniform Commercial Code, 1998 Cumulative Supplement. 320p. 1998. pap., suppl. ed. write for info. (*0-327-00398-7*, 8229012) LEXIS Pub.
— The Practical Writer. 6th ed. (C). 1995. pap. text, teacher ed. 33.75 (*0-15-501789-6*) Harcourt Coll Pubs.
— The Practical Writer. 7th ed. (C). 1998. pap. text 32.50 (*0-15-505509-7*, Pub. by Harcourt Coll Pubs) Harcourt.

— Practical Writing with Readings. 5th ed. (C). 1998. pap. text 34.00 (*0-15-505502-X*, Pub. by Harcourt Coll Pubs) Harcourt.
— Practice Writer with Readings. 3rd ed. (C). 1992. pap. text, teacher ed. 40.50 (*0-03-055844-1*, Pub. by Harcourt Coll Pubs) Harcourt.
***Bailey.** Pursuing Professional Development. (C). 2000. pap. 21.95 (*0-8384-1130-4*) Heinle & Heinle.
— 2000 GAAP Guide-Paper. 1999. pap. text 74.00 (*0-15-607061-8*) Harcourt.
— Understanding Health Insurance. LC 99-64867. (Cliffs Notes Ser.). 128p. 1999. 8.99 (*0-7645-8514-2*) IDG Bks.
Bailey. Working: Learning a Living. annot. ed. (Career Education Ser.). 1995. 54.00 (*0-8273-6563-2*) Delmar.
— Working: Learning a Living. 2nd ed. (Career Education Ser.). 1995. text 38.00 (*0-8273-6562-4*) Delmar.
— Working: Skills for a New Age. (Career Education Ser.). 1989. mass mkt., student ed., suppl. ed. 22.95 (*0-8273-3346-3*) Delmar.
— Working: Skills for a New Age. (Career Education Ser.). 1989. mass mkt., teacher ed. 18.95 (*0-8273-3345-5*) Delmar.
Bailey, ed. Forged in Fire: A History of the Fire Brigades Union. (C). 1992. text 70.00 (*0-85315-749-9*, Pub. by Lawrence & Wishart) NYU Pr.
Bailey & Koleske, J. V. Alkylene Oxides & Their Polymers. (Surfactant Science Ser.: Vol. 35). (Illus.). 272p. 1990. text 175.00 (*0-8247-8384-0*) Dekker.
Bailey & Matejka, Ladislav, eds. Sign, Semiotics Around the World. (Michigan Slavic Contributions Ser.: No. 9). 1980. pap. 10.00 (*0-930042-28-X*) Mich Slavic Pubns.
Bailey, et al. From Student to Student. (C). 1991. pap. text 23.20 (*0-536-58080-4*) Pearson Custom.
— Partnership Agencies in Brit Ur. 224p. 1995. 65.00 (*1-85728-069-5*, Pub. by UCL Pr Ltd); pap. 24.95 (*1-85728-070-9*, Pub. by UCL Pr Ltd) Taylor & Francis.
— Welding Steels Without Hydrogen Cracking. 160p. 1993. 162.00 (*1-85573-014-6*, Pub. by Woodhead Pubng) Am Educ Systs.
Bailey, jt. auth. see Draper.
Bailey, jt. auth. see Knepper.
Bailey, jt. auth. see Leiber.
Bailey, Henry. Oregon Uniform Commercial Code, 3 vols. 2nd ed. 1990. text 235.00 (*0-327-01042-8*, 82286, MICHIE) LEXIS Pub.
Bailey ßlagle, Judith, ed. see Baillie, Joanna.
Bailey, A. Explosives, Propellants & Pyrotechnics. 2nd ed. (Brassey's Land Warfare Ser.). 1998. 39.95 (*1-85753-255-4*, Pub. by Brasseys) Brasseys.
Bailey, A. E., ed. Microwave Measurements. 2nd rev. ed. (Electrical Measurement Ser.: No. 3). 1989. pap. 119.00 (*0-86341-184-3*, EL003) INSPEC Inc.
Bailey, A. Peter. The Harlem Hospital Story: One Hundred Years of Struggle Against Illness, Racism, & Genocide. LC 90-63874. 100p. (Orig.). 1991. pap. 11.98 (*0-9625169-7-X*) Native Sun Pubs.
Bailey, A. Peter & Slade, Edith J. Harlem Today: A Cultural & Visitors Guide. 2nd ed. (Illus.). 80p. pap. 7.95 (*0-936073-09-8*) Gumbs & Thomas.
Bailey, A. Peter, jt. auth. see Afley, Alvin, Jr.
Bailey, A. Peter, jt. auth. see Collins, Rodnell P.
Bailey, A. W. Fall Back Up. LC 99-990492. 365p. 1999. 25.00 (*0-7388-0430-4*); pap. 15.00 (*0-7388-0431-2*) Xlibris Corp.
Bailey, Abigail. Memoirs of Mrs. Abigail Bailey Who Had Been the Wife of Major Asa Bailey Formerly of Landoff, N. H. Baxter, Annette K., ed. LC 79-5487. (Signal Lives Ser.). 1980. reprint ed. lib. bdg. 31.95 (*0-405-12821-5*) Ayer.
Bailey, Adrian. Illustrated Dictionary of Photography. 1988. 10.98 (*0-671-08465-8*) S&S Trade.
— Okavango: Africa's Wetland Wilderness. LC 98-172947. 1999. 49.95 (*1-86872-041-1*) Struik Pubs.
Bailey, Alfred C., jt. auth. see Williamson, George H.
Bailey, Alfred G. The Conflict of European & Eastern Algonkian Cultures, 1504-1700: A Study in Canadian Civilization. 2nd ed. LC 78-434310. 241p. reprint ed. pap. 74.80 (*0-8357-6394-3*, 203575000096) Bks Demand.
— The Sun, the Wind, the Summer Field. LC 97-104846. 120p. 1996. pap. 10.95 (*0-86492-194-2*, Pub. by Goose Ln Edits) Genl Dist Srvs.
Bailey, Alfred G., jt. ed. see Klinck, Carl F.
Bailey, Alice A. A Compilation on Sex. 1980. pap. 10.00 (*0-85330-136-0*) Lucis.
— Consciousness of the Atom. LC 65-1061. 1922. 18.00 (*0-85330-001-1*) Lucis.
— Consciousness of the Atom. LC 65-1061. 1973. pap. 10.00 (*0-85330-101-8*) Lucis.
— The Consciousness of the Atom. 162p. 1997. reprint ed. pap. 19.95 (*0-7661-0046-4*) Kessinger Pub.
— Death: The Great Adventure. 1985. pap. 10.00 (*0-85330-138-7*) Lucis.
— The Destiny of the Nations. LC 89-195778. 1949. 18.00 (*0-85330-002-X*) Lucis.
— The Destiny of the Nations. LC 89-195778. 1971. pap. 10.00 (*0-85330-102-6*) Lucis.
— Discipleship in the New Age, Vol. 1. LC 44-28587. 1944. 35.00 (*0-85330-003-8*) Lucis.
— Discipleship in the New Age, Vol. 1. LC 44-28587. 1972. pap. 22.00 (*0-85330-103-4*) Lucis.
— Discipleship in the New Age, Vol. 2. LC 44-28587. 1955. 35.00 (*0-85330-004-6*) Lucis.
— Discipleship in the New Age, Vol. 2. LC 44-28587. 1972. pap. 22.00 (*0-85330-104-2*) Lucis.
— Education in the New Age. LC 54-1711. 1954. 18.00 (*0-85330-005-4*) Lucis.
— Education in the New Age. LC 54-1711. 1971. pap. 10.00 (*0-85330-105-0*) Lucis.
— Esoteric Astrology. LC 53-19914. (Treatise on the Seven Rays Ser.: Vol. III). 1975. 33.00 (*0-85330-020-8*); pap. 20.00 (*0-85330-120-4*) Lucis.
— Esoteric Healing. LC 53-19914. (Treatise on the Seven Rays Ser.: Vol. IV). 1971. pap. 20.00 (*0-85330-121-2*) Lucis.
— Esoteric Healing. LC 53-19914. (Treatise on the Seven Rays Ser.: Vol. IV). 1978. 33.00 (*0-85330-021-6*) Lucis.
— Esoteric Psychology. LC 53-19914. (Treatise on the Seven Rays Ser.: Vol. I). 1971. pap. 14.00 (*0-85330-118-2*) Lucis.
— Esoteric Psychology. LC 53-19914. (Treatise on the Seven Rays Ser.: Vol. I). 1979. 27.00 (*0-85330-018-6*) Lucis.
— Esoteric Psychology. LC 53-19914. (Treatise on the Seven Rays Ser.: Vol. II). 1981. 35.00 (*0-85330-019-4*); pap. 22.00 (*0-85330-119-0*) Lucis.
— Externalisation of the Hierarchy. LC 58-73. 1957. 33.00 (*0-85330-006-2*) Lucis.
— Externalisation of the Hierarchy. LC 58-73. 1972. pap. 20.00 (*0-85330-106-9*) Lucis.
— From Bethlehem to Calvary. 2nd ed. LC 37-23525. 1937. 21.00 (*0-85330-007-0*) Lucis.
— From Bethlehem to Calvary. 2nd ed. LC 37-23525. 1972. pap. 11.00 (*0-85330-107-7*) Lucis.
— From Intellect to Intuition. LC 32-16728. 1932. 21.00 (*0-85330-008-9*) Lucis.
— From Intellect to Intuition. LC 32-16728. 1972. pap. 11.00 (*0-85330-108-5*) Lucis.
— Glamour: A World Problem. LC 50-14189. 1950. 21.00 (*0-85330-009-7*) Lucis.
— Glamour: A World Problem. LC 50-14189. 1971. pap. 11.00 (*0-85330-109-3*) Lucis.
— Initiation, Human & Solar. LC 52-179. 1922. 21.00 (*0-85330-010-0*) Lucis.
— Initiation, Human & Solar. LC 52-179. 1972. pap. 11.00 (*0-85330-110-7*) Lucis.
— The Labours of Hercules: An Astrological Interpretation. 2nd ed. 1974. pap. 12.00 (*0-85330-130-1*) Lucis.
— Letters on Occult Meditation. LC 26-8569. 1922. 26.00 (*0-85330-011-9*) Lucis.
— Letters on Occult Meditation. LC 26-8569. 1972. pap. 13.00 (*0-85330-111-5*) Lucis.
— Light of the Soul. 1927. 35.00 (*0-85330-012-7*) Lucis.
— Light of the Soul. 1972. pap. 14.00 (*0-85330-112-3*) Lucis.
***Bailey, Alice A.** Master Index of the Books of Alice A. Bailey. 793p. 1998. pap. 25.00 (*0-85330-144-1*) Lucis.
Bailey, Alice A. Ponder on This: A Compilation. 1971. pap. 14.00 (*0-85330-131-X*) Lucis.
Bailey, Alice A. Problems of Humanity. 3rd ed. LC 53-2808. 1964. pap. 11.00 (*0-85330-113-1*) Lucis.
— The Rays & the Initiations. LC 53-19914. (Treatise on the Seven Rays Ser.: Vol. V). 1972. pap. 22.00 (*0-85330-122-0*) Lucis.
— The Rays & the Initiations. LC 53-19914. (Treatise on the Seven Rays Ser.: Vol. V). 1981. 35.00 (*0-85330-022-4*) Lucis.
— Reappearance of the Christ. LC 48-11756. 1948. 21.00 (*0-85330-014-3*) Lucis.
— Reappearance of the Christ. LC 48-11756. 1962. pap. 11.00 (*0-85330-114-X*) Lucis.
— Serving Humanity: A Compilation. 1977. pap. 14.00 (*0-85330-133-6*) Lucis.
— The Seven Rays of Life. 365p. (Orig.). 1995. pap. 13.00 (*0-85330-142-5*) Lucis.
— The Seventh Ray: Revealer of the New Age. 1995. pap. 11.00 (*0-85330-141-7*) Lucis.
— The Soul & Its Mechanism. LC 31-995. 1973. pap. 10.00 (*0-85330-115-8*) Lucis.
— Telepathy & the Etheric Vehicle. LC 50-11465. 1950. 21.00 (*0-85330-016-X*) Lucis.
— Telepathy & the Etheric Vehicle. LC 50-11465. 1971. pap. 11.00 (*0-85330-116-6*) Lucis.
— Treatise on Cosmic Fire. LC 51-6116. 1925. 60.00 (*0-85330-017-8*) Lucis.
— Treatise on Cosmic Fire. LC 51-6116. 1973. pap. 36.00 (*0-85330-117-4*) Lucis.
— Treatise on White Magic. LC 34-4815. 1934. 33.00 (*0-85330-023-2*) Lucis.
— Treatise on White Magic. LC 34-4815. 1970. pap. 20.00 (*0-85330-123-9*) Lucis.
— Unfinished Autobiography. LC 51-32284. 1951. 26.00 (*0-85330-024-0*) Lucis.
— Unfinished Autobiography. LC 51-32284. 1973. pap. 13.00 (*0-85330-124-7*) Lucis.
Bailey, Alison. Posterity & Strategic Policy: A Moral Assessment of Nuclear Policy Options. Czubaroff, Jeanine & Ginsburg, Robert N., eds. LC 89-33902. (Social Philosophy Research Institute Bks.: No. 7). 162p. (Orig.). (C). 1989. pap. text 26.00 (*0-8191-7476-9*); lib. bdg. 45.00 (*0-8191-7475-0*) U Pr of Amer.
Bailey, Allen R. EU Directive Handbook: Understanding the European Union Compliance Process & What It Means to You. (Illus.). 216p. 1997. boxed set 59.95 (*1-57444-102-7*) St Lucie Pr.
Bailey, Alton E. Bailey's Industrial Oil & Fat Products, 5 Vols. 5th ed. Hui, Yiu H., ed. LC 95-9528. 3010p. 1996. 610.00 (*0-471-59430-X*) Wiley.
Bailey, Alvin R., Jr., jt. ed. see Cummins, Light T.
Bailey, Andrew, et al. Economics, Finance, & Management. 4th rev. ed. Newton, Grant, ed. (Certified Management Accountant Review Ser.: Vol. 1). (Illus.). 479p. (C). 1995. pap. text 30.00 (*0-918937-22-1*) Malibu Pub.
— Management Reporting, Analysis, & Behavioral Issues. 4th rev. ed. Newton, Grant, ed. (Certified Management Accountant Review Ser.: Vol. 3). (Illus.). 292p. (C). 1995. pap. text 30.00 (*0-918937-23-X*) Malibu Pub.
Bailey, Andrew, jt. auth. see Zimmerman, Vernon.
Bailey, Andrew D., Jr. Statistical Auditing: Review, Concepts & Problems. 308p. (C). 1981. 2.20 (*0-15-583759-1*) Harcourt Coll Pubs.
Bailey, Andy. Shock Rock: From Iggy to Ziggy & Ozzy to Rozz. (Illus.). 288p. 1999. pap. text 18.95 (*0-8230-7668-7*) Watsn-Guptill.
***Bailey, Andy R.** Digital Audio Networks. (Illus.). 256p. 2000. pap. 49.95 (*0-240-51588-9*) Buttrwrth-Heinemann.
Bailey, Anne, jt. auth. see Servat, Annabel.
Bailey, Anne E. & Davey, Frank. Timothy Findley & the Aesthetics of Fascism: Intertextual Collaboration & Resistance. LC 99-160289. 1998. pap. 12.95 (*0-88922-386-6*) Talon Pr.
Bailey, Anne J. Between the Enemy & Texas: Parsons's Texas Cavalry in the Civil War. LC 88-31194. (Illus.). 358p. 1989. 25.95 (*0-87565-034-1*) Tex Christian.
— The Chessboard of War: Sherman & Hood in the Autumn Campaigns of 1864. LC 99-39771. (Great Campaigns of the Civil War Ser.). (Illus.). 264p. 2000. 32.00 (*0-8032-1273-9*) U of Nebr Pr.
Bailey, Anne J. & Fraser, Walter J., Jr. Portraits of Conflict: A Photographic History of Georgia in the Civil War. LC 96-21515. 1997. 75.00 (*1-55728-421-0*) U of Ark Pr.
***Bailey, Anne J. & Sutherland, Daniel E.** Civil War Arkansas: Beyond Battles & Leaders. LC 99-48841. (Illus.). 336p. 2000. pap. 22.00 (*1-55728-565-9*); text 34.00 (*1-55728-564-0*) U of Ark Pr.
***Bailey, Anthony.** America, Lost & Found: An English Boy's Wartime Adventure in the New world. LC 99-57692. 2000. pap. 12.00 (*0-226-03455-0*) U Ch Pr.
Bailey, Anthony. The Coast of Summer: Sailing New England Waters from Shelter Island to Cape Cod. LC 98-55566. 368p. 1999. pap. 14.95 (*1-57409-074-7*) Sheridan.
— Major Andre. LC 86-29577. 192p. 1987. 15.95 (*0-374-19917-5*) FS&G.
— The Outer Banks. LC 98-49043. (Chapel Hill Book Ser.). 288p. 1999. pap. 16.95 (*0-8078-4820-4*) U of NC Pr.
— Responses to Rembrandt. LC 93-15042. (Illus.). 160p. 1994. 21.95 (*0-943221-18-8*) Timken Pubs.
***Bailey, Anthony.** Routing for Beginners. 192p. 1999. pap. text 24.95 (*1-86108-101-4*) Guild Master.
Bailey, Anthony. Standing in the Sun: A Life of J. M. W. Turner. 16.00 (*0-06-118020-3*) HarpC.
— Standing in the Sun: A Life of J. M. W. Turner. LC 98-68076. (Illus.). 512p. 1999. 35.00 (*0-06-118002-5*) HarpC.
— The Thousand Dollar Yacht. (Illus.). 214p. 1996. pap. 14.95 (*1-57409-011-9*) Sheridan.
***Bailey, Arthur.** Anyone Can Dowse for Better Health: Identify Your Food Sensitivities & Mineral Supplement Need. (Illus.). 192p. 1999. pap. text 14.95 (*0-572-02461-4*) Foulsham UK.
Bailey, Arthur W., jt. auth. see Wright, Henry A.
Bailey, Audra. Hold Fast to Dreams: 60 Years in Indiana Education. (Illus.). 150p. 1996. 21.95 (*1-878208-96-9*) Guild Pr IN.
Bailey, B. & Storey, S. Stock Control Systems & Records. 132p. (C). 1984. 300.00 (*0-7855-5721-0*, Pub. by Inst Pur & Supply) St Mut.
Bailey, Barbara. When I Get Older I'll Understand. LC 99-64515. 192p. (YA). (gr. 8-12). 2000. pap. 7.95 (*1-56315-211-8*, Pub. by SterlingHse) Natl Bk Netwk.
Bailey, Barry. A Picture of God. 108p. 1994. pap. 2.69 (*0-687-31019-9*) Abingdon.
Bailey, Becky. I Love You Rituals: Activities to Build Bonds & Strengthen Relationships with Children. 2nd rev. ed. Whalen, Sarah, ed. LC 97-594. (Illus.). 208p. 1997. reprint ed. pap. 19.95 (*1-889609-05-6*) Loving Guidnce.
— There's Gotta Be a Better Way: Discipline That Works! 3rd rev. ed. Whalen, Sarah, ed. LC 97-70596. (Illus.). 326p. (Orig.). 1997. reprint ed. pap. 21.95 (*1-889609-03-X*) Loving Guidnce.
***Bailey, Becky A.** Easy To Love, Difficult To Discipline: The 7 Basic Skills For Turning Conflict Into Cooperation. LC 99-44313. 304p. 2000. 23.00 (*0-688-16116-2*, Wm Morrow) Morrow Avon.
— I Love You Rituals. (Illus.). 224p. 2000. pap. 14.00 (*0-688-16117-0*, Quil) HarperTrade.
Bailey, Bede, et al, eds. Letters of Bede Jarrett. (Dominican Sources in English Ser.: Vol. 5). 282p. 1989. write for info. (*0-9502759-6-4*, Pub. by Downside Abbey); lib. bdg. write for info. (*0-9511202-4-7*, Pub. by Downside Abbey) Parable.
Bailey, Beth L. From Front Porch to Back Seat: Courtship in Twentieth-Century America. LC 87-46312. (Illus.). 208p. 1988. 35.00 (*0-8018-3609-3*) Johns Hopkins.
— From Front Porch to Back Seat: Courtship in Twentieth-Century America. (Illus.). 208p. 1989. reprint ed. pap. 14.95 (*0-8018-3935-1*) Johns Hopkins.
— Sex in the Heartland. LC 99-21754. 320p. 1999. 27.00 (*0-674-80278-0*) HUP.
Bailey, Beth L. & Farber, David. The First Strange Place: Race & Sex in World War II Hawaii. LC 93-43661. 286p. (C). 1994. reprint ed. pap. 15.95 (*0-8018-4867-9*) Johns Hopkins.
— The First Strange Place: The Alchemy of Race & Sex in World War II Hawaii. LC 92-36559. 300p. 1992. 24.95 (*0-02-901222-8*) Free Pr.
Bailey, Betty & Hilliard, Alison. Living Stones Pilgrimage: With the Christians of the Holy Land. 128p. 1998. pap. 16.50 (*0-304-70466-0*) Continuum.
Bailey, Betty, jt. auth. see Twitchett, John.
Bailey, Betty J. From the Beginning: Resources & Study Guide to the Middle East. 1992. pap. 3.00 (*0-377-00241-0*) Friendship Pr.
Bailey, Betty J. & Tarasar, Constance J. Eyes to See, Ears to Hear: Study Guide to the Peoples & Churches of the U. S. S. R. 1987. pap. 5.95 (*0-377-00168-6*) Friendship Pr.
Bailey, Bill. America's Good News Almanac: Inspirational True Stories to Warm the Heart. LC 96-17081. 224p. 1996. pap. 12.00 (*0-671-53538-2*) S&S Trade.
— America's Good News Almanac: Inspirational True Stories to Warm the Heart. large type ed. LC 96-30308. 1996. 24.95 (*0-7862-0839-2*) Thorndike Pr.
— Fish Ohio: 100 Fishing Lakes. 112p. 1997. 16.95 (*1-881139-19-0*) Glovebox Guidebks.
— Golf Etiquette 101. LC 97-49305. 112p. 1998. per. 10.00 (*0-7615-1286-1*) Prima Pub.
— Illinois State Parks: A Guide to Illinois State Parks. 400p. 1995. pap. 14.95 (*1-881139-11-5*) Glovebox Guidebks.
— Kentucky State Parks: A Guide to Kentucky State Parks. 400p. 1995. pap. 14.95 (*1-881139-13-1*) Glovebox Guidebks.
— The Kid from Hoboken: An Autobiography. Damme, Lynn, ed. LC 94-169167. 432p. (Orig.). 1993. reprint ed. pap. 134.00 (*0-608-00301-8*, 206077100006) Bks Demand.
— Michigan: Zoos & Animal Parks. (Glovebox Guidebooks Travel Guide Ser.). 160p. 1992. write for info. (*1-881139-00-X*) Glovebox Guidebks.
— New York State Parks: A Complete Outdoor Recreation Guide. 400p. 1997. pap. 15.95 (*1-881139-18-2*) Glovebox Guidebks.
— Pennsylvania State Parks: A Guide to Pennsylvania State Parks. 375p. 1996. pap. 15.95 (*1-881139-15-8*) Glovebox Guidebks.
— Protocol & Etiquette of Golf: The Golfer's Guide to Proper Behavior on the Golf Course. (Illus.). 112p. (Orig.). 1993. pap. 9.95 (*1-55958-358-4*) Prima Pub.
— Thrill Sports in the Great Lakes Region. 1994. pap. 12.95 (*1-881139-10-7*) Glovebox Guidebks.
— Virginia State Parks: A Guide to Virginia State Parks. 300p. 1996. pap. 14.95 (*1-881139-14-X*) Glovebox Guidebks.
— What's Cheap & Free in Michigan. 2nd rev. ed. 400p. 1995. pap. 12.95 (*1-881139-05-0*) Glovebox Guidebks.
— Wisconsin State Parks: A Complete Recreation Guide. (Illus.). 400p. 1998. pap. 15.95 (*1-881139-21-2*) Glovebox Guidebks.
Bailey, Bill & Bailey, Penny. Michigan's Only Antique & Flea Market Guidebook. (Glovebox Guidebooks Travel Guide Ser.). (Illus.). 207p. 1994. 11.95 (*1-881139-02-6*) Glovebox Guidebks.
— Michigan's Only Antique & Flea Market Guidebook. 208p. 1997. pap. 11.95 (*1-881139-20-4*) Glovebox Guidebks.
Bailey, Bill & Murphy, Patrick. Thanks, Dad - You Really Were a "Wise" Guy Afterall. (Heartlines Ser.). 128p. 1994. pap. 6.95 (*1-881139-09-3*) Glovebox Guidebks.
Bailey, Bill, jt. auth. see Ainley, Patrick.
Bailey, Bill, jt. auth. see Weber, Art.
Bailey, Binnie. Managing Retail Shops in Hospitals & Other Nonprofit Institutions. LC 93-36041. (Illus.). 224p. (Orig.). 1993. pap. 32.00 (*0-87258-649-9*, 019200) Am Hospital.
***Bailey, Bob.** Minor League Fall Classics: From the Junior World Series to the Triple A World Series. 380p. 2001. spiral bd. 24.95 (*1-893392-03-1*) Baseball Pr Bks.
Bailey, Bob, ed. see Cohen, Bob.
Bailey, Bonnie S. Remembrances of Things Passed. LC 92-73647. 320p. 1993. write for info. (*0-9634316-0-9*) Highland Gourmet.
Bailey, Bren, jt. auth. see Bartholomew, Gail.
Bailey, Brenda. A Quaker Couple in Nazi Germany. 300p. 1999. pap. 32.00 (*1-85072-131-9*, Pub. by W Sessions) St Mut.
Bailey, Brent, ed. Facing the Storm: Five Years of Research in & Around Kakuh National Park, Ghana. (Illus.). 241p. 1997. pap. 10.00 (*1-881173-21-6*) Conser Intl.
Bailey, Brent, jt. ed. see Parker, Theodore A., 3rd.
Bailey, Brian. Luddite Rebellion. 1998. pap. text 33.95 (*0-7509-1353-3*, Pub. by Sutton Pub Ltd) Intl Pubs Mktg.
Bailey, Brian J. The Bride. 123p. 1992. pap. 10.00 (*0-9630837-3-2*) Zion Christ.
— Colossians & Philemon. 122p. pap. 10.00 (*0-9630837-8-3*) Zion Christ.
Bailey, Brian J. The Comforter. Caram, Paul & Caram, Betsy, eds. 265p. (Orig.). (C). 1995. pap. text. write for info. (*0-9643924-1-0*) Zion Christian.
Bailey, Brian J. Daniel. 173p. 1993. pap. 10.00 (*0-9630837-5-9*) Zion Christ.
Bailey, Brian J. Hebrews: Within the Veil. Caram, Paul G., ed. 225p. (Orig.). (C). 1995. pap. text. write for info. (*0-9643924-2-9*) Zion Christian.
Bailey, Brian J. Hitting the Mark: An Exposition of Paul's Epistle to the Philippians. 119p. 1997. pap. 8.00 (*0-9643924-5-3*) Zion Christ.
— Isaiah. 352p. 1994. pap. 14.00 (*0-9630837-7-5*) Zion Christ.
— The Journey of Israel: Our Spiritual Journey from Earth to Heaven. 133p. 1993. pap. 12.00 (*0-9630837-4-0*) Zion Christ.
Bailey, Brian J. The Luddite Rebellion. LC 98-6214. 240p. 1998. text 38.00 (*0-8147-1335-1*) NYU Pr.
Bailey, Brian J. Pillars of Faith. 147p. 1995. pap. 10.00 (*0-9630837-9-1*) Zion Christ.
Bailey, Brian J. Psalms, Bk. 1, Chapters 1-50. Caram, Paul G., ed. 256p. (Orig.). (C). 1996. pap. text. write for info. (*0-9643924-3-7*) Zion Christian.
Bailey, Brian J. Psalms Bk 2: Chapters 51-100. Alarid, Brian D., ed. 278p. pap. 12.00 (*1-890381-01-2*) Zion Christ.
— The Revelation of Jesus Christ. 256p. 1996. pap. 12.00 (*0-9643924-4-5*) Zion Christ.
— Romans: More Than Conquerors. 223p. 1994. pap. 12.00 (*0-9630837-6-7*) Zion Christ.
— Ruth: The Gentile Bride of Christ. 55p. 1992. pap. 6.00 (*0-9630837-2-4*) Zion Christ.

An Asterisk (*) at the beginning of an entry indicates that the title is appearing for the first time.

— Soldiers for Christ: An Exposition of Paul's Epistle to the Ephesians. Alarid, Brian D., ed. 147p. 1997. pap. 10.00 (*1-890381-00-4*) Zion Christ.

— Studies in the Lives of David & Solomon. 88p. 1991. pap. 10.00 (*0-9630837-0-8*) Zion Christ.

— The Three Houses of Esther. 39p. 1992. pap. 5.00 (*0-9630837-1-6*) Zion Christ.

Bailey, Brian K. Secrets to Happiness, Inner Peace & Health: Complete Guide to Optimal Wellness of Body, Mind & Spirit. (Illus.). 320p. (Orig.). 1997. pap. 15.95 (*0-9654904-0-8*) Hlth Unltd.

Bailey, Britt, jt. auth. see Lappe, Marc.

Bailey, Britt, jt. auth. see Lappe, Mark.

Bailey, Brooke. The Remarkable Lives of 100 Women Healers & Scientists. 208p. 1997. reprint ed. pap. text 12.00 (*0-7881-5061-8*) DIANE Pub.

Bailey, Bruce. We See All. 281p. 1983. 35.00 (*0-317-69293-3*) B M Bailey.

Bailey, Bruce H. & McDonald, Scott L. Wind Resource Assessment Handbook: Fundamentals for Conducting a Successful Monitoring Program. (Illus.). 96p. (C). 1998. pap. text 39.95 (*0-88016-098-5*) WindBks.

Bailey, Bruce L., jt. auth. see Bailey, Guy F.

Bailey, Bryan L., jt. auth. see Arthur, Michael J.

Bailey, Byron J. Head & Neck Surgery. 1993. text 375.00 (*0-397-51349-6*) Lppncott W & W.

— Head & Neck Surgery: Otolaryngology, 2 vols. (Illus.). 2,644p. 1993. text 350.00 (*0-397-51120-5*) Lppncott W & W.

— Head & Neck Surgery -- Otolaryngology. 2nd ed. LC 98-6115. 2900p. 1998. text 315.00 (*0-397-51805-6*) Lppncott W & W.

— Head & Neck Surgery -- Otolaryngology: Study Guide. 2nd ed. 320p. 1998. pap. text 49.50 (*0-397-51846-3*) Lppncott W & W.

— Study Guide Head & Neck Surgery. 352p. 1993. pap. text, student ed. 49.50 (*0-397-51345-3*) Lppncott W & W.

— Surgery of the Mandible. Holt, Richard, ed. (American Academy of Facial Plastic & Reconstructive Surgery Monograph). 1987. text 89.00 (*0-86577-239-8*) Thieme Med Pubs.

Bailey, Byron J., et al, eds. Atlas of Head & Neck Surgery - Otolaryngology. (Illus.). 934p. 1996. text 240.00 (*0-397-51315-1*) Lppncott W & W.

— Head & Neck Surgery - Otolarnygology, 2 vols., 1. LC 92-49766. (Illus.). 1993. write for info. (*0-397-51334-8*) Lppncott W & W.

— Head & Neck Surgery - Otolarnygology, 2 vols., 2. LC 92-49766. (Illus.). 1993. write for info. (*0-397-51335-6*) Lppncott W & W.

— Head & Neck Surgery - Otolarnygology, 2 vols., Set. LC 92-49766. (Illus.). 1993. 350.00 (*0-397-51333-X*) Lppncott W & W.

Bailey, Byron J. & Biller, Hugh F. Surgery of the Larynx. (Illus.). 471p. 1985. text 142.00 (*0-7216-1472-8*, W B Saunders Co) Harcrt Hlth Sci Grp.

***Bailey, C.** Bass Drum Control. rev. ed. 32p. 1998. pap. 17.95 incl. audio compact disk (*0-7935-9159-7*) H Leonard.

— Drum Solos - The Art of Phrasing. 48p. 1998. pap. 17.95 incl. audio compact disk (*0-7935-9160-0*) H Leonard.

Bailey, C., et al. Indonesian Marine Capture Fisheries. (ICLARM Studies & Reviews: No. 10). 196p. 1987. pap. 18.00 (*971-10-2230-3*, Pub. by ICLARM) Intl Spec Bk.

Bailey, C. A., ed. Advanced Cryogenics. LC 77-119158. (International Cryogenics Monograph Ser.). (Illus.). 537p. 1971. reprint ed. pap. 166.50 (*0-608-05480-1*, 206594900006) Bks Demand.

Bailey, C. Everett. Children in Therapy: Using the Family as a Resource. 384p. 1999. 45.00 (*0-393-70289-8*) Norton.

Bailey, C. J. Thoughts to Be Added To... How One Successful Entrepreneur Thinks. (Illus.). 93p. (Orig.). 1987. pap. 3.95 (*0-9619857-0-4*) Entrprnr Projects.

Bailey, C. P., jt. auth. see Blackman, N. S.

Bailey, C. R. & Pearce, A. MCQS for the Primary FRCA. LC 98-45216. 260p. (C). 1999. pap. text 39.00 (*0-7020-2160-1*, Pub. by W B Saunders) Saunders.

Bailey, Candace, ed. see Purcell, Henry, et al.

Bailey, Carol A. A Guide to Field Research. LC 94-45023. (Research Methods & Statistics Ser.). 1995. pap. 19.95 (*0-8039-9058-8*) Pine Forge.

Bailey, Carolyn. Woman & Home Simple Flower Arranging. (Illus.). 112p. 1994. write for info. (*1-57215-024-6*) World Pubns.

Bailey, Carolyn S. For the Story Teller, Story Telling & Stories to Tell. 1975. reprint ed. 52.00 (*1-55888-978-7*) Omnigraphics Inc.

— The Little Rabbit Who Wanted Red Wings. (All Aboard Bks.). (Illus.). 32p. (J). (ps-1). 1988. pap. 2.99 (*0-448-19089-3*, G & D) Peng Put Young Read.

— Miss Hickory. (Illus.). (J). (gr. 4-7). 1946. 16.99 (*0-670-47940-3*, Viking Child) Peng Put Young Read.

— Miss Hickory. LC 46-7275. (Illus.). (J). (gr. 4-7). 1977. pap. 4.99 (*0-14-030956-X*, PuffinBks) Peng Put Young Read.

Bailey, Carolyn S. Miss Hickory, Set. abr. ed. (J). (gr. 4-7). 1972. pap. 15.95 incl. audio (*0-670-47945-4*) Live Oak Media.

Bailey, Carolyn S. Stories for Every Holiday. LC 89-43337. 277p. 1990. reprint ed. lib. bdg. 40.00 (*1-55888-880-2*) Omnigraphics Inc.

— The Three Billy Goats Gruff. LC 93-33492. (Children's Thrift Classics Ser.). (Illus.). 96p. (J). 1994. pap. 1.00 (*0-486-28021-7*) Dover.

Bailey, Carolyn S. & Lewis, Clara M. For the Children's Hour. (Illus.). 1979. reprint ed. 54.00 (*1-55888-977-9*) Omnigraphics Inc.

Bailey, Carolyn Sherwin. Boys & Girls of Colonial Days. McHugh, Michael J., ed. (Illus.). 124p. (J). (gr. 3-6). 1990. pap. text 5.00 (*1-930092-38-5*, CLP29555) Christian Liberty.

— Boys & Girls of Colonial Days: Answer Key. McHugh, Michael J., ed. 1990. 1.00 (*1-930092-39-3*) Christian Liberty.

— Little Rabbit Who Wanted Red Wings. (Picture Puzzle Board Bks.). (Illus.). 12p. (J). (ps-3). 2000. bds. 6.99 (*0-8431-7567-2*, Price Stern) Peng Put Young Read.

Bailey, Carolyn Sherwin. Miss Hickory. (J). 1977. 10.09 (*0-606-04008-0*, Pub. by Turtleback) Demco.

Bailey, Cathy, jt. illus. see Williams, Don.

Bailey, Cecil J. Paul: Pride & Penitence. 224p. (Orig.). 1989. pap. 9.95 (*0-940999-50-1*, C-2160) Star Bible.

Bailey, Charles, Jr., jt. ed. see Hewitt, Joe A.

Bailey, Charles J. Essays on Time-Based Linguistic Analysis. (Illus.). 430p. 1996. text 99.00 (*0-19-824220-4*) OUP.

— Variation & Linguistic Theory. LC 73-84648. 170p. reprint ed. pap. 52.70 (*0-8357-3350-5*, 203958300013) Bks Demand.

Bailey, Charles-James N. English Phonetic Transcription. LC 85-50101. (Publications in Linguistics: No. 74). 291p. (Orig.). 1985. pap. 18.00 (*0-88312-000-3*) S I L Intl.

— How Grammars of English Have Missed the Boat: There's Been More Flummoxing Than Meets the Eye. (Grammar Ser.: Vol. 3). 1997. pap. 4.50 (*1-881309-14-2*) Orchid Land.

— How It Has Gone So Wrong with English Grammars. (Grammar Ser.: No. 2). 72p. (Orig.). (C). 1997. pap. write for info. (*1-881309-12-6*) Orchid Land.

— How It Has Gone So Wrong with English Grammars. (Grammar Ser.: Vol. 2). (Orig.). (C). 1998. pap. write for info. (*1-881309-00-2*) Orchid Land.

— Linguistics Series. (Orig.). (C). 1992. pap. write for info. (*1-881309-02-9*) Orchid Land.

— Variation in the Data: Can Linguistics Ever Become a Science? LC 92-90762. (Linguistics Ser.: No. 1). (Illus.). (Orig.). (C). 1993. pap. write for info. (*1-881309-03-7*) Orchid Land.

— Why More English Instruction Won't Mean Better Grammar. (Grammar Ser.: No. 1). (Orig.). (C). 1992. pap. write for info. (*1-881309-01-0*) Orchid Land.

Bailey, Charles R. The Old Regime Colleges, 1789-1795: Local Initiatives in Recasting French Secondary Education, Vol. 147. LC 93-2277. (American University Studies: History: Ser. IX, Vol. 147). X, 292p. (C). 1994. text 47.95 (*0-8204-2247-9*) P Lang Pubng.

Bailey, Charles W., jt. auth. see Knebel, Fletcher.

Bailey, Charles W., Jr., jt. ed. see Hewitt, Joe A.

Bailey, Chris H. The Battle of the Atlantic: The Corvettes & Their Crews: An Oral History. (Illus.). 192p. 1995. 31.95 (*1-55750-734-1*) Naval Inst Pr.

Bailey, Chris H., ed. Social Change in the Royal Navy, 1924-70: The Life & Times of Admiral Sir Frank Twiss. LC 97-151263. (Illus.). 236p. 1996. 44.95 (*0-7509-0610-3*, Pub. by Sutton Pub Ltd) Intl Pubs Mktg.

Bailey, Christina A., jt. auth. see Bailey, Philip S., Jr.

Bailey, Christopher, jt. auth. see Mallett, Jane.

Bailey, Christy. Can You See God?, Bk. 2. 1995. pap. write for info. (*1-888246-03-0*) Covenant IL.

— Can You See God?, Bks. 1 & 2. 1995. pap. 8.95 (*1-888246-04-9*) Covenant IL.

— Can You See God? The Pure in Heart Shall See God. 36p. (J). (gr. 4-7). 1995. pap. 10.00 (*1-888246-02-2*) Covenant IL.

Bailey, Clifford, jt. auth. see Selby, Peter.

Bailey, Clinton. Bedouin Poetry from Sinai & the Negev: Mirror of a Culture. (Illus.). 496p. 1991. text 150.00 (*0-19-826547-6*) OUP.

Bailey, Colin A., ed. Advanced Cryogenics. 1971. pap. 65.00 (*0-306-30458-9*) Da Capo.

Bailey, Colin B. The Loves of the Gods: Mythological Painting from Watteau to David. LC 91-40371. (Illus.). 588p. 1992. pap. 29.95 (*0-912804-26-2*) Kimbell Art.

Bailey, Colin B. & J. Paul Getty Museum Staff. Jean-Baptiste Greuze: The Laundress. LC 99-56026. (Studies on Art Ser.). 90p. 1999. pap. 17.50 (*0-89236-564-1*) J P Getty Trust.

Bailey, Colin B., et al. Renoir's Portraits: Impressions of an Age. LC 97-60428. (Illus.). 344p. 1998. 60.00 (*0-300-07133-7*); pap. 30.00 (*0-300-07134-5*) Yale U Pr.

Bailey, Colleen, ed. see Schnitzspahn, Karen.

Bailey, Conner. Small-Scale Fisheries of San Miguel Bay, Philippines: Occupational & Geographical Mobility. (ICLARM Technical Reports: No. 10). (Illus.). 57p. (Orig.). 1983. pap. 11.50 (*0-89955-396-6*, Pub. by ICLARM) Intl Spec Bk.

Bailey, Conner, ed. Small-Scale Fisheries of San Miguel Bay, Philippines: Social Aspects of Production & Marketing. (ICLARM Technical Reports: No. 9). (Illus.). 57p. (Orig.). 1982. pap. text 14.00 (*0-89955-397-4*, Pub. by ICLARM) Intl Spec Bk.

Bailey, Conner, et al, eds. Aquacultural Development: Social Dimensions of an Emerging Industry. 296p. (C). 1996. text 75.00 (*0-8133-8942-9*, Pub. by Westview) HarpC.

Bailey, Connor. The Sociology of Production in Rural Malay Society. (EASSM Ser.). (Illus.). 242p. (C). 1983. text 39.95 (*0-19-582530-6*) OUP.

Bailey, Cornelia & Bledsoe, Christena. God, Dr. Buzzard & the Bolito Man. 224p. 2000. 23.95 (*0-385-49376-2*) Doubleday.

Bailey, Covert. The Fit or Fat Target Diet. 144p. 1989. pap. 11.00 (*0-395-51082-1*) HM.

— The New Fit or Fat. enl. rev. ed. 180p. 1991. pap. 11.00 (*0-395-58564-3*) HM.

— Smart Eating: Choosing Wisely, Living Lean. 1996. 19.95 (*0-614-15494-4*) HM.

— Smart Exercise: Burning Fat, Getting Fit. 292p. 1996. pap. 11.00 (*0-395-66114-5*) HM.

— The Ultimate Fit or Fat. LC 99-40641. 180p. 2000. pap. 11.00 (*0-618-00204-9*) HM.

Bailey, Covert & Bishop, Lea. The Fit or Fat Woman. 152p. 1989. pap. 11.00 (*0-395-51010-4*) HM.

Bailey, Covert & Gates, Ronda. Smart Eating: Choosing Wisely, Living Lean. 246p. 1996. pap. 9.95 (*0-395-85492-X*) HM.

***Bailey, Covert & Gates, Ronda.** Smart Eating: Choosing Wisely, Living Lean. 246p. 1999. reprint ed. text 20.00 (*0-7881-6285-3*) DIANE Pub.

Bailey-Cummings, Joanne & Cummings, Alan. San Juan the Powder Keg Island: The Settlers Own Stories. (Illus.). 208p. (Orig.). 1987. pap. 7.95 (*0-944257-00-3*) San Juan Ent.

Bailey, Cyril, ed. Legacy of Rome. (Legacy Ser.). (Illus.). 1923. 49.95 (*0-19-821906-7*) OUP.

Bailey, Cyril, ed. The Legacy of Rome. xii, 512p. 1998. reprint ed. 158.00 (*1-56169-368-5*) Gaunt.

Bailey, Cyril, ed. see Lucretius.

Bailey, Cyril, tr. & notes see Epicurus.

Bailey, D. L., jt. auth. see Buhr, Raymond J. A.

Bailey, D. R. Epigrams, Vol. 1. LC 92-8234. (Loeb Classical Library: No. L094). 416p. (C). 1993. 19.95 (*0-674-99555-4*) HUP.

— Epigrams, Vol. 2. LC 92-8234. (Loeb Classical Library: No. L095). 416p. (C). 1993. text 19.95 (*0-674-99556-2*) HUP.

— Epigrams, Vol. 3. (Loeb Classical Library: No. L480). 416p. 1993. text 19.95 (*0-674-99529-5*) HUP.

— Selected Classical Papers. LC 97-3789. 388p. (C). 1997. text 54.50 (*0-472-10816-6*, 10816) U of Mich Pr.

— Two Studies in Roman Nomenclature. (APA American Classical Studies). 114p. 1976. pap. 29.95 (*1-55540-666-1*) OUP.

Bailey, D. R., ed. see Cicero, Marcus Tullius.

Bailey, D. R., tr. see Cicero, Marcus Tullius.

Bailey, D. R. Shackleton, see Shackleton Bailey, D. R.

Bailey, D. T., ed. Accounting in Socialist Countries. (International Accounting Ser.). 224p. 1988. lib. bdg. 75.00 (*0-415-00429-2*, A1458) Routledge.

Bailey, D. Waylon & Strange, John O. Biblical Hebrew Grammar. LC 85-60960. 240p. 1985. 24.00 (*0-914520-23-7*) Insight Pr.

***Bailey, Dale.** American Nightmares: The Haunted House Formula in American Popular Fiction. LC 98-49557. 8p. 1999. 40.95 (*0-87972-789-6*); pap. 20.95 (*0-87972-790-X*) Bowling Green Univ Popular Press.

Bailey, Damon & Trogdon, Wendell. Damon - Living a Dream: Life in the Limelight. 200p. 1995. pap. 14.95 (*0-9642371-2-1*) Backroads Pr.

Bailey, Dan A. Liability of Corporate Officers & Directors Vol. 1: 1998 Replacement Volume. 6th ed. LC 98-88727. 1998. 165.00 (*0-327-00731-1*) LEXIS Pub.

— Liability of Corporate Officers & Directors Vol. 2: 1998 Replacement Volume. 6th ed. LC 98-88727. 1998. 165.00 (*0-327-00732-X*, 6395811) LEXIS Pub.

Bailey, Dan A., jt. auth. see Knepper, William E.

Bailey, Dan E. WW II Wrecks of Palau. LC 90-60055. (Illus.). 246p. 1991. 42.95 (*0-911615-04-0*) North Valley.

Bailey, Daniel E., ed. Computer Science in Social & Behavioral Science Education. LC 77-25087. (Illus.). 520p. 1978. 49.95 (*0-87778-101-X*) Educ Tech Pubns.

Bailey, D'Army. Mine Eyes Have Seen: Dr. Martin Luther King Jr.'s Final Journey. Lyons, David, ed. LC 93-16660. (Illus.). 144p. 1993. 29.95 (*1-881096-02-5*) Towery Pub.

Bailey, Dave, jt. auth. see Webster, Dick.

Bailey, David. Models Close-Up. (Illus.). 192p. 1999. pap. 29.95 (*0-7893-0255-1*, Pub. by Universe) St Martin.

— Ships in the Making: A History of Ship Model Testing at Teddington & Feltham, 1910. 400p. 1995. 85.00 (*1-85044-943-0*) LLP.

Bailey, David, et al, photos by. Nine by Nine. (Illus.) 96p. 1984. pap. 12.95 (*0-912810-47-5*) Lustrum Pr.

Bailey, David, et al. Making Transnationals Accountable: A Significant Step for Britain. LC 93-38033. (Illus.) 240p. (C). 1994. pap. 25.99 (*0-415-06871-1*, B3709) Routledge.

Bailey, David, ed. see Hubert, Tony.

Bailey, David A. Mirage: Enigmas of Race, Difference & Desire. LC 96-131527. (Illus.). 112p. 1996. pap. 18.95 (*0-905263-84-7*) Dist Art Pubs.

Bailey, David C. Viva Cristo Rey: The Cristero Rebellion & the Church-State Conflict in Mexico. LC 73-17119. (Texas Pan-American Ser.). 368p. reprint ed. pap. 114.10 (*0-8357-7722-7*, 203607900002) Bks Demand.

Bailey, David H. & Gottlieb, Louise. Biblioteca Basica de Rotary. White, Willmon L. & Perlberg, Mark, eds. (SPA., Illus.). 506p. 1982. 16.75 (*0-915062-15-1*) Rotary Intl.

— Bibliotheque de Base du Rotary. White, Willmon L. & Perlberg, Mark, eds. (FRE., Illus.). 506p. 1982. 16.75 (*0-915062-10-0*) Rotary Intl.

— Honoring Our Past: The Words & Wisdom of Paul Harris. White, Willmon L. & Perlberg, Mark, eds. (ITA., Illus.). ix, 147p. 1996. pap. 6.00 (*0-915062-12-7*) Rotary Intl.

— Literature Basica de Rotary. White, Willmon L. & Perlberg, Mark, eds. (POR., Illus.). 506p. 1982. 16.75 (*0-915062-14-3*) Rotary Intl.

— Rotary Basic Library. White, Willmon L. & Perlberg, Mark, eds. (JPN., Illus.). 506p. 1982. 16.75 (*0-915062-13-5*) Rotary Intl.

— Schlag Nach Uber Rotary. White, Willmon L. & Perlberg, Mark, eds. (GER., Illus.). 506p. 1982. 16.75 (*0-915062-11-9*) Rotary Intl.

Bailey, David H., et al. Rotary Basic Library, 7 vols. White, Willmon L. & Perlberg, Mark, eds. (Illus.). 506p. 1987. 16.75 (*0-915062-08-9*) Rotary Intl.

Bailey, David H., ed. see SIAM Conference on Parallel Processing for Scientific Computing Staff.

Bailey, David N. Evaluating Commercial Antacids. Stanitski, Conrad L., ed. (Modular Laboratory Program in Chemistry Ser.). 12p. (C). 1996. pap. text 1.50 (*0-87540-478-2*, ANAL 478-2) Chem Educ Res.

— Evaluating the Calcium Ion Content in Commercial Dried Milk Powders. Neidig, H. Anthony, ed. (Modular Laboratory Program in Chemistry Ser.). 7p. (C). 1994. pap. text 1.50 (*0-87540-437-5*, ANAL 437-5) Chem Educ Res.

Bailey, David S. & Bailey, Deborah R. Therapeutic Approaches in Mental Health - Psychiatric Nursing. 4th ed. LC 96-40370. (Illus.). 481p. (C). 1997. pap. text 29.95 (*0-8036-0213-8*) Davis Co.

Bailey, Debbie. Brothers. (Talk-about-Books Ser.: Vol. 8). (Illus.). 14p. (J). (ps). 1993. bds. 5.95 (*1-55037-274-2*, Pub. by Annick) Firefly Bks Ltd.

— Clothes Talk About Books, No. 4. (Talk-about-Books Ser.: Vol. 4). (Illus.). 14p. (J). (ps-k). 1991. bds. 5.95 (*1-55037-167-3*, Pub. by Annick) Firefly Bks Ltd.

— Families. (Talk-about Books Ser.). (Illus.). 104p. (J). 1999. text 19.95 (*1-55037-594-6*, Pub. by Annick Pr) Firefly Bks Ltd.

— Feliz Cumpleanos! (Talk-about-Books Ser.). (SPA., Illus.). 14p. (J). 1999. bds. 5.95 (*1-55037-575-X*, Pub. by Annick) Firefly Bks Ltd.

— Grandma. (Talk-about-Bks.: Vol. 9). (Illus.). 14p. (J). (ps). 1994. bds. 5.95 (*1-55037-966-6*, Pub. by Annick) Firefly Bks Ltd.

— Grandpa. (Talk-about-Bks.: Vol. 10). (Illus.). 14p. (J). (ps up). 1994. bds. 5.95 (*1-55037-967-4*, Pub. by Annick) Firefly Bks Ltd.

— Happy Birthday Board Book. (Talk about Bks.: Vol. 14). (Illus.). 14p. (J). (ps). 1999. bds. 5.95 (*1-55037-559-8*, Pub. by Annick Pr) Firefly Bks Ltd.

— Hats Talk About Books, No. 2. (Talk-about-Books Ser.: Vol. 2). (Illus.). 14p. (J). (ps-k). 1991. bds. 5.95 (*1-55037-159-2*, Pub. by Annick) Firefly Bks Ltd.

— Hermanas. LC 92-94994. (Hablemos Ser.).Tr. of Sisters. (SPA., Illus.). 14p. (J). 1993. bds. 5.95 (*1-55037-307-2*, Pub. by Annick) Firefly Bks Ltd.

— Hermanos. LC 92-94993.Tr. of Brothers. (SPA., Illus.). 14p. (J). 1993. bds. 5.95 (*1-55037-308-0*, Pub. by Annick) Firefly Bks Ltd.

***Bailey, Debbie.** The Hospital. (Talk-About-Bks.: No. 15). (Illus.). 14p. (J). (ps). 2000. pap. 5.95 (*1-55037-632-2*, Pub. by Annick Pr) Firefly Bks Ltd.

Bailey, Debbie. I Hagamos De Cuenta!, Vol. 13.Tr. of Let's Pretend. (SPA., Illus.). 14p. (J). 1999. bds. 5.95 (*1-55037-574-1*, Pub. by Annick) Firefly Bks Ltd.

— Let's Pretend. (Talk about Bks.: Vol. 13). (Illus.). 14p. (J). (ps). 1999. bds. 5.95 (*1-55037-558-X*, Pub. by Annick Pr) Firefly Bks Ltd.

— Mi Mama.Tr. of My Mom. (SPA., Illus.). 14p. (J). (ps). 1992. bds. 5.95 (*1-55037-264-5*, Pub. by Annick) Firefly Bks Ltd.

— Mi Papa.Tr. of My Dad. (SPA., Illus.). 14p. (J). (ps). 1992. bds. 5.95 (*1-55037-265-3*, Pub. by Annick) Firefly Bks Ltd.

— My Dad. 6th ed. (Talk-about-Books Ser.: Vol. 6). (Illus.). 14p. (J). (ps-k). 1991. bds. 5.95 (*1-55037-164-9*, Pub. by Annick) Firefly Bks Ltd.

— My Family, No. 11. (Talk-about-Books Ser.: Vol. 11). (Illus.). 14p. (J). (ps). 1998. bds. 5.95 (*1-55037-510-5*, Pub. by Annick) Firefly Bks Ltd.

— My Mom Talk About Books, No.5. 5th ed. (Talk-about-Books Ser.: Vol. 5). (Illus.). 14p. (J). (ps-k). 1991. bds. 5.95 (*1-55037-163-0*, Pub. by Annick) Firefly Bks Ltd.

— The Playground, No. 12. (Talk about Book Ser.: Vol. 12). (Illus.). 14p. (J). (ps). 1998. bds. 5.95 (*1-55037-511-3*, Pub. by Annick) Firefly Bks Ltd.

— Shoes Talk About Books, No. 3. (Talk-about-Books Ser.: Vol. 3). (Illus.). 14p. (J). (ps-k). 1991. bds. 5.95 (*1-55037-161-4*, Pub. by Annick) Firefly Bks Ltd.

— Sisters. (Talk-about-Books Ser.: Vol. 7). (Illus.). 14p. (J). (ps). 1993. bds. 5.95 (*1-55037-275-0*, Pub. by Annick) Firefly Bks Ltd.

— Toys. (Talk about Books Ser.: 1). (Illus.). 14p. (J). (ps-k). 1991. bds. 5.95 (*1-55037-165-7*, Pub. by Annick) Firefly Bks Ltd.

Bailey, Debbie & Huszar, Susan. Ma Maman.Tr. of My Mom. (FRE., Illus.). 14p. (J). (ps). 1992. bds. 4.95 (*1-55037-267-X*, Pub. by Annick) Firefly Bks Ltd.

— Mon Papa.Tr. of My Dad. (FRE., Illus.). 14p. (J). (ps). 1992. bds. 4.95 (*1-55037-266-1*, Pub. by Annick) Firefly Bks Ltd.

Bailey, Deborah R., jt. auth. see Bailey, David S.

Bailey, Dennis. Khetho LC 97-195474. (Gap Bks.). 108p. 1994. write for info. (*1-86853-015-9*) Heinemann.

Bailey, Dennis, jt. auth. see Mixner, David.

Bailey, Derek. Improvisation: Its Nature & Practice in Music. rev. ed. LC 93-24899. (Illus.). 172p. 1993. pap. 13.95 (*0-306-80528-6*) Da Capo.

Bailey, DeWitt. Pattern Dates for British Ordnance Small Arms, 1718-1783. (Illus.). 128p. 1997. pap. 20.00 (*1-57747-016-8*) Thomas Publications.

Bailey, DeWitt, jt. auth. see Visser, H. L.

Bailey, Diana M. Ethical & Legal Dilemmas in Occupational Therapy. Schwartzberg, Sharan L., ed. LC 94-33914. 184p. 1994. 22.95 (*0-8036-0567-6*) Davis Co.

— Research for the Health Professional: A Practical Guide. 2nd ed. LC 96-36840. (Illus.). 278p. (C). 1997. pap. text 26.95 (*0-8036-0151-4*) Davis Co.

Bailey, Diane. The Natural Hair Care Specialist Braiding Book. LC 97-25161. (HAIR). 256p. 1997. pap. 37.95 (*1-56253-316-9*) Thomson Learn.

Bailey, Diane & Sproston, Clare. Choosing & Using Training Consultants. 108p. 1993. 69.95 (*0-566-07328-5*, Pub. by Gower) Ashgate Pub Co.

B

Bailey, Dimon. The Well Within: Parables for Living & Dying. pap. write for info. (*0-232-52172-7*) S Asia.

Bailey, Don & Unruh, Daile, eds. Canadian Christmas Stories in Prose & Verse. 216p. 1990. pap. 16.95 (*1-55082-001-X*, Pub. by Quarry Pr) LPC InBook.

— Great Canadian Murder & Mystery Stories. 240p. 1991. pap. 18.95 (*1-55082-019-2*, Pub. by Quarry Pr) LPC InBook.

Bailey, Don C. A Glossary of Japanese Neologisms. LC 62-17990. 184p. reprint ed. pap. 57.10 (*0-608-11069-8*, 205536300017) Bks Demand.

Bailey, Donald B., Jr. & Wolery-Allegheny, Mark. Teaching Infants & Preschoolers with Disabilities. 2nd ed. (Illus.). 592p. (C). 1992. 77.00 (*0-675-21390-8*, Merrill Coll) P-H.

Bailey, Donald B., Jr., et al. Implementing Family-Centered Services in Early Intervention: A Team-Based Model for Change. 174p. 1993. pap. text 19.95 (*0-914797-62-X*) Brookline Bks.

Bailey, Donald B., jt. auth. see Mclean, Mary E.

Bailey, Donald M., ed. Archaeological Research in Roman Egypt: The Proceeding of the Seventeenth Classical Colloquium of the Department of Greek & Roman Antiquities, British Museum. (Journal of Roman Archaeology Supplementary Ser.: No. 19). (ENG, FRE & GER., Illus.). 264p. 1996. 89.50 (*1-887829-19-9*) Jour Roman Arch.

Bailey, Donald M. & British Museum Staff. Greek & Roman Pottery Lamps. rev. ed. LC 73-151255. 1972. write for info. (*0-7141-1237-2*, Pub. by British Mus Pr) U of Pa Pr.

Bailey, Donna. Bears. LC 89-22015. (Animal World Ser.). (Illus.). 32p. (J). (gr. 4-7). 1990. pap. 4.95 (*0-8114-4614-X*) Raintree Steck-V.

— Cars, Trucks, & Trains. LC 89-21736. (Facts About Ser.). (Illus.). 48p. (J). 1990. pap. 4.95 (*0-8114-6625-6*) Raintree Steck-V.

— Cycling. LC 90-36488. (Sports World Ser.). (Illus.). 32p. (J). (ps-3). 1990. pap. 3.95 (*0-8114-4712-X*) Raintree Steck-V.

— Planes. LC 89-21737. (Facts About Ser.). (Illus.). 48p. (J). 1990. pap. 4.95 (*0-8114-6630-2*) Raintree Steck-V.

— Reptiles. LC 89-21756. (Facts About Ser.). (Illus.). 48p. (J). (gr. 2-5). 1990. pap. 4.95 (*0-8114-6627-2*) Raintree Steck-V.

Bailey, Donna & Sproule, Anna. Brazil. LC 90-30534. (Where We Live Ser.). (Illus.). 32p. (J). 1990. lib. bdg. 5.00 (*0-8114-2560-6*) Raintree Steck-V.

— Ireland. LC 90-9645. (Where We Live Ser.). (Illus.). 32p. (J). (gr. 1-4). 1990. lib. bdg. 5.00 (*0-8114-2562-2*) Raintree Steck-V.

Bailey, Dorothy, jt. auth. see Brown County Historical Society Staff.

***Bailey, Douglass W.** Balkan Prehistory: Exclusion, Incorporation & Identity. LC 99-57122. 328p. 2000. pap. 29.99 (*0-415-21598-6*) Routledge.

— Balkan Prehistory: Exclusion Incorporation & Identity. LC 99-57122. 328p. (C). 2000. text. write for info. (*0-415-21597-8*) Routledge.

Bailey, Duane. Java Structure: Data Structures in Java for the Principled Programmer. LC 98-18625. 350p. 1998. pap. 44.00 (*0-07-289179-3*) McGraw.

***Bailey, Duane A.** Java Elements: Elements of Java for the Principled Programmer. LC 99-42391. 2000. write for info. (*0-07-228357-2*) McGrw-H Hghr Educ.

Bailey, E., Sr. James Hutton: Founder of Modern Geology. 161p. 1971. 20.50 (*0-686-43854-X*) Elsevier.

Bailey, E., jt. auth. see Bailey, R.

Bailey, E. H. Astrology & the Cards. 2nd ed. (Astro-Cards Reprints Ser.). 60p. 1994. pap. text 9.00 (*1-885500-08-4*, AR6) Astro-Cards.

Bailey, Ed. Maximum RPM. LC 97-66201. 450p. 1997. 39.99 (*0-672-31105-4*) Sams.

Bailey, Edd H. A Life with the Union Pacific: The Autobiography of Edd Bailey. (Illus.). 180p. 1989. 24.95 (*0-913473-09-X*) Saltillo Pr.

Bailey, Edward & Schaw-Miller, Stephen. Insolvent Partnerships. 284p. 1994. boxed set 121.00 (*0-406-02463-4*, UK, MICHIE) LEXIS Pub.

Bailey, Edward, et al. Corporate Insolvency: Law & Practice. 2nd ed. 900p. 1996. write for info. (*0-406-08142-5*, MICHIE) LEXIS Pub.

— Corporate Insolvency - Law & Practice. 650p. 1992. boxed set 170.00 (*0-406-14501-6*, UK, MICHIE) LEXIS Pub.

— Opinion Writing, 1998-99. 3rd ed. LC 99-199646. (Inns of Court School of Law Ser.). 203p. 1998. pap. 42.00 (*1-85431-772-5*) Gaunt.

— Opinion Writing, 1997-98. 2nd ed. (Inns of Court School of Law Ser.). 197p. 1997. pap. 40.00 (*1-85431-674-5*, Pub. by Blackstone Pr) Gaunt.

Bailey, Edward, jt. auth. see Berry, Christopher.

Bailey, Edward D., jt. auth. see Winterhelt, Sigbet.

Bailey, Edward P., Jr. The Plain English Approach to Business Writing. rev. ed. LC 96-45541. (Illus.). 144p. 1997. pap. 10.95 (*0-19-511565-1*) OUP.

Bailey, Edward P. Plain English at Work: A Guide to Writing & Speaking. 304p. (C). 1996. 25.00 (*0-19-510449-8*) OUP.

— Writing & Speaking at Work: A Practical Guide for Business & Professional Communication. LC 98-14893. 237p. 1998. pap. text 34.67 (*0-13-080731-1*) P-H.

Bailey, Edward P., Jr., et al. The Practical Writer with Readings. 3rd ed. 390p. (C). 1992. teacher ed. write for info. (*0-03-055842-5*) Harcourt Coll Pubs.

Bailey, Edwin C. Past & Present of Winneshiek County: A Record of Settlement, Organization, Progress & Achievement. (Illus.). 934p. 1995. reprint ed. lib. bdg. 101.00 (*0-8328-5027-6*) Higginson Bk Co.

Bailey, Eileen. The Arizona Celebrity Cookbook. LC 97-24702. (Illus.). 160p. 1997. pap. 16.95 (*0-87358-692-1*) Northland AZ.

***Bailey, Eileen M.** The Rhodesian Ridgeback: An Owner's Guide to a Happy Healthy Pet. LC 99-47512. (Illus.). 2000. 12.95 (*1-58245-011-0*) Howell Bks.

Bailey, Elaine. Buttermilk Clouds. 89p. 1999. pap. 10.95 (*0-9628023-3-6*) Lillium Pr.

Bailey, Elaine C. Cat Tails: Some of My Best Friends Are Cats. 3rd ed. (Illus.). 96p. 1997. pap. 9.95 (*0-9680575-0-0*) Paws Pub.

Bailey, Elinor P. Mother Plays with Dolls: And Finds an Important Key to Unlocking Creativity. LC 90-3210. (Illus.). 96p. 1990. pap. 22.95 (*0-939009-39-0*, EPM) Howell Pr VA.

— The Rag Doll: From Plain to Fancy. 92p. 1994. pap. 19.95 (*1-881588-09-2*, 882670166) EZ Quilting.

Bailey, Elizabeth. A Fragile Mask. large type ed. (Mills & Boon Large Print Ser.). 350p. 1996. 23.99 (*0-263-14828-9*, Pub. by Mills & Boon) Ulverscroft.

— Friday Dreaming. large type ed. 350p. 1995. 23.99 (*0-263-14188-8*, Pub. by Mills & Boon) Ulverscroft.

***Bailey, Elizabeth.** Misfit Maid. 352p. 2000. 26.99 (*0-263-16364-4*, Pub. by Mills & Boon) Ulverscroft.

Bailey, Elizabeth. Sweet Sacrifice. (Regency Romance Ser.). 1993. per. 2.99 (*0-373-31194-X*, 1-31194-3) Harlequin Bks.

Bailey, Elizabeth E. & Peck, Janet R., eds. The Political Economy of Privatization & Deregulation. (International Library of Critical Writings in Economics: Vol. 44). 672p. 1995. 270.00 (*1-85278-831-3*) E Elgar.

Bailey, Elizabeth E., et al. Deregulating the Airlines. (Regulation of Economic Activity Ser.). (Illus.). 386p. 1985. 33.00 (*0-262-02213-3*) MIT Pr.

Bailey, Elmer J. Novels of George Meredith. LC 75-163892. (Studies in George Meredith: No. 21). 1971. reprint ed. lib. bdg. 75.00 (*0-8383-1312-4*) M S G Haskell Hse.

— Religious Thought in the Greater American Poets. LC 68-8436. (Essay Index Reprint Ser.). 1977. reprint ed. 18.95 (*0-8369-0167-3*) Ayer.

Bailey, Elsa. The Uncommon Book of Prayer. LC 87-17119. (Illus.). 80p. (Orig.). 1987. pap. 6.95 (*0-9618943-0-X*) Lord & Bilder.

Bailey, Emma. Sold to the Lady in the Green Hat. rev. ed. 228p. 1969. 8.95 (*0-914960-01-6*) Academy Bks.

Bailey, Emmanuel F. I Want to Help But How? How to Help Grieving People. (Orig.). 1993. pap. 6.95 (*1-55673-543-X*) CSS OH.

***Bailey, Eric.** Passport's Illustrated Guide to Florida. 2nd ed. (Passport's Illustrated Travel Guides from Thomas Cook Ser.). 192p. 2000. pap. 14.95 (*0-658-00505-7*, 005057) NTC Contemp Pub Co.

***Bailey, Eric & Bailey, Ruth.** Signpost Guides: Dordogne & Western France. LC 99-87816. (Thomas Cook Signpost Guides Ser.). (Illus.). 1999. pap. 22.95 (*0-7627-0683-X*) Globe Pequot.

Bailey, Eric & Bailey, Ruth, eds. On the Road around England & Wales: Driving Holidays, Short Breaks & Day Trips Across England & Wales. (On the Road Around...Ser.). (Illus.). 372p. 1998. pap. 17.95 (*0-8442-9995-2*, 99952, Passprt Bks) NTC Contemp Pub Co.

Bailey, Eric, et al. On the Road Around Capital Region U. S. A. (On the Road Around... Ser.). (Illus.). 372p. 1997. pap. 15.95 (*0-8442-4950-5*, 49505, Passprt Bks) NTC Contemp Pub Co.

Bailey, Eric J. Medical Anthropology & African American Health. LC 99-21244. 272p. 2000. 65.00 (*0-89789-592-4*, Bergin & Garvey) Greenwood.

— Urban African American Health Care. 206p. (Orig.). (C). 1991. pap. 23.50 (*0-8191-8277-X*); lib. bdg. 49.00 (*0-8191-8276-1*) U Pr of Amer.

Bailey, Eric V. A Glossary of Spanish Philatelic Terms. 86p. 1984. reprint ed. pap. 5.00 (*0-913129-12-7*) La Tienda.

***Bailey, Erroll J.** Mr. Dream Merchant. 280p. (J). (gr. 7-12). 2000. 15.95 (*1-902618-30-0*, Pub. by Element Childrns) Penguin Putnam.

Bailey, Erroll J. Mr. Dream Merchant: A Novel. LC 97-45795. 224p. 1998. 19.95 (*1-86204-192-X*, Pub. by Element MA) Penguin Putnam.

Bailey, Esther, jt. auth. see Salierno, Lori.

Bailey, Esther S., jt. auth. see Flexner, Abraham.

Bailey, Etta Lorene. Etta's Collection of Children's Stories. 48p. (J). (gr. k-6). 2000. pap. 8.00 (*0-8059-4677-2*) Dorrance.

Bailey, F. G. The Civility of Indifference: On Domesticating Ethnicity. (Illus.). 208p. 1996. text 39.95 (*0-8014-3217-0*); pap. text 16.95 (*0-8014-8308-5*) Cornell U Pr.

— Humbuggery & Manipulation: The Art of Leadership. LC 88-1177. 208p. 1988. pap. text 14.95 (*0-8014-9487-7*) Cornell U Pr.

— The Kingdom of Individuals: An Essay on Self-Respect & Social Obligation. LC 92-29723. 248p. 1993. pap. text 16.95 (*0-8014-8078-7*) Cornell U Pr.

— The Need for Enemies: A Bestiary of Political Forms. LC 97-38676. 240p. 1998. 39.95 (*0-8014-3470-X*, Comstock Pub); pap. 15.95 (*0-8014-8474-X*, Comstock Pub) Cornell U Pr.

— The Prevalence of Deceit. LC 90-42148. 168p. 1991. 35.00 (*0-8014-2542-5*); pap. text 12.95 (*0-8014-9773-6*) Cornell U Pr.

— The Witch-Hunt: or The Triumph of Morality. (Illus.). 232p. 1996. pap. text 15.95 (*0-8014-8210-0*) Cornell U Pr.

Bailey, F. L. Some Sex Beliefs & Practices in a Navaho Community. (Harvard University Peabody Museum of Archaeology & Ethnology Papers: Vol. 40, No. 1). 1950. 25.00 (*0-527-01300-5*) Periodicals Srv.

Bailey, F. Lee. The Defense Never Rests. 1972. mass mkt. 5.99 (*0-451-12640-8*, AE2640, Sig) NAL.

Bailey, F. Lee & Fishman, Kenneth. Criminal Trial Techniques, 3 vols., Set. LC 94-69191. 1994. ring bd. 345.00 (*0-614-07291-3*) West Group.

Bailey, F. Lee & Rothblatt, Henry B. Complete Manual of Criminal Forms, 3 vols., Set. 2nd ed. LC 93-72788. 1993. ring bd. 345.00 (*0-685-59831-4*) West Group.

— Crimes of Violence: Homicide & Assault. LC 72-97625. 1973. 120.00 (*0-685-59834-9*) West Group.

— Crimes of Violence: Rape & Other Sex Crimes. LC 72-97625. 1973. 120.00 (*0-685-59835-7*) West Group.

— Cross Examination in Criminal Trials. LC 78-18628. 1978. 98.00 (*0-685-59830-6*) West Group.

— Defending Business & White Collar Crimes, 2 vols., Set. 2nd ed. LC 84-80662. 1984. 220.00 (*0-685-59841-1*) West Group.

— Handling Juvenile Delinquency. LC 78-70828. 1982. 98.00 (*0-685-59846-2*) West Group.

— Handling Misdemeanor Cases. 2nd ed. LC 92-74139. 1992. 120.00 (*0-685-59832-2*) West Group.

— Handling Narcotic & Drug Cases. LC 72-84855. 1972. 120.00 (*0-685-59833-0*) West Group.

— Invest & Prep Criminal Case. 2nd ed. LC 85-80968. 1985. 89.50 (*0-685-59844-6*) West Group.

— Successful Technique for Criminal Trials. 2nd ed. LC 84-82304. 1985. 98.00 (*0-685-59849-7*) West Group.

***Bailey, F. M.** The Touch of Fear. 317p. 2000. pap. write for info. (*0-7541-1016-8*, Pub. by Minerva Pr) Unity Dist.

Bailey, F. T. Zone Chiro (Simplified) 48p. 1996. reprint ed. spiral bd. 9.00 (*0-7873-0063-2*) Hlth Research.

Bailey, Faith C. Adoniram Judson. (Golden Oldies Ser.). 128p. mass mkt. 4.99 (*0-8024-0287-9*, 374) Moody.

— D. L. Moody. (Golden Oldies Ser.). mass mkt. 4.99 (*0-8024-0039-6*, 377) Moody.

— George Mueller. (Golden Oldies Ser.). 160p. mass mkt. 4.99 (*0-8024-0031-0*, 379) Moody.

Bailey, Faye, ed. see Fitzgerald, Josephine.

Bailey, Fenton. Fall from Grace: The Untold Story of Michael Milken. (Illus.). 320p. 1992. 19.95 (*1-55972-135-9*, Birch Ln Pr) Carol Pub Group.

Bailey, Foster. Changing Esoteric Values. 2nd ed. 1970. pap. 5.00 (*0-85330-125-5*) Lucis.

— Reflections. 1979. pap. 10.00 (*0-85330-134-4*) Lucis.

— The Spirit of Masonry. 2nd ed. 1972. pap. 10.00 (*0-85330-135-2*) Lucis.

— Things to Come. 1974. pap. 9.00 (*0-85330-129-8*) Lucis.

Bailey, Francis, jt. auth. see Knowles, P. Lance.

Bailey, Frank. Another Helper. rev. ed. 134p. 1996. pap. 6.00 (*1-879451-03-4*) Carpenters Pub.

— Another Helper Workbook. 112p. 1998. wbk. ed. 10.00 (*1-879451-06-9*) Carpenters Pub.

— Joy Unspeakable: Experiencing the Glory of God. 72p. (Orig.). 1996. pap. 5.00 (*1-879451-02-6*) Carpenters Pub.

— The Promise of the Father. 76p. 1998. pap. 6.00 (*1-879451-05-0*) Carpenters Pub.

— Salvation & the Holy Spirit. 30p. (Orig.). Date not set. pap. 2.00 (*1-879451-04-2*) Carpenters Pub.

Bailey, Frank, jt. auth. see Franks, Norman.

Bailey, Frank E. British Policy & the Turkish Reform Movement: A Study in Anglo-Turkish Relations, 1826-1853. LC 74-80519. 1970. reprint ed. 45.00 (*0-86527-019-8*) Fertig.

Bailey, Frank W. French Escadrilles de Chasse War Chronology. (Illus.). 248p. 1999. 44.95 (*1-902304-34-9*, Pub. by Grub St) Seven Hills Bk.

Bailey, Frankie Y. Out of the Woodpile: Black Characters in Crime & Detective Fiction, 27. LC 90-45804. (Contributions to the Study of Popular Culture Ser.: No. 27). 208p. 1991. 55.00 (*0-313-26671-9*, BOW, Greenwood Pr) Greenwood.

Bailey, Frankie Y. & Green, Alice P. "Law Never Here" A Social History of African American Responses to Issues of Crime & Justice. LC 98-38282. 264p. 1999. 65.00 (*0-275-95303-3*, Praeger Pubs) Greenwood.

Bailey, Frankie Y. & Hale, Donna C. Popular Culture, Crime & Justice. LC 97-24853. (Criminal Justice Ser.). 450p. (C). 1997. 36.95 (*0-534-51975-X*) Wadsworth Pub.

Bailey, Fred. Practical Strategies for Stock Options. 20p. 1997. pap. 3.00 (*0-915513-82-X*) Ctr Futures Ed.

Bailey, Fred A. Class & Tennessee's Confederate Generation. LC 86-1407. (Fred W. Morrison Series in Southern Studies). (Illus.). 215p. reprint ed. pap. 66.70 (*0-608-06008-9*, 206633600008) Bks Demand.

— William Edward Dodd: The South's Yeoman Scholar. LC 96-47667. (Minds of the New South Ser.). 320p. 1997. text 42.50 (*0-8139-1708-5*) U Pr of Va.

Bailey, Fred E., jt. ed. see Eisenberg, Adi.

Bailey, Frederic W. Early Connecticut Marriages: As Found on Ancient Church Records Prior to 1800, 7 bks. in 1. LC 68-18785. 1000p. 1997. reprint ed. 55.00 (*0-8063-0007-8*) Genealog Pub.

— Early Massachusetts Marriages Prior to 1800: Plymouth County Marriages, 1892-1746, 3 vols. in 1. 661p. 1996. reprint ed. 40.00 (*0-8063-0008-6*) Genealog Pub.

— The Heirloom Publication of Bailey's Photo-Ancestral Record: The Record of My Ancestry. 7th ed. 144p. 1982. 49.95 (*0-9609488-0-5*); 75.00 (*0-9609488-1-3*) Heirloom Pubns.

Bailey, Frederick E., Jr., ed. Initiation of Polymerization. LC 83-2613. (ACS Symposium Ser.: No. 212). 500p. 1983. lib. bdg. 58.95 (*0-8412-0765-8*) Am Chemical.

— Initiation of Polymerization. LC 83-2613. (ACS Symposium Ser.: No. 212). (Illus.). 511p. 1983. reprint ed. pap. 158.50 (*0-608-03219-0*, 206373800007) Bks Demand.

Bailey, Frederick H., jt. auth. see Woods, Frederick S.

Bailey, G. D., ed. Bibliography of Soil Taxonomy, 1960-1979. 194p. (Orig.). 1987. pap. text 35.00 (*0-85198-588-2*) OUP.

Bailey, G. W., et al, eds. JMSA Proceedings: Microscopy & Microanalysis, 1995. 1132p. 1995. 225.00 (*1-56700-032-0*) Begell Hse.

— Proceedings: Microscopy & Microanalysis, 1995. 1096p. 1996. 225.00 (*0-614-16841-4*) Begell Hse.

Bailey, Garrick. History of the Navajos: The Reservation Years. LC 86-6641. (Illus.). 360p. 1999. pap. 24.95 (*0-933452-28-4*) Schol Am Res.

***Bailey, Garrick.** The Osage & the Invisible World: From the Works of Francis La Flesche, Vol. 217. 1999. pap. text 16.95 (*0-8061-3132-2*) U of Okla Pr.

Bailey, Garrick & Peoples, James G. Humanity: An Introduction to Cultural Anthropology. 3rd ed. Jucha, ed. LC 93-34740. 500p. (C). 1994. pap. text 50.75 (*0-314-02875-7*) West Pub.

Bailey, Garrick A., jt. auth. see Peoples, James G.

Bailey, Garrick A., ed. & intro. see La Flesche, Francis.

Bailey, Gary L., ed. Lake Log, 1978: An Annual Review of the Great Lakes Shipping Season. (Illus.). 80p. 1979. write for info. (*0-932690-02-5*) Ctr for Arch Collects.

Bailey, Gearld D., jt. auth. see Ross, Tweed W.

Bailey, Geoff, ed. Klithi: Palaeolithic Settlement & Quaternary Landscapes in Northwest Greece, 2 vols. (Monographs Ser.). (Illus.). 696p. 1997. 125.00 (*0-9519420-2-6*, Pub. by McDonald Inst) David Brown.

***Bailey, Geoff, et al, eds.** Human Ecodynamics. (Symposia of the Association for Environmental Archaeology Ser.: Vol. 19). (Illus.). 160p. (C). 2000. pap. 50.00 (*1-84217-001-5*, Pub. by Oxbow Bks) David Brown.

Bailey, George. The Perception Mongers: Reflections on Soviet Propaganda. (C). 1990. 35.00 (*0-907967-12-4*, Pub. by Inst Euro Def & Strat) St Mut.

Bailey, George, intro. West Side Stories: A Multicultural Anthology of Contemporary Short Stories. (Orig.). 1992. pap. 9.95 (*0-9627425-1-1*) City Stoop Pr.

Bailey, George W., jt. ed. see Schaller, Frank W.

Bailey, George W. S., jt. auth. see Danto, Arthur C.

Bailey, Gerald. Prophecies: Can You See into the Future? 96p. (J). (gr. 4 up). 1998. pap. 5.95 (*1-901881-40-7*, Pub. by Element MA) Penguin Putnam.

— Talking to Animals: Can They Really Understand? (Elements of the Extraordinary Ser.). (Illus.). 128p. (J). (gr. 4-7). 1998. pap. text 4.95 (*1-901881-97-0*, Pub. by Element Child) Penguin Putnam.

Bailey, Gerald & Lumley, Dan. Staff Development in Technology: A Sourcebook for Teachers, Technology Leaders & School Administrators. LC 98-160794. 294p. 1997. ring bd. 89.00 (*1-879639-57-2*) Natl Educ Serv.

Bailey, Gerald, jt. auth. see Lumley, Dan.

Bailey, Gerald D. Teacher Self-Assessment: A Means for Improving Classroom Instruction. 72p. 1985. pap. 7.95 (*0-8106-1687-4*) NEA.

Bailey, Gerald D., ed. Computer-Based Integrated Learning Systems. LC 92-34233. (Illus.). 176p. 1993. 34.95 (*0-87778-256-3*) Educ Tech Pubns.

Bailey, Gerald D. & Baily, Gwen L. 101 Activities for Creating Effective Technology Staff Development Programs: A Sourcebook of Games, Stories, Role Playing & Learning Exercises for Administrators. LC 93-43260. 1995. 21.95 (*0-590-49748-0*, 1028.3.b35 1994) Scholastic Inc.

Bailey, Gerald D. & Lumley, Dan. Technology Staff Development Programs: A Leadership Sourcebook for School Administrators. LC 93-29341. 1995. 39.95 (*0-590-49220-9*, 1731b25 1994) Scholastic Inc.

Bailey, Gerald D., et al. Leadership & Technology: What School Board Members Need to Know. Ward, Anne, ed. 194p. (Orig.). 1995. pap. 35.00 (*0-88364-196-8*, 03-135) Natl Sch Boards.

— 101 Tips, Traps & To-Dos for Creating Teams: A Guidebook for School Leaders. 394p. 1998. ring bd. 89.00 (*1-879639-61-0*) Natl Educ Serv.

Bailey, Gerald D., jt. auth. see Ross, Tweed W., Jr.

Bailey, Gilbert E. & Thayer, Paul S. California's Disappearing Coast: A Legislative Challenge. LC 74-170336. 115p. (Orig.). reprint ed. pap. 35.70 (*0-7837-2134-X*, 204241600004) Bks Demand.

Bailey, Graham S., ed. Enzymes from Snake Venom. LC 98-77812. 740p. 1998. 175.00 (*1-880293-08-0*) Alaken.

Bailey, Gregory J., jt. auth. see Kraus, Gary E.

Bailey, Gregory J., ed. see Brockington, John.

***Bailey, Guy.** The Ultimate Playground & Recess Game Book. LC 00-190754. (Illus.). 155p. 2001. pap. 16.95 (*0-9669727-2-4*) Educators Pr.

— The Ultimate Sport Lead-Up Game Book: The Very Best Skill-Building Game for Grades K-8. 2nd rev. ed. LC 99-90898. (Illus.). 215p. 2000. pap. 23.95 (*0-9669727-1-6*) Educators Pr.

Bailey, Guy, et al, eds. The Emergence of Black English: Text & Commentary. LC 91-13319. (Creole Language Library: Vol. 8). x, 352p. 1991. 71.00 (*1-55619-161-8*); pap. 27.95 (*1-55619-163-4*) J Benjamins Pubng Co.

Bailey, Guy, jt. ed. see Montgomery, Michael B.

Bailey, Guy F. & Bailey, Bruce L. Journey of Visions. (Illus.). 176p. 1996. 49.00 (*0-9654980-1-8*) Journey of Visions.

— Journey of Visions. deluxe ed. (Illus.). 176p. 1996. lthr. 79.00 (*0-9654980-0-X*) Journey of Visions.

***Bailey, Gwen.** Adopt the Perfect Dog. LC 99-56141. 1999. 19.95 (*0-7621-0239-X*, Pub. by RD Assn) Penguin Putnam.

— Ideal Puppy. 128p. (J). 2000. 12.95 (*0-7641-5211-4*) Barron.

Bailey, Gwen. The Perfect Puppy: How to Raise a Well-Behaved Dog. LC 95-49963. (Illus.). 192p. 1996. 19.95 (*0-89577-839-4*, Pub. by RD Assn) Penguin Putnam.

— The Well Behaved Dog. LC 97-39474. (Illus.). 128p. 1998. 12.95 (*0-7641-5066-9*) Barron.

Bailey, Gwen, ed. see Wilder, Brittian, III.

B

An Asterisk (*) at the beginning of an entry indicates that the title is appearing for the first time.

Bailey, H. C. Mr. Fortune Speaking. 269p. 1977. reprint ed. lib. bdg. 12.95 (*0-89966-276-5*) Buccaneer Bks.
***Bailey, H. C.** The Plot. 252p. 2000. pap. 9.95 (*0-594-00162-5*) Eightn Hundrd.
Bailey, H. Randolph & Snyder, Michael J. Ambulatory Anorectal Surgery. LC 98-52782. 272p. 1999. 110.00 (*0-387-98603-0*) Spr-Verlag.
***Bailey, Hale.** Murder on their Hands. (Criminal Justice Ser.). 2001. 25.00 (*0-534-53480-5*) Wadsworth Pub.
Bailey, Harold E., ed. see Symposium on Water Supply & Water Reuse Staff.
Bailey, Harold W. The Culture of the Sakas in Ancient Iranian Khotan. (Columbia Lecture Ser.: Vol. 1). xii, 114p. 1981. text 19.50 (*0-88206-053-8*) Bibliotheca Persica.
Bailey-Harris, R. J., jt. auth. see Finlay, H. A.
Bailey-Harris, Rebecca J., jt. auth. see Finlay, H. A.
Bailey, Harry P. The Weather of Southern California. (California Natural History Guides Ser.: No. 17). (Illus.). (Orig.). 1966. pap. 10.95 (*0-520-00062-5*, Pub. by U CA Pr) Cal Prin Full Svc.
Bailey, Hazel. Postal Reform in Canada: Canada Post Corporation's Universal Service & Ratemaking. (Illus.). 68p. (C). 1999. pap. text 20.00 (*0-7881-7642-0*) DIANE Pub.
Bailey, Helen M. Forty American Biographies, 2 vols., Set. large type ed. reprint ed. 10.00 (*0-89064-149-8*) NAVH.
Bailey, Henry C. Mister Fortune Speaking. LC 78-140325. (Short Story Index Reprint Ser.). 1977. 20.95 (*0-8369-3717-1*) Ayer.
Bailey, Henry J. Brady on Bank Checks, No. 1. 7th ed. 1274p. 1992. suppl. ed. 77.00 (*0-7913-1158-9*) Warren Gorham & Lamont.
— Brady on Bank Checks, No. 2. 7th ed. 1274p. 1992. suppl. ed. 77.00 (*0-7913-1272-0*) Warren Gorham & Lamont.
Bailey, Henry J., III. Oregon Uniform Commercial Code, 3 vols. 1680p. 1990. boxed set 225.00 (*0-409-24954-8*, MICHIE) LEXIS Pub.
— Oregon Uniform Commercial Code, 3 vols. 1680p. 1993. suppl. ed. 55.00 (*0-685-74297-0*, MICHIE) LEXIS Pub.
— Oregon Uniform Commercial Code, 3 vols., Set. 1993. boxed set 225.00 (*0-614-05940-2*, MICHIE) LEXIS Pub.
Bailey, Henry J. Oregon Uniform Commercial Code, 3 vols., Set. 1680p. 1995. 225.00 (*0-614-10381-9*, MICHIE) LEXIS Pub.
Bailey, Henry J., III & Hagedorn, Richard B. Secured Transactions in a Nutshell. 3rd ed. (Nutshell Ser.). 390p. (C). 1988. pap. 21.00 (*0-314-41445-2*) West Pub.
Bailey, Herb. Vitamin E: (For a Healthy Heart & Long Life) 256p. (Orig.). 1993. pap. 4.95 (*0-7867-0053-X*) Carroll & Graf.
Bailey, Herbert S., Jr. The Art & Science of Book Publishing. LC 90-7103. 234p. 1990. reprint ed. pap. text 14.95 (*0-8214-0970-0*) Ohio U Pr.
Bailey-Hughes, Brenda. The Administrative Assistant. LC 97-69693. (Fifty-Minute Ser.). (Illus.). 120p. 1997. pap. 10.95 (*1-56052-456-1*) Crisp Pubns.
Bailey, I. E. Dansk-Engelsk Handels-og Fagordbog. (DAN & ENG.). 514p. 1973. 95.00 (*0-7859-0910-9*, M8411) Fr & Eur.
— Dansk-Engelsk Handels-og Fagordbog: Danish - English Business Dictionary. (DAN & ENG.). 514p. 1979. 95.00 (*0-8288-6233-8*, M8411) Fr & Eur.
Bailey, Ian H. Construction Law in Australia. xviii, 318p. 1981. pap. 47.50 (*0-455-20260-5*, Pub. by LawBk Co) Gaunt.
Bailey, Ian L. & Hall, Amanda. Visual Impairment: An Overview. LC 90-1099. 56p. 1990. pap. 19.95 (*0-89128-174-6*) Am Foun Blind.
Bailey, Ida & Bailey, Vern. Brinnon: A Scrapbook of History. LC 97-76638. 1997. boxed set 30.00 (*0-9622337-9-X*) Perry Pub WA.
Bailey, Isabel. Pishey Thompson Man of Two Worlds. 275p. (C). 1991. 80.00 (*0-902662-96-1*, Pub. by R K Pubns) St Mut.
***Bailey, Ivor.** Furniture Facelifts: Innovative Ways to Give New Life to Tired Furniture. 2000. pap. 12.95 (*1-902617-07-X*, Pub. by Collins & Br) Sterling.
Bailey, J., et al. Nature's Mysteries. (Illus.). 32p. 91.14 (*0-7614-0856-8*) Marshall Cavendish.
Bailey, J. A. & Jeger, M. J., eds. Colletotrichum: Biology, Pathology & Control. (Illus.). 416p. 1992. text 140.00 (*0-85198-756-7*) OUP.
Bailey, J. B. A., jt. auth. see Zabecki, David T.
Bailey, J. D. History of Grindal Shoals. 86p. 1981. reprint ed. pap. 10.00 (*0-89308-233-3*) Southern Hist Pr.
Bailey, J. K. Already on Holy Ground: Experiencing the Presence in Ordinary Life. 200p. pap. 14.00 (*1-56838-107-7*) Hazelden.
Bailey, J. M. Prostaglandins, Leukotrienes, Lipoxins & PAF: Mechanisms of Action, Molecular Biology & Clinical Applications. (GWUMC Department of Biochemistry Annual Spring Symposium Ser.). (Illus.). 448p. (C). 1992. text 123.00 (*0-306-44055-5*, Kluwer Plenum) Kluwer Academic.
Bailey, J. Martin. One Thousand Years: Stories from the History of Christianity in the U. S. S. R., 988-1988. 1987. pap. 4.95 (*0-377-00167-8*) Friendship Pr.
— Spring of Nations: Churches in the Rebirth of Central & Eastern Europe. (Orig.). 1991. pap. 10.95 (*0-377-00224-0*) Friendship Pr.
Bailey, J. Martyn, ed. Prostaglandins, Leukotrienes, & Lipoxins. LC 85-16941. (GWUMC Department of Biochemistry Annual Spring Symposia Ser.). 722p. 1985. 150.00 (*0-306-41980-7*, Plenum Trade) Perseus Pubng.
Bailey, J. O. Thomas Hardy & the Cosmic Mind: A New Reading of "The Dynasts" LC 77-24118. 223p. 1977. reprint ed. lib. bdg. 55.00 (*0-8371-9743-0*, BATH, Greenwood Pr) Greenwood.
Bailey, Jack. The British Co-Operative Movement. LC 73-19302. (Illus.). 178p. 1974. reprint ed. lib. bdg. 55.00 (*0-8371-7116-4*, BABC, Greenwood Pr) Greenwood.
Bailey, Jackie, et al. Better Buildings for Better Services: Innovative Developments in Primary Care. LC 97-29165. (National Primary Care Research & Development Centre Ser.). (Illus.). viii, 105p. 1997. write for info. (*1-85775-287-2*, Radcliffe Med Pr) Scovill Paterson.
Bailey, Jackson H. Japan on the World Scene: Reflections on Uniqueness & Commonality. rev. ed. (Occasional Papers, Institute for Education on Japan: Vol. 1, No. 2). 17p. (C). 1989. pap. 5.00 (*0-9619977-4-5*) Earlham Pr.
— Ordinary People, Extraordinary Lives: Political & Economic Change in a Tohoku Village. LC 91-15781. (Illus.). 272p. 1991. text 35.00 (*0-8248-1299-9*) UH Pr.
Bailey, Jackson H., ed. see Holvik, Leonard C.
***Bailey, Jacqui.** The Story of London: From Roman River to Capital City. 32p. 2000. pap. 6.99 (*0-7136-5386-8*, Pub. by A & C Blk) Midpt Trade.
Bailey, James. After Thought: The Computer Challenge to Human Intelligence. 1997. pap. 15.00 (*0-465-00782-1*, Pub. by Basic) HarpC.
— After Thought: The Computer Challenge to Human Intelligence. (Illus.). 277p. 1998. text 25.00 (*0-7881-5659-4*) DIANE Pub.
— Three Russian Lyric Folk Song Meters. 429p. 1993. 27.95 (*0-89357-237-3*) Slavica.
Bailey, James, et al, eds. An Anthology of Russian Folk Epics. LC 98-17071. (Folklores & Folk Cultures of Eastern Europe Ser.). 464p. 1998. pap. text 32.95 (*0-87332-641-5*) M E Sharpe.
Bailey, James & Ivanova, Tatyana, eds. An Anthology of Russian Folk Epics. LC 98-17071. (Folklores & Folk Cultures of Eastern Europe Ser.). 464p. (C). (gr. 13). 1998. text 72.95 (*0-87332-640-7*) M E Sharpe.
Bailey, James & Ollis, David F. Biochemical Engineering Fundamentals. 2nd ed. (Chemical Engineering Ser.). 928p. (C). 1986. 101.56 (*0-07-003212-2*) McGraw.
Bailey, James, jt. auth. see Rowland, Desmond.
Bailey, James A. Principles of Wildlife Management. LC 83-19766. 384p. (C). 1984. text 84.95 (*0-471-01649-7*) Wiley.
Bailey, James A., et al, eds. Readings in Wildlife Conservation. LC 74-28405. (Illus.). 722p. (Orig.). (C). 1974. pap. 12.00 (*0-933564-02-3*) Wildlife Soc.
Bailey, James E., ed. Energy Systems: An Analysis for Engineers & Policy Makers. LC 78-2564. (Energy, Power, & Environment Ser.: No. 2). (Illus.). 135p. reprint ed. pap. 41.90 (*0-7837-0685-5*, 204101800019) Bks Demand.
Bailey, James E., et al, eds. Ullmann's Encyclopedia of Industrial Chemistry, 6E, 1999 Electronic Release. 600p. 1999. cd-rom 1150.00 (*3-527-20163-7*) Wiley.
Bailey, James E., jt. auth. see Bedworth, David D.
Bailey, James F., ed. Immigration & Nationality Acts: Legislative Histories & Related Documents 1977-1986, 32 vols., 33 bks. 1987. 1995.00 (*0-89941-623-3*, 301680) W S Hein.
Bailey, James F., ed. Immigration & Nationality Acts: Legislative Histories & Related Documents, 1977-1986 First Series. LC 79-50286. 1987. 1995.00 (*0-930342-91-7*) W S Hein.
Bailey, James F., jt. ed. see Trelles, Oscar M.
Bailey, James L. & Vander Broek, Lyle D. Literary Forms in the New Testament: A Handbook. 224p. (Orig.). 1992. pap. 22.95 (*0-664-25154-4*) Westminster John Knox.
Bailey, James O. Pilgrims Through Space & Time: Trends & Patterns in Scientific & Utopian Fiction. LC 76-38126. 341p. 1972. reprint ed. lib. bdg. 69.50 (*0-8371-6323-4*, BAPS, Greenwood Pr) Greenwood.
— The Poetry of Thomas Hardy: A Handbook & Commentary. LC 77-97015. 740p. reprint ed. pap. 200.00 (*0-7837-2076-9*, 204235000004) Bks Demand.
Bailey, James W. Utilitarianism, Institutions, & Justice. LC 96-41290. 224p. 1997. text 55.00 (*0-19-510510-9*) OUP.
Bailey, Jan. Heart of the Other: Island Poems. LC 97-91396. 53p. 1998. 15.00 (*1-884416-21-7*) A Press.
— Paper Clothes. Inman, Sue L. & Freeman, Keller C., eds. (Poetry Ser.). 64p. (Orig.). 1995. pap. 10.00 (*0-9645778-0-1*) Emrys Pr.
Bailey, Jane. Promising. 192p. 1996. pap. 11.95 (*0-7472-5330-7*, Pub. by Headline Bk Pub) Trafalgar.
— Tuning. LC 78-11150. 1978. pap. 4.00 (*0-918366-09-7*) Slow Loris.
***Bailey, Jane H. & Guskey, Thomas R.** Student-Led Conferences. LC 00-8784. (Experts on Assessment Kit Ser.). 2000. pap. write for info. (*0-8039-6856-6*) Corwin Pr.
Bailey, Janet. The Great San Francisco Trivia & Fact Book. LC 99-25683. (Illus.). 352p. 1999. pap. 12.95 (*1-58182-011-9*) Cumberland Hse.
Bailey, Jania. Thriving: The Journey to Success in the Business World. Hogue, Holly, ed. (Illus.). 92p. 1997. pap. 12.95 (*1-881571-10-6*) Letters Etcetera.
Bailey, Jean, jt. auth. see Freeman, Jerome.
***Bailey, Jeffery V., et al.** Controlling Misfit Risk in Multiple-Manager Investment Programs LC 99-207587. xii, 123p. 1998. write for info. (*0-943205-43-3*) RFICFA.
Bailey, Jeffrey, jt. auth. see Nishijima, Gudo.
Bailey, Jeffrey A., jt. auth. see Nishijima, Gudo.
Bailey, Jennifer. Norman Mailer: Quick-Change Artist. LC 79-14282. 160p. 1980. text 44.00 (*0-06-490284-6*, 06324) B&N Imports.
— Philippine Islands: The United States Army Campaigns of World War 2. 23p. 1992. pap. 1.00 (*0-16-035879-5*) USGPO.
Bailey, Jerry D., jt. ed. see Gallagher, Karen Symms.
Bailey, Jill. Birds. LC 91-58211. (Eyewitness Explorers Ser.). (Illus.). 64p. (J). (gr. k-3). 1997. pap. 5.95 (*0-7894-2212-3*) DK Pub Inc.
— Facts & Records. LC 92-19026. (Picture Pockets Ser.). (J). 1993. pap. 13.00 (*0-671-79149-4*) S&S Bks Yung.
— Genetics & Evolution: The Molecules of Inheritance. (The New Encyclopedia of Science Ser.). (Illus.). 160p. 1995. 39.95 (*0-19-521137-5*) OUP.
— How Caterpillars Turn into Butterflies. LC 98-15028. (Nature's Mysteries Ser.). (J). 1998. 22.79 (*0-7614-0857-6*) Benchmark Books.
— How Insects Work Together. LC 98-22669. (Nature's Mysteries Ser.). (Illus.). 32p. (J). (gr. 3-7). 1998. lib. bdg. 22.79 (*0-7614-0859-2*, Benchmark NY) Marshall Cavendish.
***Bailey, Jill.** Mosquito. LC 98-10596. (Bug Bks.). (Illus.). 32p. (J). (gr. 1-3). 1998. 13.95 (*1-57572-663-7*) Heinemann Lib.
Bailey, Jill. Worm. LC 98-10623. (Bug Bks.). (Illus.). 32p. (J). 1998. 13.95 (*1-57572-665-3*) Heinemann Lib.
Bailey, Jill, ed. Animal Life: Form & Function in the Animal Kingdom. (New Encyclopedia of Science Ser.). (Illus.). 160p. 1995. 39.95 (*0-19-521084-0*) OUP.
***Bailey, Jill, ed.** Penguin Dictionary of Plant Sciences. (Illus.). 500p. 2000. pap. 14.95 (*0-14-051403-1*, Pub. by Pnguin Bks Ltd) Trafalgar.
Bailey, Jill & Seddon, Tony. Animal Parenting. (Nature Watch Ser.). (Illus.). 64p. (YA). 1989. 15.95 (*0-8160-1654-2*) Facts on File.
— Birds of Prey. (Nature Watch Ser.). (Illus.). 64p. (J). (gr. 5 up). 1988. 15.95 (*0-8160-1655-0*) Facts on File.
Bailey, Jill & Thomas, Catherine, eds. Planet Earth. (Illus.). 160p. (J). (gr. 3-9). 1993. 40.00 (*0-19-910144-2*) OUP.
Bailey, Jill, jt. auth. see Seddon, Tony.
Bailey, Jim. Sailing to Paradise: The Discovery of the Americas in 5000 B.C. 1995. 32.50 (*0-684-81297-5*) S&S Trade.
— Santeria in the Eastern United States. 88p. 1991. pap. text 6.00 (*0-9630657-0-X*) Godolphin Hse.
Bailey, Jim, jt. auth. see Henry, Orville.
Bailey, Joan. Griffon Gun Dog Supreme: The History & the Story of How to Improve a Breed. LC 96-67220. (Illus.). 463p. (Orig.). 1996. pap. 34.95 (*0-9630127-2-X*) Swan Valley Pr.
— How to Help Gun Dogs Train Themselves: Taking Advantage of Early Conditioned Learning. LC 91-66075. (Illus.). 224p. (Orig.). 1992. pap. 19.95 (*0-9630127-0-3*) Swan Valley Pr.
— How to Help Gun Dogs Train Themselves: Taking Advantage of Early Conditioned Learning. 2nd rev. ed. LC 93-60621. (Illus.). 222p. (Orig.). 1998. reprint ed. pap. 21.95 (*0-9630127-1-1*) Swan Valley Pr.
Bailey, Joanne, jt. auth. see Palmer, Ralph A.
Bailey, Joanne I. & Nyberg, Carl O. Gunkholing in North Puget Sound: Complete Cruising Guide from Edmonds-Kingston North to the San Juans. (Gunkholing Ser.: Vol. 5). (Illus.). 320p. (Orig.). Date not set. pap. 27.50 (*0-944257-03-8*) San Juan Ent.
— Gunkholing in South Puget Sound: A Comprehensive Cruising Guide from Kingston-Edmonds South to Olympia. Cox, Sally, ed. LC 96-68526. (Gunkholing Ser.: Vol. 4). (Illus.). 352p. (Orig.). 1997. pap. 29.95 (*0-944257-02-X*) San Juan Ent.
— Gunkholing in the Gulf Islands. 4th rev. ed. (Gunkholing Ser.: Vol. 2). (Illus.). 320p. Date not set. reprint ed. pap. 29.95 (*0-944257-05-4*) San Juan Ent.
— Gunkholing in the San Juans. 8th rev. ed. (Gunkholing Ser.: Vol. 1). (Illus.). 350p. 1999. reprint ed. pap. 29.95 (*0-944257-04-6*) San Juan Ent.
Bailey, Jocelyn. The Village Blacksmith. (Album Ser.: No. 24). (Illus.). 32p. 1998. pap. 6.25 (*0-85263-511-7*, Pub. by Shire Pubns) Parkwest Pubns.
— The Village Wheelwright & Carpenter. (Album Ser.: No. 11). (Illus.). 32p. 1998. pap. 6.25 (*0-85263-394-7*, Pub. by Shire Pubns) Parkwest Pubns.
Bailey, Joe. Pessimism. 200p. 1988. text 47.50 (*0-415-00247-8*); pap. text 14.95 (*0-415-00248-6*) Routledge.
— Social Europe. (C). 1992. text 45.00 (*0-582-06801-0*); pap. text 29.95 (*0-582-06809-6*) Addison-Wesley.
— Social Europe. 274p. (C). 1995. text 66.00 (*0-582-06810-X*) Addison-Wesley.
— Social Europe. 2nd ed. LC 98-9566. (Sociology Ser.). 296p. (C). 1998. pap. text 25.20 (*0-582-31609-X*) Longman.
Bailey, John. Fishing Detective. 1994. 29.95 (*0-00-218457-5*, Pub. by HarpC) Trafalgar.
Bailey, John. Managing People & Technological Change. 256p. (Orig.). 1993. pap. 53.50 (*0-273-60027-3*, Pub. by Pitman Pub) Trans-Atl Phila.
Bailey, John. Master Angler. 1997. 29.95 (*0-00-218734-5*, Pub. by HarpC) Trafalgar.
Bailey, John. A Poacher's Way. (Illus.). 160p. 1996. 34.95 (*1-85223-859-3*, Pub. by Crolwood) Trafalgar.
— Stillwater Trout Fishing. (Illus.). 160p. 1996. 45.00 (*1-85223-860-7*, Pub. by Crolwood) Trafalgar.
— Tales from the River Bank. LC 97-74408. (Illus.). 224p. 1997. 31.95 (*0-563-38798-X*, BBC-Parkwest) Parkwest Pubns.
— Ultimate Freshwater Fishing. LC 98-7551. (Illus.). 192p. 1998. 29.95 (*0-7894-2866-0*) DK Pub Inc.
— Walt Whitman. LC 74-131615. 1970. reprint ed. 49.00 (*0-403-00502-7*) Scholarly.
— The Young Fishing Enthusiast: A Young Enthusiast's Guide to Fishing. LC 99-10042. (Young Enthusiast Ser.). 1999. 15.95 (*0-7894-3965-4*) DK Pub Inc.
Bailey, John, ed. International Scrap Directory. 577p. 1985. 153.00 (*0-947671-25-0*) Metal Bulletin.
— Quest for Space: A Celebration of America's Space Program. anniversary ed. (Illus.). 170p. 1999. pap. 8.95 (*1-891965-01-8*) Belmont Intl.
Bailey, John & Aquauo-Quezada, Sergio, eds. Strategy & Security in U. S. - Mexican Relations Beyond the Cold War. (Contemporary Perspectives Ser.: Vol. 9). (Orig.). 1996. pap. 21.95 (*1-878367-32-3*) UCSD Ctr US-Mex.
Bailey, John, et al. Parenting Skills Workshop Series: A Manual for Parent Educators. (Illus.). 108p. 1995. ring bd. 19.00 (*1-57753-004-7*, 321PSW) Corn Coop Ext.
Bailey, John C. Claims of French Poetry: Nine Studies in the Greater French Poets. LC 67-30195. (Essay Index Reprint Ser.). 1977. 20.95 (*0-8369-0168-1*) Ayer.
— Continuity of Letters. LC 67-30173. (Essay Index Reprint Ser.). 1977. 20.95 (*0-8369-0169-X*) Ayer.
— Poets & Poetry: Being Articles Reprinted from the Literary Supplement of 'The Times' LC 67-30196. (Essay Index Reprint Ser.). 1977. 18.95 (*0-8369-0170-3*) Ayer.
Bailey, John J. & Link, John E. Statecraft & Agriculture in Mexico, 1980-1982: Domestic & Foreign Policy Considerations in the Making of Mexican Agricultural Policy. (Research Reports: No. 23). 40p. (Orig.). (C). 1981. pap. 5.00 (*0-935391-22-3*, RR-23) UCSD Ctr US-Mex.
Bailey, John W. The Life & Works of General Charles King, 1844-1933: Martial Spirit. LC 98-23275. 270p. 1998. text 99.95 (*0-7734-8356-X*) E Mellen.
— Pacifying the Plains: General Alfred Terry & the Decline of the Sioux, 1866-1890, 17. LC 78-19300. (Contributions in Military History Ser.: No. 17). 236p. 1979. 59.95 (*0-313-20625-2*, BAT/, Greenwood Pr) Greenwood.
Bailey, Jonathan B., ed. Field Artillery & Fire Power. (Combined Arms Library Ser.: Vol. 1). 385p. 1989. 59.95 (*0-85066-810-7*) Taylor & Francis.
Bailey, Joseph. Serenity Principle. 1988. pap. 7.95 (*0-06-255481-6*) HarpC.
— The Serenity Principle: Finding Inner Peace in Recovery. LC 87-46195. 144p. 1990. pap. 13.00 (*0-06-250039-2*, PL 4286, Pub. by Harper SF) HarpC.
Bailey, Joseph, jt. auth. see Carlson, Richard.
Bailey, Joseph, ed. see Archiati, Pietro.
Bailey, Joseph A. Dictionary of Medical-Legal Terms: A General Guide to Interpretation & Usage. LC 97-8985. 164p. 1998. 29.95 (*1-85070-680-8*) Prthnon Pub.
Bailey, Joseph C. Seaman A. Knapp: Schoolmaster of American Agriculture. LC 73-165702. (American Education, Ser, No. 2). 1972. reprint ed. 19.95 (*0-405-03691-4*) Ayer.
Bailey, Joseph P., jt. ed. see McKnight, Lee W.
Bailey, Joseph R., jt. auth. see Miller, Rita R.
Bailey, Joseph T. Bailey. Ancestry of Joseph Trowbridge Bailey of Philadelphia, & Catherine Goddard Weaver of Newport, R. I. 54p. 1997. reprint ed. pap. 11.00 (*0-8328-7323-3*); reprint ed. lib. bdg. 21.00 (*0-8328-7322-5*) Higginson Bk Co.
Bailey, Joseph V. The Speed Trap: How to Avoid the Frenzy of the Fast Lane. LC 98-47952. 224p. 1999. pap. 9.95 (*0-06-251589-6*, Pub. by Harper SF) HarpC.
Bailey, Judith. Begin in English: Vocabulary-Expanding Short Stories for Launched Beginners, Vol. I. Ashkenas, Joan, ed. LC 87-81968. (Illus.). 112p. 1988. pap. text 10.95 (*0-943327-04-0*) JAG Pubns.
— Begin in English Vol. II: Vocabulary-Expanding Short Stories for Launched Beginners. LC 89-81968. (Illus.). 1992. pap. 10.95 (*0-943327-11-3*) JAG Pubns.
— Begin in English Vol. III: Vocabulary-Expanding Short Stories for Launched Beginners. LC 87-81968. (Illus.). 1996. pap. 10.95 (*0-943327-16-4*) JAG Pubns.
— From the Beginning: A First Reader in American History. Ashkenas, Joan, ed. (Illus.). 208p. 1990. pap. 18.95 (*0-943327-07-5*) JAG Pubns.
Bailey, Judith A. & Cottom, Robert I., eds. After Chancellorsville: The Civil War Letters of Private Walter G. Dunn & Emma Fitz Randolph. LC 98-35805. (Illus.). 256p. 1998. pap. 22.50 (*0-938420-62-3*) MD Hist.
Bailey, Judith E. Impassable Roads. 48p. (Orig.). 1989. pap. 4.75 (*0-9622314-0-1*) Rhema Ministries.
Bailey, June. Puzzles & Games for Critical & Creative Thinking. (Gifted & Talented Ser.). (Illus.). 80p. (J). (ps-1). 1994. pap. 4.95 (*1-56565-129-4*, 01294W, Pub. by Lowell Hse) NTC Contemp Pub Co.
Bailey, Jutta. Applying for a Position in Germany: How to Write a German Resume & Letter of Application. 90p. 1996. spiral bd. 16.00 (*0-942017-33-1*, 04-64401) Amer Assn Teach German.
Bailey, K. C. Death for Cause. LC 95-94049. 290p. (Orig.). 1995. pap. 12.00 (*0-9644935-0-0*) Meerkat Publ.
Bailey, Karen. Irish Proverbs. 1986. 7.95 (*0-8118-1532-3*) Chronicle Bks.
Bailey, Karen. Irish Toasts. (Little Bks.). 60p. 1996. 7.95 (*0-8118-1065-8*) Chronicle Bks.
Bailey, Katharine & Karch, Amy M. Lippincott's Need-to-Know Psychotropic Drug Facts. LC 97-42713. (Need-to-Know Ser.). 240p. 1997. pap. text 14.95 (*0-7817-1039-1*) Lppncott W & W.
Bailey, Katharine R. & Bourne, Gloria. U. S. Virgin Islands: Jewels of the Caribbean--St. Croix, St. Thomas, St. John. LC 86-82891. (Illus.). 48p. (Orig.). 1986. pap. 7.95 (*0-88714-012-2*) KC Pubns.
Bailey, Kathleen, et al, eds. Foreign Teaching Assistants in U. S. Universities. LC 84-60503. 133p. (Orig.). 1984. pap. text 15.00 (*0-912207-03-5*) NAFSA Washington.
Bailey, Kathleen & Rudney, Robert, eds. Proliferation & Export Controls. LC 92-23886. 138p. (Orig.). (C). 1992. pap. text 18.50 (*0-8191-8720-8*); lib. bdg. 44.00 (*0-8191-8719-4*) U Pr of Amer.
Bailey, Kathleen & Savage, Lance, eds. New Ways in Teaching Speaking. 365p. 1994. pap. 22.95 (*0-939791-54-4*) Tchrs Eng Spkrs.
Bailey, Kathleen C. Doomsday Weapons in the Hands of Many: The Arms Control Challenge of the '90s. 168p. 1991. 22.95 (*0-252-01826-5*) U of Ill Pr.

B

An Asterisk (*) at the beginning of an entry indicates that the title is appearing for the first time.

Bailey, Kathleen C., ed. Weapons of Mass Destruction: Costs vs. Benefits. (C). 1994. 16.00 (*81-7304-099-0*, Pub. by Manohar) S Asia.

Bailey, Kathleen M. Principles of Assessment. LC 97-30858. (Teaching Methods Ser.). 256p. (J). 1997. mass mkt. 22.95 (*0-8384-6688-5*) Wadsworth Pub.

Bailey, Kathleen M. & Nunan, David, eds. Voices from the Language Classroom: Qualitative Research in Second Language Education. (Language Teaching Library). (Illus.). 472p. (C). 1996. text 69.95 (*0-521-55127-7*); pap. text 27.95 (*0-521-55904-9*) Cambridge U Pr.

Bailey, Kathleen M., jt. auth. see Allwright, Richard.

Bailey, Kathryn. The Life of Webern. LC 97-25751. (Musical Lives Ser.). (Illus.). 238p. (C). 1998. pap. 14.95 (*0-521-57566-4*) Cambridge U Pr.

Bailey, Kathryn, ed. Webern Studies. LC 96-33834. (Illus.). 394p. (C). 1996. text 69.95 (*0-521-47526-0*) Cambridge U Pr.

Bailey, Kathryn M. The Adventures of Andria Vol. 1: On the Farm. LC 97-74546. (Illus.). 32p. (J). (gr. 1-5). 1997. write for info. (*0-9659689-0-1*) Huckleberry Hollow.

— The Magical Christmas. LC 98-72924. (Adventures of Andria Ser.). (Illus.). 35 p. 1998. write for info. (*0-9659689-1-X*) Huckleberry Hollow.

Bailey, Kathy, ed. see Kenendy, John W.

Bailey, Keith. 10 Biblical Principles for Effective Deliverance Ministry. 1998. pap. 1.99 (*0-87509-785-5*) Chr Pubns.

— Web of Heroes. (Illus.). 224p. 1996. pap. 25.95 (*1-57872-005-2*, 0005BG) Web Games.

— Web of Stars. Dykstra, Gino & Ravenswood, Fritzen, eds. (Illus.). 208p. (Orig.). 1995. pap. 25.95 (*1-57872-002-8*, 0002BG) Web Games.

— Webs Basic Gaming System. 2nd ed. Ravenswood, Fritzen, ed. & illus. by. Dykstra, Gino, illus. 86p. (Orig.). 1996. pap. 14.95 (*1-57872-001-X*, 0001BG) Web Games.

Bailey, Keith & Dykstra, Gino. Web of Horrors. (Illus.). 224p. 1996. pap. 25.95 (*1-57872-004-4*, 0004BG) Web Games.

Bailey, Keith M. Aprender a Vivir: Learning to Live. Bucher, Dorothy, tr. (SPA.). 125p. 1980. mass mkt. 3.99 (*0-87509-299-3*) Chr Pubns.

— Care of Converts. LC 97-163108. (Orig.). 1997. pap. 9.99 (*0-87509-707-3*) Chr Pubns.

— Christ's Coming & His Kingdom: A Study in Bible Prophecy. 875th ed. 1998. pap. 10.99 (*0-87509-808-8*) Chr Pubns.

— Divine Healing: The Children's Bread. LC 77-83941. 1977. pap. 10.99 (*0-87509-233-0*) Chr Pubns.

— Learning to Live. (Orig.). 1997. mass mkt. 3.99 (*0-87509-709-X*) Chr Pubns.

— Servants in Charge: A Training Manual for Elders & Deacons. 1997. pap. 9.99 (*0-87509-745-6*) Chr Pubns.

— Strange Gods: Responding to the Rise of Spirit Worship in America. 250p. 1998. pap. 11.99 (*0-87509-770-7*) Chr Pubns.

Bailey, Keith M., jt. auth. see Bubna, Paul F.

Bailey, Kenneth. Enciclopedia Infantil Molino. (SPA.). 234p. 1973. 95.00 (*0-7859-0877-3*, S22860) Fr & Eur.

— Enciclopedia Infantil Molino. (SPA.). 234p. (J). 1973. 95.00 (*0-8288-6277-X*, S22860) Fr & Eur.

— Enciclopedia Juvenil Molino en Color, 5 vols. 2nd ed. (SPA.). 510p. (J). 1985. 150.00 (*0-7859-5113-X*, S22861) Fr & Eur.

Bailey, Kenneth D. Methods of Social Research. 3rd ed. 608p. (C). 1987. 32.95 (*0-02-901450-6*) Free Pr.

— Methods of Social Research. 3rd ed. 533p. 1999. reprint ed. text 20.00 (*0-7881-6239-X*) DIANE Pub.

— Methods of Social Research. 4th ed. LC 93-36444. (Illus.). 600p. 1994. 32.95 (*0-02-901279-1*) Free Pr.

— Social Entropy Theory. LC 88-30109. 310p. (C). 1990. pap. text 24.95 (*0-7914-0057-3*) State U NY Pr.

— Social Entropy Theory. LC 88-30109. 310p. (C). 1990. text 74.50 (*0-7914-0056-5*) State U NY Pr.

— Sociology & the New Systems Theory: Toward a Theoretical Synthesis. LC 93-23718. 372p. (C). 1994. text 64.50 (*0-7914-1743-3*); pap. text 21.95 (*0-7914-1744-1*) State U NY Pr.

— Typologies & Taxonomies: An Introduction to Classification Techniques, No. 102. (Quantitative Applications in the Social Sciences Ser.: Vol. 102). (Illus.). 96p. 1994. pap. 10.95 (*0-8039-5259-7*) Sage.

Bailey, Kenneth E. Poet & Peasant: Through Peasant Eyes. 1983. pap. 25.00 (*0-8028-1947-8*) Eerdmans.

Bailey, Kenneth K. Southern White Protestantism in the Twentieth Century. 1990. 17.50 (*0-8446-1035-6*) Peter Smith.

Bailey, Kenneth W. Marketing & Pricing of Milk & Dairy Products in the United States. LC 97-5474. (Illus.). 296p. 1997. 39.95 (*0-8138-2750-7*) Iowa St U Pr.

Bailey, Kent G. Human Paleopsychology: Applications to Aggression & Pathological Processes. 568p. (C). 1986. text 115.00 (*0-89859-810-9*) L Erlbaum Assocs.

Bailey, Kent G., jt. auth. see Ahern, Susan.

Bailey, Kerry, jt. auth. see Steege, Ray.

Bailey, L. & Ball, B. Honey Bee Pathology. 2nd ed. (Illus.). 193p. 1991. text 83.00 (*0-12-073481-8*) Acad Pr.

Bailey, L. Charles, ed. see Oxley, Robert R.

Bailey, L. N. European Soccer. LC 72-181482. 234 p. 1970. write for info. (*0-7207-0190-2*, Pelham Bks) Viking Penguin.

Bailey, L. R. Indian Slave Trade in the Southwest: A Study of Slave-Taking & the Traffic in Indian Captives from 1700-1935. LC 66-2888. (Illus.). 19.95 (*0-87026-028-6*) Westernlore.

Bailey, Larry. San Poil Chronicle. LC 98-86296. 325p. 1998. 25.00 (*0-7388-0049-X*); pap. 15.00 (*0-7388-0050-3*) Xlibris Corp.

— Working: Learning a Living. 2nd ed. LC 95-70256. (CA - Career Development Ser.). 480p. 1995. mass mkt. 49.95 (*0-538-65096-6*) S-W Pub.

Bailey, Larry J. Career Education for Teachers & Counselors: A Practical Approach. LC 85-13959. 204p. 1985. pap. 13.50 (*0-910328-41-2*) Sulzburger & Graham Pub.

— The Job Ahead. 1992. mass mkt., teacher ed. 9.95 (*0-8273-4926-2*) Delmar.

— Working: Learning a Living. (CA - Career Development Ser.). 1996. mass mkt., suppl. ed. 6.95 (*0-538-66372-3*) S-W Pub.

— Working: Learning a Living. 2nd ed. (CA - Career Development Ser.). 1996. mass mkt., wbk. ed. 13.95 (*0-538-65097-4*) S-W Pub.

— Working: Learning a Living. 2nd ed. (CA - Career Development Ser.). 1996. mass mkt. 68.95 (*0-538-65098-2*) S-W Pub.

— Working: Skills for a New Age. (Career Education Ser.). 1989. 55.95 (*0-8273-3344-7*) Delmar.

— Working, Lesson Plans Guide: Learning a Living. 2nd ed. (CA - Career Development Ser.). 1997. pap. 5.95 (*0-538-65871-1*) S-W Pub.

Bailey, Larry L. Birthright. 251p. 1993. pap. 9.95 (*0-9633326-0-0*) Highland WA.

Bailey, Larry P. Governmental GAAP Guide, 1992. 1991. pap. 45.00 (*0-685-48722-9*) Harcourt.

— Miller Comprehensive Governmental GAAP Guide. (Miller Accounting Ser.). 1100p. 1988. pap. 50.00 (*0-15-601784-9*); pap. 40.00 (*0-15-601789-X*) Harcourt.

— Miller Comprehensive Governmental GAAP Guide, 1990. 1989. pap. 40.00 (*0-685-33323-X*) Harcourt.

***Bailey, Larry P.** Miller Governmental GAAP Guide. 1400p. 2000. pap. 79.00 (*0-15-607230-0*) Harcourt Prof.

Bailey, Larry P. Miller Governmental GAAP Guide: A Comprehensive Interpretation of All Current Promulgated Governmental Generally Accepted Accounting. 99th ed. (Governmental GAAP Guide (Miller) Ser.). (Illus.). 1400p. (C). 1998. pap. 69.00 (*0-15-606317-4*, Pub. by Harcourt Coll Pubs) Harcourt.

***Bailey, Larry P.** 2000 Miller GAAS Guide. (Illus.). xxv, 850p. 1999. pap. 74.00 (*0-15-607021-9*) Harcourt Prof.

Bailey, Larry P. 2000 Miller Governmental GAAP Guide. (Illus.). xxix, 3727p. 1999. pap. 74.00 (*0-15-607036-7*) Harcourt Prof.

***Bailey, Larry P.** 2001 Miller Compilations & Reviews. 900p. 2000. pap. 149.00 (*0-15-607193-2*) Harcourt.

— 2001 Miller Compilations & Reviews. (Illus.). xxxiii, 903p. 2000. pap. 131.00 (*0-15-606872-9*) Harcourt Prof.

Bailey, Larry P., jt. auth. see Miller, Martin A.

Bailey, Lawrence R. & Martz, Ron. Solitary Survivor: The First American POW in Southeast Asia. (Association of the U. S. Army Book Ser.). (Illus.). 237p. 1995. 23.95 (*1-57488-004-7*) Brasseys.

Bailey, Leaonead P., ed. Broadside Authors & Artists. LC 70-108887. 1974. 9.95 (*0-910296-25-1*) Broadside Pr.

Bailey, Lee. Lee Bailey's Cooking for Friends: Good Simple Food for Entertaining Friends Everywhere. LC 97-51779. 200p. 1998. 16.99 (*0-517-20307-3*) Random Hse Value.

— Lee Bailey's Country Flowers: Gardening & Bouquets from Spring to Fall. LC 97-12225. 176p. 1997. pap. 14.99 (*0-517-18742-6*) Random Hse Value.

— Lee Bailey's Country Weekends: Recipes for Good Food & Easy Living. LC 97-9759. 176p. 1997. 14.99 (*0-517-18746-9*) Wings Bks.

— Lee Bailey's Desserts. LC 97-23983. 184p. 1998. 14.99 (*0-517-18749-3*) Random Hse Value.

— Lee Bailey's Dinners at Home. 1995. 25.00 (*0-614-15464-2*) C Potter.

— Lee Bailey's "The Way I Cook" A Collection of All My Recipes with More Than 90 New Favorites. LC 96-20757. 1996. 32.50 (*0-517-59751-9*) C Potter.

***Bailey, Lee.** Long Weekends. LC 99-52841. 2000. 16.99 (*0-517-20899-7*) Random Hse Value.

— The Way I Cook. 2000. 12.99 (*0-517-20891-1*) Random Hse Value.

***Bailey, Lee Ross.** It's Mary Ann's Range. LC 99-91606. 1999. 25.00 (*0-7388-0940-3*); pap. 18.00 (*0-7388-0941-1*) Xlibris Corp.

Bailey, Lee W. & Yates, Jenny, eds. The Near Death Experience: A Reader. 1996. pap. 19.95 (*0-614-97727-4*) Routledge.

Bailey, Lee W., ed. see Yates, Jenny.

Bailey, Leigh H. Taking Charge of Your Career. vii, 82p. 1998. pap. 14.95 (*0-9664664-0-3*) L Bailey Assocs.

Bailey, Leon. Critical Theory & the Sociology of Knowledge: A Comparative Study in the Theory of Ideology. (Am. Univ. Studies: Vol. 62). XII, 215p. (C). 1996. pap. 39.95 (*0-8204-3654-2*) P Lang Pubng.

Bailey, Liberty Hyde. Cyclopedia of American Horticulture, 6 vols., Set. 1972. lib. bdg. 1800.00 (*0-87968-247-7*) Gordon Pr.

— The Holy Earth. LC 80-27854. (Illus.). 124p. 1980. reprint ed. pap. 6.00 (*0-9605314-6-7*) NY St Coll Ag.

— Hortus Third: A Concise Dictionary of Plants Cultivated in the United States & Canada. (Illus.). 1312p. 1976. 150.00 (*0-02-505470-8*) Macmillan.

— How Plants Get Their Names. (Illus.). 181p. 1963. pap. 5.95 (*0-486-20796-X*) Dover.

— Sketch of the Evolution of Our Native Fruits. LC 72-89072. (Rural America Ser.). 1973. reprint ed. 39.00 (*0-8420-1473-X*) Scholarly Res Inc.

— Survival of the Unlike. 1991. 60.00 (*0-936128-25-9*) De Young Pr.

Bailey, Liberty Hyde, et al, eds. Cyclopedia of American Agriculture: A Popular Survey of Agricultural Conditions, Practices & Ideals in the United States & Canada - Vol. 2, Crops Fourth Edition. LC 74-30617. (American Farmers & the Rise of Agribusiness Ser.). (Illus.). 1975. reprint ed. 71.95 (*0-405-06762-3*) Ayer.

Bailey, Linda. Gordon Loggins & the Three Bears. unabridged ed. LC 97-930197. (Illus.). 32p. (J). (ps-2). 1997. 14.95 (*1-55074-362-7*, Pub. by Kids Can Pr) Genl Dist Srvs.

***Bailey, Linda.** How Can a Brilliant Detective Shine in the Dark? (Stevie Diamond Mystery Ser.). (J). 1999. 4.95 (*1-55074-750-9*) Kids Can Pr.

Bailey, Linda. How Can a Frozen Detective Stay Hot on the Trail? Grant, Christy, ed. LC 97-107170. (Stevie Diamond Mysteries Ser.: Vol. 4). 172p. (J). (gr. 4-7). 1996. pap. 4.50 (*0-8075-3401-3*); lib. bdg. 13.95 (*0-8075-3400-5*) A Whitman.

— How Can a Frozen Detective Stay Hot on the Trail? (Stevie Diamond Mystery Ser.). 1996. 9.60 (*0-606-10308-2*, Pub. by Turtleback) Demco.

Bailey, Linda. How Can a Frozen Detective Stay Hot on the Trail?, No. 4. (Stevie Diamond Mystery Ser.). 166p. (J). 1996. pap. 4.95 (*1-55074-321-X*) Kids Can Pr.

— How Can I Be a Detective If I Have to Baby-Sit? (Stevie Diamond Mystery Ser.). (J). 1996. 9.60 (*0-606-08881-4*, Pub. by Turtleback) Demco.

Bailey, Linda. How Can I Be a Detective If I Have to Babysit? (Stevie Diamond Mystery Ser.: No. 2). 160p. (J). (gr. 4-7). 1996. lib. bdg. 13.95 (*0-8075-3404-8*) A Whitman.

— How Can I Be a Detective If I Have to Babysit? Grant, Christy, ed. LC 95-39545. (Stevie Diamond Mystery Ser.: No. 2). (Illus.). 160p. (J). (gr. 4-7). 1996. pap. 4.50 (*0-8075-3405-6*) A Whitman.

Bailey, Linda. How Can I Be a Detective If I Have to Babysit? (Stevie Diamond Mystery Ser.). 160p. (J). 1993. pap. 4.95 (*1-55074-172-1*) Kids Can Pr.

Bailey, Linda. How Come the Best Clues Are Always in the Garbage. Grant, Christy, ed. LC 95-43878. (Stevie Diamond Mystery Ser.: No. 1). (Illus.). 175p. (J). (gr. 4-7). 1996. pap. 4.50 (*0-8075-3410-2*) A Whitman.

— How Come the Best Clues Are Always in the Garbage? (Stevie Diamond Mystery Ser.: No. 1). (Illus.). 175p. (J). (gr. 4-7). 1996. lib. bdg. 13.95 (*0-8075-3409-9*) A Whitman.

Bailey, Linda. How Come the Best Clues Are Always in the Garbage? (Stevie Diamond Mystery Ser.). 176p. (J). 1992. pap. 4.95 (*1-55074-094-6*) Kids Can Pr.

— How Come the Best Clues Are Always in the Garbage? (Stevie Diamond Mystery Ser.). 1996. 9.60 (*0-606-08880-6*, Pub. by Turtleback) Demco.

Bailey, Linda. What's a Daring Detective Like Me Doing in the Dog House? LC 97-25358. (Stevie Diamond Mysteries Ser.: Vol. 5). 200p. (J). (gr. 4-7). 1997. pap. 4.50 (*0-8075-8835-0*); lib. bdg. 13.95 (*0-8075-8834-2*) A Whitman.

— What's a Daring Detective Like Me Doing in the Dog House? (Stevie Diamond Mystery Ser.). 1997. 9.60 (*0-606-13816-1*, Pub. by Turtleback) Demco.

Bailey, Linda. What's a Daring Detective Like Me Doing in the Doghouse? (Stevie Diamond Mystery Ser.). (Illus.). 192p. (J). 1997. pap. 4.95 (*1-55074-398-8*) Kids Can Pr.

— Who's Got Gertie? And How Can We Get Her Back? Grant, Christy, ed. LC 96-13692. (Stevie Diamond Mysteries Ser.: Vol. 3). 176p. (J). (gr. 4-7). 1996. pap. 4.50 (*0-8075-9063-0*); lib. bdg. 13.95 (*0-8075-9062-2*) A Whitman.

Bailey, Linda. Who's Got Gertie? And How Can We Get Her Back? (Stevie Diamond Mystery Ser.). 160p. (J). 1994. pap. 4.95 (*1-55074-217-5*) Kids Can Pr.

Bailey, Linda. Who's Got Gertie? And How Can We Get Her Back? LC 49-122010. (Stevie Diamond Mystery Ser.). 1996. 9.60 (*0-606-10307-4*, Pub. by Turtleback) Demco.

Bailey, Linda & Bailey, Wendy. When Addie Was Scared. 32p. 1999. 15.95 (*1-55074-431-3*) Kids Can Pr.

***Bailey, Linda & Slavin, Bill.** Adventures in Ancient Egypt. (Good Times Travel Agency Ser.). (Illus.). 48p. (J). (gr. 3-7). 2000. pap. 7.95 (*1-55074-548-4*, Pub. by Kids Can Press); pap. 14.95 (*1-55074-546-8*, Pub. by Kids Can Press) Genl Dist Srvs.

— Adventures in the Middle Ages. (Good Times Travel Agency Ser.). (Illus.). 48p. (J). (gr. 3-7). 2000. 14.95 (*1-55074-538-7*, Pub. by Kids Can Press); pap. 7.95 (*1-55074-540-9*, Pub. by Kids Can Press) Genl Dist Srvs.

Bailey, Lisa D., jt. compiled by see Trimble, Susan M.

***Bailey, Lonnie.** And the Beat Goes On. 1999. pap. write for info. (*1-58235-264-X*) Watermrk Pr.

Bailey, Lonnie. Heart of Fire, Soul of Light. 1998. pap. write for info. (*1-57553-988-8*) Watermrk Pr.

***Bailey, Lonnie.** The Muse of Weird. 1999. pap. write for info. (*1-58235-220-8*) Watermrk Pr.

Bailey, Lonnie. The Paradise of Frolicsome Fools. 1999. pap. write for info. (*1-58235-036-1*) Watermrk Pr.

Bailey, Lonnie D. Darkness Falls. 1997. pap. 56.95 (*1-57553-621-8*) Watermrk Pr.

— Green Is the Grass. 1998. pap. write for info. (*1-57553-748-6*) Watermrk Pr.

— Lonnie Bailey's Zoo. 1998. pap. write for info. (*1-57553-917-9*) Watermrk Pr.

— No God in the Holly. 1998. pap. write for info. (*1-57553-719-2*) Watermrk Pr.

— Scythe of the Reaper. 1998. pap. write for info. (*1-57553-820-2*) Watermrk Pr.

Bailey, Lorilyn. The Little Book of Online Romance: How to Find It, How to Keep It. (Illus.). 128p. Date not set. pap. 6.95 (*0-9641239-6-7*) Lormax Commun.

— The Original Dating Questionnaire for Teens: A Great Way to Get to Know Each Other. (Illus.). 128p. (Orig.). (YA). (gr. 7-12). pap. write for info. (*0-9641239-7-5*) Lormax Commun.

— The Original Lovers' Questionnaire Book. 128p. 1994. pap. 9.95 (*0-9641239-9-1*) Lormax Commun.

Bailey, Lorraine H. Time to Spare. (Gregg-McGraw-Hill Series for Independent Living). 1978. text 13.20 (*0-07-003223-8*) McGraw.

Bailey, Lotus, ed. see Christopher, John R.

Bailey, Louise H. From Rockhill to Connemara: The Story Before Carl Sandburg. (Illus.). 48p. 1992. pap. 2.25 (*0-915992-14-0*) Eastern National.

Bailey, Lynn. Bisbee: Queen of the Copper Camps. (Illus.). 176p. 1983. 29.95 (*0-87026-058-8*) Westernlore.

***Bailey, Lynn.** Flowers by Moonlight, 1 vol. 1999. mass mkt. 5.99 (*0-515-12448-6*, Jove) Berkley Pub.

— Kissed by Starlight, 1 vol. (Magical Love Ser.). 1999. mass mkt. 5.99 (*0-515-12505-9*, Jove) Berkley Pub.

— Magic by Daylight. (Magical Love Ser.). 1999. mass mkt. 5.99 (*0-515-12701-9*, Jove) Berkley Pub.

— Splendid You. 2000. mass mkt. 5.99 (*0-515-12868-6*, Jove) Berkley Pub.

Bailey, Lynn B., ed. Folate in Health & Disease, No. 1. LC 94-35431. (Clinical Nutrition in Health & Disease Ser.: Vol. 1). (Illus.). 488p. 1994. text 195.00 (*0-8247-9280-7*) Dekker.

Bailey, Lynn R. Bosque Redondo: The Navajo Internment at Fort Sumner, New Mexico, 1863-68. enl. rev. ed. (Great West & Indian Ser.: No. 69). (Illus.). 275p. 1998. 28.95 (*0-87026-100-2*) Westernlore.

— The Devil Has Foreclosed: the Private Journal of George Whitwell Parsons Vol. 2: The Concluding Arizona Years, 1882-87. (Great West & Indian Ser.: Vol. 68). (Illus.). 1997. 36.95 (*0-87026-099-5*) Westernlore.

— From Adze to Vermilion: A Bibliography of Writings on Historic Sites Archaeology. LC 68-29144. (Illus.). 250p. 19.95 (*0-87026-040-5*) Westernlore.

***Bailey, Lynn R.** Henry Clay Hooker & the Sierra Bonita. (Great West & Indian Ser.: Vol. 70). (Illus.). 213p. 1998. 26.95 (*0-87026-106-1*) Westernlore.

Bailey, Lynn R. If You Take My Sheep... The Evolution & Conflicts of Navajo Pastoralism, 1630-1868. (Illus.). 304p. 1979. 26.95 (*0-87026-050-2*) Westernlore.

— The Long Walk: A History of the Navajo Wars, 1846-1868. (Illus.). 300p. 1979. 24.95 (*0-87026-047-2*) Westernlore.

— Old Reliable: A History of Bingham Canyon, Utah. (Illus.). 220p. 1988. 29.95 (*0-87026-068-5*) Westernlore.

— The Search for Lopez: Utah's Greatest Manhunt. (Great West & Indian Ser.: Vol. 54). (Illus.). 1990. 24.95 (*0-87026-073-1*) Westernlore.

— Supplying the Mining World: The Mining Equipment Manufacturers of San Francisco, 1850-1900. (Illus.). 1996. 36.95 (*0-87026-096-0*) Westernlore.

***Bailey, Lynn R.** A Tale of the Unkilled: The Life, Times & Writings of Wells W. Spicer. (Mining Camp Chronicles Ser.: 3). (Illus.). 1999. per. 18.95 (*0-87026-108-8*) Westernlore.

Bailey, Lynn R. A Tenderfoot in Tombstone, the Private Journal of George Whitwell Parksons: The Turbulent Years, 1880-82. LC 96-60051. (Great West & Indian Ser.: Vol. 65). (Illus.). 1996. 36.95 (*0-87026-095-2*) Westernlore.

***Bailey, Lynn R.** The Valiants: The Tombstone Rangers & Apache War Frivolities. (Mining Camp Chronicles Ser.: Vol. 4). (Illus.). 1999. per. 18.95 (*0-87026-110-X*) Westernlore.

Bailey, Lynn R. We'll All Wear Silk Hats: The Erie & Chiricahua Cattle Companies & the Rise of Corporate Ranching in the Sulphur Spring Valley of Arizona, 1883-1909. (Great West & Indian Ser.: 61). (Illus.). 1994. 26.95 (*0-87026-088-X*) Westernlore.

Bailey, Lynn R., ed. Tombstone from a Woman's Point of View: The Letters of Clara Spalding Brown, July 7, 1880, to November 14, 1882. (Mining Camp Chronicles Ser.: 1). (Illus.). 96p. 1998. per. 16.00 (*0-87026-105-3*) Westernlore.

Bailey, Malcolm, tr. see De Singly, Francois.

Bailey, Maralyn, jt. auth. see Bailey, Maurice.

Bailey, Marcella, jt. auth. see Reynolds, Peter.

Bailey, Margaret E. Wild Streak. LC 72-106245. (Short Story Index Reprint Ser.). 1977. 20.95 (*0-8369-3281-1*) Ayer.

Bailey, Margaret J. The Grains or Passages in the Life of Ruth Rover, with Occasional Pictures of Oregon, Natural & Moral. Leasher, Evelyn & Frank, Robert J., eds. LC 85-13749. (Illus.). 352p. 1986. reprint ed. 29.95 (*0-87071-346-9*) Oreg St U Pr.

Bailey, Margaret L. Milton & Jakob Boehme. LC 65-15885. (Studies in Comparative Literature: No. 35). 1969. reprint ed. lib. bdg. 75.00 (*0-8383-0505-9*) M S G Haskell Hse.

Bailey, Margery, ed. see Boswell, James.

Bailey, Mari V. Marita - Perdida en Mexico. Keogan, Blanca & Raygoza, Mireya C., trs. (ENG & SPA., Illus.). 342p. 1998. pap. 11.95 (*1-888031-06-9*, Edit Rosa d Desierto) Liahona Dev.

Bailey, Mari V., ed. Directory of LDS Resources. (ENG & SPA., Illus.). 16p. (Orig.). 1996. pap. text 10.95 (*1-888031-02-6*, Prairie Rse) Liahona Dev.

— Directory of LDS Resources. 16p. (Orig.). 1997. pap. text 8.95 (*1-888031-04-2*, Prairie Rse) Liahona Dev.

— How to Use Forwarding Agencies to Distribute LDS Products in Mexico. De Raygoza, Mireya C., tr. (ENG & SPA.). 8p. (Orig.). 1996. pap. text 3.00 (*1-888031-01-8*, Prairie Rse) Liahona Dev.

Bailey, Mari Vawn. Marita: Missing in Mexico. 278p. 1996. 14.95 (*1-56236-227-5*, Pub. by Aspen Bks) Origin Bk Sales.

Bailey, Marilyn. Index to Southwestern Wisconsin: A History of Old Crawford County, 1932. 59p. 1983. pap. 8.50 (*0-910255-41-5*) Wisconsin Gen.

Bailey, Marilyn J. Index to "History of Southeastern Wisconsin-Old Milwaukee Country" 1932. 67p. 1984. pap. 9.00 (*0-910255-43-1*) Wisconsin Gen.

Bailey, Marilyn J., jt. auth. see Wisconsin State Department of Transportation Staff.

Bailey, Mark. New Testament Explorer, 1. LC 99-39608. 1999. 34.99 (*0-8499-1448-5*) Word Pub.

An Asterisk (*) at the beginning of an entry indicates that the title is appearing for the first time.

— New Testament Explorer: Supersaver ed., 1. 1999. 29.97 (*0-8499-1600-3*) Word Pub.
— Saint: A Novel of Intrigue & Faith. 406p. 1997. mass mkt. 6.99 (*0-515-12173-8*, Jove) Berkley Pub.
— To Follow Him: 7 Marks of a Disciple. LC 96-30049. 192p. 1997. pap. 11.99 (*1-57673-035-2*, Multnomah Bks) Multnomah Pubs.
— The Troublesome Board Member, Vol. 137. (Illus.). 25p. (Orig.). 1996. pap. text 16.00 (*0-925299-55-3*) Natl Ctr Nonprofit.
Bailey, Mark, ed. The Bailiffs' Minute Book of Dunwich, 1404-1430. (Suffolk Records Society Ser.). 159p. (C). 1992. 45.00 (*0-85115-306-2*, Boydell Pr) Boydell & Brewer.
Bailey, Martha J. American Women in Science: A Biographic Dictionary. LC 94-10096. 488p. 1994. lib. bdg. 60.00 (*0-87436-740-9*) ABC-CLIO.
***Bailey, Martha J.** American Women in Science, 1950 to the Present: A Biographical Dictionary. LC 98-22433. 496p. 1998. lib. bdg. 75.00 (*0-87436-921-5*) ABC-CLIO.
Bailey, Martha J. Supervisory & Middle Managers in Libraries. LC 80-23049. 218p. 1981. 21.00 (*0-8108-1400-5*) Scarecrow.
Bailey, Martin. Union of Tanganyika & Zanzibar: A Study in Political Integration. (Foreign & Comparative Studies Program, Eastern Africa Ser.: No. 9). 114p. 1973. pap. 3.00 (*0-915984-06-7*) Syracuse U Foreign Comp.
— Van Gogh in England: Portrait of the Artist As a Young Man. (Illus.). 144p. (C). 1992. pap. 39.95 (*0-85331-617-1*, Pub. by Lund Humphries) Antique Collect.
— Vermeer. (Color Library). (Illus.). 128p. 1995. pap. 14.95 (*0-7148-3463-7*, Pub. by Phaidon Press) Phaidon Pr.
Bailey, Martin J. Mismeasurement of Economic Growth. 27p. 1991. pap. 9.95 (*1-55815-150-8*) ICS Pr.
— Studies in Positive & Normative Economics. (Economists of the Twentieth Century Ser.). 320p. 1992. 95.00 (*1-85278-604-3*) E Elgar.
Bailey, Martin J., jt. ed. see Harberger, Arnold C.
***Bailey, Mary.** Aquarium Fish Identifier: Practical Handbook. 1999. 9.95 (*0-7548-0010-5*, Lorenz Bks) Anness Pub.
— Complete Guide to Acquarium Fish Keeping: Practical Handbook. 1999. pap. 9.95 (*0-7548-0015-6*, Lorenz Bks) Anness Pub.
Bailey, Mary. A Learning Experience. LC 89-63521. 1990. pap. 13.00 (*0-85330-139-5*) Lucis.
— Pet Owner's Guide to Tropical Fishkeeping. (Pet Owner's Guide Ser.). (Illus.). 80p. 1997. 8.00 (*1-86054-067-8*, Pub. by Ringpr Bks) Seven Hills Bk.
***Bailey, Mary.** Taking Great Photos. (Practical Handbook Ser.). 1999. pap. 9.95 (*0-7548-0019-9*, Lorenz Bks) Anness Pub.
***Bailey, Mary & Burgess, Peter.** Tropical Fishlopaedia: A Complete Guide to Tropical Fish Care. (Illus.). 320p. 2000. pap. text 29.95 (*1-58245-166-4*) Howell Bks.
***Bailey, Mary & Sanford, Gina.** Practical Fishkeeping. 2000. pap. 12.95 (*1-84215-055-3*) Anness Pub.
Bailey, Mary, et al. A Visit to a Comprehensive Guidance Program That Works. (Illus.). 138p. (C). 1997. ring bd. 17.50 (*1-56109-074-3*, EC205) CAPS Inc.
Bailey, Mary L., jt. ed. see Lin, Jason Y.
Bailey, Mary T. & Mayer, Richard T., eds. Public Management in an Interconnected World: Essays in the Minnowbrook Tradition, 293. LC 91-34160. (Contributions in Political Science Ser.: No. 293). 216p. 1992. 57.95 (*0-313-27457-6*, BYD/, Greenwood Pr) Greenwood.
Bailey, Matthew. The Poema del Cid & the Poema de Fernan Gonzalez: The Transformation of an Epic Tradition. (Spanish Ser.: No. 78). vi, 144p. 1993. 20.00 (*0-940639-88-2*) Hispanic Seminary.
Bailey, Maurice & Bailey, Maralyn. One Hundred Seventeen Days Adrift. (Illus.). 192p. 1992. pap. 14.95 (*0-924486-31-7*) Sheridan.
***Bailey, Maxine.** Sistahs. LC 99-159977. 1999. 13.95 (*0-88754-553-X*) Theatre Comm.
Bailey, Melbourne E., jt. auth. see Gray, Elliot C., Jr.
Bailey, Melinda C., ed. EU Special Medicinal Products Directive. 100p. 1996. 89.95 (*1-57172-072-3*) Intl Qual.
Bailey, Melinda C., intro. EC CE Marking. 83p. 1995. 49.95 (*1-57172-004-9*) Intl Qual.
— EC In-Vitro Diagnostic Directive. write for info. (*1-57172-020-0*) Intl Qual.
— EU Electrical & Electronic Compendium. 844p. 1996. 595.00 (*1-57172-059-6*) Intl Qual.
— EU Electro-Medical Equipment. 81p. 1996. 64.95 (*1-57172-060-X*) Intl Qual.
— EU Harmonization Directive. 25p. 1995. 29.95 (*1-57172-063-4*) Intl Qual.
— EU Human Medicinal Products Directive. 162p. 1996. 94.95 (*1-57172-064-2*) Intl Qual.
— EU Human Medicinal Products Testing Directive. 150p. 1996. 99.95 (*1-57172-065-0*) Intl Qual.
— EU Medical Device Compendium. 897p. 1996. 595.00 (*1-57172-067-7*) Intl Qual.
— EU Medicinal Product Compendium. 950p. 1996. 695.00 (*1-57172-069-3*) Intl Qual.
— EU Medicinal Product Labeling Directive. 95p. Date not set. 79.95 (*1-57172-070-7*) Intl Qual.
— EU Modules of Conformity Assessment Directive. 97p. 1996. 69.95 (*1-57172-073-1*) Intl Qual.
— EU Product Liability & Safety Directive. 128p. 1996. 89.95 (*1-57172-071-5*) Intl Qual.
— EU Technical Standards & Certification Directive. 262p. 1996. 150.00 (*1-57172-077-4*) Intl Qual.
— EU Veterinary Medicinal Products Directive. 119p. 1995. 99.95 (*1-57172-042-1*) Intl Qual.
— European Union: Active Implantable Medical Device. 75p. 1996. 64.95 (*1-57172-058-8*) Intl Qual.
— European Union: Electro-Magnetic Compatibility Directive. 94p. 1996. 64.95 (*1-57172-055-3*) Intl Qual.
— European Union: EMEA Authorization Directive. 153p. 1996. 94.95 (*1-57172-068-5*) Intl Qual.
— European Union: Good Laboratory Practices. 84p. 1996. 69.95 (*1-57172-061-8*) Intl Qual.
— European Union: Good Manufacturing Practices. 158p. 1996. 99.95 (*1-57172-062-6*) Intl Qual.
— European Union: In-Vitro Diagnostic Directive. 118p. 1996. 99.95 (*1-57172-066-9*) Intl Qual.
— European Union: Medical Device Directive. 221p. 1996. 150.00 (*1-57172-076-6*) Intl Qual.
***Bailey, Mercedes.** Delivering a Winning Job Interview. (Cliffs Notes Ser.). 128p. 1999. pap. text 8.99 (*0-7645-8548-7*) IDG Bks.
Bailey-Mershon, Glenda. Bird Talk: Poems by Glenda Bailey-Mershon. (Midwest Women Poets Ser.). 37p. 1998. 6.00 (*1-891476-11-4*) Wild Dove.
— The History of the American Women's Movement: A Study Guide. (Illus.). 33p. 1997. pap. 10.00 (*0-9639894-4-8*) Wild Dove.
***Bailey-Mershon, Glenda.** Jane's Story II: An Anthology by Midwestern Women. LC 99-75798. 170p. 2000. pap. 15.95 (*0-9639894-3-X*, 23) Wild Dove.
Bailey-Mershon, Glenda, et al, eds. Jane's Stories: An Anthology of Work by Midwestern Women. LC 94-60374. (Illus.). 131p. 1994. pap. 9.95 (*0-9639894-0-5*) Wild Dove.
***Bailey, Michael A., et al, eds.** Campaigns & Elections: Contemporary Case Studies. 212p. 1999. pap. 22.95 (*1-56802-495-9*) CQ Pr.
Bailey, Michele. The Cuckoo Case. large type ed. 304p. 31.50 (*0-7089-3695-4*) Ulverscroft.
Bailey, Michelle, ed. see Bennett, William H., et al.
Bailey, Mike. Three Finger Pickin' Banjo Songbook. 112p. 1997. spiral bd. 19.95 incl. audio compact disk (*0-7866-2887-1*, 93612BCD) Mel Bay.
— Writing Erotic Fiction: And Getting Published. LC 98-65244. (Teach Yourself Ser.). (Illus.). 192p. 1998. pap. 12.95 (*0-8442-0022-0*, 00220, Teach Yrslf) NTC Contemp Pub Co.
***Bailey, Mike & North, Tony.** Liberator Album: B-24s of the 2nd Air Division USAAF. (Illus.). 192p. 1998. 39.95 (*1-85780-060-5*) Specialty Pr.
Bailey, Mike & Smith, Michael L. Deluxe Gospel Banjo Songbook. 96p. 1982. pap. 11.95 (*0-87166-707-X*, 93891) Mel Bay.
Bailey, N., ed. Faults in Fusion Welds in Constructional Steels. (Illus.). 48p. 1986. pap. 39.95 (*0-85300-207-X*, Pub. by Woodhead Pubng) Am Educ Systs.
Bailey, N., et al. Welding Steels Without Hydrogen Cracking. 2nd ed. (Illus.). 160p. 1993. 128.00 (*0-614-02558-3*, 6324U) ASM Intl.
Bailey, N., jt. auth. see Evans, G. M.
***Bailey, N. C. & Eskeland, N. L.** Call Me Gene. (Illus.). 90p. (YA). (gr. 5-8). 1999. pap. 19.95 (*0-9673811-0-X*) ScienceTwoDiscover.
Bailey, N. C., jt. auth. see Eskeland, N. L.
Bailey, Nan, et al. The National Black Independent Political Party. 32p. pap. 5.00 (*0-87348-690-0*) Pathfinder NY.
***Bailey, Nancy.** Scottish Childhood, Vol. 2. 1998. pap. 11.00 (*0-00-472176-4*, Pub. by HarpC) Trafalgar.
Bailey, Nancy G., jt. auth. see Bailey, Walter B.
Bailey, Nancy R., jt. ed. see Gulati, Gita.
Bailey, Nathan. A Universal Etymological English Dictionary. (Anglistica & Americana Ser.: No. 52). 982p. 1969. reprint ed. 240.00 (*0-317-05068-0*, 05102625) G Olms Pubs.
Bailey, Ney. Faith Is Not a Feeling. LC 78-60077. 115p. Date not set. pap. 8.99 (*0-918956-45-5*) Integrtd Res.
— Faith Is Not a Feeling. 112p. 1979. reprint ed. pap. 7.99 (*1-57902-011-9*, 1532e) Integrtd Res.
Bailey, Norman. Weldability of Ferritic Steels. (Illus.). 304p. 1994. boxed set 171.00 (*1-85573-092-8*, 6421, Pub. by Woodhead Pubng) Am Educ Systs.
Bailey, Norman A. Strategic Economics. (Special Issue of Comparative Strategy Ser.: Vol. 7, No. 2). 75p. 1988. pap. 18.00 (*0-8448-1553-5*) Taylor & Francis.
Bailey, Norman A. & Cohen, Richard. The Mexican Time Bomb: A Twentieth Century Fund Paper. 61p. (Orig.). (C). 1987. pap. text 9.00 (*0-87078-209-6*) Century Foundation.
Bailey, Norman A., jt. auth. see Perry, William.
Bailey, Norman T. The Elements of Stochastic Processes with Applications to the Natural Sciences. (Classics Library). 264p. 1990. pap. 89.95 (*0-471-52368-2*) Wiley.
— Mathematics, Statistics & Systems for Health. LC 77-1307. (Wiley Series in Probability & Mathematical Statistics). 232p. reprint ed. pap. 72.00 (*0-608-17855-1*, 203265300080) Bks Demand.
— Statistical Methods in Biology. 3rd ed. (Illus.). 269p. (C). 1995. pap. text 19.95 (*0-521-46983-X*) Cambridge U Pr.
Bailey, Norman W. Bailey. The Baileys of Baileytown, a Genealogy of the South Jersey Bailys with Especial Reference to the Descendants of Edward Bailey, Sr., of Cumberland County, Including Descendants Through Daughters. (Illus.). 152p. 1997. reprint ed. pap. 24.00 (*0-8328-7329-2*); reprint ed. lib. bdg. 34.00 (*0-8328-7328-4*) Higginson Bk Co.
Bailey, P. Analysis of Potential Self-guarantee Tests for Demonstrating Financial Assurance by Non- Profit Colleges, Universities & Hospitals & by Business Firms That Do Not Issue Bonds. 65p. 1997. pap. 6.50 (*0-16-062848-2*) USGPO.
— Price-Anderson Act, Crossing the Bridge to the Next Century: Report to Congress. 178p. 1998. per. 15.00 (*0-16-062957-8*) USGPO.
Bailey, P., et al. Active Learning for Children with Disabilities. Fowkes, Lois, ed. (Active Learning Ser.). (Illus.). 160p. (Orig.). 1995. pap., teacher ed. 16.95 (*0-201-49402-7*) Supplementary Div.
— Multinational Enterprises & Employment in the Global Economy of the 1990s. xvi, 325p. (Orig.). 1993. pap. 40.50 (*92-2-107105-7*) Intl Labour Office.
Bailey, P. D. An Introduction to Peptide Chemistry. LC 89-22582. 240p. 1990. 170.00 (*0-471-92348-6*) Wiley.
— An Introduction to Peptide Chemistry. LC 89-22582. 240p. 1992. pap. 69.95 (*0-471-93532-8*) Wiley.
Bailey, P. H. Human Rights: Australia in an International Context. 408p. 1990. pap. 78.00 (*0-409-30057-8*, Austral, MICHIE) LEXIS Pub.
Bailey, P. L., jt. ed. see Stanley, Theodore H.
***Bailey, Patricia A., et al, eds.** Integrating Community Service into Nursing Education: A Guide to Service-Learning. LC 99-26341. (Series on the Teaching of Nursing). (Illus.). 144p. 1999. text 31.95 (*0-8261-1268-4*) Springer Pub.
***Bailey, Patricia M.** Packaging Law Europe. LC 99-72611. (Ashgate Studies in Environmental Policy & Practice). 156p. 1999. text 61.95 (*1-85972-282-2*, Pub. by Avebry) Ashgate Pub Co.
Bailey, Patrick D. Organonitrogen Chemistry. (Oxford Chemistry Primers Ser.: Vol. 38). (Illus.). 94p. (C). 1996. pap. text 12.95 (*0-19-855775-2*) OUP.
Bailey, Patty, ed. see Wilder, Donna.
Bailey, Paul. City in the Sun: The Japanese Concentration Camp at Poston, Arizona. (Illus.). 1979. 24.95 (*0-87026-026-X*) Westernlore.
— Ghost Dance Messiah: The Jack Wilson Story. LC 75-135152. 24.95 (*0-87026-025-1*) Westernlore.
— Holy Smoke: A Dissertation on the Utah War. (Great West & Indian Ser.: Vol. 44). (Illus.). 1977. 24.95 (*0-87026-037-5*) Westernlore.
***Bailey, Paul.** Kitty & Virgil. LC 99-86843. 280p. 2000. 25.95 (*1-58567-010-3*, Pub. by Overlook Pr) Penguin Putnam.
Bailey, Paul. Polygamy Was Better Than Monotony: To My Grandfathers & Their Plural Wives. LC 72-83538. (Illus.). 24.95 (*0-87026-027-8*) Westernlore.
— Reform the People: Changing the Attitudes Towards Popular Education in Early Twentieth-Century China. 320p. 1993. pap. 35.00 (*0-7486-0281-X*, Pub. by Edinburgh U Pr) Col U Pr.
— Those Kings & Queens of Old Hawaii: A Mele to Their Memory. LC 75-259. (Illus.). 381p. 1975. 31.95 (*0-87026-035-9*) Westernlore.
— An Unnatural History of Death Valley: With Reflections on the Valley's Varmints, Virgins, Vandals & Visionaries. LC 78-21578. (Illus.). 84p. 1978. pap. 5.95 (*0-912494-31-X*) Death Valley Fortyniners.
Bailey, Paul, ed. The Oxford Book of London. 400p. 1996. 30.00 (*0-19-214192-9*) OUP.
Bailey, Paul, tr. from CHI. Strengthen the Country & Enrich the People: The Reform Writings of Ma Jianzhong. LC 96-146029. (Durham East Asia Ser.). 240p. (C). 1998. text 45.00 (*0-7007-0468-X*, Pub. by Curzon Pr Ltd) UH Pr.
Bailey, Paul C., tr. see Rudin, Josef.
Bailey, Paul J. Postwar Japan: 1945 to the Present. (Historical Association Studies). (Illus.). 224p. 1996. pap. 14.95 (*0-631-17901-1*) Blackwell Pubs.
Bailey, Paul J., tr. see Bastid, Marianne.
Bailey, Pearl. Duey's Tale. LC 74-22278. (Illus.). 59p. 1975. 10.95 (*0-15-126576-3*) Harcourt.
— Hurry up, America, & Spit. LC 76-12481. 106p. 1976. 5.95 (*0-15-143000-4*) Harcourt.
— Pearl's Kitchen. LC 73-6624. 211p. 1973. 9.95 (*0-15-171600-5*) Harcourt.
— The Raw Pearl. LC 67-11963. (Illus.). 1968. 10.95 (*0-15-175930-8*) Harcourt.
— Talking to Myself. LC 78-153679. 233p. 1971. 12.95 (*0-15-187990-7*) Harcourt.
Bailey, Peg. The Lemon Lovers Cookbook. LC 96-76510. (Illus.). 160p. 1996. 18.95 (*1-56352-324-8*) Longstreet.
Bailey, Penny, jt. auth. see Bailey, Bill.
Bailey, Percival & Cushing, Harvey. Classification of the Tumors of the Glioma Group on a Histogenetic Basis with a Correlated Study of Prognosis. (Illus.). 1970. reprint ed. 20.00 (*0-87266-049-4*) Argosy.
Bailey, Percival, tr. see Bekhtereva, Natal'ia P.
Bailey, Peter. Bringing Human Rights to Life. 270p. 1993. 14.00 (*1-86287-103-5*, Pub. by Blackstone Pr) Gaunt.
— Leisure & Class in Victorian England: Rational Recreation & the Contest for Control, 1830-1885. (Illus.). 288p. 1987. pap. 16.95 (*0-416-02142-5*) Routledge.
— Popular Culture & Performance in the Victorian City. LC 99-174955. (Illus.). 320p. (C). 1998. text 59.95 (*0-521-57417-X*) Cambridge U Pr.
Bailey, Peter, ed. Music Hall: The Business of Pleasure. LC 86-12837. (Popular Music in Britain Ser.). 208p. 1987. 123.95 (*0-335-15278-3*); pap. 33.95 (*0-335-15129-9*) OpUniv Pr.
Bailey, Peter J. Passing Through. 1982. pap. 5.25 (*0-8222-0875-X*) Dramatists Play.
— Reading Stanley Elkin. LC 84-8735. 242p. 1985. text 24.95 (*0-252-01172-4*) U of Ill Pr.
***Bailey, Peter J.** The Reluctant Film Art of Woody Allen. LC 00-28308. (Illus.). 288p. 2000. 27.50 (*0-8131-2167-1*) U Pr of Ky.
Bailey, Peter K. Poplar Island - My Memories As a Boy. (Illus.). viii, 158p. 1996. 19.50 (*0-9655453-0-X*) P K Bailey.
Bailey, Peter L. Analysis with Ion-Selective Electrodes. 2nd ed. LC 80-49971. (Heyden International Topics in Science Ser.). 263p. reprint ed. pap. 81.60 (*0-8357-5443-X*, 202597600048) Bks Demand.
Bailey, Philip M. Homeopathic Psychology: Personality Profiles of the Major Constitutional Remedies. LC 95-9242. 417p. (Orig.). (C). 1995. 25.00 (*1-55643-099-X*) North Atlantic.
Bailey, Philip S. Ozone Reactions with Organic Compounds: A Symposium Sponsored by the Division of Petroleum Chemistry at the 161st Meeting of the American Chemical Society, Los Angeles, California, March 29-30, 1971. LC 72-88560. (American Chemical Society Advances in Chemistry Ser.: Vol. 112). 141p. reprint ed. pap. 43.80 (*0-608-12444-3*, 202423700036) Bks Demand.
Bailey, Philip S., Jr. & Bailey, Christina A. Organic Chemistry. 2nd ed. 1997. pap. text, student ed. 37.00 (*0-13-850348-6*) P-H.
— Organic Chemistry. 5th ed. 1995. pap. text, student ed., suppl. ed. 38.00 (*0-13-180324-7*) P-H.
***Bailey, Philip S., Jr. & Bailey, Christina A.** Organic Chemistry. 6th ed. LC 99-52987. 570p. 1999. pap. text 69.00 (*0-13-924119-1*) P-H.
Bailey, Philip S., Jr. & Bailey, Christina A. Organic Chemistry: A Brief Survey of Concepts & Applications. 4th ed. 1989. student ed. 21.00 (*0-318-40087-1*, H1781-7) P-H.
Bailey, Phillip. Proust's Self-Reader: The Pursuit of Literature As Privileged Communication. LC 97-67749. (Marcel Proust Ser.: Vol. 7). 182p. 1997. lib. bdg. 38.95 (*1-883479-15-0*) Summa Pubns.
Bailey, Qwen, ed. see Wilder, Brittian, III.
Bailey, R. & Bailey, E. Ireland. 2nd ed. (Illustrated Travel Guides from Thomas Cook Ser.). (Illus.). 192p. 1994. pap. 14.95 (*0-8442-9054-8*, Passprt Bks) NTC Contemp Pub Co.
Bailey, R. A., ed. Surveys in Combinatorics, 1997. (London Mathematical Society Lecture Note Ser.: Vol. 241). (Illus.). 351p. (C). 1997. pap. text 42.95 (*0-521-59840-0*) Cambridge U Pr.
Bailey, R. F., ed. see Maull, B.
Bailey, R. O., jt. ed. see Alspaugh, M. A.
Bailey, R. W. I Protest: The Actual Accounts of Spiritual Journeys. Steele, Wayne, ed. LC 96-83890. 200p. (Orig.). 19.99 (*1-888642-00-9*) Land-Ship Bkstore.
Bailey, Randall C. David in Love & War: The Pursuit of Power in 2 Samuel 10-12. (Journal for the Study of the Old Testament Supplement Ser.: Vol. 75). 214p. 1990. 48.00 (*1-85075-209-5*, Pub. by Sheffield Acad) CUP Services.
— The Recovery of Black Presence: An Interdisciplinary Exploration. Grant, Jacquelyn, ed. 256p. (Orig.). 1995. pap. 16.95 (*0-687-35735-7*) Abingdon.
Bailey, Raymond C. Popular Influence upon Public Policy: Petitioning in Eighteenth-Century Virginia, 10. LC 78-73792. (Contributions in Legal Studies: No. 10). (Illus.). 203p. 1979. 49.95 (*0-313-20892-1*, BPP/, Greenwood Pr) Greenwood.
Bailey, Rebecca. A Wild Kentucky Garden: Poems & Essays. Pendarvis, Edwina, ed. LC 98-26939. (New Books by New Authors Ser.: Vol. 5). 96p. 1998. pap. 9.95 (*0-945084-72-2*) J Stuart Found.
Bailey, Rebecca, ed. The Kinks: Reflections on 30 Years of Music. LC 94-60630. 208p. (Orig.). 1994. pap. 10.00 (*0-9640755-1-2*) Trillium Pub.
Bailey, Richard. The Creative Writer's Craft: Lessons in Poetry, Fiction, & Drama. annuals LC 98-23827. 1998. 10.95 (*0-8442-5716-8*) NTC Contemp Pub Co.
— Energy: The Rude Awakening. LC 77-89057. 1978. 20.00 (*0-918998-03-4*) Energy Educ.
— Neither Carpetbaggers Nor Scalawags: Black Officeholders During the Reconstruction of Alabama, 1867-1878. (Illus.). 498p. (C). 1991. 29.95 (*0-9627218-0-8*) R Bailey.
— Neither Carpetbaggers Nor Scalawags: Black Officeholders During the Reconstruction of Alabama, 1867-1878. rev. ed. (Illus.). 393p. 1997. reprint ed. 21.00 (*0-9627218-5-9*) R Bailey.
— Neither Carpetbaggers nor Scalawags: Black Officeholders During the Reconstruction of Alabama, 1867-1878. 3rd rev. ed. (Illus.). 393p. 1995. 39.95 (*0-9627218-3-2*); pap. 18.95 (*0-9627218-4-0*) R Bailey.
— Nineteenth-Century English. (Illus.). 384p. 1998. pap. text 19.95 (*0-472-08540-9*, 08540) U of Mich Pr.

Bailey, Richard. They Too Call Alabama Home: African American Profiles, 1800-1999. (Illus.). 490p. 1999. 55.00 (*0-9671883-0-X*) Pyramid Pubs AL.
They achieved in music, the arts, government service, military affairs, athletics, science, athletics, education, religion, entertainment & other areas of endeavor. But until now much of their story has not been told. They too call Alabama home: African American Profiles, 1800-1999 bridges the gap between anonymity & acclaim by offering a fresh & in-depth look at African American achievers with Alabama ties. Some of those profile in the book were born in the state, while others came to Alabama to etch their mark on history. Still others departed Alabama to make a name for themselves in various parts of the world. Alabama & other parts of the world have benefited greatly from the contributions of these people. This book builds upon the author's previous work on Alabama Reconstruction. Genealogists & students of southern history, African American history & Alabama history will find much to appreciate in this book Thirteen appendices & two lists help to illuminate the achievements of these people. One lists identifies persons by occupations & other list identifies them according to their city of birth. Mail to Pyramid Publishing, Inc., P.O. Box

1264, Montgomery, AL 36102-1264. Telephones: 1-800-484-1191, ext. 8039 (orders only); 1-334-272-7248 (inquiries only); or fax, 1-334-272-7248. You may also place orders at (alabamablackhistory.com) or through leading book outlets. The ISBN is 0-9671883-0-X. ***Publisher Paid Annotation.***

***Bailey, Richard.** They Too Call Alabama Home: African American Profiles, 1800-1999. 490p. 1999. wbk. ed. 19.95 (*0-9671883-1-8*) Pyramid Pubs AL.

Bailey, Richard, ed. New Light on George Fox & Early Quakerism. LC 92-27477. 368p. 1992. text 99.95 (*0-7734-9829-X*) E Mellen.

Bailey, Richard, et al. Le Service a la Clientele en Assurance: Perfectionnment, ACS 100. Duisit, Vivian, ed. (Associate, Customer Service Program Ser.). (FRE.). pap. 36.00 (*0-939921-52-9*, Pub. by Life Office) PBD Inc.

***Bailey, Richard, et al.** Servicio al Cliente en la Industria del Seguro: Mejorando Sus Habilidades. Vallenilla, Ines, ed. (LOMA Serie del Servicio al Cliente). Orig. Title: Customer Service in Insurance: Improving Your Skills. (SPA., Illus.). 280p. 2000. pap. 40.00 (*1-57974-089-8*, Pub. by Life Office) PBD Inc.

Bailey, Richard, jt. auth. see Somers, Frans.

B

Bailey, Richard N. & Cramp, Rosemary. Cumberland, Westmorland & Lancashire North-of-the-Sands. (Corpus of Anglo-Saxon Stone Sculpture Ser.: Vol. II). (Illus.). 466p. 1988. 189.00 (*0-19-726036-5*) OUP.

Bailey, Richard O., jt. ed. see Alspaugh, Mark A.

Bailey, Richard W. Images of English: A Cultural History of the Language. (Illus.). 344p. (C). 1993. pap. text 19.95 (*0-472-08242-6*, 08242) U of Mich Pr.

— The Seven Deadly Sins in the Contemporary Church. 21p. 1993. pap. 1.59 (*0-87509-541-0*) Chr Pubns.

Bailey, Richard W., ed. Dictionaries of English: Prospects for the Record of Our Language. 176p. (C). 1987. text 34.50 (*0-472-10087-4*, 10087) U of Mich Pr.

— Early Modern English: Additions & Antedatings to the Record of English Vocabulary 1475-1700. 380p. 1978. lib. bdg. 80.00 (*3-487-06510-X*) G Olms Pubs.

Bailey, Richard W. & Dolezel, Lubomir. An Annotated Bibliography of Statistical Stylistics. (Bibliographic Ser.: No. 2). 97p. 1968. pap. 3.00 (*0-930042-17-4*) Mich Slavic Pubns.

Bailey, Richard W. & Fosheim, Robin M., eds. Literacy for Life: The Demand for Reading & Writing. LC 83-8265. x, 272p. 1983. pap. 19.75 (*0-87352-131-5*, J303P); lib. bdg. 37.50 (*0-87352-130-7*, J303C) Modern Lang.

Bailey, Richard W. & Ghorlach, Manfred, eds. English As a World Language. LC 81-21904. 504p. reprint ed. pap. 156.30 (*0-7837-4711-X*, 205906300003) Bks Demand.

Bailey, Richard With, jt. auth. see Arthur, James.

***Bailey, Robert.** Gay Politics, Urban Politics: Identity & Economics in the Urban Setting. LC 98-22051. (Power, Conflict & Democracy Ser.). 496p. 1998. pap. 24.50 (*0-231-09663-1*); lib. bdg. 49.50 (*0-231-09662-3*) Col U Pr.

Bailey, Robert, Jr. Radicals in Urban Politics: The Alinsky Approach. LC 73-90938. xii, 200p. 1974. lib. bdg. 19.50 (*0-226-03452-6*) U Ch Pr.

Bailey, Robert. Tropical Deforestation: The Human Dimension. Sponsel, Leslie E. et al, eds. (Illus.). 352p. 1996. pap. 20.50 (*0-231-08481-1*) Col U Pr.

Bailey, Robert, ed. Wagner: Prelude & Transfiguration from Wagner's Tristan & Isolde. (Critical Scores Ser.). (C). 1985. pap. text 15.50 (*0-393-95405-6*) Norton.

Bailey, Robert & Whelan, John. The Reconstruction & Re-Equipment of Kuwait: New Business Opportunities, 3 vols., Set. 600p. 1991. pap. text 615.00 (*1-85333-585-1*) G & T Inc.

Bailey, Robert C. The Behavioral Ecology of Efe Pygmy Men in the Ituri Forest, Zaire. LC 91-10954. (Anthropological Papers Ser.: No. 86). xviii, 158p. (Orig.). 1991. pap. 15.00 (*0-915703-24-6*) U Mich Mus Anthro.

Bailey, Robert F. The Pocket Size Carpenter's Helper. (Illus.). 123p. (Orig.). (C). 1996. pap. 12.95 (*0-937635-00-6*) R S Wood.

Bailey, Robert G. Ecoregions: The Ecosystem Geography of the Oceans & Continents. LC 97-26384. 200p. 1997. write for info. (*0-387-98305-8*); pap. write for info. (*0-387-98311-2*) Spr-Verlag.

— Ecosystem Geography. LC 95-34178. (Illus.). 241p. 1996. 69.95 (*0-387-94354-4*) Spr-Verlag.

Bailey, Robert L. An Examination of Prime Time Network Television Special Programs: 1948-1966. Sterling, Christopher H., ed. LC 78-21716. (Dissertations in Broadcasting Ser.). (Illus.). 1980. lib. bdg. 30.95 (*0-405-11755-8*) Ayer.

Bailey, Robert S. Lilly Industries, Inc. A History of Success, a Future of Possibilities. LC 98-87856. (Illus.). 120p. 1998. pap. write for info. (*0-9666504-0-9*) Lilly Indust.

Bailey, Robert W. The Cervical Spine. LC 79-152020. 271p. reprint ed. pap. 84.10 (*0-608-30208-2*, 205567600029) Bks Demand.

— The Crisis Regime: The M. A. C., the E. F. C. B., & the Political Impact of the New York City Financial Crisis. LC 84-8897. 230p. (C). 1985. text 74.50 (*0-87395-850-0*); pap. text 24.95 (*0-87395-851-9*) State U NY Pr.

— Human Performance Engineering: Designing High Quality, Professional User Interfaces for Computer Products, Applications, & Systems. 3rd ed. LC 95-45147. 576p. (C). 1996. 83.00 (*0-13-149634-4*) P-H.

Bailey, Robert W., et al. Complications in Laparoscopic Surgery. 416p. 1996. write for info. (*0-683-30053-9*) Lppncott W & W.

Bailey, Roberta & English, Jean, eds. A Bountiful Year: Cooking Through the Seasons in Maine. (Cookbook Ser.). (Illus.). 220p. 1990. spiral bd. 12.00 (*0-9621498-2-9*, Robin Hood) R Hood Little.

Bailey, Robin. Shadowdance. (Illus.). (Orig.). 1996. pap. 5.99 (*1-56504-946-2*, 13403, Borealis) White Wolf.

Bailey, Robin W. Infocom, No. 3: Enchanter. 320p. (Orig.). 1989. pap. 3.95 (*0-380-75386-3*, Avon Bks) Morrow Avon.

— Infocom, No. 6: The Lost City of Zork. 304p. 1991. mass mkt. 4.50 (*0-380-75389-8*, Avon Bks) Morrow Avon.

— Swords Against the Shadowland. 244p. 1998. pap. 9.99 (*1-56504-893-8*, 12016, Borealis) White Wolf.

Bailey, Roger. Functional Programming with Hope. 1990. text 61.95 (*0-470-21649-2*) P-H.

— Irrigated Crops & Their Management. (Illus.). 214p. 1990. 37.95 (*0-85236-205-6*, Pub. by Farming Pr) Diamond Farm Bk.

Bailey, Ronald. Ecoscam: The False Prophets of Ecological Apocalypse. 256p. 1994. pap. 10.95 (*0-312-10971-7*) St Martin.

Bailey, Ronald, ed. The True State of the Planet. LC 95-937. 1995. per. 15.00 (*0-02-874010-6*) Free Pr.

Bailey, Ronald H. The Battles for Atlanta. (Civil War Ser.). (Illus.). 176p. (gr. 7). 1999. 29.95 (*0-8094-4773-8*) Time-Life.

Bailey, Ronald H. & Time-Life Books Editors. Air War in Europe. LC 99-158470. (World War II Ser.). 208p. 1998. 19.95 (*0-7835-5704-3*) Time-Life Educ.

Bailey, Ronald T. Frozen in Silver: The Life & Frontier Photography of P. E. Larson. LC 97-17883. (Illus.). 300p. 1998. pap. 24.95 (*0-8040-1000-5*); text 44.95 (*0-8040-0999-6*) Swallow.

Bailey, Ronald W., ed. Records of Oman, 1867-1965, 17 vols. (Illus.). 10800p. (C). 1988. reprint ed. lib. bdg. 3495.00 (*1-85207-120-6*, Pub. by Archive Editions) N Ross.

Bailey, Ronald W., jt. auth. see Furst, Michele.

Bailey, Rosalie. Pre-Revolutionary Dutch Houses & Families in Northern New Jersey & Southern New York. 612p. 1993. reprint ed. lib. bdg. 109.00 (*0-7812-5292-X*) Rprt Serv.

Bailey, Rosalie F. Dutch Systems in Family Naming New York-New Jersey. 1985. 6.50 (*0-915156-12-1*, SP 12) Natl Genealogical.

***Bailey, Rosalie F.** Guide to Genealogical & Biographical Sources for New York City (Manhattan), 1783-1898. 96p. 1998. reprint ed. pap. 14.00 (*0-8063-4801-1*, Pub. by Clearfield Co) ACCESS Pubs Network.

Bailey, Rosemary. Scarlet Ribbons: A Priest with AIDS. LC 97-67370. 216p. 1998. pap. 16.99 (*1-85242-521-0*) Serpents Tail.

Bailey, Roy. Fifty Activities for Developing Counselling Skills. 300p. 1991. ring bd. 245.95 (*0-566-02909-X*, Pub. by Gower) Ashgate Pub Co.

— Fifty Activities for Managing Stress. 128p. 1989. ring bd. 271.95 (*0-566-02777-1*, Pub. by Gower) Ashgate Pub Co.

Bailey, Roy & Clarke, Margaret. Stress & Coping in Nursing. 352p. 1990. pap. 32.50 (*0-412-33830-0*, A4441) Chapman & Hall.

Bailey, Roy D. Therapeutic Nursing for the Mentally Handicapped. (Illus.). 1982. pap. text 16.95 (*0-19-261314-6*) OUP.

Bailey, Ruth. I Can Do Anything... You Can Do Better! (Illus.). 138p. 1999. pap. write for info. (*0-7392-0141-7*, P03069) Morris Pubng.

Bailey, Ruth, jt. auth. see Bailey, Eric.

Bailey, Ruth, jt. ed. see Bailey, Eric.

Bailey, S. J. & Paddison, Ronan, eds. Local Government Finance: An International Comparison. 208p. 1988. lib. bdg. 59.50 (*0-415-00529-9*) Routledge.

Bailey, S. W., ed. Hydrous Phyllosilicates (Exclusive of Micas) Reviews in Mineralogy. (Reviews in Mineralogy Ser.: Vol. 19). 725p. 1988. per. 28.00 (*0-939950-23-5*) Mineralogical Soc.

— Micas. (Reviews in Mineralogy Ser.: Vol. 13). 584p. 1984. per. 28.00 (*0-939950-17-0*) Mineralogical Soc.

Bailey, Sarah L. Historical Sketches of Andover: Comprising the Present Towns of North Andover & Andover Massachusetts. (Illus.). 626p. 1995. pap. text 38.50 (*0-7884-0116-5*) Heritage Bk.

— Historical Sketches of Andover, Comprising the Present Towns of North Andover & Andover. (Illus.). 650p. 1989. reprint ed. lib. bdg. 65.00 (*0-8328-0802-4*, MA0005) Higginson Bk Co.

Bailey-Serres, Julia, et al. A Look Beyond Transcription: Mechanisms Determining MRNA Stability & Translation in Plants. LC 98-4694. 183p. 1998. pap. write for info. (*0-943088-36-4*) Am Soc of Plan.

Bailey, Shackleton. Epigrams, 2 vols., Vol. 1. LC 92-8234. (Loeb Classical Library: No. 94). 416p. 1993. text 18.95 (*0-674-99105-2*) HUP.

Bailey, Shackleton. Horati Flacci, Q. (LAT.). 1995. 29.95 (*3-519-01437-8*, T1437, Pub. by B G Teubner); pap. 24.95 (*3-519-01436-X*, T1436, Pub. by B G Teubner) U of Mich Pr.

— Lucani Bk. X: De Bello Civili. (LAT.). 1997. 95.00 (*3-519-11502-6*, T1502, Pub. by B G Teubner) U of Mich Pr.

***Bailey, Shackleton.** Valerius Maximus: Memorable Doings & Sayings, 2 vols. LC 99-89336. 2000. text. write for info. (*0-674-99542-2*) HUP.

Bailey, Shackleton, ed. Anthologia Latina Pt. I, Fasciule 1: Carmina in Codicibus Scripta - Libri Salmasiani Aliorumque Carmina. (LAT.). 1982. 100.00 (*3-519-01030-5*, T1030, Pub. by B G Teubner) U of Mich Pr.

— Martialis, M. Valerii. (LAT.). 1990. 110.00 (*3-519-01531-5*, T1531, Pub. by B G Teubner) U of Mich Pr.

— Quintiliani, M. Fabii: Declamationes Minores. (LAT.). 1989. 105.00 (*3-519-01753-9*, T1753, Pub. by B G Teubner) U of Mich Pr.

Bailey, Shackleton, ed. see Cicero, Marcus Tullius.

Bailey, Shackleton D., ed. Harvard Studies in Classical Philology, Vol. 84. LC 44-32100. 1990. 30.00 (*0-674-37931-4*) HUP.

— Harvard Studies in Classical Philology, Vol. 89. 240p. 1985. 32.50 (*0-674-37936-5*) HUP.

Bailey, Sharon O. Cinders & Sparks. (Action/Adventures in Love Ser.). 224p. 1997. pap. 14.95 (*0-9660801-0-6*) WiWy Wrld.

Bailey, Sheri & Temple, Dura. Southern Girls. 64p. 1996. pap. 5.60 (*0-87129-659-4*, SB2) Dramatic Pub.

Bailey, Sheril. The Sheril Bailey Complete Manicuring & Nailcare Guide. LC 97-41545. 1998. write for info. (*0-8362-5187-3*) Andrews & McMeel.

Bailey, Sheryl K., et al. African Americans in Alaska Resource Guide. 4th ed. 40p. (Orig.). 1992. pap. text 15.95 (*0-9630369-1-2*) A Abraham.

— African Americans in Alaska Resource Guide & Calendar 1994. 5th ed. 40p. (Orig.). 1993. pap. text 15.95 (*0-9630369-2-0*) A Abraham.

Bailey, Sican, jt. illus. see King-Smith, Dick.

Bailey, Sinead, jt. auth. see Bryant, Raymond L.

Bailey, Stanley E., jt. auth. see Wadman, Robert C.

Bailey, Stephen. Kashrut, Tefillin, Tzitzit: Studies in the Purpose & Meaning of Symbolic Mitzvot Inspired by the Commentaries of Rabbi Samson Raphael Hirsch. LC 99-23970. (Illus.). 200p. 2000. 40.00 (*0-7657-6106-8*) Aronson.

— Offices. LC 89-23944. (Briefing & Design Guide Ser.: No. 3). (Illus.). 200p. 1990. reprint ed. pap. 62.00 (*0-608-04411-3*, 206519200001) Bks Demand.

Bailey, Stephen, jt. ed. see Paddison, Ronan.

Bailey, Stephen K. Congress Makes a Law: The Story Behind the Employment Act of 1946. LC 80-12550. 282p. 1980. reprint ed. lib. bdg. 38.50 (*0-313-22407-2*, BACK, Greenwood Pr) Greenwood.

Bailey, Stephen K. & Mosher, Edith K. ESEA: The Office of Education Administers a Law. LC 68-27692. (Illus.). 411p. reprint ed. pap. 127.50 (*0-8357-3990-2*, 203668800005) Bks Demand.

Bailey, Stephen K., et al. Research Frontiers in Politics & Government. LC 72-7820. 247p. 1973. reprint ed. lib. bdg. 65.00 (*0-8371-6527-X*, BARF, Greenwood Pr) Greenwood.

Bailey, Steve. Science in the Service of Physical Education & Sport: The Story of the International Council for [Sic] Sport Science & Physical Education, 1956-1996. LC 96-22600. 360p. 1997. 196.50 (*0-471-96924-9*) Wiley.

Bailey, Sturges M. History of Columbia County, Wisconsin, Illinois, 1914: Index, 27p. (Orig.). 1982. pap. 6.00 (*0-910255-35-0*) Wisconsin Gen.

Bailey, Sturges W. Index to a Standard History of Sauk County Wisconsin, 1918. (Illus.). 55p. (Orig.). 1983. pap. text 8.50 (*0-910255-39-3*) Wisconsin Gen.

— Index to Portrait & Biographical Album of Green Lake, Marquette, & Waushara Cos., Wis., 1890. (Illus.). 44p. (Orig.). 1983. pap. text 7.25 (*0-910255-38-5*) Wisconsin Gen.

Bailey, Sturges W., ed. see International Clay Conference Staff.

Bailey, Sue, ed. see Polley, Louis E.

Bailey, Susan D. National Directory of Corporate Philanthropy for Native Americans. Meiners, Phyllis A., ed. LC 97-65770. (Multicultural Grant Guides: Vol. 5). (Illus.). 275p. (Orig.). 1999. pap. 98.95 (*0-9633694-7-4*) CRC EagleRock.

Bailey, Susan P. A & L Quick Review: Medical Record. 7th ed. LC 98-13628. 311p. (C). 1998. pap. text 32.95 (*0-8385-0353-5*) Appleton & Lange.

— Medical Record Examination Review (MEPC) 6th ed. (Illus.). 288p. (C). 1994. pap. text 25.95 (*0-8385-6192-6*, A6192-7) Appleton & Lange.

— Problems & Cases in Health Information Management. (Illus.). v, 93p. (Orig.). (C). 1997. pap. text 22.95 (*0-9657783-0-4*) Lenox Pub Co.

— Problems & Cases in Health Information Management: Instructor Guide. (Illus.). v, 93p. (Orig.). (C). 1997. pap. text, teacher ed. 26.95 (*0-9657783-1-2*) Lenox Pub Co.

Bailey, Susan P. & Muller, Joanne. Roleplays in Health Information Management: An Instructional Resource. v, 153p. 1997. pap. text 44.95 (*0-9657783-2-0*) Lenox Pub Co.

Bailey, Sydney & Daws, Sam. The Procedure of the U. N. Security Council. 3rd ed. LC KZ5038.B34 1998. (Illus.). 710p. 1998. text 165.00 (*0-19-828073-4*) OUP.

Bailey, Sydney D. British Parliamentary Democracy. 3rd ed. LC 77-18752. (Illus.). 248p. 1978. reprint ed. lib. bdg. 65.00 (*0-313-20195-1*, BABR, Greenwood Pr) Greenwood.

— The General Assembly of the United Nations: A Study of Procedure & Practice, Vol. 9. rev. ed. LC 78-2810. (Carnegie Endowment for International Peace, United Nations Studies: No. 9). (Illus.). 347p. 1978. reprint ed. lib. bdg. 65.00 (*0-313-20336-9*, BAGA) Greenwood.

— The Korean Armistice. LC 91-43998. 328p. 1992. text 55.00 (*0-312-07920-6*) St Martin.

— The Secretariat of the United Nations, Vol. 11. LC 78-2880. (Carnegie Endowment for International Peace, United Nations Studies: No. 11). 132p. 1978. reprint ed. lib. bdg. 45.00 (*0-313-20338-5*, BASU, Greenwood Pr) Greenwood.

— The U. N. Security Council & Human Rights. LC 94-19511. 1994. text 75.00 (*0-312-12324-8*) St Martin.

— Voting in the Security Council. LC 69-15990. 285p. reprint ed. 88.40 (*0-8357-9252-8*, 201301700083) Bks Demand.

Bailey, T. E. & Lundgaard, Kris. Program Design with Pseudocode. 2nd ed. LC 85-15170. 200p. (C). 1985. mass mkt. 14.50 (*0-534-05574-5*) Brooks-Cole.

Bailey, T. G. English-Punjabi Dictionary. 160p. 1987. 24.95 (*0-8288-1772-3*, F43340) Fr & Eur.

Bailey, T. Grahame & Cummings, T. Panjabi Manual & Grammar: A Guide to the Colloquial Panjabi. (C). 1994. reprint ed. text 22.00 (*81-206-0918-2*, Pub. by Asian Educ Servs) S Asia.

Bailey, T. Melville. Hamilton: Chronicle of a City. 1983. 24.95 (*0-89781-067-8*, 5057) Am Historical Pr.

Bailey, T. N. & Knapp, Anthony W., eds. Representation Theory & Automorphic Forms: Instructional Conference, International Centre for Mathematical Sciences, March 1996, Edinburgh, Scotland. LC 97-26278. (Proceedings of Symposia in Pure Mathematics Ser.: Vol. 61). 479p. 1997. text 69.00 (*0-8218-0609-2*) Am Math.

Bailey, Temple. Glory of Youth. 1975. lib. bdg. 15.30 (*0-89966-010-X*) Buccaneer Bks.

— Radiant Tree, & Other Stories. LC 73-116932. (Short Story Index Reprint Ser.). 1977. 21.95 (*0-8369-3434-2*) Ayer.

— The Tin Soldier. 1975. lib. bdg. 19.10 (*0-89966-011-8*) Buccaneer Bks.

Bailey, Terence. The Ambrosian Cantus. (Wissenschaftliche Abhandlungen-Musicological Studies: Vol. 47). (ENG.). 258p. 1987. 52.00 (*0-931902-53-3*) Inst Mediaeval Mus.

— Antiphon & Psalm in the Ambrosian Office. (Wissenschaftliche Abhandlungen-Musicological Studies: No. 50/3). 320p. 1994. 78.00 (*0-931902-83-5*) Inst Mediaeval Mus.

Bailey, Terence & Merkley, Paul. The Antiphons of the Ambrosian Office. (Wissenschaftliche Abhandlungen-Musicological Studies: Vol. 50, Pt. 1). (ENG.). 271p. 1989. 70.00 (*0-931902-60-6*) Inst Mediaeval Mus.

— The Melodic Tradition of the Ambrosian Office - Antiphons. (Wissenschaftliche Abhandlungen-Musicological Studies: Vol. 50, Pt. 2). (ENG.). 656p. 1990. 160.00 (*0-931902-64-9*) Inst Mediaeval Mus.

Bailey, Thomas. On Writing Short Stories. LC 99-35471. 352p. (C). 1999. pap. text 31.95 (*0-19-512272-0*) OUP.

Bailey, Thomas, compiled by. Favorite Alabama Jokes. 4th rev. ed. 96p. 1996. pap. 5.95 (*1-878561-52-9*) Seacoast AL.

Bailey, Thomas A. The American Spirit: American History As Seen by Contemporaries, Vol. 2. 5th ed. (C). 1984. pap. text 31.56 (*0-669-05381-3*) HM Trade Div.

— Art of Diplomacy: The American Experience. LC 68-11680. (C). 1968. 32.50 (*0-89197-032-0*); pap. text 16.95 (*0-89197-033-9*) Irvington.

— Essays Diplomatic & Undiplomatic of Thomas A. Bailey. DeConde, Alexander & Rappaport, Armin, eds. LC 69-17917. (Illus.). (C). 1969. 42.00 (*0-89197-151-3*) Irvington.

— The Man in the Street. (History - United States Ser.). 334p. 1993. reprint ed. lib. bdg. 89.00 (*0-7812-4837-X*) Rprt Serv.

— The Man in the Street: The Impact of American Public Opinion on Foreign Policy. 1964. 16.50 (*0-8446-0015-6*) Peter Smith.

— The Policy of the United States Toward the Neutrals, 1917-1918. 1979. 44.95 (*0-405-10578-9*) Ayer.

— Presidential Greatness: The Image & the Man from George Washington to the Present. LC 66-19996. reprint ed. 30.00 (*0-89197-356-7*); reprint ed. pap. text 14.95 (*0-89197-642-6*) Irvington.

— Probing America's Past: A Critical Examination of Major Myths & Misconceptions, 2 vols. 1973. pap. text 13.50 (*0-685-42171-6*) HM Trade Div.

Bailey, Thomas A. & Kennedy, David M. The American Pageant. 7th ed. (C). 1983. text 65.16 (*0-669-05270-1*); pap. text 48.76 (*0-669-05266-3*) HM Trade Div.

— The American Pageant: A History of the Republic. 8th ed. (C). 1987. teacher ed. 15.16 (*0-669-10814-6*); student ed. 25.16 (*0-669-10813-8*); student ed. 22.76 (*0-669-14023-6*); student ed. 2.66 (*0-669-11356-5*) HM Trade Div.

— The American Pageant: A History of the Republic, 2 vols. 9th ed. LC 90-81560. 1019p. (C). 1991. pap. text 22.76 (*0-669-21054-4*); 2.66 (*0-669-21058-7*); 22.76 (*0-669-21056-0*); 14.76 (*0-669-21057-9*) HM Trade Div.

— The American Pageant: A History of the Republic. 10th ed. 1038p. (C). 1994. text 65.16 (*0-669-33892-3*) HM Trade Div.

— The American Pageant: A History of the Republic, Set. 8th ed. (C). 1987. text 65.16 (*0-669-10810-3*) HM Trade Div.

— The American Pageant: A History of the Republic, 2 vols., Set. 9th ed. LC 90-81560. 390p. (C). 1991. pap. text 25.16 (*0-669-21053-6*) HM Trade Div.

— The American Pageant: A History of the Republic, Vol. 1 to 1877. 8th ed. 479p. (C). 1987. pap. text 48.76 (*0-669-10811-1*) HM Trade Div.

— The American Spirit, II. 6th ed. LC 86-82149. 565p. (C). 1987. pap. text 31.56 (*0-669-12801-5*) HM Trade Div.

— The American Spirit: United States History as Seen by Contemporaries, 2 vols., Vol. I. 7th ed. LC 90-80758. 486p. (C). 1991. pap. text 31.56 (*0-669-21472-8*) HM Trade Div.

— The American Spirit: United States History as Seen by Contemporaries, 2 vols., Vol. 2. 7th ed. LC 90-80758. 666p. (C). 1991. pap. text 31.56 (*0-669-21473-6*) HM Trade Div.

— The American Spirit Chapters 1-24: United States History as Seen by Contemporaries, 2 vols., Vol. 1. 8th ed. LC 93-71277. 542p. (C). 1994. pap. text 31.56 (*0-669-34361-7*) HM Trade Div.

— The American Spirit Chapters 24-45: United States History as Seen by Contemporaries, 2 vols., Vol. 2. 8th ed. LC 93-71277. 718p. (C). 1994. pap. text 31.56 (*0-669-34362-5*) HM Trade Div.

— The Interactive American Pageant CD-ROM for Macintosh & Windows Vol. 1: To 1877. 10th ed. 508p. (C). 1994. pap. text 48.76 (*0-669-33905-9*) HM Trade Div.

— The Interactive American Pageant CD-ROM for Macintosh & Windows Vol. 2: Since 1865. 10th ed. 551p. (C). 1994. pap. text 48.76 (*0-669-33906-7*) HM Trade Div.

Bailey, Thomas A., et al. Family Law Casenotes & Quotes, 2 vols. 875p. 1990. ring bd. 120.00 (*1-57862-004-X*) State Bar WI.

Bailey, Thomas A., jt. auth. see Berryman, Sue.

Bailey, Thomas A., jt. auth. see Kennedy, David M.

Bailey, Thomas E. The Best of the Beach: The Complete Outdoors & Travel Guide to the Alabama & NW Florida Coasts. 192p. (Orig.). 1994. pap. 9.95 (*1-878561-28-6*) Seacoast AL.

Bailey, Thomas P. Race Orthodoxy in the South & Other Aspects of the Negro Question. reprint ed. 27.50 (*0-404-00136-X*) AMS Pr.

Bailey, Thomas R., ed. Learning to Work. LC 95-77616. 105p. (C). 1995. pap. 12.95 (*0-8157-0773-8*) Brookings.

Bailey, Todd B. The Power of Choice. 94p. 1993. pap. 3.95 (*1-883155-00-2*) T Bailey Minist.

Bailey, Tom. The Grace That Keeps This World. 64p. (Orig.). 1991. pap. 3.95 (*0-9629248-0-6*) Mbira Pr.

— Reefs, Wrecks & Rigs. (Illus.). 160p. (Orig.). 1993. pap. 6.95 (*1-878561-18-9*) Seacoast AL.

— Seafood of Northern Gulf. 1994. pap. 4.95 (*1-878561-31-6*) Seacoast AL.

— Seafood of the Florida Suncoast. (Illus.). 80p. (Orig.). 1986. pap. 2.50 (*0-685-63151-6*) Seacoast AL.

— Seafood of the Northern Gulf. (Illus.). 80p. (Orig.). 1984. pap. 2.50 (*0-685-63150-8*) Seacoast AL.

Bailey, Tom, jt. auth. see Bolton, Mike.

Bailey, Trevor. Interactive Spatial Data Analysis. (C). 1996. pap. text 75.00 (*0-582-24493-5*) Addison-Wesley.

Bailey, Troy, ed. Death Records, Ashtabula County, Ohio, 1867-1908. 579p. 1998. text 65.00 (*1-888851-02-3*); pap. text 50.00 (*1-888851-03-1*) Ashtabula Cnty.

Bailey, Ura J., jt. auth. see Morris, Lorenzo.

Bailey, Ura J., jt. auth. see Washington, Valora.

Bailey, Ura J., jt. ed. see Morris, Lorenzo.

Bailey, Valerie, ed. see Harris, George H.

Bailey, Valerie M. A Gathering of Roses. (Poetry Palette Ser.: Vol. 1). (Illus.). 74p. (Orig.). 1991. pap. 5.00 (*0-945641-04-4*) Castle Hills.

— Spinning Straw into Gold. (Poetry Palette Ser.: Vol. 2). (Illus.). 96p. (Orig.). 1990. pap. 5.00 (*0-945641-03-6*) Castle Hills.

Bailey, Valerie M., ed. see Grainger, Johnie.

Bailey, Valerie M., ed. see Harris, George H.

Bailey, Vern, jt. auth. see Bailey, Ida.

Bailey, Vicky, jt. auth. see Kitzinger, Sheila.

Bailey, Victor. Delinquency & Citizenship: Reclaiming the Young Offender, 1914-1948. 360p. 1987. 69.00 (*0-19-822664-0*) OUP.

— This Rash Act: Suicide Across the Life Cycle in the Victorian City. LC 97-32785. 376p. 1998. 55.00 (*0-8047-3123-3*); pap. write for info. (*0-8047-3124-1*) Stanford U Pr.

Bailey, Vince, ed. see International SAMPE Symposium & Exhibition Staff.

Bailey, Vyn. Patanjali's Meditation Yoga. 1998. pap. text. write for info. (*0-7318-0648-4*) Simon & Schuster.

Bailey, W. G., et al, eds. The Surface Climates of Canada. (Illus.). 400p. 1997. pap. text 32.95 (*0-7735-1672-7*, Pub. by McG-Queens Univ Pr) CUP Services.

— The Surface Climates of Canada. LC 99-203403. (Illus.). 400p. 1998. text 75.00 (*0-7735-0928-3*, Pub. by McG-Queens Univ Pr) CUP Services.

Bailey, W. H. Raymond Saunders. (Illus.). 10p. 1998. pap. 15.00 (*1-885998-12-0*) Hunter College.

Bailey, W. T. Richfield Springs & Vicinity: Historical, Biographical & Descriptive. (Illus.). 227p. 1997. reprint ed. lib. bdg. 29.50 (*0-8328-6212-6*) Higginson Bk Co.

Bailey, Wade H. Applied Statics & Strength of Materials. LC 97-212171. (Illus.). 1997. write for info. (*0-934623-82-1*) Solomon Pr.

Bailey, Walter. A Short Discourse of the Three Kinds of Peppers in Common Use. LC 77-38145. (English Experience Ser.: No. 425). 48p. 1972. reprint ed. 20.00 (*90-221-0425-7*) Walter J Johnson.

— Two Treatises Concerning the Perservation of Eye-Sight. LC 74-28827. (English Experience Ser.: No. 709). 1975. reprint ed. 20.00 (*90-221-0709-4*) Walter J Johnson.

Bailey, Walter, jt. auth. see Rotter, Joseph.

Bailey, Walter, III, ed. see Murphy, Melvin.

Bailey, Walter B. Programmatic Elements in the Works of Schoenberg. LC 83-18310. (Studies in Musicology: No. 74). (Illus.). 200p. reprint ed. pap. 62.00 (*0-8357-1480-2*, 207033600085) Bks Demand.

Bailey, Walter B., ed. The Arnold Schoenberg Companion. LC 97-41923. 352p. 1998. lib. bdg. 89.50 (*0-313-28779-1*, Greenwood Pr) Greenwood.

Bailey, Walter B. & Bailey, Nancy G. Radie Britain: A Bio-Bibliography, 25. LC 89-78117. (Bio-Bibliographies in Music Ser.: No. 25). 173p. 1990. lib. bdg. 52.95 (*0-313-26277-2*, BYR/, Greenwood Pr) Greenwood.

Bailey, Walter J. & Toop, E. R. Canadian Military Postal Markings. (Illus.). 872p. 1997. boxed set 109.95 (*0-9652431-2-5*, CMPM) C G Firby.

Bailey, Waylon. As You Go. LC 81-47888. 118p. (Orig.). 1981. pap. 4.00 (*0-914520-15-6*) Insight Pr.

***Bailey, Waylon.** Josue: Valentia Ante el Futuro.Tr. of Joshua: Courage for the Future. (SPA.). 96p. 1998. pap. text 5.50 (*0-311-04038-1*) Casa Bautista.

Bailey, Waylon & Hudson, Tom. Step by Step Through the Old Testament. 228p. 1991. pap. text 12.95 (*0-7673-2619-9*, LifeWy Press) LifeWay Christian.

Bailey, Wayne & Caneva, Thomas. The Complete Marching Band Resource Manual: Techniques & Materials for Teaching, Drill Design, & Music Arranging. LC 94-7036. (Illus.). 280p. (Orig.). 1994. spiral bd. 31.95 (*0-8122-1508-7*) U of Pa Pr.

Bailey, Wayne, et al. Teaching Brass: A Resource Manual. 192p. (C). 1991. pap. 39.69 (*0-07-003266-1*) McGraw.

Bailey, Wayne, jt. ed. see Motamedi, M. Edward.

Bailey, Wayne E., ed. Proceedings of the Fifth International Symposium on Silicon-on-Insulator Technology & Devices. LC 92-81318. (Proceedings Ser.: Vol. 92-13). 452p. 1992. 55.00 (*1-56677-013-0*) Electrochem Soc.

Bailey, Wendy, jt. auth. see Bailey, Linda.

Bailey, Wilford S., et al. Athletics & Academe: An Anatomy of Abuses & a Prescription for Reform. LC 97-52772. (Ace/Oryx Series on Higher Education). (Illus.). 160p. 1991. reprint ed. pap. text 27.95 (*1-57356-209-2*) Oryx Pr.

Bailey, William. The Ethics of Kant & Brunner: An Existential Blend. (Contemporary Existentialism Ser.: Vol. 6). XI, 194p. (C). 1998. text 44.95 (*0-8204-3133-8*) P Lang Pubng.

— Man, Religion & Science: A Functional View. LC 80-65860. (Illus.). 242p. (Orig.). 1981. pap. 1150.00 (*0-9604196-0-8*) W Bailey Pub.

Bailey, William A. Bill Bailey Came Home: As a Farm Boy, As a Stowaway at the Age of Nine, a Trapper at the Age of Fifteen & a Hobo at the Age of Sixteen. Fife, Austin E. & Fife, Alta, eds. LC 73-79904. (Illus.). 195p. reprint ed. pap. 60.50 (*0-8357-6039-1*, 203460100090) Bks Demand.

***Bailey, William E.** Andrew's Legacy: Winds of Change. LC 99-61428. (Illus.). 211p. 1999. 19.95 (*0-910287-14-7*) TelShare Pub Co.

Bailey, William E. The Invisible Drug. LC 96-77886. (Illus.). 392p. 1996. 34.95 (*0-9653793-3-7*, MPI-001-76) Mosaic Publns.

Bailey, William G., compiled by. Americans in Paris, 1900-1930: A Selected, Annotated Bibliography, Vol. 19. LC 89-1924. (Bibliographies & Indexes in World Literature Ser.: No. 19). 181p. 1989. lib. bdg. 62.95 (*0-313-26442-2*, BAM, Greenwood Pr) Greenwood.

Bailey, William G., compiled by. Human Longevity from Antiquity to the Modern Lab: A Selected, Annotated Bibliography, 4. LC 86-29560. (Bibliographies & Indexes in Gerontology Ser.: No. 4). 219p. 1987. lib. bdg. 69.50 (*0-313-25371-4*, BHL/, Greenwood Pr) Greenwood.

Bailey, William G., et al, eds. Encyclopedia of Police Science. 2nd ed. LC 94-46828. (Illus.). 888p. 1995. text 100.00 (*0-8153-1331-4*, H1729) Garland.

Bailey, William G., jt. auth. see Hoffman, Frank W.

Bailey, William G., jt. auth. see Hoffmann, Frank.

Bailey, William G., jt. auth. see Hoffmann, Frank W.

Bailey, William J. Managing Self-Renewal in Secondary Education. LC 74-13352. 208p. 1975. 37.95 (*0-87778-074-9*) Educ Tech Pubns.

— Organizing Schools. LC 96-61758. (Educational Leadership for the 21st Century Ser.: Vol. 4). 243p. 1996. text 44.95 (*1-56676-486-6*) Scarecrow.

— Power to the Schools: School Leader's Guidebook to Restructuring. LC 92-335. 160p. 1992. pap. 21.95 (*0-8039-6017-4*) Corwin Pr.

— School-Site Management Applied. LC 90-71264. 195p. 1992. 44.95 (*0-87762-743-6*) Scarecrow.

Bailey, William J. & Guynn, Stephen J. Bibliographic Index of Health Education Periodicals (BIHEP) Vol. 2, 1981 Cumulative Edition. 650p. 1982. lib. bdg. 75.00 (*0-941636-01-1*) IN U Dept Health.

— Bibliographic Index of Health Education Periodicals (BIHEP) 1980 Cumulative Edition. 428p. 1982. lib. bdg. 75.00 (*0-941636-00-3*) IN U Dept Health.

Bailey, William J., et al. Seven Significant Positions in Education. (Educational Leadership for the 21st Century Ser.). 180p. 1996. 34.95 (*1-56676-236-7*, 762367) Scarecrow.

Bailey, William J., ed. see Baruth, Leroy G. & Manning, M. Lee.

Bailey, William J., ed. see Shapiro, Joan P., et al.

Bailey, William M., jt. auth. see Garrelick, Renee.

***Bailey-Williams, Nicole L.** A Little Piece of Sky. 128p. (YA). (gr. 9-12). 2000. pap. 8.95 (*0-9700186-0-6*) Sugarenes.

Bailie, Eleanor. Chopin: The Pianist's Repertoire - A Graded Practical Guide. LC 98-216011. 592p. 1998. 49.95 (*1-871082-67-6*, Pub. by Kahn & Averill) Paul & Co Pubs.

Bailie, Frances, jt. auth. see Ricardo, Catherine.

Bailie, George A. Bailey. History & Genealogy of the Family of Bailie of North of Ireland . . . Including the Parish(es) of Duneane, Ireland & Dunain, Scotland. (Illus.). 96p. 1997. reprint ed. pap. 18.00 (*0-8328-7327-6*); reprint ed. lib. bdg. 28.00 (*0-8328-7326-8*) Higginson Bk Co.

Bailie, Gil. Violence Unveiled: Humanity at the Crossroads. 312p. 1997. pap. 17.95 (*0-8245-1645-1*) Crossroad NY.

Bailie, John. The Da Capo History of Western Classical Music. LC 98-40010. (Illus.). 192p. 1999. mass mkt. 29.95 (*0-306-80885-4*, Pub. by Da Capo) HarpC.

Bailie, Marcus. Canoeing & Kayaking: Techniques, Tactics, Training. (Crowood Sports Guides Ser.). (Illus.). 128p. 1992. pap. 22.95 (*1-85223-528-4*, Pub. by Cro1wood) Trafalgar.

Bailie, Mashoed & Winseek, Dwayne, eds. Democratizing Communication? Comparative Perspectives on Information & Power. LC 97-1993. (Hampton Press Communication Ser.). 448p. 1997. text 85.00 (*1-57273-064-1*); pap. text 35.00 (*1-57273-065-X*) Hampton Pr NJ.

Bailie, Stuart. The Cranberries: In Your Head. (Illus.). 80p. pap. 19.95 (*1-873884-37-0*, VX 01000, Pub. by Indep Music Pr) Music Sales.

— Philip Lynott: The Ballad of the Thin Man. (Illus.). 256p. 1996. text 25.99 (*1-886894-83-3*, MBS Paperbk) Mus Bk Servs.

Bailie, William. Josiah Warren: The First American Anarchist. LC 78-172201. (Right Wing Individualist Tradition in America Ser.). (Illus.). 1972. reprint ed. 17.95 (*0-405-00411-7*) Ayer.

— Josiah Warren: The First American Anarchist, a Sociological Study. 1971. 250.00 (*0-87700-024-7*) Revisionist Pr.

Bailiff, John, tr. see Poggeler, Otto.

Bailin, et al. Colorado Evidentiary Foundations, 1998 Cumulative Supplement. 101p. 1998. pap., suppl. ed. write for info. (*0-327-00688-9*, 8033210) LEXIS Pub.

Bailin, D. & Love, A. Introduction to Gauge Field Theory. rev. ed. LC 92-38471. (Graduate Student Series in Physics). (Illus.). 384p. 1993. pap. 61.00 (*0-7503-0281-X*) IOP Pub.

— Supersymmetric Gauge Field Theory & String Theory. (Graduate Student Series in Physics). (Illus.). 322p. 1994. 185.00 (*0-7503-0268-2*) IOP Pub.

— Supersymmetric Gauge Field Theory & String Theory. LC 94-10522. (Graduate Student Series in Physics). (Illus.). 322p. 1994. pap. 57.00 (*0-7503-0267-4*) IOP Pub.

Bailin, Daryl, jt. auth. see Bailin, George.

Bailin, George. Counterculture. Friedman, Eric et al, eds. (C). 1982. pap. 7.50 (*0-942856-00-7*) Seaport Poets & Writers.

— Dead Reckoning. (Illus.). 64p. (Orig.). 1984. pap. 6.00 (*0-943120-00-4*) Dragonsbreath.

— First Strike. Whatley, Daryl, ed. (Illus.). 56p. (Orig.). (C). 1987. pap. 5.00 (*0-942856-01-5*) Seaport Poets & Writers.

Bailin, George & Bailin, Daryl. Sage of Ananda: Shri Brahmananda Sarasvati, Vol. I. 96p. (Orig.). 1993. pap. 9.95 (*0-942856-03-1*) Seaport Poets & Writers.

Bailin, Hao. Chaos II. 752p. (C). 1990. text 97.00 (*981-02-0095-1*); pap. text 43.00 (*981-02-0096-X*) World Scientific Pub.

Bailin, Michael T., jt. auth. see Hurford, William E.

Bailin, Roxanne, et al. Colorado Evidentiary Foundations. LC 97-66272. 413p. 1997. text 75.00 (*1-55834-460-8*, 80329-10, MICHIE) LEXIS Pub.

Bailin, Sharon. Achieving Extraordinary Ends: An Essay on Creativity. Runco, Mark A., ed. (Creativity Research Ser.: Vol. 7). 152p. (C). 1994. pap. 39.50 (*0-89391-780-X*) Ablx Pub.

Bailin, Sharon, ed. Achieving Extraordinary Ends: An Essay of Creativity. (C). 1988. text 107.50 (*90-247-3674-9*) Kluwer Academic.

Bailin, Sharon, jt. ed. see Portelli, John P.

***Bailin, Sidney C.** Libra: Learning & Inquiry-Based Reuse Adoption. LC 00-33487. 2000. write for info. (*0-7803-6009-5*) IEEE Standards.

Bailis, Lawrence N. Community Based Organizations & Vocational Education: The Path to Partnership. 50p. 1987. 6.00 (*0-318-23411-4*, IN319) Ctr Educ Trng Employ.

Bailis, Tammy. Sinostrology: A Guide to the Zoo. 87p. 1998. pap. 14.00 (*0-86690-477-8*, B3693-014) Am Fed Astrologers.

Bailkey, Nels M. Readings in Ancient History. 5th ed. LC 95-78712. 527p. (C). 2000. pap. text 27.16 (*0-669-39766-0*) HM Trade Div.

— Readings in Ancient History: Thought & Experience from Gilgamesh to St. Augustine. 4th ed. 507p. (C). pap. text 27.16 (*0-669-27744-4*) HM Trade Div.

***Bailkin, Jordanna.** Liberal Arts. 1999. pap. text 18.00 (*0-226-03551-4*); lib. bdg. 50.00 (*0-226-03550-6*) U Ch Pr.

Bailkin, Kenneth J., Jr., et al. Expansion Opportunities for Foreign Companies Doing Business in the United States. write for info. (*0-318-60804-9*) Harcourt.

***Baillargeon, Denyse.** Making Do: Women, Family & Home in Montreal During the Great Depression. Klein, Yvonne, tr. 200p. 1999. pap. 29.95 (*0-88920-326-1*) W Laurier U Pr.

***Baillargeon, Morgan & Tepper, Leslie.** Legends of Our Times: Native Cowboy Life. LC 98-3001. (Illus.). 265p. 2000. pap. 24.95 (*0-295-97729-9*) U of Wash Pr.

Baillargeon, Morgan, jt. auth. see Tepper, Leslie H.

Baillaud, Catherine. Salt Dough Models. (Crafty Hands Collection). (Illus.). 48p. 1995. pap. 9.99 (*1-85410-328-8*, Pub. by Aurum Pr) London Brdge.

Baille, Susanne, et al. Bolton. (Illus.). 96p. pap. text 10.00 (*1-55046-036-6*, Pub. by Boston Mills) Genl Dist Srvs.

Baillet, Adrien. Jugemens des Savans sur les Principaux Ouvrages des Auteurs, 8 vols. in 4, Set. cxii, 2863p. 1971. reprint ed. 680.00 (*3-487-04089-1*) G Olms Pubs.

— La Vie de Monsieur Descartes, 2 vols., Set. xlii, 1019p. 1972. reprint ed. 240.00 (*3-487-04279-7*) G Olms Pubs.

Baillet, M., et al, eds. Les "Petites Grottes" de Qumran: Planches, Vol. III. (Discoveries in the Judaean Desert Ser.: No. III). (Illus.). 80p. 1997. text 68.00 (*0-19-826947-1*) OUP.

Baillet, Maurice, ed. Qumran Grotte Four, No. III. (Discoveries in the Judaean Desert Ser.: Vol. 7). (Illus.). 320p. 1982. text 195.00 (*0-19-826321-X*) OUP.

Bailleul, Charles. Petit Dictionnaire Bambara-Francais, Francais-Bambara. (BAM & FRE.). 340p. 1994. pap. 105.00 (*0-7859-8594-8*, 086127220x) Fr & Eur.

Bailleux, Nathalie. The Book of Chocolate. (Illus.). 216p. 1996. 50.00 (*2-08-013588-0*, Pub. by Flammarion) Abbeville Pr.

Baillie, jt. auth. see Garrett.

Baillie, Alexander F. Kurrachee: Past, Present & Future. 2nd ed. (Oxford in Asia Historical Reprints Ser.). (Illus.). 320p. (C). 1998. 45.00 (*0-19-577586-4*) OUP.

Baillie, Alistar, jt. ed. see Jain, Ravi E.

Baillie, Allan. Adrift. 1994. 9.09 (*0-606-06161-4*, Pub. by Turtleback) Demco.

— Bad Boys. 96p. (J). (gr. 4-7). 1994. pap. 2.95 (*0-590-48258-0*) Scholastic Inc.

— Bad Boys. 1993. 8.05 (*0-606-06220-3*, Pub. by Turtleback) Demco.

Baillie, Allan. Little Brother. LC 91-28797. 1994. 9.09 (*0-606-06535-0*, Pub. by Turtleback) Demco.

Baillie, Donald M. A Diary of Private Prayer. 136p. 1949. 16.50 (*0-684-30997-1*, Scribners Ref) Mac Lib Ref.

Baillie, G. H. Watches, Their History Decoration & Mechanism. (Illus.). 379p. 1979. 75.00 (*0-7198-0140-0*, Pub. by NAG Press) Antique Collect.

Baillie, George. Correspondence of George Baillie of Jerviswood. Earl Of Minto, ed. LC 76-161744. (Bannatyne Club, Edinburgh. Publications: No. 72). reprint ed. 67.50 (*0-404-52792-2*) AMS Pr.

Baillie-Grohman, F., ed. see Edward of Norwich, Duke.

Baillie-Grohman, William A. Sport in Art. LC 69-18532. (Illus.). 445p. 1978. 49.95 (*0-405-08228-2*, Pub. by Blom Pubns) Ayer.

Baillie-Grohman, William A., ed. see Edward of Norwich, Duke.

Baillie, Harold W, jt. auth. see Garrett, Thomas M.

Baillie, Hugh. High Tension. LC 79-90604. (Essay Index Reprint Ser.). 1977. 29.95 (*0-8369-1543-7*) Ayer.

Baillie, I. C., et al. Revised Classification of the Soils of Belize. 71p. 1993. pap. 30.00 (*0-85954-344-7*, Pub. by Nat Res Inst) St Mut.

Baillie, J. B., tr. see Hegel, Georg Wilhelm Friedrich.

Baillie, James. Contemporary Analytic Philosophy. LC 96-8981. 436p. (C). 1996. pap. text 48.00 (*0-13-520974-9*) P-H.

— Problems in Personal Identity. 176p. 1992. pap. 16.95 (*1-55778-521-X*) Paragon Hse.

***Baillie, James.** Routledge Philosophy Guidebook to Hume on Morality. LC 99-59823. (Philosophy Guidebooks Ser.). 240p. 2000. pap. 14.95 (*0-415-18049-X*) Routledge.

— Routledge Philosophy Guidebook to Hume on Morality. LC 99-59823. (Philosophy Guidebooks Ser.). 240p. 2000. 60.00 (*0-415-18048-1*) Routledge.

Baillie, Joan P., anno. Look at the Record: An Album of Toronto's Lyric Theatres, 1825-1984. (Illus.). 300p. 1995. 39.95 (*0-88962-326-0*) Mosaic.

Baillie, Joanna. The Collected Letters of Joanna Baillie, Vol. 1. Bailey \Slagle, Judith, ed. LC 98-36605. 560p. 1999. 52.50 (*0-8386-3812-0*) Fairleigh Dickinson.

***Baillie, Joanna.** The Collected Letters of Joanna Baillie, Vol. 2. Slagle, Judith B., ed. LC 98-36605. 744p. 1999. 65.00 (*0-8386-3816-3*) Fairleigh Dickinson.

Baillie, Joanna. The Dramatic & Poetical Works Complete in One Volume. 846p. reprint ed. lib. bdg. 160.00 (*3-487-06119-8*) G Olms Pubs.

Baillie, Joanna, et al. Joanna Baillie: A Selection of Poems & Plays. Gilroy, Amanda & Hanley, Keith, eds. LC 97-27597. (Pickering Woman's Classics Ser.). 400p. Date not set. 55.00 (*1-85196-358-8*, Pub. by Pickering & Chatto) Ashgate Pub Co.

Baillie, John. A Diary of Private Prayer. 135p. 1979. pap. 7.00 (*0-684-16323-3*, Scribners Ref) Mac Lib Ref.

— A Diary of Private Prayer. 144p. 1996. per. 7.00 (*0-684-82498-1*) S&S Trade.

— A Diary of Private Prayer. large type ed. (Large Print Inspirational Ser.). 144p. 1986. pap. 8.95 (*0-8027-2519-8*) Walker & Co.

Baillie, John. Employment Attitudes in Britain. (Issues Ser.: No. 14). 70p. 1996. pap. 60.00 (*0-85292-667-7*, Pub. by IPM Hse) St Mut.

Baillie, John. God Was in Christ. 240p. 1980. 55.00 (*0-684-16470-1*, PG104HRE, Scribners Ref) Mac Lib Ref.

— Intermediate Gastrointestinal Endoscopy. LC 96-50473. (Illus.). 158p. 1997. text 66.00 (*0-7506-9555-2*) Buttrwrth-Heinemann.

Baillie, Jonathan & Groombridge, Brian, contrib. by. 1996 IUCN List of Threatened Animals. 368p. 1996. pap. text 40.00 (*2-8317-0335-2*, Pub. by IUCN) Island Pr.

Baillie, Kenneth, jt. auth. see Cotner, Robert.

Baillie, Laureen, compiled by. British Biographical Index, 4 vols. 2045p. 1991. lib. bdg. 1140.00 (*0-86291-390-X*) U Pubns Amer.

Baillie, Laureen, ed. The Catalogue of Printed Music in the British Library to 1980, 62 vols. (Illus.). 1987. text 9785.00 (*3-598-31400-0*) K G Saur Verlag.

Baillie, Laureen & K. G. Saur Verlag Staff. Indian Biographical Archive, 7 vols. LC 97-227537. 1997. write for info. (*3-598-34110-5*) K G Saur Verlag.

Baillie, M. G. Tree-Ring Dating & Archaeology. LC 81-16079. (Illus.). (C). 1982. 33.95 (*0-226-03630-8*) U Ch Pr.

— Tree-Ring Dating & Archaeology. LC 81-16079. (Illus.). (C). 1994. pap. text 14.95 (*0-226-03631-6*) U Ch Pr.

— Tree-Ring Dating & Archaeology. LC 81-16079. (Illus.). 272p. reprint ed. pap. 84.40 (*0-608-08831-5*, 206947000004) Bks Demand.

Baillie, Marilyn. Little Wonders: Animal Babies & Their Families. (Amazing Things Animals Do Ser.). (Illus.). 32p. (YA). (ps up). 1995. 14.95 (*1-895688-37-X*, Pub. by Owl Bks) Firefly Bks Ltd.

— Little Wonders: Animal Babies & Their Families. (Amazing Things Animals Do Ser.). (Illus.). 32p. (YA). (ps up). 1996. pap. 5.95 (*1-895688-31-0*, Pub. by Owl Bks) Firefly Bks Ltd.

— Little Wonders: Animal Babies & Their Families. 1995. 11.15 (*0-606-09567-5*, Pub. by Turtleback) Demco.

— My Cat.Tr. of Mon Chat. (Illus.). 32p. (J). 1993. 12.95 (*1-55074-125-X*, Pub. by Kids Can Pr); pap. 5.95 (*1-55074-206-X*, Pub. by Kids Can Pr) Genl Dist Srvs.

B

— My Dog. unabridged ed.Tr. of Mon Chien. (Illus.). 32p. (J). (gr. 2-6). 1993. 12.95 (*1-55074-127-6*, Pub. by Kids Can Pr); pap. 5.95 (*1-55074-208-6*, Pub. by Kids Can Pr) Genl Dist Srvs.

— Side by Side: Animals Who Help Each Other, Vol. 4. (Amazing Things Animals Do Ser.). (Illus.). 32p. (YA). (gr. k up). 1997. 17.95 (*1-895688-56-6*, Pub. by Owl Bks); pap. 6.95 (*1-895688-57-4*, Pub. by Owl Bks) Firefly Bks Ltd.

— Time to Eat: Animals Who Hide & Save Their Food. (Amazing Things Animals Do Ser.). (Illus.). 32p. (YA). (gr. k up). 1995. 14.95 (*1-895688-36-1*, Pub. by Owl Bks) Firefly Bks Ltd.

— Time to Eat: Animals Who Hide & Save Their Food. (Amazing Things Animals Do Ser.). (Illus.). 32p. (YA). (ps up). 1996. pap. 5.95 (*1-895688-30-2*, Pub. by Owl Bks) Firefly Bks Ltd.

— Time to Eat: Animals Who Hide & Save Their Food. 1995. 11.15 (*0-606-09974-3*, Pub. by Turtleback) Demco.

— Wild Talk: How Animals Talk to Each Other. (Illus.). 32p. (YA). (ps-3). 1996. 17.95 (*1-895688-54-X*, Pub. by Owl Bks); pap. 6.95 (*1-895688-55-8*, Pub. by Owl Bks) Firefly Bks Ltd.

Baillie, Martha. My Sister, Esther. 118p. 1997. pap. 14.95 (*0-88801-200-4*, Pub. by Turnstone Pr) Genl Dist Srvs.

Baillie, Mike. Exodus to Arthur: Catastrophic Encounters with Comets. (Illus.). 256p. 1998. 19.95 (*0-7134-8352-0*, Pub. by B T B) Branford.

Baillie, Robert. Letters & Journals, 3 vols. Laing, David, ed. LC 70-161745. (Bannatyne Club, Edinburgh. Publications: No. 73). reprint ed. 295.00 (*0-404-52800-7*) AMS Pr.

Baillie, Virginia & Trygstad, Louise. Effective Nursing Leadership: A Practical Guide. Cordoni, Tatiana I., ed. 348p. (C). 1989. 55.00 (*0-8342-0036-8*, 20036) Aspen Pub.

Baillie, William M., ed. A Choice Ternary of English Plays: Gratiae Theatrales, 1662. LC 83-1915. (Medieval & Renaissance Texts & Studies: Vol. 26). 320p. 1984. 24.00 (*0-86698-054-7*, MR26) MRTS.

Baillieres. Comprehensive Vet Dictionary. 1990. pap. text 40.95 (*0-7020-1395-1*, W B Saunders Co) Harcrt Hlth Sci Grp.

Baillieul, J., et al, eds. Essays on Mathematical Robotics. LC 98-34427. (IMA Volumes in Mathematics & Its Applications Ser.: Vol. 104). (Illus.). 391p. 1998. 69.95 (*0-387-98596-4*) Spr-Verlag.

Baillieul, John B. & Willems, J. C., eds. Essays in Mathematical Control Theory. LC 98-24740. (Illus.). 385p. 1998. 59.95 (*0-387-98317-1*) Spr-Verlag.

Baillif, Michael E. Unified Audit & Litigation Procedures for Pass-Through Entities. LC 96-61612. 1997. 130.00 (*0-7913-2965-8*) Warren Gorham & Lamont.

Baillon, J. B., jt. ed. see Thera, Michel A.

Baillot, Pierre. The Art of the Violin. Goldberg, Louise, tr. from FRE. 540p. 1991. pap. 35.00 (*0-8101-0754-6*) Northwestern U Pr.

Baillou, Jean, jt. auth. see Ronsard, Pierre De.

Bailly, Anatole. Dictionnaire Abrege Grec-Francais.Tr. of Greek - French Dictionary. (FRE & GRE.). 1012p. 1969. pap. 65.00 (*0-8288-6584-1*, M6019) Fr & Eur.

— Dictionnaire Grec-Francais.Tr. of Greek-French Dictionary. (FRE & GRE.). 2230p. 1967. pap. 125.00 (*0-8288-6680-5*, M6020) Fr & Eur.

Bailly, Antione, jt. ed. see Lever, William.

Bailly, Constantina R. Meditations on Shiva: The Shivastotravali of Utpaladeva. 133p. (C). 1995. pap. text 9.95 (*0-7914-2530-4*) State U NY Pr.

— Shaiva Devotional Songs of Kashmir: A Translation & Study of Utpaladeva's Shivastotravali. LC 87-6488. (SUNY Series in the Shaiva Traditions of Kashmir). 196p. (C). 1987. text 44.50 (*0-88706-492-2*); pap. text 14.95 (*0-88706-493-0*) State U NY Pr.

Bailly, G., et al. Talking Machines. xii524p. 1992. 263.00 (*0-444-89115-3*, North Holland) Elsevier.

***Bailly, H. C., et al, eds.** The Nuclear Fuel of Pressurized Water Reactors & Fast Reactors. (Illus.). 660p. 1999. 253.00 (*1-898298-57-2*, Pub. by Intercept UK) Spr-Verlag.

Bailly, H. C. & De Borms, C. T. Materials Flows in the Post-Consumer Waste Stream of the 1980s. 96p. 1977. pap. text 73.00 (*0-86010-080-4*) G & T Inc.

Bailly-Herzberg, Janine. Dictionnaire de l'Estampe en France 1830-1950. (FRE.). 384p. 1985. 195.00 (*0-7859-7717-1*, 2080120131) Fr & Eur.

Bailly, Jean C., jt. auth. see Tanning, Dorothea.

***Bailly, Jenny.** Mastering Direct Access Fundamentals: Understanding Market Information & Learning the Key Skills. (Direct Access Trader Ser.). 2001. 24.95 (*0-07-136249-5*) McGraw.

Bailly, Robert. Dictionnaire des Communes, Vaucluse. (FRE.). 476p. (J). 1986. 95.00 (*0-7859-8211-6*, 2903044279) Fr & Eur.

Bailly, Sharon. Pass It On! All about Notes from Secret Codes & Special Inks to Fancy Folds & Dead Man's Drops. LC 94-46949. (Illus.). 64p. (J). (gr. 4-6). 1995. lib. bdg. 23.40 (*1-56294-588-2*) Millbrook Pr.

Bailon, Jean-Paul, jt. ed. see Bathias, Claude.

Bailon, Pascal, et al, eds. Affinity Chromatography: Methods & Protocols. (Methods in Molecular Biology Ser.: Vol. 147). 240p. 2000. 79.50 (*0-89603-694-4*) Humana.

Bailowitz, Richard A. & Brock, James P. The Butterflies of Southeastern Arizona. (Illus.). 1997. pap. text 29.95 (*0-9626629-0-9*) Sonoran Arthropod.

Bailowitz, Richard A. & Danforth, Doug. 70 Common Butterflies of the Southwest. LC 97-42153. 1997. pap. 7.95 (*1-877856-84-3*) SW Pks Mnmts.

Bails, Benito. Diccionario de Arquitectura Civil. (SPA.). 152p. 1991. 55.00 (*0-7859-6050-3*, 8460605302) Fr & Eur.

Bails, Dale G. & Peppers, Larry C. Business Fluctuations: Forecasting Techniques & Applications. 2nd ed. LC 92-22926. 656p. (C). 1992. text 68.20 (*0-13-093394-5*) Prntice Hall Bks.

Bails, Roberta C. The Path of the Wise Woman: A Tale of the Spiritual & Mythic Dimensions of Menopause. 75p. 1994. pap. write for info. (*0-9644354-0-3*) Mid-Life Hse.

Bailur, Jayanti. Ruth Prawer Jhabvala: Fiction & Film. (C). 1992. text 12.00 (*0-685-63535-X*, Pub. by Arnold Pubs) S Asia.

Baily & Van Dorn. Massachusetts Practice Series - Taxation, 4 vols. 1986. 147.50 (*0-317-52107-1*) West Pub.

Baily, Albert E. The Arts & Religion. (Illus.). 180p. 1977. 27.95 (*0-8369-2889-X*) Ayer.

Baily, Auguste. Maeterlinck. LC 74-6385. (Studies in French Literature: No. 45). 1974. lib. bdg. 75.00 (*0-8383-1877-0*) M S G Haskell Hse.

Baily, B. & Farmer, D., eds. Purchasing Principles & Management. 324p. (Orig.). (C). 1990. 165.00 (*0-7855-5758-X*, Pub. by Inst Pur & Supply) St Mut.

Baily, Collins A. Evidence of Our Nation Heritage. 260p. 1998. pap. 9.95 (*0-9627989-1-6*) Grapevine ID.

Baily, Francis. The Doctrine of Interest & Annuities: Analytically Investigated & Explained; Together with Several Useful Tables Connected with the Subject. Brief, Richard P., ed. LC 80-1470. (Dimensions of Accounting Theory & Practice Ser.). 1980. reprint ed. lib. bdg. 19.95 (*0-405-13500-9*) Ayer.

Baily-Friedman. Macroeconomics Finance Market Readings Pr. 2nd ed. 1994. 22.00 (*0-256-13746-3*, Irwn McGrw-H) McGrw-H Hghr Educ.

Baily, Gwen L., jt. auth. see Bailey, Gerald D.

Baily, Jane B. Dottie, the Unfoolish Mule. LC 90-93258. (Illus.). 32p. (Orig.). (J). (gr. k-3). 1990. pap. 6.95 (*0-9626642-1-9*) J B Baily.

Baily, John. Walt Whitman. 1988. reprint ed. lib. bdg. 59.00 (*0-7812-0051-2*) Rprt Serv.

***Baily, Joseph.** Los Horoscopos y To Futuro. (SPA.). 1999. mass mkt. 4.99 (*0-7899-0789-5*) Spanish Hse Distributors.

Baily, Martin N., ed. Workers, Jobs, & Inflation. LC 82-70891. 365p. 1982. 39.95 (*0-8157-0764-9*); pap. 18.95 (*0-8157-0763-0*) Brookings.

Baily, Martin N. & Chakrabarti, Alok K. Innovation & the Productivity Crisis. LC 88-1697. 133p. 1988. 28.95 (*0-8157-0760-6*); pap. 10.95 (*0-8157-0759-2*) Brookings.

Baily, Martin N. & Friedman, Philip. Macroeconomics, Financial Markets & the International Sector. 2nd ed. LC 94-27884. (Economics Ser.). 608p. (C). 1995. text 69.75 (*0-256-12552-X*, Irwn McGrw-H) McGrw-H Hghr Educ.

— Macroeconomics Financial Markets & the International Sector: International Version. (C). 1992. text, student ed. 32.50 (*0-256-11401-3*, Irwn McGrw-H) McGrw-H Hghr Educ.

Baily, Martin N., et al. Growth with Equity: Economic Policymaking for the Next Century. 239p. (C). 1993. 38.95 (*0-8157-0766-5*) Brookings.

Baily, Mary A. & Cikins, Warren I., eds. The Effects of Litigation on Health Care Costs. LC 85-70875. (Dialogues on Public Policy Ser.). 85p. 1985. pap. 10.95 (*0-8157-0757-6*) Brookings.

Baily, P. J. Purchasing & Supply Management. 296p. (C). 1989. 150.00 (*0-7855-6111-0*, Pub. by Inst Pur & Supply) St Mut.

— Purchasing & Supply Management. 5th ed. 304p. 1987. mass mkt. 34.95 (*0-412-28940-7*) Chapman & Hall.

Baily, Peter. Purchasing Systems & Records. 3rd ed. 150p. 1991. text 49.95 (*0-566-09061-9*, Pub. by Gower) Ashgate Pub Co.

Baily, Peter & Farmer, David. Materials Management Handbook. 300p. (C). 1988. 220.00 (*0-7855-3765-1*, Pub. by Inst Pur & Supply) St Mut.

— Materials Management Handbook. 300p. (C). 1989. 450.00 (*0-7855-4616-2*, Pub. by Inst Pur & Supply) St Mut.

Baily, Peter, et al. Purchasing Principles & Management. 8th ed. LC 99-220508. 352p. 2000. pap. write for info. (*0-273-62381-8*) F T P H.

Baily, Samuel L. Immigrants in the Promised Lands: Italians in Buenos Aires & New York City, 1870-1914. LC 98-12399. (Studies in Comparative History). (Illus.). 336p. 1999. 45.00 (*0-8014-3562-5*) Cornell U Pr.

Baily, Samuel L. & Ramella, Franco, eds. One Family, Two Worlds: An Italian Family's Correspondence Across the Atlantic, 1901-1922. Lenaghan, John, tr. (Illus.). 224p. (C). 1988. text 45.00 (*0-8135-1331-6*); pap. text 16.00 (*0-8135-1354-5*) Rutgers U Pr.

Baily, Samuel L., ed. see Scobie, James R.

Baily, Thelma F. & Baily, Walter H. Child Welfare Practice. LC 82-49034. (Jossey-Bass Social & Behavioral Science Ser.). 263p. reprint ed. pap. 81.60 (*0-8357-4804-9*, 203774100009) Bks Demand.

Baily, Walter H., jt. auth. see Baily, Thelma F.

Baily, Walter L. Introductory Lectures on Automorphic Forms. LC 72-4034. (Publications of the Mathematical Society of Japan: Vol. 12, No. 2). 278p. 1973. reprint ed. pap. 86.20 (*0-608-06622-2*, 206681900009) Bks Demand.

Bailyn, Bernard. Education in the Forming of American Society: Needs & Opportunities for Study. LC 60-51488. 159p. reprint ed. pap. 49.30 (*0-7837-0280-9*, 204060100018) Bks Demand.

— Faces of Revolution: Personalities & Themes in the Struggle for American Independence. LC 92-50101. 1992. pap. 16.00 (*0-679-73623-9*) Vin Bks.

— Ideological Origins of the American Revolution. 25th enl. ed. 352p. (C). 1992. pap. 17.50 (*0-674-44302-0*) HUP.

— The New England Merchants in the 17th Century. 257p. 1979. pap. 14.95 (*0-674-61280-9*) HUP.

— The Ordeal of Thomas Hutchinson. LC 73-76379. 458p. 1976. pap. 17.95 (*0-674-64161-2*) Belknap Pr.

— The Origins of American Politics. LC 68-12665. 1970. pap. 5.56 (*0-394-70865-2*, V604) Vin Bks.

— The Peopling of British North America: An Introduction. LC 87-45916. 192p. 1988. pap. 10.00 (*0-394-75779-3*) Vin Bks.

— Voyagers to the West: A Passage in the Peopling of America on the Eve of the Revolution. LC 87-45917. 736p. 1988. reprint ed. pap. 25.00 (*0-394-75778-5*) Vin Bks.

Bailyn, Bernard, ed. The Debate on the Constitution Pt. 1: September 1787-February 1788. LC 92-25449. 1214p. 1993. 35.00 (*0-940450-42-9*, Pub. by Library of America) Penguin Putnam.

— The Debate on the Constitution Pt. 2: January-August, 1788. LC 92-25449. 1175p. 1993. 35.00 (*0-940450-64-X*, Pub. by Library of America) Penguin Putnam.

Bailyn, Bernard & Morgan, Philip D., eds. Strangers Within the Realm: Cultural Margins of the First British Empire. LC 90-40278. xii, 456p. (C). 1991. 59.95 (*0-8078-1952-2*); pap. 19.95 (*0-8078-4311-3*) U of NC Pr.

Bailyn, Bernard, et al. Glimpses of the Harvard Past. LC 85-14131. (Illus.). 162p. 1990. text 27.00 (*0-674-35443-5*) HUP.

— The Great Republic: A History of the American People, 2 vols. 3rd ed. LC 84-81193. (Illus.). 869p. (C). 1985. teacher ed. 2.66 (*0-669-07549-3*); student ed. 25.16 (*0-669-07548-5*) HM Trade Div.

— The Great Republic: A History of the American People, 2 vols. 4th ed. (C). 1992. pap. text, student ed. 16.76 (*0-669-20988-0*); teacher ed. 2.66 (*0-669-20989-9*) HM Trade Div.

— The Great Republic: A History of the American People, 2 vols., II. 3rd ed. LC 84-81193. (Illus.). 869p. (C). 1985. pap. text 48.76 (*0-669-07547-7*) HM Trade Div.

— The Great Republic: A History of the American People, 2 vols., Set. 3rd ed. LC 84-81193. (Illus.). 869p. (C). 1985. text 65.16 (*0-669-07545-0*) HM Trade Div.

— The Great Republic: A History of the American People, 2 vols., Vol. I. 4th ed. 723p. (C). 1992. pap. text 27.16 (*0-669-20986-4*) HM Trade Div.

— The Great Republic: A History of the American People, 2 vols., Vol. II. 4th ed. 656p. (C). 1992. pap. text 27.16 (*0-669-20987-2*) HM Trade Div.

Bailyn, Bernard, jt. ed. see Fleming, Donald H.

Bailyn, Lotte. Breaking the Mold: Women, Men, & Time in the New Corporate World. 275p. 1993. 24.95 (*0-02-901281-3*) Free Pr.

Bailyn, Lotte, jt. auth. see Rapoport, Rhona.

Bailyn, Martin. A Survey of Thermodynamics. LC 93-28712. 480p. 1994. text 79.95 (*0-88318-797-3*, AIP Pr) Spr-Verlag.

Baim, Dean V. The Sports Stadium As a Municipal Investment. 151. LC 93-21501. (Contributions in Economics & Economic History Ser.). 264p. 1994. 59.95 (*0-313-27816-4*, Greenwood Pr) Greenwood.

Baim, Donald S. & Grossman, William. Cardiac Catheterization, Angiography & Intervention. 5th ed. (Illus.). 786p. 1996. 85.00 (*0-683-00318-6*) Lppncott W & W.

Baim, Donald S. & Grossman, William. Grossman's Cardiac Catheterization, Angiography, & Intervention. 6th ed. 880p. text 99.00 (*0-683-30741-X*) Lppncott W & W.

Baim, Donald S., jt. auth. see Grossman, William.

***Baiman, Ron P., et al.** Political Economy & Contemporary Capitalism: Radical Perspectives on Economic Theory & Policy. LC 99-47226. (Illus.). 368p. 2000. text 69.95 (*0-7656-0529-5*) M E Sharpe.

Baimbridge, Mark, et al, eds. The Impact of the Euro: Debating Britain's Future. LC 99-15590. 241p. 2000. text 69.95 (*0-312-22573-3*) St Martin.

Bain & Engelhardt. An Introduction to Probability & Mathematical Statistics. (C). 1987. pap. 44.75 (*0-87150-067-1*, 36G0160) PWS Pubs.

Bain & Howells. Government & Economy. 1987. pap. text. write for info. (*0-582-29670-6*, Pub. by Addison-Wesley) Longman.

Bain, et al. Bank Strategies for the Nineteen Nineties. 1986. 75.00 (*0-85297-162-1*, Pub. by Chartered Bank) St Mut.

Bain, jt. auth. see Howells.

Bain, A. D. The Economics of the Financial System. 2nd ed. 320p. 1992. pap. text 33.95 (*0-631-18197-0*) Blackwell Pubs.

Bain, A. G. & Bonnington, S. T. Hydraulic Transport of Solids by Pipelines. 1970. 114.00 (*0-08-015778-5*, Pub. by Pergamon Repr) Franklin.

Bain, Alexander. The Emotions & the Will. 681p. 145.00 (*1-85506-656-4*) Thoemmes Pr.

Bain, Alexander. Emotions & the Will, 5. LC 77-72191. (Contributions to the History of Psychology Ser.: No. 5, Pt. A, Orientations). 638p. 1977. reprint ed. lib. bdg. 95.00 (*0-313-26929-7*, U6929, Greenwood Pr) Greenwood.

— English Composition & Rhetoric. fac. ed. LC 96-3518. (American Linguistics, 1700-1900 Ser.: No. 497). 372p. 1996. reprint ed. 50.00 (*0-8201-1497-9*) Schol Facsimiles.

— James Mill: A Biography. LC 66-19689. xxxii, 466p. 1967. reprint ed. 49.50 (*0-678-00214-2*) Kelley.

— John Stuart Mill: A Criticism with Personal Recollections (1882 Edition) (Key Texts Ser.). 216p. 1996. reprint ed. pap. 24.95 (*1-85506-213-5*) Bks Intl VA.

— Mental Science: A Compendium of Psychology & the History of Philosophy. LC 73-2958. (Classics in Psychology Ser.). 1977. reprint ed. 34.95 (*0-405-05132-8*) Ayer.

— Practical Essays. LC 72-4533. (Essay Index Reprint Ser.). 1977. reprint ed. 21.95 (*0-8369-2935-7*) Ayer.

Bain, Alexander. Senses & the Intellect. 650p. 145.00 (*1-85506-654-8*) Thoemmes Pr.

Bain, Alexander. Senses & the Intellect, 4. LC 77-72191. (Contributions to the History of Psychology Ser.: No. 4, Pt. A, Orientations). 605p. 1977. reprint ed. lib. bdg. 95.00 (*0-313-26928-9*, U6928, Greenwood Pr) Greenwood.

Bain, Alexander, ed. see Grote, George.

***Bain, Aly.** 50 Fiddle Solos. 2000. pap. write for info. (*0-7119-7077-7*) Music Sales.

— Fifty Fiddle Solos. 48p. 1989. pap. 15.95 incl. audio (*0-7119-2130-X*, AM 75128) Music Sales.

Bain, Ann M., ed. see Bailet, Laura L. & Moats, Louisa C.

Bain, B. J. Self-Assessment for the MRCP: Haematology. 200p. 1997. pap. text 28.00 (*1-86094-068-4*) World Scientific Pub.

Bain, Barbara. Blood Cells: A Practical Guide. 2nd ed. (Illus.). 368p. 1995. 95.00 (*0-86542-913-8*) Blackwell Sci.

Bain, Barbara J. Beginner's Guide to Blood Cells. LC 95-53136. (Illus.). 120p. (Orig.). 1996. pap. text 34.95 (*0-86542-717-8*) Blackwell Sci.

— Blood Cells: A Practical Guide. 2nd ed. (Illus.). 326p. 1996. pap. text 54.95 (*0-632-04155-2*) Blackwell Sci.

***Bain, Barbara J.** Haemoglobinopathy Diagnosis. LC 00-34309. (Illus.). 240p. 2000. 99.00 (*0-632-05577-4*) Blackwell Sci.

Bain, Barbara J. Leukaemia Diagnosis. 2nd ed. LC 98-28846. (Illus.). 1999. 99.95 (*0-632-05165-5*) Blackwell Sci.

— Picture Tests in Haematology. LC 98-10014. (Colour Guide Ser.). 1999. pap. text 19.95 (*0-443-05943-8*) Church.

Bain, Barbara J., et al. Bone Marrow Pathology. 2nd ed. 280p. 1996. text 195.00 (*0-86542-647-3*) Blackwell Sci.

Bain, Barbara J., tr. see D'Onofrio, Giuseppe & Zini, Gina.

Bain, Beverly K. & Leger, Dawn. Assistive Technology: An Interdisciplinary Approach. LC 97-8215. 1997. pap. text 44.95 (*0-443-07552-2*) Church.

Bain, Bill, ed. see Drummond, John.

Bain, Bill, jt. ed. see Drummond, John.

Bain, Bruce, ed. The Sociogenesis of Language & Human Conduct. 580p. 1983. 110.00 (*0-306-41041-9*, Plenum Trade) Perseus Pubng.

Bain, Carl E., ed. The Norton Introduction to Literature: Drama. 600p. (C). 1973. pap. text 41.75 (*0-393-09366-2*) Norton.

Bain, Carl E., et al, eds. Writing Themes about Literature: A Guide to Accompany the Norton Introduction to Literature. 3rd ed. (C). 1983. pap. text 21.75 (*0-393-95350-5*) Norton.

Bain, Caroline D. The Abenakee Club of Biddeford Pool, Maine: A Centennial History. LC 98-6912. 1998. pap. 25.00 (*1-880158-19-1*) J N Townsend.

Bain, D., jt. ed. see Neu, H.

Bain, D. M. Menander: Samia. (Classical Texts Ser.). 1983. 59.99 (*0-85668-224-1*, Pub. by Aris & Phillips); pap. 22.00 (*0-85668-225-X*, Pub. by Aris & Phillips) David Brown.

— Menander, SAMIA. (BC-AP Classical Ser.). (GER.). 200p. 1985. 49.00 (*0-86516-113-5*) Bolchazy-Carducci.

Bain, David. Actors & Audience: A Study of Asides & Related Conventions in Greek Drama. 240p. 1987. pap. 21.00 (*0-19-814724-4*) OUP.

Bain, David H. Empire Express: Building the First Transcontinental Railroad. LC 99-33375. (Illus.). 720p. 1999. 34.95 (*0-670-80889-X*, Viking) Viking Penguin.

Bain, David H. & Plum, Sydney L., eds. At an Elevation: On the Poetry of Robert Pack. LC 94-78295. 205p. (Orig.). 1994. pap. 13.95 (*0-910408-10-6*) Coll Store.

Bain, David Haward. Empire Express: Building the First Transcontinental Railroad. (Illus.). 816p. 2000. pap. 18.00 (*0-14-008499-1*, Viking) Viking Penguin.

Bain, David R., jt. auth. see Giles, Geoff A.

Bain, Donald. Brandy & Bullets: Murder, She Wrote. large type ed. LC 99-18822. 304p. 1999. 20.95 (*0-7838-8596-2*) Mac Lib Ref.

***Bain, Donald.** A Little Yuletide Murder: A Murder, She Wrote, Mystery. large type ed. LC 00-39521. 2000. write for info. (*0-7838-9101-6*, G K Hall & Co) Mac Lib Ref.

Bain, Donald. Manhattans & Murder. large type ed. LC 98-14731. 267p. 1998. 19.95 (*0-7838-0133-5*, G K Hall & Co) Mac Lib Ref.

***Bain, Donald.** Murder, She Wrote: Martinis & Mayhem. large type ed. LC 99-15669. 1999. pap. 20.95 (*0-7838-8665-9*, G K Hall Lrg Type) Mac Lib Ref.

***Bain, Donald & Fletcher, Jessica.** Murder at the Powderhorn Ranch: A Murder, She Wrote Mystery. large type ed. LC 99-56673. (Nightingale Ser.). 256p. 2000. pap. 21.95 (*0-7838-8926-7*) Mac Lib Ref.

Bain, Donald, jt. auth. see Fletcher, Jessica.

Bain, Edgar C. Pioneering in Steel Research: A Personal Record. LC 74-31126. (Illus.). 297p. reprint ed. pap. 92.10 (*0-8357-6263-7*, 203307400083) Bks Demand.

Bain, Edgar C., jt. auth. see Paxton, Harold W.

Bain, Elsbeth, ed. see Shakespeare, William.

Bain, Foster H. & Read, Thomas T. Ores & Industry in South America. Bruchey, Stuart & Bruchey, Eleanor, eds. LC 76-4767. (American Business Abroad Ser.). (Illus.). 1976. reprint ed. 35.95 (*0-405-09265-2*) Ayer.

Bain, Gabriel H. Auras 101: A Basic Study of Human Auras & the Techniques to See Them. 1998. pap. 6.95 (*1-891824-07-4*) Light Tech Pubng.

— Living Rainbows. 120p. (Orig.). 1993. pap. 14.95 (*0-929385-42-X*) Light Tech Pubng.

Bain, George. Celtic Art, 7 vols. 1997. boxed set 24.95 (*0-948474-07-6*) Celt Heritage Bks.

An Asterisk (*) at the beginning of an entry indicates that the title is appearing for the first time.

— Celtic Art. 168p. 1982. 45.00 (*0-85335-196-1*, Pub. by Stuart Titles Ltd) St Mut.
— Celtic Art: The Methods of Construction. (Illus.). 160p. 1973. reprint ed. pap. 9.95 (*0-486-22923-8*) Dover.
Bain, George S. & Woolven, G. B. A Bibliography of British Industrial Relations. LC 76-53516. 689p. reprint ed. pap. 180.00 (*0-8357-7179-2*, 2030578) Bks Demand.
Bain, Geri. Modern Bride 3 - Honeymoons & Weddings Away: The Complete Guide to Planning Your Most Romantic Trip Ever. LC 95-1298. (Modern Bride Library). 256p. 1995. pap. 16.95 (*0-471-00722-6*) Wiley.
***Bain, Gordon.** Silvered Wings: The Aerial Photography of Gordon Bain. (Illus.). 144p. 1999. 39.95 (*1-84037-024-6*) Voyageur Pr.
Bain, Iain. Celtic Knotwork. LC 91-39091. (Illus.). 136p. 1992. pap. 14.95 (*0-8069-8638-7*) Sterling.
Bain, Irene. Agricultural Reform in Taiwan: From Here to Modernity? 582p. (C). 1993. 47.50 (*962-201-543-3*, Pub. by Chinese Univ) U of Mich Pr.
Bain, J., et al, eds. Andrology: Basic & Clinical Aspects of Male Reproduction & Infertility. (Progress in Reproductive Biology & Medicine Ser.: Vol. 3). (Illus.). 1978. 85.25 (*3-8055-2807-8*) S Karger.
Bain, J. & Hafez, E. S., eds. Diagnosis in Andrology. (Clinics in Andrology Ser.: No. 4). (Illus.). 255p. 1980. text 195.50 (*90-247-2365-5*) Kluwer Academic.
***Bain, James & De Bierre, Julia.** Restoration Recipes: Techniques for Repairing & Refinishing Fine Furniture. LC 99-21074. (Illus.). 176p. 1999. pap. 19.95 (*0-8118-2510-8*) Chronicle Bks.
Bain, James, ed. & illus. see Henry, Alexander.
Bain, James R., jt. auth. see Humphrey, Stephen R.
***Bain, Jerald.** So Your Child Is Gay: A Guide for Canadian Families & Their Friends. (Phyllis Bruce Bks.). 256p. 2000. pap. 15.00 (*0-00-638492-7*) HarpC.
Bain, Joe S. Barriers to New Competition: Their Character & Consequences in Manufacturing Industries. (Reprints of Economic Classics Ser.). (Illus.). x, 329p. 1993. reprint ed. lib. bdg. 45.00 (*0-678-01467-1*) Kelley.
— Economics of the Pacific Coast Petroleum Industry, 3 vols., Set. LC 69-10067. (Illus.). 1969. reprint ed. lib. bdg. 125.00 (*0-8371-0293-6*, BAPP) Greenwood.
— Economics of the Pacific Coast Petroleum Industry, 3 vols., Vol. 1. LC 69-10067. (Illus.). 1969. reprint ed. lib. bdg. 75.00 (*0-313-21503-0*, BAPA) Greenwood.
— Economics of the Pacific Coast Petroleum Industry, 3 vols., Vol. 2. LC 69-10067. (Illus.). 1969. reprint ed. lib. bdg. 75.00 (*0-313-21504-9*, BAPB) Greenwood.
— Economics of the Pacific Coast Petroleum Industry, 3 vols., Vol. 3. LC 69-10067. (Illus.). 1969. reprint ed. lib. bdg. 75.00 (*0-313-21505-7*, BAPC) Greenwood.
— Industrial Organization. 2nd ed. LC 67-29930. (Illus.). 1968. text 21.50 (*0-471-04291-9*) Wiley.
— International Differences in Industrial Structure: Eight Nations in the 1950's, 6. LC 80-14615. (Studies in Comparative Economics: No. 6). (Illus.). 209p. 1980. reprint ed. lib. bdg. 35.00 (*0-313-22408-0*, BAID) Greenwood.
Bain, John, jt. auth. see Hart, Cyril.
Bain, John, jt. ed. see Hart, Cyril.
Bain, John A. Chess Rules for Students. Mitchell, Robert P., ed. (Illus.). 43p. (J). (gr. 2-8). 1994. pap. text 3.50 (*0-9639614-2-X*) Lrning Plus.
— Chess Tactics for Students. Mitchell, Robert P., ed. (Illus.). 228p. (Orig.). (J). (gr. 2-12). 1994. teacher ed. 14.95 (*0-9639614-1-1*); pap. 14.95 (*0-9639614-0-3*) Lrning Plus.
Bain, Joseph, ed. see Beaugue, Jean de.
Bain, Joseph, ed. see Maitland, Richard.
Bain, Joseph H. Casinos - the International Casino Guide Vol. 6: The Complete Guide to the World's Casinos & Casino Resorts. Dror, Eli, ed. (Illus.). 600p. (Orig.). 1997. pap. 27.00 (*0-9618612-9-0*) Bain Dror.
Bain, Joseph H. & Dror, Eli, eds. Spas: The International Spa Guide. 4th ed. (Illus.). 316p. 1998. pap. text 20.00 (*0-7881-5250-5*) DIANE Pub.
Bain, Joseph H., jt. auth. see Angelo, Eli.
Bain, Joseph H., ed. see Dror, Eli.
Bain, Josie G. & Herman, Joan L., eds. Making Schools Work for Underachieving Minority Students: Next Steps for Research, Policy, & Practice, 36. LC 89-48904. (Contributions to the Study of Education Ser.: No. 36). 320p. 1990. 59.95 (*0-313-26889-4*, BMH/) Greenwood.
Bain, K., jt. auth. see Howells, P. G.
Bain, Keith, jt. auth. see Howells, Peter.
Bain, Kenneth R. When the Lessons Are over the Grading Begins. 182p. 1997. pap. 8.95 (*1-884707-66-1*) Lifestyles.
Bain, Lauren. Glamorgan: He Who Would Be Cat. (Illus.). 20p. 1998. pap. 8.95 (*0-9668524-1-9*) Companion Star.
Bain, Lauren S. Glamorgan's Tales: A Cat's Garden of Verse. (Glamorgan Ser.). (Illus.). 20p. 1998. pap. 8.95 (*0-9668524-0-0*) Companion Star.
Bain, Lee J. Statistical Analysis of Reliability & Life-Testing Models: Theory & Methods. 2nd expanded rev. ed. (Statistics: Textbooks & Monographs: Vol. 115). (Illus.). 520p. 1991. text 175.00 (*0-8247-8506-1*) Dekker.
Bain, Lee J. & Englehardt, Max. An Introduction to Probability & Mathematical Statistics. 2nd ed. 664p. (C). 1991. pap. 58.50 (*0-534-92930-3*) Wadsworth Pub.
Bain, Mildred C., jt. auth. see Bain, William J.
***Bain, Neville & Mabey, Bill.** The People Advantage: Improving Results Through Better Selection & Performance. LC 99-41759. 2000. 34.95 (*1-55753-177-3*) Purdue U Pr.
Bain, Nisbet R. The Daughter of Peter the Great. 1988. reprint ed. lib. bdg. 79.00 (*0-7812-0465-8*) Rprt Serv.
Bain, Peter & Shaw, Paul, eds. Blackletter: Type & National Identity. LC 97-43579. (Illus.). 64p. 1998. pap. 14.95 (*1-56898-125-2*) Princeton Arch.
Bain, Peter, jt. auth. see Gennard, John.
Bain-Pew, Gilda, jt. auth. see Phoenix, Charlotte Y.
Bain, R. N. Slavonic Europe: A Political History of Russia & Poland, 1447-1796. 1976. lib. bdg. 59.95 (*0-8490-2615-6*) Gordon Pr.
Bain, R. Nisbet. Last King of Poland & His Contemporaries. LC 71-135789. (Eastern Europe Collection). 1979. reprint ed. 26.95 (*0-405-02731-1*) Ayer.
— Slavonic Europe: A Political History of Poland & Russia from 1447 to 1796. LC 76-135790. (Eastern Europe Collection). 1971. reprint ed. 25.95 (*0-405-02732-X*) Ayer.
Bain, R. Nisbet, tr. see Jokai, Mor.
Bain, Reginald F. Clowns' Play. 1981. 3.75 (*0-87129-424-9*, C52) Dramatic Pub.
Bain, Richard. Images of London. (Illus.). 144p. 1994. 40.00 (*1-55082-120-2*, Pub. by Quarry Pr) LPC InBook.
— Images of Waterloo County. (Illus.). 144p. 1996. 40.00 (*1-55082-159-8*, Pub. by Quarry Pr) LPC InBook.
Bain, Richard, ed. see Austen, Jane.
Bain, Richard C. & Parris, Judith H. Convention Decisions & Voting Records. 2nd ed. LC 73-1082. (Brookings Institution Studies in Presidential Selection). 480p. reprint ed. pap. 148.80 (*0-608-14525-4*, 202536000043) Bks Demand.
Bain, Robert. H. L. Davis. LC 74-1969. (Western Writers Ser.: No. 11). 46p. 1974. pap. 4.95 (*0-88430-010-2*) Boise St U W Writ Ser.
Bain, Robert, ed. Whitman's & Dickinson's Contemporaries: An Anthology of Their Verse. LC 95-9867. 504p. (C). 1996. 49.95 (*0-8093-1721-4*); pap. 19.95 (*0-8093-2031-2*) S Ill U Pr.
Bain, Robert, et al, eds. Southern Writers: A Biographical Dictionary. LC 78-25899. 1979. pap. text 22.50 (*0-8071-0390-X*) La State U Pr.
Bain, Robert & Flora, Joseph M., eds. Contemporary Poets, Dramatists, Essayists, & Novelists of the South: A Bio-Bibliographical Sourcebook. LC 93-43750. 664p. 1994. lib. bdg. 105.00 (*0-313-28765-1*, Greenwood Pr) Greenwood.
Bain, Robert & Flora, Joseph M., eds. Fifty Southern Writers Before 1900: A Bio-Bibliographical Sourcebook. LC 86-31832. 432p. 1987. lib. bdg. 105.00 (*0-313-24518-5*, BFB/, Greenwood Pr) Greenwood.
Bain, Robert, jt. ed. see Flora, Joseph M.
Bain, Robert, jt. ed. see Taylor, Beverly.
Bain, Robert N. Charles the Twelfth & the Collapse of the Swedish Empire, 1682-1719. LC 70-95062. (Select Bibliographies Reprint Ser.). 1977. 36.95 (*0-8369-5064-X*) Ayer.
— Charles the Twelfth & the Collapse of the Swedish Empire, 1682-1719. LC 73-14432. (Heroes of the Nations Ser.). reprint ed. 47.50 (*0-404-58251-6*) AMS Pr.
— Daughter of Peter the Great. 1899. 13.00 (*0-403-00002-5*) Scholarly.
— Daughter of Peter the Great. LC 72-136407. (BCL Ser.: No. II). reprint ed. 29.50 (*0-404-00447-4*) AMS Pr.
— Peter Third, Emperor of Russia. 1902. 12.00 (*0-403-00465-9*) Scholarly.
— Peter Third, Emperor of Russia: The Story of a Crisis & a Crime. LC 72-156962. (BCL Ser.: No. II). reprint ed. 29.50 (*0-404-00448-2*) AMS Pr.
Bain, Roger J., ed. Proceedings of the 5th Symposium on the Geology of the Bahamas. (Illus.). 247p. (Orig.). (C). 1991. pap. text 20.00 (*0-935909-37-0*) Bahamian.
Bain, Sherry. Benjamin Gets Saved. LC 98-91110. (Illus.). 100p. (J). 1998. pap. 9.95 (*1-889448-23-0*) NBN Publishers Group.
Bain, Steve. Fundamental Illustrator 7. LC 97-227981. (Illus.). 800p. (Orig.). 1997. pap. text 34.99 (*0-07-882415-X*, Oracle Press) Osborne-McGraw.
— Fundamental Quark Xpress 4.0. LC 98-203041. 1998. pap. text 39.99 (*0-07-882513-X*) Osborne-McGraw.
— Using CorelDRAW X: Special Ed. LC 99-61028. 1999. pap. text 39.99 (*0-7897-1971-1*) Que.
***Bain, Susanne L.** Home Schooling: A Better Education for Your Child. 2nd ed. (Illus.). 200p. 1999. pap. 14.95 (*0-9675055-0-X*) Andros Bks.
— Home Schooling: Strategies for Success. (Illus.). 200p. 2000. pap. 14.95 (*0-9675055-1-8*) Andros Bks.
Bain, Trevor. Banking the Furnace: Restructuring of the Steel Industry in Eight Countries. LC 92-18358. 190p. 1992. 25.00 (*0-88099-128-3*); pap. 15.00 (*0-88099-127-5*) W E Upjohn.
***Bain, William D.** Verses from the Heart. 88p. 1999. pap. write for info. (*1-57579-157-9*, Pub. by Pine Hill Pr) Penmarch Pub.
Bain, William G. Investment Performance Measurement. 224p. 1996. 140.00 (*1-85573-195-9*, Pub. by Woodhead Pubng) Am Educ Systs.
— Investment Performance Measurement. 224p. 1996. pap. 65.00 (*1-85573-339-0*, Pub. by Woodhead Pubng) Am Educ Systs.
Bain, William J. & Bain, Mildred C. Building Together: A Memoir of Our Lives in Seattle. Davis, Barbara A., ed. (Illus.). 224p. 1991. text. write for info. (*0-9631413-0-9*) Beckett FL.
Bain, Winifred E. Seventy-Five Years of Concerns for Children: History of the Association for Childhood Education International, 1892-1967. Rasmussen, Margaret, ed. LC 67-20740. (Illus.). 96p. reprint ed. pap. 30.00 (*0-7837-0548-4*, 204088100019) Bks Demand.
***Bainbridge, Beryl.** According to Queeney. 224p. 2000. 22.00 (*0-7867-0773-9*, Pub. by Carroll & Graf) Publishers Group.
Bainbridge, Beryl. An Awfully Big Adventure. 224p. 1995. pap. 8.95 (*0-7867-0184-6*) Carroll & Graf.
Bainbridge, Beryl. An Awfully Big Adventure. LC 91-226248. 193 p. 1989. 10.95 (*0-7156-2204-8*) G Duckworth.
Bainbridge, Beryl. An Awfully Big Adventure. large type ed. 1997. 24.95 (*1-85695-264-9*, Pub. by Isis-Oasis) Dual Dolphin.
***Bainbridge, Beryl.** An Awfully Big Adventure. large type unabridged ed. 196p. 1999. pap. 19.95 (*0-7531-5120-0*, 151200, Pub. by ISIS Lrg Prnt) ISIS Pub.
Bainbridge, Beryl. The Birthday Boys. 192p. 1994. 18.95 (*0-7867-0071-8*) Carroll & Graf.
— The Birthday Boys. 189p. 1995. pap. 9.95 (*0-7867-0207-9*) Carroll & Graf.
— The Birthday Boys. large type ed. LC 94-22433. 251p. 1995. pap. 18.95 (*0-7862-0310-2*) Thorndike Pr.
— The Bottle Factory Outing. 192p. 1994. pap. 9.95 (*0-7867-0146-3*) Carroll & Graf.
— The Dressmaker. 160p. 1996. pap. 8.95 (*0-7867-0322-9*) Carroll & Graf.
— English Journey: or The Road to Milton Keynes. LC 97-3448. 160p. 1997. pap. 9.95 (*0-7867-0420-9*) Carroll & Graf.
— Every Man for Himself. LC 97-17487. 224p. 1997. pap. 10.95 (*0-7867-0467-5*) Carroll & Graf.
— Forever England: North & South. 174p. 1999. 22.00 (*0-7867-0611-2*) Carroll & Graf.
— Master Georgie. 190p. 1998. 21.00 (*0-7867-0563-9*) Carroll & Graf.
***Bainbridge, Beryl.** Master Georgie. 190p. 1999. pap. text 11.95 (*0-7867-0697-X*) Carroll & Graf.
Bainbridge, Beryl. Master Georgie. large type ed. LC 98-41988. 1999. 30.00 (*0-7862-1681-6*) Thorndike Pr.
Bainbridge, Beryl. Mum & Mr. Armitage: Selected Stories of Beryl Bainbridge. LC 86-136242. 144 p. 1985. 7.95 (*0-7156-2080-0*) G Duckworth.
— A Quiet Life. 208p. 1999. pap. 10.95 (*0-7867-0635-X*) Carroll & Graf.
Bainbridge, Beryl. Something Happened Yesterday. (Illus.). 176p. 1998. 20.00 (*0-7867-0517-5*) Carroll & Graf.
— Watson's Apology. 224p. 1988. pap. text. write for info. (*0-07-003255-6*) McGraw.
Bainbridge, Beryl. Winter Garden. LC 80-155191. 157 p. 1980. 5.95 (*0-7156-1495-9*) G Duckworth.
Bainbridge, Beryl. Young Adolf. 208p. 1995. pap. 9.95 (*0-7867-0258-3*) Carroll & Graf.
Bainbridge, Colin. Designing for Change: A Practical Guide to Business Transformation. LC 96-28872. 264p. 1996. 87.95 (*0-471-96452-2*) Wiley.
Bainbridge, David. Bainbridge: EC Data Protection Directive. (Current EC Legal Developments Ser.). 1996. write for info. (*0-406-01447-7*, EDPD, MICHIE) LEXIS Pub.
***Bainbridge, David.** Cases & Materials on Intellectual Property: Law. 2nd ed. 384p. (Orig.). 1999. pap. 62.50 (*0-273-63556-5*, Pub. by F T P-H) Trans-Atl Phila.
— Data Protection Law & Privacy in Telecommunications: The New Law. 1999. 46.50 (*1-85811-203-6*, Pub. by CLT Prof) Gaunt.
— Intellectual Property. 4th ed. 703p. 1999. pap. 65.00 (*0-273-63156-X*, Pub. by F T P-H) Trans-Atl Phila.
Bainbridge, David. Introduction to Computer Law. 3rd ed. 355p. 1996. pap. 62.50 (*0-273-61940-3*, Pub. by Pitman Pub) Trans-Atl Phila.
***Bainbridge, David.** Introduction to Computer Law. 4th ed. 384p. 1999. pap. 57.50 (*0-273-63159-4*, Pub. by F T P-H) Trans-Atl Phila.
Bainbridge, David. Software Licensing. 212p. 1995. pap. 53.00 (*1-85811-028-9*, Pub. by CLT Prof) Gaunt.
***Bainbridge, David.** Software Licensing. 2nd ed. 1999. pap. 63.00 (*1-85811-191-9*, Pub. by CLT Prof) Gaunt.
Bainbridge, David, jt. auth. see Mitchell, Steven.
Bainbridge, David I. Patent Law. 440p. 1999. boxed set 152.00 (*1-85811-140-4*, Pub. by CLT Prof) Gaunt.
Bainbridge, Delores. The Robin. Petoskey, Eva, ed. (Illus.). 36p. (J). (gr. 1-8). 1997. 20.00 (*0-9657888-0-6*) First Amer Prev Ctr.
Bainbridge, Jim. Show Me the Money: A Century of Great Movie Lines. 1999. 10.95 (*0-942627-61-X*) Woodford Pubng.
Bainbridge, John. Astronomical Description of the Late Comet. LC 74-28828. (English Experience Ser.: No. 710). 1975. reprint ed. 20.00 (*90-221-0710-8*) Walter J Johnson.
— Huna Magic - Empowers You to Create Health, Wealth & Relationships: Learn the Secret Within the Secret. 2nd rev. ed. LC 88-70689. Orig. Title: Mana Magic. (Illus.). 212p. 1994. pap. 10.95 (*0-9620658-1-1*) Barnhart Pr.
Bainbridge, John & Elliott, Jonathan, eds. Manual of Canine & Feline Nephrology & Urology. (BSAVA Ser.). (Illus.). 232p. 1996. pap. 82.95 (*0-8138-1879-6*) Iowa St U Pr.
Bainbridge, John S. & Wood, Terry. The Study & Teaching of Law in Africa, with a Survey of Institutions of Legal Education in Africa. x, 342p. 1972. reprint ed. text 12.50 (*0-8377-0304-2*, Rothman) W S Hein.
***Bainbridge, Kathy.** Building Web Sites Constituents Will Use. Shapiro, Richard, ed. (Illus.). 27p. 1999. pap. text 20.00 (*1-930473-03-6*) Congressional Mgmt Fdnt.
Bainbridge, Margaret, ed. The Turkic Peoples of the World. 350p. 1992. 75.00 (*0-7103-0409-9*, A5105) Routledge.
Bainbridge, Reginald B. Euripides the Idealist. 206p. 1977. 16.95 (*0-8369-6845-X*) Ayer.
Bainbridge, Russ. Bert & the Candy Lady. 120p. 1998. pap. 5.25 (*1-57502-972-3*, PO2662) Morris Pubng.
Bainbridge, Simon. Napoleon & English Romanticism. (Studies in Romanticism: No. 14). (Illus.). 274p. (C). 1995. text 59.95 (*0-521-47336-5*) Cambridge U Pr.
Bainbridge, Simon, jt. ed. see Archer, Jeffrey.
***Bainbridge, Timothy.** Penguin Companion to European Union. 528p. 1999. pap. 22.95 (*0-14-026879-0*, Pub. by Pnguin Bks Ltd) Trafalgar.
Bainbridge, Virginia. Gilds in the Medieval Countryside: Social & Religious Change in Cambridgeshire, C. 1350-1558. LC 96-4785. (Studies in the History of Medieval Religion: Vol. 10). (Illus.). 192p. (C). 1997. reprint ed. 75.00 (*0-85115-617-7*) Boydell & Brewer.
Bainbridge, W. S., ed. Westminster Hymnal. (Illus.). 452p. 1996. pap. 12.95 (*0-912141-40-9*) Roman Cath Bks.
Bainbridge, Willaim Sims. Religion, Deviance & Social. 204p. (C). 1997. 70.00 (*0-415-91528-7*) Routledge.
Bainbridge, William S. Experiments in Psychology: A Microcomputer Laboratory. 80p. (C). 1986. pap. text 16.50 (*0-534-04043-8*) Brooks-Cole.
— Sociology. LC 97-6360. (Barron's College Review Ser.). 400p. 1997. pap. 12.95 (*0-8120-9920-6*) Barron.
— Spaceflight Revolution: A Sociological Study. LC 82-21725. 304p. 1983. reprint ed. 24.50 (*0-89874-501-2*) Krieger.
Bainbridge, William S. & Stark, Rodney. Religion, Deviance & Social Control. 200p. (C). 1997. pap. 20.99 (*0-415-91529-5*) Routledge.
Bainbridge, William S., jt. auth. see Stark, Rodney.
Bainbridge, William Sims. Sociology of Religious Movements. LC 96-37328. (Illus.). 488p. (C). 1996. pap. 28.99 (*0-415-91202-4*) Routledge.
***Baine, Celeste.** The Fantastical Engineer: A Thrillseeker's Guide to Careers in Theme Park Engineering. (Illus.). 128p. (C). 2000. pap. 17.95 (*0-9664763-2-8*) Bonamy Publ.
Baine, Celeste. Is There an Engineer Inside You? A Comprehensive Guide to Career Decisions in Engineering. LC 98-96216. (Illus.). 192p. (YA). (gr. 10-12). 1999. pap. 14.95 (*0-9664763-0-1*) Bonamy Publ.
Baine, David. Instructional Design for Special Education. LC 81-9693. (Illus.). 320p. 1982. 39.95 (*0-87778-179-6*) Educ Tech Pubns.
— Memory & Instruction. LC 85-16216. (Illus.). 340p. 1986. 44.95 (*0-87778-192-3*) Educ Tech Pubns.
Baine, Rodney M., ed. Creating Georgia: Minutes of the Bray Associates, 1730-1732, & Supplementary Documents. LC 94-4169. 168p. 1995. 50.00 (*0-8203-1666-0*) U of Ga Pr.
— The Publications of James Edward Oglethorpe. LC 92-38271. 528p. 1994. 65.00 (*0-8203-1546-X*) U of Ga Pr.
Baines, Carol T. Women's Caring: Feminist Perspectives on Social Welfare. 2nd ed. LC 99-177913. 264p. 1998. pap. text 24.95 (*0-19-541302-4*) OUP.
Baines, Anthony. Brass Instruments: Their History & Development. LC 93-19988. (Illus.). 320p. 1993. reprint ed. pap. 9.95 (*0-486-27574-4*) Dover.
— The Oxford Companion to Musical Instruments. LC 92-8635. (Illus.). 416p. 1992. 55.00 (*0-19-311334-1*) OUP.
— Woodwind Instruments & Their History. (Illus.). 384p. 1998. reprint ed. pap. 11.95 (*0-486-26885-3*) Dover.
***Baines, Barry K.** The Ethical Will Resource Kit: Preserving Your Legacy of Values. vi, 22p. 1998. wbk. ed. 9.45 (*0-9676794-0-0*) Josaba.
Baines, Chris. The Flower. LC 89-77652. (Ecology Story Book Ser.). (Illus.). 24p. (J). 1990. 7.95 (*0-940793-53-9*, Crocodile Bks) Interlink Pub.
— The Nest. LC 89-77653. (Ecology Story Book Ser.). (Illus.). 24p. (J). (ps-3). 1990. 7.95 (*0-940793-55-5*, Crocodile Bks) Interlink Pub.
— The Old Boot. LC 89-77747. (Ecology Story Book Ser.). (Illus.). 24p. 1990. 7.95 (*0-940793-52-0*, Crocodile Bks) Interlink Pub.
— The Picnic. LC 89-77746. (Ecology Story Book Ser.). (Illus.). 24p. (J). (ps-3). 1990. 7.95 (*0-940793-54-7*, Crocodile Bks) Interlink Pub.
Baines, Chris & Smart, Jane. A Guide to Habitat Creation. 104p. (C). 1991. text 100.00 (*1-85341-031-4*, Pub. by Surrey Beatty & Sons) St Mut.
Baines, Dominic. Samba. LC 99-43503. (Black Book Ser.). 1999. pap. text 49.99 (*1-57610-455-9*) Coriolis Grp.
Baines, Doris C. Christmas Traditions & Legends. LC 97-71614. (Illus.). 176p. 1997. 35.00 (*0-9660475-4-0*) Kendor Inc.
Baines, Dudley. Emigration from Europe, 1815-1930. (New Studies in Economic & Social History: No. 11). 96p. (C). 1995. text 34.95 (*0-521-55270-2*) Cambridge U Pr.
— Emigration from Europe, 1815-1930. (New Studies in Economic & Social History: No. 11). 95p. (C). 1995. pap. text 10.95 (*0-521-55783-6*) Cambridge U Pr.
Baines, Elizabeth, et al. Best Radio Plays of 1989. (Methuen Drama Ser.). 191p. (C). 1990. write for info. (*0-413-63240-7*, A0468, Methuen Drama) Methn.
Baines, Elizabeth M. Perspectives on Gerontological Nursing. (Illus.). 400p. 1991. text 65.00 (*0-8039-3722-9*); pap. text 28.95 (*0-8039-4237-0*) Sage.
Baines, Elizabeth M., ed. Perspectives on Gerontological Nursing. LC 91-6874. (Illus.). 430p. 1991. reprint ed. pap. 133.30 (*0-608-04297-8*, 206507600012) Bks Demand.
Baines, Francesca. Castles. (Worldwise Ser.). (Illus.). 48p. (J). (gr. 4-6). 1994. lib. bdg. 23.00 (*0-531-14334-1*) Watts.
— Castles. LC 94-24223. (Worldwise Ser.). (Illus.). 48p. (J). (gr. 4-6). 1995. pap. 7.00 (*0-531-15267-7*) Watts.
— El Mundo de las Plantas. Sanz, Maria T., tr. (Biblioteca de Descubrimientos Ser.). (SPA., Illus.). 32p. (J). (gr. k-4). 1998. 11.95 (*1-58087-010-4*) C D Stampley Ent.
— Mundo Marino. (Biblioteca de Descubrimientos Ser.).Tr. of Ocean World. (SPA., Illus.). (J). (gr. 3-6). 1997. 11.95 (*0-915741-88-1*, SY7079) C D Stampley Ent.
Baines, Francesca. Ocean World. (Launch Pad Library). (Illus.). 32p. (J). (gr. k-4). 1997. 11.95 (*0-915741-81-4*) C D Stampley Ent.
Baines, Francesca. Planes. (Worldwise Ser.). (Illus.). 48p. (J). (gr. 4-6). 1994. lib. bdg. 23.00 (*0-531-14341-4*) Watts.

B

— Planes. (Worldwise Ser.). (Illus.). 48p. (J). (gr. 4-6). 1995. pap. 7.00 (*0-531-15268-5*) Watts.
— World of Plants. (Launch Pad Library). (Illus.). 32p. (J). (gr. k-4). 1998. 11.95 (*1-58087-003-1*) C D Stampley Ent.
***Baines, Gay & Eichelberger, Mary Ann.** Storms: Stories & Poems. 132p. 1999. pap. 14.95 (*0-9675504-0-8*) July Lit Pr.
Baines, Gwendolyn L. Only My Children & Me. (Illus.). 32p. (Orig.). (YA). 1994. pap. 4.50 (*0-9614505-4-1*) Nevada Pub.
— People in the Web of Life. 2nd ed. (J). (gr. 7 up). 1992. pap. 9.95 (*0-9614505-1-7*) Nevada Pub.
— Sassy, Secure, & over Sixty. large type ed. LC 96-68369. (Illus.). 112p. (Orig.). 1997. pap. 12.95 (*0-9614505-3-3*) Nevada Pub.
— Son I Love You, But . . . (Illus.). 32p. (Orig.). (YA). 1994. pap. 4.50 (*0-9614505-2-5*) Nevada Pub.
Baines, Harold. The Nigerian Scam Masters: An Expose of a Modern International Gang. 171p. 2000. 34.00 (*1-56072-282-7*); pap. 23.95 (*1-56072-267-3*, Nova Kroshka Bks) Nova Sci Pubs.
Baines, John. Coasts. LC 98-25830. (Ecology Alert Ser.). (J). 1998. 22.83 (*0-8172-5370-X*) Raintree Steck-V.
— Environmental Disasters. LC 93-8526. (World's Disasters Ser.). (Illus.). 48p. (J). 1993. lib. bdg. 5.00 (*1-56847-086-X*) Raintree Steck-V.
— Hypsoconsciousness: Techniques for Achieving Personal Success. Bregazzi, Josephine, tr. from SPA. LC 94-96631. (Illus.). 256p. (Orig.). 1995. pap. 9.95 (*1-882692-02-0*) J Baines Inst.
— Japan. LC 93-23948. (Country Fact Files Ser.). (J). (gr. 5 up). 1994. lib. bdg. 24.26 (*0-8114-1847-2*) Raintree Steck-V.
— The Science of Love. Hipskind, Judith, ed. Bregazzi, Josephine, tr. from SPA. LC 92-97419. (Illus.). 401p. (Orig.). 1993. pap. 12.95 (*1-882692-00-4*) J Baines Inst.
— The Secret Science: For the Physical & Spiritual Transformation of Man. 3rd ed. Brown, Evelyne, tr. from SPA. LC 93-91617. (Hermetic Philosophy Ser.: Bk. 1). (Illus.). 240p. 1998. pap. 8.95 (*1-882692-01-2*) J Baines Inst.
— The Stellar Man. Hipskind, Judith, ed. Nunez, Margaret L., tr. from SPA. LC 84-48085. (Hermetic Philosophy Ser.: Bk. 2). (Illus.). 288p. (Orig.). 1985. pap. 9.95 (*0-87542-026-5*) J Baines Inst.
Baines, John & Malek, Jaromir. Cultural Atlas of Ancient Egypt. (Cultural Atlas Ser.). (Illus.). 240p. 1980. 45.00 (*0-87196-334-5*) Facts on File.
***Baines, John & Malek, Jaromir.** Cultural Atlas of Ancient Egypt. rev. ed. LC 99-57588. (Cultural Atlas Ser.). (Illus.). 240p. 2000. 50.00 (*0-8160-4036-2*, Checkmark) Facts on File.
Baines, John, tr. see Hornung, Erik.
Baines, John D. Antarctica. LC 96-52704. (Continents Ser.). 48p. (J). 1997. lib. bdg. 25.69 (*0-8172-4782-3*) Raintree Steck-V.
— Keeping the Air Clean. LC 97-17980. (Protecting Our Planet Ser.). (J). 1998. 25.69 (*0-8172-4936-2*) Raintree Steck-V.
— The United States. LC 93-26533. (Country Fact Files Ser.). (J). 1993. lib. bdg. 24.26 (*0-8114-1857-X*) Raintree Steck-V.
Baines, Keith. Malory's Le Morte D'Arthur: King Arthur & the Legends of the Round Table. (J). 1962. 13.09 (*0-606-03433-1*, Pub. by Turtleback) Demco.
***Baines, Lawrence & Kunkel, Anthony J.** Going Bohemian: Activities That Engage Adolescents in the Art of Writing Well. 192p. 1999. pap. 22.95 (*0-87207-254-1*, 254) Intl Reading.
Baines, Lawrence, jt. ed. see Simmons, Johns S.
Baines, M. J. & Morton, K. W., eds. Numerical Methods for Fluid Dynamics IV. (Illus.). 622p. 1994. text 115.00 (*0-19-853696-8*) OUP.
Baines, M. J., jt. auth. see Morton, K. W.
Baines, M. J., jt. ed. see Morton, K. W.
Baines, Micael J. Moving Finite Elements. (Monographs on Numerical Analysis). (Illus.). 240p. 1995. text 80.00 (*0-19-853467-1*) OUP.
Baines, Nicholas C., jt. auth. see Japikse, David.
Baines, Patricia. Flax & Linen. (Album Ser.: No. 133). (Illus.). 32p. 1998. pap. 6.25 (*0-85263-727-6*, Pub. by Shire Pubns) Parkwest Pubns.
— Linen: Hand Spinning & Weaving. (Illus.). 208p. (Orig.). 1990. 21.95 (*0-934026-52-1*) Interweave.
— Spinning Wheels, Spinners & Spinning. 1987. reprint ed. pap. 12.95 (*0-923150-48-X*) Robin & Russ.
Baines, Paul. The House of Forgery in Eighteenth-Century Britain. LC 98-29246. (Early Modern History Ser.). 1999. 83.95 (*1-84014-601-X*) Ashgate Pub Co.
***Baines, Paul & Burns, Edward, eds.** Five Romantic Plays 1768-1821. (Oxford World's Classics Ser.). 432p. 2000. pap. 14.95 (*0-19-283316-2*) OUP.
Baines, Peter G. Topographic Effects in Stratified Flows. (Monographs on Mechanics). (Illus.). 498p. (C). 1995. text 80.00 (*0-521-43501-3*) Cambridge U Pr.
— Topographic Effects in Stratified Flows. (Monographs on Mechanics & Applied Mathematics). (Illus.). 498p. 1997. pap. text 35.95 (*0-521-62923-3*) Cambridge U Pr.
Baines, Victor. Remember the Future: The Prophecies of Nostradamus. (Illus.). 224p. (Orig.). 1994. pap. 17.95 (*0-9631740-2-9*) Holographic Bks.
Bainham. The International Survey of Family Law, 1995, Vol. ISFL 2. 1997. 185.00 (*90-411-0374-0*) Kluwer Law Intl.
Bainham, Andrew, ed. International Survey of Family Law: Published on Behalf of the International Society of Family Law, Vol. 1. LC 96-5361. 516p. 1996. 167.50 (*90-411-0218-3*) Kluwer Law Intl.
— The International Survey of Family Law, 1996. 540p. 1998. 162.50 (*90-411-0573-5*) Kluwer Law Intl.
***Bainham, Andrew, et al, eds.** What Is a Parent? A Socio-Legal Analysis. 256p. 1999. 54.00 (*1-84113-058-3*, Pub. by Hart Pub); pap. 27.00 (*1-84113-043-5*, Pub. by Hart Pub) Intl Spec Bk.
Baini, Giuseppe. Memorie Storico-Critiche Della Vita E Delle Opere Di Giovanni Pierluigi Da Palestrina, 2 vols., Set. xxxiv, 816p. 1966. reprint ed. 225.00 (*0-318-71580-5*) G Olms Pubs.
***Bainov, D.** Proceedings of the 9th International Colloquium on Differential Equations: Plovdiv, Bulgaria, 18-23 August 1998. 460p. 1999. 210.00 (*90-6764-296-7*, Pub. by VSP) Coronet Bks.
Bainov, D., ed. Proceedings of the Seventh International Colloquium on Differential Equations: Plovdiv, Bulgaria, 18-23 August, 1996. (Illus.). 480p. 1997. 199.00 (*90-6764-233-9*, Pub. by VSP) Coronet Bks.
— Proceedings of the Sixth International Colloquium on Differential Equations. 424p. 1996. 187.50 (*90-6764-203-7*, Pub. by VSP) Coronet Bks.
Bainov, D. & Covachev, V., eds. Proceedings of the 5th International Colloquium on Differential Equations. 370p. 1995. 165.00 (*90-6764-192-8*, Pub. by VSP) Coronet Bks.
— Proceedings of the First International Colloquium on Numerical Analysis. viii, 178p. 1993. 107.50 (*90-6764-152-9*) Coronet Bks.
— Proceedings of the Fourth International Colloquium on Differential Equations. 316p. 1994. 135.00 (*90-6764-169-3*) Coronet Bks.
— Proceedings of the Second International Colloquium on Numerical Analysis. 204p. 1994. 115.00 (*90-6764-168-5*) Coronet Bks.
— Proceedings of the Third International Colloquium on Differential Equations. 236p. 1993. 125.00 (*90-6764-153-7*) Coronet Bks.
Bainov, D. & Covachev, V., eds. Proceedings of the Third International Colloquium on Numerical Analysis. 236p. 1995. 135.00 (*90-6764-193-6*, Pub. by VSP) Coronet Bks.
Bainov, D. & Simeonov, P. S. Impulse Differential Equations: Asymptotic Properties of the Solutions. LC 94-30314. (Series on Advances in Mathematics for Applied Sciences). 248p. 1995. text 74.00 (*981-02-1823-0*) World Scientific Pub.
Bainov, D. D. & Mishev, D. P. Oscillation Theory for Neutral Differential Equations with Delay. (Illus.). 288p. 1991. 149.00 (*0-7503-0142-2*) IOP Pub.
Bainov, D. D. & Simeonov, P. S. Systems with Impulse Effect: Stability, Theory & Applications. 1989. text 79.95 (*0-470-21437-6*) P-H.
Bainov, Drumi. Impulsive Differential Equations Periodic Solutions & Applications. 1993. 84.95 (*0-582-09639-1*, Pub. by Addison-Wesley) Longman.
Bainov, Drumi D. Oscillation Theory of Operator - Differential Equations. (Soviet & East European Mathematics Ser.). 280p. 1995. text 61.00 (*981-02-1100-7*) World Scientific Pub.
Bainov, Drumi D. & Covachec, V. Differential Equations: The Second Colloquium. 276p. 1992. text 81.00 (*981-02-1075-2*) World Scientific Pub.
Bainov, Drumi D. & Covachev, V. Impulsive Differential Equations with a Small Parameter: Advances in Mathematics for Applied Sciences Ser. 260p. 1994. text 53.00 (*981-02-1434-0*) World Scientific Pub.
Bainov, Drumi D. & Simeonov, Pavel S. Integral Inequalities & Applications. LC 92-9022. (Mathematics & Its Applications East European Ser.: Vol. 57). 260p. (C). 1992. text 175.00 (*0-7923-1714-9*) Kluwer Academic.
Bains, Dale. Amongst the Martian Ruins. 141p. 1998. pap. write for info. (*1-86106-953-7*, Pub. by Minerva Pr) Unity Dist.
Bains, Dick, et al. Lotus Domino for the AS/400. Heidelberg, Jelan, ed. (AS/400 Ser.). (Illus.). 374p. 1999. 59.95 (*1-889671-29-0*) Advice Pr.
Bains, Doris. A Supplement to Notae Latinae: Abbreviations in Latin MSS. of 850 to 1050 A. D. xii, 72p. reprint ed. 19.37 (*0-685-66490-2*, 05100366) G Olms Pubs.
Bains, Gurpit S. Complex Structures in Hinid-Urdu: Explorations in Government & Binding Theory. LC 94-19019. (Monographs in Linguistics & the Philosophy of Language: Vol. 3). 1995. write for info. (*0-8204-2589-3*) P Lang Pubng.
Bains, Harwant S. Blood. (Methuen New Theatrescripts Ser.). 47p. (Orig.). (C). 1989. pap. 11.95 (*0-413-19520-1*) Heinemann.
Bains, Paul, tr. see Guattari, Felix.
Bains, Paul, tr. see Stengers, Isabelle.
Bains, Rae. Benito Juarez: Hero of Modern Mexico. LC 92-2291. (Men in History Library). (Illus.). 48p. (J). (gr. 4-6). 1997. lib. bdg. 17.25 (*0-8167-2825-9*, BB214) Troll Communs.
— Benito Juarez, Hero of Modern Mexico. LC 92-2291. (Illus.). 48p. (J). (gr. 4-6). 1997. pap. 3.95 (*0-8167-2826-7*) Troll Communs.
— Clara Barton: Angel of the Battlefield. LC 81-23123. (Illus.). 48p. (J). (gr. 4-6). 1997. pap. 3.95 (*0-89375-753-5*) Troll Communs.
— Clara Barton: Angel of the Battlefield. LC 81-23123. (Illus.). 48p. (J). (gr. 4-6). 1997. lib. bdg. 17.25 (*0-89375-752-7*) Troll Communs.
— Discovering Electricity. LC 81-3339. (Illus.). 32p. (J). (gr. 2-4). 1982. pap. 3.50 (*0-89375-565-6*); lib. bdg. 17.25 (*0-89375-564-8*) Troll Communs.
— Gandhi, Peaceful Warrior. LC 89-5101. (Illus.). 48p. (J). (gr. 4-6). 1996. pap. 3.95 (*0-8167-1768-0*) Troll Communs.
— Gandhi, Peaceful Warrior. LC 89-5101. (Illus.). 48p. (J). (gr. 4-6). 1997. lib. bdg. 17.25 (*0-8167-1767-2*) Troll Communs.
— Harriet Tubman: The Road to Freedom. LC 81-23145. (Illus.). 48p. (J). (gr. 4-6). 1996. pap. 3.95 (*0-89375-761-6*) Troll Communs.
— Harriet Tubman: The Road to Freedom. LC 81-23145. (Illus.). 48p. (J). (gr. 4-6). 1997. lib. bdg. 17.25 (*0-89375-760-8*) Troll Communs.
— Indians of the Eastern Woodlands. LC 84-2664. (Illus.). 32p. (J). (gr. 3-6). 1985. pap. text 3.50 (*0-8167-0119-9*); lib. bdg. 14.50 (*0-8167-0118-0*) Troll Communs.
— Indians of the Plains. LC 84-2645. (Illus.). 32p. (J). (gr. 3-6). 1985. pap. text 3.50 (*0-8167-0189-X*); lib. bdg. 14.50 (*0-8167-0188-1*) Troll Communs.
— Indians of the West. LC 84-2600. (Illus.). 32p. (J). (gr. 3-6). 1985. pap. text 3.50 (*0-8167-0135-0*); lib. bdg. 14.50 (*0-8167-0134-2*) Troll Communs.
— Jack London: A Life of Adventure. LC 91-3927. (Illus.). 48p. (J). (gr. 4-6). 1996. pap. 3.95 (*0-8167-2514-4*) Troll Communs.
— James Monroe, Young Patriot. LC 85-1071. (Illus.). 48p. (J). (gr. 4-6). 1986. lib. bdg. 17.25 (*0-8167-0557-7*) Troll Communs.
— James Monroe, Young Patriot. LC 85-1071. (Illus.). 48p. (J). (gr. 4-6). 1997. pap. 3.95 (*0-8167-0558-5*) Troll Communs.
— Robert E. Lee: Brave Leader. LC 85-1092. (Illus.). 48p. (J). (gr. 4-6). 1997. pap. 3.95 (*0-8167-0546-1*) Troll Communs.
— Robert E. Lee: Brave Leader. LC 85-1092. (Illus.). 48p. (J). (gr. 4-6). 1997. lib. bdg. 17.25 (*0-8167-0545-3*) Troll Communs.
— Thurgood Marshall: Fight for Justice. LC 92-37302. (Illus.). 48p. (J). (gr. 4-6). 1997. pap., teacher ed. 3.95 (*0-8167-2828-3*) Troll Communs.
— Thurgood Marshall: Fight for Justice. LC 92-37302. (Men in History Library). (Illus.). 48p. (J). (gr. 4-6). 1997. 17.25 (*0-8167-2827-5*, BT279) Troll Communs.
— Wonders of Rivers. LC 81-7423. (Illus.). 32p. (J). (gr. 2-4). 1982. pap. 3.50 (*0-89375-571-0*) Troll Communs.
Bains, Ravinder S. Reservation Policy & Anti-Reservationists. (C). 1994. 20.00 (*81-7018-785-0*, Pub. by BR Pub) S Asia.
Bains, Richard & Chakravarti, Robin. Application Development Concepts for the IBM AS-400. Cozzi, Robert, Jr., ed. 360p. 1992. 56.00 (*0-9621825-4-0*) Cozzi Research.
Bains, Tara S. & Johnston, Hugh. The Four Quarters of the Night: The Life-Journey of an Emigrant Sikh. (McGill-Queen's Studies in Ethnic History). (Illus.). 304p. 1995. 65.00 (*0-7735-1265-9*, Pub. by McG-Queens Univ Pr); pap. 24.95 (*0-7735-1266-7*, Pub. by McG-Queens Univ Pr) CUP Services.
Bains, Trilochan & MacKenzie, D. Scott, eds. The 1st International Non-Ferrous Processing & Technology Conference: Conference Proceedings, 10-12 March 1997. LC 97-73689. 558p. 1997. 124.00 (*0-87170-592-3*, 6558) ASM.
Bains, William. Biotechnology from A to Z. 2nd ed. (Illus.). 420p. 1998. pap. text 27.95 (*0-19-963693-1*) OUP.
Bains, Yashdip S. Antony & Cleopatra: An Annotated Bibliography. Godshalk, William, ed. LC 98-29860. (Shakespeare Bibliographies Ser.: Vol. 27). 552p. 1998. 95.00 (*0-8153-1474-4*, H1786) Garland.
— English Canadian Theatre, 1765-1826, Vol. 27. LC 97-14021. (American University Studies XXVI). XII, 244p. (C). 1998. text 44.95 (*0-8204-3822-7*) P Lang Pubng.
Bainter, Jack J. Student Success, Everyone's Business: Twelve Imperatives & 101 Helpful Hints. LC 98-86692. 325p. 1998. 25.00 (*0-7388-0063-5*); pap. 15.00 (*0-7388-0064-3*) Xlibris Corp.
Baintner, Karoly. Intestinal Absorption of Macromolecules & Immune Transmission from Mother to Young. 288p. 1986. 144.00 (*0-8493-5589-3*, RA1231, CRC Reprint) Franklin.
Bainton. Conc Airway Management. 1994. 39.00 (*0-316-07673-2*) Little.
Bainton, Roland H. The Age of the Reformation. LC 83-25145. (Anvil Ser.). 192p. (C). 1984. reprint ed. pap. 12.50 (*0-89874-736-8*) Krieger.
— Christian Attitudes Toward War & Peace. LC 60-12064. 1979. pap. 9.95 (*0-687-07027-9*) Abingdon.
— Christianity. (American Heritage Library). 416p. 1986. pap. 15.00 (*0-8281-0489-1*) HM.
— The Church of Our Fathers. (Illus.). 222p. (C). 1978. pap. text 20.60 (*0-02-305450-6*, Macmillan Coll) P-H.
— The Church of Our Fathers. 1987. pap. 8.99 (*0-88019-211-9*) Schmul Pub Co.
— Early Christianity. LC 83-25150. 188p. (C). 1984. reprint ed. pap. text 12.50 (*0-89874-735-X*) Krieger.
— Here I Stand. 1955. pap. 5.99 (*0-451-62581-1*, Ment) NAL.
— Here I Stand: A Life of Martin Luther. LC 40-45795. 1991. pap. 5.95 (*0-687-16895-3*) Abingdon.
— Here I Stand: A Life of Martin Luther. (Illus.). 288p. 1995. pap. 12.95 (*0-452-01146-9*, Mer) NAL.
— Here I Stand: A Life of Martin Luther. 1990. 24.25 (*0-8446-6225-9*) Peter Smith.
— The Medieval Church. LC 78-11433. (Anvil Ser.). 192p. 1979. reprint ed. pap. 12.50 (*0-88275-786-5*) Krieger.
— The Reformation of the Sixteenth Century. enl. ed. (Illus.). 290p. 1985. pap. 18.50 (*0-8070-1301-3*, BP697) Beacon Pr.
Bainton, Roland H., ed. Martin Luther's Christmas Book. LC 97-28979. 96p. 1997. pap. 10.99 (*0-8066-3577-0*, 9-3577, Augsburg) Augsburg Fortress.
— Martin Luther's Easter Book. LC 97-28980. (Illus.). 96p. 1997. pap. text 10.99 (*0-8066-3578-9*, 9-3578, Augsburg) Augsburg Fortress.
Bainton, Roland H., tr. see Gedat, Gustav-Adolf.
Bainton, Roland H., tr. see Holborn, Hajo.
***Bainton, Roland Herbert.** Christianity. (Illus.). 432p. 2000. pap. 16.00 (*0-618-05687-4*, Mariner Bks) HM.
Bainton, Ronald H. The Church of Our Fathers. 1984. 32.75 (*0-8446-6120-1*) Peter Smith.
Bainum, Peter M., ed. Space in the 1980's & Beyond, 17th European Space Symposium, Jun. 4-6, 1980, London, England. (Science & Technology Ser.: Vol. 53). (Illus.). 302p. 1981. 40.00 (*0-87703-154-1*, Am Astronaut Soc); pap. 30.00 (*0-87703-155-X*, Am Astronaut Soc) Univelt Inc.
Bainum, Peter M., et al, eds. International Space Year (ISY) in the Pacific Basin, Fourth ISCOPS (formerly PISSTA) AAS/JRS/CSA Symposium, Nov. 17-20, 1991, Kyoto, Japan. LC 57-43769. (Advances in the Astronautical Sciences Ser.: Vol. 77). (Illus.). 798p. 1992. 120.00 (*0-87703-351-X*, Am Astronaut Soc) Univelt Inc.
— International Space Year (ISY) in the Pacific Basin, 4th ISCOPS (formerly PISSTA) AAS/JRS/CSA Symposium, Nov. 17-20, 1991, Kyoto, Japan. LC 57-43769. (Advances in the Astronautical Sciences Ser.: Vol. 77). (Illus.). 798p. 1992. pap. 90.00 (*0-87703-352-8*, Am Astronaut Soc) Univelt Inc.
— Space Cooperation into the 21st Century, Seventh ISCOPS (Formerly PISSTA) JRS/AAS/CSA Symposium, Jul, 15-18, 1997, Nagasaki, Japan: 7th ISCOPS (Formerly PISSTA) JRS/AAS/CSA Symposium, Nagasaki, Japan, July 15-18, 1997. LC 57-43769. (Advances in the Astronautical Sciences Ser.: Vol. 96). 1098p. 1997. 145.00 (*0-87703-438-9*, Am Astronaut Soc) Univelt Inc.
— Space Utilization & Applications in the Pacific, Third (PISSTA) AAS/JRS/CSA Symposium, Nov. 6-8, 1989, Los Angeles, CA. LC 57-43769. (Advances in the Astronautical Sciences Ser.: Vol. 73). (Illus.). 764p. 1990. 95.00 (*0-87703-325-0*, Am Astronaut Soc); pap. 80.00 (*0-87703-326-9*, Am Astronaut Soc) Univelt Inc.
— Strengthening Cooperation in the 21st Century, Sixth ISCOPS (Formerly PISSTA) AAS/JRS/CSA Symposium, Dec. 6-8, 1995, Marina Del Rey, CA: 6th ISCOPS (Formerly PISSTA) AAS/JRS/CSA Symposium, Marina Del Rey, CA, Dec. 6-8, 1995. LC 57-43769. (Advances in the Astronautical Sciences Ser.: Vol. 91). 1154p. 1996. 145.00 (*0-87703-409-5*, Am Astronaut Soc) Univelt Inc.
— Tethers in Space: Proceedings of First International Conference on Tethers in Space (NASA & PSN Sponsors; AIAA, AAS & AIDAA Co-Sponsors), Sept. 17-19, 1986, Arlington, VA. LC 57-43769. (Advances in the Astronautical Sciences Ser.: Vol. 62). (Illus.). 784p. 1987. 80.00 (*0-87703-264-5*, Am Astronaut Soc) Univelt Inc.
— Tethers in Space: Proceedings of the 1st International Conference on Tethers in Space (NASA & PSN Sponsors; AIAA, AAS & AIDAA Co-Sponsors), Sept. 17-19, 1986, Arlington, VA. LC 57-43769. (Advances in the Astronautical Sciences Ser.: Vol. 62). (Illus.). 784p. 1987. pap. 70.00 (*0-87703-265-3*, Am Astronaut Soc) Univelt Inc.
Bainum, Peter M. & Koelle, Dietrich E., eds. Spacelab Space Platforms, & the Future, Fourth AAS/DGLR Symposium & 20th Goddard Memorial Symposium, Mar. 17-19, 1982, Greenbelt, MD. LC 57-43769. (Advances in The Astronautical Sciences Ser.: Vol. 49). (Illus.). 502p. 1982. 55.00 (*0-87703-174-6*, Am Astronaut Soc) Univelt Inc.
— Spacelab Space Platforms, & the Future, Fourth AAS/DGLR Symposium & 20th Goddard Memorial Symposium, Mar. 17-19, 1982, Greenbelt, MD. LC 57-43769. (Advances in The Astronautical Sciences Ser.: Vol. 49). (Illus.). 502p. 1982. pap. 45.00 (*0-87703-175-4*, Am Astronaut Soc) Univelt Inc.
Bainum, Peter M. & Von Bun, Friedrich. Europe-United States Space Activities with a Space Propulsion Supplement. (Science & Technology Ser.: Vol. 61). (Illus.). 442p. 1985. 55.00 (*0-87703-217-3*, Am Astronaut Soc) Univelt Inc.
Bainum, Peter M. & Von Bun, Friedrich, eds. Europe/United States Space Activities - With a Space Propulsion Supplement, 23rd Goddard Memorial Symposium/19th European Space Symposium, Mar. 27-29, 1985, Greenbelt, MD. (Science & Technology Ser.: Vol. 61). 242p. 1985. 55.00 (*0-87870-321-7*, Am Astronaut Soc) Univelt Inc.
— Europe/United States Space Activities - With a Space Propulsion Supplement, 23rd Goddard Memorial Symposium/19th European Space Symposium, Mar. 27-29, 1985, Greenbelt, MD. (Science & Technology Ser.: Vol. 61). (Illus.). 442p. 1985. pap. 45.00 (*0-87703-218-1*, Am Astronaut Soc) Univelt Inc.
Bainum, Peter M., jt. ed. see Adelman, Andrew.
Bainum, Peter M., jt. ed. see Carter, Len J.
Baiocchi, Claudio & Capelo, Antonio. Variational & Quasivariational Inequalities: Applications to Free Boundary Problems. LC 83-6731. 462p. reprint ed. pap. 143.30 (*0-7837-4020-4*, 204385000011) Bks Demand.
Baiocco, Sharon A., et al. Distinguished Teaching. LC 97-37760. 320p. 1998. 36.00 (*0-205-26654-1*) P-H.
Baipai, Pratime. Enzymes in Pulp & Paper Processing. 170p. 1997. pap. 95.00 (*0-87930-523-1*) Miller Freeman.
Bair, Alisa. A Table for Two: A Mother & Her Young Daughter Face Death Together . . . LC 97-50193. 214p. 1997. pap. 8.95 (*1-56148-218-8*) Good Bks PA.
Bair, Barbara. Though Justice Sleeps: African Americans, 1880-1900. (The Young Oxford History of African Americans Ser.). (YA). (gr. 12 up). 1997. 21.00 (*0-614-25378-0*) OUP.
Bair, Barbara & Cayleff, Susan E., eds. Wings of Gauze: Women of Color & the Experience of Health & Illness. LC 92-46308. 394p. 1993. pap. text 21.95 (*0-8143-2302-2*) Wayne St U Pr.
— Wings of Gauze: Women of Color & the Experience of Health & Illness. LC 92-46308. 393p. reprint ed. pap. 121.90 (*0-608-10628-3*, 2071250) Bks Demand.

An Asterisk (*) at the beginning of an entry indicates that the title is appearing for the first time.

Bair, Barbara, ed. see Garvey, Marcus M.

Bair, Barbara, jt. ed. see Hill, Robert A.

Bair, Barbara, ed. see Rogers, Will.

Bair, Bruce. Good Land: My Life As a Farm Boy. LC 96-48710. 189p. 1997. 22.00 (*1-883642-34-5*) Steerforth Pr.

Bair, Daniel A. Generating Independent Income Vol. 1: An Outline of the Methods Used by Some of This Country's Most Outstanding Achievers. LC 94-73274. 232p. (Orig.). 1995. pap. 9.95 (*0-9644644-7-0*) DC Publ.

— Generating Independent Income Vol. 2: An Outline of the Methods Used by Some of This Country's Most Outstanding Achievers. LC 94-73274. 232p. (Orig.). 1995. pap. 9.95 (*0-9644644-8-9*) DC Publ.

Bair, Dawn, ed. see Indy Publications Staff.

Bair, Dawn, ed. see Shaffer, Jan & Robinson, Mark.

Bair, Deirdre. Anais Nin: A Biography. 672p. 1996. pap. 16.95 (*0-14-025525-7*, Penguin Bks) Viking Penguin.

— Samuel Beckett. 784p. 1990. pap. 20.00 (*0-671-69173-2*) S&S Trade.

***Bair, Diane.** Bat Watching. 1999. 19.93 (*0-516-21893-X*) Capstone Pr.

Bair, Diane. Bear Watching. LC 99-19585. (Wildlife Watching Ser.). 48p. (YA). 1999. 19.93 (*0-7368-0319-X*, Cpstone High Low) Capstone Pr.

***Bair, Diane.** Bear Watching. 1999. 19.93 (*0-516-21894-8*) Capstone Pr.

Bair, Diane. Butterfly Watching. LC 99-18299. (Wildlife Watching Ser.). 48p. (YA). 1999. 19.93 (*0-7368-0320-3*, Cpstone High Low) Capstone Pr.

***Bair, Diane.** Butterfly Watching. 1999. 19.93 (*0-516-21895-6*) Capstone Pr.

— Deer Watching. 1999. 19.93 (*0-516-21896-4*) Capstone Pr.

Bair, Diane. Eagle Watching. LC 99-22956. (Wildlife Watching Ser.). 48p. (YA). 1999. 19.93 (*0-7368-0322-X*, Cpstone High Low) Capstone Pr.

***Bair, Diane.** Eagle Watching. 1999. 19.93 (*0-516-21897-2*) Capstone Pr.

Bair, Diane. Fun Places to Go with Children in New England. 3rd ed. LC 97-34336. 1998. pap. text 11.95 (*0-8118-1865-9*) Chronicle Bks.

***Bair, Diane.** Sea Turtle Watching. 1999. 19.93 (*0-516-21898-0*) Capstone Pr.

Bair, Diane. Tide Pool Life Watching. LC 99-25189. (Wildlife Watching Ser.). 48p. (YA). 1999. 19.93 (*0-7368-0324-6*, Cpstone High Low) Capstone Pr.

***Bair, Diane.** Tide Pool Life Watching. 1999. 19.93 (*0-516-21899-9*) Capstone Pr.

Bair, Diane. Whale Watching. LC 99-22689. (Wildlife Watching Ser.). 48p. (YA). 1999. 19.93 (*0-7368-0325-4*, Cpstone High Low) Capstone Pr.

Bair, Diane & Wright, Pamela. Bat Watching. LC 99-19606. (Wildlife Watching Ser.). 48p. (YA). 1999. 19.93 (*0-7368-0318-1*, Cpstone High Low) Capstone Pr.

— Deer Watching. LC 99-14651. (Wildlife Watching Ser.). 48p. (YA). 2000. 14.95 (*0-7368-0321-1*) Capstone Pr.

— Sea Turtle Watching. LC 99-25192. (Wildlife Watching Ser.). 48p. (YA). 2000. 19.93 (*0-7368-0323-8*) Capstone Pr.

— Wild Encounters: Eco-Touring & Wildlife Watching Adventures. LC 98-15960. 1998. pap. 25.00 (*1-57223-134-3*, 1343) Willow Creek Pr.

Bair, Diane & Wright, Pamela. Wildlife Watching. (Illus.). 48p. 127.60 (*0-7368-0442-0*, Capstone Bks) Capstone Pr.

Bair, Dierdre. Simone de Beauvoir: A Biography. (Illus.). 718p. 1999. pap. text 17.00 (*0-7881-6036-2*) DIANE Pub.

Bair, Elmer O. Elmer Bair's Story, 1899-1987 Vol. 1. Mangan, Velda B., ed. LC 87-80294. (Illus.). 484p. (YA). (gr. 9 up). 1987. 20.00 (*0-9618269-0-8*) Elmer Bair.

Bair, Frank E. Alzheimer's, Stroke & Twenty-Nine Other Neurological Disorders: A Sourcebook Containing Basic Information on Types, Symptoms, Causes, Diagnostic Methods, & Treatments. (Health Reference Ser.: Vol. 2). 600p. 1993. lib. bdg. 78.00 (*1-55888-748-2*) Omnigraphics Inc.

— Climates of the States, 2 Vols., Vol. 1. 3rd ed. 1588p. 1985. 255.00 (*0-8103-1042-2*) Gale.

Bair, Frank E., ed. Cancer Sourcebook: Basic Information on Cancer Types, Symptoms, Diagnostic Methods, & Treatments, Including Statistics on Cancer Occurrences Worldwide & the Risks Associated with Known Carcinogens & Activities. (Health Reference Ser.: Vol. 1). (Illus.). viii, 932p. 1990. lib. bdg. 78.00 (*1-55888-888-8*) Omnigraphics Inc.

— Climates of the States, 2 vols. 4th ed. 1575p. 1998. 245.00 (*0-8103-0449-X*) Gale.

Bair, Frederick H., Jr. The Zoning Board Manual. LC 84-60300. 132p. 1984. pap. 24.95 (*0-918286-32-8*, Planners Press) Am Plan Assn.

***Bair, Janet.** Devotions for Young Readers. (Illus.). 224p. (J). (gr. k-3). 2000. pap. 12.99 (*0-7847-1268-9*, 23951) Standard Pub.

Bair, Janet M. Devotions for Young Readers. rev. ed. Holder, Greg, ed. (Illus.). 176p. (J). (gr. k-3). 1998. 9.99 (*0-7847-0568-2*, 24-23940) Standard Pub.

Bair, Jeanette, ed. see American Occupational Therapy Association Staff.

Bair, Johann. Republik der Philippinen: Staat - Kirchen - Religionsgesellschaften und Religionsfreiheit. (Europaische Hochschulschriften Ser.: Reihe 2, Bd. 2130). (GER.). 155p. 1997. 35.95 (*3-631-31775-1*) P Lang Pubng.

Bair, Julene. One Degree West: Reflections of a Plainsdaughter. (First Series). 192p. 2000. pap. 16.00 (*0-922811-45-8*) Mid-List.

Bair, Lillian, jt. auth. see Bair, Ray.

***Bair, Linda & Andrews, Jill.** Fiddle Dee Dee: Songs, Stories & Activities. (Illus.). 120p. 2000. pap. text, teacher ed. 15.95 (*1-57950-037-4*, Alleyside) Highsmith Pr.

Bair, Lowell, tr. see Arsan, Emmanuelle.

Bair, Lowell, tr. see Dumas, Alexandre.

Bair, Lowell, tr. see Flaubert, Gustave.

Bair, Lowell, tr. see Halter, Marek.

Bair, Lowell, tr. see Hugo, Victor.

Bair, Lowell, tr. see Leroux, Gaston.

Bair, Puran Khan. Living from the Heart: Heart Rhythm Meditation for Energy, Clarity, Peace, Joy & Inner Power. LC 97-49858. 304p. 1998. pap. 14.00 (*0-609-80313-1*) Crown.

Bair, Ray & Bair, Lillian. God's Managers. 3rd rev. ed. 48p. 1981. pap. 4.99 (*0-8361-3406-0*) Herald Pr.

Bair, W. G. Igt: The First Fifty Years. x, 155p. 1991. 50.00 (*0-910091-84-6*) Inst Gas Tech.

Bair, W. G. & Linden, H. R. Continuous Production of Natural Gas Supplements from Natural Gasoline & Petroleum Distillates in a Tube Furnace. (Research Bulletin Ser.: No.27). iv, 83p. 1960. pap. 25.00 (*1-58222-013-1*) Inst Gas Tech.

Bairacli, Juliette De, see De Bairacli, Juliette.

Bairacli Levy, Juliette de, see De Bairacli Levy, Juliette.

Bairam, Erkin I. Homogenous & Nonhomogeneous Production Functions: Theory & Applications. LC 94-19038. 152p. 1994. 68.95 (*1-85628-550-2*, Pub. by Avebry) Ashgate Pub Co.

Bairam, Erkin I., ed. Production & Cost Functions: Specification, Measurement & Applications. LC 98-71456. 144p. 1998. text 55.95 (*1-84014-378-9*, Pub. by Ashgate Pub) Ashgate Pub Co.

— Studies in Labour Economics. 159p. 1993. 66.95 (*1-85628-476-X*, Pub. by Avebry) Ashgate Pub Co.

Bairathi, Shashi. Tribal Culture: Economy & Health. (C). 1991. 18.00 (*0-8364-2803-X*, Pub. by Rawat Pubns) S Asia.

Baird. Cooking with Mickey. LC 97-80313. 96p. (J). 1998. 18.45 (*0-7868-3190-1*, Pub. by Hyperion) Time Warner.

— A Critical Concordance to the Gospel According to Matthew, Vol. 39. 1994. pap. 269.95 (*0-935106-36-7*) E Mellen.

— Environmental Chemistry. 2nd ed. LC 98-39152. 1998. pap. text 68.95 (*0-7167-3153-3*) W H Freeman.

— Environmental Chemistry. 2nd ed. 1999. pap. text 25.95 (*0-7167-3435-4*) W H Freeman.

— Environmental Chemistry. 4th ed. 1995. pap. text, student ed. 20.95 (*0-7167-2707-2*) W H Freeman.

— Hot Sites. 1999. pap. 29.95 (*0-688-15888-9*, Wm Morrow) Morrow Avon.

***Baird.** Liberal Arts Chemistry. 2001. pap. text. write for info. (*0-7167-3902-X*) W H Freeman.

Baird. Scenery of Scotland: The Structure Beneath. 3rd ed. (Illus.). 64p. 1995. pap. 6.95 (*0-948636-24-6*, 6246, Pub. by Natl Mus Scotland) A Schwartz & Co.

Baird & Bunchbinder. Bankruptcy for Paralegals. 2nd ed. LC 93-80971. 1994. lib. bdg. 32.00 (*0-316-11441-3*, Aspen Law & Bus) Aspen Pub.

— Cases, Problems & Materials on Bankruptcy. 1376p. 1994. suppl. ed. 14.95 (*0-316-07685-6*) Little.

***Baird & Lafferty.** Tele-nurse: Telephone Triage Protocols. 2000. pap. 44.75 (*0-7668-2047-5*) Delmar.

Baird, jt. auth. see Andrews, Patricia H.

Baird, jt. auth. see Thompson.

Baird, A. Craig, ed. see Goodrich, Chauncey A.

Baird, A. W. Studies in Pascal's Ethics. (Archives Internationales D'Histoire des Idees Ser.: No. 16). 108p. 1975. pap. text 62.00 (*90-247-1677-2*, Pub. by M Nijhoff) Kluwer Academic.

***Baird, Alan C. & Bartos, Aniko J.** 9TimeZones.com: An Email Screenplay Collaboration Between Hungary. LC 99-91107. 349p. 1999. 25.00 (*0-7388-0612-9*); pap. 18.00 (*0-7388-0613-7*) Xlibris Corp.

Baird, Alison, jt. auth. see Brookes, Diane.

Baird, Allen J. Family Life Course & the Economic Status of Birth Cohorts: The United States & Western Europe, 1950-1980. (Studies in Historical Demography). 336p. 1990. reprint ed. text 25.00 (*0-8240-3999-8*) Garland.

— Option Market Making: Trading & Risk Analysis for the Financial & Commodity Option Markets. LC 92-12010. (Wiley Finance Editions Ser.). 224p. 1992. 69.95 (*0-471-57832-0*) Wiley.

Baird, Andrew. Eco-Hydrology. 1999. pap. 29.99 (*0-415-16273-4*) Routledge.

Baird, Anne. Space Camp: The Great Adventures for NASA Hopefuls. LC 91-21587. (Illus.). 48p. (J). (gr. 3 up). 1992. 14.00 (*0-688-10227-1*, Wm Morrow) Morrow Avon.

— The U. S. Space Camp Book of Astronauts. LC 95-10634. 48p. (J). (gr. 4-7). 1996. 16.00 (*0-688-12226-4*, Wm Morrow) Morrow Avon.

— The U. S. Space Camp Book of Rockets. LC 93-26148. (Official U. S. & Space Camp Book). (Illus.). (J). (gr. 3 up). 1994. lib. bdg. 14.93 (*0-688-12229-9*, Wm Morrow) Morrow Avon.

Baird, Arthur J., ed. see Parunak, Van Dyke H.

Baird, Arthur J., ed. see Radday, Yehuda T. & Levi, Yaakov.

Baird, B. Joyce, jt. auth. see Maynard, Donald.

Baird, Betty S. The Legacy of the Cowbird. LC 94-67722. 280p. 1995. 22.00 (*1-886029-00-8*) Spider Hill Pr.

Baird, Bob & McBurney, Craig. Electronic Day Trading to Win. LC 99-30534. 221p. 1999. 39.95 (*0-471-35072-9*) Wiley.

Baird, Brian. Are We Having Fun Yet? Enjoying the Outdoors with Partners, Families, & Groups. LC 95-550. (Illus.). 192p. 1995. pap. 12.95 (*0-89886-449-6*) Mountaineers.

Baird, Brian N. The Internship, Practicum & Field Placement Handbook: A Guide for the Helping Professions. 2nd ed. LC 98-11860. 210p. 1998. pap. text 38.20 (*0-13-923962-6*) P-H.

Baird, Bruce F. Managerial Decisions under Uncertainty: An Introduction to the Analysis of Decision Making. 2nd ed. LC 88-33842. (Engineering Management Ser.). 544p. 1989. 130.00 (*0-471-85891-9*) Wiley.

***Baird, Carolyn & Cartwright, Roger.** Development & Growth of the Cruise Industry. 336p. 1999. 56.95 (*0-7506-4384-6*) Buttrwrth-Heinemann.

Baird, Cathryn, ed. see Abernethy, C. E.

Baird, Charles O. Gauging the Potential Investment Efficiency of the Forest Resource in a Depressed Area: A Study in Methodology with Application to the Cumberland Plateau Section of Appalachia. LC SD0436.T44B3. (Duke University, School of Forestry Bulletin Ser.: No. 17). (Illus.). 141p. reprint ed. pap. 43.80 (*0-7837-6046-9*, 204585900008) Bks Demand.

Baird, Charles W. History of the Huguenot Emigration to America, 2 vols. in 1. LC 66-29569. (Illus.). 802p. 1998. reprint ed. 45.00 (*0-8063-0554-1*) Genealog Pub.

— Huguenot Emigration to America, 2 vols., Set. (Illus.). 1801p. 1996. reprint ed. lib. bdg. 79.00 (*0-8328-4993-6*) Higginson Bk Co.

— Opportunity or Privilege: Labor Legislation in America. (Studies in Social Philosophy & Policy: No. 4). 97p. (Orig.). 1984. pap. 14.95 (*0-912051-02-7*) Transaction Pubs.

Baird, D., jt. auth. see Watkins, T. F.

Baird, D. C. Experimentation: An Introduction to Measurement Theory & Experiment Design. 3rd ed. LC 94-13384. 224p. (C). 1994. pap. 26.67 (*0-13-303298-1*) P-H.

Baird, D. T., et al, eds. Organ-Selective Actions of Steroid Hormones. LC 95-42665. (Ernst Schering Research Foundation Workshop Ser.: No. 16). 1995. write for info. (*0-387-60338-7*); 68.95 (*3-540-60338-7*) Spr-Verlag.

Baird, Dan, jt. ed. see Allanson, Brian.

Baird, David. Arty Cats. (Illus.). 96p. 1999. text 15.95 (*1-55670-884-X*) Stewart Tabori & Chang.

***Baird, David.** Arty Cats Postcard Book. (Illus.). 1999. pap. 10.95 (*1-55670-954-4*) Stewart Tabori & Chang.

— Arty Dogs. (Illus.). 96p. 1999. 15.95 (*1-55670-932-3*) Stewart Tabori & Chang.

Baird, David. Frommer's Cancun, Cozumel & the Yucatan 2000. 295p. 1999. pap. 14.95 (*0-02-863130-7*) Macmillan Gen Ref.

— Golf. (Infatuation Ser.). 1998. 12.95 (*1-897954-88-3*, Pub. by Mus Quilts Pub) Sterling.

— Job: A Story of Redemption. 110p. (Orig.). 1997. pap. 6.00 (*1-885857-19-5*) Four Wnds Pubng.

***Baird, David.** Northern Lights: Lighthouses of Canada. 260p. 1999. pap. 21.95 (*1-894073-09-6*) Lynx Images.

— Spain Trip Planner & Guide. 2nd ed. (Illus.). 2000. pap. 17.95 (*0-658-00992-3*, Passprt Bks) NTC Contemp Pub Co.

— A Thousand Paths to Enlightenment. 468p. 2000. pap. 9.95 (*1-57071-525-4*) Sourcebks.

— A Thousand Paths to Happiness. 468p. 2000. pap. 9.95 (*1-57071-526-2*) Sourcebks.

— A Thousand Paths to Tranquility. 468p. 2000. pap. 9.95 (*1-57071-527-0*) Sourcebks.

— A Thousand Paths to Wisdom. 468p. 2000. pap. 9.95 (*1-57071-528-9*) Sourcebks.

Baird, David T., et al, eds. Modern Methods of Inducing Abortion. LC 95-14056. (Illus.). 220p. 1995. 99.95 (*0-86542-819-0*) Blackwell Sci.

Baird, Davis, et al, eds. Heinrich Hertz: Classical Physicist, Modern Philosopher. LC 97-23406. (Boston Studies in the Philosophy of Science: No. 198). 318p. 1997. 128.00 (*0-7923-4653-X*) Kluwer Academic.

Baird, Donald G. Polymer Processing: Principles & Design. 346p. 1995. text 145.00 (*0-7506-9105-0*) Buttrwrth-Heinemann.

Baird, Donald G. & Collias, Dimitris I. Polymer Processing: Principles & Design. LC 98-2551. 360p. 1998. 94.95 (*0-471-25453-3*) Wiley.

Baird, Donald J., et al. Aquaculture & Water Resources Management. LC 96-5880. (Illus.). 219p. 1996. text 125.00 (*0-632-03926-4*) Blackwell Sci.

***Baird, Douglas.** Inductive Logic: Probability & Statistics. 400p. 1999. pap. text 38.00 (*0-536-02787-0*) Pearson Custom.

Baird, Douglas, et al. Excavations at Kharabeh Shattani, Vol. 2. 206p. 1996. pap. 43.50 (*0-614-21835-7*) David Brown.

Baird, Douglas G. Bankruptcy. 2nd ed. 1376p. 1990. 57.00 (*0-316-07681-3*, Aspen Law & Bus) Aspen Pub.

— The Elements of Bankruptcy. 2nd rev. ed. (University Textbook Ser.). 283p. 1993. pap. text 14.95 (*1-56662-092-9*) Foundation Pr.

Baird, Douglas G., et al, eds. Commercial & Debtor-Creditor Law: Selected Statutes. 1957p. 1995. pap. text 27.95 (*1-56662-279-4*) Foundation Pr.

Baird, Douglas G. & Jackson, Thomas H. Cases, Problems & Materials on Bankruptcy. LC 84-82546. (C). 1985. 37.00 (*0-316-07677-5*, Aspen Law & Bus) Aspen Pub.

— Cases, Problems, & Materials on Bankruptcy. 2nd ed. 1376p. 1990. teacher ed. write for info. (*0-316-07684-8*, 76848) Aspen Law.

Baird, Douglas G. & Jackson, Thomas J. Security Interests in Personal Property: Cases, Problems & Materials. (University Casebook Ser.). 889p. 1990. reprint ed. pap. text. write for info. (*0-88277-604-5*) Foundation Pr.

— Security Interests in Personal Property: Cases, Problems & Materials. 2nd ed. (University Casebook Ser.). 889p. 1990. reprint ed. text 39.50 (*0-88277-549-9*) Foundation Pr.

Baird, Douglas G., et al. Commercial & Debtor-Creditor Law: Selected Statutes, 1996. 1825p. 1996. pap. text. write for info. (*1-56662-375-8*) Foundation Pr.

— Commercial & Debtor-Creditor Law: Selected Statutes, 1997 Edition. 1860p. 1997. pap. text. write for info. (*1-56662-489-4*) Foundation Pr.

— Commercial & Debtor-Creditor Law: Selected Statutes, 1998 Edition. 1872p. 1998. pap. text 29.50 (*1-56662-627-7*) Foundation Pr.

— Game Theory & the Law. LC 94-8625. (Illus.). 320p. 1994. text 52.95 (*0-674-34119-8*, BAIGAM) HUP.

— Game Theory & the Law. (Illus.). 336p. 1998. pap. 24.95 (*0-674-34111-2*) HUP.

Baird, E. Thompson. Theobold the Iron-Hearted. rev. ed. (Character Building Ser.). (Illus.). 64p. (J). (gr. 4-6). 1990. pap. 5.25 (*1-58339-058-8*, C9) Triangle Press.

Baird, Elizabeth. Apples, Peaches & Pears. 96p. spiral bd. 12.95 (*0-88862-128-0*, Pub. by J Lorimer) Formac Dist Ltd.

— Classic Canadian Cooking: Menus For The Seasons. LC 96-132795. 200p. pap. 19.95 (*1-55028-502-5*, Pub. by J Lorimer) Formac Dist Ltd.

— Quick Suppers, No. 10. 1996. pap. 12.71 (*0-345-39807-6*) Ballantine Pub Grp.

— Weekend Pleasures, No. 9. 1996. pap. 12.71 (*0-345-39806-8*) Ballantine Pub Grp.

Baird, Ellen T. The Drawings of Sahagun's Primeros Memoriales: Structure & Style. LC 93-276. 1993. 37.95 (*0-8061-2533-0*) U of Okla Pr.

Baird, Floyd M., jt. auth. see Kyle, Robert C.

***Baird, Forrest E.** Philosophic Classics. 3rd ed. (Illus.). 526p. 1999. pap. text 34.00 (*0-13-021315-2*) P-H.

— Philosophic Classics: From Plato to Derrida. 3rd ed. LC 98-50173. 1198p. (C). 1999. pap. text 37.80 (*0-13-021532-5*) P-H.

— Philosophic Classics Vol. 1: Ancient Philosophy. 3rd ed. (Illus.). 552p. (C). 1999. pap. text 33.60 (*0-13-021314-4*) P-H.

— Philosophic Classics Vol. 3: Modern Philosophy. 3rd ed. (Illus.). 646p. (C). 1999. pap. text 33.60 (*0-13-021316-0*) P-H.

— Philosophic Classics Vol. 4: Nineteenth - Century Philosophy. 2nd ed. LC 98-32332. 499p. (C). 1999. pap. text 34.00 (*0-13-021533-3*) P-H.

Baird, Forrest E., intro. Human Thought & Action: Readings in Western Intellectual History. LC 92-14866. 322p. (Orig.). (C). 1992. pap. text 52.50 (*0-8191-8762-3*); pap. text 24.50 (*0-8191-8763-1*) U Pr of Amer.

***Baird, Forrest E. & Kaufmann, Walter, eds.** Philosophic Classics Vol.5: Twentieth Century Philosophy, Vol. 5. 2nd ed. 439p. (C). 1999. pap. text 33.60 (*0-13-021534-1*) P-H.

Baird, Frances. Action Man: The Gold Medal Doll for Boys 1966-1984. (Illus.). 144p. (Orig.). pap. 24.95 (*1-872727-36-0*, Pub. by New Cavendish) Pincushion Pr.

Baird, Frank L., ed. Mexican Americans: Political Power, Influence, or Resource. (Graduate Studies: No. 14). (Illus.). 108p. (Orig.). 1977. pap. 7.00 (*0-89672-024-1*) Tex Tech Univ Pr.

Baird, Frieda Y. Do Yourself a Favor! Now Overcome Fears, Hurts & Failures: Gain New Insights to Encourage & Appreciate Yourself, Vol. 1. Baird, Jim, ed. LC 98-91551. (Let Us Remember Ser.). (Illus.). xii, 136p. (Orig.). 1998. pap. 14.95 (*0-9664044-1-6*) New Venture SC.

Baird, George. The Space of Appearance. (Illus.). 512p. 1995. 52.50 (*0-262-02378-4*) MIT Pr.

Baird, George, et al, eds. Energy Performance of Buildings. 216p. 1984. 123.00 (*0-8493-5186-3*, TJ163, CRC Reprint) Franklin.

Baird, George, et al. Building Evaluation Techniques. LC 95-24810. 320p. 1996. 60.00 (*0-07-003308-0*) McGraw.

Baird, George W. Great American Masons. 109p. 1992. reprint ed. pap. 12.95 (*1-56459-053-4*) Kessinger Pub.

Baird, Gordon C., jt. ed. see Brett, Carlton E.

Baird, H. Gordon. Management Styles for the '90s. 140p. (Orig.). 1982. 15.00 (*0-943000-00-9*) Telstar Inc.

Baird, H. S., et al, eds. Structured Document Image Analysis. LC 92-27386. ix, 584p. 1992. 100.95 (*0-387-55141-7*) Spr-Verlag.

Baird, Helen. Mosaics. (New Crafts Ser.). (Illus.). 96p. 1997. 15.95 (*1-85967-382-1*, Lorenz Bks) Anness Pub.

Baird, Henry C., ed. The Painter, Gilder & Varnisher's Companion, Containing Rules & Regulations in Every Thing, Relating to the Arts of Painting, Gilding, Varnishing & Glass-Staining... (Illus.). 216p. 1995. reprint ed. lib. bdg. 35.00 (*0-8328-4498-5*) Higginson Bk Co.

Baird, Henry M. History of the Rise of the Huguenots of France, 2 vols. LC 79-130236. reprint ed. 110.00 (*0-404-00520-9*) AMS Pr.

— Huguenots & Henry of Navarre, 2 vols. LC 76-130987. reprint ed. 89.50 (*0-404-00540-3*) AMS Pr.

— The Huguenots & the Revocation of the Edict of Nantes, 2 vols. LC 76-161752. (C). reprint ed. 94.50 (*0-404-08003-0*) AMS Pr.

Baird, Henry S. Model-Based Image Matching Using Location. (Association for Computing Machinery Distinguished Dissertation Ser.: 1984). (Illus.). 115p. 1985. 25.00 (*0-262-02220-6*) MIT Pr.

Baird, Henry W. & Gordon, Eleanora C. The Neurological Evaluation of Infants & Children. LC 65-80419. (Clinics in Developmental Medicine Ser.: Nos. 84-85). (Illus.). 249p. (C). 1991. text 47.95 (*0-521-41205-6*, Pub. by Mc Keith Pr) Cambridge U Pr.

Baird-Holmes, Sue, jt. auth. see Childs, Sharon G.

Baird, I., jt. auth. see McLeeland, C.

Baird, J. Arthur. Audience Criticism & the Historical Jesus. 1969. pap. 49.95 (*0-664-20846-0*) E Mellen.

— A Comparative Analysis of the Gospel Genre: The

B

Synoptic Mode & Its Uniqueness. LC 91-43164. (Studies in the Bible & Early Christianity: Vol. 24). 180p. 1991. lib. bdg. 79.95 (*0-7734-9460-X*) E Mellen.

Baird, J. Arthur & Freedman, David Noel. Critical Concordance to the Synoptic Gospels, Vol. 1-A. (Computer Bible Ser.). 1971. 49.95 (*0-935106-48-0*) E Mellen.

Baird, J. Arthur & Thompson, J. David. A Critical Concordance to I, II Peter. rev. ed. Freedman, David N., ed. (Computer Bible Ser.: Vol. 32). 232p. 1989. pap. 89.95 (*0-935106-28-6*) E Mellen.

— A Critical Concordance to I, II, III John & Jude. (Computer Bible Ser.: Vol. 33). 1991. pap. 89.95 (*0-935106-29-4*) E Mellen.

— A Critical Concordance to the Letter of James. (Computer Bible Ser.: Vol. 31). 144p. 1989. pap. 89.95 (*0-935106-27-8*) E Mellen.

Baird, J. Arthur, ed. see Martin, Raymond & Scorza, Sylvio.

Baird, J. Arthur, ed. see Morton, A. Q., et al.

Baird, J. Arthur, jt. ed. see Thompson, J. David.

Baird, J. G., ed. Private Letters of the Marquess of Dalhousie. (C). 1993. 14.00 (*81-85557-18-7*, Pub. by Low Price) S Asia.

Baird, J. L. & Kane, John R., eds. Rossignol: An Edition & Translation. LC 78-38. 99p. reprint ed. pap. 30.70 (*0-7837-1349-5*, 204149700020) Bks Demand.

Baird, Jack V., jt. auth. see Sopher, Charles D.

***Baird, Jacqueline.** Cuestion de Confianza (A Question of Trust) (Bianca Ser.). (SPA.). 2000. mass mkt. 3.50 (*0-373-33579-2*, 1-33579-3) Harlequin Bks.

Baird, Jacqueline. Desir Vengeur. (Azur Ser.: No. 731). (FRE.). 1998. mass mkt. 3.50 (*0-373-34731-6*, 1-34731-9) Harlequin Bks.

— A Devious Desire. (Presents Ser.). 1996. per. 3.50 (*0-373-11827-9*, 1-11827-2) Harlequin Bks.

— A Devious Desire. large type ed. (Harlequin Romance Ser.). 1996. 20.95 (*0-263-14505-0*) Thorndike Pr.

— Dishonourable Proposal. (Presents Ser.). 1993. pap. 2.89 (*0-373-11558-X*, 1-11558-3) Harlequin Bks.

— Gamble on Passion. LC 95-4589. (Presents Ser.). 187p. 1995. per. 3.25 (*0-373-11726-4*, 1-11726-6) Harlequin Bks.

— Gamble on Passion. large type ed. (Harlequin Romance Ser.). 1994. lib. bdg. 19.95 (*0-263-13869-0*) Thorndike Pr.

— Giordanni's Proposal. (Presents Ser.: No. 2029). 1999. per. 3.75 (*0-373-12029-X*, 1-12029-4) Harlequin Bks.

— Giordanni's Proposal. 1999. 21.95 (*0-263-15844-6*, G K Hall & Co) Mac Lib Ref.

— Guilty Passion. (Presents Ser.). 1994. per. 2.99 (*0-373-11627-6*, 1-11627-6) Harlequin Bks.

— A Husband of Convenience. (Romance Ser.). 1999. per. 3.75 (*0-373-12052-4*, 1-12052-6) Harlequin Bks.

***Baird, Jacqueline.** Husband of Convenience. large type ed. (Romance Ser.). 1999. 21.95 (*0-263-16241-9*) Mills & Boon.

— Husband on Trust. (Presents Ser.). 2000. mass mkt. 3.99 (*0-373-12088-5*) Harlequin Bks.

— Marido de Conveniencia.Tr. of Husband of Convenience. (ENG & SPA.). 2000. per. 3.50 (*0-373-33539-3*) Harlequin Bks.

Baird, Jacqueline. Master of Passion. (Presents Ser.). 1994. per. 2.99 (*0-373-11683-7*, 1-11683-9) Harlequin Bks.

— Mistaken for a Mistress. 1997. per. 3.50 (*0-373-11915-1*, 1-11915-5) Harlequin Bks.

— Mistaken for a Mistress. large type ed. (Harlequin Romance Ser.). 1997. 20.95 (*0-263-15165-4*) Mac Lib Ref.

***Baird, Jacqueline.** A Most Passionate Revenge. (Presents Ser.: Bk. 2137). 2000. mass mkt. 3.99 (*0-373-12137-7*, 1-12137-5) Harlequin Bks.

Baird, Jacqueline. Nothing Changes Love. LC 95-13706. (Presents Ser.). 188p. 1995. per. 3.25 (*0-373-11757-4*, 1-11757-1) Harlequin Bks.

— Passionate Betrayal. (Presents Ser.: No. 431). 1992. pap. 2.79 (*0-373-11431-1*, 1-11431-3) Harlequin Bks.

— Paul's Revenge. large type ed. 1997. 20.95 (*0-263-14794-0*) Thorndike Pr.

— Raul's Revenge. 1997. per. 3.50 (*0-373-11876-7*, 1-11876-9) Harlequin Bks.

— The Reluctant Fiancee. (Presents Ser.). 1998. per. 3.75 (*0-373-11942-9*, 1-11942-9) Harlequin Bks.

— Reluctant Fiancee, Vol. 194. large type ed. 1998. 21.95 (*0-263-15560-9*, G K Hall & Co) Mac Lib Ref.

— Secretos de Familia: Mistaken for a Mistress. (Bianca Ser.: Vol. 113).Tr. of Family's Secrets. (SPA.). 1998. per. 3.50 (*0-373-33463-X*, 1-33463-0) Harlequin Bks.

— The Valentine Child. LC 95-23071. (Presents Ser.). 187p. 1996. per. 3.50 (*0-373-11795-7*, 1-11795-1) Harlequin Bks.

— The Valentine Child. large type ed. (Harlequin Romance Ser.). 1996. 19.95 (*0-263-14573-5*) Thorndike Pr.

Baird, James. The Dome & the Rock: Structure in the Poetry of Wallace Stevens. LC 68-19701. 368p. reprint ed. pap. 114.10 (*0-608-14483-5*, 202530100043) Bks Demand.

***Baird, James D.** The Modern Christian's Happiness Plan. LC 99-69287. 176p. 2000. pap. 11.95 (*1-57921-276-X*) WinePress Pub.

Baird, James S. Hoard's Dairyman Dairy Collectibles. 3rd ed. (Illus.). 72p. (Orig.). 1994. pap. 5.00 (*0-932147-24-0*) Hoard & Sons Co.

***Baird, Janet H.** Journey to the Edge of Nowhere. LC 99-88344. 132p. (J). (gr. 3-6). 1999. 11.95 (*1-889658-19-7*) New Canaan Pub.

— Journey to the Edge of Nowhere. LC 99-88344. (Illus.). 132p. (J). (gr. 3-7). 1999. pap. 6.95 (*1-889658-15-4*) New Canaan Pub.

Baird, Janet H., ed. These Harvest Years. LC 74-167308. (Essay Index Reprint Ser.). 1977. reprint ed. 20.95 (*0-8369-2581-5*) Ayer.

Baird, Jay W. The Mythical World of Nazi War Propaganda, 1939-1945. LC 74-83132. (Illus.). 349p. reprint ed. pap. 108.20 (*0-8357-8961-6*, 203320300085) Bks Demand.

— To Die for Germany: Heroes in the Nazi Pantheon. LC 89-45189. (Illus.). 350p. 1990. reprint ed. 35.00 (*0-253-31125-X*, MB757); reprint ed. pap. 15.95 (*0-253-20757-6*) Ind U Pr.

Baird, Jim, ed. see Baird, Frieda Y.

Baird, John. Make-Up. rev. ed. 132p. 1941. 5.00 (*0-573-69031-6*) French.

— The Power of One. LC 97-70295. 300p. (C). 1997. text 35.00 (*0-943590-90-6*) Amer College.

Baird, John B. Conducting Church Meetings: Korean Edition. Chan-hie Kim, tr. 96p. (Orig.). 1993. pap. 7.95 (*0-687-31683-9*) Abingdon.

Baird, John C. Sensation & Judgment: Complementarity Theory of Psychophysics. LC 96-26481. (Scientific Psychology Ser.). 352p. 1997. 79.95 (*0-8058-1830-8*) L Erlbaum Assocs.

Baird, John C. & Lutkus, Anthony D., eds. Mind Child Architecture. LC 81-69937. 224p. reprint ed. pap. 69.50 (*0-7837-0371-6*, 204069100018) Bks Demand.

Baird, John D. Fifteen Years in Hawken Lode. 24.95 (*0-88227-011-7*) Gun Room.

— Hawken Rifles: The Mountain Man's Choice. 29.95 (*0-88227-010-9*) Gun Room.

Baird, John D., ed. Editing Texts of the Romantic Period: Papers Given at the Conference on Editorial Problems, University of Toronto, November, 1971. LC 72-96441. (Conference on Editorial Problems Ser.: No. 7). 1987. 42.50 (*0-404-63657-8*) AMS Pr.

Baird, John D., ed. see Cowper, William.

Baird, John E. Conducting Church Meetings: Everything You Need to Know to Run an Orderly Effective Church. 1991. pap. 5.95 (*0-687-31682-0*) Abingdon.

Baird, John E., jt. auth. see Andrews, Patricia H.

Baird, John R. Collectors Guide to Kuribayashi - Petri Cameras. LC 91-71476. (Illus.). 288p. 1991. 34.95 (*0-931838-16-9*) Centennial Photo Serv.

— The Japanese Camera. 110p. 1990. write for info. (*1-879561-03-4*); pap. 19.95 (*1-879561-02-6*) Hist Camera Pubns.

Baird, John W., jt. auth. see Stull, James B.

Baird, Jonathan. Day Job: A Workplace Reader for the Restless Age. LC 97-80473. (Illus.). 160p. 1998. 24.95 (*0-9660805-2-1*) Allen & Osborne.

***Baird, Jonathan.** Day Job: A Workplace Reader for the Restless Age. 2000. pap. 17.95 (*0-312-26307-4*) St Martin.

Baird, Joseph A., Jr. Joseph Fleck, 1892-1977: A Selection of Paintings from the Estate. LC 94-65873. (Illus.). 32p. (Orig.). 1994. pap. text 15.00 (*0-935037-54-3*) G Peters Gallery.

Baird, Joseph L., ed. & tr. see Hildegard of Bingen.

Baird, Joseph L., tr. see Hildegard of Bingen.

Baird, Julianne C., ed. see Aricola, Johann Friedrich.

Baird, Karen L. Gender Justice & the Health Care System. LC 97-35313. (Health Care Policy in the United States Ser.). 286p. 1998. text 63.00 (*0-8153-3056-1*) Garland.

Baird, Keith E., intro. Commentaries on a Creative Encounter: Proceedings of a Conference on the Culture & Literature of Francophone Africa, Held on October 3, 1987, at Buffalo State College. (FRE.). (Orig.). (C). 1988. pap. text. write for info. (*0-9621537-0-2*) NY AAI.

Baird, Keith E. & Twining, Mary A. Sea Island Roots: African Presence in the Carolinas & Georgia: Testimonies of African Cultural Continuity. LC 88-70201. 325p. 1990. 45.00 (*0-86543-068-3*); pap. 12.95 (*0-86543-069-1*) Africa World.

Baird, Kristin. Customer Service in Health Care: A Grassroots Approach to Creating a Culture of Service Excellen. LC 99-36797. 1999. pap. 35.00 (*1-55648-269-8*) AHPI.

Baird, Kristin, jt. auth. see Kile, Marilyn.

Baird, L. Lawrence. Mail Order Millions: It Worked for Me . . . It Will Work for You. 1995. 15.95 (*0-9623724-2-0*) Baird-Hedges Pub.

***Baird, Leon, text.** Good Thoughts from Good Friends & Family. 32p. 2000. 9.95 (*1-929669-01-1*) Vinings Pubng.

Baird, Leonard & Hartnett, Rodney T. Understanding Student & Faculty Life. LC 79-24863. (Jossey-Bass Series in Higher Education). 217p. reprint ed. pap. 67.30 (*0-8357-4931-2*, 203786100009) Bks Demand.

Baird, Leonard L., ed. Increasing Graduate Student Retention & Degree Attainment. LC 85-645339. (New Directions for Institutional Research Ser.: No. IR 80). 95p. (Orig.). 1993. pap. 22.00 (*1-55542-675-1*) Jossey-Bass.

Baird, Ljiljana. Simple Outdoor Style. (Simple Style Ser.). 112p. 1998. 24.95 (*0-8230-4801-2*) Watsn-Guptill.

Baird, Ljiljana, jt. auth. see Wood, Dorothy.

Baird, M. Katherine, jt. ed. see Baird, Robert M.

Baird, Macaran A., jt. auth. see Doherty, William J.

Baird, Margery A., ed. see De Manchicourt, Pierre.

Baird, Marie L., tr. see De Wit, Han F.

Baird, Martha. Nice Deity. LC 55-11012. 1955. 8.95 (*0-910492-04-2*) Definition.

— Two Aesthetic Realism Papers: Opposites in the Drama; Opposites in Myself. LC 79-268159. 59p. (Orig.). 1971. pap. 5.50 (*0-910492-15-8*) Definition.

Baird, Martha, ed. see Siegel, Eli.

Baird, Martha, ed. see Siegel, Eli, et al.

Baird, Martin R. Guaranteed Results. 132p. (Orig.). (YA). (gr. 10 up). 1995. pap. 12.95 (*0-9643134-0-5*) Robinson & Assocs.

Baird, Mary & Larrivee-Cohen, Donna, eds. Painting Our Way to a Better Future: An Art-Coloring Book of Contemporary Career Options for Women. 2nd ed. (Illus.). 56p. (Orig.). (J). (gr. k-9). 1997. pap. 6.95 (*0-9627833-0-7*) Hard Hatted Women.

Baird, Mary E. Harding. Our Harding Family: Record of the Family & Descendants of Samuel Harding, Whose Ancestor was Joseph Harding, Son of John of England, & of Love Mayhew Harding, Wife of Samuel Harding, Whose Ancestor was Thos. Mayhew, Son of Joseph of England, with Historical Sketches. 179p. 1997. reprint ed. pap. 27.50 (*0-8328-8966-0*); reprint ed. lib. bdg. 37.50 (*0-8328-8965-2*) Higginson Bk Co.

Baird, Micah, et al, contrib. by. Mekong. (Illus.). 120p. 1999. pap. 22.95 (*0-9671943-1-8*) Majestic Pubg.

Baird, Michael L. Engineering Your Start-Up: A Guide for the High-Tech Entrepreneur. 294p. (Orig.). 1992. pap. 29.95 (*0-912045-48-5*) Prof Pubns CA.

— Starting a High Tech Company. LC 95-16795. (IEEE Engineers Guide to Business Ser.: vol. 7). 1995. 19.95 (*0-7803-2293-2*, EG107) Inst Electrical.

Baird-Middleton, Bruce, ed. see Coles, Robert.

Baird-Murray, Maureen. A World Overturned: A Burmese Childhood, 1933-1947. LC 98-26385. (Illus.). 192p. 1998. pap. 13.95 (*1-56656-246-5*, Interlink Bks) Interlink Pub.

Baird, Nancy D. David Wendel Yandell: Physician of Old Louisville. fac. ed. LC 77-80461. (Kentucky Bicentennial Bookshelf Ser.). 128p. 1978. pap. 39.70 (*0-7837-7586-5*, 204733900007) Bks Demand.

— Luke Pryor Blackburn: Physician, Governor, Reformer. LC 79-888. (Kentucky Bicentennial Bookshelf Ser.). 136p. reprint ed. pap. 42.20 (*0-7837-5817-0*, 204548400006) Bks Demand.

Baird, Nelle, ed. see Ray, Rose M.

Baird, Nicola. A Green World? LC 97-4302. (Viewpoints Ser.). 32p. (J). 1998. 22.00 (*0-531-14451-8*) Watts.

Baird, Norman. Criminal Law. 2nd ed. (Questions & Answers Ser.). 323p. 1995. 18.00 (*1-85941-262-9*, Pub. by Cavendish Pubng) Gaunt.

Baird, Pat. Be Good to Your Gut: Recipes & Tips for People with Digestive Problems. (Illus.). 160p. 1996. pap. 17.95 (*0-86542-472-1*) Blackwell Sci.

Baird, Pat. The Pyramid Cookbook. 1995. pap. 14.95 (*0-8050-3262-2*) H Holt & Co.

— The Pyramid Cookbook: Pleasure of the Food Guide Pyramid. 272p. 1995. 24.00 (*0-8050-2648-7*) H Holt & Co.

— Quick & Hearty: Meatless Microwave Meals Everyone Will Enjoy. LC 94-41784. 1995. pap. 14.95 (*0-8050-3743-8*, Owl) H Holt & Co.

Baird, R. & Bloomfield, S. Microbial Quality Assurance in Pharmaceuticals, Cosmetics, & Toiletries. 2nd ed. LC 96-217818. (Series in Pharmaceutical Sciences). 300p. 1996. 126.00 (*0-7484-0437-6*) Taylor & Francis.

Baird, R. M., et al. Culture Media for Food Microbiology. LC 93-15218. 508p. 1993. 201.00 (*0-444-81498-1*) Elsevier.

Baird, R. N., et al, eds. Human Disease for Dental Students. 340p. 1981. pap. 35.00 (*0-8464-1217-9*) Beekman Pubs.

Baird, Richard E. Study of the Stipitate Hydnums from the Southern Appalachian Mountains: Genera - Bankera, Hydnellum, Phellodon, Sarcodon. (Bibliotheca Mycologica: Vol. 104). (Illus.). 156p. 1986. 42.00 (*3-443-59005-5*, Pub. by Gebruder Borntraeger) Balogh.

— Type Studies of North American & Other Related Taxa of Stipitate Hydnums: Genera Bankera, Hydnellum, Phellodon, Sarcodon. (Bibliotheca Mycologica: Vol. 103). (GER., Illus.). 89p. 1986. 30.00 (*3-443-59004-7*, Pub. by Gebruder Borntraeger) Balogh.

Baird, Robert. Impressions & Experiences of the West Indies & North America in 1849. 1977. 19.95 (*0-8369-9216-4*, 9072) Ayer.

— Religion in the U. S. A., 2 vols. (Works of Rev. Robert Baird). 1985. reprint ed. lib. bdg. 89.00 (*0-932051-57-X*) Rprt Serv.

— Religion in the United States of America. LC 70-83411. (Religion in America, Ser. 1). 1975. reprint ed. 42.95 (*0-405-00232-7*) Ayer.

Baird, Robert, et al, eds. Contemporary Essays on Greek Ideas: The Kilgore Festschrift. LC 86-64032. 334p. 1987. 29.95 (*0-918954-46-0*) Baylor Univ Pr.

Baird, Robert & Rosenbaum, Stuart, eds. Bigotry, Prejudice, & Hatred: Definitions, Causes & Solutions. LC 92-26547. (Contemporary Issues Ser.). 238p. (Orig.). (C). 1992. pap. 16.95 (*0-87975-751-5*) Prometheus Bks.

***Baird, Robert & Rosenbaum, Stuart, eds.** Hatred, Bigotry, & Prejudice: Definitions, Causes & Solutions. LC 99-37902. (Contemporary Issues Ser.). 290p. 1999. pap. 18.95 (*1-57392-748-1*) Prometheus Bks.

Baird, Robert D. Category Formation & the History of Religions. 2nd ed. 192p. 1991. pap. text 25.95 (*3-11-012821-7*) Mouton.

— Essays in the History of Religions. LC 90-24985. (Toronto Studies in Religion: Vol. 11). VIII, 395p. (C). 1991. text 51.95 (*0-8204-1509-X*) P Lang Pubng.

Baird, Robert D., ed. Methodological Issues in Religious Studies. LC 75-44170. (Orig.). (C). 1976. pap. text 5.95 (*0-914914-07-3*); lib. bdg. 14.95 (*0-914914-08-1*) New Horizons.

— Religion & Law in Independent India. (C). 1993. 32.00 (*81-7304-035-4*, Pub. by Manohar) S Asia.

— Religion in Modern India. (C). 1989. 36.00 (*0-945921-03-9*) South Asia Pubns.

— Religion in Modern India. (C). 1995. reprint ed. 54.00 (*81-85054-64-9*, Pub. by Manohar) S Asia.

Baird, Robert M., ed. Same-Sex Marriage: The Moral & Legal Debate. LC 96-53057. 242p. 1997. pap. 16.95 (*1-57392-129-7*) Prometheus Bks.

***Baird, Robert M., et al, eds.** Cyberethics: Social & Moral Issues in the Computer Age. LC 99-88868. 300p. 2000. pap. 18.95 (*1-57392-790-2*) Prometheus Bks.

— The Media & Morality. LC 98-50669. (Contemporary Issues Ser.). (Illus.). 360p. 1999. pap. 18.95 (*1-57392-681-7*) Prometheus Bks.

Baird, Robert M. & Baird, M. Katherine, eds. Homosexuality: Debating the Issues. LC 95-20281. (Contemporary Issues Ser.). 282p. 1995. pap. 16.95 (*1-57392-003-7*) Prometheus Bks.

Baird, Robert M. & Rosenbaum, Stuart E. Morality & the Law. LC 88-18650. (Contemporary Issues Ser.). 148p. (C). 1988. pap. 16.95 (*0-87975-474-5*) Prometheus Bks.

Baird, Robert M. & Rosenbaum, Stuart E., eds. Animal Experimentation: The Moral Issues. LC 90-28879. (Contemporary Issues Ser.). 182p. (Orig.). (C). 1991. pap. 16.95 (*0-87975-667-5*) Prometheus Bks.

— The Ethics of Abortion: Pro-Life vs. Pro-Choice. 2nd rev. ed. LC 93-4266. (Contemporary Issues Ser.). 272p. (C). 1993. reprint ed. pap. 17.95 (*0-87975-805-8*) Prometheus Bks.

— Euthanasia: The Moral Issues. LC 89-24042. (Contemporary Issues Ser.). 216p. (Orig.). (C). 1989. pap. 16.95 (*0-87975-555-5*) Prometheus Bks.

— Pornography: Private Right or Public Menace? 2nd rev. ed. LC 98-5614. (Contemporary Issues Ser.). 286p. 1998. pap. 17.95 (*1-57392-207-2*) Prometheus Bks.

— Punishment & the Death Penalty: The Current Debate. LC 94-47521. (Contemporary Issues Ser.). 258p. 1995. pap. 16.95 (*0-87975-946-1*) Prometheus Bks.

Baird, Roiann. The Underside of Light. Date not set. write for info. (*0-9659632-1-7*) Verda Publ.

— Wyrrd Madwoman. Date not set. write for info. (*0-9659632-3-3*) Verda Publ.

Baird, Ron & Comerford, Dan. The Hammer: The King of Tools. 380p. (Orig.). 1989. pap. write for info. (*0-318-65327-3*) R Baird & D Comerford.

Baird, Russell N., et al. The Graphics of Communication: Methods, Media, & Technology. 6th ed. (Illus.). 352p. (C). 1993. text 81.00 (*0-03-074977-8*, Pub. by Harcourt Coll Pubs) Harcourt.

Baird, Russell N., jt. auth. see Click, J. William.

Baird, Scott J., ed. see Fujiwara, Yoichi.

Baird, Sean. MCSE Training Guide: SQL Server 6.5 Design & Implementation. LC 98-129835. 1997. 49.99 (*1-56205-830-4*) New Riders Pub.

— SQL Server System Administration. LC 98-87723. 1998. pap. 29.99 (*1-56205-955-6*) New Riders Pub.

Baird, Sharon, jt. compiled by see Spanks, Kim.

Baird-Smith, Robin. Living Water: An Anthology of Letters of Direction. LC 88-22096. 204p. reprint ed. pap. 63.30 (*0-7837-0510-7*, 204083400018) Bks Demand.

Baird, Spencer F. Mammals of North America: The Descriptions of Species Based Chiefly on the Collections in the Museum of the Smithsonian Institution. LC 73-17797. (Natural Sciences in America Ser.). (Illus.). 844p. 1974. reprint ed. 64.95 (*0-405-05710-5*) Ayer.

Baird, Spencer F., et al. Birds of North America: The Descriptions of Species Based Chiefly on the Collections in the Museum of the Smithsonian Institution, 2 vols. LC 73-17799. (Natural Sciences in America Ser.). (Illus.). 1974. 80.95 (*0-405-05715-6*) Ayer.

— A History of North American Birds: Land Birds, 3 vols., Set. LC 73-17798. (Natural Sciences in America Ser.). (Illus.). 1972p. 1974. reprint ed. 145.95 (*0-405-05711-3*) Ayer.

— A History of North American Birds: Land Birds, 3 vols., Vol. 1. LC 73-17798. (Natural Sciences in America Ser.). (Illus.). 1972p. 1974. reprint ed. 48.95 (*0-405-05712-1*) Ayer.

— A History of North American Birds: Land Birds, 3 vols., Vol. 2. LC 73-17798. (Natural Sciences in America Ser.). (Illus.). 1972p. 1974. reprint ed. 48.95 (*0-405-05713-X*) Ayer.

— A History of North American Birds: Land Birds, 3 vols., Vol. 3. LC 73-17798. (Natural Sciences in America Ser.). (Illus.). 1972p. 1974. reprint ed. 48.95 (*0-405-05714-8*) Ayer.

— Water Birds of North America, 2 vols. (Natural Sciences in America Ser.). (Illus.). 1974. 81.95 (*0-405-05716-4*) Ayer.

Baird, Spencer F., ed. see Copper, James G.

***Baird, Stuart T.** Performance Cycling: A Scientific Way to Get the Most Out of Your Bike. LC 00-131377. (Cycling Resources Ser.). (Illus.). 256p. 2000. pap. 29.95 (*1-892495-28-7*, Pub. by Van der Plas) Seven Hills Bk.

***Baird, Susan.** Audiobook Collections & Services: A Guide for Libraries. (Illus.). 88p. 2000. pap. 19.00 (*1-57950-034-X*) Highsmith Pr.

Baird, Susan. Behind Closed Doors: Gender, Sexuality & Touch in the Doctor/Patient Relationship. LC 97-32947. 224p. 1998. 55.00 (*0-86569-285-8*, Auburn Hse) Greenwood.

— Junking Be a Junk Millionaire: What Is Junk? The Changing Nature of Junk. LC 80-85023. (Illus.). 1984. pap. 12.95 (*0-913042-13-7*) Holland Hse Pr.

Baird, Tate, ed. Fitness & Nutrition: The Winning Combination. pap. write for info. (*0-914127-60-8*) UN.

Baird, Tate, ed. see Morgan, Judith.

Baird, Tate, ed. see Oana, Katherine.

Baird, Tate, ed. see Spataro, Lucian.

Baird, Thomas. Finding Fever. LC 81-48646. 224p. (J). (gr. 6 up). 1982. 12.95 (*0-06-020353-6*) HarpC Child Bks.

— Smart Rats. LC 90-4140. 224p. (YA). (gr. 7 up). 1990. 14.95 (*0-06-020364-1*) HarpC Child Bks.

— Where Time Ends. LC 87-45864. 288p. (YA). (gr. 7 up). 1988. 13.95 (*0-06-020359-5*) HarpC Child Bks.

Baird, Thomas B., jt. auth. see Hamblen, John W.

Baird, Timothy L. Changes in Breeding Bird Populations Between 1930 & 1985 in the Quarter Run Valley of Allegany State Park, New York. (Bulletin Ser.: No. 477). (Illus.). 41p. (Orig.). (C). 1991. pap. text 6.00 (*1-55557-189-1*) NYS Museum.

Baird, Traci L., et al. Ameu en el Tratamiento del Aborto Incompleto: Experiencia Clinica y Programatica. Orig. Title: MVA in the Treatment of Incomplete Abortion. (SPA.). 24p. (Orig.). 1996. pap. 4.00 (*1-882220-10-2*, INCMON-S95) IPAS.
— AMIU No Atendimento ao Abortamento Incompleto: Experiencia Clinica e Programatica. (POR.). 21p. (Orig.). 1996. pap. write for info. (*1-882220-09-9*) IPAS.
— MVA in the Treatment of Incomplete Abortion. LC 95-4492. 1995. pap. write for info. (*1-882220-08-0*) IPAS.
Baird, Vanessa. Eye to Eye--Women: Their Words & Worlds. 127p. 1997. pap. text 29.99 (*1-85242-581-4*) Serpents Tail.
Baird, W. David & Goble, Danney. The Story of Oklahoma. LC 93-47075. (Illus.). 528p. (J). 1994. text 28.95 (*0-8061-2650-7*) U of Okla Pr.
Baird, W. F., jt. ed. see Magoon, Orville T.
Baird, Wellesley. Guyana Gold: The Story of Wellesley Baird Guyana's Greatest Miner. LC 81-51666. 210p. (Orig.). 1982. pap. 8.00 (*1-57889-000-4*); pap. 12.00 (*1-57889-079-9*) Passeggiata.
Baird, Wilhelmina. Chaos Come Again. LC 96-209494. 320p. 1996. pap. 12.00 (*0-441-00369-9*) Ace Bks.
— Chaos Come Again. 336p. 1997. mass mkt. 5.99 (*0-441-00479-2*) Ace Bks.
— ClipJoint. 336p. (Orig.). 1994. mass mkt. 4.99 (*0-441-00090-8*) Ace Bks.
— CrashCourse. 288p. (Orig.). 1993. mass mkt. 4.99 (*0-441-12163-2*) Ace Bks.
— Psykosis. 416p. (Orig.). 1995. mass mkt. 5.99 (*0-441-00238-2*) Ace Bks.
Baird, Willard. OCP Training Guide: Oracle DBA. LC 98-84813. (OCP Training Guide Ser.). 800p. 1998. 59.99 (*1-56205-891-6*) New Riders Pub.
Baird, William. Baird: Genealogical Collections Concerning the Sir-Name of Baird & the Families of Auchmedden, Newbyth & Sauchton Hall. 120p. 1992. reprint ed. pap. 22.00 (*0-8328-2628-6*); reprint ed. lib. bdg. 32.00 (*0-8328-2627-8*) Higginson Bk Co.
— General Wauchope. LC 72-4077. (Black Heritage Library Collection). 1977. reprint ed. 21.95 (*0-8369-9094-3*) Ayer.
— History of New Testament Research: From Deism to Tubingen, Vol. 1. LC 92-22629. 488p. 1992. 58.00 (*0-8006-2626-5*, 1-2626, Fortress Pr) Augsburg Fortress.
Bairez, Jean & Hicher, P. Y. Elementary Mechanics of Soil Behaviour: Saturated Remoulded Soils. (Illus.). 184p. (C). 1994. 71.00 (*90-5410-156-3*, Pub. by A A Balkema) Ashgate Pub Co.
Bairi, B. R. Handbook of Nuclear Medical Instruments. 1994. pap. 12.95 (*0-07-462026-6*) McGraw-Hill Prof.
***Bairner, Alan.** Sports, Nationalism & Globalization: European & North American Perspectives. LC 00-32980. (C). 2001. pap. text 18.95 (*0-7914-4912-2*) State U NY Pr.
— Sports, Nationalism & Globalization: European & North American Perspectives. LC 00-32980. (C). 2001. text 57.50 (*0-7914-4911-4*) State U NY Pr.
Bairner, Alan, jt. auth. see Sugden, John.
Bairoch, Paul. Cities & Economic Development: From the Dawn of History to the Present. LC 87-35484. (Illus.). xxii, 574p. 1988. pap. text 27.00 (*0-226-03466-6*) U Ch Pr.
— Cities & Economic Development: From the Dawn of History to the Present. Braider, Christopher, tr. (Illus.). 596p. 1997. 59.95 (*0-226-03465-8*) U Ch Pr.
— Economics & World History: Myths & Paradoxes. LC 93-18729. (Illus.). xi, 177p. 1995. 32.50 (*0-226-03462-3*) U Ch Pr.
— Economics & World History: Myths & Paradoxes. xvi, 200p. 1995. pap. text 14.00 (*0-226-03463-1*) U Ch Pr.
Bairstow, Linda. How to Stop Your Toddler from Driving You Crazy. LC 85-18573. 1988. 22.95 (*0-87949-243-0*) Ashley Bks.
— More Than Meets the Eye: A Young Man's Introduction to Women. LC 89-91247. 1989. 8.95 (*0-87212-228-X*) Libra.
— Spreading Your Wings: A Young Woman's Introduction to Life. LC 87-92072. 1988. 8.95 (*0-87212-210-7*) Libra.
— Til Love's Known. LC 94-73493. 1995. pap. 12.00 (*0-87212-263-8*) Libra.
***Bairstow, Lynn.** Frommer's Cancun, Cozumel & the Yucatan 2001. (Illus.). 352p. 2000. pap. 14.99 (*0-02-863873-5*) Macmillan Gen Ref.
— Frommer's Mexico 2001. (Illus.). 752p. 2000. pap. 19.99 (*0-02-863877-8*) Macmillan Gen Ref.
Bairstow, Phillip J., jt. auth. see Laszlo, Judith I.
Bais, Alkiviadis F., jt. auth. see Zerefos, C. S.
Bais, V. S. & Gupta, U. S., eds. Environment & Pollution: Impact Assessment. (Illus.). xiv, 134p. 1991. 15.00 (*81-7211-010-3*, Pub. by Northern Bk Centre) Nataraj Bks.
Bais, V. S., jt. auth. see Chauhan, I. S.
***Baisas, Bienvenido, et al.** Bible Diary 2001. 456p. 2000. 19.95 (*0-8091-0507-1*) Paulist Pr.
Baisch, Axel. Bewirtschaftung im Wasserrecht: Die Wasserrechtliche Bewirtschaftungserlaubnis Zwischen Pravention und Repression. (Europaische Hochschulschriften: Reihe 2: Bd. 1978). (GER.). 310p. 1996. pap. 57.95 (*3-631-30016-6*) P Lang Pubng.
Baisden, Chuck. Flying Tiger to Air Commando. LC 98-86280. (Illus.). 160p. 1999. 24.95 (*0-7643-0690-1*) Schiffer.
Baisden, E. B. The Fever of the Yeals. 208p. 1990. pap. text 10.00 (*1-878433-06-7*) Caribbean Diaspora Pr.
Baisden, Greg, jt. auth. see Herbert, George.
Baisden, Greg, ed. see Loisel, Regis.
Baisden, Greg, ed. see Pratt, George.
Baisden, Greg S., ed. see Baum, L. Frank.
Baisden, Greg S., ed. see Loisel, Regis.
Baisden, Greg S., ed. see Vatine, Olivier & Clement, Alain.
Baisden, Gregory, jt. auth. see Herbert, George.
Baisden, Major J., Jr. The Dynamics of Homosexuality. LC 75-31. 199p. 1975. 6.95 (*0-912984-02-3*) Allied Res Soc.
— The World of Rosaphrenia: The Sexual Psychology of the Female. LC 72-178852. 224p. 1971. 6.95 (*0-912984-01-5*) Allied Res Soc.
***Baisden, Michael.** The Maintenance Man. Sparks, Chandra, ed. LC 94-12045. (Illus.). 320p. 1999. 22.95 (*0-9643675-3-X*) Legacy Publng.
— The Maintenance Man: A Novel. 2000. pap. 12.00 (*0-7432-0478-6*, Scribner Pap Fic) S&S Trade Pap.
Baisden, Michael. Men Cry in the Dark. (Illus.). 305p. 1999. pap. 13.95 (*0-9643675-1-3*) Legacy Publng.
— Never Satisfied: How & Why Men Cheat. 3rd ed. Wohlenhaus, Kim, ed. LC 94-96628. (Illus.). 254p. (Orig.). 1995. pap. 13.95 (*0-9643675-8-0*) Legacy Publng.
Baisden, Michael, ed. Men Cry in the Dark. LC 97-72737. 305p. 1997. 22.95 (*0-9643675-0-5*) Legacy Publng.
***Baise, Matthew R.** Beaconsfield. 248p. 2000. pap. 13.95 (*0-595-09302-7*, Writers Showcase) iUniversecom.
Baise, Melanie. Inspection & Enforcement. (Your Rights in the Coalfields Ser.). (Illus.). 26p. 1983. pap. 3.00 (*0-943724-03-1*) Illinois South.
Baishi, Qi. Likeness & Unlikeness: Selected Paintings. Chasin, Helen, ed. Caiwei, Ouyang, tr. (Illus.). 1990. 89.95 (*0-8351-2216-6*) China Bks.
Baishya, A. J. & Rao, R. R. Ferns & Fern-Allies of Meghalaya. (C). 1991. text 60.00 (*81-85046-07-7*, Pub. by Scientific Pubs) St Mut.
Baishya, A. K. & Rao, R. R. Ferns & Fern Allies of Meghalaya State (India) 1988. 40.00 (*0-7855-3019-3*, Pub. by Scientific) St Mut.
Baishya, Prabin, jt. auth. see Datta-Ray, B.
Baisier, Leon. Lapidaire Chretien: Its Composition, Its Influence, Its Sources. LC 71-94163. (Catholic University of America. Studies in Romance Languages & Literatures: No. 14). 1969. reprint ed. 37.50 (*0-404-50314-4*) AMS Pr.
Baisly, Clair. Cape Cod Architecture. LC 89-60503. (Illus.). 224p. 1989. 18.50 (*0-940160-43-9*) Parnassus Imprints.
Baisner, Richard. 101 Stupid Things Employees Do to Sabotage Success. LC 97-69478. (One Hundred One Stupid Things . . . Ser.). (Illus.). 128p. 1998. pap. 9.95 (*1-883553-97-0*) R Chang Assocs.
***Baiss, Bridget.** The Making of the Crow. 2000. 25.00 (*1-870048-54-7*, Pub. by Making Crow Inc) Making of the Crow.
Baister, Stephen & Chris, Patrick. Latvia: The Bradt Travel Guide. 2nd ed. (Illus.). 320p. 1999. pap. text 17.95 (*1-898323-90-9*) Globe Pequot.
Baitalsky, Mikhail. Notebooks for the Grandchildren: Recollections of a Trotskyist Who Survived the Stalin Terror. Vogt-Downey, Marilyn, ed. & tr. by. from RUS. LC 93-25175. (Historical Memories Ser.). 460p. (C). 1995. text 75.00 (*0-391-03829-X*) Humanities.
Baiter, J. G., jt. auth. see Orelli, J. C.
Baiter, Johann G., jt. auth. see Von Orelli, Johann C.
Baitsell, George A., ed. see Gamow, George, et al.
Baitsell, George A., ed. see Jewett, Frank B., et al.
Baitsell, George A., ed. see Lawrence, Ernest O.
Baitsell, George A., ed. see Miles, Walter R., et al.
Baitsell, George A., ed. see Patten, Bradley M., et al.
Baitsell, George A., ed. see Shapley, Harlow, et al.
Baitsell, George A., ed. see Smyth, H. D., et al.
Baitsell, George A., ed. see Snyder, Laurence H., et al.
Baitsell, George A., ed. see Stadler, L. J., et al.
Baity, W. A., ed. see Armstong, Ray.
Baitz, Jon R. A Fair Country. LC 99-214698. 1997. pap. 5.25 (*0-8222-1555-1*) Dramatists Play.
— A Fair Country. LC 96-35080. 112p. 1996. pap. 10.95 (*1-55936-127-1*) Theatre Comm.
— Mizlansky/Zilinsky or "Schmucks" 1998. pap. 5.25 (*0-8222-1680-9*) Dramatists Play.
Baitz, Jon R. The Substance of Fire: A Screenplay. LC 96-48502. 160p. (J). 1996. pap. 9.70 (*0-7868-8256-5*, Pub. by Hyperion) Time Warner.
Baitz, Jon R. The Substance of Fire & Other Plays. LC 92-16985. 224p. 1991. reprint ed. 24.95 (*1-55936-052-6*); reprint ed. pap. 12.95 (*1-55936-051-8*) Theatre Comm.
— Three Hotels: Plays & Monologues. LC 93-51492. 96p. 1994. pap. 8.95 (*1-55936-085-2*) Theatre Comm.
Baitz, Jon Robin. Mizlansky/Zilinsky or "Schmucks" 112p. 1998. pap. 10.95 (*1-55936-160-3*, Pub. by Theatre Comm) Consort Bk Sales.
Baiul, Oksana. Secrets of Skating. LC 97-26039. (Illus.). 144p. 1997. 29.95 (*0-7893-0104-0*, Pub. by Universe) St Martin.
Baiul, Oksana, mem. Oksana's Dream, 3 vols. (J). 1997. write for info. (*0-614-29289-1*) Random Bks Yng Read.
Baiul, Oksana & Alexander, Heather. Oksana: My Own Story. LC 96-69537. 1997. 16.99 (*0-679-88382-7*) Random.
Baiunco-Brindza, Marie. Bed & Breakfast Guest Houses & Inns of America: Southern Region. 8th ed. (Illus.). 350p. 1994. pap. 9.95 (*0-9629885-3-7*) B & B Guest.
— Bed & Breakfast Guest Houses & Inns of America: West Coast Region. 8th ed. (Illus.). 350p. 1994. pap. 9.95 (*0-9629885-4-5*) B & B Guest.
— Inn & Travel: Bed & Breakfast Guest Houses & Inns of America. (Illus.). 1997. cd-rom 45.00 (*0-9629885-5-3*) B & B Guest.
— Inn & Travel: Bed & Breakfast Guest Houses & Inns of America. 10th ed. (Illus.). 800p. 1997. pap. 29.95 (*0-9629885-6-1*) B & B Guest.
Baiz de Gelpi, Elsa. Meet the Essay. 180p. (C). 1987. reprint ed. pap. 5.50 (*0-8477-3110-3*) U of PR Pr.
— Meet the Short Story. 230p. (C). 1992. reprint ed. pap. 9.25 (*0-8477-3111-1*) U of PR Pr.
Baizant, Vladimir. Handbook of Organosilicon Compounds Advances since 1961, Vol. 4. Hetflejs, J. et al, trs. LC 74-21879. 1008p. reprint ed. pap. 200.00 (*0-7837-3337-2*, 204104400004) Bks Demand.
Baizant, Z. P. & Rajapakse, Y. Fracture Scaling LC 99-33162. 1999. write for info. (*0-7923-5825-2*) Kluwer Academic.
Baize, Nancy, jt. auth. see Budden, Mary.
Baize, Timothy. Broc: The Littlest Champion. LC 89-92510. (Illus.). 185p. (Orig.). (J). (gr. 6-12). 1989. pap. 9.95 (*0-9625193-0-8*) T Baize.
Baizer, Manuel M., jt. ed. see Lund, Henning.
Baizer, Richard W. & Isaacs, John A., III. Cooking in Clover, Vol. I. 4th ed. 1985. pap. 12.50 (*0-961476-2-7*) Jewish Hosp Aux MO.
Baizerman, Suzanne & Searle, Karen. Finishes in the Ethnic Tradition. 1989. 9.95 (*0-932394-12-4*) Dos Tejedoras.
***Baizerman, Suzanne, et al.** Fired by Ideals: Arequipa Pottery & the Arts & Crafts Movement. LC 00-42170. 2000. pap. write for info. (*0-7649-1399-9*) Pomegranate Calif.
Baizerman, Suzanne, jt. auth. see Lucero, Helen R.
Baizi, Denise. Treasure in the Trash, Vol. 1. 62p. 1997. pap. 10.00 (*0-9661433-0-2*) JEWELS.
Baizley, Doris. A Christmas Carol. 1991. pap. 5.25 (*0-8222-0208-5*) Dramatists Play.
— Mrs. California. 1987. pap. 5.25 (*0-8222-0784-2*) Dramatists Play.
Baj, Cesare, jt. auth. see DeRemer, Dale.
Baj, Enrico, jt. auth. see Rosemont, Penelope.
Baj, John, jt. auth. see Trott, Charles E.
Baj, Pamela & Clayton, Gloria, eds. Review of Research in Nursing Education, Vol. IV. 192p. 1991. pap. 9.95 (*0-88737-504-9*) Natl League Nurse.
Baj, Pamela, jt. ed. see Clayton, Gloria.
Baja, G. S. Di, see Arcelli, C.
Bajac, Anton & Pavle, Kalan. Italian-Slovene Dictionary: Italijansko-Slovenski Slovar. (ITA & SLV.). 843p. 1986. 39.95 (*0-8288-1135-0*, F79231) Fr & Eur.
Bajada, E. & Colomb, F. R. Observations in the Twenty-One-CM Neutral Hydrogen Line. LC QB0790.02. (Carnegie Institution of Washington Publication Ser.: No. 632). 77p. reprint ed. pap. 30.00 (*0-608-10160-5*, 200790000067) Bks Demand.
Bajaj, A. K., ed. Nonlinear & Stochastic Dynamics: 1994 International Mechanical Engineering Congress & Exposition, Chicago, Illinois - November 6-11, 1994. LC 94-27986. (AMD - Design Engineering Ser.: Vol. 192, Vol. 78). 348p. 1994. 92.00 (*0-7918-1441-6*, G00936) ASME.
Bajaj, Anil K., et al, eds. Nonlinear Dynamics & Controls: Proceedings, ASME International Mechanical Engineering Congress & Exposition, 1996, Atlanta Georgia. LC 96-78672. (DE Ser.: Vol. 91). 239p. 1996. pap. text 96.00 (*0-7918-1530-7*) ASME Pr.
Bajaj, Anil K. & Shaw, Steven W., eds. Advances in Nonlinear Dynamics: Methods & Applications. LC 95-38365. 1995. text 102.50 (*0-7923-3621-6*) Kluwer Academic.
Bajaj, Chanderjit, ed. Algebraic Geometry & It's Applications: Collection of Papers from Shreeram Abhyankar's 60th Birthday Conference. LC 93-33433. 1994. 83.95 (*0-387-94176-2*) Spr-Verlag.
Bajaj, Chandrajit & Krishnamurthy, Bala. Data Visualization Techniques. 156p. 1999. 115.00 (*0-471-96356-9*) Wiley.
Bajaj, J. L. Finance Commission & Backward States. 256p. (C). 1985. 170.00 (*81-85009-08-2*, Pub. by Print Hse) St Mut.
— Rural Poverty - Issues & Options. 252p. (C). 1985. 190.00 (*81-85009-11-2*, Pub. by Print Hse) St Mut.
Bajaj, Jasbir S. & Indian Institute of Advanced Study Staff. Medical Education & Health Care: A Pluridimensional Paradigm. LC 98-903260. xiv, 218p. 1998. write for info. (*81-85952-51-5*) Indian Inst.
Bajaj, K. K., et al, eds. Spectroscopy of Shallow Centers in Semiconductors: Selected Proceedings of the International Conference, 1st, Berkeley, CA, Aug. 2-3, 1984. 120p. 1985. pap. 28.00 (*0-08-032569-6*, Pub. by PPL) Elsevier.
Bajaj, Ramkrishna. Indian Economy: Emerging Perspectives. 1986. 24.00 (*81-7023-066-7*, Pub. by Allied Pubs) S Asia.
Bajaj, Y. P. S. Medical & Aromatic Plants VII. (Biotechnology in Agriculture & Forestry Ser.: Vol. 28). 528p. 1994. 350.95 (*0-387-57446-8*) Spr-Verlag.
— Medicinal & Aromatic Plants V. (Biotechnology in Agriculture & Forestry Ser.: Vol. 24). (Illus.). 350p. 1993. 343.95 (*0-387-56008-4*) Spr-Verlag.
— Somatic Embryogenesis & Synthetic Seed. LC 94-28237. 1995. 289.00 (*0-387-57449-2*) Spr-Verlag.
— Transgenic Crops I. LC 99-22294. (Biotechnology in Agriculture & Forestry Ser.). 390p. 1999. 242.00 (*3-540-65574-3*) Spr-Verlag.
— Transgenic Trees. LC 99-10779. (Biotechnology in Agriculture & Forestry Ser.). 330p. 1999. 219.00 (*3-540-65393-7*) Spr-Verlag.
Bajaj, Y. P. S., contrib. by. Medicinal & Aromatic Plants, Vol. 33. 1995. 369.00 (*0-387-58298-3*) Spr-Verlag.
— Plant Protoplast & Genetic Engineering, Vol. 34, Pt. VI 1995. 303.95 (*3-540-58931-7*) Spr-Verlag.
Bajaj, Y. P. S., ed. Cotton. LC 97-45484. (Biotechnology in Agriculture & Forestry Ser.: Vol. 42). (Illus.). 350p. 1998. 299.00 (*3-540-62728-6*) Spr-Verlag.
— Crops I. (Biotechnology in Agriculture & Forestry Ser.: Vol. 2). (Illus.). 625p. 1986. 379.95 (*0-387-15842-1*) Spr-Verlag.
— Crops II. (Biotechnology in Agriculture & Forestry Ser.: Vol. 6). (Illus.). 610p. 1988. 358.95 (*0-387-19064-3*) Spr-Verlag.
— Cryopreservative of Plant Germplasm No. I. LC 94-46550. (Biotechnology in Agriculture & Forestry: Vol. 32). 1995. write for info. (*3-540-57451-4*) Spr-Verlag.
— Cryopreservative of Plant Germplasm No. I. LC 94-46550. (Biotechnology in Agriculture & Forestry Ser.: Vol. 32). (Illus.). 533p. 1995. 394.00 (*0-387-57451-4*) Spr-Verlag.
— Haploids in Crop Improvement One. (Biotechnology in Agriculture & Forestry Ser.: Vol. 12). (Illus.). 592p. 1990. 398.95 (*0-387-50798-1*) Spr-Verlag.
— High-Tech & Micropropagation, Vol. VI. LC 96-36395. (Biotechnology in Agriculture & Forestry Ser.: Vol. 40). (Illus.). 424p. 1997. 339.00 (*3-540-61607-1*) Spr-Verlag.
— High-Tech & Micropropagation I. (Biotechnology in Agriculture & Forestry Ser.: Vol. 17). (Illus.). 576p. 1992. 328.95 (*0-387-53656-6*) Spr-Verlag.
— High-Tech & Micropropagation II. (Biotechnology in Agriculture & Forestry Ser.: Vol. 18). (Illus.). 520p. 1992. 382.95 (*0-387-53659-0*) Spr-Verlag.
— High-Tech & Micropropagation III. (Biotechnology in Agriculture & Forestry Ser.: Vol. 19). (Illus.). 600p. 1992. 383.95 (*0-387-53660-4*) Spr-Verlag.
— High-Tech & Micropropagation IV. (Biotechnology in Agriculture & Forestry Ser.: Vol. 20). (Illus.). 496p. 1992. 382.95 (*0-387-53661-2*) Spr-Verlag.
— High-Tech & Micropropagation V. LC 96-42362. (Biotechnology in Agriculture & Forestry Ser.: Vol. 39). (Illus.). 400p. 1997. 370.00 (*3-540-61606-3*) Spr-Verlag.
— Legumes & Oilseed Crops I. (Biotechnology in Agriculture & Forestry Ser.: Vol. 10). (Illus.). 785p. 1990. 432.95 (*0-387-50786-8*) Spr-Verlag.
— Maize. (Biotechnology in Agriculture & Forestry Ser.: No. 25). 608p. 1994. 398.95 (*0-387-56392-X*) Spr-Verlag.
— Medicinal & Aromatic Plants, No. 1, Vol. 4. (Illus.). 600p. 1988. 316.95 (*0-387-18414-7*) Spr-Verlag.
— Medicinal & Aromatic Plants VIII. (Biotechnology in Agriculture & Forestry Ser.: Vol. 33). (Illus.). 504p. 1995. 369.00 (*3-540-58298-3*) Spr-Verlag.
— Medicinal & Aromatic Plants IV. (Biotechnology in Agriculture & Forestry Ser.: Vol. 21). (Illus.). 464p. 1993. 401.95 (*0-387-54644-8*) Spr-Verlag.
— Medicinal & Aromatic Plants IX, Vol. 37. 432p. 1996. 339.00 (*3-540-60597-5*) Spr-Verlag.
— Medicinal & Aromatic Plants VI. (Biotechnology in Agriculture & Forestry Ser.: Vol. 26). (Illus.). 415p. 1994. 318.95 (*0-387-56391-1*) Spr-Verlag.
— Medicinal & Aromatic Plants III. (Biotechnology in Agriculture & Forestry Ser.: Vol. 15). (Illus.). 544p. 1991. 315.00 (*0-387-52098-8*) Spr-Verlag.
— Medicinal & Aromatic Plants II. (Biotechnology in Agriculture & Forestry Ser.: Vol. 7). (Illus.). 585p. 1989. 328.95 (*0-387-19196-8*) Spr-Verlag.
— Medicinal & Aromatic Plants X. (Biotechnology in Agriculture & Forestry Ser.: Vol. 41). (Illus.). 410p. 1998. 249.00 (*3-540-62727-8*) Spr-Verlag.
— Medicinal & Aromatic Plants XI. (Illus.). 400p. 1999. 275.00 (*3-540-63911-X*) Spr-Verlag.
— Peripheral Endovascular Interventions. 2nd ed. LC 98-44697. (Illus.). 680p. 1999. 150.00 (*0-387-98444-5*) Spr-Verlag.
— Plant Protoplasts & Genetic Engineering. (Biotechnology in Agriculture & Forestry Ser.: Vol. 8, No. 1). (Illus.). 465p. 1989. 318.95 (*0-387-19194-1*) Spr-Verlag.
— Plant Protoplasts & Genetic Engineering, Vol. VII. (Biotechnology in Agriculture & Forestry Ser.). (Illus.). xxiii, 350p. 1996. 259.00 (*3-540-60876-1*) Spr-Verlag.
— Plant Protoplasts & Genetic Engineering II. (Biotechnology in Agriculture & Forestry Ser.: Vol. 9). (Illus.). 510p. 1989. 165.95 (*0-387-50789-2*) Spr-Verlag.
— Plant Protoplasts & Genetic Engineering III. (Biotechnology in Agriculture & Forestry Ser.: Vol. 22). (Illus.). 320p. 1993. 242.95 (*0-387-56313-X*) Spr-Verlag.
— Plant Protoplasts & Genetic Engineering IV. (Biotechnology in Agriculture & Forestry Ser.: Vol. 23). (Illus.). 387p. 1994. 317.95 (*0-387-56384-9*) Spr-Verlag.
— Plant Protoplasts & Genetic Engineering V, 29. (Biotechnology in Agriculture & Forestry Ser.: Vol. 29). 426p. 1994. 334.95 (*0-387-57447-6*) Spr-Verlag.
— Potato. (Biotechnology in Agriculture & Forestry Ser.: Vol. 3). (Illus.). 535p. 1987. 309.95 (*0-387-17966-6*) Spr-Verlag.
— Rice, Vol. 14. (Biotechnology in Agriculture & Forestry Ser.). (Illus.). 648p. 1991. 330.00 (*0-387-51810-X*) Spr-Verlag.
— Somaclonal Variation in Crop Improvement I. (Biotechnology in Agriculture & Forestry Ser.: Vol. II). 720p. 1990. 423.95 (*0-387-50785-X*) Spr-Verlag.
Bajaj, Y. P. S., ed. Somaclonal Variation in Crop Improvement II, Vol. 36, Pt. II. (Biotechnology in Agriculture & Forestry Ser.: Vol. 36). (Illus.). 392p. 1996. 292.00 (*3-540-60549-5*) Spr-Verlag.
— Somatic Embryogenesis & Synthetic Seed, 2. (Biotechnology in Agriculture & Forestry Ser.: Vol. 31). 1995. 398.00 (*3-540-57449-2*) Spr-Verlag.
Bajaj, Y. P. S., ed. Somatic Embryogenesis & Synthetic Seed I. (Biotechnology in Agriculture & Forestry Ser.: Vol. 30). 494p. 1995. 345.00 (*0-387-57448-4*) Spr-Verlag.
— Somatic Hybridization in Crop Improvement. LC 94-15685. (Biotechnology in Agriculture & Forestry Ser.: Vol. 27). 1994. 390.95 (*0-387-57445-X*) Spr-Verlag.
— Transgenic Medicinal Plants. LC 98-37572. (Biotechnology in Agriculture & Forestry Ser.). (Illus.). 370p. 1999. 249.00 (*3-540-65120-9*) Spr-Verlag.
— Trees. LC 85-17309. (Biotechnology in Agriculture & Forestry Ser.: Vol. 1). (Illus.). 550p. 1985. 344.95 (*0-387-15581-3*) Spr-Verlag.

B

An Asterisk (*) at the beginning of an entry indicates that the title is appearing for the first time.

— Trees, No. III. (Biotechnology in Agriculture & Forestry Ser.). (Illus.). 512p. 1991. 405.95 (*0-387-52576-9*) Spr-Verlag.

— Trees IV, Vol. 35. 432p. 1996. 298.50 (*3-540-60547-9*) Spr-Verlag.

— Trees II. (Biotechnology in Agriculture & Forestry Ser.: Vol. 5). (Illus.). 640p. 1989. 328.95 (*0-387-19158-5*) Spr-Verlag.

— Wheat. (Biotechnology in Agriculture & Forestry Ser.: Vol. 13). (Illus.). 704p. 1991. 398.95 (*0-387-51809-6*) Spr-Verlag.

Bajaj, Y. P. S., jt. ed. see Reinert, J.

Bajaly, Stephen. The Community Networking Handbook. LC 98-45246. 216p. 1999. 32.00 (*0-8389-0745-8*) ALA.

Bajandas, Frank J., jt. auth. see Kline, Lanning B.

Bajard, Jean-Pierre & Sibieude, C. Business in French: Les Affaires En Francais. (FRE.). 224p. 1988. pap. 29.95 (*0-8288-1550-X*, F14960); pap., teacher ed. write for info. (*0-8288-1551-8*, F16350) Fr & Eur.

Bajaria, Hans J., ed. Quality Assurance: Methods, Management, & Motivation. LC 81-50392. 260p. reprint ed. pap. 80.60 (*0-608-13127-X*, 202417500035) Bks Demand.

Bajaria, Hans J. & Copp, Richard P. Statistical Problem Solving (SPS) A Team Process for Identifying & Resolving Problems. (Illus.). 300p. 1991. 44.95 (*0-9629223-0-7*) Multiface Pub.

Bajd, Tadej, jt. auth. see Kralj, Alojz R.

Bajec, A. & Kalan, P. Italian-Slovene Dictionary: Dizionario Italiano-Slovar. (ITA & SLV.). 843p. 1980. 150.00 (*0-8288-1009-5*, M9692) Fr & Eur.

Bajekal, Madhavi, jt. auth. see Jarman, Brian.

Bajema, Cliff. What Really Matters? Passing on Your Family Values. (Issues in Christian Living Ser.). 1995. pap. 7.75 (*1-56212-098-0*) CRC Pubns.

Bajema, Clifford E. At One with Jesus: Rediscovering the Secret of Lectio Divina. LC 98-23651. 61p. 1998. pap. 4.75 (*1-56212-354-8*) CRC Pubns.

Bajema, Don. Boy in the Air. 140p. (Orig.). 1990. pap. 8.00 (*1-880985-06-3*) Two Thirteen Sixty-one.

— Reach. LC 97-150438. (Illus.). 148p. (Orig.). 1996. pap. 11.00 (*1-880985-19-5*) Two Thirteen Sixty-one.

Bajema, Edith. Como Mantenerse Cuando Todo Se Derrumba. (SPA.). 48p. pap. 8.95 (*1-55883-100-2*, 6711-0010C) Libros Desafio.

Bajema, Edith. Does God Want to Spoil My Fun? (In Spirit Ser.). 1994. pap. 19.95 (*1-56212-080-8*) CRC Pubns.

***Bajema, Edith.** DYB Romans Pt. 1: Leader Guide. 95p. 1999. pap., teacher ed. 6.95 (*1-56212-509-5*, 152535) CRC Pubns.

— DYB Romans Pt. 1: Study Guide. 64p. 1999. pap., student ed. 4.25 (*1-56212-510-9*, 152530) CRC Pubns.

— DYB Romans Pt. 2: Leaders Guide. 64p. 1999. pap., teacher ed. 4.95 (*1-56212-511-7*, 152545) CRC Pubns.

— DYB Romans Pt. 2: Study Guide. 49p. 1999. pap., student ed. 3.25 (*1-56212-512-5*, 152540) CRC Pubns.

— DYB Sermon on the Mount: Leaders Guide. 56p. 1999. pap., teacher ed. 4.95 (*1-56212-514-1*, 152495) CRC Pubns.

— DYB Sermon on the Mount: Study Guide. 36p. 1999. pap., student ed. 3.25 (*1-56212-515-X*, 152490) CRC Pubns.

— Es Dios un Aguafiestas? (SPA.). 64p. pap. 8.95 (*1-55883-101-0*, 67711-0012C) Libros Desafio.

Bajema, Edith. Hank's Secret. LC 93-18465. (Open Door Bks.). 1993. pap. text 3.95 (*1-56212-030-1*) CRC Pubns.

Bajema, Edith. Jesus in John: Study Guide. (Discover Your Bible Ser.). 45p. pap., student ed. 2.95 (*1-56212-233-9*) CRC Pubns.

— Jesus-Son of God.ODB. 22p. 1993. pap. 2.95 (*1-56212-047-6*) CRC Pubns.

Bajema, Edith. Mama's Decision. (Open Door Bks.). (Illus.). 69p. 1992. pap. text 3.95 (*1-56212-014-X*, 1740-2150) CRC Pubns.

— Trapped by Memory. (Open Door Bks.). (Illus.). 68p. (Orig.). 1992. pap. text 3.95 (*1-56212-013-1*, 1740-2120) CRC Pubns.

Bajema, Edith & Averill, Diane. Toda la Verdad y Nada Mas Que la Lerdad. (SPA.). 48p. pap. 8.95 (*1-55883-102-9*, 67711-0013C) Libros Desafio.

— Up Close & Personal. 187p. pap. 19.95 (*1-56212-139-1*) CRC Pubns.

— The Whole Truth. 191p. pap. 19.95 (*1-56212-108-1*) CRC Pubns.

Bajema, Edith & Tejal, Gary. Jesus, Meeting Our Lord-Mark/Ldr.-ODB. 101p. 1987. pap. 12.25 (*1-56212-046-8*) CRC Pubns.

Bajema, Edith, jt. auth. see Averill, Diane.

Bajema, Edith, jt. auth. see Vander Griend, Alvin.

Bajenaru, George. Restless Planet: Tulburatoara Lume. 160p. (Orig.). 1993. pap. 13.99 (*0-9619930-8-1*) Moonfall Pr VA.

Bajenescu, T. I. & Bazu, M. I. Reliability of Electronic Components: A Practical Guide to Electronic Systems Manufacturing. LC 99-14933. (Illus.). 510p. 1999. 156.00 (*3-540-65722-3*) Spr-Verlag.

Baji-Holms, Karin. 101 Vacations to Change Your Life: A Guide to Wellness Centers, Spiritual Retreats & Spas. LC 99-36059. (Illus.). 208p. 1999. pap. 12.95 (*0-8065-2082-5*, Citadel Pr) Carol Pub Group.

Baji, Karin, jt. compiled by see Holmes, John P.

Bajic, B. Technical-Economical Dictionary for Business Purposes. (CRO, ENG, FRE, GER & SER.). 1700p. 1973. 150.00 (*0-8288-6332-6*, M9689) Fr & Eur.

Bajic, M., ed. Neuron, Brain & Behaviour: Proceedings of the Annual Meeting of the European Brain & Behaviour Society, Novi Sad, Yugoslavia, 19th, 23-25 August, 1987. (Advances in the Biosciences Ser.: Vol. 70). 236p. 1988. 94.00 (*0-08-035597-8*, Pergamon Pr) Elsevier.

Bajic-Poderegin, Milka. The Dawning. Poderegin, Nadja, tr. from SER. LC 94-48736. (Emerging Voices Ser.).Tr. of Svitanje. 384p. 1995. 29.95 (*1-56656-198-1*); pap. 14.95 (*1-56656-188-4*) Interlink Pub.

Bajis, J. Common Ground: An Introduction to Eastern Christianity. 1991. pap. 16.95 (*0-937032-81-6*) Light&Life Pub Co MN.

Bajkai, Louis A. Teachers Guide to Overseas Teaching: A Complete & Comprehensive Guide of English-Language Schools & Colleges Overseas. 3rd rev. ed. LC 77-81788. (Illus.). 192p. 1983. pap. 19.95 (*0-9601550-2-3*) Friends World Teach.

Bajkhaif, Mohammed O. Infant Mortality of Indian Muslims: Determinants & Implications. 1993. 14.00 (*81-7018-737-0*) S Asia.

Bajor, Dottie. Potter County Leek Cookbook. (Illus.). 80p. (Orig.). 1990. pap. 6.95 (*0-9621577-0-8*) D Bajor.

Bajorek, Lagretta Metzger, jt. auth. see Rieger, Loretta Metzger.

***Bajou, Valerie.** Eugene Carriere: Monograph (1849-1906) 1998. 70.00 (*2-940033-29-3*, Pub. by Acatos Edit) Antique Collect.

Bajpai, Avi C. FORTRAN & Algol: A Programmed Course for Students of Science & Technology. LC 73-5712. 273p. reprint ed. pap. 84.70 (*0-608-10052-8*, 201398100088) Bks Demand.

Bajpai, Avi C. & Bond. Applied Math. 1989. pap. text 49.60 (*0-13-037938-7*) P-H.

Bajpai, Avi C. & Bond, R. M. Applied Math. 349p. 1983. pap. text 26.50 (*0-471-86166-9*) P-H.

Bajpai, Avi C., et al. Numerical Methods for Engineers & Scientists: A Students' Course Book. LC QA0297.B32. (Series of Programmes on Mathematics for Engineers & Scientists). 392p. reprint ed. pap. 121.60 (*0-7837-4021-2*, 204385100011) Bks Demand.

Bajpai, K. D., ed. Glory That Was Bundelkhand: Mahendra Kumar 'Manav' Felicitation Volume. 1992. 68.00 (*0-8364-2863-3*, Pub. by Eastern Bk Linkers) S Asia.

Bajpai, K. P., et al. Brasstacks & Beyond: Perception & Management of Crisis in South Asia. (C). 1995. 28.00 (*81-7304-130-X*, Pub. by Manohar) S Asia.

***Bajpai, Kanti P., ed.** Peacock & the Dragon: India-China Relations in the 21st Century. 2000. 44.00 (*81-241-0642-8*, Pub. by Har-Anand Pubns) S Asia.

Bajpai, Kanti P., et al, eds. Interpreting World Politics: Essays for A. P. Rana. LC 94-42502. 400p. 1995. 29.95 (*0-8039-9210-6*) Sage.

Bajpai, P., et al. Biotechnology for Environmental Protection in the Pulp & Paper Industry. LC 99-30761. (Illus.). viii, 248p. 1999. 159.00 (*3-540-65677-4*) Spr-Verlag.

Bajpai, Rakesh K. & Zappi, Mark E. Bioremediation of Surface & Subsurface Contamination. LC 97-34037. (Annals of the New York Academy of Sciences Ser.). xi, 341 p. 1997. pap. 110.00 (*1-57331-065-4*) NY Acad Sci.

Bajpai, S. C. Kinnaur: A Restricted Land in the Himalaya. (C). 1991. 26.50 (*81-85182-58-2*, Pub. by Indus Pub) S Asia.

Bajpai, Shailaja, jt. auth. see Unnikrishnan, Namita.

Bajpai, U. S. India & Japan: A New Relationship? 1988. 28.00 (*81-7062-045-7*, Pub. by Lancer India) S Asia.

Bajpai, U. S., ed. Forty Years of the United Nations. 215p. (C). 1987. 24.00 (*81-7062-030-9*, Pub. by Lancer India) S Asia.

Bajpal, A. C. Advanced Engineering Mathematics. 2nd ed. LC 90-37523. 512p. 1990. pap. 115.00 (*0-471-92595-0*) Wiley.

Bajpal, Gita. Agrarian Urban Economy & Social Change. (C). 1989. 29.50 (*81-7035-053-0*, Pub. by Daya Pub Hse) S Asia.

Bajracharya, jt. auth. see Vaidya.

Bajracharya, B. R. Bahadur Shah: The Regent of Nepal (1785-1794 A. D.) (C). 1992. 50.00 (*0-7855-0172-X*, Pub. by Ratna Pustak Bhandar) St Mut.

— Bahadur Shah: The Regent of Nepal (1785-1794 A.D.) (C). 1992. text 21.00 (*81-7041-643-4*, Pub. by Anmol) S Asia.

Bajracharya, B. R., ed. Cultural History of Nepal. (C). 1993. 44.00 (*81-7041-840-2*, Pub. by Anmol) S Asia.

— Foreign Policy of Nepal. (C). 1993. 28.00 (*81-7041-842-9*, Pub. by Anmol) S Asia.

— Modernization in Nepal. (C). 1993. 22.00 (*81-7041-841-0*, Pub. by Anmol) S Asia.

— Political Development in Nepal. (C). 1993. 22.00 (*81-7041-844-5*, Pub. by Anmol) S Asia.

***Bajracharya, N. M.** Buddhism in Nepal: 465 B. C. to 1100 A. D. 1998. pap. 68.00 (*0-7855-7525-1*) St Mut.

Bajura, R. A. & Morrow, T. B., eds. Modeling of Environment Flow Systems. 88p. 1983. pap. text 20.00 (*0-317-02634-8*, H00281) ASME.

Bajura, R. A., ed. see Symposium on Polyphase Flow & Transport Technology.

Bajus, M. Sulfur Compounds in Hydrocarbon Pyrolysis, Vol.9. (Sulfur Reports). 76p. 1989. pap. text 106.00 (*3-7186-4944-6*, Harwood Acad Pubs) Gordon & Breach.

Bajusz, E. & Jasmin, C., eds. Nutritional Pathobiology. (Methods & Achievements in Experimental Pathology Ser.: Vol. 6). (Illus.). 1972. 104.50 (*3-8055-1343-7*) S Karger.

Bajusz, E. & Jasmin, G., eds. Functional Morphology of the Heart. (Methods & Achievements in Experimental Pathology Ser.: Vol. 5). 1971. 172.25 (*3-8055-1209-0*) S Karger.

Bajwa, Farooq, ed. see Khan, Syed Ahmed.

Bajwa, Sukhwinder, jt. auth. see Jason-Lloyd, Leonard.

Bajzer, Z., et al, eds. Applications of Physics to Medicine & Biology: Proceedings of the 2nd International Conference on the Applications of Physics to Medicine & Biology, Italy, November 1983. 664p. (C). 1984. 123.00 (*9971-966-81-6*) World Scientific Pub.

Bak, A., ed. see International Conference, Bielefeld, West Germany.

Bak, Anthony. K-Theory of Forms. LC 81-5176. (Annals of Mathematics Studies: No. 98). 278p. 1981. reprint ed. pap. 86.20 (*0-608-02520-8*, 206316400004) Bks Demand.

Bak, Dong H. Klagender Gott-Klagende Menschen: Studien zur Klage im Jeremiabuch. (Beiheft zur Zeitschrift fuer die Alttestamentliche Wissenschaft Ser.: Band 193). xiii, 273p. (C). 1990. lib. bdg. 80.00 (*3-11-012341-X*) De Gruyter.

Bak, Hans, ed. Multiculturalism & the Canon of American Culture. 374p. (C). 1993. pap. 49.50 (*90-5383-018-9*, Pub. by VU Univ Pr) Paul & Co Pubs.

Bak, Hans, et al, eds. Social & Secure? Politics & Culture of the Welfare State: a Comparative Inquiry. LC 97-103424. 400p. 1996. pap. 50.00 (*90-5383-458-3*, Pub. by VU Univ Pr) Paul & Co Pubs.

***Bak, Hans & Krabbendam, Hans, eds.** Writing Lives: American Biography & Autobiography. LC 99-199224. 320p. 1999. pap. 50.00 (*90-5383-617-9*, Pub. by VU Univ Pr) Paul & Co Pubs.

Bak, J. & Newman, D. J. Complex Analysis. Ewing, J. H. et al, eds. (Undergraduate Texts in Mathematics Ser.). (Illus.). x, 244p. (C). 1993. text 39.95 (*0-387-90615-0*) Spr-Verlag.

— Complex Analysis. 2nd ed. LC 96-12475. (Undergraduate Texts in Mathematics Ser.). 294p. 1996. 39.95 (*0-387-94756-6*) Spr-Verlag.

Bak, J. M., ed. see Fugedi, Erik.

Bak, James M., ed. Liberty & Socialism: Writings of Libertarian & Socialists in Hungary, 1884-1919. 224p. (C). 1991. text 57.50 (*0-8476-7680-3*) Rowman.

Bak, Janos, ed. German Peasant War of Fifteen Twenty-Five. (Library of Peasant Studies: No. 3). 135p. 1976. 32.00 (*0-7146-3063-2*, Pub. by F Cass Pubs) Intl Spec Bk.

Bak, Janos M., ed. Coronations: Medieval & Early Modern Monarchic Ritual. 1990. 50.00 (*0-520-06677-4*, Pub. by U CA Pr) Cal Prin Full Svc.

— The Laws of the Medieval Kingdom of Hungary, 1458-1490. (Laws of Hungary Ser.: Series I, Vol. 3). xxix, 230p. 1995. 75.00 (*1-884445-26-8*) C Schlacks Pub.

Bak, Janos M., et al, eds. The Laws of the Medieval Kingdom of Hungary, 1000-1301. LC 89-10492. (Laws of Hungary Ser.: Series I, Vol. 1). 320p. 1989. 95.00 (*1-884445-08-X*) C Schlacks Pub.

— The Laws of the Medieval Kingdom of Hungary, 1301-1457. LC 89-10492. (Laws of Hungary Ser.: Series I, Vol. 2). 500p. (C). 1993. 150.00 (*1-884445-09-8*) C Schlacks Pub.

Bak, Janos M. & Kiraly, Bela K., eds. From Hunyadi to Rakoczi Vol. 3: War & Society in Late Medieval & Early Modern Hungary, No. 12. 600p. 1982. text 79.50 (*0-930888-13-8*, 104) Col U Pr.

Bak, Janos M., tr. see Gurevich, Aron I.

Bak, Janos M., tr. see Litvan, Gyorgy.

***Bak, Kristine.** Treasure in the Gulch. (Illus.). 40p. 2000. pap. 5.95 (*0-89992-147-7*) Am Assn Blood.

Bak, Maren, ed. Changing Patterns of European Family Life. 320p. (C). 1989. lib. bdg. 55.00 (*0-415-00513-2*, A0443) Routledge.

Bak, Monika. Cursed Dowry. LC 98-90542. 1999. pap. 12.95 (*0-533-12834-X*) Vantage.

Bak, P. How Nature Works: The Science of Self-Organized Criticality. LC 96-16845. (Illus.). 212p. 1996. 27.00 (*0-387-94791-4*) Spr-Verlag.

Bak, Per. How Nature Works: The Science of Self-Organized Criticality. 216p. 1999. pap. text 18.00 (*0-387-98738-X*) Spr-Verlag.

Bak, Richard. Casey Stengel: A Splendid Baseball Life. LC 96-41909. 1997. 29.95 (*0-87833-929-9*) Taylor Pub.

***Bak, Richard.** Children's Crusade. 2001. write for info. (*0-670-88454-5*) Viking Penguin.

Bak, Richard. Cobb Would Have Caught It: The Golden Age of Baseball in Detroit. LC 91-4156. (Illus.). 386p. 1993. pap. 16.95 (*0-8143-2356-1*) Wayne St U Pr.

***Bak, Richard.** The CSS Hunley: The Greatest Undersea Adventure of the Civil War. LC 99-18435. (Illus.). 1999. 29.95 (*0-87833-219-7*) Taylor Pub.

Bak, Richard. The Day Lincoln Was Shot: An Illustrated Chronicle. LC 98-5311. (Illus.). 1998. 29.95 (*0-87833-200-6*) Taylor Pub.

***Bak, Richard.** The Day Lincoln Was Shot: An Illustrated Chronicle. (Illus.). 2001. pap. 18.95 (*0-87833-195-6*) Taylor Pub.

Bak, Richard. Detroit: A Postcard Album. LC 98-87328. (Postcard History Ser.). 124 p. 1999. write for info. (*0-7524-1355-4*) Arcadia Publng.

***Bak, Richard.** Detroit, 1900-1930. (Images of America Ser.). 1999. pap. 18.99 (*0-7524-1354-6*) Arcadia Publng.

Bak, Richard. Detroit Red Wings. 1998. pap. 22.95 (*0-87833-221-9*) Taylor Pub.

— The Detroit Redwings. LC 96-23714. (Illus.). 256p. 1997. 39.95 (*0-87833-975-2*) Taylor Pub.

— Joe Louis: The Great Black Hope. LC 98-6772. (Illus.). 328p. 1998. reprint ed. pap. 16.95 (*0-306-80879-X*) Da Capo.

— Lindbergh: Triumph & Tragedy. LC 99-38311. 2000. 32.95 (*0-87833-246-4*) Taylor Pub.

— Lou Gehrig: An American Classic. LC 94-46151. 208p. 1995. 29.95 (*0-87833-883-7*) Taylor Pub.

— A Place for Summer: A Narrative History of Tiger Stadium. LC 98-2509. (Illus.). 512p. 1998. 34.95 (*0-8143-2512-2*, Great Lks Bks) Wayne St U Pr.

— Turkey Stearnes & the Detroit Stars: The Negro Leagues in Detroit, 1919-1933. LC 93-34402. (Illus.). 302p. (C). 1994. text 24.95 (*0-8143-2483-5*, Great Lks Bks) Wayne St U Pr.

— Turkey Stearnes & the Detroit Stars: The Negro Leagues in Detroit, 1919-1933. LC 93-34402. (Illus.). 302p. 1995. pap. 15.95 (*0-8143-2582-3*, Great Lks Bks) Wayne St U Pr.

***Bak, Richard, et al.** The Corner: A Century of Memories at Michigan & Trumbull. 1999. pap. 39.95 (*1-57243-337-X*) Triumph Bks.

Bak, Richard, jt. auth. see Roosevelt, Theodore.

***Bak, Richard G.** Yankees Baseball, 1920-1961. (Images of America Ser.). 128p. 1999. pap. 18.99 (*0-7385-0244-8*) Arcadia Publng.

Bak, Samuel. Chess As Metaphor in the Art of Samuel Bak. Melody, David, tr. from FRE. (ENG & FRE., Illus.). 80p. 1991. 35.00 (*1-879985-02-0*) Pucker Gallery.

— The Past Continues. (Illus.). 35.00 (*0-8276-0496-3*) JPS Phila.

Bak, Samuel. Landscapes of Jewish Experience. LC 97-19468. (Tauber Institute for the Study of European Jewry Ser.: No. 25). 131p. 1997. 50.00 (*0-9635318-2-4*, Pub. by Pucker Gallery) U Pr of New Eng.

Baka, Farida & Al-Shabab, Omar S. Discourse, Structuring & Text Analysis. 146p. 1996. pap. 19.95 (*1-85756-250-X*, Pub. by Janus Pubng) Paul & Co Pubs.

Bakacs, T., jt. auth. see Voino-Yasenetsky, M. V.

Bakaitis, Vyt. City Country. 146p. 1991. pap. 11.95 (*0-9628181-2-7*) Black Thistle Pr.

Bakaitis, Vyt, tr. see Megas, Jonas.

Bakal, Curtis W., et al. Vascular & Interventional Radiology: Principles & Practices. (Illus.). 608p. 2000. 110.00 (*0-86577-678-4*) Thieme Med Pubs.

***Bakal, Donald.** Minding the Body: Clinical Uses of Somatic Awareness. LC 98-55170. 228p. 1999. 30.00 (*1-57230-435-9*) Guilford Pubns.

Bakal, Donald A. Psychology & Health. 2nd ed. LC 91-5241. Orig. Title: Psychology & Medicine, 1979. 256p. (C). 1992. text 36.95 (*0-8261-7900-2*) Springer Pub.

Bakalar, Elsa. A Garden of One's Own: Designing & Creating Your Personal Flower Garden. LC 93-32867. (Illus.). 211p. 1994. 25.00 (*0-688-12145-4*, Wm Morrow) Morrow Avon.

Bakalar, James B. & Grinspoon, Lester. Drug Control in a Free Society. 192p. 1988. pap. text 17.95 (*0-521-35772-1*) Cambridge U Pr.

— Marihuana, the Forbidden Medicine. 1995. pap. 13.00 (*0-300-05994-9*) Yale U Pr.

Bakalar, James B., jt. auth. see Grinspoon, Lester.

Bakalar, James B., jt. ed. see Grinspoon, Lester.

Bakalar, Nicholas. American Satire: An Anthology of Writings from Colonial Times to the Present. LC 96-44144. 468p. 1997. pap. 14.95 (*0-452-01174-4*, Mer) NAL.

Bakalar, Nicholas, jt. auth. see Berkman, Alan.

Bakalar, Nicholas, jt. ed. see Cournos, Francine.

Bakalar, Nick. American Satire. 1999. pap. 14.95 (*0-452-27798-1*, Plume) Dutton Plume.

— The Baseball Fan's Companion. LC 96-151432. 1996. 14.95 (*0-02-860848-8*) Macmillan.

— Gaffes & Goofs of the G. O. P. Bakalar Republican-Isms. LC 96-8451. 96p. 1996. pap. 7.95 (*0-471-16456-9*) Wiley.

Bakalar, Nick, jt. auth. see Acton, Jay.

Bakalian, Anny. Armenian Americans: From Being to Feeling Armenian. 330p. (C). 1992. 44.95 (*1-56000-025-2*) Transaction Pubs.

***Bakalian, Mary.** No More Foot Pain: How Can You Fix Your Feet & Knees. LC 00-90782. (Illus.). 104p. 2000. pap. 19.95 (*0-9700183-0-4*) Goodfoot.

Bakalinsky, Adah. Stairway Walks in San Francisco. 3rd rev. ed. LC 95-1502. (Illus.). 148p. 1995. pap. 10.95 (*0-89997-184-9*) Wilderness Pr.

Bakalinsky, Adah & Gordon, Larry. Stairway Walks in Los Angeles. LC 90-41027. (Illus.). 128p. 1990. pap. 10.95 (*0-89997-112-1*) Wilderness Pr.

Bakalis, Maria B., jt. auth. see Hjorth, Linda S.

Bakalla, M. Hassan. The Morphological & Phonological Component of the Arabic Verb. (ARA.). 700p. 1979. 30.00 (*0-86685-054-6*, Pub. by Librairie du Liban) Intl Bk Ctr.

Bakalla, Muhammad. Dictionary of Modern Linguistic Terms: English-Arabic, Arabic-English. (ARA & ENG.). 218p. 1983. 35.00 (*0-86685-304-9*, LDL3049, Pub. by Librairie du Liban) Intl Bk Ctr.

Bakalla, Muhammed H. Arabic Culture: Through Its Language & Literature. 365p. (Orig.). 1982. pap. 17.95 (*0-7103-0027-1*) Routledge.

Bakalla, Muhammed H., ed. see Ingham, Bruce.

Bakalow, Anatolij. Multilingual Dictionary of Corrosion Protection Terms: English, French, German, Russian. (ENG, FRE, GER & RUS.). 1994. 495.00 (*0-7859-9981-7*) Fr & Eur.

Bakaly, Charles G., Jr. & Grossman, Joel M. Modern Law of Employment Contracts: Formation, Operation & Remedies for Breach. 357p. 1983. suppl. ed. 70.00 (*0-15-004288-4*, H42884) Harcourt.

Bakaly, Charles G., Jr. & Kramer, Saul G. AIDS & Drug Abuse in the Workplace: Resolving the Thorny Legal-Medical Issues. LC 86-196310. 309p. 40.00 (*0-685-17695-9*) Harcourt.

Bakaly, Charles G., Jr., et al. The Modern Law of Employment Relationships. 1088p. 1989. ring bd. 118.00 (*0-13-301466-5*) Aspen Law.

— The Modern Law of Employment Relationships. 2nd ed. 1100p. ring bd. 126.00 (*0-13-595315-4*, 59533) Aspen Law.

Bakama, B., jt. auth. see Williams, Theatrice.

Bakan, Abigail B. Ideology & Class Conflict in Jamaica: The Politics of Rebellion. 192p. (C). 1990. text 60.00 (*0-7735-0745-0*, Pub. by McG-Queens Univ Pr) CUP Services.

Bakan, Abigail B., et al, eds. Imperial Power & Regional Trade: The Caribbean Basin Initiative. 272p. (C). 1993. pap. 29.95 (*0-88920-220-6*) W Laurier U Pr.

Bakan, David. On Method: Toward a Reconstruction of Psychological Investigation. LC 67-28628. (Jossey-Bass Behavioral Science Ser.). 205p. reprint ed. pap. 63.60 (*0-608-16880-7*, 202774500056) Bks Demand.

— Slaughter of the Innocents. LC 78-155168. (Jossey-Bass Behavioral Science Ser.). 142p. reprint ed. pap. 44.10 (*0-7837-6507-X*, 204561900007) Bks Demand.

Bakan, Gina, ed. see Jones, Jessica.

Bakan, Joel. Just Words: Constitutional Rights & Social Wrongs. LC 97-169880. 230p. 1997. text 50.00 (*0-8020-0461-X*, KF4483) U of Toronto Pr.

Bakan, Michael B. Music of Death & New Creation: Experiences in the World of Balinese Gamelan Beleganjur. LC 98-42727. (Chicago Studies in Ethnomusicology). 370p. 1999. pap. text 30.00 (*0-226-03488-7*) U Ch Pr.

— Music of Death & New Creation: Experiences in the World of Balinese Gamelan Beleganjur. LC 98-42727. 1999. lib. bdg. 60.00 (*0-226-03487-9*) U Ch Pr.

Bakar, Isa Bin, jt. ed. see Abdullah, Moha Asri.

Bakar, Osman. Classification of Knowledge in Islam: A Study in Islamic Philosophies of Science. 312p. 1996. pap. 18.00 (*0-614-21596-X*, 138) Kazi Pubns.

Bakar, Osman. The Classification of Knowledge in Islam: A Study in Islamic Philosophy. LC 99-487849. 1996. text 29.50 (*0-946621-71-3*) St Martin.

— History & Philosophy of Islamic Science. 2000. pap. 25.00 (*0-946621-83-7*) Islamic Texts.

Bakar, Osman. Tawhid & Science: Essays on the History & Philosophy of Islamic Science. 266p. 1996. pap. 18.00 (*0-614-21612-5*, 1217) Kazi Pubns.

Bakar, Osman, ed. Critique of Evolutionary Theory: A Collection of Essays. 155p. 1996. pap. 16.95 (*0-614-21597-8*, 185) Kazi Pubns.

Bakari, Imruh & Cham, Mbye, eds. African Experiences of Cinema. (Distributed for the British Film Institute Ser.). 224p. 1996. 49.95 (*0-85170-510-3*, Pub. by British Film Inst); pap. 24.95 (*0-85170-511-1*, Pub. by British Film Inst) Ind U Pr.

Bakari, Mtoro B. Customs of the Swahili People. Allen, J. W., tr. 340p. 1996. 19.95 (*0-614-21623-0*, 191) Kazi Pubns.

Bakas, Susan C. The Story of the Killing Dentist. 1989. pap. 4.95 (*1-55817-552-0*) Kensgtn Pub Corp.

Bakas, Tita. Black-Eyed Susan. (Illus.). 32p. (J). (gr. 1-5). 1999. 12.95 (*0-9662431-1-0*, Pub. by Viewpoint NC); pap. 7.95 (*0-9662431-2-9*, Pub. by Viewpoint NC) Quality Bks IL.

Bakay, Arpad. A Bakayak Es Rokohaik: Magyarurszagon USA E's Kulfoldon. LC 93-90896. (HUN.). 282p. 1993. 39.95 (*0-9640137-0-3*) A Bakay.

Bakay, Betty. Mother Moose & Her Whole Caboose. (Illus.). 32p. (J). (gr. k-2). 1998. pap. 12.95 (*0-8059-4358-7*) Dorrance.

***Bakay, Betty J.** Razz Ma Tazz - Classical 'n Jazz Instruments. (Illus.). 24p. (J). (gr. k-12). 1999. pap. write for info. (*0-9677268-0-8*) CopyRite Printing.

Bake, Paul M. Moments in Time Vol. 1: A Broken Field Run Through a Lifetime of Baltimore Based Sports Stories. Adornato, Gary, ed. LC 97-94565. (Illus.). 232p. 1997. pap. 17.95 (*0-9661217-0-8*) P Baker.

Bake, William A. Blue Ridge. (Illus.). 112p. 1984. pap. 12.95 (*0-8487-0631-5*) Oxmoor Hse.

Bake, William A., et al, texts. The Sierra Club Guides to the National Parks of the East & Middle West: The East & the Middle West. rev. ed. LC 95-11446. (Sierra Club Guides to the National Parks Ser.). (Illus.). 412p. 1995. pap. 24.95 (*0-679-76494-1*) Random.

Bakeer, Donald. Crips: The Story of a South Central L.A. Street Gang. 195p. 1992. reprint ed. 19.95 (*0-9634969-0-5*) Precocious.

Bakeev, N. F., jt. auth. see Volynskii, A. L.

Bakel, J. Van, see Van Bakel, J.

Bakeless, John. America As Seen by Its First Explorers: The Eyes of Discovery. (Illus.). 439p. 1989. pap. 9.95 (*0-486-26031-3*) Dover.

Bakeless, John. Christopher Marlowe. LC 75-42103. (English Literature Ser.: No. 33). (C). 1974. lib. bdg. 75.00 (*0-8383-1881-9*) M S G Haskell Hse.

— Daniel Boone, Master of the Wilderness. 1993. reprint ed. lib. bdg. 89.00 (*0-7812-5423-X*) Rprt Serv.

— Spies of the Confederacy. 1998. 23.50 (*0-8446-6930-X*) Peter Smith.

Bakeless, John, ed. see Lewis, Meriwether & Clark, William.

Bakeless, John E. Lewis & Clark: Partners in Discovery. unabridged ed. LC 96-19433. (Illus.). 498p. 1996. reprint ed. pap. text 11.95 (*0-486-29233-9*) Dover.

— Spies of the Confederacy. LC 97-23084. (Illus.). 456p. 1997. pap. 9.95 (*0-486-29865-5*) Dover.

— Turncoats, Traitors & Heroes: Espionage in the American Revolution. LC 97-31872. 408p. 1998. reprint ed. pap. 15.95 (*0-306-80843-9*) Da Capo.

Bakelman, I. Convex Analysis & Nonlinear Geometric Elliptic Equations. 613p. 1994. 139.95 (*0-387-13620-7*) Spr-Verlag.

Bakelman, I. R., et al, eds. A Tribute to Ilya Bakelman. (Discourses in Mathematics & Its Applications Ser.). vi, 138p. (Orig.). (C). 1994. pap. 12.00 (*0-9630728-2-X*) TX A&M Dept Math.

Bakelman, I. Ya. Inversions. Teller, Joan W. & Williams, Susan, trs. from RUS. LC 74-5727. (Popular Lectures in Mathematics). 82p. (C). 1975. pap. text 10.00 (*0-226-03499-2*) U Ch Pr.

Bakelman, Llya J. Geometric Analysis & Nonlinear Parial Differential Equations. (Lecture Notes in Pure & Applied Mathematics Ser.: Vol. 144). (Illus.). 336p. 1993. pap. text 176.00 (*0-8247-8897-4*) Dekker.

Bakely, Donald C. Bethy & the Mouse: A Father Remembers His Children with Disabilities. LC 97-3936. 184p. (Orig.). 1997. pap. 16.95 (*1-57129-035-4*) Brookline Bks.

Bakema, J. B. Thoughts about Architecture. Grey, Marianne, ed. (Academy Architecture Ser.). (Illus.). 160p. 1982. pap. 14.95 (*0-312-80190-4*) St Martin.

Bakeman, Mary H., et al. Ramsey County's Forgotten Cemetery. LC 98-54647. 1998. write for info. (*0-915709-65-1*) Pk Geneal Bk.

Bakeman, Mary H. A Comprehensive Index to A. T. Andreas Illustrated Historical Atlas of Minnesota 1874. LC 92-1361. (Illus.). 332p. 1992. 29.50 (*0-915709-01-5*) Pk Geneal Bk.

— A Guide to the Minnesota State Census Microfilm. LC 92-42767. 1992. pap. 4.00 (*0-915709-06-6*) Pk Geneal Bk.

— Lexington School: Its Story, Its Community. LC 98-19273. 50p. 1998. pap. 15.00 (*0-915709-62-7*) Pk Geneal Bk.

— St. Anthony of Padua Catholic Cemetery, Minneapolis, Minnesota, 1851-1995 LC 99-18170. 1999. 25.00 (*0-915709-66-X*) Pk Geneal Bk.

Bakeman, Mary H., compiled by. Every Name Index to Minnesota Genealogical Journal, Issues 5 & 6. LC 93-22867. 46p. (Orig.). 1993. pap. 12.00 (*0-915709-07-4*) Pk Geneal Bk.

— Every Name Index to Recollections of Early Days in Duluth. 1995. pap. 3.50 (*0-915709-23-6*) Pk Geneal Bk.

— Minnesota Land Owner Maps & Directories. LC 94-22062. 1994. text. write for info. (*0-915709-16-3*) Pk Geneal Bk.

Bakeman, Mary H., ed. Every Name Index to Minnesota Genealogical Journal, Issues 3 & 4. LC 93-22866. 55p. (Orig.). 1993. pap. 12.00 (*0-915709-08-2*) Pk Geneal Bk.

— Minnesota's WW Two Army War Dead. 40p. 1994. pap. 9.50 (*0-915709-14-7*) Pk Geneal Bk.

— Pensioners on the Roll As of January 1, 1883, (Living in Minnesota) with Every Name Index. LC 94-16879. 84p. 1994. reprint ed. pap. 12.50 (*0-915709-13-9*) Pk Geneal Bk.

— Pensioners on the Roll, 1 January 1883, Living in Dakota Territory. LC 96-27299. (Orig.). 1996. pap. 7.50 (*0-915709-26-0*) Pk Geneal Bk.

— Pensioners on the Rolls, 1 January 1883, Living in Wisconsin. LC 98-28939. 140p. 1998. pap. 17.50 (*0-915709-63-5*) Pk Geneal Bk.

Bakeman, Mary H., intro. Early Presbyterian Church Records from Minnesota, 1835-1871: Including the Church at Fort Snelling. LC 92-32098. (Illus.). 32p. 1992. pap. 10.00 (*0-915709-05-8*) Pk Geneal Bk.

Bakeman, Mary H. & Green, Stina, compiled by. Calvary Cemetery St. Paul Minnesota Vol. 3: 1889-1896. LC 95-621. (Illus.). 1997. pap. 22.50 (*0-915709-55-4*) Pk Geneal Bk.

***Bakeman, Mary H. & Green, Stina B., comments.** Calvary Cemetry Vol. 5: St. Paul Minnesota, 1905-1911. (Illus.). 100p. 1999. pap. 22.50 (*0-915709-74-0*, M353) Pk Geneal Bk.

Bakeman, Mary H. & Green, Stina B., compiled by. Calvary Cemetery, St. Paul, Minnesota Vol. 2: 1879-1988. LC 95-621. (Illus.). (Orig.). 1996. pap. 22.50 (*0-915709-25-2*) Pk Geneal Bk.

***Bakeman, Mary H. & Green, Stina B., compiled by.** Calvary Cemetery, St. Paul, Minnesota Vol. 4: 1897-1904. LC 98-621. (Illus.). 98p. 1998. pap. 22.50 (*0-915709-64-3*) Pk Geneal Bk.

Bakeman, Mary H. & Green, Stina B., compiled by. Calvary Cemetery St. Paul, Minnesota, 1854-1878 Vol. 1: Its Predecessors, 1841-1853, Vol. 1. LC 95-621. (Calvary Cemetery, St. Paul, Minnesota Ser.). (Illus.). 72p. 1995. pap. 17.50 (*0-915709-19-8*) Pk Geneal Bk.

Bakeman, Mary H., ed. see Park Genealogical Books Staff.

***Bakeman, Mary Hawkes, compiled by.** The Days of 1869: Springfield, Brown County, Minnesota. (Illus.). 80p. 2000. pap. 10.00 (*0-915709-75-9*, M 365) Pk Geneal Bk.

Bakeman, Roger. Understanding Social Science Statistics: A Spreadsheet Approach. 464p. 1992. pap. 55.00 (*0-8058-1117-6*); text 99.95 (*0-8058-0623-7*) L Erlbaum Assocs.

Bakeman, Roger & Gottman, John M. Observing Interaction: An Introduction to Sequential Analysis. 2nd ed. LC 96-26084. (Illus.). 220p. (C). 1997. text 69.95 (*0-521-45008-X*); pap. text 24.95 (*0-521-57427-7*) Cambridge U Pr.

Bakeman, Roger & Quera, Vicenc. Analyzing Interaction: Sequential Analysis with SDIS & GSEQ. (Illus.). 166p. (C). 1995. text 64.95 (*0-521-44451-9*); pap. text 24.95 (*0-521-44901-4*) Cambridge U Pr.

Bakeman, Roger & Robinson, Byron F. Understanding Log-Linear Analysis with ILOG: An Interactive Approach. 160p. 1994. pap. 19.95 (*0-8058-1240-7*); text 36.00 (*0-8058-1239-3*) L Erlbaum Assocs.

Bakemeier, Alice M. Hilltop Heritage: A History & Guide to a Denver Neighborhood. LC 98-70354. (Illus.). 68p. 1998. pap. write for info. (*0-9659574-0-3*) Heritage Pr CO.

— History of the University of Colorado School of Nursing. (Illus.). viii, 100p. 1998. pap. write for info. (*0-9659574-1-1*) Heritage Pr CO.

Baken, Lenore. Camp Europe by Train. 7th ed. 512p. 1991. pap. 14.95 (*0-917656-07-5*) Ariel Pubns.

Baken, Ronald J. & Orlikoff, Robert F. Clinical Measurement of Speech & Voice. 2nd ed. LC 99-24709. 864p. 1999. pap. 89.95 (*1-56593-869-0*, 1698) Thomson Learn.

Baken, Robert-Jan & Van Der Linden, Jan. Land Delivery for Low Income Groups in Third World Cities. 124p. 1992. 82.95 (*1-85628-373-9*, Pub. by Avebry) Ashgate Pub Co.

Baken, Ronald J. Clinical Measurement of Speech & Voice. (Illus.). 528p. (Orig.). 1996. reprint ed. pap. text 59.95 (*1-56593-809-7*, 1582) Thomson Learn.

Baken, Ronald J. & Daniloff, Raymond G., eds. Readings in Clinical Spectrography in Speech. (Illus.). 576p. (Orig.). (C). 1990. pap. text 55.00 (*1-879105-04-7*, 0005) Thomson Learn.

Baken, Ronald J., jt. auth. see Orlikoff, Robert F.

Baker. Advanced Financial Accounting. 4th ed. 408p. 1998. pap. 26.88 (*0-07-290825-4*) McGraw.

— Advanced Financial Accounting. 4th ed. 409p. 1998. pap. 32.81 (*0-07-290826-2*) McGraw.

— Advertising for Global Market. (Business Technology Ser.). (C). 1998. pap. 39.95 (*0-442-02624-2*, VNR) Wiley.

— The Atomic Bomb. 2nd ed. (C). 1996. pap. text 25.00 (*0-15-504449-4*) Harcourt Coll Pubs.

Baker. Brave Little Monster. LC 99-87294. (Illus.). 32p. (J). (ps-3). pap. 5.95 (*0-06-443625-X*) HarpC.

— Brave Little Monster. LC 99-87194. (Illus.). 32p. (J). (ps-3). 2001. 14.95 (*0-06-028698-9*) HarpC.

Baker. Clinical Dermatology. 4th ed. (Illus.). 320p. 1989. text 40.95 (*0-7020-1359-5*, W B Saunders Co) Harcrt Hlth Sci Grp.

— Collage: Rev De Gramm. 4th ed. 416p. 1995. pap. 44.69 (*0-07-005162-3*) McGraw.

Baker. Collecting Prints & Drawings in Europe C.1500-1750. 78.95 (*0-7546-0037-8*) Ashgate Pub Co.

Baker. Creators of the American Mind: Abraham Lincoln. (C). 1999. pap. text 19.00 (*0-15-505699-9*, Pub. by Harcourt Coll Pubs) Harcourt.

— Creators of the American Mind: Eleanor Roosevelt. (C). 1998. pap. text 19.00 (*0-15-505704-9*, Pub. by Harcourt Coll Pubs) Harcourt.

— Doing Social Reseach. 2nd ed. 1993. teacher ed. 20.00 (*0-07-003493-1*) McGraw.

— Finite Elements 1-2-3. 1992. student ed. 12.81 (*0-07-003468-0*) McGraw.

— The French Revolution, 3 vols., Vol. 1. 1987. 50.00 (*0-08-036276-1*, Pergamon Pr) Elsevier.

— Get to Know Keith Baker. (J). 1994. 40.00 incl. VHS (*0-15-200107-7*) Harcourt.

— Gullah. LC 96-80321. (Gullah Island Ser.: No. 8). (Illus.). 24p. (J). (ps-1). 1997. 3.25 (*0-689-81243-4*) S&S Childrens.

— Health. LC 97-75315. xxi, 196p. (C). 1998. pap. text 16.36 (*0-395-90247-9*) HM.

— Hollow Victory: The Cold War & Its Aftermath. 256p. Date not set. text 59.50 (*1-86064-124-5*) I B T.

— Instructors Manual for Activity-Based Costing. 1998. teacher ed. write for info. (*0-8342-1127-0*) Aspen Pub.

— Introduction to Philosophy. 2nd ed. 560p. 1998. pap. text 38.00 (*0-536-01924-X*) Pearson Custom.

***Baker.** Letters of Wilkie Collins, Vol.2. LC 99-19642. 1999. text 55.00 (*0-312-22344-7*) St Martin.

Baker. Marketing Introductory Text. 1997. text 25.95 (*0-333-55686-0*, Pub. by Macmillan) St Martin.

— Marketing Workbook: Strategy & Management. LC 98-228280. 288p. 1998. pap. text 32.95 (*0-7506-3652-1*) Buttrwrth-Heinemann.

— Montage. 3rd ed. 1996. audio 28.13 (*0-07-913240-5*) McGraw.

— A Nation in 2 States. 2000. 65.00 (*0-8133-6656-9*) Westview.

— National Gallery Complete Illustrated Catalogue. (C). 1995. 160.00 (*0-300-06362-8*) Yale U Pr.

— National Gallery Complete Illustrated Catalogue. (Illus.). (C). 1995. 80.00 (*0-300-06359-8*) Yale U Pr.

— Panache Litteraire 3e-student Tape. 3rd ed. (College French). (FRE.). (C). 1994. student ed., suppl. ed. 6.95 incl. audio (*0-8384-5512-3*) Heinle & Heinle.

— Panache Litteraire 3e-student Text. 3rd ed. (College French). (FRE.). (C). 1994. mass mkt. 37.95 (*0-8384-4234-X*) Heinle & Heinle.

— Plants & Civilization. 2nd ed. (Biology Ser.). 1970. pap. 5.50 (*0-534-02026-7*) Wadsworth Pub.

***Baker.** Practical Stylist. 8th ed. (C). 2000. pap. text. write for info. (*0-321-05507-1*) Addison-Wesley.

— Prospective Payment for Long Term Care: An Annual Guide, 2000 Edition. 2000. write for info. (*0-8342-1799-6*) Aspen Pub.

Baker. Religion & the Rise of Sport. 1994. 24.95 (*0-02-901185-X*) S&S Trade.

— The Rivalry. Date not set. 27.50 (*0-8050-5680-7*); pap. 14.00 (*0-8050-5681-5*, Owl) H Holt & Co.

***Baker.** School Counseling in 21st Century. 3rd ed. LC 99-32770. 418p. 1999. 67.00 (*0-13-645094-6*) P-H.

Baker. Some Day I'll Find You. large type ed. LC 98-40001. Date not set. 30.00 (*0-7838-8475-3*, G K Hall Lrg Type) Mac Lib Ref.

— Stargazer, Vol. 1. 1998. mass mkt. 5.99 (*0-312-96315-5*) St Martin.

— Transcription for Medical Office Assistant. 1998. 99.95 incl. audio (*0-8273-7907-2*) Delmar.

— Transcription for Medical Office Assistant. (C). 1998. teacher ed. 16.00 (*0-8273-7906-4*) Delmar.

Baker. Understanding Panic Attacks. 1995. pap. 12.95 (*0-7459-3313-0*, Pub. by Lion Pubng) Trafalgar.

Baker. You & HIV: A Day at a Time. (Illus.). 272p. (J). 1991. pap. text 25.00 (*0-7216-3606-3*, W B Saunders Co) Harcrt Hlth Sci Grp.

— You & Leukemia. rev. ed. 1988. pap. text 26.00 (*0-7216-1495-7*, W B Saunders Co) Harcrt Hlth Sc Grp.

***Baker.** You & Leukemia. 2nd ed. 2001. pap. text. write for info. (*0-7216-9067-X*) Harcourt.

Baker, ed. Introduction to Scientific Computing. (C). 2000. text, teacher ed. write for info. (*0-321-01615-7*) Addson-Wesley Educ.

Baker & Cauvin. Panache Litteraire. 3rd ed. (FRE.). 1994. pap. text 50.95 incl. audio (*0-8384-5533-6*) Heinle & Heinle.

Baker & Couvin. Panache Litteraire. 2nd ed. (C). 1989. pap. 30.95 (*0-8384-3658-7*) Heinle & Heinle.

Baker & Dewar. The Mind. (What's the Big Idea Ser.). 1996. mass mkt. 8.95 (*0-340-65588-7*, Pub. by Hodder & Stought Ltd) Trafalgar.

Baker & Lumsden. Color Atlas of Cytology for the Dog & Cat. LC 99-37111. (Illus.). 256p. (C). (gr. 13). 1999. text 99.00 (*0-8151-0402-2*, 23968) Mosby Inc.

Baker & McKenzie. Guide to Financing Power Projects. (Project Finance Strategic Reports). 1996. 225.00 (*1-85564-540-8*, Pub. by Euromoney) Am Educ Systs.

— Guide to Financing Telecommunication Projects. (Project Finance Strategic Reports). 1997. 225.00 (*1-85564-543-2*, Pub. by Euromoney) Am Educ Systs.

Baker & McKenzie. NAFTA Handbook. LC 95-106721. 276p. 1994. pap. 38.00 (*0-8080-0025-X*, BLS-3384) CCH INC.

Baker & McKenzie. Single European Market Reporter: Guide to Community Rules & Their Implementation in National Law. 1991. ring bd. 199.50 (*90-6544-934-5*) Kluwer Law Intl.

Baker & Mendelsohn. Reforming America's Schools: From Teachers & Curriculum to Glogilization & Interdiscipline. LC 97-215901. 248p. (C). 1997. per. 31.95 (*0-7872-3952-6*, 41395201) Kendall-Hunt.

Baker & Woods, Gail Baker. Mass Media Writing. 350p. (C). 1996. pap. text 53.00 (*0-13-776444-8*) P-H.

Baker, jt. auth. see Derick.

Baker, jt. auth. see Ebert.

Baker, jt. auth. see Ho.

Baker, jt. auth. see Wade.

Baker, Mark D. Religious No More: Building Communities of Grace & Freedom. LC 99-21814. 180p. 1999. pap. 14.99 (*0-8308-1592-9*, 1592) InterVarsity.

Baker & Columbia State College Staff. Elementry & Intermediate Algebra. 520p. 1998. pap. text 62.50 (*0-536-01052-8*) Pearson Custom.

Baker & Daniels Attorneys at Law Staff. Employment Law Handbook. 3rd ed. 466p. 1998. pap. 95.00 (*1-883698-20-0*) IN Chamber Comm.

— Employment Law Handbook: A Business Guide to Indiana & Federal Employment Laws. 406p. 1995. pap. 95.00 (*1-883698-05-7*) IN Chamber Comm.

Baker & Hostetler, McCutchen Black, Staff. Hospital Contracts Manual, 3 vols., Set. LC 82-16344. ring bd. 475.00 (*0-89443-828-X*) Aspen Pub.

Baker & McKenzie North American Tax Practice Group. Intercompany Pricing: Guide to the New 1993 United States Rules. LC 93-33199. 1993. write for info. (*90-6544-774-1*) Kluwer Law Intl.

Baker, A. Practical Stylist. 7th ed. (C). 1997. pap. text 11.00 (*0-06-360430-2*) HarpC.

Baker, A., et al, eds. A Tribute to Paul Erdos. (Illus.). 496p. (C). 1991. text 105.00 (*0-521-38101-0*) Cambridge U Pr.

Baker, A. A. & Jones, R., eds. Bonded Repair of Aircraft Structures. (C). 1988. text 211.50 (*90-247-3606-4*) Kluwer Academic.

Baker, A. Brad, jt. auth. see Khoshafian, Setrag.

Baker, A. C. Tidal Power. (Energy Ser.: No. 5). 260p. 1991. 82.00 (*0-86341-189-4*, EN005) INSPEC Inc.

Baker, A. D., III. Naval Institute Guide to Combat Fleets of the World, 1998: Their Ships, Aircraft & Systems. (Illus.). 1200p. 1998. 150.00 (*1-55750-111-4*) Naval Inst Pr.

***Baker, A. D., III.** The Naval Institute Guide to Combat Fleets of the World, 2000-2001: Their Ships, Aircraft & Systems. (Illus.). 960p. 2000. 175.00 (*1-55750-197-1*) Naval Inst Pr.

Baker, A. D., jt. ed. see Brundle, C. R.

Baker, A. J. Finite Element Computational Fluid Mechanics. 510p. 1983. pap. 85.00 (*1-56032-245-4*) Hemisp Pub.

Baker, A. J. & Pepper, D. W. Finite Element 1-2-3 Set. 368p. (C). 1991. 61.50 (*0-07-909975-0*) McGraw.

Baker, A. S. Bibliography of the Helminth Parasites of New Zealand. 79p. (Orig.). 1996. pap. text 19.95 (*0-85198-265-4*) OUP.

Baker, Aaron & Boyd, Todd. Out of Bounds: Sports, Media & the Politics of Identity. LC 96-19729. 1997. 39.95 (*0-253-33228-1*); pap. 17.95 (*0-253-21095-X*) Ind U Pr.

Baker, A.D. Naval Institute Guide to Combat Fleets of the World, 1998: Their Ships, Aircraft & Systems. 1998. 129.95 (*1-55750-112-2*) Naval Inst Pr.

***Baker, Adam L.** New York Graphic. LC 99-88713. 308p. 2000. pap. 13.00 (*0-385-49843-8*, Anchor NY) Doubleday.

Baker, Adolph. Modern Physics & Anti-Physics. LC 74-109506. (C). 1970. pap. text 23.16 (*0-201-00485-2*) Addison-Wesley.

Baker, Adrienne. The Jewish Woman in Contemporary Society: Transitions & Traditions. Campling, Jo, ed. LC 93-16206. 304p. (C). 1993. text 50.00 (*0-8147-1210-X*); pap. text 19.50 (*0-8147-1211-8*) NYU Pr.

***Baker, Adrienne.** Serious Shopping: Psychotherapy & Consumerism. 220p. 2000. pap. 25.00 (*1-85343-483-3*, Pub. by Free Assoc Bks) Intl Spec Bk.

***Baker, Adrienne, ed.** Serious Shopping: Psychotherapy & Consumerism. 220p. 2000. 55.00 (*1-85343-482-5*, Pub. by Free Assoc Bks) Intl Spec Bk.

Baker, Alan. Benjamin & the Box. LC 77-23870. 32p. (J). 1977. write for info. (*0-397-31774-3*) Lppncott W & W.

— Benjamin Bounces Back. (Illus.). (J). (gr. k-2). 1978. 9.95 (*0-397-31809-X*) HarpC Child Bks.

— Benjamin's Dreadful Dream. LC 79-5369. (Illus.). (J). (ps-2). 1980. 9.95 (*0-397-31902-9*) HarpC Child Bks.

— Benjamin's Dreadful Dream. LC 79-5369. (Illus.). (J). (ps-2). 1980. lib. bdg. 9.89 (*0-397-31903-7*) HarpC Child Bks.

— Black & White Rabbit's ABC. LC 93-29760. (Little Rabbit Bks.: Vol. 3). (Illus.). 24p. (J). (ps). 1994. 9.95 (*1-85697-951-2*, Kingfisher) LKC.

An Asterisk (*) at the beginning of an entry indicates that the title is appearing for the first time.

***Baker, Alan.** Black & White Rabbit's ABC. 24p. (J). 1999. pap. 3.95 (*0-7534-5253-7*) LKC.

Baker, Alan. Brown Rabbit's Day. LC 94-42007. (Little Rabbit Bks.). (Illus.). 24p. (J). (ps up). 1995. 9.95 (*1-85697-584-3*, Kingfisher) LKC.

— Brown Rabbit's Day. 24p. (J). 1999. pap. 3.95 (*0-7534-5256-1*) LKC.

— Brown Rabbit's Shape Book. LC 93-29758. (Little Rabbit Bks.: Vol. 1). (Illus.). 24p. (J). (ps-k). 1994. 9.95 (*1-85697-950-4*, Kingfisher) LKC.

***Baker, Alan.** Brown Rabbit's Shape Book. 24p. (J). 1999. pap. 3.95 (*0-7534-5255-3*) LKC.

Baker, Alan. A Concise Introduction to the Theory of Numbers. (Illus.). 112p. 1985. pap. text 18.95 (*0-521-28654-9*) Cambridge U Pr.

— Destination Earth: A History of Alleged Alien Presence. (Illus.). 200p. 1998. pap. 12.95 (*0-7137-2719-5*) Sterling.

***Baker, Alan.** The Encyclopedia of Alien Encounters: A Complete Guide from Abductions to the Yeti. (Illus.). 288p. 2000. 45.00 (*0-8160-4226-8*, Checkmark); pap. 27.95 (*0-8160-4227-6*, Checkmark) Facts on File.

Baker, Alan. Fraternity among the French Peasantry: Sociability & Voluntary Associations in the Loire Valley, 1815-1914. LC 98-35994. (Cambridge Studies in Historical Geography: No. 28). (Illus.). 390p. (C). 1999. text 74.95 (*0-521-64213-2*) Cambridge U Pr.

***Baker, Alan.** Ghosts & Spirits. 304p. 1998. pap. 12.95 (*1-57500-027-X*, Pub. by TV Bks) HarpC.

Baker, Alan. Gray Rabbit's Odd One Out. LC 94-42002. (Little Rabbit Bks.). (Illus.). 24p. (J). (ps-3). 1995. 9.95 (*1-85697-585-1*) LKC.

— Gray Rabbit's Odd One Out. 24p. (J). 1999. pap. 3.95 (*0-7534-5257-X*, Kingfisher) LKC.

— Gray Rabbit's One, Two, Three. LC 93-29759. (Little Rabbit Bks.: No. 2). (Illus.). 24p. (J). (ps). 1994. 9.95 (*1-85697-952-0*, Kingfisher) LKC.

***Baker, Alan.** Gray Rabbit's 1, 2, 3. 24p. (J). 1999. pap. 3.95 (*0-7534-5252-9*) LKC.

Baker, Alan. I Thought I Heard... LC 95-43118. (Illus.). 24p. (J). (ps-2). 1996. lib. bdg. 18.90 (*0-7613-0460-6*, Copper Beech Bks) Millbrook Pr.

— Little Rabbit's Bedtime. (Illus.). 12p. (J). (ps up). 1998. 10.95 (*0-7534-5143-3*, Kingfisher) LKC.

— Little Rabbit's First Number Book. LC 98-12836. (Little Rabbit Bks.). (J). (gr. 2 up). 1998. 11.95 (*0-7534-5167-0*, Kingfisher) LKC.

— Little Rabbit's First Time Book. LC 99-11823. (YA). (ps up). 1999. 11.95 (*0-7534-5220-0*) LKC.

— Little Rabbit's First Word Book. (Illus.). 40p. (J). (ps up). 1995. 11.95 (*0-7534-5020-8*) LKC.

— Little Rabbit's Snacktime. LC 97-39697. (Little Rabbit Bks.). (Illus.). 20p. (J). (ps-k). 1998. 10.95 (*0-7534-5144-1*, Kingfisher) LKC.

— Look Who Lives in the Arctic. LC 99-46892. (Look Who Lives in--Ser.). 32p. (J). 1999. 14.95 (*0-87226-540-4*, 65404B, P Bedrick Books) NTC Contemp Pub Co.

— Look Who Lives in the Desert. (Look Who Lives in--Ser.). 32p. (J). 1999. 14.95 (*0-87226-541-2*, 65412B, P Bedrick Books) NTC Contemp Pub Co.

— Look Who Lives in the Ocean. LC 98-37549. (Look Who Lives in--Ser.). 32p. (J). 1999. 14.95 (*0-87226-539-0*, 65390B, P Bedrick Books) NTC Contemp Pub Co.

***Baker, Alan.** Look Who Lives in the Rain Forest. LC 98-37562. (Look Who Lives in--Ser.). 32p. (J). 1999. 14.95 (*0-87226-538-2*, 65382B, P Bedrick Books) NTC Contemp Pub Co.

Baker, Alan. Mouse's Christmas. LC 96-2332. (Illus.). 24p. (J). (ps-1). 1996. 12.95 (*0-7613-0503-3*, Copper Beech Bks) Millbrook Pr.

— Mouse's Halloween. LC 97-5072. (Illus.). 32p. (J). (ps-2). 1997. 12.95 (*0-7613-0628-5*); lib. bdg. 21.40 (*0-7613-0704-4*, Copper Beech Bks) Millbrook Pr.

— Robot Wars: Technical Manual. (Illus.). 156p. 1999. pap. 27.50 (*0-7522-1361-X*) Trans-Atl Phila.

***Baker, Alan.** True Life Encounter: UFO Sightings. 1999. pap. 12.95 (*1-57500-022-9*, Pub. by TV Bks) HarpC.

Baker, Alan. White Rabbit's Color Book. LC 93-32316. (Little Rabbit Bks.: No. 4). (Illus.). 24p. (J). (ps). 1994. 9.95 (*1-85697-953-9*) LKC.

***Baker, Alan.** White Rabbit's Color Book. (Little Rabbit Bks.). (Illus.). 24p. (ps-k). 1999. pap. 3.95 (*0-7534-5254-5*) LKC.

Baker, Alan, tr. see Matschinsky, Wolfgang.

Baker, Alan A. Whales & Dolphins of New Zealand & Australia: An Identification Guide. (Illus.). 133p. (C). 1990. pap. text 20.00 (*0-86473-099-3*, Pub. by Victoria Univ Pr) Lubrecht & Cramer.

Baker, Alan A., jt. ed. see Hoskin, Brian C.

Baker, Alan J. Investment, Valuation & the Managerial Theory of the Firm. 336p. 1978. text 72.95 (*0-566-00192-6*) Ashgate Pub Co.

Baker, Alan R. & Biger, Gideon, eds. Ideology & Landscape in Historical Perspective: Essays on the Meanings of Some Places in the Past. (Cambridge Studies in Historical Geography: No. 18). (Illus.). 371p. (C). 1992. text 69.95 (*0-521-41032-0*) Cambridge U Pr.

Baker, Albert E. Prophets for a Day of Judgment. LC 72-90605. (Essay Index Reprint Ser.). 1977. 19.95 (*0-8369-1390-6*) Ayer.

***Baker, Alex.** Terry Adkins: Relay Hymn. (Illus.). 32p. (C). 1999. pap. 15.00 (*0-88454-095-2*) U of Pa Contemp Art.

Baker, Alice C. True Stories of New England Captives Carried to Canada During the Old French & Indian Wars. (Illus.). 418p. 1991. pap. 27.50 (*1-55613-420-7*) Heritage Bk.

Baker, Alison. Loving Wanda Beaver: Novella & Stories. LC 95-12600. 208p. 1995. 16.95 (*0-8118-1064-X*) Chronicle Bks.

— Loving Wanda Beaver: Novella & Stories. 1997. pap. text 11.95 (*0-8118-1788-1*) Chronicle Bks.

— Voices of Resistance: Oral Histories of Moroccan Women. LC 97-2649. (Series in Oral & Public History). (Illus.). 352p. (C). 1998. text 74.50 (*0-7914-3621-7*); pap. text 24.95 (*0-7914-3622-5*) State U NY Pr.

Baker, Amenzo W. Baker Genealogy & Collateral Branches. Stone, Merlin J., ed. (Illus.). 226p. 1997. reprint ed. pap. 34.00 (*0-8328-7339-X*); reprint ed. lib. bdg. 44.00 (*0-8328-7338-1*) Higginson Bk Co.

Baker, Amy C. & Manfredi-Petitt, Lynn A. Circle of Love: Relationships Between Parents, Providers & Children in Family Care. LC 98-4948. (Illus.). 240p. 1998. pap. 15.95 (*1-884834-42-6*) Redleaf Pr.

Baker, Amy J. Voting by Institutional Investors on Corporate Governarle Issues in the 1992 Proxy Season. O'Hara, Peg, ed. (Illus.). (Orig.). 1993. pap. text 25.00 (*1-879775-16-6*) IRRC Inc DC.

Baker, Andrew & Goodman, Lori. Working with the Intermarried: A Practical Guide for Workshop Leaders. LC 85-71160. 36p. (Orig.). 1985. pap. 4.00 (*0-87495-071-6*) Am Jewish Comm.

Baker, Andrew H., ed. Vascular Disease: Molecular Biology & Gene Transfer Protocols. LC 98-55168. (Methods in Molecular Medicine Ser.: Vol. 30). (Illus.). 456p. 1999. 99.50 (*0-89603-731-2*) Humana.

Baker, Andrew J. & Plymen, Roger J., eds. P-Adic Methods & Their Applications. (Illus.). 206p. 1992. text 65.00 (*0-19-853594-5*) OUP.

Baker, Ann. Introducing English Pronunciation: A Teacher's Guide to Tree or Three? & Ship or Sheep. 160p. 1982. pap. text 19.95 (*0-521-28580-1*) Cambridge U Pr.

— Ship or Sheep. (Cambridge English Language Learning Ser.). (Illus.). 1981. pap. 11.95 (*0-521-28354-X*) Cambridge U Pr.

Baker, Ann & Baker, Johnny. Counting on a Small Planet: Activities for Environmental Mathematics. LC 91-30571. 96p. (C). (gr. k). 1992. pap. text 17.50 (*0-435-08327-9*, 08327) Heinemann.

— Mathematics in Process. LC 90-34373. 170p. (C). (gr. k). 1990. pap. text 21.50 (*0-435-08306-6*, 08306) Heinemann.

— Maths in the Mind: A Process Approach to Mental Strategies. LC 91-7547. (Illus.). 120p. (Orig.). (C). (gr. k). 1991. pap. text 16.50 (*0-435-08316-3*) Heinemann.

Baker, Ann & Goldstein, Sharon. Pronunciation Pairs: An Introductory Course for Students of English. (Illus.). 158p. (C). 1990. pap. text, student ed. 16.95 (*0-521-34972-9*) Cambridge U Pr.

— Pronunciation Pairs: An Introductory Course for Students of English. (Illus.). 137p. (C). 1990. pap. text, teacher ed. 17.95 (*0-521-34973-7*) Cambridge U Pr.

Baker, Ann, jt. auth. see Baker, John.

Baker, Ann Sullivan, jt. ed. see Ciulla, Thomas A.

Baker, Anne. Abortion & Options Counseling: A Comprehensive Reference. rev. ed. LC 95-75149. (Illus.). 222p. 1995. pap. 25.00 (*0-9644777-0-X*) Hope Clinic for Women.

— Christmas Delights for Two Violins, Pts. Violin I-II. 25p. 1992. pap. text 5.95 (*0-87487-436-X*) Summy-Birchard.

— Christmas Delights for Two Violins, Pts. Violin I-II: Score. 25p. 1992. pap. text 8.95 (*0-87487-437-8*) Summy-Birchard.

— Moonlight on the Mersey. 512p. 1997. pap. 11.95 (*0-7472-5319-6*, Pub. by Headline Bk Pub) Trafalgar.

— A Question of Honour: The Life of Lieutenant General Valentine Baker Pasha. LC 97-131098. (Illus.). 191p. 1996. pap. 21.95 (*0-85052-496-2*, Pub. by Leo Cooper) Trans-Atl Phila.

Baker, Anne P. Beethoven. (Get a Life...Pocket Biographies Ser.). (Illus.). 128p. 1997. pap. 9.95 (*0-7509-1509-9*, Pub. by Sutton Pub Ltd) Intl Pubs Mktg.

Baker, Anthony. Long Island Country Houses, 2. Date not set. write for info. (*0-393-03900-5*) Norton.

— Long Island Country Houses, 2 vols., Set. (Illus.). 1120p. Date not set. write for info. (*0-393-03899-8*) Norton.

Baker, Anthony E., jt. auth. see Bonn, Keith E.

Baker, Anthony K., et al, eds. Long Island Country Houses & Their Architects, 1860-1940. (Illus.). 584p. 1997. 85.00 (*0-393-03856-4*) Norton.

Baker, Archibald G. & Shepherd, A. H., Jr., eds. A Short History of Christianity. LC 83-147781. (Midway Reprint Ser.). 285p. Date not set. reprint ed. pap. 88.40 (*0-608-20983-X*, 205451100003) Bks Demand.

Baker, Arnie. Bicycling Medicine: Cycling Nutrition, Physiology, Injury Prevention, & Treatment for Riders of All Levels. LC 98-27500. (Illus.). 336p. 1998. per. 14.00 (*0-684-84443-5*) S&S Trade Pap.

— The Essential Cyclist. LC 97-44824. (Essential...Ser.). (Illus.). 160p. 1998. pap. 14.95 (*1-55821-522-0*) Lyons Pr.

— Smart Cycling. LC 96-18734. 304p. 1997. per. 14.00 (*0-684-82243-1*) S&S Trade Pap.

Baker, Art. Windows NT Device Driver Book: A Guide for Programmers. LC 96-22449. 544p. (C). 1996. pap. 44.95 incl. disk (*0-13-184474-1*) P-H.

— Windows NT Device Driver Book: A Guide for Programmers. 2nd ed. 500p. 2000. pap. 49.99 (*0-13-020431-5*) P-H.

— Writing Device Drivers W. (C). 1997. pap. text 39.95 (*0-201-40715-9*) Addison-Wesley.

Baker, Arthur. Arthur Baker's Historic Calligraphic Alphabets. (Pictorial Archive Ser.). (Illus.). 96p. (Orig.). 1980. pap. 6.95 (*0-486-24054-1*) Dover.

— Calligraphic Alphabets. LC 79-8223. (Pictorial Archive Ser.). (Illus.). 157p. (Orig.). 1974. pap. 8.95 (*0-486-21045-6*) Dover.

— Calligraphic Initials. LC 78-56108. (Illus.). 1978. 12.50 (*0-910158-44-4*); pap. 8.95 (*0-910158-48-7*) Art Dir.

— Calligraphic Swash Initials. (Illus.). 96p. (Orig.). (gr. 7 up). 1984. pap. 7.95 (*0-486-24427-X*) Dover.

***Baker, Arthur.** Calligraphy. LC 99-58784. 2000. pap. 9.95 (*0-486-40950-3*) Dover.

Baker, Arthur. Celtic Hand Stroke by Stroke (Irish Half-Uncial from "The Book of Kells") (Arthur Baker Calligraphy Manual: Lettering, Calligraphy, Typography Ser.). (Illus.). 48p. (Orig.). 1983. pap. 3.95 (*0-486-24336-2*) Dover.

— Chancery Cursive Stroke by Stroke: An Arthur Baker Calligraphy Manual. (Illus.). 64p. 1982. pap. 3.95 (*0-486-24278-1*) Dover.

— Cut & Assemble Paper Airplanes That Fly. (J). 1982. pap. 4.95 (*0-486-24302-8*) Dover.

— Encyclopedia of Calligraphic Styles. 1990. 15.00 (*0-910158-95-9*) Art Dir.

— Learning Calligraphy Stroke by Stroke, 3 vols., Set. (Illus.). 1987. pap. 11.40 (*0-486-25428-3*) Dover.

— The Roman Alphabet. LC 76-44477. (Illus.). 1977. 15.00 (*0-910158-23-1*) Art Dir.

— Roman Capitals Stroke by Stroke: An Arthur Baker Calligraphy Manual. (Illus.). 32p. (Orig.). (gr. 6 up). 1983. pap. 3.50 (*0-486-24450-4*) Dover.

Baker, Arthur. Brush Calligraphy. (Lettering, Calligraphy, Typography Ser.). 96p. (Orig.). 1984. pap. 6.95 (*0-486-24533-0*) Dover.

Baker, Arthur & Barron, Don. The Script Alphabet. LC 78-56103. (Illus.). 1978. pap. 8.95 (*0-910158-47-9*) Art Dir.

Baker, Arthur, jt. auth. see Baker, Joan.

Baker, Arthur E. A Concordance to the Poetical & Dramatic Works of Alfred Lord Tennyson. (BCL1-PR English Literature Ser.). 1212p. 1992. reprint ed. lib. bdg. 119.00 (*0-7812-7691-8*) Rprt Serv.

Baker, Arthur Ernest. A Tennyson Dictionary. (BCL1-PR English Literature Ser.). 296p. 1992. reprint ed. lib. bdg. 79.00 (*0-7812-7692-6*) Rprt Serv.

— A Tennyson Directory. LC 67-30807. (Studies in Tennyson: No. 27). 1916. reprint ed. lib. bdg. 75.00 (*0-8383-0706-X*) M S G Haskell Hse.

Baker, Arthur M. Awakening Our Self-Healing Body: A Solution to the Health Care Crisis. LC 93-93516. 306p. (Orig.). 1994. pap. 12.95 (*1-883989-25-6*) Self Hlth Care.

— Bacteria, Germs, & Viruses Do Not Cause Disease: Discriminating Between Medical Myth & Biological Fact. LC 93-93558. 55p. (Orig.). 1994. pap. 8.95 (*1-883989-07-8*) Self Hlth Care.

— The Harmful Effects of Allopathic (Western) Medicine: Drugs Degenerate the Body. LC 93-93558. 42p. (Orig.). 1994. pap. 8.95 (*1-883989-29-9*) Self Hlth Care.

— Holistic Self-Health Care: The Theory & Practical Application of Natural Hygiene. LC 93-93557. 67p. (Orig.). 1994. pap. 8.95 (*1-883989-36-1*) Self Hlth Care.

— The Incredible Organizing Power of the Human Body: Phenomenal Facts of Physiology. 18p. (Orig.). 1994. pap. 5.95 (*1-883989-17-5*) Self Hlth Care.

— Organizations & Practitioners of Natural Hygiene & a Brief History of Natural Hygiene. 24p. (Orig.). 1994. pap. 5.95 (*1-883989-03-5*) Self Hlth Care.

— Our Ailing Health Care System: Health Care Is Bankrupting America & Leaving Us Increasingly Diseased. LC 93-93556. 50p. (Orig.). 1994. pap. 8.95 (*1-883989-11-6*) Self Hlth Care.

— The Scientific Basis of Vegetarianism: Determining Our Natural Dietary Needs. 30p. (Orig.). 1994. pap. 7.95 (*1-883989-46-9*) Self Hlth Care.

Baker, Augusta & Greene, Ellin. Storytelling: Art & Technique. 2nd ed. LC 77-16481. 182p. 1987. 35.00 (*0-8352-2336-1*) Bowker.

Baker, Austin. Eddy the Eagle & the Diamond. LC 98-39776. (J). 1998. write for info. (*1-56763-431-1*); pap. write for info. (*1-56763-432-X*) Ozark Pub.

Baker, B. & Gyawali, G. Promoting Proper Pesticides Use in Nepal. 1994. pap. 35.00 (*0-7855-0420-6*, Pub. by Ratna Pustak Bhandar) St Mut.

Baker, B. Granville. The Walls of Constantinople. LC 72-178513. (Medieval Studies). reprint ed. 37.50 (*0-404-56509-3*) AMS Pr.

Baker, B. O. Keeping Christmas. (Illus.). 100p. (J). 1996. write for info. (*0-614-19222-6*, Vol. 1) Stonebridge Pub.

Baker, Barbara. Digby & Kate No. 3. 48p. (J). 1997. pap. 3.50 (*0-14-038622-X*) Viking Penguin.

— Digby & Kate & the Beautiful Day. LC 98-135347. (Illus.). 48p. 1998. 13.99 (*0-525-45855-7*) NAL.

— One Saturday Afternoon. LC 98-41605. (gr. 1-4). 1999. 13.99 (*0-525-45882-4*) NAL.

— One Saturday Afternoon. 1999. pap. 3.50 (*0-14-038756-0*) Viking Penguin.

— One Saturday Morning. (Puffin Easy-To-Read. Level 2 Ser.). (J). 1997. 8.70 (*0-606-11709-1*, Pub. by Turtleback) Demco.

— One Saturday Morning. (Illus.). (J). (gr. k-3). 1997. pap. 3.50 (*0-14-038605-X*) Viking Penguin.

— Third Grade is Terrible. (J). 1989. 9.09 (*0-606-05032-9*, Pub. by Turtleback) Demco.

— Third Grade Is Terrible. MacDonald, Patricia, ed. (Illus.). 112p. (J). (gr. 2-5). 1991. reprint ed. mass mkt. 3.99 (*0-671-70379-X*, Minstrel Bks) PB.

***Baker, Barbara.** Third Grade Is Terrible: Third Grade is Terrible. (Puffin Chapters Ser.). (J). 1999. pap. 3.99 (*0-14-130103-1*, PuffinBks) Peng Put Young Read.

Baker, Barbara. The William Problem. (Puffin Chapters Ser.). (J). 1997. 9.09 (*0-606-13069-1*, Pub. by Turtleback) Demco.

— The William Problem. (Puffin Chapters Ser.). (Illus.). 128p. (J). (gr. 2-5). 1997. pap. 3.99 (*0-14-037699-2*, Viking) Viking Penguin.

Baker, Barbara, ed. Shanghai: Electric & Lurid City. (Illus.). 312p. 1998. pap. text 29.95 (*0-19-590603-9*) OUP.

Baker, Barbara & Boyington, Evelyn. Down East Puzzles & Word Games. (Illus.). 80p. (Orig.). (J). 1989. pap. 3.95 (*0-89272-272-X*) Down East.

Baker, Barbara & Slavick, Madeleine. Round: Poems & Photographs of Asia. (Illus.). 88p. 1999. 36.00 (*962-7160-65-2*, Pub. by Asia) Weatherhill.

Baker, Barbara E., et al, eds. The National Directory of Internships. 9th ed. 607p. (Orig.). 1993. write for info. (*0-937883-11-5*) NSEE.

Baker, Barbara P. Steamy Dreamer: The Saga of Dr. Hartley O. Baker & the Baker Steamer Motor Car. 176p. 1996. 29.95 (*1-882418-22-0*); pap. 22.95 (*1-882418-23-9*) Centenn Pubns.

Baker, Barbara S. Recent Advances in Psoriasis: The Role of the Immune System. 180p. 1999. 28.00 (*1-86094-120-6*) World Scientific Pub.

Baker, Barbara S., jt. auth. see Carter, Donald E.

Baker, Barbarina. The Girl from down Under. 1990. write for info. (*0-318-66793-2*) Tevis Pub.

Baker, Barrie. The Village of a Hundred Smiles: And Other Stories. (Illus.). 48p. (J). (gr. 3-5). 1998. pap. 7.95 (*1-55037-535-0*, Pub. by Annick) Firefly Bks Ltd.

— The Village of a Hundred Smiles: And Other Stories. (Illus.). 48p. (J). (gr. 1-5). 1998. lib. bdg. 18.95 (*1-55037-522-9*) Firefly Bks Ltd.

Baker, Barry, jt. auth. see Shaffer, Brian.

Baker, Barry B., ed. Cooperative Cataloging: Past, Present & Future. LC 93-44337. (Cataloging & Classification Quarterly Ser.: Vol. 17, Nos. 3-4). (Illus.). 275p. 1993. lib. bdg. 49.95 (*1-56024-582-4*) Haworth Pr.

Baker, Barry B., intro. The USMARC Format for Holdings & Locations: Development, Implementation & Use. LC 88-16383. (Technical Services Quarterly Supplement Ser.: No. 2). 231p. 1988. text 49.95 (*0-86656-695-3*) Haworth Pr.

Baker, Barry B. & Lysiak, Lynne D., eds. From Tape to Product: Some Practical Considerations on the Use of OCLC-MARC Tapes. LC 85-60594. (Library Hi Tech Monograph: No. 3). 1985. 45.00 (*0-87650-191-9*) Pierian.

Baker, Beatrice, ed. see Steele, Archibald T.

Baker, Beatrice V. & Quayle, Thomas E. Go Forth, Multiply, & Prosper: The Saga of Charles Crismon & Edmund Ellsworth: Mormon Pioneers. (Illus.). 570p. (Orig.). 1989. spiral bd. 40.00 (*0-9623144-1-2*) Vilate Pub.

Baker, Benjamin. Benjamin Baker, Forth Bridge. (Opus: Vol. 18). (Illus.). 60p. 1998. 42.00 (*3-930698-18-8*) Dist Art Pubs.

Baker, Benjamin A. Glance at New York. Meserve, Walter J., ed. & intro. by. (On Stage, America! Ser.). 34p. 1996. spiral bd. 3.95 (*0-937657-27-1*) Feedbk Theabks & Prospero.

Baker, Benjamin S. Special Occasions in the Black Church. LC 88-35601. 254p. 1989. 16.99 (*0-8054-2320-6*, 4223-20) Broadman.

Baker, Bernadette, jt. auth. see Galliers, Robert.

***Baker, Beth.** Sylvia Earle: Guardian of the Sea. LC 99-32159. (Biographies Ser.). (Illus.). 112p. (YA). (gr. 4-7). 2000. lib. bdg. 25.26 (*0-8225-4961-1*, Lerner Publctns) Lerner Pub.

Baker, Betty. Little Runner of the Longhouse. LC 62-8040. (I Can Read Bks.). (Illus.). 64p. (J). (ps-3). 1962. lib. bdg. 15.89 (*0-06-020341-2*) HarpC Child Bks.

— Little Runner of the Longhouse. LC 62-8040. (I Can Read Bks.). (Illus.). 64p. (J). (ps-3). 1989. pap. 3.95 (*0-06-444122-9*, HarpTrophy) HarpC Child Bks.

Baker, Betty. Little Runner of the Longhouse. (I Can Read Bks.). (J). (gr. 1-3). 1989. 8.95 (*0-606-12401-2*, Pub. by Turtleback) Demco.

Baker, Betty L. Aranas por Todas Partes. Romo, Alberto, tr. (Books for Young Learners).Tr. of Spiders Everywhere. (SPA., Illus.). 8p. (J). (gr. k-2). 1997. pap. text 5.00 (*1-57274-184-8*, A2825) R Owen Pubs.

— Spiders Everywhere. LC 98-227245. (Books for Young Learners). (Illus.). 8p. (J). (gr. k-2). 1997. pap. text 5.00 (*1-57274-081-7*, A2500) R Owen Pubs.

Baker, Bevan B. & Copson, E. T. The Mathematical Theory of Huygens Principle. LC 50-8926. 200p. reprint ed. pap. 62.00 (*0-608-30952-4*, 205116600080) Bks Demand.

— The Mathematical Theory of Huygens Principle. 3rd ed. vii, 195p. 1987. text 17.95 (*0-8284-0329-5*, 329) Chelsea Pub.

Baker, Bill. The Essential Road Guide for Costa Rica. (Illus.). 125p. 1992. 12.95 (*1-885557-00-0*) Intl Mrkting.

— The Rules of the Game: Buying Real Estate in Costa Rica. 139p. 1994. 29.00 (*1-885557-01-9*) Intl Mrkting.

— 2 Corinthians. LC 99-45673. (NIV Commentary Ser.). 300p. 1999. 21.99 (*0-89900-634-5*) College Pr Pub.

Baker, Bill, et al. Community Relations: Unleashing the Power of Corporate Citizenship. Kelly, Susan, ed. (Illus.). 147p. 1998. spiral bd. 495.00 (*1-928593-00-3*) Am Prodtv Qual.

Baker, Blanch M. Dramatic Bibliography. LC 68-20214. 1972. reprint ed. 24.95 (*0-405-08229-0*, Pub. by Blom Pubns) Ayer.

— Theatre & Allied Arts. LC 66-12284. 1972. reprint ed. 47.95 (*0-405-08230-4*, Pub. by Blom Pubns) Ayer.

Baker, Bo. Keeping Christmas, Vol. 1. expanded ed. (Illus.). 100p. 1996. 12.99 (*0-9653820-0-1*) Stonebridge Pub.

Baker, Bob. One-Hundred One Ways to Make Money Right Now in the Music Business: The A-Z Guide to Cashing in on Your Talents. Hustwit, Gary, ed. LC 92-82622. 140p. (Orig.). (C). 1993. pap. 14.95 (*0-9627013-4-3*) Rockpress Pub.

Baker Book House Staff, Jon. The Baker Bible Dictionary for Kids. (Illus.). (gr. 3-7). 1999. audio compact disk 9.99 (*0-8010-0268-0*, New Kids Media) Baker Bks.

— Baker Bible Encyclopedia for Kids. (Illus.). (gr. k-6). 1998. audio compact disk 39.99 (*0-8010-0253-2*, New Kids Media) Baker Bks.

***Baker Book House Staff, Jon.** The Baker Book of Bible People for Kids. (J). (ps-3). 1999. audio compact disk 9.99 (*0-8010-0282-6*) Baker Bks.

An Asterisk (*) at the beginning of an entry indicates that the title is appearing for the first time.

— The Baker Books of the Bible. (J). (ps-3). 1999. audio compact disk 9.99 (*0-8010-0283-4*) Baker Bks.
— The Birth of Jesus. (J). (ps-3). 1999. audio compact disk 9.99 (*0-8010-0281-8*) Baker Bks.
— Seeking Sammy in the New Testament. (J). (ps-3). 1999. audio compact disk 9.99 (*0-8010-0280-X*) Baker Bks.
— Seeking Sammy in the Old Testament. (J). (ps-3). 1999. audio compact disk 9.99 (*0-8010-0278-8*) Baker Bks.
***Baker Books Publishing Staff.** Bible Champions David: The Life of David. (J). (ps-3). 1999. audio compact disk 9.99 (*0-8010-0274-5*) Baker Bks.
Baker, Brant. Gospel Sermons for Children. LC 95-10471. (Gospels, Series A: Vol. 1). 128p. 1995. pap. 10.99 (*0-8066-2780-8*, 9-2780) Augsburg Fortress.
Baker, Brant D. Welcoming the Children: Experimental Children's Sermons. 96p. 1995. pap. 9.99 (*0-8066-2835-9*, 9-2835) Augsburg Fortress.
Baker, Brant D., jt. auth. see Johnson, Ben Campbell.
***Baker, Brenda J.** The Maleness of God. 240p. 1999. pap. 14.95 (*1-55050-158-5*, Pub. by Coteau) Genl Dist Srvs.
Baker, Brenda J. & Kealhofer, Lisa, eds. Bioarchaeology of Native Americans in the Spanish Borderlands. (Ripley P. Bullen Monographs). (Illus.). 288p. 1996. 49.95 (*0-8130-1464-6*) U Press Fla.
Baker, Brent & Bozell, L. Brent, III, eds. How to Identify, Expose & Correct Liberal Media Bias. 225p. (Orig.). 1994. pap. 18.95 (*0-9627348-2-9*) Media Res Ctr.
Baker, Brent D. Let the Children Come: A New Approach to Children's Sermons. LC 91-8876. 80p. (Orig.). 1991. pap. 9.99 (*0-8066-2545-7*, 9-2545, Augsburg) Augsburg Fortress.
Baker, Brent H., jt. ed. see Bozell, L. Brent, III.
Baker, Brian H., et al. Geology of the Eastern Rift System of Africa. LC 76-178774. (Geological Society of America, Special Paper: No. 136). 73p. reprint ed. pap. 30.00 (*0-608-15644-2*, 203187000077) Bks Demand.
Baker, Briant. The Radio Road Guide: Your Source for Nearly 10,000 AM & FM Stations Across the U. S. A. 160p. 1997. pap. 14.95 (*0-89896-326-5*) Larksdale.
***Baker, Bruce.** Escape from Domination: Political Disengagement & Its Consequences in Sub Saharan Africa. LC 00-41634. 2000. pap. write for info. (*0-86543-872-2*) Africa World.
Baker, Bruce L., et al. Behavior Problems. 80p. 1976. spiral bd. 12.95 (*0-87822-170-0*, 1700) Res Press.
— Steps to Independence: A Skills Training Guide for Parents & Teachers of Children with Special Needs. 3rd ed. LC 96-26889. 1996. 28.00 (*1-55766-268-1*) P H Brookes.
Baker, C. Building Simple Furniture. 1983. pap. 2.95 (*0-88266-180-9*, Storey Pub) Storey Bks.
— Chair Caning. 1983. pap. 2.95 (*0-88266-190-6*, Storey Pub) Storey Bks.
— The Eye of Needle: Prophetic Parable. 1997. pap. text 7.99 (*1-884369-62-6*, Parable Pubns) McDougal Pubng.
— Thermal Modeling of Petroleum Generation: Theory & Applications. LC 96-50381. (Developments in Petroleum Science Ser.: 45). 526p. 1996. 172.50 (*0-444-82030-2*) Elsevier.
Baker, C., tr. see Amman, J. C.
***Baker, C. D.** Journey of Souls. 2000. 22.99 (*1-887159-39-8*); pap. 16.99 (*1-887159-47-9*) Preston-Speed.
Baker, C. David. The Fencerow Tails. (Illus.). 48p. (J). (gr. k-5). 1991. 12.95 (*0-9630669-0-0*) Liberty Lines.
— Suffer the Children. (Illus.). 600p. 1998. 29.95 (*0-9630669-1-9*) Liberty Lines.
Baker, C. Edwin. Advertising & a Democratic Press. 214p. (C). 1993. pap. text 16.95 (*0-691-02116-3*, Pub. by Princeton U Pr) Cal Prin Full Svc.
— Restoring the People's Voice in Air Quality Planning: Governor Shoould Free Metro Denver from Top-Down Bullying. 10p. 1989. pap. text 8.00 (*1-57655-126-1*) Independ Inst.
Baker, C. F., ed. The Fundamentals of Papermaking Materials Vol. 1: Proceedings. 679p. 1997. 120.00 (*1-85802-209-6*, Pub. by Pira Internatl) Bks Intl VA.
— The Fundamentals of Papermaking Materials Vol. 2: Proceedings. 711p. 1997. 120.00 (*1-85802-210-X*, Pub. by Pira Internatl) Bks Intl VA.
Baker, C. J. Beyond Death. 1977. pap. 3.25 (*0-87813-953-2*) Christian Light.
Baker, C. J., et al. No-Tillage Seeding: Science & Practice. LC 97-142324. (CAB International Publication Ser.). 272p. (C). 1996. text 95.00 (*0-85199-103-3*) OUP.
Baker, C. Jean, et al. The Handbook for All Profession. rev. ed. (Illus.). 98p. (C). 1992. reprint ed. pap. text 11.95 (*1-877804-08-8*) Chandler White.
Baker, C. L. English Syntax. 2nd ed. 560p. 1995. pap. text 32.50 (*0-262-52198-9*) MIT Pr.
— English Syntax. 2nd ed. (Illus.). 560p. 1995. 60.00 (*0-262-02385-7*) MIT Pr.
Baker, C. R., ed. Stochastic Processes in Underwater Acoustics. (Lecture Notes in Control & Information Sciences: Vol. 85). v, 205p. 1986. pap. 32.00 (*0-387-16869-9*) Spr-Verlag.
Baker, Calvin. Naming New World. 128p. 1998. pap. 9.95 (*0-312-18140-X*) St Martin.
— Naming the New World. LC 96-29347. 128p. 1997. text 18.95 (*0-312-15178-0*) St Martin.
Baker, Camy. Camy Baker's Body Electric: 30 Cool Rules for a Brand-New You. (J). (gr. 4-7). 1999. pap. 3.99 (*0-553-48658-6*) BDD Bks Young Read.
— Camy Baker's It Must Be Love: 15 Cool Rules for Choosing a Better Boyfriend. 160p. (J). (gr. 4-7). 1999. pap. 3.99 (*0-553-48657-8*) BDD Bks Young Read.
— How to Be Popular in the Sixth Grade: Thirty Cool Rules to Rule the School. 144p. (J). (gr. 3-7). 1998. pap. 3.99 (*0-553-48655-1*) Bantam.
— Love You Like a Sister: Thirty Cool Rules for Making & Being a Better Best Friend. 176p. (J). (gr. 3-8). 1998. pap. 3.99 (*0-553-48656-X*) Bantam.
Baker, Carin G. Families, Phooey! No. 6: Families, Phooey! LC 96-68724. (Illus.). 24p. (ps-1). 1996. 3.25 (*0-689-80826-7*) S&S Childrens.
Baker, Carin Greenberg. Pride of the Green Mountains. (Treasured Horses Ser.). (J). (gr. 3-9). 1998. pap. text 3.99 (*0-590-31654-0*) Scholastic Inc.
— Pride of the Green Mountains, 3. (Treasured Horses Ser.). (J). 1998. 9.09 (*0-606-13863-3*, Pub. by Turtleback) Demco.
Baker, Carl T. Doc, Don't Tell Anyone: The Goofy Things That Have Happened to This Veterinarian. (Illus.). 246p. 1997. pap. 14.95 (*0-9658836-1-2*) WY Wedidit.
Baker, Carlos. The Echoing Green: Romanticism, Modernism, & the Phenomena. LC 83-43058. 390p. 1984. reprint ed. pap. 120.90 (*0-608-03348-0*, 206406000008) Bks Demand.
— Emerson: Among the Eccentrics. 1995. 30.00 (*0-201-40775-2*) Addison-Wesley.
— Emerson among the Eccentrics: A Group Portrait. LC 95-34146. (Illus.). xv, 608p. 1997. pap. 17.95 (*0-14-026029-3*) Viking Penguin.
— Ernest Hemingway: A Life Story. LC 72-428710. 702p. 1969. write for info. (*0-00-211225-6*) Collins SF.
— Ernest Hemingway Life Story. 1976. 47.50 (*0-685-45827-X*, Scribners Ref) Mac Lib Ref.
— Hemingway, the Writer As Artist. 4th rev. ed. 440p. 1972. pap. text 22.95 (*0-691-01305-5*, 86, Pub. by Princeton U Pr) Cal Prin Full Svc.
***Baker, Carnel.** Learning to Live - Living to Learn. LC 99-97546. xii, 154p. 1999. 10.95 (*1-929943-01-6*) United Pubs.
— Learning to Live - Living to Learn II. xiv, 222p. 2000. 13.95 (*1-929943-02-4*) United Pubs.
Baker, Carol. Vancouver. (Essential Guides Ser.). (Illus.). 128p. (J). (gr. k). 1994. pap. 7.95 (*0-8442-8941-8*, 89418, Passprt Bks) NTC Contemp Pub Co.
— Vancouver & British Columbia. (Illustrated Travel Guides from Thomas Cook Ser.). (Illus.). 192p. 1994. pap. 12.95 (*0-8442-9035-1*, Passprt Bks) NTC Contemp Pub Co.
— Vancouver & British Columbia. 3rd ed. (Passport's Illustrated Travel Guides from Thomas Cook Ser.). (Illus.). 192p. 1999. pap. 14.95 (*0-658-00035-7*, 000357, Passprt Bks) NTC Contemp Pub Co.
Baker, Carol, ed. see Bedwell, Randall.
Baker, Carolyn. Reclaiming the Dark Feminine: The Price of Desire. LC 96-68642. 160p. (Orig.). 1996. pap. 12.95 (*1-56184-088-2*) New Falcon Pubns.
Baker, Carolyn, jt. auth. see Johnson, Greer Cavallara.
Baker, Carolyn D. & Luke, Allan, eds. Towards a Critical Sociology of Reading Pedagogy: Papers of the XII World Congress on Reading. LC 91-7316. (Pragmatics & Beyond New Ser.: No. 19). xxi, 287p. 1991. 71.00 (*1-55619-285-1*); pap. 27.95 (*1-55619-286-X*) J Benjamins Pubng Co.
Baker, Carolyn N. The Beginner's Bible: Tales of Virtue. (Kid-Friendly Inspirational Ser.). (Illus.). 1995. 8.99 (*0-679-87637-5*, Pub. by Random Bks Yng Read) Random.
Baker, Carolyn Nabors, see Nabors Baker, Carolyn.
Baker-Carr, Sally, ed. see Fregly, Bert.
Baker, Catharine S., ed. Gather Together: A Commemorative Cookbook. (Illus.). 120p. (Orig.). 1987. pap. 6.95 (*0-9619762-0-9*) First Universalist.
***Baker, Catherine.** Winning the Academic Game: Survival Skills for Student Athletes. 3rd ed. 282p. (C). 1999. per. 39.95 (*0-7872-6485-7*, 41648501) Kendall-Hunt.
Baker, Catherine. Your Genes, Your Choices: Exploring the Issues Raised by Genetic Research. (Illus.). 84p. 1997. pap. write for info. (*0-87168-601-5*, 97-35) AAAS.
Baker, Catherine, jt. auth. see Aaron, P. G.
Baker, Catherine Anne & Batten, Lynn Margord. Finite Geometries. (Lecture Notes in Pure & Applied Mathematics Ser.: Vol. 103). (Illus.). 400p. 1985. pap. text 155.00 (*0-8247-7488-4*) Dekker.
***Baker, Cathleen.** By His Own Labor: The Biography of Dard Hunter. LC 00-20692. 2000. write for info. (*1-58456-020-7*) Oak Knoll.
Baker, Cathy. Employee Benefits in Small Private Establishments, 1994. (Illus.). 94p. (Orig.). (C). 1996. pap. text 25.00 (*0-7881-3735-2*) DIANE Pub.
***Baker, Cathy, ed.** Employee Benefits in Small Private Establishments, 1996. (Illus.). 111p. (C). 2000. pap. text 25.00 (*0-7881-8781-3*) DIANE Pub.
Baker, Champ L., Jr. The Hughston Clinic Sports Medicine Field Manual. (Illus.). 400p. 1996. write for info. (*0-683-00310-0*) Lppncott W & W.
Baker, Champ L., et al, eds. The Hughston Clinic: Sports Medicine Book. LC 94-23442. (Illus.). 732p. 1995. 125.00 (*0-683-00397-6*) Lppncott W & W.
Baker, Champ L., Jr., et al, eds. The Hughston Clinic Sports Medicine Field Manual. LC 95-25585. 1996. write for info. (*0-683-00031-4*) Lppncott W & W.
Baker, Champ L., jt. auth. see Esch, James C.
Baker, Charles. The Book of Bible History. 1980. lib. bdg. 59.95 (*0-8490-3159-1*) Gordon Pr.
***Baker, Charles.** William Faulkner's Postcolonial South. LC 98-54298. (Modern American Literature Ser.: Vol. 23). 168p. (C). 2000. text 43.95 (*0-8204-4432-4*) P Lang Pubng.
Baker, Charles & Baker, Margaret. Orchid Species Culture: Dendrobium. 875p. 1996. pap. 59.95 (*0-88192-366-4*) Timber.
Baker, Charles F. A Dispensational Theology. 688p. (C). 1971. text 19.95 (*0-912340-01-0*); pap. text 14.95 (*0-912340-02-9*) Grace Bible Coll.
— Eternal Life Insurance. 22p. 1982. 1.00 (*0-89814-055-2*) Grace Publns.
— Real Baptism. 80p. 1994. 4.25 (*0-89814-045-5*) Grace Publns.
Baker, Charles F., III. The Struggle for Freedom. Yoder, Carolyn P., ed. (Illus.). 144p. (YA). (gr. 4-9). 1990. 17.95 (*0-382-40969-8*) Cobblestone Pub Co.
Baker, Charles F. Teologia Dispensacional. 709p. 1995. 14.95 (*0-89814-025-0*) Grace Publns.
— Understanding the Body of Christ: A Pauline Trilogy. 161p. (C). 1985. text 8.95 (*0-912340-04-5*) Grace Bible Coll.
— Understanding the Book of Acts. 182p. (C). 1981. text 6.95 (*0-912340-03-7*) Grace Bible Coll.
— Understanding the Gospels. 324p. 1994. 10.99 (*0-89814-044-7*) Grace Publns.
Baker, Charles F., III & Baker, Rosalie F. The Classical Companion: The Indispensable Guide to the Study of Classical Civilization, Complete with Stories, Puzzles, Projects, Classroom Activities, & Original Plays. 2nd ed. (Illus.). 184p. 1988. pap. text 19.95 (*0-942389-04-2*) Cobblestone Pub Co.
— Classical Ingenuity: The Legacy of Greek & Roman Architects, Artists, & Inventors. (Illus.). 160p. 1994. pap. 17.50 (*0-942389-07-7*) Cobblestone Pub Co.
— Myths & Legends of Mount Olympos. 96p. 1994. pap. 12.95 (*0-942389-06-9*) Cobblestone Pub Co.
Baker, Charles F., III, jt. auth. see Baker, Rosalie F.
Baker, Charles H., Jr. Gentleman's Companion, Vol. I. 2nd ed. (Fifty Greatest Bks.). 200p. 1992. reprint ed. 50.00 (*1-56416-037-8*) Derrydale Pr.
— Gentleman's Companion, Vol. II. 2nd ed. (Fifty Greatest Bks.). 200p. 1992. reprint ed. 50.00 (*1-56416-038-6*) Derrydale Pr.
Baker, Charles J. Baker's Industrial Guide to Hazardous Materials. LC 93-77536. 330p. 1993. 39.95 (*0-9627052-1-7*) Maltese Ent.
— The Firefighter's Handbook of Hazardous Materials. 5th ed. LC 90-62551. 330p. 1990. 39.95 (*0-9627052-0-9*) Maltese Ent.
Baker, Charles O. & Baker, Margaret L. Orchid Species Culture: Dendrobium. LC 96-4992. 875p. 1996. 99.95 (*0-88192-360-5*) Timber.
Baker, Charles O., jt. auth. see Baker, Margaret L.
Baker, Charlie, jt. auth. see Gates, Alan.
Baker, Charlotte. Trail North: Stories of Texas' Yesterdays. 2nd ed. (J). (gr. 4-7). 1997. pap. 8.95 (*1-57168-066-7*) Sunbelt Media.
Baker, Charlotte & Battison, Robbin M. Sign Language & the Deaf Community: Essays in Honor of William Stokoe. (Illus.). 267p. 1981. pap. text 8.95 (*0-913072-36-2*) Natl Assn Deaf.
Baker, Cherie, ed. & illus. see Abrams, Karl J.
Baker, Chester E. Doughboy's Diary. Ragosta, Millie, ed. LC 97-48924. 138p. 1998. 19.95 (*1-57249-100-0*, Burd St Pr) White Mane Pub.
Baker, Chet. As Though I Had Wings: The Lost Memoir. LC 97-14685. 118p. 1997. text 16.95 (*0-312-16797-0*) St Martin.
— Chet Baker: As Though I Had Wings: The Lost Memoir. 128p. 1998. pap. 9.95 (*0-312-20083-8*) St Martin.
Baker, Chris. Simple Winning Chess. 1999. pap. text 18.95 (*1-85744-225-3*) Cadgn Bks.
***Baker, Chris.** Win with Black. 2000. pap. 19.95 (*1-901983-32-3*, Pub. by Gambit) BHB Intl.
Baker, Chris, tr. see Baginski, Bodo & Sharamon, Shalila.
Baker, Christena B., et al. Rebuilding Children's Lives: A Blueprint for Treatment Foster Parents. LC 96-229714. 294p. 1996. pap. 19.99 (*0-938510-76-2*, 63-003) Boys Town Pr.
Baker, Christina L. In a Generous Spirit: A First-Person Biography of Myra Page. (Women in American History Ser.). 1996. write for info. (*0-614-09497-6*) U of Ill Pr.
— In a Generous Spirit: A First Person Biography of Myra Page. 312p. 1996. text 48.95 (*0-252-02234-3*); pap. text 15.95 (*0-252-06543-3*) U of Ill Pr.
Baker, Christine D., jt. ed. see Ussher, Jane M.
Baker, Christopher. Passport's Illustrated Guide to Jamaica. 2nd ed. (Passport's Illustrated Ser.). 192p. 2000. pap. 14.95 (*0-8442-1136-2*, 11362, Passprt Bks) NTC Contemp Pub Co.
— Rembrandt. 1993. 29.98 (*1-55521-856-3*) Bk Sales Inc.
Baker, Christopher, et al, eds. The Bahamas Index & Yearbook, 1997, No. 12. 217p. 1998. text 100.00 (*0-932265-50-2*); pap. text 49.95 (*0-932265-51-0*) White Sound.
Baker, Christopher, photos by. Crabtree & Evelyn Cookbook: A Book of Light Meals & Small Feasts. LC 89-30646. (Illus.). 256p. 1989. 29.95 (*0-941434-99-0*) Stewart Tabori & Chang.
— Tulipa: A Photographer's Botanical. LC 99-32474. (Illus.). 308p. 1999. 65.00 (*1-57965-122-4*, 85122) Artisan.
Baker, Christopher, tr. see Mandel, Peter.
Baker, Christopher J. Covenant & Liberation: Giving New Heart to God's Endangered Family. (European University Studies: Theology: Ser. 23, Vol. 411). XVIII, 357p. 1991. pap. 62.00 (*3-631-43479-0*) P Lang Pubng.
Baker, Christopher J. An Indian Rural Economy, 1880 to 1955: The Tamilnad Countryside. (Illus.). 636p. 1985. text 65.00 (*0-19-821572-X*) OUP.
Baker, Christopher J. The Politics of South India, 1920-1937. LC 75-2716. (Cambridge South Asian Studies: 17). 387p. reprint ed. pap. 110.30 (*0-608-17036-4*, 2027279) Bks Demand.
Baker, Christopher P. Jamaica. (Illustrated Travel Guides from Thomas Cook Ser.). (Illus.). 192p. 1995. pap. text 12.95 (*0-8442-9092-0*, Passprt Bks) NTC Contemp Pub Co.
***Baker, Christopher P.** Jamaica. 2nd ed. (Illus.). 496p. 1999. pap. 17.95 (*0-86442-780-8*) Lonely Planet.
Baker, Christopher P. Lonely Planet Bahamas, Turks & Caicos. (Illus.). 512p. 1998. pap. 17.95 (*0-86442-482-5*) Lonely Planet.
— Lonely Planet Jamaica. LC 97-147759. (Illus.). 496p. 1996. pap. 17.95 (*0-86442-372-1*) Lonely Planet.
***Baker, Christopher P.** Mi Moto Fidel: Motorcycling Through Castro's Cuba. 2001. 26.00 (*0-7922-7961-1*) Natl Geog.
Baker, Christopher P. Moon Handbooks: Costa Rica. 3rd expanded ed. Vol. 3. (Illus.). 820p. 1999. pap. 19.95 (*1-56691-124-9*, Moon Handbks) Avalon Travel.
— Moon Handbooks: Cuba. 750p. 1997. pap. 19.95 (*1-56691-095-1*, Moon Handbks) Avalon Travel.
***Baker, Christopher P.** Moon Handbooks: Havana. (Illus.). 370p. 2000. pap. 16.95 (*1-56691-182-6*, Moon Handbks) Avalon Travel.
— Moon Handbooks - Cuba. 2nd rev. ed. (Moon Handbks.). (Illus.). 790p. 2000. pap. 19.95 (*1-56691-209-1*, Pub. by Avalon Travel) Publishers Group.
Baker, Christopher P., jt. auth. see National Geographic Society.
Baker, Christopher W. Let There Be Life! Animating with the Computer. LC 96-23289. (Illus.). 48p. (J). (gr. 3-7). 1997. 16.95 (*0-8027-8472-0*); lib. bdg. 17.85 (*0-8027-8473-9*) Walker & Co.
***Baker, Christopher W.** Scientific Visualization: The New Eyes of Science. (New Century Technology Ser.). 48p. (YA). (gr. 5-8). 2000. 22.90 (*0-7613-1351-6*) Millbrook Pr.
— Virtual Reality: Experiencing Illusion. LC 99-34200. (New Century Technology Ser.). 48p. (YA). (gr. 5-8). 2000. lib. bdg. 22.90 (*0-7613-1350-8*) Millbrook Pr.
Baker, Chuck. How Virtually Anybody Can Buy Real Estate: Even Without A Suitcase Filled with Cash. Morton, Peter, ed. (Illus.). 162p. (Orig.). 1994. pap. 14.95 (*0-9640121-0-3*) Interst Fifteen.
Baker, Clara, ed. see Walker, Jim.
Baker Clayton, Valerie L. Answering My Heart's Cry. LC 98-61051. (Illus.). 192p. 1998. pap. write for info. (*1-57921-137-2*) WinePress Pub.
***Baker, Cliff F., et al.** American Beauty (Musical) 103p. 1999. pap. 5.95 (*0-87129-929-1*, A77) Dramatic Pub.
Baker, Clyde D., jt. auth. see Shipman, James T.
Baker, Clyde N., Jr., ed. Drilled Piers & Caissons II. 153p. 1985. 19.00 (*0-87262-447-1*) Am Soc Civil Eng.
Baker-Cohen, K. F. Comparative Enzyme Histochemical Observations on Submammalian Brains. Incl. Pt. 1. Striatal Structures in Reptiles & Birds. 1968. Basal Structures of the Brainstem in Reptiles & Birds. 1968. (Advances in Anatomy Ser.: Vol. 40, Pt. 6). (Illus.). 70p. 1968. 18.90 (*0-387-04090-0*) Spr-Verlag.
Baker, Colin. Aspects of Bilingualism in Wales. 209p. 1985. 84.95 (*0-905028-51-1*, Pub. by Multilingual Matters); pap. 34.95 (*0-905028-50-3*, Pub. by Multilingual Matters) Taylor & Francis.
— Attitudes & Languages. (Multilingual Matters Ser.: No. 83). 198p. 1992. 69.00 (*1-85359-143-2*, Pub. by Multilingual Matters); pap. 24.95 (*1-85359-142-4*, Pub. by Multilingual Matters) Taylor & Francis.
— Foundations of Bilingual Education & Bilingualism. LC 92-42296. (Multilingual Matters Ser.: No. 95). 250p. 1993. 59.50 (*1-85359-178-5*, Pub. by Multilingual Matters); pap. 24.50 (*1-85359-177-7*, Pub. by Multilingual Matters) Taylor & Francis.
— Foundations of Bilingual Education & Bilingualism. 2nd ed. LC 95-26506. (Bilingual Education & Bilingualism Ser.: Vol. 1). 480p. 1996. 90.00 (*1-85359-358-3*, Pub. by Brit Inst Lrning); pap. 26.95 (*1-85359-357-5*, Pub. by Brit Inst Lrning) Taylor & Francis.
— Introduction to Papermaking. 2nd ed. 79p. 1995. pap. 95.00 (*1-85802-118-9*) Gale.
— Key Issues in Bilingualism & Bilingual Education. 1988. 69.00 (*0-905028-95-3*, Pub. by Multilingual Matters); pap. 24.95 (*0-905028-94-5*, Pub. by Multilingual Matters) Taylor & Francis.
— Organic Geochemistry in Petroleum Exploration. LC TN0870.5.A44. (AAPG Continuing Education Course Note Ser.: Vol. 10). (Illus.). 168p. reprint ed. pap. 52.10 (*0-608-08726-2*, 206936500004) Bks Demand.
— A Parents' & Teachers' Guide to Bilingualism. LC 94-49737. (Bilingual Education & Bilingualism Ser.: No. 5). 270p. 1995. 59.00 (*1-85359-265-X*, Pub. by Multilingual Matters) Taylor & Francis.
***Baker, Colin.** A Parents' & Teachers' Guide to Bilingualism. 2nd ed. LC 99-28420. (Parents' & Teachers' Guides Ser.). 2000. pap. 15.95 (*1-85359-455-5*) Taylor & Francis.
Baker, Colin. Refining Technologies: A Literature Review. (Pira Reviews of Pulp & Paper Technology Ser.). 75p. 1991. pap. 95.00 (*0-902799-86-X*, TS1120, Pub. by Pira Internatl) Bks Intl VA.
— Retreat from Empire: Sir Robert Armitage in Africa & Cyprus, Vol. 1. 432p. 1998. text 59.50 (*1-86064-223-3*, Pub. by I B T) St Martin.
Baker, Colin & Garcia, Ofelia. A Parents' & Teachers' Guide to Bilingualism. LC 94-49737. (Bilingual Education & Bilingualism Ser.: No. 5). 270p. 1995. pap. 19.95 (*1-85359-264-1*, Pub. by Multilingual Matters) Taylor & Francis.
Baker, Colin & Jones, Sylvia P. Encyclopedia of Bilingual Education & Bilingualism. LC 96-24015. (Illus.). 758p. 1999. 150.00 (*1-85359-362-1*, Pub. by Multilingual Matters) Taylor & Francis.
Baker, Colin, jt. ed. see Garcia, Ofelia.
Baker, Cozy. Kaleidorama. (Illus.). 116p. 1990. spiral bd. 20.00 (*0-9608930-3-2*) Beechcliff Bks.
— Kaleidoscope Renaissance. (Illus.). 200p. 1993. 30.00 (*0-9608930-4-0*) Beechcliff Bks.
— Kaleidoscopes: Wonders of Wonder. Rymar, Cyndy & MacFarland, Sara, eds. LC 98-37213. (Illus.). 144p. 1999. 34.95 (*1-57120-063-0*, 10188) C & T Pub.
Baker, Crump W. Introduction to Topology. LC 96-26557. 170p. (C). 1996. reprint ed. 29.50 (*1-57524-008-4*) Krieger.

Baker, Cynthia S. Good Tidings of Great Joy: Six Advent Dramas. (Orig.). 1994. pap. 6.75 (*0-7880-0097-7*) CSS OH.

— Nine Changed Lives. 1991. pap. 5.50 (*1-55673-282-1*, 9115) CSS OH.

— They Followed the Master. 1994. pap. 6.95 (*1-55673-704-1*) CSS OH.

Baker, D. Dios de la Segunda Oportunidad.Tr. of God of Second Chances. (SPA.). 144p. 1994. pap. 7.99 (*0-8297-1843-5*) Vida Pubs.

Baker, D. A., jt. auth. see Hall, John L.

Baker, D. C., et al, eds. The Digby Plays. (EETS Original Ser.: Vol. 283). (Illus.). 1982. reprint ed. 37.50 (*0-19-722285-4*) OUP.

Baker, D. C., jt. auth. see Chu, C. K.

Baker, D. E. Changing Political Leadership in an Indian Province: The Central Provinces & Berar 1919-1939. 1980. 14.95 (*0-19-561135-7*) OUP.

— Colonialism in an Indian Hinterland: The Central Provinces, 1820-1920. (Illus.). 388p. (C). 1993. 32.00 (*0-19-563049-1*, 14338) OUP.

Baker, D. E., ed. see Cibber, Colley.

Baker, D. James. Planet Earth: The View from Space. (Frontiers of Space Ser.). (Illus.). 192p. 1990. text 36.50 (*0-674-67070-1*) HUP.

— Planet Earth: The View from Space. 208p. 1993. pap. text 12.95 (*0-674-67071-X*) HUP.

***Baker, D. James, ed.** Our Ocean Future: Themes & Issues Concerning the Nation[0012]s Stake in the Oceans. 57p. 2000. reprint ed. pap. text 20.00 (*0-7881-8873-9*) DIANE Pub.

***Baker, D. James & Graykowski, John, eds.** National Ocean Conference: Oceans of Commerce, Oceans of Life. (Illus.). 240p. 2000. reprint ed. pap. text 50.00 (*0-7881-8871-2*) DIANE Pub.

Baker, D. N., et al, eds. Solar-Terrestrial Energy Program: The Initial Results from STEP Facilities & Theory Campaigns. LC 94-7968. (COSPAR Colloquia Ser.: Vol. 5). 844p. 1994. 290.00 (*0-08-042131-8*) Elsevier.

Baker, D. N., jt. auth. see Priest, E. R.

Baker, D. S. Greek Proverbs. (Illus.). 80p. 1998. 13.95 (*0-86281-556-8*, Pub. by Appletree Pr) Irish Bks Media.

— A Little Book of Table Graces. (Illus.). 60p. 1998. 9.95 (*0-86281-551-7*, Pub. by Appletree Pr) Irish Bks Media.

Baker, D. W. The Civilised Surveyor: Thomas Mitchell & Australian Aboriginals. (Illus.). 240p. 1997. pap. 29.95 (*0-522-84763-3*, Pub. by Melbourne Univ Pr) Paul & Co Pubs.

***Baker, D. W.** Preacher, Politician, Patriot: A Life of John Dunmore Lang. LC 98-201228. 240p. 1999. pap. 29.95 (*0-522-84822-2*, Pub. by Melbourne Univ Pr) Paul & Co Pubs.

Baker, D. W. Texas Scrap-Book: Made up of the History, Biography & Miscellany of Texas & Its People. 792p. 1991. 34.95 (*0-87611-108-8*) Tex St Hist Assn.

— Texas Scrap-Book: Made up of the History, Biography & Miscellany of Texas & Its People. limited ed. 792p. 1991. boxed set 85.00 (*0-87611-113-4*) Tex St Hist Assn.

Baker, Dale & Baker, Thomas. Forjemos Responsabilidad Taller para Padres e Hijos (Responsibility Building Workshop for Parents & Kids) Paquete para Los Instructores (Leader's Kit) (SPA.). 1997. ring bd. 150.00 (*1-885903-03-0*) ParentingKids.

— Forjemos Responsabilidad Taller para Padres e Hijos: Guia para Padres. (SPA.). 108p. 1997. pap. 12.00 (*1-885903-05-7*) ParentingKids.

— Motivemos a Su Hijos (A) para Que Triunte en la Escuela (Motivating Your Child for School Success) Paquete para Los Instructores (Leader's Kit) (SPA.). 1998. ring bd. 150.00 (*1-885903-06-5*) ParentingKids.

— Parenting Your Teenager: Leader's Kit. rev. ed. (SPA.). 55p. 1994. ring bd. 150.00 (*1-885903-02-2*) ParentingKids.

— Parenting Your Teenager: Parent's Guide. rev. ed. 83p. 1994. pap. 12.00 (*1-885903-00-6*, TX3882 835) ParentingKids.

— Responsibility Building Workshop for Parents & Kids: Parent's Guide. 100p. 1997. pap. 12.00 (*1-885903-04-9*) ParentingKids.

Baker, Dale R. Capillary Electrophoresis. 272p. 1995. 64.95 (*0-471-11763-3*) Wiley.

Baker, Dale R. & Piburn, Michael D. Constructing Science in Middle & Secondary School Classrooms. (C). 1997. pap., teacher ed. write for info. (*0-205-26143-4*, T6143-6) Allyn.

Baker, Dan & Weisgerber, Bill. Television Production. Duane, James E., ed. LC 80-23479. (Instructional Media Library: Vol. 15). (Illus.). 112p. 1981. 27.95 (*0-87778-175-3*) Educ Tech Pubns.

Baker, Daniel. The COTS & Rugged Defense Computer Market: A Survey & Analysis of DoD & Defense Contractor Requirements for Commercial Subsystems, Boards, & Portable Computers. 2nd rev. ed. Klein, Stanley, ed. 252p. 1997. ring bd. 4490.00 (*1-879764-08-3*) Tech Res Inst.

— Explorers & Discoverers of the World. 637p. 1993. 80.00 (*0-8103-5421-7*) Gale.

***Baker, Daniel.** Thinking Critically about Contemporary Ethical Issues. 306p. (C). 1999. pap. text 38.95 (*0-7872-6354-0*, 41635401) Kendall-Hunt.

Baker, Daniel. Wholesale Billing & Service Provisioning Systems in Telecommunications. Klein, Stanley, ed. 1997. ring bd. 4990.00 (*1-879764-09-1*) Tech Res Inst.

Baker, Daniel & Klein, Stanley. Convergence Billing Systems in Telecommunications: A Worldwide Survey & Analysis Report on Service Provider Requirements & Supplier Opportunities in the Telecom Billing Systems Market. 1996. 4990.00 (*1-879764-07-5*) Tech Res Inst.

— Data Warehousing & Decision Support Systems in Telecommunications: A Worldwide Survey & Market Analysis of Telecom Buyer Demand & Requirements. 250p. 1995. ring bd. 4990.00 (*1-879764-05-9*) Tech Res Inst.

— DoD & Defense Contractor Requirements for COTS (Commercial-Off-the-Shelf) Computers: A Survey & Strategic Analysis of Open System Market Opportunities in the Post Mil-Spec Era. 268p. 1995. ring bd. 3990.00 (*1-879764-04-0*) Tech Res Inst.

— Wireline Carrier Billing Systems in Telecommunications: Worldwide Survey & Analysis Report on Service Provider Requirements & Supplier Opportunities in the Telecom Billing Systems Market. 1996. 4990.00 (*1-879764-06-7*) Tech Res Inst.

Baker, Daniel B. Power Quotes: 4,000 Trenchant Soundbites on Leadership & Liberty, Treason & Triumph, Sacrifice & Scandal, Risk & Rebellion, Weakness & War, & Other Affaires Politiques. 402p. 1992. 15.95 (*0-8103-9416-2*) Visible Ink Pr.

Baker, Daniel B., ed. Political Quotations: A Collection of Notable Sayings on Politics from Antiquity Through 1988. 508p. 1990. 55.00 (*0-8103-4920-5*, 030121) Gale.

Baker, Daniel B., jt. auth. see Baker, Nancy.

Baker, Daniel B., jt. ed. see Saari, Peggy.

Baker, Daniel P. Customer Care Systems in Telecommunications. Klein, Stanley, ed. 1997. ring bd. 4990.00 (*1-879764-10-5*) Tech Res Inst.

***Baker, Danny & Perry, Mark.** Sniffin' Glue & Other Rock-N-Roll Habits: The Catalogue of Chaos, 1976-1977. 176p. 2000. pap. 30.00 (*1-86074-275-0*) Sanctuary Pub.

Baker, Darrell. Boo! to You, Too, Winnie the Pooh LC 97-214834. (J). 1997. write for info. (*0-7853-2413-5*) Pubns Intl Ltd.

Baker, Darrell & Publications International, Ltd. Editorial Staff. Farm Songs, 1 Vol. LC 98-182051. (Illus.). (J). 1998. write for info. (*0-7853-2670-7*) Pubns Intl Ltd.

Baker, Darryl & Kiner, Larry F. The Sir Harry Lauder Discography. LC 90-49631. (Illus.). 222p. 1990. 45.00 (*0-8108-2384-5*) Scarecrow.

Baker, Data. Flight Sim 98 Tricks of the Trade. (Illus.). 420p. 1998. pap. 34.95 (*1-55755-346-7*) Abacus MI.

Baker, Dave, et al, eds. Challenging Ways of Knowing: In English, Mathematics, & Science. 240p. 1996. 85.00 (*0-7507-0524-8*, Falmer Pr); pap. 29.95 (*0-7507-0525-6*, Falmer Pr) Taylor & Francis.

Baker, Dave, et al. How Big is the Moon: Whole Maths in Action. LC 90-5187. (Illus.). 110p. (Orig.). (J). (gr. k). 1990. pap. 15.95 (*0-435-08312-0*, 08312) Heinemann.

Baker, Dave, jt. auth. see McGill, John.

Baker, David. After the Reunion: Poems by David Baker. LC 94-1308. 80p. 1994. 24.00 (*1-55728-352-4*); pap. 16.00 (*1-55728-353-2*) U of Ark Pr.

— Believe It Or Not Space Facts, Reading Level 5. (Today's World in Space Bks.: Set I). (Illus.). 48p. (J). (gr. 3-8). 1988. 23.93 (*0-86592-407-4*) Rourke Enter.

Baker, David. Comparing Key Organizational Qualities of American Public & Private Secondary Schools. 98p. 1996. pap. 7.00 (*0-16-063588-8*) USGPO.

Baker, David. Danger on Apollo 13. (Great Adventures Ser.). (Illus.). 32p. (YA). (gr. 4 up). 1988. lib. bdg. 22.60 (*0-86592-871-1*) Rourke Enter.

— David Baker's Arranging & Composing, for the Small Ensemble: Jazz - R&B - Jazz & Rock. rev. ed. 176p. (C). 1988. pap. text 23.95 (*0-88284-469-5*, 2750) Alfred Pub.

— Earthwatch, Set II. (Today's World in Space Ser.: Set 11). (Illus.). 48p. (J). (gr. 3-8). 1989. lib. bdg. 23.93 (*0-86592-372-8*) Rourke Enter.

— Factories in Space, Set I. LC 87-16689. (Today's World in Space Ser.). (Illus.). 48p. (J). (gr. 3-8). 1987. lib. bdg. 23.93 (*0-86592-409-0*) Rourke Enter.

— Flight & Flying: A Chronology. LC 92-31491. (Illus.). 560p. 1994. 65.00 (*0-8160-1854-5*) Facts on File.

— Flight to the Stars, Set II. (Today's World in Space Ser.: Set 11). (Illus.). 48p. (J). (gr. 3-8). 1989. lib. bdg. 22.60 (*0-86592-373-6*) Rourke Enter.

— Future Fighters. (Military Aircraft Library). (Illus.). 48p. (J). (gr. 3-8). 1989. lib. bdg. 18.60 (*0-86592-535-6*) Rourke Enter.

— Grumman F-14 Tomcat. (Illus.). 200p. 1998. 44.95 (*1-86126-094-6*, Pub. by Crolwood) Motorbooks Intl.

— Haunts. (Cleveland Poets Ser.: No. 39). 53p. (Orig.). 1985. pap. 6.00 (*0-914946-53-6*) Cleveland St Univ Poetry Ctr.

— Helicopters. (Military Aircraft Library). (Illus.). 48p. (J). (gr. 3-8). 1987. 13.95 (*0-685-67593-9*) Rourke Corp.

— Helicopters. (Military Aircraft Library). (Illus.). 48p. (J). (gr. 3-8). 1987. lib. bdg. 23.93 (*0-86592-356-6*) Rourke Enter.

— The Henry Holt Guide to Astronomy. LC 89-11018. (Illus.). 288p. (Orig.). 1995. pap. 12.95 (*0-8050-1197-8*, Owl) H Holt & Co.

***Baker, David.** Heresy & the Ideal: On Contemporary Poetry. LC 99-57806. 232p. (C). 2000. 40.00 (*1-55728-602-7*); pap. 20.00 (*1-55728-603-5*) U of Ark Pr.

— The Heyday of the Shotgun. 160p. 2000. 39.95 (*1-57157-200-7*) Safari Pr.

Baker, David. Ideology of Obsession: A. K. Chesterton & British Fascism. 256p. 1996. text 65.00 (*1-86064-073-7*, Pub. by I B T) St Martin.

— Introduction to Torts. 2nd ed. LC 96-170398. 419p. 1996. pap. 75.00 (*0-455-21381-X*, Pub. by LawBk Co) Gaunt.

— Jazz Improvisation. rev. ed. (Illus.). 132p. 1988. pap. text 21.95 (*0-88284-370-2*, 2749) Alfred Pub.

— Jazz Pedagogy: A Comprehensive Method of Jazz Education for Teacher & Student. rev. ed. 208p. (C). 1988. reprint ed. pap., student ed. 24.95 (*0-88284-483-0*, 2751) Alfred Pub.

— Journey to the Outer Planets. LC 87-19888. (Today's World in Space Bks.). (Illus.). 48p. (J). 1987. 13.95 (*0-685-67599-8*) Rourke Corp.

— Journey to the Outer Planets, Set I. LC 87-19888. (Today's World in Space Ser.). (Illus.). 48p. (J). (gr. 3-8). 1987. lib. bdg. 23.93 (*0-86592-405-8*) Rourke Enter.

— Land-Based Fighters. (Military Aircraft Library). (Illus.). 48p. (J). (gr. 3-8). 1987. 13.95 (*0-685-67591-2*) Rourke Corp.

— Land-Based Fighters. (Military Aircraft Library). (Illus.). 48p. (J). (gr. 3-8). 1987. lib. bdg. 23.93 (*0-86592-351-5*) Rourke Enter.

— Laws of the Land. 2nd ed. Burmaster, Orvis C., ed. LC 81-69224. (Ahsahta Press Modern & Contemporary Poets of the West Ser.). 70p. 1981. pap. 6.95 (*0-916272-18-4*) Ahsahta Pr.

— Living in Space. (Today's World in Space Bks.: Set 11). (Illus.). 48p. (J). (gr. 3-8). 1989. 13.95 (*0-685-58639-1*) Rourke Corp.

— Living in Space. (Today's World in Space Bks.: Set 11). (Illus.). 48p. (J). (gr. 3-8). 1989. lib. bdg. 21.27 (*0-86592-401-5*) Rourke Enter.

— Living on the Moon. (Today's World in Space Bks.: Set 11). (Illus.). 48p. (J). (gr. 3-8). 1989. 13.95 (*0-685-58642-1*) Rourke Corp.

— Messerschmidt ME262. (Illus.). 192p. 1997. 44.95 (*1-86126-078-4*, Pub. by Crolwood) Motorbooks Intl.

— Military Aircraft Library, 3 bks. (Illus.). 288p. (J). (gr. 3-8). 1989. lib. bdg. 75.81 (*0-86592-350-7*) Rourke Enter.

— Military Aircraft Library, 6 bks., Set II, Reading Level 5. (Illus.). 288p. (J). (gr. 3-8). 1989. 83.70 (*0-685-58763-0*) Rourke Corp.

— Navy Fighters. (Military Aircraft Library). (Illus.). 48p. (J). (gr. 3-8). 1987. 13.95 (*0-685-67594-7*) Rourke Corp.

— Navy Strike Planes. (Military Aircraft Library). (Illus.). 48p. (J). (gr. 3-8). 1989. 13.95 (*0-685-58602-2*) Rourke Corp.

— The Organ: A Brief Guide to Its Construction, History, Usage & Music. (Illus.). 96p. 1991. pap. 10.50 (*0-7478-0131-2*, Pub. by Shire Pubns) Parkwest Pubns.

— Peace in Space. LC 87-19885. (Today's World in Space Bks.). (Illus.). 48p. (J). (gr. 3-8). 1987. 13.95 (*0-685-67601-3*) Rourke Corp.

— Peace in Space. LC 87-19885. (Today's World in Space Ser.). (Illus.). 48p. (J). (gr. 3-8). 1987. lib. bdg. 23.93 (*0-86592-408-2*) Rourke Enter.

— Research Planes. (Military Aircraft Library). (Illus.). 48p. (J). (gr. 3-8). 1987. 13.95 (*0-685-67595-5*) Rourke Corp.

— Research Planes. (Military Aircraft Ser.). (Illus.). 48p. (J). (gr. 3-8). 1987. lib. bdg. 23.93 (*0-86592-354-X*) Rourke Enter.

— Soviet Air Force. LC 88-12121. (Soviet Military Power Ser.). (Illus.). 48p. (J). (gr. 3-8). 1987. lib. bdg. 13.95 (*0-685-58301-5*) Rourke Corp.

— Soviet Air Force. LC 88-12121. (Soviet Military Power Ser.). (Illus.). 48p. (J). (gr. 3-8). 1987. lib. bdg. 18.60 (*0-86625-331-9*) Rourke Pubns.

— Soviet Forces in Space. LC 88-14050. (Soviet Military Power Ser.). (Illus.). 48p. (J). (gr. 3-8). 1987. lib. bdg. 13.95 (*0-685-58299-X*) Rourke Corp.

— Soviet Forces in Space. LC 88-14050. (Soviet Military Power Ser.). (Illus.). 48p. (J). (gr. 3-8). 1987. lib. bdg. 18.60 (*0-86625-335-1*) Rourke Pubns.

— Spy Planes. (Military Aircraft Library). (Illus.). 48p. (J). (gr. 3-8). 1987. lib. bdg. 13.95 (*0-685-67592-0*) Rourke Corp.

— Starwatch. (Today's World in Space Bks.: Set 11). (Illus.). 48p. (J). (gr. 3-8). 1989. lib. bdg. 13.95 (*0-685-58637-5*) Rourke Corp.

— Starwatch, Set II. (Today's World in Space Ser.: Set 11). (Illus.). 48p. (J). (gr. 3-8). 1989. lib. bdg. 23.93 (*0-86592-400-7*) Rourke Enter.

— Summer Sleep. (Poetry Chapbook Ser.). 32p. (Orig.). 1985. pap. 7.00 (*0-937669-19-9*) Owl Creek Pr.

— Sweet Home, Saturday Night. 96p. 1991. pap. 14.00 (*1-55728-203-X*) U of Ark Pr.

— Today's World in Space, 6 bks., Set I, Reading Level 5. (Illus.). 288p. (J). (gr. 3-8). 1988. lib. bdg. 83.70 (*0-685-58830-0*) Rourke Corp.

— Today's World in Space, 6 bks., Set I, Reading Level 5. (Illus.). 288p. (J). (gr. 3-8). 1988. lib. bdg. 111.60 (*0-86592-403-1*) Rourke Enter.

— Today's World in Space, 6 bks., Set II, Reading Level 5. (Illus.). 288p. (J). (gr. 3-8). 1989. lib. bdg. 83.70 (*0-685-58762-2*) Rourke Corp.

— Today's World in Space, 4 bks., Set II, Reading Level 5. (Illus.). 288p. (J). (gr. 3-8). 1989. lib. bdg. 95.40 (*0-86592-370-1*) Rourke Enter.

— The Truth about Small Towns: Poems. LC 98-2820. 112p. 1998. pap. 16.00 (*1-55728-517-9*) U of Ark Pr.

Baker, David, ed. Due Diligence, Disclosures & Warranties in the Corporate Acquisitions Practice. 2nd ed. 288p. 1992. lib. bdg. 139.00 (*1-85333-633-5*, Pub. by Graham & Trotman) Kluwer Academic.

— Meter in English: A Critical Engagement. LC 96-27935. 352p. 1997. pap. 20.00 (*1-55728-444-X*); text 38.00 (*1-55728-422-9*) U of Ark Pr.

— Resource Management in Academic Libraries. 237p. (C). 1997. 80.00 (*1-85604-036-4*, LAP0364, Pub. by Library Association) Bernan Associates.

Baker, David & Engel, Robert. Organic Chemistry. Pullins, ed. (Chemistry). 1200p. (C). 1992. pap. 82.25 (*0-314-93000-0*) West Pub.

Baker, David & Griffith, Jim. Key Maths GCSE: Foundation. Hogan, Paul et al, eds. 448p. 1998. pap. 32.50 (*0-7487-3387-6*, Pub. by S Thornes Pubs) Trans-Atl Phila.

— Key Maths GCSE: Higher. Hogan, Paul et al, eds. 464p. 1998. pap. 32.50 (*0-7487-3390-6*, Pub. by S Thornes Pubs) Trans-Atl Phila.

— Key Maths GCSE: Higher Teacher File. Hogan, Paul et al, eds. 336p. 1998. pap. 130.00 (*0-7487-3393-0*, Pub. by S Thornes Pubs) Trans-Atl Phila.

— Key Maths GCSE: Intermediate Teacher File. Hogan, Paul et al, eds. 336p. 1998. pap. 99.50 (*0-7487-3392-2*, Pub. by S Thornes Pubs) Trans-Atl Phila.

— Key Maths GCSE: Intermediate 1. Hogan, Paul et al, eds. 416p. 1998. pap. 32.50 (*0-7487-3388-4*, Pub. by S Thornes Pubs) Trans-Atl Phila.

— Key Maths GCSE Foundation: Teacher File. Hogan, Paul et al, eds. 336p. 1998. pap. 125.00 (*0-7487-3391-4*, Pub. by S Thornes Pubs) Trans-Atl Phila.

Baker, David & Seawright, David, eds. Britain for & Against Europe: British Politics & the Question of European Integration. (Illus.). 268p. 1998. text 68.00 (*0-19-828078-5*) OUP.

Baker, David, et al. How Different, How Similar? Comparing Key Organizational Qualities of American Public & Private Secondary Schools. (Illus.). 88p. (C). 1998. pap. text 25.00 (*0-7881-7049-X*) DIANE Pub.

— Key Maths 9 Question Bank: Licensed for Photo copying. 612p. 1998. pap. 125.00 (*0-7487-2802-3*, Pub. by S Thornes Pubs) Trans-Atl Phila.

***Baker, David, et al.** Key Maths 7-1. rev. ed. (Illus.). 410p. (YA). 2000. pap. 29.50 (*0-7487-5524-1*, Pub. by S Thornes Pubs) Trans-Atl Phila.

— Key Maths 7-1 Teacher File. (Illus.). 352p. (YA). 2000. pap. 125.00 (*0-7487-5526-8*, Pub. by S Thornes Pubs) Trans-Atl Phila.

— Key Maths 7-2. rev. ed. (Illus.). 426p. (YA). (gr. 6-9). 2000. pap. 29.50 (*0-7487-5525-X*, Pub. by S Thornes Pubs) Trans-Atl Phila.

— Key Maths 7-2 Teacher File. (Illus.). 352p. (YA). 2000. pap. 125.00 (*0-7487-5527-6*, Pub. by S Thornes Pubs) Trans-Atl Phila.

Baker, David, et al. More Light on the Path: Daily Scripture Readings in Hebrew & Greek. LC 98-40712. 384p. (C). 1999. pap. 21.99 (*0-8010-2165-0*) Baker Bks.

Baker, David, jt. auth. see Chitty, Gill.

Baker, David, jt. auth. see Monif, Gilles R.

Baker, David, jt. auth. see Scientific American Staff.

Baker, David A., ed. Acyclovir Therapy for Herpes Virus Infections. (Infectious Disease & Therapy Ser.: Vol. 4). (Illus.). 344p. 1989. text 165.00 (*0-8247-8091-4*) Dekker.

Baker, David B., jt. auth. see Hughes, Jan N.

Baker, David D., ed. The Dancing Rose. 62p. 1998. pap. 10.00 (*0-9666649-0-6*) Full Moon CT.

***Baker, David D., ed.** The Dancing Rose, No. IV. (Illus.). 90p. 1999. pap. 9.95 (*0-9666649-2-2*) Full Moon CT.

Baker, David E. Biographia Dramatica, 3 vols., Set. 1985. reprint ed. lib. bdg. 225.00 (*0-7812-0645-6*) Rprt Serv.

Baker, David E., et al. Biographia Dramatica, or Companion to the Playhouse, 4 pts. in 3 vols., Set. LC 70-159990. (BCL Ser. I). reprint ed. 265.00 (*0-404-00530-6*) AMS Pr.

Baker, David E., jt. auth. see Audette, Susan T.

Baker, David J. Between Nations: Shakespeare, Spenser, Marvell, & the Question of Britain. LC 97-8205. 268p. 1998. 39.50 (*0-8047-2997-2*) Stanford U Pr.

Baker, David J., tr. see Farnoux, Alexandre.

Baker, David L. Two Testaments, One Bible: A Study of the Theological Relationship Between the Old & New Testaments. rev. ed. LC 91-31817. 304p. 1992. pap. 19.99 (*0-8308-1765-4*, 1765) InterVarsity.

Baker, David R. Performance by Computer Modeling or Prescription by Model Code? 1986. pap. 7.50 (*0-318-22369-4*, TR 86-5) Society Fire Protect.

— Speculative High-Rise Dilemma: Fully Sprinklered or Hydraulic Fire Alarm. 1984. 4.35 (*0-318-03823-4*, TR84-6) Society Fire Protect.

Baker, David V. Race & Ethnic Relations. (C). 1999. pap. text 56.00 (*0-205-15923-0*, Macmillan Coll) P-H.

Baker, David V., jt. auth. see Aguirre, Adalberto, Jr.

Baker, David V., jt. ed. see Aguirre, Adalberto, Jr.

Baker, David V., jt. ed. see Aquirre, Adalberto.

Baker, David W. Nahum, Habakkuk, Zephaniah. LC 88-9360. (Tyndale Old Testament Commentary Ser.). 128p. 1989. pap. 12.99 (*0-87784-249-3*, 249) InterVarsity.

— Nahum, Habakkuk, Zephaniah. LC 88-9360. (Tyndale Old Testament Commentary Ser.: Vol. 23b). 128p. 1989. 19.99 (*0-8308-1427-2*, 1427) InterVarsity.

***Baker, David W. & Arnold, Bill T., eds.** The Face of Old Testament Studies: A Survey of Contemporary Approaches. LC 99-37516. 512p. 1999. 34.99 (*0-8010-2215-0*) Baker Bks.

Baker, David W., et al. Obadiah, Jonah, Micah. LC 88-9041. (Tyndale Old Testament Commentary Ser.). 208p. (Orig.). (C). 1989. pap. 12.99 (*0-87784-275-2*, 275) InterVarsity.

— Obadiah, Jonah, Micah. LC 88-9041. (Tyndale Old Testament Commentary Ser.: Vol. 23a). 208p. (Orig.). (C). 1989. 19.99 (*0-8308-1425-6*, 1425) InterVarsity.

Baker, David Weil. Divulging Utopia: Radical Humanism in Sixteenth-Century England. LC 98-53494. (Massachusetts Studies in Early Modern Culture). 232p. 1999. 35.00 (*1-55849-198-8*) U of Mass Pr.

Baker, Dean. An Evaluation of Private Alternatives to Social Security. LC 97-7569. 1997. write for info. (*0-87078-407-2*) Century Foundation.

Baker, Dean, ed. Getting Prices Right: The Debate over the Consumer Price Index. LC 97-17606. (Economic Policy Institute Ser.). 200p. (C). (gr. 13). 1997. text 56.95 (*0-7656-0221-0*); pap. text 24.95 (*0-7656-0222-9*) M E Sharpe.

Baker, Dean, et al, eds. Globalization & Progressive Economic Policy: The Real Constraints & Options. LC 98-38598. (Illus.). 544p. (C). 1998. pap. text 24.95 (*0-521-64376-7*) Cambridge U Pr.

— Globalization & Progressive Economic Policy: The Real Constraints & Options. LC 98-38598. (Illus.). 544p. (C). 1999. text 64.95 (*0-521-64360-0*) Cambridge U Pr.

***Baker, Dean & Weisbrot, Mark.** Social Security: The Phony Crisis. LC 99-28058. 152p. 2000. 22.00 (*0-226-03544-1*) U Ch Pr.

***Baker, Debbie K.** Children Are a Gift of the Lord. LC 99-224248. (Promises & Blessings Ser.). 64p. 1999. pap. 7.99 (*0-7369-0113-2*) Harvest Hse.

— A Home Built with Love. LC 99-224261. (Promises & Blessings Ser.). 64p. 1999. pap. 7.99 (*0-7369-0114-0*) Harvest Hse.

Baker, Deborah, ed. see Bobrick, Benson.

Baker, Deborah, ed. see Clark-Lewis, Elizabeth.

Baker, Deborah, ed. see De Ferrari, Gabriella.

Baker, Deborah, ed. see Glattstein, Judy.

Baker, Deborah, ed. see Hollander, Anne.

Baker, Deborah, ed. see Lobo, RuthAnn & Lobo, Rebecca.

Baker, Deborah, ed. see MacPhee, Rosalind.

Baker, Deborah, ed. see Obama, Barack.

Baker, Deborah, ed. see Shneidman, Edwin S.

Baker, Deborah, jt. ed. see Skevington, Suzanne.

Baker, Deborah J., et al. The Supper of the Lord. (Orig.). 1988. pap. 1.95 (*1-55673-023-3*, 8807) CSS OH.

Baker, Deborah L. Narcissus & the Lover: Mythic Recovery & Reinvention in Sceve's Delie. (Stanford French & Italian Studies: Vol. 46). 160p. 1987. pap. 56.50 (*0-915838-62-1*) Anma Libri.

— The Subject of Desire: Petrarchan Poetics & the Female Voice in Louise Labe. LC 96-7181. (Purdue Studies in Romance Literatures: No. 11). 240p. 1996. 41.95 (*1-55753-088-2*) Purdue U Pr.

Baker, Debra. Certain Seamless Carbon & Alloy Standard, Line, & Pressure Steel Pipe from Argentina, Brazil, Germany & Italy: An International Trade Investigation. (Illus.). 106p. (Orig.). (C). 1994. pap. text 65.00 (*0-7881-1438-7*) DIANE Pub.

Baker, Debra Ratterman & ABA, Center on Children & the Law Staff. What I Wish I'd Learned in Law School: Social Science Research for Children's Attorneys. LC 98-110618. vi, 145p. 1997. write for info. (*1-57073-484-4*) Amer Bar Assn.

Baker, Delbert W. Make Us One: Celebrating Spiritual Unity in the Midst of Cultural Diversity: Removing Barriers, Building Bridges. Thomas, Jerry D., ed. LC 95-18148. 284p. 1995. pap. 5.97 (*0-8163-1267-2*) Pacific Pr Pub Assn.

Baker, Denise N. Julian of Norwich's Showings: From Vision to Book. 226p. 1994. pap. text 16.95 (*0-691-01720-4*, Pub. by Princeton U Pr) Cal Prin Full Svc.

***Baker, Denise N., ed.** Inscribing the Hundred Years' War in French & English Cultures. LC 00-21409. (C). 2000. pap. text 22.95 (*0-7914-4702-2*) State U NY Pr.

— Inscribing the Hundred Years' War in French & English Cultures. LC 00-21409. (C). 2000. text 68.50 (*0-7914-4701-4*) State U NY Pr.

Baker, Dennis, jt. auth. see Kidder, Donna.

Baker, Dennis, jt. auth. see Stewart, Birdella.

Baker, Derek, ed. England in the Early Middle Ages. (Portraits & Documents Ser.). (Illus.). 296p. (C). 1995. pap. 19.95 (*0-85115-647-9*) Boydell & Brewer.

— England in the Later Middle Ages. (Portraits & Documents Ser.). (Illus.). 272p. (C). 1995. pap. 19.95 (*0-85115-648-7*) Boydell & Brewer.

Baker, Derek & Bovair, Keith. Making Special Schools Ordinary: Models for the Developing Special School, Vol. 1. 260p. 1989. 79.95 (*1-85000-436-6*, Falmer Pr); pap. 37.95 (*1-85000-437-4*, Falmer Pr) Taylor & Francis.

Baker, Derek & Bovair, Keith, eds. Making Special Schools Ordinary Vol. 2: Practitioners Changing Special Education. 220p. 1990. pap. 37.95 (*1-85000-439-0*, Falmer Pr) Taylor & Francis.

Baker, Derek, jt. auth. see Salmon, Nicholas.

Baker, Derrick K., ed. see Bassette, E. J.

Baker, Derrick K., ed. see Beckom, Jesse, Jr.

Baker, Derrick K., ed. see Beckom, Rosalie.

Baker, Devreaux, et al, eds. Wood, Water, Air & Fire: The Anthology of Mendocino Women Poets. LC 99-475298. 330p. 1998. pap. 22.95 (*0-9656052-3-X*, Pub. by Pot Shard) Bored Feet Pubns.

***Baker, Diane.** Jazzy Jewelry: To Make & Wear. (Kids Can Ser.). (Illus.). 160p. (J). (gr. 3-9). 2000. pap. 12.95 (*1-885593-47-3*) Williamson Pub Co.

Baker, Diane, jt. auth. see Thomas, Chris.

***Baker, Diane L., et al.** A Guide to Genetic Counseling. LC 98-5906. 433p. 1998. 84.95 (*0-471-18541-8*); pap. 54.95 (*0-471-18867-0*) Wiley.

Baker, Dianne. Ted Bear's Magic Swing. LC 91-65819. (Illus.). 32p. (J). (gr. 1-3). 1997. 6.48 (*0-87159-162-6*) Unity Bks.

Baker, Dianne, jt. auth. see Price, Courtney.

Baker, Dianne I. & Cole, Sandra S. Winning Softball Drills: A Complete Drill Book for Coaches. rev. ed. LC 91-72843. (Illus.). 262p. (Orig.). 1989. reprint ed. pap. 17.95 (*1-880138-00-X*, SB-16) Championship Bks & Vid Prodns.

Baker, Don. Beginning Blues Harp. (Illus.). 48p. (Orig.). pap. 15.95 incl. audio (*0-7119-2507-0*, AM78977) Music Sales.

— Beginning Blues Harp. (Illus.). 64p. (Orig.). 1995. pap. 19.95 incl. audio compact disk (*0-7119-5206-X*, AM932184, Pub. by Wise Publns) Omnibus NY.

— Beginning Rock Harp. (Illus.). 64p. (Orig.). 1995. pap. 17.95 incl. audio compact disk (*0-7119-3831-8*, AM91709, Pub. by Wise Publns) Omnibus NY.

— Finding Hope in Times of Crisis. (Guidelines for Living Ser.). 1992. 10.99 (*0-88486-058-2*) Arrowood Pr.

— 1 & 2 Thessalonians: How Can I Be Sure? (LifeGuide Bible Studies). 64p. (Orig.). 1991. pap., wbk. ed. 4.99 (*0-8308-1015-3*, 1015) InterVarsity.

— Ghost Towns of the Montana Prairie. Keenan, Gerry, ed. (Illus.). 98p. 1997. pap. 16.00 (*0-87108-050-8*) Pruett.

— Philippians. (LifeGuide Bible Studies). 60p. (Orig.). 1985. pap., wbk. ed. 4.99 (*0-8308-1013-7*, 1013) InterVarsity.

— Winning the Worry War. 2nd ed. 120p. 1993. pap. 7.99 (*1-56476-057-X*, 63057, Victor Bks) Chariot Victor.

Baker, Don, jt. auth. see Mellon, Steve.

Baker, Don E., jt. auth. see Needler, Marvin A.

Baker, Don R. Synthesis & Chemistry of Agrochemicals No. II. 588p. 1990. text 145.00 (*0-8412-1885-4*, Pub. by Am Chemical) OUP.

Baker, Don R., et al, eds. Synthesis & Chemistry of Agrochemicals. LC 87-22304. (Symposium Ser.: No. 355). (Illus.). ix, 571p. 1987. 94.95 (*0-8412-1434-4*, Pub. by Am Chemical) OUP.

— Synthesis & Chemistry of Agrochemicals. LC 87-22304. (ACS Symposium Ser.: Vol. 355). 488p. 1987. reprint ed. pap. 151.30 (*0-608-03878-4*, 206432500008) Bks Demand.

— Synthesis & Chemistry of Agrochemicals IV. (ACS Symposium Ser.: No. 584). (Illus.). 506p. 1995. text 140.00 (*0-8412-3091-9*, Pub. by Am Chemical) OUP.

— Synthesis & Chemistry of Agrochemicals V. (Symposium Ser.: No. 686). 352p. text 120.95 (*0-8412-3546-5*, Pub. by Am Chemical) OUP.

— Synthesis & Chemistry of Agrochemicals III. LC 92-27345. (ACS Symposium Ser.: Vol. 504). (Illus.). 468p. 1992. text 120.00 (*0-8412-2473-0*, Pub. by Am Chemical) OUP.

***Baker, Don R. & Umetsu, Norihari, eds.** Agrochemical Discovery: Insect, Weed & Fungal Control. (ACS Symposium Ser.: Vol. 774). (Illus.). 334p. 2000. text 120.00 (*0-8412-3724-7*) Am Chemical.

Baker, Donald. Functions of Folk & Fairy Tales. LC 81-2825. 24p. 1981. pap. 2.00 (*0-87173-096-0*) ACEI.

— Joshua: The Power of God's Promises. (LifeGuide Bible Studies). 61p. 1988. pap., wbk. ed. 4.99 (*0-8308-1024-2*, 1024) InterVarsity.

— Joshua: The Power of God's Promises. rev. ed. (Life Guide Bible Studies Ser.). 64p. 1999. pap. 4.99 (*0-8308-3024-3*, 3024) InterVarsity.

— Judges: Returning to God. (Life Guide Bible Studies). 64p. (Orig.). 1995. pap., wbk. ed. 4.99 (*0-8308-1040-4*, 1040) InterVarsity.

— Mas Alla del Perdon.Tr. of Beyond Forgiveness. (SPA.). 119p. 1984. pap. 4.99 (*958-95163-2-7*, 498520) Editorial Unilit.

***Baker, Donald.** Philippians. rev. ed. (Orig.). 1999. pap. 4.99 (*0-8308-3013-8*) InterVarsity.

Baker, Donald & Baker, Mary. Bible Study Guide for All Ages: For Classes, Study Groups, & Family Devotionals, 4 vols., Unit 1. (Illus.). 200p. 1981. 29.95 (*1-879614-01-4*) BSG Printing.

— Bible Study Guide for All Ages: For Classes, Study Groups, & Family Devotionals, 4 vols., Unit 2. (Illus.). 200p. 1982. 29.95 (*1-879614-02-2*) BSG Printing.

— Bible Study Guide for All Ages: For Classes, Study Groups, & Family Devotionals, 4 vols., Unit 3. (Illus.). 200p. 1983. 29.95 (*1-879614-03-0*) BSG Printing.

— Bible Study Guide for All Ages: For Classes, Study Groups, & Family Devotionals, 4 vols., Unit 4. (Illus.). 200p. 1985. 29.95 (*1-879614-04-9*) BSG Printing.

Baker, Donald C., jt. auth. see Ogilvy, J. D.

Baker, Donald C., ed. see Chaucer, Geoffrey.

Baker, Donald E., ed. see Estes, MaryBelle H.

Baker, Donald I. & Brandel, Roland E. The Law of Electronic Fund Transfer Systems. 2nd ed. 1988. 145.00 (*0-7913-0052-8*); suppl. ed. 61.00 (*0-7913-1247-X*); suppl. ed. 61.00 (*0-685-56110-0*) Warren Gorham & Lamont.

Baker, Donald I., jt. auth. see Rowley, J. W.

***Baker, Donald J., Jr.** The Last Apostle. 2000. pap. 12.95 (*1-891929-56-9*) Four Seasons.

Baker, Donald R., et al. Petroleum & Basin Evolution. LC 96-23073. 1996. write for info. (*0-387-61128-2*) Spr-Verlag.

— Petroleum & Basin Evolution. LC 96-23073. (Illus.). 530p. 1996. 129.00 (*3-540-61128-2*) Spr-Verlag.

Baker, Donald W. The Day Before. 48p. (Orig.). 1988. pap. 5.95 (*0-935306-43-9*) Barnwood Pr.

— Search Patterns: Poetry. 48p. (Orig.). 1996. pap. 7.95 (*1-884482-08-2*) Stepngstone.

— Unposted Letters. LC 83-173208. 64p. 1984. pap. 6.95 (*0-935306-23-4*) Barnwood Pr.

***Baker, Donna.** Back Room Girl. 192p. 1999. 24.00 (*0-7278-2253-5*, Pub. by Severn Hse) Chivers N Amer.

— Back Room Girl. large type ed. LC 99-46979. (Thorndike Romance Ser.). 1999. 24.95 (*0-7862-2261-1*) Thorndike Pr.

Baker, Donna. An Endless Song. 608p. 1995. mass mkt. 11.95 (*0-7472-4728-5*, Pub. by Headline Bk Pub) Trafalgar.

***Baker, Donna.** Firestorm. 224p. 2000. 25.00 (*0-7278-5436-4*, Pub. by Severn Hse) Chivers N Amer.

Baker, Donna. A Man Possessed. 192p. 1996. 22.00 (*0-7278-5175-6*) Severn Hse.

— A Man Possessed. large type ed. LC 96-52558. 318p. 1997. pap. 20.95 (*0-7862-1021-4*) Thorndike Pr.

***Baker, Donna.** Midnight Rainbow. large type ed. LC 99-14746. 1999. pap. 25.95 (*0-7838-8618-7*, G K Hall Lrg Type) Mac Lib Ref.

— Painted Lady. 224p. 25.00 (*0-7278-5512-3*) Severn Hse.

Baker, Donna. Ride for a Fall. 192p. 1998. 24.00 (*0-7278-5305-8*) Severn Hse.

***Baker, Donna.** Ride for a Fall. large type ed. LC 00-37770. 210p. 2000. pap. 25.95 (*0-7862-2648-X*) Thorndike Pr.

Baker, Donna. Some Day I'll Find You. LC 98-49001. 251p. 1999. write for info. (*0-7540-2185-8*) Chivers N Amer.

— Vintage Anheuser-Busch: An Unauthorized Collector's Guide. LC 98-87930. (Illus.). 160p. (Orig.). 1999. pap. 29.95 (*0-7643-0739-8*) Schiffer.

— Writing a Romantic Novel: And Getting Published. LC 98-65242. (Teach Yourself Ser.). (Illus.). 192p. 1998. pap. 12.95 (*0-8442-0021-2*, 00212, Teach Yrslf) NTC Contemp Pub Co.

***Baker, Donna S.** Chocolate Memorabilia. (Illus.). 160p. 2000. pap. 29.95 (*0-7643-1153-0*) Schiffer.

Baker, Donna S. Collectible Bells: Treasures of Sight & Sound. LC 98-4707. 1998. 39.95 (*0-7643-0555-7*) Schiffer.

— More Collectible Bells: Classic to Contemporay. LC 99-17656. (Illus.). 192p. 1999. 39.95 (*0-7643-0865-3*) Schiffer.

***Baker, Donna S.** Wade Miniatures; An Unauthorized Guide to Whimsies, Premiums, Villages & Characters. (Illus.). 160p. 2000. pap. 16.95 (*0-7643-1051-8*) Schiffer.

Baker, Dora, tr. & intro. see Steffen, Albert.

Baker, Doris. Gone Away. 72p. (Orig.). 1996. pap. 9.95 (*1-884707-23-8*) Lifestyles.

— Penned in the Spirit. Demings, Patricia, ed. LC 99-90524. 52p. 1999. pap. 10.95 (*1-891601-15-6*) Ladies Caliber.

Baker, Dorothee. CrossWord Sticklers Basic Pack. (CrossWord Sticklers Ser.). (J). (gr. 1-12). 1993. 19.50 (*1-883459-00-1*) Adv Methodologies.

— CrossWord Sticklers Class Pack. (CrossWord Sticklers Ser.). (J). (gr. 1-12). 1993. 49.50 (*1-883459-01-X*) Adv Methodologies.

— CrossWord Sticklers Parental Involvement Program. (CrossWord Sticklers Ser.). (J). (gr. 1-8). 1993. 250.00 (*1-883459-04-4*) Adv Methodologies.

— CrossWord Sticklers School Pack. (CrossWord Sticklers Ser.). (J). (gr. 1-8). 1993. 335.00 (*1-883459-02-8*) Adv Methodologies.

— Strip Replacement Pack. (CrossWord Sticklers Ser.). (J). (gr. 1-12). 1993. 17.50 (*1-883459-03-6*) Adv Methodologies.

Baker, Dorothy. Le Jeune Homme a la Trompette. (FRE.). 1982. pap. 10.95 (*0-7859-1957-0*, 2070373843) Fr & Eur.

— Young Man with a Horn. 1977. reprint ed. lib. bdg. 20.95 (*0-89244-025-2*, Queens House) Amereon Ltd.

Baker, Dorothy, ed. Brainwashing: A Synthesis of the Russian Textbook of Psycho Politics. 68p. (Orig.). 1991. pap. 3.00 (*0-933900-16-3*) Foun Human Under.

— Poetics in the Poem: Critical Essays on American Self-Reflexive Poetry. (American University Studies: Vol. 184, No. 4). X, 322p. (C). 1998. text 51.95 (*0-8204-3329-2*) P Lang Pubng.

Baker, Dorothy & Baker, Howard. The Ninth Day. (Lost Play Ser.). 1967. pap. 1.25 (*0-912262-05-2*) Proscenium.

Baker, Dorothy, ed. see Masters, Roy.

Baker, Dorothy, ed. see Pompelli, Jean.

Baker, Dorothy D. Trio. LC 77-5686. 234p. 1977. lib. bdg. 59.50 (*0-8371-9647-7*, BATR, Greenwood Pr) Greenwood.

Baker, Dorothy Z. Mythic Masks in Self-Reflexive Poetry: A Study of Pan & Orpheus. LC 85-16468. (Studies in Comparative Literature: No. 62). x, 186p. 1986. 29.95 (*0-8078-7062-5*) U of NC Pr.

— Mythic Masks in Self-Reflexive Poetry: A Study of Pan & Orpheus. LC 85-16468. (University of North Carolina Studies in Comparative Literature: Vol. 62). 196p. reprint ed. pap. 60.80 (*0-608-08602-9*, 206912500003) Bks Demand.

Baker, Dorthy. Young Man with a Horn. 20.95 (*0-8488-0877-0*, Queens House) Amereon Ltd.

Baker, Doug & Hutchins, Susan. American Journey: From 1865 to the Present. 964p. (C). 1995. text 52.00 (*0-536-59187-3*) Pearson Custom.

***Baker, Douglas, et al.** Now I Know Better, Too: Kids Tell Kids about Safety. 111p. (J). (gr. k-12). 1999. pap. 7.95 (*0-9676469-0-1*) Yale-New Haven.

Baker, Douglas M. Alcoholism. (C). 1977. pap. 12.50 (*0-906006-06-6*, Pub. by Baker Pubns) New Leaf Dist.

— Anthropogeny: The Esoteric History of Man's Origin. (Illus.). (C). 1975. pap. 24.00 (*0-906006-03-1*, Pub. by Baker Pubns) New Leaf Dist.

— Aquarius Rising. (Esoteric Astrology: The Rising Signs Ser.). 1981. pap. 7.50 (*0-906006-39-2*, Pub. by Baker Pubns) New Leaf Dist.

— Aquarius Sun Sign. (Astrological Sun Sign Ser.). 1972. pap. 5.50 (*0-906006-27-9*, Pub. by Baker Pubns) New Leaf Dist.

— Aries Rising. (Esoteric Astrology: The Rising Signs Ser.). 1978. pap. 7.50 (*0-906006-29-5*, Pub. by Baker Pubns) New Leaf Dist.

— Aries Sun Sign. (Astrological Sun Sign Ser.). 1972. pap. 5.50 (*0-906006-17-1*, Pub. by Baker Pubns) New Leaf Dist.

— Bach Flower Remedies Repertories, Pt. 1. 1978. pap. 11.00 (*0-906006-60-0*, Pub. by Baker Pubns) New Leaf Dist.

— Bach Flower Remedies Repertories, Pt. 2. 1981. pap. 11.00 (*0-906006-61-9*, Pub. by Baker Pubns) New Leaf Dist.

— Beyond the Intellect. 1979. pap. 25.00 (*0-906006-45-7*, Pub. by Baker Pubns) New Leaf Dist.

— Biomagnetism. 1977. pap. 21.00 (*0-906006-84-8*, Pub. by Baker Pubns) New Leaf Dist.

— Cancer Rising. (Esoteric Astrology: The Rising Signs Ser.). 1978. pap. 7.50 (*0-906006-32-5*, Pub. by Baker Pubns) New Leaf Dist.

— Cancer Sun Sign. (Astrological Sun Sign Ser.). 1972. pap. 5.50 (*0-906006-20-1*, Pub. by Baker Pubns) New Leaf Dist.

— Capricorn Rising. (Esoteric Astrology: The Rising Signs Ser.). 1981. pap. 7.50 (*0-906006-38-4*, Pub. by Baker Pubns) New Leaf Dist.

— Capricorn Sun Sign. (Astrological Sun Sign Ser.). 1972. pap. 5.50 (*0-906006-26-0*, Pub. by Baker Pubns) New Leaf Dist.

— Diary of an Alchemist. 1967. pap. 23.00 (*0-906006-09-0*, Pub. by Baker Pubns) New Leaf Dist.

— Dictionary of Astrology, 3 vols. 1994. 500.00 (*0-906006-80-5*, Pub. by Baker Pubns) New Leaf Dist.

— The Egoic Lotus. 1977. pap. 7.00 (*0-906006-07-4*, Pub. by Baker Pubns) New Leaf Dist.

— Esoteric Anatomy, Pt. 1. (Illus.). (C). 1976. pap. 27.00 (*0-906006-04-X*, Pub. by Baker Pubns) New Leaf Dist.

— Esoteric Anatomy, Pt. 2. (C). 1979. pap. 25.00 (*0-906006-48-1*, Pub. by Baker Pubns) New Leaf Dist.

— Esoteric Astrology Vol. 1: Introduction. (C). 1975. pap. 32.00 (*0-906006-01-5*, Pub. by Baker Pubns) New Leaf Dist.

— Esoteric Astrology Vol. 2: Introduction. (C). 1987. pap. 25.50 (*0-906006-12-0*, Pub. by Baker Pubns) New Leaf Dist.

— Esoteric Astrology Vol. 3: The Houses. (C). 1979. pap. 21.00 (*0-906006-41-4*, Pub. by Baker Pubns) New Leaf Dist.

— Esoteric Astrology Vol. 4: Rising Signs, Aries-Virgo. (C). 1979. pap. 29.00 (*0-906006-42-2*, Pub. by Baker Pubns) New Leaf Dist.

— Esoteric Astrology Vol. 5: Rising Signs, Libra-Pisces. (Illus.). (C). 1982. pap. 25.00 (*0-906006-64-3*, Pub. by Baker Pubns) New Leaf Dist.

— Esoteric Astrology Vol. 6: Colloqualisms. (C). 1980. pap. 21.00 (*0-906006-51-1*, Pub. by Baker Pubns) New Leaf Dist.

— Esoteric Astrology Vol. 7: Soul's Purpose, Part 1. (C). 1981. pap. 25.50 (*0-906006-63-5*, Pub. by Baker Pubns) New Leaf Dist.

— Esoteric Astrology Vol. 8: Soul's Purpose, Part 2. (C). 1982. pap. 25.50 (*0-906006-67-8*, Pub. by Baker Pubns) New Leaf Dist.

— Esoteric Astrology Vol. 9: Intercepted Signs, Aries-Virgo. (C). 1982. pap. 25.50 (*0-906006-65-1*, Pub. by Baker Pubns) New Leaf Dist.

— Esoteric Astrology Vol. 10: Intercepted Signs, Libra - Pisces. 1984. pap. 25.50 (*0-906006-66-X*, Pub. by Baker Pubns) New Leaf Dist.

— Esoteric Astrology Vol. 11: Retrograde Planets. 1991. pap. 35.00 (*0-906006-79-1*, Pub. by Baker Pubns) New Leaf Dist.

— Esoteric Healing, Vol. 1. 1975. pap. 25.50 (*0-906006-00-7*, Pub. by Baker Pubns) New Leaf Dist.

— Esoteric Healing, Vol. 2. 1983. pap. 25.50 (*0-906006-55-4*, Pub. by Baker Pubns) New Leaf Dist.

— Esoteric Healing, Vol. 3. 1978. pap. 48.00 (*0-906006-14-7*, Pub. by Baker Pubns) New Leaf Dist.

— Esoteric Psychology: The Seven Rays. (C). 1979. pap. 25.00 (*0-906006-02-3*, Pub. by Baker Pubns) New Leaf Dist.

— Gemini Rising. (Esoteric Astrology: The Rising Signs Ser.). 1978. pap. 7.50 (*0-906006-31-7*, Pub. by Baker Pubns) New Leaf Dist.

— Gemini Sun Sign. (Astrological Sun Sign Ser.). 1972. pap. 5.50 (*0-906006-19-8*, Pub. by Baker Pubns) New Leaf Dist.

— Greek & Roman Mythology, Vol. D-I. (C). 1988. pap. 21.00 (*0-906006-08-2*, Pub. by Baker Pubns) New Leaf Dist.

— Greek & Roman Mythology, Vol. M-Pom. (C). 1987. pap. 21.00 (*0-906006-13-9*, Pub. by Baker Pubns) New Leaf Dist.

— Greek & Roman Mythology, Vol. A-C. 1987. pap. 21.00 (*0-906006-56-2*, Pub. by Baker Pubns) New Leaf Dist.

— Greek & Roman Mythology, Vol. Pom-Z. (C). 1987. pap. 21.00 (*0-906006-15-5*, Pub. by Baker Pubns) New Leaf Dist.

— A Handbook of the Seven Rays. (C). 1984. pap. 12.50 (*0-906006-69-4*, Pub. by Baker Pubns) New Leaf Dist.

— The Horoscope of the United States. 1994. pap. 17.00 (*0-906006-86-4*, Pub. by Baker Pubns) New Leaf Dist.

— The Human Aura. 1986. pap. 12.00 (*0-906006-73-2*, Pub. by Baker Pubns) New Leaf Dist.

— In the Steps of the Master. 1977. pap. 22.00 (*0-906006-70-8*, Pub. by Baker Pubns) New Leaf Dist.

— The Jewel in the Lotus. (C). 1975. pap. 32.00 (*0-906006-71-6*, Pub. by Baker Pubns) New Leaf Dist.

— Karmic Laws. 1977. pap. 11.50 (*0-906006-10-4*, Pub. by Baker Pubns) New Leaf Dist.

— Leo Rising. (Esoteric Astrology: The Rising Signs Ser.). 1978. pap. 7.50 (*0-906006-33-3*, Pub. by Baker Pubns) New Leaf Dist.

— Leo Sun Sign. (Astrological Sun Sign Ser.). 1972. pap. 5.50 (*0-906006-21-X*, Pub. by Baker Pubns) New Leaf Dist.

— Libra Rising. (Esoteric Astrology: The Rising Signs Ser.). 1980. pap. 7.50 (*0-906006-53-8*, Pub. by Baker Pubns) New Leaf Dist.

— Libra Sun Sign. (Astrological Sun Sign Ser.). 1972. pap. 5.50 (*0-906006-23-6*, Pub. by Baker Pubns) New Leaf Dist.

— Life after Death. 1982. pap. 12.50 (*0-906006-58-9*, Pub. by Baker Pubns) New Leaf Dist.

— Meditation, the Theory & Practice. 1975. pap. 32.00 (*0-906006-74-0*, Pub. by Baker Pubns) New Leaf Dist.

— Nuclear Fallout. 1982. pap. 9.00 (*0-906006-68-6*, Pub. by Baker Pubns) New Leaf Dist.

— Occult Significance of UFO's. 1979. pap. 12.50 (*0-906006-43-0*, Pub. by Baker Pubns) New Leaf Dist.

— The Opening of the Third Eye. 1977. pap. 12.00 (*0-906006-85-6*, Pub. by Baker Pubns) New Leaf Dist.

— Paracelsus, His Methods of Healing. 1982. pap. 11.00 (*0-906006-72-4*, Pub. by Baker Pubns) New Leaf Dist.

— The Phenomena of Materialisation. 1978. pap. 11.00 (*0-906006-62-7*, Pub. by Baker Pubns) New Leaf Dist.

— Pisces Rising. (Esoteric Astrology: The Rising Signs Ser.). 1981. pap. 7.50 (*0-906006-40-6*, Pub. by Baker Pubns) New Leaf Dist.
— Pisces Sun Sign. (Astrological Sun Sign Ser.). 1972. pap. 5.50 (*0-906006-28-7*, Pub. by Baker Pubns) New Leaf Dist.
— Powers Latent in Man. 1977. pap. 12.00 (*0-906006-76-7*, Pub. by Baker Pubns) New Leaf Dist.
— The Psychology of Discipleship. (C). 1976. 26.50 (*0-906006-05-8*, Pub. by Baker Pubns) New Leaf Dist.
— Reincarnation. 1981. pap. 12.50 (*0-906006-57-0*, Pub. by Baker Pubns) New Leaf Dist.
— Sagitarius Rising. (Esoteric Astrology: The Rising Signs Ser.). 1981. pap. 7.50 (*0-906006-37-6*, Pub. by Baker Pubns) New Leaf Dist.
— Sagitarius Sun Sign. (Astrological Sun Sign Ser.). 1972. pap. 5.50 (*0-906006-25-2*, Pub. by Baker Pubns) New Leaf Dist.
— Scorpio Rising. (Esoteric Astrology: The Rising Signs Ser.). 1980. pap. 7.50 (*0-906006-54-6*, Pub. by Baker Pubns) New Leaf Dist.
— Scorpio Sun Sign. (Astrological Sun Sign Ser.). 1972. pap. 5.50 (*0-906006-24-4*, Pub. by Baker Pubns) New Leaf Dist.
— Shakespeare: The True Authorship. 1976. pap. 25.00 (*0-906006-90-2*, Pub. by Baker Pubns) New Leaf Dist.
— The Spiritual Diary. 1976. pap. 22.00 (*0-906006-88-0*, Pub. by Baker Pubns) New Leaf Dist.
— Stress Disorders. 1977. pap. 12.50 (*0-906006-11-2*, Pub. by Baker Pubns) New Leaf Dist.
— Superconsciousness Through Meditation. 1978. pap. 12.50 (*0-906006-75-9*, Pub. by Baker Pubns) New Leaf Dist.
— Taurus Rising. (Esoteric Astrology: The Rising Signs Ser.). 1978. pap. 7.50 (*0-906006-30-9*, Pub. by Baker Pubns) New Leaf Dist.
— Taurus Sun Sign. (Astrological Sun Sign Ser.). 1972. pap. 5.50 (*0-906006-18-X*, Pub. by Baker Pubns) New Leaf Dist.
— The Techniques of Astral Projection. 1978. pap. 12.50 (*0-906006-89-9*, Pub. by Baker Pubns) New Leaf Dist.
— The Third Eye. (C). 1980. pap. 12.50 (*0-906006-59-7*, Pub. by Baker Pubns) New Leaf Dist.
— Virgo Rising. (Esoteric Astrology: The Rising Signs Ser.). 1978. pap. 7.50 (*0-906006-34-1*, Pub. by Baker Pubns) New Leaf Dist.
— Virgo Sun Sign. (Astrological Sun Sign Ser.). 1972. pap. 5.50 (*0-906006-22-8*, Pub. by Baker Pubns) New Leaf Dist.
— The Wheel of Rebirth. 1978. pap. 12.00 (*0-906006-16-3*, Pub. by Baker Pubns) New Leaf Dist.
Baker, Douglas S., ed. see Fundacion Ecologista Staff, et al.
Baker, Douglas S., ed. see Iremonger, Susan & Sayre, Roger.
Baker, Douglas S., ed. see Muchoney, Douglas M., et al.
Baker, Douglas S., ed. see Sullivan, Kathleen M. & Chiappone, Mark.
Baker, Duck. Celtic Airs, Jigs, Hornpipes, & Reels. 1994. vdisk 39.95 (*1-56222-789-0*, 94872VX) Mel Bay.
Baker, Duck. Classic American Folk Blues Themes. 80p. 1995. pap. 9.95 (*0-7866-0269-4*, 95068); pap. 24.95 incl. audio compact disk (*0-7866-1192-8*, 95068CDP) Mel Bay.
— Complete Gospel Guitar CD Package. 168p. 1997. 34.95 (*0-7866-2786-7*, 96321COP) Mel Bay.
— Guitar of Duck Baker: Fingerstyle Jazz Composition: Intermediate Level. 80p. 1998. pap. 22.95 incl. audio compact disk (*0-7866-3004-3*, 96990BCD) Mel Bay.
Baker, Dusty, Jr., et al. You Can Teach Hitting. (Illus.). 256p. 1993. pap. 24.95 (*0-940279-73-8*, 79738H, Mstrs Pr) NTC Contemp Pub Co.
Baker, Dwight C. T'ai Shan: An Account of the Sacred Eastern Peak of China. 1973. lib. bdg. 250.00 (*0-87968-474-7*) Krishna Pr.
Baker, Dwight L. Understanding Islam: An Approach to Witness. 125p. (Orig.). 1989. pap. 4.63 (*0-685-29349-1*) Baptist Literacy.
Baker, E. Solaraust Microcomputer Solar Analysis Package. 1986. 41.50 (*0-08-029860-5*) Elsevier.
Baker, E., et al. Solar Heating & Cooling Systems: Design for Australian Conditions. (Illus.). 332p. 1984. pap. text 46.00 (*0-08-029852-4*, Pergamon Pr) Elsevier.
Baker, E. C. Fighter Aces of the R. A. F., 1939-45. (Illus.). 1965. pap. 4.95 (*0-913076-00-7*) Beachcomber Bks.
Baker, E. Charlotte. On Eagle's Wings. 154p. 1990. 9.99 (*1-56043-853-3*) Destiny Image.
Baker, E. H., et al. Structural Analysis of Shells. LC 79-27250. 364p. 1981. reprint ed. lib. bdg. 49.95 (*0-89874-118-1*) Krieger.
Baker, E. Rob, ed. see Luke, Helen M.
Baker, E. W., ed. Organic Geochemistry No. 2: A Selection of Papers from the Second Australian Geochemistry Conference, University of Melbourne, 28-29 May 1984. 98p. 1985. pap. 40.00 (*0-08-032640-4*, Pub. by PPL) Elsevier.
Baker, Ed. Blues Riffs for Piano. 30p. (YA). Date not set. pap., pap. text 14.95 incl. audio (*0-89524-928-6*); pap., pap. text 17.95 incl. audio compact disk (*0-89524-929-4*, Pub. by Cherry Lane) H Leonard.
***Baker, Ed & Busick, Chris.** Is He Gay? LC 99-89997. 80p. 2000. pap. 10.00 (*0-684-86793-1*, Fireside) S&S Trade Pap.
Baker, Ed & Williams, Art. Woodstock: Bits & Pieces. (Illus.). 144p. 1990. pap. 24.95 (*1-55046-013-7*, Pub. by Boston Mills) Genl Dist Srvs.
Baker, Edgar. A Guide to Study. (C). 1975. 40.00 (*0-85171-057-3*, Pub. by IPM Hse) St Mut.
Baker, Edward. Small Animal Allergy: A Practical Guide. LC 90-5615. (Illus.). 144p. 1990. pap. 42.50 (*0-8121-1240-7*) Lppncott W & W.
— Writer's Guide to Overcoming Rejection: A Practical Sales Course for the as Yet Unpublished. 1998. pap. 12.95 (*1-84024-010-5*, Pub. by Summers) Howell Pr VA.
Baker, Edward, jt. auth. see Aldaraca, Bridget.
Baker, Edward, tr. see Retamar, Roberto F.
Baker, Edward A. A Dead Man's Apartment, Rosemary with Ginger, Face Divided: Three Plays. 1996. pap. 5.25 (*0-8222-1513-6*) Dramatists Play.
— North of Providence - Dolores - Lady of Fadima. 1991. pap. 5.25 (*0-8222-0091-0*) Dramatists Play.
Baker, Edward L., jt. ed. see Halperin, William.
Baker, Edwart Martin. Scoring a Whole In One: People in Enterprise Playing in Concert. Christopher, William F., ed. LC 98-74743. (Management Library: Vol. 25). 96p. 1999. pap. 12.95 (*1-56052-549-5*, Pub. by Crisp Pubns) Natl Bk Netwk.
Baker, Edwin. Advertising & a Democratic Press. LC 93-2177. 208p. 1993. text 39.50 (*0-691-03258-0*, Pub. by Princeton U Pr) Cal Prin Full Svc.
Baker, Edwin & Swanby, Gordon. Clearing the Air on Carbon Monxide: Fatal Scientific Flaws in the EDA Crackdown on Denver & Other Cities. 22p. 1988. pap. text 8.00 (*1-57655-110-5*) Independ Inst.
Baker, Elizabeth. Cherokee Country. (Illus.). 326p. (C). 1968. pap. 9.95 (*0-937766-24-0*) Drelwood Comns.
— Does the Bible Teach Nutrition? LC 97-60974. 128p. 1997. pap. 11.99 (*1-57921-035-X*, Pub. by WinePress Pub) BookWorld.
— The Gourmet Uncook Book. LC 93-72256. (YA). (gr. 11 up). 1994. pap. 13.95 (*0-937766-15-1*) Drelwood Comns.
— Printers & Technology. LC 74-12847. (Illus.). 545p. 1974. reprint ed. lib. bdg. 79.50 (*0-8371-7763-4*, BAPT, Greenwood Pr) Greenwood.
— Protective Labor Legislation. 467p. 1993. reprint ed. lib. bdg. 99.00 (*0-7812-5243-1*) Rprt Serv.
— Protective Labor Legislation, with Special Reference to Women in the State of New York. LC 76-82239. (Columbia University. Studies in the Social Sciences: No. 259). reprint ed. 22.50 (*0-404-51259-3*) AMS Pr.
— The Undiet Book. 210p. 1992. pap. 9.95 (*0-937766-17-8*) Intl Promotions.
— The Unmedical Miracle - Oxygen. 119p. 1996. pap. 12.95 (*1-57901-010-5*) Intl Promotions.
— The Unmedical Miracle - Oxygen. rev. ed. 150p. 1994. pap. 11.95 (*0-937766-12-7*) Drelwood Comns.
Baker, Elizabeth & Baker, Elton. The Uncook Book: Raw Food Adventures to a New Health High. (Illus.). 208p. 1980. pap. 11.95 (*0-937766-05-4*) Drelwood Comns.
— The Unmedical Book. 263p. (Orig.). 1987. pap. 11.95 (*0-918880-14-9*) Intl Promotions.
Baker, Elizabeth, et al. Plays of Today, Vol. 1. LC 76-132137. (Play Anthology Reprint Ser.). 1977. 19.95 (*0-8369-8214-2*) Ayer.
Baker, Elizabeth F. Displacement of Men by Machines: Effects of Technological Change in Commercial Printing. Stein, Leon, ed. LC 77-70481. (Illus.). 1977. reprint ed. lib. bdg. 25.95 (*0-405-10155-4*) Ayer.
Baker, Ellen K., jt. ed. see Hornyak, Lynne M.
Baker, Ellis B. Genealogy of the Benjamin Family in the United States of America from 1632 to 1898. (Illus.). 88p. 1988. reprint ed. pap. 17.50 (*0-8328-0237-9*); reprint ed. lib. bdg. 25.50 (*0-8328-0236-0*) Higginson Bk Co.
Baker, Elsa J. Sit down & Play. Baker, Kenneth W., ed. LC 87-90545. (Illus.). 203p. (Orig.). 1987. pap. 9.95 (*0-9620178-0-9*) Sycamore WA.
Baker, Elton, jt. auth. see Baker, Elizabeth.
Baker, Elwood T. Baker. Genealogy of Eber & Lydia Smith Baker of Marion Oh. & Their Descendants to Oct. 1909. 87p. 1997. reprint ed. pap. 16.50 (*0-8328-7343-8*); reprint ed. lib. bdg. 26.50 (*0-8328-7342-X*) Higginson Bk Co.
Baker, Emanuel R., jt. auth. see Connell, Nancy D.
Baker, Emanuel R., jt. auth. see Kenett, Ron.
Baker, Emerson W. The New England Knight: Enrichment, Advancement & the Life of Sir William Phillips, 1651-1695. LC 98-204088. (Illus.). 400p. 1998. pap. 19.95 (*0-8020-8171-1*); text 65.00 (*0-8020-0925-5*) U of Toronto Pr.
Baker, Emerson W., Jr., ed. Maine in the Age of Discovery: Christopher Levett's Voyage, 1623-1624 & a Guide to Sources. 1988. pap. 14.00 (*0-318-42474-6*) Maine Hist.
Baker, Emerson W., et al, eds. American Beginnings: Exploration, Culture, & Cartography in the Land of Norumbega. LC 93-4380. (Illus.). xxxiv, 396p. 1995. text 50.00 (*0-8032-4554-8*) U of Nebr Pr.
Baker, Eric & Blik, Tyler. Trademarks of the '20s & '30s. LC 85-11355. (Illus.). 144p. 1985. pap. 14.95 (*0-87701-360-8*) Chronicle Bks.
Baker, Eric, et al. Trademarks of the '40s & '50s. LC 88-6142. (Illus.). 144p. 1988. pap. 14.95 (*0-87701-485-X*) Chronicle Bks.
Baker, Ernest. Essays on Government. LC 86-18290. 312p. 1986. reprint ed. lib. bdg. 92.50 (*0-313-25221-1*, BSSG, Greenwood Pr) Greenwood.
— Revivals of the Bible. 1997. pap. 6.99 (*0-907927-30-0*) Emerald House Group Inc.
Baker, Ernest A. Guide to Historical Fiction. LC 68-9157. 1968. reprint ed. 20.00 (*0-87266-001-X*) Argosy.
— A History of the English Novel: Edgeworth, Austen, & Scott, 11 vols., Vol. 6. 277p. 1979. reprint ed. 34.50 (*0-06-480051-2*, 06331) B&N Imports.
— A History of the English Novel: From the Brontes to Meredith, Romanticism in the English Novel, 11 vols., Vol. 8. 411p. 1972. reprint ed. 34.50 (*0-06-480053-9*, 06333) B&N Imports.
— A History of the English Novel: The Age of Romance, 11 vols., Vol. 1. (History of the English Novel Ser.). 336p. 1977. reprint ed. 34.50 (*0-06-480046-6*, 06326) B&N Imports.
— A History of the English Novel: The Day Before Yesterday, 11 vols., Vol. 9. 364p. 1975. reprint ed. 34.50 (*0-06-480054-7*, 06334) B&N Imports.
— A History of the English Novel: The Elizabethan Age & After, 11 vols., Vol. 2. 303p. 1966. reprint ed. 34.50 (*0-06-480047-4*, 06327) B&N Imports.
— A History of the English Novel: The Later Romances & the Establishment of Realism, 11 vols., Vol. 3. 278p. 1969. reprint ed. 34.50 (*0-06-480048-2*, 06328) B&N Imports.
***Baker, Ernest W.** A 50-Year Adventure in the Advertising Business. 250p. 2000. 24.95 (*0-8143-2910-1*) Wayne St U Pr.
Baker, Eugene, III & Paulson, Steven K. Experimental Exercises in Organization Theory. LC 94-16782. 192p. 1994. pap. text 51.00 (*0-13-051229-X*, Pub. by P-H) S&S Trade.
Baker, Eva H. & Johnson, Lucy D. Harrington Family in Rhode Island. 105p. 1997. reprint ed. pap. 18.00 (*0-8328-8986-5*); reprint ed. lib. bdg. 28.00 (*0-8328-8985-7*) Higginson Bk Co.
Baker, Eva L. & O'Neil, Harold F., eds. Technology Assessment, 2 vols., Set. 1994. pap. 55.00 (*0-8058-1709-3*) L Erlbaum Assocs.
— Technology Assessment, 2 vols., Vol. I. 272p. 1994. 69.95 (*0-8058-1246-6*); pap. 36.00 (*0-8058-1247-4*) L Erlbaum Assocs.
— Technology Assessment, 2 vols., Vol. II. 296p. 1994. 59.95 (*0-8058-1248-2*) L Erlbaum Assocs.
— Technology Assessment, 2 vols., Vol. II. 296p. 1994. pap. 36.00 (*0-8058-1249-0*) L Erlbaum Assocs.
Baker, Eve. Paths in Solitude. 127p. 1994. pap. 39.95 (*0-85439-513-X*, Pub. by St Paul Pubns) St Mut.
Baker, F. A., jt. auth. see Tainter, F. H.
Baker, F. C. The Fresh Water Mollusca of Wisconsin. 1973. reprint ed. lib. bdg. 150.00 (*3-7682-0764-1*) Lubrecht & Cramer.
Baker, F. Mervin, ed. Proposing a New Scientific Method & Biosocial Theory to Explain Western Society. LC 98-8629. 176p. 1998. text 79.95 (*0-7734-8310-1*) E Mellen.
***Baker, F. Scott.** Access X Power Programming. 1999. pap. 49.99 (*0-7897-1538-4*) Que.
Baker, F. W., ed. Drought Resistance in Cereals. 240p. 1996. text 60.00 (*0-85198-641-2*) OUP.
Baker, F. W. & Terry, P. J., eds. Tropical Grassy Weeds. 203p. 1991. 70.00 (*0-85198-709-5*) OUP.
Baker, Felicity, tr. see Levi-Strauss, Claude.
Baker, Finn, jt. tr. see Schjoldager, Harold.
***Baker, Fiona.** C20th Furniture: Over 230 Classics of Modern Design. (Illus.). 256p. 2000. 50.00 (*1-85868-875-2*, Pub. by Carlton Bks Ltd) Natl Bk Netwk.
— Furniture. (Twentieth-Century Ser.). 2000. pap. text 16.95 (*1-85868-759-4*) Carlton Bks Ltd.
Baker-Fletcher, Garth. Somebodyness: Martin Luther King, Jr. & the Theory of Dignity. LC 93-19847. (Harvard Theological Studies: Vol. 31). 160p. (C). 1996. pap. 12.00 (*0-8006-7087-6*) TPI PA.
Baker-Fletcher, Garth, jt. auth. see Baker-Fletcher, Karen.
Baker-Fletcher, Garth K. Xodus: An African-American Male Journey. 224p. 1995. pap. 20.00 (*0-8006-2918-3*, 1-2918) Augsburg Fortress.
Baker-Fletcher, Karen. A Singing Something: Anna J. Cooper & the Foundations of Womanist Theology. LC 94-22622. 160p. 1994. 19.95 (*0-8245-1399-1*) Crossroad NY.
— Sisters of Dust, Sisters of Spirit: A Creation-Centered Womanist Spirituality. LC 98-34570. 1998. pap. text 16.00 (*0-8006-3077-7*, 1-3077, Fortress Pr) Augsburg Fortress.
Baker-Fletcher, Karen & Baker-Fletcher, Garth. My Sister, My Brother: Womanist & Xodus God-Talk. LC 97-12080. (Bishop Henry McNeal Turner/Sojourners Truth Series in Black Religion: No. 12). 325p. (Orig.). 1996. pap. 18.00 (*1-57075-099-8*) Orbis Bks.
Baker, Fran. King of the Mountain. 1995. mass mkt. 2.95 (*0-553-55038-1*) Bantam.
— Once a Warrior. LC 98-92659. 344p. 1998. pap. 12.95 (*0-9663397-0-3*, 16579330) Delphi Bks.
Baker, Frances A. Keeper of the Idiom of the People: The Duquesne University Tamburitzans. LC 80-51690. (Illus.). 110p. 1981. per. 10.00 (*0-918660-15-7*) Ragusan Pr.
Baker, Frank. Charles Wesley's Verse. 1988. pap. 10.00 (*0-7162-0446-0*) Epworth Pr.
Baker, Frank. From Wesley to Asbury: Studies in Early American Methodism. LC 75-39454. xiv, 223p. 1976. text 35.95 (*0-8223-0359-0*) Duke.
Baker, Frank, ed. The Heart of True Spirituality: John Wesley's Own Choice, Vol. 1. 2nd ed. 112p. 1985. pap. 3.70 (*0-310-39621-2*, 17064P) Zondervan.
— The Heart of True Spirituality: John Wesley's Own Choice, Vol. 2. 94p. 1985. pap. 3.95 (*0-310-45101-9*, 17079P) Zondervan.
Baker, Frank, jt ed. see Green, Gareth M.
Baker, Frank B. Computer Managed Instruction: Theory & Practice. LC 77-24006. (Illus.). 440p. 1978. 44.95 (*0-87778-099-4*) Educ Tech Pubns.
Baker, Frank B., ed. Item Response Theory: Parameter Estimation Techniques. (Statistics: Textbooks & Monographs: Vol. 129). (Illus.). 456p. 1992. text 185.00 (*0-8247-8636-X*) Dekker.
Baker, Frank C. Life of the Pleistocene or Glacial Period. LC 74-80996. (BCL Ser. I). 1969. reprint ed. 49.50 (*0-404-00449-0*) AMS Pr.
Baker, Frank J. How to Make Your Camera Pay for Your Vacation. LC 81-10843. 1991. 14.95 (*0-87949-208-2*) Ashley Bks.
Baker, Fred A. Baker. Genealogical Record of Rev. Nicholas Baker (1610-78) & His Descendants. 147p. 1997. reprint ed. pap. 25.00 (*0-8328-7345-4*); reprint ed. lib. bdg. 35.00 (*0-8328-7344-6*) Higginson Bk Co.
Baker, Frederick. Ways of Co-Existing: Urban, Suburban & Global Communities. 260p. (C). 1997. per. 44.95 (*0-7872-3887-2*, 41388701) Kendall-Hunt.
Baker, G. Construction: Techniques. 1976. 10.48 (*0-13-169417-0*); pap. 10.16 (*0-13-169409-X*) P-H.
— Design Strategies in Architecture. (Illus.). 292p. (Orig.). 1989. pap. text 39.95 (*0-419-15950-9*, E & FN Spon) Routledge.
***Baker, G. & Easley, J. A., eds.** Equine Dentistry. (Illus.). 315p. 1998. text. write for info. (*0-7020-2392-2*) W B Saunders.
Baker, G. & Freire, A., eds. Nonlinear Partial Differential Equations in Geometry & Physics: The 1995 Barrett Lectures. LC 96-51031. (Progress in Nonlinear Differential Equations & Their Applications Ser.: Vol. 29). 153p. 1997. 58.00 (*3-7643-5493-3*) Spr-Verlag.
Baker, G. & Karihaloo, B. L., eds. Fracture of Brittle Disordered Materials: Concrete, Rock & Ceramics. (Illus.). 592p. (C). 1994. 150.00 (*0-419-19050-3*, E & FN Spon) Routledge.
Baker, G., et al. Community Nursing: Research & Recent Developments. 240p. (Orig.). 1986. pap. 25.00 (*0-7099-4415-2*, Pub. by C Helm) Routldge.
Baker, G., tr. see Simotta, George.
Baker, G. H. The Biology & Control of White Snails (mollusca, Helicidae), Introduced Pests in Australia. LC 86-229493. 31 p. 1986. write for info. (*0-643-04053-6*, Pub. by CSIRO) Accents Pubns.
***Baker, G. P.** Augustus: The Golden Age of Rome. LC 00-34540. 2000. reprint ed. pap. 18.95 (*0-8154-1089-1*, Pub. by Cooper Sq) Natl Bk Netwk.
— Hannibal. LC 99-34894. (Illus.). 366p. 1999. pap. 16.95 (*0-8154-1005-0*) Cooper Sq.
Baker, G. P. & Hacker, P. M. An Analytical Commentary on Wittgenstein's Philosophical Investigations. LC 85-20837. xxvi, 374p. 1985. pap. text 13.95 (*0-226-03539-5*) U Ch Pr.
— Wittgenstein: Meaning & Understanding: Essays on the Philosophical Investigations. LC 85-20838. xxvi, 374p. 1985. pap. text 14.95 (*0-226-03540-9*) U Ch Pr.
— Wittgenstein, Understanding & Meaning: An Analytical Commentary on the Philosophical Investigations, Vol. 1. LC 79-15740. 1980. lib. bdg. 60.00 (*0-226-03526-3*) U Ch Pr.
Baker, Garth & Freire, Alexandre S. Nonlinear Partial Differential Equations in Geometry & Physics: The 1995 Barrett Lectures. LC 96-51031. (Progress in Nonlinear Differential Equations & Their Applications Ser.). 1997. 58.00 (*0-8176-5493-3*) Birkhauser.
Baker, Gary L. Understanding Uwe Johnson. LC 98-40217. (Understanding Modern European & Latin Literature Ser.). 160p. 1999. 29.95 (*1-57003-282-3*) U of SC Pr.
Baker, Gary R. Cadets in Gray: The Story of the Cadets of the South Carolina Military Academy & Cadet Rangers in the Civil War. LC 89-61483. (Illus.). 242p. 1990. 21.95 (*0-9623065-0-9*) Palmetto Bookworks.
Baker, Geoff. Trade Winds on the Niger: The Saga of the Royal Niger Company 1830-1971. 224p. 1997. text 39.50 (*1-86064-014-1*) St Martin.
Baker, Geoffrey. Antoine Predock. (Architectural Monographs: Vol. 51). (Illus.). 128p. (Orig.). 1997. pap. 38.00 (*0-471-97772-1*) Wiley.
— Design Strategies for Architecture. 2nd ed. (Illus.). 344p. (C). 1996. pap. 39.99 (*0-419-16130-9*, E & FN Spon) Routledge.
— Le Corbusier: An Analysis of Form. 2nd ed. (Illus.). 336p. (C). (gr. 13). 1991. pap. text 51.95 (*0-7476-0028-7*) Chapman & Hall.
Baker, Geoffrey H. Le Corbusier - Creative Search: The Formative Years of Charles-Edouard Jeanneret. LC 94-66155. 1995. 77.00 (*0-419-17730-2*) Routledge.
— Le Corbusier: An Analysis of Form. 3rd ed. (Illus.). 368p. 1996. pap. 34.95 (*0-442-02432-0*, VNR) Wiley.
Baker, Geoffrey H. Le Corbusier: An Analysis of Form. 3rd ed. 385p. 1996. text 34.95 (*0-471-28813-6*, VNR) Wiley.
Baker, Geoffrey H. Le Corbusier: The Creative Search. LC 94-66155. (Architecture Ser.). (Illus.). 320p. 1996. text 64.95 (*0-442-02128-3*, VNR) Wiley.
Baker, Geoffrey H. & Gubler, Jacques. Le Corbusier: Early Works at la Chaux-de-Fonds. (Academy Architecture Ser.). (Illus.). 128p. 1987. 45.00 (*0-312-47582-9*); pap. 30.00 (*0-312-47583-7*) St Martin.
Baker, George. Oleum Magistrale. LC 72-171. (English Experience Ser.: No. 123). 104p. 1969. reprint ed. 16.00 (*90-221-0123-1*) Walter J Johnson.
— The Sad Sack. LC 83-46010. (Classics of Modern American Humor Ser.). reprint ed. 30.00 (*0-404-19926-7*) AMS Pr.
Baker, George, jt. ed. see Needleman, Jacob.
Baker, George A., III. Managing Change: A Model for Community College Leaders, 4 bks. LC 99-163031. 32p. 1998. pap. 20.00 (*0-87117-312-3*, 1417) Comm Coll Pr Am Assn Comm Coll.
Baker, George A., Jr. Point Lace & Diamonds. LC 74-103080. (Granger Index Reprint Ser.). 1977. 17.95 (*0-8369-6095-5*) Ayer.
Baker, George A., ed. A Handbook on the Community College in America: Its History, Function, & Management. LC 92-45081. 720p. 1993. lib. bdg. 135.00 (*0-313-28028-2*, BHZ, Greenwood Pr) Greenwood.
Baker, George A., Jr. & Graves-Morris, Peter. Pade Approximants. 2nd ed. (Encyclopedia of Mathematics & Its Applications Ser.: No. 59). (Illus.). 762p. (C). 1996. text 120.00 (*0-521-45007-1*) Cambridge U Pr.

An Asterisk (*) at the beginning of an entry indicates that the title is appearing for the first time.

Baker, George A., III, et al. Cultural Leadership: Inside America's Community Colleges. 1992. pap. 33.00 (*0-87117-241-0*, 1333) Comm Coll Pr Am Assn Comm Coll.
— Teaching As Leading: Profiles of Excellence in the Open-Door College. 300p. 1990. 33.00 (*0-87117-199-6*, 1211) Comm Coll Pr Am Assn Comm Coll.
Baker, George A., III, jt. auth. see Roueche, John E.
Baker, George C., Jr. Introduction to the History of Early New England Methodism. LC 70-95393. 1969. reprint ed. 31.50 (*0-404-00466-0*) AMS Pr.
Baker, George P. Development of Shakespeare as a Dramatist. LC 71-160010. (BCL Ser. I). reprint ed. 39.50 (*0-404-00467-9*) AMS Pr.
— The Development of Shakespeare As a Dramatist. (BCL1-PR English Literature Ser.). 329p. 1992. reprint ed. lib. bdg. 89.00 (*0-7812-7302-1*) Rprt Serv.
— Dramatic Technique. LC 77-77706. (Theatre, Film & the Performing Arts Ser.). 532p. 1976. reprint ed. pap. 15.95 (*0-306-80030-6*); reprint ed. lib. bdg. 55.00 (*0-306-71344-6*) Da Capo.
— Dramatic Technique. LC 74-100220. 531p. 1970. reprint ed. lib. bdg. 65.00 (*0-8371-3005-0*, BADT, Greenwood Pr) Greenwood.
— Modern American Plays. LC 73-4868. (Play Anthology Reprint Ser.). 1977. reprint ed. 31.95 (*0-8369-8247-9*) Ayer.
Baker, George P. & Smith, George D. The New Financial Capitalists: Kohlberg Kravis Roberts & the Creation of Corporate Value. LC 98-28007. 240p. (C). 1998. 24.95 (*0-521-64260-4*) Cambridge U Pr.
Baker, Georgette. Bilingual Songs & Fingerplays for the Mitt: Cantemos Chiquitos. (Illus.). 12p. (Orig.). (J). (gr. k-2). 1995. pap. text 29.95 (*0-9623930-3-7*) Cantemos.
— Cantemos Chiquitos. (Cantemos Ser.: Vol. 2). (SPA., Illus.). (J). (gr. k-12). Date not set. pap. 10.95 (*0-9623930-2-9*) Cantemos.
— Cantemos Chiquitos No. I: Songs & Fingerplays from Mexico & South America. (Illus.). 20p. (Orig.). (J). (gr. k-3). 1994. pap. 6.95 (*0-9623930-1-0*) Cantemos.
— Cuentos y Canciones. (Cantemos Chiquitos Ser.).Tr. of Songs & Stories. (ENG & SPA.). 29p. (Orig.). (J). (gr. k-3). 1995. pap. 12.95 incl. audio (*0-9623930-5-3*) Cantemos.
— You Too Can Be in TV Commercials. Doughty, Mark, ed. (Illus.). 86p. (Orig.). 1988. pap. 7.95 (*0-9623930-0-2*) Cantemos.
***Baker, Georgia O.** A Handbook of Costume Drawing: A Guide to Drawing the Period Figure. 2nd ed. LC 99-87664. 192p. 2000. pap. 36.95 (*0-240-80403-1*, Focal) Buttrwrth-Heinemann.
Baker, Georgia O. & Pullen, Helen R. A Handbook of Costume Drawing. 168p. 2000. pap. text 42.95 (*0-240-80112-1*, Focal) Buttrwrth-Heinemann.
Baker, Ginny A., jt. auth. see Tickner, Jan.
Baker, Glen B., jt. ed. see Boulton, Alan A.
Baker, Glenda, ed. see Jansen, Verna A.
Baker, Glenn, jt. auth. see Tester, Jerry.
Baker, Glenn A. The Beatles Down Under: The 1964 Australia & New Zealand Tour. (Rock & Roll Remembrances Ser.: No. 7). (Illus.). 130p. 1985. reprint ed. 34.50 (*0-87650-186-2*) Popular Culture.
— Monkeemania! The Story of the Monkees. 2nd ed. 1997. pap. text 15.95 (*0-85965-256-4*, Pub. by Plexus) Publishers Group.
***Baker, Glenn A.** Monkeemania: The Story of the Monkees. 3rd ed. (Illus.). 2000. pap. 15.95 (*0-85965-292-0*) Plexus.
Baker, Glenn E. & Crow, Leonard R. Electricity Fundamentals. LC 73-131131. 1971. 16.95 (*0-672-97506-8*, Bobbs) Macmillan.
Baker, Glenn E. & Miller, Rex. Carpentry Fundamentals. (Contemporary Construction Ser.). (Illus.). 512p. (gr. 10-12). 1981. text 35.96 (*0-07-003361-7*) McGraw.
Baker, Glenn E. & Yeager, L. Dayle. Wood Technology. LC 72-83817. 1974. write for info. (*0-672-97507-6*); lab manual ed. write for info. (*0-672-97107-0*) Macmillan.
Baker, Glenn E., jt. auth. see Miller, Rex.
Baker, Gloria. Sacred Sounds for All Seasons. (Illus.). 121p. (Orig.). (C). pap. 14.95 (*1-56516-034-7*) H Leonard.
Baker-Gonzalez, Joan & Blau, Eileen K. Building on Basics: A Thematic Approach to Reading Comprehension. LC 98-34159. 272p. 1998. pap. text 11.96 (*0-201-34052-6*) Addison-Wesley.
Baker-Gonzalez, Joan & Blau, Eileen K. Building Understanding: A Thematic Approach to Reading Comprehension. LC 94-31208. 1995. pap. text 23.08 (*0-201-82528-7*) Addison-Wesley.
Baker, Gordon & Morris, Katherine. Descartes' Dualism. 256p. (C). 1995. 70.00 (*0-415-10121-2*) Routledge.
Baker, Gordon E. Rural Versus Urban Political Power: The Nature & Consequences of Unbalanced Representation. LC 78-12263. 70p. 1979. reprint ed. lib. bdg. 38.50 (*0-313-21223-6*, BARV, Greenwood Pr) Greenwood.
Baker, Gordon E., jt. auth. see Mason, Alpheus T.
Baker, Gordon P. A Cloud of Witnesses: Cameos of Ten Who Jesus Touched. LC 93-30841. 72p. (Orig.). 1994. pap. 8.50 (*1-55673-516-2*, 9403) CSS OH.
Baker, Gregory L. Religion & Science: From Swedenborg to Chaotic Dynamics. 172p. pap. (*0-934623-09-0*) Solomon Pr.
Baker, Gregory L. & Gollub, Jerry P. Chaotic Dynamics: An Introduction. 2nd ed. (Illus.). 270p. (C). 1996. text 74.95 (*0-521-47106-0*); pap. text 27.95 (*0-521-47685-2*) Cambridge U Pr.
***Baker, Gregory S.** Processing Near-Surface Seismic-Reflection Data: A Primer. Young, Roger A., ed. (Course Notes Ser.: Vol. 11). (Illus.). 77p. 1999. 75.00 (*1-56080-090-9*) Soc Expl Geophys.
Baker, Guy E. Baker's Dozen: 13 Effective Principles for Financial Success. (Illus.). 163p. 1994. mass mkt. 20.00 (*0-9647721-1-6*) Standel Pub.
— Why People Buy. (Illus.). 115p. 1995. 25.00 (*0-9647721-0-8*) Standel Pub.
Baker, Guy E. & Jensen, Rick. Investment Alchemy: Managing Financial Risk. (Illus.). 1998. mass mkt. 25.00 (*0-9647721-3-2*) Standel Pub.
***Baker, Gwendolyn.** Days on the Porch: The Friendship of Betty Nelson & Ellie Green. (Illus.). 114p. 1998. pap. 9.95 (*0-9669295-0-0*) Royal Crest.
Baker, Gwendolyn C. Planning & Organizing for Multicultural Instruction. 2nd ed. 1993. pap. 20.95 (*0-201-86112-7*) Addison-Wesley.
— Redesigning the Nonprofit Organization: How Vision, Leadership, & Planning Helped One Non-Profit Redefine Itself, No. 53. 23p. 1993. pap. text 16.00 (*0-925299-30-8*) Natl Ctr Nonprofit.
Baker, H. A. Visions of Heaven. 139p. 1973. mass mkt. 5.99 (*0-88368-401-2*) Whitaker Hse.
Baker, H. B. Zonitid Snails from Pacific Islands, 4 pts. in 3 vols., Pt. 1. (BMB Ser.). 1974. reprint ed. 25.00 (*0-527-02266-7*) Periodicals Srv.
— Zonitid Snails from Pacific Islands, 4 pts. in 3 vols., Pt. 2. (BMB Ser.). 1974. reprint ed. 25.00 (*0-527-02273-X*) Periodicals Srv.
— Zonitid Snails from Pacific Islands, 4 pts. in 3 vols., Pt. 3. (BMB Ser.). 1974. reprint ed. 25.00 (*0-527-02274-8*) Periodicals Srv.
Baker, H. Barton. History of the London Stage & Its Famous Players 1576-1903. LC 72-81971. (Illus.). 572p. 1972. reprint ed. 27.95 (*0-405-08231-2*, Pub. by Blom Pubns) Ayer.
Baker, H. D. Hugo Chinese: Simplified Language Course. LC 98-31747. (CHI & ENG.). 1999. pap. 29.95 incl. audio (*0-7894-4220-5*) DK Pub Inc.
Baker, H. D. R. Mardarin Chinese in Three Months. LC 98-31747. (Hugo's Simplified Language Course Ser.). 304p. 1999. pap. text 14.95 (*0-7894-4214-0*) DK Pub Inc.
Baker, H. F. Abelian Functions: Abel's Theorem & the Allied Theory of Theta Functions. (Cambridge Mathematical Library). 720p. (C). 1996. pap. text 47.95 (*0-521-49877-5*) Cambridge U Pr.
Baker, H. H. A Classified French Vocabulary. (ENG & FRE.). 96p. 1982. pap. 5.95 (*0-8288-1212-8*, M10841) Fr & Eur.
Baker, H. Kent, et al. Ethics in the Investment Profession: An International Survey. 49p. (Orig.). 1995. pap. text 20.00 (*0-943205-29-8*) RFICFA.
Baker Hanna, Beulah, tr. see Zum Brunnen, Mary H.
Baker, Harold. Mikhail Bakhtin: An Annotated Bibliography. Cain, William, ed. (Bibliographies of Modern Critics & Critical Schools Ser.). 300p. Date not set. text 45.00 (*0-8153-1172-9*) Garland.
Baker, Harold R., et al, eds. Dignity & Growth: Citizen Participation in Social Change. 276p. (Orig.). (C). 1991. pap. text 17.95 (*1-55059-023-5*) Temeron Bks.
Baker, Harry F. & Ridley, Rosalind M., eds. Prion Diseases. LC 96-3408. (Methods in Molecular Medicine Ser.: Vol. 3). (Illus.). 336p. 1996. 99.00 (*0-89603-342-2*) Humana.
Baker, Harry F., jt. auth. see Ridley, Rosalind M.
Baker, Harvey W., jt. auth. see Wise, Robert A.
Baker, Hattie M. The Fallacy of Medicine. 9p. 1996. reprint ed. spiral bd. 8.00 (*0-7873-0064-0*) Hlth Research.
Baker, Helen & Pearson, Alan, eds. The Subjective Experience of Admission to a Nursing Unit: An Interpretive Study. (Research Monographs: No. 6). 1995. pap. 20.00 (*0-7300-1518-1*, Pub. by Deakin Univ) St Mut.
Baker, Helen, jt. auth. see Pearson, Alan.
Baker, Helen W. No Shame in Love. 330p. 1998. pap. 7.98 (*1-57502-672-4*, PO1905) Morris Pubng.
Baker, Hendrik. Stage Management & Theatrecraft: A Stage Manager's Handbook. 4th ed. LC 68-16449. (Illus.). 392p. 1988. pap. 20.00 (*0-85343-556-1*, Pub. by J G Miller Ltd) Empire Pub Srvs.
***Baker, Henry A.** History of Montville, Connecticut, Formerly the North Parish of New London, 1640-1896. fac. ed. 726p. 1999. reprint ed. 75.00 (*0-7404-0022-3*) Higginson Bk Co.
Baker, Henry E. The Colored Inventor: A Record of Fifty Years. LC 71-75851. 18p. reprint ed. pap. 12.95 (*0-88143-068-4*) Ayer.
— The Colored Inventor: A Record of Fifty Years. LC 71-75851. (American Negro: His History & Literature. Series 2). 1969. reprint ed. pap. 1.00 (*0-405-01943-2*) Ayer.
Baker, Henry E. & Wilson, James. The Microscope Made Easy: The Description & Manner of Using Mr. Wilson's Set of Pocket Microscopes. (History of Microscopy Ser.). 390p. 1987. reprint ed. 29.00 (*0-940095-03-3*) Sci Heritage Ltd.
Baker, Henry G., ed. Memory Management: Proceedings International Workshop, IWMM '95, Kinross, U. K., September 27-29, 1995. (Lecture Notes in Computer Science Ser.: Vol. 986). 417p. 1995. 68.00 (*3-540-60368-9*) Spr-Verlag.
Baker, Henry J., et al, eds. The Laboratory Rat, Vol. 2: Research & Applications. LC 79-51688. (American College of Laboratory Animal Medicine Ser.). 1980. text 146.00 (*0-12-074902-5*) Acad Pr.
Baker, Henry M., ed. see Kidder, Frederic.
Baker, Herbert. Cecil Rhodes. LC 77-102223. (Select Bibliographies Reprint Ser.). 1977. 26.95 (*0-8369-5108-5*) Ayer.
Baker, Herman & Frank, Oscar. Clinical Vitaminology: Methods & Interpretation. LC 68-24678. 250p. reprint ed. pap. 77.50 (*0-608-13682-4*, 205132600095) Bks Demand.
Baker, Herschel, jt. ed. see Rollins, Hyder.
Baker, Herschel C. Hyder Edward Rollins: A Bibliography. LC 60-10032. (Illus.). 64p. 1964. 9.95 (*0-674-43001-8*) HUP.
— John Philip Kemble: The Actor in His Theatre. LC 76-90701. 414p. 1970. reprint ed. lib. bdg. 75.00 (*0-8371-2279-1*, BAJK, Greenwood Pr) Greenwood.
— The Race of Time: Three Lectures on Renaissance Historiography. LC 66-29031. (Alexander Lectures: No. 1965). 110p. reprint ed. pap. 34.10 (*0-608-18036-X*, 201412200093) Bks Demand.
Baker, Herschel C., ed. Four Essays on Romance. LC 77-152269. 100p. 1971. pap. 5.95 (*0-674-31475-1*) HUP.
Baker, Hershel. The Later Renaissance in England: Nondramatic Verse & Prose, 1600-1660. (Illus.). 962p. 1996. reprint ed. pap. text 39.95 (*0-88133-842-7*) Waveland Pr.
Baker, Houston A., Jr. Afro-American Poetics: Revisions of Harlem & the Black Aesthetic. LC 88-2724. (Illus.). 212p. 1996. pap. 14.95 (*0-299-11504-6*) U of Wis Pr.
— The Betrayal of Race. 1999. write for info. (*0-8052-4163-9*) Schocken.
— Black Literature in America. 443p. (C). 1971. 41.88 (*0-07-003365-X*) McGraw.
— Black Studies, Rap & the Academy. LC 92-42997. (Black Literature & Culture Ser.). (Illus.). 128p. (C). 1993. 16.95 (*0-226-03520-4*) U Ch Pr.
— Black Studies, Rap & the Academy. (Illus.). xii, 122p. 1995. pap. 9.95 (*0-226-03521-2*) U Ch Pr.
— Blues, Ideology & Afro-American Literature: A Vernacular Theory. LC 84-2655. (Illus.). 288p. 1985. lib. bdg. 22.00 (*0-226-03536-0*) U Ch Pr.
— Blues, Ideology & Afro-American Literature: A Vernacular Theory. LC 84-2655. (Illus.). 240p. 1987. pap. text 13.00 (*0-226-03538-7*) U Ch Pr.
— Blues Journeys Home. LC 85-80142. (Illus.). 59p. (Orig.). (YA). (gr. 7-12). 1985. pap., per. 5.00 (*0-916418-61-8*) Lotus.
— The Journey Back: Issues in Black Literature & Criticism. LC 79-20861. 213p. 1984. pap. text 14.00 (*0-226-03535-2*) U Ch Pr.
— Long Black Song: Essays in Black American Literature & Culture. 156p. 1990. pap. text 14.50 (*0-8139-1301-2*) U Pr of Va.
— Long Black Song: Essays in Black American Literature & Culture. LC 72-77261. 168p. reprint ed. pap. 52.10 (*0-608-17191-3*, 202699800053) Bks Demand.
— A Many Colored Coat: Countee Cullen. (Broadside Critics Ser.: No. 4). (YA). (gr. 12 up). 1974. pap. 3.00 (*0-910296-36-7*) Broadside Pr.
— Modernism & the Harlem Renaissance. LC 87-5014. (Illus.). 144p. 1987. 19.95 (*0-226-03524-7*) U Ch Pr.
— Modernism & the Harlem Renaissance. LC 87-5014. (Illus.). 144p. 1989. pap. text 10.95 (*0-226-03525-5*) U Ch Pr.
— No Matter Where You Travel, You Still Be Black. LC 78-61608. 58p. 1979. per. 5.00 (*0-916418-18-9*) Lotus.
— Singers of Daybreak: Studies in Black American Literature. LC 82-23280. 107p. 1975. 19.95 (*0-88258-017-5*); pap. 12.95 (*0-88258-025-6*) Howard U Pr.
— Spirit Run. LC 81-82664. 38p. (YA). (gr. 9-12). 1982. pap. 3.00 (*0-916418-38-3*) Lotus.
— Workings of the Spirit: The Poetics of Afro-American Women's Writing. (Illus.). 239p. (C). 1998. pap. text 15.00 (*0-7881-5287-4*) DIANE Pub.
— Workings of the Spirit: The Poetics of Afro-American Women's Writing. LC 90-41980. (Black Literature & Culture Ser.). (Illus.). 256p. 1990. 29.95 (*0-226-03522-0*) U Ch Pr.
— Workings of the Spirit: The Poetics of Afro-American Women's Writing. LC 90-41980. (Black Literature & Culture Ser.). (Illus.). xvi, 256p. 1992. pap. text 13.95 (*0-226-03523-9*) U Ch Pr.
Baker, Houston A., Jr., ed. Three American Literatures: Essays in Chicano, Native American, & Asian-American Literature for Teachers of American Literature. LC 82-63420. iii, 265p. 1982. pap. 19.75 (*0-87352-353-9*, B103P) Modern Lang.
Baker, Houston A., Jr., et al, eds. Black British Cultural Studies: A Reader. LC 95-42672. (Black Literature & Culture Ser.). (C). 1996. lib. bdg. 48.00 (*0-226-14480-1*) U Ch Pr.
Baker, Houston A., Jr. & Redmond, Patricia, eds. Afro-American Literary Study in the 1990s. LC 89-31971. (Black Literature & Culture Ser.). 252p. 1989. 29.95 (*0-226-03537-9*) U Ch Pr.
— Afro-American Literary Study in the 1990s. LC 89-31971. (Black Literature & Culture Ser.). 252p. 1991. pap. text 11.95 (*0-226-03543-3*) U Ch Pr.
Baker, Houston A., Jr., jt. ed. see Fiedler, Leslie A.
Baker, Houston A., Jr., jt. ed. see Weixlmann, Joe.
Baker, Houston A., Jr., ed. & intro. see Douglass, Frederick.
Baker, Howard. And the Cheat Goes On: An Expose on How Students Are Cheating in School. Schiller, David, ed. LC 89-84658. (Illus.). 202p. (Orig.). 1989. pap. 12.95 (*0-9623660-0-5*) Forum Pr Intl.
Baker, Howard, Jr The One Minute Communicator: Tips, Techniques & Observations for Better Business Communication. LC 91-71063. (Illus.). 75p. (Orig.). (C). 1991. pap. 5.95 (*0-9623660-1-3*) Forum Pr Intl.
— One Minute Listener. 125p. 1991. pap. write for info. (*0-318-68594-9*) Forum Pr Intl.
— The One Minute Meeting. 135p. 1991. pap. write for info. (*0-318-68593-0*) Forum Pr Intl.
Baker, Howard. Soul Keeping: Ancient Paths of Spiritual Direction. LC 98-28275. 1998. pap. 10.00 (*1-57683-049-7*) NavPress.
Baker, Howard, jt. auth. see Baker, Dorothy.
Baker, Howard H., Jr. No Margin for Error: America in the Eighties. 1980. 10.95 (*0-686-65902-3*, Times Bks) Crown Pub Group.
Baker, Howard J., jt. ed. see Hall, Denis R.
Baker, Hugh. Chinese Family & Kinship. LC 78-26724. 272p. 1980. pap. text 19.00 (*0-231-04769-X*) Col U Pr.
— Hong Kong Images: On Chinese Customs, Folklore & Traditional Life. 180p. (Orig.). 1990. pap. 42.50 (*962-209-255-1*, Pub. by HK Univ Pr) Coronet Bks.
Baker, Hugh & Ho, Hanson. Teach Yourself Cantonese, 2 cass. (CHI.). 336p. 1996. pap. 21.95 incl. audio (*0-8442-3897-X*, Teach Yrslf) NTC Contemp Pub Co.
— Teach Yourself Cantonese: A Complete Course for Beginners. LC 95-68140. (Teach Yourself Ser.). (CHI., Illus.). 336p. 1996. pap. 14.95 (*0-8442-3892-9*, Teach Yrslf) NTC Contemp Pub Co.
Baker, Hugh, jt. ed. see Avedesian, Michael.
Baker, Hugh D. A Chinese Lineage Village: Sheung Shui. LC 68-23023. 251p. 1968. reprint ed. pap. 30.00 (*0-8357-2747-5*, 203985900013) Bks Demand.
Baker, I. L. George Orwell's Animal Farm. rev. ed. (Brodie's Notes Ser.). 64p. 1992. pap. 5.95 (*0-333-58159-8*, Pub. by Macmillan) Trans-Atl Phila.
***Baker, Ian & Laird, Thomas.** The Dalai Lama's Secret Temple: Tantric Wall Paintings from Tibet. LC 00-100630. (Illus.). 216p. 2000. 65.00 (*0-500-51003-2*, Pub. by Thames Hudson) Norton.
Baker, Ian, et al. Interstitial & Substitutional Solute Effects in Intermetallics: International Symposium on Interstitial & Substitutional Solute Effects in Internetallics (2nd: 1998: Rosemont,IL) Proceedings of the Second International Symposium : Held At The 1998 Tms Fall Meeting In Rosemont, Illinois on October 11-15 1998. LC 98-67358. 374p. 1998. 86.00 (*0-87339-413-5*) Minerals Metals.
Baker, Ian A. Tibetan Art of Healing. LC 97-26110. 192p. 1997. 50.00 (*0-8118-1897-7*) Chronicle Bks.
— Tibetan Art of Healing. LC 97-26110. (Illus.). 192p. 1997. pap. text 29.95 (*0-8118-1871-3*) Chronicle Bks.
Baker, J. Selected International Investment Portfolios for the New Decade. LC 98-22590. 220p. 1998. 63.00 (*0-08-043064-3*, Pergamon Pr) Elsevier.
Baker, J. & Murphy, V. Handbook of Marine Science: Compounds from Marine Organism. LC 74-30747. 1976. 136.00 (*0-87819-391-X*, CRC Reprint) Franklin.
Baker, J., tr. see Eichrodt, Walther.
Baker, J. A. Le Pelerin. (FRE.). 256p. 1989. pap. 10.95 (*0-7859-2124-9*, 2070381692) Fr & Eur.
Baker, J. A., tr. see Von Campenhausen, Hans.
Baker, J. C. Baptist History of the North Pacific Coast. Gaustad, Edwin S., ed. LC 79-52589. (Baptist Tradition Ser.). (Illus.). 1980. reprint ed. lib. bdg. 53.95 (*0-405-12456-2*) Ayer.
Baker, J. David. The Postal History of Indiana, 2 vols., Set. Hartmann, Leonard H., ed. LC 76-10531. (Illus.). 1100p. 1976. 75.00 (*0-917528-03-4*) L H Hartmann.
— The Postal History of Indiana, Vol. 1. Hartmann, Leonard H., ed. (Illus.). 1976. write for info. (*0-917528-01-8*) L H Hartmann.
— The Postal History of Indiana, Vol. 2. Hartmann, Leonard H., ed. (Illus.). 1976. write for info. (*0-917528-02-6*) L H Hartmann.
Baker, J. G. Flora of Mauritius & the Seychelles. 1971. reprint ed. 160.00 (*3-7682-0677-7*) Lubrecht & Cramer.
— Handbook of Fern Allies. (C). 1988. 30.00 (*0-7855-3265-X*, Pub. by Scientific) St Mut.
— Handbook of the Amaryllideae: Including the Alstromeriae & Agaveae. (Plant Monograph: No.7). 1972. reprint ed. 30.00 (*3-7682-0751-X*) Lubrecht & Cramer.
— Handbook of the Bromeliaceae. (Plant Monograph: No.8). 1972. reprint ed. 32.00 (*3-7682-0752-8*) Lubrecht & Cramer.
— Handbook of the Irideae. (Plant Monograph: No.9). 1972. reprint ed. 30.00 (*3-7682-0753-6*) Lubrecht & Cramer.
Baker, J. H. The Legal Profession & the Common Law: Historical Essays. 450p. 1986. 70.00 (*0-907628-62-1*) Hambledon Press.
— Manual of Law French. 2nd ed. (Illus.). 160p. 1990. text 86.95 (*0-85967-745-1*, Pub. by Scolar Pr) Ashgate Pub Co.
— Sources of English Legal History: Private Law to 1750. 698p. 1986. pap. 39.50 (*0-614-05966-6*, MICHIE) LEXIS Pub.
Baker, J. H. & Ringrose, J. S., eds. A Catalogue of English Legal Manuscripts in Cambridge University Library: With Codicological Descriptions of the Early Manuscripts by J. S. Ringrose. 918p. 1996. 215.00 (*0-85115-376-3*) Boydell & Brewer.
***Baker, J. Keith & Smith Baker, Pamela.** The Morning After: Surviving Your Year 2000 Solution. Strategies to Keep Pace with the Technological Evolution. large type ed. LC 99-70370. 128p. 1999. 22.95 (*0-9668049-2-9*, 1-2-9) Electec Pr.
Baker, J. M. A Treatise on Elders. 24p. 1992. pap. 0.95 (*1-56794-011-0*, D2275) Star Bible.
Baker, J. M., ed. Durability Of Building Materials & Components: Proceedings of the Fifth International Conference. 768p. (C). (gr. 13). 1990. text 215.00 (*0-419-15480-9*) Chapman & Bkman.
Baker, J. P., jt. ed. see Best, E. P.
Baker, J. Robert, et al, eds. A Baptism Sourcebook. LC 93-4123. (Seasonal Sourcebook Ser.). (Illus.). 224p. 1993. pap. 15.00 (*0-929650-93-X*, BAPTSB) Liturgy Tr Pubns.
— A Marriage Sourcebook. LC 94-25324. (Illus.). 236p. (Orig.). 1994. pap. 15.00 (*1-56854-039-6*, MARRSB) Liturgy Tr Pubns.
Baker, J. Robert & Budde, Barbara, eds. A Eucharist Sourcebook. LC 98-49838. 200p. (Orig.). 1999. pap. 15.00 (*1-56854-182-1*, EUCHSB) Liturgy Tr Pubns.

B

An Asterisk (*) at the beginning of an entry indicates that the title is appearing for the first time.

Baker, J. Stannard & Fricke, Lynn B. Traffic Accident Investigation Manual. 9th ed. 420p. 1986. 55.00 (0-912642-06-8) Traffic Inst.

Baker, J. T. Baker's Maneuvering Card. (C). 1987. 35.00 (0-85174-192-4) St Mut.

Baker, J. Wayne, jt. auth. see Riede, David C.

Baker, Jack, et al. Basic Mathematics: A Review. 2nd ed. 670p. (C). 1985. text 71.00 (0-03-071588-1, Pub. by SCP) Harcourt.

Baker, James. Leadership 101: 20 Solid Lessons in Leadership for the New Leader. 250p. 1998. pap. 15.95 (1-878208-74-8) Guild Pr IN.

— Studs Terkel. (Twayne's United States Authors Ser.). 160p. 1992. 32.00 (0-8057-7638-9) Macmillan.

Baker, James & Blair, Maxine. Here Am I: Send Me. 180p. (Orig.). 1995. pap. 10.00 (1-884295-09-6) Ananta Prnting.

Baker, James, jt. auth. see Reisman, W. Michael.

Baker, James, ed. see Howell, John M.

Baker, James C. Foreign Direct Investment in Less Developed Countries: The Role of ICSID & MIGA. LC 99-10384. 256p. 1999. 65.00 (1-56720-312-4, Q312, Quorum Bks) Greenwood.

— International Business Expansion into Less-Developed Countries: The International Finance Corporation & Its Operations. LC 91-23251. (Illus.). 328p. 1992. lib. bdg. 79.95 (1-56024-201-9) Haworth Pr.

Baker, James Calvin. International Finance. LC 97-23781. 538p. 1997. pap. text 61.00 (0-02-305891-9) P-H.

Baker, James F. I Don't Want to Live Anymore: Thoughts on Suicide & It's Prevention. 26p. 1992. pap. 4.95 (0-916780-33-3) CES Assocs.

— Professional Resume Writing Techniques. (Illus.). 105p. (C). 1984. 37.95 (0-916780-26-0) CES Assocs.

Baker, James L., ed. see Society of Environmental Toxicology & Chemistry (S.

Baker, James M., ed. Baldwin's Kentucky Practice, 4 vols. 2006p. 1980. 299.50 (0-8322-0056-5) Banks-Baldwin.

Baker, James M., et al, eds. Music Theory in Concept & Practice. LC 96-53956. (Eastman Studies in Music: Vol. 8). 544p. 1997. 130.00 (1-878822-79-9) Univ Rochester Pr.

Baker, James N., ed. & illus. see Stresau, Frederic B.

Baker, James R. Women's Rights in Old Testament Times. LC 92-4953. 198p. 1998. 17.95 (1-56085-029-9) Signature Bks.

Baker, James R. & Siegler, Arthur B., Jr., eds. Lord of the Flies: Text, Notes & Criticism. 1964. mass mkt. 6.95 (0-399-50643-8, Perigee Bks) Berkley Pub.

***Baker, James Robert.** Adrenaline. 232p. 2000. reprint ed. pap. 11.95 (1-55583-565-1, Pub. by Alyson Pubns) Consort Bk Sales.

— Testosterone: A Novel. 232p. 2000. 22.95 (1-55583-567-8, Pub. by Alyson Pubns) Consort Bk Sales.

Baker, James T. Ayn Rand. (United States Authors Ser.: No. 501). 184p. 1987. 21.95 (0-8057-7497-1, Twyne) Mac Lib Ref.

— Nat Turner: Cry Freedom in America. LC 97-74389. 160p. (C). 1997. pap. text 25.00 (0-15-503855-9, Pub. by Harcourt Coll Pubs) Harcourt.

— Thomas Merton: Social Critic: A Study. LC 76-132827. 183p. reprint ed. pap. 56.80 (0-608-18506-X, 203152100075) Bks Demand.

— Under the Sign of the Waterbearer: A Life of Thomas Merton. 1976. pap. 2.95 (0-915216-15-9) Marathon Intl Bk.

Baker, James W. Illusions Illustrated: A Professional Magic Show for Young Performers. LC 83-19549. (Illus.). 120p. (J). (gr. 6 up). 1984. pap. 6.95 (0-8225-9512-5, Lerner Publctns) Lerner Pub.

Baker, James W. & Brabb, E. Thanksgiving Cookery. LC 93-70949. (Traditional Country Life Recipe Ser.). (Illus.). 96p. (Orig.). 1994. pap. 9.95 (1-883283-03-5) Brick Tower.

Baker, James W., et al. Thanksgiving by the (Cook) Book. (Illus.). 52p. (Orig.). 1996. pap. 9.95 (0-940628-53-8) Pilgrim Soc.

Baker, Jane. Jewels of Thought. 1991. 16.95 (1-878096-06-0) Best E TX Pubs.

Baker, Janet. Seeking Immortality: Chinese Tomb Sculpture from the Schloss Collection. (Illus.). 72p. 1996. pap. 24.95 (0-9633959-5-5) Bowers Mus.

— Solicitors' Accounts: A Student's Guide. 4th ed. x, 392p. 1992. 36.00 (1-85431-238-3, Pub. by Blackstone Pr) Gaunt.

Baker, Janet, jt. auth. see Kay, Dale.

Baker, Janet, tr. see Xin, Yang & Chengru, Zhu.

***Baker, Janita.** Blues & Ragtime for Fretted Dulcimer: Beginning-Intermediate Level. 104p. 1998. 14.95 (0-7866-3008-6, 96754) Mel Bay.

***Baker-Jarvis, James.** Dielectric & Magnetic Properties of Printed Wiring Boards & Other Substrate Materials. 78p. 1999. pap. 7.00 (0-16-056958-3) USGPO.

— Electrical Properties & Dielectric Relaxation of DNA in Solution. 71p. 1999. pap. 6.25 (0-16-060887-2) USGPO.

***Baker, Jason D.** Baker's Guide to Christian Distance Education: Online Learning for All Ages. 196p. 2000. pap. 13.99 (0-8010-6341-8) Baker Bks.

Baker, Jason D. Christian Cyberspace Companion: A Guide to the Internet & Christian Online Resources. 2nd ed. LC 96-32032. (Illus.). 256p. (gr. 11 up). 1997. pap. 15.99 (0-8010-5738-8) Baker Bks.

***Baker, Jason D.** Parent's Computer Companion: A Guide to Software & Online Resources. LC 99-32104. 144p. 1999. pap. 9.99 (0-8010-6077-X) Baker Bks.

Baker, Jay. Night of the Fair. large type ed. (Linford Mystery Library). 560p. 1997. pap. 16.99 (0-7089-5020-5, Linford) Ulverscroft.

Baker, Jean. Mary Todd Lincoln. Date not set. reprint ed. pap. write for info. (0-393-31599-1) Norton.

Baker, Jean H. Affairs of Party: The Political Culture of Northern Democrats in the Mid-Nineteenth Century. LC 98-14327. (North's Civil War Ser.: No. 7). 367p. 1998. 32.50 (0-8232-1864-3); pap. 19.95 (0-8232-1865-1) Fordham.

— Ambivalent Americans: The Know-Nothing Party in Maryland. LC 76-51813. 224p. reprint ed. pap. 69.50 (0-8357-5342-5, 202582600046) Bks Demand.

— Mary Todd Lincoln: A Biography. LC 86-23757. (Illus.). 500p. 1989. pap. 17.95 (0-393-30586-4) Norton.

— The Politics of Continuity: Maryland Political Parties from 1858 to 1870. LC 72-12354. (Goucher College Ser.). (Illus.). 254p. 1973. 40.00 (0-8018-1418-9) Johns Hopkins.

— The Stevensons: A Biography of an American Family. 592p. (C). 1997. pap. 16.95 (0-393-31598-3) Norton.

Baker, Jean L. A Free Country. 348p. 1993. 22.00 (0-9633646-0-X) Natale Pub.

Baker, Jean M. Family Secrets: Gay Sons - A Mother's Story. LC 97-18839. (Illus.). 241p. 1997. 39.95 (0-7890-0248-5, Harrington Park); pap. 14.95 (1-56023-915-8, Harrington Park) Haworth Pr.

Baker, Jeanette. Catriona. 1997. per. 5.99 (0-671-53675-3, Pocket Books) PB.

***Baker, Jeanette.** Irish Fire. 400p. 2000. mass mkt. 6.50 (0-671-03407-3, Pocket Star Bks) PB.

Baker, Jeanette. Irish Lady. 1998. per. 5.99 (0-671-01734-9) PB.

— The Legacy. 1996. mass mkt. 5.99 (0-671-53674-5) PB.

— Nell. 418p. 1999. per. 6.50 (0-671-01735-7) S&S Trade.

— The Reckoning. 304p. 1997. mass mkt. 5.50 (0-7860-0441-X, Pinncle Kensgtn) Kensgtn Pub Corp.

***Baker, Jeanne.** An Undercover Story: Covered Bridges of California. (Illus.). 80p. 2000. pap. 12.95 (1-880849-23-2) Chapel Hill NC.

Baker, Jeanne C. & Madera, Joseph A. Journey into Light. Lilly, Don, ed. LC 92-85488. (Illus.). 212p. (Orig.). 1993. pap. text 9.95 (0-925078-01-8) Moonbeam Pub.

***Baker, Jeannie.** The Hidden Forest. LC 99-23175. (Illus.). 32p. (J). (gr. k-3). 2000. 16.95 (0-688-15760-2, Grenwillow Bks); lib. bdg. 16.89 (0-688-15761-0, Grenwillow Bks) HarpC Child Bks.

— The Story of Rosy Dock. abr. ed. LC 94-4677. (Illus.). 32p. (J). (ps-3). 1995. 14.89 (0-688-11493-8, Grenwillow Bks) HarpC Child Bks.

Baker, Jeannie. Where the Forest Meets the Sea. LC 87-7551. (Illus.). 32p. (J). (gr. 2 up). 1988. 16.00 (0-688-06363-2, Grenwillow Bks) HarpC Child Bks.

Baker, Jeannie. Where the Forest Meets the Sea. LC 87-7551. (Illus.). 32p. (J). (gr. 2 up). 1988. 15.93 (0-688-06364-0, Grenwillow Bks) HarpC Child Bks.

Baker, Jeannie. Window. LC 90-3922. (Illus.). 32p. (J). (gr. 2 up). 1991. 16.89 (0-688-08918-6, Grenwillow Bks) HarpC Child Bks.

Baker, Jeannine, et al. Conscious Conception: Elemental Journey Through the Labyrinth of Sexuality. LC 86-26994. (Illus.). 411p. 1986. pap., lib. bdg. 20.00 (0-938190-83-0) North Atlantic.

Baker, Jeannine P. Prenatal Yoga & Natural Birth. 2nd expanded ed. LC 74-19553. (Illus.). 1986. reprint ed. pap. text 10.00 (0-913512-52-4) Freestone Pub Co.

Baker, Jeff. Warblers of Europe & Asia. LC 97-23921. 360p. 1997. text 49.50 (0-691-01169-9, Pub. by Princeton U Pr) Cal Prin Full Svc.

— Windows CE Application Programming: Developing Applications for the Handheld PC. LC 96-79358. 466p. 1997. pap. 49.99 incl. cd-rom (1-57870-005-1) Macmillan Tech.

Baker, Jeff & Tribble, Thomas H. Homemade Mortar Construction Manual. (Illus.). 56p. 1989. pap. 8.00 (0-87364-501-4) Paladin Pr.

Baker, Jeffrey. Time & Mind in Wordsworth's Poetry. LC 80-11947. 213p. reprint ed. pap. 66.10 (0-608-10619-4, 207124100009) Bks Demand.

Baker, Jeffrey A. Cheque Mate: The Game of Princes. 339p. 1995. pap. 12.99 (0-88368-383-0) Whitaker Hse.

Baker, Jeffrey J. & Allen, Garland A. The Study of Biology. 4th ed. LC 81-17550. (Illus.). 1040p. 1982. text. write for info. (0-201-10180-7); student ed. write for info. (0-201-10182-3) Addison-Wesley.

Baker, Jeffrey J. & Allen, Garland E. Course in Biology. 3rd ed. LC 78-67451. (Life Sciences Ser.). 1979. text. write for info. (0-201-00308-2) Addison-Wesley.

— Matter, Energy, & Life: An Introduction to Chemical Concepts. 4th ed. LC 80-17946. (Life Sciences Ser.). 256p. (C). 1981. pap. text 23.00 (0-201-00169-1) Addison-Wesley.

Baker, Jeffrey P. The Machine in the Nursery: Incubator Technology & the Origins of Newborn Intensive Care. LC 95-40320. (Illus.). 256p. (C). 1996. text 45.00 (0-8018-5173-4) Johns Hopkins.

Baker, Jennifer. At Midnight: Once upon a Dream. 192p. (gr. 7-9). 1995. mass mkt. 3.99 (0-590-25947-4) Scholastic Inc.

— At Midnight a Novel Based on Cinderella. (Once Upon a Dream Ser.). (J). 1995. 9.09 (0-606-07968-8, Pub. by Turtleback) Demco.

— Calm Before the Storm. (Dawson's Creek Ser.: No. 2). 176p. (YA). (gr. 8 up). 1998. per. 4.99 (0-671-02475-2, Archway) PB.

— Cher Negotiates New York. (Clueless Ser.: No. 2). (YA). (gr. 7 up). 1995. mass mkt. 4.99 (0-671-56868-X, PB Trade Paper) PB.

***Baker, Jennifer.** Enchanted Hearts: Eternally Yours, Vol. 2. (Enchanted Hearts Ser.: No. 2). 176p. (YA). (gr. 7-12). 1999. mass mkt. 4.50 (0-380-80073-X) Morrow Avon.

Baker, Jennifer. 501 Practical Ways to Love Your Husband & Kids. LC 95-53686. 208p. 1996. pap. 10.99 (0-570-04846-X, 12-3283) Concordia.

— Good-Bye to Love, Bk. 2. 240p. (J). (gr. 7-9). 1994. pap. 3.95 (0-590-48324-2) Scholastic Inc.

— He Said/She Said: Her Secret. (YA). (gr. 7 up). 1997. pap. 3.99 (0-614-28882-7, Archway) PB.

— He Said/She Said: His Story. (YA). (gr. 7 up). 1997. pap. 3.99 (0-614-28883-5, Archway) PB.

— Her Secret He Said She Said. (YA). 1997. per. 3.99 (0-671-00222-8, Archway) PB.

— His Secret He Said She Said, Vol. 2. (He Said-She Said Ser.). (YA). 1997. per. 3.99 (0-671-00223-6, Archway) PB.

— In Sickness & in Health. (First Comes Love Ser.). 308p. (YA). (gr. 7-9). 1993. pap. 3.50 (0-590-46315-2) Scholastic Inc.

— Jack Frost Digest. (Illus.). 128p. (gr. 3-7). 1998. pap. text 3.99 (0-590-63983-8) Scholastic Inc.

— Just Like Sisters. (Class Secrets Ser.: No. 02). (YA). (gr. 7 up). 1995. per. 3.99 (0-671-51034-7, Archway) PB.

— The Lying Game. (Class Secrets Ser.: No. 4). (YA). (gr. 7 up). 1996. mass mkt. 3.99 (0-671-51036-3, Pocket Books) PB.

— Most Likely to Decieve. (Class Secrets Ser.: No. 01). 188p. (YA). (gr. 7 up). 1995. mass mkt. 3.99 (0-671-51033-9, Archway) PB.

— Rose: Once upon a Dream: Based on Beauty & the Beast. (J). 1996. mass mkt. 3.99 (0-590-25948-2) Scholastic Inc.

— Sworn to Silence. (Class Secrets Ser.: No. 3). (YA). (gr. 7 up). 1995. mass mkt. 3.99 (0-671-51035-5) PB.

Baker, Jennifer & Williamson, Kevin. The Beginning of Everything Else. (YA). (gr. 8 up). 1998. per. 4.99 (0-671-02473-6) PB.

Baker, Jenny. Simple French Cuisine: From Provence & Languedoc. (Illus.). 272p. 1992. pap. 12.95 (0-571-14454-3) Faber & Faber.

— Simply Fish: A Guide to Identifying, Buying & Eating Fish. (Illus.). 288p. 1994. pap. 13.95 (0-571-14966-9) Faber & Faber.

Baker, Jerry. Flower Power! LC SB405.B24697 1999. 1999. pap. 12.95 (0-345-43415-3) Ballantine Pub Grp.

— Happy, Healthy Houseplants, 1 vol. 1999. pap. 14.95 (0-452-28106-7) NAL.

— The Impatient Gardener. 240p. (Orig.). 1983. pap. 12.95 (0-345-30949-9) Ballantine Pub Grp.

***Baker, Jerry.** The Impatient Gardener. (Orig.). 1999. pap. 12.95 (0-345-91566-6) Ballantine Pub Grp.

Baker, Jerry. Impatient Gardener. 240p. 1998. pap. text 12.00 (0-345-91136-9) Ballantine Pub Grp.

— The Impatient Gardener's Lawn Book. 208p. 1999. pap. 12.00 (0-345-34094-9) Ballantine Pub Grp.

— The Impatient Gardener's Lawn Book. 1999. pap. write for info. (0-345-91296-9, Ballantine) Ballantine Pub Grp.

***Baker, Jerry.** Jerry Baker's Lawn Book. 1999. pap. 12.95 (0-345-91565-8) Ballantine Pub Grp.

Baker, Jerry. Plants Are Still Like People. (Orig.). 1999. pap. 18.95 (0-452-28105-9) NAL.

Baker, Jim. Benjamin Franklin: The Uncommon Man. (Illus.). 1976. pap. 1.00 (0-914482-13-0) Ohio Hist Soc.

— Billie Jean King. LC 74-7690. 90 p. 1974. 1.50 (0-448-07436-2) Putnam Pub Group.

— Forts in the Forest: Kentucky in the Year of the Bloody Sevens. LC 75-39915. (Illus.). 48p. (Orig.). 1975. pap. 1.00 (0-914482-11-4) Ohio Hist Soc.

Baker, Jim. Media Inc.'s Northwest Production Index. 18th ed. (Illus.). 400p. Date not set. pap. 25.00 (0-940317-45-1) Media Index Pub.

— Media Inc.'s Western Canada Production Index. 2nd ed. (Illus.). 320p. Date not set. pap. 25.00 (0-940317-46-X) Media Index Pub.

Baker, Joan & Baker, Arthur. Walker's Companion to the Wade Roads. 120p. (C). 1987. 95.00 (0-906664-18-7, Pub. by Mercat Pr Bks) St Mut.

Baker, Joan B. & Tobin, Judith. Symbols of Faith: A Visual Journey to Historic Churches of New Mexico. (Illus.). 56p. (Orig.). 1993. pap. 22.00 (0-9637342-0-2); 15.00 (0-9637342-1-0) Bunbury Pr.

Baker, JoAnn. The View from My House. Orloff, Erica, ed. 224p. 1998. pap. 12.95 (1-885843-07-0) Saturn Press.

Baker, JoAnn, jt. auth. see Orloff, Erica.

Baker, Joe, Jr. Causes of Failure in Performance Appraisal & Supervision: A Guide to Analysis & Evaluation for Human Resources Professionals. LC 87-37571. 172p. 1988. 49.95 (0-89930-348-X, BKA/, Quorum Bks) Greenwood.

Baker, Joe. Coping with Drug Abuse: A Lifeline for Parents. LC 82-12723. (Illus.). 60p. 1982. pap. 7.95 (0-943690-00-5) DARE.

Baker, Joel E., ed. Atmospheric Deposition of Contaminants to the Great Lakes & Coastal Waters: Proceedings from a Session at SETAC's 15th Annual Meeting, 30 October-3 November 1994, Denver, Colorado. LC 97-17289. (SETAC Technical Publications Ser.). (Illus.). 451p. 1997. 80.00 (1-880611-10-4, SETAC Pr) SETAC.

Baker, John. Henry Lee McFee & Formalist Realism in American Still Life. LC 86-47721. (Illus.). 152p. 1987. 50.00 (0-8387-5110-5) Bucknell U Pr.

— Mauchline Ware. (Album Ser.: No. 140). (Illus.). 32p. 1998. pap. 6.25 (0-85263-734-9, Pub. by Shire Pubns) Parkwest Pubns.

— The Peregrine. LC 67-23049. 191p. 1987. reprint ed. pap. 16.95 (0-89301-115-0) U of Idaho Pr.

— Practical Indonesian: A Communication Guide. (IND.). 70p. 1992. pap. 2.95 (0-945971-52-4) Periplus.

— Practical Indonesian: A Communication Guide. Stachels, Michael, tr. from IND. (GER.). 70p. 1992. pap. 2.95 (0-945971-53-2) Periplus.

— Practical Indonesian: A Communication Guide. (DUT.). 70p. 1992. pap. 2.95 (0-945971-54-0); pap. 2.95 (0-945971-55-9) Periplus.

***Baker, John.** Why the History of English Law Has Not Been Finished: An Inaugural Lecture. 31p. (C). 1999. pap. text 9.95 (0-521-66397-0) Cambridge U Pr.

Baker, John & Baker, Ann. From Puzzles to Projects: Solving Problems All the Way. LC 92-46099. (Illus.). 129p. (C). 1993. reprint ed. pap. text 19.50 (0-435-08337-6, 08337) Heinemann.

Baker, John, jt. auth. see Wade, Michael G.

Baker, John, jt. auth. see Warren, Rick.

Baker, John A. The Faith of a Christian. pap. write for info. (0-232-51739-8) S Asia.

— Italian Communism: The Road to Legitimacy & Autonomy. (Illus.). 283p. (Orig.). (C). 1994. pap. text 45.00 (0-7881-1112-4) DIANE Pub.

Baker, John A. & Collins, Mary S. A Bibliography of Completed Research on Administration of Physical Education & Athletics 1971-1982. Zeigler, Earle F., ed. (Monograph Series on Sport & Physical Education Management). 77p. (C). 1995. pap. text 5.80 (0-87563-562-8) Stipes.

Baker, John A. & Zarriello, Jean. A Bibliography of Completed Research & Scholarly Endeavor Relating to Management in the Allied Professions (1980-1990 Inclusive) Zeigler, Earle F., ed. (Monograph Series on Sport & Physical Education Management). 47p. (C). 1995. pap. text 5.60 (0-87563-565-2) Stipes.

Baker, John C. Directors & Their Functions. LC 73-1990. (Big Business; Economic Power in a Free Society Ser.). 1973. reprint ed. 12.95 (0-405-05074-7) Ayer.

— Farm Broadcasting: The First Sixty Years. LC 80-24623. 354p. reprint ed. pap. 109.80 (0-608-16689-8, 202706400053) Bks Demand.

— John C. Baker: An Oral History. LC 96-7363. 1996. write for info. (0-9650743-0-7); pap. write for info. (0-9650743-1-5) Ohio Univ Lib.

— Non-Proliferation Incentives for Russia & Ukraine. LC 98-101324. (Adelphi Papers: No. 309). (Illus.). 92p. (Orig.). 1997. pap. text 32.00 (0-19-829371-2) OUP.

— Trading Away Security? The Clinton Administration's 1994 Decision on Satellite Imaging Exports. (Pew Case Studies in International Affairs). 50p. (C). 1997. pap. text 3.50 (1-56927-222-0) Geo U Inst Dplmcy.

***Baker, John C., et al.** Commercial Observation Satellites: At the Leading Edge of Global Transparency. LC 00-42512. 2000. write for info. (0-8330-2872-3) Rand Corp.

Baker, John C., jt. auth. see Berman, Robert P.

Baker, John D., jt. auth. see Gardner, Floyd M.

Baker, John F. Federal Constitution: An Essay. vi, 126p. 1987. reprint ed. 27.50 (0-8377-1944-5, Rothman) W S Hein.

***Baker, John F.** Literary Agents: A Writer's Introduction. LC 98-50769. 256p. 1999. pap. 14.95 (0-02-861740-1, Pub. by Macmillan) S&S Trade.

Baker, John F., et al. The Steel Skeleton, Vol. 2: Plastic Behaviour & Design. LC 54-3769. 447p. reprint ed. pap. 127.40 (0-608-12283-1, 2024427) Bks Demand.

Baker, John H. The Common Law Tradition: Lawyers, Books & the Law. LC 99-32559. 1999. 70.00 (1-85285-181-3) Hambledon Press.

— Monuments of Endlesse Labours: English Canonists & Their Work, 1300-1900. LC 97-45674. 1998. 45.00 (1-85285-167-8) Hambledon Press.

Baker, John M. American House Styles: A Concise Guide. 160p. 1994. 21.95 (0-393-03421-6) Norton.

***Baker, John R.** Advances in Parasitology. 448p. (C). 1999. 109.95 (0-12-031742-7) Acad Pr.

— Advances in Parasitology, Vol. 45. Vol. 45. (Illus.). 272p. 2000. 139.95 (0-12-031745-1) Acad Pr.

— Advances in Parasitology, Vol. 46. Vol. 46. (Illus.). 224p. 2000. 109.95 (0-12-031746-X) Acad Pr.

Baker, John R. The Freedom of Science: An Original Anthology. LC 74-25150. (History, Philosophy & Sociology of Science Ser.). 1975. reprint ed. 23.95 (0-405-06636-8) Ayer.

— Race. (Illus.). 643p. (C). 1981. reprint ed. 25.00 (0-936396-04-0) Natl Vanguard.

Baker, John R., et al, eds. Advances in Parasitology, Vol. 34. (Illus.). 299p. 1994. text 104.00 (0-12-031734-6) Acad Pr.

— Advances in Parasitology, Vol. 35. (Illus.). 387p. 1995. text 90.00 (0-12-031735-4) Acad Pr.

— Advances in Parasitology, Vol. 36. (Illus.). 440p. 1995. text 95.00 (0-12-031736-2) Acad Pr.

— Advances in Parasitology, Vol. 37. (Illus.). 360p. 1996. text 69.95 (0-12-031737-0) Acad Pr.

— Advances in Parasitology, Vol. 38. (Illus.). 384p. 1996. text 75.00 (0-12-031738-9) Acad Pr.

— Advances in Parasitology, Vol. 39. (Illus.). 368p. 1997. text 99.95 (0-12-031739-7) Morgan Kaufmann.

— Advances in Parasitology, Vol. 40. (Illus.). 448p. 1998. boxed set 99.95 (0-12-031740-0) Morgan Kaufmann.

— Advances in Parasitology, Vol. 41. (Illus.). 352p. (C). 1998. text 99.95 (0-12-031741-9) Acad Pr.

***Baker, John R., et al, eds.** Advances in Parasitology Vol. 44. 330p. 1999. 99.95 (0-12-031744-3) Acad Pr.

Baker, John R. & Muller, J. R., eds. Advances in Parasitology, Vol. 33. (Illus.). 299p. 1994. text 104.00 (0-12-031733-8) Acad Pr.

Baker, John R. & Muller, Ralph, eds. Advances in Parasitology, Vol. 28. (Serial Publication Ser.). 300p. 1989. text 104.00 (0-12-031728-1) Acad Pr.

Baker, John R. & Muller, Ralph L., eds. Advances in Parasitology, Vol. 25. (Serial Publication Ser.). 352p. 1986. text 104.00 (0-12-031725-7) Acad Pr.

— Advances in Parasitology, Vol. 26. (Serial Publication Ser.). 300p. 1987. text 104.00 (0-12-031726-5) Acad Pr.

— Advances in Parasitology, Vol. 31. (Illus.). 444p. 1992. text 104.00 (0-12-031731-1) Acad Pr.

— Advances in Parasitology, Vol. 32. (Illus.). 455p. 1993. text 104.00 (0-12-031732-X) Acad Pr.

Baker, John R., et al. Advances in Parasitology, Vol. 43. (Advances in Parasitology Ser.). (Illus.). 344p. 1999. 109.95 (0-12-031743-5) Acad Pr.

Baker, John R., jt. auth. see Bach, Peter H.

Baker, John R., jt. auth. see Kreier, Julius P.

Baker, John R., jt. ed. see Kreier, Julius P.

Baker, John S., et al. Halls Criminal Law: 1993 Statutory Appendix. 5th ed. 217p. 1993. pap. text 10.00 (*0-87215-671-0*, 11729-10, MICHIE) LEXIS Pub.

Baker, John S., jt. ed. see Levasseur, Alain A.

Baker, Johnny, jt. auth. see Baker, Ann.

Baker, Jon. Brothers Keeper 3. (J). 1999. pap. 3.99 (*0-671-03549-5*) S&S Trade.

Baker, Jon & Illiff, Peter. Varsity Blues. 1999. per. 5.99 (*0-671-03568-1*) PB.

Baker, Jonathan. Step-by-Step Art School: Still Life. 144p. 1993. 14.98 (*1-55521-829-6*) Bk Sales Inc.

Baker, Jonathan, ed. Rural-Urban Dynamics in Francophone Africa. 199p. 1997. pap. text. write for info. (*91-7106-401-X*) Transaction Pubs.

— Small Town Africa: Studies in Rural-Urban Interaction. (Scandinavian Institute of African Studies). 268p. 1990. 55.00 (*91-7106-305-6*) Coronet Bks.

Baker, Jonathan & Pedersen, Poul, eds. The Rural-Urban Interface in Africa: Expansion & Adaptation. (Seminar Proceedings Ser.: 27). 318p. (Orig.). 1992. pap. text 29.95 (*91-7106-376-5*) Transaction Pubs.

Baker, Jonathan & Pedersen, Poul O., eds. The Rural-Urban Interface in Africa: Expansion & Adaptation. (Scandinavian Institute of African Studies: No. 27). 320p. (Orig.). 1992. pap. 77.50 (*91-7106-329-3*) Coronet Bks.

Baker-Jones, Leslie. The Tivyside Gentry. 1997. pap. 67.95 (*0-8464-4582-4*) Beekman Pubs.

— The Tivyside Gentry. 1997. 68.00 (*1-85902-381-9*, Pub. by Gomer Pr) St Mut.

Baker, Joseph E. Past & Present of Alameda County, California, Vol. I. (Illus.). 456p. 1993. reprint ed. lib. bdg. 48.00 (*0-8328-2935-8*) Higginson Bk Co.

— Past & Present of Alameda County, California, Vol. II. (Illus.). 589p. 1993. reprint ed. lib. bdg. 59.50 (*0-8328-2936-6*) Higginson Bk Co.

Baker, Joseph O. The Ethics of Life & Death with Heinrich von Kleist. LC 91-2973. (American University Studies: Germanic Languages & Literature: Ser. I, Vol. 96). 124p. (C). 1992. text 36.95 (*0-8204-1687-8*) P Lang Pubng.

Baker, Joseph O., jt. ed. see Stott, Michelle.

Baker, Joseph T. & Murphy, Vreni. Compounds from Marine Organisms, Vol. 2. (Section B, Handbook of Marine Science Ser.). 240p. 1981. 135.00 (*0-8493-0214-5*, GC24, CRC Reprint) Franklin.

Baker, Joseph T. & Murphy, Vreni, eds. Handbook of Marine Science: Section B, Compounds from Marine Organisms, Vol. 1. 216p. 1976. 121.95 (*0-8493-0213-7*, GC24) CRC Pr.

Baker, Josephine & Bouillon, Jo. Josephine. (Illus.). 302p. 1995. pap. 12.00 (*1-56924-978-4*) Marlowe & Co.

Baker, Judith, ed. Group Rights. (Studies in Philosophy). 208p. (C). 1994. text 45.00 (*0-8020-2975-2*); pap. text 17.95 (*0-8020-6945-2*) U of Toronto Pr.

Baker, Judith H. The Year 2000 Project Office Handbook: Year 2000 & Beyond. (Illus.). 100p. 1998. 25.00 (*1-57914-030-0*) Campbell-Smith.

Baker, Judith J. Activity-Based Costing & Activity-Based Management in Health Care. LC 97-38539. 416p. 1998. 69.00 (*0-8342-1115-7*) Aspen Pub.

— Prospective Payment for Home Health Agencies. 522p. Date not set. ring bd. 159.00 (*0-8342-1313-3*, 13133) Aspen Pub.

— Prospective Payment for Home Health Agencies. LC 98-38051. 300p. 1998. 69.00 (*0-8342-1111-4*, 11114) Aspen Pub.

— Prospective Payment for Long Term Care: An Annuel Guide. 300p. 1998. 69.00 (*0-8342-1142-4*, 11424) Aspen Pub.

***Baker, Judith J. & Baker, R. W.** Health Care Finance. LC 99-38261. 263p. 1999. 59.00 (*0-8342-1206-4*) Aspen Pub.

Baker, Judy L. Poverty Reduction & Human Development in the Caribbean. LC HC1551.Z9P613. (World Bank Discussion Papers: No. 366). 229p. 1997. pap. 22.00 (*0-8213-3970-2*, 13970) World Bank.

Baker, Judy L. & Grosh, Margaret E. Measuring the Effects of Geographic Targeting on Poverty Reduction. LC 93-33092. (Living Standards Measurement Study Working Papers: No. 99). 42p. 1994. pap. 22.00 (*0-8213-2666-X*, 12666) World Bank.

Baker, Judy L., jt. auth. see Grosh, Margaret E.

***Baker, Julie.** Time Out for Holiness at Home. 2000. pap. 7.99 (*0-7814-3461-0*) Chariot Victor.

— Time Out for Holiness at Work. 2000. pap. 7.99 (*0-7814-3462-9*) Chariot Victor.

— Time Out for Prayer. (Time Out for Women Ser.). 2000. 12.99 (*0-7814-3409-2*); write for info. (*0-7814-3466-1*) Chariot Victor.

Baker, Julie P., jt. auth. see Baker, T. Lindsay.

Baker, Julie P., jt. ed. see Baker, T. Lindsay.

Baker, Juliette, adapted by. The Pope Answers: John Paul II's Encyclical Letter "The Mission of Christ the Redeemer" adapted ed. 70p. (C). 1990. 29.00 (*0-85439-405-2*, Pub. by St Paul Pubns) St Mut.

Baker, Justine C. & Martin, Francis G. A Neural Network Guide to Teaching. LC 98-65079. (Fastback Ser.: No. 431). 50p. 1998. pap. 3.00 (*0-87367-631-9*, FB#431) Phi Delta Kappa.

Baker, K., ed. The French Revolution & the Creation of Modern Political Culture Vol. 1: The Political Culture of the Old Regime. 583p. 1987. 172.00 (*0-08-034258-2*, Pergamon Pr) Elsevier.

Baker, K., et al, eds. The French Revolution & the Creation of Modern Political Culture, 4 vols. 1994. 535.00 (*0-08-042409-0*) Elsevier.

Baker, K. & Fane, Xenia F. Understanding & Guiding Young Children. 3rd ed. LC 67-4932. 1975. 26.48 (*0-13-935825-0*) P-H.

Baker, Kage. In the Garden of Iden: A Novel of the Company. LC 97-23284. 336p. 1998. 23.00 (*0-15-100299-1*) Harcourt.

— In the Garden of Iden: A Novel of the Company. 1998. mass mkt. 5.99 (*0-380-73179-7*, Eos) Morrow Avon.

— Mendoza in Hollywood: A Novel of the Company. LC 99-14949. 352p. 2000. 24.00 (*0-15-100448-X*, Harvest Bks) Harcourt.

***Baker, Kage.** Sky Coyote. 304p. 2000. mass mkt. 5.99 (*0-380-73180-0*, Avon Bks) Morrow Avon.

Baker, Kage. Sky Coyote: A Novel of the Company. LC 98-16833. 352p. (C). 1999. 23.00 (*0-15-100354-8*) Harcourt.

***Baker, Kage.** Sometimes. LC 98-15561. (Illus.). 352p. (J). (gr. k-2). 1999. pap. text 24.00 (*0-15-100449-8*) Harcourt.

***Baker, Karen & Manzi, Nina.** Major State Aids & Taxes (In Minnesota) A Comparative Analysis (1997 Update) (Illus.). 230p. 1999. pap. text 35.00 (*0-7881-8160-2*) DIANE Pub.

Baker, Karen L. Seneca. LC 95-35846. (Illus.). 32p. (J). (ps up). 1997. 15.00 (*0-688-14030-0*, Grenwillow Bks) HarpC Child Bks.

Baker, Katherine. Twenty-Six World Travel Adventures. Reiter, Irene, ed. LC 97-76358. (Illus.). 192p. 1998. pap. 12.95 (*1-883294-62-2*) Masthof Pr.

Baker, Katherine H. Bioremediation. 1993. 69.95 (*0-07-003360-9*) McGraw.

***Baker, Kathleen.** Indigenous Land Management in West Africa. (Oxford Geographical & Environmental Studies). (Illus.). 260p. 2000. text 65.00 (*0-19-823393-0*) OUP.

Baker, Kathleen M., jt. ed. see Chapman, Graham P.

Baker, Keith. Big Fat Hen. LC 93-19160. (Illus.). 32p. (J). (ps-1). 1994. 15.00 (*0-15-292869-3*) Harcourt.

— Big Fat Hen. LC 93-19160. (Illus.). 32p. (J). 1997. pap. 5.95 (*0-15-201331-8*, Harcourt Child Bks) Harcourt.

— Big Fat Hen. LC 93-19160. (Illus.). 32p. (J). 1999. pap. 6.00 (*0-15-201951-0*) Harcourt.

— Cat Tricks. LC 96-47240. (Illus.). 44p. (J). (ps-1). 1997. 15.00 (*0-15-292857-X*) Harcourt.

***Baker, Keith.** Cat Tricks. (Illus.). 44p. (ps up). 2000. pap. 7.00 (*0-15-202416-6*, Harcourt Child Bks) Harcourt.

Baker, Keith. The Dove's Letter. LC 87-8530. (Illus.). 32p. (J). (ps-3). 1988. 14.95 (*0-15-224133-7*, Harcourt Child Bks) Harcourt.

— The Dove's Letter. LC 87-8530. (Illus.). 32p. (J). (ps-3). 1993. reprint ed. pap. 5.95 (*0-15-224134-5*, Voyager Bks) Harcourt.

— Hide & Snake. LC 90-19967. (Illus.). 32p. (J). (ps-3). 1991. 12.95 (*0-15-233986-8*) Harcourt.

— Hide & Snake. LC 90-19967. (Illus.). 32p. (J). (ps-3). 1995. pap. 6.00 (*0-15-200225-1*, Voyager Bks) Harcourt.

***Baker, Keith.** Hide & Snake. 30p. (J). 1999. 5.95 (*0-15-202229-5*, Red Wagon Bks) Harcourt.

Baker, Keith. Hide & Snake. 1991. 11.20 (*0-606-07646-8*, Pub. by Turtleback) Demco.

— Inheritance: A Novel. LC 97-32028. 288p. 1998. 24.00 (*0-688-15321-6*, Wm Morrow) Morrow Avon.

— The Magic Fan. LC 88-18727. (Illus.). 32p. (J). (gr. k-3). 1989. 14.95 (*0-15-250750-7*) Harcourt.

— The Magic Fan. (Illus.). 32p. (J). (gr. k-5). 1997. pap. 7.00 (*0-15-200983-3*, Voyager Bks) Harcourt.

— The Magic Fan. 1997. 12.20 (*0-606-12408-X*, Pub. by Turtleback) Demco.

— The Magic Fan. 93rd ed. 1993. pap. text 17.10 (*0-15-300334-0*, Harcourt Child Bks) Harcourt.

— Public Budgeting Using One-Two-Three. 1988. 49.95 incl. disk (*1-55828-143-6*, MIS Pr) IDG Bks.

— Quack & Count! LC 98-7924. 24p. (J). 1999. 14.00 (*0-15-292858-8*, Harcourt Child Bks) Harcourt.

— Quien Es la Bestia? Ada, Alma Flor, tr. from ENG. LC 93-49341.Tr. of Who Is the Beast?. (SPA., Illus.). 32p. (J). (ps-3). 1994. pap. 6.00 (*0-15-200185-9*) Harcourt.

— Sometimes. LC 98-15561. (Green Light Readers Ser.). (Illus.). 20p. (J). 1999. pap. 3.95 (*0-15-202002-0*) Harcourt.

***Baker, Keith.** Sometimes. (Green Light Readers Ser.). (Illus.). (J). 2000. 10.95 (*0-15-202387-9*) Harcourt.

Baker, Keith. Who Is the Beast? LC 89-29365. (Illus.). 32p. (J). (ps-2). 1990. 14.95 (*0-15-296057-0*) Harcourt.

— Who Is the Beast? LC 89-29365. (Illus.). 32p. (J). (ps-3). 1994. pap. 6.00 (*0-15-200122-0*) Harcourt.

— Who Is the Beast? LC 89-29365. (Big Bks.). (Illus.). 32p. (J). (ps-3). 1991. reprint ed. pap. 23.95 (*0-15-296059-7*) Harcourt.

Baker, Keith, jt. auth. see Rossell, Christine H.

Baker, Keith F. & Daublon, Georges. Buying & Selling a Residence in France. 130p. (C). 1993. 210.00 (*0-85459-809-X*, Pub. by Tolley Pubng) St Mut.

Baker, Keith M. Condorcet: From Natural Philosophy to Social Mathematics. LC 74-5725. 538p. (C). 1982. pap. text 20.50 (*0-226-03533-6*) U Ch Pr.

— Condorcet: From Natural Philosophy to Social Mathematics. LC 74-5725. 552p. Date not set. reprint ed. pap. 171.20 (*0-608-20982-1*, 205451000003) Bks Demand.

Baker, Keith M., ed. Condorcet: Selected Writings. LC 75-38680. (Library of Liberal Arts: No. 159). 1976. pap. 12.81 (*0-672-60381-0*, Bobbs) Macmillan.

Baker, Keith M., et al, eds. The French Revolution & the Creation of Modern Political Culture Vol. 4: The Terror: International Conference on the Terror in the French Revolution, Stanford University, CA, 10-13 December, 1992. 424p. 1994. 46.00 (*0-08-041387-0*) Elsevier.

Baker, Keith M., ed. see Chartier, Roger.

Baker, Keith M., ed. see Forrest, Alan.

Baker, Keith M., ed. see Popkin, Jeremy D.

***Baker, Ken.** The Brave Little Monster. 32p. (J). (ps-3). 2001. lib. bdg. 14.89 (*0-06-028699-7*) HarpC Child Bks.

— A Man Made. 2001. 18.95 (*1-58542-083-2*, Tarcher Putnam) Putnam Pub Group.

Baker, Kendall L., et al. Germany Transformed: Political Culture & the New Politics. LC 80-18244. (Illus.). 384p. (C). 1981. 46.50 (*0-674-35315-3*) HUP.

Baker, Kenneth. Chords & Progressions for Jazz & Popular Keyboard. 128p. pap. 17.95 (*0-8256-2286-7*, AM 31584) Omnibus NY.

— Classical Themes. (Home Organist Library; Vol. 13). (Illus.). 80p. 1992. pap. 17.95 (*0-7119-2963-7*, AM88924) Music Sales.

***Baker, Kenneth.** Climbing Back to America. LC 99-63239. (Illus.). 202p. 1999. pap. 17.95 (*1-891601-14-8*) Ladies Caliber.

Baker, Kenneth. The Complete Keyboard Player, Bk. 1. (Illus.). 48p. 1985. pap. 9.95 (*0-8256-2445-2*, AM38308) Music Sales.

— The Complete Keyboard Player, Bk. 2. (Illus.). 48p. 1985. pap. 9.95 (*0-8256-2446-0*, AM38316) Music Sales.

— The Complete Keyboard Player, Bk. 3. (Illus.). 48p. 1985. pap. 9.95 (*0-8256-2447-9*, AM38324) Music Sales.

— The Complete Keyboard Player: Chord Book. (Illus.). 32p. 1987. pap. 7.95 (*0-7119-1189-4*, AM66507) Music Sales.

— The Complete Keyboard Player: Classics. (Illus.). 40p. 1987. pap. 7.95 (*0-7119-1288-2*, AM67661) Music Sales.

— The Complete Keyboard Player: Omnibus Edition (Included Soundsheet), 3 bks., set. (Illus.). 144p. pap. 21.95 (*0-8256-1063-X*, AM 60476) Omnibus NY.

— The Complete Keyboard Player: Richard Clayderman. (Illus.). 40p. 1987. pap. 7.95 (*0-8256-1159-8*, AM66002) Music Sales.

— Complete Keyboard Player Christmas Songs. (Illus.). 40p. pap. 7.95 (*0-8256-1169-5*, AM65954) Music Sales.

— The Complete Organ Player: Hymn Book. (Illus.). 48p. 1985. pap. 11.95 (*0-7119-0565-7*, AM37680) Music Sales.

— The Complete Organ Player: Marches. (Illus.). 48p. 1985. pap. 8.95 (*0-7119-1129-0*, AM65822) Music Sales.

***Baker, Kenneth.** Complete Organ Player Songbook. Vol. 2. Vol. 2. (Illus.). 2000. pap. 10.95 (*0-7119-0360-3*) Music Sales.

Baker, Kenneth. The Complete Piano Player, Bk. 1. Vol. 1. (Illus.). 48p. 1984. pap. 9.95 (*0-8256-2434-7*, AM34828) Music Sales.

— The Complete Piano Player, Bk. 2. (Illus.). 48p. 1984. pap. 9.95 (*0-8256-2435-5*, AM34836) Music Sales.

— The Complete Piano Player, Bk. 3. Vol. 3. (Illus.). 48p. 1984. pap. 9.95 (*0-8256-2436-3*, AM34844) Music Sales.

— The Complete Piano Player, Bk. 4. (Illus.). 48p. 1984. pap. 9.95 (*0-8256-2437-1*, AM34851) Music Sales.

— The Complete Piano Player, Bk. 5. Vol. 5. (Illus.). 48p. 1984. pap. 9.95 (*0-8256-2438-X*, AM34869) Music Sales.

— The Complete Piano Player: Children's Pieces. (Illus.). 48p. 1988. pap. 12.95 (*0-7119-1132-0*, AM65855) Music Sales.

— The Complete Piano Player: Omnibus Edition. (Illus.). 240p. 1996. pap. 21.95 (*0-8256-2439-8*, AM 39645) Music Sales.

— The Complete Piano Player: Style Book. (Illus.). 48p. 1984. pap. 15.95 (*0-7119-0461-8*, AM35338) Music Sales.

— Fundamentals of Catholicism: Grace, the Church, the Sacraments, Eschatology, Vol. 3. LC 82-80297. 388p. (Orig.). 1983. pap. 14.95 (*0-89870-027-2*) Ignatius Pr.

— Fundamentals of Catholicism: The Creed, the Commandments, Vol. I. LC 82-80297. 282p. (Orig.). 1982. pap. 14.95 (*0-89870-017-5*) Ignatius Pr.

— Minimalism: Art of Circumstance. (Illus.). 144p. 1997. 45.00 (*0-89659-887-X*) Abbeville Pr.

— The U. C. System for Producing Healthy Container-Grown Plants. 332p. (C). 1985. text 80.00 (*0-7855-0034-0*, Pub. by Surrey Beatty & Sons) St Mut.

Baker, Kenneth, ed. Complete Organ Player: Songbook Three. (Illus.). 48p. 1988. pap. 8.95 (*0-8256-1159-7*, AM34083) Music Sales.

Baker, Kenneth, selected by. The Complete Keyboard Player Songbook, No. 1. (Illus.). 40p. 1986. pap. 7.95 (*0-8256-1075-3*, AM39116) Music Sales.

— The Complete Keyboard Player Songbook, No. 2. (Illus.). 40p. 1986. pap. 7.95 (*0-8256-1188-1*, AM39124) Music Sales.

— The Complete Keyboard Player Songbook, No. 3. (Illus.). 40p. 1986. pap. 7.95 (*0-8256-1189-X*, AM39132) Music Sales.

— The Complete Organ Player: Classical Pieces. (Illus.). 48p. 1985. pap. 8.95 (*0-7119-0757-9*, AM60559) Music Sales.

— Complete Organ Player: Songbook Two. (Illus.). 48p. 1988. pap. 8.95 (*0-8256-1198-9*, AM33739) Music Sales.

— Complete Organ Player Songbook: Songbook One. (Illus.). 48p. 1988. pap. 10.95 (*0-8256-1197-0*, AM33721) Music Sales.

— The Joy of Organ Music, Bk. 2. (Illus.). 80p. 1979. pap. 11.95 (*0-7119-0130-9*, AM34380) Music Sales.

— Twenty-Five Favourite Classics Everybody Loves to Hear. (Illus.). 160p. 1975. pap. 19.95 (*0-8256-2688-9*, AM21569) Music Sales.

— Twenty-Five Favourite Classics Everybody Loves to Hear, Vol. 2. (Illus.). 160p. 1975. pap. 19.95 (*0-8256-2689-7*, AM21577) Music Sales.

Baker, Kenneth, jt. auth. see Armstrong, Richard.

Baker, Kenneth, jt. auth. see Plous, Phyllis.

Baker, Kenneth A. Ephesians: Uniting Against Evil. (Revelation Ser.). 64p. (Orig.). 1996. pap., teacher ed. 6.75 (*1-56212-224-X*, 1310-0440) CRC Pubns.

Baker, Kenneth F. Inside the Bible. LC 98-71260. 1998. pap. text 14.95 (*0-89870-665-3*) Ignatius Pr.

Baker, Kenneth F. & Cook, R. James. Biological Control of Plant Pathogens. LC 73-18420. (Biology of Plant Pathogens Books Ser.). 451p. reprint ed. pap. 139.90 (*0-8357-7230-6*, 205554800028) Bks Demand.

Baker, Kenneth F., jt. auth. see Cook, R. James.

Baker, Kenneth P., et al, eds. Annual Review of Phytopathology, Vol. 10. LC 63-8847. (Illus.). 1972. text 42.00 (*0-8243-1310-0*) Annual Reviews.

— Annual Review of Phytopathology, Vol. 11. LC 63-8847. (Illus.). 1973. text 42.00 (*0-8243-1311-9*) Annual Reviews.

— Annual Review of Phytopathology, Vol. 12. LC 63-8847. (Illus.). 1974. text 42.00 (*0-8243-1312-7*) Annual Reviews.

— Annual Review of Phytopathology, Vol. 13. LC 63-8847. (Illus.). 1975. text 42.00 (*0-8243-1313-5*) Annual Reviews.

— Annual Review of Phytopathology, Vol. 14. LC 63-8847. (Illus.). 1976. text 42.00 (*0-8243-1314-3*) Annual Reviews.

— Annual Review of Phytopathology, Vol. 15. LC 63-8847. (Illus.). 1977. text 42.00 (*0-8243-1315-1*) Annual Reviews.

Baker, Kenneth R. Elements of Sequencing & Scheduling. 2nd ed. (C). 1995. pap. text 45.00 (*0-9639746-1-0*) K R Baker.

Baker, Kenneth R. & Kropp, Dean H. Management Science: An Introduction to the Use of Decision Models. LC 84-21959. (Illus.). 662p. reprint ed. pap. 200.00 (*0-8357-7523-2*, 203603000097) Bks Demand.

Baker, Kenneth S. Fundamentals of Catholicism: God, Trinity, Creation, Christ, Mary, Vol. 2. LC 82-80297. 387p. (Orig.). 1983. pap. 14.95 (*0-89870-019-1*) Ignatius Pr.

Baker, Kenneth W. Alone in the Valley. LC 91-42101. 296p. 1992. 22.00 (*1-877946-17-6*) Permanent Pr.

Baker, Kenneth W., ed. see Baker, Elsa J.

Baker, Kent. Financial Management. (College Outline Ser.). 483p. (C). 1987. pap. text 14.50 (*0-15-601645-1*) Harcourt Coll Pubs.

— Finster Frets. (Illus.). 32p. (J). (ps-3). 1994. pap. 6.95 (*0-19-540899-3*) OUP.

— Finster Frets. (Illus.). (J). (gr. k-3). 1994. audio. write for info. (*0-614-17735-9*) Stoddart Publ.

— Finster Frets. unabridged ed. (Illus.). 32p. (J). (ps up). 1996. pap. 11.75 incl. audio (*0-19-541055-6*); pap. 5.95 (*0-7737-5698-1*) STDK.

— A Man Wanders Sometimes. 228p. 1989. 22.95 (*0-7737-2296-3*) Genl Dist Srvs.

Baker, Kevin. Dreamland. LC 98-39205. 528p. 1999. 26.00 (*0-06-019309-3*) HarpC.

— Dreamland. 2000. write for info. (*0-06-099580-7*) HarpC.

***Baker, Kevin.** Dreamland. 2000. mass mkt. 6.99 (*0-06-103082-1*) HarpC.

Baker, Kevin. Dreamland. 672p. 2000. mass mkt. 6.99 (*0-06-093121-3*, Torch) HarpC.

***Baker, Kevin.** Dreamland: A Novel, Set. abr. ed. 1999. audio. write for info. (*0-694-52108-6*, 694567, Pub. by HarperAudio) Lndmrk Audiobks.

— Dreamland: Australian Edition. 1999. pap. 15.50 (*0-06-095343-8*) HarpC.

Baker, Kevin. Dreamland Mobile. 1999. write for info. (*0-06-099590-4*) HarpC.

Baker, Kevin X. Message to the Incarcerated Blackman & Woman in America. 72p. (Orig.). 1997. pap. 7.00 (*1-56411-162-8*) Untd Bros & Sis.

Baker, Kim. The RVer's Bible: Everything You Need to Know about Choosing, Using, & Enjoying Your RV. LC 96-54031. 416p. 1997. pap. 19.95 (*0-684-82267-9*) Simon & Schuster.

Baker, Kim & Baker, Sunny. The Complete Idiot's Guide to Project Management. LC 97-71187. 352p. 1997. pap. 16.95 (*0-02-861745-2*, Alpha Ref) Macmillan Gen Ref.

— Eastside Eats: A Comprehensive Guide to Eastside Dining & Wineries. Chieger, Bob, ed. & intro. by. (Poor Man's Guide Ser.). (Illus.). 112p. (Orig.). 1988. pap. 8.95 (*0-930180-11-9*) Homestead Bk.

— How to Promote, Publicize & Advertise Your Growing Business: Getting the Word Out Without Spending a Fortune. LC 91-29669. 336p. 1992. 107.50 (*0-471-55194-5*); pap. 12.95 (*0-471-55193-7*) Wiley.

***Baker, Kim & Baker, Sunny.** How to Say It Online. 2001. pap. 16.00 (*0-7352-0164-1*) PH Pr.

Baker, Kim & Baker, Sunny. PageMaker 5 for Windows: A Self-Teaching Guide. 304p. 1993. pap. 22.95 (*0-471-58953-5*) Wiley.

— The Professional's Guide to QuarkXPress3 3.3 for the Macintosh: The Essential Sourcebook for Designers, Typographers, & Creative Directors. LC 94-25276. 624p. 1995. pap. 39.95 incl. cd-rom (*0-471-11439-1*) Wiley.

Baker, Kim, jt. auth. see Baker, Sunny.

Baker, Kitty, jt. auth. see Wagner, Jearnine.

Baker-Kline, Christina. Desire Lines: A Novel. LC 98-19509. 320p. 1999. 24.00 (*0-688-15107-8*, Wm Morrow) Morrow Avon.

***Baker-Kline, Christina.** Four-way Stop. 2001. write for info. (*0-688-17724-7*, Wm Morrow) Morrow Avon.

Baker-Kline, Christina, ed. Room to Grow: 22 Writers Encounter the Pleasures & Paradoxes of Raising Young Children. LC 98-56270. 1999. pap. 23.00 (*1-58238-032-5*, Whitman Coin) St Martin.

Baker-Kreuger, Sherry. Toy Fox Terrier. 192p. 1994. 9.95 (*0-86622-868-3*, KW-222) TFH Pubns.

Baker, Krystyna. Masks. 150p. 1981. pap. 20.00 (*0-89672-085-3*) Tex Tech Univ Pr.

B

— Masks. deluxe limited ed. 150p. 1981. 50.00 (*0-89672-086-1*) Tex Tech Univ Pr.

Baker, Kyle. The Cowboy Wally Show. rev. ed. (Illus.). 150p. 1996. pap. 14.95 (*1-56924-834-6*) Marlowe & Co.

— Why I Hate Saturn. Nevelow, Mark, ed. (Illus.). 208p. 1998. mass mkt. 17.95 (*0-930289-72-2*, Pub. by Warner Bks) Little.

— You Are Here. LC 99-162328. (Illus.). 160p. 1998. pap. text 19.95 (*1-56389-442-4*, Pub. by DC Comics) Time Warner.

Baker, Kyle, et al. Residents: Freak Show, the Residents. (Illus.). 80p. (Orig.). 1992. pap. 9.95 (*1-878574-32-9*) Dark Horse Comics.

— Residents: Freak Show, the Residents. limited ed. (Illus.). 80p. (Orig.). 1992. 79.95 (*1-56971-001-5*) Dark Horse Comics.

Baker, Kyle, jt. auth. see Carroll, Lewis, pseud.

Baker, L. C. History of the United States Secret Service. (Illus.). 810p. 1992. reprint ed. pap. text 45.00 (*1-55613-660-9*) Heritage Bk.

Baker, L. D., ed. see Duncan, Jerry R., et al.

Baker, L. E., jt. auth. see Geddes, Leslie A.

Baker, L. F., et al. Collage, Vol. 4. 3rd ed. 1990. pap. text, student ed. write for info. (*0-07-540838-4*) McGraw.

Baker, L. O., jt. ed. see Ryan, J. R.

Baker, L. R. I., et al. Practical Procedures in Nephrology. (Illus.). 160p. 1999. text 45.00 (*0-340-74083-3*, Pub. by E A) OUP.

Baker, L. Richard. Eternal Boundary. (Advanced Dungeons & Dragons, 2nd Edition: Planescape Adventures Ser.). 1994. 9.95 (*1-56076-843-6*) TSR Inc.

— Player's Option: Combat & Tactics; Advanced Dungeons & Dragons Rulebook. 2nd ed. 1995. 20.00 (*0-7869-0096-2*, Pub. by TSR Inc) Random.

Baker, Lafayette C. History of the United States Secret Service. LC 70-156006. (Foundations of Criminal Justice Ser.). reprint ed. 52.75 (*0-404-09106-7*) AMS Pr.

Baker, Larry. The Flamingo Rising. LC 97-73822. 309p. 1997. 4.99 (*0-375-40050-8*) Knopf.

— Flamingo Rising. 320p. 1998. pap. 12.95 (*0-345-42702-5*) Ballantine Pub Grp.

Baker, Laura. Broken in Two. 320p. 1999. pap. 5.99 (*0-312-97175-3*, St Martins Paperbacks) St Martin.

— Legend, Vol. 1. 288p. 1998. pap. 5.99 (*0-312-96662-8*, Pub. by Tor Bks) St Martin.

Baker, Laura, jt. auth. see Simmons, Suzanne.

Baker, Laurence. Nephrology. (Medico-Legal Practitioner Ser.). xv, 166p. 1998. 72.00 (*1-85941-025-1*, Pub. by Cavendish Pubng) Gaunt.

Baker, Laurence C., jt. auth. see Spetz, Joanne.

Baker, Laurence H., ed. Soft Tissue Sarcomas. (Cancer Treatment & Research Ser.). 1983. text 98.00 (*0-89838-584-9*) Kluwer Academic.

Baker, Lawrence A., ed. Environmental Chemistry of Lakes & Reservoirs. LC 93-31891. (Advances in Chemistry Ser.: No. 237). 627p. 1994. text 165.00 (*0-8412-2526-5*, Pub. by Am Chemical) OUP.

Baker, Lawrence H., et al. Biology & Therapy of Acute Leukemia. (Developments in Oncology Ser.). 1985. text 120.00 (*0-89838-728-0*) Kluwer Academic.

***Baker, Lawrence W., contrib. by.** American Civil War Reference Library: Cumulative Index. LC 99-46921. (J). 2000. 5.00 (*0-7876-3819-6*) Gale.

Baker, Lawrence W., jt. auth. see Bruno, Leonard C.

Baker, Lawrence W., ed. see Bruno, Leonard C.

Baker, Lawrence W., ed. see Hillstrom, Kevin & Hillstrom, Laurie Collier.

Baker, Lee D. From Savage to Negro: Anthropology & the Construction of Race, 1896-1954. LC 97-31602. (Illus.). 313p. 1998. 40.00 (*0-520-21167-7*, Pub. by U CA Pr); pap. 17.95 (*0-520-21168-5*, Pub. by U CA Pr) Cal Prin Full Svc.

Baker, Leonard. The Recipe for Success in Network Marketing. Fuller, Linda, ed. 128p. (Orig.). 1992. pap. text 12.00 (*0-910973-04-0*) Arrowhead AZ.

Baker, Leslie. Employee-Employer Rights: A Guide for the British Columbia Work Force. 11th ed. (Legal Ser.). 144p. 1997. pap. 10.95 (*1-55180-107-8*) Self-Counsel Pr.

Baker, Leslie, ed. see Korte, Diana & Scaer, Roberta.

Baker, Leslie A. Paris Cat. LC 97-42169. (Illus.). 32p. (J). (gr. k-3). 1999. 15.95 (*0-316-07309-1*) Little.

Baker Library Staff, ed. 1999 Harvard Business School Core Collection. 464p. 1999. pap. 65.00 (*0-87584-888-5*) Harvard Busn.

Baker Library Staff & Marsh, Sue, eds. Harvard Business School Core Collection, 1998: An Author, Title, & Subject Guide. (Reference Ser.). 430p. 1998. pap. 65.00 (*0-87584-774-9*) Harvard Busn.

Baker, Lida R., jt. auth. see Tanka, Judith.

Baker, Liliane L. The Common Doom. LC 91-67442. 183p. (Orig.). 1991. pap. text 12.95 (*1-878815-01-6*) Reflected Images.

Baker, Lillian. American & Japanese Relocation in World War II Fact, Fiction & Fallacy: The Lillian Baker Memorial Edition. Webber, Bert, ed. LC 96-43108. (Illus.). 237p. 1996. pap. 29.95 (*0-936738-03-0*) Webb Research.

— Art Nouveau & Art Deco Jewelry. (Illus.). 176p. 1997. pap. 9.95 (*0-89145-158-7*, 1278) Collector Bks.

— Baker's Encyclopedia of Hatpins & Hatpin Holders. LC 97-39205. 204p. 1998. 39.95 (*0-7643-0485-2*) Schiffer.

— Dishonoring America: The Falsification of World War II History. LC 94-30725. (Illus.). 168p. 1994. pap. 13.95 (*0-936738-84-7*) Webb Research.

— Fifty Years of Collectible Fashion Jewelry. (Illus.). 192p. 1995. 19.95 (*0-89145-319-9*, 1716) Collector Bks.

— Hatpins & Hatpins Holders. (Illus.). 160p. 1995. pap. 9.95 (*0-89145-224-9*, 1424) Collector Bks.

— The Japanning of America: Redress & Reparations Demands by Japanese-Americans. LC 89-49617. (Illus.). 254p. 1991. pap. 14.95 (*0-936738-14-6*) Webb Research.

— One Hundred Years of Collectible Jewelry. (Illus.). 169p. 1997. pap. 9.95 (*0-89145-066-1*, 1181) Collector Bks.

Baker, Linda. Modern Toys, 1930-1980. (Illus.). 270p. 1996. 19.95 (*0-89145-277-X*, 1540) Collector Bks.

— Soul Contracts: How They Affect Your Life & Your Relationships. LC 98-67602. 180p. 1998. pap. 12.95 (*1-892193-01-9*, Patchwrk Pr) Tenacity Pr.

Baker, Linda, et al, eds. Developing Engaged Readers in School & Home Communities. 336p. 1995. text 79.95 (*0-8058-1596-1*) L Erlbaum Assocs.

— Developing Engaged Readers in School & Home Communities. 336p. 1996. pap. 39.95 (*0-8058-1976-2*) L Erlbaum Assocs.

***Baker, Linda, et al, eds.** Engaging Young Readers: Promoting Achievement & Motivation. LC 99-56748. (Solving Problems in the Teaching of Literacy Ser.). 328p. 2000. lib. bdg. 45.00 (*1-57230-554-1*, C0554) Guilford Pubns.

Baker, Linda, jt. auth. see Garing, Ward.

Baker, Linda F., jt. auth. see Curro, Michael J.

Baker, Linda P. The Irda. (DragonLance Lost Histories Ser.). (Illus.). 320p. (Orig.). 1995. pap. 5.99 (*0-7869-0138-1*, Pub. by TSR Inc) Random.

— Tears of the Night Sky. (DragonLance Chaos War Ser.). 1998. pap. 5.99 (*0-7869-1185-9*, Pub. by TSR Inc) Random.

Baker, Lionel, ed. Selected Papers on Optical Transfer Function - Foundation & Theory. LC 92-19409. (Milestone Ser.: Vol. 59). 1992. pap. 45.00 (*0-8194-0994-4*) SPIE.

— Selected Papers on Optical Transfer Function - Foundation & Theory. LC 92-19409. (Milestone Ser.: Vol. MS 59/HC). 1992. 55.00 (*0-8194-0993-6*) SPIE.

— Selected Papers on Optical Transfer Function - Measurement. LC 92-19408. (Milestone Ser.: Vol. 60). 1992. pap. 45.00 (*0-8194-0996-0*) SPIE.

Baker, Lisa S. The Losers Club. 288p. 2000. text 23.95 (*0-312-24216-6*, Minotaur) St Martin.

Baker, Liza, ed. see Mouse Works Staff.

Baker, Lois & Anderson, Beth. Inpatient Pediatric Nursing. LC 94-34478. (Plans of Care for Specialty Practice Ser.). 600p. (C). 1994. pap. 51.95 (*0-8273-6005-3*) Delmar.

Baker, Lois, tr. see Fan Cheng-da.

Baker, Lori. Crazy Water: Six Fictions. LC 95-50172. 192p. (C). 1996. pap. 14.95 (*0-8147-1284-3*); text 25.00 (*0-8147-1283-5*) NYU Pr.

— Minor Archeologies. (Isthmus Project Ser.). 24p. 1999. pap. 5.00 (*0-945926-52-9*) Paradigm RI.

— Scraps. 96p. 1996. pap. 10.00 (*0-945926-33-2*, Pub. by Paradigm RI) SPD-Small Pr Dist.

— Scraps. aut. ed. 96p. 1996. pap. 25.00 (*0-945926-34-0*, Pub. by Paradigm RI) SPD-Small Pr Dist.

Baker, Lorian, jt. auth. see Cantwell, Dennis.

Baker, Lou & Smith, Bradley J. Parallel Programming. (Illus.). 352p. 1996. 55.00 (*0-07-912259-0*) McGraw.

Baker, Louis. Artificial Intelligence in the Ada Environment. (Illus.). 320p. 1989. text 39.95 (*0-07-003350-1*) McGraw.

— C-Tools for Scientists & Engineers. (Illus.). 320p. 1989. text 34.95 (*0-07-003355-2*) McGraw.

— Math Function Handbook. 1991. pap. text 49.95 incl. disk (*0-07-911158-0*) McGraw.

— More C Tools for Scientists & Engineers. (Computing That Works Ser.). 304p. 1991. pap. 34.95 (*0-07-003358-7*) McGraw.

Baker, Louise. Out on a Limb. (American Autobiography Ser.). 213p. 1995. reprint ed. lib. bdg. 79.00 (*0-7812-8446-5*) Rprt Serv.

Baker, Lucia F. Collage: Lectures Litteraires, Vol. 2. 4th ed. (C). 1995. pap. 34.38 (*0-07-005167-4*) McGraw.

Baker, Lucia F. & Moran, Ruth A. Collage de Grammaire, Vol. 1. 4th ed. (C). 1995. pap., wbk. ed., lab manual ed. 28.13 (*0-07-005163-1*) McGraw.

Baker, Lucia F., et al. Collage: Lectures Litteraires. 4th ed. LC 95-22290. 1995. write for info. (*0-614-32357-6*) McGraw.

— Collage: Varietes Culturelles, Vol. 3. 4th ed. LC 95-20365. 244p. (C). 1995. pap. 34.38 (*0-07-005168-2*) McGraw.

— Montage. 2nd ed. (C). 1991. text 39.25 (*0-07-003469-9*) McGraw.

— Montage, Deuxieme Niveau. 3rd ed. (C). 1996. pap., wbk. ed., lab manual ed. 31.25 (*0-07-006029-0*) McGraw.

— Montage, Deuxieme Niveau. 3rd ed. 528p. (C). 1997. pap. 50.31 (*0-07-006020-7*) McGraw.

Baker, Lucinda. The Painted Lady. LC 98-96335. 192p. 1998. lib. bdg. 18.95 (*0-8034-9315-0*, Avalon Bks) Bouregy.

Baker, Lucy. Ancient Greece. LC 98-74919. (Interfact Ser.). (Illus.). 48p. (J). (gr. 2-8). 1999. spiral bd. 15.00 incl. cd-rom (*0-7166-7234-0*) World Bk.

***Baker, Lucy.** Birds of the Caribbean. (Illus.). 70p. 1999. pap. 10.00 (*976-9501-60-3*) NoHo Inc.

— Chez Lucy. (Illus.). 77p. 1988. pap. 12.95 (*976-9501-63-8*) NoHo Inc.

— Deserts. (Interfact Ser.). (Illus.). 48p. (J). (gr. 2-8). 1999. spiral bd. write for info. incl. cd-rom (*0-7166-7203-0*) World Bk.

— Heart of Stone. (Illus.). 300p. 1999. pap. 12.95 (*976-9501-64-6*) NoHo Inc.

Baker, Lucy. Life in Rainforests. 32p. (J). (gr. 3-7). 1993. pap. 4.95 (*0-590-46131-1*) Scholastic Inc.

— Life in the Deserts. 32p. (J). (gr. 4-7). 1993. pap. 4.95 (*0-590-46129-X*) Scholastic Inc.

— Life in the Deserts. (Life in the . . . Ser.). (J). 1990. 10.15 (*0-606-05425-1*, Pub. by Turtleback) Demco.

— Life in the Oceans. 32p. (J). (gr. 4-7). 1993. pap. 4.95 (*0-590-46132-X*) Scholastic Inc.

— Life in the Oceans. (Life in the . . . Ser.). (J). 1990. 10.15 (*0-606-05426-X*, Pub. by Turtleback) Demco.

— Life in the Rainforests. (J). 1990. 10.15 (*0-606-05427-8*, Pub. by Turtleback) Demco.

***Baker, Lucy.** Oceans. (Interfact Ser.). (Illus.). (J). (gr. 2-7). 2000. spiral bd. 14.95 (*1-58728-459-6*) Two Can Pub.

Baker, Lucy. Oceans. LC 98-6814. (Interfact Ser.). (Illus.). 48p. (J). (gr. 2-8). 1997. spiral bd. 15.00 incl. cd-rom (*0-7166-7212-X*) World Bk.

— Rain Forests. LC 98-6813. (Interfact Ser.). (Illus.). 48p. (J). (gr. 2-8). 1997. write for info. incl. cd-rom (*0-7166-7230-8*) World Bk.

***Baker, Lucy.** Rainforests. (Interfact Ser.). (Illus.). (J). (gr. 2-7). 2000. 14.95 incl. cd-rom (*1-58728-461-8*) Two Can Pub.

— Senses. LC 98-74918. (Interfact Ser.). (Illus.). 48p. (J). (gr. 2-8). 1999. spiral bd. write for info. incl. cd-rom (*0-7166-7233-2*) World Bk.

— Treating Ailments with Plants & Herbs. (Illus.). 160p. 1999. pap. 12.95 (*976-9501-62-X*) NoHo Inc.

Baker, Lynda A. & Crandall, Sharon Olexa. Sick Bay, 1. LC 97-78276. 1999. 24.95 (*0-9662378-0-3*) Astoria Prodns.

Baker, Lynn A., jt. auth. see Gillette, Clayton P.

Baker, Lynne R. Explaining Attitudes: A Practical Approach to the Mind. (Cambridge Studies in Philosophy). 260p. (C). 1995. text 64.95 (*0-521-42053-9*); pap. text 23.95 (*0-521-42190-X*) Cambridge U Pr.

— Saving Belief: A Critique of Physicalism. 192p. 1988. pap. text 14.95 (*0-691-02050-7*, Pub. by Princeton U Pr) Cal Prin Full Svc.

— Saving Belief: A Critique of Physicalism. LC 87-25926. 190p. 1987. reprint ed. pap. 58.90 (*0-608-04631-0*, 206531800003) Bks Demand.

***Baker, Lynne Rudder.** Persons & Bodies: A Constitution View. (Studies in Philosophy). 256p. (C). 2000. text 49.95 (*0-521-59263-1*); pap. text 18.95 (*0-521-59719-6*) Cambridge U Pr.

Baker, M. Dinosaurs. 1996. pap. text 19.95 (*0-9647283-0-3*) Mace Baker.

Baker, M., ed. see Reiner, M.

Baker, M. F. & Williams, W. M., eds. White Clover. 534p. (Orig.). 1987. pap. text 115.00 (*0-85198-529-7*) OUP.

Baker, M. J. Marketing: An Introductory Text. 503p. (C). 1985. 175.00 (*0-7855-5657-5*, Pub. by Inst Pur & Supply) St Mut.

— Marketing: An Introductory Text. 503p. (C). 1988. 70.00 (*0-7855-3781-3*, Pub. by Inst Pur & Supply) St Mut.

— Marketing: An Introductory Text. 503p. (C). 1989. 135.00 (*0-7855-4627-8*, Pub. by Inst Pur & Supply) St Mut.

Baker, M. J. & Ughanwa, D. O. The Role of Design in International Competitiveness. 448p. 1989. 87.50 (*0-415-00013-0*, A2516) Routledge.

Baker, M. Joyce. Images of Women in Film: The War Years, 1941-1945. Berkhofer, Robert, ed. LC 80-39795. (Studies in American History & Culture: No. 21). (Illus.). 196p. 1981. reprint ed. pap. 60.80 (*0-8357-1153-6*, 207008300064) Bks Demand.

Baker, M. Pauline, jt. auth. see Hearn, D. Donald.

Baker, M. Pauline, jt. auth. see Hearn, Donald.

Baker, Madeline. The Angel & the Outlaw. 448p. (Orig.). 1996. mass mkt. 5.99 (*0-8439-3931-1*) Dorchester Pub Co.

— Apache Flame, 1 vols. 352p. 1999. mass mkt. 5.99 (*0-451-40820-9*) NAL.

— Apache Runaway. 448p. (Orig.). 1995. pap. text, mass mkt. 5.99 (*0-8439-3742-4*) Dorchester Pub Co.

— Apache Runaway. 448p. (Orig.). 1998. mass mkt. 5.99 (*0-8439-4464-1*, Leisure Bks) Dorchester Pub Co.

— Beneath a Midnight Moon. 448p. (Orig.). 1994. pap. text, mass mkt. 4.99 (*0-8439-3649-5*) Dorchester Pub Co.

— Chase the Wind. 400p. 1996. mass mkt. 5.99 (*0-8439-4069-7*) Dorchester Pub Co.

***Baker, Madeline.** Chase the Wind. 400p. 2000. mass mkt. 5.99 (*0-505-52401-5*, Love Spell) Dorchester Pub Co.

Baker, Madeline. Cheyenne Surrender. 448p. (Orig.). 1995. mass mkt. 5.99 (*0-8439-4031-X*) Dorchester Pub Co.

— Comanche Flame. 448p. 1995. mass mkt. 5.99 (*0-8439-4032-8*) Dorchester Pub Co.

— Feather in the Wind. 400p. (Orig.). 1997. mass mkt. 5.99 (*0-8439-4197-9*) Dorchester Pub Co.

— First Love, Wild Love. 448p. 1995. reprint ed. mass mkt. 5.99 (*0-8439-4033-6*) Dorchester Pub Co.

— Forbidden Fires. 448p. (Orig.). 1995. mass mkt. 5.99 (*0-8439-4034-4*) Dorchester Pub Co.

— Hawk's Woman. (Topaz Historical Romance Ser.). 384p. 1998. mass mkt. 5.99 (*0-451-40819-5*, Topaz) NAL.

— Lacey's Way. 448p. (Orig.). 1990. pap. text 4.50 (*0-8439-2918-9*) Dorchester Pub Co.

***Baker, Madeline.** Lacey's Way, 1. 448p. (Orig.). 1999. reprint ed. mass mkt. 5.99 (*0-8439-4587-7*, Leisure Bks) Dorchester Pub Co.

Baker, Madeline. Lacey's Way. rev. ed. 448p. (Orig.). 1996. mass mkt. 5.99 (*0-8439-3956-7*) Dorchester Pub Co.

— Lakota Renegade. 448p. (Orig.). 1995. pap. text 5.99 (*0-8439-3832-3*) Dorchester Pub Co.

***Baker, Madeline.** Lakota Renegade, 1. 448p. (Orig.). 1999. reprint ed. mass mkt. 5.99 (*0-8439-4588-5*, Leisure Bks) Dorchester Pub Co.

Baker, Madeline. Love Forevermore. 432p. 1997. mass mkt. 5.99 (*0-8439-4267-3*, Leisure Bks) Dorchester Pub Co.

— Love in the Wind. 448p. (Orig.). 1997. mass mkt. 5.99 (*0-8439-4227-4*) Dorchester Pub Co.

— Love in the Wind, 1. 432p. (Orig.). 1999. reprint ed. mass mkt. 5.99 (*0-8439-4589-3*, Leisure Bks) Dorchester Pub Co.

— Midnight Fire. 448p. 1996. mass mkt. 5.99 (*0-8439-4056-5*, Leisure Bks) Dorchester Pub Co.

— Midnight Fire, 1. 448p. 1999. reprint ed. mass mkt. 5.99 (*0-8439-4590-7*, Leisure Bks) Dorchester Pub Co.

— Paradise, 1. 368p. 1999. mass mkt. 5.50 (*0-8439-4552-4*) Dorchester Pub Co.

— Prairie Heat. 448p. 1991. pap. text 4.99 (*0-8439-3161-2*) Dorchester Pub Co.

— Prairie Heat. 448p. 1995. mass mkt. 5.99 (*0-8439-4036-0*) Dorchester Pub Co.

— Reckless Desire. 448p. 1995. pap. text 4.99 (*0-8439-3727-0*) Dorchester Pub Co.

— Reckless Desire, 1. 448p. 1999. reprint ed. mass mkt. 5.99 (*0-8439-4591-5*, Leisure Bks) Dorchester Pub Co.

***Baker, Madeline.** Reckless Heart. 480p. (Orig.). 1999. mass mkt. 5.99 (*0-8439-4527-3*, Leisure Bks) Dorchester Pub Co.

Baker, Madeline. Reckless Love. 480p. (Orig.). 1995. pap. text 5.99 (*0-8439-3869-2*) Dorchester Pub Co.

— Renegade Heart. 480p. 1996. mass mkt. 5.99 (*0-8439-4085-9*, Leisure Bks) Dorchester Pub Co.

— The Spirit Path. 448p. (Orig.). 1995. mass mkt. 5.99 (*0-8439-4037-9*) Dorchester Pub Co.

— Spirit's Song. 400p. 1999. mass mkt. 5.99 (*0-8439-4476-5*) Dorchester Pub Co.

***Baker, Madeline.** Unforgettable. 400p. 2000. pap. 5.99 (*0-8439-4762-4*, Leisure Bks) Dorchester Pub Co.

Baker, Madeline. Warrior's Lady. 448p. (Orig.). 1997. mass mkt. 5.99 (*0-8439-4305-X*, Leisure Bks) Dorchester Pub Co.

— A Whisper in the Wind. 432p. 1995. mass mkt. 5.99 (*0-8439-4035-2*) Dorchester Pub Co.

***Baker, Madeline, et al.** Enchanted Crossings. 448p. 2000. pap. 5.99 (*0-505-52380-9*, Love Spell) Dorchester Pub Co.

Baker, Madeline, et al. A Frontier Christmas. 400p. 1995. pap. text, mass mkt. 5.99 (*0-8439-3889-7*) Dorchester Pub Co.

***Baker, Madeline, et al.** A Frontier Christmas. 400p. 1999. reprint ed. pap. 5.99 (*0-8439-4664-4*, Leisure Bks) Dorchester Pub Co.

Baker, Madeline, et al. Love's Legacy. Graham, Heather et al, eds. 448p. 1996. pap. text 6.99 (*0-8439-4000-X*) Dorchester Pub Co.

— A Wilderness Christmas. 448p. 1995. reprint ed. pap. text, mass mkt. 5.99 (*0-8439-3919-2*) Dorchester Pub Co.

***Baker, Madeline, et al.** A Wilderness Christmas. 448p. 1999. reprint ed. pap. 5.99 (*0-8439-4665-2*, Leisure Bks) Dorchester Pub Co.

Baker, Maggie, ed. see Scatchard, Bill.

***Baker, Malcolm.** Figured in Marble: The Making & Viewing of Eighteenth-Century Sculpture. (Illus.). 224p. 2000. 80.00 (*0-89236-606-0*) J P Getty Trust.

Baker, Malcolm & Richardson, Brenda, eds. A Grand Design: The Art of the Victoria & Albert Museum. (Illus.). 1997. pap. 16.60 (*0-8109-2792-6*, Pub. by Abrams) Time Warner.

Baker, Marcia L. Flower Patch. 24p. 1998. pap. 10.00 (*0-9651439-3-7*) Royal Pubns Inc.

— Not Your Grandmother's Flower Garden: A Strip-Pieced Quilt Method. LC 97-146463. (Not Your Grandmother's Quilts Ser.: Vol. 1). (Illus.). 36p. (Orig.). 1996. pap. 14.95 (*0-9651439-0-2*) Alicias Attic.

— Not Your Grandmother's Stars: A Strip-Pieced Quilt Method. (Not Your Grandmother's Quilts Ser.: Vol. 3). (Illus.). 48p. (Orig.). Date not set. pap. write for info. (*0-9651439-2-9*) Alicias Attic.

— Not Your Grandmother's Tumbling Blocks: A Strip-Pieced Quilt Method. (Not Your Grandmother's Quilts Ser.: Vol. 2). (Illus.). 24p. (Orig.). 1997. pap. 10.00 (*0-9651439-1-0*) Alicias Attic.

Baker, Marcus. Extract from Geographic Dictionary of Alaska. (Shorey Historical Ser.). 75p. reprint ed. pap. 10.00 (*0-8466-0100-1*, S100) Shoreys Bkstore.

Baker, Margaret. Discovering Christmas Customs & Folklore. 1989. pap. 25.00 (*0-7478-0175-4*, Pub. by Shire Pubns) St Mut.

— Discovering Christmas Customs & Folklore: A Guide to Seasonal Rites. enl. rev. ed. 1992. reprint ed. pap. 7.95 (*0-913714-56-9*, Pub. by Shire Pubns) Parkwest Pubns.

— Discovering the Folklore of Plants. 96p. 1996. pap. 10.50 (*0-7478-0178-9*, Pub. by Shire Pubns) St Mut.

— Food & Cooking. (Junior Reference Ser.). (Illus.). 64p. (J). (gr. 6 up). 1979. 14.95 (*0-7136-1465-X*) Dufour.

— London Statues & Monuments. (Illus.). 128p. pap. 12.50 (*0-7478-0284-X*, Pub. by Shire Pubns) Parkwest Pubns.

— London Statues & Monuments. 128p. 1989. pap. 30.00 (*0-7478-0162-2*, Pub. by Shire Pubns) St Mut.

Baker, Margaret, jt. auth. see Baker, Charles.

Baker, Margaret J., et al. Controlling Movement: A Therapeutic Approach to Early Intervention. 352p. 1991. 92.00 (*0-8342-0192-5*) Aspen Pub.

Baker, Margaret L. & Baker, Charles O. Orchid Species Culture: Pescatorea to Pleione. LC 90-22011. 264p. 1991. 32.95 (*0-88192-189-0*); pap. 19.95 (*0-88192-208-0*) Timber.

Baker, Margaret L., jt. auth. see Baker, Charles O.

***Baker, Margaret Rogers.** The Man Who Brought Me Roses. LC 00-190445. 2000. 25.00 (*0-7388-1750-3*); pap. 18.00 (*0-7388-1751-1*) Xlibris Corp.

Baker, Mark. Cops. 1989. pap. 6.99 (*0-671-68551-1*) PB.

***Baker, Mark.** D. A. Prosecutors in Their Own Words. LC 98-53425. 255p. 1999. pap. 23.50 (*0-684-83156-2*) Simon & Schuster.

Baker, Mark. I Hate Videots. 1982. 3.80 (*0-671-45688-1*) S&S Trade.

— Making Sense of the New NHS White Paper. LC 98-195926. 143 p. 1998. write for info. (*1-85775-239-2*) Scovill Paterson.

— Sanders Sports Autograph Price Guide, 1994. 3rd ed. 1993. pap. 19.95 (*0-89487-198-6*) Scott Pub Co.

— SCD Baseball Autograph Handbook: A Comprehensive Guide to Authentication & Valuation of Hall of Fame Autographs. 2nd ed. LC 89-83583. (Illus.). 352p. 1991. pap. 19.95 (*0-87341-169-2*, BA02) Krause Pubns.

An Asterisk (*) at the beginning of an entry indicates that the title is appearing for the first time.

— Sex Lives: A Sexual Self-Portrait of America. LC 96-42941. 1997. per. 14.00 (0-671-70254-8) PB.
— What Men Really Think: About Women, Love, Sex, Themselves. Rubenstein, Julie, ed. 352p. 1993. reprint ed. mass mkt. 5.99 (0-671-79592-9) PB.
Baker, Mark A. Collectors Guide to Celebrity Autographs. LC 96-76692. (Illus.). 416p. 1996. pap. 19.95 (0-87341-464-0, CAU) Krause Pubns.
***Baker, Mark A.** Collectors Guide to Celebrity Autographs. 2nd rev. ed. LC 96-76692. (Illus.). 352p. 2000. pap. 24.95 (0-87341-838-7, CAU2) Krause Pubns.
Baker, Mark A. Goldmine Price Guide to Rock 'n' Roll Memorabilia. LC 97-73040. (Illus.). 768p. 1997. pap. 24.95 (0-87341-490-X, RRM) Krause Pubns.
***Baker, Mark Allen.** Advanced Autograph Collecting. LC 99-67510. (Illus.). 352p. 2000. pap. 24.95 (0-87341-632-5, ADAC) Krause Pubns.
Baker, Mark Allen. All-Sport Autograph Guide. LC 94-77502. (Illus.). 304p. 1994. pap. 12.95 (0-87341-316-4, AG01) Krause Pubns.
— Auto Racing Memorabilia & Price Guide. LC 95-82424. (Illus.). 304p. 1996. pap. 19.95 (0-87341-437-3, ARC) Krause Pubns.
Baker, Mark C. Incorporation: A Theory of Grammatical Function Changing. vii, 544p. 1994. pap. text 21.95 (0-226-03542-5) U Ch Pr.
— Incorporation: A Theory of Grammatical Function Changing. vii, 552p. 1999. lib. bdg. 72.00 (0-226-03541-7) U Ch Pr.
— Incorporation: A Theory of Grammatical Function Changing. LC 87-16181. (Chicago Original Paperback Ser.). (Illus.). 551p. Date not set. reprint ed. pap. 170.90 (0-608-20984-8, 205451200003) Bks Demand.
— The Polysynthesis Parameter. (Oxford Studies in Comparative Syntax). (Illus.). 576p. 1996. text 95.00 (0-19-509307-0) OUP.
Baker, Mark R. & Kirk, Simon, eds. Making Sense of Research & Development. 1995. write for info. (1-85775-094-2, Radcliffe Med Pr) Scovill Paterson.
Baker, Mark R., et al. Clinical Effectiveness & Primary Care. LC 97-6232. 1997. write for info. (1-85775-129-9, Radcliffe Med Pr) Scovill Paterson.
— Seismic Pavement Analyzer Operations Manual with Technical Specifications. 61p. (C). 1993. pap. text 10.00 (0-309-05752-3, SHRP-H-374) SHRP.
***Baker, Mark V.** Private Murphy's Law. (Illus.). 96p. 1999. pap. 5.95 (0-9679357-0-9, Pub. by Flat Earth) Byrrd Ent Inc.
Baker, Mark W., jt. auth. see Berry, Carmen R.
Baker, Martha. Garden Ornaments. LC 98-18876. 1999. 40.00 (0-609-60264-0) Crown Pub Group.
Baker, Martha, jt. auth. see Evans, Lee.
Baker, Martha, jt. compiled by see Cassidy, David.
***Baker, Mary.** Bible Study Guide for All Ages: Beginner Level Activity Pages -- Lessons 105-130. (Illus.). 26p. (J). (ps-2). 2000. pap. text 4.95 (1-879614-63-4) BSG Printing.
— Bible Study Guide for All ages: Beginner Level Activity Pages -- Lessons 131-156. (Illus.). 26p. (J). 2000. pap. text 4.95 (1-879614-64-2) BSG Printing.
— Bible Study Guide for All Ages: Beginner Level Activity Pages -- Lessons 157-182. (Illus.). 26p. (J). 2000. pap. text 4.95 (1-879614-65-0) BSG Printing.
— Bible Study Guide for All Ages: Beginner Level Activity Pages -- Lessons 183-208. (Illus.). 26p. (J). 2000. pap. text 4.95 (1-879614-66-9) BSG Printing.
— Bible Study Guide for All Ages: Intermediate Level Activity Pages -- Lesson 131-156. (Illus.). 26p. (J). 2000. pap. text 4.95 (1-879614-68-5) BSG Printing.
— Bible Study Guide for All Ages: Intermediate Level Activity Pages -- Lessons 105-130. 26p. (J). (gr. 3-7). 2000. pap. text 4.95 (1-879614-67-7) BSG Printing.
— Bible Study Guide for All Ages: Intermediate Level Activity Pages -- Lessons 157-182. (Illus.). 26p. (J). 2000. pap. text 4.95 (1-879614-69-3) BSG Printing.
— Bible Study Guide for All Ages: Intermediate Level Activity Pages -- Lessons 183-208. (Illus.). 26p. (J). 2000. pap. text 4.95 (1-879614-70-7) BSG Printing.
— Bible Study Guide for All Ages: Low Reading Level Teaching Plan - First Year - First Quarter. (Illus.). 55p. 1994. teacher ed. 11.95 (1-879614-12-X) BSG Printing.
— Bible Study Guide for All Ages: Low Reading Level Teaching Plan - First Year - Fourth Quarter. (Illus.). 53p. 1998. teacher ed. 11.95 (1-879614-31-6) BSG Printing.
— Bible Study Guide for All Ages: Low Reading Level Teaching Plan - First Year - Second Quarter. (Illus.). 55p. 1994. teacher ed. 11.95 (1-879614-20-0) BSG Printing.
— Bible Study Guide for All Ages: Low Reading Level Worksheets - First Year - First Quarter. (Illus.). 54p. (J). (gr. 2-4). 1994. wbk. ed. 4.95 (1-879614-09-X) BSG Printing.
— Bible Study Guide for All Ages: Low Reading Level Worksheets - First Year - Fourth Quater. (Illus.). 54p. 1998. wbk. ed. 4.95 (1-879614-30-8) BSG Printing.
— Bible Study Guide for All Ages: Low Reading Level Worksheets - First Year - Second Quarter. (Illus.). 54p. (J). (gr. 2-4). 1998. wbk. ed. 4.95 (1-879614-17-0) BSG Printing.
— Bible Study Guide for All Ages: Multi-Level Worksheets - First Year - Third Quarter. (Illus.). (J). (gr. 5-7). 1999. wbk. ed. 4.95 (1-879614-45-6) BSG Printing.
— Bible Study Guide for All Ages: Non-Reading Level Teaching Plan - First Year - Third Quarter. (Illus.). 1998. wbk. ed. 11.95 (1-879614-40-5) BSG Printing.
— Bible Study Guide for All Ages: Non-Reading Level Teaching Visuals - First Year - First Quarter. (Illus.). 55p. 1994. teacher ed. 11.95 (1-879614-11-1) BSG Printing.
— Bible Study Guide for All Ages: Non-Reading Level Teaching Visuals - First Year - Second Quarter. (Illus.). 55p. 1994. teacher ed. 11.95 (1-879614-19-7) BSG Printing.
— Bible Study Guide for All Ages: Non-Reading Level Wall Time Line. (Illus.). 28p. (J). (ps-1). 1994. ring bd. 19.95 (1-879614-14-6) BSG Printing.
— Bible Study Guide for All Ages: Non-Reading Level Worksheets - First Year - First Quarter. (Illus.). 54p. (J). (ps-1). 1994. wbk. ed. 4.95 (1-879614-08-1) BSG Printing.
— Bible Study Guide for All Ages: Non-Reading Level Worksheets - First Year - Second Quarter. (Illus.). 54p. (J). (ps-1). 1998. wbk. ed. 4.95 (1-879614-16-2) BSG Printing.
— Bible Study Guide for All Ages: Non-Reading Level Worksheets - First Year - Third Quarter. (Illus.). 54p. (J). (ps-1). 1998. wbk. ed. 4.95 (1-879614-39-1) BSG Printing.
— Bible Study Guide for All Ages: Regular Reading Level Teaching Plan - First Year - First Quarter. (Illus.). 55p. 1994. teacher ed. 11.95 (1-879614-13-8) BSG Printing.
— Bible Study Guide for All Ages: Regular Reading Level Teaching Plan - First Year - Second Quarter. (Illus.). 54p. 1998. teacher ed. 11.95 (1-879614-21-9) BSG Printing.
— Bible Study Guide for All Ages: Regular Reading Level Worksheets - First Year - First Quarter. (Illus.). 55p. (J). (gr. 5-7). 1994. wbk. ed. 4.95 (1-879614-10-3) BSG Printing.
— Bible Study Guide for All Ages: Regular Reading Level Worksheets - First Year - Second Quarter. (Illus.). 54p. (J). (gr. 5-7). 1998. wbk. ed. 4.95 (1-879614-18-9) BSG Printing.
— Bible Study Guide for All Ages: Unlabeled Wall Maps/Time-Line. (Illus.). 5p. 1998. ring bd. 19.95 (1-879614-07-3) BSG Printing.
— Bible Study Guide for All Ages Labels 105-156: Pictures & Names Label Packet. (Illus.). 4p. 1998. ring bd. 5.95 (1-879614-29-4) BSG Printing.
— Bible Study Guide for All Ages Lessons 157-208: Pictures & Names Label Packet. (Illus.). 4p. 1998. ring bd. 5.95 (1-879614-34-0) BSG Printing.
— Bible Study Guide for All Ages Lessons 209-260: Pictures & Names Label Packet. (Illus.). 5p. 1998. ring bd. 5.95 (1-879614-35-9) BSG Printing.
— Bible Study Guide for All Ages Lessons 1-26: Beginner Level Activity Pages. (Illus.). 26p. (J). (ps-2). 1999. wbk. ed. 4.95 (1-879614-47-2) BSG Printing.
— Bible Study Guide for All Ages Lessons 1-26: Intermediate Level Activity Pages. (Illus.). 26p. (J). (gr. 3-7). 1999. wbk. ed. 4.95 (1-879614-48-0) BSG Printing.
— Bible Study Guide for All Ages Lessons 1-52: Pictures & Names Label Packet. (Illus.). 7p. 1994. ring bd. 9.95 (1-879614-15-4) BSG Printing.
— Bible Study Guide for All Ages Lessons 27-52: Beginner Level Activity Pages. (Illus.). 26p. (J). (ps-2). 1999. wbk. ed. 4.95 (1-879614-50-2) BSG Printing.
— Bible Study Guide for All Ages Lessons 27-52: Intermediate Level Activity Pages. (Illus.). 26p. (J). (gr. 3-7). 1999. wbk. ed. 4.95 (1-879614-49-9) BSG Printing.
— Bible Study Guide for All Ages Lessons 53-78: Beginner Level Activity Pages. (Illus.). 26p. (J). (ps-2). 1999. wbk. ed. 4.95 (1-879614-52-9) BSG Printing.
— Bible Study Guide for All Ages Lessons 53-78: Intermediate Level Activity Pages. (Illus.). 26p. (J). (gr. 3-7). 1999. wbk. ed. 4.95 (1-879614-51-0) BSG Printing.
— Bible Study Guide for All Ages Lessons 53-104: Pictures & Names Label Packet. (Illus.). 4p. 1998. ring bd. 5.95 (1-879614-28-6) BSG Printing.
— Bible Study Guide for All Ages Lessons 79-104: Beginner Level Activity Pages. (Illus.). 26p. (J). (ps-2). 1999. wbk. ed. 4.95 (1-879614-54-5) BSG Printing.
— Bible Study Guide for All Ages Lessons 79-104: Intermediate Level Activity Pages. (Illus.). 26p. (J). (gr. 3-7). 1999. wbk. ed. 4.95 (1-879614-53-7) BSG Printing.
— Bible Study Guide for All Ages Lessons 261-312: Pictures & Names Label Packet. (Illus.). 4p. 1998. ring bd. 5.95 (1-879614-36-7) BSG Printing.
— Bible Study Guide for All Ages Lessons 313-364: Pictures & Names Label Packet. (Illus.). 3p. 1998. ring bd. 5.95 (1-879614-37-5) BSG Printing.
— Bible Study Guide for All Ages Lessons 365-416: Pictures & Names Label Packet. (Illus.). 5p. 1998. ring bd. 5.95 (1-879614-38-3) BSG Printing.
Baker, Mary. God's Answers to Single Parenting. 2nd ed. (Illus.). 91p. 1998. reprint ed. pap. 10.00 (1-891951-09-2) By the Grace of God.
Baker, Mary, jt. auth. see Baker, Donald.
Baker, Mary, ed. see Page, Randy, et al.
Baker, Mary, tr. see Henaff, Marcel.
Baker, Mary A., ed. Sex Differences in Human Performance. fac. ed. LC 86-9182. (Wiley Series on Studies in Human Performance). (Illus.). 218p. 1987. reprint ed. pap. 67.60 (0-608-00969-5, 206181600011) Bks Demand.
Baker, Mary T., jt. ed. see Cardamone, Jeanette M.
Baker, Maryn. The Short Change Game: How to Stop the School from Depriving Your Retarded or Handicapped Child. LC 81-3653. 1983. 13.95 (0-87949-211-2) Ashley Bks.
Baker, Matt. Phantom Lady. 64p. 1994. pap. 9.95 (1-885730-02-0) Verotik.
Baker, Maurice. Shetland Sheepdogs Today. (Illus.). 160p. 1993. 24.95 (0-948955-40-6, Pub. by Ringpr Bks) Seven Hills Bk.
Baker, Maurice, ed. see Lunde, Joyce P.
Baker, Maurice E., jt. ed. see Lawson, Merlin P.
Baker, MeeCee & Mikesell, Robert E., Jr. Animal Science Biology & Technology. (AgriScience & Technology Ser.). 428p. 1995. text 62.50 (0-8134-3040-2) Interstate.
— Animal Science Biology & Technology. 500p. 1995. teacher ed. 12.95 (0-8134-3041-0) Interstate.
— Animal Science Biology & Technology. (AgriScience & Technology Ser.). 1996. text, teacher ed. 89.95 (0-8134-3113-1) Interstate.
Baker, Michael. Critical Thinking Activities to Improve Writing Skills A1: Arguments. 68p. (YA). (gr. 7 up). 1989. pap. 1.95 (0-89455-385-2) Crit Think Bks.
— Marketing Theory. (ITBP Textbooks Ser.). 1933. text. write for info. (1-86152-593-1, Pub. by ITBP) Thomson Learn.
Baker, Michael. Product Management/Marketing. LC 96-25428. 550p. (C). 1998. pap. 49.00 (0-13-065368-3) P-H.
***Baker, Michael, et al.** Marketing Managerial Foundations. 560p. 2000. pap. 64.95 (0-7329-5211-5, Pub. by Macmill Educ) Paul & Co Pubs.
Baker, Michael J. Dictionary of Marketing & Advertising. 2nd ed. (Illus.). 1990. 57.50 (0-89397-372-6) Nichols Pub.
***Baker, Michael J.** IEBM Encyclopedia of Marketing. (Illus.). 865p. 1999. write for info. (1-86152-304-1) Thomson Learn.
Baker, Michael J., ed. Companion Encyclopedia of Marketing. LC 95-44469. 1070p. 1996. pap. 156.95 (0-415-09395-3) Thomson Learn.
***Baker, Michael J., ed.** Marketing Book. 4th ed. 718p. 1999. pap. text 49.95 (0-7506-4114-2) Buttrwrth-Heinemann.
Baker, Michael K. The Sword. LC 84-90678. 303p. (J). (gr. 5). 1985. pap. 8.00 (0-932543-00-6); text 8.00 (0-932543-01-4) M B Pub.
Baker, Michael O. What Would You Do? B1: Character Education. 32p. (Orig.). (YA). (gr. 7 up). 1989. pap. 9.95 (0-89455-349-6) Crit Think Bks.
Baker, Michael O. What Would You Do? Bk. A-1: Developing &/or Applying Ethical Standards. (J). (gr. 7-8). 1989. pap. text 11.00 (0-89455-348-8) CSEE.
— What Would You Do? Bk. B-1: Developing &/or Applying Ethical Standards. (YA). (gr. 9-12). 1989. 11.00 (0-614-24448-X) CSEE.
Baker, Mickey. Mickey Baker's Jazz Guitar. (Illus.). 72p. pap. 12.95 (0-86001-016-3, CL10158) Music Sales.
Baker, Mickey. Study of the Many Shades of the Blues. 48p. 1997. pap. 17.95 incl. audio compact disk (0-7866-2500-7, 96318BCD) Mel Bay.
***Baker, Mike.** My Favorite Horror Story. 2000. mass mkt. 6.99 (0-88677-914-6, Pub. by DAW Bks) Penguin Putnam.
Baker, Mike. Strike It Rich on eBAY. 74p. 1999. pap. 14.95 (0-9671646-0-5) Mike Baker.
Baker, Molly. High-Flying Adventures in the Stock Market. LC 00-38216. 286p. 2000. 24.95 (0-471-35936-X) Wiley.
Baker, Mona. In Other Words: A Coursebook on Translation. LC 91-33898. 320p. (C). 1992. pap. 24.99 (0-415-03086-2, A9571) Routledge.
Baker, Mona, ed. Routledge Encyclopedia of Translation Studies. LC 96-44586. 654p. (C). 1998. 165.00 (0-415-09380-5) Routledge.
Baker, Mona, et al, eds. Text & Technology: In Honour of John Sinclair. LC 93-17441. xii, 361p. 1993. 74.00 (1-55619-494-3) J Benjamins Pubng Co.
***Baker, Murray.** The Debt-Free Graduate: How to Survive College Without Going Broke. 320p. 2000. pap. 13.99 (1-56414-472-0) Career Pr Inc.
Baker, N., jt. auth. see Turrent, D.
Baker, N. C., ed. see Structural Division Staff of the American Society.
Baker, N. R. & Bowyer, J. R., eds. Photoinhibition of Photosynthesis: From Molecular Mechanisms to the Field. 500p. 1994. 177.50 (1-872748-03-1, Pub. by Bios Sci) Coronet Bks.
Baker, N. R. & Thomas, H., eds. Crop Photosynthesis: Spatial & Temporal Determinants. LC 92-18712. (Topics in Photosynthesis Ser.: Vol. 12). xviii, 452p. 1992. 247.00 (0-444-41596-3); 263.00 (0-444-89608-2) Elsevier.
Baker, N. V., ed. see Theodoulou, Stella Z.
Baker, Nancy. The Night Inside. 1999. pap. write for info. (0-451-18327-4, Sig) NAL.
***Baker, Nancy & Baker, Daniel B.** Explorers & Discoverers: From Alexander the Great to Sally Ride, Vol. 7. 225p. 1999. text 39.00 (0-7876-3681-9, GML00299-113309, UXL) Gale.
Baker, Nancy & Christensen, Thomas, eds. Aesthetics & the Art of Musical Composition in the German Enlightenment: Selected Writings of Johann Georg Sulzer & Heinrich Christoph Koch. (Cambridge Studies in Music Theory & Analysis: No. 7). (Illus.). 222p. (C). 1996. text 64.95 (0-521-36035-8) Cambridge U Pr.
Baker, Nancy & Hoffman, Richard L. Exploring Virginia Insects: An Activity Book. 32p. (J). (gr. 4-6). Date not set. pap. 4.95 (0-9625801-8-X) VA Mus Natl Hist.
Baker, Nancy, jt. auth. see Fenker, Dayna.
Baker, Nancy, ed. see Marino, Martha.
Baker, Nancy, ed. see Women Crowned in Glory Staff.
Baker, Nancy K. & Hanning, Barbara R., eds. Musical Humanism & Its Legacy: Essays in Honor of Claude V. Palisca. LC 91-45586. (Festschrift Ser.: No. 11). (Illus.). 525p. 1992. lib. bdg. 54.00 (0-945193-29-7) Pendragon NY.
Baker, Nancy L. & Huling, Nancy. A Research Guide for Undergraduates: English & American Literature. 4th ed. LC 95-31637. (Illus.). viii, 88p. 1995. pap. 10.00 (0-87352-566-3, S2013) Modern Lang.
Baker, Nancy V. Conflicting Loyalties: Law & Politics in the Attorney General's Office, 1789-1990. LC 91-42344. viii, 250p. 1992. 25.00 (0-7006-0530-4) U Pr of KS.
Baker, Naomi & Young, Tammy. Craft an Elegant Wedding. LC 94-38728. (Illus.). 144p. 1995. pap. 17.95 (0-8019-8575-7) Krause Pubns.
— Know Your Baby Lock. 2nd rev. ed. LC 90-55324. (Illus.). 182p. 1994. pap. 17.95 (0-8019-8592-7) Krause Pubns.
— Sew Sensational Gifts. LC 92-56584. (Illus.). 160p. 1993. pap. 16.95 (0-8019-8237-5) Krause Pubns.
— Simply Serged Fabrics: A Handbook for Overlocking Today's Varied Textiles. LC 89-83400. (Illus.). 200p. 1990. pap. text 14.95 (0-8019-8104-2) NP-Chilton.
Baker, Naomi, et al. The Ultimate Serger Answer Guide: Troubleshooting for Any Overlock Brand or Model. LC 95-33546. (Creative Machine Arts Ser.). (Illus.). 96p. 1996. pap. 16.95 (0-8019-8645-1) Krause Pubns.
Baker, Natalie. Masters of Art: The World's Great Artists, Their Lives & Works. 1987. 17.98 (0-88365-716-3) Galahad Bks.
Baker, Neil J. Behavioral Health in Primary Care: A Guide for Clinical Integration. Cummings, Nicholas A. et al, eds. LC 97-19722. 464p. 1997. 65.00 (1-887841-10-5, 60505, Psychosocial) Intl Univs Pr.
Baker, Neil R., ed. Photosynthesis & the Environment. LC 96-49526. (Advances in Photosynthesis Ser.). 508p. (C). 1996. lib. bdg. 292.50 (0-7923-4316-6) Kluwer Academic.

B

Baker, Nelson M. A Genealogy of the Descendants of Edward Baker of Lynn, Mass., 1630. 99p. 1988. reprint ed. pap. 13.00 (0-8328-0161-5); reprint ed. lib. bdg. 21.00 (0-8328-0160-7) Higginson Bk Co.
Baker, Newton D. Why We Went to War. LC 72-1278. (Select Bibliographies Reprint Ser.). 1977. reprint ed. 15.95 (0-8369-6820-4) Ayer.
Baker, Nicholson. The Everlasting Story of Nory: A Novel. 1999. pap. 12.00 (0-679-76375-9) Vin Bks.
— Fermata. 1995. pap. 13.00 (0-679-75933-6) Vin Bks.
— The Mezzanine. (Vintage Contemporaries Ser.). 1990. pap. 11.00 (0-679-72576-8) Vin Bks.
— Room Temperature. LC 90-55705. 128p. 1991. pap. 10.00 (0-679-73440-6) Vin Bks.
— The Size of Thoughts: Essays & Other Lumber. 368p. 1997. pap. 13.00 (0-679-77624-9) Random.
— U & I: A True Story. 1992. pap. 11.00 (0-679-73575-5) Vin Bks.
— Vox: A Novel. LC 92-56365. 1993. pap. 11.00 (0-679-74211-5) Random.
Baker, Nick. Energy & Environment in Architecture. LC 98-54418. 1998. pap. 55.00 (0-419-22770-9, E & FN Spon) Routledge.
— 101 Winning Ways. 1995. pap., per. write for info. (0-9643367-4-X) Peak Performance.
Baker, Nicola, ed. Building a Relational Society: New Priorities for Public Policy. 300p. (Orig.). 1996. pap. 32.95 (1-85742-349-6, Pub. by Arena); text 64.95 (1-85742-348-8, Pub. by Arena) Ashgate Pub Co.
Baker, Nicole, ed. see Toeschi, Carl J. & Cannabich, Christian.
Baker, Nikki. In the Game. (Virginia Kelly Mystery Ser.). 224p. (Orig.). 1991. pap. 9.95 (1-56280-004-3) Naiad Pr.
Baker, Noel S. Hard Core Roadshow: A Screenwriter's Diary. LC 97-175897. (Illus.). 256p. 1998. pap. 15.95 (0-88784-584-3, Pub. by Hse of Anansi Pr) Genl Dist Srvs.
Baker, Norman. The Way It Was in North Rockland. 1973. pap. 5.00 (0-911183-10-8) Rockland County Hist.
Baker, North & Ellis Staff. Swallow: Genealogy of the Swallow Family, 1666-1910. (Illus.). 217p. 1992. reprint ed. pap. 34.50 (0-8328-2202-7); reprint ed. lib. bdg. 44.50 (0-8328-2201-9) Higginson Bk Co.
Baker, Olaf. Where the Buffaloes Begin. LC 85-5682. (Illus.). 48p. (J). (ps-3). 1985. pap. 6.99 (0-14-050560-1, Viking Child) Peng Put Young Read.
— Where the Buffaloes Begin. (Picture Puffin Ser.). (Illus.). (J). 1981. 11.19 (0-606-00542-0, Pub. by Turtleback) Demco.
Baker, Ovid, et al. Gas Liquid Two-Phase Flow in Pipelines: II-Design Manual. 53p. 1970. 3.00 (0-318-12632-X, L20269) Am Gas Assn.
Baker, P., et al. Dictionary of Mauritian Creole. (CRP & FRE.). 365p. 1987. 59.95 (0-8288-7296-1, 2858029733) Fr & Eur.
Baker, P. L. Islamic Textiles. LC 96-153812. 1995. 54.00 (0-7141-2522-9, Pub. by Textile Inst) St Mut.
Baker, P. N., et al. Case Commentaries in Obstetrics & Gynecology. (Illus.). 265p. 1997. pap. text 32.95 (0-7020-2235-7, Pub. by W B Saunders) Saunders.
Baker, P. Randall. King Husain & the Kingdom of Hejaz. (Arabia Past & Present Ser.: Vol. 10). (Illus.). 1979. 29.95 (0-900891-48-3) Oleander Pr.
Baker, P. W., et al. Jones & Buckle Vol. I: The Civil Practice of the Magistrates' Courts in South Africa: The Act. 8th ed. 548p. 1988. 76.00 (0-7021-2175-4, Pub. by Juta & Co) Gaunt.
— Jones & Buckle Vol. II: The Civil Practice of the Magistrates' Courts in South Africa: The Rules. 8th ed. 705p. 1991. 86.00 (0-7021-2431-1, Pub. by Juta & Co) Gaunt.
***Baker, Pam.** Columbus Celebrates the Millennium, an International Quest. LC 99-14818. (Millennium Ser.). (Illus.). 1999. 39.00 (1-885352-98-0) Community Comm.
Baker, Pam. Houston County: In Our Own Words. LC 98-42410. (Illus.). 128p. 1998. 28.00 (1-885352-25-5) Community Comm.
Baker, Pam, ed. see Blansfeld, Joseph, et al.
Baker, Pam, ed. see Jacobs, Barbara B., et al.
Baker, Pamela, et al. ENPC Pocket Review. (Illus.). 1994. spiral bd. 22.00 (0-935890-37-8) Emerg Nurses IL.

— Essentials in Emergency Nursing, 2 vols. (Illus.). 145p. Date not set. pap. text 250.00 (*0-935890-26-2*) Emerg Nurses IL.

Baker, Pamela C. & Keene, Pamela A. Columbus: The Spirit, the People, the Promise. Turner, James E. & Hughes, Mary S., eds. LC 92-73250. 264p. 1992. text 39.00 (*0-9630029-2-9*) Community Comm.

Baker, Pamela J. My First Book of Sign. (Awareness & Caring Ser.). (Illus.). 76p. (J). (gr. k up). 1992. reprint ed. lib. bdg. 18.95 (*1-878363-92-1*) Forest Hse.

Baker, Pamela J., jt. auth. see Mikoff, Eli C.

Baker, Patricia. EAEDC Advocacy Guide. LC 94-79759. 108p. 1994. pap. text 5.00 (*0-944490-78-6*) Mass CLE.

— EAEDC Advocacy Guide: An Advocate's Guide to Emergency Aid to Elders, Disabled & Children in Massachusetts. LC 98-88689. 173 p. 1998. write for info. (*1-57589-110-7*) Mass CLE.

— Fashions of a Decade: The 1940s. Cumming, Valerie & Feldman, Elane, eds. (Illus.). 64p. (J). (gr. 4-9). 1992. 19.95 (*0-8160-2467-7*) Facts on File.

— Fashions of a Decade: The 1950s. Cumming, Valerie & Feldman, Elane, eds. (Illus.). 64p. (J). (gr. 4-9). 1991. 19.95 (*0-8160-2468-5*) Facts on File.

Baker, Patricia A., jt. auth. see Weber, Valerie.

Baker, Patrick L. Centring the Periphery: Chaos, Order & the Ethnohistory of Dominica. (Illus.). 280p. 1994. 60.00 (*0-7735-1134-2*, Pub. by McG-Queens Univ Pr) CUP Services.

Baker, Patsy. Wigs & Make-Up for Theatre, Television, & Film. LC 93-150928. (Illus.). 248p. reprint ed. pap. 76.90 (*0-608-07416-0*, 206764300009) Bks Demand.

— Wigs & Make-Up for Theatre, TV & Film. (Illus.). 286p. 1993. pap. text 59.95 (*0-7506-0431-X*) Buttrwrth-Heinemann.

Baker, Patty, ed. & creator see Samuel, Lynette M.

Baker, Paul. Hamlet Esp. 1971. pap. 5.25 (*0-8222-0492-4*) Dramatists Play.

— Integration of Abilities: Exercises for Creative Growth. (Illus.). 1977. pap. 24.00 (*0-87602-030-9*) Anchorage.

— South Africa. 2nd ed. (Passport's Illustrated Travel Guides). (Illus.). 192p. 1999. pap. 14.95 (*0-8442-1207-5*, 12075, Passprt Bks) NTC Contemp Pub Co.

Baker, Paul A., jt. ed. see Shukla, Vijai.

Baker, Paul G. A Reassessment of D. H. Lawrence's "Aaron's Rod" Litz, A. Walton, ed. LC 83-9224. (Studies in Modern Literature: No. 31). 223p. reprint ed. 69.20 (*0-8357-1470-5*, 207049200097) Bks Demand.

Baker, Paul J. & Anderson, Louis E. Social Problems: A Critical Thinking Approach. 414p. (C). 1987. pap. write for info. (*0-534-07428-6*) Wadsworth Pub.

Baker, Paul J., et al. Social Problems: A Critical Thinking Approach. 2nd ed. 530p. (C). 1992. pap. 36.50 (*0-534-19014-6*) Wadsworth Pub.

***Baker, Paul M.** Practice Management for Complementary Therapists. (Illus.). 256p. 2000. pap. 45.00 (*0-7506-4510-5*) Buttrwrth-Heinemann.

Baker, Paul R., ed. see D'Arusmont, Frances W.

***Baker, Paula, et al.** Prescriptions for a Healthy House: A Practical Guide for Architects, Builders, & Homeowners. (Illus.). 250p. 1998. pap. 29.95 (*0-9702107-0-1*) Baker Laporte.

Baker, Paula, et al. Prescriptions for a Healthy House: A Practical Guide for Architects, Builders & Homeowners. LC 97-42428. 280p. 1997. pap. 29.95 (*1-56690-355-6*, InWord Pr) High Mtn.

Baker, Pauline. Espanol para los Hispanos. (SPA.). 128p. 1994. pap. 12.95 (*0-8442-7116-0*, Natl Textbk Co) NTC Contemp Pub Co.

Baker, Pauline. Spanish Verb Drills. 2nd ed. (SPA., Illus.). 176p. 1990. pap. 8.95 (*0-8442-7034-2*, 70342, Natl Textbk Co) NTC Contemp Pub Co.

Baker, Pauline H. South Africa & the World Economy in the 1990's. 1993. pap. 16.95 (*0-8157-0775-4*) Brookings.

Baker, Pearl. Robbers Roost Recollections. (Western Experience Ser.). (Illus.). 204p. 1991. pap. 14.95 (*0-87421-154-9*) Utah St U Pr.

— The Wild Bunch at Robbers Roost. LC 88-38635. (Illus.). ix, 224p. 1989. reprint ed. pap. 9.95 (*0-8032-6089-X*, Bison Books) U of Nebr Pr.

***Baker, Peter.** The Breach: Inside the Impeachment & Trial of William Jefferson Clinton. (Illus.). 464p. 2000. 27.50 (*0-684-86813-X*) Scribner.

Baker, Peter. Deconstruction & The Ethical Turn. LC 95-5313. 184p. 1995. 49.95 (*0-8130-1365-8*) U Press Fla.

— An Explanation of How the Brain Works. 190p. 1997. pap. 16.95 (*1-85756-376-X*, Pub. by Janus Pubng) Paul & Co Pubs.

***Baker, Peter.** Jesus. 2000. pap. text 12.95 (*1-873741-34-0*) Millivres Bks.

Baker, Peter. Obdurate Brilliance: Exteriority & the Modern Long Poem. 252p. (C). 1991. 49.95 (*0-8130-1064-0*) U Press Fla.

***Baker, Peter, ed.** The Anglo-Saxon Chronicle: 8: MS F. (Anglo-Saxon Chronicle). 256p. 2000. 75.00 (*0-85991-490-9*) Boydell & Brewer.

Baker, Peter, ed. Onward: Contemporary Poetry & Poetics. X, 439p. (C). 1996. pap. text 29.95 (*0-8204-3032-3*) P Lang Pubng.

Baker, Peter, et al, eds. The Scope of Words: In Honor of Albert S. Cook. LC 90-27661. X, 424p. (C). 1991. text 54.00 (*0-8204-1417-4*) P Lang Pubng.

Baker, Peter, jt. ed. see Lapidge, Michael.

Baker, Peter S. Beowulf: Basic Readings. 2nd ed. 1994. pap. 34.65 (*0-8153-3666-7*) Garland.

Baker, Peter S. Words & Works: Studies in Medieval English Language & Literature in Honour of Fred C. Robins. LC 98-209493. (Illus.). 368p. 1998. text 60.00 (*0-8020-4153-1*) U of Toronto Pr.

Baker, Peter S., ed. Beowulf: Basic Readings. LC 94-28245. (Basic Readings in Anglo-Saxon England Ser.: Vol. 1). 328p. 1995. text 50.00 (*0-8153-0098-0*, H1431) Garland.

Baker, Philip, jt. auth. see Kingdom, John.

Baker, Phyllis L. Bored & Busy: An Analysis of Formal & Informal Organization in the Automated Office. LC 90-25698. (American University Studies: Anthropology & Science: Ser. XI, Vol. 52). (Illus.). 145p. (C). 1991. text 35.95 (*0-8204-1362-3*) P Lang Pubng.

Baker, Piers. Matching Colors. (Build-a-Block Bks.). (Illus.). 16p. (J). (ps-1). 1998. 9.99 (*0-689-81568-9*) Litle Simon.

— Matching Shapes. (Build-a-Block Bks.). (Illus.). 16p. (J). (ps-1). 1998. 9.99 (*0-689-81569-7*) Litle Simon.

Baker, Quentin, ed. see Lane, Mary B.

Baker, R. Advanced dBASE III Application. 1991. 24.95 (*0-8306-6625-7*) McGraw-Hill Prof.

— dBASE III Plus: Advanced. 1991. 29.95 (*0-8306-6639-7*) McGraw-Hill Prof.

— The dBASE III Plus Multiuser. 1991. 29.95 (*0-8306-6646-X*) McGraw-Hill Prof.

— Inventors & Inventions That Have Changed the Modern World. (History of Science & Technology Ser.). 168p. 1976. 17.50 (*0-7141-0380-2*, Pub. by SRIS) L Erlbaum Assocs.

— Panic Disorder: Theory, Research & Therapy. (Clinical Psychology Ser.). 364p. 1992. pap. 119.95 (*0-471-93317-1*) Wiley.

Baker, R., et al, eds. Radioactive Waste Management & Environmental Remediation: Proceedings, International Conference on Radioactive Waste Mangement & Environmental. 1036p. 1997. pap. 250.00 (*0-7918-1242-1*) ASME.

Baker, R. & Stepanova, E. Russian for Everybody: American Edition, Set. 6th ed. Kostomarov, V. G., ed. 544p. (C). 1992. 25.95 (*0-8285-3001-7*) Firebird NY.

Baker, R. A. Compendio de la Historia Cristiana: A Summary of Christian History. Almanza, Francisco G., tr. (SPA.). 372p. 1974. reprint ed. pap. 21.99 (*0-311-15032-2*) Casa Bautista.

Baker, R. D. Concrete Sun: Poems by R. D. Baker. 2nd expanded rev. ed. (Poetry Chapbook Ser.). (Illus.). 28p. 1995. pap. 4.00 (*1-887641-01-7*) Argonne Hotel Pr.

— Crazy Shotgun Guy: Poems by R. D. Baker. 2nd expanded rev. ed. (Poetry Chapbook Ser.). (Illus.). 28p. 1995. pap. 4.00 (*1-887641-00-9*) Argonne Hotel Pr.

— My Blue Goddess: Poems by R. D. Baker. (Poetry Chapbook Ser.). (Illus.). 28p. (Orig.). 1995. pap. 4.00 (*1-887641-10-6*) Argonne Hotel Pr.

— My War Against Sleep: Poems. (Poetry Chapbook Ser.). (Illus.). 28p. (Orig.). 1995. pap. 4.00 (*1-887641-02-5*) Argonne Hotel Pr.

— Panther Passing Across: Poems by R. D. Baker. (Poetry Chapbook Ser.). (Illus.). 28p. (Orig.). 1995. pap. 4.00 (*1-887641-03-3*) Argonne Hotel Pr.

Baker, R. D., ed. Collected WordWrights 1995: Poetry & Prose from the Magazine for People Who Love Written Word. (Illus.). 128p. (Orig.). 1995. pap. 25.00 (*1-887641-16-5*) Argonne Hotel Pr.

— Collected WordWrights 1996: Poetry & Prose from the Magazine for People Who Love the Written Word. (Illus.). 128p. (Orig.). 1996. pap. 25.00 (*1-887641-17-3*) Argonne Hotel Pr.

— Collected WordWrights 1997: Poetry & Prose from the Magazine for People Who Love the Written Word. (Illus.). 128p. (Orig.). 1997. pap. 25.00 (*1-887641-18-1*) Argonne Hotel Pr.

Baker, R. D., ed. see Biggar, Joanna.

Baker, R. D., ed. see Brown, Jamie.

Baker, R. D., ed. see Franks, David.

Baker, R. D., ed. see Goudreau, Ron.

Baker, R. D., ed. see Hazen, Elizabeth.

Baker, R. D., ed. see Kosow, Lisa.

Baker, R. D., ed. see Levy, Sara.

Baker, R. D., ed. see Negri, Sharon.

Baker, R. D., ed. see Reinke, Michael.

Baker, R. D., ed. see Williford, Rhonda.

Baker, R. J. & Nelder, J. A. Glim Manual Release 3. (Orig.). 1978. pap. 14.00 (*0-317-52204-3*, Pub. by Numer Algo) Princeton Bk Co.

Baker, R. Jacob, et al. CMOS Circuit Design, Layout & Simulation. LC 97-21906. (IEEE Press on Microelectronic Systems Ser.). 944p. 1997. 89.95 (*0-7803-3416-7*, PC 5689) Inst Electrical.

Baker, R. Jerry, et al. Policy & Procedures Manual for Purchasing & Materials Control. 2nd ed. LC 92-20166. 480p. (C). 1992. pap. 79.95 (*0-13-689969-2*) P-H.

Baker, R. Lisle & Wolfe, Norman H. Negotiated Development & Open Space Preservation: A Case Study of Neighborhood Purchase & Ultimate City Aquisition Involving Partial Development, Betterment Assessments & Federal Tax Benefits. LC HD0266.M37. (Lincoln Institute Monograph: No. 84-1). 66p. reprint ed. pap. 30.00 (*0-7837-5772-7*, 204543700006) Bks Demand.

Baker, R. M., et al, eds. Animal Welfare in the Twenty-First Century: Ethical, Educational & Scientific Challenges. 129p. 1994. pap. 125.00 (*0-9590540-6-5*, Pub. by Univs Fed Animal Welfare) St Mut.

— Animals & Science in the Twenty First Century: New Technologies & Challenges. 112p. 1994. pap. 125.00 (*0-646-22484-0*, Pub. by Univs Fed Animal Welfare) St Mut.

— Effective Animal Experimentation Ethics Committees. 136p. 1994. pap. 125.00 (*0-7855-2845-8*, Pub. by Univs Fed Animal Welfare) St Mut.

— Improving the Well-Being of Animals in the Research Environment. 146p. 1994. pap. 125.00 (*0-646-18116-5*, Pub. by Univs Fed Animal Welfare) St Mut.

Baker, R. Ray. Before Man in Michigan. 1936. 12.50 (*0-911586-52-0*) Wahr.

— Red Brother. (J). 1927. 12.50 (*0-911586-03-2*) Wahr.

Baker, R. Robin. Bird Navigation: The Solution of a Mystery? 256p. (C). 1984. 40.00 (*0-8419-0946-6*); pap. 26.95 (*0-8419-0947-4*) Holmes & Meier.

— Migration: Paths Through Time & Space. (Illus.). 248p. (C). 1983. 39.95 (*0-8419-0868-0*) Holmes & Meier.

Baker, R. Robinson & Niederhuber, John. The Operative Management of Breast Disease. (Illus.). 147p. 1992. text 179.00 (*0-7216-2960-1*, W B Saunders Co) Harcrt Hlth Sci Grp.

Baker, R. S. Woodrow Wilson & the World Settlement, 2 vols. (Illus.). 1958. 16.50 (*0-8446-1039-9*) Peter Smith.

Baker, R. Terry, et al, eds. Strong Metal-Support Interactions. LC 85-30708. (ACS Symposium Ser.: Vol. 298). 248p. 1986. reprint ed. pap. 76.90 (*0-608-03844-X*, 206429100008) Bks Demand.

Baker, R. Terry & Murrell, Larry L., eds. Novel Materials in Heterogeneous Catalysis. LC 90-1209. (Symposium Ser.: No. 437). (Illus.). 376p. 1990. 98.00 (*0-8412-1863-3*, Pub. by Am Chemical) OUP.

Baker, R. Terry, jt. ed. see Albright, Lyle F.

Baker, R. W., et al. Membrane Separation Systems: Recent Developments & Future Directions. LC 90-23675. (Illus.). 451p. 1991. 129.00 (*0-8155-1270-8*) Noyes.

Baker, R. W., jt. auth. see Baker, Judith J.

Baker, R. W., jt. auth. see Feldman, Janet I.

Baker, Rachel. The First Woman Doctor. (Scholastic Biography Ser.). (Illus.). 192p. (J). (gr. 4-7). 1987. reprint ed. pap. 3.99 (*0-590-44767-X*) Scholastic Inc.

Baker, Rachel. First Woman Doctor: The Story of Elizabeth Blackwell, M. D. (Scholastic Biography Ser.). (J). 1971. 9.09 (*0-606-03581-8*, Pub. by Turtleback) Demco.

Baker, Rachel, jt. auth. see Freedman, Marc.

Baker, Ralph, jt. ed. see Meyer, Fred.

Baker, Ralph H. The National Bituminous Coal Commission Administration of the Bituminous Coal Act, 1937-1941. LC 78-64183. (Johns Hopkins University. Studies in the Social Sciences. Thirtieth Ser. 1912: 3). (Illus.). 360p. reprint ed. 28.50 (*0-404-61291-1*) AMS Pr.

Baker, Ralph R., ed. Current Trends in the Management of Breast Cancer. LC 76-49094. 175p. reprint ed. pap. 54.30 (*0-608-15102-5*, 202307900032) Bks Demand.

Baker, Ralph S., et al, eds. Soil & Water Science: Key to Understanding Our Global Environment. LC 94-31646. (SSSA Special Publications: No. 41). 103p. 1994. pap. 15.00 (*0-89118-816-9*) Soil Sci Soc Am.

Baker, Rance G. & Phillips, Billie R. The Sampler: Patterns for Composition. 2nd ed. LC 85-80169. 203p. (C). 1986. pap. text 31.96 (*0-669-07684-8*) HM Trade Div.

Baker, Randall. Environmental Management in the Tropics. 240p. 1992. lib. bdg. 99.95 (*0-87371-661-2*, L661) Lewis Pubs.

— Scale & Administrative Performance: The Governance of Small States & Microstates. Conway, Dennis, ed. (Series on Environment & Development). 41p. (Orig.). 1992. pap. 2.00 (*1-881157-08-3*) In Ctr Global.

— Summer in the Balkans: Laughter & Tears after Communism. LC 94-21108. (Books for a World That Works). (Illus.). vi, 202p. 1994. 30.00 (*1-56549-037-1*); pap. 14.95 (*1-56549-036-3*) Kumarian Pr.

Baker, Randall, ed. Comparative Public Management: Putting U. S. Public Policy & Implementation in Context. LC 93-43438. 296p. 1994. 69.50 (*0-275-94347-X*, Praeger Pubs); pap. 26.95 (*0-275-94348-8*, Praeger Pubs) Greenwood.

— Environmental Law & Policy in the European Union & the United States. LC 97-9176. 280p. 1997. 65.00 (*0-275-95262-2*, Praeger Pubs) Greenwood.

— Public Administration in Small & Island States. LC 91-44015. (Library of Management for Development, New Direction). (Illus.). xv, 310p. 1992. 35.00 (*1-56549-001-0*); pap. 12.95 (*1-56549-000-2*) Kumarian Pr.

Baker, Ray S. Following the Color Line: An Account of Negro Citizenship in the American Democracy. (BCL1 - U. S. History Ser.). 314p. 1991. reprint ed. lib. bdg. 89.00 (*0-7812-6086-8*) Rprt Serv.

— New Industrial Unrest: Reasons & Remedies. LC 78-156402. (American Labor Ser., No. 2). 1977. reprint ed. 19.95 (*0-405-02912-8*) Ayer.

— Woodrow Wilson: Life & Letters, 8 vols., Set. (History - United States Ser.). 1992. reprint ed. lib. bdg. 720.00 (*0-7812-6226-7*) Rprt Serv.

Baker, Ray S., see Grayson, David, pseud.

Baker, Raymond. Forts of Old San Juan: San Juan National Historic Site, Puerto Rico. 80p. 1997. pap. 5.50 (*0-16-061674-3*) USGPO.

Baker, Raymond C., ed. Handbook of Pediatric Primary Care. LC 95-20030. 304p. 1995. pap. text 32.00 (*0-316-07825-5*) Lppncott W & W.

Baker, Raymond C. & Schmitt, Barton D. Pediatric Telephone Advice. 2nd ed. LC 97-3048. 300p. 1998. spiral bd. 35.95 (*0-316-77390-5*) Lppncott W & W.

Baker, Raymond W. Sadat & After: Struggles for Egypt's Political Soul. 392p. 1990. 49.50 (*0-674-78497-9*) HUP.

Baker, Rhonda. Media Law: A User's Guide for Film & Programme Makers LC 99-168078. 292p. 1997. write for info. (*0-415-13670-9*) Routledge.

Baker, Rich. Player's Option. 1996. 22.00 (*0-7869-0394-5*, Pub. by TSR Inc) Random.

Baker, Richard. Arms & Equipment Guide. 1998. 16.95 (*0-7869-1214-6*, Pub. by TSR Inc) Random.

***Baker, Richard.** City of Ravens. 2000. mass mkt. 6.99 (*0-7869-1401-7*) Wizards Coast.

Baker, Richard. Los Dos Mundos: Rural Mexican Americans, Another America. LC 94-28073. 294p. 1994. pap. 24.95 (*0-87421-184-0*) Utah St U Pr.

***Baker, Richard.** Dungeons & Dragons 3rd Core Rules Player's Handbook. 288p. 2000. 19.95 (*0-7869-1550-1*) TSR Inc.

— Forge of Fury. 2000. pap. 9.96 (*0-7869-1644-3*) Wizards Coast.

— Implementing Change with Clinical Audit. LC 98-35855. 208p. 1999. pap. 39.95 (*0-471-98257-1*) Wiley.

Baker, Richard. The Last Warhulk. 1998. 13.95 (*0-7869-1217-0*, Pub. by TSR Inc) Random.

— Meditations & Disquisitions. 1995. 23.99 (*0-87377-997-5*) GAM Pubns.

— Mexican American Students. LC 98-75415. 180p. (C). 1999. per. 31.95 (*0-7872-5623-4*, 41562301) Kendall-Hunt.

— Mozart: An Illustrated Biography. (Illus.). 149p. 1997. (*0-316-64133-2*) Little.

— Richard Baker's Companion to Music: A Personal A-Z Guide to Classical Music. (Illus.). 208p. 1995. 27.95 (*0-563-36414-9*, BBC-Parkwest) Parkwest Pubns.

— Schubert: A Life in Words & Pictures. 160p. 1999. pap. 17.00 (*0-316-07889-1*, Pub. by Little) Time Warner.

— The Shadow Stone. 1998. pap. 5.99 (*0-7869-1186-7*, Pub. by TSR Inc) Random.

***Baker, Richard.** Terror of Tobermory: An Informal Biography of Vice-Admiral Sir Gilbert. 188p. 2000. pap. 15.95 (*1-84158-031-7*, Pub. by Birlinn Ltd) Dufour.

Baker, Richard. Zero Point. 1999. pap. 5.99 (*0-7869-1367-3*, Pub. by TSR Inc) Random.

Baker, Richard & Slavicsek, Bill. Alien Compendium: Creatures of the Verge. (Illus.). 128p. (YA). (gr. 7 up). 1998. per. 21.95 (*0-7869-0778-9*, Pub. by TSR Inc) Random.

Baker, Richard A. Conservation Politics: The Senate Career of Clinton P. Anderson. LC 85-8748. 352p. reprint ed. pap. 109.20 (*0-7837-5865-0*, 204558400006) Bks Demand.

— Marie Lloyd: Queen of the Music-Halls. large type ed. (Lythway Ser.). 240p. 1992. 21.50 (*0-7451-1410-5*, G K Hall Lrg Type) Mac Lib Ref.

— The Senate of the United States. LC 87-3740. (Anvil Ser.). 272p. 1987. pap. 15.00 (*0-89874-865-8*, (K)) Krieger.

Baker, Richard A. & Davidson, Roger H. First among Equals: Senate Leaders of the 20th Century. 1991. 46.95 (*0-87187-581-0*); pap. 28.95 (*0-87187-586-1*) Congr Quarterly.

Baker, Richard Duck. Complete Gospel Guitar. 168p. 1997. pap. 19.95 incl. cd-rom (*0-7866-2503-1*, 96321) Mel Bay.

Baker, Richard E. Controlled Release of Biological Active Agents. LC 86-22422. 279p. 1987. 189.00 (*0-471-83724-5*) Wiley.

— The Dynamics of the Absurd in the Existentialist Novel. LC 92-38883. (American University Studies: General Literature: Ser. XIX, Vol. 31). 152p. (C). 1993. text 34.95 (*0-8204-2079-4*) P Lang Pubng.

— The Killing Place. 65p. (Orig.). 1984. pap. 3.00 (*0-685-42666-1*) Vardaman Pr.

— Shattered Visage. 103p. (Orig.). 1982. pap. 3.50 (*0-942648-01-3*) Vardaman Pr.

— Shell Burst Pond. (Illus.). 1982. pap. 3.00 (*0-942648-02-1*) Vardaman Pr.

Baker, Richard E. & Lembke, Valdean C. Advanced Financial Accounting. 3rd ed. (C). 1995. pap. text, student ed. 26.88 (*0-07-005728-1*) McGraw.

— Advanced Financial Accounting: Worksheets. 3rd ed. (C). 1996. pap. text 25.50 (*0-07-005727-3*) McGraw.

Baker, Richard E., et al. Advanced Financial Accounting. 3rd ed. LC 95-41295. (C). 1995. text 98.25 (*0-07-005414-2*) McGraw.

— Advanced Financial Accounting. 4th ed. LC 98-21047. 1224p. 1998. 90.31 (*0-07-290472-0*) McGraw.

Baker, Richard H. Advanced dBASE III Applications. (Illus.). 448p. (Orig.). 1985. 28.95 (*0-8306-0418-9*, 2618); pap. 21.95 (*0-8306-0318-2*, 2618) McGraw-Hill Prof.

— The Computer Security Handbook. LC 85-20580. (Illus.). 288p. 1985. 32.95 (*0-8306-0308-5*, 2608H) McGraw-Hill Prof.

— Extranets: The Complete Reference. LC 97-70565. (Illus.). 528p. 1997. pap. 39.95 (*0-07-006302-8*) McGraw.

— Framework II Applications. 2nd ed. (Illus.). 336p. (Orig.). 1987. 26.95 (*0-8306-2198-9*, 2798) McGraw-Hill Prof.

— Network Security: How to Plan for It & Achieve It. LC 94-20430. 1994. 45.00 (*0-07-005119-4*); pap. 34.95 (*0-07-005141-0*) McGraw.

***Baker, Richard H., ed.** The Federal Housing Board's Responsibility for Safety & Soundness & Mission Regulation of the Federal Home Loan Bank System: Congressional Hearing. (Illus.). 322p. (C). 2000. reprint ed. pap. text 35.00 (*0-7881-8960-3*) DIANE Pub.

— The Operation of Hedge Funds & Their Role in the Financial System: Congressional Hearing. 141p. (C). 2000. pap. text 35.00 (*0-7567-0036-1*) DIANE Pub.

— Technology & Banking: Congressional Hearing. 289p. 2000. pap. text 40.00 (*0-7567-0137-6*) DIANE Pub.

Baker, Richard L. World Builder's Guide Book. 1996. 20.00 (*0-7869-0434-8*, Pub. by TSR Inc) Random.

Baker, Richard S. Man of the Trees: Selected Writings of Richard St. Barbe Baker. (Illus.). 144p. (Orig.). 1989. 17.50 (*0-9600772-0-0*); pap. 12.50 (*0-9600772-1-9*) Ecology Action.

***Baker, Richard W.** Membrane Technology & Applications. 528p. 1999. 99.95 (*0-07-135440-9*) McGraw.

Baker, Richard W., ed. The ANZUS States & Their Region: Regional Policies of Australia, New Zealand, & the United States. LC 93-14121. 248p. 1994. 65.00 (*0-275-94693-2*, C4693, Praeger Pubs) Greenwood.

— Australia, New Zealand, & the United States: Internal Change & Alliance Relations in the Anzus States. LC 90-45198. 304p. 1991. 65.00 (*0-275-93797-6*, C3797, Praeger Pubs) Greenwood.

Baker, Richard W. & Hawke, Gary R., eds. ANZUS Economics: Economic Trends & Relations among Australia, New Zealand & the United States. LC 92-16558. 276p. 1992. 59.95 (*0-275-94381-X*, C4381, Praeger Pubs) Greenwood.

An Asterisk (*) at the beginning of an entry indicates that the title is appearing for the first time.

***Baker, Rick.** Mangroves to Major League: A Timeline of St. Petersburg, Florida (Pre-History to 2000 A.D.) (Illus.). 400p. 2000. 34.95 (*0-941072-38-X*) Southern Herit.

Baker, Rob. Planning Memorial Celebrations: A Sourcebook. LC 99-13085. 224p. 1999. pap. 12.00 (*0-609-80404-9*) Crown.

Baker, Rob, tr. see Nicolescu, Basarab.

Baker, Robert. Amos: A Study Guide. 152p. 1995. pap. 12.00 (*1-57312-020-0*) Smyth & Helwys.

— Successful Surgery: A Doctor's Mind & Body Guide to Help You Through Surgery. 288p. 1996. pap. 12.00 (*0-671-51900-X*, PB Trade Paper) PB.

Baker, Robert, ed. The Codification of Medical Morality. (Philosophy & Medicine Ser.: No. 49). 240p. 1995. pap. text 55.50 (*0-7923-3529-5*, Pub. by Kluwer Academic) Kluwer Academic.

— The Codification of Medical Morality, Vol. 2. (Philosophy & Medicine Ser.: No. 49). 240p. 1995. lib. bdg. 122.00 (*0-7923-3528-7*, Pub. by Kluwer Academic) Kluwer Academic.

— Legislating Medical Ethics: A Study of the New York State Do-Not-Resuscitate Law. LC 94-19575. (Philosophy & Medicine Ser.: 48). 476p. (C). 1995. lib. bdg. 220.50 (*0-7923-2995-3*, Pub. by Kluwer Academic) Kluwer Academic.

Baker, Robert, et al, eds. The Codification of Medical Morality Vol. 1: Historical & Philosophical Studies of the Formalization of Western Medical Morality in the Eighteenth & Nineteenth Centuries, No. 45. LC 92-49845. 238p. (C). 1993. lib. bdg. 124.50 (*0-7923-1921-4*, Pub. by Kluwer Academic) Kluwer Academic.

***Baker, Robert & Carey, Kimball.** Baker's Handbook of Ohio School Law, 199899. 2nd rev. ed. 674p. 1998. pap. 57.50 (*1-58360-001-9*) Anderson Pub Co.

Baker, Robert & Hair, P. E. Travails in Guinea: Robert Baker's "Brefe Dyscourse" (?1568) LC 93-199129. 48 p. 1990. write for info. (*0-85323-007-2*) Liverpool Univ Pr.

Baker, Robert & London, Barbara. Instant Projects: A Handbook of Demonstrations & Assignments for Photography Classes. Horenstein, Henry, ed. 272p. (Orig.). 1986. pap. 20.00 (*0-9616459-1-1*) Polaroid Corp.

Baker, Robert & Nietzel, Michael T. Private Eyes: One Hundred & One Knights. LC 85-70857. 385p. 1985. 30.95 (*0-87972-329-7*); pap. 18.95 (*0-87972-330-0*) Bowling Green Univ Popular Press.

Baker, Robert, jt. auth. see Adams, Ansel.

Baker, Robert, jt. auth. see Nyhus, Lloyd M.

Baker, Robert A. Child Sexual Abuse & False Memory Syndrome. LC 97-40899. 479p. 1998. 34.95 (*1-57392-182-3*) Prometheus Bks.

— Hidden Memories: Voices & Visions from Within. LC 96-8961. 390p. 1996. pap. 17.95 (*1-57392-094-0*) Prometheus Bks.

— Mind Games: Are We Obsessed with Therapy? LC 96-3035. (Illus.). 476p. 1996. 29.95 (*1-57392-071-1*) Prometheus Bks.

— Organic Substances & Sediments in Water Vol. 1: Huumics/Soils. 408p. 1991. lib. bdg. 110.00 (*0-87371-342-7*) CRC Pr.

— Organic Substances/Sediments in Water Vol. 3: Biological. 344p. 1991. lib. bdg. 110.00 (*0-87371-529-2*) CRC Pr.

— Relations Between Northern & Southern Baptists. rev. ed. Gaustad, Edwin S., ed. LC 79-52590. (Baptist Tradition Ser.). 1980. reprint ed. lib. bdg. 25.95 (*0-405-12457-0*) Ayer.

— They Call It Hypnosis. LC 90-33490. (Illus.). 313p. (C). 1990. 28.95 (*0-87975-576-8*) Prometheus Bks.

Baker, Robert A., ed. Organic Substances/Sediments in Water Vol. 2: Processes/Analysis. 560p. 1991. lib. bdg. 110.00 (*0-87371-528-4*) CRC Pr.

Baker, Robert A. & Landers, John M. A Summary of Christian History. rev. ed. LC 93-11779. 29.99 (*0-8054-1064-3*, 4210-64) Broadman.

Baker, Robert A. & Nickell, Joe. Missing Pieces: How to Investigate Ghosts, UFOs, Psychics, & Other Mysteries. LC 92-3439. 339p. (C). 1992. 27.95 (*0-87975-729-9*) Prometheus Bks.

Baker, Robert B. Philosophy & Sex. 3rd ed. LC 97-46446. 671p. 1998. pap. text 24.95 (*1-57392-184-X*) Prometheus Bks.

***Baker, Robert B., et al, eds.** The American Medical Ethics Revolution: How the AMA's Code of Ethics Has Transformed Physicians' Relationships to Patients, Professionals, & Society. LC 99-29636. 448p. 1999. 59.95 (*0-8018-6170-5*) Johns Hopkins.

Baker, Robert C. Linear Electronics in Control Systems. (Illus.). 240p. 1988. text 49.95 (*0-943876-03-6*) Barks Pubns.

Baker, Robert D., et al. Pediatric Parenteral Nutrition. LC 96-34371. (Clinical Nutrition Ser.). 465p. 1997. 79.00 (*0-412-07441-9*) Kluwer Academic.

Baker, Robert E., jt. auth. see Frank, Sandra J.

Baker, Robert F., ed. Handbook of Highway Engineering. LC 82-8922. 904p. 1982. reprint ed. lib. bdg. 115.00 (*0-89874-482-2*) Krieger.

Baker, Robert J. County Road Thirteen. LC 90-45933. 152p. (Orig.). 1990. pap. 7.99 (*0-8361-3540-7*) Herald Pr.

— Selection Indices in Plant Breeding. 240p. 1986. 132.00 (*0-8493-6377-2*, SB123, CRC Reprint) Franklin.

Baker, Robert J., et al, eds. Biology of Bats of the New World Family Phyllostomatidae, Pt. I. (Special Publications: No. 10). (Illus.). 218p. (Orig.). 1976. pap. 8.00 (*0-89672-036-5*) Tex Tech Univ Pr.

— Biology of Bats of the New World Family Phyllostomatidae, Pt. II. (Special Publications: No. 13). (Illus.). 364p. (Orig.). 1977. pap. 16.00 (*0-89672-039-X*) Tex Tech Univ Pr.

— Biology of Bats of the New World Family Phyllostomatidae, Part III, Part III. (Special Publications: No. 16). (Illus.). 441p. (Orig.). 1979. pap. 20.00 (*0-89672-068-3*) Tex Tech Univ Pr.

Baker, Robert J., jt. ed. see Genoways, Hugh H.

Baker, Robert K. Doing Library Research: An Introduction for Community College Students. LC 80-22943. (Guides to Library Research Ser.). 260p. 1981. text 42.50 (*0-89158-778-0*) Westview.

Baker, Robert L. Russian for Everybody. 288p. 1984. 49.95 (*0-7855-0912-7*, Pub. by Collets) St Mut.

Baker, Robert L. & Mednick, Birgitte R. Influences on Human Development: A Longitudinal Perspective. 1984. lib. bdg. 91.00 (*0-89838-130-4*) Kluwer Academic.

Baker, Robert P. Joshua's Way. Laborde, Karen, ed. 204p. 1997. 22.95 (*1-57579-070-X*) Pine Hill Pr.

Baker, Robert S. Brave New World: History, Science & Dystopia. (Masterwork Studies: No. 39). 160p. 1989. 23.95 (*0-8057-8077-7*, Twayne); per. 13.95 (*0-8057-8121-8*, Twayne) Mac Lib Ref.

— The Dark Historic Page: Social Satire & Historicism in the Novels of Aldous Huxley, 1921-1939. LC 81-70004. 253p. 1982. reprint ed. pap. 81.60 (*0-608-01926-7*, 206258100003) Bks Demand.

Baker, Robert S., ed. see Huxley, Aldous.

Baker, Robert W., jt. auth. see Trzepacz, Paula T.

Baker, Robin. Fantastic Journeys, the Marvels of Animal Migration. LC 92-170666. 25.00 (*1-85391-185-2*) Sterling.

— Guerras de Espermas Infelidad, Conflictos Sexuales y Otras Batallas de Alcoba. (SPA.). 356p. 1997. pap. 40.98 (*968-890-199-7*) Edivision Comp.

***Baker, Robin.** Sex in the Future: The Reproductive Revolution & How it Will Change Us. 336p. 2000. 25.95 (*1-55970-521-3*, Pub. by Arcade Pub Inc) Time Warner.

Baker, Robin. Sperm Wars: The Science of Sex. 319p. 1999. pap. text 18.00 (*0-7881-6004-4*) DIANE Pub.

***Baker, Robin & Oram, Elizabeth.** Baby Wars: Parenthood & Family Strife. 294p. 2000. reprint ed. pap. text 20.00 (*0-7881-6867-3*) DIANE Pub.

— Baby Wars: The Dynamics of Family Conflict. LC 98-35619. 320p. 1999. 25.00 (*0-88001-658-2*) HarpC.

***Baker, Robin & Oram, Elizabeth.** Baby Wars: The Dynamics of Family Conflict. 320p. 2000. pap. 14.00 (*0-06-095797-2*, Ecco Press) HarperTrade.

Baker, Rodney & Leonard, Alan. A Maritime History of Southampton in Picture Postcards. (C). 1989. 39.00 (*1-85455-032-2*, Pub. by Ensign Pubns & Print) St Mut.

Baker-Rodof, Mina, ed. Dandy Dutch Recipes. 160p. 1991. spiral bd. 6.95 (*0-941016-84-6*) Penfield.

Baker, Roger. Drag: A History of Female Impersonation in the Performing Arts. LC 94-37485. (Illus.). 268p. (C). 1995. text 45.00 (*0-8147-1253-3*); pap. text 18.50 (*0-8147-1254-1*) NYU Pr.

Baker, Roger A. Neural Repair, Transplantation & Rehabilitation. 336p. 1999. 54.95 (*0-86377-628-0*) L Erlbaum Assocs.

***Baker, Roger C.** Flow Measurement Handbook: Industrial Designs, Operating Principles, Applications & Performance. LC 99-14190. (Illus.). 600p. (C). 2000. 110.00 (*0-521-48010-8*) Cambridge U Pr.

Baker, Roger G., ed. The Bible As Literature: Out of the Best Book. 304p. (C). 1995. pap. text 14.95 (*1-886632-06-5*) Snow Coll Eng.

— Snow Faculty Studies: The Journal of the Faculty of Snow College, Vol. 1. 101p. (C). 1991. text 14.95 (*1-886632-01-4*) Snow Coll Eng.

— Snow Faculty Studies: The Journal of the Faculty of Snow College, Vol. 2. 99p. (C). 1992. text 14.95 (*1-886632-02-2*) Snow Coll Eng.

— Snow Faculty Studies: The Journal of the Faculty of Snow College, Vol. 3. 84p. (C). 1993. text 14.95 (*1-886632-03-0*) Snow Coll Eng.

— Snow Faculty Studies: The Journal of the Faculty of Snow College, Vol. 4. 113p. (C). 1994. text 14.95 (*1-886632-04-9*) Snow Coll Eng.

Baker, Ron. Oil & Gas: The Production Story. (Illus.). 91p. (Orig.). 1983. pap. text 25.00 (*0-88698-002-X*, 3.90010) PETEX.

— A Primer of Offshore Operations. 3rd ed. Bork, Kathy, ed. Clardy, Jonell, tr. (Illus.). 132p. 1997. pap. text 35.00 (*0-88698-178-6*, 1.10030) PETEX.

Baker, Ron. A Primer of Oilwell Drilling. 5th rev. ed. Bork, Kathy, ed. LC 92-46408. (Illus.). 151p. 1996. pap. text 25.00 (*0-88698-159-X*, 2.00050) PETEX.

Baker, Ron. A Primer of Oilwell Drilling Workbook. (Illus.). 60p. 1994. ring bd., wbk. ed. 20.00 (*0-88698-174-3*, 2.00056) PETEX.

— Treating Oil Field Emulsions. 4th ed. Bork, Kathy, ed. (Illus.). 115p. 1990. pap. text 25.00 (*0-88698-137-9*, 3.50040) PETEX.

Baker, Ron, ed. Well Logging Methods: Well Servicing & Workover, Lesson 3. 2nd ed. (Illus.). 54p. (Orig.). 1992. pap text 16.00 (*0-88698-151-4*, 3-70320) PETEX.

***Baker, Ron & International Association of Drilling Contractors.** Diesel Engines & Electric Power. 3rd ed. LC 98-18155. (Rotary Drilling Ser.). Orig. Title: Power & Power Transmission; Diesel Engines & Electric Power. (Illus.). 248p. 1998. pap. 20.00 (*0-88698-169-7*, 2.108301) PETEX.

Baker, Ron, jt. auth. see Ebert, Gary.

Baker, Ron, ed. see Fitzpatrick, Jim.

Baker, Ron, ed. see Van Dyke, Kate.

Baker, Ronal J. Biblical Dinosaurs. rev. ed. (Illus.). 307p. 199_. pap. 12.95 (*0-9629531-3-X*) Biblical Dinos.

Baker, Ronald J. Pricing for Value: A Professional's Guide 1998. 98th ed. (C). 1998. pap. 79.00 (*0-15-606291-7*, Pub. by Harcourt Coll Pubs) Harcourt.

***Baker, Ronald J.** Professional's Guide to Value Pricing with CD-ROM. 400p. 2000. pap. 99.00 incl. cd-rom (*0-15-607224-6*) Harcourt Prof.

Baker, Ronald J. The Professional's Guide to Value Pricing 2000. 400p. 1999. pap. text 99.00 (*0-15-606993-8*) Harcourt.

***Baker, Ronald J.** Professional's Guide to Value Pricing 2000. 460p. 1999. pap. 99.00 (*0-15-606992-X*) Harcourt.

Baker, Ronald L. From Needmore to Prosperity: Hoosier Place Names in Folklore & History. LC 94-44707. 1995. 29.95 (*0-253-32866-7*); pap. 15.95 (*0-253-20955-2*) Ind U Pr.

— Hoosier Folk Legends. LC 81-47568. 288p. (Orig.). 1982. 27.50 (*0-253-32844-6*) Ind U Pr.

— Hoosier Folk Legends. LC 81-47568. 288p. (Orig.). 1984. pap. 12.95 (*0-253-20334-1*, MB 334) Ind U Pr.

— Jokelore: Humorous Folktales from Indiana. LC 84-43174. 236p. 1986. 31.95 (*0-253-33163-3*); pap. 12.95 (*0-253-20406-2*, MB 406) Ind U Pr.

Baker, Ronald L. & Carmony, Marvin. Indiana Place Names. LC 74-17915. 224p. 1976. 27.50 (*0-253-14167-2*) Ind U Pr.

— Indiana Place Names. LC 74-17915. 218p. Date not set. reprint ed. pap. 67.60 (*0-608-20580-X*, 205449500002) Bks Demand.

***Baker, Ronald L. & Federal Writers' Project Staff.** Homeless, Friendless & Penniless: The WPA Interviews with Former Slaves Living in Indiana. LC 00-32004. 2000. 29.95 (*0-253-33803-4*) Ind U Pr.

Baker, Rosalie F. & Baker, Charles F., III. Ancient Greeks: Creating the Classical Tradition. LC 95-26637. (Oxford Profiles Ser.). (Illus.). 256p. (J). (gr. 5). 1997. 35.00 (*0-19-509940-0*) OUP.

— Ancient Romans: Expanding the Classical Tradition. LC 97-21531. (Oxford Profiles Ser.). (Illus.). 272p. (YA). (gr. 9 up). 1998. 35.00 (*0-19-510884-1*) OUP.

Baker, Rosalie F., jt. auth. see Baker, Charles F., III.

***Baker, Rosaria F.** The Soul of a Poet. 24p. 2000. pap. 7.00 (*0-8059-4691-8*) Dorrance.

Baker, Roscoe. The American Legion & American Foreign Policy. LC 74-39. (Illus.). 329p. 1974. reprint ed. lib. bdg. 75.00 (*0-8371-7360-4*, BAAL, Greenwood Pr) Greenwood.

Baker, Ross K. Friend & Foe in the U. S. Senate. LC 98-73897. 334p. (C). 1999. pap. text 17.95 (*1-58390-002-0*) Copley Pub.

— House & Senate. 2nd ed. LC 95-5367. (C). 1995. pap. text 14.75 (*0-393-96318-7*) Norton.

— The New Fat Cats: Members of Congress As Political Benefactors - A Twentieth Century Fund Paper. 92p. 1989. write for info. (*0-87078-301-7*); pap. 8.95 (*0-87078-300-9*) Century Foundation.

Baker, Russell. The Good Times. large type ed. (General Ser.). 300p. 1990. lib. bdg. 22.95 (*0-8161-4919-2*, G K Hall Lrg Type) Mac Lib Ref.

— The Good Times. 352p. 1991. reprint ed. pap. 9.95 (*0-452-25289-X*, Plume) Dutton Plume.

— Growing Up. LC 83-8213. 288p. 1983. pap. 13.95 (*0-452-25550-3*, Plume) Dutton Plume.

— Growing Up. 1992. mass mkt. 6.99 (*0-451-16838-0*, Sig) NAL.

Baker, Russell. Growing Up. 1982. 11.09 (*0-606-00805-5*, Pub. by Turtleback) Demco.

— Making Your Way to an Access in Mathematics. 38p. (C). 1994. text 9.40 (*0-536-58619-5*) Pearson Custom.

Baker, Russell. So This Is Depravity. 1987. pap. 4.95 (*0-317-56882-5*) PB.

— There's a Country in My Cellar. 432p. 1991. pap. 8.95 (*0-380-71451-5*, Avon Bks) Morrow Avon.

Baker, Russell, ed. The Norton Book of Light Verse. 1986. 29.95 (*0-393-02366-4*) Norton.

— Russell Baker's Book of American Humor. 598p. 1993. 30.00 (*0-393-03592-1*) Norton.

Baker, Russell P. Marriages & Obituaries from the Tennessee Baptist, 1844-1862. 137p. 1979. 18.50 (*0-89308-127-2*) Southern Hist Pr.

Baker, Ruth. G. H. & Friends Learn about Jesus. 1995. 6.95 (*0-911866-27-2*) LifeSprings Res.

Baker, Ruth T. Summer Storms, Winter Skies. 1999. pap. 4.50 (*1-57514-330-5*, 1179) Encore Perform Pub.

Baker, S. Josephine. Fighting for Life. LC 74-1664. (Children & Youth Ser.). (Illus.). 280p. 1974. reprint ed. 26.95 (*0-405-05945-0*) Ayer.

Baker, Sally. Color Me Love. LC 75-27766. (Illus.). 1975. pap. 4.50 (*0-930422-08-2*) Dennis-Landman.

Baker, Samm S., jt. auth. see Bellak, Leopold.

Baker, Samm S., jt. auth. see Tarnower, Herman.

Baker, Samuel. Wild Beasts & Their Ways. 1988. 35.00 (*0-935632-75-1*) Wolfe Pub Co.

Baker, Samuel, jt. auth. see Langer, Lawrence L.

Baker, Samuel H. Reading in Public Sector Economics. 2nd ed. LC 96-44861. (Fe - Public Finance Ser.). 1996. mass mkt. 38.95 (*0-538-86524-5*) S-W Pub.

Baker, Samuel H. & Elliott, Catherine S., eds. Readings in Public Sector Economics. LC 89-84052. 603p. (C). 1990. pap. text 30.36 (*0-669-18027-0*) HM Trade Div.

Baker, Samuel W. Albert N'yanzu: Great Basins of the Nile & Explorations of the Nile Sources, 2 vols. reprint ed. text 79.00 (*0-7812-0732-0*) Rprt Serv.

— In the Heart of Africa. LC 73-109310. 1970. reprint ed. lib. bdg. 45.00 (*0-8371-3567-2*, BHA&) Greenwood.

Baker, Sandy. Drawing DoodleLoops: Creative Whole Language Activities for Beginning Writers. (DoodleLoops Ser.). (Illus.). 96p. teacher ed. 10.95 (*0-86653-789-9*, GA1483) Good Apple.

— Math DoodleLoops. (DoodleLoops Ser.). 96p. 1996. teacher ed. 11.99 (*1-56417-842-0*, GA1549) Good Apple.

— Spelling DoodleLoops. (DoodleLoops Ser.). 96p. 1996. teacher ed. 11.99 (*1-56417-843-9*, GA1550) Good Apple.

Baker, Sanna. Grandpa Is a Flyer. LC 94-22008. (Illus.). (J). (gr. k up). 1995. lib. bdg. 15.95 (*0-8075-3033-6*) A Whitman.

Baker, Sanna A. Mississippi Going North. LC 95-52923. (Illus.). 32p. (J). (gr. k-4). 1996. lib. bdg. 15.95 (*0-8075-5164-3*) A Whitman.

Baker, Sarah. Fighting for Life. (American Autobiography Ser.). 264p. 1995. reprint ed. lib. bdg. 79.00 (*0-7812-8447-3*) Rprt Serv.

Baker, Scott. Ancestral Hungers. 1996. pap. 14.95 (*0-312-86305-5*) St Martin.

— Ancestral Hungers. 320p. mass mkt. 5.99 (*0-8125-0259-0*, Pub. by Tor Bks) St Martin.

— Ancestral Hungers. LC 94-44447. 320p. 1995. 21.95 (*0-312-85868-X*) Tor Bks.

— Ancestral Hungers. 320p. 1996. mass mkt. write for info. (*0-614-05543-1*) Tor Bks.

Baker, Sean. CORBA Distributed Objects: Using ORBIX. LC 97-14386. 544p. (C). 1997. 49.95 (*0-201-92475-7*) Addison-Wesley.

Baker, Selwyn J. & Ramachandran, K. The Design & Analysis of Iron Supplementation Trials. DeMaeyer, Edouard M. & Kahn, Samuel G., eds. (Illus.). 38p. (Orig.). 1984. pap. text 3.50 (*0-935368-44-2*) ILSI.

Baker, Shan R., ed. Microsurgical Reconstruction of the Head & Neck. (Illus.). 366p. 1989. text 171.00 (*0-443-08587-0*) Church.

Baker, Shan R. & Swanson, Neil A., eds. Local Flaps in Facial Reconstruction. (Illus.). 656p. (C). (gr. 13). 1994. text 196.00 (*0-8016-6925-1*, 06925) Mosby Inc.

Baker, Sharlene. Finding Signs. 256p. 1991. mass mkt. 4.99 (*0-446-36198-4*) Warner Bks.

Baker, Sharon. Burning Tears of Sassurum. 288p. (Orig.). 1988. pap. 3.50 (*0-380-75113-5*, Avon Bks) Morrow Avon.

— Journey to Membliar. 256p. (Orig.). 1987. pap. 3.50 (*0-380-75114-3*, Avon Bks) Morrow Avon.

— Who's in Charge Here? For LTC Charge Nurses: A Guidebook for the Long Term Care Charge Nurse. 132p. (C). 1998. 18.00 (*1-877735-26-4*, 2157PP) Prof Prnting & Pub.

Baker, Sharon L., jt. auth. see Lancaster, F. Wilfrid.

Baker, Sheena. There's a Worm in My Apple. (Illus.). 111p. 1985. pap. 6.95 (*0-7737-5029-0*) Genl Dist Srvs.

Baker, Shelli J. The Travail of the Flag. LC 89-63069. (Illus.). 96p. 1989. pap. 6.95 (*0-89221-176-8*) New Leaf.

Baker-Shenk, Charlotte. American Sign Language: A Look at Its History, Structure & Community. 1978. pap. 3.95 (*0-932666-01-9*) T J Pubs.

Baker-Shenk, Charlotte, jt. auth. see Cokely, Dennis.

Baker, Sheridan. The Practical Stylist: Canadian Edition. 3rd ed. (C). 1991. pap. 20.93 (*0-06-040449-3*) Addson-Wesley Educ.

Baker, Sheridan, et al. The Canadian Practical Stylist with Reading. 2nd ed. 432p. (C). 1986. pap. 22.81 (*0-06-040466-3*) Addson-Wesley Educ.

Baker, Sheridan W. The Practical Stylist with Readings & Handbook. 8th ed. LC 96-49817. 540p. (C). 1997. pap. text 49.00 (*0-321-01182-1*) Longman.

Baker, Sheridan Warner. The Practical Stylist. 8th ed. LC 97-22126. 268p. (C). 1997. pap. text 40.00 (*0-321-01975-X*) Addison-Wesley.

Baker, Shirley. Street Photographs: Manchester & Salford. (Illus.). 1989. pap. 21.00 (*1-85224-058-X*, Pub. by Bloodaxe Bks) Dufour.

Baker, Shirley K. & Jackson, Mary E., eds. The Future of Resource Sharing. LC 95-35946. (Journal of Library Administration: Vol. 21, Nos. 1-2). 202p. 1995. 49.95 (*1-56024-773-8*) Haworth Pr.

Baker, Shirley R., ed. see American Family Records Association Staff.

Baker, Sidney M. Detoxification & Healing: The Key to Optimal Health. Barilla, Jean, ed. LC 96-46373. 200p. (Orig.). 1997. pap. 14.95 (*0-87983-709-8*, 37098K, Keats Publng) NTC Contemp Pub Co.

— Folic Acid. (Good Health Guides Ser.). 50p. 1995. pap. 3.95 (*0-87983-662-8*, 36628K, Keats Publng) NTC Contemp Pub Co.

***Baker, Sidney M. & Baar, Karen.** The Circadian Prescription: Get in Step with Your Body's Natural Rhythms to Maximize Energy, Vitality & Longevity. 240p. 2000. 24.95 (*0-399-14596-6*) Putnam Pub Group.

Baker-Smith, Dominic. More's Utopia. 224p. 1991. 69.95 (*0-04-800078-7*, A8191) Routledge.

Baker-Smith, Dominic & Erasmus, Desiderius. Expositions of the Psalms. Smith, Michael J., tr. (Collected Works of Erasmus: Vol. 63). 480p. 1997. text 100.00 (*0-8020-4308-9*) U of Toronto Pr.

Baker-Smith, Veronica P. A Life of Anne of Hanover, Princess Royal. (Publications of the Sir Thomas Browne Institute, Leiden, New Ser.). xi, 190p. 1995. 83.00 (*90-04-10198-5*) Brill Academic Pubs.

Baker, Sorelle, jt. auth. see Rosenberg, Donna.

Baker, Stanley. Railroad Collectibles. 4th ed. (Illus.). 198p. 1996. pap. 14.95 (*0-89145-410-1*, 2026) Collector Bks.

Baker, Stanley B., ed. School Counsel in 21st Century Report. 2nd ed. 1996. 51.80 (*0-13-026031-2*) P-H.

***Baker, Stephen.** The Fiction of Postmodernity. 224p. 2000. pap. 25.95 (*0-7425-0199-X*) Rowman.

Baker, Stephen. How to Live with a Neurotic Cat. LC 99-24728. 1999. pap. text 7.99 (*0-517-20734-6*) Random Hse Value.

— How to Live with a Neurotic Cat. (Illus.). 128p. 1989. mass mkt. 10.95 (*0-446-38640-5*, Pub. by Warner Bks) Little.

— How to Live with a Neurotic Cat Owner. (Illus.). 144p. (Orig.). 1993. mass mkt. 7.99 (*0-446-39391-6*, Pub. by Warner Bks) Little.

— How to Live with a Neurotic Dog. LC 95-51145. (Illus.). 128p. (Orig.). 1988. pap. 12.95 (*0-8092-4628-7*, 462870, Contemporary Bks) NTC Contemp Pub Co.

— How to Live with a Neurotic Dog. LC 94-17120. (Illus.). 144p. (Orig.). 1994. 7.99 (*0-517-11842-4*) Random.

B

An Asterisk (*) at the beginning of an entry indicates that the title is appearing for the first time

— Me & My Cat: A Feline Family Album. (Illus.). 144p. 1992. mass mkt. 12.99 (*0-446-39455-6*, Pub. by Warner Bks) Little.

— Systematic Approach to Advertising Creativity. LC 78-23814. (Illus.). 288p. reprint ed. pap. 89.30 (*0-8357-3612-1*, AU0039700004) Bks Demand.

Baker, Stephen A. Effects of Law Enforcement Accreditation: Officer Selection, Promotion, & Education. LC 95-30541. 184p. 1995. 59.95 (*0-275-95311-4*, Praeger Pubs) Greenwood.

Baker, Stephen H. Macintosh Programming Faqs. 656p. 1996. pap. 39.99 (*0-7645-4001-7*) IDG Bks.

Baker, Stephen R. The Abdominal Plain Film. (Illus.). 431p. (C). 1990. pap. text 140.00 (*0-8385-7896-9*, A7896-2) Appleton & Lange.

— The Abdominal Plain Film. 2nd ed. LC 98-6879. 431p. 1999. 165.00 (*0-8385-0275-X*, Apple Lange Med) McGraw.

***Baker, Steve.** The Postmodern Animal. (Essays in Art & Culture Ser.). (Illus.). 224p. 2000. pap. 24.95 (*1-86189-060-5*, Pub. by Reaktion Bks) Consort Bk Sales.

Baker, Steve & Tabor, Amy. Human Rights Committees: Keeping Organizations on Course. (High Tide Disability Series). 57p. 1999. spiral bd. 10.95 (*1-892696-04-5*) High Tide Pr.

B

Baker, Steve & Ward, Neil. Trophy Stripers & Hybrids. LC 89-82206. (Illus.). 268p. (Orig.). 1990. pap. 14.50 (*0-937866-22-9*) Atlantic Pub Co.

Baker, Steve J. California Co-op Directory & Resource Guide. 55p. 1984. pap. text 5.50 (*0-910427-00-3*) Calif Dept Co.

***Baker, Steven.** Stairway to the Stars. 2000. pap. write for info. (*1-58235-284-4*) Watermrk Pr.

Baker, Stewart A. & Davis, Mark D. The UNCITRAL Arbitration Rules in Practice: The Experience of the Iran-United States Claims Tribunal. LC 92-17357. 1992. 80.00 (*90-6544-628-1*) Kluwer Law Intl.

Baker, Stewart A. & Hurst, Paul R. The Limits of Trust: Cryptography, Governments, & Electronic Commerce. LC 98-26470. 1998. 125.00 (*90-411-0635-9*) Kluwer Law Intl.

Baker, Stuart. Birds, Vol. I. 2nd ed. (Fauna of British India Ser.). (Illus.). xxiv, 484p. 1974. reprint ed. 30.00 (*0-88065-198-9*) Scholarly Pubns.

— Birds: Passeres fam. IX Cinelida XVII regulida. (Fauna of British India Ser.: Vol. 2). xxiii, 561p. 1985. 75.00 (*1-55528-014-5*, Pub. by Today Tomorrow) Scholarly Pubns.

— Birds: Passeres fam XVII Irenida XXXIII Eurylamida, Vol. 3. (Fauna of British India Ser.). xx, 480p. 1985. 75.00 (*1-55528-015-3*, Pub. by Today Tomorrow) Scholarly Pubns.

Baker, Stuart, ed. Oke's Magisterial Formulist. ring bd. write for info. (*0-406-99835-3*, OMFASET, MICHIE) LEXIS Pub.

— Oke's Magisterial Formulist, 2 vols., Set. ring bd. 380.00 (*0-406-32400-X*, UK, MICHIE) LEXIS Pub.

Baker, Stuart & Bazell, Christopher. Endorsement & Disqualification. 235p. 1989. pap. 66.00 (*0-406-13801-X*, UK, MICHIE) LEXIS Pub.

Baker, Stuart, jt. auth. see Nowinski, Joseph.

Baker, Sue. The Birds & the Bees. LC 91-39758. 32p. (J). (gr. 3 up). 1991. 9.99 (*0-85953-400-6*) Childs Play.

— Child's Play Weather. (J). (ps-3). write for info. (*0-85953-929-6*) Childs Play.

Baker, Sue, et al. Ottawa: A Contemporary Portrait. LC 97-36178. 224p. 1997. 39.00 (*1-885352-74-3*) Community Comm.

— Principles of Hotel Front Office Operations: A Study Guide. LC 93-3152. (Hotel & Catering Ser.). 304p. 1994. pap. 35.00 (*0-304-32729-8*) Continuum.

Baker, Sue, jt. auth. see Hibbert, Vicky.

Baker, Sue, jt. illus. see Kubler, Annie.

Baker, Sunny. From Book Idea to Bestseller. LC 96-51455. 432p. 1997. per. 18.00 (*0-7615-0630-6*) Prima Pub.

Baker, Sunny & Baker, Kim. Marketing Yearbook. (C). 1992. 79.95 (*0-13-554486-6*, Macmillan Coll) P-H.

— Million Dollar Home-Based Businesses: Successful Entrepreneurs. 228p. 1993. pap. 9.95 (*1-55850-246-7*) Adams Media.

— On Time - On Budget: A Step-by-Step Guide for Managing Any Project. LC 92-12298. 320p. (C). 1992. text 39.95 (*0-13-633447-4*) P-H.

— On Time - On Budget: A Step-by-Step Guide for Managing Any Project. (Illus.). 304p. 1997. reprint ed. text 20.00 (*0-7881-5087-1*) DIANE Pub.

— The Ultimate Home Office Survival Guide. LC 98-13278. (Ultimate Survival Guide Ser.). 400p. 1998. pap. 18.95 incl. cd-rom (*0-7689-0007-7*) Petersons.

Baker, Sunny & Sbraga, Michelle. The Pasta Gourmet: Creative Pasta Recipes from Appetizers to Desserts. LC 96-148597. (Illus.). 304p. pap. 14.95 (*0-89529-663-2*, Avery) Penguin Putnam.

Baker, Sunny, jt. auth. see Baker, Kim.

Baker, Susan. How to Humiliate Your Peeping Tom. 1988. 15.00 (*0-614-18199-2*) Visual Studies.

***Baker, Susan.** Provincetown Dogs. LC 99-44080. (Illus.). 40p. 2000. pap. 12.95 (*1-58465-037-0*) U Pr of New Eng.

Baker, Susan, photos by. The History of Provincetown. (Illus.). 64p. 1999. 20.00 (*0-9660352-2-4*) Verve Edtns.

Baker, Susan & Gibson, Steve. Gore Vidal. LC 96-26809. (Critical Companions to Popular Contemporary Writers Ser.). 232p. 1997. 29.95 (*0-313-29579-4*) Greenwood.

Baker, Susan & Jehlicka, Petr, eds. Dilemmas of Transition: The Environment, Democracy & Economic Reform in East Central Europe. LC 98-17800. 160p. 1998. 52.50 (*0-7146-4764-0*, Pub. by F Cass Pubs); pap. 24.50 (*0-7146-4310-6*, Pub. by F Cass Pubs) Intl Spec Bk.

Baker, Susan & Kousis, Maria, eds. Politics of Sustainable Development. LC 96-29598. 288p. (C). 1997. 85.00 (*0-415-13873-6*); pap. 25.99 (*0-415-13874-4*) Routledge.

Baker, Susan & Van Doorne-Huiskes, Anneke, eds. Women & Public Policy: The Shifting Boundaries Between the Public & Private Spheres. 248p. 1999. text 65.95 (*1-84014-936-1*, Pub. by Ashgate Pub) Ashgate Pub Co.

Baker, Susan, jt. ed. see Kehler, Dorothea.

Baker, Susan, ed. see Yearly, Steven.

Baker, Susan Gonzalez. The Cautious Welcome: The Legalization Programs of the Immigration Reform & Control Act. LC 90-43203. (Urban Institute Report: No. 90-9). 205p. (C). 1990. pap. text 20.00 (*0-87766-494-3*); lib. bdg. 39.00 (*0-87766-493-5*) Urban Inst.

Baker, Susan J., jt. auth. see Adams, Laurie S.

Baker, Susan K. Managing Patient Expectations: The Art of Finding & Keeping Loyal Patients. LC 98-15900. (Business & Management Ser.). 256p. 1998. 34.95 (*0-7879-4158-1*) Jossey-Bass.

Baker, Susan P., et al. The Injury Fact Book. 2nd ed. (Illus.). 368p. 1991. text 39.95 (*0-19-506194-2*) OUP.

Baker, Susan S. Radical Beginnings: Richard Hofstadter & the 1930s, 112. LC 84-27930. (Contributions in American History Ser.: No. 112). 268p. 1985. 62.95 (*0-313-24713-7*, BHO/, Greenwood Pr) Greenwood.

Baker, Susan S. & Davis, Anne. Pediatric Enteral Nutrition. 1993. text 69.95 (*0-442-01341-8*) Chapman & Hall.

Baker, Susan S., et al. In-Home Breastfeeding Support Program: Guide for Implementation & Management. 82p. 1997. ring bd. 38.16 (*0-9659498-2-6*) N C Coop Ext.

— In-Home Breastfeeding Support Program: Guide for Training Breastfeeding Support Counselors: Teaching Materials, Vols. 1 & 2. large type ed. 1997. 168.00 (*0-9659498-0-X*) N C Coop Ext.

— In-Home Breastfeeding Support Program Vol. 2: Guide for Training Breastfeeding Counselors: Teaching Materials, Vols. 1 & 2. large type ed. 1997. 168.00 (*0-9659498-1-8*) N C Coop Ext.

Baker, Susan S., jt. auth. see Norris, Joye A.

Baker, Sylvia. Endangered Vertebrates: A Selected, Annotated Bibliography, 1981-1988. LC 90-2863. 216p. 1990. text 10.00 (*0-8240-4796-6*) Garland.

Baker, Sylvia. A Certain Seduction. 256p. 1996. mass mkt. 10.95 (*0-7472-5123-1*, Pub. by Headline Bk Pub) Trafalgar.

— Evolution: Bone of Contention. 1976. pap. 4.99 (*0-85234-226-8*, Pub. by Evangelical Pr) P & R Pubng.

— The Loving Game. 288p. 1997. pap. 11.95 (*0-7472-5124-X*, Pub. by Headline Bk Pub) Trafalgar.

— The Loving Game. large type ed. (Black Satin Romance Ser.). 442p. 1997. 27.99 (*1-86110-027-2*, Pub. by Mgna Lrg Print) Ulverscroft.

Baker, T., tr. see Bree, Malwine.

Baker, T. F. A History of the County of Middlesex Vol. X: Hackney Parish. (Victoria History of the Counties of England Ser.). (Illus.). 232p. 1995. 160.00 (*0-19-722782-1*) OUP.

Baker, T. F., ed. A History of the County of Middlesex, Vol. 6. (Victoria History of the Counties of England Ser.). (Illus.). 248p. 1980. 135.00 (*0-19-722750-3*) OUP.

— A History of the County of Middlesex: Islington & Stoke Newington Parishes, Vol. 8. (Victoria History of the Counties of England Ser.). (Illus.). 250p. 1985. 145.00 (*0-19-722762-7*) OUP.

Baker, T. Harri & Browning, Jane. An Arkansas History for Young People. 2nd ed. (YA). (gr. 8 up). 1997. student ed. 36.00 (*1-55728-399-0*) U of Ark Pr.

Baker, T. Lindsay. Blades in the Sky: Windmilling through the Eyes of B. H. "Tex" Burdick. LC 92-17903. 128p. 1992. pap. 20.00 (*0-89672-294-5*) Tex Tech Univ Pr.

— Building the Lone Star: An Illustrated Guide to Historic Sites. LC 86-5860. (Centennial Series of the Association of Former Students: No. 20). (Illus.). 360p. 1986. 34.95 (*0-89096-289-8*) Tex A&M Univ Pr.

— The Early History of Panna Maria, Texas. (Graduate Studies: No. 9). (Illus.). 69p. (Orig.). 1975. pap. 4.00 (*0-89672-016-0*) Tex Tech Univ Pr.

— A Field Guide to American Windmills. LC 84-40272. (Illus.). 516p. 1985. 75.00 (*0-8061-1901-2*) U of Okla Pr.

— The First Polish Americans: Silesian Settlements in Texas. LC 78-6373. (Illus.). 320p. 1996. reprint ed. pap. 16.95 (*0-89096-725-3*) Tex A&M Univ Pr.

— Ghost Towns of Texas. LC 86-40067. (Illus.). 208p. 1991. pap. 19.95 (*0-8061-2189-0*) U of Okla Pr.

— The Polish Texans. (Illus.). 120p. 1982. pap. 7.95 (*0-933164-99-8*) U of Tex Inst Tex Culture.

***Baker, T. Lindsay.** The 702 Model Windmill: Its Assembly, Installation & Use. (Illus.). 65p. 1999. pap. 19.95 (*0-9679480-0-2*) Amer Wind.

Baker, T. Lindsay, ed. North American Windmill Manufacturers' Trade Literature: A Descriptive Guide. LC 98-6908. (Illus.). 608p. 1998. 37.50 (*0-8061-3045-8*) U of Okla Pr.

— The Texas Red River Country: The Official Surveys of the Headwaters, 1876. LC 98-4859. (Illus.). 256p. 1998. 29.95 (*0-89096-803-9*) Tex A&M Univ Pr.

Baker, T. Lindsay & Baker, Julie P. The WPA Oklahoma Slave Narratives. LC 95-16222. (Illus.). 544p. 1996. pap. 24.95 (*0-8061-2859-3*) U of Okla Pr.

Baker, T. Lindsay & Baker, Julie P., eds. Till Freedom Cried Out: Memories of Texas Slave Life. LC 96-38575. (Clayton Wheat Williams Texas Life Ser.: Vol. 6). (Illus.). 192p. (C). 1997. text 29.95 (*0-89096-736-9*) Tex A&M Univ Pr.

— The WPA Oklahoma Slave Narratives. LC 95-16222. 1996. 49.95 (*0-8061-2792-9*) U of Okla Pr.

Baker, T. N., ed. Titanium Technology in Microalloyed Steels. (Illus.). 240p. 1997. 100.00 (*1-86125-015-0*, Pub. by Inst Materials) Ashgate Pub Co.

Baker, Terri. I'm Not Dancing Anymore. 320p. 1998. pap. 6.99 (*0-7860-0534-3*, Pinncle Kensgtn) Kensgtn Pub Corp.

— I'm Not Dancing Anymore: O. J. Simpson's Niece Speaks Her Mind. LC 97-73755. 304p. 1997. 24.95 (*1-57566-256-6*) Kensgtn Pub Corp.

Baker, Terry L. Colonial Pennsylvania: The Pennsylvania Legacy. Myers, Susan, ed. LC 96-42964. (Proud to Be an American Ser.). (Illus.). 64p. 1997. pap. 5.95 (*0-87905-748-3*) Gibbs Smith Pub.

Baker, Theodore. Baker's Biographical Dictionary of Musicians. 143p. reprint ed. lib. bdg. 69.00 (*0-7812-9190-9*) Rprt Serv.

— Dictionary of Musical Terms. (Music Book Index Ser.). 257p. 1993. reprint ed. lib. bdg. 79.00 (*0-7812-9712-5*) Rprt Serv.

— A Dictionary of Musical Terms. 257p. 1990. reprint ed. lib. bdg. 69.00 (*0-7812-9007-4*) Rprt Serv.

— Dictionary of Musical Terms: Containing an English-Italian Vocabulary for Composers & Students. (ENG & ITA.). 47.50 (*0-87557-053-4*) Saphrograph.

— Dictionnaire Biographique des Musiciens, 32 vols. (FRE.). 4830p. 1995. 250.00 (*0-7859-9946-9*) Fr & Eur.

— On the Music of the North American Indians. Buckley, Ann, tr. from GER. (Music Reprint Ser.: 1977). 1978. lib. bdg. 25.00 (*0-306-70888-4*) Da Capo.

— Uber die Musik der Nordamerikanischen Wilden. LC 71-38496. reprint ed. 31.50 (*0-404-08337-4*) AMS Pr.

Baker, Theodore, jt. auth. see Slonimsky, Nicolas.

Baker, Theodore, tr. see D'Indy, Vincent.

Baker, Therese L. Doing Social Research. 2nd ed. LC 93-4267. 512p. (C). 1993. 65.63 (*0-07-003492-3*) McGraw.

— Doing Social Research. 2nd ed. LC 93-4267. (C). 1993. pap., wbk. ed. 22.81 (*0-07-003494-X*) McGraw.

— Doing Social Research. 3rd ed. LC 98-3563. 552p. 1998. 65.63 (*0-07-006002-9*) McGraw.

Baker, Thomas & Ferone, Frank. The Liturgy Committee Handbook. 112p. (Orig.). 1998. pap. 14.95 (*0-89622-955-6*) Twenty-Third.

Baker, Thomas & Murphy, Frank. Que Puede Hacer para Ayudar a Su Hijos (A) a Trivnter en la Escuelai (What You Can Do to Help Your Child Succeed in School - While Keeping Your Child Safe & Drug Free: Paquete para Los Instructores (Leader's Kit) (SPA.). 1998. ring bd. 150.00 (*1-885903-07-3*) ParentingKids.

Baker, Thomas, jt. auth. see Baker, Dale.

Baker, Thomas, jt. auth. see Dale, D. D.

Baker, Thomas A. Second Chance in Centerville. 96p. (J). (gr. 3-9). 1991. pap. 11.00 (*0-87879-908-7*) High Noon Bks.

Baker, Thomas E. Another Such Victory: The Story of the American Defeat at Guilford Courthouse That Helped Win the War for Independence. 90p. 1981. pap. 3.25 (*0-915992-06-X*) Eastern National.

— The Most Wonderful Work: Our Constitution Interpreted. 706p. 1996. 26.95 (*0-314-20339-7*) West Pub.

Baker, Thomas E., ed. Rationing Justice on Appeal: The Problems of the U. S. Courts of Appeals. 426p. 1994. text. write for info. (*0-314-03494-3*) West Pub.

Baker, Thomas E. & Floyd, Timothy W. Can a Good Christian Be a Good Lawyer? Homilies, Witnesses, & Reflections. LC 97-37197. (Studies in Law & Contemporary Issues Ser.). 218p. 1998. 35.00 (*0-268-00825-6*); pap. 20.00 (*0-268-00826-4*) U of Notre Dame Pr.

***Baker, Thomas Edward.** Effective Police Leadership. LC 99-88164. 250p. 2000. pap. 29.95 (*1-889031-25-9*) Looseleaf Law.

Baker, Thomas J. & Gordon, Howard L. Surgical Rejuvenation of the Face. 2nd ed. (Illus.). 640p. (C). (gr. 13). 1995. text 272.00 (*0-8016-0153-3*, 00153) Mosby Inc.

Baker, Thomas J., et al. Facial Skin Resurfacing. LC 97-28725. 1997. 230.00 (*0-942219-77-5*) Quality Med Pub.

— Facial Skin Resurfacing. (Illus.). 250p. 1997. 275.00 incl. VHS (*1-57626-085-2*, QMP) Quality Med Pub.

Baker, Thomas N. Sentiment & Celebrity: Nathaniel Parker Willis & the Trials of Literary Fame. LC 98-5728. (Illus.). 272p. 1998. 49.95 (*0-19-512073-6*) OUP.

Baker, Thomas R. Weather in the Lab: Simulate Nature's Phenomena. LC 92-34050. (Illus.). 146p. 1993. write for info. (*0-8306-4309-5*) McGraw-Hill Prof.

— Weather in the Lab: Simulate Nature's Phenomena. LC 92-34050. (Illus.). 146p. (YA). (gr. 9-12). 1993. pap. 11.95 (*0-8306-4307-9*) McGraw-Hill Prof.

***Baker, Tim.** Extreme Faith: Twelve Radical Young Believer's in the Bible Who Changed Our World. 192p. (YA). 2000. pap. 10.99 (*0-7852-6757-3*) Nelson.

— Home & Family, Vol. 9. (Pulse Ser.). 2000. pap. 14.99 (*0-8307-2510-5*) Gospel Lght.

— Teachings of Jesus. (Pulse Ser.: No. 4). 1999. pap. text 14.99 (*0-8307-2409-5*) Gospel Lght.

Baker, Tim, ed. A Victoria History of the County of Middlesex Vol. XI: Early Stepney with Bethnal Green. (Victoria History of the Counties of England Ser.). (Illus.). 320p. 2000. text 110.00 (*0-19-722791-0*) OUP.

***Baker, Tim & Gowensmith, Debbie.** Catholic Student Plan-It Calendar, 2000-2001. 128p. (YA). (gr. 6-9). 2000. 8.95 (*0-88489-681-1*) St Marys.

***Baker, Tim & Simpson, Amy.** Living Beyond Belief: 13 Bible Studies to Help Teenagers Experience God. LC 99-30359. 1999. 16.99 (*0-7644-2099-2*) Group Pub.

Baker, Timothy B. & Cannon, Dale S., eds. Assessment & Treatment of Addictive Disorders. LC 87-30537. 318p. 1988. 75.00 (*0-275-92388-6*, C2388, Praeger Pubs) Greenwood.

Baker, Timothy D. & Perlman, Mark. Health Manpower in a Developing Economy: Taiwan, a Case Study in Planning. LC 67-22892. (Johns Hopkins Monographs in International Health). 219p. reprint ed. pap. 67.90 (*0-608-11864-8*, 202308100032) Bks Demand.

Baker, Tod A., et al, eds. Political Parties in the Southern States: Party Activists in Partisan Coalitions. LC 89-26557. 264p. 1990. 55.00 (*0-275-93027-0*, C3027, Greenwood Pr) Greenwood.

Baker, Todd M. Professional Liability Insurance in Texas. (Working Paper Ser.: No. 68). 27p. 1992. pap. 5.50 (*0-89940-550-9*) LBJ Sch Pub Aff.

Baker, Tom. Corporate Time Out. 75p. 1998. pap. write for info. (*0-9617676-5-0*) Jhnsn & Jhnsn.

— High School Highways, 5 novels in ea. set, 48p.ea., Set 1. (Illus.). (J). (gr. 2-7). 1988. pap. 17.00 (*0-87879-536-7*) High Noon Bks.

Baker, Toni. Mastering Machine Code on Your ZX-81. 176p. 1982. 18.41 (*0-685-08667-4*) P-H.

Baker, Tonya S. Home Is Where You Least Expect It. LC 98-88290. 325p. 1998. 25.00 (*0-7388-0141-0*); pap. 15.00 (*0-7388-0142-9*) Xlibris Corp.

Baker, Tracey & Kennedy, Barbara. Writing Synthesis. LC 92-26176. 350p. (C). 1997. pap. text 41.40 (*0-673-38964-2*) Addson-Wesley Educ.

Baker, V. Historical Archaeology at Black Lucy's Garden, Andover Massachusetts: Ceramics from the Site of a 19th Century Afro-American, Vol. 8. 1978. pap. 10.00 (*0-939312-09-3*) Peabody Found.

Baker, Vaughan B. & Kreamer, Jean T. Louisiana Tapestry: Ethnicity in St. Landry Parish. (Illus.). (Orig.). (gr. 7-12). 1983. pap. text 10.00 (*0-940984-07-5*) Univ LA Lafayette.

***Baker, Vaughan Burdin & Conrad, Glenn R., eds.** Visions & Revisions Vol. 15: Perspectives on Louisiana's Society & Culture. LC 96-84494. (Louisiana Purchase Bicentennial Series in Louisiana History). 802p. (C). 2000. 45.00 (*1-887366-36-9*) Univ LA Lafayette.

Baker, Vernon. Lasting Valor. 1997. 24.95 (*1-885478-30-5*) Genesis Press.

Baker, Vernon J. & Olsen, Ken. Lasting Valor. 1999. 55.00 (*1-885478-51-8*, Pub. by Genesis Press) BookWorld.

Baker, Vernon J. & Olson, Ken. Lasting Valor. 320p. 1999. reprint ed. mass mkt. 6.50 (*0-553-58062-0*) Bantam.

***Baker, Vicki.** Timber Hills. LC 98-87017. 192p. 1999. pap. 11.95 (*1-56315-165-0*) SterlingHse.

Baker, Vicki, jt. ed. see Deppe, Gunter.

Baker, Vicki V. & Deppe, Gunter. Management of Perioperative Complications in Gynecology. Schmitt, Bill, ed. LC 96-15894. (Illus.). 288p. 1996. text 78.95 (*0-7216-5881-4*, W B Saunders Co) Harcrt Hlth Sci Grp.

Baker, Vickie. Surprised by Hope: From Circus Girl to Quadriplegic Journey of Terror & Joy. LC 99-80159. Date not set. pap. 12.99 (*0-88965-161-2*, Pub. by Horizon Books) Chr Pubns.

Baker, Victor R. The Channels of Mars. LC 81-7549. (Illus.). 212p. reprint ed. pap. 65.80 (*0-608-20097-2*, 207136900011) Bks Demand.

— Paleohydrology & Sedimentology of Lake Missoula Flooding in Eastern Washington. LC 72-89463. (Geological Society of America. Special Paper Ser.). vii, 79p. 1973. write for info. (*0-8137-2144-X*) Geol Soc.

Baker, Victor R., et al. Flood Geomorphology. LC 87-27920. 528p. 1988. 260.00 (*0-471-62558-2*) Wiley.

Baker, Victor R., jt. auth. see Costa, John E.

Baker, Victoria J. A Sinhalese Village in Sri Lanka: Coping with Uncertainty. 208p. (C). 1997. pap. text 23.50 (*0-15-505176-8*) Harcourt Coll Pubs.

Baker, Virginia. History of Warren in the War of the Revolution, 1776-1783. (Illus.). 68p. 1997. reprint ed. pap. 14.50 (*0-8328-6487-0*) Higginson Bk Co.

***Baker, Vivian Violet West.** Diary: The Story of the "Trip Out West" (Illus.). 16p. 1999. pap. 12.00 (*0-9677980-0-0*) R W Baker.

Baker, W. Buck. Celtic Mythological Influences on American Theatre, 1750-1875: Chwedioniaeth Geltaidd Dylanwad ar Chwaraedy Americanaidd, 1750-1875. LC 93-22181. 92p. (Orig.). (C). 1993. pap. text 19.50 (*0-8191-9225-2*); lib. bdg. 39.50 (*0-8191-9224-4*) U Pr of Amer.

Baker, W. D. Dare to Win: The Story of New Zealand Air Service. 10th ed. (Elite Unit Ser.). 124p. 1987. 29.95 (*0-89839-102-4*) Battery Pr.

Baker, W. E. Explosion Hazards & Evaluation. (Fundamental Studies in Engineering: Vol. 5). 808p. 1983. 418.00 (*0-444-42094-0*) Elsevier.

Baker, W. E. & Tang, M. J. Gas, Dust & Hybrid Explosions. (Fundamental Studies in Engineering: No. 13). xx,256p. 1991. 135.00 (*0-444-88150-6*) Elsevier.

Baker, W. E., et al. Similarity Methods in Engineering Dynamics: Theory & Practice of Scale Modeling. 2nd ed. (Fundamental Studies in Engineering: No. 12). xii,384p. 1991. 184.00 (*0-444-88156-5*) Elsevier.

Baker, W. J., et al, eds. Recent Trends in Theoretical Psychology. (Recent Research in Psychology Ser.). (Illus.). 380p. 1988. 61.95 (*0-387-96757-5*) Spr-Verlag.

— Recent Trends in Theoretical Psychology: Proceedings of the Third Biennial Conference of the International Society for Theoretical Psychology April 17-21, 1989, Vol. 2. (Illus.). xix, 465p. 1990. 71.95 (*0-387-97311-7*) Spr-Verlag.

Baker, W. R. My Divided Brain. LC 98-41210. 80p. 1999. pap. 11.00 (*1-56474-298-9*) Fithian Pr.

Baker, W. S. Bibliotheca Washingtoniana. 1973. 59.95 (*0-87968-746-0*) Gordon Pr.

Baker, Wallace H., ed. Grouting in Geotechnical Engineering. LC 81-71798. 1028p. 1982. pap. 82.00 (*0-87262-295-9*) Am Soc Civil Eng.

An Asterisk (*) at the beginning of an entry indicates that the title is appearing for the first time.

***Baker, Wayne E.** Achieving Success Through Social Capital: Tapping the Hidden Resources in Your Personal & Business Networks. LC 00-9554. (University of Michigan Business School Management Ser.). 2000. 25.00 (*0-7879-5309-1*) Jossey-Bass.

***Baker, Wendy.** The Curtain & Fabric Selector: The Easy-to-Use Guide to Selecting Curtains & Fabrics. 2000. 24.95 (*1-85585-804-5*, Pub. by Collins & Br) Sterling.

Baker, Wendy. Experimenta con la Electricidad. (Illus.). 48p. 1995. 18.50 (*84-348-3813-3*) T R Bks.

***Baker, Wendy.** Insects. (Make It Work! Science Ser.). (Illus.). (J). (gr. 4-7). 2000. pap. 6.95 (*1-58728-356-5*) Two Can Pub.

— Sound. (Make It Work! Science Ser.). (Illus.). (J). 2000. 12.95 (*1-58728-374-3*) Two Can Pub.

Baker, Wendy & Haslam, Andrew. Earth: A Creative Hands-on Approach to Science. LC 92-27573. (Make It Work! Ser.). (Illus.). 48p. (J). (gr. 2-5). 1993. 12.95 (*0-689-71662-1*) Aladdin.

— Electricity. (Make It Work! Ser.). (Illus.). 48p. (J). 15.95 (*0-590-74521-2*) Scholastic Inc.

— Electricity: A Creative Hands-on Approach to Science. LC 92-24566. (Make It Work! Ser.). (Illus.). 48p. (J). (gr. 2-5). 1993. 12.95 (*0-689-71663-X*) Aladdin.

— Insects. (Make It Work! Ser.). (Illus.). 48p. (J). 15.95 (*0-590-24204-0*); pap. 9.99 (*0-590-24330-6*) Scholastic Inc.

— Plants. (Make It Work! Ser.). (Illus.). (J). 15.95 (*0-590-74523-9*); pap. 9.99 (*0-590-24331-4*) Scholastic Inc.

— Plants: A Creative Hands-On Approach to Science. LC 92-24559. (Make It Work! Ser.). (Illus.). 48p. (J). (gr. 2-5). 1993. 12.95 (*0-689-71664-8*) Aladdin.

— Sound: A Creative Hands-on Approach to Science. LC 92-30104. (Make It Work! Ser.). (Illus.). 48p. (J). (gr. 2-5). 1993. 12.95 (*0-689-71665-6*) Aladdin.

Baker, Wendy, et al. Electricity. (Make It Work! (Eureka!) Ser.). (FRE., Illus.). (J). pap. 9.99 (*0-590-74806-8*) Scholastic Inc.

Baker, Wendy, et al. Sound. (Make It Work! Ser.). (Illus.). 48p. (J). 15.95 (*0-590-74522-0*); pap. 9.99 (*0-590-24631-3*) Scholastic Inc.

***Baker, Wendy, et al.** Sound. LC 00-25671. (Make It Work Ser.). (Illus.). (J). 2000. pap. write for info. (*1-58728-361-1*) Two Can Pub.

Baker, Wheeler L. Crisis Management: A Model for Managers. (Illus.). 112p. (Orig.). (C). 1994. pap. write for info. (*0-9641182-0-3*) Foot Hill Con.

Baker-White, Robert. The Text in Play: Representations of Rehearsal in Modern Drama. LC 98-45334. 216p. 1999. 37.50 (*0-8387-5381-7*) Bucknell U Pr.

Baker, Will. Shadow Hunter. Zion, Claire, ed. 512p. 1994. reprint ed. mass mkt. 5.50 (*0-671-79045-5*, Pocket Star Bks) PB.

***Baker, Will.** Tony & the Cows: A True Story from the Range Wars. 122p. 2000. 20.00 (*1-881090-35-3*) Confluence Pr.

Baker, Will. What a Piece of Work: Stories. LC 92-14336. 200p. 1992. 24.95 (*0-8262-0853-3*) U of Mo Pr.

Baker, William. The Early History of the London Library. LC 92-3065. 168p. 1992. 79.95 (*0-7734-9473-1*) E Mellen.

— Kashmir: Happy Valley of Death. 77p. 1994. pap. 15.00 (*1-871031-42-7*) Defenders Pubns.

***Baker, William.** Letters of Wilkie Collins. LC 99-19642. 1999. text 55.00 (*0-312-22343-9*) St Martin.

Baker, William. Sanctification. 160p. 1986. pap. 7.70 (*0-310-35301-7*, 11140P) Zondervan.

Baker, William. South Slavic Writers since World War II Vol. 181: South Slavic Writers since World War II. LC 97-15112. (Dictionary of Literary Biography Ser.). 400p. 1997. text 155.00 (*0-7876-1070-4*) Gale.

Baker, William & Kay, Gary. Becoming a Successful Student. 224p. (C). 1996. per. 33.95 (*0-7872-2242-9*, 41224201) Kendall-Hunt.

***Baker, William & Womack, Kenneth.** Ernest Hemingway-Documentary. LC 99-16782. (Dictionary of Literary Biography Ser.). 400p. 1999. text 155.00 (*0-7876-3106-X*) Gale.

Baker, William & Womack, Kenneth. Recent Work in Critical Theory, 1989-1995: An Annotated Bibliography, 51. LC 96-18346. (Bibliographies & Indexes in World Literature Ser.: Vol. 51). 608p. 1996. lib. bdg. 110.00 (*0-313-29434-8*, Greenwood Pr) Greenwood.

***Baker, William & Womack, Kenneth, compiled by.** Twentieth-Century Bibliography & Textual Criticism: An Annotated Bibliography. Vol. 13. 2000. lib. bdg. write for info. (*0-313-30537-4*) Greenwood.

Baker, William, ed. see Eliot, George, pseud.

Baker, William, ed. see Scott, Sir Walter.

Baker, William, jt. ed. see Wolfreys, Julian.

Baker, William A. A Maritime History of Bath, Maine & the Kennebec River Regions, 2 vols., 1. LC 73-85867. (Illus.). 564p. 1973. write for info. (*0-937410-08-X*) ME Maritime Mus.

— A Maritime History of Bath, Maine & the Kennebec River Regions, 2 vols., 2. LC 73-85867. (Illus.). 596p. 1973. write for info. (*0-937410-09-8*) ME Maritime Mus.

— A Maritime History of Bath, Maine & the Kennebec River Regions, 2 vols., Set. LC 73-85867. (Illus.). 1160p. 1973. 60.00 (*0-937410-10-1*) ME Maritime Mus.

Baker, William A., jt. auth. see Kluger, Miriam P.

Baker, William C., jt. auth. see Kelly, James C.

Baker, William E. Jacques Prevert. LC 67-19347. (Twayne's World Authors Ser.). 1967. lib. bdg. 15.95 (*0-685-02667-1*) Irvington.

Baker, William F. & Dessart, George. Down the Tube: An Inside Account of the Failure of American Television. 352p. 1999. pap. 14.00 (*0-465-00723-6*, Pub. by Basic) HarpC.

Baker, William H., et al. Communication & Technology: Today & Tomorrow. Williams, Al & Goings, Douglas, eds. 236p. (Orig.). (C). 1994. pap. text 14.95 (*0-931874-20-3*) Assn Busn Comm.

Baker, William H., jt. auth. see Lewis, Philip V.

Baker, William J. Beyond Port & Prejudice: Charles Lloyd of Oxford, 1784-1829. LC 76-24243. 1981. 20.00 (*0-89101-032-7*) U Maine Pr.

***Baker, William J.** If Christ Came to the Olympics: New College Lectures. 192p. 2000. pap. 19.95 (*0-86840-579-5*, Pub. by Univ of West Aust Pr) Intl Spec Bk.

Baker, William J. Sports in the Western World. rev. ed. (Sport & Society Ser.). (Illus.). 368p. 1988. pap. text 15.95 (*0-252-06042-3*) U of Ill Pr.

Baker, William J. & Mangan, James A., eds. Sport in Africa: Essays in Social History. LC 87-1804. 320p. 1987. 49.50 (*0-8419-0906-7*) Holmes & Meier.

Baker, William J. & Rog, James A., eds. Sports & the Humanities: A Symposium. LC 83-50027. 126p. (Orig.). (C). 1983. pap. 10.95 (*0-89101-055-6*) U Maine Pr.

Baker, William J., jt. auth. see Prideaux, Gary D.

***Baker, William K., Jr. & Guerrero, Diana L.** Crisis Management Resources for Zoos & Other Animal Care Facilities. Chan, Susan D., ed. (Illus.). 416p. 1999. pap. write for info. (*1-929672-02-0*) Am Assn Zoo Keep.

Baker, William L., jt. ed. see Mladenoff, David J.

***Baker, William M.** Making Many Glad: The Life & Labours of Daniel Baker. 2000. pap. 10.99 (*0-85151-781-1*) Banner of Truth.

Baker, William P. The English Village. LC 72-138199. 224p. 1971. reprint ed. lib. bdg. 59.50 (*0-8371-5552-5*, BAEV, Greenwood Pr) Greenwood.

Baker, William R. Personal Speech - Ethics in the Epistle of James. LC 95-161221. (WissUNT Zum Neuen Testament Ser.). 350p. (Orig.). 1994. pap. text 87.50 (*3-16-145958-X*, Pub. by JCB Mohr) Coronet Bks.

— Sticks & Stones: The Discipleship of Our Speech. LC 96-8120. 180p. (Orig.). 1996. pap. 11.99 (*0-8308-1986-X*, 1986) InterVarsity.

Baker, William S. Itinerary of General Washington. 334p. 1985. reprint ed. 59.00 (*0-932051-79-0*) Rprt Serv.

Baker, William W. More in Common Than You Think: The Bridge Between Islam & Christianity. LC 99-164157. (Illus.). vii, 136p. (Orig.). 1998. pap. 15.00 (*0-910643-01-6*) Defenders Pubns.

— Theft of a Nation. 3rd rev. ed. 192p. (Orig.). 1989. pap. 15.00 (*0-910643-00-8*); pap. 10.00 (*0-317-99885-4*) Defenders Pubns.

Baker, Winona. Beyond the Lighthouse. 1992. pap. 9.95 (*0-88982-114-3*, Pub. by Oolichan Bks) Genl Dist Srvs.

Baker Wolf, Mona, jt. ed. see Chambers, Edgar, 4th.

Baker-Woods, Gail, et al. Mass Media Writing: An Introduction. (C). 1996. pap. text, teacher ed. write for info. (*0-13-776451-0*, 77645-0) Allyn.

Baker, Yaba. Just Like Me. Alexander, Jarda, ed. (Illus.). 26p. (Orig.). (J). 1996. reprint ed. pap. 4.95 (*1-55411-147-4*) Untd Bros & Sis.

— Just Like Me: Coloring Book of Careers. (Illus.). 28p. (gr. k-6) 1998. pap. 4.95 (*1-928889-03-4*) DBW Inc.

— Just Like Me: How African American Inventions Changed America. 3rd ed. Alexander, Jarda, ed. (Illus.). 36p. (gr. k-6). 1996. reprint ed. pap. 4.95 (*1-928889-00-X*) DBW Inc.

— Just Like Me: The Beginning of Civilization. (Illus.). 28p. (gr. k-6). 1998. pap. 4.95 (*1-928889-01-8*) DBW Inc.

Bakerjian, R., ed. see SME Staff.

Bakerjian, Ramon, jt. ed. see Boyes, William.

Bakerman, Jane S., ed. And Then There Were Nine: More Women of Mystery. (Illus.). 219p. 1985. 20.95 (*0-87972-319-X*) Bowling Green Univ Popular Press.

Bakerman, Paul & Bakerman, Seymour. Bakerman's ABC's of Adult & Pediatric Drug Therapy. 1992. pap. text 28.50 (*0-945577-05-2*) Interpret Lab Data.

Bakerman, Paul, ed. see Bakerman, Seymour.

Bakerman, Seymour. Bakerman's ABCs of Interpretive Laboratory Data. 3rd ed. Bakerman, Paul & Strausbauch, Paul, eds. 543p. 1994. 28.50 (*0-945577-06-0*) Interpret Lab Data.

— Clinical Chemistry Review Notes & Clinical Chemistry Review Questions, 2 vols., Set. 1182p. 1986. pap. text 90.00 (*0-945577-02-8*) Interpret Lab Data.

Bakerman, Seymour, jt. auth. see Bakerman, Paul.

Bakerman, Theodore. Anthracite Coal: A Study in Advanced Industrial Decline. Bruchey, Stuart, ed. LC 78-22556. (Energy in the American Economy Ser.). (Illus.). 1979. lib. bdg. 25.95 (*0-405-11960-7*) Ayer.

Bakerna, Lucy. Life in the Deserts. World Book Staff, ed. LC 96-61738. (World Book Ecology Ser.). (Illus.). 32p. (J). (gr. 3-8). 1997. 9.95 (*0-7166-5200-5*) World Bk.

— Life in the Oceans. LC 96-61736. (World Book Ecology Ser.). (Illus.). 32p. (J). (gr. 3-8). 1999. write for info. (*0-7166-5202-1*) World Bk.

— Life in the Rain Forests. LC 96-61737. (World Book Ecology Ser.). (Illus.). 32p. (J). (gr. 3-8). 1999. write for info. (*0-7166-5204-8*) World Bk.

Bakerroshi, Richard. Original Mind: The Practice of Zen in the West. 256p. 1999. 23.95 (*1-57322-110-4*, Riverhead Books) Putnam Pub Group.

Bakers. Fund Chemistry. 3rd ed. 1999. pap. text, student ed. 31.67 (*0-13-080174-7*) P-H.

Bakerville, Peter. Victoria: Beyond the Island: An Illustrated History. 144p. 1986. 27.95 (*0-89781-192-5*) Am Historical Pr.

Bakescu, R., tr. see Klimontovich, Yu L.

***Bakewell & Mullins.** Victorian Architectural Sheet-Metal Ornaments: A Reprint of the 1887 Catalog. LC 99-41610. 196p. 1999. pap. text 14.95 (*0-486-40725-X*) Dover.

Bakewell, Charles M. Source Book in Ancient Philosophy (1907) 400p. 1998. reprint ed. pap. 29.95 (*0-7661-0147-9*) Kessinger Pub.

Bakewell, Dennis. The Black Experience in the United States: A Bibliography Based on Collections of the California State University, Northridge Library. 1970. 12.00 (*0-937048-11-9*) Santa Susana.

Bakewell, Elizabeth, ed. see Getty Art History Information Program Staff.

Bakewell, K. G., et al. Managing User-Centred Libraries & Information Services. 2nd rev. ed. (Illus.). 290p. (C). 1996. text 110.00 (*0-7201-2270-8*) Continuum.

Bakewell, K. G., jt. auth. see Dare, Gillian A.

Bakewell, Liza, jt. ed. see Bright, Brenda J.

Bakewell, Michael. Fitzrovia: London's Bohemia. 1999. 11.95 (*1-85514-256-2*) Natl Port Gall.

— Lewis Carroll: A Biography. LC 95-472. (Illus.). 400p. 1996. 27.50 (*0-393-03906-4*) Norton.

Bakewell, Nicholas. Santa & the Christ Child. (Illus.). 32p. 1984. 10.95 (*0-9616286-0-X*) Santa Chrst Child.

Bakewell, Peter. Silver & Entrepreneurship in Seventeenth-Century Potosi: The Life & Times of Antonio Lopez de Quiroga. LC 94-41720. (Illus.). 272p. 1995. pap. 14.95 (*0-87074-386-4*) SMU Press.

Bakewell, Peter, ed. Mines of Silver & Gold in the Americas. LC 96-237. (Expanding World Ser.: Vol. 19). 420p. 1997. 138.95 (*0-86078-513-0*, Pub. by Variorum) Ashgate Pub Co.

Bakewell, Peter J. A History of Latin America: Empires & Sequels, 1450-1930. LC 96-38512. (History of the World Ser.). (Illus.). 640p. 1997. text 73.95 (*0-631-16791-9*); pap. text 26.95 (*0-631-20547-0*) Blackwell Pubs.

— Silver & Entrepreneurship in Seventeenth-Century Potosi: The Life & Times of Antonio Lopez de Quiroga. LC 88-14227. 268p. reprint ed. pap. 83.10 (*0-7837-5862-6*, 204558100006) Bks Demand.

Bakewell, Robert. An Introduction to Geology. Albritton, Claude C., Jr., ed. LC 77-6508. (History of Geology Ser.). 1978. reprint ed. lib. bdg. 44.95 (*0-405-10431-6*) Ayer.

Bakewell-Sachs, Susan, et al. Assessment of Risk in the Term Newborn. LC 97-8218. 1997. write for info. (*0-86525-074-X*) March of Dimes.

Bakewell, Siam, jt. auth. see Kendrick, Donald.

Bakewell, T. Q. Ball Bearings for Enclosed Gear Drives. (Technical Papers: Vol. P269.01A). (Illus.). 12p. 1964. pap. text 30.00 (*1-55589-367-8*) AGMA.

Bakewell, William. Hollywood Be Thy Name: Random Recollections of a Movie Veteran from Silents to Talkies to TV. LC 90-28171. (Filmmakers Ser.: No. 25). (Illus.). 267p. 1991. 39.50 (*0-8108-2388-8*) Scarecrow.

Bakhash, Shaul. The Reign of the Ayatollahs: Iran & the Islamic Revolution. LC 86-166958. x, 292 p. 1986. 9.95 (*0-465-06888-X*) Basic.

Bakhash, Shaul B. The Politics of Oil & Revolution in Iran. LC 82-72116. 37p. 1982. pap. 6.95 (*0-8157-0781-9*) Brookings.

Bakhaus, Rebecca P., ed. see American Association of Equine Practitioners Staff.

Bakhit, Michelle A. & Shay, Kevin J. How to Work with the Media in Promoting Your Business or Organization: A Guide for the Small Business Owner or Organization Director for Promotion on a Shoestring Budget. 24p. (Orig.). 1994. pap. 3.95 (*1-881365-70-0*) Shay Pubns.

— Observations from the Edge: Deeper Than Deep Thoughts. (Illus.). 24p. (Orig.). 1995. pap. 3.95 (*1-881365-68-9*) Shay Pubns.

Bakhit, Michelle A., ed. see Shay, Kevin J.

Bakhle, Y. S. & Vane, John R., eds. Metabolic Functions of the Lung. LC 76-41467. (Lung Biology in Health & Disease Ser.: No. 4). (Illus.). 373p. reprint ed. pap. 115.70 (*0-7837-3379-8*, 204333700008) Bks Demand.

Bakhshi, Taj M. Mathematics & Graphics. (Orig.). 1995. pap. 19.13 (*1-56870-175-6*) RonJon Pub.

Bakht, Baidar, ed. Query of the Road: Selected Poems of Akhtar-ul-iman with Extensive Commentary. 1996. 36.00 (*81-7167-303-1*, Pub. by Rupa) S Asia.

Bakhtiar, Cyrus, tr. see Sadiq, Jafar.

Bakhtiar, Cyrus, tr. see Shariati, Ali.

Bakhtiar, Laleh. Encyclopedia of Islamic Law: A Compendium of the Major Schools. LC 99-200837. 676p. (Orig.). (J). 1997. pap. 39.95 (*1-56744-498-9*) Kazi Pubns.

— Encyclopedia of Muhammad's Women Companions & the Tradition They Related: A Sourcebook for Gender Studies. 550p. (C). 1996. pap. text 39.95 (*1-871031-43-5*) Kazi Pubns.

— God's Will Be Done Vol. 1: Traditional Psychoethics & Personality Paradigm. 175p. (C). 1993. pap. 19.95 (*1-56744-429-6*) Kazi Pubns.

— Moral Healer's Handbook: The Psychology of Spiritual Chivalry. (God's Will Be Done Ser.: Vol. 2). 320p. (C). 1994. pap. 19.95 (*1-871031-39-7*) Kazi Pubns.

— Moral Healing Through the Most Beautiful Names: The Practice of Spiritual Chivalry. (God's Will Be Done Ser.: Vol. 3). 276p. (C). 1994. pap. 19.95 (*1-871031-40-0*) Kazi Pubns.

— Muhammad's Companions: Essays on Those Who Bore Witness, Pt. I. 210p. (YA). (gr. 10-12). 1993. pap. 15.95 (*1-56744-426-1*) Kazi Pubns.

— Muhammad's Companions: Essays on Those Who Bore Witness, Pt. II. 205p. (YA). (gr. 10-12). 1993. pap. 12.95 (*1-56744-318-4*) Kazi Pubns.

— Muslim Woman Believer: The Journey of Becoming. 80p. 1989. pap. text 5.60 (*1-871031-08-7*) Abjad Bk.

— Shariati on Shariati: An Autobiographical Biography & English Guide to the Collected Works. 144p. (Orig.). (C). 1989. pap. text 14.00 (*1-871031-05-2*) Abjad Bk.

— Sufi: Expressions of the Mystic Quest. LC 87-50252. (Art & Imagination Ser.). (Illus.). 120p. 1997. reprint ed. pap. 16.95 (*0-500-81015-X*, Pub. by Thames Hudson) Norton.

— Sufi Expressions of the Mystic Quest. 128p. 1996. pap. 14.95 (*0-614-21356-8*, 1185) Kazi Pubns.

— Sufi Women: Angels in the Making. 112p. 1996. pap. 12.95 (*0-614-21559-5*, 1471) Kazi Pubns.

— Sufi Women of America: Angels in the Making. 114p. (Orig.). (C). 1997. pap. 12.05 (*1-871031-44-3*) Kazi Pubns.

— Traditional Psychoethics & Personality Paradigm, God's Will Be Done, Vol. I. 174p. 1996. pap. 19.95 (*0-614-21562-5*, 348) Kazi Pubns.

Bakhtiar, Laleh, adapted by. Encyclopedia of Islamic Law: A Compendium of the Major Schools. 664p. (Orig.). 1995. 65.00 (*1-56744-532-2*); pap. 39.95 (*1-56744-511-X*) Kazi Pubns.

Bakhtiar, Laleh, ed. Ramadan: Motivating Believers to Action. 320p. (Orig.). 1994. pap. 19.95 (*0-934905-25-8*) Kazi Pubns.

Bakhtiar, Laleh, tr. Ayatullah Ruhullah Khomeini: A Short Biography. 24p. 1989. pap. text 1.70 (*1-871031-26-5*) Abjad Bk.

Bakhtiar, Laleh & Ardalan, Nader. The Sense of Unity: The Sufi Tradition in Persian Architecture. 155p. 1996. pap. 29.95 (*0-614-21589-7*, 1121) Kazi Pubns.

Bakhtiar, Laleh, jt. auth. see Ardalan, Nader.

Bakhtiar, Laleh, ed. see Rauf, A.

Bakhtiar, Laleh, tr. see Ayatullah Ruhullah Khomeini.

Bakhtiar, Laleh, tr. see Dar Rah Haqq.

Bakhtiar, Laleh, tr. see Khomeini, Ayatullah R.

Bakhtiar, Laleh, tr. see Mutahhari, Murtaza.

Bakhtiar, Laleh, tr. see Sayyid, Muhammad T.

Bakhtiar, Laleh, tr. see Shariati, Ali.

Bakhtiar, Laleh, tr. see Tabataba'i, Sayyid M.

***Bakhtiar-van Dillen, Lailee.** Harem Letters. Levine, Becky, ed. LC 99-70998. (Illus.). 254p. 1999. pap. 16.95 (*1-891165-09-7*) Sera Pub.

***Bakhtiari, S.** Advanced Non Destructive Evaluation for Steam Generator Tubing. 69p. 2000. pap. 7.00 (*0-16-059080-9*) USGPO.

Bakhtin, Mikhail M. Art & Answerability: Early Philosophical Essays. Holquist, Michael, ed. Liapunov, Vadim, ed. & tr. by. Brostrom, Kenneth, tr. (Slavic Ser.: No. 9). 384p. (C). 1990. text 35.00 (*0-292-70411-9*) U of Tex Pr.

— The Dialogic Imagination: Four Essays. Holquist, Michael, ed. & tr. by. from RUS. Emerson, Caryl, tr. from RUS. LC 80-15450. (Slavic Ser.: No. 1). 477p. 1981. pap. 16.95 (*0-292-71534-X*) U of Tex Pr.

— Rabelais & His World. Iswolsky, Helene, tr. from RUS. LC 84-47792. 510p. 1984. 39.95 (*0-253-34830-7*); pap. 16.95 (*0-253-20341-4*, MB 341) Ind U Pr.

— Speech Genres & Other Late Essays. Emerson, Caryl & Holquist, Michael, eds. McGee, Vern W., tr. from RUS. (Slavic Ser.: No. 8). 203p. (C). 1986. text 25.00 (*0-292-72046-7*); pap. text 14.95 (*0-292-77560-1*) U of Tex Pr.

— Toward a Philosophy of the Act. Liapunov, Vadim, ed. & tr. by. from RUS. Holquist, Michael, ed. LC 93-7557. (Slavic Ser.: No. 10). 128p. (C). 1993. pap. 12.95 (*0-292-70805-X*); text 25.00 (*0-292-76534-7*) U of Tex Pr.

***Bakhtin, Mikhail M.** Unknown Bakhtin. 2000. 45.00 (*0-87501-155-1*) Ardis Pubs.

Bakhtin, Mikhail M. & Medvedev, Pavel N. The Formal Method in Literary Scholarship: A Critical Introduction to Sociological Poetics. Wehrle, Albert J., tr. from RUS. LC 77-15529. 224p. 1991. reprint ed. pap. text 15.95 (*0-8018-4318-9*) Johns Hopkins.

Bakhtin, Mikhail M., jt. auth. see Medvedev, Pavel N.

Bakhtine. L' Oeuvre de Francois Rabelais et la Culture Populaire au Moyen Age et sous Renaissance. Robel, tr. (Bibliotheque des Idees Ser.). 26.95 (*0-685-34193-3*, F31460) Fr & Eur.

BaKhufu, Auset. The Six Black Presidents: Black Blood, White Masks: A Little Bit of Melanin: The Six Black President (U. S. A.) LC 91-90486. 365p. (C). 1993. per. 19.95 (*1-880187-00-0*) PIKK Pubns.

Bakhuizen, J. N., ed. Ratramnus, de Corpore et Sanguine Domini. (Verhandelingen der Koninklijke Nederlandse Akademie van Wetenschappen, Afd. Letterkunde, Nieuwe Reeks Ser.: No. 87). 156p. 1974. pap. 40.75 (*0-7204-8288-7*) Elsevier.

Bakhurst, David. Consciousness & Revolution in Soviet Philosophy: From the Bolsheviks to Evald Ilyenkov. (Modern European Philosophy Ser.). 304p. (C). 1991. text 80.00 (*0-521-38534-2*); pap. text 22.95 (*0-521-40710-9*) Cambridge U Pr.

Bakhurst, David & Sypnowich, Christine, eds. The Social Self: Inquiries in Social Construction. LC 95-78829. 192p. 1995. pap. 14.99 (*0-8039-7597-X*) Sage.

Bakhvalov, N. & Panasenko, G. Homogenisation - Averaging Process in Periodic Media: Mathematical Problems in the Mechanics of Composite Materials. (C). 1989. text 303.50 (*0-7923-0049-1*) Kluwer Academic.

Bakich, Michael E. The Cambridge Guide to the Constellations. (Illus.). 334p. (C). 1995. pap. 22.95 (*0-521-44921-9*) Cambridge U Pr.

***Bakich, Michael E.** The Cambridge Planetary Handbook. LC 99-10171. 1999. pap. write for info. (*0-521-63415-6*) Cambridge U Pr.

Bakich, Michael E. The Cambridge Planetary Handbook. LC 99-10171. (Illus.). 346p. 2000. 29.95 (*0-521-63280-3*) Cambridge U Pr.

Bakies, Anna L. Coaching with Kids. 2nd rev. ed. LC 98-73892. (Illus.). viii, 58p. 1999. spiral bd. 5.00 (*1-892365-06-5*) Epic Conver.

Bakija, Jon, jt. auth. see Slemrod, Joel.

Bakija, Jon M., jt. auth. see Steuerle, C. Eugene.

B

Bakirtzis, Charalambos & Koester, Helmut, eds. Philippi at the Time of Paul & after His Death. LC 98-39837. 128p. 1998. pap. 16.00 (*1-56338-263-6*) TPI PA.

Bakis, Henry, jt. ed. see Roche, Edward M.

Bakis, Kirsten. Lives of the Monster Dogs. LC 96-25017. 320p. 1997. 23.00 (*0-374-18987-0*) FS&G.

***Bakis, Kirsten.** Lives of the Monster Dogs. LC 97-48550. 304p. 1998. mass mkt. 12.99 (*0-446-67416-8*, Pub. by Warner Bks) Little.

Bakish, David. Jimmy Durante: His Show Business Career, with an Annotated Filmography & Discography. LC 94-32141. (Illus.). 303p. 1994. lib. bdg. 35.00 (*0-89950-968-1*) McFarland & Co.

Bakish, R. Proceedings of Second International Conference on Pervaporation Processes in the Chemical Industry. (Illus.). 210p. 1987. pap. 100.00 (*0-939997-01-0*) Bakish Mat.

Bakish, R., ed. Proceedings of 10th International Conference on Vacuum Web Coating. (Proceedings of the Internaitonal Conferences on Vacuum Web Coating Ser.: Vol. 10). (Illus.). 325p. (Orig.). (C). 1997. pap. write for info. (*0-939997-20-7*) Bakish Mat.

Bakish, Robert. Proceedings of the 12th International Vacuum Web Coating Conference. (Illus.). 1999. pap. 70.00 (*0-939997-22-3*) Bakish Mat.

Bakish, Robert, ed. Proceedings, Eleventh International Conference on Vacuum Web Coating, No. 11. (Illus.). 300p. 1998. pap. 70.00 (*0-939997-21-5*) Bakish Mat.

— Proceedings of the 13th International Vacuum Web Coating Conference, Vol. 13. (Illus.). 250p. 2000. pap. 80.00 (*0-939997-23-1*) Bakish Mat.

Bakish, Robert & White, S. S. Handbook of Electron Beam Welding. LC 64-7538. (Wiley Series on the Science & Technology of Materials). 279p. reprint ed. pap. 86.50 (*0-608-30427-1*, 200739800062) Bks Demand.

Bakish, Robert, ed. see International Conference on Electron & Ion Beam Sc.

Bakit, Muhammad A. Ottoman Province of Damascus in the 16th Century. 308p. 1982. 48.00 (*0-86685-322-7*, LDL3227) Intl Bk Ctr.

Bakitas,R.N., Marie & Wujcik, Debra. Blood & Marrow Stem Cell Transplant. 2nd ed. LC 97-2860. (Nursing Ser.). 608p. 1997. 68.75 (*0-7637-0356-7*) Jones & Bartlett.

Bakk, Karl R. Man & His Deities. LC 89-91059. (Orig.). 1989. pap. 9.95 (*0-922958-15-7*) H W Parker.

Bakke, Corean. Let the Whole World Sing: The Story Behind the Music of Lausanne II. LC 94-24994. 286p. 1994. pap. 13.00 (*0-940895-18-8*) Cornerstone IL.

***Bakke, David.** God Knows His Name: The True Story of John Doe No. 24. LC 00-20070. 2000. pap. 15.95 (*0-8093-2327-3*) S Ill U Pr.

Bakke, David, jt. auth. see Hamm, Dale.

Bakke, Diane & Davis, Jackie. Places Around the Bases: A Historic Tour of the Coors Field Neighborhood. (Illus.). 160p. 1995. pap. text 16.95 (*1-56579-117-7*) Westcliffe Pubs.

Bakke, E. Wight, jt. auth. see Noland, William E.

Bakke, Gary L., et al. Wisconsin Attorney's Desk Reference, 2 vols. 960p. 1999. ring bd. 115.00 (*1-57862-028-7*) State Bar WI.

***Bakke, Jeannette A.** Holy Invitations: Exploring Spiritual Direction. LC 00-27896. 320p. (gr. 13). 2000. pap. 16.99 (*0-8010-6327-2*) Baker Bks.

Bakke, Ray. A Theology As Big As the City. LC 96-29820. 240p. 1997. pap. 12.99 (*0-8308-1890-1*, 1890) InterVarsity.

Bakke, Raymond. The Urban Christian. LC 87-30861. 202p. 1987. reprint ed. pap. 11.99 (*0-87784-523-9*, 523) InterVarsity.

Bakke, Raymond J. & Roberts, Samuel K. The Expanded Mission of City Center Churches. rev. ed. Orig. Title: The Expanded Mission of Old First Churches. 136p. 1998. pap. 13.00 (*0-9664671-0-8*) Intl Urban Assocs.

***Bakke, Robert.** The Power of Extraordinary Prayer. LC 00-25256. 224p. 2000. pap. 10.99 (*1-58134-154-7*) Crossway Bks.

Bakke, Timothy O., ed. Kitchens: Design, Remodel, Build. 3rd rev. ed. LC 96-84687. (Illus.). 192p. 1992. pap. 14.95 (*1-880029-68-5*) Creative Homeowner.

Bakke, Timothy O., ed. see Baldwin, Ed.

Bakke, Timothy O., ed. see Beneke, Jeff.

Bakke, Timothy O., ed. see Cory, Steve.

Bakke, Timothy O., ed. see Hingley, Brian.

Bakke, Timothy O., ed. see Jacobs, David, et al.

Bakke, Timothy O., ed. see Jones, Jack P.

Bakke, Timothy O., ed. see Presutti, Michael.

Bakke, Timothy O., jt. ed. see Quinn, Patrick.

Bakke, Timothy O., ed. see Schultz, Mort.

Bakke, Timothy O., ed. see Wagner, John.

Bakkeby, William M., Jr. It's a New Way of Living. LC 98-217218. vi, 45p. 1998. pap. 3.95 (*0-9661069-0-3*) Word of Grace.

— Living in God's Abundance. 120p. 1999. pap. 7.00 (*0-9661069-1-1*) Word of Grace.

***Bakken, Borge.** The Exemplary Society: Human Improvement, Social Control, & the Dangers of Modernity in China. LC 99-42802. (Studies on Contemporary China). 456p. 2000. write for info. (*0-19-829523-5*) OUP.

Bakken, Borge, ed. Migration in China. LC 98-216544. 160p. 1998. pap. 19.95 (*87-87062-57-7*, Pub. by NIAS) Paul & Co Pubs.

Bakken, Dick. Feet with the Jesus. LC 86-27625. 52p. 1989. 15.00 (*0-89924-056-9*); pap. 8.00 (*0-89924-054-2*) Lynx Hse.

Bakken, Gary & Abele, Jon R. Innkeeper's Liability Management. 448p. 1995. 65.00 (*0-913875-06-6*, 5056) Lawyers & Judges.

Bakken, Gordon & Farrington, Brenda. Learning California History: Essential Skills for the Survey Course & Beyond. (Illus.). 186p. (C). 1999. pap. text, wbk. ed. 15.95 (*0-88295-945-X*) Harlan Davidson.

Bakken, Gordon M. The Development of Law in Frontier California: Civil Law & Society, 1850-1890, 33. LC 84-25202. (Contributions in Legal Studies: No. 33). (Illus.). 162p. 1985. 47.95 (*0-313-24725-0*, BFC/, Greenwood Pr) Greenwood.

— The Development of Law on the Rocky Mountain Frontier: Civil Law & Society, 1850-1912, 27. LC 82-20984. (Contributions in Legal Studies: No. 27). 200p. 1983. 49.95 (*0-313-23285-7*, BDL/, Greenwood Pr) Greenwood.

— Practicing Law in Frontier California. LC 90-40646. (Law in the American West Ser.). (Illus.). xviii, 192p. 1991. text 50.00 (*0-8032-1219-4*) U of Nebr Pr.

— Rocky Mountain Constitution Making, 1850-1912, 35. LC 86-12143. 194p. 1987. 52.95 (*0-313-25538-5*, BKC/, Greenwood Pr) Greenwood.

***Bakken, Gordon Morris, ed.** Law in the Western United States. LC 00-32610. Vol. 6. 448p. 2000. 49.95 (*0-8061-3215-9*) U of Okla Pr.

Bakken, Henry H. Basic Concepts, Principles, & Practices of Cooperation. 1963. 3.00 (*0-912084-05-7*) Mimir.

— The Hills of Home-A Family History. 1976. 13.50 (*0-912084-11-1*) Mimir.

***Bakken, Kenneth L.** The Journey into God: Healing & Christian Faith. 2000. pap. 15.99 (*0-8066-4048-0*, Augsburg) Augsburg Fortress.

Bakken, Larry A. Justice in the Wilderness: A Study of Frontier Courts in Canada & the United States, 1670-1870. LC 86-17889. (Illus.). xiii, 266p. 1986. reprint ed. 37.50 (*0-8377-0354-9*, Rothman) W S Hein.

Bakken, Peter W., et al. Ecology, Justice, & Christian Faith: A Critical Guide to the Literature, 36. LC 95-36040. (Bibliographies & Indexes in Religious Studies: No. 36). 256p. 1995. lib. bdg. 59.95 (*0-313-29073-3*, BT695, Greenwood Pr) Greenwood.

Bakken, Peter W., ed. see Sittler, Joseph.

Bakken, Roger. The Coach's Pocket Planner. (Illus.). 72p. 1983. per. 5.95 (*0-930097-00-9*) Sportsrite Pub Co.

Bakken, Turina R., ed. see Marien, Edward J.

Bakkenist, Gisele. Environmental Information: Law, Policy & Experience. (Environmental Law Ser.). 250p. 1994. 105.00 (*1-874698-15-5*, Pub. by Cameron May) Gaunt.

Bakker. Dutch-English, English-Dutch Dictionary of Information Science. (DUT & ENG.). 366p. 1985. 45.00 (*0-8288-4024-5*, F116490) Fr & Eur.

— Sport Psychology. 1999. pap. text 61.95 (*0-471-93913-7*) Wiley.

Bakker, A., ed. Mechanical Behavior of Materials: Invited Papers Presented at the 7th International Conference, the Hague, the Netherlands, May 28-June 2, 1995. (Illus.). 164p. (Orig.). 1996. pap. 77.50 (*90-407-1126-7*, Pub. by Delft U Pr) Coronet Bks.

Bakker, A. F. International Financial Institutions. LC 95-33970. 232p. (C). 1996. pap. 32.46 (*0-582-27763-9*) Longman.

Bakker, A. R. Approaches of Assessment of Information Technology. LC 94-73350. 336p. (gr. 12). 1994. 93.00 (*90-5199-200-9*) IOS Press.

Bakker, Ad, jt. ed. see Kirk, Mark.

Bakker, Age, ed. Monetary Stability Through International Cooperation: Essays in Honour of Andre' Szasz Presented on the Occasion of His Retirement from the Governing Board. 412p. (C). 1994. lib. bdg. 106.00 (*0-7923-3004-8*) Kluwer Academic.

Bakker, Age F. The Liberalization of Capital Movements in Europe: The Monetary Committee & Financial Integration, 1958-1994. LC 95-20404. (Financial & Monetary Policy Studies: Vol. 29). 340p. (C). 1996. lib. bdg. 110.50 (*0-7923-3591-0*) Kluwer Academic.

Bakker-Arkema, F. & Maier, P. E. Handbook of Agricultural Crop Drying & Storage. (Illus.). Date not set. text. write for info. (*0-8247-9437-0*) Dekker.

***Bakker-Arkema, F. W., et al, eds.** CIGR Handbook of Agricultural Engineering Vol. IV: Agro Processing Engineering. LC 98-93767. 540p. 1999. text 58.75 (*1-892769-03-4*, M0998) Am Soc Ag Eng.

Bakker, B. L. G. & Dantzig, L. van, eds. Few-Body Problems in Physics '93: Proceedings of the XIVth European Conference on Few-Body Problems in Physics, Amsterdam, the Netherlands, August 23-27, 1993. LC 94-1450. (Few-Body Systems Ser.: Suppl. 7). (Illus.). xv, 486p. 1994. 129.95 (*0-387-82550-9*) Spr-Verlag.

Bakker, Boudewijn, et al. Landscapes of Rembrandt. (Illus.). 392p. 69.95 (*90-6868-204-0*, Pub. by U Thoth) Bks Nippan.

Bakker, Brit, et al. Norsk - Serbokroatisk Ordbok. (CRO, NOR & SER.). 688p. 1992. lib. bdg. 275.00 (*0-7859-3672-6*, 8200075850) Fr & Eur.

Bakker, C. M., et al. Neural Aspects of Human Movement: Implications for Control & Coordination. viii, 96p. 1993. pap. 44.00 (*90-265-1322-4*) Swets.

Bakker, D. J., ed. Proceedings of the Tenth International Congress on Hyperbaric Medicine. 201p. (C). 1992. 35.50 (*0-941332-24-1*, D450) Best Pub Co.

Bakker, D. J., et al, eds. Developmental Dyslexia & Learning Disorders: Child Health & Development, Vol. 5. (Illus.). vi, 166p. 1987. 61.00 (*3-8055-4585-1*) S Karger.

Bakker, Dave, ed. see Pennington, M. J.

Bakker, Dirk J. Neuropsychological Treatments of Dyslexia. (Illus.). 112p. 1990. pap. text 19.95 (*0-19-506132-2*) OUP.

— Specific Reading Disability. Satz, Paul, ed. (Modern Approaches to the Diagnosis & Instruction of Multi-Handicapped Children Ser.: Vol. 3). xii, 166p. 1970. 25.00 (*90-237-4103-X*) Taylor & Francis.

Bakker, Dirk J., ed. Learning Diabilities Vol. 1: Neuropsychological Correlates & Treatment. x, 202p. 1989. 55.50 (*90-265-0983-9*) Swets.

Bakker, Egbert J. Linguistics & Formulas in Homer: Scalarity & Description of the Particle Per. LC 88-10110. x, 306p. (C). 1988. 65.00 (*1-55619-046-8*) J Benjamins Pubng Co.

— Poetry in Speech: Orality & Homeric Discourse. LC 96-3197. (Myth & Poetics Ser.). 256p. 1996. text 49.95 (*0-8014-3295-2*) Cornell U Pr.

Bakker, Egbert J., ed. Grammar As Interpretation: Greek Literature in Its Linguistic Contexts. LC 97-8213. (Mnemosyne, Supplements Ser.: No. 171). viii, 262p. 1997. 114.00 (*90-04-10730-4*) Brill Academic Pubs.

Bakker, Egbert J. & Kahane, Ahuvia. Written Voices, Spoken Signs: Tradition, Performance, & the Epic Text. LC 96-46776. (Center for Hellenic Studies Colloquia Ser.). (Illus.). 304p. 1997. 39.95 (*0-674-96260-5*) HUP.

Bakker, Elna S. An Island Called California: An Ecological Introduction to Its Natural Communities. exp. rev. ed. LC 82-17453. (Illus.). 400p. (C). 1985. pap. 18.95 (*0-520-04948-9*, Pub. by U CA Pr) Cal Prin Full Svc.

— An Island Called California: An Ecological Introduction to Its Natural Communities. LC 82-17453. (Illus.). 500p. reprint ed. pap. 155.00 (*0-7837-4759-4*, 204450600003) Bks Demand.

Bakker, Evert P., ed. Alkali Cation Transport Systems in Prokaryotes. 464p. 1992. lib. bdg. 232.00 (*0-8493-6982-7*, QH509) CRC Pr.

Bakker, F. C., jt. auth. see G. H. I. M. Walenkamp.

Bakker, Frans. Praying Always. Pronk, Cornelis & Pronk, Fredrika, trs. from DUT. 114p. 1987. reprint ed. pap. 7.99 (*0-85151-514-2*) Banner of Truth.

Bakker, Gerald & Clark, Len. Explanation: An Introduction to the Philosophy of Science. LC 87-31538. x, 213p. (C). 1988. pap. text 31.95 (*0-87484-838-5*, 838) Mayfield Pub.

Bakker, H., ed. Enthalpies in Alloys: Miedema's Semi-Empirical Model. (Materials Science Foundations Ser.: Vol. I). (Illus.). 92p. (C). 1998. text 48.00 (*0-87849-783-8*, Pub. by Scitec Pubns) Enfield Pubs NH.

***Bakker, H. J. C. & Helmink, J. W. A.** Successfully Integrating Two Businesses. LC 00-39392. 228p. 2000. 104.95 (*0-566-08368-X*) Ashgate Pub Co.

Bakker, Hans. Ayodhya, Pt. 1: The History of Ayodhya from the 7th c. B. C. to the Middle of the 18th c., Its Development into a Sacred Centre with Special Reference to the Ayodhyamahatmya & to the Worship of Rama According to the Agastyasamhita. (Illus.). 872p. (C). 1986. 146.00 (*90-6980-007-1*, Pub. by Egbert Forsten) Hod1der & Stoughton.

— The Vakatakas: An Essay in Hindu Iconology. LC 97-221451. (Gonda Indological Studies: No. 5). (Illus.). xiv, 212p. 1997. lib. bdg. 112.00 (*90-6980-100-0*, Pub. by Egbert Forsten) Hod1der & Stoughton.

Bakker, Hans, ed. The Sacred Centre As the Focus of Political Interest: Proceedings of the Symposium Held on the Occasion of the 375th Anniversary of the University of Groningen, 5-8 March 1989. (Groningen Oriental Studies: Vol. VI). ix, 268p. 1992. pap. 52.00 (*90-6980-036-5*, Pub. by Egbert Forsten) Hod1der & Stoughton.

***Bakker, Henk.** Sugar Cane Cultivation & Management. LC 99-31318. 679p. (C). 1999. text. write for info. (*0-306-46119-6*, Kluwer Plenum) Kluwer Academic.

Bakker, Isabel, ed. The Strategic Silence: Gender & Economic Policy. LC 94-35309. 170p. (C). 1994. text 19.95 (*1-85649-262-1*, Pub. by Zed Books) St Martin.

Bakker, Isabella, ed. Rethinking Restructuring: Gender & Change in Canada. 320p. 1996. text 55.00 (*0-8020-0702-3*); pap. text 22.95 (*0-8020-7651-3*) U of Toronto Pr.

Bakker, J. The Role of the Mythic West in Some Representative Examples of Classic & Modern American Literature: The Shaping Force of the American Frontier. LC 91-20378. (Studies in American Literature: Vol. 13). 284p. 1991. lib. bdg. 89.95 (*0-7734-9713-7*) E Mellen.

Bakker, J. T. Living & Working with the Gods: Studies of Evidence for Private Religion & Its Material Environment in the City of Ostia (100-500 AD) LC 94-132791. 383p. 1992. 100.00 (*90-5063-056-1*, DMAHA, Pub. by Gieben) J Benjamins Pubng Co.

Bakker, J. T., ed. The Mills-Bakeries of Ostia: Description & Interpretation. (Dutch Monographs on Ancient History & Archaeology: Vol. 21). 225p. 1999. 135.00 (*90-5063-058-8*, Pub. by Gieben) J Benjamins Pubng Co.

Bakker, J. W. De, see De Bakker, J. W.

Bakker, Jan A. The Dutch Hunebedden: Megalithic Tombs of the Funnel Beaker Culture. (Archaeological Ser.: No. 2). (Illus.). xiv, 214p. (Orig.). 1992. pap. 34.00 (*1-879621-02-9*) Intl Mono Prehstry.

Bakker, Jan W. The Philippine Justice System: The Independence & Impartiality of the Judiciary & Human Rights from 1986 till 1997. LC 98-164482. 234p. Date not set. reprint ed. pap. 72.60 (*0-608-20633-4*, 207206900003) Bks Demand.

Bakker, Jim. I Was Wrong: The Untold Story of the Shocking Journey from PTL Power to Prison & Beyond. LC 97-102988. (Illus.). 224p. 1996. 24.99 (*0-7852-7425-1*, J Thoma Bks) Nelson.

— I Was Wrong: The Untold Story of the Shocking Journey from PTL Power to Prison & Beyond. (Illus.). 480p. 1997. pap. 15.99 (*0-7852-7136-8*) Nelson.

— Prosperity & the Coming Apocalypse. LC 98-39749. 256p. 1998. 19.99 (*0-7852-7458-8*) Nelson.

***Bakker, Jim.** The Refuge: The Joy of Christian Community in a Torn-Apart World. 256p. 2000. 19.99 (*0-7852-7459-6*) Nelson.

Bakker, Kees, ed. Joris Ivens & the Documentary Context. (Film Culture in Transition Ser.). (Illus.). 300p. (C). text 49.50 (*90-5356-425-X*, Pub. by Amsterdam U Pr); pap. text 24.95 (*90-5356-389-X*, Pub. by Amsterdam U Pr) U of Mich Pr.

***Bakker, Klaas-Jan.** Soil Retaining Structures: Development of Models for Structural Analysis. (Illus.). 236p. 2000. 75.00 (*90-5809-321-2*, Pub. by A A Balkema) Ashgate Pub Co.

***Bakker, Maaike.** Cups & Saucers: Paper-Pieced Kitchen Designs. (Illus.). 80p. 2000. pap. 22.95 (*1-56477-333-7*) Martingale & Co.

Bakker, Marilyn. The Wiley Encyclopedia of Packaging Technology. LC 86-4041. 768p. 1986. 275.00 (*0-471-80940-3*) Wiley.

Bakker, Martijn, jt. ed. see Kroes, Peter.

Bakker, Martinus A. & Morrison, Beverly H., eds. Studies in Netherlandic Culture & Literature. (Publications of the American Association for Netherlandic Studies). (Illus.). 260p. 1994. lib. bdg. 49.50 (*0-8191-9466-2*) U Pr of Amer.

Bakker, Onno. Lumi-Imager F1: Lab Protocols. LC 98-39227. 1998. pap. write for info. (*3-540-64794-5*) Spr-Verlag.

Bakker, P. G., jt. ed. see Henkes, R. A.

Bakker, Paul J. J. M., jt. ed. see Hoenen, Maarten J.F. M.

Bakker, Peter. A Language of Our Own: The Genesis of Michif, the Mixed Cree-French Language of the Canadian Metis. LC 97-7301. (Oxford Studies in Anthropological Linguistics: No. 10). (Illus.). 336p. 1997. text 85.00 (*0-19-509711-4*) OUP.

— A Language of Our Own: The Genesis of Michif, the Mixed Cree-French Language of the Canadian Metis. rev. ed. LC 97-7301. (Oxford Studies in Anthropological Linguistics: No. 10). (Illus.). 336p. 1997. pap. 49.95 (*0-19-509712-2*) OUP.

***Bakker, Peter, et al.** What Is the Romani Language? (Interface Collection: Vol. 21). 137p. 2000. pap. 23.95 (*1-902806-06-9*, Pub. by Univ of Herfordshire) Bold Strummer Ltd.

Bakker, Robert T. The Dinosaur Heresies. 480p. 1988. pap. 12.95 (*0-8217-2859-8*, Zebra Kensgtn) Kensgtn Pub Corp.

— Dinosaur Heresies. 1996. pap. text 15.00 (*0-8217-5608-7*, Zebra Kensgtn) Kensgtn Pub Corp.

— Dinosaur Heresies. 1995. pap. 12.95 (*0-8217-5032-1*) NAL.

— Raptor Red. 1996. mass mkt. 8.99 (*0-553-54252-4*) Bantam.

— Raptor Red. 272p. 1996. mass mkt. 6.50 (*0-553-57561-9*) Bantam.

Bakker, Ron, et al, eds. Judicial Control: Comparative Essays on Judicial Review. LC 96-200540. 165p. 1995. pap. 48.00 (*90-6215-508-1*, Pub. by Maklu Uitgev) Gaunt.

Bakker, Suzanne, ed. Health Information Management: What Strategies? LC 97-13932. 364p. 1997. text 184.00 (*0-7923-4546-0*) Kluwer Academic.

Bakker, Suzanne, ed. see Third European Conference of Medical Libraries.

Bakker, Tammy F. & Rudnitsky, David. When the Spirit Moves You: The Autobiography of Tammy Faye Bakker. 1996. pap. 22.00 (*0-614-15433-2*) Villard Books.

Bakker, W. F., et al, eds. Cretan Studies, Vol. 1. vii, 270p. (Orig.). 1988. pap. 98.00 (*90-256-0952-X*, Pub. by AM Hakkert) BookLink Distributors.

— Cretan Studies, Vol. 2. (Illus.). 230p. (Orig.). 1990. pap. 82.00 (*90-256-0998-8*, Pub. by AM Hakkert) BookLink Distributors.

— Cretan Studies, Vol. 3. (Illus.). 232p. (Orig.). 1992. pap. 82.00 (*90-256-1041-2*, Pub. by AM Hakkert) BookLink Distributors.

— Cretan Studies, Vol. 4. (Illus.). 174p. (Orig.). 1995. pap. 82.00 (*90-256-0949-X*, Pub. by AM Hakkert) BookLink Distributors.

Bakker, W. T., et al, eds. Materials for Coal Gasification: Proceedings of a Conference Held in Conjunction with ASM's Materials Week '87, Cincinnati, OH, 10-15 October 1987. LC 88-70075. (Illus.). 268p. reprint ed. pap. 83.10 (*0-8357-4090-0*, 203685600005) Bks Demand.

Bakkers, A., ed. Applying Transputer Based Parallel Machines: Proceedings of the 10th Occam User Group Technical Meeting, Enschede, Netherlands, April 3-5, 1989. (Transputer & Occam Engineering Ser.). 317p. (YA). (gr. 12). 1989. pap. 65.00 (*90-5199-011-1*, Pub. by IOS Pr) IOS Press.

Bakkers, A. & Welch, P., eds. Architectures, Languages & Patterns for Parallel & Distributed Applications. LC 98-72607. (Concurrent Science Engineering Ser.: Vol. 52). 285p. 1998. 80.00 (*90-5199-391-9*, Pub. by IOS Pr) IOS Press.

Bakkhurst, David & Sypnowich, Christine, eds. The Social Self: Inquiries in Social Construction. LC 95-78829. 192p. 1995. 45.00 (*0-8039-7596-1*) Sage.

Bakkum, Maria. Love's Subtle Signature. Leih, janet, ed. (Illus.). 66p. 1993. pap. 5.00 (*1-877649-17-1*) Tesseract SD.

— Portraits in Sun & Shadow. (Illus.). 66p. 1995. pap. 5.00 (*0-614-24751-9*) Tesseract SD.

— Woman to Woman. 71p. 1994. per. 5.00 (*0-614-24752-7*) Tesseract SD.

Bakland, Leif K., jt. auth. see Ingle, John I.

***Baklanoff, Eric N. & Moseley, Edward H., eds.** Competing for Latin American Markets: A Business Perspective on the Spanish-American War Centennial. 1999. pap. 7.95 (*0-943394-13-9*) U of Ala Ctr Bus.

Baklanov, Grigory. South of the Main Offensive. Ainsztein, R., tr. from RUS. LC 64-25464. 192p. 1963. 24.95 (*0-8023-1006-0*) Dufour.

An Asterisk (*) at the beginning of an entry indicates that the title is appearing for the first time.

***Bako-Arifari, Nassirou & Laurent, Pierre-Joseph, eds.** Social & Economic Dimensions of Local Development & Decentralization in Sub-Saharan Africa. 176p. 1999. 23.95 (*3-8258-3960-5*, Pub. by CE24) Transaction Pubs.

Bako, Elemer. Finland & the Finns: A Selected Bibliography. (Illus.). 276p. (Orig.). (C). 1994. pap. text 50.00 (*0-7881-0326-1*) DIANE Pub.

— Finland & the Finns: A Selective Bibliography. LC 93-16151. 1993. write for info. (*0-8444-0780-1*) Lib Congress.

***Bakon, Shimon & Berlyn, Patricia.** The Adventures of Shani in the Land of Beyond-Sambatyon. 1999. 15.00 (*965-90235-0-2*) En-gedi Books.

Bakos. Pushing Sexual Limits. 1995. mass mkt. write for info. (*0-312-95424-7*) St Martin.

***Bakos.** Still Sexy. LC 99-13299. 320p. 1999. mass mkt. 6.99 (*0-312-97151-6*) St Martin.

Bakos, jt. auth. see Block, Joel D.

Bakos, Adrianna E. Images of Kingship in Early Modern France: Louis XI in Political Thought, 1560-1789. LC 96-42013. 280p. (C). 1997. 80.00 (*0-415-15478-2*) Routledge.

Bakos, Adrianna E., ed. Politics, Ideology & the Law in Early Modern Europe: Essays in Honor of J. H. M. Salmon. LC 94-20552. (Illus.). 208p. (C). 1995. 85.00 (*1-878822-39-X*) Univ Rochester Pr.

Bakos, F. Rumanian-Hungarian Concise Dictionary. 835p. 1991. 50.00 (*963-05-5877-7*, Pub. by Akade Kiado) St Mut.

Bakos, Joan B. & Karrick, Guy E. Dining in Corporate America: Handbook of Noncommercial Foodservice Management. LC 89-6608. 249p. (C). 1989. 65.00 (*0-8342-0065-1*) Aspen Pub.

Bakos, Susan C. Appointment for Murder. 1989. mass mkt. 3.95 (*1-55817-238-6*, Pinncle Kensgtn) Kensgtn Pub Corp.

Bakos, Susan C. Female Superior Position. 320p. 1994. 18.95 (*0-8217-4582-4*, Zebra Kensgtn) Kensgtn Pub Corp.

Bakos, Susan C. The Female's Superior Position. 1995. pap. 4.99 (*0-8217-4964-1*) NAL.

— Kink: The Hidden Sex Lives of Americans. 1995. mass mkt. 6.99 (*0-312-95684-3*, Pub. by Tor Bks) St Martin.

— Secrets of Better Sex. 304p. (C). 1996. 18.95 (*0-13-606666-6*, Macmillan Coll) P-H.

— Sexational Secrets, Vol. 1. 1998. mass mkt. 6.99 (*0-312-96341-6*) St Martin.

— Sexational Secrets: Exotic Advice Your Mother Never Told You. 240p. 1996. 22.95 (*0-312-14413-X*) St Martin.

— Sexsational Secrets: Things Your Mother Never Told You. 1996. 22.95 (*0-614-97013-X*) St Martin.

— Sexual Pleasures: A Groundbreaking Book That Shows Women How to Claim the Sexual Passion They... 1992. mass mkt. 4.99 (*0-312-92847-5*) St Martin.

— What Men Really Want: Straight Talk from Men about Sex. 256p. 1991. mass mkt. 5.99 (*0-312-92638-3*) St Martin.

Bakos, Susan Crain. Still Sexy. LC 99-13299. 1999. text 23.95 (*0-312-20591-0*) St Martin.

Bakos, Susan Crain, jt. auth. see Block, Joel.

Bakoulis, Marion G., jt. auth. see Breitkopf, Lyle J.

Bakr, A. A. The Boundary Integral Equation Method in Axisymmetric Stress Analysis Problems. (Lecture Notes in Engineering Ser.: Vol. 14). 213p. 1986. 31.00 (*0-387-16030-2*) Spr-Verlag.

Bakr, M. Elsevier's Dictionary of the Environment. LC 98-48785. 800p. 1998. write for info. (*0-444-82966-0*) Elsevier.

— Elsevier's Maritime Dictionary. (ARA, ENG & FRE.). 664p. 1987. 305.75 (*0-444-42737-6*) Elsevier.

— Elsevier's Maritime Dictionary in English, French & Arabic. (ARA, ENG & FRE.). 664p. 1987. 350.00 (*0-8288-9263-6*, M1515) Fr & Eur.

Bakr, Salwa. The Wiles of Men & Other Stories. Johnsom-Daview, Denys, tr. from ARA. LC 93-4648. 190p. (C). 1993. reprint ed. pap. 14.95 (*0-292-70800-9*) U of Tex Pr.

Bakre, A. B. Religion in Social Flux: As Seen in the Main Purearnea-s LC 98-905764. xviii, 337 p. 1998. write for info. (*81-86339-37-X*, Pub. by Eastern Bk Linkers) S Asia.

Bakris, George L., ed. Renin-Angiotensin System in Diabetic Nephropathy: From Bench to Bedside. (Mineral & Electrolyte Metabolism Ser.: Vol. 24, No. 6 (1998)). (Illus.). iv, 94p. 1998. pap. 34.00 (*3-8055-6816-9*) S Karger.

Bakris, George L., jt. ed. see Sobel, Barry J.

Bakry, D., et al. Lectures on Probability Theory. (Lecture Notes in Mathematics Ser.). 411p. 1994. 79.95 (*0-387-58208-8*) Spr-Verlag.

Bakshee, Igor. Graphica 2. (Illus.). 1999. pap. 34.95 (*1-57955-010-X*) Wolfram Media.

Bakshi, D. N. Hindu Divinities in Japanese Buddhist Pantheon. 200p. 1979. 29.95 (*0-318-37161-8*) Asia Bk Corp.

— Iconography of the Buddha Images in Japan. (C). 1988. 18.50 (*0-8364-2280-5*, Pub. by Ctr Jpns Studies) S Asia.

Bakshi, G. D. The Indian Military Revival. (C). 1987. 19.00 (*81-7062-023-6*, Pub. by Lancer India) S Asia.

Bakshi, Guba D. Flora of Murshidabad. 316p. (C). 1984. 240.00 (*81-85046-11-5*, Pub. by Scientific) St Mut.

Bakshi, Om. The Crisis of Political Theory: An Inquiry into Contemporary Thought. 144p. 1988. 21.00 (*0-19-562094-1*) OUP.

Bakshi, P. M. The Constitution of India. (C). 1990. 40.00 (*0-89771-210-2*) St Mut.

Bakshi, Parminder K. Distant Desire: Homoerotic Codes & the Subversion of the English Novel in E. M. Forster's Fiction. LC 94-19454. (Sexuality & Literature Ser.: Vol. 5). XII, 250p. (C). 1996. text 47.95 (*0-8204-2544-3*) P Lang Pubng.

Bakshi, R. Gandhi & Civil Disobedience Movement. 230p. 1985. 37.95 (*0-318-36582-0*) Asia Bk Corp.

***Bakshi, Rajni.** Bapu Kuti: Journeys in Rediscovery of Gandhi. LC 98-915450. 334p. 1998. 18.50 (*0-14-027838-9*, Penguin Classics) Viking Penguin.

Bakshi, S. R. Abdul Ghaffar Khan: The Frontier Gandhi. (C). 1992. 34.00 (*0-685-61703-3*, Pub. by Anmol) S Asia.

— Abul Kalam Azad: The Secular Leader. 1991. 38.50 (*81-7041-432-6*, Pub. by Anmol) S Asia.

— Annie Besant: Founder of Home Rule Movement. 1990. 42.00 (*81-7041-259-5*, Pub. by Anmol) S Asia.

— Arya Samaj: Swami Dayanand & His Ideology. (C). 1991. text 52.00 (*81-7041-461-X*, Pub. by Anmol) S Asia.

— Aurobindo Ghose: Revolutionary & Reformer. (C). 1994. text 26.00 (*81-7041-702-3*, Pub. by Anmol) S Asia.

— B. R. Ambedkar: Statesman & Constitutionalist. (C). 1992. 30.00 (*0-685-59602-8*, Pub. by Anmol) S Asia.

— Bal Gangadhar Tilak: Struggle for Swaraj. 1990. 42.00 (*81-7041-262-5*, Pub. by Anmol) S Asia.

— Bhagat Singh: Patriot & Martyr. (C). 1990. 42.00 (*81-7041-258-7*, Pub. by Anmol) S Asia.

— C. Rajagopalachari. (C). 1991. 56.00 (*81-7041-433-4*, Pub. by Anmol) S Asia.

— Documents of Muslim Politics: A Study of Khilafat Movement. (C). 1990. 135.00 (*0-89771-154-8*) St Mut.

***Bakshi, S. R.** Encyclopaedia of Punjab, 10 vols. 1998. pap. 5000.00 (*81-7415-016-1*, Pub. by Print Hse) St Mut.

Bakshi, S. R. Gandhi & Civil Disobedience Movement. 230p. 1986. 29.00 (*0-8364-1820-4*, Pub. by Gitanjali Prakashan) S Asia.

— Gandhi & Hindu-Muslim Unity. 1987. 37.95 (*0-318-36644-4*) Asia Bk Corp.

— Gandhi & Khilafat. 1985. 18.00 (*0-8364-1491-8*, Pub. by Gitanjali Prakashan) S Asia.

— Gandhi & Status of Harijans. 1987. 37.95 (*0-318-36645-2*) Asia Bk Corp.

— Govind Ballabh Pant: The True Gandhian. (C). 1991. 31.00 (*81-7041-430-X*, Pub. by Anmol) S Asia.

— Har Dayal: Role in Freedom Struggle. (C). 1994. text 28.00 (*81-7041-706-6*, Pub. by Anmol) S Asia.

— History of the Punjab: Maharaja Ranjit Singh. (C). 1991. 31.00 (*0-685-53622-X*, Pub. by Anmol) S Asia.

— Jagivan Ram: The Harijan Leader. (Indian Freedom Fighters Ser.: No. 25). (C). 1992. 24.00 (*81-7041-496-2*, Pub. by Anmol) S Asia.

— Jawaharlal Nehru: Role in Freedom Struggle. 1990. 42.00 (*81-7041-261-7*, Pub. by Anmol) S Asia.

— KM Munshi: Role in Freedom Movement. (Indian Freedom Fighters Ser.: No. 34). (C). 1993. 36.00 (*0-685-68077-0*, Pub. by Anmol) S Asia.

— Madan Mohan Malaviya the Man & His Ideology. (C). 1991. 45.00 (*81-7041-429-6*, Pub. by Anmol) S Asia.

— Mahadev Govind Ranade: Socio-Economic Ideology. (Indian Freedom Fighters Ser.: No. 41). 1993. 34.00 (*81-7041-605-1*, Pub. by Anmol) S Asia.

— Mahatma Gandhi: Congress & Its Leadership. (C). 1990. text 26.00 (*81-7041-256-0*, Pub. by Anmol) S Asia.

— The Making of India & Pakistan: Selected Documents, 6 vols. 4100p. 1997. 4000.00 (*81-7100-913-1*, Pub. by Print Hse) St Mut.

— Moorarji Desai: The Man & His Ideas. (Indian Freedom Fighters Ser.: No. 23). (C). 1992. 27.00 (*81-7041-494-6*, Pub. by Anmol) S Asia.

— Motilal Nehru: The Man & His Ideology. 1990. 42.00 (*81-7041-257-9*, Pub. by Anmol) S Asia.

— Pherozeshah Mehta: Socio-Political Ideology. (C). 1991. 37.50 (*81-7041-427-X*, Pub. by Anmol) S Asia.

— Rafi Ahmad Kidwai: The True Nationalist. (Indian Freedom Fighters Ser.: No. 42). 1993. 34.00 (*81-7041-606-X*, Pub. by Anmol) S Asia.

— Rajendra Prasad: A True Gandhian. (C). 1990. 40.00 (*81-7041-255-2*, Pub. by Anmol) S Asia.

— Sardar Patel: His Political Ideology. 1990. 42.00 (*81-7041-263-3*, Pub. by Anmol) S Asia.

— Syama Prasad Mookerjee: Founder of Jana Sangh. (C). 1992. 32.00 (*0-685-59773-3*, Pub. by Anmol) S Asia.

— V. K. Krishna Menon: India & Kashmir Problem. (C). 1994. text 50.00 (*81-7041-705-8*, Pub. by Anmol) S Asia.

***Bakshi, S. R., ed.** Encyclopaedia of Gurus, 6 vols. 1998. pap. 5000.00 (*81-7415-015-3*, Pub. by Print Hse) St Mut.

***Bakshi, S. R. & Bala, Kiran, eds.** Development of Women, Children & Weaker Sections, 5 Vols. 1999. 198.50 (*81-7629-120-X*, Pub. by Deep & Deep Pubns) S Asia.

Bakshi, S. R. & Ram Sharma, Sita. Contemporary Political Leadership in India: Bansi Lal: Chief Minister of Haryana. 1998. 36.00 (*81-7024-985-6*) Ashish Pub Hse.

Bakshi, S. R. & Ram Sharma, Sitaram. Contemporary Political Leadership in India: Parkash Singh Badal: Chief Minister of Punjab. 1998. 36.00 (*81-7024-987-2*) Ashish Pub Hse.

Bakshi, S. R., et al. Contemporary Political Leadership in India: Prafulla Kumar Mahanta: Chief Minister of Assam. 1998. 36.00 (*81-7648-008-8*) Ashish Pub Hse.

Bakshi, S. R., jt. ed. see Sharma, Suresh K.

Bakshi, Trilochan S. & Naveh, Zev, eds. Environmental Education: Principles, Methods & Applications. LC 80-11837. (Environmental Science Research Ser.: Vol. 18). 298p. 1980. 75.00 (*0-306-40433-8*, Plenum Trade) Perseus Pubng.

Bakshian, Aram, Jr., ed. The American Speaker: Your Guide to Successful Speaking. 400p. 1992. ring bd. 297.00 (*0-9634672-0-4*) Georgetwn Pub Hse.

Bakshtein, Joseph, et al. The Aesthetic Arsenal: Socialist Realism under Stalin. LC 93-61431. (Illus.). 300p. 1993. write for info. (*1-884229-00-X*) Inst For Contemp.

Bakshy, Alexander. Soviet Scene: Six Plays of Russian Life. 348p. 1977. 22.95 (*0-8369-8200-2*) Ayer.

— The Theatre Unbound. LC 68-56535. 1972. reprint ed. 23.95 (*0-405-08232-0*, Pub. by Blom Pubns) Ayer.

Bakshy, Alexander, tr. see Gor'kii, Maksim.

Bakshy, Alexander, tr. see Gorky, Maxim.

Bakshy, Alexander, tr. see Solovyov, Vladimir.

Baksi, Arun K., et al, eds. Diabetes Education. LC 83-25976. (Wiley-Medical Publication). 149p. reprint ed. pap. 46.20 (*0-8357-8631-5*, 203505500092) Bks Demand.

Bakst, Aaron. Arithmetic for the Modern Age. LC 60-53374. 349p. reprint ed. pap. 108.20 (*0-8357-5737-4*, 200724300063) Bks Demand.

Bakst, Daren & Fuller, Carol. SPEEDE Implementation Guide. 4th ed. 108p. 1998. write for info. (*1-57858-013-7*, 6006) Am Assn Coll Registrars.

***Bakst, Daren L.** Student Privacy on Campus. LC 99-64562. (Illus.). 100p. 1999. pap. 39.95 (*0-9673344-0-3*, 202.363.3149) Council on Law.

Bakst, Daren L., ed. Hopwood, Bakke, & Beyond: Diversity on Our Nation's Campuses. LC 98-5264. 211p. 1998. pap., per. 45.00 (*1-57858-014-5*, 3012) Am Assn Coll Registrars.

Bakst, Daren L., jt. ed. see Coyle, Betsy.

Bakst, James. A History of Russian-Soviet Music. LC 76-55406. (Illus.). 406p. 1977. reprint ed. lib. bdg. 75.00 (*0-8371-9422-9*, BARS, Greenwood Pr) Greenwood.

Bakst, Leon. The Decorative Art of Leon Bakst. LC 68-57183. (Illus.). 1972. reprint ed. 33.95 (*0-405-08234-7*, Pub. by Blom Pubns) Ayer.

Bakst, Leon, Jr. Designs of Leon Bakst for "The Sleeping Princess" LC 68-56514. (Illus.). 1972. 36.95 (*0-405-08235-5*, Pub. by Blom Pubns) Ayer.

Bakst, M. R. & Cecil, H. C. Techniques for Semen Evaluation, Semen Storage, & Fertility Determination. (Illus.). 98p. (Orig.). 1997. pap. text, lab manual ed. 12.00 (*0-9649811-1-4*) Poultry Sci.

Bakst, M. R. & Wishart, G. J. Proceedings - First International Symposium on the Artificial Insemination of Poultry. (Illus.). 300p. (Orig.). (C). 1995. pap. text 35.00 (*0-9649811-0-6*) Poultry Sci.

***Baktash, Cyrus, ed.** Nuclear Structure 98. (Conference Proceedings Ser.: Vol. 481). (Illus.). 632p. 1999. 165.00 (*1-56396-858-4*, Pub. by Am Inst Physics) Spr-Verlag.

Baktiari, Bahman. Parliamentary Politics in Revolutionary Iran: The Institutionalization of Factional Politics. (Illus.). 312p. 1996. 49.95 (*0-8130-1461-1*) U Press Fla.

Bakule, Paula D., ed. Rodale's Book of Practical Formulas. (Illus.). 456p. 1994. 12.98 (*1-56731-046-X*, MJF Bks) Fine Comms.

***Bakuli, Stephen N.** Literature in English: African Literature in Novels, Oral Literature, Drama, Short Stories. 160p. (C). 2000. pap. 29.95 (*1-891016-34-2*) Esparto Pr.

Bakunin, Jack. Pierre Leroux & the Birth of Democratic Socialism. 1976. lib. bdg. 250.00 (*0-87700-221-5*) Revisionist Pr.

Bakunin, Michael. God & the State. LC 75-105664. 89p. 1970. pap. 5.95 (*0-486-22483-X*) Dover.

— God & the State. LC 78-148871. (Select Bibliographies Reprint Ser.). (Illus.). 1977. reprint ed. 15.95 (*0-8369-5643-5*) Ayer.

— Marxism, Freedom & the State. 64p. (Orig.). 1984. reprint ed. pap. 3.50 (*0-900384-27-1*) Left Bank.

— Statism & Anarchy. Shatz, Marshall S., ed. (Cambridge Texts in the History of Political Thought Ser.). 293p. (C). 1990. text 59.95 (*0-521-36182-6*); pap. text 19.95 (*0-521-36973-8*) Cambridge U Pr.

Bakunin, Mikhail. Statism & Anarchy. Harrison, J. Frank, ed. 1974. lib. bdg. 300.00 (*0-87700-219-3*) Revisionist Pr.

Bakus, Gerald J. Quantitative Ecology & Marine Biology. (Illus.). 165p. (C). 1991. text 60.00 (*90-6191-917-7*, Pub. by A A Balkema) Ashgate Pub Co.

Bakus, Gerald J., et al. Coral Reef Ecosystems. (Illus.). 260p. (C). 1994. text 45.00 (*90-6191-953-3*, Pub. by A A Balkema) Ashgate Pub Co.

Bakus, Gerald J., jt. auth. see Green, Karen D.

Bakushinskii, A. B. & Goncharskii, A. V. Ill-Posed Problems, 301. LC 94-30306. (Mathematics & Its Applications Ser.). 1994. text 166.50 (*0-7923-3073-0*) Kluwer Academic.

***Bakut tswah Bakut & Dutt, Sagarika.** Africa at the Millennium: An Agenda for Mature Development. LC 00-33325. 2000. write for info. (*0-312-23519-4*) St Martin.

Bakuzis, Egolfs V. & Hansen, H. L. Balsam Fir, Abies Balsamea (Linnaeus) Miller: A Monographic Review. LC 65-17539. (Illus.). 467p. reprint ed. pap. 144.80 (*0-8357-5954-7*, 203320400084) Bks Demand.

Bakvis, Herman. Catholic Power in the Netherlands. (Illus.). 254p. 1981. 60.00 (*0-7735-0361-7*, Pub. by McG-Queens Univ Pr) CUP Services.

— Regional Ministers: Power & Influence in the Canadian Cabinet. 416p. 1991. pap. 22.95 (*0-8020-6698-4*); text 60.00 (*0-8020-2622-2*) U of Toronto Pr.

Bakvis, Herman & Chandler, William M., eds. Federalism & the Role of the State. viii, 328p. (Orig.). 1987. pap. 20.95 (*0-8020-6621-6*) U of Toronto Pr.

Baky, Meredith P., jt. auth. see Blass, Laurie.

Bakytova, jt. auth. see Trup.

Bal. Quoting Caravaggio. LC 98-46907. (Illus.). 328p. 1999. 45.00 (*0-226-03556-5*) U Ch Pr.

Bal, Gurprett, jt. auth. see Judge, Paramjit S.

Bal, H. E. Programming Distributed Systems. 290p. (Orig.). 1990. pap. 29.95 (*0-929306-05-8*) Silicon Pr.

***Bal, H. E., et al, eds.** Internet Programming Languages: Proceedings of the ICCL'98 Workshop, Chicago, IL, U. S. A., May 13, 1998. LC 99-52213. (Lecture Notes in Computer Science Ser.: Vol. 1686). ix, 143p. 1999. pap. 45.00 (*3-540-66673-7*) Spr-Verlag.

Bal, Meike & Boer, Inge. The Point of Theory: Practices of Cultural Analysis. (Illus.). 326p. 1994. 34.95 (*0-8264-0657-2*) Continuum.

Bal, Mieke. Death & Dissymmetry: The Politics of Coherence in the Book of Judges. (Chicago Studies in the History of Judaism). (Illus.). 324p. 1988. pap. text 19.95 (*0-226-03555-7*); lib. bdg. 60.00 (*0-226-03554-9*) U Ch Pr.

— Double Exposures: The Subject of Cultural Analysis. (Illus.). 352p. (C). 1996. 80.00 (*0-415-91703-4*); pap. 25.99 (*0-415-91704-2*) Routledge.

— Lethal Love: Feminist Literary Readings of Biblical Love Stories. LC 86-45592. (Illus.). 152p. 1987. pap. 11.95 (*0-253-20434-8*, MB 434) Ind U Pr.

— The Mottled Screen: Reading Proust Visually. LC 96-49839. 272p. 1997. 45.00 (*0-8047-2807-0*); pap. 17.95 (*0-8047-2808-9*) Stanford U Pr.

— Murder & Difference: Gender, Genre & Scholarship on Sisera's Death. LC 86-42995. (Indiana Studies in Biblical Literature). (Illus.). 160p. 1988. 35.00 (*0-253-33905-7*) Ind U Pr.

— Murder & Difference: Gender, Genre & Scholarship on Sisera's Death. LC 86-42995. (Indiana Studies in Biblical Literature). (Illus.). 160p. 1992. pap. 11.95 (*0-253-20741-X*, MB 741) Ind U Pr.

— Narratology: Introduction to the Theory of Narrative. 176p. 1985. pap. text 14.95 (*0-8020-6557-0*) U of Toronto Pr.

— Narratology: Introduction to the Theory of Narrative. 2nd ed. LC 98-117283. 240p. 1998. text 40.00 (*0-8020-0759-7*) U of Toronto Pr.

— On Meaning-Making: Essays in Semiotics. 320p. (C). 1994. pap. 29.95 (*0-944344-39-9*) Polebridge Pr.

— On Story-Telling: Essays in Narratology. LC 90-26587. (Illus.). 288p. (C). 1991. pap. 29.95 (*0-944344-17-8*) Polebridge Pr.

Bal, Mieke, et al, eds. Acts of Memory: Cultural Recall in the Present. LC 98-47540. (Illus.). 268p. 1998. pap. 19.95 (*0-87451-889-X*); text 45.00 (*0-87451-886-5*) U Pr of New Eng.

Bal, Mieke & Gonzales, Bryan. The Practice of Cultural Analysis: Exposing Interdisciplinary Interpretation. LC 98-35018. (Cultural Memory in the Present Ser.). 1999. 65.00 (*0-8047-3066-0*); pap. 24.95 (*0-8047-3067-9*) Stanford U Pr.

Bal, Mieke, et al. Looking In: The Art of Viewing. (Illus.). 240p. 1999. text 60.00 (*90-5701-102-6*); pap. text 24.95 (*90-5701-112-3*) Gordon & Breach.

Bal, Mike. Narratology: Introduction to the Theory of Narrative. 2nd ed. 240p. 1997. pap. text 16.95 (*0-8020-7806-0*) U of Toronto Pr.

Bal, Peggy. Pebbles in the Stream: A History of Beale Air Force Base & Neighboring Areas. rev. ed. LC 93-20345. (Illus.). x, 118p. 1993. pap. 11.95 (*0-915641-05-4*) Nevada County Hist Society.

Bal, Roland & Halffman, Willem. The Politics of Chemical Risk: Scenarios for a Regulatory Future. LC 98-23057. 367p. 1998. 175.00 (*0-7923-4891-5*) Kluwer Academic.

Bal, S. N. Catalogue of Medicinal Plant Exhibits. 121p. (C). 1984. 35.00 (*0-7855-3303-6*, Pub. by Scientific) St Mut.

Bal, Sharanjit S. & Douglas, Johnson E. Designing Successful Farmer-Managed Seed Systems. (Discussion Paper Ser.). 28p. (Orig.). 1991. pap. 6.00 (*0-933595-62-X*) Winrock Intl.

Bal, Sukhwant. The Interactive Manager. 192p. 1995. pap. 29.95 incl. disk (*0-7494-1708-0*, Kogan Pg Educ) Stylus Pub VA.

Bala, jt. auth. see Bruno, G.

Bala, B. K. Drying & Storage of Cereals. (Illus.). 310p. (C). 1997. 49.50 (*1-886106-93-2*) Science Pubs.

— Energy & Environment: Modelling & Simulation. LC 98-35904. 1998. 95.00 (*1-56072-608-3*) Nova Sci Pubs.

***Bala, Iwan, ed.** Certain Welsh Artists: Custodial Aesthetics in Contemporary Welsh Art. (Illus.). 200p. 1999. (*1-85411-251-1*, Pub. by Seren Bks) Dufour.

Bala, Juan L., Jr., jt. auth. see Yamayee, Zia A.

Bala, Juan L., jt. auth. see Yamayee, Zia M.

Bala, Kiran, jt. ed. see Bakshi, S. R.

Bala, Nicholas C. & Clarke, Kenneth L. The Child & the Law. LC 81-179630. (Illus.). 1981. write for info. (*0-07-077868-X*) McG-H Ryerson.

Bala, Poonam. Imperialism & Medicine in Bengal: A Socio-Historical Perspective. (Illus.). 172p. 1992. 28.00 (*0-8039-9100-2*) Sage.

Bala, Raghuram. Using Optima++ Special Edition. LC 96-69959. 656p. 1996. pap. text 49.99 incl. cd-rom (*0-7897-0894-9*) Que.

Bala, Raj. Trends in Urbanisation in India. 1986. 49.50 (*81-7033-012-2*, Pub. by Rawat Pubns) S Asia.

Bala, Suman. Joseph Conrad's Fiction. 1991. text 30.00 (*81-7076-029-1*, Pub. by Intellect Pub Hse) Advent Bks Div.

Balaam, David & Veseth, Michael. Introduction to International Political Economy. LC 95-34435. 504p. 1995. pap. text 55.00 (*0-13-149592-5*) P-H.

***Balaam, David & Veseth, Michael.** Introduction to International Political Economy. 2nd ed. 504p. 2000. pap. 44.00 (*0-13-018349-0*) P-H.

Balaam, David N. & Carey, Michael J., eds. Food Politics: The Regional Conflict. LC 79-48097. 254p. 1981. text 61.50 (*0-916672-52-2*, R3328); pap. text 16.00 (*0-86598-070-5*, R3831) Rowman.

Balaban, A. T., ed. Science & Technology Management. LC 97-77022. 243p. 1998. 97.00 (*90-5199-372-2*) IOS Press.

Balaban, A. T., et al, eds. Steric Fit in Quantitative Structure-Activity Relations. (Lecture Notes in Chemistry Ser.: Vol. 15). (Illus.). 178p. 1980. 27.95 (*0-387-09755-4*) Spr-Verlag.

Balaban, Alexandru T. Annulenes, Benzo-Hetero-, Homoderivatives & Their Valence Isomers, 3 Vols. 272p. 1987. 149.00 (*0-8493-6880-4*, CRC Reprint); 131.00 (*0-8493-6882-0*, CRC Reprint) Franklin.

— Annulenes, Benzo-Hetero-, Homoderivatives & Their Valence Isomers, 3 Vols., Set. 1987. 156.00 (*0-8493-6879-0*, QD341) CRC Pr.

— Annulenes, Benzo-Hetero-, Homoderivatives & Their Valence Isomers, 3 Vols., Vol. 2. 248p. 1987. Apple II 139.00 (*0-8493-6881-2*, CRC Reprint) Franklin.

Balaban, Alexandru T., ed. From Chemical Topology to Three-Dimensional Geometry. LC 96-51630. (Topics in Applied Chemistry Ser.). 438p. (C). 1997. text 125.00 (*0-306-45462-9*, Kluwer Plenum) Kluwer Academic.

Balaban, Alexandru T., et al. Labelled Compounds & Radiopharmaceuticals Applied in Nuclear Medicine. LC 84-5262. 744p. reprint ed. pap. 200.00 (*0-7837-6365-4*, 204607700010) Bks Demand.

Balaban, Alexandru T., jt. ed. see Devillers, James.

Balaban, Avraham. Between God & Beast: An Examination of Amos Oz's Prose. 272p. (C). 1993. 40.00 (*0-271-00851-2*) Pa St U Pr.

***Balaban, Bob.** Programming Domino 4.6 Java: Groupware for the Internet. LC 98-10610. 480p. 1998. 49.99 (*1-55851-583-6*, MIS Pr) IDG Bks.

Balaban, Carey, et al. The Skilful Physician. 266p. 1997. text 69.00 (*90-5702-531-0*, Harwood Acad Pubs); pap. text 29.95 (*90-5702-532-9*, Harwood Acad Pubs) Gordon & Breach.

Balaban, E., jt. ed. see Short, R. V.

Balaban, Gheorghe, jt. auth. see Comanescu, Sorin.

Balaban, Jocelyn, jt. auth. see Otto, Ramona.

Balaban, John. Blue Mountain. LC 81-7505. 88p. 1982. 24.95 (*0-87775-143-9*); pap. 9.95 (*0-87775-144-7*) Unicorn Pr.

— The Hawk's Tale. LC 87-14938. (Illus.). 148p. (J). (gr. 3-7). 1988. 14.95 (*0-15-200462-9*, Gulliver Bks) Harcourt.

— Locusts at the Edge of Summer: New & Selected Poems. 150p. 1997. pap. 15.00 (*1-55659-123-3*) Copper Canyon.

— Words for My Daughter. LC 90-85090. (National Poetry Ser.). 80p. (Orig.). 1991. pap. 10.00 (*1-55659-037-7*) Copper Canyon.

Balaban, John, ed. Ca Dao Vietnam: A Bilingual Anthology of Vietnamese Folk Poetry. (VIE & ENG.). 1992. 15.95 (*0-88962-118-7*); pap. 8.95 (*0-88962-117-9*) Mosaic.

— Ca Dao Vietnam: Bilingual Anthology of Vietnamese Folk Poetry. (ENG & VIE., Illus.). 1980. 19.95 (*0-87775-128-5*); pap. 13.95 (*0-87775-129-3*) Unicorn Pr.

Balaban, John & Duc, Nguyen Q., eds. Vietnam: A Traveler's Literary Companion. LC 95-46930. (Travelers' Literary Companions Ser.: Vol. 3). (Illus.). 256p. 1996. pap. 12.95 (*1-883513-02-2*) Whereabouts.

Balaban, John, tr. see Huong, Ho Xuan.

Balaban, Majer. Historia i Literatura Zydowska, 3 vols., Set. (Illus.). 1978. reprint ed. 120.00 (*0-318-23357-6*) Szwede Slavic.

Balaban, Mira, et al, eds. Understanding Music with AI: Perspectives on Music Cognition. (AAAI Press Ser.). (Illus.). 490p. 1992. pap. text 45.00 (*0-262-52170-9*) MIT Pr.

Balaban, Miriam, ed. Desalination Directory. 5th ed. 350p. 1992. lib. bdg. 210.00 (*0-86689-031-9*) Balaban Intl Sci Serv.

— Scientific Information Transfer: The Editor's Role. 1978. lib. bdg. 247.50 (*90-277-0917-3*) Kluwer Academic.

Balaban, Murat O. Food Engineering Principles & Applications. (Food Engineering & Manufacturing Ser.). 2000. 59.95 (*0-8493-4286-4*) CRC Pr.

Balaban, Nancy. Starting School: From Separation to Independence - a Guide for Early Childhood Teachers. (Early Childhood Education Ser.). 160p. (C). 1985. pap. text 15.95 (*0-8077-2793-8*) Tchrs Coll.

***Balaban, Oded.** Plato & Protagoras: Truth & Relativism in Ancient Greek Philosophy. LC 99-37747. 368p. 1999. 75.00 (*0-7391-0075-0*) Lxngtn Bks.

Balaban, Oded. Politics & Ideology: A Philosophical Approach. 304p. 1995. 69.95 (*1-85972-020-X*, Pub. by Avebry) Ashgate Pub Co.

— Subject & Consciousness: A Philosophical Inquiry into Self-Consciousness. LC 89-39313. 234p. (C). 1990. lib. bdg. 58.00 (*0-8476-7616-1*) Rowman.

Balaban, Oded & Erev, Anan. The Bounds of Freedom: About the Eastern & Western Approaches to Freedom. (American University Studies: Vol. 165). X, 186p. (C). 1995. pap. text 41.95 (*0-8204-2514-1*) P Lang Pubng.

Balaban, Robert S., jt. ed. see Schaefer, Saul.

Balaban, T. On the Mixed Problem for a Hyperbolic Equation. LC 52-42839. (Memoirs Ser.: No. 1/112). 117p. 1971. pap. 16.00 (*0-8218-1812-0*, MEMO/1/112) Am Math.

Balabane, M., et al, eds. Integrable Systems & Applications. (Lecture Notes in Physics Ser.: Vol. 342). viii, 342p. 1989. 48.00 (*0-387-51615-8*) Spr-Verlag.

Balabanian, Norman. Electric Circuits. LC 93-26186. (McGraw-Hill Series in Electrical & Computer Engineering). 864p. (C). 1993. 100.31 (*0-07-004804-5*) McGraw.

— Electric Circuits. LC 93-26186. (McGraw-Hill Series in Electrical & Computer Engineering). (C). 1995. pap., student ed. 22.81 (*0-07-004806-1*) McGraw.

Balabanian, Norman, jt. auth. see Bickart, Theodore A.

Balabanov, Ivan, jt. auth. see Duet, Karen F.

Balabanski, Vicky. Eschatology in the Making: Mark, Matthew & the Didache. (Society for New Testament Studies Monograph Ser.: Vol. 97). 260p. (C). 1997. text 59.95 (*0-521-59137-6*) Cambridge U Pr.

Balabkins, Nicholas. Indigenization & Economic Development: The Nigerian Experience. Altman, Edward I. & Walter, ingo I., eds. LC 81-81654. (Contemporary Studies in Economic & Financial Analysis: Vol. 33). 325p. 1982. 78.50 (*0-89232-227-6*) Jai Pr.

Balabukha, V. & Greaves, J. Chemical Protection: The Body Against Ionizing Radiation. LC 63-10104. (International Series of Monographs on Pure & Applied Mathematics: Vol. 17). 1963. 80.00 (*0-08-009996-3*, Pub. by Pergamon Repr) Franklin.

Balachandran, A. P., et al. Classical Topology & Quantum States. 376p. (C). 1991. text 66.00 (*981-02-0329-2*); pap. text 36.00 (*981-02-0330-6*) World Scientific Pub.

— The Hubbard Model & Anyon Superconductivity. 148p. (C). 1990. text 43.00 (*981-02-0348-9*); pap. text 21.00 (*981-02-0349-7*) World Scientific Pub.

Balachandran, B., et al, eds. Advances in Cryogenic Engineering (Materials), Vol. 44. (Illus.). 1128p. (C). 1998. text 225.00 (*0-306-45918-3*, Kluwer Plenum) Kluwer Academic.

***Balachandran, Bala V. & Thiagarajan, S. Ramu.** Reengineering Revisited. 107p. 1999. pap. 39.75 (*1-885065-16-7*) E Elgar.

Balachandran, Balakumar, jt. auth. see Nayfeh, Ali H.

Balachandran, G. John Bullion's Empire: Britain's Gold Problem & India Between the Wars. (SOAS London Studies on South Asia: No. 10). 220p. (C). 1996. text 40.00 (*0-7007-0428-0*, Pub. by Curzon Pr Ltd) UH Pr.

— The Reserve Bank of India: 1951-1967. (Illus.). 1,208p. 1998. text 70.00 (*0-19-564468-9*) OUP.

Balachandran, I., jt. auth. see Sivarajan, V. V.

Balachandran, Indira, jt. auth. see Sivarajan, V. V.

Balachandran, M. Knowledge-Based Optimum Design. 176p. 1992. 95.00 (*1-85312-113-4*) Computational Mech MA.

Balachandran, M. Knowledge-Based Optimum Design. LC 90-84918. (Topics in Engineering Ser.: Vol. 10). 182p. 1992. 95.00 (*0-945824-96-3*, 1134) Computational Mech MA.

Balachandran, M., ed. A Guide to Trade & Securities Statistics. LC 77-73818. 1977. 29.50 (*0-87650-077-7*) Pierian.

Balachandran, M. & Balachandran, S. Subject Guide to Reference Books, 1970-1975. LC 79-83698. 1980. 60.00 (*0-87650-102-1*) Pierian.

Balachandran, M. & Balachandran, S., eds. Reference Book Review Index, 1973-1975. LC 79-83697. 1980. 60.00 (*0-87650-073-4*) Pierian.

Balachandran, M., jt. auth. see Balachandran, S.

Balachandran, M., jt. ed. see Balachandran, S.

***Balachandran, S.** Customer-Driven Services Management. LC 99-37980. 1999. write for info. (*0-7619-9372-X*) Sage.

Balachandran, S. & Balachandran, M. Reference Sources, 1981. LC 77-79318. 1992. 75.00 (*0-87650-134-X*) Pierian.

Balachandran, S. & Balachandran, M., eds. Reference Sources, 1980. LC 77-79318. 1981. 75.00 (*0-87650-127-7*) Pierian.

Balachandran, S., jt. auth. see Balachandran, M.

Balachandran, S., jt. ed. see Balachandran, M.

Balachandran, Sarojini. Airport Planning: 1965-1975. No. 1140. 1976. 5.00 (*0-686-20412-3*, Sage Prdcls Pr) Sage.

— State & Local Statistics Sources. 2nd ed. 1993. 150.00 (*0-8103-5468-3*) Gale.

— Technical Writing: A Bibliography. 1977. pap. 3.90 (*0-931874-07-6*) Assn Busn Comm.

Balachandran, Sarojini, ed. Energy Statistics: A Guide to Information Sources. LC 80-13338. (Natural World Information Guide Ser.: Vol. 1). 288p. 1980. 68.00 (*0-8103-1016-3*) Gale.

Balachandran, U., et al, eds. High Temperature Superconductors: Synthesis, Processing, & Large-Scale Applications. (Illus.). 356p. 1996. 20.00 (*0-87339-326-0*) Minerals Metals.

Balachandran, U. & McGinn, P. J., eds. High-Temperature Superconductors: Synthesis, Processing, & Applications II. LC 97-212911. (Illus.). 227p. 1997. 102.00 (*0-87339-401-1*, 4011) Minerals Metals.

Balacheff, Nicolas, ed. & tr. see Brousseau, Guy.

Balachi, Shiva, ed. Reconstructing Gender in the Middle East: Tradition, Identity, & Power. LC 94-3733. 272p. 1995. 52.50 (*0-231-10122-8*); pap. 19.50 (*0-231-10123-6*) Col U Pr.

Baladi, G. Y., jt. auth. see Chen, Wai-Fah.

Baladi, Gilbert, jt. ed. see Bush, Albert J., III.

Baladi, Viviane. Positive Transfer Operators & Decay of Correlations. (Advanced Series in Nonlinear Dynamics). 230p. 1998. 48.00 (*981-02-3328-0*) World Scientific Pub.

Balado, Carl R. & Oteiza, Esther I., eds. Cultural & Linguistic Diversity in American Schools. 324p. (Orig.). (C). 1995. pap. text 37.50 (*0-9644512-2-0*) IntraCoast Pub.

Balado, J. L. The Story of Taize. (Illus.). 144p. (Orig.). 1982. 4.95 (*0-8164-2321-0*) Harper SF.

Baladouni, Vahe & Makepeace, Margaret. Armenian Merchants of the Seventeenth & Early Eighteenth Centuries: English East India Company Sources. LC 98-43975. (Transactions of the American Philosophical Society Ser.: Vol. 88, Pt. 5). 1999. pap. 22.00 (*0-87169-885-4*) Am Philos.

Balady, Gary J. & Pina, Ileana L., eds. Exercise & Heart Failure. LC 97-6841. (American Heart Association Monograph Ser.). (Illus.). 368p. 1997. 75.00 (*0-87993-667-3*) Futura Pub.

Balafoutis, Constantinos A. & Patel, Rajnikant V. Dynamic Analysis of Robot Manipulators: A Cartesian Tensor Approach. (C). 1991. text 114.50 (*0-7923-9145-4*) Kluwer Academic.

Balagangadhara, S. N. The Heathen in His Blindness: Asia, the Western Culture & the Dynamic of Religion. (Studies in the History of Religions: No. 64). 563p. 1993. 163.00 (*90-04-09943-3*, NLG230) Brill Academic Pubs.

Balageas, D., et al, eds. Quantitative Infrared Thermography QIRT 94. (Proceedings of the Eurotherm Seminar Ser.: No. 42). 370p. 169.00 (*2-85933-042-9*) Elsevier.

Balagopal, Padmini & American Dietetic Association Staff. Indian & Pakistani Food Practices, Customs, & Holidays. LC 96-21638. 1996. write for info. (*0-88091-151-4*) Am Dietetic Assn.

***Balagopal, Padmini & American Dietetic Association Staff.** Indian & Pakistani Food Practices, Customs & Holidays. 2nd ed. LC 00-38036. (Ethnic & Regional Food Practices - A Ser.). (Illus.). 2000. write for info. (*0-88091-186-7*) Am Dietetic Assn.

Balagopal, Tara. Learn to Play on Veena. (Illus.). 84p. 1982. 12.95 (*0-318-36329-1*) Asia Bk Corp.

***Balagopal, Tara.** Pancha Ratna Kritis of Saint Thyagaraja. LC 98-900856. 1998. 438.00 (*81-85151-60-1*, Pub. by Harman Pub Hse) S Asia.

Balagopalan, C., et al. Cassava in Food, Feed & Industry. LC 88-2626. 224p. 1988. 125.00 (*0-8493-4560-X*, TP416, CRC Reprint) Franklin.

Balagopalan, Mohan. Air Quality Permitting. Date not set. 55.00 (*1-56670-152-X*) Lewis Pubs.

***Balague, Lin & Long, Robert.** Ali Baba y los 40 Ladrones (Ali Baba & the 40 Thieves) LC 00-39455. (Cuentos y Leyendas Bilinghues Ser.). (SPA & ENG., Illus.). (J). 2000. write for info. (*0-658-01024-7*) NTC Contemp Pub Co.

— La Dama y el Leon (The Princess & the Lion) LC 00-39454. (Cuentos y Leyendas Bilinghues Ser.). (ENG & SPA., Illus.). (J). 2000. pap. write for info. (*0-658-01015-8*) NTC Contemp Pub Co.

— Hansel y Gretel (Hansel & Gretel) LC 00-39456. (Cuentos y Leyendas Bilinghues Ser.). (SPA & ENG., Illus.). (J). 2000. write for info. (*0-658-01038-7*) NTC Contemp Pub Co.

Balaguer, Mark. Platonism & Anti-Platonism in Mathematics. 240p. 1998. text 45.00 (*0-19-512230-5*) OUP.

Balaguer, Miguel. Diccionario Griego-Espanol. 2nd ed. (GRE & SPA.). 940p. 1977. 29.95 (*0-8288-5342-8*, S50344) Fr & Eur.

Balagurusamy, E. Artificial Intelligence Technology Applications & Management. 1994. 16.25 (*0-07-462036-3*) McGraw-Hill Prof.

Balahoutis, Linda, jt. auth. see Fleming, Don.

Balaji, K. P. Abhimanyu. 1978. pap. 2.00 (*0-8364-0227-8*) S Asia.

Balakian, Anna. Andre Breton: Magus of Surrealism. LC 78-83006. 1971. 20.00 (*0-19-501298-4*) Hawkshead Bk.

Balakian, Anna. The Symbolist Movement in the Literature of European Languages. (Comparative History of Literatures in European Language Ser.: Vol. 2). 732p. 1984. pap. 75.00 (*963-05-3895-4*, Pub. by Akade Kiado) St Mut.

Balakian, Anna, et al. Selected Essays from the International Conference on Surrealism & the Oneiric Process. 202p. 1993. per. 13.00 (*1-883199-00-X*) St U W Georgia.

Balakian, Anna A. The Snowflake on the Belfry: Dogma & Disquietude in the Critical Arena. LC 93-7762. 1994. 19.95 (*0-253-31132-2*) Ind U Pr.

— Surrealism: The Road to the Absolute. LC 76-87200. (Illus.). 33p. (C). 1987. pap. text 17.00 (*0-226-03560-3*) U Ch Pr.

Balakian, Nona. The World of William Saroyan: A Literary Interpretation. LC 97-4379. (Illus.). 296p. 1998. 45.00 (*0-8387-5368-X*) Bucknell U Pr.

Balakian, Nona & Simmons, Charles. The Creative Present: Notes on Contemporary American Fiction. rev. ed. LC 77-189247. 302p. (C). 1973. reprint ed. 40.00 (*0-87752-158-1*) Gordian.

Balakian, Peter. Black Dog of Fate: A Memoir. LC 98-10530. 304p. 1998. reprint ed. pap. 14.00 (*0-7679-0254-8*) Broadway BDD.

— Dyer's Thistle. LC 95-69473. (Poetry Ser.). 78p. (C). 1996. 20.95 (*0-88748-232-5*); pap. 11.95 (*0-88748-233-3*) Carnegie-Mellon.

— Reply from Wilderness Island. 89p. 1988. pap. 12.95 (*0-935296-73-5*, Pub. by Sheep Meadow) U Pr of New Eng.

— Sad Days of Light. LC 92-74529. (Classic Contemporaries Ser.). 1993. pap. 12.95 (*0-88748-160-4*) Carnegie-Mellon.

Balakian, Peter & Yaghlian, Nevart, trs. from ARM. Bloody News from My Friend: Poems by Siamanto. LC 96-3047. 72p. (Orig.). 1996. pap. 14.95 (*0-8143-2640-4*) Wayne St U Pr.

Balakier, Ann S. & Balakier, James J. The Spatial Infinite at Greenwich in Works by Christopher Wren, James Thornhill, & James Thomson: The Newton Connection. LC 94-38758. (Illus.). 172p. 1995. text 79.95 (*0-7734-9057-4*) E Mellen.

Balakier, James J., jt. auth. see Balakier, Ann S.

Balakina, Natalia M. & Bowlt, John E. Art from Russia's Turning Point: Isaak Brodsky & His Collection. (Illus.). 48p. 1998. pap. 15.00 (*0-9668494-0-X*) Yellowstone Art.

***Balakirev, Mily.** Islamey & Other Favorite Russian Piano Works. 2000. pap. 12.95 (*0-486-41160-5*) Dover.

Balakirev, Mily. Piano Complete Works (Music Scores Ser.). 1998. pap. text 7.98 (*963-8303-76-X*) Kone Music.

— Piano Complete Works IV, 1. 1998. pap. text 7.95 (*963-9059-62-5*) Konemann.

***Balakirev, Mily.** Piano Complete Works III. (Music Scores Ser.). 1998. pap. 7.98 (*963-9059-61-7*) Kone Music.

Balakrishman, N., jt. auth. see Aggarwala, R.

Balakrishman, N. P. Flora of Jawai, Vols. 1 & 2. (C). 1988. 40.00 (*0-7855-7060-8*, Pub. by Scientific); 40.00 (*0-7855-7061-6*, Pub. by Scientific) St Mut.

Balakrishna, jt. ed. see Subramanian, A. P.

Balakrishnan, A. R. Heat & Mass Transfer. 1994. 28.50 (*0-07-462041-X*) McGraw-Hill Prof.

Balakrishnan, A. V. Elements of State Space Theory of Systems. LC 83-8343. (University Series in Modern Engineering). 194p. (C). 1983. pap. text 28.50 (*0-911575-27-8*) Optimization Soft.

— Elements of State Space Theory of Systems. (University Series in Modern Engineering). ix, 187p. 1983. 69.95 (*0-387-90904-4*) Spr-Verlag.

— Introduction to Random Processes in Engineering. LC 95-2742. 416p. 1995. 120.00 (*0-471-12487-7*) Wiley.

— Kalman Filtering Theory. (University Series in Modern Engineering). xii, 222p. 1984. 69.95 (*0-387-90903-6*) Spr-Verlag.

— Kalman Filtering Theory. 2nd enl. rev. ed. LC 87-31312. (Series in Communication & Control Systems). 267p. (C). 1987. text 72.00 (*0-911575-49-9*) Optimization Soft.

— State Space Theory of Systems. 2nd enl. rev. ed. LC 88-25591. (Series in Communication & Control Systems). 224p. 1988. text 65.00 (*0-911575-54-5*) Optimization Soft.

Balakrishnan, A. V., et al, eds. Detection of Changes in Random Processes. LC 86-17970. (Translations Series in Mathematics & Engineering).Tr. of Statisticheskie problemy upravleniia, otobrazhenie izmenenii svoistv sluchainykh protsessov. 240p. 1986. text 86.00 (*0-911575-20-0*) Optimization Soft.

— Vistas in Applied Mathematics: Numerical Analysis, Atmospheric Sciences, Immunology. LC 86-8340. (Translations Series in Mathematics & Engineering). 396p. 1986. text 98.00 (*0-911575-38-3*) Optimization Soft.

Balakrishnan, A. V., intro. Computational Techniques in Identification & Control of Flexible Flight Structures: Proceedings of the NASA-UCLA Workshop, Lake Arrowhead, CA, Nov. 2-4, 1989. LC 90-44391. 304p. (Orig.). 1990. pap. text 99.00 (*0-911575-59-6*) Optimization Soft.

Balakrishnan, A. V. & Borovkov, A. A., eds. Advances in Probability Theory: Limit Theorems & Related Problems. LC 84-2366. (Translations Series in Mathematics & Engineering). 392p. 1984. text 98.00 (*0-911575-03-0*) Optimization Soft.

— Advances in Probability Theory: Limit Theorems for Sums of Random Variables. LC 85-27931. (Translations Series in Mathematics & Engineering). 313p. 1985. text 80.00 (*0-911575-17-0*) Optimization Soft.

Balakrishnan, A. V. & Butts, Russell, eds. The Proceedings of the NASA-UCLA Workshop on Laser Propagation in Atmospheric Turbulence. (COMCON Conferences Proceedings Ser.). (Illus.). 200p. 1996. pap. text 68.00 (*0-911575-68-5*) Optimization Soft.

Balakrishnan, A. V. & Zolesio, J. P., eds. Stabilization of Flexible Structures: Proceedings of the Comcon Workshop, Montpellier, France, December 1987. LC 88-34517. (Comcon Conferences Proceedings Ser.). 320p. (Orig.). 1988. pap. text 90.00 (*0-911575-37-5*) Optimization Soft.

Balakrishnan, A. V., ed. see Benveniste, A., et al.

Balakrishnan, A. V., ed. see Boguslavskij, I. A.

Balakrishnan, A. V., ed. see Chistyakov, V. P., et al.

Balakrishnan, A. V., ed. see Dembo, Amir & Zeitouni, Ofer.

Balakrishnan, A. V., ed. see Dem'yanov, V. F. & Rubinov, A. M.

Balakrishnan, A. V., ed. see Dem'yanov, V. F. & Vasil'ev, L. V.

Balakrishnan, A. V., ed. see Dubovitskij, V. A.

Balakrishnan, A. V., ed. see Fleming, Wendall H. & Soner, H. Mete.

Balakrishnan, A. V., ed. see Gabasov, R. F. & Kirillova, F. M.

Balakrishnan, A. V., ed. see Ivanishchev, V. V. & Krasnoshchekov, A. D.

Balakrishnan, A. V., jt. ed. see Joshi, Mohan C.

Balakrishnan, A. V., ed. see Kloeden, Peter E. & Platen, Eckhard.

Balakrishnan, A. V., ed. see Kolchin, V. F.

Balakrishnan, A. V., ed. see Lions, J. L.

Balakrishnan, A. V., ed. see Maitra, A. P. & Sudderth, William D.

Balakrishnan, A. V., ed. see Marchuk, Gurii I.

Balakrishnan, A. V., ed. see Polyak, B. T.

Balakrishnan, A. V., ed. see Prabhu, N. U.

Balakrishnan, A. V., ed. see Serfozo, Richard.

Balakrishnan, A. V., ed. see Yadrenko, Mikhail I.

***Balakrishnan, Gopal.** The Enemy: An Intellectual Portrait of Carl Schmitt. 320p. (C). 2000. 35.00 (*1-85984-760-9*, Pub. by Verso) Norton.

Balakrishnan, Gopal, ed. Mapping the Nation. (Mappings Ser.). 288p. (C). 1996. pap. 22.00 (*1-85984-060-4*, B4636, Pub. by Verso) Norton.

Balakrishnan, Mundanthra, ed. Environmental Problems & Prospects in India. (C). 1993. 44.00 (*81-204-0771-7*, Pub. by Oxford IBH) S Asia.

— Tropical Ecosystems: A Synthesis of Tropical Ecology & Conservation. (C). 1994. text 58.00 (*81-204-0873-X*, Pub. by Oxford IBH) S Asia.

Balakrishnan, Mundanthra, et al, eds. Tropical Ecosystems: A Synthesis of Tropical Ecology & Conservation. (Illus.). 452p. (C). 1994. text 69.00 (*1-881570-24-X*) Science Pubs.

Balakrishnan, N. Advances in Combinatorial Methods & Applications to Probability & Statistics. LC 97-6185. (Statistics for Industry & Technology Ser.). 1997. write for info. (*3-7643-3908-X*) Birkhauser.

***Balakrishnan, N.** Handbook of Applied Industrial Statistics. 656p. 1999. 79.95 (*0-8493-8973-9*) CRC Pr.

Balakrishnan, N. Order Statistics & Inference Estimation Methods. LC 96-2811. (Statistical Modeling & Decision Science Ser.). 377p. 1990. text 116.00 (*0-12-076948-4*) Acad Pr.

***Balakrishnan, N.** Statistical Distribution Theory Inference. 2000. 89.95 (*1-58488-124-0*, Chap & Hall CRC) CRC Pr.
Balakrishnan, N., ed. Handbook of the Logistic Distribution. (Statistics: Textbooks & Monographs: Vol. 123). (Illus.). 616p. 1991. text 180.00 (*0-8247-8587-8*) Dekker.
Balakrishnan, N., ed. Recent Advances in Life-Test & Reliability Statistics. 672p. 1995. boxed set 134.95 (*0-8493-8972-0*) CRC Pr.
***Balakrishnan, N., et al, eds.** Advances in Stochastic Simulation Methods. (Statistics for Industry & Technology Ser.). (Illus.). 416p. 2000. 79.95 (*0-8176-4107-6*) Birkhauser.
Balakrishnan, N. & Basu, Asit P., eds. The Exponential Distribution: Theory, Methods & Applications. 664p. 1996. text 72.00 (*2-88449-192-9*) Gordon & Breach.
Balakrishnan, N. & Chen, William S. CRC Handbook of Tables for Order Statistics from Inverse Gaussian Distributions with Applications. LC 97-22215. 704p. 1997. boxed set 104.95 (*0-8493-3118-8*) CRC Pr.
Balakrishnan, N. & Chen, William W. Handbook of Tables for Order Statistics from Lognormal Distributions With Applications LC 99-18121. 1999. write for info. (*0-7923-5634-9*) Kluwer Academic.
Balakrishnan, N. & Rao, C. R. Order Statistics: Applications. LC 98-226116. (Handbook of Statistics Ser.: No. 17). 800p. 1998. write for info. (*0-444-82922-9*) Elsevier.
— Order Statistics: Theory & Methods. LC 98-220801. (Handbook of Statistics Ser.: No. 16). 1998. write for info. (*0-444-82091-4*) Elsevier.
Balakrishnan, N., et al. Computer Systems & Education. 1994. pap. 13.95 (*0-07-462044-4*) McGraw-Hill Prof.
Balakrishnan, N., jt. auth. see Arnold, Barry C.
Balakrishnan, N., jt. auth. see Harter, H. Leon.
Balakrishnan, N., jt. auth. see Johnson, Norman L.
Balakrishnan, N., jt. auth. see Panchapakesan, S.
Balakrishnan, N., ed. see Denker, M., et al.
Balakrishnan, N., jt. ed. see Glaz, J.
Balakrishnan, N. P., jt. auth. see Ansari, R.
Balakrishnan, Pulapre. Pricing & Inflation in India. (Illus.). 290p. 1992. text 29.95 (*0-19-562833-0*) OUP.
***Balakrishnan, R. & Ranganathan, K. S.** A Textbook of Graph Theory. LC 99-15016. (Universitext Ser.). (Illus.). 264p. 1999. 59.95 (*0-387-98859-9*) Spr-Verlag.
Balakrishnan, T. R., et al. Fertility & Family Planning in a Canadian Metropolis. LC 75-332127. 233p. reprint ed. pap. 72.30 (*0-608-12529-6*, 202385600034) Bks Demand.
Balakrishnan, V. & Bottani, C. E., eds. Mechanical Properties & Behavior of Solids: Plastic Instabilities. 380p. 1986. text 89.00 (*9971-5-0040-X*) World Scientific Pub.
Balakrishnan, V. K. Introductory Discrete Mathematics. (Illus.). 248p. 1996. reprint ed. pap. text 9.95 (*0-486-69115-2*) Dover.
— Schaum's Outline of Combinatorics. (Schaum's Outline Ser.). 288p. (C). 1995. pap. 15.95 (*0-07-003575-X*) McGraw.
— Schaum's Outline of Graph Theory. 288p. (C). 1997. pap. 14.95 (*0-07-005489-4*) McGraw.
Balamore, Usha, tr. see Muhaiyaddeen, M. R.
Balan, Bruce. Blackout in the Amazon. (Cyber.Kdz Ser.). (J). 1997. 9.09 (*0-606-13296-1*, Pub. by Turtleback) Demco.
***Balan, Bruce.** Buoy, Home at Sea. LC 97-28233. (Illus.). 80p. (gr. 2-3). 1998. 14.95 (*0-385-32539-8*) Delacorte.
— Great NASA Flu. (Cyber.Kdz Ser.). 1997. 9.09 (*0-606-11232-4*, Pub. by Turtleback) Demco.
Balan, Bruce. Great NASA Flu. 3rd ed. (Cyber Kdz Ser.: No. 3). 144p. (J). 1997. pap. 3.99 (*0-380-78516-1*, Avon Bks) Morrow Avon.
— In Pursuit of Picasso. (Cyber Kdz Ser.). 176p. 1998. pap. 3.99 (*0-380-79499-3*) Morrow Avon.
— In Pursuit of Picasso, 5. (Cyber.Kdz Ser.). (J). 1998. 9.09 (*0-606-13297-X*, Pub. by Turtleback) Demco.
— In Search of Scum, Vol. 1. 160p. (J). (gr. 3-7). 1997. pap. 3.99 (*0-380-78514-5*, Avon Bks) Morrow Avon.
— Picture's Worth. (Cyber.Kdz Ser.). 1997. 9.09 (*0-606-11231-6*, Pub. by Turtleback) Demco.
— Pie in the Sky. 1999. pap. 4.99 (*0-14-055533-1*) NAL.
— When the Chips Are Down, 6. (Cyber.Kdz Ser.). (J). 1998. 9.09 (*0-606-13298-8*, Pub. by Turtleback) Demco.
Balan, Ioanichie, jt. auth. see Archimandrite I. Balan.
Balan, J., jt. ed. see Zelinka, J.
Balan, Jorge, et al. Men in a Developing Society: Geographic & Social Mobility in Monterrey, Mexico. LC 72-6282. (Latin American Monographs: No. 30). 406p. reprint ed. pap. 125.90 (*0-8357-7747-2*, 203610400002) Bks Demand.
Balan, K. Education & Employment. (C). 1992. 12.00 (*81-7024-476-5*, Pub. by Ashish Pub Hse) S Asia.
— Socio-Economic Change in India. (C). 1992. text 11.00 (*81-7024-474-9*, Pub. by Ashish Pub Hse) S Asia.
Balan, K. R. Dictionary of Management. (C). 1995. pap. write for info. (*81-207-1657-4*) Sterling Pubs.
***Balan, S.** Productivity in the Age of Competitiveness. 1998. pap. 125.00 (*81-86982-78-7*, Pub. by Business Pubns) St Mut.
Balanced Products, Inc. Staff & Haskell, Nikki. Nikki Haskell's Star Diet: Look & Feel Like a Star. 256p. 1998. 20.00 (*1-57566-283-3*, Knsington) Kensgtn Pub Corp.
Balanchine, George. Choreography by George Balanchine: A Catalogue of Works. 1983. 125.00 (*0-87130-050-8*) Eakins.
Balanchine, George & Mason, Francis. One Hundred One Stories of the Great Ballets. LC 73-9140. 560p. 1975. pap. 14.00 (*0-385-03398-2*) Doubleday.
Baland, Jean-Marie & Platteau, Jean-Phillipe. Halting Degradation of Natural Resources. (Illus.). 440p. 1996. text 85.00 (*0-19-828921-9*) OUP.
***Baland, Jean-Marie & Platteau, Jean-Phillipe.** Halting Degradation of Natural Resources. (Illus.). 440p. 2000. pap. text 35.00 (*0-19-829061-6*) OUP.
Balandier, Georges. Ambiguous Africa. 225p. 1976. pap. 2.25 (*0-380-00560-3*, Avon Bks) Morrow Avon.
Balandin, I. G., et al. Virology Reviews: Interferon & Its Inducers, Vol. 3. Lvov, Dmitri K., ed. (Soviet Medical Reviews Ser.: Vol. 3, Pt. 2). vi, 168p. 1989. pap. text 150.00 (*3-7186-4921-7*) Gordon & Breach.
Balandina, N., jt. ed. see Bokstein, B.
Balandrin, Manuel F., jt. ed. see Kinghorn, A. Douglas.
Balanis, Constantine A. Antenna Theory: Analysis & Design. 2nd ed. LC 96-12134. 960p. 1996. text 111.95 (*0-471-59268-4*) Wiley.
— Engineering Electromagnetics. 1008p. 1989. text 102.95 (*0-471-62194-3*) Wiley.
Balanis, George N. English-Greek Picture Book. Balanis, Toula, ed. (Illus.). 96p. 1996. lab manual ed. 33.00 (*0-9650747-0-6*) Anotek.
— Greek-English Picture Book. Balanis, Toula, ed. (ENG & GRE., Illus.). 96p. 1996. lab manual ed. 33.00 (*0-9650747-1-4*) Anotek.
Balanis, Toula, ed. see Balanis, George N.
Balano, James W., ed. The Log of the Skipper's Wife. LC 79-52446. (Illus.). 160p. 1979. pap. 10.95 (*0-89272-062-X*) Down East.
Balanoff, Howard R. Public Administration, 1999-2000. 6th ed. (Annual Ser.). (Illus.). 240p. 1998. pap. text 12.25 (*0-07-039227-7*, Dshkn McG-Hill) McGrw-H Hghr Educ.
Balanoff, Howard. Annual Editions: Public Administration, 96-97. 4th ed. 256p. (C). 1995. per. write for info. (*1-56134-436-2*) Brown & Benchmark.
Balanov, Zalman, jt. auth. see Kushkuley, Alexander.
Balanshi, P. & Druk, V. Moldavian Art, 14th-19th Centuries. (Illus.). (C). 1985. text 195.00 (*0-7855-5813-6*, Pub. by Collets) St Mut.
Balant, Luc P., jt. ed. see Welling, Peter G.
Balanvskiy, Leonid, et al. Telecommunications Network Architecture in the Former Soviet Union, Vol. II. (Foreign Technology Assessment Ser.). xviii, 155p. (Orig.). 1994. pap. 200.00 (*1-881874-10-9*) Global Cnslts.
***Balanya, Belen, et al.** Europe Inc. LC 99-40487. 224p. 2000. 69.95 (*0-7453-1496-1*, Pub. by Pluto GBR); pap. 19.95 (*0-7453-1491-0*, Pub. by Pluto GBR) Stylus Pub VA.
Balarajan. Health Statistics U. K. 1996. 96th ed. 1997. text 21.00 (*0-443-05571-8*, W B Saunders Co) Harcrt Hlth Sci Grp.
Balaram, Mahant K. Srimad Bhagavatam Canto 10 Vol. 6: The Beautiful Narrations of the Supreme Lord. (Illus.). 360p. (YA). Date not set. write for info. (*0-9631403-7-X*) H H K B S.
Balard, Michel. La Mer Noire et la Romanie Genoise (XIIIE-XVE Siecles) (Collected Studies: No. CS294). (FRE.). 334p. (C). 1989. lib. bdg. 119.95 (*0-86078-242-5*, Pub. by Variorum) Ashgate Pub Co.
Balarezo, Martin. Suenos de un ilegal. MBG Publications Staff, ed. (SPA.). 376p. (Orig.). 1994. pap. text 6.95 (*0-9635531-0-0*) GEMATEXT.
Balari, Eugenio R. Cuba, la Revolucion Acosada? (Cuba, the Hounded Revolution?) (SPA.). 171p. 1993. pap. 6.99 (*968-16-4057-8*, Pub. by Fondo) Continental Bk.
Balari, Sergio & Dini, Luca, eds. Romance in HPSG. LC 96-50436. (CSLI Lecture Notes Ser.: Vol. 75). 425p. (C). 1998. text 69.95 (*1-57586-083-X*); pap. text 26.95 (*1-57586-082-1*) Cambridge U Pr.
Balarin, Felice. Hardware-Software Co-Design of Embedded Systems: The Polis Approach, Vol. 404. LC 97-11862. (VLSI, Computer Architecture, & Digital Signal Processingience Ser.). 1997. text 121.00 (*0-7923-9936-6*) Kluwer Academic.
Balarkrishnan, T. R. Family & Childbearing in Canada: A Demographic Analysis. LC 93-93050. 1993. pap. text 19.95 (*0-8020-7356-5*) U of Toronto Pr.
Balas, E., et al, eds. Integer Programming & Combinatorial Optimization: 4th International Conference, IPCO '95, Copenhagen, Denmark, May 29-31, 1995, Proceedings. (Lecture Notes in Computer Science Ser.: Vol. 920). 463p. 1995. 75.00 (*3-540-59408-6*) Spr-Verlag.
***Balas, E. A., et al, eds.** Information Technology Strategies from the United States & the European Union: Transferring Research to Practice for Health Care Improvement. (Studies in Health Technology & Informatics: Vol. 76). 134p. 2000. 67.00 (*1-58603-054-X*) IOS Press.
Balas, Edith. Joseph Csaky: A Pioneer of Modern Sculpture. LC 98-4154. (Memoirs Ser.: No. 230). (Illus.). xvii, 237 p. 1999. 30.00 (*0-87169-230-9*, M230-bae) Am Philos.
— Michelangelo's Medici Chapel: A New Interpretation. LC 94-78511. (Memoirs Ser.: Vol. 216). (Illus.). 195p. (C). 1995. 40.00 (*0-87169-216-3*, M216-bae) Am Philos.
***Balas, Egon.** Will to Freedom: A Perilous Journey Through Facism & Communism. LC 99-37873. 336p. 1999. 29.95 (*0-8156-0603-6*) Syracuse U Pr.
Balas, Egon & Clausen, Jens, eds. Integer Programming & Combinatorial Optimization: 4th International Conference, IPCO '95, Copenhagen, Denmark, May 1995 Proceedings. LC 95-17870. (Lecture Notes in Computer Science Ser.: Vol. 920). 1995. write for info. (*0-387-59408-6*) Spr-Verlag.
Balas, Robert S. & Rice, Donald. Qu'Est-Ce Qui se Passe, 3 vols. 3rd ed. (C). 1990. pap. 37.16 (*0-395-52586-1*) HM.
— Qu'Est-Ce Qui se Passe, 3 vols. 3rd ed. (C). 1990. pap. 38.36 (*0-395-52626-4*) HM.
— Qu'Est-Ce Qui se Passe, 3 vols. 3rd ed. (C). 1990. audio 24.36 (*0-395-52905-0*) HM.
— Qu'Est-Ce Qui se Passe, 3 vols. 3rd ed. (C). 1990. pap., teacher ed. 5.96 (*0-395-52875-5*) HM.
Balasco, Dianne. Hair Flair. (J). (gr. 4-7). 1994. pap. 6.95 (*0-8167-3366-X*) Troll Communs.
Balashov, V. Interaction of Particles & Radiation with Matter. Pontecorvo, G., tr. from RUS. (Illus.). 250p. 1997. 69.95 (*3-540-60871-0*) Spr-Verlag.
Balashov, Y. S. An Atlas of Ixodid Tick Ultrastructure. 289p. 1983. pap. 8.25 (*0-685-08073-0*, ESAATLAS) Entomol Soc.
Balashova, Elena, tr. see Dragomoschenko, Arkadii.
Balashova, Elena, tr. see Dragomoschenko, Arkadil.
Balaskas, Janet. Active Birth: The New Approach to Giving Birth Naturally. rev. ed. Ziedrich, Linda, ed. LC 91-32334. (Illus.). 272p. 1992. 19.95 (*1-55832-037-7*); pap. 14.95 (*1-55832-038-5*) Harvard Common Pr.
— Easy Excercises for Pregnancy. (Orig.). 1997. pap. 16.00 (*0-614-27360-9*) Macmillan USA.
— Easy Exercises for Pregnancy. LC 96-51126. (Illus.). 96p. 1997. 16.00 (*0-02-861661-8*) Macmillan.
— New Natural Pregnancy: Practical Wellbeing from Conception to Birth. 1999. pap. 15.00 (*1-56656-311-9*) Interlink Pub.
— Preparing for Birth with Yoga: Exercises for Pregnancy & Childbirth. (Home Library of Alternative Medicine). (Illus.). 192p. 1994. pap. 18.95 (*1-85230-431-6*, Pub. by Element MA) Penguin Putnam.
Balasov, L. A., et al. Fourteen Papers on Series & Approximation. LC 51-5559. (Translations Ser. 2: Vol. 77). 266p. 1969. 49.00 (*0-8218-1777-9*, TRANS2/77) Am Math.
Balassa, Bela. Essays in Development Strategy. 64p. 1988. pap. 9.95 (*1-55815-018-8*) ICS Pr.
Balassa, Bela & Williamson, John. Adjusting to Success: Balance of Payments Policy in the East Asian NICs. rev. ed. LC 90-4373. (Policy Analyses in International Economics Ser.: No. 17). 158p. reprint ed. pap. 49.00 (*0-7837-4221-5*, 204391000012) Bks Demand.
Balassa, Bela A. Development Strategies in Semi-Industrial Economies. LC 81-15558. (World Bank Research Publications). 408p. reprint ed. pap. 126.50 (*0-7837-5379-9*, 204514300005) Bks Demand.
Balassa, Bela A. The Structure of Protection in Developing Countries. LC 77-147366. 395p. reprint ed. pap. 122.50 (*0-7837-5380-2*, 204514400005) Bks Demand.
Balassa, Bela A. The Theory of Economic Integration. LC 82-2971. (Irwin Series in Economics). 304p. 1982. reprint ed. lib. bdg. 55.00 (*0-313-23543-0*, BATY, Greenwood Pr) Greenwood.
Balassa, Bela A. & Kreinin, M. E. Studies in Trade Liberalization: Problems & Prospects for the Industrial Countries. LC 67-22889. 362p. reprint ed. pap. 112.30 (*0-608-11865-6*, 202308000032) Bks Demand.
Balassa, Bela A., et al. Toward Renewed Economic Growth in Latin America. LC 86-15253. 207p. (Orig.). reprint ed. pap. 64.20 (*0-7837-4216-9*, 204390500012) Bks Demand.
***Balassanian, Sergiei, et al.** Earthquake Hazard & Seismic Risk Reduction. LC 00-33048. (Advances in Natural & Technological Hazard Research Ser.). 2000. write for info. (*0-7923-6390-6*) Plenum.
Balassanian, Sergiei, jt. auth. see Giardini, Domenico.
Balassanian, Sonia. Portraits. (Illus.). 24p. (Orig.). 1983. pap. 10.00 (*0-9608388-1-3*) S Balassanian.
— There Might Have Been an Insane Heart: Selected Poems in Armenian Language. (ARM.). 80p. (Orig.). 1982. pap. 5.00 (*0-9608388-0-5*) S Balassanian.
Balassi, William, et al, eds. This Is about Vision: Interviews with Southwestern Writers. LC 89-70428. 210p. 1990. reprint ed. pap. 65.10 (*0-608-04145-9*, 206487800011) Bks Demand.
Balaster, G. A., ed. see Steiner, Rudolf.
Balasubrahmanyan, Vimal. In Search of Justice, Women, Law, Landmark Judgements, & Media. (C). 1990. 65.00 (*0-89771-320-6*) St Mut.
Balasubramaniam, A. S. Soil Mechanics 9th Asian, Vol. 2. 1993. 388.00 (*974-07-7289-7*) Ashgate Pub Co.
Balasubramaniam, A. S., ed. Developments in Deep Foundations & Ground Improvement Schemes: Proceedings Symposia on Geotextiles, Geomembranes & Other Geosynthetics in Ground Improvement, Bangkok, Thailand 1994. (Illus.). 293p. 1996. 149.00 (*90-5410-593-3*, Pub. by A A Balkema) Ashgate Pub Co.
Balasubramaniam, A. S., et al, eds. Computer & Physical Modelling in Geotechnical Engineering: Proceedings of the International Symposium, Bankok, 3-6 December 1986. 550p. (C). 1989. text 220.00 (*90-6191-864-2*, Pub. by A A Balkema) Ashgate Pub Co.
— Developments in Geotechnical Aspects of Embankments, Excavations & Buried Structures: Proceedings of the Symposium Held in 1988 & 1990 in Bangkok on Underground Excavations in Soils & Rocks. (Illus.). 608p. (C). 1991. text 181.00 (*90-5410-019-2*, Pub. by A A Balkema) Ashgate Pub Co.
— Geotechnical Aspects of Mass & Material Transportation: Proceedings of the International Symposium, Bangkok, 3-14 December 1984. 544p. (C). 1984. text 246.00 (*90-6191-686-0*, Pub. by A A Balkema) Ashgate Pub Co.
— Geotechnical Aspects of Restoration Works on Infrastructures & Monuments: Proceedings of a Symposium, Bangkok, December 1988. (Illus.). 384p. (C). 1990. text 168.00 (*90-6191-116-8*, Pub. by A A Balkema) Ashgate Pub Co.
— Geotechnical Engineering in Southeast Asia: A Commemorative Volume of the Southeast Asian Geotechnical Society. 352p. (C). 1985. text 252.00 (*90-6191-599-6*, Pub. by A A Balkema) Ashgate Pub Co.
— Geotechnical Problems & Practice of Dam Engineering: Proceedings of the International Symposium Held at Asian Institute of Technology, Bangkok, 1-15 December 1980. 400p. (C). 1982. text 168.00 (*90-6191-265-2*, Pub. by A A Balkema) Ashgate Pub Co.
— Prediction vs. Performance in Geotechnical Engineering: Proceedings of the Symposium, Bangkok, November-December 1992. (Illus.). 450p. (C). 1994. text 136.00 (*90-5410-355-8*, Pub. by A A Balkema) Ashgate Pub Co.
— Recent Developments in Ground Improvement Techniques: Proceedings of the International Symposium Held at Asian Institute of Technology, Bangkok, 29 November - 3 December 1982. 598p. (C). 1985. text 220.00 (*90-6191-568-6*, Pub. by A A Balkema) Ashgate Pub Co.
Balasubramaniam, A. S., ed. see Chandra, S. & Bergado, D. T.
Balasubramaniam, A. S., jt. ed. see Yudhibir.
***Balasubramaniam, Ambikaipakan.** Neuropeptide Y Protocols. (Methods in Molecular Biology Ser.: Vol. 153). (Illus.). 324p. 2000. 99.50 (*0-89603-662-6*) Humana.
Balasubramaniam, K. S., et al, eds. Solar Drivers of Interplanetary & Terrestrial Disturbances. (ASP Conference Series Proceedings: Vol. 95). 628p. 1996. 34.00 (*1-886733-16-3*) Astron Soc Pacific.
— Synoptic Solar Physics. LC 98-71228. (Conference Series Proceedings: Vol. 140). 587p. 1998. 52.00 (*1-886733-60-0*) Astron Soc Pacific.
Balasubramanian, D. Cats Have Nine Lives. 1993. write for info. (*81-7236-078-9*, Pub. by Wiley Estrn) Franklin.
Balasubramanian, Krishnan. Relativistic Effects in Chemistry, 2 vols. 828p. 1997. 180.00 (*0-471-18184-6*) Wiley.
— Relativistic Effects in Chemistry Pt. A: Theory & Techniques. LC 96-36641. 301p. 1997. 105.00 (*0-471-30400-X*) Wiley.
— Relativistic Effects in Chemistry Pt. B: Applications. LC 96-36641. 527p. 1997. 105.00 (*0-471-17991-4*) Wiley.
Balasubramanian, M. Nehru: A Study in Secularism. 120p. 1980. 14.95 (*0-940500-32-9*) Asia Bk Corp.
Balasubramanian, R. Continuous Time Controller Design. (Control Engineering Ser.: No. 39). 298p. 1989. 99.00 (*0-86341-162-2*, CE039) INSPEC Inc.
— Primal Spirituality of the Vedas: Its Renewal & Renaissance. LC 96-902382. (C). 1996. 23.00 (*81-215-0721-9*, Pub. by M Manoharial) Coronet Bks.
— Tradition of Advaita: Essays in Honour of Bhasyabhavajna VR Kalyanasundara Sastri. LC 94-900800. (C). 1994. 28.00 (*81-215-0588-7*, Pub. by M Manoharial) Coronet Bks.
Balasubramanian, R., ed. Perspectives in Philosophy, Religion & Art: Essays in Honour of Margaret Chatterjee. (C). 1993. 18.00 (*81-85636-05-2*, Pub. by Manohar Bk Srv) S Asia.
Balasubramanian, R. & Sibjivan, Bhattacharya. Freedom, Progress & Society. 483p. 1986. 38.00 (*81-208-0262-4*, Pub. by Motilal Bnarsidass) S Asia.
Balasubramanian, Radha. The Poetics of Korolenko's Fiction. LC 96-2775. (Middlebury Studies in Russian Language & Literature: No. 12). 146p. (C). 1997. text 39.95 (*0-8204-3305-5*) P Lang Pubng.
Balasubramanian, V., et al. Resource Management in Rice Systems: Nutrients: Papers Presented at the International Workshop on Natural Resource Management in Rice Systems: Technology Adaptation for Efficient Nutrient Use, Bogor, Indonesia, 2-5 December 1996. LC 98-27942. (Developments in Plant & Soil Sciences Ser.). 1998. write for info. (*0-7923-5199-1*) Kluwer Academic.
***Balasubramanyam, Rajeev.** In Beautiful Disguises. 2001. pap. 13.95 (*1-58234-127-3*) Bloomsbury Pubg.
Balasubramanyam, V. N. International Transfer of Technology to India. LC 73-163952. (Special Studies in International Economics & Development). 1973. 42.50 (*0-275-28245-7*) Irvington.
Balasubramanyam, V. N. & Sapsford, David, eds. The Economics of International Investment. 240p. 1994. text 90.00 (*1-85278-889-5*) E Elgar.
Balasubramanyam, V. N., jt. auth. see Togan, Shubidey.
Balasubramanyam, V. N., ed. see Bhagwati, Jagdish.
Balasubramniam, A. S., ed. see Symposium on Developments in Geotechnical Engineer.
Balasubrmaniam, A. S., et al, eds. Recent Developments in Laboratory & Field Tests & Analysis of Geotechnical Problems: Proceedings of International Symposium, Bangkok, 6-9 December 1983. 632p. (C). 1986. text 246.00 (*90-6191-623-2*, Pub. by A A Balkema) Ashgate Pub Co.
Balasundaram, F. J. Dalits & Christian Mission in the Tamil Country: The Dalit Movement & Protestant Christians in the Tamil Speaking Districts of Madras Presidency, 1919-1939 with Special Reference to London Mission Society Area in Salem, Attur, Coimbatore & Erode. LC 98-903033. 192 p. 1997. write for info. (*81-7086-200-0*) Asian Trad Corp.
Balasuriya, Tissa. The Eucharist & Human Liberation. LC 78-9160. 192p. (Orig.). reprint ed. pap. 59.60 (*0-8357-4055-2*, 203674500005) Bks Demand.
— Mary & Human Liberation: The Story & the Text. LC 97-23821. 256p. 1997. pap. 20.00 (*1-56338-225-3*) TPI PA.
— Planetary Theology. LC 83-19339. 288p. (Orig.). reprint ed. pap. 89.30 (*0-8357-2665-7*, 204020100015) Bks Demand.
Balat, Michel, et al, eds. Signs of Humanity (L'Homme et Ses Signes) Proceedings of the IVth IASS Congress. LC 92-31588. (Approaches to Semiotics Ser.: Vol. 107). (FRE., Illus.). 1804p. 1992. lib. bdg. 536.95 (*3-11-011675-8*) Mouton.
Balata, Bill. Being the Ball: The Cart Path Toward Golf-Awareness. LC 99-22895. 112p. 1999. 9.88 (*0-9670877-0-8*) BTB Ent.
***Balawanta, Aisa & Atwal, Jasbir.** English-Panjabi (Roman Script) Gurmukhi-Dictionary LC 99-933954. 286p. 1999. write for info. (*81-202-0446-8*, Pub. by Ajanta Pubns) S Asia.

***Balawyder, Aloysius.** In the Clutches of the Kremlin: Canadian-East European Ralations, 1945-1962. 2000. 36.00 (0-88033-444-4, 546, Pub. by East Eur Monographs) Col U Pr.

Balawyder, Aloysius. The Maple Leaf & the White Eagle: Canadian-Polish Relations, 1918-1978. (East European Monographs: No. 66). 300p. 1980. text 68.50 (0-914710-59-1, Pub. by East Eur Monographs) Col U Pr.

Balawyder, Aloysius, ed. Canadian-Soviet Relations, 1936-1980. 222p. 1994. pap. 14.95 (0-88962-160-8) Mosaic.

Balay, Diane H. The Man from Nazareth: Life of Christ - From the Annunciation to the Resurrection. 128p. 1997. spiral bd. 11.95 (0-687-05318-8) Abingdon.

Balay, Richard H. User's Introduction to UNIX V. 128p. 1988. spiral bd. 17.95 (0-8403-4671-9) Kendall-Hunt.

Balay, Robert, ed. Guide to Reference Books: Covering Materials from 1985-1990, Supplement to the 10th Edition. LC 92-6463. 623p. reprint ed. pap., suppl. ed. 193.20 (0-608-06019-4, 206634700008) Bks Demand.

Balay, Robert, et al, eds. Guide to Reference Books. 11th ed. LC 95-26322. 2040p. 1996. 275.00 (0-8389-0669-9) ALA.

Balayan, M. Virology Reviews Vol. 4, Pt. 4: Chemoprophylaxis & Chemotherapy of Viral Infections, Vol. 4. (Soviet Medical Reviews Ser.: Section E). 78p. 1992. pap. text 104.00 (3-7186-5284-6, Harwood Acad Pubs) Gordon & Breach.

Balaye, Simone, ed. see Stael, Madame de.

Balazard, Sylvestre, jt. auth. see Marks, Anthony.

Balazs & Hervonet. Sung Bibliography. 1979. text 65.00 (0-9622011-5-4, CH1586) Col U Pr.

Balazs, Andras, et al. Reproduction & Aging. 331p. (C). 1974. text 32.50 (0-8422-7159-7) Irvington.

Balazs, Andre. The Chateau Marmont's Hollywood Handbook. LC 96-11998. (Illus.). 256p. 1996. pap. 25.00 (0-7893-0023-0, Pub. by Universe) St Martin.

Balazs, Anna C., jt. ed. see Stroeve, Pieter.

Balazs, Anne L., et al, eds. An Annotated Bibliography for Marketing to an Older Population. LC 89-18278. 69p. 1989. pap. text 25.00 (0-87757-202-X) Am Mktg.

Balazs, Anne L., et al. An Annotated Bibliography for Marketing to an Older Population. LC 89-18278. (Bibliography Ser.). 87p. 1989. reprint ed. pap. 30.00 (0-7837-9759-1, 206048700005) Bks Demand.

Balazs, Bela. Theory of the Film: Character & Growth of a New Art. LC 71-169347. (Arno Press Cinema Program Ser.). (Illus.). 312p. 1978. reprint ed. 23.95 (0-405-03910-7) Ayer.

Balazs, Bela, jt. ed. see Szebehely, Victor G.

Balazs, Ervin, jt. ed. see Tepfer, Mark.

Balazs, Etienne. Chinese Civilization & Bureaucracy: Variations on a Theme. Wright, Arthur F., ed. Wright, H. M., tr. LC 64-20909. 331p. reprint ed. pap. 102.70 (0-8357-8712-5, 203366500087) Bks Demand.

Balazs, Eva H. Hungary & the Habsburgs, 1765-1800: An Experiment in Enlightened Absolutism. 430p. 1998. 29.95 (963-9116-03-3) Ctrl Europ Univ.

***Balazs, Geza.** The Story of Hungarian: A Guide to the Language. 190p. 1999. pap. 21.00 (963-13-4362-6, Pub. by Corvina Bks) St Mut.

Balazs, Istvan. A Musical Guide to Hungary. 160p. 1999. pap. 21.00 (963-13-3399-X, Pub. by Corvina Bks) St Mut.

Balazs, Judit & Wiberg, Hakan, eds. Changes, Chances & Challenges Europe 2000. LC 96-147839. 274p. 1995. pap. 175.00 (963-05-6932-9, Pub. by Akade Kiado) St Mut.

— Peace Research for the 1990s. 271p. (C). 1994. 35.00 (963-05-6620-6, Pub. by Akade Kiado) Intl Spec Bk.

Balazs, Tibor. Cardiac Toxicology, Vol. I. 240p. 1981. 134.00 (0-8493-5555-9, RC682, CRC Reprint) Franklin.

— Cardiac Toxicology, Vol. II. 240p. 1981. 138.00 (0-8493-5556-7, RC682, CRC Reprint) Franklin.

— Cardiac Toxicology, Vol. III. 232p. 1981. 133.00 (0-8493-5558-3, RC682, CRC Reprint) Franklin.

Balba, A. Monem. Management of Problem Soils in Arid Ecosystems. 272p. 1995. lib. bdg. 110.00 (0-87371-811-9, L811) Lewis Pubs.

Balbach, Edith D., jt. auth. see Glantz, Stanton A.

Balbach, Margaret & Bliss, Lawrence C. A Laboratory Manual for Botany. 7th ed. (Illus.). 413p. (C). 1991. pap. text, student ed. 49.00 (0-03-030184-X, Pub. by SCP) Harcourt.

***Balbaiz, Peter.** Extractive Metallurgy of Activated Minerals. LC 00-28770. (Process Metallurgy Ser.). (Illus.). 2000. write for info. (0-444-50206-8) Elsevier.

Balbaki, M. Al-Mawrid: Dictionary. 1997. 69.00 (0-935782-34-6) Kazi Pubns.

— Al-Mawrid Al-Qareb Pocket Size Dictionary. 1989. 8.95 (0-935782-32-X) Kazi Pubns.

— Al-Mawrid Al-Sagher Pocket Size Dictionary. 1992. 6.75 (0-935782-33-8) Kazi Pubns.

Balbani, Niccolo. Newes from Italy of a Second Moses: or The Life of Galeacius Carracciolus the Noble Marquese of Vico. Crashaw, W., tr. LC 79-84085. (English Experience Ser.: No. 905). 92p. 1979. reprint ed. lib. bdg. 15.00 (90-221-0905-4) Walter J Johnson.

Balbas, L. T., ed. see Pidal, Ramon M.

***Balbazs, Ervin, et al, eds.** Biological Resource Management: Connecting Science & Policy. LC 00-28452. (Illus.). 320p. 2000. 169.00 (3-540-67117-X) Spr-Verlag.

Balber, Susanrachel & Greenspan, Joshua. The Book of Joshua: An Historical Biography. (Illus.). 206p. 1989. write for info. (0-318-64308-1) Galen Pr.

Balbert, Peter. D. H. Lawrence & the Psychology of Rhythm: The Meaning of Form in the Rainbow. (Studies in English Literature: No. 99). 1974. pap. 33.85 (90-279-3032-5) Mouton.

Balbin, I. & Lecot, K., compiled by. Logic Programming. 1985. pap. text 98.50 (0-908069-15-4) Kluwer Academic.

Balbin, Julius. Bitch of Buchenwald. Barkan, Stanley H., ed. Rizzuto, Charlz, tr. (Review Holocaust Chapbook Ser.: No. 1, CCC180).Tr. of Esperanto & Eng.. 48p. 1986. 15.00 (0-89304-300-1); pap. 5.00 (0-89304-301-X) Cross-Cultrl NY.

— Strangled Cries. Barkan, Stanley H., ed. Rizzuto, Charlz, tr. (Cross-Cultural Review Chapbook Ser.: No. 8: Esperanto Poetry 1). (ENG & ESP.). 24p. 1980. 15.00 (0-89304-848-8, CCC134); pap. 5.00 (0-89304-807-0) Cross-Cultrl NY.

Balbir. General Hindi-French Dictionary. (FRE & HIN.). 1104p. 1992. 195.00 (0-8288-6921-9, 2901795463) Fr & Eur.

Balbir Singh, ed. English-Punjabi Dictionary. 1984. 18.50 (0-8364-1241-9, Pub. by Punjabi U) S Asia.

Balbirer, jt. auth. see Shapiro, Alan.

Balbo, G., jt. ed. see Azema, P.

Balbo, Ned C. Galileos Banquet. Armitage, Barri, ed. LC 98-12285. 1998. pap. 12.00 (0-931846-52-8) Wash Writers Pub.

Balboa, Celso R. On Christian Dogma: An Interview with Josefina Chacin Ducharne. Gonzales, Bertha, tr. from SPA. LC 87-71301.Tr. of Sobre el Dogma Cristiano. 42p. 1987. pap. 4.00 (0-9607590-6-9) Action Life Pubns.

Balboni, Alan. Beyond the Mafia: Italian Americans & the Development of Las Vegas. LC 95-51534. (Wilbur S. Shepperson Series in History & Humanities). (Illus.). 192p. 1996. 27.95 (0-87417-243-8) U of Nev Pr.

Balboni, Alan & Tomlinson, Larry K. A Critical Inquiry into American Politics. 432p. (C). 1995. pap. text, per. 44.95 (0-8403-9579-5) Kendall-Hunt.

Balbuena, Perla B. & Seminario, J. M. Molecular Dynamics: From Classical to Quantum Methods. LC 99-22300. (Theoretical & Computational Chemistry Ser.). 970p. 1999. 421.50 (0-444-82910-5) Elsevier.

Balbus, Isaac D. The Dialectics of Legal Repression: Black Rebels Before the American Criminal Courts. LC 73-76762. 270p. 1973. 35.00 (0-87154-081-9) Russell Sage.

— Emotional Rescue: The Theory & Practice of a Feminist Father. LC 97-28024. (Thinking Gender Ser.). 256p. (C). 1997. pap. 20.99 (0-415-91918-5) Routledge.

— Emotional Rescue: The Theory & Practice of a Feminist Father. LC 97-28024. (Thinking Gender Ser.). 256p. (C). 1997. 75.00 (0-415-91917-7) Routledge.

— Marxism & Domination: A Neo-Hegelian, Feminist, Psychoanalytic Theory of Sexual, Political, & Technological Liberation. LC 82-47582. 432p. 1982. reprint ed. pap. 134.00 (0-608-00002-7, AU004680006) Bks Demand.

Balby, Richard. Ghosts for Christmas. 1992. 7.98 (1-55521-805-9) Bk Sales Inc.

Balcar, Ewald & Lovesey, Stephen W. Theory of Magnetic Neutron & Photon Scattering. (Oxford Series on Neutron Scattering in Condensed Matter: No. 2). (Illus.). 236p. 1989. text 65.00 (0-19-851006-3) OUP.

Balcar, Gerald P. Consent of the Governed. 531p. 1999. 28.95 (0-9672357-0-7) O Frederick Inc.

Balcarres, Colin L. Memoirs Touching the Revolution in Scotland. LC 73-161754. (Bannatyne Club, Edinburgh. Publications: No. 71). reprint ed. 44.50 (0-404-52791-4) AMS Pr.

***Balcavage, Dynise.** Chicago Fire of 1871. (Great Disasters Ser.). (Illus.). 128p. 2000. 19.95 (0-7910-5269-9) Chelsea Hse.

— Janis Joplin. (They Died Too Young Ser.). 2000. 16.95 (0-7910-5856-5) Chelsea Hse.

Balcavage, Walter X. Biochemistry: Examination & Board Review. 420p. (C). 1995. pap. text 32.95 (0-8385-0661-5, A0661-7, Apple Lange Med) McGraw.

Balcazar, Jose L., et al. Structural Complexity, No. II. (EATCS Monographs on Theoretical Computer Science: Vol. 22). (Illus.). 296p. 1990. 55.95 (0-387-52079-1) Spr-Verlag.

— Structural Complexity I. (EATCS Monographs on Theoretical Computer Science: Vol. 11). (Illus.). ix, 191p. 1988. 39.00 (0-387-18622-0) Spr-Verlag.

— Structural Complexity I. 2nd ed. LC 94-36688. (Texts in Theoretical Computer Science Ser.). 248p. 1995. 39.00 (3-540-58384-X) Spr-Verlag.

Balcells, Albert. Catalan Nationalism: Past & Present. Walker, Geoffrey J., ed. & intro. by. LC 94-47389. Orig. Title: Nationalismo Catalan. (SPA.). 240p. 1995. text 59.95 (0-312-12611-5) St Martin.

Balcells, Jacqueline. The Enchanted Raisin. Miller, Elizabeth G., tr. from SPA. LC 88-28587. (Discoveries Ser.). (Illus.). 104p. (J). (gr. 3-7). 1988. pap. 11.00 (0-935480-38-2) Lat Am Lit Rev Pr.

Balcer, Bernadette & O'Byrne-Pelham, Fran. Philadelphia. LC 88-20198. (Downtown America Ser.). (Illus.). 60p. (J). (gr. 3 up). 1988. pap. 7.95 (0-382-24795-7, Dillon Silver Burdett); lib. bdg. 13.95 (0-87518-388-3, Dillon Silver Burdett) Silver Burdett Pr.

Balcer, Jack M. A Prosopographical Study of the Ancient Persians Royal & Noble, 550-450 B.C. LC 93-27367. 380p. 1993. write for info. (0-7734-9372-7) E Mellen.

Balcerowicz, Leszek. Socialism, Capitalism, Transformation. LC 96-221255. (Central European University Press Bks.). (Illus.). 384p. 1996. pap. 26.95 (1-85866-026-2) Ctrl Europ Univ.

— Socialism, Capitalism, Transformation. LC 96-221255. (Illus.). 384p. (C). 1996. 49.95 (1-85866-025-4) Ctrl Europ Univ.

Balcerowicz, Leszek, et al, eds. Enterprise Exit Processes in Transition Economies: Downsizing, Workouts, & Liquidation. (Illus.). 320p. (C). 1998. 49.95 (963-9116-07-6); pap. 16.95 (963-9116-16-5) Ctrl Europ Univ.

Balcerzak, Edwin A., ed. Group Care of Children: Transitions Toward the Year 2000. 1989. pap. 9.95 (0-87868-287-2) Child Welfare.

Balcerzyk, Stanislaw & Josefiak, Tadeusz. Commutative Rings: Dimension Multiplicity, Homological Methods. 1989. text 59.95 (0-470-21348-5) P-H.

Balcerzyk, Stanislaw & Jozefiak, Tadeusz. Commutative Notherian & Krull Rings. 1989. text 59.95 (0-470-21391-4) P-H.

Balch. Math Applications. 1995. 47.95 (0-02-824625-X) McGraw.

— Psychology of Memory. (C). Date not set. pap. text. write for info. (0-15-507163-7) Harcourt Coll Pubs.

Balch, Adrian M. Airline Nostalgia: Classic Aircraft in Color. 112p. 1999. pap. text 29.95 (1-882663-42-X) Plymouth VT.

— Vintage Glory: Airline Color Schemes of the '50s & '60s. (Illus.). 112p. 1995. pap. 21.95 (1-85310-436-1) MBI Pubg.

Balch, C. M., ed. Surgical Approaches to Cutaneous Melanoma. (Pigment Cell Ser.: Vol. 7). (Illus.). viii, 212p. 1985. 148.00 (3-8055-4055-8) S Karger.

Balch, Charles M., et al, eds. Cutaneous Melanoma. 3rd ed. LC 97-29168. (Illus.). 650p. 1997. text 130.00 (0-942219-85-6) Quality Med Pub.

***Balch, David L., ed.** Homosexuality, Science & the "Plain Sense" of Scripture. LC 99-55787. 310p. 2000. pap. 20.00 (0-8028-4698-X) Eerdmans.

Balch, David L., jt. auth. see Osiek, Carolyn A.

Balch, David L., jt. auth. see Stambaugh, John E.

Balch, Emily G. Occupied Haiti. LC 75-14988. 186p. 1970. reprint ed. lib. bdg. 45.00 (0-8371-2785-8, BAL&) Greenwood.

— Our Slavic Fellow Citizens. LC 69-18758. (American Immigration Collection. Series 1). (Illus.). 1969. reprint ed. 29.95 (0-405-00506-7) Ayer.

Balch, Galusha. Genealogy of the Balch Families in America. (Illus.). 585p. 1988. reprint ed. pap. 87.00 (0-8328-0165-8); reprint ed. lib. bdg. 105.00 (0-8328-0164-X) Higginson Bk Co.

Balch, Glenn. Buck, Wild. LC 75-44168. (Illus.). (J). (gr. 5 up). 1976. 11.95 (0-690-01055-9) HarpC Child Bks.

— Christmas Horse. (Illus.). (J). 1990. reprint ed. pap. 12.00 (0-931659-10-8) Limberlost Pr.

Balch Institute for Ethnic Studies Staff. Civil Rights & Social Wrongs: Black-White Relations since World War II. Higham, John, ed. LC 97-8568. 224p. 1997. 28.50 (0-271-01709-0) Pa St U Pr.

— Rites of Passage in America: Traditions of the Life Cycle. LC 92-72033. (Illus.). 70p. 1992. 8.50 (0-937437-10-7) Balch IES Pr.

Balch Institute for Ethnic Studies Staff & Anti-Defamation League of B'nai B'rith Staff. Ethnic Images in Advertising. (Illus.). 1984. 4.25 (0-614-32309-6) Balch IES Pr.

***Balch, Jack S.** Lamps at High Noon. (Radical Novel Reconsidered Ser.). 448p. 2000. reprint ed. pap. 19.95 (0-252-06939-0) U of Ill Pr.

Balch, James & Walker, Morton. Indigestion & What to Do about It: A Guide to Overcoming the Discomforts of Indigestion Using Drug-Free Remedies. 1997. pap. 10.95 (0-614-27341-2) Penguin Putnam.

Balch, James, jt. auth. see Balch, Phyllis.

Balch, James, jt. auth. see Balch, Phyllis A.

Balch, James F., Jr. Dietary Wellnes - RX for Cooking: Healing Forces Within for Obesity & Disease. Balch, Phyllis & Kean, Sharon, eds. (Illus.). 282p. 1987. pap. 19.95 (0-942023-00-5) P A B Bks.

Balch, James F. The Super Anti-Oxidants: Why They Will Change the Face of Healthcare in the 21st Century. LC 99-232631. 320p. 1998. pap. 21.95 (0-87131-851-2) M Evans.

— The Super Antioxidants: Why They Will Change the Face of Healthcare in the 21st Century. 256p. 1999. pap. 14.95 (0-87131-894-6, Pub. by M Evans) Natl Bk Netwk.

— 10 Natural Remedies That Can Save Your Life. LC 99-13160. 272p. 1999. 19.95 (0-385-49349-5) Doubleday.

***Balch, James F.** Ten Natural Remedies That Can Save Your Life. 272p. 2000. pap. 11.95 (0-385-49350-9) Doubleday.

Balch, James F., Jr. & Balch, Phyllis. Nutritional Outline for the Professional & the Wise Man. 7th rev. ed. 329p. 1987. pap. 21.95 (0-942023-25-0) P A B Bks.

Balch, James F. & Balch, Phyllis. Prescription for Cooking & Dietary Wellness. 317p. 1993. pap. 16.95 (0-942023-02-1) P A B Bks.

Balch, James F. & Balch, Phyllis A. Prescription for Nutritional Healing: A Practical A-Z Reference to Drug-Free Remedies Using Vitamins, Minerals, Herbs & Food Supplements. LC 90-452. (Illus.). 340p. 1990. pap. 16.95 (0-89529-429-X, Avery) Penguin Putnam.

— Prescription for Nutritional Healing: A Practical A-Z Reference to Drug-Free Remedies Using Vitamins, Minerals, Herbs & Food Supplements. 2nd ed. 1999. 29.95 (0-13-025447-9) P-H.

— Prescription for Nutritional Healing: A Practical A-Z Reference to Drug-Free Remedies Using Vitamins, Minerals, Herbs & Food Supplements. 2nd ed. LC 97-157317. (Illus.). 608p. 1996. pap. 19.95 (0-89529-727-2, Avery) Penguin Putnam.

— Prescription for Nutritional Healing: A-to-Z Guide to Supplements : A Handy Resource to Today's Most Effective Nutritional Supplements. LC 98-156431. 256p. 1997. mass mkt. 6.95 (0-89529-816-3, Avery) Penguin Putnam.

Balch, James F. & Walker, Morton. Heartburn & What to Do About It: A Guide to Overcoming the Discomforts of Indigestion Using Drug-Free Remedies. LC 97-46876. 190p. Date not set. pap. 10.95 (0-89529-792-2, Avery) Penguin Putnam.

Balch, James F., Jr., jt. auth. see Balch, Phyllis.

Balch, James F., jt. auth. see Balch, Phyllis A.

Balch, Pamela M. & Balch, Patrick E. The Cooperating Teacher: A Practical Approach for the Supervision of Student Teachers. LC 87-10585. 196p. (Orig.). (C). 1987. lib. bdg. 43.50 (0-8191-6424-0) U Pr of Amer.

Balch, Patrick E., jt. auth. see Balch, Pamela M.

Balch, Phyllis & Balch, James. Prescription for Dietary Wellness: Using Food to Heal. 330p. Date not set. pap. 16.95 (0-89529-868-6, Avery) Penguin Putnam.

Balch, Phyllis & Balch, James F., Jr. Prescription for Cooking: Designer Diets for the Healing Force Within. rev. ed. 306p. (Orig.). 1987. reprint ed. pap. text 14.95 (0-685-55184-9) P A B Bks.

Balch, Phyllis, jt. auth. see Balch, James F.

Balch, Phyllis, jt. auth. see Balch, James F., Jr.

Balch, Phyllis, jt. auth. see Rister, Robert.

Balch, Phyllis, ed. see Balch, James F., Jr.

Balch, Phyllis A. & Balch, James. Recetas Nutritivas Que Curan: Prescription for Nutritional Healing-Spanish-English Edition. LC 00-26638. (SPA.). 640p. 2000. pap. 24.95 (1-58333-010-0, Avery) Penguin Putnam.

***Balch, Phyllis A. & Balch, James F.** Prescription for Nutritional Healing: A Practical A-to-Z Reference to Drug-Free Remedies Using Vitamins, Minerals, Herbs & Food Supplements. 3rd ed. 704p. 2000. pap. 22.95 (1-58333-077-1, Avery); spiral bd. 27.95 (1-58333-083-6, Avery) Penguin Putnam.

Balch, Phyllis A., jt. auth. see Balch, James F.

Balch, Si & Society of American Foresters Staff. The Land Ethic: Meeting Human Needs for the Land & Its Resources. LC 98-39583. (Forestry Forum Ser.). 1998. pap. write for info. (0-939970-76-7) Soc Am Foresters.

Balch, Stephen H. & Zurcher, Rita C. The Dissolution of General Education: 1914-1993. (Illus.). 70p. (Orig.). 1996. pap. 12.00 (0-9653143-0-8) Natl Assn Scholars.

Balch, Thomas. The French in America During the War of Independence of the United States, 2 vols., Set. LC 72-8702. (American Revolutionary Ser.). reprint ed. lib. bdg. 75.00 (0-8398-0185-8) Irvington.

Balch, Thomas, ed. The Examination of Joseph Galloway, Esq., by a Committee of the House of Commons. LC 72-8749. (American Revolutionary Ser.). reprint ed. lib. bdg. 32.00 (0-8398-0183-1) Irvington.

Balch, Thomas W. Alabama Arbitration. LC 74-95063. (Select Bibliographies Reprint Ser.). 1977. 21.95 (0-8369-5065-8) Ayer.

— World Court in the Light of the United States Supreme Court. 165p. 1983. reprint ed. 32.50 (0-8377-0340-9, Rothman) W S Hein.

Balch, Thomas W., ed. see Blanchard, Claude.

Balch, Trudy, tr. see Garcia Pinto, Magdalena.

Balch, W. E., et al, eds. Small GTPases & Their Regulators Pt. A: Ras Family. (Methods in Enzymology Ser.: Vol. 255). (Illus.). 548p. 1995. text 104.00 (0-12-182156-0) Acad Pr.

Balch, W. E., ed. see Simon, Melvin I.

Balchen, Jens G., ed. Dynamics & Control of Chemical Reactors, Distillation Columns, & Batch Processes: Selected Papers from the 3rd IFAC Symposium, Maryland, U. S. A. LC 92-44352. (IFAC Symposia Ser.). 386p. 1993. 167.00 (0-08-041711-6, Pergamon Pr) Elsevier.

Balchin, Jody. Decorative Painting on Glass, Ceramics & Metal. (Illus.). 80p. 1998. pap. 15.95 (0-85532-838-X, 838X, Pub. by Srch Pr) A Schwartz & Co.

Balchin, John. The Compact Survey of the Bible. LC 87-15124. 288p. (Orig.). 1987. pap. 9.99 (0-87123-964-7) Bethany Hse.

***Balchin, Judy.** Celtic Glass Painting. 64p. 2000. pap. 15.95 (0-85532-927-0, Pub. by Srch Pr) Midpt Trade.

Balchin, Judy. Classic Glass Painting: Inspirations from the Past. (Illus.). 96p. 1999. pap. 19.95 (0-85532-879-7, 8797, Pub. by Srch Pr) A Schwartz & Co.

***Balchin, Judy.** Paper Mache. LC 00-38889. (Step-by-Step Ser.). (Illus.). 2000. write for info. (1-57572-328-X) Heinemann Lib.

— Papier Mache. (Step-by-Step Children's Crafts Ser.). 32p. (J). 2000. pap. 8.95 (0-85532-912-2, Pub. by Srch Pr) Midpt Trade.

Balchin, Nigel C. Welding & Cutting. (Safety Instruction Booklet Ser.). (Illus.). 16p. 1991. 45.00 (1-85573-055-3, Pub. by Woodhead Pubng) Am Educ Systs.

Balchin, Nigel C. & Castner, Harvey R., eds. Health & Safety in Welding & Allied Processes. 4th ed. LC 93-25420. 1993. 50.00 (0-07-004669-7) McGraw.

Balchin, Paul N. Housing Policy: An Introduction. 3rd ed. LC 94-39859. 1995. write for info. (0-04-150932-3) Routledge.

— Regional Policy & Planning in Europe. 1999. 85.00 (0-415-16009-X); pap. 25.99 (0-415-16010-3) Routledge.

Balchin, Paul N., ed. Housing Policy in Europe. (Illus.). 368p. (C). 1996. 85.00 (0-415-13512-5); pap. 25.99 (0-415-13513-3) Routledge.

Balchin, Paul N. & Rhoden, Maureen. Housing: The Essential Foundations. LC 97-28274. (Illus.). 352p. (C). 1998. 90.00 (0-415-16007-3); pap. 27.99 (0-415-16008-1) Routledge.

Balchum, Oscar J., jt. ed. see Sharma, Om P.

Balci, Osman, et al, eds. Computer Science & Operations Research: New Developments in Their Interfaces. LC 92-10675. 548p. 1992. 146.00 (0-08-040806-0, Pergamon Pr) Elsevier.

— Proceedings, 1990 Winter Simulation Conference: New Orleans, Louisiana. 1024p. 1990. 130.00 (0-911801-72-3, WSC-90) Soc Computer Sim.

Balckett, Ruth, et al. Berry Patch. Shreves, Kathey, ed. (Illus.). 104p. (C). 1981. spiral bd. 5.95 (0-940158-02-7) Zucchini Patch.

An Asterisk (*) at the beginning of an entry indicates that the title is appearing for the first time.

Balcom, Leah. Christian Clown Skits. LC 97-204967. 1997. pap. 9.95 (*0-7880-0929-X*, Fairway Pr) CSS OH.

Balcom, William T. Serving Readers. LC 96-38513. (Highsmith Press Handbook Ser.). 120p. 1997. pap. 19.00 (*0-917846-74-5*, 95643) Highsmith Pr.

Balcomb, F. W. Balcombe: First Book of the Balcombe Family. 95p. 1993. reprint ed. pap. 17.00 (*0-8328-3257-X*); reprint ed. lib. bdg. 27.00 (*0-8328-3256-1*) Higginson Bk Co.

— Witt Genealogy. 40p. 1993. reprint ed. lib. bdg. write for info. (*0-8328-6586-9*) Higginson Bk Co.

Balcomb, J. Douglas. Passive Solar Buildings. (Solar Heat Technologies: Fundamentals & Applications Ser.: Vol. 7). (Illus.). 583p. 1992. 65.00 (*0-262-02341-5*) MIT Pr.

***Balcomb, Janissa R., et al, eds.** Proceedings & Papers of the Sixteenth Trumpeter Swan Society Conference. (Illus.). 136p. 1999. pap. text 15.00 (*1-888377-01-1*) Trumpeter Swan Soc.

Balcomb, Marcy, jt. auth. see Witt, Kevin.

Balcomb, Mary N. Robin-Robin: A Journal. LC 95-22236. 80p. 1995. pap. 19.95 (*1-887532-05-6*) Cody Pub.

— Robin-Robin: A Journal. limited ed. LC 95-22236. 80p. 1995. boxed set 125.00 (*1-887532-06-4*) Cody Pub.

— William F. Reese. LC 83-72443. (Illus.). 176p. 1984. 70.00 (*0-916029-00-X*) Blue Raven Pub Co.

— William F. Reese. limited ed. LC 83-72443. (Illus.). 176p. 1984. 600.00 (*0-916029-01-8*) Blue Raven Pub Co.

Balcomb, Philip E. The Clock Book: An Overview of Heirloom & Contemporary Clocks in American Homes. (Illus.). 192p. (Orig.). 1996. pap. 18.95 (*0-9620456-3-2*) Tempus Pr.

— The Clock Repair First Reader: Second Steps for the Beginner. (Illus.). 160p. (Orig.). 1989. pap. 16.95 (*0-9620456-1-6*) Tempus Pr.

— The Clock Repair Primer: The Beginner's Handbook. 7th rev. ed. (Illus.). 158p. (Orig.). 1998. pap. 15.95 (*0-9620456-0-8*) Tempus Pr.

— Radio Controlled Model Airplane Basic Flight Training: Course Manual & Instructor's Guide. (Illus.). 78p. (Orig.). 1992. pap. 10.00 (*0-9620456-2-4*) Tempus Pr.

Balcombe, Betty. Everyone's Guide for Using Psychic Ability. LC 95-3102. 192p. (Orig.). 1995. pap. 11.00 (*0-87728-835-6*) Weiser.

***Balcombe, Betty F.** The Psychic Handbook. 192p. 2000. pap. 12.95 (*1-57863-213-7*) Weiser.

Balcombe, Dennis, tr. see Avanzini, John F.

Balcombe, Jonathan. The Use of Animals in Higher Education: Problems, Alternatives & Recommendations. 60p. Date not set. pap. write for info. (*0-9658942-1-5*, Humane) Humane Soc.

Balcombe, Terry. Men of Death. 136p. 1998. pap. 16.00 (*0-8059-4283-1*) Dorrance.

Balcon, Jill, ed. The Pity of War: Poems of the 1st World War. (Illus.). 80p. 1985. 18.95 (*0-85683-083-6*, Pub. by Shepheard-Walwyn Pubs) Paul & Co Pubs.

Balcon, Michael, et al. Twenty Years of British Film, 1925-1945. LC 73-169326. (National Cinema Ser.). (Illus.). 120p. 1975. reprint ed. 16.95 (*0-405-03890-9*) Ayer.

Balczewski, Leszek. Propagation of Light. LC 97-90062. 42p. 1998. pap. 10.95 (*0-533-12698-3*) Vantage.

Balcziak, Bill. Movies. (Communication Today & Tomorrow Ser.). (Illus.). 48p. (J). (gr. 4-8). 1989. lib. bdg. 25.27 (*0-86592-058-3*) Rourke Enter.

— Music. (Communication Today & Tomorrow Ser.). (Illus.). 48p. (J). (gr. 4-8). 1989. lib. bdg. 25.27 (*0-86592-056-7*) Rourke Enter.

— Newspapers. (Communication Today & Tomorrow Ser.). (Illus.). 48p. (J). (gr. 4-8). 1989. lib. bdg. 25.27 (*0-86592-069-9*) Rourke Enter.

— Radio. (Communication Today & Tomorrow Ser.). (Illus.). 48p. (J). (gr. 4-8). 1989. lib. bdg. 25.27 (*0-86592-057-5*) Rourke Enter.

— Television. (Communication Today & Tomorrow Ser.). (Illus.). 48p. (J). (gr. 4-8). 1989. lib. bdg. 25.27 (*0-86592-059-1*) Rourke Enter.

Balcziak, Bill, jt. auth. see Frisch, Carlienne.

Bald & Cobb. Active Grammar. Date not set. pap. text. write for info. (*0-582-51738-9*, Pub. by Addison-Wesley) Longman.

Bald, G. Timeless Tripod. 1993. 16.99 (*0-89906-131-1*); pap. 12.99 (*0-89906-132-X*) Mesorah Pubns.

Bald, Kenneth B. Dark Shadows - The Comic Strip Book. 152p. 1996. pap. 15.95 (*0-938817-39-6*) Pomegranate Pr.

Bald, Margaret. Literature Suppressed on Religious Grounds, 4 vols. LC 97-43638. (Banned Bks.). 352p. 1998. 35.00 (*0-8160-3306-4*) Facts on File.

Bald, Robert C. Donne & the Drurys. LC 86-22754. 186p. 1986. reprint ed. lib. bdg. 59.50 (*0-313-25226-2*, BADO, Greenwood Pr) Greenwood.

— Donne's Influence in English Literature. 1932. 16.50 (*0-8446-1040-2*) Peter Smith.

Bald, Robert C., ed. see Shakespeare, William.

Bald, W. B. & Robards, Anthony W., eds. Food Freezing: Today & Tomorrow. (Series in Applied Biology: Vol. 3). (Illus.). 216p. 1991. 129.95 (*0-387-19668-4*) Spr-Verlag.

Balda, Diane. Fearsome Foursome. 97p. (YA). 1999. pap. 6.99 (*1-57532-177-7*) Press-Tige Pub.

Balda, Russell P., et al. Animal Cognition in Nature: The Convergence of Psychology & Biology in Laboratory & Field. LC 99-211220. (Illus.). 480p. 1998. boxed set 79.95 (*0-12-077030-X*) Acad Pr.

Balda, Russell P., jt. auth. see Marzluff, John M.

Baldacchino, Godfrey. Global Tourism & Informal Labour Relations: The Small Scale Syndrome at Work. LC 96-39585. (Employment & Work Relations in Context Ser.). (Illus.). 288p. 1998. 110.00 (*0-7201-2248-1*) Continuum.

***Baldacchino, Godfrey & Milne, David.** Lessons from the Political Economy of Small Islands: The Resourcefulness of Jurisdiction. LC 99-55726. 2000. 69.95 (*0-312-23195-4*) St Martin.

Baldacchino, John. Post-Marxist Marxism: Questioning the Answer: Difference & Realism after Lukacs & Adorno. LC 96-85191. (Avebury Series in Philosophy). 179p. 1996. text 62.95 (*1-85972-438-8*, Pub. by Avebury) Ashgate Pub Co.

Baldacchino, John M. Easels of Utopia: Art's Fact Returned. LC 97-77388. (Avebury Series in Philosophy). 174p. 1998. text 64.95 (*1-84014-114-X*, Pub. by Ashgate Pub) Ashgate Pub Co.

Baldacchino, Joseph. Economics & the Moral Order. LC 84-62819. 43p. (Orig.). 1985. pap. 6.00 (*0-932783-00-7*) Natl Human Inst.

Baldacchino, Joseph, ed. Educating for Virtue. (Orig.). 1988. pap. 7.00 (*0-932783-02-3*) Natl Human Inst.

Baldacchino, Lewis. A Study in Kant's Metaphysics of Aesthetic Experience: Reason & Feeling. LC 91-44832. (Studies in the History of Philosophy: Vol. 25). 156p. 1992. lib. bdg. 69.95 (*0-7734-9468-5*) E Mellen.

Baldacci, David. Absolute Power. large type ed. 1997. pap. 22.95 (*0-614-25107-9*, G K Hall Lrg Type) Mac Lib Ref.

— Absolute Power. 528p. 1996. reprint ed. mass mkt. 7.99 (*0-446-60358-9*, Pub. by Warner Bks) Little.

— The Executive Power. 1996. write for info. (*0-614-15471-5*) Warner Bks.

***Baldacci, David.** Saving Faith. 480p. 1999. 26.95 (*0-446-52577-4*, Pub. by Warner Bks); mass mkt. 16.00 (*0-446-67647-0*, Pub. by Warner Bks) Little.

— Saving Faith. 528p. 2000. mass mkt. 7.99 (*0-446-60889-0*, Warner Vision) Warner Bks.

— Saving Faith. LC 99-36764. 1999. 25.00 (*0-375-40866-5*) Wheeler Pub.

— Saving Faith. large type ed. 2000. pap. 12.95 (*0-375-72798-1*) Random.

Baldacci, David. The Simple Truth. LC 98-44512. 680p. 1999. write for info. (*0-7540-2178-5*) Chivers N Amer.

— The Simple Truth. LC 98-22548. 470p. 1998. 25.00 (*0-446-52332-1*, Pub. by Warner Bks) Little.

— The Simple Truth. 544p. 1999. mass mkt. 7.99 (*0-446-60771-1*, Pub. by Warner Bks) Little.

— The Simple Truth. large type ed. LC 98-44512. 690p. 1999. 30.00 (*0-7862-1696-4*) Thorndike Pr.

— Total Control. 720p. 1997. reprint ed. mass mkt. 7.99 (*0-446-60484-4*, Pub. by Warner Bks) Little.

— Total Control: A Novel. 528p. 1996. mass mkt. 12.00 (*0-446-67374-9*, Pub. by Warner Bks) Little.

— Total Control: A Novel. large type ed. LC 96-47710. 846p. 1997. 26.95 (*0-7862-0963-1*) Thorndike Pr.

— Total Control: A Novel. large type ed. 846p. 1998. pap. 24.95 (*0-7862-0964-X*) Thorndike Pr.

— The Winner. LC 97-34569. 528p. 1998. 25.00 (*0-446-52259-7*, Pub. by Warner Bks) Little.

— The Winner. large type ed. LC 97-32306. (Basic Ser.). 1998. pap. 28.95 (*0-7862-1281-0*) Thorndike Pr.

— The Winner. 656p. 1998. reprint ed. mass mkt. 7.99 (*0-446-60632-4*, Pub. by Warner Bks) Little.

***Baldacci, David.** Wish You Well. 368p. 2000. 24.95 (*0-446-52716-5*) Warner Bks.

Baldacci, Paolo. De Chirico. (Illus.). 440p. 1998. 95.00 (*0-8212-2499-9*, Pub. by Bulfinch Pr) Little.

Baldaev, D. S. Dictionary of Criminal Jargon, 2 vols. (RUS.). 703p. (C). 1997. 32.95 (*0-8285-5521-4*) Firebird NY.

Baldaia, Peter J. Breaking the Mold: New Directions in Glass. (Illus.). 20p. 1996. pap. text 7.50 (*1-885820-02-X*) Huntsville.

Baldaia, Peter J., contrib. by. Boston 1990: The Sixth Triennial Exhibition. (Illus.). 6p. 1990. 2.00 (*0-934358-27-3*) Fuller Mus Art.

— Gail Chase-Bien. (Illus.). 24p. 1989. 10.00 (*0-934358-23-0*) Fuller Mus Art.

Baldaia, Peter J., jt. auth. see Brockton Art Museum Publications Staff.

Baldaia, Peter J, ed. see Brockton Art Museum Publications Staff.

Baldamus, C. A., et al, eds. Biocompatibility in Hemodialysis. (Contributions to Nephrology Ser.: Vol. 36). (Illus.). viii, 140p. 1983. pap. 83.50 (*3-8055-3601-1*) S Karger.

— Improvements in Dialysis Therapy. (Contributions to Nephrology Ser.: Vol. 74). (Illus.). viii, 242p. 1990. 29.75 (*3-8055-4981-4*) S Karger.

Baldamus, C. A. & Koch, K. M., eds. Erythropoietin: From Molecular Structure to Clinical Application. (Contributions to Nephrology Ser.: Vol. 76). (Illus.). x, 350p. 1989. 29.75 (*3-8055-5035-9*) S Karger.

Baldani. Mathematical Economics. (C). 1996. pap. text, student ed. write for info. (*0-03-011579-5*) Harcourt Coll Pubs.

Baldani, Jeffrey. Mathematical Economics. (C). 1995. text 91.50 (*0-03-098145-X*, Pub. by Harcourt Coll Pubs) Harcourt.

Baldanza, Frank. Ivy Compton-Burnett. LC 64-8325. (Twayne's English Authors Ser.). 142p. (C). 1964. text 20.95 (*0-8290-1728-3*) Irvington.

Baldasano, J. H., et al, eds. Air Pollution II Vol. 2: Pollution Control & Monitoring. LC 94-72961. (Air Pollution Ser.). 576p. 1994. 224.00 (*1-56252-285-X*, 3617) Computational Mech MA.

Baldasano, J. M., et al, eds. Air Pollution II Vol. 1: Computer Simulation. 608p. 1994. 236.00 (*1-85312-360-9*) Computational Mech MA.

— Air Pollution II Vol. 2: Pollution Control & Monitoring. 576p. 1994. 224.00 (*1-85312-361-7*) Computational Mech MA.

Baldasano, J. M. & Power, H., eds. Environmental Engineering & Management. 346p. 1999. 196.00 (*1-85312-602-0*, 6020, Pub. by WIT Pr) Computational Mech MA.

Baldasano, J. M., jt. ed. see Power, H.

Baldasano, J. M., jt. ed. see Sucharov, L. J.

***Baldasare, Linda.** How to Start a Profitable Home-Based Dealer Shuttle Service: The Road to Success Starts Here. (Illus.). 176p. 1999. pap. 22.95 (*0-9672784-0-6*) Road Runner Pubg.

Baldasono, J. H., et al, eds. Air Pollution II Vol. 1: Computer Simulation. LC 94-72961. (Air Pollution Ser.). 608p. 1994. 236.00 (*1-56252-284-1*, 3609) Computational Mech MA.

***Baldassare, Mark.** California in the New Millennium: The Changing Social & Political Landscape. LC 99-55785. (Illus.). 440p. 2000. 27.50 (*0-520-22512-0*, Pub. by U CA Pr) Cal Prin Full Svc.

— Risky Business: Providing Local Public Services in Los Angeles County. LC 00-29346. 2000. write for info. (*1-58213-022-1*) Pub Policy Inst.

Baldassare, Mark. Trouble in Paradise: The Suburban Transformation & Its Challenges. LC 85-19499. 267p. 1986. text 52.50 (*0-231-06014-9*) Col U Pr.

— Trouble in Paradise: The Suburban Transformation in America. 251p. 1988. pap. text 19.50 (*0-231-06015-7*) Col U Pr.

— When Government Fails: The Orange County Bankruptcy. LC 97-32806. 320p. 1998. 48.00 (*0-520-21485-4*, Pub. by U CA Pr); pap. 18.95 (*0-520-21486-2*, Pub. by U CA Pr) Cal Prin Full Svc.

Baldassari, Anne. Picasso & Photography: The Dark Mirror. Dusinberre, Deke, tr. LC 97-34000. (Illus.). 256p. 1997. 55.00 (*2-08-013646-1*, Pub. by Flammarion) Abbeville Pr.

— Picasso & Photography: The Dark Mirror. LC 97-34000. (Illus.). 256p. 1998. pap. 39.95 (*2-08-013649-6*) Tex A&M Univ Pr.

***Baldassari, Anne.** Picasso Working on Paper. 2000. 45.00 (*1-85894-107-5*) Merrell Holberton.

Baldassari, Butch. Evergreen/Mandolin Music for Christmas. 32p. 1995. pap. 5.95 (*0-7866-0627-4*, 95535); pap. 15.95 incl. audio (*0-7866-0629-0*, 95535P); pap. 20.95 incl. audio compact disk (*0-7866-0631-2*, 95535CDP) Mel Bay.

Baldassari, F., et al, eds. P-Acid Analysis: Proceedings of the International Conference Held in Trento, Italy, May 29-June 2, 1989. (Lecture Notes in Mathematics Ser.: Vol. 1454). v, 382p. 1991. 59.95 (*0-387-53477-6*) Spr-Verlag.

Baldassaro. Carlo Levi. 2001. 47.50 (*1-85973-181-3*, Pub. by Berg Pubs); pap. 19.50 (*1-85973-186-4*, Pub. by Berg Pubs) NYU Pr.

Baldassaro, Lawrence, jt. auth. see Pickering-Iazzi, Robin.

Baldassarre, Angela. The Great Directors: Interviews with Filmmakers of Italian Descent. (Essay Ser.: Vol. 42). 128p. 1999. pap. 13.00 (*1-55071-094-X*) Guernica Editions.

Baldassarre, Guy A. & Bolen, Eric. Waterfowl Ecology & Management. 632p. 1994. 150.00 (*0-471-59770-8*) Wiley.

Baldassarri, Mario. Maffeo Pantaleoni. LC 96-38023. 212p. 1997. text 79.95 (*0-312-17358-X*) St Martin.

Baldassarri, Mario, et al, eds. Equity, Efficiency & Growth: The Future of the Welfare State. (Central Issues in Contemporary Economic Theory & Policy Ser.). 432p. 1996. text 85.00 (*0-312-16014-3*) St Martin.

— The International System Between Integration & Neo-Protectionism. LC 95-53122. (Central Issues in Contemporary Economic Theory & Policy Ser.). 192p. 1996. text 75.00 (*0-312-15961-7*) St Martin.

— The 1990s Slump: Causes & Cures. 400p. 1996. text 85.00 (*0-312-16012-7*) St Martin.

— The Privatization of Public Utilities: The Case of Italy. LC 96-46621. (Central Issues in Contemporary Economic Theory & Policy Ser.). (Illus.). 320p. 1997. text 79.95 (*0-312-17258-3*) St Martin.

— World Saving, Prosperity & Growth. LC 92-40362. (Central Issues in Contemporary Economic Theory & Policy Ser.). 403p. 1993. text 79.95 (*0-312-09582-1*) St Martin.

Baldassarri, Mario & Modigliani, Franco, eds. The Italian Economy: What Next? LC 95-14922. (Central Issues in Contemporary Economic Theory & Policy Ser.). 1995. text 75.00 (*0-312-12475-9*) St Martin.

Baldassarri, Mario & Roberti, Paolo, eds. Fiscal Problems in the Single-Market Europe. LC 93-31488. (Central Issues in Contemporary Economic Theory & Policy Ser.). 1994. text 85.00 (*0-312-12013-3*) St Martin.

Baldassarri, Mario, et al. Institution & Economic Organization in the Advanced Economies: The Governance Perspective. LC 97-41071. (Central Issues in Contemporary Economic Theory & Policy Ser.). 288p. 1998. text 79.95 (*0-312-21276-3*) St Martin.

— Institutions & Economic Organization in the Advanced Economies: The Governance Perspective. LC 97-41071. (Central Issues in Contemporary Economic Theory & Policy Ser.). 284p. 79.95 (*0-333-71575-6*) Macmillan.

Baldassarri, Mario, jt. ed. see Annunziato, Paolo.

***Baldassarri, Stefano U. & Saiber, Arielle.** Images of Quattrocentro Florence: Selected Writings in Literature, History & Art. LC 99-52702. (Italian Literature & Thought Ser.). (Illus.). 384p. 2000. pap. 18.00 (*0-300-08052-2*) Yale U Pr.

Baldasty, Gerald J. The Commercialization of News in the Nineteenth Century. LC 92-10590. 256p. (Orig.). (C). 1992. pap. 19.95 (*0-299-13404-0*) U of Wis Pr.

— E. W. Scripps & the Business of Newspapers. LC 98-25357. (History of Communication Ser.). 272p. 1999. 42.50 (*0-252-02255-6*); pap. 16.95 (*0-252-06750-9*) U of Ill Pr.

Baldauf-Berdes, Jane J. Women Musicians of Venice: Musical Foundations, 1525-1855. 2nd rev. ed. (Oxford Monographs on Music). 329p. 1996. pap. text 26.00 (*0-19-816604-4*) OUP.

Baldauf, Gretchen S., compiled by. Career Index: A Selective Bibliography for Elementary Schools, 7. LC 89-28611. (Bibliographies & Indexes in Education Ser.: No. 7). 224p. 1990. lib. bdg. 59.95 (*0-313-24832-X*, BCX/, Greenwood Pr) Greenwood.

Baldauf, J. G., jt. ed. see Ramsey, A. T.

***Baldauf, Ken.** Learn Windows NT 4.0 Workstation. LC 97-68880. (Illus.). 164p. 1999. pap. 32.00 incl. cd-rom (*1-58076-242-5*) Que Educ & Trng.

Baldauf, Ken. Windows NT 4.0 Workstation Essentials. LC 97-69641. 1997. 22.99 (*1-57576-993-X*) Que Educ & Trng.

— Windows NT 4.0 Workstation Essentials. annot. ed. 256p. 1998. teacher ed. 49.99 (*1-57576-999-9*) Sams.

— Windows 98 Essentials. 181p. (C). 1998. spiral bd. 22.99 (*1-58076-088-0*) Que Educ & Trng.

***Baldauf, Richard B. & Kaplan, Robert B.** Language Planning in Nepal, Taiwan & Sweden. LC 99-54927. 2000. write for info. (*1-85359-483-0*) Taylor & Francis.

Baldauf, Richard B. & Luke, Allan, eds. Language Planning & Education in Australia & the South Pacific. 290p. 1990. 99.00 (*1-85359-048-7*, Pub. by Multilingual Matters); pap. 44.95 (*1-85359-047-9*, Pub. by Multilingual Matters) Taylor & Francis.

Baldauf, Richard B., jt. auth. see Kaplan, Robert B.

Baldauski, Karen. Cat-Coloring Book. (J). 1950. pap. 2.95 (*0-486-24011-8*) Dover.

Baldauski, Karen, jt. auth. see Gos, Francois.

Balde, J. Electronic Packaging Tradeoffs. 1989. text. write for info. (*0-442-31839-1*, VNR) Wiley.

Balde, Jacob. Carmina Lyrica. (Illus.). xviii, 610p. 1977. reprint ed. 120.00 (*3-487-06236-4*) G Olms Pubs.

Baldegger, Markus, et al. Kontaktschwelle Deutsch als Fremdsprache. 504p. 1993. pap. 54.95 (*3-468-49450-5*) Langenscheidt.

Baldelli, Pia G. Power Politics, Diplomacy, & the Avoidance of Hostilities Between England & the United States in the Wake of the Civil War. Bertozzi, Elena & Ipsen, Cynthia D., trs. from ITA. LC 98-17754. (Studies in American History: Vol. 21). 390p. 1998. 109.95 (*0-7734-8398-5*) E Mellen.

Baldeosingh, Kevin. The Autobiography of Paras P. (Caribbean Writers Ser.). 192p. 1996. pap. 10.95 (*0-435-98818-2*) Heinemann.

— Virgin's Triangle. (Caribbean Writers Ser.). 1997. pap. 13.95 (*0-435-98947-2*) Heinemann.

Balder, A. P. Long Island Sound & the South Shore. (Illus.). 80p. 1994. pap. 39.95 (*0-930151-11-9*) Chartcrafters Pubs.

— Marine Atlas of the Hawaiian Islands. LC 91-45699. (Illus.). 120p. 1992. pap. text 39.00 (*0-8248-1444-4*) UH Pr.

***Balder, A. P.** Mariner's Atlas: South Florida, the Keys & the Bahama Islands the Dry Tortugas, Shark River & Okeechobee Waterway. 132p. 2000. pap. 59.95 (*0-930151-23-2*, Pub. by Chartcrafters Pubs) Firefly Bks Ltd.

— Mariner's Atlas: Southern New England, Long Island Sound & the South Shore. 132p. 2000. pap. 59.95 (*0-930151-22-4*, Pub. by Chartcrafters Pubs) Firefly Bks Ltd.

Balderas, Eduardo, tr. see Dean, Bessie.

Baldereschi, A., ed. The Physics of Latent Image Formation in Silver Halides: Proceedings of the 3rd Symposium, Trieste Italy, 1983. 313p. 1984. 46.00 (*9971-966-34-4*) World Scientific Pub.

Baldereschi, A. & Paorici, C., eds. Epitaxial Electronic Materials. 336p. (C). 1988. text 108.00 (*9971-5-0506-1*) World Scientific Pub.

Balderjahn, I., et al, eds. Classification, Data Analysis & Data Highways. (Studies in Classification, Data Analysis, & Knowledge Organization). (Illus.). x, 414p. 1998. pap. 99.00 (*3-540-63909-8*) Spr-Verlag.

Balderman, Bobbi. Buying Creative Services. (Illus.). 240p. 1995. 39.95 (*0-8442-3497-4*, NTC Business Bks) NTC Contemp Pub Co.

Balderose, Nancy W. Once upon a Pony: A Mountain Christmas. LC 92-13814. (Illus.). 32p. (J). (ps up). 1994. pap. 9.95 (*0-8192-7001-6*) Morehouse Pub.

Balderrama, Francisco E. In Defense of la Raza, the Los Angeles Mexican Consulate, & the Mexican Community, 1929 to 1936. LC 82-11121. 149p. reprint ed. pap. 46.20 (*0-8357-8589-0*, 203496100091) Bks Demand.

Balderrama, Francisco E., et al. Decade of Betrayal: Mexican Repatriation in the 1930's. LC 94-48682. (Illus.). 293p. 1995. reprint ed. pap. 18.95 (*0-8263-1575-5*) U of NM Pr.

***Baldersheim, Harald, ed.** Nordic Region-Building in a European Perspective. LC 98-74704. 7p. 1999. text 61.95 (*0-7546-1001-2*) Ashgate Pub Co.

Baldersheim, Harald & Stahlberg, Krister, eds. Towards the Self-Regulating Municipality: Free Communes & Administrative Modernization in Scandinavia. 242p. 1994. 81.95 (*1-85521-553-5*, Pub. by Dartmth Pub) Ashgate Pub Co.

Balderson, D. Small Business Management: Cases & Incidents: Canadian Version. (C). 1989. text 36.95 (*0-256-07834-3*, Irwn McGrw-H) McGrw-H Hghr Educ.

Balderson, John L., jt. auth. see Davis, Reba B.

Balderson, Robert H. The Official Guide to Gunmarks. 3rd ed. (Illus.). 352p. 1996. pap. 15.00 (*0-676-60039-5*) Hse Collectbls.

— The Official Price Guide to Antique & Modern Firearms. 9th ed. 672p. 1996. pap. 17.00 (*0-87637-907-2*) Hse Collectbls.

— Official Price Guide to Collector Handguns. 5th ed. 560p. 1997. pap. 17.00 (*0-676-60038-7*) Random.

Balderston, Daniel. Out of Context: Historical Reference & the Representation of Reality in Borges. LC 92-23417. 231p. 1993. text 49.95 (*0-8223-1289-1*); pap. text 18.95 (*0-8223-1316-2*) Duke.

Balderston, Daniel, compiled by. The Latin American Short Story: An Annotated Guide to Anthologies & Criticism, 34. LC 92-7336. (Bibliographies & Indexes in World Literature Ser.: No. 34). 552p. 1992. lib. bdg. 79.50 (*0-313-27360-X*, BLJ, Greenwood Pr) Greenwood.

— The Literary Universe of Jorge Luis Borges: An Index to References & Allusions to Persons, Titles & Places in His Writings, 9. LC 86-14947. (Bibliographies & Indexes in World Literature Ser.: No. 9). 306p. 1986. lib. bdg. 75.00 (*0-313-25083-9*, BWS/) Greenwood.

Balderston, Daniel & Guy, Donna J., eds. Sex & Sexuality in Latin America. LC 96-35697. 320p. (C). 1997. text 55.00 (*0-8147-1289-4*); pap. text 20.00 (*0-8147-1290-8*) NYU Pr.

*__Balderston, Daniel, et al.__ Encyclopedia of Contemporary Latin American & Caribbean Cultures. LC 00-32303. 2000. write for info. (*0-415-22973-1*) Routledge.

Balderston, Daniel, ed. see Jitrik, Noe, et al.

Balderston, Daniel, tr. see Bianco, Jose.

Balderston, Daniel, tr. see Molloy, Sylvia.

Balderston, Daniel, tr. see Piglia, Ricardo.

Balderston, David. The Harbour Ferries of Auckland. 104p. (C). 1988. 75.00 (*1-86934-004-3*, Pub. by Grantham Hse) St Mut.

Balderston, Frederick E. Managing Today's University. LC 74-9111. (Jossey-Bass Higher Education Ser.). 325p. 1974. reprint ed. pap. 100.80 (*0-608-14785-0*, 202564900045) Bks Demand.

— Managing Today's University: Strategies for Viability, Change, & Excellence. 2nd ed. LC 94-25143. 421p. 1995. text 36.95 (*0-7879-0072-9*) Jossey-Bass.

Balderston, Judith, et al. Malnourished Children of the Rural Poor: The Web of Food, Health, Education, Fertility, & Agricultural Production. LC 81-3483. 223p. 1981. 24.95 (*0-86569-071-5*, Auburn Hse) Greenwood.

Balderston, Katharine C. The History & Sources of Percy's Memoir of Goldsmith. (BCL1-PR English Literature Ser.). 61p. 1992. reprint ed. lib. bdg. 59.00 (*0-7812-7358-7*) Rprt Serv.

Balderston, Katherine C. The History & Sources of Percy's Memoir of Goldsmith, 1926. 1928. 29.00 (*0-527-04700-7*) Periodicals Srv.

Balderston, Katherine G., ed. see Goldsmith, Oliver.

Balderston, Marion, ed. see Claypoole, James.

Balderston, Marion R., et al. Passengers & Ships Prior to 1684, Penn's Colony, Vol. 1. Sheppard, Walter Lee, Jr., ed. 245p. 1992. reprint ed. pap. 21.00 (*1-55613-664-1*) Heritage Bk.

Balderston, Richard A., et al, eds. The Hip. (Illus.). 544p. 1991. 149.50 (*0-8121-1302-0*) Lppncott W & W.

Balderston, Richard A. & An, Howard S. Complications in Spinal Surgery. (Illus.). 208p. 1990. text 70.00 (*0-7216-3522-9*, W B Saunders Co) Harcrt Hlth Sci Grp.

Balderston, Theo, tr. see Holtfrerich, Carl-Ludwig.

Balderstone, David, jt. auth. see Lambert, David.

Balderstone, Steven J., jt. auth. see Mabin, Victoria J.

Baldes, Maria. The Annihilator of Diabetes: The Propeller from Hell. LC 99-90486. 365p. 1999. 25.00 (*0-7388-0416-9*); pap. 15.00 (*0-7388-0417-7*) Xlibris Corp.

Baldeschwieler, John D., ed. Chemistry & Chemical Engineering in the People's Republic of China. LC 79-11217. 266p. 1979. pap. 14.95 (*0-8412-0502-7*) Am Chemical.

*__Baldessari, John.__ Metaphor Problem: Again. 2000. pap. 35.00 (*3-88375-404-8*) Walther Konig.

— While Something Is Happening Here... 2000. 30.00 (*3-88375-396-3*) Walther Konig.

Baldessarini, Ross J. Chemotherapy in Psychiatry. enl. rev. ed. (Illus.). 416p. 1985. 44.00 (*0-674-11383-7*) HUP.

Baldev, B., jt. auth. see Mahajan.

Baldeweg, Juan N. & Bonet, Juan M. Juan Navano Baldeweg. 176p. 2000. 45.00 (*1-58423-013-4*) Gingko Press.

*__Baldi, Philip.__ The Foundations of Latin. LC 98-51324. xviii, 534p. 1999. 192.30 (*3-11-016294-6*) De Gruyter.

Baldi, Philip. An Introduction to the Indo-European Languages. LC 82-19218. 208p. 1983. pap. 24.95 (*0-8093-1091-0*) S Ill U Pr.

Baldi, Philip, ed. Linguistic Change & Reconstruction Methodology. (Trends in Linguistics, Studies & Monographs: No. 45). (Illus.). xii, 752p. (C). 1990. lib. bdg. 213.85 (*0-89925-546-9*) Mouton.

Baldi, Philip & Werth, Ronald N., eds. Readings in Historical Phonology: Chapters in the Theory of Sound Change. LC 77-13895. (C). 1978. pap. 18.95 (*0-271-00539-4*) Pa St U Pr.

Baldi, Phillip, ed. Patterns of Change, Change of Patterns: Linguistic Change & Reconstruction Methodology. LC 91-34032. xii, 343p. (Orig.). (C). 1991. pap. text 43.60 (*3-11-013405-5*) Mouton.

Baldi, Pierre & Brunak, Soren. Bioinformatics: The Machine Learning Approach. LC 97-36102. (Adaptive Computation & Machine Learning Ser.). (Illus.). 360p. 1998. 44.00 (*0-262-02442-X*, Bradford Bks) MIT Pr.

Baldi, Roberto. Distributorship, Franchising, Agency. 280p. 1987. 84.00 (*90-6544-329-0*) Kluwer Law Intl.

Baldi, T. Mid-Tertiary Stratigraphy & Paleogeographic Evolution of Hungary. rev. ed. (Illus.). 201p. (C). 1986. 60.00 (*963-05-3945-4*, Pub. by Akade Kiado) St Mut.

Baldi, T. & Senes, Jan. Om Egerien. Die Egerer, Pouzdraner, Puchkirchener Schichtengruppe und die Bretkaer Formation, Band V. (Chronostratigraphie und Neostratotypen Ser.). (DUT.). 580p. 1975. 38.00 (*3-510-60005-3*, Pub. by E Schweizerbartsche) Balogh.

Baldick. Imaginary Muslims. Date not set. text. write for info. (*1-85043-497-2*) I B T.

Baldick, Chris. The Concise Oxford Dictionary of Literary Terms. (Oxford Paperback Reference Ser.). 256p. 1992. reprint ed. pap. 13.95 (*0-19-282893-2*) OUP.

— Criticism Literary Theory. LC 95-40515. (Literature in English Ser.). 304p. (C). 1996. pap. text 24.38 (*0-582-03383-7*, Pub. by Addison-Wesley) Longman.

— In Frankenstein's Shadow: Myth, Monstrosity & Nineteenth-Century Writing. (Illus.). 218p. 1990. reprint ed. pap. text 18.95 (*0-19-812249-7*) OUP.

— The Social Mission of English Criticism, 1848-1932. (Oxford English Monographs). 255p. 1983. 65.00 (*0-19-812821-5*) OUP.

— The Social Mission of English Criticism, 1848-1932. (Oxford English Monographs). 260p. 1987. pap. text 24.00 (*0-19-812979-3*) OUP.

Baldick, Chris, ed. The Oxford Book of Gothic Tales. LC 92-41146. 566p. 1993. pap. 15.95 (*0-19-283117-8*) OUP.

Baldick, Chris, ed. see Polidori, John W.

Baldick, Julian. Black God. 245p. 1997. text 59.50 (*1-86064-123-7*, Pub. by I B T) St Martin.

— Black God: An Afroasiatic Roots of the Jewish, Christian & Muslim Religions. LC 98-15229. 1998. pap. text 19.95 (*0-8156-0522-6*) Syracuse U Pr.

— Imaginary Muslims: The Uwaysi Mystics of Central Asia. LC 92-36918. 300p. (C). 1993. pap. text 22.50 (*0-8147-1207-X*) NYU Pr.

— Imaginary Muslims: The Uwaysi Mystics of Central Asia. LC 92-36918. 300p. (C). 1993. text 55.00 (*0-8147-1206-1*) NYU Pr.

— Mystical Islam: An Introduction to Sufism. 192p. (C). 1989. text 50.00 (*0-8147-1138-3*); pap. text 18.50 (*0-8147-1139-1*) NYU Pr.

Baldick, Robert, tr. see Barbusse, Henri.

Baldick, Robert, tr. see Flaubert, Gustave.

Baldick, Robert, tr. see Huysmans, J. K.

Baldick, Robert, tr. see Simenon, Georges.

Baldin, A. M., et al, eds. Relativistic Nuclear Physics & Quantum Chromodynamics. 670p. (C). 1991. text 118.00 (*981-02-0785-9*) World Scientific Pub.

Baldin, Lou. In League with a UFO. LC 97-72781. (Orig.). 1997. pap. 12.95 (*1-890622-03-6*) Leathers Pub.

Balding, K. M., jt. auth. see Gaeta, B. A.

Baldinger, Jo Ann, ed. see Duran, Laurel.

Baldinger, Kathleen O. The World's Oldest Health Plan: Health, Nutrition & Healing from the Bible. LC 93-85138. 352p. 1994. pap. 14.95 (*0-914984-57-8*) Starburst.

Baldinger, Kathleen O'Bannon. Health & Nutrition. Richards, Larry, ed. (God's Word for the Biblically-Inept Ser.). (Illus.). 352p. 1999. pap. 16.95 (*0-914984-05-5*, Pub. by Starburst) Natl Bk Netwk.

*__Baldinger, Pam.__ Distribution of Goods in China: Regulatory Framework & Business Options. (Special Report Ser.). 54p. 1998. pap. 75.00 (*1-929892-01-2*) US-China Bus Cnl.

Baldinger, Sandra, jt. auth. see Smith, Katherine P.

Baldini, Baccio. Discorso Sopra la Mascherata Della Genealogia Delg'Iddei, Repr. of 1565 Ed. LC 75-27852. (Renaissance & the Gods Ser.: Vol. 10). (Illus.). 1976. lib. bdg. 88.00 (*0-8240-2059-6*) Garland.

Baldini, Enrico, jt. auth. see Freedberg, David.

Baldini, Francesco, et al, eds. Biomedical Systems & Technologies II, Vol. 3199. LC 98-162135. (Europto Ser.). 316p. 1998. 80.00 (*0-8194-2631-8*) SPIE.

Baldini, Pier R., ed. Italian Renaissance Studies in Arizona. 211p. (C). 1989. pap. 15.00 (*0-685-26158-1*) Rosary IL.

Baldini, Pier R., jt. auth. see Lebano, Edoardo A.

Baldini, Umberto & Casazza, Ornella. The Brancacci Chapel. (Illus.). 378p. 1992. 125.00 (*0-8109-3120-6*, Pub. by Abrams) Time Warner.

*__Baldino, Rachel Greene.__ Welcome to Methadonia: A Social Worker's Candid Account of Life in a Methadone Clinic. LC 00-9137. 206p. (C). 2000. pap. 15.95 (*1-929109-02-4*) White Hat.

Baldinucci, Filippo. Vocabolario Toscano Dell'arte Del Disegno. fac. ed. (Documents of Art & Architectural History Ser. 1: Vol. 5). (ITA., Illus.). 1980. lib. bdg. 45.00 (*0-89371-105-5*) Broude Intl Edns.

Baldizonne, Gianni. Timeless Earth: Journey Across India. 1996. 45.00 (*0-944142-72-9*, Pub. by Mapin Pubng) Antique Collect.

Baldizzone, Gianni, jt. auth. see Baldizzone, Tiziana.

Baldizzone, Tiziana & Baldizzone, Gianni. Tibet: Journey to the Forbidden City. (Illus.). 160p. 1997. 40.00 (*1-55670-511-5*) Stewart Tabori & Chang.

Baldizzoni, Gianni, jt. auth. see Baldizzoni, Tiziana.

Baldizzoni, Tiziana & Baldizzoni, Gianni. Tales from the River Brahmaputra. LC 98-23050. (Illus.). 1998. 65.00 (*1-57062-401-1*, Pub. by Shambhala Pubns) Random.

Baldner, Jean V. Pebbles in the Wind. (Illus.). 52p. (Orig.). (YA). (gr. 7 up). pap. 5.95 (*0-9615317-0-3*) Baldner J V.

Baldner, Ralph W. Bibliography of Seventeenth-Century French Prose Fiction. LC 67-28711. xiv, 197p. 1967. lib. bdg. 37.50 (*0-87352-016-5*, Z0030) Modern Lang.

Baldo, B. A., ed. Molecular Approaches to the Study of Allergens. (Monographs in Allergy: Vol. 28). (Illus.). viii, 166p. 1990. 185.25 (*3-8055-5213-0*) S Karger.

Baldo, B. A. & Tovey, E. R., eds. Protein Blotting: Methodology, Research & Diagnostic Application. (Illus.). viii, 168p. 1989. 97.50 (*3-8055-4881-8*) S Karger.

Baldo, Jonathan. The Unmasking of Drama: Contested Representation in Shakespeare's Tragedies. 240p. 1996. 39.95 (*0-8143-2598-X*) Wayne St U Pr.

Baldo, M. Nuclear Methods & Nuclear Equations of State. LC 99-30643. 600p. 1997. text 109.00 (*981-02-2165-7*) World Scientific Pub.

Baldo, S., et al. Fractals in Engineering: Proceedings of the Conference on Fractals in Engineering '94. 296p. 1995. text 99.00 (*981-02-1835-4*) World Scientific Pub.

Baldock. Cube Route. LC 99-53073. (Illus.). 270p. 2000. 32.95 (*0-471-72032-1*) Wiley.

*__Baldock, Carole.__ How to Raise Confident Children. 2000. pap. 10.95 (*0-85969-828-9*, Pub. by Sheldon Pr) Intl Pubs Mktg.

Baldock, Carole. How to Succeed as a Single Parent. 1999. pap. text 11.95 (*0-85969-805-X*) S C K Pubns.

— Making Money from Writing: How to Become a Freelance Writer. 144p. 1998. pap. 19.95 (*1-85703-244-6*, Pub. by How To Bks) Trans-Atl Phila.

— Writing Reviews: How to Write about Arts & Leisure for Pleasure & Profit. (Successful Writing Ser.). (Illus.). 128p. 1996. pap. 19.95 (*1-85703-441-4*, Pub. by How To Bks) Trans-Atl Phila.

Baldock, Cora V. & Lally, James. Sociology in Australia & New Zealand: Theory & Methods, 16. LC 72-778. (Contributions in Sociology Ser.: No. 16). (Illus.). 328p. 1974. 75.00 (*0-8371-6126-6*, BSA/, Greenwood Pr) Greenwood.

Baldock, John. Alternative Gospel. LC 97-43906. 1998. pap. 14.95 (*1-86204-165-2*, Pub. by Element MA) Penguin Putnam.

— Elements of Christian Symbolism. (Elements of...Ser.). 144p. 1997. pap. 9.95 (*1-86204-139-3*, Pub. by Element MA) Penguin Putnam.

— The Little Book of Bible. (Little Bks.). (Illus.). 48p. 1993. pap. 5.95 (*1-85230-447-2*, Pub. by Element MA) Penguin Putnam.

— The Little Book of Love. LC 98-188282. (Little Bks.). (Illus.). 48p. 1997. pap. 5.95 (*1-86204-050-8*, Pub. by Element MA) Penguin Putnam.

— The Little Book of Sufi Wisdom. LC 95-30359. (Illus.). 48p. 1995. pap. 5.95 (*1-85230-717-X*, Pub. by Element MA) Penguin Putnam.

— Little Book of Zen Wisdom. 48p. 1994. pap. 5.95 (*1-85230-563-0*, Pub. by Element MA) Penguin Putnam.

*__Baldock, John.__ Social Policy. LC 99-12998. 1999. write for info. (*0-19-878173-3*); write for info. (*0-19-878174-1*) OUP.

Baldock, Marion. Greek Tragedy: An Introduction. (Classical World Ser.). (Illus.). 104p. (C). 1989. pap. 18.95 (*1-85399-119-8*, Pub. by Brist Class Pr) Focus Pub-R Pullins.

*__Baldock, Richard & Graham, Jim, eds.__ Image Processing & Analysis. (The Practical Approach Ser.: 219). (Illus.). 320p. 2000. text 120.00 (*0-19-963701-6*) OUP.

— Image Processing & Analysis. (The Practical Approach Ser.: No. 219). (Illus.). 320p. 2000. pap. text 60.00 (*0-19-963700-8*) OUP.

Baldock, Robert. Destination Z: The History of the Future. LC 98-35070. (Illus.). 296p. 1999. 29.95 (*0-471-98462-0*) Wiley.

*__Baldock, Robert.__ Introduction to Modern German Poetry. 296p. 2000. pap. 19.95 (*0-471-86161-8*) Wiley.

Baldomir, D. & Hammond, P. Geometry of Electromagnetic Systems, Vol. 33. (Monographs in Electrical & Electronic Engineering: No. 39). (Illus.). 250p. (C). 1996. text 100.00 (*0-19-859187-X*, Clarendon Pr) OUP.

Baldoni, V. Representations of Lie Groups & Quantum Groups. 1994. pap. 89.95 (*0-582-23179-5*) Longman.

Baldor, Juan A. A Beginning Course in Spanish. (Illus.). viii, 358p. (Orig.). 1990. pap. text 24.99 (*0-9673147-0-4*) Allied Pubg.

— A Beginning Course in Spanish. 375p. (Orig.). (C). 1990. pap. text 24.95 (*0-9625897-0-5*) DonMar Pub.

— A Beginning Course in Spanish: Activity Manual. (Illus.). v, 238p. 1999. pap. text. write for info. (*0-9673147-1-2*) Allied Pubg.

Baldor, Robert A. Managed Care Made Simple. LC 95-9515. 1995. pap. 21.95 (*0-86542-474-8*) Blackwell Sci.

*__Baldor, Robert A.__ Managed Care Made Simple. 2nd ed. LC 97-43321. (Illus.). 1998. pap. 23.95 (*0-632-04378-4*) Blackwell Sci.

Baldovin, John F. City, Church & Renewal. (Worship Ser.). 1991. pap. 14.95 (*0-912405-78-3*, Pastoral Press) OR Catholic.

Baldovin, John F., ed. see Hovda, Robert W.

Baldovin, John F., jt. ed. see Mitchell, Nathan D.

Baldrich, Juan J. Sembraron la No Siembra: Los Cosecheros de Tabaco Puertorriquenos Frente a las Corporaciones Tabacaleras, 1920-1934. LC 88-81126. (Coleccion Semilla). (SPA.). 194p. 1988. pap. 7.50 (*0-940238-08-X*) Ediciones Huracan.

Baldridge, Alan, jt. auth. see Davis, John.

Baldridge, Blanche J. Hamlett. My Virginia Kin, Comprising the Hamlett, Witt, Giles, Wills, Eubank-Furtune, Mullenix, Lynchard, Talbot & Kight Families, with a Short Treatise on the Loving Family. (Illus.). 240p. 1997. reprint ed. pap. 37.00 (*0-8328-8936-9*); reprint ed. lib. bdg. 47.00 (*0-8328-8935-0*) Higginson Bk Co.

Baldridge, Carol. Illinois Through the Decades Fact Cards. (Illus.). 70p. (J). (gr. 4-8). 2000. ring bd. 34.00 (*1-884925-73-1*) Toucan Valley.

— Texas Indians Fact Cards. (Illus.). 64p. (J). (gr. 4-8). 1997. ring bd. 29.00 (*1-884925-53-7*) Toucan Valley.

— Texas Missions Fact Cards. (Illus.). 86p. (J). (gr. 4-8). 1998. ring bd. 34.00 (*1-884925-58-8*) Toucan Valley.

Baldridge, Cates. The Dialogics of Dissent in the English Novel. LC 93-41021. 219p. (C). 1994. text 40.00 (*0-87451-666-8*) U Pr of New Eng.

— Graham Greene's Fictions: The Virtues of Extremity. LC 99-47291. 224p. 2000. 34.95 (*0-8262-1251-4*) U of Mo Pr.

Baldridge, Cyrus L., jt. auth. see Singer, Caroline.

Baldridge, Gary. Keith Parks: Breaking Barriers & Opening Frontiers. LC 99-14808. 112p. 1999. 12.00 (*1-57312-286-6*) Smyth & Helwys.

Baldridge, J. Victor. Power & Conflict in the University: Research in the Sociology of Complex Organizations. LC 70-140548. 254p. reprint ed. 78.80 (*0-8357-9957-3*, 201311300085) Bks Demand.

Baldridge, J. Victor & Deal, Terrence E., eds. The Dynamics of Organizational Change in Education. rev. ed. LC 82-62033. 504p. 1983. 44.00 (*0-8211-0134-X*) McCutchan.

Baldridge, J. Victor, et al. Policy Making & Effective Leadership. LC 77-82909. (Jossey-Bass Series in Higher Education). 318p. reprint ed. pap. 98.60 (*0-8357-4932-0*, 203786200009) Bks Demand.

Baldridge, J. Victor, jt. auth. see Kemerer, Frank R.

Baldridge, Joy. Fast Forward MBA in Self-Managed Selling. 216p. 1999. pap. 16.95 (*0-471-34854-6*) Wiley.

Baldridge, Melissa, ed. Visions of the West: Art & Artifacts From the Private Collections of J. P. Bryan, Torch Energy Advisors Incorporated, & Others. LC 99-11445. (Illus.). 320p. 1999. 60.00 (*0-87905-854-4*) Gibbs Smith Pub.

Baldridge, Robert C. Spearfishing Diaries, 1959-61. (Illus.). 51p. 1997. 19.95 (*1-57638-099-8*) Merriam Pr.

— Victory Road. 3rd ed. LC 95-80653. (World War II Memoir Ser.: No. 212). (Illus.). 156p. 1998. pap. 24.95 (*1-57638-000-9*, M212-S) Merriam Pr.

— Victory Road. 3rd rev. ed. LC 95-80653. (World War II Memoir Ser.: Vol. 212). (Illus.). 156p. 1997. 31.95 (*1-57638-043-2*, M212H) Merriam Pr.

Baldridge, Victor J., jt. ed. see Riley, Gary L.

Baldridge, W. S., et al, eds. Rio Grande Rift: Northern New Mexico. (Guidebook Ser.: No. 35). (Illus.). 379p. 1984. 45.00 (*1-58546-070-2*) NMex Geol Soc.

Baldrige, Alan, jt. auth. see Gordon, David G.

Baldrige, Letitia. Amy Vanderbilt's Everyday Etiquette: Answers to Today's Etiquette Questions. 12.09 (*0-606-02055-1*, Pub. by Turtleback) Demco.

*__Baldrige, Letitia.__ Legendary Brides: The World's Most Celebrated Weddings & How to Recreate Their Magic. 176p. 2000. 50.00 (*0-06-019559-2*, HarpCollins) HarperTrade.

Baldrige, Letitia. Letitia Baldrige's Complete Guide to the New Manners for the '90s. (Illus.). 672p. 1990. 30.00 (*0-89256-320-6*) S&S Trade.

— Letitia Baldrige's More Than Manners. LC 96-50980. 1997. 23.00 (*0-684-81875-2*, Scribners Ref) Mac Lib Ref.

— Letitia Baldrige's New Complete Guide to Executive Manners. rev. ed. 672p. 1993. 40.00 (*0-89256-362-1*, Rawson Assocs) Macmillan.

Baldrige, Letitia, ed. In the Kennedy Style: The Most Memorable Occasions of the JFK White House. LC 97-39466. (Illus.). 144p. 1998. 29.95 (*0-385-48964-1*) Doubleday.

Baldry, C. Computers, Jobs, & Skills: The Industrial Relations of Technological Change. LC 88-23384. (Approaches to Information Technology Ser.). (Illus.). 212p. (C). 1988. pap. 49.50 (*0-306-42963-2*, Plenum Trade) Perseus Pubng.

Baldry, Cherith. Cradoc's Quest. Reck, Sue, ed. (Saga of the Six Worlds Ser.). 160p. (YA). (gr. 8-12). 1994. pap. 4.99 (*0-7814-0093-7*, Chariot Bks) Chariot Victor.

*__Baldry, Cherith.__ Exiled from Camelot. 320p. 2000. pap. 14.95 (*1-928999-16-6*) Green Knight.

— Mutiny in Space. (Illus.). 128p. (J). pap. 7.95 (*0-14-038489-8*, Pub. by Pnguin Bks Ltd) Trafalgar.

Baldry, Cherith. Rite of Brotherhood. Reck, Sue, ed. LC 94-17037. (Saga of the Six Worlds Ser.: Vol. 3). 160p. (J). (gr. 5-9). 1994. pap. 4.99 (*0-7814-0094-5*, Chariot Bks) Chariot Victor.

— Storm Wind. Reck, Sue, ed. LC 94-30488. (Saga of the Six Worlds Ser.: Vol. 1). 160p. (J). (gr. 4-7). 1994. pap. 4.99 (*0-7814-0095-3*, Chariot Bks) Chariot Victor.

Baldry, David, et al. Environmental Impact Assessment of Settlement & Development in the Upper Leraba Basin: Burkina Faso, Cote d'Ivoire, & Mali. LC 95-37033. (Technical Papers: No. 302). 56p. 1995. pap. 22.00 (*0-8213-3435-2*, 13435) World Bank.

Baldry, H. C. The Voice of Greece: The First Great Literature & Its Living Context. rev. ed. (Illus.). 64p. (C). 1991. pap. text 1.75 (*1-877891-25-8*) Paperbook Pr Inc.

Baldry, P. E. The Battle Against Heart Disease: A Physician Traces the History of Man's Achievements in this Field for the General Reader. LC 75-108098. 200p. reprint ed. pap. 57.00 (*0-8357-5996-2*, 2022434) Bks Demand.

Balducci, Carolyn, jt. ed. see Balducci, Gioacchino.

Balducci, Corrado. The Devil: Alive & Active in Our World. Aymann, Jordan, tr. LC 90-39458. 197p. (Orig.). 1990. pap. 9.95 (*0-8189-0586-7*) Alba.

Balducci, Gioacchino & Balducci, Carolyn, eds. Eyewear & Contact Lenses for Sports. Orig. Title: Occhiali e Lenti a Contatto Nello Sport. (Illus.). 64p. 1996. pap. 19.95 (*0-9652465-5-8*) Leonardo MI.

Balducci, Lodovico, et al, eds. Comprehensive Geriatric Oncology. 824p. 1997. text 120.00 (*90-5702-225-7*, Harwood Acad Pubs) Gordon & Breach.

Balducci, Lodovico, et al. Geriatric Oncology. (Illus.). 496p. 1992. text 103.00 (*0-397-51210-4*) Lppncott W & W.

*__Balducci, Rita.__ Amber. (Jelly Tale Bks.). (Illus.). 5p. (J). (ps-k). 2000. bds. 4.99 (*1-57584-687-X*, Pub. by Rdrs Digest) S&S Trade.

Balducci, Rita. Barbie & Kelly's Special Day. (Barbie Lift & Learn Flap Book Ser.). (Illus.). 10p. (J). (gr. k-3). 1999. bds. 8.99 (*1-57584-337-4*, Pub. by Rdrs Digest) Random.

*__Balducci, Rita.__ Bouncy. (Jelly Tale Bks.). (Illus.). 5p. (J). (ps). 2000. bds. 4.99 (*1-57584-686-1*, Pub. by Rdrs Digest) S&S Trade.

Balducci, Rita. Eddie's New Whistle. (Fisher-Price Sidesqueaker Play Bks.). (Illus.). 16p. (J). 1998. bds. 3.99 (*1-57584-085-5*, Pub. by Rdrs Digest) Random.

An Asterisk (*) at the beginning of an entry indicates that the title is appearing for the first time.

— Engineering Mechanics: Combined Statics & Dynamics. 8th ed. 34p. (C). 1999. write for info. (*0-13-016608-1*) S&S Trade.
— I Can Button ! (I Can Do It! Bks.: Vol. 2). (Illus.). 10p. (J). (gr. k-3). 1999. bds. 4.99 (*1-57584-276-9*, Pub. by Rdrs Digest) Random.
— I Can Lace! (I Can Do It! Bks.: Vol. 1). (Illus.). 10p. (J). (gr. k-3). 1999. bds. 4.99 (*1-57584-275-0*, Pub. by Rdrs Digest) Random.
— Kelly's Super Saturday. (Barbie Lift & Learn Ser.). (Illus.). 5p. (J). (gr. k-3). 2000. bds. 8.99 (*1-57584-410-9*, RD Childrens) Rdrs Digest.
***Balducci, Rita.** Magic Holiday: Storybook, Necklace & Gift Box Mini Craft Kit. (Barbie Ser.). (Illus.). 16p. (J). (gr. 1-4). 2000. bds. 6.99 (*1-57584-449-4*, Pub. by Rdrs Digest) S&S Trade.
Balducci, Rita. Mix & Match Fashions: Story Book & Key Chain Craft Kit. (Barbie Mix & Match Bks.). (Illus.). 16p. (J). (gr. k-3). 1999. spiral bd. 7.99 (*1-57584-334-X*, Pub. by Rdrs Digest) S&S Trade.
— The Nutcracker. (Little Golden Storybks.). (J). 1997. 3.99 (*0-307-16177-3*, 16177, Goldn Books) Gldn Bks Pub Co.
— The Poky Little Puppy's Busy Counting Book. (Super Shape Bks.). (Illus.). 24p. (J). (ps-3). 1994. pap. 3.29 (*0-307-10015-4*, 10015) Gldn Bks Pub Co.
— Scarecrow Mix: Halloween Pigs/Happy Scarecrow. (J). 1999. pap. text 4.50 (*1-55254-089-8*) Brighter Vision.
— Shopping Surprise. (Barbie Glittery Window Bks.). (Illus.). 12p. (J). (gr. k-3). 2000. bds. 4.99 (*1-57584-408-7*, RD Childrens) Rdrs Digest.
— What Shall I Be? (Barbie Carry Along Ser.). (Illus.). 20p. (J). (gr. k-3). 1999. bds. 11.99 (*1-57584-336-6*, Pub. by Rdrs Digest) S&S Trade.
Balducci, Rita & Reader's Digest Editors. Fire Chief Ladybug. (Pull Back & Go Bks.: No. 1). (Illus.). 10p. (J). (gr. k-3). 1998. bds. 7.99 (*1-57584-211-4*, Pub. by Rdrs Digest) Random.
— Mail Carrier Spider: I'm a Book with Wheels. (Pull-Back 'n Go Ser.: No. 3). (Illus.). 10p. (J). (gr. k-3). 1998. bds. 7.99 (*1-57584-213-0*, Pub. by Rdrs Digest) Random.
— Officer Beetle: I'm a Book with Wheels. (Pull-Back 'n Go Bks.: No. 4). (Illus.). 10p. (J). (gr. k-3). 1998. bds. 7.99 (*1-57584-214-9*, Pub. by Rdrs Digest) Random.
— Pilot Bee: I'm a Book with Wheels. (Pull-Back 'n Go Bks.: No. 2). (Illus.). 10p. (J). (gr. k-3). 1998. bds. 7.99 (*1-57584-212-2*, Pub. by Rdrs Digest) Random.
Balducci, Rita, jt. auth. see Miller, Sara.
Balducci, Rita W. Cinderella. LC 97-80132. (Wonderful World of Disney Ser.). 80p. (J). (gr. 3-7). 1997. pap. 3.25 (*0-7868-4209-1*, Pub. by Disney Pr) Time Warner.
— Halloween Pigs. LC 97-224940. (Illus.). 32p. (J). 1997. pap. 3.50 (*0-8167-4373-8*) Troll Communs.
Balduini, C., jt. ed. see Zwilling, R.
Baldus, Christian. Regelhafte Vertragsauslegung Nach Parteirollen Im Klassischen Romischen Recht Und in der Modernen Volkerrechtswissenschaft: Zur Rezeptionsfahigkeit Romischen Rechtsdenkens. XIV, 930p. 1998. 113.95 (*3-631-34296-9*) P Lang Pubng.
Baldus, David C. & Cole, James L. Statistical Proof of Discrimination. 386p. 1980. text 95.00 (*0-07-003470-2*) Shepards.
Baldus, David C., et al. Equal Justice & the Death Penalty: A Legal & Empirical Analysis. 752p. 1990. text 70.00 (*1-55553-056-7*) NE U Pr.
Baldus, Harold L., jt. auth. see Baldus, Phil.
Baldus, Harold L., jt. auth. see Baldus, Phillip R.
Baldus, Phil & Baldus, Harold. Homage to the Alphabet: Over Fourteen Hundred Large-Format Complete Showings of Headline Typefaces. 2nd ed. LC 85-60114. (Illus.). 652p. 1985. 68.00 (*0-685-10300-5*); pap. 35.00 (*0-933107-00-5*) Phils Photo.
Baldus, Phillip R. & Baldus, Harold L. You Can Teach Old Type New Tricks. (Illus.). 24p. 1985. pap. 10.00 (*0-933107-01-3*) Phils Photo.
Baldus, Wolfgang. Schwarze Post. 696p. 1998. 124.00 (*1-885184-02-6*) Album Pubng.
Balduzzi, D., et al. Libro Degli Esercizi 1. (GER.). 128p. 1997. pap. write for info. (*3-468-96771-3*) Langenscheidt.
Baldwin, et al. The Romance of the Book. deluxe ed. Brooks, Marshall, ed. LC 95-76146. 192p. 1995. 75.00 (*0-913559-32-6*) Birch Brook Pr.
— The Romance of the Book. limited ed. Brooks, Marshall, ed. LC 95-76146. (Illus.). 200p. (Orig.). 1995. pap. 18.00 (*0-913559-28-8*) Birch Brook Pr.
Baldwin, A. Facing Heads on Ancient Greek Coins. (Illus.). 1982. reprint ed. pap. 8.00 (*0-942666-06-2*) S J Durst.
Baldwin, A., et al. International Bid Preparation. LC 96-113426. (International Construction Management Ser.: Vol. 4). ix, 106p. (Orig.). 1995. pap. 13.50 (*92-2-108752-2*) Intl Labour Office.
— International Bidding Case-Study. LC 96-113424. (International Construction Management Ser.: Vol. 2). x, 133p. 1995. pap. 13.50 (*92-2-108268-7*) Intl Labour Office.
Baldwin, A. Dwight, Jr., et al. Beyond Preservation: Restoring & Inventing Landscapes. 256p. 1993. pap. 19.95 (*0-8166-2347-3*); text 49.95 (*0-8166-2346-5*) U of Minn Pr.
Baldwin, A. R., ed. Proceedings of the Seventh International Conference on Jojoba & Its Uses. 453p. 1989. 40.00 (*0-935315-22-5*) Am Oil Chemists.
— The Second World Conference on Detergents: Proceedings. 302p. 1987. 95.00 (*0-935315-14-4*) Am Oil Chemists.
— The World Conference on Emerging Technologies in the Fats & Oils Industry: Proceedings. 432p. 1986. 40.00 (*0-935315-13-6*) Am Oil Chemists.
Baldwin, Agnes. The Electrum & Silver Coins of Chios, Issued During the Sixth, Fifth & Fourth Centuries B.C. A Chronological Study. (Illus.). 60p. 1979. reprint ed. 20.00 (*0-916710-61-0*) Obol Intl.
— Symbolism on Greek Coins. LC 76-62839. (Illus.). 1977. reprint ed. lib. bdg. 30.00 (*0-915262-10-X*) S J Durst.
Baldwin, Agnes, jt. auth. see Baldwin, William P., Jr.
Baldwin, Agnes L. First Settlers of South Carolina, 1670-1700. 264p. 1985. 25.00 (*0-89308-551-0*) Southern Hist Pr.
Baldwin, Alexinia Y. Baldwin Identification Matrix 2. 2nd ed. 22p. 1984. pap., teacher ed. 10.00 (*0-89824-125-1*); pap., student ed. 12.50 (*0-89824-126-X*) Trillium Pr.
Baldwin, Alexinia Y. & Vialle, Wilma. The Many Faces of Giftedness: Lifting the Mask. LC 98-10691. (C). 1998. pap. 46.95 (*0-7668-0006-7*) Delmar.
Baldwin, Alex, pseud. The Last Heroes. (Men at War Ser.: Vol. 1). 1988. mass mkt. 5.99 (*0-671-67822-1*) PB.
— Soldier Spies. (Men at War Ser.: No. 3). 1989. mass mkt. 4.50 (*0-671-68444-2*) PB.
Baldwin, Alicia. Cruisin' No. 6. (Baywatch Sprinter Ser.). (YA). 1996. pap. 3.99 (*0-679-88231-6*, Bullseye Bks) Random Bks Yng Read.
— Heartbreak Hotel. (Baywatch Sprinter Ser.). 1997. pap. 3.99 (*0-679-88418-1*, Bullseye Bks) Random Bks Yng Read.
Baldwin, Allen A. Redeem Us from Virtue. 157p. 1993. pap. 8.95 (*1-880365-36-7*) Prof Pr NC.
Baldwin, Anna & Hutton, Sarah, eds. Platonism & the English Imagination. LC 93-9341. 373p. (C). 1994. text 74.95 (*0-521-40308-1*) Cambridge U Pr.
Baldwin, Anne B. Catherine of Siena: A Biography. LC 86-63595. 192p. (Orig.). 1987. pap. 8.95 (*0-87973-510-4*, 510) Our Sunday Visitor.
Baldwin, Anne R., jt. auth. see Teague, Lynn S.
Baldwin, B., jt. ed. see Kottlowski, F. E.
Baldwin, Barbara. Speak Your Mind: A Public Speaking Program for Middle School Students. Coy, Stanley C., ed. 44p. (C). 1992. teacher ed. 6.50 (*1-881459-03-9*) Eagle Pr SC.
Baldwin, Barbara & Donnelly, Margarita, eds. Calyx International Anthology. (Illus.). 200p. (C). 1997. pap. 12.00 (*0-934971-59-5*) Calyx Bks.
Baldwin, Barry. An Anthology of Byzantine Poetry. (London Studies in Classical Philology: Vol. 14). vii, 241p. 1985. 57.00 (*90-70265-27-3*, Pub. by Gieben) J Benjamins Pubng Co.
— An Anthology of Later Latin Literature. (London Studies in Classical Philology: Vol. 19). 397p. (C). 1987. 60.00 (*90-70265-98-2*, Pub. by Gieben) J Benjamins Pubng Co.
— The Philogelos: or Laughter Lover. (London Studies in Classical Philology: Vol. 10). xii, 134p. (C). 1983. 44.00 (*90-70265-45-1*, Pub. by Gieben) J Benjamins Pubng Co.
— Roman & Byzantine Papers. (London Studies in Classical Philology: Vol. 21). 708p. 1989. 147.00 (*90-5063-017-0*, Pub. by Gieben) J Benjamins Pubng Co.
— Studies in Aulus Gellius. 130p. 1975. 10.00 (*0-87291-071-7*) Coronado Pr.
— Studies on Greek & Roman History & Literature. (London Studies in Classical Philology: Vol. 15). 602p. (C). 1985. lib. bdg. 94.00 (*90-70265-09-5*, Pub. by Gieben) J Benjamins Pubng Co.
— Studies on Late Roman & Byzantine History, Literature & Language. (London Studies in Classical Philology: Vol. 12). 517p. (C). 1984. 94.00 (*90-70265-56-7*, Pub. by Gieben) J Benjamins Pubng Co.
Baldwin, Barry, tr. & intro. see Timarion, English.
Baldwin, Ben C. & Baldwin, Ben S. AFRA Member Directory & Ancestral Surname Registry, Vol. 4. Karns, Kermit B., ed. iv, 26p. 1987. pap. 5.00 (*0-913233-11-0*) AFRA.
Baldwin, Ben G. The Complete Book of Insurance: Protecting Your Life, Health, Property & Income. 275p. 1991. per. 24.95 (*1-55738-235-2*, Irwn Prfssnl) McGraw-Hill Prof.
— The Complete Book of Insurance: The Consumer's Guide to Insuring Your Life, Health, Property & Income. rev. ed. 275p. 1996. pap. 24.95 (*1-55738-880-6*, Irwn Prfssnl) McGraw-Hill Prof.
— New Life Insurance Investment Advisor: Achieving Financial Security for You & Your Family Through Today's Insurance Product, Revised Edition. 2nd rev. ed. LC 94-172094. 350p. 1994. text 24.95 (*1-55738-512-2*, Irwn Prfssnl) McGraw-Hill Prof.
Baldwin, Ben G. & American Bar Association Staff. Lawyers Guide to Insurance. LC 99-25996. 1999. write for info. (*1-57073-671-5*) Amer Bar Assn.
Baldwin, Ben S., ed. AFRA Pedigree Tables, 1991 Vol. 2: American Family Records Association Members. 56p. 1991. pap. 5.00 (*0-913233-19-6*) AFRA.
— AFRA Pedigree Tables, 1991 Vol. 4: American Family Records Association Members. 56p. 1991. pap. 5.00 (*0-913233-21-8*) AFRA.
Baldwin, Ben S., jt. auth. see Baldwin, Ben C.
Baldwin, Ben S., ed. see American Family Records Association Staff.
Baldwin, Bernard. Mountain Ash & Penrhiwceiber Remembered in Pictures. 80p. (C). 1989. 65.00 (*0-905928-50-4*, Pub. by D Brown & Sons Ltd) St Mut.
Baldwin, Betty C., ed. see American Family Records Association Staff.
Baldwin, Bill. Canby's Legion. 368p. (Orig.). 1995. mass mkt. 5.50 (*0-446-60174-8*, Pub. by Warner Bks) Little.
— The Defenders. 320p. (Orig.). 1992. mass mkt. 5.50 (*0-446-36250-6*, Aspect) Warner Bks.
— The Defiance. 368p. (Orig.). 1996. mass mkt. 5.99 (*0-446-60334-1*, Pub. by Warner Bks) Little.
— Galactic Convoy. 320p. 1987. mass mkt. 5.50 (*0-445-20408-7*) Warner Bks.
— The Helmsman. 320p. 1985. mass mkt. 4.99 (*0-445-20027-8*) Warner Bks.
— Mercenaries. 1991. mass mkt. 4.95 (*0-446-36139-9*) Warner Bks.
— The Siege. 320p. (Orig.). 1994. mass mkt. 5.50 (*0-446-36503-3*, Aspect) Warner Bks.
***Baldwin, Bill, ed.** The Trading Game: Inside Lobbying for the North American Free Trade Agreement. (Illus.). 108p. (C). 1999. reprint ed. pap. text 20.00 (*0-7881-8242-0*) DIANE Pub.
Baldwin, Bill, et al. Wings of Freedom: Ghost Squadron of the Confederate Air Force. (Illus.). 61p. (Orig.). 1987. pap. 8.95 (*0-929726-00-6*) Confederate Air.
Baldwin, Billy & Gardine, Michael. Billy Baldwin: An Autobiography. 1985. 24.95 (*0-316-30357-7*) Little.
Baldwin, Bird T., et al. Farm Children: Investigation of Rural Child Life in Selected Areas of Iowa. LC 75-169372. (Family in America Ser.). (Illus.). 1972. reprint ed. 24.95 (*0-405-03848-8*) Ayer.
Baldwin, Bobby. Tales Out of Tulsa. 1984. pap. 6.95 (*0-89746-006-5*) Gambling Times.
Baldwin, Brent, ed. see Zweifel, Karyn.
Baldwin, Bruce. Annual Report Project & Reading. 2nd ed. (Miscellaneous/Catalogs Ser.). (C). 1998. mass mkt. 20.95 (*0-538-87940-8*) S-W Pub.
— Annual Report, Projects/Readings, Financial Accounting. 2nd ed. (AB - Accounting Principles Ser.). 1995. mass mkt. 15.00 (*0-538-85150-3*) S-W Pub.
— Annual Report Supplement. (AB - Accounting Principles Ser.). (C). 1994. pap. 17.95 (*0-538-84290-3*) S-W Pub.
— Financial Accounting Score Builders. 3rd ed. 268p. (C). 1994. pap. text 20.50 (*1-56226-193-2*) CAT Pub.
— Horizons, Tutorial: Linkway. (DA - Computer Education Ser.). (J). (gr. k-8). 1995. pap. 25.95 (*0-538-62596-1*) S-W Pub.
— Scorebuilder for Principles of Accounting, Vol. I. 181p. (C). 1989. pap. text 19.95 (*0-256-07831-9*, 01-3037-01, Irwn McGrw-H) McGraw-H Hghr Educ.
— Scorebuilder for Principles of Accounting, Vol. II. 179p. (C). 1989. pap. text 19.95 (*0-256-07832-7*, 01-3038-01, Irwn McGrw-H) McGraw-H Hghr Educ.
Baldwin, Bruce & Pattison, Diana. Managerial Accounting Score Builders. 3rd ed. 224p. (C). 1994. pap. text 18.65 (*1-56226-194-0*) CAT Pub.
Baldwin, Bruce & Pattison, Diane. Managerial Accounting Score Builders. 2nd ed. (C). 1994. pap. text, student ed. 13.25 (*0-256-17604-3*, Irwn McGrw-H) McGrw-H Hghr Educ.
Baldwin, Bruce, jt. auth. see Ingram.
Baldwin, Bruce A. Beyond the Cornucopia Kids: How to Raise Healthy Achieving Children. LC 88-70117. 286p. (Orig.). 1988. pap. 12.95 (*0-933583-07-9*) Direction Dynamics.
— Financial Accounting: Information for Decisions. 3rd ed. 1997. 15.50 (*0-538-87063-X*) Thomson Learn.
— Getting Better Together: Living the Good Life with Someone You Love. LC 93-90785. 318p. (Orig.). 1993. pap. 12.95 (*0-933583-20-6*) Direction Dynamics.
— It's All in Your Head: Lifestyle Management Strategies for Busy People! (Illus.). 270p. (Orig.). 1985. pap. 12.95 (*0-933583-00-1*) Direction Dynamics.
Baldwin, C. Candee Genealogy, with Notices of Allied Families. (Illus.). 240p. 1989. reprint ed. pap. 32.00 (*0-8328-1303-6*); reprint ed. lib. bdg. 42.00 (*0-8328-1302-8*) Higginson Bk Co.
Baldwin, C. & Paul, H. G., eds. English Poems. (Granger Poetry Library). 416p. 1985. reprint ed. 45.00 (*0-89609-244-5*) Roth Pub Inc.
Baldwin, C. S. Renaissance Literary Theory & Practice. 1959. 16.50 (*0-8446-1042-9*) Peter Smith.
Baldwin, Carl R. Captains of the Wilderness. 317p. 1986. 21.95 (*0-318-22522-0*) Tiger Rose Pub.
— Immigration Questions & Answers. 2nd ed. LC 95-76694. 176p. 1997. pap. 14.95 (*1-880559-32-3*) Allworth Pr.
— Immigration Questions & Answers. 2nd rev. ed. LC 97-72219. 184p. 1997. pap. 14.95 (*1-880559-84-6*) Allworth Pr.
— Inmigracion Preguntas y Respuestas. Dominquez, Humberto S., tr. LC 96-84659. (SPA.). 176p. (Orig.). 1996. pap. 14.95 (*1-880559-53-6*) Allworth Pr.
— Inmigracion Preguntas y Respuestas (Immigration Questions & Answers) 2nd rev. ed. Dominguez, Humberto S., tr. LC 96-84659. (SPA.). 176p. 1997. pap. 14.95 (*1-58115-001-6*) Allworth Pr.
Baldwin, Carliss Y. & Clark, Kim B. Design Rules: The Power of Modularity, Vol. 1. LC 99-16204. (Illus.). 432p. 1999. 45.00 (*0-262-02466-7*) MIT Pr.
Baldwin, Carol. The Buses Roll. Underhill, Linn, ed. (Illus.). 112p. (C). 1974. pap. 4.95 (*0-393-05535-3*) Norton.
Baldwin, Carol L. Friendship Counseling: Biblical Foundations for Helping Others. 320p. (Orig.). 1988. pap. 12.50 (*0-310-39041-9*, 18386P) Zondervan.
Baldwin, Carol M. Language & the Document Revolution. 2nd ed. (Illus.). 172p. 1999. pap. 25.00 (*0-9666358-2-5*) Lamp Lighter.
— Peace Makers. LC 99-187137. (Illus.). 75p. 1998. pap. 19.95 (*0-9666358-1-7*) Lamp Lighter.
Baldwin, Cathy, ed. see Youngs, Bettie B. & Tracy, Brian S.
Baldwin, Charles. An Ambassador's Journey: An Exploration of People & Culture. (American Values Projected Abroad Ser.: Vol. XV). 148p. 1984. pap. text 15.00 (*0-8191-3807-X*) U Pr of Amer.
Baldwin, Charles C. The Baldwin Genealogy, from 1500 to 1881. (Illus.). 974p. 1988. reprint ed. pap. 146.00 (*0-8328-0167-4*); reprint ed. lib. bdg. 156.00 (*0-8328-0166-6*) Higginson Bk Co.
— The Baldwin Genealogy Supplement. (Illus.). 498p. 1988. reprint ed. pap. 68.00 (*0-8328-0169-0*); reprint ed. lib. bdg. 78.00 (*0-8328-0168-2*) Higginson Bk Co.
— Men Who Make Our Novels. rev. ed. LC 67-30174. (Essay Index Reprint Ser.). 1977. 22.95 (*0-8369-0171-1*) Ayer.
— Stanford White. LC 78-150512. (Architecture & Decorative Art Ser.: Vol. 39). 1971. reprint ed. pap. 6.95 (*0-306-80031-4*); reprint ed. lib. bdg. 49.50 (*0-306-70138-3*) Da Capo.
Baldwin, Christina. Calling the Circle: The First & Future Culture. LC 97-26911. 256p. 1998. pap. 13.95 (*0-553-37900-3*) Bantam.
— Life's Companion: Journal Writing As a Spiritual Quest. 368p. 1990. pap. 14.95 (*0-553-35202-4*) Bantam.
— One to One: Self-Understanding Through Journal Writing. LC 91-4142. 180p. 1991. pap. 9.95 (*0-87131-652-8*) M Evans.
Baldwin, Cinda K. Great & Noble Jar: Traditional Stoneware of South Carolina. LC 92-12029. (Illus.). 240p. 1993. 39.95 (*0-8203-1371-8*) U of Ga Pr.
Baldwin, Clare C. Organization & Administration of Substitute-Teaching Service in City-School Systems. LC 75-176533. (Columbia University. Teachers College. Contributions to Education Ser.: No. 615). reprint ed. 37.50 (*0-404-55615-9*) AMS Pr.
Baldwin, Craig. Tribulation 99: Alien Anomalies under America. 72p. 1992. pap. 9.99 (*0-9642284-1-6*) Ediciones La Calavera.
***Baldwin, D.** An Atlas of Depression. (Illus.). 140p. 2001. 88.00 (*1-85070-942-4*) Prthnon Pub.
Baldwin, D. & Hopcroft, K. I. A Handbook for Housemen. 2nd ed. (Illus.). 208p. 1993. pap. 29.95 (*0-632-03334-7*) Blackwell Sci.
***Baldwin, Dan.** Preventive Home Maintenance Manual. (Illus.). 171p. 2000. pap. 24.95 (*0-9701918-0-4*) Baldwin & Assocs.
Baldwin, David. Track & Field Record Holders: Profiles of the Men & Women Who Set World, Olympic & American Marks, 1946 Through 1995. LC 96-3026. 344p. 1996. lib. bdg. 52.50 (*0-7864-0249-0*) McFarland & Co.
Baldwin, David, jt. auth. see Merson, Stephen.
Baldwin, David, jt. auth. see Weis, Margaret.
Baldwin, David A. The Academic Librarian's Human Resources Handbook: Employer Rights & Responsibilities. LC 96-19888. 167p. 1996. lib. bdg. 30.00 (*1-56308-345-0*) Libs Unl.
— Economic Statecraft. LC 85-42672. 456p. 1985. pap. text 21.95 (*0-691-10175-2*, Pub. by Princeton U Pr) Cal Prin Full Svc.
— The Public Librarian's Human Resources Handbook: Employer Rights & Responsibilities. LC 98-15020. 185p. 1998. pap. 30.00 (*1-56308-618-2*) Libs Unl.
— Supervising Student Employees in Academic Libraries: A Handbook. xvii, 194p. 1991. pap. text 32.00 (*0-87287-869-4*) Libs Unl.
Baldwin, David A., ed. America in an Interdependent World: Problems of United States Foreign Policy. LC 75-41909. 372p. reprint ed. pap. 115.40 (*0-8357-5350-6*, 202323200032) Bks Demand.
— Key Concepts in International Political Economy, 2 vol. (Library of International Political Economy: Vol. 5). 1072p. 1993. 385.00 (*1-85278-614-0*) E Elgar.
— Neorealism & Neoliberalism: The Contemporary Debate. LC 93-17701. (New Directions in World Politics Ser.). 377p. 1993. pap. 22.00 (*0-231-08441-2*) Col U Pr.
Baldwin, David A. & Migneault, Robert L. Humanistic Management by Teamwork: An Organizational & Administrative Alternative for Academic Libraries. 180p. 1996. lib. bdg. 38.00 (*0-87287-981-X*) Libs Unl.
Baldwin, David A., et al. Effective Management of Student Employment: Organizing for Student Employment in Academic Libraries. LC 99-46277. 300p. 1999. pap. 45.00 (*1-56308-688-3*) Libs Unl.
Baldwin, David G., et al. Chemical Safety Handbook: For the Semiconductor/electronics Industry. 2nd ed. LC 98-206180. ix, 438 p. 1996. 19.95 (*1-883595-07-X*) OEM Health.
— Semiconductor Industrial Hygiene Handbook: Monitoring, Ventilation, Equipment, & Ergonomics. LC 94-31248. (Illus.). 348p. 1995. 125.00 (*0-8155-1369-0*) Noyes.
***Baldwin, David M. & Walls, Gail W.** Turner County, Georgia: A Pictorial History. LC 99-50159. 1999. write for info. (*1-57864-089-X*) Donning Co.
Baldwin, Dawn A. Safety & Environmental Training: Using Compliance to Improve Your Company. LC 92-15212. 256p. 1992. text 60.95 (*0-442-01066-4*, VNR) Wiley.
Baldwin, Dawn A. Safety Environmental Training: Using Compliance to Improve Your Company. (Industrial Health & Safety Ser.). 237p. 1992. 69.95 (*0-471-28470-X*, VNR) Wiley.
Baldwin, Dean R. H. E. Bates: A Literary Life. LC 85-63640. (Illus.). 272p. 1987. 42.50 (*0-941664-24-4*) Susquehanna U Pr.
— V. S. Pritchett. (Twayne's English Authors Ser.: No. 445). 152p. 1987. 32.00 (*0-8057-6942-0*) Macmillan.
Baldwin, Dean R. & Morris, Gregory. The Short Story in English: Britain & North America - An Annotated Bibliography. LC 94-15580. (Magill Bibliographies). 371p. 1920. 50.00 (*0-8108-2834-0*) Scarecrow.
Baldwin, Deborah. Protestants & the Mexican Revolution: Missionaries, Ministers & Social Change. 216p. 1990. text 26.95 (*0-252-01659-9*) U of Ill Pr.
Baldwin, Debra L. Taco Titan: The Glen Bell Story. LC 98-58150. (Illus.). 286p. 1999. pap. 22.99 (*1-56530-299-0*) Summit TX.
Baldwin, Deirdra. Totemic: Poems. deluxe ed. (Burning Deck Poetry Chapbooks Ser.). 32p. 1983. pap. 15.00 (*0-930901-13-4*) Burning Deck.
Baldwin, Diane & Whiteside, Frances. Introduction to Business Organizations. 2nd ed. 272p. (C). 1999. per. 29.95 (*0-929563-52-2*) Pearson Pubns.

An Asterisk (*) at the beginning of an entry indicates that the title is appearing for the first time.

Baldwin, Dirk & Paradice, David. Applications Development in Microsoft Access 2000. 656p. (C). 2000. pap. text 49.95 (*0-7600-7108-X*) Course Tech.

Baldwin, Dirk, jt. auth. see Paradice, David.

Baldwin, Dorothy. Health & Exercise. (Your Health Ser.). (Illus.). 32p. (J). (gr. 3-8). 1987. 12.95 (*0-685-67611-0*) Rourke Corp.

— Health & Exercise. (Your Health Ser.). (Illus.). 32p. (J). (gr. 3-8). 1987. lib. bdg. 16.95 (*0-86592-293-4*) Rourke Enter.

— Health & Feelings. (Your Health Ser.). (Illus.). 32p. (J). (gr. 3-8). 1987. 12.95 (*0-685-58167-5*) Rourke Corp.

— Health & Friends. (Your Health Ser.). (Illus.). 32p. (J). (gr. 3-8). 1987. 12.95 (*0-685-67612-9*) Rourke Corp.

— Health & Friends. (Your Health Ser.). (Illus.). 32p. (J). (gr. 3-8). 1987. lib. bdg. 22.60 (*0-86592-289-6*) Rourke Enter.

— Health & Hygiene. (Your Health Ser.). (Illus.). 32p. (J). (gr. 3-8). 1987. 12.95 (*0-685-67610-2*) Rourke Corp.

Baldwin, Douglas. Land of the Red Soil. (Illus.). 90p. 1990. 9.95 (*0-920304-96-6*, Pub. by Gynergy-Ragweed) U of Toronto Pr.

Baldwin, Ed. Bird Feeders. Bakke, Timothy O., ed. LC 94-69654. (Illus.). 104p. 1996. pap. 10.95 (*1-880029-46-4*) Creative Homeowner.

Baldwin, Edgar M., ed. Fairmount TWP: The Making of a Township: Being an Account of the Early Settlement & Subsequent Development of Fairmount Twp., Grant Co., 1829-1917. (Illus.). 503p. 1997. reprint ed. lib. bdg. 52.50 (*0-8328-6650-4*) Higginson Bk Co.

Baldwin, Edith E. Toward a Theory of Family Well-Being I. 36p. 1996. 12.50 (*1-929083-04-1*) Kappa Omi Nu.

Baldwin, Edith E., jt. auth. see Brown, Marjorie M.

Baldwin, Edward A. Backyard Building Projects. (Illus.). 256p. 1993. 25.95 (*0-8306-2114-8*, 3766); pap. 16.95 (*0-8306-2114-8*, 3766) McGraw-Hill Prof.

— Bird Feeders, Shelters & Baths. (Illus.). 128p. 1990. 24.95 (*0-88266-625-8*, Garden Way Pub); pap. 14.95 (*0-88266-623-1*, Garden Way Pub) Storey Bks.

— Building Birdhouses & Feeders. Rae, Norman, ed. LC 89-85929. (Illus.). 112p. (Orig.). 1990. pap. 9.95 (*0-89721-213-4*, Ortho Bks) Meredith Bks.

— Country Elegance: Projects for Woodworkers. (Illus.). 256p. 1991. 26.95 (*0-8306-0579-7*, 3768); pap. 14.95 (*0-8306-0527-4*) McGraw-Hill Prof.

— PVC Furniture. (Weekend Woodworker Ser.). 144p. 1992. 24.95 (*0-8306-4077-0*, 4202); pap. 12.95 (*0-8306-4076-2*, 4202) McGraw-Hill Prof.

— Woodshop Accessories You Can Make. (Illus.). 224p. 1993. 24.95 (*0-8306-2126-1*, 3767); pap. 14.95 (*0-8306-2124-5*, 3767) McGraw-Hill Prof.

Baldwin-Edwards, Martin & Arango, Joaquin. Immigrants & the Informal Economy in Southern Europe. LC 99-30821. 216p. 1999. pap. 24.50 (*0-7146-4484-6*, Pub. by F Cass Pubs) Intl Spec Bk.

***Baldwin-Edwards, Martin & Arango, Joaquin.** Immigrants & the Informal Economy in Southern Europe. LC 99-30821. 216p. 1999. 57.50 (*0-7146-4925-2*, Pub. by F Cass Pubs) Intl Spec Bk.

Baldwin-Edwards, Martin & Schain, Martin A., eds. The Politics of Immigration in Western Europe. LC 94-11485. (Illus.). 216p. (C). 1994. 49.50 (*0-7146-4593-1*, Pub. by F Cass Pubs); pap. 19.50 (*0-7146-4137-5*, Pub. by F Cass Pubs) Intl Spec Bk.

Baldwin, Elaine. Introducing Cultural Studies. LC 98-27056. 1998. write for info. (*0-13-433301-2*) P-H.

***Baldwin, Elaine.** Introducing Cultural Studies. LC 99-87218. 2000. pap. text 25.00 (*0-8203-2245-8*) U of Ga Pr.

Baldwin, Elisa Moore, jt. auth. see Jordan, Mattie May.

Baldwin, Elizabeth, et al, eds. Edible Coatings & Films to Improve Food Quality. LC 94-60493. 365p. 1994. text 159.95 (*1-56676-113-1*) Technomic.

Baldwin, Elizabeth L., tr. see Groos, Karl.

Baldwin, Elizabeth W., tr. see Nasu, Masamoto.

Baldwin, Elizabeth W., tr. see Nasu, Masamotot.

Baldwin, Elmer. History of La Salle County, Illinois. 552p. 1993. reprint ed. lib. bdg. 57.50 (*0-8328-3489-0*) Higginson Bk Co.

— History of LaSalle Co, IL. (Illus.). 578p. (Orig.). 1994. reprint ed. pap. text 35.00 (*1-55613-936-5*) Heritage Bk.

Baldwin, Emily, jt. auth. see Glade, William P.

Baldwin, Ernest. An Introduction to Comparative Biochemistry. 4th ed. LC 64-21524. 199p. reprint ed. pap. 56.80 (*0-608-12305-6*, 2024418) Bks Demand.

Baldwin, Faith. Adam's Eden. 202p. reprint ed. lib. bdg. 19.95 (*0-88411-630-1*) Amereon Ltd.

— Alimony. 1976. reprint ed. 23.95 (*0-88411-616-6*) Amereon Ltd.

— American Family. 390p. reprint ed. lib. bdg. 23.95 (*0-88411-629-8*) Amereon Ltd.

— Arizona Star. large type ed. LC 93-34587. 474p. 1994. pap. 18.95 (*1-56054-319-1*) Thorndike Pr.

— Arizona Star. 1976. reprint ed. lib. bdg. 24.95 (*0-88411-601-8*) Amereon Ltd.

***Baldwin, Faith.** Blue Horizons. large type ed. 303p. 2000. lib. bdg. 25.95 (*1-58547-033-3*) Ctr Point Pubg.

Baldwin, Faith. Blue Horizons. 1976. reprint ed. lib. bdg. 23.95 (*0-88411-618-2*) Amereon Ltd.

— Breath of Life. 1976. reprint ed. lib. bdg. 23.95 (*0-88411-617-4*) Amereon Ltd.

— Change of Heart. 1974. reprint ed. lib. bdg. 23.95 (*0-88411-606-9*) Amereon Ltd.

— Deadly Legacy. LC 99-11204. 1999. 21.95 (*0-7862-1874-6*) Mac Lib Ref.

— District Nurse. large type ed. LC 92-44776. (General Ser.). 322p. 1993. reprint ed. lib. bdg. 17.95 (*1-56054-316-7*) Thorndike Pr.

— Face Toward the Spring. large type ed. LC 93-13141. (Illus.). 228p. 1993. lib. bdg. 16.95 (*1-56054-317-5*) Thorndike Pr.

— Face Toward the Spring. 219p. reprint ed. lib. bdg. 21.95 (*0-88411-625-X*) Amereon Ltd.

— Garden Oats. 1976. reprint ed. lib. bdg. 23.95 (*0-88411-607-7*) Amereon Ltd.

— Give Love the Air. 286p. reprint ed. lib. bdg. 23.95 (*0-88411-626-3*) Amereon Ltd.

— The Heart Has Wings. 317p. reprint ed. lib. bdg. 24.95 (*0-88411-627-1*) Amereon Ltd.

— The Heart Remembers. large type ed. LC 96-38776. 378p. 1997. 20.95 (*0-7862-0917-8*) Thorndike Pr.

— The High Road. 1976. reprint ed. lib. bdg. 23.95 (*0-88411-608-5*) Amereon Ltd.

— Hotel Hostess. 1976. reprint ed. lib. bdg. 23.95 (*0-88411-609-3*) Amereon Ltd.

— Judy: A Story of Divine Corners. 1976. reprint ed. lib. bdg. 22.95 (*0-88411-619-0*) Amereon Ltd.

— Letty & the Law. 1976. reprint ed. lib. bdg. 22.95 (*0-88411-610-7*) Amereon Ltd.

— Look Out for Liza. 1976. reprint ed. lib. bdg. 22.95 (*0-88411-620-4*) Amereon Ltd.

— Make-Believe. large type ed. LC 90-44506. 371p. 1990. reprint ed. lib. bdg. 19.95 (*1-56054-053-2*) Thorndike Pr.

— Marry for Money. 1976. reprint ed. lib. bdg. 22.95 (*0-88411-621-2*) Amereon Ltd.

— Men Are Such Fools. 1976. reprint ed. lib. bdg. 23.95 (*0-88411-611-5*) Amereon Ltd.

— The Moon's Our Home. 1976. reprint ed. lib. bdg. 24.95 (*0-88411-602-6*) Amereon Ltd.

— No Private Heaven. 1976. reprint ed. lib. bdg. 21.95 (*0-88411-622-0*) Amereon Ltd.

— The Office Wife. large type ed. LC 93-26416. 378p. 1993. pap. 17.95 (*1-56054-318-3*) Thorndike Pr.

— The Office Wife. 1976. reprint ed. lib. bdg. 23.95 (*0-88411-603-4*) Amereon Ltd.

— Rehearsal for Love. 1976. reprint ed. lib. bdg. 24.95 (*0-88411-612-3*) Amereon Ltd.

— Rich Girl, Poor Girl. large type ed. 323p. 1993. reprint ed. lib. bdg. 19.95 (*1-56054-274-8*) Thorndike Pr.

— Skyscraper. 1976. reprint ed. lib. bdg. 24.95 (*0-88411-623-9*) Amereon Ltd.

— Sleeping Beauty. 1976. reprint ed. lib. bdg. 22.95 (*0-88411-624-7*) Amereon Ltd.

— Something Special. large type ed. LC 91-8484. 324p. 1991. reprint ed. lib. bdg. 19.95 (*1-56054-161-X*) Thorndike Pr.

— Station Wagon Set. 1976. reprint ed. lib. bdg. 27.95 (*0-88411-604-2*) Amereon Ltd.

— That Man Is Mine. 1976. reprint ed. lib. bdg. 24.95 (*0-88411-613-1*) Amereon Ltd.

— Twenty-Four Hours a Day. large type ed. LC 91-34433. 345p. 1992. reprint ed. lib. bdg. 18.95 (*1-56054-273-X*) Thorndike Pr.

— Twenty-Four Hours a Day. 1976. reprint ed. 24.95 (*0-88411-605-0*) Amereon Ltd.

— The West Wind. large type ed. 1998. 19.95 (*0-7862-1548-8*) Thorndike Pr.

— White Collar Girl. 1976. reprint ed. lib. bdg. 24.95 (*0-88411-614-X*) Amereon Ltd.

— White Magic. 1976. reprint ed. lib. bdg. 24.95 (*0-88411-615-8*) Amereon Ltd.

— Woman on Her Way. LC 97-35447. 1997. 25.95 (*0-7862-1257-8*) Five Star.

— You Can't Escape. 1976. reprint ed. lib. bdg. 22.95 (*0-88411-625-5*) Amereon Ltd.

Baldwin, Fletcher N., Jr. & Munro, Robert J. Money Laundering: Asset Forfeiture & International Financial Crimes, Commentary, Analysis & Treaties, 5 vols. 1993. ring bd. 600.00 (*0-379-20156-9*) Oceana.

Baldwin, Frances E. Sumptuary Legislation & Personal Regulation in England. LC 78-64119. (Johns Hopkins University. Studies in the Social Sciences. Thirtieth Ser. 1912: 1). reprint ed. 41.50 (*0-404-61233-4*) AMS Pr.

Baldwin, Frank. Balling the Jack. LC 97-6124. 1997. 21.50 (*0-684-83360-3*) S&S Trade.

— Balling the Jack. 288p. 1998. pap. 11.00 (*0-684-84581-4*) S&S Trade.

Baldwin, Frank, tr. see Ienaga, Saburo.

Baldwin, Frank, tr. see Mohamad, Mahathir & Ishihara, Shintaro.

Baldwin, Fred, jt. photos by see Watriss, Wendy V.

Baldwin, Fred D. The Camelot Contract: Ripping Off the Government under Good King Arthur. LC 86-61941. 124p. (Orig.). 1987. pap. 6.95 (*0-937941-00-X*) Pennon Pr.

— Conflicting Interests: Corporate-Governance Controversies. LC 83-48400. 224p. 1984. text 30.00 (*0-669-07123-4*) Pennon Pr.

Baldwin, G. Wyoming, 5 vols. , Set. LC 97-38590. (Celebrate the States Ser.: Group 5). (Illus.). 144p. (YA). (gr. 4 up). 1998. lib. bdg. 35.64 (*0-7614-0662-X*, Benchmark NY) Marshall Cavendish.

Baldwin, Gary D. Moser Artistic Glass. LC 98-105107. (Illus.). 192p. 1997. 44.95 (*1-57080-038-3*) Antique Pubns.

— Moser Artistic Glass. 2nd rev. ed. LC 98-105107. (Illus.). 192p. 1997. pap. 34.95 (*1-57080-037-5*) Antique Pubns.

Baldwin, Gene. A Matter of Destiny. LC 98-89479. 375p. 1998. text 25.00 (*0-7388-0271-9*); pap. text 15.00 (*0-7388-0272-7*) Xlibris Corp.

Baldwin, George B. Beyond Nationalization: The Labor Problems of British Coal. LC 55-10966. (Wertheim Publications in Industrial Relations). (Illus.). 346p. 1955. 24.95 (*0-674-06900-5*) HUP.

— Planning & Development in Iran. LC 67-18377. 231p. reprint ed. pap. 71.70 (*0-608-11863-X*, 202308200032) Bks Demand.

Baldwin, George B., jt. ed. see Upper, Jack L.

Baldwin, George C. An Introduction to Nonlinear Optics. LC 73-23074. (Illus.). 156p. (C). 1969. pap. text 33.00 (*0-306-20004-X*, Kluwer Plenum) Kluwer Academic.

Baldwin, George C. An Introduction to Nonlinear Optics. LC 73-23074. (Illus.). 156p. (C). 1969. 54.00 (*0-306-30388-4*, Plenum Trade) Perseus Pubng.

Baldwin, George E. Baldwin. Descendants of Dea. Aaron Baldwin of N. Branford, Ct., 1724-1800, with Brief Account of His Ancestors. 102p. 1997. reprint ed. pap. 17.00 (*0-8328-7351-9*); reprint ed. lib. bdg. 27.00 (*0-8328-7350-0*) Higginson Bk Co.

— The Descendants of Deacon Aaron Baldwin of North Branford, Connecticut 1724-1800 with a Brief Account of His Ancestors. 108p. 1995. pap. 11.50 (*0-7884-0319-2*) Heritage Bk.

Baldwin, George H. Seeing England from the Fifty-Yard Line: A Rewarding Season Spent Coaching American Football & Touring the Land of Cricket & Rugby. LC 97-145673. (Illus.). 150p. 1996. 14.95 (*0-930753-20-8*) Spect Ln Pr.

Baldwin, Gordon. Looking at Photographs: A Guide to Technical Terms. LC 90-28861. (Looking at...Ser.). (Illus.). 97p. 1991. pap. 12.95 (*0-89236-192-1*, Pub. by J P Getty Trust) OUP.

— Roger Fenton: Pasha & Bayadere. LC 96-1755. (Getty Museum Studies on Art). (Illus.). 122p. (Orig.). 1996. pap. 17.50 (*0-89236-367-3*, Pub. by J P Getty Trust) OUP.

***Baldwin, Gordon & Keller, Judith.** Nadar/Warhol: Paris/New York: Photography & Fame. LC 99-21007. (Illus.). 240p. 1999. 60.00 (*0-89236-560-9*, Pub. by J P Getty Trust) OUP.

***Baldwin, Gordon, et al.** Nadar--Warhol, Paris--New York: Photography & Fame LC 99-21007. 1999. write for info. (*0-89236-565-X*) J P Getty Trust.

Baldwin, Gratia E. New Beatrice: or The Virtue That Counsels. LC 75-160011. reprint ed. 24.50 (*0-404-00469-5*) AMS Pr.

Baldwin, Gregory A. Handbook of Pediatric Emergencies. 3rd ed. 608p. pap. text 39.95 (*0-7817-2236-5*) Lppncott W & W.

Baldwin, Gregory A., ed. Handbook of Pediatric Emergencies. 2nd ed. LC 93-1239. (Handbook Ser.). (Illus.). 592p. 1993. pap. text 37.95 (*0-316-07918-9*) Lppncott W & W.

Baldwin, Grover H. School Site Management & School Restructuring. 92p. (C). 1993. text 25.00 (*1-56534-055-8*) Ed Law Assn.

Baldwin, Guy. The Leather Contest Guide: A Handbook for Promoters, Contestants, Judges & Titleholders. LC 93-70456. 144p. (Orig.). 1993. pap. 12.95 (*1-881943-08-9*) Daedalus Pub.

***Baldwin, Guy.** Oklahoma. (Celebrate the States Ser.). (Illus.). (J). 2000. 35.64 (*0-7614-1067-8*, Benchmark NY) Marshall Cavendish.

Baldwin, Guy. Ties That Bind: The SM - Leather - Fetish Erotic Style Issues, Commentaries & Advice. Bean, Joseph, ed. LC 93-70930. 244p. (Orig.). 1993. pap. 14.95 (*1-881943-09-7*) Daedalus Pub.

Baldwin, H. A. Holiness & the Human Element. 1996. pap. 6.99 (*0-88019-041-8*) Schmul Pub Co.

***Baldwin, H. Burnell.** Promises Made Clear: A Modern Day Catechism Companion. 44p. 1999. pap. 6.00 (*0-7880-1525-7*) CSS OH.

Baldwin, H. I. Forest Tree Seeds. (C). 1989. 230.00 (*81-7136-013-0*, Pub. by Periodical Expert) St Mut.

***Baldwin, Harmon A.** Planning for Disaster: A Guide for School Administrators. 2nd ed. LC 99-68091. 1999. pap. 8.00 (*0-87367-818-4*) Phi Delta Kappa.

Baldwin, Harrison C. The History of Hillsborough, NH. (Illus.). 201p. 1993. reprint ed. lib. bdg. 27.50 (*0-8328-3179-4*) Higginson Bk Co.

Baldwin, Harry G. & Holz, William B. Accounting for Value As Well As Original Cost: A Solution to the Appreciation Problem, 2 vols. Brief, Richard P., ed. LC 77-87263. (Development of Contemporary Accounting Thought Ser.). 1978. reprint ed. lib. bdg. 24.95 (*0-405-10892-3*) Ayer.

Baldwin, Harry L., Jr. Essential Geometry. LC 92-18140. 144p. (C). 1993. pap. 15.63 (*0-07-004537-2*) McGraw.

— Essential Geometry. LC 92-18140. (C). 1993. pap. text, teacher ed. 9.68 (*0-07-004538-0*) McGraw.

Baldwin, Helen G., tr. see Binet, Alfred.

Baldwin, Helene L. Samuel Beckett's Real Silence. LC 80-21465. 184p. (C). 1981. 28.50 (*0-271-00301-4*) Pa St U Pr.

Baldwin, Henry. A General View of the Origin & Nature of the Constitution & Government of the United States. LC 72-118027. (American Constitutional & Legal History Ser). 1970. reprint ed. lib. bdg. 27.50 (*0-306-71944-4*) Da Capo.

***Baldwin, Henry.** A General View of the Origin & Nature of the Constitution & Government of the United States: Deduced from the Political History & Condition of the Colonies & States... LC 00-26728. 2000. write for info. (*1-58477-098-8*) Lawbk Exchange.

Baldwin, Henry I. Forest Leaves: How to Identify Trees & Shrubs of Northern New England. 2nd rev. ed. (Illus.). 272p. 1993. pap. 12.95 (*0-914339-43-5*, Pub. by P E Randall Pub) U Pr of New Eng.

***Baldwin, Howard & Epler, Anita.** Teach Yourself Macintosh in 24 Hours. 392p. 1999. pap. text 20.00 (*0-7881-6809-6*) DIANE Pub.

Baldwin, Huntley. Creating Effective TV Commercials. 245p. 1988. 29.95 (*0-8442-3063-4*, NTC Business Bks) NTC Contemp Pub Co.

Baldwin, Ian T., jt. auth. see Karban, Richard.

Baldwin, J. Fuzzy Logic. LC 96-177157. 278p. 1996. 155.00 (*0-471-96281-3*) Wiley.

Baldwin, J., jt. auth. see Schacht, R. M.

Baldwin, J. D. & Clift, W. A Record of the Descendants of George Denison of Stonington, Conn. (Illus.). 424p. 1989. reprint ed. pap. 63.50 (*0-8328-0471-1*); reprint ed. lib. bdg. 71.50 (*0-8328-0470-3*) Higginson Bk Co.

Baldwin, J. E., ed. see Mukaiyama, Teruaki.

Baldwin, J. F. Harvest after the Fall. 200p. (Orig.). 1994. pap. 8.95 (*0-936163-18-6*) Summit Pr CO.

Baldwin, J. F., jt. auth. see Nash, Ronald H.

Baldwin, J. H. Environmental Planning & Management. 352p. 1988. pap. 325.00 (*81-7089-093-4*, Pub. by Intl Bk Distr) St Mut.

Baldwin, J. J. Environmental Planning & Management. 336p. 1988. 130.00 (*0-7855-6549-3*, Pub. by Intl Bk Distr) St Mut.

Baldwin, J. T. Fundamentals of Stability Theory. (Perspectives in Mathematical Logic Ser.). (Illus.). 465p. 1987. 149.95 (*0-387-15298-9*) Spr-Verlag.

Baldwin, J. T., ed. Classification Theory. (Lecture Notes in Mathematics Ser.: Vol. 1292). 500p. 1988. 69.95 (*0-387-18674-3*) Spr-Verlag.

***Baldwin, Jack.** Baldwin's Guide to Inns of Mississippi. LC 99-86887. 2000. write for info. (*1-56554-663-6*) Pelican.

Baldwin, Jack & Baldwin, Winnie. Baldwin's Guide to Inns of Louisiana. 2nd ed. LC 97-22439. (Illus.). 304p. 1998. pap. 14.95 (*1-56554-320-3*) Pelican.

— Baldwin's Guide to Museums of Louisiana. LC 97-49815. (Illus.). 304p. 1999. pap. text 14.95 (*1-56554-272-X*) Pelican.

— Baldwin's Guide to Museums of Louisiana. LC 97-49815. 1998. pap. write for info. (*1-56555-427-2*) Pelican Pubs.

Baldwin, Jack, jt. ed. see Ferland, Gary.

Baldwin, James. The Amen Corner. 160p. 1990. mass mkt. 5.99 (*0-440-20662-6*, LE) Dell.

— The Amen Corner. LC 97-35624. 1998. pap. 10.00 (*0-375-70188-5*) Vin Bks.

— Another Country. LC 92-50564. 448p. 1993. pap. 13.00 (*0-679-74471-1*) Vin Bks.

— Blues for Mister Charlie: A Play. LC 94-23842. 1995. pap. 10.00 (*0-679-76178-0*) Vin Bks.

— The Devil Finds Work. 160p. 1990. mass mkt. 6.99 (*0-440-20661-8*, LE) Dell.

— The Devil Finds Work. 144p. 2000. pap. 11.95 (*0-385-33460-5*) Dell.

— Early Novels & Stories: Go Tell It on the Mountain; Giovanni's Room; Another Country; Going to Meet the Man. Morrison, Toni, ed. LC 97-23028. (Library of America Ser.). 970p. 1998. 35.00 (*1-883011-51-5*, Pub. by Library of America) Penguin Putnam.

— The Evidence of Things Not Seen. 1998. lib. bdg. 29.95 (*1-56849-575-7*) Buccaneer Bks.

— The Evidence of Things Not Seen. LC 94-49040. 1995. reprint ed. pap. 9.95 (*0-8050-3939-2*, Owl) H Holt & Co.

— The Fire Next Time. LC 94-23228. 126p. 1995. 13.50 (*0-679-60151-1*) Modern Lib NY.

— The Fire Next Time. LC 92-50566. 128p. 1993. pap. 9.00 (*0-679-74472-X*) Vin Bks.

— Giovanni's Room. 224p. 1988. mass mkt. 6.99 (*0-440-32881-0*, LE) Dell.

— Giovanni's Room. 176p. 2000. pap. 11.95 (*0-385-33458-3*) Dell.

— Go Tell It on the Mountain. 224p. 1985. mass mkt. 6.99 (*0-440-33007-6*, LE) Dell.

— Go Tell It on the Mountain. 240p. 2000. pap. 11.95 (*0-385-33457-5*) Dell.

— Go Tell It on the Mountain. 336p. 1995. 14.95 (*0-679-60154-6*) Random.

— Go Tell It on the Mountain. 1985. 11.09 (*0-606-01584-1*, Pub. by Turtleback) Demco.

— Going to Meet the Man. LC 94-41586. 1995. pap. 11.00 (*0-679-76179-9*) Vin Bks.

— If Beale Street Could Talk. 224p. 1986. mass mkt. 6.99 (*0-440-34060-8*, LE) Dell.

— If Beale Street Could Talk. 176p. 2000. pap. 11.95 (*0-385-33459-1*) Dell.

— If Beale Street Could Talk. 1986. 11.60 (*0-606-01598-1*, Pub. by Turtleback) Demco.

— If Beale Street Could Talk. large type ed. LC 96-14703. 229 p. 1996. 22.95 (*0-7838-1817-3*) Mac Lib Ref.

— Jimmy's Blues: Selected Poems. 64p. 1986. text 11.95 (*0-312-44247-5*) St Martin.

— Jimmy's Blues: Selected Poems. 80p. 1990. pap. 9.95 (*0-312-05104-2*) St Martin.

— Just above My Head. 592p. 2000. pap. 11.95 (*0-385-33456-7*) Dell.

— No Name in the Street. 208p. 1986. mass mkt. 6.99 (*0-440-36461-2*, LE) Dell.

— Nobody Knows My Name: More Notes of a Native Son. LC 92-50565. 192p. 1993. pap. 11.00 (*0-679-74473-8*) Vin Bks.

— Notes of a Native Son. 2nd ed. LC 90-52598. (African-American Studies). 176p. 1984. reprint ed. pap. 13.00 (*0-8070-6431-9*) Beacon Pr.

— One Day When I Was Lost: A Scenario Based on Alex Haley's "The Autobiography of Malcolm X" 272p. 1990. mass mkt. 6.50 (*0-440-20660-X*, LE) Dell.

— The Price of the Ticket: Collected Nonfiction, 1948-1985. 704p. 1985. text 35.00 (*0-312-64306-3*) St Martin.

— Tell Me How Long the Train's Been Gone: A Novel. 384p. 1986. mass mkt. 6.99 (*0-440-38581-4*, LE) Dell.

— Tell Me How Long the Train's Been Gone: A Novel. LC 97-35625. 1998. pap. 14.00 (*0-375-70189-3*) Random.

Baldwin, James & University of Massachusetts Staff. A Tribute to James Baldwin: Black Writers Redefine the Struggle. Chametzky, Jules, ed. LC 88-29585. 92p. 1989. pap. 10.95 (*0-87023-677-6*) U of Mass Pr.

Baldwin, James, jt. auth. see Hansberry, Lorraine.

Baldwin, James, jt. auth. see Marr, John S.

Baldwin, James, ed. see McCally, Regina W.

Baldwin, James J., 3rd. The Struck Eagle: Micah Jenkins of the 5th South Carolina Volunteers & the "Palmetto Sharpshooters" LC 96-14115. (Illus.). 455p. 1996. 34.95 (*1-57249-017-9*) White Mane Pub.

An Asterisk (*) at the beginning of an entry indicates that the title is appearing for the first time.

Baldwin, James M. Between Two Wars, Eighteen Sixty-One to Nineteen Twenty-One: Being Memories, Opinion & Letters Received by James Mark Baldwin, 2 vols., Set. LC 75-3020. reprint ed. 115.00 (*0-404-59013-6*) AMS Pr.
— Darwin & the Humanities. LC 75-3021. reprint ed. 29.50 (*0-404-59016-0*) AMS Pr.
— Development & Evolution: Including Psychophysical Evolution, Evolution by Orthoplasy & the Theory of Genetic Modes. LC 75-3022. (Philosophy in America Ser.). reprint ed. 56.00 (*0-404-59017-9*) AMS Pr.
— Dictionary of Philosophy & Psychology, Vol. 3, Pt. 1. 1960. 24.50 (*0-8446-1049-6*) Peter Smith.
— Dictionary of Philosophy & Psychology, Vol. 3, Pt. 2. 1960. 24.50 (*0-8446-1050-X*) Peter Smith.
— Fragments in Philosophy & Science: Being Collected Essays & Addresses. LC 75-3023. (Philosophy in America Ser.). reprint ed. 59.50 (*0-404-59018-7*) AMS Pr.
— Genetic Theory of Reality. LC 75-3024. (Philosophy in America Ser.). reprint ed. 59.50 (*0-404-59019-5*) AMS Pr.
— Handbook of Psychology, 2 vols. LC 75-3025. (Philosophy in America Ser.). reprint ed. 145.00 (*0-404-59020-9*) AMS Pr.
— The Individual & Society: Or, Psychology & Sociology. LC 75-3026. (Philosophy in America Ser.). reprint ed. 39.50 (*0-404-59023-3*) AMS Pr.
— The Individual & Society: Psychology & Sociology. LC 73-14147. (Perspectives in Social Inquiry Ser.). 214p. 1974. reprint ed. 13.95 (*0-405-05492-0*) Ayer.

Baldwin, James M. Social & Ethical Interpretations in Mental Development. 592p. 120.00 (*1-85506-687-4*) Thoemmes Pr.

Baldwin, James M. Social & Ethical Interpretations in Mental Development. 2nd ed. LC 73-2960. (Classics in Psychology Ser.). 1977. reprint ed. 40.95 (*0-405-05133-6*) Ayer.
— Thought & Things: A Study of the Development & Meaning of Thought or Genetic Logic, 3 vols., Set. LC 75-3029. (Philosophy in America Ser.). reprint ed. 275.00 (*0-404-59025-X*) AMS Pr.
— Thought & Things: Study of the Development & Meaning of Thought or Genetic Logic, 4 vols. LC 74-21397. (Classics in Child Development Ser.). 1975. reprint ed. 103.95 (*0-405-06451-9*) Ayer.

Baldwin, James M., ed. Dictionary of Philosophy & Psychology: 1901-1902 Edition, 2 vols. 2nd ed. (Illus.). 1576p. 1998. 295.00 (*1-85506-596-7*) Thoemmes Pr.

Baldwin, James Mark. Mental Development in the Child & the Race. 496p. 120.00 (*1-85506-683-1*) Thoemmes Pr.

Baldwin, James T. Buckyworks: Buckminster Fuller's Ideas for Today. LC 95-26003. 243p. 1996. text 29.95 (*0-471-12953-4*) Wiley.
— Buckyworks: Buckminster Fuller's Ideas for Today. LC 95-26003. (Illus.). 256p. 1997. pap. 24.95 (*0-471-19812-9*) Wiley.

Baldwin, Janice I. Behavior Principles in Everyday Life. 3rd ed. LC 97-770. 390p. (C). 1997. pap. text 59.00 (*0-13-084096-3*) P-H.

Baldwin, Jean. George. (Illus.). 39p. (J). (gr. 1-4). 1997. pap. 5.95 (*1-879418-82-7*) Audenreed Pr.

Baldwin, Jeduthan. Revolutionary Journal of Colonel Jeduthan Baldwin, 1775-1778. Baldwin, Thomas W., ed. LC 73-140853. (Eyewitness Accounts of the American Revolution Ser.). (Illus.). 1971. reprint ed. 36.00 (*0-405-01223-3*) Ayer.

Baldwin, Jeff. Cycling Hawaii. LC 97-38895. (Bicycle Bks.). (Illus.). 224p. 1997. pap. 14.95 (*0-933201-85-0*, Bicycle Bks) MBI Pubg.

***Baldwin, Joel.** The Survivor's Guide: An Orderly Step-by-step Method To Help You Help Your Beneficiaries, 1. LC 97-93832. (Illus.). 157p. 1998. pap. 14.95 (*0-9665304-0-3*) Linden Point.

Baldwin, John. Best of the Bowies of the American Frontier. (Illus.). 80p. 1999. 75.00 (*0-9651146-2-7*) Early Am Artistry.
— Early Knives & Beaded Sheaths of the American Frontier. (Of the American Frontier Ser.). (Illus.). 82p. 1997. 75.00 (*0-9651146-1-9*) Early Am Artistry.
— Edinburgh, Lothians & the Borders: Exploring Scotland's Heritage. (Exploring Scotland's Heritage Ser.). (Illus.). 228p. 1997. pap. 22.00 (*0-11-495292-2*, Pub. by Statnry Office) Balogh.

***Baldwin, John.** Mountains of the Coast: Travels to Remote Corners of the Pacific Ranges. (Illus.). 112p. 1999. 36.95 (*1-55017-213-1*) Harbour Pub Co.

Baldwin, John. Rethinking Police Interrogation in England & Wales. Hughes, Graham, ed. (Occasional Papers: Vol. XI). 24p. (Orig.). 1992. pap. 5.00 (*1-878429-60-4*) NYU Ctr for Rsch in Crime Justice.
— Small Claims in the Country Courts in England & Wales: The Bargain Basement of Civil Justice. (Oxford Socio-Legal Studies). (Illus.). 190p. 1998. text 67.00 (*0-19-826477-1*) OUP.
— Tomahawks *Pipe Axes* of the American Frontier. (Of the American Frontier Ser.). (Illus.). 128p. 1995. 75.00 (*0-9651146-0-0*) Early Am Artistry.

Baldwin, John & French, Peter. Forensic Phonetics. 224p. 1990. text 47.50 (*0-86187-786-1*, Pub. by P P Pubs) Cassell & Continuum.

Baldwin, John, et al. Judging Social Security: The Adjudication of Claims for Benefit in Britain. (Illus.). 236p. 1994. text 39.95 (*0-19-825720-1*) OUP.

Baldwin, John, jt. auth. see Marr, John S.

Baldwin, John D. Ancient America in Notes on America Archaeology. 301p. 1996. reprint ed. spiral bd. 18.50 (*0-7873-0065-9*) Hlth Research.
— Ancient America in Notes on American Archaeology. (Works of John D. Baldwin). xii, 299p. reprint ed. lib. bdg. 49.00 (*0-932051-06-5*) Rprt Serv.
— Ancient America, in Notes on American Archaeology. 300p. 1996. reprint ed. pap. 17.50 (*1-56459-657-5*) Kessinger Pub.

***Baldwin, John D.** Ancient America, in Notes on American Archaeology. (LC History-America-E). 299p. 1999. reprint ed. lib. bdg. 89.00 (*0-7812-4304-1*) Rprt Serv.

Baldwin, John D. George Herbert Mead: A Unifying Theory for Sociology. (Masters of Social Theory Ser.: Vol. 6). (Illus.). 160p. 1986. text 48.00 (*0-8039-2321-X*); pap. text 19.95 (*0-8039-2320-1*) Sage.
— George Herbert Mead: A Unifying Theory for Sociology. LC 85-30249. (Masters of Social Theory Ser.: No. 6). 168p. reprint ed. pap. 52.10 (*0-7837-4564-8*, 204409300003) Bks Demand.
— Pre-Historic Nations. (Works of John D. Baldwin). vii, 411p. reprint ed. lib. bdg. 59.00 (*0-932051-07-3*) Rprt Serv.
— Pre-Historic Nations: or Inquiries Concerning Some of the Great People: The Works of John D. Baldwin. 414p. reprint ed. text 79.00 (*0-7812-0734-7*) Rprt Serv.
— Pre-Historic Nations: or Inquiries Concerning Some of the Great Peoples & Civilizations of Antiquity. 414p. 1988. reprint ed. spiral bd. 41.50 (*0-7873-1280-0*) Hlth Research.
— Pre-Historic Nations or Inquiries Concerning Some of the Great Peoples & Civilizations of Antiquity & Their Probable Relation to a Still Older Civilization of the Ethiopians or Cushites of Arabia (1869) 400p. 1998. reprint ed. pap. 29.95 (*0-7661-0143-6*) Kessinger Pub.

***Baldwin, John Denison & Clift, William.** A Record of the Descendants of Capt. George Denison of Stonington, Connecticut: With Notices of His Father & Brothers, & Some Account of Other Denisons Settled in America in the Colony Times. (Illus.). 440p. 1999. pap. 30.50 (*0-7884-1346-5*, B040) Heritage Bk.

***Baldwin, John H.** Left Handed Through Time. LC 00-190670. 191p. 2000. 25.00 (*0-7388-1726-0*); pap. 18.00 (*0-7388-1727-9*) Xlibris Corp.

Baldwin, John H., jt. auth. see Jones, L. R.

Baldwin, John R. The Dynamics of Industrial Competition: A North American Perspective. (Illus.). 480p. (C). 1995. text 69.95 (*0-521-46561-3*) Cambridge U Pr.

Baldwin, John R. The Dynamics of Industrial Competition: A North American Perspective. (Illus.). 480p. (C). 1998. pap. 24.95 (*0-521-63357-5*) Cambridge U Pr.

***Baldwin, John S.** Currency Paper Procurement: Meaningful Competition Unlikely under Current Conditions. 124p. 2000. reprint ed. pap. text 25.00 (*0-7881-8886-0*) DIANE Pub.

***Baldwin, John W.** Aristocratic Life in Medieval France: The Romances of Jean Renart &Gerbert de Montreuil, 1190. LC 99-29030. 312p. 1999. 49.95 (*0-8018-6188-8*) Johns Hopkins.

Baldwin, John W. The Government of Philip Augustus: Foundations of French Royal Power in the Middle Ages. 632p. 1991. pap. 19.95 (*0-520-07391-6*, Pub. by U CA Pr) Cal Prin Full Svc.
— The Language of Sex: Five Voices from Northern France Around 1200. (Chicago Series on Sexuality, History, & Society). (Illus.). 332p. 1995. reprint ed. pap. text 17.95 (*0-226-03614-6*) U Ch Pr.
— The Scholastic Culture of the Middle Ages, 1000-1300. (Illus.). 125p. (C). 1997. reprint ed. pap. text 12.50 (*0-88133-942-3*) Waveland Pr.

Baldwin, John W. & Goldthwaite, Richard A., eds. Universities in Politics: Case Studies from the Late Middle Ages & Early Modern Period. LC 73-183041. (Johns Hopkins Symposia in Comparative History Ser.). 144p. reprint ed. pap. 44.70 (*0-608-14657-9*, 202582900046) Bks Demand.

Baldwin, Joseph. Wind in the Willows - Straight. 118p. 1966. pap. 5.50 (*0-87129-160-6*, W35) Dramatic Pub.

Baldwin, Joseph G. The Flush Times of Alabama & Mississippi. 1989. reprint ed. lib. bdg. 90.00 (*0-7812-1877-2*) Rprt Serv.
— Party Leaders. 1989. reprint ed. lib. bdg. 79.00 (*0-7812-1878-0*) Rprt Serv.
— Party Leaders: Sketches of Thomas Jefferson, Alexander Hamilton, Andrew Jackson, Henry Clay, John Randolph of Roanoke; Including Notices of Many Other Distinguished American Statesmen. LC 72-39654. (Essay Index Reprint Ser.). 1977. reprint ed. 25.95 (*0-8369-2741-9*) Ayer.

Baldwin, Joyce. DNA Pioneer: James Watson & the Double Helix. LC 93-31090. 160p. (J). (gr. 4-6). 1994. 14.95 (*0-8027-8297-3*); lib. bdg. 15.85 (*0-8027-8298-1*) Walker & Co.
— Lamentations-Daniel. (Bible Study Commentaries Ser.). 128p. 1984. pap. 4.95 (*0-87508-162-2*) Chr Lit.
— To Heal the Heart of a Child: Helen Taussig, M.D. 128p. (J). 1992. 14.95 (*0-8027-8166-7*); lib. bdg. 15.85 (*0-8027-8167-5*) Walker & Co.

Baldwin, Joyce G. Daniel. Wiseman, Donald J., ed. LC 78-18547. (Tyndale Old Testament Commentary Ser.: Vol. 21). 210p. 1978. pap. 12.99 (*0-87784-273-6*, 273) InterVarsity.
— Esther. Wiseman, Donald J., ed. LC 84-15670. (Tyndale Old Testament Commentary Ser.: Vol. 12). 126p. 1984. pap. 12.99 (*0-87784-262-0*, 262) InterVarsity.
— 1 & 2 Samuel. Wiseman, Donald J., ed. LC 88-32895. (Tyndale Old Testament Commentary Ser.: Vol. 8). 299p. (Orig.). (C). 1989. 19.99 (*0-8308-1426-4*, 1426) InterVarsity.
— Haggai, Zechariah, Malachi. LC 72-75980. (Tyndale Old Testament Commentary Ser.). 253p. 1972. pap. 12.99 (*0-87784-276-0*, 276) InterVarsity.
— Samuel First & Second. Wiseman, Donald J., ed. LC 88-32895. (Tyndale Old Testament Commentary Ser.). 299p. (Orig.). (C). 1989. pap. 12.99 (*0-87784-258-2*, 258) InterVarsity.

Baldwin, Juanitta. The Callico Tree. 280p. 1992. pap. 13.95 (*1-880308-03-7*); lib. bdg. 19.95 (*1-880308-02-9*) Suntop.

***Baldwin, Juanitta.** Kudzu Cuisine. LC 99-58618. (Illus.). 2000. pap. 16.00 (*1-880308-23-1*) Suntop.
— Website Weaving for Greenhorns. 20p. 2000. pap. 9.00 (*1-880308-15-0*) Suntop.

Baldwin, Juanitta, jt. auth. see Almy, Virginia.

Baldwin, Juanitta, jt. auth. see Grubb, Esther.

Baldwin, Juanitta, jt. auth. see Hoots, Diane.

Baldwin, Juanitta, ed. see Almy, Virginia.

***Baldwin, Judith A.** The Inner Knower. rev. ed. 132p. 1999. pap. 11.95 (*1-56519-003-3*) Human Relations.
— Let the Inner Knower Lead the Way. 132p. 1996. pap. 11.95 (*1-56519-000-9*) Human Relations.

Baldwin, Judith A. & Baldwin, William J. From My Heart to Yours: A Transformational Guide to Unlocking the Power of Love. LC 96-75022. 96p. (Orig.). 1996. pap. 19.95 (*0-929915-17-8*) Headline Bks.

Baldwin, Judith M. What Your Little Black Book Reveals: The Incredible Secret Power of the Addresses You Keep. Clark, Merry, ed. LC 96-92434. (Illus.). 112p. 1997. pap. 9.95 (*0-9652969-0-3*) S F C Communs.

Baldwin, Kathleen M., et al. Davis's Manual of Critical Care Therapeutics. LC 94-37605. (Illus.). 757p. (C). 1995. pap. text 33.95 (*0-8036-0574-9*) Davis Co.

Baldwin, Kenneth, ed. Modern Methods for Automating Finite Element Mesh Generation. (Sessions Proceedings Ser.). 84p. 1986. 14.00 (*0-87262-564-8*) Am Soc Civil Eng.

Baldwin, Kenneth H. & Kirby, David K., eds. Individual & Community: Variations on a Theme in American Fiction. LC 74-75476. xvii, 222p. 1975. text 38.95 (*0-8223-0319-1*) Duke.

Baldwin, Kenneth L. Stop Hurtful Words & Harmful Habits: A Life Therapy Guide to Personal Growth. LC 96-27982. 176p. (Orig.). 1997. pap. 14.95 (*1-56825-034-7*) Rainbow Books.

Baldwin, Kenny. The Unconverted Me. 152p. 1999. pap. 13.00 (*0-8059-4421-4*) Dorrance.

***Baldwin, Kieran.** Managing Individual Performance: A Systematic, Seven Step Approach to Enhancing Employee Performance & Results. (Illus.). 144p. (Orig.). 1999. pap. 19.95 (*1-85703-438-4*, Pub. by How To Bks) Trans-Atl Phila.

Baldwin, Laura H. & Gotz, Glenn A. Transfer Pricing for Air Force Depot-Level Reparables. LC 97-41617. 97p. 1997. pap. 15.00 (*0-8330-2557-0*, MR-808-AF) Rand Corp.

Baldwin, Laura H., et al. Incentives to Undertake Sourcing Studies in the Air Force. LC 99-176685. 66p. 1998. pap. text 6.00 (*0-8330-2638-0*, DB-240-AF) Rand Corp.

***Baldwin, Laura H., et al.** Strategic Sourcing: Measuring & Managing Performance. (Illus.). xv, 88p. (C). 1999. pap. 8.00 (*0-8330-2788-3*, DB-287-AF) Rand Corp.

Baldwin, Lawrence. Open VMS System Management Guide. LC 95-14965. (Illus.). 416p. 1995. pap. 59.95 (*1-55558-143-9*, Digital DEC) Buttrwrth-Heinemann.

***Baldwin, Lawrence & Hoffman, Steve.** OpenVMS System Management Guide. 2nd ed. 480p. 2001. pap. 49.95 (*1-55558-243-5*, Digital DEC) Buttrwrth-Heinemann.

Baldwin-LeClair, Jack. I Sing the Law Electric: Computer Source Manual for Legal Assistants. 160p. (C). 1992. pap. text 24.95 (*0-8403-7822-X*) Kendall-Hunt.

Baldwin, Leland. Pittsburgh: The Story of a City. 1993. reprint ed. lib. bdg. 89.00 (*0-7812-5424-8*) Rprt Serv.

Baldwin, Leland D. The Keelboat Age on Western Waters. LC 41-10342. (Illus.). 288p. 1980. reprint ed. pap. 14.95 (*0-8229-5319-6*) U of Pittsburgh Pr.
— Pittsburgh: The Story of a City, 1750-1865. rev. ed. LC 73-104172. (Illus.). 360p. 1970. reprint ed. pap. 14.95 (*0-8229-5216-5*) U of Pittsburgh Pr.
— Whiskey Rebels: The Story of a Frontier Uprising. LC 39-11763. 336p. (C). 1968. reprint ed. pap. 14.95 (*0-8229-5151-7*) U of Pittsburgh Pr.

Baldwin, Lewis L. Yatra of a Sometime Maverick. (Illus.). 210p. 1989. write for info. (*0-9622551-0-6*) Sea Este Pubs.

Baldwin, Lewis L., ed. see Williams, Richard K.

Baldwin, Lewis V. There Is a Balm in Gilead: The Cultural Roots of Martin Luther King, Jr. LC 90-13837. 352p. (Orig.). 1991. pap. 23.00 (*0-8006-2457-2*, 1-2457, Fortress Pr) Augsburg Fortress.
— To Make the Wounded Whole: The Cultural Legacy of Martin Luther King, Jr. LC 91-34739. 344p. 1992. pap. 22.00 (*0-8006-2543-9*, 1-2543) Augsburg Fortress.
— Toward the Beloved Community: Martin Luther King, Jr. & South Africa. LC 95-18073. (Illus.). 296p. 1995. 24.95 (*0-8298-1102-8*); pap. 18.95 (*0-8298-1108-7*) Pilgrim OH.

Baldwin-Lima-Hamilton Corporation Staff. The Narrow-Gauge Locomotive: The Baldwin Catalog of 1877. LC 67-24619. 57p. reprint ed. pap. 30.00 (*0-608-16173-X*, 201625200002) Bks Demand.

Baldwin, Lindley. Samuel Morris. LC 86-72978. 96p. 1987. mass mkt. 4.99 (*0-87123-950-7*) Bethany Hse.

Baldwin, Linton. The Big Round. 1995. pap. 11.95 (*1-881471-09-8*) S Duyvil.

Baldwin, Lionel. High Technology & the Future of Education. (Occasional Paper Ser.). 20p. 1986. 3.00 (*0-318-22364-3*, OC 122) Ctr Educ Trng Employ.

Baldwin, Loammi. Thoughts on the Study of Political Economy: With an Appendix: Drydocks. 105p. 1968. 37.50 (*0-678-00374-2*) Kelley.

Baldwin, Louis. Loves of Their Lives: Enduring Romantic Relationships from Antony & Cleopatra to Today. (Illus.). 320p. 1993. 21.95 (*1-55972-190-1*, Birch Ln Pr) Carol Pub Group.
— Triumph over the Odds: Inspirational Success Stories. LC 94-20162. 256p. 1994. 19.95 (*1-55972-238-X*, Birch Ln Pr) Carol Pub Group.

***Baldwin, Louis.** Turning Points: Pivotal Moments in the Careers of 83 Famous Figures. LC 99-29852. 216p. 1999. pap. 22.50 (*0-7864-0626-7*) McFarland & Co.
— Women of Strength: Biographies of 106 Who Have Excelled in Traditionally Male Fields, A. D. 61 to the Present. 242p. 1999. reprint ed. pap. text 20.00 (*0-7881-6743-X*) DIANE Pub.

Baldwin, Louis. Women of Strength: Biographies of 106 Who Have Excelled in Traditionally Male Fields, 61 A.D. to the Present. LC 96-38693. 254p. 1996. pap. 28.50 (*0-7864-0250-4*) McFarland & Co.

Baldwin, Louis & Baldwin, Virginia. One Woman's Liberation: The Story of Fanny Burney. LC 90-5988. 1991. 29.95 (*0-89341-600-2*, Longwood Academic); pap. 14.95 (*0-89341-601-0*, Longwood Academic) Hollowbrook.

Baldwin, Louise. A Teacher's Guide to Patty Reed's Doll: The Story of the Donner Party. (Illus.). 64p. (Orig.). 1996. pap., teacher ed. 11.95 (*0-9617357-7-5*) Tomato Enter.

Baldwin, Lydia W. A Yankee School-Teacher in Virginia. LC 70-37583. (Black Heritage Library Collection). 1977. reprint ed. 22.95 (*0-8369-8959-7*) Ayer.

Baldwin, M. Simon Evans: An Anthology. 269p. (C). 1989. 45.00 (*0-907083-03-X*, Pub. by S A Baldwin) St Mut.

Baldwin, Malcolm F. The Southwest Energy Complex: A Policy Evaluation. LC 73-79429. 79p. reprint ed. pap. 30.00 (*0-608-11749-8*, 201578700097) Bks Demand.

Baldwin, Marc D. Reading "The Sun Also Rises" Hemingway's Political Unconscious. 2nd ed. (Modern American Literature: Vol. 4). 153p. 1998. pap. 24.95 (*0-8204-4264-X*) P Lang Pubng.

Baldwin, Mark & Burton, Tony, eds. Canals - a New Look. 198p. (C). 1989. 70.00 (*0-85033-516-7*, Pub. by S A Baldwin) St Mut.

Baldwin, Mark, jt. auth. see Henderson, Stevie.

Baldwin, Mark, jt. ed. see Studwell, William E.

Baldwin, Marshall W. Raymond III of Tripolis & the Fall of Jerusalem, 1140-1187. LC 76-29830. reprint ed. 45.00 (*0-404-15411-5*) AMS Pr.

Baldwin, Marshall W., tr. see Erdmann, Carl.

Baldwin, Mart. A Busy Day in Loafer's Glory: A Rambler's Guide to the Mostly Off-the-Beaten Path Carolina Places. LC 96-79547. 156p. 1996. pap. 13.95 (*1-888549-01-7*) Appalachan Pr.
— Drifting the River: Growing up Wild in the South. (Illus.). 172p. 1999. 18.00 (*1-888715-03-0*, Pub. by Wolfhnd Pr) Parnassus Bk Dist.
— Kill the Benefactor. 336p. 1995. pap. 7.95 (*1-57087-166-3*) Prof Pr NC.
— Kill the Benefactor. LC 98-89773. 312p. 2000. reprint ed. pap. 16.00 (*1-892323-13-3*) Vivisphere.

Baldwin, Martha. Self-Sabotage: How to Stop it & Soar to Success. 160p. 1990. mass mkt. 13.95 (*0-446-39108-5*, Pub. by Warner Bks) Little.

Baldwin, Martin. Contemporary Painting in Canada. (Illus.). 64p. (Orig.). 1942. pap. 40.00 (*1-879886-07-3*) Addison Gallery.

Baldwin, Marva, jt. auth. see McBride, Michael B.

***Baldwin, Marvin E.** Observed Minima Timings of Eclipsing Binaries, No. 5. (Illus.). 59p. 1999. pap. text 3.00 (*1-878174-31-2*) Am Assn Var Star.

Baldwin, Marvin E. & Samolyk, Gerard, compiled by. Observed Minima Timings of Eclipsing Binaries, No. 1. (Illus.). 58p. 1993. pap. text 3.00 (*1-878174-10-X*) Am Assn Var Star.
— Observed Minima Timings of Eclipsing Binaries, No. 2. (Illus.). 58p. 1995. pap. text 3.00 (*1-878174-26-6*) Am Assn Var Star.
— Observed Minima Timings of Eclipsing Binaries, No. 3. (Illus.). 58p. 1996. pap. text 3.00 (*1-878174-27-4*) Am Assn Var Star.
— Observed Minima Timings of Eclipsing Binaries, No. 4. (Illus.). 58p. 1997. pap. text 3.00 (*1-878174-24-X*) Am Assn Var Star.

Baldwin, Matthew W. The Hell You Say! (Illus.). 100p. (Orig.). 1992. pap. 5.95 (*0-9633471-0-1*) M Baldwin.

Baldwin, Maureen. On Winning the Lottery. LC 98-90490. (Illus.). 120p. 1998. pap. 12.95 (*0-9664676-0-4*) Winners Pr.

Baldwin, Michael. Exit Wounds. 304p. 1989. pap. 3.95 (*0-380-70657-1*, Avon Bks) Morrow Avon.
— The Rape of OC. 656p. 1996. pap. 11.95 (*0-7515-0624-9*) Trafalgar.

Baldwin, Michael & Miller, Keith. The Gunners' Favourite: The 25-Pounder Gun: A Brief History. 1997. pap. 22.00 (*0-901721-27-1*, Pub. by Natl Army Mus) St Mut.

Baldwin, Michael J., jt. auth. see McCarthy, Leo J.

Baldwin, Michael L. & Jefferies, Leigh C., eds. Irradiation of Blood Components. LC 92-49758. 78p. 1992. 43.00 (*1-56395-012-X*) Am Assn Blood.

Baldwin, Michael L. & Kurtz, Sanford R. Transfusion Practice in Cardiac Surgery. LC 91-4865. (Illus.). 58p. (C). 1991. text 9.00 (*1-56395-005-7*) Am Assn Blood.

***Baldwin, Michele, ed.** The Use of Self in Therapy. abr. ed. LC 99-36719. 306p. 1999. pap. 24.95 (*0-7890-0745-2*) Haworth Pr.
— The Use of Self in Therapy. 2nd abr. ed. LC 99-36719. 295p. 1999. 49.95 (*0-7890-0744-4*) Haworth Pr.

Baldwin, Michele, jt. auth. see Satir, Virginia M.

Baldwin, Michele, jt. auth. see Schwab, Johanna.

Baldwin, Michelle, jt. auth. see Satir, Virginia M.

***Baldwin, Mitchell C.** Surviving Corporate Downsizing with Dignity & Grace! 1999. pap. 13.95 (*0-9669080-0-7*) Smart Pubg.

Baldwin, N. A. Baldwin. Brief Genealogy of the Baldwins. 70p. 1997. reprint ed. pap. 14.00 (*0-8328-7349-7*); reprint ed. lib. bdg. 24.00 (*0-8328-7348-9*) Higginson Bk Co.

B

Baldwin, Neil. Edison: Inventing the Century. (Illus.). 544p. (J). 1995. 27.45 (*0-7868-6041-3*, Pub. by Hyperion) Time Warner.
— Edison: Inventing the Century. (Illus.). 544p. (J). 1996. pap. 14.45 (*0-7868-8119-4*, Pub. by Hyperion) Time Warner.
— Legends of the Plumed Serpent: Biography of a Mexican God. LC 98-36524. (Illus.). 224p. 1998. text 37.50 (*1-891620-03-7*, Pub. by PublicAffairs NY) HarpC.
— Man Ray: American Artist. (Quality Paperbacks Ser.). (Illus.). 449p. 1991. reprint ed. pap. 16.95 (*0-306-80423-9*) Da Capo.
— A Separate Peace (Knowles) (Barron's Book Notes Ser.). (C). 1984. pap. 3.95 (*0-8120-3441-4*) Barron.
— Tracking the Plumed Serpent. 1999. write for info. (*0-7868-6146-0*) Disney Pr.
— The Writing Life. Osen, Diane, ed. LC 95-42500. (Illus.). 128p. 1995. pap. 15.00 (*0-679-76983-8*) Random.
Baldwin, Nick. A-Z of Cars of the '20s. (Illus.). 224p. 1998. pap. 24.95 (*1-901432-09-2*, Bay View Bks) MBI Pubg.
— Classic Tractors of the World. LC 98-2944. (Illus.). 192p. 1998. 29.95 (*0-89658-394-5*) Voyageur Pr.
— Four Wheel Drive & Land-Rover. 1989. pap. 25.00 (*0-85263-964-3*, Pub. by Shire Pubns) St Mut.
— Four-Wheel Drive & Land-Rover. (Album Ser.: No. 221). (Illus.). 32p. pap. 5.25 (*0-7478-0342-0*, Pub. by Shire Pubns) Parkwest Pubns.
— Old Delivery Vans. 1989. pap. 30.00 (*0-85263-845-0*, Pub. by Shire Pubns) St Mut.
— The Wolseley. (Album Ser.: No. 322). (Illus.). 32p. 1995. pap. 4.75 (*0-7478-0297-1*, Pub. by Shire Pubns) Parkwest Pubns.
Baldwin, Nick, jt. auth. see Georgano, Nick.
Baldwin, Nick, jt. auth. see Morland, Andrew.
Baldwin, Nina H., ed. see Hazard, Ann.
Baldwin, Norma. Power to Care? 210p. 1990. text 66.95 (*1-85628-092-6*, Pub. by Avebry) Ashgate Pub Co.
***Baldwin, Norma & Carruthers, Lyn.** Developing Neighbourhood Support & Child Protection Strategies. LC 98-72850. (Illus.). 165p. 1998. text 59.95 (*1-84014-312-6*) Ashgate Pub Co.
Baldwin, Norman, et al. Residents' Rights: A Strategy for Action in Houses for Older People. 215p. 1993. 66.95 (*1-85628-366-6*, Pub. by Avebry) Ashgate Pub Co.
Baldwin, Pat, ed. see Shakespeare, William.
Baldwin, Patricia L. Covering the Campus: The History of the Chronicle of Higher Education. LC 95-8936. 1995. 24.95 (*0-929398-96-3*); pap. 16.95 (*0-929398-97-1*) UNTX Pr.
***Baldwin, Paul, ed.** The 365 Most Important Events of the 20th Century. LC 99-18702. 304p. 1999. pap. 14.00 (*0-688-15628-2*, Wm Morrow) Morrow Avon.
***Baldwin, Peter.** Contagion & the State in Europe, 1830-1930. LC 98-39337. 614p. (C). 1999. 64.95 (*0-521-64288-4*) Cambridge U Pr.
Baldwin, Peter. The Politics of Social Solidarity: Class Bases of the European Welfare State, 1875-1975. 367p. (C). 1992. pap. text 24.95 (*0-521-42893-9*) Cambridge U Pr.
— Toy Theatres of the World. (Illus.). 176p. 1993. 39.95 (*0-302-00614-1*, Pub. by Zwemmer Bks) Intl Spec Bk.
Baldwin, Peter A. Four & Twenty Blackbirds: Personality Theory & the Understanding of Our Multiple Selves. LC 97-4111. 290p. 1997. pap. text 16.95 (*1-883647-06-1*) Bramble Co.
Baldwin, Peter C. Domesticating the Street: The Reform of Public Space in Hartford, 1850-1930. Miller, Zane L., ed. LC 99-28008. (Urban Life & Urban Landscape Ser.). (Illus.). 336p. 1999. pap. text 19.95 (*0-8142-5026-2*) Ohio St U Pr.
***Baldwin, Peter C.** Domesticating the Street: The Reform of Public Space in Hartford, 1850-1930. Miller, Zane L., ed. LC 99-28008. (Urban Life & Urban Landscape Ser.). (Illus.). 336p. 1999. text 50.00 (*0-8142-0824-X*) Ohio St U Pr.
Baldwin, Petie W. Winds of Imagination. LC 76-17537. 1976. pap. 5.00 (*0-917166-01-9*) Creative Vent.
***Baldwin, Phil N.** Statistics: Know-How Made Easy. LC 96-96898. (Know-How Made Easy Ser.: Vol. 1). (Illus.). 407p. 1999. pap. 39.00 incl. disk (*0-9672274-0-2*) Lrnlt Educ Div.
Baldwin, Philip. In Search of Clear Lines, 1. 1999. 65.00 (*3-7165-1163-3*) Benteli Verlag.
Baldwin, R. E. & McGarry, Thomas W. Last Hope: The Blood Chit Story. LC 96-70415. (Illus.). 224p. 1997. 49.95 (*0-7643-0222-1*) Schiffer.
Baldwin, R. W., jt. ed. see Byers, Vera S.
Baldwin, Rachel Y. My Psalms. Harris-Charity, Elizabeth, ed. (Illus.). 35p. 1998. pap. 9.95 (*0-9651866-4-4*) Youth Corp.
Baldwin, Rahima. Special Delivery. LC 78-61611. 192p. 1995. pap. 17.95 (*0-89087-934-6*) Celestial Arts.
— You Are Your Child's First Teacher. LC 88-3983. (Illus.). 380p. 1995. 19.95 (*0-89087-569-3*) Celestial Arts.
Baldwin, Rahima & Palmarini, Terra. Pregnant Feelings: Developing Trust in Birth. LC 85-62305. (Illus.). 208p. (Orig.). 1995. pap. 17.95 (*0-89087-423-9*) Celestial Arts.
Baldwin, Ralph B. The Measure of the Moon. LC 62-20025. 546p. reprint ed. pap. 169.30 (*0-608-30856-0*, 202002300016) Bks Demand.
— They Never Knew What Hit Them. Hoyem, George A., ed. (Illus.). 247p. 1999. 39.95 (*0-939683-15-6*) Armory Pubns.
Baldwin, Rebecca. Dartwood's Daughters. large type ed. LC 90-10730. 267p. 1990. lib. bdg. 17.95 (*0-89621-969-0*) Thorndike Pr.
— Peerless Theodosia. 224p. 2000. 19.95 (*1-929085-12-5*); lib. bdg. 17.95 (*1-929085-13-3*); mass mkt. 4.95 (*1-929085-11-7*) Rgncy Pr.
— Peerless Theodosia. large type ed. 336p. 2000. lib. bdg. 23.95 (*1-929085-14-1*); per. 19.95 (*1-929085-15-X*) Rgncy Pr.
— A Royal Visit. large type ed. LC 97-1179. (Candlelights Ser.). 191p. 1997. 18.95 (*0-7862-1089-3*) Thorndike Pr.
Baldwin, Richard. Is Bigger Better? The Economics of EC Enlargement. 1994. pap. 14.95 (*1-898128-06-5*, Pub. by Ctr Econ Policy Res) Brookings.
Baldwin, Richard, et al, eds. Expanding Membership of the European Union. (Illus.). 288p. (C). 1995. text 59.95 (*0-521-48134-1*) Cambridge U Pr.
Baldwin, Richard, jt. auth. see Harvey, Richard.
Baldwin, Richard E. Making Europe Work: Intergovernmental Conference, 1996. 134p. 1995. pap. text 14.95 (*1-898128-23-5*, Pub. by Ctr Econ Policy Res) Brookings.
— Towards an Integrated Europe. 234p. (C). 1994. pap. 19.95 (*1-898128-13-8*) Brookings.
***Baldwin, Richard E., et al, eds.** Market Integration, Regionalism & the Global Economy. LC 99-11548. (Illus.). 352p. (C). 1999. 69.95 (*0-521-64181-0*); pap. 25.95 (*0-521-64589-1*) Cambridge U Pr.
Baldwin, Richard E. & Francois, Joseph F., eds. Dynamic Issues in Commercial Policy Analysis. LC 98-29540. (Illus.). 300p. (C). 1999. text 80.00 (*0-521-64171-3*) Cambridge U Pr.
Baldwin, Richard F. Managing Mill Maintenance: The Emerging Realities. LC 89-85008. (Illus.). 302p. 1990. 45.00 (*0-87930-220-8*, 471) Miller Freeman.
***Baldwin, Richard F.** Maximizing Forest Product Resources for the 21st Century. LC 99-43322. 232p. 1999. pap. 49.00 (*0-87930-599-1*) Miller Freeman.
Baldwin, Richard F. Operations Management in the Forest Products Industry. LC 84-61889. (Illus.). 264p. 1984. pap. 45.00 (*0-87930-160-0*) Miller Freeman.
— Plywood & Veneer-Based Products: Manufacturing Practices. (Illus.). 388p. 1995. 59.00 (*0-87930-371-9*, 417) Miller Freeman.
***Baldwin, Richard L.** Administration Can Be Murder. Sasso, Holly, ed. (Louis Searing & Margaret McMillan Mystery Ser.). 246p. 2000. pap. 12.95 (*0-9660685-4-8*, Pub. by Buttonwood) Partners Pubs Grp.
— Growing Alaska Natives: The Propagation of Alaska's Native Plants. (ENG.). 105p. 1997. spiral bd. 19.00 (*1-57833-062-9*) Todd Commns.
— Kaligruak An Alaskan Salmon. (ENG.). 51p. (J). 1986. pap. 6.00 (*1-57833-061-0*) Todd Commns.
Baldwin, Richard L. A Lesson Plan for Murder. LC 97-78341. (Louis Searing & Margaret McMillan Mystery Ser.). 253p. 1998. pap. 12.95 (*0-9660685-0-5*) Buttonwood.
— The Piano Recital. LC 98-229708. (Illus.). 24p. 1999. pap. 6.95 (*0-9660685-1-3*) Buttonwood.
***Baldwin, Richard L.** The Principal Cause of Death. (Louis Searing & Margaret McMillan Mystery Ser.). 264p. 1999. pap. 12.95 (*0-9660685-2-1*) Buttonwood.
— Unity & the Children. 1999. write for info. (*0-9660685-3-X*) Buttonwood.
Baldwin, Rick. Creating Opportunities: Activity Book. (Illus.). 80p. 1996. pap. text 7.95 (*0-19-458875-0*) OUP.
— Creating Opportunities: Video Guide. (Illus.). 36p. 1996. pap. text 3.95 (*0-19-458876-9*) OUP.
Baldwin, Robert. Door of Water. LC 96-219434. 64p. (Orig.). 1996. pap. 7.95 (*0-9653567-0-1*) Blck Wolf.
***Baldwin, Robert.** A Reader on Regulation. LC 98-30990. (Illus.). 536p. 1998. text 60.00 (*0-19-876529-0*); pap. text 35.00 (*0-19-876530-4*) OUP.
Baldwin, Robert. Rules & Government. (Oxford Socio-Legal Studies). 352p. 1997. pap. text 35.00 (*0-19-826489-5*) OUP.
Baldwin, Robert, ed. Harmonization & Hazard: Regulating Workplace Health & Safety in the European Community. (European Business Law & Practice Ser.). 304p. (C). 1992. lib. bdg. 126.50 (*1-85333-723-4*, Pub. by Graham & Trotman) Kluwer Academic.
Baldwin, Robert & Cane, Peter. Law & Uncertainty: Risks & Legal Processes. LC 96-37304. 1997. 146.00 (*90-411-0942-0*) Kluwer Law Intl.
***Baldwin, Robert & Cave, Martin.** Understanding Regulation. LC 98-47348. (Illus.). 378p. 1999. text 82.00 (*0-19-877437-0*); pap. text 35.00 (*0-19-877438-9*) OUP.
Baldwin, Robert & McCrudden, Christopher, eds. Regulation & Public Law. (Law in Context Ser.). xx, 399p. 1987. reprint ed. 47.50 (*0-297-78780-2*) W S Hein.
Baldwin, Robert & McPeek, James A. An Introduction to Philosophy Through Literature. LC 50-8252. 596p. 1980. 39.50 (*0-471-07000-9*) Krieger.
Baldwin, Robert, jt. auth. see Thrush, Emily A.
Baldwin, Robert A. Making It in the Construction Business: The Contractor's Survival Guide. 1993. pap. 19.95 (*0-8306-3991-8*) McGraw-Hill Prof.
Baldwin, Robert E. Geography & Ownership. LC 98-3324. Vol. 59. (Illus.). 328p. 1998. 48.00 (*0-226-03572-7*) U Ch Pr.
— The Inefficacy of Trade Policy. LC 82-23425. (Essays in International Finance Ser.: No. 150). 26p. 1982. pap. text 10.00 (*0-88165-057-9*) Princeton U Int Finan Econ.
Baldwin, Robert E. Nontariff Distortions of International Trade. LC 78-109436. 222p. reprint ed. pap. 68.90 (*0-608-13342-6*, 205577900038) Bks Demand.
Baldwin, Robert E. The Philippines. LC 74-82373. (Foreign Trade Regimes & Economic Development Ser.: No. 5). 187p. reprint ed. pap. 58.00 (*0-8357-7581-X*, 205690200096) Bks Demand.
— The Philippines. (Special Conference Series on Foreign Trade Regimes & Economic Development: No. 5). 187p. 1975. reprint ed. 48.70 (*0-87014-505-3*) Natl Bur Econ Res.
— Trade Policy in a Changing World Economy. LC 88-20881. (Illus.). xii, 288p. 1989. 47.95 (*0-226-03611-1*) U Ch Pr.
Baldwin, Robert E., ed. Empirical Studies of Commercial Policy. (National Bureau of Economic Research Conference Report Ser.). (Illus.). 332p. 1991. 57.50 (*0-226-03569-7*) U Ch Pr.
— Trade Policy Issues & Empirical Analysis. (National Bureau of Economic Research Conference Report Ser.). (Illus.). 392p. 1988. lib. bdg. 55.50 (*0-226-03607-3*) U Ch Pr.
Baldwin, Robert E. & Krueger, Anne O., eds. The Structure & Evolution of Recent U. S. Trade Policy. LC 84-2560. (National Bureau of Economic Research Conference Report Ser.). 448p. 1985. lib. bdg. 60.00 (*0-226-03604-9*) U Ch Pr.

Baldwin, Robert E. & Magee, Christopher S. Congressional Trade Votes: From NAFTA to Fast Track. 150p. (C). 2000. pap. 18.95 (*0-88132-267-9*) Inst Intl Eco.
The unwillingness of the US House of Representatives to renew fast-track authority in 1997 & 1998 means that further trade liberalization for the United States is likely to slow down to grind to a halt, since negotiators elsewhere know that any agreements reached could be modified by the US Congress. This political impasse raises several overarching questions: Does the status of fast track represent a temporary or a permanent setback in the postwar trend toward freer trade? is it due simply to lax efforts in mobilizing groups that support trade liberalization, or is US trade policy becoming more protectionist? More generally, what were the most economic & social factors shaping congressional voting on trade legislation in the 1990s. How do these factors differ for the various trade bills Congress considered over this period? Baldwin & Magee attempt to answer these questions by analyzing three key trade bills: NAFTA in 1993; the legislation implementing the Uruguay Round agreements in 1994; & the House bill seeking to renew fast-track authority in 1998. The authors provide a brief legislative history of each & then outline a conceptual framework for their analysis. Focusing on district & state economic conditions, ideological leanings & campaign contributions, they find both predictable & surprising relationships in the data. *Publisher Paid Annotation.*

Baldwin, Robert E., et al. Issues in U. S.-EC Trade Relations. (National Bureau of Economic Research Conference Report Ser.). (Illus.). xii, 412p. 1988. lib. bdg. 59.00 (*0-226-03608-1*) U Ch Pr.
— Political Economy of U. S.-Taiwan Trade. LC 95-13471. (Studies in International Trade Policy). 232p. 1995. text 75.00 (*0-472-10551-5*, 10551) U of Mich Pr.
Baldwin, Robert F. Daily Life in Ancient & Modern Beijing. LC 98-17769. (Cities Through Time Ser.). (Illus.). 64p. (J). (gr. 4-7). 1999. lib. bdg. 23.93 (*0-8225-3214-X*, Runestone Pr) Lerner Pub.
— New England Whaler. LC 95-14542. (American Pastfinder Ser.). (Illus.). 48p. (J). (gr. 4-7). 1996. lib. bdg. 19.95 (*0-8225-2978-5*, Lerner Publctns) Lerner Pub.
— This Is the Sea That Feeds Us. LC 97-42916. (Illus.). 36p. (YA). (ps up). 1998. 16.95 (*1-883220-69-6*); pap. 7.95 (*1-883220-70-X*) Dawn CA.
Baldwin, Rodney, ed. Developing the Future Aviation System. LC 98-28581. 19p. 1998. text 65.95 (*0-291-39843-X*, Pub. by Avebry) Ashgate Pub Co.
Baldwin, Roger. Inside a Cop: The Tensions in the Public & Private Lives of the Police. (Illus.). 1977. pap. 3.95 (*0-910286-55-8*) Boxwood.
***Baldwin, Roger G. & Chronister, Jay L.** Teaching Without Tenure: Policies & Practices for a New Era. LC 00-8845. (Illus.). 224p. 2001. write for info. (*0-8018-6502-6*) Johns Hopkins.
Baldwin, Roger G., jt. auth. see Austin, Ann E.
Baldwin, Roger N., ed. see Kropotkin, Piotr A.
Baldwin, Rollin P. & Hughes, Jonathan T. Boards at Their Best: A New Approach Toward Improved Board Effectiveness. LC 95-74860. (Illus.). 208p. (Orig.). 1995. pap. 24.95 (*1-884280-00-5*) Connolly-Cormack.
Baldwin, Rosalia, tr. Una Guia para el I Ching. 3rd ed.Tr. of Guide to the I Ching. (SPA.). 360p. (Orig.). 1997. pap. 18.95 (*0-9603832-9-8*) Anthony Pub Co.
Baldwin, S. Alcohol Education & Young Offenders: Medium & Short Term Effectiveness of Education Programs. (Recent Research in Psychology Ser.). (Illus.). ix, 152p. 1991. 63.95 (*0-387-97507-1*) Spr-Verlag.
Baldwin, Sallie. Beautiful Christmas Jewelry. (Illus.). 16p. (J). (gr. 4-7). 1996. pap. 6.95 (*0-8167-3526-3*) Troll Communs.
Baldwin, Sally, et al, eds. Quality of Life: Perspectives & Policies. LC 93-25921. 272p. (C). 1993. pap. 27.99 (*0-415-09581-6*) Routledge.
Baldwin, Sam. Biomass Stoves: Engineering, Design, Development, & Dissemination. Crouch, Margaret, ed. 287p. 1987. 35.75 (*0-86619-274-3*) Vols Tech Asst.
— Lab Tests of Fired Clay & Metal One-Pot Chimneyless Stoves. 37p. 1988. 8.75 (*0-86619-237-9*) Vols Tech Asst.
Baldwin, Sarah, ed. see Shahro, Eileen.
Baldwin, Scott. Art of Advocacy Vol. 1: Direct Examination. 1981. ring bd. 160.00 (*0-8205-1036-X*) Bender.
Baldwin, Scott & Hare, Francis H. Scott Baldwin on Jury Arguments, 1. LC 97-13281. (Trial Practice Library Ser.). 312p. 1997. boxed set 135.00 (*0-471-16462-3*) Wiley.
Baldwin, Scott & McGovern, Frances E. The Preparation of a Product Liability Case. 2nd ed. 1066p. boxed set 125.00 (*0-316-07973-1*, 79731) Aspen Law.
Baldwin, Scott, et al. The Preparation of a Product Liability Case. 1054p. 1981. 80.00 (*0-316-07925-1*, Aspen Law & Bus) Aspen Pub.
— The Preparation of a Product Liability Case. 2nd ed. 1072p. 1992. 125.00 (*0-316-07962-6*, Aspen Law & Bus) Aspen Pub.
— The Preparation of a Product Liability Case, 1. 3rd ed. LC 98-20960. 1066p. 1998. ring bd. 145.00 (*0-7355-0145-9*) Panel Pubs.
— Product Liability Case Digest. annuals 400p. pap. 60.00 (*0-316-08015-2*, 80152) Aspen Law.
Baldwin, Shauna S. English Lessons & Other Stories. 165p. 1996. pap. text 13.95 (*0-86492-183-7*, Pub. by Goose Ln Edits) Genl Dist Srvs.
***Baldwin, Shauna S.** What the Body Remembers. LC 99-30320. 496p. 1999. 25.95 (*0-385-49604-4*, N A Talese) Doubleday.
***Baldwin, Shauna Singh.** What the Body Remembers. 2001. reprint ed. pap. 15.00 (*0-385-49605-2*, Anchor NY) Doubleday.
Baldwin, Sherman. Ironclaw: A Navy Carrier Pilot's Gulf War Experience. 320p. 1997. mass mkt. 5.99 (*0-553-57748-4*) Bantam.
— Ironclaw: A Navy Carrier Pilot's Gulf War Experience. LC 96-2287. 288p. 1996. 24.00 (*0-688-14303-2*, Wm Morrow) Morrow Avon.
Baldwin, Shirley & Boas, Sarah. Conversational French in Seven Days. LC 99-31524. (Language in Seven Days Ser.). (FRE., Illus.). 96p. 1995. pap. 6.95 (*0-8442-4467-8*, 44678, Passprt Bks) NTC Contemp Pub Co.
Baldwin, Shirley & Boas, Sarah. Conversational French in Seven Days. (Language in 7 Days Ser.). (Illus.). 96p. 1995. 12.95 incl. audio (*0-8442-4466-X*, 326150, Passprt Bks) NTC Contemp Pub Co.
Baldwin, Shirley & Boas, Sarah. Conversational German in Seven Days. LC 97-50367. (Language in Seven Days Ser.). (GER., Illus.). 96p. 1995. pap. 7.95 (*0-8442-4484-8*, 44848, Passprt Bks) NTC Contemp Pub Co.
Baldwin, Shirley & Boas, Sarah. Conversational German in Seven Days. (Language in 7 Days Ser.). (Illus.). 96p. 1995. 12.95 incl. audio (*0-8442-4483-X*, 326163, Passprt Bks) NTC Contemp Pub Co.
Baldwin, Shirley & Boas, Sarah. Conversational Italian in Seven Days. (Language in Seven Days Ser.). (ITA., Illus.). 96p. 1995. pap. 7.95 (*0-8442-4498-8*, 44988, Passprt Bks) NTC Contemp Pub Co.
Baldwin, Shirley & Boas, Sarah. Conversational Italian in Seven Days. (Language in 7 Days Ser.). (Illus.). 96p. 1995. 12.95 incl. audio (*0-8442-4497-X*, 326176, Passprt Bks) NTC Contemp Pub Co.
Baldwin, Shirley & Boas, Sarah. Conversational Russian in Seven Days. LC 98-10779. (Language in Seven Days Ser.). (RUS., Illus.). 96p. 1994. pap. 8.95 (*0-8442-4534-8*, 45348, Passprt Bks) NTC Contemp Pub Co.
Baldwin, Shirley & Boas, Sarah. Conversational Russian in Seven Days. (Language in 7 Days Ser.). (Illus.). 96p. 1995. 12.95 incl. audio (*0-8442-4533-X*, 326202, Passprt Bks) NTC Contemp Pub Co.
— Conversational Spanish in Seven Days. LC 97-50365. (Language in Seven Days Ser.). (SPA., Illus.). 96p. 1994. pap. 6.95 (*0-8442-4453-8*, 44538, Passprt Bks) NTC Contemp Pub Co.
Baldwin, Shirley & Boas, Sarah. Conversational Spanish in Seven Days. (Language in 7 Days Ser.). (Illus.). 96p. 1995. 12.95 incl. audio (*0-8442-4452-X*, 326137, Passprt Bks) NTC Contemp Pub Co.
Baldwin, Shirley, et al. French Conversational. (Conversational Ser.). (FRE., Illus.). 96p. 1995. pap. 14.95 incl. audio (*0-8442-9132-3*, Natl Textbk Co) NTC Contemp Pub Co.
— German Conversational. (Conversational Ser.). (GER.). 96p. 1995. pap. 14.95 incl. audio (*0-8442-9133-1*, Natl Textbk Co) NTC Contemp Pub Co.
— Greek Conversational. (Conversational Ser.). (ENG & GRE.). 96p. 1997. pap. 14.95 incl. audio (*0-8442-9140-4*, Natl Textbk Co) NTC Contemp Pub Co.
— Italian Conversational. (Conversational Ser.). (ITA.). 96p. 1995. pap. 14.95 incl. audio (*0-8442-9135-8*, Natl Textbk Co) NTC Contemp Pub Co.
— Russian Conversational, Set. (Conversational Ser.). (RUS.). 96p. 1995. pap. 14.95 incl. audio (*0-8442-9137-4*, Natl Textbk Co) NTC Contemp Pub Co.
— Spanish Conversational, Set. (Conversational Ser.). (SPA.). 96p. 1995. pap. 14.95 incl. audio (*0-8442-9130-7*, Natl Textbk Co) NTC Contemp Pub Co.
Baldwin, Shirley M. First Aid for the Office & Workplace. (Illus.). 192p. 1991. pap. 15.00 (*0-87527-483-8*) Green.
Baldwin, Simeon E. The American Judiciary. LC 91-55366. (American State Ser.). xiii, 403p. 1991. reprint ed. 95.00 (*0-912004-92-4*) Gaunt.
— American Judiciary. (American State Ser.). xiii, 403p. 1992. reprint ed. 47.50 (*0-8377-1922-4*, Rothman) W S Hein.
Baldwin, Spurgeon, ed. & tr. see Latini, Brunetto.
Baldwin, Spurgeon, tr. see Latini, Brunetto.
Baldwin, Stanley. On England, & Other Addresses. LC 70-156609. (Essay Index Reprint Ser.). 1977. reprint ed. 23.95 (*0-8369-2305-7*) Ayer.

— This Torch of Freedom: Speeches & Addresses. LC 73-157962. (Essay Index Reprint Ser.). 1977. reprint ed. 23.95 (*0-8369-2213-1*) Ayer.

Baldwin, Stanley C. 1999. LC 94-16540. 220p. (Orig.). 1994. pap. 9.99 (*0-8308-1363-2*, 1363) InterVarsity.

— 1999. LC 98-53616. (Orig.). 1999. pap. 23.95 (*0-7862-1807-X*) Thorndike Pr.

— What Did Jesus Say about That? rev. ed. LC 74-28510. 224p. 1975. pap. 9.99 (*0-88207-718-X*, 6-2718, Victor Bks) Chariot Victor.

Baldwin, Stanley C., jt. auth. see MacGregor, Malcolm.

Baldwin, Stanley S. Forward Everywhere: Her Majesty's Territorials. 288p. 1994. text 49.00 (*0-08-040716-1*, Pub. by Brasseys) Brasseys.

***Baldwin, Stephen A., ed.** Membrane Transport: A Practical Approach. (The Practical Approach Ser.: Vol. 230). (Illus.). 352p. 2000. text 110.00 (*0-19-963705-9*); pap. text 55.00 (*0-19-963704-0*) OUP.

Baldwin, Stephen C. Pictures in the Air: The Story of the National Theatre of the Deaf. (Illus.). 176p. 1994. 24.95 (*1-56368-025-4*) Gallaudet Univ Pr.

Baldwin, Steve. The Myth of Community Care: An Alternative Neighbourhood Model of Care. LC 93-30442. 186p. 1993. pap. 31.75 (*1-56593-225-0*, 0563) Singular Publishing.

Baldwin, Steve & Barker, Philip. Needs Assessment of Human Problems. LC 97-41334. (Illus.). 256p. 1998. pap. text 35.00 (*0-7506-2435-3*) Buttrwrth-Heinemann.

Baldwin, Steve & Holgate, Karen, eds. Political Correctness Invades the Classroom: The Public Speaks Out! LC 98-56505. 304p. 1999. pap. 15.00 (*0-938453-07-6*) Small Helm Pr.

Baldwin, Steve & Oxlad, Melissa. Electroshock & Minors: A Fifty Year Review. LC 99-16141. 2000. lib. bdg. write for info. (*0-313-30861-6*) Greenwood.

Baldwin, Steve, jt. auth. see Lessard, Bill.

Baldwin, Steve, jt. compiled by see Rogers, Pamela.

Baldwin, Steve, jt. ed. see Barker, Philip J.

Baldwin, Stuart & Halstead, Beverly. Dinosaur Stamps of the World. (Illus.). 128p. (C). 1989. pap. 79.00 (*0-9508063-4-X*, Pub. by S A Baldwin) St Mut.

Baldwin, Stuart A. John Ray Essex Naturalist. 80p. (C). 1986. 35.00 (*0-9508063-3-1*, Pub. by S A Baldwin) St Mut.

Baldwin, Sue. Lifesavers: Tips for Success & Sanity for Early Childhood Managers. Whelan, Mary S., ed. LC 96-35829. (Illus.). 150p. (Orig.). 1996. pap. 14.00 (*0-9654439-0-6*) Insights Trning.

***Baldwin, Sue.** Lighten up & Live Longer: A Collection of Jokes, Antidotes & Stories Guaranteed to Tickle Your Soul. Steiner-Whelan, Mary, ed. (Illus.). 160p. 1999. pap. 12.00 (*0-9654439-1-4*) Insights Trning.

Baldwin, T. O., et al, eds. Chemical Aspects of Enzyme Biotechnology: Fundamentals. LC 91-10371. (Industry-University Cooperative Chemistry Program Symposia Ser.). (Illus.). 368p. (C). 1991. text 132.00 (*0-306-43815-1*, Kluwer Plenum) Kluwer Academic.

Baldwin, T. O., jt. auth. see Kelly, J. W.

Baldwin, T. W. Patten Genealogy: William Patten of Cambridge, 1635 & His Descendants. (Illus.). 300p. 1989. reprint ed. pap. 45.00 (*0-8328-0941-1*); reprint ed. lib. bdg. 53.00 (*0-8328-0940-3*) Higginson Bk Co.

Baldwin, Thomas, ed. see Moore, G. E.

Baldwin, Thomas B. The Cabin. 120p. 1993. 12.00 (*0-9636032-0-5*) Baldwin PA.

Baldwin, Thomas F., et al. Convergence: Integrating Media, Information, & Communication. LC 95-37638. 440p. 1995. 58.00 (*0-8039-5904-4*); pap. 26.95 (*0-8039-5905-2*) Sage.

Baldwin, Thomas O., jt. ed. see Larimer, George H.

Baldwin, Thomas W. Bacon Genealogy: Michael Bacon of Dedham, 1640, & His Descendants. 422p. 1993. reprint ed. pap. 44.00 (*0-8328-3012-7*); reprint ed. lib. bdg. 54.00 (*0-8328-3011-9*) Higginson Bk Co.

— Vital Records of Natick, Massachusetts, to 1850. 249p. 1991. reprint ed. pap. 19.00 (*1-55613-457-6*) Heritage Bk.

Baldwin, Thomas W., ed. see Baldwin, Jeduthan.

Baldwin, Tony, jt. ed. see Appleton, Richard E.

***Baldwin, U. Bernell.** Ordination. LC 99-93692. (Illus.). vii, 210p. 1999. pap. 15.00 (*0-9670514-0-1*) U & W Pub.

Baldwin, Vicki H. Administrator's Guide to the U. S. Department of Education Including Technology Resources. 145p. 1996. reprint ed. pap. text 30.00 (*0-7881-3620-8*) DIANE Pub.

Baldwin, Virginia, jt. auth. see Baldwin, Louis.

Baldwin, Virginia J. Pathology of Multiple Pregnancy. LC 92-48343. 1993. 193.00 (*0-387-94011-1*) Spr-Verlag.

Baldwin, W. E., ed. see Bouvier, John.

Baldwin, W. W. The Price of Power. LC 76-990. (FDR & the Era of the New Deal Ser.). 361p. 1976. reprint ed. lib. bdg. 39.50 (*0-306-70803-5*) Da Capo.

Baldwin, William. Suede Holloway. 1978. pap. 3.95 (*0-9602170-0-2*) Ars Eterna.

— Treatise of Morall Philosophie. rev. ed. LC 67-10126. 414p. 1967. reprint ed. 50.00 (*0-8201-1003-5*) Schol Facsimiles.

***Baldwin, William J.** CE-VI - Close Encounters of the Possession Kind: A Different Kind of Interference of Otherworldly Beings. 128p. 1998. pap. 10.95 (*0-929915-22-4*) Headline Bks.

Baldwin, William J. Spirit Releasement Therapy: A Technical Manual. (Illus.). 480p. 1993. pap. 39.95 (*1-882658-00-0*) Human Potent Fnd.

— Spirit Releasement Therapy: A Technique Manual. 2nd ed. (Illus.). 480p. 1995. pap. 39.95 (*0-929915-16-X*) Headline Bks.

Baldwin, William J., jt. auth. see Baldwin, Judith A.

Baldwin, William L. Antitrust & the Changing Corporation. LC 61-16905. 315p. reprint ed. pap. 97.70 (*0-8357-5641-6*, 201787900010) Bks Demand.

Baldwin, William L. Structure of the Defense Market, 1955-1964. LC 67-23730. 257p. reprint ed. 79.70 (*0-608-16107-1*, 201788000010) Bks Demand.

— The World Tin Market: Political Pricing & Economic Competition. LC 83-8888. (Duke Press Policy Studies). xii, 273p. 1983. text 58.95 (*0-8223-0505-4*) Duke.

Baldwin, William L. & Scott, John T. Market Structure & Technological Change, Vol. 17. (Fundamentals of Pure & Applied Economics Ser.: Vol. 1). viii, 170p. 1987. pap. text 58.00 (*3-7186-0375-6*) Gordon & Breach.

Baldwin, William P., III. Charleston. LC 97-74350. (Illus.). 80p. 1997. 34.95 (*0-933101-17-1*); pap. 19.95 (*0-933101-18-X*) Legacy Pubns.

Baldwin, William P., Jr. Lowcountry Daytrips. (Illus.). 237p. (Orig.). 1995. pap. 9.95 (*0-933101-07-4*) Legacy Pubns.

Baldwin, William P., Jr. & Baldwin, Agnes. Plantations of the Low Country: South Carolina, 1697-1865. LC 84-82499. (Illus.). 144p. 1986. pap. 19.95 (*0-933101-03-1*) Legacy Pubns.

Baldwin, William P., jt. auth. see Whaley, Emily.

Baldwin, Winnie, jt. auth. see Baldwin, Jack.

Baldy, C. & Stigter, C. J. Agrometeorology of Multiple Cropping in Warm Climates. (Illus.). 264p. 1997. pap. 44.00 (*1-886106-92-4*, 6924) Science Pubs.

Baldy, Marian. The University Wine Course. (Illus.). 380p. 1992. pap. 24.95 (*0-932664-67-9*) Wine Appreciation.

— The University Wine Course: A Comprehensive Text & Self Tutorial. LC 92-50668. (Illus.). 426p. 1993. pap. 35.00 (*0-932664-69-5*) Wine Appreciation.

Baldy, Marian W. Teacher's Manual for the University Wine Course. 86p. 1993. pap., teacher ed. 12.95 (*0-932664-68-7*, 6680M) Wine Appreciation.

Baldy-Moulinier. Cerebral Blood Flow, Metabolism & Epilepsy. (Current Problems in Epilepsy Ser.: Vol. 1). (Illus.). 1983. 79.95 (*0-86196-038-6*, Pub. by J Libbey Med) Bks Intl VA.

Baldy-Moulinier, M., et al. Clinical Use of Emission Tomography in Focal Epilepsy. (Current Problems in Epilepsy Ser.: Vol. 7). 192p. 1989. 74.95 (*0-86196-206-0*, Pub. by J Libbey Med) Bks Intl VA.

Baldy, Tom F. Battle for Ulster: A Study of Internal Security. 153p. (Orig.). 1987. pap. 3.75 (*0-317-62826-7*, S-N 008-020-01101-1) US HHS.

— Battle for Ulster: A Study of Internal Security. (Illus.). 136p. (Orig.). (C). 1997. reprint ed. pap. text 40.00 (*0-7881-4145-7*) DIANE Pub.

Baldyga, Daniel G. A Sailor Remembers: His Voyage from Darkness into Light. 320p. (Orig.). 1989. pap. 9.95 (*0-924142-00-6*) Mystic Hse.

Bale, Chris. Faces in the Crowd: A Journey in Hope. (Illus.). 224p. 1999. pap. 27.50 (*962-201-885-8*, Pub. by Chinese Univ) U of Mich Pr.

Bale, Chris, jt. auth. see Nutt, Tim.

Bale, Don, Jr. The Fabulous Investment Potential of Singles. 4th rev. ed. 1980. pap. 5.00 (*0-912070-13-7*) Bale Bks.

— Fabulous Investment Potential of Uncirculated Singles. 4th rev. ed. 1980. pap. 5.00 (*0-912070-11-0*) Bale Bks.

— Gold Mine in Your Pocket. 4th rev. ed. 1980. pap. 5.00 (*0-912070-07-2*) Bale Bks.

— How to Find Valuable Old & Scarce Coins. 4th rev. ed. 1980. pap. 5.00 (*0-912070-15-3*) Bale Bks.

— How to Invest in Uncirculated Singles. 4th rev. ed. 1980. pap. 5.00 (*0-912070-10-2*) Bale Bks.

— Out of Little Coins, Big Fortunes Grow. 4th rev. ed. 1980. pap. 5.00 (*0-912070-08-0*) Bale Bks.

Bale, Don, Jr., ed. Fabulous Investment Potential of Liberty Walking Half Dollars. 4th rev. ed. 1980. pap. 5.00 (*0-912070-05-6*) Bale Bks.

Bale, John. The Brawn Drain: Foreign Student Athletes in American Universities. 248p. 1991. text 29.95 (*0-252-01732-3*) U of Ill Pr.

— Chief Promises of God. LC 70-133635. (Tudor Facsimile Texts. Old English Plays Ser.: No. 21). reprint ed. 59.50 (*0-404-53321-3*) AMS Pr.

— The Dramatic Writings. (BCL1-PR English Literature Ser.). 347p. 1992. reprint ed. lib. bdg. 89.00 (*0-7812-7234-3*) Rprt Serv.

— The First Two Partes of the Acts or Unchaste Examples of the Englyshe Votaryes. LC 79-84086. (English Experience Ser.: No. 906). 540p. 1979. reprint ed. lib. bdg. 40.00 (*90-221-0906-2*) Walter J Johnson.

— Index Britanniae Scriptorum. xxxvi, 580p. reprint ed. write for info. (*0-318-71734-4*) G Olms Pubs.

— Index Brittanie Scriptorum: John Bale's Index of British & Other Writers. Poole, Reginald L., ed. 656p. 1990. 99.00 (*0-85991-297-3*) Boydell & Brewer.

— John Bale's Index of British & Other Writers. Poole, Reginald L., ed. (Anecdota Oxoniensia Ser.: No. 9). 1988. reprint ed. 97.50 (*0-404-63959-3*) AMS Pr.

— King Johan. Adams, Barry B., ed. & intro. by. LC 67-12048. (Huntington Library Publications). 221p. 1969. reprint ed. pap. 68.60 (*0-608-03165-8*, 206361800007) Bks Demand.

— Kynge Johan: A Play in Two Parts. Collier, J. Payne, ed. LC 79-160012. (Camden Society, London. Publications, First Ser.: No. 2). reprint ed. 32.00 (*0-404-50102-8*) AMS Pr.

— Landscapes of Modern Sport. LC 94-16005. 1994. 49.00 (*0-7185-1458-0*); pap. 24.00 (*0-7185-1464-5*) St Martin.

— Temptation of Christ. LC 74-133636. (Tudor Facsimile Texts. Old English Plays Ser.: No. 22). reprint ed. 59.50 (*0-404-53322-1*) AMS Pr.

— Three Laws. LC 78-133637. (Tudor Facsimile Texts. Old English Plays Ser.: No. 23). reprint ed. 59.50 (*0-404-53323-X*) AMS Pr.

Bale, John & Maguire, Joseph A., eds. The Global Sports Arena: Athletic Talent Migration in an Interdependent World. LC 93-24340. 304p. 1994. 52.50 (*0-7146-3489-1*, Pub. by F Cass Pubs); pap. 22.50 (*0-7146-4116-2*, Pub. by F Cass Pubs) Intl Spec Bk.

Bale, John & Sang, Joe. Kenyan Running: Movement Culture, Geography & Global Change. LC 96-12789. (Illus.). 224p. (C). 1996. 49.50 (*0-7146-4684-9*, Pub. by F Cass Pubs); pap. 24.50 (*0-7146-4218-5*, Pub. by F Cass Pubs) Intl Spec Bk.

Bale, John, jt. auth. see Weilgart, W. John.

Bale, Karen A. & Duey, Kathleen. Hurricane: New Bedford, Massachusetts, 1784. LC 98-50386. (Survival Ser.). 160p. 1999. per. 3.99 (*0-689-82544-7*) S&S Childrens.

Bale, Karen A. Desire's Promise. 320p. 1997. mass mkt. 4.99 (*0-8217-5706-7*, Zebra Kensgtn) Kensgtn Pub Corp.

— Love's Promise. 416p. 1996. mass mkt. 4.99 (*0-8217-5234-0*, Zebra Kensgtn) Kensgtn Pub Corp.

— Sun Dancer's Passion. (Sweet Medicine's Prophecy Ser.: No. 1). 1981. mass mkt. 3.95 (*0-8217-2790-7*, Zebra Kensgtn) Kensgtn Pub Corp.

Bale, Karen A., jt. auth. see Duey, Kathleen.

Bale, Sue & Jones, Vanessa. Wound Care Nursing: A Patient-Centered Approach. (Illus.). 255p. 1996. pap. text 34.00 (*0-7020-1870-8*, Pub. by W B Saunders) Saunders.

***Bale, Tim.** Sacred Cows & Common Sense: The Symbolic Statecraft & Political Culture of the British Labour Party. 286p. 1999. text 70.95 (*1-84014-769-5*, Pub. by Ashgate Pub) Ashgate Pub Co.

Bale, Tim, jt. auth. see Brivati, Brian.

Balee, William. Advances in Historical Ecology. LC 97-34863. (Illus.). 416p. 1998. 65.00 (*0-231-10632-7*) Col U Pr.

— Footprints of the Forest: Ka'apor Ethnobotany - Historical Ecology of Plant Utilization by an Amazonian People. LC 93-11044. 1994. 75.50 (*0-231-07484-0*) Col U Pr.

Balee, William, jt. ed. see Posey, Darrell A.

Balee, William L. Footprints of the Forest. (Biology & Resource Management Ser.). (Illus.). 416p. 1999. pap. 25.00 (*0-231-07485-9*) Col U Pr.

Balek, Jaroslav. Groundwater Resources Assessment. (Developments in Water Science Ser.: No. 38). 250p. 1989. 181.50 (*0-444-98895-5*) Elsevier.

Balek, Jaroslav, et al. Remediation of Soil & Groundwater Opportunities in Eastern Europe: Proceedings of the NATO Advanced Research Workshop on Remediation of Soil & Groundwater As a Technical, Institutional & Socio-Economic Problem - Opportunities in Eastern Europe, Prague, Czech Republic, November 6-10, 1995. McBean, Edward A., ed. LC 96-30278. (NATO ASI Series, Partnership SubSeries 2). 480p. (C). 1995. text 250.00 (*0-7923-4182-1*) Kluwer Academic.

Balek, V. & Tolgessy, J. Thermal Analysis Pt. C: Emanation Thermal Analysis & Other Radiometric Emanation Methods. (Comprehensive Analytical Chemistry Ser.: Vol. XII C). 304p. 1984. 196.50 (*0-444-99659-1*) Elsevier.

Balemi, S., et al, eds. Discrete Event Systems: Modeling & Control: Proceedings of a Joint Workshop Held in Prague, August 1992. LC 93-9970. (Progress in Systems & Control Theory Ser.: No. 13). vii, 230p. 1993. 81.50 (*0-8176-2845-2*) Birkhauser.

Balen, A. T. Van, see Van Balen, A. T.

Balen, Adam & Smith, John. The CTG in Practice. (Illus.). 203p. (Orig.). 1992. pap. text 38.95 (*0-443-04675-1*) Church.

Balen, Adam H. & Jacobs, Howard S. Infertility in Practice. LC 97-7775. 1997. pap. text 55.00 (*0-443-05356-1*) Church.

Balen, Henry. Distributed Object Architectures with CORBA. (Managing Object Technology Ser.: No. 21). 352p. 2000. pap. 39.95 (*0-521-65418-1*) Cambridge U Pr.

Balena, Francesco. Programming Microsoft Visual Basic 6.0. LC 99-20381. (Programming Ser.). (Illus.). 1276p. 1999. pap. 59.99 (*0-7356-0558-0*) Microsoft.

Balendra, Thambirajah. Vibration of Buildings to Wind & Earthquakes. LC 93-15460. 1995. 159.00 (*0-387-19833-4*) Spr-Verlag.

Balensiefer, Frank. The Job Search Game & How to Score, Vol. 1. LC 86-90499. (Illus.). 166p. 1986. pap. 6.95 (*0-9617228-0-0*) F H Balenseifer.

***Balensiefer, Ronald.** God's One-Sided Mirror. 184p. 1999. pap. 15.00 (*0-8059-4607-1*) Dorrance.

Balensuela, C. Matthew, ed. Ars Cantus Mensurabilis Mensurata Per Modos Iuris. LC 94-10656. (Greek & Latin Music Theory Ser.). xii, 331p. 1994. text 45.00 (*0-8032-1245-3*) U of Nebr Pr.

Balent, Matthew. Compendium of Weapons, Armor & Castles. Marciniszyn, Alex & Siembieda, Kevin, eds. (Illus.). 224p. (Orig.). 1989. pap. 19.95 (*0-916211-38-X*, 411) Palladium Bks.

Balent, Matthew, jt. auth. see Siembieda, Kevin.

Balent, Matthew, jt. auth. see Wujcik, Erick.

Balentine, Bruce & Morgan, David P. How to Build a Speech Recognition Application: A Style Guide for Telephony Dialogues. 319p. 1999. pap. 95.00 (*0-9671278-1-5*) Enterp Integ Grp.

Balentine, F. J. Freund & Bro. Pioneer Gunmakers to the West. LC 95-75009. (Illus.). 400p. 1997. 69.95 (*1-882824-13-X*) Graphic Pubs.

Balentine, Samuel E. Prayer in the Hebrew Bible: The Drama of Divine-Human Dialogue. LC 92-20553. (Overtures to Biblical Theology Ser.). 328p. 1993. pap. 21.00 (*0-8006-2615-X*, 1-2615) Augsburg Fortress.

— The Torah's Vision of Worship. LC 99-12063. (Overtures to Biblical Theology Ser.). 240p. 1999. pap. 26.00 (*0-8006-3155-2*, 1-3155, Fortress Pr) Augsburg Fortress.

Balentine, Samuel F., jt. ed. see Barton, John.

Balerna, A., jt. ed. see Burattini, E.

Balerna, M., jt. ed. see Colpi, G. M.

Bales. Burpee American Gardening Series: Gardening with Children. 1994. pap. 9.00 (*0-671-87465-9*) S&S Trade.

Bales, Barry V., jt. auth. see Hadden, Susan G.

***Bales, David.** Gospel Subplots: Story Sermons of God's Grace. LC 99-55644. 2000. pap. 13.50 (*0-7880-1584-2*) CSS OH.

Bales, Don, ed. Correctional Officer Resource Guide. 3rd ed. LC 97-9814. (Illus.). 165p. 1997. pap. 29.95 (*1-56991-064-2*) Am Correctional.

***Bales, Donnie & Milan, Garth.** Freestyle Motocross: Jump Tricks from the Pros. (Illus.). 128p. 2000. pap. 19.95 (*0-7603-0926-4*, 130526AP, Pub. by MBI Pubg) Motorbooks Intl.

***Bales, Donnie & Semics, Gary.** Pro Motocross & Off-Road Riding Techniques. 2nd ed. LC 99-87809. (Illus.). 224p. 2000. pap. 24.95 (*0-7603-0831-4*, Pub. by MBI Pubg) Motorbooks Intl.

Bales, Erv, et al, eds. Building Applications of Heat Flux Transducers-STP 885. LC 85-22863. (Illus.). 267p. 1985. text 34.00 (*0-8031-0438-3*, STP885) ASTM.

Bales, Eugene F. A Ready Reference to Philosophy East & West. 314p. (C). 1988. lib. bdg. 44.00 (*0-8191-6640-5*) U Pr of Amer.

Bales, Eugene H. Rudolph, Encouraged by His Therapist. Coop, Mahlon, ed. 114p. 1997. pap. 7.00 (*0-939391-22-8*) B Woodley Pr.

Bales, Jack. Esther Forbes: A Bio-Bibliography of the Author of Johnny Tremain. LC 97-27707. (Author Bibliographies Ser.). 173p. 1998. 45.00 (*0-8108-3370-0*) Scarecrow.

— Kenneth Roberts. (United States Authors Ser.). 184p. 1993. 22.95 (*0-8057-7643-5*) Macmillan.

— Kenneth Roberts: The Man & His Works. LC 89-34008. (Author Bibliographies Ser.). (Illus.). 354p. 1989. 45.00 (*0-8108-2227-X*) Scarecrow.

***Bales, Jack, ed.** Conversations with Willie Morris. LC 99-54749. 225p. 2000. pap. 18.00 (*1-57806-237-3*); text 45.00 (*1-57806-236-5*) U Pr of Miss.

Bales, Jack, jt. auth. see Scharnhorst, Gary.

Bales, Jack, ed. see Roberts, Kenneth.

Bales, James D. Instrumental Music & New Testament Worship. 406p. 1996. reprint ed. pap. write for info. (*0-945441-24-X*) Res Pubns AR.

Bales, John. Guide to Owning a Parakeet: Budgie. (Illus.). 64p. 1997. pap. 6.95 (*0-7938-2008-1*, RE-208) TFH Pubns.

— Guide to Owning Amazon Parrots. (Illus.). 1997. pap. 6.95 (*0-7938-2000-6*, RE-200) TFH Pubns.

***Bales, Kevin.** Disposable People; New Slavery in the Global Economy. LC 98-47869. 288p. 2000. pap. text 14.95 (*0-520-22463-9*, Pub. by U CA Pr) Cal Prin Full Svc.

— New Slavery: A Reference Handbook. 2000. lib. bdg. 45.00 (*1-57607-239-8*) ABC-CLIO.

Bales, Michael C. Launch Ramps of Baja California. LC 92-90030. (Illus.). 112p. (Orig.). 1992. pap. 6.95 (*0-9632188-0-8*) Cortez Pubns.

Bales, Norman. He Died to Make Men Holy. 352p. (Orig.). 1991. 14.99 (*0-89900-271-4*) College Pr Pub.

Bales, Peter. The Art of Brachygraphie: That Is, to Write As Fast As a Man Speaketh Treatably, Writing but One Letter for a Word. LC 70-38146. (English Experience Ser.: No. 426). 120p. 1972. reprint ed. 20.00 (*90-221-0426-5*) Walter J Johnson.

Bales, Richard. Persuasion in the French Personal Novel: Studies of Chateaubriand, Constant, Balzac, Nerval, & Fromentin. LC 96-70889. 154p. 1997. lib. bdg. 34.95 (*1-883479-16-9*) Summa Pubns.

Bales, Richard, ed. see Proust, Marcel.

Bales, Richard A. Compulsory Arbitration: The Grand Experiment in Employment. LC 97-25729. 248p. 1997. 29.95 (*0-8014-3446-7*) Cornell U Pr.

Bales, Robert F. The Fixation Factor, in Alcohol Addition: An Hypothesis Derived from a Comparative Study of Irish-Jewish Social Norms. Zuckerman, Harriet & Merton, Robert K., eds. LC 79-8971. (Dissertations on Sociology Ser.). 1980. lib. bdg. 44.95 (*0-405-12948-3*) Ayer.

— Interaction Process Analysis: A Method for the Study of Small Groups. LC 76-15042. (Midway Reprint Ser.). (Illus.). 221p. Date not set. reprint ed. pap. 68.60 (*0-608-20990-2*, 205451800003) Bks Demand.

— Social Interaction Systems: Theory & Measurement. LC 98-53727. 455p. 1998. 49.95 (*1-56000-267-0*) Transaction Pubs.

— Symlog Case Study Kit: With Instructions for a Group Self-Study. LC 79-7480. 1980. pap. 19.95 (*0-02-901310-0*) Free Pr.

Bales, Robert F., et al. Symlog: A Manual for the Case Study of Groups. LC 79-7480. (Illus.). 1979. 50.00 (*0-02-901300-3*) Free Pr.

Bales, Suzanne F. Annuals. (Illus.). 96p. 1991. per. 9.00 (*0-671-86394-0*, P-H Gardening) Prntice Hall Bks.

— Ready, Set, Grow: A Guide to Gardening with Children. 144p. 1996. 17.95 (*0-02-860399-0*) Macmillan.

— Roses. LC 92-43069. (Burpee American Gardening Ser.). (Illus.). 1994. pap. 9.00 (*0-671-85044-X*) P-H.

— Vines. LC 94-5195. (Burpee American Gardening Ser.). (Illus.). 1995. pap. 8.00 (*0-671-85045-8*, P-H Gardening) Prntice Hall Bks.

***Bales, Suzy.** A Garden of Fragrance. LC 99-58698. 192p. 2000. 29.95 (*0-06-039341-6*, ReganBks) HarperTrade.

Bales, W. I. Tso Tsung T'ang: Soldier & Statesman of Old China. 1972. lib. bdg. 250.00 (*0-87968-475-5*) Krishna Pr.

Bales, William A. & Fearon, Harold E. CEOs' - Presidents' Perceptions & Expectations of the Purchasing Function. Ketchum, Carol L., ed. LC 93-71180. 38p. (Orig.). (C). 1993. pap. text 20.00 (*0-945968-14-0*) Ctr Advanced Purchasing.

Bales, William A., jt. auth. see Fearon, Harold E.

B

An Asterisk (*) at the beginning of an entry indicates that the title is appearing for the first time.

Balescu, Radu. Statistical Dynamics. 350p. 1997. 48.00 (*1-86094-045-5*); pap. text 24.00 (*1-86094-046-3*) World Scientific Pub.

Balesi, Charles J. The Time of the French in the Heart of North America, 1673-1818. (Illus.). (Orig.). (C). 1992. pap. text 17.00 (*1-881370-00-3*) Alliance Francaise.

Balester & Gibson. Preparing for the English 104 Equivalency Exam. 44p. (C). 1998. pap. 6.95 (*0-7872-4898-3*) Kendall-Hunt.

Balester, Valerie. Cultural Divide: A Study of African-American College-Level Writers. LC 93-18826. 168p. (C). 1993. pap. text 21.50 (*0-86709-325-0*, 0325, Pub. by Boynton Cook Pubs) Heinemann.

Balester, Valerie, jt. auth. see Kells, Michelle Hall.

Balestra, Dominic & Schrenk, Lawrence P., eds. Ways to World Meaning Vol. 64: Annual ACPA Proceedings, 1990. 1991. pap. 20.00 (*0-918090-24-5*) Am Cath Philo.

***Balestra, Mark.** Complete Idiot's Guide to Online Gambling. 380p. 2000. 16.99 (*0-7897-2207-0*) Que.

Balestracci, Duccio. The Renaissance in the Fields: Family Memoirs of a 15th-Century Tuscan Peasant. LC 98-41052. 1999. 48.50 (*0-271-01878-X*) Pa St U Pr.

— The Renaissance in the Fields: Family Memoirs of a 15th-Century Tuscan Peasant. abr. rev. ed. LC 98-41052. (Illus.). 220p. 1999. pap. 14.95 (*0-271-01879-8*) Pa St U Pr.

Balestri, Diane P., et al, eds. Learning to Design, Designing to Learn: Using Technology to Transform the Curriculum. 225p. 1992. 75.00 (*0-8448-1706-6*) Taylor & Francis.

Balestrieri, Elizabeth. Beatitudes/Poems: Poems. LC 96-45644. 112p. 1997. pap. 19.95 (*0-7734-2701-5*, Mellen Poetry Pr) E Mellen.

Balestrino, Philip. El Esqueleto Dentro de Ti. 1995. 10.15 (*0-606-08512-2*, Pub. by Turtleback) Demco.

— Fat & Skinny. LC 74-12306. (Let's-Read-&-Find-Out Science Bks.). (Illus.). (J). (gr. k-3). 1975. lib. bdg. 12.89 (*0-690-00665-9*) HarpC Child Bks.

— Skeleton Inside You. LC 72-132290. (Let's-Read-&-Find-Out Science Bks.). (Illus.). (J). (gr. k-3). 1971. pap. 4.95 (*0-690-01263-2*); lib. bdg. 12.89 (*0-690-74123-5*) HarpC Child Bks.

— Skeleton Inside You. LC 85-42982. (Trophy Let's-Read-&-Find-Out Bk.). (Illus.). 40p. (J). (ps-3). 1986. pap. 4.95 (*0-06-445039-2*, HarpTrophy) HarpC Child Bks.

— Skeleton Inside You. (Let's Read-&-Find-Out Science Ser.). 1989. 10.15 (*0-606-09862-3*, Pub. by Turtleback) Demco.

— The Skeleton Inside You. rev. ed. LC 88-24600. (Trophy Let's-Read-&-Find-Out Bk.). (Illus.). 32p. (J). (ps-3). 1989. pap. 4.95 (*0-06-445087-2*, HarpTrophy) HarpC Child Bks.

Baletibc, Zvonimir & Nikibc, Gozard. Croatia Between Aggression & Peace. LC 95-130802. 80 p. 1994. write for info. (*953-174-019-4*) ADA Publng.

Balewa, Alhaji S. Shaihu Umar: A Historical Novel about Slavery in Africa. Hisket, Mervin, tr. LC 89-5765. (Topics in World History Ser.). (Illus.). 144p. 1989. 18.95 (*1-55876-012-1*); pap. 9.95 (*1-55876-006-7*) Wiener Pubs Inc.

Baley. Algebra: A First Course. 3rd ed. (Mathematics Ser.). 1990. pap., student ed. 20.95 (*0-534-10333-2*) PWS Pubs.

— S.m. Algebra: A First Course. 2nd ed. (Math). 1984. student ed. 10.50 (*0-534-02762-8*) Brooks-Cole.

Baley, ed. 4 Problems Analysis Introduction to Philosphy. 278p. 1999. pap. text 38.00 (*0-536-02635-1*) P-H.

Baley & Holstege. Sm-algebra-a First Course. (Math). 1980. student ed. 7.50 (*0-534-00764-3*) Brooks-Cole.

Baley, John D. Trigonometry: Student Solutions Manual. 3rd ed. (C). 1995. pap. text, student ed. 31.25 (*0-07-005721-4*) McGraw.

Baley, John D. & Holstege, Martin. Algebra: A First Course. 2nd ed. (Math). 505p. (C). 1984. mass mkt. 31.25 (*0-534-02761-X*) PWS Pubs.

— Trigonometry. 2nd ed. (C). 1991. pap. text, teacher ed. 21.50 (*0-07-003568-7*) McGraw.

— Understanding Algebra. (C). 1991. text 52.00 (*0-07-003566-0*) McGraw.

Baley, John D. & Sarell. Trigonometry. 3rd ed. 416p. (C). 1995. pap. 48.13 (*0-07-005188-7*) McGraw.

Baley, John D., et al. Basic Mathematics: A Program for Semi-Independent Study. 370p. (C). 1978. 2.66 (*0-669-01020-0*) HM Trade Div.

Baleyete, Jean. Economic & Legal Dictionary, French-English/English-French. 4th ed. (FRE.). 663p. 1995. 150.00 (*0-7859-9945-0*) Fr & Eur.

Baleyte, Jean, et al. Dictionnaire Economique et Juridique. 3rd rev. ed. (FRE.). 1992. write for info. (*0-7859-7883-6*, 2-275-00643-5) Fr & Eur.

— Dictionnaire Economoqie et Juridique: Francais-Anglais, Anglais-Francais. 3rd ed. (ENG & FRE.). 725p. 1992. pap. 150.00 (*0-8288-0381-1*, M8442) Fr & Eur.

Balf, Thomas & Sims, David L., eds. Hazardous Waste Regulation & the Small Quantity Generator. 505p. ring bd. 99.95 (*0-317-65537-X*, 323) Busn Legal Reports.

***Balf, Todd.** The Last River: The Tragic Race for Shangri-la. 288p. 2000. 24.00 (*0-609-60625-5*, Crown) Crown Pub Group.

Balfe, Alan. CorelDRAW! 3.0: A User's Guide. LC 92-18189. 480p. (C). 1992. pap. text 34.95 (*0-13-014581-5*) P-H.

Balfe, Dennis M. & Slone, Richard. Review of Whole Body. LC 99-23503. (Illus.). 672p. 1999. 75.00 (*0-07-058219-X*) McGraw-Hill HPD.

Balfe, Dennis M., et al. Gastrointestinal Disease (Fifth Series) Test & Syllabus. (Profession Self-Evaluation Program Ser.: Vol. 39). (Illus.). 750p. 1995. 220.00 (*1-55903-039-9*) Am Coll Radiology.

Balfe, Donna. The Last Housewife in America. 32p. (Orig.). 1996. pap. 6.00 (*0-9644333-7-0*) CrosslusRds.

Balfe, Judith & Wyszomirski, Jane, eds. Art, Ideology & Politics. LC 84-26325. 384p. 1985. 69.50 (*0-275-90055-X*, C0055, Praeger Pubs) Greenwood.

Balfe, Judith H., ed. Paying the Piper: Causes & Consequences of Art Patronage. LC 92-38280. 344p. 1993. text 45.95 (*0-252-02005-7*); pap. text 17.95 (*0-252-06310-4*) U of Ill Pr.

***Balfe, Judith Huggins. Passing It On: The Inheritance & Use of Summer Houses. 304p. 1999. (*1-57087-486-7*) Prof Pr NC.**

A family summer house can be the repository of generations of family experiences. It simultaneously can be the source of great family discord as new generations increase family size & diversity. Judith Huggins Balfe, a professional sociologist & summer house heir, has interviewed 125 families who share time & ownership at family summer homes in 18 states & Canada. Her book is a professional assessment of the various factors that determine the parameters of summer house inheritance, & their consequences for both families & individuals. These include differences of social class or status, & issues of authority over the summer house & the legacy it preserves. In separate chapters, Balfe describes several family roles & organizing structures. She also explains a variety of formal, legal arrangements, suggests mediation principles, & presents some tested methods of fair division of time at the summer house. Using scores of interview excerpts, she illustrates the difficulties & solutions multi-generational families have had with family summer houses. Each situation is unique, but how relatives perceive legacy, stewardship & family commitment will determine how successful is the passing on of summer houses. ***Publisher Paid Annotation.***

Balfe, Judith Huggins, jt. auth. see Huggins, Kenneth.

Balflour, E. The Timber Trees of India & of Eastern & Southern Asia, 1870. 370p. (C). 1988. 80.00 (*0-7855-3253-6*, Pub. by Scientific) St Mut.

Balfoort, John P. Always Look Back. (Illus.). 322p. 1996. 24.95 (*0-945199-13-9*); pap. 14.95 (*0-945199-06-6*) Double SS Pr.

Balfour. Shanghai. write for info. (*0-471-87733-6*) Wiley.

— World Cities. text. write for info. (*0-471-48945-X*) Wiley.

Balfour, Alan. Informatics of Architectures. pap. text 35.00 (*0-471-98251-2*) Wiley.

Balfour, Alan, ed. Berlin. LC 98-113379. (World Cities Ser.: No. 3). (Illus.). 369p. 1995. 95.00 (*1-85490-374-8*, Pub. by Wiley) Wiley.

***Balfour, Angus.** Lorna Barrett. 224p. 1999. mass mkt. 7.95 (*1-56201-159-6*, Pub. by Blue Moon Bks) Publishers Group.

Balfour, Angus. Shades of Singapore Vol. 1: Sister Sarah Balfour's Memoirs of Judicial Caning in South Africa. 304p. (Orig.). 1994. mass mkt. 7.95 (*1-56201-071-9*) Blue Moon Bks.

Balfour, Arthur J. Essays & Addresses. LC 72-3422. (Essay Index Reprint Ser.). 1977. reprint ed. 20.95 (*0-8369-2890-3*) Ayer.

— Essays, Speculative & Political. LC 76-142604. (Essay Index Reprint Ser.). 1977. reprint ed. 23.95 (*0-8369-2306-5*) Ayer.

— Theism & Thought: A Study in Familiar Beliefs. LC 77-27208. (Gifford Lectures: 1922-23). reprint ed. 45.00 (*0-404-60469-2*) AMS Pr.

***Balfour, Arthur James & Perry, Michael W.** Theism & Humanism: The Book That Influenced C. S. Lewis, 1, 1. LC 00-101331. 200p. (YA). (gr. 9-13). 2000. pap. 14.95 (*1-58742-000-7*) Inkling Bks.

Balfour, Betty. Lord Lytton's Indian Administration, 1876-80: The Untold Story. (C). 1988. 58.50 (*81-212-0137-3*, Pub. by Gian Publng Hse) S Asia.

Balfour-Browne, F. Water Beetles & Other Things (Half a Century's Work) 226p. 1962. 50.00 (*0-7855-0680-2*) St Mut.

Balfour, Bruce. Outpost Official Strategy Guide. LC 93-87075. (Illus.). 300p. 1994. pap. 19.95 (*1-55958-508-0*) Prima Pub.

— Star Crusader: A Novel. 312p. 1995. mass mkt. 5.99 (*0-7615-0067-7*) Prima Pub.

Balfour, C. M. County Folklore Vol. IV: Printed Extracts No. 6, Examples of Printed Folklore Concerning Northumberland. Thomas, Northcote W., ed. (Folk-Lore Society, London Monographs). 1972. reprint ed. pap. 25.00 (*0-8115-0524-3*) Periodicals Srv.

Balfour, Christopher. Roads to Oblivion: Triumphs & Tragedies of British Car Makers 1946-56. (Illus.). 208p. 1996. 39.95 (*1-870979-82-6*, Bay View Bks) MBI Pub.

Balfour, Conrad. Black Men Still Singing: Poetry. 1990. 8.00 (*0-940248-38-7*) Guild Pr.

Balfour, Conrad, ed. The Butterfly Tree. 190p. 1985. pap. 7.00 (*0-89823-068-3*) New Rivers Pr.

Balfour, D. J. K. Psychotropic Drugs of Abuse. (International Encyclopedia of Pharmacology & Therapeutics Ser.). (Illus.). 384p. 1990. 193.00 (*0-08-036851-4*, Pergamon Pr) Elsevier.

Balfour, Daniel T. Thirteenth Virginia Cavalry. (Virginia Regimental Histories Ser.). (Illus.). 115p. 1986. 19.95 (*0-930919-29-7*) H E Howard.

Balfour, Danny L., jt. auth. see Adams, Guy B.

Balfour, Daryl. Etosha: A Visual Souvenir. LC 98-101189. 1998. 22.95 (*1-86872-045-4*, Pub. by New5 Holland) Sterling.

Balfour, Daryl & Balfour, Sharna. African Elephants: A Celebration of Majesty. (Illus.). 168p. 1998. 45.00 (*0-7892-0389-8*) Abbeville Pr.

— Rhino. (Illus.). 176p. 1992. text 39.95 (*1-56757-001-1*) Appleton Comms.

Balfour, David. Ancient Orkney Melodies. (C). 1986. 60.00 (*0-907618-12-X*, Pub. by Orkney Pr) St Mut.

Balfour, David, ed. Oppressions of the Sixteenth Century in the Islands of Orkney & Zetland: From Original Documents. (Maitland Club, Glasgow. Publications: No. 75). reprint ed. 39.50 (*0-404-53114-8*) AMS Pr.

Balfour, David W. & Koutsogiane, Joyce H. Cumberland by the Blackstone: 250 Years of Heritage. LC 97-35818. 1997. write for info. (*1-57864-008-3*) Donning Co.

Balfour, Derek. Re-Upholstery Techniques. 1986. 9.95 (*0-316-07932-4*) Little.

Balfour, Dianne, jt. ed. see Davis, Hank.

Balfour, E. The Cyclopaedia of India, Set. Vols. 1-5. 1985. reprint ed. 5000.00 (*0-7855-6643-0*, Pub. by Intl Bk Distr) St Mut.

— The Cyclopaedia of India, Vol. 1. 1985. reprint ed. write for info. (*0-7855-2576-9*, Pub. by Intl Bk Distr); reprint ed. write for info. (*0-7855-2618-8*, Pub. by Intl Bk Distr) St Mut.

— The Cyclopaedia of India, Vol. 2. 1131p. 1985. reprint ed. write for info. (*0-7855-2577-7*, Pub. by Intl Bk Distr); reprint ed. write for info. (*0-318-68681-3*, Pub. by Intl Bk Distr) St Mut.

— The Cyclopaedia of India, Vol. 3. 1228p. 1985. reprint ed. write for info. (*0-7855-2578-5*, Pub. by Intl Bk Distr); reprint ed. write for info. (*0-7855-2619-6*, Pub. by Intl Bk Distr) St Mut.

— The Cyclopaedia of India, Vol. 4. 931p. 1985. reprint ed. write for info. (*0-7855-2620-X*, Pub. by Intl Bk Distr) St Mut.

— The Cyclopaedia of India, Vol. 5. 1198p. 1985. reprint ed. write for info. (*0-7855-2621-8*, Pub. by Intl Bk Distr) St Mut.

— The Cyclopaedia of India, Vol.4. 1985. reprint ed. write for info. (*0-7855-2579-3*, Pub. by Intl Bk Distr) St Mut.

— The Cyclopaedia of India, Vols. 1-5. 1985. reprint ed. write for info. (*0-7855-2580-7*, Pub. by Intl Bk Distr) St Mut.

— Cyclopedia of India & of Eastern & Southern Asia, 5 vols., Set. 2nd ed. (C). 1988. 1600.00 (*0-7855-3237-4*, Pub. by Scientific) St Mut.

***Balfour, E. G.** Encyclopaedia Asiatica, 9 vols. 1998. pap. 6250.00 (*81-7020-325-2*, Pub. by Print Hse) St Mut.

Balfour, Edward. The Cyclopaedia of India, 5 vols., Set. 5596p. 1986. reprint ed. pap. 7500.00 (*81-7089-060-8*, Pub. by Intl Bk Distr) St Mut.

— Cyclopaedia of India & of Eastern & Southern Asia. 3rd ed. 3800p. 1967. reprint ed. 409.00 (*3-201-00028-0*) Balogh.

Balfour, Edward G. Encyclopaedia Asiatica: Comprising Indian Subcontinent, Eastern & Southern Asia, 9 vols., Set. (C). 1988. 995.00 (*0-7855-0051-0*, Pub. by Print Hse) St Mut.

Balfour, Edward H. Notes on a House in Westconnaug, It's People & History. LC 98-92911. (Illus.). 114p. 1998. pap. 9.95 (*1-57502-818-2*) Morris Pubng.

Balfour, Frederic H. Taoist Texts. 1973. lib. bdg. 300.00 (*0-87968-191-8*) Krishna Pr.

Balfour, Graham. The Life of Robert Louis Stevenson, 2 vols., Set. (BCL1-PR English Literature Ser.). 1992. reprint ed. lib. bdg. 150.00 (*0-7812-7670-5*) Rprt Serv.

— The Life of Robert Louis Stevenson, 2 vols., Set. LC 01-25406. 1968. reprint ed. 29.00 (*0-403-00143-9*) Scholarly.

Balfour, Henry, et al. Anthropological Essays Presented to Edward Burnett Tyler: In Honour of His 75th Birthday. LC 76-44683. reprint ed. 57.50 (*0-404-15900-1*) AMS Pr.

Balfour, Ian. Famous Diamonds. 1998. 125.00 (*0-903432-51-X*) CMW Ltd.

— Northrop Frye. (World Authors Ser.). 160p. 1988. 28.95 (*0-8057-8235-4*, TWAS 806 (CANADA), Twyne) Mac Lib Ref.

Balfour, Issac B., tr. see Goebel, K.

Balfour, James. Philosophical Dissertations: 1782 Edition. 240p. 1996. reprint ed. 68.00 (*1-85506-323-9*) Bks Intl VA.

— Reminiscences of Golf on St. Andrews. rev. ed. 1987. 28.00 (*0-940889-14-5*) Classics Golf.

Balfour, James A. Computer Analysis of Structural Framework. 2nd ed. LC 92-10845. 1992. 55.00 (*0-632-02912-9*) Blackwell Sci.

Balfour-Lynn, I. M. & Valman, H. B. Practical Management of the Newborn. 5th ed. LC 92-49491. 304p. 1993. pap. 36.95 (*0-632-03571-4*, Pub. by Blckwll Scitfc UK) Blackwell Sci.

Balfour, M. Mysterious Scotland. LC 97-136345. 1997. text 35.00 (*1-85158-695-4*, Pub. by Mainstream Pubng) Trafalgar.

***Balfour, Michael.** Bangkok. (Illus.). 96p. 2000. 20.00 (*1-85995-740-4*) Parkstone Pr.

— Sydney. (Great Cities Ser.). (Illus.). 96p. 2000. 20.00 (*1-85995-730-7*) Parkstone Pr.

Balfour, Michael, tr. see Von Meding, Dorothee.

Balfour-Paul, Glen. The End of Empire in the Middle East: Britain's Relinquishment of Power in the Last Three Arab Dependencies. (Cambridge Middle East Library: No. 25). (Illus.). 302p. (C). 1994. pap. text 21.95 (*0-521-46636-9*) Cambridge U Pr.

Balfour-Paul, Jenny. Indigo in the Arab World. (Illus.). 330p. 1996. 75.00 (*0-7007-0373-X*, Pub. by Curzon Pr Ltd) Paul & Co Pubs.

Balfour, R. C., jt. frwd. see Beales, Peter.

Balfour, Sebastian. Castro. (Profiles in Power Ser.). 184p. (C). 1990. 56.00 (*0-582-02971-6*, 78608); pap. text 20.50 (*0-582-02972-4*, 78607) Longman.

— Castro: Profiles in Power. 2nd ed. LC 94-36634. (Profiles in Power Ser.). 198p. (C). 1995. pap. 31.20 (*0-582-24558-3*, 76983) Longman.

Balfour, Sebastian. Dictatorship, Workers, & the City: Labour in Greater Barcelona since 1939. (Illus.). 300p. 1989. text 75.00 (*0-19-822740-X*) OUP.

— The End of the Spanish Empire, 1898-1923. LC 96-26833. (Illus.). 280p. 1997. text 68.00 (*0-19-820507-4*) OUP.

***Balfour, Sebastian & Preston, Paul.** Spain & the Great Powers in the Twentieth Century. LC 98-39238. (Canada Blanch Studies in Contemporary Spain). 1999. write for info. (*0-415-18077-5*); pap. write for info. (*0-415-18078-3*) Routledge.

Balfour, Sharna, jt. auth. see Balfour, Daryl.

Balfour, Susan. Managing Stress in a Changing World. (Illus.). 144p. (Orig.). 1997. pap. 19.95 incl. audio (*1-85410-448-9*, Pub. by Aurum Pr) London Brdge.

Balfour, Thelma. Black Love Signs: An Astrological Guide to Passion Romance & Relationships for African-Americans. LC 98-33240. 320p. 1999. per. 12.00 (*0-684-84783-3*) S&S Trade Pap.

— Black Sun Signs: An African-American Guide to the Zodiac. 240p. 1996. per. 11.00 (*0-684-81209-6*, Fireside) S&S Trade Pap.

Balfour, Vivian V., ed. The Perimeter of Light: Writings about the Vietnam War. LC 92-60239. (Illus.). 280p. (Orig.). 1992. pap. 15.95 (*0-89823-140-X*) New Rivers Pr.

Balfour, Vivian V., ed. see Jarvenpa, Diane.

Balgassi, Haemi. Peacebound Trains. LC 94-26797. (Illus.). 32p. (J). (gr. 2-5). 1996. 14.95 (*0-395-72093-1*, Clarion Bks) HM.

***Balgassi, Haemi.** Peacebound Trains. (Illus.). 48p. (J). (gr. 2-5). 2000. pap. 5.95 (*0-618-04030-7*, Clarion Bks) HM.

Balgassi, Haemi. Tae's Sonata. LC 96-29081. (Illus.). 128p. (J). (gr. 4-7). 1997. 14.00 (*0-395-84314-6*, Clarion Bks) HM.

Balge, Marci Z., jt. auth. see Krieger, Gary R.

Balge, Richard. Acts. (People's Bible Commentary Ser.). 304p. (Orig.). 1993. pap. 10.99 (*0-570-04594-0*, 12-8012) Concordia.

Balge, Richard, jt. auth. see Gerlach, Joel C.

Balge, Richard D. Acts. LC 87-63118. (People's Bible Ser.). 292p. 1987. pap. 11.99 (*0-8100-0286-8*, 15N0451) Northwest Pub.

— Acts. LC 87-63118. (People's Bible Ser.). 1988. student ed. 4.00 (*0-938272-63-2*, 22-2205) Northwest Pub.

Balge, Richard D., ed. Sermon Studies on the Epistles: Series B. LC 98-83035. 332p. 1993. 27.99 (*0-8100-0486-0*, 15N0552) Northwest Pub.

— Sermon Studies on the Epistles: Series C. LC 91-61108. 355p. 1991. 27.99 (*0-8100-0381-3*, 15N0530) Northwest Pub.

— Sermon Studies on the Gospels: Series A. LC 89-60651. 380p. 1989. 27.99 (*0-8100-0312-0*, 15N0484) Northwest Pub.

Balgette, Joseph. Great Stink of London. 1999. 36.95 (*0-7509-1975-2*) A Sutton.

Balgooy, M. M. Van, see Van Balgooy, M. M., ed.

***Balgopal, Pallassana R., ed.** Social Work Practice with Immigrants & Refugees. 288p. 2000. text 49.50 (*0-231-10856-7*); pap. text 21.00 (*0-231-10857-5*) Col U Pr.

Balgos, M. C., jt. ed. see Munro, J. L.

***Balheimer, David.** Icons of Sport. (Illus.). 224p. 2000. 29.95 (*1-871349-74-5*, Pub. by Kensington West) Midpt Trade.

Balhoff, Michael J. Strategic Planning for Pastoral Ministry. (Illus.). 136p. 1992. student ed. 19.95 (*0-912405-87-2*, Pastoral Press) OR Catholic.

Balhorn, Linda. The Professional Model's Handbook: A Comprehensive Guide to Modeling & Related Fields. (Career Development Ser.). (Illus.). 512p. 1990. 34.50 (*0-87350-376-7*) Thomson Learn.

Balhuisen, Anne R. Searching on Location: Planning a Research Trip. LC 92-3207. 112p. 1992. pap. 9.95 (*0-916489-43-4*) Ancestry.

Bali, Mrinal. Space Exploration. LC 90-19204. (Contemporary World Issues Ser.). 240p. 1990. lib. bdg. 39.50 (*0-87436-578-3*) ABC-CLIO.

Bali, Yogendra. Chandra Shekhar: A Political Biography. (C). 1991. 27.95 (*0-7069-5798-9*, Pub. by Vikas) S Asia.

Balia, Daryl M., ed. Perspectives in Theology & Mission from South Africa: Signs of the Times. LC 93-21574. 1993. pap. 39.95 (*0-7734-1950-0*) E Mellen.

Balia, Mimma, jt. auth. see Lovric, Michelle.

Balian, Edward S. The Graduate Research Guidebook: A Practical Approach to Doctoral - Masters Research. 3rd ed. 306p. (Orig.). (C). 1994. pap. text 49.50 (*0-8191-9471-9*); lib. bdg. 74.50 (*0-8191-9470-0*) U Pr of Amer.

Balian, Edward S., compiled by. Shutterbug's Guide to Better Photography. 96p. 1992. pap. 9.95 (*0-9634576-0-8*) Patch Pub.

Balian, Lecia, jt. auth. see Balian, Poppy.

Balian, Lorna. Amelia's Nine Lives. (Illus.). 32p. (J). (ps-3). 1986. lib. bdg. 13.95 (*0-687-01250-3*) Abingdon.

— Amelia's Nine Lives. (Illus.). 32p. (J). (ps-3). 1986. reprint ed. 12.95 (*0-687-37096-5*) Humbug Bks.

— The Aminal. (Illus.). 48p. (J). (ps-3). 1994. lib. bdg. 14.95 (*1-881772-19-5*) Humbug Bks.

— Bah! Humbug? (Illus.). 32p. (J). (ps-3). 1988. reprint ed. 12.95 (*0-687-37107-4*) Humbug Bks.

— A Garden for a Groundhog. 48p. 1985. 13.95 (*0-687-14009-9*) Abingdon.

— Garden for a Groundhog. (Illus.). 32p. (J). (gr. k up). 1994. reprint ed. lib. bdg. 14.95 (*1-881772-20-9*) Humbug Bks.

— Humbug Potion: An A-B-Cipher. (Illus.). 32p. (J). (ps-3). 1984. reprint ed. 12.95 (*0-687-37102-3*) Humbug Bks.

An Asterisk (*) at the beginning of an entry indicates that the title is appearing for the first time.

— Humbug Rabbit. (Illus.). 32p. (J). (ps-3). 1997. 16.95 (*1-881772-04-7*) Humbug Bks.

— Humbug Witch. (Illus.). 32p. (J). (gr. k up). 1994. reprint ed. lib. bdg. 14.95 (*1-881772-24-1*) Humbug Bks.

— I Love You, Mary Jane. (Illus.). 32p. (J). (ps-3). 1988. reprint ed. 12.95 (*0-687-37100-7*) Humbug Bks.

— Leprechauns Never Lie. (Illus.). 32p. (J). (ps-5). 1994. lib. bdg. 14.95 (*1-881772-07-1*) Humbug Bks.

— Mother's, Mother's Day. (Illus.). 32p. (J). (ps-3). 1987. reprint ed. 12.95 (*0-687-37097-3*) Humbug Bks.

— The Socksnatchers. (Illus.). 32p. (J). (ps-3). 1988. 14.95 (*0-687-39047-8*) Humbug Bks.

— Sometimes It's Turkey, Sometimes It's Feathers. (Illus.). 32p. (J). (ps-3). 1994. lib. bdg. 14.95 (*1-881772-15-2*) Humbug Bks.

— The Sweet Touch. (Illus.). 52p. (J). (ps-6). 1994. reprint ed. lib. bdg. 14.95 (*1-881772-26-8*) Humbug Bks.

— A Sweetheart for Valentine. (Illus.). 32p. (J). (ps-3). 1987. reprint ed. 12.95 (*0-687-37109-0*) Humbug Bks.

— Wilbur's Space Machine. LC 90-55095. (Illus.). 32p. (J). (gr. k-5). 1990. lib. bdg. 19.95 (*0-8234-0836-1*) Humbug Bks.

Balian, Poppy & Balian, Lecia. Humbug Handbook: The Lorna Balian Educational Activity Book. (Illus.). 32p. (Orig.). (J). 1994. pap. 5.00 (*1-881772-33-0*) Humbug Bks.

Balian, R., ed. Fluid Dynamics. (Houches Lectures: 1973). 1977. 165.00 (*0-677-10170-8*) Gordon & Breach.

Balian, R. & Weill, G., eds. Les Houches Lectures, 1973: Molecular Fluids, Vol. 73. xvi, 460p. 1976. text 483.00 (*0-677-16020-8*) Gordon & Breach.

Balian, R., ed. see Blaszak, Maaiej & Mickiewicz, A.

Balian, R., ed. see Dobado, Antonio, et al.

Balian, R., ed. see Henkel, Malte.

Balian, R., ed. see Lavis, D. A. & Bell, G. M.

Balian, R., ed. see Mosel, U.

Balian, R. M. From Microphysics to Macrophysics I: Methods & Applications of Statistical Physics. Beiglbock, W. et al, eds. Ter Haar, D. & Gregg, J. F., trs. from FRE. (Texts & Monographs in Physics). (Illus.). xxii, 465p. 1991. 64.95 (*0-387-53266-8*) Spr-Verlag.

— From Microphysics to Macrophysics II: Methods & Applications of Statistical Physics. Beiglbock, W. et al, eds. (Texts & Monographs in Physics). (Illus.). 624p. 1992. 89.00 (*0-387-53599-3*) Spr-Verlag.

Balian, R. M., et al, eds. ILL-Condensed Matter: Les Houches Session XXXI. 636p. 1984. text 98.00 (*9971-950-59-6*); pap. text 46.00 (*9971-950-60-X*) World Scientific Pub.

Balian, R. M. & Zinn-Justin, J., eds. Methods in Field Theory: Les Houches Session XXVIII. 406p. 1981. pap. text 26.00 (*9971-83-015-9*) World Scientific Pub.

— Methods in Field Theory: Les Houches Session XXVIII. 406p. 1993. text 33.00 (*9971-83-078-7*) World Scientific Pub.

Balibar, Etienne. Masses, Classes, Ideas: Studies on Politics & Philosophy before & after Marx. Swenson, James, tr. LC 93-19168. (ENG & FRE.). 272p. (C). 1994. pap. 20.99 (*0-415-90602-4*, A7328) Routledge.

— The Philosophy of Marx. Turner, Chris, tr. 160p. (C). (gr. 13). 1995. 60.00 (*1-85984-951-2*, C0515, Pub. by Verso) Norton.

— Politics & the Other Scene. Hahn, Daniel, tr. 60.00 (*1-85984-725-0*) Norton.

***Balibar, Etienne.** Politics & the Other Scene. Hahn, Daniel, tr. 1999. pap. 20.00 (*1-85984-267-4*, Pub. by Verso) Norton.

Balibar, Etienne. Race, Nation & Class. LC 91-27500. 232p. (C). 1991. pap. 20.00 (*0-86091-542-5*, A5525, Pub. by Verso) Norton.

— Race, Nation & Class: Ambiguous Identities. LC 91-27500. 232p. (C). (gr. 13). 1991. 60.00 (*0-86091-327-9*, A5521, Pub. by Verso) Norton.

— Spinoza & Politics. 1998. pap. 18.00 (*1-85984-102-3*) Norton.

Balibar, F., jt. auth. see Levy-Leblond, Jean-Marc.

***Balick, Don.** Animal Survival. Marson, Ron, ed. (Science with Simple Things Ser.: No. 37). (Illus.). 64p. 1999. teacher ed. 15.00 (*0-941008-50-9*) Tops Learning.

Balick, M. J., jt. auth. see Pinheiro, C. U.

Balick, Michael J. The Systematics & Economic Botany of the Oenocarpus - Jessenia (Palmae) Complex. LC 86-23455. (Advances in Economic Botany Ser.: Vol. 3). (Illus.). 148p. 1986. pap. 24.65 (*0-89327-311-2*) NY Botanical.

Balick, Michael J., ed. The Palm - Tree of Life: Biology, Utilization & Conservation. LC 87-36900. (Advances in Economic Botany Ser.: Vol. 6). (Illus.). 296p. (C). 1988. pap. text 45.70 (*0-89327-326-0*) NY Botanical.

Balick, Michael J., et al, eds. Medicinal Resources of the Tropical Forest: Biodiversity & Its Importance to Human Health. LC 95-13809. (Biology & Resource Management in the Tropics Ser.). (Illus.). 464p. 1996. 79.00 (*0-231-10170-8*) Col U Pr.

— Medicinal Resources of the Tropical Forest: Biodiversity & its Importance to Human Health. (Biology & Resource Management in the Tropics Ser.). (Illus.). 440p. 1996. pap. 37.00 (*0-231-10171-6*) Col U Pr.

Balick, Michael J. & Cox, Paul A. Plants, People & Culture: The Science of Ethnobotany, a Scientific American Library Book. (Illus.). 256p. 1996. pap. text 32.95 (*0-7167-5061-9*) W H Freeman.

***Balick, Michael J., et al.** Checklist of the Vascular Plants of Belize, with Common Names & Uses. LC 99-16042. 1999. write for info. (*0-89327-434-8*) NY Botanical.

Balick, Michael J., jt. auth. see Arvigo, Rosita.

Balick, Michael J., jt. ed. see Prance, Ghillean T.

Balicki, Alan. Preservation Guide No. 6: Matting & Framing. LC 84-106237. (Illus.). ii, 14p. (Orig.). 1989. pap. 3.95 (*0-917860-28-4*) Historic New Orleans.

Balido, Paul, jt. auth. see Appell, David.

Baliga. MCQs in Clinical Medicine. 2nd ed. LC 99-29016. 1999. pap. text 16.00 (*0-7020-2296-9*, W B Saunders Co) Harcrt Hlth Sci Grp.

— MRCP: 500 MCQ's for MRCP, Pt. 1. 1997. pap. text 28.00 (*0-7020-2243-8*) Harcourt.

— Semiconductor Power Devices. 1995. teacher ed. 21.75 (*0-534-94099-4*) PWS Pubs.

— 250 Short Cases in Clinical Medicine. 1997. pap. text 32.00 (*0-7020-2205-5*) Bailliere Tindall.

Baliga, B. Jayant. Modern Power Devices. LC 92-29624. 496p. (C). 1992. reprint ed. lib. bdg. 67.50 (*0-89464-799-7*) Krieger.

— Power Semiconductor Devices. (General Engineering Ser.). 528p. 1995. mass mkt. 109.95 (*0-534-94098-6*) PWS Pubs.

Baliga, B. Jayant, jt. auth. see Singh, Ranbir.

Baliga, M., jt. auth. see Kapur, N.

Baliga, Sanjay S., jt. auth. see Repetto, Robert C.

Balikci, Asen. The Netsilik Eskimo. rev. ed. (Illus.). 264p. (C). 1989. reprint ed. pap. text 12.95 (*0-88133-435-9*) Waveland Pr.

Baliles, Gerald L. Preserving the Chesapeake Bay. LC 95-62287. (Illus.). 64p. 1996. 14.95 (*1-884549-02-0*) VA Mus Natl Hist.

***Baliles, Gerald L.** Preserving the Chesapeake Bay: Lessons in the Political Reality of Natural Resource Stewardship. (Illus.). 60p. 2000. reprint ed. text 25.00 (*0-7881-9097-0*) DIANE Pub.

Balim, Cigdem, et al, eds. Turkey: Political, Social & Economic Challenges in the 1990s. LC 95-12128. (Social, Economic & Political Studies of the Middle East: No. 53). 280p. 1995. 110.50 (*90-04-10283-3*) Brill Academic Pubs.

***Balim-Harding, Cidgem.** Turkey. 2nd rev. ed. Vol. 27. 350p. 1999. lib. bdg. 112.00 (*1-85109-295-1*) ABC-CLIO.

Balin, Arthur K., ed. Practical Handbook of Human Biologic Age Determination. 544p. 1994. lib. bdg. 165.00 (*0-8493-0129-7*, QP86) CRC Pr.

***Balin, Carole B.** To Reveal Our Hearts: Jewish Women Writers in Tsarist Russia. LC 00-39545. (Monographs of the Hebrew Union College). 2000. write for info. (*0-87820-423-7*) Hebrew Union Coll Pr.

— To Reveal Our Hearts: Jewish Women Writers in Tsarist Russia. 224p. 2000. 39.95 (*0-8143-2936-5*) Wayne St U Pr.

Balin, Jane. Community & Contagion: A Neighborhood's Reception to a Nursing Home for People with AIDS. LC 98-36506. 1999. write for info. (*0-8014-3606-0*); pap. 14.95 (*0-8014-8579-7*) Cornell U Pr.

Balin, Peter. Flight of the Feathered Serpent. LC 78-64357. (Illus.). 184p. 1983. reprint ed. pap. 15.95 (*0-910261-01-6*, Arcana Pubng) Lotus Pr.

— Xultun (Mayan) Tarot Deck: A Maya Tarot Deck. 2nd ed. (Illus.). 78p. (Orig.). 1982. pap. 15.95 (*0-910261-00-8*, Arcana Pubng) Lotus Pr.

Balina, Marina, et al, eds. Endquote: Sots-Art Literature & Soviet Grand Style. (Illus.). 336p. 1999. 69.95 (*0-8101-1653-7*); pap. 24.95 (*0-8101-1767-3*) Northwestern U Pr.

Balingasa, Eduardo, jt. auth. see Balingasa, Nancy.

Balingasa, Nancy & Balingasa, Eduardo. The Food Jungle: Your Guide to Healthy Eating. (Illus.). 288p. 1999. pap. 14.95 (*0-9672087-0-X*) Print Matters TX.

Balino, Thomas J. & Cottarelli, Carlo, eds. Frameworks for Monetary Stability: Policy Issues & Country Experiences. 766p. 1994. pap. 35.00 (*1-55775-419-5*) Intl Monetary.

Balino, Tomas. Monetary Policy in Dollarized Economies, 171. LC 98-43299. 1998. write for info. (*1-55775-757-7*) Intl Monetary.

Balino, Tomas J., et al. Currency Board Arrangements: Issues & Experiences, Vol. 151. LC 97-31294. (Occasional Paper). 1997. write for info. (*1-55775-668-6*) Intl Monetary.

Balino, Tomas T., jt. ed. see Sundararajan, V.

Balinska, Marta A. For the Good of Humanity: Ludwik Rajchman, Medical Statesman. LC 98-45333. (Illus.). 293p. 1998. 36.95 (*963-9116-17-3*) Ctrl Europ Univ.

Balinski, Rebecca, tr. see Manent, Pierre.

Balinski, Rebecca, tr. see Poirier, Jean-Pierre.

Balinsky, Benjamin. Improving Personnel Selection Through Effective Interviewing: Essentials for Management. LC 77-94944. (Orig.). 1978. pap. 17.05 (*0-935198-05-9*); per. 18.25 (*0-935198-04-0*) M M Bruce.

Balint, Andor. Physiological Genetics of Agricultural Crops. 166p. (C). 1984. 50.00 (*963-05-3288-3*, Pub. by Akade Kiaco) St Mut.

***Balint, Anna.** Auszug Deutscher Studenten in Den Freiheitskrieg Von, 1813 (1908-1909) Ferdinand Hodlers Jenaer Historiengemalde: Auftragsgeschichte, Werkgenese, Nachleben. 336p. 1999. 51.95 (*3-631-34658-1*) P Lang Pubng.

Balint, David L., ed. CPCM Candidate's Workbook: Commercial Purchasing. rev. ed. 60p. 1993. pap. 15.00 (*0-940343-51-7*, CPCOM) Natl Contract Mgmt.

— CPCM Candidate's Workbook: Contracting. rev. ed. 176p. 1993. pap. 22.50 (*0-940343-52-5*, CPCNC) Natl Contract Mgmt.

— CPCM Candidate's Workbook: Finance, Economics, & Accounting. rev. ed. 146p. 1993. pap. 22.50 (*0-940343-53-3*, CPFEA) Natl Contract Mgmt.

— CPCM Candidate's Workbook: General Examination. rev. ed. 170p. 1993. pap. 22.50 (*0-940343-50-9*, CPGEX) Natl Contract Mgmt.

— CPCM Candidate's Workbook: Legal. rev. ed. 126p. 1993. pap. 22.50 (*0-940343-54-1*, CPLGL) Natl Contract Mgmt.

— CPCM Candidate's Workbook: Logistics. rev. ed. 98p. 1993. pap. 22.50 (*0-940343-55-X*, CPLOG) Natl Contract Mgmt.

— CPCM Candidate's Workbook: Production. rev. ed. 126p. 1993. pap. 22.50 (*0-940343-57-6*, CPPRD) Natl Contract Mgmt.

— CPCM Candidate's Workbook: State & Local Government. rev. ed. 60p. 1993. pap. 15.00 (*0-940343-56-8*, CPSLG) Natl Contract Mgmt.

Balint, Enid. Before I Was I: Psychoanalysis & the Imagination. Mitchell, Juliet & Parsons, Michael, eds. 248p. 1998. reprint ed. 35.00 (*1-892746-10-7*, 46107) Other Pr LLC.

***Balint, Enid, et al.** Before I Was I: Psychoanalysis & the Imagination. LC 00-27702. 2000. pap. write for info. (*1-892746-61-1*) Other Pr LLC.

Balint, Enid, et al. The Doctor, the Patient & the Group: Balint Revisited. LC 92-49166. 176p. 1993. pap. write for info. (*0-415-08053-3*) Routledge.

Balint, Michael. The Basic Fault: Therapeutic Aspects of Regression. 205p. 1992. reprint ed. pap. 16.95 (*0-8101-1025-3*) Northwestern U Pr.

— The Doctor, His Patient & the Illness. 2nd ed. 395p. (Orig.). 1963. 62.50 (*0-8236-1380-1*) Intl Univs Pr.

— Problems of Human Pleasure & Behavior. 1973. pap. 3.95 (*0-87140-279-3*, Pub. by Liveright) Norton.

— Thrills & Regressions. 148p. (Orig.). 1959. 27.50 (*0-8236-6540-2*) Intl Univs Pr.

Balint, Michael, tr. see Ferenczi, Sandor.

Balint, Peter J., jt. auth. see Zilinskas, Raymond A.

Balint, Peter J., jt. ed. see Zilinskas, Raymond A.

Balio, Tino. Grand Design: Hollywood As a Modern Business Enterprise, 1930-1939. LC 95-30572. (History of the American Cinema Ser.: Vol. 5). (Illus.). 483p. 1995. pap. 22.95 (*0-520-20334-8*, Pub. by U CA Pr) Cal Prin Full Svc.

— United Artists: The Company Built by the Stars. LC 75-12208. (Illus.). 339p. reprint ed. pap. 105.10 (*0-608-20415-3*, 207166800002) Bks Demand.

Balio, Tino, ed. The American Film Industry. rev. ed. LC 84-40143. (Illus.). 677p. 1985. reprint ed. pap. 200.00 (*0-608-07478-0*, 206770000009) Bks Demand.

— The American Film Industry. rev. ed. LC 84-40143 (Illus.). 680p. 1985. pap. 24.95 (*0-299-09874-5*) U of Wis Pr.

Balio, Tino, jt. ed. see Cripps, Thomas.

Balio, Tino T. Grand Design: History of the American Cinema. Harpole, Charles H., ed. (History of the American Cinema Ser.: Vol. 5). (Illus.). 340p. 1993. 85.00 (*0-684-19115-6*, Scribners Ref) Mac Lib Ref.

Baliozian, Ara. The Armenians. LC 80-19619. 250p. 1980. pap. 6.95 (*0-933706-22-7*) Ararat Pr.

— From Plato to Sartre: Wisdom for Armenians. LC 95-22809. 1995. 10.00 (*0-931539-12-9*) Armenian Ref Bks.

Baliozian, Ara, ed. Zohrab: An Introduction. 79p. 1985. pap. 3.95 (*0-920553-00-1*) Natl Assn Arm.

Baliozian, Ara, ed. see Pushkin, Aleksandr, et al.

Balirwa, John S. Lake Victoria Wetlands & the Ecology of the Nile Tilapia, Oreochromis Niliticus Linne. LC 99-496402. (IHE Thesis Ser.: Vol. 11). (Illus.). 247p. (C). 1998. text 42.00 (*90-5410-411-2*, Pub. by A A Balkema) Ashgate Pub Co.

Balisacan, Arsenio M. Poverty, Urbanization & Development Policy: A Philippine Perspective. LC 94-945501. 188p. (Orig.). (C). 1995. pap. text 15.00 (*971-542-041-9*, Pub. by U of Philippines Pr) UH Pr.

***Balisok, Russell S., et al.** California Elder Law: An Advocate's Guide - 5-99 Update, 2 vols. Gerber, Mary, ed. LC 93-71394. 708p. 1999. ring bd. 99.00 (*0-7626-0322-4*, ES-32056) Cont Ed Bar-CA.

— California Elder Law: An Advocate's Guide: May 2000 Update, 2 vols. Gerber, Mary, ed. LC 93-71394. 876p. 2000. 68.00 (*0-7626-0423-9*, ES-32057) Cont Ed Bar-CA.

Balisterri, W. F. & Stocker, J. Thomas. Pediatric Hepatology. 1990. 250.00 (*0-89116-738-2*) Hemisp Pub.

Balistreri, W. F., et al, eds. Hepatobiliary, Pancreatic & Splenic Disease in Children: Medical & Surgical Management. LC 97-901. 632p. 1997. 284.50 (*0-444-82052-3*) Elsevier.

***Balit, Christina, adapted by.** Atlantis: The Legend of a Lost City: Adapted & Retold from Plato's Timaeus & Critias. LC 99-27943. 32p. 2000. 16.95 (*0-8050-6334-X*) H Holt & Co.

Balitres, Z. The Cosmic Experience: A Collection of Poems in the Nineteen-Nineties. LC 97-90247. 83p. 1998. 12.95 (*0-533-12344-5*) Vantage.

***Baljekar, Mridula.** Quick Vegetarian Curries. 224p. 1999. pap. 13.00 (*0-7225-3845-6*) Thorsons PA.

Baljekar, Mridula. The Real Balti Cookbook: Over 100 Quick & Authentic Recipes. (Illus.). 128p. 1997. 24.95 (*0-09-180975-4*, Pub. by Ebury Pr) Trafalgar.

***Baljekar, Mridula.** Secrets from an Indian Kitchen. (Secrets from a Kitchen Ser.). (Illus.). 160p. 2000. 27.50 (*1-86205-143-7*, Pub. by Pavilion Bks Ltd) Trafalgar.

Baljinnyam, I., et al. Ruptures of Major Earthquakes & Active Deformation in Mongolia & Its Surroundings. LC 93-17406. (Geological Society of America, Memoir Ser.: No. 181). (Illus.). 66p. Date not set. reprint ed. pap. 30.00 (*0-608-20641-5*, 207207700003) Bks Demand.

Baljon, Lodwijk. Designing Parks: An Examination of Contemporary Approaches to Design in Landscape Architecture. (Illus.). 322p. 1995. pap. 39.50 (*1-870673-15-8*, Pub. by Garden Art Pr) Antique Collect.

Balk, Alfred. The Free List: Property Without Taxes. LC 78-129147. 276p. 1971. 35.00 (*0-87154-083-5*) Russell Sage.

— Movie Palace Masterpiece: Saving Syracuse's Loew's State/Landmark Theater. 80p. 1999. 24.95 (*0-8156-8123-2*) Syracuse U Pr.

— The Myth of American Eclipse: The New Global Age. 246p. (C). 1990. 39.95 (*0-88738-369-6*) Transaction Pubs.

Balk, B. M. Industrial Price, Quantity, & Productivity Indices: The Micro-Economic Theory & an Application. LC 98-29051. 1998. 99.95 (*0-7923-8244-7*) Kluwer Academic.

Balk, C. L., jt. ed. see Fitzsimmons, J. P.

Balk, Christianne. Desiring Flight. LC 94-38209. 104p. (Orig.). 1995. pap. 14.95 (*1-55753-062-9*) Purdue U Pr.

Balk, David E., jt. ed. see Corr, Charles A.

Balk, H. Wesley. The Complete Singer-Actor: Training for Music Theatre. 2nd ed. LC 85-1146. xiv, 248p. 1985. pap. 18.95 (*0-8166-1418-0*) U of Minn Pr.

— The Radiant Performer: The Spiral Path to Performing Power. (Illus.). 352p. (C). 1990. pap. 19.95 (*0-8166-1868-2*) U of Minn Pr.

Balk, M. B. Polyanalytic Functions. (Mathematical Research Ser.: Vol. 63). 1991. pap. text 73.45 (*3-05-501292-5*, Pub. by Akademie Verlag) Wiley.

Balk, Walter L. Managerial Reform & Professional Empowerment in the Public Service. LC 95-19463. 216p. 1996. 55.00 (*1-56720-011-7*, Quorum Bks) Greenwood.

Balka, Christie & Rose, Andy, eds. Twice Blessed: On Being Lesbian or Gay & Jewish. LC 89-42598. 320p. 1991. pap. 16.00 (*0-8070-7909-X*) Beacon Pr.

***Balka, Ellen & Smith, Richard.** Women, Work & Computerization: Charting a Course to the Future I. LC 00-38433. (IFIP Ser.: Vol. 44). (Illus.). 2000. write for info. (*0-7923-7864-4*, Kluwer Plenum) Kluwer Academic.

Balka, Marie. La Nuit. (FRE.). 1978. pap. 12.95 (*0-7859-1875-2*, 2070370380) Fr & Eur.

— La Rancon du Silence. (FRE.). 192p. 1975. pap. 10.95 (*0-7859-1797-7*, 2070366502) Fr & Eur.

Balka, Miroslaw. Miroslaw Balka: 36,6. (Illus.). 44p. 1993. pap. 15.00 (*0-941548-25-2*) Ren Soc U Chi.

***Balkan, Eric.** City of Tears. unabridged ed. 221p. 1999. pap. 10.00 (*0-934741-04-2*) Packet Pr.

Balkan, Erol M. International Bank Lending & Country Risk. (Illus.). 202p. (C). 1994. lib. bdg. 115.00 (*1-56072-171-5*) Nova Sci Pubs.

Balkan, N., et al. Negative Differential Resistance & Instabilities in 2-D Semiconductors. LC 93-15664. (NATO ASI Series B, Physics: Vol. 307). (Illus.). 454p. (C). 1993. 125.00 (*0-306-44490-9*, Plenum Trade) Perseus Pubng.

Balkan, Naci, ed. Hot Electrons in Semiconductors: Phsyics & Devices. (Series on Semiconductor Science & Technology: No. 5). (Illus.). 528p. 1998. text 150.00 (*0-19-850058-0*) OUP.

Balkanski, M., et al, eds. Festschrift in Honor of Rogerio Cerqueira Leite. 384p. (C). 1991. text 99.00 (*981-02-0572-4*) World Scientific Pub.

Balkanski, M., et al, eds. Solid State Ionics II Vol. 210: Materials Research Society Symposium Proceedings. 722p. 1991. text 17.50 (*1-55899-102-6*) Materials Res.

Balkanski, M. & Moss, T. S., eds. Optical Properties of Semiconductors. enl. rev. ed. (Handbook on Semiconductors Ser.: Vol. 2). 874p. 1994. 340.25 (*0-444-89101-3*) Elsevier.

***Balkanski, M. & Wallis, R. F.** Semiconductor Physics. 8. (Illus.). 528p. 2000. pap. text 60.00 (*0-19-851740-8*) OUP.

— Semiconductor Physics. Vol. 8. (Illus.). 528p. 2000. text 125.00 (*0-19-851741-6*) OUP.

Balkanski, M., jt. ed. see Akridge, J. R.

Balkanski, M., jt. ed. see Averous, M.

Balkanski, M., jt. ed. see Tuller, H. L.

Balkanski, Minko, ed. Devices Based on Low-Dimensional Semiconductor Structures: Proceedings of the NATO Advances Study Institute, Sozopol, Bulgaria, Sept. 19-30, 1995. (NATO Advanced Science Institutes, Partnership Sub-Series). 424p. (C). 1996. text 217.50 (*0-7923-4102-3*) Kluwer Academic.

— Fabrication, Properties & Applications of Low-Dimensional Semiconductors: Proceedings of the NATO Advanced Study Institute, Sozopol, Bulgaria, September 19-29, 1994. (NATO ASI - Partnership Sub-Series 3). 480p. (C). 1995. text 240.00 (*0-7923-3569-4*) Kluwer Academic.

Balkanski, Minko & Andreev, Nikolai, eds. Advanced Electronic Technologies & Systems Based on Low-Dimensional Quantum Devices. LC 97-43110. (NATO ASI Ser.). 291p. 1998. text 197.50 (*0-7923-4875-3*) Kluwer Academic.

Balkay, B., tr. see Assonyi, Cs. & Richter, R.

Balke, Fred. Vom Verlust der Kosmologie . . . Und Den Versuchen Sie Wiederzugewinnen. (Europaische Hochschulschriften Ser.: Reihe 23, Bd. 478). (GER.). 269p. 1993. 49.80 (*3-631-45966-1*) P Lang Pubng.

Balke, Kevin N. & Ullman, Gerald L. Advanced Technologies for Communicating with Motorists: A Synthesis of Human Factors & Traffic Management Issues. 54p. (Orig.). (C). 1994. pap. text 35.00 (*0-7881-0189-7*) DIANE Pub.

Balke, Willem. Calvin & the Anabaptist Radicals. 350p. 1999. pap. 32.00 (*1-57910-073-2*) Wipf & Stock.

Balke, William. Calvin & the Anabaptist Radicals. Heynen, William, tr. LC 81-12438. 350p. reprint ed. pap. 108.50 (*0-8357-7977-7*, 202531500043) Bks Demand.

Balkema, A. A. Safety & Environmental Issues in Rock Engineering, 1. 928p. 1993. pap. text 123.00 (*90-5410-340-X*, Pub. by A A Balkema) Ashgate Pub Co.

Balkema, A. A., jt. ed. see Correia, A. Gomes.

Balkema, Sandra, ed. see Leary, Patty, et al.

Balken, Deborah, et al. Arthur Dove: A Retrospective. Laing, M. E., ed. LC 97-13748. (Illus.). 208p. (Orig.). 1997. pap. text 39.95 (*0-262-52240-3*) MIT Pr.

B

— Arthur Dove: A Retrospective. Laing, M. E., ed. LC 97-13748. (Illus.). 208p. (Orig.). 1997. 60.00 (*0-262-02433-0*) MIT Pr.

Balken, Debra B. Arthur G. Dove: Pastels, Charcoals, Watercolors. (Illus.). 15p. 1993. pap. text 15.00 (*0-9635932-0-X*) T Dintenfass Gal.

— Natural Spectacles. (Illus.). 30p. 1996. 16.00 (*0-933519-33-8*) D W Bell Gallery.

Balken, Debra B., contrib. by. Bryan Hunt: Sculpture & Drawings. LC 98-65879. (Illus.). 34p. 1998. pap. 20.00 (*1-879173-37-9*) Locks Gallery.

Balken, Debra B., text. Edna Andrade: Paintings, 1960's-1990's. LC 97-220815. (Illus.). 30p. 1997. pap. 20.00 (*1-879173-33-6*) Locks Gallery.

Balken, Debra B. & Rothschild, Deborah M. Suzy Frelinghuysen & George L. K. Morris: American Abstract Artists Aspects of Their Work & Collection. LC 92-50485. (Illus.). 64p. (Orig.). 1993. pap. 18.95 (*0-913697-14-1*) U of Pa Pr.

Balken, Debra B., et al. Muntadas: Between the Frames, the Forum. LC 94-31860. 1994. pap. 15.00 (*0-938437-49-6*) MIT List Visual Arts.

***Balken, Debra Bricker.** Philip Gustons Poor Richard. 1999. pap. 17.00 (*0-226-03622-7*); lib. bdg. 55.00 (*0-226-03621-9*) U Ch Pr.

***Balken, Debra Bricker, text.** Gregory Amenoff. (Illus.). 27p. 2000. pap. 20.00 (*1-58821-078-2*) Salander OReilly.

Balkenbush, Susan. What's New in Nevada Schools? A Case Study: Jacobson Elementary School. 7p. 1993. 7.00 (*1-886306-01-X*) Nevada Policy.

Balkenende, William P. Love in Times of Reformation. Den Hertog, Judy, tr. from DUT. (Illus.). 105p. (Orig.). (YA). 1991. pap. 7.90 (*0-921100-32-9*) Inhtce Pubns.

Balkie, William, jt. auth. see Healy, Phyllis F.

Balkin, J. M. Cultural Software: A Theory of Ideology. LC 97-37011. 352p. 1998. 35.00 (*0-300-07288-0*) Yale U Pr.

Balkin, Jack. Legal Canons. 1999. text 50.00 (*0-8147-9857-8*) NYU Pr.

Balkin, Jack & Lev. Legal Canons. pap. text. write for info. (*0-8147-9870-5*) NYU Pr.

Balkin, Richard. A Writer's Guide to Book Publishing. 3rd rev. ed. LC 93-46730. 288p. 1994. pap. 14.95 (*0-452-27021-9*, Plume) Dutton Plume.

Balkin, Richard, ed. see Gregory, Ross.

Balkin, Richard, ed. see Purvis, Thomas L.

Balkin, Rick, ed. see Shifflett, Crandall A.

Balkin, Steven. Self-Employment for Low Income People. LC 88-35735. 258p. 1989. 59.95 (*0-275-92807-1*, C2807, Praeger Pubs) Greenwood.

Balkir, Canan & Williams, Allan M., eds. Turkey & Europe. LC 92-41816. 224p. 1993. text 59.00 (*1-85567-012-7*) St Martin.

Balko, B., et al, eds. Gamma-Ray Lasers. (Quantitative Spectroscopy & Radiative Transfer Ser.: No. 39). 250p. 1989. 77.00 (*0-08-037015-2*, Pergamon Pr) Elsevier.

Balkoski, Joseph. Beyond the Beachhead: The Twenty-Ninth Infantry Division in Normandy. LC 88-21903. (Illus.). 320p. 1989. 19.95 (*0-8117-0221-9*) Stackpole.

— Beyond the Beachhead: The 29th Division in Normandy. 2nd ed. LC 98-53788. (Illus.). 320p. 1999. pap. text 14.95 (*0-8117-2682-7*) Stackpole.

Balkoski, Victoria, jt. ed. see Glezerman, Tatyana B.

Balkovek, James. Alice Dunbar-Nelson: Great American Short Stories III. LC 95-76749. (Classic Short Stories Ser.). 80p. (YA). (gr. 6-12). 1995. pap. 5.95 (*0-7854-0599-2*, 40085) Am Guidance.

— Alphonse Daudet: Great Short Stories from Around the World I. LC 94-75344. (Classic Short Stories Ser.). 80p. 1994. pap. 5.95 (*0-7854-0649-2*, 40065) Am Guidance.

— Bret Harte: Great American Short Stories I. LC 94-75015. (Classic Short Stories Ser.). 80p. 1994. pap. 5.95 (*0-7854-0623-9*, 40004) Am Guidance.

— Charlotte Perkins Gilman: Great American Short Stories II. LC 94-75027. (Classic Short Stories Ser.). 80p. 1994. pap. 5.95 (*0-7854-0586-0*, 40026) Am Guidance.

— Edna Ferber: Great American Short Stories III. LC 95-76750. (Classic Short Stories Ser.). 80p. (YA). (gr. 6-12). 1995. pap. 5.95 (*0-7854-0625-5*, 40086) Am Guidance.

— Fyodor Dostoevsky: Great Short Stories from Around the World I. LC 94-75348. (Classic Short Stories Ser.). 80p. 1994. pap. 5.95 (*0-7854-0650-6*, 40069) Am Guidance.

— Hamlin Garland: Great American Short Stories II. LC 94-75029. (Classic Short Stories Ser.). 80p. 1994. pap. 5.95 (*0-7854-0585-2*, 40028) Am Guidance.

— Henry James: Great American Short Stories III. LC 95-76752. (Classic Short Stories Ser.). 80p. (YA). (gr. 6-12). 1995. pap. 5.95 (*0-7854-0627-1*, 40088) Am Guidance.

— Herman Melville: Great American Short Stories II. LC 94-75022. (Classic Short Stories Ser.). 80p. 1994. pap. 5.95 (*0-7854-0589-5*, 40021) Am Guidance.

— Honore de Balzac: Great Short Stories from Around the World I. LC 94-75349. (Classic Short Stories Ser.). 80p. 1994. pap. 5.95 (*0-7854-0647-6*, 40070) Am Guidance.

— Irvin S. Cobb: Great American Short Stories III. (Classic Short Stories Ser.). 80p. (YA). (gr. 6-12). 1995. 5.95 (*0-7854-0596-8*, 40082) Am Guidance.

— Jack London: Great American Short Stories II. LC 94-75025. (Classic Short Stories Ser.). 80p. 1994. pap. 5.95 (*0-7854-0588-7*, 40024) Am Guidance.

— Leopoldo Alas: Great Short Stories from Around the World I. (Classic Short Stories Ser.). 80p. 1994. pap. 5.95 (*0-7854-0646-8*, 40067) Am Guidance.

— Mary Wilkins Freeman: Great American Short Stories III. LC 95-76751. (Classic Short Stories Ser.). 80p. (YA). (gr. 6-12). 1995. pap. 5.95 (*0-7854-0626-3*, 40087) Am Guidance.

— Mori Ogwai: Great Short Stories from Around the World I. LC 94-75345. (Classic Short Stories Ser.). 80p. 1994. pap. 5.95 (*0-7854-0653-0*, 40066) Am Guidance.

— O. Henry: Great American Short Stories II. LC 94-75030. (Classic Short Stories Ser.). 80p. 1994. pap. 5.95 (*0-7854-0587-9*, 40029) Am Guidance.

— Rabindranath Tagore: Great Short Stories from Around the World I. LC 94-75347. (Classic Short Stories Ser.). 80p. 1994. pap. 5.95 (*0-7854-0654-9*, 40068) Am Guidance.

— Rebecca Harding Davis: Great American Short Stories III. LC 95-76747. (Classic Short Stories Ser.). 80p. (YA). (gr. 6-12). 1995. pap. 5.95 (*0-7854-0597-6*, 40083) Am Guidance.

— Richard Harding Davis: Great American Short Stories II. LC 94-75031. (Classic Short Stories Ser.). 80p. 1994. pap. 5.95 (*0-7854-0584-4*, 40030) Am Guidance.

— Ring Lardner: Great American Short Stories III. LC 95-76753. (Classic Short Stories Ser.). 80p. (YA). (gr. 6-12). 1995. pap. 5.95 (*0-7854-0628-X*, 40089) Am Guidance.

— Sarah Orne Jewett: Great American Short Stories I. LC 94-75019. (Classic Short Stories Ser.). 80p. 1994. pap. 5.95 (*0-7854-0576-3*, 40008) Am Guidance.

— Sherwood Anderson: Great American Short Stories I. LC 94-75020. (Classic Short Stories Ser.). 80p. 1994. pap. 5.95 (*0-7854-0619-0*, 40009) Am Guidance.

— Theodore Dreiser: Great American Short Stories III. LC 95-76748. (Classic Short Stories Ser.). 80p. (YA). (gr. 6-12). 1995. pap. 5.95 (*0-7854-0598-4*, 40084) Am Guidance.

— Thomas Bailey Aldrich: Great American Short Stories III. LC 95-76745. (Classic Short Stories Ser.). 80p. (YA). (gr. 6-12). 1995. pap. 5.95 (*0-7854-0595-X*, 40081) Am Guidance.

— Wilbur Daniel Steele: Great American Short Stories III. LC 95-76754. (Classic Short Stories Ser.). 80p. (YA). (gr. 6-12). 1995. pap. 5.95 (*0-7854-0629-8*, 40090) Am Guidance.

— Willa Cather: Great American Short Stories I. LC 94-75018. (Classic Short Stories Ser.). 80p. 1994. pap. 5.95 (*0-7854-0620-4*, 40007) Am Guidance.

***Balkow, Dieter.** Glass Construction Manual. LC 99-44600. 1999. write for info. (*0-8176-6077-1*) Birkhauser.

Balkowski, C. & Kraan-Korteweg, R. C., eds. Unveiling Large-Scale Structures Behind the Milky Way. (ASP Conference Series Proceedings: Vol. 67). 318p. 1994. 34.00 (*0-937707-86-4*) Astron Soc Pacific.

***Balkumar, K. C.** Trends, Patterns & Implications of Rural to Urban Migration in Nepal. 1999. pap. 43.00 (*0-7855-7650-9*) St Mut.

Balkun, Stephen J. My Father's Greatest Gift: A Father & Son Share an Extraordinary Journey. 110p. 1995. pap. 12.95 (*0-9649184-0-4*) Lionbird Pr.

Balkuv-Ulutin, S. & Yardimci, T., eds. International Congress on Thrombosis: 15th Congress, Antalya, Turkey, October 1998: Abstracts. (Haemostasis Ser.: Vol. 28, Suppl. 2 (1998)). viii, 310p. 1998. pap. 45.25 (*3-8055-6800-2*) S Karger.

Balkwill. The Incredible Human Body: A Book of Discovery & Learning. (Illus.). 128p. 1998. pap. 12.95 (*0-8069-8691-3*) Sterling.

Balkwill, F. R., ed. Cytokines: A Practical Approach. 2nd ed. (The Practical Approach Ser.: No. 155). (Illus.). 456p. 1995. text 105.00 (*0-19-963567-6*); pap. text 55.00 (*0-19-963566-8*) OUP.

Balkwill, F. R., jt. auth. see Waxman, J. H.

Balkwill, Fran. Amazing Schemes Within Your Genes. (Illus.). 32p. (J). (gr. 3-6). 1993. pap. 8.95 (*0-87614-635-3*, Carolrhoda) Lerner Pub.

— Amazing Schemes Within Your Genes. LC 92-42942. (Cells & Things Ser.). (Illus.). (J). (gr. 3-6). 1993. lib. bdg. 19.93 (*0-87614-804-6*, Carolrhoda) Lerner Pub.

Balkwill, Fran. Amazing Schemes within Your Genes. (Illus.). (J). 1994. 14.40 (*0-606-18813-4*) Turtleback.

— Cell Wars. LC 92-6377. (Illus.). 28p. (J). (gr. 3-6). 1992. lib. bdg. 19.93 (*0-87614-761-9*, Carolrhoda) Lerner Pub.

Balkwill, Fran. Cell Wars. (Illus.). 32p. (J). (gr. 3-6). 1994. pap. 8.95 (*0-87614-637-X*, Carolrhoda) Lerner Pub.

Balkwill, Fran. Cell Wars. (Illus.). (J). 1994. 14.30 (*0-606-18815-0*) Turtleback.

Balkwill, Fran. Cells Are Us. (Illus.). 32p. (J). (gr. 3-6). 1994. pap. 8.95 (*0-87614-636-1*, Carolrhoda) Lerner Pub.

— Cells Are Us. (Cells & Things Ser.). (Illus.). 32p. (J). (gr. 3-6). 1996. lib. bdg. 19.93 (*0-87614-762-7*, Carolrhoda) Lerner Pub.

Balkwill, Fran. Cells Are Us. (Illus.). (J). 1993. 14.40 (*0-606-18816-9*) Turtleback.

Balkwill, Fran. DNA Is Here to Stay. (Cells & Things Ser.). (Illus.). 32p. (J). (gr. 3-6). 1993. lib. bdg. 19.93 (*0-87614-763-5*, Carolrhoda) Lerner Pub.

— DNA is Here to Stay. (Illus.). 32p. (J). (gr. 3-6). 1993. pap. 8.95 (*0-87614-638-8*, First Ave Edns) Lerner Pub.

— Microbes, Bugs & Wonder Drugs. Darley-Ujmar, Victor, ed. (Making Sense of Science Ser.: Vol. 1). (Illus.). 128p. (YA). (gr. 7-11). 1995. 20.00 (*1-85578-065-8*, Pub. by Portland Pr Ltd) Ashgate Pub Co.

***Balkwill, Fran, ed.** The Cytokine Network. (Frontiers in Molecular Biology Ser.: Vol. 25). (Illus.). 224p. 2000. text 110.00 (*0-19-963703-2*) OUP.

Balkwill, Fran & Rolph, Mic. The Incredible Human Body: A Book of Discovery & Learning. LC 96-25745. (Illus.). 128p. (J). 1996. 19.95 (*0-8069-6125-2*) Sterling.

Balkwill, Fran, ed. see Bellamy, David.

Balkwill, Fran, ed. see Bett, Brian.

Balkwill, Fran, ed. see Painter, Mike.

Balkwill, Fran, ed. see Phillips, David.

Balkwill, Fran, ed. see Rose, Steven & Lichtenfels, Alexander.

Balkwill, Fran, ed. see Sharman, Helen.

Balkwill, Fran, ed. see Walker, David.

***Balkwill, Frances R.** The Cytokine Network. LC 99-46595. 224p. 2000. pap. text 50.00 (*0-19-963702-4*) OUP.

Balkwill, Frances R. Cytokines in Cancer Therapy. (Illus.). 320p. 1989. 37.50 (*0-19-261797-4*) OUP.

Balkwill, H. R., jt. ed. see Tankard, A. J.

Balkwill, John. An Attack on the National Security State. 132p. (Orig.). 1995. pap. 10.00 (*0-9648241-0-8*) Dreamstoker.

***Balkwill, Richard.** Best Book of Trains. LC 99-12757. 32p. (J). (gr. k-3). 1999. 12.95 (*0-7534-5200-6*) LKC.

Balkwill, Richard. Clothes & Crafts in Ancient Egypt. LC 97-31850. (J). 1998. pap. write for info. (*0-382-39704-5*, Dillon Silver Burdett); lib. bdg. 22.00 (*0-382-39703-7*, Dillon Silver Burdett) Silver Burdett Pr.

— Food & Feasts in Ancient Egypt. 1994. pap. text 5.95 (*0-382-24734-5*, New Dscvry Bks) Silver Burdett Pr.

— Trafalgar. LC 93-2650. (Great Battles & Sieges Ser.). (Illus.). 32p. (YA). (gr. 6 up). 1993. lib. bdg. 13.95 (*0-02-726326-6*, New Dscvry Bks) Silver Burdett Pr.

Balkwill, Richard, ed. Multilingual Dictionary of Copyright, Rights & Contracts. 256p. 1994. 49.95 (*0-948905-88-3*) Chapman & Hall.

***Ball.** Analog Interfacing to Microprocessors. 2001. 29.95 (*0-7506-7339-7*, Newnes) Buttrwrth-Heinemann.

Ball. Ancient Settlement in the Zummar Region Vol. 1: Excavations in the Saddam Dam Salvage Project, 1985-86. (Iraq Archaeological Reports). (Illus.). 240p. Date not set. pap. write for info. (*0-85668-545-3*, Pub. by Aris & Phillips) David Brown.

***Ball.** Automotive Service Management. (Automotive Technology Ser.). 2001. pap. 35.25 (*0-7668-1998-1*) Delmar.

Ball. Bach Flower Remedies Workbook. pap. 29.95 (*0-85207-311-9*) Beekman Pubs.

— Birthrate Plus: A Framework for Workforce Planning & Decision Making for Midwifery Services. LC 97-142349. 176p. 1997. pap. text 34.00 (*1-898507-41-4*) Buttrwrth-Heinemann.

— The Clinician's Guide to Linguistic Profiling of Language Impairment. 134p. 1992. 41.50 (*1-56593-559-4*, 0486) Singular Publishing.

— Conservative Party since 1945. LC 99-231191. 272p. 1998. pap. 27.95 (*0-7190-4013-2*, Pub. by Manchester Univ Pr); text 74.95 (*0-7190-4012-4*, Pub. by Manchester Univ Pr) St Martin.

— Educations. 1986. pap. text. write for info. (*0-582-35532-X*, Pub. by Addison-Wesley) Longman.

— Infectious Disease Color Guide. 2nd ed. LC 99-28873. (Illus.). (C). 1999. pap. text 16.95 (*0-443-05883-0*) Church.

Ball. Middle School Advisement. (J). (gr. 5-8). 1996. pap. text, wbk. ed. 24.95 (*1-55734-193-1*) Tchr Create Mat.

— Pediatric Nursing & Drugs Package. 1996. pap. 75.95 (*0-8385-8105-6*, Prentice Hall) P-H.

Ball. Phonetics for Speech Pathology. 2nd ed. 314p. 1993. pap. 62.25 (*1-56593-240-4*, 0560) Singular Publishing.

***Ball.** Political Ideologies & the Democratic Ideal. 3rd ed. 1999. 45.93 (*0-201-66695-2*); 46.87 (*0-201-66696-0*); 48.75 (*0-201-66697-9*); 46.87 (*0-201-66698-7*) Addison-Wesley.

Ball. Political Ideologies & the Democratic Ideal. 3rd ed. LC 98-7260. 320p. (C). 1998. pap. text 51.00 (*0-321-00541-4*) Addison-Wesley Educ.

***Ball.** Political Ideology. 3rd ed. 1999. 48.75 (*0-201-66694-4*) Addison-Wesley.

Ball. Reading Classical Latin: Second Year. 2nd ed. 1998. pap. 45.00 (*0-07-006070-3*) McGraw.

— Some Aspects of Technological Economics. 1989. 8.00 (*0-85186-879-7*) CRC Pr.

— Task Maths 5. (Um - International Math Ser.). 1991. 72.95 (*0-538-62769-7*) S-W Pub.

— Task Maths 4. (Um - International Math Ser.). 1991. text, teacher ed. 72.95 (*0-538-62781-6*) S-W Pub.

— Task Math's 4-Teacher Resource. 2nd ed. (UM - International Math Ser.). 1991. 30.95 (*0-17-431428-0*) S-W Pub.

***Ball.** 10,000 Dreams Interpreted. 560p. 2000. 10.99 (*0-517-20947-0*) Random Hse Value.

Ball, et al. Ideas & Ideologies: A Reader. 3rd ed. LC 98-7258. 320p. (C). 1998. pap. text 48.00 (*0-321-00539-2*) Addison-Wesley Educ.

Ball, jt. auth. see Cannon.

Ball, jt. auth. see Enoch, M. David.

Ball, A. The Price Guide to Pot-Lids. (Price Guide Ser.). (Illus.). 320p. 1980. 59.50 (*0-902028-56-1*) Antique Collect.

Ball, A. H., ed. see Ruskin, John.

Ball, A. P. Infectious Diseases. (Color Guide Ser.). (Illus.). 120p. (Orig.). 1992. pap. text 16.95 (*0-443-04594-1*) Church.

— Infectious Diseases. 2nd ed. LC 98-45256. (Colour Aids Ser.). (Orig.). 1998. write for info. (*0-443-05771-0*) Church.

Ball, A. R., tr. see Fitzpatrick, Edward A., ed.

Ball, A. S. Bacterial Cell Culture: Essential Data. LC 97-1970. (Essential Data Ser.). 110p. 1997. pap. 39.95 (*0-471-96973-7*) Wiley.

Ball, Adrian. The Last Day of the Old World. LC 77-18896. 278p. 1978. reprint ed. lib. bdg. 65.00 (*0-313-20202-8*, BALD, Greenwood Pr) Greenwood.

Ball, Aimee Lee, jt. auth. see Shepherd, Cybill.

***Ball, Alan.** American Beauty: The Shooting Script. LC 99-52235. (Shooting Script Ser.). (Illus.). 128p. 1999. pap. text 16.95 (*1-55704-404-X*) Newmarket.

Ball, Alan. Five One Act Plays by Alan Ball. 1993. pap. 5.25 (*0-8222-1368-0*) Dramatists Play.

— Five Women Wearing the Same Dress. 1993. pap. 5.25 (*0-8222-1367-2*) Dramatists Play.

***Ball, Alan & Mendes, Sam.** American Beauty: The Shooting Script. (Illus.). 128p. 2000. 22.95 (*1-55704-423-6*, Newmarket Shooting) Newmarket.

Ball, Alan M. Now My Soul Is Hardened: Abandoned Children in Soviet Russia, 1918-1930. LC 92-46236. 1994. 60.00 (*0-520-08010-6*, Pub. by U CA Pr) Cal Prin Full Svc.

— Now My Soul Is Hardened: Abandoned Children in Soviet Russia, 1918-1930. (Illus.). 356p. 1996. pap. 19.95 (*0-520-20694-0*, Pub. by U CA Pr) Cal Prin Full Svc.

— Russia's Last Capitalists: The Nepmen, 1921-1929 with a New Preface. 243p. 1988. pap. 18.95 (*0-520-07174-3*, Pub. by U CA Pr) Cal Prin Full Svc.

Ball, Alan R. Modern Politics & Government. 5th ed. LC 94-3063. 288p. (C). 1994. pap. text 19.95 (*1-56643-002-X*, Chatham House Pub) Seven Bridges.

Ball, Alan R. & Peters, B. Guy. Modern Politics & Government. 6th ed. LC 99-51531. (Illus.). 320p. (C). 2000. pap. text 27.95 (*1-889119-07-5*, Chatham House Pub) Seven Bridges.

Ball, Amy & Uzamere, Pius A. Consumer's Guide to Legal Research. 128p. 1998. pap. 16.95 (*1-892662-01-9*) Natl Intermedia.

Ball, Andrew, et al, eds. Drug Injecting & HIV Infection: Global Dimensions & Local Responses. 294p. 1998. 72.00 (*1-85728-824-6*); pap. 26.95 (*1-85728-825-4*, Pub. by UCL Pr Ltd) Taylor & Francis.

Ball, Andrew & Narain, Lakshimi. Deloitte Ross: VAT - A Business by Business Guide. 2nd ed. 477p. 1996. pap. 62.00 (*0-406-99087-5*, MICHIE) LEXIS Pub.

Ball, Andrew & Narain, Lakshmi. Touche-Ross: VAT - A Business by Business Guide, 1994. 1994. pap. 32.95 (*0-406-04477-5*, MICHIE) LEXIS Pub.

Ball, Angela. Kneeling Between Parked Cars. 1990. pap. 12.00 (*0-937669-41-5*) Owl Creek Pr.

— The Museum of the Revolution. LC 97-76752. (Poetry Ser.). 72p. 1999. pap. 12.95 (*0-88748-275-9*) Carnegie-Mellon.

— Possession. 96p. 1995. pap. 9.95 (*0-9639528-6-2*, Red Hen Press) Valentine CA.

— Quartet. LC 94-70464. (Poetry Ser.). 72p. 1995. pap. 11.95 (*0-88748-189-2*) Carnegie-Mellon.

Ball, Ann. Blessed Miguel Pro: 20th-Century Mexican Martyr. LC 96-60532. (Illus.). 119p. 1996. pap. 6.00 (*0-89555-542-5*, 1340) TAN Bks Pubs.

— Catholic Book of the Dead. LC 94-68928. 1995. pap. 12.95 (*0-87973-744-1*) Our Sunday Visitor.

— Catholic Traditions in Cooking. LC 93-83238. 180p. (Orig.). 1993. pap. 15.95 (*0-87973-531-7*, 531) Our Sunday Visitor.

— Catholic Traditions in Crafts. LC 96-70434. 1997. pap. 16.95 (*0-87973-711-5*) Our Sunday Visitor.

— Catholic Traditions in the Garden. LC 97-69355. (Illus.). 160p. 1998. pap. 15.95 (*0-87973-556-2*) Our Sunday Visitor.

— Faces of Holiness: Modern Saints in Photos & Words. LC 98-65863. 272p. 1998. pap. 14.95 (*0-87973-950-9*) Our Sunday Visitor.

— A Handbook of Catholic Sacramentals. LC 91-60013. (Illus.). (Orig.). 1991. pap. 8.95 (*0-87973-448-5*, 448) Our Sunday Visitor.

— A Litany of Saints. LC 92-61546. 224p. (Orig.). 1993. pap. 8.95 (*0-87973-460-4*, 460) Our Sunday Visitor.

— Modern Saints: Their Lives & Faces, 2 vols., Bk. 1. LC 82-50357. (Illus.). 457p. 1994. pap. 18.00 (*0-89555-222-1*) TAN Bks Pubs.

— Modern Saints: Their Lives & Faces, 2 vols., Bk. 2. LC 82-50357. (Illus.). 457p. 1993. pap. 20.00 (*0-89555-223-X*) TAN Bks Pubs.

— Set of 2 Modern Saints Books. 38.00 (*0-89555-221-3*, 1130) TAN Bks Pubs.

***Ball, Armand & Ball, Beverly.** Basic Camp Management: An Introduction to Camp Administration. 5th rev. ed. LC 99-41510. 350p. 2000. per. 42.95 (*0-87603-165-3*) Am Camping.

Ball, Avis J. Caring for an Aging Parent: Have I Done All I Can. LC 86-18664. 134p. (Orig.). 1986. 27.95 (*0-87975-368-4*) Prometheus Bks.

— Caring for an Aging Parent: Have I Done All I Can. LC 86-18664. 134p. (Orig.). 1986. pap. 17.95 (*0-87975-364-1*) Prometheus Bks.

Ball, B., jt. auth. see Bailey, L.

Ball, Barbara, jt. auth. see Ball, Frederick W.

Ball, Barbara, jt. auth. see Bright, Vonette.

Ball, Barbara, jt. ed. see Bright, Vonette.

Ball, Barbara B., jt. auth. see Ball, Frederick W.

Ball, Beverly, jt. auth. see Ball, Armand.

Ball, Bill. How to Use Linux. LC 98-89192. (How to Use ... (Que) Series). 1999. pap. text 24.99 (*0-672-31545-9*) Sams.

***Ball, Bill.** Linux for Your Laptop. 2000. pap. 39.99 (*0-7615-2816-4*) Prima Pub.

Ball, Bill. Sams Teach Yourself Linux in 24 Hours. 380p. 1998. 24.99 (*0-672-31162-3*, Pub. by Macmillan) S&S Trade.

— Teach Yourself Linux in 24 Hours. 2nd ed. LC 98-88372. (Teach Yourself Ser.). (Illus.). 574p. 1999. pap. 24.99 incl. cd-rom (*0-672-31526-2*) Sams.

***Ball, Billy.** SUSE Linux 6.1 Unleashed. (Unleashed Ser.). (Illus.). 1999. pap. 49.99 (*0-672-31780-X*) Sams.

Ball, Bob. Western Memorabilia & Collectibles. (Illus.). 160p. 1993. pap. 19.95 (*0-88740-484-7*) Schiffer.

Ball, Bonnie. The Melungeons. Mintz, James W., ed. (Illus.). 114p. 1992. pap. 8.95 (*0-932807-74-7*) Overmountain Pr.

Ball, Braden L. Around West Florida in 80 Years. LC 97-60867. (West Florida Pioneer Ser.). (Illus.). 224p. 1997. 19.95 (*0-9659142-0-8*) U of West Fla.

Ball, Braden L., jt. auth. see Belin, J. C.

Ball, Brian. Hop It Duggy Dog. (Illus.). 32p. (J). pap. 7.95 (*0-14-038158-9*, Pub. by Pnguin Bks Ltd) Trafalgar.

Ball, Bryan W. The Seventh-Day Men: Sabbatarians & Sabbatarianism in England & Wales, 1600-1800. LC 92-30811. (Illus.). 414p. 1994. text 75.00 (*0-19-826752-5*) OUP.

Ball, C. East European Cookbook. 160p. 1996. 15.98 (*0-7858-0558-3*) Bk Sales Inc.

Ball, Caroline. Identifying Guide to Horse & Pony Breeds. 80p. 1994. 6.98 (*0-7858-0051-4*) Bk Sales Inc.

— Law for Social Workers. 3rd ed. LC 96-84398. 192p. 1996. 55.95 (*1-85742-326-7*, Pub. by Arena); pap. 29.95 (*1-85742-324-0*, Pub. by Arena) Ashgate Pub Co.

***Ball, Caroline.** USA 2001. (Independent Traveller's Guide Ser.). (Illus.). 2000. pap. 19.95 (*0-7627-0767-4*) Globe Pequot.

***Ball, Caroline & Rogers, Barbara, eds.** U. S. A. 2000: The Budget Travel Guide. LC 99-56579. (Thomas Cook Independent Traveler's Guides Ser.). (Illus.). 1999. pap. 19.95 (*0-7627-0673-2*) Globe Pequot.

Ball, Caroline, ed. see Gray, Peter.

Ball, Carolyn. Blessings in Disguise. 256p. 1996. pap. 12.95 (*0-89087-799-8*) Celestial Arts.

Ball, Carolyn M. Claiming Your Self-Esteem: A Guide Out of Codependency, Addiction, & Other Useless Habits. 224p. 1995. reprint ed. pap. 11.95 (*0-89087-645-2*) Celestial Arts.

Ball, Charles. Fifty Years in Chains: or The Life of an American Slave. LC 70-89426. (Black Heritage Library Collection). 1977. 36.95 (*0-8369-8507-9*) Ayer.

— Slavery in the United States: A Narrative of the Life & Adventures of Charles Ball, a Black Man. LC 71-92414. 1970. reprint ed. 11.00 (*0-403-00178-1*) Scholarly.

Ball, Charles E. The Finishing Touch. 1992. text 29.95 (*0-318-14564-2*) Trafton Printing.

***Ball, Charles E., et al.** Building the Beef Industry: A Century of Commitment. LC 97-66850. xv, 296 p. 1998. write for info. (*1-879894-16-5*) Saratoga Pub.

Ball, Charles F. The Life & Times of the Apostle Paul. rev. ed. 200p. 1996. pap. 9.99 (*0-8423-3500-5*) Tyndale Hse.

Ball, Charles T. From Old Main to a New Century: A History of Phi Kappa Tau. 240p. 1996. 49.95 (*0-929690-29-X*) Herit Pubs AZ.

Ball, Chris & Lipsedge, Maurice. Multiple Choice Questions in Psychiatry. LC 97-30184. (An Arnold Publication). 144p. 1998. pap. text 16.95 (*0-340-69227-8*) OUP.

Ball, Chris, jt. auth. see Airs, John.

Ball, Christopher, ed. Genetics in Breeding of Industrial Microorganisms. 216p. 1984. lib. bdg. 159.00 (*0-8493-5672-5*, QR53) CRC Pr.

Ball, Christopher & Urwin, Dorma, eds. Fitness for Purpose: Essays in Higher Education. 134p. 1985. pap. 28.00 (*1-85059-007-9*) OpUniv Pr.

Ball, Christopher A. Take Charge of Your Worker's Compensation Claim: An A to Z Guide. 2nd rev. ed. Warner, Ralph E., ed. LC 97-20972. (Illus.). 400p. 1997. pap. 29.95 (*0-87337-393-6*) Nolo com.

Ball, Colin & Ball, Mary. Fit for Work? Youth, School & (un) Employment. 144p. pap. 5.95 (*0-906495-12-1*) Writers & Readers.

Ball, Colin & Ball, Mog. Water Supplies for Rural Communities. 64p. (Orig.). 1991. pap. 15.00 (*1-85339-112-3*, Pub. by Intermed Tech) Stylus Pub VA.

Ball, D. Air Power: Global Developments & Australian Perspectives. (Illus.). 659p. 1989. 40.00 (*0-08-034417-8*, Pergamon Pr) Elsevier.

— You Can Play the Ukulele. 40p. 1986. pap. 4.95 (*0-7935-3764-9*) H Leonard.

Ball, D., jt. ed. see Langtry, J. O.

Ball, D. W. Loitering in the Lakes. 1987. 42.00 (*0-7223-2174-0*, Pub. by A H S Ltd) St Mut.

Ball, David. Animal Farm (Orwell) (Barron's Book Notes Ser.). (C). 1984. pap. 3.95 (*0-8120-3402-3*) Barron.

— Backwards & Forwards: A Technical Manual for Reading Plays. LC 82-19333. 128p. (Orig.). 1983. pap. 10.95 (*0-8093-1110-0*) S Ill U Pr.

— Theater Tips & Strategies for Jury Trials. LC 97-164111. 166p. 1997. pap. 37.95 (*1-55681-531-X*) Natl Inst Trial Ad.

Ball, David, tr. see Michaux, Henri.

Ball, David M. I Am in John's Gospel: Literary Function, Background & Theological Implications. LC 96-134257. (JSNT Supplement Ser.: No. 124). 309p. 1996. 85.00 (*1-85075-587-6*, Pub. by Sheffield Acad) CUP Services.

Ball, David W. Empires of Sand. LC 99-24798. 576p. 1999. 23.95 (*0-553-11014-4*) Bantam.

— Essential Math for Chemistry Students. 150p. 1996. pap. 31.95 (*0-314-09604-3*) West Pub.

Ball, DeAnn & Ball, Terry. Each One a Miracle. 172p. 1994. 10.95 (*0-910523-41-X*) Grandin Bk Co.

Ball, Deborah, jt. auth. see Lampert, Magdalene.

Ball, Deborah l., jt. auth. see Lampert, Magdalene.

Ball, Derek. Advanced Powerbuilder 5.0: Tools for the Enterprise. LC 96-2909. (ITCP-UK Computer Science Ser.). (Illus.). 400p. 1996. mass mkt. 41.95 incl. cd-rom (*1-85032-855-2*) ITCP.

— Official Powerbuilder 6.0. 2nd ed. LC 97-62045. (ITCP - US Computer Science Ser.). (C). 1998. mass mkt. 49.99 (*1-85032-918-4*) ITCP.

Ball, Derek, jt. auth. see Richmond, Ian.

Ball, Derrick F., et al. Agglomeration of Iron Ores. LC 74-168614. 408p. reprint ed. pap. 126.50 (*0-8357-5256-9*, 205089000069) Bks Demand.

Ball, Desmond. Developments in U. S. Strategic Nuclear Policy under the Carter Administration. (CISA Working Papers: No. 21). 23p. (Orig.). 1980. pap. 15.00 (*0-86682-020-5*) Ctr Intl Relations.

Ball, Desmond, ed. The Transformation of Security of the Asia-Pacific Region. LC 95-20638. (Illus.). 220p. (C). 1996. 45.00 (*0-7146-4661-X*, Pub. by F Cass Pubs); pap. 24.50 (*0-7146-4190-1*, Pub. by F Cass Pubs) Intl Spec Bk.

Ball, Desmond & Downs, Cathy, eds. Security & Defence: Pacific & Global Perspectives. 512p. 1991. pap. text 24.95 (*0-04-442161-3*, Pub. by Allen & Unwin Pty) Paul & Co Pubs.

***Ball, Desmond & Horner, David.** Breaking the Codes: Australias's KGB Network. (Illus.). 488p. 1999. pap. 29.95 (*1-86448-578-7*, Pub. by Allen & Unwin Pty) Paul & Co Pubs.

Ball, Desmond & Kerr, Pauline. Presumptive Engagement: Australia's Asia-Pacific Security Policy in the 1990s. LC 96-176162. 200p. 1997. pap. text 24.95 (*1-86373-977-7*, Pub. by Allen & Unwin Pty) Paul & Co Pubs.

***Ball, Desmond & McDonald, Hamish.** Death in Balibo, Lies in Canberra. (Illus.). 208p. 2000. pap. 22.50 (*1-86508-369-0*, Pub. by Allen & Unwin Pty) Paul & Co Pubs.

Ball, Desmond & Wilson, Helen, eds. Strange Neighbours: The Australia-Indonesia Relationship. 288p. 1991. pap. 24.95 (*0-04-442233-4*, Pub. by Allen & Unwin Pty) Paul & Co Pubs.

Ball, Desmond J. Aborigines in the Defence of Australia. (Illus.). 240p. 1991. pap. text 31.01 (*0-08-034419-4*, Pergamon Pr) Elsevier.

Ball, Desmond J. & Babbage, Ross. Geographic Information Systems: Defense Applications. (Illus.). 220p. 1990. 38.00 (*0-08-034444-5*, Pergamon Pr) Elsevier.

Ball, Desmond J., jt. auth. see Richelson, Jeffrey T.

Ball, Doc. California Surfriders, 1946. 2nd ed. 116p. 1946. 29.95 (*0-911449-05-1*) Mountain Sea.

Ball, Don, Jr. America's Railroads: The Second Generation. (Illus.). 224p. 1980. 55.00 (*0-393-01416-9*) Norton.

— The Pennsylvania Railroad: The 1940s & 1950s. 1986. 50.00 (*0-393-02357-5*) Norton.

Ball, Donald A. International Business. 7th ed. 1998. text 66.50 (*0-256-26206-3*) McGraw.

Ball, Donald A. & McCulloch, Wendell. International Business: The Challenge of Global Competition. 7th ed. LC 98-23852. 1998. 77.00 (*0-07-154006-7*) McGraw.

Ball, Donald A. & McCulloch, Wendell H., Jr. International Business: The Challenge of Competition. annot. ed. LC 95-18497. 1995. teacher ed. write for info. (*0-256-16606-4*, Irwn Prfssnl) McGraw-Hill Prof.

— International Business: The Challenge of Competition. 6th ed. LC 95-18497. 752p. (C). 1995. text 68.50 (*0-256-16601-3*, Irwn Prfssnl) McGraw-Hill Prof.

Ball, Donald B., jt. auth. see Kessler, John S.

Ball, Donald B., jt. ed. see Kessler, John S.

Ball, Donald L. Fighting Amphibs: The LCS(L) in World War II. LC 97-73465. (Illus.). 338p. 1997. pap. 19.95 (*0-9659055-0-0*) Mill Neck Pubns.

— The Genealogy of the Locomobile Steam Carriage, 1899-1904. (Illus.). 55p. (Orig.). 1994. pap. 15.95 (*1-886727-00-7*) Stanley Mus.

Ball, Donald M. Practical Forage Concepts. LC 98-97018. (Illus.). viii, 160p. 1999. pap. 10.00 (*0-9616023-1-7*) AL Cattlemen.

Ball, Donald M., et al. Southern Forages. 2nd ed. (Illus.). 264p. (C). 1996. pap. text. write for info. (*0-9629598-2-0*) PPI.

Ball, Donald W. Microecology: Social Situations & Intimate Space. LC 72-10541. (Studies in Sociology). 40p. (C). 1973. pap. text. write for info. (*0-672-61209-7*, Bobbs) Macmillan.

— Microecology: Social Situations & Intimate Space. reprint ed. pap. text 7.95 (*0-8290-0238-2*) Irvington.

Ball, Donna. The Darkest Hour. 288p. 1992. mass mkt. 4.50 (*0-8217-3774-0*, Zebra Kensgtn) Kensgtn Pub Corp.

Ball, Douglas. Financial Failure & Confederate Defeat. 344p. 1991. text 29.95 (*0-252-01755-2*) U of Ill Pr.

— Victorian Publishers' Bindings. (Illus.). 214p. 1985. 38.50 (*0-916271-01-3*) BkPr Ltd.

Ball, Douglas B. Comprehensive Catalog & History of Confederate Bonds. (Illus.). 288p. 1998. 40.00 (*0-931960-58-4*) BNR Pr.

— Confederate States of America Currency, 1861-1865 No. 5: Handbook. 35p. 1986. 6.00 (*0-685-72027-6*); boxed set 20.00 incl. sl. (*0-685-72028-4*) Am Numismatic.

Ball, Douglas H., et al. Stories Worth Reading. (Triumph Ser.: Vol. I). (Illus.). 192p. (Orig.). (YA). (gr. 8-11). 1989. pap. text. write for info. (*0-9621844-0-3*) Printemps Bks.

Ball, Duncan. Selby Speaks, More Adventures of a Talking Dog. 1997. 9.60 (*0-606-11827-6*, Pub. by Turtleback) Demco.

— Selby, the Secret Adventures of a Talking Dog. 1997. 9.60 (*0-606-11828-4*, Pub. by Turtleback) Demco.

Ball, E. F., et al. The Middletown Photographs. Sargent, T. A., ed. (Illus.). 68p. (Orig.). 1984. pap. 5.00 (*0-915511-01-0*) Ball St U Mus Art.

Ball, E. Michael. The Effective Organization's Workbook. LC 96-44873. 1997. pap. write for info. (*0-07-709220-1*) McGraw.

Ball, Edmund E. Rambling Recollections of Flying & Flyers, Vol. 2. 208p. (Orig.). 1993. pap. write for info. (*0-9623291-9-3*) Minnetrista.

Ball, Edmund F. Rambling Recollections of Flying & Flyers, Vol. 1. 240p. (Orig.). 1993. pap. write for info. (*0-9623291-7-7*) Minnetrista.

***Ball, Edward.** Slaves in the Family. 2000. 15.95 (*0-345-91763-4*) Ballantine Pub Grp.

***Ball, Edward, ed.** In Search of True Wisdom: Essays in Old Testament Interpretation in Honour of Ronald E. Clements. (Journal for the Study of the Old Testament Supplement Ser.: No. 300). 292p. 2000. 85.00 (*1-84127-071-7*, Pub. by Sheffield Acad) CUP Services.

Ball, Edward D. & Lister, John. Practical Guide to Bone Marrow Transplantation. (Illus.). 795p. 2000. text. write for info. (*0-443-07622-7*, W B Saunders Co) Harcrt Hlth Sci Grp.

Ball, Eve. In the Days of Victorio. 1972. pap. text 13.95 (*0-8165-0401-6*) U of Ariz Pr.

— Ma'am Jones of the Pecos. LC 68-9336. 265p. reprint ed. pap. 82.20 (*0-608-13353-1*, 202555000044) Bks Demand.

Ball, Eve, et al. Indeh: An Apache Odyssey. LC 88-40212. (Illus.). 356p. 1988. pap. 16.95 (*0-8061-2165-3*) U of Okla Pr.

Ball, Eve, ed. see Klasner, Lily.

Ball, Everett J. Little Blaine Creek is Rising: Memories from Kentucky. 242p. 1991. 35.00 (*0-9628918-0-0*) J R Ball.

Ball, F. Carlton. Decorating Pottery. LC 67-19833. (Ceramics Monthly Handbooks Ser.). (Illus.). 64p. 1967. pap. 7.95 (*0-934706-05-0*) Am Ceramic.

— Syllabus for Advanced Ceramics. LC 77-187486. (C). pap. 3.95 (*0-935066-03-9*) Keramos Bks.

Ball, F. Nolan. God's Plan for Financing the Ministry. LC 91-91548. 250p. 1995. reprint ed. 12.00 (*0-9631898-0-8*) The Rock Panama Cty.

***Ball, Frederick W. & Ball, Barbara.** Impact Hiring: The Secrets of Hiring a Superstar. LC 99-88006. (Illus.). 300p. 1999. 21.95 (*0-8281-1439-0*) Forb Custom Pub.

Ball, Frederick W. & Ball, Barbara B. Killer Interviews. 192p. 1996. pap. 10.95 (*0-07-005756-7*) McGraw.

Ball, G. H., jt. auth. see Warren, F. D.

Ball, Gene V. & Koopman, William J. Clinical Rheumatology. (Illus.). 367p. 1986. text 79.00 (*0-7216-1451-5*, W B Saunders Co) Harcrt Hlth Sci Grp.

Ball, George E., ed. Taxonomy, Phylogeny & Zoogeography of Beetles & Ants. (Entomologica Ser.). 1985. text 366.50 (*90-6193-511-3*) Kluwer Academic.

Ball, George W. The Past Has Another Pattern: Memoirs. (Illus.). 540p. 1983. pap. 9.95 (*0-393-30142-7*) Norton.

Ball, George W., ed. Global Companies: The Political Economy of World Business. LC 75-5557. 1975. 8.95 (*0-13-357145-9*); pap. 2.95 (*0-13-357137-8*) Am Assembly.

Ball, George W., ed. see American Assembly Staff.

Ball, Gerald T., jt. auth. see Owens, Elisabeth A.

Ball, Gordon. '66 Frames: A Memoir. (Illus.). 288p. 1999. pap. 15.95 (*1-56689-082-9*, Pub. by Coffee Hse) Consort Bk Sales.

Ball, Gordon, ed. see Ginsberg, Allen.

Ball, Graham, jt. auth. see Bohaychuk, Wendy.

Ball, Gregory, tr. from DUT. Aldo van Eyck: Works 1944-1999. LC 99-43794. (Illus.). 312p. 1999. 70.00 (*3-7643-6012-7*, Pub. by Birkhauser) Princeton Arch.

Ball, Gregory, tr. see Worldviews Group Staff.

Ball, Guy, ed. A Victorian Reclaimed: Pre-Restoration Images of the Dr. Howe-Waffle House. LC 98-86094. (Illus.). 54p. 1998. 34.95 (*1-888840-01-3*, 1888840013) Wilson-Barnett.

Ball, Guy & Flamm, Bruce. Collector's Guide to Pocket Calculators. LC 96-90758. (Illus.). 204p. (Orig.). 1997. pap. 23.95 (*1-888840-14-5*) Wilson-Barnett.

***Ball, Guy, et al.** Neighborhood Organization Starter Guide. 2nd rev. ed. LC 99-60331. 1999. 19.95 (*1-888840-04-8*) Wilson-Barnett.

***Ball, H. A.** The Side Door: A Story of Action, Tension, Suspense. LC 99-203169. 244p. 1999. pap. 18.95 (*1-85756-309-3*, Pub. by Janus Pubng) Paul & Co Pubs.

Ball, Harry P. Of Responsible Command: A History of the U. S. Army War College. rev. ed. LC 94-79283. (Illus.). 538p. 1994. 29.00 (*0-9613301-1-2*) Alumni Assn US.

Ball, Helen B., jt. auth. see Ball, William G.

***Ball, Howard.** The Bakke Case: Race, Education & Affirmative Action. LC 00-41163. (Landmark Law Cases & American Society Ser.). 2000. pap. 12.95 (*0-7006-1046-4*) U Pr of KS.

— Bakke Case: Race, Education & Affirmative Action. (Landmark Law Cases & American Society Ser.). 2000. 29.95 (*0-7006-1045-6*) U Pr of KS.

Ball, Howard. Cancer Factories: America's Tragic Quest for Uranium Self-Sufficiency, 37. LC 92-32225. (Contributions in Medical Studies: No. 37). 216p. 1993. 55.00 (*0-313-27566-1*, BFJ, Greenwood Pr) Greenwood.

— Controlling Regulatory Sprawl: Presidential Strategies from Nixon to Reagan, 105. LC 83-8541. (Contributions in Political Science Ser.: No. 105). 206p. 1984. 55.00 (*0-313-23525-2*, BCF/, Greenwood Pr) Greenwood.

— Courts & Politics: The Federal Judicial System. 2nd ed. (Illus.). 320p. (C). 1986. pap. text 36.00 (*0-13-184664-7*) P-H.

— A Defiant Life: Thurgood Marshall & the Persistence of Racism in America. LC 98-23031. (Illus.). 448p. 1999. 30.00 (*0-517-59931-7*) Crown Pub Group.

— Hugo L. Black: Cold Steel Warrior. (Illus.). 328p. 1996. 39.95 (*0-19-507814-4*) OUP.

— Judicial Craftsmanship or Fiat? Direct Overturn by the United States Supreme Court, 7. LC 77-91102. (Contributions in Political Science Ser.: No. 7). 160p. 1978. 49.95 (*0-313-20035-1*, BJC/, Greenwood Pr) Greenwood.

— Prosecuting War Crimes & Genocide: The Twentieth-Century Experience. LC 99-22186. (Illus.). 304p. 1999. 35.00 (*0-7006-0977-6*) U Pr of KS.

— We Have a Duty: The Supreme Court & the Watergate Tapes Litigation, 60. LC 90-3135. (Contributions in Legal Studies: No. 60). 184p. 1990. 52.95 (*0-313-26565-8*, BWB, Greenwood Pr) Greenwood.

Ball, Howard, et al, eds. Multicultural Education in Colleges & Universities: A Transdisciplinary Approach. LC 97-31207. 200p. 1998. write for info. (*0-8058-1693-3*); pap. write for info. (*0-8058-1694-1*) L Erlbaum Assocs.

Ball, Howard & Mzamane, Mbulelo V. Race, Ethnicity, & the American Context. (C). 1995. 50.00 (*0-205-16660-1*, Macmillan Coll) P-H.

Ball, Howard, et al. Compromised Compliance: Implementation of the 1965 Voting Rights Act, 66. LC 81-6342. (Contributions in Political Science Ser.: No. 66). (Illus.). 300p. 1982. 65.00 (*0-313-22037-9*, BCM/, Greenwood Pr) Greenwood.

Ball, Hugo. Critique of the German Intelligentsia. Harris, Brian L., tr. from GER. LC 93-7111.Tr. of Zur Kritik der Deutschen Intelligenz. 273p. 1993. 60.00 (*0-231-07526-X*) Col U Pr.

— Flight Out of Time: A Dada Diary. Elderfield, John, ed. Raimes, Ann, tr. from GER. (Documents of Twentieth Century Art Ser.). (Illus.). 324p. (C). 1996. pap. 17.95 (*0-520-20440-9*, Pub. by U CA Pr) Cal Prin Full Svc.

Ball, Hugo, et al. Blago Bung, Blago Bung, Bosso Fatakal: The First Texts of the German Dada. Green, Malcolm, tr. from GER. LC 96-143908. (Atlas Anti-Classics Ser.). 176p. (Orig.). 1995. pap. 15.99 (*0-947757-86-4*, Pub. by Atlas Pr) Serpents Tail.

***Ball, Ian.** Traditional Beer & Cider Making. 2nd ed. (Illus.). 128p. 2001. pap. 6.95 (*0-7160-2045-9*, Pub. by Elliot RW Bks) Midpt Trade.

Ball, Ian R., jt. ed. see Schockaert, Ernest R.

Ball, J. & DeTar, C., eds. Salt Lake City Meeting: Regular Meetings of the Division of Particles & Fields APS. 680p. 1987. pap. 70.00 (*9971-5-0244-5*); text 148.00 (*9971-5-0243-7*) World Scientific Pub.

Ball, J. & Moore, A. Essential Physics for Radiographers. 2nd ed. 296p. 1986. pap. 19.00 (*0-632-01482-2*) Blackwell Sci.

Ball, J. & Torem, Dorothy H. Masterpieces of Costume Jewelry. LC 95-31294. 208p. (gr. 10). 1996. 49.95 (*0-88740-900-8*) Schiffer.

Ball, J. A., et al. Interpolation of Rational Matrix Functions. (Operator Theory Ser.: Vol. 45). 605p. 1990. 221.00 (*0-8176-2476-7*) Birkhauser.

Ball, J. C. & Ross, A. The Effectiveness of Methadone Maintenance Treatment: Patients, Programs, Services & Outcome. (Illus.). 312p. 1991. 92.00 (*0-387-97423-7*) Spr-Verlag.

Ball, J. J., et al, eds. Healthcare Information Management Systems: A Practical Guide. (Computers in Health Care Ser.). (Illus.). 384p. 1994. 44.00 (*0-387-97434-2*) Spr-Verlag.

Ball, J. M., ed. Systems of Nonlinear Partial Differential Equations. 1983. text 222.50 (*90-277-1629-3*) Kluwer Academic.

Ball, J. M., ed. see Gurtin, Morton E.

Ball, J. Michael. Encyclopedia of Investigative Information Sources: City, County, State, Federal Records, Financial, Private & Directory Sources. 2nd ed. 100p. (Orig.). 1997. pap. text 35.00 (*0-918487-10-2*) Thomas Investigative.

— Private Investigator's Book of Legal Forms & Contracts. 80p. 1997. spiral bd. 29.95 (*0-918487-01-3*) Thomas Investigative.

Ball, Jacqueline A. Let's Party. (Looking Good Ser.). (Illus.). 32p. (J). (gr. 5 up). 1990. lib. bdg. 11.95 (*0-685-36382-1*) Rourke Corp.

— Looking Good, 8 bks., Set. (Illus.). 64p. (J). (gr. 5 up). 1990. lib. bdg. 127.52 (*0-86625-287-8*) Rourke Pubns.

— Looking Good, 8 bks., Set 11. (Illus.). 64p. (J). (gr. 5 up). 1990. 95.60 (*0-685-58754-1*) Rourke Corp.

— Riddles about Baby Animals. Brook, Bonnie, ed. (What Can It Be? Ser.). (Illus.). 32p. (J). (ps-3). 1989. pap. 4.95 (*0-382-24385-4*); lib. bdg. 6.95 (*0-671-68576-7*, Silver Pr NJ) Silver Burdett Pr.

— Riddles about Our Bodies. Brook, Bonnie, ed. (What Can It Be? Ser.). (Illus.). 32p. (J). (ps-3). 1989. pap. 4.95 (*0-382-24386-2*, Silver Pr NJ) Silver Burdett Pr.

— Riddles about Our Bodies. Brook, Bonnie, ed. (What Can It Be? Ser.). (Illus.). 32p. (J). (ps-3). 1989. lib. bdg. 6.95 (*0-671-68578-3*, Silver Pr NJ) Silver Burdett Pr.

— Riddles about the Seasons. Brook, Bonnie, ed. (What Can It Be? Ser.). (Illus.). 32p. (J). (ps-3). 1989. pap. 4.95 (*0-382-24387-0*, Silver Pr NJ) Silver Burdett Pr.

— Riddles about the Seasons. Brook, Bonnie, ed. (What Can It Be? Ser.). (Illus.). 32p. (J). (ps-3). 1989. lib. bdg. 6.95 (*0-671-68582-1*, Silver Pr NJ) Silver Burdett Pr.

— Riddles about the Senses. Brook, Bonnie, ed. (What Can It Be? Ser.). (Illus.). 32p. (J). (ps-3). 1989. pap. 2.95 (*0-382-24388-9*); lib. bdg. 6.95 (*0-671-68580-5*, Silver Pr NJ) Silver Burdett Pr.

Ball, Jacqueline A. Hygiene. (Looking Good Ser.: Set II). 32p. (J). 1989. lib. bdg. 19.93 (*0-86625-285-1*) Rourke Pubns.

— Let's Party. (Looking Good Ser.: Set II). (Illus.). 32p. (YA). (gr. 5 up). 1990. lib. bdg. 19.93 (*0-86625-418-8*) Rourke Pubns.

— Puberty. (Looking Good Ser.: Set II). 32p. (J). 1989. lib. bdg. 19.93 (*0-86625-283-5*) Rourke Pubns.

— What Can It Be?, 8 bks., Seet. (Illus.). 32p ea.p. (J). (gr. k-3). 1990. lib. bdg. 27.80 (*0-671-94103-8*, Silver Pr NJ) Silver Burdett Pr.

Ball, James. The British Economy at the Crossroads: Ball on Britain. (Illus.). 282p. 1998. 47.50 (*0-273-63702-9*, Pub. by Pitman Pbg) Trans-Atl Phila.

Ball, James, ed. The Economics of Wealth Creation. (British Association for the Advancement of Science Ser.). 256p. 1992. 95.00 (*1-85278-642-6*) E Elgar.

Ball, James & Ball, William. Stockport Grammar School, 1487-1987: The Quincentenary History. 128p. (C). 1982. text 60.00 (*0-947818-06-5*, Pub. by Old Vicarage); pap. text 39.00 (*0-947818-05-7*, Pub. by Old Vicarage) St Mut.

Ball, James R. The Anacondas in Life. Shannon, Vicki, ed. (Illus.). 40p. 1993. pap. 2.75 (*0-9633184-1-1*) Goals Inst.

— DNA Leadership Through Goal-Driven Management. unabridged ed. LC 97-70642. (Illus.). 448p. 1997. 29.95 (*1-887570-00-4*) Goals Inst.

— The Entrepreneur's Tool Kit. 2nd unabridged ed. 54p. 1993. pap. 29.95 (*0-9633184-5-4*) Goals Inst.

— The Power of Your Actions. Shannon, Vicki, ed. (Illus.). 40p. 1993. pap. 2.75 (*0-9633184-2-X*) Goals Inst.

— Soar...If You Dare: And Use Your Secret Powers for Success to Make Your Dreams Come True. 2nd rev. ed. LC 98-93566. (Illus.). 270p. 1999. pap. 12.95 (*1-887570-02-0*) Goals Inst.

— Your Ultimate Secret Power. Shannon, Vicki, ed. (Illus.). 24p. 1993. pap. 2.75 (*0-9633184-0-3*) Goals Inst.

***Ball, James T.** McGraw-Hill Civil Engineering PE Exam Guide: Breadth & Depth. (Illus.). 2000. 99.95 (*0-07-136177-4*) McGraw.

Ball, Jane. Pediatric Nursing Transparencies. (C). 1994. pap. text 225.00 (*0-8385-8076-9*, A8076-0) Appleton & Lange.

Ball, Jane & Bindler, Ruth M. Pediatric Nursing: Caring for Children. 2nd ed. LC 98-25825. 1083p. (C). 1998. pap. text 62.95 (*0-8385-8123-4*) Appleton & Lange.

Ball, Jane A., jt. auth. see Littlefield, Robert S.

Ball, Jane W. Mosby's Pediatric Patient Teaching Guides. LC 97-37998. (Illus.). 224p. (C). (gr. 13). 1998. text 74.95 (*0-8151-1558-X*, 29994) Mosby Inc.

— Mosby's Pediatric Patient Teaching Guides on CD-Rom. LC 97-37607. (Illus.). 225p. (C). (gr. 13). 1998. text 129.00 (*0-8151-2577-1*) Mosby Inc.

Ball, Jeff & Ball, Liz. Rodale's Flower Garden Problem Solver. (Illus.). 432p. 1994. 9.98 (*1-56731-045-1*, MJF Bks) Fine Comms.

— Rodale's Flower Garden Problem Solver: Annuals, Perennials, Bulbs & Roses. (Illus.). 432p. 1995. pap. 14.95 (*0-87596-698-5*) Rodale Pr Inc.

— Rodale's Landscape Problem Solver: A Plant by Plant Guide. (Illus.). 448p. 1995. pap. 14.95 (*0-87596-692-6*, 01-185-0) Rodale Pr Inc.

— Smart Yard: The Guide to 60-Minute Lawn Care. (Illus.). 208p. (Orig.). 1995. pap. 16.95 (*1-55591-138-2*) Fulcrum Pub.

***Ball, Jeff & Whitten, Bruce A.** Trailhead of the American Indian Courting Flute. (Illus.). 22p. 1999. pap. 11.00 (*0-9672383-0-7*) Four Winds Trad.

Ball, Jennifer, ed. see Petersen, Bernie.

***Ball, Jeremy.** The Green Spectacles. 256p. (C). 1999. per. 42.95 (*0-7872-6371-0*) Kendall-Hunt.

Ball, Jeri L. The Great Communitarian Hoax: The Hidden Agenda of the Clinton-Gore Administration. 52p. (Orig.). 1998. pap. 5.00 (*0-9653226-6-1*) Am Freedom Pr.

— The Voices of America's Destruction: And the Life-Giving, Life-Celebrating Antidote. (Illus.). 189p. 1998. pap. 15.00 (*0-9653226-4-5*) Am Freedom Pr.

Ball, Joanne D. Jewelry of the Stars: Creations from Joseff of Hollywood. LC 90-63500. (Illus.). 192p. 1991. 44.95 (*0-88740-294-1*) Schiffer.

Ball, Joanne D. & Torem-Craig, Caroline D. Wedding Traditions: Here Comes the Bride. LC 97-72681. (Illus.). 176p. 1997. 29.95 (*0-930625-63-3*) Krause Pubns.

Ball, Joanne D. & Torem, Dorothy H. The Art of Fashion Accessories. LC 92-63102. (Illus.). 240p. 1993. 59.95 (*0-88740-461-8*) Schiffer.

— Commercial Fragrance Bottles. LC 93-85222. (Illus.). 256p. 1993. 79.95 (*0-88740-556-8*) Schiffer.

— Fragrance Bottle Masterpieces. LC 96-17243. (Illus.). 256p. 1996. 69.95 (*0-88740-985-7*) Schiffer.

***Ball, Joanne Dubbs.** Costume Jewelers: The Golden Age of Design. 3rd ed. (Illus.). 208p. 2000. 39.95 (*0-7643-1084-4*) Schiffer.

Ball, Jody. The Bible on Worker's Comp Investigation. 1997. spiral bd. 35.00 (*1-891247-07-7*) Thomas Investigative.

— Check Mate: The Book of Premarital & Divorce Investigations. 125p. 1998. spiral bd. 35.00 (*1-891247-21-2*) Thomas Investigative.

— Conducting Crimes Against Persons Investigations in the Private Sector: The Private Sectors Guide to Conducting Homicide, Suicide, Rape & Child Abuse Investigations. 1997. pap. 35.00 (*1-891247-02-6*) Thomas Investigative.

— Private Investigative Agency Start-Up Manual. 1998. spiral bd. 45.00 (*1-891247-14-X*) Thomas Investigative.

— Process Server's Handbook & Legal Reference Directory: Technical & Legal Aspects of Successfully Serving Legal Papers. 1997. spiral bd. 38.00 (*1-891247-01-8*) Thomas Investigative.

***Ball, Jody & Parker, Anne.** Providing Security Services & Consulting. 1999. spiral bd. 24.95 (*1-891247-32-8*) Thomas Investigative.

Ball, Jody M. Conducting Child Abuse Investigations. 65p. (Orig.). 1997. pap. text 19.95 (*0-918487-12-9*) Thomas Investigative.

Ball, John. Ananda: Where Yoga Lives. LC 82-82100. 240p. 1982. 16.95 (*0-87972-207-X*) Bowling Green Univ Popular Press.

— Ananda: Where Yoga Lives. LC 82-82100. (Illus.). 232p. 1982. pap. 9.95 (*0-87972-208-8*, DS1) Bowling Green Univ Popular Press.

— Born to Wander: The Autobiography of John Ball. Burbridge, Gary, ed. & intro. by. LC 94-77965. (Illus.). 160p. (YA). (gr. 8 up). 1994. 24.95 (*0-9617708-4-8*) GRMI Hist Comm.

— Escape from Dixie, Vol. 1. LC 97-159556. (Illus.). 109p. (Orig.). 1996. pap. 12.95 (*0-929214-08-0*) Goldstar Enterprises.

— In the Heat of the Night. (Mystery Scene Bk.). 208p. 1992. mass mkt. 4.50 (*0-88184-887-5*) Carroll & Graf.

— In the Heat of the Night. 158p. 1992. reprint ed. lib. bdg. 14.95 (*0-89966-916-6*) Buccaneer Bks.

— The Kiwi Target. 185p. 1991. mass mkt. 3.95 (*0-88184-671-6*) Carroll & Graf.

— Radiographic Imaging. 6th rev. ed. Price, Tony, ed. LC 95-5293. 1995. pap. 39.95 (*0-632-03901-9*) Blackwell Sci.

— Then Came Violence. large type ed. 352p. 1982. 27.99 (*0-7089-0870-5*) Ulverscroft.

— Understanding Disease. 111p. 1991. pap. 19.95 (*0-85207-229-5*, Pub. by C W Daniel) Natl Bk Netwk.

— Understanding Disease: A Health Practitioner's Handbook. (Illus.). 264p. (Orig.). pap. 29.95 (*0-8464-4307-4*) Beekman Pubs.

Ball, John & Moore, Adrian D. Essential Physics for Radiographers. 3rd ed. LC 97-16872. 388p. 1997. 39.95 (*0-632-03902-7*) Blackwell Sci.

Ball, John & Plant, Richard. Bibliography of Theatre History in Canada: The Beginnings to 1984. 400p. (C). 1993. text 85.00 (*1-55022-120-5*, Pub. by ECW) Genl Dist Srvs.

Ball, John, jt. auth. see McDonnell, Leo.

Ball, John, tr. see Gilles, Peter.

Ball, John C. Social Deviancy & Adolescent Personality. LC 72-12308. (Illus.). 119p. 1973. reprint ed. lib. bdg. 49.50 (*0-8371-6687-X*, BASD, Greenwood Pr) Greenwood.

***Ball, John C. & Jonnes, Jill.** Fame at Last: Who Was Who According to the New York Times Obituaries. LC 00-31484. 320p. 2000. 24.95 (*0-7407-0940-2*) Andrews & McMeel.

Ball, John D., jt. auth. see Peake, Thomas H.

Ball, John D., ed. see Roma, Tom J.

Ball, John D., ed. see Roma, Tom J. & Farnell, Kim.

Ball, John E. Carpenters & Builders Library. 5th ed. 1982. 35.95 (*0-672-23244-8*, G K Hall & Co) Mac Lib Ref.

— Carpenters & Builders Library. 5th ed. 1987. pap. 47.95 (*0-02-506450-9*) Macmillan.

— Carpenters & Builders Library, Set: Vol. 1-4. 5th ed. LC 82-133279. 1983. pap. 43.95 (*0-672-23369-X*) Macmillan.

— Carpenters & Builders Library, Vol. 1. 5th ed. 1984. pap. 11.95 (*0-672-23365-7*) Macmillan.

— Carpenters & Builders Library, Vol. 2. 5th ed. 1984. 11.95 (*0-672-23366-5*) Macmillan.

— Carpenters & Builders Library, Vol. 3. 5th ed. 1984. pap. 11.95 (*0-672-23367-3*) Macmillan.

— Carpenters & Builders Library, Vol. 4. 5th ed. 1985. per. 11.95 (*0-672-23368-1*) Macmillan.

— Exterior & Interior Trim. LC 75-6060. 192p. (C). 1975. pap. 25.95 (*0-8273-1120-6*) Delmar.

— Practical Problems in Mathematics for Masons. 2nd ed. LC 78-74431. (Mathematics - Construction Ser.). 200p. (C). 1980. teacher ed. 14.00 (*0-8273-1284-9*); pap. text 15.75 (*0-8273-1283-0*) Delmar.

Ball, John E. & Leeke, John. Carpenters & Builders Library, 4 vols. rev. ed. 1991. write for info. (*0-318-68344-X*) Macmillan.

— Carpenters & Builders Library, 4 vols. 6th ed. Incl. Vol. 4. Carpenters & Builders Library: Millwork, Power Tools, Painting. 6th rev. ed. (Illus.). 360p. 1991. 21.95 (*0-02-506454-1*); Vol. 1. Tools, Steel Square, Joinery. 6th rev. ed. (Illus.). 400p. 1991. 21.95 (*0-02-506451-7*); 89.95 (*0-02-506455-X*) Macmillan.

Ball, John F. Mazda RX-7: The 1st Generation, 1979-1985. (Illus.). 218p. 1990. 19.95 (*0-929214-04-8*) Goldstar Enterprises.

— Taming the Taildragger. 5th ed. 107p. 1994. pap. 9.95 (*0-929214-06-4*) Goldstar Enterprises.

Ball, John H., III. Chronicling the Soul's Windings: Thomas Hooker & His Morphology of Conversion. 280p. (C). 1991. lib. bdg. 48.00 (*0-8191-8362-8*) U Pr of Amer.

Ball, John H., III & Rollinson, Philip, eds. The Westminster Confession of Faith: A Modern Study Edition. v, 53p. (Orig.). 1991. pap. text 4.00 (*0-9614303-4-6*) Summertown.

Ball, John M. Saints of Another God. LC 88-62794. 254p. (Orig.). 1989. pap. 10.99 (*0-8100-0304-X*, 15N0462) Northwest Pub.

Ball, John T. Barefoot in the Palace. 1985. 6.55 (*0-89536-748-3*, 5854) CSS OH.

Ball, John W., ed. Jockey's Guild Yearbook. 152p. 1995. 45.00 (*0-9647765-0-2*) Horse Star Cards.

— Jockeys' Guild Yearbook, 1996. 160p. 1996. 45.00 (*0-9647765-1-0*) Horse Star Cards.

Ball, Joseph. Factorization & Model Theory for Contraction Operators with Unitary Part. LC 77-25161. (Memoirs Ser.: No. 13/198). 68p. 1991. pap. 19.00 (*0-8218-2198-9*, MEMO/13/198) Am Math.

Ball, Joseph A. Factorization & Model Theory for Contraction Operators with Unitary Part. LC 77-25161. (American Mathematical Society Ser.: No. 198). 76p. reprint ed. pap. 30.00 (*0-608-09214-2*, 205271800005) Bks Demand.

Ball, Joseph W. The Archaeological Ceramics of Becan, Campeche, Mexico. (Publications: No. 43). (Illus.). xiv, 190p. 1977. 25.00 (*0-939238-48-9*) Tulane MARI.

— Cahal Pech, the Ancient Maya, & Modern Belize: The Story of an Archaeological Park. (University Research Lectures: No. 9). (Illus.). 116p. 1994. 30.00 (*1-879691-17-5*) SDSU Press.

Ball, Judy & Danich, John. The Brain, the Soul, God. 174p. 1986. pap. 6.95 (*0-88144-064-7*) Christian Pub.

Ball, K. Randall. Easyriders: Ultimate Custom Bikes. LC 98-164975. (Illus.). 176p. 1997. 24.95 (*1-56025-151-4*, Thunders Mouth) Avalon NY.

— Out Law Justice. 272p. 1997. pap. text. write for info. (*0-9651605-1-3*) Five Ball.

— Prize Possession. pap. 5.99 (*0-9651605-0-5*) Five Ball.

Ball, Karen. Reunion. LC 99-22189. 352p. 1999. pap. 6.99 (*1-57673-597-4*) Multnomah Pubs.

— Wilderness. LC 99-40049. 384p. 1999. mass mkt. 6.99 (*1-57673-552-4*, Multnomah Wom Fict) Multnomah Pubs.

Ball, Karen, et al. Fools for Love. LC 97-43804. 1997. pap. 9.99 (*1-57673-235-5*) Multnomah Pubs.

— Mistletoe. LC 96-222597. 300p. 1996. pap. 9.99 (*1-57673-013-1*, Palisades OR) Multnomah Pubs.

Ball, Kay. Lasers: The Perioperative Challenge. 2nd ed. LC 94-47036. (Illus.). 448p. (C). (gr. 13). 1995. pap. text 35.95 (*0-8151-0524-X*, 24568) Mosby Inc.

Ball, Kay A. Lasers: The Perioperative Challenge. 256p. 1990. 44.95 (*0-685-51072-7*) Laser Inst.

Ball, Keith & Milman, Vitali, eds. Convex Geometry Analysis. LC 98-51729. (Mathematical Sciences Research Institute Publications: No. 34). xx, 236 p. (C). 1999. text 39.95 (*0-521-64259-0*) Cambridge U Pr.

Ball, Ken. Xeriscape Programs for Water Utilities. 104p. 1990. pap. 47.00 (*0-89867-525-1*, 20253) Am Water Wks Assn.

Ball, Kenneth. BMW 1800, 1964-70 Autobook: Workshop Manual for All Models of the BMW 1800, 1964-70. 2nd ed. LC 74-176434. (Autobook Series of Workshop Manuals). 169p. 1970. write for info. (*0-85147-180-3*) A & C Blk.

Ball, Kenneth R., jt. auth. see Willcutt, J. Robert.

Ball-Kilbourne, Debra, compiled by. Mudpie Olympics & Ninety-Nine Other Nonedible Games. LC 93-37816. 112p. (Orig.). 1994. pap. 13.95 (*0-687-78095-0*) Abingdon.

Ball-Kilbourne, Gary L. Get Acquainted with Your Bible. 72p. (Orig.). 1993. pap., student ed. 5.95 (*0-687-14046-3*) Abingdon.

Ball-Kilbourne, Gary L. Get Acquainted with Your Bible: Korean Student Book. 5.00 (*0-687-01570-7*) Abingdon.

Ball-Kilbourne, Gary L. Get Acquainted with Your Bible Leader's Guide. 48p. (Orig.). 1993. pap., teacher ed. 5.95 (*0-687-14047-1*) Abingdon.

Ball, L. A., jt. ed. see Miller, Lois K.

Ball, Larry A. From Travel Air to Baron: How Beech Created a Classic. LC 94-94265. (Illus.). 503p. 1994. 39.95 (*0-9641514-0-5*) Ball Pubns.

— The Immortal Twin Beech. LC 94-94266. (Illus.). 240p. 1995. 39.95 (*0-9641514-2-1*) Ball Pubns.

— They Called Me "Mr. Bonanza" LC 90-63687. (Illus.). 321p. 1990. 39.95 (*0-911978-05-4*) Ball Pubns.

— Those Incomparable Bonanzas. 9th ed. LC 73-187284. (Illus.). 219p. 1971. reprint ed. 39.95 (*0-9641514-1-3*) Ball Pubns.

— Those Remarkable Mooneys. limited ed. LC 97-93261. (Illus.). 251p. 1998. 39.95 (*0-9641514-9-9*) Ball Pubns.

***Ball, Larry D.** Ambush at Bloody Run: The Wham Paymaster Robbery of 1889: A Story of Politics, Religion, Race & Banditry in Arizona Territory. LC 00-26670. 2000. pap. write for info. (*0-910037-41-8*) AZ Hist Soc.

— Ambush at Bloody Run: The Wham Paymaster Robbery of 1889: A Story of Politics, Religion, Race & Banditry in Arizona Territory. (Illus.). 280p. 2000. 34.95 (*0-910037-40-X*) AZ Hist Soc.

Ball, Larry D. Desert Lawmen: The High Sheriffs of New Mexico & Arizona, 1846-1912. (Illus.). 414p. (C). 1996. reprint ed. pap. 19.95 (*0-8263-1700-6*) U of NM Pr.

Ball, Larry D. & Clements, William M. Voices from State: An Oral History of Arkansas State University. Hawkins, Ruth, ed. 208p. 1985. 19.95 (*0-930677-00-5*) Ark St Univ.

Ball, Larry L. Multimedia Network Integration & Management. (McGraw-Hill Computer Communications Series). (Illus.). 416p. 1996. 50.00 (*0-07-005227-1*) McGraw.

Ball, Linda. Look, Look! I Wrote A Book! Reproducible Little Books for Emergent Readers. (Illus.). 176p. (J). 1997. pap. text 12.95 (*0-673-36357-0*, GoodYrBooks) Addson-Wesley Educ.

***Ball, Liz.** Hidden Treasures: Hidden Picture Puzzles. (Illus.). 56p. 1999. 4.50 (*0-9678159-0-8*) Hidden Pic.

— My New York Garden: A Gardener's Journal. (Illus.). 128p. 2000. spiral bd. 19.95 (*1-930604-10-6*) Cool Springs Pr.

— My Pennsylvania Garden: A Gardener's Journal. (Illus.). 128p. 2000. spiral bd. 19.95 (*1-930604-06-8*) Cool Springs Pr.

Ball, Liz. The Philadelphia Garden Book: A Gardener's Guide for the Delaware Valley. LC 99-18614. (Illus.). 440p. 1999. pap. 24.95 (*1-888608-46-3*) Cool Springs Pr.

— Smith & Hawken Composting. LC 97-32748. (Illus.). 160p. 1998. pap. 10.95 (*0-7611-0732-0*) Workman Pub.

Ball, Liz, jt. auth. see Ball, Jeff.

Ball, Louise B. The International Medical Graduate's Guide to U. S. Medicine: Negotiating the Maze. LC 95-13724. 220p. (Orig.). 1995. pap. 28.95 (*1-883620-16-3*) Galen AZ.

Ball, Lucille. I Love Lucy. 1997. mass mkt. 6.99 (*1-57297-323-4*) Blvd Books.

— Love, Lucy. large type ed. LC 96-48275. 1999. pap. 24.95 (*0-7862-0966-6*) Thorndike Pr.

Ball, Lucille & Hoffman, Betty H. Love, Lucy. large type ed. LC 96-48275. (Americana Series). 368p. 1997. lib. bdg. 26.95 (*0-7862-0965-8*) Thorndike Pr.

Ball, Lyle V., ed. The Art of Lyle V. Ball. deluxe ed. (Illus.). 80p. 1984. 250.00 (*0-930083-01-6*) J Bacon Co.

Ball, M. A. Mathematics in the Social & Life Sciences: Theories, Models & Methods. (Mathematics & Its Applications Ser.). 1985. text 69.95 (*0-470-20191-6*) P-H.

Ball, M. G. European Rail Atlas: Scandinavia & Eastern Europe. (European Rail Atlas Ser.). (Illus.). 128p. (Orig.). 1994. pap. 15.95 (*0-7110-3172-X*) Hunter NJ.

Ball, M. H., et al, eds. Aspects of the Computer-Based Patient Record. (Computers in Health Care Ser.). (Illus.). xx, 316p. 1996. 49.50 (*0-387-97723-6*) Spr-Verlag.

Ball, M. H., ed. see Weed, L. L.

Ball, M. J., et al, eds. Healthcare Information Management Systems: A Practical Guide. 2nd ed. LC 95-6682. (Computers in Health Care Ser.). (Illus.). 358p. 1995. text 48.00 (*0-387-94477-X*) Spr-Verlag.

— Nursing Informatics. (Computers in Health Care Ser.). (Illus.). 450p. 1993. 44.00 (*0-387-96639-0*) Spr-Verlag.

***Ball, M. J., et al, eds.** Nursing Informatics: Where Caring & Technology Meet. 3rd ed. (Illus.). 456p. 2000. 59.00 (*0-387-98923-4*) Spr-Verlag.

Ball, M. L., jt. auth. see Kelly, D. S.

Ball, M. L., jt. auth. see St. Leger Kelly, D.

Ball, M. Margaret. NATO & the European Union Movement. LC 74-9319. (Library of World Affairs, London, Institute of World Affairs Ser.: No. 45). (Illus.). 486p. 1974. reprint ed. lib. bdg. 79.50 (*0-8371-7642-5*, BANA, Greenwood Pr) Greenwood.

— Open Commonwealth. LC 78-171937. 300p. reprint ed. 93.00 (*0-8357-9113-0*, 201788200010) Bks Demand.

Ball, M. O., et al, eds. Network Routing. LC 95-41879. (Handbooks in Operations Research & Management Science Ser.: Vol. 8). 796p. 1995. 165.00 (*0-444-82141-4*) Elsevier.

Ball, Madaleine & Mann, Jim. Lipids & Heart Diseases: A Guide for the Primary Care Team. 2nd ed. (Illus.). 184p. 1995. pap. text 39.50 (*0-19-262495-4*) OUP.

Ball, Margaret. Changeweaver. (Fantasy Ser.). 304p. (Orig.). 1993. pap. 4.99 (*0-671-72173-9*) Baen Bks.

— Lost in Translation. 1995. per. 5.99 (*0-671-87688-0*) Baen Bks.

— Mathemagics. 352p. 1996. mass mkt. 5.99 (*0-671-87755-0*) Baen Bks.

— No Earthly Sunne. 1994. per. 5.99 (*0-671-87633-3*) S&S Trade.

— The Shadow Gate. (Fantasy Ser.). 1991. mass mkt. 5.99 (*0-671-72032-5*) Baen Bks.

Ball, Margaret, jt. auth. see McCaffrey, Anne.

Ball, Marion J., ed. How to Select a Computerized Hospital Information System. (Data Processing in Medicine Ser.: Vol. 2). (Illus.). 1972. 51.50 (*3-8055-1465-4*) S Karger.

Ball, Marion J. & Hannah, Kathryn J. Using Computers in Nursing. (Illus.). 303p. (C). 1984. pap. text 25.95 (*0-8359-8129-0*) Appleton & Lange.

Ball, Marion J., et al. Strategies & Technologies for Health Care Information: Theory into Practice. LC 98-30324. (Health Informatics Ser.). 1999. 49.95 (*0-387-98442-9*) Spr-Verlag.

Ball, Marion J., ed. see Douglas, Judith V.

Ball, Marshall Stewart. Kiss of God: The Wisdom of a Silent Child. LC 99-41265. 1999. pap. 9.95 (*1-55874-743-5*) Health Comm.

Ball, Martim, jt. auth. see Clutton-Brock, Tim.

***Ball, Martin.** Vowel Disorders. (Illus.). 280p. 2000. 50.00 (*0-7506-7249-8*) Buttrwrth-Heinemann.

Ball, Martin J. The New Phonologies: Developments in Clinical Linguistics. Kent, Raymond D., ed. LC 96-53434. 282p. 1997. pap. 49.95 (*1-56593-082-7*, 0387) Thomson Learn.

Ball, Martin J., ed. Phonetics for Speech Pathology. 300p. 1989. 45.00 (*0-85066-667-8*) Taylor & Francis.

— The Use of Welsh. 1988. 99.00 (*0-905028-99-6*, Pub. by Multilingual Matters); pap. 39.95 (*0-905028-98-8*, Pub. by Multilingual Matters) Taylor & Francis.

Ball, Martin J., et al, eds. Celtic Linguistics Ieithyddiaeth Geltaidd: Readings in the Brythonic Languages. Festschrift for T. Arwyn Watkins. LC 90-31745. (Current Issues in Linguistic Theory Ser.: Vol. 68). xxiv, 470p. 1990. 118.00 (*90-272-3565-1*) J Benjamins Pubng Co.

Ball, Martin J. & Code, Chris, eds. Instrumental Clinical Phonetics. 304p. 1997. 59.95 (*1-56593-317-6*, 1250) Thomson Learn.

Ball, Martin J. & Duckworth, Martin, eds. Advances in Clinical Phonetics. LC 96-28906. (Studies in Speech Pathology & Clinical Linguistics: No. 6). xiv, 258p. 1996. lib. bdg. 69.00 (*1-55619-393-9*) J Benjamins Pubng Co.

Ball, Martin J. & Jones, Glyn E., eds. The Celtic Languages. LC 92-38316. (Language Family Descriptions Ser.). (Illus.). 672p. (C). (gr. 13). 1993. 160.00 (*0-415-01035-7*, A7189) Routledge.

Ball, Martin J. & Muller, Nicole. Mutation in Welsh. LC 91-30393. 288p. (C). (gr. 13). 1992. text 89.95 (*0-415-03165-6*, A6067) Routledge.

Ball, Martin J. & Rahilly, Joan. Phonetics: The Science of Speech. 1999. 65.00 (*0-340-70009-2*, Pub. by E A); pap. 19.95 (*0-340-70010-6*, Pub. by E A) OUP.

Ball, Martin J., et al. The Phonetic Transcription of Disordered Speech. (Illus.). 224p. (Orig.). 1996. pap. text 45.00 (*1-56593-206-4*, 0529) Thomson Learn.

Ball, Martin J., jt. ed. see Dent, Raymond D.

Ball, Mary, jt. auth. see Ball, Colin.

Ball, Mary M. & Whittington, Frank. Surviving Dependence: Voices of African American Elders. (Society & Aging Ser.). 287p. 1995. 46.95 (*0-89503-125-6*) Baywood Pub.

Ball, Max W., et al. This Fascinating Oil Business. LC 64-15660. (Illus.). 1979. reprint ed. pap. 11.95 (*0-672-52584-4*) Macmillan.

Ball, Michael. Decorative Glasswork. (New Crafts Ser.). (Illus.). 96p. 1997. 14.95 (*1-85967-375-9*, Lorenz Bks) Anness Pub.

— Housing Policy & Economic Power: The Political Economy of Owner Occupation. LC 83-13070. 448p. (C). 1983. pap. 24.99 (*0-416-35280-4*, NO. 3967) Routledge.

— Understanding Basic Horse Care: Your Guide to Horse Health Care & Management. Duke, Jacqueline, ed. (Horse Health Care Library). (Illus.). 108p. 1998. pap. text 14.95 (*1-58150-004-1*) Blood-Horse.

***Ball, Michael.** Wire Magic. (Illus.). 80p. 2000. pap. 16.99 (*1-58180-089-4*, North Lght Bks) F & W Pubns Inc.

Ball, Michael & Lizieri, Colin. Economics of Commercial Property Markets. LC 99-172637. 400p. (C). 1998. 110.00 (*0-415-14992-4*); pap. 37.99 (*0-415-14993-2*) Routledge.

An Asterisk (*) at the beginning of an entry indicates that the title is appearing for the first time.

Ball, Michael, et al. Housing & Social Change in Europe & the U. S. A. 256p. 1988. lib. bdg. 53.00 (*0-415-00510-8*) Routledge.
— Housing & Social Change in Europe & the U. S. A. 240p. (C). 1990. pap. text 18.95 (*0-415-04994-6*, AA4488) Routledge.
Ball, Michael A. Understanding Equine First Aid - Emergency Care: Your Guide to Horse Health Care & Management. (Horse Health Care Library). (Illus.). 108p. 1998. pap. 14.95 (*0-939049-95-3*) Blood-Horse.
— Understanding the Equine Eye. 1999. pap. text 14.95 (*1-58150-032-7*, Pub. by Blood-Horse) IPG Chicago.
Ball, Michael R. Professional Wrestling As Ritual Drama in American Popular Culture. LC 90-44431. (Studies in Sociology: Vol. 8). 200p. 1990. lib. bdg. 79.95 (*0-88946-112-0*) E Mellen.
Ball, Michael S. & Smith, Gregory W. Analyzing Visual Data. (Qualitative Research Methods Ser.: Vol. 24). 96p. (C). 1992. text 24.00 (*0-8039-3434-3*); pap. text 10.50 (*0-8039-3435-1*) Sage.
***Ball, Michelle & Morris, Barbara.** Wake up, Brain Grade 5. 2000. write for info. (*1-57022-228-2*) ECS Lrn Systs.
— Wake up, Brain Grade 4. 2000. write for info. (*1-57022-227-4*) ECS Lrn Systs.
— Wake up, Brain Grade 1. 2000. write for info. (*1-57022-224-X*) ECS Lrn Systs.
— Wake up, Brain Grade 6. 2000. write for info. (*1-57022-229-0*) ECS Lrn Systs.
— Wake up, Brain Grade 3. 2000. write for info. (*1-57022-226-6*) ECS Lrn Systs.
— Wake up, Brain Grade 2. 2000. write for info. (*1-57022-225-8*) ECS Lrn Systs.
***Ball, Milner S.** Called by Stories: Biblical Sagas & Their Challenge for Law. LC 99-56925. 264p. 2000. 49.95 (*0-8223-2501-2*); pap. 17.95 (*0-8223-2524-1*) Duke.
Ball, Milner S. Lying Down Together: Law, Metaphor & Theology. LC 85-40361. (Rhetoric of the Human Sciences Ser.). 224p. 1985. text 24.00 (*0-299-10450-8*) U of Wis Pr.
— The Word & the Law. LC 92-28701. 224p. (C). 1993. 29.95 (*0-226-03625-1*) U Ch Pr.
— The Word & the Law. viii, 224p. 1995. pap. text 14.95 (*0-226-03627-8*) U Ch Pr.
Ball, Mog, jt. auth. see Ball, Colin.
Ball, Moya A. Vietnam-on-the Potomac. LC 91-31690. (Political Communication Ser.). 232p. 1992. 59.95 (*0-275-93881-6*, Praeger Pubs) Greenwood.
Ball, Myron D. I Am the Secret: The Richter Manuscript. LC 94-96048. (Illus.). 346p. (Orig.). 1994. pap. 15.95 (*0-9640476-0-8*) Hudson Yard.
Ball, Nancy. Shy Ann. LC 88-51305. (Illus.). 55p. (Orig.). (J). (gr. k-4). 1989. pap. 3.95 (*0-931563-03-8*) Wishing Rm.
Ball, Nelson. Bird Tracks on Hard Snow. LC 95-102823. 61p. 1994. pap. 12.00 (*1-55022-222-8*, Pub. by ECW) Genl Dist Srvs.
— With Issa: Poems, 1964-71. 120p. (C). 1991. pap. 12.00 (*1-55022-146-9*, Pub. by ECW) Genl Dist Srvs.
Ball, Nelson, ed. Frank Harrington's Kristmiss Book. (Illus.). 64p. 19.95 (*1-55128-006-X*, Pub. by Mercury Bk) LPC InBook.
Ball, Nicole. The Military in the Development Process: A Guide to Issues. LC 81-21009. (Guides to Contemporary Issues Ser.: No. 2). 124p. (C). 1981. 17.95 (*0-941690-02-4*); pap. 10.95 (*0-941690-03-2*) Regina Bks.
— Pressing for Peace: Can Aid Induce Reform? LC 92-31498. (Policy Essay Ser.: No. 6). 96p. (C). 1992. pap. 13.95 (*1-56517-006-7*) Overseas Dev Council.
— Security & Economy in the Third World. LC 88-9875. (Illus.). 459p. (Orig.). 1988. reprint ed. pap. 142.30 (*0-608-02584-4*, 206323000004) Bks Demand.
Ball, Nicole & Halevy, Tammy. Making Peace Work: The Role of the International Development Community. LC 96-33786. (Overseas Development Council Ser.: Vol. 18). 132p. (Orig.). 1996. pap. text 13.95 (*1-56517-022-9*) Overseas Dev Council.
Ball, Nicole, tr. see Clement, Catherine.
Ball, Nicole, tr. see Conde, Maryse.
Ball, Nigel & Hugh, Nick. The Sleep Solution: A 21-Night Program for Restful Sleep. LC 98-85071. (Illus.). 252p. 1998. reprint ed. pap. 14.95 (*1-56975-154-4*) Ulysses Pr.
Ball, Norman & Vardalas, John. Ferranti-Packard: Pioneers in Canadian Electrical Manufacturing. (Illus.). 352p. 1994. 75.00 (*0-7735-0983-6*, Pub. by McG-Queens Univ Pr) CUP Services.
Ball, Norman R., ed. Building Canada: A History of Public Works. (Illus.). 352p. 1988. pap. text 24.95 (*0-8020-6898-7*) U of Toronto Pr.
Ball, Pam, et al. Fiction South - Fiction North. Milazzo, Richard, ed. LC 91-90447. (Illus.). 184p. (Orig.). 1992. pap. 8.95 (*0-9631022-0-6*) Ridgefld Pr.
***Ball, Pamela.** Complete Dream Dictionary. 2000. 9.99 (*0-7858-1214-8*) Bk Sales Inc.
Ball, Pamela. Lava. LC 97-44194. 192p. 1998. pap. 12.00 (*0-8050-5776-5*, Owl) H Holt & Co.
— Lava: A Novel. LC 96-31660. 192p. 1997. 21.00 (*0-393-04024-0*) Norton.
Ball, Patricia. Animals. (Hands-On Minds-On Science Ser.). (Illus.). 96p. 1994. pap., teacher ed. 11.95 (*1-55734-630-5*) Tchr Create Mat.
— Plants. (Hands-On Minds-On Science Ser.). (Illus.). 96p. 1994. pap., teacher ed. 11.95 (*1-55734-629-1*) Tchr Create Mat.
Ball, Patricia A. Straight Talk Is More Than Words: Persuasive Communications: The Key to Achieving Your Goals. Politella, Sue, ed. (Illus.). (Orig.). 1996. pap. 20.00 (*1-887373-00-4*) T Knox Pub.
***Ball, Patrick, et al.** State Violence in Guatemala, 1960-1996: A Quantitative Reflection. LC 99-168991. 154p. 1999. write for info. (*0-87168-630-9*) AAAS.
Ball, Paul, jt. auth. see Nicholls, Paul.
Ball, Peter. Anglican Spiritual Direction. LC 98-26793. 1998. 12.95 (*1-56101-159-2*) Cowley Pubns.
— Endoscopic Surgery. LC 96-44663. (Perioperative Nursing Ser.). (Illus.). 224p. (C). (gr. 13). 1997. text 54.95 (*0-8151-0600-9*, 27473) Mosby Inc.
Ball, Phil. Ghosts & Shadows: A Marine in Vietnam, 1968-1969. LC 98-6074. (Illus.). 224p. 1998. pap. 26.50 (*0-7864-0505-8*) McFarland & Co.
Ball, Philip. Designing the Molecular World: Chemistry at the Frontier. LC 93-38151. 376p. 1994. text 47.50 (*0-691-00058-1*, Pub. by Princeton U Pr); pap. text 17.95 (*0-691-02900-8*, Pub. by Princeton U Pr) Cal Prin Full Svc.
***Ball, Philip.** Life's Matrix: A Biography of Water. LC 99-59110. (Illus.). 400p. 2000. text 25.00 (*0-374-18628-6*) FS&G.
Ball, Philip. Made to Measure: New Materials for the 21st Century. LC 97-4027. 445p. 1997. 29.95 (*0-691-02733-1*, Pub. by Princeton U Pr) Cal Prin Full Svc.
***Ball, Philip.** Made to Measure: New Materials for the 21st Century. 1999. pap. 17.95 (*0-691-00975-9*, Pub. by Princeton U Pr) Cal Prin Full Svc.
Ball, Philip. The Self-Made Tapestry: Pattern Formation in Nature. LC 98-16650. (Illus.). 312p. 1999. 37.50 (*0-19-850244-3*) OUP.
Ball, R. H. Ball: Conquering the Frontiers, a Biography & History of One Branch of the Ball Family. (Illus.). 102p. 1994. reprint ed. pap. 18.50 (*0-8328-4192-7*); reprint ed. lib. bdg. 28.50 (*0-8328-4191-9*) Higginson Bk Co.
Ball, Randy. Backroads: A Portfolio of Mountain Images. 2nd ed. 48p. 1992. pap. 6.50 (*0-9631936-0-0*) R Ball Photo.
— Time Passages. (Illus.). 60p. (Orig.). 1992. pap. 5.00 (*0-9631936-1-9*) R Ball Photo.
Ball, Randy N. Abandoned: Forgotten Places of East Tennessee. (Illus.). 32p. (Orig.). 1995. pap. 10.00 (*0-9631936-2-7*) R Ball Photo.
Ball, Raphael, jt. auth. see Wild, Aloysius.
***Ball, Raymond F.** Flying to Marcy: Early Aviation History of Oneida County, N. Y. LC 00-90410. (Illus.). 307p. 2000. pap. 24.95 (*0-9668178-2-6*) Oneida Cty Hist.
Ball, Raymond J. & Kothari, S. P., eds. Financial Statement Analysis. LC 93-40433. (Series in Advanced Topics in Finance & Accounting). 800p. (C). 1994. 48.13 (*0-07-004645-X*) McGraw.
Ball, Richard. Mask of Aeschylus. LC 81-66410. 88p. (Orig.). 1981. pap. 3.00 (*0-940066-00-9*) Dalmas & Ricour.
— One Hundred Sonnets for St. Augustine. 100p. 1986. pap. 8.00 (*0-940066-04-1*) Dalmas & Ricour.
Ball, Richard A., et al. House Arrest & Correctional Policy: Doing Time at Home. LC 87-28349. (Studies in Crime, Law & Justice: No. 3). 180p. 1988. reprint ed. pap. 55.80 (*0-608-01530-X*, 205957400002) Bks Demand.
Ball, Richard T. Legal Issues in Athletic Training. 300p. 2000. pap. 19.95 (*0-8036-0339-8*) Davis Co.
Ball, Rick. Making Space: Design for Compact Living. LC 88-22431. (Illus.). 136p. 1990. pap. 15.95 (*0-87951-365-9*, Pub. by Overlook Pr) Penguin Putnam.
Ball, Rick & NBC News Staff. Meet the Press: 50 Years of History in the Making. LC 97-73866. (Illus.). 240p. 1997. 39.95 (*0-07-046614-9*) McGraw.
Ball, Rick & Pratt, Andy, eds. Industrial Property: Policy & Economic Development. LC 94-171881. 256p. (C). 1993. pap. 81.95 (*0-415-09152-7*) Thomson Learn.
Ball, Robdy. The French-Speaking World: A Practical Introduction to Sociolinguistic Issues. LC 96-43951. (Routledge Language in Society Ser.). (Illus.). 248p. (C). 1997. 65.00 (*0-415-12986-9*) Routledge.
Ball, Robert. Performance Review in Local Government. LC 98-71408. 214p. 1998. text 63.95 (*1-84014-123-9*, Pub. by Ashgate Pub) Ashgate Pub Co.
— Texaco Collectibles with Price Guide. LC 94-65616. (Illus.). 128p. (Orig.). 1994. pap. 24.95 (*0-88740-656-4*) Schiffer.
— Walking on Water. LC 92-64376. 230p. 1992. pap. 12.95 (*0-8314-0079-X*) Sci & Behavior.
Ball, Robert & Peters, Paul. Military Medals, Decorations & Orders of the United States & Europe: A Photographic Study to the Beginning of WW II. (Illus.). 184p. 1994. 45.00 (*0-88740-579-7*) Schiffer.
Ball, Robert E. The Fundamentals of Aircraft Combat Survivability: Analysis & Design. LC 85-15722. (Educ Ser.). (Illus.). 398p. 1985. 57.95 (*0-930403-02-9*, 02-9) AIAA.
Ball, Robert Edward. Barbara Broughel: Storytelling Chairs. (Illus.). 4p. (Orig.). 1991. pap. 2.50 (*0-938437-37-2*) MIT List Visual Arts.
— Slaves in the Family. LC F279.C453A2 . 512p. 1999. pap. 15.95 (*0-345-43105-7*) Ballantine Pub Grp.
— Slaves in the Family. LC 97-34640. (Illus.). 504p. 1998. 30.00 (*0-374-26582-8*) FS&G.
Ball, Robert Edward & Ball, Whitlock. The Harleston Family. 1924. write for info. (*0-688-16840-X*, Wm Morrow) Morrow Avon.
***Ball, Robert Edward & Ballard, Edward G.** Slaves in the Family. large type ed. LC 99-14745. 774p. 1999. 29.95 (*0-7838-8628-4*, G K Hall & Co) Mac Lib Ref.
Ball, Robert H., jt. auth. see Bowman, Walter P.
Ball, Robert J. Reading Classical Latin: The Second Year. 510p. 1990. pap. 45.00 (*0-87291-203-5*) Coronado Pr.
Ball, Robert J., ed. The Classical Papers of Gilbert Highet. LC 83-7181. 416p. 1983. text 72.50 (*0-231-05104-2*) Col U Pr.
Ball, Robert J., ed. see Highet, Gilbert.
Ball, Robert M. Straight Talk about Social Security. LC 98-22807. 79p. 1998. pap. 9.95 (*0-87078-422-6*) Century Foundation.
Ball, Robert M. & Bethell, Thomas N. Because We're All in This Together: The Case for a National Long Term Care Insurance Policy. (Illus.). 119p. 1989. pap. 10.00 (*0-685-35416-4*) Fam USA Found.
Ball, Robert S. Great Astronomers. LC 74-994. (Essay Index Reprint Ser.). (Illus.). 1977. reprint ed. 24.95 (*0-518-10142-8*) Ayer.
— A Treatise on the Theory of Screws. LC 98-229030. (Mathematical Library). (Illus.). 576p. (C). 1998. pap. text 34.95 (*0-521-63650-7*) Cambridge U Pr.
Ball, Robert W. American Shelf & Wall Clocks: A Pictorial History for Collectors. LC 92-60630. (Illus.). 288p. 1992. text 69.95 (*0-88740-427-8*) Schiffer.
— Nautical Antiques. LC 94-65429. (Illus.). 240p. 1994. 39.95 (*0-88740-602-5*) Schiffer.
Ball, Robert W. & Vebell, Edward. Cowboy Collectibles & Western Memorabilia. rev. ed. LC 91-65654. (Illus.). 160p. 1993. pap. 29.95 (*0-88740-505-3*) Schiffer.
Ball, Robert W. D. American Shelf & Wall Clocks: A Pictorial History for Collectors. 2nd rev. ed. (Illus.). 288p. 1999. 69.95 (*0-7643-0905-6*) Schiffer.
— Collector's Guide to British Army Campaign Medals. LC 96-86493. (Illus.). 160p. 1996. 29.95 (*0-930625-64-1*) Krause Pubns.
***Ball, Robert W. D.** Mauser Military Rifles of the World. 2nd rev. ed. LC 95-82422. (Illus.). 304p. 2000. 44.95 (*0-87341-828-X*) Krause Pubns.
Ball, Robert W. D. Remington Firearms: The Golden Age of Collecting. LC 95-79727. (Illus.). 194p. 1995. 29.95 (*0-87341-360-1*, GAR01) Krause Pubns.
— Springfield Armory Shoulder Weapons, 1795-1968. (Illus.). 264p. 1997. 34.95 (*0-930625-74-9*, Antique Trader) Krause Pubns.
Ball, Rodney. The French-Speaking World: A Practical Introduction to Sociolinguistic Issues. LC 96-43951. (Routledge Language in Society Ser.). (Illus.). 248p. (C). 1997. pap. 20.99 (*0-415-12987-7*) Routledge.
Ball-Rokeach, Sandra J., et al. The Great American Values Test: Influencing Behavior & Belief Through Television. LC 83-48468. 208p. (C). 1984. 29.95 (*0-02-926850-8*) Free Pr.
Ball-Rokeach, Sandra J. & Cantor, Muriel G., eds. Media, Audience & Social Structure. LC 85-27871. 448p. (Orig.). (C). 1986. text 49.95 (*0-8039-2581-6*); pap. text 24.00 (*0-8039-2582-4*) Sage.
— Media, Audience & Social Structure. LC 85-27871. 400p. (Orig.). 1986. reprint ed. pap. 124.00 (*0-608-04298-6*, 206507700012) Bks Demand.
Ball-Rokeach, Sandra J., jt. auth. see DeFleur, Melvin L.
Ball, Ron, jt. auth. see Yager, Dexter R., Sr.
Ball, Ronnie. Hymns & Prayers for Children. (Illus.). 64p. 1984. pap. 10.95 (*0-8256-0304-8*, AM38639) Music Sales.
Ball, Roscoe L. Harkness. Some Descendants of John & Margaret Harkness of Newton, Massachusetts. (Illus.). 55p. 1997. reprint ed. pap. 11.00 (*0-8328-8976-8*); reprint ed. lib. bdg. 21.00 (*0-8328-8975-X*) Higginson Bk Co.
Ball, S., ed. Jurisprudence. 192p. (C). 1990. pap. 70.00 (*1-85352-780-7*, Pub. by HLT Pubns) St Mut.
Ball, S. C. Jungle Fowls from Pacific Islands. (BMB Ser.). 1969. reprint ed. 25.00 (*0-527-02214-4*) Periodicals Srv.
Ball, S. C., jt. auth. see Fowler, H. W.
Ball, S. H. Mines of the Silver Peak Range, Kawich Range & Other Southwestern Nevada Districts. 218p. 1983. pap. 14.95 (*0-913814-61-X*) Nevada Pubns.
Ball, S. J. The Cold War: An International History, 1947-1991. LC 97-15378. (Contemporary History Ser. ; An Arnold Publication). 272p. 1997. text 49.95 (*0-340-64546-6*, Pub. by E A) OUP.
— The Cold War: An International History, 1947-1991. 2nd ed. LC 97-15378. (Contemporary History Ser. ; An Arnold Publication). 272p. 1997. pap. text 19.95 (*0-340-59168-4*, Pub. by E A) OUP.
Ball, Samuel, jt. auth. see Anderson, Scarvia B.
Ball, Sara. The Animal Show Mix & Match Book. (Illus.). (J). (ps-1). 1992. 3.00 (*1-56021-141-5*) W J Fantasy.
— Estan Solos en Casa Dos Ositos (Two Bears Are Home Alone) Segovia, Francisco, tr. (SPA., Illus.). 8p. (J). (gr. 1-3). 1994. 12.99 (*968-16-4557-X*, Pub. by Fondo) Continental Bk.
Ball, Sara & Walbrecker, Dirk. Has Visto? Por Ahi Anda una Zorra (Have You Seen a Fox Around Here?) Segovia, Francisco, tr. (SPA., Illus.). 8p. (J). 1994. 10.99 (*968-16-4558-8*, Pub. by Fondo) Continental Bk.
Ball, Simon & Bell, Stuart. Environmental Law. 2nd ed. 469p. 1994. pap. 48.00 (*1-85431-287-1*, Pub. by Blackstone Pr) Gaunt.
— Environmental Law. 3rd ed. 546p. 1995. pap. 44.00 (*1-85431-443-2*, Pub. by Blackstone Pr) Gaunt.
Ball, Stanley C. The Distribution & Behavior of the Spadefoot Toad in Connecticut. (Connecticut Academy of Arts & Sciences Ser., Trans.: Vol. 32). 1936. pap. 39.50 (*0-685-44367-1*) Elliots Bks.
Ball State University. Ball Point. 17th ed. 264p. 1999. pap. text 8.00 (*0-536-01725-5*) P-H.
***Ball, Stefan.** Bach Flower Gardener. (Illus.). 2000. pap. 9.95 (*0-85207-329-1*) C W Daniel.
Ball, Stefan. Bach Flower Remedies for Men. 208p. 1997. pap. 13.95 (*0-85207-302-X*, Pub. by C W Daniel) Natl Bk Netwk.
***Ball, Stefan.** Principles of Bach Flower Remedies: The Only Introduction You'll Ever Need. 2000. pap. 11.00 (*0-7225-3919-3*) Thorsons PA.
Ball, Stefan & Howard, Judy. Bach Flower Remedies for Animals. 1999. 24.95 (*0-85207-296-1*) C W Daniel.
***Ball, Stefan & Howard, Judy.** Emotional Healing for Cats. 2000. pap. 12.95 (*0-85207-336-4*, Pub. by C W Daniel) Natl Bk Netwk.
Ball, Stephen. Web TCL Complete. LC 99-18117. (The Complete Reference Ser.). 500p. 1998. pap. text 49.95 incl. cd-rom (*0-07-913713-X*) McGraw.
***Ball, Stephen, ed.** A Policeman's Ireland: Recollections of Samuel Waters, R. I. C. LC 99-197984. 96p. 1999. pap. 12.95 (*1-85918-189-9*, Pub. by Cork Univ) Intl Spec Bk.
Ball, Stephen G., ed. Myocardial Infarction: From Trials to Practice. 224p. 1995. 75.00 (*1-871816-26-2*, Pub. by Wrightson Biomed) Taylor & Francis.
Ball, Stephen J. Education Reform: A Critical & Post Structural Approach. LC 94-12242. 176p. 1994. 94.00 (*0-335-19273-4*); pap. 33.95 (*0-335-19272-6*) OpUniv Pr.
— The Micro-Politics of the School Towards a Theory of School Organization. 256p. 1988. pap. 15.95 (*0-416-00112-2*) Routledge.
***Ball, Stephen J.** Sociology of Education: Major Themes. LC 99-89253. 2000. pap. write for info. (*0-415-19812-7*) Routledge.
Ball, Stephen J. & Goodson, Ivor F., eds. Teachers' Lives & Careers. LC 85-4562. (Issues in Education & Training Ser.: Vol. 3). 247p. 1985. pap. 34.95 (*1-85000-029-8*, Falmer Pr) Taylor & Francis.
Ball, Stephen J., jt. auth. see Galloway, D.
Ball, Steve & Dunham, Scott. Playing with Fire: A Search for the Hidden Heart of Rock & Roll. LC 97-5420. 304p. (Orig.). 1997. pap. 16.95 (*0-934252-72-6*, Pub. by Hohm Pr) SCB Distributors.
Ball, Steven, ed. The HIV-Negative Gay Man: Developing Strategies for Survival & Emotional Well-Being. LC 98-12623. 115p. 1998. 29.95 (*0-7890-0522-0*) Haworth Pr.
— The HIV Negative Gay Man: Developing Strategies for Survival & Emotional Well-Being. LC 98-12623. 115p. 1998. pap. 12.95 (*1-56023-114-9*, Harrington Park) Haworth Pr.
Ball, Stuart. Baldwin & the Conservative Party: The Crisis of 1929-31. LC 87-22405. 320p. (C). 1988. 52.50 (*0-300-03961-1*) Yale U Pr.
— Conservative Party British Politics 1902-52. LC 94-31525. (Seminar Studies in History). (C). 1995. pap. text 14.00 (*0-582-08002-9*, Pub. by Addison-Wesley) Longman.
— Embedded Microprocessor Systems: Real World Design. LC 96-13188. 184p. 1996. text 34.95 (*0-7506-9791-1*) Buttrwrth-Heinemann.
Ball, Stuart & Seldon, Anthony, eds. The Heath Government, 1970-1974. LC 95-49157. 432p. (C). 1996. pap. text 22.25 (*0-582-25991-6*, Pub. by Addison-Wesley) Longman.
— Health Government 1970 74. 2nd ed. LC 94-36634. (Profiles in Power Ser.). 432p. (C). 1996. text 56.75 (*0-582-25992-4*, Pub. by Addison-Wesley) Longman.
Ball, Stuart, jt. auth. see Headlam, Cuthbert Morley.
Ball, Stuart F. & Franklin, Rudolph M., eds. Glaucoma - Diagnosis & Therapy: Transactions of the New Orleans Academy of Ophthalmology. 216p. 1993. pap. text 60.00 (*90-6299-105-X*, Pub. by Kugler) Kugler Pubns.
Ball, Stuart M., Jr. The Backpackers Guide to Hawai'i. LC 95-41359. 1996. pap. 15.95 (*0-8248-1785-0*, Kolowalu Bk) UH Pr.
— The Hikers Guide to O'ahu. LC 93-5507. (Illus.). 264p. 1993. pap. 17.95 (*0-8248-1513-0*, Kolowalu Bk) UH Pr.
***Ball, Stuart M., Jr.** The Hikers Guide to the Hawaiian Islands. LC 99-36621. 280p. 1999. pap. 19.95 (*0-8248-2223-4*, Latitude Twenty) UH Pr.
Ball, Stuart R. Debugging Embedded Microprocessor Systems. LC 97-44582. 256p. 1998. pap. text 29.95 (*0-7506-9990-6*) Buttrwrth-Heinemann.
***Ball, Stuart R.** Embedded Microprocessor Systems: Real World Design. 2nd ed. LC 99-86910. (Illus.). 516p. 2000. pap. 34.95 (*0-7506-7234-X*, Newnes) Buttrwrth-Heinemann.
Ball, Stuart W. Programs for the TI-81 & TI-82 Calculators. (Illus.). 1995. pap. text 14.95 (*0-914534-12-2*) Stokes.
Ball, Susie, ed. Strategies in Genetic Counseling: The Challenge of the Future. (National Society of Genetic Counselors Ser.: Vol. 1). 216p. 1988. 35.95 (*0-89885-388-5*, Kluwer Acad Hman Sci) Kluwer Academic.
Ball, T. H. Dinwiddie: Genealogical Records of the Dinwiddie Clan of Northwestern Indiana. 120p. 1997. reprint ed. pap. 21.00 (*0-8328-8316-6*); reprint ed. lib. bdg. 31.00 (*0-8328-8315-8*) Higginson Bk Co.
— Northwestern Indiana, from 1800 to 1900: A View of Our Region Through the Nineteenth Century. (Illus.). 570p. 1995. reprint ed. lib. bdg. 59.00 (*0-8328-5013-6*) Higginson Bk Co.
Ball, T. H., ed. Encyclopedia of Genealogy & Biography of Lake County Indiana. (Illus.). 674p. 1992. reprint ed. lib. bdg. 68.00 (*0-8328-2573-5*) Higginson Bk Co.
— Lake County, 1884: Account of the Semi-Centennial of Lake Co., with Historical Papers & Other Interesting Records. (Illus.). 488p. 1997. reprint ed. lib. bdg. 49.50 (*0-8328-6657-1*) Higginson Bk Co.
Ball, T. H. & Halbert, H. S. The Creek War of 1813 & 1814. Owsley, rank L., Jr., ed. LC 94-37440. (Library of Alabama Classics). (Illus.). 400p. 1995. pap. 29.95 (*0-8173-0775-3*) U of Ala Pr.
Ball, Terence. Reappraising Political Theory. 328p. 1995. pap. text 19.95 (*0-19-827995-7*) OUP.
— Rousseau's Ghost: A Novel. LC 97-47561. 224p. (C). 1998. text 31.50 (*0-7914-3933-X*) State U NY Pr.
— Rousseau's Ghost: A Novel. LC 97-47561. (C). 1999. pap. text 19.95 (*0-7914-3934-8*) State U NY Pr.
Ball, Terence, ed. Idioms of Inquiry: Critique & Renewal in Political Science. LC 86-23033. (SUNY Series in Political Theory: Contemporary Issues). 255p. (C). 1987. pap. text 21.95 (*0-88706-458-2*) State U NY Pr.
— Political Theory & Praxis: New Perspectives. LC 77-73320. 291p. reprint ed. pap. 90.30 (*0-8357-7664-6*, 205699100097) Bks Demand.

Ball, Terence & Pocock, J. G., eds. Conceptual Change & the Constitution. LC 88-203. x, 222p. 1988. pap. 14.95 (*0-7006-0456-1*) U Pr of KS.

Ball, Terence, ed. see Jefferson, Thomas.

Ball, Terence, ed. see Mill, James.

Ball, Terri. OOTI, a Child of the Nisenan. Smith, Jo & ARNHA Publication Committee, eds. (Illus.). 32p. (J). (gr. 3-4). 1996. pap. 4.95 (*1-887815-02-3*) Amer River Nat Hist.

Ball, Terrie, ed. see O'Diear, James.

Ball, Terry & Crooks, Alan. GNVQ Advanced Electrical & Electronic Engineering. (GNVQ Ser.). (Illus.). 544p. (Orig.). (C). 1998. pap. 52.50 (*0-7487-2870-8*, Pub. by S Thornes Pubs) Trans-Atl Phila.

Ball, Terry, jt. auth. see Ball, DeAnn.

Ball, Thomas. My Fourscore Years: Autobiography by Sculptor Thomas Ball. St. Leon, Shirley, ed. LC 93-1771. (Illus.). 200p. (C). 1993. 34.95 (*0-9620635-2-5*) TreCavalli Pr.

Ball, Thomas E., ed. Sunday Morning Atlanta, Preaching, Vol. I. (Illus.). 120p. (Orig.). 1995. pap. 9.95 (*0-9621362-2-0*) T E Balls Pubns.

Ball, Tom. Blues Harmonica: A Crash Course & Overview. (Illus.). 72p. (Orig.). 1993. pap. text 16.95 incl. audio (*0-931759-72-2*) Centerstream Pub.

— Sonny Terry Licks for Blues Harmonica. (Illus.). 48p. 1995. pap. text 19.95 incl. audio compact disk (*1-57424-018-8*) Centerstream Pub.

B

***Ball, Tricia.** Rain Forest: Hands-On Minds-On Science. Forbes, Evan D., ed. (Illus.). 96p. (J). 1999. pap., teacher ed. 11.95 (*1-57690-386-9*, TCM2386) Tchr Create Mat.

***Ball, Trisha.** Rain Forest: Primary. (Illus.). 96p. 1999. pap., teacher ed. 11.95 (*1-57690-385-0*, TCM 2385) Tchr Create Mat.

Ball, V. Travels in India: Jean-Baptiste Tavernier, 2 vols., Set. Crooke, William, ed. (C). 1995. 58.00 (*81-215-0682-4*, Pub. by M Manoharial) Coronet Bks.

— Tribal & Peasant Life in Nineteenth Century India. 1986. reprint ed. 60.00 (*0-8364-1583-3*, Pub. by Usha) S Asia.

Ball, Vic, ed. Ball RedBook. 16th rev. ed. LC 97-6832. (Illus.). 816p. (C). 1997. text 71.95 (*1-883052-15-7*, B032) Ball Pub.

Ball, Victoria K. Opportunities in Interior Design Careers. LC 94-47112. (Opportunities In . . . Ser.). (Illus.). 160p. pap. 11.95 (*0-8442-4441-4*, 44414, VGM Career) NTC Contemp Pub Co.

— Opportunities in Interior Design Careers. (Illus.). 144p. 1990. 13.95 (*0-8442-6481-4*, VGM Career) NTC Contemp Pub Co.

— Opportunities in Interior Design Careers. LC 94-47112. (Illus.). 160p. 1995. 14.95 (*0-8442-4440-6*, 44406, VGM Career) NTC Contemp Pub Co.

— Opportunities in Interior Design Careers. 2nd ed. (Illus.). 144p. 1993. pap. 10.95 (*0-8442-6482-2*, VGM Career) NTC Contemp Pub Co.

Ball, W. E., jt. auth. see Brysch, O. P.

Ball, W. P., jt. auth. see Foote, G. W.

Ball, W. P., jt. ed. see Foote, G. W.

Ball, W. Valentine. Law of Libel As Affecting Newspapers & Journalists. (Legal Reprint Ser.). xiii, 165p. 1986. reprint ed. 35.00 (*0-8377-1939-9*, Rothman); reprint ed. 25.00 (*0-421-37560-4*) W S Hein.

Ball, W. W. Fun with String Figures. LC 76-173664. (Illus.). 89p. (J). (gr. k-3). 1999. reprint ed. pap. 2.95 (*0-486-22809-6*) Dover.

— Short Account of the History of Mathematics. 4th ed. 522p. (C). 1960. pap. 11.95 (*0-486-20630-0*) Dover.

Ball, W. W. Rouse & Coxeter, H. S. M. Mathematical Recreations & Essays. 448p. 1987. reprint ed. pap. 8.95 (*0-486-25357-0*) Dover.

***Ball, Wanda H. & Brewer, Pamela B.** Socratic Seminars in the Block. LC 99-32739. 2000. 29.95 (*1-883001-79-X*) Eye On Educ.

Ball, Warwick. Rome in East: The Transformation of an Empire. LC 99-21402. 1999. text. write for info. (*0-415-11376-8*) Routledge.

— Syria: A Historical & Architectural Guide. LC 97-21909. 256p. 1998. pap. 19.95 (*1-56656-225-2*) Interlink Pub.

Ball, Whitlock, jt. auth. see Ball, Robert Edward.

Ball, William. Red Hat Linux 6 Unleashed. 1200p. 1999. 39.99 (*0-672-31689-7*) Macmillan.

— A Sense of Direction: Some Observations on the Art of Directing. LC 84-8104. 196p. (C). 1984. pap. 19.95 (*0-89676-082-0*, Drama Pubs) QSMG Ltd.

— Using Linux. LC 97-81344. 1998. pap. text 29.99 (*0-7897-1623-2*) Que.

Ball, William, jt. auth. see Ball, James.

Ball, William G. & Ball, Helen B. A Workout. 76p. (Orig.). 1992. pap. 7.95 (*1-880322-07-2*) Champions Christ.

Ball, William M. Nationalism & Communism in East Asia. LC 75-30044. (Institute of Pacific Relations Ser.). reprint ed. 39.50 (*0-404-59502-2*) AMS Pr.

Ball, William S. Pediatric Neurimaging. LC 97-7705. 816p. 1997. text 175.00 (*0-316-07987-1*) Lppncott W & W.

Ball, Zachary. Bristle Face. LC 62-2219. 206p. (J). (gr. 4-6). 1991. 14.95 (*0-8234-0915-5*) Holiday.

Balla. Hooray for English, Bk. 1. 96p. 1997. text 13.99 (*0-673-19577-5*) Addison-Wesley.

— Hooray for English, Bk. 2. 96p. 1997. text 13.99 (*0-673-19578-3*) Addison-Wesley.

— Hooray for English, Bk. 4. 1997. text 13.99 (*0-673-19580-5*) Addison-Wesley.

— Hooray for English, Bk. 5. 96p. 1997. text 13.99 (*0-673-19581-3*) Addison-Wesley.

— Hooray for English, Bk. 6. 1993. text 13.99 (*0-673-19582-1*) Addison-Wesley.

— WKBK HOORAY ENGLISH BK1. 64p. 1997. pap. text, wbk. ed. 7.72 (*0-673-19416-7*) Addison-Wesley.

— WKBK HOORAY ENGLISH BK2. 1997. pap. text, wbk. ed. 7.72 (*0-673-19417-5*) Addison-Wesley.

— WKBK HOORAY ENGLISH BK3. 2nd ed. 64p. 1997. pap. text, wbk. ed. 7.72 (*0-673-19418-3*) Addison-Wesley.

— WKBK HOORAY ENGLISH BK6. 6th ed. 1997. pap. text, wbk. ed. 7.72 (*0-673-19421-3*) Addison-Wesley.

— Workbook Hooray English Bk5. 5th ed. 64p. 1997. pap. text, wbk. ed. 7.72 (*0-673-19420-5*) Addison-Wesley.

Balla, ed. Hooray for English, Bk 6. 1997. pap. text 13.99 (*0-673-19409-4*) Addison-Wesley.

Balla, et al. Hooray English Book, Vol. 5. 1997. 28.95 (*0-673-19434-5*) Addison-Wesley.

— SONG CST HOORAY ENG BK 4, Vol. 4. 1997. 28.95 (*0-673-19431-0*) Addison-Wesley.

— SONG CST HOORAY ENG BK 6, Vol. 6. 1997. 28.95 (*0-673-19437-X*) Addison-Wesley.

— SONG CST HOORAY ENG BK2, Vol. 2. 1997. 28.95 (*0-673-19425-6*) Addison-Wesley.

— SONG CST HOORAY ENG BK3, Vol. 3. 1997. 28.95 (*0-673-19428-0*) Addison-Wesley.

Balla, D. & Zigler, Edward F. Mental Retardation: The Developmental-Difference Controversy. (Illus.). 352p. (C). 1982. text 69.95 (*0-89859-170-8*) L Erlbaum Assocs.

***Balla, Ellen M.** Ten Tales for Teaching English. (Illus.). 152p. 1999. pap., teacher ed. 14.95 (*0-673-59240-5*, GoodYrBooks) Addson-Wesley Educ.

Balla, George E. The Four Centuries Between the Testaments: A Survey of Israel & the Diaspora from 336BC to 94AD. LC 93-39347. 94p. 1993. pap. 7.95 (*0-941037-27-4*, BIBAL Press) D & F Scott.

Balla, M. I., jt. auth. see Podvesko, M. L.

Balla, M. J., jt. auth. see Podvesko, M. L.

Balla, Mark. Brazilian Phrasebook. 2nd ed. (Lonely Planet Phrasebooks). (Illus.). 96p. (Orig.). 1993. pap. 5.95 (*0-86442-176-1*) Lonely Planet.

***Balla, Peter.** Challenges to New Testament Theology: An Attempt to Justify the Enterprise. 280p. (C). 1998. reprint ed. pap. 19.95 (*1-56563-394-6*) Hendrickson MA.

Ballabh, Vishwa, jt. ed. see Saxena, N. C.

Ballabh, Vishwa, jt. ed. see Singh, Katar.

Ballabio, E., et al. Rehabilitation Technology: Strategies for the European Union; Proceedings of the First Tide Congress, Apr 6-7, 1993, Brussels. LC 93-78138. (Studies in Health Technology & Informatics: Vol. 9). 271p. (gr. 12). 1993. 105.00 (*90-5199-131-2*, Pub. by IOS Pr) IOS Press.

Ballabon, M., ed. Economics Selections, 2 vols. Incl. Vol. 2. 1963-1970. 402p. 1974. text 224.00 (*0-677-01070-2*); write for info. (*0-318-52700-6*) Gordon & Breach.

Ballabon, M. B., ed. Economic Perspectives: An Annual Survey of Economics, Vol. 1. xviii, 262p. 1979. text 174.00 (*3-7186-0001-3*) Gordon & Breach.

— Economic Perspectives: An Annual Survey of Economics, Vol. 2. xii, 272p. 1981. text 223.00 (*3-7186-0036-6*) Gordon & Breach.

Ballabon, Maurice, ed. Economic Perspectives. (Annual Survey of Economics Ser.: Vol. 3). xii, 200p. 1983. text 147.00 (*3-7186-0165-6*) Gordon & Breach.

Ballabriga, Angel, ed. Feeding from Toddlers to Adolescence. LC 96-10796. (Nestle Nutrition Workshop Ser.: Vol. 37). 336p. 1996. text 77.00 (*0-397-51792-0*) Lppncott W & W.

Ballabriga, Angel & Rey, Jean, eds. Weaning: Why, What, & When? (Nestle Nutrition Workshop Ser.: Vol. 10). 240p. 1987. 45.50 (*0-685-38974-X*, 1699) Lppncott W & W.

— Weaning: Why, What, & When? LC 86-230234. (Nestle Nutrition Workshop Ser.: Vol. 10). (Illus.). 239p. 1987. reprint ed. pap. 74.10 (*0-608-07220-6*, 206744500009) Bks Demand.

Ballachanda, Bopanna B. The Human Ear Canal: Theoretical Implications & Clinical Considerations Including Cerumen Management. (Illus.). 276p. (C). 1995. 85.00 (*1-56593-169-6*, 0478) Thomson Learn.

Ballad Society. Publications of the Ballad Society, 14 vols., Set, Nos. 1-38. (Ballad Society Ser.: Nos. 1-38). reprint ed. 1315.00 (*0-404-50820-0*) AMS Pr.

***Balladelli, Micky & de Clercq, Jan.** Mission Critical Active Directory: Architecting a Secure & Scalable Infrastructure. 512p. 2000. pap. 44.95 (*1-55558-240-0*, Digital DEC) Buttrwrth-Heinemann.

Ballagas, Emilio, ed. Mapa de la Poesia Negra Americana. (B. E. Ser.: No. 8). (SPA.). 1946. 35.00 (*0-8115-2959-2*) Periodicals Srv.

Ballagh, James C. A History of Slavery in Virginia. LC 78-64269. (Johns Hopkins University. Studies in the Social Sciences. Thirtieth Ser. 1912: 24). reprint ed. 39.50 (*0-404-61371-3*) AMS Pr.

— White Servitude in the Colony of Virginia: A Study of the System of Indentured Labor in the American Colonies. LC 78-63840. (Johns Hopkins University. Studies in the Social Sciences. Thirtieth Ser. 1912: 6-7). reprint ed. 39.50 (*0-404-61098-6*) AMS Pr.

Ballagh, James H., ed. Employee Relations Outlook: Impact of Foreign & Domestic Competition. (Current Issues Ser.: No. 1). 53p. 1993. reprint ed. 7.50 (*0-89215-130-7*) U Cal LA Indus Rel.

— Retiree Health Care Crisis. (Current Issues Ser.: No. 12). 100p. (Orig.). 1989. pap. 10.00 (*0-89215-159-5*) U Cal LA Indus Rel.

Ballahue. Fitness Wellness. 3rd ed. 1995. 36.74 (*0-697-23731-1*, WCB McGr Hill) McGrw-H Hghr Educ.

Ballaira, Guglielmo, ed. Hermogenes: Index Nominum et Locorum Hermogenianus. write for info. (*0-318-71979-7*) G Olms Pubs.

Ballam, Harry & Morton, Phyllis D., eds. The Christmas Book. LC 89-63104. (Illus.). 260p. 1990. reprint ed. lib. bdg. 42.00 (*1-55888-854-3*) Omnigraphics Inc.

Ballan, Dorothy. Feminism & Marxism. 68p. 1976. pap. 3.50 (*0-89567-006-2*) World View Forum.

— El Marxismo y la Liberacion de la Mujer. (Illus.). vii, 108p. 1986. pap. 4.95 (*0-89567-081-X*) World View Forum.

Ballan, Hussein & Declerc, Michel. High Voltage Devices & Circuits in Standard CMOS Technologies. LC 98-11622. 1998. write for info. (*0-7923-8234-X*) Kluwer Academic.

Ballance, Alton. Ocracokers. LC 89-4886. (Illus.). xvi, 255p. (C). 1989. 27.50 (*0-8078-1878-X*); pap. 13.95 (*0-8078-4265-6*) U of NC Pr.

Ballance, C. History of Peoria. (Illus.). 271p. 1997. reprint ed. lib. bdg. 35.00 (*0-8328-5779-3*) Higginson Bk Co.

Ballance, Craigg, jt. auth. see Keen, Peter G.W.

***Ballance, David K.** Birds in Counties: An Ornithological Bibliography of the Counties of England, Wales, Scotland & LC 99-41135. 1999. 98.00 (*1-86094-157-5*) World Scientific Pub.

Ballance, Nancy, ed. Active Parenting Family Guide: Tobacco, Alcohol & Other Drugs. (Illus.). 32p. (Orig.). 1993. pap. text 2.50 (*1-880283-05-0*) Active Parenting.

Ballance, P. E., et al. Phosphorus-32: Practical Radiation Protection. (Handbook Ser.: No. 9). 82p. (C). 1992. 130.00 (*0-948237-08-2*, Pub. by H&H Sci Cnslts) St Mut.

— Tritium: Radiation Protection in the Laboratory. 77p. 1994. pap. 150.00 (*0-948237-12-0*, Pub. by H&H Sci Cnslts) St Mut.

Ballance, P. F., ed. South Pacific Sedimentary Basins. (Sedimentary Basins of the World Ser.: Vol. 2). 434p. 1993. 222.50 (*0-444-88287-1*) Elsevier.

Ballance, Richard, jt. ed. see Bartram, Jamie.

Ballance, Robert, et al. The World's Pharmaceutical Industries: An International Perspective on Innovation, Competition & Policy. 288p. 1992. 100.00 (*1-85278-646-9*) E Elgar.

Ballance, Robert H. International Industry & Business: Structural Change, Industrial Policy & Industry Strategies. LC 86-28793. (Illus.). 256p. (C). 1987. text 60.00 (*0-04-339037-4*); pap. text 27.95 (*0-04-339038-2*) Routledge.

***Ballanche, Pierre-Simon.** Vie de Madame Recamier: Edition Etablie, Presentee et Annotee Sous la Direction de Kurt Kloocke. (FRE., Illus.). VII, 184p. 1999. 38.00 (*3-631-33939-9*) P Lang Pubng.

Ballanger, Edgard G., ed. see American Urological Association Staff.

Ballantine. Cpa Review Guide. 350p. 1999. pap. 20.00 (*0-13-085909-5*) S&S Trade.

Ballantine, jt. auth. see Spade.

Ballantine, Betty, ed. The Captain's Garden: A Reflective Journey Home Through the Art of Paul Landry. LC 96-14092. (Illus.). 152p. 1996. 35.00 (*0-86713-033-4*, 85068) Greenwich Wrkshop.

Ballantine Books Publishing Staff. Complete Guide to Pills. 1998. mass mkt. 6.99 (*0-345-91315-9*) Ballantine Pub Grp.

***Ballantine Books Publishing Staff.** Phantom Menace: Star Wars Art of Epic One. (Art of Star Wars Ser.). (Illus.). (J). 2000. pap. 22.95 (*0-345-43109-X*, Del Rey) Ballantine Pub Grp.

— Smart Alec's Knock Knock Jokes for Kids. (J). 1987. 9.09 (*0-606-03923-6*, Pub. by Turtleback) Demco.

Ballantine Books Publishing Staff. Stupid Jokes for Kids: Selections from the Great Big Fat Giant Joke Book. (J). 1991. 10.09 (*0-606-01289-3*, Pub. by Turtleback) Demco.

— Transportation. 1998. pap. write for info. (*0-676-54717-6*) Ballantine Pub Grp.

Ballantine Books Publishing Staff & Slaviscek, Bill. Guide to the New Star Wars Universe. 3rd ed. (Illus.). Date not set. pap. 16.00 (*0-345-43145-6*, Ballantine) Ballantine Pub Grp.

Ballantine, Christopher. Marabi Nights: Early South African Jazz & Vaudeville. (Illus.). 116p. (Orig.). (C). 1994. pap. text 24.95 (*0-86975-439-4*, Pub. by Ravan Pr) Ohio U Pr.

— Music & Its Social Meanings. (Monographs on Musicology: Vol. 2). xx, 202p. (C). 1984. pap. text 25.00 (*0-677-22000-6*) Gordon & Breach.

Ballantine, Colin. Vintage Russian: Props & Jets of the Iron Curtain. LC 98-55452. (Illus.). 112p. 1998. pap. 24.95 (*0-7603-0668-0*) MBI Pubg.

***Ballantine, David.** Chalk's Woman. 2000. text 23.95 (*0-312-87348-4*) St Martin.

Ballantine, David & Weinberg, Sylvia. The Book of Our House. LC 86-18231. (Illus.). 288p. 1987. 21.95 (*0-87951-267-9*, Pub. by Overlook Pr) Penguin Putnam.

Ballantine, Jeanne H. The Sociology of Education: A Systematic Analysis. 4th ed. LC 96-42921. 443p. 1997. 65.00 (*0-13-476037-9*) P-H.

Ballantine, Jeanne H., ed. Our Social World: An Introduction to Sociology. (C). 1998. text. write for info. (*0-321-01179-1*) Addson-Wesley Educ.

— Schools & Society: A Unified Reader. LC 88-33384. 593p. (Orig.). (C). 1989. pap. text 43.95 (*0-87484-907-1*, 907) Mayfield Pub.

Ballantine, Jeanne H., jt. auth. see Cargan.

Ballantine, Jeanne H., jt. auth. see Cargan, Leonard.

Ballantine, Jeanne H., jt. ed. see Cargan, Leonard.

Ballantine, John W. The Human Side of Economics: Its Significance for Enterprise Management. (Illus.). 176p. 1973. text 8.00 (*0-912084-08-1*) Mimir.

***Ballantine, Kathleen.** According to His Word: Prayers from God's Word. 240p. 1999. pap. write for info. (*0-7392-0331-2*, PO3499) Morris Pubng.

Ballantine, Larry G., et al, eds. Triazine Herbicides: Risk Assessment. (ACS Symposium Ser.: No. 683). (Illus.). 502p. 1998. text 140.00 (*0-8412-3542-2*) OUP.

Ballantine, Richard. The Sawtooth Wolves. LC 96-83437. (Illus.). 192p. 1996. 40.00 (*0-9649915-0-0*) Rufus Pubns Inc.

Ballantine, Richard & Grant, Richard. Richards' Ultimate Bicycle Repair Manual. LC 93-29836. (Illus.). 96p. 1994. pap. 8.95 (*1-56458-484-4*) DK Pub Inc.

— Ultimate Bicycle Book. LC 91-31540. (DK Living Ser.). 192p. 1998. pap. 13.95 (*0-7894-2252-2*) DK Pub Inc.

Ballantine, Todd. Tideland Treasure. LC 91-37185. (Illus.). 222p. 1991. reprint ed. pap. 15.95 (*0-87249-795-X*) U of SC Pr.

Ballantyne. Atlas of Laparoscopic Surgery. LC 99-31883. 1999. text 95.00 (*0-7216-6326-5*, W B Saunders Co) Harcrt Hlth Sci Grp.

— Deafness. 5th ed. 340p. 1993. pap. 63.50 (*1-56593-517-9*, 0426) Singular Publishing.

Ballantyne, A., jt. auth. see Von Karman, Theodore.

Ballantyne, Andrew. Architecture, Landscape & Liberty: Richard Payne Knight & the Picturesque. (Illus.). 329p. (C). 1997. text 99.95 (*0-521-46200-2*) Cambridge U Pr.

Ballantyne, Archibald. Voltaire's Visit to England, Seventeen Twenty-Six to Seventeen Twenty-Nine. (Works of Archibald Ballantyne). 338p. 1985. reprint ed. lib. bdg. 49.00 (*0-685-10498-2*) Rprt Serv.

Ballantyne, B. & Von Karman, Theodore. Advances in Aeronautical Sciences, 2 vols., Set, Vols. 3 & 4. LC 59-6840. (International Series of Monographs in Aeronautics & Astronautics). 1962. reprint ed. 468.00 (*0-08-009696-4*, Pub. by Pergamon Repr) Franklin.

Ballantyne, Bill. Wesakejack & the Bears. 2nd ed. (Illus.). 32p. (J). 1997. reprint ed. pap. 6.95 (*0-921368-72-0*, Pub. by Bain & Cox) Genl Dist Srvs.

— Wesakejack & the Flood. LC 96-126268. (Illus.). (J). 1995. 12.95 (*0-921368-45-3*, Pub. by Bain & Cox) Genl Dist Srvs.

— Wesakejack & the Flood. (Illus.). 32p. 1997. pap. 12.95 incl. audio (*0-921368-73-9*, Pub. by Bain & Cox) Genl Dist Srvs.

— Wesakejack & the Flood. (J). 1995. write for info. incl. audio (*0-921368-47-X*) Blizzard Publ.

— Wesakejack & the Flood. 2nd ed. (Illus.). 32p. (J). 1997. reprint ed. pap. 6.95 (*0-921368-71-2*, Pub. by Bain & Cox) Genl Dist Srvs.

Ballantyne, Bob. Out in the Open: Life on the Street. LC 96-910691. (Illus.). 96p. 1997. pap. 15.95 (*1-55145-099-2*) NStone Publ.

***Ballantyne, Bryan, et al, eds.** General & Applied Toxicology, 3 vols. 2nd ed. 2224p. 1999. 575.00 (*1-56159-242-0*) Groves Dictionaries.

Ballantyne, C. K., jt. auth. see Gray, J. M.

Ballantyne, Colin K. & Harris, Charles. The Periglaciation of Britain. LC 92-43477. (Illus.). 340p. (C). 1994. text 105.00 (*0-521-32459-9*) Cambridge U Pr.

— The Periglaciation of Britain. LC 92-43477. (Illus.). 340p. (C). 1995. pap. text 44.95 (*0-521-31016-4*) Cambridge U Pr.

Ballantyne, D. L. & Converse, John M. Experimental Skin Grafts & Transplantation Immunity. (Illus.). 196p. 1979. 127.00 (*0-387-90425-5*) Spr-Verlag.

Ballantyne, David. The Cunninghams. (New Zealand Classics Ser.). 240p. 1987. pap. 9.95 (*0-19-558158-X*) OUP.

Ballantyne, Donald B. Minimizing Earthquake Damage: A Guide for Water Utilities. (Illus.). 98p. 1994. pap. 30.00 (*0-89867-750-5*, 20326) Am Water Wks Assn.

Ballantyne, Donald B., ed. Lifeline Earthquake Engineering in the Central & Eastern U. S. Proceedings of Three Sessions Sponsored by the Technical Council on Lifeline Earthquake Engineering Research at the ASCE National Convention in New York, New York, September 1992. LC 92-26364. 200p. 1992. 26.00 (*0-87262-902-3*) Am Soc Civil Eng.

***Ballantyne, Duncan & Mazingo, Christopher.** Measuring Dispute Resolution Outcomes: A Literature Review with Implications for Workers Compensation. LC 99-26092. 140p. 1999. 75.00 (*0-935149-78-3*, WC-99-1) Workers Comp Res Inst.

Ballantyne, Duncan S. Dispute Prevention & Resolution in Workers' Compensation: A National Inventory, 1997-1998. LC 98-4018. 256p. 1998. 80.00 (*0-935149-74-0*, WC-98-3) Workers Comp Res Inst.

— Revisiting Workers' Compensation in Connecticut: Administrative Inventory. LC 98-36239. 136p. 1998. 29.00 (*0-935149-75-9*, WC-98-4) Workers Comp Res Inst.

— Revisiting Workers' Compensation in Pennsylvania: Administrative Inventory. LC 96-54811. 1997. 35.00 (*0-935149-65-1*, WC-97-1) Workers Comp Res Inst.

***Ballantyne, Duncan S.** Workers' Compensation in Louisiana: Administrative Inventory. LC 99-36507. 130p. 1999. 35.00 (*0-935149-77-5*, WC-99-4) Workers Comp Res Inst.

— Workers' Compensation in Ohio Administrative Inventory. 120p. 2000. pap. 35.00 (*0-935149-91-0*, WC-99-6) Workers Comp Res Inst.

Ballantyne, Duncan S. & Dunleavy, James F. Workers' Compensation in New Jersey: Administrative Inventory. LC 93-47994. 1994. 35.00 (*0-935149-44-9*, WC-94-2) Workers Comp Res Inst.

— Workers' Compensation in Oregon: Administrative Inventory. LC 95-6284. 1995. 35.00 (*0-935149-52-X*, WC-95-2) Workers Comp Res Inst.

Ballantyne, Duncan S. & Eccleston, Stacey M. Workers' Compensation in Georgia: Administrative Inventory. LC 92-20983. 1992. 35.00 (*0-935149-34-1*, WC-92-4) Workers Comp Res Inst.

Ballantyne, Duncan S. & Joyce, Karen M. Workers' Compensation in Illinois: Administrative Inventory. LC 96-43125. 1996. 35.00 (*0-935149-63-5*, WC-96-9) Workers Comp Res Inst.

An Asterisk (*) at the beginning of an entry indicates that the title is appearing for the first time.

Ballantyne, Duncan S. & Shiman, Lawrence. Revisiting Workers' Compensation in Michigan: Administrative Inventory. LC 97-27483. 1997. 35.00 (*0-935149-69-4*, WC-97-4) Workers Comp Res Inst.

Ballantyne, Duncan S. & Telles, Carol A. Workers' Compensation in Minnesota: Administrative Inventory. LC 71-17044. 1991. 35.00 (*0-935149-27-9*, WC-91-1) Workers Comp Res Inst.

— Workers' Compensation in Missouri: Administrative Inventory. LC 93-7235. 1993. 35.00 (*0-935149-40-6*, WC-93-1) Workers Comp Res Inst.

— Workers' Compensation in New York: Administrative Inventory. LC 92-26511. 1992. 35.00 (*0-935149-36-8*, WC-92-6) Workers Comp Res Inst.

— Workers' Compensation in Pennsylvania: Administrative Inventory. LC 91-38317. 1991. 35.00 (*0-935149-30-9*, WC-91-4) Workers Comp Res Inst.

— Workers' Compensation in Wisconsin: Administrative Inventory. LC 92-33151. 1992. 35.00 (*0-935149-37-6*, WC-92-7) Workers Comp Res Inst.

Ballantyne, Duncan S., jt. auth. see Eccleston, Stacey M.

Ballantyne, Duncan S., jt. auth. see Telles, Carol A.

Ballantyne, Garth H., et al. Laparoscopic Surgery. (Illus.). 736p. 1994. text 230.00 (*0-7216-6648-5*, W B Saunders Co) Harcrt Hlth Sci Grp.

Ballantyne, Iain & Povah, Nigel. Assessment & Development Centres. 186p. 1995. 78.95 (*0-566-07484-2*, Pub. by Gower) Ashgate Pub Co.

Ballantyne, J. K. The Resident Engineer. 2nd ed. 51p. 1986. 10.00 (*0-7277-0355-2*, Pub. by T Telford) RCH.

Ballantyne, J. R. & Mitra, Pramada D., trs. Sahitya-Darpana: or Mirror of Composition of Visvanatha: A Treatise on Poetical Criticism. (C). 1994. reprint ed. text 32.00 (*81-208-1145-3*, Pub. by Motilal Bnarsidass) S Asia.

Ballantyne, James R. Principles of Persian Calligraphy. 1977. lib. bdg. 59.95 (*0-8490-2480-3*) Gordon Pr.

Ballantyne, James R., tr. see Varadaraja.

Ballantyne, Janet. Joy of Gardening Cookbook. Haar, Amanda, ed. LC 94-1835. (Illus.). 336p. 1984. reprint ed. 25.00 (*0-88266-356-9*, Garden Way Pub); reprint ed. pap. 19.95 (*0-88266-355-0*, Garden Way Pub) Storey Bks.

Ballantyne, John. Bedside Manners: An Anthology of Medical Wit & Wisdom. 266p. 1998. pap. text 16.00 (*0-7881-5650-0*) DIANE Pub.

Ballantyne, John, et al, eds. DNA Technology & Forensic Science. (Banbury Reports: No. 32). (Illus.). 430p. 1989. lib. bdg. 95.00 (*0-87969-232-4*) Cold Spring Harbor.

Ballantyne, John W. Manual of Antenatal Pathology & Hygiene: The Embryo. (Classics in Human Development Ser.: Issue 1). 697p. 1991. reprint ed. text 75.00 (*1-879554-00-3*) Greenwood-Gene.

Ballantyne, Kay, et al. Hands-On Science: Ten Themes for the Whole Year. (Illus.). 96p. (J). (gr. 1-3). 1993. pap. 12.95 (*1-55799-250-9*, EMC 828) Evan-Moor Edu Pubs.

Ballantyne, R. M. The Coral Island. (Illus.). (YA). (gr. 5 up). 1995. pap. 3.99 (*0-14-036761-6*, Viking) Viking Penguin.

— Hudson Bay. 322p. 1985. reprint ed. lib. bdg. 59.00 (*0-932051-89-8*) Rprt Serv.

***Ballantyne, R. M.** The Prairie Chief. (Illus.). 256p. 2000. reprint ed. 18.00 (*1-889128-72-4*) Mantle Ministries.

Ballantyne, R. M. Twice Bought. (Old West Ser.). (Illus.). 240p. 1999. reprint ed. 18.00 (*1-889128-56-2*) Mantle Ministries.

Ballantyne, Roy, jt. auth. see Uzzell, David.

Ballantyne, W. M. Essays & Addresses on Arab Laws. 288p. 1998. 85.00 (*0-7007-1094-9*, Pub. by Curzon Pr Ltd) Paul & Co Pubs.

— Legal Development in Arabia: A Selection of Addresses & Articles. 148p. 1980. lib. bdg. 84.50 (*0-86010-167-3*) Kluwer Law Intl.

— Register of Laws of the Arabian Gulf: Basic Work & 1988 Supplement Service. (C). 1988. 935.00 (*1-85333-089-2*, Pub. by Graham & Trotman); ring bd. 935.00 (*1-85333-090-6*, Pub. by Graham & Trotman) Kluwer Academic.

— Register of Laws of the Arabian Gulf: 1989 Basic Work & 1989 Supplement Service. (C). 1989. pap. text 27.00 (*1-85333-253-4*, Pub. by Graham & Trotman) Kluwer Academic.

— Register of Laws of the Arabian Gulf: 1991 Main Work & 1991 Supp Service. (C). 1991. ring bd. 1230.00 (*1-85333-491-X*, Pub. by Graham & Trotman); suppl. ed. 267.00 (*0-685-39302-X*, Pub. by Graham & Trotman) Kluwer Academic.

— Register of Laws of the Arabian Gulf: 1992 Main Work & 1992 Supplement Service. 700p. 1992. ring bd. 1185.00 (*1-85333-639-4*, Pub. by Graham & Trotman) Kluwer Academic.

Ballantyne, W. M., ed. Register of Laws of the Arabian Gulf: Main Work & Supplement Service, 1990. (C). 1990. 1528.00 (*1-85333-333-6*, Pub. by Graham & Trotman) Kluwer Academic.

— Register of Laws of the Arabian Gulf: 1993 Main Work & 1993 Supplement Service. (C). 1993. ring bd. 2023.00 (*1-85333-810-9*, Pub. by Graham & Trotman) Kluwer Academic.

Ballapragada, Bhaskar & Water Environment Research Foundation Staff. Toxic Chlorinated Compounds: Fate & Biodegradation in Anaerobic Digestion. LC 98-60054. 1998. write for info. (*0-9662553-0-5*) Wtr Environ Res.

Ballara, Angela. Iwi: The Dynamics of Meaori Tribal Organisation from C.1769 to C.1945 LC 98-197995. 400 p. 1998. write for info. (*0-86473-328-3*) Victoria Univ Pr.

Ballara, Angela, intro. Te Kingitanga: Selected Essays from the Dictionary of New Zealand Biography. LC 97-168554. (Illus.). 136p. 1997. pap. 19.95 (*1-86940-202-2*, Pub. by Auckland Univ) Paul & Co Pubs.

***Ballarati, Michele, et al.** Caffelletto's High Quality Bed & Breakfast in Italy. 239p. 1999. pap. 22.50 (*88-7166-452-3*, Pub. by Le Lettere) Kesend Pub Ltd.

Ballard. Angel at Troublesome Creek. LC 99-33543. 224p. 1999. text 22.95 (*0-312-24175-5*) St Martin.

Ballard, Adolphus, ed. British Borough Charters, 1042-1216. LC 80-2236. reprint ed. 49.50 (*0-404-18750-1*) AMS Pr.

***Ballard, Allen B.** Where I'm Bound: A Novel. 320p. 2000. 24.00 (*0-684-87031-2*) S&S Trade.

Ballard, Bambi, tr. see Beaucour, Fernand, et al.

Ballard, Barry. A Darker Art: A Journal for Poetry from the Dark Side. 58p. (Orig.). 1997. pap. 3.00 (*1-57502-492-6*, PO1461) Morris Pubng.

Ballard, Beverly. Grandma's ABCs of Fruits & Vegetables. (Illus.). 128p. 1996. pap. 9.95 (*1-881316-97-1*) A&B Bks.

Ballard, Beverly J. Falling Acorns. 365p. 1998. mass mkt. 7.95 (*0-9667364-0-0*) Novelle Publ.

— Final Vengeance. 181p. 1999. 16.95 (*0-9667364-1-9*) Novelle Publ.

— Maria - A Woman of Valor. 206p. 1999. 18.95 (*0-9667364-2-7*) Novelle Publ.

Ballard, Bobbie. My Kwanzaa Story. (Illus.). 48p. (J). (gr. k-6). 1993. 6.95 (*0-9639349-0-2*) Ujamaa Ent.

Ballard, Brigid, jt. auth. see Clanchy, John.

Ballard, Bruce W. The Role of Mood in Heidegger's Ontology. 154p. (Orig.). (C). 1990. pap. text 20.50 (*0-8191-7979-5*); lib. bdg. 35.50 (*0-8191-7978-7*) U Pr of Amer.

***Ballard, Bruce W.** Understanding MacIntyre. LC 99-50163. 104p. 2000. 44.00 (*0-7618-1561-9*); pap. 24.50 (*0-7618-1562-7*) U Pr of Amer.

Ballard, Bryan L., jt. auth. see Ballard, Carol L.

Ballard, C., jt. ed. see Goldman, L. R.

Ballard, C. R. Hearts in the Web. 248p. (Orig.). 1997. pap. 12.95 (*0-9658639-0-5*) Wolfe Pub.

Ballard, Carol. The Heart & Circulatory System. LC 96-31764. (Human Body Ser.). (Illus.). 48p. (J). (gr. 5-10). 1997. lib. bdg. 25.68 (*0-8172-4800-5*) Raintree Steck-V.

— How Do Our Ears Hear? LC 97-9063. (How Our Bodies Work Ser.). (J). 1998. lib. bdg. 22.83 (*0-8172-4737-8*) Raintree Steck-V.

— How Do Our Eyes See? LC 97-7708. (How Our Bodies Work Ser.). (J). 1998. lib. bdg. 22.83 (*0-8172-4736-X*) Raintree Steck-V.

— How Do We Feel & Touch? LC 97-3261. (How Our Bodies Work Ser.). (J). 1998. 22.83 (*0-8172-4739-4*) Raintree Steck-V.

— How Do We Move? LC 97-17986. (How Your Body Works Ser.). 1998. 22.83 (*0-8172-4741-6*) Raintree Steck-V.

— How Do We Taste & Smell? LC 97-3258. (How Our Bodies Work Ser.). (J). (ps-4). 1998. 22.83 (*0-8172-4738-6*) Raintree Steck-V.

— How Do We Think? LC 97-17984. (How Your Body Works Ser.). (ps-4). 1998. 22.83 (*0-8172-4740-8*) Raintree Steck-V.

— The Stomach & Digestive System. LC 96-31769. (Human Body Ser.). (Illus.). 48p. (J). (gr. 5-10). 1997. lib. bdg. 25.68 (*0-8172-4801-3*) Raintree Steck-V.

Ballard, Carol L. & Ballard, Bryan L. Nikki's Adventures. (Illus.). 40p. (J). (gr. k-6). 1999. pap. 18.00 (*0-8059-4675-6*) Dorrance.

Ballard, Charles, jt. ed. see Duminy, Andrew.

Ballard, Charles L. A General Equilibrium Model for Tax Policy Evaluation. LC 84-28096. (National Bureau of Economic Research Monograph). (Illus.). 274p. Date not set. reprint ed. pap. 85.00 (*0-608-20985-6*, 205451300003) Bks Demand.

— Winter Count Poems. 1997. pap. text 12.95 (*0-912678-96-8*) Greenfld Rev Lit.

Ballard, Charles L., et al. A General Equilibrium Model for Tax Policy Evaluation. LC 84-28096. (National Bureau of Economic Research Monographs). x, 264p. 1985. lib. bdg. 36.00 (*0-226-03632-4*) U Ch Pr.

***Ballard, Chester A.** Keeper of the Woods. 160p. 2000. pap. 12.45 (*1-58500-981-4*) First Bks Lib.

Ballard, Chet, et al, eds. The Student's Companion to Sociology. LC 96-33056. (Illus.). 320p. 1997. text 66.95 (*0-631-19947-0*); pap. text 25.95 (*0-631-19948-9*) Blackwell Pubs.

Ballard, Chris. Hoops Nation. LC 97-28106. (Illus.). 320p. 1998. pap. 12.95 (*0-8050-4877-4*) H Holt & Co.

Ballard, Colin R. Napoleon: An Outline. LC 76-179503. (Select Bibliographies Reprint Ser.). 1977. reprint ed. 23.95 (*0-8369-6632-5*) Ayer.

Ballard, Dana H. An Introduction of Natural Computation. LC 96-44545. (Complex Adaptive System Ser.). (Illus.). 304p. 1997. 50.00 (*0-262-02420-9*, Bradford Bks) MIT Pr.

— Introduction to Natural Computation. 1999. pap. 32.50 (*0-262-52258-6*) MIT Pr.

Ballard, Darlene. God's Rose: A Testimony of God's Love. 2nd ed. 82p. 1997. reprint ed. pap. write for info. (*0-9670536-0-9*) Teen Chall GA.

Ballard, David. Foundation Aspects of Non Standard Mathematics. LC 94-30811. (Contemporary Mathematics Ser.: Vol. 176). 135p. 1994. pap. 40.00 (*0-8218-0293-3*, CONM/176) Am Math.

Ballard, David N., Jr., jt. auth. see Zeimet, Denis.

Ballard, Debbi A. How to Succeed in Your Own Network Marketing Business. LC 91-70936. 169p. 1991. 14.95 (*0-9629109-0-2*) IMLC.

Ballard, Delores. Barbeque & Butterbeans: (And Other Essentials of Life) (Orig.). 1992. pap. 7.35 (*0-9618910-1-7*) Jackson Sun.

Ballard, Dianna. Whole Wheat Breadmaking: Secrets of the Masters Made Easy. 1993. pap. 9.95 (*1-55517-120-6*) CFI Dist.

Ballard, Donna. Doing It for Ourselves: Success Stories of African-American Women in Business. LC 97-1 8067. 224p. (Orig.). 1997. pap. 12.00 (*0-425-15613-3*) Berkley Pub.

Ballard, E. G., ed. Contributions by E. G. Ballard; R. L. Barber; J. K. Feibleman; C. H. Hamburg; H. N. Lee; P. G. Morrison; L. N. Roberts; R. C. Whittemore. (Tulane Studies in Philosophy: No. 5). 93p. 1967. pap. text 57.00 (*90-247-0279-8*, Pub. by M Nijhoff) Kluwer Academic.

Ballard, Edward G. Art & Analysis. (Works of Edward G. Ballard). xiv, 219p. 1985. reprint ed. 49.00 (*0-932051-76-6*) Rprt Serv.

— Art & Analysis: An Essay Toward Theory in Aesthetics. 219p. 1957. reprint ed. 25.00 (*0-403-08903-4*) Somerset Pub.

— Philosophy & the Liberal Arts. (C). 1989. lib. bdg. 160.00 (*0-7923-0241-9*) Kluwer Academic.

Ballard, Edward G. Philosophy at the Crossroads. LC 72-130663. 317p. 1971. pap. 98.30 (*0-7837-8501-1*, 204930900011) Bks Demand.

Ballard, Edward G. Principles of Interpretation. LC 83-4281. (Series in Continental Thought : Vol. 5). 261p. 1983. text 36.95 (*0-8214-0688-4*); pap. text 19.95 (*0-8214-0689-2*) Ohio U Pr.

Ballard, Edward G., jt. auth. see Ball, Robert Edward.

Ballard, Edward G, tr. see Ricoeur, Paul.

Ballard, F. J. Gene Expression Regulation at the RNA & Protein Levels. Kay, J. et al, eds. (Biochemical Society Symposium Ser.: Symposia 55). (Illus.). 203p. 1989. text 110.50 (*0-904498-24-7*, Pub. by Portland Pr Ltd) Ashgate Pub Co.

***Ballard, F. Mignon.** An Angel to Die For. 2000. text 23.95 (*0-312-24174-7*) St Martin.

Ballard, Frank, jt. auth. see Fijan, Carol.

Ballard, Frederic L., Jr. ABCs of Arbitrage: Tax Rules for Investment of Bond Proceeds by Municipalities. 406p. 1994. pap. 94.95 (*1-57073-044-X*, 533-0056) Amer Bar Assn.

Ballard, Frederic L. ABC's of Arbitrage: Tax Rules for Investment of Bond Proceeds by Municipalities: 1998 Edition. LC 98-16130. 1998. 109.95 (*1-57073-566-2*) Amer Bar Assn.

Ballard, G. A. Rulers of the Indian Ocean. LC 98-9049-2. xv, 319 p. 1998. 39.50 (*81-206-1314-7*, Pub. by Asian Educ Servs) S Asia.

Ballard, Geneva, et al. Appreciation Literature Workshops. 240p. (C). 1995. spiral bd. 30.95 (*0-7872-0741-1*) Kendall-Hunt.

Ballard, George. Memoirs of Several Ladies of Great Britain: Who Have Been Celebrated for Their Writings or Skill in the Learned Languages, Arts & Sciences. Perry, Ruth, ed. LC 84-10385. 487p. reprint ed. pap. 151.00 (*0-608-10589-9*, 207121000009) Bks Demand.

— Memoirs of Several Ladies of Great Britain Who Have Been Celebrated for Their Writings or Skill in the Learned Languages, Arts & Sciences. Perry, Ruth, ed. LC 84-10385. 488p. 1985. 49.95 (*0-8143-1747-2*) Wayne St U Pr.

Ballard, George A. The Influence of the Sea on the Political History of Japan. LC 74-136516. (Illus.). 311p. 1972. reprint ed. lib. bdg. 35.00 (*0-8371-5435-9*, BAIS, Greenwood Pr) Greenwood.

Ballard, Harlan H. Tiler's Jewel (1921) 142p. 1999. reprint ed. pap. 14.95 (*0-7661-0738-8*) Kessinger Pub.

Ballard, J., jt. ed. see Bergan, J. J.

Ballard, J., jt. ed. see Hunt, Garry E.

Ballard, J. G. The Atrocity Exhibition. (Illus.). 140p. 1990. pap. 13.99 (*1-889307-03-3*) RE Search.

Ballard, J. G. The Best Short Stories of J. G. Ballard. LC 94-42290. (Illus.). 1995. pap. 15.95 (*0-8050-3876-0*, Owl) H Holt & Co.

— Cocaine Nights. (Illus.). 336p. 1998. 23.00 (*1-887178-66-X*, Pub. by Counterpt DC) HarpC.

— Cocaine Nights. 336p. 1999. pap. text 15.00 (*1-58243-017-9*, Pub. by Counterpt DC) HarpC.

— Concrete Island. 176p. 1994. pap. 12.00 (*0-374-52413-0*, Noonday) FS&G.

— Crash. 224p. 1994. pap. 12.00 (*0-374-52412-2*, Noonday) FS&G.

— The Day of Creation. 256p. 1999. pap. 13.00 (*0-374-52577-3*) FS&G.

— The Drowned World. 175p. 1987. mass mkt. 3.95 (*0-88184-324-5*) Carroll & Graf.

— Empire of the Sun. 384p. 1987. mass mkt. 5.99 (*0-671-64877-2*) PB.

— Empire of the Sun. 1997. reprint ed. lib. bdg. 39.95 (*1-56849-663-X*) Buccaneer Bks.

— J. G. Ballard. Vale, Vale, ed. (RE-Search Ser.: Vols. 8 & 9). (Illus.). 176p. (Orig.). 1984. pap. 17.99 (*0-9650469-7-4*) RE Search.

— The Kindness of Women. LC 92-39420. 352p. 1993. pap. 13.00 (*0-15-647114-0*) Harcourt.

— Memories of the Space Age. LC 88-15075. (Illus.). 224p. 1988. 18.95 (*0-87054-157-9*) Arkham.

— Running Wild. 112p. 1998. pap. 10.00 (*0-374-52546-3*, Noonday) FS&G.

— Rushing to Paradise. LC 96-65. 240p. 1996. pap. 12.00 (*0-312-13415-0*, Picador USA) St Martin.

— The Terminal Beach. 1987. reprint ed. mass mkt. 3.50 (*0-88184-370-9*) Carroll & Graf.

— The Unlimited Dream Company. 1993. reprint ed. lib. bdg. 27.95 (*0-89968-391-6*, Lghtyr Pr) Buccaneer Bks.

— Users Guide to Millenium. 320p. 1997. pap. 14.00 (*0-312-15683-9*) St Martin.

— A User's Guide to the Millennium: Essays & Reviews. 1996. 23.00 (*0-614-96854-2*, Picador USA) St Martin.

— A User's Guide to the Millennium: Essays & Reviews. 1997. pap. 14.00 (*0-614-27420-6*, Picador USA) St Martin.

— Vermilion Sands. 208p. 1988. mass mkt. 3.95 (*0-88184-422-5*) Carroll & Graf.

— War Fever. 1991. 18.95 (*0-374-28645-0*) FS&G.

— War Fever. 176p. 1999. pap. 10.00 (*0-374-52576-5*) FS&G.

Ballard, J. P. Remember Sometimes the Seekers of Dreams. 63p. (Orig.). 1988. pap. text 6.95 (*0-9620563-1-6*) Common Mans Symposium.

— Summer Days Gone: Thoughts & Reflections. 37p. (Orig.). 1987. pap. text 5.00 (*0-9620563-0-8*) Common Mans Symposium.

Ballard, Jack S. United States Air Force in Southeast Asia, Development & Employment of Fixed-wing Gunships, 1962-1972. 342p. 1982. per. 21.00 (*0-16-061378-7*) USGPO.

Ballard, James. What's the Rush? Step Out of the Race, Free Your Mind, Change Your Life. LC 98-28980. (Illus.). 224p. 1999. 20.00 (*0-7679-0310-2*) Broadway BDD.

Ballard, James G. Empire Du Soleil. (FRE.). 438p. 1990. pap. 12.95 (*0-7859-2145-1*, 2070382680) Fr & Eur.

Ballard, James O., jt. ed. see Hawkins, Anne H.

Ballard, Jane. Gordon's Print Price Annual, 1997. 1376p. 1997. 155.00 (*0-931036-03-8*) Gordon s Art.

Ballard, Jim. Boo! A Parable for Children over & under 21. LC 75-25393. (Mandala Series in Education). (Illus.). 1975. pap. 3.50 (*0-916250-08-3*) Irvington.

— Circlebook: A Leader Handbook for Conducting Circletime - A Curriculum of Affect. LC 75-25396. (Mandala Series in Education). (Illus.). 60p. (Orig.). 1981. reprint ed. pap. 7.95 (*0-8290-0150-6*) Irvington.

— Dibble & the Great Blob: A Parable for Children Over & Under 21. LC 75-25393. (Mandala Series in Education). 1975. pap. 3.50 (*0-916250-06-7*) Irvington.

— Handbook for Star Trackers. (Illus.). 128p. (Orig.). 1988. pap. 12.95 (*0-933346-47-6*) Sky Pub.

— Seeing Circle: A Parable for Children over & under 21. LC 75-25393. (Mandala Series in Education). 1975. pap. 6.50 (*0-916250-07-5*) Irvington.

— Stop a Moment: A Group Leader's Handbook of Energizing Experiences. LC 77-81459. (Mandala Series in Education). (Illus.). 73p. 1982. reprint ed. pap. 8.95 (*0-8290-0981-7*) Irvington.

— Stories with Holes: A Collection of Open-Ended Stories for Conducting Inquiry Training in the Classroom, Vol. 1. LC 75-25392. (Mandala Series in Education). 32p. (Orig.). 1996. 7.50 (*0-8290-0355-X*) NL Assocs.

— Warm Snuggles & Cold Ouchies: A Parable for Children over & under 21. LC 75-25393. (Mandala Series in Education). 1975. pap. 7.50 (*0-916250-05-9*) Irvington.

— Why Not? How to Be Doing What You Really Like...And Getting Paid. LC 76-14016. (Mandala Series in Education). 180p. (Orig.). 1976. pap. 8.95 (*0-916250-10-5*) Irvington.

Ballard, Jim, jt. auth. see Timmermann, Tim.

Ballard, Jimmy & Quinn, Brennan. How to Perfect Your Golf Swing. LC 86-186. (Illus.). 160p. 1990. mass mkt. 15.00 (*0-671-72310-3*) Golf Digest.

Ballard, Joe N., ed. The History of the U. S. Army Corps of Engineers. (Illus.). 159p. (C). 1999. pap. text 35.00 (*0-7881-7666-8*) DIANE Pub.

Ballard, John. African American Consciousness: Reclaiming Your History! LC 92-63383. (Soul to Soul Guides Ser.: Vols. I & II). (Illus.). 304p. 1993. 14.95 (*0-932279-99-6*) World Citizens.

— Annotated Commonwealth Employees' Rehabilitation & Compensation Act, 1988. 260p. 1991. pap. 48.00 (*1-86287-069-1*, Pub. by Federation Pr) Gaunt.

— Annotated Safety, Rehabilitation & Compensation Act 1988. 2nd ed. 360p. 1995. pap. 54.00 (*1-86287-177-9*, Pub. by Federation Pr) Gaunt.

— Brothers & Sisters: Real Love Knows No Boundaries!, 2 bks. in 1. LC 93-12119. (Soul to Soul Adventure Ser.: Bk. 2). (Illus.). 1993. pap. 14.95 (*0-932279-11-2*) World Citizens.

— The Girl Who Couldn't Wait for Christmas. (Illus.). 64p. (J). (ps-5). 2000. write for info. (*0-932279-50-3*) World Citizens.

— The Guide to End World Hunger. Ghose, Prema, ed. LC 84-63141. (Soul to Soul Guides Ser.). (Illus.). 72p. 1985. pap. 3.95 (*0-932279-25-2*, New Horiz CA) World Citizens.

— India Revealed! The True Roots of Hinduism & the World's Oldest Democracy. (Soul to Soul Guides Ser.: Vol. 1). (Illus.). (C). 1999. 14.95 (*0-932279-26-0*) World Citizens.

— Monsoon: A Novel to End World Hunger. Ghose, Prema, ed. LC 84-62121. (MacBurnie King Adventure Ser.). (Illus.). 242p. 1985. 14.95 (*0-932279-00-7*, New Horiz CA); pap. 9.95 (*0-932279-01-5*, New Horiz CA) World Citizens.

— Monsoon: A Novel to End World Hunger. LC 84-62121. (MacBurnie King Adventure Ser.). (Illus.). 240p. (YA). (gr. 7 up). 1986. pap. text 29.95 (*0-932279-02-3*, Clsrm Classics) World Citizens.

— Skateman: In the City of Angels. (Skateman: 1). (Illus.). (YA). 1999. write for info. (*0-932279-60-0*) World Citizens.

— Soul Survivors: Real Love Knows No Boundaries. (Soul to Soul Adventure Ser.: 3). (Illus.). (YA). (gr. 7-13). 1999. write for info. (*0-932279-13-9*) World Citizens.

— Soul to Soul: A Daring Adventure, 2 bks. in 1. LC 93-6649. (Soul to Soul Adventure Ser.: Bk. I). (Illus.). 1993. pap. 14.95 (*0-932279-10-4*) World Citizens.

***Ballard, John & Suff, Paul.** World Soccer: The Dictionary of Football: The Complete A-Z of International Football. (Illus.). 608p. 1999. pap. 39.50 (*0-7522-2434-4*, Pub. by Boxtree) Trans-Atl Phila.

Ballard, John, et al. Annotated Safety Rehabilitation & Compensation Act, 1988. 3rd ed. 467p. 1997. pap. 64.00 (*1-86287-250-3*, 15146, Pub. by Federation Pr) Gaunt.

B

An Asterisk (*) at the beginning of an entry indicates that the title is appearing for the first time.

***Ballard, John, et al.** Annotated Safety, Rehabilitation & Compensation Act 1988. 4th ed. 526p. 1999. pap. 69.95 (*1-86287-336-4*, Pub. by Federation Pr) Gaunt.

Ballard, John, jt. auth. see Glaumann, Hans.

***Ballard, John H.** SoulMates: A Novel to End World Hunger, with an Introduction by Mother Teresa & The Gandhi Foundation, 2 bks. in 1. Ellen, Joan, ed. LC 97-41770. (Soul to Soul Adventure Ser.). 524p. (YA). (gr. 7 up). 1998. 19.95 (*0-932279-06-6*) World Citizens.

Ballard, John H. SoulMates: A Novel to End World Hunger, with an Introduction by Mother Teresa & The Gandhi Foundation, 2 bks. in 1. Ellen, Joan, ed. LC 97-41770. (Soul to Soul Adventure Ser.). (Illus.). 524p. (YA). (gr. 7 up). 1998. pap. 14.95 (*0-932279-05-8*) World Citizens.

***Ballard, John R.** Continuity during the Storm: Boissy d'Anglas & the Era of the French Revolution, 74. LC 99-462064. (Contributions to the Study of World History Ser.: Vol. 74). 224p. 2000. 62.50 (*0-313-31508-6*, GM1508, Greenwood Pr) Greenwood.

Ballard, John R. Upholding Democracy: The United States Military Campaign in Haiti, 1994-1997. LC 98-5239. 292p. 1998. 59.95 (*0-275-96237-7*, Praeger Pubs) Greenwood.

Ballard, Jon. 1-4-3 Means I Love You. LC 98-94377. 188p. 1999. pap. text 14.95 (*0-9668850-0-7*) CNC Pubg.

Ballard, Karen A., ed. see Copel, Linda.

Ballard, Keith. Inclusive Education: International Voices On Disability & Justice. LC 99-211191. 192p. 1999. pap. 29.95 (*0-7507-0934-0*, Falmer Pr) Taylor & Francis.

— Inclusive Education: International Voices on Disability & Justice. LC 99-211191. 1999. 85.00 (*0-7507-0935-9*, Falmer Pr) Taylor & Francis.

Ballard, Keith, jt. auth. see Heshusius, Lous.

Ballard, L. S., jt. auth. see Warren, Thomas B.

Ballard, Linda M. Forgetting Frolic: Marriage Traditions in Ireland. LC 98-181584. (Illus.). 176p. 1998. pap. 19.95 (*0-85389-666-6*, Pub. by Inst Irish Studies) Irish Bks Media.

Ballard, Lisa, jt. auth. see Siebert, Lori.

Ballard, Lois. Reptiles. LC 81-38525. (New True Books Ser.). (Illus.). 48p. (J). (gr. k-4). 1982. pap. 5.50 (*0-516-41644-8*); lib. bdg. 21.00 (*0-516-01644-X*) Childrens.

Ballard, M. Russell. Counseling with Our Councils: Learning to Minister Together in the Church & in the Family. LC 97-38121. xi, 188p. 1997. 5.95 (*1-57345-209-2*) Deseret Bk.

— The Law of Sacrifice & What Came from Kirtland LC 98-72585. (Classic Talk Ser.). 91 p. 1998. write for info. (*1-57345-403-6*) Deseret Bk.

— Nuestra Busqueda de la Felicidad: Una Invitacion Para Conocer la Iglesia De Jesucristo De los Santos De los Ultimos Dias. (SPA.). xii, 141p. 1994. pap. 6.95 (*0-87579-915-9*) Deseret Bk.

— Our Search for Happiness: An Invitation to Understand the Church of Jesus Christ of Latter-Day Saints. LC 93-29353. 124p. 1993. 11.95 (*0-87579-804-7*) Deseret Bk.

— Our Search for Happiness: An Invitation to Understand the Church of Jesus Christ of Latter-Day Saints. LC 93-29353. 124p. 1995. pap. 6.95 (*0-87579-917-5*) Deseret Bk.

— Suicide: Some Things We Know, & Some We Don't. 56p. 1993. 5.95 (*0-87579-766-0*) Deseret Bk.

Ballard, Margaret B. Ballard. William Ballard, a Genealogical Record of His Descendants in Monroe County, WV. (Illus.). 410p. 1997. reprint ed. pap. 62.00 (*0-8328-7359-4*); reprint ed. lib. bdg. 72.00 (*0-8328-7358-6*) Higginson Bk Co.

Ballard, Michael. Civil War Mississippi: A Guide. LC 99-30825. (Illus.). 112p. 2000. 25.00 (*0-87805-870-2*); pap. 14.95 (*1-57806-196-2*) U Pr of Miss.

Ballard, Michael B. The Campaign for Vicksburg. (Civil War Ser.). (Illus.). 56p. 1996. pap. 4.95 (*0-915992-92-2*) Eastern National.

— A Long Shadow: Jefferson Davis & the Final Days of the Confederacy. LC 97-6957. 1997. pap. 15.95 (*0-8203-1941-4*) U of Ga Pr.

— Pemberton: The General Who Lost Vicksburg. Orig. Title: Pemberton: A Biography. (Illus.). 250p. 1999. reprint ed. pap. 18.00 (*1-57806-226-8*) U Pr of Miss.

Ballard, Michael B., jt. ed. see Cockrell, Thomas D.

***Ballard, Mignon F.** Aunt Matilda's Ghost. 144p. 2000. 22.50 (*1-57072-116-5*); pap. 12.50 (*1-57072-132-7*) Overmountain Pr.

Ballard, Mignon F. Deadly Promise. 1991. reprint ed. mass mkt. 3.99 (*0-373-26086-5*) Harlequin Bks.

Ballard, Mignon F. Final Curtain. 192p. 1992. 18.95 (*0-88184-799-2*) Carroll & Graf.

***Ballard, Mignon F.** Raven Rock. 2000. 24.50 (*1-57072-119-X*); pap. 15.00 (*1-57072-135-1*) Overmountain Pr.

***Ballard, Mignon Franklin.** Angel at Troublesome Creek. large type ed. LC 00-26117. 2000. 24.95 (*1-57490-275-X*, Beeler LP Bks) T T Beeler.

Ballard, Mike, jt. auth. see Thomas, Richard.

Ballard, Nancy J. The First Friend Would Have to Be the Best. (Dear Cee Cee Picture Bk.). (Illus.). 44p. 1990. text 14.95 (*0-9627864-0-3*) Dear Cee-Cee.

Ballard, Newton A. Ballard History, 1635-1935. (Illus.). 35p. 1997. reprint ed. pap. 7.00 (*0-8328-7357-8*); reprint ed. lib. bdg. 17.00 (*0-8328-7356-X*) Higginson Bk Co.

***Ballard, Patricia.** By Honor Bound. LC 99-17959. 295p. 1999. 24.95 (*0-7862-1871-1*) Five Star.

Ballard, Patricia. Fine Wine in Food. (Illus.). 144p. 1988. pap. 9.95 (*0-932664-56-3*) Wine Appreciation.

— Wine in Every Day Cooking: Cooking with Wine for Family & Friends. 1998. pap. 8.95 (*0-932664-84-9*) Wine Appreciation.

— Wine in Everyday Cooking: Cooking with Wine for Family & Friends. 128p. pap. 8.95 (*0-932664-45-8*) Wine Appreciation.

Ballard, Patti, jt. auth. see Carden, Connie.

Ballard, Paul, ed. Facing Death. 208p. 1996. pap. 18.95 (*0-7083-1331-0*, Pub. by Univ Wales Pr) Paul & Co Pubs.

***Ballard, Peg.** Chad Checks: The Sound of CH. LC 99-15890. (Wonder Books Ser.). (Illus.). 24p. (J). (ps-2). 1999. lib. bdg. 21.41 (*1-56766-727-9*) Childs World.

Ballard, Peg. Gifts for Gus: The Sound of "G" LC 99-20962. (Wonder Books Ser.). (Illus.). 24p. (J). 1999. lib. bdg. 21.41 (*1-56766-701-5*) Childs World.

***Ballard, Peg.** Shoes: The Sound of SH. LC 99-31460. (Wonder Books Ser.). (Illus.). 23p. (J). (ps-2). 1999. lib. bdg. 14.99 (*1-56766-726-0*) Childs World.

— This & That: The Sound of TH. LC 99-15888. (Wonder Books Ser.). (Illus.). 24p. (J). (ps-2). 1999. lib. bdg. 21.41 (*1-56766-728-7*) Childs World.

Ballard, Peg. Vets: The Sound of "V" LC 99-25549. (Wonder Books Ser.). (Illus.). 24p. (J). 1999. lib. bdg. 21.41 (*1-56766-700-7*) Childs World.

Ballard, Peg & Klingel, Cynthia F. Little Bit: The Sound of "Short L" LC 99-25499. (Wonder Books Ser.). (Illus.). 24p. (J). 1999. lib. bdg. 21.41 (*1-56766-698-1*) Childs World.

Ballard, Peg, jt. auth. see Klingel, Cynthia Fitterer.

***Ballard, Peggy.** You're Already a Success: Thoughts on Beginning Your New Career. LC 99-57368. 2000. 10.95 (*0-7407-0466-4*) Andrews & McMeel.

Ballard, Phillipa, et al. Community Attitudes to Adult Material on Pay Television. LC 98-206493. 12 p. 1997. write for info. (*0-477-01810-6*) Horticult & Food Res.

Ballard, Rhea, compiled by. The Right to Die No. 35: A Selective Bibliography. (Tarlton Law Library Legal Bibliography Ser.: No. 35). 40p. 1992. 20.00 (*0-935630-40-6*) U of Tex Tarlton Law Lib.

***Ballard, Robert.** Exploring the Titanic. (Illus.). 1999. 14.50 (*0-8335-5914-1*) Econo-Clad Bks.

— Finding the Titanic. (Illus.). (J). (gr. 2-4). 1999. pap. 11.10 (*0-7857-2438-9*) Econo-Clad Bks.

Ballard, Robert Duane. Coastal Images of America: At the Water's Edge. LC 97-42919. (Illus.). 196p. 1998. 45.00 (*0-7892-0313-8*) Abbeville Pr.

— The Discovery of the Titanic. 1988. 35.00 (*0-446-51385-7*, Pub. by Warner Bks) Little.

Ballard, Robert Duane. The Discovery of the Titanic. rev. ed. LC 87-8211. (Illus.). 288p. 1995. mass mkt. 13.99 (*0-446-67174-6*, Pub. by Warner Bks) Little.

— Explorations: From the Man Who Discovered the Titanic: A Life of Underwater Adventure. (Illus.). 24p. 1998. pap. 14.45 (*0-7868-8389-8*, Pub. by Hyperion) Time Warner.

Ballard, Robert Duane. Exploring the Bismarck. (Time Quest Bks.). (J). 1991. 12.15 (*0-606-05271-2*, Pub. by Turtleback) Demco.

— Exploring the Bismarck: The Real-Life Quest to Find Hitler's Greatest Battleship. 64p. (J). (gr. 4-7). 1993. pap. 6.95 (*0-590-44269-4*) Scholastic Inc.

— Exploring the Titanic. LC 88-6478. (Illus.). 64p. (J). (gr. 4-7). 1988. 14.95 (*0-590-41953-6*) Scholastic Inc.

— Finding the Titanic. LC 93-19203. (Illus.). 48p. (J). (gr. 2-3). 1993. pap. 3.99 (*0-590-47230-5*, Cartwheel) Scholastic Inc.

— Lost Liners: From the Titanic to the Andrea Doria: The Ocean Floor Reveals Its Greatest Lost Ships. 224p. (J). 1998. pap. 29.45 (*0-7868-8384-7*, Pub. by Hyperion) Time Warner.

— Lost Wreck of the Isis. (J). (gr. 4-7). 1994. pap. 4.95 (*0-590-43853-0*) Scholastic Inc.

Ballard, Robert Duane & Archbold, Rick. Exploring the Bismarck. 64p. (J). (gr. 3-7). 1991. 15.95 (*0-590-44268-6*, Scholastic Hardcover) Scholastic Inc.

— Ghost Liners. LC 98-3412. (Illus.). 64p. (J). (gr. k-3). 1998. 18.95 (*0-316-08020-9*) Little.

— Lost Liners: From the Titanic to the Andrea Doria: The Ocean Floor Reveals It's Greatest Lost Ships. LC 97-15270. (Illus.). 224p. (J). 1997. 60.00 (*0-7868-6296-3*, Pub. by Hyperion) Time Warner.

***Ballard, Robert Duane & Archbold, Rick.** Return to Midway: The Quest to Find the Lost Ships from the Greatest Battle of the Pacific War. LC 99-10831. 192p. 1999. per. 40.00 (*0-7922-7500-4*) Natl Geog.

***Ballard, Robert Duane & Hively, Will.** The Eternal Darkness: A Personal History of Deep-Sea Exploration. 314p. 2000. 29.95 (*0-691-02740-4*, Pub. by Princeton U Pr) Cal Prin Full Svc.

Ballard, Robert Duane & McConnell, Malcolm. Explorations: My Quest for Adventure & Discovery under the Sea. (Illus.). 416p. (J). 1995. 24.45 (*0-7868-6042-1*, Pub. by Hyperion) Time Warner.

Ballard, Robert Duane & McConnell, Malcolm. Explorations: My Quest for Adventure & Discovery under the Sea. LC 94-48507. (Illus.). 416p. (J). 1996. reprint ed. pap. 14.45 (*0-7868-8181-X*, Pub. by Hyperion) Time Warner.

Ballard, Robert Duane & Moore, J. G. Atlas of the Mid-Atlantic Ridge Rift Valley. (Illus.). 1977. 73.00 (*0-387-90247-3*) Spr-Verlag.

Ballard, Roberta A. Pediatric Care of the ICN Graduate. (Illus.). 368p. 1988. text 75.00 (*0-7216-1404-3*, W B Saunders Co) Harcrt Hlth Sci Grp.

Ballard, Roberta A., jt. auth. see Taeusch, H. William.

Ballard, Robin. Cat & Alex & the Magic Flying Carpet. LC 90-33229. (Illus.). 32p. (J). (ps-1). 1991. 14.95 (*0-06-020389-7*); lib. bdg. 14.89 (*0-06-020390-0*) HarpC Child Bks.

Ballard, Robin. Good-Bye, House. LC 93-252. (Illus.). 24p. (J). (ps-3). 1994. 13.93 (*0-688-12526-3*, Grenwillow Bks) HarpC Child Bks.

— My Day, Your Day. (J). 2001. write for info. (*0-688-17796-4*, Grenwillow Bks); lib. bdg. write for info. (*0-06-029187-7*, Grenwillow Bks) HarpC Child Bks.

Ballard, Robin. Tonight & Tomorrow. LC 98-50789. (Illus.). 24p. (J). (ps-3). 2000. 15.95 (*0-688-16790-X*, Grenwillow Bks) HarpC Child Bks.

— When I Am a Sister. LC 97-6326. (Illus.). 24p. (J). (ps-3). 1998. 15.00 (*0-688-15397-6*, Grenwillow Bks) HarpC Child Bks.

***Ballard, Robin.** When I Am a Sister. LC 97-6326. (Illus.). 24p. (J). (ps-3). 1998. 14.93 (*0-688-15398-4*, Grenwillow Bks) HarpC Child Bks.

Ballard, Robin. When We Get Home. 1999. lib. bdg. write for info. (*0-688-16169-3*, Grenwillow Bks) HarpC Child Bks.

— When We Get Home. LC 98-3446. (Illus.). 24p. (J). (ps-3). 1999. 16.00 (*0-688-16168-5*, Grenwillow Bks) HarpC Child Bks.

Ballard, Roger, ed. Desh Pardesh: The South Asian Presence in Britain. 1996. 36.00 (*81-7018-911-X*, Pub. by BR Pub) S Asia.

Ballard, Ron. When a Father Abandons His Children. (Christian Living Ser.). 1997. pap. 1.59 (*0-87509-596-8*) Chr Pubns.

Ballard, Ronn, jt. auth. see Sandbach, John.

Ballard, Scott. The Complete Guide to Designing Your Own Home. (Illus.). 144p. (Orig.). 1995. pap. 17.99 (*1-55870-334-9*, Betrwy Bks) F & W Pubns Inc.

Ballard, Scott L. Georgia Standards of Appellate Review. Roy, Vijayesh D., ed. LC 95-79340. 200p. 1995. text. write for info. (*0-7620-0003-1*) West Group.

Ballard, Sebastian. Namibia Handbook. (Illus.). 240p. 1997. 19.95 (*0-8442-4905-X*) NTC Contemp Pub Co.

***Ballard, Sebastian.** Namibia Handbook. 2nd ed. LC 98-68295. (Footprint Handbooks Ser.: Vol. 2). (Illus.). 352p. 1999. pap. text 21.95 (*0-8442-2133-3*, 21333, NTC Business Bks) NTC Contemp Pub Co.

— South Africa Handbook 2000: With Lesotho & Swasiland. 4th ed. (Footprints Bks.). 816p. 1999. pap. 22.95 (*0-8442-4810-X*, 4810X, Natl Textbk Co) NTC Contemp Pub Co.

Ballard, Sebastian. South Africa Handbook, 1999. 3rd ed. (Footprint Handbooks Ser.). (Illus.). 816p. (Orig.). 1998. 24.95 (*0-8442-4966-1*) NTC Contemp Pub Co.

— Zimbabwe & Malawi Handbook with Botswana, Mozambique & Zambia. 1997. 19.95 (*0-8442-4912-2*) NTC Contemp Pub Co.

Ballard, Sebastian & Linton, Rupert. South Africa Handbook, 1998: With Lesotho & Swaziland. 2nd ed. (Footprint Handbks.). (Illus.). 816p. 1997. 24.95 (*0-8442-4786-3*, Passprt Bks) NTC Contemp Pub Co.

Ballard, Sebastian & Linton, Rupert, eds. 1997 South Africa Handbook. rev. ed. (Footprint Handbks.). 600p. 1996. 21.95 (*0-8442-4913-0*, Passprt Bks) NTC Contemp Pub Co.

Ballard, Steven. Groundwater Management: Key Poetry Issues. (C). 1989. pap. text 27.50 (*0-8133-7299-2*) Westview.

Ballard, Steven, et al. Innovation Through Technical & Scientific Information: Government & Industry Cooperation. LC 88-18518. 210p. 1989. 62.95 (*0-89930-412-5*, BIA/, Quorum Bks) Greenwood.

Ballard, Steven C. & James, Thomas E., Jr., eds. The Future of the Sunbelt: Managing Growth & Change. LC 83-13890. 241p. 1983. 55.00 (*0-275-90941-7*, C0941, Praeger Pubs) Greenwood.

Ballard, Susan. Fairy Tales from Far Japan. 1972. lib. bdg. 250.00 (*0-87968-477-1*) Krishna Pr.

Ballard, Susan D. Count on Reading Handbook. 1997. pap. text 19.95 (*0-8389-7892-4*) ALA.

Ballard, Terry. Innopac: A Reference Guide to the System. LC 96-185837. 216p. 1995. 39.50 (*1-57387-015-3*) Info Today Inc.

Ballard, Todhunter. Blood & Gold. large type ed. LC 98-48142. 1999. 18.95 (*1-57490-168-0*, Sagebrush LP West) T T Beeler.

— Incident at Sun Mountain. 320p. 1996. reprint ed. mass mkt. 4.99 (*0-8439-3935-4*) Dorchester Pub Co.

***Ballard, Todhunter.** Loco & the Wolf. large type ed. LC 99-46304. 215p. 1999. 21.95 (*0-7838-8793-0*) Mac Lib Ref.

— The Long Trail Back. 1999. 19.00 (*0-7540-8070-6*, Gunsmoke) Chivers N Amer.

Ballard, Todhunter. The Marshal from Deadwood. large type ed. LC 97-40245. (Sagebrush Large Print Westerns Ser.). 1997. lib. bdg. 18.95 (*1-57490-094-3*) T T Beeler.

— Night Riders. large type ed. LC 98-15051. (Sagebrush Large Print Westerns Ser.). 1998. 18.95 (*1-57490-125-7*) T T Beeler.

— Plunder Canyon. large type ed. (Sagebrush Large Print Westerns Ser.). 1996. lib. bdg. 17.95 (*1-57490-048-X*, Sagebrush LP West) T T Beeler.

***Ballard, Todhunter.** Round-Up. large type ed. LC 99-29288. 1999. pap. 20.95 (*0-7838-8650-0*, G K Hall & Co) Mac Lib Ref.

Ballard, Vaughn. Solomon Mangham: His Ancestors & Descendants. (Illus.). 369p. 1989. 45.00 (*0-685-26973-6*) Family Arlington.

Ballardie, Francis W., ed. Autoimmunity in Nephritis. LC 91-35410. 130p. 1992. text 88.00 (*3-7186-5195-5*) Gordon & Breach.

Ballardini, Kerstin & Stjarnlof, Sune, eds. Essentials of Swedish Grammar. (SWE & ENG., Illus.). 160p. 1990. pap. 14.95 (*0-8442-8539-0*, Natl Textbk Co) NTC Contemp Pub Co.

Ballare, Antonia & Lampros, Angelique. Behavior Smart! Ready-to-Use Activities for Building Personal & Social Skills in Grades K-4. LC 93-42750. (Illus.). 224p. 1994. pap. text 27.95 (*0-87628-172-2*) Ctr Appl Res.

Ballarin, Eduard. Commercial Banks Amid the Financial Revolution: Developing a Competitive Strategy. LC 85-23299. 272p. 1986. text 34.95 (*0-88730-081-2*, HarpBusn) HarpInfo.

Ballas, Jack. Apache Blanco. 208p. (Orig.). 1994. mass mkt. 4.50 (*0-515-11452-9*, Jove) Berkley Pub.

— Bandido Caballero. 304p. 1997. mass mkt. 5.99 (*0-425-15956-6*) Berkley Pub.

— Granger's Claim. 1998. mass mkt. 5.99 (*0-425-16453-5*) Berkley Pub.

— Hard Land. 1996. mass mkt. 5.99 (*0-425-15519-6*) Berkley Pub.

— Maverick Guns. 208p. (Orig.). 1993. pap. 4.99 (*0-515-11162-7*, Jove) Berkley Pub.

— Powder River. 208p. 1995. mass mkt. 4.50 (*0-515-11727-7*, Jove) Berkley Pub.

— Rugged Trail, 1 vol. 1999. mass mkt. 5.99 (*0-425-16855-7*) Berkley Pub.

***Ballas, Jack.** Trail Brother. 2000. mass mkt. 5.99 (*0-425-17304-6*) Berkley Pub.

Ballas, Robert, jt. auth. see Ginzburg, Vladimir B.

Ballas, Samir K. Sickle Cell Pain. LC 98-2595. (Progress in Pain Research & Management Ser.: Vol. 11). (Illus.). 389p. 1998. 87.00 (*0-931092-22-1*) Intl Assn Study Pain.

Ballas, Shimon. The Shoes of Tanboury. 40p. 1970. 4.95 (*0-88482-767-4*) Hebrew Pub.

Ballas, Toula, tr. see Dister, Alain.

Ballast, David K. Architect's Handbook of Formulas, Tables & Mathematical Calculations. 544p. (C). 1988. text 60.00 (*0-13-044686-6*, Busn) P-H.

— Architecture Exam Review: Site Planning & Building Design Graphic Divisions. 3rd ed. LC 99-24759. 1999. pap. 38.95 (*1-888577-42-8*) Prof Pubns CA.

— Architecture Exam Review Vol. II: Nonstructural Topics, 4th ed. (Illus.). 452p. 1998. pap. 49.95 (*1-888577-27-4*, AREN3) Prof Pubns CA.

— The Denver Chronicle: From a Golden Past to a Mile-High Future. LC 94-24411. 210p. 1995. pap. 18.95 (*0-88415-201-4*, 5201) Gulf Pub.

— Encyclopedia of Associations & Information Sources for Architects, Designers & Engineers. LC 97-20300. 832p. 1998. text 157.95 (*0-7656-0035-8*, Sharpe Prof) M E Sharpe.

— Handbook of Construction Tolerances. 357p. 1994. 49.50 (*0-07-003553-9*) McGraw.

— Handbook Of Construction Tolerances. (C). 1993. 69.95 (*0-13-374026-9*, Macmillan Coll) P-H.

— Interior Construction & Detailing for Designers & Architects. (Illus.). 398p. 1994. 54.95 (*0-912045-67-1*) Prof Pubns CA.

— Interior Design Reference Manual: A Guide to the NCIDQ Exam. 326p. (Orig.). 1992. pap. 56.95 (*0-912045-41-8*) Prof Pubns CA.

***Ballast, David Kent.** Architecture Exam Review Vol. 1: Structural Topics. 4th ed. (Illus.). 264p. 1999. pap. 46.95 (*1-888577-45-2*, ARES4) Prof Pubns CA.

Ballaster, Ros. Seductive Forms: Women's Amatory Fiction from 1684-1740. 240p. (C). 1992. 55.00 (*0-19-811244-0*) OUP.

— Seductive Forms: Women's Amatory Fiction from 1684-1740. 240p. 1998. reprint ed. pap. text 24.95 (*0-19-818477-8*) OUP.

Ballaster, Ros, et al. Women's Worlds: Ideology, Femininity, & the Woman's Magazine. 196p. (C). 1992. pap. text 15.00 (*0-333-49236-6*) NYU Pr.

Ballaster, Ros, ed. & intro. see Austen, Jane.

Ballaster, Rosalind, ed. see Manley, Delarivier.

Ballata, Phyllis. Writing from Life: Collecting & Connecting. LC 96-38642. 422p. (C). 1997. pap. text 32.95 (*1-55934-555-1*, 1555) Mayfield Pub.

— Writing from Life Instructor's Manual. 107p. (Orig.). (C). 1997. pap. text. write for info. (*1-55934-556-X*, 1556) Mayfield Pub.

Ballato, Arthur, jt. ed. see Gerber, Eduard A.

***Ballator, Nada.** NAEP 1996 Trends in Writing: Fluency & Writing Conventions, Holistic & Mechanics Scores in 1984 & 1996. LC 99-460649. 67p. 1999. pap. 6.00 (*0-16-050042-7*) USGPO.

Ballatore, Ron & Miller, William. Swimming & Aquatics Today. Perlee, Clyde, ed. 227p. (C). 1990. mass mkt. 24.50 (*0-314-50329-3*) West Pub.

Ballatori, N. Toxicology of Metals: Biochemical Aspects, No. 115. Goyer, Robert & Cherian, George M., eds. LC 94-26484. (Illus.). xxii, 467p. 1995. 393.95 (*0-387-58281-9*) Spr-Verlag.

Ballauff, M. Polymer Latexes, Epoxide Resins, Polyampholytes. LC 99-177490. (Advances in Polymer Science Ser.). 212 p. 1998. 149.00 (*3-540-64911-5*) Spr-Verlag.

Ballay. Water Quality International, '94 Pt. 1: Combined Sewer Overflows & Urban Storm Drainage. (Water Science & Technology Ser.). 212p. 1995. pap. 96.50 (*0-08-042547-X*, Pergamon Pr) Elsevier.

Ballay, et al. Water Quality International, '94 Pt. 4: Design & Operation of Wastewater. (Water Science & Technology Ser.: 30). (Illus.). 290p. 1995. pap. 147.00 (*0-08-042549-6*, Pergamon Pr) Elsevier.

— Water Quality International, '94 Pt. 5: Water Quality Management in Central Eastern Europe. (Water Science & Technology Ser.). 280p. 1995. pap. 147.00 (*0-08-042553-4*, Pergamon Pr) Elsevier.

— Water Quality International, '94 Pt. 10: Water Quality Monitoring. (Water Science & Technology Ser.). 304p. 1995. pap. 138.50 (*0-08-042638-7*, Pergamon Pr) Elsevier.

— Water Quality International, '94 Pt. 11: Petrochemical Waste Management. 2nd ed. (Water Science & Technology Ser.: 30). 274p. 1995. pap. 122.50 (*0-08-042632-8*, Pergamon Pr) Elsevier.

— Water Quality International, '94 - WST 30-3 Pt. 3:

An Asterisk (*) at the beginning of an entry indicates that the title is appearing for the first time.

Chemical & Petrochemical Waste Management. (Water Science & Technology Ser.: 30). 290p. 1995. pap. 147.00 (*0-08-042550-X*, Pergamon Pr) Elsevier.

Ballay, D., et al, eds. Water Quality International, '94 Pt. 7: Groundwater Contamination, Environmental Restoration & Diffuse Source Pollution. (Water Science & Technology Ser.: Vol. 30). 184p. 1995. pap. 73.50 (*0-08-042617-4*) Elsevier.

— Water Quality International, '96 Pt. 5: Innovative Treatment Technologies; Membrane Technology. Selected Proceedings of the 18th Biennial Conference of the International Association on Water Quality, Held in Singapore, 23-28 June 1996. (Water Science & Technology Ser.: 34). 270p. 1996. pap. 130.00 (*0-08-043088-0*, Pergamon Pr) Elsevier.

— Water Quality International, '94 Pt. 2: Watermatex 94 - Systems Analysis & Computing in Water Quality Management. (Water Science & Technology Ser.: Vol. 30). 234p. 1994. pap. 107.50 (*0-08-042548-8*, Pergamon Pr) Elsevier.

— Water Quality International, '94 Pt. 6: Nutrient Removal. (Water Science & Technology Ser.: Vol. 30). 378p. 1995. pap. 160.50 (*0-08-042554-2*, Pergamon Pr) Elsevier.

— Water Quality International '96: River Basin Management; Management & Institutional Affairs; Environmental Engineering Education. Selected Proceedings of the 18th Biennial Conference of the International Association on Water Quality, Held in Singapore, 23-28 June 1996. 214p. 1997. pap. 128.00 (*0-08-043092-9*, Pergamon Pr) Elsevier.

— Water Quality International, '96: Wet Weather Pollution Control, Sewage Design, Operation & Maintenance, Instrumentation, Control & Automation, Large Wastewater Treatment Plants, Sludge Management, Cross Media Pollution & Volatile Organic Emissions. (Water Science & Technology Ser.). 594p. 1996. pap. text 258.00 (*0-08-043086-4*, Pergamon Pr) Elsevier.

— Water Quality International, '96 Pt. 1: Nutrient Removal. Selected Proceedings of the 18th Biennial Conference of the International Association on Water Quality, Held in Singapore, 23-28 June 1996. 504p. 1996. pap. 258.50 (*0-08-043081-3*, Pergamon Pr) Elsevier.

— Water Quality International, '96 Pt. 3: Modelling of Activated Sl. 544p. 1996. pap. 255.00 (*0-08-043085-6*, Pergamon Pr) Elsevier.

— Water Quality International, '96 Pt. 4: Environmental Contaminants; Health-Related Water Microbiology; Coastal. 474p. 1996. pap. 258.50 (*0-08-043087-2*, Excerpta Medica) Elsevier.

— Water Quality International, '96 Pt. 6: Chemical, Petrochemical & Hazardous Waste Management. Selected Proceedings of the 18th Biennial Conference of the International Association on Water Quality, Held in Singapore, 23-28 June 1996. 196p. 1997. pap. 130.00 (*0-08-043089-9*, Pergamon Pr) Elsevier.

— Water Quality International, '96 Pt. 7: Agro-Industries Technologies & Waste Stabilization Ponds; Wastewater Reclamation & Reuse. Selected Proceedings of the 18th Biennial Conference of the International Association on Water Quality, Held in Singapore, 23-28 June 1996. (Water Science & Technology Ser.: 34). 270p. 1996. pap. 130.00 (*0-08-043091-0*, Pergamon Pr) Elsevier.

Ballay, D. & IAWQ Programme Committee. Water Quality International, '94 Pt. 9: Special Applications & Emerging Technologies; Specific Pollutants & Treatment Technologies; Water Reuse - Industrial & Municipal Applications. (Water Science & Technology Ser.: Vol. 30). 260p. 1995. 122.50 (*0-08-042630-1*, Pergamon Pr) Elsevier.

Ballay, D., et al. Water Quality International, '94 Pt. 8: Anaerobic Digestion; Sludge Management; Appropriate Technologies. (Water Science & Technology Ser.: Vol. 30). 314p. 1995. 138.50 (*0-08-042629-8*, Pergamon Pr) Elsevier.

Ballbach, Jane & Slater, Jan. Making Career Transitions: Ensuring a Successful Career Change. (Personal Growth & Development Collection). (Illus.). 106p. 1996. pap. 14.95 (*1-883553-79-2*) R Chang Assocs.

Ballbach, Nathan A. The Gooseneck Tidings. LC 75-28578. 1977. 4.50 (*0-918808-01-4*) Northlands MI.

Ballback, Jane & Slater, Jan. Managing Your Career in a Changing Workplace: Taking Control of Your Career. LC 96-85724. (Personal Growth & Development Collection). (Illus.). 123p. 1996. pap. 14.95 (*1-883553-76-8*) R Chang Assocs.

— Marketing Yourself & Your Career: Promoting Your Skills & Accomplishments. LC 96-85830. (Personal Growth & Development Collection). (Illus.). 106p. 1996. pap. 14.95 (*1-883553-78-4*) R Chang Assocs.

— Unlocking Your Career Potential: Fulfilling Your Career Desires. LC 96-85835. (Personal Growth & Development Collection). (Illus.). 118p. (Orig.). 1996. pap. 14.95 (*1-883553-77-6*) R Chang Assocs.

Balle, Michael. Managing with Systems Thinking: Making Dynamics Work for You in Business Decision Making. LC 94-7631. 1994. 21.95 (*0-07-707951-5*) McGraw.

Ballech, Susan & Connelly, Naomi, eds. Buying & Selling Social Care Social Services Policy Forum Paper No. 5: Report of a Seminar Held on 12 November, 1996. 1996. pap. 23.00 (*1-899942-15-7*, Pub. by Natl Inst Soc Work) St Mut.

Ballem, Hugh, tr. see Niosi, Jorge.

Ballem, John B. The Oil & Gas Lease in Canada. LC 72-75734. 344p. reprint ed. pap. 106.70 (*0-608-16539-5*, 202635600049) Bks Demand.

— The Oil & Gas Lease in Canada. 2nd ed. LC 86-221667. 363p. 1985. text 75.00 (*0-8020-2550-1*) U of Toronto Pr.

Ballen, Kate, jt. auth. see Shimm, Patricia H.

Ballendorf, Dirk A., jt. auth. see Bartlett, Merrill L.

Ballendorf, Dirk A., jt. auth. see Wuerch, William L.

Ballendorf, Dirk A., ed. see Wang, Chih.

Ballenger, Bruce & Lane, Barry. Discovering the Writer Within: 40 Days to More Imaginative Writing. 192p. 1996. pap. 15.99 (*0-89879-739-X*, Wrtrs Digest Bks) F & W Pubns Inc.

Ballenger, Bruce G. Ballengers of Tryon. LC 96-86205. (Illus.). 300p. 1996. 42.00 (*0-9653773-0-X*) B G Ballenger.

Ballenger, Bruce P. Curious Researcher. 2nd ed. LC 97-19428. 352p. 1997. pap. text 20.00 (*0-205-27328-9*) P-H.

— The Curious Researcher: A Guide to Writing Research Papers. 2nd rev. ed. 340p. 1998. pap. text 23.00 (*0-205-29702-1*) Allyn.

Ballenger, Craig. Shasta's Headwaters: An Angler's Guide to the Upper Sacramento & McCloud Rivers. LC 99-174959. 160p. 1998. pap. 19.95 (*1-57188-136-0*) F Amato Pubns.

Ballenger, Cynthia. Teaching Other People's Children: Literacy & Learning In A Bilingual Classroom, Vol. 8. LC 98-47545. 8. 120p. 1998. pap. 17.95 (*0-8077-3789-5*) Tchrs Coll.

Ballenger, Cynthia. Teaching Other People's Children: Literacy & Learning in a Bilingual Classroom. LC 98-47545. (Practioner Inquiry Ser.). 120p. 1999. text 38.00 (*0-8077-3790-9*) Tchrs Coll.

Ballenger, James C., ed. Biology of Agoraphobia. LC 84-6157. (Clinical Insights Ser.). 125p. reprint ed. pap. 38.80 (*0-8357-7823-1*, 203619600002) Bks Demand.

— Clinical Aspects of Panic Disorder. (Frontiers of Clinical Neuroscience Ser.). 342p. 1990. 325.00 (*0-471-56694-2*) Wiley.

Ballenger, John J. Diseases of the Nose, Throat, Ear, Head & Neck. 14th ed. LC 90-6143. (Illus.). 1376p. 1991. text 199.50 (*0-8121-1345-4*) Lppncott W & W.

Ballenger, John J. & Snow, James B., eds. Otorhinolaryngology: Head & Neck Surgery. 15th rev. ed. LC 95-7241. (Illus.). 1296p. 1996. 179.00 (*0-683-00315-1*) Lppncott W & W.

***Ballenger, John Jacob.** Otolaryngology Head & Neck Surgery. 16th ed. 2002. pap. 236.00 (*0-7693-0172-X*, Pub. by Singular Publishing) Thomson Learn.

— Otolaryngology Head & Neck Surgery Pocket Manual. 16th ed. 2002. pap. 64.00 (*0-7693-0173-8*, Pub. by Singular Publishing) Thomson Learn.

***Ballenger, Lee.** The Outpost War: The U. S. Marine Corps in Korea, 1952. LC 99-86415. 2000. 24.95 (*1-57488-241-4*) Brasseys.

Ballenger, Sally, jt. auth. see Taylor, Joyce.

Ballenger, Seale. Hell's Belles Vol. 1: A Tribute to the Spitfires, Bad Seeds & Steel Magnolias of the New & Old South. LC 97-14776. (Illus.). 304p. 1997. pap. 14.95 (*1-57324-096-6*) Conari Press.

***Ballenger, Seale.** Hell's Belles Vol. 1: A Tribute to the Spitfires, Bad Seeds & Steel Magnolias of the New & Old South. 288p. 1999. 7.98 (*1-56731-308-6*, MJF Bks) Fine Comms.

Ballenger, Sharon. Adventures of the Ballenger Bears. (Illus.). 62p. (Orig.). (J). (ps-6). 1992. spiral bd. 11.95 (*1-880734-00-1*) SharLew Ent.

Ballentine, David J., Jr., et al. Acoustic Wave Sensors: Theory, Design & Physico-Chemical Applications. LC 96-21931. (Applications of Modern Acoustics Ser.). (Illus.). 436p. 1996. text 85.00 (*0-12-077460-7*) Acad Pr.

Ballentine, George. Your Voice in Speech or Song. (Illus.). 64p. 1999. reprint ed. 19.95 (*0-938075-24-1*) Ocean View Bks.

Ballentine, Henry A., jt. auth. see Sherman, Francis T.

Ballentine, J. Gregory. Equity, Efficiency, & the U. S. Corporation Income Tax. LC 79-26226. (AEI Studies: No. 263). 119p. reprint ed. pap. 36.90 (*0-8357-4473-6*, 203732000008) Bks Demand.

Ballentine, Kathryn. California Family Law Trial Preparation Handbook. iv, 116p. 1998. ring bd. 75.00 (*0-932663-96-6*) CA Fam Law.

Ballentine, Lee. Dream Protocols. (Illus.). 96p. (Orig.). 1992. 19.95 (*0-9626708-2-0*); pap. 9.95 (*0-9626708-1-2*) Talisman IN.

— Dream Protocols. deluxe limited ed. LC 92-2846. (Illus.). (Orig.). 1992. 59.95 (*0-938075-50-0*) Ocean View Bks.

— Phase Language. 80p. (Orig.). 1995. pap. 8.95 (*1-880766-07-8*) Pantograph Pr.

— Phase Language. deluxe limited ed. LC 94-36984. 96p. (Orig.). 1995. 59.95 (*0-938075-62-4*) Ocean View Bks.

— Renounce the Emerald Piety. 8p. 1999. pap. 5.00 (*0-938075-76-4*) Ocean View Bks.

Ballentine, Lee, ed. Poly: New Speculative Writing. LC 87-19827. (Illus.). 336p. 1989. 59.95 (*0-938075-08-X*); pap. 24.95 (*0-938075-05-5*) Ocean View Bks.

Ballentine, Martha. Himalayan Mountain Cookery: A Vegetarian Cookbook. LC 84-29055. (Illus.). 203p. 1976. spiral bd. 12.95 (*0-89389-015-4*) Himalayan Inst.

Ballentine, R. Diet & Nutrition: A Holistic Approach. LC 78-110274. (Illus.). 634p. (C). 1978. pap. 19.95 (*0-89389-048-0*) Himalayan Inst.

***Ballentine, R., ed.** Joints & Glands Exercises I. unabridged ed. 1999. pap. text 9.95 incl. audio (*0-89389-172-X*) Himalayan Inst.

Ballentine, Richard. Ultimate Bicycling. 192p. 1992. 35.00 (*0-385-25318-4*) Doubleday.

***Ballentine, Rudolph.** Radical Healing: Integrating the World's Great Therapeutic Traditions to Create a New Transformation. 2000. pap. 17.00 (*0-609-80484-7*, Three Riv Pr) Crown Pub Group.

Ballentine, Rudolph. Transition to Vegetarianism: An Evolutionary Step. LC 87-23618. (Illus.). 300p. 1999. pap. 16.95 (*0-89389-175-4*) Himalayan Inst.

Ballentine, Rudolph M. Radical Healing: Integrating the World's Great Therapeutic Traditions to Create a New Transformative Medicine. LC 98-28802. (Illus.). 640p. 1999. 27.50 (*0-609-60137-7*) Harmony Bks.

Ballentine, Rudolph M., ed. The Theory & Practice of Meditation. 2nd ed. LC 86-9802. 165p. 1986. pap. 12.95 (*0-89389-075-8*) Himalayan Inst.

Ballentine, Rudolph M., ed. see Himalayan International Institute Staff.

Baller, F. W. The Sacred Edict of K'ang Hsi. LC 79-89636. 1979. 18.00 (*0-915032-25-2*) Natl Poet Foun.

Baller, F. W. The Sacred Edict of K'ang Hsi. LC 79-89636. 1979. pap. 14.95 (*0-915032-28-7*) Natl Poet Foun.

Baller, Karen. Beginning with Me. LC 98-7818. 91p. 1998. pap. 3.95 (*1-56212-355-6*) CRC Pubns.

***Ballerini, Andrea & Rota, Luciana.** Extreme Diving. (Illus.). 128p. 2000. pap. 22.50 (*0-7893-0510-0*) Universe.

Ballerini, Julia, jt. auth. see Castle, Ted.

Ballerini, Luigi. The Cadence of the Neighboring Tribe, Vol. 92. (Sun & Moon Classics Ser.). 120p. 1997. pap. text 10.95 (*1-55713-327-1*) Sun & Moon CA.

— Che Figurato Muore. Harrison, Thomas J., tr. from ITA. LC 78-58982. 1986. 12.95 (*0-915570-11-4*) Oolp Pr.

— La Linea Longobarda. (Stanford French & Italian Studies: Vol. 82). (ITA.). 125p. (Orig.). 1996. pap. 56.50 (*0-915838-48-6*) Anma Libri.

Ballerini, Luigi, et al, eds. The Promised Land: Italian Poetry after 1975, Vol. 156. (Sun & Moon Classics Ser.). 1999. pap. text 25.95 (*1-55713-316-6*, Pub. by Sun & Moon CA) Consort Bk Sales.

Ballerini, Luigi, tr. see Giuliani, Alfredo, ed.

Ballerstedt, Elke & Glatzer, Wolfgang. Soziologischer Almanach. (GER.). 616p. (C). 1982. text 37.50 (*3-593-32419-9*) Irvington.

Ballester, Gonzalo Forrente. Los Anos Indecisos. 1999. pap. text 9.95 (*84-08-02814-6*) Planeta.

Ballester, Gonzalo T. Gozos y las Sombras, Vol. 2. 496p. 1991. pap. 18.95 (*0-7859-5173-3*) Fr & Eur.

— Gozos y las Sombras, Vol. 3. 1991. pap. 18.95 (*0-7859-5171-7*) Fr & Eur.

— Gozos y las Sombras: El Senor Ilega, Vol. 1. 464p. 1991. pap. 18.95 (*0-7859-5174-1*) Fr & Eur.

— The King Amaz'd: A Chronicle. Smith, Colin, tr. LC 96-172575. 320p. 1996. pap. 7.95 (*0-460-87730-5*, Everyman's Classic Lib) Tuttle Pubng.

Ballester, Mariano. Introduction to Profound Prayer. Lane, Bethany, tr. from ITA. LC 97-1543. 120p. (Orig.). 1997. pap. text 9.95 (*0-8146-2430-8*, Liturg Pr Bks) Liturgical Pr.

Ballester y Marquez, Jose A., jt. auth. see Gray, Robin F.

Ballestero, Carl. How High My Mountain. 344p. 1992. pap. 14.95 (*0-9633118-0-8*) C Ballestero Pub.

Ballestero, Enrique & Romero, Carlos. Multiple Criteria Decision Making & Its Applications to Economic Problems. LC 98-36003. 1998. write for info. (*0-7923-8238-2*) Kluwer Academic.

Ballesteros, A., et al. Stability & Stabilization of Biocatalysts: Proceedings of an International Symposium. LC 98-31093. (Progress in Biotechnology Ser.). 1998. 316.00 (*0-444-82970-9*) Elsevier.

Ballesteros, Antonio M. Tres Farsas Contemporaneas y un Secuestro. Maroto, Angel R. & Whitehead, Charles E., eds. (Orig.). (YA). (gr. 10-12). 1980. pap. text 5.95 (*0-88334-125-5*) Longman.

Ballesteros, Isolina. Escritura Feminina y Discurso Autobiografico en la Nueva Novela Espanola. LC 93-14188. (American University Studies II, Romance Language & Literature: Vol. 207). (SPA.). VIII, 202p. (C). 1994. text 39.95 (*0-8204-2250-9*) P Lang Pubng.

Ballesteros, M. & Alborg, J. L. Historia Universal, 2 vols. 5th ed. (SPA., Illus.). 1094p. 1993. 150.00 (*84-249-3003-7*) Elliots Bks.

Ballesteros, Maria D., jt. auth. see Ballesteros, Octavio A.

Ballesteros, Octavio A. & Ballesteros, Maria D. Mexican Sayings: The Treasure of a People. (ENG & SPA., Illus.). 95p. 1992. 14.95 (*0-89015-810-X*) Sunbelt Media.

Ballesteros, S., jt. auth. see Shepp, Bryan E.

Ballesteros, Seve & Andrisani, John. Natural Golf. (Illus.). 240p. 1991. reprint ed. pap. 16.95 (*0-02-048361-9*) Macmillan.

Ballesteros, Soledad, ed. Cognitive Approaches to Human Perception. LC 93-6805. 304p. 1994. 69.95 (*0-8058-1043-9*) L Erlbaum Assocs.

Ballestrem, K. G. Russian Philosophical Terminology. (Sovietica Ser.: No. 19). (ENG, FRE, GER & RUS.). 117p. 1965. lib. bdg. 119.00 (*90-277-0036-2*) Kluwer Academic.

— Die Sowjetische Erkenntnismetaphysik und ihr Verhaeltnis zu Hegel. (Sovietica Ser.: No. 27). (GER.). 189p. 1968. lib. bdg. 132.50 (*90-277-0037-0*) Kluwer Academic.

Ballestrero, Anastasio. Martha & Mary: Meeting Christ As Friend. 118p. 1996. pap. 22.00 (*0-85439-483-4*, Pub. by St Paul Pubns) St Mut.

Ballet, Arthur H., ed. Playwrights for Tomorrow, Vol. 13. LC 66-19124. 314p. pap. 97.40 (*0-8357-6527-X*, 203589600013) Bks Demand.

— Playwrights for Tomorrow: A Collection of Plays, 5. LC 66-19124. 166p. 1969. reprint ed. pap. 51.50 (*0-608-08307-0*, 205583800005) Bks Demand.

— Playwrights for Tomorrow: A Collection of Plays, 6. LC 66-19124. 148p. 1969. reprint ed. pap. 45.90 (*0-608-08308-9*, 205583800006) Bks Demand.

— Playwrights for Tomorrow: A Collection of Plays, Vol. 1. LC 66-19124. 280p. 1966. reprint ed. pap. 86.80 (*0-8357-6528-8*, 203589600001) Bks Demand.

— Playwrights for Tomorrow: A Collection of Plays, Vol. 3. LC 66-19124. 352p. reprint ed. pap. 109.20 (*0-8357-6529-6*, 203589600003) Bks Demand.

— Playwrights for Tomorrow: A Collection of Plays, Vol. 4. LC 66-19124. 349p. reprint ed. pap. 108.20 (*0-8357-6530-X*, 203589600004) Bks Demand.

— Playwrights for Tomorrow: A Collection of Plays, Vol. 7. LC 66-19124. 221p. reprint ed. pap. 68.60 (*0-8357-6531-8*, 203589600007) Bks Demand.

— Playwrights for Tomorrow: A Collection of Plays, Vol. 8. LC 66-19124. 220p. reprint ed. pap. 68.20 (*0-8357-6532-6*, 203589600008) Bks Demand.

— Playwrights for Tomorrow: A Collection of Plays, Vol. 9. LC 66-19124. 216p. reprint ed. pap. 67.00 (*0-8357-6533-4*, 203589600009) Bks Demand.

— Playwrights for Tomorrow: A Collection of Plays, Vol. 10. LC 66-19124. 201p. reprint ed. pap. 62.40 (*0-8357-6534-2*, 203589600010) Bks Demand.

— Playwrights for Tomorrow: A Collection of Plays, Vol. 11. LC 66-19124. 237p. reprint ed. pap. 73.50 (*0-8357-6525-3*, 203589600011) Bks Demand.

— Playwrights for Tomorrow: A Collection of Plays, Vol. 12. LC 66-19124. 274p. reprint ed. pap. 85.00 (*0-8357-6526-1*, 203589600012) Bks Demand.

Ballet Caravan, Inc. Staff. Dance Index Vols. 1-7: Nos. 7, 8; Jan. 1942 to Aug. 1948. 1971. 42.95 (*0-405-00791-4*, 11312) Ayer.

Balletta, Patricia W. The Wilkinson Book: Being the Ancestry & Descendants of Major General James Wilkinson of Calvert Co., MD et ux, Ann Biddle of Philadelphia, PA. (Illus.). 530p. 1994. text 85.00 (*0-9640893-2-7*) P W W Balletta.

Ballew, Arlette C., jt. auth. see Pfeiffer, J. William.

***Ballew, Bill.** Tough Enough to Be Vikings: Minnesota's Purple Pride from A to Z. (Illus.). 256p. 1999. 26.95 (*0-9670393-0-4*) Old Norse Pub.

Ballew, Julius R. & Mink, George. Case Management in Social Work: Developing the Professional Skills Needed for Work with Multiproblem Clients. 2nd ed. LC 96-15866. (Illus.). 334p. 1996. text 55.95 (*0-398-06659-0*); pap. text 41.95 (*0-398-06660-4*) C C Thomas.

Ballew, K. M., tr. see Valenzuela, Luisa.

Ballew, Scott. Managing IP Networks with Cisco Routers. Loukides, Michael, ed. LC 97-223524. 352p. (Orig.). 1997. reprint ed. pap. 34.95 (*1-56592-320-0*) OReilly & Assocs.

Ballew, William. Openstep Programming: Step Two - A New Foundation. 400p. 1997. 44.95 (*0-387-94144-4*) Spr-Verlag.

Ballew, William & Eatherly, Denise. OpenStep Programming. 1997. 49.95 incl. disk (*0-614-20325-2*) Spr-Verlag.

Ballew-Wood, Juanita. Wooden Images: Misericords & Medieval England. LC 98-36202. 184p. 1999. 55.00 (*0-8386-3779-5*) Fairleigh Dickinson.

Balley, A. Peter & Slade, Edith J. Harlem Today: A Cultural & Visitors Guide. 2nd ed. (Illus.). 72p. 1998. pap. text 7.00 (*0-7881-5228-9*) DIANE Pub.

Ballhagen, J. Kid's Pumpkin Fun. (Illus.). 176p. (J). 1997. spiral bd. 5.95 (*1-57166-105-0*) Hearts N Tummies.

Ballhatchet, H. & Kaiser, S. Teach Yourself Japanese: A Complete Course for Beginners. (ENG & JPN., Illus.). 348p. 1994. pap. 9.95 (*0-8442-3807-4*, Teach Yrslf) NTC Contemp Pub Co.

— Teach Yourself Japanese Complete, Set 2. (JPN.). 348p. 1995. pap. 19.95 incl. audio (*0-8442-3868-6*, Teach Yrslf) NTC Contemp Pub Co.

Ballhatchet, H. & Kaiser, Stefan. Teach Yourself Japanese. (Teach Yourself Ser.). 1992. 15.95 (*0-8288-8368-8*); 45.00 incl. audio (*0-8288-8370-X*) Fr & Eur.

Ballhatchet, Kenneth. Caste, Class & Catholicism in India, 1789-1914. LC 98-193093. (SOAS London Studies on South Asia: Vol. 17). 288p. 1998. text 48.00 (*0-7007-1095-7*, Pub. by Curzon Pr Ltd) UH Pr.

Ballhaus, W. F. & Hussaini, M. Yousuff. Advances in Fluid Dynamics. (Illus.). x, 315p. 1989. 98.95 (*0-387-97163-7*, 3533) Spr-Verlag.

Ballhaus, William F. A Nation in Trouble & Many Didn't Care. LC 96-28196. (Illus.). 224p. 1996. 24.95 (*0-9653066-0-7*) W F Ballhaus.

Ballico, E., et al, eds. Classification of Irregular Varieties: Minimal Models & Abelian Varieties. (Lecture Notes in Mathematics Ser.: Vol. 1515). (Illus.). 149p. 1992. 37.95 (*0-387-55295-2*) Spr-Verlag.

Ballico, E. & Ciliberto, Ciro. Algebraic Curves & Projective Geometry. (Lecture Notes in Mathematics Ser.: Vol. 1389). v, 288p. 1989. 41.95 (*0-387-51509-7*, 3437) Spr-Verlag.

Ballico, E., ed. see Colliot-Thelene, J. L., et al.

Ballico, Edoardo. Projective Geometry with Applications. LC 94-27247. (Lecture Notes in Pure & Applied Mathematics Ser.: Vol. 166). (Illus.). 256p. 1994. pap. text 125.00 (*0-8247-9278-5*) Dekker.

Ballie, Kate. Provence & the Cote D'Azur. 4th ed. 576p. 1999. pap. 17.95 (*1-85828-420-1*, Pub. by Rough Guides) Penguin Putnam.

Balliet & Armstrong-West. Shaping a Life: Douglass College First Year Course 090:101. 2nd ed. 132p. (C). 1997. per. 29.95 (*0-7872-4284-5*) Kendall-Hunt.

Balliet & Fitzgerald. Frommer's Irreverent Guide to Chicago. 2nd ed. (Frommer's Irreverent Guides Ser.). 224p. 1998. 12.95 (*0-02-862572-2*) Macmillan.

Balliet, jt. auth. see Rutgers University Staff.

***Balliet & Fitzgerald Staff.** Irreverent Guide to Chicago. 3rd ed. (Irreverent Guides Ser.). (Illus.). 2000. pap. 12.99 (*0-7645-6230-4*, Frommer) Macmillan Gen Ref.

— Irreverent Guide to New Orleans. 3rd ed. (Irreverent Guides Ser.). (Illus.). 2000. pap. 12.99 (*0-7645-6226-6*, Frommer) Macmillan Gen Ref.

Balliet & Fitzgerald Staff. Miami. (Edge Guide to . . . Ser.). 256p. 1999. pap. 14.00 (*1-56352-519-4*) Longstreet.

— New Orleans. (Edge Guide to . . . Ser.). 256p. 1999. pap. 14.00 (*1-56352-520-8*) Longstreet.

Balliet & Fitzgerald Staff, ed. see Fitzgerald, F. Stop.

Balliet, Barbara. Women, Culture & Society. (C). 1998. pap. text. write for info. (*0-393-96889-8*) Norton.

B

B

— Women, Culture & Society. (C). 1998. pap., teacher ed. write for info. (*0-393-96890-1*) Norton.

Balliet, Barbara & Armstrong-West, Suzan. Shaping a Life: Douglass College First Year Course. 250p. (C). 1996. pap. text, per. 29.95 (*0-7872-2793-5*) Kendall-Hunt.

Balliet, Conrad A. W. B. Yeats: A Census of the Manuscripts. LC 89-17226. 498p. 1990. text 20.00 (*0-8240-6629-4*, 772) Garland.

Balliet, Edgar, jt. auth. see Balliet, Gay.

Balliet, Emil. Acts: To the Ends of the Earth. (Spiritual Discovery Ser.). 124p. 1996. pap., teacher ed. 9.95 (*0-88243-212-5*, 02-0212); pap., student ed. 4.95 (*0-88243-112-9*, 02-0112) Gospel Pub.

Balliet, Gay & Balliet, Edgar. Touched by All Creatures: Doctoring Animals in the Pennsylvania Dutch Country. LC 98-66169. (Illus.). 340p. (YA). 1999. 25.95 (*0-88282-169-5*) New Horizon NJ.

Balliet, Gay L. Henry Miller & Surrealist Metaphor: Riding the Ovarian Trolley. (Modern American Literature Ser.: Vol. 3). XIV, 187p. (C). 1996. text 45.95 (*0-8204-2831-0*) P Lang Pubng.

***Balliet, Gay L.** Lowell: The True Story of an Existential Pig. LC 99-75938. (Illus.). 260p. 2000. 23.95 (*0-88282-193-8*) New Horizon NJ.

Balliet, Gay L. Such Agreeable Friends. 266p. (Orig.). 1987. pap. write for info. (*0-910119-33-3*) SOCO Pubns.

Balliet, L. Dow. The Day of Wisdom According to Number Vibration. 188p. 1996. reprint ed. spiral bd. 16.00 (*0-7873-0066-7*) Hlth Research.

Balliet, Lee. Survey of Labor Relations. 2nd ed. LC 87-864. 224p. 1987. reprint ed. pap. 69.50 (*0-608-00709-9*, 206148200009) Bks Demand.

Balliett & Fitzgerald, Inc. Staff. Edge Atlanta. LC 98-66367. (Edge Guide to . . . Ser.: Vol. 1). 192p. 1998. pap. 14.00 (*1-56352-517-8*) Longstreet.

— Edge Austin. LC 98-66368. (Edge Guide to . . . Ser.: Vol. 2). 247p. 1998. pap. 14.00 (*1-56352-518-6*) Longstreet.

Balliett, Blue. The Ghosts of Nantucket: Twenty-Three True Accounts. LC 84-70015. (Illus.). 128p. (Orig.). 1984. pap. 9.95 (*0-89272-191-X*) Down East.

— Nantucket Hauntings: Twenty-One Firsthand Encounters with the Supernatural. LC 90-81834. 176p. 1990. pap. 10.95 (*0-89272-279-7*) Down East.

Balliett, Dee & Balliett, Gene. Your Financial Plan. LC 97-69079. 1997. pap. 29.95 (*0-9636537-1-7*) PCI-Prof Comm.

Balliett, Deo & Balliett, Gene. Your Financial Plan Is a Vision of Riches. (Illus.). viii, 268p. 1998. pap. 29.95 (*0-9636537-2-5*) PCI-Prof Comm.

***Balliett, Fitzgerald.** Frommer's Irreverent Guide to Boston. 3rd ed. (Frommer's Irreverent Guides Ser.). (Illus.). 240p. 2000. pap. 12.99 (*0-7645-6228-2*) IDG Bks.

— Frommer's Irreverent Guide to Walt Disney World. 3rd ed. (Frommer's Irreverent Guides Ser.). (Illus.). 272p. 2000. pap. 12.99 (*0-7645-6229-0*) IDG Bks.

Balliett, Gene. Make Your Kid Rich: A Financial Guide for the Whole Family. 201p. (Orig.). 1993. pap. 12.95 (*0-9636537-0-9*) PCI-Prof Comm.

Balliett, Gene, jt. auth. see Balliett, Dee.

Balliett, L. Dow. The Day of Wisdom According to Number Vibration (1917) 188p. 1996. reprint ed. pap. 15.95 (*1-56459-848-9*) Kessinger Pub.

— How to Attain Success Through the Strength of Vibration of Numbers (1913) 82p. 1996. reprint ed. pap. 12.95 (*1-56459-901-9*) Kessinger Pub.

— Nature's Symphony: Lessons in Number Vibration. 127p. 1996. reprint ed. spiral bd. 11.50 (*0-7873-0068-3*) Hlth Research.

—Nature's Symphony, 1911: Lessons in Number Vibration. 127p. 1996. reprint ed. pap. 10.95 (*1-56459-649-4*) Kessinger Pub.

— Number Vibration in Questions & Answers. 104p. 1983. pap. 9.00 (*0-89540-139-8*, SB-139) Sun Pub.

— The Philosophy of Numbers: Their Tone & Colors. 165p. 1996. reprint ed. spiral bd. 15.00 (*0-7873-0067-5*) Hlth Research.

— Vibration: A System of Numbers As Taught by Pythagoras. 80p. 1983. pap. 7.00 (*0-89540-138-X*, SB-138) Sun Pub.

— Vibration: How to Attain Success Through the Strength of Vibration. 81p. 1996. reprint ed. spiral bd. 12.50 (*0-7873-1182-0*) Hlth Research.

Balliett, Whitney. Alec Wilder & His Friends. LC 82-1467. (Roots of Jazz Ser.). (Illus.). 205p. 1983. reprint ed. lib. bdg. 27.50 (*0-306-76153-X*) Da Capo.

— American Musicians II: Seventy-One Portraits in Jazz. LC 96-21232. 528p. 1996. 39.95 (*0-19-509538-3*) OUP.

— American Musicians II: Seventy-Two Portraits in Jazz. (Illus.). 528p. 1998. reprint ed. pap. 18.95 (*0-19-512116-3*) OUP.

***Balliett, Whitney.** Collected Works on Jazz 1957-1998. (Illus.). 352p. 2000. text 35.00 (*0-312-20288-1*) St Martin.

Balliett, Will. Trucker's Road Atlas. 1990. pap. 16.95 (*0-13-931104-1*) P-H.

Balliett, Will, ed. The Little Book of Fishing: An Anthology. LC 93-46760. (Illus.). 160p. 1994. 16.00 (*0-87113-568-X*, Atlntc Mnthly) Grove-Atltic.

***Balliett, Will & Dyja, Thomas, eds.** The Hard Way: Writing by the Rebels Who Changed Sports. LC 99-23962. (Illus.). 360p. 1999. pap. 16.95 (*1-56025-230-8*, Thunders Mouth) Avalon NY.

Balliett, Will & Fitzgerald, F-Stop. Trucker's Road Atlas. 208p. 1992. pap. 16.95 (*0-13-948241-5*, H M Gousha) Prntice Hall Bks.

Balliett, Will, jt. auth. see McDonald, George.

Balliett, Will, ed. see Fitzgerald, F-Stop.

Ballieux, Rudy E., jt. ed. see Fauci, Anthony S.

***Ballif, Michelle.** Seduction, Sophistry & the Woman with the Rhetorical Figure. LC 99-86609. (Rhetorical Philosophy & Theory Ser.). 2001. write for info. (*0-8093-2333-8*) S Ill U Pr.

Ballif, Michelle, jt. auth. see Moran, Michael G.

Ballim, Afzal & Wilks, Yorick. Artificial Believers: The Ascription of Belief. 288p. 1991. text 69.95 (*0-8058-0453-6*) L Erlbaum Assocs.

Ballin, Albert. The Deaf Mute Howls. LC 98-38153. (Gallaudet Classics in Deaf Studies). (Illus.). 112p. 1998. pap. 18.95 (*1-56368-073-4*) Gallaudet Univ Pr.

Ballin, Amy, et al. Trash Conflicts: A Science & Social Studies Curriculum on the Ethics of Disposal. (Illus.). 220p. (Orig.). 1993. pap. 28.00 (*0-942349-06-7*) Eductrs Soc Respons.

Ballin, Enid, jt. auth. see Deng, Dean Y.

Ballin, Hartmut. Satsanga Veda. 128p. 1996. write for info. (*0-9649408-0-9*) Trillenium Pubng.

Ballin-Smith, Beverley, ed. Howe: Four Millenia of Orkney Prehistory. (Society of Antiquaries of Scotland, Monograph Ser.: No. 9). (Illus.). 292p. 1994. pap. 58.00 incl. mic. film (*0-903903-09-1*, Pub. by Soc Antiquaries) David Brown.

Ballinder, Peter, ed. see Bach, Johann Sebastian.

Balling, Adalbert L. Fundamentals Structural Analys. 2000. 76.74 (*0-07-234550-0*) McGraw.

Balling, Frederick J. Sister Carrie Notes. (Cliffs Notes Ser.). 104p. 1967. pap. 4.95 (*0-8220-1201-4*, Cliff) IDG Bks.

Balling, L. Christian. A Game of Pawns. Brady, Upton, ed. LC 85-47785. 324p. 1985. 15.95 (*0-685-10490-7*) Little.

— Revelation. 48p. 1999. mass mkt. 6.99 (*0-8125-7177-0*, Pub. by Forge NYC) St Martin.

— Revelation. LC 97-34390. 1998. text 24.95 (*0-312-86314-4*) St Martin.

Balling, Michael, ed. see Wagner, Richard.

Balling, Morten, et al, eds. Corporate Governance, Financial Markets & Global Convergence. LC 97-38341. 368p. 1998. lib. bdg. 154.00 (*0-7923-4825-7*) Kluwer Academic.

Balling, Robert C., Jr. The Heated Debate: Greenhouse Predictions vs. Climate Reality. LC 91-29747. (Bureaucracy vs. the Environment Ser.). (Illus.). 250p. 1992. 21.95 (*0-936488-47-6*); pap. 14.95 (*0-936488-48-4*) PRIPP.

Balling, Robert C., Jr. & Nasrallah, Hassan A. The Heated Debate: Greenhouse Predictions vs. Climate Reality, Middle Eastern Edition. LC 94-46524. 194p. 1995. 21.95 (*0-936488-68-9*) PRIPP.

Balling, Robert C., Jr., jt. auth. see Michaels, Patrick J.

Balling, Robert C., Jr., jt. auth. see Williams, Martin A. J.

Ballingall, Peter. The DK Pocket Guide to Golf Drills & Practices. deluxe ed. (Illus.). 128p. 1995. pap. 18.95 (*0-7894-0193-2*, 6-70507) DK Pub Inc.

— Learn Golf in a Weekend. 95p. 1991. 16.00 (*0-394-58747-2*) Knopf.

Ballinger, Anne & Patchett, Stephen. Pocket Essentials of Clinical Medicine. 2nd ed. LC 99-23407. (Illus.). 600p. 1998. pap. write for info. (*0-7020-2289-6*) W B Saunders.

— Saunder's Pocket Essentials of Clinical Medicine. (Illus.). 547p. 1995. pap. text 27.00 (*0-7020-1921-6*, Pub. by W B Saunders) Saunders.

Ballinger, Barbara. Bathrooms. (For Your Home Ser.). 72p. 1995. pap. 12.95 (*1-56799-281-1*, Friedman-Fairfax) M Friedman Pub Grp Inc.

***Ballinger, E., et al, eds.** Environmental Assessment in Countries in Transition. 208p. (C). 2000. pap. 32.00 (*963-9116-92-0*) Ctrl Europ Univ.

Ballinger, Elizabeth. Dog Training & Communication: A Guide to a More Compatible Relationship with Your Dog. (Illus.). 80p. (Orig.). 1987. pap. text 4.00 (*0-614-32321-2*, Classc Pub) Marciel Pub & Print.

— The Magic Bird. (Illus.). 64p. (J). (gr. 3-5). 1994. pap. 6.95 (*1-879331-45-4*, Classc Pub) Marciel Pub & Print.

— Prairie Stories of the West. (Illus.). 124p. (Orig.). (J). (gr. k-8). 1993. reprint ed. pap. text 8.95 (*1-879331-39-X*, Classc Pub) Marciel Pub & Print.

— To Be a Clown. 96p. (J). (gr. 5-8). 1994. pap. 7.95 (*1-879331-44-6*, Classc Pub) Marciel Pub & Print.

— Training Your Dog: A Guide to a More Compatible Relationship. 120p. 1983. pap. write for info. (*0-318-57590-6*) Old Farm Ken.

Ballinger, Erich. Detective Dictionary: A Handbook for Aspiring Sleuths. LC 93-11882. (Late-Night Library). (Illus.). 144p. (YA). (gr. 5 up). 1994. lib. bdg. 19.93 (*0-8225-0721-8*, Lerner Publctns) Lerner Pub.

— The Learning Gym. (Illus.). 29p. 1996. pap. 9.95 (*0-942143-09-4*) Edu-Kinesthetics.

— Monster Manual: A Complete Guide to Your Favorite Creatures. LC 93-34219. (Late-Night Library). (Illus.). 144p. (YA). (gr. 5 up). 1994. lib. bdg. 19.93 (*0-8225-0722-6*, Lerner Publctns) Lerner Pub.

— Monster Manual: A Complete Guide to Your Favorite Creatures. (Illus.). 144p. (J). (gr. 5-9). 1997. reprint ed. pap. text 8.95 (*0-8225-9771-3*) Lerner Pub.

Ballinger, Jack T. Chemical Operator's Portable Handbook. 496p. 1999. pap. 54.95 (*0-07-006369-9*) McGraw.

Ballinger, Jack T., jt. auth. see Shugar, Gershon J.

Ballinger, James K. Beyond the Endless River: Western American Drawings & Watercolors of the Nineteenth Century. LC 78-59557. (Illus.). 181p. (Orig.). 1979. pap. 12.00 (*0-910407-23-1*) Phoenix Art.

Ballinger, James K. & Horton, Tonia L. Peter Hurd: Insight to a Painter. 84p. 1983. pap. 10.00 (*0-910407-02-9*) Phoenix Art.

Ballinger, James K., jt. auth. see Library of American Art Staff.

Ballinger, James K., ed. see Hildreth, Jean C.

Ballinger, Jim. Singalong with Sherlock Holmes. (Illus.). 276p. 1995. pap. 24.00 (*0-9695673-7-5*, Pub. by Grg A Vanderburgh) Battered Silicon.

Ballinger, K., et al. EEG Technician Curriculum: EEG 110, 111, 112, 114, 120. 515p. (C). 1994. ring bd. write for info. (*0-933195-76-1*) CA College Health Sci.

***Ballinger, Keith.** Fundamentals of COM & DCOM. 400p. 2000. pap. text 49.99 (*0-13-013984-X*) P-H.

***Ballinger, Lee.** Lynyrd Skynyrd: An Oral History. 256p. 1999. pap. 13.50 (*0-380-80154-X*, Avon Bks) Morrow Avon.

Ballinger, Pamela. Claim-Making & Large Scale Historical Processes in the Late Twentieth Century. 41p. 1997. pap. 5.00 (*0-935371-46-X*) CFISAC.

Ballinger, Peter. Fantasia: Fantasia for Charney Manor for Four Viols. (Charney Manor Ser.: Vol. CM008). ii, 15p. (Orig.). 1995. pap. text 10.00 (*1-56571-125-4*) PRB Prods.

— Trio for Viole da Gamba: Opus 3. (Contemporary Consort Ser.: No. 8). i, 22p. 1989. pap. text 10.00 (*1-56571-011-8*) PRB Prods.

— Variations for Pianoforte. (Contemporary Keyboard Ser.: No. 3). 7p. 1990. pap. text 6.00 (*1-56571-016-9*) PRB Prods.

Ballinger, Peter, ed. see Bach, Johann Sebastian.

Ballinger, Peter, ed. see Brahms, Johannes.

Ballinger, Peter, ed. see Pepping, Ernst.

Ballinger, Peter, ed. see Salvatore, Giovanni.

Ballinger, Philip W. Merrill's Atlas of Radiographic Positions & Radiologic Procedures. 9th ed. LC 98-52916. (Illus.). 608p. 1999. text 67.00 (*0-8151-2651-4*, 31649) Mosby Inc.

— Merrill's Atlas of Radiographic Positions & Radiologic Procedures, 3. 9th ed. (Illus.). 400p. 1999. text 67.00 (*0-8151-2653-0*, 31651) Mosby Inc.

— Merrill's Atlas of Radiographic Positions & Radiologic Procedures, Set. 9th ed. (Illus.). 1696p. 1999. text 169.00 (*0-8151-2650-6*, 31648) Mosby Inc.

— Merrill's Atlas of Radiographic Positions & Radiologic Procedures, Vol.2. 9th ed. LC 98-52916. (Illus.). 688p. 1999. text 67.00 (*0-8151-2652-2*, 31650) Mosby Inc.

Ballinger, Philip W. Merrill's Atlas-Radiographic Positions & Radiologic Procedures. 8th ed. 1995. teacher ed. write for info. (*0-8151-6219-7*) Mosby Inc.

Ballinger, Philip W. Pocket Guide to Radiography. 3rd ed. LC 95-6295. (Illus.). 400p. (C). (gr. 13). 1995. spiral bd. 22.95 (*0-8151-0401-4*, 24273) Mosby Inc.

***Ballinger, Phillip A.** Poem as Sacrament: The Theological Aesthetic of Gerard Manley Hopkins. 272p. 2000. pap. text 30.00 (*0-8028-4737-4*) Eerdmans.

Ballinger, Raymond A. Layout & Graphic Design. LC 72-90309. 96 p. 1970. write for info. (*0-289-79634-2*) SVista Bks.

Ballinger, Rex E., ed. see Usigli, Rodolfo.

Ballinger, Rex E., ed. see Zunzunegui, Juan A.

Ballinger, Richard A. A Treatise on the Property Rights of Husband & Wife, under the Community or Ganancial System: Adapted to the Statutes & Decisions of Louisiana, Texas, California, Nevada, Washington, Idaho, Arizona & New Mexico. xiii, 543p. 1981. reprint ed. lib. bdg. 85.00 (*0-8377-0320-4*, Rothman) W S Hein.

Ballinger, Rodolfo, ed. see Visigli, R.

Ballinger, Royce E., et al. Amphibians & Reptiles. 240p. (C). 1983. text. write for info. (*0-697-04786-5*, WCB McGr Hill) McGrw-H Hghr Educ.

Ballington, Don A. Pharmacy Practice for Technicians. LC 98-27634. 377p. 1998. 27.95 (*0-7638-0099-6*); teacher ed. write for info. (*0-7638-0100-3*); wbk. ed. write for info. (*0-7638-0098-8*) Paradigm MN.

Ballington, Don A. & Laughlin, Mary M. Pharmacology for Technicians. LC 98-11383. 1998. write for info. (*0-7638-0096-1*) Paradigm MN.

Ballington, Don A. & Laughlin, Mary M. Pharmacology for Technicians: Instructor's Guide. text 14.00 (*0-7638-0097-X*) EMC-Paradigm.

Ballington, Don A. & Laughlin, Mary M. Pharmacy Math for Technicians. LC 98-9872. 1998. 27.44 (*0-7638-0101-1*) Paradigm MN.

Ballington, Don A. & Laughlin, Mary M. Pharmacy Math for Technicians: Instructor's Guide. text, teacher ed. 14.00 (*0-7638-0102-X*) EMC-Paradigm.

Balliro, Lenore. Riding Bicycles in the Rain. Sherman, Alana & DeGennaro, Lorraine, eds. 20p. (Orig.). 1993. pap. 5.00 (*0-939689-16-2*) Alms Hse Pr.

Ballis, George Elfie, ed. Dream What We Can Become & Rejoice: Sonar Lo Que Podemos Ser y Gozar. deluxe ed. (Illus.). 18p. 1995. ring bd. (*1-930023-02-2*) Food & Land Fndt.

Ballis, Pamela M. Diary in Poetry. 1997. pap. write for info. (*1-57553-516-5*) Watermrk Pr.

Ballis, Peter H. Leaving the Adventist Ministry. LC 98-33607. (Religion in the Age of Transformation Ser.). 256p. 1999. 59.95 (*0-275-96229-6*, Praeger Pubs) Greenwood.

Ballister, Barry. Barry Ballister's Fruit & Vegetable Stand. (Illus.). 496p. 1990. pap. 15.95 (*0-87951-363-2*, Pub. by Overlook Pr) Penguin Putnam.

— Barry Ballister's Fruit & Vegetable Stand: A Complete Guide to the Selection, Preparation & Nutrition of Fresh Produce. LC 86-43061. (Illus.). 432p. 1987. 29.95 (*0-87951-272-5*, Pub. by Overlook Pr) Penguin Putnam.

Ballister-Howells, Pegi. New Jersey Gardener's Guide: The What, Where, When, How & Why of Gardening in New Jersey. (Illus.). 400p. 1998. pap. 19.95 (*1-888608-47-1*) Cool Springs Pr.

Ballistocardiograph Research Society Staff. Ballistocardiography - Research & Computer Diagnosis: Proceedings of the Ballistocardiograph Research Society, 16th Annual Meeting, Atlantic City, 1972. Franke, E. K., ed. (Bibliotheca Cardiologica Ser.: No. 32). (Illus.). 160p. 1973. pap. 36.75 (*3-8055-1376-3*) S Karger.

— Ballistocardiography & Clinical Studies: Proceedings of the Ballistocardiograph Research Society, 14th Annual Meeting, Atlantic City, 1970. Harrison, W. K., ed. (Bibliotheca Cardiologica Ser.: No. 27). 1971. pap. 21.75 (*3-8055-1188-4*) S Karger.

— Circulatory Assist & Ballistocardiographic Studies: Proceedings of the Ballistocardiograph Research Society Annual Meeting, 15th, Atlantic City, 1971. Jackson, D. H., ed. (Bibliotheca Cardiologica Ser.: No. 29). 1972. pap. 34.00 (*3-8055-1323-2*) S Karger.

— Ultrasound & Ballistocardiography in Cardiovascular Research: Proceedings of the Ballistocardiography & Cardiovascular Dynamics Congress, 3rd World, 9th European, Sofia, 1973. Baan, Jan, ed. (Bibliotheca Cardiologica Ser.: No. 34). (Illus.). 120p. 1974. 47.00 (*3-8055-1763-7*) S Karger.

Ballistocardiography & Cardiovascular Dynamics Con. Ballistocardiographic Methods & Cardiovascular Dynamics: Proceedings of the Ballistocardiography & Cardiovascular Dynamics Congress, 3rd World, 9th European Sofia, 1973. Talakov, A., ed. (Bibliotheca Cardiologica Ser.: No. 33). 300p. 1975. pap. 121.00 (*3-8055-1701-7*) S Karger.

Ballivy, Gerard, ed. The Pressuremeter & Its New Avenues: Proceedings of the 4th International Symposium, 17-19 May 1995, Sherbrooke, Quebec, Canada. (Illus.). 502p. (C). 1995. text 149.00 (*90-5410-545-3*, Pub. by A A Balkema) Ashgate Pub Co.

Ballman, Ray E. The How & Why of Home Schooling. expanded rev. ed. LC 95-7422. 176p. 1995. pap. 10.99 (*0-89107-859-2*) Crossway Bks.

***Ballman, Swanee.** Tamarind, 4 vols. 1999. pap. 11.95 (*0-9628733-4-9*, Pub. by Legacy Pub FL) BookWorld.

Ballmann, Doug, ed. see McBride, William E.

Ballmann, Josef. Continuum Mechanics with Applications. (Engineering Mathematics Ser.). 352p. 1999. 95.00 (*0-8493-8511-3*) CRC Pr.

Ballmann, Werner. Lectures on Spaces of Nonpositive Curvature. LC 95-38397. (DMV Seminar Ser.: Vol. 25). 112p. 1995. pap. 32.00 (*3-7643-5242-6*) Birkhauser.

— Lectures on Spaces of Nonpositive Curvature. (DMV Seminar Ser.: Vol. 25). 1995. 32.00 (*0-8176-5242-6*) Birkhauser.

Ballmer, T. T. & Brennenstuhl, W. Speech Art Classification. (Language & Communication Ser.: Vol. 8). (Illus.). 274p. 1980. 46.95 (*0-387-10294-9*) Spr-Verlag.

Ballmer, Thomas T. Biological Foundations of Linguistic Communication: Towards a Biocybernetics of Language. (Pragmatics & Beyond Ser.: Vol. III, No. 7). x, 161p. (Orig.). 1983. pap. 52.00 (*90-272-2520-6*) J Benjamins Pubng Co.

Ballmer, Thomas T., ed. Linguistic Dynamics: Discourses, Procedures & Evolution. (Research in Text Theory Ser.: Vol. 9). (Illus.). viii, 366p. 1985. 146.15 (*3-11-010115-7*) De Gruyter.

Ballner, Maryjean. Cat Massage. LC 97-7596. 1997. pap. 10.95 (*0-312-15492-5*) St Martin.

***Ballner, Maryjean.** Dog Massage: A Whiskers-to-Tail Guide to Your Dog's Ultimate Massage Experience. LC 00-40259. (Illus.). 2000. write for info. (*0-312-26727-4*) St Martin.

Ballocchi, S., jt. ed. see Scarpioni, L. L.

Balloch, Sue. Working in the Social Services. 1995. pap. 75.00 (*0-902789-98-8*, Pub. by Natl Inst Soc Work) St Mut.

Ballola, Giovanni C., ed. see Rossini, Gioachino.

***Ballon, Hilary.** Louis le Vau: Mazarin's Collaege, Colbert's Revenge LC 99-25747. 1999. write for info. (*0-691-04895-9*) Princeton U Pr.

Ballon, Hilary. The Paris of Henri IV: Architecture & Urbanism. (Illus.). 304p. 1991. 48.00 (*0-262-02309-1*) MIT Pr.

— The Paris of Henri IV: Architecture & Urbanism. (Illus.). 378p. 1994. pap. text 24.00 (*0-262-52197-0*) MIT Pr.

***Ballon, Hillary.** Louis Le Vau: Mazarin's College, Colbert's Revenge. LC 99-25747. 1999. 45.00 (*0-691-00186-3*, Pub. by Princeton U Pr) Cal Prin Full Svc.

Ballon, Rachel F. The Writer's Sourcebook: From Writing Blocks to Writing Blockbusters. 272p. 1996. 26.00 (*1-56565-466-8*) Lowell Hse.

Ballon, Robert J. Foreign Competition in Japan: Human Resource Strategies. (Illus.). 192p. (C). (gr. 13). 1991. pap. 78.95 (*0-415-06980-7*, A6549) Thomson Learn.

Ballonoff, Paul. Energy: Ending the Never-Ending Crisis. LC 97-42891. 224p. 1997. 18.95 (*1-882577-45-0*); pap. text 9.95 (*1-882577-46-9*) Cato Inst.

Balloon. Vroom Vroom: Sports Cars. (J). 1998. 9.95 (*0-8069-9555-6*) Sterling.

— Vroom Vroom: Work Vehicles. (J). 1998. 9.95 (*0-8069-9557-2*) Sterling.

Balloon Books Staff. Dictionary for 2-Year-Olds. (Tiny the Mouse Dictionaries Ser.). 1999. 4.95 (*0-8069-5933-9*) Sterling.

— Dictionary for 1-Year-Olds. (Tiny the Mouse Dictionaries Ser.). 1999. 4.95 (*0-8069-5932-0*) Sterling.

— Dictionary for 3-Year-Olds. (Tiny the Mouse Dictionaries Ser.). 1999. 4.95 (*0-8069-5934-7*) Sterling.

— Dictionary for 4-Year-Olds. (Tiny the Mouse Dictionaries Ser.). 1999. 4.95 (*0-8069-5935-5*) Sterling.

— Division. (Play & Learn Ser.). 1999. pap. text 3.95 (*0-8069-7825-2*) Sterling.

***Balloon Books Staff.** First Words Coloring Book. (Illus.). (J). 2000. pap. 2.95 (*0-8069-2661-9*); pap. 2.95 (*0-8069-2663-5*) Sterling.

Balloon Books Staff. Fun Learning for 3- & 4-Year-Olds. (Tiny the Mouse Fun Learning Ser.). 1999. pap. text 4.95 (*0-8069-3940-0*) Sterling.

— Fun Learning for 4- & 5-Year-Olds. (Tiny the Mouse Fun Learning Ser.). 1999. pap. text 4.95 (*0-8069-3938-9*) Sterling.

— Go to Sleep: Book & Doll. 1999. pap. text 6.95 (*0-8069-5925-8*) Sterling.

An Asterisk (*) at the beginning of an entry indicates that the title is appearing for the first time.

— Let's Go: Book & Doll. 1999. pap. text 6.95 (*0-8069-5926-6*) Sterling.
— Make a Doll House. 1999. pap. text 5.95 (*0-8069-3792-0*) Sterling.
— Multiplication. 1999. pap. text 3.95 (*0-8069-7823-6*) Sterling.
— Sticker Book for 5-Year-Olds: Reusable Stickers. 1999. pap. text 3.95 (*0-8069-5761-1*) Sterling.
***Balloon Books Staff.** Sticker Book for 3-Year-Olds: Reusable Stickers. 1999. pap. text 3.95 (*0-8069-5751-4*) Sterling.
Balloon Books Staff. Sticker Book for 2-Year-Olds: Reusable Stickers. 1999. pap. text 3.95 (*0-8069-5936-3*) Sterling.
— Sticker Book for 4-Year-Olds: Reusable Stickers. 1999. pap. text 3.95 (*0-8069-5759-X*) Sterling.
Ballor, Ginny & Newmann, Carrie, eds. Playmates. 40p. (Orig.). 1997. pap. 3.00 (*1-882294-23-8*) Green Gate.
Ballor, Ginny, jt. ed. see Neumann, Carrie.
Ballor, Ginny, jt. ed. see Newmann, Carrie.
Ballor, Ginny, ed. see Schmidt, Rosemary.
Ballor, Ginny L. & Neumann, Carrie. Candy Apple Red. 40p. (Orig.). 1993. pap. 3.00 (*1-882294-13-0*) Green Gate.
Ballor, Ginny L. & Neumann, Carrie, eds. Autumn's Frailties. 40p. (Orig.). (C). 1996. pap. 3.00 (*1-882294-15-7*) Green Gate.
— Midnight Garden. 40p. (Orig.). (C). 1996. pap. 3.00 (*1-882294-14-9*) Green Gate.
— A Paler Shade of White. 40p. (Orig.). (C). 1996. pap. 3.00 (*1-882294-18-1*) Green Gate.
— Pensive Thoughts. 40p. (Orig.). (C). 1996. pap. 3.00 (*1-882294-16-5*) Green Gate.
Ballor, Ginny L., ed. see Gilliland, Brian.
Ballor, Ginny L., ed. see Haskin, Connie.
Ballor, Ginny L., ed. see Hay, C. David.
Ballor, Ginny L., ed. see Henson, Grant E.
Ballor, Ginny L., jt. ed. see Neumann, Carrie.
Ballor, Ginny L., ed. see Wise, Norma.
Ballord, Esek S. Ballord. Some of the Descendants of Zaccheus Ballord, a Private in the Revolutionary War; Also in the Last French & Indian War. 74p. 1997. reprint ed. pap. 15.00 (*0-8328-7361-6*); reprint ed. lib. bdg. 25.00 (*0-8328-7360-8*) Higginson Bk Co.
Ballot, Christian. Density of Prime Divisors of Linear Recurrences. LC 95-2679. (Memoirs Ser.: Vol. 115/551). 102p. 1995. pap. 34.00 (*0-8218-2610-7*, MEMO/115/551) Am Math.
Ballot, Michael. Labor-Management Relations in a Changing Environment. 2nd ed. LC 95-35394. 656p. 1995. text 95.95 (*0-471-11185-6*) Wiley.
Ballou, A. History of the Town of Milford, from Its First Settlement to 1881, 2 pts., Pt. 2. (Illus.). 646p. 1989. reprint ed. lib. bdg. 65.00 (*0-8328-0564-5*) Higginson Bk Co.
— History of the Town of Milford, from Its first Settlements to 1881, 2 pts., Pt. 1. (Illus.). 511p. 1989. reprint ed. lib. bdg. 52.00 (*0-8328-0563-7*) Higginson Bk Co.
Ballou, Adin. Autobiography of Adin Ballou, 1803-1890. Heywood, William S., ed. LC 74-26603. (American Utopian Adventure Ser.). (Illus.). xviii, 586p. 1975. reprint ed. lib. bdg. 57.50 (*0-87991-033-X*) Porcupine Pr.
— Christian Non-Resistance in All Its Important Bearings, Illustrated & Defended. LC 76-137527. (Peace Movement in America Ser.). 240p. 1972. reprint ed. lib. bdg. 29.95 (*0-89198-054-7*) Ozer.
— An Elaborate History & Genealogy of the Ballous in America. (Illus.). 1338p. 1988. reprint ed. pap. 166.00 (*0-8328-0175-5*); reprint ed. lib. bdg. 176.00 (*0-8328-0174-7*) Higginson Bk Co.
— History of the Hopedale Community: From its Inception to its Virtual Submergence in the Hopedale Parish. Heywood, W. S., ed. LC 76-187467. (American Utopian Adventure Ser.). xvii, 415p. 1972. reprint ed. lib. bdg. 49.50 (*0-87991-007-0*) Porcupine Pr.
— History of the Hopedale Community, from Its Inception to Its Virtual Submergence in the Hopedale Parish. Heywood, William S., ed. LC 72-2935. (Communal Societies in America Ser.). reprint ed. 37.50 (*0-404-10701-X*) AMS Pr.
— Practical Christian Socialism. LC 72-2936. (Communal Societies in America Ser.). reprint ed. 61.50 (*0-404-10702-8*) AMS Pr.
— Practical Christian Socialism, 2 vols. 655p. 1985. reprint ed. lib. bdg. 79.00 (*0-932051-86-3*) Rprt Serv.
Ballou, Dale & Podgursky, Michael. Teacher Pay & Teacher Quality. LC 96-39941. (C). 1997. text 35.00 (*0-88099-177-1*) W E Upjohn.
Ballou, Dale & Podgursky, Michael J. Teacher Pay & Teacher Quality. LC 96-39941. (C). 1997. pap. text 17.00 (*0-88099-176-3*) W E Upjohn.
Ballou, David, ed. Essays in Biochemistry Vol. 34: Metalloproteins. (Essays in Biochemistry Ser.: No. 33). 200p. 1998. pap. text 30.50 (*1-85578-106-9*, Pub. by Portland Pr Ltd) Ashgate Pub Co.
***Ballou, David P.** Metalloproteins. (Essays in Biochemistry Ser.: Vol. 34). 180p. 2000. pap. text 29.95 (*0-691-05048-1*) Princeton U Pr.
Ballou, David P., jt. auth. see Ninfa, Alexander J.
Ballou, Glen M. Handbook for Sound Engineers: The New Audio Encyclopedia. 2nd ed. LC 98-153928. 1506p. 1991. 120.00 (*0-240-80331-0*, Focal) Buttrwrth-Heinemann.
Ballou, H. S. Starr: Early Starrs in Kent & New England. (Illus.). 140p. 1992. reprint ed. pap. 23.00 (*0-8328-2739-8*); reprint ed. lib. bdg. 33.00 (*0-8328-2738-X*) Higginson Bk Co.
Ballou, J. D., et al, eds. Population Management for Survival & Recovery. LC 94-25126. (Methods & Cases in Conservation Science Ser.). (Illus.). 512p. 1995. 72.00 (*0-231-10176-7*); pap. 32.50 (*0-231-10177-5*) Col U Pr.
Ballou, John E., ed. Radiation & the Lymphatic System: Proceedings. LC 75-38685. (ERDA Symposium Ser.). 265p. 1976. pap. 14.50 (*0-87079-030-7*, CONF-740930); fiche 9.00 (*0-87079-317-9*, CONF-740930) DOE.
Ballou, Mary, ed. Psychological Interventions: A Guide to Strategies. LC 95-6939. 232p. 1995. 59.95 (*0-275-94851-X*, Praeger Pubs) Greenwood.
Ballou, Mary & Gabalac, Nancy W. A Feminist Position on Mental Health. 190p. 1985. 37.95 (*0-398-05040-6*); pap. 25.95 (*0-398-06013-4*) C C Thomas.
Ballou, Mary, jt. ed. see Brown, Laura S.
Ballou, Maturin M. Aztec Land (1890) 370p. 1998. reprint ed. pap. 27.95 (*0-7661-0574-1*) Kessinger Pub.
— Due South, Cuba, Past & Present. LC 72-91661. 316p. 1969. reprint ed. lib. bdg. 59.50 (*0-8371-2071-3*, BAD&) Greenwood.
— History of Cuba: Or Notes of a Traveler in the Tropics. LC 70-161756. (Illus.). reprint ed. 31.50 (*0-404-00488-1*) AMS Pr.
Ballou, Patricia K. Women: A Bibliography of Bibliographies. 2nd ed. (Reference Bks. - Women's Studies). 349p. 1986. 40.00 (*0-8161-8729-0*, Hall Reference) Macmillan.
Ballou, Ralph. Badminton for Beginners. 2nd ed. (Health Sciences Ser.). (Illus.). 112p. (C). 1997. pap. text 16.95 (*0-89582-395-0*) Wadsworth Pub.
Ballou, Robert O. The Portable World Bible. (Portable Library). 1977. pap. 15.95 (*0-14-015005-6*, Penguin Bks) Viking Penguin.
Ballou, Robert O., ed. see James, William.
Ballou, Ronald H. Business Logistics Management: Planning, Organizing, & Controlling the Supply Chain. 4th ed. LC 97-52254. 681p. 1998. 100.00 (*0-13-795659-2*) P-H.
Ballou, Tim & Higgins, Linda. The O'Dooles of Reseda: A Year in the Life of America's Most Dysfunctional Family. 224p. 1995. pap. 14.95 (*0-8065-1609-7*, Citadel Pr) Carol Pub Group.
Ballough, Charles A. The Power That Heals. 62p. 1996. reprint ed. spiral bd. 9.00 (*0-7873-0069-1*) Hlth Research.
— The Power That Heals & How to Use It. 1991. lib. bdg. 79.00 (*0-8490-4545-2*) Gordon Pr.
Ballow, Mark, ed. IVIG Therapy Today. LC 91-20896. (Illus.). 160p. 1992. 99.50 (*0-89603-223-X*) Humana.
Ballow, Willard. Billy the Kid: A Graphic History. LC 98-96331. x, 188 p. 1998. write for info. (*0-9666381-0-7*) Owlhoot Trail.
Balls, Ashley. Law Firms Managing for Profit. 152p. 1998. pap. 39.00 (*1-86287-280-5*, Pub. by Federation Pr) Gaunt.
Balls, Edward K. Early Uses of California Plants. (California Natural History Guides Ser.: No. 10). (Illus.). (Orig.). 1962. pap. 11.95 (*0-520-00072-2*, Pub. by U CA Pr) Cal Prin Full Svc.
Balls, M., ed. see British Society for Developmental Biology Staff.
Balls, M., jt. ed. see Van Zutphen, L. F.
Balls, Michael. Animals & Alternatives in Toxicology: Present Status & Future Prospects. 390p. 1991. 95.00 (*1-56081-511-6*, Wiley-VCH) Wiley.
Balls, Michael, ed. Animals & Alternatives in Toxicology Present Status & Future Prospects. 1991. 125.00 (*0-471-19929-X*) Wiley.
Balls, Michael, et al. Animals & Alternatives in Toxicity Testing. 1983. text 104.00 (*0-12-077480-1*) Acad Pr.
***Balls, Michael, et al.** Progress in the Reduction, Refinement & Replacement of Animal Experimentation. LC 00-42978. (Developments in Animal & Veterinary Science Ser.). (Illus.). 2000. write for info. (*0-444-50529-6*) Elsevier.
Balls, Michael, jt. ed. see Fentem, Julia.
Balls Organista, Pamela & Chun, Kevin M., eds. Readings in Ethnic Psychology. LC 97-44675. 432p. (C). (gr. 13). 1998. 80.00 (*0-415-91962-2*) Routledge.
Balls-Organista, Pamela & Chun, Kevin M., eds. Readings in Ethnic Psychology. LC 97-44675. 384p. (C). (gr. 13). 1998. pap. 29.99 (*0-415-91963-0*) Routledge.
Ballsey, B. Things on the Net Newt Wouldn't Want You to See. (Illus.). 160p. (Orig.). 1996. pap. 8.95 (*1-887652-28-0*) Off Color Pr.
Ballstadt, Carl, ed. The Search for English-Canadian Literature: An Anthology of Critical Articles from the Nineteenth & Early Twentieth Centuries. LC 75-15779. (Literature of Canada, Poetry & Prose in Reprint Ser.: No. 16). 263p. reprint ed. pap. 81.60 (*0-608-12792-2*, 202349000033) Bks Demand.
Ballstadt, Carl, et al, eds. Letters of Love & Duty: The Correspondence of Susanna & John Moodie. LC 92-95697. 360p. 1993. text 35.00 (*0-8020-5708-X*) U of Toronto Pr.
— Susanna Moodie: Letters of a Lifetime. (Illus.). 400p. 1993. pap. 19.95 (*0-8020-7385-9*) U of Toronto Pr.
Ballstadt, Carl, et al. Susanna Moodie: Letters of a Lifetime. 400p. 1985. 35.00 (*0-8020-2580-3*) U of Toronto Pr.
Ballstadt, Carl, ed. see Traill, Catharine Parr.
***Ballton, Lula Bailey.** Sittin' Around Bein' Brown. LC 00-90214. 2000. pap. 7.95 (*0-533-13499-4*) Vantage.
Balluffi, R. W., jt. auth. see Sutton, A. P.
Ballve, Faustino. Essentials of Economics: A Brief Survey of Principles & Policies. 3rd ed. LC 97-61136. 108p. 1997. pap. 9.95 (*1-57246-069-5*) Foun Econ Ed.
Ballweber, Hettie L. Archaeology! LC 95-25618. (Illus.). 74p. (J). (gr. 4-12). 1996. 14.75 (*0-917882-42-3*); pap. 9.95 (*0-917882-43-1*) MD Hist Pr.
***Ballweg, Judy K.** KI Pix Digital Gallery: Cameras, Scanners & Computers. (Illus.). 120p. (J). (gr. k-2). 2000. spiral bd. 26.95 (*1-56484-156-1*) Intl Society Tech Educ.
— Kid Pix ABC: Art, Books & Computers. (Illus.). 150p. (J). (gr. k-2). 2000. spiral bd. 25.95 (*1-56484-155-3*) Intl Society Tech Educ.
Ballweg, Mary Lou, jt. auth. see Endometriosis Association Staff.
Ballweg, Ruth, et al, eds. Physician Assistant: A Guide to Clinical Practice. LC 93-12579. 1994. pap. text. write for info. (*0-7216-4586-0*, W B Saunders Co) Harcrt Hlth Sci Grp.
***Ballweg, Ruth, et al.** Physician Assistant: A Guide to Clinical Practice. 2nd ed. Sullivan, Edward M. & Kuhn, Shirley, eds. LC 98-24848. (Illus.). 860p. (C). 1999. text 69.00 (*0-7216-7653-7*) Harcourt.
Bally, A. W., ed. Seismic Expression of Structural Styles: A Picture & Work Atlas, Vol. 3. (Studies in Geology: No. 15). (Illus.). ix, 388p. 1996. ring bd. 44.00 (*0-614-00768-2*) Fodors Travel.
Bally, A. W., et al, eds. Dynamics of Plate Interiors. LC 80-28968. (Geodynamics Ser.: Vol. 1). 168p. 1980. 20.00 (*0-87590-508-0*, G00100) Am Geophysical.
Bally, A. W. & Palmer, A. R., eds. Geology of North America: An Overview. (DNAG, Geology of North America Ser.: Vol. A). (Illus.). 629p. 1989. 35.00 (*0-8137-5207-8*) Geol Soc.
Bally, Charles, ed. see De Saussure, Ferdinand.
Bally, G. V. & Greguss, P. Optics in Biomedical Sciences: Graz Austria, 1981 Proceedings. (Optical Sciences Ser.: Vol. 31). (Illus.). 274p. 1982. 73.95 (*0-387-11666-4*) Spr-Verlag.
Bally, G. Von, see Dirksen, D. & Von Bally, G., eds.
Bally, Gert Von, see Von Bally, Gert, ed.
Bally, Scott J., jt. ed. see Moseley, Mary J.
Balm, Paul H. M. Stress Physiology in Animals. 1999. write for info. (*0-8493-9741-3*) CRC Pr.
Balm, A. J. & Kroon, B. B., eds. Cutaneous Head & Neck Melanoma: Diagnosis & Treatment. (Journal: Diagnostic Oncology: Vol. 3, No. 5, 1994). (Illus.). 58p. 1994. pap. 23.50 (*3-8055-6000-1*) S Karger.
Balm, Donald S., jt. auth. see Grossman, William.
Balm, Paul H., ed. Stress Physiology in Animals Vol. 2: Sheffield Biological Sciences. (Sheffield Biological Sciences Ser.: Vol. 2). 288p. 1999. write for info. (*1-85075-908-1*, Pub. by Sheffield Acad) CUP Services.
Balm, Roger. Malta. LC 95-42380. (American Geographical Society Around the World Program Ser.). 1996. 18.95 (*0-939923-58-0*); pap. 13.95 (*0-939923-57-2*) M & W Pub Co.
***Balmaceda, Margarita, ed.** On the Edge: Ukrainian-Central European-Russian Security Triangle. 300p. (C). 2000. 49.95 (*963-9116-80-7*) Ctrl Europ Univ.
Balmain, Aleksandr. Napoleon in Captivity: Reports of Count Balmain Russian Commissioner on the Island of St. Helena 1816-1820. Park, Julian, ed. & tr. by. LC 72-160955. (Select Bibliographies Reprint Ser.). 1977. reprint ed. 25.95 (*0-8369-5822-5*) Ayer.
Balmain, Julianne. The Queen's Amulet. (Illus.). 24p. 1999. 12.95 (*0-8118-2462-4*) Chronicle Bks.
Balmain, Julianne, jt. auth. see Traig, Jennifer.
***Balmain, Lydia.** No Doctors, Please. large type ed. 320p. 2000. pap. 20.99 (*1-85389-905-4*, Dales) Ulverscroft.
Balmain, Lydia. Surgeon in the Snow. large type ed. (Magna Romance Ser.). 250p. 1992. 27.99 (*0-7505-0400-5*) Ulverscroft.
— Theatre of Love. large type ed. 328p. 1993. 27.99 (*0-7505-0471-4*) Ulverscroft.
Balmain, Melissa. Just Us: Adventure Travels of a Mother & Daughter. LC 97-43688. (Illus.). 208p. 1998. 24.95 (*0-571-19948-8*) Faber & Faber.
Balman, F. E. & Dolan, A. G. Labour Employment in Private Forestry in England & Wales till 1976. 1983. 60.00 (*0-7855-7180-9*) St Mut.
Balmand, Pascal. Histoire de la France. (FRE.). 445p. 1992. pap. 42.95 (*2-218-03170-1*, Pub. by Ed Hatier) Hatier Pub.
Balmary, Marie. Psychoanalyzing Psychoanalysis: Freud & the Hidden Fault of the Father. LC 81-18568. 208p. reprint ed. pap. 64.50 (*0-7837-2194-3*, 204253200004) Bks Demand.
Balmas, Enea. Dictionnaire Francais-Italien, Italien-Francais. (FRE & ITA.). 1993. write for info. (*0-7859-7617-5*, 2010206541) Fr & Eur.
Balmaseda, Charlie, ed. see Gonzalez, Orlando.
Balme, Christopher B. Decolonizing the Stage: Theatrical Syncretism & Post-Colonial Drama. LC 98-36573. (Illus.). 328p. 1999. text 85.00 (*0-19-818444-1*) OUP.
Balme, D. M., ed. & tr. see Aristotle.
Balme, D. M., tr. & notes see Aristotle.
***Balme, Maurice & Morwood, James.** Latin Course Part I. 2nd ed. (Oxford Latin Course Ser.). (Illus.). 160p. (C). 1999. text 24.95 (*0-19-521550-8*) OUP.
— Latin Course Part II. 2nd ed. (Oxford Latin Course Ser.). (Illus.). 176p. (C). 1999. text 24.95 (*0-19-521551-6*) OUP.
— Latin Course Part III. 2nd ed. (Oxford Latin Course Ser.). (Illus.). 224p. (C). 1999. text 25.95 (*0-19-521552-4*) OUP.
— Oxford Latin Course Cassette II: Recordings for Part III & the Reade. (Oxford Latin Course Ser.). (C). 1999. audio 19.95 (*0-19-840562-6*) OUP.
Balme, Maurice & Morwood, James. Oxford Latin Reader, Pt. IV. 2nd ed. LC 97-189694. (Oxford Latin Course Ser.). (Illus.). 256p. (C). 1997. pap. text 22.95 (*0-19-521209-6*); pap. text, teacher ed. 15.95 (*0-19-912233-4*) OUP.
Balme, Maurice G. The Millionaire's Dinner Party: An Adaptation of the Cena Trimalchionis of Petronius. (Illus.). 96p. 1974. pap. text 18.95 (*0-19-912025-0*) OUP.
Balme, Maurice G. & Lawall, Gilbert. Athenaze, Vol. 1. 128p. (C). 1990. pap. text, teacher ed. 16.95 (*0-19-506384-8*) OUP.
— Athenaze, Vol 2. rev. ed. 144p. (C). 1991. pap. text, teacher ed. 16.95 (*0-19-506930-7*, 9056) OUP.
— Athenaze: An Introduction to Ancient Greek, Vol. 1. rev. ed. (Illus.). 288p. (C). 1990. pap. text 21.95 (*0-19-505621-3*) OUP.
— Athenaze: An Introduction to Ancient Greek, Vol. 2. rev. ed. (Illus.). 312p. (C). 1991. pap. text 21.95 (*0-19-505622-1*, 8344) OUP.
Balme, Maurice G. & Morwood, James. Oxford Latin Course. 2nd ed. (Illus.). 64p. (C). 1996. pap. text, teacher ed. 15.95 (*0-19-912230-X*) OUP.
— Oxford Latin Course, Pt. I. 2nd ed. LC 96-209131. (Illus.). 157p. (C). 1996. pap. text 21.95 (*0-19-521203-7*) OUP.
— Oxford Latin Course, Pt. II. 2nd ed. (Illus.). 176p. (C). 1996. pap. text 21.95 (*0-19-521205-3*) OUP.
— Oxford Latin Course, Pt. III. (Illus.). 256p. (C). 1988. pap. text 20.95 (*0-19-912092-7*) OUP.
— Oxford Latin Course, Pt. III. 2nd ed. LC 96-209131. (Illus.). 224p. (C). 1997. pap. text 23.95 (*0-19-521207-X*) OUP.
Balme, Maurice G. & Morwood, James H. Oxford Latin Course, Pt. I. 2nd ed. LC 97-201005. (Illus.). 102p. 1997. pap. text, teacher ed. 15.95 (*0-19-912232-6*) OUP.
— Oxford Latin Course Pt. 2, Pt. II. 2nd ed. (Illus.). 76p. 1997. pap. text, teacher ed. 15.95 (*0-19-912231-8*) OUP.
Balme, Maurice G., ed. see Apuleius, Lucius.
Balmer, Alden J. Mouse Trap Cars: The Secrets to Success. 4th rev. ed. Cotter, Chris, ed. (Illus.). 90p. 1998. pap. 14.00 (*0-9656674-1-3*) Doc Fizzix.
— MouseTrap Cars: A Teachers Guide. 3rd rev. ed. Cotter, Chris, ed. (Illus.). 145p. (gr. 6 up). 1999. pap. 18.00 (*0-9656674-0-5*) Doc Fizzix.
Balmer, Carol, jt. ed. see Finley, Rebecca S.
Balmer, Ceci, ed. see Shankar, Sri Sri Ravi.
Balmer, Edwin, jt. auth. see Wylie, Philip.
***Balmer, Helen.** Ghostorama: 3-D Diorama. LC 99-162427. 6p. (J). (ps-3). 1998. 9.98 (*0-7651-0884-4*) Smithmark.
Balmer, Joe, ed. see Junkin, Hattie M.
Balmer, Josephine, tr. from GRE. Classical Women Poets. 160p. 1996. pap. 16.95 (*1-85224-342-2*, Pub. by Bloodaxe Bks) Dufour.
Balmer, Josephine, tr. see Sappho.
Balmer, Les, et al. Signals & Systems: An Introduction. 2nd ed. 496p. 1997. pap. 74.00 (*0-13-495672-9*) P-H.
Balmer, P., et al, eds. Sludge Rheology & Sludge Management: Selected Proceedings of the International Workshop on the Rheology of Sludges, Held in Bari, Italy, 17 March 1997 & the International Specialized Conference on Sludge Management, Held in Czestochowa, Poland, 26-28 June 1997. 300p. 1997. pap. write for info. (*0-08-043377-4*) Elsevier.
***Balmer, Randall.** Blessed Assurance: A History of Evangelicalism in America. 2000. pap. 15.00 (*0-8070-7711-9*) Beacon Pr.
Balmer, Randall. Grant Us Courage: Travels Along the Mainline of American Protestantism. LC 95-16205. 176p. 1996. 30.00 (*0-19-510086-7*) OUP.
Balmer, Randall & Fitzmier, John R. The Presbyterians. LC 92-17840. (Religious Traditions in American Culture Ser.). 152p. 1994. pap. 18.95 (*0-275-94847-1*, Praeger Pubs) Greenwood.
Balmer, Randall, jt. ed. see Blumhofer, Edith L.
Balmer, Randall H. Blessed Assurance: A History of Evangelicalism in America. LC 99-24838. 160p. 1999. 23.00 (*0-8070-7710-0*) Beacon Pr.
— Mine Eyes Have Seen the Glory: A Journey into the Evangelical Subculture in America. 264p. 1989. 19.95 (*0-685-47315-5*) OUP.
— Mine Eyes Have Seen the Glory: A Journey into the Evangelical Subculture in America. enl. ed. 320p. 1993. pap. text 14.95 (*0-19-507985-X*) OUP.
Balmer, Randall H. & Fitzmier, John R. The Presbyterians: Denominations in America, 5. LC 92-17840. 288p. 1993. lib. bdg. 69.50 (*0-313-26084-2*, BPD, Greenwood Pr) Greenwood.
Balmer, Robert T. Thermodynamics. (West Engineering Ser.). 1990. pap., student ed. 14.25 (*0-534-93867-1*) PWS Pubs.
***Balmer, Robert T.** Thermodynamics. 2nd ed. (General Engineering Ser.). (C). 1999. pap. 63.00 (*0-534-95434-0*) PWS Pubs.
— Thermodynamics with Disk. (West Engineering Ser.). (C). 1990. 69.50 (*0-534-93811-6*) PWS Pubs.
Balmer, Wayne T. & Davis, Drew K. Groundwater Resources of Delaware County, Pennsylvania. (Water Resource Reports: Vol. 66). (Illus.). 67p. (Orig.). 1996. pap. 11.50 (*0-8182-0127-4*) Commonweal PA.
Balmforth, David N. America's Coming Crisis: Prophetic Warnings, Divine Destiny. 192p. 1998. 18.98 (*0-88290-631-3*, 1088) Horizon Utah.
— New Age Menace: The Secret War Against the Followers of Christ. 1996. pap. 13.98 (*0-88290-535-X*, 1067) Horizon Utah.
Balmforth, Michael B., ed. Eastern Edition. annuals (C). 1989. 69.00 (*0-7855-5949-3*, Pub. by Laurie Norie & Wilson Ltd) St Mut.
— Western Edition. (C). 1989. 105.00 (*0-7855-5950-7*, Pub. by Laurie Norie & Wilson Ltd) St Mut.
— The Yachtsman's Almanac, 1992. (C). 1989. 80.00 (*0-7855-6722-4*, Pub. by Laurie Norie & Wilson Ltd) St Mut.
Balmforth, R. The Problem-Play. LC 76-52915. (Studies in Drama: No. 39). 1977. lib. bdg. 75.00 (*0-8383-2129-1*) M S G Haskell Hse.

B

Balmin, David B. Time Schedule Modeling: Programming in Web & Local Computers Using Java. (Computational Science Ser.). (C). 1999. pap. 24.95 (*0-9636817-0-2*) Intl Univ Line.

***Balmond, Cecil.** Informal. Brensing, Christian, ed. (Illus.). 400p. 2001. 45.00 (*3-7913-2400-4*) Prestel Pub NY.

Balmond, Cecil. Number Nine: The Search for the Sigma Code. LC 98-11906. (Illus.). 220p. 1998. 19.98 (*3-7913-1933-7*) te Neues.

Balmont, V., tr. see Alfutov, N. A.

Balmori, Diana. Las Alianzas de Familias en America Latina. (SPA.). pap. 12.99 (*968-16-3405-5*, Pub. by Fondo) Continental Bk.

— Process Architecture No. 134: Landscape of Balmori. (Illus.). 144p. 1997. pap. 37.95 (*4-89331-134-4*, Pub. by Process Archit) Bks Nippan.

— Transitory Gardens, Uprooted Lives. 1995. pap. 18.00 (*0-300-06301-6*) Yale U Pr.

Balmori, Diana & Morton, Margaret. Transitory Gardens. (Illus.). 160p. 1993. 35.00 (*0-300-05772-5*) Yale U Pr.

Balmori, Diana, et al. Beatrix Farrand's American Landscapes: Her Gardens & Campuses. LC 85-1969. (Illus.). 215p. (Orig.). 1986. pap. 24.95 (*0-89831-003-2*) Sagapr.

— Notable Family Networks in Latin America. LC 84-2423. (Illus.). 264p. 1984. 32.50 (*0-226-03639-1*) U Ch Pr.

Balmuth, Bernard. The Language of the Cutting Room: A Primary Reference Manual for the Assistant Editor of 35mm Film. 9th rev. ed. LC 81-84920. (Illus.). 97p. (C). 1996. pap. text 13.50 (*0-9607486-0-1*) Rosallen Pubns.

Balmuth, Deborah, ed. Herb Mixtures & Spicy Blends. (Illus.). 160p. 1996. pap. 12.95 (*0-88266-918-4*, 918-4) Storey Bks.

Balmuth, Deborah, ed. see Bethmann, Laura D.

Balmuth, Deborah, ed. see Burch, Monte.

Balmuth, Deborah, ed. see Hill, Cherry.

Balmuth, Deborah, ed. see K.Dodt, Colleen.

Balmuth, Deborah, ed. see Makela, Casey.

Balmuth, Deborah, ed. see Makela, Casey & Booth, Nancy M.

Balmuth, Deborah, ed. see Milne, Wendy H.

Balmuth, Deborah, ed. see Oppenheimer, Betty.

Balmuth, Deborah, ed. see Pleasant, Barbara.

Balmuth, Deborah, ed. see Reppert, Bertha.

Balmuth, Deborah, ed. see Sexton, Althea.

Balmuth, Deborah, ed. see Stovel, Edith & Wakefield, Pamela.

Balmuth, Deborah, ed. see Woodson, R. Dodge.

Balmuth, Miriam. The Roots of Phonics: A Historical Introduction. LC 92-35885. 251p. 1992. pap. 23.50 (*0-912752-32-7*) York Pr.

Balmuth, Miriam S., ed. Studies in Sardinian Archaeology Vol. II: Sardinia in the Mediterranean. (Illus.). 296p. 1986. text 47.50 (*0-472-10081-5*, 10081) U of Mich Pr.

Balmuth, Miriam S., et al, eds. Encounters & Transformations: The Archaeology of Iberia in Transition. (MMA Ser.: No. 7). 170p. 1997. 74.00 (*1-85075-593-0*, Pub. by Sheffield Acad) CUP Services.

Balnap, Barbara P., jt. auth. see Hall, Michael.

Balner, Ceci, ed. see Shankar, Sri Sri Ravi.

Balner, H. Bone Marrow Transplantation & Other Treatment After Radiation Injury. 1977. pap. text 73.50 (*90-247-2056-7*) Kluwer Academic.

— A New Medical Model: A Challenge for Biomedicine? 96p. 1989. pap. 18.00 (*90-265-1067-5*) Swets.

Balner, H. & Van Rood, Y., eds. Conceptual & Methodological Issues in Cancer Psychotherapy Intervention Studies. (Publications of the Helen Dowling Institute for Biopsychosocial Medicine). 100p. 1990. pap. 18.00 (*90-265-1138-8*) Swets.

Balner, H., jt. ed. see Labije, J. Ten.

Balny, Claude, jt. auth. see Hayashi, Rikimaru.

Balo, Bob, ed. Bob's Joint: A Poetry Collection. 1994. write for info. (*1-884391-05-2*) Bobs Joint.

Baloche, Lynda A. Cooperative Classroom. LC 97-31563. 272p. 1997. pap. text 33.00 (*0-13-360090-4*) P-H.

Balodis, Janis. The Ghosts Trilogy. 1997. pap. 24.95 (*0-86819-504-9*, Pub. by Currency Pr) Accents Pubns.

Balog, A. European Congress of Mathematics: Budapest, July 22-26, 1996. LC 98-27945. (Progress in Mathematics Ser.). 1998. 199.00 (*0-8176-5496-8*); 109.00 (*0-8176-5497-6*) Birkhauser.

— European Congress of Mathematics: Budapest, July 22-26, 1996. LC 98-27945. (Progress in Mathematics Ser.). 1998. 109.00 (*0-8176-5498-4*) Birkhauser.

Balog, A., et al, eds. European Congress of Mathematics Vol. I: Budapest, July 22-26, 1996. (Progress in Mathematics Ser.: Vol. 168). 360p. 1998. 109.00 (*3-7643-5497-6*) Birkhauser.

— European Congress of Mathematics Vol. II: Budapest, July 22-26, 1996. (Progress in Mathematics Ser.: Vol. 169). 416p. 1998. 109.00 (*3-7643-5498-4*) Birkhauser.

***Balog, Emily.** Afraid. 2000. 13.95 (*0-533-13206-1*) Vantage.

Balog, James. James Balog's Animals A to Z. LC 95-49519. (Illus.). 26p. (J). (ps). 1996. bds. 7.95 (*0-8118-1339-8*) Chronicle Bks.

— Wildlife Requiem. (C). 1984. 30.00 (*0-933642-06-7*); pap. 20.00 (*0-933642-07-5*) Intl Ctr Photo.

***Balog, James & Pedersen, B. Martin, eds.** Animal. (Illus.). 192p. 1999. text 60.00 (*1-888001-80-1*) Graphis US.

Balog, John N., et al. Guidebook for Attracting Paratransit Patrons to Fixed-Route Services. LC 97-61131. (Report/Transit Cooperative Research Program Ser.). 1997. write for info. (*0-309-06068-0*) Natl Acad Pr.

Balog, Paul. Coinage of the Ayyubids. (Illus.). 380p. 1980. lib. bdg. 60.00 (*0-901405-13-2*) S J Durst.

Balog, Paul. Umayyad, Abbasid & Tulunid Glass Weights & Vessel Stamps. (Numismatic Studies: No. 13). (Illus.). 377p. 1976. 60.00 (*0-89722-066-8*) Am Numismatic.

Balog, Zoltan & Sauter, Gerhard, eds. Mitarbeiter des Zeitgeistes? Die Auseinandersetzung Uber die Zeitgemabheit Als Kriterium Kirchlichen Handelns und die Kriterien Theologischer Entscheidungen in der Reformierten Kirche Ungarns, 1967-1992. (Beitrage zur Theologischen Urteilsbildung Ser.: Bd. 3). (GER.). 277p. 1997. 54.95 (*3-631-31636-4*) P Lang Pubng.

Balogh, A. G. & Walter, G. Materials Science Applications of Ion Beam Techniques: Proceedings of the International Symposium on Materials Science Applications of Ion Beam Techniques Incorporating the 1st German-Australian Workshop on Ion Beam Analysis, Seeheim, Germany, September 1996. (Materials Science Forum Ser.: Vols. 248 & 249). (Illus.). 512p. (C). 1997. text 176.00 (*0-87849-767-6*, Pub. by Trans T Pub) Enfield Pubs NH.

Balogh, Brian. Chain Reaction: Expert Debate & Public Participation in American Commercial Nuclear Power, 1945-1975. 352p. (C). 1991. text 54.95 (*0-521-37296-8*) Cambridge U Pr.

— Chain Reaction: Expert Debate & Public Participation in American Commercial Nuclear Power, 1945-1975. 352p. (C). 1993. pap. text 19.95 (*0-521-45736-X*) Cambridge U Pr.

Balogh, Brian, ed. Integrating the Sixties: The Origins, Structures, & Legitimacy of Public Policy in a Turbulent Decade. (Issues in Policy History Ser.: Vol. 6). 184p. 1996. pap. 16.95 (*0-271-01624-8*) Pa St U Pr.

Balogh, F., jt. auth. see Renyi-Vamos, F.

Balogh, I. Gesellschaftliche Information Philosophische Angalyse. 264p. (C). 1991. pap. 85.00 (*963-05-6014-3*, Pub. by Akade Kiado) St Mut.

Balogh, James C. Golf Course Management & Construction. 976p. 1992. lib. bdg. 95.00 (*0-87371-742-2*, L742) Lewis Pubs.

Balogh, Judy M., et al. Beyond a Dream: An Instructor's Guide for Small Business Exploration. 228p. 1985. 25.00 (*0-318-17848-6*, LT 68) Ctr Educ Trng Employ.

Balogh, M. & Laszlo, Pierre. Organic Chemistry Using Clays. LC 92-38522. (Reactivity & Structure Ser.: Vol. 29). 1993. 151.95 (*0-387-55710-5*) Spr-Verlag.

***Balogh, Mary.** A Chance Encounter. 224p. 1999. 25.00 (*0-7278-2254-3*, Pub. by Severn Hse) Chivers N Amer.

— A Chance Encounter. large type ed. 344p. 2000. write for info. (*0-7089-4177-X*) Ulverscroft.

Balogh, Mary. A Christmas Promise. large type ed. (Orig.). 1995. 27.99 (*0-7089-3406-4*) Ulverscroft.

— Dancing with Clara. 224p. 20.00 (*0-7278-4543-8*) Severn Hse.

— Dancing with Clara. large type ed. 416p. 1995. 27.99 (*0-7089-3370-X*) Ulverscroft.

— Daring Masquerade. 1989. mass mkt. 4.50 (*0-451-15886-5*, Sig) NAL.

— Deceived. 384p. (Orig.). 1993. pap. 4.99 (*0-685-62547-8*, Onyx) NAL.

— The Double Wager. 224p. 1990. pap. 3.50 (*0-451-16477-6*, Sig) NAL.

— Heartless. 400p. (Orig.). 1995. mass mkt. 5.99 (*0-425-15011-9*) Berkley Pub.

— Indiscreet. 352p. 1997. mass mkt. 5.99 (*0-515-12001-4*, Jove) Berkley Pub.

— Irresistible. 320p. 1998. mass mkt. 6.99 (*0-515-12367-6*, Jove) Berkley Pub.

— The Last Waltz. (Regency Romance Ser.). 223p. 1998. mass mkt. 4.99 (*0-451-19147-1*, Sig) NAL.

— Masked Deception. 1999. 25.00 (*0-7278-5460-7*, Pub. by Severn Hse) Chivers N Amer.

***Balogh, Mary.** More Than a Mistress. LC 99-462117. 352p. 2000. 16.95 (*0-385-33531-8*) Delacorte.

Balogh, Mary. One Night for Love. 384p. 1999. mass mkt. 6.50 (*0-440-22600-7*) Dell.

***Balogh, Mary.** One Night for Love. large type ed. LC 99-48206. 1999. 22.95 (*1-56895-795-5*, Wheeler) Wheeler Pub.

— The Rake's Mistress. 2000. mass mkt. 6.50 (*0-440-22601-5*) Bantam Dell.

Balogh, Mary. Silent Melody. 368p. 1997. mass mkt. 5.99 (*0-425-15862-4*) Berkley Pub.

— Thief of Dreams. 329p. 1998. mass mkt. 6.99 (*0-515-12274-2*, Jove) Berkley Pub.

— Thief of Dreams. large type ed. LC 99-19342. 1999. pap. write for info. (*1-56895-717-3*) Wheeler Pub.

— Truly. 352p. 1996. mass mkt. 5.99 (*0-425-15329-0*) Berkley Pub.

— Unforgiven. 320p. 1998. mass mkt. 6.99 (*0-515-12206-8*, Jove) Berkley Pub.

Balogh, Mary, et al. A Regency Christmas Carol. LC 97-14804. (Super Regency Anthologies Ser.). 352p. 1997. mass mkt. 5.99 (*0-451-19387-3*, Sig) NAL.

— Timeswept Brides. 352p. 1996. mass mkt. 5.99 (*0-515-11891-5*, Jove) Berkley Pub.

Balogh, Thomas. The Dollar Crisis, Causes & Cure. Wilkins, Mira, ed. LC 78-3896. (International Finance Ser.). 1979. reprint ed. lib. bdg. 29.95 (*0-405-11202-5*) Ayer.

Balogun & Trapa, B. B. Agricultural Statistics in Nepal: A User's Assessment. 1994. pap. 40.00 (*0-7855-0424-9*, Pub. by Ratna Pustak Bhandar) St Mut.

Balogun, F. Odun. Adjusted Lives: Stories of Structural Adjustments. LC 95-6644. 125p. 1995. 29.95 (*0-86543-486-7*) Africa World.

— Adjusted Lives: Stories of Structural Adjustments. LC 95-6644. 125p. 1995. pap. 9.95 (*0-86543-487-5*) Africa World.

— Tradition & Modernity in the African Short Story: An Introduction to a Literature in Search of Critics, 141. LC 90-42616. (Contributions in Afro-American & African Studies: No. 141). 208p. 1991. 55.00 (*0-313-27637-4*, BTM/, Greenwood Pr) Greenwood.

Balogun, M. Jide & Mutahaba, Gelase, eds. Economic Restructuring & African Public Administration: Issues, Actions, & Future Choices. LC 89-2677. (Kumarian Press Library of Management for Development Ser.). 274p. Date not set. reprint ed. pap. 85.00 (*0-608-20739-X*, 205449800003) Bks Demand.

Baloh, Robert W. Dizziness, Hearing Loss, & Tinnitus. LC 97-42657. (Illus.). 240p. (C). 1997. text 49.50 (*0-8036-0330-4*) OUP.

Baloh, Robert W. & Honrubia, Vicente. Clinical Neurophysiology of the Vestibular System. 2nd ed. LC 89-16897. (Contemporary Neurology Ser.: No. 32). (Illus.). 336p. (C). 1990. text 72.00 (*0-8036-0584-6*); pap. text 37.50 (*0-8036-0585-4*) OUP.

Baloh, Robert W., ed. see Halmagyi, M.

Baloian, Bruce E. Anger in the Old Testament. (American Univ. Studies: Theology & Religion: Ser. 7, Vol. 99). 225p. 1992. 40.95 (*0-8204-1514-6*) P Lang Pubng.

Baloian, James C. The Ararat Papers. LC 79-50729. 1979. 6.95 (*0-933706-06-5*); pap. 3.95 (*0-933706-07-3*) Ararat Pr.

Balok, Becki. Bouncer & the Stream of Life. (Illus.). 64p. (J). (gr. 3-12). 1999. pap. 9.99 (*0-9662759-1-8*, BCP-0999) Becalm Pub.

— Wake Up! Awaken the Spirit Within & You'll Never Be the Same Again. 120p. 1998. pap. 12.95 (*0-9662759-0-X*, BCP-0198) Becalm Pub.

Balokovic, Joyce B. Towards the Center. 1956. 3.95 (*0-910664-23-4*) Gotham.

Balon, Brett & Resch, Peter, eds. Survival of the Imagination: The Mary Donaldson Memorial Lectures. 328p. 1993. pap. 21.95 (*1-55050-051-1*, Pub. by Coteau) Genl Dist Srvs.

Balon, E. K. Lake Kariba. 1974. text 389.50 (*90-6193-076-6*) Kluwer Academic.

Balon, Eugene K., ed. Charrs: Salmonid Fishes of the Genus Salvelinus. (Perspectives in Vertebrate Science Ser.: No. 1). (Illus.). 919p. 1980. text 565.50 (*90-6193-701-9*) Kluwer Academic.

Balon, Eugene K., et al, eds. The Biology of Latimeria Chalumnae & Evolution of Coelacanths. (Developments in Environmental Biology of Fishes Ser.). 424p. 1991. lib. bdg. 283.00 (*0-7923-1224-4*) Kluwer Academic.

— Women in Ichtyology: An Anthology in Honour of ET, Roland & Genie. LC 94-31170. (Developments in Environmental Biology of Fishes Ser.: No. 15). 448p. 1995. text 382.50 (*0-7923-3165-6*) Kluwer Academic.

***Balon, Richard, ed.** Practical Management of the Side Effects of Psychotropic Drugs. LC 98-44760. (Medical Psychiatry Ser.: Vol. 12). (Illus.). 304p. 1998. text 150.00 (*0-8247-1926-3*) Dekker.

Balon, Richard, jt. ed. see Riba, Michelle B.

Balon, Robert. New Rules of the Ratings Game. 156p. 1995. pap. 59.95 (*0-89324-227-6*, 3792) Natl Assn Broadcasters.

Balon, Robert E. Rules of the Radio Ratings Game. 130p. 1988. pap. 24.95 (*0-8058-1048-X*) L Erlbaum Assocs.

Balona, Luis A., ed. Pulsation, Rotation & Mass Loss in Early-Type Stars: Proceedings of the 162nd Symposium of the International Astronomical Union Held in Antibes-Juan-Les-Pins, France, October 5-8, 1993. 572p. (C). 1994. pap. text 95.00 (*0-7923-3045-5*); lib. bdg. 186.50 (*0-7923-3044-7*) Kluwer Academic.

Balonek, Thomas, ed. Proceedings of the 1997 Undergraduate Symposium on Research in Astronomy. (C). 1998. pap. text. write for info. (*1-882334-07-8*) Keck NE Astron.

Balonov, M. I., jt. ed. see Merwin, S.

Balor, Paul. Manual of the Mercenary Soldier: A Guide to Mercenary War, Money & Adventure. 320p. 1988. text 29.95 (*0-87364-474-3*) Paladin Pr.

Balos, Beverly & Fellows, Mary L. Law & Violence Against Women: Cases & Materials on Systems of Oppression. LC 93-74421. 714p. (C). 1994. boxed set 75.00 (*0-89089-567-8*) Carolina Acad Pr.

Balos, Beverly, jt. auth. see Fellows, Mary L.

Balossino, Nello. The Image on the Shroud. 1996. pap. 39.95 (*0-85439-536-9*, Pub. by St Paul Pubns) St Mut.

Balota, D. A., et al, eds. Comprehension Processes in Reading. 680p. (C). 1990. 135.00 (*0-8058-0653-9*); pap. 69.95 (*0-8058-0654-7*) L Erlbaum Assocs.

Balotti, F. Franklin & Finkelstein, Jesse A. The Delaware Law of Corporations & Business Organizations: Text - Forms - Law, 5 vols. 2nd ed. 5744p. ring bd. 510.00 (*0-13-200486-0*, 43873) Aspen Law.

Balotti, R. Franklin & Finkelstein, Jesse A. The Delaware Law of Corporations & Business Organizations. 3rd ed. LC 97-37284. 1997. write for info. (*1-56706-671-2*); write for info. (*1-56706-672-0*); write for info. (*1-56706-673-9*); pap. write for info. (*1-56706-670-4*) Aspen Law.

— The Delaware Law of Corporations & Business Organizations. 3rd ed. LC 97-37284. 1998. ring bd. 595.00 (*1-56706-669-0*) Aspen Law.

— The Delaware Law of Corporations & Business Organizations: Text, Forms, & Law, 3 vols. 1985. 300.00 (*0-317-29371-0*, #H43872) Harcourt.

— The Delaware Law of Corporations & Business Organizations: Text-Forms-Law, 5 vols. 1988. write for info. (*0-318-65478-4*, H43872) P-H.

— The Delaware Law of Corporations & Business Organizations: Text, Forms, Law, 6 vols. 2nd ed. 5628p. 1995. ring bd. 450.00 (*0-13-288888-2*) Aspen Law.

Balotti, R. Franklin, et al. Meetings of Shareholders. 2nd ed. 568p. 1991. ring bd. 110.00 (*0-13-109349-5*) Aspen Law.

— Meetings of Stockholders. 3rd ed. 591p. 1996. ring bd. 160.00 (*1-56706-276-8*, 62768) Panel Pubs.

***Balouch, Kristen.** The King & the Three Thieves. LC 00-8764. (Illus.). 32p. (J). (ps-3). 2000. 15.99 (*0-670-88059-0*, Viking Child) Peng Put Young Read.

Balouch, Kristen. Listen to the Storyteller: A Trio of Musical Tales from Around the World. LC 97-43615. 32p. (J). 1999. 16.99 (*0-670-88054-X*) Viking Penguin.

Balouet, Jean-Christophe. Lost Forever, 4 bks. Incl. Extinct Animals of the Islands. Behm, Barbara J. LC 96-50238. (Illus.). 32p. (J). (gr. 3 up). 1997. lib. bdg. 21.27 (*0-8368-1525-4*); Extinct Animals of the Northern Continents. Behm, Brenda. LC 96-37610. (Illus.). 32p. (J). (gr. 3 up). 1997. lib. bdg. 21.27 (*0-8368-1526-2*); Extinct Animals of the Southern Continents. Behm, Barbara J. LC 96-37608. (Illus.). 32p. (J). (gr. 3 up). 1997. lib. bdg. 21.27 (*0-8368-1527-0*); Extinct Wildlife. Behm, Barbara J. LC 96-37603. (Illus.). 32p. (J). (gr. 3 up). 1997. lib. bdg. 21.27 (*0-8368-1524-6*); (Illus.). (J). 1997. Set lib. bdg. 85.07 (*0-8368-1523-8*) Gareth Stevens Inc.

Balouet, Jean-Christopher & Behm, Barbara J. In Peril, 2 bks. Incl. Endangered Animals of the Northern Continents. LC 94-11675. (Illus.). 32p. (J). (gr. 3 up). 1994. lib. bdg. 21.27 (*0-8368-1079-1*); (Illus.). (J). Set lib. bdg. 42.53 (*0-8368-1076-7*) Gareth Stevens Inc.

Balough, et al. The Gifts of Christmas. 1998. per. 5.99 (*0-373-83372-5*, 1-83372-2) Harlequin Bks.

***Balough, Linda & Bartley, Betty.** A Pictorial History of Hendricks County, Indiana LC 99-29868. (Illus.). 1999. write for info. (*1-57864-074-1*) Donning Co.

Baloun, Calvin H., ed. Corrosion in Natural Waters. LC 90-665. (Special Technical Publication (STP) Ser.: No. 1086). (Illus.). 160p. 1990. text 45.00 (*0-8031-1383-8*, STP1086) ASTM.

Balousek, M. William, jt. auth. see Jaeger, Richard W.

Balousek, Marv. Honey, This Is Trudy. Faster, Karen, ed. 226p. (Orig.). 1994. pap. 12.95 (*1-878569-17-1*) Badger Bks Inc.

— House of Alex: A True Story of Architecture & Art, Greed, Deception & Blackmail. (Illus.). 193p. (Orig.). 1990. pap. 9.95 (*1-878569-06-6*) WI State Journal.

— More Wisconsin Crimes of the Century. Snell, Barbara, ed. (Illus.). 174p. (Orig.). 1993. pap. 12.95 (*1-878569-11-2*, Waubesa Pr) Badger Bks Inc.

***Balousek, Marv.** 101 Wisconsin Unsolved Mysteries. (Illus.). 224p. 2000. pap. 12.95 (*1-878569-70-8*) Badger Bks Inc.

Balousek, Marv. Wisconsin Heroes. Kirsch, J. Allen, ed. (Illus.). 200p. (Orig.). 1995. pap. 12.95 (*1-878569-28-7*) Badger Bks Inc.

— Wisconsin's Historic Courthouses. Kirsch, J. Allen, ed. (Heritage Ser.). (Illus.). 1998. 35.00 (*1-878569-56-2*) Badger Bks Inc.

Balousek, Marv & Balousek, Mary. 50 Wisconsin Crimes of the Century. Kirsch, J. Allen, ed. (Illus.). 384p. (Orig.). 1997. pap. 16.95 (*1-878569-47-3*) Badger Bks Inc.

Balousek, Marv, jt. auth. see Kirsch, J. Allen.

Balousek, Marv, ed. see Gale, Zona.

Balousek, Marv, ed. see Hopkins, Steve.

Balousek, Marv, ed. see Phillips, Larry W.

Balousek, Mary, jt. auth. see Balousek, Marv.

Balovnev, V. I. Methods of Scale Modeling of Operating Processes of Highway Construction Machines. 1986. 21.50 (*81-205-0046-6*, Pub. by Oxford IBH) S Asia.

Balow, Tom, jt. auth. see Carpenter, Allan.

Balows, A., et al, eds. Laboratory Diagnosis of Infectious Diseases. (Illus.). 1160p. 1988. 423.00 (*0-387-96755-9*) Spr-Verlag.

— The Prokaryotes: A Handbook on the Biology of Bacteria: Ecophysiology, Isolation, Identification, Applications, 4 vols., Set. (Illus.). clxxii, 4770p. 1991. 2635.95 (*0-387-97258-7*) Spr-Verlag.

Balows, Albert. Essays in Microbiology. LC 68-29639. 144p. reprint ed. 44.70 (*0-8357-9784-8*, 201351400086) Bks Demand.

— Topley & Wilson's Microbiology & Microbial Infections Vol. 2: Systematic Bacteriology. 9th ed. (Illus.). 750p. 1998. text 195.00 (*0-340-66317-0*, Pub. by E A) OUP.

Baloyra, Enrique A. El Salvador in Transition. LC 82-4815. xviii, 236p. (C). 1982. pap. 12.95 (*0-8078-4093-9*) U of NC Pr.

— El Salvador in Transition. LC 82-4815. 254p. 1982. reprint ed. pap. 78.80 (*0-608-00197-X*, 206098000006) Bks Demand.

Baloyra, Enrique A. & Martz, John D. Political Attitudes in Venezuela: Societal Cleavages & Political Opinion. LC 78-14241. (Texas Pan-American Ser.). 320p. reprint ed. pap. 99.20 (*0-8357-7723-5*, 203608000002) Bks Demand.

Baloyra, Enrique A., jt. auth. see Morris, J. A.

Balrow, Tani E. & Lowe, Donald M. Chinese Reflections: Americans Teaching in the People's Republic. LC 85-6467. (Illus.). 256p. 1985. 59.95 (*0-275-91759-2*, C1759, Praeger Pubs) Greenwood.

Balsai, Michael. General Care & Maintenance of Popular Monitors & Tegus. (Illus.). 170p. (Orig.). 1997. pap. text 16.00 (*1-882770-39-0*) Adv Vivarium.

Balsam, Alan, jt. auth. see Balsam, Rosemary M.

Balsam, Betty. The Crescent Moon. LC 98-60399. 550p. 1998. pap. 14.95 (*1-881636-07-0*) Windsor Hse Pub Grp.

— My Sins upon You All. LC 98-61469. 546p. 1999. pap. 17.95 (*1-881636-62-3*) Windsor Hse Pub Grp.

Balsam, Charles & Balsam, Elizabeth. Family Planning: A Guide for Exploring the Issues. 3rd ed. LC 93-79880. 48p. (Orig.). 1994. pap. 1.95 (*0-89243-592-5*) Liguori Pubns.

— La Planificacion Familiar: Guia para Investigar el Tema. LC 96-77378. (SPA.). 64p. 1997. pap. 2.95 (*0-7648-0027-2*) Liguori Pubns.

Balsam, Elizabeth, jt. auth. see Balsam, Charles.

Balsam, M. S. & Sagarin, Edward, eds. Cosmetics: Science & Technology, 3 vols., Set. 2nd ed. LC 90-5276. 2128p. (C). 1992. reprint ed. lib. bdg. 375.00 (*0-89464-528-5*) Krieger.

B

An Asterisk (*) at the beginning of an entry indicates that the title is appearing for the first time.

— Cosmetics: Science & Technology, 3 vols., Vol. 1. 2nd ed. LC 90-5276. 624p. (C). 1992. reprint ed. lib. bdg. 135.00 (*0-89464-525-0*) Krieger.

— Cosmetics: Science & Technology, 3 vols., Vol. 2. 2nd ed. LC 90-5276. 704p. (C). 1992. reprint ed. lib. bdg. 143.50 (*0-89464-526-9*) Krieger.

— Cosmetics: Science & Technology, 3 vols., Vol. 3. 2nd ed. LC 90-5276. 800p. (C). 1992. reprint ed. lib. bdg. 163.50 (*0-89464-527-7*) Krieger.

Balsam, Peter & Tomie, Arthur, eds. Context & Learning. 432p. (C). 1984. text 89.95 (*0-89859-442-1*) L Erlbaum Assocs.

Balsam, Rosemary M. On Being a Clinical Supervisor: Psychodynamic Psychotherapy Teaching & Learning. 250p. 2000. 40.00 (*0-8236-5642-X*, 05642) Intl Univs Pr.

Balsam, Rosemary M. & Balsam, Alan. Becoming a Psychotherapist: A Clinical Primer. LC 83-24301. xxii, 370p. (C). 1984. pap. text 17.00 (*0-226-03636-7*) U Ch Pr.

Balsama, Joseph J. & Chaston, Peter R. Weather Basics. unabridged ed. (Illus.). 384p. 1997. pap. 34.00 (*0-9645172-5-6*) Chaston Scient.

Balsamo, Anne. Technologies of the Gendered Body: Reading Cyborg Women. LC 95-22648. (Illus.). 232p. 1995. text 49.95 (*0-8223-1686-2*); pap. text 17.95 (*0-8223-1698-6*) Duke.

Balsamo, Anne, ed. Science, Technology & Culture. (Cultural Studies: Vol. 12, Issue 3). 160p. (C). 1998. pap. 14.00 (*0-415-18427-4*, D5955) Routledge.

Balsamo, Gian. Pruning the Genealogical Tree: Procreation & Lineage in Literature, Law & Religion. LC 99-13997. 320p. 1999. 46.50 (*0-8387-5409-0*) Bucknell U Pr.

Balsamo, Kathy. Daily Doses of Thinking: March - April - May. (Illus.). 95p. 1998. pap. 5.95 (*1-880505-30-4*, GGA2012) Pieces of Lrning.

— Dinosaurs. (Questivities Ser.: Set 1). 1995. pap. 6.95 (*1-880505-62-2*, CLC0171) Pieces of Lrning.

— Weather. (Questivities Ser.). 1995. pap. 6.95 (*1-880505-65-7*, CLC0177) Pieces of Lrning.

Balsamo, Kathy L. My State. (Illus.). 144p. 1997. pap. 14.95 (*1-880505-50-9*, CLC0202) Pieces of Lrning.

— Thematic Activities for Student Portfolios. (Illus.). 112p. 1994. pap. 12.95 (*1-880505-11-8*, CLC0169) Pieces of Lrning.

Balsamo, Kathy L., jt. auth. see Johnson, Nancy L.

Balsamo, Larry & Bergeson, Sandra. Everything You Never Wanted to Know about Sex. (Conversation Bks.). 122p. 1995. pap. 9.95 (*1-884057-09-8*) Trivial Development Corp.

— Indecent Proposals. (Conversation Bks.). 122p. 1995. pap. 9.95 (*1-884057-10-1*) Trivial Development Corp.

Balsamo, Luigi. Bibliography, History of Tradition. Pettas, William A., tr. from ITA. 212p. 1990. pap. 35.00 (*0-9600094-2-6*, 30553) Oak Knoll.

Balsamo, William & Carpozi, George, Jr. Crime, Inc. The Inside Story of the Mafia's First 100 Years. Dunphy, Joan S., ed. Orig. Title: Under the Clock. 391p. 1991. pap. 15.95 (*0-88282-073-7*) New Horizon NJ.

Balsara, Nauzer J. Money Management Strategies for Futures Traders. LC 91-38287. (Financial Editions Ser.). 288p. 1992. 69.95 (*0-471-52215-5*) Wiley.

Balsdon, John P. The Emperor Gaius (Caligula) LC 77-7328. (Illus.). 243p. 1977. reprint ed. lib. bdg. 35.00 (*0-8371-9074-6*, BAEG, Greenwood Pr) Greenwood.

Balse, M. The Indian Female: Attitude Towards Sex. 124p. 1976. 9.95 (*0-318-37081-6*) Asia Bk Corp.

Balse, Mayah. Mystics & Men of Miracles in India. (Illus.). 1976. 7.95 (*0-913244-10-4*) Hapi Pr.

***Balseiro, Isabel.** Running Toward Us: New Writing from South Africa. LC 99-49243. 216p. 2000. pap. write for info. (*0-325-00211-8*); lib. bdg. write for info. (*0-325-00231-2*) Greenwood.

Balseiro, Jose A. Novelistas Espanoles Modernos. 8th enl. rev. ed. LC 76-27662. (SPA.). 403p. 1977. 8.00 (*0-8477-3173-1*) U of PR Pr.

— Obra Selecta. LC 89-46602. (SPA.). 760p. 1990. 75.00 (*0-8477-3643-1*) U of PR Pr.

Balseiro, Jose A., ed. see Casona, Alejandro.

Balseiro, Maria L., tr. see Sackville-West, Vita.

Balseiro, Maria L., tr. see Steig, William.

***Balsekar, Ramesh.** Who Cares?! The Unique Teaching of Ramesh S. Balsekar. Bardo, Blayne, ed. LC 99-62314. 215p. 1999. pap. 16.00 (*0-929448-18-9*) Advaita Pr CA.

Balsekar, Ramesh S. Consciousness Speaks: Conversations with Ramesh S. Balsekar. Liquorman, Wayne, ed. LC 92-74534. 392p. (Orig.). 1993. pap. 19.00 (*0-929448-14-6*) Advaita Pr CA.

— A Duet of One: The Ashtavakra Gita Dialogue. LC 89-84929. 224p. (Orig.). 1989. pap. 16.00 (*0-929448-11-1*) Advaita Pr CA.

— Experiencing the Teaching. LC 88-71633. 124p. (Orig.). 1988. pap. 14.00 (*0-929448-07-3*) Advaita Pr CA.

— Explorations into the Eternal: Forays into the Teaching of Nisargadatta Maharaj. Dikshit, Sudhakar, ed. LC 89-81300. xv, 261p. 1996. reprint ed. pap. 15.95 (*0-89386-023-9*) Acorn NC.

— The Final Truth: A Guide to Ultimate Understanding. LC 89-94930. 240p. (Orig.). 1989. pap. 16.00 (*0-929448-09-X*) Advaita Pr CA.

— From Consciousness to Consciousness. LC 89-84768. 80p. 1989. pap. 11.00 (*0-929448-10-3*) Advaita Pr CA.

— A Net of Jewels: Daily Meditations for Seekers of Truth. Starbuck, Gary, ed. LC 96-79929. 384p. 1997. 25.00 (*0-929448-15-4*) Advaita Pr CA.

Balsekar, Ramesh s. Pointers from Nisargadatta Maharaj. LC 82-71505. xiv, 223p. 1998. reprint ed. pap. 14.95 (*0-89386-033-6*) Acorn NC.

Balsekar, Ramesh S. Ripples. rev. ed. Liquorman, Wayne, ed. LC 98-71392. 42p. 1998. pap. 6.00 (*0-929448-16-2*) Advaita Pr CA.

— Your Head in the Tiger's Mouth. Bardo, Blayne, ed. LC 98-71393. 472p. 1998. pap. 24.00 (*0-929448-17-0*) Advaita Pr CA.

Balser, Benjamin H., ed. Psychotherapy of the Adolescent: At Different Levels of Psychiatric Practice with Special Emphasis on the Role of the School. LC 57-9326. 270p. (Orig.). 1959. reprint ed. pap. 24.95 (*0-8236-8249-8*, 225400) Intl Univs Pr.

Balser, Diane. Sisterhood & Solidarity: Feminism & Labor in Modern Times. LC 87-4733. 248p. (Orig.). 1987. 35.00 (*0-89608-278-4*); pap. 10.00 (*0-89608-277-6*) South End Pr.

***Balser, Werner.** Formal Power Series & Linear Systems of Meromorphic ODE. LC 99-31350. (Universitext Ser.). 300p. 1999. 49.95 (*0-387-98690-1*) Spr-Verlag.

Balser, Werner. From Divergent Power Series to Analytic Functions: Theory & Application of Multisummable Power Series, 1582. LC 94-28232. (Lecture Notes in Mathematics Ser.). 1994. 29.95 (*0-387-58268-1*) Spr-Verlag.

Balsera, Viviana Diaz, see Diaz Balsera, Viviana.

Balshaw-Biddle, Katharine, et al. Steam Remediation of Contaminated Soils. LC 99-29056. 410p. ring bd. 69.95 (*1-56670-465-0*) Lewis Pubs.

Balshaw-Biddle, Katherine, et al. Subsurface Contamination Monitoring Using Laser Fluorescence LC 99-26361. (Aatdf Monograph Ser.). 1999. write for info. (*0-8493-4153-1*) CRC Pr.

Balshaw, Maggie. Help in the Classroom, Vol. 1. 2nd ed. 1999. pap. 25.95 (*1-85346-476-7*) David Fulton.

***Balshaw, Maria.** Looking for Harlem: Urban Aesthetics in African-American Literature. 192p. 2000. 59.95 (*0-7453-1339-6*, Pub. by Pluto GBR); pap. 19.95 (*0-7453-1334-5*, Pub. by Pluto GBR) Stylus Pub VA.

***Balshaw, Maria & Kennedy, Liam.** Urban Space & Representation LC 99-37925. 2000. write for info. (*0-7453-1349-3*) Pluto GBR.

Balshem, Martha. Cancer in the Community: Class & Medical Authority. LC 92-48963. (Series in Ethnographic Inquiry). (Illus.). 192p. 1993. text 42.00 (*1-56098-250-0*); pap. text 16.95 (*1-56098-251-9*) Smithsonian.

Balshone, Benjamin. Determined! 1984. 15.95 (*0-8197-0494-6*) Bloch.

Balsiger, David, jt. auth. see Andre, Wayne.

Balsiger, David W., et al, contrib. by. The Incredible Power of Prayer Videos. 1997. pap. 74.99 incl. VHS (*0-7644-3038-6*) Group Pub.

Balsiger, David W. & Sellier. The Lincoln Conspiracy. 1994. reprint ed. lib. bdg. 29.95 (*1-56849-531-5*) Buccaneer Bks.

Balsiger, David W., et al. The Incredible Power of Prayer. LC 98-182702. 300p. 1997. pap. 5.99 (*0-8423-1579-9*) Tyndale Hse.

Balski, Grzegorz. Directory of Eastern European Film-Makers & Films, 1945-1991. LC 91-22023. 540p. 1992. lib. bdg. 89.50 (*0-313-28278-1*, BOG, Greenwood Pr) Greenwood.

Balslev, Anindita N., ed. Cross-Cultural Conversation: Initiation. LC 96-30768. (AAR Cultural Criticism Ser.). 236p. 1996. pap. 29.95 (*0-7885-0308-1*, 010705) OUP.

***Balslev, Anindita Niyogi.** Cultural Otherness: Correspondence with Richard Rorty. 2nd ed. LC 99-38046. (AAR Cultural Criticism Ser.: Vol. 4). 125p. 2000. pap. 16.95 (*0-7885-0300-6*, 010704) OUP.

— A Study of Time in Indian Philosophy. 2nd ed. 188p. 2000. 26.50 (*81-215-0893-2*, Pub. by Munshiram) S Asia.

Balslev, E., ed. Eighteenth Scandinavian Congress of Mathematicians. (Progress in Mathematics Ser.: No. 11). 528p. (C). 1981. 62.50 (*0-8176-3040-6*) Birkhauser.

— Schrodinger Operators, Aarhus, 1985. (Lecture Notes in Mathematics Ser.: Vol. 1218). v, 222p. 1986. pap. 25.30 (*0-387-16826-5*) Spr-Verlag.

Balslev, Erik, et al, eds. Schrodinger Operators: The Quantum Mechanical Many-Body Problem: Proceedings of a Workshop Held at Aarhus, Denmark, 15 May-1 August 1991. LC 92-14018. (Lecture Notes in Physics Ser.: Vol. 403). viii, 264p. 1992. 66.95 (*0-387-55490-4*) Spr-Verlag.

Balslev, H. Flora of Ecuador No. 208: Juncaceae. (Opera Botanica Series B). 44p. 1979. pap. 15.00 (*91-546-0271-8*, Pub. by Coun Nordic Pubs) Balogh.

Balslev, H. & Mena, Patricio V. Comparacion Entre la Vegetacion de los Paramos y el Cinturon Afroalpino. (Illus.). 54p. 1996. 12.95 (*87-87600-15-3*, Pub. by Aarhus Univ Pr) David Brown.

Balslev, H., et al. Flowering Plants of Amazonian Ecuador: A Checklist. (AAU Reports: No. 24). (Illus.). 220p. (C). 1991. pap. 12.95 (*87-87600-31-5*, Pub. by Aarhus Univ Pr) David Brown.

Balslev, H., jt. auth. see Pedersen, H. B.

Balslev, H., jt. auth. see Velasquez, E. Bravo.

Balslev, Henrik. Juncaceae. (Flora Neotropica Monographs: No. 68). (Illus.). 1996. 29.50 (*0-89327-403-8*, FLN 68) NY Botanical.

Balslev, Henrik, ed. Neotropical Montane Forests: Biodiversity & Conservation Abstracts from a Symposium at the New York Botanical Garden, June 21 - 26, 1993. LC 97-156073. (AAU Reports: No. 31). 112p. (C). 1993. pap. 12.95 (*87-87600-40-4*, Pub. by Aarhus Univ Pr) David Brown.

Balslev, Henrik, ed. see Churchill, Steven P.

Balslev, Henrik, ed. see Jorgensen, Peter M. & Ulloa, Carmen U.

Balslev, I., jt. auth. see Stahl, A.

Balslev, Lisbet B. & Porphyrios, Demetri, eds. Danish Classicists in Copenhagen & Athens: An Architectural Design Profile. (Academy Architecture Ser.). (Illus.). 80p. 1987. pap. 19.95 (*0-312-18223-6*) St Martin.

***Balsley, Bob.** Understanding Guitar Chords. 80p. 1998. pap. 10.95 (*0-7866-3265-8*, 96932) Mel Bay.

Balsley, Howard L. & Conway, James J. Acquiring a Fortune: Financial Novice to Millionaire. LC 91-11856. 128p. 1991. lib. bdg. 18.95 (*0-931541-18-2*) Mancorp Pub.

Balsley, Irol W. Where on Earth? 144p. (J). (gr. 4-8). 1986. student ed. 11.99 (*0-86653-336-2*, GA 691) Good Apple.

Balsley, Ronald D., jt. auth. see Birsner, E. Patricia.

***Balsom, Denis & Jones, J. Barry, eds.** The Road to the National Assembly for Wales. 240p. 2000. 55.00 (*0-7083-1492-9*, Pub. by U Wales Pr); 29.95 (*0-7083-1483-X*, Pub. by U Wales Pr) Paul & Co Pubs.

Balson, Maurice. Becoming Better Parents. (C). 1990. 65.00 (*0-86431-076-5*) St Mut.

— Understanding Classroom Behaviour. 3rd ed. 248p. 1997. pap. 31.95 (*1-85742-386-0*, Pub. by Arena) Ashgate Pub Co.

— Understanding Classroom Behaviour. 3rd ed. (C). 1992. pap. 70.00 (*0-86431-098-6*, Pub. by Aust Council Educ Res) St Mut.

Balster, Brigitte. Los Americanos. San Miguel-Carmona, Soledad, tr. from FRE. (Illus.). 399p. 1993. 24.95 (*2-7005-0175-6*, Pub. by Assimil) Distribks Inc.

Balster, Brigitte, et al. Los Americanos, 3 cass., Incl. 3 60-min. cassettes. (SPA.). pap. 59.95 incl. audio (*2-7005-1334-7*, Pub. by Assimil) Distribks Inc.

Balston, D. M. & Macario, Raymond C., eds. Cellular Radio Systems. LC 93-31141. 380p. 1993. text 89.00 (*0-89006-646-9*) Artech Hse.

Balston, Tommy. To the Edge: Confessions of a Lifeboat Coxswain. 196p. 1990. pap. 27.00 (*1-898218-64-1*) St Mut.

Balswick, Jack. Men at the Crossroads: Beyond Traditional Roles & Modern Options. LC 92-20599. 180p. (Orig.). 1992. pap. 10.99 (*0-8308-1385-3*, 1385) InterVarsity.

***Balswick, Jack.** Two-Paycheck Marriage: Making It Work. 208p. 1999. mass mkt. 5.99 (*0-8007-8667-X*) Revell.

***Balswick, Jack & Balswick, Judith.** Authentic Human Sexuality: An Integrated Christian Approach. LC 99-38845. 1999. 24.99 (*0-8308-1595-3*) InterVarsity.

Balswick, Jack & Balswick, Judith. Families in Pain: Working through the Hurts. LC 96-46250. 256p. (gr. 12 up). 1997. pap. 12.99 (*0-8007-5621-5*) Revell.

Balswick, Jack, jt. auth. see Lee, Cameron.

Balswick, Jack O. & Balswick, Judith K. The Family: A Christian Perspective on the Contemporary Home. 2nd ed. LC BV4526.2.B357 1999. (Illus.). 386p. (C). (gr. 13). 1999. pap. 17.99 (*0-8010-2185-5*) Baker Bks.

Balswick, Judith & Piper, Boni. Life Ties: Cultivating Relationships That Make Life Worth Living. LC 95-40448. 168p. (Orig.). 1995. pap. 9.99 (*0-8308-1614-3*, 1614) InterVarsity.

Balswick, Judith, jt. auth. see Balswick, Jack.

Balswick, Judith K., jt. auth. see Balswick, Jack O.

Balswick, Judith K., jt. auth. see Piper, Boni.

Balta-Calleja, F. J. & Vonk, C. G. X-Ray Scattering of Synthetic Polymers. (Polymer Science Library: No. 8). 318p. 1989. 238.50 (*0-444-87385-6*) Elsevier.

Balta, E., jt. auth. see Balta, P.

Balta, P. & Balta, E. An Introduction to the Physical Chemistry of the Vitreous State. (Abacus Bks.). 288p. 1976. text 110.00 (*0-85626-088-6*) Gordon & Breach.

Baltagi. Econometric Analysis of Panel Data. 80p. 1995. pap. text, teacher ed. 9.95 (*0-471-95544-2*) Wiley.

Baltagi, B. H. Econometrics. LC 97-48776. (Illus.). xiv, 3918p. (C). 1997. pap. 42.00 (*3-540-63617-X*) Spr-Verlag.

— Econometrics. 2nd ed. LC 99-17484. xiv, 398p. 1999. pap. 44.95 (*3-540-65417-8*) Spr-Verlag.

— Solutions Manual for Econometrics. (Illus.). viii, 321p. 1997. pap. 29.95 (*3-540-63896-2*) Spr-Verlag.

Baltagi, Badi H. Econometric Analysis of Panel Data. LC 94-22812. 270p. 1995. 110.00 (*0-471-95299-0*); pap. 75.00 (*0-471-95300-8*) Wiley.

***Baltagi, Badi H., ed.** A Companion to Theoretical Econometrics. 2000. 124.95 (*0-631-21254-X*) Blackwell Pubs.

Baltake, Joe. The Films of Jack Lemmon. 1977. 14.95 (*0-8065-0560-5*, Citadel Pr) Carol Pub Group.

— Jack Lemmon: His Films & Career. (Illus.). 288p. 1986. reprint ed. pap. 12.95 (*0-8065-1001-3*, Citadel Pr) Carol Pub Group.

***Baltas, Joyce Nessel.** Easy Mini-Lessons: Reading. 96p. 1999. pap. 12.95 (*0-439-04092-2*) Scholastic Inc.

— Follow the Direction! 180 Daily Exercises That Help Kids Learn to Follow Written Directions...I, Vol. 1. (Illus.). 64p. 1999. pap. 10.95 (*0-590-66131-0*) Scholastic Inc.

Baltas, N. K., et al, eds. Economic Interdependence & Cooperation in Europe. LC 97-52197. (Studies in International Economics & Institutions). (Illus.). vi, 200p. 1998. 84.95 (*3-540-64008-8*) Spr-Verlag.

Baltay, Charles, ed. see American Institute of Physics.

Baltazar, Eulalio. Liberation Theology & Teilhard de Chardin. (Teilhard Studies: No. 20). 1989. pap. 3.50 (*0-89012-057-9*) Am Teilhard.

Baltazzi, Evan S. Dog Gone West: A Western for Dog Lovers. (Illus.). 115p. (Orig.). (YA). (gr. 7 up). 1994. pap. 3.95 (*0-918948-05-3*) Evanel.

— Self-Protection Complete: The A.S.P. System: A Complete System of Holistic Body-Mind Self-Protection, for Mental & Physical Fitness, for Self-Defense & Prevention for Sport. deluxe ed. Baltazzi, Nellie D., ed. (Illus.). 334p. (C). (gr. 13 up). 1991. text 37.00 (*0-918948-04-5*) Evanel.

Baltazzi, Nellie D., ed. see Baltazzi, Evan S.

***Baltba Calleja, Francisco J. & Rosaniec, Zbigniew.** Block Copolymers. LC 00-37683. 2000. pap. write for info. (*0-8247-0382-0*) Dekker.

Baltch, Aldona L. & Smith, Raymond P., eds. Pseudomonas Aeruginosa - Infections & Treatment, No. 12. (Infectious Disease & Therapy Ser.: Vol. 12). (ITA., Illus.). 640p. 1994. text 215.00 (*0-8247-9210-6*) Dekker.

Balteanu, Dan & Slaymaker, Olav, eds. Geomorphology & Land Management. (Annals of Gemorphology Supplement Ser.: No. 58). (Illus.). 197p. (Orig.). 1986. pap. text 79.50 (*0-317-63557-3*) Lubrecht & Cramer.

Baltema, Patrick, ed. see Ziek, Peter J. & Schrecengost, Fred.

Baltensperger, Bradley H. Nebraska. (C). 1996. pap. text 20.00 (*0-86531-471-3*) Westview.

Balter, Alison. Alison Balter's Mastering Access 97 Development: Premier Edition. 2nd ed. LC 96-72230. 1168p. 1997. 49.99 (*0-672-30999-8*) Sams.

***Balter, Alison.** Mastering Access 2000 Development. LC 98-87340. (Illus.). 1342p. 1999. pap. 49.99 incl. cd-rom (*0-672-31484-3*) Sams.

Balter, Charles. India on a Thousand Dollars a Day: The Official Guide for Buying Your Way into Enlight'ment. (Illus.). 312p. (Orig.). 1995. pap. 15.95 (*0-9646244-0-0*) Stillpt Pr.

Balter, Frances. The River's Bend. 59p. 1998. pap. 12.95 (*0-941895-15-7*) Amherst Wri Art.

Balter, Harry G. Tax Fraud & Evasion. 5th ed. 920p. 1982. suppl. ed. 150.00 (*0-88262-796-1*, TFE) Warren Gorham & Lamont.

— Tax Fraud & Evasion, No. 1. 5th ed. 920p. 1991. suppl. ed. 66.50 (*0-7913-0836-7*) Warren Gorham & Lamont.

— Tax Fraud & Evasion, No. 2. 5th ed. 920p. 1991. suppl. ed. 150.00 (*0-7913-0967-3*) Warren Gorham & Lamont.

Balter, J. Deborah. Aeronautical Dictionary: With Emphasis on A. T. C. Communications, 2 vols., 1. 653p. (Orig.). 1994. pap. text. write for info. (*0-941456-08-0*) Aviation Lang Sch.

— Aeronautical Dictionary: With Emphasis on A. T. C. Communications, 2 vols., 2. 653p. (Orig.). 1994. pap. text. write for info. (*0-941456-09-9*) Aviation Lang Sch.

— Aeronautical Dictionary: With Emphasis on A. T. C. Communications, 2 vols., Set. 653p. (Orig.). 1994. pap. text. write for info. (*0-941456-10-2*) Aviation Lang Sch.

— Air Traffic Control Communications V. F. R. Directives & Explanations, Vol. 2. (Illus.). 48p. (Orig.). 1997. pap. text. write for info. incl. audio (*0-941456-14-5*) Aviation Lang Sch.

— Air Traffic Control Communications V. F. R. Directives with Explanations, Vol. 1. (Illus.). 31p. (Orig.). 1997. pap. text. write for info. incl. audio (*0-941456-13-7*) Aviation Lang Sch.

— A Foreigner's Guide to Comfortable Living in the United States: Everyday Etiquette & Procedures for Conducting Personal Business. 61p. (Orig.). 1996. pap. text 20.00 (*0-941456-11-0*) Aviation Lang Sch.

— Intermediate Aeronautical Language Manual, Vol. I. 183p. (Orig.). 1992. pap. text. write for info. (*0-941456-16-1*) Aviation Lang Sch.

— Workbook for Airline Pilots. 195p. 1993. pap. text. write for info. (*0-941456-20-X*) Aviation Lang Sch.

***Balter, Lawrence.** Parenthood in America: An Encyclopedia, 2 Vols. 2001. lib. bdg. 150.00 (*1-57607-213-4*) ABC-CLIO.

Balter, Lawrence & Shreve, Anita. Dr. Balter's Baby Sense. 1985. 16.95 (*0-317-49627-1*) PB.

— Who's in Control? Dr. Balter's Guide to Discipline Without Combat. LC 88-34145. 187p. 1989. pap. 10.00 (*0-671-68227-X*) S&S Trade.

Balter, Marie. Nobody's Child: The Marie Balter Story. 1991. 17.95 (*0-201-57073-4*) Addison-Wesley.

Balter, Marie & Katz, Richard. Nobody's Child. 1992. reprint ed. pap. 13.00 (*0-201-60816-2*) Addison-Wesley.

Balter, Rochelle, jt. auth. see Robin, Mitchell W.

***Baltes, Gerhard & Eckert, Brigitta.** Differente Bildungsorte In Systemischer Vernetzung: Eine Antwort auf das Problem der Funktionellen Differenzierung In der Kooperation Zwischen Jugendarbeit und Schule. (Erziehungskonzeptionen und Praxis. Bd. 40 Ser.u). Xi, 331p. 1999. 48.95 (*3-631-35092-9*) P Lang Pubng.

Baltes, H., et al, eds. Sensors Update: A Comprehensive Survey, Vol. 2. (Sensors Ser.). 313p. 1996. 425.00 (*3-527-29432-5*) Wiley.

Baltes, H., et al, eds. Sensors Update, Vol. 5. 294p. 1999. 250.00 (*3-527-29551-8*) Wiley.

Baltes, H., jt. auth. see Nathan, A.

Baltes, H. P., ed. Inverse Scattering Problems in Optics. (Topics in Current Physics Ser.: Vol. 20). (Illus.). 313p. 1980. 69.95 (*0-387-10104-7*) Spr-Verlag.

Baltes, Henry, et al, eds. Sensors Update: A Comprehensive Survey, Vol. 4. (Sensors Ser.). (Illus.). 230p. 1998. 275.00 (*3-527-29552-6*) Wiley.

***Baltes, Henry, et al, eds.** Sensors Update, Vol. 6, Special Volume: Sensor Research in Japan. 436p. 2000. 240.00 (*3-527-29820-7*) Wiley.

Baltes, M. Die Weltentstehung des Platonischen Timaios Nach den Antiken Interpreten. (GER.). 1978. pap. 25.00 (*90-04-05799-4*, PHA, 35) Brill Academic Pubs.

Baltes, Margaret M., jt. ed. see Baltes, Paul B.

Baltes, Margret M. The Many Faces of Dependency in Old Age. (Illus.). 203p. (C). 1996. text 54.95 (*0-521-49684-5*); pap. text 16.95 (*0-521-49804-X*) Cambridge U Pr.

Baltes, Margret M. & Baltes, Paul B., eds. The Psychology of Control & Aging. LC 85-25363. 449p. reprint ed. pap. 139.20 (*0-7837-5184-2*, 204491700004) Bks Demand.

Baltes, Paul B., et al, eds. Alter und Altern: Ein Interdisziplinaerer Studientext zur Gerontologie. (Sonderausgabe des 1992 Ershienenen 5. Forschungsberichtes der Akademie der Wissenschaft zu Berlin Ser.). (GER.). 822p. (C). 1994. pap. text 36.95 (*3-11-014408-5*) De Gruyter.

— Life-Span Development & Behavior, Vol. 7. 352p. (C). 1986. text 99.95 (*0-89859-692-0*) L Erlbaum Assocs.

B

An Asterisk (*) at the beginning of an entry indicates that the title is appearing for the first time.

Baltes, Paul B. & Baltes, Margaret M., eds. Successful Aging: Perspectives from the Behavioral Sciences. (European Network on Longitudinal Studies on Individual Development). (Illus.). 413p. (C). 1993. pap. text 22.95 (*0-521-43582-X*) Cambridge U Pr.

Baltes, Paul B. & Mayer, Karl U., eds. The Berlin Aging Study: Aging from 70 to 100. LC 98-8082. (Illus.). 544p. (C). 1999. write for info. (*0-521-62134-8*) Cambridge U Pr.

Baltes, Paul B. & Staudinger, Ursula, eds. Interactive Minds: Life-Span Perspectives on the Social Foundation of Cognition. (Illus.). 469p. (C). 1996. pap. text 24.95 (*0-521-48567-3*) Cambridge U Pr.

— Interactive Minds: Life-Span Perspectives on the Social Foundation of Cognition. (Illus.). 469p. (C). 1996. text 64.95 (*0-521-48106-6*) Cambridge U Pr.

Baltes, Paul B., et al. Life-Span Development & Behavior, Vol. 9. Featherman, David L. et al, eds. 400p. 1988. 99.95 (*0-8058-0272-X*) L Erlbaum Assocs.

— Life-Span Development & Behavior, Vol. 10. Featherman, David L. et al, eds. 384p. 1990. 105.00 (*0-8058-0609-1*) L Erlbaum Assocs.

— Life-Span Developmental Psychology: Introduction to Research Methods. 280p. 1988. reprint ed. pap. text 34.50 (*0-8058-0235-5*) L Erlbaum Assocs.

Baltes, Paul B., jt. auth. see Smelser, Neil J.

Baltes, Paul B., jt. ed. see Baltes, Margret M.

Baltes, Paul B., ed. see Featherman, David L., et al.

Baltes, Paul B., ed. see Mittelstrass, Juergen.

Baltes, Werner, ed. Rapid Methods for Analysis of Food & Food Raw Material. LC 90-71262. 320p. 1990. 39.95 (*0-87762-794-0*) Technomic.

Balthasar, Hans Urs Von. Elucidations. 1998. pap. 16.95 (*0-89870-621-1*) Ignatius Pr.

— Theo-Drama: Theological Dramatic Theory LC 88-80725. 1988. 40.00 (*0-89870-689-0*) Ignatius Pr.

Balthasar, Hans Urs Von & Von Balthasar, Hans U. Mary for Today. LC 87-83506. 75p. pap. 9.95 incl. audio (*0-89870-190-2*, 120) Ignatius Pr.

Balthasar, Hans Urs Von, see Urs Von Balthasar, Hans, ed.

Balthaser, William F. Call for Help: How to Raise Philanthropic Funds with Phonothons. LC 82-20958. (Illus.). 152p. 1983. 26.95 (*0-930807-11-1*, 600174) Fund Raising.

Balthazar, Judith W. Copper & Bronze Working in Early Through Middle Bronze Age Cyprus. (Studies in Mediterranean Archaeology & Literature: No. 84). (Illus.). 459p. (Orig.). 1990. pap. 57.50 (*91-85058-46-7*, Pub. by P Astroms) Coronet Bks.

Balthazar, Louis. French-Canadian Civilization. rev. ed. LC 97-127553. (ACSUS Papers Ser.). 50p. 1996. pap. 7.50 (*0-87013-395-0*, 0-87013-395-0) Mich St U Pr.

Balthazar, Louis, jt. auth. see Hero, Alfred O., Jr.

Balthazart, J., ed. Hormones, Brain & Behaviour in Vertebrates: Pt. 1: Sexual Differentiation, Neuroanatomical Aspects, Neurotransmitters & Neuropeptides. (Comparative Physiology Ser.: Vol. 8). viii, 226p. 1990. 185.25 (*3-8055-5184-3*) S Karger.

— Hormones, Brain & Behaviour in Vertebrates: Pt. 2: Behavioural Activation in Males & Females - Social Interactions & Reproductive Endocrinology. (Comparative Physiology Ser.: Vol. 9). viii, 230p. 1990. 185.25 (*3-8055-5185-1*) S Karger.

— Molecular & Cellular Basis of Social Behavior in Vertebrates. (Advances in Comparative & Environmental Physiology Ser.: Vol. 3). (Illus.). 380p. 1989. 152.95 (*0-387-19429-0*) Spr-Verlag.

Balthazart, J., et al, eds. Hormones & Behavior in Higher Vertebrates. (Proceedings in Life Sciences Ser.). (Illus.). 500p. 1983. 128.95 (*0-387-12576-0*) Spr-Verlag.

Balthazor, Thomas J., jt. auth. see Way, Ineke F.

Balthis, Frank, ed. see Beach-Balthis, Judy.

Balthis, Frank S., ed. see Beach-Balthis, Judy.

Balthis, Frank S., ed. & photos by see Howe, Sheri.

***Baltikas, Linda B. & Piercy, Robert W.** Give Your Gifts: The Prayer Services. 144p. 1999. pap. 24.95 (*1-57999-059-2*, G-4946) GIA Pubns.

Baltimo. Preparation for Confirmation: According to the Baltimore Catechism. 26p. (J). (gr. 5-12). 1996. pap. 3.45 (*0-935952-34-9*) Angelus Pr.

Baltimore Conference Staff. Human Gene Mapping Three: Proceedings - Journal: Cytogenetics & Cell Genetics, Vol. 16, Nos. 1-5. Bergsma, Daniel, ed. (Illus.). 420p. 1976. pap. 95.75 (*3-8055-2345-9*) S Karger.

Baltimore Country Club Staff. Baltimore Country Club: One Hundred Years. LC 98-49705. 1998. write for info. (*1-57864-057-1*) Donning Co.

Baltimore County Public Library's Blue Ribbon Commission. Give 'Em What They Want: Managing the Public's Library. LC 92-13756. (Public Library Administration Ser.). (Illus.). 183p. 1992. reprint ed. pap. 56.80 (*0-608-01734-5*, 206239100002) Bks Demand.

Baltimore, David, et al. Molekular Zellbiologie. 2nd ed. (GER., Illus.). xlii, 1448p. (C). 1996. text 94.85 (*3-11-014460-3*, 126/96) De Gruyter.

Baltimore Museum of Art Staff. American Prints, 1860-1950. Johnson, Robert F., ed. LC 76-13195. 40p. 1977. lib. bdg. 18.00 (*0-226-68824-0*) U Ch Pr.

Baltimore Plenary Council Staff. Baltimore Catechism, No. 1. 1977. reprint ed. pap. 3.50 (*0-89555-010-5*) TAN Bks Pubs.

— Baltimore Catechism, No. 2. 1977. reprint ed. pap. 4.50 (*0-89555-008-3*) TAN Bks Pubs.

— Baltimore Catechism: Cathechism of Christian Doctrine, No. 3. 1994. reprint ed. pap. 8.00 (*0-89555-007-5*, 147) TAN Bks Pubs.

Baltimore Region Institutional Studies Center Staff, et al, eds. The Urban Information Thesaurus: A Vocabulary for Social Documentation. LC 76-52604. 375p. 1977. lib. bdg. 65.00 (*0-8371-9483-0*, UTH, Greenwood Pr) Greenwood.

Baltimore, Robert S., jt. auth. see Jenson, Hal.

Baltimore Sun Company Staff. Cal Touches Home. Gibbons, Jack, ed. 100p. (Orig.). 1995. pap. 10.95 (*0-9649819-0-4*) Baltimore Sun.

***Baltin, Mark & Collins, Chris, eds.** The Handbook of Contemporary Syntactic Theory. LC 99-87402. (Handbooks in Linguistics Ser.). (Illus.). 880p. 2000. text 124.95 (*0-631-20507-1*) Blackwell Pubs.

Baltin, Mark R. & Kroch, Anthony S. Alternative Conceptions of Phrase Structure. LC 88-34327. (Illus.). 328p. 1989. pap. text 24.00 (*0-226-03642-1*); lib. bdg. 72.00 (*0-226-03641-3*) U Ch Pr.

Balton, Michael, ed. European Policing: The Law Enforcement News Interviews. (Orig.). 1978. pap. 2.95 (*0-89444-011-X*) John Jay Pr.

Baltrock, Thomas, intro. Kiki Smith: Works 1988-1995. LC 99-176811. (Illus.). 46p. 1998. 29.95 (*3-932189-77-9*, 810501, Pub. by Salon-Verlag) Dist Art Pubs.

Baltrusaitis, Jurgis. Anamorphic Art. Strachan, W. J., tr. (Illus.). 182p. 1977. write for info. (*0-85964-029-9*) Chadwyck-Healey.

— The Fantastic in the Middle Ages: Classical & Exotic Influences on Gothic Art. (Illus.). 256p. 2001. 45.00 (*0-85991-528-X*) Boydell & Brewer.

Baltrusch, Burghard. Bewubtsein und Erzahlungen der Moderne im Werk Fernando Pessoas. (Bonner Romanistische Arbeiten Ser.: Bd. 61). (GER., Illus.). 421p. 1997. 63.95 (*3-631-31406-X*) P Lang Pubng.

Baltrusch, Ernst. Symmachie Und Spondai: Untersuchungen Zum Griechischen Voelkerrecht der Archaischen Und Klassischen Zeit (8. - 5. Jahrhundert V. Chr.) (Untersuchungen zur Antiken Literatur und Geschichte Ser.: No. 43). (GER.). xi, 274p. (C). 1994. lib. bdg. 144.65 (*3-11-013745-3*) De Gruyter.

Baltrush, Libby, ed. see Johnston, John P.

Baltrush, Tim, ed. see Johnston, John P.

Baltsan, Hayim. Webster's New World Hebrew Dictionary. 1994. per. 18.00 (*0-671-88991-5*, Webstrs New) Macmillan Gen Ref.

Baltscheffsky, H., ed. Origin & Evolution of Biological Energy Conversion. 328p. 1997. 135.00 (*0-471-18581-7*) Wiley.

Baltscheffsky, Herrick, ed. Origin & Evolution of Biological Energy Conversion. (Illus.). 350p. 1996. 125.00 (*1-56081-614-7*, Wiley-VCH) Wiley.

Baltscheffsky, Herrick, et al, eds. Molecular Evolution of Life. (Illus.), 384p. 1987. text 100.00 (*0-521-33642-2*) Cambridge U Pr.

Baltscheffsky, M., ed. Current Research in Photosynthesis: Proceedings of the VIIIth International Congress on Photosynthesis, Stockholm, Sweden, August 6-11, 1989. 4 vols., Set. (C). 1990. text 1754.50 (*0-7923-0587-6*) Kluwer Academic.

Baltuck, Naomi. Apples from Heaven: Multicultural Folktales about Stories & Storytellers. LC 95-21890. xvi, 144p. 1995. pap. 17.50 (*0-208-02434-4*, Linnet Bks) Shoe String.

— Apples from Heaven: Multicultural Folktales about Stories & Storytellers. LC 95-21890. xvi, 144p. 1995. lib. bdg. 25.00 (*0-208-02424-7*, Linnet Bks) Shoe String.

— Crazy Gibberish & Other Story Hour Stretches from a Storyteller's Bag of Tricks. LC 93-20681. (Illus.). 152 p. (J). 1993. pap. text 22.50 (*0-208-02337-2*, Linnet Bks); lib. bdg. 25.00 (*0-208-02336-4*, Linnet Bks) Shoe String.

***Baltuck, Naomi.** Keeper of the Crystal Spring. 448p. 1999. pap. 12.95 (*0-14-027611-4*) Viking Penguin.

***Baltus, Rita.** Personal Psychology for Life & Work. 5th ed. 1999. teacher ed. 14.95 (*0-02-804295-6*); text 31.28 (*0-02-804294-8*) Glencoe.

Baltus, Rita K. Personal Psychology for Life & Work. 4th ed. LC 93-41127. 1994. 19.50 (*0-02-801096-5*) Glencoe.

***Baltussen, Han.** Theophrastus against the Presocratics & Plato: Peripatetic Dialectic in the de Sensibus. (Philosophia Antiqua Ser.). 232p. 2000. text 81.00 (*90-04-11720-2*) Brill Academic Pubs.

Balty, Jean C., jt. auth. see Van Rengen, Wilfried.

Baltz, E. H., jt. ed. see Weir, J. E., Jr.

Baltz, Elmer H. & Myers, Donald A. Stratigraphic Framework of Upper Paleozoic Rocks, Southeastern Sangre de Cristo Mountains, New Mexico. LC 99-492641. (Memoir Ser.). (Illus.). 269p. 1999. pap. write for info. (*1-883905-03-6*) NM Bureau Mines.

Baltz, Frederick W. As of First Importance: A Theology & Practice of Evangelism for Mainline Churches. 184p. 1996. pap. 14.95 (*0-7880-0675-4*, Fairway Pr) CSS OH.

— Lazarus & the Fourth Gospel Community. LC 95-14581. (Biblical Press Ser.: Vol. 37). 120p. 1996. 59.95 (*0-7734-2428-8*, Mellen Biblical Pr) E Mellen.

Baltz, George E., jt. auth. see Baltz, Shirley V.

Baltz, Jennifer, jt. ed. see Lindgren, C. E.

***Baltz, Lewis.** Politics of Bacteria, Docile Bodies, Ronde de Nuit. (Illus.). 60p. 1998. 26.00 (*0-914357-57-3*, Pub. by Los Angeles Mus Contemp) RAM Publications.

Baltz, Lewis. Rule Without Exception. Turrell, Julia B., ed. LC 90-71711. (Illus.). 154p. 1988. pap. 50.00 (*0-8263-1270-5*) U of NM Pr.

— Rule Without Exception. Turrell, Julia B., ed. LC 90-71711. (Illus.). 154p. 1991. 75.00 (*0-8263-1269-1*) U of NM Pr.

***Baltz, Lewis, photos by.** Lewis Baltz: New Industrial Parks Near Irvine, California. 2nd ed. (Illus.). 112p. 2000. reprint ed. 35.00 (*0-9630785-6-9*) RAM Publications.

Baltz, Louis J., III. The Battle of Cold Harbor. (Virginia Civil War Battles & Leaders Ser.). (Illus.). 282p. 1994. 25.00 (*1-56190-060-5*) H E Howard.

Baltz, Richard H. Industrial Microorganisms: Basis & Applied Molecular Genetics. LC 93-24172. 309p. reprint ed. pap. 95.80 (*0-608-08633-9*, 206915600003) Bks Demand.

Baltz, Shirley V. & Baltz, George E. Prince George's Co. MD Marriages & Deaths in Nineteenth Century Newspapers, Vol. 1 A-J. (Illus.). 331p. (Orig.). 1995. pap. 25.00 (*0-7884-0626-4*) Heritage Bk.

— Prince George's County, Maryland Vol. 2: Marriages & Deaths in Nineteenth Century Newspapers, K-Z. 291p. (Orig.). 1995. pap. 25.00 (*0-7884-0282-X*) Heritage Bk.

Baltz, Terry & Baltz, Wayne. The Invisible Kid & Dr. Poof's Magic Soap. LC 93-87287. (Invisible Kid Ser.: No. 1). 136p. (Orig.). (J). (gr. 2-6). 1993. pap. 6.50 (*1-884610-11-0*) Prairie Divide.

— The Invisible Kid & the Intergalactic RV. LC 97-76601. (Invisible Kid Ser.: No. 3). 127p. (J). (gr. 2-6). 1997. pap. 6.50 (*1-884610-13-7*) Prairie Divide.

— The Invisible Kid & the Killer Cat. LC 94-69516. (The Invisible Kid Ser.: No. 2). 127p. (Orig.). (J). (gr. 2-6). 1994. pap. 6.50 (*1-884610-12-9*) Prairie Divide.

— Night of the Falling Stars. LC 95-70986. 181p. (Orig.). (YA). (gr. 5 up). 1995. pap. 6.50 (*1-884610-51-X*) Prairie Divide.

Baltz, Wayne, jt. auth. see Baltz, Terry.

Baltzarek, Franz, ed. see Lee, Sun-Jae.

Baltzell, D. Catherine. Head Start: Research Provides Little Information on Impact of Current Program. (Illus.). 56p. 1998. pap. text 20.00 (*0-7881-3851-0*) DIANE Pub.

Baltzell, D. Catherine & Doughty, Sherri, eds. Head Start Programs: Participant Characteristics, Services, & Funding. (Illus.). 91p. 1999. pap. text 20.00 (*0-7881-7878-4*) DIANE Pub.

Baltzell, E. D. Sporting Gentlemen: Men's Tennis from the Age of Honor to the Cult of the Superstar. (Illus.). 420p. 1998. text 30.00 (*0-7881-5660-8*) DIANE Pub.

Baltzell, E. Digby. Judgement & Sensibility: Religion & Stratification. LC 93-41656. 313p. (C). 1994. text 39.95 (*1-56000-048-1*) Transaction Pubs.

— Philadelphia Gentlemen: The Making of a National Upper Class. LC 89-4362. (Illus.). 476p. 1989. pap. 24.95 (*0-88738-789-6*) Transaction Pubs.

— The Protestant Establishment. LC 86-24678. 429p. 1987. pap. 20.00 (*0-300-03818-6*) Yale U Pr.

— The Protestant Establishment Revisited. Schneiderman, Howard G., ed. 336p. (C). 1991. 44.95 (*0-88738-419-6*) Transaction Pubs.

— The Protestant Establishment Revisited. Schneiderman, Howard G., ed. 265p. 1999. pap. 24.95 (*0-7658-0664-9*) Transaction Pubs.

— Puritan Boston & Quaker Philadelphia. LC 79-7581. (Illus.). 1980. 45.00 (*0-02-901320-8*) Free Pr.

— Sporting Gentlemen: Men's Tennis from the Age of Honor to the Cult of the Superstar. (Illus.). 420p. 1995. 30.00 (*0-02-901315-1*) Free Pr.

Baltzell, E. Digby, intro. Puritan Boston & Quaker Philadelphia. 608p. (C). 1996. pap. text 24.95 (*1-56000-830-X*) Transaction Pubs.

Baltzell, Martha P. Bridging Diversity: Confessions of a Yankee Catholic. LC 97-36421. 272p. 1997. pap. 14.95 (*1-55612-914-9*, LL1914) Sheed & Ward WI.

Baltzell, Richard, ed. see Penner, James.

Baltzell Wright, Linda. Crossing over Time Sampler. LC 96-71092. (Illus.). 48p. 1997. pap. 9.95 (*0-8487-1289-7*) Oxmoor Hse.

Baltzer, Dieter. Ezechiel und Deuterojesaja: Beruehrungen in der Heilserwartung der beiden grossen Exilspropheten. (Beiheft zur Zeitschrift fuer die Alttestamentliche Wissenschaft Ser.: No. 121). (C). 1971. 76.15 (*3-11-001756-3*) De Gruyter.

Baltzer, Friedrich. Theodor Boveri: Life & Work of a Great Biologist, 1862-1915. LC 67-21996. (Illus.). 187p. reprint ed. pap. 58.00 (*0-608-17462-9*, 202994300066) Bks Demand.

Baltzer, Klaus. Deutero-Isaiah: A Commentary. Machinist, Peter, ed. Kohl, Margaret, tr. LC 98-35306. 400p. 2000. 48.00 (*0-8006-6039-0*, 1-6039) Augsburg Fortress.

Baltzer, Klaus, ed. see Zimmerli, Walther.

Baltzer, Rebecca A., et al, eds. The Union of Words & Music in Medieval Poetry. (Illus.). 167p. (C). 1991. text 45.00 incl. audio (*0-292-78519-4*) U of Tex Pr.

Baltzer, Rebecca A., jt. auth. see Fassler, Margot E.

***Balu.** Divine Glory. 1998. pap. 18.50 (*81-7030-640-X*, Pub. by Sri Satguru Pubns) S Asia.

Balu, K. & Holden, Patrick W. Guidance for Field-Scale Ground-Water Monitoring Studies. (Illus.). 464p. 1999. text 130.00 (*0-8412-3662-3*, Pub. by Am Chemical) OUP.

Balu, Neal J., jt. auth. see Kundur, P.

Balucani, Umberto & Zoppi, Marco. Dynamics of the Liquid State. (Illus.). 352p. 1995. text 115.00 (*0-19-851739-4*) OUP.

Baluhkin, A. V. Morphological Bases of the Systematics & Phylogeny of the Notothenoid. (C). 1989. 28.00 (*81-7087-048-8*) S Asia.

Balukhaty, S. D., ed. see Stanislavski, Constantin.

Balukhovsky, A. N., jt. auth. see Khain, V. E.

Balun, Charles. Lucio Fulci: Beyond the Gates of Hell - A Tribute to the Maestro. 2nd ed. LC 97-60427. (Illus.). 80p. 1997. reprint ed. pap. 12.95 (*1-888214-07-4*) Fantasma Bks.

***Balun, Paul.** Disgraceful Archaeology. (Illus.). 128p. 1999. pap. 16.99 (*0-7524-1476-3*, Pub. by Tempus Pubng) Arcadia Pubing.

Balushkin, A. V. Morphological Bases of the Systematics & Phylogeny of the Nototheniid Fishes. Kohli, I., tr. (Russian Translation Ser.: No. 73). 160p. (C). 1990. text 91.00 (*90-6191-960-6*, Pub. by A A Balkema) Ashgate Pub Co.

Baluska, F., ed. see International Symposium on Structure & Function of.

Balutanski, Kathleen, ed. The Novels of Alex La Guma: The Representation of a Political Conflict. LC 86-51304. 142p. 1990. reprint ed. 25.00 (*0-89410-557-4*, Three Contnts); reprint ed. pap. 12.50 (*0-89410-558-2*, Three Contnts) L Rienner.

Balutansky, Kathleen M. & Sourieau, Marie-Agnes, eds. Caribbean Creolization: Reflections on the Cultural Dynamics of Language, Literature, & Identity. LC 97-34954. 1998. 49.95 (*0-8130-1558-8*) U Press Fla.

Balutis, Alan P. & Honan, Joseph C., eds. Public Affairs Internships: Theory & Practice. 297p. 1984. 22.95 (*0-87073-727-9*); pap. 16.95 (*0-87073-728-7*) Schenkman Bks Inc.

Baluyut, Butch. Baluyut: A Collection of Ninety Portraits. 96p. write for info. (*0-9635453-7-X*); pap. write for info. (*0-9635453-2-9*) B Baluyut.

Balvay, Gerard & International Congress of Limnology & Oceanography, eds. Space Partition Within Aquatic Ecosystems: Proceedings of the Second International Congress of Limnology & Oceanography, Held in Evian, May 25-28, 1993. LC 94-43528. (Developments in Hydrobiology Ser.: Vol. 104). 1995. text 349.50 (*0-7923-3293-8*) Kluwer Academic.

Balvet, Barbara B., tr. see French Oil & Gas Industry Association Staff, et al, eds.

Balwada, Ravi, jt. auth. see Devraj, Venkat S.

Baly, Denis. Basic Biblical Geography. LC 86-45206. 80p. 1987. pap. 12.00 (*0-8006-1922-6*, 1-1922, Fortress Pr) Augsburg Fortress.

Baly, Monica. Florence Nightingale & the Nursing Legacy: Building the Foundation of Modern Nursing & Midwifery. 2nd ed. LC 98-70738. (Illus.). 256p. 1998. 19.95 (*1-891696-01-7*) BainBridgeBooks.

Balyeat Nash, Joy. White Leaves. LC 90-71567. (Illus.). 80p. (Orig.). 1990. pap. 8.95 (*0-9623026-1-9*) Stonehaven TX.

***Balyi, Istvan.** A Coaches/Parents Guide: Developing the Young Soccer Player Ages 6 to 21. (Illus.). 36p. 1999. pap. 5.95 (*1-891200-09-7*) Performance Conditioning.

Balykin, V. I. & Letokhov, V. S. Atom Optics with Laser Light. (Laser Science & Technology Ser). 128p. 1995. otabind 50.00 (*3-7186-5697-3*, Harwood Acad Pubs) Gordon & Breach.

Balyoz, Harold. Discovering Torkom's Teachings. LC 97-72956. 420p. pap. 21.00 (*0-9609710-3-3*) Altai Pub.

— Discovering Torkom's Teachings. 420p. 1997. pap. 21.00 (*0-9609710-2-5*) Altai Pub.

— Signs of Christ. LC 79-64608. 436p. 21.00 (*0-9609710-0-9*) Altai Pub.

— Three Remarkable Women. (Illus.). 285p. pap. 14.95 (*0-9609710-1-7*) Altai Pub.

Balyuzi, H. M. Abdu'l-Baha: The Centre of the Covenant of Baha'u'llah. rev. ed. (Illus.). 576p. 1971. reprint ed. pap. 17.25 (*0-85398-043-8*, 331-037) G Ronald Pub.

— Baha'u'llah: Shams-i-Haqiqat. Sabet, Minu, tr. (PEO., Illus.). 648p. 1991. 74.95 (*0-85398-320-8*) G Ronald Pub.

— Baha'u'llah: The King of Glory. (Illus.). 552p. 1980. pap. 33.95 (*0-85398-328-3*) G Ronald Pub.

— Eminent Baha'is in the Time of Baha'u'llah. (Illus.). 400p. 1986. 37.95 (*0-85398-151-5*) G Ronald Pub.

Balz, Albert G. Idea & Essence in the Philosophies of Hobbes & Spinoza. LC 70-161737. reprint ed. 37.50 (*0-404-00489-X*) AMS Pr.

Balz, Dan & Brownstein, Ronald. Storming the Gates: Protest Politics & the Republican Revival. 424p. 1996. 24.95 (*0-614-12887-0*) Little.

Balz, Horst. Exegetical Dictionary of the New Testament, 3 vols., Set. 1993. 150.00 (*0-8028-2412-9*) Eerdmans.

Balz, Horst & Schneider, Gerhard, eds. Exegetical Dictionary of the New Testament, Vol. 1. 1990. 50.00 (*0-8028-2409-9*) Eerdmans.

— Exegetical Dictionary of the New Testament, Vol. 2. xxiv, 556p. 1991. text 50.00 (*0-8028-2410-2*) Eerdmans.

— Exegetical Dictionary of the New Testament, Vol. 3. 584p. 1993. 50.00 (*0-8028-2411-0*) Eerdmans.

***Balz, Horst, et al.** Theologische Realenzyklopadie (TRE) iv, 800p. 1999. 287.00 (*3-11-016243-1*) De Gruyter.

Balz, Rodolphe. The Healing Power of Essential Oils: Fragrance Secrets for Everyday Use. (Illus.). 203p. (Orig.). 1996. pap. 14.95 (*0-941524-89-2*) Lotus Pr.

***Balz, Rodolphe.** The Healing Power of Essential Oils: Fragrance Secrets for Everyday Use. 203p. (Orig.). 1999. pap. 100.00 (*81-208-1612-9*, Pub. by Motilal Bnarsidass) St Mut.

Balza, Jose. Este Mar Narrativo. (SPA.). pap. 10.99 (*968-16-2570-6*, Pub. by Fondo) Continental Bk.

Balzac, Honore de. Annette et le Criminel, ou Suite du Vicaire des Ardennes. 10.95 (*0-8288-9325-X*, 2080703919) Fr & Eur.

— Annette et le Criminel, ou Suite du Vicaire des Ardennes. (FRE.). 446p. 1982. pap. 10.95 (*0-7859-3479-0*, F118145) Fr & Eur.

— Balzac's Short Stories. 1991. lib. bdg. 75.00 (*0-8490-4179-1*) Gordon Pr.

— Beatrix. (Class. Garnier Ser.). 1962. pap. 11.95 (*0-8288-9337-3*) Fr & Eur.

— Beatrix. (FRE.). 535p. 1979. pap. 13.95 (*0-7859-1897-3*, 2070371239) Fr & Eur.

— Beatrix. (Folio Ser.: No. 1123). (FRE.). 1962. 12.95 (*2-07-037123-9*) Schoenhof.

— The Black Sheep. Adamson, Donald, tr. LC 77-357255. (Classics Ser.). 344p. 1970. pap. 13.95 (*0-14-044237-5*) Viking Penguin.

— The Bureaucrats. Foulkes, Charles, tr. from FRE. (European Classics Ser.). 300p. 1993. 39.95 (*0-8101-0973-5*) Northwestern U Pr.

— The Bureaucrats. Foulkes, Charles, tr. from FRE. (European Classics Ser.). 300p. 1993. pap. 14.95 (*0-8101-0987-5*) Northwestern U Pr.

— Le Cabinet des Antiques. Castex, Pierre-Georges, ed. (Coll. Prestige). 1958. 49.95 (0-685-34071-6); pap. 29.95 (0-8288-9361-6) Fr & Eur.
— The Centenarian: Or, the Two Beringhelds. Menville, Douglas A. & Reginald, R., eds. Slusser, George E., tr. LC 75-46250. (Supernatural & Occult Fiction Ser.). (Illus.). 1976. lib. bdg. 34.95 (0-405-08110-3) Ayer.
— Cesar Birotteau. 10.95 (0-8288-9362-4, 2070367037) Fr & Eur.
— Cesar Birotteau. (Folio Ser.: No. 703). (FRE.). pap. 9.95 (2-07-036703-7) Schoenhof.
— Cesar Birotteau. (Illus.). 320p. 1994. pap. 9.95 (0-14-044600-1, Penguin Classics) Viking Penguin.
— Le Chef-d'Oeuvre Inconnu. large type ed. (FRE.). 29.95 (0-7859-6520-3) Fr & Eur.
— Le Chef-d'Oeuvre Inconnu. (FRE.). 443p. 1991. reprint ed. pap. 10.95 (0-7859-3397-2) Fr & Eur.
— Les Chouans. (FRE.). 1972. pap. 12.95 (0-7859-1694-6, 2070360849) Fr & Eur.
— Les Chouans. (Folio Ser.: No. 84). (FRE.). pap. 9.95 (2-07-036084-9) Schoenhof.
— Les Chouans. unabridged ed. (FRE.). pap. 7.95 (2-87714-292-2, Pub. by Bookking Intl) Distribks Inc.
— Colonel Chabert. 1964. 10.95 (0-685-58341-4, 207036593X) Fr & Eur.
— Colonel Chabert. Cosman, Carol, tr. from FRE. LC 97-10790. 128p. 1997. pap. 9.95 (0-8112-1359-5, NDP847, Pub. by New Directions) Norton.
— Colonel Chabert. (Folio Ser.: No. 593). (FRE.). 1964. pap. 9.95 (2-07-036593-X) Schoenhof.
— Le Colonel Chabert: Le Contrat de Marriage. (FRE.). 1984. pap. 10.95 (0-7859-3119-8) Fr & Eur.
— Le Colonel Chabert: Suivi de Le Contrat de Mariage. (FRE.). (C). 1974. pap. 11.95 (0-8442-1827-8, VF1827-8) NTC Contemp Pub Co.
— Le Colonel Chabert, el Verdugo, Adieu, le Requisitionnaire. (FRE.). 320p. 1974. pap. 11.95 (0-7859-2207-5, 207036593X) Fr & Eur.
— Colonel Chabert, les Peines de Coeur... unabridged ed. (FRE.). pap. 5.95 (2-87714-199-3, Pub. by Bookking Intl) Distribks Inc.
— La Comedie Humaine, Vol. 1. (FRE.). 1712p. 125.00 (0-7859-7575-6) Fr & Eur.
— La Comedie Humaine, Vol. 1. deluxe ed. (Pleiade Ser.). (FRE.). 1574p. 1976. 85.95 (2-07-010851-1) Schoenhof.
— La Comedie Humaine, Vol. 2. deluxe ed. (Pleiade Ser.). (FRE.). 1176p. 1971. 85.95 (2-07-010852-X) Schoenhof.
— La Comedie Humaine, Vol. 3. deluxe ed. (Pleiade Ser.). (FRE.). 1680p. 1976. 88.95 (2-07-010858-9) Schoenhof.
— La Comedie Humaine, Vol. 4. deluxe ed. (Pleiade Ser.). (FRE.). 1072p. 88.95 (2-07-010862-7) Schoenhof.
— La Comedie Humaine, Vol. 5. 5th deluxe ed. (Pleiade Ser.). (FRE.). 1574p. 1977. 85.95 (2-07-010849-X) Schoenhof.
— La Comedie Humaine, Vol. 6. (Pleiade Ser.). (FRE.). 1577p. 1977. 84.95 (2-07-010850-3) Schoenhof.
— La Comedie Humaine, Vol. 7. deluxe ed. (Pleiade Ser.). (FRE.). 1760p. 1970. 88.95 (2-07-010874-0) Schoenhof.
— La Comedie Humaine, Vol. 8. deluxe ed. (Pleiade Ser.). (FRE.). 1852p. 93.95 (2-07-010866-X) Schoenhof.
— La Comedie Humaine, Vol. 9. (Pleiade Ser.). (FRE.). 1762p. 89.95 (2-07-010869-4) Schoenhof.
— La Comedie Humaine, Vol. 10. deluxe ed. (Pleiade Ser.). (FRE.). 1856p. 85.95 (2-07-010868-6) Schoenhof.
— La Comedie Humaine, Vol. 11. deluxe ed. (Pleiade Ser.). (FRE.). 1952p. 89.95 (2-07-010876-7) Schoenhof.
— La Comedie Humaine, Vol. 12. deluxe ed. (Pleiade Ser.). (FRE.). 1984p. 98.95 (2-07-010877-5) Schoenhof.
— La Comedie Humaine: Etudes de Moeurs (Scenes de la Vie Privee-1), Vol. 1. deluxe ed. (FRE.). 1574p. 1976. 110.00 (0-7859-4750-7, M2119) Fr & Eur.
— La Comedie Humaine: Scenes de la Vie de Province-2, Vol. 3. deluxe ed. (FRE.). 1680p. 1976. 115.00 (0-7859-4752-3, M2121) Fr & Eur.
— La Comedie Humaine: Scenes de la Vie Militaire, Scenes de la Vie de Campagne, Vol. 6. deluxe ed. (FRE.). 1577p. 1977. 105.00 (0-7859-4755-8, M2124) Fr & Eur.
— La Comedie Humaine: Scenes de la Vie Parisienne-1, Vol. 4. deluxe ed. (FRE.). 1072p. 1970. 110.00 (0-7859-4753-1, M2121) Fr & Eur.
— La Comedie Humaine: Scenes de la Vie Parisienne-2, Vol. 5. 5th deluxe ed. (FRE.). 1574p. 1977. 110.00 (0-7859-4754-X, M2123) Fr & Eur.
— La Comedie Humaine: Scenes de la Vie Privee-2, Scenes de la Vie de Province-1, Vol. 2. deluxe ed. (FRE.). 1176p. 1971. 110.00 (0-7859-4751-5, M2120) Fr & Eur.
— Contes Drolatiques. (FRE.). 189p. 1985. 29.95 (0-7859-4582-2, 2868810098) Fr & Eur.
— Le Contrat du Mariage, une Double Famille, l'Interdiction. (FRE.). 440p. 1973. pap. 10.95 (0-7859-1726-8, 2070363023) Fr & Eur.
— Le Contrat du Mariage, une Double Famille, l'Interdiction. (Folio Ser.: No. 302). (FRE.). 1973. pap. 8.95 (2-07-036302-3) Schoenhof.
— Correspondance, Vol. 1. (FRE.). 851p. 1960. 49.95 (0-8288-7466-2) Fr & Eur.
— Correspondance, Vol. 3. (FRE.). 927p. 1964. 49.95 (0-8288-7467-0) Fr & Eur.
— Correspondance, Vol. 4. (FRE.). 930p. 1966. 49.95 (0-8288-7468-9) Fr & Eur.
— Correspondance, Vol. 5. (FRE.). 1009p. 1969. 49.95 (0-8288-7469-7) Fr & Eur.
— Correspondances a l'Exception Ides Lettres de Mme. Hanska, 5 vols. Pierrot, ed. write for info. (0-8288-9326-8); write for info. (0-8288-9327-6); write for info. (0-8288-9328-4); write for info. (0-8288-9329-2); write for info. (0-8288-9330-6) Fr & Eur.
— Correspondances a l'Exception Ides Lettres de Mme. Hanska, 5 vols., Set. Pierrot, ed. pap. 65.00 (0-685-57707-4) Fr & Eur.
— Cousin Bette. 1998. 20.00 (0-375-40076-1) Everymns Lib.
— Cousin Bette. Raphael, Sylvia, tr. (Oxford World's Classics Ser.). (Illus.). 518p. 1998. pap. 9.95 (0-19-283668-4) OUP.
— Cousin Bette. LC 98-165915. 1998. pap. 10.95 (0-14-026821-9) Viking Penguin.
— Le Cousin Pons. Allem, ed. (Coll. Prestige). 1977. pap. 12.95 (0-7859-3468-5) Fr & Eur.
— Le Cousin Pons. (Folio Ser.: No. 380). 1962. pap. 9.95 (2-07-036380-5, 989) Schoenhof.
— Le Cousin Pons. Hunt, Herbert J., tr. (Classics Ser.). 336p. 1978. pap. 11.95 (0-14-044205-7, Penguin Classics) Viking Penguin.
— Le Cousin Pons. unabridged ed. (FRE.). pap. 7.95 (2-87714-190-X, Pub. by Bookking Intl) Distribks Inc.
— La Cousine Bette. Allem, Maurice, ed. (Coll. Prestige). (FRE.). 1984. 49.95 (0-685-34079-1); pap. 10.95 (0-7859-3466-9, 2070361381) Fr & Eur.
— La Cousine Bette. (Folio Ser.: No. 138). (FRE.). 1955. pap. 10.95 (2-07-036138-1, 952) Schoenhof.
— La Cousine Bette. Crawford, Marion A., tr. (Classics Ser.). 448p. 1965. pap. 10.95 (0-14-044160-3, Penguin Classics) Viking Penguin.
— La Cousine Bette. unabridged ed. (FRE.). pap. 7.95 (2-87714-154-3, Pub. by Bookking Intl) Distribks Inc.
— Le Cure de Tours. (Folio Ser.: No. 747). (FRE.). pap. 9.95 (2-07-036717-7) Schoenhof.
— Le Cure de Tours, La Grenadiere, L'Illustre Gaudissart. Berard, ed. (Coll. GF). pap. 11.95 (0-8288-9340-3) Fr & Eur.
— Le Cure de Tours, Pierette. Meininger, Anne-Marie, ed. (Coll. Prestige). (FRE.). 1976. pap. 12.95 (0-7859-1152-9, 2070367177) Fr & Eur.
— Le Cure de Village. 1965. 10.95 (0-685-58342-2, 2070366596) Fr & Eur.
— Le Cure de Village. (FRE.). 384p. 1975. pap. 12.95 (0-7859-1800-0, 2070366596) Fr & Eur.
— Le Cure de Village. (Folio Ser.: No. 659). (FRE.). 1965. pap. 9.95 (2-07-036659-6) Schoenhof.
— Un Debut dans la Vie. (FRE.). 251p. 1991. pap. 10.95 (0-7859-3480-4) Fr & Eur.
— Un Debut dans la Vie: Avec: un Homme d'Affairs, Un Prince de la Boheme. pap. 14.95 (0-686-53862-5) Fr & Eur.
— La Derniere Fee Ou la Nouvelle Lampe Merveilleuse, Paris, 1825. (FRE.). 186p. 1990. pap. 31.95 (0-7859-4583-0) Fr & Eur.
— La Duchesse de Langeais - La Fille aux Yeux d'Or. (FRE.). 1976. pap. 11.95 (0-7859-1834-5, 2070368467) Fr & Eur.
— La Duchesse de Langeais - une Tenebreuse Affaire. unabridged ed. (FRE.). 1996. pap. 7.95 (2-87714-331-7, Pub. by Bookking Intl) Distribks Inc.
— La Duchesse de Langeais & la Fille aux Yeux d'Or. (Folio Ser.: No. 846). (FRE.). 1958. pap. 9.95 (2-07-036846-7, 356) Schoenhof.
— L' Eglise. (FRE.). 108p. 1947. pap. 14.95 (0-7859-7574-8) Fr & Eur.
— Les Employes. (FRE.). 337p. 1985. pap. 16.95 (0-7859-2017-X, 2070376699) Fr & Eur.
— Les Employes. (Folio Ser.: No. 1669). (FRE.). 377p. 1970. 12.95 (2-07-037669-9) Schoenhof.
— L' Envers de l'Histoire Contemporaine. (FRE.). 340p. 1978. pap. 12.95 (0-7859-1879-5, 2070370569) Fr & Eur.
— Eugenie Grandet. LC 92-52896. 1992. 15.00 (0-679-41716-8) Everymns Lib.
— Eugenie Grandet. Caster, Pierre-Georges, ed. (Class. Garnier Ser.). (FRE.). 1964. pap. 10.95 (0-7859-3544-4, F55639) Fr & Eur.
— Eugenie Grandet. Castex, ed. (Coll. Prestige). (FRE.). 432p. 1979. 24.95 (0-7859-4661-6, F55628) Fr & Eur.
— Eugenie Grandet. (FRE.). (C). 1983. pap. 7.95 (0-8442-1958-4, VF1958-4) NTC Contemp Pub Co.
— Eugenie Grandet. Raphael, Sylvia, tr. (World's Classics Ser.). 234p. 1991. pap. 9.95 (0-19-282605-0) OUP.
***Balzac, Honore de.** Eugenie Grandet. Raphael, Sylvia, tr. (Exford World's Classics Ser.). 240p. 2000. pap. 9.95 (0-19-283834-2) OUP.
Balzac, Honore de. Eugenie Grandet. (Folio Ser.: No. 31). (FRE.). 1965. pap. 8.95 (2-07-036031-8) Schoenhof.
— Eugenie Grandet. Crawford, Marion A., tr. (Classics Ser.). 256p. 1955. pap. 10.95 (0-14-044050-X, Penguin Classics) Viking Penguin.
— Eugenie Grandet. unabridged ed. (FRE.). pap. 5.95 (2-87714-129-2, Pub. by Bookking Intl) Distribks Inc.
— La Femme de Trente. (Coll. GF). 1962. pap. 11.95 (0-8288-9332-2, 2201) Fr & Eur.
— La Femme de Trente Ans. Allem, Maurice, ed. (Class. Garnier Ser.). pap. 29.95 (0-685-34084-8) Fr & Eur.
— La Femme de Trente Ans. (FRE.). 371p. 1977. pap. 11.95 (0-7859-2212-1, 207036951X) Fr & Eur.
— La Femme de Trente Ans. (Folio Ser.: No. 951). (FRE.). pap. 9.95 (2-07-036951-X) Schoenhof.
— Ferragus: La Fille aux Yeux d'Or. (FRE.). 353p. 1988. pap. 12.95 (0-7859-2989-4) Fr & Eur.
— Une Fille d'Eve: La Fausse Maitresse. (Folio Ser.: No. 1202). (FRE.). pap. 9.95 (2-07-037202-2) Schoenhof.
— Une Fille d'Eve Suivi de la Fausse Maitresse. (FRE.). 1980. pap. 11.95 (0-7859-1918-X, 2070372022) Fr & Eur.
— Five Plays, 2 vols. in 1. 1976. reprint ed. 54.00 (0-86527-291-3) Fertig.
— Gambara. (FRE.). 200p. 1964. pap. 18.95 (0-7859-5320-5) Fr & Eur.
***Balzac, Honore de.** Gillette or the Unknown Masterpiece. 64p. 1999. 9.00 (0-903400-99-5, Pub. by Menard Pr.) SPD-Small Pr Dist.
Balzac, Honore de. The Girl with the Golden Eyes. Cosman, Carol, tr. 128p. 1998. 16.95 (0-7867-0561-2) Carroll & Graf.
***Balzac, Honore de.** The Girl with the Golden Eyes. LC 99-48840. 145p. 1999. 24.95 (1-56000-462-2) Transaction Pubs.
Balzac, Honore de. Gobseck une Double Famille. (FRE.). 256p. 1984. pap. 10.95 (0-7859-3398-0) Fr & Eur.
— Gosbeck: Maitre Cornelius, Facino Cane. 251p. 1969. 10.95 (0-8288-9355-1, F55491) Fr & Eur.
— Harlot High & Low. Heppenstall, Rayner, tr. (Ping Classic Ser.). 558p. 1970. pap. 13.95 (0-14-044232-4, Penguin Classics) Viking Penguin.
— Illusions Perdues. Adam, ed. (Class. Garnier Ser.). pap. 29.95 (0-685-34086-4) Fr & Eur.
— Illusions Perdues. (FRE.). 1972. pap. 17.95 (0-7859-1691-1, 2070360628) Fr & Eur.
— Illusions Perdues. Adam, ed. (Folio Ser.: No. 62). (FRE.). 13.95 (2-07-036062-8) Schoenhof.
— Illusions Perdues. unabridged ed. (FRE.). pap. 7.95 (2-87714-172-1, Pub. by Bookking Intl) Distribks Inc.
— The Last Fay. Du Plessis, Eric H., tr. from FRE. & intro. by. LC 95-47380. (Studies in French Literature: Vol. 23). (Illus.). 216p. 1996. text 89.95 (0-7734-8861-8) E Mellen.
— The Lily of the Valley. 2nd ed. Hill, Lucienne, tr. LC 97-17484. 256p. 1997. pap. 11.95 (0-7867-0471-3) Carroll & Graf.
— Lost Illusions. Raine, Kathleen, tr. LC 97-2727. 1997. 21.00 (0-679-60264-X) Modern Lib NY.
— Lost Illusions. Hunt, Herbert J., tr. LC 79-29738. (Classics Ser.). 384p. 1971. pap. 18.99 (0-14-044251-0, Penguin Classics) Viking Penguin.
— Louis Lambert. 272p. 1968. 10.95 (0-8288-9357-8) Fr & Eur.
— Louis Lambert - Les Proscrits - Jesus-Christ en Flandres. (FRE.). 320p. 1980. pap. 11.95 (0-7859-1905-8, 2070371611) Fr & Eur.
— Le Lys dans la Vallee. (Coll. Prestige). 49.95 (0-685-34088-0) Fr & Eur.
— Le Lys dans la Vallee. (FRE.). 1972. pap. 12.95 (0-7859-1698-9, 2070361128) Fr & Eur.
— Le Lys dans la Vallee. (Folio Ser.: No. 112). (FRE.). 1965. pap. 9.95 (2-07-036112-8) Schoenhof.
— Le Lys dans la Vallee. unabridged ed. (FRE.). pap. 7.95 (2-87714-170-5, Pub. by Bookking Intl) Distribks Inc.
— La Maison du Chat-Qui-Pelote: Avec: La Vendetta, la Bourse, le Bal de Sceaux. write for info. (0-318-63484-8) Fr & Eur.
— La Maison du Chat-Qui-Pelote & la Vendetta, la Bourse & le Bal de Sceaux. (Folio Ser.: No. 1441). (FRE.). pap. 12.95 (2-07-037441-6) Schoenhof.
— La Maison du Chat-Qui Pelote & le Bal de Sceaux & la Vendetta. (FRE.). 1985. pap. 16.95 (0-7859-1969-4, 2070374416) Fr & Eur.
— Maison Nucingen & Melmoth Reconcilie. (Folio Ser.: No. 1957). (FRE.). (Orig.). pap. 10.95 (2-07-038052-1) Schoenhof.
— Massimilla Doni. (FRE.). 264p. 1964. pap. 19.95 (0-7859-5321-3) Fr & Eur.
— Maximes et Pensees. 159p. 19.95 (0-686-53894-3) Fr & Eur.
— Le Medecin de Campagne. Allem, Maurice, ed. (Coll. Prestige). 49.95 (0-685-34089-9) Fr & Eur.
— Le Medecin de Campagne. Citron, Pierre, ed. (Coll. GF). pap. 9.95 (0-685-34090-2) Fr & Eur.
— Le Medecin de Campagne. (Class. Garnier Ser.). (FRE.). 1974. pap. 12.95 (0-7859-3470-7) Fr & Eur.
— Le Medecin de Campagne. (Folio Ser.: No. 636). (FRE.). pap. 10.95 (2-07-036636-7) Schoenhof.
— Memoires de Deux Jeunes Mariees. (FRE.). 352p. 1981. pap. 11.95 (0-7859-1932-5, 2070372685) Fr & Eur.
— Memoires de Deux Jeunes Mariees. (Folio Ser.: No. 1268). (FRE.). 380p. 1969. 9.95 (2-07-037268-5) Schoenhof.
— Mercadet. Cornthwaite, Robert, tr. LC 94-26759. (Great Translations for Actors Ser.). 128p. 1994. pap. 11.95 (1-880399-63-6) Smith & Kraus.
— Modeste Mignon. 382p. 1967. 10.95 (0-685-58344-9, 2070373606) Fr & Eur.
— Modeste Mignon. (FRE.). 382p. 1982. pap. 12.95 (0-7859-3474-X, 2070373606) Fr & Eur.
— Modeste Mignon. (Folio Ser.: No. 1360). (FRE.). 382p. 1967. pap. 9.95 (2-07-037360-6) Schoenhof.
— La Muse du Departement & un Prince de la Boheme. (FRE.). (Orig.). 1984. pap. 16.95 (0-7859-1992-9, 2070375420) Fr & Eur.
— La Muse du Departement & un Prince de la Boheme. (Folio Ser.: No. 1542). (FRE.). (Orig.). pap. 13.95 (2-07-037542-0) Schoenhof.
— Nouvelles Revolutionnaires. (FRE.). 1989. pap. 12.95 (0-7859-3431-6) Fr & Eur.
— Oeuvres Completes, 24 tomes, Set. 2500.00 (0-685-34067-8) Fr & Eur.
— Oeuvres Completes: Cambara, la Recherche de l'Absolu, l'Enfant Maudit, Vol. 15. (FRE., Illus.). 1970. 50.00 (0-7859-5331-0) Fr & Eur.
— Oeuvres Completes: Contes Drolatiques, Vol. 18. (FRE., Illus.). 1970. 50.00 (0-7859-5334-5) Fr & Eur.
— Oeuvres Completes: Enquete sur la Politique des deux Ministeres, Ecrits et Articles Legitimistes, Enchantillon de Causerie Francaise, Vol. 23. (FRE., Illus.). 1971. 50.00 (0-7859-5338-8) Fr & Eur.
— Oeuvres Completes: Facino Cane, Sarrasine, Pierre Grassau, Vol. 9. (FRE., Illus.). 1969. 150.00 (0-7859-5328-0) Fr & Eur.
— Oeuvres Completes: Falthurne, Stenie, la Seconde Falthurne, Vol. 21. (FRE., Illus.). 1970. 150.00 (0-7859-5553-4) Fr & Eur.
— Oeuvres Completes: Ferragus, la Duchessa de Langeais, la Fille aux yeur d'Or, Vol. 8. (FRE., Illus.). 1969. 150.00 (0-7859-5327-2) Fr & Eur.
— Oeuvres Completes: La Femme Abandonee, Honorine, Beatrix, Vol. 3. (FRE., Illus.). 1968. 150.00 (0-7859-5323-X) Fr & Eur.
— Oeuvres Completes: La Maison du Chat-Qui-Pelote, le Bal de Sceaux, Memoires de deux Jeunes Maries, Vol. 1. (FRE., Illus.). 1712p. 1968. 150.00 (0-7859-5322-1) Fr & Eur.
— Oeuvres Completes: La Medicin de Capagne, le Cure de Village, Les Paysans, Vol. 13. (FRE., Illus.). 1969. 150.00 (0-7859-5332-9) Fr & Eur.
— Oeuvres Completes: La Peau de Chagrin, Jesus-Christ en Flanders, Melmoth Reconcile, Vol. 14. (FRE., Illus.). 1969. 150.00 (0-7859-5330-2) Fr & Eur.
— Oeuvres Completes: La Pere Goriot, le Colonel Chabert, la Messe de l'Athee, Vol. 4. (FRE., Illus.). 1600p. 1968. 150.00 (0-7859-5324-8) Fr & Eur.
— Oeuvres Completes: L'Auberge Rouge, sur Catherine de Medicis, L'Elexir de Longue Vie, Vol. 16. (FRE., Illus.). 1970. 150.00 (0-685-73314-9) Fr & Eur.
— Oeuvres Completes: Le Cabinet des Antiques, Illusions Perdues, Vol. 7. (FRE., Illus.). 1968. 150.00 (0-7859-5552-6) Fr & Eur.
— Oeuvres Completes: Le Cousin Pons, un Prince de la Boheme, Vol. 11. (FRE., Illus.). 1969. 150.00 (0-685-73315-7) Fr & Eur.
— Oeuvres Completes: Le Cure de Tours, la Rabouilleuse, l'Illustre Gaudissart, Vol. 6. (FRE., Illus.). 1968. 150.00 (0-7859-5326-4) Fr & Eur.
— Oeuvres Completes: L'Epicier, la Femme comme Il Faut, le Notaire, Vol. 24. (FRE., Illus.). 1971. 150.00 (0-685-73316-5) Fr & Eur.
— Oeuvres Completes: Physiologie du Mariage, Petites Miseres de la Vie Conjugale, Vol. 17. (FRE., Illus.). 1970. 150.00 (0-7859-5333-7) Fr & Eur.
— Oeuvres Completes: Theatre, la Moratre, le Faiseur, l'Ecole des Menages, Vol. 20. (FRE., Illus.). 1970. 150.00 (0-7859-5336-1) Fr & Eur.
— Oeuvres Completes: Theatre, Vautrin, les Ressources de Quinola, Pamela Giraud, Vol. 19. (FRE., Illus.). 1970. 150.00 (0-7859-5335-3) Fr & Eur.
— Oeuvres Completes: Un Debut dans la Vie, Albert Savarus, La Vendetta, Vol. 2. (FRE., Illus.). 1968. 150.00 (0-7859-5551-8) Fr & Eur.
— Oeuvres Completes: Un Episode sous la Terrel, une Tenebreuse Affaire, le Depute d'Arcis, les Chouans, Vol. 12. (FRE., Illus.). 1969. 150.00 (0-685-73317-3) Fr & Eur.
— Oeuvres Completes: Un Homme d'Affaires, les Employes, la Cousine Bette, Vol. 10. (FRE., Illus.). 1969. 150.00 (0-7859-5329-9) Fr & Eur.
— Oeuvres Completes: Ursule Mirouet, Eugenie Grandet, la Lys dans la Vallee, Vol. 5. (FRE., Illus.). 1968. 150.00 (0-7859-5535-6) Fr & Eur.
— Oeuvres Completes: Vie de Moliere, Vie de la Fontane, Souvenirs d'un Paria, Vol. 22. (FRE., Illus.). 1971. 150.00 (0-7859-5337-X) Fr & Eur.
— Oeuvres Diverses. deluxe ed. Castex, Pierre-Georges, ed. (FRE.). 1904p. 1990. lib. bdg. 165.00 (0-7859-3811-7) Fr & Eur.
— Old Goriot. Crawford, Marion A., tr. (Classics Ser.). 304p. 1951. pap. 10.95 (0-14-044017-8, Penguin Classics) Viking Penguin.
— Les Paysans. (Folio Ser.: No. 675). (FRE.). pap. 9.95 (2-07-036675-8) Schoenhof.
— La Peau de Chagrin. Allem, Maurice, ed. (Class. Garnier Ser.). pap. 29.95 (0-685-34091-0) Fr & Eur.
— La Peau de Chagrin. (Coll. GF). 1960. pap. 10.95 (0-8288-9335-7, 1701) Fr & Eur.
— La Peau de Chagrin. (FRE.). 448p. 1966. pap. 10.95 (0-7859-3469-3, 2070365557) Fr & Eur.
— La Peau de Chagrin. 1999. pap. 9.95 (2-266-08332-5) Midwest European Pubns.
— La Peau de Chagrin. (Folio Ser.: No. 555). (FRE.). pap. 8.95 (2-07-036555-7) Schoenhof.
— Peines de Coeur d'une Chatte Anglaise. (FRE.). 1985. pap. 10.95 (0-7859-2988-6) Fr & Eur.
— Le Pere Goriot. 21.95 (0-88411-598-4) Amereon Ltd.
— Le Pere Goriot. Castex, Pierre-Georges, ed. (Coll. Prestige). 49.95 (0-685-34093-7); pap. 29.95 (0-685-34092-9) Fr & Eur.
— Le Pere Goriot. 1960. 10.95 (0-685-58345-7, 2070367843); pap. 10.95 (0-8288-9365-9, 2070367843) Fr & Eur.
— Le Pere Goriot. (Modern Library College Editions). (C). 1950. pap. text 6.25 (0-07-553572-6, T2) McGraw.
— Le Pere Goriot. 1962. mass mkt. 6.95 (0-451-52190-0, Sig Classics) NAL.
— Le Pere Goriot. (FRE.). (C). 1983. pap. 7.95 (0-8442-1764-6, VF1764-6) NTC Contemp Pub Co.
— Le Pere Goriot. (Folio Ser.: No. 784). (FRE.). 1960. pap. 9.95 (2-07-036784-3) Schoenhof.
— Pere Goriot. Krailsheimer, A. J., tr. (Oxford World's Classics Ser.). (Illus.). 300p. 1999. pap. 9.95 (0-19-283569-6) OUP.
— Le Pere Goriot. 1992. reprint ed. lib. bdg. 24.95 (0-89968-260-X, Lghtyr Pr) Buccaneer Bks.
— Le Pere Goriot. unabridged ed. (FRE.). pap. 7.95 (2-87714-123-3, Pub. by Bookking Intl) Distribks Inc.
Balzac, Honore de. Le Pere Goriot: D Level. text 8.95 (0-88436-043-1) EMC-Paradigm.
Balzac, Honore de. Physiologie du Mariage. (FRE.). 448p. 1987. pap. 11.95 (0-7859-2063-3, 2070378322) Fr & Eur.
— Physiologie du Mariage. (Folio Ser.: No. 1832). (FRE.). pap. 7.95 (2-07-037809-8) Schoenhof.
— Physiologie du Mariage. Regard, Maurice, ed. (Folio Ser.: No. 1832). (FRE.). 320p. 1968. 9.95 (2-07-037832-2) Schoenhof.

B

— Physiology of Marriage. LC 97-1641. 358p. (C). 1997. reprint ed. pap. text 15.95 (*0-8018-5550-0*) Johns Hopkins.

— The Quest of the Absolute. 1997. pap. 11.99 (*1-873982-58-5*, Pub. by Dedalus) Subterranean Co.

— La Rabouilleuse. 1960. 10.95 (*0-685-58346-5*, 2070361632) Fr & Eur.

— La Rabouilleuse. (FRE.). 448p. 1972. pap. 12.95 (*0-7859-1705-5*, 2070361632) Fr & Eur.

— La Rabouilleuse. (Folio Ser.: No. 163). (FRE.). 1960. pap. 9.95 (*2-07-036163-2*) Schoenhof.

— La Rabouilleuse. unabridged ed. (FRE.). pap. 7.95 (*2-87714-223-X*, Pub. by Bookking Intl) Distribks Inc.

— La Recherche de L'Absolu. (Folio Ser.: No. 739). (FRE.). pap. 9.95 (*2-07-036739-8*, 2163) Schoenhof.

— La Recherche de l'Absolu, la Messe de L'Athee. (FRE.). 1976. pap. 12.95 (*0-7859-1816-7*, 2070367398) Fr & Eur.

— The Rise & Fall of Cesar Birotteau. Furey, Francis T., tr. (Illus.). 449p. 1989. pap. 8.95 (*0-88184-448-9*) Carroll & Graf.

— Les Secrets de la Princesse de Cadignan et Autres Etudes. (FRE.). 416p. 1981. pap. 12.95 (*0-7859-1928-7*, 2070372502) Fr & Eur.

— Les Secrets de la Princesse de Cadignan et Autres Etudes de Femme. (Folio Ser.: No. 1250). (FRE.). pap. 9.95 (*2-07-037250-2*) Schoenhof.

— Selected Short Stories. 22.95 (*0-8488-0422-8*); lib. bdg. 22.95 (*0-8488-2132-7*) Amereon Ltd.

— Selected Short Stories. Raphael, Sylvia, ed. & tr. by. (Classics Ser.). 272p. 1977. pap. 12.95 (*0-14-044325-8*, Penguin Classics) Viking Penguin.

— Selected Short Stories: A Dual-Language Book. LC 99-39916. 256p. 1999. pap. text 9.95 (*0-486-40895-7*) Dover.

— Seraphita. LC 73-134961. (Short Story Index Reprint Ser.). 1980. 20.95 (*0-8369-3691-4*) Ayer.

— Seraphita. (FRE.). 172p. 1986. pap. 29.95 (*0-7859-4756-6*, M2149) Fr & Eur.

— Seraphita. 176p. 1997. reprint ed. pap. 19.95 (*0-7661-0113-4*) Kessinger Pub.

— Seraphita: (And Hours Lambert & the Esciles) 3rd ed. Blow, David, ed. Bell, Clara, tr. from FRE. (European Classics). (Illus.). 316p. 1999. reprint ed. pap. 11.95 (*1-873982-41-0*, Pub. by Dedalus) Hippocrene Bks.

— Serrasine: L'Hermaphrodite. (FRE.). 1989. pap. 11.95 (*0-7859-2997-5*) Fr & Eur.

— Splendeurs et Miseres des Courtisanes. (Coll. GF). pap. 9.95 (*0-685-34094-5*) Fr & Eur.

— Splendeurs et Miseres des Courtisanes. (FRE.). 704p. 1973. pap. 16.95 (*0-7859-1724-1*, 2070364054) Fr & Eur.

— Splendeurs et Miseres des Courtisanes. (Folio Ser.: No. 405). (FRE.). 698p. 1973. pap. 12.95 (*2-07-036405-4*) Schoenhof.

— Splendeurs et Miseres des Courtisanes. unabridged ed. (FRE.). pap. 7.95 (*2-87714-149-7*, Pub. by Bookking Intl) Distribks Inc.

— Une Tenebreuse Affaire. 1973. 11.95 (*0-685-58347-3*, 2070364682); pap. 11.95 (*0-7859-1760-8*, 2070364682) Fr & Eur.

— Une Tenebreuse Affaire. (Folio Ser.: No. 468). (FRE.). 1973. 9.95 (*2-07-036468-2*) Schoenhof.

***Balzac, Honore de.** The Unknown Masterpiece & Other Stories. Appelbaum, Stanley, tr. from FRE. LC 98-49245. 80p. 1999. pap. text 1.50 (*0-486-40649-0*) Dover.

Balzac, Honore de. Ursule Mirouet. write for info. (*0-318-63612-3*, 2449) Fr & Eur.

— Ursule Mirouet. (FRE.). 1981. pap. 12.95 (*0-7859-1937-6*, 2070373002) Fr & Eur.

— Ursule Mirouet. (Folio Ser.: No. 1300). (FRE.). pap. 9.95 (*2-07-037300-2*) Schoenhof.

— La Vieille Fille. (FRE.). 348p. 1990. pap. 11.95 (*0-7859-1154-5*, 2070370240) Fr & Eur.

— La Vieille Fille. (Folio Ser.: No. 1024). (FRE.). pap. 9.95 (*2-07-037024-0*) Schoenhof.

— La Vielle Fille: Le Cabinet des Antiques. (FRE.). 1990. reprint ed. pap. 13.95 (*0-7859-2990-8*) Fr & Eur.

— The Wild Ass's Skin. Hunt, Herbert J., tr. (Classics Ser.). 288p. 1977. pap. 10.95 (*0-14-044330-4*, Penguin Classics) Viking Penguin.

— Works: With Introductions by George Saintsbury, 18 Vols., Set. LC 78-150468. (Short Story Index Reprint Ser.). reprint ed. 550.00 (*0-8369-3791-0*) Ayer.

Balzac, Honore de & Brooks, Peter. Le Pere Goriot: A New Translation: Responses, Contemporaries & Other Novelists, Twentieth-Century Criticism. Raffel, Burton, tr. LC 97-19938. (Norton Critical Editions Ser.). (C). 1997. pap. text 12.50 (*0-393-97166-X*) Norton.

Balzac, Honore de & Castex, Pierre-G. L' Histoire des Treize: Avec: Ferragus, La Duchesse de Langeais, La Fille aux Yeux d'Or. (FRE., Illus.). 513p. 1992. pap. 14.95 (*0-7859-3239-9*, 2266043102) Fr & Eur.

Balzac, Honore de & Charpak, A. Monsieur Vautrin. (FRE.). 46p. 1963. pap. 14.95 (*0-8288-9058-7*, FA530) Fr & Eur.

Balzac, Honore de & Citron, Pierre. Une Fille d'Eve. 10.95 (*0-8288-9354-3*) Fr & Eur.

— Pierrette. 9.95 (*0-686-53924-9*) Fr & Eur.

Balzac, Honore de & Franck, Pierre. La Doulou. (FRE.). 280p. 1992. 29.95 (*0-7859-1205-3*, 2883820171) Fr & Eur.

Balzac, Honore de & Guyon, Bernard. L' Illustre Gaudissart: Avec: La Muse de Depatement. 576p. 1970. 28.95 (*0-8288-9356-X*) Fr & Eur.

Balzac, Honore de & Pommier, Jean. L' Eglise. 108p. 1947. 14.95 (*0-686-53864-1*) Fr & Eur.

Balzac, Honore de & Regard, Maurice. L' Envers de l'Histoire Contemporaine. (Folio Ser.: No. 1056). (FRE.). 1959. 9.95 (*2-07-037056-9*) Schoenhof.

Balzac, Honore de & Sacy, Samuel S. de. Les Paysans. 512p. 1975. 12.95 (*0-8288-9358-6*) Fr & Eur.

Balzac, Irma, tr. see Beller, William S., ed.

Balzac, Jean L. Les Oeuvres, 2 vols. lxviii, 1996p. reprint ed. write for info. (*0-318-71314-4*) G Olms Pubs.

Balzani, Ugo. Le Cronache Italiane Nel Medio Evo. xiv, 333p. 1973. reprint ed. 70.00 incl. 3.5 hd (*3-487-04671-7*) G Olms Pubs.

Balzani, Vincenzo, ed. Supramolecular Photochemistry. (C). 1987. text 247.50 (*90-277-2593-4*) Kluwer Academic.

Balzani, Vincenzo & De Cola, Lee. Supramolecular Chemistry: Proceedings of the Second NATO Science Forum, Taormina (Sicily), Italy, December 15-18, 1991. LC 92-5813. (NATO Advanced Study Institutes Series C, Mathematical & Physical Sciences: No. 371). 476p. (C). 1992. text 247.50 (*0-7923-1759-9*) Kluwer Academic.

***Balzano, Frederica J.** Why Should Extroverts Make All the Money? Networking Made Easy for the Introvert. 256p. 2000. pap. 14.95 (*0-8092-9787-6*, Contemporary Bks) NTC Contemp Pub Co.

Balzano, Frederica J. & Kelly, Marsha B. Why Should Extroverts Make All the Money? LC 98-49521. 256p. 1999. 21.95 (*0-8092-2816-5*, 281650, Contemporary Bks) NTC Contemp Pub Co.

Balzano, Gerald J., jt. ed. see McCabe, Vickie.

Balzar, John. Yukon Alone: The World's Toughest Adventure Race. LC 99-10313. (Illus.). 304p. 2000. 25.00 (*0-8050-5949-0*) H Holt & Co.

— Yukon Alone: The World's Toughest Adventure Race. (Illus.). 320p. 2001. pap. 14.00 (*0-8050-5950-4*, Owl) H Holt & Co.

Balzarotti, A., et al, eds. Spectroscopies of Semiconductors & Insulators, Highlights On: Proceedings of International School. 532p. (C). 1989. text 141.00 (*9971-5-0959-8*) World Scientific Pub.

Balzatti, James D. U. S. Stabling Guide, Vol. 6. Maimone, Donella, ed. (Illus.). 300p. Date not set. pap. 24.95 (*0-9655278-2-4*) Balzotti Pubns.

Balzer, Cary, jt. auth. see Balzer, Tracy.

Balzer, D. & Luders, H. Alkypolyglucosides as a Nonionic Surfactant. (Surfactant Science Ser.). 2000. write for info. (*0-8247-9390-0*) Dekker.

***Balzer, Donna.** The Prairie Rock Garden. (Prairie Garden Bks.). (Illus.). 96p. 2000. pap. 9.95 (*0-88995-195-0*, Pub. by Red Deer) Genl Dist Srvs.

Balzer, Elizabeth. Hercules. LC 96-71817. (Illus.). (J). 1997. lib. bdg. 14.89 (*0-7868-5050-7*, Pub. by Disney Pr) Little.

— Hercules Illustrated Classic, Vol. 1. LC 96-71817. (Illus.). 96p. (J). 1997. 14.95 (*0-7868-3126-X*, Pub. by Disney Pr) Time Warner.

Balzer, Harley D., ed. Russia's Missing Middle Class: The Professions in Russian History. LC 95-42117. 352p. (YA). (gr. 13). 1996. text 87.95 (*1-56324-707-0*); pap. text 36.95 (*1-56324-748-8*) M E Sharpe.

***Balzer, Howard.** Kurt Warner: The Quarterback. LC 00-101251. (Sport Snaps Ser.). 2000. pap. text 12.95 (*1-892920-34-4*) G H B Pubs.

Balzer, Isabel, tr. see Cachin, Charles.

Balzer, Isabel, tr. see Thompson, Lauri, ed.

Balzer, John E. Buck's Book: A View of the Third Vermont Infantry Regiment. 80p. 1992. pap. 9.95 (*0-9634722-2-4*) Balzer & Assocs.

Balzer, Marjorie M., ed. Culture Incarnate: Native Anthropology from Russia. LC 94-33956. 284p. (gr. 13). 1995. 81.95 (*1-56324-534-5*) M E Sharpe.

— Culture Incarnate: Native Anthropology from Russia. LC 94-33956. 284p. (C). (gr. 13). 1995. pap. 36.95 (*1-56324-535-3*) M E Sharpe.

— Russian Traditional Culture: Religion, Gender & Customary Law. LC 92-4775. (Illus.). 332p. (C). (gr. 13). 1992. pap. text 38.95 (*1-56324-040-8*) M E Sharpe.

— Shamanic Worlds: Rituals & Lore of Siberia & Central Asia. LC 96-28497. (Illus.). 292p. (gr. 13). 1996. pap. 21.95 (*1-56324-973-1*, N Castle) M E Sharpe.

— Shamanism: Soviet Studies of Traditional Religion in Siberia & Central Asia. LC 89-77158. 216p. (C). (gr. 13). 1990. 79.95 (*0-87332-624-5*) M E Sharpe.

Balzer, Marjorie M., ed. Russian Traditional Culture: Religion, Gender & Customary Law. LC 92-4775. (Illus.). 332p. (C). (gr. 13). 1992. text 85.95 (*1-56324-039-4*) M E Sharpe.

***Balzer, Marjorie Mandelstam.** The Tenacity of Ethnicity: A Siberian Saga in Global Perspective. LC 99-22818. (Illus.). 280p. 1999. 55.00 (*0-691-00674-1*, Pub. by Princeton U Pr) Cal Prin Full Svc.

Balzer, Marjorie Mandelstam. The Tenacity of Ethnicity: A Siberian Saga in Global Perspective. LC 99-22818. 280p. 1999. pap. 19.95 (*0-691-00673-3*, Pub. by Princeton U Pr) Cal Prin Full Svc.

Balzer, Nadine, ed. see Betters, Fran.

Balzer, Pamela, jt. ed. see Schoengrund, Lynn.

Balzer, Ralf & Strauss, Dieter. Alles Gute: Companion Guide. (GER.). 176p. 1989. 15.95 (*3-468-96870-1*) Langenscheidt.

— Alles Gute: Workbook Study Guide. (GER.). 176p. 1989. student ed. 22.95 (*3-468-96880-9*) Langenscheidt.

Balzer, Richard. Peepshows: A Visual History. LC 97-33267. (FRE & ENG., Illus.). 160p. 1998. 45.00 (*0-8109-6349-3*, Pub. by Abrams) Time Warner.

— Peepshows: An Eye to the World. (Illus.). 160p. (Orig.). 1997. write for info. (*0-9656676-0-X*); pap. write for info. (*0-9656676-1-8*) Eye Wndr Pr.

Balzer-Riley, Julia. Communications in Nursing: Communicating Assertively & Responsibly in Nursing. 3rd ed. (Illus.). 496p. (C). (gr. 13). 1995. pap. text 35.00 (*0-8151-0562-2*, 25467) Mosby Inc.

— Customer Service from A to Z: Making the Connection. (Illus.). 170p. 1998. pap. 29.95 (*1-888343-17-6*) Hartman Pub.

Balzer, Robert L. Wines of the World, 2 vols., Set. (Learn in Your Car - Discovery Ser.). 1992. pap. 29.95 incl. audio (*1-56015-206-0*) Penton Overseas.

— Wines of the World, Vol. 1, set. (Learn in Your Car - Discovery Ser.). 1992. pap. 15.95 incl. audio (*1-56015-200-1*) Penton Overseas.

— Wines of the World, Vol. 2, set. abr. ed. (Learn in Your Car - Discovery Ser.: Vol. 2). 1992. pap. 15.95 incl. audio (*1-56015-205-2*) Penton Overseas.

Balzer, Tracy & Balzer, Cary. The Way Cool Bible: Topical Selection Teac. 55p. 1993. pap. 4.95 (*0-917851-61-7*) Bristol Hse.

Balzer, William K., et al. Users' Manual for the Job Descriptive Index (JD1; 1997 Revision) & the Job in General (JIG) Scales. 2nd rev. ed. (Illus.). 273p. (Orig.). 1997. pap. 35.00 (*0-9627727-0-4*) BGSU Dept Psy.

Balzer, Wolfgang. Soziale Institutionen. (Philosophie & Wissenschaft - Transdisziplinaere Studien: No. 4). (GER.). x, 306p. (Orig.). 1993. pap. 36.95 (*3-11-013850-6*) De Gruyter.

Balzer, Wolfgang, et al, eds. Reduction in Science: Structure, Examples, Philosophical Problems. (Synthese Library: 175). 453p. 1984. text 179.50 (*90-277-1811-3*) Kluwer Academic.

Balzer, Wolfgang & Dawe, Chris M. Models for Genetics. (Illus.). 183p. 1997. pap. 42.95 (*3-631-31876-6*) P Lang Pubng.

— Models for Genetics. LC 97-19725. (Illus.). 183p. 1997. pap. 42.95 (*0-8204-3283-0*) P Lang Pubng.

Balzer, Wolfgang & Hamminga, Bert, eds. Philosophy of Economics. 272p. (C). 1989. lib. bdg. 132.00 (*0-7923-0157-9*, Pub. by Kluwer Academic) Kluwer Academic.

Balzer, Wolfgang & Heidelberger, Michael, eds. Zur Logik Empirischer Theorien. 331p. 1983. 66.95 (*3-11-008236-5*); pap. 32.35 (*3-11-009711-7*) De Gruyter.

Balzer, Wolfgang & Moulines, C. Ulises, eds. Structuralist Theory of Science: Focal Issues, New Results. LC 95-45839. (Perspektiven der Analytischen Philosophie - Perspectives in Analytical Philosophy Ser.: Vol. 6). xi, 295p. (C). 1996. lib. bdg. 155.60 (*3-11-014075-6*) De Gruyter.

Balzer, Wolfgang, et al. An Architectonic for Science. 468p. (C). 1987. text 237.50 (*90-277-2403-2*, D Reidel) Kluwer Academic.

Balzert, Monika. Die Komposition Des Claudianischen Gotenkriegsgedichtes c. 26. (Spudasmata Ser.: Bd. 23). (GER.). vii, 158p. 1974. 35.00 (*3-487-05134-6*) G Olms Pubs.

Balzhiser, R. E., et al. Chemical Engineering Thermodynamics. (International Physical & Chemical Engineering Sciences Ser). (Illus.). (C). 1972. text 68.20 (*0-13-128603-X*) P-H.

Balzola, Asun. La Primavera. (Cuatro Estaciones Ser.). (SPA.). 1986. 12.15 (*0-606-02306-2*, Pub. by Turtleback) Demco.

Balzora, Renaud, tr. see Brock, Charles.

***Balzotti, Jim.** Jim Balzotti's Best Guest Ranches & Horseback Riding Vacations. 2nd ed. 2000. pap. text 22.95 (*0-9655278-1-6*) Balzotti Pubns.

***Balzouman, Paul.** The Adventures of Bustum & Bookum. LC 99-93620. (Illus.). 1999. pap. 7.95 (*0-533-13090-5*) Vantage.

***Bama.** Karukku - Translated from the Tamil. 2000. pap. 7.95 (*0-333-93190-4*, Pub. by Macmillan) S Asia.

Baman Das Basu, ed. The Sacred Books of the Hindus, 47 vols. reprint ed. 1575.50 (*0-404-57800-4*) AMS Pr.

Bamat, Thomas & Wiest, Jean-Paul, eds. Popular Catholicism in a World Church: Seven Case Studies in Inculturation. LC 98-55523. (Faith & Cultures Ser.). xii, 315p. 1999. pap. 24.00 (*1-57075-252-4*) Orbis Bks.

Bambace, Anthony, compiled by. Will H. Bradley: A Reference Guide. LC 94-43788. 1995. 75.00 (*1-884718-08-6*) Oak Knoll.

— Will H. Bradley: A Reference Guide. deluxe ed. LC 94-43788. 1995. 450.00 (*1-884718-09-4*) Oak Knoll.

Bambach, Carmen C. Drawing & Painting in the Italian Renaissance Workshop: Theory & Practice, 1300-1600. LC 98-51727. (Illus.). 480p. (C). 1999. 125.00 (*0-521-40218-2*) Cambridge U Pr.

Bambach, Carmen C., et al. Genoa: Drawings & Prints, 1530-1800. LC 96-155. (Illus.). 96p. (Orig.). 1996. pap. 14.95 (*0-87099-772-6*) Metro Mus Art.

Bambach, Charles R. Heidegger, Dilthey, & the Crisis of Historicism. 304p. 1995. text 47.50 (*0-8014-3079-8*); pap. text 19.95 (*0-8014-8260-7*) Cornell U Pr.

Bambach, Richard K., ed. see Erwin, Douglas H.

***Bambah, R. P. & Hans-Gill, R. J., eds.** Number Theory. (Trends in Mathematics Ser.). 536p. 2000. 115.00 (*3-7643-6259-6*) Birkhauser.

***Bambah, R. P., et al.** Number Theory. LC 00-21717. (Trends in Mathematics Ser.). (Illus.). 2000. write for info. (*0-8176-6259-6*) Birkhauser.

Bambakidis, Gust & Bowmannn, R. C., Jr., eds. Hydrogen in Disordered & Amorphous Solids. LC 86-8154. (NATO ASI Series B, Physics: Vol. 136). 438p. 1986. 110.00 (*0-306-42275-1*, Plenum Trade) Perseus Pubng.

Bambara, Joseph, jt. auth. see Allen, Paul R.

***Bambara, Joseph J.** SQL Server 7 Developer's Guide. (Illus.). 850p. 2000. pap. 39.99 (*0-7645-4672-4*) IDG Bks.

Bambara, Linda M. & Knoster, Tim. Designing Positive Behavior Support Plans. LC 98-10503. (Innovations Ser.). 1998. 21.95 (*0-940898-55-1*) Am Assn Mental.

Bambara, Linda M. & Koger, Freya. Opportunities for Daily Choice Making. Browder, Diane M., ed. LC 96-35425. (Innovations Ser.: Vol. 8). (Illus.). 48p. (Orig.). 1996. pap. 21.95 (*0-940898-44-6*) Am Assn Mental.

Bambara, Richard J. MVS & UNIX: A Survival Handbook for Multi-Platform Users, Developers & Managers. LC 98-6457. (Illus.). 608p. 1998. pap. 65.00 (*0-07-006663-9*) McGraw.

Bambara, Toni Cade. Gorilla, My Love. 192p. 1992. pap. 11.00 (*0-679-73898-3*) Vin Bks.

— The Salt Eaters. 304p. 1992. pap. 12.00 (*0-679-74076-7*) Vin Bks.

— The Sea Birds Are Still Alive. LC 82-40018. 224p. 1982. pap. 12.00 (*0-394-71176-9*) Random.

***Bambara, Toni Cade.** Those Bones Are Not My Child. 2000. pap. 16.00 (*0-679-77408-4*) Vin Bks.

— Those Bones Are Not My Child: A Novel, 1 vol. LC 99-21534. 944p. 1999. 27.50 (*0-679-44261-8*) Pantheon.

Bambara, Toni Cade & Wise, Leah, eds. Southern Black Utterances Today. (Southern Exposure Ser.). (Illus.). 120p. (Orig.). (C). 1975. pap. 4.50 (*0-943810-04-3*) Inst Southern Studies.

***Bambaren, Sergio.** The Dolphin. (Illus.). 112p. 1999. reprint ed. pap. 10.95 (*1-56170-398-2*, 800T) Hay House.

Bambaren, Sergio. The Dolphin: Story of a Dreamer. 2nd rev. ed. LC 97-14212. (Illus.). 112p. 1997. 14.95 (*1-56170-391-5*, 800) Hay House.

Bambauer, H. U., et al. Optische Bestimmung der Gesteinsbildenden Minerale Teil 1: Bestimmungstabellen. 188p. 1982. 32.00 (*3-510-65106-5*, Pub. by E Schweizerbartsche) Balogh.

Bambeck, Manfred. Goettliche Komoedie & Exegese. viii, 253p. (C). 1975. pap. 129.25 (*3-11-004874-4*) De Gruyter.

Bamber, B. & Lansbury. International & Comparative Industrial Relations. 2nd ed. 1993. pap. text 29.95 (*1-86152-197-9*) Thomson Learn.

Bamber, C. J. Plants of the Punjab. (C). 1976. text 350.00 (*0-89771-546-2*, Pub. by Intl Bk Distr) St Mut.

Bamber, C. J., ed. Plants of the Punjab. 676p. 1976. reprint ed. 225.00 (*0-7855-6642-2*, Pub. by Intl Bk Distr) St Mut.

Bamber, Chrissie, et al. Learning from Others: Good Programs & Successful Campaigns. LC 96-84978. 358p. 1996. pap. text 50.00 (*0-912585-11-0*) Ctr Law & Ed.

Bamber, Greg J. & Lansbury, Russell, eds. International & Comparative Industrial Relations. 276p. 1987. text 39.95 (*0-04-327097-2*); pap. text 18.95 (*0-04-327096-4*) Routledge.

Bamber, Greg J. & Lansbury, Russell D. International & Comparative Employment Relations: A Study of Industrialised Market Economies. rev. ed. LC 98-60249. xiii, 442 p. 1998. write for info. (*0-7619-5591-7*) Sage.

Bamber, Linda. Comic Women, Tragic Men: A Study of Gender & Genre in Shakespeare. LC 81-51903. 224p. 1982. 39.50 (*0-8047-1126-7*) Stanford U Pr.

Bamberg, Christian. Franzoezich fur Mediziner: Medizinisches Woerterbuch. (FRE & GER.). 398p. 1992. 75.00 (*0-7859-7113-0*, 382431181X) Fr & Eur.

Bamberg, Corona. Cost of Being Human. 1984. 14.95 (*0-87193-128-1*) Dimension Bks.

Bamberg, David. Illusion Show: A Life in Magic. 2nd enl. rev. ed. (Illus.). 440p. 1991. 49.50 (*0-916638-48-0*, D M Magic Bks) Meyerbooks.

Bamberg, Dorothy L., jt. auth. see Rapp, Doris J.

Bamberg, E. & Schoner, W., eds. The Sodium Pump: Structure Mechanism Hormonal Control & Its Role in Disease. 906p. 1994. 87.95 (*0-387-91466-8*) Spr-Verlag.

Bamberg, Ernst & Passow, Hermann, eds. The Band Three Proteins: Anion Transporters, Binding Proteins, & Senescent Antigenes. LC 92-22096. (Progress in Cell Research Ser.: Vol. 2). xvi,358p. 1992. 237.50 (*0-444-89547-7*) Elsevier.

Bamberg, G. Agency Theory, Information, & Incentives. Spremann, Klaus, ed. (Illus.). 555p. 1987. 83.70 (*0-387-18422-8*) Spr-Verlag.

Bamberg, G. & Spremann, A., eds. Risk & Capital: Proceedings of the 2nd Summer Workshop on Risk & Capital Held at the University of Ulm, West Germany, June 20-24, 1983. (Lecture Notes in Economics & Mathematical Systems Ser.: Vol. 227). 320p. 1984. 41.00 (*0-387-12923-5*) Spr-Verlag.

Bamberg, G. & Spremann, Klaus, eds. Capital Market Equilibria. (Illus.). x, 228p. 1986. 59.00 (*0-387-16248-8*) Spr-Verlag.

***Bamberg, J. H.** British Petroleum & the Political Economy of International Oil, 1950-1975: The Challenge of Nationalism. LC 99-51453. 2000. write for info. (*0-521-25951-7*) Cambridge U Pr.

— The History of the British Petroleum Company: British Petroleum & Global Oil, 1950-1975, Vol. 3. (History of British Petroleum). (Illus.). 500p. (C). 2000. pap. text Price not set. (*0-521-78515-4*) Cambridge U Pr.

Bamberg, J. H. The History of the British Petroleum Company, Vol. 2: The Anglo-Iranian Years, 1928-1954. (Illus.). 667p. (C). 1994. text 100.00 (*0-521-25950-9*) Cambridge U Pr.

Bamberg, Michael. The Acquisition of Narratives: Learning to Use Language. (New Babylon Studies in the Social Sciences: No. 49). 245p. (C). 1988. text 113.10 (*0-89925-285-0*) Mouton.

Bamberg, Michael G. Narrative Development: Six Approaches. LC 97-2352. 1997. 69.95 (*0-8058-2057-4*); pap. 32.50 (*0-8058-2058-2*) L Erlbaum Assocs.

Bamberg, Michael G., ed. Oral Versions of Personal Experience - Three Decades of Narrative Analysis: A Special Issue of the Journal of Narrative & Life History. 415p. 1997. pap. write for info. (*0-8058-9865-4*) L Erlbaum Assocs.

Bamberg, Paul & Sternberg, Shlomo. A Course in Mathematics for Students of Physics, 2 vols., Vol. 1. 423p. (C). 1991. pap. text 32.95 (*0-521-40649-8*) Cambridge U Pr.

Bamberg, Robert D., ed. see James, Henry.

An Asterisk (*) at the beginning of an entry indicates that the title is appearing for the first time.

Bamberger, Carl, ed. The Conductor's Art. 334p. 1989. text 69.00 (*0-231-07128-0*) Col U Pr.

Bamberger, David. Judaism & the World's Religions. (J). (gr. 7-8). pap. 9.95 (*0-87441-461-X*) Behrman.

— My People: Abba Eban's History of the Jews, Vol. II. (Illus.). 1979. pap. 10.95 (*0-87441-280-3*) Behrman.

— My People: Abba Eban's History of the Jews Genesis to 1776, Vol. I. LC 77-10667. (Illus.). 1978. pap. text 10.95 (*0-87441-263-3*) Behrman.

— A Young Person's History of Israel. 2nd ed. Mandelkern, Nicholas D., ed. (Illus.). 150p. (Orig.). (J). (gr. 5-7). 1985. pap. 7.95 (*0-87441-393-1*) Behrman.

Bamberger, David & Bedor, Deborah. Judaism & the World's Religions. pap., teacher ed. 14.95 (*0-87441-481-4*) Behrman.

Bamberger, David & Horn, Geoffrey. My People: Abba Eban's History of the Jews Genesis to 1776, Vol. I. LC 77-10667. (Illus.). 1978. pap., teacher ed. 14.95 (*0-87441-296-X*) Behrman.

Bamberger, David & Kurinsky, Miriam P. My People: Abba Eban's History of the Jews Genesis to 1776, Vol. I. LC 77-10667. (Illus.). 1978. pap., wbk. ed. 4.95 (*0-87441-329-X*) Behrman.

Bamberger, David, jt. auth. see Horn, Geoffrey.

Bamberger, David, jt. auth. see Siegel, Seymour.

Bamberger, Fred. Your Computer Can Kill You. 1984. ring bd. 74.95 (*0-917194-15-2*) Prog Studies.

Bamberger, Honi. Logic Posters, Problems & Puzzles: 4 Big Posters & Dozens of Brain Boosting Reproducibles. (J). 1999. pap. 12.95 (*0-590-64273-1*) Scholastic Inc.

— Super Graphs, Venns & Glyphs: Hundreds of Great Data Collecting Activities to Build Real... 1996. pap. text 16.95 (*0-590-67477-3*) Scholastic Inc.

Bamberger, I. Nathan. Timely Torah Twinkles. LC 88-43161. 110p. 1988. pap. 8.95 (*0-88400-131-8*, Shengold Bks) Schreiber Pub.

Bamberger, Ib N. The Viking Jews. (Illus.). 162p. 1990. reprint ed. pap. 9.95 (*1-871055-60-1*) Soncino Pr.

Bamberger, Ingold, ed. Product/Market Strategies of Small & Medium-Sized Enterprises. 435p. 1994. 96.95 (*1-85628-963-X*, Pub. by Avebry) Ashgate Pub Co.

Bamberger, Jeanne. The Mind Behind the Musical Ear: How Children Develop Musical Intelligence. 304p. (C). 1991. text 52.00 (*0-674-57607-1*) HUP.

— The Mind Behind the Musical Ear: How Children Develop Musical Intelligence. (Illus.). 304p. 1995. pap. text 20.50 (*0-674-57606-3*, BAMMIX) HUP.

***Bamberger, Jeanne Shapiro.** Developing Musical Intuitions: A Project-Based Introduction to Making & Understanding Music. LC 99-11123. 320p. 1999. write for info. (*0-19-510571-0*) OUP.

Bamberger, John E., tr. from GRE. Praktikos & Chapters on Prayer. LC 76-152483. (Cistercian Studies: No. 4). xciv, 88p. 1972. pap. 6.95 (*0-87907-904-5*) Cistercian Pubns.

Bamberger, Michael. Integrating Quantitative & Qualitative Research: Lessons from the Field. LC 99-12980. (Directions in Development Ser.). 1999. write for info. (*0-8213-4431-5*) World Bank.

— To the Linksland. 208p. 1993. pap. 12.95 (*0-14-015941-X*, Penguin Bks) Viking Penguin.

Bamberger, Michael, et al, eds. The Design & Management of Poverty Reduction Programs & Projects in Anglophone Africa: Proceedings of a Seminar Sponsored Jointly by the Economic Development Institute of the World Bank & the Uganda Management Institute. LC 94-354. (EDI Seminar Ser.). 218p. 1996. pap. 22.00 (*0-8213-2767-4*, 12767) World Bank.

Bamberger, Michael & Aziz, Abdul, eds. The Design & Management of Sustainable Projects to Alleviate Poverty in South Asia: EDI Seminar Report Ser. LC 93-8237. 350p. 1993. pap. 22.00 (*0-8213-2472-1*, 12472) World Bank.

Bamberger, Michael & Cheema, G. Shabbir. Case Studies of Project Sustainability: Implications for Policy & Operations from Asian Experience. (EDI Seminar Ser.). 122p. 1990. pap. 22.00 (*0-8213-1614-1*, 11614) World Bank.

Bamberger, Michael, jt. auth. see Valadez, Joseph.

Bamberger, Michael A. Reckless Legislation: How Legislators Ignore the Constitution. LC 99-32376. 224p. 2000. text 32.00 (*0-8135-2732-5*) Rutgers U Pr.

Bamberger, Michael A., et al, eds. State Limited Partnership Laws, 10 vols. 6469p. 1987. ring bd. 795.00 (*0-13-108523-9*) Aspen Law.

Bamberger, Michael A. & Basile, Joseph J. State Limited Partnership Laws: Practice Guides, Statutes, Annotations & Official Forms. LC 86-30532. 497.00 (*0-15-004391-0*) P-H.

Bamberger, Michael A. & Jacobson, Arthur J., eds. State Limited Liability Company Laws: Practice Guides, Annotations, Statutes, Forms, 3 vols., Set. LC 94-191. 3800p. 1994. 250.00 (*0-13-124892-8*) Aspen Law.

— State Limited Partnership Laws, 7 vols. 9458p. 1998. ring bd. 520.00 (*1-56706-257-1*, 62571) Panel Pubs.

Bamberger, Michael A.l & Jacobson, Arthur J., eds. State Limited Liability Company & Partnership Laws, 5 vols. 5354p. 1999. ring bd. 325.00 (*1-56706-256-3*, 62563) Panel Pubs.

Bamberger, Michelle. Help! The Quick Guide to First Aid for Your Dog. (Illus.). 160p. 1993. per. 9.95 (*0-87605-557-9*) Howell Bks.

— Help! The Quick Guide to First Aid for Your Cat: The Quick Guide to First Aid for Your Cat. LC 94-37313. (Illus.). 160p. 1995. per. 9.95 (*0-87605-794-6*) Howell Bks.

***Bamberger, Peter & Meshoulam, Ilan.** Human Resource Strategy: Formulation, Implementation & Impact. LC 99-50419. (Advanced Topics in Organizational Behavior Ser.). 214p. 2000. 56.00 (*0-7619-1424-2*) Sage.

Bamberger, Phylis S. & Gottlieb, David J., eds. Practice under the Federal Sentencing Guidelines, 3 vols. 3rd ed. 2690p. 1993. ring bd. 260.00 (*0-13-126905-4*) Aspen Law.

Bamberger, Seligman B. Kisvei Rabbeinu Yitzchak Dov Halevi. 2nd ed. LC 93-826529. (Illus.). 1992. write for info. (*0-9635295-0-1*) Z B Bamberger.

Bamberger, Tom. An American Story: Photography from the Permanent Collection. (Illus.). 32p. (Orig.). 1992. pap. 9.95 (*0-944110-29-0*) Milwauk Art Mus.

— Blood Relatives: The Family in Contemporary Photography. (Illus.). 16p. (Orig.). 1991. pap. 4.95 (*0-944110-10-X*) Milwauk Art Mus.

— New Wisconsin Photography. (Illus.). 27p. 1994. pap. 5.00 (*0-944110-49-5*) Milwauk Art Mus.

Bamberger, Tom & Brehmer, Debra. Nathan Lerner: Photographs, 1932-1944. (Illus.). 16p. 1995. pap. 5.00 (*0-944110-54-1*) Milwauk Art Mus.

Bamberger, Tom & Marvel, Terrence L. H. H. Bennett: A Sense of Place. (Illus.). 32p. (Orig.). 1992. pap. 12.00 (*0-944110-26-6*) Milwauk Art Mus.

Bamberger, Tom, et al. Generation X: New Art from Milwaukee. (Illus.). 24p. (Orig.). 1995. pap. 5.00 (*0-944110-75-4*) Milwauk Art Mus.

Bamberger, Tom, jt. auth. see Freudenheim, Tom L.

Bamberger, W. C. A Jealousy for Aesop. LC 86-63357. 112p. (Orig.). 1987. pap. 9.95 (*0-930501-12-8*) Livingston U Pr.

— A Jealousy for Aesop. LC 86-63357. (Illus.). 112p. (Orig.). (C). 1987. pap. 9.95 (*0-930501-13-6*) Swallows Tale Pr.

— Kenward Elmslie: A Bibliographical Profile. (Illus.). 138p. 1993. pap. 15.00 (*0-917453-29-8*) Bamberger.

— Riding Some Kind of Unusual Skull Sleigh: On the Arts of Don Van Vliet. limited ed. (Illus.). 210p. 1999. pap. 17.00 (*0-917453-35-2*) Bamberger.

— William Eastlake: High Desert Interlocutor. LC 92-24444. (Milford Series: Popular Writers of Today: Popular Writers of Today: Vol. 65). 136p. 1993. pap. 19.00 (*0-89370-296-X*) Millefleurs.

— The Work of William Eastlake: An Annotated Bibliography & Guide. Clarke, Boden & Mallett, Daryl F., eds. LC 93-340. (Bibliographies of Modern Authors Ser.: No. 21). 104p. 1994. pap. 17.00 (*0-89370-498-9*) Millefleurs.

Bamberger, W. C., jt. auth. see Elmslie, Kenward.

Bamberger, William J. & Bryan, Nora Sherwood, eds. Marketing Government Geographic Information: Issues & Guidelines. (Illus.). vii, 108p. 1993. pap. 45.00 (*0-916848-00-0*) Urban & Regional Information Systems.

Bamberger, William L. & Davidson, Cathy N. Closing: The Life & Death of an American Factory. LC 97-36923. (Illus.). 224p. 1998. 27.50 (*0-393-04568-4*) Norton.

— Closing: The Life & Death of an American Factory. (Illus.). 228p. 1999. pap. 19.95 (*0-393-31922-9*) Norton.

Bambery, Annecke. Old Sheffield Plate. 1989. pap. 50.00 (*0-85263-965-1*, Pub. by Shire Pubns) St Mut.

Bambi. Are We Having Fun Yet? LC 97-90677. 1998. pap. 8.95 (*0-533-12451-4*) Vantage.

***Bambola, Sylvia.** Refiner's Fire. LC 00-8204. 192p. 2000. pap. 10.99 (*1-57673-694-6*, Pub. by Multnomah Pubs) GL Services.

Bamborough, J. B., ed. see Burton, Robert.

Bambrick, Susan, ed. The Cambridge Encyclopedia of Australia. (Illus.). 394p. (C). 1994. 69.95 (*0-521-36511-2*) Cambridge U Pr.

Bambridge, Vicky. Weimaraner Today. (Illus.). 160p. 1993. 24.95 (*0-948955-17-1*, Pub. by Ringpr Bks) Seven Hills Bk.

Bambrough, Paul J. Simulations in English Teaching. LC 94-12227. (English, Language & Education Ser.). 128p. 1994. pap. 31.95 (*0-335-19151-7*) OpUniv Pr.

Bambrough, Renford. Philosophy of Aristotle. 1963. mass mkt. 6.99 (*0-451-62783-0*, Sig) NAL.

Bamburak, Gary. The Distorted Bamburak. (Illus.). 96p. (Orig.). 1989. pap. 5.89 (*0-9622560-1-3*) Bamburak Designs.

— The Portable Bamburak. (Illus.). 72p. (Orig.). 1989. pap. 4.95 (*0-9622560-0-5*) Bamburak Designs.

Bamburak, Gary P. In the Grand Scheme of Things: A Collection of Short & Amusingly Quirky Stories. Lundquist, Karen, ed. & frwd. by. Coxhill, Deidre C., frwd. (Illus.). 48p. (Orig.). 1996. pap. 5.95 (*0-9622560-3-X*) Bamburak Designs.

Bamburak, Michael, ed. see Rappaport, Theodore S.

Bamburger, Claude P. Breaking the Mold: A Memoir. (Illus.). 316p. (Orig.). 1996. pap. 16.95 (*0-9653827-0-2*) C P Bamberger.

Bame, E. Allen. Activities, Techknowledge Reference Series. (TP - Technology Education Ser.). (J). (gr. k-12). 1997. 20.95 (*0-538-64483-4*) S-W Pub.

— Experiencing Technology. (Tech & Industrial Education Ser.). 1994. text 16.70 (*0-8273-5779-6*) Delmar.

Bame, E. Allen & Cummings, Paul. Exploring Technology. 2nd ed. (Technology Ser.). 288p. (C). 1989. mass mkt., student ed. 20.95 (*0-87192-218-5*) Delmar.

— Exploring Technology. 2nd ed. (Technology Education K-12). 288p. (C). 1987. pap. 24.48 (*0-87192-196-0*) Thomson Learn.

— Exploring Technology: Activity Manual. LC 79-53783. (Technology Education K-12). (Illus.). 288p. 1980. 17.75 (*0-87192-113-8*) Thomson Learn.

Bame, Kwabena N. Come to Laugh: A Study of African Traditional Theatre in Ghana. LC 84-6259. (Illus.). 192p. (C). 1985. text 23.50 (*0-936508-07-8*); pap. text 12.95 (*0-936508-08-6*) Barber Pr.

Bamer, Donald. Cure That Headache Naturally. 11p. 1989. pap. 2.00 (*0-913923-69-9*) Woodland UT.

— Practical Iridology. 1996. pap. text 18.95 (*1-885670-02-8*) Woodland UT.

Bamer, Donald R. Introduction to Iridology: The Beginner's Guide to Iris Study. 1997. pap. text 5.95 (*1-885670-46-X*) Woodland UT.

Bamesberger, Velda C. An Appraisal of a Social Studies Course, in Terms of Its Effect upon the Achievement, Activities & Interests of Pupils. LC 72-176535. (Columbia University. Teachers College. Contributions to Education Ser.: No. 328). reprint ed. 37.50 (*0-404-55328-1*) AMS Pr.

Bamfield. Fine Chemicals for the Electronics Industry, No. 60. 1987. 76.00 (*0-85186-636-0*) CRC Pr.

Bamfield, Peter. Research & Development Management in the Chemical Industry. LC 96-17520. (Illus.). 17?p. 1996. 110.00 (*3-527-28778-7*, Wiley-VCH) Wiley.

Bamford. Distorted Images 1920s: British National Identity & Film in the 1920's. 224p. 1999. text 49.50 (*1-86064-358-2*, Pub. by I B T) St Martin.

Bamford, C. H., et al, eds. Comprehensive Chemical Kinetics Vol. 25: Diffusion-Limited Reactions. 404p. 1985. 353.75 (*0-444-42354-0*) Elsevier.

Bamford, C. H. & Compton, R. G. Comprehensive Chemical Kinetics: Electrode Kinetics: Principles & Methodology, Vol. 26. xviii,450p. 1986. 408.00 (*0-444-42550-0*) Elsevier.

Bamford, C. H. & Tipper, C. F. Reactions of Solids with Gases. (Comprehensive Chemical Kinetics Ser.: Vol. 21). xiv,238p. 1984. 208.00 (*0-444-42288-9*, I-450-84) Elsevier.

— Simple Processes at the Gas-Solid Interface. (Comprehensive Chemical Kinetics Ser.: Vol. 19). xiv,436p. 1984. 362.00 (*0-444-42287-0*, I-147-84) Elsevier.

Bamford, C. H. & Tipper, C. F., eds. Comprehensive Chemical Kinetics, Vols. 1-18. Incl. Addition & Elimination Reactions of Aliphatic Compounds. Compton, R. G., ed. xiv,516p. 1973. 320.00 (*0-444-41051-1*); Vol. 1. Practice of Kinetics. 450p. 1969. 264.25 (*0-444-40673-5*); Vol. 2. Theory of Kinetics. 486p. 1969. 264.25 (*0-444-40674-3*); Vol. 3. Formation & Decay of Excited Species: Formation & Decay of Excited Species. xii,300p. 1970. 241.50 (*0-444-40802-9*); Vol. 4. Decomposition of Inorganic & Organometallic Compounds. xii,272p. 1972. 241.50 (*0-444-40936-X*); Vol. 5. Decomposition & Isomerization of Organic Compounds. xvi,780p. 1972. 370.50 (*0-444-40861-4*); Vol. 6. Reactions of Non-Metallic Inorganic Compounds. 518p. 1972. 227.25 (*0-444-40944-0*); Vol. 7. Reactions of Metallic Salts & Complexes & Organometallic Compounds. xvi,616p. 1972. 349.00 (*0-444-40913-0*); Vol. 8. Proton Transfer of Related Reactions. xii,262p. 1977. 237.50 (*0-444-41512-2*); Vol. 10. Ester Formation & Hydrolysis & Related Reactions. 310p. 1972. 241.50 (*0-444-40957-2*); Vol. 12. Electrophilic Substitution at a Saturated Carbon Atom. xiv,256p. 1973. 237.50 (*0-444-41052-X*); Vol. 13. Reactions of Aromatic Compounds. xii,508p. 1972. 320.00 (*0-444-40937-8*); Vol. 14. Degradation of Polymers. xvi,564p. 1975. 342.00 (*0-444-41155-0*); Vol. 14A. Free Radical Polymerization. xiv,594p. 1976. 333.00 (*0-444-41486-X*); Vol. 15. Nonradial Polymerization. xvi,660p. 1976. 365.50 (*0-444-41252-2*); Vol. 16. Liquid Phase Oxidation. xii,264p. 1980. 237.50 (*0-444-41860-1*); Vol. 17. Gas Phase Combustion. xiv,520p. 1977. 342.00 (*0-444-41513-0*); Vol. 18. Selected Elementary Reactions. 486p. 1976. 350.00 (*0-444-41294-8*); write for info. (*0-318-51818-X*) Elsevier.

— Comprehensive Chemical Kinetics: Complex Catalytic Processes, Vol. 20. xii,414p. 1978. 333.00 (*0-444-41651-X*) Elsevier.

— Comprehensive Chemical Kinetics Vol. 11: Reactions of Carbonyl Compounds. write for info. (*0-444-88167-0*) Elsevier.

— Modern Methods in Kinetics. (Comprehensive Chemical Kinetics Ser.: Vol. 24). xvi,528p. 1983. 424.50 (*0-444-42028-2*) Elsevier.

— Reactions in the Solid State, Vol. 22. (Comprehensive Chemical Kinetics Ser.: 22). xiv,340p. 1980. 274.50 (*0-444-41807-5*) Elsevier.

Bamford, C. H., et al. Comprehensive Chemical Kinetics. LC 70-420111. 1969. write for info. (*0-444-41631-5*) Elsevier.

— Kinetics & Chemical Technology. (Comprehensive Chemical Kinetics Ser.: Vol. 23). 288p. 1985. 259.25 (*0-444-42441-5*) Elsevier.

***Bamford, Christopher & Eriugena, John Scotus.** The Voice of the Eagle: The Heart of Celtic Christianity. 2nd ed. 228p. 2000. pap. 16.95 (*0-9701097-0-9*) Anthroposophic.

Bamford, Christopher & Marsh, William P., eds. Celtic Christianity: Ecology & Holiness. 144p. 1987. pap. text 10.95 (*0-940262-07-X*, Lindisfarne) Anthroposophic.

Bamford, Christopher, jt. auth. see Steiner, Rudolf.

Bamford, Christopher, ed. see Steiner, Rudolf.

Bamford, Christopher, ed. & intro. see Harrison, C. G.

Bamford, Christopher, tr. see Floride, Athys.

Bamford, Christopher, tr. see Kuhlewind, Georg.

Bamford, Christopher, tr. see Steiner, Rudolf.

Bamford, Francis, ed. see Oglander, John.

Bamford, G. J., jt. auth. see Coldwell, R. L.

Bamford, Hal. Florida History. 2nd ed. (Illus.). 84p. 1984. pap. 6.95 (*0-8200-1032-4*) Great Outdoors.

Bamford, Hal, ed. see VanKirk, Jacques, et al.

Bamford, Holly A. Review of Methods & Measurements of Selected Hydrophobic Organic Contaminant Aqueous Solubilities, Vapor Pressures & Air-Water Partition Coefficients. 101p. 1998. per. 8.00 (*0-16-056695-9*) USGPO.

***Bamford, James.** Body of Secrets: Anatomy of the Ultra-Secret National Security Agency. 2001. 27.50 (*0-385-49907-8*) Doubleday.

Bamford, James. The Puzzle Palace: A Report on America's Most Secret Agency. 656p. 1983. pap. 15.95 (*0-14-006748-5*, Penguin Bks) Viking Penguin.

— The Puzzle Palace: Inside the National Security Agency, America's Most Secret Intelligence Organization. rev. ed. 656p. 1999. pap. 13.95 (*0-14-023116-1*, Penguin Bks) Viking Penguin.

Bamford, Janet. Consumer Reports Money Book: How to Get It, Save It & Spend It Wisely. 1997. 29.95 (*0-89043-883-8*) Consumer Reports.

***Bamford, Janet.** Consumer Reports Money Book: How to Get It, Save It & Spend It Wisely. 2000. pap. 19.95 (*0-89043-946-X*) Consumer Reports.

Bamford, Janet. Smarter Insurance Solutions. LC 96-84216. (Bloomberg Personal Bookshelf Ser.). (Illus.). 256p. 1996. pap. 19.95 (*1-57660-003-3*, Pub. by Bloomberg NJ) Norton.

Bamford, Janet. Street Wise: A Guide for Teen Investors. pap. 16.95 (*1-57660-039-4*, Pub. by Bloomberg NJ) Norton.

Bamford, Janet, et al. Consumer Reports Money Book: How to Get It, Save It & Spend It Wisely. rev. ed. LC 94-23327. 1995. 29.95 (*0-89043-763-7*) Consumers Union.

Bamford, John & Saunders, Elaine. Hearing Impairment. 2nd ed. (Illus.). 304p. (C). 1991. pap. text 41.50 (*1-879105-07-1*, A007) Thomson Learn.

Bamford, Julian, jt. auth. see Day, Richard R.

***Bamford, Karen.** Sexual Assault in Jacobean Drama. LC 99-87928. 1999. text 45.00 (*0-312-21976-8*) St Martin.

Bamford, Kathleen, jt. auth. see Gillespie, S. H.

Bamford, Lawrence Von, see Von Bamford, Lawrence.

Bamford, Lawrence Von, see Tremblay, Kenneth R., Jr. & Von Bamford, Lawrence, eds.

Bamford, M. Work & Health: An Introduction to Occupational Health Care. (Illus.). 208p. 1994. pap. text 35.00 (*1-56593-199-8*, 0514) Singular Publishing.

Bamford, Paul W. Forests & French Sea Power, 1660-1789. LC 57-226. (Scholarly Reprint Ser.). 252p. reprint ed. pap. 78.20 (*0-608-30121-3*, 205545500022) Bks Demand.

— Privilege & Profit: A Business Family in Eighteenth-Century France. LC 88-26127. 373p. 1988. reprint ed. pap. 115.70 (*0-608-03630-7*, 206445700009) Bks Demand.

***Bamford, Rosemary & Kristo, Janice V.** Checking Out Nonfiction K-8: Good Choices for Best Learning. LC 99-66215. (Bill Harp Professional Teachers Library). 128p. 1999. pap. 15.95 (*1-929024-02-9*) CG Pubs Inc.

Bamford, Rosemary & Kristo, Janice V., eds. Making Facts Come Alive: Choosing Quality Nonfiction Literature K-8. LC 97-69085. (Illus.). 384p. (J). (gr. k-8). 1998. pap. text, teacher ed. 39.95 (*0-926842-67-6*) CG Pubs Inc.

Bamford, Samuel. Autobiography, 2 vols., Vol. 1. Chaloner, William H., ed. 364p. 1967. 35.00 (*0-7146-1055-0*, Pub. by F Cass Pubs) Intl Spec Bk.

— Autobiography, 2 vols., Vol. 2. Chaloner, William H., ed. 580p. 1967. 35.00 (*0-7146-1056-9*, Pub. by F Cass Pubs) Intl Spec Bk.

Bamford, Susannah. Blind Trust. large type ed. LC 90-45201. 456p. 1990. reprint ed. lib. bdg. 18.95 (*1-56054-066-4*) Thorndike Pr.

Bamford, Terry. Managing Social Work. 200p. 1983. 25.00 (*0-422-77960-1*, NO. 3802, Pub. by Tavistock) Routldge.

Bamford, W. H., ed. Service Experience & Design in Pressure Vessels & Piping Including High Pressure Technology. LC 96-85160. 261p. 1996. pap. text 110.00 (*0-7918-1782-2*, TS283) ASME Pr.

— Service Experience & Life Management - Nuclear, Fossil, & Petrochemical Plants. (PVP Ser.: Vol. 261). 352p. 1993. 70.00 (*0-7918-0988-9*, H00820) ASME.

— Service Experience & Reliability Improvement: Nuclear, Fossil & Petrochemical Plants: Proceedings of the Pressure Vessels & Piping Conference, Minneapolis, MN, 1994. LC 94-71758. (PVP Ser.: Vol. 288). 430p. 1994. pap. 70.00 (*0-7918-1361-4*) ASME.

Bamforth, Charles. Beer: Tap into the Art & Science of Brewing. LC 98-5697. (Illus.). 270p. (C). 1998. 27.95 (*0-306-45797-0*, Plen Insight) Perseus Pubng.

Bamforth, D. B. Ecology & Human Organization on the Great Plains. LC 88-22520. (Interdisciplinary Contributions to Archaeology Ser.). (Illus.). 232p. (C). 1988. 42.50 (*0-306-42956-X*, Plenum Trade) Perseus Pubng.

Bamforth, Iain. Open Workings. LC 97-131675. 96p. 1997. pap. 14.95 (*1-85754-257-6*, Pub. by Carcanet Pr) Paul & Co Pubs.

Bamforth, Nicholas. Sexuality, Morals & Justice: A Theory of Lesbian & Gay Rights & the Law. LC 96-164121. (Lesbian & Gay Studies). 320p. 1997. 69.95 (*0-304-33145-7*); pap. 27.50 (*0-304-33147-3*) Continuum.

Bamforth, Nick. AIDS & the Healer Within. 2nd rev. ed. 172p. (Orig.). 1993. reprint ed. pap. 9.95 (*0-944256-27-9*) ACCESS Pubs Network.

— Trusting the Healer Within. 2nd ed. 176p. (Orig.). 1989. pap. 9.95 (*0-944256-26-0*) ACCESS Pubs Network.

Bamforth, P. B. & Price, W. F. Concreting Deep Lifts & Large Volume Pours. LC 95-152835. (CIRIA Reports: No. 135). 84p. 1995. pap. 57.60 (*0-7277-2025-2*, Pub. by T Telford) RCH.

Bamfylde, C. A., jt. auth. see Baring-Gould, Sabine.

Bamgaertner, Jill P. & Dover, Linda A. Poetry. 703p. (C). 1989. pap. text 41.50 (*0-15-570680-2*) Harcourt Coll Pubs.

— Poetry. 703p. (C). 1990. pap. text 34.00 (*0-15-570681-0*) Harcourt Coll Pubs.

Bamgbosa, Ayo, et al. New Englishes: A West African Perspective. LC 97-25143. 1997. pap. write for info. (*0-86543-592-8*) Africa World.

An Asterisk (*) at the beginning of an entry indicates that the title is appearing for the first time.

B

Bamgbose, Ayo. Language & the Nation: The Language Question in Sub-Saharan Africa. 160p. 1992. pap. 27.50 (*0-7486-0306-9*, Pub. by Edinburgh U Pr) Col U Pr.

Bamgbose, Ayo, et al. New Englishes: A West African Perspective. LC 97-25143. 1997. write for info. (*0-86543-591-X*) Africa World.

Bamidbar. Linear Chumash. LC 97-3090. (ENG & HEB.). 1997. 16.95 (*0-87306-797-5*) Feldheim.

Bamidele, Ojo. Nigeria's Third Republic. LC 98-28665. 1999. 75.00 (*1-56072-580-X*) Nova Sci Pubs.

***Bamiro, Edmund Olushina.** The English Language & the Construction of Cultural & Social Identity in Zimbabwean & Trinbagonian Literatures. LC 99-13321. (Berkeley Insights in Linguistics & Semiotics Ser.: Vol. 40). 264p. (C). 2000. text 51.95 (*0-8204-4495-2*) P Lang Pubng.

Bamlett, Doug, jt. auth. see Shilmover, Barry.

Bamman, Catherine, ed. see Armitage, Merle.

Bamman, Gale W. Research in Tennessee. LC 93-37251. (Research in the States Ser.). 1993. 6.50 (*0-915156-72-5*) Natl Genealogical.

Bamman, Gerry, tr. see Ibsen, Henrik.

Bammate, Haidar. Muslim Contribution to Civilization. 1985. 2.75 (*0-89259-029-7*) Am Trust Pubns.

Bammel, C. P. Tradition & Exegesis in Early Christian Writers. (Collected Studies: Vol. 500). 328p. 1995. 101.95 (*0-86078-494-0*, Pub. by Variorum) Ashgate Pub Co.

Bammel, Caroline P., jt. auth. see Wickham, Lionel R.

Bammel, E. & Moule, Charles F., eds. Jesus & the Politics of His Day. 523p. 1985. pap. text 29.95 (*0-521-31344-9*) Cambridge U Pr.

Bammel, Gene. Leisure & Human Behavior. 4th ed. 1999. pap. text 35.78 (*0-697-29496-X*) McGraw.

Bammel, Gene & Bammel, Lei L. Leisure & Human Behavior. 3rd ed. LC 95-75475. 528p. (C). 1995. text. write for info. (*0-697-23330-8*) Brown & Benchmark.

Bammel, Lei L., jt. auth. see Bammel, Gene.

Bammer, Angelika, ed. Displacements: Cultural Identities in Question. LC 94-1182. (Theories of Contemporary Culture Ser.). 288p. 1994. 29.95 (*0-253-31138-1*); pap. 14.95 (*0-253-20897-1*) Ind U Pr.

— The Question of "Home" (New Formations Ser.: No. 17). (Illus.). 192p. (C). 1992. pap. 19.95 (*0-85315-758-8*, Pub. by Lawrence & Wishart) NYU Pr.

Bammes, Gottfied. Korper und Gewand: Gesetzmaigkeiten - zeichnerische Durchdringung -kunstlerischer Ausdruck. (GER., Illus.). 240p. 1997. text 75.00 (*90-5705-027-7*) Gordon & Breach.

Bammes, Gottfried. Animal Anatomy: An Illustrated Reference to Drawing Animals. 144p. 1994. 14.98 (*0-7858-0055-7*) Bk Sales Inc.

— Human Anatomy: An Illustrated Reference to Drawing Humans. 1994. 14.98 (*0-7858-0054-9*) Bk Sales Inc.

Bamonte, Suzanne S., jt. auth. see Bamonte, Tony.

Bamonte, Suzanne Schaeffer, jt. auth. see Bamonte, Tony.

Bamonte, Tony. Sheriffs: 1911-1989: A History of Murders in the Wilderness of Washington's Last County. 2nd ed. LC 91-70632. (Illus.). 251p. 1996. 26.00 (*0-87062-206-4*) A H Clark.

Bamonte, Tony & Bamonte, Suzanne S. History of Newport, Washington. LC 98-61453. (Illus.). 96p. 1998. 18.95 (*0-9652219-3-8*) Tornado Creek.

— History of Pend Oreille County. LC 96-60610. (Illus.). 288p. 1996. 29.95 (*0-9652219-1-1*) Tornado Creek.

— Manito Park: A Reflection of Spokane's Past. LC 98-90257. (Illus.). 128p. 1998. 21.95 (*0-9652219-2-X*) Tornado Creek.

***Bamonte, Tony & Bamonte, Suzanne Schaeffer.** Spokane & the Inland Northwest: Historical Images. LC 99-96906. (Illus.). 336p. 1999. 49.95 (*0-9652219-4-6*) Tornado Creek.

Bamonte, Tony, ed. see Ladd, Dean.

Bamossy, Gary J., jt. auth. see Costa, Janeen A.

Bampfylde, C. A., jt. auth. see Baring-Gould, S.

Bampi, Franco, ed. see Boffi, V. C., et al.

Bampton, Bob. Animal Friends Little Duck Board Book. (Illus.). 14p. (ps-k). 1999. 7.95 (*1-58185-223-1*) Quadrillion Media.

— Animal Friends Little Kitten Board Book. 1999. 7.95 (*1-58185-221-5*) Quadrillion Media.

***Bampton, Bob.** Animal Friends Little Pony Board Book. (Illus.). 14p. (J). (ps-3). 1999. 7.95 (*1-58185-222-3*) Quadrillion Media.

Bampton, Bob. Animal Friends Little Puppy Board Book. (Illus.). 14p. (ps-k). 1999. 7.95 (*1-58185-220-7*) Quadrillion Media.

Bampton, Claire & Hawcock, David. Solar System. (Zoomers Ser.). (Illus.). 4p. (J). (gr. 4-6). 1999. pap. 2.99 (*1-57584-283-1*, Pub. by Rdrs Digest) Random.

— Your Amazing Body. (Zoomers Ser.). (Illus.). 4p. (J). (gr. 4-6). 1999. pap. 2.99 (*1-57584-282-3*, Pub. by Rdrs Digest) Random.

Bampton, Clare, jt. auth. see Hawcock, David.

Bamser, Ian, ed. see Smith, Carroll.

Bamsey, Ian. Porsche Turbo Race Cars. (Illus.). 160p. 1989. 49.95 (*0-85429-780-4*, F780, Pub. by GT Foulis) Haynes Manuals.

— Vanwell 2. 5 Litre F1: A Technical Appraisal. (Haynes Constructors Ser.). (Illus.). 96p. 1991. 12.95 (*0-85429-838-X*, Pub. by GT Foulis) Haynes Manuals.

Bamton, Claire & Hawcock, David. Fantastic Frogs, 1. (Zoomers Ser.). 4p. (J). (gr. 2-5). 1999. 2.99 (*1-57584-284-X*) RD Assn.

***Bamyeh, Mohammed A.** The Ends of Globalization. LC 00-8035. 2000. pap. write for info. (*0-8166-3593-5*) U of Minn Pr.

— Social Origins of Islam: Mind, Economy & Discourse. LC 98-42289. 1999. pap. text 18.95 (*0-8166-3264-2*) U of Minn Pr.

— Social Origins of Islam: Mind, Economy, Discourse. LC 98-42289. 1999. write for info. (*0-8166-3263-4*) U of Minn Pr.

Bamzai, P. N. Culture & Political History of Kashmir: Medieval Kashmir, Vol. 2. (C). 1994. 85.00 (*81-85880-33-6*, Pub. by Print Hse) St Mut.

— Culture & Political History of Kashmir: Modern Kashmir, Vol. 3. (C). 1994. 75.00 (*81-85880-34-4*, Pub. by Print Hse) St Mut.

— Culture & Political History of Kashmir Vols. 1-3: Ancient Kashmire; Medieval Kashmir; Modern Kashmire, 3 vols. 882p. 1994. pap. 600.00 (*81-85880-31-X*, Pub. by Print Hse) St Mut.

Bamzai, P. N., ed. Culture & Political History Vol. 1: Ancient Kashmir. (C). 1994. 150.00 (*81-85880-32-8*, Pub. by Print Hse) St Mut.

Ban, jt. auth. see Swift-Bandin, Nancy.

Ban Breathnach, Sarah. Hold That Thought. 370p. 1997. 12.95 (*0-446-91207-7*, Pub. by Warner Bks) Little.

***Ban Breathnach, Sarah.** The Illustrated Discovery Journal: Creating a Visual Autobiography of Your Authentic Self. 160p. 1999. 22.95 (*0-446-52144-2*, Pub. by Warner Bks) Little.

Ban Breathnach, Sarah. Simple Abundance: A Daybook of Comfort & Joy. 752p. 1998. 24.00 (*0-446-52538-3*, Pub. by Warner Bks) Little.

— Simple Abundance: A Daybook of Comfort & Joy, Vol. 1. 528p. 1995. 21.00 (*0-446-51913-8*, Pub. by Warner Bks) Little.

— Simple Abundance Journal of Gratitude. 1997. 12.95 (*0-446-52395-X*, Pub. by Warner Bks) Little.

— The Simple Abundance Journal of Gratitude: Living By Your Own Lights. 144p. 1996. 12.95 (*0-446-52106-X*, Pub. by Warner Bks) Little.

***Ban Breathnach, Sarah.** Something More: Excavating Your Authentic Self. large type ed. LC 99-23296. (Nonfiction Ser.). 1999. 28.95 (*0-7838-8652-7*, G K Hall Lrg Type) Mac Lib Ref.

Ban Breathnach, Sarah, et al. Something More: Excavating Your Authentic Self. LC 98-27040. 351p. 1998. 20.00 (*0-446-52413-1*, Pub. by Warner Bks) Little.

Ban, Carolyn. How Do Public Managers Manage? Bureaucratic Constraints, Organizational Culture, & the Potential for Reform. LC 94-47405. (Public Administration Ser.). 320p. 1995. 28.95 (*0-7879-0098-2*) Jossey-Bass.

— Public Personnel Management. 2nd ed. LC 96-25492. 275p. (C). 1996. pap. text 52.00 (*0-8013-1699-5*) Addison-Wesley.

Ban, Carolyn & Riccucci, Norma M. Public Personnel Management: Current Concerns, Future Challenges. 256p. (Orig.). (C). 1991. pap. text 40.95 (*0-8013-0508-X*, 78402) Longman.

Ban, Carolyn, jt. ed. see Ingraham, Patricia W.

Ban, Eliezer G. The Constant Feud: Forest Versus Desert. LC 98-56067. 300p. 1999. write for info. (*965-229-197-8*, Pub. by Gefen Pub Hse) Gefen Bks.

Ban, Eva. An Act of God? 174p. mass mkt. 4.99 (*1-55197-237-9*) Picasso Publ.

Ban, Istvan. Mathematical Exploration of the Environment. LC 95-236915. 115p. 1995. pap. 75.00 (*963-05-6820-9*, Pub. by Akade Kiado) St Mut.

Ban, Jeno. The Tactics of End-Games. LC 97-22514. (Illus.). 214p. 1997. reprint ed. pap. text 7.95 (*0-486-29705-5*) Dover.

Ban, John R. Parents Assuring Student Success (PASS) Achievement Made Easy by Learning Together. 141p. (Orig.). 1995. pap. text 23.95 (*1-879639-25-4*) Natl Educ Serv.

Ban, Karen Le, see Le Ban, Karen.

Ban, Shigeru, jt. auth. see Ambasz, Emilio.

Ban, T. & Silvestrini, B., eds. Trazodone, New Avenues in Psycho-Pharmaco-Therapy: Proceedings of the International Symposium, Montreal, October, 1973. (Modern Problems of Pharmacopsychiatry Ser.: Vol. 9). 250p. 1974. 65.25 (*3-8055-1718-1*) S Karger.

Ban, T. A. & Freyhan, F. A., eds. Drug Treatment of Sexual Dysfunction. (Modern Problems of Pharmacopsychiatry Ser.: Vol. 15). (Illus.). vi, 194p. 1980. 85.25 (*3-8055-2906-6*) S Karger.

Ban, T. A. & Hippius, H., eds. Thirty Years CINP. (Illus.). xviii, 138p. 1988. 34.00 (*0-387-50117-7*) Spr-Verlag.

Ban, T. A. & Hollender, M. H. Psychopharmacology for Everyday Practice. x, 198p. 1981. pap. 32.75 (*3-8055-2241-X*) S Karger.

Ban, T. A. & Lehmann, H. Peter, eds. Diagnosis & Treatment of Old Age Dementias. (Modern Problems of Pharmacopsychiatry Ser.: Vol. 23). (Illus.). viii, 112p. 1989. 62.75 (*3-8055-4844-3*) S Karger.

Ban, T. H., ed. Psychopharmacology for the Aged. xii, 216p. 1980. pap. 34.00 (*3-8055-1204-X*) S Karger.

Ban, Thomas A., jt. ed. see McGuigan, F. J.

Bana e Costa, C. A., ed. Readings in Multiple Criteria Decision Aid. (Illus.). xii, 660p. 1990. 129.95 (*0-387-52950-0*) Spr-Verlag.

Banabhatta. Harshacarita: Text of Uchchhvasas 1-VIII. Kane, P. V., ed. 645p. 1986. reprint ed. 22.00 (*81-208-0032-X*, Pub. by Motilal Bnarsidass) S Asia.

— Kadambari: A Classic Sanskrit Story of Magical Transformations. Layne, Gwendolyn, tr. from SAN. LC 89-39521. (Library of World Literature in Translation: Vol. 12). 460p. 1991. text 20.00 (*0-8240-2998-4*) Garland.

Banac, Ivo. Eastern Europe in Revolution. LC 91-57903. 264p. 1992. pap. text 15.95 (*0-8014-9997-6*) Cornell U Pr.

— The Effects of World War I: The Class War after the Great War: The Rise of Communist Parties in East Central Europe, 1918-1921. (East European Monographs: No. 137). 277p. 1983. text 57.00 (*0-88033-028-7*, Pub. by East Eur Monographs) Col U Pr.

— The National Question in Yugoslavia: Origins, History, Politics. LC 83-45931. (Illus.). 456p. 1984. pap. text 19.95 (*0-8014-9493-1*) Cornell U Pr.

— With Stalin Against Tito: Cominformist Splits in Yugoslav Communism. LC 88-47717. 320p. 1988. text 42.50 (*0-8014-2186-1*) Cornell U Pr.

Banac, Ivo, et al, eds. Nation & Ideology. (East European Monographs: No. 95). 479p. 1981. text 84.00 (*0-914710-89-3*, Pub. by East Eur Monographs) Col U Pr.

Banac, Ivo & Verdery, Katherine, creators. National Character & National Ideology in Interwar Eastern Europe. LC 95-679. 1995. write for info. (*0-936586-13-3*, Pub. by Yale Russian) Slavica.

***Banach, Daniel T.** Mechanical Desktop 4: Applying Designer & Assembly Modules. LC 99-53881. (Student Material TV Ser.). (Illus.). 536p. (C). 1999. text 59.95 (*0-7668-1946-9*) Delmar.

Banach, Daniel T. Mechanical Desktop 2.0: Applying Designer & Assembly Modules. abr. rev. ed. LC 98-14979. 700p. (C). 1998. pap. 70.95 (*0-7668-0068-7*, AutoDesk Pr) Delmar.

— Mechanical Desktop 3.0 Update Guide. LC 98-31478. 144p. (C). 1998. pap. 17.95 (*0-7668-1125-5*) Delmar.

Banach, Stefan. Theorie des Operations Lineaires. 2nd ed. LC 63-21849. 14.95 (*0-8284-0110-1*) Chelsea Pub.

— Theory of Linear Operations. (Mathematical Library: No. 38). x,238p. 1987. 159.00 (*0-444-70184-2*, North Holland) Elsevier.

Banach, William J. The ABC Complete Book of School Marketing. 2nd rev. ed. (Illus.). 275p. 1998. pap. text 75.00 (*0-9663735-0-2*) Banach MI.

Banachowski, Lesek. Analysis of Algorithms & Data & Structures. 1991. text 36.75 (*0-201-41693-X*) Addison-Wesley.

Banack, Sandra A., jt. ed. see Cox, Paul.

Banacki, Raymond. Boys Night Out. (Illus.). 84p. 1994. mass mkt. 5.95 (*1-58193-094-1*) Brown Bag Prods.

Banaga, Abdelgadir, et al. External Audit & Corporate Governance in Islamic Banks: A Joint Practitioner-Academic Research Study. 288p. 1994. 72.95 (*1-85628-441-7*, Pub. by Avebry) Ashgate Pub Co.

Banahan, Benjamin F. Marketing to Pharmacists: Understanding Their Role & Influence. LC 98-33324. 165p. 1998. 69.95 (*0-7890-0686-3*, Pharmctl Prods) Haworth Pr.

***Banahan, Benjamin F., III, ed.** Marketing to Pharmacists: Understanding Their Role & Influence. 165p. 2000. pap. 29.95 (*0-7890-1009-7*, Pharmctl Prods) Haworth Pr.

Banahan, Michael. C Book: Featuring the ANSI C Standard. 2nd ed. 1991. 31.25 (*0-685-40064-6*) Addison-Wesley.

***Banaian, King.** The Ukrainian Economy since Independence. LC 99-38282. 192p. 1999. 70.00 (*1-85898-990-6*) E Elgar.

Banaji, Jairus. Beyond Multinationalism: Management Policy & Bargaining Relationships in International Companies. 200p. (C). 1990. text 25.00 (*0-8039-9637-3*) Sage.

Banakar, Reza. The Doorkeepers of the Law: A Socio-Legal Study of Ethnic Discrimination in Sweden. LC 98-24498. (Socio-Legal Studies). 161p. 1998. text 68.95 (*1-84014-485-8*, Pub. by Dartmth Pub) Ashgate Pub Co.

Banakar, Umesh V. Bioavailability, Bioequivalence & Therapeutic Substitutions. 248p. 1995. ring bd. 149.95 (*1-56676-350-9*) Technomic.

— Pharmaceutical Dissolution Testing. (Drugs & the Pharmaceutical Sciences Ser.: Vol. 49). (Illus.). 454p. 1991. text 199.00 (*0-8247-8567-3*) Dekker.

— Transdermal Drug Delivery: Seminar Notes - October 1994. 1994. 149.95 (*1-56676-237-5*) Technomic.

Banakar, Unmesh V., et al. Advances in New Drug Delivery Systems: Technology, Materials & Effective Management. 484p. 1994. ring bd. 144.95 (*1-56676-177-8*) Technomic.

Banakas, E. K., ed. United Kingdom National Committee of Comparative Law Vol. 8: United Kingdom Law in the 1980s. 344p. 1988. pap. 60.00 (*0-406-50186-6*, Pub. by UK Natl Committee) St Mut.

Banakas, Efstathios K. Civil Liability for Pure Economic Loss. LC 96-44869. 1996. lib. bdg. 95.00 (*90-411-0908-0*) Kluwer Academic.

Banales, Eddie. From Gangs to Grace: The Story of Pomona's Eddie Banales. 115p. 1991. pap. 8.95 (*0-9630375-0-1*) Fam Comm Educ.

***Bananafish Publishing Staff, ed.** Bananafish: Short Fiction. 122p. 1998. pap. write for info. (*0-9661539-1-X*) bananafish.

Banani, Amin. The Modernization of Iran, 1921-1941. LC 61-5504. (Illus.). 205p. 1961. reprint ed. pap. 30.00 (*0-608-00250-X*, 206076500006) Bks Demand.

Banani, Amin, ed. Tahirih: The Poetry of Qurratu'l-'Ayn. Date not set. 19.95 (*0-933770-55-3*) Kalimat.

Banani, Amin, et al, eds. Poetry & Mysticism in Islam: The Heritage of Rumi. (Levi Della Vida Symposia Ser.: No. 11). 214p. (C). 1994. text 69.95 (*0-521-45476-X*) Cambridge U Pr.

Banani, Amin & Sabagh, Georges. Poetry & Mysticism in Islam: The Heritage of Rumi. 214p. 1996. 59.95 (*0-614-21327-4*, 1439) Kazi Pubns.

Banani, Amin, jt. tr. see Kessler, Jascha.

Banaphula, et al. Wildfire & Other Stories. LC 99-933666. x, 240 p. 1999. write for info. (*81-7046-152-9*, Pub. by Seagull Bks) S Asia.

Banas, Anne M., jt. ed. see Greeley, Hugh P.

Banas, Josef. The Scapegoats: The Exodus of the Remnants of Polish Jewry. Szafar, Tadeusz, tr. 221p. 1979. 40.00 (*0-8419-6303-7*) Holmes & Meier.

Banas, Jozef & Goebel. Measures of Noncompactness in Banach Spaces. (Lecture Notes in Pure & Applied Mathematics Ser.: Vol. 60). (Illus.). 112p. 1980. pap. text 115.00 (*0-8247-1248-X*) Dekker.

Banas, Norma. WISC-III Prescriptions. LC 78-12881. 96p. 1992. pap. 12.00 (*0-87879-206-6*) Acad Therapy.

***Banasch, Darren.** Which Fly Do I Use? A Guide to Choosing Flies That Catch Trout. (Illus.). 48p. 2000. pap. 8.95 (*1-57188-202-2*) F Amato Pubns.

Banash, Stan & Brown, Dee, eds. Best of Dee Brown's West: An Anthology. LC 96-6237. (Illus.). 384p. 1997. 24.95 (*0-940666-76-6*); pap. 14.95 (*0-940666-77-4*) Clear Light.

Banashak, Brian. The Little Book of Business Wisdom: Practical Insights for Entrepreneurs, Professionals, & Business Owners. 160p. 1997. pap. 5.95 (*0-9637311-6-5*) Genesis Comm Inc.

***Banashak, Brian.** The Little Book of Business Wisdom: Practical Insights for Entrepreneurs, Professionals, & Business Owners. 96p. 2000. pap. 5.95 (*1-58169-041-X*, Evergrn Pr AL) Genesis Comm Inc.

Banasiak, J., jt. auth. see Mika, J. R.

Banasik, Jacquelyn L. Lectureview for Pathophysiology: Biological & Behavioral Perspectives. 2nd ed. Date not set. text. write for info. (*0-7216-7180-2*, W B Saunders Co) Harcrt Hlth Sci Grp.

— Pathophysiology: Biological & Behavioral Perspectives: Instructor's Manual. 2nd ed. (Illus.). 335p. Date not set. teacher ed. write for info. (*0-7216-7179-9*, W B Saunders Co) Harcrt Hlth Sci Grp.

Banasik, Jacquelyn L., jt. auth. see Copstead, Lee-Ellen C.

***Banasik, Michael, ed.** Serving with Honor: The Diary of Captain Eathan Allen Pinnell Eighth Missouri (Confederate) LC 99-70729. (Unwritten Chapters of the Civil War West of the River Ser.: Vol. 3). (Illus.). 448p. 1999. pap. 19.95 (*0-9628936-9-2*) Pr Camp Pope.

Banasik, Michael E. Embattled Arkansas: The Prairie Grove Campaign of 1862. (Illus.). 580p. 1996. 40.00 (*1-56837-308-2*) Broadfoot.

Banasik, Michael E., ed. Missouri Brothers in Gray: The Reminiscences & Letters of William J. & John P. Bull. LC 97-77924. (Unwritten Chapters of the Civil War West of the River Ser.: No. 1). (Illus.). 190p. 1998. pap. 12.95 (*0-9628936-8-4*) Pr Camp Pope.

Banaszak, Grzegorz, et al. Algebraic K-Theory, Vol. 199. LC 96-9185. (Contemporary Mathematics Ser.). 210p. 1996. pap. 49.00 (*0-8218-0511-8*, CONM/199) Am Math.

Banaszak, Lee A. Why Movements Succeed or Fail: Opportunity, Culture, & the Struggle for Woman Suffrage. LC 96-2190. (Studies in American Politics). 296p. 1996. text 49.50 (*0-691-02640-8*, Pub. by Princeton U Pr); pap. text 19.95 (*0-691-02639-4*, Pub. by Princeton U Pr) Cal Prin Full Svc.

Banaszak, Leonard, jt. auth. see Bernlohr, David A.

***Banaszak, Leonard J.** Foundations of Structural Biology. (Illus.). 184p. (C). 1999. pap. text 64.95 (*0-12-077700-2*) Acad Pr.

Banaszak, Ronald A., jt. ed. see Callahan, William T., Jr.

Banaszczyk, W. Additive Subgroups of Topological Vector Spaces. (Lecture Notes in Mathematics Ser.: Vol. 1466). vii, 178p. 1991. 35.95 (*0-387-53917-4*) Spr-Verlag.

Banathy, Bela. Developing a Systems View of Education. (Systems Inquiry Ser.). 92p. (Orig.). 1980. pap. text 10.95 (*0-914105-01-9*) Intersystems Pubns.

Banathy, Bela, ed. Design Inquiry. 150p. 1987. text 15.95 (*0-318-32524-1*) Intersystems Pubns.

Banathy, Bela H. Designing Social Systems in a Changing World. LC 96-36781. (Contemporary Systems Thinking Ser.). (Illus.). 387p. (C). 1997. 69.50 (*0-306-45251-0*, Plenum Trade) Perseus Pubng.

***Banathy, Bela H.** Guided Evolution of Society: A Systems View. LC 00-33113. (Contemporary Systems Thinking Ser.). 2000. pap. write for info. (*0-306-46382-2*, Kluwer Plenum) Kluwer Academic.

Banathy, Bela H. Systems Design of Education: A Journey to Create the Future. LC 90-19155. (Illus.). 240p. 1991. 37.95 (*0-87778-229-6*) Educ Tech Pubns.

— A Systems View of Education: Concepts & Principles for Effective Practice. LC 92-7928. (Illus.). 224p. (Orig.). 1992. 34.95 (*0-87778-245-8*) Educ Tech Pubns.

Banathy, Bela H., ed. Evolutionary Visions of the Future. (Illus.). 96p. 1985. pap. 18.25 (*0-08-032563-7*, Pub. by PPL) Elsevier.

— Systems Education: Perspectives, Programs, & Methods. (Systems Inquiry Ser.). 177p. 1983. pap. 16.95 (*0-914105-02-7*) Intersystems Pubns.

— Systems Inquiring - Applications, Theory, Philosophy & Methodology: Proceedings of the Society for General Systems Research, 1985, Set. 1200p. 1985. pap. text 86.00 (*0-914105-36-1*) Intersystems Pubns.

Banatre, J. P., et al, eds. Research Directions in High-Level Parallel Programming Languages: Mont Saint-Michel, France, June 17-19, 1991 Proceedings. (Lecture Notes in Computer Science Ser.: Vol. 574). viii, 387p. 1992. 52.95 (*0-387-55160-3*) Spr-Verlag.

Banatre, J. P., et al. Prospects for Functional Programming in Software Engineering. Commission of the European Community Staff, ed. (Research Reports ESPRIT, Project 302: Vol. 1). ix, 210p. 1991. 34.95 (*0-387-53852-6*) Spr-Verlag.

Banatre, Michel & Lee, Peter A., eds. Hardware & Software Architectures for Fault Tolerance: Experience & Perspectives. LC 94-2916. (Lecture Notes in Computer Science Ser.: Vol. 774). xiii, 311p. 1994. 50.95 (*0-387-57767-X*) Spr-Verlag.

Banatvala, J. E. Viral Infections of the Heart. 304p. 1993. text 85.00 (*0-340-55737-0*, Pub. by E A) OUP.

Banavar, Jayanth R., et al, eds. Physics & Chemistry of Porous Media II. LC 83-73640. (AIP Conference Proceedings Ser.: No. 154). 336p. 1987. lib. bdg. 65.00 (*0-88318-354-4*) Am Inst Physics.

Banbery, Alan, jt. auth. see Huber, Martin.

An Asterisk (*) at the beginning of an entry indicates that the title is appearing for the first time.

Banbery, Jane B., et al. Insider's Guide to Getting into Print for A-E-P & Environmental Consulting Firms. (Insider's Guide Ser.: No. 3). 128p. (Orig.). 1994. pap. text 79.00 (*1-885002-01-7*) Zweig White.

Banbury, Catherine M. Surviving Technological Innovation in the Pacemaker Industry, 1959-1990. rev. ed. LC 96-46669. (Studies on Industrial Productivity). (Illus.). 201p. 1997. text 54.00 (*0-8153-2796-X*) Garland.

Banbury, Gisela. Christian Cross Stitch. (Illus.). 48p. 1999. pap. 14.95 (*0-85532-839-8*, 8398, Pub. by Srch Pr) A Schwartz & Co.

Banbury, Gisela, ed. from GER. The Art of Painting on Silk, Vol. 1. (Illus.). 96p. 1987. pap. 19.95 (*0-85532-597-6*, 597-6, Pub. by Srch Pr) A Schwartz & Co.

Banbury, Gisela, jt. auth. see Dewar, Angela.

Banbury, Jen. Like a Hole in the Head: A Novel. LC 97-16935. 304p. (gr. 8). 1998. 21.95 (*0-316-17110-7*) Little.

— Like a Hole in the Head: A Novel. LC 98-52920. 296p. 1999. mass mkt. 12.00 (*0-446-67517-2*, Pub. by Warner Bks) Little.

***Bancalari, Robert.** Celtic Encyclopedia - Mandolin Edition. 144p. 1999. pap. 19.95 (*0-7866-4809-0*, 98197) Mel Bay.

— J. S. Bach for Mandolin. 104p. 1998. spiral bd. 19.94 incl. audio compact disk (*0-7866-2796-4*, 95770BCD) Mel Bay.

— Mandolin Classics in Tablature. 56p. 1995. pap. 8.95 (*0-7866-0197-3*, 95353) Mel Bay.

— Recorder in the Baroque Era. 32p. 1999. pap. 7.95 (*0-7866-2548-1*, 96331) Mel Bay.

Bancel, Daniel & Signore, Monique, eds. Problems of Collapse & Numerical Relativity. 1984. text 185.50 (*90-277-1816-4*) Kluwer Academic.

***Bancel, Marilyn.** Planning Your Capital Campaign. (Excellence in Fund Raising Workbooks Ser.). 2000. pap. 25.95 (*0-7879-5247-8*) Jossey-Bass.

Bancewicz, J., jt. auth. see Morris, A. I.

Banchek, Linda. Snake In, Snake Out. LC 78-51935. (Illus.). (J). (ps-1). 1978. 9.82 (*0-690-03852-6*); lib. bdg. 11.89 (*0-690-03853-4*) HarpC Child Bks.

Banchereau, J., et al. Imunne Tolerance. 264p. pap. 72.00 (*2-906077-92-5*) Elsevier.

Banchereau, Jacques, et al, eds. Dendritic Cells in Fundamental & Clinical Immunology Vol. 2: Proceedings; International Symposium on Dendritic Cells in Fundamental & Clinical Immunology (3d: 1994: Annecy, France), Vol. 2. (Advances in Experimental Medicine & Biology Ser.: Vol. 378). 592p. 1995. 145.00 (*0-306-45078-X*, Kluwer Plenum) Kluwer Academic.

Bancheri, Salvatore. Ultimate Italian: Basic-Intermediate. 1998. pap. 18.00 (*0-609-80257-7*) Liv Lang.

Bancheri, Salvatore & Lettieri, Michael. Living Language Italian All the Way Cassette/Book: Learn at Home & on the Go. LC 93-8975. 1994. 60.00 (*0-517-58375-5*) Crown Pub Group.

— Living Language Italian All the Way Manual: Learn at Home & on the Go. LC 93-8975. 1994. pap. 16.00 (*0-517-58376-3*) Crown Pub Group.

Bancheri, Salvatore, et al. Lettura e Conversazione. 116p. (Orig.). (C). 1987. pap. text 17.95 (*0-8020-6641-0*) U of Toronto Pr.

Banchich, Thomas. Cebes' Pinax. 47p. 1997. pap. 5.00 (*0-929524-90-X*) Bryn Mawr Commentaries.

Banchieri, Adriano. Adriano Banchieri: Canzoni & Francese (of 1596) Bartholomew, Leland, ed. (Recent Researches in Music of the Renaissance Ser.: Vol. RRR20). (Illus.). 99p. 1975. pap. 35.00 (*0-89579-056-4*) A-R Eds.

— Conclusioni nel Suono dell'Organo. fac. ed. (Monuments of Music & Music Literature in Facsimile Ser., Series II: Vol. 101). 1975. lib. bdg. 35.00 (*0-8450-2301-2*) Broude.

Banchoff, T. F. & Wermer, J. Linear Algebra through Geometry. (Undergraduate Texts in Mathematics Ser.). (Illus.). 257p. 1983. 32.00 (*0-387-90787-4*) Spr-Verlag.

— Linear Algebra Through Geometry. 2nd ed. (Undergraduate Texts in Mathematics Ser.). (Illus.). xii, 305p. 1995. 43.95 (*0-387-97586-1*) Spr-Verlag.

Banchoff, Thomas. The German Problem Transformed: Institutions, Politics & Foreign Policy, 1945-1995. LC 98-58102. (Social History, Popular Culture, & Politics in Germany Ser.). 232p. 1999. text 44.50 (*0-472-11008-X*, 11008) U of Mich Pr.

Banchoff, Thomas & Smith, Mitchell, eds. Legitimacy & the European Union. LC 98-38355. 208p. (C). 1999. pap. 24.99 (*0-415-18189-5*, D6207) Routledge.

— Legitimacy & the European Union. LC 98-38355. (Illus.). 208p. (C). (gr. 13). 1999. 80.00 (*0-415-18188-7*, D6203) Routledge.

Banchoff, Thomas F. Beyond the Third Dimension: Geometry, Computer Graphics & Higher Dimensions. (Illus.). 210p. 1996. pap. text 19.95 (*0-7167-6015-0*) W H Freeman.

Banci, Lewis & Smith, Milburn. The Ten O'Clock Scholar. 1969. pap. 5.25 (*0-8222-1117-3*) Dramatists Play.

Banci, Lucia & Comba, Peter, eds. Molecular Modeling & Dynamics of Bioinorganic Systems. LC 97-31748. (NATO ASI Ser.). 470p. 1997. text 234.00 (*0-7923-4824-9*, D Reidel) Kluwer Academic.

Bancilhon, Francois, et al, eds. Advances in Database Technology - EDBT 1990. (Lecture Notes in Computer Science Ser.: Vol. 416). ix, 452p. 1990. 49.95 (*0-387-52291-3*) Spr-Verlag.

— Building an Object-Oriented Database System: The Story of O2. (Series in Data Management Systems). 640p. 1990. pap. 59.95 (*1-55860-169-4*) Morgan Kaufmann.

Banco Credito Industriel Staff. Diccionario Comercial Exterior. (SPA.). 120p. 1990. pap. write for info. (*0-7859-6041-4*, 8440488378) Fr & Eur.

Bancoff, Carl. A Forgotten Man: A Novel. 1988. 15.95 (*0-940461-03-X*) Seth Pr.

Bancom, John, jt. auth. see Wagner, Barry.

Bancquart, Marie-Claire, ed. see France, Anatole, pseud.

Bancquart, Marie-Claire, ed. see Maupassant, Guy de.

Bancroft. Human Sexuality & Its Problems. 3rd ed. 1999. text 83.00 (*0-443-05161-5*, W B Saunders Co) Harcrt Hlth Sci Grp.

— Theory & Practice of Histological Techniques. 4th ed. 1995. text 156.00 (*0-443-04760-X*, B0971) Church.

Bancroft, Ann, jt. auth. see Loewen, Nancy.

Bancroft, Ann, jt. auth. see Madigan, Dan.

Bancroft, Anne. Element Classics: Dhammapada. LC 96-44605. (Element Classics of World Spirtuality Ser.). 176p. 1997. pap. 14.95 (*1-85230-921-0*, Pub. by Element MA) Penguin Putnam.

— The Spiritual Journey. 160p. 1991. pap. 13.95 (*1-85230-239-9*, Pub. by Element MA) Penguin Putnam.

— Women in Search of the Sacred. LC 96-209852. 1997. pap. 11.95 (*0-14-019494-0*, Penguin Bks) Viking Penguin.

— Zen: Direct Pointing to Reality. (Art & Imagination Ser.). (Illus.). 1987. pap. 15.95 (*0-500-81018-4*, Pub. by Thames Hudson) Norton.

***Bancroft, Anne, ed.** The Buddha Speaks. LC 99-48885. 112p. 2000. 16.95 (*1-57062-493-3*, Pub. by Shambhala Pubns) Random.

Bancroft, Brenda, et al. Historical Collection Vol. 2: Dream Spinner, Shores of Promise, the Sure Promise, & When Comes. LC 97-155107. (Inspirational Romance Reader Ser.). 500p. 1997. pap. 4.97 (*1-55748-952-1*) Barbour Pub.

Bancroft, Bronwyn. Dirrangun. 1998. pap. 6.95 (*0-207-19185-9*) HarpC.

— Minah. 1998. pap. 6.95 (*0-207-19169-7*) HarpC.

— Whalers. 1998. pap. 6.95 (*0-207-19177-8*) HarpC.

Bancroft, Bronwyn. Dreamtime: Aboriginal Stories. LC 93-79375. 96p. (J). (gr. 3 up). 1994. 16.00 (*0-688-13296-0*) Lothrop.

Bancroft, Bronwyn, jt. auth. see Morgan, Sally.

Bancroft, Caroline. Colorado's Lost Gold Mines & Buried Treasure. (Illus.). 56p. 1961. pap. 4.95 (*0-933472-16-1*) Johnson Bks.

— Colorful Colorado: Its Dramatic History. (Illus.). 96p. 1959. pap. 5.95 (*0-933472-13-7*) Johnson Bks.

— Silver Queen: The Fabulous Story of Baby Doe Tabor. (Illus.). 80p. 1955. pap. 4.95 (*0-933472-21-8*) Johnson Bks.

— Six Racy Madams of Colorado. (Illus.). 64p. 1965. pap. 4.95 (*0-933472-22-6*) Johnson Bks.

— Unique Ghost Towns & Mountain Spots. (Illus.). 96p. 1961. pap. 5.95 (*0-933472-24-2*) Johnson Bks.

— The Unsinkable Mrs. Brown. (Illus.). 44p. 1963. pap. 4.95 (*0-933472-25-0*) Johnson Bks.

Bancroft, Caroline, jt. auth. see Wills, May B.

Bancroft, Catherine & Gruenberg, Hannah C. Felix's Hat. LC 92-10868. (Illus.). 32p. (J). (ps-2). 1993. lib. bdg. 14.95 (*0-02-708325-X*, Four Winds Pr) S&S Childrens.

Bancroft, Colette M. The Arizona Daily Star Dining Guide. LC 94-24261. 1994. pap. write for info. (*0-9607758-3-8*) Ariz Daily Star.

Bancroft, Dennis & Carr, Ronnie, eds. Influencing Children's Development. (Child Development Ser.). (Illus.). 352p. (C). 1995. 60.95 (*0-631-19421-5*) Blackwell Pubs.

— Influencing Children's Development. (Child Development Ser.). (Illus.). 352p. (C). 1995. pap. 27.95 (*0-631-19422-3*) Blackwell Pubs.

Bancroft, Edward. An Essay on the Natural History of Guiana. (Illus.). 402p. Date not set. 18.95 (*0-405-01729-4*) Arno Press.

Bancroft, Emery H. Elemental Theology: An Introductory Survey of Conservative Doctrine. LC 95-37481. 400p. 1996. pap. 16.99 (*0-8254-2152-7*) Kregel.

— Fundamentos de Teologia Biblica.Tr. of Elemental Theology. (SPA.). 496p. 1987. pap. 12.99 (*0-8254-1050-9*, Edit Portavoz) Kregel.

***Bancroft, Fedric, text.** Josef Sudek: Into Modernism. (Illus.). 44p. 1999. 15.00 (*1-58821-071-5*) Salander OReilly.

Bancroft, Frances, ed. see Elliott, Tom.

Bancroft, Frederic. A Sketch of the Negro in Politics, Especially in South Carolina & Mississippi. LC 70-160007. reprint ed. 39.50 (*0-404-00003-7*) AMS Pr.

— Slave Trading in the Old South. LC 95-20493. (Southern Classics Ser.). (Illus.). 464p. 1996. pap. text 18.95 (*1-57003-103-7*) U of SC Pr.

***Bancroft, Fredric, text.** Josef Sudek: An Overview. (Illus.). 40p. 1998. pap. 15.00 (*1-58821-073-1*) Salander OReilly.

— Josef Sudek: Still Lifes. (Illus.). 44p. 1999. pap. 15.00 (*1-58821-074-X*) Salander OReilly.

Bancroft, G. Thomas & Woolfenden, Glen E. Molt of Scrub Jays & Blue Jays in Florida. 51p. 1982. 10.00 (*0-943610-29-X*) Am Ornithologists.

Bancroft, George. History of the Formation of the Constitution of the United States. (Works of George Bancroft). 1989. reprint ed. lib. bdg. 150.00 (*0-7812-0294-9*) Rprt Serv.

— History of the Formation of the Constitution of the United States of America. 1977. 56.95 (*0-8369-7151-5*, 7983) Ayer.

— History of the Formation of the Constitution of the United States, 1882. 2nd ed. LC 99-23946. 2000. reprint ed. write for info. (*1-58477-002-3*) Lawbk Exchange.

— History of the United States of America: From the Discovery of the Continent, 6 vols., Set. rev. ed. (BCL1 - U. S. History Ser.). 1991. reprint ed. lib. bdg. 540.00 (*0-7812-6034-5*) Rprt Serv.

— The History of the United States of America from the Discovery of the Continent. Nye, Russel B., ed. LC 66-23683. (Classic American Historians Ser.). 414p. reprint ed. pap. 128.40 (*0-608-16514-X*, 202676300052) Bks Demand.

— The Life & Letters of George Bancroft, 2 vols. in . Howe, Mark D., ed. LC 78-106990. (American Public Figures Ser.). 1970. reprint ed. lib. bdg. 79.50 (*0-306-71877-4*) Da Capo.

— Literary & Historical Miscellanies. 1977. 22.95 (*0-8369-7208-2*, 8007) Ayer.

— Literary & Historical Miscellanies. (Works of George Bancroft). 1989. reprint ed. lib. bdg. 79.00 (*0-685-27846-8*) Rprt Serv.

— Poems. (Works of George Bancroft). 1989. reprint ed. lib. bdg. 79.00 (*0-685-27844-1*) Rprt Serv.

— The Principal Works of George Bancroft. 1989. reprint ed. lib. bdg. 65.00 (*0-685-27842-5*) Rprt Serv.

Bancroft, George O. A Practical Guide to Credit & Collection. LC 88-83151. 276p. 1989. 29.95 (*0-8144-5953-6*) AMACOM.

Bancroft, Gordon. Improve You Math! LC 98-3584. (C). 1998. pap. text. write for info. (*0-201-33130-6*) Addison-Wesley.

— Mathematics for Management Science. (C). 1998. pap. text. write for info. (*0-201-17846-X*) Addison-Wesley.

Bancroft, Gordon & O'Sullivan, George. Quantitative Methods for Accounting & Business Studies. 3rd ed. LC 93-10243. 1993. 15.95 (*0-07-707731-8*) McGraw

***Bancroft, Gwendolyn Adele.** Make Room for Jesus in Your Inn. (Illus.). 180p. 1999. pap. write for info. (*0-7392-0460-2*, PO3770) Morris Pubng.

Bancroft, H. H. History of Nevada, 1540-1888. (Illus.). 332p. 1982. 49.95 (*0-913814-44-X*) Nevada Pubns.

— History of Utah, 1840-1886. (Illus.). 808p. 1981. 49.95 (*0-913814-49-0*) Nevada Pubns.

Bancroft, Henrietta. Animals in Winter: Stage 1. (Let's Read-&-Find-Out Science Ser.). 1997. 10.15 (*0-606-11046-1*, Pub. by Turtleback) Demco.

Bancroft, Henrietta & Van Gelder, Richard G. Animals in Winter: Newly Illustrated Edition. rev. ed. LC 95-36246. (Let's-Read-&-Find-Out Science Bks.: Stage 1). (Illus.). 32p. (J). (ps-1). 1997. 14.95 (*0-06-027157-4*); pap. 4.95 (*0-06-445165-8*); lib. bdg. 15.89 (*0-06-027158-2*) HarpC Child Bks.

Bancroft, Hubert. History of Texas & the North Mexican States. 1993. reprint ed. lib. bdg. 180.00 (*0-7812-5862-6*) Rprt Serv.

***Bancroft, Hubert.** The Native Races of the Pacific States of North America, 5 vols. (LC History-America-E). 1999. reprint ed. lib. bdg. 450.00 (*0-7812-4233-9*) Rprt Serv.

***Bancroft, Hubert H.** American Antiquities, Being the Entire Section Devoted to the Subject in the Author's Series of the Native Races. (LC History-America-E). 807p. 1999. reprint ed. lib. bdg. 240.00 (*0-7812-4305-X*) Rprt Serv.

Bancroft, Hubert H. California Inter Pocula. fac. ed. LC 67-29422. (Works of Hubert Howe Bancroft Ser.). 1967. reprint ed. 60.00 (*0-914888-28-5*) Bancroft Pr.

— California Pioneer Register & Index, 1542-1848: Including Inhabitants... 1769-1800 & a List of Pioneers. 392p. 1990. reprint ed. 20.00 (*0-8063-4893-3*) Clearfield Co.

— Essays & Miscellany. fac. ed. LC 67-29422. (Works of Hubert Howe Bancroft Ser.). 1967. reprint ed. 50.00 (*0-914888-42-0*) Bancroft Pr.

— History of California, 7 vols. 1992. reprint ed. lib. bdg. 525.00 (*0-7812-5004-8*) Rprt Serv.

— History of California, 7 vols., Set. fac. ed. LC 67-29422. (Works of Hubert Howe Bancroft Ser.). 1963. reprint ed. 495.00 (*0-914888-20-X*) Bancroft Pr.

— History of Central America, 3 vols., Set. fac. ed. LC 67-29422. (Works of Hubert Howe Bancroft Ser.). 1967. reprint ed. 250.00 (*0-914888-06-4*) Bancroft Pr.

— History of Mexico, 5 vols., No. 5. fac. ed. LC 67-29422. (Works of Hubert Howe Bancroft Ser.). 1967. reprint ed. 200.00 (*0-914888-10-2*) Bancroft Pr.

— Literary Industries. fac. ed. LC 67-29422. (Works of Hubert Howe Bancroft Ser.). 1967. reprint ed. 50.00 (*0-914888-43-9*) Bancroft Pr.

— Popular Tribunals. 1992. reprint ed. lib. bdg. 75.00 (*0-7812-5005-6*) Rprt Serv.

— Popular Tribunals, 2 vols., Set. fac. ed. LC 67-29422. (Works of Hubert Howe Bancroft Ser.). 1967. reprint ed. 100.00 (*0-914888-39-0*) Bancroft Pr.

— Works, 39 vols., Set. (BCL1 - United States Local History Ser.). 1991. reprint ed. lib. bdg. 3510.00 (*0-7812-6334-4*) Rprt Serv.

***Bancroft, Hubert Howe.** California Inter Pacula. (Works of Hubert Howe Bancroft: Vol. 35). 1999. reprint ed. lib. bdg. 90.00 (*0-7812-7828-7*) Rprt Serv.

— California Pastoral. (Works of Hubert Howe Bancroft: Vol. 34). 814p. 1999. reprint ed. lib. bdg. 90.00 (*0-7812-7827-9*) Rprt Serv.

— Essays & Miscellany. (Works of Hubert Howe Bancroft: Vol. 38). 770p. 1999. reprint ed. lib. bdg. 90.00 (*0-7812-7831-7*) Rprt Serv.

— History of Alaska, 1730-1885. (Works of Hubert Howe Bancroft: Vol. 33). 814p. 1999. reprint ed. lib. bdg. 90.00 (*0-7812-7826-0*) Rprt Serv.

— History of Arizona & New Mexico. (Works of Hubert Howe Bancroft: Vol. 17). 868p. 1999. reprint ed. lib. bdg. 90.00 (*0-7812-7817-1*) Rprt Serv.

— History of British Columbia, 1792-1887. (Works of Hubert Howe Bancroft: Vol. 32). 1999. reprint ed. lib. bdg. 90.00 (*0-7812-7825-2*) Rprt Serv.

— History of Central America Pt. 1: 1501-1530. (Works of Hubert Howe Bancroft: Vol. 6). 1999. reprint ed. lib. bdg. 90.00 (*0-7812-7806-6*) Rprt Serv.

— History of Central America Pt. 2: 1530-1800. (Works of Hubert Howe Bancroft: Vol. 7). 782p. 1999. reprint ed. lib. bdg. 90.00 (*0-7812-7807-4*) Rprt Serv.

— History of Central America Pt. 3: 1801-1887. (Works of Hubert Howe Bancroft: Vol. 8). 792p. 1999. reprint ed. lib. bdg. 90.00 (*0-7812-7808-2*) Rprt Serv.

— The History of Mexico Pt. 1: 1516-1521. (Works of Hubert Howe Bancroft: Vol. 9). 814p. 1999. reprint ed. lib. bdg. 90.00 (*0-7812-7809-0*) Rprt Serv.

— The History of Mexico Pt. 2: 1521-1600. (Works of Hubert Howe Bancroft: Vol. 10). 783p. 1999. reprint ed. lib. bdg. 90.00 (*0-7812-7810-4*) Rprt Serv.

— The History of Mexico Pt. 3: 1600-1803. (Works of Hubert Howe Bancroft: Vol. 11). 796p. 1999. reprint ed. lib. bdg. 90.00 (*0-7812-7811-2*) Rprt Serv.

— The History of Mexico Pt. 4: 1804-1824. (Works of Hubert Howe Bancroft: Vol. 12). 844p. 1999. reprint ed. lib. bdg. 90.00 (*0-7812-7812-0*) Rprt Serv.

— The History of Mexico Pt. 6: 1861-1887. (Works of Hubert Howe Bancroft: Vol. 14). 1999. reprint ed. lib. bdg. 90.00 (*0-7812-7814-7*) Rprt Serv.

— The History of Nevada, Colorado & Wyoming Pt. 1: 1540-1888. (Works of Hubert Howe Bancroft: Vol. 25). 860p. 1999. reprint ed. lib. bdg. 90.00 (*0-7812-7818-X*) Rprt Serv.

— History of Oregon Pt. 1: 1834-1848. (Works of Hubert Howe Bancroft: Vol. 29). 828p. 1999. reprint ed. lib. bdg. 90.00 (*0-7812-7822-8*) Rprt Serv.

— History of Oregon Pt. 2: 1848-1883. (Works of Hubert Howe Bancroft: Vol. 30). 820p. 1999. reprint ed. lib. bdg. 90.00 (*0-7812-7823-6*) Rprt Serv.

— The History of the Northwest Coast Pt. 1: 1543-1800. (Works of Hubert Howe Bancroft: Vol. 27). 1999. reprint ed. lib. bdg. 90.00 (*0-7812-7820-1*) Rprt Serv.

— History of the Northwest Coast Pt. 2: 1800-1846. (Works of Hubert Howe Bancroft: Vol. 28). 785p. 1999. reprint ed. lib. bdg. 90.00 (*0-7812-7821-X*) Rprt Serv.

— History of United States & Texas Pt. 1: 1531-1800. (Works of Hubert Howe Bancroft: Vol. 15). 1999. reprint ed. lib. bdg. 90.00 (*0-7812-7815-5*) Rprt Serv.

— The History of Utah, 1540-1886. (Works of Hubert Howe Bancroft: Vol. 26). 856p. 1999. reprint ed. lib. bdg. 90.00 (*0-7812-7819-8*) Rprt Serv.

— History of Washington, Idaho, & Montana. (Works of Hubert Howe Bancroft: Vol. 31). 863p. 1999. reprint ed. lib. bdg. 90.00 (*0-7812-7824-4*) Rprt Serv.

— Literary Industries. (Works of Hubert Howe Bancroft: Vol. 39). 814p. 1999. reprint ed. lib. bdg. 90.00 (*0-7812-7832-5*) Rprt Serv.

— The Native Races Pt. 1: Wile Tribes. (Works of Hubert Howe Bancroft: Vol. 1). 1999. reprint ed. lib. bdg. 90.00 (*0-7812-7801-5*) Rprt Serv.

— The Native Races Pt. 2: Civilized Nations. (Works of Hubert Howe Bancroft: Vol. 2). 818p. 1999. reprint ed. lib. bdg. 90.00 (*0-7812-7802-3*) Rprt Serv.

— The Native Races Pt. 3: Myths & Languages. (Works of Hubert Howe Bancroft: Vol. 3). 808p. 1999. reprint ed. lib. bdg. 90.00 (*0-7812-7803-1*) Rprt Serv.

— The Native Races Pt. 4: Antiquities. (Works of Hubert Howe Bancroft: Vol. 4). 1999. reprint ed. lib. bdg. 90.00 (*0-7812-7804-X*) Rprt Serv.

— The Native Races Pt. 5: Primative History. (Works of Hubert Howe Bancroft: Vol. 5). 1999. reprint ed. lib. bdg. 90.00 (*0-7812-7805-8*) Rprt Serv.

— Popular Tribunals, Pt. 1. (Works of Hubert Howe Bancroft: Vol. 36). 764p. 1999. reprint ed. lib. bdg. 90.00 (*0-7812-7829-5*) Rprt Serv.

— Popular Tribunals, Pt. 1. (Works of Hubert Howe Bancroft: Vol. 37). 782p. 1999. reprint ed. lib. bdg. 90.00 (*0-7812-7830-9*) Rprt Serv.

Bancroft-Hunt, Norman. Native Americans. 1998. pap. 12.99 (*0-7858-0880-9*) Bk Sales Inc.

Bancroft, Iris, ed. see Lange, Ed.

Bancroft, Iris, ed. see Lange, Ed & Sohler, Stan.

Bancroft, Iris, ed. see Smith, Dennis C. & Sparks, Bill.

Bancroft, J., ed. The Pharmacology of Sexual Function & Dysfunction. LC 95-7067. (International Congress Ser.: Vol. 1075). 366p. 1995. 212.50 (*0-444-82040-X*, Excerpta Medica) Elsevier.

Bancroft, J. D., jt. auth. see Horobin, R. W.

Bancroft, James, jt. auth. see Abbott-Smith, George.

Bancroft, James W. Rorke's Drift: The Zulu War, 1879. (Illus.). 176p. 1994. 40.00 (*1-885119-09-7*) Sarpedon.

— Rorke's Drift: The Zulu War, 1879. 176p. (C). 1997. 80.00 (*0-946771-94-4*, Pub. by Spellmnt Pubs) St Mut.

— The Zulu War, 1879: The Terrible Night at Rorke's Drift. 1988. 40.00 (*0-946771-48-0*) Spellmnt Pubs.

Bancroft, John. The Pharmacology of Sexual Function & Dysfunction: Proceedings of the Esteve Foundation Symposium VI, Son Vida, Mallorca, 9-12 October 1994. LC 95-7067. (International Congress Ser.: No. 1075). 1995. write for info. (*0-614-32277-4*, Excerpta Medica) Elsevier.

Bancroft, John, ed. Annual Review of Sex Research. (C). 1991. text 45.00 (*0-9628266-0-X*) Soc Sci Study Sex.

***Bancroft, John, ed.** The Role of Theory in Sex Research. LC 99-56971. (Kinsey Institute Ser.). 368p. 2000. 49.95 (*0-253-33706-2*) Ind U Pr.

Bancroft, John & Machover, Reinisch J., eds. Adolescence & Puberty. (Kinsey Institute Ser.: No. 3). (Illus.). 320p. 1990. text 60.00 (*0-19-505336-2*) OUP.

Bancroft, John, ed. see Kinsey Institute for Research in Sex, Gender, & Re.

Bancroft, John, ed. see Moratto, Michael J.

***Bancroft, John C.** A Practical Understanding of Pre- & Poststack Migraitons Vol. 2: (Prestack) Young, Roger A., ed. (Course Notes Ser.: No. 9). (Illus.). 388p. 1998. pap. text 60.00 (*1-56080-084-4*) Soc Expl Geophys.

— A Practical Understanding of Pre- & Poststack Migrations Vol. 1: (Poststack) Young, Roger A., ed. (Course Notes Ser.: No. 7). (Illus.). 380p. 1997. pap. text 47.00 (*1-56080-045-3*) Soc Expl Geophys.

Bancroft, John C. Writing That Sells. (Illus.). 180p. 1975. pap. 10.95 (*0-686-11023-4*) J C Bancroft.

B

Bancroft, John D. Human Sexuality & Its Problems. 2nd ed. (Illus.). 748p. 1989. pap. text 83.00 (0-443-03455-9) Church.

Bancroft, John D. & Cook, Harry C. Manual of Histological Techniques. (Illus.). 274p. (Orig.). 1984. pap. text 32.00 (0-443-02870-2) Church.

— Manual of Histological Techniques & Their Diagnostic Applications. 2nd ed. LC 93-35533. 1994. text 59.95 (0-443-04534-8) Church.

Bancroft, John D. & Stevens, Alan, eds. Theory & Practice of Histological Techniques. 3rd ed. (Illus.). 726p. 1990. text 132.00 (0-443-03559-8) Church.

Bancroft, Keith, ed. see Goodson, Aileen.

Bancroft Library, University of California, Berkeley Staff. Index to Printed Maps, 1st Supplement. 1975. 160.00 (0-8161-1172-3, G K Hall & Co) Mac Lib Ref.

Bancroft-Marcus, Rosemary, ed. see Chortatsis, Georgios.

Bancroft, Margaret A. & Stoller, Lawrence B. Avoiding Classification As an Investment Company: Exemptions & Exclusions for Business Corporations. (Corporate Practice Ser.: No. 65). 1995. 95.00 (1-55871-321-2) BNA.

Bancroft, Marie & Bancroft, Squire. The Bancrofts: Recollections of Sixty Years. LC 70-87117. (Illus.). 1972. reprint ed. 36.95 (0-405-08236-3, Pub. by Blom Pubns) Ayer.

Bancroft, N. Blue Flames. mass mkt. 6.95 (0-7472-5206-8, Pub. by Headline Bk Pub) Trafalgar.

Bancroft, Nancy. New Partnerships for Managing Technological Change. LC 91-16748. 288p. 1991. 128.95 (0-471-54674-7) Wiley.

Bancroft, Nancy H. The Feminine Quest for Success: How to Prosper in Business & Be True to Yourself. LC 95-34422. (Illus.). 232p. 1995. 22.95 (1-881052-62-1) Berrett-Koehler.

Bancroft, Nancy H., et al. Implementing SAP R3. 2nd ed. LC 97-25858. 336p. (C). 1997. 46.00 (0-13-889213-X) P-H.

Bancroft, Page, tr. see Barreda, Pedro.

Bancroft, Peter. Gem & Crystal Treasures. (Illus.). 488p. 1984. 60.00 (0-9613461-1-6) Western Enter.

Bancroft, R. J., jt. auth. see Rockey, J. L.

***Bancroft, Randy.** Schrodingers Cat & the Golden Bough: Reflections on Science, Mythology & Magic. 256p. 2000. 37.50 (0-7618-1749-2) U Pr of Amer.

Bancroft, Randy. Understanding Electromagnetic Scattering Using the Moment Method: A Practical Approach. 254p. 1996. 93.00 (0-89006-859-3) Artech Hse.

Bancroft, Richard. Dangerous Positions & Proceedings. LC 74-38147. (English Experience Ser.: No. 427). 192p. 1972. reprint ed. 35.00 (90-221-0427-3) Walter J Johnson.

— A Survey of the Pretended Holy Dicipline. LC 78-38148. (English Experience Ser.: No. 428). 472p. 1972. reprint ed. 75.00 (90-221-0428-1) Walter J Johnson.

Bancroft, Squire, jt. auth. see Bancroft, Marie.

Bancroft, Theodore A. Topics in Intermediate Statistical Methods. LC 68-17487. 143p. 1968. reprint ed. pap. 44.40 (0-608-00156-2, 206093700001) Bks Demand.

Bancroft, W. Jane. Suggestopedia & Language Acquisition: Variations on a Theme. 320p. 1999. text 41.00 (90-5700-524-7, ECU54); pap. text 22.00 (90-5700-525-5, ECU29) Gordon & Breach.

Bancroft-Whitney Staff. California Family Law Service: A Practical Step-by-Step Treatment of California Family Law Incorporating the Expertise of Leading Practitioners. write for info. (0-318-61958-X) West Group.

— Uniform Commercial Code of the State of California: Annotated. 7p. write for info. (0-318-62081-2) West Group.

Bancroft, William W. Joseph Conrad - His Philosophy of Life. LC 65-15867. (Studies in Conrad: No. 8). 1969. reprint ed. lib. bdg. 75.00 (0-8383-0506-7) M S G Haskell Hse.

Band, Arnold. Nahman of Bratslav, the Tales. LC 78-53433. (Classics of Western Spirituality Ser.). 368p. 1978. pap. 21.95 (0-8091-2103-4) Paulist Pr.

Band, Ora, ed. Hebrew: A Language Course, Level 3 (Shalav Gimel) 326p. 1987. pap. text 12.95 (0-87441-381-8) Behrman.

— Reader: Modern Hebrew Prose & Poetry. 1996. pap. 14.95 (0-87441-480-6) Behrman.

Band, Ora, et al. Hebrew: A Language Course, Level I. 256p. (C). 1982. pap. text, teacher ed. 16.95 (0-87441-380-X) Behrman.

— Hebrew: A Language Course, Level I, Primer. 256p. (C). 1982. pap. text 6.95 (0-87441-463-6) Behrman.

— Hebrew: A Language Course, Level 1 (Shalav Aleph) 256p. (C). 1982. pap. text 12.95 (0-87441-331-1) Behrman.

Band, Ora, ed. see Bergman, Bella.

Band, P. R., ed. Early Detection & Localization of Lung Tumors in High Risk Groups. (Recent Results in Cancer Research Ser.: Vol. 82). (Illus.). 210p. 1982. 76.00 (0-387-11249-9) Spr-Verlag.

Band, William. Touchstones: Ten New Ideas Revolutionizing Business. 306p. 1994. 24.95 (0-471-31096-4) Wiley.

Band, William F. Warriors Who Ride the Wind. (American Heroes Ser.). (Illus.). 267p. 1993. 19.95 (0-916693-20-1) Castle Bks.

***Band, Yehuda B., ed.** Optical Pulse & Beam Propagation. 302p. 1999. pap. text 92.00 (0-8194-3079-X) SPIE.

Banda, E., et al, eds. Rifted Ocean-Continent Boundaries. LC 95-15545. (NATO ASI Ser.: Series C, Mathematical & Physical Sciences: Vol. 463). 1995. text 191.50 (0-7923-3505-8) Kluwer Academic.

Banda, Guillermo R., ed. see Gould, Roberta.

Bandal, Suresh K., ed. The Pesticide Chemist & Modern Toxicology. LC 81-10790. (ACS Symposium Ser.: Vol. 160). 593p. 1981. reprint ed. pap. 183.90 (0-608-03050-3, 206350300007) Bks Demand.

Bandal, Suresh K., et al, eds. The Pesticide Chemist & Modern Toxicology. LC 81-10790. (ACS Symposium Ser.: No. 160). 1981. 54.95 (0-8412-0636-8) Am Chemical.

Bandarage, Asoka. Colonialism in Sri Lanka: The Political Economy of the Kandyan Highlands, 1833-1886. LC 83-17274. (Studies in the Social Sciences: No. 39). xiv, 404p. 1983. 120.00 (90-279-3080-5) Mouton.

— Women, Population & Global Crisis: A Political-Economic Analysis. LC 96-36915. 400p. (C). 1997. text 25.00 (1-85649-428-4, Pub. by Zed Books) St Martin.

Bandaranayake, Senake. The Rock & Wall Paintings of Sri Lanka. (Illus.). 300p. 1986. 80.00 (955-9029-00-2) Lake Hse Bkshop.

Bandaranayake, Senake & Fonseka, Manel. Ivan Peries Paintings, 1938-88. (Illus.). 179p. 1986. write for info. (955-9458-00-0) Tamarind Pubns.

Bandaruk, William, jt. ed. see Epstein, George.

Bandat, H. Von, see Von Bandat, H.

Banday & Shah. Dictionary of Statistics. 342p. 1989. 80.00 (81-7041-228-5, Pub. by Scientific Pubs) St Mut.

Banday, Shabir H. Application of Probability in Decision Making. 200p. 1992. 80.00 (81-7041-590-X, Pub. by Scientific Pubs) St Mut.

— Linear Programming in Decision Making. 150p. 1992. 60.00 (81-7041-582-9, Pub. by Scientific Pubs) St Mut.

Bande, Usha. The Novels of Anita Desai. 191p. 1988. text 25.00 (81-85218-01-3, Pub. by Prestige) Advent Bks Div.

Bandeira, Manuel. Recife - Manual Bandeira. Flintoff, Eddie, tr. 56p. (C). 1988. pap. 30.00 (0-947612-04-1, Pub. by Rivelin Grapheme Pr) St Mut.

Bandel, Betty. Sing the Lord's Song in a Strange Land: The Life of Justin Morgan. LC 78-73309. 264p. 1981. 35.00 (0-8386-2411-1) Fairleigh Dickinson.

***Bandel, David A.** Linux Security Toolkit. 480p. 2000. pap. text 39.99 (0-7645-4690-2) IDG Bks.

Bandele, Ajamu. A Book of Poems: A Black Man's View. (Illus.). 212p. 1996. pap. 14.99 (1-57502-332-6, PO1114) Morris Pubng.

— A Personal Diary of Poetry: A Black Man's View. 115p. pap. 10.00 (1-891143-50-6) Fantom Pubns.

— Poetry of the Reincarnation of a King: A Black Man's View. 360p. 1997. pap. 16.00 (1-57502-428-4, PO1309) Morris Pubng.

Bandele, Asha. Absence in the Palm of My Hands. LC 96-20896. 128p. 1996. pap. 12.00 (0-86316-013-1) Writers & Readers.

***Bandele, Asha.** The Prisoner's Wife. 240p. 2000. reprint ed. pap. 12.95 (0-671-02148-6, WSP) PB.

Bandele, Asha. The Prisoner's Wife: A Memoir. LC 99-12117. 224p. 1999. 22.50 (0-684-85073-7) S&S Trade.

Bandele, Biyi. The Sympathetic Undertaker. (African Writers Ser.). 208p. 1993. pap. 9.95 (0-435-90592-9, 90592) Heinemann.

Bandele, Gabriel. The Noble Art of Vending: An African Centered Guide to Vending Success. LC 92-97193. 100p. (Orig.). 1992. pap. 10.00 (1-882706-01-3) Bandele Pubns.

Bandele, Gabriel & Bandele, Kai. How to Market & Sell Your Crafts: From Making It To Making It Big In the Crafts Business. LC 92-97196. 100p. (Orig.). 1992. pap. 7.95 (1-882706-03-X) Bandele Pubns.

Bandele, Gabriel & Hooper, L. Do for Self: One Hundred of the Best Businesses for Africans in the 21st Century. LC 92-75200. 130p. 1992. pap. 10.00 (1-882706-02-1) Bandele Pubns.

Bandele, Kai. Cultural Caravans: A Guide to Sharing Cultural Activities & Events with your Family. LC 92-97194. 125p. (Orig.). 1992. pap. 10.00 (1-882706-05-6) Bandele Pubns.

Bandele, Kai, jt. auth. see Bandele, Gabriel.

Bandele Publications. Bandele's Annual Small Business Guide to African-American Events. 150p. (Orig.). 1992. pap. 15.00 (1-882706-00-5) Bandele Pubns.

— Bandele's Festival Goers' Guide to African-American Events. LC 92-75201. 100p. (Orig.). 1992. pap. 8.00 (1-882706-04-8) Bandele Pubns.

Bandele, Ramla. Nzinga. (J). 1992. pap. 6.95 (0-88378-023-2) Third World.

Bandele-Thomas, Biyi. The Man Who Came in from the Back of Beyond. (African Writers Ser.). 140p. (C). 1992. pap. 9.95 (0-435-90587-2, 90587) Heinemann.

Bandelier, Adolf F. The Delight Makers. LC 70-28000. 524p. 1971. reprint ed. pap. 15.00 (0-15-625264-3, Harvest Bks) Harcourt.

— Final Report of Investigations among the Indians of the Southwestern U. S., 2 vols., Set. LC 74-7918. reprint ed. 132.50 (0-404-58054-8) AMS Pr.

— Hemenway Southwestern Archaeological Expedition. LC 74-7922. reprint ed. 40.00 (0-404-58057-2) AMS Pr.

— Historical Introduction to Studies among the Sedentary Indians of New Mexico & a Report on the Ruins of the Pueblo at Pecos. LC 76-20788. reprint ed. 31.50 (0-404-58051-3) AMS Pr.

— Pioneers in American Anthropology: The Bandelier-Morgan Letters, 1873-1883, 2 vols. White, Leslie Alvin, ed. LC 74-7921. reprint ed. 81.50 (0-404-11806-2) AMS Pr.

— Report of an Archaeological Tour in Mexico in 1881. LC 76-24822. reprint ed. 42.50 (0-404-58052-1) AMS Pr.

— Scientist on the Trail. Hammond, George P., ed. LC 67-24721. (Quivira Society Publications, Vol. 10). 1967. reprint ed. 19.95 (0-405-00084-7) Ayer.

Bandelier, Adolf F. & Hewett, Edgar H. Indians of the Rio Grande Valley. LC 74-7920. reprint ed. 46.50 (0-404-11805-4) AMS Pr.

Bandelier, Adolf F., ed. see Nunez Cabeza de Vaca, Alvar.

Bandelier, Adolph F. The Discovery of New Mexico by the Franciscan Monk Friar Marcos de Niza in 1539. Rodack, Madeleine T., tr. from FRE. LC 80-25083. 135p. (C). 1981. 28.95 (0-8165-0717-1) U of Ariz Pr.

— Papers of the Archaeological Institute of America, 6 vols., Set. (American Ser.). reprint ed. 177.00 (0-404-19502-4); reprint ed. 278.00 (0-404-58050-5) AMS Pr.

***Bandelier, Adolph F.** Pioneers in American Anthropology: The Bandelier-Morgan Letters, 1873-1883, 2 vols. (LC History-America-E). 1999. reprint ed. lib. bdg. 180.00 (0-7812-4234-7) Rprt Serv.

— The Romantic School in American Archaeology. (LC History-America-E). 14p. 1999. reprint ed. lib. bdg. 69.00 (0-7812-4235-5) Rprt Serv.

Bandelier, Adolph F. Scientist on the Trail. (American Autobiography Ser.). 142p. 1995. reprint ed. lib. bdg. 69.00 (0-7812-8448-1) Rprt Serv.

— The Southwestern Journals of Adolf F. Bandelier, 1880-1882. Lange, Charles H. & Riley, Carroll L., eds. LC 65-17862. 502p. reprint ed. pap. 155.70 (0-608-12628-4, 202543000043) Bks Demand.

— The Southwestern Journals of Adolph F. Bandelier, 1883-1884. Lange, Charles H. & Riley, Carroll L., eds. LC 65-17862. 562p. reprint ed. pap. 174.30 (0-608-12631-4, 202543100043) Bks Demand.

— The Southwestern Journals of Adolph F. Bandelier, 1885-1888. Lange, Charles H. & Riley, Carroll L., eds. LC 65-17862. 720p. reprint ed. pap. 200.00 (0-608-12632-2, 202543200043) Bks Demand.

Bandelier, Adolph F. & Ten Kate, Herman F. An Outline of the Documentary History of the Zuni Tribe: Somatological Observations of Indians of the Southwest. LC 76-21219. (Journal of American Ethnology & Archaeology: Vol. 3). reprint ed. 47.50 (0-404-58043-2) AMS Pr.

Bandelier, Fanny, tr. see Nunez Cabeza de Vaca, Alvar.

Bandello, Matteo. Certain Tragical Discourses of Bandello, 2 vols. Fenton, Geffraie, tr. LC 73-160008. (Tudor Translations, First Ser.: Nos. 19-20). reprint ed. 115.00 (0-404-51900-8) AMS Pr.

***Bandelow, Borwin.** Panic & Agoraphobia Scale (PAS) LC 99-71758. (Illus.). 88p. 1999. pap. 49.00 (0-88937-216-0) Hogrefe & Huber Pubs.

Bandem, I. Made & DeBoer, Frederick E. Balinese Dance in Transition: Kaja & Kelod. 2nd ed. (Illus.). 180p. 1996. text 45.00 (967-65-3071-9) OUP.

Bandemer, Hans. Fuzzy Sets, Fuzzy Logic, Fuzzy Methods with Applications. LC 96-177884. 250p. 1996. 139.95 (0-471-95636-8) Wiley.

Bandemer, Hans, ed. Modelling Uncertain Data. 171p. 1993. pap. 69.95 (3-05-501578-9) Wiley.

Bandemer, Hans & Nather, Wolfgang. Fuzzy Data Analysis. LC 92-14042. (Theory & Decision Library, Mathematical & Statistical Methods Series B: Vol. 20). 352p. (C). 1992. text 171.00 (0-7923-1772-6) Kluwer Academic.

Bandemer, Mary A. The Poetry I Write! 48p. (Orig.). 1994. pap. 4.00 (1-884257-05-4) AGEE Keyboard.

Bander, Edward, ed. Justice Holmes Ex Cathedra. LC 91-73010. xix, 430p. 1991. reprint ed. 48.50 (0-89941-772-8, 307240) W S Hein.

Bander, Edward J., jt. auth. see Doyle, Francis R.

Bander, Edward J., ed. see Shakespeare, William.

Bander, Karen L., jt. auth. see Hill, Lowell D.

Bander, M., ed. see American Institute of Physics.

Bander, Peter. The Prophecies of St. Malachy. LC 74-125419. (Illus.). 1993. reprint ed. pap. 7.00 (0-89555-038-5) TAN Bks Pubs.

Bander, Peter, et al. The Prophecies of St. Malachy & St. Columbkille. 5th ed. 142p. 1995. pap. 9.95 (0-86140-386-X, Pub. by Smyth) Dufour.

Bander, Robert G. Sentence Making: A Writing Workbook in English As a Second Language. 248p. (C). 1982. pap. text 12.95 (0-03-058072-2) Harcourt Coll Pubs.

Bandera, Cesareo. The Sacred Game: The Role of the Sacred in the Genesis of Modern Literary Fiction. LC 93-6295. (Studies in Romance Literatures). 304p. (C). 1994. 50.00 (0-271-01301-X); pap. text 18.95 (0-271-01302-8) Pa St U Pr.

Bandera, Mark J. The Tsymbaly Maker & His Craft: The Ukrainian Hammered Dulcimer in Alberta. (Illus.). xii, 62p. pap. 14.95 (0-920862-80-2) Ukrainian Acad.

Banderet, Louis E., jt. ed. see Krueger, Gerald P.

Banderjee, Mrityunjoy. Essentials of Modern Marketing. (C). 1988. 10.00 (81-204-0335-5, Pub. by Oxford IBH) S Asia.

Bandes, Susan J., ed. see Halsted, Elizabeth, et al.

Bandes, Susan J., ed. see North, Bill.

Bandettini, P. A., jt. ed. see Moonen, C. T.

Bandey, Brian. International Copyright in Computer Program Technology. 300p. 1996. 125.00 (1-85811-098-X, Pub. by CLT Prof) Gaunt.

Bandhauer-Schöffmann, Irene, jt. auth. see Duchen, Claire.

Bandholtz, Harry H. Undiplomatic Diary. LC 77-160009. reprint ed. 49.50 (0-404-00494-6) AMS Pr.

***Bandholtz, Harry Hill & Kruger, Fritz-Konrad.** An Undiplomatic Diary: Hungary & W. W. I. Simon, Andrew L., ed. LC 00-102297. 300p. 2000. 39.95 (0-9665734-6-3) Simon Publns.

Bandhopadhyay, Sekhar. Caste, Politics & the Raj: Bengal, 1872-1937. 1990. 22.00 (81-7074-066-5, Pub. by KP Bagchi) S Asia.

Bandhopadhyaya, Jayantanuja, ed. Dimensions of Strategy: Some Indian Perspectives. 1989. 21.50 (81-85195-25-0, Pub. by Minerva) S Asia.

Bandhu, Desh, et al, eds. Current Trends in Indian Environment. 240p. 1990. reprint ed. 25.00 (0-685-59948-5) Scholarly Pubns.

Bandhu, Desh, jt. auth. see Gupta, K. M.

Bandiera, M. Research in Science Education in Europe. LC 99-20462. 1999. write for info. (0-7923-5699-3) Kluwer Academic.

Bandieramonte, Gaetano, et al, eds. Photothermal Therapies in Medicine. LC 98-164978. (Europto Ser.: Vol. 3193). 196p. 1998. 89.00 (0-8194-2625-3) SPIE.

Bandieramonte, Gaetano, jt. auth. see Bellina, Joseph H.

Bandila, Ratna K. Food Problems in India. (Illus.). xvii, 184p. (C). 1992. 20.00 (81-7024-465-X, Pub. by Ashish Pub Hse) Nataraj Bks.

Bandini, Carol, jt. auth. see Cancelmo, Joseph A.

Bandini, Lydia, ed. see Devi-Doolin, Daya.

Bandini, S. & Mauri, Giancarlo. ACRI '96: Proceedings of the Second Conference on Cellular Automate for Research & Industry, Milan, Italy, 16-18 October 1996. LC 96-29972. 1997. pap. 69.95 (3-540-76091-1) Spr-Verlag.

Bandishte, D. D. A Study of the Ethics of Bertrand Russell. 160p. 1984. 12.95 (0-318-37010-7) Asia Bk Corp.

Bandle, C. Elliptic & Parabolic. 1995. pap. 67.95 (0-582-23961-3, Pub. by Addison-Wesley) Longman.

Bandle, Catherine. Elliptic & Parabolic. 1992. lib. bdg. 74.95 (0-582-07252-2, Pub. by Addison-Wesley) Longman.

Bandle, Catherine, ed. see European Conference on Elliptic & Parabolic Proble.

Bandle, Catherine, Conference on General Inequalit. General Inequalities 7: 7th International Conference on General Inequalities, Oberwolfach, November 13-18, 1995. LC 97-8158. (International Series of Numerical Mathematics). 1997. write for info. (0-8176-5722-3); write for info. (3-7643-5722-3) Birkhauser.

Bandler, Faith. Turning the Tide: A Personal History of the Federal Council for the Advancement of Aborigines & Torres Strait Islanders. LC 89-175034. xvii, 173 p. 1989. write for info. (0-85575-196-7) AIB & TSIS.

Bandler, James. How to Use Financial Statements: A Guide to Understanding the Numbers. 160p. 1994. text 18.95 (0-7863-0197-X, Irwn Prfssnl) McGraw-Hill Prof.

***Bandler, James P.** A Quick Killing. LC 99-65319. 192p. 2000. pap. 11.95 (1-56315-253-3, Pub. by SterlingHse) Natl Bk Netwk.

Bandler, Richard. Adventures of Anybody. LC 93-84506. 1993. pap. 12.95 (0-916990-29-X) META Pubns.

— Magic in Action. rev. ed. LC 84-61646. 1985. 22.95 (0-916990-14-1) META Pubns.

— Time for a Change. LC 93-84505. 1993. 19.95 (0-916990-28-1) META Pubns.

Bandler, Richard & Grinder, John. Patterns of Hypnotic Techniques of Milton H. Erickson, M. D., Vol. 1. LC 75-24584. 1975. pap. 19.95 (0-916990-01-X) META Pubns.

— Patterns of the Hypnotic Techniques of Milton H. Erickson, M.D., Vol. I. LC 96-25682. 280p. 1997. pap. 18.95 (1-55552-052-9) Metamorphous Pr.

— The Structure of Magic, Vol. 1. LC 75-12452. 1975. pap. 16.95 (0-8314-0044-7) Sci & Behavior.

Bandler, Richard & LaValle, John. Persuasion Engineering. LC 95-76816. 1996. 24.95 (0-916990-36-2) META Pubns.

Bandler, Richard, jt. auth. see Grinder, John.

Bandler, Richard, jt. ed. see Depaulis, A.

Bandler, W., jt. auth. see Kohout, L. J.

Bandley, Michale J., jt. auth. see Buchanan, Clive J.

Bandlow, W., et al, eds. Genetics, Biogenetics & Bioenergetics of Mitochondria: Symposium, Sept. 1975, University of Munich, Germany. (C). 1976. 107.70 (3-11-006865-6) De Gruyter.

— Mitochondria 1977: Genetics & Biogenesis of Mitochondria. (C). 1977. 215.40 (3-11-007321-8) De Gruyter.

Bandman, Bertram. Children's Right to Freedom, Care & Enlightenment. LC 99-26255. (Reference Books on Family Issues). 250p. 1999. text 37.00 (0-8153-2131-7) Garland.

Bandman, Elsie L. Critical Thinking in Nursing. 2nd ed. LC 94-29377. (C). 1994. pap. text 37.95 (0-8385-1374-3, A1374-6) Appleton & Lange.

— Nursing Ethics Through the Life Span. 3rd ed. (C). 1995. pap. text 32.95 (0-8385-6638-3, A6638-9) Appleton & Lange.

Bando, Flavia & Raven, Arlene. Nancy Azara: Sacred Dwellings: The Work of Nancy Azara. (Illus.). 32p. (Orig.). 1994. pap. 10.00 (1-889523-09-7) Tweed Mus.

Bando, Mark A. Breakout at Normandy: The 2nd Armored Division in the Land of the Dead. LC 99-36475. (Illus.). 160p. 1999. pap. 19.95 (0-7603-0654-0, Pub. by MBI Pubg) Motorbooks Intl.

Bando, Yoshichika & Yamauchi, Hisao, eds. Advances in Superconductivity 5: Proceedings of the 5th International Symposium on Superconductivity (ISS '92), November 16-19, 1992, Kobe. LC 93-1409. 1993. 264.95 (0-387-70122-2) Spr-Verlag.

Bandon, Alexandra. Asian Indian Americans. LC 94-41698. (Footsteps to America Ser.). (YA). (gr. 6 up). 1995. lib. bdg. 13.95 (0-02-768144-0, New Dscvry Bks) Silver Burdett Pr.

— Chinese Americans. LC 93-32711. (Footsteps to America Ser.). (Illus.). 112p. (YA). (gr. 6 up). 1994. lib. bdg. 13.95 (0-02-768149-1, New Dscvry Bks) Silver Burdett Pr.

— Date Rape. LC 93-24063. (Update Ser.). 48p. (YA). (gr. 10 up). 1994. lib. bdg. 13.95 (0-382-24755-8) Silver Burdett Pr.

Bandon, Alexandra. Date Rape. LC 93-24063. (Update Ser.). 1994. 10.15 (0-606-10350-3, Pub. by Turtleback) Demco.

Bandon, Alexandra. Dominican Americans. (Footsteps to America Ser.). (J). 1999. 22.00 (*0-02-768152-1*, Mac Bks Young Read) S&S Childrens.

— Filipino Americans. LC 92-42205. (Footsteps to America Ser.). (Illus.). 112p. (YA). (gr. 6 up). 1993. lib. bdg. 13.95 (*0-02-768143-2*, New Dscvry Bks) Silver Burdett Pr.

— Korean Americans. LC 93-31059. (Footsteps to America Ser.). 112p. (J). 1994. pap. 7.95 (*0-382-24736-1*, New Dscvry Bks) Silver Burdett Pr.

— Korean Americans. LC 93-31059. (Footsteps to America Ser.). (J). 1999. text 22.00 (*0-02-768147-5*, New Dscvry Bks) Silver Burdett Pr.

— Mexican Americans. LC 92-41001. (Footsteps to America Ser.). (Illus.). 112p. (YA). (gr. 6 up). 1993. lib. bdg. 14.95 (*0-02-768142-4*, New Dscvry Bks) Silver Burdett Pr.

— Vietnamese Americans. LC 93-45497. 112p. (J). 1994. pap. 7.95 (*0-382-24763-9*) Silver Burdett Pr.

— Vietnamese Americans. LC 93-45497. (J). 1999. lib. bdg. 22.00 (*0-02-768146-7*, New Dscvry Bks) Silver Burdett Pr.

— West Indian Americans. LC 93-27201. (Footsteps to America Ser.). (Illus.). 112p. (YA). (gr. 6 up). 1994. lib. bdg. 13.95 (*0-02-768148-3*, New Dscvry Bks) Silver Burdett Pr.

***Bandon, Alexandra & O'Brien, Patrick.** Marco Polo. LC 99-48893. (Explorers & Exploration Ser.). 48p. (J). 2000. lib. bdg. write for info. (*0-7398-1485-0*) Raintree Steck-V.

Bandopadhyay, B. Survey of Indian Metal Sculpture. 217p. 1987. 99.95 (*0-318-36259-7*) Asia Bk Corp.

Bandopadhyay, Bhwanicharan. Kalikata Kamalalaya: Calcutta in the Early 19th Century. (C). 1990. text 11.00 (*0-8364-2591-X*, Pub. by Firma KLM) S Asia.

Bandopadhyay, Sukumar & Nelson, Michael G., eds. Mining in the Arctic: Proceedings of the 2nd International Symposium on Mining in the Arctic, Fairbanks, Alaska, 19-22 July 1992. (Illus.). 326p. (C). 1992. text 128.00 (*90-5410-078-8*, Pub. by A A Balkema) Ashgate Pub Co.

Bandopadhyay, Sukumar & Skudrzyk, F. J., eds. Mining in the Arctic: Proceedings of the 1st International Symposium on Mining in the Arctic, Fairbanks, 17-19 July 1989. 256p. (C). 1989. text 168.00 (*90-6191-899-5*, Pub. by A A Balkema) Ashgate Pub Co.

Bandopadhyaya, Arun. The Agrarian Economy of Tamilnadu, 1820-1855. (C). 1992. 28.00 (*81-7074-108-4*, Pub. by KP Bagchi) S Asia.

Bandopadhyaya, J. Climate & the World Order. 178p. 1983. 23.95 (*0-318-37227-4*) Asia Bk Corp.

— North over South: A NonWestern Perspective of International Relations. 1982. 26.00 (*0-8364-0894-2*) S Asia.

Bandopadhyaya, S. The Music of India. 80p. 1978. 7.95 (*0-318-36332-1*) Asia Bk Corp.

Bandow, Doug. Beyond Good Intentions: A Biblical View of Politics. LC 88-70698. (Turning Point Christian Worldview Ser.). 271p. 1988. pap. 15.99 (*0-89107-498-8*) Crossway Bks.

— The Politics of Envy: Statism As Theology. 322p. (C). 1994. 39.95 (*1-56000-171-2*) Transaction Pubs.

— The Politics of Plunder: Misgovernment in Washington. 385p. 1990. 34.95 (*0-88738-309-2*) Transaction Pubs.

— Tripwire: Korea & U. S. Foreign Policy in a Changed World. 140p. 1996. 19.95 (*1-882577-29-9*); pap. text 9.95 (*1-882577-30-2*) Cato Inst.

Bandow, Doug, ed. Perpetuating Poverty: The World Bank, the IMF, & the Developing World. LC 93-48499. 320p. 1993. 25.95 (*1-882577-06-X*) Cato Inst.

Bandow, Doug & Carpenter, Ted G., eds. The U. S. South Korean Alliance: Time for a Change. 206p. (C). 1992. 39.95 (*1-56000-018-X*); pap. 24.95 (*1-56000-583-1*) Transaction Pubs.

Bandrauk, A. D. & Wallace, S. C. Coherence Phenomena in Atoms & Molecules in Laser Fields. (NATO ASI Ser.: Vol. 287). (Illus.). 416p. (C). 1992. text 129.50 (*0-306-44190-X*, Kluwer Plenum) Kluwer Academic.

Bandrauk, Andre D., ed. Molecules in Laser Fields. LC 93-40776. (Illus.). 480p. 1993. text 225.00 (*0-8247-9175-4*) Dekker.

Bandrowski, James F. Corporate Imagination. 1990. 32.95 (*0-02-901501-4*) Free Pr.

***Bandrowski, James F.** Corporate Imagination Plus. 2000. per. 19.95 (*0-7432-0549-9*) S&S Trade.

Bandrowski, Juliusz K., ed. Great Battle on the Vistula. LC 73-151603. (BCL Ser. I). reprint ed. 37.50 (*0-404-00495-4*) AMS Pr.

Bandruk, A. D., ed. Atomic & Molecular Processes with Short Intense Laser Pulses. LC 88-2509. (NATO ASI Series B, Physics: Vol. 171). (Illus.). 492p. 1988. 135.00 (*0-306-42826-1*, Plenum Trade) Perseus Pubng.

Bandsma, Arend & Brandt, Robin. Flatweaves of Turkey. (Illus.). 168p. 1997. 50.00 (*0-85667-490-7*, Pub. by P Wilson) Antique Collect.

Bandstra, Andrew. In the Company of Angels: What the Bible Teaches, What You Need to Know. LC 94-44899. 1995. pap. 9.95 (*1-56212-081-6*) CRC Pubns.

Bandstra, Andrew J. In the Company of Angels. 12.99 (*0-08-923922-9*) Brasseys.

— In the Company of Angels: What the Bible Teaches, What You Need to Know. (Illus.). 1995. pap., student ed. 11.95 (*1-56212-090-5*) CRC Pubns.

Bandstra, Barry L. Reading the Old Testament: An Introduction to the Hebrew Bible. LC 94-13210. 576p. 1994. 45.00 (*0-534-21354-5*) Wadsworth Pub.

— Reading the Old Testament: Intro to the Hebrew Bible. 2nd ed. LC 98-35207. (Religion Ser.). 1999. pap. 75.95 (*0-534-52727-2*) Wadsworth Pub.

Bandt, Christoph, et al, eds. Fractal Geometry & Stochastics. (Progress in Probability Ser.: Vol. 37). 264p. 1996. 89.50 (*3-7643-5263-9*) Birkhauser.

— Fractal Geometry & Stochastics, Vol. 37. LC 95-23670. (Progress in Probability Ser.). 1995. 89.50 (*0-8176-5263-9*) Birkhauser.

***Bandt, Christoph, et al, eds.** Fractal Geometry & Stochastics II. LC 99-51723. (Progress in Probability Ser.: Vol. 46). 296p. 1999. 98.00 (*0-8176-6215-4*, Pub. by Birkhauser) Spr-Verlag.

— Fractal Geometry & Stochastics II. LC 99-51723. (Progress in Probability Ser.: Vol. 46). 296p. 2000. 79.95 (*3-7643-6215-4*) Birkhauser.

Bandtock, Peter & Knowles, Peter. White Water Europe: The North Alps, Bk. 1. (Illus.). 256p. 1996. pap. 24.95 (*0-89732-212-6*) Menasha Ridge.

Banducci, Don, ed. see Bourne, Heidi L.

Bandura, Albert. Self Efficacy: The Exercise of Control. LC 96-52118. 500p. 1997. pap. text 40.95 (*0-7167-2850-8*); pap. text 62.95 (*0-7167-2626-2*) W H Freeman.

— Self-Efficacy in Changing Societies. 352p. 1997. pap. text 22.95 (*0-521-58696-8*) Cambridge U Pr.

— The Social Foundations of Thought & Action: A Social Cognitive Theory. (Illus.). 544p. 1985. 110.00 (*0-13-815614-X*) P-H.

Bandura, Albert. Social Learning Theory. 247p. 1976. pap. text 33.00 (*0-13-816744-3*) P-H.

Bandura, Albert, ed. Self-Efficacy in Changing Societies. (Illus.). 350p. (C). 1995. text 59.95 (*0-521-47467-1*) Cambridge U Pr.

Bandura, Albert & Ribes-Inesta, Emilio, eds. Analysis of Delinquency & Aggression. 256p. 1976. text 59.95 (*0-89859-360-3*) L Erlbaum Assocs.

Bandura, Albert & Walters, Richard H. Adolescent Aggression: A Study of the Influence of Child-Training Practices & Family Inter-Relationships. LC 59-12125. 489p. reprint ed. 151.60 (*0-8357-9518-7*, 201240400081) Bks Demand.

Bandy, A. R., ed. The Chemistry of the Atmosphere - Oxidants & Oxidation in the Earth's Atmosphere: Proceedings. 228p. 1995. 87.00 (*0-85404-765-4*, QC879) CRC Pr.

Bandy, D. Brent, jt. ed. see Raymond, Bruce C.

Bandy, Dale D. Prentice-Hall Federal Tax Course, 1983. (Illus.). 368p. (C). 1982. pap. text, student ed. 9.95 (*0-13-312637-4*) P-H.

— Prentice-Hall Federal Tax Course, 1984: Student Guide. (Illus.). 368p. (C). 1983. pap. 10.95 (*0-13-312736-2*) P-H.

— Prentice-Hall Federal Tax Course, 1986: Student Guide. (Illus.). 352p. (C). 1985. 11.95 (*0-13-312802-4*) P-H.

— Prentice-Hall 1985 Federal Tax Course. 1985th ed. (Illus.). 368p. (C). 1984. 11.95 (*0-13-312778-8*) P-H.

— Prentice-Hall, 1987. (Illus.). 352p. (C). 1986. student ed. 11.95 (*0-317-46064-1*) P-H.

Bandy, JoAnne. The Complete Guide to Retirement Housing: Central Florida Edition. LC 98-218563. 171p. 1998. pap. 19.95 (*0-9664668-0-2*) Sr Educ Assocs.

Bandy, Ken & Freeland, Florence, compiled by. The Gettysburg Papers, Vols. I & II. 1103p. 1988. 50.00 (*0-89029-044-X*) Morningside Bkshop.

Bandy, Marcia & Bandy, Maurice. Saddleback Ancestors: Rancho Families of Orange County California. 2nd rev. ed. Heinz, Sharon & Cohen, Patricia F., eds. LC 98-68429. (Illus.). xxi, 327p. 1998. 30.00 (*0-9667946-0-5*) Orange Cty Geneal Soc.

Bandy, Maurice, jt. auth. see Bandy, Marcia.

Bandy, Susan J., ed. Coroebus Triumphs: The Alliance of Sport & the Arts. (Illus.). 303p. 1989. pap. 18.75 (*0-916304-76-0*) SDSU Press.

Bandy, Susan J. & Darden, Anne S., eds. Crossing Boundaries: An International Anthology of Women's Experiences in Sports. LC 99-13733. 328p. 1999. pap. text 21.95 (*0-7360-0088-7*, BBAN0088) Human Kinetics.

Bandy, Thomas. Moving off the Map: A Field Guide to Changing the Congregation. LC 98-40758. 240p. 1998. pap. 17.00 (*0-687-06800-2*) Abingdon.

Bandy, Thomas, jt. auth. see Easum, William M.

Bandy, Thomas G. Kicking Habits: Welcome Relief for Addicted Churches. LC 96-48670. (Illus.). 232p. 1997. pap. 14.95 (*0-687-03189-3*) Abingdon.

Bandyk. Varicose Veins: A Guide for Patients. Ellis & Carey, Larry, eds. (Surgery Ser.). (Illus.). 24p. (Orig.). 1995. pap. 2.95 (*1-885274-22-X*) Health InfoNet Inc.

Bandyoapadhyay, Jayanata K. QS-9000 Handbook: A Guide to Registration & Audit. 256p. 1996. boxed set 74.95 (*1-57444-011-X*) St Lucie Pr.

Bandyopadhyay, Bholanath. The Political Ideas of Benoy Kumar Sarkar. 1985. 15.00 (*0-8364-1336-9*, Pub. by KP Bagchi) S Asia.

— Studies in Indian Metal Sculptures. 250p. (C). 1987. 44.00 (*0-8364-2180-9*, Pub. by Sundeep Prak) S Asia.

Bandyopadhyay, Gitasree. Constraints in Bengal Politics, Nineteen Twenty-One to Nineteen Forty-One: Gandhian Leadership. 1985. 20.00 (*0-8364-1448-9*, Pub. by Sarat) S Asia.

Bandyopadhyay, K. K. Evaluation of Methodology for Seismic Qualification of Equipment, Cable Trays & Ducts in ALWR Plants by Use of Experience Data. 135p. 1997. per. 14.00 (*0-16-062857-1*) USGPO.

Bandyopadhyay, Mridula & MacPherson, Stewart. Women & Health: Tradition & Culture in Rural India. LC 97-77384. 228p. 1998. text 63.95 (*1-84014-349-5*, Pub. by Ashgate Pub) Ashgate Pub Co.

***Bandyopadhyay, Nanda.** Computing for Non-Specialists. LC 99-54345. 312p. 2000. pap. 49.00 (*0-201-64861-X*) Addisn-Wesley Iberoamer.

Bandyopadhyay, P. R., et al, eds. Application of Microfabrication to Fluid Mechanics 1994: Proceedings: International Mechanical Engineering Congress & Exposition (1994: Chicago, IL) LC 94-78965. (FED Ser.: Vol. 197). 87p. 1995. pap. 48.00 (*0-7918-1391-6*, G00886) ASME Pr.

Bandyopadhyay, Pranab. The Goddess of Tantra. rev. ed. (C). 1990. text 52.00 (*81-85094-30-6*, Pub. by Punthi Pus) S Asia.

— Hindu Faith & Religion. (C). 1987. 21.00 (*0-8364-2131-0*) S Asia.

— Mother Goddess Durga. 1987. 13.00 (*0-8364-2065-9*) S Asia.

— Shankaracharya. (C). 1990. text 11.00 (*81-85328-09-9*, Pub. by Firma KLM) S Asia.

— Tantra: Occultism & Spirituality. (C). 1994. 18.00 (*0-8364-2893-5*, Pub. by Firma KLM) S Asia.

— Yoga, Sadhana & Samadhi. (C). 1987. 16.00 (*0-8364-2132-9*) S Asia.

— Yogis & Mystics. (C). 1988. 32.50 (*81-85094-13-6*) S Asia.

Bandyopadhyay, Pratul. Geometry, Topology & Quantization. LC 96-36620. (Mathematics & Its Applications Ser.). 240p. (C). 1996. text 144.00 (*0-7923-4305-0*) Kluwer Academic.

Bandyopadhyay, S., et al, eds. Quantum Confinement: Quantum Confinement & Dots: 3rd International Symposium. (Proceedings Ser.: Vol. 95-17). (Illus.). 367p. 1996. 78.00 (*1-56677-112-9*) Electrochem Soc.

Bandyopadhyay, Samik, tr. from BEN. Mother of 1084: Mahasweta Devi. LC 97-901803. (C). 1997. pap. 14.00 (*81-7046-139-1*, Pub. by Seagull Bks) S Asia.

Bandyopadhyay, Sekhar. Burma Today. 120p. 1987. 17.95 (*0-318-37226-6*) Asia Bk Corp.

— Caste, Protest & Identity in Colonial India: The Nama Sudras of Bengal, 1872-1947. (SOAS London Studies on South Asia: 15). 288p. (C). 1997. text 48.00 (*0-7007-0626-7*, Pub. by Curzon Pr Ltd) UH Pr.

Bandyopadhyay, Sekhar, ed. Bengal: Communities, Development, & States. (C). 1994. text 30.00 (*81-7304-089-3*, Pub. by Manohar) S Asia.

Bandyopadhyay, Subir. Calcutta Cycle Rickshaw Pullers: A Sociological Study. 1990. 14.50 (*81-85195-27-7*, Pub. by Minerva) S Asia.

Bandyopadhyay, Taradas & Ghatek, Subrata, eds. Current Issues in Monetary Economics. 352p. (C). 1990. lib. bdg. 59.50 (*0-389-20911-2*) B&N Imports.

Bandyopadhyay, Tirthanath, jt. auth. see Sengupta, Kalyan K.

Bandyopadhyaya, Jayantanuja. The Making of India's Foreign Policy. 362p. 1991. 19.95 (*0-940500-35-3*) Asia Bk Corp.

Bandyopadhyaya, Kalyani. Political Economy of Nonalignment: Indonesia & Malaysia. (C). 1990. 24.00 (*81-7003-113-3*, Pub. by S Asia Pubs) S Asia.

Bandyopadhyaya, Narayan C. Development of Hindu Polity & Political Theories. 1980. text 28.50 (*0-685-13695-7*) Coronet Bks.

Bandyopadhyaya, Sekhar. Ada-Chowtal on Sitar (Anthology of Poorav Baj) (C). 1990. 10.00 (*81-7018-595-5*, Pub. by BR Pub) S Asia.

— Origin of Raga. (C). 1995. 12.50 (*81-215-0261-6*, Pub. by M Manoharial) Coronet Bks.

Bandyopadyaya, Manik. The Puppets' Tale. Ghosh, Sachindralal, tr. (C). 1995. reprint ed. 8.00 (*81-7201-655-7*, Pub. by Indian Pubs) S Asia.

Bandyopahyay, B. Survey of Indian Metal Sculpture. 217p. 1987. 65.00 (*0-8364-2035-7*, Pub. by Usha) S Asia.

Bane, Adele F. & Lear, Amy C. Technology & Adult Learning: A Selected Bibliography. LC 93-38477. (Educational Technology Selected Bibliography Ser.: Vol. 11). 55p. 1994. pap. 24.95 (*0-87778-273-3*) Educ Tech Pubns.

Bane, Andy. Intelligent Compassion for the Homeless: Colorado Could Lead Nation. (Issue Papers: No. 10-91). 15p. 1991. pap. text 8.00 (*1-57655-054-0*) Independ Inst.

Bane, Bernard M. The Bane in Kennedy's Existence. LC 66-30557. 169p. 1967. pap. 10.95 (*0-9600164-0-6*) BMB Pub Co.

— Controlled Brinkmanship. 8p. 1968. pap. 0.35 (*0-9600164-1-4*) BMB Pub Co.

— The "Figure Eight" Schematic: Towards Codifying Bodily Functions. 3rd ed. 100p. 1980. pap. 4.00 (*0-930924-05-3*) BMB Pub Co.

— The Grand Model of Mind. LC 62-13784. 73p. 1962. pap. 10.00 (*0-9600164-2-2*) BMB Pub Co.

— Guidelines to Authenticity Stepping Stones to Health. LC 77-87980. 60p. 1977. pap. 3.00 (*0-9600164-6-5*) BMB Pub Co.

— Is President John F. Kennedy Alive...& Well? 15th rev. ed. LC 88-116961. 220p. 1993. pap. 15.00 (*0-930924-33-9*) BMB Pub Co.

— On the Impact of Morality in Our Times. 113p. 1985. pap. 5.00 (*0-930924-22-3*) BMB Pub Co.

— A Schematic Replica of the Cardiac Cycle. 45p. 1981. pap. 3.00 (*0-930924-11-8*) BMB Pub Co.

— Tramp, Tramp, Tramp, the Girls Are Marching: A Self-Styled Report on the Women's Liberation Movement. 80p. 1982. pap. 5.00 (*0-930924-15-0*) BMB Pub Co.

— Vatican "One" The Fault Line of Vatican II. 86p. 1986. pap. 5.00 (*0-930924-25-8*) BMB Pub Co.

Bane, Leni L., jt. auth. see Marsh, G. Alex.

Bane, Mary J. & Ellwood, David T. Welfare Realities: From Rhetoric to Reform. LC 93-45029. 208p. 1994. 37.95 (*0-674-94912-9*) HUP.

Bane, Mary J., jt. auth. see Masnick, George.

Bane, Mary J., jt. ed. see Carballo, Manuel.

Bane, Mary Jo & Ellwood, David T. Welfare Realities: From Rhetoric to Reform. 240p. 1996. pap. 18.00 (*0-674-94913-7*) HUP.

Bane, Michael. Acceptable Risks. 288p. 1996. 21.95 (*0-02-860426-1*) Macmillan.

— Diving on the Edge: A Guide for New Divers. LC 97-44823. (Illus.). 198p. 1998. pap. 14.95 (*1-55821-540-9*) Lyons Pr.

— Over the Edge: An Odyssey in Extreme Sports. 256p. 1998. pap. text 12.95 (*0-02-862280-4*) Macmillan.

***Bane, Michael.** Over the Edge: An Odyssey in Extreme Sports. LC 00-35175. 243p. 2000. pap. 19.95 (*0-89997-265-9*) Wilderness Pr.

— Trail Safe: Averting Threatening Human Behavior in the Outdoors. 180p. 2000. pap. 14.95 (*0-89997-264-0*) Wilderness Pr.

Bane, Michael. White Boy Singin' the Blues: The Black Roots of White Rock. rev. ed. (Illus.). 286p. 1992. reprint ed. pap. 12.95 (*0-306-80479-4*) Da Capo.

Bane, Michael, jt. auth. see Garwood, Dave.

Bane, Michael, jt. auth. see Tritt, Travis.

Bane, Ros Ann, ed. see Heikens, Steve G.

Bane, Rosanne. Dancing in the Dragon's Den: Rekindling the Creative Fire in Your Shadow. LC 99-31855. (Illus.). 320p. 1999. pap. 19.95 (*0-89254-047-8*) Nicolas-Hays.

Bane, Rosemary C., jt. auth. see Poffenberger, Nancy.

Bane, Vickie. Dr . Laura Schlessinger. 2nd ed. LC 99-22077. 225p. 1999. text 23.95 (*0-312-20530-9*) St Martin.

***Bane, Vickie.** Dr. Laura: The Unauthorized Biography. (Illus.). 240p. 1999. mass mkt. 6.99 (*0-312-97122-2*) St Martin.

Bane, Vickie, et al. The Lives of Danielle Steel. 1995. mass mkt. 5.99 (*0-312-95575-8*, Pub. by Tor Bks) St Martin.

Bane, William F. We Did It Their Way. unabridged ed. Matson, Mary K. & Negley, Oka, eds. (Illus.). 230p. 1996. 19.62 (*0-9652452-0-9*) Bane-Clene.

Banek, Yvette. New Baby's Prayers. (First Bible Collection). 6p. (J). (gr. k-3). 1999. text 10.99 (*1-57584-279-3*, Pub. by Rdrs Digest) Random.

— New Baby's Prayers. 8p. (J). (ps). 1999. 9.99 (*0-7847-0846-0*, 03499) Standard Pub.

Baneke, Joost, et al. Dutch Art & Character: Psychoanalytical Perspectives on Bosch, Brueghel, Rembrandt, Van Gogh, Mondrian, Willink, Queen Wilhelmina. 228p. 1993. 73.00 (*90-265-1369-0*); pap. 44.00 (*90-265-1373-9*) Swets.

Baneres, Enric. Diccionari de l'Esport Catala-Castella, Castella-Catala. (CAT & SPA.). 408p. 1989. 41.95 (*0-7859-6494-0*, 847739072X) Fr & Eur.

Banerian, James. Losers Are Pirates: A Close Look at the PBS Series "Vietnam: A Television History" rev. ed. LC 85-61423. 416p. 1985. pap. 14.95 (*0-932729-01-0*) Sphinx Pub.

Banerjea, Akshaya K. Philosophy of Gorakhnath with Goraksha-Vacana-Sangraha. 355p. (C). 1999. 21.00 (*81-208-0534-8*, Pub. by Motilal Bnarsidass); pap. 15.50 (*81-208-0535-6*, Pub. by Motilal Bnarsidass) St Mut.

Banerjea, H. N. Technology of Portland Cement & Blended Cements. 154p. 1980. 15.95 (*0-318-37338-6*) Asia Bk Corp.

Banerjee. Chemical Plant Safety. 1998. 85.00 (*1-56032-069-9*) Hemisp Pub.

Banerjee. Under the Raj. text 22.00 (*1-58367-035-1*) Monthly Rev.

Banerjee. Virtual Manufacturing. text 79.95 (*0-471-35443-0*) Wiley.

***Banerjee, A., ed.** An Historical Evaluation of Thomas Hardy's Poetry. LC 00-33952. (Studies in British Literature: Vol. 49). 432p. 2000. 109.95 (*0-7734-7721-7*) E Mellen.

Banerjee, A. C. The Khalsa Raj. 1985. 17.50 (*0-8364-1355-5*, Pub. by Abhinav) S Asia.

— New History of Medieval India. 1983. text 23.00 (*0-685-14083-0*) Coronet Bks.

— The Splendour of Buddhism. (C). 1991. text 12.75 (*0-685-50091-8*, Pub. by M Manoharial) S Asia.

Banerjee, Ajit K. Rehabilitation of Degraded Forests in Asia. LC 94-40154. (World Bank Technical Papers: No. 270). 62p. 1995. pap. 22.00 (*0-8213-3119-1*, 13119) World Bank.

Banerjee, Amalesh & Kar, Biman. Economic Planning & Development of North-Eastern States. LC 99-931893. 441 p. 1999. write for info. (*81-7391-290-4*) S Asia.

Banerjee, Anil C. Annexation of Burma. LC 77-87007. reprint ed. 34.50 (*0-404-16793-4*) AMS Pr.

— The Constitutional History of India, Vol. I. 586p. 1987. 34.95 (*0-318-36619-3*) Asia Bk Corp.

Banerjee, Anil Chandra, see Chandra Banerjee, Anil.

Banerjee, Anindya. Econometrics of Economic Policy. 1997. pap. text 28.95 (*0-631-20343-5*) Blackwell Pubs.

Banerjee, Anindya, et al. Co-Integration, Error Correction, & the Econometric Analysis of Non-Stationary Data. LC 92-27344. (Advanced Texts in Econometrics Ser.). (Illus.). 342p. (C). 1993. pap. text 28.00 (*0-19-828810-7*) OUP.

Banerjee, Anuradha. Environment, Population, & Human Settlements of Sundarban Delta. LC 98-915287. 424p. 1998. write for info. (*81-7022-739-9*) Concept.

Banerjee, Archana. Models of Metaphilosophy. (C). 1989. 22.50 (*81-85195-21-8*, Pub. by Minerva) S Asia.

***Banerjee, Arpan.** Radiology Made Easy. (Illus.). 184p. 1999. pap. text 39.95 (*1-84110-014-5*) OUP.

Banerjee, Ashis. Accident & Emergency Medicine: Survival. 1996. pap. text 31.50 (*0-7020-2210-1*, W B Saunders Co) Harcrt Hlth Sci Grp.

Banerjee, B. Criminal Pleading, Law, Practice & Procedure with Model Forms. 3rd ed. (C). 1990. 160.00 (*0-89771-190-4*) St Mut.

— Digest, Cases & Materials, Land Acquisition & Compensation Cases. (C). 1990. 110.00 (*0-89771-302-8*) St Mut.

— Essential of Medical Microbiology, 2 vols. 2nd ed. (C). 1988. 80.00 (*0-7855-6118-8*, Pub. by Current Dist) St Mut.

Banerjee, B. G. & Bhatia, Kiran. Tribal Demography of Gonds. (C). 1988. 21.50 (*81-212-0237-X*, Pub. by Gian Publng Hse) S Asia.

Banerjee, B. N. India on the Threshold of the 21st Century. 388p. 1986. 49.95 (*0-318-36577-4*) Asia Bk Corp.

B

Banerjee, B. N., jt. auth. see Islam, M. M.

Banerjee, Bani P. Corporate Strategies: A Comprehensive Handbook Based on the Indian Experience. LC 99-935754. (Illus.). 552p. 1999. text 60.00 (*0-19-564763-7*) OUP.

Banerjee, Brojendra N. Can the Ganga be Cleaned. (C). 1989. 27.50 (*81-7018-544-0*) S Asia.

Banerjee, D. & Jacobson, Loren, eds. Metastable Microstructures. 351p. 1993. text 75.00 (*1-881570-06-1*) Science Pubs.

Banerjee, D., jt. auth. see Gambhir, R. S.

Banerjee, Deb K., ed. Marx & His Legacy: A Centennial Appraisal. (C). 1988. 17.50 (*81-7074-012-6*, Pub. by KP Bagchi) S Asia.

***Banerjee, Dillon.** So, You Want to Join the Peace Corps... What to Know Before You Do. LC HC60.5.B34. (Illus.). 192p. 2000. pap. 12.95 (*1-58008-097-9*) Ten Speed Pr.

***Banerjee, Dipankar.** Security in South Asia: Comprehensive & Cooperative. LC 99-936959. 309p. 1999. 29.00 (*81-7049-101-0*, Pub. by Manas Pubns) Nataraj Bks.

Banerjee, Dipek, ed. Essays in Economic Analysis & Policy: A Tribute to Bhabatosh Datta. 284p. 1991. 15.95 (*0-19-562734-2*) OUP.

Banerjee, G. India As Known to the Ancient World. 1990. reprint ed. 14.00 (*81-206-0561-6*, Pub. by Asian Educ Servs) S Asia.

B

Banerjee, G. C. Textbook of Animal Husbandry. 7th rev. ed. (C). 1991. 27.00 (*81-204-0066-6*, Pub. by Oxford IBH) S Asia.

Banerjee, Gauranga N. Hellenism in Ancient India. (C). 1995. reprint ed. 34.00 (*0-8364-2910-9*, Pub. by Mittal Pubs Dist) S Asia.

Banerjee, Hasi. Sarojini Naidu: The Traditional Feminist. LC 99-931555. (Monograph - Department of History, University of Calcutta Ser.). 122 p. 1998. 14.00 (*81-7074-208-0*, Pub. by K P Bagchi) S Asia.

Banerjee, Himadri. Agrarian Society of the Punjab, 1849-1901. 1983. 24.00 (*0-8364-0968-X*, Pub. by Manohar) S Asia.

Banerjee, Hiranmay. Rabindranath Tagore - Builders of Modern India. 195p. 1981. 9.95 (*0-318-36913-3*) Asia Bk Corp.

Banerjee, J. N. The Development of Hindu Iconography. 3rd ed. (Illus.). 1974. text 47.50 (*0-685-13702-3*) Coronet Bks.

Banerjee, Jacqueline. Through the Northern Gate Vol. 6: Childhood & Growing up in British Fiction, 1719-1901. (Studies in Nineteenth-Century British Literature). XXIX, 244p. (C). 1996. text 49.95 (*0-8204-3010-2*) P Lang Pubng.

Banerjee, Jitendra N. The Development of Hindu Iconography. 3rd enl. rev. ed. 1986. 47.50 (*81-215-0069-9*, Pub. by M Manoharial) Coronet Bks.

Banerjee, K., et al. Flare Gas Systems Pocket Handbook. fac. ed. LC 85-12665. (Illus.). 143p. 1985. reprint ed. pap. 44.40 (*0-608-00974-1*, 206182800012) Bks Demand.

Banerjee, Kali S. Cost of Living Index Numbers: Practice, Precision, & Theory. LC 75-985. (Statistics, Textbooks & Monographs: No. 11). 197p. reprint ed. pap. 61.10 (*0-7837-0734-7*, 204105800019) Bks Demand.

Banerjee, L. K. & Rao, T. A. Mangroves of Orissa Coast & Their Ecology. (Illus.). 118p. 1990. text 17.50 (*81-211-0028-3*, Pub. by Mahendra Pal Singh) Lubrecht & Cramer.

Banerjee, M. L. Orchids of Nepal. (International Bioscience Ser.: No. 4). 134p. (C). 1978. 24.00 (*0-7855-3291-9*, Pub. by Scientific) St Mut.

Banerjee, Maria N. Terminal Paradox: The Novels of Milan Kundera. 304p. 1991. pap. 12.95 (*0-8021-3233-2*, Grove) Grove-Atltic.

Banerjee, Mrityunjoy. Planning in India. rev. ed. (C). 1988. 16.00 (*81-204-0334-7*, Pub. by Oxford IBH) S Asia.

***Banerjee, Mukulika.** The Pathan Unarmed: Opposition & Memory in the Khudai Khidmatgar Movement. (World Anthropology Ser.). 320p. 2000. 65.00 (*0-933452-68-3*); pap. 29.95 (*0-933452-69-1*) Schol Am Res.

Banerjee, Nikunja V. Chaitanya & Vaisnavism. (C). 1992. 9.50 (*0-8364-2794-7*, Pub. by RDDHI) S Asia.

— The Dhammapada. (C). 1989. 19.50 (*0-685-37834-9*, Pub. by M Manoharial) S Asia.

— Knowledge Reason & Human Anatomy. 1986. 32.00 (*0-8364-1657-0*, Pub. by Somaiya) S Asia.

— Towards Perpetual Peace. 1988. 21.00 (*81-208-0536-4*, Pub. by Motilal Bnarsidass) S Asia.

Banerjee, Nirmala, ed. Indian Women in a Changing Industrial Scenario. (IDPAD Ser.: No. 5). (Illus.). 344p. 1991. 35.00 (*0-8039-9659-4*) Sage.

Banerjee, P. The Life of Krishna in Indian Art. (Illus.). 348p. 1978. 94.95 (*0-318-36269-4*) Asia Bk Corp.

Banerjee, P. & Gupta, S. K., eds. Man, Society & Nature. (C). 1988. 21.50 (*81-208-0566-6*, Pub. by Motilal Bnarsidass) S Asia.

Banerjee, P. K. Biophysical Chemistry Metal Ions DNA: Interactions. (International Bioscience Monographs: No. 8). 1979. 10.00 (*0-88065-022-2*) Scholarly Pubns.

— Boundary Element Methods in Engineering. LC 93-13475. 496p. (C). 1994. 98.75 (*0-07-707769-5*) McGraw.

Banerjee, P. K. & Morino, L., eds. Boundary Element Methods in Nonlinear Fluid Dynamics: Developments in Boundary Element Methods, No. 6. 358p. 1990. mass mkt. 161.50 (*1-85166-429-7*) Elsevier.

Banerjee, P. K. & Mukherjee, S. Developments in Boundary Element Methods, Vol. 3. 328p. 1984. mass mkt. 136.50 (*0-85334-253-9*, I-167-84) Elsevier.

Banerjee, P. K. & Shaw, R. P., eds. Developments in Boundary Element Methods, Vol. 2. (Illus.). 288p. 1982. pap. 157.50 (*0-85334-112-5*) Thomson Learn.

Banerjee, P. K. & Watson, J. O., eds. Developments in Boundary Element Methods, Vol. 4. 360p. 1986. mass mkt. 123.50 (*0-85334-376-4*) Elsevier.

Banerjee, Paramita, jt. auth. see Debi, Mahasveta.

Banerjee, Partha P., jt. auth. see Jarem, John M.

***Banerjee, Prithviraj, et al, eds.** High Performance Computing - HiPC'99: 6th International Conference, Calcutta, India, December 17-20, 1999, Proceedings. LC 99-58843. (Lecture Notes in Computer Science Ser.: Vol. 1745). xxii, 412p. 1999. pap. 69.00 (*3-540-66907-8*) Spr-Verlag.

Banerjee, Projesh. Dance in Thumri. 114p. 1986. 35.00 (*81-7017-212-8*, Pub. by Abhinav) S Asia.

Banerjee, R. N., ed. Theory of Pricing & Monetary Economics. (C). 1989. 50.00 (*0-89771-425-3*, Pub. by Current Dist) St Mut.

Banerjee, Romen. Wahrnehmung-Perception. 48p. 1996. 29.00 incl. audio compact disk (*3-931126-10-2*, Pub. by Die Gestalten) Consort Bk Sales.

Banerjee, Ron. Poetry from Bengal. LC 89-82066. 160p. (Orig.). 1990. pap. 19.95 (*0-948259-79-5*, Pub. by Forest Bks) Dufour.

***Banerjee, Ruma.** Chemistry & Biochemistry of B12. LC 98-51778. 921p. 1999. 295.00 (*0-471-25390-1*) Wiley.

Banerjee, S. & Mukhopadhyay, P. Phase Transformations in Titanium & Zicronium-Based Alloys. (Pergamon Materials Ser.: Vol. 5). 1999. write for info. (*0-08-042145-8*, Pergamon Pr) Elsevier.

Banerjee, S. & Ramanujan, R. V., eds. Advances in Physical Metallurgy. 550p. 1996. pap. text 72.00 (*2-88449-210-0*) Gordon & Breach.

Banerjee, S., jt. ed. see Singh, J. P.

Banerjee, S. B. & Jha, S. S., eds. Recent Trends in Raman Spectroscopy. 408p. (C). 1989. pap. 40.00 (*9971-5-0794-3*); text 109.00 (*9971-5-0786-2*) World Scientific Pub.

Banerjee, S. C. A Brief History of Tantra Literature. 576p. (C). 1986. 42.00 (*81-85109-46-X*, Pub. by Naya Prokash) S Asia.

— Folklore in Buddhist & Jaina Literatures: An Account of the Life of the Common People As Reflected in Pali, Prakrit & Apabhramsa Works. (Bibliotheca Indo Buddhica Ser.: No. 37). 118p. (C). 1987. text 13.00 (*81-7030-116-5*) S Asia.

Banerjee, S. C., ed. Manusmrti with Sanskrit Commentary Manvarthamuktavali of Kulluka Bhatta. (C). 1990. reprint ed. 26.00 (*81-208-0765-0*, Pub. by Motilal Bnarsidass) S Asia.

***Banerjee, S. K.** Diplomatic Encounter: A Novel. 238p. 1999. 24.00 (*81-241-0635-5*, Pub. by Har-Anand Pubns) Nataraj Bks.

Banerjee, S. K. Economic Life in the Great Epic. (C). 1990. text 44.00 (*81-85094-26-8*, Pub. by Punthi Pus) S Asia.

Banerjee, S. P. A Textbook of Analytical Chemistry. 1985. text 79.00 (*0-7855-0752-3*, Pub. by Current Dist) St Mut.

Banerjee, S. P. & Moitra, Shefali, eds. Communication, Identity, & Self-Expression: Essays in Memory of S. N. Ganguly. 1985. 24.95 (*0-19-561683-9*) OUP.

Banerjee, Sanjay, jt. ed. see Streetman, Ben G.

***Banerjee, Sanjoy & Eaton, John K.** Turbulence & Shear Flow Phenomena: First International Symposium, September 12-15, 1999, Santa Barbara, California. LC 99-35612. 1368p. 1999. 165.00 (*1-56700-135-1*) Begell Hse.

Banerjee, Satarupa. Book of Indian Sweets. (C). 1994. 34.00 (*81-7167-150-0*, Pub. by Rupa) S Asia.

— Cooking with Yogurt. (C). 1995. 12.50 (*81-86112-19-7*, Pub. by UBS Pubs Dist) S Asia.

Banerjee, Seyit, jt. ed. see Yalkowsky, Samuel H.

Banerjee, Shibnath. The Chinese Government & Politics. 175p. (C). 1980. 13.95 (*0-940500-04-3*) Asia Bk Corp.

***Banerjee, Sikata.** Warriors in Politics: Hindu Nationalism, Violence & the Shiv Sena in Mumbai. LC 99-45103. 224p. 1999. 62.00 (*0-8133-3699-6*) Westview.

Banerjee, Sikhar N., jt. ed. see Basmajian, John V.

Banerjee, Srivastava. One Hundred Indian Feature Films: An Annotated Filmography. LC 88-22716. 214p. 1988. text 10.00 (*0-8240-9483-2*, H728) Garland.

Banerjee, Sube, jt. auth. see Prince, Martin R.

Banerjee, Subrata. Monolithic Refractories: A Comprehensive Handbook. LC 98-19043. (Illus.). 350p. 1998. 68.00 (*981-02-3120-2*, G046) World Scientific Pub.

Banerjee, Sudhish C., ed. Spontaneous Combustion of Coal & Mine Fires. 180p. (C). 1985. text 136.00 (*90-6191-574-0*, Pub. by A A Balkema) Ashgate Pub Co.

Banerjee, Sujit, jt. ed. see Conners, Terrance E.

Banerjee, Sumanta. The Parlour & the Streets: Elite & Popular Culture in 19th Century Calcutta. 1989. 26.50 (*81-7046-063-8*, Pub. by Seagull Bks) S Asia.

— The Parlour & the Streets: Elite & Popular Culture in 19th Century Calcutta. 1998. 29.50 (*81-7046-099-9*, Pub. by Seagull Bks) S Asia.

Banerjee, Surabhi. Modern Poems from Bengal. 1996. pap. 12.00 (*81-7476-089-X*, Pub. by UBS Pubs Dist) S Asia.

— Satyajit Ray: Beyond the Frame. 1996. 18.00 (*81-7023-545-6*, Pub. by Allied Pubs) S Asia.

Banerjee, Surabhi, tr. Jyoti with the People: A Political Memoir. 1997. 20.00 (*81-7476-172-1*, Pub. by UBS Pubs) S Asia.

Banerjee, Tapas K. Background to Indian Criminal Law. (C). 1990. 85.00 (*0-89771-189-0*) St Mut.

Banerjee, Tarasankar. Historiography in Modern Indian Languages 1800-1947. (C). 1987. 31.00 (*81-85109-68-0*, Pub. by Naya Prokash) S Asia.

— Various Bengal: Aspects of Modern History. 328p. 1986. 27.50 (*0-8364-1669-4*, Pub. by Popular Prakashan) S Asia.

***Banerjee, Timir.** The Braying Donkey: Reflections on a Life. LC 00-37907. (Illus.). 136p. 2000. 22.00 (*1-883911-43-5*) Brandylane.

Banerjee, Timir & Dominges da Silva, Alvaro A., eds. Signs, Syndromes & Eponyms: Our Legacy. 283p. 45.00 (*1-879284-68-5*) Am Assn Neuro.

Banerjee, Tridib & Baer, William. Beyond the Neighborhood Unit: Residential Environments & Public Policy. LC 84-11619. (Environment, Development, & Public Policy: Public Policy & Social Services Ser.). (Illus.). 270p. (C). 1984. 90.00 (*0-306-41555-0*, Plenum Trade) Perseus Pubng.

Banerjee, Tridib, jt. auth. see Loukaitou-Sideris, Anastasia.

Banerjee, Tridib, ed. see Lynch, Kevin.

Banerjee, Uptal. Dependence Analysis for Supercomputing. (C). 1988. text 98.00 (*0-89838-289-0*) Kluwer Academic.

— Loop Transformations for Restructuring Compilers: The Foundations. LC 92-41647. 328p. (C). 1993. text 141.50 (*0-7923-9318-X*) Kluwer Academic.

Banerjee, Uptal, et al, eds. Languages & Compilers for Parallel Computing: 6th International Workshop, Portland, Oregon, U. S. A., August 12-14, 1993: Proceedings. LC 93-46748. (Lecture Notes in Computer Science Ser.: Vol. 768). 1994. 93.95 (*0-387-57659-2*) Spr-Verlag.

Banerjee, Uptal, et al. Languages & Compilers for Parallel Computing: 4th International Workshop, Santa Clara, California, U. S. A., August 7-9, 1991: Proceedings. Nicolau, Alexander et al, eds. LC 92-13947. (Lecture Notes in Computer Science Ser.: Vol. 589). x, 419p. 1992. 63.95 (*0-387-55422-X*); pap. 53.00 (*3-540-55422-X*) Spr-Verlag.

Banerjee, Uptal, ed. see Nicolau, Alexander.

Banerjee, Utpal. Dependence Analysis. LC 96-34497. (Loop Transformation for Restructuring/Compilers Ser.). 232p. (C). 1996. text 115.00 (*0-7923-9809-2*) Kluwer Academic.

— Loop Parallelization. LC 94-5029. (International Series in Engineering & Computer Science, VLSI, Computer Architecture, & Digital Screen Processing). 192p. (C). 1994. text 133.50 (*0-7923-9455-0*) Kluwer Academic.

Banerjee, Utpal K. Indian Performing Arts. (C). 1992. 60.00 (*0-7069-5948-5*, Pub. by Vikas) S Asia.

— Indian Performing Arts. (C). 1994. text 48.00 (*0-7069-8671-7*, Pub. by Vikas) S Asia.

Banerji, A. K. Digest, Cases & Materials on Limitation Act. (C). 1990. 125.00 (*0-89771-251-X*) St Mut.

Banerji, Arun. Aspects of Indo-British Economic Relations, 1858-98. (Illus.). 1982. text 27.00 (*0-19-561341-4*) OUP.

— Finances in the Early Raj: Investments & the External Sector. LC 94-49089. (Illus.). 338p. 1995. 45.00 (*0-8039-9223-8*) Sage.

Banerji, Arun K., ed. Arms Race, Disarmament & Security. (C). 1991. 16.50 (*81-7074-107-6*, Pub. by KP Bagchi) S Asia.

— Gulf War & the Energy Crisis in India. (C). 1993. 24.00 (*81-7074-120-3*, Pub. by KP Bagchi) S Asia.

Banerji, Arundhati. Early Indian Terracotta Art. LC 93-910404. (C). 1995. 68.50 (*81-85151-81-4*, Pub. by Harman) S Asia.

— Images, Attributes & Motifs: Studies in Early Indian Art & Numismatics, 2 vols. (C). 1993. 185.00 (*81-85067-85-6*, Pub. by Sundeep Prak) S Asia.

Banerji, Arup. Merchants & Markets in Revolutionary Russia, 1917-1930. LC 96-21858. 304p. 1997. text 69.95 (*0-312-16293-6*) St Martin.

Banerji, B. Pathar Panchali. 166p. 1987. 10.95 (*0-318-36919-2*) Asia Bk Corp.

Banerji, Chitrita. Bengali Cooking: Seasons & Festivals. (Illus.). 208p. 2000. pap. 15.95 (*1-897959-29-X*, Pub. by Serif) IPG Chicago.

Banerji, Christiane & Donald, Diana, eds. Gillray Observed: The Earliest Accounts of His Caricatures in "London und Paris" LC 98-26521. (Illus.). 272p. (C). 1999. text 75.00 (*0-521-58075-7*) Cambridge U Pr.

Banerji, Christiane, tr. see Siemann, Wolfram.

Banerji, Dilip & Raymond, Jacque. Elements of Microprogramming. (Illus.). 416p. (C). 1982. pap. text 51.00 (*0-13-267146-8*) P-H.

Banerji, H. C. Colebrooke's Translation of the Lilavati. (C). 1993. 17.00 (*81-206-0840-2*, Pub. by Asian Educ Servs) S Asia.

Banerji, M. L. Orchids of Nepal. (Illus.). 135p. (Orig.). 1982. text 15.00 (*0-934454-95-7*) Lubrecht & Cramer.

Banerji, M. L. & Pradhan, Prabha. The Orchids of Nepal Himalaya. (Illus.). 640p. 1983. lib. bdg. 385.00 (*3-7682-1366-8*) Lubrecht & Cramer.

Banerji, P. Handbook of Snake Bites. 430p. 1985. pap. 175.00 (*0-7855-0365-X*, Pub. by Intl Bks & Periodicals) St Mut.

Banerji, R. B. Artificial Intelligence: A Theoretical Approach. 254p. 1980. 48.75 (*0-444-00334-7*) P-H.

Banerji, Ranan, jt. auth. see Wood, Raquel.

***Banerji, S. C.** Brief History of Dharmasastra. 1999. write for info. (*81-7017-370-1*, Pub. by Abhinav Pubns) S Asia.

Banerji, S. C. A Companion of Sanskrit Literature. 1000p. (C). 1987. 44.00 (*81-208-0063-X*, Pub. by Motilal Bnarsidass) S Asia.

— Tantra in Bengal. (C). 1992. reprint ed. 29.50 (*81-85425-63-9*, Pub. by Manohar) S Asia.

Banerji, S. K., ed. see International Symposium on Boron Steels (September.

Banerji, S. K., jt. ed. see Krauss, G.

Banerji, S. K., ed. see Metallurgical Society of AIME Staff.

Banerji, Sanjukta. Deferred Hopes: Blacks in Contemporary America. LC 86-73077. 399p. (C). 1987. text 40.00 (*0-89891-013-7*) Advent Bks Div.

Banerji, Sures C. Companion to Indian Philosophy. 1996. 52.00 (*81-7018-743-5*, Pub. by BR Pub) S Asia.

***Banerji, Sures C.** Cultural Reciprocation Between India & the World. LC 99-931563. x, 496p. 1999. 64.00 (*81-85616-59-0*, Pub. by Sharada Pub Hse) S Asia.

Banerji, Sures C. Folklore in Ancient & Medieval India. 2nd ed. (C). 1991. 37.50 (*81-85094-38-1*, Pub. by Punthi Pus) S Asia.

— Society in Ancient India. (Reconstructing Indian History & Culture Ser.: No. 1). (C). 1993. text 40.00 (*81-246-0000-7*, Pub. by DK Pubs Ind) S Asia.

***Banerji, Sures Chandra.** The Cultural Glory of Ancient India. xiv, 546p. 2000. 39.00 (*81-246-0137-2*, Pub. by D K Printwrld) Nataraj Bks.

— Society in Ancient India: Evolution since the Vedic Times Based on Sanskrit, Pali, Prakrt & Other Classical Sources. 423p. 1997. 32.00 (*81-246-0079-1*, Pub. by D K Printwrld) Nataraj Bks.

Banes, Bradford, ed. see Walecka, J. Dirk & Fetter, Alexander L.

Banes, Charles H. History of the Philadelphia Brigade. 34.50 (*0-8488-0910-6*) Amereon Ltd.

Banes, Daniel. Shakespeare, Shylock & Kabbalah. LC 78-58912. 1978. 9.99 (*0-686-10284-3*); pap. 3.60 (*0-686-10285-1*) Malcolm Hse.

Banes, F. Dominico. Scholastica Commentaria in Primam Partem Summae Theologicae S. Thomae Aquinatis, De Deo Uno. Urbano, Luis, ed. (Medieval Studies Reprint). (LAT & SPA.). reprint ed. lib. bdg. 48.00 (*0-697-00028-1*) Irvington.

Banes, Sally. Dancing Women: Female Bodies on Stage. LC 97-24496. (Illus.). 296p. 1998. pap. 27.99 (*0-415-11162-5*) Routledge.

— Dancing Women: Female Bodies on Stage. LC 97-24496. (Illus.). 296p. (C). 1998. 85.00 (*0-415-09671-5*) Routledge.

— Democracy's Body: Judson Dance Theater, 1962-1964. LC 83-15920. (Studies in the Fine Arts: The Avant-Garde: No. 43). 288p. reprint ed. pap. 89.30 (*0-8357-1481-0*, 207062600009) Bks Demand.

— Democracy's Body: Judson Dance Theater, 1962-1964. LC 93-21760. (Illus.). 288p. 1993. reprint ed. pap. text 17.95 (*0-8223-1399-5*) Duke.

— Greenwich Village, 1963: Avant-Garde Performance & the Effervescent Body. LC 93-18393. (Illus.). 352p. 1993. text 54.95 (*0-8223-1357-X*); pap. text 17.95 (*0-8223-1391-X*) Duke.

— Subversive Expectations: Performance Art & Paratheater in New York, 1976-85. LC 98-6969. 312p. (C). 1998. pap. 19.95 (*0-472-06678-1*, 06678); text 47.50 (*0-472-09678-8*, 09678) U of Mich Pr.

— Terpsichore in Sneakers: Post-Modern Dance. rev. ed. LC 86-7829. (Illus.). 311p. 1987. reprint ed. pap. 19.95 (*0-8195-6160-6*, Wesleyan Univ Pr) U Pr of New Eng.

— Writing Dancing in the Age of Postmodernism. LC 93-8225. (Illus.). 428p. 1994. pap. 25.00 (*0-8195-6268-8*, Wesleyan Univ Pr) U Pr of New Eng.

Banes, Sally, et al, intros. Art Performs Life: Merce Cunningham, Meredith Monk, Bill T. Jones. LC 98-7401. (Illus.). 176p. 1998. pap. 29.95 (*0-935640-56-8*) Walker Art Ctr.

Banes, Sally, ed. & tr. see Souritz, Elizabeth.

Banet, Gary T., jt. auth. see Heck, Cary.

Banet-Weiser, Sarah. The Most Beautiful Girl in the World: Beauty Pageants & National Identity. LC 99-19922. 280p. 1999. 48.00 (*0-520-21789-6*, Pub. by U CA Pr) Cal Prin Full Svc.

— The Most Beautiful Girls in the World: Beauty Pageants & National Identity. LC 99-19922. 290p. 1999. 17.95 (*0-520-21791-8*, Pub. by U CA Pr) Cal Prin Full Svc.

Baneth, Jean. Fortress Europe & Other Myths about Trade: Policies Toward Merchandise Imports in the EC & Other Major Industrial Economies (& What They Mean for Developing Countries) LC 93-44524. (Discussion Paper Ser.: No. 225). 56p. 1994. 6.95 (*0-8213-2738-0*, 12738) World Bank.

— Selecting Development Projects for the World Bank. LC 96-16613. (Discussion Paper Ser.: Vol. 322). 94p. 1996. pap. 22.00 (*0-8213-3625-8*) World Bank.

***Baney, Douglas M., et al, eds.** Optical Amplifiers & Their Applications. LC 98-85587. (Trends in Optics & Photonics Ser.: Vol. 25). (Illus.). 318p. 1998. pap. 55.00 (*1-55752-559-5*) Optical Soc.

Baney, R., et al, eds. Submicron Multiphase Materials. (Materials Research Society Symposium Proceedings Ser.: Vol. 274). 185p. 1992. text 30.00 (*1-55899-169-7*) Materials Res.

Baney, Terry A. Yankees & the City: Struggling over Urban Representation in Connecticut, 1880 to World War I. LC 92-27523. (Modern American History: New Studies & Outstanding Dissertations). 288p. 1992. text 20.00 (*0-8153-1098-6*) Garland.

Baneyx, Francois, jt. auth. see Lucotte, Gerald.

Baneyx, Francois, jt. ed. see Lucotte, G.

Banfe, Charles. Airline Management. 240p. (C). 1991. text 52.60 (*0-13-019183-3*, 320701) P-H.

Banff Conference on Theoretical Psychology Staff. Toward Unification in Psychology: The Banff Conference on Theoretical Psychology. Royce, Joseph R., ed. LC 72-505050. 314p. reprint ed. pap. 97.40 (*0-608-30631-2*, 201439300089) Bks Demand.

***Banffy, Miklos.** They Were Found Wanting. 2000. pap. 15.99 (*1-900850-29-X*) Arcadia Bks.

Banfichi Ferrari, Paola & Secondo, Adriana. Dictionnaire Collins Super Gem Francais-Italien, Italien-Francais. (FRE & ITA.). 216p. 1985. 23.95 (*0-7859-7605-1*, 2010116631) Fr & Eur.

Banfield. Here the People Rule: Selected Essays. 2nd ed. 180p. (C). 1991. 24.75 (*0-8447-3769-0*) Am Enterprise.

Banfield, A. F. Mammals of Canada. LC 73-92298. (Illus.). 1974. text 47.50 (*0-8020-2137-9*) U of Toronto Pr.

An Asterisk (*) at the beginning of an entry indicates that the title is appearing for the first time.

*Banfield, Ann. The Phantom Table: Woolf, Fry, Russell & the Epistemology of Modernism. LC 99-51626. (Illus.). 420p. (C). 2000. text 49.95 (0-521-77347-4) Cambridge U Pr.

Banfield, Edward C. Here the People Rule: Selected Essays. LC 85-9504. (Environment, Development, & Public Policy: Public Policy & Social Services Ser.). 366p. 1985. 65.00 (0-306-41969-6, Plenum Trade) Perseus Pubng.

— Political Influence. LC 82-6245. 354p. 1982. lib. bdg. 41.50 (0-313-22645-8, BAPF, Greenwood Pr) Greenwood.

— The Unheavenly City Revisited: A Revision of the Unheavenly City. 358p. (C). 1990. reprint ed. pap. text 18.95 (0-88133-529-0) Waveland Pr.

Banfield, Edward C., intro. Civility & Citizenship in Liberal Democratic Societies. LC 91-11662. 165p. 1991. 24.95 (0-943852-94-3) Prof World Peace.

Banfield, Edward C. & Banfield, L. F. The Moral Basis of a Backward Society. LC 58-9398. 1967. pap. 14.95 (0-02-901510-3) Free Pr.

Banfield, Edward C. & Wilson, James Q. City Politics. LC 63-19134. (Joint Center for Urban Studies). (Illus.). 374p. 1963. 35.00 (0-674-13250-5) HUP.

Banfield, Edward C., jt. auth. see Meyerson, Martin.

Banfield, Edwin. The Banfield Family Collection of Barometers. (Illus.). 313p. 1997. pap. 14.95 (0-948382-10-4, Pub. by Baros Bks) Antique Collect.

— Barometer Makers & Retailers 1660-1900. (Illus.). 256p. 1997. pap. 19.95 (0-948382-06-6, Pub. by Baros Bks) Antique Collect.

— Barometers: Aneroid & Barographs. (Illus.). 160p. 1997. 24.95 (0-948382-02-3, Pub. by Baros Bks) Antique Collect.

— Barometers: Stick or Cistern Tube. (Illus.). 256p. 1997. 29.95 (0-948382-00-7, Pub. by Baros Bks) Antique Collect.

— Barometers: Wheel or Banjo. (Illus.). 160p. 1997. 24.95 (0-948382-01-5, Pub. by Baros Bks) Antique Collect.

— The Italian Influence on English Barometers from 1780. (Illus.). 160p. 1997. pap. 14.95 (0-948382-07-4, Pub. by Baros Bks) Antique Collect.

Banfield, Emiko. Harnessing Value in the Supply Chain: Strategic Sourcing in Action. LC 99-17589. 384p. 1999. 55.00 (0-471-34975-5) Wiley.

Banfield, Jillian F. & Nealson, Kenneth H., eds. Geomicrobiology: Interactions Between Microbes & Minerals. (Reviews in Mineralogy Ser.: Vol. 35). (Illus.). 448p. (C). 1997. pap. 32.00 (0-939950-45-6) Mineralogical Soc.

Banfield, L. F., jt. auth. see Banfield, Edward C.

Banfield, Laura, tr. see Machiavelli, Niccolo.

Banfield, Laura F., tr. see Machiavelli, Niccolo.

*Banfield, Stephen. Gerald Finzi: An English Composer. 576p. 2000. pap. 25.00 (0-571-19598-9, Pub. by Faber & Faber) Penguin Books.

Banfield, Stephen. Sondheim's Broadway Musicals. LC 93-12818. 472p. (C). 1995. pap. 28.95 (0-472-08083-0, 08083) U of Mich Pr.

Banfield, Stephen, intro. The Blackwell History of Music in Britain Vol. 6: The Twentieth Century. (Illus.). 560p. 1995. 143.95 (0-631-17424-9) Blackwell Pubs.

*Banfield, Susan. The Andersonville Prison Civil War Crimes Trial: A Headline Court Case. (Headline Court Cases Ser.). (Illus.). 104p. (YA). (gr. 6 up). 2000. lib. bdg. 20.95 (0-7660-1386-3) Enslow Pubs.

Banfield, Susan. The Bakke Case: Quotas in College Admissions. LC 97-21309. (Landmark Supreme Court Cases Ser.). (Illus.). 128p. (YA). (gr. 6 up). 1998. lib. bdg. 20.95 (0-89490-968-1) Enslow Pubs.

— Charlemagne. (World Leaders Past & Present Ser.). (Illus.). 120p. (YA). (gr. 5 up). 1986. lib. bdg. 19.95 (0-87754-592-8) Chelsea Hse.

— The Fifteenth Amendment: African-American Men's Right to Vote. LC 97-26318. (Constitution Ser.). (Illus.). 128p. (YA). (gr. 6 up). 1998. lib. bdg. 20.95 (0-7660-1033-3) Enslow Pubs.

— Inside Recovery: How the Twelve-Step Program Can Work for You. LC 98-11797. (Drug Abuse Prevention Library). (Illus.). 64p. (YA). (gr. 7-12). 1998. lib. bdg. 16.95 (0-8239-2634-6, DRINRE) Rosen Group.

— Joan of Arc. (World Leaders Past & Present Ser.). (Illus.). 120p. (YA). (gr. 5 up). 1985. lib. bdg. 19.95 (0-87754-556-1) Chelsea Hse.

— The Rights of Man, the Reign of Terror: The Story of the French Revolution. LC 89-2742. 224p. (YA). (gr. 7 up). 1990. 15.00 (0-397-32353-0) HarpC Child Bks.

— The Rights of Man, the Reign of Terror: The Story of the French Revolution. LC 89-2742. 224p. (YA). (gr. 7 up). 1990. lib. bdg. 14.89 (0-397-32354-9) HarpC Child Bks.

Banfield, Thomas C. Industry of the Rhine, 2 vols. in 1, Series 1 (Agriculture), Series 2 (Manufactures) LC 68-55470. (Reprints of Economic Classics Ser.). 1969. reprint ed. 67.50 (0-678-00568-0) Kelley.

— The Organization of Industry. 2nd ed. LC 68-55469. (Reprints of Economic Classics Ser.). 1973. reprint ed. 35.00 (0-678-00964-3) Kelley.

*Banfield, William C. Musical Landscapes in Color: Conversations with Black American Composers. 480p. 1999. 59.50 (0-8108-3706-4) Scarecrow.

Banfill, ed. Rheology of Fresh Cement & Concrete: Proceedings of an International Conference, Liverpool, 1990. (Illus.). 384p. (C). 1990. 125.00 (0-419-15360-8, E & FN Spon) Routledge.

Bang. The Shrimper. LC 99-33348. (Illus.). 48p. (gr. 6 up). 2000. 15.95 (0-8050-5396-4) H Holt & Co.

Bang, Betsy. Old Woman & the Red Pumpkin: Level 4, Green. LC 98-88095. (Reading Together Ser.). (Illus.). 32p. (J). 1999. pap. write for info. (0-7636-0857-2) Candlewick Pr.

Bang, Betsy G. Functional Anatomy of the Olfactory System in 23 Orders of Birds. (Acta Anatomica Ser.: Suppl. 58, Vol. 79). 1971. pap. 19.25 (3-8055-1193-0) S Karger.

Bang, Derrick, jt. auth. see Podley, Andrea.

Bang, Elizabeth. Delightful Doughcrafts: Over 80 Cute & Whimsical Projects. LC 98-101339. (Illus.). 128p. 1997. 27.95 (0-7063-7558-0, Pub. by WrLock) Sterling.

Bang, Herman. Katinka. Nunnally, Tiina, tr. from DAN. LC 90-45560. (Modern Classics Ser.: No. 3).Tr. of Ved Vejen. 174p. (Orig.). 1990. 17.95 (0-940242-47-8); pap. 8.95 (0-940242-46-X) Fjord Pr.

— Tina. Christopherson, Paul, tr. LC 84-12286. 224p. (C). 1984. text 18.95 (0-485-11254-X, Pub. by Athlone Pr) Humanities.

Bang, Hyochoong, jt. auth. see Kwon, Young W.

*Bang-Jensen, Jorgen & Gutin, Gregory. Digraphs: Theory, Algorithms, & Applications. LC 00-44032. 2000. write for info. (1-85233-268-9) Spr-Verlag.

Bang, Katherine G., jt. auth. see Greenstein, David.

Bang, M. Violin Method, Bk. 4. (Illus.). 96p. 1922. pap. 13.95 (0-8258-0252-0, 0-45) Fischer Inc NY.

Bang, Mary Jo. Apology for Want. LC 97-1760. (Bakeless Literary Publication Prize for Poetry, Bread Loaf Writer's Conference Ser.). 80p. 1997. pap. 12.95 (0-87451-822-9) U Pr of New Eng.

Bang, Mary Jo, et al, eds. Columbia Poetry Review, No. 6. 96p. (Orig.). 1992. pap. 6.00 (0-932026-32-X) Columbia College Chi.

Bang, Molly. Common Ground: The Water, Earth & Air We Share. LC 96-49618. (Illus.). 32p. (J). (gr. 1-7). 1997. write for info. (0-590-10056-4) Scholastic Inc.

Bang, Molly. Delphine. LC 87-34958. (Illus.). 32p. (J). (ps-3). 1988. 12.95 (0-688-05636-9, Wm Morrow) Morrow Avon.

Bang, Molly. Goose. LC 95-47616. (Illus.). (J). 1996. write for info. (0-614-11089-0) Blue Sky Pr Inc.

— Goose. LC 95-47616. (Illus.). 32p. (J). (ps-3). 1996. 10.95 (0-590-89005-0, Blue Sky Press) Scholastic Inc.

— The Grey Lady & the Strawberry Snatcher. LC 85-29224. (Illus.). 48p. (J). (ps-3). 1984. text 16.00 (0-02-708140-0, Mac Bks Young Read) S&S Childrens.

— The Grey Lady & the Strawberry Snatcher. LC 85-29224. 1996. 11.19 (0-606-09369-9, Pub. by Turtleback) Demco.

— One Fall Day. LC 93-36490. (Illus.). 24p. (J). (ps up). 1994. 15.00 (0-688-07015-9, Grenwillow Bks) HarpC Child Bks.

— The Paper Crane. LC 84-13546. (Illus.). 32p. (J). (ps-3). 1985. 16.00 (0-688-04108-6, Grenwillow Bks) HarpC Child Bks.

Bang, Molly. The Paper Crane. (J). 1985. 10.15 (0-606-04295-4, Pub. by Turtleback) Demco.

— The Paper Crane. LC 84-13546. 32p. (J). (gr. k up). 1987. reprint ed. mass mkt. 5.95 (0-688-07333-6, Wm Morrow) Morrow Avon.

— Picture This: How Pictures Work. (Illus.). 2000. 19.95 (1-58717-029-9) SeaStar.

— Picture This: How Pictures Work. LC 00-24402. (Illus.). (J). 2000. pap. 12.95 (1-58717-030-2) SeaStar.

— Ten, Nine, Eight. LC 81-20106. (Illus.). 24p. (J). (ps-1). 1983. 15.89 (0-688-00907-7, Grenwillow Bks) HarpC Child Bks.

Bang, Molly. Ten, Nine, Eight. LC 81-20106. (Illus.). 24p. (J). (ps-3). 1983. 16.00 (0-688-00906-9, Grenwillow Bks) HarpC Child Bks.

— Ten, Nine, Eight. (Illus.). 13p. (J). 1996. pap. 6.95 (0-688-14901-4, Grenwillow Bks) HarpC Child Bks.

— Ten, Nine, Eight. 1991. 10.15 (0-606-00872-1, Pub. by Turtleback) Demco.

— Ten, Nine, Eight. large type ed. (J). (ps-2). 1989. 19.95 (0-590-73313-3) Scholastic Inc.

Bang, Molly. Ten, Nine, Eight. LC 81-20106. (Illus.). 24p. (J). (ps up). 1991. reprint ed. mass mkt. 5.95 (0-688-10480-0, Wm Morrow) Morrow Avon.

Bang, Molly. Ten, Nine, Eight (Spanish edition) Diez, Nueve, Ocho. Cohen, Clarita, tr. LC 81-20106. (ENG & SPA., Illus.). 24p. (J). (ps-3). 1997. 15.00 (0-688-15596-0, Grenwillow Bks) HarpC Child Bks.

— Ten, Nine, Eight (Spanish edition) Diez, Nueve, Ocho. LC 81-20106. (ENG & SPA., Illus.). 24p. (ps-3). 1997. mass mkt. 4.95 (0-688-15468-9, Wm Morrow) Morrow Avon.

— Tye May & the Magic Brush. (J). 1992. 10.15 (0-606-01339-3, Pub. by Turtleback) Demco.

— Wiley & the Hairy Man: Adapted from an American Folk Tale. (Ready-to-Read Ser.). (J). 1987. 9.15 (0-606-03506-0, Pub. by Turtleback) Demco.

— Yellow Ball. LC 90-46077. (Illus.). 24p. (J). (ps up). 1991. lib. bdg. 15.93 (0-688-06315-2, Wm Morrow) Morrow Avon.

— Yellow Ball. LC 92-40722. (Picture Puffin Ser.). (Illus.). (J). 1993. 9.70 (0-606-05713-7, Pub. by Turtleback) Demco.

Bang, Molly, ed. The Goblins Giggle & Other Stories. (J). (gr. 3-5). 1988. 23.25 (0-8446-6360-3) Peter Smith.

Bang, Molly, et al. From Sea to Shining Sea: A Treasury of American Folklore & Folk Songs. LC 92-30598. 416p. (J). (gr. 2 up). 1993. 29.95 (0-590-42868-3) Scholastic Inc.

Bang, Molly. The Grey Lady & the Strawberry Snatcher. 48p. (J). (ps-3). 1996. per. 5.99 (0-689-80381-8) Aladdin.

Bang, Molly G. Tye May & the Magic Brush. LC 80-16488. (Illus.). 56p. (J). (ps-3). 1992. mass mkt. 5.95 (0-688-11504-7, Wm Morrow) Morrow Avon.

— Wiley & the Hairy Man. 1996. pap. 3.99 (0-689-81142-X) S&S Childrens.

— Wiley & the Hairy Man. (Illus.). 64p. (J). (gr. k-4). 1996. 14.00 (0-689-81141-1) S&S Childrens.

Bang, Molly Garrett. Diez, Nueve, Ocho/Ten, Nine, Eight. (Mulberry En Espanol Ser.). 1997. 10.15 (0-606-11256-1, Pub. by Turtleback) Demco.

— When Sophie Gets Angry - Really, Really Angry... LC 97-42209. (Illus.). 40p. (J). (ps-2). 1998. 15.95 (0-590-18979-4) Scholastic Inc.

— Wiley & the Hairy Man. 1998. pap. 3.99 (0-87628-337-7) Ctr Appl Res.

Bang, Nils U., ed. Thrombosis & Atherosclerosis. LC 81-11708. (Illus.). 484p. reprint ed. pap. 150.10 (0-8357-7606-9, 205692900096) Bks Demand.

Bang, Yong H. One Dollar a Day: Poverty in Indonesia. 240p. 1998. pap. 16.00 (0-8059-4443-5) Dorrance.

Banga, Ajay K. Electrically Assisted Transdermal & Topical Drug Delivery Metabolism & Molecular Physiology of Saccharomyces. LC 98-214657. (Series in Pharmaceutical Sciences). 1998. 95.00 (0-7484-0687-5) Taylor & Francis.

— Therapeutic Peptides & Proteins: Formulation, Processing, & Delivery Systems. LC 95-61206. 340p. 1995. 110.95 (1-56676-329-0) Technomic.

Banga, Indu. Agrarian System of the Sikhs Seventeen Fifty-Nine to Eighteen Forty-Nine. 1979. 18.50 (0-88386-758-3) S Asia.

— Ports & Their Hinterlands in India, 1700-1950. (C). text 32.00 (81-85425-86-8, Pub. by Manohar) S Asia.

Banga, Indu, ed. Five Punjabi Centuries: Polity, Economy, Society & Culture c. 1500-1990, Essays for J. S. Grewal. LC 97-901024. (C). 1997. 68.00 (81-7304-175-X, Pub. by Manohar) S Asia.

Banga, S. K., jt. ed. see Banga, S. S.

Banga, S. S. & Banga, S. K., eds. Hybrid Cultivar Development. 420p. 1998. 159.00 (3-540-63523-8) Spr-Verlag.

Bangalore, Nirmala & Carter, Judith, eds. Guide to Searching the Bibliographic Utilities for Conference Proceedings. 15p. (C). 1994. pap. 8.00 (0-8389-7734-0) Assn Coll & Res Libs.

Bangash, M. Y. H. Impact & Explosion: Structural Analysis & Design. 1993. 270.00 (0-8493-7742-0, T) CRC Pr.

*Bangash, M. Y. H. & Bangash, T. Staircases: Structural Analysis & Design. 337p. (C). 1999. 95.00 (90-5410-607-7, Pub. by A A Balkema) Ashgate Pub Co.

Bangash, T., jt. auth. see Bangash, M. Y. H.

Bangash, Y. Concrete & Concrete Structures: Numerical Modelling Applications Ser. 660p. 1990. mass mkt. 242.00 (1-85166-294-4) Elsevier.

Bange, David W., jt. auth. see Schelin, Charles W.

Bange, Oliver. The EEC Crisis of 1963: Kennedy, MacMillan, de Gaulle & Andenauer in Conflict. LC 98-51153. 240p. 1999. text 65.00 (0-312-22018-9) St Martin.

*Bangemann, Martin, ed. How to Benefit from the Information Society: A Selection of Case Studies. (Illus.). 62p. (C). 1999. reprint ed. pap. text 25.00 (0-7881-7571-8) DIANE Pub.

Bangert, Albrecht. Eighties Style: Designs of the Decade. (Illus.). 240p. 1990. pap. 29.95 (1-55859-117-6) Abbeville Pr.

Bangert, Mark P. Leading the Church's Song: A Practical Introduction to Leading Congregational Song. Farley, Robert Buckley, ed. LC 98-33961. 1999. pap. 20.00 incl. audio compact disk (0-8066-3591-6, 3-402, Augsburg) Augsburg Fortress.

— Symbols & Terms of the Church. 24p. 1990. pap. 2.50 (0-8066-2522-8, 23-1957) Augsburg Fortress.

Bangert, Sharon, tr. & intro. see Eberhardt, Isabelle.

Bangert, Stephen K., jt. ed. see Marshall, William J.

Bangert, William V. A Bibliographical Essay on the History of the Society of Jesus. Ganss, George E., ed. LC 76-12667. (Studies on Jesuit Topics IV: No. 6). xvi, 75p. 1976. pap. 0.75 (0-912422-16-5) Inst Jesuit.

— A History of the Society of Jesus. 2nd rev. ed. Ganss, George E., ed. LC 85-80693. (Original Studies Composed in English III: No. 3). xii, 578p. (C). 1986. 21.00 (0-912422-73-4) Inst Jesuit.

Bangerter, Alisa D. & Bedell, Mella W. Sweet Surprises for the Holidays. LC 97-73819. (Illus.). vi, 138p. 1997. pap. 10.95 (0-9659101-0-5) Gingerbread Grdn.

Bangerter, Brad. The National Managed Care Leadership Directory: Key Contacts in Today's Leading Managed Care Organization. 11th rev. ed. Bangerter, Laura & Weidner, Mirid, eds. 426p. 1999. pap. 185.00 (0-9639238-3-8) HlthQuest Pubs.

— Who's Who in Managed Healthcare: Profiles of Key Decision Makers in Today's Leading Health Care Organizations. 5th rev. ed. Bangerter, Laura, ed. 287p. 1999. pap. 119.00 (0-9639238-6-2) HlthQuest Pubs.

Bangerter, Brad & Healthquest Editors. Who's Who in Managed Health Care: 1999 Edition. 5th rev. ed. 287p. 1999. pap. 119.00 (0-9639238-7-0) HlthQuest Pubs.

Bangerter, Laura, ed. see Bangerter, Brad.

Bangerter, Lowell A., jt. auth. see Kerschbaumer, Marie-Therese.

Bangerter, Lowell A., tr. see Giese, Alexander.

Bangerter, Lowell A., tr. see Glas-Larsson, Margareta.

Bangerter, Lowell A., tr. see Kaiser, Gloria.

Bangerter, Lowell A., tr. see Mitgutsch, Anna.

Bangerter, Lowell A., tr. & afterword by see Ebner, Jeannie.

Bangerter, Lowell A., tr. & afterword by see Ferk, Janko.

Bangerter, Lowell A., tr. & afterword by see Kaiser, Gloria.

Bangerter, Lowell A., tr. & afterword by see Marginter, Peter.

Bangerter, Lowell A., tr. & afterword by see Weigel, Hans.

Bangerter, Lowell A., tr. & afterword by see Zweig, Stefan.

Bangham, Ralph V. A Resurvey of the Fish Parasites of Western Lake Erie. (Bulletin New Ser.: Vol. 4, No. 2). 1972. pap. text 2.00 (0-86727-061-6) Ohio Bio Survey.

Banghart, Bob & Banghart, Love. The Proper Care of Chow Chows, AKC Rank No. 17. (Illus.). 256p. 1996. 16.95 (0-7938-1967-9, TW138) TFH Pubns.

Banghart, Love, jt. auth. see Banghart, Bob.

Bangia, B. Mama Bangia's Magic Kitchen. (Illus.). 48p. (Orig.). 1994. pap. 6.95 (0-9637255-2-1) Dancing Unicorn.

Bangjie, Tan. Into the Wild: The Rare & Endangered Species of China. 108p. 1996. pap. 24.95 (7-80005-298-2, Pub. by New World Pr) Cheng & Tsui.

Bangjiu, Peter Z. The Mountain Pierces the Blue Sky: Second Collection of Poems, 1960-1993. Moeller, Jim et al, eds. LC 94-12045. (Illus.). 240p. Date not set. write for info. (1-881614-02-6) Serenity CA.

— The Mountain Pierces the Blue Sky: Second Collection of Poems, 1960-1993. Moeller, Jim et al, eds. LC 94-12045. (Illus.). 1995. pap. 11.95 (1-881614-01-8) Serenity CA.

Bangla, Rupasi. The Beauteous Bengal, Jibanananda Das. 1987. 11.00 (0-8364-2239-2, Pub. by Mittal Pubs Dist) S Asia.

Bangley. Si Estoy Perdonado, Por que Me Siento Culpable? - If I'm Forgiven Why Do I...? (SPA.). 101p. 1995. write for info. (1-56063-523-1) Editorial Unilit.

Bangley, Bernard. If I'm Forgiven, Why Do I Still Feel Guilty? rev. ed. 130p. 1992. reprint ed. pap. 8.99 (0-87788-397-1, H Shaw Pubs) Waterbrook Pr.

— Morning & Evening with the Spiritual Classics. 90p. 1999. pap. 2.99 (0-87788-534-6, H Shaw Pubs) Waterbrook Pr.

Bangley, Bernard, selected by. Near to the Heart of God: Daily Insights from the Spiritual Classics. LC 98-24970. 393p. 1998. pap. 11.99 (0-87788-824-8, H Shaw Pubs) Waterbrook Pr.

Bango, Guillermo De, see De Bango, Guillermo.

Bango Torviro, I. G. Camino de Santiago. (SPA., Illus.). 368p. 1993. 295.00 (84-239-5294-0) Elliots Bks.

— Romanico en Espana. (SPA., Illus.). 416p. 1993. 295.00 (84-239-5295-9) Elliots Bks.

Bangs. Pursuit of the Houseboat. 1995. per. 8.00 (1-57283-002-6) S&S Trade.

Bangs & Pinson. The Real World Entrepreneur Field Guide. LC 98-31848. 1999. pap. 59.95 (1-57410-113-7, 61013901) Dearborn.

Bangs, A. Marie. The Spider in My Sink: On Politics, Love & Children. rev. ed. (Illus.). 162p. reprint ed. pap. 11.95 (0-9641427-0-8) Orphyn Annie.

*Bangs, Carl. Arminius: A Study in the Dutch Reformation. 388p. 1998. pap. 30.00 (1-57910-150-X) Wipf & Stock.

Bangs, Carl. Arminius: A Study in the Dutch Reformation. rev. ed. Allison, Joseph D., ed. 384p. 1985. pap. 12.95 (0-310-29481-9, 18368P) Zondervan.

— Phineas F. Bresee: His Life in Methodism, the Holiness Movement, & the Church of the Nazarene. LC 95-35010. 320p. 1995. kivar 36.99 (0-8341-1621-9) Beacon Hill.

Bangs, Carol J. The Bones of the Earth. LC 83-12128. 64p. 1983. pap. 6.95 (0-8112-0883-4, NDP563, Pub. by New Directions) Norton.

Bangs, Charles, ed. The Spectrum Anthology of Short Classics, 2 Vols. LC 86-60606. (Orig.). pap. write for info. (0-938555-02-2) Spectrum Music.

— The Spectrum Anthology of Short Classics, 2 Vols., Vol. 1. LC 86-60606. 226p. (Orig.). write for info. (0-938555-00-6) Spectrum Music.

— The Spectrum Anthology of Short Classics, 2 Vols., Vol. 2. LC 86-60606. 219p. (Orig.). write for info. (0-938555-01-4) Spectrum Music.

Bangs, Christopher. The Lear Collection: A Study of Copper Alloy Socket Candlesticks AD 200-1700. LC 94-77257. 398p. 1996. 120.00 (0-9642224-0-X) Kings Hill Pubns.

Bangs, David. The Business Planning Guide. 8th ed. LC 98-13586. 240p. 1998. pap. 24.95 (1-57410-099-8) Dearborn.

Bangs, David H. Business Planning Guide. 1995. pap. text 39.95 incl. cd-rom (0-7931-1655-4, 1800-0101) Dearborn.

Bangs, David H., Jr. Cash Flow: Mas Que un Problema Contable. 2nd ed.Tr. of Cash Flow Control Guide. (SPA.). 80p. (Orig.). 1997. pap. 15.95 (0-7931-2701-7, 1700-1001) Dearborn.

— Cash Flow Control Guide: Methods to Understand & Control Small Business's Number One Problem. 88p. 1989. pap. text 14.95 (0-936894-02-4, 6100-0402) Dearborn.

— The Market Planning Guide. 4th ed. LC 94-46609. 240p. 1994. pap. 19.95 (0-936894-72-5, 610003-04) Dearborn.

Bangs, David H. The Market Planning Guide: Creating a Plan to Successfully Market Your Business, Products or Service. 5th ed. LC 97-44730. 224p. 1998. write for info. (1-57410-098-X) Dearborn.

Bangs, David H., Jr. The Market Planning Guide: Gaining & Maintaining the Competitive Edge. 164p. 1989. pap. 19.95 (0-936894-03-2, 6100-0303) Dearborn.

— El Plan de Negocios. 7th ed.Tr. of Business Planning Guide. (SPA.). 192p. 1997. pap. 19.95 (0-7931-2696-7, 1700-0501) Dearborn.

— Smart Steps to Smart Choices: Testing Your Business Idea. 144p. 1996. pap. 22.95 (1-57410-021-1, 6100-9301) Dearborn.

Bangs, David H. The Start-Up Guide: A One-Year Plan for Entrepreneurs. 3rd ed. LC 98-39695. 192p. 1998. pap. 22.95 (1-57410-115-3, 61000203) Dearborn.

— Tengo una Excelente Idea: Como Saber Si Tendra Exito Como Negocio.Tr. of Smart Steps to Smart Choices. (SPA.). 1998. pap. text 19.95 (0-7931-2902-8) Dearborn.

*Bangs, David H. & Axman, Andi. A Crash Course in Marketing. LC 99-59670. 224p. 2000. pap. 10.95 (1-58062-254-2) Adams Media.

Bangs, David H., Jr. & Axman, Andi. Launching Your Home-Based Business: How to Successfully Plan, Finance & Grow Your New Venture. LC 97-27091. 272p. 1997. pap. 22.95 (*1-57410-053-X*, 5614-5001) Dearborn.

Bangs, David H., Jr. & Pellecchia, Michael, eds. Financial Troubleshooting: An Action Plan for Money Management in the Small Business. 183p. 1999. pap. 15.95 (*1-880394-92-8*) Thomson Learn.

Bangs, David H., Jr., jt. auth. see Rainsford, Peter.

Bangs, David H., Jr., jt. auth. see Rogak, Lisa A.

Bangs, Edward. Steven Kellogg's Yankee Doodle. LC 94-23603. (J). 1996. 11.19 (*0-606-10097-0*, Pub. by Turtleback) Demco.

Bangs, Frank S., Jr., ed. Land-Use Controls Annual, 1971. Incl. Land-Use Controls Annual, 1972. 232p. 1973. pap. 5.00 212p. 1972. Set pap. 5.00 (*0-318-13017-3*) Am Plan Assn.

***Bangs, Gregory.** Different Directions. 1999. pap. write for info. (*1-58235-321-2*) Watermrk Pr.

Bangs, Isaac. Journal of Lieutenant Isaac Bangs, April 1 to July 29, 1776. LC 67-29021. (Eyewitness Accounts of the American Revolution Ser.). 1975. reprint ed. 16.95 (*0-405-01104-0*) Ayer.

Bangs, Jeremy D. Church Architecture & Art in the Low Countries Before 1566. LC 96-47051. (Sixteenth Century Essays & Studies: Vol. 37). (Illus.). 244p. 1997. 65.00 (*0-940474-39-5*, SCJP) Truman St Univ.

Bangs, Jeremy D. & New England Historic Genealogical Society Staff. Town Records of Scituate, Massachusetts, Vol. 1. LC 97-32457. 1997. 50.00 (*0-88082-058-6*) New Eng Hist.

Bangs, John K. Booming of Acre Hill & Other Reminiscences of Urban & Suburban Life. LC 79-98558. (Short Story Index Reprint Ser.). (Illus.). 1977. 20.95 (*0-8369-3132-7*) Ayer.

— Dreamers, a Club. LC 72-98559. (Short Story Index Reprint Ser.). (Illus.). 1977. 20.95 (*0-8369-3133-5*) Ayer.

— The Enchanted Type-Writer. LC 77-104410. reprint ed. pap. text 5.95 (*0-89197-746-5*); reprint ed. lib. bdg. 14.00 (*0-8290-2397-6*) Irvington.

— Enchanted Typewriter. LC 73-94702. (Short Story Index Reprint Ser.). 1977. 19.95 (*0-8369-3080-0*) Ayer.

— Ghosts I Have Met & Others. (Works of John Kendrick Bangs). 191p. 1985. reprint ed. lib. bdg. 59.00 (*0-932051-12-X*) Rprt Serv.

— A House-Boat on the Styx. (Works of John Kendrick Bangs). 171p. reprint ed. lib. bdg. 59.00 (*0-932051-13-8*) Rprt Serv.

— A Houseboat on the Styx. reprint ed. lib. bdg. 19.95 (*0-89190-625-8*, Rivercity Pr) Amereon Ltd.

— A Houseboat on the Styx. LC 78-131616. 171p. 1899. reprint ed. 4.00 (*0-403-00503-5*) Scholarly.

— Houseboat on the Styx. LC 71-112788. (BCL Ser. II). 1970. reprint ed. 37.50 (*0-404-00496-2*) AMS Pr.

— Little Book of Christmas. LC 77-116933. (Short Story Index Reprint Ser.). (Illus.). 1977. 19.95 (*0-8369-3435-0*) Ayer.

— Mantel-Piece Minstrels, & Other Stories. LC 78-85689. (Short Story Index Reprint Ser.). 1977. 16.95 (*0-8369-3030-4*) Ayer.

— Mister Bonaparte of Corsica. LC 70-166657. (Illus.). 1971. reprint ed. 19.00 (*0-403-01416-6*) Scholarly.

— Mister Munchausen. LC 78-81261. (Short Story Index Reprint Ser.). 1977. 19.95 (*0-8369-3013-4*) Ayer.

— Over the Plum Pudding. LC 70-86136. (Short Story Index Reprint Ser.). 1977. 20.95 (*0-8369-3040-1*) Ayer.

— Paste Jewels. LC 70-96035. (Short Story Index Reprint Ser.). 1977. 19.95 (*0-8369-3081-9*) Ayer.

— The Pursuit of the House-Boat. (BCL1-PS American Literature Ser.). 204p. 1992. reprint ed. lib. bdg. 69.00 (*0-7812-6672-6*) Rprt Serv.

— Pursuit of the Houseboat. 1897. 5.00 (*0-403-00474-8*) Scholarly.

— Pursuit of the Houseboat. LC 79-89550. (Illus.). reprint ed. 34.50 (*0-404-00497-0*) AMS Pr.

— Pursuit of the Houseboat. reprint ed. lib. bdg. 20.95 (*0-89190-626-6*, Rivercity Pr) Amereon Ltd.

— R. Holmes & Co. Being the Remarkable Adventure of Raffles Holmes. LC 78-91073. (American Humorists Ser.). reprint ed. lib. bdg. 47.50 (*0-8398-0151-3*) Irvington.

— The Time Shop. LC 98-16587. (Illus.). (J). 1999. 16.95 (*1-57102-137-X*, Ideals Child) Hambleton-Hill.

— The Water Ghost & Others. 1972. reprint ed. pap. text 12.95 (*0-8290-0677-X*); reprint ed. lib. bdg. 32.50 (*0-8422-8005-7*) Irvington.

Bangs, John K., ed. Potted Fiction: Being a Series of Extracts from the World's Best Sellers, Put up in Thin Slices for Hurried Consumers. LC 70-178436. (Short Story Index Reprint Ser.). 1977. reprint ed. 15.95 (*0-8369-4036-9*) Ayer.

Bangs, John K., ed. see Witherup, Anne W.

Bangs, Lester. Psychotic Reactions & Carburetor Dung: An Anthology. Marcus, Greil, ed. 1988. reprint ed. pap. 16.00 (*0-679-72045-6*) Vin Bks.

Bangs, Merwin, & Co. Staff, ed. Catalogue of Books on Hermetic Philosophy: The E. A. Hitchcock Collection. 1985. reprint ed. pap. 7.95 (*0-916411-33-8*) Holmes Pub.

Bangs, Nina. Original Sin, 1 vol. (Love Spell Ser.). 400p. 1999. mass mkt. 5.99 (*0-505-52324-8*) Dorchester Pub Co.

***Bangs, Nina, et al.** Seduction by Chocolate. 368p. (Orig.). 2000. pap. 5.50 (*0-8439-4667-9*, Leisure Bks) Dorchester Pub Co.

***Bangs, Richard.** The Lost River. LC 99-13287. 266p. (YA). 1999. 25.00 (*1-57805-026-X*, Pub. by Sierra) Random.

***Bangsbo, Jens & Peitersen, Birger.** Soccer Systems & Strategies. LC 00-20657. (Illus.). 144p. 2000. pap. 16.95 (*0-7360-0300-2*) Human Kinetics.

Bangsund, Esther & Grimsrud, Wanda. World Class Tours. (Illus.). 96p. (Orig.). 1992. pap., teacher ed. 10.00 (*1-895411-39-4*) Peguis Pubs Ltd.

Bangura, Abdul K. The Effects of American Foreign Aid to Egypt, 1957-1987. LC 94-27130. 255p. 1994. text 89.95 (*0-7734-2287-0*) E Mellen.

— Kipsigis. LC 94-16188. (Heritage Library of African Peoples). (Illus.). 64p. (YA). (gr. 7-12). 1994. lib. bdg. 16.95 (*0-8239-1765-7*) Rosen Group.

— Political Presuppositions & Implicatures of the Most Popular African-American Hymns. (Illus.). 189p. (C). 1996. lib. bdg. 85.00 (*1-56072-351-3*) Nova Sci Pubs.

— The Presuppositions & Implicatures of the Founding Fathers. LC 97-142650. 194p. (Orig.). (C). 1996. pap. text 14.95 (*0-943025-84-2*) Cummngs & Hath.

Bangura, Abdul K., ed. Research Methodology & African Studies, Vol. 1. LC 93-45512. 274p. (C). 1994. pap. text 32.50 (*0-8191-9394-1*) U Pr of Amer.

— Research Methodology & African Studies, Vol. 1. LC 93-45512. 274p. (C). 1994. lib. bdg. 59.00 (*0-8191-9393-3*) U Pr of Amer.

Bangura, Abdul K., et al. Political Behavior. 176p. (C). 1996. pap. text 29.00 (*0-7618-0223-1*); lib. bdg. 39.00 (*0-7618-0222-3*) U Pr of Amer.

***Bangura, Abdul Karim, ed.** Historical Political Economy of Washinton, D. C. 104p. 2000. 37.50 (*0-7618-1707-7*) U Pr of Amer.

***Bangura, Ahmed S.** Islam & the West African Novel: The Politics of Representation. LC 99-56007. 176p. 2000. 49.95 (*0-89410-863-8*, Three Contnts) L Rienner.

Banham, Debby, ed. Monasteriales Indicia: The Anglo-Saxon Monastic Sign Language. 96p. 1993. pap. 14.95 (*0-9516209-4-0*, Pub. by Anglo-Saxon Bks) Paul & Co Pubs.

***Banham, Gary.** Kant & the Ends of Aesthetics. LC 99-36060. 1999. text 59.95 (*0-312-22748-5*) St Martin.

Banham, Joanna, ed. Encyclopedia of Interior Design, 2 vols. LC 97-149314. (Illus.). 1600p. 1997. lib. bdg. 270.00 (*1-884964-19-2*) Fitzroy Dearborn.

***Banham, Lorna.** In My Weakness: My Prayer Book. Bell, Pearl T., ed. 34p. 2000. write for info. (*0-9660456-7-X*) Manchestr Pubs.

Banham, Martin, ed. The Cambridge Guide to Theatre. 2nd ed. (Illus.). 1232p. (C). 1995. 49.95 (*0-521-43437-8*) Cambridge U Pr.

Banham, Martin, et al, eds. The Cambridge Guide to African & Caribbean Theatre. LC 93-36900. (Illus.). 269p. (C). 1994. 59.95 (*0-521-41139-4*) Cambridge U Pr.

Banham, Martin & Wake, Clive. African Theatre Today. LC 77-350062. 111p. reprint ed. pap. 34.50 (*0-8357-5241-0*, 203248800080) Bks Demand.

***Banham, Martin, et al.** African Theatre in Development. LC 99-29414. 1999. pap. write for info. (*0-253-21341-X*) Ind U Pr.

Banham, Martin, jt. ed. see Stanton, Sarah.

Banham, Mary, ed. see Banham, Reyner.

Banham, P., jt. ed. see Andrews, P.

Banham, Reyner. The Architecture of the Well-Tempered Environment. rev. ed. LC 84-156. (Illus.). 320p. (C). 1984. pap. text 33.00 (*0-226-03698-7*) U Ch Pr.

— The Architecture of the Well-Tempered Environment. 2nd rev. ed. LC 84-156. (Illus.). 320p. (C). 1984. lib. bdg. 36.00 (*0-226-03697-9*) U Ch Pr.

— A Critic Writes: Essays by Reyner Banham. Banham, Mary et al, eds. LC 96-14255. (Illus.). 378p. 1996. 45.00 (*0-520-08855-7*, Pub. by U CA Pr) Cal Prin Full Svc.

— A Critic Writes: Essays by Reyner Banham. 300p. 1999. pap. 22.50 (*0-520-21944-9*, Pub. by U CA Pr) Cal Prin Full Svc.

— Scenes in America Deserta. (Illus.). 224p. 1989. reprint ed. pap. text 12.00 (*0-262-52143-1*) MIT Pr.

— Theory & Design in the First Machine Age. 340p. 1980. pap. text 19.50 (*0-262-52058-3*) MIT Pr.

Banham, Reyner, et al. Buffalo Architecture: A Guide. (Illus.). 352p. 1981. pap. text 20.00 (*0-262-52063-X*) MIT Pr.

***Banham, Russ.** Conoco: 125 Years of Energy. LC 99-68222. (Illus.). 176p. 2000. write for info. (*0-944641-38-5*) Greenwich Pub Group.

Banham, Russ. Coors: A Rocky Mountain Legend. LC 97-81376. (Illus.). 128p. 1998. write for info. (*0-944641-29-6*) Greenwich Pub Group.

— Heading in New Directions: A History of Boatmen's Bancshares. LC 98-84299. (Illus.). 120p. 1998. write for info. (*0-944641-30-X*) Greenwich Pub Group.

— Legacy & Leadership: USF&G's First Century. LC 95-82396. (Illus.). 112p. 1995. write for info. (*0-944641-18-0*) Greenwich Pub Group.

Bani, Kay M. Called to Duty: The Christian Nurse's Resource Book. LC 97-91199. 1998. 19.95 (*0-533-12592-8*) Vantage.

Bani-Sadr, Abol H. My Turn to Speak: Iran, the Revolution & Secret Deals with the U. S. 240p. 1991. 24.95 (*0-08-040563-0*, 3883M) Brasseys.

Banich, Marie T. Neuropsychology: The Neural Bases of Mental Function. 640p. (C). 1997. pap. text 61.16 (*0-395-66699-6*) HM.

Banichuk, N. V. Introduction to Optimization of Structures. Komkov, Vadim, tr. from RUS. (Illus.). 328p. 1990. 118.95 (*0-387-97212-9*) Spr-Verlag.

— Problems & Methods of Optimal Structural Design. LC 83-8103. (Mathematical Concepts & Methods in Science & Engineering Ser.: Vol. 26). (Illus.). 336p. 1983. 85.00 (*0-306-41284-5*, Plenum Trade) Perseus Pubng.

Banichuk, N. V., et al, eds. Dynamical Problems of Rigid-Elastic Systems & Structures: IUTAM Symposium, Moscow, USSR, May 23-27, 1990. (Illus.). xvi, 236p. 1991. 75.00 (*0-387-53788-0*) Spr-Verlag.

Banick, Steve. Using Photoshop X. (Using... Ser.). 1998. pap. 29.99 (*0-7897-1656-9*) Que.

Banicki, Patsy & Staige, Pat. Farmer Carpenter's Barn & the Cow's Saturday Night Dance. (Illus.). (Orig.). (J). (gr. k-4). Date not set. pap. write for info. (*0-9641375-1-8*) Staige Prods.

Banieqbal, B., et al, eds. Temporal Logic in Specification. (Lecture Notes in Computer Science Ser.: Vol. 398). vi, 448p. 1989. 54.00 (*0-387-51803-7*) Spr-Verlag.

Banier, Francois-Marie. Balthazar, Fils De Famille. (FRE.). 264p. 1985. pap. 11.95 (*0-7859-2184-2*, 2070704718) Fr & Eur.

— Past-Present. LC 96-42082. 1997. write for info. (*0-06-881516-6*, Wm Morrow); 50.00 (*0-688-15156-6*, Wm Morrow) Morrow Avon.

— Private Heroes. 193p. 1999. 49.95 (*3-89322-507-2*, Pub. by Dr Cantz sche Druckerei GmbH) Dist Art Pubs.

Banigan, John J., jt. auth. see Richards, Phil.

Banigan, Rae L. A Family-Centered Approach to Developing Communication: Prevention, Screening, Facilitation. LC 97-26064. 120p. 1997. pap. text 35.00 (*0-7506-9881-0*) Buttrwrth-Heinemann.

Banik, Allen E. The Choice Is Clear. 40p. 1995. reprint ed. pap. 3.00 (*0-911311-31-9*) Acres USA.

— La Eleccion Es Clara.Tr. of Choice Is Clear. (ENG & SPA.). 40p. 1995. reprint ed. pap. 3.00 (*0-911311-38-6*) Acres USA.

Banik, Allen E. & Wade, Carlson. Your Water & Your Health. rev. ed. (Illus.). 144p. 1990. pap. 4.95 (*0-87983-514-1*, 35141K, Keats Publng) NTC Contemp Pub Co.

Banik Capuzzo, Teresa, jt. auth. see Capuzzo, Michael.

Ba'Nikongo, Nikongo, ed. Debt & Development in the Third World: Trends & Strategies. LC 91-72097. (Studies in the Development of the Afro-Diaspora). 230p. (Orig.). (C). 1991. pap. text 19.95 (*1-879893-00-2*) IAAS Pubs.

BaNikongo, Nikongo, ed. Leading Issues in African-American Studies. LC 97-5379. 1997. pap. 29.95 (*0-89089-669-0*) Carolina Acad Pr.

Banim, John. The Anglo-Irish of the Nineteenth Century 1828. LC 97-6477. (Hibernia Ser.). 248p. 1998. 105.00 (*1-85477-221-X*) Continuum.

— The Croppy: A Tale of 1798, 3 vols., 2 bks., Set. LC 79-8230. reprint ed. 84.50 (*0-404-61765-4*) AMS Pr.

Banim, Lisa. American Dreams. LC 93-22573. (Stories of the States Ser.). (Illus.). 80p. (J). (gr. 4-6). 1993. lib. bdg. 14.95 (*1-881889-34-3*) Silver Moon.

Banim, Lisa. American Dreams. (Stories of the States Ser.). (Illus.). 108p. (J). (gr. 4-7). 1995. pap. 5.95 (*1-881889-68-8*) Silver Moon.

Banim, Lisa. Drums at Saratoga. LC 93-16460. (Stories of the States Ser.). (Illus.). 64p. (J). (gr. 4-7). 1993. lib. bdg. 14.95 (*1-881889-20-3*) Silver Moon.

— Drums at Saratoga. (Stories of the States Ser.). (Illus.). 108p. (J). (gr. 4-7). 1995. pap. 5.95 (*1-881889-70-X*) Silver Moon.

— The Hessian's Secret Diary. (Mysteries in Time Ser.). (Illus.). 100p. (J). (gr. 4-6). 1998. pap. text 5.95 (*1-893110-00-1*) Silver Moon.

— The Hessian's Secret Diary - Brooklyn, N. Y., 1776. LC 96-757. (Mysteries in Time Ser.). (Illus.). 80p. (J). (gr. 4-7). 1996. lib. bdg. 14.95 (*1-881889-86-6*) Silver Moon.

— A Spy in the King's Colony. LC 93-42389. (Mysteries in Time Ser.). (Illus.). (J). (gr. 4-6). 1994. text 14.95 (*1-881889-54-8*) Silver Moon.

— A Spy in the King's Colony. (Mysteries in Time Ser.). (Illus.). 116p. (J). (gr. 4-6). 1998. pap. text 5.95 (*1-893110-01-X*) Silver Moon.

— A Thief on Morgan's Plantation. LC 94-34961. (Mysteries in Time Ser.). (Illus.). 80p. (J). (gr. 4-7). 1995. text 14.95 (*1-881889-62-9*) Silver Moon.

***Banim, Lisa, et al.** Winner Take All. (Two of a Kind Ser.: No. 10). 112p. (J). (gr. 4-7). 2000. mass mkt. 4.25 (*0-06-106580-3*) HarpC.

Banis, Robert, ed. 24-Point Gospel - The Big News for Today: The Gospel According to Matthew, Mark, Luke & John (KJV) large type ed. LC 98-85937. 512p. 1998. pap. 38.95 (*1-888725-11-7*) Sci & Human Pr.

Banis, Robert J., ed. Copyright Issues for Librarians, Teachers & Authors. 60p. 1998. 4.95 (*1-888725-21-4*) Sci & Human Pr.

Banis, Robert J., ed. see NIAID Staff.

Banis, William J., jt. auth. see Krannich, Ronald L.

Banisar, David, ed. Cryptography & Privacy Sourcebook, 1998. 8th ed. 310p. (C). 1998. pap. text 50.00 (*0-7881-7439-8*) DIANE Pub.

— Cryptography & Privacy Sourcebook, 1994: Primary Documents on U. S. Encryption Policy, the Clipper Chip, the Digital Telephony Proposal & Export Controls. (Illus.). 450p. (Orig.). (C). 1994. pap. text 75.00 (*0-7881-0837-9*) DIANE Pub.

— Cryptography & Privacy Sourcebook, 1995: Documents on Encryption Policy, Wiretapping, & Information Warfare. (Illus.). 330p. (Orig.). 1995. pap. text 50.00 (*0-7881-2606-7*) DIANE Pub.

— Cryptography & Privacy Sourcebook, 1996, 2 vols. 306p. 1996. pap. text 75.00 (*1-57979-107-7*) DIANE Pub.

— Cryptography & Privacy Sourcebook, 1996: Documents on Wiretapping, Cryptography, the Clipper Chip, Key Escrow & Export Controls. 6th ed. (Illus.). 324p. 1996. pap. text 50.00 (*0-7881-3276-8*) DIANE Pub.

Banisar, David & Rotenberg, Marc, eds. Cryptography & Privacy Sourcebook, 1993: The 3rd CPSR Conference. (Illus.). 325p. (Orig.). (C). 1994. pap. text 60.00 (*0-7881-0836-0*) DIANE Pub.

Banisar, David, jt. auth. see Schneier, Bruce.

Banister & Mekjavic. Laboratory Experiments, Human Structure. (Applied Science Ser.). 1993. text 27.75 (*0-314-02574-X*) S-W Pub.

Banister, Claire. The Midwife's Pharmacopeia. LC 98-134173. 178p. 1997. pap. text 25.00 (*1-898507-61-9*) Buttrwrth-Heinemann.

Banister, D. Transport Policy & the Environment. LC 98-166829. 1998. 85.00 (*0-419-23140-4*, E & FN Spon) Routledge.

Banister, D. & Pickup, L. Urban Transport & Planning: A Bibliography with Abstracts. 360p. 1989. text 120.00 (*0-7201-1627-9*) Continuum.

Banister, David. Transport Planning: An International Appraisal. LC 93-33231. (Illus.). 264p. (C). 1994. 85.00 (*0-419-18930-0*, E & FN Spon) Routledge.

Banister, David, et al, eds. The Environment, Land Use & Urban Policy. LC 99-21909. 583p. (C). 1999. 220.00 (*1-85898-722-9*) E Elgar.

— European Transport & Communication Networks: Policy Evolution & Change. LC 95-237927. 372p. 1995. 145.00 (*0-471-95737-2*) Wiley.

***Banister, David & Berechman, Joseph.** Transport Investment & Economic Development. (Illus.). 352p. 2000. 100.00 (*0-419-25590-7*, E & FN Spon) Routledge.

— Transport Investment & Economic Development. (Illus.). 352p. (C). 2000. pap. 29.99 (*0-419-25600-8*, E & FN Spon) Routledge.

Banister, David & Berechman, Joseph, eds. Transport in a Unified Europe: Policies & Challenges. LC 93-36449. (Studies in Regional Science & Urban Economics: Vol. 24). 446p. 1993. 127.00 (*0-444-81702-6*, North Holland) Elsevier.

Banister, David, jt. ed. see Button, Kenneth J.

Banister, Doug. Word & Power in Church. LC 99-31133. 192p. 2000. 16.99 (*0-310-22710-0*) Zondervan.

— Word & Power in Life. 2000. 16.99 (*0-310-22833-6*) Zondervan.

Banister, Eric, et al. Contemporary Health Issues. (Orig.). (C). 1987. pap. text 40.00 (*0-86720-077-4*) Jones & Bartlett.

Banister, Henry C. Musical Analysis. 81p. 1991. reprint ed. lib. bdg. 59.00 (*0-7812-9362-6*) Rprt Serv.

Banister, John. The Historie of Man. LC 74-26164. (English Experience Ser.: No. 122). (Illus.). 250p. 1969. reprint ed. 60.00 (*90-221-0122-3*) Walter J Johnson.

— A Needful, New & Necessarie Treatise of Chyrugerie. LC 73-171732. (English Experience Ser.: No. 300). 276p. 1971. reprint ed. 22.00 (*90-221-0300-5*) Walter J Johnson.

***Banister, Joseph R.** Investigating the Federal Income Tax: A Preliminary Report. (Illus.). 95p. 1999. pap. 20.00 (*0-9678449-0-8*) J R Banister.

Banister, Judith. China's Changing Population. LC 82-60105. xviii, 488p. 1987. 67.50 (*0-8047-1155-0*); pap. 22.50 (*0-8047-1887-3*) Stanford U Pr.

— Vietnam Population Dynamics & Prospects. LC 92-32674. (Indochina Research Monographs: No. 6). 1993. pap. 10.00 (*1-55729-038-5*) IEAS.

Banister, Judith, ed. English Silver Hallmarks. 118p. 1995. pap. 4.95 (*0-572-01181-4*, Pub. by Foulsham UK) Assoc Pubs Grp.

Banister, Judith, jt. auth. see Eberstadt, Nicholas.

Banister, Keith. Sharks: A Unique First Visual Reference. (Look Inside Ser.). (Illus.). 20p. (J). (gr. 4-6). 1995. 10.99 (*0-89577-690-1*, Pub. by Rdrs Digest) S&S Trade.

Banister, Keith & Campbell, Andrew, eds. The Encyclopedia of Aquatic Life. (Illus.). 384p. 1985. 45.00 (*0-8160-1257-1*) Facts on File.

Banister, Manly. The Craft of Bookbinding. LC 93-34492. (Illus.). 160p. 1994. reprint ed. pap. 7.95 (*0-486-27852-2*) Dover.

— Making Picture Frames in Wood. LC 81-50985. (Home Craftsman Bks.). (Illus.). 128p. (YA). (gr. 10-12). 1982. pap. 10.95 (*0-8069-7542-3*) Sterling.

— Practical Guide to Etching & Other Intaglio Printmaking Techniques. 128p. 1986. reprint ed. pap. 7.95 (*0-486-25165-9*) Dover.

Banister, Peter, et al. Qualitative Methods in Psychology: A Research Guide. LC 94-25724. 160p. 1994. pap. 30.95 (*0-335-19181-9*) OpUniv Pr.

Banister, Richard. A Treatise of 113 Diseases of the Eyes. LC 79-37135. (English Experience Ser.: No. 297). 480p. 1971. reprint ed. 35.00 (*90-221-0297-1*) Walter J Johnson.

Banja, Judith, jt. auth. see Munroe, Mary H.

Banjak, Stephen. Sokol Gymnastic Manual: New & Revised Version. LC 93-83580. 364p. 1993. write for info. (*0-912981-23-7*) Hse BonGiovanni.

Banjura, Abdul K. The Limitations of Survey Research Methods in Assessing the Problem of Minority Student Retention in Higher Education: The Focus-Group Method As One Alternative. LC 92-4670. 144p. 1992. lib. bdg. 69.95 (*0-7734-9830-3*) E Mellen.

Bank, Aaron, jt. auth. see Nathanson, E. M.

Bank Administration Institute Staff. Standardized RFPs: Effective Tools for Selecting Cash Management Banks. LC 96-84784. 149p. (Orig.). 1996. pap. 100.00 (*0-614-30099-1*) Treasry Mgmt.

Bank, Adrianne, jt. ed. see Wolfson, Ronald.

Bank, B., et al, eds. Non-Linear Parametric Optimization. 224p. 1983. 66.50 (*0-8176-1375-7*) Birkhauser.

Bank, Barbara J., ed. see Curators of University of Missouri Staff.

***Bank, David.** Breaking Windows: The Rise & Fall of Microsoft. 2001. 25.00 (*0-7432-0315-1*) Free Pr.

Bank, Flemming. How to Profit from Your Ideas. 100p. 1997. pap. write for info. (*0-9665482-0-5*) Fl Bank.

Bank, Frank & Twyman, Gib. Call Me Lumpy: My Leave It to Beaver Days. Breon, Brad, ed. LC 97-41563. 220p. 1997. 21.95 (*1-886110-29-8*, Pub. by Addax Pubng) Midpt Trade.

Bank, J., jt. auth. see Banks, S.

Bank, Jodrell, jt. auth. see Lovell, Bernard.

Bank, John. Essence of Total Quality Management. 128p. (C). 1993. pap. text 19.95 (*0-13-284902-X*) P-H.

— Essence of TQM. 2nd ed. 224p. (C). 1999. pap. 19.95 (*0-13-573114-3*) P-H.

— Outdoor Development for Managers. 2nd ed. LC 93-48694. 192p. 1994. 74.95 (*0-566-07395-1*, Pub. by Gower) Ashgate Pub Co.

Bank, Julie & Stern, Christina, eds. Kids, Animals & Literature: An Annotated Bibliography of Children's Books with a Positive, Humane Theme. rev. ed. (Illus.). 60p. 1998. pap. text 25.00 (*0-7881-7168-2*) DIANE Pub.

***Bank, Lawrence C., ed.** Materials & Construction: Exploring the Connection. LC 99-13265. 928p. 1999. 99.00 (*0-7844-0423-2*) Am Soc Civil Eng.

Bank, Lawrence H. Seventeen Farrington Way. LC 87-19344. 1988. 22.95 (*0-87949-267-8*) Ashley Bks.

Bank Marketing Association Staff. The Analysis of 1994 Bank Marketing Expenditures. 1995. 145.00 (*0-89982-442-0*) Am Bankers.

— Inside Bank Marketing: Organizing, Staffing, Recruiting, Retaining. (Illus.). 104p. (Orig.). 1990. 110.00 (*1-55695-002-0*) Bank Mktg Assn.

— One Hundred One Marketing Ideas, Vol. IV. 212p. (Orig.). 1990. 45.00 (*1-55695-001-2*) Bank Mktg Assn.

Bank, Melissa. The Girls' Guide to Hunting & Fishing. LC 98-48590. 288p. 1999. 23.95 (*0-670-88300-X*) Viking Penguin.

***Bank, Melissa.** Girl's Guide to Hunting & Fishing. LC 98-48590. (Illus.). 274p. (YA). 1999. pap. 12.95 (*0-14-029324-8*) Viking Penguin.

— The Girls' Guide to Hunting & Fishing. large type ed. LC 99-37937. (Thorndike Basic Ser.). (Illus.). 1999. 29.95 (*0-7862-2168-2*) Thorndike Pr.

Bank, Mirra. Anonymous Was a Woman: A Celebration in Words & Images of Traditional American Art & the Women Who Made It. (Illus.). 128p. 1995. pap. 13.95 (*0-312-13430-4*, St Martin Griffin) St Martin.

***Bank of Canada Staff & Institute of Internal Auditors Staff.** Risk-Based Internal Auditing & Dynamic Control Assessment: Revolutionizing Internal Audit Services. Campbell, Lee A., ed. LC 98-186439. (CSA Library). v, 24 p. 1998. write for info. (*0-89413-396-9*) Inst Inter Aud.

Bank of England Staff. The Development & Opportunity of Monetary Policy. 1984. pap. 13.95 (*0-19-877233-5*) OUP.

— The Economics of Pension Arrangements: Papers Presented at the 20th Meeting of the Panel of Academic Consultants on 4 March, 1983. LC HD7106.G73. (Bank of England. Panel Paper: No. 20). 32p. reprint ed. pap. 30.00 (*0-608-13368-X*, 202252100027) Bks Demand.

— Employment, Real Wages & Unemployment in the United Kingdom. LC HC0256.Z99. (Bank of England. Panel of Academic Consultants. Panel Papers: No. 24). 33p. reprint ed. pap. 30.00 (*0-608-15542-X*, 202972300064) Bks Demand.

— Monetary Trends in the United Kingdom: Papers Presented at the Twenty-Second Meeting of the Panel of Academic Consultants on 28 October, 1983. Includes Part 2 & Appendix B to the Paper by Professor D. F. Hendry & N. R. Ericsson. LC HG0935.. 140p. reprint ed. pap. 43.40 (*0-8357-3732-2*, 203645800003) Bks Demand.

Bank One Community Writers Staff. Sand Dollar $ucce$$ large type ed. (WeWrite Kids! Ser.: No. 40). (Illus.). 45p. (J). (gr. 2-5). 1998. pap. 3.95 (*1-57635-022-3*) WeWrite.

Bank, R. E. Computational Aspects of VLSI Design with an Emphasis on Semiconductor Device Simulation Bank. LC 89-18355. 190p. 1990. text 58.00 (*0-8218-1132-0*, LAM/25) Am Math.

Bank, R. E., et al, eds. Mathematical Modelling & Simulation of Electrical Circuits & Semiconductor Devices. LC 94-21583. (International Numerical Mathematics Ser.: Vol. 117). 336p. 1994. 99.50 (*0-8176-5053-9*) Birkhauser.

— Mathematical Modelling & Simulation of Electrical Circuits & Semiconductor Devices: Proceedings of a Conference Held at the Mathematisches Forschunginstitut, Oberwolfach, Oct. 30-Nov. 5, 1988. (International Series of Numerical Mathematics: Vol. 93). 312p. 1990. 87.50 (*0-8176-2439-2*) Birkhauser.

Bank, Randy. PLTMG: A Software Package for Solving Elliptic Partial Differential Equations Users' Guide 8.0. 3rd rev. ed. LC 98-11767. (Software, Environments & Tools Ser.: Vol. 5). (Illus.). xi, 110p. 1998. pap. 32.50 (*0-89871-409-5*, SE05) Soc Indus-Appl Math.

Bank, Richard. Why Be Jewish & How to Do It. Date not set. write for info. (*0-7657-6169-6*) Aronson.

Bank, Rosemari K. Theatre Culture in America, 1825-1860. (Studies in American Theatre & Drama: No. 7). (Illus.). 304p. (C). 1997. text 64.95 (*0-521-56387-9*) Cambridge U Pr.

Bank, Simmy, jt. ed. see Burns, Gerard P.

Bank, Stephen P. & Kahn, Michael D. The Sibling Bond: 15th Anniversary Edition: The First Major Account of the Powerful Emotional Connections Among Brothers & Sisters Throughout Life. rev. ed. LC 97-9634. 384p. 1997. 30.00 (*0-465-07817-6*, Pub. by Basic) HarpC.

Bank Street College Media Group Staff, ed. see Brenner, Barbara, et al.

Bank Street Staff. Jacques Cousteau. 128p. 2000. pap. 8.95 (*0-07-135741-6*) McGraw.

— Killer Games. 122p. 2000. pap. 8.95 (*0-07-134334-2*) McGraw.

— The Lady Is a Doctor. 124p. 2000. pap. 8.95 (*0-07-134335-0*) McGraw.

— Rachel Carson. 128p. 2000. pap. 8.95 (*0-07-135742-4*) McGraw.

— Sally Ride. 121p. 2000. pap. 8.95 (*0-07-135740-8*) McGraw.

Bank, Ted, ed. Readings in Anthropology: People of the Bering Sea. 1971. pap. text 9.95 (*0-8422-0137-8*) Irvington.

Banka, Jozef. Time & Method in Recentivism. LC 98-28999. (Studia Philosophica et Historica: Vol. 24). 123p. 1998. pap. text 31.95 (*0-8204-3581-3*) P Lang Pubng.

BANKAI Workshop Staff. Adaptive Intelligent Systems: Proceedings of the Third BANKAI Workshop, Brussels, Belgium, 12-14 October 1992. LC 93-9382. 250p. 1993. 150.00 (*0-444-89838-7*) Elsevier.

Bankaitis, Vytas A. Phospholipid Transfer Proteins: Emerging Roles in Vesicle Trafficking, Signal Transduction & Metabolic Regulation. (Molecular Biology Intelligence Unit Ser.). 163p. 1995. 99.00 (*1-57059-330-2*) Landes Bioscience.

Bankart, A. S. Manipulative Surgery. 150p. 1997. reprint ed. spiral bd. 12.50 (*0-7873-0070-5*) Hlth Research.

Bankart, C. Peter. Talking Cures: A History of Western & Eastern Psychotherapies. LC 96-2816. (Counseling Ser.). 544p. (C). 1996. mass mkt. 68.95 (*0-534-34383-X*) Brooks-Cole.

— Talking Cures: A History of Western & Eastern Psychotherapies. (C). 1997. text, teacher ed. write for info. (*0-534-34384-8*) Brooks-Cole.

Bankel, Hansgeorg. Der Spaetarchaische Tempel der Aphaia auf Aegina. (Denkmaeler Antiker Architektur Ser.: Bd 19). (GER., Illus.). xi, 180p. (C). 1993. lib. bdg. 229.25 (*3-11-012808-X*) De Gruyter.

Banker, jt. auth. see Atkinson.

Banker, Bev & Tanner, Karen. Sillysongs: For Phonology & Sound Awareness. LC 98-5570. 1998. 59.00 (*1-888222-18-2*) Thinking Pubns.

***Banker, David E. & Sobel, Estelle.** Beautiful Skin: Every Womens Guide to Looking Her Best at Any Age. 256p. 2000. pap. 16.95 (*1-58062-325-5*) Adams Media.

Banker, Gary & Goslin, Kimberly, eds. Culturing Nerve Cells. 2nd ed. LC 97-17167. (Cellular & Molecular Neuroscience Ser.). (Illus.). 580p. 1998. 70.00 (*0-262-02438-1*, Bradford Bks) MIT Pr.

Banker, Gilbert S. & Rhodes, Christopher T., eds. Modern Pharmaceutics, No. 72. 3rd ed. LC 95-33238. (Drugs & the Pharmaceutical Sciences Ser.: Vol. 72). (Illus.). 960p. 1995. text 195.00 (*0-8247-9371-4*) Dekker.

Banker, H. J., ed. see Underwood, L. M.

Banker, Howard J. A Partial History & Genealogical Record of the Bancker or Banker Families of America & in Particular the Descendants of Laurens Mattyse Bancker. (Illus.). 458p. 1988. reprint ed. pap. 68.00 (*0-8328-0179-8*); reprint ed. lib. bdg. 76.00 (*0-8328-0178-X*) Higginson Bk Co.

Banker, J. Stanley. Walk Cheerfully: The Middleroad. LC 94-7299. (Illus.). 159p. 1994. 10.00 (*0-944350-33-X*) Friends United.

Banker, John. A Semantic & Structural Analysis of Philemon. 64p. 1990. pap. 12.00 (*0-88312-934-5*) S I L Intl.

— A Semantic & Structural Analysis of Philippians. LC 96-67037. 199p. 1996. pap. 13.60 (*1-55671-020-8*) S I L Intl.

— A Semantic & Structural Analysis of Titus. Callow, John, ed. 124p. 1987. pap. 10.20 (*0-88312-916-7*) S I L Intl.

Banker, Karen L. Brick by Brick Vol. 2: The Intricacy of Building Relationships. LC 97-194804. (Rose Cottage Papers). (Illus.). 80p. (Orig.). 1996. pap. 12.00 (*1-887106-14-6*) McRae Banker.

Banker, Karen L. Sunlight & Brickwork Vol. 1: Artistic Impressions of Augusta, GA. (Rose Cottage Papers). 80p. 1995. pap. 12.00 (*1-887106-05-7*) McRae Banker.

Banker, Mark T. Presbyterian Missions & Cultural Interaction in the Far Southwest, 1850-1950. (Illus.). 248p. (C). 1992. text 36.95 (*0-252-01929-6*) U of Ill Pr.

Banker, Rajiv D. Management Accounting. 2nd ed. Atkinson, Anthony A., ed. LC 96-34705. 741p. (C). 1996. 93.00 (*0-13-255761-4*) P-H.

Banker-Riskin, Anita, jt. auth. see Riskin, Michael.

Banker, V. K. Bank Fraud of the Century: Bank of Credit & Commerce International: The Inside Story. vii, 186p. 1992. pap. 8.95 (*81-220-0253-6*, Pub. by Konark Pubs Pvt Ltd) Advent Bks Div.

Bankers Books Staff. Financial Institutions: Directory of the United Kingdom & Republic of Ireland, 1987 Edition. 1997. pap. 225.00 (*0-85297-400-0*, Pub. by Chartered Bank) St Mut.

Bankert, Jan A., ed. Digges' Choice. LC 96-39670. 140p. (Orig.). 1996. 19.50 (*0-89725-243-8*, 1635) Picton Pr.

Bankes, George. Peruvian Pottery. (Ethnography Ser.: No. 15). (Illus.). 72p. pap. 10.50 (*0-7478-0013-8*, Pub. by Shire Pubns) Parkwest Pubns.

Bankes, James. Jack London Stories of Boxing. 208p. 1991. text 19.95 (*0-697-13805-4*, WCB McGr Hill) McGrw-H Hghr Educ.

Bankes, James L. Clinical Ophthalmology: A Text & Colour Atlas. 3rd ed. LC 93-35577. 138p. 1994. text 44.95 (*0-443-04819-3*) Church.

Bankes, Tim, jt. auth. see Hatter, David.

***Bankhead, Betty, et al.** Write It: A Guide for Research, MLA Version. 2nd ed. LC 98-55987. 60p. 1999. pap. 10.00 (*1-56308-689-1*) Libs Unl.

***Bankhead, Donna & Blas, Lynette.** Last Minute Weddings: It's Still Not Too Late to Plan the Celebration of Your Dreams. LC 99-22503. 128p. 1999. pap. 10.99 (*1-56414-415-1*) Career Pr Inc.

Bankhead, Donna, jt. auth. see Flowers, Michael.

Banki, Judith H. What Viewers Should Know about the Oberammergau Passion Play. 20p. 1980. pap. 1.50 (*0-87495-024-4*) Am Jewish Comm.

Banki, L. Bioessay of Pesticides in the Laboratory: Research & Quality Control. 490p. (C). 1978. 90.00 (*963-05-1306-4*, Pub. by Akade Kiado) St Mut.

Bankier, David. The Germans & the Final Solution: Public Opinion under Nazism. (Jewish Society & Culture Ser.). 224p. 1996. pap. text 26.95 (*0-631-20100-9*) Blackwell Pubs.

***Bankier, David, ed.** Probing the Depths of German Antisemitism: German Society & the Persecution of the Jews, 1933-1941. LC 99-56222. 600p. 2000. 39.95 (*1-57181-238-5*) Berghahn Bks.

Bankier, William. The Mount St. Helens Volcano. Parker, Liz, ed. (Take Ten Bks.). (YA). (gr. 6-12). 1993. pap. text 3.95 (*1-56254-098-X*) Saddleback Pubns.

***Bankier, William.** The Mount St. Helens Volcano. rev. ed. (Take Ten Ser.). (Illus.). 45p. (YA). (gr. 4-12). 1999. pap. 3.95 (*1-58659-023-5*) Artesian.

Bankier, William. Selected Short Stories of William Bankier. 250p. 1995. pap. 16.95 (*0-88962-553-0*) Mosaic.

Banking & Currency Committee. Commercial Banks & Their Trust Activities, 2 vols., Set. LC 75-81987. 1969. reprint ed. 39.95 (*0-405-00011-1*) Ayer.

— Commercial Banks & Their Trust Activities, 2 vols., Vol. 1. LC 75-81987. 1969. reprint ed. 20.95 (*0-405-00012-X*) Ayer.

— Commercial Banks & Their Trust Activities, 2 vols., Vol. 2. LC 75-81987. 1969. reprint ed. 20.95 (*0-405-00013-8*) Arno Press.

— Growth of Unregistered Bank Holding Companies: Problems & Prospects. LC 75-81988. 1969. reprint ed. 23.95 (*0-405-00019-7*) Ayer.

— Report of the Committee Appointed Pursuant to House Resolutions 429 & 504 to Investigate the Concentration of Control of Money & Credit. LC 75-2677. (Wall Street & the Security Market Ser.). 1975. reprint ed. 23.95 (*0-405-07239-2*) Ayer.

— Stock Exchange Practices: Proceedings of the Committee on Banking & Currency, U. S. Senate, 1934. LC 75-2678. (Wall Street & the Security Market Ser.). 1975. reprint ed. 34.95 (*0-405-07240-6*) Ayer.

Banking Law Journal Editors, ed. Banking Law Journal Digest: Annual Supplement, 2 vols. 7th ed. 1982. 135.00 (*0-685-55627-1*) Warren Gorham & Lamont.

***Bankman, Issac.** Handbook of Medical Image Processing. (Biomedical Engineering Ser.). (Illus.). 1100p. 2000. 119.00 (*0-12-077790-8*) Acad Pr.

Bankman, Joseph, et al. Federal Income Tax: Examples & Explanations. (Examples & Explanations Ser.). 591p. 1996. pap. 26.95 (*0-316-08040-3*, 80403) Aspen Law.

— Federal Income Tax: Examples & Explanations. 2nd ed. LC 98-28966. 1998. pap. text 33.95 (*0-7355-0059-2*) Panel Pubs.

Bankman, Joseph, jt. auth. see Klein, William A.

***Banko, Stephen T., III.** Memories of War Dreams of Peace: Echoes of the Vietnam War. (Illus.). 36p. 1998. pap. 12.95 (*0-9673458-0-4*, BT-01198-MOW) SHS Pubs.

Banko, William, jt. ed. see Devine, T. M.

Banko, Winston E. The Trumpeter Swan: Its History, Habits, & Population in the United States. LC 80-12533. (Illus.). 224p. reprint ed. pap. 69.50 (*0-7837-4651-2*, 204437500002) Bks Demand.

Bankoff, Greg. Crime, Society, & the State in Nineteenth-Century Philippines. LC 96-946362. 260p. 1997. pap. text 22.00 (*971-550-203-2*, Pub. by Ateneo de Manila Univ Pr) UH Pr.

Bankoff, Greg & Elston, Kylie. Environmental Regulation in Malaysia & Singapore. (Asia Papers: No. 2). pap. 14.95 (*1-875560-49-1*, Pub. by Univ of West Aust Pr) Intl Spec Bk.

Bankoff, Peter N. A Soviet Assignment. LC 88-18563. 192p. 1988. 14.75 (*0-930950-19-4*); pap. 8.75 (*0-930950-20-8*) Nopoly Pr.

Bankoff, S. G., ed. Topics in Two-Phase Heat Transfer & Flow: Presented at the Winter Annual Meeting of ASME, San Francisco, CA, Dec. 10-15, 1978. LC 78-68087. 239p. reprint ed. pap. 74.10 (*0-608-30765-3*, 201387600087) Bks Demand.

Bankoff, S. G., ed. see National Heat Transfer Conference Staff.

Bankole, Katherine K. Slavery & Medicine: Enslavement & Medical Practices in Antebellum Louisiana. LC 97-35394. (Studies in African American History & Culture). 274p. 1998. 56.00 (*0-8153-3059-6*) Garland.

Bankowski, Z., et al, eds. Ethics & Epidemiology: International Guidelines. (Proceedings of the XXVth CIOMS Conference Ser.). (ENG & FRE.). viii, 191p. 1991. pap. text 25.00 (*92-9036-048-8*, 1830025) World Health.

Bankowski, Z. & Ada, G. L., eds. Health Technology Transfer: Whose Responsibility? (Proceedings of the XXIIIrd CIOMS Round Table Conference Ser.). 165p. 1990. pap. text 20.00 (*92-9036-043-7*, 1830023) World Health.

Bankowski, Z. & Bernardelli, J. Medical Ethics & Medical Education: XIVth CIOMS Round Table Conference Bilingual English/Spanish. (CIOMS Round Table Proceedings Ser.: No. 14). 1981. pap. text 20.00 (*92-9036-006-2*) World Health.

Bankowski, Z. & Bryant, J. Health Policy, Ethics & Human Values - An International Dialogue: Highlights of the XVIIIth CIOMS Round Table Conference. (CIOMS Publication Ser.). 1985. pap. text 10.00 (*92-9036-021-6*) World Health.

— Health Policy, Ethics & Human Values: European & North American Perspectives: Conference Highlights, Papers & Conclusions, XXIst CIOMS Conference. (CIOMS Round Table Proceedings Ser.: No. 21). 1988. pap. text 20.00 (*92-9036-034-8*) World Health.

Bankowski, Z. & Bryant, J. H., eds. Health Policy, Ethics & Human Values: Proceedings of the CIOMS Round Table Coference, an International Dialogue, XVIIth. 336p. 1985. pap. text 25.00 (*92-9036-023-2*, 1830018) World Health.

— Poverty, Vulnerability, & the Value of Human Life: A Global Agenda for Bioethics. (Highlights & Papers of the XXVIIth CIOMS Conference, Ixtapa, Guerrero State, Mexico). xi, 246p. 1994. pap. text 25.00 (*92-9036-060-7*, 1830028) World Health.

Bankowski, Z. & Carballo, M., eds. Battered Children & Child Abuse: Proceedings of the CIOMS Round Table Conference, XIXth. 187p. 1986. pap. text 20.00 (*92-9036-026-7*, 1830019) World Health.

Bankowski, Z. & Dunne, J. F., eds. Drug Surveillance: International Cooperation Past, Present, & Future: Proceedings of the XXVIIth CIOMS Conference. LC 95-155443. viii, 198p. 1994. pap. text 25.00 (*92-9036-059-3*, 1830027) World Health.

Bankowski, Z. & Howard-Jones, N. Biomedical Research Involving Animals: Proposed International Guiding Principles. (CIOMS Round Table Proceedings Ser.: No. 17). 1984. pap. text 25.00 (*92-9036-017-8*) World Health.

— Human Experimentation & Medical Ethics: XVth CIOMS Round Table Conference. (CIOMS Round Table Proceedings Ser.: No. 15). 1982. text 30.00 (*92-9036-009-7*) World Health.

Bankowski, Z. & Levine, R. J., eds. Ethics & Research on Human Subjects: International Guidelines. (Proceedings of the XXVth CIOMS Conference Ser.). ix, 291p. 1993. pap. text 25.00 (*92-9036-054-2*, 1830026) World Health.

Bankowski, Z. & Mijia, A., eds. Health Manpower Out of Balance: Conflicts & Prospects, Proceedings of the 20th CIOMS Round Table Conference, Acapulco, Mexico, 7-12 Sept. 1987. 210p. 1987. pap. text 20.00 (*92-9036-030-5*, 1830020) World Health.

Bankowski, Z., jt. auth. see Howard-Jones, N.

Bankowski, Zenon. European Union & Its Order: The Legal Theory of European Integration. 1999. pap. text 39.95 (*0-631-21504-2*) Blackwell Pubs.

Bankowski, Zenon, ed. Revolutions in Law & Legal Thought. (Enlightenment Rights & Revolution Ser.: No. 6). 212p. 1991. pap. 37.90 (*0-08-040924-5*, Pub. by Aberdeen U Pr) Macmillan.

Bankowski, Zenon, et al, eds. Informatics & the Foundations of Legal Reasoning. LC 95-8280. (Law & Philosophy Library: Vol. 21). 388p. (C). 1995. lib. bdg. 147.00 (*0-7923-3455-8*, Pub. by Kluwer Academic) Kluwer Academic.

Bankowski, Zenon, ed. see Wroblewski, Jerzy.

Bankowsky, Jack, et al. Investigations 1988. (Illus.). 25p. 1988. pap. 7.50 (*0-88454-047-2*) U of Pa Contemp Art.

***Banks.** Activities for Older People Needing Care. 2000. pap. text 35.00 (*0-7506-4741-8*) Buttrwrth-Heinemann.

Banks. Anatomy & Physiology of Farm Animals. 1994. 32.50 (*0-8016-6395-4*) Mosby Inc.

Banks. Black Children & Therapeutic Identity Work. 61.95 (*1-85742-307-0*) Ashgate Pub Co.

Banks. Delphi: Off GD Tandy. 1989. pap. 19.95 (*0-13-200429-1*) P-H.

— Dist Law Set. 1990. 145.00 (*0-316-08027-6*, Aspen Law & Bus) Aspen Pub.

— Education Psychology. Date not set. pap. text, teacher ed. write for info. (*0-314-04797-2*) West Pub.

— English Changing World: Level 2 (Teacher's Edition) 2nd ed. 232p. (C). 1997. text, teacher ed. 25.47 (*0-673-14508-5*) Addson-Wesley Educ.

— English Changing World: Level 3 (Teacher's Edition) (C). 1997. text, teacher ed. 25.47 (*0-673-14509-3*) Addson-Wesley Educ.

— English Changing World: Level 5 (Teacher's Edition) (C). 1997. text, teacher ed. 19.10 (*0-673-14511-5*) Addson-Wesley Educ.

— English Changing World: Level 6 (Teacher's Edition) (C). 1997. text, teacher ed. 19.10 (*0-673-14512-3*) Addson-Wesley Educ.

— English for a Changing World: Level 1, Part A. 1984. pap. text, student ed. 9.10 (*0-673-14550-6*) Addison-Wesley.

— Getting the Most Out of Deskmate: Tandy X Version. 2nd ed. 1990. pap. 19.95 (*0-13-353004-3*) P-H.

— A New Introduction to Management. (GC - Principles of Management Ser.). Date not set. text 54.95 (*0-538-83380-7*) S-W Pub.

— The Pancreas: A Text & Atlas. 1998. text. write for info. (*0-7216-6670-1*, W B Saunders Co) Harcrt Hlth Sci Grp.

Banks. Prosperity & Parenthood. 248p. 1993. 56.95 (*0-7512-0267-3*) Ashgate Pub Co.

— Teaching Strategies for the Social Studies. 5th ed. 1999. 65.62 (*0-201-66664-2*) Addison-Wesley.

Banks. Ukraine: Restructuring for Growth. (Euromoney Country Guide Ser.). 1998. 170.00 (*1-85564-570-X*, Pub. by Euromoney) Am Educ Systs.

Banks. Victorian Values. 208p. 1994. 53.95 (*0-7512-0269-X*) Ashgate Pub Co.

Banks, ed. English Changing World. 1997. pap. text, student ed. 13.72 (*0-673-14501-8*); pap. text, student ed. 13.72 (*0-673-14502-6*) Addison-Wesley.

— English Changing World. 3rd ed. 1997. pap. text, student ed. 13.72 (*0-673-14503-4*) Addison-Wesley.

— English for a Changing World: LV5. 5th ed. 1997. pap. text, student ed. 13.72 (*0-673-14505-0*) Addison-Wesley.

— Workbook English Changing World 1. 96p. 1997. pap. text, wbk. ed. 7.59 (*0-673-14513-1*) Addison-Wesley.

Banks & Orlando. Night & Day, Bk. 1. (C). 1993. pap. text 21.27 (*0-13-043696-8*) S&S Trade.

Banks & Rowe. Readings in English. 96p. 1990. pap. text 15.80 (*0-13-635228-6*) P-H.

— Readings in English, No. 2. (C). 1990. pap. text 15.80 (*0-13-815069-9*) P-H.

Banks & Rowe. Readings in English 1. 112p. 1990. pap. text 11.80 (*0-13-199845-5*) P-H.

Banks, jt. auth. see Rasool.

Banks, Alan S., et al. Mcglamry's Comprehensive Textbook of Foot Surgery. 3rd ed. 2,256p. text 325.00 (*0-683-30471-2*) Lppncott W & W.

Banks, Amanda C. Birth Chairs, Midwives, & Medicine. LC 99-27105. (Illus.). 176p. 1999. 48.00 (*1-57806-171-7*); pap. 18.00 (*1-57806-172-5*) U Pr of Miss.

Banks-Anderson, Yolanda, jt. ed. see Sexton, Ken.

B

An Asterisk (*) at the beginning of an entry indicates that the title is appearing for the first time.

Banks, Ann. Children's Travel Journal. (Illus.). 48p. (J). (gr. 1-12). 1995. 19.95 (*0-9641262-0-6*) Little Bkrm.

— First Person America. 1991. pap. 10.95 (*0-393-30781-6*) Norton.

— It's My Money: A Kid's Guide to the Green Stuff. LC 93-12618. (Illus.). (J). (gr. 3-7). 1993. 3.99 (*0-670-36086-4*, PuffinBks) Peng Put Young Read.

Banks, Ann, ed. Harlem: Photographs by Aaron Siskind, 1932-1940. rev. ed. LC 90-63168. (Illus.). 80p. (C). 1991. reprint ed. pap. 15.95 (*1-56098-041-9*) Smithsonian.

Banks, Ann & Evans, Nancy. Goodbye, House: A Kid's Guide to Moving. LC 98-35995. (Illus.). 48p. (J). 1999. pap. 9.95 (*0-517-88574-3*) Crown Pub Group.

Banks, Anna & Banks, Stephen P., eds. Fiction & Social Research: By Ice or Fire. LC 98-19693. (Ethnographic Alternatives Ser.: Vol. 4). 272p. (C). 1998. pap. 24.95 (*0-7619-9035-6*) AltaMira Pr.

— Fiction & Social Research: By Ice or Fire. LC 98-19693. (Ethnographic Alternatives Ser.: Vol. 4). 272p. (C). 1998. 62.00 (*0-7619-9034-8*) AltaMira Pr.

Banks, Anne. A Guy Thing: How to Be a Man Without (Necessarily) Becoming a Father. rev. ed. 2000. pap. 0.50 (*0-89230-196-1*) Do It Now.

Banks, Arnold J. Oscilloscope Guide. (Illus.). 336p. 1997. pap. 29.95 (*0-7906-1124-4*) Prompt Publns.

Banks, Arthur. A Military Atlas of the First World War. (Illus.). 1997. 29.95 (*0-85052-563-2*, Pub. by Leo Cooper) Combined Pub.

B

***Banks, Arthur.** Wings of the Dawning. 416p. 1998. 24.95 (*0-947993-74-6*, Pub. by Mlvrn Pubg Co) Brit Bk Co Inc.

Banks, Arthur. A World Atlas of Military History, 1861-1945. (Quality Paperbacks Ser.). (Illus.). 180p. 1988. reprint ed. pap. 12.95 (*0-306-80332-1*) Da Capo.

Banks, Arthur S., ed. Political Handbook of the World, 1994-1995. 60th ed. LC 81-643916. (Political Handbook of the World Ser.). 1226p. (C). 1995. 104.95 (*0-933199-10-4*) CSA Pubn.

— Political Handbook of the World, 1988: 1988. LC 81-643916. (Illus.). 877p. 1988. 89.95 (*0-933199-04-X*) CSA Pubn.

Banks, Arthur S., et al, eds. Political Handbook of the World, 1986. LC 81-643916. (Illus.). 803p. 1986. 79.95 (*0-933199-01-5*) CSA Pubn.

— Political Handbook of the World, 1987. LC 81-643916. (Illus.). 850p. 1987. 84.95 (*0-933199-03-1*) CSA Pubn.

— Political Handbook of the World, 1990. LC 81-643916. (Illus.). 956p. 1990. 89.95 (*0-933199-06-6*) CSA Pubn.

— Political Handbook of the World, 1991. LC 81-643916. (Illus.). 1016p. 1991. 89.95 (*0-933199-07-4*) CSA Pubn.

— Political Handbook of the World, 1995-1996. 61st ed. LC 81-643916. (Political Handbook of the World Ser.). 1322p. (C). 1996. 109.95 (*0-933199-11-2*) CSA Pubn.

— Political Handbook of the World, 1997. 62nd rev. ed. LC 81-643916. 1220p. 1997. 115.00 (*0-933199-12-0*) CSA Pubn.

***Banks, Arthur S. & Muller, Thomas C.** Political Handbook of the World, 2000. 64th ed. LC 81-643916. (Political Handbook of the World Ser.). (Illus.). 1375p. (C). 2000. 130.00 (*0-933199-15-5*) CSA Pubn.

Banks, Arthur S. & Muller, Thomas C., eds. Political Handbook of the World, 1998. 63rd rev. ed. LC 81-643916. (Political Handbook of the World Ser.). (Illus.). 1297p. 1998. 119.00 (*0-933199-13-9*) CSA Pubn.

***Banks, Arthur S. & Muller, Thomas C., eds.** Political Handbook of the World, 1999. 64th ed. LC 81-643916. (Illus.). 1325p. 2000. 125.00 (*0-933199-14-7*) CSA Pubn.

Banks, Arthur S., et al. Economic Handbook of the World, 1982. 640p. 1982. text 53.00 (*0-07-003692-6*) McGraw.

— Political Handbook of the World, 1984-1985. LC 81-643916. (Illus.). 768p. 1985. 79.95 (*0-933199-00-7*) CSA Pubn.

— Political Handbook of the World, 1993. LC 81-643916. (Illus.). 1224p. 1993. 104.50 (*0-933199-09-0*) CSA Pubn.

— Political Handbook of the World, 1992: 1992. LC 81-643916. (Illus.). 1120p. 1992. 94.95 (*0-933199-08-2*) CSA Pubn.

Banks, B. Three Kinds of Faith for Healing. 1992. pap. 4.95 (*0-89228-103-0*) Impact Christian.

Banks, B. H., ed. see Turner, J. J.

Banks-Baldwin Law Publishing Company Staff, jt. auth. see Kentucky Staff.

***Banks, Bernard W.** Differential Equations with Graphical & Numerical Methods. LC 00-22175. (Illus.). 464p. 2000. 91.00 (*0-13-084376-8*) P-H.

Banks, Bernard W. A Primer for Modern Mathematics. 144p. (C). 1993. text 23.13 (*0-697-21494-X*, WCB McGr Hill) McGrw-H Hghr Educ.

Banks, Bill. Alive Again! 168p. (Orig.). 1977. pap. 4.95 (*0-89228-048-4*) Impact Christian.

— Breaking Unhealthy Soul-Ties. 1999. pap. text 7.95 (*0-89228-139-1*) Impact Christian.

Banks, Bill. Complete Price Guide for Victorian Opalescent Glass. 108p. 1995. pap., spiral bd. 13.50 (*0-9649459-0-8*) Banks Pubng.

Banks, Bill. Complete Price Guide for Victorian Opalescent Glass. 3rd ed. 108p. 1998. pap. 13.50 (*0-9649459-2-4*) Banks Pubng.

— Complete Price Guide for Victorian Opalescent Glass. 4th rev. ed. 108p. 1999. pap. 13.50 (*0-9649459-3-2*) Banks Pubng.

— Complete Price Guide for Victorian Opalescent Glass: 1996. 2nd rev. ed. 108p. 1997. pap., spiral bd. 13.50 (*0-9649459-1-6*) Banks Pubng.

— Complete Price Guide for Victorian Opalescent Glass, 2000. 5th ed. 108p. 2000. pap. 15.00 (*0-9649459-4-0*) Banks Pubng.

— Deliverance for Children & Teens, Vol. 3. (Power for Deliverance Ser.). (Orig.). 1989. pap. 6.95 (*0-89228-034-4*) Impact Christian.

— Deliverance from Childlessness. 140p. 1990. pap. 5.95 (*0-89228-037-9*) Impact Christian.

— Deliverance from Fat & Eating, Vol. 2. (Power for Deliverance Ser.). (Orig.). 1988. pap. 5.95 (*0-89228-032-8*) Impact Christian.

— Everything Is Possible with God: (The Martin Hlastan Story) LC 98-170352. 224p. (Orig.). 1995. pap. 9.95 (*0-89228-119-7*) Impact Christian.

— Songs of Deliverance, Vol. 1. (Power for Deliverance Ser.). (Orig.). 1987. pap. 5.95 (*0-89228-031-X*) Impact Christian.

***Banks, Bill.** WWF Attitude, Get It: Official Acclaim Strategy Guide. (Illus.). 1999. pap. 12.99 (*1-57840-986-1*) Acclaim Bks.

Banks, Bill & Banks, Sue. Ministering to Abortion's Aftermath. 144p. (Orig.). 1982. pap. 5.95 (*0-89228-057-3*) Impact Christian.

Banks, Brian. The Beatitudes, for a Cappella SATB Chorus & SATB Soloists. (University Choral Ser.: No. 1). 14p. 1992. pap. text 2.50 (*1-56571-062-2*, UC001) PRB Prods.

— Canada from Space. (Illus.). 120p. 1995. pap. 19.95 (*1-55158-000-4*, Pub. by Camden Hse) Firefly Bks Ltd.

— The Image of Huysmans. LC 89-45874. (Studies in the Nineteenth Century: No. 7). 1990. 39.50 (*0-404-61487-6*) AMS Pr.

— "Quam Pulchra Es", for a Cappella SATB Chorus: After Dunstable. (University Choral Ser.: No. 3). 6p. 1992. pap. text 2.00 (*1-56571-065-7*, UC003) PRB Prods.

— "Voces Super Speciosa Facta Est" for ATB Chorus. (University Choral Ser.: No. 4). 4p. 1994. pap. text 1.50 (*1-56571-101-7*) PRB Prods.

Banks, Bruce A., ed. see Minerals, Metals & Materials Society Staff.

Banks, Caroline. Night & Day: Reading for the Adult Learner of ESL - EFL, Bk. 2. 144p. 1993. pap. text 21.27 (*0-13-043704-2*) P-H.

— Night & Day Book 3: Reading for the Adult Learner of ESL EFL, Bk. 3. 128p. 1993. pap. text 21.27 (*0-13-043712-3*) P-H.

Banks, Caroline G. Warm under the Cat: Haiku & Senryu Poems. 40p. (Orig.). 1995. pap. 5.00 (*0-9645254-0-2*) Wllngtn Pr.

Banks, Carolyn. Death by Dressage. 1993. mass mkt. 4.50 (*0-449-14843-2*, GM) Fawcett.

— Death on the Diagonal. 1996. mass mkt. 4.99 (*0-449-14968-4*) Fawcett.

— Groomed for Death. 1995. mass mkt. 4.99 (*0-449-14913-7*) Fawcett.

— A Horse to Die For. 1996. mass mkt. 5.50 (*0-449-14969-2*, GM) Fawcett.

— Mr. Right. LC 98-34202. 352p. 1999. 25.00 (*0-933256-91-4*) Second Chance.

— Tart Tales: Elegant Erotic Stories. 224p. 1995. 6.98 (*0-7858-0466-8*) Bk Sales Inc.

— Tart Tales: Elegant Erotic Stories. 224p. 1994. pap. 8.95 (*0-7867-0079-3*) Carroll & Graf.

Banks, Carolyn & Rizzo, Janis, eds. A Loving Voice: A Caregiver's Book of Read-Aloud Stories for the Elderly. LC 91-34876. 320p. 1992. pap. 14.95 (*0-914783-59-9*) Charles.

— A Loving Voice: A Caregiver's Book of Read-Aloud Stories for the Elderly. large type ed. LC 92-42562. (General Ser.). 417p. 1993. lib. bdg. 21.95 (*0-8161-5620-4*, G K Hall Lrg Type) Mac Lib Ref.

— A Loving Voice: A Caregiver's Book of Read-Aloud Stories for the Elderly. large type ed. LC 92-42562. (General Ser.). 417p. 1994. 18.95 (*0-8161-5621-2*, G K Hall Lrg Type) Mac Lib Ref.

— A Loving Voice Vol. II: A Caregiver's Book of More Read-Aloud Stories for the Elderly. LC 94-1593. 296p. (Orig.). 1994. pap. 14.95 (*0-914783-70-X*) Charles.

Banks, Carolyn, ed. see Torres, Eliseo, et al.

***Banks, Cate & Douglas, Heather.** Law on the Internet. 128p. 2000. pap. 29.95 (*1-86287-354-2*, Pub. by Federation Pr) Gaunt.

***Banks, Charles E.** Colonial Families of Martha's Vineyard. 571p. 1999. pap. 45.00 (*0-8063-4933-6*) Clearfield Co.

Banks, Charles E. English Ancestry & Homes of the Pilgrim Fathers Who Came to Plymouth on the Mayflower in 1620, the Fortune in 1621, & the Anne & the Little James in 1623. 187p. 1997. reprint ed. 18.50 (*0-8063-0708-0*) Genealog Pub.

— The History of Martha's Vineyard, Mass., Vol. 2: Town Annals. (Illus.). 645p. 1989. reprint ed. lib. bdg. 64.50 (*0-8328-0844-X*, MA0201) Higginson Bk Co.

— The History of Martha's Vineyard, Massachusetts, Vol. 1: General History. (Illus.). 535p. 1989. reprint ed. lib. bdg. 53.00 (*0-8328-0843-1*, MA0200) Higginson Bk Co.

— History of York: Successively Known As Bristol (1632), Agamenticus (1641), Gorgeana (1642) & York (1652), 2 vols. (Illus.). 938p. 1997. reprint ed. lib. bdg. 99.00 (*0-8328-5935-4*) Higginson Bk Co.

— The Planters of the Commonwealth in Massachusetts: A Study of the Emigrants & Emigration in Colonial Times. LC 67-30794. (Illus.). xiii, 231p. 1997. reprint ed. 20.00 (*0-8063-0018-3*) Genealog Pub.

— Winthrop Fleet of 1630: An Account of the Vessels, the Voyage, the Passengers & Their English Homes, from Original Authorities. LC 68-57951. (Illus.). ix, 119p. 1999. reprint ed. 15.00 (*0-8063-0020-5*, 306) Genealog Pub.

Banks, Charles W. The Life & Times of John Calvin: With an Earnest Appeal for the Adoption of Open-Air Preaching. LC 83-45599. reprint ed. 42.50 (*0-404-19867-8*) AMS Pr.

Banks, Cherry A. Teaching Strategy Ethnic Studies. 6th ed. 574p. 1996. pap. text 57.00 (*0-205-18940-7*) Allyn.

Banks, Cherry A., jt. ed. see Banks, James A.

***Banks, Chris, ed.** Big Canyon Country Guide to Mountain Biking in WV. deluxe ed. (Illus.). 80p. 2001. pap. 16.95 (*0-9700165-2-2*) Twin Rivers NC.

Banks, Christiana, jt. auth. see Bliss, Michael.

Banks, Christopher P. Judicial Politics in the D. C. Circuit Court. LC 99-14371. (Illus.). 200p. 1999. 38.00 (*0-8018-6184-5*) Johns Hopkins.

Banks, Cicely & Alvarado, Noemi. Manual del Maestro - Progresa con las Matematicas. (SPA.). 80p. 1998. pap. text 12.00 (*0-9624192-3-0*) N Bacchus.

— Progresa con las Matematicas. 80p. 1999. pap. text, teacher ed. 12.00 (*0-9624192-4-9*) N Bacchus.

Banks, Cicely, jt. auth. see Alvarado, N.

Banks, Cliff. Tunnel Rats. 208p. (Orig.). 1989. mass mkt. 3.95 (*0-445-20944-5*, Pub. by Warner Bks) Little.

— Tunnel Rats: Mud & Blood. 192p. 1990. mass mkt. 3.95 (*0-445-20946-1*, Pub. by Warner Bks) Little.

Banks, Cundi. Women in Transition: Social Control in Papua New Guinea. 171p. 1993. pap. 30.00 (*0-642-18635-9*, Pub. by Aust Inst Criminology) Advent Bks Div.

Banks, Dale. Tattoo. 352p. 1995. mass mkt. 4.99 (*0-7860-0169-0*, Pinncle Kensgtn) Kensgtn Pub Corp.

***Banks, Daniel E.** Occupational Lung Disease. LC 99-21662. (Illus.). 538p. 1999. text 110.00 (*0-412-73630-6*) OUP.

Banks, David. Sarah Ferguson: The Royal Redhead. LC 87-15567. (Taking Part Ser.). (Illus.). 64p. (J). (gr. 3 up). 1988. lib. bdg. 13.95 (*0-87518-369-7*, Dillon Silver Burdett) Silver Burdett Pr.

Banks, David, jt. auth. see Purdy, Michael.

Banks, David, ed. see Hanley, Ken.

Banks, David, ed. see Mason, Bill.

Banks, David, ed. see Streit, Jackson.

Banks, David, ed. see Streit, Taylor.

Banks, David, ed. see Tinnin, Glenn.

Banks, David, ed. see Zeller, Bob.

Banks, David H., Jr. Como Arrancar Tu Propio Negocio: The Start up Guide. 2nd ed.Tr. of Start up Guide. (SPA.). 160p. 1997. pap. 19.95 (*0-7931-2700-9*, 1700-0901) Dearborn.

Banks, David J. From Class to Culture: Social Conscience in Malay Novels since Independence. LC 86-51497. (Monographs: No. 29). x, 200p. (C). 1988. pap. 17.00 (*0-938692-29-1*) Yale U SE Asia.

Banks, David J., ed. Changing Identities in Modern Southeast Asia. (World Anthropology Ser.). (Illus.). x, 358p. 1976. 35.40 (*90-279-7949-9*) Mouton.

Banks, David P. Tropical Orchids: Of Malaysia & Singapore. (Nature Guides Ser.). (Illus.). 64p. 1999. 9.95 (*962-593-156-2*) Tuttle Pubng.

Banks, Dennis, ed. see Seals, David.

Banks, Diana, jt. auth. see Rosier, Malcolm E.

Banks, Doris, ed. see Hollenbeck, Joan W.

Banks, Doris H. Medieval Manuscript Bookmaking: A Bibliographic Guide. LC 89-27935. (Illus.). 290p. 1989. 36.00 (*0-8108-2274-1*) Scarecrow.

Banks, Eddie. Anti-Personnel Mines: A Recognition Guide. LC 97-22216. (Brassey's Essential Guides Ser.). (Illus.). 512p. 1997. 120.00 (*1-85753-228-7*, Pub. by Brasseys) Brasseys.

***Banks, Elizabeth.** The Remaking of an American. 352p. 2000. reprint ed. pap. 19.95 (*0-8130-1776-9*) U Press Fla.

Banks, Ellen. Maple Leaf Rag. 1989. 50.00 (*0-932526-63-2*) Nexus Pr.

Banks, Emma D., ed. Original Recitations with Lesson-Talks. enl. ed. LC 79-51959. (Granger Poetry Library). 1980. reprint ed. 20.00 (*0-89609-176-7*) Roth Pub Inc.

Banks, Enoch M. The Economics of Land Tenure in Georgia. LC 68-56647. (Columbia University. Studies in the Social Sciences: No. 58). reprint ed. 41.50 (*0-404-51058-2*) AMS Pr.

Banks, Erik. Complex Derivatives: Understanding & Managing the Risks of Exotic Options Complex Swaps. LC 94-143928. 300p. 1993. text 75.00 (*1-55738-550-5*, Irwn Prfssnl) McGraw-Hill Prof.

— Emerging Fixed-Income Markets in Asia: A-Country-by-Country Guide to the Structure, Practices. (C). 1994. text 70.00 (*1-55738-827-X*, Irwn Prfssnl) McGraw-Hill Prof.

***Banks, Erik.** Rise & Fall of the Merchant Bank: The Evolution of the Global Investment Bank. LC 99-491040. 1999. 80.00 (*0-7494-2821-X*, Kogan Pg Educ) Stylus Pub VA.

Banks, Erik. Volatility & Credit Risk in the Capital Markets: Assessing & Managing the Risk of Financial Instruments & Off-Balance Sheet Operations. 300p. 1993. text 70.00 (*1-55738-509-2*, Irwn Prfssnl) McGraw-Hill Prof.

Banks, Erma D. & Byerman, Keith. Alice Walker: An Annotated Bibliography. LC 89-1251. 242p. 1989. text 15.00 (*0-8240-5734-1*, H889) Garland.

Banks, F. Coins of Bible Days. LC 84-71643. 1985. reprint ed. pap. 18.00 (*0-942666-41-0*) S J Durst.

***Banks, Ferdinand E.** Global Finance & Financial Markets: A Modern Introduction. 230p. 2000. 48.00 (*981-02-4326-X*); pap. 26.00 (*981-02-4327-8*) World Scientific Pub.

— A Modern Introduction to Energy Economics. 288p. 1999. 125.00 (*0-7923-7700-1*) Kluwer Academic.

Banks, G. V. L' Etranger, Camus: Critical Monographs in English. 64p. 1993. pap. 45.00 (*0-85261-318-0*, Pub. by Univ of Glasgow) St Mut.

Banks, Gary & Kinley, Eddie. Sharing Christ with Black Muslims: An Introduction to the Orientation of Black Muslims. Thomas, Teri, ed. 64p. (Orig.). 1996. pap. 7.95 (*0-9651234-0-5*) BKin Lght Minist.

Banks, Gary & Tumlir, Jan. Economic Policy & the Adjustment Problems: Thames Essays. 120p. 1987. pap. 19.95 (*0-566-05332-2*, Pub. by Avebry) Ashgate Pub Co.

Banks, George. The Human Diversity Workshop. 1994. ring bd. 149.95 (*0-87425-984-3*) HRD Press.

Banks, Granger. The Third Prototype. 100p. 1998. pap. write for info. (*1-57502-746-1*, P02071) Morris Pubng.

Banks, H. T., ed. Control & Estimation of Distributed Parameter Systems. LC 92-27712. (Frontiers in Applied Mathematics Ser.: Vol. 11). xii, 227p. 1992. pap. 74.50 (*0-89871-297-1*) Soc Indus-Appl Math.

Banks, H. T., et al, eds. Identification & Control in Systems Governed by Partial Differential Equations. (Proceedings in Applied Mathematics Ser.: No. 68). ix, 234p. 1993. pap. 60.50 (*0-89871-317-X*) Soc Indus-Appl Math.

Banks, H. T. & Kunisch, K. Estimation Techniques for Distributed Parameter Systems. (Systems & Control: Foundations & Applications Ser.: No. 1). 350p. 1989. 56.50 (*0-8176-3433-9*) Birkhauser.

***Banks, H. T., et al.** Electromagnetic Material Interrogation Using Conductive Interfaces & Acoustic Waveforms. (Frontiers in Applied Mathematics Ser.: Vol. 21). 2000. 56.00 (*0-89871-459-1*) Soc Indus-Appl Math.

Banks, H. T., et al. Smart Material Structures: Modeling, Estimation & Control. LC 96-223099. 310p. 1996. 159.95 (*0-471-97024-7*) Wiley.

Banks, Heywood. Fly's Eyes: Looking at the World Through Fly's Eyes. large type ed. (Illus.). 28p. (J). (gr. 1-6). 1997. pap. 7.95 (*0-9661407-0-2*) Maverick Projs.

— Toast! (Illus.). 28p. 1999. text 14.95 (*0-9661407-1-0*) Maverick Projs.

Banks, Iain M. Against a Dark Background. 1996. write for info. (*1-85723-179-1*) Little.

Banks, Iain M. Bridge, The (TP) LC 96-53369. 256p. 1997. pap. 13.00 (*0-06-105358-9*, HarperPrism) HarpC.

***Banks, Iain M.** The Business: A Novel. LC 00-30785. 2000. write for info. (*0-7432-0014-4*) S&S Trade.

Banks, Iain M. Classic Glamour Photography. (Illus.). 176p. 1989. pap. 24.95 (*0-8174-3672-3*, Amphoto) Watsn-Guptill.

— Excession. 512p. 1998. mass mkt. 5.99 (*0-553-57537-6*, Spectra) Bantam.

***Banks, Iain M.** Inversions. LC 99-51901. 352p. 2000. 23.95 (*0-671-03668-8*) PB.

Banks, Iain M. Player of Games, The TP. LC 96-35028. 288p. 1997. pap. 13.00 (*0-06-105356-2*, HarperPrism) HarpC.

— A Song of Stone. LC 98-13076. 288p. 1998. 23.00 (*0-684-85353-1*); 23.00 (*0-684-85725-1*) S&S Trade.

***Banks, Iain M.** A Song of Stone. 288p. 1999. per. 12.00 (*0-684-85536-4*, Scribner Pap Fic) S&S Trade Pap.

Banks, Iain M. State of the Art. 1989. 16.00 (*0-929480-06-6*) Mark Ziesing.

— State of the Art. limited ed. 1989. 40.00 (*0-929480-07-4*) Mark Ziesing.

— The Wasp Factory. LC 98-8355. 192p. 1998. per. 12.00 (*0-684-85315-9*) Simon & Schuster.

Banks, Iain M., et al. Ask Dr. Ian about Men's Health. 206p. 1997. pap. 17.95 (*0-85640-592-2*, Pub. by Blackstaff Pr) Dufour.

***Banks, Ingrid.** Hair Matters: Beauty, Power & Black Women's Consciousness. LC 99-50485. 2000. pap. text 17.50 (*0-8147-1337-8*) NYU Pr.

— Hair Matters: Beauty, Power, & Black Women's Consciousness. 192p. 2000. text 55.00 (*0-8147-1336-X*) NYU Pr.

Banks, J. Persuasive Technical Writing. LC 65-28552. 1966. 36.00 (*0-08-011668-X*, Pub. by Pergamon Repr) Franklin.

Banks, J. A. The Strange Death of Capitalist Individualism. LC 93-22659. 132p. 1993. 72.95 (*1-85521-407-5*, Pub. by Dartmth Pub) Ashgate Pub Co.

Banks, J. A. & Banks, Olive. Feminism & Family Planning in Victorian England. (Modern Revivals in Economic & Social History Ser.). 160p. (C). 1993. text 49.95 (*0-7512-0268-1*, Pub. by Gregg Revivals) Ashgate Pub Co.

Banks, J. Houston, jt. auth. see Sobel, Max A.

Banks, Jacqueline T. Egg-Drop Blues. LC 94-4917. 128p. (J). (gr. 3-6). 1995. 15.00 (*0-395-70931-8*) HM.

Banks, James. Teaching Strategies for the Social Studies. 5th ed. LC 98-38664. 528p. (C). 1998. 74.00 (*0-8013-1165-9*) Addison-Wesley.

— Wing of Scarlet. (American Autobiography Ser.). 144p. 1995. reprint ed. lib. bdg. 69.00 (*0-7812-8449-X*) Rprt Serv.

Banks, James, jt. auth. see Stokes, Robert.

***Banks, James A.** Cultural Diversity & Education: Foundations, Curriculum, & Teaching. 4th ed. 352p. 2000. pap. text 46.67 (*0-205-30865-1*) Allyn.

Banks, James A. Educating Citizens in a Multicultural Society. LC 97-3895. (Multicultural Studies). 192p. 1997. text 50.00 (*0-8077-3632-5*); pap. text 22.95 (*0-8077-3631-7*) Tchrs Coll.

— An Introduction to Multicultural Education. 2nd ed. LC 98-14915. 150p. 1998. pap. 27.00 (*0-205-27750-0*) Allyn.

— Multicultural Education. 3rd ed. 446p. 1996. pap. text 52.00 (*0-205-18896-6*) Allyn.

Banks, James A. Multicultural Education: Issues & Perspectives. 3rd ed. 464p. 1997. pap. 56.95 (*0-471-36457-6*) Wiley.

Banks, James A. Multicultural Education, Transformative Knowledge & Action: Historical & Contemporary Perspectives. LC 96-1069. (Multicultural Education Ser.). 384p. (C). 1996. text 57.00 (*0-8077-3532-9*); pap. text 26.95 (*0-8077-3531-0*) Tchrs Coll.

— Multiethnic Education 1987: Theory & Practice. 3rd ed. LC 93-15713. 350p. 1993. pap. 57.00 (*0-205-14745-3*) Allyn.

An Asterisk (*) at the beginning of an entry indicates that the title is appearing for the first time.

Banks, James A., ed. Handbook of Research on Multicultural Education. 882p. 1999. reprint ed. text 40.00 (*0-7881-6393-0*) DIANE Pub.

Banks, James A. & Banks, Cherry A., eds. Handbook of Research on Multicultural Education. LC 94-28862. 1995. 75.00 (*0-02-895797-0*) Macmillan.

— Multicultural Education: Issues & Perspectives. 400p. 1989. pap. text 33.00 (*0-205-11791-0*, H17916) Allyn.

Banks, James A. & Clegg, Ambrose A., Jr. Teaching Strategies for the Social Studies: Inquiry, Valuing & Decision-Making. 4th ed. LC 84-14388. 505p. (C). 1990. text 62.81 (*0-8013-0472-5*, 78302) Longman.

***Banks, James A. & McGee Banks, Cheryl A., eds.** Multicultural Education: Issues & Perspectives. 4th ed. 464p. (C). 2000. pap. 108.95 (*0-471-38379-1*) Wiley.

***Banks, James E.** Alferd Packer's Wilderness Cookbook. (Wild & Woolly West Ser.: No. 9). (Illus.). 48p. 1998. pap. 4.95 (*0-86541-036-4*) Filter.

Banks, James E. Naming the Organic Compunds PB. 2nd ed. LC 75-291. (C). 1976. pap. text 34.50 (*0-7216-1536-8*, W B Saunders Co) Harcrt Hlth Sci Grp.

Banks, James G., jt. auth. see Hawkesford, John.

Banks, James H. Introduction to Transportation Engineering. LC 97-31111. 381p. 1997. 82.81 (*0-07-005789-3*) McGraw.

Banks, Janet C. Creating & Assessing Performance-Based Curriculum Projects: A Teacher's Guide to Project-Based Learning & Performance Assessment. LC 97-68404. (Illus.). 140p. (Orig.). 1997. pap., teacher ed. 19.95 (*1-886753-19-9*) CATS Publ.

— Creating the Multi-Age Classroom. rev. ed. LC 95-68876. (Illus.). 144p. 1995. pap., teacher ed. 19.95 (*1-886753-03-2*) CATS Publ.

— Creative Projects for Independent Learners. rev. ed. LC 95-68877. (Illus.). 144p. 1995. pap., teacher ed. 19.95 (*1-886753-02-4*) CATS Publ.

— Developing Research Skills: Independent Research Projects on Animals & Plants. rev. ed. LC 95-70739. (Illus.). 136p. 1995. pap., teacher ed. 19.95 (*1-886753-00-8*) CATS Publ.

— Enhancing Research Skills: A Thematic Research Unit on the Civil War. rev. ed. LC 95-72210. 124p. 1995. pap., teacher ed. 19.95 (*1-886753-01-6*) CATS Publ.

— Essential Learnings of Mathematics: What Students Should Know & Be Able to Do. LC 96-83247. (Illus.). 148p. (Orig.). 1996. pap., teacher ed. 19.95 (*1-886753-04-0*) CATS Publ.

Banks, Jay. House Calls in the Hills: Memoirs of a Country Doctor. LC 96-78488. 135p. (Orig.). 1996. pap. 10.95 (*0-941092-35-6*) Mtn St Pr.

Banks, Jeffrey. Signaling Games in Political Science, Vol. 46. (Fundamentals of Pure & Applied Economics Ser.). viii, 90p. 1991. pap. text 55.00 (*3-7186-5087-8*, Harwood Acad Pubs) Gordon & Breach.

Banks, Jeffrey S. & Hanushek, Eric A., eds. Modern Political Economy: Old Topics, New Directions. (Political Economy of Institutions & Decisions Ser.). (Illus.). 283p. (C). 1995. text 64.95 (*0-521-47233-4*); pap. text 19.95 (*0-521-47810-3*) Cambridge U Pr.

Banks, Jeffrey S., jt. auth. see Austen-Smith, David.

Banks, Jennifer S. Preservation Planning Program Resource Guides: Options for Replacing & Reformatting Deteriorated Materials. 51p. 1993. pap. 15.00 (*0-918006-63-5*) ARL.

Banks, Jeri. All of Us Together: The Story of Inclusion at the Kinzie School. LC 94-7508. 200p. 1994. 24.95 (*1-56368-028-9*) Gallaudet Univ Pr.

***Banks, Jerry.** Handbook of Simulation. LC 97-51533. 864p. 1998. 150.00 (*0-471-13403-1*, Wiley-Interscience) Wiley.

Banks, Jerry. Principles of Quality Control. LC 88-22763. 672p. 1989. text 102.95 (*0-471-63551-0*) Wiley.

Banks, Jerry, et al. Discrete-Event System Simulation. 2nd ed. LC 95-30801. (Prentice Hall International Series in Industrial & Systems Engineering). 548p. (C). 1995. 99.00 (*0-13-217449-9*) P-H.

— Introduction to SIMAN V & CINEMA V. 480p. 1994. pap. 89.95 (*0-471-30960-5*) Wiley.

Banks, Jimmy. The Darrell Royal Story: Collector's Edition. LC 94-231361. (Illus.). 192p. 1997. 19.95 (*0-89015-981-5*, Eakin Pr) Sunbelt Media.

Banks, Joan. Peter Stuyvesant. LC 99-24901. (Colonial Leaders Ser.). (Illus.). 80p. (J). 1999. 16.95 (*0-7910-5346-6*) Chelsea Hse.

— Peter Stuyvesant. (Colonial Leaders Ser.). (Illus.). 80p. (J). (gr. 3 up). 1999. pap. 8.95 (*0-7910-5689-9*) Chelsea Hse.

— Song of La Selva: A Story of a Costa Rican Rain Forest. LC 98-13023. (Habitat Ser.: No. 9). (Illus.). 36p. (J). (gr. 1-4). 1998. 15.95 (*1-56899-586-5*) Soundprints.

— Song of La Selva: A Story of a Costa Rican Rain Forest. (Habitat Ser.: Vol. 9). (Illus.). 36p. (J). (gr. 1-4). 1998. 19.95 incl. audio (*1-56899-588-1*, BC7009); pap. 5.95 (*1-56899-587-3*); pap. 10.95 incl. audio (*1-56899-589-X*) Soundprints.

— Song of La Selva: A Story of a Costa Rican Rain Forest, Incl. toy. (Habitat Ser.: Vol. 9). (Illus.). 36p. (J). (gr. 1-4). 1998. 26.95 (*1-56899-590-3*); 31.95 incl. audio (*1-56899-592-X*); pap. 16.95 (*1-56899-591-1*); pap. 19.95 incl. audio (*1-56899-593-8*) Soundprints.

***Banks, Joan.** U. S. Constitution. (Your Government Ser.). 2000. 17.95 (*0-7910-5991-X*) Chelsea Hse.

Banks, Joanne Trautmann, ed. see Woolf, Virginia.

Banks, John. The Island Queens: or The Death of Mary Queen of Scotland. (Augustan Reprints Ser.: Nos. 265-266 (1991)). reprint ed. 18.50 (*0-404-70265-1*) AMS Pr.

— Vertue Betray'd: or Anna Bullen: A Tragedy. LC 92-25500. (Augustan Reprints Ser.: Nos. 205-206). 1981. reprint ed. 21.50 (*0-404-70205-8*, PR3316) AMS Pr.

Banks, John, et al. Turn of the Century Home. (Illus.). 125p. 1995. pap. 25.00 (*0-941548-29-5*) Ren Soc U Chi.

Banks, John A. Dancing Guide: Basic Art of the Dance. LC 99-94028. 145p. 1999. pap. 9.50 (*0-9629833-2-2*, Pub. by Jordan Bk Co) ACCESS Pubs Network.

— The Nature of Human Well-Being: The Constructive Conduct of a Society & a Person. (Conceptual Model of Humanity Ser.: No. 3). 450p. 1995. pap. text 12.00 (*0-9629833-1-4*) Jordan Bk Co.

— Statistics: A First Course. (C). 1995. pap. text, student ed. 27.50 (*0-07-054942-7*) McGraw.

— Superior Living: Handbook for the Conduct of Life. 352p. (Orig.). 1992. 10.00 (*0-9629833-0-6*) Jordan Bk Co.

Banks, John L. Administrative Needs for Educational Reform in Guidance & Counseling. LC 93-3924. 125p. 1993. pap. 44.95 (*1-880921-29-4*) Austin & Winfield.

— Administrative Needs for Educational Reform in Guidance Counseling. LC 93-3924. 125p. 1994. 54.95 (*1-880921-31-6*) Austin & Winfield.

— Greater Is He That Prophesieth. (Illus.). 24p. 1995. 5.00 (*0-9648655-0-5*) Banks Ink.

Banks, Joyce R. Selecting a Thinking Skills Program. LC 90-72123. 120p. 1991. pap. 24.95 (*0-87762-788-6*) Scarecrow.

Banks, Julia, jt. auth. see Banks, Robert.

Banks, Kate. Alphabet Soup. (Dragonfly Bks.). (Illus.). 32p. (J). (ps-2). 1994. pap. 4.99 (*0-679-86723-6*, Pub. by Knopf Bks Yng Read) Random.

Banks, Kate. Alphabet Soup. LC 87-3191. 1994. 10.19 (*0-606-06176-2*, Pub. by Turtleback) Demco.

Banks, Kate. And If the Moon Could Talk. LC 97-29770. (Illus.). 32p. (J). (ps-k). 1998. 15.00 (*0-374-30299-5*) FS&G.

— Baboon. LC 96-20888. (Illus.). 32p. (J). (ps-1). 1997. 14.00 (*0-374-30474-2*) FS&G.

***Banks, Kate.** Baboon. 2000. pap. write for info. (*0-374-40473-9*) FS&G.

Banks, Kate. The Bird, the Monkey & the Snake in the Jungle. LC 98-3860. (Illus.). 32p. (J). (ps up). 1999. text 16.00 (*0-374-30729-6*) FS&G.

***Banks, Kate.** Close Your Eyes. LC 99-46430. 2001. text. write for info. (*0-374-31382-2*) FS&G.

— Great Blue House. 2002. text (*0-374-32769-6*) FS&G.

— Howie Bowles, Secret Agent. LC 98-55144. (Illus.). 64p. (J). (gr. 3-7). 1999. 15.00 (*0-374-33500-1*, Frances Foster) FS&G.

— Night Worker. LC 99-27595. 2000. text 16.00 (*0-374-35520-7*) St Martin.

Banks, Kate. Spider, Spider. LC 96-11653. (Illus.). 32p. (J). (ps-3). 1996. 14.00 (*0-374-37151-2*) FS&G.

***Banks, Kate.** Spider Spider. (Illus.). 32p. (J). (ps-k). 2000. pap. 5.95 (*0-374-46986-5*, Sunburst Bks) FS&G.

Banks, Kathy. REAL Home School. LC 99-93864. (Illus.). iv, 132p. 1999. pap. 17.95i (*0-9672192-0-5*) Five Pnt Pubg.

Banks, Katy, ed. see Hodges, Meredith S.

Banks, Kenneth C., et al. The Company of Neighbours: Revitalizing Community Through Action Research. 144p. 1999. text 40.00 (*0-8020-0936-0*); pap. text 16.95 (*0-8020-7905-9*) U of Toronto Pr.

Banks, Kerry. Babe Ruth Era: Old-Time Baseball Trivia. 144p. 1998. 9.95 (*1-55054-613-9*) Sterling.

— The Glory Years: Old-Time Baseball Trivia. LC 96-910901. (ENG & CHI., Illus.). 144p. 1997. pap. 9.95 (*1-55054-531-0*, Pub. by Greystone Bks) Sterling.

— Mats Sundin. (Hockey Heroes Ser.). 1998. pap. text 6.95 (*1-55054-642-2*, Pub. by DGL) Sterling.

— Old-Time Baseball Trivia The Stormy Years 1969-89. 1999. pap. text 5.95 (*1-55054-675-9*) DGL.

— Pavel Bure: The Riddle of the Russian Rocket. 208p. 1999. 19.95 (*1-55054-714-3*, Greystone) DGL.

***Banks, Kerry.** The Stormy Years, 1969-1989. (Old-Time Baseball Trivia Ser.). (Illus.). 144p. (gr. 3-7). 1999. pap. 9.95 (*1-55054-673-2*) DGL.

— Teemu Selanne. (Hockey Heroes Ser.). (Illus.). 48p. (J). 1999. pap. 6.95 (*1-55054-678-3*) DGL.

Banks, Kerry, jt. auth. see Weekes, Don.

***Banks, Kevin & Maitland, G. D.** The Maitland Concept of Manipulative Therapy. 6th ed. (Illus.). 352p. 2000. pap. text 65.00 (*0-7506-3911-3*) Buttrwrth-Heinemann.

Banks, Laura, jt. auth. see Barber, Janette.

***Banks, Leanne.** Bride of Fortune. (Desire Ser.). 2000. mass mkt. 3.99 (*0-373-76311-5*, 1-76311-9) Silhouette.

Banks, Leanne. A Date with Dr. Frankenstein. (Congratulations Ser.). 1995. per. 3.75 (*0-373-09983-5*) Harlequin Bks.

***Banks, Leanne.** De Si Douces Retrouvailles. (Rouge Passion Ser.: No. 525). (FRE.). 1999. mass mkt. 3.99 (*0-373-37525-5*, 1-37525-2) Harlequin Bks.

— Doctor Wore Spurs. (Desire Ser.: Vol. 128). 2000. per. 3.99 (*0-373-76280-1*) Silhouette.

— Expecting the Boss's Baby. 2001. mass mkt. 3.99 (*0-373-76338-7*, 1-76338-2) Silhouette.

Banks, Leanne. The Five Minute Bride. (Desire Ser.). 1997. per. 3.50 (*0-373-76058-2*, 1-76058-6) Silhouette.

***Banks, Leanne.** Five-Minute Bride. large type ed. (Silhouette Ser.). 1999. 21.95 (*0-373-59649-9*) Harlequin Bks.

— Her Forever Man: (Man of the Month) (Desire Ser.: No. 1267). 2000. mass mkt. 3.75 (*0-373-76267-4*, 1-76267-4) Harlequin Bks.

Banks, Leanne. The Lone Rider Takes a Bride: The Rulebreakers. (Desire Ser.: No. 1172). 1998. per. 3.75 (*0-373-76172-4*, 1-76172-5) Harlequin Bks.

— Millionaire Dad. (Desire Ser.). 1998. per. 3.75 (*0-373-76166-X*, 1-76166-7) Silhouette.

***Banks, Leanne.** Una Mujer Unica. (Harlequin Deseo Ser.: Vol. 159).Tr. of Unique Woman. (SPA.). 156p. 1999. per. 3.50 (*0-373-35289-1*, 1-35289-7) Harlequin Bks.

— Un Padre Millonario. (Harlequin Deseo Ser.: Vol. 157).Tr. of Millionaire Dad. (SPA.). 156p. 1999. per. 3.50 (*0-373-35287-5*, 1-35287-1) Harlequin Bks.

Banks, Leanne. Ridge: The Avenger (Sons & Lovers) LC 96-7347. (Desire Ser.). 185p. 1996. per. 3.50 (*0-373-05987-6*, 1-05987-2) Silhouette.

— The Secretary & the Millionaire. 1999. per. 3.75 (*0-373-76208-9*, 1-76208-7) Silhouette.

— Sin Ataduras: The You-Can't-Make-Me Bride. (Deseo Ser.: Vol. 113).Tr. of No Strings. (SPA.). 1998. per. 3.50 (*0-373-35243-3*, 1-35243-4) Harlequin Bks.

— Thirty-Day Fiance: The Rulebreakers. (Desire Ser.: No. 1179). 1998. per. 3.75 (*0-373-76179-1*, 0-76179-1) Silhouette.

— The Troublemaker Bride. (How to Catch a Princess Ser.). 1997. per. 3.50 (*0-373-76070-1*, 1-76070-1) Silhouette.

— The You-Can't-Make-Me Bride. (Desire Ser.: No. 1082). 1997. per. 3.50 (*0-373-76082-5*, 1-76082-6) Silhouette.

***Banks, Leanne.** You-Can't-Make-Me Bride. large type ed. 280p. 2000. 22.95 (*0-373-46499-1*) Thorndike Pr.

Banks, Leo. They Left Their Mark: Heros & Rogues of Arizona History. (Arizona Highways Wild West Collection). 144p. 1999. pap. 7.95 (*0-916179-70-2*) Ariz Hwy.

Banks, Leo, et al. Days of Destiny: 20 Stories of Desperados & Lawmen. 141p. 1999. pap. 7.95 (*0-916179-56-7*) Ariz Hwy.

Banks, Leo W. Manhunts & Massacres. (Wild West). 144p. 1999. pap. 7.95 (*0-916179-63-X*) Ariz Hwy.

***Banks, Leo W.** Rattlesnake Blues: Dispatches from a Snakebit Territory. (Wild West Collection: 8). (Illus.). 144p. 2000. 7.95 (*1-893860-12-4*) Ariz Hwy.

— Stalwart Women: Frontier Stories of Indomitable Spirit. LC 99-61929. (Wild West Collection). 144p. 1999. pap. 7.95 (*0-916179-77-X*) Ariz Hwy.

***Banks, Leo W., et al.** Travel Arizona II: A Guide to the Best Tours & Sites. LC 98-87497. (Illus.). 1999. 15.95 (*0-916179-80-X*) Ariz Hwy.

Banks, Leo W., jt. auth. see Childs, Craig.

Banks, Lydia. Motivation in the Workplace: Inspiring Your Employees. Miller, Karen M., ed. LC 97-70993. (How-to Book Ser.). 110p. (Orig.). 1997. pap. 12.95 (*1-884926-46-0*, MOTIV) Amer Media.

***Banks, Lynne R.** Fair Exchange. LC 99-203227. 262p. 1998. write for info. (*0-7499-0424-0*, Pub. by Piatkus Bks) London Brdge.

Banks, Lynne Reid. The Adventures of King Midas. LC 92-3795. (Illus.). 160p. (J). (gr. 4-7). 1992. 14.00 (*0-688-10894-6*, Wm Morrow) Morrow Avon.

— The Adventures of King Midas. 160p. (J). (gr. 4). 1993. mass mkt. 4.50 (*0-380-71564-3*, Avon Bks) Morrow Avon.

Banks, Lynne Reid. Adventures of King Midas. 1992. 9.60 (*0-606-05106-6*, Pub. by Turtleback) Demco.

— Adventures of King Midas. 153p. pap. 4.50 (*0-8072-1468-X*) Listening Lib.

— Alice-by-Accident. LC 99-41647. 144p. (J). (gr. 4-7). 2000. 14.95 (*0-380-97865-2*) Morrow Avon.

Banks, Lynne Reid. Angela & Diabola. LC 96-41682. 160p. (J). (gr. 3-7). 1997. 14.00 (*0-380-97562-9*, Avon Bks) Morrow Avon.

— Angela & Diabola. LC 96-41682. 176p. (J). (gr. 3-7). 1998. mass mkt. 4.50 (*0-380-79409-8*, Avon Bks) Morrow Avon.

— Angela & Diabola. (J). 1998. 9.60 (*0-606-13124-8*, Pub. by Turtleback) Demco.

Banks, Lynne Reid. Angela & Diabola. 163p. (J). (gr. 4-6). pap. 4.50 (*0-8072-1515-5*) Listening Lib.

Banks, Lynne Reid. Behind Scenes Indian. 32p. (J). (gr. 4-7). 1995. pap. 3.95 (*0-590-50984-5*) Scholastic Inc.

— Broken Bridge. LC 94-26636. (Illus.). 336p. (YA). (gr. 5 up). 1995. 16.00 (*0-688-13595-1*, Wm Morrow) Morrow Avon.

— Broken Bridge. LC 94-26636. 272p. (YA). (gr. 7 up). 1996. mass mkt. 4.50 (*0-380-72384-0*, Avon Bks) Morrow Avon.

Banks, Lynne Reid. Broken Bridge. LC 94-26636. 1996. 9.60 (*0-606-09105-X*, Pub. by Turtleback) Demco.

Banks, Lynne Reid. The Fairy Rebel. LC 87-28740. (Illus.). 128p. (YA). (gr. 5 up). 1988. 15.95 (*0-385-24483-5*) Doubleday.

— Fairy Rebel. 128p. (J). (gr. 4-7). 1989. mass mkt. 4.50 (*0-380-70650-4*, Avon Bks) Morrow Avon.

— Fairy Rebel. 1985. 9.60 (*0-606-00995-7*, Pub. by Turtleback) Demco.

Banks, Lynne Reid. Fairy Rebel. 118p. (J). (gr. 4-6). pap. 4.50 (*0-8072-1480-9*) Listening Lib.

Banks, Lynne Reid. Farthest-Away Mountain. 144p. (J). (gr. 4-7). 1991. 14.95 (*0-385-41534-6*) Doubleday.

— Farthest-Away Mountain. 144p. (J). (gr. 4-7). 1992. mass mkt. 4.50 (*0-380-71303-9*, Avon Bks) Morrow Avon.

Banks, Lynne Reid. Farthest-Away Mountain. (Illus.). (J). 1992. 9.85 (*0-606-17970-4*) Turtleback.

— Farthest Away Mountain. 130p. (J). (gr. 3-5). pap. 4.50 (*0-8072-1499-X*) Listening Lib.

Banks, Lynne Reid. Harry the Poisonous Centipede. LC 96-16048. (Illus.). 160p. (J). (gr. 3-7). 1997. 15.00 (*0-688-14711-9*, Wm Morrow) Morrow Avon.

***Banks, Lynne Reid.** Harry the Poisonous Centipede. LC 96-16048. (Illus.). 128p. (J). (gr. 3-7). 1998. pap. 4.95 incl. audio (*0-380-72734-X*, Avon Bks) Morrow Avon.

— Harry the Poisonous Centipede. 118p. (J). (gr. 1-3). pap. 4.50 (*0-8072-1523-6*) Listening Lib.

— Harry the Poisonous Centipede II. (J). 2001. write for info. (*0-06-029139-7*) Morrow Avon.

— I, Houdini. 128p. (J). 1989. mass mkt. 4.99 (*0-380-70649-0*, Avon Bks) Morrow Avon.

— I, Houdini. 127p. (J). (gr. 4-5). pap. 4.99 (*0-8072-1493-0*) Listening Lib.

Banks, Lynne Reid. I, Houdini: The Amazing Story of an Escape-Artist Hamster. (J). 1978. 9.60 (*0-606-04254-7*, Pub. by Turtleback) Demco.

— I, Houdini: The Autobiography of a Self-Educated Hamster. LC 87-22284. (Illus.). 128p. (J). (gr. 5 up). 1988. 15.95 (*0-385-24482-7*) Doubleday.

— The Indian in the Cupboard. (Indian in the Cupboard Ser.: No. 1). (Illus.). (J). (gr. 4-7). 1980. 15.95 (*0-385-17060-2*, 088464) Doubleday.

— The Indian in the Cupboard. (Indian in the Cupboard Ser.: No. 1). (Illus.). 192p. (J). (gr. 4-7). 1985. 16.95 (*0-385-17051-3*) Doubleday.

Banks, Lynne Reid. The Indian in the Cupboard. (Indian in the Cupboard Ser.: No. 1). 181p. (J). (gr. 4-7). pap. 4.99 (*0-8072-1433-7*) Listening Lib.

Banks, Lynne Reid. The Indian in the Cupboard. (Indian in the Cupboard Ser.: No. 1). (J). (gr. 4-7). 1999. pap. 4.95 (*5-553-81211-9*, Avon Bks) Morrow Avon.

Banks, Lynne Reid. The Indian in the Cupboard. (Indian in the Cupboard Ser.: No. 1). (J). (gr. 4-7). 1982. 9.60 (*0-606-02215-5*, Pub. by Turtleback) Demco.

Banks, Lynne Reid. The Indian in the Cupboard. (Indian in the Cupboard Ser.: No. 1). 44p. (J). (gr. 4-7). 1998. 11.95 (*1-56137-693-0*, NU6930SP) Novel Units.

***Banks, Lynne Reid.** The Indian in the Cupboard. (Indian in the Cupboard Ser.: No. 1). 44p. (J). (gr. 4-7). 1999. 9.95 (*1-56137-225-0*) Novel Units.

— Indian in the Cupboard. (Indian in the Cupboard Ser.: No. 1). (Illus.). 192p. (J). (gr. 4-7). 1999. mass mkt. 4.99 (*0-380-60012-9*, Avon Bks) Morrow Avon.

Banks, Lynne Reid. Indian in the Cupboard. (Indian in the Cupboard Ser.). (Illus.). 208p. (J). (gr. 3-7). 1995. reprint ed. mass mkt. 4.99 (*0-380-72558-4*, Avon Bks) Morrow Avon.

— The Indian in the Cupboard: Mystery of the Cupboard, Secret of the Indian, Return of the Indian. (Indian in the Cupboard Ser.: Nos. 1, 2, 3). (J). (gr. 4-7). 1995. pap., boxed set 15.96 (*0-380-72643-2*, Avon Bks) Morrow Avon.

Banks, Lynne Reid. The Indian in the Cupboard Boxed Set. (Indian in the Cupboard Ser.: Nos. 1, 2, 3). (J). (gr. 4-7). 1994. boxed set 15.96 (*0-380-72404-9*, Avon Bks) Morrow Avon.

Banks, Lynne Reid. The Indian in the Cupboard Scrapbook. (Indian in the Cupboard Ser.). 32p. (J). (gr. 4-7). 1995. pap. 2.95 (*0-590-50983-7*) Scholastic Inc.

— The Indian in the Cupboard Study Guide. (Scholastic Literature Guide Ser.). 16p. (J). 1997. pap. text 3.95 (*0-590-37364-1*) Scholastic Inc.

— The Key to the Indian. LC 98-24972. (Indian in the Cupboard Ser.: No. 5). 240p. (J). (gr. 3-7). 1998. 16.00 (*0-380-97717-6*, Avon Bks) Morrow Avon.

— The Key to the Indian. LC 98-24972. (Indian in the Cupboard Ser.: No. 5). (Illus.). 240p. (J). (gr. 4-7). 1999. mass mkt. 4.99 (*0-380-80373-9*, Avon Bks) Morrow Avon.

Banks, Lynne Reid. The Key to the Indian. (Indian in the Cupboard Ser.: No. 5). 240p. (J). (gr. 5-7). pap. 4.99 (*0-8072-1551-1*) Listening Lib.

Banks, Lynne Reid. La Llave Magica. 1995. 15.05 (*0-606-10440-2*, Pub. by Turtleback) Demco.

— La Llave Magica: The Indian in the Cupboard. (ENG & SPA.). (J). 1996. pap. 8.95 (*84-241-3266-1*) Lectorum Pubns.

— Lynne Reid Banks, 3 vols. (J). (gr. 4-7). 1991. pap., boxed set 11.97 (*0-380-71680-1*, Avon Bks) Morrow Avon.

— The Magic Hare. LC 92-10585. (Illus.). 64p. (J). 1993. 15.00 (*0-688-10895-4*, Wm Morrow) Morrow Avon.

— The Magic Hare. LC 92-10585. 64p. (J). (gr. 4-7). 1994. mass mkt. 5.99 (*0-380-71562-7*, Avon Bks) Morrow Avon.

Banks, Lynne Reid. Magic Hare. LC 92-10585. 1993. 11.19 (*0-606-06551-2*, Pub. by Turtleback) Demco.

Banks, Lynne Reid. Maura's Angel. LC 97-50350. (Little Women Journals). 128p. (J). (gr. 3-7). 1998. 14.00 (*0-380-97590-4*, Avon Bks) Morrow Avon.

— Maura's Angel. LC 97-50350. 160p. (YA). (gr. 3-7). 1999. mass mkt. 4.99 (*0-380-79514-0*, Avon Bks) Morrow Avon.

Banks, Lynne Reid. Melusine. 256p. (YA). (gr. 5 up). 1997. mass mkt. 4.99 (*0-380-79135-8*, Avon Bks) Morrow Avon.

Banks, Lynne Reid. Melusine: A Mystery. LC 88-32798. (Charlotte Zolotow Bk.). 256p. (YA). (gr. 7 up). 1989. 12.95 (*0-06-020394-3*) HarpC Child Bks.

— Melusine: A Mystery. LC 88-32798. (Charlotte Zolotow Bk.). 224p. (YA). (gr. 7 up). 1991. mass mkt. 3.95 (*0-06-447054-7*, HarpTrophy) HarpC Child Bks.

— Melusine: A Mystery. 1997. 9.60 (*0-606-13604-5*, Pub. by Turtleback) Demco.

— Moses in Egypt: A Novel. (Prince of Egypt Ser.). (J). (gr. 2-5). 1998. pap. text 4.99 (*0-8499-5898-9*) Tommy Nelson.

— My Darling Villain. LC 76-58718. 240p. (YA). (gr. 7 up). 1977. 11.25 (*0-06-020392-7*) HarpC Child Bks.

Banks, Lynne Reid. The Mystery of the Cupboard. LC 92-39295. (Indian in the Cupboard Ser.: No. 4). (Illus.). 256p. (J). (gr. 4-7). 1993. 16.95 (*0-688-12138-1*, Wm Morrow); 15.93 (*0-688-12635-9*, Wm Morrow) Morrow Avon.

— The Mystery of the Cupboard. (Indian in the Cupboard Ser.: No. 4). 256p. (J). (gr. 4-7). 1999. mass mkt, 4.95 (*0-380-72013-2*, Avon Bks) Morrow Avon.

Banks, Lynne Reid. The Mystery of the Cupboard. (Indian in the Cupboard Ser.: No. 4). (J). (gr. 4-7). 1993. 9.60 (*0-606-05934-2*, Pub. by Turtleback) Demco.

Banks, Lynne Reid. The Mystery of the Cupboard. (Indian in the Cupboard Ser.: No. 4). 246p. (J). (gr. 4-7). pap. 4.99 (*0-8072-1459-0*) Listening Lib.

Banks, Lynne Reid. The Mystery of the Cupboard. (Indian in the Cupboard Ser.: No. 4). 224p. (J). (gr. 4-7). 1995. reprint ed. mass mkt. 4.50 (*0-380-72595-9*, Avon Bks) Morrow Avon.

B

B

Banks, Lynne Reid. One More River. 256p. (YA). (gr. 5 up). 1993. mass mkt. 4.99 (*0-380-71563-5*, Avon Bks) Morrow Avon.

Banks, Lynne Reid. One More River. 256p. (YA). (gr. 7 up). 1996. mass mkt. 4.50 (*0-380-72755-2*, Avon Bks) Morrow Avon.

Banks, Lynne Reid. One More River. 1992. 9.09 (*0-606-05525-8*, Pub. by Turtleback) Demco.

Banks, Lynne Reid. One More River. rev. ed. 256p. (YA). (gr. 5 up). 1992. 14.00 (*0-688-10893-8*, Wm Morrow) Morrow Avon.

— Prince of Egypt: The Novel. 128p. 1998. pap. 4.99 (*0-14-130217-8*, PuffinBks) Peng Put Young Read.

— The Return of the Indian. LC 85-31119. (Indian in the Cupboard Ser.: No.2). (Illus.). 192p. (J). (gr. 4-7). 1986. 15.95 (*0-385-23497-X*) Doubleday.

Banks, Lynne Reid. The Return of the Indian. (Indian in the Cupboard Ser.: No. 2). 189p. (J). (gr. 4-7). pap. 4.99 (*0-8072-1434-5*) Listening Lib.

— The Return of the Indian. (Indian in the Cupboard Ser.: No. 2). (Illus.). 208p. (J). (gr. 4-7). 1999. mass mkt. 4.99 (*0-380-70284-3*, Avon Bks) Morrow Avon.

— The Return of the Indian. (Indian in the Cupboard Ser.: No. 2). (J). (gr. 4-7). 1986. 9.09 (*0-606-03644-X*, Pub. by Turtleback) Demco.

— The Return of the Indian. (Indian in the Cupboard Ser.). (J). (gr. 4-7). 1999. 9.95 (*1-56137-232-3*) Novel Units.

— The Return of the Indian. large type unabridged ed. (Indian in the Cupboard Ser.). (J). (gr. 4-7). 1989. 22.95 incl. audio (*0-8161-9284-7*, G K Hall & Co) Mac Lib Ref.

Banks, Lynne Reid. The Return of the Indian. (Indian in the Cupboard Ser.: No. 2). 192p. (J). (gr. 4-7). 1995. reprint ed. mass mkt. 4.50 (*0-380-72593-2*, Avon Bks) Morrow Avon.

— The Secret of the Indian. LC 89-1272. (Indian in the Cupboard Ser.: No. 3). 160p. (J). (gr. 4-7). 1989. 15.95 (*0-385-26292-2*) Doubleday.

*__Banks, Lynne Reid.__ The Secret of the Indian. LC 89-1272. (Indian in the Cupboard Ser.: No. 2). (Illus.). 160p. (J). (gr. 3-7). 1999. mass mkt. 4.99 (*0-380-71040-4*, Avon Bks) Morrow Avon.

— The Secret of the Indian. (Indian in the Cupboard Ser.: No. 3). (J). (gr. 4-7). 1989. 9.60 (*0-606-04795-6*, Pub. by Turtleback) Demco.

Banks, Lynne Reid. The Secret of the Indian. (Indian in the Cupboard Ser.: No. 3). 176p. (J). (gr. 4-7). 1995. reprint ed. mass mkt. 4.50 (*0-380-72594-0*, Avon Bks) Morrow Avon.

— The Writing on the Wall. LC 81-47796. (Charlotte Zolotow Bk.). 256p. (YA). (gr. 7 up). 1982. 12.95 (*0-06-020388-9*) HarpC Child Bks.

Banks, M. M., ed. Alphabetum Narrationum: An Alphabet of Tales. (EETS, OS Ser.: Nos. 126-7). 1972. reprint ed. 75.00 (*0-527-00122-8*) Periodicals Srv.

— British Calendar Customs, Orkney & Shetland. (Folk-Lore Society, London Monographs: Vol. 112). 1972. reprint ed. 40.00 (*0-8115-0543-X*) Periodicals Srv.

— British Calendar Customs, Scotland Vol. I: Movable Festivals, Harvest, March Ridings & Wappynshaws, Wells, Fairs. (Folk-Lore Society, London Monographs: Vol. 100). 1972. reprint ed. pap. 30.00 (*0-8115-0537-5*) Periodicals Srv.

— British Calendar Customs, Scotland Vol. II: Fixed Festivals, The Quarters, Hogmanay, January to March, Inclusive. (Folk-Lore Society, London Monographs: Vol. 104). 1972. reprint ed. pap. 30.00 (*0-8115-0539-1*) Periodicals Srv.

Banks, Marcus. Ethnicity: Anthropological Constructions. LC 95-33348. 224p. (C). 1996. pap. 22.99 (*0-415-07801-6*) Routledge.

— Organizing Jainism in India & England. (Oxford Studies in Social & Cultural Anthropology). (Illus.). 282p. 1992. text 75.00 (*0-19-827388-6*) OUP.

— Rethinking Visual Anthropology. (Illus.). 304p. 1999. pap. text 18.00 (*0-300-07854-4*) Yale U Pr.

Banks, Marcus & Morphy, Howard. Rethinking Visual Anthropology. LC 96-35202. (Illus.). 304p. 1997. 40.00 (*0-300-06691-0*) Yale U Pr.

*__Banks, Martin.__ Chimpanzee. (Natural World Ser.). (J). 2000. pap. 7.95 (*0-7398-1817-1*) Raintree Steck-V.

— Chimpanzee: Habitats, Life Cycles, Food Chains, Threats. LC 99-35397. (Natural World Ser.). 48p. (J). 2000. lib. bdg. 25.69 (*0-7398-1062-6*) Raintree Steck-V.

Banks, Martin. How Monkeys "Talk" LC 98-20530. (Nature's Mysteries Ser.). (J). 1998. lib. bdg. 22.79 (*0-7614-0858-4*) Marshall Cavendish.

Banks, Mary M. Coffee. (World Encyclopedia of ... Ser.). 1999. 40.00 (*0-7548-0197-7*, Lorenz Bks) Anness Pub.

— Coffee: A Gourmet's Guide. 1999. 14.95 (*1-85868-610-5*, Pub. by Carlton Bks Ltd) Natl Bk Netwk.

Banks, Mary M., ed. see Robert of Thornton.

Banks, Melvin. Is Anything Too Hard for God? pap. 6.99 (*0-551-02105-5*) Zondervan.

— Power for Living. pap. 5.99 (*0-551-01881-X*) Zondervan.

Banks, Melvin E., Sr. Wisdom from Above. 1998. pap. text 7.95 (*0-940955-43-1*) Urban Ministries.

*__Banks, Melvin E., Sr., ed.__ God Delivers on His Promise: Based on Old Testament Scriptures. 116p. 1999. pap. text 7.95 (*0-940955-56-3*, 1-11) Urban Ministries.

— Good News about Jesus Christ: Based on Selected New Testament Scriptures. 164p. 1998. pap. text 7.95 (*0-940955-49-0*, 1-11) Urban Ministries.

— In the Beginning: Based on the Book of Genesis. 105p. 1999. pap. text 7.95 (*0-940955-52-0*, 1-11) Urban Ministries.

— Jesus, King of Kings: 13 Life-Changing Group Studies. 118p. 1999. pap. text 7.95 (*0-940955-58-X*) Urban Ministries.

— Life in Jesus, God's Son: Based on the Gospel of John. 162p. 1999. pap. text 7.95 (*0-940955-51-2*, 1-11) Urban Ministries.

*__Banks, Melvin E., ed.__ The Unfolding Story of God's Salvation Plan: Based on Old Testament Scriptures. 110p. 1998. text 7.95 (*0-940955-48-2*, 1-11) Urban Ministries.

Banks, Melvin E., Sr., jt. auth. see Trimiew, Oliver, Jr.

Banks, Merry. Animals of the Night. LC 89-6194. (Illus.). 32p. (J). (ps). 1990. text, lib. bdg. 13.95 (*0-684-19093-1*) Scribner.

Banks, Michael. Malibu. LC 91-33456. 160p. (Orig.). 1992. pap. 6.95 (*1-56474-014-5*) Fithian Pr.

— Microsoft Word 97. 10th ed. LC 98-4560. (Exam Cram Ser.). xxv, 437 p. (C). 1999. mass mkt. 26.99 (*1-57610-222-X*) Coriolis Grp.

— One-Stop CompuServe for Windows. 89p. 1995. pap. 34.95 incl. cd-rom (*1-55828-463-X*, MIS Pr) IDG Bks.

— Web Psychos, Stalkers, & Pranksters: How to Protect Yourself in Cyberspace. 1997. pap. 24.99 (*0-614-28446-5*) Coriolis Grp.

— Welcome to Compuserve for Windows. LC 94-14528. 1994. pap. 24.95 incl. disk (*1-55828-353-6*, MIS Pr) IDG Bks.

Banks, Michael, jt. auth. see Coulter, William.

Banks, Michael, jt. auth. see Mitchell, Chris.

Banks, Michael A. Delphi: The Official Guide. 2nd rev. ed. Matthes, Chip, ed. 300p. 1990. reprint ed. pap. text 19.95 (*0-9625623-0-0*) Genl Videotex.

— The Internet Unplugged: Utilities & Techniques for Internet Productivity...Online & Off. Eamon, Donald, ed. LC 98-138319. (Illus.). 251p. (Orig.). 1997. pap. 29.95 (*0-910965-24-2*) Info Today Inc.

— The Modem Reference: The Complete Guide to PC Communications. 4th ed. (C). 2000. pap. 29.95 (*0-910965-36-6*) Info Today Inc.

*__Banks, Michael A.__ PC Confidential: Secure Your PC & Privacy from Snoops, Spies, Spouses, Supervisors & Credit Card Thieves. 288p. 2000. pap. 24.99 incl. cd-rom (*0-7821-2747-9*) Sybex.

Banks, Michael A., et al. Careers & Identities. 224p. 1991. 123.00 (*0-335-09715-4*); pap. 34.95 (*0-335-09714-6*) OpUniv Pr.

Banks, Michael A., jt. auth. see Cannon, Robert L.

Banks, Mike. Mountain Climbing for Beginners. 1978. 8.95 (*0-8128-2448-2*, Scrbrough Hse) Madison Bks UPA.

Banks, Nannette E. Black Etc. And Everything Else My Soul Has to Offer. Johnson, Brian A., ed. (Illus.). 32p. 1999. lib. bdg. 12.00 (*0-9650204-6-0*) Neurotechtonics.

Banks, Natalie N. The Golden Thread: The Continuity of Esoteric Teaching. 2nd ed. 62p. 1999. reprint ed. pap. 5.00 (*0-85330-127-1*) Lucis.

Banks, Nathaniel. The Curate's Play. 1962. pap. 3.25 (*0-8222-0259-X*) Dramatists Play.

Banks, Nathaniel P., et al. Report of a General Plan for the Promotion of Public & Personal Health. LC 70-180589. (Medicine & Society in America Ser.). 554p. 1972. reprint ed. 31.95 (*0-405-03971-9*) Ayer.

Banks, Nick & University of Birmingham,UK Staff. White Counsellors - Black Clients: Theory, Research & Practice. LC HV3177.G7B36 1999. (Interdisciplinary Research Series in Ethnic, Gender & Class Relations). 312p. 1999. text 65.95 (*1-84014-146-8*) Ashgate Pub Co.

Banks, Olive, jt. auth. see Banks, J. A.

Banks, Oliver. The Politics of British Feminism, 1918-1970. 160p. 1993. 85.00 (*1-85278-108-4*) E Elgar.

Banks, Orianna & Tanqueray, Rebecca. Lofts: Living in Space. 192p. 1999. pap. 29.95 (*0-7893-0361-2*, Pub. by Universe) St Martin.

Banks, P. M. & Kockarts, G. Aeronomy. Incl. Set. 1973. 50.50 write for info. (*0-318-50223-2*) Acad Pr.

Banks, Pat & Davidson, Carolyn. Where Grandma Lives, Love Is Forever. (Illus.). 34p. (J). (gr. 3-6). 1998. 7.50 (*1-56469-033-4*) Harmony Hse Pub.

*__Banks, Paul, ed.__ The Making of Peter Grimes: Essays. (Aldeburgh Studies in Music). (Illus.). 298p. 2000. pap. 35.00 (*0-85115-791-2*) Boydell & Brewer.

Banks, Paul, ed. The Making of Peter Grimes: The Facsimile of Britten's Composition Draft. 256p. (C). 1996. 170.00 (*0-85115-632-0*) Boydell & Brewer.

Banks, Paul, ed. see Mitchell, Donald.

Banks-Payne, Ruby. Ruby's Low-Fat Soul Food Cookbook. 192p. 1996. pap. 12.95 (*0-8092-3153-0*, 315300, Contemporary Bks) NTC Contemp Pub Co.

Banks, Peter, et al. The Biochemistry of the Tissues. 2nd ed. LC 75-26739. 509p. reprint ed. pap. 157.80 (*0-8357-7221-7*, 205224100069) Bks Demand.

Banks, Peter A., jt. auth. see Lankisch, P. G.

Banks, Peter A., ed. see National Foundation for Ileitis & Colitis Staff.

Banks, Peter M. & Doupnik, J. R. Introduction to Computer Science. LC 75-20407. (Illus.). 378p. reprint ed. pap. 117.20 (*0-7837-3425-5*, 205774600008) Bks Demand.

Banks, Peter M. & Kraybill, William G. Pathology for the Surgeon. McGrew, Larry, ed. LC 95-11487. 416p. 1996. text 77.00 (*0-7216-5288-3*, W B Saunders Co) Harcrt Hlth Sci Grp.

Banks, Phyllis M. & Burke, Virginia M., eds. Black Americans: Images in Conflict. LC 72-121891. (Composition & Rhetoric Ser.). (Orig.). (C). 1970. pap. write for info. (*0-672-61177-5*, CR4, Bobbs) Macmillan.

Banks-Pye, Roger. Colefax & Fowler's Interior Inspirations. LC 96-78531. 192p. 1997. 45.00 (*0-8212-2333-X*, Pub. by Bulfinch Pr) Little.

*__Banks, R. E.__ Fluorine Chemistry at the Millennium: Fascinated by Fluorine. LC 00-26273. 2000. write for info. (*0-08-043405-3*) Elsevier.

Banks, R. E., et al, eds. Sir Joseph Banks: A Global Perspective. (Illus.). ii, 235p. 1994. pap. 24.00 (*0-947643-61-3*, Pub. by Royal Botnic Grdns) Balogh.

Banks, R. E., et al. Organofluorine Chemistry: Principles & Commercial Applications. (Topics in Applied Chemistry Ser.). (Illus.). 670p. (C). 1994. text 135.00 (*0-306-44610-3*, Kluwer Plenum) Kluwer Academic.

Banks, Ridgway. Echoes, for Voice & Piano. (Contemporary Vocal Ser.: No. 2). 4p. 1990. pap. text 3.00 (*1-56571-021-5*) PRB Prods.

— Maacama Trio for ATB Recorders. (Contemporary Consort Ser.: No. 1). 21p. 1989. pap. text 8.00 (*1-56571-006-1*) PRB Prods.

— Thirteen Propositions for Piano Solo. (Contemporary Keyboard Ser.: No. 4). i, 9p. 1990. pap. text 10.00 (*1-56571-017-7*) PRB Prods.

— Three Chanteys for Violin, Clarinet & Piano. (Contemporary Instrumental Ser.: No. 2). i, 19p. 1989. pap. text 10.00 (*1-56571-019-3*) PRB Prods.

*__Banks, Robert.__ Faith Goes to Work: Reflections from the Marketplace. 190p. (Orig.). 1999. pap. 19.00 (*1-57910-329-4*) Wipf & Stock.

Banks, Robert. Going to Church in the First Century. (Illus.). 60p. (Orig.). 1990. pap. 5.95 (*0-940232-37-5*) Seedsowers.

— Paul's Idea of Community: The Early House Churches in Their Cultural Setting. rev. ed. LC 94-30999. 234p. 1994. pap. 12.95 (*1-56563-050-5*) Hendrickson MA.

— Redeeming the Routines: Bringing Theology to Life. LC 92-41788. 200p. (C). 1993. pap. text 15.99 (*0-8010-2116-2*, Bridgept Bks) Baker Bks.

— Reenvisioning Theological Education: Exploring a Missional Alternative to Current Models. LC 99-32101. 272p. 1999. pap. 20.00 (*0-8028-4620-3*) Eerdmans.

— Slicing Pizzas, Racing Turtles & Further Adventures in Applied Mathematics. LC 98-53513. 1999. 24.95 (*0-691-05947-0*, Pub. by Princeton U Pr) Cal Prin Full Svc.

— The Tyranny of Time: When 24 Hours Is Not Enough. 265p. 1997. pap. 20.00 (*1-57910-029-5*) Wipf & Stock.

Banks, Robert, ed. Faith Goes to Work: Reflections from the Marketplace. LC 93-71925. 190p. (Orig.). 1993. pap. 16.95 (*1-56699-115-3*, AL144) Alban Inst.

Banks, Robert & Banks, Julia. The Church Comes Home: Building Community & Mission Through Home Churches. LC 97-16954. 260p. 1998. pap. 14.95 (*1-56563-179-X*) Hendrickson MA.

Banks, Robert & Entman, June. Tennessee Civil Procedure. LC 99-60819. 950p. 1999. 105.00 (*0-327-00949-7*, 60135-10) LEXIS Pub.

*__Banks, Robert & Powell, Kimberly, eds.__ Faith in Leadership: How Leaders Live Out Their Faith in Their Work - And Why It Matters. 272p. 2000. 24.00 (*0-7879-4586-2*, Pfiffr & Co) Jossey-Bass.

Banks, Robert B. Towing Icebergs, Falling Dominoes & Other Adventures in Applied Mathematics. LC 98-4557. (Illus.). 326p. 1998. 29.95 (*0-691-05948-9*, Pub. by Princeton U Pr) Cal Prin Full Svc.

Banks, Robert J. & Stevens, R. Paul, eds. The Complete Book of Everyday Christianity: An A-To-Z Guide to Following Christ in Every Aspect of Life. xiv, 1166p. 1999. pap. 24.99 (*0-8308-1454-X*, 1454) InterVarsity.

Banks, Robert O., jt. ed. see Sperelakis, Nicholas.

Banks, Roderick L. Lindley & Banks on Partnerships. 17th ed. 1994. 232.00 (*0-421-48260-5*, Pub. by Sweet & Maxwll) Gaunt.

Banks, Ronald. Rights: You Pay the Bills. 88p. 1997. 11.95 (*1-901647-09-9*, Pub. by Othila Pr) Intl Spec Bk.

Banks, Ronald, ed. Costing the Earth. 196p. (Orig.). 1989. pap. 10.00 (*0-85683-111-5*, Pub. by Shepheard-Walwyn Pubs) Paul & Co Pubs.

Banks, Russell. Affliction. LC 89-45075. 368p. 1990. pap. 13.00 (*0-06-092007-6*, Perennial) HarperTrade.

— The Angel on the Roof: The Stories of Russell Banks. LC 99-55738. 512p. 2000. 27.50 (*0-06-017396-3*) HarpC.

— The Book of Jamaica. LC 95-53321. 1996. write for info. (*0-614-95864-4*, Perennial) HarperTrade.

— Book of Jamaica. LC 95-53321. 352p. 1996. pap. 13.00 (*0-06-097707-8*) HarpC.

*__Banks, Russell.__ Cloudsplitter: A Novel. LC 97-22163. 768p. 1998. 27.50 (*0-06-016860-9*, HarperFlamingo) HarpC.

Banks, Russell. Cloudsplitter: A Novel. LC 97-22163. 768p. 1999. pap. 15.00 (*0-06-093086-1*) HarpC.

— Continental Drift. LC 84-48137. 384p. 1994. pap. 13.50 (*0-06-092574-4*) HarperTrade.

*__Banks, Russell.__ Continental Drift. 400p. 2000. pap. 14.00 (*0-06-095673-9*, Perennial) HarperTrade.

Banks, Russell. Family Life. LC 95-53323. 144p. (Orig.). 1996. pap. 12.00 (*0-06-097704-3*) HarpC.

— Family Life. (Orig.). 1996. write for info. (*0-614-96296-X*, Perennial) HarperTrade.

— Hamilton Stark. LC 95-53320. 320p. 1996. pap. 13.00 (*0-06-097705-1*) HarpC.

— Hamilton Stark. LC 95-53320. 1996. write for info. (*0-614-95863-6*, Perennial) HarperTrade.

— The Invisible Stranger: The Patten, Maine, Photographs of Arturo Patten. LC 98-49395. (Illus.). 80p. 1999. 32.50 (*0-06-019234-8*) HarpC.

— The New World: Stories. LC 78-10646. (Illinois Short Fiction Ser.). 144p. 1996. 11.95 (*0-252-00722-0*) U of Ill Pr.

— The Relation of My Imprisonment. LC 83-17873. 121p. 1984. 12.95 (*0-940650-25-8*) Sun & Moon CA.

— The Relation of My Imprisonment. deluxe limited ed. LC 83-17873. 124p. 1984. 20.00 (*0-940650-24-X*) Sun & Moon CA.

— Relation of My Imprisonment: Fiction By, A. LC 96-143049. 128p. 1996. pap. 11.00 (*0-06-097680-2*) HarpC.

— Rule of the Bone: Novel, A. LC 95-11701. 400p. 1996. pap. 13.00 (*0-06-092724-0*) HarpC.

— Stories. Date not set. 14.00 (*0-06-093125-6*) HarpC.

— Success Stories. LC 95-53322. 208p. 1996. pap. 12.00 (*0-06-092719-4*) HarpC.

— Success Stories. LC 95-53322. 1996. write for info. (*0-614-95865-2*, Perennial) HarperTrade.

— Sweet Hereafter Movie Tie-In: A Novel. LC 90-56404. 272p. 1997. pap. 13.00 (*0-06-092324-5*, Perennial) HarperTrade.

— Trailerpark. LC 95-53310. 288p. 1996. pap. 13.00 (*0-06-097706-X*) HarpC.

— Trailerpark. LC 95-53310. 1996. write for info. (*0-614-95862-8*, Perennial) HarperTrade.

Banks, Russell & Twichell, Chase, eds. Ploughshares Winter, 1993-94: Borderlands. 231p. (Orig.). (C). 1993. pap. 8.95 (*0-933277-09-1*) Ploughshares.

*__Banks, Ryan C.__ Brace Yourself. 72p. 1999. pap. 12.95 (*0-9673480-0-5*) R C Banks.

Banks, S. & Bank, J. 1001 Ways to Pass Organic Chemistry. 2nd ed. (One Thousand One Ways to Pass Ser.). 312p. (C). 1997. pap. text, suppl. ed. 9.50 (*0-03-020692-8*) SCP.

Banks, Samuel L., ed. The Education of Black Children & Youths: A Framework for Educational Excellence. LC 85-80933. 91p. (Orig.). (C). 1985. pap. 9.95 (*0-935132-04-X*) C H Fairfax.

Banks, Sara H. A Net to Catch Time. (Illus.). (J). 1996. lib. bdg. 17.99 (*0-679-96673-0*) Random.

Banks, Sara H. Tomo-Chi-Chi: Gentle Warrior. pap. 12.95 (*0-913720-79-8*) Beil.

Banks, Sara H. Under the Shadow of Wings. LC 96-21180. 160p. (J). 1999. mass mkt. 4.50 (*0-689-82436-X*) Aladdin.

— The Way Was Through Woods: The Story of Tomo-Chi-Chi. 2nd ed. LC 93-85477. 92p. (J). (gr. 5 up). 1993. pap. 7.95 (*1-879373-59-9*) Roberts Rinehart.

Banks, Sarah. Ethical Issues in Youth Work. LC 98-38315. (Professional Ethics Ser.). 1999. 75.00 (*0-415-16500-8*); pap. 24.99 (*0-415-16501-6*) Routledge.

Banks, Sarah Harrell. Abraham's Battle: A Novel of Gettysburg. LC 98-21108. 96p. (J). (gr. 4-6). 1999. 15.00 (*0-689-81779-7*) S&S Childrens.

— Under the Shadow of Wings. LC 96-21180. 160p. (J). 1997. 15.00 (*0-689-81207-8*) S&S Childrens.

Banks, Smith C., jt. auth. see Presley, Delma E.

*__Banks, Stephen.__ Multicultural Public Relations: A Social-Interpretive Approach. 2nd ed. (Illus.). 184p. 2000. 39.95 (*0-8138-2940-2*) Iowa St U Pr.

Banks, Stephen G., et al. New Fitness Formula. (Orig.). 1990. pap. text 7.95 (*0-9627708-0-9*) NordicPress.

Banks, Stephen P. Multicultural Public Relations: A Social-Interpretive Approach. (Communicating Effectively in Multicultural Contexts Ser.: Vol. 4). 145p. 1995. text 36.00 (*0-8039-4840-9*); pap. text 17.95 (*0-8039-4841-7*) Sage.

Banks, Stephen P., et al. Foundations of Organizational Communication: A Reader. 2nd ed. LC 94-28286. 389p. (C). 1994. pap. text 52.00 (*0-8013-1252-3*) Longman.

Banks, Stephen P., jt. ed. see Banks, Anna.

Banks, Stephen P., ed. see IFAC Symposium Staff.

Banks, Steve. Janis' Garden Party. limited ed. (Illus.). 75p. (Orig.). 1997. write for info. (*0-9658205-1-3*) Bugiganga Pr.

— Janis' Garden Party. limited ed. (Illus.). 68p. (Orig.). 1998. pap. 19.95 (*0-9658205-0-5*) Bugiganga Pr.

*__Banks, Steven & Galan, Manny.__ A Space Oddity. (Catdog Tales Ser.). 144p. (gr. 4-7). 2000. 3.99 (*0-689-83363-6*, Simon Spot) Litle Simon.

*__Banks, Steven R.__ Catdog: Undercover. 64p. 2000. pap. 3.99 (*0-689-83009-2*) S&S Childrens.

— Catdog's Vacation. 64p. 2000. pap. 3.99 (*0-689-83008-4*) S&S Childrens.

Banks, Steven R. & Thompson, Charles L. Educational Psychology: For Teachers in Training. LC 94-34058. 450p. (C). 1995. 79.95 (*0-314-04443-4*) West Pub.

Banks, Sue. Fun with the Autoharp. (Fun Bks.). 32p. 1971. pap. 4.95 (*0-87166-431-3*, 93289) Mel Bay.

Banks, Sue & Bay, William. Easy Way Christmas Song Folio - Piano. 20p. 1972. pap. 4.95 (*0-87166-845-9*, 93313) Mel Bay.

Banks, Sue, jt. auth. see Banks, Bill.

Banks, Susan B. The Little Skunk. (Illus.). 40p. (J). (ps-7). 1995. 10.99 (*0-89228-120-0*) Impact Christian.

Banks, Susan V. & Orr, Carol A. The Beginning of Something Good: 25 Romantic Recipes. (Illus.). 52p. 1997. spiral bd. 7.95 (*0-9656177-0-X*) C & S Books.

Banks, Syd. In Quest of the Pearl. 113p. 1990. 10.95 (*0-937713-02-3*) Duval-Bibb.

— Second Chance. 2nd ed. 91p. 1989. reprint ed. pap. 6.95 (*0-937713-04-X*) Duval-Bibb.

— Second Chance. 2nd ed. 91p. 1990. reprint ed. 10.95 (*0-937713-01-5*) Duval-Bibb.

Banks, Sydney. Missing Link: Reflections on Philosophy & Spirit. 160p. 1998. 12.95 (*0-9681645-0-1*); lthr. 19.95 (*0-9681645-2-8*) Lone Pine.

Banks, Theodore H. Wild Geese. LC 73-144741. (Yale Series of Younger Poets: No. 7). reprint ed. 18.00 (*0-404-53807-X*) AMS Pr.

Banks, Theodore L. Antitrust Law, Set. 1792p. 1992. 295.00 (*0-316-08034-9*, Aspen Law & Bus) Aspen Pub.

— Distribution Law. 1989. 145.00 (*0-316-08023-3*, Aspen Law & Bus) Aspen Pub.

— Distribution Law: Antitrust Principles & Practice 2nd ed. LC 98-43651. 1993. ring bd. 310.00 (*0-7355-0268-4*) Panel Pubs.

Banks, Theodore M. Distribution Law for the Practitioner. write for info. (*0-318-59310-6*, Aspen Law & Bus) Aspen Pub.

Banks, Theodore R., jt. auth. see Molnar, J. J.

An Asterisk (*) at the beginning of an entry indicates that the title is appearing for the first time.

B

An Asterisk (*) at the beginning of an entry indicates that the title is appearing for the first time.

Bannerji, Kaushalya. The Faces of Five O'Clock. LC 97-113268. 64p. Date not set. pap. 9.95 (*1-896705-10-3*) Sister Vis Pr.

Bannerman, Carol, ed. see Pitman, Bonnie.

Bannerman, Colin. A Friend in the Kitchen: Old Australian Cookery Books. LC 97-103753. (Illus.). 192p. 1997. pap. 16.95 (*0-86417-805-0*, Pub. by Kangaroo Pr) Seven Hills Bk.

Bannerman, Elizabeth, ed. see Chase, Emily.

Bannerman, Gary. Bon Voyage! The Cruise Traveler's Handbook. (Illus.). 256p. 1991. pap. 9.95 (*0-8442-9547-7*, Passprt Bks) NTC Contemp Pub Co.

Bannerman, Glenn Q. & Fakkema, Robert E. Guide for Recreation Leaders. 2nd rev. ed. Graham, Mary, ed. LC 98-2659. (Illus.). 172p. 1998. pap. 9.95 (*1-57895-023-6*, Bridge Res) Curriculm Presbytrn KY.

Bannerman, Glenn Q. & Pugsley, M. Neil. Recreation with Dance, Movement, & Music. LC 98-33190. 1999. 11.95 (*1-57895-026-0*, Bridge Res) Curriculm Presbytrn KY.

Bannerman, Helen. Cotillion. 64p. 1983. reprint ed. lib. bdg. 26.95 (*0-89966-127-0*) Buccaneer Bks.

— The Little Black Sambo Story Book. 64p. 1983. reprint ed. lib. bdg. 25.95 (*0-89966-298-6*) Buccaneer Bks.

— The Story of Little Babaji. LC 96-84139. (Michael di Capua Bks.). (Illus.). 72p. (J). (ps-3). 1996. 14.95 (*0-06-205064-8*); lib. bdg. 14.89 (*0-06-205065-6*) HarpC Child Bks.

— The Story of Little Black Mingo. (Illus.). 72p. (J). (ps-4). 1990. reprint ed. 12.95 (*0-9616844-5-3*) Greenhouse Pub.

— The Story of Little Black Quibba. (Illus.). 68p. (J). (ps-4). 1990. reprint ed. 12.95 (*0-9616844-4-5*) Greenhouse Pub.

— The Story of Little Black Sambo. (Illus.). 24p. (J). (gr. k-4). 1994. 16.95 (*0-87797-265-6*) Cherokee.

— The Story of Little Black Sambo. (Illus.). 58p. (J). 1996. 25.00 (*0-9616844-8-8*) Greenhouse Pub.

— The Story of Little Black Sambo. LC 58-88. (Illus.). 64p. (J). (gr. k-3). 1923. 15.95 (*0-397-30006-9*) HarperTrade.

— The Story of Little Black Sambo. large type ed. (Illus.). 58p. (J). 1986. pap. 12.95 (*0-9616844-1-0*) Greenhouse Pub.

— The Story of Little Black Sambo. LC 95-82095. (Wee Books for Wee Folks). (Illus.). 61p. (J). (gr. 4-7). 1996. reprint ed. 6.95 (*1-55709-414-4*) Applewood.

— Tigers for Supper. LC 98-60515. (Domino Readers Ser.). (Illus.). 24p. (J). (ps-1). 1998. pap. 5.95 (*1-887734-36-8*) Star Brght Bks.

Bannerman, J. W. M., jt. auth. see Steer, K. A.

Bannerman, John. The Beatons: A Medical Kindred in the Classical Gaelic Tradition. 176p. 1998. pap. 45.00 (*0-85976-489-3*, Pub. by J Donald) St Mut.

— Studies in the History of Dalriada. LC 75-301815. ix, 178p. 1974. write for info. (*0-7011-2040-1*) Chatto & Windus.

***Bannerman, Mark.** The Beckoning Noose. large type ed. 240p. 1999. pap. 18.99 (*0-7089-5550-9*, Linford) Ulverscroft.

— The Early Lynching. large type ed. 240p. pap. 18.99 (*0-7089-5413-8*) Ulverscroft.

Bannerman, Mark. Escape to Purgatory. large type ed. (Linford Western Large Print Ser.). 272p. 1998. pap. 17.99 (*0-7089-5280-1*, Linford) Ulverscroft.

***Bannerman, Mark.** Grand Valley Feud. large type ed. 264p. 2000. pap. 18.99 (*0-7089-5622-X*, Linford) Ulverscroft.

— Man Without a Yesterday. large type ed. 256p. 1999. pap. 18.99 (*0-7089-5515-0*, Linford) Ulverscroft.

— Renegade Rose. 264p. 2000. 18.99 (*0-7089-5682-3*) Ulverscroft.

Bannerman, Patrick. Islam in Perspective: A Guide to Islamic Society, Politics Law. 304p. 1989. 35.00 (*0-415-01015-2*, A3440) Routledge.

Bannerman, R. LeRoy. Norman Corwin & Radio: The Golden Years. LC 85-1028. (Illus.). 294p. 1986. pap. 91.20 (*0-608-05128-4*, 206568700005) Bks Demand.

Bannerman, R. LeRoy & Barnouw, Erik. On a Note of Triumph: Norman Corwin & the Golden Years of Radio. (Illus.). 275p. reprint ed. pap. 8.95 (*0-8184-0512-0*) Carol Pub Group.

***Bannerot, Scott & Bannerot, Wendy.** The Cruiser's Handbook of Fishing. LC 99-47114. (Illus.). 352p. 1999. 34.95 (*0-07-134560-4*) McGraw-Hill Prof.

Bannerot, Wendy, jt. auth. see Bannerot, Scott.

Bannet, J., jt. ed. see Belmaker, R. H.

Bannett, Eve T. Postcultural Theory. 240p. 1994. pap. 15.95 (*1-56924-891-5*) Marlowe & Co.

Bannikov, Aleksandre F. & Tyler, James C. Phylogenetic Revision of the Fish Families Luvaridae & Kushlukiidae (Acanthuroidei), with a New Genus & Two New Species of Eocene Luvarids. LC 95-1795. (Smithsonian Contributions to Paleobiology Ser.: Vol. 81). 49p. 1995. reprint ed. pap. 30.00 (*0-608-00513-4*, 206133400008) Bks Demand.

Bannikov, Alexandre F., jt. auth. see Tyler, James C.

Banning, Bill. Heritage Years: Second Marine Division Commemorative Anthology 1940-1949. LC 88-50051. (Illus.). 192p. 1989. 39.95 (*0-938021-58-3*) Turner Pub KY.

Banning, James H., jt. auth. see Strange, C. Carney.

Banning, Kent. Opportunities in Purchasing Careers. 160p. 1989. 14.95 (*0-8442-8669-9*, VGM Career) NTC Contemp Pub Co.

— Opportunities in Purchasing Careers. LC 97-29044. (Opportunities in . . . Ser.). 160p. 1997. 14.95 (*0-8442-2327-1*, VGM Career); pap. 12.95 (*0-8442-8670-2*, 297OIPUR, VGM Career); pap. 11.95 (*0-8442-2329-8*, VGM Career) NTC Contemp Pub Co.

***Banning, Kent & Friday, Ardelle.** Change Your Career. LC 98-8253. (Here's How Ser.). 192p. 1998. pap. 16.95 (*0-8442-6628-0*, 66280) NTC Contemp Pub Co.

Banning, Kent, jt. auth. see Shivell, Kirk.

Banning, Kent B. Opportunities in Franchising Careers. rev. ed. LC 95-30141. (VGM Opportunities Ser.). (Illus.). 160p. 1995. 14.95 (*0-8442-4433-3*, 44333, VGM Career) NTC Contemp Pub Co.

Banning, Kent B. & Friday, Ardelle. How to Change Your Career. 192p. 1993. pap. 9.95 (*0-8442-8685-0*, VGM Career) NTC Contemp Pub Co.

— Planning Your Career Change. 1995. pap. 6.95 (*0-8442-6688-4*, Passprt Bks) NTC Contemp Pub Co.

Banning, Kent B. & Friday, Ardelle F. Time for a Change: The Re-Entry & Re-Career Workbook. LC 95-2573. (Illus.). 192p. 1995. pap. 9.95 (*0-8442-4396-5*, 43965, VGM Career) NTC Contemp Pub Co.

Banning, Lance. Jefferson & Madison: Three Conversations from the Founding. (Merril Jensen Lectures). 256p. 1995. text 27.95 (*0-945612-42-7*); pap. text 17.95 (*0-945612-48-6*) Madison Hse.

— The Jeffersonian Persuasion: Evolution of a Party Ideology. LC 77-14666. 307p. 1978. text 47.50 (*0-8014-1151-3*); pap. text 17.95 (*0-8014-9200-9*) Cornell U Pr.

— The Sacred Fire of Liberty: James Madison & the Founding of the Federal Republic. LC 95-14369. (Illus.). 536p. 1995. text 45.00 (*0-8014-3152-2*) Cornell U Pr.

— The Sacred Fire of Liberty: James Madison & the Founding of the Federal Republic. (Illus.). 536p. 1998. pap. 17.95 (*0-8014-8524-X*) Cornell U Pr.

Banning, Leroy F. Banning Branches. LC 94-209900. 414p. (Orig.). 1994. pap. text 30.00 (*1-55613-957-8*) Heritage Bk.

— Banning Branches. rev. ed. iv, 189p. (Orig.). 1997. pap. 33.00 (*0-7884-0726-0*, B056) Heritage Bk.

— Regimental History of the 35th Alabama Infantry, 1862-1865. (Illus.). 152p. 1999. pap. 18.00 (*0-7884-1133-0*, B057) Heritage Bk.

Banning, Lynna. Lost Acres Bride. 1998. per. 4.99 (*0-373-29037-3*, 1-29037-8) Harlequin Bks.

— Plum Creek Bride. 1999. per. 4.99 (*0-373-29074-8*, 1-29074-1) Harlequin Bks.

— Western Rose (March Madness) (Historical Ser.). 1996. per. 4.50 (*0-373-28910-3*, 1-28910-7) Harlequin Bks.

— Wildwood. (Historical Ser.: No. 374). 1997. per. 4.99 (*0-373-28974-X*, 1-28974-3) Harlequin Bks.

Banning, Margaret C. Country Club People. 1976. lib. bdg. 14.85 (*0-89968-006-2*, Lghtyr Pr) Buccaneer Bks.

— Spellbinders. 1976. lib. bdg. 14.35 (*0-89968-008-9*, Lghtyr Pr) Buccaneer Bks.

Banning, William. Six Horses. 1992. reprint ed. lib. bdg. 75.00 (*0-7812-5006-4*) Rprt Serv.

Banninga, Simon & Sarig, Oded. Corporate Finance: A Valuation Approach. LC 96-7925. (Series in Finance). (Illus.). 446p. (C). 1996. 75.63 (*0-07-005099-6*) McGraw.

Bannink, B. A., ed. Integration of Ecological Aspects in Coastal Engineering Projects: Proceedings of a Symposium Held in Rotterdam, The Netherlands, June 6-10, 1983, Set, Vol. 16: 1-4. LC 83-25745. (Illus.). 800p. 1984. pap. 175.00 (*0-08-031036-2*, Pergamon Pr) Elsevier.

Banninster, Jim E. & Bawcutt, Paul A. Practical Risk Management. 240p. (C). 1981. 140.00 (*0-900886-22-6*, Pub. by Witherby & Co) St Mut.

Bannish, Sally, ed. see Ludwig, Ray & Morrison, Ivy.

Bannister, A. Solvg Probs in Surveying. 2nd ed. (C). 1994. pap. 34.95 (*0-582-23644-4*, Pub. by Addison-Wesley) Longman.

Bannister, A. J. Shall Suffer Death. LC 95-81160. (Illus.). 200p. (Orig.). 1996. pap. 15.00 (*1-879418-93-2*) Audenreed Pr.

Bannister, Anne. From Hearing to Healing: Working with the Aftermath of Child Sexual Abuse. 2nd ed. LC 98-5758. (NSPCC/Wiley Child Protection & Policy Ser.). 212p. 1998. pap. 48.50 (*0-471-98298-9*) Wiley.

— The Healing Drama. LC 98-129945. 1997. 49.50 (*1-85343-382-9*, Pub. by Free Assoc Bks); pap. 19.50 (*1-85343-383-7*, Pub. by Free Assoc Bks) NYU Pr.

Bannister, Anthony, jt. photos by see Johnson, Peter.

Bannister, Arthur. Surveying. 7th ed. LC 98-148629. 502p. (C). 1998. pap. text 77.95 (*0-582-30249-8*, Prentice Hall) P-H.

Bannister, B. R. Instrumentacion, Transductores E Interfaces. (SPA.). 176p. (C). 1994. pap. text 12.33 (*0-201-62561-X*) Addison-Wesley.

Bannister, B. R. Management & Control of Viral Haemorrhagic Fevers. xii, 65p. 1996. 22.00 (*0-11-321860-5*, Pub. by Statnry Office) Balogh.

Bannister, Barbara & Ford, Edna P., eds. State Capitals Quilt Blocks: Fifty Patchwork Patterns from "Hearth & Home Magazine" 1912-1916. 80p. (Orig.). 1977. pap. 5.95 (*0-486-23557-2*) Dover.

— The United States Patchwork Pattern Book: Fifty Quilt Blocks for Fifty States from "Hearth & Home" 1907-1912. LC 75-2821. 80p. (Orig.). 1976. pap. 5.95 (*0-486-23243-3*) Dover.

***Bannister, Barbara, et al.** Infectious Disease. 2nd ed. (Illus.). 552p. (C). 2000. pap. 53.95 (*0-632-05319-4*) Blackwell Sci.

Bannister, Barbara A., et al. Infectious Disease. (Illus.). 450p. 1996. pap. text 74.95 (*0-632-03251-0*) Blackwell Sci.

Bannister, Barbara F. New Elementary School Librarian's Almanac: Practical Ideas, Tips, Techniques & Activities for Every Month of the School Year. LC 91-252. 256p. 1991. text 32.95 (*0-87628-605-8*) Ctr Appl Res.

Bannister, Barbara J. & Carlile, Janice B. Elementary School Librarian's Survival Guide. LC 93-17556. (Illus.). 224p. 1993. pap. text 27.95 (*0-87628-297-4*) Ctr Appl Res.

***Bannister, Bronwyn.** Haunt. 160p. 2000. pap. 24.95 (*1-877133-84-1*, Pub. by Univ Otago Pr) Intl Spec Bk.

Bannister, Carys M. & Tew, Brian, eds. Current Concepts in Spina Bifida & Hydrocephalus. (Clinics in Developmental Medicine Ser.: No. 122). 215p. (C). 1992. text 57.95 (*0-521-41279-X*) Cambridge U Pr.

Bannister, Dan W. Lincoln & the Common Law. 261p. (Orig.). 1992. pap. 12.95 (*0-9623335-1-4*) HSP IL.

— Lincoln & the Illinois Supreme Court. Hughett, Barbara, ed. LC 94-96808. (Illus.). 224p. 1995. 23.95 (*0-9644649-0-X*) D W Bannister.

Bannister, David, jt. auth. see Moreland, Carl.

Bannister, Don, ed. Issues & Approaches in Psychological Therapies. LC 74-6996. 300p. reprint ed. 93.00 (*0-8357-9918-2*, 201780000008) Bks Demand.

Bannister, Geoffrey J. & Stolp, Chandler. Spatial Concentration in Mexican Industry: A Test of the Benefits Versus the Costs. (U. S. - Mexican Occasional Papers). 40p. (C). 1993. pap. 7.00 (*0-89940-586-X*) LBJ Sch Pub Aff.

Bannister, Geoffrey J., jt. auth. see Glickman, Norman J.

Bannister, Hank & Crane, Tim. The Guide to Computing Around Portland. rev. ed. Berard, Barbara, ed. (Illus.). 1984. pap. 8.95 (*0-916241-01-7*) Microconsulting NW.

Bannister, J., jt. ed. see Wildsmith, J. A. W.

Bannister, J. V. Life Chemistry Reports Vol. 6, No. 3: A Special Issue, Vol. 6, No. 3. 118p. 1988. pap. text 94.00 (*3-7186-4885-7*) Gordon & Breach.

— Symposium on Polyamines, 1-3 June 1990, Albere, Trento, Italy, Vol. 9. (Life Chemistry Reports). 273p. 1991. pap. text 350.00 (*3-7186-5225-0*, Harwood Acad Pubs) Gordon & Breach.

Bannister, J. V., ed. Life Chemistry Reports, Vol. 7. 48p. 1989. pap. text 63.00 (*3-7186-4982-9*) Gordon & Breach.

— Life Chemistry Reports, Vol. 8. 48p. 1990. pap. text 69.00 (*3-7186-5037-1*) Gordon & Breach.

— Life Chemistry Reports, Vol. 12. (Life Chemistry Reports: Vol. 12, No. 2). 102p. 1994. pap. text 211.00 (*3-7186-5640-X*) Gordon & Breach.

— Life Chemistry Reports Vol. 7, No. 1: Temperature Dependent Proteins, Vol. 7, No. 1. 64p. 1989. pap. text 92.00 (*3-7186-4969-1*) Gordon & Breach.

— Life Chemistry Reports Vol. 7, No. 3: Heavy Metal Toxicity Contents, Vol. 7, No. 3. 176p. 1989. pap. text 244.00 (*3-7186-4998-5*) Gordon & Breach.

— Life Chemistry Reports Vol. 12, No. 3. (Life Chemistry Reports). 196p. 1995. pap. text 580.00 (*3-7186-5735-X*, Harwood Acad Pubs) Gordon & Breach.

Bannister, J. V., et al, eds. Bioreductive Activation of Quinoid Compounds: Chemical, Biochemical & Toxicological Aspects. (Free Radical Research Communications Ser.). 214p. 1990. pap. text 318.00 (*3-7186-5028-2*) Gordon & Breach.

Bannister, J. V. & Cocco, D. Symposium on Polyamines, 2-4 May 1991, Alghero, Sardinia, Vol. 10. (Life Chemistry Reports). 170p. 1993. pap. text 481.00 (*3-7186-5339-7*) Gordon & Breach.

Bannister, J. V. & Michelson, A. M., eds. Life Chemistry Reports, Vol. 1, Part 3. 114p. 1983. pap. text 112.00 (*3-7186-0171-0*) Gordon & Breach.

— Life Chemistry Reports, Vol. 2. 120p. 1984. pap. text 98.00 (*3-7186-0270-9*) Gordon & Breach.

— Life Chemistry Reports, Vol. 3. 52p. 1985. pap. text 43.00 (*3-7186-0298-9*) Gordon & Breach.

— Life Chemistry Reports, Vol. 3. 78p. 1986. pap. text 58.00 (*3-7186-0340-3*) Gordon & Breach.

— Life Chemistry Reports, Vol. 4. 112p. 1986. text 190.00 (*3-7186-0379-9*) Gordon & Breach.

— Life Chemistry Reports, Vol. 4. 106p. 1987. pap. text 71.00 (*3-7186-0417-5*); pap. text 129.00 (*3-7186-0451-5*); pap. text 192.00 (*3-7186-0461-2*) Gordon & Breach.

— Life Chemistry Reports, Vol. 6. 142p. 1987. pap. text 203.00 (*3-7186-4803-2*) Gordon & Breach.

— Life Chemistry Reports, Vol. 6. 122p. 1988. pap. text 145.00 (*3-7186-4810-5*) Gordon & Breach.

— Life Chemistry Reports Vol. 5, Pts. 1-4: The Active Site of Copper Proteins, Vol. 5, Nos. 1-4. ii, 341p. 1987. pap. text 431.00 (*3-7186-0462-0*) Gordon & Breach.

Bannister, J. V., et al. Free Radicals in Biological Medicine, Vol. 3. x, 266p. 1985. pap. text 252.00 (*3-7186-0285-7*) Gordon & Breach.

Bannister, J. V., jt. ed. see Michelson, A. M.

Bannister, J. V., ed. see Sies, Helmut & De Groot, H.

Bannister, Jay. Building Construction Inspection: A Guide for Architects. LC 90-13028. 320p. 1991. 80.00 (*0-471-53004-2*) Wiley.

Bannister, Jim. How to Manage Risk. (DYP Textbook Ser.). 289p. 1993. pap. 170.00 (*1-870255-81-X*) LLP.

— Practical Insurance Security Analysis. (DYP Textbook Ser.). 134p. 1993. pap. 155.00 (*1-870255-51-8*) LLP.

Bannister, Jo. A Bleeding of Innocents. LC 98-35739. 304p. 1999. pap. write for info. (*0-7540-3482-8*) Chivers N Amer.

— A Bleeding of Innocents. (Worldwide Library Mysteries: No. 241). 1997. per. 4.99 (*0-373-26241-8*, 1-26241-9, Wrldwide Lib) Harlequin Bks.

— A Bleeding of Innocents. large type ed. LC 98-35739. 319p. 1999. 30.00 (*0-7862-1610-7*, G K Hall Lrg Type) Mac Lib Ref.

***Bannister, Jo.** Broken Lines. 272p. 2000. per. 4.99 (*0-373-26338-4*) Harlequin Bks.

Bannister, Jo. Broken Lines. LC 98-50899. 304p. 1999. text 22.95 (*0-312-19842-6*) St Martin.

— Broken Lines. large type ed. LC 98-42034. Date not set. 30.00 (*0-7862-1682-4*) Thorndike Pr.

***Bannister, Jo.** Changelings. 2000. text 22.95 (*0-312-26567-0*) St Martin.

Bannister, Jo. Charisma. 1997. per. 4.99 (*0-373-26253-1*, 1-26253-4, Wrldwide Lib) Harlequin Bks.

— Critical Angle. 224p. 1999. 25.00 (*0-7278-2288-8*, Pub. by Severn Hse) Chivers N Amer.

— The Hireling's Tale. LC 99-47638. 320p. 1999. text 23.95 (*0-312-24400-2*, Minotaur) St Martin.

***Bannister, Jo.** The Hireling's Tale. large type ed. 1999. 22.95 (*0-7862-2163-1*) Thorndike Pr.

Bannister, Jo. The Lazarus Hotel. 1999. per. 4.99 (*0-373-26307-4*, 1-26307-8, Wrldwide Lib) Harlequin Bks.

— The Lazarus Hotel. large type ed. (Ulverscroft Large Print Ser.). 432p. 1997. 27.99 (*0-7089-3858-2*) Ulverscroft.

— No Birds Sing. (WWL Mystery Ser.). 1998. per. 4.99 (*0-373-26283-3*, 1-26283-1, Wrldwide Lib) Harlequin Bks.

— No Birds Sing. 240p. 1996. text 21.95 (*0-312-14382-6*) St Martin.

— No Birds Sing. large type ed. (Ulverscroft Large Print Ser.). 464p. 1997. 27.50 (*0-7089-3732-2*) Ulverscroft.

— The Primrose Convention. LC 97-51169. 272p. 1998. text 22.95 (*0-312-18157-4*) St Martin.

— The Primrose Convention. large type ed. LC 97-52115. 263p. 1998. pap. write for info. (*0-7540-3253-1*) Chivers N Amer.

— The Primrose Convention. large type ed. 1998. 22.95 (*0-7862-1383-3*) Thorndike Pr.

***Bannister, Jo.** Promise Switchback. 1999. 25.00 (*0-7278-5489-5*, Pub. by Severn Hse) Chivers N Amer.

Bannister, Jo. A Taste for Burning. (Castlemere Mystery Ser.). 1997. per. 4.99 (*0-373-26259-0*, 1-26259-1, Wrldwide Lib) Harlequin Bks.

— An Uncertain Death. 192p. 1998. 24.00 (*0-7278-5262-0*) Severn Hse.

— Unlawful Entry. 192p. 1998. 24.00 (*0-7278-5359-7*) Severn Hse.

***Bannister, Jo.** Unlawful Entry. large type ed. 368p. 1999. 31.99 (*0-7505-1329-2*, Pub. by Mgna Lrg Print) Ulverscroft.

Bannister, Ken. Energy Reduction Through Improved Maintenance. LC 98-43882. (Illus.). 128p. 1998. pap. 27.95 (*0-8311-3082-2*) Indus Pr.

Bannister, Kenneth E. Lubrication for Industry. 200p. 1996. text 32.95 (*0-8311-3061-X*) Indus Pr.

Bannister, Linda. AP Examination in English Language & Composition. (Illus.). 270p. 2000. pap. text 19.95 (*0-87891-923-6*) Res & Educ.

— Writing Apprehension & Anti-Writing: A Naturalistic Study of Composing Strategies Used by College Freshmen. LC 92-9604. 220p. 1992. lib. bdg. 89.95 (*0-7734-9832-X*) E Mellen.

Bannister, Mary. Storybook Connections. (Illus.). 320p. (Orig.). 1995. pap., teacher ed. 24.95 (*1-878279-78-5*, MM1999) Monday Morning Bks.

Bannister, Mary, et al. Reading Connections. (Illus.). 336p. (Orig.). (J). (ps-1). 1996. pap. 24.95 (*1-878279-97-1*, MM2026) Monday Morning Bks.

Bannister, Polly. Blue Ribbon Recipes: Award-Winning Recipes from America's Country Fairs. Old Farmers Almanac Editors, ed. LC 97-8173. (Old Farmer's Almanac Home Library). (Illus.). 160p. (YA). (gr. 11). 1997. pap. 12.95 (*0-7835-4935-0*) Time-Life.

Bannister, Robert C. Jessie Bernard: The Making of a Feminist. LC 90-34390. (Illus.). 285p. (C). 1991. text 38.00 (*0-8135-1614-5*) Rutgers U Pr.

— Social Darwinism: Science & Myth. rev. ed. LC 79-615. (American Civilization Ser.). 292p. (C). 1989. 19.95 (*0-87722-566-4*) Temple U Pr.

— Sociology & Scientism: The American Quest for Objectivity, 1880-1940. LC 86-24985. 311p. 1987. reprint ed. pap. 96.50 (*0-608-08012-8*, 206797700001) Bks Demand.

Bannister, Robert C., ed. see Sumner, William G.

Bannister, Roberta. Math: Grade 1. Hoffman, Joan, ed. (I Know It! Book Ser.). (Illus.). 32p. (J). (ps-3). 1979. student ed. 2.25 (*0-938256-28-9*, 02028) Sch Zone Pub Co.

— Math: Grade 2. Hoffman, Joan, ed. (I Know It! Book Ser.). (Illus.). 32p. (J). (ps-3). 1979. student ed. 2.49 (*0-938256-30-0*, 02030) Sch Zone Pub Co.

— Math: Grade 3. Hoffman, Joan, ed. (I Know It! Book Ser.). (Illus.). 32p. (J). (ps-3). 1979. student ed. 2.49 (*0-938256-31-9*, 02031) Sch Zone Pub Co.

— Math: Grade 4. Hoffman, Joan, ed. (I Know It! Book Ser.). (Illus.). 32p. (J). (ps-3). 1979. student ed. 2.25 (*0-938256-33-5*, 02033) Sch Zone Pub Co.

— Math: Grades 5-6. Hoffman, Joan, ed. (I Know It! Book Ser.). (Illus.). 32p. (J). (ps-3). 1980. student ed. 2.49 (*0-938256-35-1*, 02035) Sch Zone Pub Co.

Bannister, Roger. The Four-Minute Mile. (Illus.). 256p. 1994. reprint ed. pap. 14.95 (*1-55821-027-X*) Lyons Pr.

Bannister, Roger, ed. Brain & Bannister's Clinical Neurology. 7th ed. (Illus.). 634p. 1992. pap. text 52.50 (*0-19-261913-6*) OUP.

Bannister, Roger, jt. ed. see Mathias, C. J.

Bannister, Saxe, ed. see Paterson, William.

Bannister, Shala M. Family Treasures: Videotaping Your Family History, a Guide for Preserving Your Family's Living History As an Heirloom for Future Generations. LC 94-241865. (Illus.). 97p. pap. 11.95 (*0-8063-1438-9*, Pub. by Clearfield Co) ACCESS Pubs Network.

Bannister, Ursula, et al. Jugendbucher im DaF-Unterricht: Damals War Es Friedrich. (GER., Illus.). 69p. 1996. ring bd. 12.00 (*0-942017-38-2*, 04-64405) Amer Assn Teach German.

Banno, Junji. The Establishment of the Japanese Constitutional System. Stockwin, J. A., tr. LC 91-25699. (Nissan Institute/Routledge Japanese Studies Ser.). (Illus.). 272p. (C). (gr. 13). 1992. 90.00 (*0-415-00497-7*, A6895) Routledge.

— Establishment of the Japanese System. 272p. (C). 1995. pap. 29.99 (*0-415-13475-7*) Routledge.

An Asterisk (*) at the beginning of an entry indicates that the title is appearing for the first time.

Banno, Junji, ed. The Political Economy of Japanese Society: Internationalization & Domestic Issues, Vol. 2. (The Political Economy of Japanese Society Ser.). (Illus.). 382p. 1998. text 85.00 (*0-19-828034-3*) OUP.

— The Political Economy of Japanese Society: The State or the Market?, Vol. 1. LC 97-23116. (The Political Economy of Japanese Society Ser.). (Illus.). 376p. 1998. text 90.00 (*0-19-828033-5*) OUP.

Banno, Masataka. China & the West, 1858-1861: The Origins of the Tsungli Yamen. LC 64-13419. (Harvard East Asian Ser.: No. 15). 427p. reprint ed. pap. 132.40 (*0-608-30751-3*, 200641300059) Bks Demand.

***Bannock, Graham, et al, eds.** Dictionary of Economics. (Economist Ser.). 439p. 1998. 29.95 (*0-471-29599-X*) Wiley.

Bannock, Graham & Doran, Alan. Going Public: The Markets in Unlisted Securities. 128p. (C). 1987. 80.00 (*0-06-318370-6*, Pub. by P Chapman) St Mut.

Bannock, Graham & Manser, William. The International Dictionary of Finance. LC 99-47266. 290p. 1999. 29.95 (*0-471-36328-6*) Wiley.

Bannock, Graham & Peacock, Alan. Governments & Small Business: Changing Viewpoints. 224p. (C). 1988. 160.00 (*1-85396-035-7*, Pub. by P Chapman) St Mut.

Bannock, Graham, et al. The Penguin Dictionary of Economics. 6th ed. LC 99-214064. (Illus.). 438p. 1999. pap. 16.95 (*0-14-051376-0*) Viking Penguin.

Bannock, Graham, jt. auth. see Peacock, Alan.

Bannon, John Frances. Spanish Borderlands Frontier: 1513-1821. LC 74-110887. (Histories of the American Frontier Ser.). (Illus.). 308p. 1974. reprint ed. pap. 17.95 (*0-8263-0309-9*) U of NM Pr.

Bannon, Alexander L., jt. auth. see Depper, Estelle M.

Bannon, Ann. I Am a Woman. 224p. 1986. pap. 5.95 (*0-930044-84-3*) Naiad Pr.

— Journey to a Woman. 224p. 1989. pap. 5.95 (*0-930044-86-X*) Naiad Pr.

— Women in the Shadows. 176p. 1986. pap. 5.95 (*0-930044-85-1*) Naiad Pr.

Bannon, B., et al. Titanium the Choice . . . rev. ed. (Illus.). 17p. (Orig.). text 5.00 (*0-935297-07-3*, 9608) Intl Titanium.

Bannon, Cynthia J. The Brothers of Romulus: Fraternal Pietas in Roman Law, Literature, & Society. LC 97-7562. 288p. 1997. text 35.00 (*0-691-01571-6*, Pub. by Princeton U Pr) Cal Prin Full Svc.

Bannon, Edwin. Refractory Men, Fanatical Women. 219p. 1993. pap. 14.95 (*0-85244-226-2*, 959, Pub. by Gra1cewing) Morehouse Pub.

Bannon, J., jt. auth. see Gebhardt, Richard H.

Bannon, J. S., ed. Reviews in Weed Science, Vol. 1. 74p. 1985. text 9.00 (*0-318-32863-1*) Weed Sci Soc.

Bannon, James. North Carolina: A Guide to Backcountry Travel & Adventure. LC 95-71155. (Illus.). 387p. (Orig.). 1995. pap. 16.00 (*0-9648584-0-1*) Out There Pr.

— Sea Kayaking Florida & the Georgia Sea Islands. LC 98-65065. (Illus.). 180p. 1998. pap. 15.00 (*0-9648584-5-2*) Out There Pr.

— Virginia: A Guide to Backcountry Travel & Adventure. LC 98-66747. 388p. (Orig.). 1998. pap. 16.00 (*0-9648584-8-7*) Out There Pr.

— West Virginia: A Guide to Backcountry Travel & Adventure. LC 97-69894. 266p. 1997. pap. 15.00 (*0-9648584-4-4*) Out There Pr.

Bannon, James & Giffen, Morrison. Sea Kayaking the Carolinas. LC 97-65863. (Illus.). 220p. (Orig.). 1997. pap. 15.00 (*0-9648584-3-6*) Out There Pr.

Bannon, Jan. Oregon State Parks: A Complete Recreation Guide. LC 93-41780. (State Parks Ser.). 250p. 1994. pap. 14.95 (*0-89886-380-5*) Mountaineers.

Bannon, John F. Herbert Eugene Bolton: The Historian & the Man, 1870-1953. LC 77-20951. (Illus.). 316p. 1978. pap. 98.00 (*0-608-05631-6*, 206608700006) Bks Demand.

Bannon, Joseph. 911 Management. 1999. pap. 29.95 (*1-57167-132-3*) Sagamore Pub.

Bannon, Joseph J. Take Charge! A "How-To" Approach for Solving Every Day Problems. LC 91-61668. (Illus.). 152p. 1992. pap. 3.00 (*0-915611-46-5*) Sagamore Pub.

Bannon, Joseph J., ed. Current Issues in Leisure Services: Looking Ahead in a Time of Transition. LC 87-2792. (Practical Management Ser.). 180p. (C). 1987. pap. 23.95 (*0-87326-050-3*) Intl City-Cnty Mgt.

Bannon, Joseph J. & Busser, James A. Problem Solving in Recreation & Parks. 3rd ed. LC 91-68237. (Illus.). 440p. (C). 1992. text 44.95 (*0-915611-50-3*) Sagamore Pub.

***Bannon, Kay T.** Yonder Mountain: A Cherokee Legend. (Illus.). (J). 1999. pap. write for info. (*0-9669946-0-4*) Lob Cove.

Bannon, Liam. Proceedings of the Second European Conference on Computer-Supported Cooperative Work - ECSCW 1991. 364p. (C). 1991. pap. text 171.00 (*0-7923-1439-5*) Kluwer Academic.

Bannon, Lois & Clark, Taylor. Handbook of Audubon Prints. LC 79-1319. (Illus.). 128p. 1991. 16.95 (*0-88289-862-0*) Pelican.

Bannon, Lois Elmer, jt. auth. see Clark, Taylor.

Bannon, Race. Learning the Ropes: A Basic Guide to Safe & Fun S-M Lovemaking. LC 92-73484. 159p. (Orig.). 1993. pap. 12.95 (*1-881943-07-0*) Daedalus Pub.

Bannon, Richard J., jt. auth. see Zerga, Joseph F.

Bannour, A. Logics Dictionary German-English-French. (ENG, FRE & GER.). 231p. 1995. 65.00 (*2-85319-260-1*, Pub. by Conseil Intl Lang) IBD Ltd.

Bannour, Abderrazak. Dictionnaire de Logique pour Linguistes. (FRE.). 231p. 1995. 125.00 (*0-7859-9944-2*) Fr & Eur.

Bano, Sayeeda S. Intra-Industry International Trade: The Canadian Experience. 202p. 1991. text 82.95 (*1-85628-127-2*, Pub. by Avebry) Ashgate Pub Co.

Banoczy, J. Oral Leukoplakia. 1982. text 137.50 (*90-247-2655-7*) Kluwer Academic.

***Banomyong, Pridi.** The King of the White Elephant. 2000. pap. 12.00 (*974-7449-22-6*, Pub. by CPNCOCAPB) Lantern Books.

— National Economic Policy of Luang Pradist Manudharm. 2000. pap. 12.00 (*974-7449-23-4*, Pub. by CPNCOCAPB) Lantern Books.

Banos, A. & Cullen, A. Dipole Radiation Presence of a Conducting Half Space. LC 65-14781. (International Series of Monographs in Electromagnetic Waves: Vol. 9). 1966. 118.00 (*0-08-011171-8*, Pub. by Pergamon Repr) Franklin.

Banos, Mona L. Interludes. 64p. 1993. pap. 7.95 (*1-883612-01-2*) Bks Unltd.

Banovetz, James M. Managing Human Resources Local Government Cases. LC 98-40339. 1998. write for info. (*0-87326-162-3*) Intl City-Cnty Mgt.

***Banovetz, James M., ed.** Governing Illinois: Your Connection to State & Local Government. 2nd rev. ed. LC 99-32266. Orig. Title: Governing Illinois: Of the People, by the People & for the People. 1999. pap. text 12.00 (*0-938943-16-2*) U IL Spgfld Pub Affrs.

Banovetz, James M., ed. Managing Local Government: Cases in Decision Making. LC 82-26829. (Municipal Management Ser.). 244p. 1990. pap. 28.95 (*0-87326-060-0*) Intl City-Cnty Mgt.

— Managing Local Government: Cases in Decision Making. 2nd ed. LC 98-22838. (Municipal Management Ser.). 242p. 1998. pap. text 29.95 (*0-87326-157-7*) Intl City-Cnty Mgt.

— Managing Local Government Finance: Cases in Decision Making. (Municipal Management Ser.). 75p. 1996. pap. 15.95 (*0-87326-111-9*) Intl City-Cnty Mgt.

— Managing Small Cities & Counties: A Practical Guide. rev. ed. (Municipal Management Ser.). (Illus.). 350p. (C). 1994. pap. text 34.00 (*0-87326-093-7*) Intl City-Cnty Mgt.

Banowetz, Joseph. The Pianist's Guide to Pedaling. LC 84-47534. (Illus.). 320p. 1992. reprint ed. pap. 15.95 (*0-253-20732-0*) Ind U Pr.

Banque de France Staff. Dictionnaire Economique de l'Anglais et du Francais: Systeme Banquaire. (ENG & FRE.). 232p. 1992. pap. 125.00 (*0-7859-1005-0*, 2717822798) Fr & Eur.

— Dictionnaire Economique de l'Anglais et du Francais Vol. 2: Credit, Taux D'Interet. (ENG & FRE.). 1992. pap. 105.00 (*0-7859-7956-5*, 2717823581) Fr & Eur.

Bansa, Helmut & Hofer, Hans-H. Artificial Aging As a Predictor of Paper's Future Useful Life, 1989. (Monograph to Abbey Newsletter: Suppl. 1). (Illus.). v, 23p. 1989. pap. 5.00 (*0-9622071-0-1*) Abbey Pubns.

Bansak, Edmund G. Fearing the Dark: The Val Lewton Career. LC 94-23271. (Illus.). 581p. 1995. lib. bdg. 55.00 (*0-89950-969-X*) McFarland & Co.

Bansal & Howard. Business & the Natural Environment. 304p. 1997. pap. text 42.95 (*0-7506-2051-X*) Buttrwrth-Heinemann.

Bansal, B. L. Bon Its Encounter with Buddhism in Tibet. (C). 1994. 22.00 (*81-86339-03-5*, Pub. by Eastern Bk Linkers) S Asia.

— Digest of Motor Accident Claims & Compensation. (C). 1989. 250.00 (*0-7855-4798-3*) St Mut.

Bansal, I. J. Human Biology-Recent Advances: Proceedings of the International Symposium on Human Growth, Vol. 1. 307p. 1982. 39.00 (*0-88065-249-7*, Pub. by Today Tomorrow) Scholarly Pubns.

Bansal, I. J., ed. Anthropology in Indian Context. 278p. 1983. 59.00 (*1-55528-069-2*, Pub. by Today Tomorrow) Scholarly Pubns.

Bansal, I. J. & Sidhu. Human Biology-Recent Advances: Proceedings of the International Symposium on Human Growth, Vol. 2. xxxvi, 609p. 1983. 59.00 (*0-317-64527-7*, Pub. by Today Tomorrow) Scholarly Pubns.

Bansal, I. J., et al. New Horizons in Human Biology. (Illus.). 250p. 1991. 59.00 (*1-55528-254-7*, Pub. by Today Tomorrow) Scholarly Pubns.

Bansal, N. P. Handbook of Glass Properties. (Academic Press Handbook Ser.). 1986. text 262.00 (*0-12-078140-9*) Acad Pr.

Bansal, Narenda K., et al. Passive Building Design: A Handbook of Natural Climatic Control. LC 93-38991. 340p. 1994. 1874.00 (*0-444-81745-X*) Elsevier.

Bansal, Narottam P., ed. Advances in Ceramic-Matrix Composites. LC 93-33159. (Ceramic Transactions Ser.: No. 38). 854p. 1994. 74.00 (*0-944904-69-6*, CT038) Am Ceramic.

Bansal, Narottam P., et al, eds. Innovative Processing & Synthesis of Ceramics, Glasses, & Composites. LC 97-43769. (Ceramic Transactions Ser.: No. 85). 433p. 1997. 95.00 (*1-57498-030-0*) Am Ceramic.

***Bansal, Narottam P. & Singh, J. P., eds.** Innovative Processing & Synthesis of Ceramics, Glasses, & Composites II. (Ceramic Transactions Ser.: Vol. 94). 24p. 1999. text 95.00 (*1-57498-060-2*, CT094) Am Ceramic.

Bansal, Narottam P. & Singh, Jitendra P. Advances in Ceramic-Matrix Composites III. LC 96-31022. (Ceramic Transactions Ser.: No. 74). 656p. 1996. 95.00 (*1-57498-020-3*, CT074) Am Ceramic.

Bansal, Narottam P., jt. ed. see Singh, J. P.

Bansal, Raj K. Nomenclature of Organic Compounds. (Illus.). 1979. text. write for info. (*0-07-096370-3*) McGraw.

— Synthetic Approaches in Organic Chemistry. LC 98-124016. (Chemistry Ser.). 458p. 1997. pap. 40.00 (*0-7637-0665-5*) Jones & Bartlett.

Bansal, Roop Chand. Active Carbons. Donnet, Stoeckl, ed. (Illus.). 504p. 1988. text 225.00 (*0-8247-7842-1*) Dekker.

Bansal, S. K. Financial Problems of Small Scale Industries. 250p. 1992. 100.00 (*81-7041-556-X*, Pub. by Scientific Pubs) St Mut.

Bansal, Vipul K., jt. auth. see Penza, Pietro.

Banse, M., jt. ed. see Tangermann, Stefan.

Banse, Timothy P. The Fuels Book. (Illus.). 192p. 1987. pap. 19.99 (*0-934523-22-3*) Middle Coast Pub.

— Home Applications & Games for the Coleco Adam. LC 84-23353. 132p. 1985. pap. 14.95 (*0-934523-01-0*); lib. bdg. 15.95 (*0-934523-00-2*) Middle Coast Pub.

— How to Keep Your Powerboat Shipshape. (Illus.). 198p. 1987. 14.95 (*0-934523-75-4*); pap. 12.95 (*0-934523-76-2*) Middle Coast Pub.

— New Car Reports, 1993. (Illus.). 1992. pap. 9.95 (*0-934523-04-5*) Middle Coast Pub.

— What to Do When Leaded Fuel Becomes Extinct. (Illus.). 64p. 1986. pap. 4.95 (*0-934523-21-5*) Middle Coast Pub.

— What to Do When Leaded Fuel Becomes Extinct. rev. ed. LC 86-5459. (Illus.). 71p. 1989. pap. 9.95 (*0-934523-20-7*) Middle Coast Pub.

Banse, Tom. Marine Engine Lay-Up: A Step-by-Step Guide to Decommissioning Inboards, Stern Drives, & Outboard Motors. LC 95-30192. 1995. write for info. (*0-934523-39-8*) Middle Coast Pub.

Bansemer, Richard F. O Lord, Teach Me to Pray: A Catechetical Prayer Book for Personal Use. (Illus.). 96p. (YA). (gr. 7 up). 1995. 7.50 (*0-9633142-8-9*) Am Luth Pub Bur.

— Praying on the Journey with Christ: A Commitment to Encounter Christ Through the Gospel of John. 1997. pap. text 19.25 (*0-7880-1179-0*) CSS OH.

— Praying on the Journey with Christ: A Committment to Encounter Christ Through the Gospel of John. LC 97-39506. 222p. 1997. pap. 19.25 (*0-7880-1176-6*) CSS OH.

— We Believe Vol. 2: A Prayer Book Based on the Augsburg Confession. 148p. 1999. 9.50 (*1-892921-00-6*) Am Luth Pub Bur.

Bansemer, Roger. The Art of Hot-Air Ballooning. (Illus.). 165p. 1987. 34.95 (*0-944201-00-8*) Gollum Pr.

***Bansemer, Roger.** Bansemer's Book of Carolina & Georgia Lighthouses. LC 99-53480. (Illus.). 128p. 2000. 24.95 (*1-56164-194-4*) Pineapple Pr.

Bansemer, Roger. Bansemer's Book of Florida Lighthouses. LC 98-42532. (Illus.). 144p. 1999. 29.95 (*1-56164-172-3*) Pineapple Pr.

— Mountains in the Mist: Impressions of the Great Smokies. LC 93-19261. 184p. 1993. 26.95 (*0-87833-839-X*) Taylor Pub.

— Southern Shores. Kasper, Dixie, ed. (Illus.). 256p. 1997. reprint ed. 35.00 (*0-944428-43-6*) Cruising Guide.

Bansemer, Roger & Renc, Bill. At Water's Edge: The Birds of Florida. LC 92-37447. (Illus.). 128p. 1993. 24.95 (*0-87833-821-7*) Taylor Pub.

Bansemer, Roger, jt. auth. see May, Daryl.

***Bansen, Norman C.** Passages from India: Letters, Essays & Poems. Nielsen, John W., ed. xvi, 201p. 1999. pap. 19.95 (*0-930697-05-7*) Lur Pubns.

Bansil, P. C. Agricultural Statistics in India. 3rd rev. ed. 14.00 (*0-8364-1500-0*, Pub. by Oxford IBH) S Asia.

Banskota, Purushottam. The Gurkha Connection: A History of the Burkha Recruitment in the British Indian Army. 221p. 1994. 20.00 (*81-85693-22-6*, Pub. by Nirala Pubns) Nataraj Bks.

Bansleben, Manfred. Neue Perspektiven. 2nd ed. (C). Date not set. pap. text, teacher ed., suppl. ed. write for info. (*0-15-501101-4*) Harcourt Coll Pubs.

— Neue Perspektiven. 2nd ed. (C). 1996. pap. text. write for info. (*0-03-072461-9*) Harcourt Coll Pubs.

— Neue Perspektiven. 2nd ed. (C). 1997. pap. text, wbk. ed., lab manual ed. write for info. (*0-03-072466-X*) Harcourt Coll Pubs.

— Perspektiven: Texte zur Kultur und Literatur. 272p. (C). 1987. pap. text 40.50 (*0-03-063238-2*) Harcourt Coll Pubs.

— Perspektiven: Ubungen zur Grammatik. (C). 1987. pap. text 53.00 (*0-03-063239-0*) Harcourt Coll Pubs.

— Perspektiven: Ubungen Zur Grammatik & Texte Zur Kultur & Literatur. (C). 1987. pap. text, student ed. 30.00 (*0-03-063241-2*) Harcourt Coll Pubs.

Banta. Ohio. text. write for info. (*0-8050-6110-X*) St Martin.

Banta, Christopher C. Bass Marimba Designs. (Illus.). 312p. (Orig.). (C). 1992. pap. text, per. 35.00 (*0-942742-01-X*) Funhouse Pr.

— The Fundamentals of Marimba Bar Fabrication & Tuning. (Illus.). 148p. (Orig.). (C). 1992. per. 20.00 (*0-942742-00-1*) Funhouse Pr.

— Seeing Is Believing? Haunted Shacks, Mystery Spots, & Other Delightful Phenomena. rev. ed. LC 95-92322. (Illus.). 224p. (Orig.). 1996. pap. 21.95 (*0-942742-14-1*) Funhouse Pr.

***Banta Corporation Staff & GATF Staff.** Technovation Handbook: A Review of Current Imaging Technologies Affecting Major Print Markets. (Illus.). 96p. (C). 1999. pap. 25.00 (*0-88362-250-5*, 1571) GATFPress.

Banta, D. D. Historical Sketch of Johnson County. (Illus.). 170p. 1997. reprint ed. lib. bdg. 24.50 (*0-8328-6656-3*) Higginson Bk Co.

Banta, Elsa M. Banta Pioneers: And Records of the Wives & Allied Families. (Illus.). 303p. 1995. reprint ed. pap. 45.00 (*0-8328-4900-6*); reprint ed. lib. bdg. 55.00 (*0-8328-4899-9*) Higginson Bk Co.

Banta, H. David. Anticipating & Assessing Health Care Technology: General Considerations & Policy Conclusions. a Report Commissioned by the Steering Committee on Future Health Scenarios, Vol. 1. (C). 1987. pap. text 105.00 (*0-89838-897-X*) Kluwer Academic.

Banta, H. David, ed. Resources for Health: Technology Assessment for Policy Makings. LC 81-21079. 235p. 1982. 59.95 (*0-275-91358-9*, C1358, Praeger Pubs) Greenwood.

Banta, H. David, et al, eds. Health Care Technology & Its Assessment in Eight Countries. (Illus.). 368p. (Orig.). (C). 1995. pap. text 65.00 (*0-7881-2501-X*) DIANE Pub.

Banta, H. David, jt. auth. see Scenario Commission on Future Health Care Technolo.

Banta, James E., ed. Contemporary Issues in Public Health: A Special Issue of Journal of Community Health. 132p. 1987. pap. 16.95 (*0-89885-375-3*, Kluwer Acad Hman Sci) Kluwer Academic.

Banta, Ken. Reinventing Ketchup: How Heinz is Creating a New Global Brand. 320p. 1999. 27.50 (*0-670-87684-4*) Viking Penguin.

Banta, Kim C., jt. auth. see Dunton, Loren.

Banta, Margrit A. Parish Reconciliation Services: Seasonal Celebrations for Adults & Children. LC 93-61483. 80p. (Orig.). 1994. pap. 12.95 (*0-89622-586-0*) Twenty-Third.

Banta, Martha. Henry James & the Occult: The Great Extension. LC 72-75386. 287p. (C). reprint ed. 89.00 (*0-8357-9215-3*, 201301000083) Bks Demand.

— Taylored Lives: Narrative Productions in the Age of Taylor, Veblen, & Ford. LC 92-38609. (Illus.). 464p. (C). 1993. 37.50 (*0-226-03701-0*) U Ch Pr.

— Taylored Lives: Narrative Productions in the Age of Taylor, Veblen, & Ford. LC 92-38609. (Illus.). 446p. (C). 1995. pap. text 18.95 (*0-226-03702-9*) U Ch Pr.

— A Time to Be Free: Daily Meditations for Enhancing Self-Esteem. 432p. 1990. pap. 9.95 (*0-553-35203-2*) Bantam.

Banta, Martha, ed. New Essays on "The American" (American Novel Ser.). 192p. 1987. text 32.95 (*0-521-30730-9*); pap. text 14.95 (*0-521-31449-6*) Cambridge U Pr.

Banta, Martha, ed. & intro. see Wharton, Edith.

Banta, Marvin H. After the Grasshopper: A Collection of Poems. LC 86-80226. (Illus.). 64p. (Orig.). 1986. pap. 10.00 (*0-937139-00-9*) Grasshopper Pubns.

— A Certain Voice: A Collection of Poems. LC 95-80293. (Illus.). 124p. (Orig.). 1995. pap. 10.00 (*0-937139-03-3*) Grasshopper Pubns.

— Six-Sixty-Six: The Number of a Man. LC 87-91121. 64p. (Orig.). 1987. pap. 7.95 (*0-937139-01-7*) Grasshopper Pubns.

Banta, Melissa. Colin Powell: Military Leader. LC 94-8349. (Junior Black Americans of Achievement Ser.). (Illus.). 76p. (J). (gr. 3-6). 1994. pap. 4.95 (*0-7910-2142-4*); lib. bdg. 14.95 (*0-7910-1770-2*) Chelsea Hse.

***Banta, Melissa.** A Curious & Ingenious Art: Reflections on Daguerreotypes at Harvard. LC 00-29927. (Illus.). 208p. 2000. 55.00 (*0-87745-724-7*) U of Iowa Pr.

Banta, Melissa & Wayson, Anne. Essence & Persuasion: The Power of Black & White. (Illus.). 64p. (Orig.). 1995. pap. text 10.00 (*0-922668-13-2*) SUNYB Poetry Rare Bks.

Banta, R. E. Fuller. Benjamin Fuller & Some of His Descendants, 1765-1958. (Illus.). 143p. 1997. reprint ed. pap. 22.50 (*0-8328-8672-6*); reprint ed. lib. bdg. 32.50 (*0-8328-8671-8*) Higginson Bk Co.

— The Ohio. LC 98-30104. (Ohio River Valley Ser.). (Illus.). 608p. 1998. reprint ed. 39.95 (*0-8131-2098-5*); reprint ed. pap. 19.95 (*0-8131-0959-0*) U Pr of Ky.

Banta, Ray. Indiana's Laughmakers. (Illus.). 176p. (Orig.). 1988. pap. 12.95 (*0-317-91346-8*) PennUltimate Pubs.

Banta, Theodore M. A Frisian Family: The Banta Genealogy: Descendants of Epke Jacobse, Who Came from Friesland, Netherlands, to New Amsterdam, Feb., 1659. (Illus.). 427p. 1988. reprint ed. pap. 67.00 (*0-8328-0181-X*); reprint ed. lib. bdg. 77.00 (*0-8328-0180-1*) Higginson Bk Co.

— Sayre Family: Lineage of Thomas Sayre, a Founder of Southampton. (Illus.). 774p. 1989. reprint ed. lib. bdg. 124.00 (*0-8328-1050-9*) Higginson Bk Co.

Banta, Theordore M. Sayre Family: Lineage of Thomas Sayre, a Founder of Southampton. (Illus.). 774p. 1989. reprint ed. pap. 116.00 (*0-8328-1051-7*) Higginson Bk Co.

Banta, Trudy W., ed. Implementing Outcomes Assessment: Promise & Perils. LC 85-645339. (New Directions for Institutional Research Ser.: No. IR 59). 1988. pap. 22.00 (*1-55542-888-6*) Jossey-Bass.

Banta, Trudy W., et al. Assessment in Practice: Putting Principles to Work on College Campuses. LC 95-18627. (Higher & Adult Education Ser.). 411p. 1995. pap. 36.95 (*0-7879-0134-2*) Jossey-Bass.

Banta, Trudy W., jt. auth. see Palomba, Cathrine A.

Banta, Trudy W., jt. ed. see Borden, Victor M.

Banta, William F. AIDS in the Workplace: Legal Questions & Practical Answers. enl. rev. ed. LC 86-46309. 422p. 1993. 37.00 (*0-669-28056-9*) Lxngtn Bks.

Bantam Books Inc. Editors. Bank Street Level 3, 4 vols., Set. 1991. pap., boxed set 14.00 (*0-553-61842-3*) Bantam.

— Disturbing Behavior. (Illus.). 192p. (YA). 1998. mass mkt. 4.99 (*0-553-57139-7*) Bantam.

— Medical Reference, 3 vols., Set. 1992. mass mkt., boxed set 20.95 (*0-553-62870-4*) Bantam.

Bantam Books Inc. Editors, ed. The Pill Book Guide to Medication for Your Dog & Cat. LC 99-159362. 624p. 1998. mass mkt. 6.99 (*0-553-57989-4*) Bantam.

Bantam Doubleday Staff & Evans. The Horse Whisperer: An Illustrated Companion to the Major Motion Picture. (Illus.). 160p. 1998. pap. 19.95 (*0-440-50840-1*, Dell Trade Pbks) Dell.

Bantas, Andrei. NTC's Romanian & English Dictionary. LC 97-49454. (ENG & RUM., Illus.). 672p. 1997. 29.95 (*0-8442-4976-9*, 49769, Natl Textbk Co) NTC Contemp Pub Co.

B

Bantel, Linda, et al. A Proud Heritage. Neff, Terry A. & Sanden, Michael, eds. (Two Centuries of American Art Ser.). (Illus.). 1987. write for info. (*0-932171-01-X*) Terra Found Arts.

Bantens, Robert J. Eugene Carriere: His Work & His Influence. LC 82-4919. (Studies in the Fine Arts: The Avant-Garde: No. 29). (Illus.). 289p. 1983. reprint ed. pap. 89.60 (*0-8357-1329-6*, 207048800096) Bks Demand.

Bantens, Robert J., jt. auth. see Rosenblum, Robert.

Banthin, Richard. CADD Desktop Tutor: Automanager Workflow 4.0. 2nd unabridged ed. Allen, Richard, ed. Angelini, Mike, tr. (Illus.). 175p. 1996. wbk. ed. 249.00 incl. cd-rom (*1-891502-19-0*, CDTAMW0596) Tech Learn Co.

Banthiya, Ruchi. From Historicity to Postmodernity: A Case of South Asia. (C). 1994. 18.00 (*81-7033-230-3*, Pub. by Rawat Pubns) S Asia.

Banti, Anna. Artemisia. Caracciolo, Shirley D., tr. LC 88-6498. (European Women Writers Ser.). v, 222p. 1988. pap. 12.00 (*0-8032-6119-5*, Bison Books) U of Nebr Pr.

— A Piercing Cry: Translation of Anna Banti's Un Grido Lacerante. Lewis, S. Mark & Valentini, Daria, trs. from ITA. LC 96-1195. XV, 119p. (C). 1997. pap. 24.95 (*0-8204-3001-3*) P Lang Pubng.

Banting. Business Marketing, 2 vols. 2nd ed. (C). Date not set. text 71.16 (*0-395-87102-6*) HM.

Banting, Keith, et al, eds. Degrees of Freedom: Canada & the United States in a Changing World. 512p. 1997. 65.00 (*0-7735-1447-3*, Pub. by McG-Queens Univ Pr); pap. 24.95 (*0-7735-1448-1*, Pub. by McG-Queens Univ Pr) CUP Services.

Banting, Keith & Simeon, Richard, eds. Redesigning the State: The Politics of Constitutional Change. 269p. 1985. pap. 17.95 (*0-8020-6569-4*) U of Toronto Pr.

Banting, Keith G. The Welfare State & Canadian Federalism. rev. ed. 280p. 1987. pap. 24.95 (*0-7735-0631-4*, Pub. by McG-Queens Univ Pr) CUP Services.

Banting, Keith G. & Simeon, Richard, eds. Redesigning the State: The Politics of Constitutional Change. LC JF0031.R43. 269p. reprint ed. pap. 83.40 (*0-8357-3629-6*, 203635700003) Bks Demand.

Banting, Keith S., et al, eds. Reform of Retirement Income Policy: International & Canadian Perspectives. 1996. text 49.95 (*0-88911-759-4*, Pub. by McG-Queens Univ Pr) CUP Services.

Banting, Keith S. & Broadway, Robin, eds. Reform of Retirement Income Policy: International & Canadian Perspectives. LC 96-932027. 1996. pap. text 22.95 (*0-88911-739-X*, Pub. by McG-Queens Univ Pr) CUP Services.

Banting, Pamela. Body, Inc. A Theory of Translation Poetics. 1997. pap. 14.95 (*0-88801-190-3*, Pub. by Turnstone Pr) Genl Dist Srvs.

Bantjes, A., jt. ed. see Dawids, Steen.

Bantjes, Adrian A. As If Jesus Walked on Earth: Cardenismo, Sonora, & the Mexican Revolution. LC 97-12365. (Latin American Silhouettes Ser.). (Illus.). 300p. 1998. 50.00 (*0-8420-2653-3*, SR Bks) Scholarly Res Inc.

***Bantjes, Adrian A.** As If Jesus Walked on Earth: Cardenismo, Sonora, & the Mexican Revolution. LC 97-12365. (Illus.). 300p. 2000. pap. 21.95 (*0-8420-2751-3*) Scholarly Res Inc.

Bantle, Gawain, jt. auth. see Powers, Rhea.

Bantle, Lee F. Diving for the Moon. LC 94-35207. 176p. (J). (gr. 4-7). 1995. per. 14.00 (*0-689-80004-5*, Mac Bks Young Read) S&S Childrens.

Bantlin, Marguerite, ed. see Heald, Weldon F.

Bantly, Francisca C. Embracing Illusion: Truth & Fiction in "The Dream of the Nine Clouds" LC 96-3284. (SUNY Series, Toward a Comparative Philosophy of Religions). 262p. (C). 1996. text 68.50 (*0-7914-2969-5*); pap. text 22.95 (*0-7914-2970-9*) State U NY Pr.

Bantly, Harold A., jt. compiled by see Freedman, Janet L.

Bantock, G. A. Studies in the History of Educational Theory: Artifice & Nature, 1350-1765, Vol. 1. 1980. text 55.00 (*0-04-370092-6*) Routledge.

Bantock, G. H. Studies in the History of Educational Theory: The Minds & Masses, 1760-1980, Vol. 2. (Illus.). 368p. 1984. text 55.00 (*0-04-370119-1*) Routledge.

Bantock, Gavin. Anhaga. Date not set. pap. 7.95 (*0-900977-34-5*, Pub. by Anvil Press) Dufour.

— Dragons. 104p. 1979. pap. 14.95 (*0-85646-049-4*, Pub. by Anvil Press) Dufour.

— Eirenikon. 32p. 1972. 14.95 (*0-900977-87-6*, Pub. by Anvil Press) Dufour.

— A New Thing Breathing. Date not set. 14.95 (*0-900977-03-5*, Pub. by Anvil Press) Dufour.

***Bantock, Nick.** The Artful Dodger: Images & Reflections. LC 99-53952. (Illus.). 2000. 40.00 (*0-8118-2752-6*) Chronicle Bks.

Bantock, Nick. Capolan: Travels of a Vagabond Country. (Illus.). 48p. 1997. 18.95 (*0-8118-1545-5*) Chronicle Bks.

— The Forgetting Room. LC 96-51665. (Illus.). 112p. 1999. pap. 14.00 (*0-06-093126-4*) HarpC.

— The Golden Mean: In Which the Extraordinary Correspondence of Griffin & Sabine Concludes. LC 92-47350. (Illus.). 48p. 1993. 17.95 (*0-8118-0298-1*) Chronicle Bks.

— Griffin & Sabine: An Extraordinary Correspondence. LC 90-26484. (Illus.). 48p. 1991. 17.95 (*0-87701-788-3*) Chronicle Bks.

— The Griffin & Sabine Trilogy, 3 bks. (Illus.). 1994. boxed set 49.95 (*0-8118-0696-0*) Chronicle Bks.

— Magic Carpets. 1999. pap. 18.95 (*0-670-85589-8*) Viking Penguin.

— The Museum at Purgatory. LC 98-53766. (Illus.). 128p. 1999. 25.00 (*0-06-757546-3*) HarpC.

— Sabine's Notebook: In Which the Extraordinary Correspondence of Griffin & Sabine Continues. (Illus.). 48p. 1992. 17.95 (*0-8118-0180-2*) Chronicle Bks.

— The Venetian's Wife: A Strangely Sensual Tale of a Renaissance Explorer, a Computer, & a Metamorphosis. LC 95-47243. 132p. 1996. 22.95 (*0-8118-1140-9*) Chronicle Bks.

Bantock, Nick & Strong, Stacie. Runners, Sliders, Bouncers, Climbers: A Pop-Up Look at Animals in Motion. (Illus.). 15p. (J). (gr. 1-5). 1992. 14.95 (*1-56282-219-5*, Pub. by Hyprn Child) Time Warner.

Banton, Michael. Racial Theories. 2nd rev. ed. LC 97-32115. 264p. (C). 1998. pap. text 19.95 (*0-521-62945-4*) Cambridge U Pr.

Banton, Michael P. International Action Against Racial Discrimination. LC 95-47057. (Illus.). 378p. 1996. text 65.00 (*0-19-828061-0*, Clarendon Pr) OUP.

— Promoting Racial Harmony. 146p. 1985. text 54.95 (*0-521-30082-7*) Cambridge U Pr.

— Racial & Ethnic Competition. (Modern Revivals in Sociology Ser.). 1993. 72.95 (*0-7512-0110-3*, Pub. by Gregg Pub) Ashgate Pub Co.

— Racial Consciousness. (Illus.). 176p. (C). 1989. pap. text 69.00 (*0-582-02385-8*, 70445); pap. text 41.00 (*0-582-02384-X*, 70445) Longman.

— Racial Consciousness. 2nd ed. LC 96-28506. 1p. (C). 1997. pap. 22.26 (*0-582-29911-X*) Longman.

— White & Coloured: The Behavior of the British People Towards Coloured Immigrants. LC 76-43335. 223p. 1977. reprint ed. lib. bdg. 59.50 (*0-8371-9290-0*, BAWAC, Greenwood Pr) Greenwood.

Banton, Michael P., ed. Social Anthropology of Complex Societies. (Orig.). 1968. pap. 15.95 (*0-422-72520-X*, NO. 2069, Pub. by Tavistock) Routldge.

Banu (Sons of) Musa Bin Shakir Staff. The Book of Ingenious Devices. Hill, Donald R., tr. 1978. lib. bdg. 220.00 (*90-277-0833-9*) Kluwer Academic.

Banu, U. A. Razia Akter, see Razia Akter Banu, U. A., ed.

Banu, Zenab. Politics of Communalism. (C). 1989. 32.00 (*0-86132-183-9*, Pub. by Popular Prakashan) S Asia.

Banuazizi, Ali & Weiner, Myron, eds. The New Geopolitics of Central Asia. LC 94-11996. 288p. 1995. 39.95 (*0-253-31139-X*); pap. 15.95 (*0-253-20918-8*) Ind U Pr.

— The State, Religion, & Ethnic Politics: Afghanistan, Iran, & Pakistan. LC 86-6048. (Contemporary Issues in the Middle East Ser.). 464p. 1988. reprint ed. pap. text 19.95 (*0-8156-2448-4*) Syracuse U Pr.

Banuazizi, Ali, jt. ed. see Weiner, Myron.

Banuelas, Arturo J., ed. Mestizo Christianity: Theology from the Latino Perspective. LC 95-23232. 250p. (Orig.). 1995. 17.00 (*1-57075-032-7*) Orbis Bks.

Banuelos, Gary, jt. auth. see Terry, Norman.

***Banuelos, R. & Moore, C. N.** Probabilistic Behavior of Harmonic Functions. (Progress in Mathematics Ser.: Vol. 175). 224p. 1999. 75.00 (*3-7643-6062-3*, Pub. by Birkhauser) Spr-Verlag.

Banuet-Alvers, Yvonne. Fitness & Good Health Text & Workbook, Set. 176p. (C). 1996. pap. text 23.95 (*0-7872-2418-9*, 41241801) Kendall-Hunt.

— Yoga the College Way. 216p. (C). 1996. boxed set 23.69 (*0-7872-2443-X*) Kendall-Hunt.

Banuri, T., jt. ed. see Amalric, F.

Banuri, Tariq, et al, eds. Just Development: Beyond Adjustment with a Human Face. LC 97-930633. (Illus.). 224p. (C). 1997. text 27.00 (*0-19-577830-8*) OUP.

Banuri, Tariq & Schor, Juliet B., eds. Financial Openness & National Autonomy: Opportunities & Constraints. (WIDER Studies in Development Economics). (Illus.). 302p. 1992. text 75.00 (*0-19-828364-4*) OUP.

Banus, Maria. Across Bucharest after Rain. Der-Hovanessian & Mattfield, trs. (QRL Poetry Bks.: Vol. XXXV). 1996. 20.00 (*0-614-15853-2*) Quarterly Rev.

Banus, Maria, et al. Demon in Brackets. Dutescu, D. et al, trs. from RUM. LC 93-71945. (ENG & RUM.). 228p. 1994. pap. 18.95 (*1-85610-031-6*, Pub. by Forest Bks) Dufour.

Banvard, Theodore J. Goodenows Who Originated in Sudbury Massachusetts, 1638 A. D. They Came from Wilts & Dorset England Across America They Roamed & Multiplied. LC 94-76043. (Illus.). 952p. 1994. 78.50 (*0-9641209-0-9*) Goodnow Fam Assn.

Banville, John. Athena. 1996. pap. 12.00 (*0-679-73685-9*) Random.

— The Book of Evidence. 1991. mass mkt. 8.99 (*0-446-39253-7*) Warner Bks.

— The Broken Jug: After Heinrich Von Kleist. LC 94-185541. 84p. 1994. pap. 14.95 (*1-85235-145-4*) Dufour.

— Doctor Copernicus: A Novel. LC 93-10924. 1993. pap. 12.00 (*0-679-73799-5*) Vin Bks.

— Ghosts. 1994. pap. 13.00 (*0-679-75512-8*) Vin Bks.

— Kepler. LC 93-13108. 1993. pap. 12.00 (*0-679-74370-7*) Vin Bks.

— Mefisto. 240p. 1999. pap. 13.95 (*1-56792-097-7*) Godine.

— Mefisto. 1991. mass mkt. 8.99 (*0-446-39282-0*, Pub. by Warner Bks) Little.

— The Newton Letter. 96p. 1987. pap. 10.95 (*1-56792-096-9*) Godine.

— The Newton Letter. 1991. pap. 8.99 (*0-446-39283-9*) Warner Bks.

— Nightspawn. 200p. 1993. pap. 16.95 (*1-85235-126-8*) Dufour.

— The Untouchable. LC 96-49637. 368p. 1997. 25.00 (*0-679-45108-0*) Knopf.

— The Untouchable. 384p. 1998. pap. 13.00 (*0-679-76747-9*) Vin Bks.

— The Untouchable. large type ed. LC 97-24568. 1997. lib. bdg. 21.95 (*0-7862-1213-6*) Thorndike Pr.

Banville, Theodore De. Poesies de Theodore De Banville, "Odes Funambulesques" LC 75-41016. (BCL Ser. II). reprint ed. 45.00 (*0-404-14505-1*) AMS Pr.

Banville, Theodore De, see De Banville, Theodore.

Banwart, Don. Rails, Rivalry, & Romance: Railroad History of Bourbon Co. (Illus.). 512p. 1982. 40.00 (*0-9601568-7-9*) Historic Pres Bourbon.

Banwart, Donald D., ed. Footprints of Bourbon County Families. (Illus.). 460p. 1991. 55.00 (*0-9601568-5-2*) Historic Pres Bourbon.

Banwart, L., jt. ed. see Stucki, J. W.

Banwart, Mary E. Hume's Imagination. LC 93-37636. (Studies in European Thought: Vol. 8). XIV, 179p. (C). 1994. text 41.95 (*0-8204-2356-4*) P Lang Pubng.

Banwart, Wayne L., jt. auth. see Hassett, John J.

Banwarth, Francine, ed. see Lazar, Edward.

Banwell, Barbara F. & Gall, Victoria, eds. Physical Therapy Management of Arthritis, No. 16. (Clinics in Physical Therapy Ser.: Vol. 16). (Illus.). 212p. 1987. pap. text 50.00 (*0-443-08438-6*) Church.

Bany-Winters, Lisa. On Stage! Theater Games & Activities for Kids. LC 97-14018. (Illus.). 160p. (J). (gr. 1-7). 1997. pap. 14.95 (*1-55652-324-6*) Chicago Review.

Banya, Kingsley. Implementing Educational Innovation in the Third World: A West African Experience. LC 93-18881. 208p. 1993. 89.95 (*0-7734-2234-X*) E Mellen.

***Banyaga, A., et al, eds.** Topics in Low-Dimensional Topology. 130p. 1999. 28.00 (*981-02-4050-3*) World Scientific Pub.

Banyaga, Augustin. The Structure of Classical Diffeomorphism Groups. LC 97-3534. 1997. text 120.50 (*0-7923-4475-8*) Kluwer Academic.

Banyai, Istvan. Re-Zoom. (Picture Puffin Ser.). (J). (gr. k up). 1998. pap. 5.99 (*0-14-055694-X*, PuffinBks) Peng Put Young Read.

— Re-Zoom. LC 95-14265. (Illus.). 64p. (J). 1995. 15.99 (*0-670-86392-0*, Viking) Viking Penguin.

— REM: Rapid Eye Movement. 1997. 14.99 (*0-614-29141-0*) Viking Penguin.

— Zoom. LC 94-33181. (Illus.). 64p. (J). (gr. k-3). 1995. 15.99 (*0-670-85804-8*, Viking) Viking Penguin.

— Zoom. (Picture Puffin Ser.). (Illus.). 64p. (J). (gr. k-3). 1998. pap. 6.99 (*0-14-055774-1*) Viking Penguin.

Banyai, L. & Koch, Stephan W. Semiconductor Quatum Dots. (Atomic, Molecular & Optical Ser.). 256p. 1993. text 48.00 (*981-02-1390-5*) World Scientific Pub.

Banyai, L., jt. ed. see Haug, Hartmut.

Banyal, S. S., ed. see Singh, Bhim.

***Banyard.** The Birder's Journal. (Illus.). 144p. 1998. 9.95 (*1-55110-773-2*) Whitecap Bks.

Banyard, Philip. Controversies in Psychology. LC 98-35362. (Modular Psychology Ser.). 1999. write for info. (*0-415-19496-2*); pap. write for info. (*0-415-19497-0*) Routledge.

— Introduction to Psychological Research. (C). 1997. pap. text 20.00 (*0-8147-1276-2*) NYU Pr.

Banyard, Philip & Grayson, Andrew. Introducing Psychological Research: Sixty Studies That Shape Psychology. LC 95-42254. (Illus.). 528p. (C). 1996. text 55.00 (*0-8147-1275-4*) NYU Pr.

Banyard, Victoria L., jt. auth. see Williams, Linda M.

***Banyas, Rebecca, et al.** Westside Light Rail Public Art Guide. LC 98-61132. 80 p. 1998. write for info. (*0-9666762-0-3*) Tri-County Metro.

Banyasz. Robust Control Design. LC 97-50627. (IFAC Postprint Ser.). 1997. pap. text 100.00 (*0-08-042606-9*, Pergamon Pr) Elsevier.

Banyasz, C., ed. Adaptive Systems in Control & Signal Processing 1995. (IFAC Postprint Ser.). 490p. 1995. pap. write for info. (*0-08-042375-2*, Pergamon Pr) Elsevier.

Banyasz, C. & Keviczky, L. Identification & System Parameter Estimation: Selected Papers from the 9th IFAC/IFORS Syposium, Budapest, Hungary, 8-12 July 1991, 2 vols. 1300p. 1992. 518.50 (*0-08-041271-8*, Pergamon Pr) Elsevier.

— Identification & System Parameter Estimation 1991, 2 vols. (IFAC Symposia Ser.: Vol. 9203). 1300p. 1992. pap. 197.00 (*0-08-043040-6*, Pergamon Pr) Elsevier.

Banyasz, Cs., ed. Intelligent Components & Instruments for Control Applications 1994: 2nd IFAC Symposium, Budapest, Hungary, 8-10 June 1994. LC 94-33839. 412p. 1994. pap. 99.00 (*0-08-042234-9*, Pergamon Pr) Elsevier.

***Banz, Stefan.** I Built This Garden for Us. (Illus.). 260p. 2000. 19.95 (*3-905509-23-7*, Pub. by Patrick Frey) Dist Art Pubs.

Banzet, P., et al, eds. Proceedings of the 3rd International Congress on Neo-Adjuvant Chemotherapy. (Illus.). 477p. 1992. 174.00 (*0-387-55039-9*) Spr-Verlag.

Banzhaf, H. Spencer, et al. Environmental Policy Analysis with Limited Information: Principles & Applications of the Transfer Method. LC 98-9844. (New Horizons in Environmental Economics Ser.). 256p. 1999. 85.00 (*1-85898-655-9*) E Elgar.

Banzhaf, Hajo. The Crowley Tarot: The Handbook of the Cards. (Illus.). 224p. 1997. pap. 17.95 (*0-88079-715-0*, BK129) US Games Syst.

***Banzhaf, Hajo.** Tarot & the Journey of the Hero. LC 99-59294. (Illus.). 224p. 2000. pap. 19.95 (*1-57863-117-3*) Weiser.

Banzhaf, Hajo. The Tarot Handbook, Vol. 1. LC 93-60077. (Illus.). 184p. 1994. pap. 17.95 (*0-88079-511-5*, BK113) US Games Syst.

Banzhaf, Hajo & Haebler, Anna. Key Words for Astrology. 304p. (Orig.). 1996. pap. 16.95 (*0-87728-875-5*) Weiser.

***Banzhaf, Hajo & Hemmerlein, Elisa.** Tarot as Your Companion: A Practical Guide to the Rider-Waite & Crowley Tarot Decks. LC 99-36075. 1999. 17.95 (*1-57281-217-6*) US Games Syst.

Banzhaf, Hajo & Theler, Brigitte. Secrets of Love & Partnership: The Astrological Guide for Finding Your "One & Only" LC 98-19023.Tr. of Du Bist Alles Was Mir Fehlt Suchbild und Selbstbild Im Horoskop. (Illus.). 272p. 1998. pap. 14.95 (*1-57863-040-1*) Weiser.

Banzhaf, Robert A. Screen Process Printing. 1983. text 18.62 (*0-02-672270-4*) Glencoe.

Banzhaf, W., et al, eds. Genetic Programming: Proceedings of the First European Workshop, EuroGP'98, Paris, France, April 14-15, 1998. LC 98-4168. (Lecture Notes in Computer Science Ser.: Vol. 1391). x, 232p. 1998. pap. 43.00 (*3-540-64360-5*) Spr-Verlag.

Banzhaf, W. & Eeckman, F. H., eds. Evolution & Biocomputation. (Lecture Notes in Computer Science Ser.: Vol. 899). 277p. 1995. 49.00 (*3-540-59046-3*) Spr-Verlag.

Banzhaf, Wolfgang & Eeckman, Frank H., eds. Evolution & Biocomputation: Computational Models of Evolution. LC 95-5970. (Lecture Notes in Computer Science Ser.: No. 899). 1995. write for info. (*0-387-59046-3*) Spr-Verlag.

***Banzhaf, Wolfgang & Reeves, Colin R.** Foundations of Genetic Algorithms, Vol. 5. LC 99-201701. 400p. 1999. 79.95 (*1-55860-559-2*, Pub. by Morgan Kaufmann) Harcourt.

Banzhaf, Wolgang, et al. Genetic Programming: An Introduction. LC 97-51603. 470p. 1998. pap. text 59.95 (*1-55860-510-X*) Morgan Kaufmann.

Bao, C. Synoptic Meteorology in China. (Illus.). vi, 269p. 1988. 103.95 (*0-387-16715-3*) Spr-Verlag.

Bao, Dalizhabu, jt. auth. see Di Cosmo, Nicola.

Bao, David D., et al. Finsler Geometry: Joint Summer Research Conference on Finsler Geometry, July 16-20, 1995, Seattle, Washington. LC 96-21779. (Contemporary Mathematics Ser.: Vol. 196). 310p. 1996. pap. 61.00 (*0-8218-0507-X*, CONM/61) Am Math.

***Bao, David Dai-Wai, et al.** An Introduction to Riemann-Finsler Geometry. LC 99-49808. (Graduate Texts in Mathematics Ser.: Vol. 200). (Illus.). 400p. 2000. 49.95 (*0-387-98948-X*) Spr-Verlag.

Bao, Yuheng. The Concept of the Relationship Between Painting & Poetry. LC 99-22944. (Studies in Art History: Vol. 1). 228p. 1999. text 89.95 (*0-7734-8043-9*) E Mellen.

Bao, Zhiming. The Structure of Tone. LC 99-19275. 264p. 1999. text 55.00 (*0-19-511880-4*) OUP.

***Baofu, Peter.** The Future of Human Civilization LC 99-41420. 1999. write for info. (*0-7734-7945-7*) E Mellen.

— The Future of Human Civilization. LC 99-41420. 476p. 1999. text 99.95 (*0-7734-7901-5*) E Mellen.

Baogang He. The Democratization of China. LC 96-10515. (China in Transition Ser.). 296p. (C). 1996. 75.00 (*0-415-14764-6*) Routledge.

Baoill, Colm O. The Harps' Cry: An Anthology of 17th Century Gaelic Poetry. 256p. pap. 21.95 (*1-874744-13-0*, Pub. by Birlinn Ltd) Dufour.

Baolin, Ma & Mao, Cindy. Sing Chinese II: China's Best Folk Songs. 96p. 1997. pap. 21.95 incl. audio, audio compact disk (*0-8351-2595-5*); pap. 29.95 incl. audio compact disk (*0-8351-2597-1*); spiral bd. 15.95 incl. audio, audio compact disk (*0-8351-2594-7*) China Bks.

Baoqi, Qin, jt. auth. see Murray, Diane H.

Baosworth, A. S. History of Randolph County: From Its Earliest Exploration & Settlement to the Present Time (1916) (Illus.). 448p. 1997. reprint ed. lib. bdg. 47.00 (*0-8328-6952-X*) Higginson Bk Co.

Baoudndi, M. Salah, et al. Microlocal Analysis. Beals, Richards & Preiss, Linda, eds. LC 84-2852. (Contemporary Mathematics Ser.: No. 27). 252p. 1984. pap. 37.00 (*0-8218-5031-8*, CONM/27) Am Math.

***Baouendi, M. Salah.** Real Submanifolds in Complex Space & Their Mappings. LC 98-44235. 1998. 69.50 (*0-691-00498-6*, Pub. by Princeton U Pr) Cal Prin Full Svc.

Baouendi, M. Salah, et al, eds. Microlocal Analysis. LC 84-2852. (Contemporary Mathematics Ser.: No. 27). (Illus.). 260p. reprint ed. pap. 80.60 (*0-608-09193-6*, 205269700003) Bks Demand.

Baowen, Wei, jt. ed. see Shen, W. Q.

Baowersox, U. S. Bauersachs Family History & Chronology. (Illus.). 168p. 1997. reprint ed. pap. 25.00 (*0-8328-7425-6*); reprint ed. lib. bdg. 35.00 (*0-8328-7424-8*) Higginson Bk Co.

Bapat. Shanty Town City: The Case of Poona. (Progress in Planning Ser.: Vol. 15, Pt. 3). 85p. 1981. pap. 16.25 (*0-08-026811-0*, Pergamon Pr) Elsevier.

Bapat, R. B. Linear Algebra & Linear Models. 2nd ed. LC 99-30383. (Universitext Ser.). 184p. 1999. 44.95 (*0-387-98871-8*) Spr-Verlag.

Bapat, R. B. & Raghavan, T. E. Nonnegative Matrices & Applications. (Encyclopedia of Mathematics & Its Applications Ser.: No. 64). (Illus.). 349p. (C). 1997. text 69.95 (*0-521-57167-7*) Cambridge U Pr.

Bapes, Robert. IdeaDoc's Rx for Creativity. 72p. 1996. pap. 17.00 (*1-57502-329-6*, P01100) Morris Pubng.

Bapna, Ashok, ed. One World One Future: New International Strategies for Development. 364p. 1985. 65.00 (*0-275-90056-8*, C0056, Praeger Pubs) Greenwood.

Bapna, S. L. & Rao, K. R. Supply & Price Outlook for Crops. 262p. 1987. 18.50 (*81-204-0218-9*, Pub. by Oxford IBH) S Asia.

Bappu, M. K., ed. see International Astronomical Union Staff.

***Bapsar, Yavuz & Weichert, Dieter.** Nonlinear Continuum Mechanics of Solids: Fundamental Mathematical & Physical Concepts. LC 99-55461. x, 204p. 2000. pap. 59.95 (*3-540-66601-X*) Spr-Verlag.

Baptie, David. Musical Scotland Past & Present. 253p. 1972. reprint ed. lib. bdg. 60.00 (*3-487-04292-4*) G Olms Pubs.

Baptist, C. Tanker Handbook for Deck Officers. (Illus.). (C). 1987. 140.00 (0-85174-386-2) St Mut.
— Tanker Handbook for Deck Officers. 7th ed. (Illus.). 200p. 1993. text 95.00 (0-85174-587-3) Sheridan.
Baptist, Claire, et al, eds. Computers in the Medical Office: Using MediSoft. LC 94-20025. 1995. 50.88 (0-02-803042-7) Glencoe.
Baptist, Claire, et al. Computers in the Medical Office: Using MediSoft (DOS Version) 1995. teacher ed. 12.21 (0-02-803043-5) Glencoe.
Baptist, Jane. The Flight of the Eagle: The View Through Minority Group Eyes. 170p. mass mkt. 4.99 (1-55197-082-1) Picasso Publ.
Baptist-Metz, Johannes, jt. auth. see Schillebeeckx, Edward.
Baptist, Oren C. The Baptista Megafamily: Ten Centuries in Europe, Madeira & America. LC 90-71034. (Illus.). 266p. 1990. 35.95 (0-9617956-0-3) Madeira Pubns.
***Baptist Spanish Publishing House Staff.** La Biblia Libro por Libro Bk. 9: Condensed Edition. (SPA.). 1999. pap. 3.40 (0-311-11289-7) Baptist Spanish.
— La Biblia Libro por Libro Bk. 9: Youth Pupils Edition. (SPA.). 1999. pap. 5.99 (0-311-11279-X) Baptist Spanish.
— Ezra, Nehemiah, Esther, Colossians, 1 & 2 Timothy, Titus, Joel, Obadiah, Nahum, Zephaniah, Hagga: LA Biblia Libro Por Libro #9 Maestros Javenes y Adultos. (Bible Book by Book (Spanish) Ser.: Vol. 9). 1999. pap. 9.50 (0-311-11259-5) Baptist Spanish.
— Ezra, Nehemiah, Esther, Colossians, 1 & 2 Timothy, Titus, Joel, Obadiah, Nahum, Zephaniah, Hagga: LA Biblia Libro Por Libro # 9 Maestros Jovenes y Adultos. (Bible Book by Book (Spanish) Ser.: Vol. 9). 1999. pap. 5.99 (0-311-11269-2) Baptist Spanish.
— Santa Biblia Para Familias RVA.Tr. of Family Bible. 2000. 42.99 (0-311-48790-4) Baptist Spanish.
— Santa Biblia RVA Ultra Fina Ultrathin Bible. 2000. 25.99 (0-311-48831-5); 25.99 (0-311-48833-1); 53.99 (0-311-48835-8) Baptist Spanish.
— Santa Biblia RVA Ultra Fine Ultrathin Bible. 2000. 25.99 (0-311-48832-3); 47.99 (0-311-48834-X) Baptist Spanish.
***Baptist Spanish Publishing House Staff, ed.** Sermones Para el Nuevo Milenio. (SPA.). 96p. 2000. pap. 5.95 (0-311-43051-1) Baptist Spanish.
Baptist Theological Seminary Faculty Staff. Festschrift Gunter Wagner. Ruschlikon & Schwiez, eds. LC 95-209415. (International Theological Studies - Contributions of Baptist Scholars: Vol. 1). (GER.). xviii, 251p. 1994. pap. 39.95 (3-906752-07-0, Pub. by P Lang) P Lang Pubng.
Baptista, Alessandra R. & Mathis, Wayne N. A Revision of New World Cyamops Melander (Diptera: Periscelididae) LC 94-26880. (Smithsonian Contributions to Zoology Ser.: No. 563). 29p. reprint ed. pap. 30.00 (0-7837-8766-9, 204951100012) Bks Demand.
Baptista, Joao, jt. auth. see Gertz, Dwight L.
Baptista, Luis, jt. auth. see Welty, Carl.
Baptista, Lynne H. & Rosenthal, Mark, contrib. by. Discover Animal Life. (Discover Ser.). (Illus.). 48p. (J). (gr. 3-6). 1996. lib. bdg. 15.95 (1-56674-106-8, HTS Bks) Forest Hse.
Baptista Mantuanus. The Eclogues of Mantuan. Bush, Douglas, ed. Turberville, George, tr. LC 38-12665. 208p. 1977. reprint ed. 50.00 (0-8201-1181-3) Schol Facsimiles.
Baptista, Maria. Spanish, Just Enough Book. (Hugo's Language Courses Ser.). 128p. (Orig.). 1995. pap. 5.95 (0-85285-224-X) Hunter NJ.
Baptista, Todd R. Group Harmony: Behind the Rhythm & the Blues. LC 96-96294. (Illus.). 232p. (Orig.). 1996. pap. text 19.95 (0-9631722-5-5) Hamilton Print.
***Baptiste, Claire.** Building Bridges. LC 99-65304. 192p. 2000. pap. 11.95 (1-56315-258-4, Pub. by SterlingHse) Natl Bk Netwk.
Baptiste, Fitzroy A. War, Cooperation, & Conflict: The European Possessions in the Caribbean, 1939-1945, 23. LC 87-8643. (Contributions in Comparative Colonial Studies: No. 23). 365p. 1988. 65.00 (0-313-25472-9, BWC/, Greenwood Pr) Greenwood.
Baptiste, Gurline J., ed. see Lykins, Elizabeth M.
Baptiste, H. Prentice, Jr. Multicultural Education: A Synopsis. LC 79-89924. 1979. pap. text 16.00 (0-8191-0851-0) U Pr of Amer.
Baptiste, H. Prentice, Jr., et al, eds. Leadership, Equity, & School Effectiveness. LC 89-37459. 279p. 1990. pap. 86.50 (0-608-05604-9, 206606200006) Bks Demand.
Baptiste, H. Prentice, Jr & Baptiste, Mira L. Developing the Multicultural Process in Classroom Instruction: Competencies for Teachers. LC 79-89993. 1979. pap. text 26.00 (0-8191-0855-3) U Pr of Amer.
Baptiste, H. Prentice, jt. auth. see Boyer, James B.
Baptiste, Mira L., jt. auth. see Baptiste, H. Prentice, Jr.
Baptiste, Sandra. The Caribbean & the European Union Development. (Illus.). 72p. (C). 1998. pap. text 20.00 (0-7881-7171-2) DIANE Pub.
Baptiste, Victor N. Bartolome de las Casas & Thomas More's "Utopia" Connections & Similarities - A Translation & Study. LC 89-84022. 76p. 1990. pap. 20.00 (0-911437-43-6) Labyrinthos.
Bapty, Ian & Yates, Tim, eds. Archaeology after Structuralism. 352p. (C). 1991. text 85.00 (0-415-04500-2, A5539) Routledge.
Baqir, M. Lahore: Past & Present. (C). 1993. 14.00 (81-85557-22-5, Pub. by Low Price) S Asia.
Baqli, Ruzbihan. The Unveiling of Secrets: Diary of a Sufi Master. Ernst, Carl W., tr. from ARA. xi, 150p. (Orig.). 1997. pap. 15.95 (0-9644362-1-3) Parvardigar Pr.
***Baquedano, Elizabeth.** Aztec, Inca & Maya. (Eyewitness Books). (Illus.). (J). (gr. 4-7). 2000. 19.99 (0-7894-6596-5) DK Pub Inc.
— Aztec, Inca & Maya. (Eyewitness Books). (J). (gr. 4-7). 2000. 15.95 (0-7894-6115-3) DK Pub Inc.
— Aztec, Inca & Maya. (Eyewitness Books). (Illus.). 64p. (YA). (gr. 5 up). 1993. lib. bdg. 20.99 (0-679-93883-4, Pub. by Knopf Bks Yng Read) Random.
— Los Aztecas. 1997. pap. text 9.98 (968-38-0304-0) Panorama Edit.
Baquedano, Sarah. Rombo y Otros Momentos. LC 83-82850. (Coleccion Caniqui). (SPA.). 309p. 1984. pap. 9.95 (0-89729-345-2) Ediciones.
Baquero, Gaston. Palabras en la Arena. Hiriart, Rosario, ed. (SPA.). 102p. (Orig.). 1997. pap. 15.00 (1-887175-03-2) ECV NY.
Baquero, R. Manifestations of the Electron-Phonon Interaction - 2nd Cinvestav Superconductivity Sym. 224p. 1994. text 109.00 (981-02-1545-2) World Scientific Pub.
Baquiran, Delia C. & Gallagher, Jean. Lippincott's Cancer Chemotherapy Handbook. LC 97-34705. 384p. 1997. pap. text 27.00 (0-397-55470-2) Lppncott W & W.
Bar-Adon, Aaron. The Rise & Decline of a Dialect: A Study in the Revival of Modern Hebrew. LC 74-80121. (Janua Linguarum, Ser. Practica: No. 197). 116p. (Orig.). 1975. pap. text 36.95 (90-279-3206-9) Mouton.
Bar Am, Meir. The Parnas. Van Handel, Esther, tr. 1986. pap. 6.95 (0-87306-400-3) Feldheim.
Bar, Antonio. Syndicalism & Revolution in Spain. (History of Anarchism Ser.). 1981. lib. bdg. 250.00 (0-8490-3208-3) Gordon Pr.
***Bar-Asher, Meir Mikhael.** Scripture & Exegesis in Early Imeamei-Shiism. LC 99-24377. (Islamic Philosophy, Theology & Science Ser.). 1999. 94.00 (90-04-11495-5) Brill Academic Pubs.
Bar-Asher, Moshe, ed. Studies in Hebrew & Jewish Languages: Presented to Shelomo Morag. (ENG & HEB.). 741p. 1996. text 32.00 (965-342-659-1, Pub. by Bialik) Eisenbrauns.
Bar-Avi, Patrick & Benaroya, Haym. Nonlinear Dynamics of Compliant Offshore Structures. LC 97-19331. (Advances in Engineering Ser.: Vol. I). (Illus.). 182p. 1997. 88.00 (90-265-1499-9) Swets.
Bar, Christian Von, see Von Bar, Christian.
Bar, Christian Von, see Spier, Jaap & Von Bar, Christian.
Bar, Christian Von, see Hartkamp, A. S. & Von Bar, Christian.
Bar-Cohen, A., ed. see AIAA-ASME Thermophysics & Heat Transfer Conference.
Bar-Cohen, Avram & Kraus, Allan D., eds. Advances in Thermal Modeling of Electronic Components & Systems, Vol. 2. 448p. 1993. 99.00 (0-7918-0015-6, 800156) ASME Pr.
Bar-Cohen, Avram, jt. auth. see Kraus, Allan D.
***Bar-Cohen, Yoseph, ed.** Electroactive Polymer Actuators & Devices. 426p. 1999. pap. text 92.00 (0-8194-3143-5) SPIE.
Bar, Edwig Von, see Von Bar, Edwig, ed.
Bar-Efrat, S. Narrative Art in the Bible. (JSOTS Ser.: Vol. 70). 295p. 1989. pap. 19.95 (1-85075-133-1, Pub. by Sheffield Acad) CUP Services.
Bar-Eli, Michael, jt. ed. see Lidor, Ronnie.
Bar-Elli, Gilead. The Sense of Reference: Intentionality in Frege. LC 96-32718. (Perspektiven der Analytischen Philosophie - Perspectives in Analytical Philosophy Ser.: Vol. 10). xxvi, 251p. 1996. lib. bdg. 124.50 (3-11-015059-X) De Gruyter.
Bar Hebraeus. The Laughable Stories. Budge, E. A. Wallis, tr. from SYR. LC 73-18852. (Luzac's Semitic Text & Translation Ser.: No. 1). (ENG.). reprint ed. 49.50 (0-404-11347-8) AMS Pr.
Bar-Ilan, Ruth, tr. see Hallamish, Moshe.
Bar-Itzhak, Haya. Jewish Poland - Legends of Origin: Ethnopoetics & Legendary Chronicles. (Illus.). 216p. 2000. 34.95 (0-8143-2789-3) Wayne St U Pr.
Bar-Itzhak, Haya & Shenhar, Aliza. Jewish Moroccan Folk Narratives from Israel. Widman, Miriam, tr. LC 92-44747. (Jewish Folklore & Anthropology Ser.). (Illus.). 206p. 1993. pap. text 21.95 (0-8143-2443-6) Wayne St U Pr.
Bar-Itzhak, Haya & Shenhar, Aliza, eds. Jewish Moroccan Folk Narratives from Israel. Widmann, Miriam, tr. LC 92-44747. (Jewish Folklore & Anthropology Ser.). (Illus.). 205p. reprint ed. pap. 63.60 (0-608-10520-1, 2054431) Bks Demand.
***Bar, Jochen A.** Sprachreflexion der Deutschen Fruhromantik: Konzepte Zwischen Universalpoesie Und Grammatischem Kosmopolitismus Mit Lexikographischem Anhang. ix, 582p. 1999. 165.35 (3-11-016372-1) De Gruyter.
Bar-Joseph, Uri. Best of Enemies: Israel & Trans-Jordan in the 1948 War. 224p. 1986. 49.50 (0-7146-3211-2, Pub. by F Cass Pubs) Intl Spec Bk.
— Intelligence Intervention in the Politics of Democratic States: The United States, Israel, & Great Britain. LC 93-43352. 384p. 1995. 60.00 (0-271-01331-1); pap. 19.95 (0-271-01332-X) Pa St U Pr.
Bar, Jurgen. Der Assyrische Tribut und Seine Darstellung: Eine Untersuchung zur Imperialen Ideologie im Neuassyrischen Reich. (Alter Orient und Altes Testament Ser.: Vol. 243). (GER.). xiii, 279p. 1996. text 82.50 (3-7887-1572-3) NeukirchenerV.
***Bar, Jurgen.** Optionsewertung Und Asicherungsstrategien. (Illus.). IX, 220p. 1999. 45.95 (3-631-33546-6) P Lang Pubng.
Bar-Kana, I., jt. auth. see Kaufman, H.
Bar-Kochva, Bezalal. The Seleucid Army. (Cambridge Classical Studies). 318p. 1976. text 64.95 (0-521-20667-7) Cambridge U Pr.
Bar-Kochva, Bezalel. Pseudo-Hecateus "On the Jews" Legitimizing the Jewish Diaspora. LC 95-20939. (Hellenistic Culture & Society Ser.: Vol. XXI). (Illus.). 287p. (C). 1997. 60.00 (0-520-20059-4, Pub. by U CA Pr) Cal Prin Full Svc.
Bar, Laurel B. & Galluzzo, Judith D. The Accessible School: Universal Design for Educational Settings. LC 98-51671. (Illus.). 80p. (Orig.). 1998. pap. text 39.95 (0-944661-20-3) MIG Comns.
Bar-Lev, Geoffrey. Jewish Amerian Struggle for Equality. LC 92-7473. (Discrimination Ser.). 112p. (J). 1992. lib. bdg. 18.95 (0-86593-182-8) Rourke Corp.
Bar-Lev, Geoffrey & Sakkal, Joyce. Jewish Amerian Struggle for Equality. LC 92-7473. (Discrimination Ser.). (YA). 1992. 16.95 (0-685-59291-X) Rourke Corp.
Bar-Levav, Reuven. Every Family Needs a C.E.O. What Mothers & Fathers Can Do about Our Deteriorating Families & Values. LC 94-61637. 288p. 1995. 19.95 (0-9644177-0-7) Fathering.
Bar, Michael Zohar. Bitter Scent. 1999. pap. write for info. (0-452-27534-2, Plume) Dutton Plume.
***Bar, Moshe.** Linux Internals. (Application Development Ser.). (Illus.). 2000. pap. 49.99 (0-07-212598-5) Osborne-McGraw.
Bar-Niv, Justice. International Labour Law Reports, Vol. 10. 584p. 1992. lib. bdg. 273.50 (0-7923-1388-7) Kluwer Academic.
Bar-Niv, Ran, jt. auth. see Bickelhaupt, David L.
Bar-Niv, Zvi H. International Labour Law Reports, Vol. 6. (C). 1988. lib. bdg. 174.50 (90-247-3605-6) Kluwer Academic.
— International Labour Law Reports, Vol. 8. (C). 1990. lib. bdg. 238.50 (0-7923-0429-2, Pub. by Graham & Trotman) Kluwer Academic.
Bar-Niv, Zvi H., ed. International Labor Law Reports, Vol. 9. (C). 1990. lib. bdg. 254.00 (0-7923-0848-4) Kluwer Academic.
Bar Niv, Zvi H., ed. International Labour Law Reports, Vol. II. 560p. (C). 1993. lib. bdg. 266.00 (0-7923-1889-7) Kluwer Academic.
Bar-Niv, Zvi H., ed. International Labour Law Reports, Vol. 7. (C). 1989. lib. bdg. 246.00 (0-7923-0099-8) Kluwer Academic.
***Bar-Niv, Zvi H., et al, eds.** International Labour Law Reports, Vol. 17. 524p. 1998. 224.00 (90-411-1060-7) Kluwer Law Intl.
***Bar-Niv, Zvi H., et al.** International Labour Law Reports, Vol. 18. 584p. 2000. 262.00 (90-411-1363-0) Kluwer Academic.
Bar-On, A. Z. The Categories & the Principle of Coherence: Whitehead's Theory of Categories in Historical Perspective. (Nijhoff International Philosophy Ser.: No. 26). 258p. 1987. lib. bdg. 139.00 (90-247-3478-9, Pub. by M Nijhoff) Kluwer Academic.
Bar-on, A. Zvie. Ontological Analysis: The Classical Model. 244p. (C). Date not set. lib. bdg. 42.50 (0-7618-0029-8) U Pr of Amer.
Bar On, Bat-Ami, ed. Engendering Origins: Critical Feminist Readings in Plato & Aristotle. LC 92-36046. (SUNY Series in Feminist Philosophy). 247p. (C). 1993. text 54.50 (0-7914-1643-7); pap. text 18.95 (0-7914-1644-5) State U NY Pr.
— Modern Engendering: Critical Feminist Readings in Modern Western Philosophy. LC 92-36047. (SUNY Series in Feminist Philosophy). 280p. 1993. text 64.50 (0-7914-1641-0); pap. text 21.95 (0-7914-1642-9) State U NY Pr.
Bar-On, Dan. Fear & Hope: Three Generations of the Holocaust. LC 94-42016. 416p. 1995. text 44.50 (0-674-29522-6, BARFEA) HUP.
— The Indescribable & the Undiscussable: Reconstructing Human Discourse after Trauma. 310p. 1998. 49.95 (963-9116-34-3); pap. 19.95 (963-9116-33-5) Ctrl Europ Univ.
Bar-On, Dan, jt. auth. see Niv, Amittai.
Bar-On, Dorit, tr. see Kalechofsky, Roberta, ed.
Bar-On, Mordechai. The Gates of Gaza: Israel's Road to Suez & Back, 1955-1957. 432p. 1994. text 39.95 (0-312-10586-X) St Martin.
— The Gates of Gaza: Israel's Road to Suez & Back, 1955-57. 336p. 1995. pap. 19.95 (0-312-12340-X) St Martin.
— In Pursuit of Peace: A History of the Israeli Peace Movement. LC 96-4787. 1996. 37.50 (1-878379-54-2); pap. text 24.95 (1-878379-53-4) US Inst Peace.
Bar-On, Reuven & Handley, Rich. The Last Corporate Secret: Applying Emotional-Social-Behavioral Audit to Augment to Collective EQ & Improve Organizational Effectiveness. 208p. 1998. 24.95 (0-9664546-2-6) Pro-Philes.
***Bar-On, Reuven & Parker, James D. A.** Handbook of Emotional Intelligence. LC 00-31550. 2000. 69.95 (0-7879-4984-1) Jossey-Bass.
Bar-Or, O. The Health Implications of Exercise & Sports in the School Aged Child & Adolescent. (Journal: Pediatrician: Vol.13, No. 1). (Illus.). 60p. 1986. pap. 35.75 (3-8055-4469-3) S Karger.
Bar-Or, Oded, et al, eds. The Child & Adolescent Athlete. LC 95-182. (Encyclopedia of Sports Medicine Ser.: Vol. 6). 672p. 1995. 95.00 (0-86542-904-9) Blackwell Sci.
Bar-Or, Oded, jt. ed. see Blimkie, Cameron J.
Bar-Or, Roman. Prikhodiat Veka I Ukhodiat Veka: The Ages Arrive & Go. LC 90-47354. (RUS.). 128p. (Orig.). 1991. pap. 8.00 (1-55779-037-X) Hermitage Pubs.
Bar, Peter Rudolf & Beal, M. Flint, eds. Neuroprotection. LC 97-12545. (Illus.). 584p. 1997. text 185.00 (0-8247-9876-7) Dekker.
Bar-Sagi, Dafna, ed. Transmembrane Signaling Protocols. LC 97-45056. (Methods in Molecular Biology Ser.: Vol. 84). (Illus.). 320p. 1998. 99.50 (0-89603-488-7); spiral bd. 74.50 (0-89603-432-1) Humana.
Bar-Shalom, Yaakov. Multitarget-Multisensor Tracking Vol. I: Applications & Advances. (Illus.). 365p. (C). 1998. reprint ed. ring bd. 60.00 (0-9648312-2-8, MTAA1) YBS Pubng.
— Multitarget-Multisensor Tracking Vol. II: Applications & Advances. (Illus.). 488p. (C). 1998. reprint ed. ring bd. 60.00 (0-9648312-3-6, MTAA2) YBS Pubng.
***Bar-Shalom, Yaakov.** Multitarget/Multisensor Tracking Vol. III: Applications & Advances. (Radar Library). 2000. 109.00 (1-58053-091-5) Artech Hse.
Bar-Shalom, Yaakov & Li, Xiao-Rong. Estimation & Tracking: Principles, Techniques & Software. (Illus.). 536p. 1998. reprint ed. ring bd. 65.00 (0-9648312-1-X, ET) YBS Pubng.
Bar-Shalom, Yaakov & Xiao-Rong Li. Multitarget-Multisensor Tracking: Principles & Techniques. 630p. (C). 1995. pap. text 120.00 (0-9648312-0-1) YBS Pubng.
Bar-Siman-Tov, Yaacov. Israel & the Peace Process, 1977-1982: In Search of Legitimacy for Peace. LC 93-50589. (SUNY Series in Israeli Studies). 338p. (C). 1994. pap. text 21.95 (0-7914-2220-8) State U NY Pr.
— Israel & the Peace Process, 1977-1982: In Search of Legitimacy for Peace. LC 93-50589. (SUNY Series in Israeli Studies). 338p. (C). 1994. text 64.50 (0-7914-2219-4) State U NY Pr.
Bar-Simon-Tov, Yaacov. The Israeli-Egyptian War of Attrition, 1969-1970: A Case-Study of Limited Local War. LC 80-11124. 256p. 1980. text 57.50 (0-231-04982-X) Col U Pr.
Bar-Tal, Daniel. Group Beliefs. (Social Psychology Ser.). 175p. 1989. 90.95 (0-387-97085-1) Spr-Verlag.
***Bar-Tal, Daniel.** Security Concerns: Insights for the Israeli Experience. LC 98-52739. (Contemporary Studies in Sociology: Vol. 17). 1999. 78.50 (0-7623-0468-5) Jai Pr.
— Shared Beliefs in a Society: Social Psychological Analysis. LC 00-8359. 2000. pap. write for info. (0-7619-0659-2) Sage.
Bar-Tal, Daniel, et al, eds. Stereotyping & Prejudice. (Social Psychology Ser.). (Illus.). 275p. 1989. 44.00 (0-387-96883-0) Spr-Verlag.
Bar-Tal, Raviv. How Children Understand War & Peace: A Call for International Peace Education. Raviv, Amiran et al, eds. LC 98-40154. 352p. 1999. text 44.95 (0-7879-4169-7) Jossey-Bass.
Bar-Tura, Maggie, tr. see Oz, Amos.
Bar, W. & Zurich, eds. Advances in Forensic Haemogenetics, Vol. 5. 677p. 1994. 105.00 (0-387-57643-6) Spr-Verlag.
Bar-Yaacov, Nissim. The Israel-Syrian Armistice: Problems of Implementation, 1949-1966. LC 68-988. (Illus.). 382p. reprint ed. pap. 118.50 (0-608-13686-7, 205159300097) Bks Demand.
Bar-Yam, Yaneer. Dynamics of Complex Systems. Jeffrey, Robbin S., ed. LC 96-52033. 953p. (C). 1997. 59.00 (0-201-55748-7) Addison-Wesley.
— Unifying Themes in Complex Systems: Proceedings of the First NECSI International Conference. (New England Complex Systems Institute Ser.). 704p. 2000. text 60.00 (0-7382-0049-2, Pub. by Perseus Pubng) HarpC.
Bar Yohai, Shimon. Hashmotot Zohar: Hebrew Text. 1969. write for info. (0-943688-20-5) Res Ctr Kabbalah.
— Zohar: Hebrew Text, 10 vols. 1981. write for info. (0-943688-68-X) Res Ctr Kabbalah.
— Zohar: Hebrew Text, 24 vols. 1992. 345.00 (0-943688-67-1) Res Ctr Kabbalah.
Bar-Yosef, O., jt. ed. see Phillips, J. L.
***Bar-Yosef, Ofer.** The Geography of Neanderthals & Modern Humans in Europe & the Greater Mediterranean. Pilbeam, David, ed. LC 00-91057. (Peabody Museum Bulletins Ser.: Vol. 8). (Illus.). 220p. 2000. pap. text 25.00 (0-87365-958-9) Peabody Harvard.
Bar-Yosef, Ofer & Gopher, Avi, eds. An Early Neolithic Village in the Jordan Valley Pt. I: The Archaeology of Netiv Hagdud. LC 96-71485. (American School of Prehistoric Research Bulletins Ser.: Vol. 43). (Illus.). 280p. (C). 1997. pap. 45.00 (0-87365-547-8, A43) Peabody Harvard.
Bar-Yosef, Ofer & Valla, Francois R., eds. The Natufian Culture in the Levant. (Archaeological Ser.: No. 1). (Illus.). vi, 644p. (Orig.). 1991. pap. 55.00 (1-879621-01-0); lib. bdg. 75.00 (1-879621-03-7) Intl Mono Prehstry.
Bar-Yosef, Ofer, jt. ed. see Rocek, Thomas R.
Bar-Ziv, Jacob, jt. auth. see Meizner, Israel.
Bar-Zohar, Michael. Ben-Gurion: A Biography. Kidron, Peretz, tr. from HEB. LC 86-10741. (Illus.). 342p. 1986. 17.95 (0-915361-59-0); pap. 12.95 (0-915361-60-4) Lambda Pubs.
— Beyond Hitler's Grasp: The Heroic Rescue of Bulgaria's Jews. LC 98-8407. (Illus.). 288p. 1998. 24.95 (1-58062-060-4) Adams Media.
— Bitter Scent: The Case of L'Oreal, Nazis & the Arab Boycott. 264p. 1999. reprint ed. pap. text 25.00 (0-7881-6268-3) DIANE Pub.
— Brothers. 1995. mass mkt. 5.99 (0-449-14678-2, GM) Fawcett.
Bar-Zohar, Michael, ed. Lionhearts: Heroes of Israel. LC 98-84483. (Illus.). 352p. 1998. 30.00 (0-446-52358-5, Pub. by Warner Bks) Little.
— Lionhearts: Heroes of Israel. 352p. 1999. pap. write for info. (0-446-67528-8) Warner Bks.
***BAR/BRI Staff.** 2001 Patent Law in Practice: Discovery. 2000. pap. text. write for info. (0-15-607168-1) Harcourt.
***Bara, Craig.** Sebring. (Images of America Ser.). 128p. 1999. pap. 18.99 (0-7385-0180-8) Arcadia Publng.
Bara, Craig & Crist, Lyle. Alliance. LC 98-87443. (Images of America Ser.). (Illus.). 128p. 1998. pap. 16.99 (0-7524-1328-7) Arcadia Publng.
Baraban. Restaurant. 2nd ed. text 59.95 (0-471-35935-1) Wiley.
Baraban, Regina S. & Durocher, Joseph F. Restaurant Design. 272p. 1992. pap. 49.95 (0-471-28488-2, VNR) Wiley.

B

Baraban, Regina S. & Durocher, Joseph F. Successful Restaurant Design. (Illus.). 262p. 1992. pap. text 39.95 (*0-442-01152-0*, VNR) Wiley.

Barabas, Christine. Technical Writing in a Corporate Culture: A Study of the Nature of Information. Farr, Marcia, ed. LC 90-32194. (Writing Research Ser.: Vol. 18). 272p. (C). 1990. pap. 39.50 (*0-89391-664-1*); text 73.25 (*0-89391-603-X*) Ablx Pub.

Barabas, Gabor, jt. auth. see Barabas, SuzAnne.

Barabas, Kathy. Let's Find Out about Money. LC 96-44077. (Let's Find Out Library Ser.). (Illus.). 24p. (J). (ps-2). 1997. 4.95 (*0-590-73803-8*) Scholastic Inc.

— Let's Find Out about Toothpaste. LC 96-47546. (Let's Find Out Library Ser.). (Illus.). (J). 1997. write for info. (*0-590-73804-6*) Scholastic Inc.

Barabas, SuzAnne & Barabas, Gabor. Gunsmoke: A Complete History & Analysis of the Legendary Broadcast Series with a Comprehensive Episode-by-Episode Guide to Both the Radio & Television Programs. LC 89-42703. (Illus.). 848p. 1990. lib. bdg. 85.00 (*0-89950-418-3*) McFarland & Co.

Barabashev, Alexei. Long Cycles in the History of Mathematics. Anellis, Irving H., ed. Crowe, Gregory, tr. from RUS. (Russian Philosophy & History of Logic, Mathematics & Science Ser.). (Illus.). xii, 176p. (Orig.). 1996. pap. 29.95 (*1-884905-02-1*) Modern Logic.

Barabasi, Albert-Laszlo. Fractal Concepts in Surface Growth. 386p. 1995. pap. text 32.95 (*0-521-48318-2*) Cambridge U Pr.

Barabasi, Albert-Laszlo & Barabasi, Eugene H. Fractal Concepts in Surface Growth. 386p. 1995. text 80.00 (*0-521-48308-5*) Cambridge U Pr.

Barabasi, Eugene H., jt. auth. see Barabasi, Albert-Laszlo.

Barabasz, Arreed F. & Barabasz, Marianne, eds. Clinical & Experimental Restricted Environmental Stimulation: New Developments & Perspectives. 1993. write for info. (*0-318-69808-0*) Spr-Verlag.

Barabasz, Marianne, jt. ed. see Barabasz, Arreed F.

Barabba, Vincent P. Meeting of the Minds. 1995. 27.95 (*0-07-103629-6*) McGraw.

— Meeting of the Minds: Creating the Market-Based Enterprise. LC 95-13342. 224p. 1995. 27.95 (*0-87584-577-0*) Harvard Busn.

Barabba, Vincent P. & Zaltman, Gerald. Hearing the Voice of the Market. 250p. 1991. 39.95 (*0-07-103285-1*) McGraw.

— Hearing the Voice of the Market: Competitive Advantage Through Creative Use of Market Information. 320p. 1990. 35.00 (*0-87584-241-0*) Harvard Busn.

Barabe, Denis, jt. ed. see Jean, Roger V.

Barabey d'Aurevilly, Jules. Une Vielle Maitresse. (FRE.). 1979. pap. 16.95 (*0-7859-1893-0*, 2070371158) Fr & Eur.

Barabtarlo, G., ed. Solzhenitsyn: What a Pity! & Other Short Stories. (Russian Texts Ser.). (RUS.). 1996. pap. 18.95 (*1-85399-425-1*, Pub. by Brist Class Pr) Focus Pub-R Pullins.

Barabtarlo, G., tr. see Nabokov, Vladimir.

***Barabtarlo, Gennady.** Cold Fusion: Aspects of the German Cultural Presence in Russia. LC 99-40047. 288p. 2000. 69.95 (*1-57181-188-5*) Berghahn Bks.

Barabtarlo, Gennady. Phantom of Fact: A Guide to Nabokov's PNIN. 1989. 37.95 (*0-87501-060-1*) Ardis Pubs.

Barabtarlo, Gennady, jt. ed. see Nicol, Charles.

Barac, Antun. A History of Yugoslav Literature. (Joint Committee on Eastern Europe Publication Ser.: No. 1). 1972. 15.00 (*0-930042-19-0*); pap. 10.00 (*0-930042-49-2*) Mich Slavic Pubns.

Baracca, Angelo, et al. Statistical Mechanics: Foundations, Problems, Perspectives. 700p. 1998. text 78.00 (*981-02-1693-9*) World Scientific Pub.

Baracchi, Paolo, tr. see Parrini, Paolo.

Barach, Jeffrey A. & Eckhardt, D. Reed. Leadership & the Job of the Executive. LC 96-590. 280p. 1996. 59.95 (*0-89930-991-7*, Quorum Bks) Greenwood.

Barach, Kathleen, jt. auth. see Greenbacker, Liz.

Barach, Roland. Mindtraps: Unlocking the Key to Investment Success. 2nd ed. 260p. Date not set. reprint ed. 34.95 (*0-935219-07-2*) Intl Trading Mastery.

Barackman, Floyd H. Practical Christian Theology: Examining the Great Doctrines of the Faith. 3rd ed. LC 97-49304. 576p. 1998. pap. text 22.99 (*0-8254-2374-0*) Kregel.

— Victors, Not Victims: The Christian's Secret of Overcoming the Power of Sin. LC 92-39332. 128p. 1993. pap. 8.99 (*0-8254-2273-6*) Kregel.

Baracks, Clarence A. Growing up in New City, New York, in the Early 1920s. LC 95-14795. 1996. pap. 5.00 (*0-911183-41-8*) Rockland County Hist.

Baracus, Audrey. Hidden Secrets. 144p. (J). (gr. 3-7). 1996. pap. 3.99 (*0-380-78369-X*, Avon Bks) Morrow Avon.

Barad, Judith. Consent: The Means to an Active Faith According to St. Thomas Aquinas. LC 91-27565. (American University Studies: Philosophy: Ser. V, Vol. 126). 124p. (C). 1992. text 35.95 (*0-8204-1596-0*) P Lang Pubng.

***Barad, Judith.** Ethics of Star Trek. (Illus.). 2000. 22.00 (*0-06-019530-4*) HarpC.

Barad, Judith A. Aquinas on the Nature & Treatment of Animals. LC 95-23836. (Catholic Scholars Press Ser.). 195p. 1995. 64.95 (*1-57309-007-7*); pap. 44.95 (*1-57309-006-9*) Intl Scholars.

Barad, Leona G., jt. auth. see Levien, Alisa.

***Baradar, Majid.** Seismic Principles Practice Exams for the California Special Civil Engineer Examination. 2nd ed. LC 99-14451. (Illus.). 69p. 1999. pap. 29.95 (*1-888577-34-7*, SPPE2) Prof Pubns CA.

Baradar, Majid. 345 Solved Seismic Design Problems. 4th ed. LC 99-14452. (Illus.). 167p. 1999. pap. 34.95 (*1-888577-35-5*, SESP4) Prof Pubns CA.

Baradas, David. Land of the Morning: Treasures of the Philippines. (Orig.). 1995. pap. write for info. (*1-877742-04-X*) SF Craft & Folk.

Baradat, P. H., et al. Population Genetics & Genetic Conservation of Forest Trees. (Illus.). 479p. 1996. 150.00 (*90-5103-109-2*, Pub. by SPB Acad Pub) Balogh.

Baradat, Sergio. A Year in the Life of a Rose. 1997. pap. write for info. (*0-609-80013-2*) Derrydale.

Baradat, Sergio & Holt, Saxon. All-America Roses. LC 97-30400. 1998. 14.95 (*0-8118-1845-4*) Chronicle Bks.

— Miniature Roses. LC 97-30393. 1998. 14.95 (*0-8118-1844-6*) Chronicle Bks.

Baraff, Carol. A New Theory of Arthritis Based on the Edgar Cayce Readings. 43p. 1981. 2.00 (*1-882545-01-X*) Herit Pubns.

Baraff, Carol, ed. The Edgar Cayce Products: Twenty Years of Research. 79p. 1979. 2.50 (*1-882545-02-8*) Herit Pubns.

Baraga, Frederic. A Dictionary of the Ojibway Language. 3rd ed. LC 92-28915. xvii, 731p. 1992. reprint ed. pap. 24.95 (*0-87351-281-2*, Borealis Book) Minn Hist.

Baragar, W. R., et al, eds. Volcanic Regimes in Canada: The Proceedings of a Symposium Sponsored by the Volcanology Division of the Geological Association of Canada & Held at the University of Waterloo in Waterloo, Ontario, May 16-17. 1975. LC 79-305269. (Geological Association of Canada. Special Paper: No. 16). 482p. reprint ed. pap. 149.50 (*0-608-17198-0*, 202784500056) Bks Demand.

Baragary, Ray. Billboard Guide to Home Recording. rev. ed. (Illus.). 288p. 1996. pap. text 19.95 (*0-8230-8300-4*, Billboard Bks) Watsn-Guptill.

Baragiola, R. A. Ionization of Solids by Heavy Particles. LC 93-8373. (NATO ASI Ser.: Vol. 306). (Illus.). 470p. (C). 1993. text 135.00 (*0-306-44489-5*, Kluwer Plenum) Kluwer Academic.

***Baragwanath, Mark.** Unfair Dismissal in New South Wales. 1999. pap. 56.00 (*0-455-21601-0*, 18156, Pub. by LBC Info Servs) Gaunt.

Barah, M., et al, eds. Critical Current Limitation in High Temperature Superconductors. (Progress in High Temperature Superconductivity Ser.: Vol. 30). 500p. (C). 1992. text 121.00 (*981-02-0803-0*) World Scientific Pub.

Baraheni, Reza. God's Shadow: Prison Poems. LC 75-34731. 103p. reprint ed. pap. 32.00 (*0-608-13278-0*, 205602300044) Bks Demand.

Barahona, Ana. Genetica: La Continuidad de la Vida. (Ciencia para Todos Ser.). (SPA.). pap. 6.99 (*968-16-4534-0*, Pub. by Fondo) Continental Bk.

Barahona, P., et al, eds. EPIA '91: Fifth Portuguese Conference on Artificial Intelligence Albufeira, Portugal, October 1-3, 1991 Proceedings. (Lecture Notes in Artificial Intelligence: Vol. 541). viii, 292p. 1991. 32.95 (*0-387-54535-2*) Spr-Verlag.

***Barahona, P. & Alferes, J. J., eds.** Progress in Artificial Intelligence: 9th Portuguese Conference on Artificial Intelligence, EPIA '99, Evora, Portugal, September 22-24, 1999, Proceedings. LC 99-49082. (Lecture Notes in Artificial Intelligence Ser.: Vol. 1695). xi, 385p. 1999. pap. 62.00 (*3-540-66548-X*) Spr-Verlag.

Barahona, Pedro, et al, eds. Artificial Intelligence in Medicine: 5th Conference on Artificial Intelligence in Medicine, Europe, AIME '95, Pvia, Italy, June 1995. LC 95-30443. (Lecture Notes in Computer Science Ser.: Vol. 934). 1995. write for info. (*0-387-60025-6*) Spr-Verlag.

Barahona, Pedro & Christensen, J. P. Knowledge & Decisions in Health Care Telematics. LC 93-81157. (Studies in Health Technology & Informatics: Vol. 12). 251p. (YA). (gr. 12). 1994. 95.00 (*90-5199-152-5*) IOS Press.

Barahona, Renato. Vizcaya on the Eve of Carlism: Politics & Society, 1800-1833. (Basque Ser.). (Illus.). 352p. 1989. text 44.95 (*0-87417-122-9*) U of Nev Pr.

Barai, Kumudini. Role of Women in the History of Orissa. (C). 1994. 32.00 (*81-85094-78-0*, Pub. by Punthi Pus) S Asia.

Baraith, Roop S. Transit Politics in South Asia. 1989. 36.00 (*0-8364-2539-1*, Commonwealth) S Asia.

Baraitser. Color Atlas of Congenital Malformation Syndromes. 1995. 81.95 (*0-7234-2073-4*) Mosby Inc.

Baraitser, Francis & Winter, Robin. A Colour Atlas of Clinical Genetics. (Illus.). 159p. 1988. text 55.00 (*0-7234-1547-1*) Wolfe Pub.

***Baraitser, Marion.** Theatre of Animation: Contemporary Adult, 19. 4th ed. 86p. 1999. pap. text 21.00 (*90-5755-008-3*, Harwood Acad Pubs) Gordon & Breach.

— Theatre of Animation: Contemporary Adult Plays. 86p. 1999. pap. text 21.00 (*90-5755-009-1*, Harwood Acad Pubs) Gordon & Breach.

Baraitser, Marion, ed. Plays by Mediterranean Women. 296p. 1999. pap. 16.00 (*0-9515877-3-0*) Theatre Comm.

Baraitser, Michael. The Genetics of Neurological Disorders. 2nd ed. (Oxford Monographs on Medical Genetics: No. 18). (Illus.). 752p. 1990. text 125.00 (*0-19-261814-8*) OUP.

— The Genetics of Neurological Disorders. 3rd ed. LC 97-8304. (Oxford Monographs on Medical Genetics: No. 34). (Illus.). 450p. 1997. text 89.50 (*0-19-262814-3*) OUP.

Baraitser, Michael, jt. auth. see Winter, Robin M.

Barajas, Felipe, tr. see Underwood, Paula.

Barak, Amnon, et al. The MOSIX Distributed Operation System: Load Balancing for UNIX. LC 93-3663. (Lecture Notes in Computer Science Ser.: Vol. 672). 1993. 39.95 (*0-387-56663-5*) Spr-Verlag.

Barak, Anthony J. The Mongrel: A Story of Logan Fontanelle of the Omaha Indians. Reisdorff, James J., ed. (Illus.). 152p. (Orig.). 1988. pap. 9.95 (*0-942035-09-7*) South Platte.

***Barak, Gregg.** Crime & Crime Control: A Global View. LC 99-49044. 288p. 2000. 49.95 (*0-313-30681-8*, Greenwood Pr) Greenwood.

Barak, Gregg. Gimme Shelter: A Social History of Homelessness in Contemporary America. LC 90-24567. 232p. 1991. 55.00 (*0-275-93320-2*, C3320, Praeger Pubs) Greenwood.

— Gimme Shelter: A Social History of Homelessness in Contemporary America. LC 90-24567. 232p. 1992. pap. 16.95 (*0-275-94401-8*, B4401, Praeger Pubs) Greenwood.

— Integrating Criminologies. LC 96-53560. 330p. 1997. pap. text 52.00 (*0-205-16557-5*) Allyn.

— Integrating Criminologies: Instructor's Manual & Test Bank. 112p. (C). 1997. pap. text, teacher ed. write for info. (*0-205-27596-6*, T7596-4) Allyn.

Barak, Gregg, ed. Crimes by the Capitalist State: An Introduction to State Criminality. LC 90-9889. (SUNY Series in Radical, Social & Political Theory). 301p. (C). 1991. text 24.50 (*0-7914-0584-2*) State U NY Pr.

— Integrative Criminology. LC 98-12102. (International Library of Criminology, Criminal Justice, & Penology). 599p. 1998. text 171.95 (*1-84014-008-9*, Pub. by Ashgate Pub) Ashgate Pub Co.

— Media, Process, & the Social Construction of Crime: Issues in Criminal Justice. LC 93-39423. (Current Issues in Criminal Justice Ser.: Vol. 10). (Illus.). 344p. 1995. pap. text 24.95 (*0-8153-1855-3*, H1690) Garland.

— Varieties of Criminology: Readings from a Dynamic Discipline. LC 93-14138. (Criminology & Crime Control Policy Ser.). 320p. 1993. 75.00 (*0-275-94485-9*, C4485, Praeger Pubs); pap. 26.95 (*0-275-94774-2*, Praeger Pubs) Greenwood.

Barak, Gregg, ed. Media, Criminal Justice & Mass Culture. 2nd rev. ed. LC KF224.S485R46 1996. 240p. 2000. pap. text 26.50 (*0-911577-37-8*, Pub. by Willow Tree NY) Lib Res.

***Barak, Gregg, et al.** Class, Race, Gender & Crime: Realities of Criminal Justice in America. 310p. (C). 2001. pap. text. write for info. (*1-891487-34-5*) Roxbury Pub Co.

Barak, M., ed. Electrochemical Power Sources: Primary & Secondary Batteries. (Energy Ser.: No. 1). (Illus.). 516p. 1980. 139.00 (*0-906048-26-5*, EN001) INSPEC Inc.

Barak, Robert J. & Breier, Barbara E. Successful Program Review: A Practical Guide to Evaluating Programs in Academic Settings. (Higher Education Ser.). 160p. 1990. text 30.95 (*1-55542-241-1*) Jossey-Bass.

Barak, Ronald S., ed. Real Estate Issues in the Health Care Industry: Proceedings of the First Annual Conference of the Health Care Real Estate Institute. (Current Topics in Real Estate Finance & Economics Ser.). 184p. (C). 1996. lib. bdg. 78.50 (*0-7923-9696-0*) Kluwer Academic.

Barak, Yoshua. Black Men Say Goodbye to Misery, Say Hello to Love: The Black Man's Alternative to the American Black Women. 184p. 1992. pap. text 10.00 (*1-881316-10-6*) A&B Bks.

Baraka, Amiri Imamu, pseud. The Autobiography of Leroi Jones. LC 97-173698. 476p. (Orig.). 1997. pap. 16.95 (*1-55652-231-2*, Lawrence Hill) Chicago Review.

— The Autobiography of Leroi Jones- Amiri Baraka. 329p. 1984. 16.95 (*0-88191-000-7*) Freundlich.

— Black Music. LC 97-41725. (Illus.). 228p. 1998. reprint ed. pap. 14.95 (*0-306-80814-5*) Da Capo.

— Black Music. LC 80-15439. (Illus.). 221p. 1980. reprint ed. lib. bdg. 49.50 (*0-313-22518-4*, JOBK, Greenwood Pr) Greenwood.

— Blues People: Negro Music in White America. LC 80-15648. 244p. 1980. reprint ed. lib. bdg. 55.00 (*0-313-22519-2*, JOBP, Greenwood Pr) Greenwood.

— Digging Afro American Classical Music. 1999. pap. 18.95 (*1-56886-069-2*, Pub. by Marsilio Pubs) Consort Bk Sales.

***Baraka, Amiri Imamu, pseud.** Eulogies. 1999. pap. text 14.95 (*1-56886-070-6*, Pub. by Marsilio Pubs) Consort Bk Sales.

Baraka, Amiri Imamu, pseud. Four Black Revolutionary Plays. LC 97-51767. (Orig.). 1997. pap. 11.00 (*0-7145-3005-0*) M Boyars Pubs.

— Funk Lore: New Poems, 1984-1994. 96p. (Orig.). 1996. pap. text 11.95 (*1-55713-296-8*) Sun & Moon CA.

— LeRoi Jones - Amiri Baraka Reader. Harris, William J., ed. 544p. 1991. pap. 16.95 (*1-56025-007-0*, Thunders Mouth) Avalon NY.

***Baraka, Amiri Imamu, pseud.** The LeRoi Jones - Amiri Baraka Reader. 2nd ed. LC 99-32364. 560p. 1999. pap. 16.95 (*1-56025-238-3*, Thunders Mouth) Avalon NY.

Baraka, Amiri Imamu, pseud. Reggae or Not! (Chapbook Ser.). (Illus.). 32p. 1982. pap. 3.00 (*0-936556-04-8*) Contact Two.

— The Sidney Poet Heroical. LC 78-66005. 1979. pap. 5.95 (*0-918408-12-1*) Ishmael Reed.

— Transbluesency: The Selected Poems of Amiri Baraka/Leroi Jones. Vangelisti, Paul, ed. 292p. 1995. 32.95 (*1-56886-013-7*) Marsilio Pubs.

— Wise Why's Y's: The Griot's Tale. 86p. 1994. 14.95 (*0-88378-150-6*) Third World.

— Wise Why's Y's: The Griot's Tale. 132p. 1995. pap. text 12.00 (*0-88378-047-X*) Third World.

Baraka, Amiri Imamu, pseud & Jones, LeRoi. The Fiction of Leroi Jones - Amiri Baraka. LC 99-25770. 450p. 2000. pap. 19.95 (*1-55652-353-X*, Pub. by Chicago Review) IPG Chicago.

Baraka, Magda. Egyptian Upper Class Between Revolutions: 1919-1952. 300p. 1998. 45.00 (*0-86372-230-X*, Pub. by Garnet-Ithaca) LPC InBook.

Barakan, Mayumi & Greer, Judith C. Tokyo City Guide. rev. ed. (Illus.). 364p. 1995. pap. 14.95 (*0-8048-1964-5*) Tuttle Pubng.

Barakat, Gamal. English-Arabic Dictionary of Diplomacy & Related Terminology. (ARA & ENG.). 1982. 25.00 (*0-86685-290-5*) Intl Bk Ctr.

Barakat, Halim. The Arab World. 339p. 1996. 25.00 (*0-614-21619-2*, 48) Kazi Pubns.

— Arab World: Society, Culture, & State. (C). 1993. pap. 18.95 (*0-520-08427-6*, Pub. by U CA Pr) Cal Prin Full Svc.

— Days of Dust. 2nd ed. Le Gassick, Trevor, tr. from ARA. LC 82-74265.Tr. of Awdat al-Ta'ir ila'l'Bahr. (Illus.). 179p. (C). 1983. reprint ed. pap. 14.50 (*0-89410-360-1*, Three Contnts) L Rienner.

— Six Days. Frangieh, Bassam & McGehee, Scott, trs. LC 90-11283. 121p. 1990. 22.00 (*0-89410-661-9*, Three Contnts); pap. 12.00 (*0-89410-662-7*, Three Contnts) L Rienner.

Barakat, Halim, intro. Toward a Viable Lebanon. 395p. 1988. 27.95 (*0-614-02965-1*); pap. text 17.95 (*0-932568-13-0*) GU Ctr CAS.

Barakat, Halim I. Lebanon in Strife: Student Preludes to the Civil War. LC 76-50046. (Modern Middle East Ser.: No. 2). 256p. reprint ed. pap. 79.40 (*0-8357-7724-3*, 203608100002) Bks Demand.

Barakat, Hoda. The Stone of Laughter: A Novel. Bennett, Sophie, tr. LC 95-14090. (Emerging Voices Ser.).Tr. of Hajar al-Dahk. 240p. 1995. 29.95 (*1-56656-197-3*); pap. 12.95 (*1-56656-190-6*) Interlink Pub.

Barakat, N. & Hamza, A. A. Interferometry of Fibrous Materials. (Optics & Optoelectronics Ser.). (Illus.). 180p. 1990. 126.00 (*0-85274-100-6*) IOP Pub.

Barakat, Robert. Cistercian Sign Language. LC 70-152476. (Cistercian Studies: No. 11). 1976. 5.00 (*0-87907-811-1*) Cistercian Pubns.

Barake, Bassam. Linguistic French & Arabic Dictionary: Dictionnaire de Linguistique Francais-Arabe. (ARA & FRE.). 298p. 1986. 39.95 (*0-8288-1586-0*, M2310) Fr & Eur.

Baral, Chitta, ed. Theories of Action, Planning, & Robot Control: Bridging the Gap: Papers from the 1996 Workshop. (Technical Reports). (Illus.). 130p. 1996. spiral bd. 25.00 (*1-57735-021-9*) AAAI Pr.

Baral, J. K. Gender Politics. 1990. 19.00 (*81-7141-103-7*) S Asia.

— International Politics: Dynamics & Dimensions. 347p. 1987. 29.95 (*81-7003-080-3*) Asia Bk Corp.

Baral, J. K., jt. ed. see Jena, B. B.

Baral, Lok R. Nepal: Problems of Governance. (Governance in South Asia Ser.). 1993. text 30.00 (*81-220-0304-4*, Pub. by Konark Pubs Pvt Ltd) Advent Bks Div.

— Opposition Politics in Nepal. 1977. 12.00 (*0-8364-0049-6*) S Asia.

— The Politics of Balanced Interdependence: Nepal & SAARC. 1988. 50.00 (*0-7855-0294-7*, Pub. by Ratna Pustak Bhandar) St Mut.

— The Politics of Balanced Interdependence: Nepal & Saarc. 140p. (C). 1988. 150.00 (*0-89771-089-4*, Pub. by Ratna Pustak Bhandar) St Mut.

Baraldi, Severino, jt. auth. see Montgomery, Mary.

Barale, Michele A. & Rabinovitz, Rubin. A KWIC Concordance to Samuel Beckett's Murphy. LC 90-3312. 560p. 1990. text 25.00 (*0-8240-4603-X*, 1079) Garland.

Barale, Michele A. & Rabinovitz, Rubin, eds. A KWIC Concordance to Beckett's Trilogy Molloy, Malone Dies, & The Unnamable, 2 vols. LC 87-38471. 1988. text 20.00 (*0-8240-8394-6*, 753) Garland.

Barale, Michele A., ed. see Rand, Erica.

Barale, Vittorio & Schlittenhardt, Peter M., eds. Ocean Color - Theory & Applications in a Decade of CZCS Experience: Based on the Lectures Given During the Eurocourse Held at the Joint Research Centre Ispra, Italy, October 21, 1991. LC 92-46130. (Eurocourses: Remote Sensing Ser.: No. 3). 384p. (C). 1993. text 188.00 (*0-7923-1586-3*) Kluwer Academic.

Baralt, Guillermo A. La Buena Vista: Estancia de Frutos Menores, Fabrića de Harinas y Hacienda Cafetalera (1833-1904) CARIMAR Staff, tr. (SPA., Illus.). 141p. (Orig.). (C). 1988. pap. 22.00 (*0-9622083-1-0*); text 35.00 (*0-9622083-0-2*) Cnsrvation Trust PR.

— Buena Vista: Life & Work on a Puerto Rican Hacienda, 1833-1904. LC 98-37128. (Illus.). 208p. 1999. pap. 21.95 (*0-8078-4801-8*); lib. bdg. 49.95 (*0-8078-2474-7*) U of NC Pr.

— Esclavos Rebeldes. LC 81-70982. (Coleccion Semilla). (SPA.). 190p. 1982. pap. 7.50 (*0-940238-07-1*) Ediciones Huracan.

***Baram, A.** Easy Walks in Jerusalem. (Illus.). 2000. 32.50 (*965-90048-6-9*, Pub. by Israel Shalem) Shalom.

— Israel's Southern Landscape: Guide to Eilat & the Neger. (Illus.). 2000. 35.00 (*965-90048-4-2*, Pub. by Israel Shalem) Shalom.

Baram, Amatzia. Building Toward Crisis: Saddam Hussein's Strategy for Survival. LC 98-3313. (Policy Papers: No. 47). 176p. 1998. pap. 19.95 (*0-944029-25-6*) Wash Inst NEP.

Baram, Amatzia & Rubin, Barry, eds. Iraq's Road to War. LC 93-24709. 304p. 1994. text 49.95 (*0-312-10171-6*) St Martin.

— Iraq's Road to War. 304p. 1996. pap. 19.95 (*0-312-16446-7*) St Martin.

Baram, Amatzia, et al. Iran & the West: Is There a Need to Reconsider Policies? Contributions to a Friedrich Ebert Foundation Issue Seminar. (Illus.). 65p. 1998. pap. write for info. (*0-9647348-4-2*) Friedrich-Ebert Found.

Baram, Michael S. & Partan, Daniel G. Corporate Disclosure of Environmental Risks: U. S. & European Law. 320p. 1990. boxed set 105.00 (*0-88063-258-5*, 80331-10, MICHIE) LEXIS Pub.

Baram, Michael S., jt. auth. see Hale, Andrew R.

Baram, Micheal S. Managing Chemical Risks: Corporate Response to Sara Title III. 2nd ed. 288p. 1992. lib. bdg. 99.95 (*0-87371-725-2*) CRC Pr.

An Asterisk (*) at the beginning of an entry indicates that the title is appearing for the first time.

Baram, Robert, ed. Spiritual Journeys. LC 87-6668. 436p. 1987. pap. 12.95 (*0-8198-6876-0*) Pauline Bks.

***Baram, Uzi & Carroll, Lynda.** The Historical Archaeology of the Ottoman Empire: Breaking New Ground. LC 00-22108. (Contributions to Global Historical Archaeology Ser.). 2000. write for info. (*0-306-46311-3*, Kluwer Plenum) Kluwer Academic.

Baramki, D. C. & Sellers, Ovid R. A Roman-Byzantine Burial Cave in Northern Palestine. (American Schools of Oriental Research, Supplement Ser.: Vols. 15-16). 55p. 1953. pap. text 10.00 (*0-89757-315-3*) Am Sch Orient Res.

Baramki, Dimitri. Coins Exhibited in the Archaeological Museum of the American University of Beirut. (Illus.). 1968. pap. 22.95 (*0-8156-6010-3*, Pub. by Am U Beirut) Syracuse U Pr.

Baramki, Dimitri C., jt. auth. see Kelso, James L.

Baramki, Dimtri C., ed. Coin Collection of the American University of Beirut Museum: Palestine & Phoenicia. 1974. 49.95 (*0-8156-6043-X*, Pub. by Am U Beirut) Syracuse U Pr.

Baran, Alexander. Synthesis of Polymers for Plastic Optical Fibers, 3 vols., Vols. 1-3. 1995. 495.00 (*0-614-18422-3*) Info Gatekeepers.

***Baran, Annette & Pannor, Reuben.** Lethal Secrets. rev. ed. LC 93-20015. (Illus.). 187p. 1999. reprint ed. pap. 11.95 (*1-56743-020-1*, Amistad) HarperTrade.

Baran, Daniel T. Contemporary Diagnosis & Management of Osteoporosis. (Illus.). 160p. (C). 2000. pap. 29.95 (*1-884065-48-1*) Assocs in Med.

Baran, Elaine V. Italian, Modern Spoken, Set-8. unabridged ed. (Self-Instructional Language Courses). 124p. (C). pap. 185.00 incl. audio (*0-88432-073-1*, AFZ501) Audio-Forum.

— Modern Spoken Italian, Pt. B. unabridged ed. (Self-Instructional Language Courses). 136p. (C). pap. 185.00 incl. digital audio (*0-88432-074-X*, AFZ551) Audio-Forum.

Baran, Gary L. Philosophy - Love of Wisdom: Selections & Study Questions. 3rd ed. 230p. (C). 1994. text 30.80 (*0-536-58730-2*) S&S Trade.

— Philosophy Love of Wisdom: Selections & Study Questions. (C). 1991. text 25.80 (*0-536-57920-2*) Pearson Custom.

Baran, Henryk, ed. see Pomorska, Krystyna.

***Baran, Jan W.** The Election Law Primer for Corporations. LC 99-34480. 1999. pap. write for info. (*1-57073-689-8*) Amer Bar Assn.

Baran, Paul. Potential Market Demand for Two-Way Information Services to the Home, 1970-1990. 139p. 1971. 10.50 (*0-318-14418-2*, R26) Inst Future.

Baran, Paul A. Longer View: Essays Toward a Critique of Political Economy. LC 68-13656. 464p. 1972. pap. 10.00 (*0-85345-220-2*, Pub. by Monthly Rev) NYU Pr.

— Political Economy of Growth. LC 57-7953. 352p. 1968. pap. 15.00 (*0-85345-076-5*, Pub. by Monthly Rev) NYU Pr.

Baran, Paul A. & Sweezy, Paul M. Monopoly Capital: An Essay on the American Economic & Social Order. LC 65-15269. 416p. 1968. reprint ed. pap. 18.00 (*0-85345-073-0*, Pub. by Monthly Rev) NYU Pr.

Baran, Paula. Today's Woman: Prenatal Care & Beyond. Zagury, Carolyn S. & Ciocco, Margaret C., eds. LC 97-62502. 128p. 1998. pap. 12.95 (*1-880254-53-0*) Vista.

Baran, R. Color Atlas of the Hair, Scalp & Nails. (Illus.). 192p. (C). (gr. 13). 1991. text 69.00 (*0-8151-0417-0*, 21727) Mosby Inc.

***Baran, Robert.** Onychomycosis: The Current Approach to Diagnosis & Therapy. 74p. 1999. 49.95 (*1-85317-767-9*, Pub. by Martin Dunitz) Blackwell Sci.

Baran, Robert. Texas Atlas of Nail Disorders: Diagnosis & Treatment. 224p. 1996. write for info. (*1-85317-201-4*) Martin Dunitz.

— Text Atlas Nail Disorders. 1997. write for info. (*1-85317-436-X*) Martin Dunitz.

Baran, Robert & Dawber, R. P. R., eds. Diseases of the Nails & Their Management. 2nd ed. LC 93-41599. (Illus.). 528p. 1994. 195.00 (*0-632-03754-7*) Blackwell Sci.

Baran, Robert & Maibach, Howard I. Cosmetic Dermatology. (Illus.). 584p. 1994. write for info. (*0-683-00321-6*) Lppncott W & W.

Baran, Robert, et al. Manual of Nail Disease & Surgery. 2nd ed. LC 97-5904. (Illus.). 112p. 1997. pap. text 69.95 (*0-86542-638-4*) Blackwell Sci.

Baran, Robert, et al. Nail Disorders: Common Presenting Signs, Differential Diagnosis & Treatment. (Illus.). 188p. 1991. text 39.95 (*0-443-08800-4*) Church.

Baran, Robert H., jt. auth. see Coughlin, James P.

Baran, Robert J. A Bonsai Coloring Book: A Guide to Your First Dwarf Potted Trees. (Illus.). 40p. (J). (gr. 2-12). 1999. pap. 3.95 (*0-9659913-4-2*) Pyramid Dancer.

— Designing Dwarfs in the Desert: Up Through the First 35 Years of the Phoenix Bonsai Society. LC 98-107797. (Illus.). 82p. 1997. pap. 12.95 (*0-9659913-3-4*) Pyramid Dancer.

Baran, Roger, et al, eds. International Joint Ventures in East Asia. LC 95-50892. (Journal of Euromarketing: Vol. 4, Nos. 3/4). 165p. (C). 1996. 39.95 (*1-56024-771-1*, Intl Busn Pr) Haworth Pr.

Baran, Stanley J. Introduction to Mass Communication: Media Literacy & Culture. LC 98-34578. xxiv, 518p. 1998. pap. text 51.95 (*1-55934-960-3*, 960-3) Mayfield Pub.

— Mass Communication Theory: Foundations, Ferment, & Future. 2nd ed. LC 99-34363. (Mass Communication Ser.). 1999. pap. 56.95 (*0-534-56088-1*) Wadsworth Pub.

Baran, Stanley J. & Davis, Dennis K. Mass Communication Theory: Foundations, Ferment & Future. LC 94-16637. 407p. 1994. pap. 36.25 (*0-534-17670-4*) Wadsworth Pub.

Baran, Stanley J. & Massey, Kimbery B. Introduction to Mass Communication Instructor's Resource Guide. xiii, 191p. (C). 1998. pap. text. write for info. (*0-7674-0990-6*, 0990-6) Mayfield Pub.

— Introduction to Mass Communication Media Literacy Worksheets. 80p. (C). 1998. pap. text 7.95 (*0-7674-0984-1*, 0984-1) Mayfield Pub.

Baran, Stanley J. & Wallis, Roger. The Known World of Broadcast News: International News & the Electronic Media. LC 89-49327. (Comedia Bk.). (Illus.). 272p. (C). 1990. pap. 24.99 (*0-415-03604-6*, A4587) Routledge.

Baran, Stanley J., jt. auth. see Massey, Kimberley B.

***Baran, Susan.** The Necessary Boat. LC 99-41318. 2000. 12.00 (*1-891305-19-0*) Painted Leaf.

Baran, Vaclav. Uranium (VI) -Oxygen Chemistry: Uranyl Hydroxo Complexes, Uranates, Oxides. 135p. (Orig.). 1993. pap. text 60.00 (*0-911767-62-2*) Hadronic Pr Inc.

Baranczak, Stanisaw, tr. see Szymborska, Wislawa.

Baranczak, Stanislaw. Breathing under Water & Other East European Essays. 264p. 1990. 35.50 (*0-674-08125-0*) HUP.

— Breathing under Water & Other East European Essays. 272p. 1992. pap. text 11.95 (*0-674-08126-9*) HUP.

— A Fugitive from Utopia: The Poetry of Zbigniew Herbert. LC 86-25818. 176p. 1987. 36.50 (*0-674-32685-7*) HUP.

— Under My Own Roof. Kujawinski, Frank, tr. (Poetry Chapbook Ser.). 1980. 3.95 (*0-932191-03-7*) Mr Cogito Pr.

Baranczak, Stanislaw, selected by. Citizen R. K. Does Not Live: Poems of Ryszard Krynicki. (Poetry Chapbook Ser.). 36p. 1985. 10.00 (*0-932191-06-1*, PG7170) Mr Cogito Pr.

Baranczak, Stanislaw & Cavanagh, Clare, eds. Polish Poetry of the Last Two Decades of Communist Rule: Spoiling Cannibals' Fun. 204p. (Orig.). 1991. 29.95 (*0-8101-0968-9*); pap. 12.95 (*0-8101-0982-4*) Northwestern U Pr.

Baranczak, Stanislaw, tr. see Kochanowski, Jan.

Baranczak, Stanislaw, tr. see Szymborska, Wislawa.

Baranek, Patricia M., jt. auth. see Ericson, Richard V.

***Baranescu, Rodica & Challen, Bernard.** Diesel Engine Reference Book. 2nd ed. 700p. 1999. 99.00 (*0-7680-0403-9*, R-183) Soc Auto Engineers.

Baraness, Marc & Richards, Larry, eds. Toronto Places: Elements of Urban Design. (Illus.). 108p. 1992. text 50.00 (*0-8020-2834-9*) U of Toronto Pr.

Baranik, Rudolph, ed. see Thompson, Glenn.

Baranishyn, Barbara, jt. auth. see Wernig, Julie K.

Baranoff, Timy. Kindergarten Minute by Minute. LC 78-72076. (J). (gr. k). 1979. pap. 10.99 (*0-8224-4100-4*) Fearon Teacher Aids.

Baranov, A. Basic Latin for Plant Taxonomists. 1971. pap. text 45.00 (*3-7682-0727-7*) Lubrecht & Cramer.

Baranov, A. E., et al. Clinical Pre-Computer Proforma for the International Computer Database for Radiation Exposure Case Histories. LC 94-211290. (Illus.). 128p. 1994. 62.95 (*0-387-57596-0*) Spr-Verlag.

Baranov, Alvin B. How to Evict a Tenant. 14th rev. ed. (Illus.). 156p. (C). 1992. pap. text 18.95 (*0-910531-18-8*) Wolcotts.

— Incorporation Made Easy. 12th ed. (Illus.). 156p. (C). 1988. pap. text 19.95 (*0-910531-17-X*) Wolcotts.

Baranov, E. G., et al. Mining & Industrial Applications of Low Density Explosives. LC 99-226661. (Illus.). 126p. (C). 1996. text 65.00 (*90-5410-295-0*, Pub. by A A Balkema) Ashgate Pub Co.

Baranov, K. K. Arabic - Russian Dictionary. 6th ed. (ARA & RUS.). 944p. 1984. reprint ed. 34.95 (*0-8285-5422-6*) Firebird NY.

Baranov, Samary. Logic Synthesis for Control Automata. LC 94-12288. 408p. (C). 1994. text 173.50 (*0-7923-9458-5*) Kluwer Academic.

Baranov, V. B. Astrophysics & Space Physics Reviews Vol. 8, Pt. 5: Gas Dynamics of Solar Wind Interaction with Interstellar Gas, Vol. 8. (Soviet Scientific Reviews Ser.: Section E). 55p. 1993. text 114.00 (*3-7186-5447-4*, Harwood Acad Pubs) Gordon & Breach.

Baranov, V. S., jt. auth. see Dyban, A. P.

Baranov, Valeriy I., jt. auth. see Stechkin, Boris S.

Baranov, Vladislva, et al, eds. European Cytogenetics Conference: 1st Conference, Athens, June 1997: Abstracts. (Cytogenetics & Cell Genetics Ser.: Vol. 77, No. 1-2, 1997). 168p. 1997. pap. 64.50 (*3-8055-6549-6*) S Karger.

Baranov, Wladimir. Potential Fields & Their Transformations in Applied Geophysics. Van Nostrand, R. G. & Saxov, S., eds. (Geoexploration Monographs: No. 6). (Illus.). xv, 121p. 1975. 38.00 (*3-443-13008-9*, Pub. by Gebruder Borntraeger) Balogh.

Baranov, Z. Arabic-Russian Dictionary. (ARA & RUS.). 1984. 49.95 (*0-8288-0787-6*, F47635) Fr & Eur.

Baranova, Z. I., et al. Chinese - Russian Dictionary. 2nd ed. (CHI & RUS.). 528p. 1988. reprint ed. 34.95 (*0-8285-5410-2*) Firebird NY.

Baranovic, T. M., et al. Eleven Papers on Topology & Algebra. LC 51-5559. (Translations Ser.: Series 2, Vol. 55). 304p. 1966. 51.00 (*0-8218-1755-8*, TRANS2/55) Am Math.

Baranovskii, E. P., jt. auth. see Ryskov, S. S.

Baranovsky, Vladmir, ed. Russia & Europe: The Emerging Security Agenda. LC 97-180593. (SIPRI Publication). 600p. 1997. text 85.00 (*0-19-829201-5*) OUP.

Baranow, Joan. Morning: Two Poems. (Tanbark Ser.). 16p. (Orig.). 1997. pap. 6.00 (*1-887853-14-6*) Radiolarian.

Baranowski, Anne-Marie. Conquete du Mouvement et Recherche de Soi: L'Imaginaire de Karl Philipp Moritz. (Contacts Ser.: Series III, Vol. 35). (FRE.). 438p. 1996. 60.95 (*3-906754-52-9*, Pub. by P Lang) P Lang Pubng.

Baranowski, Arthur R. Compartiendo la fe para las Pequenas Comunidades Eclesiales. Frank, Jerry tr. (Llamados a ser Iglesia Ser.). 104p. 2000. pap. 9.95 (*0-86716-406-9*) St Anthony Mess Pr.

— Creando Pequenas Comunidades de Fe: Un Plan para Reestructurar la Parroquia y Renovar la Vida... Frank, Jerry, tr. (Llamados a ser Iglesia Ser.). 88p. 2000. pap. 7.95 (*0-86716-404-2*) St Anthony Mess Pr.

—Creating Small Church Communities: A Plan for Restructuring the Parish & Renewing Catholic Life. 3rd rev. ed. 120p. (Orig.). 1996. pap. 7.95 (*0-86716-275-9*, B2759) St Anthony Mess Pr.

— Faith Sharing for Small Church Communities: Questions & Commentaries on the Sunday Readings. 132p. 1993. pap. 9.95 (*0-86716-166-3*) St Anthony Mess Pr.

— Orando Solos y Juntos. Frank, Jerry, tr. (Llamados a ser Iglesia Ser.). 120p. 2000. pap. 6.95 (*0-86716-403-4*) St Anthony Mess Pr.

— Pastoreando a los Pastores. Frank, Jerry, tr. (Llamados a ser Iglesia Ser.). 80p. 2000. pap. 6.95 (*0-86716-405-0*) St Anthony Mess Pr.

— Pastoring the 'Pastors' Resources for Training & Supporting Pastoral Facilitators for Small Faith Communities. 68p. 1988. pap. text 6.95 (*0-86716-597-9*) St Anthony Mess Pr.

— Praying Alone & Together: An 11-Session Prayer Module for Small Faith Communities. 107p. 1988. pap. 6.95 (*0-86716-897-8*) St Anthony Mess Pr.

Baranowski, Shelley. The Confessing Church, Conservative Elites, & the Nazi State. LC 86-12575. (Texts & Studies in Religion: Vol. 28). 200p. 1986. lib. bdg. 79.95 (*0-88946-816-8*) E Mellen.

— The Sanctity of Rural Life: Nobility, Protestantism, & Nazism in Weimar Prussia. (Illus.). 280p. 1995. text 60.00 (*0-19-506881-5*) OUP.

Baranowski, Shelley O. & Furlough, Ellen, eds. Being Elsewhere: Tourism, Consumer Culture, & Identity in Modern Europe & North America. (Illus.). 352p. (C). text 57.50 (*0-472-11167-1*, 11167) U of Mich Pr.

Baranowski, Willa. Love to Quilt Penny Squares. (Illus.). 56p. (Orig.). 1996. pap. 12.95 (*0-89145-879-4*, 4753, Am Quilters Soc) Collector Bks.

Baranowski, Zane. Colloidal Silver: The Natural Antibiotic Alternative. (Orig.). 1995. pap. 3.50 (*0-9647080-1-9*) Healing Wisdom.

Baranowski, Zdzislaw. The International Horseman's Dictionary. 176p. (C). 1990. 35.00 (*0-85131-262-4*, Pub. by J A Allen) St Mut.

— Woerterbuch Pferd und Reiter: Dictionary of Horses & Horsemanship. (ENG, FRE & GER.). 1977. 16.95 (*0-8288-5570-6*, M6910) Fr & Eur.

Baranska, Halina, et al. Laser Raman Spectrometry: Analytical Applications. (Analytical Chemistry Ser.). 392p. 1988. text 74.00 (*0-470-20829-5*) P-H.

Baranskaya, Natalya. Just Another Week. Paperno, Lora et al, eds. (RUS.). 92p. (Orig.). (C). 1989. pap. text 9.95 (*0-89357-202-0*) Slavica.

— A Week Like Any Other: Novellas & Stories. Monks, Pieta, tr. LC 89-34486. 231p. 1989. pap. 10.95 (*0-931188-80-6*) Seal Pr WA.

Baranski, Anton. Geschichte der Thierzucht und Thiermedicin im Altertum. (Documenta Hippologica Ser.). 245p. 1997. reprint ed. 60.00 (*3-487-04180-1*) G Olms Pubs.

Baranski, Johnny. Fish Pond Moon. (Sunburst Matchbooks Ser.: No. 2). (Illus.). 16p. (Orig.). 1986. pap. 3.00 (*0-934648-11-5*) Sunburst Pr.

— Hitch Haiku. (Sunburst Matchbooks Ser.: No. 3). 20p. (Orig.). 1987. pap. 4.00 (*0-934648-12-3*) Sunburst Pr.

— Pencil Flowers. LC 82-12057. (Kestrel Ser.). 24p. 1983. 3.00 (*0-914974-36-X*) Holmgangers.

— Poems from Prison. (Sunburst Originals Ser.: No 7). 16p. (Orig.). 1979. pap. 2.00 (*0-934648-02-6*) Sunburst Pr.

— Silent Silos: A Counterbomb Haiku Sequence. (Sunburst Matchbooks Ser.: No. 1). (Illus.). 16p. (Orig.). 1985. pap. 3.00 (*0-934648-10-7*) Sunburst Pr.

Baranski, Zygmunt G. The New Italian Novel. (Toronto Italian Studies). 272p. 1997. pap. text 19.95 (*0-8020-8080-4*) U of Toronto Pr.

Baranski, Zygmunt G. & Boyde, Patrick, eds. The Fiore in Context: Dante, France, Tuscany. LC 95-50449 (William & Katherine Devers Series in Dante Studies: Vol. 2). 544p. (C). 1997. pap. text 30.00 (*0-268-00995-3*) U of Notre Dame Pr.

Baranski, Zygmunt G. & Pertile, Lino, eds. The New Italian Novel. (Writers of Italy Ser.). 300p. (C). 1994. text 60.00 (*0-7486-0414-6*, Pub. by Edinburgh U Pr) Col U Pr.

Baranski, Zymunt G., ed. Pasolini Old & New: Surveys & Studies. 440p. 1999. boxed set 45.00 (*1-85182-436-7*, Pub. by Four Cts Pr) Intl Spec Bk.

Baranskii, V. A., et al. Sixteen Papers on Logic & Algebra. LC 51-5559. (Translations Ser.: Series 2, Vol. 94). 276p. 1970. 45.00 (*0-8218-1794-9*, TRANS2/94) Am Math.

Baranson, Jack. Automotive Industries in Developing Countries. LC 77-85339. (World Bank Staff Occasional Papers: No. 8). 120p. reprint ed. pap. 37.20 (*0-8357-5925-3*, 202173300022) Bks Demand.

— Manufacturing Problems in India: The Cummins Diesel Experience. LC 67-26917. 168p. reprint ed. pap. 52.10 (*0-608-15216-1*, 202741000055) Bks Demand.

— North-South Technology Transfer: Financing & Institution Building. LC 81-80543. 160p. 1981. 25.75 (*0-912338-27-X*); fiche 12.75 (*0-912338-28-8*) Lomond.

— Robots in Manufacturing: Key to International Competitiveness. LC 83-81240. 168p. 1983. 32.50 (*0-912338-39-3*); fiche 16.50 (*0-912338-40-7*) Lomond.

Baranson, Jack, et al. Soviet Automation: Perspectives & Prospects. LC 86-83289. 1986. 49.50 (*0-912338-61-X*) Lomond.

Barante, Amable G. Histoire de la Convention Nationale, 6 vols. LC 77-161739. reprint ed. 455.00 (*0-404-07780-3*) AMS Pr.

— Histoire du directoire de la Republique francaise, 3 vols., Set. LC 71-161740. reprint ed. 225.00 (*0-404-07770-6*) AMS Pr.

Barany, Anders, et al. The Nobel Prizes, 1996. (Illus.). 401p. 1997. 92.50 (*91-85848-26-3*, Pub. by Nobel Fnd) Coronet Bks.

Barany, Franz R., et al, eds. Gastrointestinal Emergencies Two: Proceedings of the 2nd International Symposium on Gastrointestinal Emergencies, Rome, 7-8 June 1979. (Advances in the Biosciences Ser.: Vol. 27). (Illus.). 184p. 1980. 35.50 (*0-08-024927-2*, Pergamon Pr) Elsevier.

Barany, George. The Anglo-Russian Entente Cordiale of Sixteen Ninety-Seven to Sixteen Ninety-Eight: Peter I & William III at Utrecht. (East European Monographs: No. 207). 101p. 1986. text 48.50 (*0-88033-104-6*, Pub. by East Eur Monographs) Col U Pr.

Barany, Michael, ed. Biochemistry of Smooth Muscle Contraction. LC 95-23967. (Illus.). 434p. 1995. text 115.00 (*0-12-078160-3*) Acad Pr.

Barany, Ronald. The Psalms. LC 97-91812. x, 286p. 1997. 23.00 (*0-9657767-0-0*) Psilam Pub.

Barany Society Meeting Staff. Current Studies in Otoneurology: Proceedings of the Barany Society Meeting, Toronto, Aug. 1971. Barber, H. O. & Frederickson, J. M., eds. (Advances in OtoRhinoLaryngology Ser.: Vol. 19). (Illus.). 1973. 134.00 (*3-8055-1448-4*) S Karger.

Barany, Zoltan & Volgyes, Ivan, eds. The Legacies of Communism in Eastern Europe. LC 94-43245. 272p. 1995. text 48.00 (*0-8018-4997-7*); pap. text 15.95 (*0-8018-4998-5*) Johns Hopkins.

Barany, Zoltan, jt. ed. see Braun, Aurel.

Baranzini, Marlene S., jt. auth. see Egger-Bovet, Howard.

Baranzini, Mauro. A Theory of Wealth Distribution & Accumulation. (Illus.). 288p. 1991. text 75.00 (*0-19-823313-2*) OUP.

Baranzini, Mauro, jt. ed. see Cencini, Alvaro.

Baras, F., jt. ed. see Nicolis, G.

Baras, J. S. & Mirelli, V., eds. Recent Advances in Stochastic Calculus. (Progress in Automation & Information Systems Ser.). ix, 217p. 1990. 71.95 (*0-387-97273-0*) Spr-Verlag.

Baras, Victor, jt. ed. see Himmelfarb, Milton.

Barasanti, Jeanne, jt. auth. see Stone, Elizabeth.

Barasch, Frances. Monarch Notes on Shakespeare's Henry Fourth, Pt. 2. (Orig.). (C). 3.95 (*0-671-00634-7*, Arco) Macmillan Gen Ref.

Barasch, Lynne. Old Friends. LC 97-4987. (Illus.). 32p. (J). (gr. k-3). 1998. 16.00 (*0-374-35611-4*) FS&G.

Barasch, Lynne. The Reluctant Flower Girl. (Illus.). 40p. (J). (ps-3). 14.95 (*0-06-028809-4*); lib. bdg. 14.89 (*0-06-028810-8*) HarpC Child Bks.

***Barasch, Marc Ian.** Healing Dreams: Exploring the Dreams That Can Transform Your Life. 336p. 2000. 24.95 (*1-57322-167-8*) Putnam Pub Group.

Barasch, Marcian, jt. auth. see Hirshberg, Caryle.

***Barasch, Moshe.** From Impressionism to Kandinsky. (Theories of Art Ser.: Vol. 3). 2000. pap. 25.00 (*0-415-92627-0*) Routledge.

— From Plato to Winckelmann. 2000. pap. 25.00 (*0-415-92625-4*) Routledge.

— From Winckelmann to Baudelaire. (Theories of Art Ser.: Vol. 2). 25.00 (*0-415-92626-2*) Routledge.

Barasch, Moshe. Icon: Studies in the History of an Idea. 296p. (C). 1992. text 50.00 (*0-8147-1172-3*) NYU Pr.

— Icon: Studies in the History of an Idea. 296p. (C). 1993. pap. text 19.50 (*0-8147-1214-2*) NYU Pr.

— Language of Art. LC 96-45828. (C). 1997. text 67.50 (*0-8147-1255-X*) NYU Pr.

— Modern Theories of Art Vol. 2: From Impressionism to Kandinsky. 384p. 1998. text 60.00 (*0-8147-1272-X*); pap. text 20.00 (*0-8147-1273-8*) NYU Pr.

— Modern Theories of Art, One: From Winckelmann to Baudelaire. 416p. (C). 1990. text 47.50 (*0-8147-1133-2*) NYU Pr.

— Theories of Art: From Plato to Winckelmann. 352p. (C). 1985. pap. text 18.50 (*0-8147-1061-1*) NYU Pr.

Barasch, Seymour. Arco GED: High School Equivalency Examination. 14th ed. 864p. 1996. pap. 12.95 (*0-02-860315-X*, Arco) Macmillan Gen Ref.

— GED: High School Equivalency Examinations. 15th ed. 752p. 1997. pap. 14.95 (*0-02-862204-9*, Arc) IDG Bks.

Barash, Carol. English Women's Poetry, 1649-1714: Politics, Community & Linguistic Authority. (Illus.). 360p. 1997. text 55.00 (*0-19-811973-9*, Clarendon Pr) OUP.

— English Women's Poetry, 1649-1714: Politics, Community & Linguistic Authority. 368p. 2000. pap. 24.95 (*0-19-818686-X*) OUP.

— Myth of Monogamy Clothbound. 2001. pap. text. write for info. (*0-7167-4004-4*) W H Freeman.

Barash, Carol. Olive Schreiner Reader: Writings on Women & South Africa. 1987. pap. 12.95 (*0-86358-118-8*, Pub. by Pandora) Routldge.

Barash, Carol, jt. ed. see Greenfield, Susan C.

Barash, Cathy, ed. see Roth, Susan A.

***Barash, Cathy W.** Choosing Plant Combinations: 501 Beautiful Ways to Mix & Match Color & Shape in the Garden. LC 99-70562. (Illus.). 264p. 1999. 29.95 (*0-696-21014-2*) Meredith Bks.

Barash, Cathy W. Edible Flowers: Desserts & Drinks. LC 97-11851. (Illus.). 96p. (Orig.). 1997. pap. 16.95 (*1-55591-389-X*) Fulcrum Pub.

— Edible Flowers: From Garden to Palate. (Illus.). 264p. 1995. pap. 24.95 (*1-55591-246-X*) Fulcrum Pub.

B

— Evening Gardens: Planning & Planting a Landscape to Dazzle the Senses after Sundown. (Illus.). 176p. (Orig.). 1998. pap. 20.00 (*0-7881-5602-0*) DIANE Pub.

— Taylor's Weekend Gardening Guide to Kitchen Gardens. LC 98-11771. (Taylor's Weekend Gardening Guides Ser.). (Illus.). 128p. 1998. pap. 12.95 (*0-395-82749-3*) HM.

***Barash, Cathy Wilkinson.** The Climbing Garden. (Illus.). 128p. 2000. 20.00 (*1-56799-964-6*, Friedman-Fairfax) M Friedman Pub Grp Inc.

Barash, Cathy Wilkinson, ed. see Rushing, Felder.

Barash, Dany, tr. see Calle, Sophie & Baudrillard, Jean.

Barash, David P. Aging: An Exploration. LC 82-48868. 232p. 1983. 25.00 (*0-295-95993-2*) U of Wash Pr.

— Approaches to Peace: A Reader in Peace Studies. LC 98-27847. (Illus.). 288p. (C). 1999. pap. 22.50 (*0-19-512386-7*) OUP.

— Beloved Enemies: Our Need for Opponents. LC 94-3468. 309p. (C). 1994. 27.95 (*0-87975-908-9*) Prometheus Bks.

— Gives Peas a Chance: Enjoying Our Natural Environment. 1991. pap. 12.95 (*0-8184-0549-X*) Carol Pub Group.

— The Great Outdoors: A Book about Gardening, Star Gazing, Mountain Climbing & Other Pleasures of Nature. 1989. 17.95 (*0-8184-0496-5*) Carol Pub Group.

— Ideas of Human Nature. LC 97-36775. 294p. (C). 1998. pap. text 33.40 (*0-13-647587-6*) P-H.

— Marmots: Social Behavior & Ecology. LC 89-4284. (Illus.). 384p. 1989. 55.00 (*0-8047-1534-3*) Stanford U Pr.

Barash, David P., ed. Approaches to Peace: A Reader in Peace Studies. LC 98-27847. (Illus.). 288p. (C). 1999. text 49.95 (*0-19-512385-9*) OUP.

Barash, David P. & Barash, Ilona A. The Mammal in the Mirror: Understanding Our Place in the Natural World. LC QP34.5.B34 1999. 336p. 1999. text 24.95 (*0-7167-3391-9*, Sci Am Lib) W H Freeman.

***Barash, David P. & Barash, Ilona A.** The Mammal in the Mirror: Understanding Our Place in the Natural World. 2000. pap. 14.95 (*0-7167-4166-0*) W H Freeman.

Barash, David P. & Lipton, Judith E. Making Sense of Sex: How Genes & Gender Influence Our Relationships. LC 97-25746. 240p. 1997. 24.95 (*1-55963-452-9*) Island Pr.

Barash, Harvey L. & Dicker, Eva B. Our Father Abe: The Story of a Deaf Shoe Repairman. (Illus.). 272p. (Orig.). 1991. 12.95 (*0-9629634-1-0*) Abar Pr.

Barash, Ilona A., jt. auth. see Barash, David P.

Barash, Melanee L., jt. auth. see Richmond, Mardi.

Barash, Moshe. Imago Hominis: Studies in the Language of Art. LC 94-4874. (Illus.). 292p. (C). 1994. text 65.00 (*0-8147-1231-2*) NYU Pr.

Barash, Paul G., et al, eds. Clinical Anesthesia. 3rd ed. LC 96-10243. 1,568p. 1996. text 145.00 (*0-397-51482-4*) Lppncott W & W.

— Handbook of Clinical Anesthesia. 3rd ed. 750p. 1996. spiral bd. 39.95 (*0-397-58733-3*) Lppncott W & W.

Barash, Paul G., et al. Clinical Anesthesia. 4th ed. 1504p. text 165.00 (*0-7817-2268-3*) Lppncott W & W.

— Handbook of Clinical Anesthesia. 4th ed. 900p. pap. text 39.95 (*0-7817-2918-1*) Lppncott W & W.

***Barash, Susan Shapiro.** Second Wives: The Pitfalls & Rewards of marrying Widowers & Divorced Men. LC 99-75939. 256p. 2000. pap. 15.95 (*0-88282-182-2*) New Horizon NJ.

***Barashkov, A. S.** Smaller Parameter Method in Multidimensional Inverse Problems. (Inverse & Ill-Posed Problems Ser.). 144p. 1998. 122.50 (*90-6764-295-9*, Pub. by VSP) Coronet Bks.

Barashkov, E. V. The State Art Museum of the Moldavian SSR. (Illus.). 1982. 175.00 (*0-7855-1666-2*) St Mut.

Barasi, Stephen, jt. auth. see Barker, Roger A.

Barata, Joao C., et al, eds. Particles & Fields: Proceedings of the 9th Jorge Andre Swieca Summer School Brazil 16 - 28 February 1997. LC 98-213675. 500p. 1998. 84.00 (*981-02-3453-8*) World Scientific Pub.

***Barata, Joao C. A., et al, eds.** Particle & Fields. 500p. 2000. 96.00 (*981-02-4254-9*) World Scientific Pub.

Barata, Sharyn & Christianson, Robbin C. Chartwell's Guide to Billing in a New Era. Smith, L. Dennis, ed. & illus. by. 356p. 1999. spiral bd. 975.00 (*1-891790-21-8*) Chartwell Inc.

Barata, Sharyn, jt. ed. see Shrine, Jim.

Baratham, Gopal. A Candle or the Sun. 224p. (Orig.). 1992. pap. 15.99 (*1-85242-225-4*) Serpents Tail.

— Moonrise, Sunset. (Mask Noir Ser.). 256p. (Orig.). 1996. pap. 12.99 (*1-85242-501-6*) Serpents Tail.

Baratier, David. A Run of Letters. (Poetry New York Pamphlet Ser.: Vol. 5). 26p. 1998. pap. 5.00 (*0-923389-31-8*) Meet Eyes Bind.

Baratier, David, ed. see Massman, Gordon.

Baratier, David, ed. see Miller, Errol.

Baratier, David, ed. see Stenhouse, Shelley.

Baratieri, Luiz N., et al. Advanced Operative Dentistry. Monteiro, Sylvio, Jr. & Volkmer, Fernando J., trs. from SPA. (POR., Illus.). 510p. 1993. text 126.00 (*85-7288-002-X*, B9997) Quint Pub Co.

Baratloo, Balch & Moji, Clifton C. Angst: Cartography. 103p. 1990. pap. 9.95 (*0-930829-10-7*) Lumen Inc.

Baratt, Olivia Elton. Basket Making. 1999. pap. text. write for info. (*1-85974-206-8*) New5 Holland.

Baratta, Don. The Sicilian Gentleman's Cookbook. 2nd rev. ed. (Illus.). 272p. (Orig.). 1992. pap. 15.95 (*1-55958-230-8*) Prima Pub.

Baratta, Francis I., jt. ed. see Brown, Kevin R.

Baratta, Joseph P., compiled by. Strengthening the United Nations: A Bibliography on U. N. Reform & World Federalism, 7. LC 87-134. (Bibliographies & Indexes in World History Ser.: No. 7). 359p. 1987. lib. bdg. 69.50 (*0-313-25840-6*, BSU/) Greenwood.

— United Nations System: An Annotated Bibliography. LC 94-41759. (International Organizations Ser.: Vol. 10). 542p. 1995. text 89.95 (*1-56000-216-6*) Transaction Pubs.

Baratta-Lorton, Mary. Mathematics Their Way. 1976. pap. text 38.95 (*0-201-04320-3*) Addison-Wesley.

— Mathematics...a Way of Thinking. 1977. text 28.00 (*0-201-04322-X*) Addison-Wesley.

— Twentieth Anniversary Edition Math Their Way Package. anniversary ed. 1994. pap. 59.00 (*0-201-86153-4*) Addison-Wesley.

— Workjobs: Activity-Centered Learning for Early Childhood. 1972. pap. text 17.95 (*0-201-04311-4*) Addison-Wesley.

— Workjobs for Parents: Activity-Centered Learning in the Home. 1975. pap. text 12.95 (*0-201-04303-3*) Addison-Wesley.

Baratta-Lorton, Robert. Baratta-Lorton Reading Program: Teacher's Manual. (Illus.). 447p. 1985. ring bd. write for info. (*0-9614646-1-5*) Ctr Innovation.

— Dekodiphukan. LC 85-70308. (Illus.). 116p. 1985. pap. 24.95 (*0-9614646-0-7*) Ctr Innovation.

Baratta, Mary. Mathematics Their Way: 20th Anniversary Edition. anniversary ed. 1995. pap. 39.95 (*0-201-86149-6*) Addison-Wesley.

Baratta, Marylou, jt. auth. see Baratta, Tommy.

Baratta, Tommy & Baratta, Marylou. Cooking for Jack. 1997. per. 14.00 (*0-671-53561-7*, PB Trade Paper) PB.

— Cooking for Jack (Nicholson) Delicious Low-Fat Italian Recipes from the Star's Kitchen. (Illus.). 176p. 1999. reprint ed. text 20.00 (*0-7881-6186-5*) DIANE Pub.

Baratti, David G., jt. auth. see Jackson, F. Scott.

Baratz, Joan C. & Shuy, Roger W., eds. Teaching Black Children to Read. LC 72-3760. (Urban Language Ser.: No. 4). 233p. reprint ed. pap. 72.30 (*0-8357-3342-4*, 203957000013) Bks Demand.

Baratz, Lewis, jt. auth. see Place, Irene M.

Baratz, Lewis R. International Directory of Current Early-Music Periodicals. MacCracken, Thomas G., ed. LC 95-209762. (Early Music America Information Resource Ser.). 24p. (Orig.). 1994. pap. 5.00 (*1-878206-07-9*) Early Music.

Baratz, Mark E. Orthopedic Surgery: The Essentials. LC 98-45052. 1999. 125.00 (*3-13-116291-0*) Thieme Med Pubs.

Baratz, Mark E., et al. Orthopedic Surgery: The Essentials. LC 98-45052. (Illus.). 992p. 1999. 99.00 (*0-86577-779-9*) Thieme Med Pubs.

Baratz, Morton S. Corporate Giants & the Power Structure. (Reprint Series in Social Sciences). (C). 1993. reprint ed. pap. text 5.00 (*0-8290-3141-3*, PS-13) Irvington.

— The Investor's Guide to Futures Money Management. (Illus.). 160p. (Orig.). 1984. pap. 19.95 (*0-936624-28-0*) Futures Pub.

— The Investor's Guide to Futures Money Management. (Orig.). 1990. 29.95 (*0-936624-04-3*) Futures Pub.

— The Union & the Coal Industry, 4. LC 82-25141. (Yale Studies in Economics: No. 4). 170p. (C). 1983. reprint ed. lib. bdg. 59.50 (*0-313-23698-4*, BAUC, Greenwood Pr) Greenwood.

Baratz, Sharon R., ed. see Council on Health Care Technology Institute of Med.

Barauh, Sanjib. India Against Itself: Assam & the Politics of Nationality. LC 99-12909. 1999. 36.50 (*0-8122-3491-X*) U of Pa Pr.

Barav, A., et al, eds. The Yearbook of European Law, 1996, Vol. 16. 820p. 1998. text 210.00 (*0-19-876499-5*) OUP.

Barav, A. & Wyatt, D. A., eds. Yearbook of European Law, 1995, 15. 680p. 1997. text 215.00 (*0-19-825783-X*) OUP.

Barav, A. & Wyatt, Derrick, eds. Yearbook of European Law 1997, Vol. 17. 856p. 1999. text 195.00 (*0-19-826883-1*) OUP.

Barav, Ami. Yearbook of European Law, 1988, Vol. 8. Wyatt, Derrick A., ed. 394p. 1990. text 130.00 (*0-19-825263-3*) OUP.

Barav, Ami, ed. Commentary on the EC Treaty & the Single European Act. LC 92-33884. 200p. 1998. 195.00 (*0-19-825615-9*) OUP.

Barav, Ami & Philip, Christian. Dictionnaire Juridique des Communautes Europeennes. (FRE.). 1993. write for info. (*0-7859-7748-1*, 2130449123) Fr & Eur.

Barav, Ami & Wyatt, D. A., eds. Yearbook of European Law, Vol. 12. (Illus.). 868p. 1994. text 175.00 (*0-19-825780-5*) OUP.

Barav, Ami & Wyatt, Derrick A. Yearbook of European Law, 1989, Vol. 9. 502p. 1991. text 150.00 (*0-19-825423-7*) OUP.

Barav, Ami & Wyatt, Derrick A., eds. Yearbook of European Law, 1990, Vol. 10. 674p. 1992. text 175.00 (*0-19-825705-8*) OUP.

— Yearbook of European Law, 1991, Vol. 11. 700p. 1993. text 160.00 (*0-19-825779-1*) OUP.

— Yearbook of European Law, 1994, Vol. 14. 782p. 1996. text 195.00 (*0-19-825782-1*) OUP.

Baravalle, Herman Von, see Von Baravalle, Herman.

Baravalle, Hermann V. The Waldorf Approach to Arithmetic. Booth, David, ed. LC 95-72205. (Illus.). 175p. (Orig.). 1996. pap. 15.75 (*1-888182-51-2*, WAA, Parker Courtney) Sci & Math Assn.

Baravykas, V. English - Lithuanian Dictionary. (ENG & LIT.). lib. bdg. 39.95 (*0-8288-2625-0*, F64172) Fr & Eur.

— Lithuanian - English Dictionary. (ENG & LIT.). 39.95 (*0-8288-2486-X*) Fr & Eur.

Barazandeh, Alex. A Window of Opportunity in the U.S.A. The Story of My Life. Barazandeh, Marie, ed. 241p. 1994. 20.00 (*0-9640364-0-1*) A Barazandeh.

Barazandeh, Marie, ed. see Barazandeh, Alex.

Barazangi, Nimat H., ed. Islamic Identity & the Struggle for Justice. 136p. 1996. 34.95 (*0-614-21433-5*, 1423) Kazi Pubns.

Barazangi, Nimat H., et al, eds. Islamic Identity & the Struggle for Justice. LC 95-23907. 136p. (C). 1996. 49.95 (*0-8130-1382-8*) U Press Fla.

Barb, Alwyn. Reconstruction to Reform: Texas Politics, 1876-1906. LC 99-41948. (Illus.). 340p. 1999. reprint ed. pap. text 14.95 (*0-87074-444-5*) SMU Press.

Barba. Introduction to Educational Technology. (Education Ser.). 1910. pap. 42.00 (*0-534-52812-0*) Wadsworth Pub.

Barba, Eugenio. The Paper Canoe: Guide to Theatre Anthropology. Fowler, Richard, tr. LC 94-7809. 224p. (C). 1995. pap. 22.99 (*0-415-11674-0*, B3202) Routledge.

Barba, Eugenio & Savarese, Nicola. The Dictionary of Theatre Anthropology: The Secret Art of the Performer. Fowler, Richard, tr. (Illus.). 232p. (C). (gr. 13). 1991. pap. 50.00 (*0-415-05308-0*, A6232) Routledge.

Barba, Gustau B. Diccionari Politic. (CAT.). 144p. 1990. pap. 13.95 (*0-7859-6393-6*, 8486175119) Fr & Eur.

Barba, Harry. The Case for Socially Functional Art Culture & Education, 4 vols., Set. Incl. Vol. 1. How to Teach Writing in the Time It Takes to Consume a Glass - a Quart - a Barrel of Wine. 1969. pap. 7.95 (*0-911906-02-9*); Vol. 2. Teaching in Your Own Write. 1970. pap. text 7.95 (*0-911906-06-1*); Vol. 3. Two Connecticut Yankees Teaching in Appalachia. 1974. pap. text 7.95 (*0-911906-10-X*); Vol. 4. Case for Socially Functional Education. 1973. pap. text 30.00 (*0-911906-04-5*); (Barba-Cue Ser.). (Orig.). 1973. Set pap. 30.00 (*0-911906-17-7*) Harian Creative Bks.

— The Day the World Went Sane: A Fictive Ballet & a Dramatic Opera. LC 78-70762. 1979. 17.95 (*0-911906-14-2*); pap. 12.95 (*0-911906-13-4*) Harian Creative Bks.

— Love in the Persian Way. (C). 1970. pap. 5.95 (*0-911906-07-X*) Harian Creative Bks.

— Mona Lisa Smiles: Faces of Love. LC 90-93457. 252p. 1993. 19.95 (*0-911906-30-4*); pap. 12.95 (*0-911906-31-2*) Harian Creative Bks.

— Mona Lisa Smiles: Faces of Love. 1993. 19.95 (*0-614-06134-2*) Harian Creative Bks.

— One of a Kind (the Many Faces & Voices of America) LC 75-41743. 1976. pap. 9.95 (*0-911906-11-8*) Harian Creative Bks.

— Round Trip to Byzantium. LC 84-80153. 379p. 1985. pap. 15.95 (*0-911906-29-0*); lib. bdg. 22.95 (*0-911906-28-2*) Harian Creative Bks.

— Three by Harry Barba. LC 67-27073. (Orig.). 1967. pap. 35.00 (*0-911906-00-2*) Harian Creative Bks.

— Trip a Go-Go. (Mini-Book Ser.). 1970. pap. 5.95 (*0-911906-03-7*) Harian Creative Bks.

— What's Cooking in Congress?, Vol. I. Barba, Marian, ed. LC 79-83777. (Illus.). 144p. (J). (gr. 5 up). 1979. pap. 9.95 (*0-911906-15-0*) Harian Creative Bks.

— What's Cooking in Congress? Collector's Edition, Vol. II. Barba, Marian, ed. LC 79-83777. (What's Cooking Ser.). (Illus.). 250p. 1982. 50.00 (*0-911906-20-7*, 0278-4947); pap. 30.00 (*0-911906-21-5*) Harian Creative Bks.

Barba, Harry, et al. Three by Three: Barba, Bond, Hamalian. LC 77-78963. 115p. (Orig.). 1969. 30.00 (*0-911906-01-0*) Harian Creative Bks.

Barba, Harry, ed. see Avila, Kay, et al.

Barba, Harry, ed. see Bendick, Candy, et al.

Barba, J. The Use of Steel. (Works of J. Barba). ix, 110p. 1985. reprint ed. lib. bdg. 39.00 (*0-932051-61-8*) Rprt Serv.

Barba, James & Leonard, William. Radiographic Positioning Competency: Based Applications. 340p. (C). 1993. mass mkt., student ed. 32.75 (*0-8273-4456-2*) Delmar.

— Radiographic Positioning Competency-Based Applications: Instructor's Guide. 48p. 1992. pap., teacher ed. 14.00 (*0-8273-4457-0*) Delmar.

Barba, Luis. Radiografia de un Sitio Arqueologico. 138p. 1990. pap. 5.70 (*968-36-1378-0*, UN001) UPLAAP.

Barba, Luis, et al. Manual de Tecnicas Microquimicas de Campo para la Arqueologia. 36p. 1991. pap. 2.50 (*968-36-2184-8*, UN002) UPLAAP.

Barba, Marian, ed. see Barba, Harry.

Barba, Marybeth. Rules of Etiquette for Very Young Ladies, Incl. doll. 10p. (J). 1996. pap. 19.90 (*1-890414-10-7*) Bow Tie.

Barba, Rick. CD-ROM Classics, Vol. 2. LC 96-69049. 384p. 1997. per. 19.99 (*0-7615-1152-0*) Prima Pub.

Barba, Rick. CD-ROM Classics: Cheats & Hints to Your Favorite Games. LC 96-69049. 408p. 1996. pap., per. 19.95 (*0-7615-0804-X*) Prima Pub.

Barba, Rick. CD-ROM Game Secrets, Vol. 1. (Illus.). 350p. 1994. pap. 19.95 (*1-55958-526-9*) Prima Pub.

— Doom BattleBook the Authorized Strategy Guide, Vol. 1. LC 94-66791. 1994. pap. 14.95 (*1-55958-651-6*) Prima Pub.

— Gabriel Knight 3: Prima's Official Strategy Guide, Vol. 3. LC 98-65448. (Illus.). 244p. 1999. per. 19.99 (*0-7615-1578-X*, Prima Games) Prima Pub.

***Barba, Rick.** Homeworld: Prima's Official Strategy Guide. LC 98-65450. (Illus.). 244p. 2000. pap. 19.99 (*0-7615-1576-3*) Prima Pub.

Barba, Rick. Jedi Knight: Official Strategy Guide. LC 96-70082. 424p. 1997. pap. 19.99 (*0-7615-0922-4*) Prima Pub.

— King's Quest VIII Mask of Eternity: The Official Strategy Guide. LC 97-68845. 244p. 1998. per. 19.99 (*0-7615-1115-6*) Prima Pub.

— The Last Express: The Official Strategy Game. LC 96-71683. 216p. 1997. per. 19.99 (*0-7615-0989-5*) Prima Pub.

— Mission Critical: The Official Strategy Guide. 1995. pap. text 19.95 (*0-7615-0177-0*) Prima Pub.

— Outlaws: The Official Strategy Guide. LC 96-70481. 264p. 1997. pap., per. 19.99 (*0-7615-0939-9*) Prima Pub.

— The Pandora Directive: The Official Strategy Guide. LC 95-74690. 1996. pap. text 19.99 (*0-7615-0373-0*) Prima Pub.

Barba, Rick. Phantasmagoria Puzzle of Flesh: The Official Strategy Guide. LC 96-70079. 192p. 1996. pap., per. 19.99 (*0-7615-0877-5*) Prima Pub.

— Quest for Glory 5: The Official Strategy Guide. LC 97-69340. (Secrets of the Game Ser.). 240p. 1998. per. 19.99 (*0-7615-1189-X*) Prima Pub.

— Rama: The Official Strategy Guide. 288p. 1996. pap., per. 19.99 (*0-7615-0879-1*) Prima Pub.

Barba, Rick. Riven: The Mini Guide. LC 97-69948. 64p. 1997. per. 5.99 (*0-7615-1334-5*) Prima Pub.

***Barba, Rick.** Riven: The Sequel to Myst: Prima's Official Strategy Guide. (Value Ser.). 2000. pap. 9.99 (*0-7615-2897-0*) Prima Pub.

Barba, Rick. The Sequel to Myst: The Official Strategy Guide. LC 96-72316. 208p. 1997. pap. 19.99 (*0-7615-0830-9*) Prima Pub.

— The Sims: Prima's Official Strategy Guide. (Official Strategy Guides Ser.). 2000. pap. 14.99 (*0-7615-2339-1*) Prima Pub.

— SimTower: The Vertical Empire: The Official Strategy Guide. 1995. pap. 19.95 (*0-7615-0042-1*) Prima Pub.

— Stonekeep: The Official Strategy Guide. 1995. pap. 19.95 (*1-55958-733-4*) Prima Pub.

— Stunt Island: The Official Strategy Guide. (Illus.). 256p. 1993. pap. 19.95 (*1-55958-247-2*) Prima Pub.

— Tex Murphy: Overseer: The Official Strategy Guide. (Secrets of the Game Ser.). 240p. 1998. per. 19.99 (*0-7615-1314-0*) Prima Pub.

— Timelapse: Ancient Civilizations: The Official Strategy Guide. LC 95-73072. 264p. 1996. per. 19.99 (*0-7615-0497-4*) Prima Pub.

— Tribes: Prima's Official Strategy Guide. (Prima Games Ser.). 240p. 1998. per. 19.99 (*0-7615-1908-4*) Prima Pub.

— Under a Killing Moon: Official Strategy Guide. LC 94-67740. 272p. 1994. pap. 19.95 (*1-55958-679-6*) Prima Pub.

— Warlords III: The Official Strategy Guide. LC 97-68841. 240p. 1997. per. 19.99 (*0-7615-1199-7*) Prima Pub.

— Warlords III - Dark Lords Rising: Prima's Official Strategy Guide. LC 98-66896. 96p. 1998. per. 19.99 (*0-7615-1770-7*) Prima Pub.

Barba, Rick. Zork Nemesis. 160p. 1996. pap., per. 14.99 (*0-7615-0711-6*) Prima Pub.

***Barba, Rick & DeMaria, Rusel.** Myst: Prima's Official Strategy Guide. (Value Ser.). 2000. pap. 9.99 (*0-7615-2894-6*) Prima Pub.

Barba, Rick & DeMaria, Rusel. Myst: The Official Strategy Guide. expanded rev. ed. (Illus.). 192p. 1997. pap. 19.95 (*0-7615-0102-9*, Prima Games) Prima Pub.

***Barba, Rick & Honeywell, Steve.** Star Wars: Force Commander. (Official Strategy Guides Ser.). 256p. 2000. pap. 19.99 (*0-7615-2194-1*) Prima Pub.

Barba, Rick & Hutchins, Blake. Starsiege Vol. 3: Prima's Official Strategy Guide. LC 97-69346. 240p. 1998. per. 19.99 (*0-7615-1190-3*) Prima Pub.

Barba, Rick & Reese, Andrew. DOOM Battlebook. expanded rev. ed. 288p. 1995. per. 19.95 (*0-7615-0362-5*) Prima Pub.

Barba, Roberta H. Science in the Multicultural Classroom: A Guide to Teaching & Learning. 2nd ed. LC 97-10531. 450p. 1997. pap. text 62.00 (*0-205-26737-8*) Allyn.

Barba, Roberta R., jt. auth. see Reynolds, Karen E.

Barba, William C., ed. Higher Education in Crisis: New York in National Perspective. LC 94-37750. (Reference Library of Social Science: Vol. 963). 216p. 1995. text 42.00 (*0-8153-1708-5*, SS963) Garland.

Barbach, Lonnie. The Erotic Edge: Erotica for Couples. 274p. 1996. pap. 13.95 (*0-452-27464-8*, Plume) Dutton Plume.

— Falling in Love Again: Sexual Enrichment Program. 1997. 100.00 (*0-87630-852-3*) Brunner-Mazel.

— The Pause: Positive Approaches to Menopause. 304p. 1994. mass mkt. 6.99 (*0-451-18035-6*, Sig) NAL.

***Barbach, Lonnie.** Seductions: Tales of Erotic Persuasion. 288p. 2000. pap. 13.95 (*0-452-28059-1*, Plume) Dutton Plume.

Barbach, Lonnie. Seductions: Tales of Erotic Persuasion. LC 98-26993. 304p. 1999. 23.95 (*0-525-94462-1*) NAL.

— Turn Ons: Pleasing Yourself While You Please Your Lover. 96p. 1998. pap. 10.95 (*0-452-27759-0*, Plume) Dutton Plume.

Barbach, Lonnie, ed. Erotic Interludes: Tales Told by Women. LC 95-2766. 1995. pap. 12.95 (*0-452-27398-6*, Plume) Dutton Plume.

Barbach, Lonnie G. For Each Other: Sharing Sexual Intimacy. 1982. 13.95 (*0-385-17296-6*, Anchor NY) Doubleday.

— For Each Other: Sharing Sexual Intimacy. LC 83-8804. (Illus.). 320p. 1983. pap. 14.95 (*0-385-17297-4*, Anchor NY) Doubleday.

— For Each Other: Sharing Sexual Intimacy. 1984. mass mkt. 6.99 (*0-451-15271-9*, Sig) NAL.

— For Yourself: Fulfillment of Female Sexuality & Guide to Orgasmic Response. 1976. mass mkt. 6.99 (*0-451-16681-7*, Sig) NAL.

— For Yourself: The Fulfillment of Female Sexuality. LC 74-4873. 240p. 1975. pap. 12.95 (*0-385-11245-9*, Anchor NY) Doubleday.

***Barbach, Lonnie G.** The Pause: Positive Approaches to Perimenopause & Menopause. LC 99-32063. 2000. pap. 13.95 (*0-452-28110-5*, Plume) Dutton Plume.

Barbach, Lonnie G. Pleasures: Women Write Erotica. LC 85-42550. 368p. 1985. reprint ed. pap. 13.50 (*0-06-097002-2*, PL 7002, Perennial) HarperTrade.

An Asterisk (*) at the beginning of an entry indicates that the title is appearing for the first time.

Barbach, Lonnie G. & Geisinger, David L. Going the Distance: Finding & Keeping Lifelong Love. 320p. 1993. pap. 13.95 (*0-452-26948-2*, Plume) Dutton Plume.

Barbadillo, Pedro, tr. see Cole, Brock.

Barbadillo, Pedro, tr. see L'Engle, Madeleine.

Barbagallo, Cathy, ed. see Carlson, Glenn E., et al.

Barbagallo, Mario, et al, eds. Recent Advances in Geriatrics: Proceedings of the 8th Course of the International School of Gerontology & Geriatrics on Advances in Geriatrics: Cardiovascular System, Arterial Hypertension & Osteoporosis Held in Erice, Italy, March 20-25, 1997. LC 97-46470. (Illus.). 302p. 1998. 95.00 (*0-306-45779-2*, Kluwer Plenum) Kluwer Academic.

*__Barbagallo, Vera.__ A Thief's Way to Heaven: The 7 Minute Prayer Book. unabridged ed. (Illus.). 32p. 1999. pap. 3.00 (*0-9675830-0-4*) J Zajac.

Barbakadze, V., contrib. by. Durability of Building Structures & Constructions. LC 99-227044. (Illus.). 264p. (C). 1995. 123.00 (*90-5410-249-7*, Pub. by A A Balkema) Ashgate Pub Co.

Barbalet, J. M. Citizenship. LC 88-27718. (Concepts in Social Thought Ser.). 119p. (Orig.). 1989. pap. 13.95 (*0-8166-1776-7*) U of Minn Pr.

— Emotion, Social Theory & Social Structure: A Macrosociological Approach. LC 97-25639. 220p. (C). 1998. text 54.95 (*0-521-62190-9*) Cambridge U Pr.

Barbalet, Jack. Citizenship. Parkin, Frank, ed. (Concepts in the Social Sciences Ser.). 128p. 1988. 32.50 (*0-335-15571-5*); pap. 9.99 (*0-335-15570-7*) OpUniv Pr.

Barban, Arnold M., et al. Essentials of Media Planning: A Marketing Viewpoint. 3rd ed. LC 92-13907. (Illus.). 176p. 1993. pap. 17.95 (*0-8442-3523-7*) NTC Contemp Pub Co.

— Essentials of Media Planning: A Marketing Viewpoint. 3rd ed. (Illus.). 176p. 1993. 29.95 (*0-8442-3522-9*, NTC Business Bks) NTC Contemp Pub Co.

Barbanel, Edward, jt. ed. see Garrett, Don.

Barbanel, Linda. Sex, Money & Power. LC 96-20129. 304p. 1996. 14.95 (*0-02-861120-9*) Macmillan.

Barbanell. Global Art Resource Guide: Latino, American Art. 1996. 40.00 (*0-7838-2111-5*, G K Hall Lrg Type) Mac Lib Ref.

— Global Art Resource Guide: Latino, American Art. 1998. 20.00 (*0-7838-2112-3*, Hall Reference) Macmillan.

Barbanell, Edward, jt. auth. see Garrett, Don.

Barbanti-Brodano, Giuseppe, et al, eds. DNA Tumor Viruses: Oncogenic Mechanisms. (Infectious Agents & Pathogenesis Ser.). (Illus.). 452p. (C). 1996. text 115.00 (*0-306-45151-4*, Kluwer Plenum) Kluwer Academic.

Barbanti, Tullia. Al Dente: Italian Cooking Done Just Right. (ITA., Illus.). 209p. (Orig.). 1987. pap. 15.95 (*0-614-29576-9*) T Barbanti.

— Al Dente: Italian Cooking Done Just Right. (Illus.). 209p. (Orig.). 1987. pap. text 15.99 (*0-9620558-0-8*) T Barbanti.

Barbantini, Constance. Scriviamo, Scriviamo: Advanced Beginning. (ITA.). 104p. (C). Date not set. pap., wbk. ed. 9.95 (*0-8442-8037-2*, X80372) NTC Contemp Pub Co.

— Si Scrive Cosi: Beginning. (ITA.). 100p. (C). Date not set. pap., wbk. ed. 9.95 (*0-8442-8035-6*, X80356) NTC Contemp Pub Co.

Barbara, Agustin. Marriage Across Frontiers. 104p. 1989. 59.00 (*1-85359-042-8*, Pub. by Multilingual Matters); pap. 24.95 (*1-85359-041-X*, Pub. by Multilingual Matters) Taylor & Francis.

Barbara, Bernard, et al. Lectures on Modern Magnetism. (Illus.). 240p. 1988. 86.95 (*0-387-17558-X*) Spr-Verlag.

Barbara, Bernard, jt. ed. see Gunther, Leon.

Barbara, Daniel, ed. Databases & Mobile Computing. LC 96-22305. 96p. (C). 1996. text 103.00 (*0-7923-9749-5*) Kluwer Academic.

Barbara, Leila & Scott, Mike, eds. Reflections on Language Learning. LC 94-30329. 240p. 1994. 74.95 (*1-85359-258-7*); pap. 29.95 (*1-85359-257-9*) Taylor & Francis.

Barbara Lowenstein Association Staff. The 100 Best Small Towns. 1995. pap. 12.00 (*0-671-89300-9*) Prntice Hall Bks.

Barbara, Luigi, et al, eds. Nutrition in Gastrointestinal Disease. LC 86-31316. 320p. 1987. reprint ed. pap. 99.20 (*0-608-04685-X*, 206540600004) Bks Demand.

— Recent Advances in Bile Acid Research. LC 85-25797. (Illus.). 347p. 1985. reprint ed. pap. 107.60 (*0-7837-9557-2*, 206030600005) Bks Demand.

Barbara, M., jt. ed. see Filipo, R.

Barbara, Maurizio, jt. ed. see Filipo, R.

Barbara, Paul F. Ultrafast Phenomena IX: Proceedings of the 9th International Conference, Dana Point, CA, May 1-5, 1994. LC 94-39999. (Series in Chemical Physics: Vol. 60). 1994. 119.95 (*3-540-58455-2*) Spr-Verlag.

Barbara, Paul F. & Fujimoto, J. G. Ultrafast Phenomena X: Proceedings of the 10th International Conference, Del Coronado, CA, May 28-June 1, 1996. LC 96-35229. (Springer Series in Chemical Physics: Vol. 62). (Illus.). 473p. 1996. 109.00 (*3-540-61704-3*) Spr-Verlag.

Barbara Sinatra Children's Center Staff. The Sinatra Celebrity Cookbook: Barbara, Frank & Friends. LC 96-92543. 300p. 1996. 24.95 (*0-9646756-0-9*) B Sinatra Chldrns.

Barbarash, Lorraine. Are We Having Fun Yet? A Guide to Games & Activities. 255p. (Orig.). 1992. pap. 27.95 (*0-9632364-0-7*) Barbarash Pubns.

— Multicultural Games. LC 96-33062. (Illus.). 152p. (Orig.). 1996. pap. text 14.95 (*0-88011-565-3*, BBAR0565) Human Kinetics.

Barbaree, Howard E., et al, eds. The Juvenile Sex Offender. LC 93-5209. 329p. 1993. lib. bdg. 40.00 (*0-89862-120-8*) Guilford Pubns.

Barbaree, James M., et al, eds. Legionella: Current Status & Emerging Perspectives. LC 92-48890. (Illus.). 390p. 1993. 79.00 (*1-55581-055-1*) ASM Pr.

Barbaree, James M., ed. see Freije, Matthew R.

*__Barbarello, James.__ Handbook for Parallel Port Design. LC 98-68488. 1999. pap. 29.95 (*0-7906-1177-5*) Prompt Publns.

Barbarello, James. PC Hardware Projects, Vol. 2. (Illus.). 191p. 1997. pap. 29.95 (*0-7906-1109-0*) Prompt Publns.

— PC Hardware Projects, Vol. 3. 205p. 1998. pap. 29.95 (*0-7906-1151-1*) Prompt Publns.

— PC Hardware Projects Vol. 1: A Complete Guide to Building Practical Addons to Your Computer. LC 97-173507. (Illus.). 256p. 1997. pap. 29.95 (*0-7906-1104-X*) Prompt Publns.

Barbares, E., jt. ed. see Pfeiffer, S. E.

Barbarese, J. T. New Science: Poems. LC 88-26080. (Contemporary Poetry Ser.). 96p. 1989. pap. 14.95 (*0-8203-1117-0*) U of Ga Pr.

Barbaresi. Flower ABC Coloring Book. (Illus.). (J). pap. 1.00 (*0-486-27309-1*) Dover.

— Spelling Fun. (Illus.). 32p. (J). pap. text 1.00 (*0-486-40044-1*) Dover.

Barbaresi, Lavinia M., jt. auth. see Dressler, Wolfgang U.

Barbaresi, Nina. Animal Alphabet Coloring Book. (Illus.). (J). (gr. k-3). 1991. pap. 2.50 (*0-486-26698-2*) Dover.

— Animal Word Puzzles Coloring Book. 81st ed. (Illus.). (J). (gr. k-3). 1991. pap. 2.50 (*0-486-26848-9*) Dover.

— Bird Stickers. (Illus.). (J). (gr. k-3). 1991. pap. 1.00 (*0-486-26813-6*) Dover.

Barbaresi, Nina. Birthday Sticker Book. (Illus.). (J). 1991. pap. text 1.00 (*0-486-26391-6*) Dover.

— Cat Stickers. (Illus.). (J). 1991. pap. text 1.00 (*0-486-26786-5*) Dover.

Barbaresi, Nina. Circus Stickers. (Illus.). (J). (gr. k-3). 1991. pap. 1.00 (*0-486-26814-4*) Dover.

— Clown Faces Stickers. (Illus.). (J). (gr. k-3). 1998. pap. 1.00 (*0-486-27248-6*) Dover.

— Dinosaur Sticker Paper Doll, Vol. 108. (Illus.). (J). (gr. k-3). 1990. pap. 1.00 (*0-486-26224-3*) Dover.

— Easter Sticker Book. (Illus.). (J). (ps). 1990. pap. 1.00 (*0-486-26225-1*) Dover.

— Easy Crossword Puzzles. 1989. pap. 1.00 (*0-486-26128-X*) Dover.

— Forest Animals Stickers. (Little Activity Bks.). (J). (ps up). 1996. pap. 1.00 (*0-486-29090-5*) Dover.

— French Alphabet Coloring Book. (Illus.). (J). (gr. k-3). 1992. pap. 2.50 (*0-486-27247-8*) Dover.

— Funny Animals Sticker Book. 80th ed. (Illus.). (J). (ps-1). 1991. pap. 1.00 (*0-486-26602-8*) Dover.

Barbaresi, Nina. Halloween Party. (Little Activity Bks.). (Illus.). (J). 1989. pap. 1.00 (*0-486-26053-4*) Dover.

— Irish Sticker Book. (Illus.). (J). 1991. pap. text 1.00 (*0-486-26590-0*) Dover.

Barbaresi, Nina. Little Animal ABC Coloring Book. 80th ed. (Illus.). (J). (gr. k-3). 1998. pap. 1.00 (*0-486-25834-3*) Dover.

— Little Animal Activity Book. (Illus.). (J). (gr. k-3). 1990. pap. 1.00 (*0-486-26272-3*) Dover.

Barbaresi, Nina. Little Awards Sticker Book. (Little Activity Bks.). (Illus.). (J). 1991. pap. 1.00 (*0-486-26388-6*) Dover.

Barbaresi, Nina. Little Butterfly Stickers, Vol. 80. (Illus.). (J). (gr. k-3). 1993. pap. 1.00 (*0-486-27663-5*) Dover.

— Little German ABC Coloring Book. (Illus.). (J). (gr. k-3). 1993. pap. 1.00 (*0-486-27463-2*) Dover.

Barbaresi, Nina. Little Halloween Sticker Book. (Little Activity Bks.). (Illus.). (J). 1991. pap. 1.00 (*0-486-26390-8*) Dover.

— Little Search: A Word Puzzle. (Illus.). (J). 1990. pap. 1.00 (*0-486-26455-6*) Dover.

— Merry Christmas Sticker Book. (Little Activity Bks.). (Illus.). (J). 1993. pap. 1.00 (*0-486-27150-1*) Dover.

Barbaresi, Nina. Night Before Christmas Coloring Book. 80th ed. (Illus.). (J). 1990. pap. 1.00 (*0-486-25737-1*) Dover.

Barbaresi, Nina. Pegatinas de los Animales de la Granja. (SPA., Illus.). (J). 1995. pap. 1.00 (*0-486-28838-2*) Dover.

— Pets Sticker Book. (Little Activity Bks.). (Illus.). (J). 1991. pap. 1.00 (*0-486-26389-4*) Dover.

— Search-A-Word-Coloring Book. (J). 1991. pap. 2.50 (*0-486-26327-4*) Dover.

Barbaresi, Nina. Shark Stickers. (Illus.). (J). (gr. k-3). 1993. pap. 1.00 (*0-486-27664-3*) Dover.

— Snow White & the Seven Dwarfs: Coloring Book. (J). 1989. pap. 1.00 (*0-486-25911-0*) Dover.

— Spanish Alphabet Coloring Book. (Illus.). (J). (gr. k-3). 1998. pap. 2.50 (*0-486-27249-4*) Dover.

— Valentine Sticker Book. (Illus.). (J). (gr. k-3). 1989. pap. 1.00 (*0-486-26192-1*) Dover.

— Whales & Dolphins Stickers. 1992. pap. text 1.00 (*0-486-26978-7*) Dover.

Barbaresi, Nina. Zoo Animals Stickers. (Illus.). (J). 1992. pap. 1.00 (*0-486-26979-5*) Dover.

Barbaresi, Nina, jt. auth. see Appelbaum, Stanley.

Barbaresi, Nina, jt. auth. see Applebaum, Stanley.

Barbaric, Slavko. El Ayuno. 60p. 1988. pap. 2.95 (*0-940535-18-1*, UP116) Franciscan U Pr.

— Fasting. 56p. 1988. pap. 2.95 (*0-940535-12-2*, UP110) Franciscan U Pr.

— In the School of Love. Riehle Foundation Staff, ed. Sarcevic, tr. LC 95-60456. (Orig.). 1995. pap. 4.50 (*1-880033-18-6*) Queenship Pub.

— Oren Con el Corazon.Tr. of Pray with the Heart. 55p. 1988. pap. 4.50 (*0-940535-15-7*, UP113) Franciscan U Pr.

— Pray with the Heart. rev. ed. 235p. (C). 1990. 4.50 (*0-940535-34-3*, UP112) Franciscan U Pr.

— Way of the Cross. 62p. 1991. pap. 4.95 (*0-940535-29-7*, UP129) Franciscan U Pr.

Barbaric, Z. L. Principles of Genitourinary Radiology Vol. 2: Nervous System & Sensory Organs. 2nd rev. ed. (Flexibook Ser.). (Illus.). 520p. 1994. 99.00 (*0-86577-493-5*) Thieme Med Pubs.

*__Barbarich, Steve S.__ Complete Manual on How to Make Money from Your Inventions & Patterns. 320p. 2000. pap. 16.95 (*1-58062-298-4*) Adams Media.

Barbarin, B., jt. auth. see Didier, Jean-Pierre.

Barbarin, Georges. Je et Moi. 155p. 1991. 9.95 (*2-920083-52-X*) Edns Roseau.

— Le Livre de Chevet. 180p. 1984. 18.50 (*2-920083-05-8*) Edns Roseau.

*__Barbarin, Oscar A. & Richter, Linda M.__ Mandela's Children: Growing-Up in a Post-Apartheid South Africa. LC 00-31134. 2000. pap. write for info. (*0-415-92469-3*) Routledge.

Barbarinde, Olufemi A. The Lome Conventions & Development: An Empirical Assessment. LC 94-1145. 1994. 77.95 (*1-85628-678-9*, Pub. by Avebry) Ashgate Pub Co.

Barbarito & D'Amico. Modules for Medication Administration. 190p. (C). 1998. spiral bd. 39.95 (*0-7872-4691-3*, 41469102) Kendall-Hunt.

Barbaro, Sarafino. Seazar & Cleo's Pet Food Cookbook: Pet Cookbook. 70p. Date not set. pap. 19.95 (*0-9670446-0-X*) S E B.

Barbarossa, Fred. The Car Care Book. (Automotive Technology Ser.). 1983. pap., teacher ed. 16.50 (*0-538-33031-7*) S-W Pub.

— The Car Care Book. 2nd ed. LC 88-3697. (Automotive Technology Ser.). 1988. mass mkt. 30.75 (*0-8273-3375-7*) Delmar.

— The Car Care Book. 2nd ed. (Automotive Technology Ser.). 1988. pap., teacher ed. 13.50 (*0-8273-3376-5*) Delmar.

— The Car Care Book. 3rd ed. (Automotive Technology Ser.). 1997. text 31.00 (*0-8273-6669-8*) Delmar.

— The Car Care Book. 3rd ed. (Automotive Technology Ser.). 1997. teacher ed. 11.50 (*0-8273-6670-1*, VNR) Wiley.

*__Barbarossa, Fred.__ Car Care Book. 3rd ed. (Primarily Tech Material). (C). 2001. pap. 22.50 (*0-7668-1969-8*) Delmar.

*__Barbarossa, James.__ Do You Know God's Will for Your Life? (Illus.). 120p. 1999. pap. 8.00 (*0-9676380-0-3*) Step By Step Min.

Barbaroux, Charles O. Memoires de Robert Guillemard, Sergent en Retraite, Suivis de Documents Historiques, 2 vols. reprint ed. 30.00 (*0-404-07537-1*) AMS Pr.

Barbarow, Peter. Give Peas a Chance. LC 90-5838. (Illus.). 256p. 1989. pap. 12.95 (*0-87961-205-3*) Naturegraph.

Barbarski, Krzysztof. Polish Armour, 1939-45. (Vanguard Ser.: No. 30). (Illus.). 48p. pap. 10.95 (*0-85045-467-0*, 9319, Pub. by Ospry) Stackpole.

Barbas, Bernd. Aircraft of the Luftwaffe Fighter Aces, Vol. I. LC 95-68642. (Illus.). 256p. 1995. 49.95 (*0-88740-751-X*) Schiffer.

— Aircraft of the Luftwaffe Fighter Aces, Vol. II. LC 95-68642. (Illus.). 256p. 1995. 49.95 (*0-88740-752-8*) Schiffer.

*__Barbas, Carlos F.__ Phage Display: A Laboratory Manual. LC 00-30834. (Illus.). 2000. pap. write for info. (*0-87969-545-5*) Cold Spring Harbor.

Barbas, Donald J. Miami Beach Models' Diet. (Illus.). 202p. 1996. pap. 14.95 (*0-9658346-0-3*) Miami Beach.

*__Barbas, Kerren.__ Name the Baby: Search Through over 3000 Baby Names & Their Meanings in This Charming & Unique Book. (Illus.). 1999. 9.95 (*0-7667-2977-X*) Gibson.

*__Barbas, Kerren.__ Best Friends Petite Photo Album. 1999. pap. 4.95 (*0-88088-659-5*) Peter Pauper.

Barbas, Kerren. Conversations with Remarkable Children on Friendship. (Keepsakes Ser.). 56p. 1999. 7.99 (*0-88088-900-4*) Peter Pauper.

Barbash, Barry P., et al. The '40 Act Institute. LC 98-173166. (Corporate Law & Practice Course Handbook Ser.). 456 p. 1998. 129.00 (*0-87224-464-4*) PLI.

Barbash, Ilisa. Cross-Cultural Filmmaking: A Handbook for Making Documentary & Ethnographic Films & Videos. LC 96-17662. (Illus.). 380p. 1997. pap. 29.95 (*0-520-08760-7*, Pub. by U CA Pr) Cal Prin Full Svc.

Barbash, Ilisa & Taylor, Lucien. Cross-Cultural Filmmaking: A Handbook for Making Documentary & Ethnographic Films & Videos. LC 96-17662. (Illus.). 380p. 1997. 70.00 (*0-520-08759-3*, Pub. by U CA Pr) Cal Prin Full Svc.

Barbash, Jack. The Elements of Industrial Relations. LC 83-40258. 167p. reprint ed. pap. 51.80 (*0-608-09843-4*, 206923100003) Bks Demand.

— Labor's Grass Roots: A Study of the Local Union. LC 73-11839. 250p. 1974. reprint ed. lib. bdg. 65.00 (*0-8371-7064-8*, BALG, Greenwood Pr) Greenwood.

Barbash, Jack & Barbash, Kate, intros. Theories & Concepts in Comparative Industrial Relations. LC 88-21443. 281p. 1989. text 34.95 (*0-87249-580-9*) U of SC Pr.

Barbash, Jack E. & Resek, Elizabeth A. Pesticides in Ground Water: Distribution, Trends & Governing Factors. Gilliom, Robert J., ed. (Pesticides in the Hydrologic System Ser.). 616p. (C). 1997. boxed set 84.95 (*1-57504-005-0*) CRC Pr.

Barbash, Kate, jt. intro. see Barbash, Jack.

*__Barbash, Robert W., ed.__ Pennsylvania Guidelines for School Library Information Programs. 66p. (C). 2000. pap. text 20.00 (*0-7567-0002-7*) DIANE Pub.

Barbash, Shephard. Oaxacan Woodcarving: The Magic in the Trees. (Illus.). 120p. 1993. 27.50 (*0-8118-0316-3*); pap. 18.95 (*0-8118-0250-7*) Chronicle Bks.

Barbashov, B. M. & Nesterenko, V. V. Introduction to the Relativistic String Theory. Dumbrajs, T. Y., tr. 264p. 1990. text 59.00 (*9971-5-0687-4*); pap. text 36.00 (*981-02-0411-6*) World Scientific Pub.

Barbasiewicz, Robert. Auto Mag Vol. 1: The Pasadena Days: The Years 1966-1972. unabridged ed. Ottemoeller, Sylvia, ed. (Illus.). 146p. 1998. pap. 45.00 (*0-9662695-0-0*) Krats Pub.

Barbasin, E. A., et al. Twelve Papers on Analysis, Applied Mathematics & Algebraic Topology. (Translations Ser.: Series 2, Vol. 25). 334p. 1963. 38.00 (*0-8218-1725-6*, TRANS2/25) Am Math.

*__Barbato, Joseph.__ Writing for a Good Cause: The Complete Guide to Crafting Proposals & Other Persuasive Pieces for Nonprofits. 2000. per. 15.00 (*0-7432-0578-2*) S&S Trade.

*__Barbato, Joseph & Furlich, Danielle S.__ Writing for a Good Cause: The Complete Guide to Crafting Proposals & Other Persuasive Pieces for Nonprofits. LC 00-25248. 336p. 2000. pap. 15.00 (*0-684-85740-5*, Fireside) S&S Trade Pap.

Barbato, Joseph & Horak, Lisa W., eds. Off the Beaten Path: Stories of Place. LC 98-66419. 224p. 1998. 24.00 (*0-86547-530-X*) N Point Pr.

*__Barbato, Joseph & Horak, Lisa W., eds.__ Off the Beaten Path: Stories of Place. 272p. 1999. pap. 13.00 (*0-86547-538-5*) N Point Pr.

Barbato, Joseph & Weinerman, Lisa, eds. Heart of the Land: Essays on Last Great Places. 320p. 1996. pap. 13.00 (*0-679-75501-2*) Random.

Barbato, Joseph, jt. auth. see Luks, Allan.

Barbato, Joseph, jt. ed. see Sklar, Morty.

Barbatti, Joseph R. A Quest for Ultimate Truth. unabridged ed. (Illus.). 192p. 1999. pap. 13.50 (*0-9671931-0-9*, 01) Barbatti.

Barbauld, Anna L. Eighteen Hundred & Eleven, 1812. LC 94-44535. (Revolution & Romanticism, 1789-1834 Ser.). 1995. 48.00 (*1-85477-176-0*) Continuum.

— Poems, 1792. LC 93-17413. (Revolution & Romanticism Ser.). 168p. 1993. reprint ed. 48.00 (*1-85477-127-2*) Continuum.

Barbauld, Anna L., ed. see Richardson, Samuel.

Barbazette, Jean. Successful New Employee Orientation: Assess, Plan, Conduct, & Evaluate Your Program. LC 93-37070. 128p. 1994. ring bd. 89.95 (*0-88390-417-9*, Pffr & Co) Jossey-Bass.

Barbe, B. F., ed. Very Large Scale Integration (VLSI) Fundamentals & Applications. 2nd ed. (Electrophysics Ser.: Vol. 5). (Illus.). 302p. 1982. 63.95 (*0-387-11368-1*) Spr-Verlag.

Barbe, D. F., ed. Charge-Coupled Devices. (Topics in Applied Physics Ser.: Vol. 38). (Illus.). 1980. 61.00 (*0-387-09832-1*) Spr-Verlag.

Barbe, Dominique. Grace & Power: Basic Communities & Nonviolence in Brazil. enl. ed. Brown, John P., tr. LC 86-23572.Tr. of La Grace et le Pouvoir. 160p. (Orig.). 1987. reprint ed. pap. 49.60 (*0-7837-9826-1*, 206055500005) Bks Demand.

— A Theology of Conflict & Other Writings on Nonviolence. LC 89-8827.Tr. of Uma Teologia de Conflito: A Nao-Violencia Ativa. 199p. 1989. reprint ed. pap. 61.70 (*0-7837-9832-6*, 206056100005) Bks Demand.

Barbe, Jean-Maurice. Nouveau Dictionnaire de Prenoms. (FRE.). 448p. 1985. pap. 45.00 (*0-7859-8112-8*, 2858827958) Fr & Eur.

Barbe, Katharina. Irony in Context. LC 95-36113. (Pragmatics & Beyond New Ser.: No. 34). x, 208p. 1995. 57.00 (*1-55619-327-0*) J Benjamins Pubng Co.

Barbe-Marboi, Francois. History of Louisiana 1977. Lyon, E. Wilson, ed. LC 77-5665. (Louisiana Bicentennial Reprint Ser.). xviii, 460p. 1930. reprint ed. 42.50 (*0-8071-0186-9*, BHISLO) Claitors.

Barbe-Marbois, Francois. Our Revolutionary Forefathers: The Letters of Francois, Marquis De Barbe-Marbois During His Residence in the United States As Secretary of the French Legation 1779-1785. LC 71-99659. (Select Bibliographies Reprint Ser.). 1977. 25.95 (*0-8369-5088-7*) Ayer.

Barbe, Philippe & Bartail, Patrice. The Weighted Bootstrap. LC 95-5885. (Lecture Notes in Statistics Ser.: Vol. 98). 1995. 48.95 (*0-387-94478-8*) Spr-Verlag.

Barbe, Richard H., jt. auth. see McKee, Patrick W.

Barbe, Waitman. Famous Poems Explained. 1976. lib. bdg. 59.95 (*0-8490-1803-X*) Gordon Pr.

Barbe, Walter. Consonant Blends & Digraphs, Bk. D. (Linking Learning to Sound/Symbol Correspondence Ser.). 48p. (J). (gr. 2-3). 1998. wbk. ed. 2.50 (*1-56762-086-8*) Modern Learn Pr.

— Final & Middle Sounds, Bk. C. (Linking Learning to Sound/Symbol Correspondence Ser.). 48p. (J). (gr. 2-3). 1998. wbk. ed. 2.50 (*1-56762-085-X*) Modern Learn Pr.

— Vowel Combinations, Bk. E. (Linking Learning to Sound/Symbol Correspondence Ser.). 48p. (J). (gr. 2-3). 1998. wbk. ed. 2.50 (*1-56762-087-6*) Modern Learn Pr.

Barbe, Walter B. Growing up Learning: Identifying & Teaching Children with Different Learning Styles. (Illus.). 203p. 1998. reprint ed. pap. 12.95 (*1-56762-088-4*) Modern Learn Pr.

— Initial Consonant Sounds. (Linking Learning to Sound - Symbol Relationships Ser.: Bk. A). 48p. (J). (gr. 2-3). 1997. pap., wbk. ed. 2.50 (*1-56762-078-7*) Modern Learn Pr.

— Long & Short Vowel Sounds. (Linking Learning to Sound - Symbol Relationships Ser.: Bk. B). 48p. (J). (gr. 2-3). 1997. pap., wbk. ed. 2.50 (*1-56762-079-5*) Modern Learn Pr.

*__Barbe, Walter B.__ Reading Skills Competency Tests: Advanced Level. LC LB1050.75.R43A45. (Competency Tests for Basic Reading Skill Ser.). 1999. spiral bd. 29.95 (*0-13-021333-0*) P-H.

B

B

— Reading Skills Competency Tests: Fifth Level. LC 98-51643. (Competency Tests for Basic Reading Skill Ser.). (Illus.). 123p. 1999. spiral bd. 29.95 (*0-13-021331-4*) P-H.
— Reading Skills Competency Tests: First Level. LC 98-51643. (Competency Tests for Basic Reading Skill Ser.). (Illus.). 123p. 1999. spiral bd. 29.95 (*0-13-021326-8*) P-H.
— Reading Skills Competency Tests: Fourth Level. (Competency Tests for Basic Reading Skill Ser.). 1999. spiral bd. 29.95 (*0-13-021329-2*) P-H.
— Reading Skills Competency Tests: Second Level. (Competency Tests for Basic Reading Skill Ser.). 1999. spiral bd. 29.95 (*0-13-021327-6*) P-H.
— Reading Skills Competency Tests: Sixth Level. (Competency Tests for Basic Reading Skill Ser.). 1999. spiral bd. 29.95 (*0-13-021332-2*) P-H.
— Reading Skills Competency Tests: Third Level. (Competency Tests for Basic Reading Skill Ser.). 1999. spiral bd. 29.95 (*0-13-021328-4*) P-H.
Barbe, Walter B. Resource Book for the Kindergarten Teacher. (Illus.). (C). 1980. 39.95 (*0-88309-103-8*) Zaner-Bloser.
***Barbe, Walter B., ed.** Signposts Language Arts Activities for Grade 2. (Illus.). 64p. (J). (gr. 2-3). 2000. 2.95 (*1-56762-119-8*) Modern Learn Pr.
— Signposts Language Arts Activities for Kindergarten. (Illus.). 32p. (J). 2000. wbk. ed. 6.95 (*1-56762-117-1*) Modern Learn Pr.
— Signposts Language Arts Activities Kindergarten Teacher's Manual, 2 vols. (Illus.). 80p. 2000. teacher ed. 16.95 (*1-56762-121-X*) Modern Learn Pr.
Barbe, Walter B., et al, eds. Spelling: Basic Skills for Effective Communication. 1982. 14.95 (*0-88309-118-6*) Zaner-Bloser.
Barbe, Walter B. & Renzulli, Joseph S., eds. Psychology & Education of the Gifted. 3rd ed. LC 80-11174. 544p. 1981. pap. text 22.95 (*0-8290-0234-0*) Irvington.
Barbe, Walter B. & Swassing, Raymond H. Teaching Through Modality Strengths: Concepts & Practices. LC 79-66953. (C). 1979. 12.95 (*0-88309-100-3*) Zaner-Bloser.
Barbe, Walter B., et al. Basic Skills in Kindergarten: Foundations for Formal Learning. (C). 1980. 12.95 (*0-88309-104-6*) Zaner-Bloser.
Barbe, Walter B., jt. auth. see Lucas, Virginia H.
Barbe, Walter B., ed. see Dale, Edgar & O'Rourke, Joseph.
Barbe, Walter B., ed. see Green, Joan.
Barbe, Walter B., ed. see Ramirez, Raul.
Barbe, Walter B., ed. see Ramirez, Raul C., Jr.
Barbe, Walter B., ed. see Reichert, Gwen.
Barbe, Walter B., ed. see Young, Barbara A.
Barbeau, Anne T. Intellectual Design of John Dryden's Heroic Plays. LC 71-81412. 232p. reprint ed. pap. 72.00 (*0-8357-9288-9*, 201319100085) Bks Demand.
Barbeau, Arthur E. & Henri, Florette. The Unknown Soldiers: African-American Troops in World War I. LC 95-45862. (Illus.). 320p. 1996. reprint ed. pap. 14.95 (*0-306-80694-0*) Da Capo.
Barbeau, Clayton C. Dante & Gentucca: A Love Story. 2nd ed. LC 97-139599. (Illus.). 43p. 1996. reprint ed. pap. 5.95 (*0-9633157-4-9*) Ikon Pr.
— Delivering the Male: Out of the Tough Guy Trap into a Better Marriage. 136p. 1992. reprint ed. pap. 12.95 (*0-9633157-1-4*) Ikon Pr.
— How to Raise Parents: Questions & Answers for Teens & Parents. (Illus.). 221p. 1992. reprint ed. pap. 14.95 (*0-9633157-3-0*) Ikon Pr.
— The Ikon. 2nd ed. LC 95-234033. 256p. 1995. 19.95 (*0-9633157-0-6*) Ikon Pr.
— Joy of Marriage. Orig. Title: Creative Marriage: the Middle Years. 121p. 1992. reprint ed. pap. 12.95 (*0-9633157-2-2*) Ikon Pr.
Barbeau, E. J. Polynomials. LC 96-29451. (Problem Books in Mathematics). (FRE., Illus.). 465p. 1995. 59.95 (*0-387-96919-5*) Spr-Verlag.
***Barbeau, Edward J.** Mathematical Fallacies, Flaws & Filmflam. LC 99-67971. 152p. 1999. pap. 24.95 (*0-88385-529-1*) Math Assn.
Barbeau, Edward J. Power Play. LC 96-79983. (Spectrum Ser.). 212p. 1997. pap. text 31.95 (*0-88385-523-2*, POPL) Math Assn.
Barbeau, Edward J., et al. Five Hundred Mathematical Challenges. LC 95-878644. (Spectrum Ser.). 300p. 1995. pap. text 36.95 (*0-88385-519-4*, CHMP) Math Assn.
Barbeau, Marius. Totem Poles Vol. 1: According to Crests & Topics, Vol. I. (Illus.). 460p. 1993. pap. 27.95 (*0-660-12902-7*, Pub. by CN Mus Civilization) U of Wash Pr.
— Totem Poles Vol. 2: According to Location, Vol. II. (Illus.). 470p. 1994. pap. 27.95 (*0-660-12903-5*, Pub. by CN Mus Civilization) U of Wash Pr.
Barbeau, Maurice. Art of the Totem. (Illus.). 64p. 1984. 8.95 (*0-88839-168-4*) Hancock House.
Barbee, A. H. Behind the Iron Curtain: The Story of John Visser. 74p. 1985. reprint ed. pap. 6.95 (*0-89084-280-9*, 024984) Bob Jones Univ.
— Who is Really Your Radio or T. V. Preacher? 99 Important Questions Before You Donate. 60p. 1997. spiral bd. 12.95 (*0-925291-12-9*, 09-03-97-110437) Advocacy Servs Pr.
Barbee, Anita P., jt. auth. see Derlega, Valerian J.
Barbee, Evelyn E. Cooking with Booze: Your House or Mine. 102p. 1995. 14.95 (*0-9647146-0-4*) Pleasure Foods.
Barbee, Frederick C. & Zahl, Paul F., eds. The Collects of Thomas Cranmer. 144p. 1918. 17.00 (*0-8028-3845-6*) Eerdmans.
Barbee, G. A. The Road Best Traveled: Through the Bible in 365 Devotions. 1996. 8.25 (*1-55673-994-X*, Fairway Pr) CSS OH.
— Values: A Book of Family Devotions. LC 96-96375. 190p. 1996. pap. write for info. (*0-7880-0682-7*, Fairway Pr) CSS OH.
Barbee, Jack. Can Little Donkeys Really Talk? (Illus.). 20p. (Orig.). (J). (gr. 1-7). 1996. pap. 8.00 (*0-9656259-0-7*) Foerstel Design.
Barbee, Robert, intro. Yellowstone in the Eagle's Eye. (FRE, GER & JPN.). 100p. (Orig.). 1991. pap. 14.95 (*0-9627618-2-6*) Billings Gazette.
Barbee, Robert A. & Bloom, John W. Asthma in the Elderly. LC 97-22376. (Lung Biology in Health & Disease Ser.: Vol. 108). (Illus.). 312p. 1997. text 145.00 (*0-8247-9870-8*) Dekker.
Barbee, S. Diane, ed. see Miller, Patrizia & Fairbanks, Linda C.
Barbee, Sam. Changes of Venue. (Illus.). 48p. 1997. pap. 8.00 (*1-880994-35-6*) Mt Olive Coll Pr.
Barbee, T. W., Jr., et al, eds. Multilayers: Synthesis, Properties, & Nonelectronic Applications. (Materials Research Society Symposium Proceedings Ser.: Vol. 103). 1988. text 17.50 (*0-931837-71-5*) Materials Res.
Barbehenn, Frank W. Finding God in the Ashes: Rebuilding Faith in Wake of Family Trauma. 1999. pap. 14.99 (*0-8054-1840-7*) Broadman.
Barbeito, Carol L. Management Assistance Services for Nonprofit Organizations: A Planning Manual. 110p. 1998. pap. 39.95 (*1-893014-00-2*) Applied Resrch & Dev.
***Barbell, Kathy & Wright, Lois M.** Family Foster Care in the Next Century. LC 00-27302. 2000. pap. 24.95 (*0-7658-0712-2*) Transaction Pubs.
Barbellion, W. N. Enjoying Life & Other Literary Remains. 1973. 75.00 (*0-87968-257-4*) Gordon Pr.
— Journal of a Disappointed Man. 1972. lib. bdg. 250.00 (*0-87968-150-0*) Gordon Pr.
— A Last Diary. 1973. 250.00 (*0-87968-382-1*) Gordon Pr.
Barbello, James. Real-World Interfacing with Your PC: A Hands-On Guide to Parallel Port Projects. 2nd ed. 119p. 1997. pap. text 29.95 incl. audio compact disk (*0-7906-1145-7*) Prompt Publns.
Barber. Advanced Civil Procedure. (LQ-Paralegal Ser.). (C). 1998. pap. text, teacher ed. 14.95 (*0-8273-8093-3*) Delmar.
— Advanced Civil Procedure. (Paralegal). (C). 1999. mass mkt. 48.95 (*0-8273-8092-5*) Delmar.
— Gilbert Basic Accounting for Lawyers. 2nd ed. 1997. pap. text 16.95 (*0-15-900343-1*) Harcourt Legal.
— Global Past Readings, Vol. VII. LC 97-80446. 1998. pap. text 12.95 (*0-312-17192-7*) St Martin.
— Legal Research. (C). 1996. text 39.95 (*0-8273-7971-4*) Delmar.
— Legal Research. (Paralegal Ser.). 128p. 1996. teacher ed. 12.95 (*0-8273-7475-5*) Delmar.
— Legal Writing. 2nd ed. (Paralegal Ser.). 1997. teacher ed. 16.95 (*0-8273-7541-7*) Delmar.
— 1947: When All Hell Broke Loose. 31.95 (*0-8488-1564-5*) Amereon Ltd.
***Barber.** Noah & the Ark. 2000. 17.95 (*0-385-40566-9*, Pub. by Transworld Publishers Ltd) Trafalgar.
Barber, ed. Pneumatic Handbook. 8th ed. LC 97-33006. 650p. 1997. text 230.00 (*1-85617-249-X*) Elsevier.
Barber & Lampert, Junko. The Tofu Gourmet. 1996. 39.95 (*4-07-975109-5*) Shufu No.
Barber, jt. auth. see Grauer.
Barber, jt. auth. see Grauer, Robert T.
Barber, jt. auth. see Smia.
Barber & Barber Staff. The Word Nerd Party: A Book of Word Plays. (J). 1996. 17.00 (*0-689-80491-1*) S&S Childrens.
Barber, Alfred W. Handbook of HiFi-Audio Systems & Projects. (Illus.). 1984. 18.95 (*0-685-08102-8*, Busn) P-H.
— Practical Guide to Integrated Circuits. 2nd ed. write for info. (*0-318-58193-0*) P-H.
Barber, Alison E. Individual & Organizational Perspectives. LC 97-45383. (Foundations for Organizational Science Ser.). 172p. 1998. write for info. (*0-7619-0942-7*); pap. write for info. (*0-7619-0943-5*) Sage.
Barber, Allen H. Celestial Symbols: Symbolism in Doctrine, Religous Traditions & Temple Architecture. LC 89-83436. 176p. 1989. 14.98 (*0-88290-344-6*) Horizon Utah.
Barber, Andrew V. Fundamentals of Christianity: A Bible Study & Guide. LC 99-70759. (Illus.). 520p. 1999. pap. 24.95 (*0-9669702-0-9*, 10) Spec Del.
Barber, Anne & Waymon, Lynne. 52 Ways to Re-Connect, Follow up & Stay in Touch: When You Don't Have Time to Network. LC 94-75139. 160p. 1994. per. 14.95 (*0-8403-9224-9*) Kendall-Hunt.
***Barber, Anne, et al.** Tips for Growing Your Practice. 88p. 1999. pap. 20.00 (*0-943599-32-6*) OEPF.
Barber, Anne, et al. Vision Therapist Vol. 34-3: Amblyopia. (Illus.). 120p. (Orig.). 1992. pap. text 18.00 (*0-943599-52-0*) OEPF.
— Vision Therapist Vol. 36-1: Behavioral Issues. (Illus.). 70p. (Orig.). 1994. pap. text 18.00 (*0-943599-68-7*) OEPF.
— Vision Therapy Vol. 37-1: Training Laterality & Directionality. (Illus.). 87p. (Orig.). 1994. pap. text 18.00 (*0-943599-75-X*) OEPF.
Barber, Anne, tr. see Ofer, Dalia & Weiner, Hannah.
Barber, Anthony. Great Britain's Tax Credit Income Supplement. LC 74-32639. (Illus.). 36p. 1975. pap. 3.00 (*0-915312-00-X*) Inst Socioecon.
Barber, Anthony, ed. Handbook of Noise & Vibration Control. 6th ed. 600p. 1993. 184.00 (*1-85617-079-9*) Elsevier.
Barber, Antonia. Apollo & Daphne: Masterpieces of Mythology. LC 97-42834. 48p. (YA). (gr. 5 up). 1998. 16.95 (*0-89236-504-8*, Pub. by J P Getty Trust) OUP.
— Catkin. LC 94-10565. (Illus.). 48p. (J). (gr. 2-6). 1994. 17.99 (*1-56402-485-7*) Candlewick Pr.
— Catkin. LC 94-10565. (Illus.). 48p. (J). (gr. 2-6). 1996. reprint ed. pap. 7.99 (*1-56402-976-X*) Candlewick Pr.
Barber, Antonia. Dancing Shoes: Into the Spotlight. (Illus.). 96p. (J). pap. 5.95 (*0-14-038683-1*, Pub. by Pnguin Bks Ltd) Trafalgar.
— Dancing Shoes: Lessons for Lucy. (Illus.). 96p. (J). pap. 5.95 (*0-14-038681-5*, Pub. by Pnguin Bks Ltd) Trafalgar.
— Dancing Shoes: Lucy's Next Step. (Illus.). 96p. (J). pap. 5.95 (*0-14-038685-8*, Pub. by Pnguin Bks Ltd) Trafalgar.
— Dancing Shoes: Lucy's Next Step. 6th ed. (Illus.). 96p. (J). pap. 5.95 (*0-14-130150-3*, Pub. by Pnguin Bks Ltd) Trafalgar.
— Dancing Shoes: Making the Grade. (Illus.). 96p. (J). pap. 5.95 (*0-14-130149-X*, Pub. by Pnguin Bks Ltd) Trafalgar.
— Dancing Shoes Friends & Rivals. (Illus.). 96p. (J). pap. 5.95 (*0-14-038684-X*, Pub. by Pnguin Bks Ltd) Trafalgar.
Barber, Antonia. The Enchanter's Daughter. (Illus.). 32p. (J). (ps-3). 1994. pap. 5.95 (*0-374-42143-9*) FS&G.
— Enchanter's Daughter. 1988. 11.15 (*0-606-07482-1*, Pub. by Turtleback) Demco.
— The Ghosts. Ashby, Ruth, ed. 224p. (YA). (gr. 6 up). 1989. mass mkt. 3.50 (*0-671-70714-0*, Archway) PB.
***Barber, Antonia.** The Monkey & the Panda. (Illus.). (J). (ps-4). 1999. pap. text 7.99 (*0-7112-1085-3*) F Lincoln.
Barber, Antonia. The Mousehole Cat. (Illus.). 40p. 1996. mass mkt. 5.99 (*0-689-80837-2*) S&S Childrens.
Barber, Antonia. Mousehole Cat. 1996. 11.19 (*0-606-10882-3*, Pub. by Turtleback) Demco.
— Tales from Grimm. (Illus.). 112p. (J). (ps-4). 1999. pap. 13.99 (*0-7112-1341-0*) F Lincoln.
Barber, Antonia. Tales from the Ballet. LC 99-33618. 96p. (YA). 1999. pap. 11.95 (*0-7534-5262-6*) LKC.
Barber, Antonia, et al, eds. Shoes of Satin, Ribbons of Silk: Tales from the Ballet. LC 95-1352. (Illus.). 96p. (J). (gr. 1 up). 1995. 17.95 (*1-85697-593-2*) LKC.
Barber, Arnold. The County Agent. (UED 85 Ser.). (Illus.). 1989. pap. 5.00 (*0-933842-11-2*, UED85) Extension Div.
Barber, B., et al, eds. Towards Security in Medical Telematics: Legal & Technical Aspects. (Studies in Health Technology & Informatics: Vol. 27). 262p. (YA). (gr. 12). 1996. 98.00 (*90-5199-246-7*, 246-7) IOS Press.
Barber, Barbara. Broderie Perse: The Elegant Quilt. LC 96-49791. (Love to Quilt Ser.). 1996. 14.95 (*0-89145-875-1*, 4833, Am Quilters Soc) Collector Bks.
— Solos for Young Violinists, Vol. 1. 48p. (J). 1997. pap. 12.95 (*0-87487-988-4*, 0988) Summy-Birchard.
— Solos for Young Violinists, Vol. 2. 56p. (J). 1997. pap. 12.95 (*0-87487-989-2*, 0989) Summy-Birchard.
— Solos for Young Violinists, Vol. 3. 48p. (J). 1997. pap. 12.95 (*0-87487-990-6*, 0990) Summy-Birchard.
— Solos for Young Violinists, Vol. 4. 48p. (J). 1997. pap. 12.95 (*0-87487-991-4*, 0991) Summy-Birchard.
— Solos for Young Violinists, Vol. 5. 56p. (J). 1997. pap. 12.95 (*0-87487-992-2*, 0992) Summy-Birchard.
— Solos for Young Violinists, Vol. 6. (J). 1997. pap. 12.95 (*0-87487-993-0*, 0993) Summy-Birchard.
Barber, Barbara E. Allie's Basketball Dream. LC 96-33845. (Illus.). 32p. (J). (ps-6). 1996. 14.95 (*1-880000-38-5*) Lee & Low Bks.
— Allie's Basketball Dream. LC 96-33845. (Illus.). 32p. (J). (ps-5). 1998. pap. 6.95 (*1-880000-72-5*) Lee & Low Bks.
— Saturday at the New You. LC 93-5165. (Illus.). 32p. (J). (ps up). 1994. 14.95 (*1-880000-06-7*) Lee & Low Bks.
— Saturday at the New You. 1994. 11.15 (*0-606-09819-4*, Pub. by Turtleback) Demco.
— Saturday at The New You. (Illus.). 32p. (J). (ps up). 1996. reprint ed. pap. 5.95 (*1-880000-43-1*) Lee & Low Bks.
Barber, Benjamin R. An Aristocracy of Everyone: The Politics of Education & the Future of America. LC 92-53157. 320p. 1994. reprint ed. pap. 14.95 (*0-19-509154-X*) OUP.
— The Conquest of Politics: Liberal Philosophy in Democratic Times. LC 87-37687. 231p. reprint ed. pap. 71.70 (*0-608-08020-9*, 206798500001) Bks Demand.
— The Death of Communal Liberty: A History of Freedom in a Swiss Mountain Canton. LC 72-14018. (Illus.). 320p. reprint ed. pap. 99.20 (*0-7837-6766-8*, 204659600003) Bks Demand.
— Education for Democracy. Battistoni, Richard M., ed. 692p. (C). 1999. per. 59.95 (*0-7872-5156-9*, 41515603) Kendall-Hunt.
— Jihad vs. McWorld: How Globalism & Tribalism Are Re-Shaping the World. LC 96-96061. 400p. 1996. pap. 12.95 (*0-345-38304-4*) Ballantine Pub Grp.
— Living in a Democracy. 24p. 2000. pap. 16.00 (*0-87117-324-7*) Comm Coll Pr Am Assn Comm Coll.
— A Passion for Democracy: American Essays. LC 97-52582. 282p. 1998. text 26.95 (*0-691-05766-4*, Pub. by Princeton U Pr) Cal Prin Full Svc.
***Barber, Benjamin R.** Passion for Democracy: Amrerican Essays. 2000. pap. text 16.95 (*0-691-05024-4*) Princeton U Pr.
Barber, Benjamin R. A Place for Us: How to Make Society Civil & Democracy Strong. LC 97-44914. 172p. 1998. 22.00 (*0-8090-7657-8*) Hill & Wang.
— Strong Democracy: Participatory Politics for a New Age. LC 83-4842. 320p. (C). 1984. pap. 17.95 (*0-520-05616-7*, Pub. by U CA Pr) Cal Prin Full Svc.
Barber, Benjamin R. & McGrath, Michael J., eds. The Artist & Political Vision. LC 80-80317. 408p. (C). 1981. 44.95 (*0-87855-380-0*) Transaction Pubs.
Barber, Benjamin R. & Watson, Patrick. The Struggle for Democracy. 1989. 29.95 (*0-316-08058-6*) Little.
Barber, Bernard. Constructing the Social System. 500p. (C). 1993. text 54.95 (*1-56000-102-X*) Transaction Pubs.
— Effective Social Science: Eight Cases in Economics, Political Science & Sociology. LC 87-23416. 224p. 1988. 22.50 (*0-87154-091-6*) Russell Sage.
— Intellectual Pursuits: Toward an Understanding of Culture. 160p. 1998. 55.00 (*0-8476-8859-3*); pap. 18.95 (*0-8476-8860-7*) Rowman.
— Mass Apathy & Voluntary Social Participation in the United States. Zuckerman, Harriet & Merton, Robert K., eds. LC 79-8972. (Dissertations on Sociology Ser.). 1980. lib. bdg. 28.95 (*0-405-12949-1*) Ayer.
— Science & the Social Order. LC 78-1569. 288p. 1978. reprint ed. lib. bdg. 65.00 (*0-313-20356-3*, BASSO, Greenwood Pr) Greenwood.
— Social Studies of Science. 265p. 1990. 44.95 (*0-88738-329-7*) Transaction Pubs.
Barber, Bernard & Barber, Elinor G. European Social Class: Stability & Change. LC 77-13508. (Main Themes in European History). 145p. 1978. reprint ed. lib. bdg. 38.50 (*0-8371-9860-7*, BAEU, Greenwood Pr) Greenwood.
Barber, Bernard, et al. Research on Human Subjects: Problems of Social Control in Medical Experimentation. LC 70-83831. 264p. 1973. 40.00 (*0-87154-090-8*) Russell Sage.
— Research on Human Subjects: Problems of Social Control in Medical Experimentation. LC 78-55938. 263p. 1979. reprint ed. pap. text 24.95 (*0-87855-649-4*) Transaction Pubs.
Barber, Bernard, ed. see Henderson, L. J.
***Barber, Brandon.** Sam Teach Yourself e-Music Today: Playing, Recording, Researching & Promoting MP3 & Online. (Teach Yourself Today Ser.). 300p. 2000. pap. 17.99 (*0-672-31855-5*) Sams.
Barber, Brenda. Joy in Winter Bk. 1: Seasons of Love Scenes. 180p. (Orig.). 1996. pap. 7.99 (*1-57502-337-7*, P1120) Morris Pubng.
Barber, Brian K. & Rollins, Boyd C., eds. Parent-Adolescent Relationships. 254p. (Orig.). (C). 1989. pap. text 25.00 (*0-8191-7744-X*) U Pr of Amer.
Barber, Bruce, et al, eds. Voices of Fire: Art, Rage, Power & the State. (Theory/Culture Ser.). (Illus.). 224p. 1996. text 55.00 (*0-8020-0754-6*) U of Toronto Pr.
— Voices of Fire: Art, Rage, Power & the State. (Theory/Culture Ser.). (Illus.). 224p. 1996. pap. text 24.95 (*0-8020-7803-6*) U of Toronto Pr.
***Barber, C., et al, eds.** Functional Neuroscience: Evoked Potentials & Magnetic Fields. LC 99-37657. (Supplements to Electroencephalography & Clinical Neurophysiology Ser.: Vol. 49). 350p. 1999. 200.50 (*0-444-50062-6*) Elsevier.
Barber, C., et al. Functional Neuroscience. LC 96-48525. (Electroencephalography & Clinical Neurophysiology Ser.). 380p. 1996. 215.50 (*0-444-82430-8*) Elsevier.
Barber, C. J. The Minister's Library, Vol. 2. 1985. 24.99 (*0-8024-5299-X*) Loizeaux.
Barber, C. L. Creating Elizabethan Tragedy: The Theater of Marlowe & Kyd. Wheeler, Richard P., ed. 184p. 1994. pap. text 11.95 (*0-226-03704-5*) U Ch Pr.
— Shakespeare's Festive Comedy. 266p. 1972. pap. text 17.95 (*0-691-01304-7*, 271, Pub. by Princeton U Pr) Cal Prin Full Svc.
Barber, Cesar L. Creating Elizabethan Tragedy: The Theater of Marlowe & Kyd. Wheeler, Richard P., ed. & intro. by. LC 87-19052. (A Chicago Original Paperback Ser.). 181p. Date not set. reprint ed. pap. 56.20 (*0-608-20986-4*, 205451400003) Bks Demand.
Barber, Charles. Early Modern English. 272p. 1997. 28.00 (*0-7486-0835-4*, Pub. by Edinburgh U Pr) Col U Pr.
— The English Language: A Historical Introduction. 3rd ed. LC 92-18555. (Cambridge Approaches to Linguistics Ser.). (Illus.). 311p. (C). 1993. pap. text 18.95 (*0-521-42622-7*) Cambridge U Pr.
***Barber, Charles.** The English Language: A Linguistic Introduction. (Canto Book Ser.). (Illus.). 320p. (C). 2000. pap. text 13.95 (*0-521-78570-7*) Cambridge U Pr.
Barber, Charles V., et al. Breaking the Logjam: Obstacles to Forest Policy Reform in Indonesia & the United States. LC 94-60225. 120p. 1994. pap. 20.00 (*0-915825-39-2*) World Resources Inst.
— Tiger by the Tail: Reorienting Biodiversity Conservation & Development in Indonesia. (Illus.). 150p. 1995. pap. 20.00 (*1-56973-043-1*) World Resources Inst.
Barber, Chris & Pykitt, David. Journey to Avalon: The Final Discovery of King Arthur. LC 97-17273. (Illus.). 376p. 1997. pap. 19.95 (*1-57863-024-X*) Weiser.
Barber, Cyril J. The Books of Samuel, Vol. 1. LC 94-337. 383p. 1994. 24.99 (*0-87213-027-4*) Loizeaux.
— The Books of Samuel, Vol. 2. 1998. 24.99 (*0-87213-029-0*) Loizeaux.
— Habakkuk & Zephaniah. (Everyman's Bible Commentaries Ser.). pap. 9.99 (*0-8024-2069-9*, 479) Moody.
— Judges: A Narrative of God's Power. LC 89-77360. 293p. 1990. 24.99 (*0-87213-025-8*) Loizeaux.
***Barber, Cyril.** Minister's Library. 1999. 79.99 (*1-57822-050-5*) Bible Companion.
Barber, Cyril. The Minister's Library, Vol. 1. LC 84-25500. 510p. 1974. 24.99 (*0-8024-5296-5*) Loizeaux.
— Nehemiah & the Dynamics of Effective Leadership. rev. ed. LC 91-21697. 191p. 1991. pap. 9.99 (*0-87213-026-6*) Loizeaux.
— Ruth: A Story of God's Grace. LC 89-2763. 192p. 1989. 19.99 (*0-87213-024-X*) Loizeaux.
***Barber, Cyril J. & Krauss, Robert M., Jr.** An Introduciton to Theological Research: A Guide for College & Seminary Students. 2nd rev. expanded ed. 192p. 2000. pap. 24.50 (*0-7618-1659-3*) U Pr of Amer.

An Asterisk (*) at the beginning of an entry indicates that the title is appearing for the first time.

Barber, Cyril J. & Strauss, Gary H. Leadership: The Dynamics of Success. 126p. 1982. pap. 4.95 (*0-87921-068-0*) Attic Pr.

Barber, Cyril J., et al. New Unger's Bible Dictionary. Harrison, R. K., ed. (Illus.). 1416p. 39.99 (*0-8024-9037-9*, 228) Moody.

Barber, D. E. Doses to the Hand During the Administration of Radiolabeled Antibodies Containing Y-90, TC- 99m, I-131 & LU-177. 65p. 1997. pap. 6.50 (*0-16-062814-8*) USGPO.

Barber, D. K. Baldy & the Mohawks. LC 98-90736. 1999. pap. 12.95 (*0-533-12897-8*) Vantage.

Barber, Dan & Peterson, Charles J., eds. Indexes to the Airpost Journal Volumes 1-60, 1929-1989 & Aero Philatelist Annals, Volumes 1-25, 1953-1971 & 1975-1982. 194p. 1992. 12.00 (*0-939429-02-0*) Am Air Mail.

Barber, Daniel L. How to Protect Yourself until the Police Arrive. LC 95-94793. (Illus.). 152p. (Orig.). (C). 1996. pap. text 15.95 (*0-938895-10-9*) D L Barber Ventures.

— Law Enforcement Firearms Training. 4th rev. ed. LC 86-50683. (Illus.). 205p. (Orig.). 1988. reprint ed. pap. text 12.95 (*0-938895-04-4*) D L Barber Ventures.

Barber, Daniel M. Finding Funding: The Comprehensive Guide to Grantwriting. 200p. 1994. pap. 29.95 incl. disk (*0-9638091-0-5*) D M Barber.

Barber, Dave. How to Publish a How-to Book. Hearn, Bonnie, ed. 38p. (Orig.). 1993. pap., student ed. 14.95 (*0-9637594-1-8*) Kick-Start Pr.

— You Can Be the Best Chiropractor in Your Town: The Nuts & Bolts of Running a Successful Practice. (Illus.). 224p. (Orig.). 1993. pap. 49.95 (*0-9637594-0-X*) Kick-Start Pr.

Barber, David. The Spirit Level. LC 95-31659. 76p. 1995. pap. 12.95 (*0-8101-5024-7*); text 29.95 (*0-8101-5023-9*) Northwestern U Pr.

Barber, David H. Answering Law Exams: Power Think. (Winning in Law School Ser.: Bk. 2). 148p. 1986. 12.95 (*0-915667-13-4*) Spectra Pub Co.

— How to Study Law: Fast Learn. (Winning in Law School Ser.: Bk. 9). 116p. (Orig.). 1987. pap. text 12.95 (*0-915667-14-2*) Spectra Pub Co.

— The Productivity Principle. 140p. (Orig.). (C). 1986. pap. text. write for info. (*0-915667-08-8*) Spectra Pub Co.

— Stress Reduction. 2nd rev. ed. (Winning in Law School Ser.: Bk. 1). (Illus.). 52p. 1986. pap. text 12.95 (*0-915667-06-1*) Spectra Pub Co.

— Surviving Your Role As a Lawyer. 2nd rev. ed. (Illus.). 166p. 1987. pap. text 17.95 (*0-915667-07-X*) Spectra Pub Co.

Barber, David H. & Eades, Ronald W. Questions & Answers: Torts. (Winning in Law School Ser.: Bk. 7). 236p. (Orig.). 1986. pap. text 12.95 (*0-915667-12-6*) Spectra Pub Co.

Barber, David H., et al. Federal Courts: Adaptable to Courses Utilizing Materials by McCormick. LC 87-122495. (Legalines Ser.). 247p. 12.95 (*0-685-19022-6*) Harcourt.

Barber, David W. Bach, Beethoven & the Boys: Music History As It Ought to Be Taught. 10th rev. anniversary ed. (Illus.). 160p. 1986. pap. 14.95 (*0-920151-10-8*, Pub. by Sound & Vision) Firefly Bks Ltd.

— Better Than It Sounds: A Dictionary of Humorous Musical Quotations. (Illus.). 128p. 1998. pap. 11.95 (*0-920151-22-1*, Pub. by Sound & Vision) Firefly Bks Ltd.

— Getting a Handle on Messiah. (Illus.). 128p. 1994. pap. 11.95 (*0-920151-17-5*, Pub. by Sound & Vision) Firefly Bks Ltd.

— If It Ain't Baroque: More Music History as It Ought to Be Taught. Donald, Dave, tr. (Illus.). 160p. 1992. pap. 15.95 (*0-920151-15-9*, Pub. by Sound & Vision) Firefly Bks Ltd.

— A Musician's Dictionary. 2nd rev. ed. (Illus.). 96p. (Orig.). 1997. pap. 11.95 (*0-920151-21-3*, Pub. by Sound & Vision) Firefly Bks Ltd.

— Tenors, Tantrums & Trills: An Opera Dictionary from Aida to Zzzz. (Illus.). 96p. (Orig.). 1996. pap. 11.95 (*0-920151-19-1*, Pub. by Sound & Vision) Firefly Bks Ltd.

— Tutus, Tights & Tiptoes: Ballet History As It Ought to Be Taught. (Illus.). 136p. 1999. pap. 14.95 (*0-920151-30-2*, Pub. by Sound & Vision) Firefly Bks Ltd.

— When the Fat Lady Sings: Opera History As It Ought to Be Taught. (Illus.). 160p. (Orig.). 1990. pap. 12.95 (*0-920151-11-6*, Pub. by Sound & Vision) Firefly Bks Ltd.

***Barber, David W.** When the Fat Lady Sings: Opera History As It Ought to Be Taught. rev. expanded ed. (Illus.). 176p. (Orig.). 2000. pap. 16.95 (*0-920151-34-5*, Pub. by Sound & Vision) Firefly Bks Ltd.

Barber, Derbish. Being a Medical Insurance Clerk. 240p. 1994. pap. 23.40 (*0-89303-223-9*) P-H.

Barber, Derek L., jt. auth. see Davies, Donald W.

Barber, E. A., ed. Carmina. 2nd ed. (Oxford Classical Texts Ser.). 188p. 1954. text 24.95 (*0-19-814630-2*) OUP.

Barber, E. A., jt. ed. see Powell, J. U.

Barber, E. J. Prehistoric Textiles: The Development of Cloth in the Neolithic & Bronze Ages with Special Reference to the Aegean. (Illus.). 416p. 1991. text 95.00 (*0-691-03597-0*, Pub. by Princeton U Pr); pap. text 35.00 (*0-691-00224-X*, Pub. by Princeton U Pr) Cal Prin Full Svc.

Barber, E. J., et al. Varia on the Indo-European Past: Papers in Memory of Marjia Gimbutas. Dexter, Miriam R. & Polome, Edgar C., eds. LC 97-71018. (Journal of Indo-European Studies Monograph Ser.: No. 19). 255p. (C). 1997. pap. 48.00 (*0-941694-58-5*) Inst Study Man.

Barber, Edward A., et al. The Ceramic Furniture & Silver Collectors' Glossary. (Architecture & Decorative Art Ser.). 1976. pap. 6.95 (*0-306-80049-7*) Da Capo.

Barber, Edwin A. Genealogical Record of the Atlee Family, of Lancaster County, Penn. (Illus.). 130p. 1988. reprint ed. pap. 26.00 (*0-8328-0137-2*); reprint ed. lib. bdg. 34.00 (*0-8328-0136-4*) Higginson Bk Co.

— Marks of American Potters. (Illus.). 1976. reprint ed. 37.95 (*0-89344-001-9*) Ars Ceramica.

— Marks of American Potters - With Facsimilies of 1000 Marks & Illustrations of Rare Examples of American Wares. 1976. reprint ed. 59.00 (*0-403-06291-8*, Regency) Scholarly.

Barber, Elinor, et al, eds. Bridges to Knowledge: Foreign Students in Comparative Perspective. LC 84-16374. 264p. 1985. pap. text 17.00 (*0-226-03709-6*); lib. bdg. 33.00 (*0-226-03708-8*) U Ch Pr.

Barber, Elinor G., jt. auth. see Barber, Bernard.

Barber, Elizabeth W. The Mummies of Urumchi. LC 98-18958. (Illus.). 240p. 1999. 35.00 (*0-393-04521-8*) Norton.

— Women's Work: The First 20,000 Years: Women, Cloth & Society in Early Times. (Illus.). 336p. 1995. pap. 13.95 (*0-393-31348-4*, Norton Paperbks) Norton.

***Barber, Elizabeth Wayland.** The Mummies of Urumchi. (Illus.). 256p. 2000. pap. text 17.95 (*0-393-32019-7*) Norton.

Barber, Eric A., jt. auth. see Butler, Harold E.

Barber, Ezekiel. Instant Encyclopedia of Indian History. Narang, Rajanini, ed. (Illus.). 413p. (YA). (gr. 8-9). 1981. write for info. (*0-911799-01-X*) Simplex Ent.

Barber, Flavel C. Holding the Line: The Third Tennessee Infantry, 1861-1864. Ferrell, Robert H., ed. LC 94-8653. (Illus.). 281p. 1994. 35.00 (*0-87338-504-7*) Kent St U Pr.

Barber, Frances, ed. see Shakespeare, William.

Barber, G. A., compiled by. Sullivan County Gravestone Inscriptions (Taken from Various Cemeteries), 10 vols. 1596p. 1997. reprint ed. lib. bdg. 59.50 (*0-8328-6255-X*) Higginson Bk Co.

Barber, G. G. The Livre d'Artiste. (Illus.). 96p. 1995. pap. 15.00 (*0-907849-54-7*, 547, Pub. by Ashmolean Mus) A Schwartz & Co.

Barber, Gerald M., jt. auth. see Burt, James E.

Barber, Godfrey L. The Historian Ephorus. LC 76-29429. (BCL Ser. II). reprint ed. 34.50 (*0-404-15343-7*) AMS Pr.

— The Historian Ephorus. rev. ed. Miller, M. C., ed. xii, 259p. (C). 1993. reprint ed. text 25.00 (*0-89005-501-7*) Ares.

Barber, H. O., ed. see Barany Society Meeting Staff.

Barber, H. R. Ovarian Carcinoma: Etiology, Diagnosis & Treatments. 3rd ed. (Illus.). 424p. 1992. 119.00 (*0-387-97824-0*) Spr-Verlag.

Barber, Harry L., jt. auth. see Barber, Hoyt L.

Barber, Henry. British Family Names: Their Origin & Meaning. enl. ed. 286p. 1997. pap. 25.00 (*0-8063-0021-3*, 315) Clearfield Co.

Barber, Hoyt L. Copyrights, Patents & Trademarks. 2nd ed. 1996. text 32.95 (*0-07-005103-8*) McGraw.

— Copyrights, Patents & Trademarks: Protect Your Rights Worldwide. 256p. 1989. pap. 16.95 (*0-8306-0233-X*) McGraw-Hill Prof.

— How to Incorporate Your Business. 1989. pap. 9.95 (*0-8306-9444-7*) McGraw-Hill Prof.

— How to Incorporate Your Business in Any State. (Illus.). 120p. 1988. pap. 8.95 (*0-685-17658-4*, 8243) Petrocelli.

— Tax Havens: How to Bank, Invest, & Do Business-Offshore & Tax Free. 256p. 1993. 24.95 (*0-07-003659-4*) McGraw.

Barber, Hoyt L. & Barber, Harry L. The Book of Bond, James Bond. (Illus.). 176p. 1999. pap. 19.95 (*1-890723-20-7*, Pub. by Cyclone Bks) SCB Distributors.

Barber, Hugh O., jt. ed. see Sharpe, James A.

Barber, Hugh R. A Crisis of Conscience: A Catholic Doctor Speaks Out. LC 92-39827. 1993. 17.95 (*1-55972-162-6*, Birch Ln Pr) Carol Pub Group.

— Perimenopausal & Geriatric Gynecology. 640p. 1988. 75.00 (*0-02-305880-3*, Macmillan Coll) P-H.

Barber, J., et al, eds. Advances in Molecular & Cell Biology Vol. 10: Molecular Processes of Photosynthesis. 456p. 1995. 128.50 (*1-55938-710-6*) Jai Pr.

Barber, J. & Malkin, R., eds. Techniques & New Developments in Photosynthesis Research. (NATO ASI Series A, Life Sciences: Vol. 168). (Illus.). 622p. 1989. 155.00 (*0-306-43220-X*, Plenum Trade) Perseus Pubng.

Barber, J. R. Elasticity. (C). 1992. lib. bdg. 153.00 (*0-7923-1609-6*) Kluwer Academic.

Barber, Jack. War, the Whores & the Afrika Korps. 1998. pap. 14.95 (*0-86417-903-0*, Pub. by Kangaroo Pr) Seven Hills Bk.

Barber, Jacqueline. Bubble-ology. rev. ed. Bergman, Lincoln & Fairwell, Kay, eds. (Great Explorations in Math & Science (GEMS) Ser.). (Illus.). 80p. (YA). (gr. 5-8). 1992. reprint ed. pap. 10.50 (*0-912511-11-7*, GEMS) Lawrence Science.

— Chemical Reactions. rev. ed. Bergman, Lincoln & Fairwell, Kay, eds. (Great Explorations in Math & Science (GEMS) Ser.). (Illus.). 40p. (YA). (gr. 6-8). 1998. pap. 9.00 (*0-924886-06-4*, GEMS) Lawrence Science.

***Barber, Jacqueline.** Crime Lab Chemistry. Bergman, Lincoln et al, eds. (Great Explorations in Math & Science (GEMS) Ser.). (Illus.). 36p. (J). (gr. 4-8). 1999. pap., teacher ed. 9.00 (*0-924886-34-X*, GEMS) Lawrence Science.

— Leader's Handbook. (Illus.). (J). 2000. pap. 13.50 (*0-924886-52-8*, GEMS) Lawrence Science.

— Of Cabbages & Chemistry. rev. ed. Bergman, Lincoln & Fairwell, Kay, eds. (Great Explorations in Math & Science (GEMS) Ser.). (Illus.). 88p. 1999. pap., teacher ed. 10.50 (*0-924886-28-5*, GEMS) Lawrence Science.

— Once upon a Guide: Connecting Young People's Literature to Great Explorations in Math & Science. (Illus.). (J). 2000. pap. 13.50 (*0-924886-53-6*, GEMS) Lawrence Science.

— Parent Partners: Workshops to Foster School/Home/ Family Partnerships. (Illus.). 2000. pap. 19.95 (*0-924886-54-4*, GEMS) Lawrence Science.

— Solids, Liquids & Gases. rev. ed. Bergman, Lincoln & Fairwell, Kay, ed. (Great Explorations in Math & Science (GEMS) Ser.). (Illus.). 64p. (Orig.). 1999. pap., teacher ed. 16.00 (*0-924886-27-7*, GEMS) Lawrence Science.

— Vitamin C Testing. rev. ed. Bergman, Lincoln & Fairwell, Kay, eds. (Great Explorations in Math & Science (GEMS) Ser.). (Illus.). 64p. (J). (gr. 4-8). 1999. pap., teacher ed. 10.50 (*0-924886-31-5*, GEMS) Lawrence Science.

Barber, Jacqueline & Willard, Carolyn. Bubble Festival: Presenting Bubble Activities in a Learning Station Format. rev. ed. Bergman, Lincoln & Babcock, Carl, eds. (Great Explorations in Math & Science (GEMS) Ser.). (Illus.). 176p. (Orig.). (J). (gr. k-6). 1994. reprint ed. pap., teacher ed. 16.00 (*0-912511-80-X*, GEMS) Lawrence Science.

Barber, Jacqueline, et al. Discovering Density. rev. ed. Bergman, Lincoln & Fairwell, Kay, eds. (Great Explorations in Math & Science (GEMS) Ser.). (Illus.). 80p. (YA). (gr. 6-8). 1993. reprint ed. pap. 10.50 (*0-912511-17-6*, GEMS) Lawrence Science.

***Barber, Jacqueline, et al.** Dry Ice Investigations. Stone, Florence et al, eds. (Great Explorations in Math & Science (GEMS) Ser.). (Illus.). 212p. (YA). (gr. 6-8). 1999. pap. 21.00 (*0-924886-15-3*, Pub. by Lawrence Science) Consort Bk Sales.

Barber, Jacqueline, et al. GEMS Leader's Handbook. rev. ed. Babcock, Carl et al, eds. (Great Explorations in Math & Science (GEMS) Ser.). (Illus.). 80p. 1997. reprint ed. pap., teacher ed. 13.50 (*0-912511-73-7*, GEMS) Lawrence Science.

— GEMS Teacher's Handbook. Babcock, Carl & Fairwell, Kay, eds. (Great Explorations in Math & Science (GEMS) Ser.). (Illus.). 60p. 1998. pap., teacher ed. 10.50 (*0-924886-07-2*, GEMS) Lawrence Science.

— Insights & Outcomes: Assessments for Great Explorations in Math & Science. Babcock, Carl et al, eds. (Great Explorations in Math & Science (GEMS) Ser.) (Illus.). 284p. 1995. teacher ed., spiral bd. 31.50 (*0-912511-90-7*, GEMS) Lawrence Science.

— Learning about Learning. Bergman, Lincoln et al, eds. (Great Explorations in Math & Science (GEMS) Ser.). (Illus.). 220p. (Orig.). (J). (gr. 6-8). 1996. teacher ed., spiral bd. 25.50 (*0-912511-95-8*, GEMS) Lawrence Science.

— Once upon a GEMS Guide: Connecting Young People's Literature to Great Explorations in Math & Science. rev. ed. Babcock, Carl & Stone, Florence, eds. (Great Explorations in Math & Science (GEMS) Ser.). (Illus.). 412p. 1994. reprint ed. pap., teacher ed. 31.50 (*0-912511-78-8*, GEMS) Lawrence Science.

***Barber, Jacqueline, et al.** A Parent's Guide to Great Explorations in Math & Science (GEMS) rev. ed. Babcock, Carl, ed. (Great Explorations in Math & Science (GEMS) Ser.). (illus.). 52p. 1999. pap., teacher ed. 10.50 (*0-924886-26-9*, GEMS) Lawrence Science.

Barber, Jacqueline, jt. auth. see Ahouse, Jeremy J.

Barber, Jacqueline, jt. auth. see Hosoume, Kimi.

Barber, Jacqueline, jt. auth. see Sneider, Cary.

Barber, Jacques P. & Crits-Christoph, Paul, eds. Dynamic Therapies for Psychiatric Disorders: Axis I. LC 94-42944. 1995. 55.00 (*0-465-01742-8*, Pub. by Basic) HarpC.

Barber, Jacques P., jt. ed. see Crits-Christoph, Paul.

Barber, James. South Africa in the Twentieth Century: From Empire to Rainbow Nation. LC 99-11161. (History of the Contemporary World Ser.). 304p. 1999. pap. 59.95 (*0-631-19101-1*); pap. 29.95 (*0-631-19102-X*) Blackwell Pubs.

— Theodore Roosevelt, Icon of the American Century. LC 98-23378. (Illus.). 3p. 1999. pap. text 22.95 (*0-295-97753-1*) U of Wash Pr.

Barber, James. Uneasy Relationship. 1983. 77.95 (*0-435-83042-2*) Ashgate Pub Co.

Barber, James D. The Book of Democracy. LC 94-36188. 432p. (C). 1995. pap. text 33.20 (*0-13-340068-9*) P-H.

— Erasmus: A Play on Words. LC 81-40002. 80p. (Orig.). 1982. pap. text 12.50 (*0-8191-1869-9*) U Pr of Amer.

— The Lawmakers: Recruitment & Adaptation to Legislative Life, 11. LC 79-26379. 314p. 1980. reprint ed. lib. bdg. 65.00 (*0-313-22200-2*, BALA, Greenwood Pr) Greenwood.

— Politics by Humans: Research on American Leadership. LC 87-36593. xii, 517p. 1988. text 64.95 (*0-8223-0837-1*); pap. text 25.95 (*0-8223-0848-7*) Duke.

— The Presidential Character: Predicting Performance in the White House. 4th ed. 544p. (C). 1992. pap. text 18.00 (*0-13-718123-X*) P-H.

— The Pulse of Politics: Electing Presidents in the Media Age. 345p. (C). 1992. pap. 24.95 (*1-56000-589-0*) Transaction Pubs.

Barber, James D., ed. Race for the Presidency: The Media & the Nominating Process. LC 78-111878. (American Assembly Guides Ser.). 1978. 11.95 (*0-13-750141-2*) Am Assembly.

Barber, James G. Alexandria in the Civil War. (Virginia Civil War Battles & Leaders Ser.). (Illus.). 130p. 1988. 19.95 (*0-930919-62-9*) H E Howard.

— Beyond Casework. 1997. pap. 17.95 (*0-333-54876-0*) St Martin.

***Barber, James G.** Presidents. LC 99-43281. (Eyewitness Books). (Illus.). 64p. (J). (gr. 4-7). 2000. 15.95 (*0-7894-5243-X*, D K Ink) DK Pub Inc.

Barber, James G. Social Work with Addictions. LC 94-25331. (C). 1994. text 45.00 (*0-8147-1241-X*); pap. text 18.50 (*0-8147-1242-8*) NYU Pr.

— To the President: Folk Portraits by the People. Smithsonian Institution, National Portrait Gallery, ed. (Illus.). 96p. (Orig.). 1993. pap. 19.95 (*1-56833-023-5*) Madison Bks UPA.

Barber, Janette & Banks, Laura. Breaking the Rules. LC 96-39972. 1997. pap. write for info. (*0-15-644296-5*) Harcourt.

Barber, Jennifer, et al. Take Three: 3. Melnyczuk, Askold, ed. (AGNI New Poets Ser.: No. 3). 96p. 1998. pap. 12.95 (*1-55597-282-9*) Graywolf.

***Barber, Joel D.** Wild Fowl Decoys. (Illus.). 151p. 2000. pap. 24.95 (*1-56833-145-2*, Pub. by Derrydale Pr) Natl Bk Netwk.

Barber, John. Soviet Historians in Crisis, 1928-1932. LC 80-13798. 194p. 1981. 39.50 (*0-8419-0614-9*) Holmes & Meier.

Barber, John & Harrison, Mark. SOVIET HOME FRONT1941 45. (Illus.). 264p. (C). 1995. 87.00 (*0-582-00964-2*, 78912); pap. text 45.00 (*0-582-00965-0*, 78913) Longman.

***Barber, John, et al.** The Soviet Defence-Industry Complex from Stalin to Khrushchev LC 99-16308. (Studies in Russian & East European History & Society). 2000. text 79.95 (*0-312-22602-0*) St Martin.

B

Barber, John R. Modern European History. LC 90-56009. (Outline Ser.). (Illus.). 416p. (Orig.) (C). 1993. pap. 13.00 (*0-06-467112-7*) HarpC.

***Barber, John T. & Tait, Alice A., eds.** The Information Society & the Black Community. LC 00-23547. 2000. write for info. (*0-275-95724-1*, Praeger Pubs) Greenwood.

Barber, John W. Historical Collections, Relating to the History & Antiquities of Every Town in Massachusetts. (Illus.). 624p. 1994. reprint ed. lib. bdg. 62.50 (*0-8328-3956-6*) Higginson Bk Co.

— Historical Collections... Relating to the History & Antiquities of Every Town in Massachusetts: With Geographical Descriptions. (Illus.). 631p. 1995. reprint ed. pap. 49.95 (*0-8063-4578-0*, 9036) Clearfield Co.

— History of the Amistad Captives. LC 76-82168. (Anti-Slavery Crusade in America Ser.). 1976. reprint ed. 13.95 (*0-405-00608-X*) Ayer.

Barber, John W. & Howe, Henry. Early Woodcut Views of New York & New Jersey: 304 Illustrations from the "Historical Collection" 1990. 15.00 (*0-8446-5156-7*) Peter Smith.

— Historical Collections of the State of New Jersey: Containing Geographical Descriptions of Every Township in the State. (Illus.). 582p. 1990. reprint ed. pap. 32.50 (*1-55613-307-3*) Heritage Bk.

— Historical Collections of the State of New Jersey, Containing a General Collection of the Most Interesting Facts, Traditions, Biographical Sketches, Etc. (Illus.). 520p. 1992. reprint ed. lib. bdg. 52.00 (*0-8328-2380-5*) Higginson Bk Co.

***Barber, John W. & Howe, Henry.** Historical Collections of the State of New York. (Illus.). 672p. 1999. pap. 39.50 (*0-7884-1338-4*, B063) Heritage Bk.

Barber, John W., jt. auth. see Howe, Henry.

Barber, John Warner. Connecticut Historical Collections: Containing a General Collection of Interesting Facts, Traditions, Biographical Sketches, Anecdotes, etc. Relating to the History & Antiquity of Every Town in Connecticut with Geographical Descriptions. abr. ed. (Illus.). 584p. 1999. reprint ed. pap. 24.95 (*0-939883-05-8*, Pub. by Bibliopola Pr) U Pr of New Eng.

Barber, Joseph, et al. Hypnosis & Suggestive Management of Pain: A Clinical Guide. 413p. 1996. 45.00 (*0-393-70216-2*) Norton.

Barber, Joseph A., ed. Francesco Petrarch's Rime Disperse. LC 91-11150. (Library of Medieval Literature: Ser. A). 216p. 1991. text 12.00 (*0-8153-0144-8*) Garland.

Barber, Joseph E., jt. auth. see Horowitz, Leonard G.

Barber, Josephine. German for Musicians. LC 84-48545. (Illus.). 294p. 1985. pap. 29.95 (*0-253-21260-X*) Ind U Pr.

***Barber, Joyce.** Vignettes: Amusing Stories from My Life. (Illus.). 150p. 2000. pap. 14.95 (*0-9643958-2-7*) Assoctd W Palm Bch.

Barber, K. E. Peat Stratigraphy & Climatic Change. 242p. (C). 1981. text 123.00 (*90-6191-087-0*, Pub. by A A Balkema) Ashgate Pub Co.

Barber, Karen. Ready, Set . . . Wait! Help for Life on Hold. LC 95-10264. 160p. (YA). (gr. 10). 1996. pap. 12.99 (*0-8010-5712-4*) Baker Bks.

Barber, Karen, ed. Afterglow: More Stories of Lesbian Desire. 189p. (Orig.). 1993. pap. 11.95 (*1-55583-315-2*) Alyson Pubns.

— Bushfire: Stories of Lesbian Desire. 206p. (Orig.). 1991. pap. 11.95 (*1-55583-312-8*) Alyson Pubns.

Barber, Karen, jt. ed. see Yamaguchi, Lynne.

***Barber, Karin.** The Generation of Plays: Yoruba Popular Life in Theater. LC 00-40740. 2000. write for info. (*0-253-33807-7*) Ind U Pr.

— Readings in African Popular Culture. LC 97-11211. 194p. 1997. pap. text 22.95 (*0-253-21140-9*) Ind U Pr.

Barber, Karin, ed. Readings in African Popular Culture. LC 97-11211. 1997. 45.00 (*0-253-33294-X*) Ind U Pr.

Barber, Karin, et al. West African Popular Theatre. LC 96-42321. (Drama & Performance Studies). 1997. 39.95 (*0-253-33204-4*); pap. 17.95 (*0-253-21077-1*) Ind U Pr.

Barber, Katherine, ed. The Canadian Oxford Dictionary. 1600p. 1999. 39.95 (*0-19-541120-X*) OUP.

***Barber, Kathleen L.** A Right to Representation: Proportional Election Systems for the Twenty-First Century. (Urban Life & Urban Landscape Ser.). 240p. 2000. 55.00 (*0-8142-0854-1*); pap. 21.95 (*0-8142-5058-0*) Ohio St U Pr.

Barber, Kenneth F. & Gracia, Jorge J., eds. Individuation & Identity in Early Modern Philosophy: Descartes to Kant. LC 93-38028. 275p. (C). 1994. text 59.50 (*0-7914-1967-3*); pap. text 19.95 (*0-7914-1968-1*) State U NY Pr.

Barber, Kim. Career Success with Pets: How to Get Started, Get Going, Get Ahead. LC 95-38134. (Illus.). 256p. (Orig.). 1996. per. 17.95 (*0-87605-768-7*) Macmillan.

Barber, Kristen, jt. auth. see Shea, Dennis.

Barber, Laurence. When South Yarmouth Was Quaker Village. (Illus.). 52p. 1988. pap. 4.00 (*0-9625068-2-6*) Hist Soc Yarmouth.

Barber, Lawrence. Tango Around the Horn: The World War II Voyage of America's Last Large Sailing Ship. enl. rev. ed. (Illus.). 256p. 1991. pap. 13.95 (*1-880827-01-8*) OR Maritime Ctr & Mus.

Barber, Lilian S., et al, eds. The New Complete Italian Greyhound. (Illus.). 1993. 21.95 (*0-9611986-2-1*) Ital Greyhnd.

Barber, Linda & Gabriel, Nancy. I Can Write! I Can Read! My Writing Book for Names & Telephone Numbers. (My Writing Book Ser.). (Illus.). 128p. (Orig.). (J). (ps-2). 1994. student ed. 9.95 (*0-9632868-0-3*) Going Places.

Barber, Linda & Garwood, Ruth. Being a Medical Admitting Clerk. 144p. (C). 1994. pap. 17.75 (*0-89303-072-4*) P-H.

Barber, Lou. The Baker Affair. LC 99-61370. 256p. 2000. pap. 14.95 (*0-88739-264-4*) Creat Arts Bk.

— Dropout to Test Pilot: Lou Barber's Autobiography. (Illus.). 163p. 1997. pap. 15.00 (*0-9660434-0-5*) Barbers Retail.

Barber, Lucie W. Celebrating the Second Year of Life: A Parent's Guide for a Happy Child. LC 78-21484. 148p. (Orig.). 1979. pap. 10.95 (*0-89135-015-2*) Religious Educ.

— The Religious Education of Preschool Children. LC 80-27623. 196p. (Orig.). 1981. pap. 16.95 (*0-89135-026-8*) Religious Educ.

— Teaching Christian Values. LC 83-22981. 250p. (Orig.). (C). 1984. pap. 16.95 (*0-89135-041-1*) Religious Educ.

Barber, Lucius I. A Record & Documentary History of Simsbury, Ct. 429p. 1993. reprint ed. lib. bdg. 45.00 (*0-8328-2853-X*) Higginson Bk Co.

Barber, Luke, jt. auth. see Weinstein, Matt W.

Barber, M. The Learning Game. 1997. pap. text 19.95 (*0-575-40100-1*, Pub. by V Gollancz) Trafalgar.

Barber, M. J. Handbook of Power Cylinders, Valves & Controls. viii,364p. 1986. 172.00 (*0-85461-100-2*) Elsevier.

Barber, M. N. & Ninham, B. W. Random & Restricted Walks: Theory & Applications, Vol. 10. (Mathematics & Its Applications Ser.). xiv, 176p. 1970. text 173.00 (*0-677-02620-X*) Gordon & Breach.

Barber, M. P. Public Administration. 245p. (C). 1984. 120.00 (*0-7855-5652-4*, Pub. by Inst Pur & Supply) St Mut.

***Barber, Malcolm.** The Cathars in Languedoc. LC 00-22125. (Medieval World Ser.). 256p. 2000. pap. 25.33 (*0-582-25661-5*) Addison-Wesley.

— The Cathers in Languedoc. 256p. 2001. 79.95 (*0-582-25662-3*) Longman.

Barber, Malcolm. Crusaders & Heretics, Twelfth to Fourteenth Centuries. (Collected Studies: Vol. 498). 364p. 1995. 97.95 (*0-86078-476-2*, Pub. by Variorum) Ashgate Pub Co.

Barber, Malcolm, ed. The Military Orders: Fighting for the Faith & Caring for the Sick. (Illus.). 432p. 1994. text 98.95 (*0-86078-438-X*, Pub. by Variorum) Ashgate Pub Co.

Barber, Malcolm C. The New Knighthood: A History of the Order of the Temple. (Canto Book Ser.). (Illus.). 465p. (C). 1995. pap. 12.95 (*0-521-55872-7*) Cambridge U Pr.

— The Trial of the Templars. (Canto Book Ser.). 320p. (C). 1993. pap. 12.95 (*0-521-45727-0*) Cambridge U Pr.

— The Two Cities: Medieval Europe 1050-1320. (Illus.). 612p. (C). (gr. 13). 1998. pap. 25.99 (*0-415-09682-0*, B2556) Routledge.

Barber, Marcia, jt. ed. see Stephens-Peck, Inc. Staff.

***Barber, Margaret.** The Longman Guide to Columbia Online Style. 32p. (C). 1999. pap. 2.80 (*0-321-06745-2*) Addison-Wesley.

Barber, Margaret F. Grey Brethren, & Other Fragments in Prose & Verse. LC 75-125202. (Short Story Index Reprint Ser.). 1977. 15.95 (*0-8369-3569-1*) Ayer.

***Barber, Marianne.** Food Allergies. 2001. pap. text 15.00 (*0-8050-6600-4*) St Martin.

Barber, Marie. Cross-Stitch the Special Moments in Your Life. LC 97-2479. (Illus.). 128p. 1997. 27.95 (*0-8069-9612-9*) Sterling.

— Cross-Stitch the Speical Moments of Your Life. 1999. pap. text 14.95 (*0-8069-9668-4*) Sterling.

***Barber, Marie.** 515 Inspirational Cross-Stitch Designs. (Illus.). 2000. pap. 14.95 (*0-8069-5598-8*) Sterling.

Barber, Marie. Heavenly Cross-Stitch: Designs with a Christian Theme. LC 98-18737. (Illus.). 128p. 1998. 27.95 (*0-8069-0349-X*) Sterling.

***Barber, Marie.** Heavenly Cross-Stitch: Designs with Christian Theme. 128p. 1999. pap. text 14.95 (*0-8069-2023-8*) Sterling.

— Marie Barber's 515 Inspirational Cross Stitch Designs. LC 98-46796. 1999. 24.95 (*0-8069-6255-0*) Sterling.

Barber, Marie-Claire, tr. see Ferraris, Luigi V., ed.

Barber, Martha. El Viejito Chiflado y La Viejita Chiflada. (SPA., Illus.). 32p. (J). (ps-3). 1998. pap. 4.95 (*1-57255-504-1*) Mondo Pubng.

Barber, Mary C. Smoothies: 50 Recipes for High-Energy Refreshment. LC 97-1124. 1997. pap. 15.95 (*0-8118-1648-6*) Chronicle Bks.

— Wraps: Easy Recipes for Handheld Meals. LC 97-17111. 1997. pap. text 14.95 (*0-8118-1812-8*) Chronicle Bks.

***Barber, Mary C., et al.** The Smoothies Deck: 50 Recipes for High-Energy Refreshment. (Illus.). 1999. 12.95 (*0-8118-2380-6*) Chronicle Bks.

Barber, Mary Corpening, et al. Cocktail Food: 50 Recipes with Attitude. LC 98-55736. (Illus.). 132p. 1999. 16.95 (*0-8118-2418-7*) Chronicle Bks.

***Barber, Mary Corpening, et al.** Skewer It! 50 Recipes for Stylish Entertaining. LC 00-27307. (Illus.). 2000. 17.95 (*0-8118-2815-8*) Chronicle Bks.

— Super Smoothies: 50 Recipes for Health & Energy. LC 99-39549. (Illus.). 108p. 2000. pap. 16.95 (*0-8118-2540-X*) Chronicle Bks.

Barber, Maryann, jt. auth. see Bauer, Robert T.

Barber, Maryann, jt. auth. see Grauer, Robert.

Barber, Maryann, jt. auth. see Grauer, Robert T.

Barber, Maryann M., jt. auth. see Grauer, Robert T.

Barber, Michael. Education & the Teacher Unions. Hills, Philip, ed. (Issues in Education Ser.). 140p. 1992. text 100.00 (*0-304-32359-4*); pap. text 27.95 (*0-304-32364-0*) Continuum.

— The Learning Game: Arguments for an Education Revolution. 320p. 1998. pap. 24.95 (*0-575-06364-5*, Pub. by Indigo) Trafalgar.

— The Making of the 1944 Education Act. LC 93-42667. (Education Ser.). 144p. 1995. 90.00 (*0-304-32659-3*) Continuum.

— The Making of the 1944 Education Act. LC 93-42667. (Education Ser.). 144p. 1995. pap. 29.95 (*0-304-32661-5*) Continuum.

Barber, Michael, ed. Education in the Capital. 160p. 1992. text 99.50 (*0-304-32603-8*) Continuum.

Barber, Michael & Dann, Ruth, eds. Raising Educational Standards in the Inner Cities: Practical Initiatives in Action. (School Development Ser.). (Illus.). 208p. 1996. 99.50 (*0-304-33136-8*); pap. 37.95 (*0-304-33138-4*) Continuum.

Barber, Michael & Graham, Duncan, eds. Sense, Nonsense, & the National Curriculum. LC 92-39724. 1993. 85.00 (*0-7507-0160-9*, Falmer Pr); pap. 29.95 (*0-7507-0161-7*, Falmer Pr) Taylor & Francis.

Barber, Michael & Pearce, Paul. Yang-Baxter Equations, Conformal Invariance & Integrability in Statistical Mechanics & Field Theory. 426p. 1990. text 92.00 (*981-02-0067-5*) World Scientific Pub.

Barber, Michael B., et al, contrib. by. Upland Archeology in the East - A Symposium, Vol. 38, No. 1. (Illus.). 458p. 1996. pap. 22.00 (*1-884626-29-7*) Archeolog Soc.

— Upland Archeology in the East - A Symposium, Vol. 38, No. 2. (Illus.). 290p. 1996. pap. 16.00 (*1-884626-30-0*) Archeolog Soc.

— Upland Archeology in the East - A Symposium, Vol. 38, No. 3. (Illus.). 356p. 1996. pap. 20.00 (*1-884626-31-9*) Archeolog Soc.

— Upland Archeology in the East - A Symposium, Vol. 38, No. 4. (Illus.). 336p. 1996. pap. 18.00 (*1-884626-32-7*) Archeolog Soc.

— Upland Archeology in the East - A Symposium, Vol. 38, No. 5. (Illus.). 241p. 1996. pap. 14.00 (*1-884626-33-5*) Archeolog Soc.

— Upland Archeology in the East - A Symposium, Vol. 38, No. 6. (Illus.). 256p. 1996. pap. 12.00 (*1-884626-34-3*) Archeolog Soc.

Barber, Michael D. Equality & Alterity: Phenomenological Investigations of Discrimination. LC 97-13529. 240p. 1998. 55.00 (*0-391-04049-9*) Humanities.

— Ethical Hermeneutics: Rationalist Enrique Dussel's Philosophy of Liberation. LC 96-37190. (Perspectives in Continental Philosophy Ser.: Vol. 3). xvi, 298p. (C). 1996. pap. 19.00 (*0-8232-1704-3*); text 37.50 (*0-8232-1703-5*) Fordham.

— Guardian of Dialogue: Max Scheler's Phenomenology, Sociology of Knowledge, & Philosophy of Love. LC 92-52715. 208p. (C). 1993. 33.50 (*0-8387-5228-4*) Bucknell U Pr.

— Social Typifications & the Elusive Other: Alfred Schutz's Phenomenology & the Sociology of Knowledge. LC 86-73241. 144p. 1988. 32.50 (*0-8387-5123-7*) Bucknell U Pr.

***Barber, Michael E., et al.** Stormwater Runoff Cost-Benefit Project: Proiritzing Stormwater Outfalls. (Illus.). 99p. (C). 2000. reprint ed. pap. text 25.00 (*0-7881-8615-9*) DIANE Pub.

Barber, Mike. Athletic Scholarships: A Guide. 1993. pap. text 13.95 (*0-9662996-0-4*) BACA Pubg.

Barber, N. What They Don't Tell You about Living. (Illus.). (J). mass mkt. 7.95 (*0-340-69349-5*, Pub. by Hodder & Stought Ltd) Trafalgar.

— What They Don't Tell You about Music. (J). mass mkt. 8.95 (*0-340-68995-1*, Pub. by Hodder & Stought Ltd) Trafalgar.

***Barber, Nathan.** Master AP European History. 2000. pap. 15.99 (*0-7645-6185-5*, Arco) Macmillan Gen Ref.

Barber, Ned. Quality Assessment for Healthcare: A Baldrige-Based Handbook. LC 95-41103. 204p. 1995. pap. 29.95 (*0-527-76305-5*) Productivity Inc.

***Barber, Nicky.** Fire & Flood. (Natural Disasters Ser.). (Illus.). 32p. (YA). (gr. 5 up). 1999. pap. 5.95 (*0-7641-1058-6*) Barron.

Barber, Nicola. Deserts. (Alpha Bks.). (Illus.). 45p. (gr. 5-8). 1996. write for info. (*0-237-51662-4*) EVN1 UK.

Barber, Nicola. Fires & Floods. (J). 1997. write for info. (*0-237-51770-1*) EVN1 UK.

Barber, Nicola. Hurricanes & Storms. (Alpha Bks.). (Illus.). 45p. (J). (gr. 5-8). 1996. write for info. (*0-237-51325-0*) EVN1 UK.

— Pollution. (Illus.). 44p. (J). (gr. 5-8). 1996. write for info. (*0-237-51513-X*) EVN1 UK.

— Rainforests. (Illus.). 45p. (J). (gr. 5-8). 1996. write for info. (*0-237-51324-2*) EVN1 UK.

— Rivers, Ponds & Lakes. (Illus.). 44p. (J). (gr. 5-8). 1996. write for info. (*0-237-51323-4*) EVN1 UK.

— The Search for Lost Cities. LC 96-40495. (Treasure Hunters Ser.). (Illus.). 48p. (J). (gr. 4 up). 1998. lib. bdg. 25.69 (*0-8172-4840-4*) Raintree Steck-V.

— Seas & Oceans. (Alpha Bks.). (Illus.). 45p. (J). (gr. 5-8). 1996. write for info. (*0-237-51685-3*) EVN1 UK.

Barber, Nicola & Ganeri, Anita. The Search for Sunken Treasure. LC 97-5403. (Treasure Hunters Ser.). (Illus.). 48p. (J). (gr. 4 up). 1998. lib. bdg. 25.69 (*0-8172-4838-2*) Raintree Steck-V.

Barber, Nicola & Mure, Mary. The World of Art. LC 97-20487. (J). 1998. pap. write for info. (*0-382-39811-4*); lib. bdg. 19.95 (*0-382-39812-2*) Silver Burdett Pr.

— The World of Music. LC 95-1394. (J). (gr. 5-7). 1995. lib. bdg. 15.95 (*0-382-39116-0*) Silver Burdett Pr.

— The World of Music. LC 95-1394. (Illus.). 94p. (J). (gr. 5-7). 1995. pap. 8.95 (*0-382-39117-9*) Silver Burdett Pr.

Barber, Nigel. Parenting: Roles, Styles & Outcomes. LC 98-7502. 159p. 1998. 34.00 (*1-56072-573-7*) Nova Sci Pubs.

***Barber, Nigel.** Why Parents Matter: Parental Investment & Child Outcomes. LC 99-55886. 256p. 2000. 27.95 (*0-89789-725-0*, Bergin & Garvey) Greenwood.

***Barber, Noel.** The Black Hole of Calcutta: A Reconstruction. (Common Reader Edition Ser.). 2000. pap. 17.95 (*1-58579-007-9*, Pub. by Akadine Pr) Trafalgar.

Barber, Noel. Farewell to France. 1983. 17.95 (*0-02-506830-X*) Macmillan.

— The Natives Were Friendly. 2.95 (*0-86072-021-7*, Pub. by Quartet) Charles River Bks.

— Sakkara. 1985. 18.95 (*0-02-506820-2*) Macmillan.

— Sakkara. 1985. pap. 3.95 (*0-380-70091-3*, Avon Bks) Morrow Avon.

***Barber, Noel.** The Week France Fell: June 10- June 16, 1940. 2000. reprint ed. pap. 18.95 (*0-8154-1091-3*) Cooper Sq.

Barber, Noel, jt. auth. see Lioger, Richard.

Barber, Olive. Meet Me in Juneau. LC 60-53461. (Illus.). 258p. 1960. 12.95 (*0-8323-0079-9*); pap. 9.95 (*0-8323-0256-2*) Binford Mort.

Barber, Olive. Meet Me in Juneau. 175p. pap. text 13.00 (*1-57833-024-6*) Todd Commns.

Barber, P. W. & Hill, S. C. Light Scattering by Particles: Computational Methods. (Advanced Series in Applied Physics: Vol. 2). 276p. 1990. pap. 40.00 (*9971-5-0832-X*); text 85.00 (*9971-5-0813-3*) World Scientific Pub.

Barber, P. W., jt. auth. see Chang, R. K.

Barber, Paul. Vampires, Burial & Death: Folklore & Reality. 244p. (C). 1990. reprint ed. pap. 14.00 (*0-300-04859-9*) Yale U Pr.

Barber, Paul J. Applied Cognitive Psychology: An Information Processing Approach. (Illus.). 170p. 1988. pap. 15.95 (*0-416-08762-0*, 9181) Routledge.

Barber, Paul J. & Legge, David. Information & Human Performance. (New Essential Psychology Ser.). 194p. 1986. pap. 14.95 (*0-416-34950-1*, NO. 9181) Routledge.

Barber, Peter M., et al. Switzerland 700. LC 93-108510. 111p. 1991. write for info. (*0-7123-0258-1*) B23tish Library.

***Barber, Phil.** Insiders' Guide to California's Wine Country. 3rd ed. 528p. 2000. pap. text 16.95 (*1-57380-167-4*) IPBI.

Barber, Phil, text. Superstars of the NFL: Featuring the 35 Best Players in the NFL. LC 99-162325. (Lionheart Book Ser.). (Illus.). 160p. 1998. pap. 19.95 (*0-8362-7115-7*) Andrews & McMeel.

Barber, Phyllis. And the Desert Shall Blossom: A Novel. LC 90-42363. 285p. reprint ed. pap. 88.40 (*0-7837-3965-6*, 204379400011) Bks Demand.

— How I Got Cultured: A Nevada Memoir. LC 91-23324. (Associated Writing Programs Award for Creative Nonfiction Ser.). (Illus.). 216p. 1992. 24.95 (*0-8203-1413-7*) U of Ga Pr.

— How I Got Cultured: A Nevada Memoir. LC 93-38160. (Illus.). 206p. 1994. pap. 12.95 (*0-87417-233-0*) U of Nev Pr.

— Legs: The Story of a Giraffe. LC 90-47679. (Illus.). 80p. (J). (gr. 4-7). 1991. text 13.95 (*0-689-50526-4*) McElderry Bks.

***Barber, Phyllis.** Parting the Veil: Stories from a Mormon Imagination. LC 98-47294. 142p. 1999. pap. 16.95 (*1-56085-120-1*) Signature Bks.

Barber, Phyllis N. Smiley Snake's Adventure. Jordan, Alton, ed. (Buppet Bks.). (Illus.). (J). (gr. 1-4). 1980. 9.95 (*0-89868-098-0*, Read Res); pap. 3.95 (*0-89868-109-X*, Read Res) ARO Pub.

Barber, Preston, jt. auth. see Heiserman, Russell L.

Barber, Raymond G. History of the Barbers of Java, New York. Swinson, Gary E., ed. LC 92-81529. (Illus.). 96p. (Orig.). 1992. pap. 9.95 (*0-9629573-3-X*) G E Swinson.

***Barber, Raymond G.** The Model Father. 22p. 1999. pap. write for info. (*0-87398-571-0*) Sword of the Lord.

Barber, Raymond G. & Swinson, Gary E. The Civil War Letters of Charles Barber, Private, 104th New York Volunteer Infantry. LC 91-909058. 256p. 1991. pap. 20.00 (*0-9629573-2-1*) G E Swinson.

Barber, Red. 1947: When All Hell Broke Loose in Baseball. (Quality Paperbacks Ser.). 380p. 1984. pap. 14.95 (*0-306-80212-0*) Da Capo.

Barber, Red & Creamer, Robert W. Rhubarb in the Catbird Seat. LC 96-41632. 338p. 1997. pap. 14.95 (*0-8032-6136-5*, Bison Books) U of Nebr Pr.

Barber, Richard. Arthurian Literature XI. 168p. (C). 1992. 75.00 (*0-85991-350-3*) Boydell & Brewer.

— Bestiary. fac. ed. (Illus.). 205p. 1999. pap. 35.00 (*0-85115-753-X*, Suffolk Records Soc) Boydell & Brewer.

— The Companion Guide to Gascony (NE) (Illus.). 368p. 1999. pap. 24.95 (*1-900639-27-0*) Boydell & Brewer.

— The Devil's Crown: A History of Henry II & His Sons. LC 96-19308. (Illus.). 176p. 1996. pap. 16.95 (*0-938289-78-0*, 289780) Combined Pub.

***Barber, Richard.** Earl Spencer: Saint or Sinner? large type unabridged ed. 280p. 1999. 26.95 (*0-7531-5087-5*, 150875, Pub. by ISIS Lrg Prnt) ISIS Pub.

Barber, Richard. King Arthur: Hero & Legend. (Illus.). 234p. 1994. 35.00 (*0-85115-419-0*); pap. 17.95 (*0-85115-254-6*) Boydell & Brewer.

— Myths & Legends of the British Isles. LC 99-21492. (Illus.). 640p. 1999. 55.00 (*0-85115-748-3*, Suffolk Records Soc) Boydell & Brewer.

— Pilgrimages. (Illus.). 168p. 1998. pap. 22.95 (*0-85115-471-9*, Boydell Pr) Boydell & Brewer.

Barber, Richard, ed. The Arthurian Legends: An Illustrated Anthology. (Illus.). 286p. 1996. pap. 17.95 (*0-85115-252-X*, Boydell Pr) Boydell & Brewer.

— The Arthurian Legends: An Illustrated Anthology. (Illus.). 269p. (C). 1996. 45.00 (*0-85115-110-8*) Boydell & Brewer.

— Arthurian Literature, Vol. 1. (Illus.). 181p. 1981. reprint ed. 72.00 (*0-85991-081-4*) Boydell & Brewer.

— Arthurian Literature, Vol. III. 142p. 1983. 75.00 (*0-85991-149-7*) Boydell & Brewer.

— Arthurian Literature, Vol. V. 157p. 1985. 75.00 (*0-85991-191-8*) Boydell & Brewer.

— Arthurian Literature, Vol. VI. 172p. 1992. 75.00 (*0-85991-226-4*) Boydell & Brewer.

— Arthurian Literature, Vol. VII. (Illus.). 1987. 75.00 (*0-85991-242-6*) Boydell & Brewer.

— Arthurian Literature, Vol. X. 168p. 1991. 75.00 (*0-85991-308-2*) Boydell & Brewer.

— The Pastons: A Family in the War of the Roses. LC 93-11789. 208p. (C). 1999. reprint ed. pap. 22.95 (*0-85115-338-0*, Boydell Pr) Boydell & Brewer.

Barber, Richard, et al, eds. Arthurian Literature, Vol. VIII. 212p. 1989. 75.00 (*0-85991-283-3*) Boydell & Brewer.

— Arthurian Literature, Vol. IX. (Arthurian Literature Ser.). 151p. (C). 1989. 75.00 (*0-85991-291-4*) Boydell & Brewer.

Barber, Richard, tr. The Life & Campaigns of the Black Prince. LC 97-23498. (Illus.). 152p. 1997. pap. 24.95 (*0-85115-469-7*, Boydell Pr) Boydell & Brewer.

***Barber, Richard & Barker, Juliet.** Tournaments: Jousts, Chivalry & Pageants in the Middle Ages. (Illus.). 240p. 2000. pap. 29.95 (*0-85115-781-5*) Boydell & Brewer.

Barber, Richard, ed. see Aubrey, John.

Barber, Richard E., Sr. The Economic Emancipation of African-Americans: Let the Church Say "Amen" 176p. (Orig.). 1992. pap. 7.95 (*0-9634704-0-X*) Penny Lovers.

Barber, Robin. Athens. 4th ed. (Blue Guide Ser.). (Illus.). 288p. 1999. pap. 22.95 (*0-393-31930-X*) Norton.

— Greece. 6th ed. (Blue Guide Ser.). 1995. pap. 25.00 (*0-393-31273-9*, Norton Paperbks) Norton.

— Rhodes & the Dodecanese. (Blue Guide Ser.). (Illus.). 256p. 1997. pap. 18.95 (*0-393-31582-7*) Norton.

Barber, Rowland. The Night They Raided Minsky's. 23.95 (*0-88411-097-4*) Amereon Ltd.

— Rhubarb in the Catbird Seat. 27.95 (*0-8488-1565-3*) Amereon Ltd.

Barber, Rowland, jt. auth. see Marx, Harpo.

Barber, Russell . Doing Historical Archaeology: Exercises Using Documentary, Oral & Material Evidence. LC 93-39035. 248p. 1994. pap. text 21.00 (*0-13-176033-5*) P-H.

Barber, Russell J. & Berdan, Frances F. The Emperor's Mirror: Concepts, Methods, & Strategies in Ethnohistory. LC 97-45412. (Illus.). 430p. 1998. pap. 24.95 (*0-8165-1848-3*) U of Ariz Pr.

— The Emperor's Mirror: Understanding Cultures Through Primary Sources. LC 97-45412. (Illus.). 430p. 1998. 45.00 (*0-8165-1847-5*) U of Ariz Pr.

Barber, Russell J., et al. Reading the Global Past, Vol. I. LC 97-80446. 1998. pap. text 12.95 (*0-312-17184-6*) St Martin.

Barber, Russell J., jt. auth. see Berdan, Frances F.

Barber, S. Adagio: For Strings Flute Quartet. 1991. pap. 12.00 (*0-7935-0756-1*) H Leonard.

— Agnus Dei: From Adagio for Strings Opus 11. (LAT.). 12p. 1986. pap. 1.25 (*0-7935-5493-4*, 50313910) H Leonard.

— Canzone for Flute & Piano: From Opus 38 Transcribed from the Second Movement of the Piano Concerto. 12p. 1986. pap. 4.95 (*0-7935-3816-5*, 50289400) H Leonard.

— Canzonetta for Oboe & Piano. 12p. 1993. pap. 8.95 (*0-7935-3075-X*) H Leonard.

— Collected Songs High Voice & Piano. (American Composers Ser.). 140p. 1986. per. 19.95 (*0-7935-5337-7*, 50328790) H Leonard.

— Complete Piano Music of Samuel Barber. (American Composer Ser.). 120p. 1986. pap. 12.95 (*0-7935-2462-8*, 50336700) H Leonard.

— Concerto for Violin & Orchestra Opus 14: Study Score, No. 75. 84p. 1987. pap. 18.00 (*0-7935-5562-0*, 50339370) H Leonard.

— Concerto Violin Opus 14: Orchestra. 36p. 1986. pap. 17.95 (*0-7935-5458-6*, 50337010) H Leonard.

— Dover Beach: Medium Voice & String Quartet for Voice & Piano. 16p. 1986. pap. 4.95 (*0-7935-3723-1*, 50279610) H Leonard.

— Essay for Orchestra Score. 48p. 1990. pap. 15.00 (*0-7935-1020-1*) H Leonard.

— Hermit Songs: High Voice Piano. 32p. 1987. pap. 8.95 (*0-7935-5209-5*, 50328820) H Leonard.

— Knoxville Summer, 1915 Now 151: Vocal/Orchestra Opus 24 Study Score. 52p. 1986. pap. 20.00 (*0-7935-4081-X*, 50339220) H Leonard.

— Medea: Chamber Orchestra Score. 144p. 1991. pap. 40.00 (*0-7935-0913-0*) H Leonard.

— Piano Concerto: 2 Pianos, 4 Hands. 88p. 1987. pap. 17.95 (*0-7935-3812-2*, 50289380) H Leonard.

— Piano Concerto Opus 38: Study Score. 144p. 1986. per. 35.00 (*0-7935-3946-3*, 50339520) H Leonard.
— Souvenirs Ballet Suite Opus 28: One Piano, Four Hands Original. 68p. 1986. pap. 19.95 (*0-7935-4991-4*, 50286370) H Leonard.
— String Quartet Opus 11: Study Score, No. 28. 20p. 1986. pap. 15.00 (*0-7935-5560-4*, 50338950) H Leonard.
— Sure on This Shining Night Opus 13, No. 3. 8p. 1986. pap. 1.25 (*0-7935-5481-0*, 50308930) H Leonard.
— Ten Early Songs for Middle Voice & Piano. 32p. 1994. pap. 8.95 (*0-7935-3709-6*) H Leonard.
— Third Essay: For Orchestra Full Score. 56p. 1991. pap. 25.00 (*0-7935-0934-3*, 50481210) H Leonard.
— Three Songs Opus 45 Low Voice & Piano. 20p. 1995. pap. 8.95 (*0-7935-3837-8*, 50333030) H Leonard.
— Two Scenes Antony & Cleopatra: Soprano Piano: Scene 1. Give Me Some Music; Scene 2. Death of Cleopatra. 64p. 1986. pap. 10.00 (*0-7935-1796-6*, 50339660) H Leonard.
— Vanessa: Vocal Score. 272p. 1986. pap. 45.00 (*0-7935-5125-0*, 50338080) H Leonard.
— Vanessa Libretto. 48p. 1986. pap. 4.95 (*0-7935-2922-0*, 50340390) H Leonard.

Barber, S. A. & Bouldin, D. R., eds. Roots, Nutrient & Water Influx, & Plant Growth. (ASA Special Publications: No. 49). 136p. 1984. 12.00 (*0-89118-082-6*) Am Soc Agron.

Barber, Sara, ed. see Maradona, Remigio M.

***Barber, Sarah.** A Revolutionary Rogue: Henry Marten & the Immoral English Republic. (Illus.). 224p. 2000. 39.95 (*0-7509-2304-0*) Sutton Publng.

Barber, Sarah, jt. auth. see Ellis, Steven G.

Barber, Sarah L. Connections: Using Multicultural, Racial, & Ethnic Short Stories to Promote Better Writing. rev. ed. 272p. (C). 1994. pap. text, per. 27.95 (*0-8403-8033-X*) Kendall-Hunt.

Barber, Sotirios A. The Constitution & the Delegation of Congressional Power. LC 74-16688. x, 154p. 1975. lib. bdg. 17.50 (*0-226-03705-3*) U Ch Pr.
— The Constitution & the Delegation of Congressional Power. LC 74-16688. 162p. Date not set. reprint ed. pap. 50.30 (*0-608-20987-2*, 205451500003) Bks Demand.
— The Constitution of Judicial Power. LC 93-20096. (Constitutional Thought Ser.). 304p. (C). 1993. 30.00 (*0-8018-4587-4*) Johns Hopkins.
— The Constitution of Judicial Power: Defending the Activist Tradition. LC 93-20096. (Series in Constitutional Thought). 296p. 1997. reprint ed. pap. text 15.95 (*0-8018-5790-2*) Johns Hopkins.
— On What the Constitution Means. LC 83-48049. 256p. 1983. 38.00 (*0-8018-3020-6*) Johns Hopkins.
— On What the Constitution Means. LC 83-48049. 240p. 1986. reprint ed. pap. text 14.95 (*0-8018-3344-2*) Johns Hopkins.

Barber, Sotirios A., jt. ed. see Kommers, Donald P.

Barber, Stanley A. Soil Nutrient Bioavailability: A Mechanistic Approach. 2nd ed. LC 94-22899. (Illus.). 414p. 1995. 110.00 (*0-471-58747-8*) Wiley.

Barber-Starkey, Joe. Winter of Raven. 432p. 1996. mass mkt. 5.99 (*0-8125-2435-7*) Tor Bks.

Barber, Stephen. Antonin Artaud: Blows & Bombs. (Illus.). 176p. 1994. pap. 10.95 (*0-571-17252-0*) Faber & Faber.

***Barber, Stephen.** Artaud: The Screaming Body. 1999. pap. text 19.95 (*1-84068-009-1*) Creation Books.

Barber, Stephen. Edmund White: The Burning World. LC 98-33116. 224p. 1999. text 25.95 (*0-312-19974-0*) St Martin.
— Edmund White: The Burning World: The Authorized Biography. (Illus.). 224p. 1999. 27.50 (*0-330-34966-X*) Trans-Atl Phila.
— Fragments of the European City. LC 96-189235. (Topographics Ser.). 108p. 1997. pap. 18.95 (*0-948462-66-3*, Pub. by Reaktion Bks) Consort Bk Sales.

Barber, Steve. Legal Writing. 2nd ed. LC 96-21164. (Paralegal Ser.). 416p. (C). 1997. mass mkt. 42.95 (*0-8273-7539-5*) Delmar.
— Legal Writing for Paralegals. 1993. 48.00 (*0-538-70631-7*) S-W Pub.

Barber, Steve & McCormick, Mark. Legal Research. rev. ed. LC 95-21728. (Paralegal Ser.). 448p. (C). 1995. mass mkt. 44.95 (*0-8273-7474-7*) Delmar.

Barber, Sue. Hysterectomy, Woman to Woman. LC 95-80366. 212p. 1996. pap. 14.95 (*1-885221-15-0*) BookPartners.

Barber, Susanna. News Cameras in the Courtroom: A Free Press-Fair Trial Debate. Voigt, Melvin J., ed. LC 86-10858. (Communication & Information Science Ser.). 176p. 1987. text 73.25 (*0-89391-349-9*) Ablx Pub.

***Barber, Terri.** Garden Ponds for Dummies. (For Dummies Ser.). (Illus.). 2000. pap. 19.99 (*0-7645-5256-2*) IDG Bks.

Barber, Terry. The Complete Idiot's Guide to Garden Ponds. (Illus.). 352p. Date not set. pap. 16.95 (*1-58245-064-1*) Howell Bks.

***Barber, Terry, ed.** Welcome Home! Stories of Men & Women Who Were Raised Catholic, Left the Church & then Returned. 221p. 2000. pap. 12.95 (*0-89870-792-7*, Pub. by Ignatius Pr) Midpt Trade.

Barber, Theodore X. Hypnosis: A Scientific Approach. LC 95-37615. 298p. 1995. pap. 55.00 (*1-56821-740-4*) Aronson.

Barber, Theodore X., et al, eds. Advances in Altered States of Consciousness & Human Potentialities, Vol. 1. LC 76-42132. 700p. 1980. 69.95 (*0-88437-002-X*) Psych Dimensions.

Barber, Theodore X. & Goldstein, A. Pitfalls in Human Research: 10 Pivotal Points. LC 76-13488. (General Psychology Ser.: No. 67). 128p. 1976. 64.00 (*0-08-020935-1*, BF76, Pub. by Pergamon Repr) Franklin.

Barber, Theodore X., et al. Hypnosis, Imagination & Human Potentialities. LC 73-19539. 1974. pap. text 22.00 (*0-08-017931-2*, Pergamon Pr) Elsevier.

Barber, Thomas. Pharmaceutical Particulate Matter: Analysis & Control. (Illus.). 531p. 1993. 126.75 (*0-935184-29-5*) Interpharm.

Barber, Thomas A. Control of Particulate Matter Contamination in Healthcare Manufacturing, Vol. 1. LC 99-18307. (Illus.). 500p. 1998. 193.00 (*1-57491-072-8*) Interpharm.

Barber, Thomas H. Where We Are At. (Right Wing Individualist Tradition in America Ser.). 1972. reprint ed. 21.95 (*0-405-00412-5*, 71-172202) Ayer.

***Barber, Thomas M.** The Cabin by the Creek. 696p. 2000. 19.95 (*1-886699-29-1*) Five Corners.

***Barber, Tom.** The Gospel According to the Serpent. 105p. 2000. pap. 9.95 (*1-891429-08-6*) Armadillo Pubng.

Barber, V. C. & Mascorro, J. A., eds. Electron Microscopy Safety Handbook. 2nd ed. (Illus.). 1994. pap. 20.00 (*0-911302-72-7*) San Francisco Pr.

***Barber, Wayne.** Following God Bible Study. 1999. pap., wbk. ed. 79.99 (*0-89957-305-3*) AMG Pubs.

Barber, Wayne. Life Principles from the Old Testament. (Following God Ser.). 1998. pap. text 16.99 (*0-89957-300-2*) AMG Pubs.
— The Rest of Grace: Entering into the Wonder of the Christ Life. LC 98-6164. 224p. 1998. pap. 9.99 (*1-56507-944-2*) Harvest Hse.

Barber, Wendy, jt. auth. see Hinchcliffe, John.

Barber, Will. The Monsters' Tea Party, Vol. 4353. Graves, Kimberlee, ed. (Fun & Fantasy Ser.). (Illus.). 16p. (J). (ps-1). 1997. pap. 2.75 (*1-57471-250-0*, 4353) Creat Teach Pr.
— People Say Hello, Vol. 3904. Williams, Rozanne L., ed. (Social Studies Learn to Read Ser.). (Illus.). 8p. (J). (ps-2). 1996. pap. 1.75 (*1-57471-123-7*, 3904) Creat Teach Pr.
— People Say Hello, Vol. 3961. Williams, Rozanne L., ed. (Social Studies Big Bks.). (Illus.). 8p. (J). (ps-2). 1997. pap. 8.98 (*1-57471-169-5*, 3961) Creat Teach Pr.

Barber, Will, ed. Texas Court Charge Series, 8 vols., Vols. 1-8. Date not set. ring bd. 544.00 (*0-409-25689-7*, 82492, MICHIE) LEXIS Pub.
— Texas Court's Charge Series Vol. 7: Probate/Family Law, Vol. 7. (Texas Court's Charge Ser.). 240p. Date not set. ring bd. 85.00 (*0-409-25687-0*, 82523, MICHIE) LEXIS Pub.

Barber, Will G., ed. Court's Charge Reporter (TX) 100p. Date not set. ring bd. 200.00 (*0-409-25340-5*, 82658, MICHIE) LEXIS Pub.
— Texas Court's Charge Series: Banking & Debtor-Creditor, Vol. 5. 370p. Date not set. ring bd. 85.00 (*0-409-25683-8*, 82513, MICHIE) LEXIS Pub.
— Texas Court's Charge Series: Commercial Contracts. 240p. Date not set. ring bd. 85.00 (*0-409-25681-1*, 82508, MICHIE) LEXIS Pub.
— Texas Court's Charge Series: Commercial Torts & DTPA, Vol. 3. 300p. Date not set. ring bd. 85.00 (*0-409-25680-3*, 82503, MICHIE) LEXIS Pub.
— Texas Court's Charge Series: Insurance, Vol. 2. 240p. Date not set. ring bd. 85.00 (*0-409-25679-X*, 82498, MICHIE) LEXIS Pub.
— Texas Court's Charge Series: Negligence Actions, Vol. 8. 350p. Date not set. ring bd. 85.00 (*0-409-25677-3*, 82528, MICHIE) LEXIS Pub.
— Texas Court's Charge Series: Real Property/Landlord Tenant, Vol. 6. 450p. Date not set. ring bd. 85.00 (*0-409-25682-X*, 82518, MICHIE) LEXIS Pub.
— Texas Courts Series: Labor & Employment, Vol. 1. 250p. Date not set. ring bd. 85.00 (*0-409-25678-1*, 82493, MICHIE) LEXIS Pub.

Barber, William A. The Impressed Duty Stamps of the British Colonial Empire. (Illus.). 164p. 1998. pap. text 30.00 (*0-9613725-2-4*) W A Barber.

Barber, William J. Designs Within Disorder: Franklin D. Roosevelt, the Economists, & the Shaping of American Economic Policy, 1933-1945. (Historical Perspectives on Modern Economics Ser.). 190p. (C). 1996. text 52.95 (*0-521-56078-0*) Cambridge U Pr.
— The Economy of British Central Africa: A Case Study of Economic Development in a Dualistic Society. LC 84-19119. 271p. 1984. reprint ed. lib. bdg. 69.50 (*0-313-24619-X*, BBCA, Greenwood Pr) Greenwood.

Barber, William J., ed. Perspectives on the History of Economic Thought: Themes in Keynesian Criticism & Supplementary Modern Topics, Vol. VI. (Perspectives on the History of Economic Thought Ser.). 176p. 1991. text 90.00 (*1-85278-364-8*) E Elgar.
— Perspectives on the History of Economic Thought Vol. 5: Themes in Pre-Classical & Marxian Economics. (Perspectives on the History of Economic Thought Ser.). 176p. 1991. text 90.00 (*1-85278-363-X*) E Elgar.

Barber, William J., intro. Economists & Higher Learning in the Nineteenth Century: Breaking the American Academic Mold. rev. ed. LC 92-32939. 556p. (C). 1993. pap. 29.95 (*1-56000-656-0*) Transaction Pubs.

Barber, William J., ed. see Fisher, Irving.

Barber, Williams J., ed. see Jeffery, David, et al.

Barbera, Andre. The Euclidean Division of the Canon: Greek & Latin Sources. LC 91-35207. (Greek & Latin Music Theory Ser.). (Illus.). xii, 316p. 1991. text 45.00 (*0-8032-1220-8*) U of Nebr Pr.

Barbera, Andre, ed. Music Theory & Its Sources: Antiquity & the Middle Ages. LC 89-40390. (Conferences in Medieval Studies: Vol. 1). (C). 1990. text 57.50 (*0-268-01379-9*) U of Notre Dame Pr.

Barbera, Greg, et al. Stovepiper. (Illus.). 144p. (Orig.). 1994. pap. 12.95 (*0-9642339-0-8*) Stovepiper Bks.

Barbera, Hanna. My First Box of Prayers, 4 bks. (Illus.). (J). (gr. 2 up). 1988. 8.95 (*0-687-27539-3*) Abingdon.

Barbera, Henry. The Military Factor in Social Change Vol. 1: From Provincial to Political Society. LC 97-20090. (State As Revolution Ser.). 280p. 1997. text 39.95 (*1-56000-342-1*) Transaction Pubs.
— The Military Factor in Social Change Vol. 2: The State As Revolution. LC 97-20090. 370p. 1998. text 45.95 (*1-56000-356-1*) Transaction Pubs.

Barbera, Jack & McBrien, William. Stevie: A Biography of Stevie Smith. LC 87-673122. 378 p. 1986. 7.95 (*0-333-42671-1*) Macmillan.

Barbera, Jack, et al. Stevie Smith: A Bibliography. (Twentieth Century Literary Bibliographies Ser.). 183p. 1987. lib. bdg. 55.00 (*0-313-27666-8*) Greenwood.

***Barbera, Joe.** My Life in 'Toons: From Flatbush to Bedrock in Under a Century. 250p. 2000. reprint ed. 20.00 (*0-7881-9308-2*) DIANE Pub.

***Barbera, Maria & Coyte, Rodney.** Shareholder Value Demystified: An Explanation of Methodologies & Use. 80p. 1999. pap. 19.95 (*0-86840-697-X*, Pub. by New South Wales Univ Pr) Intl Spec Bk.

***Barbera, Maria, et al.** Innovative Management Accounting: Insights from Practice. 80p. 1999. pap. 19.95 (*0-86840-705-4*, Pub. by New South Wales Univ Pr) Intl Spec Bk.

***Barbera, Mia.** Washington & Oregon. (Rails-to-Trails Ser.). (Illus.). 256p. 2000. pap. 14.95 (*0-7627-0696-.*) Globe Pequot.

Barbera, Thomas V., et al. Death & Dying: A Guide for Staff Serving Adults with Mental Retardation. 392p. 1989. lib. bdg. 15.95 (*0-313-28385-0*) Greenwood.

Barberis, Bruno. Shroud, Carbon-Dating & Calculus of Probabilities. 1996. pap. 39.95 (*0-85439-537-7*, Pub. by St Paul Pubns) St Mut.

Barberis, Daniele. Negotiating Mining Agreements: Past, Present & Future Trends. LC 98-30195. (International Energy & Resources Law & Policy Ser.). 288p. 1998. 111.00 (*90-411-9673-0*) Kluwer Academic.

Barberis, France. Would You Like a Parrot? LC 67-28671. (Illus.). 32p. (J). (ps). 16.95 (*0-87592-060-8*) Scroll Pr.

Barberis, Peter. The Elite of the Elite: Permanent Secretaries in the British Higher Civil Service. (Illus.). 304p. 1996. text 83.95 (*1-85521-479-2*, Pub. by Dartmth Pub) Ashgate Pub Co.
— Encyclopedia of British & Irish Political Organizations: Parties, Groups, & Movements of the Twentieth Century. LC 98-52555. 1999. 150.00 (*1-85567-264-2*) P P Pubs.
— The Whitehall Reader: The U. K.'s Administrative Machine in Action. LC 95-24921. 256p. 1996. 103.95 (*0-335-19312-9*); pap. 34.95 (*0-335-19311-0*) OpUniv Pr.

Barberis, Peter, ed. The Civil Service in an Era of Change. LC 96-35394. (Illus.). 192p. 1997. text 72.95 (*1-85521-805-4*, Pub. by Dartmth Pub) Ashgate Pub Co.

Barberis, Peter & May, Timothy. Government, Industry & Political Economy. LC 93-10130. 1993. 123.00 (*0-335-15681-9*); pap. 40.95 (*0-335-15680-0*) OpUniv Pr.

Barbernitz, Patricia. Parish Ministry for Returning Catholics. LC 93-5901. 128p. (Orig.). 1994. pap. 6.95 (*0-8091-3441-1*) Paulist Pr.
— RCIA Team Manual: How to Implement the Rite of Christian Initiation of Adults in Your Parish. 88p. 1986. pap. 8.95 (*0-8091-2814-4*) Paulist Pr.

Barbero, B. J., jt. ed. see Martinez, J. R.

Barbero, Ever J. Introduction to Composite Materials Design. LC 98-21968. 336p. 1998. 65.00 (*1-56032-701-4*) Hemisp Pub.

Barbero, G., et al, eds. Optics of Liquid Crystals: Optics & Interfacial Phenomena in Liquid Crystals & Polymers: Proceedings of the 2nd International Topical Meeting, Italy, October 1988, A Special Issue of the Journal Molecular Crystals & Liquid Crystals. xiv, 470p. 1990. pap. text 1382.00 (*2-88124-403-3*) Gordon & Breach.

Barbero, G. & Evangelista, L. R. Elementary Course on the Continuum Theory for Nematic Liquid Crystals. 400p. 1997. text 46.00 (*981-02-3224-1*) World Scientific Pub.

Barbero, Luca M. Conrad Marca-Relli. (Illus.). 188p. 1999. 75.00 (*0-295-97802-3*) U of Wash Pr.

Barberousse. Writing about Literature. (C). 1993. pap. text 3.96 (*0-395-67166-3*) HM.

Barberousse, Michel, ed. Dictionnaire de la Voile: Dictionary of Flight. (FRE.). 256p. 1970. pap. 19.95 (*0-8288-6514-0*, M6606) Fr & Eur.

Barbery, Willard S. Brother Sheffey. 1979. pap. 8.99 (*0-88019-005-1*) Schmul Pub Co.

Barbet, Jean. Architecture of Altars & Chimneys: Livre d'Architecture d'Auteb et Te Cheminees, 1633, 2 vols. (Printed Sources of Western Art Ser.). (FRE., Illus.). 1981. reprint ed. pap., boxed set 55.00 (*0-915346-59-1*) A Wofsy Fine Arts.

Barbet, Pierre. A Doctor at Calvary: The Passion of Our Lord Jesus Christ As Described by a Surgeon. Earl of Wicklow, tr. from FRE. (Illus.). 192p. 1993. reprint ed. text 15.75 (*0-912141-04-2*) Roman Cath Bks.

Barbett, Samuel. Current Funds Revenues & Expenditures of Institutions of Higher Education: Fiscal Years 1987 Through 1995. 62p. 1997. pap. 5.00 (*0-16-049209-2*) USGPO.
— Residence & Migration of First Time Freshmen Enrolled in Higher Education Institutions: Fall 1994. 43p. 1996. pap. 3.50 (*0-16-063578-0*) USGPO.

Barbett, Samuel & National Center for Education Statistics Staff. Fall Enrollment in Postsecondary Institutions, 1996. LC 98-229311. (Education Department Publication NCES 99 Ser.: Vol. 239) (Illus.). 169p. 1998. pap. 14.00 (*0-16-049835-X*) USGPO.

Barbett, Samuel F. Enrollment in Higher Education: Fall 1995. LC 97-214093. 186p. 1997. per. 16.00 (*0-16-049131-2*) USGPO.

Barbetta, Gian P. Defining the Nonprofit Sector: Italy. Salamon, Lester M. & Anheier, Helmut K., eds. (Working Papers of the Johns Hopkins Comparative Nonprofit Sector Project: No. 8). (Illus.). 16p. 1993. pap. text 6.00 (*1-886333-10-6*) JH Univ Inst Pol Studies.
— The Nonprofit Sector in Italy. LC 97-12999. (Johns Hopkins Nonprofit Sector Ser.). 1997. text. write for info. (*0-7190-5086-3*) Manchester Univ Pr.
— The Nonprofit Sector in Italy. LC 97-12999. (Johns Hopkins Nonprofit Sector Ser.). 1997. text 59.95 (*0-7190-5085-5*, Pub. by Manchester Univ Pr) St Martin.

Barbetta, Sue. Nilla's Big Adventure. (Illus.). 32p. (J). (gr. k-3). 1998. pap. 4.95 (*1-892774-00-3*) Bullfrog Pubg.

***Barbetta, Sue.** Surprise under the Sea. (Undersea Adventure Ser.). (Illus.). 48p. (J). (gr. 1-2). 1999. pap. 6.95 (*1-892774-01-1*) Bullfrog Pubg.

Barbey d'Aurevilly, Jules. Le Cachet d'Onyx. Lea. (FRE.). 1991. pap. 15.95 (*0-7859-3331-X*, 2905964553) Fr & Eur.
— Le Chevalier des Touches. (FRE.). 192p. 1965. pap. 10.95 (*0-7859-2185-0*, 2080700634) Fr & Eur.
— Dandyism. Ainslie, Douglas, tr. from FRE. (Illus.). 96p. (C). 1988. reprint ed. pap. 8.95 (*1-55554-035-X*) PAJ Pubns.
— Les Diaboliques. (FRE.). 1987. pap. 11.95 (*0-7859-1736-5*, 2070363422) Fr & Eur.
— L' Ensorcelee. (FRE.). 309p. 1987. pap. 10.95 (*0-7859-1842-6*, 2070369102) Fr & Eur.
— Une Histoire sans Nom. (FRE.). 192p. 1990. pap. 10.95 (*0-7859-2186-9*, 2080705881) Fr & Eur.
— Oeuvres Romanesque Completes, 2 vols., Vol. 1. deluxe ed. Petit, Marcel, ed. (FRE.). 1536p. 1964. lib. bdg. 115.00 (*0-7859-3740-4*, 2070100480) Fr & Eur.
— Oeuvres Romanesques Completes, 2 vols., Vol. 2. deluxe ed. Petit, Jacques, ed. (FRE.). 1712p. 1966. lib. bdg. 120.00 (*0-7859-3741-2*, 2070100499) Fr & Eur.
— Un Pretre Marie. (FRE.). 1980. pap. 16.95 (*0-7859-1913-9*, 2070371832) Fr & Eur.

Barbey, Dorine. Giant Works: Underground, over Water, in the Air. (Young Discovery Library). (Illus.). 40p. (J). (gr. k-6). 1993. lib. bdg. 2.99 (*1-56674-059-2*, HTS Bks) Forest Hse.
— Giant Works: Underground, over Water, in the Air. Bogard, Vicki, tr. from FRE. LC 91-48167. (Illus.). 38p. (J). (gr. k-5). 1992. 5.95 (*0-944589-44-8*) Young Discovery Lib.
— People at Work. LC 97-23938. (Illus.). 80p. (YA). (gr. 4 up). 2000. lib. bdg. 25.30 (*0-88682-954-2*, Creat Educ) Creative Co.

Barbey, Dorine, et al. Animals Around Us. Gibson, Sarah et al, trs. LC 97-27541. (Illus.). 80p. (J). (gr. 2-9). 1998. lib. bdg. 23.95 (*0-88682-943-7*, Creat Educ) Creative Co.
— Creative Discoveries, 8 vols. (Illus.). 640p. (J). lib. bdg. 191.60 (*0-88682-942-9*) Creative Co.

Barbey, Graham J., jt. auth. see Tetlow, Roger T.

Barbezat, Daniel, jt. auth. see Neal, Larry D.

Barbi, Michele. Chaos & Noise in Biology & Medicine. (Series on Biophysics & Biocybernetics). 1998. 76.00 (*981-02-3600-X*) World Scientific Pub.

***Barbi, Sia.** Barbi Twins-Dying to Be Healthy: Millennium Dieting & Nutrition. 208p. 2000. pap. 12.95 (*1-892676-11-7*, Pub. by ICD Inc) ACCESS Pubs Network.

Barbi Twins. History of the Barbi Twins. Conte, Robert V., ed. (Illus.). 48p. 1998. pap. 19.95 (*1-890313-01-7*, RCTP9702) Studio Chikara.

Barbich, Sheryl L. The Quick & Easy Guide to Delegation: Key to Profitability & Growth. LC 95-48471. 1996. write for info. (*0-87051-173-4*) Am Inst CPA.
— The Quick & Easy Guide to Delegation: Key to Profitability & Growth. LC 96-6142. 1996. write for info. (*0-87051-176-9*) Am Inst CPA.
— Strategic Planning: A Step-by-Step Guide to Building a Successful CPA Firm. LC 93-31677. 1993. 41.25 (*0-87051-140-8*) Am Inst CPA.

Barbie, Richard. Shrew! - Musical. 110p. 1977. pap. 5.95 (*0-87129-108-8*, S03) Dramatic Pub.

Barbier, Abigail. Quick Patchwork Projects. LC 98-115177. (Illus.). 128p. 1998. 24.95 (*0-7063-7562-9*, Pub. by WrLock) Sterling.

Barbier, Antoine-Alexandre. Dictionnaire des Ouvrages Anonymes. 3rd ed. (FRE.). 1646p. 1964. lib. bdg. 995.00 (*0-8288-2493-2*, F12410) Fr & Eur.
— Dictionnaire des Ouvrages Anonymes, 4 vols., Set. (FRE.). xlv, 2533p. 1986. reprint ed. 650.00 (*3-487-00550-6*) G Olms Pubs.

Barbier, E., ed. The Application of Nuclear Techniques in Geothermal Investigations. 192p. 1983. pap. 61.00 (*0-08-030269-6*, 2304, 1506, 1901, Pergamon Pr) Elsevier.
— The Application of Nuclear Techniques to Geothermal Studies: Proceedings. 1978. pap. 94.00 (*0-08-021670-6*, Pergamon Pr) Elsevier.
— Cerro Prieto Geothermal Field: Proceedings of the First Symposium Held at San Diego, California, Sept. 1978. (Illus.). 300p. 1981. pap. 94.00 (*0-08-026241-4*, Pergamon Pr) Elsevier.
— Cerro Prieto Geothermal Field: Proceedings of the Second Symposium, 17-19 October 1979, Mexicali, Mexico-Selected Papers. 144p. 1982. pap. 46.00 (*0-08-028746-8*, Pergamon Pr) Elsevier.

Barbier, E. & Trindade, M., eds. Utilization of Geothermal Energy for Electric Power Production & Space Heating. (Selected Papers from the UNECE Seminar Held in Florence, Italy 14-17 May 1984). 392p. 1985. pap. 61.00 (*0-08-032638-2*, Pergamon Pr) Elsevier.

Barbier, E., et al. Paradise Lost. 1994. 32.00 (*1-85383-181-6*, Pub. by Escan Pubns) Island Pr.

B

Barbier, Edward B. The Economics of Environment & Development: Selected Essays. LC 97-33566. 576p. 1998. 120.00 (*1-85898-685-0*) E Elgar.

Barbier, Edward B., jt. auth. see Pearce, David.

Barbier, Edward B., jt. ed. see Swanson, Timothy M.

Barbier, George. The Illustrations of George Barbier in Full Color. LC 76-42589. (Illus.). 47p. (Orig.). 1977. pap. 7.95 (*0-486-23476-2*) Dover.

Barbier, J. & Henry, J. F., eds. Primary Hyperparathyroidism: Report Presented at the 93rd French Surgical Congress, Paris, September 1991. 168p. 1993. 96.95 (*0-387-59578-3*) Spr-Verlag.

***Barbier, Jean P., ed.** A Guide to Pre-Columbian Art. (Illus.). 98p. 1999. pap. 12.95 (*88-8118-252-1*, Pub. by Skira IT) Abbeville Pr.

Barbier, Jean P., et al, eds. Islands & Ancestors: Indigenous Styles of Southeast Asia. (Illus.). 364p. 1988. 85.00 (*3-7913-0899-8*, Pub. by Prestel) te Neues.

Barbier, Jean P. & Hugues, Francois C. Dictionnaires des Maladies. (FRE.). 528p. 1973. 59.95 (*0-7859-0725-4*, M6022) Fr & Eur.

Barbier, John. Eastern Sierra Fishing Guide for Day Hikers. (Illus.). 125p. 1998. pap. 14.95 (*0-9651967-1-2*) J Barbier.

— Trout Man of the Sierra: Life As a Fishing Bum. 1999. pap. 12.95 (*0-9651967-2-0*) J Barbier.

Barbier, John & Perkins, William P. Guide to Employee Recruitment & Hiring. 500p. 1996. 186.00 (*0-7913-2609-8*) Warren Gorham & Lamont.

Barbier, Maurice. Dictionary of Construction & Public Works: Dictionnaire du Batiment et des Travaux Publics. (ENG & FRE.). 176p. 1985. 69.95 (*0-8288-1325-6*, M4642) Fr & Eur.

Barbier, Maurice, et al. Diccionario Tecnico Ilustrado de Edificacion y Obras Publicas. (SPA.). 177p. 1981. pap. 29.95 (*0-8288-1327-2*, S50273) Fr & Eur.

Barbier, Patrick. The World of the Castrati: The History of an Extraordinary Operatic Phenomenon. 1999. pap. text 17.95 (*0-285-63460-7*) IPG Chicago.

Barbier, Yves. Oil Dictionary: Dictionnaire du Petrole. (ENG & FRE.). 272p. 1980. pap. 175.00 (*0-8288-0696-9*, M15455) Fr & Eur.

Barbieri, Cesare, et al, eds. The Three Galileos: The Man, the Spacecraft, the Telescope: Proceedings of the Conference Held in Padova, Italy on January 7-10, 1997. LC 97-45515. (Astrophysics & Space Science Library). 480p. 1998. text 217.50 (*0-7923-4861-3*) Kluwer Academic.

Barbieri, E., jt. auth. see DiGregorio, G. John.

***Barbieri, Edward J., et al.** Handbook of Commonly Prescribed Pediatric Drugs. 6th ed. 250p. 1998. 18.50 (*0-942447-27-1*) Med Surveill.

Barbieri, Edward J., jt. auth. see DiGregorio, G John.

Barbieri, Elaine. Amber Fire. 512p. (Orig.). 1998. mass mkt. 5.99 (*0-505-52290-X*, Love Spell) Dorchester Pub Co.

***Barbieri, Elaine.** Amber Treasure. 496p. (Orig.). 2000. pap. 5.99 (*0-505-52370-1*, Leisure Bks) Dorchester Pub Co.

Barbieri, Elaine. Captive Ecstasy. 1981. mass mkt. 2.75 (*0-89083-738-4*, Zebra Kensgtn) Kensgtn Pub Corp.

— Captive Ecstasy. 432p. 1997. reprint ed. mass mkt. 5.50 (*0-505-52224-1*, Love Spell) Dorchester Pub Co.

— Chastity. (Dangerous Virtues Ser.: Vol. 3). 384p. (Orig.). 1998. mass mkt. 5.99 (*0-8439-4339-4*, Leisure Bks) Dorchester Pub Co.

***Barbieri, Elaine.** Eagle. 400p. 1999. mass mkt. 5.99 (*0-8439-4469-2*, Leisure Bks) Dorchester Pub Co.

— Hawk. 400p. (Orig.). 1999. mass mkt. 5.99 (*0-8439-4646-6*, Leisure Bks) Dorchester Pub Co.

— Love's Fiery Jewel. 512p. 2000. pap. 5.99 (*0-505-52391-4*, Love Spell) Dorchester Pub Co.

— Night Raven. 400p. 2000. mass mkt. 5.99 (*0-8439-4723-3*, Leisure Bks) Dorchester Pub Co.

Barbieri, Elaine. Race for Tomorrow. (Orig.). 1993. per. 3.99 (*0-373-83243-5*, 1-83243-5) Harlequin Bks.

— Stark Lightning. (Men at Work Ser.). 224p. 1999. per. 4.50 (*0-373-81038-5*) Harlequin Bks.

— Tarnished Angel. 448p. 1998. reprint ed. mass mkt. 5.50 (*0-505-52250-0*, Love Spell) Dorchester Pub Co.

— Wings of a Dove, 1 vol. (Love Spell Ser.). 464p. 1999. mass mkt. 5.99 (*0-505-52323-X*) Dorchester Pub Co.

***Barbieri, Elaine.** Wishes on the Wind. 432p. 1999. mass mkt. 5.50 (*0-505-52348-5*, Love Spell) Dorchester Pub Co.

Barbieri, Elaine, et al. Mistletoe Marriages: Rendezvous; The Wolf & the Lamb; Christmas in the Valley; Keeping Christmas. 1994. per. 4.99 (*0-373-83309-1*, 1-83309-4) Harlequin Bks.

***Barbieri, Elaine, et al.** Something Borrowed, Something Blue. 400p. 2000. mass mkt. 5.99 (*0-8439-4725-X*, Leisure Bks) Dorchester Pub Co.

***Barbieri, Gian P.** Equator. 1999. 29.99 (*3-8228-6623-7*) Taschen Amer.

Barbieri, Gian P. Madagascar. (Photo & Sexy Bks.). 1997. 29.99 (*3-8228-8262-3*) Taschen Amer.

— Tahiti Tattoos. 1998. 29.99 (*3-8228-7763-8*) Taschen Amer.

***Barbieri, Gian Paolo.** Tahiti Tattoos. (SPA.). 128p. 1998. 38.99 (*3-8228-8038-8*) Benedikt Taschen.

Barbieri, Heather D. Seattle Emergency Espresso: The Insider's Guide to Neighborhood Coffee Spots. LC 92-20627. (Illus.). 180p. (Orig.). 1992. pap. 9.95 (*0-88240-399-0*, Alaska NW Bks) Gr Arts Ctr Pub.

Barbieri, I., et al. Topics on Biomathematics: Proceedings of the Second International Conference. 352p. 1993. text 105.00 (*981-02-1490-1*) World Scientific Pub.

Barbieri, Louis. First & Second Peter. (Everyman's Bible Commentaries Ser.). pap. 9.99 (*0-8024-2061-3*, 496) Moody.

— Mark. LC 96-207803. (Gospel Commentaries Ser.). pap. 21.99 (*0-8024-5450-X*, 516) Moody.

Barbieri, Louis A. Primera y Segunda Pedro. (Comentario Biblico Portavoz Ser.). Orig. Title: First & Second Peter, (Everyman's Bible Commentary). (SPA.). 144p. 1981. pap. 6.99 (*0-8254-1051-7*, Edit Portavoz) Kregel.

Barbieri, M. The Semantic Theory of Evolution. Hahn, R. et al, eds. (Models of Scientific Thought Ser.: Vol. 2). 188p. 1985. pap. text 53.00 (*3-7186-0397-7*) Gordon & Breach.

Barbieri, Marcello. The Semantic Theory of Evolution. (Models of Scientific Thought Ser.: Vol. 2). xii, 188p. 1985. text 96.00 (*3-7186-0243-1*) Gordon & Breach.

Barbieri, Maureen. Sounds from the Heart: Learning to Listen to Girls. LC 94-45705. 249p. 1995. pap. text 21.00 (*0-435-08843-2*, 08843) Heinemann.

Barbieri, Maureen & Rief, Linda, eds. Workshop 6: The Teacher As Writer. (Workshops by & for Teachers Ser.). 113p. 1994. pap. text 18.50 (*0-435-08816-5*, 08816) Heinemann.

Barbieri, Maureen & Tateishi, Carol. Meeting the Challenges in Today's Classroom. LC 96-20397. 1996. pap. text 24.00 (*0-435-07225-0*) Heinemann.

Barbieri, Maureen, jt. ed. see Rief, Linda.

Barbieri, Nello, tr. see Wilson, Blake, ed.

Barbieri, Paula. The Other Woman: My Years with O. J. Simpson: Story of Love, Trust & Betrayal. LC 97-73861. (Illus.). 304p. 1997. 23.45 (*0-316-65113-3*) Little.

Barbieri, Renzo. The Fashion Show. Neugroschel, Joachim, tr. 288p. 1986. 16.95 (*0-8184-0409-4*) Carol Pub Group.

Barbieri, Robert L., et al. Gynecology in Primary Care: A Step-by-Step Approach. LC 99-26450. (Illus.). 100p. 1999. pap. 34.95 (*0-89454-032-7*) Sci Am Medicine.

Barbieri, William A. Ethics of Citizenship: Immigration & Group Rights in Germany. LC 97-40979. 1998. 49.95 (*0-8223-2057-6*); pap. 16.95 (*0-8223-2071-1*) Duke.

Barbieri, William M. Sidewalk: Reflections & Images. LC 79-99433. (Illus.). 95p. reprint ed. pap. 30.00 (*0-8357-7020-6*, 203353900086) Bks Demand.

Barbillon, Claire, jt. auth. see Aghion, Irene.

Barbir, Karl K., et al. Modernization in the Middle East: The Ottoman Empire & Its Afro-Asian Successors. Black, Cyril E. et al, eds. LC 91-44788. (Illus.). 392p. 1992. 29.95 (*0-87850-085-5*); pap. 17.95 (*0-87850-084-7*) Darwin Pr.

Barbiroli, Giancarlo. The Dynamics of Technology: A Methodological Framework for Techno-Economic Analyses. LC 97-29155. (Theory & Decision Library: No. 25). 347p. 1997. 160.50 (*0-7923-4756-0*) Kluwer Academic.

Barbisio, Gallo. Bruno Martinazzi, Symbolic Jewelry. 1997. 75.00 (*3-925369-75-9*, Pub. by Arnoldsche Art Pubs) Antique Collect.

Barbo, Beverly. The Walking Wounded. LC 87-72944. (Illus.). 248p. (Orig.). 1987. 13.95 (*0-944996-00-0*); pap. 9.95 (*0-944996-01-9*) Carlsons.

Barbo, John. Cleveland Fishing Guide: Including the Lake Erie Shoreline, Inland Lakes, Reservoirs, Ponds, Rivers & Streams. LC 98-25347. (Illus.). 240p. 1998. pap. 13.95 (*1-886228-13-2*) Gray & Co Pubs.

***Barbo, Maria S.** Catnapped Caper. Vol. 1. (Illus.). 32p. (ps-3). 2000. pap. text 3.99 (*0-439-16010-3*) Scholastic Inc.

— Official Pokemon Collector's Sticker Book. (Illus.). 48p. (J). (gr. 2-5). 1999. pap. 5.99 (*0-439-10659-1*) Scholastic Inc.

— The Official Pokemon Handbook, Nos. 151-250. (Illus.). (J). 2000. pap. 10.99 (*0-439-15422-7*) Scholastic Inc.

Barbo, Maria S., jt. auth. see Scholastic, Inc. Staff.

Barbo, Thereas. Murder Hill: A True Story of 19th Century Crime & Punishment on Cape Cod. 1999. pap. text 16.95 (*0-940160-81-1*) Parnassus Imprints.

Barbold, M. Hymns in Prose for Children. 24p. (J). (gr. 2-3). 1995. pap. 6.95 (*1-882427-24-6*) Aspasia Inc.

Barbolet, Herb, et al. Farm Folk, City Folk. (Illus.). 172p. 1999. pap. 24.95 (*1-55054-651-1*, Pub. by DGL) Orca Bk Pubs.

Barbon, Nicholas. A Discourse of Trade. LC 05-24876. 39p. 1987. pap. 5.00 (*0-942153-20-0*) Entropy Conserv.

Barbor, Marcus. The Human Brain. (Illus.). 24p. (gr. 2 up). 1999. 19.95 (*0-7624-0491-4*) Running Pr.

Barborcai, Nina. Animales de la Jungla. 1994. 1.00 (*0-486-28380-1*) Dover.

***Barborka, Geoff R.** The Divine Plan. 564p. 1998. pap. 22.50 (*81-7059-291-7*, Pub. by Theos Pub Hse) Natl Bk Netwk.

Barborka, Geoffrey. Divine Plan: Commentary on the Secret Doctrine. 3rd ed. 1998. 35.00 (*81-7059-184-8*, Pub. by Theos Pub Hse) Natl Bk Netwk.

— Mahatmas & Their Letters. 1989. 24.95 (*0-8356-7062-7*) Theos Pub Hse.

Barborka, Geoffrey A. Glossary of Sanskrit Terms & Key to Their Correct Pronunciation. 76p. 1972. pap. 6.50 (*0-913004-04-9*); audio 6.50 (*0-913004-89-8*) Point Loma Pub.

— H. P. Blavatsky: Tibet & Tulku. (Illus.). 1986. 19.25 (*0-8356-7159-3*) Theos Pub Hse.

Barbosa-Canovas, et al. Nonthermal Preservation of Foods. LC 97-35932. (Food Science & Technology Ser.: Vol. 82). (Illus.). 296p. 1997. text 145.00 (*0-8247-9979-8*) Dekker.

Barbosa-Canovas, G. V., et al. Food Engineering Laboratory Manual. LC 97-60700. 155p. 1997. pap. text 41.95 (*1-56676-541-2*) Technomic.

***Barbosa-Canovas, Gustave V. & Gould, Grahame W., eds.** Innovations in Food Processing. LC 00-104017. (Food Preservation Technology Ser.). 288p. 2000. text 124.95 (*1-56676-782-2*) Technomic.

Barbosa-Canovas, Gustavo V. Preservation of Foods with Pulsed Electric Fields. LC 99-60092. (Food Science & Technology International Ser.). 197p. 1999. 89.95 (*0-12-078149-2*) Acad Pr.

Barbosa-Canovas, Gustavo V. & Okos, Martin R., eds. Food Dehydration. LC 93-35990. 126p. 1993. 35.00 (*0-8169-0621-1*, P-68) Am Inst Chem Eng.

Barbosa del Rosario, Pilar. Historia del Pacto Sagastino a Traves de un Epistolario Inedito: El Pacto Produce Desconcierto, 1897-1890. LC 80-22173. 218p. 1981. 9.60 (*0-8477-0866-7*); pap. 7.20 (*0-8477-0867-5*) U of PR Pr.

Barbosa, Duarte. A Description of the Coasts of East Africa & Malabar in the Beginning of the Sixteenth Century. Stanley, Henry E., tr. (C). 1995. 42.00 (*81-206-1020-2*, Pub. by Asian Educ Servs) S Asia.

Barbosa, J. L. & Colares, A. G. Minimal Surfaces in IR Cube. (Lecture Notes in Mathematics Ser.: Vol. 1195). x, 124p. 1990. 31.95 (*0-387-16491-X*) Spr-Verlag.

Barbosa-Lima, Carlos. Brazilian Music for Acoustic Guitar. 68p. 1993. 8.95 (*1-56222-558-8*, 94840); audio 10.98 (*1-56222-794-7*, 94840C); audio compact disk 15.98 (*0-7866-0371-2*, 95397CD) Mel Bay.

Barbosa-Lima, Carlos. Brazilian Music for Acoustic Guitar. 68p. 1993. pap. 18.95 incl. audio (*0-7866-1151-0*, 94840P); pap. 23.95 incl. audio compact disk (*0-7866-1150-2*, 94840CDP) Mel Bay.

Barbosa-Lima, Carlos. More Brazilian Music Acoustic Guitar. 1993. 18.95 incl. audio (*0-7866-1194-4*, 95073P); pap. 8.95 (*1-56222-892-7*, 95073) Mel Bay.

— More Brazilian Music Acoustic Guitar. 1993. audio 10.98 (*1-56222-901-X*, 95073C) Mel Bay.

Barbosa-Lima, Carlos. More Brazilian Music for Acoustic Guitar. 64p. 1993. pap. 23.95 incl. audio compact disk (*0-7866-1193-6*, 95073CDP) Mel Bay.

Barbosa-Lima, Carlos & Griggs, John. Brazilian Jazz Guitar Styles. 72p. 1996. 19.95 incl. audio compact disk (*0-7866-2719-0*, 95111BCD) Mel Bay.

***Barbosa-Lima, Carlos & Griggs, John.** Carlos Barbosa-Lima: Contemp Etudes, Preludes & Pcs for Guitar. 120p. 1998. pap. 19.95 (*0-7866-3478-2*, 95341BCD) Mel Bay.

— Carlos Barbosa-Lima - Elements of Technique for Guitar. 104p. 1998. 19.95 (*0-7866-3480-4*, 95369BCD) Mel Bay.

— Carlos Barbosa-Lima Guitar Scales. 20p. 1995. pap. 6.95 (*0-7866-0112-4*, 95270) Mel Bay.

— Carlos Barbosa-Lima/Arpeggio Studies for Guitar. 36p. 1995. pap. 7.95 (*0-7866-0320-8*, 95380) Mel Bay.

Barbosa-Lima, Carlos, jt. auth. see Griggs, John.

***Barbosa, Luiz C.** The Brazilian Amazon Rainforest: Global Ecopolitics, Development, & Democracy. LC 99-72967. 208p. 1999. 49.00 (*0-7618-1521-X*) U Pr of Amer.

— The Brazilian Amazon Rainforest: Global Ecopolitics, Development & Democracy. LC 99-72967. 208p. 1999. pap. 27.50 (*0-7618-1522-8*) U Pr of Amer.

Barbosa, M. A. & Campilho, A., eds. Imaging Techniques in Biomaterials: Digital Image Processing Applied to Orthopaedic & Dental Implants. LC 94-13351. 402p. 1994. 187.50 (*0-444-89774-7*) Elsevier.

Barbosa, Manuel Bernardo Martins, jt. see Farsi, Mohammad.

Barbosa, Pedro. Conservation Biological Control. LC 97-80315. (Illus.). 396p. (C). 1998. boxed set 69.95 (*0-12-078147-6*) Acad Pr.

Barbosa, Pedro & Letourneau, Deborah K., eds. Novel Aspects of Insect-Plant Interactions. LC 88-5494. 362p. 1988. 150.00 (*0-471-83276-6*) Wiley.

Barbosa, Pedro & Schultz, Jack C., eds. Insect Outbreaks. 578p. 1987. text 142.00 (*0-12-078148-4*) Acad Pr.

Barbosa, Pedro & Wagner, Michael R. Introduction to Forest & Shade Tree Insects. 639p. 1989. text 104.00 (*0-12-078146-8*) Acad Pr.

Barbosa, Pedro, et al. Microbial Mediation of Plant-Herbivore Interactions. LC 90-42726. 530p. 1991. 190.00 (*0-471-61324-X*) Wiley.

Barbosa, Pilar, et al, eds. Is the Best Good Enough? Optimality & Competition in Syntax. LC 97-45557. (Illus.). 440p. 1998. 55.00 (*0-262-02448-9*) MIT Pr.

— Is the Best Good Enough? Optimality & Competition in Syntax. LC 97-45557. (Illus.). 440p. 1998. pap. text 27.50 (*0-262-52249-7*) MIT Pr.

Barbosa, Rogerio A. African Animal Tales. Guthrie, Feliz, tr. from POR. LC 92-42378. (Illus.). 62p. (J). (gr. 1-3). 1993. 17.95 (*0-912078-96-0*) Volcano Pr.

***Barbosa, Valmir C.** An Atlas of Edge-Reversal Dynamics. LC 00-43020. (Chapman & Hall/CRC Research Notes in Mat). (Illus.). 2000. write for info. (*1-58488-209-3*, Chap & Hall CRC) CRC Pr.

Barbosa, Valmir C. An Introduction to Distributed Algorithms. (Illus.). 392p. 1996. 45.00 (*0-262-02412-8*) MIT Pr.

Barbot, Daniel. A Bicycle for Rosaura. (Illus.). 24p. (J). (ps-3). 1991. 9.95 (*0-916291-34-0*) Kane-Miller Bk.

— A Bicycle for Rosaura. (Illus.). 24p. (J). (ps-3). 1994. pap. 5.95 (*0-916291-51-0*) Kane-Miller Bk.

Barbot, Jacques, jt. auth. see Baggish, Michael S.

***Barbotin, Jean-Noel & Portais, Jean-Charles.** NMR in Microbiology: Theory & Applications. 500p. 2000. 169.99 (*1-898486-21-2*, Pub. by Horizon Sci) Intl Spec Bk.

Barbotin, Maurice, jt. auth. see Tourneux, Henry.

Barbottin, G. & Vapaille, A., eds. Instabilites in Silicon Device Vol. 2: Silicon Passivation & Related Instabilites. 852p. 1989. 300.00 (*0-444-70016-1*, North Holland) Elsevier.

***Barbottin, G. & Vapaille, A., eds.** Instabilities in Silicon Devices. 964p. 1999. 200.50 (*0-444-81801-4*, North Holland) Elsevier.

Barbottin, G. & Vapaille, A., eds. Instabilities in Silicon Devices: Silicon Passivation & Related Instabilities, Vol. 1. xxiv,518p. 1986. 233.00 (*0-444-87944-7*, North Holland) Elsevier.

Barbour. A Blue Night. 1998. 6.50 (*0-15-201526-4*) Harcourt.

— Environmental Science in Buildings. 192p. 1997. text write for info. (*0-419-21910-2*, E & FN Spon) Routledge.

— A Yellow Day. 1998. 6.50 (*0-15-201525-6*) Harcourt.

Barbour, jt. auth. see Rost.

Barbour, A. D., et al. Poisson Approximation. (Studies in Probability: No. 2). 288p. 1992. text 55.00 (*0-19-852235-5*) OUP.

Barbour, Alan G. Lyme Disease: The Cause, the Cure, the Controversy. (Health Bks.). (Illus.). 272p. (C). 1996. 35.95 (*0-8018-5224-2*); pap. 15.95 (*0-8018-5245-5*) Johns Hopkins.

Barbour, Allen. Caring for Patients: A Critique of the Medical Model. LC 94-27113. 418p. 1995. 59.50 (*0-8047-2389-3*) Stanford U Pr.

— Caring for Patients: A Critique of the Medical Model. 418p. 1997. pap. 59.50 (*0-8047-3153-5*) Stanford U Pr.

Barbour, Amy L., ed. Selections from Herodotus. (Illus.). 1977. reprint ed. pap. 19.95 (*0-8061-1427-4*) U of Okla Pr.

Barbour, Anita, photos by. Wild Flora of the Northeast. (Illus.). 196p. 1991. 35.00 (*0-87951-344-6*, Pub. by Overlook Pr) Penguin Putnam.

Barbour, Anita, jt. auth. see Barbour, Spider.

***Barbour, Anne.** Buried Secrets. (Regency Romance Ser.). 224p. 2000. mass mkt. 4.99 (*0-451-20023-3*, Sig) NAL.

Barbour, Anne. Lord Glenraven's Return. large type ed. LC 94-48915. 336p. 1995. pap. 20.95 (*0-7862-0417-6*) Thorndike Pr.

— Man of Affairs, 1 vol. (Signet Regency Romance Ser.). 224p. 1999. mass mkt. 4.99 (*0-451-19693-7*) NAL.

***Barbour, Anne, et al.** Grand Hotel. 352p. 2000. mass mkt. 6.50 (*0-451-20036-5*, Sig) NAL.

Barbour, Barbara, jt. auth. see Frankel, Sheila.

***Barbour Bargain Books Staff.** Criss Cross Your Way Through the Bible: 40 Bible Crossword Puzzles for Kids. (J). 1999. pap. text 0.99 (*1-57748-440-1*) Barbour Pub.

Barbour, Barton H., ed. & anno. see Larkin, James R.

Barbour, Bill & Barbour, Mary. Home Exchange Vacationing: Your Guide to Free Accommodations. LC 95-51059. (Illus.). 316p. 1996. pap. text 14.95 (*1-55853-389-3*) Rutledge Hill Pr.

Barbour, Chandler. Families, Schools & Communities: Building Partnerships for Educating the Children. 327p. 1996. pap. text 46.00 (*0-02-305861-7*, Macmillan Coll) P-H.

***Barbour, Chandler & Barbour, Nita H.** Families, Schools, & Communities: Building Partnerships for Educating Children. 2nd ed. 452p. 2000. pap. 46.00 (*0-13-018552-3*) P-H.

Barbour, Charlotte & Rankin, H. C. Inheritance Tax in Scotland. 224p. 1994. pap. text 55.00 (*0-406-02978-4*, UK, MICHIE) LEXIS Pub.

Barbour, Daphne & Sturman, Shelley, eds. Saint-Porchaire Ceramics. LC 96-208077. (Studies in the History of Art Ser.: No. 52). (Illus.). 162p. 1996. pap. 35.00 (*0-89468-213-X*) Natl Gallery Art.

Barbour, Daphne S. & Sturman, Shelley G., eds. Saint-Porchaire Ceramics. (Illus.). 1996. 25.00 (*0-300-07693-2*) Yale U Pr.

***Barbour, David.** Shadows Bend: A Novel of the Fantastic & Unspeakable. 2000. pap. 13.00 (*0-441-00765-1*) Ace Bks.

Barbour, Douglas. B. P. Nichol & His Works. 95p. (C). 1992. pap. 9.95 (*1-55022-066-7*, Pub. by ECW) Genl Dist Srvs.

— Daphne Marlatt & Her Works. (Canadian Author Studies). 71p. (C). 1992. pap. 9.95 (*1-55022-065-9*, Pub. by ECW) Genl Dist Srvs.

— John Newlove & His Works. (Canadian Author Studies). 58p. (C). 1992. pap. 9.95 (*1-55022-070-5*, Pub. by ECW) Genl Dist Srvs.

— Michael Ondaatje. (Twayne's World Authors Ser.). 170p. 1993. pap. 32.00 (*0-8057-8290-7*, Twyne) Mac Lib Ref.

Barbour, Durwood, jt. auth. see Johnson, Todd.

Barbour, Elisa, jt. auth. see Lewis, Paul George.

Barbour, Elisa, jt. auth. see Silva, J. Fred.

Barbour, F. C. The English Ancestry & American Descendants of Richard Spelman of Middletown, Connecticut, 1700. (Illus.). 559p. 1989. reprint ed. pap. 86.00 (*0-8328-1097-5*); reprint ed. lib. bdg. 96.00 (*0-8328-1096-7*) Higginson Bk Co.

Barbour, Floyd B., ed. Black Power Revolt. LC 67-31432. (Extending Horizons Ser.). 288p. (C). 1968. 5.95 (*0-87558-038-6*) Porter Sargent.

Barbour, Frederick K. & Barbour, Margaret R. Frederick K. & Margaret R. Barbour's Furniture Collection. (Illus.). 1963. suppl. ed. 3.00 (*0-940748-16-9*) Conn Hist Soc.

Barbour, Haley. Agenda for America: A Republican Direction for the Future. 318p. 1996. 24.95 (*0-89526-721-7*) Regnery Pub.

Barbour, Hugh. Margaret Fell Speaking. LC 76-4224. (Orig.). 1976. pap. 4.00 (*0-87574-206-8*) Pendle Hill.

Barbour, Hugh, et al, eds. Quaker Crosscurrents: 300 Years of New York Yearly Meetings. LC 94-48761. (Illus.). 432p. 1995. 59.95 (*0-8156-2651-7*); pap. 19.95 (*0-8156-2664-9*) Syracuse U Pr.

Barbour, Hugh & Frost, J. William. The Quakers, 3. LC 88-10240. (Denominations in America Ser.). (Illus.). 421p. 1988. reprint ed. lib. bdg. 75.00 (*0-313-22816-7*, BSF/) Greenwood.

Barbour, Hugh C. The Byzantine Thomism of Gennadios Scholarios: And His Translation of the Commentary of Armandus de Bellovisu on the "De Ente et Essentia" of Thomas Aquinas. 128p. 1996. pap. 69.95 (*1-57309-189-8*, Cath Scholar Pr) Intl Scholars.

An Asterisk (*) at the beginning of an entry indicates that the title is appearing for the first time.

Barbour, Hugh S., ed. William Penn on Religion & Ethics: The Emergence of Liberal Quakerism, 2 vols., 1. LC 90-29146. (Studies in American Religion: Vol. 53). (Illus.). 704p. 1991. lib. bdg. 139.95 (*0-88946-687-4*) E Mellen.

Barbour, Ian G. Energy & American Values. Brooks, Harvey et al, eds. LC 82-13174. 239p. 1982. 55.00 (*0-275-90758-9*, C0758, Praeger Pubs); pap. 17.95 (*0-275-91526-3*, B1526, Praeger Pubs) Greenwood.

Barbour, Ian G. Ethics in Age Techno. 320p. 1992. pap. 19.00 (*0-334-00408-X*) HarpC.

Barbour, Ian G. Ethics in an Age of Technology: Gifford Lectures, Volume Two. LC 91-59045. 336p. 1992. pap. 21.00 (*0-06-060935-4*, Pub. by Harper SF) HarpC.

— Religion & Science: Historical & Contemporary Issues. LC 97-6294. Vol. 1. 384p. 1997. pap. 19.00 (*0-06-060938-9*, Pub. by Harper SF) HarpC.

— Technology, Environment & Human Values. LC 80-12330. 331p. 1980. 27.95 (*0-275-90448-2*, C0448, Praeger Pubs); pap. 26.95 (*0-275-91483-6*, B1483, Praeger Pubs) Greenwood.

***Barbour, Ian G.** When Science Meets Religion: Enemies, Strangers or Partners? 224p. 2000. pap. 16.00 (*0-06-060381-X*, Pub. by Harper SF) HarpC.

Barbour, J. & Pfister, H., eds. Mach's Principle: From Newton's Bucket to Quantum Gravity. (Einstein Studies: Vol. 6). 536p. 1996. 64.50 (*0-8176-3823-7*) Birkhauser.

Barbour, J. B. Absolute or Relative Motion? A Study from a Machian Point of View of the Discovery & the Structure of Dynamical Theories - the Discovery of Dynamics, pt. 1. 768p. 1989. text 129.95 (*0-521-32467-X*) Cambridge U Pr.

Barbour, J. C., et al, eds. Atomistic Mechanisms in Beam Synthesis & Irradiation of Materials Vol. 504: Materials Research Society Symposium Proceedings. LC 99-17074. 461p. 1999. text 76.00 (*1-55899-409-2*) Materials Res.

Barbour, James & Quick, Thomas. Romanticism: Critical Essays. LC 85-20649. 354p. 1985. pap. text 23.95 (*0-8240-9349-6*) Garland.

Barbour, James & Quirk, Thomas. Romanticism: Critical Essays. LC 85-20649. 354p. 1986. text 39.00 (*0-8240-9348-8*) Garland.

Barbour, James & Quirk, Tom. Writing the American Classics. LC 89-16648. xvi, 288p. (C). 1990. 59.95 (*0-8078-1896-8*); pap. 19.95 (*0-8078-4280-X*) U of NC Pr.

Barbour, James & Quirk, Tom, eds. Biographies of Books: The Compositional Histories of Notable American Writings. 344p. (C). 1995. 49.95 (*0-8262-1044-9*) U of Mo Pr.

Barbour, James, ed. see Liebling, A. J.

Barbour, James M. The Church Music of William Billings. LC 72-39000. 167p. 1972. reprint ed. lib. bdg. 27.50 (*0-306-70434-X*) Da Capo.

Barbour, James Murray. Tuning & Temperament: A Historical Survey. LC 74-37288. (Illus.). 228p. 1972. reprint ed. lib. bdg. 35.00 (*0-306-70422-6*) Da Capo.

Barbour, John. The Bruce. Duncan, A. A., ed. 736p. 1997. pap. 14.95 (*0-86241-681-7*, Pub. by Canongate Books) Interlink Pub.

— The Bruce. 384p. 1996. pap. 48.00 (*1-873644-58-2*, Pub. by Mercat Pr Bks) St Mut.

— The Buik of the Most Noble & Vailzeand Conquerour Alexander the Great. Laing, David, ed. LC 70-161748. (Bannatyne Club, Edinburgh. Publications: No. 46). reprint ed. 62.50 (*0-404-52756-6*) AMS Pr.

— Selections from Barbour's Bruce, Set, Pts. 1 & 4. Skeat, Walter W., ed. (EETS, ES Ser.: No. 11). 1974. reprint ed. 30.00 (*0-527-00225-9*) Periodicals Srv.

Barbour, John D. Versions of Deconversion: Autobiography & the Loss of Faith. 238p. (C). 1994. text 35.00 (*0-8139-1546-5*) U Pr of Va.

Barbour, Joseph. Growing As a Blended Family. LC 96-165096. (Family Life Issues Ser.). 1994. pap. 4.50 (*0-570-09510-7*, 20-2708) Concordia.

Barbour, Judy. Colorado Foods & More... 64p. (Orig.). 1990. pap. text 5.95 (*0-9611746-2-5*) J Barbour Bks.

— Cowboy Chow. 80p. (Orig.). 1988. pap. text 14.95 (*0-9611746-0-9*) J Barbour Bks.

— Elegant Elk: Delicious Deer. 3rd ed. LC 78-50099. (Illus.). 196p. 1983. reprint ed. 13.95 (*0-686-33178-8*) P Peters Studio.

— Gathering of the Game. 138p. 1996. write for info. (*0-9611746-9-2*) J Barbour Bks.

— Wonderful Wyoming Facts & Foods. 2nd ed. 64p. (Orig.). 1989. pap. text 5.95 (*0-9611746-1-7*) J Barbour Bks.

***Barbour, Julian B.** Absolute or Relative Motion?: The Deep Structure Of General Relativity. (Illus.). 480p. 2001. text 95.00 (*0-19-513203-3*) OUP.

— Absolute or Relative Motion?: The Discovery Of Dynamics. (Illus.). 768p. 2001. pap. text 49.95 (*0-19-513202-5*) OUP.

Barbour, Julian B. The End of Time. LC 99-44319. (Illus.). 384p. 2000. 30.00 (*0-19-511729-8*) OUP.

Barbour, Julian B. & Pfister, Herbert, eds. Mach's Principle: From Newton's Bucket to Quantum Gravity. (Einstein Studies: Vol. 6). 1995. pap. write for info. (*3-7643-3823-7*) Birkhauser.

Barbour, Julian B., tr. see Al'pert, Iakov L.

Barbour, Julian B., tr. see Skobel'tsyn, D. V., ed.

Barbour, Julian B., tr. see Vizgin, Vladimir P.

Barbour, K. M., ed. see Oguntoyinbo, J. S., et al.

Barbour, Karen. Little Nino's Pizzeria. LC 86-32006. (Illus.). 32p. (J). (ps-3). 1990. pap. 6.00 (*0-15-246321-6*, Voyager Bks) Harcourt.

— Little Nino's Pizzeria. LC 86-32006. (Big Bks.). (Illus.). 32p. (J). (ps-3). 1991. pap. 19.95 (*0-15-246322-4*, Harcourt Child Bks) Harcourt.

— Nancy. (Illus.). 30p. (J). (ps-3). 1989. 13.95 (*0-15-256675-9*) Harcourt.

Barbour, Kathryn. The Quest: A Guide to the Job Interview. 112p. (C). 1993. pap. text 18.95 (*0-8403-6984-0*) Kendall-Hunt.

Barbour, Lucius B. Burlington, Connecticut, Epitaphs. 32p. 1997. reprint ed. pap. 6.00 (*0-8328-5626-6*) Higginson Bk Co.

— Clinton Epitaphs. 58p. 1997. reprint ed. pap. 12.00 (*0-8328-5628-2*) Higginson Bk Co.

— Genealogical Data from Farmington Cemeteries. 63p. 1997. reprint ed. pap. 12.50 (*0-8328-5645-2*) Higginson Bk Co.

— Genealogical Data from Guilford Cemeteries. 104p. 1997. reprint ed. pap. 15.00 (*0-8328-5652-5*) Higginson Bk Co.

— Genealogical Data from New London Connecticut Cemeteries. 207p. 1997. reprint ed. pap. 22.50 (*0-8328-5671-1*) Higginson Bk Co.

— Haddam Epitaphs. 82p. 1997. reprint ed. pap. 15.00 (*0-8328-5653-3*) Higginson Bk Co.

Barbour, M., et al. Waterborne & Solvent Based Surface Coatings Resins & Their Applications Vol. 1: Vinyl Acrylic. 504p. 1996. 250.00 (*0-471-97882-5*) Wiley.

— Waterborne & Solvent Based Surface Coatings Resins & Their Applications Vol. 2: Epoxies. 528p. 1998. 250.00 (*0-471-97883-3*) Wiley.

Barbour, Margaret R., jt. auth. see Barbour, Frederick K.

Barbour, Mary, jt. auth. see Barbour, Bill.

Barbour, Mary, tr. see Saint Louis Grignon de Montfort.

Barbour, Michael, et al. California's Changing Landscape: The Diversity, Ecology & Conservation of California Vegetation. (Illus.). 1993. pap. 24.95 (*0-943460-17-4*) Calif Native.

Barbour, Michael G. Terrestrial Plant Ecology. 3rd ed. LC 98-30070. 688p. (C). 1998. 74.00 (*0-8053-0004-X*) Benjamin-Cummings.

Barbour, Michael G. & Billings, William Dwight, eds. North American Terrestrial Vegetation. 2nd rev. ed. LC 97-29061. (Illus.). 621p. (C). 2000. text 120.00 (*0-521-55027-0*); pap. text 49.95 (*0-521-55986-3*) Cambridge U Pr.

Barbour, Michael G. & Major, Jack, eds. Terrestrial Vegetation of California. 2nd ed. (Special Publications: No. 9). 1040p. (Orig.). 1988. 50.00 (*0-943460-13-1*) Calif Native.

Barbour, Nancy. Palau. 3rd rev. ed. DeMan, Elaine, ed. (Illus.). 175p. 2000. pap. 24.95 (*0-9626344-2-5*) Full Court CA.

Barbour, Nelson H. Three Worlds: Plan of Redemption. 199p. 1985. reprint ed. pap. 7.95 (*1-883858-30-5*) Witness CA.

Barbour, Nita, jt. auth. see Seefeldt, Carol.

Barbour, Nita H. & Seefeldt, Carol. Developmental Continuity Across Preschool & Primary Grades. LC 93-599. 1993. 15.00 (*0-87173-128-2*) ACEI.

Barbour, Nita H., jt. auth. see Barbour, Chandler.

***Barbour, Oliver L.** Treatise on the Criminal Law & Criminal Courts of the State New York & Upon the Jurisdiction, Duty & Authority of Justices of the Peace & of the Magistrates & on the Power & Duty of Sheriffs, Constables..., 2 vols. 1463p. 1999. reprint ed. 315.00 (*1-56169-453-3*) Gaunt.

***Barbour, Paul.** Who Wants to Be a Contestant? The Ultimate Insider's Guide to Getting on America's Hottest Game Show. (Illus.). 192p. 2000. pap. 10.95 (*1-57500-182-9*, Pub. by TV Bks) HarpC.

Barbour, Philip L., ed. see Smith, John, et al.

Barbour, Philip L., tr. & notes see Pushkin, Aleksandr.

Barbour, Philippe, ed. The European Union Handbook. LC 97-147140. 359p. 1996. lib. bdg. 75.00 (*1-884964-28-1*, 64-28-1) Fitzroy Dearborn.

Barbour, Phillipe. Brittany. (Cadogan Guides). (Illus.). 576p. 1998. pap. text 18.95 (*1-86011-044-4*, Pub. by Cadgn Bks) Globe Pequot.

— France: The Loire. (Cadogan Guides Ser.). (Illus.). 480p. 1997. pap. text 19.95 (*1-86011-091-6*, Pub. by Cadgn Bks) Globe Pequot.

Barbour Publishing, Inc. Editors. Bible Crosswords Collection. (Bible Crosswords Collection: Vol. 11). 112p. 1998. pap. 2.49 (*1-57748-370-7*) Barbour Pub.

— Bible Crosswords Collection. (Bible Crosswords Collection: Vol. 12). 112p. 1998. pap. 2.49 (*1-57748-371-5*) Barbour Pub.

— Bible Crosswords Collection 5. 112p. 1996. pap. 2.49 (*1-55748-885-1*) Barbour Pub.

— Bible Crosswords Collection 2, No. 2. 112p. 1995. pap. 2.49 (*1-55748-595-X*) Barbour Pub.

***Barbour Publishing, Inc. Editors.** The Bible Promise Book: King James Version, Graduate's Edition. 176p. 2000. 3.97 (*1-57748-692-7*) Barbour Pub.

— The Bible Promise Book: New International Version, Graduates Edition. 176p. 2000. 3.97 (*1-57748-705-2*); 3.97 (*1-57748-706-0*) Barbour Pub.

Barbour Publishing, Inc. Editors. Bible Word Search. (Bible Word Search Collection: Vol. 11). 112p. 1998. pap. 2.49 (*1-57748-372-3*) Barbour Pub.

— Bible Word Search Collection, No. 1. 112p. 1996. pap. 2.49 (*1-55748-881-9*) Barbour Pub.

Barbour Publishing, Inc. Editors. Bible Word Search Collection, No. 2. 112p. 1996. pap. 2.49 (*1-55748-882-7*) Barbour Pub.

Barbour Publishing, Inc. Editors. Bible Word Search Collection, No. 4. 1997. pap. 2.49 (*1-55748-948-3*) Barbour Pub.

— Crosswood Collection, Vol. 1. large type ed. 1998. pap. 2.97 (*1-57748-169-0*) Barbour Pub.

— Crosswood Collection, Vol. 2. large type ed. 1998. pap. 2.97 (*1-57748-170-4*) Barbour Pub.

— Faith's Greatest Heroes, Vol. 1. Lindstedt, David, ed. & intro. by. LC 99-193790. (Essential Christian Library Ser.). 319p. 1999. 9.97 (*1-57748-445-2*) Barbour Pub.

— Feast. 96p. 1999. 9.97 incl. audio compact disk (*1-57748-580-7*) Barbour Pub.

— First & Ten. 1999. pap. 0.99 (*1-57748-435-5*) Barbour Pub.

— Friends. 96p. 1999. 9.97 incl. audio compact disk (*1-57748-579-3*) Barbour Pub.

***Barbour Publishing, Inc. Editors.** Fun Bible Trivia 2. 1999. pap. text 1.39 (*1-57748-599-8*) Barbour Pub.

Barbour Publishing, Inc. Editors. He Is Risen. LC 99-229513. 1999. pap. 0.99 (*1-57748-430-4*) Barbour Pub.

— Heart of Purest Gold: A Celebration of a Mother's Love. LC 99-215466. 40p. 1999. 1.99 (*1-57748-496-7*) Barbour Pub.

— Holiday Ideas. 1997. pap. text 0.99 (*1-55748-962-9*) Barbour Pub.

Barbour Publishing, Inc. Editors. Jumbo Bible Coloring Fun, Vol. 2. (Illus.). (J). 1997. pap. text 4.97 (*1-57748-036-8*) Barbour Pub.

Barbour Publishing, Inc. Editors. Jumbo Bible Crossword Collection, Vol. 1. 448p. 1995. pap. 4.97 (*1-55748-832-0*) Barbour Pub.

***Barbour Publishing, Inc. Editors.** Jumbo Bible Crossword Collection, Vol. 2. 448p. 1998. pap. 4.97 (*1-57748-206-9*) Barbour Pub.

Barbour Publishing, Inc. Editors. Jumbo Bible Word Search Collection, Vol. 1. 1997. pap. 4.97 (*1-57748-017-1*) Barbour Pub.

— The KJV Bible for Toddlers. (Illus.). 192p. (J). (ps-k). 1999. pap. 4.97 (*1-57748-583-1*) Barbour Pub.

— The Lord Is Come. 1999. pap. 0.99 (*1-57748-437-1*) Barbour Pub.

— Play Ball. 1999. pap. 0.99 (*1-57748-429-0*) Barbour Pub.

— Romance. 96p. 1999. 9.97 incl. audio compact disk (*1-57748-582-3*) Barbour Pub.

***Barbour Publishing, Inc. Editors.** Selections from Stepping Heavenward. 96p. 2000. 9.97 (*1-57748-717-6*) Barbour Pub.

— Selections from the Bible Promise Book. 96p. 2000. 9.97 (*1-57748-719-2*) Barbour Pub.

Barbour Publishing, Inc. Editors. Spring's Memory. 1999. pap. 4.97 (*1-57748-502-5*) Barbour Pub.

— Sunday. 96p. 1999. 9.97 incl. audio compact disk (*1-57748-581-5*) Barbour Pub.

— What Do You Know? 1999. pap. 0.99 (*1-57748-434-7*) Barbour Pub.

— Wisdom from the Proverbs: A Daily Devotional. 365p. 1997. 12.95 (*1-57748-015-5*) Barbour Pub.

— With a Greatful Heart. 1999. pap. 0.99 (*1-57748-436-3*) Barbour Pub.

— Word Search Collection, No. 1. large type ed. 1998. pap. text 2.97 (*1-57748-171-2*) Barbour Pub.

— Word Search Collection, Vol. 2. large type ed. 1998. pap. 2.97 (*1-57748-172-0*) Barbour Pub.

Barbour Publishing, Inc. Editors, compiled by. Bible Promises. (Little Library Ser.). 48p. 1994. pap. text 0.99 (*1-55748-520-8*) Barbour Pub.

Barbour Publishing, Inc. Editors, ed. Bible Crosswords Collection 4. 112p. 1995. pap. 2.49 (*1-55748-656-5*) Barbour Pub.

— Bible Word Search Collection, No. 5. 1997. pap. 2.49 (*1-55748-981-5*) Barbour Pub.

— Bible Word Search Collection, No. 6. 1997. pap. 2.49 (*1-55748-982-3*) Barbour Pub.

***Barbour Publishing, Inc. Editors & Livingstone Corp. Staff.** Ultimate Guide to the Internet for the Christian Family. 448p. 2000. pap. 4.97 (*1-57748-731-1*) Barbour Pub.

***Barbour Publishing, Inc. Editors & Sanna, Ellyn.** Just the Girls: A Celebration of Mothers & Daughters. 40p. 2000. 1.99 (*1-57748-715-X*) Barbour Pub.

Barbour Publishing, Inc. Editors & Sanna, Ellyn. Mother's Heart. LC 99-215454. 94p. 1999. pap. 0.99 (*1-57748-431-2*) Barbour Pub.

***Barbour Publishing, Inc. Editors & Sanna, Ellyn.** Still the One: A Celebration of a Journey Shared. 40p. 2000. 1.99 (*1-57748-733-8*) Barbour Pub.

Barbour Publishing, Inc. Editors, et al. Bible Clues for the Clueless: God's Word in Your World. (Clues for the Clueless Ser.). 245p. 1999. pap. 8.99 (*1-57748-490-8*) Barbour Pub.

***Barbour Publishing, Inc. Editors, et al.** Inspirational Romance Reader No. 4: Contemporary Collection. (Contemporary Collection: No. 4). 464p. 2000. pap. 4.97 (*1-57748-734-6*) Barbour Pub.

— Inspirational Romance Reader No. 4: Historical Collection. Vol. 4. 464p. 2000. pap. 4.97 (*1-57748-736-2*) Barbour Pub.

Barbour Publishing, Inc. Editors, ed. see Dickens, Charles.

Barbour Publishing Staff. Mountaintop. 1997. pap. text 1.66 (*1-57748-246-8*) Barbour Pub.

***Barbour Publishing Staff, ed.** On Wings Like Eagles Quote Book: Inspiration from Scripture for the Golf Enthusiast. 1998. pap. 3.97 (*1-57748-297-2*) Barbour Pub.

Barbour, R. Glassblowing for Laboratory Technicians. 2nd ed. 1979. 123.00 (*0-08-022155-6*, Pub. by Pergamon Repr) Franklin.

Barbour, R. James & SKog, Kenneth E., eds. Role of Wood Production in Ecosystem Management: Proceedings of the Sustainable Forestry Working Group at the IUFRO All Division 5 Conference, Pullman, Washington, July 1997. (Illus.). 110p. 1997. reprint ed. 16.00 (*0-89904-673-8*, Ecosytems Resrch); reprint ed. pap. 12.00 (*0-89904-674-6*, Ecosytems Resrch Crumb Elbow Pub.

Barbour, R. James, jt. ed. see Rowell, Roger M.

Barbour, R. S., ed. The Kingdom of God & Human Society: Essays by Members of the Scripture, Theology & Society Group. 308p. 1994. pap. text 29.95 (*0-567-29228-2*, Pub. by T & T Clark) Bks Intl VA.

Barbour, R. W., jt. auth. see Ernst, C. H.

Barbour, Randall L., et al, eds. Computational, Experimental & Numerical Methods for Solving Ill-Posed Inverse Imaging Problems Vol. 3171: Medical & Nonmedical Applications. LC 98-143983. 250p. 1997. 69.00 (*0-8194-2593-1*) SPIE.

Barbour, Reid. Deciphering Elizabethan Fiction. LC 91-51139. 176p. (C). 1993. 31.50 (*0-87413-450-1*) U Delaware Pr.

— English Epicures & Stoics: Ancient Legacies in Early Stuart Culture. LC 98-21413. (Massachusetts Studies in Early Modern Culture). 328p. (C). 1998. 45.00 (*1-55849-171-6*) U of Mass Pr.

Barbour, Roger W. & Davis, Wayne H. Bats of America. fac. ed. LC 73-80086. (Illus.). 311p. 1994. pap. 96.50 (*0-7837-7587-3*, 204734000007) Bks Demand.

— Mammals of Kentucky. LC 74-7870. (Illus.). 368p. 1974. 29.00 (*0-8131-1314-8*) U Pr of Ky.

Barbour, Roger W. & Wharton, Mary E. Trees & Shrubs of Kentucky. 2nd ed. (Illus.). 592p. 1994. 34.95 (*0-8131-1294-X*) U Pr of Ky.

Barbour, Roger W., et al. Kentucky Birds: A Finding Guide. LC 72-91662. (Illus.). 326p. reprint ed. 101.10 (*0-8357-9787-2*, 201618400001) Bks Demand.

Barbour, Roger W., jt. auth. see Ernst, Carl H.

Barbour, Roger W., jt. auth. see Wharton, Mary E.

Barbour, Rosaline S. Developing Focus Group Research: Politics, Theory & Practice. LC 98-61656. 225 p. 1999. 25.95 (*0-7619-5568-2*) Sage.

Barbour, Rosaline S. & Huby, Guro. Meddling with Mythology: AIDS & the Social Construction of Knowledge. LC 97-49216. 304p. (C). 1998. 85.00 (*0-415-16389-7*); pap. 25.99 (*0-415-16390-0*) Routledge.

***Barbour, Rosaline S. & Kitzinger, Jenny, eds.** Developing Focus Group Research: Politics, Theory & Practice. LC 98-61656. 256p. 1999. 74.00 (*0-7619-5567-4*) Sage.

Barbour, Ross. Now You Know: The Story of the Four Freshmen (Golden Anniversary Edition) 2nd anniversary ed. LC 98-29601. (Illus.). 320p. 1998. pap. 24.95 (*0-936653-83-3*) Tiare Pubns.

Barbour, Sarah. Nathalie Sarraute & the Feminist Reader: Identities in Process. LC 92-52716. 304p. (C). 1993. 46.50 (*0-8387-5235-7*) Bucknell U Pr.

Barbour, Scott. American Modernism. LC 99-25707. (Literary Companion Ser.). 144p. (YA). (gr. 9-12). 2000. pap. 17.45 (*0-7377-0200-1*) Greenhaven.

***Barbour, Scott.** American Modernism. LC 99-25707. (Literary Movements & Genres Ser.). 144p. (YA). (gr. 9-12). 2000. lib. bdg. 27.95 (*0-7377-0201-X*) Greenhaven.

— Drug Legalization. LC 99-48084. (Current Controversies Ser.). 320p. 2000. 17.45 (*0-7377-0336-9*) Greenhaven.

— Drug Legalization. LC 99-48084. (Current Controversies Ser.). 320p. 2000. pap. 13.96 (*0-7377-0335-0*) Greenhaven.

— The Environment. (Opposing Viewpoints Digests Ser.). (Illus.). 144p. (YA). (gr. 6-10). 2000. pap. 14.95 (*1-56510-872-8*); lib. bdg. 23.70 (*1-56510-873-6*) Greenhaven.

— Free Speech. LC 99-29107. (Current Controversies Ser.). 320p. (J). (gr. 9-12). 2000. pap. 17.45 (*0-7377-0142-0*); lib. bdg. 27.45 (*0-7377-0143-9*) Greenhaven.

— Lyndon B. Johnson. LC 00-28333. 2000. pap. write for info. (*0-7377-0500-0*) Greenhaven.

Barbour, Scott. Violence. Swisher, Karin L., ed. LC 95-35628. (Opposing Viewpoints Ser.). (Illus.). 306p. (J). (gr. 5-12). 1996. pap. text 16.20 (*1-56510-354-8*) Greenhaven.

Barbour, Scott, ed. Alcohol: Opposing Viewpoints. LC 97-14487. (Opposing Viewpoints Ser.). (Illus.). (J). (gr. 5-12). 1997. pap. 16.20 (*1-56510-674-1*); lib. bdg. 26.20 (*1-56510-675-X*) Greenhaven.

— Hunger. (Current Controversies Ser.). 224p. 1995. pap. text 16.20 (*1-56510-238-X*, 238X) Greenhaven.

Barbour, Scott, ed. Hunger. LC 94-43376. (Current Controversies Ser.). 224p. 1995. lib. bdg. 26.20 (*1-56510-239-8*, 2398) Greenhaven.

Barbour, Scott, ed. Teen Violence. LC 98-36949. (Opposing Viewpoints Digests Ser.). (J). (gr. 4-12). 1998. pap. 14.95 (*1-56510-864-7*); lib. bdg. 23.70 (*1-56510-865-5*) Greenhaven.

***Barbour, Scott, et al, eds.** Violence Against Women. LC 98-35007. (Current Controversies Ser.). 294p. (YA). (gr. 9-12). 1998. pap. 17.45 (*0-7377-0014-9*); lib. bdg. 27.45 (*0-7377-0015-7*) Greenhaven.

— Work: Opposing Viewpoints. (Opposing Viewpoints Ser.). (Illus.). 312p. (YA). (gr. 10 up). 1995. pap. text 16.20 (*1-56510-218-5*) Greenhaven.

Barbour, Scott, et al, eds. Work: Opposing Viewpoints. (Opposing Viewpoints Ser.). (Illus.). 312p. (YA). (gr. 10 up). 1995. lib. bdg. 26.20 (*1-56510-219-3*) Greenhaven.

Barbour, Scott & Swisher, Karin L., eds. Health & Fitness. LC 96-7203. (Opposing Viewpoints Ser.). 1996. 26.20 (*1-56510-403-X*); pap. 16.20 (*1-56510-402-1*) Greenhaven.

Barbour, Scott, jt. auth. see Torr, James D.

Barbour, Scott, jt. ed. see Sadler, A. E.

Barbour, Spider & Barbour, Anita. Wild Flora of the Northeast. (Illus.). 196p. 1995. pap. 19.95 (*0-87951-584-8*, Pub. by Overlook Pr) Penguin Putnam.

***Barbour, Stephen & Carmichael, Cathie, eds.** Language & Nationalism in Europe. (Illus.). 400p. 2000. text 70.00 (*0-19-823671-9*) OUP.

Barbour, Stephen & Stevenson, Patrick. Soziolinguistische Variation im Deutschsprachigen Raum. 400p. 1998. text 30.00 (*3-11-014581-2*) De Gruyter.

B

— Variation in German: A Critical Approach to German Sociolinguistics. (Illus.). 322p. (C). 1990. text 69.95 (0-521-35397-1) Cambridge U Pr.

Barbour, Violet. Capitalism in Amsterdam in the Seventeenth Century. LC 78-64208. (Johns Hopkins University. Studies in the Social Sciences. Thirtieth Ser. 1912: 1). reprint ed. 39.50 (0-404-61313-6) AMS Pr.

Barbour, William, ed. Illegal Immigration. LC 93-1808. (Current Controversies Ser.). 224p. (YA). 1994. pap. 16.20 (1-56510-071-9); lib. bdg. 26.20 (1-56510-072-7) Greenhaven.

Barbour, William S., ed. Immigration Policy. (At Issue Ser.). 128p. 1995. lib. bdg. 18.70 (1-56510-300-9) Greenhaven.

— Immigration Policy. (At Issue Ser.). 128p. (C). 1995. pap. text 11.20 (1-56510-267-3) Greenhaven.

Barboza, Betty B. Maxie. LC 97-77339. (Illus.). 80p. 1998. pap. 12.95 (0-944851-12-6) Earth Star.

Barboza, Ronald. Cape Verdean-American Coloring Book. (Illus.). 1995. 6.95 (0-9647284-1-9) Barika Photo & Prodns.

— Cape Verdean Coloring Book. (Illus.). 1995. 6.95 (0-9647284-0-0) Barika Photo & Prodns.

Barboza, Ronald, ed. A Salute to Cape Verdean Musicians & Their Music. (Illus.). 48p. (YA). (gr. 9-12). 1989. pap. 10.00 (0-9627637-0-5) D&C Cape Verdeans.

Barboza, Steve. American Jihad: Islam after Malcolm X. 254p. 1996. 25.00 (0-614-21478-5, 31) Kazi Pubns.

Barboza, Steven. Amer Jihad. 384p. 1995. pap. 14.00 (0-385-47694-9) Doubleday.

— Sugar Hill. (J). 1998. write for info. (0-7868-0130-1) Hyperion.

Barboza, Steven, ed. The African American Book of Values: Classic Moral Stories. LC 97-25628. (Illus.). 960p. 1998. 32.50 (0-385-48259-0, Anchor NY) Doubleday.

Barbre, Sylvia J., ed. see Dupre, Dalmation D.

Barbree, Jay. Day I Died: One Man's Successful Battle Back from the Dead. LC 90-53405. 296p. 1990. 19.95 (0-88282-061-3) New Horizon NJ.

Barbree, Jay & Caidin, Martin. A Journey Through Time: Exploring the Universe with the Hubble Space Telescope. LC 95-6758. (Illus.). 256p. 1995. 32.95 (0-670-86018-2, Viking Studio) Studio Bks.

Barbrook. Media Freedom: The Contradictions of Communication in the Age of Modernity. LC 95-1908. (C). 54.95 (0-7453-0944-5, Pub. by Pluto GBR); pap. 19.95 (0-7453-0943-7) Pluto GBR.

Barbu, Marian. Aspects of the Actual Novel. 300p. 1994. pap. text 9.95 (1-879585-67-7) Erhus Univ Pr.

Barbu, V., ed. Differential Equations & Control Theory. 368p. 1992. ring bd. 94.95 (0-582-06691-3, LM6691, Chap & Hall CRC) CRC Pr.

Barbu, V. & Precupanu, T. Convexity & Optimization in Banach Spaces. (Mathematics & Its Applications East European Ser.). 1986. text 211.50 (90-277-1761-3) Kluwer Academic.

Barbu, Viorel. Mathematical Methods in Optimization of Differential Systems. LC 94-37359. (Mathematics & Its Applications Ser.: Vol. 310).Tr. of Methode Matematice in Optimizarea Sistemelor Diferentiale. 259p. (C). 1994. text 178.50 (0-7923-3176-1) Kluwer Academic.

— Partial Differential Equations & Boundary Value Problems. LC 98-6571. (Mathematics & Its Applications Ser.). 1998. 129.00 (0-7923-5056-1) Kluwer Academic.

Barbu, Viorel, et al, eds. Optimization, Optimal Control, & Partial Differential Equations: First Franco-Romanian Conference, Iasi, September 7-11, 1992. LC 92-25607. (International Series of Numerical Mathematics: Vol. 107). xiii, 347p. 1992. 122.00 (0-8176-2788-X, Pub. by Birkhauser) Princeton Arch.

Barbu, Zevedei. Democracy & Dictatorship: Their Psychology & Patterns of Life. 1956. 69.50 (0-614-01802-1) Elliots Bks.

— Problems of Historical Psychology. LC 75-28659. 222p. 1976. reprint ed. lib. bdg. 55.00 (0-8371-8476-2, BAHP, Greenwood Pr) Greenwood.

Barbu, Zevedei. Society, Personality & Culture. (Blackwell's Sociology Ser.). 183p. (C). 1971. pap. 17.95 (0-8464-1162-8) Beekman Pubs.

Barbules, Nicholas, ed. Philosophy of Education, 1986: Proceedings of the 42nd Meeting of the Philosophy of Education Society. annuals 352p. 1983. 30.00 (0-318-16177-X) Phil Ed Soc.

Barbusse, Henri. Hell. Baldick, Robert, tr. LC 94-61776. 270p. (Orig.). 1995. pap. 12.95 (1-885983-01-8) Turtle Point Pr.

Barbut, Erol, jt. auth. see Brandal, Willy.

Barbuto, Domenica. American Settlement Houses & Progressive Social Reform: An Encyclopedia of the American Settlement Movement. LC 99-28054. (Illus.). 280p. 1999. boxed set 74.95 (1-57356-146-0) Oryx Pr.

***Barbuto, Domenica M.** The American Settlement Movement: A Bibliography, 42. LC 99-33433. (Bibliographies & Indexes in American History Ser.). 136p. 1999. lib. bdg. 59.95 (0-313-30756-3) Greenwood.

Barbuto, Domenica M. The International Financial Statistics Locator: A Research & Information Guide. LC 94-19999. (Research & Information Guides in Business, Industry, & Economic Institutions Ser.: Vol. 11). 352p. 1994. text 20.00 (0-8153-1483-3, SS924) Garland.

Barbuto, Domenica M. & Kreisel, Martha. Guide to Civil War Books: An Annotated Selection of Modern Works on the War Between the States. LC 95-40623. 221p. 1995. pap. 32.00 (0-8389-0672-9, 0672-9-2045) ALA.

***Barbuto, Richard V.** Niagara 1814: America Invades Canada. 2000. 39.95 (0-7006-1052-9) U Pr of KS.

Barbuy, B., ed. The Stellar Populations of Galaxies: Proceedings of the 149th Symposium of the International Astronomical Union, Held in Angro dos Reis, Brazil, August 5-9, 1991. (International Astronomical Union Symposia Ser.). 540p. (C). 1992. pap. text 94.00 (0-7923-1699-1); lib. bdg. 188.00 (0-7923-1698-3) Kluwer Academic.

Barbuzza, Tite. Barcelona Club Flyers. 360p. 1999. pap. 30.00 (84-89698-25-2, Pub. by Actar) Dist Art Pubs.

Barca, jt. auth. see Cobb.

Barca, Frances Calderon De La, see Calderon de la Barca, Frances.

Barca, Michele & Cobb, Kate. 10 Teambuilders: Ready-to-Use Games for Team Development. LC 98-4001. 500p. 1999. 393.95 (0-566-07907-0, Pub. by Gower) Ashgate Pub Co.

***Barca, Pedro & FitzGerald, Edward.** Eight Dramas of Pedro Calderbon de la Barca. LC 99-87264. 2000. pap. 14.95 (0-252-06903-X) U of Ill Pr.

Barcalow. Moral Philosophy: Theory & Issues. (Philosophy Ser.). 1993. teacher ed. 25.25 (0-534-21037-6) Wadsworth Pub.

— Open Questions: An Introduction to Philosophy. 3rd ed. (Philosophy Ser.). 2000. pap. text 36.00 (0-534-51907-5) Thomson Learn.

Barcalow, Emmett. Moral Philosophy: Theory & Issues. 378p. 1993. mass mkt. 30.25 (0-534-21036-8) Wadsworth Pub.

— Moral Philosophy: Theory & Issues. 2nd ed. LC 97-28869. (C). 1997. 51.95 (0-534-52645-4) Wadsworth Pub.

— Open Questions: An Introduction to Philosophy. 476p. (C). 1991. mass mkt. 27.75 (0-534-16512-5) Wadsworth Pub.

— Open Questions: An Introduction to Philosophy. 296p. (C). 1992. 23.50 (0-534-16514-1) Wadsworth Pub.

— Open Questions: An Introduction to Philosophy. 2nd ed. LC 95-48129. (Philosophy Ser.). (C). 1996. 52.95 (0-534-50473-6) Wadsworth Pub.

Barcan, Alan. Sociological Theory & Educational Reality: The Sociology of Education in Australia. 1992. pap. 46.95 (0-86840-125-0, Pub. by New South Wales Univ Pr) Intl Spec Bk.

— Two Centuries of Education in New South Wales. 1988. pap. 29.95 (0-86840-322-9, Pub. by New South Wales Univ Pr) Intl Spec Bk.

***Barcan, Ruth & Buchanan, Ian, eds.** Imagining Australian Space: Cultural Studies & Spiritual Inquiry. 218p. 1999. 34.95 (1-876268-37-9, Pub. by Univ of West Aust Pr) Intl Spec Bk.

Barcanova. Diccionari Barcanova de la Llengua. (CAT.). 816p. 1991. 55.00 (0-7859-6231-X, 8475332250) Fr & Eur.

— Diccionari Barcanova de la Llengua Basic. (CAT.). 592p. 1991. 24.95 (0-7859-6232-8, 8475334210) Fr & Eur.

— Diccionari Barcanova d'Historia de Catalunya. (CAT.). 320p. 1990. 35.00 (0-7859-6234-4, 8475334571) Fr & Eur.

Barce, Elmore. Land of the Miamis: Account of the Struggle to Secure Possession of the North West from the End of the Revolution until 1812. (Illus.). 422p. 1997. reprint ed. lib. bdg. 45.00 (0-8328-7090-0) Higginson Bk Co.

***Barcelbo, John J. & Cramton, Roger C.** Lawyer's Practice & Ideals: A Comparative View. LC 99-33764. 1999. 125.00 (90-411-9392-8) Kluwer Law Intl.

Barcellos, Anthony & Hickerson. Calculus with Analytic Geometry. (C). 1985. pap. text, student ed. 32.00 (0-07-057529-0) McGraw.

Barcellos, Anthony, jt. auth. see Stein, Sherman K.

Barcelo, D., ed. Applications of LC/MS in Environmental Chemistry. 566p. 1996. 258.50 (0-444-82067-1) Elsevier.

Barcelo, D. & Hennion, M.-C. Trace Determination of Pesticides & Their Degradation in Water. 1996. write for info. (0-614-17889-4) Elsevier.

Barcelo, Dami A. & Hennion, Marie C. Trace Determination of Pesticides & Their Degradation Products in Water, Vol. 19. LC 97-38632. (Techniques & Instrumentation in Analytical Chemistry Ser.). 542p. 1997. 273.00 (0-444-81842-1) Elsevier.

Barcelo, Damia, ed. Environmental Analysis: Techniques, Applications, & Quality Assurance. LC 93-28296. (Techniques & Instrumentation in Analytical Chemistry Ser.: 13). 658p. 1993. 315.50 (0-444-89648-1) Elsevier.

Barcelo, Helene & Kalai, Gil, eds. Jerusalem Combinatorics, '93: An International Conference in Combinatorics, May 9-17, 1993, Jerusalem, Israel. LC 94-34723. (Contemporary Mathematics Ser.: Vol. 178). 360p. 1994. pap. 64.00 (0-8218-0294-1, CONM/178) Am Math.

Barcelo, J. English-Spanish, Spanish-English Vocabulary of Chemistry: Vocabulario Ingles-Espanol-Ingles de Quimica. (ENG & SPA.). 111p. 1983. pap. 19.95 (0-8288-0175-4, S35566) Fr & Eur.

Barcelo, Joan. Pas de Dansa. limited ed. (Ediciones Especiales y de Bibliofilo Ser.). (CAT., Illus.). 1993. 500.00 (84-343-0321-3) Elliots Bks.

Barcelo, John J., 3rd, et al. Document Supplement to International Commercial Arbitration. (American Casebook Ser.). 300p. 1998. pap. 22.50 (0-314-23073-4) West Pub.

Barcelo Miller, Maria de F. La Lucha Por El Sufragio Femenino En Puerto Rico, 1896-1935. LC 97-60512. write for info. (0-929157-45-1) Ediciones Huracan.

Barcelo, Miquel. Miquel Barcelo: Il Cristo della Vucciria. (Illus.). 176p. 1999. 45.00 (88-8158-190-6) Charta.

Barcelo, Miquel, jt. auth. see Juncosa, Enrique.

Barcelo, Randy. Canciones de la Vellonera. 48p. 1996. pap. 3.95 (1-885901-19-4) Presbyters Peartree.

Barcelona, M. J., et al. Practical Guide for Groundwater Sampling. 156p. (C). 1988. 160.00 (0-7855-6712-7, Pub. by Scientific) St Mut.

Barcelona, Michael, et al, eds. Handbook of Groundwater Protection. (Science Information Resource Center Ser.). 212p. 1988. 165.00 (0-89116-821-4) Hemisp Pub.

Barcelona, Michael, et al. Contamination of Ground Water: Prevention, Assessment, Restoration. LC 90-31404. (Pollution Technology Review Ser.: No. 184). (Illus.). 213p. 1990. 89.00 (0-8155-1243-0, 900124) Noyes.

Barcena, Theresa L. & Donofrio, William. Barcena's Clinical Reference Pocket Guide to Abbreviations & Symbols Used in Hospitals. (Reference Pocket Guide Ser.). 116p. (C). 1994. pap. text 10.00 (0-9643995-0-4) Barcena & Co.

Barcenes, Greg, tr. see McIntyre, Sally.

Barch, Margaret J. Act Cytogenetics. 3rd ed. LC 96-37936. 650p. 1997. text, lab manual ed. 142.00 (0-397-51651-7) Lppncott W & W.

Barcham, William L., text. Tiepolo. (Masters of Art Ser.). (Illus.). 128p. 1992. 24.95 (0-8109-3858-8, Pub. by Abrams) Time Warner.

***Barcham, William L., et al.** Paintings in the National Gallery, London. (Illus.). 608p. 2000. 135.00 (0-8212-2695-9) Bulfinch Pr.

Barchas, Elizabeth. Just a Handful: Poems of Rare & Endangered Wildlife. unabridged ed. (Illus.). 24p. (J). (gr. 5-10). 1995. pap. 9.95 incl. audio (0-9632621-5-7) High Haven Mus.

Barchas, Jack D., jt. ed. see Korenman, Stanley G.

Barchas, Jack D., jt. ed. see Martin, Joseph B.

Barchas, Patricia R., ed. Social Hierarchies: Essays Toward a Sociophysiological Perspective, 47. LC 83-22600. (Contributions in Sociology Ser.: No. 47). (Illus.). 160p. 1984. 45.00 (0-313-23165-6, BSH/, Greenwood Pr) Greenwood.

Barchas, Patricia R. & Mendoza, Sally P., eds. Social Cohesion: Essays Toward a Sociophysiological Perspective, 49. LC 83-22594. (Contributions in Sociology Ser.: No. 49). (Illus.). 203p. 1984. 57.95 (0-313-24395-6, BCH/) Greenwood.

***Barchas, Sarah.** Bridges Across the World: A Multicultural Songfest. 60p. (J). (gr. k-6). 1999. pap. 16.98 incl. audio compact disk (1-889686-14-X) High Haven Mus.

— Bridges Across the World: A Multicultural Songfest. (Illus.). 60p. (J). (gr. k-6). 1999. pap. 14.98 incl. audio (1-889686-13-1); pap. 5.95 (1-889686-16-6) High Haven Mus.

Barchas, Sarah. Get Ready, Get Set, Sing! Songs for Early Childhood. (Illus.). 40p. (J). (ps-3). 1994. pap. 12.95 incl. audio (0-9632621-1-4); pap. 15.98 incl. audio compact disk (0-9632621-2-2) High Haven Mus.

— If I Had a Pony: Animal Activity Songs. (Illus.). (J). (gr. k-4). 1996. pap. 12.95 incl. audio (0-9632621-7-3); pap. 15.98 incl. audio compact disk (0-9632621-8-1) High Haven Mus.

— Pinata & More! Bilingual Songs for Children. 2nd rev. ed. (ENG & SPA., Illus.). 36p. (J). (gr. k-6). 1997. pap. 12.95 incl. audio (1-889686-06-9) High Haven Mus.

Barchas, Sarah. Pinata & More! Bilingual Songs for Children. 2nd rev. ed. (ENG & SPA., Illus.). 36p. (J). (gr. k-6). 1997. pap. 15.98 incl. audio compact disk (1-889686-07-7) High Haven Mus.

Barchas, Sarah. Todos, Listos, CANTEN! Canciones para Ninos y para Aprender el Espanol. McClure, Marilyn et al, trs.Tr. of Get Ready, Get Set, SING!. (SPA., Illus.). 40p. (Orig.). (J). (ps-3). 1995. pap. 15.98 incl. audio compact disk (0-9632621-4-9) High Haven Mus.

— Todos, Listos, Canten! Canciones para Ninos y para Aprender el Espanol. McClure, Marilyn et al, trs. (SPA & ENG., Illus.). 40p. (J). (ps-3). 1995. pap. 12.95 incl. audio (0-9632621-3-0) High Haven Mus.

Barchas, Sarah, ed. This Old Man (Este Viejito) McClure, Marilyn et al, trs. (Singing Your Way to English & Spanish Ser.). (ENG & SPA., Illus.). 32p. (Orig.). (J). (ps-2). 1997. pap. 3.95 (1-889686-01-8) High Haven Mus.

Barchas, Sarah, ed. The Giant & the Rabbit: Six Bilingual Folktales from Hispanic Culture. (ENG & SPA., Illus.). 36p. (J). (gr. k-5). 1996. pap. 12.95 incl. audio (0-9632621-6-5) High Haven Mus.

Barchas, Sarah E. I Was Walking down the Road. (J). (ps-2). 1993. 19.95 (0-590-71883-5) Scholastic Inc.

— I Was Walking Down the Road. 1989. pap. text 22.00 (0-590-64788-1) Scholastic Inc.

Barchatowa, Jelena. Russischer Kontruktivismus - Plakatkunst. Glier, Erhard, tr. from FRE. (GER.). 216p. (C). 1992. 50.00 (3-8170-2024-4, Pub. by Knstvrlag Weingrtn) Intl Bk Import.

Barchers, Suzanne. Creating & Managing the Literate Classroom: Making the Whole Language Transition. xv, 187p. 1990. pap. text 23.00 (0-87287-705-1) Teacher Ideas Pr.

Barchers, Suzanne. Leap Hops, Pops, & Mops. (Illus.). 12p. (J). write for info. (1-58605-017-6) Knowledge Kids.

***Barchers, Suzanne I.** Bridges to Reading, K-3: Teaching Reading Skills with Children's Literature. LC 99-10209. 5p. 1999. pap. 23.00 (1-56308-758-8) Teacher Ideas Pr.

Barchers, Suzanne I. Bridges to Reading, 3-6: Teaching Reading Skills with Children's Literature. LC 99-10209. 5p. 1999. pap. 23.50 (1-56308-759-6) Teacher Ideas Pr.

— Fifty Fabulous Fables: Beginning Readers Theatre. LC 97-23132. (Illus.). 130p. 1997. lib. bdg. 21.50 (1-56308-553-4) Teacher Ideas Pr.

***Barchers, Suzanne I.** Multicultural Folktales: Readers Theatre for Elementary Students. 225p. 2000. pap. 24.50 (1-56308-760-X, TIP) Libs Unl.

Barchers, Suzanne I. Readers Theatre for Beginning Readers. LC 92-45813. (Illus.). vii, 97p. 1993. pap. text 19.00 (1-56308-136-9) Teacher Ideas Pr.

— Reading Methods: From Process to Practice. LC 97-37398. (C). 1997. 71.95 (0-534-53856-8) Wadsworth Pub.

— Scary Readers Theatre. (Illus.). xiii, 157p. 1994. pap. text 22.00 (1-56308-292-6) Teacher Ideas Pr.

— Teaching Language Arts: An Integrated Approach. Jucha, ed. LC 93-36299. 530p. (C). 1994. 45.75 (0-314-02503-0) West Pub.

— Wise Women: Folk & Fairy Tales from Around the World. (Illus.). 400p. 1997. lib. bdg. 22.00 (1-56308-592-5) Libs Unl.

***Barchers, Suzanne I. & Marden, Patricia C.** Cooking up U. S. History: Recipes & Research to Share with Children. 2nd ed. LC 98-55921. 16p. 1999. pap. 24.00 (1-56308-682-4) Teacher Ideas Pr.

Barchers, Suzanne I. & Rauen, Peter J. Holiday Storybook Stew: Cooking Through the Year with Books Kids Love. LC 98-14700. (Illus.). 128p. (J). (gr. k-6). 1998. pap. 15.95 (1-55591-972-3) Fulcrum Pub.

— Storybook Stew: Cooking with Books Kids Love. LC 96-13780. (Illus.). 128p. (J). 1996. pap. 15.95 (1-55591-944-8) Fulcrum Pub.

***Barchers, Suzanne I., et al.** 365 Reading Activities LC 99-179628. 240p. 1998. write for info. (0-7853-2812-2) Pubns Intl Ltd.

Barchers, Suzanne I., jt. auth. see Marden, Patricia C.

Barchiesi, Alessandro. The Poet & the Prince: Ovid & Augustan Discourse. LC 96-49230. 285p. 1997. 48.00 (0-520-20223-6, Pub. by U CA Pr) Cal Prin Full Svc.

Barchilon, Jacques, jt. auth. see Holman, Robyn.

***Barchok, Charles, Jr.** Aviation Safety: New Airlines Illustrate Long-Standing Problems in FAA[0012]s Inspection Program. (Illus.). 51p. 2000. reprint ed. pap. text 20.00 (0-7881-8912-3) DIANE Pub.

Barchowsky, Nan J. BFH, a Manual for Fluent Handwriting. Barchowsky, Paul & McGrath, Sally V., eds. LC 97-91564. (Illus.). 85p. (Orig.). 1997. text 39.95 incl. cd-rom (0-9656745-7-6) Swansbury.

Barchowsky, Paul, ed. see Barchowsky, Nan J.

Barci, Rosalie. Tambourine Interweave. 150p. 1994. 6.95 (0-9643777-0-5) R G Barci.

Barcia, Jose R., tr. see Vallejo, Cesar.

Barcia, Roque. Sinonimus Castellanos. 17th ed. (SPA.). 590p. 1978. 15.95 (0-8288-5271-5, S11889) Fr & Eur.

***Barciauskas, Jonas.** Landscapes of Wisdom: In Search of Spirituality. 240p. 2000. 49.00 (0-7618-1731-X) U Pr of Amer.

***Barciauskas, Jonas Vladas.** Landscapes of Wisdom: In Search of a Spirituality of Knowing. LC 00-30286. 240p. 2000. pap. 29.50 (0-7618-1732-8) U Pr of Amer.

Barcikowski, Robert S., ed. Computer Packages & Research Design: Vol. 1-BMDP with Annotations of Input & Output from the BMDP, SAS, SPSS & SPSSX Statistical Packages. (Illus.). 572p. (Orig.). 1983. pap. text 47.50 (0-8191-3494-5) U Pr of Amer.

Barcikowski, Robert S., et al. Assessment, Testing & Evaluation in Teacher Education. (Social & Policy Issues in Education Ser.). (Illus.). 1995. pap. 24.95 (1-56750-154-0); text 73.25 (1-56750-153-2) Ablx Pub.

Barcinas, Josefina, ed. see Salas, Marilyn C.

Barcio, Robert, et al. The Story of Gannon University: Education on the Square. LC 85-81770. 208p. (Orig.). 1985. 10.00 (0-936063-00-9); pap. text 5.00 (0-685-12412-6) Gannon U Pr.

Barciszewski, Jan, ed. see NATO Advanced Research Workshop on RNA: Biochemistry & Biotechnology Staff.

Barck, Christophorus. Wort und Tat Bei Homer. (Spudasmata Ser.: Bd. XXXIV). (GER.). 180p. 1976. 35.00 (3-487-06233-X) G Olms Pubs.

Barck, Karlheinz, et al, contrib. by. Werner Kraus Das Wissenschaftliche Werk: Band: 4 Essays zur Spanischen und Franzosischen Literatur- und Ideologiegeschichte der Moderne. 804p. 1997. 146.00 (3-11-015521-4) De Gruyter.

Barck, Oscar T., Jr. & Lefler, Hugh T. History of the United States-Since 1865. LC 68-12884. (Illus.). 655p. reprint ed. 200.00 (0-8357-9907-7, 201246600081) Bks Demand.

Barcker-McKee, Steven, et al. A Student's Guide to the Federal Rules of Civil Procedure. LC 98-161897. 650p. (C). 1997. pap. 23.25 (0-314-22679-6) West Pub.

Barclay. History of Balmville. 3.98 (0-686-14962-9) T E Henderson.

— How to Relate to Your Pastor. rev. ed. 1995. pap. 5.00 (0-944802-26-5) M Barclay Pubns.

— King & the Kingdom. 1993. pap. 7.00 (0-7152-0006-2) St Mut.

— Midwifery in Australia. (C). 1998. pap. text 42.00 (0-443-05429-0) Harcourt.

— Trigonometry. 3rd ed. (C). 1993. pap. text, student ed. 25.00 (0-03-096638-8) Harcourt Coll Pubs.

Barclay, et al. New Product Development. 196p. pap. 65.95 (0-7506-4998-4) Buttrwrth-Heinemann.

Barclay, A. Neil, et al, eds. The Leucocyte Antigen Factsbook. 2nd ed. LC 97-15939. (Illus.). 640p. 1997. pap. text 49.95 (0-12-078185-9) Morgan Kaufmann.

Barclay, Alexander. Practical View of the Present State of Slavery in the West Indies. LC 74-83955. (Black Heritage Library Collection). 1977. 36.95 (0-8369-8508-7) Ayer.

Barclay, Alexander, tr. see Brant, Sebastian.

***Barclay, Alistair & Halpin, Clair.** Excavations at Barrow Hills, Radley, Oxfordshire Vol. 1: The Neolithic & Bronze Age Monument Complex. (Thames Valley Landscapes Ser.: Vol. 11). (Illus.). 335p. 1999. pap. 86.50 (0-947816-89-5, Pub. by Oxford Univ Comm Arch) David Brown.

***Barclay, Alistair & Halpin, Claire.** Excavations at Barrow Hills, Radley, Oxfordshire: The Neolithic & Bronze Age Monument Complex. Healy, Frances & Durden, Theresa, eds. (Thames Valley Landscapes Ser.: Vol. 11). (Illus.). 390p. (C). 1998. pap. 86.50 (0-947816-88-7, Pub. by Oxford Univ Comm Arch) David Brown.

Barclay, Alistair, et al. Excavations at the Devil's Quoits, Stanton Harcourt. (Thames Valley Landscapes Ser.: Vol. 3). (Illus.). 140p. 1995. pap. 32.00 (0-947816-84-4, Pub. by Oxford Univ Comm Arch) David Brown.

An Asterisk (*) at the beginning of an entry indicates that the title is appearing for the first time.

*Barclay, Alistar & Harding, Jan, eds. Pathways & Ceremonies: The Cursus Monuments of Britian & Ireland. (Neolithic Studies Group Seminar Papers: Vol. 4). 154p. 1999. pap. 45.00 (1-900188-42-2, Pub. by Oxbow Bks) David Brown.

Barclay, Allan G., jt. ed. see McNamara, Regis.

Barclay, Barbara, jt. auth. see Cole, Malcolm S.

Barclay, Byrna. Crosswinds. 216p. 1995. pap. 12.95 (1-55050-087-2, Pub. by Coteau) Genl Dist Srvs.

Barclay, C. & Walmsley, A. D. Dental Prosthetics. 2nd ed. LC 97-18739. (Colour Guide Ser.). 1997. write for info. (0-443-05813-X) Harcrt Hlth Sci Grp.

Barclay, Ceylon. Red Rum Punch. LC 94-60436. (Illus.). 350p. (Orig.). 1994. pap. text 14.95 (0-940121-15-8, P201, Cross Roads Bks) Cross Cultural Pubns. This work is a tangled story of a communist-to-capitalist venture in the Caribbean. A truly heart-breaking account authored by a businessman & educator who was deeply involved in this effort to assist a small emerging third world nation. This skillfully crafted story of hope & betrayal will haunt you. It is a true account of an attempt to establish a capitalist toehold in Grenada & will quietly weave its way into your heart. ***Publisher Paid Annotation.***

Barclay, Cornelia B. Barclay. Our Branch of Barclays. 78p. 1997. reprint ed. pap. 15.50 (0-8328-7373-X); reprint ed. lib. bdg. 25.50 (0-8328-7372-1) Higginson Bk Co.

Barclay, David E. Frederick William IV & the Prussian Monarchy, 1840-1861. (Illus.). 350p. 1995. text 89.00 (0-19-820430-2) OUP.

Barclay, David E. & Glaser-Schmidt, Elisabeth, eds. Transatlantic Images & Perceptions: Germany & America since 1776. LC 96-31667. (Publications of the German Historical Institute, Washington, D. C.). (Illus.). 381p. (C). 1997. text 74.95 (0-521-58091-9) Cambridge U Pr.

Barclay, David E. & Weitz, Eric D., eds. Between Reform & Revolution: German Socialism & Communism from 1840 to 1990. LC 97-22088. 592p. 1998. 85.00 (1-57181-000-5) Berghahn Bks.

Barclay, David R., et al. Encountering the Glass Ceiling: Gender, Values, & the Structure of Work. unabridged ed. Glass, Judith, ed. (Dynamics of Gender in the Workplace Ser.: Vol. 2). 71p. 1995. pap. text 18.50 (0-89215-187-0) U Cal LA Indus Rel.

Barclay, Dolores. Believe in Yourself. 1989. 6.95 (0-8378-1874-5) Gibson.

Barclay, Dolores, jt. auth. see Perry, Joan.

***Barclay, Donald.** Managing Public Access Computers: A How-to-Do-It Manual for Librarians. 225p. 1999. pap. 59.95 (1-55570-361-5) Neal-Schuman.

Barclay, Donald A. Teaching Electronic Information Literacy: A How-To-Do-It Manual. LC 95-31401. 179p. (Orig.). 1995. pap. 65.00 incl. disk (1-55570-299-6) Neal-Schuman.

Barclay, Donald A., ed. Teaching Electronic Information Literacy: A How-To-Do-It Manual. LC 95-31401. (Illus.). 179p. (Orig.). 1995. pap. 49.95 (1-55570-186-8) Neal-Schuman.

Barclay, Donald A., et al, eds. Into the Wilderness Dream: Exploration Narratives of the American West, 1500-1805. 408p. (C). 1994. pap. 19.95 (0-87480-444-2) U of Utah Pr.

Barclay, F. H. Primer of Pelvicology, Pt. 1. 31p. 1985. reprint ed. spiral bd. 10.00 (0-7873-1154-5) Hlth Research.

Barclay, Frederica, jt. auth. see Santos-Granero, Fernando.

Barclay, Frederico, jt. auth. see Santos-Granero, Fernando.

Barclay, Glen S. Friends in High Places: Australian-American Diplomatic Relations Since 1945. LC E 0183.8.A8. 253p. reprint ed. pap. 78.50 (0-8357-6826-0, 203551200095) Bks Demand.

— Friends in High Places: The Australian-American Security Relationship since 1945. 1985. text 29.00 (0-19-554608-3) OUP.

— A Very Small Insurance Policy: The Politics of Australian Involvement in Vietnam, 1954-1967. LC 86-27284. 199p. (Orig.). (C). 1988. pap. text 29.95 (0-7022-2069-8, Pub. by Univ Queensland Pr) Intl Spec Bk.

Barclay, Gwen, jt. auth. see Hill, Madalene.

Barclay, Harold. People Without Government: An Anthology of Anarchy. 162p. 1996. reprint ed. pap. 12.95 (1-871082-16-1, Pub. by Kahn & Averill) Paul & Co Pubs.

— The Role of the Horse in Man's Culture. 398p. 1990. 58.00 (0-85131-329-9, Pub. by J A Allen) St Mut.

Barclay, I., et al. New Product Development: A Practical Workbook for Improving Performance. 192p. Date not set. text 170.00 (1-85573-447-8, Pub. by Woodhead Pubng) Am Educ Systs.

***Barclay, Ian, et al.** Improving Product Development Performance: A Practical Workbook & Software Package. LC 99-39003. 1999. write for info. (0-8493-2385-1) CRC Pr.

Barclay, Ian, jt. auth. see Olford, Stephen F.

***Barclay, James A.** The Toronto Terror: The Life & Works of Stanley Thompson, Golf Course Architect. (Illus.). 176p. 2000. 35.00 (1-886947-93-7) Sleepng Bear.

Barclay, James R. Psychological Assessment: A Theory Systems Approach. LC 89-37230. 458p. (C). 1991. lib. bdg. 47.00 (0-89464-405-X) Krieger.

Barclay, James T. The City of the Great King: Jerusalem As It Was, As It Is, & As It Is to Be. Davis, Moshe, ed. LC 77-70664. (America & the Holy Land Ser.). 1977. reprint ed. lib. bdg. 54.95 (0-405-10225-9) Ayer.

Barclay, Janet M., ed. Emily Bronte Criticism Nineteen Hundred to Nineteen Eighty: An Annotated Check List. LC 83-17433. 162p. 1984. lib. bdg. 55.00 (0-313-27667-6) Greenwood.

***Barclay, Janet M., ed.** How Cold Was It? (Illus.). 24p. (J). (ps-4). 2000. pap. 11.95 (1-894222-19-9) LOB4.

Barclay, John. The Seventy-Year Ebb & Flow of Chinese Library & Information Services: May 4, 1919 to the Late 1980s. LC 94-27784. 351p. 1995. 48.00 (0-8108-2713-1) Scarecrow.

Barclay, John, ed. Early Christian Thought in Its Jewish Context. (Illus.). 314p. (C). 1996. text 64.95 (0-521-46285-1) Cambridge U Pr.

Barclay, John M. Colossians & Philemon. (New Testament Guides Ser.). 131p. 1997. pap. 12.50 (1-85075-818-2, Pub. by Sheffield Acad) CUP Services.

— Jews in the Mediterranean Diaspora: From Alexander to Trajan (323 B. C. E. - 117 C. E.) LC 96-197557. 538p. 59.95 (0-567-08500-7, Pub. by T & T Clark) Bks Intl VA.

— Jews in the Mediterranean Diaspora: From Alexander to Trajan (323 B. C. E. -117 C. E.) 544p. 1999. pap. 24.95 (0-520-21843-4, Pub. by U CA Pr) Cal Prin Full Svc.

— Obeying the Truth: A Study of Paul's Ethics in Galatians. Riches, John E., ed. (Studies of the New Testament & Its World). 320p. text 49.95 (0-567-09493-6, Pub. by T & T Clark) Bks Intl VA.

Barclay, Juliet. Havana: A Portrait of a City. (Illus.). 192p. 1996. pap. 19.95 (0-304-34554-7, Pub. by Cassell) Sterling.

Barclay, Kathy & Boone, Elizabeth. Building a Three-Way Partnership: The Leader's Role in Linking School, Families & Community. LC 94-25224. (Illus.). 240p. 1999. 24.95 (0-590-49720-0) Scholastic Inc.

— The Parent Difference: Uniting School, Family, & Community. 2nd rev. ed. LC 96-78398. (Illus.). 263p. 1996. pap. 32.95 (1-57517-073-6, 1467) SkyLght.

— Supporting the Move to Whole Language: A Handbook for School Leaders. LC 92-40245. 1995. 24.95 (0-590-49222-5, 1576b296 1993) Scholastic Inc.

Barclay, Kenneth A. C++ Problem Solving & Programming. LC 93-44647. 350p. 1994. pap. 60.00 (0-13-126673-X, Prentice Hall) P-H.

Barclay, Laurie, ed. Clinical Geriatric Neurology. LC 92-20248. (Illus.). 513p. 1993. text 98.00 (0-8121-1610-0) Lppncott W & W.

Barclay, Lesley, jt. auth. see Lupton, Deborah.

Barclay, Leslie & Barkley, Carolyn L. History of the Scottish Barclays. 229p. 1995. pap. 20.00 (1-888265-00-0) Willow Bend.

Barclay, Linwood. Father Knows Zilch: A Guide for Dumbounded Dads. (Illus.). 224p. 1996. pap. 17.95 (0-7737-5808-9) Stoddart Publ.

Barclay, Linwood. This House Is Nuts: Surviving the Absurdities of Everyday Life. LC 97-931930. (Illus.). 204p. 1998. 17.95 (0-7737-3056-7) Stoddart Publ.

***Barclay, Lou Anne.** Foreign Direct Investment in Emerging Economies: Corporate Strategy & Investment Behaviour in the Caribbean. LC 99-45122. 272p. 2000. 90.00 (0-415-22023-8) Routledge.

Barclay, M. A. Real Truth about Tithing. LC 96-122344. 1994. pap. 5.00 (0-944802-20-6) M Barclay Pubns.

— Six Ways to Check Your Leadings. LC 98-144087. 1997. pap. 5.00 (0-944802-18-4) M Barclay Pubns.

— Warring Mental Warfare. LC 96-163029. 1996. pap. 5.00 (0-944802-28-1) M Barclay Pubns.

— What about Death. 1997. pap. 5.00 (0-944802-21-4) M Barclay Pubns.

Barclay, Mark T. Avoiding Pitfalls of Familiarity. 1998. pap. 5.99 (0-944802-30-3) M Barclay Pubns.

— Beware of Seducing Spirits. 2nd ed. LC 96-163073. 1995. pap. 6.00 (0-944802-25-7) M Barclay Pubns.

— Building a Supernatural Church. 50p. 1991. reprint ed. pap. 5.00 (0-944802-11-7) M Barclay Pubns.

— Charging the Year Two Thousand. 86p. (Orig.). (C). 1991. pap. 6.00 (0-944802-13-3) M Barclay Pubns.

— Enduring Hardness. rev. ed. 50p. (C). 1992. pap. 5.00 (0-944802-10-9) M Barclay Pubns.

— How to Always Reap a Harvest. LC 96-163031. pap. 5.00 (0-944802-12-5) M Barclay Pubns.

— How to Relate to Your Pastor. pap. 5.00 (0-944802-05-2) M Barclay Pubns.

— The Making of a Man of God. 80p. (Orig.). (C). pap. 5.00 (0-944802-19-2) M Barclay Pubns.

— The Remnant. 73p. (Orig.). 1988. pap. 5.00 (0-944802-00-1) M Barclay Pubns.

— Seven Bible Ways to Properly Relate to Your Pastor. 32p. 1982. pap. 2.25 (0-88144-024-8) Christian Pub.

— Sheep, Goats & Wolves. 54p. (Orig.). 1985. pap. 5.00 (0-944802-06-0) M Barclay Pubns.

— The Sin of Familiarity: Those Practicing Excessive Familiarity - a Devastating Sin. 64p. (Orig.). 1989. pap. 5.00 (0-944802-04-4) M Barclay Pubns.

— The Sin of Lawlessness: A Lethal Practice. 57p. (Orig.). 1989. pap. 5.00 (0-944802-01-X) M Barclay Pubns.

Barclay, Michael R. Catalogue of the Works of Charles Ricketts R.A. 69p. 1985. pap. 15.00 (0-938768-50-6, Pub. by Catalpa Pr Ltd) Oak Knoll.

— A Catalogue of the Works of Charles Ricketts RA. 1985. write for info. (0-904995-08-9) Battledore Ltd.

Barclay, Oliver R. The Intellect & Beyond: Developing a Christian Mind. 144p. (Orig.). 1985. pap. 3.95 (0-310-33291-5, 12280P) Zondervan.

Barclay, Olivia. Horary Astrology Rediscovered. LC 89-51779. (Illus.). 349p. 1990. pap. 18.95 (0-914918-99-0, Whitford) Schiffer.

Barclay, Peter J., ed. see British Computer Society Staff, et al.

Barclay, Peter M., contrib. by. The Barclay Report: Social Workers - Their Role & Tasks. (C). 1982. 110.00 (0-7855-0067-7, Pub. by Natl Inst Soc Work) St Mut.

Barclay, R. J., et al. Disturbance Index Method for Assessing Severity of Procedures on Rodents. (C). 1988. pap. 30.00 (0-900767-51-0, Pub. by Univs Fed Animal Welfare) St Mut.

Barclay, R. Mary, tr. see Kraepelin, Emil.

Barclay, Robert. The Art of the Trumpet-Maker: The Materials, Tools, & Techniques of the Seventeenth & Eighteenth Centuries in Nuremberg. LC 95-47888. (Early Music Ser.: Vol. 14). (Illus.). 198p. (C) 1996. pap. text 32.00 (0-19-816605-2, Clarendon Pr) OUP.

— Barclay's Apology in Modern English: An Apology for the True Christian Divinity. Freiday, Dean, ed. 465p. 1991. reprint ed. pap. 18.00 (0-913342-69-6) Barclay Pr.

***Barclay, Robert O.** A Gift Once Given. LC 99-9432. 1999. 25.00 (0-7388-0766-4); pap. 18.00 (0-7388-0767-2) Xlibris Corp.

Barclay, Ronald. An Alphabet of Barclay. 112p. 1993. pap. 11.90 (0-7152-0692-3) St Mut.

Barclay, Scott. Appealing Act: Why People Appeal in Civil Cases. LC 99-28704. 1999. 35.00 (0-8101-1656-0) Northwestern U Pr.

Barclay, Shinan N. Inner Marriage: A Way to Wholeness, Empowerment & Bliss. (Illus.). 200p. (Orig.). (C). 1990. pap. 12.95 (0-945086-29-6) Sunlight Prodns.

— Rebonding with the Natural World: A Primer for Inter-Species Communication. (Illus.). 200p. (Orig.). (C). 1991. pap. 11.95 (0-685-35728-7) Sunlight Prodns.

— Who Am I? What Am I? Where Do I Belong? The Storytale about the Search for Meaning, Identity & Purpose. (Illus.). 40p. (J). (ps-4). 1990. 5.95 (0-317-89505-2); pap. write for info. (0-945085-08-3) Sunlight Prodns.

Barclay, Shinan N., ed. Moontime Anthology: Menesis, a Call to Power, a Return to the Sacred. (Illus.). 250p. (Orig.). 1991. pap. 13.95 (0-945086-89-X) Sunlight Prodns.

Barclay, Shinan N., jt. auth. see Dillon, Mary.

Barclay, Shinan N., jt. auth. see Johansen, Gayle.

Barclay-Smith, Phyllis, jt. auth. see Pollard, H. B. C.

***Barclay, Steven.** The Motion Picture Image: From Film to Digital. LC 99-45476. 224p. 1999. pap. 34.95 (0-240-80390-6, Focal) Buttrwrth-Heinemann.

Barclay, Steven, ed. A Place in the World Called Paris. LC 94-2089. (Illus.). 176p. 1994. 18.95 (0-8118-0286-7) Chronicle Bks.

Barclay, Suzanne. Knights Divided. (Sommerville Brothers Ser.). 1997. per. 4.99 (0-373-28959-6, 1-28959-4) Harlequin Bks.

***Barclay, Suzanne.** Knights of the Black Rose, 49. (Historical Ser.). 2000. per. 4.99 (0-373-29091-8) Harlequin Bks.

Barclay, Suzanne. Knight's Ransom. (Historical Ser.). 1996. per. 4.99 (0-373-28935-9, 1-28935-4) Harlequin Bks.

— Knight's Rebellion: The Sommerville Brothers. (Historical Ser.: No. 391). 1997. per. 4.99 (0-373-28991-X, 1-28991-7) Harlequin Bks.

— Lion of the North. LC 95-15859. (Historical Ser.). 299p. 1995. per. 4.50 (0-373-28872-7, 1-28872-9) Harlequin Bks.

— Lion's Heart. LC 95-7108. (Historical Ser.). 299p. 1995. per. 3.99 (0-373-28852-2, 1-28852-1) Harlequin Bks.

— Lion's Lady: The Sutherland Series. (Historical Ser.). 1998. per. 4.99 (0-373-29011-X, 0-29011-4) Harlequin Bks.

— Lion's Legacy. LC 96-7292. (Historical Ser.). 295p. 1996. per. 4.50 (0-373-28904-9, 1-28904-0) Harlequin Bks.

— Man with a Mission. (Intimate Moments Ser.). 1993. mass mkt. 3.39 (0-373-07483-2, 5-07483-6) Silhouette.

— Pride of Lions. 1998. per. 4.99 (0-373-29043-8, 1-29043-6, Mira Bks) Harlequin Bks.

— Taming the Lion: The Sutherland Series. (Historical Ser.: No. 463). 1999. per. 4.99 (0-373-29063-2, 1-29063-4, Harlequin) Harlequin Bks.

Barclay, Suzanne, et al. The Knights of Christmas: Kara's Gift; The Twelfth Day of Christmas; A Wish for Noel, 3 bks. 1997. per. 4.99 (0-373-28987-1, 1-28987-5) Harlequin Bks.

Barclay, Tessa. The Champagne Girls. large type ed. 1993. 39.95 (0-7066-1016-4, Pub. by Remploy Pr) St Mut.

— Her Father's Child. large type ed. (Charnwood Large Print Ser.). 544p. 1996. 27.99 (0-7089-8884-9, Charnwood) Ulverscroft.

— A Hidden Beauty. large type ed. (Charnwood Large Print Ser.). 848p. 1995. 27.99 (0-7089-8854-7, Charnwood) Ulverscroft.

— The Last Heiress. large type ed. 1993. 39.95 (0-7066-1020-2, Pub. by Remploy Pr) St Mut.

— The Millionaire's Woman. large type ed. (Charnwood Large Print Ser.). 1996. 27.99 (0-7089-8886-5, Charnwood) Ulverscroft.

— The Saturday Girl. large type ed. LC 97-43859. 533 p. 1998. write for info. (0-7540-2082-7) Chivers N Amer.

— The Saturday Girl. large type ed. LC 97-43859. 590p. 1998. 24.95 (0-7838-8416-8, G K Hall & Co) Mac Lib Ref.

— The Wine Widow. large type ed. 1993. 39.95 (0-7066-1012-1, Pub. by Remploy Pr) St Mut.

Barclay, Thomas & Douglas, Carstaairs. Chinese-English Dictionary of the Vernacular or Spoken Language of Amoy. 276p. reprint ed. suppl. ed. 98.00 (957-9482-32-2, RFE007, Pub. by SMC Pub) Farkwest Pubns.

Barclay, W. Intro to the Bible. 1987. 6.95 (0-687-19489-X) Abingdon.

Barclay, William. Acts of the Apostles. 1993. pap. 24.00 (0-7152-0276-6) St Mut.

— All Sufficient Christ: Studies in Paul's Letters to the Colossians. 142p. 1993. pap. 30.00 (0-7152-0389-4) St Mut.

— Ambassador for Christ: The Life & Teaching of Paul. 176p. 1993. pap. 24.00 (0-7152-0694-X) St Mut.

— And He Had Compassion: The Miracles of Jesus. 2725p. 1994. pap. 16.00 (0-8170-0686-9) Judson.

— And He Had Compassion: The Miracles of Jesus. 272p. (C). 1992. pap. 35.00 (0-7855-6831-X, Pub. by St Andrew) St Mut.

— And He Had Compassion: The Miracles of Jesus. 272p. 1993. pap. 21.00 (0-7152-0667-2) St Mut.

— And Jesus Said: The Parables of Jesus. 208p. 1993. pap. 22.00 (0-7152-0666-4) St Mut.

— The Apostles Creed. (William Barclay Library). 320p. 1999. pap. 18.00 (0-664-25826-3) Westminster John Knox.

— At the Last Trumpet: Jesus Christ & the End of Time. LC 98-37925. 112p. 1999. pap. 10.00 (0-664-25806-9) Westminster John Knox.

— A Barclay Prayer Book. LC 90-39209. 352p. (Orig.). (C). 1990. pap. 13.00 (0-334-02460-9) TPI PA.

***Barclay, William.** Barclay's Life of Jesus. LC 99-49160. (William Barclay Library). 384p. 2000. pap. 18.95 (0-664-22226-9, Pub. by Westminster John Knox) Presbyterian Pub.

Barclay, William. A Beginner's Guide to the New Testament. 160p. (C). 1992. pap. 40.00 (0-7855-6846-8, Pub. by St Andrew) St Mut.

— A Beginner's Guide to the New Testament. 128p. 1993. pap. 22.00 (0-7152-0669-9) St Mut.

— A Beginner's Guide to the New Testament. LC 95-2523. 128p. 1995. pap. 12.00 (0-664-25598-1) Westminster John Knox.

— Communicating the Gospel. 1978. reprint ed. pap. 5.00 (0-7152-0401-7) Outlook.

— Corinthians. 288p. 1993. pap. 30.00 (0-7152-0278-2) St Mut.

— Daily Study Bible for the New Testament, 18 vols. rev. ed. Incl. Acts of the Apostles. 1975. pap. 12.95 (0-664-24106-9); Gospel of Luke. 1975. pap. 12.95 (0-664-24103-4); Gospel of Mark. 1975. pap. 12.95 (0-664-24102-6); Letter to the Hebrews. 1976. pap. 12.95 (0-664-24112-3); Letter to the Romans. 1975. pap. 12.95 (0-664-24107-7); Letters of James & Peter. 1975. pap. 12.95 (0-664-24113-1); Letters of John & Jude. 1976. pap. 12.95 (0-664-24114-X); Letters to the Corinthians. 1975. pap. 12.95 (0-664-24108-5); Letters to the Galatians & Ephesians. 1976. pap. 12.95 (0-664-24109-3); Letters to the Philippians, Colossians & Thessalonians. 1975. pap. 12.95 (0-664-24110-7); Letters to Timothy, Titus & Philemon. 1975. pap. 12.95 (0-664-24111-5); Vol. 1. Gospel of John. 1975. pap. 12.95 (0-664-24104-2); Vol. 1. Gospel of Matthew. 1975. pap. 12.95 (0-664-24100-X); Vol. 1. Revelation of John. 1976. pap. 12.95 (0-664-24115-8); Vol. 2. Gospel of John. 1975. pap. 12.95 (0-664-24105-0); Vol. 2. Gospel of Matthew. 1975. pap. 12.95 (0-664-24101-8); Vol. 2. Revelation of John. 1976. pap. 12.95 (0-664-24116-6); 189.95 (0-664-24098-4) Westminster John Knox.

***Barclay, William.** Discovering Jesus. (William Barclay Library). (Illus.). 140p. 2000. pap. 14.95 (0-664-22192-0) Westminster John Knox.

Barclay, William. Flesh & Spirit. 142p. 1993. pap. 30.00 (0-7152-0396-7) St Mut.

— Galatians & Ephesians. 208p. 1993. pap. 21.00 (0-7152-0279-0, Pub. by St Andrew) St Mut.

— God's Young Church: A Study of the Early Church. 144p. (C). 1992. pap. 30.00 (0-7855-6829-8, Pub. by St Andrew) St Mut.

— God's Young Church: A Study of the Early Church. 144p. 1993. pap. 21.00 (0-7152-0061-5, Pub. by St Andrew) St Mut.

— Good Tidings of Great Joy: The Birth of Jesus the Messiah. LC 99-23300. (William Barclay Library). 96p. 1999. pap. 12.95 (0-664-25850-6) Westminster John Knox.

***Barclay, William.** Growing in Christian Faith: A Book of Daily Readings. (William Barclay Library). 96p. 2000. pap. 9.95 (0-664-22227-7, Pub. by Westminster John Knox) Presbyterian Pub.

Barclay, William. Hebrews. 212p. 1993. pap. 21.00 (0-7152-0282-0, Pub. by St Andrew) St Mut.

— Index. 224p. 1993. pap. 21.00 (0-7152-0378-9, Pub. by St Andrew) St Mut.

— Introducing the Bible. LC 90-35763. 1990. pap. 5.95 (0-687-19490-3) Abingdon.

— Introducing the Bible. 176p. 1997. pap. 9.95 (0-687-36590-2) Abingdon.

— Introducing the Bible. large type ed. LC 85-6397. 304p. 1985. reprint ed. pap. 9.95 (0-8027-2495-7) Walker & Co.

— James & Peter. 368p. 1993. pap. 25.00 (0-7152-0283-9, Pub. by St Andrew) St Mut.

— Jesus As They Saw Him. LC 78-18224. 1978. pap. 20.00 (0-8028-1775-0) Eerdmans.

— John, No. 1. 272p. 1993. pap. 22.00 (0-7152-0274-X, Pub. by St Andrew) St Mut.

— John, No. 2. 304p. 1993. pap. 21.00 (0-7152-0275-8, Pub. by St Andrew) St Mut.

— John - Jude. 196p. 1993. pap. 24.00 (0-7152-0284-7, Pub. by St Andrew) St Mut.

— King & the Kingdom. 208p. 1993. pap. 30.00 (0-7152-0695-8, Pub. by St Andrew) St Mut.

— The Lord's Prayer. (William Barclay Library). 128p. 1999. pap. 12.00 (0-664-25815-8) Westminster John Knox.

— Luke. 312p. 1993. pap. 24.00 (0-7152-0273-1, Pub. by St Andrew) St Mut.

— The Making of the Bible. 106p. (C). 1992. pap. 35.00 (0-7855-6828-X, Pub. by St Andrew) St Mut.

B

— The Making of the Bible. 106p. 1993. pap. 30.00 (*0-7152-0420-3*, Pub. by St Andrew) St Mut.
— Mark. 384p. 1993. pap. 25.00 (*0-7152-0272-3*, Pub. by St Andrew) St Mut.
— The Master's Men. large type ed. LC 85-6395. 224p. 1985. reprint ed. pap. 8.95 (*0-8027-2496-5*) Walker & Co.
— Matthew, No. 1. 416p. 1993. pap. 30.00 (*0-7152-0270-7*, Pub. by St Andrew) St Mut.
— Matthew, No. 2. 392p. 1993. pap. 22.00 (*0-7152-0271-5*, Pub. by St Andrew) St Mut.
— The Mind of Jesus. (C). 1990. pap. 30.00 (*0-85305-291-3*, Pub. by Arthur James) St Mut.
— The Mind of Jesus. LC 61-7332. 352p. 1976. reprint ed. pap. 18.00 (*0-06-060451-4*, RD143, Pub. by Harper SF) HarpC.
— More Prayers for Plain People. (Abingdon Classics Ser.). 160p. (Orig.). 1993. pap. 5.95 (*0-687-27187-8*) Abingdon.
— The New Testament: A Translation by William Barclay. (William Barclay Library). 598p. 1999. pap. 18.95 (*0-664-22174-2*) Westminster John Knox.
— New Testament Words. LC 73-12737. (William Barclay Library). 96p. 2000. pap. 17.95 (*0-664-24761-X*, Pub. by Westminster John Knox) Presbyterian Pub.
— The Old Law & the New Law: The Ten Commandments & the Sermon on the Mount. 128p. 1993. pap. 30.00 (*0-7152-0197-2*, Pub. by St Andrew) St Mut.
— Palabras Griegas Del Nuevo Testamento: New Testament Words. Marin, Javier-Jose, tr. 220p. 1976. reprint ed. pap. 10.50 (*0-311-42052-4*) Casa Bautista.
— The Parables of Jesus. (William Barclay Library). 222p. 1999. reprint ed. pap. 15.00 (*0-664-25828-X*) Westminster John Knox.
— Philippians, Colossians, & Thessalonians. 240p. 1993. pap. 21.00 (*0-7152-0280-4*, Pub. by St Andrew) St Mut.
— The Plain Man's Book of Prayers. LC 90-83632. 144p. 1959. pap. 8.95 (*0-87061-180-1*) Chr Classics.
— Plain People Look at the Beatitudes. (Abingdon Classics Ser.). 128p. (Orig.). 1993. pap. 4.95 (*0-687-31550-6*) Abingdon.
— Prayers for Help & Healing. LC 94-39634. 1994. pap. 10.99 (*0-8066-2784-0*, 9-2784, Augsburg) Augsburg Fortress.
— Prayers for Young People. LC 92-38164. (Abingdon Classics Ser.). 96p. (Orig.). (YA). 1993. pap. 1.49 (*0-687-33328-8*) Abingdon.
— Revelation, No. 1. 196p. 1993. pap. 30.00 (*0-7152-0285-5*, Pub. by St Andrew) St Mut.
— Revelation, No. 2. 244p. 1993. pap. 30.00 (*0-7152-0286-3*, Pub. by St Andrew) St Mut.
— Romans. 240p. 1993. pap. 24.00 (*0-7152-0277-4*, Pub. by St Andrew) St Mut.
— The Ten Commandments. (William Barclay Library). 208p. 1999. pap. 15.00 (*0-664-25816-6*) Westminster John Knox.
— Timothy, Titus & Philemon. 304p. 1993. pap. 21.00 (*0-7152-0281-2*, Pub. by St Andrew) St Mut.
— We Have Seen the Lord! The Passion & Resurrection of Jesus Christ. LC 98-35961. 112p. 1999. pap. 10.00 (*0-664-25807-7*) Westminster John Knox.
— William Barclay: A Spiritual Autobiography. LC 73-76528. 127p. reprint ed. pap. 39.40 (*0-7837-0511-5*, 204083500018) Bks Demand.

Barclay, William, ed. And Jesus Said: The Parables of Jesus. 208p. (C). 1992. pap. 35.00 (*0-7855-6830-1*, Pub. by St Andrew) St Mut.
— Every Day with William Barclay. (C). 1990. pap. 45.00 (*0-85305-253-0*, Pub. by Arthur James) St Mut.
— Marching Orders. (C). 1990. pap. 30.00 (*0-85305-251-4*, Pub. by Arthur James) St Mut.
— The Old Law & the New Law: The Ten Commandments & the Sermon on the Mount. 128p. (C). 1992. pap. 35.00 (*0-7855-6827-1*, Pub. by St Andrew) St Mut.
— Seven Fresh Wineskins. (C). 1990. pap. 24.00 (*0-85305-276-X*, Pub. by Arthur James) St Mut.
— Through the Year with William Barclay. (C). 1990. pap. 35.00 (*0-85305-252-2*, Pub. by Arthur James) St Mut.

Barclay, William, et al, eds. Racial Conflict, Discrimination, & Power: Historical & Contemporary Studies. LC 75-11964. (Studies in Modern Society: Political & Social Issues: No. 9). 1976. pap. 11.95 (*0-404-13144-1*); lib. bdg. 32.50 (*0-404-13140-9*) AMS Pr.

Barclay, William R. & McIntosh, Robins P., eds. Algal Biomass Technologies: An Interdisciplinary Perspective. Proceedings of a Workshop on the Present Status & Future Directions for Biotechnologies Based on Algal Biomass Production, April 5-7, 1984, University of Colorado, Boulder. (Nova Hedwigia, Beihefte/ Supplementary Issues Ser.: Beih 83). (Illus.). viii, 273p. 1984. pap. 71.00 (*3-443-51003-5*, Pub. by Gebruder Borntraeger) Balogh.

Barcley, Alexander, tr. see Brant, Sebastian.

***Barcley, William B.** Christ in You: A Study in Paul's Theology & Ethics. LC 99-44146. 1999. pap. write for info. (*0-7618-1512-0*) U Pr of Amer.
— Christ in You: A Study in Paul's Theology & Ethics. LC 99-44146. 184p. 1999. 42.50 (*0-7618-1511-2*) U Pr of Amer.

Barcliff, Boris C., ed. see Shabazz, Tariq A.

Barcomb, David. Office Automation: A Survey of Tools & Technology. 2nd ed. 350p. 1988. pap. text 28.00 (*0-13-631094-X*) P-H.

Barcons, X. & Fabian, Andrew C., eds. The X-Ray Background. (Illus.). 324p. (C). 1992. text 74.95 (*0-521-41651-5*) Cambridge U Pr.

Barcott, Bruce. The Measure of a Mountain. 288p. 1998. pap. 12.95 (*0-345-42633-9*) Ballantine Pub Grp.
— The Measure of a Mountain: Beauty & Terror on Mount Rainier. LC 97-22029. 288p. 1997. 23.95 (*1-57061-074-6*) Sasquatch Bks.

Barcott, Bruce, ed. Northwest Passages: A Literary Anthology of the Pacific Northwest from Coyote Tales to Roadside Attractions. LC 94-2939. 320p. (Orig.). 1994. pap. 15.95 (*1-57061-005-3*) Sasquatch Bks.

Barcroft, Alasdair. Aloe Vera: Nature's Legendary Healer. 128p. 1997. pap. 10.95 (*0-285-63352-X*, Pub. by Souvenir Pr Ltd) IPG Chicago.

Barcus. Functions in College Algebra. 224p. (C). 1998. pap. text 34.80 (*0-201-34734-2*) Addison-Wesley.

***Barcus.** Functions of College Algebra Class Test II. 1998. pap. text 28.00 (*0-201-34728-8*) Addison-Wesley.

Barcus, Alexandra. College Algebra: Preview Edition. 176p. (C). 1997. pap. 31.60 (*0-201-34710-5*) Addison-Wesley.

Barcus, Audrey. Dangerous Secrets. 1996. 9.09 (*0-606-09180-7*, Pub. by Turtleback) Demco.
— Hidden Secrets. 1996. 9.09 (*0-606-09409-1*, Pub. by Turtleback) Demco.

Barcus, F. Earle. Images of Life on Children's Television: Sex Roles, Minorities & Families. LC 83-4131. 217p. 1983. 52.95 (*0-275-90942-5*, C0942, Praeger Pubs) Greenwood.

Barcus, Francis Earle. Images of Life on Children's Television: Sex Roles, Minorities & Families. LC 83-4131. 1983. 21.95 (*0-03-063883-6*) Holt R&W.

Barcus, Frank. Freshwater Fury. LC 86-15799. (Great Lakes Bks.). (Illus.). 182p. reprint ed. pap. 56.50 (*0-608-10644-5*, 2071266) Bks Demand.
— Freshwater Fury: Yarns & Reminiscences of the Greatest Storm in Inland Navigation. LC 86-15799. (Great Lakes Bks.). (Illus.). 182p. 1986. pap. 16.95 (*0-8143-1828-2*) Wayne St U Pr.

Barcus, James E., ed. Shelley: The Critical Heritage. (Critical Heritage Ser.). 1975. 69.50 (*0-7100-8148-0*, Routledge Thoemms) Routledge.

Barcus, Nancy. Discover Waco: Reflections & Images. unabridged ed. (Illus.). 62p. 1993. pap. 12.95 (*0-9650227-0-6*) Arcway Pubns.
— Waco People . . . Making a Difference: Representative Wacoans. (Illus.). 214p. (Orig.). 1996. pap. 15.95 (*0-9650227-1-4*) Arcway Pubns.

Barcus, Sam W. Handbook of Management Consulting Services. 2nd ed. Wilkinson, Joseph W., ed. LC 94-23359. 768p. 1994. 64.95 (*0-07-003686-1*) McGraw.

Barcus, Sam W., ed. Financial Information Systems Manual. 2nd ed. 1993. ring bd. 150.00 (*0-685-69585-9*, FISM) Warren Gorham & Lamont.

Barcus, Sam W., III, ed. see Brooks, Rebecca, et al.

***Barczewski, Stephanie L.** Myth & National Identity in Nineteenth Century Britain: The Legends of King Arthur & Robin Hood. LC 99-40054. 288p. 2000. write for info. (*0-19-820728-X*) OUP.

Barczy, P., ed. Solidification & Microgravity. (Materials Science Forum Ser.: Vol. 77). 342p. 1992. text 100.00 (*0-87849-624-6*, Pub. by Trans T Pub) Enfield Pubs NH.

Bard, jt. auth. see Engkent.

Bard, Allan J. & Lund, Henning, eds. Encyclopedia of Electrochemistry of the Elements: Organic Section, Vol. 11. LC 73-88796. 360p. 1978. reprint ed. pap. 111.60 (*0-608-08198-1*, 202671300011) Bks Demand.

Bard, Allen J. Electroanalytical Chemistry, Vol. 4. (Illus.). 344p. 1970. text 199.00 (*0-8247-1038-X*) Dekker.
— Electroanalytical Chemistry, Vol. 5. (Illus.). 400p. 1971. text 199.00 (*0-8247-1041-X*) Dekker.
— Electroanalytical Chemistry, Vol. 14. (Illus.). 464p. 1986. text 199.00 (*0-8247-7608-9*) Dekker.

Bard, Allen J. Electroanalytical Chemistry, Vol. 15. (Illus.). 392p. 1988. text 199.00 (*0-8247-7646-1*) Dekker.
— Electroanalytical Chemistry, Vol. 16. (Illus.). 360p. 1988. text 199.00 (*0-8247-7994-0*) Dekker.

Bard, Allen J. Electroanalytical Chemistry, Vol. 18. (Illus.). 416p. 1993. text 199.00 (*0-8247-9092-8*) Dekker.
— Electroanalytical Chemistry Vol. 13: A Series of Advances. LC 66-11287. (Illus.). 408p. 1984. pap. 126.50 (*0-608-04803-8*, 204098200013) Bks Demand.
— Encyclopedia of Electrochemicals of the Elements, Vol. 13. 400p. 1979. 195.00 (*0-8247-2513-1*) Dekker.
— Encyclopedia of Electrochemistry of the Elements, Vol. 3. 328p. 1975. 195.00 (*0-8247-6137-5*) Dekker.
— Encyclopedia of Electrochemistry of the Elements, Vol. 5. 400p. 1976. 195.00 (*0-8247-2505-0*) Dekker.
— Encyclopedia of Electrochemistry of the Elements, Vol. 15. 344p. 1985. 195.00 (*0-8247-2515-8*) Dekker.
— Encyclopedia of the Electrochemistry of the Elements, Vol. 9B. 696p. 1986. 195.00 (*0-8247-2519-0*) Dekker.
— Integrated Chemical Systems: A Chemical Approach to Nanotechnology. (Baker Lectures). 324p. 1994. 74.95 (*0-471-00733-1*) Wiley.

Bard, Allen J., ed. Electroanalytical Chemistry: A Series of Advances, Vol. 1. LC 66-11287. 436p. 1966. reprint ed. pap. 135.20 (*0-608-04779-1*, 202150400022) Bks Demand.
— Electroanalytical Chemistry: A Series of Advances, Vol. 2. LC 66-11287. 282p. 1967. reprint ed. pap. 87.50 (*0-608-04780-5*, 205506600002) Bks Demand.
— Electroanalytical Chemistry: A Series of Advances, Vol. 3. LC 66-11287. (Illus.). 322p. 1969. reprint ed. pap. 99.90 (*0-608-04778-3*, 202150500022) Bks Demand.
— Electroanalytical Chemistry: A Series of Advances, Vol. 6. LC 66-11287. 383p. 1973. reprint ed. pap. 118.80 (*0-608-04784-8*, 202709300006) Bks Demand.
— Electroanalytical Chemistry: A Series of Advances, Vol. 7. LC 66-11287. (Illus.). 304p. 1974. pap. 94.30 (*0-8357-8392-8*, 202709300007) Bks Demand.
— Electroanalytical Chemistry: A Series of Advances, Vol. 8. LC 66-11287. 392p. 1975. reprint ed. pap. 121.60 (*0-608-04783-X*, 202671500008) Bks Demand.
— Electroanalytical Chemistry: A Series of Advances, Vol. 10. LC 66-11287. 318p. 1977. reprint ed. pap. 98.60 (*0-608-04782-1*, 202671200010) Bks Demand.
— Electroanalytical Chemistry: A Series of Advances, 2 vols., Vol. 11. LC 66-11287. (Illus.). 384p. 1982. reprint ed. pap. 119.10 (*0-7837-0640-5*, 204098200011) Bks Demand.
— Electroanalytical Chemistry: A Series of Advances, 2 vols., Vol. 12. LC 66-11287. (Illus.). 267p. 1982. reprint ed. pap. 82.80 (*0-608-04781-3*, 204098200012) Bks Demand.
— Encyclopedia of Electrochemistry of the Elements, Vol. 1. LC 73-88796. 511p. 1973. reprint ed. pap. 158.50 (*0-608-08201-5*, 202798400001) Bks Demand.
— Encyclopedia of Electrochemistry of the Elements, Vol. 6. LC 73-88796. 359p. 1976. reprint ed. pap. 111.30 (*0-608-08202-3*, 202798600006) Bks Demand.
— Encyclopedia of Electrochemistry of the Elements, Vol. 8. LC 73-88796. 512p. 1978. reprint ed. pap. 158.80 (*0-608-08199-X*, 203087300008) Bks Demand.
— Encyclopedia of Electrochemistry of the Elements, Vol. 9, Pt. A. LC 73-88796. 630p. 1982. reprint ed. pap. 195.30 (*0-608-04615-9*, 206538400003) Bks Demand.
— Encyclopedia of Electrochemistry of the Elements, Vol. 10. LC 73-88796. 464p. 1976. reprint ed. pap. 143.90 (*0-608-08200-7*, 203087400010) Bks Demand.

Bard, Allen J. & Faulkner, Larry R. Electrochemical Methods: Fundamentals & Applications. LC 79-24712. 736p. 1980. text 108.95 (*0-471-05542-5*) Wiley.
— Electrochemical Methods: Fundamentals & Applications. 2nd ed. 940p. 2000. write for info. (*0-471-04372-9*) Wiley.

Bard, Allen J. & Rubenstein, Israel, eds. Electroanalytical Chemistry. (Illus.). 336p. 1998. text 175.00 (*0-8247-5996-8*) Dekker.
— Electroanalytical Chemistry Vol. 19: A Series of Advances. (Illus.). 544p. 1996. text 199.00 (*0-8247-9379-X*) Dekker.

Bard, Allen J. & Rubinstein, Israel, eds. Electroanalytical Chemistry Vol. 21: A Series of Advances. (Illus.). 349p. 1999. text 175.00 (*0-8247-7399-3*) Dekker.

Bard, Allen J., et al. Standard Potentials in Aqueous Solution. (Monographs in Electroanalytical Chemistry & Electrochemistry: Vol. 6). (Illus.). 848p. (C). 1985. text 65.00 (*0-8247-7291-1*) Dekker.

Bard, Chantal, et al, eds. Development of Eye-Hand Coordination Across the Life Span. LC 89-22560. (Physical Activity, Growth & Motor Development Across the Lifespan Ser.). 396p. 1990. text 34.95 (*0-87249-628-7*) U of SC Pr.

Bard, E. & Broecker, W. S., eds. The Last Deglaciation: Absolute & Radiocarbon Chronologies. (NATO ASI Series I: Global Environmental Change: Vol. 2). (Illus.). xiv, 344p. 1992. 159.00 (*0-387-53123-8*) Spr-Verlag.

Bard, Edmond B. Never in Doubt: Remembering Iowa Jima. Kessler, Lynn S., ed. LC 98-47672. (Illus.). 248p. 1999. 32.95 (*1-55750-463-6*) Naval Inst Pr.

Bard, Erwin W. Port of New York Authority. LC 68-58547. (Columbia University. Studies in the Social Sciences: No. 468). reprint ed. 34.50 (*0-404-51468-5*) AMS Pr.

Bard, F. X., ed. see Orstrom.

Bard Graduate Center for Studies in the Decorative Arts Staff, et al. Finnish Modern Design: Utopian Ideals & Everyday Realities, 1930-97. Aav, Marianne & Stritzler-Levine, Nina, eds. LC 97-44402. (Illus.). 412p. 1998. 75.00 (*0-300-07504-9*) Yale U Pr.

Bard Hall, Susan, see Hall, Susan Bard.

Bard, J. C., et al. Wildcat Gorge Cave. fac. ed. (Basin Research Associates Occasional Papers: No. 4). (Illus.). 258p. 1981. reprint ed. pap. text 26.88 (*1-55567-565-4*) Coyote Press.

Bard, J. P. Microtextures of Igneous & Metamorphic Rocks. 1986. pap. text 69.00 (*90-277-2313-3*); lib. bdg. 143.00 (*90-277-2220-X*) Kluwer Academic.

Bard, Jim, jt. auth. see Gough, David.

Bard, Jonathan. A Colour Atlas of Developing Embryos. LC 92-48738. 1993. 24.95 (*0-8151-0412-X*) Mosby Inc.

Bard, Jonathan, ed. Embryos: Color Atlas of Development. (Illus.). 224p. 1993. text 89.00 (*0-7234-1740-7*) CRC Pr.

Bard, Jonathan B. Morphogenesis: The Cellular & Molecular Processes of Developmental Anatomy. (Developmental & Cell Biology Monographs: No. 23). (Illus.). 315p. (C). 1990. text 95.00 (*0-521-36196-6*) Cambridge U Pr.
— Morphogenesis: The Cellular & Molecular Processes of Developmental Anatomy. (Developmental & Cell Biology Monographs: No. 23). (Illus.). 325p. (C). 1992. pap. text 42.95 (*0-521-43612-5*) Cambridge U Pr.

Bard, Jonathan B.L. The Anatomical Basis of Mouse Development. LC 99-60459. 304p. 1999. 99.95 (*0-12-402060-7*) Acad Pr.

Bard, Jonathan F. Practical Bilevel Optimization: Algorithms & Applications. LC 98-45182. (Nonconvex Optimization & Its Applications Ser.). 19p. 1999. 225.00 (*0-7923-5458-3*) Kluwer Academic.

Bard, Karoly, tr. see Wiener, Imre A.

Bard, Katheryn, ed. Encyclopedia of the Archeology of Ancient Egypt. LC 98-16350. (Illus.). 968p. (C). 1999. 250.00 (*0-415-18589-0*) Routledge.

Bard, Kathryn Ann. From Farmers to Pharaohs: Mortuary Evidence for the Rise of Complex Society in Egypt. (Monographs in Mediterranean Archaeology: No. 2). 150p. 1994. 60.00 (*1-85075-387-3*, Pub. by Sheffield Acad) CUP Services.

Bard, M. & Laredo, J. D., eds. Interventional Radiology in Bone & Joint. (Illus.). 300p. 1988. 213.00 (*0-387-82029-9*) Spr-Verlag.

Bard, Margaret. Show & Tell. Chelius, Jane, ed. 400p. (Orig.). 1995. mass mkt. 5.99 (*0-671-86592-7*) PB.

Bard, Marjorie. Organizational & Community Response to Domestic Abuse & Homelessness. LC 93-47244. (Children of Poverty Ser.). 192p. 1994. text 20.00 (*0-8153-1597-X*) Garland.
— Shadow Women: Homeless Women's Survival Stories. LC 90-60897. 236p. (Orig.). (C). 1990. pap. 9.95 (*1-55612-358-2*) Sheed & Ward WI.

Bard, Martin L. The Peril of Faith. 2nd ed. LC 89-49523. 175p. (Orig.). 1989. pap. 6.50 (*0-910309-64-7*, 5012) Am Atheist.

Bard, Mary. Doctor Wears Three Faces. (American Autobiography Ser.). 254p. 1995. reprint ed. lib. bdg. 79.00 (*0-7812-8575-5*) Rprt Serv.

Bard, Maureen. Getting Organized for Your New Baby: A Checklist & Planning Guide for Busy Parents to Be. LC 86-8485. 122p. 1986. pap. 5.00 (*0-88166-081-7*) Meadowbrook.
— Getting Organized for Your New Baby: A Checklist & Planning Guide for Busy Parents-To-Be. rev. ed. 196p. 1995. pap. 9.00 (*0-671-53477-7*) Meadowbrook.

Bard, Mitchell. The Complete Idiot's Guide to World War II. (Complete Idiot's Guides Ser.). 416p. 1998. pap. 17.95 (*0-02-862735-0*) Macmillan Gen Ref.

Bard, Mitchell G. The Complete Idiot's Guide to Middle East Conflict. 400p. 1999. pap. text 16.95 (*0-02-863261-3*, Pub. by Macmillan Gen Ref) S&S Trade.
— The Water's Edge & Beyond: Defining the Limits to Domestic Influence on United States Middle East Policy. 176p. (C). 1990. 44.95 (*0-88738-346-7*) Transaction Pubs.

Bard, Rachel. Editing Guide: A Handbook for Writers & Editors. rev. ed. LC 89-92409. 104p. (C). 1989. reprint ed. pap. 10.95 (*0-929838-02-5*) Blue Zoo.
— Newswriting Guide: A Handbook for Student Reporters. 2nd rev. ed. LC 79-55986. 96p. 1988. reprint ed. pap. 10.95 (*0-9603666-4-4*) Blue Zoo.
— Newswriting Guide: A Handbook for Student Reporters. 3rd ed. LC 79-55986. write for info. (*0-929838-09-2*) Blue Zoo.

***Bard, Rachel.** Queen Without a Country. (Illus.). 367p. 2000. 29.95 (*0-7541-1205-5*, Pub. by Minerva Pr) Unity Dist.

***Bard, Rachel, ed.** Olympic Peninsula: Best Places Destinations. 2nd ed. (Best Places Destinations Ser.). (Illus.). 208p. 2000. pap. 12.95 (*1-57061-235-8*) Sasquatch Bks.

Bard, Rachel, ed. Olympic Peninsula Best Places: A Destination Guide. 128p. (Orig.). 1996. pap. 9.95 (*1-57061-059-2*) Sasquatch Bks.

Bard, Rachel & Kellogg, Caroline. Zucchini & All That Squash. 2nd ed. LC 84-52215. 104p. (Orig.). 1990. pap. 7.95 (*0-9603666-6-0*) Blue Zoo.

Bard, Ray & Henderson, Sheila. Own Your Own Franchise: Everything You Need to Know about the 160 Best Opportunities in America. 1987. pap. 22.95 (*0-201-11438-0*) Addison-Wesley.

Bard, Ray, et al. The Trainer's Professional Development Handbook. LC 87-45507. (Management Ser.). 346p. 1987. text 46.95 (*1-55542-067-2*) Jossey-Bass.

Bard, Richard, ed. see Miami Herald Staff.

Bard, Robert L. & Kurantzick, Lewis. Copyright Duration: Duration, Term Extension, & the Making of Copyright Policy. LC 99-12060. 286p. 1998. 75.00 (*1-57292-131-5*) Austin & Winfield.

Bard, Ronald J., ed. Excellence in the Constructed Project. 576p. 1989. pap. 7.00 (*0-87262-740-3*) Am Soc Civil Eng.

Bard, Ruth, ed. see Larson, Wanda Z.

Bard, Samuel. A Discourse upon the Duties of a Physician. LC 96-9412. 32p. 1996. reprint ed. 9.95 (*1-55709-446-2*) Applewood.

Bard, Tate, ed. see Buch, Jane.

Bard, Tate, ed. see McClure, Patricia.

Bard, Terry R. Medical Ethics in Practice: The Ethics Advisory Group at Boston's Beth Israel Hospital: A Case Study. (Death Education, Aging & Health Care Ser.). 128p. 1990. 53.95 (*1-56032-056-7*) Hemisp Pub.

Bard, Therese B. Student Assistants in the School Library Media Center. LC 98-49267. 230p. 1999. pap. 30.00 (*1-56308-406-6*) Teacher Ideas Pr.

Barda, Rick. X-Files: The Official Strategy Guide. LC 98-65317. 244p. 1998. per. 19.99 (*0-7615-1572-0*) Prima Pub.

Bardach, Eugene. Managerial Craftsmanship: Getting Agencies to Work Together. LC 98-25467. 1998. 44.95 (*0-8157-0798-3*); pap. 19.95 (*0-8157-0797-5*) Brookings.

***Bardach, Eugene.** A Practical Guide for Policy Analysis: The Eightfold Path to More Effective Problem Solving. 2nd ed. LC 99-50621. (Illus.). 144p. (C). 2000. pap. text 12.95 (*1-889119-29-6*) Seven Bridges.

Bardach, Eugene & Kagan, Robert A., eds. Social Regulation: Strategies for Reform. LC 81-85279. 420p. 1982. text 39.95 (*0-917616-47-2*) Transaction Pubs.
— Social Regulation: Strategies for Reform. LC 81-85279. 420p. 1999. pap. 24.95 (*0-917616-46-4*) Transaction Pubs.

***Bardach, Eugene, et al.** North Richmond Gets Its Buses Back: How a Poor Community & an Urban Transit Agency Struck up a Partnership. LC 99-31684. 1999. 5.00 (*0-87772-389-3*) UCB IGS.

Bardach, Janusz & Gleeson, Kathleen. Man Is Wolf to Man: A Story of Survival. LC 98-5402. 397p. 1998. 29.95 (*0-520-21352-1*, Pub. by U CA Pr) Cal Prin Full Svc.
— Man is Wolf to Man: Surviving the Gulag. LC 98-5402. 397p. 1999. pap. 17.95 (*0-520-22152-4*, Pub. by U CA Pr) Cal Prin Full Svc.

Bardach, Janusz & Sayler, Kenneth. Atlas of Craniofacial & Cleft Surgery. LC 98-13316. 1200p. 1998. text 399.00 (*0-397-51807-2*) Lppncott W & W.

Bardach, Janusz, jt. auth. see Salyer, Kenneth E.

Bardach, Janusz, jt. auth. see Sprintzen, Robert J.

Bardach, John E. Sustainable Aquaculture. LC 96-44727. 251p. 1997. 99.00 (*0-471-14829-6*) Wiley.

An Asterisk (*) at the beginning of an entry indicates that the title is appearing for the first time.

Bardach, John E., et al. Aquaculture: The Farming & Husbandry of Freshwater & Marine Organisms. 884p. 1974. pap. 100.00 (*0-471-04826-7*) Wiley.

Bardack, David. Localities of Fossil Vertebrates Obtained from the Niobrara Formation (Cretaceous) of Kansas. (Museum Ser.: Vol. 17,No. 1). 14p. 1965. 1.00 (*0-317-04783-3*) U KS Nat Hist Mus.

Bardacke, Frank. Good Liberals & Great Blue Herons: Land Labor & Politics in the Pajaro Valley. (Local Ecological History Ser.). (Illus.). 160p. (Orig.). 1994. pap. 9.95 (*0-9641094-0-9*) Ctr for Polit.

— Tramping out the Vintage. Date not set. pap. write for info. (*0-8050-4444-2*) H Holt & Co.

— Tramping out the Vintage. 1999. write for info. (*0-8050-4443-4*) H Holt & Co.

Bardacke, Frank, tr. Shadows of Tender Fury: The Letters & Communiques of Subcomandante Marcos & the Zapatista Army of National Liberation. (Illus.). 272p. 30.00 (*0-85345-917-7*, Pub. by Monthly Rev) NYU Pr.

Bardacke, Frank, et al, trs. Shadows of Tender Fury: The Letters & Communiques of Subcomandante Marcos & the Zapatista Army of National Liberation. 288p. 1995. pap. 15.00 (*0-85345-918-5*, Pub. by Monthly Rev) NYU Pr.

Bardaglio, Peter W. Reconstructing the Household: Families, Sex, & the Law in the Nineteenth-Century South. LC 95-11798. (Studies in Legal History). 384p. 1995. 49.95 (*0-8078-2222-1*) U of NC Pr.

— Reconstructing the Household: Families, Sex, & the Law in the Nineteenth-Century South. (Studies in Legal History). (Illus.). 384p. 1998. reprint ed. pap. 18.95 (*0-8078-4712-7*) U of NC Pr.

Bardakigian, K. D. & Thompson, Robert W. Western Armenian. (ARM.). 319p. (YA). pap. 185.00 incl. audio (*0-88432-444-3*, AFAR15) Audio-Forum.

Bardakjian, Kevork B. Reference Guide to Modern Armenian Literature, 1500-1920: With an Introductory History. LC 98-43139. 608p. 2000. 49.95 (*0-8143-2747-8*) Wayne St U Pr.

Bardakjian, Kevork B. & Thomson, Robert W. Textbook of Modern Western Armenian. LC 77-1774. 328p. 1985. pap. 15.00 (*0-88206-504-1*) Caravan Bks.

***Bardakjian, Kevork B. & Vaux, Bert.** Eastern Armenian: A Textbook LC 99-28448. 1999. write for info. (*0-88206-095-3*) Caravan Bks.

Bardana, Emil J., Jr., et al, eds. Occupational Asthma. LC 91-58457. 328p. 1991. text 69.00 (*1-56053-017-0*) Hanley & Belfus.

Bardana, Emil J. & Montanaro, Anthony, eds. Indoor Air Pollution & Health. LC 96-36591. (Clinical Allergy & Immunology Ser.: Vol. 9). (Illus.). 528p. 1996. text 215.00 (*0-8247-9479-6*) Dekker.

Bardanouve, Venus E. Angels in the Bible. Rinden, David, ed. 48p. 1996. wbk. ed. 4.95 (*0-943167-34-5*) Faith & Fellowship Pr.

Bardeche. Marcel Proust: Romancier, 2 tomes, Set. 31.95 (*0-685-37073-9*, F119810) Fr & Eur.

Bardeche, Maurice & Brasillach, Robert. History of Motion Pictures. LC 70-112565. (Literature of Cinema Ser.). 1974. reprint ed. 23.95 (*0-405-01602-6*) Ayer.

Bardeen, W. A. & White, A. R., eds. Anomalies, Geometry & Topology: Proceedings of the Symposium, Argonne, Illnois March 28-30, 1985. 558p. 1985. 104.00 (*9971-978-69-5*); pap. 55.00 (*9971-978-72-5*) World Scientific Pub.

Bardeen, W. A., et al. Electroweak Symmetry Breaking: International Workshop. 464p. 1992. text 106.00 (*981-02-1061-2*) World Scientific Pub.

Bardeleben, Renate Von, see Von Bardeleben, Renate, ed.

Bardell, Paul H., et al. Built-in Test for VLSI: Pseudorandom Techniques. LC 87-23013. 368p. 1987. 155.00 (*0-471-62463-2*) Wiley.

Bardelli, F., ed. see Green, M., et al.

Barden. Communications Technology. (Tech & Industrial Education Ser.). 1990. pap., teacher ed. 10.00 (*0-8273-3226-2*) Delmar.

***Barden, Christine.** Etude Toccata. 8p. 1999. pap. 2.95 (*0-7390-0392-5*, 18533) Alfred Pub.

— Santa's Helpers. 1999. mass mkt. 2.50 (*0-7390-0308-9*, 18542) Alfred Pub.

Barden, Cindy. Dinosaurs: Easy Readers Science. (Easy Readers Ser.). 16p. (J). (ps-1). 1997. pap. 2.49 (*1-57690-277-3*) Tchr Create Mat.

— Great States! Over 200 First-Rate Reproducible Activity Sheets to Fascinate & Educate. Mitchell, Judy, ed. (Illus.). 256p. (Orig.). (J). (gr. 3-6). 1995. pap. 19.95 (*1-57310-018-8*) Teachng & Lrning Co.

— Love to Read! Activities to Foster a Love of Reading. Mitchell, Judy, ed. (Illus.). 160p. (Orig.). (J). (gr. 3-6). 1995. pap., teacher ed. 14.95 (*1-57310-032-3*) Teachng & Lrning Co.

— Love to Write! Activities to Sharpen Creative Writing Skills. Mitchell, Judy, ed. (Illus.). 144p. (Orig.). (gr. 3-6). 1995. pap. 13.95 (*1-57310-017-X*) Teachng & Lrning Co.

— Meet the First Ladies. Mitchell, Judy, ed. (Illus.). 144p. (Orig.). (J). (gr. 3-6). 1996. pap., teacher ed. 13.95 (*1-57310-042-0*) Teachng & Lrning Co.

— Meet the Presidents. Mitchell, Judy, ed. (Illus.). 144p. (Orig.). (J). (gr. 3-6). 1996. pap., teacher ed. 13.95 (*1-57310-041-2*) Teachng & Lrning Co.

— Mighty Maps! Facts, Fun & Trivia to Develop Map Skills. Mitchell, Judy, ed. (Illus.). 96p. (Orig.). (J). (gr. 3-6). 1995. pap., teacher ed. 9.95 (*1-57310-037-4*) Teachng & Lrning Co.

— Numbers 0 to 20. (Basic Skills Ser.). (Illus.). 32p. (J). (gr. 1-2). 1997. pap. text 4.95 (*0-88724-388-6*, CD-2123) Carson-Dellos.

— Our Solar System: Easy Readers Science. (Easy Readers Ser.). 16p. (J). (ps-1). 1997. pap. 2.49 (*1-57690-280-3*) Tchr Create Mat.

— Plants & Seeds: Easy Readers Science. (Easy Readers Ser.). 16p. (J). (ps-1). 1997. pap. 2.49 (*1-57690-281-1*) Tchr Create Mat.

— Rain Forest. (Easy Readers Ser.). 16p. (J). (ps-1). 1997. pap. 2.49 (*1-57690-282-X*) Tchr Create Mat.

— Super States! Puzzles, Games & Fascinating Trivia about the United States: Grades 3-6. Mitchell, Judy, ed. (Illus.). 192p. 1995. pap., teacher ed. 16.95 (*1-57310-029-3*) Teachng & Lrning Co.

— Whales: Easy Theme Reader. (Easy Readers Ser.). 16p. (J). 1997. pap. 2.49 (*1-57690-279-X*) Tchr Create Mat.

Barden, Cindy, et al. Celebrate the Months Vol. 2370: March. Johnson, Kristine, ed. (Illus.). 96p. (J). (gr. k-3). 1997. pap. 9.98 (*1-57471-304-3*) Creat Teach Pr.

— Celebrate the Months Vol. 2371: April. Thrall Cicciarelli, Joellyn, ed. 96p. (J). (gr. k-3). 1997. pap. 9.98 (*1-57471-305-1*) Creat Teach Pr.

Barden, Dan. John Wayne: A Novel. 192p. 1998. pap. 11.00 (*0-385-48710-X*, Anchor NY) Doubleday.

***Barden, Garrett.** Essays on a Philosophic Interpretation of Justice: The Virtue of Justice. LC 95-53712. (Problems in Contemporary Philosophy Ser.: Vol. 41). 24p. 1999. text 79.95 (*0-7734-8180-X*) E Mellen.

Barden, James E., jt. auth. see Theodore, Louis.

Barden, Janet K., ed. see Barden, William, Jr.

Barden, John A., jt. auth. see Halfacre, R. Gordon.

Barden, John G. A Suggested Program of Teacher Training for Mission Schools Among the Batetela. LC 75-176517. (Columbia University. Teachers College. Contributions to Education Ser.: No. 853). reprint ed. 37.50 (*0-404-55853-4*) AMS Pr.

Barden, John R., ed. Letters to the Home Circle: The North Carolina Service of Pvt. Henry A. Clapp, 1862-1863. LC 99-229793. (Illus.). 252p. 1999. pap. 28.00 (*0-86526-270-5*) NC Archives.

Barden, Karl A. The Activated Church. 182p. (Orig.). 1992. pap. 10.99 (*1-56043-067-2*) Destiny Image.

— Satan Who/Enlightened Church. LC 95-161400. 224p. (Orig.). 1994. pap. 10.99 (*1-56043-135-0*) Destiny Image.

Barden, L. W. The Ruy Lopez: Winning Chess with 1P-K4. 185p. 1963. 13.00 (*0-08-013006-2*, Pergamon Pr); pap. 8.50 (*0-08-009997-1*, Pergamon Pr) Elsevier.

Barden, Leonard. How Good Is Your Chess? LC 75-28848. 112p. 1976. reprint ed. pap. 4.95 (*0-486-23294-8*) Dover.

— Introduction to Chess Moves & Tactics Simply Explained. (Illus.). 102p. (Orig.). 1998. pap. 3.95 (*0-486-21210-6*) Dover.

Barden, Leonard, jt. auth. see Harding, Tim.

Barden, Louise C. Tea Leaves. (Harperprints Chapbook Ser.). 24p. (Orig.). 1996. pap. 5.00 (*1-883314-06-2*) NC Writers Network.

Barden, R. Christopher & Jackson, Bruce K. Optimal Performance in Tennis: Mental Skills for Maximum Achievement in Athletics & Life. Ford, Martin E., ed. (Illus.). 204p. 1993. 59.95 incl. audio (*0-9640543-0-2*) Optimal Perform.

Barden, Renardo. All Time Greats. LC 92-12053. (Basketball Heroes Ser.). (J). 1992. 17.26 (*0-86593-163-1*) Rourke Corp.

— Base Stealers. (Baseball Heroes Ser.). (J). 1991. 12.50 (*0-86593-126-7*) Rourke Corp.

— Base Stealers, 8 bks., Set. (Baseball Heroes Ser.). 48p. (J). (gr. 3-8). 1991. lib. bdg. 15.95 (*0-86593-125-9*) Rourke Corp.

— Cults. (Troubled Society Ser.). (Illus.). 64p. (YA). (gr. 7 up). 1990. lib. bdg. 17.95 (*0-86593-070-8*) Rourke Corp.

— The Discovery of America: Opposing Viewpoints. LC 89-11709. (Great Mysteries Ser.). (Illus.). 112p. (J). (gr. 5-8). 1989. lib. bdg. 22.45 (*0-89908-071-5*) Greenhaven.

— Gangs. (Troubled Society Ser.). (Illus.). 64p. (YA). (gr. 7 up). 1990. lib. bdg. 17.95 (*0-86593-073-2*) Rourke Corp.

— Gun Control. (Troubled Society Ser.). (Illus.). 64p. (YA). (gr. 7 up). 1990. lib. bdg. 17.95 (*0-86593-072-4*) Rourke Corp.

— MVPs. (Baseball Heroes Ser.). (J). 1991. 12.50 (*0-685-66095-8*) Rourke Corp.

— MVPs. (Baseball Heroes Ser.). 48p. (J). (gr. 3-8). 1991. lib. bdg. 15.95 (*0-86593-127-5*) Rourke Corp.

— Playoff Pressure. LC 92-9143. (Basketball Heroes Ser.). 48p. (J). (gr. 3-8). 1992. lib. bdg. 15.95 (*0-86593-162-3*) Rourke Corp.

— Prisons. (Troubled Society Ser.: Set II). 64p. (J). 1991. lib. bdg. 17.95 (*0-86593-110-0*) Rourke Corp.

Barden, Robert & Hacker, Michael. Communications Technology. 1989. pap. 36.95 (*0-8273-3225-4*) Delmar.

Barden, Robert, jt. auth. see Hacker, Michael.

Barden, Samuel, ed. Fiber Optics in Astronomy. LC 88-72327. (Astronomical Society of the Pacific Conference Ser.: Vol. 3). (Illus.). 312p. 1988. 34.00 (*0-937707-20-1*) Astron Soc Pacific.

Barden, Thomas E., intro. Virginia Folk Legends. 348p. 1991. pap. 16.95 (*0-8139-1335-7*) U Pr of Va.

Barden, William, Jr. Buying & Setup Guide to High-Tech Electronics. Barden, Janet K., ed. (Illus.). 1988. write for info. (*0-318-63255-1*) W Barden Inc.

— How to Do It on the TRS-80. 352p. 1983. 29.95 (*0-936200-08-1*) Blue Cat.

— Power Printing with PCL: For the HP LaserJet & Compatibles. (Bantam Book-Software Library). 400p. 1988. pap. 39.95 incl. disk (*0-553-34588-5*) Bantam.

Bardenhewer, Otto. Patrology: The Lives & Works of the Fathers of the Church, 3 vols. 1994. pap. text 37.50 (*0-89981-069-1*) Eastern Orthodox.

Bardenouve, Venus E. When the Almond Tree Blossoms: A Bible Study for Seniors. Rinden, David, ed. 48p. 1996. wbk. ed. 4.95 (*0-943167-31-0*) Faith & Fellowship Pr.

Bardens, Ann. Stone & Water. (Illus.). 96p. 1992. pap. 12.50 (*0-945950-08-X*) Canoe Pr MI.

Bardens, Dennis. Psychic Animals: A Fascinating Investigation of Paranormal Behaviour. (Illus.). 203p. (Orig.). 1995. pap. 21.95 (*1-898307-39-3*) Ho mes Pub.

Barder, Richard C. The Georgian Bracket Clock, 1714-1830. (Illus.). 236p. 1993. 89.50 (*1-85149-158-9*) Antique Collect.

Bardes, B. American Government & Politics Today: Essentials. 8th ed. (Political Science Ser.). (C). 1998. student ed. 15.25 (*0-534-53902-5*) Wadsworth Pub.

— The Clinton Year Elections, Policies & Scandals. 9th ed. (Political Science Ser.). 1999. pap. text 6.00 (*0-534-56956-0*) Wadsworth Pub.

— Public Opinion: Measuring the American Mind. LC 99-16353. (Political Science Ser.). 1999. pap. 40.95 (*0-534-56043-1*) Brooks-Cole.

Bardes, B. & Schmidt. American Government & Politics Today: Essentials 2000-2001. 9th ed. (Political Science Ser.). 1999. pap. 59.95 (*0-534-56943-9*) Wadsworth Pub.

— American Government/Politics Today: Essentials, 2000-2001. 9th ed. (Political Science Ser.). 1999. pap. text, student ed. 17.25 (*0-534-56945-5*) Wadsworth Pub.

Bardes, B. & Shelley. American Government. (Adaptable Courseware-Softside Ser.). Date not set. pap. 51.00 (*0-534-56574-3*) Wadsworth Pub.

Bardes, Barbara. American Government: 1994-1995. Date not set. pap. text, student ed. 17.75 (*0-314-03520-6*) West Pub.

— American Government: 1996-97. Date not set. pap. text, teacher ed. write for info. (*0-314-09416-4*) West Pub.

— American Government: 1996-97. 7th ed. 1996. pap., student ed. 15.25 (*0-314-09417-2*) West Pub.

— Government Enrichment Lectures. 3rd ed. Date not set. pap. text. write for info. (*0-314-70741-7*) West Pub.

— The War in the Gulf. Date not set. pap. text. write for info. (*0-314-92938-X*) West Pub.

— WINDS OF CHANGE: ELECTION 1992. 6th ed. (Political Science). 1993. mass mkt. 5.00 (*0-314-02271-6*) West Pub.

Bardes, Barbara & Gossett, Suzanne. Declarations of Independence: Women & Political Power in Nineteenth-Century American Fiction. 266p. (C). 1990. text 40.00 (*0-8135-1500-9*); pap. text 17.00 (*0-8135-1501-7*) Rutgers U Pr.

Bardes, Barbara, ed. see Burrell, Barbara C.

Bardes, Barbara A., et al. American Government & Politics Today: Essentials 1996-1997. 7th ed. 550p. 1996. pap. 34.75 (*0-314-06948-8*) West Pub.

— American Government & Politics Today: The Essentials, 1998-1999 Edition. 8th ed. (Political Science Ser.). (C). 1997. pap. 37.75 (*0-534-53901-7*) Wadsworth Pub.

Bardes, Charles L. Essential Skills in Clinical Medicine. LC 95-19189. (Illus.). 397p. (C). 1995. pap. text 28.95 (*0-8036-0014-3*) Davis Co.

Bardet, Jean-Pierre. Experimental Soil Mechanics LC 96-320. 583p. (C). 1997. text 70.00 incl. audio compact disk (*0-13-374935-5*) P-H.

***Bardey, Catherine.** Making Soaps & Scents: Perfumes, Soaps, Splashes & Shampos That You Can Make at Home. LC 99-40548. (Life's Litte Luxuries Ser.: Vol. 2). (Illus.). 192p. 1999. pap. 10.98 (*1-57912-059-8*) Blck Dog & Leventhal.

***Bardey, Catherine.** Lingerie: A History & Celebration of Silks, Satins, Laces, Linens & Other Bare Essentials. LC 00-24400. (Illus.). 192p. 2000. 10.98 (*1-57912-105-5*, 81105) Blck Dog & Leventhal.

— Making Candles & Potpourri: Illuminate & Infuse Your Home. LC 99-41225. (Illus.). 192p. 1999. pap. text 10.98 (*1-57912-076-8*, Pub. by Blck Dog & Leventhal) Workman Pub.

— Secrets of the Spas: Pamper & Vitalize Yourself at Home. LC 98-50121. (Illus.). 192p. 1999. pap. 10.98 (*1-57912-063-6*) Blck Dog & Leventhal.

Bardfeld, Sam. Latin Violin: How to Play Charanga, Salsa & Latin Jazz Violin. 1999. pap. 25.00 incl. audio compact disk (*0-9628467-7-5*, Pub. by Gerard Sarzin Pub) Music Sales.

Bardhan, Gul, ed. Rhythm Incarnate: Tribute to Shanti Bardhan. (C). 1992. 58.00 (*81-7017-261-6*, Pub. by Abhinav) S Asia.

Bardhan, K. K., et al, eds. Non-Linearity & Breakdown in Soft Condensed Matter: Proceedings of a Workshop Held at Calcutta, India, 1-9 December, 1993. LC 94-40085. (Lecture Notes in Physics Ser.: Vol. 437). 1994. 79.95 (*3-540-58652-0*) Spr-Verlag.

Bardhan, Kalpana, ed. Of Women, Outcastes, Peasants, & Rebels: A Selection of Bengali Short Stories. 1990. 55.00 (*0-520-06713-4*, Pub. by U CA Pr); pap. 18.95 (*0-520-06714-2*, Pub. by U CA Pr) Cal Prin Full Svc.

Bardhan, Kalpana, tr. see Majumdar, Amiya Bhushan.

Bardhan, Kalpana, tr. & afterword by see Mallabarman, Adwaita.

Bardhan, Pranab. Political Economic Development. (C). 35.00 (*0-691-04280-2*, Pub. by Princeton U Pr) Cal Prin Full Svc.

— Political Economic Development. (C). 1992. pap. text 10.95 (*0-691-00389-0*, Pub. by Princeton U Pr) Cal Prin Full Svc.

— The Political Economy of Development in India: Expanded Edition with an Epilogue on the Political Economy of Reform in India. LC 99-220256. 162p. 1999. pap. text 9.95 (*0-19-564770-X*) OUP.

— The Role of Governance in Economic Development: A Political Economy Approach. LC 97-224499. 96p. 1997. pap. 18.00 (*92-64-15559-7*, 41-97-09-1, Pub. by Org for Econ) OECD.

***Bardhan, Pranab & Udry, Christopher.** Readings in Development Economics Vol. I: Micro-Theory. (Illus.). 376p. (C). 2000. 70.00 (*0-262-02484-5*); pap. 27.95 (*0-262-52282-9*) MIT Pr.

— Readings in Development Economics Vol. II: Empirical Microeconomics. (Illus.). 456p. (C). 2000. 75.00 (*0-262-02485-3*); pap. 29.95 (*0-262-52283-7*) MIT Pr.

Bardhan, Pranab K. Land, Labor, & Rural Poverty: Essays in Development Economics. LC 83-10082. 288p. 1984. text 63.00 (*0-231-05388-6*) Col U Pr.

— Land, Labor, & Rural Poverty: Essays in Development Economics. LC 83-10082. 288p. 1987. pap. 21.00 (*0-231-05389-4*, W3894) Col U Pr.

Bardhan, Pranab K., ed. The Economic Theory of Agrarian Institutions. (Illus.). 416p. 1992. pap. text 32.00 (*0-19-828762-3*) OUP.

***Bardhan, Pranab K. & Udry, Christopher.** Development Microeconomics. LC 99-20554. 256p. 1999. write for info. (*0-19-877370-6*); write for info. (*0-19-877371-4*) OUP.

Bardhan-Roy, B. K., jt. auth. see Abeles, P. W.

Bardi, jt. auth. see Coyle, John J.

Bardi, Carol A. & Bates, Georgia. Who Loves You. (Illus.). 34p. (J). (ps-k). 1997. pap. 9.95 (*0-9660498-0-2*, Bardi Pr) Bardi Consult.

Bardi, Edward J., jt. auth. see Coyle, John J.

Bardi, James. Hotel Front Office Management. 2nd ed. LC 96-17743. (Hospitality, Travel & Tourism Ser.). 368p. 1996. text 44.95 (*0-442-02084-8*, VNR) Wiley.

— Hotel Front Office Management. 2nd ed. (Hospitality, Travel & Tourism Ser.). 1997. pap., teacher ed. write for info. (*0-442-02463-0*, VNR) Wiley.

Bardi, James A. Hotel Front Office Management. 2nd ed. (Hospitality, Travel & Tourism Ser.). 480p. 1996. 54.95 (*0-471-28712-1*, VNR) Wiley.

Bardi, Lina B. Lina Bo Bardi. (Illus.). 336p. 1996. pap. text 55.00 (*88-86158-80-7*, Pub. by Charta) Dist Art Pubs.

Bardi, Luciano & Rhodes, Martin. Italian Politics: Mapping the Future. (Italian Politics Ser.). 304p. 1998. text 65.00 (*0-8133-3606-6*, Pub. by Westview) HarpC.

Bardi, M. & Dolcetta, I. Optimal Control & Viscosity Solutions of Hamilton-Jacobi-Bellman Equations. Byrnes, C. I., ed. LC 97-23275. (Systems & Control). 500p. 1996. 89.50 (*0-8176-3640-4*) Birkhauser.

Bardi, M. & Dolcetta, I. C. Optimal Control & Viscosity Solutions of Hamilton-Jacobi-Bellman Equations. LC 97-23275. (Systems & Control). 500p. 1997. write for info. (*3-7643-3640-4*) Birkhauser.

Bardi, M., et al. Stochastic & Differential Games: Theory & Numerical Methods. (Annals of the International Society of Dynamic Games Ser.). 350p. 1998. 89.50 (*0-8176-4029-0*) Birkhauser.

— Viscosity Solutions & Applications: Lectures Given at the 2nd Session of the Centro Internazionale Matematico Estivo (C. I. M. E.) Held in Montecatini Terme, Italy, June, 12-20, 1995. Dolcetta, I. Capuzzo et al, eds. LC 97-16479. (Lecture Notes in Mathematics Ser.: No. 1660). ix, 259p. 1997. pap. 48.00 (*3-540-62910-6*) Spr-Verlag.

Bardi, Pieri. The Atlas of the Classical World: Ancient Greece & Ancient Rome. LC 97-41581. (Illus.). 64p. (YA). (gr. 5-9). 1997. 19.95 (*0-87226-369-X*, 6369XB, P Bedrick Books) NTC Contemp Pub Co.

Bardige, Betty, jt. auth. see Segal, Marilyn.

Bardill. Family Therapy. (C). 1989. pap. text 34.00 (*0-536-57363-8*) Pearson Custom.

Bardill, Donald R. The Relational Systems Model for Family Therapy: Living in the Four Realities. LC 96-4072. (Illus.). 274p. (C). 1996. pap. text 24.95 (*0-7890-0183-7*) Haworth Pr.

— The Relational Systems Model for Family Therapy: Living in the Four Realities. LC 96-4072. (Illus.). 294p. (C). 1996. 49.95 (*0-7890-0074-1*) Haworth Pr.

Bardin, C. Wayne. Current Therapy in Endocrinology & Metabolism, Vol. 6. 6th ed. (Illus.). 704p. (C). (gr. 13). 1997. text 93.00 (*0-8151-2016-8*, 30566) Mosby Inc.

Bardin, C. Wayne, ed. Recent Progress in Hormone Research, Vol. 5. (Illus.). 497p. 1995. text 95.00 (*0-12-571150-6*) Acad Pr.

— Recent Progress in Hormone Research, Vol. 49. (Illus.). 400p. 1994. text 94.00 (*0-12-571149-2*) Acad Pr.

Bardin, C. Wayne, jt. ed. see Sitruk-Ware, Regine.

***Bardin, Dima & Passarino, Giampiero.** The Standard Model in the Making: Precision Study of the Electroweak Interactions. LC 99-28972. (International Series of Monographs on Physics: 104). (Illus.). 704p. 1999. pap. 150.00 (*0-19-850280-X*) OUP.

Bardin, Rodney N., jt. auth. see Jura, Jean-Jacques.

Bardin, Shlomo, ed. Self-Fulfillment Through Zionism: A Study in Jewish Adjustment. LC 70-142605. (Biography Index Reprint Ser.). 1977. reprint ed. 19.95 (*0-8369-8076-X*) Ayer.

Bardinet, Claude & Royer, J. J. Geosciences & Water Resources: Environmental Data Modeling. LC 97-880. (Data & Knowledge in a Changing World Ser.). 1997. write for info. (*3-540-61947-X*) Spr-Verlag.

Bardis, P. D., jt. auth. see Das, M. S.

Bardis, Panos. Dictionary of Quotations in Sociology. LC 85-943. 356p. 1985. lib. bdg. 75.00 (*0-313-23778-6*, BDQ/, Greenwood Pr) Greenwood.

Bardis, Panos D. South Africa & the Marxist Movement: A Study in Double Standards. LC 89-12433. (African Studies: Vol. 13). 250p. 1989. lib. bdg. 89.95 (*0-88946-174-0*) E Mellen.

Bardo, Blayne, ed. see Balsekar, Ramesh.

Bardo, Blayne, ed. see Balsekar, Ramesh S.

Bardo, Harold R., jt. auth. see Jackson, Evelyn W.

Bardo, Pamela P. English & Continental Portrait Miniatures: The Latter-Schlesinger Collection. LC 78-59762. (Illus.). 120p. 1978. pap. 7.95 (*0-89494-006-6*) New Orleans Mus Art.

Bardo, Susan. Feminist Interpretations of Descartes. LC 98-39332. 320p. 1999. 60.00 (*0-271-01857-7*); pap. 19.95 (*0-271-01858-5*) Pa St U Pr.

Bardocz, Susan, jt. ed. see Pusztai, Arpad.

Bardolph, Richard. The Negro Vanguard. LC 77-135592. 388p. 1972. reprint ed. lib. bdg. 49.75 (*0-8371-5183-X*, BNV&) Greenwood.

B

An Asterisk (*) at the beginning of an entry indicates that the title is appearing for the first time.

Bardon, ed. Catulli. 1973. pap. 24.95 (*3-519-01133-6*, T1133, Pub. by B G Teubner) U of Mich Pr.

Bardon, ed. see Lesage, Alain-Rene.

Bardon, Carol & Bardon, Jonathan. If You Ever Go to Dublin Town: A Historic Guide to the City's Street Names. (Illus.). 124p. 1988. pap. 7.95 (*0-85640-397-0*, Pub. by Blackstaff Pr) Dufour.

Bardon, Doris, jt. auth. see Laurie, Murray.

Bardon, Franz. Frabato the Magician. Dimai, Peter A., tr. from GER. (Illus.). 165p. 1982. 19.95 (*0-914732-13-7*) Bro Life Inc.

— Frabato the Magician. rev. ed. Hanswille, Gerhard, tr. from GER. (Illus.). 173p. 1996. 19.95 (*1-885928-03-3*) Merkur Pubng.

— Initiation into Hermetics. rev. ed. Hanswille, Gerhard & Gallo, Franca, trs. 360p. 1999. 32.95 (*1-885928-06-8*) Merkur Pubng.

— The Key to the True Kabbalah. Hanswille, Gerhard, tr. from GER. 279p. 1996. 35.95 (*1-885928-05-X*) Merkur Pubng.

— The Practice of Magical Evocation. 4th ed. Dimai, Peter A., tr. from GER. (Illus.). 435p. 1984. 44.00 (*0-914732-11-0*) Bro Life Inc.

Bardon, Jane E. A Cord of Light: A True Story of Courage, Healing, & Timeless Love. 200p. 1998. pap. 13.95 (*0-9667964-0-3*) J E Bardon.

***Bardon, Jonathan.** Belfast: A Century. (Illus.). 216p. 2000. 49.95 (*0-85640-659-7*, Pub. by Blackstaff Pr) Dufour.

Bardon, Jonathan. Belfast: An Illustrated History. (Illus.). 322p. 1983. 40.00 (*0-85640-272-9*, Pub. by Blackstaff Pr) Dufour.

— A History of Ulster. (Illus.). 924p. 1993. 65.00 (*0-85640-466-7*, Pub. by Blackstaff Pr); pap. 32.00 (*0-85640-476-4*, Pub. by Blackstaff Pr) Dufour.

— A Shorter Illustrated History of Ulster. LC 97-101068. 326p. 1997. pap. 29.95 (*0-85640-586-8*, Pub. by Blackstaff Pr) Dufour.

Bardon, Jonathan & Burnett, David. Belfast: A Pocket History. LC 97-102413. 170p. 1997. pap. 15.95 (*0-85640-588-4*, Pub. by Blackstaff Pr) Dufour.

Bardon, Jonathan & Conlin, Stephen. Dublin: One Thousand Years of Wood Quay. 34p. 1988. 23.00 (*0-85640-318-0*, Pub. by Blackstaff Pr) Dufour.

Bardon, Jonathan, jt. auth. see Bardon, Carol.

Bardon, Ruth, ed. see Howells, William Dean.

Bardonnet, Daniel, ed. The Peaceful Settlement of International Disputes in Europe: Future Prospects. 704p. (C). 1992. pap. text 155.00 (*0-7923-1573-1*) Kluwer Academic.

— The Peaceful Settlement of International Disputes in Europe: Future Prospects: Colloque, 1990 - Workshop 1990. (Hague Academy of International Law Recueil des Cours, Colloque Ser.). 704p. (C). 1992. lib. bdg. 215.00 (*0-7923-1572-3*) Kluwer Academic.

***Bardos, Carolyn M.** Earthen Wonders: Hungarian Ceramics Today. (Illus.). 130p. 2000. 29.95 (*0-9676808-0-8*) Lake Hse Bks NH.

Bardos, Claude, ed. see NATO Advanced Study Institute Staff.

***Bardos, Phil.** Cold War Warriors: The Story of the Achievements & Leadership of the Men of the West Point Class of 1950. LC 00-190074. 2000. 25.00 (*0-7388-1476-8*); pap. 18.00 (*0-7388-1477-6*) Xlibris Corp.

Bardosi, Vilmos. Redewendungen Tranzosisch - Deutsch: Thematisches Woerterbuch und Ubungsbuch. (FRE & GER.). 259p. 1992. 49.95 (*0-7859-8510-7*, 3825217035) Fr & Eur.

Bardossy, Andras & Duckstein, Lucien. Fuzzy Rule-Based Modeling in Geophysical, Economic, Biological & Engineering Systems. 256p. 1995. boxed set 214.95 (*0-8493-7833-8*, 7833) CRC Pr.

Bardossy, Gy & Aleva, G. J. Lateritic Bauxites. (Developments in Economic Geology Ser.: No. 27). 624p. 1990. 242.00 (*0-444-98811-4*) Elsevier.

Bardossy, Gyula, et al. Bauxites of Peninsular Italy - Composition, Origin & Geotectonic Significance. (Monograph Series on Mineral Deposits: No. 15). viii, 61p. 1977. 28.00 (*3-443-12015-6*, Pub. by Gebruder Borntraeger) Balogh.

Bardot, Andre, jt. auth. see Bouysset, Maurice.

Bardou, Jean P., et al. The Automobile Revolution: The Impact of an Industry. Laux, James M., tr. from FRE. LC 81-11571. (Illus.). 352p. reprint ed. pap. 109.20 (*0-8357-3903-1*, 203663700004) Bks Demand.

***Bardovi-Harlig, Kathleen.** Tense & Aspect in Second Language Acquisition: Form, Meaning & Use Language Learning Monograph. (Language Learning Monographs Ser.: Vol. 2). 300p. 2000. pap. 34.95 (*0-631-22149-2*) Blackwell Pubs.

Bardovi-Harlig, Kathleen, ed. see Hartford, Beverly S.

Bardoza, Jose T. Carbon Monoxide--Accidents, Poisoning & Suicide Attempts Via Car Exhaust. 160p. 1997. 47.50 (*0-7883-1706-7*); pap. 44.50 (*0-7883-1707-5*) ABBE Pubs Assn.

— Carbon Monoxide--Accidents, Poisoning & Suicide Attempts Via Car Exhaust: Index of New Information for Reference & Research. rev. ed. 167p. 1998. pap. 44.50 (*0-7883-2119-6*) ABBE Pubs Assn.

Bardsley, Beverly, tr. see Ritsos, Yannis.

Bardsley, Charles W. A Dictionary of English & Welsh Surnames: With Special American Instances. rev. ed. LC 67-25404. xvi, 837p. 1996. 50.00 (*0-8063-0022-1*) Genealog Pub.

Bardsley, Herbert J. Reconstructions of Early Christian Documents. 1977. lib. bdg. 59.95 (*0-8490-2504-4*) Gordon Pr.

Bardsley, J. N., jt. ed. see Capitelli, M.

Bardsley, Jo. Sisters of the Past: Atlantis. 256p. 1998. pap. 12.95 (*1-56167-400-1*) Am Literary Pr.

— Sisters of the Past: Atlantis. 253p. 1998. pap. 12.95 (*0-9671966-0-4*) J Bardsley.

Bardsley, L. Your Animal Life Heritage. 79p. (C). 1989. pap. 40.00 (*0-7223-2261-5*, Pub. by A H S Ltd) St Mut.

***Bardsley, Michael.** Murder for Sale. large type ed. 264p. 1999. pap. 18.99 (*0-7089-5598-3*, Linford) Ulverscroft.

— Murder on Fire. large type ed. 264p. 1999. pap. 18.99 (*0-7089-5586-X*, Linford) Ulverscroft.

— Murder on Ice. large type ed. 240p. 1999. pap. 18.99 (*0-7089-5556-8*, Linford) Ulverscroft.

Bardsley, Sandra, jt. auth. see Capacchione, Lucia.

***Bardsley, Sharon S.** Letters from the Front. 80p. 2000. pap. text 9.95 (*0-89827-207-6*) Wesleyan Pub Hse.

Bardsley, Sharon S., tr. see Connor, John.

Bardwell, J. A., ed. Surface Oxide Films. LC 97-137469. (Proceedings Ser.: Vol. 96-18). (Illus.). 322p. 1996. 52.00 (*1-56677-168-4*) Electrochem Soc.

Bardwell, John D. The Isles of Shoals: A Visual History. (Portsmouth Marine Society Ser.: No. 14). (Illus.). 220p. 1989. 35.00 (*0-915819-13-9*) Portsmouth Marine Soc.

— Ogunquit by-the-Sea. LC 95-188693. (Images of America Ser.). 1994. pap. 14.99 (*0-7524-0080-0*) Arcadia Publng.

— Old Kittery. (Images of America Ser.). 1995. pap. 16.99 (*0-7524-0088-6*) Arcadia Publng.

— Old York. LC 95-188151. (Images of America Ser.). 1994. pap. 14.99 (*0-7524-0064-9*) Arcadia Publng.

— Old York Beach. LC 95-180892. (Images of America Ser.). 1994. pap. 16.99 (*0-7524-0004-5*) Arcadia Publng.

— Old York Beach, Vol. II. LC 95-180892. (Images of America Ser.). 128p. 1996. pap. 16.99 (*0-7524-0267-6*) Arcadia Publng.

Bardwell, Leland. Dostoevsky's Grave: (New & Selected Poems) 70p. (C). 1991. 25.00 (*0-948268-91-3*, Pub. by Dedalus); pap. 15.00 (*0-7855-6862-X*, Pub. by Dedalus) St Mut.

— There We Have Been. (Orig.). (C). 1989. 39.00 (*0-946211-81-7*) St Mut.

— The White Beach: New & Selected Poems, 1960-1998. 96p. 1998. pap. 14.95 (*1-897648-07-3*, Pub. by Salmon Poetry) Dufour.

Bardwell, Lisa V., jt. auth. see Pennock, Margaret T.

Bardwell, Lorena. Modern Meatless Menus Cookbook. 1963. spiral bd. 4.95 (*0-87511-002-9*) Claitors.

***Bardwell, Sandra.** Walking in France. (Walking Guides Ser.). (Illus.). 400p. 2000. pap. 19.95 (*0-86442-601-1*) Lonely Planet.

Bardwell, Sandra, et al. Lonely Planet Walking in Ireland. 352p. 1999. pap. 17.95 (*0-86442-602-X*) Lonely Planet.

Bardwick, J., et al. Change As the Status Quo: Implications for HR Professionals, No. 2. 80p. 1993. pap. 24.95 (*1-881115-01-1*) Human Res Plan.

Bardwick, Judith M. Danger in the Comfort Zone: From Boardroom to Mailroom-How to Break the Entitlement Habit That's Killing American Business. 200p. 1991. 21.95 (*0-8144-5059-8*, 040531) AMACOM.

— Danger in the Comfort Zone: From Boardroom to Mailroom-How to Break the Entitlement Habit That's Killing American Business. LC 94-24020. 200p. 1995. pap. 16.95 (*0-8144-7886-7*) AMACOM.

***Bardwick, Judith M.** In Praise of Good Business: How Optimizing Risk Rewards Both Your Bottom Line & Your People. LC 97-41089. 368p. 1998. 24.95 (*0-471-25407-X*) Wiley.

Bardwick, Judith M., et al. Feminine Personality & Conflict. LC 80-24191. (Contemporary Psychology Ser.). 102p. 1981. reprint ed. lib. bdg. 35.00 (*0-313-22504-4*, BAFP, Greenwood Pr) Greenwood.

Bardy, Benoit, et al, eds. Studies in Perception & Action III, Vol. III. 464p. 1995. text 99.95 (*0-8058-1867-7*) L Erlbaum Assocs.

Bardy, Raymond. Parents, Adolescents & Their Faith. 1989. pap. 22.00 (*0-86217-163-6*, Pub. by Veritas Pubns) St Mut.

Bare, Brenda G. & Smeltzer, Suzanne C., eds. Brunner & Suddarth's Textbook of Medical-Surgical Nursing. 8th ed. LC 95-2835. 2,176p. 1995. text 74.95 (*0-397-55073-1*) Lppncott W & W.

Bare, Brenda G., jt. auth. see Smeltzer, Suzanne C.

Bare, Charles L. & Pursell, Donald E. The Nebraska Economy in the 1980's. 1982. 7.50 (*0-318-42809-1*) Bur Busn Res U Nebr.

Bare, Charles L., jt. auth. see Schmidt, James R.

Bare, Colleen S. Guinea Pigs Don't Read Books. (Illus.). 32p. (J). (ps-2). 1993. pap. 5.99 (*0-14-054995-1*, PuffinBks) Peng Put Young Read.

— Guinea Pigs Don't Read Books. (Picture Puffin Ser.). (Illus.). (J). 1993. 10.19 (*0-606-05853-2*, Pub. by Turtleback) Demco.

— McHenry Mansion Mystery. (Illus.). 24p. (Orig.). (J). (gr. 1-6). 1996. 2.95 (*0-9654556-0-2*) McHenry Mansion.

— Sammy, the Dog Detective. LC 97-3881. (Illus.). 32p. (J). (gr. k-3). 1998. 15.99 (*0-525-65253-1*, Dutton Child) Peng Put Young Read.

***Bare, Colleen Stanley.** Modesto: Then & Now. (Illus.). 200p. 1999. 27.50 (*0-930349-05-9*); pap. 14.95 (*0-930349-06-7*) McHenry Mus Pr.

Bare, Colleen Stanley. Never Kiss an Alligator! LC 92-62835. (Illus.). 32p. (J). (ps-3). 1994. pap. 4.99 (*0-14-055257-X*, PuffinBks) Peng Put Young Read.

Bare, Colleen Stanley. Never Kiss an Alligator! LC 92-62835. (Picture Puffin Ser.). (J). 1994. 9.19 (*0-606-06614-4*, Pub. by Turtleback) Demco.

Bare, Colleen Stanley. Sea Lions. LC 88-34062. (Skylight Bks.). 1998. 10.99 (*0-399-61235-1*, Perigee Bks) Berkley Pub.

Bare, D. M. & Bare, R. B. Baer: Genealogy of Johannes Baer, 1749-1910. (Illus.). 288p. 1992. reprint ed. pap. 44.00 (*0-8328-2624-3*); reprint ed. lib. bdg. 54.00 (*0-8328-2623-5*) Higginson Bk Co.

Bare, Harold L. They Call Me Pentecostal. LC 92-63343. 135p. 1993. pap. 8.99 (*0-87148-862-0*) Pathway Pr.

Bare Leaning & Bare West Quantity Survey, Staff, ed. Griffith's Building Price Book 1995. 41st ed. (Illus.). 848p. (C). 1994. text. write for info. (*0-900417-27-7*) Chapman & Hall.

Bare, Lloyd. High Country Hunting. LC 89-63098. (Hunter's Information Ser.). 279p. 1989. write for info. (*0-914697-26-9*) N Amer Outdoor Grp.

Bare, R. B., jt. auth. see Bare, D. M.

***Bare, Richard L.** The Film Director. 2nd rev. ed. 288p. 1999. pap. 16.95 (*0-02-863819-0*) Macmillan.

Bare, Richard L. The Film Director: A Practical Guide to Motion Pictures & Television Techniques. LC 76-130944. (Illus.). 243p. 1973. pap. 15.00 (*0-02-012130-X*) Macmillan.

Bare, Wanda, ed. see Landgraf, Sherry.

Bare, William K. Introduction to Fire Science & Fire Prevention. 299p. (C). 1987. 39.80 (*0-13-483827-0*, Macmillan Coll) P-H.

Barea, Ilsa, tr. see Schnitzler, Arthur.

Bareall, Juliet W. Manet by Himself. 1995. 32.98 (*0-7858-0429-3*) Bk Sales Inc.

Bareau, Juliet W. Manet, Monet, & the Gare Saint-Lazare. LC 97-44389. 224p. 1998. 40.00 (*0-300-07510-3*); pap. write for info. (*0-89468-230-X*) Yale U Pr.

Barefield, Carr B., jt. auth. see Barefield, Marilyn D.

Barefield, Jesse T. Desktop Publishing in the Bag. (DF - Computer Applications Ser.). 1990. mass mkt. 19.95 (*0-538-60707-6*) S-W Pub.

Barefield, Marilyn. The History of Mountain Brook & Incidentally of Shades Valley. 264p. (Orig.). 1989. 29.95 (*0-87651-990-7*) Southern U Pr.

***Barefield, Marilyn.** Researching in Alabama: A Genealogical Guide. 150p. 1999. pap. text 19.95 (*0-8173-1042-8*) U of Ala Pr.

Barefield, Marilyn D. Alabama Mortality Schedule, 1860: Eighth Census of the United States : Original Returns of the Assistant Marshalls, Third Series : Persons Who Died During the Year Ending June 30, 1860. LC 98-183666. vi, 188p. 1987. write for info. (*0-89308-603-7*) Southern Hist Pr.

— Butler County, Alabama Obituaries. (Illus.). 158p. 1985. pap. 17.50 (*0-89308-549-9*) Southern Hist Pr.

— Historical Records of Randolph County, Alabama, 1832-1900. (Illus.). 230p. 1985. 22.50 (*0-89308-548-0*) Southern Hist Pr.

— Old Demopolis Land Office Records & Military Warrants, 1818-1860, & Records of the Vine & Olive Colony. (Illus.). 172p. 1988. 20.00 (*0-89308-637-1*, BH 16) Southern Hist Pr.

— Old Montgomery Land Office Records. 1991. write for info. (*0-87651-945-1*) Southern U Pr.

— Wilcox County, Alabama, Records Of. (Illus.). 219p. 1988. 22.50 (*0-89308-636-3*, BH 17) Southern Hist Pr.

Barefield, Marilyn D., compiled by. Civil War Records of Jefferson County, Alabama. LC 93-19970. 1993. 20.00 (*0-942301-22-6*) Birm Pub Lib.

Barefield, Marilyn D. & Barefield, Carr B. Pickens County, Alabama, 1841-1861. 120p. 1984. pap. 15.00 (*0-89308-533-2*) Southern Hist Pr.

***Barefield, Marilyn Davis.** Researching in Alabama: A Genealogical Guide. 2nd rev. ed. Crumpler, Yvonne Shelton, ed. (Illus.). 144p. 1998. pap. 25.00 (*0-942301-24-2*) Birm Pub Lib.

Barefield, Russell M. The Impact of Audit Frequency on the Quality of Internal Control, Vol. 11. (Studies in Accounting Research). 86p. 1975. 12.00 (*0-86539-023-1*) Am Accounting.

Barefield, Russell M. & Holstrum, Gary L., eds. Disclosure Criteria & Segment Reporting: Proceedings of a Conference Sponsored by the Accounting Research Center & the Public Policy Research Center of the College of Business, University of Florida. LC 79-21130. (University of Florida Accounting Ser.: No. 10). 167p. reprint ed. pap. 51.80 (*0-7837-4957-0*, 204462300004) Bks Demand.

Barefield, Sandra L. Learning to Use IBM Linkway. (Illus.). 165p. (YA). (gr. 9-12). 1993. lib. bdg. 24.95 (*0-9637412-0-9*) Clicker Pub.

Barefoot. The Compliance Review Tool Kit: An Internal Control System for Auditing & Monitoring. 4th ed. (C). 1995. ring bd. 225.00 (*1-55738-783-4*, Irwn Prfssnl) McGraw-Hill Prof.

Barefoot, Betsy O., ed. Exploring the Evidence: Reporting Outcomes of Freshman Seminars. (Freshman Year Experience Monograph: No. 11). 77p. (Orig.). 1993. pap. 20.00 (*1-889271-08-X*) Nat Res Ctr.

***Barefoot, Betsy O., ed.** Exploring the Evidence Vol. II: Reporting Outcomes of First-Year Seminars. (Freshman Year Experience Monograph Ser.: No. 25). 120p. 1998. pap. 30.00 (*1-889271-25-X*) Nat Res Ctr.

Barefoot, Betsy O. & Fidler, Paul P. The 1994 National Survey of Freshman Seminar Programs: Continuing Innovations in the Collegiate Curriculum. (Freshman Year Experience Monograph: No. 20). 92p. (Orig.). 1996. pap. 35.00 (*1-889271-17-9*) Nat Res Ctr.

Barefoot, Betsy O., jt. ed. see Knowlton, Steven R.

Barefoot, Brian, tr. see Navarro, J. & Schmitz, J., eds.

Barefoot Contessa Store Staff, jt. auth. see Garten, Ina.

***Barefoot, Coy.** The Corner. 2001. 39.95 (*1-57427-113-X*) Howell Pr VA.

— The Quixtar Revolution: Discover the New High-Tech, High Touch World of Marketing. LC 99-49380. 2000. pap. 15.95 (*0-7615-2338-3*) Prima Pub.

Barefoot, Daniel. Touring the Backroads of North Carolina's Lower Coast. LC 94-47828. (Touring the Backroads Ser.). (Illus.). 363p. (Orig.). 1996. pap. 15.95 (*0-89587-126-2*) Blair.

— Touring the Backroads of North Carolina's Upper Coast. LC 94-40668. (Touring the Backroads Ser.). (Illus.). 365p. (Orig.). 1996. pap. 15.95 (*0-89587-125-4*) Blair.

Barefoot, Daniel W. General Robert F. Hoke: Lee's Modest Warrior. LC 96-2702. (Illus.). 442p. 1996. 24.95 (*0-89587-150-5*) Blair.

— Touring North Carolina's Revolutionary War Sites. LC 98-27003. (Touring the Backroads Ser.). 1998. pap. 21.95 (*0-89587-217-X*) Blair.

— Touring South Carolina's Revolutionary War Sites. LC 99-33338. (Touring the Backroads Ser.). (Illus.). 1999. pap. 19.95 (*0-89587-182-3*) Blair.

Barefoot, J. Kirk. Employee Theft Investigation. 2nd rev. ed. (Illus.). 240p. 1990. text 39.95 (*0-409-90211-X*) Buttrwrth-Heinemann.

— Undercover Investigations. 3rd ed. LC 95-38. 208p. 1995. 39.95 (*0-7506-9645-1*, BH Security) Buttrwrth-Heinemann.

Barefoot, J. Kirk & Maxwell, David. Corporate Security Administration & Management. (Illus.). 288p. 1987. 44.95 (*0-409-95106-4*) Buttrwrth-Heinemann.

Barefoot, Kevin, ed. Higher Grounds: The Little Book of Coffee Culture. 96p. 1995. pap. 4.95 (*1-55152-018-4*, Pub. by Arsenal Pulp) LPC InBook.

Barefoot, Marrinan & Associates, Inc. Staff. The Compliance Review Toolkit: An Internal Control System for Auditing & Monitoring Consumer Regulatory Compliance. rev. ed. 225p. 1994. 225.00 (*1-55738-741-9*, Irwn Prfssnl) McGraw-Hill Prof.

Barefoot, R. R., jt. auth. see Van Loon, Jon C.

Barefoot, Robert R. Death by Diet. 144p. 1996. pap. 14.95 (*0-9633703-3-2*) Bokar Cnslts.

Barefoot, Robert R. & Reich, Carl M. The Calcium Factor: The Scientific Secret of Health & Youth. 110p. (Orig.). 1992. pap. 14.95 (*0-9633703-2-4*) Bokar Cnslts.

Bareh, Hamlet. The Art History of Meghalaya. 1991. 68.00 (*0-8364-2596-0*, Pub. by Agam) S Asia.

Bareham, J. R. The Behaviour of Lambs on the First Day after Birth. 1976. 25.00 (*0-7855-1121-0*) St Mut.

Bareham, Jon R. Consumer Behavior in the Food Industry: A European Perspective. LC 95-56514. (Illus.). 234p. 1995. reprint ed. pap. 72.60 (*0-608-07966-9*, 206793800012) Bks Demand.

Bareham, Lindsey. Celebration of Soup. 416p. 1996. 29.95 (*0-470-23624-8*) Wiley.

***Bareham, Lindsey.** Celebration of Soup. 416p. 1999. pap. 14.95 (*0-471-31876-0*) Wiley.

Bareham, Lindsey. In Praise of the Potato. 324p. 1993. pap. 13.95 (*0-87951-497-3*, Pub. by Overlook Pr) Penguin Putnam.

***Bareham, Lindsey.** In Praise of the Potato. 320p. 1998. pap. 14.95 (*0-14-027093-0*, Pub. by Pnguin Bks Ltd) Trafalgar.

Bareham, Lindsey. In Praise of the Potato: Recipes from Around the World. 320p. 1992. 22.95 (*0-87951-410-8*, Pub. by Overlook Pr) Penguin Putnam.

Bareham, Tony, ed. Charles Lever: New Evaluations. 128p. (C). 1991. text 49.50 (*0-389-20964-3*) B&N Imports.

Bareikis, V. & Katilius, R. Noise in Physical Systems & 1/f Fluctuations: Proceedings of the 13th International Conference. 768p. 1995. text 148.00 (*981-02-2278-5*) World Scientific Pub.

Bareis, Charles J. & Porter, James W., eds. American Bottom Archaeology: A Summary of the FAI-270 Project Contribution to the Culture History of the Mississippi River Valley. LC 83-15366. (Illus.). 304p. 1984. pap. text 24.95 (*0-252-06346-5*) U of Ill Pr.

Bareis, George F. History of Madison Township, Ohio. (Illus.). 515p. 1993. reprint ed. lib. bdg. 52.00 (*0-8328-2966-8*) Higginson Bk Co.

Bareiss. Case-Based Reasoning. (C). 1991. pap. text 40.00 (*1-55860-199-6*) Morgan Kaufmann.

Bareither, Terry, ed. see Spring, Harry.

***Bareket, Elinoar.** Fustat on the Nile: The Jewish Elite in Medieval Egypt. LC 99-30518. (Medieval Mediterranean, 24 Ser.). (Illus.). 296p. 1999. 103.00 (*90-04-11439-4*) Brill Academic Pubs.

Barel, M. Van, see Kravanja, P. & Van Barel, M.

Barel, Marc Van, see Bultheel, Adhemar & Van Barel, Marc.

Barela. New Covenant of Clinton & Gore. 1992. pap. 7.95 (*0-9617286-2-0*) Today Bible & You.

Barela, J. Antichrist Associates & Cosmic. 1995. pap. text 7.45 (*0-9617286-0-4*) Today Bible & You.

Barela, Tim. Domesticity Isn't Pretty: A Leonard & Larry Collection. 160p. 1993. pap. 12.95 (*1-884568-00-9*) Palliard Pr.

— Kurt Cobain & Mozart Are Both Dead: Leonard & Larry 2. (Leonard & Larry Ser.: No. 2). (Illus.). 90p. 1996. pap. 9.95 (*1-884568-04-1*) Palliard Pr.

Barell, John. PBL: An Inquiry Approach. LC 98-60465. (Illus.). 181p. 1998. pap. 32.95 (*1-57517-048-5*, 1592) SkyLght.

— Playgrounds of Our Minds. LC 79-27084. 207p. 1980. pap. 64.20 (*0-7837-7447-8*, 204903900010) Bks Demand.

— Teaching for Thoughtfulness: Classroom Strategies to Enhance Intellectual Development. 2nd rev. ed. LC 94-27770. 328p. (Orig.). (C). 1994. pap. text 53.00 (*0-8013-1302-3*) Longman.

Barella, A., jt. auth. see Campos, J. G.

Barella Campos, Ana G., jt. auth. see Barella Campos, Juana.

Barella Campos, Juana & Barella Campos, Ana G. Diccionario de Refranes. (SPA.). 534p. 1975. pap. 54.95 (*0-8288-5815-2*, S50116) Fr & Eur.

Barelvi, Mahmud. Islam & World Religions. 320p. (Orig.). 1996. pap. 10.50 (*0-614-21668-0*, 569) Kazi Pubns.

Baremdt, Eric, et al, eds. The Yearbook of Media & Entertainment Law, 1997-1998, Vol. 3. 584p. 1998. text 235.00 (*0-19-826597-2*) OUP.

Baren. Libel Law & the Media: The Chilling Effect. LC 96-40026. 220p. 1997. pap. text (*0-19-826234-5*) OUP.

Baren, Martin. Hyperactivity & Attention Disorders in Children. (Pediatrics Ser.). 32p. 1999. pap. text 2.95 (*1-885274-01-7*) Health InfoNet Inc.

***Baren, Martin.** Learning Disorders & Disabilities: A Guide for Parents. unabridged large type ed. Stein, Martin & Kneel, Dennis, eds. (Pediatric & Behavioral Health Ser.: No. 1025). (Illus.). 32p. 1999. pap. 2.95 (*1-885274-59-9*) Health InfoNet Inc.

***Baren, Maurice.** Victorian Shopping. (Illus.). 144p. 1999. pap. 19.95 (*1-85479-302-0*, Pub. by M OMara) Trafalgar.

Baren, Nick. Castle of the Undead. (Endless Quest, Ravenloft Ser.: No. 2). 192p. (Orig.). 1994. pap. 3.95 (*1-56076-836-3*, Pub. by TSR Inc) Random.

Baren, William S., see Dutton, John, pseud.

Barenbaum, Michel. Reb Michel's Shmuessen: The Inspiring Ethical Lectures of a Patriarch of Mussar, the Mashgiach of Mesivtha Tifereth Jerusalem. 18.99 (*0-89906-638-0*, RMWH); pap. 15.99 (*0-89906-639-9*, RMWP) Mesorah Pubns.

Barenbaum, Ruth, ed. see Barrows, Clifford.

Barenberg, Russ. Beginning Bluegrass Guitar. (Illus.). 64p. 1989. pap. 12.95 (*0-8256-2368-5*, AM35213) Music Sales.

— Teach Yourself Bluegrass Guitar, EFS184. (Illus.). 64p. pap. 12.95 (*0-8256-2184-4*, AM21627) Music Sales.

Barenberg, Sumner A., ed. Degradable Materials. 776p. 1990. per. 99.95 (*0-8493-4274-0*, QP801) CRC Pr.

Barenblat, Rachel. The Skies Here. (Illus.). 65p. 1995. pap. 9.95 (*1-877603-31-7*) Pecan Grove.

Barenblat, Scot G. & Mesler, Donald T. Stock Index Options: How to Use & Profit from Indexed Options in Volatile & Uncertain Markets. rev. ed. 230p. 1991. 29.95 (*1-55738-181-X*, Irwn Prfssnl) McGraw-Hill Prof.

Barenblatt, G. I. Dimensional Analysis. Makinen, Paul, tr. x, 135p. 1987. text 150.00 (*2-88124-226-X*); pap. text 75.00 (*2-88124-227-8*) Gordon & Breach.

— Scaling, Self-Similarity & Intermediate Asymptotics. LC 95-48212. (Cambridge Texts in Applied Mathematics Ser.: No. 14). 408p. (C). 1996. text 95.00 (*0-521-43516-1*); pap. text 34.95 (*0-521-43522-6*) Cambridge U Pr.

— Similarity, Self-Similarity & Intermediate Asymptotics. Stein, Norman, tr. from RUS. LC 79-14621. (Illus.). 236p. 1979. reprint ed. pap. 73.20 (*0-608-05753-3*, 205971700007) Bks Demand.

Barenblatt, G. I., et al. Theory of Fluid Flows Through Natural Rocks. (C). 1990. text 304.50 (*0-7923-0167-6*) Kluwer Academic.

Barendregt, H. P. The Lambda Calculus: Its Syntax & Semantics. rev. ed. (Studies in Logic & the Foundations of Mathematics: No. 103). 622p. 1984. pap. 56.75 (*0-444-87508-5*, North Holland) Elsevier.

— The Lambda Calculus: Its Syntax & Semantics. 2nd rev. ed. (Studies in Logic & the Foundations of Mathematics: No. 103). xvi,622p. 1984. 104.00 (*0-444-86748-1*, I-127-84, North Holland) Elsevier.

Barendregt, Hank & Nipkow, Tobias, eds. Types for Proofs & Programs: International Workshop TYPES '93, Nijmegen, the Netherlands, May 1993: Selected Papers. LC 94-12368. (Lecture Notes in Computer Science Ser.: Vol. 806). 1994. write for info. (*0-387-58085-9*) Spr-Verlag.

Barendregt, Joanne, tr. see Erkelens, L.

Barends, F. B., et al, eds. Geotechnical Engineering for Transportation Infrastructure - Theory & Practice, Planning & Design, Construction & Maintenance: Proceedings of the XIIth European Conference, Amsterdam 7-10 June 1999, 3 vols. (Illus.). 2500p. 1999. 525.00 (*90-5809-047-7*, Pub. by A A Balkema) Ashgate Pub Co.

Barends, F. B., jt. ed. see Verruijt, A.

Barends, Frans B., et al, eds. Land Subsidence: Natural Causes, Measuring Techniques, the Groningen Gasfields: Proceedings: International Symposium (5th: 1995: The Hague, Netherlands) (Illus.). 426p. (C). 1995. text 110.00 (*90-5410-589-5*, TP715, Pub. by A A Balkema) Ashgate Pub Co.

Barends, Frans J., ed. Application of Stress Wave Theory to Piles: Proceedings of the Fourth International Conference on the Application of Stress-Wave Theory to Piles The Hague - The Netherlands 21-24 September 1992. (Illus.). 726p. (C). 1992. 149.00 (*90-5410-082-6*, Pub. by A A Balkema) Ashgate Pub Co.

***Barendt, E. M. & Hitchens, Lesley.** Media Law: Cases & Materials. LC 00-27283. (Law Ser.). 2000. write for info. (*0-582-31719-3*) Longman.

Barendt, E. M., jt. auth. see Ogus, Anthony I.

Barendt, Eric. Broadcasting Law: A Comparative Study. 294p. 1995. pap. text 32.00 (*0-19-826021-0*) OUP.

— An Introduction to Constitutional Law. 214p. 1998. pap. text (*0-19-876254-2*) OUP.

— An Introduction to Constitutional Law. (Clarendon Law Ser.). 214p. 1998. text 65.00 (*0-19-876253-4*, Clarendon Pr) OUP.

Barendt, Eric, ed. Media Law. LC 93-25714. (International Library of Essays in Law & Legal Theory: Vol. 21). (C). 1994. lib. bdg. 150.00 (*0-8147-1215-0*) NYU Pr.

— The Yearbook of Media & Entertainment Law, 1996, Vol. 2. 634p. 1997. text 245.00 (*0-19-826277-9*) OUP.

***Barendt, Eric, et al, eds.** Yearbook of Copyright & Media Law Vol. IV; 1999. 480p. 2000. text 165.00 (*0-19-826873-4*) OUP.

Barendt, Eric, et al, eds. The Yearbook of Media & Entertainment Law, 1995, Vol. 1. 608p. 1995. text 225.00 (*0-19-825927-1*) OUP.

Barendt, Eric & Lustgarten, Laurence. Libel Law & the Media: The Chilling Effect. LC 96-40026. (Illus.). 224p. 1997. text 56.00 (*0-19-826227-2*) OUP.

Barendt, Eric M. Broadcasting Law: A Comparative Study. 280p. (C). 1993. 55.00 (*0-19-825254-4*, 2001) OUP.

— Freedom of Speech. 366p. 1987. pap. text 32.00 (*0-19-825603-5*) OUP.

Barenholtz, Manny. Walden in the Western Reserve. (Illus.). 68p. 1989. 19.95 (*0-9617637-1-X*) CL Stock Images.

Barenholz, Yechezkel, jt. ed. see Lasic, Danilo D.

Barents, Rene. Agricultural Law of the EC. 1994. pap. text 101.00 (*90-6544-867-5*) Kluwer Academic.

Barentsz, Jelle O. Magnetic Resonance Imaging of Carcinoma of the Urinary Bladder. (Series in Radiology). (C). 1990. text 206.50 (*0-7923-0838-7*) Kluwer Academic.

Barer, Barbara M., jt. auth. see Johnson, Colleen L.

***Barer, Burl.** Headlock. (Jeff Reynolds Mystery Ser.). 2000. pap. 18.99 (*1-886199-09-4*, Deadly Alibi Pr) Madison Pubng.

— Murder In The Family. 2000. mass mkt. 6.50 (*0-7860-1135-1*) Kensgtn Pub Corp.

Barer, Burl. The Saint. 1997. per. 5.99 (*0-671-00951-6*, Pocket Books) PB.

— The Saint: A Complete History in Print, Radio, Film & Television of Leslie Charteris' Robin Hood of Modern Crime, Simon Templar, 1928-1992. LC 92-53509. (Illus.). 431p. 1993. lib. bdg. 58.50 (*0-89950-723-9*) McFarland & Co.

***Barer, M. L., et al.** Health, Health Care & Health Economics: Perspectives on Distribution. LC 98-19860. 576p. 1998. 120.00 (*0-471-97879-5*) Wiley.

Barer, R. D. & Peters, B. F. Why Metals Fail-Selected Case Histories. x, 346p. 1970. text 214.00 (*0-677-02630-7*) Gordon & Breach.

***Barer, Shlomo.** The Doctors of Revolution: 19th Century Thinkers Who Changed the World. LC 99-65583. 1200p. 2000. 49.95 (*0-500-01884-7*, Pub. by Thames Hudson) Norton.

Barer-Stein, Thelma. You Eat What You Are: People, Culture & Food Traditions. 2nd rev. expanded ed. (Illus.). 544p. 1999. 35.00 (*1-55209-365-4*) Firefly Bks Ltd.

Barer-Stein, Thelma & Draper, James A., eds. The Craft of Teaching Adults. 2nd ed. LC 93-33837. 272p. (C). 1994. reprint ed. lib. bdg. 31.50 (*0-89464-867-5*) Krieger.

Bares, Jan, ed. Electronic Imaging: Processing, Printing & Publishing in Color. (Europto Ser.: Vol. 3409). 470p. 1998. 89.00 (*0-8194-2861-2*) SPIE.

Bares, Jan, et al, eds. Imaging Sciences & Display Technologies. LC 96-70282. (Europto Ser.: Vol. 2949). 478p. 1997. 85.00 (*0-8194-2353-X*) SPIE.

Bares, Kathryn & Craddock, Jerry R., eds. Text & Concordance of the Libro de los Fueros de Castiella, MS431: Biblioteca Nacional, Madrid. (Spanish Legal Texts Ser.: No. 5). (SPA.). 8p. 1989. 10.00 incl. fiche (*0-940639-41-6*) Hispanic Seminary.

Bares, R., ed. see Lucignani, G.

Baret, Carlo, et al. The Three D Stress Analysis of Spur & Helical Gears: An Integrated System Based on the P-FEM Approach. (Nineteen Eighty-Eight Fall Technical Meeting Ser.: Vol. 88FTM7). (Illus.). 22p. 1988. pap. text 30.00 (*1-55589-512-3*) AGMA.

***Baret, Christophe, et al, eds.** Flexible Working in Food Retailing: A Comparison Between France, Germany, Great Britain & Japan. (Studies in Retailing). 256p. 2000. 90.00 (*0-415-21220-0*) Routledge.

Baret, Jack. The Falling Sky. 48p. 1999. pap. 8.00 (*0-8059-4473-7*) Dorrance.

Baretta-Bekker, H. G. Encyclopedia of Marine Sciences. Duursma, E. K. et al, eds. (Illus.). viii, 311p. 1995. reprint ed. 42.95 (*0-387-54501-8*) Spr-Verlag.

Baretta-Bekker, H. J., et al, eds. Encyclopedia of Marine Sciences. 2nd enl. ed. LC 98-18272. x, 358p. 1998. pap. 29.95 (*3-540-62675-1*) Spr-Verlag.

Baretta, J. W. & Ruardij, P., eds. Tidal Flat Estuaries. (Ecological Studies: Vol. 71). (Illus.). 360p. 1988. 158.95 (*0-387-19323-5*) Spr-Verlag.

Baretter, P. & Schramel, Peter, eds. Trace Element Analytical Chemistry in Medicine & Biology Vol. 4: Proceedings of the 4th International Workshop, Neuherberg, Federal Republic of Germany, 1986. xiii, 630p. 1987. lib. bdg. 240.00 (*3-11-010905-0*) De Gruyter.

Baretto, Alina, jt. auth. see Lederkremer, Javier.

Bareuther, Carol. Sport Fishing in the Virgin Islands: Everything You Need to Know. (Illus.). 113p. (Orig.). 1992. pap. 10.00 (*0-9631060-3-1*) Am Paradise.

— Virgin Islands Cooking. (Illus.). 184p. (Orig.). 1994. pap. text 20.00 (*0-9631060-6-6*) Am Paradise.

Barey, Pat. Bandelier National Monument. Priehs, T. J. & Burson, Therese, eds. LC 90-60724. (Illus.). 48p. (Orig.). 1990. pap. 7.95 (*0-911408-88-6*) SW Pks Mnmts.

Barey, Patricia, jt. auth. see Morella, Joe.

Barfield. Cost Accounting. 3rd ed. LC 96-32426. 1996. pap. text. write for info. (*0-314-09625-6*) West Pub.

— Cost Accounting: Readings. Date not set. pap. text 13.75 (*0-314-03514-1*) West Pub.

***Barfield.** Designing Multi Media & the Web. (C). 2000. pap. text. write for info. (*0-201-59609-1*) Addison-Wesley.

Barfield & Raiborn, Cecily A. Managerial Accounting. (AQ - Managerial Accounting Ser.). 1993. pap., teacher ed. write for info. (*0-314-02319-4*) West Pub.

Barfield, et al. Cost Accounting: Traditions &... 3rd ed. 1997. pap. 6.75 (*0-538-88062-7*) S-W Pub.

— Cost Accounting: Traditions & Innovations. 3rd ed. 1997. 20.25 (*0-538-88059-7*) Thomson Learn.

— Cost Accounting: Traditions & Innovations. 3rd ed. 1997. 21.00 (*0-538-88057-0*) Thomson Learn.

***Barfield, et al.** Cost Accounting: Traditions & Innovations. 4th ed. 2000. pap. 75.00 (*0-324-02645-5*); pap., student ed. 20.25 (*0-324-02646-3*) Thomson Learn.

Barfield, et al. Weston Manufacturing: An Activity Based Costing Case. 3rd ed. 1997. 12.50 (*0-538-88056-2*) S-W Pub.

Barfield, James, ed. see Colewsworthy, Robert & Eickel, Jerry.

Barfield, Claude E. Expanding U. S. - Asian Trade & Investment: New Challenges & Policy Options 180p. 1996. 29.95 (*0-8447-3934-0*) Am Enterprise.

— International Financial Markets: Harmonization Versus Competition. LC 96-41171. 180p. 1996. 29.95 (*0-8447-3926-X*) Am Enterprise.

— Rethinking Federalism: Block Grants & Federal, State, & Local Responsibilities. LC 81-17602. 111p. reprint ed. pap. 34.50 (*0-7837-1087-9*, 204161900021) Bks Demand.

Barfield, Claude E., ed. Science for the Twenty-First Century: The Vannevar Bush Report. LC 97-29133. 125p. 1997. pap. 14.95 (*0-8447-4015-2*) Am Enterprise.

— Science for the Twenty-First Century: The Vannevar Bush Report Revisited. LC 97-29133. 100p. 1997. 29.95 (*0-8447-4014-4*) Am Enterprise.

Barfield, Claude E. & Smith, Bruce L., eds. The Future of Biomedical Research. LC 97-34604. 125p. 1997. pap. 14.95 (*0-8447-4037-3*) Am Enterprise.

— The Future of Biomedical Research. LC 97-34604. 100p. 1997. 29.95 (*0-8447-4036-5*) Am Enterprise.

***Barfield, Claude E., et al.** Tiger by the Tail: China & the World Trade Organization. LC 99-31188. 120p. 1999. 35.00 (*0-8447-4107-8*, Pub. by Am Enterprise); pap. 17.00 (*0-8447-4108-6*, Pub. by Am Enterprise) Pub Resources Inc.

Barfield, Claude E., jt. ed. see Smith, Bruce L.

Barfield, James, ed. & photos by see Colesworthy, Robert & Reher, David.

Barfield, Jesse T. & Raiborn. Cost Accounting. 2nd ed. (SWC-Accounting). 1994. pap., student ed. 19.25 (*0-314-03508-7*) S-W Pub.

Barfield, Jesse T., et al. Cost Accounting: Traditions & Inovation. 3rd ed. LC 96-32426. 1997. pap. text 108.95 (*0-538-88047-3*) Thomson Learn.

— Cost Accounting: Traditions & Innovations 2e. 2nd ed. Leyh, ed. LC 93-41871. (SWC-Accounting). 1131p. (C). 1993. mass mkt. 64.00 (*0-314-02904-4*) West Pub.

— Laser Logos Inc. An Accounting Simulation. 3rd ed. 1997. pap. 18.25 (*0-538-88060-0*) S-W Pub.

Barfield, Jesse T., jt. auth. see Raiborn.

Barfield, Joe. The Cajun. Trujillo, Becky, ed. (Illus.). 220p. (Orig.). Date not set. pap. 9.95 (*1-884797-01-6*) Moran Pub.

— Chem Storm. 220p. Date not set. pap. 9.95 (*1-884797-03-2*) Moran Pub.

— Moon Shadow. 220p. Date not set. pap. 9.95 (*1-884797-02-4*) Moran Pub.

— Urban Kill. 220p. 1996. pap. 9.95 (*1-884797-04-0*) Moran Pub.

Barfield, Joe & Sharp, Kyler. Formula 2000 - The Dream: A Novel of a Promise & a Dream. Trujillo, Becky, ed. (Illus.). 220p. (Orig.). Date not set. pap. 9.95 (*1-884797-00-8*) Moran Pub.

Barfield, John, jt. auth. see Craven, Henry.

Barfield, Kenny. The Prophet Motive: Examining the Reliability of the Biblical Prophets. 340p. 1995. pap. 12.99 (*0-89225-458-0*, G54580) Gospel Advocate.

— Why the Bible Is Number 1: The World's Sacred Writings in the Light of Science. 242p. 1997. pap. 17.00 (*1-57910-050-3*) Wipf & Stock.

***Barfield, Norman.** Vickers Aircraft. (Transport Ser.). 1999. pap. 18.99 (*0-7524-0606-X*) Arcadia Publng.

Barfield, Owen. A Barfield Reader: Selections from the Writings of Owen Barfield. Tennyson, G. B., ed. & intro. by. LC 98-29555. 231p. 1999. pap. 18.95 (*0-8195-6361-7*, Wesleyan Univ Pr); text 45.00 (*0-8195-6351-X*, Wesleyan Univ Pr) U Pr of New Eng.

— A Barfield Sampler: Poetry & Fiction by Owen Barfield. Hunter, Jeanne C. & Kranidas, Thomas, eds. LC 92-30926. 181p. (C). 1993. text 59.50 (*0-7914-1587-2*); pap. text 19.95 (*0-7914-1588-0*) State U NY Pr.

— Orpheus: A Poetic Drama. LC 82-83247. 160p. (Orig.). 1983. pap. 6.95 (*0-940262-01-0*, Lindisfarne) Anthroposophic.

— Owen Barfield & the Origin of Language. 1979. pap. 2.50 (*0-916786-42-0*, Saint George Pubns) R Steiner Col.

— Poetic Diction: A Study in Meaning. 2nd ed. LC 87-22985. 238p. 1984. pap. 17.95 (*0-8195-6026-X*, Wesleyan Univ Pr) U Pr of New Eng.

— Saving the Appearances: A Study in Idolatry. 2nd ed. LC 88-5563. 191p. 1988. pap. 14.95 (*0-8195-6205-X*, Wesleyan Univ Pr) U Pr of New Eng.

Barfield, Owen, jt. auth. see Oudel, Solomon.

Barfield, Owen, ed. see Harwood, A. C.

Barfield, Raiborn. Management Accounting. (Miscellaneous/Catalogs Ser.). 1993. text, teacher ed. write for info. (*0-314-01273-7*) S-W Pub.

Barfield, Ray. Listening to Radio, 1920-1950. LC 95-52706. 248p. 1996. 49.95 (*0-275-95492-7*, Praeger Pubs) Greenwood.

Barfield, Ray E. & Titus, Sylvia S. Business Communications. deluxe ed. Friedlob, George T., ed. (Barron's Business Library). 320p. (Orig.). 1992. pap. text 14.95 (*0-8120-4639-0*) Barron.

Barfield, Rhonda. Eat Healthy for $50. 1996. pap. 12.00 (*0-8217-5255-3*) NAL.

Barfield, Rhonda. Eat Healthy for 50 Dollars a Week. 240p. 1996. pap. 12.00 (*1-57566-018-0*) Kensgtn Pub Corp.

— 15-Minute Cooking. 162p. (Orig.). 1996. spiral bd. 12.95 (*0-9635782-1-9*) Lilac Pub.

Barfield, Richard E. & Morgan, James N. Early Retirement: The Decision & the Experience & A Second Look. LC 70-626137. 349p. reprint ed. pap. 108.20 (*0-608-15453-9*, 202930400060) Bks Demand.

Barfield, Rodney. Seasoned by Salt: A Historical Album of the Outer Banks. LC 95-9914. (Illus.). 206p. (C). 1995. 39.95 (*0-8078-2231-0*); pap. 19.95 (*0-8078-4537-X*) U of NC Pr.

Barfield, Thomas. The Dictionary of Anthropology. LC 96-37337. 626p. (Orig.). 1997. pap. 29.95 (*1-57718-057-7*) Blackwell Pubs.

Barfield, Thomas, ed. The Dictionary of Anthropology. LC 96-37337. 672p. (Orig.). 1997. 94.95 (*1-55786-282-6*) Blackwell Pubs.

Barfield, Thomas J. The Nomadic Alternative. LC 92-15067. 224p. (C). 1993. pap. text 20.00 (*0-13-624982-5*) P-H.

— The Perilous Frontier. 1992. pap. 29.95 (*1-55786-324-5*) Blackwell Pubs.

Barfield, Thomas J., jt. auth. see Szabo, Albert.

***Barfield, Woodrow & Caudell, Thomas.** Fundamentals of Wearable Computers & Augumented Reality. LC 00-39311. (Illus.). 2000. pap. write for info. (*0-8058-2902-4*) L Erlbaum Assocs.

***Barfield, Woodrow & Caudell, Thomas, eds.** Fundamentals of Wearable Computers & Augemented Reality. 424p. 2000. write for info. (*0-8058-2901-6*) L Erlbaum Assocs.

Barfield, Woodrow & Dingus, Tom, eds. Human Factors in Intelligent Vehicle Highway Systems. LC 97-14434. (Human Factors in Transportation Ser.). 400p. (C). 1997. text 80.00 (*0-8058-1433-7*) L Erlbaum Assocs.

Barfield, Woodrow & Furness, Tom, III, eds. Virtual Environments & Advanced Interface Design. (Illus.). 600p. 1995. text 85.00 (*0-19-507555-2*) OUP.

Barfknecht, A., et al, eds. Advanced Electronic Packaging Materials Vol. 167: Materials Research Society Symposium Proceedings. 381p. 1990. text 17.50 (*1-55899-055-0*) Materials Res.

Barfknecht, Gary W. Mich-Again's Day. (Illus.). 265p. (Orig.). 1984. pap. 7.95 (*0-9608588-2-2*) Friede Pubns.

— The Michigan Book of Bests: An Eclectic Barrage of Great Places to Go & Things to Know. (Illus.). 120p. 1999. pap. 13.95 (*0-923756-20-5*) Friede Pubns.

— Ultimate Michigan Adventures: Ninety-Eight One-of-a-Kind Destinations & Diversions. rev. ed. (Illus.). 288p. 1994. pap. 14.95 (*0-923756-10-8*) Friede Pubns.

— Unexplained Michigan Mysteries. 192p. (Orig.). 1993. pap. 11.95 (*0-923756-05-1*) Friede Pubns.

Barfod, A., jt. auth. see Skog, L. E.

Barfod, Anders, jt. ed. see Skov, Flemming.

Barfoot, Joan. Some Things about Flying LC 98-201284. 208p. 1997. write for info. (*0-7043-4549-8*) Womens Press.

Barfoot, K. M., jt. auth. see Mitchell, I. V.

Barford, Charlotte, et al. Breaking the Habits of a Lifetime: Poland's First Steps Toward the Market. Norman, Jesse, ed. & frwd. by. 234p. (Orig.). 1994. pap. 15.95 (*0-938864-17-3*) Ipswich Pr.

Barford, D. W., jt. ed. see Tunstall, D. P.

Barford, J. P., et al, eds. Fundamental & Applied Aspects of Animal Cell Cultivation. 286p. 1995. pap. 44.50 (*9971-69-194-9*, Pub. by Sngapore Univ Pr) Coronet Bks.

Barford, N. C. Mechanics. LC 72-2639. (Illus.). 407p. reprint ed. pap. 126.20 (*0-608-18411-X*, 203042600069) Bks Demand.

Barford, Philip. Keyboard Music of C. P. E. Bach. 1966. 17.50 (*0-8079-0072-9*) October.

Barford, Robert A., jt. ed. see Cherry, John P.

Barfuss, DeLon. Human Physiology Lab: BIO 225/325/725. 1996. text 10.88 (*1-56870-256-6*) RonJon Pub.

Barfuss, Gerald. David Stone in Sunset Valley: The Story of the KSTP Sunset Valley Barn Dance. (Illus.). 1983. 19.95 (*0-911506-17-9*) Thueson.

Barfuss, Matto. My Cheetah Family. LC 98-33998. 48p. (J). (gr. 4-6). 1999. 23.93 (*1-57505-377-2*, Carolrhoda) Lerner Pub.

Barg, Barbara. The Origin of the Species. 1994. pap. 7.00 (*1-57027-007-4*) Autonomedia.

Barg, Barbara, ed. see Friedman, Ed.

Bargad, Warren. To Write the Lips of Sleepers: The Poetry of Amir Gilboa. LC 93-49756. (Monographs of the Hebrew Union College: No. 17). 300p. 1994. 44.95 (*0-87820-416-4*) Hebrew Union Coll Pr.

Bargad, Warren & Chyet, Stanley F., trs. from HEB. Israeli Poetry: A Contemporary Anthology. LC 84-48247. (Jewish Literature & Culture Ser.). 280p. 1986. 32.50 (*0-253-33140-4*) Ind U Pr.

— Israeli Poetry: A Contemporary Anthology. LC 84-48247. (Jewish Literature & Culture Ser.). 280p. 1988. pap. 14.95 (*0-253-20356-2*, MB 356) Ind U Pr.

***Bargagli, R.** Trace Elements in Terrestrial Plants: An Ecophysiological Approach to Biomonitoring & Biorecovery. (Environmental Intelligence Unit Ser.). xx, 324p. 1998. 189.00 (*3-540-64551-9*) Spr-Verlag.

Bargagli, Roberto. Trace Elements in Terrestrial Plants: An Ecophysiological Approach to Biomonitoring & Biorecovery. LC 98-22661. (Environmental Intelligence Unit Ser.). 1998. 189.00 (*1-57059-532-1*) Spr-Verlag.

Bargai, Uri, et al. Bovine Radiology. (Venture Series in Veterinary Medicine). (Illus.). 206p. (C). 1989. pap. text 49.95 (*0-8138-0185-0*) Iowa St U Pr.

Bargain Books Staff. Wisdom from the Proverbs. 384p. 1997. lthr. 9.97 (*1-57748-097-X*) Barbour Pub.

Bargain Books Staff. Wisdom from the Psalms. 384p. 1997. lthr. 9.97 (*1-57748-098-8*) Barbour Pub.

Bargain Books Staff, jt. auth. see Chambers, Oswald.

***Bargain Box Staff.** Twice Treasured Recipes. 224p. 2000. 19.95 (*0-9678119-0-2*, Pub. by Bargain Box) Wimmer Bks.

Bargainnier, Earl, ed. Comic Crime. LC 87-71031. 202p. (Orig.). (C). 1987. 29.95 (*0-87972-383-1*); pap. 14.95 (*0-87972-384-X*) Bowling Green Univ Popular Press.

B

Bargainnier, Earl F. The Gentle Art of Murder: The Detective Fiction of Agatha Christie. LC 80-83187. 232p. 1981. 23.95 (*0-87972-158-8*) Bowling Green Univ Popular Press.

Bargainnier, Earl F., ed. 10 Women of Mystery. LC 80-85393. 1981. 22.95 (*0-87972-172-3*); pap. 11.95 (*0-87972-173-1*) Bowling Green Univ Popular Press.

— Twelve Englishmen of Mystery. LC 83-72499. 1984. 23.95 (*0-87972-249-5*); pap. 12.95 (*0-87972-250-9*) Bowling Green Univ Popular Press.

Bargainnier, Earl F. & Dove, George N. Cops & Constables: American & British Fictional Policemen. LC 86-71642. 204p. 1986. pap. 12.95 (*0-87972-334-3*) Bowling Green Univ Popular Press.

Bargal, David, jt. auth. see Mor-Barak, Michal E.

Bargal, David, jt. ed. see Mor-Barak, Michal E.

Barganier, Jeff S. Slash Brokers: And It Shall Come to Pass in the Last Days. LC 98-70960. 256p. (Orig.). 1998. pap. 14.99 (*1-56384-150-9*) Huntington Hse.

***Barganier, Linda, ed.** The Heritage of Lowndes County, Alabama. (Heritage of Alabama Ser.: Vol. 43). 320p. 2001. 50.00 (*1-891647-56-3*) Herit Pub Consult.

Bargar, Sherie & Johnson, L. Copperheads. (J). 1997. pap. 2.50 (*0-8167-1257-3*) Troll Communs.

— Coral Snakes. (J). 1997. pap. 2.50 (*0-8167-1447-9*) Troll Communs.

— Mambas. (J). 1997. pap. 2.50 (*0-8167-1259-X*) Troll Communs.

— Pythons. (J). 1997. pap. 2.50 (*0-8167-1449-5*) Troll Communs.

— Tree Vipers. (J). 1997. pap. 2.50 (*0-8167-1451-7*) Troll Communs.

Bargar, Sherie & Johnson, Linda. Anacondas. (Snake Discovery Library: Set II). (Illus.). 24p. (J). (gr. k-4). 1987. lib. bdg. 14.60 (*0-86592-249-7*) Rourke Enter.

— Boa Constrictors. (Snake Discovery Library: Set I). (Illus.). 24p. (J). (gr. k-4). 1986. lib. bdg. 14.60 (*0-86592-959-9*) Rourke Enter.

— Boas Constrictoras. LC 93-8391. (Culebras Ser.).Tr. of Boa Constrictors. (SPA., Illus.). 24p. (J). (gr. k-4). 1993. lib. bdg. 10.95 (*0-86593-333-2*) Rourke Corp.

— Cabezas Cobrizas. (Culebras Ser.).Tr. of Copperheads. 24p. (J). (gr. k-4). 1994. lib. bdg. 10.95 (*0-86593-329-4*) Rourke Corp.

— Cobras. (Culebras Ser.). 24p. (J). (gr. k-4). 1994. lib. bdg. 10.95 (*0-86593-334-0*) Rourke Corp.

— Cobras. (Snake Discovery Library: Set I). (Illus.). 24p. (J). (gr. k-4). 1986. lib. bdg. 14.60 (*0-86592-955-6*) Rourke Enter.

— Copperheads. (Snake Discovery Library: Set I). (Illus.). 24p. (J). (gr. k-4). 1986. lib. bdg. 14.60 (*0-86592-957-2*) Rourke Enter.

— Coral Snakes. (Snake Discovery Library: Set II). (Illus.). 24p. (J). (gr. k-4). 1987. lib. bdg. 14.60 (*0-86592-246-2*) Rourke Enter.

— Cottonmouths. (Snake Discovery Library: Set I). (Illus.). 24p. (J). (gr. k-4). 1986. lib. bdg. 14.60 (*0-86592-958-0*) Rourke Enter.

— Culebras de Cascabel. (Culebras Ser.).Tr. of Rattlesnakes. 24p. (J). (gr. k-4). 1994. lib. bdg. 10.95 (*0-86593-330-8*) Rourke Corp.

— King Snakes. (Snake Discovery Library: Set II). (Illus.). 24p. (J). (gr. k-4). 1987. lib. bdg. 14.60 (*0-86592-248-9*) Rourke Enter.

— Mambas. (Culebras Ser.). 24p. (J). (gr. k-4). Date not set. lib. bdg. 10.95 (*0-86593-331-6*) Rourke Corp.

— Mambas. (Snake Discovery Library: Set I). (Illus.). 24p. (J). (gr. k-4). 1986. lib. bdg. 14.60 (*0-86592-960-2*) Rourke Enter.

— Mocsines de Agua. (Culebras Ser.).Tr. of Cottonmouths. 24p. (J). (gr. k-4). 1994. lib. bdg. 10.95 (*0-86593-332-4*) Rourke Corp.

— Pythons, Set II. (Snake Discovery Library). (Illus.). 24p. (J). (gr. k-4). 1987. lib. bdg. 14.60 (*0-86592-244-6*) Rourke Enter.

— Rat Snakes. (Snake Discovery Library: Set II). (Illus.). 24p. (J). (gr. k-4). 1987. lib. bdg. 14.60 (*0-86592-247-0*) Rourke Enter.

— Rattlesnakes. (Snake Discovery Library: Set I). (Illus.). 24p. (J). (gr. k-4). 1986. lib. bdg. 14.60 (*0-86592-956-4*) Rourke Enter.

— Tree Vipers. (Snake Discovery Library: Set II). (Illus.). 24p. (J). (gr. k-4). 1987. lib. bdg. 14.60 (*0-86592-245-4*) Rourke Enter.

Bargas, Kita. Valiente! Heritage of Texas, New Mexico, & Arizona to Statehood. (Illus.). 271p. (Orig.). 1985. pap. text 9.75 (*0-9618500-0-0*) Saxon Pubns.

— Valiente: Heritage of Texas, New Mexico, & Arizona to Statehood. 271p. (Orig.). 1985. pap. 20.00 (*1-887116-10-9*) Saxon West Pubns.

***Bargatze, Gary F.** Exploring Corporate DNA in the Age of People: A Business Handbook for the New Millennium. 192p. 1999. pap. 19.95 (*1-58000-051-7*, Pub. by Griffin CA) LPC InBook.

Bargatzky, Thomas & Kuschel, Rolf, eds. The Invention of Nature. LC 93-49696. (Illus.). 282p. 1994. write for info. (*3-631-45369-8*) P Lang Pubng.

Bargauanu, Grigore, jt. auth. see Tanasescu, Dragos.

Barge, Bruce N. & Carlson, John G. The Executive's Guide to Controlling Health Care & Disability Costs: Strategy-Based Solutions. LC 93-14655. 352p. 1993. 34.95 (*0-471-58497-5*) Wiley.

Barge, Fred H. Wryneck Vol. IX: The Neck Has Gone Awry - Torticollis. (Illus.). 315p. (C). 1998. text 59.95 (*1-885048-11-4*); pap. text 34.95 (*1-885048-12-2*) Barge Chiropract.

Barge, Frederick H. Are You the Doctor, Doctor? The Philosophy of Successful Practice, Vol. IV. 3rd ed. 157p. 1993. pap. 19.95 (*1-885048-09-2*) Barge Chiropract.

— Life Without Fear: Chiropractice Major Philosophical Tenet, Vol. V. deluxe ed. LC 94-73474. 147p. 1995. pap. 19.95 (*1-885048-10-6*) Barge Chiropract.

Barge, Fredrick H. Giant vs. Pygmy Plus Thots: Chiropractic Metaphysical Concepts, Vol. VII. LC 94-94214. 136p. 1995. text 37.95 (*1-885048-06-8*) Barge Chiropract.

— One Cause One Cure: The Health & Life Philosophy of Chiropractic, Vol. VI. LC 94-79233. 177p. 1996. reprint ed. text 37.95 (*1-885048-05-X*) Barge Chiropract.

— Scoliosis: Identifiable Causes Detection & Correction, Vol. III. 2nd expanded ed. 347p. 1996. text 75.95 (*1-885048-02-5*) Barge Chiropract.

— Tortipelvis: The Slipped Disc Syndrome, Its Cause & Correction, Vol. I. 4th ed. LC 94-72716. 164p. 1994. text 37.95 (*1-885048-00-9*) Barge Chiropract.

Barge, Fredrick H. & Palmer, B. J. It Is As Simple As That & More: Chiropractic Philosophy, Vol. 8. LC 96-83297. 208p. 1996. 37.95 (*1-885048-08-4*) Barge Chiropract.

Barge, J. Kevin. Leadership: Communication Skills for Organizations & Groups. 304p. 1994. pap. text 24.95 (*0-312-08117-0*) St Martin.

***Barge, Marcy & Kuperberg, Krystyna, eds.** Geometry & Topology in Dynamics. LC 99-48007. (Contemporary Mathematics Ser.: Vol. 246). 250p. 1999. 59.00 (*0-8218-1958-5*) Am Math.

Barge, Maureen S., jt. ed. see Garner, Willa Y.

Bargebuhr, Fredrick P. The Alhambra: A Cycle of Studies on the Eleventh Century in Moorish Spain. (C). 1968. 215.40 (*3-11-000524-7*) De Gruyter.

Bargellini, Clara, et al. Mexican Silver. (Exhibitions International Ser.). (Illus.). 176p. 1994. pap. 40.00 (*90-6988-059-8*) U of Wash Pr.

Bargellini, P. L., ed. Communications Satellite Systems. LC 73-15613. (PAAS Ser.: Vol. 32). (Illus.). 480p. 1974. 54.95 (*0-262-02100-5*, V-32) AIAA.

— Communications Satellite Technology. LC 73-15612. (PAAS Ser.: Vol. 33). (Illus.). 540p. 1974. 65.95 (*0-262-02101-3*, V-33) AIAA.

Bargen, Doris G. A Woman's Weapon: Spirit Possession in the Tale of Genji. LC 96-25663. 1997. text 50.00 (*0-8248-1801-6*); pap. text 24.95 (*0-8248-1858-X*) UH Pr.

Bargen, Walter. Mysteries in the Public Domain. LC 89-15049. (Target Poetry Ser.). 64p. (Orig.). 1990. pap. 6.50 (*0-933532-74-1*) BkMk.

— Water Breathing Air. 51p. 1999. pap. 10.00 (*0-944048-12-9*) Timberline Missouri.

Bargen, Walter L. At the Dead Center of Day. LC 97-25350. (Roy Fox Memorial Chapbook Ser.: Vol. 2). 32p. (Orig.). 1997. pap. 6.00 (*1-886157-08-1*) BkMk.

Barger. In the Charge of an Angel. 1997. 8.95 (*0-7459-3737-3*, Pub. by Lion Pubng) Trafalgar.

Barger, et al. Protocols for Gynecologic & Obstetric Health Care. 1987. pap. text 43.00 (*0-8089-1897-4*, Grune & Strat) Harcrt Hlth Sci Grp.

Barger, Alvan L., ed. Barger Journal: The Genealogy & History of the Bargers & Allied Kindred. (Illus.). 588p. 1997. reprint ed. pap. 89.50 (*0-8328-7375-6*); reprint ed. lib. bdg. 99.50 (*0-8328-7374-8*) Higginson Bk Co.

Barger, Amy & Barger, Andrew. MacFroggy Teaches BASIC. LC 93-9551. 127p. (J). (gr. 5-10). 1993. pap. text 8.95 (*0-944838-39-1*) Med Physics Pub.

Barger, Andrew, jt. auth. see Barger, Amy.

Barger, Charles. Communication Equipment of the German Army: Nineteen Thirty-Three - Nineteen Forty-Five. (Illus.). 192p. 1989. pap. 40.00 (*0-87364-534-0*) Paladin Pr.

Barger, Charles J. Radio Equipment of the Third Reich, 1933-1945. (Illus.). 112p. 1991. 25.00 (*0-87364-592-8*) Paladin Pr.

Barger, Gerald L., jt. ed. see Wang, Jen Y.

Barger, Harold. American Agriculture, Eighteen Ninety-Nine to Nineteen Thirty-Nine: A Study of Output, Employment & Productivity. LC 75-41017. (BCL Ser. II). reprint ed. 24.50 (*0-404-14640-6*) AMS Pr.

— Distrbution's Place in the American Economy Since 1869. 1975. 20.95 (*0-405-07584-7*, 16412) Ayer.

— Distribution's Place in the American Economy since 1869. (General Ser.: No. 58). 240p. 1955. reprint ed. 62.20 (*0-87014-057-4*) Natl Bur Econ Res.

— The Transportation Industries, 1889-1946: A Study of Output, Employment & Productivity. LC 75-19692. (National Bureau of Economic Research Ser.). (Illus.). 1975. reprint ed. 23.95 (*0-405-07573-1*) Ayer.

— The Transportation Industries, 1889-1946: A Study of Output, Employment, & Productivity. (General Ser.: No. 51). 304p. 1951. reprint ed. 79.10 (*0-87014-050-7*) Natl Bur Econ Res.

Barger, Harold & Landsberg, Hans H. American Agriculture, Eighteen Ninety-Nine to Nineteen Thirty-Nine: A Study of Output, Employment, & Productivity. LC 75-19693. (National Bureau of Economic Research Ser.). (Illus.). 1975. reprint ed. 36.95 (*0-405-07574-X*) Ayer.

— American Agriculture, 1899-1939: A Study of Output, Employment & Productivity. (General Ser.: No. 42). 462p. 1942. reprint ed. 120.20 (*0-87014-041-8*) Natl Bur Econ Res.

Barger, Harold & Schurr, Sam H. The Mining Industries, 1899-1939: A Study of Output, Employment, & Productivity. LC 72-2833. (Use & Abuse of America's Natural Resources Ser.). 474p. 1972. reprint ed. 33.95 (*0-405-04502-6*) Ayer.

— The Mining Industries, 1899-1939: A Study of Output, Employment, & Productivity. LC 75-19694. (National Bureau of Economic Research Ser.). (Illus.). 1975. reprint ed. 35.95 (*0-405-07575-8*) Ayer.

— The Mining Industries, 1899-1939: A Study of Output, Employment, & Productivity. (General Ser.: No. 43). 474p. 1944. reprint ed. 123.30 (*0-87014-042-6*) Natl Bur Econ Res.

***Barger, M. Susan & White, William B.** The Daguerreotype: Nineteenth-Century Technology & Modern Science. LC 99-86934. 2000. pap. 21.50 (*0-8018-6458-5*) Johns Hopkins.

Barger, Millie. Like Abigail. Hermanson, Renee, ed. LC 98-14074. 196p. (Orig.). 1998. pap. 12.95 (*1-880292-58-0*) LangMarc.

Barger, Norval. Birds Tomorrow: Their Management & Enjoyment. LC 89-3442. (Illus.). 350p. 1989. pap. 12.95 (*0-87961-193-6*) Naturegraph.

Barger, Sherie & Johnson, L. Anacondas. (J). 1997. pap. 2.50 (*0-8167-1446-0*) Troll Communs.

***Barger, Sonny, et al.** Hell's Angel: The Life & Times of Sonny Barger & the Hells Angels Motorcycle Club. (Illus.). 288p. 2000. 24.00 (*0-688-17693-3*, Wm Morrow) Morrow Avon.

***Barger, Thomas C.** Out in the Blue - Letters from Arabia 1937-1940: A Young American Geologist Explores the Deserts of Early Saudi Arabia. LC 00-90642. (Illus.). xvi, 304p. 2000. 34.95 (*0-9701157-3-3*, Selwa) T V T.

Barger, V., et al, eds. Neutrino Masses & Neutrino Astrophysics: Proceedings of the 4th Telemark Workshop, Neutrinos from Supernova 1987. 544p. (C). 1987. pap. 51.00 (*9971-5-0370-0*); text 137.00 (*9971-5-0367-0*) World Scientific Pub.

— Physics Simulations at High Energy: Proceedings of the Workshop Sponsored by the Institute for Elementary Particle Physics Research Madison, Wisconsin, 5-16 May 1986. 668p. 1987. text 144.00 (*9971-5-0181-3*) World Scientific Pub.

Barger, V. & Cline, D. B. Neutrino Mass & Low Energy Weak Interactions: Proc. of the Conference on Neutrino Mass Miniconference. 400p. 1985. 75.00 (*9971-5-0069-8*) World Scientific Pub.

Barger, V. & Halzen, Francis, eds. From Colliders to Supercolliders: Proceedings of the Conference on From Colliders to Supercolliders, Madison, Wisconsin 11-12 May, 1987. 568p. 1987. pap. 49.00 (*9971-5-0464-2*); text 125.00 (*9971-5-0428-6*, ZA0478PP) World Scientific Pub.

— New Particles, '85: Proceedings of the Conference on New Particles, Madison, Wisconsin, May 8-11, 1985. 360p. 1986. text 124.00 (*9971-5-0045-0*) World Scientific Pub.

Barger, V., ed. see American Institute of Physics.

Barger, Vernon. Classical Mechanics: A Modern Perspective. 2nd ed. 384p. (C). 1994. 90.63 (*0-07-003734-5*) McGraw.

Barger, Vernon & Cline, David. Neutrino Mass & Gauge Structure of Weak Interactions (Telemark, 1982) AIP Conference Proceedings 99, Particles & Fields Subseries 30. LC 83-71072. 283p. 1983. lib. bdg. 34.50 (*0-88318-198-3*) Am Inst Physics.

Barger, Vernon & Olsson. Classical Electricity & Magnetism. 1986. teacher ed. write for info. (*0-318-61488-X*, H87596) P-H.

Barger, W. K. The Farm Labor Movement in the Midwest: Social Change & Adaptation among Migrant Farmworkers. LC 93-3962. (Illus.). 248p. (C). 1993. pap. 15.95 (*0-292-70797-5*); text 35.00 (*0-292-70796-7*) U of Tex Pr.

Bargerstock, Andrew S. The Right Person for the Job: How to Develop a Powerful Interview Questioning Plan Using Behavior-Based Techniques. 60p. 1996. ring bd. 29.00 (*0-9639557-2-1*, Jacob-Cameron) A R K Co.

— Vanguard Staffing Practices: How Leading Employment Managers Achieve Exceptional Results. 84p. 1996. ring bd. 29.00 (*0-9639557-6-4*, Jacob-Cameron) A R K Co.

— Waking up the Organization to Internal Customer Service: Tools to Measure & Improve Human Resources & Other Internal Services. 140p. 1996. ring bd. 59.95 (*0-9639557-5-6*, Jacob-Cameron) A R K Co.

Bargerstock, Andrew S., jt. auth. see Engel, Hank.

Bargerstock, Charles T. A Tool Kit for Re-Energizing Your Organization's TQM Program. 114p. 1996. ring bd. 29.00 (*0-9639557-7-2*, Jacob-Cameron) A R K Co.

Bargh, Bernard. Pet Owner's Guide to the Golden Retriever. LC 93-9744. (Pet Owner's Guides Ser.). (Illus.). 80p. 1993. pap. 8.00 (*0-87605-979-5*) Howell Bks.

— Pet Owner's Guide to the Golden Retriever. (Pet Owner's Guide Ser.). (Illus.). 80p. 1997. 8.00 (*0-948955-43-0*, Pub. by Ringpr Bks) Seven Hills Bk.

Bargh, Catherine, et al. Governing Universities: Changing the Culture? LC 96-21853. 195p. 1996. 118.00 (*0-335-19539-3*); pap. 36.95 (*0-335-19538-5*) OpUniv Pr.

Bargh, John A., jt. ed. see Gollwitzer, Peter M.

Bargh, John A., jt. ed. see Uleman, James S.

***Bargh, Peter.** A to Z of Photoshop. (Illus.). 144p. 2000. pap. 22.95 (*0-240-51631-1*, Focal) Buttrwrth-Heinemann.

Barghini, Sandra. Palm Beach Panorama: Turn-of-Century PHotographs by E. W. Hazard. (Illus.). 36p. (Orig.). 1996. pap. 10.00 (*0-9651333-0-3*) Flagler Mus.

— A Society of Painters--Flagler's St. Augustine Art Colony. Blades, John, ed. (Illus.). 48p. (Orig.). 1998. pap. write for info. (*0-9651333-1-1*) Flagler Mus.

***Barghini, Sandra.** A Young Man's Legacy: Rare Photographs of the Titanic. (Illus.). 16p. 1999. pap. 5.00 (*0-9651333-2-X*) Flagler Mus.

Barghoorn, Frederick C. The Soviet Cultural Offensive. LC 78-17891. 353p. 1976. reprint ed. lib. bdg. 75.00 (*0-8371-8334-0*, BASCO, Greenwood Pr) Greenwood.

— The Soviet Cultural Offensive: The Role of Cultural Diplomacy in Soviet Foreign Policy. LC 60-12227. 361p. reprint ed. pap. 112.00 (*0-608-30118-3*, 200089300050) Bks Demand.

— Soviet Foreign Propaganda. LC 63-12667. 341p. reprint ed. pap. 105.80 (*0-608-17852-7*, 203263900080) Bks Demand.

Barghouti, Shawki, et al, eds. Agricultural Technologies for Market-Led Development Opportunities in the 1990's. LC 93-13669. (Technical Papers: No. 204). 180p. 1993. pap. 22.00 (*0-8213-2462-4*, 12462) World Bank.

Barghouti, Shawki, ed. see Le Moigne, Guy J.

Barghusen, J. D. The Oriental Institute Museum Teacher's Kit: Advanced Level. (Museum Publications). 195p. 1991. 12.00 (*0-918986-81-8*) Orient Inst.

— The Oriental Institute Museum Teacher's Kit: Elementary Level. (Museum Publications). 166p. 1991. 12.00 (*0-918986-80-X*) Orient Inst.

Barghusen, J. D. & Hives, J. Art Projects from the Oriental Institute Museum. (Museum Publications). 86p. 1991. 10.00 (*0-918986-82-6*) Orient Inst.

***Barghusen, Joan D.** The Aztecs. LC 99-46849. (History's Great Defeats Ser.). 133p. (J). 2000. lib. bdg. 18.96 (*1-56006-620-2*) Lucent Bks.

— The Bald Eagle. LC 98-19034. (Overview Ser.). (Illus.). 128p. (YA). (gr. 4-12). 1998. lib. bdg. 23.70 (*1-56006-254-1*) Lucent Bks.

Barghusen, Joan D. Cults. LC 97-26652. (Overview Ser.). (Illus.). 96p. (YA). (gr. 7 up). 1997. lib. bdg. 22.45 (*1-56006-199-5*) Lucent Bks.

***Barghusen, Joan D.** Daily Life in Ancient & Modern Cairo. LC 99-47839. (Cities Through Time Ser.). (Illus.). 64p. (J). (gr. 4-7). 2000. lib. bdg. 25.26 (*0-8225-3221-2*, Runestone Pr) Lerner Pub.

Barghusen, Joan D. Daily Life in Ancient & Modern Rome. LC 98-18311. (Cities Through Time Ser.). 64p. (J). (gr. 4-7). 1999. lib. bdg. 23.93 (*0-8225-3213-1*, Runestone Pr) Lerner Pub.

Barghusen, Laura. The Bear. LC 98-50214. (Overview Ser.). (Illus.). 128p. (YA). (gr. 4-12). 1999. lib. bdg. 23.70 (*1-56006-394-7*) Lucent Bks.

***Bargiela-Chiappini, Francesca.** Writing Business: Genres, Media & Discourses. LC 98-49111. (Language in Social Life Ser.). 360p. 1999. pap. 34.65 (*0-582-31985-4*) Longman.

Bargiela-Chiappini, Francesca & Harris, Sandra. The Languages of Business. LC 98-173145. 264p. 1998. pap. 30.00 (*0-7486-0833-8*, Pub. by Edinburgh U Pr) Col U Pr.

Bargiela-Chiappini, Francesca & Harris, Sandra J. Managing Language: The Discourse of Corporate Meetings. LC 97-6894. (Pragmatics & Beyond, New Ser.: Vol. 44). ix, 295p. 1997. lib. bdg. 86.00 (*1-55619-806-X*) J Benjamins Pubng Co.

Bargmann, Dale & Moyer, Robert M. Classy Clip Art. (Illus.). 122p. 1991. pap. 16.99 (*1-55945-020-7*, Group Bks) Group Pub.

Bargmann, Dale A. For the Least of These: Banners with a Conscience. LC 96-28453. 1996. 8.99 (*0-570-04897-4*, 12-3310) Concordia.

— His Banner Over Me Is Love: More Dynamic Designs for Worship Settings. LC 95-11376. (Illus.). 96p. 1995. pap. 9.99 (*0-570-04818-4*, 12-3260) Concordia.

— Raise a Banner to the Lord: 60 Dynamic Banner Designs for Worship Settings. LC 93-31200. (Illus.). 96p. (Orig.). 1994. pap. 9.99 (*0-570-04626-2*, 12-3207) Concordia.

Bargmann, Jay, ed. see Vinoly, Rafael.

Bargmann, Valentine. Studies in Mathematical Physics: Essays in Honor of Valentine Bargmann. Lieb, E. H. et al, eds. LC 76-4057. (Princeton Series in Physics). (Illus.). 475p. reprint ed. pap. 147.30 (*0-608-06628-1*, 206682500009) Bks Demand.

***Bargna, Ivan.** African Art. (Illus.). 240p. 1999. 95.00 (*88-16-69005-4*, Pub. by Jaca) Antique Collect.

Bargone, Charles. Useless Hands. LC 74-15969. (Science Fiction Ser.). 300p. 1975. reprint ed. 28.95 (*0-405-06289-3*) Ayer.

Bargrave, John. Pope Alexander the Seventh & the College of Cardinals. Robertson, James C., ed. LC 78-160001. (Camden Society, London. Publications, First Ser.: No. 92). reprint ed. 37.50 (*0-404-50192-3*) AMS Pr.

Bargyla, ed. see Corley, Hugh.

Bargyla, ed. see Hainsworth, P. H.

Bargyla, ed. see Leatherbarrow, Margaret.

Bargyla, ed. see Stephenson, W. A.

Bargyla, ed. see Turner, F. Newman.

Barham. Fire Engineering & Emergency Planning: Research & Applications. (Illus.). 616p. (C). 1996. 140.00 (*0-419-20180-7*, E & FN Spon) Routledge.

Barham, Allan. Strange to Relate. 191p. 1984. 19.95 (*0-86140-186-7*, Pub. by Smyth) Dufour.

Barham, Andrea. Dolls' House Accessories, Fixtures & Fittings. 1999. pap. text 19.95 (*1-86108-103-0*) Guild Master.

— Easy to Make Dolls' House Accessories. (Illus.). 176p. 1996. pap. 19.95 (*0-946819-37-8*, Pub. by Guild Master) Sterling.

— Making Period Dolls' House Accessories. (Illus.). 176p. 1997. pap. 17.95 (*1-86108-014-X*, Pub. by Guild Master) Sterling.

Barham, Bradford L., et al, eds. States, Firms, & Raw Materials: The World Economy & Ecology of Aluminum. LC 94-14005. 1995. 50.00 (*0-299-14110-1*); pap. 24.95 (*0-299-14114-4*) U of Wis Pr.

Barham, Bradford L. & Coomes, Oliver T. Prosperity's Promise: The Amazon Rubber Boom & Distorted Economic Development. LC 96-8820. (Dellplain Latin American Studies). (C). 1996. pap. 75.00 (*0-8133-8996-8*, Pub. by Westview) HarpC.

Barham, Charles S. Down by Willow Creek Pond: Tales Inspired by the Book of James. LC 97-66598. (Illus.). 64p. (J). (gr. 2-4). 1997. 14.95 (*1-57736-039-7*) Providence Hse.

Barham, Henry. Essay upon the Silkworm. 1988. reprint ed. 12.95 (*1-56659-010-8*) Robin & Russ.

An Asterisk (*) at the beginning of an entry indicates that the title is appearing for the first time.

Barham, J. & Field, G. Turkey Financial Markets: An Engine for Growth. (Euromoney Country Guide Ser.). 149p. 1997. 170.00 (*1-85564-616-1*, Pub. by Euromoney) Am Educ Systs.

Barham, Kevin & Heimer, Claudia. ABB - The Dancing Giant: Creating the Globally Connected Corporation. 260p. 1998. 26.95 (*0-273-62861-5*, Pub. by F T P H) Natl Bk Netwk.

***Barham, Larry.** In Search of Cheddar Man. (Illus.). 160p. 1999. pap. 16.99 (*0-7524-1401-1*, Tempus Publng) Arcadia Publng.

Barham, Martha, jt. auth. see Greene, James T.

Barham, Marti & Greene, Tom. The Silver Cord. LC 85-63215. 197p. (Orig.). 1986. pap. 12.00 (*0-87516-562-1*) DeVorss.

Barham, Mary. Love All. large type ed. (Linford Romance Library). 256p. 1998. pap. 17.99 (*0-7089-5226-7*, Linford) Ulverscroft.

Barham, Otha H., Jr. Here Where We Belong: A Collection of Outdoor Memories & Musings, Vol. 1. LC 97-92273. (Illus.). 192p. 1997. pap. 11.22 (*0-9659618-0-X*) Old Ben Pubns.

Barham, Patte B., jt. auth. see Brown, Peter H.

Barham, Peter. Closing the Asylum. 224p. 1997. pap. 15.95 (*0-14-026580-5*, Pub. by Pnguin Bks Ltd) Trafalgar.

Barham, Peter & Hayward, Robert. Relocating Madness: From the Mental Patient to the Person. 180p. (C). 1995. pap. 21.95 (*1-85343-307-1*) NYU Pr.

Barham, Robert W. The Healing. 420p. 1996. pap. 16.95 (*0-9649599-0-9*) New Ave Prodns.

Barham, Rosie. Fishing Widow's Guide. 212p. 1996. 21.95 (*1-86105-007-0*, Robson-Parkwest) Parkwest Pubns.

Barhydt, Elizabeth & Barhydt, Hamilton. Accurate Muscle Testing for Foods & Supplements Plus Balancing Meridians. 2nd ed. (Illus.). 64p. 1992. pap. 15.00 (*0-9605346-3-6*) Loving Life.

— Self-Help for Children: Improving Performance & Building Self-Esteem in School Home & Sports, Learning Blocks, Repetitive Muscle Stress, Environmental Sensitivity. 2nd ed. (Illus.). 64p. 1992. pap. 15.00 (*0-9605346-2-8*) Loving Life.

— Self-Help for Stress & Pain Plus Learning Blocks: Simple Energy Balancing Exercises for Home, School, Office & Athletics. expanded ed. (Illus.). 80p. (Orig.). 1997. pap. 15.00 (*0-9605346-4-4*) Loving Life.

Barhydt, Fran & Morgan, Paul W. The Science Teacher's Book of Lists. LC 92-26920. 528p. (C). 1993. pap. text 29.95 (*0-13-793381-9*) P-H.

Barhydt, Frances B. Science Discovery Activities Kit: Ready-to-Use Lessons & Worksheets for Grades 3-8. LC 89-712. 304p. 1989. pap. text 27.95 (*0-87628-785-2*) Ctr Appl Res.

Barhydt, Hamilton, jt. auth. see Barhydt, Elizabeth.

Barhyte, Diana Y., jt. auth. see LeSage, Joan.

Bari, G. A. Di, see Harding, W. B. & Di Bari, G. A., eds.

Bari, Judy. Timber Wars. LC 94-12124. 300p. (Orig.). 1994. pap. 14.95 (*1-56751-026-4*); lib. bdg. 29.95 (*1-56751-027-2*) Common Courage.

Bari, Karoly. Winter Diary: The Poetry of Bari Karoly. Benedek, Dezso et al, trs. LC 96-52221. 1997. pap. 22.00 (*1-56279-091-9*) Mercury Hse Inc.

Bari, N. K., et al. Series & Approximation. (Translations Ser.: Series 1, Vol. 3). 391p. 1962. text 35.00 (*0-8218-1603-9*, TRANS1/3) Am Math.

Bari, R. A., jt. ed. see Mosleh, A.

Bari, Sheldon. Beatrice: The Untold Story of a Legendary Woman of Mystery. 1998. 34.95 (*0-9660285-0-3*) Newpt Legends.

Bari, Zohurul. Re-Emergence of the Muslim Brothers in Egypt. LC 95-901601. (C). 1995. 18.50 (*81-7095-052-X*, Pub. by Lancer India) S Asia.

Bariakhtar, Viktor G., et al. Frontiers in Magnetism of Reduced Dimension Systems. LC 98-14447. (NATO ASI Ser.). 1998. 268.00 (*0-7923-5026-X*) Kluwer Academic.

Bariand, Pierre, et al. Larousse Dictionary of Precious Stones: Larousse des Pierres Precieuses. (FRE.). 262p. 1985. 75.00 (*0-8288-1467-8*, F12290) Fr & Eur.

Barias, Bob & Cheng, Pang G. Culture Shock! A Student's Guide. 240p. 1995. pap. text 12.95 (*1-55868-244-9*) Gr Arts Ctr Pub.

Barica, J. & Mur, L., eds. Hypertrophic Ecosystems. (Developments in Hydrobiology Ser.: No. 2). 330p. 1980. text 234.00 (*90-6193-752-3*) Kluwer Academic.

Baricco, Alessandro. Ocean Sea. McEwen, Alastair, tr. from ITA. LC 98-14213. 241p. 1999. 23.00 (*0-375-40423-6*) Knopf.

— Ocean Sea. (International Ser.). 256p. 2000. pap. 12.00 (*0-375-70395-0*) Vin Bks.

— Silk. Waldman, Guido, tr. 96p. 15.00 (*1-86046-310-X*, Pub. by Harvill Press) HarpC.

— Silk. Waldman, Guido, tr. LC 97-179758. 96p. 1997. 15.00 (*1-86046-258-8*) Harvill Press.

— Silk. Waldman, Guido, tr. from ITA. LC 98-7129. 112p. 1998. pap. 10.00 (*0-375-70382-9*) Vin Bks.

Barich, Bill. Big Dreams: Into the Heart of California. 1995. pap. 15.00 (*0-679-76035-0*) Vin Bks.

— Carson Valley. 352p. 1998. pap. 14.00 (*0-679-75857-7*) Vin Bks.

— Carson Valley. large type ed. (Niagara Large Print Ser.). 528p. 1997. 29.50 (*0-7089-5885-0*) Ulverscroft.

— Crazy for Rivers. LC 98-20273. (Illus.). 96p. 1999. 16.95 (*1-55821-705-3*) Lyons Pr.

— Hard to Be Good. 192p. 1987. 15.95 (*0-374-16812-1*) FS&G.

— Laughing in the Hills. LC 97-78223. 228p. 1998. reprint ed. pap. 14.00 (*1-886913-20-X*) Ruminator Bks.

***Barich, Bill.** The Sporting Life: Horses, Boxers, Rivers & a Russian Ballclub. LC 99-28206. 1999. 22.95 (*1-55821-935-8*) Lyons Pr.

— Traveling Light: A Year of Wandering, from California & England to Tuscany & Back Again. 2000. pap. 16.95 (*1-58574-185-X*) Lyon Press.

Barich, Dewey F. & Smith, Leonard C. Metal Work for Industrial Arts Shops. LC 52-8345. 103p. reprint ed. pap. 32.00 (*0-608-10060-9*, 200457000043) Bks Demand.

***Barich, Thomas E.** ACT! 4 Bible. LC HD69.T54B38 1998. (Bible Ser.). 768p. 1998. pap. 39.99 (*0-7645-3240-5*) IDG Bks.

Barich, Thomas E. How to Use Quicken X. 1997. 24.99 (*1-56276-555-8*, Ziff-Davis Pr) Que.

Barich, Thomas E., jt. auth. see Ivens, Kathy.

Barickman, Amy. Forever Yours: Wedding Quilts, Clothing & Keepsakes. Aneloski, Liz & Lytle, Joyce, eds. LC 97-37164. (Illus.). 128p. 1998. pap. 24.95 (*1-57120-042-8*, 10167) C & T Pub.

Barickman, B. J. A Bahian Counterpoint: Sugar, Tobacco, Cassava, & Slavery in the Rec Oncavo, 1780-1860. LC 97-42643. 1998. 55.00 (*0-8047-2632-9*) Stanford U Pr.

Barickman, Donald. Magnolias Southern Cuisine. LC 95-12066. (Illus.). 152p. 1995. 19.95 (*0-941711-31-5*) Wyrick & Co.

Barickman, Joan E. Schoolwise: Teaching Academic Patterns of Mind. LC 92-22088. 136p. (YA). 1992. pap. text 19.50 (*0-86709-309-9*, 0309, Pub. by Boynton Cook Pubs) Heinemann.

Barickman, Richard B., jt. auth. see Paludi, Michele A.

Barie, Philip S., jt. ed. see Shires, George T.

Barielle, Scott. Clustering Windows NT. 350p. 1998. pap. 39.95 (*1-55558-217-6*) DEC.

Barik, Bishnu C. Class Formation & Peasantry. (C). 1988. 24.50 (*81-7033-045-9*, Pub. by Rawat Pubns) S Asia.

Baril, jt. auth. see Cats.

Baril, Gilberte. The Feminine Face of the People of God: Biblical Symbols of the Church As Bride & Mother. 240p. (Orig.) (C). 1996. pap. 39.95 (*0-85439-350-1*, Pub. by St Paul Pubns) St Mut.

Baril, Jacques. Dictionnaire de Danse. (FRE.). 288p. 1964. pap. 24.95 (*0-8288-6762-3*, M6590) Fr & Eur.

Baril, Richard. Modern Machining Technology. 672p. 1987. pap., teacher ed. 14.00 (*0-8273-2579-7*); pap., student ed. 25.95 (*0-8273-2580-0*) Delmar.

***Baril, Tom, photos by.** Tom Baril: Botanica. (Illus.). 2000. 75.00 (*1-892041-20-0*, Pub. by Arena Editions) Dist Art Pubs.

Barile, A., jt. auth. see Masciocchi, C.

Barile, Andrew, jt. auth. see Monti, R. George.

Barile, Elizabeth & Laroze, Catherine. The Book of Perfume. (Illus.). 216p. 1995. 50.00 (*2-08-013590-2*, Pub. by Flammarion) Abbeville Pr.

Barile, Frank A. Introduction to In Vitro Toxicology. 240p. 1994. boxed set 104.95 (*0-8493-8659-4*) CRC Pr.

Barile, James J. Why Didn't Someone Tell Me Sooner? A How-to Guide for the Restoration & Maintenance of Health. LC 97-73943. 304p. 1997. pap. 15.95 (*0-9659411-0-8*) Autumn Press.

Barile, Louise. Meet the Stars of Dawson's Creek. (Illus.). (J). (gr. 5-9). 1998. pap. 4.99 (*0-590-64269-3*) Scholastic Inc.

Barile, Mary. Catskill Cookery: Highlights from Two Centuries. (Illus.). 95p. 1986. pap. 6.00 (*0-937213-00-4*) Heritage NY.

— Cookbooks Worth Collecting. LC 93-31761. (Illus.). 240p. 1993. pap. 17.95 (*0-87069-686-6*, Wllce-Homestd) Krause Pubns.

— Food from the Heart: Creating a Heritage Cookbook. (Illus.). 120p. 1993. student ed., ring bd. 12.95 (*0-937213-06-3*) Heritage NY.

— Let's Take the Kids: Great Places to Go with Children in New York's Hudson Valley. 5th ed. LC 97-8949. 1997. pap. 14.95 (*0-312-15559-7*) St Martin.

— Spiders & Switchel. (Illus.). 62p. 1992. pap. 6.95 (*0-9622903-3-5*) DCHA.

— Tried & True: A Century of Rural Recipes. (Illus.). 120p. 1987. spiral bd. write for info. (*0-937213-03-9*) Heritage NY.

— Waffles & Wafers: Traditional Recipes for Today's Kitchen. (Illus.). 66p. 1987. pap. 6.00 (*0-937213-01-2*) Heritage NY.

Barile, Mary, jt. auth. see Michaels, Joanne.

Barile, Mary-Margaret, jt. auth. see Michaels, Joanne.

Barile, Susan P. The Bookworm's Big Apple: A Guide to Manhattan's Booksellers. LC 94-8968. (Illus.). 400p. 1994. 46.50 (*0-231-08494-3*); pap. 18.00 (*0-231-08495-1*) Col U Pr.

Barilla, Bruce. Is the Pope Going to Heaven? A Conversation with Jesus. 24p. (Orig.). 1993. pap. 1.50 (*1-56794-032-3*, C2291) Star Bible.

Barilla, Jean. Andrographis Paniculata. (Good Health Guides Ser.). 48p. 1998. pap. 3.95 (*0-87983-884-1*, 38841K, Keats Publng) NTC Contemp Pub Co.

— Natural Health Secrets from Around the World. Geelhoed, Glenn W., ed. LC 97-13973. 112p. 1997. pap. 19.95 (*0-87983-805-1*, 38051K, Keats Publng) NTC Contemp Pub Co.

— Olive Oil Miracle. (Good Health Guides Ser.). 48p. 1997. pap. 3.95 (*0-87983-763-2*, 37632K, Keats Publng) NTC Contemp Pub Co.

Barilla, Jean, jt. auth. see Bagchi, Debasis.

Barilla, Jean, jt. auth. see Geelhoed, Glenn W.

Barilla, Jean, ed. see Baker, Sidney M.

Barillari, Diana & Godoli, Ezio. Istanbul, 1900: Art-Nouveau Architecture & Interiors. LC 96-3407. (Illus.). 220p. 1996. 75.00 (*0-8478-1989-2*, Pub. by Rizzoli Intl) St Martin.

Barillas, William D. Autoapprenticeship. LC 86-91046. (Illus.). (Orig.). 1987. pap. 7.00 (*0-940311-00-3*) Merganser Pr.

Barille, Elisabeth. Corps De Jeune Fille. (FRE.). 182p. 1988. pap. 10.95 (*0-7859-2091-9*, 2070380394) Fr & Eur.

— Lanvin LC 98-160732. (Fashion Memoir Ser.). 79 p. 1997. write for info. (*0-500-01816-2*) Thames Hudson.

Barille, Judy A. Introduction to Business. 1989. pap. 7.95 (*0-07-003733-7*) McGraw.

Barilleaux. Theme of Times American Government. 1996. pap. text. write for info. (*0-13-509804-1*) Allyn.

Barilleaux, Rene P. & Beck, Victoria J. G. Ruger Donoho: A Painter's Path. LC 95-13391. (Illus.). 96p. 1995. pap. 20.00 (*0-87805-798-6*); text 45.00 (*0-87805-797-8*) U Pr of Miss.

Barilleaux, Rene P. & Chave, Anna C. Valerie Jaudon. Tucker, Ginger, ed. (Illus.). 96p. (Orig.). 1996. pap. 25.00 (*1-887422-00-5*) Miss Mus Art.

Barilleaux, Rene P. & Grand, Stanley I. Wisconsin Triennial. (Illus.). 76p. 1987. pap. 5.00 (*0-913883-15-8*) Madison Art.

Barilleaux, Rene P. & Heartney, Eleanor. Fred Stonehouse. Ryan, Kathryn H., ed. (Illus.). 64p. (Orig.). 1992. pap. 20.00 (*0-913883-19-0*) Madison Art.

Barilleaux, Rene P. & Taylor, Sue. Don Baum: Domus. (Illus.). 64p. (Orig.). 1988. pap. 15.95 (*0-913883-17-4*) Madison Art.

Barilleaux, Rene P., et al. Abstraction at Work: Drawings by Valerie Jaudon, 1973-1999. LC 99-20868. 1999. write for info. (*1-887422-03-X*) Miss Mus Art.

— Mississippi Invitational. Greenberg, Kathy L., ed. LC 99-10848. (Illus.). 48p. 1999. pap. 10.00 (*1-887422-02-1*) Miss Mus Art.

— Wisconsin Triennial. (Illus.). 64p. 1990. pap. 10.00 (*0-913883-18-2*) Madison Art.

Barilleaux, Rene P., ed. see Felshin, Nina.

Barilleaux, Ryan J. American Government in Action: Principle, Process, Politics. 478p. 1995. pap. text 33.00 (*0-13-078924-0*) P-H.

— The Post-Modern Presidency: The Office after Ronald Reagan. LC 87-25861. 192p. 1988. 39.95 (*0-275-92721-0*, C2721, Praeger Pubs) Greenwood.

— The President & Foreign Affairs: Evaluation, Performance & Power. LC 84-26282. 224p. 1985. 49.95 (*0-275-90057-6*, C0057, Praeger Pubs) Greenwood.

Barilleaux, Ryan J., ed. Presidential Frontiers: Underexplored Issues in White House Politics. LC 97-43955. (Praeger Series in Presidential Studies). 256p. 1998. 59.95 (*0-275-96107-9*, Praeger Pubs) Greenwood.

Barilleaux, Ryan J. & Stuckey, Mary E., eds. Leadership & the Bush Presidency: Prudence or Drift in an Era of Change? LC 92-12107. (Praeger Series in Presidential Studies). 256p. 1992. 55.00 (*0-275-94418-2*, C4418, Praeger Pubs) Greenwood.

***Barillet, F.** Milking & Milk Production of Dairy Sheep & Goats. (Illus.). 571p. 1999. 114.00 (*90-74134-64-5*) Wageningen Pers.

Barilli, Benato, et al. Art in Arcadia: The Gori Collection at Celle. (Illus.). 504p. 1995. 85.00 (*88-422-0505-2*) Dist Art Pubs.

Barilli, Renato. A Course on Aesthetics. Pinkus, Karen, tr. LC 93-21779. 186p. (C). 1993. pap. 16.95 (*0-8166-2119-5*); text 44.95 (*0-8166-2118-7*) U of Minn Pr.

— Rotella. 1997. pap. 29.95 (*88-8158-088-8*, Pub. by Charta) Dist Art Pubs.

***Barillo, Madeline.** The Budget Wedding Sourcebook. LC 99-88248. 336p. 2000. pap. 17.95 (*0-7373-0307-7*, 03077W, Pub. by Lowell Hse) NTC Contemp Pub Co.

Barillo, Madeline. The Wedding Sourcebook. LC 95-43582. (Illus.). 336p. 1996. 30.00 (*1-56565-448-X*) Lowell Hse.

***Barillo, Madeline.** Wedding Sourcebook. 368p. 1999. 35.95 (*0-7373-0262-3*, 02623W) NTC Contemp Pub Co.

Barillo, Madeline. The Wedding Sourcebook. 2nd rev. ed. (Illus.). 368p. 1998. pap. 18.00 (*0-7373-0009-4*, 00094W) NTC Contemp Pub Co.

— The Wedding Sourcebook Planner. 192p. Date not set. pap. 15.00 (*1-56565-649-0*) NTC Contemp Pub Co.

***Barillo, Madeline.** The Wedding Sourcebook Planner. 2nd ed. (Illus.). 384p. 2000. pap. 22.95 (*0-7373-0384-0*, 03840W, Pub. by Lowell Hse) NTC Contemp Pub Co.

Barin, I. Thermochemical Data of Pure Substances. 3rd ed. 1885p. 1995. 535.00 (*0-471-18815-8*) Wiley.

Barineau, R. Maurice. The Theodicy of Alfred North Whitehead: A Logical & Ethical Vindication. 212p. (Orig.). (C). 1991. lib. bdg. 46.50 (*0-8191-8167-6*) U Pr of Amer.

Baring, Anne & Cashford, Jules. The Myth of the Goddess: The Evolution of an Image. 800p. 1993. pap. 24.95 (*0-14-019292-1*, Arkana) Viking Penguin.

Baring, Anne, jt. auth. see Harvey, Andrew.

Baring, Arnulf, ed. Germany's New Position in Europe: Problems & Perspectives. LC 96-22220. 160p. 1994. 39.50 (*1-85973-091-4*, Pub. by Berg Pubs); pap. 17.50 (*1-85973-096-5*, Pub. by Berg Pubs) NYU Pr.

Baring, Francis. Observations on the Establishment of the Bank of England. LC 66-21659. 81p. 1967. reprint ed. 29.50 (*0-678-00281-9*) Kelley.

Baring-Gould, S. Curious Myths of the Middle Ages. 255p. 1996. reprint ed. spiral bd. 15.50 (*0-7873-0071-2*) Hlth Research.

— Curious Myths of the Middle Ages. (Works of S. Baring-Gould). 254p. 1985. reprint ed. lib. bdg. 59.00 (*0-7812-0907-2*) Rprt Serv.

— Curious Myths of the Middle Ages 1867. 257p. 1996. reprint ed. pap. 14.95 (*1-56459-651-6*) Kessinger Pub.

Baring-Gould, S. & Bampfylde, C. A. A History of Sarawak under Its Two White Rajahs, 1839-1908. (Oxford in Asia Hardback Reprints Ser.). (Illus.) 500p. 1989. reprint ed. 35.00 (*0-19-588926-6*) OUP.

Baring-Gould, Sabine. A Book of Ghosts. (Illus.). 383p. 1977. 20.95 (*0-8369-3014-2*) Ayer.

— The Book of Were-Wolves: Being an Account of a Terrible Superstition. LC 89-61544. 266p. 1989. reprint ed. lib. bdg. 44.00 (*1-55888-818-7*) Omnigraphics Inc.

— Curious Myths of the Middle Ages. 1972. 250.00 (*0-87968-261-2*) Gordon Pr.

— Curious Myths of the Middle Ages. 1976. reprint ed. 55.00 (*0-403-06309-4*, Regency) Scholarly.

— Eastern Orthodox Saints. 1975. pap. 1.25 (*0-89981-019-5*) Eastern Orthodox.

— Family Names & Their Story. LC 68-54868. 432p. 1996. reprint ed. pap. 32.50 (*0-8063-0023-X*) Clearfield Co.

— Family Names & Their Story. LC 89-63015. xii, 431p. 1990. reprint ed. lib. bdg. 42.00 (*1-55888-843-8*) Omnigraphics Inc.

— Mehalah, a Story of the Salt Marshes, 2 vols., 1 bk. LC 79-8231. reprint ed. 44.50 (*0-404-61769-7*) AMS Pr.

— Myths of the Middle Ages. Matthews, John, ed. LC 96-225932. (Illus.). 176p. 1996. 27.95 (*0-7137-2607-5*, Pub. by Blandford Pr) Sterling.

— Red Spider, 2 vols., 1 bk. LC 79-8232. reprint ed. 44.50 (*0-404-61772-7*) AMS Pr.

— Saints of the Eastern Orthodox Church. large type ed. 1994. pap. 5.00 (*0-89981-301-1*) Eastern Orthodox.

Baring-Gould, Sabine & Bamfylde, C. A. A History of Sarawak under Its Two White Rajas. LC 77-86981. reprint ed. 54.00 (*0-404-16696-2*) AMS Pr.

Baring, Maurice. The Collected Poems of Maurice Baring. LC 75-41018. 28.50p. reprint ed. 28.50 (*0-404-14756-9*) AMS Pr.

— Diminutive Dramas. 4th ed. LC 77-70343. (One-Act Plays in Reprint Ser.). 1977. reprint ed. 25.00 (*0-8486-2012-7*) Roth Pub Inc.

— Half a Minute's Silence & Other Stories. LC 71-113647. (Short Story Index Reprint Ser.). 1977. 19.95 (*0-8369-3376-1*) Ayer.

— Punch & Judy & Other Essays. LC 68-16904. (Essay Index Reprint Ser.). 1977. reprint ed. 23.95 (*0-8369-0172-X*) Ayer.

— Sarah Bernhardt. LC 78-91893. 1972. 20.95 (*0-405-08237-1*, Pub. by Blom Pubns) Ayer.

— Sarah Bernhardt. LC 70-98809. 162p. 1970. reprint ed. lib. bdg. 55.00 (*0-8371-3018-2*, BASB, Greenwood Pr) Greenwood.

Baring, R., jt. auth. see Rogerson, Barnaby.

Baring, Rose. Moscow & St. Petersburg. LC 93-47109. (Cadogan City Guides Ser.). (Illus.). 608p. (Orig.). 1995. pap. 17.95 (*1-56440-274-6*) Globe Pequot.

***Baring, Rose.** St. Petersburg. 256p. 1999. pap. text 17.95 (*1-86011-922-0*, Pub. by Cadgn Bks) Globe Pequot.

Baringer, William. Lincoln's Rise to Power. (Illus.). xi, 373 p. 1971. reprint ed. 59.00 (*0-403-00853-0*) Scholarly.

Baringer, William E., et al. Politics & the Crisis of 1860. LC 61-14350. 170p. reprint ed. pap. 52.70 (*0-608-13738-3*, 202024300016) Bks Demand.

Barinov, Zelma. How to Make Instant Decisions & Remain Happy & Sane: Using Your Inner Compass. LC 97-97211. (Illus.). ix, 218p. 1998. pap. 24.95 (*0-9661071-8-7*) Access Pr PA.

Barinsky, E. F. Virology Reviews Vol. 4, Pt. 1: Chemoprophylaxis & Chemotheraphy of Viral Infections, Vol. 4. (Soviet Medical Reviews Ser.: Section E). ii, 152p. 1991. pap. text 160.00 (*3-7186-5150-5*, Harwood Acad Pubs) Gordon & Breach.

Barinsky, I. & Cheshik, S. Herpes Viruses, Vol. 5. (Soviet Medical Reviews Series, Section E: Virology Review: Vol. 5, Pt. 2). 165p. 1993. pap. text 239.00 (*3-7186-5394-X*) Gordon & Breach.

Barios, Nancy, jt. auth. see Todd, Karen.

***Baris, David, et al.** Bank Founder's Guidebook: SNL's Guide to Establishing a Community Bank. ii, 352p. 1999. pap. 895.00 (*0-9675122-0-4*) S N L.

***Baris, Mitchell.** Working with High-Conflict Families of Divorce: A Guide for Professionals. 2001. 50.00 (*0-7657-0292-4*) Aronson.

Baris, Mitchell A. & Garrity, Carla B. Children of Divorce: A Developmental Approach to Residence & Visitation. LC 87-63449. 104p. (Orig.). 1988. pap. 14.95 (*0-940929-06-6*, 5018) Psytec Inc.

Baris, Mitchell A., jt. auth. see Garrity, Carla B.

Barisas, Mylinda, et al. Environments for People with Dementia: Annotated Bibliography. viii, 96p. (C). 1995. per. 15.00 (*0-938744-82-8*, R93-2) U of Wis Ctr Arch-Urban.

Barisbak, Y. R. Embryology of the Eye & Its Adnexae. (Developments in Ophthalmology Ser.: Vol. 24). (Illus.). viii, 142p. 1992. 143.50 (*3-8055-5511-3*) S Karger.

Barish, Eileen. Doin' Arizona with Your Pooch! Eileen's Directory of Dog-Friendly Lodging & Outdoor Adventures in Arizona. LC 95-73088. (Illus.). 688p. (Orig.). 1996. pap. 19.95 (*1-884465-03-X*) Pet-Friendly.

— Doin' California with Your Pooch! Eileen's Directory of Dog-Friendly Lodging & Outdoor Adventure in California. 3rd ed. LC 97-75916. (Illus.). 720p. 1998. pap. 19.95 (*1-884465-10-2*) Pet-Friendly.

— Doin' New York with Your Pooch! Eileen's Directory of Dog-Friendly Lodging & Outdoor Adventures in New York. LC 96-71671. (Illus.). 672p. (Orig.). 1997. pap. 19.95 (*1-884465-08-0*) Pet-Friendly.

— Doin' Texas with Your Pooch! Eileen's Directory of Dog-Friendly Lodging & Outdoor Adventures in Texas. LC 96-92145. (Illus.). 640p. (Orig.). 1996. pap. 19.95 (*1-884465-05-6*) Pet-Friendly.

— Doin' the Northwest with Your Pooch! Eileen's Directory of Dog-Friendly Lodging & Outdoor Adventures in the Northwest. LC 96-70501. (Illus.). 672p. (Orig.). 1997. pap. 19.95 (*1-884465-06-4*) Pet-Friendly.

— The Drs. Foster & Smith Guide to Traveling with Your Pet. (Illus.). 720p. (Orig.). 1997. pap. 19.99 (*1-884465-09-9*) Pet-Friendly.

— The Guide to Lodging in Italy's Monasteries. LC 98-68528. 524p. 1999. pap. 19.95 (*1-884465-13-7*) Pet-Friendly.

— Vacationing with Your Pet! Eileen's Directory of

B

Pet-Friendly Lodging in the United States & Canada. 3rd ed. LC 96-70502. (Illus.). 720p. (Orig.). 1997. pap. 19.95 (*1-884465-07-2*) Pet-Friendly.

***Barish, Eileen.** Vacationing with Your Pet! Eileen's Directory of Pet-Friendly Lodging in the United States & Canada. 4th ed. LC 99-70631. (Illus.). 720p. (Orig.). 1999. pap. 19.95 (*1-884465-12-9*, Pub. by Pet-Friendly) SCB Distributors.

Barish, Evelyn. Emerson: The Roots of Prophecy. 281p. 1990. text 42.50 (*0-691-06787-2*, Pub. by Princeton U Pr) Cal Prin Full Svc.

Barish, Jonas. The Antitheatrical Prejudice. LC 78-59445. 1981. pap. 18.95 (*0-520-05216-1*, Pub. by U CA Pr) Cal Prin Full Svc.

Barish, Jonas A. Jonson: Volpone. LC 73-150745. (Casebook Ser.). 255 p. 1972. write for info. (*0-333-08896-4*) Macmillan.

Barish, Jonas A., ed. see Jonson, Ben.

Barish, Robert J. The Invisible Passenger: Radiation Risks for People Who Fly. (Illus.). 124p. 1996. pap. 12.00 (*1-883526-06-X*) Advan Med Pub.

Barish, Shirley. The Big Book of Great Teaching Ideas: For Jewish Schools, Youth Groups, Camps & Retreats. LC 96-43410. (Illus.). 1997. pap. 15.00 (*0-8074-0555-8*, 571205) UAHC.

Barish, T. A Theoretical Comparison of Ball & Roller Bearings. (Technical Papers: Vol. P174). (Illus.). 32p. (Orig.). 1938. pap. text 30.00 incl. audio compact disk (*1-55589-363-5*) AGMA.

Barish, Tzvi, tr. & adapted by see Adler, Sinai.

Barish, Wendy, ed. I Can Draw Horses. (I Can Draw Ser.). (Illus.). (J). (gr. 1-4). 1983. pap. 3.95 (*0-671-46447-7*) Litle Simon.

***Barish, Wendy & Jeunesse, Gallimard.** Trains. Miller, Heather, tr. from ENG. LC 97-15428. (First Discovery Book). (Illus.). 24p. (J). (ps-2). 1998. 11.95 (*0-590-38156-3*) Scholastic Inc.

Barish, Wendy, jt. auth. see Lawson, Don.

Barish, Wendy, ed. see Appleton, Victor.

Barish, Wendy, ed. see Beal, George.

Barish, Wendy, ed. see Benton, Michael J.

Barish, Wendy, ed. see Heck, Joseph.

Barish, Wendy, ed. see Hope, Laura Lee.

Barish, Wendy, ed. see Keene, Carolyn.

Barish, Wendy, ed. see Keene, Carolyn & Dixon, Franklin W.

Barish, Wendy, ed. see Sheldon, Ann.

Barish, Wendy, tr. see Gallimard Jeunesse Publishing Staff & Delafosse, Claude.

Barish, Wendy, tr. see Gallimard Jeunesse Publishing Staff & Moignot, Daniel.

Barisi, Mary E. Human Nutrition: A Health Perspective. LC 97-218916. (Arnold Publication). (Illus.). 336p. 1997. pap. text 34.50 (*0-340-64567-9*) OUP.

Barisse, Rita, tr. see Pagnol, Marcel.

Barisse, Rita, tr. see Vercors, Jean.

Barist, Jeffrey. Commercial Arbitration Law & Clauses: A Drafter's Guide. LC 94-18900. 1994. 95.00 (*0-13-312901-2*) Aspen Law.

***Baritaud, T., ed.** Multi-Dimensional Simulation of Engine Internal Flows. (Oil & Gas Science & Technology Ser.: Vol. 54, No. 2). 310p. 1999. 57.00 (*2-7108-0771-8*) Edits Technip.

Baritz, Loren. Backfire: A History of How American Culture Led Us into Vietnam & Made Us Fight the Way We Did. LC 97-51947. 416p. 1998. reprint ed. pap. 16.95 (*0-8018-5953-0*) Johns Hopkins.

— City on a Hill: A History of Ideas & Myths in America. LC 80-11468. 367p. 1980. reprint ed. lib. bdg. 35.00 (*0-313-22268-1*, BACI, Greenwood Pr) Greenwood.

— The Servants of Power. LC 73-17924. 273p. (C). 1974. reprint ed. lib. bdg. 72.50 (*0-8371-7275-6*, BASP, Greenwood Pr) Greenwood.

Baritz, Tony. AS/400 Client/Server Systems: Business Applications & Solutions. LC 95-32900. (Illus.). 408p. 1996. 50.00 (*0-07-018311-2*) McGraw.

Baritz, Tony & Dunne, David. AS/400 Concepts & Facilities. 2nd ed. (IBM Ser.). 408p. 1993. 45.00 (*0-07-018303-1*) McGraw.

Barjac, Huguette De, see De Barjac, Huguette, ed.

Barjansky, Catherine. Portraits with Backgrounds. (American Autobiography Ser.). 223p. 1995. reprint ed. lib. bdg. 79.00 (*0-7812-8450-3*) Rprt Serv.

Barjavel, Rene. La Charette Bleue. (FRE.). 256p. 1982. pap. 10.95 (*0-7859-1963-5*, 2070374068) Fr & Eur.

— Colomb De la Lune. (FRE.). 185p. 1977. pap. 10.95 (*0-7859-1853-1*, 2070369552) Fr & Eur.

— L' Enchanteur. (FRE.). 480p. 1987. pap. 11.95 (*0-7859-2065-X*, 2070378411) Fr & Eur.

— La Faim du Tigre. (FRE.). 214p. 1976. pap. 10.95 (*0-7859-1835-3*, 2070368475) Fr & Eur.

— La Peau de Cesar. (FRE.). 243p. 1987. pap. 10.95 (*0-7859-2069-2*, 2070378578) Fr & Eur.

— Ravage. (FRE.). 320p. 1972. pap. 11.95 (*0-7859-1713-6*, 2070362388) Fr & Eur.

— Tarendol. (FRE.). 512p. 1972. pap. 11.95 (*0-7859-1707-1*, 2070361691) Fr & Eur.

— La Tempete. (FRE.). 277p. 1985. pap. 10.95 (*0-7859-2022-6*, 2070376966) Fr & Eur.

— Le Voyageur Imprudent. (FRE.). 256p. 1973. pap. 10.95 (*0-7859-1764-0*, 2070364852) Fr & Eur.

Bark, Conrad V. & Restall, Eric. New Encyclopedia of Fly Fishing. rev. ed. (Illus.). 320p. 1999. 45.00 (*0-7090-6308-3*, Pub. by R Hale Ltd) Seven Hills Bk.

Bark, Dennis L. Berlin-Frage, 1949-1955: Verhandlungsgrundlagen und Eindaemmungspolitik. (Veroeffentlichungen der Historischen Kommission zu Berlin, Band 67, Beitraege zu Inflation und Wiederaufbau in Deutschland und Europa 1914-1924: Vol. 36). xiv, 544p. 1972. 146.15 (*3-11-003639-8*) De Gruyter.

Bark, Dennis L., ed. The Red Orchestra: The Case of Africa. (Publication Ser.: No. 374). 231p. (C). 1988. pap. text 5.18 (*0-8179-8742-8*) Hoover Inst Pr.

— Reflections on Europe. LC 97-23825. (Publication Ser.: No. 441). 136p. 1997. pap. 16.95 (*0-8179-9492-0*) Hoover Inst Pr.

— To Promote Peace: U. S. Foreign Policy in the Mid-1980's. (Publication Ser.: No. 294). 298p. 1984. 7.98 (*0-8179-7941-7*) Hoover Inst Pr.

Bark, Dennis L. & Harries, Owen, eds. The Red Orchestra: The Case of the Southwest Pacific. (Publication Ser.: No. 376). 271p. (C). 1989. pap. text 5.98 (*0-8179-8762-2*) Hoover Inst Pr.

Bark, Gay. Letters to My Angel. 85p. 1999. pap. 7.99 (*1-57532-183-1*) Press-Tige Pub.

Bark, Joseph. Your Skin: An Owner's Guide. 284p. (C). 1995. pap. 12.95 (*0-13-199663-0*) P-H.

Bark, Joseph P. Retin-A & Other Youth Miracles. 272p. 1990. reprint ed. pap. 9.95 (*1-55958-029-1*) Prima Pub.

Bark, Linda, jt. auth. see Riley, Ranny.

Bark, William C. Origins of the Medieval World. xiv, 162p. 1958. pap. 12.95 (*0-8047-0514-3*) Stanford U Pr.

Barkai, Avraham. Branching Out: German-Jewish Immigration to the United States, 1820-1914. LC 92-10833. (Ellis Island Ser.). (Illus.). 346p. 1994. 44.95 (*0-8419-1152-5*) Holmes & Meier.

— German-Jewish History in Modern Times: Renewal & Destruction, 1918-1945. (Illus.). 479p. 1998. 52.50 (*0-231-07478-6*) Col U Pr.

Barkai, Haim. The Evolution of Israel's Social Security System: Structure, Time Pattern & Macroeconomic Impact. LC 97-76948. (Illus.). 192p. 1998. text 59.95 (*1-84014-338-X*, Pub. by Ashgate Pub) Ashgate Pub Co.

Barkai, Haim. The Lessons of Israel's Great Inflation. LC 95-7984. 264p. 1995. 69.50 (*0-275-95146-4*, Praeger Pubs) Greenwood.

Barkai, Ron. A History of Medieval Jewish Gynaecological Texts. LC 97-52122. (Jewish Studies). 1998. 87.50 (*90-04-10995-1*) Brill Academic Pubs.

***Barkakati, Naba.** Red Hat Linux Secrets. 3rd ed. LC 99-48117. 1000p. 1999. pap. 39.99 (*0-7645-4639-2*) IDG Bks.

Barkakati, Naba, jt. auth. see Jamsa, Kris.

Barkakati, Nabajyoti. Java Annotated Archives. 880p. 1999. pap. text 49.99 (*0-07-211902-0*) Osborne-McGraw.

***Barkan.** Collective Violence. LC 98-20203. 152p. 2000. pap. 32.00 (*0-205-26782-3*) Allyn.

Barkan. Competitive Product Design for Manufacturability. 432p. (C). 1994. 54.00 (*0-02-305871-4*, Macmillan Coll) P-H.

— 5 Greatest Weather Disasters of All Time. (J). 2000. 4.99 (*0-689-82066-6*) S&S Childrens.

— Rainbows. (Weather Channel Ser.). (J). 1999. 3.99 (*0-689-82019-4*) S&S Childrens.

— The Sun. (Weather Channel Ser.). (J). 1999. 3.99 (*0-689-82020-8*) S&S Childrens.

— Weather Channel Weather Pop-up Book. 2000. 25.00 (*0-689-82065-8*) S&S Childrens.

Barkan, Bebe, ed. see Van Loon, Alfred.

Barkan, Bebe, tr. see Ignatow, Rose G.

Barkan, Christopher P., et al, eds. Principles & Practices for Diesel Contaminated Soils, Vol. 7. 120p. 1998. text 49.95 (*1-884940-21-8*) Amherst Sci Pubs.

Barkan, Diana Kormos. Walther Nernst & the Transition to Modern Physical Science. (Illus.). 300p. (C). 1998. text 64.95 (*0-521-44456-X*) Cambridge U Pr.

***Barkan, Elazar.** The Guilt of Nations: Restitution & Negotiating Historical Injustices. LC 99-88238. 464p. 2000. 29.95 (*0-393-04886-1*) Norton.

Barkan, Elazar. The Retreat of Scientific Racism: Changing Concepts of Race in Britain & the United States Between the World Wars. 395p. (C). 1993. pap. text 21.95 (*0-521-45875-7*) Cambridge U Pr.

Barkan, Elazar & Bush, Ronald, eds. Prehistories of the Future: The Primitivist Project & the Culture of Modernism. LC 94-28152. (Cultural Sitings Ser.). (Illus.). 472p. 1995. 55.00 (*0-8047-2390-7*); pap. 18.95 (*0-8047-2486-5*) Stanford U Pr.

Barkan, Elazar & Shelton, Marie-Denise. Borders, Exiles, Diasporas. LC 97-16108. (Cultural Sitings Ser.). 1998. write for info. (*0-8047-2905-0*); pap. write for info. (*0-8047-2906-9*) Stanford U Pr.

Barkan, Elliott R. And Still They Come: Immigrants & American Society, 1920 to the 1990s. Eisenstadt, A. S. & Franklin, John H., eds. (American History Ser.). (Illus.). 270p. (C). 1996. pap. text 14.95 (*0-88295-928-X*) Harlan Davidson.

— Asian & Pacific Islander Migration to the United States: A Model for New Global Patterns, 30. LC 92-10619. (Contributions in Ethnic Studies: No. 30). 280p. 1992. 59.95 (*0-313-27538-6*, BAZ/, Greenwood Pr) Greenwood.

***Barkan, Elliott R.** Making It in America: A Biographical Sourcebook of Eminent Ethnic Americans. 2001. lib. bdg. 65.00 (*1-57607-098-0*) ABC-CLIO.

Barkan, Elliott Robert, ed. A Nation of Peoples: A Sourcebook on America's Multicultural Heritage. LC 98-41061. 600p. 1999. lib. bdg. 99.50 (*0-313-29961-7*, Greenwood Pr) Greenwood.

Barkan, Elliott Robert, jt. ed. see LaMay, Michael Robert.

Barkan, Hans, ed. Johannes Brahms & Theodor Billroth: Letters from a Musical Friendship. LC 77-798. 264p. 1977. reprint ed. lib. bdg. 38.50 (*0-8371-9500-4*, BRJB, Greenwood Pr) Greenwood.

Barkan, Irving, jt. auth. see Lofbarg, John O.

Barkan, Joanne. Abraham Lincoln. Brook, Bonnie, ed. (Let's Celebrate Ser.). (Illus.). 32p. (J). (gr. k-2). 1990. lib. bdg. 6.95 (*0-671-69107-4*) Silver Burdett Pr.

— Abraham Lincoln & President's Day. LC 89-49542. (Let's Celebrate Ser.). (J). 1990. 10.15 (*0-606-10118-7*, Pub. by Turtleback) Demco.

— Abraham Lincoln & President's Day: Let's Celebrate. 32p. (J). (ps-3). 1996. pap. text 4.95 (*0-382-39477-1*) Silver Burdett Pr.

— Air, Air All Around. Brook, Bonnie, ed. (First Facts Ser.). (Illus.). 32p. (J). (ps-1). 1990. lib. bdg. 6.95 (*0-671-68655-0*, Silver Pr NJ) Silver Burdett Pr.

— Animal Car. (Circus Train Come Aboard Bks.). (Illus.). 12p. (J). (ps). 1993. bds. 3.50 (*0-689-71676-1*) Aladdin.

— Barnum's Animals: A B C: Counting 1 to 10: Shapes: Opposites, 4 vols. (Illus.). 12p. (J). (ps-k). 1998. boxed set, bds. 8.99 (*0-689-81918-8*) Litle Simon.

***Barkan, Joanne.** Barnum's Animals ABC Puzzle Pack. (Illus.). (J). (ps-k). 1999. pap. 8.99 (*0-689-82591-9*) Litle Simon.

Barkan, Joanne. Big Fire Trucks. (Illus.). 32p. (Orig.). (J). (ps-3). 1996. pap. 3.50 (*0-8167-3819-X*) Troll Communs.

— Binyah Binyah Hide-&-Seek! A Lift-the-Flap Book. (Illus.). 20p. (J). (ps-2). 1996. pap. 9.99 (*0-689-80840-2*) S&S Childrens.

— Boxcar. (Come Aboard Bks.). (Illus.). 12p. (J). (ps). 1992. pap. 3.50 (*0-689-71573-0*) Aladdin.

— Circus Locomotive. (Circus Train Come Aboard Bks.). (Illus.). 12p. (J). (ps). 1993. pap. 3.50 (*0-689-71674-5*) Aladdin.

— Clown Caboose. (Circus Train Come Aboard Bks.). (Illus.). 12p. (J). (ps). 1993. bds. 3.50 (*0-689-71675-3*) Aladdin.

— Donkey Kong Country. (My Very First Nintendo Game Boy Ser.). (Illus.). 16p. (J). (ps-2). 1997. 10.95 (*0-689-81578-6*) S&S Childrens.

— Easter Egg Fun. (J). (ps-8). 1991. 2.95 (*1-55782-368-5*) Little.

— Easter Surprise. (J). (ps-8). 1991. 2.95 (*1-55782-369-3*) Little.

— Fire, Fire Burning Bright. Brook, Bonnie, ed. (First Facts Ser.). (Illus.). 32p. (J). (ps-1). 1990. lib. bdg. 6.95 (*0-671-68654-2*, Silver Pr NJ) Silver Burdett Pr.

— Fire Truck. (Truckin' Board Bks.). (Illus.). 12p. (J). (ps-k). 1996. 4.99 (*0-689-81147-0*) S&S Childrens.

— Help! It's Halloween!, No. 2. Vol. 2. (Illus.). 24p. (J). (ps-3). 1996. 3.99 (*0-689-80929-8*) S&S Childrens.

— Lost Little Bunny. (Sparkle & Glow Bks.). (Illus.). 24p. (J). (ps-3). 1995. pap. 3.95 (*0-590-48932-1*, Cartwheel) Scholastic Inc.

— Merry Christmas, Santa. (J). 1995. pap. 3.95 (*0-8167-3736-3*) Troll Communs.

— Passenger Car. (Come Aboard Bks.). (Illus.). 12p. (J). (ps). 1992. pap. 3.50 (*0-689-71575-7*) Aladdin.

— Performers' Car. (Circus Train Come Aboard Bks.). (Illus.). 12p. (J). (ps). 1993. pap. 3.50 (*0-689-71673-7*) Aladdin.

— Recycler. (Truckin' Board Bks.). 12p. (J). (ps-k). 1996. per. 4.99 (*0-689-81149-7*) S&S Childrens.

***Barkan, Joanne.** Riddle of the Lost Lake. LC 99-63431. (Wishbone Super Mysteries Ser.: Vol. 4). (Illus.). 256p. (J). (gr. 3-7). 2000. mass mkt. 3.99 (*1-57064-540-X*, Big Red) Lyrick Pub.

Barkan, Joanne. Rocks, Rocks Big & Small. Brook, Bonnie, ed. (First Facts Ser.). (Illus.). 32p. (J). (ps-1). 1990. lib. bdg. 6.95 (*0-671-68656-9*, Silver Pr NJ) Silver Burdett Pr.

***Barkan, Joanne.** Santa Claus Nutcracker. (Nutcracker Board Bks.). (Illus.). 12p. (J). (ps-k). 1999. 4.99 (*0-689-82672-9*) Litle Simon.

Barkan, Joanne. Scrub-a-Dub-Dub. (J). 1998. 4.99 (*0-679-89021-1*, Pub. by Random Bks Yng Read) Random.

— Splish! Splash! (J). 1998. 4.99 (*0-679-89022-X*, Pub. by Random Bks Yng Read) Random.

— The Strangest Halloween, No. 1. Vol. 1. (Illus.). 24p. (J). (ps-3). 1996. 3.99 (*0-689-80928-X*) S&S Childrens.

— Super Mario's Adventures. (My Very First Nintendo Game Boy Ser.). (Illus.). 16p. (J). (ps-2). 1997. 10.95 (*0-689-81579-4*) S&S Childrens.

— Switching Hour Real Monsters Novelization #1. LC 96-2965. (Real Monsters: 1). 64p. (J). (gr. 2-5). 1996. 3.99 (*0-689-80851-8*) S&S Trade.

— A Tale of Two Sitters. LC 97-73760. (Adventures of Wishbone Ser.: No. 9). (Illus.). 144p. (J). (gr. 3-6). 1998. mass mkt. 3.99 (*1-57064-277-X*, Big Red) Lyrick Pub.

— Tanker. (Truckin' Board Bks.). 12p. (J). (ps-k). 1996. per. 4.99 (*0-689-81150-0*) S&S Childrens.

— That Fat Hat. LC 92-7414. (Hello Reader! Ser.). (Illus.). (J). (ps-3). 1992. 2.95 (*0-590-45643-1*) Scholastic Inc.

Barkan, Joanne. That Fat Hat. (Hello, Reader! Ser.). (J). 1992. 9.19 (*0-606-02945-1*, Pub. by Turtleback) Demco.

Barkan, Joanne. Tooth Fairy Magic. (Sparkle & Glow Bks.). (Illus.). 24p. (J). (ps-3). 1995. mass mkt. 3.95 (*0-590-48933-X*, Cartwheel) Scholastic Inc.

***Barkan, Joanne.** Toy Soldier. (Illus.). 12p. (J). (ps-k). 1999. 4.99 (*0-689-82673-7*) Litle Simon.

Barkan, Joanne. Tractor Trailer. (Truckin' Board Bks.). (Illus.). 12p. (J). (ps-k). 1996. per. 4.99 (*0-689-81148-9*) S&S Childrens.

— A Very Merry Santa Story. 24p. (J). (ps-3). 1992. 3.95 (*0-590-46020-X*, Cartwheel) Scholastic Inc.

— A Very Merry Snowman Story. 24p. (J). (ps-3). 1992. 3.95 (*0-590-46021-8*, Cartwheel) Scholastic Inc.

— A Very Scary Haunted House. (Illus.). 24p. (J). (ps-2). 1991. pap. 3.95 (*0-590-44497-2*) Scholastic Inc.

— A Very Scary Witch Story. 24p. (J). (ps-3). 1992. mass mkt. 3.95 (*0-590-45936-8*) Scholastic Inc.

— Visions of Emancipation: The Italian Workers' Movement since 1945. LC 84-6762. 265p. 1984. 55.00 (*0-275-91123-3*, C1123, Praeger Pubs) Greenwood.

— Visions of Emancipation: The Italian Workers' Movement since 1945. LC 84-6762. 289p. 1986. pap. 16.95 (*0-275-92597-8*, B2597, Praeger Pubs) Greenwood.

— Water, Water Everywhere. Brook, Bonnie, ed. (First Facts Ser.). (Illus.). 32p. (J). (ps-1). 1990. lib. bdg. 6.95 (*0-671-68653-4*, Silver Pr NJ) Silver Burdett Pr.

— Whiskerville Bakery. (GRE.). (J). 1990. 5.99 (*0-85953-857-5*); 5.99 (*0-85953-645-9*) Childs Play.

— Whiskerville Firestation. (GRE.). (J). 1990. 5.99 (*0-85953-858-3*); 5.99 (*0-85953-646-7*) Childs Play.

— Whiskerville Post Office. (GRE.). (J). 1990. 5.99 (*0-85953-856-7*); 5.99 (*0-85953-647-5*) Childs Play.

— Whiskerville School. (GRE.). (J). 1990. 5.99 (*0-85953-855-9*); 5.99 (*0-85953-644-0*) Childs Play.

— Witch's Hat. (Trick-or-Treat Bks.). (Illus.). 16p. (J). (ps-1). 1997. 3.99 (*0-689-81693-6*) Litle Simon.

— Zeena's Cat. (Trick-or-Treat Glow-in-the-Dark Bks.). (Illus.). 16p. (J). (ps-1). 1997. 3.99 (*0-689-81694-4*) S&S Childrens.

Barkan, Joanne & Strickland, Brad. A Pup in King Arthur's Court. LC 97-81263. (Adventures of Wishbone Ser.: Vol. 14). (Illus.). 164p. (J). (gr. 3-7). 1998. pap. 3.99 (*1-57064-325-3*) Lyrick Pub.

Barkan, Joel D. Beyond Capitalism vs. Socialism in Kenya & Tanzania. 296p. 1994. pap. text 22.00 (*1-55587-530-0*) L Rienner.

***Barkan, Joshua.** Before Hiroshima: The Confession of Murayama Kazuo & Other Stories. 148p. 2000. write for info. (*1-902881-08-7*, Pub. by Toby Pr Ltd); pap. 12.95 (*1-902881-13-3*, Pub. by Toby Pr Ltd) Toby Pr.

***Barkan, Julie Picard.** I Love Kitties! LC 99-63110. (Illus.). 18p. (ps-k). 2000. 3.99 (*0-307-10715-9*) Gldn Bks Pub Co.

— I Love Puppies! LC 99-63111. (Illus.). 18p. (ps-k). 2000. 3.99 (*0-307-10716-7*) Gldn Bks Pub Co.

— Say Please! Learn about Manners. (My First Barbie Ser.: Vol. 6). (Illus.). (J). 2000. 4.99 (*0-307-10668-3*, Goldn Books) Gldn Bks Pub Co.

— Surprises Big & Small: Learn about Opposites. (My First Barbie Ser.: Vol. 5). (J). 2000. 4.99 (*0-307-10667-5*, Goldn Books) Gldn Bks Pub Co.

Barkan, Leonard. The Gods Made Flesh: Metamorphosis & the Pursuit of Paganism. LC 86-1325. 401p. 1986. 55.00 (*0-300-03561-6*) Yale U Pr.

— The Gods Made Flesh: Metamorphosis & the Pursuit of Paganism. LC 86-1325. (Illus.). 414p. 1986. reprint ed. pap. 128.40 (*0-608-07854-9*, 205403100011) Bks Demand.

— Nature's Work of Art: The Human Body As Image of the World. LC 74-77067. 301p. reprint ed. pap. 93.40 (*0-8357-8743-5*, 203366600087) Bks Demand.

— Transuming Passion: Ganymede & the Erotics of Humanism. LC 90-37800. (Illus.). 168p. 1991. 27.50 (*0-8047-1851-2*) Stanford U Pr.

***Barkan, Leonard.** Unearthing the Past: Archaeology & Aesthetics in the Making of Renaissance Culture. LC 99-24893. (Illus.). 448p. 1999. 35.00 (*0-300-07677-0*) Yale U Pr.

Barkan, Paul. Chemical Research - 2000 & Beyond: Challenges & Visions. LC 98-4293. (An American Chemical Society Publication). (Illus.). 240p. 1998. text 35.00 (*0-8412-3575-9*) OUP.

Barkan, Rhoda & Sinclaire, Peter. From Santa Fe to O'Keeffe Country: A One Day Journey Through the Soul of New Mexico. (Adventure Roads Travel Ser.: Vol. 4). (Illus.). 144p. 1997. pap. 14.95 (*0-943734-32-0*) Ocean Tree Bks.

Barkan, S. H., et al. Baltic Heritage. 1991. boxed set 75.00 (*0-89304-952-2*) Cross-Cultrl NY.

Barkan, Sandra, et al, eds. African Literatures: Retrospective Assessments. (African Literature Association Annuals Ser.: No. 11). 160p. 1989. 22.00 (*0-89410-588-4*); pap. text 14.00 (*0-89410-589-2*) Cornell AS&RC.

Barkan, Stanley H. The Blacklines Scrawl. (Poetry Ser.). (Illus.). 1976. 15.00 (*0-89304-017-7*); pap. 7.50 (*0-89304-010-X*) Cross-Cultrl NY.

— Jewish Writers. 1991. boxed set 75.00 (*0-685-49045-9*); boxed set 50.00 (*0-685-49046-7*) Cross-Cultrl NY.

— O Jerusalem. LC 97-170911. (Illus.). 48p. 1996. 15.00 (*0-89304-469-5*); pap. 7.50 (*0-89304-470-9*) Cross-Cultrl NY.

— O Jerusalem. deluxe limited ed. LC 97-170911. (Illus.). 48p. 1996. 400.00 (*0-89304-472-5*) Cross-Cultrl NY.

— O Jerusalem. limited ed. LC 97-170911. (Illus.). 48p. 1996. 50.00 (*0-89304-471-7*) Cross-Cultrl NY.

Barkan, Stanley H., ed. And Suddenly Spring. Szyper, Adam, tr. (Review Chapbook Ser.: No. 26). (ENG & POL.). 48p. 1991. 15.00 (*0-89304-859-3*); pap. 5.00 (*0-89304-860-7*) Cross-Cultrl NY.

— And Suddenly Spring. Szyper, Adam, tr. (Review Chapbook Ser.: No. 26: Polish Poetry). (ENG & POL.). 48p. 1991. audio 10.00 (*0-685-26550-1*) Cross-Cultrl NY.

— And Suddenly Spring: Mini. Szyper, Adam, tr. (Review Chapbook Ser.: No. 26). (ENG & POL.). 48p. 1991. 15.00 (*0-89304-861-5*); pap. 5.00 (*0-89304-862-3*) Cross-Cultrl NY.

— Box of Broadsides' International Poets & Writers. 1991. boxed set 250.00 (*0-89304-955-7*) Cross-Cultrl NY.

— Cross-Cultural Review Chapbook Anthology: Volume 1 (Chapbooks 1-10) 252p. 1983. 50.00 (*0-89304-925-5*) Cross-Cultrl NY.

— Cross-Cultural Review Chapbooks, Vol. 1. 1991. pap. write for info. (*0-318-65333-8*); boxed set 40.00 (*0-89304-901-8*) Cross-Cultrl NY.

— Fifty Dutch & Flemish Novelists. LC 79-87646. (Illus.). (Orig.). 1979. 25.00 (*0-89304-031-2*, CCC118); pap. 15.00 (*0-89304-032-0*) Cross-Cultrl NY.

— Five Contemporary Dutch Poets. Nijmeijer, Peter & Rollins, Scott, trs. LC 78-87649. (Cross-Cultural Review

B

An Asterisk (*) at the beginning of an entry indicates that the title is appearing for the first time.

Chapbook Ser.: No. 2). (DUT & ENG., Illus.). 48p. 1979. 15.00 (0-89304-602-7, CCC119); pap. 5.00 (0-89304-603-5) Cross-Cultrl NY.
— Five Contemporary Flemish Poets. Holmes, James S. et al, trs. LC 79-87650. (Cross-Cultural Review Chapbook Ser.: No. 3). (DUT & ENG., Illus.). 48p. (Orig.). 1979. 15.00 (0-89304-604-3, CCC120); pap. 5.00 (0-89304-605-1) Cross-Cultrl NY.
— Four Contemporary Swedish Poets. Fulton, Robin, tr. (Cross-Cultural Review Chapbook Ser.: No. 5). (ENG & SWE., Illus.). 48p. 1981. 15.00 (0-89304-608-6); pap. 5.00 (0-89304-609-4) Cross-Cultrl NY.
— German Poetry. 1991. boxed set 75.00 (0-89304-930-1) Cross-Cultrl NY.
— Hebrew Poetry. 1991. boxed set 75.00 (0-89304-956-5) Cross-Cultrl NY.
— Staten Island Ferry International Poetry Festival. 48p. 1989. pap. 5.00 (0-89304-068-1) Cross-Cultrl NY.
— To Struga with Love. LC 78-67775. (Illus.). (Orig.). 1978. 25.00 (0-89304-098-3, CCC115); 15.00 (0-685-01276-X); boxed set 30.00 (0-89304-050-9) Cross-Cultrl NY.
Barkan, Stanley H., et al, eds. Americana Anthology: Bicentennial Edition 1776-1976, Vol. 1. LC 76-47154. (New York Poetry Forum Ser.). (Illus.). 96p. 1976. 20.00 (0-89304-011-8, CCC107); pap. 10.00 (0-89304-009-6) Cross-Cultrl NY.
— Latin American Writers. 1991. boxed set 75.00 (0-89304-940-9); boxed set 50.00 (0-685-49048-3) Cross-Cultrl NY.
Barkan, Stanley H. & Boss, Laura, eds. Women Writers: Chapbooks 1-5, Vol. I. 1991. boxed set 75.00 (0-89304-903-4); boxed set 50.00 (0-89304-902-6) Cross-Cultrl NY.
— Women Writers: Chapbooks 6-10, Vol. II. 1991. boxed set 75.00 (0-89304-905-0); boxed set 50.00 (0-89304-904-2) Cross-Cultrl NY.
Barkan, Stanley H. & Bruchac, Joseph, eds. Native American Writers. 1991. boxed set 75.00 (0-89304-912-3); boxed set 50.00 (0-685-49058-0) Cross-Cultrl NY.
Barkan, Stanley H. & Cedering, Siv. Swedish Writers. 1991. boxed set 75.00 (0-89304-949-2); boxed set 50.00 (0-685-49069-6) Cross-Cultrl NY.
Barkan, Stanley H. & Cedering, Siv, eds. Scandinavian Writers. 1991. boxed set 75.00 (0-89304-951-4); boxed set 50.00 (0-685-49067-X) Cross-Cultrl NY.
Barkan, Stanley H. & Chang, Diana. Asian Heritage. 1991. boxed set 75.00 (0-89304-941-7) Cross-Cultrl NY.
Barkan, Stanley H. & Curzon, David, eds. Box of Broadsides: Poets & Writers at the United Nations. 1991. boxed set 250.00 (0-89304-954-9) Cross-Cultrl NY.
Barkan, Stanley H. & Feiler, Eva, eds. International Festival of Poetry & Art. (International Poetry Festival Ser.: No. 2). (Illus.). 1973. 15.00 (0-89304-019-3, CCC101); pap. 7.50 (0-89304-002-9) Cross-Cultrl NY.
Barkan, Stanley H. & Mikasinovich, Branko, eds. East European Writers. 1991. 75.00 (0-685-49059-9); 50.00 (0-685-49060-2) Cross-Cultrl NY.
Barkan, Stanley H. & Patterson, Raymond R. African Heritage. 1991. boxed set 75.00 (0-89304-947-6); boxed set 50.00 (0-89304-976-X) Cross-Cultrl NY.
Barkan, Stanley H. & Poom, Ritva, eds. Finnish Writers. 1991. boxed set 75.00 (0-89304-935-2); boxed set 50.00 (0-89304-948-4) Cross-Cultrl NY.
Barkan, Stanley H. & Sait, Talat, compiled by. Five Contemporary Turkish Poets. (Cross-Cultural Review Chapbook Ser.: No. 6). (ENG & TUR., Illus.). 48p. 1992. 15.00 (0-89304-610-8); pap. 5.00 (0-89304-611-6) Cross-Cultrl NY.
Barkan, Stanley H. & Scammacca, Nat. Sicilian Writers. 1991. boxed set 75.00 (0-89304-917-4); boxed set 50.00 (0-89304-916-6) Cross-Cultrl NY.
Barkan, Stanley H. & Scammacca, Saverio A., eds. Sicilian Antigruppo. (Illus.). 30p. 1976. 25.00 (0-89304-099-1, CCC106); boxed set 30.00 (0-89304-008-8); 15.00 (0-89304-096-7) Cross-Cultrl NY.
Barkan, Stanley H. & Van De Waarsenburg, Hans, eds. Dutch & Flemish Writers. 1991. 50.00 (0-89304-910-7); boxed set 75.00 (0-89304-911-5) Cross-Cultrl NY.
Barkan, Stanley H. & Wallace, George, eds. Long Island Writers. 1991. boxed set 75.00 (0-685-49049-1) Cross-Cultrl NY.
Barkan, Stanley H., ed. see Akpalu, Vinoko.
Barkan, Stanley H., ed. see Ali, Agha S.
Barkan, Stanley H., ed. see Alkalay-Gut, Karen.
Barkan, Stanley H., ed. see Andersson, Claes.
Barkan, Stanley H., ed. see Aspenstrom, Werner.
Barkan, Stanley H., ed. see Axelrod, David B.
Barkan, Stanley H., ed. see Balbin, Julius.
Barkan, Stanley H., ed. see Berk, Ilhan.
Barkan, Stanley H., ed. see Boss, Laura.
Barkan, Stanley H., ed. see Bruchac, Joseph.
Barkan, Stanley H., ed. see Bruchac, Joseph, et al.
Barkan, Stanley H., ed. see Butscher, Edward.
Barkan, Stanley H., ed. see Cassian, Nina.
Barkan, Stanley H., ed. see Certa, Rolando.
Barkan, Stanley H., ed. see Chang, Diana.
Barkan, Stanley H., ed. see Cosme, Flavia.
Barkan, Stanley H., ed. see Daglarca, Fazil Husnu.
Barkan, Stanley H., ed. see Dame, Enid.
Barkan, Stanley H., ed. see De Moraes, Vinicius.
Barkan, Stanley H., ed. see Dobrin, Arthur.
Barkan, Stanley H., ed. see Egan, Desmond.
Barkan, Stanley H., ed. see Gershator, David.
Barkan, Stanley H., ed. see Gillan, Maria M.
Barkan, Stanley H., ed. see Hallman, Talat S.
Barkan, Stanley H., ed. see Hand, J. C.
Barkan, Stanley H., ed. see Hartman, Steven.
Barkan, Stanley H., ed. see Hartman, Susan.
Barkan, Stanley H., ed. see Henson, Lance.
Barkan, Stanley H., ed. see Ignatow, Yeedi.
Barkan, Stanley H., ed. see Ivask, Astrud.
Barkan, Stanley H., ed. see Katz, Menke.
Barkan, Stanley H., ed. see Kozer, Jose.
Barkan, Stanley H., ed. see Labra, Carilda O.
Barkan, Stanley H., ed. see Lekatsas, Barbara.
Barkan, Stanley H., ed. see Lev, Donald.
Barkan, Stanley H., ed. see Manner, Eeva L.
Barkan, Stanley H., ed. see Mohr, Marilyn.
Barkan, Stanley H., ed. see Moutet, Fernand.
Barkan, Stanley H., ed. see Mulisch, Harry.
Barkan, Stanley H., ed. see Neruda, Pablo.
Barkan, Stanley H., ed. see Ozer, Kemal.
Barkan, Stanley H., ed. see Patterson, Raymond R.
Barkan, Stanley H., ed. see Pelaccio, Mario.
Barkan, Stanley H., ed. see Popa, Vasco.
Barkan, Stanley H., ed. see Preil, Gabriel.
Barkan, Stanley H., ed. see Rabassa, Gregory.
Barkan, Stanley H., ed. see Reich, Asher.
Barkan, Stanley H., ed. see Rilke, Rainer Maria.
Barkan, Stanley H., ed. see Rinkwich, Randy.
Barkan, Stanley H., ed. see Rummo, Paul-Eerik.
Barkan, Stanley H., ed. see Scammacca, Nat.
Barkan, Stanley H., ed. see Shopov, Vladimir A.
Barkan, Stanley H., ed. see St. Germain, Sheryl.
Barkan, Stanley H., ed. see Stiller, Nikki.
Barkan, Stanley H., ed. see Van de Waarsenburgh, Hans.
Barkan, Stanley H., ed. see Van Loen, Alfred.
Barkan, Stanley H., ed. see Vroman, Leo.
Barkan, Stanley H., ed. see Wallace, George.
Barkan, Stanley H., ed. see Weissbort, Daniel.
Barkan, Stanley H., ed. see White, Claire N.
Barkan, Stanley H., ed. see Won, Ko.
Barkan, Stanley H., ed. see Yonetan, Netan.
Barkan, Steven. Discovering Sociology: An Introduction Using Explorit. (Illus.). 246p. (C). 1998. pap., wbk. ed. 18.00 (0-922914-31-1) Thomson Learn.
Barkan, Steven E. Protesters on Trial: Criminal Justice in the Southern Civil Rights & Vietnam Antiwar Movements. (Crime, Law & Deviance Ser.). 190p. (C). 1985. text 35.00 (0-8135-1108-9) Rutgers U Pr.
Barkan, Steven F. Criminology. LC 96-16095. 622p. (C). 1996. 75.00 (0-13-341603-8) P-H.
Barkanic, Stephen. Ring. 1999. pap. 23.95 (0-525-94118-5) NAL.
***Barkas, Seth A.** In the Great Together: One-Act Plays. LC 97-73497. 125p. 2000. pap. 18.95 (1-889262-51-X) Hannacroix.
Barkas, Seth A. In the Great Together: One-Act Plays. LC 97-73497. 125p. 2000. 28.95 (1-889262-07-2) Hannacroix.
Barkat, Mourad. Signal Detection & Estimation. LC 91-13451. 449p. reprint ed. pap. 139.20 (0-7837-5847-2, 204556600006) Bks Demand.
— Solutions Manual for Signal Detection & Estimation. LC 91-13451. 116p. reprint ed. pap. 36.00 (0-7837-5848-0, 204556700006) Bks Demand.
Barkatt, A., et al, eds. Materials Stability & Environmental Degradation. (Symposium Proceedings Ser.: Vol. 125). 1988. text 17.50 (0-931837-95-2) Materials Res.
Barkatt, A. & Van Konynenburg, R., eds. Scientific Basis for Nuclear Waste Management XVII: Materials Research Society Symposium Proceedings, Vol. 333. 969p. 1994. text 30.00 (1-55899-232-4) Materials Res.
***Barkauskas.** Health & Physical Assessment. 3rd ed. 2001. pap. text. write for info. (0-323-01214-0) Mosby Inc.
***Barkauskas, Violet, et al.** Health & Physical Assessment: Includes Testbank. 2nd ed. (Illus.). 816p. 1998. teacher ed. write for info. (0-8151-2802-9) Mosby Inc.
Barkauskas, Violet H. Quick References to Cultural Assessment. LC 95-230936. (Illus.). 56p. 1993. pap. text 8.95 (0-8151-0408-1) Mosby Inc.
Barkauskas, Violet H., et al. Health & Physical Assessment. 2nd ed. LC 97-14864. (Illus.). 816p. (C). (gr. 13). 1997. text 56.00 (0-8151-2776-6, 31045) Mosby Inc.
Barkauskas, Violet H., et al. Health & Physical Assessment. (Illus.). teacher ed. write for info. (0-8151-0407-3) Mosby Inc.
***Barkauskas, Violet H., et al.** Health & Physical Assessment. 2nd ed. (Illus.). 816p. 1998. student ed. write for info. (0-323-00032-0) Mosby Inc.
***Barkawi, Tarak & Laffey, Mark, eds.** Democracy, Liberalism & War: Rethinking the Relationships. 250p. 2001. 52.00 (1-55587-955-1) L Rienner.
Barkdoll, Gerald L. & Bell, James B., eds. Evaluation & the Federal Decision Maker. LC 85-644749. (New Directions for Evaluation Ser.: No. PE 41). 1989. pap. 22.00 (1-55542-874-6) Jossey-Bass.
Barkdull, Larry. The Mourning Dove: A Story of Love. 96p. 1996. pap. write for info. (1-889025-00-3, KenningHse) HomeStar Corp.
— Praise to the Man. LC 97-39831. viii, 134p. 1997. pap. 6.95 (1-57345-320-X) Deseret Bk.
— The Touch of the Master's Hand. unabridged ed. LC 98-7151. 96p. 1998. text 9.95 (0-307-44010-9, Whitman Coin) St Martin.
Barkdull, Larry & Payne, Marvin. The Prodigal. rev. ed. (Keepsake Bookcards Ser.). 16p. (Orig.). 1988. pap. 1.95 (0-929985-04-4) Jackman Pubng.
Barkdull, Larry, et al. Zion Vol. 1: Seeking the City of Enoch. 272p. 1998. 19.95 (1-889025-01-1, KenningHse) HomeStar Corp.
Barke. The Third World Diversity Change Independence. 2nd ed. 1991. pap. text. write for info. (0-05-004485-0) Addison-Wesley.
***Barke, Jack.** Traveler's South Africa Companion. (Traveler's Companion Ser.). (Illus.). 320p. 2000. pap. 24.95 (0-7627-0728-3) Globe Pequot.
Barke, James. The Land of the Leal. (Canongate Classics Ser.). 614p. 1997. pap. 13.95 (0-86241-142-4) Interlink Pub.
— The Song in the Green Thorn Tree: A Novel of the Life & Loves of Robert Burns. 512p. 1993. pap. 13.95 (0-85640-484-5, Pub. by Blackstaff Pr) Dufour.
— The Wind That Shakes the Barley: A Novel of the Life & Loves of Robert Burns. 384p. 1993. pap. 14.95 (0-85640-488-8) Dufour.
Barke, Patricia H. Barnegat Bay Decoys & Gunning Clubs 1880-1920. 2nd ed. (Illus.). 48p. 1993. reprint ed. pap. text 12.00 (0-941965-04-X) Ocean Cnty Hist.
Barkema, G. T., jt. auth. see Newman, Mark.
Barkemeyer, Erica. Eighty Plus Great Ideas for Making Money at Home: A Guide for the First-Time Entrepreneur. 256p. (Orig.). 1992. 24.95 (0-8027-1190-1); pap. 14.95 (0-8027-7378-8) Walker & Co.
Barken, Aaron H. Murder at Stonehenge: An Oxford Mystery. LC 97-12299. 1997. 25.00 (0-912526-78-5) Lib Res.
Barken, Israel, jt. auth. see Fillon, Michael.
Barken, Stanley H., ed. Cross-Cultural Review Minichapbooks, Vol. 1. 1991. boxed set 40.00 (0-89304-900-X) Cross-Cultrl NY.
Barken, Stanley H. & Gillan, Maria M. Italian Heritage. 1991. boxed set 75.00 (0-685-49044-0); boxed set 50.00 (0-89304-962-X) Cross-Cultrl NY.
Barken, Stanley H., jt. auth. see Alkalay-Gut, Karen.
Barken, Stanley H., ed. see Alberti, Rafael.
Barken, Stanley H., ed. see Huang, Parker P.
Barken, Stanley H., ed. see Oliver, Louis.
Barkenbus, Jack N., et al, eds. The Nuclear Connection: A Reassessment of Nuclear Power & Nuclear Proliferation. LC 84-26786. (Illus.). 295p. (C). 1985. 19.95 (0-88702-204-9) Washington Inst Pr.
Barkenbus, Jack N., intro. Ethics, Nuclear Deterrence & War. LC 90-32838. 348p. 1992. 24.95 (0-943852-87-0) Prof World Peace.
Barkenbus, Jack N. & Weinberg, Alvin M., eds. Stability & Strategic Defenses. LC 88-39748. (Illus.). 305p. 1989. pap. 13.95 (0-88702-050-X); text 22.95 (0-88702-046-1) Washington Inst Pr.
— Strategic Defenses & Arms Control. LC 87-2280. 263p. 1987. pap. 12.95 (0-88702-219-7) Washington Inst Pr.
Barker. Art of Texturing & Covering. 1997. 42.95 (1-85032-037-3) ITCP.
— Automation in Mining, Mineral & Metal Processing, 1995. LC 97-37601. (IPV Ser.). 450p. 1997. pap. 79.50 (0-08-042364-7, Pergamon Pr) Elsevier.
— Business Skills Improvement Exercises. 2nd ed. (KM - Office Procedures Ser.). 1992. mass mkt. 12.00 (0-538-60775-0) S-W Pub.
Barker. Communication. 7th ed. 1996. pap. text, teacher ed. write for info. (0-205-18580-0) Allyn.
Barker. Elementary Algebra. 2nd ed. (C). 1992. pap. text, teacher ed., suppl. ed. 27.00 (0-03-072884-3, Pub. by Harcourt Coll Pubs) Harcourt.
— Elementary Algebra. 2nd ed. (C). 1992. pap. text, teacher ed. 14.75 (0-03-072882-7) Harcourt Coll Pubs.
— Elements of Logic. 5th ed. 1988. teacher ed. 17.81 (0-07-003731-0) McGraw.
— Engineering Quality by Design. (Statistics: Textbooks & Monographs). (Illus.). 264p. 1990. text 69.75 (0-8247-8246-1) Dekker.
— Essentials of Math, 4 vols. 4th ed. (C). 1995. pap. text, suppl. ed. 48.36 (0-395-77613-9) HM.
— Essentials of Mathematics, 3 vols. 3rd ed. (C). 1990. pap. text, suppl. ed. 2.76 (0-395-57083-2) HM.
— Fundamentals. 6th ed. (C). 1994. pap. text 40.00 (0-03-012918-4, Pub. by Harcourt Coll Pubs) Harcourt.
— Fundamentals of Math. 5th ed. (C). 1991. pap. text 5.50 (0-03-051053-8) Harcourt Coll Pubs.
— Fundamentals of Math, Testbank. 5th ed. (C). 1991. pap. text, teacher ed., suppl. ed. 14.00 (0-03-051039-2, Pub. by Harcourt Coll Pubs) Harcourt.
— Fundamentals of Math: Prepared Tests. 5th ed. (C). 1991. pap. text 6.00 (0-03-051044-9, Pub. by Harcourt Coll Pubs) Harcourt.
— Fundamentals of Mathematics. 6th ed. (C). 1994. pap. text, teacher ed. 33.75 (0-03-003157-5) Harcourt Coll Pubs.
— Fundamentals of Mathematics. 6th ed. (C). 1994. pap. text, teacher ed. 40.00 (0-03-003248-2, Pub. by Harcourt Coll Pubs) Harcourt.
— Fundamentals of Mathematics. 6th ed. (C). 1995. pap. text, student ed. 27.00 (0-03-003158-3) Harcourt Coll Pubs.
— Intermediate Algebra. 2nd ed. (C). 1992. pap. text, teacher ed., suppl. ed. 36.00 (0-03-072859-2, Pub. by Harcourt Coll Pubs) Harcourt.
— Intermediate Algebra. 2nd ed. (C). 1992. pap. text, teacher ed. 20.75 (0-03-072857-6) Harcourt Coll Pubs.
— Intermediate Algebra. 4th ed. (C). 1995. pap. text 70.00 (0-03-009119-5, Pub. by Harcourt Coll Pubs); pap. text, teacher ed. 28.00 (0-03-009122-5); 3.5 hd 209.50 (0-03-010271-5); 5.25 hd 209.50 (0-03-010272-3) Harcourt Coll Pubs.
— Law Made Simple. 464p. Date not set. pap. text 19.95 (0-7506-2680-1) Buttrwrth-Heinemann.
Barker. Making of a Moonie. 1993. 69.95 (0-7512-0136-7) Ashgate Pub Co.
Barker. Math Cue for College Graph(MAC) 5th ed. (C). 1995. student ed. 276.50 (0-03-010197-2, Pub. by Harcourt Coll Pubs) Harcourt.
— MATHCUE SOL FNDR BASIC ALG 3E+ 3rd ed. (C). 1991. 28.50 (0-03-055237-0) Harcourt Coll Pubs.
— MATHCUE SOL FNDR INTM ALG 3E+ 3rd ed. (C). 1991. 49.50 (0-03-055234-6) Harcourt Coll Pubs.
***Barker.** Modelling & Control Dynamic. (C). 1999. pap. text. write for info. (0-582-08377-X, Pub. by Addison-Wesley) Longman.
Barker. Nutrition & Dietetics for Health. 9th ed. 1996. pap. text 33.00 (0-443-05252-2, W B Saunders Co) Harcrt Hlth Sci Grp.
***Barker.** The Philosophy: Practice of Psychology. 1999. pap. text 31.95 (0-443-06004-5) Mosby Inc.
Barker. Prepared Tests. 4th ed. (C). 1995. pap. text, teacher ed. 37.50 (0-03-010264-2, Pub. by Harcourt Coll Pubs) Harcourt.
— Prepared Tests & Printed. 4th ed. (C). 1995. pap. text 35.50 (0-03-010269-3, Pub. by Harcourt Coll Pubs) Harcourt.
— Proto Thinker. 1997. 3.5 hd 11.00 (0-534-53487-2) Brooks-Cole.
Barker. Research & Evaluation in Clinic. text. write for info. (0-471-49087-3); pap. text. write for info. (0-471-49089-X) Wiley.
Barker. A Self-Help Guide to Managing Depression. 78p. 1993. pap. 16.00 (1-56593-216-1, 0575) Singular Publishing.
***Barker.** Sharp Stuff. (J). 2000. pap. 7.95 (0-552-54642-9, Pub. by Transworld Publishers Ltd) Trafalgar.
Barker. SSM - INTERMEDIATE ALGEBRA, 4/ 4th ed. (C). 1995. pap. text, student ed. 27.00 (0-03-010244-8) Harcourt Coll Pubs.
— ST SM ELEMENTARY ALGEBRA 2E. 2nd ed. (C). 1992. pap. text, student ed. 27.00 (0-03-072883-5) Harcourt Coll Pubs.
— ST SM INTMD ALG2E(HD COV VER) 2nd ed. (C). 1992. pap. text, student ed. 27.00 (0-03-072858-4) Harcourt Coll Pubs.
— ST SOL MAN BASIC ALGEBRA 3E. 3rd ed. (C). 1991. pap. text, teacher ed. 26.50 (0-03-052179-3) Harcourt Coll Pubs.
— Student Solutions Manual -Basic. 4th ed. (C). 1994. pap. text, student ed. 27.00 (0-03-010243-X) Harcourt Coll Pubs.
— Working with Windows 95. (DF - Computer Applications Ser.). 1997. mass mkt. 24.95 (0-7895-0656-4) Course Tech.
***Barker.** WWW Featuring Netscape Communicator 5: An Introduction. (Illustrated Ser.). (C). 2000. text 21.95 (0-7600-6145-9) Course Tech.
Barker & Harrigan. Introduction to Performance: Beginning the Creative Process. 3rd ed. 128p. (C). 1997. per. 15.00 (0-7872-4249-7) Kendall-Hunt.
Barker & Kain, eds. Maps & History in South West England. 159p. 1991. pap. text 24.95 (0-85989-373-1) Northwestern U Pr.
Barker & Taylor. Your Future as a Consumer. 1990. pap. text. write for info. (0-582-66250-8, Pub. by Addison-Wesley) Longman.
Barker, et al. Gangs: An Integrated Approach. LC 99-26803. 479p. 1999. pap. 45.00 (0-13-324856-9) P-H.
Barker, A. E., ed. see Milton, John.
Barker, A. J. Introduction to Metamorphic Textures & Microstructures. 224p. 1990. 69.95 (0-412-02131-5, A3610, Chap & Hall NY); pap. 29.95 (0-412-02141-2, A3614, Chap & Hall NY) Chapman & Hall.
***Barker, A. J.** Introduction to Metamorphic Textures & Microstructures. 2nd ed. LC 98-70912. xiii, 264p. 1998. write for info. (0-412-61200-3) Chapman & Hall.
Barker, A. J. Introduction to Metamorphic Textures & Microstructures. 2nd ed. 280p. 1998. pap. 49.95 (0-7487-3985-8) St Mut.
— World of Dogs. 1988. 4.98 (0-671-06147-X) S&S Trade.
***Barker, A. L.** The Haunt. 192p. 2001. 22.95 (0-7867-0784-4, Pub. by Carroll & Graf) Publishers Group.
Barker, A. Trevor, compiled by. The Letters of H. P. Blavatsky to A. P. Sinnett. LC 73-84138. 420p. 1973. reprint ed. 23.95 (0-911500-23-5) Theos U Pr.
— The Mahatma Letters to A. P. Sinnett. 2nd ed. LC 75-10574. 590p. 1993. reprint ed. 24.95 (0-911500-20-0); reprint ed. pap. 16.95 (0-911500-21-9) Theos U Pr.
Barker, Adele M. Consuming Russia: Popular Culture, Sex & Society since Gorbachev. LC 98-50856. (Illus.). 473p. 1999. pap. 19.95 (0-8223-2313-3) Duke.
— Consuming Russia: Popular Culture, Sex & Society since Gorbachev. LC 98-50856. 450p. 1999. 59.95 (0-8223-2281-1) Duke.
— The Mother Syndrome in the Russian Folk Imagination. (Illus.). 180p. (Orig.). 1986. pap. 19.95 (0-89357-160-1) Slavica.
Barker, Alan. How to Be a Better Decision Maker. (How to Be a Better...Ser.). 1996. pap. 15.95 (0-7494-1950-4) Kogan Page Ltd.
***Barker, Alex.** Egg Bible: The Definitive Guide to Choosing, Cooking & Enjoying Eggs. (Illus.). 2000. 35.00 (0-7548-0506-9, Lorenz Bks) Anness Pub.
Barker, Alex & Mansfield, Sally. Potato: The Definitive Guide to Potatoes & Potato Cooking. 256p. 1999. 30.00 (0-7548-0172-1, Lorenz Bks) Anness Pub.
Barker, Amanda. Bangladesh. LC 95-35860. (Worldfocus Ser.). (J). 1998. 18.50 (1-57572-031-0) Heinemann Lib.
— India. (Worldfocus Ser.). (J). 1998. 18.50 (1-57572-028-0) Heinemann Lib.
— India. (World Focus Ser.). (Illus.). (J). (gr. 3-7). pap. 3.99 (0-431-07258-2, Pub. by Oxfam Pub) Stylus Pub VA.
***Barker, Amanda.** Wind Surfing. LC 99-24022. (Radical Sports Ser.). (J). 1999. lib. bdg. write for info. (1-57572-948-2) Heinemann Lib.
Barker, Andrew. A Report of Captain Ward & Danseker, Pirates. LC 68-54615. (English Experience Ser.: No. 21). 56p. 1968. reprint ed. 15.00 (90-221-0021-9) Walter J Johnson.

B

An Asterisk (*) at the beginning of an entry indicates that the title is appearing for the first time.

— Telegrams from the Soul: Peter Altenberg & the Culture of Fin-de-Siecle Vienna. (GERM Ser.). xx, 260p. 1996. 65.00 (*1-57113-079-9*) Camden Hse.

Barker, Andrew, ed. Greek Musical Writings, Vol. 2: Harmonic & Acoustic Theory. (Cambridge Readings in the Literature of Music Ser.). (Illus.). 592p. (C). 1990. text 115.00 (*0-521-30220-X*) Cambridge U Pr.

Barker, Annabelle. Morocco. 2nd ed. 1997. reprint ed. mass mkt. 6.50 (*1-56333-541-7*, Rosebud) Masquerade.

Barker, Anne M. Transformational Nursing Leadership: A Vision for the Future. 288p. (C). 1992. reprint ed. pap. text 15.95 (*0-88737-551-0*, 15-2473) Natl League Nurse.

Barker, Anne M., et al. Leadership in Dietetics: Achieving a Vision for the Future. LC 94-31016. 1994. pap. 28.00 (*0-88091-137-9*) Am Dietetic Assn.

Barker, Anthony. What Happened When? 504p. 1996. pap. 24.95 (*1-86373-986-6*, Pub. by Allen & Unwin Pty) Paul & Co Pubs.

Barker, Anthony J. & Jackson, Lisa. A Social History of Fleeting Attraction. LC 96-224331. 296p. 1996. pap. 29.95 (*1-875560-74-2*, Pub. by Univ of West Aust Pr) Intl Spec Bk.

Barker, Arthur. From Start to Finish: A Corporal's View of the RAF. LC 98-203152. 170p. 1997. write for info. (*1-85756-302-6*) Janus Pubng.

Barker, Arthur E. Beyond Political Correctness: Toward the Inclusive University. Richer, Stephen & Weir, Lorna, eds. LC 58-3195. 232p. 1995. text 45.00 (*0-8020-5025-5*) U of Toronto Pr.

— Milton & the Puritan Dilemma, 1641-1660. LC 58-3195. (University of Toronto, Department of English Studies & Texts: No. 1). 464p. reprint ed. pap. 143.90 (*0-608-16544-1*, 202635700049) Bks Demand.

— The Seventeenth Century: Bacon Through Marvell. LC 76-4657. (Goldentree Bibliographies Series in Language & Literature). (C). 1980. pap. text 14.95 (*0-88295-548-9*) Harlan Davidson.

Barker, Barbara. Ballet or Ballyhoo: The American Careers of Maria Bonfanti, Rita Sangalli, & Giuseppina Morlachi. LC 82-83629. 269p. 1984. 39.95 (*0-87127-136-2*, Dance Horizons) Princeton Bk Co.

Barker, Barbara M., ed. Bolossy Kiralfy, Creator of Great Musical Spectacles: An Autobiography. LC 88-1278. (Theater & Dramatic Studies: No. 50). (Illus.). 320p. 1988. reprint ed. pap. 99.20 (*0-8357-1862-X*, 207078100005) Bks Demand.

Barker, Barbara M., jt. auth. see Barker, Harry R.

Barker, Barry, ed. see National Institute for Explication Staff.

Barker, Barry W. & Barnett, Charles R., eds. Haciendas of Ecuador: A Travel Guide. (Caravan of Adventure Ser.). (Illus.). 1994. pap. 10.95 (*1-884960-00-6*) Earthwrld Pr.

Barker, Becky. Answers. If I Should Die Before I Wake... 4th rev. ed. Hart, Suzi S., ed. 80p. 1998. ring bd. 24.95 (*0-917875-02-8*) answers period.

— Back in His Arms. large type ed. (Black Satin Romance Ser.). 298p. 1996. 27.99 (*1-86110-018-3*) Ulverscroft.

— The Last Real Cowboy. 1995. per. 3.75 (*0-373-07684-3*, 1-07684-3) Silhouette.

— Sassy Lady. large type ed. (Black Satin Romance Ser.). 289p. 1997. 27.99 (*1-86110-024-8*) Ulverscroft.

***Barker, Ben & Barker, Karen.** Not Afraid of Flavor: Recipes from Magnolia Grill. (Illus.). 336p. 2000. 29.95 (*0-8078-2585-9*) U of NC Pr.

Barker-Benfield, G. J. The Culture of Sensibility: Sex & Society in Eighteenth-Century Britain. LC 91-47945. (Illus.). 554p. 1992. 54.95 (*0-226-03713-4*) U Ch Pr.

— The Culture of Sensibility: Sex & Society in Eighteenth-Century Britain. (Illus.). xxxiv, 554p. 1995. pap. text 22.95 (*0-226-03714-2*) U Ch Pr.

***Barker-Benfield, G J.** Horrors of the Half-known Life: Male Attitudes Toward Women & Sexuality in 19th Century America. LC 99-40334. 1999. pap. 19.99 (*0-415-92500-2*) Routledge.

Barker-Benfield, G. J. & Clinton, Catherine. Portraits of American Women: From Settlement to the Present. (Illus.). 624p. 1998. reprint ed. pap. 18.95 (*0-19-512048-5*) OUP.

Barker, Bernard, ed. The Cambridgeshire Management Workshop Professional Development & Practical Guidance for School Life in the Nineties. 176p. 1990. 90.00 (*1-870167-24-4*, Pub. by P Francis) St Mut.

Barker, Bette M., et al. Guide to Family History Sources in the New Jersey State Archives. 3rd ed. LC 94-8671. (Illus.). 32p. (Orig.). (C). 1994. pap. 7.00 (*0-944313-02-7*) NJ Dept State.

Barker, Betty, ed. Stilwell: The First 100 Years. (Illus.). 174p. (Orig.). 1997. pap. 15.00 (*0-938041-29-0*) Arc Pr AR.

Barker, Bill. Counter Schwa. (Schwa Ser.). (Illus.). 78p. (Orig.). 1994. pap. 6.00 (*0-9635914-2-8*) Schwa Pr.

— Schwa. (Illus.). 38p. 1993. pap. 6.00 (*0-9635914-1-X*) Schwa Pr.

Barker, Bob. Livestock Entomology. 2nd ed. 216p. (C). 1999. pap. text, lab manual ed. 38.95 (*0-7872-5463-0*, 41546301) Kendall-Hunt.

Barker, Brendan. Quality Promotion in Europe. 300p. 1994. 113.95 (*0-566-07512-1*, Pub. by Gower) Ashgate Pub Co.

***Barker, Brett.** Master AP Chemistry. 3rd ed. 2000. pap. 15.99 (*0-7645-6182-0*, Arco) Macmillan Gen Ref.

Barker, Britt. Letters Home. (Illus.). 64p. (Orig.). 1990. pap. 5.50 (*0-945097-09-3*) Home Educ Pr.

Barker, C. J. How You Can Achieve Total Success Through Self-Hypnosis. 32p. 1997. pap. 7.95 (*0-934650-05-5*) Sunnyside.

— Pre-Requisites for the Study of Jacob Boehme. 1987. reprint ed. pap. 6.95 (*1-55818-104-0*, Sure Fire) Holmes Pub.

— Pre-Requisites for the Study of Jacob Boehme. 34p. 1997. reprint ed. pap. 4.95 (*0-7661-0062-6*) Kessinger Pub.

Barker, C. J., ed. see Boehme, Jacob.

Barker, Carol. The Health Care Policy Process. 176p. 1996. 65.00 (*0-8039-7627-5*); pap. 24.95 (*0-8039-7628-3*) Sage.

— The Tibetans: Exile in India. (Illus.). 50p. (J). 1996. pap. 17.95 (*0-85692-205-6*, Pub. by Gallery Chldrns) Assoc Pubs Grp.

Barker, Carol, ed. see Savannah Junior Auxiliary Staff.

Barker, Charles A. Henry George. LC 91-661. 714p. 1992. 15.00 (*0-911312-85-4*) Schalkenbach.

Barker, Charles A., ed. Power & Law: American Dilemma in World Affairs, Papers of the Conference on Peace Research in History. LC 76-135660. 219p. 1971. reprint ed. pap. 67.90 (*0-608-05924-2*, 206626000008) Bks Demand.

Barker, Chia-Ling, jt. auth. see Barker, Don.

Barker, Chia-Ling, jt. auth. see Barker, Donald.

Barker, Chia Ling H. & Barker, Donald I. World Wide Web Featuring Netscape. 1997. pap. 9.50 (*0-7600-5953-5*) Course Tech.

Barker, Chia-Ling H., jt. auth. see Barker, Donald I.

Barker, Chris. Global Television: An Introduction. 256p. (Orig.). 1997. text 62.95 (*0-631-20149-1*); pap. text 34.95 (*0-631-20150-5*) Blackwell Pubs.

— Possessive Descriptions. (Dissertations in Linguistics Ser.). 200p. (C). 1996. 49.95 (*1-881526-73-9*); pap. 22.95 (*1-881526-72-0*) CSLI.

***Barker, Chris.** Television, Globalization, & Cultural Identities. LC 99-17601. (Issues in Cultural & Media Studies). 195p. 1999. 85.00 (*0-335-19955-0*) OpUniv Pr.

Barker, Chris. Television, Globalization, & Cultural Identities. LC 99-17601. (Issues in Cultural & Media Studies). 160p. 1999. 24.95 (*0-335-19954-2*) OpUniv Pr.

Barker, Chris, et al. Research Methods in Clinical & Counselling Psychology. LC 94-15972. (Clinical Psychology Ser.). 300p. 1996. pap. 54.95 (*0-471-96297-X*) Wiley.

Barker, Chris A. Teakwood Decks. (Illus.). 775p. 15.00 (*0-9609382-1-4*) Susquehanna.

Barker, Christine R., et al, eds. Gender Perceptions & the Law. 147p. 1998. text 78.95 (*1-85521-984-0*, Pub. by Ashgate Pub) Ashgate Pub Co.

Barker, Christine R. & Last, Rex W. Erich Maria Remarque. LC 79-10837. 174p. 1979. text 44.00 (*0-06-490308-7*, 06339) B&N Imports.

Barker, Cicely M. The Complete Book of Flower Fairies. (J). 1997. write for info. (*0-614-29328-6*, F Warne) Peng Put Young Read.

— Flower Fairies Activity Book. (Flower Fairies Collection). (Illus.). 24p. (J). (gr. 3 up). 1992. pap. 6.99 (*0-7232-3994-0*, F Warne) Peng Put Young Read.

— Flower Fairies Activity Book. 24p. 1993. pap. 6.99 (*0-7232-4138-4*, F Warne) Peng Put Young Read.

— Flower Fairies Address Book. (J). 1992. 6.95 (*0-7232-3762-X*, F Warne) Peng Put Young Read.

— The Flower Fairies Alphabet Coloring Book. (Flower Fairies Collection). (Illus.). 24p. (J). (ps-3). 1994. pap. 4.99 (*0-7232-4117-1*, F Warne) Peng Put Young Read.

— Flower Fairies Birthday Book. (J). 1992. 6.95 (*0-7232-3785-9*, F Warne) Peng Put Young Read.

— Flower Fairies Magical Painting Activity Book: With Magic Painting & Mystic Pencil Pictures. (Flower Fairies Collection). (Illus.). 24p. (J). 1996. pap. 5.99 (*0-7232-4227-5*, F Warne) Peng Put Young Read.

— Flower Fairies of the Garden. LC 97-224746. (Illus.). (J). (ps-3). 1991. 6.99 (*0-7232-3758-1*, F Warne) Peng Put Young Read.

— Flower Fairies of the Spring. LC 99-462566. (Illus.). (J). (ps-3). 1991. 5.95 (*0-7232-3753-0*, F Warne) Peng Put Young Read.

— Flower Fairies of the Trees. LC 85-70558. (Illus.). (J). (ps-3). 1991. 5.99 (*0-7232-3760-3*, F Warne) Peng Put Young Read.

— Flower Fairies of the Wayside. LC 98-115909. (Illus.). (J). (ps-3). 1991. 5.95 (*0-7232-3757-3*, F Warne) Peng Put Young Read.

— Flower Fairies Year: A Frieze. (J). 1992. 6.99 (*0-7232-3761-1*, F Warne) Peng Put Young Read.

— A Flower Fairy Alphabet. LC 97-224733. (Illus.). (J). 1991. 5.95 (*0-7232-3759-X*, F Warne) Peng Put Young Read.

— The Little Yellow Book. (Flower Fairies Collection). (Illus.). 64p. (J). 1995. 2.99 (*0-7232-4216-X*, F Warne) Peng Put Young Read.

— The Pink Book. (Illus.). 64p. (J). 1995. 2.99 (*0-7232-0025-4*, F Warne) Peng Put Young Read.

— A Treasury of Flower Fairies. deluxe ed. (Illus.). 128p. (J). 1992. 20.00 (*0-7232-3796-4*, Viking Child) Peng Put Young Read.

— A World of Flower Fairies. (Illus.). 128p. (J). (gr. 2 up). 1993. 20.00 (*0-7232-4002-7*, F Warne) Peng Put Young Read.

Barker, Cicely M. A Flower Fairies Postcard Book. 30p. (J). (gr. 2 up). 1991. pap. 7.99 (*0-7232-3710-7*, F Warne) Peng Put Young Read.

— The Flowers Fairies Decoupage Book. 1997. pap. 5.99 (*0-7232-4366-2*, F Warne) Peng Put Young Read.

Barker, Cicely Mary. Flower Fairies Flower Press Kit. (J). (gr. 2-5). 1999. pap. 15.00 (*0-7232-4435-9*, F Warne) Peng Put Young Read.

Barker, Claudia. Ya/Ya! Young New Orleans Artists & Their Storytelling Chairs (& How to Ya/Ya in Your Neighborhood) LC 96-31548. (Illus.). 152p. 1996. 34.95 (*0-8071-2092-8*) La State U Pr.

***Barker, Clive.** Book of Abarat. 256p. 2001. 19.95 (*0-06-028092-1*, J Cotler) HarpC Child Bks.

— Book of Hours. 256p. mass mkt. 9.95 (*0-06-440733-0*) HarpC.

Barker, Clive. Books of Blood, Vols. 1-3. LC 99-160604. 528p. 1998. reprint ed. pap. 14.00 (*0-425-16558-2*) Berkley Pub.

— Cabal Nightbreed. 1991. per. 6.99 (*0-671-74288-4*) PB.

— Clive Barker's A-Z Horror. (Illus.). 256p. 1998. pap. 20.00 (*0-06-105367-8*, HarperPrism) HarpC.

— Clive Barker's Books of Blood, Vol. 1. 224p. 1986. mass mkt. 6.99 (*0-425-08389-6*) Berkley Pub.

— Clive Barker's Books of Blood, Vol. 2. 208p. 1986. mass mkt. 6.99 (*0-425-08739-5*) Berkley Pub.

— Clive Barker's Books of Blood, Vol. 3. 208p. 1986. mass mkt. 6.99 (*0-425-09347-6*) Berkley Pub.

***Barker, Clive.** Coldheart Canyon. 2000. 26.00 (*0-06-018297-0*, HarpCollins) HarperTrade.

— Coldheart Canyon. 2001. write for info. (*0-06-018299-7*, HarpCollins) HarperTrade.

— The Essential Clive Barker: Selected Fiction. LC 99-32574. 608p. 1999. 27.50 (*0-06-019529-0*) HarpC.

Barker, Clive. Everville. 656p. 1995. mass mkt. 7.50 (*0-06-109308-4*, Harp PBks) HarpC.

***Barker, Clive.** Everville. 704p. 1999. pap. 16.00 (*0-06-093315-1*, Perennial) HarperTrade.

Barker, Clive. Everville Limited Ed. limited ed. LC 94-27296. 704p. 1994. 150.00 (*0-06-017603-2*) HarperTrade.

— Galilee. 656p. 1999. mass mkt. 7.50 (*0-06-109200-2*) HarpC.

— Galilee. limited ed. 582p. 1998. boxed set 150.00 (*1-890885-05-3*) B E Trice.

***Barker, Clive.** Galilee: Rees,&Roger, Set. abr. ed. 1998. audio 25.00 (*0-694-51985-5*, 693412) HarperAudio.

Barker, Clive. The Great & Secret Show. 704p. 1990. mass mkt. 7.50 (*0-06-109901-5*, Perennial) HarperTrade.

***Barker, Clive.** The Great & Secret Show. 672p. 1999. pap. 16.00 (*0-06-093316-X*, Perennial) HarperTrade.

— The Hellbound Heart. 176p. 1991. mass mkt. 5.99 (*0-06-100282-8*, Harp PBks) HarpC.

Barker, Clive. Imagica. 1997. pap. 14.00 (*0-614-27313-7*, HarperPrism) HarpC.

— Imajica I: The Fifth Dominion. 544p. 1995. mass mkt. 6.50 (*0-06-109414-5*, Harp PBks) HarpC.

— Imajica II: The Reconciliation. 544p. 1995. mass mkt. 6.50 (*0-06-109415-3*, Harp PBks) HarpC.

— Imajica TP: Imajica TP. 832p. 1997. pap. 16.00 (*0-06-105371-6*, HarperPrism) HarpC.

— In the Flesh. 1991. per. 6.99 (*0-671-74387-2*) PB.

— The Inhuman Condition. 1991. per. 6.99 (*0-671-74289-2*) PB.

— Sacrament. 1995. 24.00 (*0-614-96262-5*) HarpC.

— Sacrament. 624p. 1997. mass mkt. 6.99 (*0-06-109199-5*, Harp PBks); mass mkt. 6.99 (*0-614-27744-2*, Harp PBks) HarpC.

— Sacrifice. 1996. write for info. (*0-614-24245-2*) HarpC.

— Theatre Games. 226p. (C). 1988. pap. 13.95 (*0-413-45380-4*, A0285) Heinemann.

— The Thief of Always. 288p. 1993. mass mkt. 5.99 (*0-06-109146-4*, Harp PBks) HarpC.

— The Thief of Always. 240p. (gr. 4-7). 1997. mass mkt. 4.50 (*0-06-105769-X*, Harp PBks) HarpC.

— Weaveworld. 1989. per. 6.99 (*0-671-70418-4*) PB.

— Weaveworld. 1996. per. 6.99 (*0-671-31152-2*) S&S Trade.

***Barker, Clive & Trussler, Simon, eds.** New Theatre Quarterly, Vol. 62. (Illus.). 96p. 2000. pap. write for info. (*0-521-78902-8*) Cambridge U Pr.

— New Theatre Quarterly, Vol. 63. (Illus.). 96p. 2000. pap. write for info. (*0-521-78903-6*) Cambridge U Pr.

Barker, Clive, et al. Primal: From the Cradle to the Grave. (Primal Ser.). (Illus.). 64p. 1992. pap. 9.95 (*1-878574-30-2*) Dark Horse Comics.

Barker, Colin & Kennedy, Paul, eds. To Make Another World. LC 95-83279. 256p. 1996. 72.95 (*1-85972-326-8*, Pub. by Avebry) Ashgate Pub Co.

Barker, Cornelius & Searchwell, Claudette. Evaluations. 148p. 1995. pap. text, spiral bd. 25.00 (*0-7872-1195-8*) Kendall-Hunt.

***Barker, Cornelius L. & Searchwell, Claudette J.** And Yet He Lived? (Illus.). 100p. (YA). (gr. 7-12). 1999. pap. text 19.99 (*0-9678378-0-4*) Cordet Bks.

— Government by the Children for the Children. (Illus.). 35p. (YA). (gr. 7-12). 2000. pap. text 12.95 (*0-9678378-1-2*) Cordet Bks.

— Professor Eli & the Bible Bunch. rev. ed. Orig. Title: Professor Wyser & the Applic Bunch. (Illus.). 38p. 2000. pap. 15.95 (*0-9678378-2-0*) Cordet Bks.

Barker, Cornelius L. & Searchwell, Claudette J. Writing Meaningful Teacher Evaluations - Right Now! The Principal's Quick-Start Reference Guide. LC 98-9080. (Illus.). 80p. 1998. wbk. ed. 55.95 (*0-8039-6732-2*, 83075); pap., wbk. ed. 24.95 (*0-8039-6733-0*, 83076) Corwin Pr.

***Barker, Craig.** International Law & International Relations. 224p. 2000. 74.95 (*0-8264-5029-6*); pap. 24.95 (*0-8264-5028-8*) Continuum.

Barker, Craig. Starting a Marine Aquarium. 96p. 1972. 8.95 (*0-87666-751-5*, PS-305) TFH Pubns.

Barker, D. J. Mothers, Babies & Health in Later Life. 2nd ed. LC 98-14947. ix, 217p. 1998. write for info. (*0-443-06165-3*) Church.

Barker, D. J., ed. Fetal & Infant Origins of Adult Disease. (Illus.). 343p. 1992. text 53.00 (*0-7279-0743-3*, Pub. by BMJ Pub) Login Brothers Bk Co.

Barker, D. J. & Hall, A. J. Practical Epidemiology. 4th ed. (Illus.). 176p. 1991. pap. text 19.95 (*0-443-03787-6*) Church.

Barker, D. J., et al. Epidemiology in Medical Practice. 5th ed. LC 97-29782. 1997. pap. text 21.00 (*0-443-05620-X*) Church.

Barker, D. J., ed. see Coggin, D.

Barker, Dan. Just Pretend: A Freethought Book for Children. (Illus.). 72p. (Orig.). (J). (ps-6). 1988. pap. 10.00 (*1-877733-05-9*) Freedom Rel Found.

— Maybe Right, Maybe Wrong: A Guide for Young Thinkers. LC 92-416. (Young Readers Ser.). (Illus.). 76p. (J). 1992. pap. 14.95 (*0-87975-731-0*) Prometheus Bks.

— Maybe Yes, Maybe No: A Guide for Young Skeptics. LC 90-43058. (Young Readers Ser.). (Illus.). 80p. (Orig.). (J). (gr. 8-12). 1990. pap. 14.95 (*0-87975-607-1*) Prometheus Bks.

Barker, Dan A. Warrior of the Heart. (Vietnam Generation Ser.). 278p. (Orig.). (C). 1992. pap. 15.00 (*0-9628524-7-3*) Burning Cities Pr.

Barker, Daniel E. Losing Faith in Faith: From Preacher to Atheist. 392p. (Orig.). 1992. pap. 20.00 (*1-877733-07-5*) Freedom Rel Found.

Barker, Daniel S. Igneous Rocks. (Illus.). 431p. (C). 1990. reprint ed. text 90.00 (*1-878907-18-2*) TechBooks.

***Barker, Danny.** Buddy Bolden: And the Last Days of Storyville. 2000. pap. text 19.95 (*0-8264-4743-0*) Continuum.

Barker, Danny & Shipton, Alyn. Buddy Bolden & the Last Days of Storyville. LC 98-12250. 160p. 1998. 30.00 (*0-304-70106-8*) Continuum.

Barker, David. Inside the Big O. 1975. 3.00 (*0-917554-03-5*) Maelstrom.

— Slipware. (Album Ser.: No. 297). (Illus.). 32p. 1989. pap. 4.75 (*0-7478-0221-1*, Pub. by Shire Pubns) Parkwest Pubns.

— William Greatbatch. (Illus.). 288p. 1991. 95.00 (*0-9512140-3-9*, Pub. by J Horne) Antique Collect.

Barker, David & Barker, Tracy. Pythons of the World, Australia. 171p. 1994. 59.95 (*1-882770-34-X*); pap. 39.95 (*1-882770-27-7*) Adv Vivarium.

Barker, David, jt. auth. see Robertson, Kirk.

Barker, David K. The K Wave: Profiting from the Cyclical Booms & Busts in the Global Economy. LC 95-223112. 300p. 1995. text 35.00 (*1-55738-881-4*, Irwn Prfssnl) McGraw-Hill Prof.

Barker, Dean T., jt. auth. see Weinschenk, Susan.

***Barker, Deborah.** Aesthetics & Gender in American Literature: Portraits of the Woman Artist. LC 98-47704. (Illus.). 264p. 2000. 42.50 (*0-8387-5408-2*) Bucknell U Pr.

Barker, Deborah R. & Zimmerman, Julie B. Julie & Debbie's Guide to Getting Rich on Just $10 a Week. LC 96-9689. 128p. 1997. pap. 9.95 (*0-440-50781-2*) Dell.

***Barker, Dennis.** Craft of the Media Interview. 240p. 1999. 24.95 (*0-7090-6131-5*, Pub. by R Hale Ltd) Seven Hills Bk.

Barker, Dennis. Parian Ware. (Album Ser.: No. 142). (Illus.). 32p. 1998. pap. 6.25 (*0-85263-737-3*, Pub. by Shire Pubns) Parkwest Pubns.

Barker, Dennis, jt. auth. see Anderson, Alan H.

Barker, Diane, jt. auth. see McClary, Clebe.

Barker, Don. World Wide Web Featuring Netscape Communicator Software. 1997. pap. text 19.99 (*0-7600-5619-6*) Course Tech.

Barker, Don & Barker, Chia-Ling. World Wide Web Featuring Microsoft Internet Explorer 4. 256p. (C). 1997. pap. 21.95 (*0-7600-5304-9*) Course Tech.

Barker, Don, et al. Working with Windows 95. LC 96-216298. (New Perspectives Ser.). 432p. 1996. pap. 35.95 (*0-7600-4313-2*) Course Tech.

— Working with WordPerfect for Windows. 272p. 1993. pap. 28.95 (*0-87835-855-2*) Course Tech.

Barker, Donald. World Wide Web Featuring Microsoft Internet Explorer 5: Illustrated Standard Edition. (Illus.). (C). 1999. pap. 21.95 (*0-7600-6053-3*) Course Tech.

— World Wide Web Featuring Netscape Communicator 5: Illustrated Standard Edition. (Illus.). (C). 2000. pap. 19.95 (*0-7600-6045-2*) Course Tech.

Barker, Donald & Barker, Chia-Ling. World Wide Web - Illustrated (Featuring Netscape 1.1), Incl. Online companion, files. (Illustrated Ser.). (Illus.). 148p. 1995. text. write for info. (*0-7600-3504-0*) Course Tech.

— World Wide Web Featuring Netscape Navigator 2.0/3.0 Software, Incl. Online companion, files. (Illustrated Ser.). (Illus.). 192p. 1996. pap. 20.95 (*0-7600-4051-6*) Course Tech.

Barker, Donald I. & Barker, Chia-Ling H. Publishing on the Web: Featuring Netscape Navigator Gold 3 Software - Illustrated Brief Edition. 10th ed. (Illustrated Ser.). (Illus.). 96p. (C). 1996. pap. write for info. (*0-7600-4650-6*) Course Tech.

— The World Wid Web: Featuring Netscape Navigator 4.0 - Illustrated. 10th ed. (Illustrated Ser.). (Illus.). 168p. (C). 1997. pap. 21.95 (*0-7600-5178-X*) Course Tech.

Barker, Donald I. & Barker, Chia-Ling H. World Wide Web Featuring Microsoft Internet Explorer 5 - Illustrated Brief. (Illus.). 112p. per. 12.95 (*0-7600-6054-1*, Pub. by Course Tech) Thomson Learn.

Barker, Donald I., jt. auth. see Barker, Chia Ling H.

Barker, Dudley. G. K. Chesterton: A Biography. LC 72-95988. 304 p. 1973. write for info. (*0-8128-1544-0*) Madison Bks UPA.

***Barker, Dudley, et al, photos by.** Cowboy up for Jesus. (Illus.). 167p. 1999. pap. 10.00 (*0-9675474-0-7*) M Moulder.

Barker, E. Greek Political Theory. 5th ed. 468p. 1960. 17.95 (*0-416-67530-1*, NO. 2070) Routledge.

Barker, E. F. Barker Family. 553p. 1992. reprint ed. lib. bdg. 88.50 (*0-8328-2303-1*) Higginson Bk Co.

Barker, E. F. Barker Family. 553p. 1992. reprint ed. pap. 78.50 (*0-8328-2304-X*) Higginson Bk Co.

Barker, Earnest, ed. see Heath, Thomas L.

Barker, Edward, jt. auth. see Wilkinson, Allen P.

Barker, Edward B., ed. Syria & Egypt under the Last Five Sultans of Turkey, 2 vols. LC 73-6269. (Middle East Ser.). 1979. reprint ed. 56.95 (*0-405-05324-X*) Ayer.

Barker, Edwin N., jt. auth. see Pepitone, James S.

Barker, Eileen. On Freedom. LC 97-3860. 357p. 1997. pap. text 24.95 (*1-56000-976-4*) Transaction Pubs.

An Asterisk (*) at the beginning of an entry indicates that the title is appearing for the first time.

B

An Asterisk (*) at the beginning of an entry indicates that the title is appearing for the first time.

— Mountain Treasures. (Colorado Heritage Ser.). (Illus.). 44p. (J). (gr. k-6). reprint ed. pap. 7.95 (*1-878611-01-1*) Silver Rim Pr.

Barker, Jane V., jt. auth. see Downing, Sybil.

Barker, Jeff. Cross Purposes. 1992. 9.99 (*0-685-72865-X*, MP-682) Lillenas.

Barker, Jeff. Cross Purposes. 41p. 1992. pap. 8.99 (*0-8341-9790-1*) Lillenas.

Barker, Jeff. Unspoken for Time. 86p. 1996. pap. 5.50 (*0-87129-646-2*, U21) Dramatic Pub.

Barker, Jeffery L. & McKelvy, Jeffrey F., eds. Current Methods in Cellular Neurobiology. LC 83-1282. (Wiley-Interscience Publications: Vol. 1). 339p. reprint ed. pap. 105.10 (*0-7837-2384-9*, 204007000001) Bks Demand.

Barker, Jeffery L. & Smith, T. G., Jr., eds. The Role of Peptides in Neuronal Function. LC 80-24658. (Illus.). 769p. reprint ed. pap. 200.00 (*0-7837-0962-5*, 204126700019) Bks Demand.

Barker, Jeffrey H. Individualism & Community: The State in Marx & Early Anarchism, 143. LC 85-17707. (Contributions in Political Science Ser.: No. 143). 249p. 1986. 49.95 (*0-313-24706-4*, BIV/, Greenwood Pr) Greenwood.

Barker, Jeffrey L., jt. ed. see Rogawski, Michael A.

Barker, Jennifer S. The Morning Hill Cookbook: A Whole Foods Vegetarian Cookbook. LC 94-96617. 192p. 1995. pap. 11.95 (*0-9642977-0-1*) Morning Hill Assocs.

— The Morning Hill Solar Cookery Book. LC 99-70204. (Illus.). x, 102p. 1999. pap. 14.95 (*0-9642977-1-X*) Morning Hill Assocs.

Barker, Jerry & Tingey, David T., eds. Air Pollution Effects on Biodiversity. (Illus.). 304p. (gr. 13). 1992. mass mkt. 84.95 (*0-442-00748-5*) Chapman & Hall.

Barker, Joan C. Danger, Duty & Disillusion: The Worldview of Los Angeles Police Officers. LC 99-192674. (Illus.). 228p. (C). 1999. pap. text 12.95 (*1-57766-041-2*) Waveland Pr.

Barker, Joel A. Discovering the Future: The Business of Paradigms. 135p. 1985. 15.00 (*0-932183-01-8*) ILI Pr.

— Paradigms: The Business of Discovering the Future. LC 92-54950. Orig. Title: Future Edge. (Illus.). 256p. 1993. pap. 14.00 (*0-88730-647-0*, HarpBusn) HarpInfo.

Barker, John. British in Boston: Being the Diary of Lieutenant John Barker of the King's Own Regiment from Nov. 15, 1774-May 31, 1776. Decker, Peter, ed. LC 72-76555. (Eyewitness Accounts of the American Revolution Ser.). (Illus.). 1975. reprint ed. 17.95 (*0-405-01144-X*) Ayer.

— The Flight of the Liberators: The Story of the Four Hundred & Fifty-Four Bombardment Groups. 6th ed. (Aviation Ser.). 172p. 1987. 39.95 (*0-89839-096-6*) Battery Pr.

— Missouri Lawyer. (American Autobiography Ser.). 391p. 1995. reprint ed. lib. bdg. 89.00 (*0-7812-8451-1*) Rprt Serv.

Barker, John, ed. Christianity in Oceania: Ethnographic Perspectives. (ASAO Monographs: No. 12). 330p. (C). 1990. lib. bdg. 51.00 (*0-8191-7906-X*) U Pr of Amer.

Barker, John & Kellen, Jim. Career Education. LC 97-25590. 320p. 1997. pap. text 30.00 (*0-02-305884-6*) Macmillan.

Barker, John C. Strange Contrarieties: Pascal in England During the Age of Reason. LC 74-81661. (Illus.). 352p. reprint ed. pap. 109.20 (*0-7837-1163-8*, 204169200022) Bks Demand.

Barker, John H. This Is the Will of God. pap. 5.99 (*0-88019-116-3*) Schmul Pub Co.

Barker, John H., et al, eds. Clinically Applied Microcirculation Research. LC 95-1029. 512p. 1995. boxed set 289.95 (*0-8493-4870-6*, 4870) CRC Pr.

Barker, John L. River Phoenix: Into the Sun. (Illus.). 148p. (J). (gr. 4-12). 1999. pap. 9.95 (*0-9665612-3-6*) Phoenix Literary.

— Running on Empty: The Life & Career of River Phoenix LC 98-91567. 274 p. 1998. write for info. (*0-9665612-0-1*) Phoenix Literary.

Barker, John M. Saloon Problem & Social Reform. LC 76-112521. (Rise of Urban America Ser.). 1970. reprint ed. 25.95 (*0-405-02434-7*) Ayer.

Barker, John N. & Bray, John. The Indian Princess, 2 vols. in 1. LC 77-169587. (Earlier American Music Ser.: No. 11). 1973. reprint ed. 27.50 (*0-306-77311-2*) Da Capo.

Barker, John R. Progress Problems in Atmospheric Chemistry. (Advanced Series in Physical Chemistry). 1000p. 1995. text 177.00 (*981-02-1868-0*) World Scientific Pub.

Barker, John R., ed. Advances in Chemical Kinetics & Dynamics Vol. 2: Vibrational Energy Transfer Involving Large & Small Molecules, 2 pts., Set. 533p. 1995. 219.00 (*1-55938-702-5*) Jai Pr.

Barker, John S. Christmasana: Ten Short Stories for Holiday Reading. (Illus.). 144p. 1998. 14.95 (*0-9668060-3-4*) Dana Scott.

Barker, John W. Justinian & the Later Roman Empire. LC 66-11804. (Illus.). 344p. 1966. reprint ed. pap. 106.70 (*0-7837-9774-5*, 206050300005) Bks Demand.

— Justinian & the Later Roman Empire. LC 66-11804. (Illus.). 336p. (C). 1975. reprint ed. pap. text 24.95 (*0-299-03944-7*) U of Wis Pr.

***Barker, Jonathan.** Street-Level Democracy: Political Settings at the Margins. LC 99-45383. 288p. 1999. pap. 23.95 (*1-56549-106-8*) Kumarian Pr.

Barker, Jonathan, ed. Easier Living Products for the Dining Room. (Orig.). 1989. pap. text 2.75 (*0-940429-04-7*) M B Glass Assocs.

— The Politics of Agriculture in Tropical Africa. LC 84-2013. (Sage Series in African Modernization & Development: No. 9). 320p. 1984. reprint ed. pap. 99.20 (*0-608-01499-0*, 205954300001) Bks Demand.

Barker, Joseph H., et al, eds. Designing a Laboratory. 210p. 1989. 40.00 (*0-87553-150-4*) Am Pub Health.

***Barker, Judith.** Stenciling & Embossing Stunning Greeting Cards. LC 00-20011. (Illus.). 128p. 2000. pap. 22.99 (*0-89134-997-9*, North Lght Bks) F & W Pubns Inc.

Barker, Juliet. The Brontes. LC 97-24201. (Illus.). 448p. 1998. 35.00 (*0-87951-838-3*, Pub. by Overlook Pr) Penguin Putnam.

Barker, Juliet, jt. auth. see Barber, Richard.

Barker, Juliet, jt. auth. see Devitt, Peter.

Barker, Justice. New Zealand Forms & Precedents, 5 vols., Set. ring bd. write for info. (*0-409-70208-0*, NZ, MICHIE) LEXIS Pub.

Barker, Karen, jt. auth. see Barker, Ben.

Barker, Karen, jt. auth. see Jones, Kim.

Barker, Kathleen & Christensen, Kathleen, eds. Contingent Work: American Employment Relations in Transition. LC 98-11445. (Illus.). 344p. 1998. 49.95 (*0-8014-3369-X*, ILR Press); pap. 18.95 (*0-8014-8405-7*, ILR Press) Cornell U Pr.

Barker, Kathy. At the Bench: A Laboratory Navigator. LC 98-15662. 1998. 47.00 (*0-87969-523-4*) Cold Spring Harbor.

Barker, Keith. Information Books for Children. 2nd ed. 283p. 1995. 69.95 (*1-85928-072-2*, Pub. by Scolar Pr) Ashgate Pub Co.

— Outstanding Books for Children & Young People: The LA Guide to Carnegie/Greenaway Medal. 135p. 1998. pap. 35.00 (*1-85604-287-1*, LAP2871, Pub. by Library Association) Bernan Associates.

Barker, Ken. Michah-Zephaniah. LC 98-40576. (New American Commentary Ser.: Vol. 20). 320p. 1998. 29.99 (*0-8054-0120-2*, 4201-20) Broadman.

Barker, Kenneth. Religious Education, Catechesis & Freedom. LC 81-13962. 255p. (Orig.). 1981. pap. 16.95 (*0-89135-028-4*) Religious Educ.

Barker, Kenneth, ed. The NIV: The Making of a Contemporary Translation. 240p. 1986. pap. 9.95 (*0-310-24181-2*, 12080P) Zondervan.

***Barker, Kenneth L.** Balance of the NIV. LC 99-52526. 144p. 2000. pap. 13.99 (*0-8010-6239-X*) Baker Bks.

— Journal. 1997. pap. 12.99 (*0-8054-0225-X*) Broadman.

Barker, Kenneth L., ed. The Making of the NIV. 192p. (gr. 12). 1997. reprint ed. pap. 12.99 (*0-8010-5742-6*) Baker Bks.

Barker, Kerry & Hamilton, David. Betting Gaming & Lotteries. 235p. 1993. 84.00 (*1-85190-186-8*, Pub. by Tolley Pubng) St Mut.

Barker, Kerry & Sturges, John. Decision Making in Magistrates' Courts. 95p. 1990. 45.00 (*1-85190-017-9*, Pub. by Tolley Pubng) St Mut.

Barker, L. Angel Crafts. 128p. 1996. 14.98 (*0-7858-0665-2*) Bk Sales Inc.

Barker, L. Randol, et al, eds. Principles of Ambulatory Medicine. 4th ed. LC 93-46869. (Illus.). 1584p. 1995. 115.00 (*0-683-00438-7*) Lppncott W & W.

Barker, L. Randol, et al. Principles of Ambulatory Medicine. 3rd ed. 1487p. 1990. 109.00 (*0-683-00437-9*) Lppncott W & W.

— Principles of Ambulatory Medicine. 5th ed. LC 97-40570. 1600p. 1998. 109.00 (*0-683-30352-X*) Lppncott W & W.

Barker, Larry L. Communication Skills: Objectives & Criterion Referenced Exercises for Grades 7-12. (Illus.). 321p. (Orig.). (YA). 1988. pap. text 39.95 (*0-685-27248-6*) SPECTRA Inc.

— Listening Behavior. 154p. (C). 1991. reprint ed. pap. text 18.95 (*0-685-27249-4*) SPECTRA Inc.

— Listening Skills: Objectives & Criterion Referenced Exercises for Grades K-12. (Illus.). 115p. (Orig.). 1988. pap. text 27.95 (*0-685-27247-8*) SPECTRA Inc.

***Barker, Larry L. & Wahlers, Kathy J.** Groups in Process: An Introduction to Small Group Communication. 6th ed. 288p. 2000. pap. 42.00 (*0-205-32850-4*) Allyn.

***Barker, Larry L. & Watson, Kittie W.** Listen Up: How to Improve Relationships, Reduce Stress & Be More Productive by Using the Power. (Illus.). 288p. 2000. 25.95 (*0-312-24265-4*) St Martin.

Barker, Larry L., et al. Communication. 7th ed. LC 95-19524. 492p. 1995. pap. 48.00 (*0-205-17865-0*) Allyn.

Barker, Larry L., et al. Groups in Process: An Introduction to Small Group Communication. 5th ed. LC 94-38490. 268p. 1994. pap. text 48.00 (*0-205-16887-6*) Allyn.

Barker, Larry L., jt. auth. see Watson, Kittie W.

Barker, Leo R. & Costello, Julia, eds. The Archaeology of Alta California. LC 91-45783. (Spanish Borderlands Sourcebooks Ser.: Vol. 15). 544p. 1992. text 30.00 (*0-8240-1964-4*) Garland.

Barker, Lewis M. Learning & Behavior: Biological, Psychological & Sociocultural Perspectives. 2nd ed. LC 96-23094. 566p. (C). 1996. 79.00 (*0-13-256975-2*) P-H.

Barker, Lewis M., et al, eds. Learning Mechanisms in Food Selection. LC 77-76779. 632p. 1977. 40.00 (*0-918954-19-3*) Baylor Univ Pr.

Barker, Linda. Changing Rooms: Designer Makeovers. LC 98-70038. (Illus.). 160p. 1998. 29.95 (*0-563-38382-8*, Pub. by Robson Bks) Parkwest Pubns.

— Contemporary Decoupage: Fresh Ideas for Gifts, Keepsakes & Home Furnishings. LC 96-217255. (Illus.). 112p. 1996. pap. 19.95 (*0-8019-8875-6*) Krause Pubns.

— The Home Decorator's Stamping Book. LC 97-46892. Orig. Title: The Home Decorator's Stamping Kit. (Illus.). 128p. 1998. 27.95 (*1-56477-191-1*, DB338, PasTimes) Martingale & Co.

***Barker, Linda.** Home-Made Style: 100 Great Decorating Ideas. (Illus.). 2000. 24.95 (*1-85585-691-3*) Collins & Br.

Barker, Linda. Jazz up Your Junk with Linda Barker. (Illus.). 1999. pap. 24.95 (*0-7153-0832-7*, Pub. by D & C Pub) Sterling.

— Just Junk: New Looks for Old Furniture. LC 97-31685. (Illus.). 144p. 1998. 18.95 (*0-7621-0017-6*, Pub. by RD Assn) Penguin Putnam.

Barker, Lorenzo A. With the Western Sharpshooters: Michigan Boys of Company D, 66th Illinois. (Illus.). 192p. 1994. 22.95 (*1-885033-02-8*) Blue Acorn Pr.

Barker, Lucious J., et al. Civil Liberties & the Constitution: Cases & Commentaries. 8th ed. LC 98-54160. 878p. (C). 1999. pap. text 63.00 (*0-13-082897-1*) P-H.

Barker, Lucius J. Our Time Has Come: A Delegate's Diary of Jesse Jackson's 1984 Presidential Campaign. LC 87-24357. 256p. 1988. 21.95 (*0-252-01426-X*) U of Ill Pr.

Barker, Lucius J., ed. Black Electoral Politics: Participation, Performance, Promise. (National Political Science Review Ser.: Vol. II). 250p. 1999. pap. 21.95 (*0-88738-821-3*) Transaction Pubs.

— Ethnic Politics & Civil Liberties. (National Political Science Review Ser.: Vol. 3). 224p. (C). 1992. pap. text 24.95 (*1-56000-564-5*) Transaction Pubs.

— New Perspectives in American Politics: The National Political Science Review, Vol. 1. 300p. 1989. 39.95 (*0-88738-744-6*) Transaction Pubs.

Barker, Lucius J. & Barker, Twiley W., Jr. Civil Liberties & the Constitution: Cases & Commentaries. 7th ed. LC 93-23785. 784p. 1994. pap. text 69.00 (*0-13-137209-2*) P-H.

Barker, Lucius J. & Jones, Mack H. African-Americans & the American Political System. 1994. write for info. (*0-318-72280-1*) P-H.

Barker, Lucius J. & Walters, Ronald W., eds. Jesse Jackson's 1984 Presidential Campaign: Challenge & Change in American Politics. 272p. 1989. text 37.50 (*0-252-01537-1*); pap. text 14.95 (*0-252-06014-8*) U of Ill Pr.

Barker, Lucius Jefferson, et al. African Americans & the American Political System. 4th ed. LC 98-25287. 372p. 1998. pap. text 38.60 (*0-13-779562-9*) P-H.

Barker, Lynton & Rubycz, Rom. Performance Improvement in Public Service Delivery: A Toolkit for Managers. 1996. pap. 77.50 (*0-273-61663-3*) F T P-H.

Barker, M. A., et al. Reader of Modern Irdu. 334p. 1968. pap. 19.95 (*0-7735-9066-8*, Pub. by McG-Queens Univ Pr) CUP Services.

— Urdu-English Vocabulary: Student's Dictionary. LC 79-92847. (ENG & URD.). 382p. 1980. pap. text 15.00 (*0-87950-438-2*) Spoken Lang Serv.

Barker, Malcolm E. Bummer & Lazarus: San Francisco's Famous Dogs. LC 84-15491. (Illus.). 96p. (Orig.). 1984. pap. 6.95 (*0-930235-01-0*) Londonborn Pubns.

Barker, Malcolm E., compiled by. More San Francisco Memoirs, 1852-1899: The Ripening Years. (Illus.). 320p. (Orig.). 1996. pap. 16.95 (*0-930235-05-3*) Londonborn Pubns.

— San Francisco Memoirs, 1835-1851: Eyewitness Accounts of the Birth of a City. (Illus.). 320p. (Orig.). 1994. pap. 16.95 (*0-930235-04-5*) Londonborn Pubns.

— Three Fearful Days: San Francisco Memoirs of the 1906 Earthquake & Fire. LC 98-13704. (Illus.). 336p. 1998. pap. 16.95 (*0-930235-06-1*) Londonborn Pubns.

Barker, Malcolm J. & Sobey, Timothy C. Living with the Queen: Behind the Scenes at Buckingham Palace. LC 92-11345. 1992. 18.95 (*0-942637-75-5*) Barricade Bks.

Barker, Malina, tr. see Chetverikov, S. S.

Barker, Margaret. Bedside Manners. large type ed. 229p. 1995. 27.99 (*0-7505-0779-9*, Pub. by Mgna Lrg Print) Ulverscroft.

***Barker, Margaret.** A Familiar Feeling. 288p. 2000. 26.99 (*0-263-16358-X*, Pub. by Mills & Boon) Ulverscroft.

Barker, Margaret. I'd Love a Baby. large type ed. 288p. 1998. 24.99 (*0-263-15350-9*, Pub. by Mills & Boon) Ulverscroft.

— Impossible Secret. large type ed. 288p. 1996. 23.99 (*0-263-14632-4*, Pub. by Mills & Boon) Ulverscroft.

— Intimate Prescription. large type ed. (Mills & Boon Large Print Ser.). 288p. 1998. 24.99 (*0-263-15343-6*, Pub. by Mills & Boon) Ulverscroft.

— Lakeside Hospital. large type ed. 288p. 1995. 23.99 (*0-263-14177-2*, Pub. by Mills & Boon) Ulverscroft.

— The Lost Prophet: The Book of Enoch & Its Influence on Christianity. LC 88-35121. 128p. 1989. pap. 9.95 (*0-687-22779-8*) Abingdon.

— Loving Care. large type ed. 1995. 27.99 (*0-7505-0746-2*, Pub. by Mgna Lrg Print) Ulverscroft.

— Monsoon Surgeon. large type ed. (Magna Large Print Ser.). 264p. 1996. 27.99 (*0-7505-0998-8*, Pub. by Mgna Lrg Print) Ulverscroft.

— On Earth As It Is in Heaven: Temple Symbolism in the New Testament. 112p. 1996. pap. 19.95 (*0-567-29278-9*, Pub. by T & T Clark) Bks Intl VA.

— The Risen Lord: The Jesus of History As the Christ of Faith. LC 96-35849. 192p. 1996. pap. 20.00 (*1-56338-191-5*) TPI PA.

— Surgeon Royal. large type ed. 274p. 1993. 27.99 (*0-7505-0552-4*) Ulverscroft.

***Barker, Margaret.** Valentine Magic. large type ed. 288p. 1999. 25.99 (*0-263-16029-7*, Pub. by Mills & Boon) Ulverscroft.

Barker, Margaret, jt. auth. see Griggs, Jack.

Barker, Marie E. Espanol para el Bilingue. (SPA.). 352p. 1994. pap. 19.95 (*0-8442-7107-1*, Natl Textbk Co) NTC Contemp Pub Co.

Barker, Marjorie. Magical Hands. LC 89-31373. (Illus.). 28p. (J). (ps up). 1991. 16.00 (*0-88708-103-7*, Picture Book Studio) S&S Childrens.

Barker, Martin. A Haunt of Fears: The Strange History of the British Horror Comics Campaign LC 84-121188. 227p. 1984. write for info. (*0-86104-751-6*) Pluto GBR.

Barker, Martin. A Haunt of Fears: The Strange History of the British Horror Comics Campaign. LC 92-17769. (Studies in Popular Culture). (Illus.). 225p. 1992. reprint ed. text 35.00 (*0-87805-593-2*); reprint ed. pap. text 15.95 (*0-87805-594-0*) U Pr of Miss.

***Barker, Martin & Austin, Thomas.** From Antz to Titanic: A Student Guide to Film Analysis. LC 00-23268. (Illus.). (J). 2000. write for info. (*0-7453-1584-4*, Pub. by Pluto GBR) Stylus Pub VA.

Barker, Martin & Beezer, Anne, eds. Reading into Cultural Studies. LC 92-33391. 240p. (C). 1992. pap. 22.99 (*0-415-06377-9*, A7916) Routledge.

Barker, Martin & Petley, Julian. Ill Effects: The Media Violence Debate. LC 96-25087. (Communication & Society Ser.). 176p. (C). 1997. 65.00 (*0-415-14672-0*); pap. 20.99 (*0-415-14673-9*) Routledge.

Barker, Martin & Sabin, Roger. The Lasting of the Mohicans: History of an American Myth. LC 95-29991. (Studies in Popular Culture). (Illus.). 224p. 1996. 45.00 (*0-87805-858-3*); pap. 16.95 (*0-87805-859-1*) U Pr of Miss.

Barker, Maryl. Gracie. (Gracie's Great Adventures Ser.: Vol. 1). (Illus.). 40p. (J). (ps-4). 1997. pap. 12.95 (*0-9662234-0-3*) GraceMar Prodns.

— My Own Backyard. LC 99-94045. (Gracie's Great Adventures Ser.: Vol. 3). (Illus.). 40p. (J). (ps-4). 1999. pap. 14.95 (*0-9662234-2-X*) GraceMar Prodns.

— Wild Country Animal Park. (Gracie's Great Adventures Ser.: Vol. 2). (Illus.). 36p. (J). (ps-4). 1998. pap. 12.95 (*0-9662234-1-1*) GraceMar Prodns.

Barker, Maxine W. The Third Arrow: A Story of Moshulatubbee, Choctaw Chief. 166p. 1997. pap. 18.00 (*1-885480-18-0*) Pioneer Pubng.

Barker, Michael. Acrostic Journey: Poems in the Key of Life. 98p. 1998. pap. write for info. (*1-57502-939-1*, P02579) Morris Pubng.

Barker, Michael, ed. State Taxation Policy & Economic Growth. LC 83-1551. (Duke Press Policy Studies). xix, 284p. 1983. text 49.95 (*0-8223-0535-6*) Duke.

Barker, Michael & Wise, Robert N., eds. Financing State & Local Economic Development. LC 83-1561. (Duke Press Policy Studies). xxvii, 480p. 1983. text 69.95 (*0-8223-0536-4*) Duke.

— State Employment Policy in Hard Times. LC 83-5674. (Duke Press Policy Studies). xxix, 252p. 1983. text 49.95 (*0-8223-0538-0*) Duke.

Barker, Michael, ed. see Litvak, Lawrence.

Barker, Michael, ed. see Vaughan, Roger J. & Hill, Edward W.

***Barker, Michael J.** Acrostic Journey: Poems in the Key of Life. 96p. (YA). 1999. pap. write for info. (*0-7392-0452-1*, PO3750) Morris Pubng.

Barker, Michael L. Policing in Indian Country. LC 97-52328. 150p. (C). 1998. pap. text 22.50 (*0-911577-44-0*, Criminal Justice) Willow Tree NY.

Barker, Molly. Secret Language. LC 97-4108. (Illus.). 200p. 1997. boxed set 11.95 (*0-87286-328-X*) City Lights.

Barker, Muhammad A. Spoken Urdu, Bk. 1. LC 75-15183. (Spoken Language Ser.). 530p. (YA). (gr. 9-12). 1975. pap. 20.00 (*0-87950-340-8*) Spoken Lang Serv.

— Spoken Urdu, Bk. 2. LC 75-15183. (Spoken Language Ser.). 576p. (YA). (gr. 9-12). 1975. pap. 20.00 (*0-87950-341-6*) Spoken Lang Serv.

— Spoken Urdu, Bk. 3. LC 75-15183. (Spoken Language Ser.). 230p. (YA). (gr. 9-12). 1975. pap. 10.00 (*0-87950-342-4*) Spoken Lang Serv.

— Spoken Urdu, Nos. 1, 2 & 3. 1000p. 1996. pap. 59.95 (*0-614-21655-9*, 1162) Kazi Pubns.

— Spoken Urdu, 3 bks., Set. LC 75-15183. (Spoken Language Ser.). 530p. (YA). (gr. 9-12). 1975. 50.00 (*0-87950-343-2*) Spoken Lang Serv.

Barker, Muhammad A., et al. A Reader of Modern Urdu Poetry. LC 78-396470. (ENG & URD.). 334p. reprint ed. pap. 103.60 (*0-7837-6894-X*, 204672400003) Bks Demand.

— Spoken Urdu, Bks. 1 & 2. Incl. Bk. 1. Spoken Urdu. LC 75-15183. 530p. (YA). (gr. 9-12). audio 100.00 (*0-87950-344-0*); Bk. 1. Spoken Urdu. LC 75-15183. 530p. (YA). (gr. 9-12). pap. 120.00 incl. audio (*0-87950-347-5*); Bk. 2. Spoken Urdu. LC 75-15183. 530p. (YA). (gr. 9-12). audio 85.00 (*0-87950-345-9*); Bk. 2. Spoken Urdu. LC 75-15183. 530p. (YA). (gr. 9-12). pap. 105.00 incl. audio (*0-87950-348-3*); LC 75-15183. (Spoken Language Ser.). 530p. (YA). (gr. 9-12). Set pap. 225.00 incl. audio (*0-87950-349-1*) Spoken Lang Serv.

— Urdu Newspaper Reader. LC 74-21940. (Spoken Language Ser.). (Illus.). 472p. reprint ed. pap. 85.00 incl. audio (*0-87950-339-4*) Spoken Lang Serv.

Barker, Muhammad A., et al. Urdu Newspaper Reader. LC 74-21940. (Spoken Language Ser.). (Illus.). 472p. reprint ed. audio 65.00 (*0-87950-338-6*) Spoken Lang Serv.

Barker, Muhammad A., et al. Urdu Newspaper Reader. LC 74-21940. (Spoken Language Ser.). (Illus.). 472p. 1974. reprint ed. pap. 20.00 (*0-87950-337-8*) Spoken Lang Serv.

Barker, Myrtie. I Am Only One. LC 63-11615. 1963. 2.95 (*0-672-50711-0*, Bobbs) Macmillan.

Barker, Nancy N. The French Experience in Mexico, 1821-1861: A History of Constant Misunderstanding. LC 78-12935. (Illus.). 284p. reprint ed. pap. 88.10 (*0-8357-3891-4*, 203662300004) Bks Demand.

Barker, Nancy N., ed. French Legation in Texas, Vol. 1. (Illus.). 357p. 1970. 29.95 (*0-87611-026-X*) Tex St Hist Assn.

— French Legation in Texas, Vol. 2. (Illus.). 345p. 1970. 29.95 (*0-87611-030-8*) Tex St Hist Assn.

Barker, Narviar. Child Abuse & Neglect. 2nd ed. LC 98-233014. 278p. (C). 1998. per. 47.95 (*0-7872-5241-7*, 41524101) Kendall-Hunt.

Barker, Nicholas. De Triplici Nodo, Triplex Cuneus James I. (The/Books of the Monarchs of England). 256p. 1998. reprint ed. pap. 240.00 (*1-85297-007-3*, Pub. by Archival Facs) St Mut.

— Hortus Eystettensis: The Bishop's Garden & Besler's Magnificent Book. LC 94-7106. (Illus.). 152p. 1994. 60.00 (*0-8109-3424-8*, Pub. by Abrams) Time Warner.

An Asterisk (*) at the beginning of an entry indicates that the title is appearing for the first time.

— Unmade Beds. (Illus.). 96p. 1998. pap. 20.00 (*1-899235-26-4*, 810631, Pub. by Dewi Lewis) Dist Art Pubs.

***Barker, Nicholas, intro.** Botanical Prints from the Hortus Eystettensis: Selections from the Most Beautiful Botanical Book in the World. (Illus.). 64p. 2000. pap. 19.95 (*0-8109-2743-8*, Pub. by Abrams) Time Warner.

***Barker, Nicola.** The Three Button Trick And Other Stories. LC PR6052.A64876A6 1999. 1998. 23.00 (*0-88001-677-9*) HarpC.

Barker, Nicola. Wide Open. LC 98-14083. 304p. 1998. reprint ed. 23.95 (*0-88001-632-9*) HarpC.

Barker, Nicolas. Aldus Mantius & the Development of Greek Script & Type in the Fifteenth Century. 2nd rev. ed. LC 90-84329. xiii, 138p. 1992. 150.00 (*0-8232-1247-5*) Fordham.

Barker, Nicolas, ed. A Potency of Life: Books in Society. (The British Library Studies in the History of the Book). (Illus.). 216p. 1993. 80.00 (*0-7123-0287-5*, Pub. by B23tish Library) U of Toronto Pr.

Barker, Nicolas, et al, eds. Robert Burns: The Poet's Progress. LC 95-71919. (Illus.). 64p. (Orig.). 1995. pap. 12.50 (*0-939084-28-7*) R Mus & Lib.

Barker, Nicolas & Collins, John. A Sequel to an Enquiry into the Nature of Certain Nineteenth Century Pamphlets. (Illus.). 394p. 1992. reprint ed. 55.00 (*0-938768-32-8*) Oak Knoll.

Barker, Nicolas, ed. see Carter, John & Pollard, Graham.

Barker, Nicolas, ed. see Morison, Stanley.

Barker, Nicolas, ed. & rev. see Carter, John.

Barker, Nicolas J. Stanley Morison. LC 76-189157. (Illus.). 566p. 1972. 45.00 (*0-674-83425-9*) HUP.

Barker, Norman, jt. auth. see Foster, Giraud.

Barker, P. Greek We Speak. 25p. 1990. pap. 8.95 (*1-85399-176-7*, Pub. by Brist Class Pr) Focus Pub-R Pullins.

— Latin in Our Language. 78p. (C). 1993. pap. text 8.95 (*1-85399-376-X*, Pub. by Brist Class Pr) Focus Pub-R Pullins.

— Patient Assessment: A Guide for Health Professionals. 2nd ed. (Illus.). 320p. 1997. pap. 49.95 (*1-56593-329-X*, 0659) Singular Publishing.

Barker, P. E., jt. ed. see Ganetsos, G.

Barker, Pat. Another World. pap. write for info. (*0-374-90271-2*) FS&G.

— Another World. LC 99-230285. 278p. 1999. text 25.00 (*0-374-10525-1*) FS&G.

— Another World. 2000. pap. 13.00 (*0-312-20397-7*) St Martin.

— Another World. large type ed. LC 99-38414. 264p. 1999. 29.95 (*0-7838-8750-7*, G K Hall Lrg Type) Mac Lib Ref.

— Blow Your House Down. (Modern Classics). 170p. 2000. reprint ed. pap. 13.00 (*0-86068-398-2*, Pub. by Virago) Trafalgar.

— Border Crossing. 352p. 2001. 24.00 (*0-374-18115-2*) FS&G.

Barker, Pat. Dragon Boats: A Celebration. LC 96-178319. 1996. 24.95 (*0-8348-0365-8*) Weatherhill.

— The Eye in the Door. 280p. 1995. pap. 11.95 (*0-452-27272-6*, W Abrahams Bks) Dutton Plume.

— The Eye in the Door. large type ed. 1996. 25.95 (*1-56895-350-X*, Compass) Wheeler Pub.

— The Ghost Road. 288p. 1996. pap. 12.95 (*0-452-27672-1*, Plume) Dutton Plume.

— The Ghost Road, Vol. 3. large type ed. LC 96-35541. 1996. 25.95 (*1-56895-380-1*, Compass) Wheeler Pub.

— Regeneration. LC 92-44872. (William Abrahams Bks.). 252p. 1993. pap. 12.95 (*0-452-27007-3*, W Abrahams Bks) Dutton Plume.

— Regeneration. large type ed. LC 96-5286. 1996. 25.95 (*1-56895-320-8*, Compass) Wheeler Pub.

— Union Street & Blow Your House Down. LC 99-19836. 416p. 1999. pap. 15.00 (*0-312-24089-9*, Picador USA) St Martin.

***Barker, Patricia, et al, eds.** TRAC 98: Proceedings of the Eighth Annual Theoretical Roman Archaeology Conference, Leicester 1998. (Illus.). 171p. 1999. pap. 28.00 (*1-900188-86-4*, Pub. by Oxbow Bks) David Brown.

Barker, Patrick. Created Rich: How Spiritual Attitudes & Material Means Work Together to Achieve Prosperity. LC 95-35994. (Illus.). 208p. (Orig.). (C). 1995. pap. 9.95 (*0-87961-241-X*) Naturegraph.

***Barker, Paul.** Birthday Stars, Celebration Stars: At Home in the Universe. LC 00-190512. (Illus.). 173p. 2000. 19.95 (*0-9678197-6-8*) Crow Pubng Co.

Barker, Paul, ed. Living As Equals. (Illus.). 172p. (C). 1997. text 24.95 (*0-19-829205-8*) OUP.

— Living as Equals. (Illus.). 176p. 1999. pap. text 16.95 (*0-19-829518-9*) OUP.

Barker, Paul, et al. Naming & Structuring Guidelines for X.500 Directory Pilots. 26p. (Orig.). (C). 1995. pap. text 15.00 (*0-7881-1953-2*) DIANE Pub.

Barker, Paul, ed. see Barker, Robert A.

Barker, Peggy. What Happened When Grandma Died? (Illus.). 32p. 1984. 6.99 (*0-570-04090-6*, 56-1458) Concordia.

Barker, Penelope, ed. Genetics & Society. LC 95-10332. (Reference Shelf Ser.: Vol. 67, No. 3). 1995. 25.00 (*0-8242-0870-6*) Wilson.

***Barker, Peter.** Slavs in Germany--The Sorbian Minority & the German States since 1945. LC 00-32449. (Studies in German Thought & History: Vol. 20). (Illus.). 256p. 2000. 89.95 (*0-7734-7704-7*) E Mellen.

Barker, Peter, ed. German Monitor: The Party of Democratic Socialism in Germany - Modern Post-Communism or Nostalgic Populism? LC 98-196675. (German Monitor Ser.: No. 42). 222p. 1998. pap. 19.50 (*90-420-0350-2*) Editions Rodopi.

Barker, Peter & Ariew, Roger, eds. Revolution & Continuity: Essays in the History & Philosophy of Early Modern Science. LC 90-19633. (Studies in Philosophy & the History of Philosophy: Vol. 24). 222p. 1991. text 42.95 (*0-8132-0738-X*) Cath U Pr.

Barker, Peter, tr. see Duhem, Pierre.

***Barker, Phil & Stevenson, Chris.** The Construction of Power & Authority in Psychiatry. LC 99-44466. 243p. 2000. text 67.50 (*0-7506-3839-7*) Buttrwrth-Heinemann.

Barker, Philip. Basic Child Psychiatry. 6th ed. LC 94-1898. (Illus.). 416p. 1994. pap. 42.95 (*0-632-03772-5*) Blackwell Sci.

— Basic Family Therapy. 4th ed. LC 98-11191. (Illus.). 320p. 1998. pap. text 36.50 (*0-632-04259-1*) OUP.

***Barker, Philip.** Michel Foucault: An Introduction. 176p. 2000. pap. text 19.00 (*0-7486-1038-3*) Col U Pr.

Barker, Philip. Michel Foucault: Subversions of the Subject. LC 93-23231. 1993. text 45.00 (*0-312-10587-8*) St Martin.

— Psychotherapeutic Metaphors: A Guide to Theory & Practice. LC 95-20643. (Basic Principles into Practice Ser.: Vol. 5). 176p. 1996. pap. text 21.95 (*0-87630-776-4*) Brunner-Mazel.

***Barker, Philip.** Top 1000 Scientists: From the Beginning of Time to 2000 AD. 447p. 1999. 55.00 (*1-85776-405-6*, Pub. by Book Guild Ltd) Trans-Atl Phila.

Barker, Philip. Using Metaphors in Psychotherapy. LC 85-15171. 236p. 1992. pap. text 28.95 (*0-87630-716-0*) Brunner-Mazel.

Barker, Philip, jt. auth. see Baldwin, Steve.

Barker, Philip, jt. auth. see White, Roger.

Barker, Philip, jt. ed. see Yazdani, Masoud.

Barker, Philip J. Severe Depression: A Practitioner's Guide. LC 92-33173. 296p. 1992. 42.50 (*1-56593-051-7*, 0299) Thomson Learn.

Barker, Philip J. & Baldwin, Steve, eds. Ethical Issues in Mental Health. 200p. (C). 1991. pap. text 29.95 (*0-412-32950-6*, A5586) Chapman & Hall.

Barker, Philip J. & Davidson, Ben, eds. Psychiatric Nursing: Ethical Strife. (Illus.). 272p. (Orig.). 1997. pap. 38.25 (*1-56593-762-7*, 1482) Singular Publishing.

Barker, Philip J. & Fraser, Douglas, eds. The Nurse As Therapist: A Behavioural Model. LC 85-10935. 250p. (Orig.). 1985. pap. 25.00 (*0-7099-3253-7*, Pub. by C Helm) Routldge.

Barker, Phyllis. The Church School Teacher's Thirty Minute Craft Book. 36p. (Orig.). 1989. pap. 4.95 (*0-8192-4107-5*) Morehouse Pub.

Barker, R., et al. Agricultural Policy Analysis for Transition to a Market - Oriented Economy in Viet Nam. LC 95-131055. (Economic & Social Development Papers: No. 123). 146p. 1994. pap. 16.00 (*92-5-103492-3*, F34923, Pub. by FAO) Bernan Associates.

Barker, R-Lou, ed. see Lindsay, Vachel.

Barker, R. Mildred. Holy Land: A History of the Alfred Shakers. 2nd ed. 53p. 1986. pap. 3.50 (*0-915836-03-3*) United Soc Shakers.

— The Sabbathday Lake Shakers: An Introduction to the Shaker Heritage. 2nd ed. (Illus.). 26p. 1985. pap. 3.00 (*0-915836-04-1*) United Soc Shakers.

Barker, Rachel M. Collecting Rocks. 12p. 1995. pap. 1.25 (*0-16-061615-8*) USGPO.

Barker, Raffaella. The Hook. LC 98-115816. 185p. 1996. write for info. (*0-7475-2749-0*) AMACOM.

***Barker, Ralph.** The Hurricats. (Illus.). 160p. 2000. 29.99 (*0-7524-2005-4*, Pub. by Tempus Pubng) Arcadia Publng.

Barker, Ralph, jt. auth. see Cotton, Sidney.

Barker, Randolph, et al. The Rice Economy of Asia. LC 84-43086. 324p. 1985. pap. text 29.95 (*0-915707-15-2*); lib. bdg. 39.95 (*0-915707-14-4*) Resources Future.

Barker, Ray. The Crown Devon Collectors' Handbook. (Illus.). 120p. 1996. pap. 19.95 (*1-870703-22-7*, Pub. by Francis Jos Pubns) Krause Pubns.

Barker, Raymond C. Collected Essays of Raymond Charles Barker. LC 86-871939. (Mentors of New Thought Ser.). 106p. 1986. pap. 8.95 (*0-87516-578-8*) DeVorss.

— Collected Wisdom. Kramer, Jill, ed. LC 94-32867. 256p. (Orig.). 1994. pap. 10.95 (*1-56170-097-5*, 160) Hay House.

— Money Is God in Action. 16p. pap. 3.50 (*0-87516-502-8*) DeVorss.

— The Power of Decision. LC 87-32058. 165p. 1996. reprint ed. pap. 10.95 (*0-87516-699-7*) DeVorss.

— The Science of Successful Living. LC 57-11392. 145p. 1984. reprint ed. pap. 8.95 (*0-87516-536-2*) DeVorss.

— Spiritual Healing for Today. LC 88-70091. 136p. (Orig.). 1988. pap. 8.95 (*0-87516-607-5*) DeVorss.

— Treat Yourself to Life. LC 87-30216. 120p. 1996. reprint ed. pap. 9.95 (*0-87516-700-4*) DeVorss.

— Treatment: What It Is & How to Do It. 16p. pap. 3.50 (*0-87516-504-4*) DeVorss.

— You Are Invisible. 2nd enl. ed. LC 73-1654. 160p. 1986. reprint ed. pap. 8.95 (*0-87516-576-1*) DeVorss.

Barker, Reginald W. Taxonomic Notes on the Species, Figured by H. B. Brady in His Report on the Foraminifera ...During the Years 1873-1876. LC 62-6771. (Society of Economic Paleontologists & Mineralogists, Special Publication Ser.: No. 9). 262p. reprint ed. pap. 81.30 (*0-608-12958-5*, 202473500038) Bks Demand.

***Barker-Revell, Lindel.** The Goddess: Myths & Stories. LC 98-75031. (Illus.). 160p. 1999. 8.98 (*0-7651-1025-3*) Smithmark.

Barker, Richard. Case Method: Entity Relationship Modeling. (C). 1991. pap. text. write for info. (*0-201-56549-8*) Addison-Wesley.

— Case Method: Entity Relationship Modelling. 240p. (C). 1990. 59.95 (*0-201-41696-4*) Addison-Wesley.

— CASE Method Tasks & Deliverables. LC 89-48834. 352p. (C). 1990. 59.95 (*0-201-41697-2*) Addison-Wesley.

— Metodo Case: Modelo Relacional. (SPA.). 256p. (C). 1994. pap. text 20.00 (*0-201-60111-7*) Addison-Wesley.

— Oracle Case: Method Function & Process Modelling. 400p. (C). 1992. 64.95 (*0-201-56525-0*) Addison-Wesley.

Barker, Richard H. Mr. Cibber of Drury Lane. LC 71-160002. reprint ed. 32.50 (*0-404-00654-X*) AMS Pr.

Barker, Richard H., jt. auth. see Boyd, Marie A.

Barker, Richard H., ed. see MacCurdy, Rahno M., et al.

Barker, Richard M. & Puckett, Jay A. Design of Highway Bridges: Based on AASHTO LRFD, Bridge Design Specifications. LC 96-23741. 1192p. 1997. 120.00 (*0-471-30434-4*) Wiley.

Barker, Richard W. Lone Fathers & Masculinities. 304p. 1994. 72.95 (*1-85628-522-7*, Pub. by Avebry) Ashgate Pub Co.

Barker, Robert A. Philippine Diary: A Journal of Life As a Japanese Prisoner of War. Barker, Paul & Gordon, Harry, eds. (Illus.). 180p. 1990. 27.50 (*0-9624999-1-9*) R A Barker Found.

Barker, Robert A. & Alexander, Vincent C. Evidence in New York State & Federal Courts. 1050p. (C). 1996. pap. text, student ed. write for info. (*0-314-09725-2*) West Pub.

— New York Practice Vol. 5: Evidence in New York State & Federal Courts. LC 95-62237. xxxv, 1050p. 1996. 99.00 (*0-314-08636-6*) West Pub.

Barker, Robert A., jt. auth. see Chase, Oscar G.

Barker, Robert L. The Business of Psychotherapy. LC 82-1307. (Illus.). 376p. 1982. text 57.50 (*0-231-05438-6*) Col U Pr.

— Milestones in the Development of Social Work & Social Welfare. LC 99-11809. 1999. write for info. (*0-87101-309-6*, NASW Pr) Natl Assn Soc Wkrs.

— The Resource Book: Directory of Organizations, Associations, Self Help Groups & Hotlines for Mental Health & Human Services Professionals & Their Clients. LC 86-25765. 165p. 1987. text 4.95 (*0-86656-622-8*) Haworth Pr.

— The Social Work Dictionary. 3rd ed. 448p. (C). 1995. lib. bdg. 34.95 (*0-87101-253-7*, 2537) Natl Assn Soc Wkrs.

— The Social Work Dictionary. 4th ed. LC 98-8333. 32p. 1998. 34.95 (*0-87101-298-7*) Natl Assn Soc Wkrs.

— Social Work in Private Practice. 2nd ed. LC 91-35705. 209p. (C). 1991. 26.95 (*0-87101-198-0*) Natl Assn Soc Wkrs.

***Barker, Robert L. & Branson, Douglas M.** Forensic Social Work: Legal Aspects of Professional Practice. 2nd ed. LC 99-39464. 262p. 2000. pap. 24.95 (*0-7890-0868-8*) Haworth Pr.

***Barker, Robert L. & Branson, Douglas M., eds.** Forensic Social Work: Legal Aspects of Professional Practice. 2nd ed. LC 99-39464. 262p. (C). 2000. 49.95 (*0-7890-0867-X*) Haworth Pr.

Barker, Robert L. & Branson, Dougls M. Forensic Social Work: Legal Aspects of Professional Practice. LC 92-31570. 150p. 1993. 39.95 (*1-56024-351-1*); pap. 19.95 (*1-56024-352-X*) Haworth Pr.

Barker, Rocky. Saving All the Parts: Reconciling Economics & the Endangered Species Act. LC 93-4640. 220p. 1993. pap. 17.95 (*1-55963-201-1*); text 38.00 (*1-55963-202-X*) Island Pr.

Barker, Rocky, jt. auth. see Retallic, Ken.

Barker, Rodney. And the Waters Turned to Blood. 1998. per. 13.00 (*0-684-83845-1*) S&S Trade.

— And the Waters Turned to Blood: The Ultimate Biological Threat. LC 97-86. (Illus.). 334p. 1997. 23.50 (*0-684-83126-0*) S&S Trade.

— The Broken Circle: A True Story of Murder & Magic in Indian Country. 1993. mass mkt. 4.99 (*0-8041-1147-2*) Ivy Books.

— Dancing with the Devil: Sex, Espionage & the U.S. Marines: The Clayton Lonetree Story. (Illus.). 336p 1996. 24.00 (*0-684-81099-9*) Ivy Books.

— Political Ideas in Modern Britain: In & after the 20th Century. 2nd ed. 360p. (C). 1997. 85.00 (*0-415-16166-5*); pap. 25.99 (*0-415-07121-6*) Routledge.

— Political Legitimacy & the State. 224p. 1990. 55.00 (*0-19-827495-5*) OUP.

— Politics, Peoples, & Government: Themes in British Political Thought since the Nineteenth Century. LC 93-30828. 1994. text 49.95 (*0-312-10382-4*) St Martin.

Barker, Roger, et al. Frustration & Regression: An Experiment with Young Children. LC 75-34765. (Studies in Play & Games). (Illus.). 1976. reprint ed. 28.95 (*0-405-07934-6*) Ayer.

***Barker, Roger A.** A Practical Guide to Movement Disorders: Diagnosis, Investigation & Treatment. (Illus.). 224p. 2000. pap. text 57.50 (*0-7506-4469-9*) Buttrwrth-Heinemann.

***Barker, Roger A. & Barasi, Stephen.** Neuroscience at a Glance. LC 98-22073. (At a Glance Ser.). (Illus.). 96p. 1999. pap. text 21.95 (*0-86542-869-7*) Blackwell Sci.

Barker, Roger G. Ecological Psychology: Concepts & Methods for Studying the Environment of Human Behavior. LC 68-21287. vi, 242p. 1968. 37.50 (*0-8047-0658-1*) Stanford U Pr.

— Habitats, Environments, & Human Behavior. LC 77-82912. (Jossey-Bass Social & Behavioral Science Ser.). 351p. reprint ed. pap. 108.90 (*0-608-17773-3*, 205655800072) Bks Demand.

Barker, Roger G. & Gump, Paul V. Big School, Small School: High School Size & Student Behavior. LC LB3013.B3. (Illus.). 260p. 1972. reprint ed. pap. 30.00 (*0-608-00859-1*, 206165000010) Bks Demand.

Barker, Roger G. & Schoggen, Phil. Qualities of Community Life. LC 72-13601. (Jossey-Bass Behavioral Science Ser.). (Illus.). 576p. reprint ed. pap. 178.60 (*0-8357-4696-8*, 205235100008) Bks Demand.

Barker, Roger L. & Coletta, Gerard C., eds. Performance of Protective Clothing, STP 900. LC 86-10706. (Special Technical Publication Ser.). (Illus.). 625p. 1986. text 60.00 (*0-8031-0461-8*, STP900) ASTM.

Barker, Ronald & Harding, Anthony. Automobile Design: Twelve Great Designers & Their Work. 2nd ed. (Illus.). 411p. 1992. 29.00 (*1-56091-210-3*, R-115) Soc Auto Engineers.

Barker, Ronnie. Dancing in the Moonlight: Early Years on the Stage. (Illus.). 160p. 1994. 34.95 (*0-340-59104-8*, Pub. by Hodder & Stought Ltd) Trafalgar.

— It's Hello from Him. large type ed. 206p. 1989. reprint ed. 20.95 (*1-85089-341-1*, Pub. by ISIS Lrg Prnt) Transaction Pubs.

Barker, Ruth L. Caballeros. Cortes, Carlos E., ed. Van Sweringen, Norma, tr. LC 76-1237. (Chicano Heritage Ser.). (Illus.). 1977. reprint ed. lib. bdg. 33.95 (*0-405-09484-1*) Ayer.

Barker, S. Omar. Ol' S. O. B. Sez: Cowboy Limericks. LC 98-23260. (Illus.). 96p. 1998. pap. 9.95 (*1-56044-641-2*) Falcon Pub Inc.

Barker, Sandy. It Began with an Island: A True Story of Love & Adventure in a Tropical Paradise. 2nd rev. ed. (Illus.). 213p. 1985. reprint ed. pap. 8.30 (*0-9635943-7-0*) S Barker.

Barker, Sarah & Harrigan, Peter. Introduction to Performance: Beginning the Creative Process of the Actor. 2nd ed. 128p. (C). 1996. pap. text 14.95 (*0-8403-9161-7*) Kendall-Hunt.

Barker, Scott. Arizona: Off the Beaten Path: A Guide to Unique Places. 2nd ed. Tripp, Steve, ed. LC 98-41949. (Off the Beaten Path Ser.). (Illus.). 192p. 1999. pap. 12.95 (*0-7627-0262-1*, Pub. by Globe Pequot) Sterling.

Barker, Sebastian. Guarding the Border: Selected Poems. 125p. 1993. pap. 18.95 (*1-870612-76-0*, Pub. by Enitha Pr) Dufour.

— The Hand in the Well. LC 96-223587. 64p. 1996. pap. 15.95 (*1-870612-22-1*, Pub. by Enitha Pr) Dufour.

Barker, Shane R. Magnifying Your Aaronic Priesthood Calling. 1995. pap. 7.95 (*0-88494-977-X*) Bookcraft Inc.

Barker, Shirley. Dark Hills Under. LC 76-144739. (Yale Series of Younger Poets: No. 32). reprint ed. 18.00 (*0-404-53832-0*) AMS Pr.

Barker, Simon. 'Tis Pity She's a Whore. (Routledge English Texts Ser.). 240p. (C). 1997. pap. 20.99 (*0-415-04947-4*) Routledge.

Barker, Stephen, ed. Excavations & Their Objects: Freud's Collection of Antiquity. LC 94-8842. 183p. (C). 1996. text 44.50 (*0-7914-2293-3*); pap. text 14.95 (*0-7914-2294-1*) State U NY Pr.

— Signs of Change: Premodern--Modern--Postmodern. LC 94-25974. (SUNY Series in Contemporary Studies in Philosophy & Literature: No. 4). 440p. (C). 1996. pap. text 24.95 (*0-7914-2434-0*) State U NY Pr.

— Signs of Change: Premodern--Modern--Postmodern. LC 94-25974. (SUNY Series in Contemporary Studies in Philosophy & Literature: No. 4). 440p. (C). 1996. text 74.50 (*0-7914-2433-2*) State U NY Pr.

Barker, Stephen, photos by. Nightswimming: Stephen Barker. (Illus.). 96p. 1999. 60.00 (*0-944092-54-3*) Twin Palms Pub.

— Nightswimming: Stephen Barker. limited ed. (Illus.). 96p. 1999. 400.00 (*0-944092-55-1*) Twin Palms Pub.

Barker, Stephen F. The Elements of Logic. 5th ed. 291p. (C). 1988. 66.88 (*0-07-003730-2*); pap., student ed. 28.13 (*0-07-003732-9*) McGraw.

Barker, Stephen F., ed. Proof & Explanation: The Virginia Lectures by John Wisdom. 242p. (Orig.). (C). 1991. pap. text 26.50 (*0-8191-8042-4*); lib. bdg. 49.00 (*0-8191-8041-6*) U Pr of Amer.

Barker, Stephen F., jt. ed. see Achinstein, Peter.

Barker, Susan & Ward, Brian J. Explore the Barossa State Print & RGSA (SA Adelaide 1991) 160p. (C). 1991. 50.00 (*0-7855-0326-9*, Pub. by Royal Geograp Soc) St Mut.

Barker, T. C. & Harris, J. R. A Mersyside Town in the Industrial Revolution: St. Helens, 1750-1900. LC 93-30817. 1993. 35.00 (*0-7146-4555-9*, Pub. by F Cass Pubs) Intl Spec Bk.

Barker, T. E., et al, eds. Perspectives on Economic Development: Essays in the Honour of W. Arthur Lewis. LC 81-43790. (Illus.). 324p. (Orig.). (C). 1982. pap. text 27.00 (*0-8191-2382-X*) U Pr of Amer.

Barker, Tara. The Woman's Book of Orgasm: A Guide to the Ultimate Sexual Pleasure. LC 97-32606. 1998. 12.00 (*0-8065-1966-5*) Carol Pub Group.

Barker, Teresa. A Woman's Own Guide to Pregnancy & Childbirth. 64p. (Orig.). 1989. pap. 6.95 (*0-9626223-0-3*) Womens Hlthcare Pr.

Barker, Terrence S. & Lecomber, Richard. Economic Planning for 1972: An Appraisal of "The Task Ahead" LC 79-503098. (PSI Report Ser.). iv, 707p. 1969. write for info. (*0-85374-018-6*) Pol Studies Inst.

***Barker, Terry.** After Acorn: Meditations on the Message of Canada's People's Poet. LC 00-21663. 2000. pap. write for info. (*1-884206-07-7*, UnMon America) Unfinish Monumnt.

Barker, Terry, et al, eds. Global Warming & Energy Demand. (Global Environmental Change Ser.). (Illus.). 352p. (Orig.). (C). 1995. pap. 29.99 (*0-415-11601-5*, B4726) Routledge.

Barker, Terry & Kohler, Jonathan, eds. International Competitiveness & Environmental Policies. LC 97-39248. (International Studies in Environmental Policy Making Ser.). 304p. 1998. 90.00 (*1-85898-778-4*) E Elgar.

Barker, Terry & Peterson, William, eds. The Cambridge Multisectoral Dynamic Model. (Cambridge Studies in Applied Econometrics: No. 5). (Illus.). 536p. 1988. text 85.00 (*0-521-33004-1*) Cambridge U Pr.

B

Barker, Theo & Gerhold, Dorian. The Rise & Rise of Road Transport, 1700-1900. (New Studies in Economic & Social History: No. 21). 100p. (C). 1995. text 34.95 (*0-521-55280-X*) Cambridge U Pr.

— The Rise & Rise of Road Transport, 1700-1900. (New Studies in Economic & Social History: No. 21). 100p. (C). 1996. pap. text 10.95 (*0-521-55773-9*) Cambridge U Pr.

Barker, Theo & Sutcliffe, Anthony, eds. Megalopolis: The Giant City in History. LC 92-33445. 200p. 1993. text 65.00 (*0-312-09147-8*) St Martin.

***Barker, Thomas & Britz, Marjie.** Jokers Wild: Legalized Gambling in the Twenty-First Century. LC 99-59852. 2000. write for info. (*0-275-96587-2*, Praeger Pubs) Greenwood.

Barker, Thomas & Carter, David L. Police Deviance. 3rd ed. LC 90-82315. 442p. (C). 1994. pap. 35.95 (*0-87084-714-7*) Anderson Pub Co.

Barker, Thomas, et al. Police Systems & Practices: An Introduction. LC 93-39495. 354p. 1994. 63.80 (*0-13-682865-5*) P-H.

Barker, Thomas B. Greenberg's American Flyer S Gauge Operating & Repair Manual, 1945-1965. 2nd ed. Greenberg, Linda, ed. (Illus.). 80p. 1995. pap. 15.95 (*0-89778-017-5*, 10-6434, Greenberg Books) Kalmbach.

— Quality by Experimental Design. 2nd expanded rev. ed. LC 94-18956. (Quality & Reliability Ser.: Vol. 43). (Illus.). 504p. 1994. text 65.00 (*0-8247-8910-5*) Dekker.

Barker, Thomas C. Essentials of Materials Management. 335p. (C). 1989. 180.00 (*0-7855-4620-0*, Pub. by Inst Pur & Supply) St Mut.

Barker, Thomas M. Army, Aristocracy, Monarchs: War, Society & Government in Austria, 1618-1780. LC 81-85645. (Studies on Society in Change, No. 16 - War & Society in East Central Europe: Vol.7). 1982. text 55.50 (*0-930888-14-6*, EE8146) Col U Pr.

— Double Eagle & Crescent: Vienna's 2nd Turkish Siege & Its Historical Setting. LC 67-63760. (Illus.). 465p. reprint ed. pap. 144.20 (*0-8357-9592-6*, 201010400068) Bks Demand.

— Social Revolutionaries & Secret Agents: The Carinthian Slovene Partisans & Britain's Special Operations Executive. (East European Monographs). 272p. 1990. text 63.00 (*0-88033-173-9*, Pub. by East Eur Monographs) Col U Pr.

Barker, Thomas M., ed. Frederick the Great & the Making of Prussia. LC 76-23215. (European Problem Studies). 116p. 1976. reprint ed. pap. 8.50 (*0-88275-456-4*) Krieger.

Barker, Thomas M. & Martinez, Rafael B., eds. Armed Forces & Society in Spain Past & Present: A Collaborative Study. 379p. 1988. text 64.50 (*0-88033-959-4*, Pub. by East Eur Monographs) Col U Pr.

Barker, Thomas M. & Moritsch, Andreas. The Slovenes of Carinthia. LC 84-80620. (East European Monographs: No. 169). 415p. 1984. text 79.00 (*0-88033-061-9*, Pub. by East Eur Monographs) Col U Pr.

— The Slovenes of Carinthia. 2nd ed. LC 79-15399. (Eastern European Studies of Columbia University). 59.00 (*0-685-42094-9*) East Eur Monographs.

Barker, Thomas T. Writing Software Documentation: A Task-Oriented Approach. LC 97-22198. 484p. 1997. pap. 48.00 (*0-205-19576-8*) Allyn.

— Writing Software Documentation: A Task Oriented Approach. Dragga, Sam, ed. (Series in Technical Communication). 128p. (C). 1998. pap., teacher ed. write for info. (*0-205-27502-8*, T7502-2) Allyn.

Barker, Thomas T., ed. Perspectives on Software Documentation: Inquiries & Innovations. (Technical Communications Ser.). 279p. 1991. text 38.95 (*0-89503-069-1*); pap. text 29.22 (*0-89503-068-3*) Baywood Pub.

Barker, Tom. Police Ethics: Crisis in Law Enforcement. LC 96-3551. 94p. 1996. 36.95 (*0-398-06613-2*); pap. 20.95 (*0-398-06614-0*) C C Thomas.

Barker, Tracy, jt. auth. see Barker, David.

Barker, Trevor A., jt. ed. see Zulueta, J. R.

Barker, Twiley W., Jr., jt. auth. see Barker, Lucius J.

Barker, Vernon C. & Aufmann, Richard N. Essential Mathematics with Applications, 4 vols. 4th ed. 362p. (C). 1994. pap. text 35.96 (*0-395-71229-7*) HM.

— Essential Mathematics with Applications. 4th annot. ed. (C). 1995. text, teacher ed. write for info. (*0-614-25392-6*) HM.

Barker, Vernon C., et al. Essential Mathematics with Applications. 5th ed. LC 98-71982. 1 vp. 1999. pap. text 35.97 (*0-395-90710-1*) HM.

Barker, Vernon C., jt. auth. see Aufmann, Richard N.

Barker, Victor. Posture Makes Perfect Health. (Illus.). 206p. (Orig.). 1993. pap. 22.00 (*0-87040-871-2*) Japan Pubns USA.

Barker, Virgil. From Realism to Reality in Recent American Painting. LC 68-57301. (Essay Index Reprint Ser.). 1977. 13.95 (*0-8369-0173-8*) Ayer.

Barker, W. L to the P Harmonic Analysis on SL(2,R) LC 88-22227. (Memoirs Ser.: No. 76/393). 110p. 1988. pap. 17.00 (*0-8218-2456-2*, MEMO/76/393) Am Math.

Barker, W. & Sally, P., eds. Harmonic Analysis on Reductive Groups: Proceedings of the Bowdoin Conference, 1989. (Progress in Mathematics Ser.: Vol. 101). xii, 388p. 1991. 80.50 (*0-8176-3514-9*) Birkhauser.

Barker, W. A., et al, eds. Documents of English History, 1832-1950. 1954. 49.50 (*0-317-07647-7*) Elliots Bks.

Barker, W. A., et al. General History of England, 1688-1832. 3rd ed. 329p. 1963. 69.50 (*0-614-01818-8*) Elliots Bks.

Barker, W. H. West African Folk-Tales. (B. E. Ser.: No. 41). (Illus.). 1917. 25.00 (*0-8115-2992-4*) Periodicals Srv.

Barker, Wayne G. Cryptanalysis of an Enciphered Code Problem: Where an "Additive" Method of Encipherment Has Been Used. 174p. 1979. pap. 26.80 (*0-89412-037-9*) Aegean Park Pr.

— Cryptanalysis of Shift-Register Generated Stream Cipher Systems. 243p. (Orig.). (C). 1984. pap. 48.80 (*0-89412-062-X*) Aegean Park Pr.

— Cryptanalysis of the Double Transposition Cipher. 163p. 1994. pap. 34.80 (*0-89412-254-1*) Aegean Park Pr.

— Cryptanalysis of the Hagelin Cryptograph. 223p. 1978. pap. 32.80 (*0-89412-022-0*) Aegean Park Pr.

— Cryptanalysis of the Simple Substitution Cipher with Word Divisions. LC 75-18083. 132p. 1975. pap. 16.80 (*0-89412-000-X*) Aegean Park Pr.

— Cryptanalysis of the Single Columnar Transposition Cipher - with Added Computer Program Written in Basic. rev. ed. 146p. (C). 1992. pap. 28.80 (*0-89412-192-8*) Aegean Park Pr.

— Cryptograms in Spanish. 127p. 1987. pap. 4.95 (*0-89412-058-1*) Aegean Park Pr.

Barker, Wayne G. Cryptograms, One Hundred Ten Cryptograms to Be Solved. 125p. 1980. lib. bdg. 14.45 (*0-89412-090-5*) Aegean Park Pr.

Barker, Wayne G. Cryptograms, One Hundred Ten Cryptograms to Be Solved. 119p. (gr. 9 up). 1980. pap. 4.95 (*0-89412-043-3*) Aegean Park Pr.

— Introduction to the Analysis of the Data Encryption Standard (DES) 190p. (C). 1991. pap. 48.80 (*0-89412-169-3*) Aegean Park Pr.

Barker, Wayne G., ed. The History of Codes & Ciphers in the U. S. During the Period Between the World Wars Pt. I: 1919-1929. 186p. 1979. pap. 26.80 (*0-89412-039-5*); lib. bdg. 36.30 (*0-89412-102-2*) Aegean Park Pr.

— The History of Codes & Ciphers in the United States During World War I. (Illus.). 263p. 1979. pap. 26.80 (*0-89412-031-X*) Aegean Park Pr.

— History of Codes & Ciphers in the United States Prior to World War I. 140p. 1979. pap. 26.80 (*0-89412-026-3*) Aegean Park Pr.

— History of Codes & Ciphers in U. S. During the Period Between the World Wars, Pt. II: 1930-1939. 112p. 1989. pap. 26.80 (*0-89412-165-0*) Aegean Park Pr.

Barker, Wayne G. & Coffman, Rodney E. The Anatomy of Two Traitors: The Defection of Bernon F. Mitchell & William H. Martin. LC 81-69674. 131p. 1981. pap. 4.95 (*0-89412-041-7*) Aegean Park Pr.

Barker, Wendy. Let the Ice Speak: Poems by Wendy Barker. 72p. 1990. 9.95 (*0-87886-134-3*) Greenfld Rev Lit.

— Lunacy of Light: Emily Dickinson & the Experience of Metaphor. LC 86-6455. (Ad Feminam Ser.). 235p. 1991. pap. 16.95 (*0-8093-1707-9*) S Ill U Pr.

***Barker, Wendy.** Way of Whiteness. 72p. 2000. pap. (*0-930324-55-2*) Wings Pr.

Barker, Wendy & Gilbert, Sandra M., eds. The House Is Made of Poetry: The Art of Ruth Stone. LC 95-17839. (Ad Feminam Ser.). 232p. 1996. 34.95 (*0-8093-2012-6*) S Ill U Pr.

Barker, Wiley F., ed. The Arteries. 503p. 1993. 89.95 (*1-879702-07-X*, LN0207) CRC Pr.

Barker, Will. Be an Angel: An Alphabetical Inspiration. LC 95-90675. (Illus.). 60p. 1995. write for info. (*0-9648718-0-7*) Wills Wrks.

Barker, William. Puritan Profiles: 54 Influential Puritans When the Westminster Confession of Faith Was Written. unabridged ed. 320p. 1996. 23.99 (*1-85792-191-7*, Pub. by Christian Focus) Spring Arbor Dist.

Barker, William, ed. see Mulcaster, Richard.

Barker, William C. Language of the Mayas: Structure of Maya Speech & Writing. 200p. 1991. pap. write for info. (*1-880365-00-6*) Prof Pr NC.

Barker, William E. Aryan America: Race, Revolution & the Hitler Legacy. 484p. 1993. pap. 19.95 (*0-9634434-0-2*) Falcon Ridge Pub.

Barker, William H. Adding Life to Years: Organized Geriatrics Services in Great Britain & Implications for the United States. LC 86-46279. (Johns Hopkins Series in Contemporary Medicine & Public Health). (Illus.). 262p. 1987. reprint ed. pap. 81.30 (*0-608-06702-4*, 206689900009) Bks Demand.

Barker, William P. Do You Know Me? 370p. 1996. pap. 11.99 (*0-529-10636-1*, DYKM) World Publng.

Barker, William S. & Godfrey, W. Robert, eds. Theonomy: A Reformed Critique. 252p. 1990. pap. 17.99 (*0-310-52171-8*) Zondervan.

Barker, William V. Early Families of Herkimer County, New York: Descendants of the Burnetsfield Patentees. 384p. 1999. reprint ed. pap. 32.50 (*0-8063-1078-2*, 350, Pub. by Clearfield Co) ACCESS Pubs Network.

Barker, William W. SEC Registration of Public Offerings under the Securities Act of 1933. LC 97-32952. 1997. write for info. (*1-57073-490-9*) Amer Bar Assn.

Barker, Windy, ed. see Moore, Michael.

Barkeri, E. H., ed. see Etymologicum.

Barkeshli, Kasra & Volakis, John L. Applications of the Conjugate Gradient FFT Method in Scattering & Radiation Including Simulations with Impedance Boundary Conditions. LC QC0670.. (University of Michigan Reports: No. 025921-21-T). 287p. reprint ed. pap. 89.00 (*0-7837-1389-4*, 204156700021) Bks Demand.

Barket, James, tr. see Planyavsky, Alfred.

Barkey, Henri J. Reluctant Neighbor: Turkey's Role in the Middle East. LC 96-39739. 1996. pap. text 17.95 (*1-878379-64-X*) US Inst Peace.

Barkey, Henri J. & Fuller, Graham E. Turkey's Kurdish Question. LC 97-30696. (Carnegie Commission on Preventing Deadly Conflict Ser.). 264p. 1997. pap. 22.95 (*0-8476-8553-5*) Rowman.

— Turkey's Kurdish Question. LC 97-30696. (Carnegie Commission on Preventing Deadly Conflict Ser.). 264p. 1998. 65.00 (*0-8476-8552-7*) Rowman.

Barkey, Karen. Bandits & Bureaucrats: The Ottoman Route of State Centralization. LC 94-6099. (Wilder House Series in Politics, History, & Culture). (Illus.). 1994. text 39.95 (*0-8014-2944-7*) Cornell U Pr.

— Bandits & Bureaucrats: The Ottoman Route to State Centralization. (Wilder House Series in Politics, History, & Culture). (Illus.). 304p. 1996. pap. text 16.95 (*0-8014-8419-7*) Cornell U Pr.

Barkey, Karen & Von Hagen, Mark. After Empire: Multiethnic Societies & Nation-Building:The Soviet Union & Russian, Ottoman & Habsburg Empires. LC 96-50066. 208p. (C). 1997. pap. text 24.00 (*0-8133-2964-7*, Pub. by Westview) HarpC.

Barkey, Tom. Amazing Grace: An Understanding of God's Great Love for Us. (Illus.). 80p. (Orig.). 1993. pap. write for info. (*0-9626910-2-X*) Power Liv Min.

— Forbid Not Prophecy. 125p. (Orig.). (YA). (gr. 8). 1991. pap. 5.95 (*0-9626910-1-1*) Power Liv Min.

— God Is ... My Strength. Mackall, Phyllis, ed. 86p. (Orig.). (J). (gr. 8). 1990. pap. 6.95 (*0-9626910-0-3*) Power Liv Min.

Barkham, Richard, et al. The Determinants of Small Firm Growth: An Inter-Regional Study in the U. K. 1986-90. 270p. 1995. pap. 34.95 (*1-85302-331-0*, Pub. by Jessica Kingsley) Taylor & Francis.

Barkhausen, Hans. Filmpropaganda Fur Deutschland Im Ersten und Zweiten Weltkrieg. (Weitere Monographien Zur Filmgeschichte Ser.). (GER.). 328p. 1982. write for info. (*3-487-08243-8*) G Olms Pubs.

Barkhordar-Nahai, Gina. Moonlight on the Avenue of Faith. LC 98-33767. 384p. 1999. 24.00 (*0-15-100388-2*) Harcourt.

***Barkhordar-Nahai, Gina.** Moonlight on the Avenue of Faith. 400p. 2000. reprint ed. per. 13.95 (*0-671-04283-1*, WSP) PB.

Barkhouse, Joyce, jt. auth. see Atwood, Margaret.

Barkhudarov, S. Dictionary of Eighteenth Century Russian Language, Vol. 3. (ENG & RUS.). 296p. (C). 1987. 90.00 (*0-7855-6437-3*, Pub. by Collets) St Mut.

— Dictionary of Eighteenth Century Russian Language, Vol. 5. (ENG & RUS.). 256p. (C). 1989. 90.00 (*0-7855-5051-8*, Pub. by Collets) St Mut.

— Orthographical Dictionary of the Russian Language. (RUS.). 480p. (C). 1980. 90.00 (*0-7855-5048-8*, Pub. by Collets) St Mut.

Barkhudarov, S., ed. Dictionary of Eighteenth Century Russian Language, VOL. 4. (ENG & RUS.). 256p. (C). 1988. 90.00 (*0-7855-5052-6*, Pub. by Collets) St Mut.

Barkhudarova, S. G., et al, eds. Orthograhic Dictionary of the Russian Language. 25th ed. (RUS.). 400p. 1987. reprint ed. 12.95 (*0-8285-5444-7*) Firebird NY.

***Barkhuysen, T., et al.** The Execution of Strasbourg & Geneva Human Rights Decisions in the National Legal Order. LC 99-11417. (International Studies in Human Rights). xxiii, 384p. 1999. 117.00 (*90-411-1152-2*) Kluwer Law Intl.

Barkie, Karen E. Fancy, Sweet & Sugarfree. 176p. 1985. pap. 7.95 (*0-312-28164-1*) St Martin.

— Sweet & Sugar Free: Nutritional Sweets Cookbook. 5.95 (*0-317-05971-8*) Hypoglycemia Foun.

Barkin, Anya, ed. see Lavenia, George P.

Barkin, Carol. When Your Kid Goes to College: A Parent's Survival College. LC 99-11099. 176p. 1999. pap. 12.00 (*0-380-79840-9*, Eos) Morrow Avon.

Barkin, Carol & James, Elizabeth. The Holiday Handbook. LC 92-29846. 256p. (J). 1994. 17.00 (*0-395-65011-9*, Clarion Bks) HM.

— The New Complete Babysitter's Handbook. LC 93-39345. (Illus.). 160p. (J). (gr. 4-8). 1995. 16.95 (*0-395-66557-4*, Clarion Bks); pap. 7.95 (*0-395-66558-2*, Clarion Bks) HM.

— Social Smarts: Manners for Today's Kids. LC 95-35613. (Illus.). 112p. (J). (gr. 4-8). 1996. 15.00 (*0-395-66585-X*, Clarion Bks) HM.

Barkin, Carol, jt. auth. see James, Elizabeth.

Barkin, David. Distorted Development. 2nd ed. (C). 1929. text 45.00 (*0-8133-8675-6*); pap. text 15.95 (*0-8133-8676-4*) Westview.

— El Uso de la Tierra Agricola en Mexico: The Use of Agricultural Land in Mexico. (Research Reports: No. 17). (SPA.). 37p. (Orig.). (C). 1981. pap. 5.00 (*0-935391-16-9*, RR-17) UCSD Ctr US-Mex.

Barkin, George, ed. see Bierce, Ambrose.

Barkin, J. Samuel & Shambaugh, George E. Anarchy & the Environment: The International Relations of Common Pool Resources. LC 98-41202. 256p. (C). 1999. text 54.50 (*0-7914-4183-0*); pap. text 17.95 (*0-7914-4184-9*) State U NY Pr.

Barkin, Jamie S. & O'Phelan, Cesar A., eds. Advanced Therapeutic Endoscopy. LC 90-8645. (Illus.). 383p. 1990. pap. 118.80 (*0-7837-8355-8*, 204914500010) Bks Demand.

— Advanced Therapeutic Endoscopy. 2nd ed. 434p. 1994. text 158.00 (*0-7817-0155-4*) Lppncott W & W.

Barkin, Kenneth & Pelzel, Thomas. European Pewter in Everyday Life, 1600-1900. (Illus.). 71p. 1987. 15.00 (*0-932173-02-0*) Sweeney Art Gallery.

Barkin, Kenneth D. The Controversy over German Industrialization, 1890-1902. LC 78-101359. (Illus.). 317p. reprint ed. pap. 98.30 (*0-8357-8852-0*, 205675000085) Bks Demand.

— Folk Art & Function in Europe: 1600-1900. (University Art Gallery, 1993 Ser.). (Illus.). 36p. (Orig.). 1993. pap. text. write for info. (*0-932173-12-8*) Sweeney Art Gallery.

Barkin, Kenneth D., contrib. by. Arts & Crafts of Late Medieval Europe: 1350-1550. (Illus.). 32p. (Orig.). 1996. pap. 7.00 (*0-932173-15-2*) Sweeney Art Gallery.

Barkin-Leeds, Temme. John Portman: A Retrospective. LC 98-61880. (Illus.). 64p. 1999. pap. 15.00 (*0-9651743-2-8*) Barkin-Leeds.

Barkin-Leeds, Temme, ed. see Kuspit, Donald.

Barkin, Leonard, jt. ed. see Grolnick, Simon A.

Barkin, Roger M. Problem-Oriented Pediatric Diagnosis. 320p. 1990. spiral bd. 32.00 (*0-316-08102-7*) Lppncott W & W.

— Problem Oriented with Pediatric Diagnosis. 1990. 15.95 (*0-316-08104-3*, Little Brwn Med Div) Lppncott W & W.

— Problem Oriented with Pediatric Diagnosis. 1990. 10.95 (*0-316-08103-5*, Little Brwn Med Div) Lppncott W & W.

— 2000 Year Book of Medicine. (Illus.). 629p. 2000. text 82.00 (*0-8151-2903-3*, 31814) Mosby Inc.

Barkin, Roger M. & Rosen, Peter. Emergency Medicine: Concepts & Clinical Practice. 4th ed. LC 97-33346. (Illus.). 3312p. (C). (gr. 13). 1997. text 255.00 (*0-8151-3774-5*, 29223) Mosby Inc.

— Emergency Pediatrics: A Guide to Ambulatory Care. 5th ed. LC 98-26889. 1998. pap. text 169.00 (*0-323-00326-5*) Mosby Inc.

Barkin, Roger M. & Rosen, Peter. Pediatric Emergency Medicine Package. 1997. write for info. (*0-8151-2125-3*) Mosby Inc.

Barkin, Roger M., jt. auth. see Rubin, David H.

Barkin, Solomon, ed. Worker Militancy & Its Consequences: The Changing Climate of Western Industrial Relations. 2nd ed. LC 83-9564. 440p. 1983. 85.00 (*0-275-90943-3*, C0943, Praeger Pubs) Greenwood.

Barkinq, Roger M. Pediatric Emergency Medicine: Concepts & Clinical Practice. 2nd ed. LC 97-106461. (Illus.). 1328p. (C). (gr. 13). 1996. text 169.00 (*0-8151-1002-2*, 29256) Mosby Inc.

Barklage, Chris. Remembering Allen. (Illus.). 64p. 1999. pap. write for info. (*0-9672908-9-9*) C Barklage.

Barklay. Solutions Finder (IBM 3.5")-EL. 2nd ed. (C). 1992. pap. text, student ed. 21.00 (*0-03-096620-5*) Harcourt Coll Pubs.

Barklem, Jill. Autumn Story. (Brambly Hedge Ser.). (Illus.). 32p. (J). (gr. k-3). 1999. 9.95 (*0-689-83054-8*) Atheneum Yung Read.

***Barklem, Jill.** The High Hills. (Brambly Hedge Ser.). 32p. (J). (gr. k-3). 1999. 9.95 (*0-689-83091-2*) Atheneum Yung Read.

— Poppy's Babies. 32p. (J). 2000. 9.95 (*0-689-83172-2*) S&S Trade.

Barklem, Jill. Sea Story. (Brambly Hedge Ser.). 32p. (J). 2000. 9.95 (*0-689-83171-4*) S&S Trade.

***Barklem, Jill.** The Secret Staircase. (Brambly Hedge Ser.). (Illus.). 32p. (J). (gr. k-3). 1999. 9.95 (*0-689-83090-4*) Atheneum Yung Read.

— Winter Story. (Brambly Hedge Ser.). (Illus.). 32p. (J). (gr. k-3). 1999. 9.95 (*0-689-83057-2*) Atheneum Yung Read.

Barklem, Jill, jt. auth. see Simon & Schuster Children's.

Barkley. Economic Growth & the Environment. (C). 1998. pap. text 47.50 (*0-03-009597-2*) Harcourt Coll Pubs.

***Barkley.** Protocols Acute Care Nurse Practice. 2001. pap. text. write for info. (*0-7216-8536-6*, W B Saunders Co) Harcrt Hlth Sci Grp.

Barkley, Bill, jt. auth. see Green, Thad.

Barkley, Brad. Circle View: Stories. LC 96-33238. 240p. 1996. 22.50 (*0-87074-410-0*); pap. 12.95 (*0-87074-411-9*) SMU Press.

***Barkley, Brad.** Money, Love. 320p. 2000. 24.95 (*0-393-04929-9*) Norton.

Barkley, Bruce T. Customer-Driven Project Management: A New Paradigm in Managing Total Quality Implementation. 508p. 1992. 53.00 (*0-07-003739-6*) McGraw.

Barkley, Carolyn L. Princess Anne County, Virginia Marriage Bonds, 1822-1850. 277p. 1997. pap. 19.00 (*1-888265-15-9*) Willow Bend.

Barkley, Carolyn L., jt. auth. see Barclay, Leslie.

Barkley, Charles & Johnson, Roy S. Outrageous! 376p. 1993. mass mkt. 5.99 (*0-380-72101-5*, Avon Bks) Morrow Avon.

Barkley, David S., ed. see Atkinson, Daniel E., et al.

Barkley, David S., ed. see Atkinson, David E., et al.

Barkley, David S., ed. see Potter, Frank & Peck, Charles.

Barkley, David S., ed. & illus. see Potter, Frank & Peck, Charles.

Barkley, Elizabeth. Woman to Woman: Seeing God in Daily Life. LC 98-120186. 112p. 1997. pap. text 7.95 (*0-86716-226-0*) St Anthony Mess Pr.

Barkley, Elizabeth B. Loving the Everyday: Meditations for Moms. LC 94-207366. 206p. 1994. pap. 8.95 (*0-86716-191-4*) St Anthony Mess Pr.

Barkley, Frederick R., jt. auth. see Tucker, Ray T.

Barkley, Gary W., tr. see Origen.

Barkley, Katherine T. The Ambulance: The Story of Emergency Transportation of Sick & Wounded Through the Centuries. LC 90-62107. 1990. 25.00 (*0-9626357-1-5*); pap. 16.00 (*0-9626357-2-3*) Load N Go Pr.

Barkley, Kristen M., ed. see Jorgenson, Cathleen.

Barkley-Lewis, Constance. Fairy Garden: A Guide to the Fairies of the Flowers. LC 98-20628. (Illus.). 96p. 1998. 18.95 (*0-8362-6786-9*) Andrews & McMeel.

Barkley, Miriam, ed. see Moser, Joann & Dreishpoon, Douglas.

Barkley, Nella. How to Help Your Child Land the Right Job: (Without Being a Pain in the Neck) 350p. 1999. reprint ed. pap. text 10.00 (*0-7881-6228-4*) DIANE Pub.

— How to Help Your Child Land the Right Job (Without Being a Pain in the Neck) LC 92-50929. (Illus.). 360p. 1993. pap. 9.95 (*1-56305-152-4*, 3152) Workman Pub.

Barkley, Nella & Sandburg, Eric. The Crystal-Barkley Guide to Taking Charge of Your Career. LC 95-105. (Illus.). 240p. 1995. pap. 9.95 (*1-56305-495-7*, 3495) Workman Pub.

***Barkley, Roy.** The Mysteries of the Rosary: Mirror of Scripture & Gateway to Prayer. (Illus.). 2000. pap. 16.95 (*0-8189-0848-3*, Saint Pauls) Alba.

An Asterisk (*) at the beginning of an entry indicates that the title is appearing for the first time.

***Barkley, Roy R., et al.** The Portable Handbook of Texas. LC 00-36368. 2000. write for info. (*0-87611-180-0*) Tex St Hist Assn.

Barkley, Russell A. ADHD & the Nature of Self-Control. LC 97-25931. 410p. 1997. lib. bdg. 44.00 (*1-57230-250-X*, o250) Guilford Pubns.

— Attention-Deficit Hyperactivity Disorder: A Handbook for Diagnosis & Treatment. 2nd ed. LC 97-52762. 628p. 1998. lib. bdg. 59.00 (*1-57230-275-5*) Guilford Pubns.

— Defiant Children: A Clinician's Manual for Parent Training. 2nd ed. LC 96-47746. 264p. 1997. pap. text 35.00 (*1-57230-123-6*, 0123) Guilford Pubns.

— Hyperactive Children: A Handbook for Diagnosis & Treatment. LC 81-1382. 478p. 1981. reprint ed. pap. 148.20 (*0-7837-1640-0*, 204193400024) Bks Demand.

— Ninos Desafiantes (Defiant Children) Materiales de Evaluacion y Folletos para los Padres (A Clinician's Manual for Assessment & Parent Training), Spanish Supplement. 2nd ed. LC 89-1862. (School Practitioner Ser.). (SPA.). 87p. 1997. pap. text 19.95 (*1-57230-226-7*, 0226) Guilford Pubns.

— Taking Charge of ADHD: The Complete, Authoritative Guide for Parents. LC 95-37424. (Illus.). 294p. 1995. pap. text 17.95 (*0-89862-099-6*, 2099) Guilford Pubns.

***Barkley, Russell A.** Taking Charge of ADHD: The Complete, Authoritative Guide for Parents. rev. ed. 332p. 2000. pap. text 18.95 (*1-57230-560-6*, C0560); lib. bdg. 37.95 (*1-57230-600-9*, C0600) Guilford Pubns.

Barkley, Russell A. & Benton, Christine M. Your Defiant Child: Eight Steps to Better Behavior. LC 98-24231. 239p. 1998. pap. 14.95 (*1-57230-321-2*); lib. bdg. 29.95 (*1-57230-405-7*) Guilford Pubns.

Barkley, Russell A. & Murphy, Kevin R. Attention-Deficit Hyperactivity Disorder: A Clinical Workbook. 2nd ed. 134p. 1998. pap. text, wbk. ed. 29.95 (*1-57230-301-8*) Guilford Pubns.

Barkley, Russell A., et al. Defiant Teens: A Clinician's Manual for Assessment & Family Intervention. LC 98-52420. 250p. 1999. pap. 33.00 (*1-57230-440-5*) Guilford Pubns.

— Trastorno por Deficit de Atencion e Hiperactividad: Un Manual de Trabajo Clinico. Jose J. Bauermeister & Associates Staff, tr. from SPA. 174p. 1998. pap. text 29.95 (*1-57230-388-3*) Guilford Pubns.

Barkley, Russell A., jt. ed. see Mash, Eric J.

Barkley, Stephen G. A Mosaic of Learning Styles: Participant. (Illus.). 60p. 1995. pap., wbk. ed. 9.95 (*1-892334-05-4*) Perf Lrn Systs.

— A Mosaics of Learning Styles: Facilitator Guide. (Illus.). 133p. 1995. pap. 99.50 (*1-892334-04-6*) Perf Lrn Systs.

Barkley, Steve. Collection of Educational Insights. (Illus.). 36p. 1992. pap. 8.00 (*1-892334-01-1*) Perf Lrn Systs.

Barkley, T. M. Field Guide to the Common Weeds of Kansas. LC 82-21914. (Illus.). xii, 164p. 1983. 19.95 (*0-7006-0233-X*); pap. 9.95 (*0-7006-0224-0*) U Pr of KS.

Barkley, W. Emmett, jt. ed. see Richardson, John H.

Barkley, William D., jt. auth. see Martin, Alexander C.

Barkley, William M., jt. auth. see Jeffrey, Ed.

Barklon, L. I., et al. Eighteen Papers on Analysis & Quantum Mechanics. (Translations Ser.: Series 2, Vol. 91). 310p. 1970. 52.00 (*0-8218-1791-4*, TRANS2/91) Am Math.

Barklow, Irene. From Trails to Rails: The Post Offices, Stage Stops, & Wagon Roads of Union County, Oregon. Evans, Jack, ed. (Illus.). 306p. (YA). (gr. 8). 1987. pap. 15.95 (*0-9618185-0-6*) Enchant Pub Oregon.

— The Old & the New: History of the Post Offices of Wallowa County. (Illus.). 184p. (Orig.). (YA). (gr. 8 up). 1987. reprint ed. pap. 14.95 (*0-9618185-1-4*) Enchant Pub Oregon.

— School Days in the Wallowas: A History of the Ninety-One Schools & Communities That Have Been in Wallowa County Oregon. Sterbentz, Kathy, ed. (Illus.). 567p. (Orig.). 1992. 49.95 (*0-9618185-4-9*); pap. write for info. (*0-9618185-3-0*) Enchant Pub Oregon.

Barkman, Alma. Light Reflections. (Quiet Time Books for Women). pap. 4.99 (*0-8024-4787-2*, 412) Moody.

— Purrables: Words of Wisdom from the World of a Cat. LC 93-84309. 160p. 1993. pap. 6.95 (*0-914984-53-5*) Starburst.

— Rise & Shine. (Quiet Time Books for Women). pap. 4.99 (*0-8024-7387-3*, 415) Moody.

— Sunny-Side Up. (Quiet Time Books for Women). pap. 4.99 (*0-8024-8431-X*, 418) Moody.

Barkman, Betty & Barkman, Paul. A Well Trained Llama: A Trainers Guide. rev. ed. LC 88-93027. (Illus.). 95p. (Orig.). (YA). (gr. 9 up). 1989. pap. text 25.00 (*0-945860-01-3*) Birch Bark Pr.

Barkman, Bruce. Seven Sinners in Grand Opera: Level 6. McConochie, Jean A., ed. (Regents Readers Ser.). 1987. pap. text. write for info. (*0-13-807389-9*, 21066) Prentice ESL.

Barkman, Carl. Ambassador in Athens. (C). 1989. text 29.95 (*0-85036-343-8*, Pub. by MRLN) Paul & Co Pubs.

Barkman, Don. Biz Wiz, 6 vols. (Illus.). 144p. (Orig.). 1997. pap. 49.95 (*1-883655-11-0*) Busn Ctr.

— Start-Up! A Guide to Getting off on the Right Foot. 2nd rev. ed. (Illus.). 72p. 1999. pap. 14.95 (*1-883655-14-5*) Busn Ctr.

Barkman, Donald F. Building Better Meetings. 51p. 1991. 19.95 (*1-883655-02-1*) Busn Ctr.

— Designing Skill-Based Pay: Satisfying the Yearning for Earning by Learning. 2nd ed. (Illus.). 139p. 1994. 56.95 (*1-883655-01-3*) Busn Ctr.

— Open Book Management: You EZ Intro to OBM. 2nd ed. (Illus.). 52p. 1999. pap. 9.95 (*1-883655-05-6*) Busn Ctr.

— Training Others: Learning On-the-Job. 65p. 1992. 19.95 (*1-883655-03-X*) Busn Ctr.

Barkman, J. J. & Sykora, K., eds. Dependent Plant Communities: Proceedings of the 28th International Symposium of the International Association of Veetation Science (IAS), Held at Wageningen, the Netherlands, 16-19 April 1984. (Illus.). x, 174p. 1988. 65.00 (*90-5103-015-0*, Pub. by SPB Acad Pub) Balogh.

***Barkman, Lorlie.** Remember Dad? A Journey into Memory Loss. (Illus.). 74p. 1999. pap. 7.95 (*0-921788-61-4*) Kindred Prods.

Barkman, Paul, jt. auth. see Barkman, Betty.

Barkman, Robert C. Science Through Multiple Intelligences: Patterns That Inspire Inquiry. LC 99-18331. 1999. 39.00 (*1-56976-096-9*) Zephyr Pr AZ.

Barkman, William E. In-Process Quality Control for Manufacturing. (Industrial Engineering Ser.: Vol. 16). (Illus.). 296p. 1989. text 150.00 (*0-8247-8054-X*) Dekker.

Barkoff, Rupert M., et al. The Fundamentals of Franchising. LC 96-50881. 1997. pap. 89.95 (*1-57073-384-8*) Amer Bar Assn.

Barkovich, A. James. Pediatric Neuroimaging. 2nd ed. LC 94-9720. 688p. 1994. text 175.00 (*0-7817-0179-1*) Lppncott W & W.

Barkovich, A. James & Truwit, Charles L. Practical MRI Atlas of Neonatal Brain Development. LC 90-8860. (Illus.). 83p. 1990. reprint ed. pap. 30.00 (*0-608-07234-6*, 206745900009) Bks Demand.

Barkovich, Barbara R. Regulatory Interventionism in the Utility Industry: Fairness, Efficiency, & the Pursuit of Energy Conservation. LC 88-15392. 181p. 1989. 57.95 (*0-89930-383-8*, BVY/, Quorum Bks) Greenwood.

Barkovsky, E. V., et al. Hematology Reviews: Immune Mechanisms of the System Regulating the Aggregate State of Blood, Vol. 3. (Soviet Medical Reviews Ser.: Vol. 3, Pt. 2). iv, 60p. 1990. pap. text 75.00 (*3-7186-4962-4*) Gordon & Breach.

***Barkow, Al.** Gettin' to the Dance Floor: An Oral History of Professional Golf. LC 99-59058. (Illus.). 304p. 2000. reprint ed. pap. 16.95 (*1-58080-043-2*) Burford Bks.

— The Golden Era of Golf: How America Rose to Dominate the Old Scots Game. (Illus.). 272p. 2000. 24.95 (*0-312-25238-2*, Thomas Dunne) St Martin.

— Golf's Golden Grind: A History of the PGA Tour. LC 99-58452. (Illus.). 320p. 2000. reprint ed. pap. 16.95 (*1-58080-044-0*) Burford Bks.

Barkow, Al & Barrett, David. Golf Greats. LC 99-168337. 288p. 1998. mass mkt. 5.99 (*0-451-19454-3*, Sig) NAL.

Barkow, Al & Low, George. The Master of Putting. LC 96-39940. (Illus.). 96p. 1997. reprint ed. pap. 12.95 (*1-58080-012-2*) Burford Bks.

Barkow, Al, jt. auth. see Low, George.

Barkow, Al, jt. auth. see Stockton, Dave.

Barkow, Al, jt. auth. see Venturi, Ken.

Barkow, Ben. Alfred Wiener & the Making of the Holocaust Library. LC 96-49266. 210p. 1997. 45.00 (*0-85303-329-3*, Pub. by M Vallentine & Co); pap. 22.50 (*0-85303-328-5*, Pub. by M Vallentine & Co) Intl Spec Bk.

Barkow, Ben, jt. auth. see Zeidenitz, Stefan.

Barkow, Ben, ed. see De La Motte, Fouque.

Barkow, Ben, ed. see Voltaire.

Barkow, Jerome H. Darwin, Sex, & Status: Biological Approaches to Mind & Culture. 1990. pap. 20.95 (*0-8020-6855-3*) U of Toronto Pr.

— Darwin, Sex, & Status: Biological Approaches to Mind & Culture. LC GN0365.9B38. (Illus.). 473p. reprint ed. pap. 146.70 (*0-7837-0605-7*, 204095300019) Bks Demand.

Barkow, Jerome H., et al, eds. The Adapted Mind: Evolutionary Psychology & the Generation of Culture. (Illus.). 688p. 1995. reprint ed. pap. 35.00 (*0-19-510107-3*) OUP.

Barkow, Michael. Beauties & the Best: Behind the Red Door - A Memoir. LC 98-89875. 365p. 1999. 25.00 (*0-7388-0307-3*); pap. 15.00 (*0-7388-0308-1*) Xlibris Corp.

Barkow, N. I., ed. Ice Shelves of Antarctica: Soviet Antarctic Expedition. Datta, P., tr. from RUS. (ENG.). 270p. 1985. text 105.00 (*90-6191-435-3*, Pub. by A A Balkema) Ashgate Pub Co.

Barks. The Illuminated Rumi. 128p. 1997. pap. 30.00 (*0-7679-0270-X*) Broadway BDD.

Barks, Carl. The Carl Barks Library of Uncle Scrooge Comics Walt Disney's Uncle Scrooge. LC 93-187869. 1992. 8.95 (*0-944599-48-6*) Archaeol Ctr.

— Uncle Scrooge McDuck: His Life & Times. Summer, Edward, ed. LC 81-66953. (Illus.). 376p. (J). (ps-3). 1995. 59.95 (*0-89087-511-1*) Celestial Arts.

Barks, Coleman. The Essential Rumi. Moyne, John, tr. 310p. 1997. 7.98 (*0-7858-0871-X*) Bk Sales Inc.

— Gourd Seed: Poems. 140p. 1993. pap. 9.00 (*0-9618916-6-1*) Maypop.

— Naked Song: Poems. 140p. (Orig.). (C). 1992. pap. 8.00 (*0-9618916-4-5*) Maypop.

Barks, Coleman, compiled by. Xenia: A Hoard of Lost Words. 179p. 1994. pap. 7.50 (*0-9618916-9-6*) Maypop.

Barks, Coleman, tr. The Essential Rumi. 256p. 1996. pap. 18.00 (*0-614-21272-3*, 265) Kazi Pubns.

— Feeling the Shoulder of the Lion. 104p. 1996. pap. 9.00 (*0-614-21277-4*, 295) Kazi Pubns.

— The Glance: Rumi's Songs of Soul-Meeting. LC 99-25074. 112p. 1999. pap. 18.00 (*0-670-88755-2*) Viking Penguin.

— The Illuminated Rumi. LC 97-2534. (Illus.). 128p. 1997. 30.00 (*0-7679-0002-2*) Broadway BDD.

***Barks, Coleman & Green, Michael.** The Illuminated Prayer: The Five-Times Prayer of the Sufis. 144p. 2000. 18.95 (*0-345-43545-1*) Ballantine Pub Grp.

Barks, Coleman & Moyne, John, trs. The Essential Rumi. 320p. 1995. 21.00 (*0-06-250958-6*) HarperTrade.

— This Longing. LC 88-40221. 96p. 1988. pap. 10.00 (*0-939660-29-6*) Threshold CA.

Barks, Coleman, et al. The Essential Rumi. LC 94-44995. 336p. 1997. pap. 12.00 (*0-06-250959-4*) HarperTrade.

Barks, Coleman, tr. see Breton, Denise & Largent, Christopher.

Barks, Coleman, tr. see Khan, Inayat, et al.

Barks, Coleman, tr. see Maulana, Jalal al-Din Rumi.

Barks, Coleman, tr. see Rumi, Jalal Al-Din.

Barks, Coleman, tr. see Rumi, Melvana.

Barks, Coleman, tr. & intro. see Dalai Lama, VI.

Barks, Coleman, tr. & intro. see Rumi, Jalal Al-Din.

Barks, Ronald E., ed. see Intersociety Symposium on Machining of Advanced Ce.

Barksdale. Conquering Quicken. 1996. pap. text 29.95 (*0-538-67186-6*) Thomson Learn.

Barksdale. Corporate View: Orientation. (General Office Procedures Ser.). 1998. pap. 28.50 (*0-538-68474-2*) S-W Pub.

Barksdale & Kinnamon. Black Writers of America. 944p. (C). 1997. pap. text 47.00 (*0-13-779399-5*) P-H.

***Barksdale & Rutter.** Corporate Marketing Level 2: Text. (C). 2000. text 38.95 (*0-538-69154-9*) Sth-Wstrn College.

Barksdale & Rutter. Internet Concepts & Activities. (Computer Applications Ser.). 1998. pap. 23.00 (*0-538-72166-9*) S-W Pub.

— Internet Concepts & Activities. (Computer Applications Ser.). (C). 1998. pap. 34.95 (*0-538-72088-3*) S-W Pub.

***Barksdale & Rutter.** On-line Testing Certificate Level 2. 2000. pap. 6.00 (*0-538-69169-7*) S-W Pub.

Barksdale & Turner. HTML & Javascript: Programming Concepts. (Computer Applications Ser.). 1999. pap. 31.95 (*0-538-68822-X*) S-W Pub.

Barksdale, et al. Retail User's Book. (Computer Applications Ser.). 1999. pap. write for info. (*0-538-69456-4*) Thomson Learn.

Barksdale, Almina, jt. auth. see Barksdale, Karl.

Barksdale, E. C. Cosmologies of Consciousness. LC 79-23268. 148p. 1980. text 18.95 (*0-87073-969-7*); pap. text 11.95 (*0-87073-970-0*) Schenkman Bks Inc.

— Daggers of the Mind: The Russian Literary Imagination. 212p. 1979. 15.00 (*0-87291-099-7*) Coronado Pr

— Enchanted Paths & Magic Words: The Quantum Mind & Time Travel in Science & in Literary Myth. LC 97-22340. (Ars Interpretandi Ser.: Vol. 8). XXI, 424p. (C). 1998. text 60.95 (*0-8204-3850-2*) P Lang Pubng.

Barksdale, E. C., jt. auth. see Pace, David P.

Barksdale, Hiram C., jt. ed. see Reynolds, Fred D.

Barksdale Inclan, Jessica, jt. auth. see Frank Ballentine, Susan.

Barksdale, Jo, jt. auth. see Furrh, Mary L.

Barksdale, John A. Barksdale Family History & Genealogy: With Collateral Lines. 634p. 1993. reprint ed. pap. 95.00 (*0-8328-3940-X*); reprint ed. lib. bdg. 105.00 (*0-8328-3939-6*) Higginson Bk Co.

Barksdale, Julian D., et al. Laboratory Manual for Elementary Geology. 2nd ed. (Illus.). ii, 93p. (Orig.). (C). 1969. pap. text 8.95 (*0-87015-175-4*) Pacific Bks.

Barksdale, Karl. Conquering Quicken. LC 97-23822. 1997. write for info. (*0-538-68319-8*) S-W Pub.

— Java Activities: Applets on the Superhigh. LC 97-31336. (DF - Computer Applications Ser.). 240p. 1998. mass mkt. 29.95 (*0-538-68012-1*) S-W Pub.

Barksdale, Karl & Barksdale, Almina. Conquering Quicken: Personal, Business & Internet Financial Skills. 224p. 1997. pap. 24.95 (*0-538-68305-8*) Sth-Wstrn College.

Barksdale, Karl & Baumgaarten, J. Alan. Exploring the Internet: Cyberspace Odyssey. (Da - K-8 Computer Education Ser.). 1997. pap. 23.95 (*0-538-66759-1*) S-W Pub.

Barksdale, Karl & Paulsen, Eugene. HTML Activities: Webtop Publishing on the Superhighway. LC 97-16394. 192p. 1997. pap. 27.95 (*0-538-67458-X*) S-W Pub.

***Barksdale, Karl & Steffee, John.** Social Studies with Computers. 272p. 1998. spiral bd. 30.60 (*1-57426-060-X*) Computer Lit Pr.

Barksdale, Karl & Steffee, John. Writing with Computers. (Illus.). 316p. 1998. spiral bd. 30.60 (*1-57426-054-5*) Computer Lit Pr.

***Barksdale, Karl & Turner, E. Shane.** HTML Programming Concepts: Brief Course. 1999. pap. 19.95 (*0-538-69118-2*) Thomson Learn.

Barksdale, Karl, et al. Math with Computers. (Illus.). 240p. 1998. spiral bd. 30.60 (*1-57426-056-1*) Computer Lit Pr.

— Paws Presents the Internet & the World Wide Web. (Illus.). 192p. 1997. pap. 23.95 (*0-538-66765-6*) S-W Pub.

Barksdale, Lilburn S. Barksdale Stress Control Program Participant's Kit. (Illus.). 1980. pap., student ed. 34.95 incl. audio (*0-918588-23-5*, 205) Barksdale Foun.

— Barksdale Stress Control Program Script for Seminar Instructor. 91p. 1980. pap., teacher ed. 80.00 incl. audio (*0-918588-18-9*, 204) Barksdale Foun.

— Barksdale Stress Control Seminar Instructor's Kit. (Illus.). 1980. pap., vinyl bd. 80.00 incl. audio (*0-918588-21-9*, 204) Barksdale Foun.

— Building Self-Esteem. 2nd ed. LC 88-7661. 69p. 1989. pap. 5.95 (*0-918588-11-1*, 112) Barksdale Foun.

— Building Sound Self-Esteem: Instructor's Guide. 145p. 1978. pap. 105.00 (*0-918588-04-9*, 201) Barksdale Foun.

— Building Sound Self-Esteem Instructor's Kit. (Illus.). 1978. pap. 105.00 (*0-918588-13-8*, 201) Barksdale Foun.

— Building Sound Self-Esteem Participant's Kit. 86p. 1978. pap., student ed. 39.95 (*0-918588-15-4*, 203) Barksdale Foun.

— Essays on Self-Esteem. LC 77-73169. 1977. pap. 8.95 (*0-918588-00-6*, 114) Barksdale Foun.

— Home Study Course for Self-Esteem & Stress Control. 2nd unabridged rev. ed. (Illus.). 1989. pap. 39.95 incl. audio (*0-918588-16-2*, 115) Barksdale Foun.

— Manual for Building Sound Self-Esteem. 86p. 1978. pap. 39.95 (*0-918588-03-0*, 203) Barksdale Foun.

— Self-Esteem Facilitator's Kit. unabridged ed. 1978. pap., student ed., vinyl bd. 105.00 incl. audio (*0-918588-14-6*, 200) Barksdale Foun.

— Self-Esteem Study Group Package. 2nd rev. ed. (Illus.). 1989. pap. 21.95 (*0-918588-17-0*, 116) Barksdale Foun.

— Stress-Free Living. LC 93-44360. 1994. pap. 5.95 (*0-918588-27-8*, 210) Barksdale Foun.

Barksdale, Lilburn S. Stress-Free Living Kit, Incl. Handbook for Achieving Stress-Free Living. unabridged ed. 1980. pap., vinyl bd. 43.95 incl. audio (*0-918588-24-3*, 207) Barksdale Foun.

Barksdale, Lilburn S. Study Guide for Building Self-Esteem. 2nd ed. LC 88-7661. 54p. 1989. pap. 6.95 (*0-918588-12-X*, 113) Barksdale Foun.

Barksdale, Richard K. Langston Hughes: The Poet & His Critics. LC 77-8599. 167p. reprint ed. pap. 51.80 (*0-608-13298-5*, 202561000044) Bks Demand.

— Praisesong of Survival: Lectures & Essays, 1957-89. 280p. (C). 1992. text 45.00 (*0-252-01898-2*); pap. text 18.95 (*0-252-06286-8*) U of Ill Pr.

Barksdale, Thomas. It's All about You. (Illus.). (Orig.). (YA). (gr. 4 up). 1997. pap. 9.95 (*1-887798-09-9*) APU Pub Grp.

Barksdale, W. J. Practical Computer Data Communications. (Applications of Communications Theory Ser.). (Illus.). 470p. (C). 1986. 110.00 (*0-306-42323-5*, Plenum Trade) Perseus Pubng.

Barksted, William, et al. Four Jacobean Sex Tragedies: William Barsted & Lewis Machin: The Insatiate Countess; Francis Beaumont & John Fletcher: The Maid's Tragedy; Thomas Middleton: The Maiden's Tragedy; John Fletcher: The Tragedy of Valentinian. Wiggins, Martin, ed. & intro. by. (Oxford World's Classics Ser.). 470p. 1998. pap. 14.95 (*0-19-282320-5*) OUP.

Barkstrom, Jack. Poverty, Wealth Dictatorship, Democracy: Resource Scarcity & the Origins of Dictatorship. LC 98-96403. 535p. 1998. pap. 21.95 (*0-9610224-0-X*) Pericles Pr.

Barkun, Michael. Crucible of the Millennium: The Burned-Over District of New York in the 1840s. LC 86-5777. (New York State Bks.). (Illus.). 240p. 1986. pap. text 19.95 (*0-8156-2378-X*) Syracuse U Pr.

— Disaster & the Millennium. LC 73-86884. 256p. reprint ed. pap. 79.40 (*0-8357-8706-0*, 203366700087) Bks Demand.

— Disaster & the Millennium. LC 86-5969. 256p. 1974. reprint ed. pap. 79.40 (*0-608-07630-9*, 205994500010) Bks Demand.

— Disaster & the Millennium. LC 86-5979. 256p. 1986. reprint ed. pap. text 16.95 (*0-8156-2392-5*) Syracuse U Pr.

— Religion & the Racist Right: The Origins of the Christian Identity Movement. rev. ed. LC 96-28347. 352p. (C). (gr. 13). 1996. 49.95 (*0-8078-2328-7*); pap. 18.95 (*0-8078-4638-4*) U of NC Pr.

Barkun, Michael, ed. Millennialism & Violence. (Political Violence Ser.). 177p. (Orig.). 1996. 35.00 (*0-7146-4708-X*, Pub. by F Cass Pubs); pap. 18.50 (*0-7146-4250-9*, Pub. by F Cass Pubs) Intl Spec Bk.

Barkus, Homer A. Proper Use of the Watchmaker's Graver. (Illus.). 1992. pap. 5.00 (*0-930163-29-X*) Arlington Bk.

***Barkus, Philip.** How to Prepare for the Comprehensive Postal Exam: Series Test Battery 460/470. 2nd ed. LC 99-32387. 480p. 2000. 14.95 (*0-7641-0774-7*) Barron.

Barkus, Philip. How to Prepare for the Comprehensive U. S. Postal Service Examination. LC 95-18410. (Illus.). 432p. 1995. pap. 13.95 (*0-8120-9397-6*) Barron.

Barkwell, Tom. How to Become a U. S. Naval Officer: The Complete Guide to Commissioning Programs. LC 98-91546. vii, 226p. 1998. pap. 14.00 (*0-9665189-0-X*) Shipshape Pubns.

Barkwill, Linda. Finding Inner Peace in a World of Accelerating Change: A Spiritual Path to Connecting with the "Inner" Self. LC 95-94202. 1997. write for info. (*0-9645760-0-7*) In the Light.

Barkworth, Peter. The Complete "About Acting" 274p. (C). 1992. pap. 12.95 (*0-413-66110-5*, A0640, Methuen Drama) Methn.

Barla, Giovanni. Eurock 96: Prediction & Performance in Rock Media, Vol. 2. 820p. 1996. 123.00 (*90-5410-842-8*) Ashgate Pub Co.

Barla, Giovanni, ed. Prediction & Performance in Rock Mechanics & Rock Engineering: Proceedings/Comptes-Rendus/Sitzungsberichte/SPE/ISRM International Conference, EUROCK '96, Turin, 2-5.09.1996, 3 vols. (Illus.). 1000p. (C). 1996. 362.00 (*90-5410-843-6*, Pub. by A A Balkema) Ashgate Pub Co.

Barlach, Ernst. A Selftold Life. Groves, Naomi J., tr. from GER. (Illus.). 104p. 1990. pap. 15.95 (*0-921254-07-5*, Pub. by Penumbra Pr) U of Toronto Pr.

***Barlanti, A. J.** As My Mind Took in the Ghetto. 2000. pap. 7.95 (*0-533-13547-8*) Vantage.

Barlas, Aqlim, jt. auth. see Thomson, Robert S.

Barlas, Dilek. Etatism & Diplomacy in Turkey: Economic & Foreign Policy Strategies in an Uncertain World, 1929-1939. LC 97-36031. (Ottoman Empire & Its Heritage Ser.). 1998. write for info. (*90-04-10855-6*) Brill Academic Pubs.

Barlas, R., et al. World Cultures: Group 20. (Illus.). 128p. (YA). (gr. 5 up). 213.86 (*0-7614-0991-2*) Marshall Cavendish.

***Barlas, Robert.** Bahamas, 6 vols. , Set. LC 99-88028. (Cultures of the World Ser.: Vol. 20). 128p. (YA). (gr. 4-7). 2000. lib. bdg. 35.64 (*0-7614-0992-0*, Benchmark NY) Marshall Cavendish.

Barlas, Robert. Culture Shock! Canada. LC 91-77243. (Illus.). 256p. 1992. 12.95 (1-55868-087-X) Gr Arts Ctr Pub.

*Barlas, Robert. Latvia, 6 vols. , Set. LC 99-30168. (Cultures of the World Ser.: Vol. 19). 128p. (YA). (gr. 5-9). 2000. lib. bdg. 35.64 (0-7614-0977-7, Benchmark NY) Marshall Cavendish.

— Uganda, 6 vols. , Set. LC 99-27577. (Cultures of the World Ser.: Vol. 19). (Illus.). 128p. (YA). (gr. 5-9). 2000. lib. bdg. 35.64 (0-7614-0981-5, Benchmark NY) Marshall Cavendish.

Barlass, Gail. Dinosquares: A Modern Dinosaur Book for Imaginative Children. Hansen, Ron, ed. & illus. by. LC 87-62124. 24p. (J). (ps-3). 1988. pap. 3.95 (0-943925-07-X) Purple Turtle Bks.

Barlaud, M. Wavelets in Image Communication. LC 94-36820. (Advances in Image Communication Ser.: Vol. 5). 270p. 1994. 165.00 (0-444-89281-8) Elsevier.

Barlay, Stephen. Cleared for Take-Off: Behind the Scenes of Air Travel. 262p. 1996. pap. 13.95 (1-85626-173-5, Pub. by Cathie Kyle) Trafalgar.

Barlaz, Morton A., jt. ed. see Palmisano, Anna C.

Barlee, N. L. Gold Creeks & Ghost Towns. (Illus.). 190p. 1997. reprint ed. pap. 14.95 (0-88839-988-X) Hancock House.

— The Guide to Gold Panning. 3rd rev. ed. (Illus.). 192p. 1984. 17.95 (0-88839-986-3) Hancock House.

— Lost Mines & Historic Treasures. Bryce, Herb, ed. 96p. (Orig.). 1987. pap. 11.95 (0-88839-992-8) Hancock House.

— Similkameen Treasure. 96p. 1989. reprint ed. pap. 9.95 (0-88839-990-1) Hancock House.

*Barlet, Olivier. African Cinemas. 2000. pap. 29.95 (1-85649-743-7, Pub. by Zed Books); text 69.95 (1-85649-742-9, Pub. by Zed Books) St Martin.

Barlett, jt. auth. see Bona.

Barlett, Bruce. Tax Reform's "Third Rail" Mortgage Interest. 9p. 1996. pap. 5.00 (1-56808-070-0, BG139) Natl Ctr Pol.

Barlett, Christopher A. & Ghoshal, Sumantra. Transnational Management: Text Cases & Readings in Cross Border Management. 2nd ed. 200p. (C). 1995. text 72.25 (0-256-14138-X, Irwn McGrw-H) McGrw-H Hghr Educ.

Barlett, Donald L. & Steele, James B. America: What Went Wrong? 252p. 1992. pap. 6.95 (0-8362-7001-0) Andrews & McMeel.

— America: Who Stole the Dream? 276p. (Orig.). 1996. pap. 9.95 (0-8362-1314-9) Andrews & McMeel.

— Empire: The Life, Legend & Madness of Howard Hughes. (Illus.). 1981. pap. 19.95 (0-393-00025-7) Norton.

Barlett, John G. & Finkbeiner, Ann K. Guia Para Vivir con la Infeccion VIH: Desarrollado por la Clinica Johns Hopkins del SIDA. 3rd ed. LC 96-32867. 1996. pap. 15.95 (0-8018-5420-2) Johns Hopkins.

Barlett, Kenneth G. The Evening College & Its Relationship to "Community Politics" 1960. 2.50 (0-87060-082-6, PUC 16) Syracuse U Cont Ed.

Barlett, Neil. Night after Night. 80p. 1994. pap. 11.95 (0-413-68500-4, A0709, Methuen Drama) Methn.

Barlett, Peggy F. Agricultural Choice & Change: Decision Making in a Costa Rican Community. LC 81-13835. (Illus.). 208p. 1982. reprint ed. pap. 64.50 (0-8357-7940-8, 205701300002) Bks Demand.

— American Dreams, Rural Realities: Family Farms in Crisis. LC 92-18027. (Rural Culture Studies). xviii, 328p. (C). 1993. pap. 22.50 (0-8078-4399-7) U of NC Pr.

Barlett, Richard A. Exploring the American West, 1803-1879. LC 82-12483. 128p. 1983. pap. 7.00 (0-16-003449-3, S/N 024-005-00834-9) USGPO.

*Barlett, Rosamund, ed. Shostakovich in Context. LC 99-47564. 240p. 2000. 70.00 (0-19-816666-4) OUP.

Barlett, Tom. Ducks & Geese: A Guide to Management. (Illus.). 112p. 1991. 22.95 (1-85223-650-7, Pub. by Crolwood) Trafalgar.

Barletta, Barbara A. Ionic Influence in Archaic Sicily: The Monumental Art. (Studies in Mediterranean Archaeology & Literature: No. 23). (Illus.). 380p. (Orig.). 1983. pap. 52.50 (91-86098-11-X, Pub. by P Astroms) Coronet Bks.

Barletta, W. The Physics of Beams: Andrew Sessler Symposium, Los Angeles, CA December 5-6, 1993. (CP Ser.: No. 351). (Illus.). 144p. 1995. 120.00 (1-56396-376-0) Am Inst Physics.

Barletta, W. & Leutz, H. Supercolliders & Superdetectors: Proceedings of the 19th & 25th Workshops of the Information Eloisatron Project. (Science & Culture Series - Physics). 400p. 1994. text 121.00 (981-02-1595-9) World Scientific Pub.

Barletta, William A., jt. ed. see Bonifacio, Rodolfo.

Barlex, et al. Nuffield Desgin & Technology. 1995. pap. text, student ed. write for info. (0-582-21266-9, Pub. by Addison-Wesley) Longman.

— Nuffield Design & Technology. 1995. pap. text, student ed. write for info. (0-582-21265-0, Pub. by Addison-Wesley) Longman.

Barley, Chris S. Trading with the Natives: A Guide to the Small Shops of Albuquerque. Mayer, Elise, ed. (Illus.). 160p. (Orig.). 1990. pap. 9.95 (0-9627497-0-2) Dancing Desert.

Barley, Janet C. Winter in July: Visits with Children's Authors Down Under. LC 94-33216. 227p. 1995. 31.00 (0-8108-2945-2) Scarecrow.

Barley, Margaret, jt. auth. see Jeffers, Janet.

*Barley, Nick. Breathing Cities: Visualising Urban Movement. (Illus.). 128p. 2000. pap. write for info. (3-7643-6236-7, Pub. by Birkhauser) Spr-Verlag.

*Barley, Nick, ed. City Levels. (Illus.). 128p. 2000. pap. 35.00 (3-7643-6315-0) Birkhauser.

*Barley, Nick & British Council Staff. Lost & Found: Critical Voices in New British Design. LC 99-42385. 1999. write for info. (0-8176-6095-X) Birkhauser.

Barley, Nigel. Dancing on the Grave. LC 97-19052. (Illus.). 256p. 1995. 25.00 (0-8050-4824-3) H Holt & Co.

Barley, R. W., jt. auth. see Wills, B. A.

Barley, Stephen R. & Orr, Julian E., eds. Between Craft & Science: Technical Work in the United States. LC 96-32077. (ILR Press Book). (Illus.). 280p. 1996. text 47.50 (0-8014-3296-0); pap. text 19.95 (0-8014-8366-2) Cornell U Pr.

Barley, W. J. Wycliffe & Winsor Blue. 1988. mass mkt. 2.95 (0-380-70633-4, Avon Bks) Morrow Avon.

Barlin, Anne L. & Kalev, Nurit. Goodnight Toes! Bedtime Stories, Lullabies, & Movement Games. LC 93-8560. (Illus.). 152p. (ps-3). 1993. pap. 10.95 (0-87127-190-7, Dance Horizons) Princeton Bk Co.

— Hello Toes: Movement Games for Children. LC 89-35995. (Illus.). 128p. 1989. pap. 9.95 (0-916622-88-6) Princeton Bk Co.

Barling, J. Kurt, jt. ed. see Akinrinade, Olusola.

Barling, Julian & Kelloway, E. Kevin, eds. Young Workers: Varieties of Experience. LC 98-37411. 282p. 1998. 39.95 (1-55798-563-4, 431-614A) Am Psychol.

Barling, Julian, et al. Organizational Behavior & the Psychology of Unions. (Industrial-Organizational Psychology Ser.). (Illus.). 264p. 1992. text 70.00 (0-19-507336-3) OUP.

Barling, Julian, jt. ed. see Tetrick, Lois.

*Barlingay, Surendra Sheodas. Reunderstanding Indian Philosophy: Some Glimpses. LC 98-907220. x, 371p. 1998. 32.00 (81-246-0107-0, Pub. by D K Printwrld) Nataraj Bks.

Barlog, J. M. Dark Side: The Haunting. 300p. 1999. pap. 6.99 (0-9654716-1-6) BAK Books.

— Necessary Measures. 448p. 1997. pap. 6.99 (0-9654716-0-8) BAK Books.

— Windows to the Soul. LC 96-94981. 268p. (Orig.). 1996. pap. 7.99 (0-9654716-6-7) BAK Books.

Barlog, James M. Red Hearts. 392p. 1999. mass mkt. 6.99 (0-9654716-2-4) BAK Books.

Barlog, Yvonne. Living with Art Glass. (Illus.). 48p. 1998. pap. 18.95 (0-935133-66-6, 20133666) CKE Pubns.

Barlotta, Michael. Distributed Application Development with PowerBuilder 6. LC 98-29936. 512p. 1998. pap. 44.95 (1-884777-68-6) Manning Pubns.

*Barlotta, Michael J. & Weiss, Jason R. Taming Jaguar. (Power Builder Developer's Library Ser.). (Illus.). 300p. 2000. pap. 42.95 (1-930110-03-0, Pub. by Manning Pubns) IPG Chicago.

*Barlotta, Mike. Jaguar Development with Powerbuilder 7. LC 99-40227. (Illus.). 514p. 1999. pap. 44.95 (1-884777-86-4) Manning Pubns.

Barlotti, A., et al, eds. Generators & Relations in Groups & Geometries. (C). 1991. text 215.00 (0-7923-1161-2) Kluwer Academic.

*Barlough, Jeffrey E. Dark Sleeper. 2000. 14.95 (0-441-00730-9) Ace Bks.

Barloutand, R., ed. Grand Unification: Ninth Workshop. 484p. (C). 1989. text 125.00 (9971-5-0765-X) World Scientific Pub.

Barlow. Abnormal Psychology: An Integrated Approach. 2nd ed. (Psychology Ser.). 1998. pap., student ed. 19.25 (0-534-35996-5) Brooks-Cole.

— Criminal Justice in America. LC 99-12555. (Illus.). 746p. 1999. 71.00 (0-13-083271-5) P-H.

— Differential Growth. (JEEB Ser.: Vol. 29). 1989. 54.50 (0-08-036841-7, Pergamon Pr) Elsevier.

Barlow. Ghosts of Evolution. 25.00 (0-465-00551-9, Pub. by Basic); pap. 15.00 (0-465-00552-7, Pub. by Basic) HarpC.

Barlow. History of Criminal Justice. (Criminal Justice Ser.). 2002. pap. 35.00 (0-534-54784-2) Wadsworth Pub.

— Leyendas Latinoamericanas. 2nd ed. (SPA.). 176p. 1996. pap. 15.50 (0-8442-7239-6) NTC Contemp Pub Co.

Barlow. Tales of Regional Development. 59.95 (1-85972-515-5) Ashgate Pub Co.

Barlow. Wheel to Storm. 1999. text 19.95 (0-670-83902-7) Viking Penguin.

Barlow, ed. Introduction to Criminal Justice. (C). 1998. text. write for info. (0-321-01376-X) Addson-Wesley Educ.

Barlow & Duncan. Success & Failure in Housing Provision. (Policy, Planning & Critical Theory Ser.). 189p. 1994. pap. text 64.95 (0-08-041029-4, Prgamon Press) Buttrwrth-Heinemann.

Barlow & Durand. Abnormal Psychology: An Integrative Approach. 2nd ed. LC 98-20270. (Psychology). 1998. pap. 59.25 (0-534-34742-8) Brooks-Cole.

*Barlow & Durand. Abnormal Psychology: Integrative Approach. 2nd ed. (Psychology Ser.). 1999. pap. 61.50 (0-534-50676-3) Wadsworth Pub.

Barlow & Voncannon. Legal Elements of Boundaries. 2nd ed. LC 97-76677. 675p. 1997. 65.00 (1-55834-676-7, 66925-11, MICHIE) LEXIS Pub.

*Barlow & Waite. Stepping Through My Nightmares. 1998. mass mkt. 13.95 (0-340-69456-4, Pub. by Hodder & Stought Ltd) Trafalgar.

Barlow, jt. auth. see Durand.

Barlow, Teresa, jt. auth. see Scott, Julian.

Barlow, A., jt. auth. see Gee, R.

Barlow, Adrian. Answers for My Murdered Self. 28p. 1987. 30.00 (0-930126-20-3) Typographeum.

*Barlow, Adrian. The Great War in British Literature. (Cambridge Contexts in Literature Ser.). 128p. (C). 2000. pap. text 13.95 (0-521-64420-8) Cambridge U Pr.

Barlow, Alan. Fifty Activities for Developing Management Skills, Vol. 9. 300p. 1993. ring bd. 245.95 (0-566-07285-8, Pub. by Gower) Ashgate Pub Co.

— Value Cards: Creating a Culture for Team Effectiveness. LC 94-67266. 72p. 1994. ring bd. 99.95 (0-88390-444-6, Pfffr & Co) Jossey-Bass.

*Barlow, Amanda. ABC. (Baby Board Bks.). (Illus.). 12p. (J). (ps up). 2000. bds. 4.95 (0-7460-4100-4, Usborne) EDC.

— Animals. (Baby Board Bks.). (Illus.). 12p. (J). (ps up). 2000. bds. 4.95 (0-7460-4102-0, Usborne) EDC.

— 123. (Baby Board Bks.). (Illus.). 12p. (J). (ps up). 2000. bds. 4.95 (0-7460-4099-7, Usborne) EDC.

— Things That Go. (Baby Board Bks.). (Illus.). 12p. (J). (ps up). 2000. bds. 4.95 (0-7460-4101-2, Usborne) EDC.

Barlow, Andy & Chinodoros, Sandra, eds. InLine Skating in Greater Boston: Official Skating Guide of the InLine Club of Boston. 2nd ed. (Illus.). 94p. 1996. pap. 6.95 (0-9650817-0-2) InLine Club of Boston.

Barlow, Anna M. Ferryboat. 1971. pap. 3.25 (0-8222-0397-9) Dramatists Play.

— A Limb of Snow & the Meeting: Two Short Plays. 1969. pap. 5.25 (0-8222-0668-4) Dramatists Play.

Barlow, Anne. The Children Act 1989: The Private Law. 78p. 1991. 55.00 (1-85190-146-9, Pub. by Tolley Pubng) St Mut.

— Cohabitants & the Lawabitation 2nd ed. LC 97-102518. xxx, 326 p. 1997. write for info. (0-406-89621-6) LEXIS Pub.

— The Law Relating to Cohabitation. 250p. 1995. pap. 120.00 (1-86012-047-4, Pub. by Tolley Pubng) St Mut.

— Living Together: A Guide to the Law. 259p. (C). 1992. 110.00 (1-85190-151-5, Pub. by Tolley Pubng) St Mut.

*Barlow, Anne & Finn, Margaret L. Complete Work Experience. 128p. 2000. pap. 24.95 (0-86431-337-3, Pub. by Aust Council Educ Res) Stylus Pub VA.

Barlow, Annette C., jt. auth. see Celorio, Marta.

*Barlow, Anthony M., et al. Anderson's Ohio Probate Practice & Procedure, 2 vols. 1999. 195.00 (0-87084-390-7) Anderson Pub Co.

Barlow, Bernyce. Sacred Sites of the West. LC 96-28359. (Illus.). 240p. (Orig.). 1999. pap. 19.95 (1-56718-056-6) Llewellyn Pubns.

Barlow, Betty. Easy Baroque Duets. 32p. 1984. pap. text 5.95 (0-87487-262-6) Summy-Birchard.

— Fiddle Tunes for the Violinist, EFS198. (Illus.). 48p. 1977. pap. 12.95 (0-8256-2198-4, AM40882) Music Sales.

Barlow, Bob. Bob Barlows Book of Brain Boosters. LC 98-126279. (J). 1998. 8.95 (0-590-37510-5) Scholastic Inc.

Barlow, Brent A. Dealing with Differences in Marriage. LC 93-11070. x, 161p. 1993. 14.95 (0-87579-732-6) Deseret Bk.

— Just for Newlyweds. LC 92-15334. 163p. 1992. 17.95 (0-87579-623-0) Deseret Bk.

— Making Marriage Meaningful. viii, 117p. (C). 1980. pap. text 2.95 (0-8425-1828-2, Friends of the Library) Brigham.

— Twelve Traps in Today's Marriage: And How to Avoid Them. LC 86-13429. 1994. pap. 9.95 (0-87579-947-7) Deseret Bk.

— What Wives Expect of Husbands. LC 82-70919. xi, 164p. 1989. reprint ed. pap. 9.95 (0-87579-198-0) Deseret Bk.

— Worth Waiting For: Sexual Abstinence Before Marriage. LC 94-40476. 1995. 13.95 (0-87579-920-5) Deseret Bk.

Barlow, Charles F. Headaches & Migraines in Childhood. (Clinics in Developmental Medicine Ser.: No. 91). (Illus.). 288p. (C). 1991. text 52.95 (0-521-41211-0, Pub. by Mc Keith Pr) Cambridge U Pr.

Barlow, Cheri A. Charts & Forms for Coaching Families & Groups: A Companion Book for Coaching Families & Groups Toward Excellence. (Coaching Forms Ser.). (Illus.). 25p. 1997. pap., wbk. ed. 30.00 (0-9662022-1-X) Quest CA.

— Coaching Forms for Families & Groups. (Coaching Forms Ser.). (Illus.). 110p. 1997. pap., wbk. ed. 30.00 (0-9662022-0-1) Quest CA.

— Coaching Toward Excellence No. 1: Families & Groups: Theories & Techniques. LC 97-95066. (Illus.). 150p. 1998. pap. 35.00 (0-9662022-3-6) Quest CA.

Barlow, Claude W., ed. see Martinus.

Barlow, Claude W., ed. see Seneca, Lucius Annaeus.

Barlow, Claude W., tr. see Iberian Fathers.

Barlow, Cleve. Key Concepts in Maori Culture. (Illus.). 204p. 1991. pap. text 24.95 (0-19-558212-8) OUP.

Barlow, Clive & Wacher, Tim. A Field Guide to Birds of the Gambia & Senegal. LC 97-80156. (Illus.). 408p. 1998. 40.00 (0-300-07454-9) Yale U Pr.

Barlow, Colin, ed. Institutions & Economic Change in Southeast Asia: The Context of Development from the 1960's to the 1990's. LC 99-41670. 224p. 2000. 80.00 (1-85898-726-1) E Elgar.

Barlow, Connie. Green Space, Green Time: The Way of Science. LC 97-15704. 232p. 1997. 25.00 (0-387-94794-9) Spr-Verlag.

Barlow, Connie, ed. Evolution Extended: Biological Debates on the Meaning of Life. (Illus.). 300p. 1994. 38.00 (0-262-02373-3) MIT Pr.

— Evolution Extended: Biological Debates on the Meaning of Life. (Illus.). 352p. 1995. pap. text 19.00 (0-262-52206-3) MIT Pr.

— From Gaia to Selfish Genes: Selected Writings in the Life Sciences. (Illus.). 313p. 1991. 42.00 (0-262-02323-7) MIT Pr.

— From Gaia to Selfish Genes: Selected Writings in the Life Sciences. (Illus.). 288p. 1992. reprint ed. pap. text 21.00 (0-262-52178-4) MIT Pr.

Barlow, Constance A., et al. Handbook of Interactive Exercises for Groups. LC 99-178845. 168p. 1998. pap. text 24.00 (0-205-27854-X) P-H.

*Barlow, Dan. Play Cribbage to Win. 2000. pap. 7.95 (0-8069-4313-0) Sterling.

Barlow, Daniel L. Educational Psychology. (Illus.). 540p. (C). 1992. reprint ed. 85.00 (1-878907-50-6) TechBooks.

*Barlow, David E. & Barlow, Melissa Hickman. Police in a Multicultural Society: An American Story. 313p. (C). 2000. 21.95 (1-57766-129-X) Waveland Pr.

Barlow, David E., jt. auth. see Brandl, Steven G.

Barlow, David H. Abnormal Psychology. (Psychology Ser.). 1994. pap., student ed. 17.00 (0-534-20360-4) Brooks-Cole.

*Barlow, David H. Abnormal Psychology: An Integrative Approach with InfoTrac. 2nd ed. (Psychology Ser.). 1998. 53.25 incl. cd-rom (0-534-36330-X) Brooks-Cole.

Barlow, David H. Anxiety & Its Disorders: The Nature & Treatment of Anxiety & Panic. LC 87-24842. 698p. 1988. lib. bdg. 69.95 (0-89862-720-6) Guilford Pubns.

Barlow, David H., ed. Behavioral Assessment of Adult Disorders. LC 80-14673. (Guilford Behavioral Assessment Ser.). (Illus.). 512p. 1981. reprint ed. pap. 158.80 (0-608-07812-3, 205988000010) Bks Demand.

— Clinical Handbook of Psychological Disorders: A Step-by-Step Treatment Manual. 2nd ed. LC 93-849. 534p. 1993. lib. bdg. 60.00 (0-89862-129-1) Guilford Pubns.

— Diagnosis, Dimensions, & the DSM IV Special Issues Journal of Abnormal Psychology: The Science of Classification, Vol. 100, No. 3. 150p. 1991. text 20.00 (1-55798-135-3) Am Psychol.

Barlow, David H. & Cerny, Jerome A. Psychological Treatment of Panic. LC 87-19682. (Treatment Manuals for Practitioners Ser.). 227p. 1988. pap. text 22.00 (0-89862-507-6) Guilford Pubns.

Barlow, David H. & Durand, Mark. Abnormal Psychology: An Integrated Approach. LC 94-35287. 806p. 1994. pap. 61.00 (0-534-20358-2) Brooks-Cole.

Barlow, David H. & Durand, V. Mark. Abnormal Psychology: An Integrative Approach. 1995. pap., teacher ed. write for info. (0-534-20361-2) Brooks-Cole.

— Abnormal Psychology: An Integrative Approach, Test Items. 1995. pap. write for info. (0-534-20362-0) Brooks-Cole.

*Barlow, David H. & Durand, V. Mark. Abnormal Psychology: Integrative Approach. 2nd ed. (Psychology Ser.). 1999. pap. 61.50 incl. cd-rom (0-534-50677-1) Wadsworth Pub.

Barlow, David H. & Hersen, M. Single Case Experimental Designs. 2nd ed. 432p. (C). 1992. pap. text 52.00 (0-205-14271-0, H4271) Allyn.

Barlow, David H., jt. auth. see Brown, Timothy A.

Barlow, David H., jt. auth. see Durand, V. Mark.

Barlow, David H., jt. auth. see Mostofsky, David I.

Barlow, David H., ed. see Goddard, Perilou.

Barlow, David H., jt. ed. see Mavissaka, Matig.

Barlow, David H., jt. ed. see Rapee, Ronald M.

Barlow, E. R. & Wender, Ira T. Foreign Investment & Taxation. LC 55-9771. (Illus.). 508p. 1955. 4.00 (0-915506-01-7) Harvard Law Intl Tax.

Barlow, Eleanor Poe. The Master's Cat: The Story of Charles Dickens as Told by His Cat. (Illus.). 132p. (YA). (gr. 7 up). 1998. 24.00 (0-9518525-3-1) Dickens Bks.

— The Master's Cat: The Story of Charles Dickens as Told by His Cat. (YA). 1999. pap. 16.50 (1-880158-22-1) J N Townsend.

Barlow, Elizabeth, jt. auth. see Epstein, Jason.

Barlow, Frank. Feudal Kingdom of England 1042-1216. 4th ed. (History of England Ser.). (Illus.). 478p. (C). 1989. pap. text 45.00 (0-582-49504-0, 73627) Longman.

— Feudal Kingdom of England 1042-1216. 5th ed. LC 98-51308. 400p. 1999. pap. 32.86 (0-582-38117-7) Longman.

— Feudel Kingdom England. 4th ed. 1988. text 37.75 (0-582-03081-1, Pub. by Addison-Wesley) Longman.

— The Life of King Edward Who Rests at Westminster: Attributed to a Monk of St. Bertin. 2nd ed. (Oxford Medieval Texts Ser.).Tr. of Vita Aedwardi Regis Qui Apud Westmonasterium Requiescit. (Illus.). 254p. 1992. text 85.00 (0-19-820203-2) OUP.

— The Norman Conquest & Beyond. 318p. (C). 1983. 55.00 (0-907628-19-2) Hambledon Press.

— Thomas Becket. 384p. 1990. pap. 18.95 (0-520-07175-1, Pub. by U CA Pr) Cal Prin Full Svc.

*Barlow, Frank. William Rufus. (Illus.). 512p. 2000. pap. 20.00 (0-300-08291-6) Yale U Pr.

Barlow, Frank. Winchester in the Early Middle Ages: An Edition & Discussion of the Winton Domesday. (Winchester Studies). (Illus.). 646p. 1977. text 99.00 (0-19-813169-0) OUP.

Barlow, Frank, ed. English Episcopal Acta Vol. XI: Exeter, 1046-1184. (English Episcopal Acta Ser.; British Academy: Vol. XI). (Illus.). 232p. 1996. text 70.00 (0-19-726144-2) OUP.

— English Episcopal Acta Vol. XII: Exeter, 1186-1257. (English Episcopal Acta Ser.; British Academy: No. XII). 382p. 1996. text 90.00 (0-19-726145-0) OUP.

— The Life of King Edward Who Rests at Westminster: Attributed to a Monk of St. Bertin. LC 80-2170. (Norman Conquest Ser.).Tr. of Vita Aedwardi Regis Qui Apud Westmonasterium Requiescit. (ENG & LAT.). 312p. 1984. reprint ed. 37.50 (0-404-18751-X) AMS Pr.

Barlow, Frank, ed. see Bishop of Amiens, Guy.

Barlow, Fred D., jt. auth. see Elshabini-Riad, Aicha.

Barlow, Fred M. Timeless Truth for Twentieth Century Times. 123p. 1970. 3.25 (0-87398-838-8) Sword of Lord.

Barlow, Fred W. Rubber Compounding: Principles, Materials & Techniques. 2nd ed. (Illus.). 312p. 1993. text 190.00 (0-8247-8968-7) Dekker.

Barlow, G. The Genius of Dickens. LC 75-22401. (Studies in Dickens: No. 52). 1975. lib. bdg. 75.00 (0-8383-2091-0) M S G Haskell Hse.

Barlow, Galon L., Jr. The Adventures of Levi & Nathan at Bassett's Island. large type ed. (Illus.). 78p. (gr. 6 up). 1998. pap. 7.95 (0-9666020-0-5, 98-002) Farewell Pr.

— The Adventures of Levi & Nathan from the Cape of Cod to the Outer Banks, No. 3. large type ed. (Illus.). (YA). (gr. 6 up). 1998. mass mkt. 7.95 (0-9666020-2-1) Farewell Pr.

An Asterisk (*) at the beginning of an entry indicates that the title is appearing for the first time.

— The Battle of Nantucket. large type ed. (Illus.). 54p. 1998. pap. 7.95 (*0-9666020-1-3*, 98-001) Farewell Pr.

Barlow, Genevieve. Leyendas de Espana. (SPA.). 128p. 1989. pap. 15.50 (*0-8442-7243-4*) NTC Contemp Pub Co.

— Side by Side Bilingual Books - Latin America. (Stories From... Ser.). (SPA & ENG., Illus.). 280p. 1995. pap. 11.95 (*0-8442-0812-4*, Passprt Bks) NTC Contemp Pub Co.

Barlow, Genevieve & Stivers, William N. Stories from Mexico (Historias de Mexico) LC 95-68243. (BBC Phrase Books for Teenagers). (SPA & ENG., Illus.). 256p. 1995. pap. 11.95 (*0-8442-0811-6*, Passprt Bks) NTC Contemp Pub Co.

— Stories from Spain (Historias de Espana) LC 99-10382. (ENG & SPA.). 176p. 1998. pap. 11.95 (*0-8442-0499-4*, 04994, Teach Yrslf) NTC Contemp Pub Co.

Barlow, Geoffrey K. The Labour Movement in Thatcher's Britain: Conservative Macro- & Microeconomic Strategies & the Associated Labour Relations Legislation: Their Impact on the British Labour Movement During the 1980s. (European University Studies, Series 31: Vol. 320). (Illus.). xiii, 224p. 1997. pap. 44.95 (*3-631-31370-5*) P Lang Pubng.

— The Labour Movement in Thatcher's Britain: Conservative Macro- & Microeconomic Strategies & the Associated Labour Relations Legislation: Their Impact on the British Labour Movement During the 1980s. (European University Studies, Series 31: Vol. 320). (Illus.). XIII, 224p. 1997. pap. 44.95 (*0-8204-3246-6*) P Lang Pubng.

Barlow, George. Family Genealogy Comprising the Ancestry & Descendants of Jonathan Barlow & Plain Rogers, of Delaware County, N. Y. (& Allied Families) (Illus.). 508p. 1988. reprint ed. pap. 76.00 (*0-8328-0191-7*); reprint ed. lib. bdg. 86.00 (*0-8328-0190-9*) Higginson Bk Co.

— Gabriel. (Broadside Poets Ser.). 63p. 1974. pap. 2.00 (*0-685-00864-9*) Broadside Pr.

***Barlow, George W.** The Cichlid Fishes: Nature's Grand Experiment in Evolution. 256p. 2000. text 27.50 (*0-7382-0376-9*, Pub. by Perseus Pubng) HarpC.

Barlow, Gillian, jt. auth. see Pollock, Penny.

Barlow, H. B., ed. see Braitenberg, V. & Schuz, A.

Barlow, H. S. Swettenham. LC 95-949088. (Illus.). 783p. 1997. 69.95 (*983-99915-1-5*, Pub. by Southdene Sendirian) SE Asia.

— Tropical Planting & Gardening. rev. ed. 1994. pap. 120.00 (*81-7233-095-2*, Pub. by Scientific Pubs) St Mut.

Barlow, H. S. & Enoch, L. H. F. MacMillan's Tropical Planting & Gardening. 6th ed. 767p. 1994. 300.00 (*81-7233-011-1*, Pub. by Scientific Pubs) St Mut.

Barlow, Harold & Morgenstern, Sam. A Dictionary of Musical Themes. 642p. 1990. reprint ed. lib. bdg. 109.00 (*0-7812-9266-2*) Rprt Serv.

Barlow, Horace, et al, eds. Images & Understanding: Thoughts about Images: Ideas about Understanding. (Illus.). 414p. 1990. pap. text 32.95 (*0-521-36944-4*) Cambridge U Pr.

Barlow, Hugh D. Crime & Public Policy: Putting Theory to Work. Hagan, John G., ed. (Crime & Society Ser.). 288p. (C). 1995. pap. 30.00 (*0-8133-2678-8*, Pub. by Westview) HarpC.

— Criminology. 6th ed. (C). 1992. text 55.50 (*0-673-52265-2*) Addson-Wesley Educ.

— Criminology. 7th ed. LC 95-31707. 672p. (C). 1997. 74.00 (*0-673-52421-3*) Addson-Wesley Educ.

Barlow, Hugh D. & Ferdinand, Theodore N. Understanding Delinquency. 260p. (C). 1997. pap. 37.00 (*0-06-042028-6*) Addson-Wesley Educ.

Barlow, I. & Smith, R. J. The Uniforms of the British Yeomanry Force, 1794-1914 Vol. 1: The Sussex Yeomanry Cavalry. (C). 1988. 125.00 (*0-7855-7574-X*) St Mut.

— The Uniforms of the British Yeomanry Force, 1794-1914 Vol. 8: Lovat Scounts & the Scottish Horse. (C). 1988. 150.00 (*0-7855-7573-1*) St Mut.

Barlow, I. M. Spatial Dimensions of Urban Government. LC 80-41972. (Geographical Research Studies: No. 3). (Illus.). 209p. reprint ed. pap. 64.80 (*0-8357-7032-X*, 203332800085) Bks Demand.

Barlow II, John R., jt. auth. see VonCannon, Donald M.

Barlow, J., et al. Planning for Affordable Housing. 102p. 1994. pap. 30.00 (*0-11-752969-X*, HM29699, Pub. by Statnry Office) Bernan Associates.

Barlow, J. Jackson, et al, eds. The American Founding: Essays on the Formation of the Constitution, 205. LC 87-29558. (Contributions in Political Science Ser.: No. 205). 363p. 1988. 65.00 (*0-313-25610-1*, LMS/, Greenwood Pr) Greenwood.

— The New Federalist Papers. LC 88-22500. (Illus.). 480p. (Orig.). (C). 1988. pap. text 29.00 (*0-8191-7176-X*); lib. bdg. 63.00 (*0-8191-7175-1*) U Pr of Amer.

Barlow, J. W. Pharmacotherapeutics of the Thyroid Gland. Weetman, Anthony P. et al, eds. (Handbook of Experimental Pharmacology Ser.: No. 128). (Illus.). 400p. 1997. 321.00 (*3-540-62499-6*) Spr-Verlag.

Barlow, James. Public Participation in Urban Development: The European Experience. LC 95-212298. 86p. (C). 1995. pap. 17.95 (*0-85374-644-3*, Pub. by Pol Studies Inst) Brookings.

Barlow, James & Duncan, Simon. Markets, States & Housing Provision: Four European Growth Regions Compared. (Progress in Planning Ser.: Vol. 38). 88p. 1992. 64.00 (*0-08-042059-1*, Pergamon Pr) Elsevier.

Barlow, Jane. Creel of Irish Stories. LC 70-116934. (Short Story Index Reprint Ser.). 1977. 21.95 (*0-8369-3436-9*) Ayer.

— Irish Idylls. LC 77-94703. (Short Story Index Reprint Ser.). 1977. 21.95 (*0-8369-3082-7*) Ayer.

— Irish Ways. LC 77-121521. (Short Story Index Reprint Ser.). (Illus.). 1977. 24.95 (*0-8369-3477-6*) Ayer.

— Maureen's Fairing. LC 72-4418. (Short Story Index Reprint Ser.). (Illus.). 1977. reprint ed. 21.95 (*0-8369-4169-1*) Ayer.

— Strangers at Lisconnel: A Second Series of Irish Idylls. LC 73-150535. (Short Story Index Reprint Ser.). 1977. reprint ed. 18.95 (*0-8369-3832-1*) Ayer.

Barlow, Jane A., et al, eds. Cypriot Ceramics: Reading the Prehistoric Record. (University Museum Monographs: University Museum Symposium Ser.: Nos. 74 & II). (Illus.). ix, 256p. (C). 1992. text 50.00 (*0-924171-10-3*) U Museum Pubns.

***Barlow, Janelle & Maul, Dianna.** Emotional Value: Creating Strong Bonds with Your Customers. LC 99-86124. 300p. 2000. 27.95 (*1-57675-079-5*, Pub. by Berrett-Koehler) Publishers Group.

Barlow, Janelle & Moller, Claus. A Complaint Is a Gift: Using Customer Feedback As a Strategic Tool. LC 95-52763. 200p. (Orig.). 1996. pap. 16.95 (*1-881052-81-8*) Berrett-Koehler.

Barlow, Jeanine, jt. auth. see Kuehn, Lynn.

Barlow, Jeffrey & Richardson, Christine. China Doctor of John Day. LC 79-3300. (Illus.). 128p. 1997. reprint ed. pap. 12.95 (*0-8323-0346-1*) Binford Mort.

Barlow, Jeffrey G. Revolt of the Admirals: The Fight for Naval Aviation, 1945-1950. LC 98-18237. (Illus.). 448p. 1998. pap. 23.95 (*1-57488-170-1*) Brasseys.

— Revolt of the Admirals: The Fight for Naval Aviation, 1945-1950. LC 94-1937. 1994. 30.00 (*0-945274-24-6*) Naval Hist Ctr.

— Revolt of the Admirals: The Fight for Naval Aviation, 1945-1950. 444p. 1995. boxed set 30.00 (*0-16-042094-6*) USGPO.

— Sun Yat-Sen & the French, 1900-1908. LC 79-620017. (China Research Monographs: No. 14). 93p. 1979. pap. 4.00 (*0-912966-19-X*) IEAS.

***Barlow, Jerry N.** Studying & Serving with Success: Integrating Academics & Ministry. 128p. 1999. pap. text 11.95 (*1-56554-634-2*) Pelican.

***Barlow, Jewel B., et al.** Low Speed Wind Tunnel Testing. 3rd ed. LC 98-28891. 728p. 1999. 89.95 (*0-471-55774-9*) Wiley.

Barlow, Joel. Works Vols. 1 & 2: Prose & Poetry, 2 vols., Set. LC 68-17012. 1970. 150.00 (*0-8201-1062-0*) Schol Facsimiles.

***Barlow, John.** Gather Round down in Dad's Neighborhood. (Illus.). 202p. 1999. pap. 12.95 (*0-9675405-0-X*) Davis Boyce Pubng.

Barlow, John & King, Lesley. Wills, Executorship & Tax Planning. (C). 1991. text 18.00 (*1-85431-126-3*, Pub. by Blackstone Pr) Gaunt.

Barlow, John, jt. auth. see King, Anthony.

Barlow, John D., tr. see Ambery, Jean.

Barlow, John D., tr. see Amery, Jean.

Barlow, John P. Everything We Know. 1999. 21.95 (*0-670-83060-7*) Viking Penguin.

Barlow, John S. A Chinese-Russian-English Dictionary. LC 94-45600. 856p. 1995. text 100.00 (*0-8248-1729-X*) UH Pr.

— The Electroencephalogram: Its Patterns & Origins. LC 92-48443. 236p. 1993. 95.00 (*0-262-02354-7*, Bradford Bks) MIT Pr.

***Barlow, John S.** A Pocket Chinese-Russian-English Dictionary: Arranged by the Rosenberg Graphical System. (CHI, RUS & ENG.). 406p. 2000. pap. text 25.00 (*0-8248-2294-3*) UH Pr.

Barlow, John S., tr. see Beritashvili, Ivan S.

Barlow, John S., tr. see Livanov, M. N. & Rusinov, V. S., eds.

Barlow, Joseph W. Basic Spanish. (Illus.). 1939. text 18.50 (*0-89197-044-4*) Irvington.

Barlow, Judith E., ed. Plays by American Women, 1900-1930. rev. ed. LC 84-24606. 304p. 1985. reprint ed. 24.95 (*1-55783-007-X*); reprint ed. pap. 10.95 (*1-55783-008-8*) Applause Theatre Bk Pubs.

Barlow, Judith E., ed. see Luce, Clare Boothe, et al.

Barlow, Keith A., ed. see Bunker, Paul D.

Barlow, Lawrence E. Job-Search Training Activity Book. 56p. (Orig.). 1982. pap. text, student ed. 2.00 (*0-940150-02-6*) Voc Career Assess.

— Job-Search Training Instructor's Guide. 24p. (Orig.). 1982. pap. text, teacher ed. 1.75 (*0-940150-01-8*) Voc Career Assess.

— The Job-Seekers' Bible. rev. ed. LC 81-11494. 320p. (Orig.). (C). 1996. pap. 9.95 (*0-940150-00-X*) Voc Career Assess.

— Ten-Hour Job Search Training Mini Course for Vocational-Occupational Skills Program. 14p. (Orig.). 1985. 1.75 (*0-940150-03-4*) Voc Career Assess.

Barlow, Linda. Her Sister's Keeper. 576p. (Orig.). 1993. mass mkt. 5.50 (*0-446-36331-6*, Pub. by Warner Bks) Little.

— Her Sister's Keeper. (Orig.). 1994. reprint ed. lib. bdg. 22.00 (*0-7278-4701-5*) Severn Hse.

— Hunter's Bride. (Desire Ser.). 1993. per. 2.99 (*0-373-05788-1*, 5-05788-0) Silhouette.

— Intimate Betrayal. 400p. 1996. 26.00 (*0-7278-4940-9*) Severn Hse.

Barlow, Lyde & Gilbert, Reinsurance Division Staff. Reinsurance Practice & the Law. ring bd. 250.00 (*1-85044-390-4*) LLP.

Barlow, M. T. & Nualart, D. Lectures in Probability Theory & Statistics. Pierre, B. et al, eds. (Lecture Notes in Mathematics Ser.: Vol. 1690). viii, 237p. 1998. pap. 41.00 (*3-540-64620-5*) Spr-Verlag.

Barlow, Margaret. Women Artists. (Illus.). 320p. 1999. 75.00 (*0-88363-398-1*, Pub. by H L Levin) Publishers Group.

Barlow, Marjorie D. Notes on Woman Printers in Colonial America & the United States, 1639-1975. LC 76-46686. 103p. reprint ed. pap. 32.00 (*0-7837-4344-0*, 204405400012) Bks Demand.

Barlow, Maude. Big Black Book: The Essential Views of Conrad Black & Barbara Amiel. LC 98-107842. 248p. 1998. pap. text 14.95 (*0-7737-5904-2*) Stoddart Publ.

Barlow, Maude & Clarke, Tony. MAI: The Multilateral Agreement on Investment & the Threat to American Democracy. LC 98-232312. 120p. 1998. pap. 9.95 (*0-7737-5979-4*) Stoddart Publ.

***Barlow, Melinda.** Mary Lucier. LC 99-87601. 2000. 45.00 (*0-8018-6379-1*) Johns Hopkins.

— A Quilters Cookbook! Who Feeds the Family When a Quilter Quilts? (Illus.). 184p. 1999. pap. 12.00 (*0-7392-0431-9*, PO3714) Morris Pubng.

***Barlow, Melinda, ed.** Mary Lucier. LC 99-87601. 2000. pap. 19.95 (*0-8018-6380-5*) Johns Hopkins.

Barlow, Melissa Hickman, jt. auth. see Barlow, David E.

Barlow, Merlem A., jt. auth. see King, Clinton P.

Barlow, Michael. Whom the Gods Love: The Life & Music of George Butterworth. LC 99-187961. (Illus.). 1997. write for info. (*0-907689-42-6*); write for info. (*0-907689-43-4*) Toccata Pr.

Barlow, Michael. Working with Computers: Computer Orientation for Foreign Students. LC 86-83418. (Illus.). 320p. (Orig.). 1987. 23.95 (*0-940753-07-3*); pap. 15.95 (*0-940753-08-1*) Athelstan Pubns.

Barlow, Michael & Ferguson, Charles A., eds. Agreement in Natural Language: Approaches, Theories, Descriptions. LC 86-71109. 355p. 1988. 44.95 (*0-937073-02-4*) CSLI.

***Barlow, Michael & Kemmer, Suzanne, eds.** Usage-Based Models of Language. LC 99-59368. 296p. 2000. pap. text 24.95 (*1-57586-220-4*, Pub. by CSLI) Cambridge U Pr.

— Usage-Based Models of Language. LC 99-59368. 296p. (C). 2000. text 64.95 (*1-57586-219-0*, Pub. by CSLI) Cambridge U Pr.

Barlow, Nora, ed. & notes see Darwin, Charles.

Barlow, Patricia M. Aviation Antitrust: The Extraterritorial Application of the United States Antitrust Laws & International Air Transportation. LC 87-3795. 1987. 88.00 (*90-6544-293-6*) Kluwer Law Intl.

***Barlow, Patrick.** Love upon the Throne. 1999. pap. 15.95 (*1-85459-421-4*, Pub. by Theatre Comm) Consort Bk Sales.

Barlow, Patrick. Shakespeare: The Truth. 224p. 1995. pap. 11.95 (*0-413-69260-4*, A0755) Heinemann.

Barlow, Paul, ed. see Helberg, Stephen, et al.

***Barlow-Perez, Sally.** A History of Aspen. Ohlrich, Warren H., ed. LC 99-75721. (Illus.). 112p. 2000. pap. 14.95 (*1-882426-14-2*) W H O Pr.

Barlow, Philip L. Mormons & the Bible: The Place of the Latter-Day Saints in American Religion. (Religion in America). (Illus.). 296p. 1997. reprint ed. pap. 13.95 (*0-19-510971-6*) OUP.

Barlow, Philip L., ed. A Thoughtful Faith: Essays on Belief by Mormon Scholars. LC 86-71882. 310p. 1986. 16.95 (*0-939651-00-9*) Canon Pr.

Barlow, Priscilla. Wise Enough to Play the Fool: A Biography of Duncan Macrae. 258p. 1996. 45.00 (*0-85976-418-4*, Pub. by J Donald) St Mut.

***Barlow, R.** The Great American Antique Toy Bazaar, 1879-1945: 5,000 Old Engravings from Original Trade Catalogs, the Evolution of Dolls & Toys. (Pictorial Archive Ser.). 2000. pap. 9.95 (*0-486-41189-3*) Dover.

Barlow, R. A. & Bowen, H. V., eds. A Dear & Noble Boy: The Life & Letters of Louis Stokes 1897-1916. LC 95-161989. (Illus.). 200p. 1995. 26.95 (*0-85052-425-3*, Pub. by Leo Cooper) Trans-Atl Phila.

Barlow, R. J., jt. auth. see Loveless, W.

Barlow, Raymond E. & Kaiser, Joan B. A Guide to Sandwich Glass, Vol. 4. abr. ed. Nickerson, Lloyd C., ed. LC 85-72433. (Illus.). 224p. 1985. pap. 25.00 (*0-9610166-4-7*) Kaiser Pub Co.

Barlow, Raymond E. & Kaiser, Joan E. The Glass Industry in Sandwich, Vol. 1. (Illus.). 328p. 1993. 120.00 (*0-88740-551-7*) Schiffer.

— The Glass Industry in Sandwich, Vol. 3. LC 88-63065. 280p. 1987. 79.95 (*0-88740-081-7*) Schiffer.

— The Glass Industry in Sandwich, Vol. 4. Nickerson, Lloyd C., ed. LC 82-73582. (Illus.). 1983. 95.00 (*0-9610166-0-4*) Kaiser Pub Co.

— The Glass Industry in Sandwich, Vol. 4. deluxe ed. Nickerson, Lloyd C., ed. LC 82-73582. (Illus.). 1983. lthr. 125.00 (*0-9610166-1-2*) Kaiser Pub Co.

— The Glass Industry in Sandwich Vol. 2: Lighting Devices. LC 88-64002. (Illus.). 300p. 1989. 95.00 (*0-88740-170-8*) Schiffer.

— Guide to Sandwich Glass: Blown Tableware, Pressed Cup Plates, & Salts. LC 93-84876. (Illus.). 208p. 1993. pap. 29.95 (*0-88740-553-3*) Schiffer.

— A Guide to Sandwich Glass: Kerosene Lamps & Accessories. LC 88-63999. (Illus.). 144p. 1989. pap. 24.95 (*0-88740-172-4*) Schiffer.

— Guide to Sandwich Glass: Pressed Tableware. LC 93-84876. (Illus.). 96p. 1993. pap. 29.95 (*0-88740-552-5*) Schiffer.

— Guide to Sandwich Glass: Vases, Colognes & Stoppers. LC 86-63065. 108p. 1987. pap. 23.50 (*0-88740-082-5*) Schiffer.

— A Guide to Sandwich Glass: Whale Oil Lamps & Accessories. LC 88-63998. (Illus.). 144p. 1989. pap. 24.95 (*0-88740-171-6*) Schiffer.

— Guide to Sandwich Glass: Witch Balls, Containers & Toys. LC 86-63065. 100p. 1987. pap. 23.50 (*0-88740-083-3*) Schiffer.

— Price Guide for Volumes One, Two, Three & Four of the Glass Industry in Sandwich. 40p. 1993. pap. 15.00 (*0-88740-554-1*) Schiffer.

Barlow, Raymond E., jt. auth. see Kaiser, Joan E.

Barlow, Richard. Engineering Reliability. LC 97-44019. (ASA-SIAM Series on Statistics & Applied Probability: Vol. 2). (Illus.). xx, 199p. (C). 1998. pap. text 48.00 (*0-89871-405-2*, SA02) Soc Indus-Appl Math.

— Team Librarianship: The Advent of Public Library Team Structures. LC 90-107485. (Illus.). 175p. reprint ed. pap. 54.30 (*0-608-09592-3*, 205439400006) Bks Demand.

Barlow, Richard & Proschan, Frank. Mathematical Theory of Reliability. LC 96-13952. (Classics in Applied Mathematics Ser.: No. 17). xv, 258p. 1996. pap. 37.00 (*0-89871-369-2*, CL17) Soc Indus-Appl Math.

Barlow, Richard E., et al. Statistical Inference under Order Restrictions: The Theory & Application of Isotonic Regression. LC 74-39231. (Wiley Series in Probability & Mathematical Statistics: No. 8). 400p. reprint ed. pap. 124.00 (*0-608-16335-X*, 202668000051) Bks Demand.

Barlow, Richard G. The Fifth Directory of Periodicals: Publishing Articles on American & English Language & Literature, Criticism & Theory, Film, American Studies, Poetry & Fiction. LC 65-9218. 384p. (C). 1992. text 49.95 (*0-8040-0958-9*); pap. text 24.95 (*0-8040-0962-7*) Swallow.

Barlow, Robert, et al. The Biological Century: Friday Evening Talks at the Marine Biological Laboratory. (Illus.). 248p. 1993. text 45.00 (*0-674-07403-3*) HUP.

Barlow, Robert H. La Extension del Imperio de los Culhua Mexica. 262p. 1992. pap. 18.00 (*968-6254-17-X*, IN013) UPLAAP.

— The Extent of the Empire of the Culhua Mexico. LC 76-43645. (Ibero-Americana Ser.: No. 28). reprint ed. 37.50 (*0-404-15480-8*) AMS Pr.

Barlow, Robert H. & Smisor, George T., eds. Nombre de Dios, Durango. LC 76-44684. 136p. 1983. reprint ed. 32.50 (*0-404-15901-X*) AMS Pr.

Barlow, Robin & Brown, Joseph W., eds. Reproductive Health & Infectious Disease in the Middle East. LC 98-72620. 228p. 1998. text 63.95 (*1-84014-384-3*, Pub. by Ashgate Pub) Ashgate Pub Co.

Barlow, Robin, et al. Economic Behavior of the Affluent. LC 76-57713. (Brookings Institution, Studies of Government Finance Ser.). 285p. 1978. reprint ed. lib. bdg. 65.00 (*0-8371-9454-7*, BAEB, Greenwood Pr) Greenwood.

Barlow, Roger. Statistics: A Guide & Reference to the Use of Statistical Methods in the Physical Sciences. LC 88-33908. (Manchester Physics Ser.). 222p. 1989. 139.95 (*0-471-92294-3*) Wiley.

— Statistics: A Guide to the Use of Statistical Methods in the Physical Sciences. LC 88-33908. (Manchester Physics Ser.). 222p. 1993. pap. 59.95 (*0-471-92295-1*) Wiley.

Barlow, Ronald S. The Antique Tool Collector's Guide to Value. rev. ed. LC 99-174779. (Illus.). 240p. 1999. pap. 14.95 (*0-89538-099-4*) L-W Inc.

— The Great American Antique Toy Bazaar, 1879-1945: 5,000 Old Engravings from Original Trade Catalogs, the Evolution of Dolls & Toys. (Illus.). 312p. 1998. pap. 19.95 (*0-933846-06-1*) Windmill Pub Co.

— The Vanishing American Barber Shop. LC 96-76415. (Illus.). 224p. (Orig.). 1996. pap. 19.95 (*0-9652373-0-3*) W Marvy.

***Barlow, Ronald S.** Vanishing American Outhouse: Privy Plans, Photographs, Poems & Folklore. (Illus.). 135p. 2000. pap. 19.95 (*0-14-028868-6*, Viking Studio) Studio Bks.

Barlow, Ronald S. & Reynolds, Ray. The Insider's Guide to Old Books, Magazines, Newspapers & Trade Catalogs: 21,000 Items Priced by Dealers & Collectors. LC 96-103812. (Illus.). 456p. (Orig.). 1995. pap. 19.95 (*0-933846-05-3*) Windmill Pub Co.

Barlow, Sally H., jt. auth. see Byrd, A. Dean.

Barlow, Sean. Afropop! An Illustrated Guide to Contemporary African Music. LC 96-140841. (Illus.). 1995. 10.98 (*0-7858-0443-9*) Bk Sales Inc.

Barlow, Sean & Eyre, Banning. Afropop! Illustrated Guide to Contemporary African Music. (Illus.). 80p. 1995. write for info. (*1-887354-02-6*) Saraband CT.

Barlow, Shirley A. The Imagery of Euripides. 192p. 1987. 29.50 (*0-8453-4513-3*) Assoc Univ Prs.

— The Imagery of Euripides: A Study in the Dramatic Use of Pictorial Language. LC 78-596134. xii, 169p. 1971. write for info. (*0-416-08130-4*) Routledge.

— The Imagery of Euripides: A Study in the Dramatic Use of Pictorial Language LC 75-307257. (University Paperbacks Ser.). xii, 169p. 1974. write for info. (*0-416-81310-0*) Routledge.

Barlow, Shirley A., ed. see Euripides.

Barlow, Shirley A., ed. & tr. see Euripides.

Barlow, Steve. Mad Myths Stone Me. (Illus.). 124p. (J). 1997. pap. 7.95 (*0-14-037108-7*, Pub. by Pnguin Bks Ltd) Trafalgar.

— Star Bores: The Novel. (J). 1999. mass mkt. 4.95 (*1-902618-76-9*, Pub. by Element Childrns) Penguin Putnam.

— Surfer's Mad Myths: A Touch of Wind. (Illus.). 128p. (J). pap. 7.95 (*0-14-038346-8*, Pub. by Pnguin Bks Ltd) Trafalgar.

— Surfers' Mad Myths Must Fly. (Illus.). 128p. (J). pap. 7.95 (*0-14-038347-6*, Pub. by Pnguin Bks Ltd) Trafalgar.

***Barlow, Steve L.** Mad Myths Mind the Door. (Illus.). 128p. (J). 1998. pap. 7.95 (*0-14-037725-5*, Pub. by Pnguin Bks Ltd) Trafalgar.

Barlow, Steven M. Handbook of Clinical Speech Physiology. (Speech Sciences Ser.). (Illus.). 9p. (Orig.). 1999. pap. 87.95 (*1-56593-267-6*, 0589) Thomson Learn.

Barlow, Tani E. Nationalism Question. 1994. pap. 12.00 (*0-8223-6411-5*) Duke.

Barlow, Tani E., ed. Formations of Colonial Modernity in East Asia. LC 96-43148. (Positions Bks.). (Illus.). 456p. 1997. lib. bdg. 54.95 (*0-8223-1937-3*) Duke.

Barlow, Tani E., ed. Formations of Colonial Modernity in East Asia. LC 96-43148. (Positions Bks.). (Illus.). 456p. 1997. pap. text 18.95 (*0-8223-1943-8*) Duke.

B

Barlow, Tani E., ed. Gender Politics in Modern China: Writing & Feminism. LC 93-2401. 296p. 1993. text 49.95 (*0-8223-1376-6*); pap. text 18.95 (*0-8223-1389-8*) Duke.
— Marxist Scholarship, Vol. 3, No. 2. 390p. 1996. pap. 12.00 (*0-8223-6438-7*) Duke.
— Modern Sex. (Special Issue of Positions Ser.: Vol. 2, No. 3). 275p. 1995. pap. 12.00 (*0-8223-6424-7*) Duke.
Barlow, Tani E. & Lowe, Donald M. Teaching China's Lost Generation. 1987. reprint ed. 8.95 (*0-8351-1818-5*) China Bks.
Barlow, Tani E., jt. auth. see Wang, Jing.
Barlow, Tani E., ed. see Ling, Ding.
Barlow, Tani E., jt. ed. see Wang, Jing.
Barlow, Tani E., jt. ed. see Zito, Angela.
Barlow, Thomas L., jt. auth. see McNair, John F.
***Barlow, Tracie, et al.** The COTA in the Schools. (Illus.). 86p. 1999. pap. 39.00 (*0-12-784461-9*) Acad Pr.
Barlow, Virginia & Doyle, Chris. The Nature of the Islands: Plants & Animals of the Eastern Caribbean. (Illus.). 148p. (Orig.). 1993. pap. 14.95 (*0-944428-13-4*) Cruising Guide.
Barlow, Wayne E., et al. Advising California Employers, 2 vols. 2nd ed. Peyerwold, David, ed. LC 96-85305. 1596p. 1996. ring bd. 189.00 (*0-7626-0007-1*, BU-32030) Cont Ed Bar-CA.
Barlow, Wilfred. The Alexander Technique: How to Use Your Body Without Stress. (Illus.). 240p. 1991. pap. 12.95 (*0-89281-385-7*) Inner Tradit.
Barlow, William. A Briefe Discovery of the Idle Animadversions of Mark Ridley, Doctor of Phisicke. LC 71-38149. (English Experience Ser.: No. 429). 16p. 1972. reprint ed. 20.00 (*90-221-0429-X*) Walter J Johnson.
— A Dyaloge Descrybyng the Orygynall Ground of These Lutheran Saccyons, That Is, Faccyons. LC 74-80161. (English Experience Ser.: No. 641). 200p. 1974. reprint ed. 20.00 (*90-221-0641-1*) Walter J Johnson.
— Looking up at Down: The Emergence of Blues Culture. 464p. 1990. pap. 22.95 (*0-87722-722-5*) Temple U Pr.
— The Navigators Supply. LC 76-38150. (English Experience Ser.: No. 430). 100p. 1972. reprint ed. 30.00 (*90-221-0430-3*) Walter J Johnson.
— Summe & Substance of the Conference. LC 65-10395. 110p. 1965. reprint ed. 50.00 (*0-8201-1004-3*) Schol Facsimiles.
— The Summe & Substance of the Conference at Hampton Court, January 14, 1603. LC 74-28829. (English Experience Ser.: No. 711). 1975. reprint ed. 30.00 (*90-221-0711-6*) Walter J Johnson.
— Voice Over: The Making of Black Radio. LC 98-29943. (Illus.). 304p. 1998. pap. 22.95 (*1-56639-667-0*); text 49.95 (*1-56639-666-2*) Temple U Pr.
Barlow, William & Finley, Cheryl. From Swing to Soul: An Illustrated History of African American Popular Music from 1930 to 1960. LC 93-40961. 1994. 32.50 (*1-880216-18-3*, Elliott Clark) Black Belt Communs.
Barlow, William, jt. auth. see Morgan, Thomas L.
Barlow, William, jt. ed. see Dates, Jannette L.
Barlow-Williams, Katheryn. Haven't We Met Before? A Closer Look at Biblical Friends. LC 98-44912. (Study Ser.). 68p. 1999. pap. 7.95 (*0-7880-1340-8*) CSS OH.
Barlowe. Illustrating Nature: How to Paint & Draw Plants & Animals. LC 97-23766. (Illus.). 64p. pap. 12.95 (*0-486-29921-X*) Dover.
— Learning about Minerals. (Learning about Ser.). pap. 1.00 (*0-486-40017-4*) Dover.
— Learning about Wildflowers. (Learning about Ser.). pap. text 1.00 (*0-486-40016-6*) Dover.
— Long Island Nature Preserves Col. Book. 1998. pap. 2.95 (*0-486-29406-4*) Dover.
Barlowe, Amy. Happy Listening Guide. (Illus.). 20p. 1992. pap. text 5.95 (*0-87487-433-5*) Summy-Birchard.
Barlowe, Dorothy, et al. Dinosaurs. LC 77-70862. (Pop-Up Bks.: No. 3). (J). (ps-3). 1977. 10.00 (*0-394-83538-7*, Pub. by Random Bks Yng Read) Random.
***Barlowe, Dot.** Backyard Nature Coloring Book. 48p. (J). 1999. pap. 2.95 (*0-486-40560-5*) Dover.
— Beginners Book of Wildflowers. (Illus.). 2000. pap. 4.95 (*0-486-41060-9*) Dover.
— Seashore Plants & Animals. (Illus.). (J). 2000. pap. 2.95 (*0-486-41033-1*) Dover.
Barlowe, Jamie. The Scarlet Mob of Scribblers: Rereading Hester Prynne. LC 99-20051. 192p. 2000. 39.95 (*0-8093-2273-0*) S Ill U Pr.
Barlowe, Jerome & Roye, William. Rede Me & Be Nott Wrothe. Parker, Douglas H., ed. 272p. 1992. text 50.00 (*0-8020-2681-8*) U of Toronto Pr.
Barlowe, Louis Ellenwood. Cathedral of the New Age. LC 96-70979. 64p. (Orig.). 1996. pap. 9.00 (*1-886094-41-1*) Chicago Spectrum.
Barlowe, Raleigh. Land Resource Economics: The Economics of Real Estate. 4th ed. (Illus.). 672p. (C). 1985. text 65.20 (*0-13-522541-8*) P-H.
Barlowe, Raleigh, jt. auth. see Johnson, V. Webster.
***Barlowe, Raleigh Bruce.** Saint's Second Season. 264p. 1999. 23.95 (*0-7541-0512-1*, Pub. by Minerva Pr) Unity Dist.
***Barlowe, Sy.** Beginning Birdwatcher's Book. (Illus.). 2000. pap. 4.95 (*0-486-41059-5*) Dover.
Barlowe, Sy. Birds of Prey. (Learning about Ser.). 16p. (J). 1998. pap. 1.00 (*0-486-40332-7*) Dover.
— Botanical Gardens Coloring Book. (Illus.). (J). pap. 2.95 (*0-486-29858-2*) Dover.
— Desert Animals. (Learning about Ser.). (J). pap. 1.00 (*0-486-40333-5*) Dover.
— Flowers. (Learning about Ser.). (Illus.). 16p. (Orig.). pap. 1.00 (*0-486-29523-0*) Dover.
— Frogs & Toads. (Learning about Ser.). (J). pap. 1.00 (*0-486-40121-9*) Dover.
— Learning about African Animals. (Learning about Ser.). (Illus.). 16p. 1999. pap. text 1.00 (*0-486-40533-8*) Dover.
— Learning about Backyard Animals. (Learning about Ser.). (Illus.). 16p. 1999. pap. text 1.00 (*0-486-40534-6*) Dover.
— Learning about Rain Forest Animals. (Learning about Ser.). (Illus.). 16p. 1999. pap. text 1.00 (*0-486-40535-4*) Dover.
— Leaves. (Learning about Ser.). 16p. (J). pap. 1.00 (*0-486-29762-4*) Dover.
— Monkeys & Apes. (Learning about Ser.). pap. 1.00 (*0-486-40018-2*) Dover.
— 101 Questions about the Seashore. LC 97-20552. 1998. pap. 2.00 (*0-486-29914-7*) Dover.
— Sea Animals. (Learning about Ser.). (J). pap. 1.00 (*0-486-40122-7*) Dover.
— Shells. (Learning about Ser.). 16p. (J). pap. 1.00 (*0-486-29761-6*) Dover.
— Whales. (Learning about Ser.). 16p. (J). pap. 1.00 (*0-486-29787-X*) Dover.
Barlowe, W. Terry, ed. see Shaffer, Charles.
Barlowe, Wayne. The Alien Life of Wayne Barlowe. (Illus.). 72p. 1995. pap. 24.95 (*1-883398-10-X*) Morpheus Intl.
— The Alien Life of Wayne Barlowe. 72p. 1997. 95.00 (*1-883398-20-7*) Morpheus Intl.
— Barlowe's Inferno. (Illus.). 80p. 1998. 24.95 (*1-883398-36-3*) Morpheus Intl.
Barlowe, Wayne D. Expedition: Being an Account in Words & Artwork of the A. D. 2358 Voyage to Darwin IV. LC 88-40228. (Illus.). 192p. 1990. pap. 18.95 (*0-89480-629-7*, 1629) Workman Pub.
Barlowe, Wayne D. & Duskis, Neil. Barlowe's Guide to Fantasy TP: Barlowes G to Fantasy TP. LC 96-3056. 144p. 1996. pap. 19.95 (*0-06-100817-6*, Pub. by Harper SF) HarpC.
Barlowe, Wayne D., et al. Barlowe's Guide to Extraterrestrials. rev. ed. LC 86-40609. (Illus.). 144p. 1987. pap. 13.95 (*0-89480-324-7*, 1324) Workman Pub.
Barltrop, J. A. & Coyle, J. D. Excited States in Organic Chemistry. LC 74-22400. (Illus.). 398p. reprint ed. pap. 123.40 (*0-608-17670-2*, 203038700069) Bks Demand.
— Principles of Photochemistry. LC 78-16622. 223p. reprint ed. pap. 69.20 (*0-608-12207-6*, 202479600038) Bks Demand.
Barltrop, Robert. Yes, Mush: A Cockney Dictionary: The Cockney Language & Its World. (Illus.). 240p. (C). 1995. pap. 17.50 (*0-485-12047-X*, Pub. by Athlone Pr) Humanities.
— Yes, Mush: A Cockney Dictionary: The Cockney Language & Its World. (Illus.). 240p. (C). 1995. text 49.95 (*0-485-11253-1*, Pub. by Athlone Pr) Humanities.
Barman, Alicerose S. Mental Health in Classroom & Corridor. LC 68-25763. 1968. 9.20 (*0-672-75107-0*, Bobbs) Macmillan.
Barman, Jean. The West Beyond the West: A History of British Columbia. rev. ed. LC 96-215678. (Illus.). 520p. 1996. pap. text 21.95 (*0-8020-7185-6*) U of Toronto Pr.
Barman, Jean, et al, eds. Children, Teachers & Schools: In the History of British Columbia. LC 95-196051. (Illus.). 426p. (Orig.). 1995. pap. text. write for info. (*1-55059-103-7*) Detselig Ents.
Barman, Roderick J. Brazil: The Forging of a Nation, 1798-1852. LC 88-2299. 352p. 1988. 55.00 (*0-8047-1437-1*) Stanford U Pr.
— Brazil: The Forging of a Nation, 1798-1852. xii, 334p. 1994. pap. 17.95 (*0-8047-2330-3*) Stanford U Pr.
***Barman, Roderick J.** Citizen Emperor: Pedro II & The Making of Brazil. LC 99-36776. 1999. write for info. (*0-8047-3510-7*) Stanford U Pr.
***Barmann, Matthias.** Chillida. 2000. pap. 15.00 (*88-8158-247-3*) Charta.
***Barme, Geremie R.** In the Red: On Contemporary Chinese Culture. LC 98-39734. 480p. 1999. 30.00 (*0-231-10614-9*) Col U Pr.
— In the Red: On Contemporary Chinese Culture. 2000. pap. text 22.50 (*0-231-10615-7*) Col U Pr.
Barme, Geremie R. Shades of Mao: The Posthumous Cult of the Great Leader. LC 95-25979. (Illus.). 334p. (gr. 13). 1996. text 77.95 (*1-56324-678-3*, East Gate Bk); pap. text 27.95 (*1-56324-679-1*, East Gate Bk) M E Sharpe.
Barmeier, Jim. The Brain. (Overview Ser.). (Illus.). 112p. (J). (gr. 5-12). 1996. lib. bdg. 22.45 (*1-56006-107-3*) Lucent Bks.
Barmeister, George. The Energy Policy Act of Nineteen Ninety-Two. (State Legislative Reports: Vol. 17, No. 23). 6p. 1992. pap. text 15.00 (*1-55516-296-7*, 7302-1723) Natl Conf State Legis.
Barmenkov, A. Freedom of Conscience in the U. S. S. R. 182p. 1983. 25.00 (*0-7855-1218-7*, Pub. by Collets) St Mut.
Barmier, James. Manners & Customs. (Life in America 100 Years Ago Ser.). (Illus.). 104p. (YA). (gr. 5 up). 1995. lib. bdg. 19.95 (*0-7910-2844-5*) Chelsea Hse.
Barmin, A. A., ed. Current Mathematical Problems of Mechanics & Their Applications. LC 91-17128. (Proceedings of the Steklov Institute of Mathematics Ser.: Vol. 186). 267p. 1991. reprint ed. pap. 159.00 (*0-8218-3138-0*, STEKLO/186) Am Math.
Barn, Ravinder, et al. Acting on Principle: An Examination of Race & Ethnicity in Social Services Provision for Children & Families. 110p. 1997. pap. 65.00 (*1-873868-40-5*) BAAF.
Barna, Arpad. High Speed Pulse Circuits. LC 76-121904. 181p. reprint ed. pap. 56.20 (*0-608-30419-0*, 200737000061) Bks Demand.
Barna, Arpad & Porat, Dan I. Integrated Circuits in Digital Electronics. 2nd ed. LC 86-15690. 371p. 1987. 148.00 (*0-471-01145-2*) Wiley.
Barna, Dorothy, jt. auth. see Barna, Theodore.
Barna, Ed. Covered Bridges of Vermont. LC 95-53031. (Illus.). 172p. 2000. reprint ed. pap. 17.00 (*0-88150-373-8*, Pub. by Countryman) Norton.
Barna, George. Baby Busters: Disillusioned Generation. pap. 9.99 (*0-8024-7319-9*) Northfield Pub.
— Baby Busters: Disillusioned Generation. LC 94-217768. 158p. 1994. pap. 9.99 (*1-881273-19-9*) Northfield Pub.
— Finding a Church You Can Call Home: A Complete Guide to Making One of the Most Significant Decisions of Your Life. rev. ed. Woodard, Virginia, ed. LC 92-25797. Orig. Title: How to Find Your Church. 150p. 1992. reprint ed. pap. 9.99 (*0-8307-1500-2*, 5422113, Regal Bks) Gospel Lght.
— The Frog in the Kettle: What Christians Need to Know about Life in the Year 2000. Durham, Ron, ed. LC 90-37367. (Illus.). 235p. 1990. pap. 10.99 (*0-8307-1427-8*, 5420608, Regal Bks) Gospel Lght.
— Generation Next: A Probing Examination of America's Teenagers. LC 95-195545. 107p. (Orig.). 1995. spiral bd. 22.00 (*1-882297-06-7*) Barna Res Grp.
***Barna, George.** The Habits of Highly Effective Churches. Simon, Wil, ed. LC 99-49020. 2000. 17.99 (*0-8307-1865-9*, Regal Bks); pap. write for info. (*0-8307-1860-5*, Regal Bks) Gospel Lght.
Barna, George. How to Increase Giving in Your Church: A Practical Guide to the Difficult Task of Raising Funds for Your Church. LC 97-3212. 275p. 1997. pap. 12.99 (*0-8307-1921-0*, 5423038, Regal Bks) Gospel Lght.
— The Index of Leading Spiritual Indicators. 176p. 1996. pap. 10.99 (*0-8499-3603-9*) Word Pub.
— Leaders on Leadership: Wisdom, Advice & Encouragement on the Art of Leading God's People. LC 96-52238. 318p. 1997. 14.99 (*0-8307-1862-1*, Regal Bks) Gospel Lght.
— Marketing the Church: What They Never Taught You about Church Growth. LC 88-60625. 175p. (Orig.). 1988. pap. 9.00 (*0-89109-250-1*) NavPress.
— The Mind of the Donor. LC 94-227088. 85p. (Orig.). 1993. pap., spiral bd. 129.00 (*1-882297-04-0*) Barna Res Grp.
— Raising Money for Your Church. 99p. (Orig.). 1994. spiral bd. 28.00 (*1-882297-05-9*) Barna Res Grp.
— The Second Coming of the Church. LC 97-44341. 224p. 1997. 18.99 (*0-8499-1490-6*) Word Pub.
— Ten Years Later: Personal Lessons from a Decade of Research & Ministry. 150p. 1992. pap. 10.00 (*1-882297-01-6*) Barna Res Grp.
***Barna, George & Hatch, Mark.** Frog in the Kettle 2. 2001. 17.99 (*0-8307-2650-0*, Regal Bks) Gospel Lght.
***Barna, George, et al.** Experiencing God in Worship: Perspectives on the Future of Worship in the Church from Today's Most Prominent Leaders. LC 99-42148. 2000. text 24.99 (*0-7644-2133-6*) Group Pub.
Barna, George, ed. see Work, Telford.
Barna, Gordon L., jt. auth. see Carniglia, Stephen C.
Barna, Joel W. The See-Through Years: Creation & Destruction in Texas Architecture, 1981-1991. LC 92-5336. (Illus.). 300p. 1992. 27.50 (*0-89263-316-6*) Tex A&M Univ Pr.
Barna, Redd. Facilitation: Techniques in Training Workbook. (Illus.). 23p. 1991. write for info. (*0-936731-08-7*) Devel Self Rel.
Barna, Theodore & Barna, Dorothy. Ninuch & Caguch. LC 94-74842. (Illus.). 44p. (Orig.). 1994. pap. 6.00 (*1-878149-31-8*) Counterpoint Pub.
Barnaal, Dennis. Analog Electronics for Scientific Application. (Illus.). 366p. (C). 1989. reprint ed. pap. text 26.95 (*0-88133-422-7*) Waveland Pr.
— Digital & Microprocessor Electronics for Scientific Application. (Illus.). 384p. (C). 1989. reprint ed. pap. text 26.95 (*0-88133-421-9*) Waveland Pr.
Barnabas. Gospel of Barnabas. 1981. pap. 15.50 (*0-935782-12-5*) Kazi Pubns.
Barnabee, Henry C. Reminiscences of Henry Clay Barnabee. Varney, George L., ed. LC 73-169779. (Select Bibliographies Reprint Ser.). 1977. reprint ed. 46.95 (*0-8369-5999-X*) Ayer.
Barnabee, Laura W. Genealogy & Relative Factors, Conditions & Displays: Index of New Information Including Heraldry, Emblems & Insignia. rev. ed. 119p. 1997. 39.50 (*0-7883-1510-2*); pap. 34.50 (*0-7883-1511-0*) ABBE Pubs Assn.
Barnaby, David. The Elephant Who Walked to Manchester. (C). 1989. 55.00 (*0-946873-96-8*, Pub. by Basset Pubns) St Mut.
Barnaby, Frank. The Automated Battlefield. (Illus.). 180p. 1998. reprint ed. text 19.00 (*0-7881-5579-2*) DIANE Pub.
— Building a More Democratic United Nations: Proceedings of the First International Conference on a More Democratic UN. 1991. text 47.50 (*0-7146-3442-5*, Pub. by F Cass Pubs); pap. text 22.50 (*0-7146-4080-8*, Pub. by F Cass Pubs) Intl Spec Bk.
— Dictionary of Modern Military Technology. 400p. 1991. 54.50 (*0-685-38705-4*, Pub. by I B T) St Martin.
— How Nuclear Weapons Spread: Nuclear - Weapon Proliferation in the 1990s. LC 92-45847. 192p. (C). (gr. 13). 1994. 65.00 (*0-415-07674-9*) Routledge.
— Instruments of Terror: Mass Destruction Has Never Been So Easy. (Illus.). 197p. 1999. pap. 14.95 (*1-883319-81-1*) Frog Ltd CA.
— The Invisible Bomb: The Nuclear Arms Race in the Middle East. 240p. 1990. text 59.50 (*1-85043-078-0*, Pub. by I B T) St Martin.
Barnaby, Frank, et al, eds. Arms Uncontrolled. LC 75-2815. (Stockholm International Peace Research Institute Ser.). 269p. 1975. 31.00 (*0-674-04655-2*) HUP.
Barnaby, Frank & Schaerf, Carlo. Disarmament & Arms Control. viii, 414p. 1972. text 191.00 (*0-677-15230-2*) Gordon & Breach.
Barnaby, Frank, jt. ed. see Holdstock, Douglas.
Barnaby, Karen. Pacific Passions Cookbook: Celebrating the Cuisine of the Pacific Northwest. (Illus.). 224p. 1995. pap. 16.95 (*1-55110-380-X*) Whitecap Bks.
— Screamingly Good Food! Personal Favorites & Seasonal Feasts. 224p. 1997. pap. text 16.95 (*1-55110-619-1*) Whitecap Bks.
***Barnaby, Karen, et al, texts.** The Girls Who Dish! Seconds Anyone? (Illus.). 208p. 1999. pap. 16.95 (*1-55110-945-X*) Whitecap Bks.
Barnaby, Karen, et al. The Girls Who Dish! Top Women Chefs Cook Their Best. (Illus.). 208p. 1998. pap. 16.95 (*1-55110-717-1*) Whitecap Bks.
Barnaby, Karin & D'Acierno, Pellegrino, eds. C. G. Jung & the Humanities: Toward a Hermeneutics of Culture. (Illus.). 338p. (C). 1990. text 65.00 (*0-691-08616-8*, Pub. by Princeton U Pr) Cal Prin Full Svc.
***Barnaby, Wendy.** The Plague Makers: The Secret World of Biological Warfare. (Illus.). 202p. 1999. pap. 15.95 (*1-883319-85-4*) Frog Ltd CA.
— The Plague Makers: The Secret World of Biological Warfare. rev. ed. 2000. pap. text. write for info. (*0-8264-1258-0*) Continuum.
Barnack, Robert, tr. see Savenko, Nina.
***Barnacle, Hugo.** Day One. 2000. 12.95 (*0-7043-8114-1*, Pub. by Quartet) Interlink Pub.
Barnai, Jacob. The Jews in Palestine in the Eighteenth Century: Under the Patronage of the Istanbul Committee of Officials for Palestine. Weinberger, Leon J., ed. Goldblum, Naomi, tr. LC 91-31051. (Judaic Studies). (HEB.). 320p. (Orig.). 1992. pap. text 29.95 (*0-8173-0572-6*) U of Ala Pr.
Barnao, Jack. Timelocke. large type ed. LC 92-314. 325p. 1992. reprint ed. lib. bdg. 20.95 (*1-56054-394-9*) Thorndike Pr.
Barnard. Art Design & Visual Culture. LC 98-21474. 1998. pap. 21.95 (*0-312-21692-0*); text 65.00 (*0-312-21691-2*) St Martin.
***BARNARD.** An Introduction to Literature. (C). 2002. pap. text. write for info. (*0-15-506966-7*) Harcourt Coll Pubs.
Barnard. J. M. Coetzee. 1999. 22.95 (*0-8057-7815-2*, Twyne) Mac Lib Ref.
Barnard, jt. auth. see Wheeler.
Barnard, A. J., ed. Chelates in Analytical Chemistry, Vol. 2. LC 67-17003. 412p. reprint ed. pap. 117.50 (*0-608-31016-6*) Bks Demand.
Barnard, A. J., jt. ed. see Flaschka, Hermenegild A.
Barnard, Alan. Encyclopedia of Social & Cultural Anthropology. LC 99-188249. 1998. pap. 39.99 (*0-415-20318-X*) Routledge.
***Barnard, Alan.** History & Theory in Anthropology. LC 99-45362. (Illus.). 262p. (C). 2000. 54.95 (*0-521-77333-4*); pap. 19.95 (*0-521-77432-2*) Cambridge U Pr.
Barnard, Alan. Hunters & Herders of Southern Africa: A Comparative Ethnography of Khoisan Peoples. (Cambridge Studies in Social & Cultural Anthropology: No. 85). 379p. (C). 1992. text 69.95 (*0-521-41188-2*); pap. text 25.95 (*0-521-42865-3*) Cambridge U Pr.
Barnard, Alan & Spence, Jonathan D., eds. Encyclopedia of Social & Cultural Anthropology. LC 97-177211. (Illus.). 688p. (C). 1996. 160.00 (*0-415-09996-X*) Routledge.
Barnard, Alfred, jt. auth. see Picton Publishing Staff.
Barnard, Amanda. Gemology: Diamond Formula - Diamond Synthesis: A Gemological Perspective. 192p. 2000. pap. text 39.95 (*0-7506-4244-0*) Buttrwrth-Heinemann.
Barnard, Andrew. New Zealand International Visitors Survey, 1986-87: Demographic Report LC 88-209795. (NZTP International Visitors Research Ser.). 171 p. 1988. write for info. (*0-478-02079-1*, Pub. by Manaaki Whenua) Balogh.
Barnard, Andy & Burgess, Terry. Sociology Explained. 496p. (C). 1997. pap. text 38.95 (*0-521-42671-5*) Cambridge U Pr.
Barnard, Anne L. Auld Robin Gray. Scott, Sir Walter, ed. LC 79-144414. (Bannatyne Club. Edinburgh Pubns.: No. 9). reprint ed. 28.00 (*0-404-52709-4*) AMS Pr.
— South Africa a Century Ago. Wilkins, W. H., ed. LC 71-116271. x, 316p. 1972. reprint ed. 29.00 (*0-403-00461-6*) Scholarly.
Barnard, Bets, ed. see Ericson, Lois & Wakefield, Linda.
Barnard, Bill & Wallace, Tom F. The Innovation Edge: Breaking Through Performance Barriers with QFD. LC 93-60670. 180p. 1994. 75.00 (*0-939246-41-4*) Wiley.
Barnard, C. J. & Behnke, J. M., eds. Parasitism & Host Behaviour. 220p. 1990. 142.00 (*0-85066-498-5*) Taylor & Francis.
Barnard, C. J. & Thompson, D. B. Gulls & Plovers: The Ecology of Mixed-Species Feeding Groups. LC 85-12581. 320p. 1985. text 62.50 (*0-231-06262-1*) Col U Pr.
Barnard, Caroline K. Sylvia Plath. (United States Authors Ser.: No. 309). 136p. 1978. 28.95 (*0-8057-7219-7*) Macmillan.
Barnard, Catherine. EC Employment Law. 3rd ed. (Oxford European Community Law Library Ser.). 450p. 2000. text 105.00 (*0-19-876564-9*) OUP.
***Barnard, Catherine.** Employment Law. LC 96-34873. 624p. 1999. pap. 56.00 (*0-471-96665-7*) Wiley.
Barnard, Charles F. Magic Sign: The Electric Art - Architecture of Las Vegas. (Illus.). 323p. 1993. 25.00 (*0-911380-91-4*) ST Pubns.
Barnard, Charles P. & Corrales, Ramon G. The Theory & Technique of Family Therapy. (Illus.). 352p. 1981. pap. 43.95 (*0-398-06014-2*); text 55.95 (*0-398-03859-7*) C C Thomas.
Barnard, Charles P., jt. auth. see Brock, Gregory.
Barnard, Charles P., jt. auth. see Brock, Gregory W.

An Asterisk (*) at the beginning of an entry indicates that the title is appearing for the first time.

Barnard, Chester I. Functions of the Executive. 30th anniversary ed. LC 68-28690. 370p. 1971. pap. 18.95 (*0-674-32803-5*) HUP.

Barnard, Chris, et al. Asking Questions in Biology: Design, Analysis & Presentation in Practical Work. LC 92-39167. 168p. (C). 1996. pap. text 63.00 (*0-582-08854-2*) Longman.

Barnard, Cynthia, jt. auth. see Eisenberg, Jodi.

Barnard, David. The Criminal Court in Action. 3rd ed. 1988. pap. 44.00 (*0-406-55615-6*, U.K., MICHIE); boxed set 72.00 (*0-406-55614-8*, MICHIE) LEXIS Pub.

— The Family Court in Action. 1983. pap. 42.00 (*0-406-55651-2*, U.K., MICHIE); boxed set 52.00 (*0-406-55650-4*, UK, MICHIE) LEXIS Pub.

Barnard, David & Houghton, Mark. The New Civil Court in Action: The New Civil Court. 528p. 1993. pap. text 44.00 (*0-406-00268-1*, UK, MICHIE) LEXIS Pub.

***Barnard, David, et al.** Crossing Over: Narratives of Palliative Care. LC 99-29317. (Illus.). 464p. 2000. pap. text 39.95 (*0-19-512343-3*) OUP.

Barnard, David, jt. auth. see Murphy, Peter.

Barnard, David T. & Skillicorn, David B. Effective FORTRAN 77 for Engineers & Scientists. 2nd ed. 528p. (C). 1991. text 52.50 (*0-697-08546-5*, WCB McGr Hill) McGrw-H Hghr Educ.

Barnard, David T., et al. Engineering Programming Using the C Language. 496p. 1994. pap. text. write for info. (*0-697-20779-X*, WCB McGr Hill) McGrw-H Hghr Educ.

Barnard, Douglas P. & Hetzel, Robert W. Selecting a Basal Reading Program: Making the Right Choice. LC 88-51816. 103p. 1989. pap. 24.95 (*0-87762-633-2*) Scarecrow.

Barnard, E. A. & Burgen, Arnold S., eds. Receptor Subunits & Complexes. (Illus.). 480p. (C). 1992. text 120.00 (*0-521-36612-7*) Cambridge U Pr.

Barnard, E. L. Kent - Letters & Other Papers of Daniel Kent, Emigrant & Redemptioner, to Which Have Been Added a Few Interesting Hawley & Spackman Papers. (Illus.). 135p. 1994. reprint ed. 25.00 (*0-8328-6566-4*) Higginson Bk Co.

Barnard, Edward C. Naked & a Prisoner: Captain Edward C. Bernard's Narrative of Shipwreck in Palau, 1832-33. Martin, Kenneth R., ed. LC 80-83347. (Illus.). 60p. (Orig.). 1980. pap. 7.00 (*0-937854-01-8*) Kendall Whaling.

Barnard, Ellsworth. In a Wild Place. LC 97-516. (Illus.). 1998. 12.95 (*0-932691-22-6*) MA Audubon Soc.

— Wendell Willkie: Fighter for Freedom. LC 66-19668. 628p. 1971. 45.00 (*0-87023-088-3*) U of Mass Pr.

Barnard, Etwell A. New Links with Shakespeare. LC 73-153301. reprint ed. 32.50 (*0-404-00655-8*) AMS Pr.

Barnard, F. L. Three Years' Cruize in the Mozambique Channel: For the Suppression of the Slave Trade. LC 79-149863. (Black Heritage Library Collection). 1977. 27.95 (*0-8369-8745-4*) Ayer.

Barnard, F. M. Pluralism, Socialism, & Political Legitimacy: Reflections on Opening up Communism. 203p. (C). 1992. text 52.95 (*0-521-40252-2*) Cambridge U Pr.

— Self-Direction & Political Legitimacy: Rousseau & Herder. 340p. 1989. text 74.00 (*0-19-827327-4*) OUP.

Barnard, Frederick A., ed. see American Unitarian Association Staff.

Barnard, Frederick A., ed. see Campbell, Thomas M.

Barnard, Frederick A., jt. ed. see Cremin, Lawrence A.

Barnard, G. A., ed. see Pearson, Egon Sharpe.

Barnard, G. William. Exploring Unseen Worlds: William James & the Philosophy of Mysticism. LC 96-13103. 422p. (C). 1997. text 65.50 (*0-7914-3223-8*); pap. text 21.95 (*0-7914-3224-6*) State U NY Pr.

***Barnard, G. William & Kripal, Jeffrey J., eds.** Crossing Boundaries: Ethics in the History of Mysticism. (Illus.). 352p. (C). 1999. pap. text 23.95 (*1-889119-25-3*) Seven Bridges.

Barnard, George N. Photographic Views of Sherman's Campaign. LC 76-45964. (Illus.). 80p. 1977. reprint ed. pap. 8.95 (*0-486-23445-2*) North South Trader.

Barnard, Gregory. A Practical Guide to Cross-Cultural Communication. (Illus.). 144p. 1995. 90.00 (*0-304-33152-X*); pap. 25.95 (*0-304-33154-6*) Continuum.

Barnard, Guy C. Samuel Beckett: A New Approach: A Study of the Novels & Plays. LC 79-490338. xii, 144p. 1970. write for info. (*0-460-03918-0*) J M Dent & Sons.

Barnard, Harry. Eagle Forgotten: Life of John Peter Altgeld. 496p. 1973. 15.00 (*0-88286-100-X*) C H Kerr.

— Forging of an American Jew: The Life & Times of Judge Julian W. Mack. 1974. 7.95 (*0-685-52984-3*) Herzl Pr.

— Rutherford B. Hayes: And His America. Speirs, Katherine E., ed. LC 92-73458. (Signature Ser.). (Illus.). 606p. 1992. reprint ed. 32.50 (*0-945707-05-3*) Amer Political.

Barnard, Harvey F. Draining the Swamp: Monetary & Fiscal Policy Reform. LC 96-83164. (Illus.). vi, 330p. 1996. 22.95 (*0-9651124-0-3*) Allodial Pub.

***Barnard, Helen.** Exit Eden. LC 99-91205. 160p. 2000. pap. 8.95 (*1-56167-545-8*) Am Literary Pr.

Barnard, Henry. Education & Employment: Education & Labor... (Works of Henry Barnard). 1985. reprint ed. lib. bdg. 49.00 (*0-932051-82-0*) Rprt Serv.

— Normal Schools, 2 vols. 1985. reprint ed. lib. bdg. 79.00 (*0-932051-87-1*) Rprt Serv.

Barnard, Henry, compiled by. Military Schools & Courses of Instruction in the Science & Art of War. LC 68-54786. 960p. 1970. reprint ed. lib. bdg. 145.00 (*0-8371-1325-3*, BAMS, Greenwood Pr) Greenwood.

Barnard, Henry, ed. Memoirs of Teachers, Educators, & Promoters & Benefactors of Education, Literature, & Science. LC 74-89147. (American Education: Its Men, Institutions, & Ideas. Series 1). 1977. reprint ed. 35.95 (*0-405-01384-1*) Ayer.

Barnard, Hollinger F., ed. Outside the Magic Circle: The Autobiography of Virginia Foster Durr. LC 84-2556. (Illus.). 384p. 1990. pap. 19.95 (*0-8173-0517-3*) U of Ala Pr.

Barnard, Howard C. The French Tradition in Education: Ramus to Mme. Necker de Saussure. LC 74-170367. (Cambridge University Press Library Editions). 333p. reprint ed. pap. 95.00 (*0-608-17030-5*, 2027278) Bks Demand.

Barnard, Ian, jt. auth. see McArthur, Colin.

Barnard, J. L. Gammaridean Amphipoda in the Collections of Bishop Museum. (BMB Ser.: No. 215). 1955. pap. 25.00 (*0-527-02323-X*) Periodicals Srv.

Barnard, Jack, ed. see Pash, Mark.

Barnard, James W. Trailriders Guide to Cowboy Action Shooting. (Illus.). 135p. 2001. pap. 24.95 (*1-877704-31-8*) Pioneer Pr.

Barnard, Jerry L. & Ingram, Camilla. Lysianassoid Amphipoda (Crustacea) from Deepsea Thermal Vents. LC 90-9991. (Smithsonian Contributions to Zoology Ser.: No. 499). 84p. reprint ed. pap. 30.00 (*0-8357-2750-5*, 203986400013) Bks Demand.

Barnard, John. Ashton's Memorial: A History of the Strange Adventure, & Signal Deliverances of Mr. Philip Ashton, Sun of Marblehead. Knight, Russell W., ed. 1976. 12.95 (*0-87577-051-7*, PEMP105, Peabody Museum) Peabody Essex Mus.

Barnard, John, ed. Pope: The Critical Heritage. (Critical Heritage Ser.). 550p. 1973. 69.50 (*0-7100-7390-9*, Routledge Thoemms) Routledge.

Barnard, John, ed. see Bremner, Robert H.

Barnard, John, ed. see Etherege, George.

Barnard, John, ed. see Keats, John.

Barnard, Judith. The Past & Present of Solomon Sorge. 1987. pap. 5.95 (*0-317-56808-6*) PB.

***Barnard, Julia.** New Decorator. (Living Ser.). (Illus.). 192p. 2000. pap. 13.95 (*0-7894-6146-3*) DK Pub Inc.

Barnard, Julian. The Guide to Bach Flower Remedies. 106p. 1979. pap. 5.95 (*0-85207-144-2*, Pub. by C W Daniel) Natl Bk Netwk.

— Guide to the Bach Flower Remedies. 8th ed. 52p. pap. 8.95 (*0-8464-4221-3*) Beekman Pubs.

— Healing Herbs of Edward Bach: An Illustrated Guide to the Flower Remedies. (Illus.). 336p. 1997. pap. text 19.95 (*1-85398-086-2*, Pub. by Ashgrove Pr) Words Distrib.

Barnard, Julian, ed. see Bach, Edward.

Barnard, Juliana, tr. see Grandgeorge, Didier.

Barnard, Kathryn E. & Brazelton, T. Berry, eds. Touch: The Foundation of Experience. (Clinical Infant Reports: No. 4). 610p. 1990. 75.00 (*0-8236-6605-0*, BN 06605) Intl Univs Pr.

Barnard, Kevin F., et al. Demutualization: The New Conversion Options for Savings Banks, Savings & Loans, & Insurance Companies. (Illus.). write for info. (*0-318-58925-7*) Harcourt.

Barnard-King, Caroline H. Anne Sexton. (United States Authors Ser.). 208p. 1989. 32.00 (*0-8057-7538-2*, Twyne) Mac Lib Ref.

Barnard, L. W. John Potter: An Eighteenth Century Archbishop. 147p. (C). 1989. 40.00 (*0-7223-2383-2*, Pub. by A H S Ltd) St Mut.

Barnard, Laura B. Biblical Basis of Missions. 32p. 1973. pap. 1.95 (*0-89265-100-8*) Randall Hse.

Barnard, Laura S. Aristophanes' Clouds. (Greek Commentaries Ser.). 130p. (Orig.). (C). 1987. pap. text 7.00 (*0-929524-02-0*) Bryn Mawr Commentaries.

Barnard, Leo. Sir De Villiers Graaff. 1990. 39.95 (*0-86984-973-5*) Buttrwrth-Heinemann.

Barnard, Leslie W. St. Justin Martyr: The First & Second Apologies. LC 96-3012. (Ancient Christian Writers Ser.: No. 56). 192p. 1996. 29.95 (*0-8091-0472-5*) Paulist Pr.

Barnard, Malcolm. Fashion As Communication. LC 95-38743. (Illus.). 208p. (C). 1996. 65.00 (*0-415-11157-9*); pap. 18.99 (*0-415-11158-7*) Routledge.

Barnard, Marina U., jt. auth. see McKeganey, Neil.

Barnard, Marjorie. Miles Franklin: The Story of a Famous Australian. 2nd ed. (Illus.). 174p. 1989. pap. text 16.95 (*0-7022-2146-5*, Pub. by Univ Queensland Pr) Intl Spec Bk.

Barnard, Martha U., jt. auth. see Hymovich, Debra P.

Barnard, Mary. Collected Poems, 1979. LC 79-54693. 101p. 1979. pap. 8.95 (*0-932576-09-5*) Breitenbush Bks.

— The Myth of Apollo & Daphne from Ovid to Quevedo: Love, Agon, & the Grotesque. LC 86-29142. (Duke Monographs in Medieval & Renaissance Studies: No. 8). (Illus.). xi, 222p. 1987. text 34.95 (*0-8223-0701-4*) Duke.

— The Mythmakers. LC 66-20061. 213p. 1986. reprint ed. 12.95 (*0-932576-36-2*) Breitenbush Bks.

— Nantucket Genesis. LC 88-12133. 80p. 1988. 14.95 (*0-932576-64-8*); pap. 8.95 (*0-932576-65-6*) Breitenbush Bks.

— Three Fables. LC 83-19719. 56p. 1984. 10.00 (*0-932576-20-6*); pap. 4.95 (*0-932576-21-4*) Breitenbush Bks.

— Time & the White Tigress. LC 85-31353. (Illus.). 96p. 1986. 19.95 (*0-932576-31-1*) Breitenbush Bks.

Barnard, Mary, tr. see Sappho.

Barnard, Melaine. Everybody Loves Meatloaf: More Than 100 Recipes for Loaves & Fixings. LC 97-4134. 176p. 1997. pap. 14.95 (*0-06-095219-9*, Perennial) HarperTrade.

Barnard, Melanie. Low-Fat Grilling. LC 94-33253. 192p. 1995. pap. 10.00 (*0-06-095073-0*, Perennial) HarperTrade.

— Marinades: The Secret of Great Grilling. LC 96-26200. 176p. (Orig.). 1997. pap. 11.00 (*0-06-095162-1*, Perennial) HarperTrade.

— Short & Sweet: Sophisticated Desserts in No Time at All. LC 99-12463. (Illus.). 238p. 1999. 25.00 (*0-395-90145-6*) HM.

— 365 More Ways to Cook Chicken. LC 96-14265. 288p. 1996. 17.95 (*0-06-017139-1*) HarpC.

Barnard, Melanie, et al. The American Medical Association Family Health Cookbook. LC 97-2684. 1997. 30.00 (*0-671-53667-2*, PB Hardcover) PB.

Barnard, Michael. Dictionary of Advertising Terms: French - English. (ENG & FRE.). 160p. 1992. 95.00 (*0-7859-0503-0*, 2852068184) Fr & Eur.

— Dictionnaire des Termes d'Imprimerie de Reliure et de Papeterie: French - English. (ENG & FRE.). 232p. 1992. 125.00 (*0-7859-0502-2*, 2852067994) Fr & Eur.

— Dictionnaire des Termes Typographiques et de Design: French - English. (ENG & FRE.). 192p. 1992. 95.00 (*0-7859-0504-9*, 2852068192) Fr & Eur.

— Making Electronic Manuscripts. (Blueprint Ser.). 32p. (C). 1990. pap. 13.95 (*0-948905-38-7*) Chapman & Hall.

Barnard, Michael & Shobbrook, Robin. Print Buyer's Bible Promotional & Marketing Print. 2nd ed. 320p. (C). 1997. ring bd. 169.95 (*0-415-15117-1*) Routledge.

Barnard, Michael A., ed. Global Financial Strategies. 1998. ring bd. 695.00 (*0-9666637-0-5*) AFT Pub Co.

Barnard, N. Dynamic Energy Storage in the Building Fabric. 97p. (C). 1994. pap. 60.00 (*0-86022-372-8*, Pub. by Build Servs Info Assn) St Mut.

— The Shan-Fu Liang Ch'i Kuei & Associated Inscribed Vessels. 545p. 1996. 95.00 (*957-638-396-X*) Oriental Bk Store.

Barnard, N. & Starr, A. Vibration Monitoring for Building Services. BSRIA Staff, ed. 1995. pap. 95.00 (*0-86022-398-1*, Pub. by Build Servs Info Assn) St Mut.

Barnard, N., jt. auth. see Pearson, C. C.

***Barnard, Neal.** Foods That Cause You to Lose Weight: The Negative Calorie Effect. LC 98-91010. (Illus.). 352p. 1999. mass mkt. 6.99 (*0-380-80797-1*, Avon Bks) Morrow Avon.

Barnard, Neal. Foods that Fight Pain. 1999. pap. 14.00 (*0-609-80436-7*) Random Hse Value.

— Foods That Fight Pain: Revolutionary New Strategies. LC 97-43242. 352p. 1998. 25.00 (*0-609-60098-2*) Harmony Bks.

Barnard, Neal D. Eat Right, Live Longer: Using the Natural Power of Foods to Age-Proof Your Body. 400p. 1996. pap. 13.00 (*0-517-88778-9*) Crown Pub Group.

— Food for Life: How the New Four Food Groups Can Save Your Life. 320p. 1994. pap. 13.00 (*0-517-88201-9*) Crown Pub Group.

— Food Is a Wonder Medicine: The Power to Heal Is on Your Plate. abr. ed. (C). Date not set. pap. write for info. (*1-882330-07-2*) Magni Co.

— Foods Can Save Your Life: Leading Experts Tell You Why. abr. ed. (Illus.). 96p. Date not set. pap. write for info. (*1-882330-09-9*) Magni Co.

— Foods That Can Cause You to Lose Weight II: While You Watch TV. rev. ed. 192p. 1996. pap. 12.95 (*1-882330-48-X*) Magni Co.

— Foods That Cause You to Lose Weight: The Negative Calorie Effect. (GER.). 176p. 1992. pap. write for info. (*1-882330-05-6*) Magni Co.

— Foods That Cause You to Lose Weight: The Negative Calorie Effect. (FRE.). 176p. (C). 1992. pap. write for info. (*1-882330-03-X*) Magni Co.

— Foods That Cause You to Lose Weight: The Negative Calorie Effect. Brandao, Robert H., tr. from SPA. (ENG.). 174p. 1995. pap. text 12.95 (*1-882330-10-2*) Magni Co.

— Foods That Cause You to Lose Weight: The Negative Calorie Effect. rev. ed. 192p. (C). 1997. pap. 12.95 (*1-882330-35-8*) Magni Co.

— A Physician's Slimming Guide: For Permanent Weight Control. LC 92-9631. (Illus.). 80p. 1992. pap. 5.95 (*0-913990-91-4*) Book Pub Co.

— The Power of Your Plate: Eating Well for Better Health - 20 Experts Tell You How. rev. ed. LC 94-43222. 256p. (C). 1995. pap. 12.95 (*1-57067-003-X*) Book Pub Co.

***Barnard, Neal D.** Turn off the Fat Genes! LC 00-33466. 2001. 23.95 (*0-609-60631-X*) Harmony Bks.

Barnard, Neal D., ed. The Best in the World: Fast, Healthful Recipes from Exclusive & Out-of-the-Way Restaurants. (Illus.). 70p. 1998. 11.95 (*0-9664081-0-1*) Physcns Comm Resp Med.

Barnard, Neal D., et al. Foods That Cause You to Lose Weight: The Negative Calorie Effect. (Illus.). 172p. 1992. pap. 12.95 (*1-882330-00-5*) Magni Co.

Barnard, Neal D., ed. see Bates, Dorothy R.

Barnard, Nicholas. Arts & Crafts of India. deluxe ed. (Illus.). 192p. 1995. pap. 24.95 (*1-85029-705-3*, Pub. by Conran Octopus) Trafalgar.

— The Complete Home Decorating Book: The New Complete Step-by-Step Guide to Decorating Your Home. LC 94-639. (Illus.). 288p. 1994. 29.95 (*1-56458-667-7*) DK Pub Inc.

— Living with Decorative Textiles. LC 94-61397. (Illus.). 192p. 1995. pap. 24.95 (*0-500-27821-0*, Pub. by Thames Hudson) Norton.

— Living with Folk Art: Ethnic Styles from Around the World. LC 93-113284. (Illus.). 192p. 1998. pap. 24.95 (*0-500-28021-5*, Pub. by Thames Hudson) Norton.

***Barnard, Nicholas.** Step-by-Step Home Decorating Book. 376p. 2000. 29.95 (*0-7894-5186-7*, D K Ink) DK Pub Inc.

Barnard, Nicholas, jt. auth. see Adler, Peter.

Barnard, Nicholas, jt. auth. see Gillow, John.

Barnard, Nicholas, jt. auth. see Hull, Alastair.

Barnard, Noel. Ancient Chinese Bronzes & Southeast Asian Metal & Other Archaeological Artifacts. (Illus.). 467p. 1975. 60.00 (*0-89986-371-X*) Oriental Bk Store.

Barnard, Osbert H., jt. auth. see Biorklund, George.

Barnard, Paul. Florida Criminal Defense Trial Manual, 5 vols. 1997. ring bd. write for info. (*0-327-03906-X*, 80614-10, MICHIE) LEXIS Pub.

***Barnard, Paul W.** Children, Bereavement & Trauma: Nurturing Resillence. 1999. pap. text 24.95 (*1-85302-785-5*) Jessica Kingsley.

Barnard, Paul W. & Warda, Mark. How to Start a Business in New York. LC 97-38489. (Legal Survival Guides Ser.). 176p. 1997. pap. 16.95 (*1-57071-185-2*) Sourcebks.

Barnard, Peter C., ed. Identifying British Insects & Arachnids: An Annotated Bibliography of Key Works. annot. ed. LC 98-36132. (Illus.). 385p. (C). 1999. text 80.00 (*0-521-63241-2*) Cambridge U Pr.

Barnard, Phil & Quarton, Bill. Troubleshooters Pre-Purchase Home Inspection System: Opens the Door to a Building's Hidden Secrets. 104p. (Orig.). 1990. pap. 19.95 (*0-9626026-0-4*) Troubleshooters Pub.

Barnard, Philip, ed. see Brown, Charles Brockden.

Barnard, Philip, tr. see Lacoue-Labarthe, Philippe & Nancy, Jean-Luc.

Barnard, Philip, tr. & pref. see Sarduy, Severo.

Barnard, Phillip, tr. see Sollers, Phillipe.

Barnard, R. H. Road Vehicle Aerodynamic Design. (C). 1996. pap. text. write for info. (*0-582-24522-2*, Pub. by Addison-Wesley) Longman.

Barnard, R. H. & Philpott, D. R. Aircraft Flight Method. 2nd ed. (Illus.). 385p. (C). 1996. pap. text 59.95 (*0-582-23656-8*) Addison-Wesley.

Barnard-Ray, Mary & Cox, Barbara J. Beyond the Basics: A Text for Advanced Legal Writing. 427p. (C). 1991. reprint ed. 28.00 (*0-314-85410-X*) West Pub.

Barnard, Richard & Hertogs, Sam. The Children Most of All. Field, Barbara, ed. (Jacob's Star Trilogy Ser.: Vol. 2). ix, 548p. 1999. pap. 7.50 (*0-9644751-4-6*) L Hubbard Pub.

— Jakob's Star. Field, Barbara, ed. (Jakob's Star Trilogy Ser.: Vol. 3). ix, 596p. 1999. pap. 7.50 (*0-9644751-5-4*) L Hubbard Pub.

— The Price of Ashes. LC 95-75128. 625p. 1995. 21.95 (*0-9644751-1-1*); pap. write for info. (*0-9644751-0-3*) L Hubbard Pub.

— The Price of Ashes. Field, Barbara, ed. (Jacob's Star Trilogy Ser.: Vol. 1). ix, 502p. 1999. pap. 7.50 (*0-9644751-3-8*) L Hubbard Pub.

Barnard, Rita. The Great Depression & the Culture of Abundance: Kenneth Fearing, Nathanael West, & Mass Culture in the 1930s. (Cambridge Studies in American Literature & Culture: No. 87). (Illus.). 283p. (C). 1995. text 59.95 (*0-521-45034-9*) Cambridge U Pr.

Barnard, Robert. The Bad Samaritan. 240p. 1995. 21.00 (*0-684-81334-3*) S&S Trade.

— The Corpse at the Haworth Tandoori. LC 98-39263. 288p. 1999. 21.50 (*0-684-85532-1*) S&S Trade.

***Barnard, Robert.** The Corpse at the Haworth Tandoori. large type ed. 352p. 2000. write for info. (*0-7505-1502-3*, Pub. by Mgna Lrg Print) Ulverscroft.

Barnard, Robert. Corpse in a Gilded Cage. 224p. 1996. pap. 5.95 (*0-14-023788-7*, Penguin Bks) Viking Penguin.

— Death by Sheer Torture. 1993. Not sold separately (*0-614-32002-X*) Random.

— Death in a Cold Climate. 1993. Not sold separately (*0-614-32004-6*) Random Hse Value.

— Death of a Mystery Writer. 1993. Not sold separately (*0-614-32005-4*) Random Hse Value.

— Death of a Perfect Mother. 1993. Not sold separately (*0-614-32003-8*) Random.

— Death on the High C's. large type ed. 298p. 1992. 27.99 (*0-7505-0341-6*) Ulverscroft.

***Barnard, Robert.** Emily Bronte. (British Library Writers' Lives Ser.). (Illus.). 128p. (YA). 2000. text 22.95 (*0-19-521656-3*) OUP.

Barnard, Robert. A Fatal Attachment. 288p. 1992. text 20.00 (*0-684-19412-0*, Scribners Ref) Mac Lib Ref.

— A Fatal Attachment. 240p. 1994. mass mkt. 4.99 (*0-380-71998-3*, Avon Bks) Morrow Avon.

— A Fatal Attachment. large type ed. 384p. 1992. reprint ed. lib. bdg. 20.95 (*1-56054-577-1*) Thorndike Pr.

— Fete Fatale. LC 94-241182. 184p. 1994. reprint ed. pap. 7.95 (*0-88150-319-3*, Foul Play) Norton.

— The Habit of Widowhood. LC 96-6952. 224p. 1996. 21.00 (*0-684-82648-8*) S&S Trade.

— The Habit of Widowhood. large type ed. LC 97-3566. 1997. pap. 22.95 (*1-56895-423-9*) Wheeler Pub.

— A Hovering of Vultures. 224p. 1995. mass mkt. 6.99 (*0-552-14119-4*) Bantam.

— A Hovering of Vultures. LC 93-19371. 224p. 1993. text 20.00 (*0-684-19625-5*, Scribners Ref) Mac Lib Ref.

— A Hovering of Vultures. 224p. 1995. mass mkt. 4.99 (*0-380-77653-7*, Avon Bks) Morrow Avon.

— A Hovering of Vultures. 1993. 22.00 (*0-684-19666-2*) S&S Trade.

— A Hovering of Vultures. large type ed. LC 93-42056. 334p. 1994. lib. bdg. 21.95 (*0-7862-0141-X*) Thorndike Pr.

— Imagery & Theme in the Novels of Dickens LC 75-316935. (Norwegian Studies in English Ser.). 163p. 1974. write for info. (*0-391-00263-5*) Humanities.

— A Little Local Murder. 192p. 1995. pap. 7.95 (*0-88150-325-8*, Foul Play) Norton.

— The Masters of the House: A Novel of Suspense. LC 94-5853. 224p. 1994. 20.00 (*0-684-19728-6*, Scribners Ref) Mac Lib Ref.

— The Masters of the House: A Novel of Suspense. 224p. 1996. mass mkt. 4.99 (*0-380-72511-8*, Avon Bks) Morrow Avon.

— The Masters of the House: A Novel of Suspense. large type ed. 319p. 1994. lib. bdg. 22.95 (*0-7862-0329-3*) Thorndike Pr.

***Barnard, Robert.** A Murder in Mayfair. LC 99-46962. (Illus.). 288p. 2000. 23.00 (*0-684-86445-2*) Scribner.

B

— A Murder in Mayfair. large type ed. LC 00-37797. 379p. 2000. pap. 27.95 (0-7862-2656-0) Thorndike Pr.

Barnard, Robert. No Place of Safety. LC 97-32909. 192p. 1998. 21.50 (0-684-84503-2) Scribner.

— No Place of Safety. large type ed. LC 98-14590. (Basic Ser.). 1998. 26.95 (0-7862-1452-X) Thorndike Pr.

— Out of the Blackout. 188p. 1995. reprint ed. pap. 6.00 (0-88150-327-4, Foul Play) Norton.

— Political Suicide. 224p. 1995. pap. 7.95 (0-88150-326-6, Foul Play) Norton.

— School for Murder. 208p. 1994. reprint ed. pap. 7.95 (0-88150-320-7, Foul Play) Norton.

— A Short History of English Literature. 2nd ed. 282p. 1994. pap. 19.95 (0-631-19088-0) Blackwell Pubs.

— A Short History of English Literature. 2nd ed. 238p. 1995. 27.00 (82-00-03993-5) Scandnvan Univ Pr.

Barnard, Robert L. Intrusion Detection Systems. 2nd ed. (Illus.). 480p. 1988. 39.95 (0-7506-9427-0) Buttrwrth-Heinemann.

Barnard, Robert L., jt. ed. see Dubey, Abinash C.

Barnard, Roger. Good News, Bad News. LC 97-9465. (Illus.). 80p. 1997. pap. text, student ed. 11.95 (0-19-434873-3) OUP.

Barnard, Roger & Cady, Jeff. Business Venture. (Illus.). 96p. 1993. pap. text, student ed. 12.95 (0-19-457036-3) OUP.

Barnard, Roger, jt. auth. see Wilson, Warren.

Barnard, Sally, jt. auth. see Thornhill, Linda.

***Barnard, Sandie.** Rise Up: A New Guide to Public Speaking. 254p. 1999. reprint ed. pap. text 14.00 (0-7881-6237-3) DIANE Pub.

Barnard, Sandy. Custer's First Sergeant, John Ryan. LC 95-83240. (Illus.). 304p. 1996. 24.95 (0-9618087-3-X) AST Pr.

— Digging into Custer's Last Stand. (Illus.). 72p. (Orig.). 1986. pap. 10.00 (0-9618087-0-5) AST Pr.

— Digging into Custer's Last Stand. rev. ed. LC 97-94583. (Illus.). 184p. (Orig.). 1998. 24.95 (0-9618087-4-8); pap. 14.95 (0-9618087-5-6) AST Pr.

— I Go with Custer: The Life & Death of Reporter Mark Kellogg. 240p. (Orig.). 1996. 24.95 (0-9628857-1-1); pap. 14.95 (0-9628857-2-X) Bismarck Trib.

— Shovels & Speculation - Archeologists Hunt Custer. (Illus.). 64p. (Orig.). 1990. pap. 10.00 (0-9618087-1-3) AST Pr.

Barnard, Sandy, ed. Speaking about Custer, a Collection of Lectures. (Illus.). 104p. (Orig.). 1991. pap. 10.00 (0-9618087-2-1) AST Pr.

Barnard, Simon & Edgar, David, eds. Pediatric Eye Care. (Illus.). 288p. 1995. 125.00 (0-632-03979-5) Blackwell Sci.

Barnard, Stephen. The Illustrated History of Rock. (Illus.). 256p. (YA). (gr. 7 up). 1987. 75.00 (0-02-870251-4, Schirmer Books) Mac Lib Ref.

— On the Radio: Music Radio in Britain. 176p. 1989. 113.00 (0-335-15284-8); pap. 41.95 (0-335-15130-2) OpUniv Pr.

Barnard, Sue & Hartigan, Gayle. Clinical Audit in Physiotherapy: From Theory into Practice. LC 98-20594. 144p. 1998. pap. text 45.00 (0-7506-3779-X) Buttrwrth-Heinemann.

Barnard, Sue, jt. auth. see Seale, Jane.

Barnard, Susan B., jt. ed. see Jurow, Susan.

Barnard, Susan M. Reptile Keeper's Handbook. (Illus.). 262p. (Orig.). (C). 1996. pap. 58.50 (0-89464-933-7) Krieger.

Barnard, Susan M. & Durden, Lance A. A Veterinary Guide to the Parasites of Reptiles Vol. 2: Arthropods (Excluding Mites) 298p. 2000. lib. bdg. 46.50 (0-89464-908-6) Krieger.

Barnard, Susan M. & Upton, Steve J. A Veterinary Guide to the Parasites of Reptiles: Protozoa, Vol. 1. LC 93-20082. 164p. 1994. lib. bdg. 26.50 (0-89464-832-2) Krieger.

***Barnard, T. C.** Cromwellian Ireland: English Government & Reform in Ireland 1649-1660. (Oxford Historical Monographs). 376p. 2000. pap. 29.95 (0-19-820857-X) OUP.

— The English Republic, 1649-1660. 2nd ed. LC 97-22093. (Seminar Studies in History). 120p. (C). 1998. pap. 15.93 (0-582-08003-7) Addison-Wesley.

Barnard, Tanya, jt. auth. see Kramer, Sarah.

Barnard, Timothy & Rist, Peter, eds. South American Cinema: A Critical Filmography, 1915-1994. LC 95-48076. (Illus.). 432p. 1996. text 70.00 (0-8240-4574-2, H1077) Garland.

— South American Cinema: A Critical Filmography, 1915-1994. LC 98-39528. (Illus.). 432p. 1998. pap. 19.95 (0-292-70871-8) U of Tex Pr.

Barnard, Toby. Lord Burlington: Architecture, Art & Life. 328p. 1995. 65.00 (1-85285-094-9) Hambledon Press.

***Barnard, Toby & Fenlon, Jane, eds.** The Dukes of Ormonde, 1610-1745. LC 99-37404. (Illus.). 352p. 2000. 90.00 (0-85115-761-0) Boydell & Brewer.

Barnard, Toby C., et al, eds. A Miracle of Learning: Irish Manuscripts, Their Uses & Their Owners, 800-1760. LC 97-14761. (Illus.). 303p. 1997. text 86.95 (1-85928-293-8, Pub. by Ashgate Pub) Ashgate Pub Co.

Barnard, Tom. How to Grow an Adult Class. 88p. (Orig.). 1983. pap. 4.99 (0-8341-0840-2) Beacon Hill.

Barnard, Tony. The Abduction of a Limerick Heiress: Social & Political Relations in Mid-Eighteenth Century Ireland. (Maynooth Studies in Local History). 64p. 1998. pap. 9.95 (0-7165-2715-4) Intl Spec Bk.

Barnard, Tony & Neill, Hugh. Teach Yourself Mathematical Groups. (Illus.). 224p. 1997. pap. 12.95 (0-8442-3077-4, Teach Yrslf) NTC Contemp Pub Co.

Barnard, William & Wallace, Thomas F. The Innovation Edge: Creating Strategic Breakthroughs Using the Voice of the Customer. 180p. 1995. 29.95 (0-471-13196-2) Wiley.

Barnard, William, et al. Customer Integration: The QFD Leader's Guide for Decision Making. 256p. 1994. 37.50 (0-939246-67-8) Wiley.

Barnard, William D. Dixiecrats & Democrats: Alabama Politics, 1942-1950. LC 73-22711. pap. text 14.50 (0-8173-4820-4) U of Ala Pr.

Barnartt, Sharon N., jt. auth. see Christiansen, John B.

Barnas, Andrew, tr. see Levelt, Willem J.

Barnatan, Marcos Ricardo, ed. see Borges, Jorge Luis.

Barnatt, Christopher. Challenging Reality: In Search of the Future. LC 96-39899. 318p. 1997. pap. 54.95 (0-471-97072-7) Wiley.

— Cyber Business: Mindsets for a Wired Age. LC 94-48425. 256p. 1995. pap. 89.95 (0-471-95605-8) Wiley.

— Management Strategy & Information Technology: Text & Readings. 240p. 1996. mass mkt. 34.95 (0-412-74950-5) Chapman & Hall.

— Management Strategy & Information Technology: Text & Readings. 240p. 1996. pap. 34.95 (1-86152-025-5, Pub. by ITBP) Thomson Learn.

— Valueware: Technology, Humanity & Organization. LC 99-24163. (Praeger Studies on the 21st Century). 248p. 1999. 59.95 (0-275-96714-X); pap. 22.95 (0-275-96715-8, Praeger Pubs) Greenwood.

Barnavi, Eli. Historical Atlas of the Jewish People: From the Time of the Patriarchs to the Present. (Illus.). 1994. 40.00 (0-8052-4127-2) Schocken.

Barnbaum, Bruce. The Art of Photography: An Approach to Personal Expression. 2nd ed. 230p. per. write for info. (0-7872-6316-8) Kendall-Hunt.

***Barnbaum, Deborah R. & Byron, Michael.** Research Ethics Text & Readings. 368p. 2000. pap. 34.67 (0-13-021264-4, Prentice Hall) P-H.

Barnbrook, Geoff. Language & Computers: A Practical Introduction to the Computer Analysis of Language. (Edinburgh Textbooks in Empirical Linguistics Ser.). 256p. 1996. 70.00 (0-7486-0848-6, Pub. by Edinburgh U Pr); pap. 24.50 (0-7486-0785-4, Pub. by Edinburgh U Pr) Col U Pr.

Barndorff-Nielsen, O. E. Information & Exponential Families: In Statistical Theory. LC 77-9943. (Wiley Series in Probability & Mathematical Statistics). 248p. reprint ed. pap. 76.90 (0-8357-3391-2, 203964800013) Bks Demand.

— Networks & Chaos - Statistical & Probabilistic Aspects. LC 93-3333. 320p. (gr. 13). 1993. ring bd. 73.95 (0-412-46530-2, Chap & Hall CRC) CRC Pr.

Barndorff-Nielsen, O. E., et al, eds. Stochastic Geometry: Likelihood & Computation. LC 98-46543. 408p. 1998. boxed set 65.95 (0-8493-0396-6) CRC Pr.

Barndorff-Nielsen, O. E. & Cox, D. R. Asymptotic Techniques for Use in Statistics. (Monographs on Statistics & Applied Probability). 240p. (gr. 13). 1989. ring bd. 73.95 (0-412-31400-2, Chap & Hall CRC) CRC Pr.

— Inference & Asymptotics. (Monographs on Statistics & Applied Probability). (Illus.). 360p. (C). (gr. 13). 1994. ring bd. 73.95 (0-412-49440-X, Chap & Hall CRC) CRC Pr.

Barndorff-Nielsen, O. E. & Willets, B. B. Aeolian Grain Transport, Vol. 1: Mechanics. (Acta Mechanical, Supplementum Ser.: No. 1-2). (Illus.). ix, 181p. 1991. 175.95 (0-387-82269-0) Spr-Verlag.

— Aeolian Grain Transport, Vol. 2: The Erosional Environment. (Acta Mechanical, Supplementum Ser.: No. 1-2). (Illus.). ix, 181p. 1991. 175.95 (0-387-82274-7) Spr-Verlag.

***Barndorff-Nielsen, O. E., et al.** Complex Stochastic Systems. LC 00-34064. (Monographs on Statistics & Applied Probability). 2000. write for info. (1-58488-158-5, Chap & Hall CRC) CRC Pr.

Barndorff-Nielsen, O. E., et al. Decomposition & Invariance of Measures with a View to Statistical Transformation Models. (Lecture Notes in Statistics Ser.: Vol. 58). 191p. 1989. 32.95 (0-387-97131-9, 3368) Spr-Verlag.

Barndorff-Nielsen, Ole E., et al, eds. Stochastic Methods in Hydrology: Rain, Landforms & Floods Guanajuato, Mexico 25-28 March, 1996. LC 97-46911. (Advanced Series on Statistical Science & Applied Probability). 250p. 1998. 56.00 (981-02-3367-1) World Scientific Pub.

Barndorff-Nielsen, Ole E. & Vedel Jensen, Eva B., eds. Geometry in Present Day Science: Proceedings of the Conference University of Aarhus, Denmark 16-18 January 1998. 200p. 1999. 44.00 (981-02-3672-7) World Scientific Pub.

Barnds, Mary L., jt. auth. see Hughes, Jane W.

Barnds, William J., et al. Pakistan: The Long View. Ziring, Lawrence, ed. LC 76-4320. (Duke University Center for Commonwealth & Comparative Studies Publication: No. 43). 503p. reprint ed. pap. 156.00 (0-608-12778-7, 202347700033) Bks Demand.

***Barndt, Deborah, ed.** Women Working the NAFTA Food Chain: Women, Food & Globalization. LC 99-491970. (Illus.). 280p. 1999. pap. 16.95 (1-896764-19-3, Pub. by Sec Story Pr) LPC InBook.

Barndt, Walter D., Jr. The Demand Side of Competitive Intelligence: The Missing Link. 75p. 1997. pap. 20.00 (0-9621241-6-8) SCIP.

Barndt, Walter D. User-Directed Competitive Intelligence: Closing the Gap Between Supply & Demand. LC 93-49030. 208p. 1994. 57.95 (0-89930-781-7, Quorum Bks) Greenwood.

Barne, jt. auth. see Tanenbaum.

Barne, Arpad. Operational Amplifiers. LC 70-150608. (Illus.). 159p. reprint ed. pap. 49.30 (0-608-10232-6, 205552500026) Bks Demand.

Barne, David. Multiple Sclerosis - Questions & Answers. (Illus.). 120p. 2000. pap. 17.95 (1-873413-86-6) Merit Pub Intl.

Barne, Kitty. Listening to the Orchestra. LC 72-13098. (Essay Index Reprint Ser.). 1977. reprint ed. 21.95 (0-8369-8146-4) Ayer.

Barnea, Eytan R., et al, eds. Implantation & Early Pregnancy in Humans: A Combined Research & Clinical Approach. LC 93-34659. 506p. 1994. 75.00 (1-85070-513-5) Prthnon Pub.

Barneby. Silk Tree, Guanacaste, Monkey's Earring Pt. III: Ageneric System for the Synandrous Mimosaceae of the Americas - Calliandra. (Memoirs of the New York Botanical Garden Ser.: Vol. 74(3)). 224p. 1998. 45.00 (0-89327-420-8, MEM74(3)) NY Botanical.

Barneby, Rupert C. Daleae Imagines. LC 66-6394. (Memoirs Ser.: Vol. 27). (Illus.). 891p. 1977. pap. 50.00 (0-89327-002-4) NY Botanical.

— Intermountain Flora Vol. 3, Pt. B: The Fables. Cronquist, A. et al, eds. LC 73-134298. (Illus.). 292p. 1989. text 58.00 (0-89327-346-5) NY Botanical.

— Sensitivae Censitae: A Description of the Genus Mimosa (Mimosaceae) in the New World. (Memoirs Ser.: No. 65). (Illus.). 835p. 1991. text 130.00 (0-89327-366-X) NY Botanical.

Barneby, Rupert C. & Grimes, Jim. Silk Tree, Guanacaste, Monkey's Earring: A Generic System for the Synandrous Mimosacene of the Americas, Pt. I: Aberima, Albizia, & Allies. (Memoirs of the New York Botanical Garden Ser.: No. 74). (Illus.). 292p. 1996. 45.00 (0-89327-395-3, MEM 74(1)) NY Botanical.

Barneby, Rupert C., jt. auth. see Irwin, Howard S.

Barneby, Rupert C., jt. auth. see Krukoff, B. A.

Barnecut, Edith, ed. Journey with the Fathers: Commentaries on the Sunday Gospels, Year A. 3rd ed. 168p. (Orig.). 1992. pap. 9.95 (1-56548-013-9) New City.

Barnecut, Edith, ed. Journey with the Fathers: Commentaries on the Sunday Gospels, Year B. 3rd ed. 168p. (Orig.). 1993. pap. 9.95 (1-56548-056-2) New City.

Barnecut, Edith, ed. Journey with the Fathers: Commentaries on the Sunday Gospels, Year C. 3rd ed. (Word of God Throughout the Ages Ser.). 168p. (Orig.). 1994. pap. 9.95 (1-56548-064-3) New City.

Barnecut, Edith, tr. see Rotelle, John E., ed.

Barnefield, George, jt. auth. see Carpenter, Edward.

Barnekov, Timothy K., et al. Privatism & Urban Policy in Britain & the U. S. (Illus.). 288p. 1989. pap. 22.00 (0-19-823274-8) OUP.

Barnell, Hal. Instant France. Lathrop, Thomas, ed. (Illus.). 177p. 1992. spiral bd. 7.95 (0-942566-12-2) LinguaText.

Barnell, Jack M. Positive Parenting. (Christian Living Ser.). 44p. 1990. pap. 3.50 (0-8341-1366-X) Beacon Hill.

Barner-Barry, Carol & Hody, Cynthia A. The Politics of Change: The Soviet Union & Its Successor States. 372p. 1995. pap. text 34.95 (0-312-09079-X) St Martin.

— The Politics of Change: The Transformation of the Former Soviet Union. 384p. 1995. text 45.00 (0-312-12264-0) St Martin.

Barner-Barry, Carol & Rosenwein, Robert. Psychological Perspectives on Politics. (Illus.). 342p. (C). 1991. reprint ed. pap. text 22.95 (0-88133-619-X) Waveland Pr.

Barner, Bob. Bugs! Bugs! Bugs! LC 98-39604. (Illus.). 32p. (J). (ps-3). 1999. 12.95 (0-8118-2238-9) Chronicle Bks.

***Barner, Bob.** Fish Wish. LC 99-44491. (Illus.). 32p. (J). (ps-1). 2000. 16.95 (0-8234-1482-5) Holiday.

Barner, Bob. To Everything. LC 98-11107. (J). 1998. 14.95 (0-8118-2086-6) Chronicle Bks.

***Barner, Bob.** Walk the Dog. LC 99-6858. (Illus.). 32p. (J). 2000. 14.95 (0-8118-2087-4) Chronicle Bks.

Barner, Bob. Which Way to the Revolution? A Book about Maps. LC 97-34043. (Illus.). 32p. (J). (ps-3). 1998. lib. bdg. 16.95 (0-8234-1352-7) Holiday.

Barner, Bob. Dem Bones. LC 95-29. 32p. (J). (ps-3). 1996. 14.95 (0-8118-0827-0) Chronicle Bks.

Barner, Herbert E. & Scheuerman, Ricard V. Handbook of Thermochemical Data for Compounds & Aqueous Species. LC 77-20244. 166p. reprint ed. pap. 51.50 (0-7837-3426-3, 205774700008) Bks Demand.

***Barner, Robert.** Lifeboat Strategies: How to Keep Your Career above Water During Tough Times - Or Any Time. (Illus.). 192p. 2000. 16.95 (0-595-00206-4, toExcel) iUniversecom.

— Lifeboat Strategies: How to Keep Your Career Above Water During Tough Times - Or Any Time. 173p. 1999. reprint ed. pap. text 17.00 (0-7881-6819-3) DIANE Pub.

Barner, Robert W. Crossing the Minefield: Tactics for Overcoming Today's Toughest Management Challenges. 2nd ed. LC 94-25592. 256p. 1994. 24.95 (0-8144-0241-0) AMACOM.

***Barner, Robert W.** Executive Resource Management: Building & Retaining an Exceptional Leadership Team. LC 99-89257. 416p. 2000. 49.95 (0-89106-140-1, Pub. by Consulting Psychol) Consulting Psychol.

Barner, Wilfried. Neuere Alkaios-Papyri Aus Oxyrhynchus. (GER.). viii, 243p. 1967. 50.00 (0-318-70619-9) G Olms Pubs.

Barner, Wilfried & Reh, Albert M., eds. Nation & Gelehrtenrepublik: Supplement to the Lessing Yearbook. 363p. 1984. 16.00 (3-88377-190-2) Lessing Soc.

***Barnes.** Amistad Penguin Lev 3. 144p. 1999. pap. text 7.00 (0-582-40165-8) Addison-Wesley.

Barnes. Cold & Distant Stars Star Trek Deep Space Nine. 1998. per. 6.50 (0-671-02430-2) PB.

— History Atlas of Europe. (Illus.). 1998. write for info. (0-02-865342-4) Macmillan.

— Law for Business. 6th rev. ed. 1997. 32.50 (0-256-26897-5) McGraw.

— Monitoring the Health of Buildings. (Illus.). 256p. 1997. text. write for info. (0-419-20460-1, E & FN Spon) Routledge.

— Patriot Game. 1999. text. write for info. (0-312-00668-3) St Martin.

— Statistical Analysis for Engineers & Scientists. 1994. 29.37 (0-07-005094-5) McGraw.

— Story I Tell Myself. 1998. pap. 17.00 (0-226-03733-9) U Ch Pr.

— Surgical Pathology of the Head & Neck, Pt. B. (Illus.). 1896p. 1985. text 510.00 (0-8247-7269-5) Dekker.

— Teaching Case Method. 3rd ed. 416p. 1994. 35.00 (0-07-103601-6) McGraw.

***Barnes.** Telecommunications Systems & Technology. LC 98-56382. (Illus.). 519p. 1999. 101.00 (0-13-660705-5) P-H.

— Visual Communication. 2000. pap. text. write for info. (0-312-25097-5) St Martin.

Barnes. Wastewater Treatment. 3rd ed. 1987. pap. text. write for info. (0-582-29726-5, Pub. by Addison-Wesley) Longman.

— Wopert & Barnes' Pediatric Neuroradiology: Imaging of the Developing Brain. (Illus.). 576p. 2000. text 139.00 (0-8151-9355-6, 28697) Mosby Inc.

Barnes, et al, eds. James P. Cannon As We Knew Him. LC 76-25382. (Illus.). 288p. 1976. pap. 19.95 (0-87348-500-9); lib. bdg. 50.00 (0-87348-474-6) Pathfinder NY.

Barnes & Bloor. Scientific Knowledge: A Sociological Analysis. LC 96-172254. (C). Date not set. text. write for info. (0-485-11404-6) Humanities.

Barnes & Christen. Teaching & Case Method. 1994. pap. 16.95 (0-87584-565-7) Harvard Busn.

Barnes & Davison. European Business: Text & Cases. 288p. 1998. pap. text 39.95 (0-7506-1836-1) Buttrwrth-Heinemann.

Barnes & Foreman. Exploring Diversity: Readings in Sociology. LC 96-172104. 364p. 1996. pap. text 23.00 (0-536-58921-6) Pearson Custom.

Barnes & Forman. Exploring Diversity: Readings in Sociology. 2nd ed. 376p. (C). 1998. pap. text 20.00 (0-536-01580-5) Pearson Custom.

Barnes, jt. auth. see Curtis.

Barnes, jt. auth. see Frolik.

Barnes, jt. auth. see Smith.

Barnes, jt. ed. see Bua.

***Barnes & Thornburg Staff.** The Guide to Understanding Federal & Indiana Employment Laws. 387p. 1999. pap. 79.95 (0-9668710-1-4) Indiana Busn.

Barnes & Thornburg Staff. Indiana Environmental Law Handbook. 167p. 1992. pap. text 79.00 (0-86587-307-0) Gov Insts.

Barnes, A. C., tr. see Sheng-Tao, Yeh.

Barnes, A. C., tr. see Ts'ao Yu.

***Barnes, A. James.** Law for Business. 7th ed. LC 99-27985. 1200p. 1999. 86.25 (0-07-365917-7) McGraw.

Barnes, A. James, et al, eds. Molecular Liquids: Dynamics & Interactions. 1984. text 256.50 (90-277-1817-2) Kluwer Academic.

Barnes, A. James & Dworkin, Terry M. Law for Business. 6th ed. 1080p. (C). 1996. text 68.95 (0-256-19355-X, Irwn McGrw-H) McGrw-H Hghr Educ.

Barnes, A. James, et al. Essentials of Business Law & the Regulatory Environment. LC 94-21866. (Legal Studies in Business). 580p. (C). 1994. text 53.95 (0-256-14614-4, Irwn McGrw-H) McGrw-H Hghr Educ.

— Law for Business. 5th ed. LC 93-12225. (Legal Studies in Business). 1080p. (C). 1993. text 68.95 (0-256-11594-X, Irwn McGrw-H) McGrw-H Hghr Educ.

Barnes, A. James, jt. auth. see Mallor, Jane.

Barnes, A. Keith. Management Maturity: Prerequisite to Total Quality. LC 94-22125. 182p. (C). 1994. pap. text 26.50 (0-8191-9646-0); lib. bdg. 52.50 (0-8191-9645-2) U Pr of Amer.

Barnes, A. R., Jr. The Mortality Mortgage: Pricing Practices & Reform in the Life Insurance Industry. LC 95-19464. 216p. 1995. 57.95 (1-56720-003-6, Quorum Bks) Greenwood.

***Barnes, Agnes.** Waco, Texas, in Vintage Postcards. (Postcard History Ser.). (Illus.). 128p. 1999. pap. 18.99 (0-7385-0297-9) Arcadia Publng.

***Barnes, Al.** Let's Fly Backward: Barnstorming the Grand Traverse Bay Region. LC 75-39182. (Illus.). 206p. 2000. pap. 14.95 (0-915937-07-7) Hor Bks MI.

Barnes, Al. Supper in the Evening: Pioneer Tales of Michigan. 2nd rev. ed. LC 67-26278. (Illus.). 254p. 1985. pap. 10.95 (0-915937-01-8) Hor Bks MI.

— Vinegar Pie & Other Tales of the Grand Traverse Region. LC 58-12684. (Illus.). 184p. 1984. 14.50 (0-915937-00-X) Hor Bks MI.

***Barnes, Al.** Vinegar Pie & Other Tales of the Grand Traverse Region. LC 58-12684. (Illus.). 200p. 2000. 15.95 (0-915937-06-9) Hor Bks MI.

Barnes, Alan. Historic Organs in Historic Places the Eighteenth Century: Chamber Organ in Kedleston Hall. 1993. 60.00 (0-948653-01-9, Pub. by A Barnes) St Mut.

***Barnes, Alan.** Sherlock Holmes on Screen. 2000. text 22.95 (0-7134-8463-2) B T B.

Barnes, Alan & Hearn, Marcus. Kiss Kiss Bang Bang: The Secret History of James Bond. LC 98-10937. (Illus.). 192p. 1998. pap. 23.95 (0-87951-874-X, Pub. by Overlook Pr) Penguin Putnam.

Barnes, Alan & Renshaw, Martin. The Life & Work of John Snetzler. LC 93-1812. 1994. 113.95 (0-85967-932-2, Pub. by Scolar Pr) Ashgate Pub Co.

Barnes, Albert. Barnes' Notes on the New Testament. LC 62-8727. 1766p. 1966. 54.99 (0-8254-2200-0, Kregel Class) Kregel.

— Barnes' Notes on the Old & New Testaments, 14. 10,724p. (gr. 10). 1983. text 450.00 (0-8010-0834-4) Baker Bks.

— Church & Slavery. LC 79-82416. 15.00 (0-403-00150-1) Scholarly.

— Church & Slavery. LC 71-98714. 204p. 1970. reprint ed. lib. bdg. 49.50 (0-8371-2771-8, BAC&) Greenwood.

An Asterisk (*) at the beginning of an entry indicates that the title is appearing for the first time.

— Inquiry into Scriptural Views of Slavery. LC 75-92415. 1855. 23.00 (*0-403-00151-X*) Scholarly.

Barnes, Alberta C. & Weidenbach, Nell C. Early Fort Myers: Tales of Two Sisters. LC 93-72711. (Illus.). 200p. (Orig.). 1993. pap. 12.95 (*0-9638968-0-6*) Foxcord Hse.

Barnes, Alison. Counseling Older Clients: 1999 Supplement. LC 97-70989. 64p. 1999. pap. text 25.00 (*0-8318-0808-X*, B808) Am Law Inst.

***Barnes, Alison.** 2000 Supplement to Counseling Older Clients. LC 97-70989. 104p. 2000. pap. text 25.00 (*0-8318-1408-X*, BK07) Am Law Inst.

***Barnes, Alison M. & Frolik, Lawrence A.** Elderlaw, Cases & Materials: Teacher's Manual. 2nd ed. 140p. 1999. pap., teacher ed. write for info. (*0-327-01340-0*, 1146911) LEXIS Pub.

Barnes, Alison P., et al. Counseling Older Clients. LC 97-70989. 490p. 1997. text 170.00 (*0-8318-0661-3*) Am Law Inst.

Barnes, Alison P., jt. auth. see Frolik, Lawrence A.

Barnes, Allan C., ed. The Social Responsibility of Gynecology & Obstetrics. LC 65-24793. (Illus.). 224p. reprint ed. pap. 69.50 (*0-608-30508-1*, 201543100001) Bks Demand.

Barnes, Allen & Barnes, Patti. Christian Apparel. 2nd ed. LC 95-60022. 64p. 1995. per. 4.95 (*1-57258-029-1*) Teach Servs.

***Barnes, Althemese & Roberts, Ann.** Tallahassee. (Black America Ser.). (Illus.). 128p. 2000. pap. 18.99 (*0-7385-0551-X*) Arcadia Publng.

Barnes, Andrew E. & Stearns, Peter N. Social History & Issues in Human Consciousness. 272p. (C). 1990. pap. text 22.50 (*0-8147-1144-8*) NYU Pr.

Barnes, Ann & Powell, Bob. Developing Advanced Reading Skills in Modern Foreign Language Languages. (Handbooks for Language Teachers Ser.: Concepts 8). 47p. 1996. pap. 24.00 (*0-7487-2605-5*, Pub. by S Thornes Pubs) Trans-Atl Phila.

Barnes, Ann, jt. ed. see Berkeley, A. E.

Barnes, Anne & Graham, Suzanne. Target Language Testing. 1998. pap. 34.00 (*0-7487-3787-1*, Pub. by S Thornes Pubs) Trans-Atl Phila.

Barnes, Annette. Seeing Through Self-Deception. LC 97-20457. (Studies in Philosophy). 192p. (C). 1998. text 54.95 (*0-521-62014-7*) Cambridge U Pr.

Barnes, Annie S. The Black Middle Class Family: Family, Home, Interaction. 2nd ed. LC 85-51369. 147p. (C). 1989. text 40.00 (*1-55605-087-9*); pap. text 20.00 (*0-932269-50-8*) Wyndham Hall.

— Black Woman: A Sociological Study of Work, Home & the Community. LC 85-51989. (Illus.). 149p. (C). 1988. text 40.00 (*1-55605-085-2*); pap. text 20.00 (*0-932269-72-9*) Wyndham Hall.

***Barnes, Annie S.** Everyday Racism. 2000. reprint ed. pap. 14.95 (*1-57071-653-6*) Sourcebks.

Barnes, Annie S. Research Skills. 308p. 1994. per. 41.95 (*0-8403-9030-0*) Kendall-Hunt.

— Retention of African-American Males in High School: A Study of African-American Male High School Dropouts, African-American Seniors & White Male Seniors. 172p. (C). 1992. lib. bdg. 47.50 (*0-8191-8508-6*) U Pr of Amer.

***Barnes, Annie S.** Say It Loud: Middle-Class Blacks Talk about Racism & What to Do about It. LC 99-34474. 192p. 1999. pap. 19.95 (*0-8298-1336-5*) Pilgrim OH.

Barnes, Annie S. Single Parents in Black America: A Study in Culture & Legitimacy. LC 87-51006. (Illus.). 175p. (C). 1987. text 40.00 (*1-55605-023-2*); pap. text 20.00 (*1-55605-024-0*) Wyndham Hall.

Barnes, Anthony & Andrews, David, eds. Developing Careers Education & Guidance in the Curriculum. 160p. 1995. pap. 24.95 (*1-85346-323-X*, Pub. by David Fulton) Taylor & Francis.

Barnes, Arthur. God Broke His Promise? Traditional Beliefs Challenged by Scriptural Truths. LC 97-76658. 83p. 1998. pap. 9.95 (*1-880451-26-3*) Rainbows End.

Barnes, Arthur S. Christianity at Rome in the Apostolic Age. LC 72-114462. (Illus.). 222p. 1971. reprint ed. lib. bdg. 59.50 (*0-8371-4760-3*, BACR, Greenwood Pr) Greenwood.

Barnes, Austin, et al, eds. Matrix Isolation Spectroscopy. x, 606p. 1981. text 226.00 (*90-277-1328-6*) Kluwer Academic.

Barnes, B. The Elements of Social Theory. LC 95-24097. 272p. 1996. text 32.50 (*0-691-02723-4*, Pub. by Princeton U Pr) Cal Prin Full Svc.

Barnes, B. & Edge, D. Science in Context. 384p. 1982. pap. 41.95 (*0-335-10054-6*) OpUniv Pr.

***Barnes, B. Kim.** Exercising Influence: A Guide for Making Things Happen at Work, at Home & in Your Community. LC 00-190730. (Illus.). 152p. 2000. pap. 14.95 (*0-9700710-0-0*) Barnes & Conti.

Barnes, Barbara. EFG Learning Projects. (Learning Architecture for the 21st Century Ser.: Bk. 1). 32p. 1998. pap., wbk. ed. 6.95 (*1-58000-031-2*) Griffin CA.

— EFG Learning Projects. (Learning Architecture for the 21st Century Ser.: Bk. 2). 32p. 1998. pap., wbk. ed. 6.95 (*1-58000-032-0*) Griffin CA.

— EFG Learning Projects. (Learning Architecture for the 21st Century Ser.: Bk. 3). 32p. 1998. pap., wbk. ed. 6.95 (*1-58000-033-9*) Griffin CA.

— EFG Learning Projects. (Learning Architecture for the 21st Century Ser.: Bk. 4). 32p. 1998. pap., wbk. ed. 6.95 (*1-58000-034-7*) Griffin CA.

— EFG Learning Projects. (Learning Architecture for the 21st Century Ser.: Bk. 5). 32p. 1998. pap., wbk. ed. 6.95 (*1-58000-035-5*) Griffin CA.

— Learning Architecture for the 21st Century: The Ecological, Futures & Global Education Field Book. (Illus.). 288p. 1998. pap. text 34.95 (*1-58000-029-0*) Griffin CA.

***Barnes, Barbara.** Schools Transformed for the 21st Century: The Abc's of EFG. 112p. 1999. pap. 9.95 (*1-58000-052-5*, Pub. by Griffin CA) LPC InBook.

***Barnes, Barnabe.** Devil's Charter. (Tudor Facsimile Texts. Old English Plays Ser.). 1999. pap. 15.00 (*0-87830-100-3*) Routledge.

Barnes, Barnabe. Devil's Charter. LC 71-133638. (Tudor Facsimile Texts. Old English Plays Ser.: No. 121). reprint ed. 59.50 (*0-404-53421-X*) AMS Pr.

— Foure Bookes of Offices: Enabling Privat Persons for the Service of All Good Princes & Policies. LC 74-28830. (English Experience Ser.: No. 712). 1975. reprint ed. 24.00 (*90-221-0712-4*) Walter J Johnson.

Barnes, Barry. The Nature of Power. 224p. 1988. text 29.95 (*0-252-01582-7*) U of Ill Pr.

— Scientific Knowledge & Sociological Theory. (Monographs in Social Theory). 204p. 1975. pap. 13.95 (*0-7100-7962-1*, Routledge Thoemms) Routledge.

Barnes, Barry, et al, eds. Scientific Knowledge: A Sociological Analysis. 288p. 1996. pap. text 15.95 (*0-226-03731-2*) U Ch Pr.

Barnes, Barry, et al. Scientific Knowledge: A Sociological Analysis. 1996. lib. bdg. 38.00 (*0-226-03730-4*) U Ch Pr.

***Barnes, Belinda.** His Special Delivery. 2001. mass mkt. 3.50 (*0-373-19491-9*) Silhouette.

Barnes, Ben E., jt. auth. see Gay, Kathlyn.

Barnes, Bernadine A. Michelangelo's Last Judgment: The Renaissance Response. LC 97-82. (California Studies in the History of Art Ser.). 160p. 1998. 50.00 (*0-520-20549-9*, Pub. by U CA Pr) Cal Prin Full Svc.

Barnes, Beth, jt. auth. see Schultz, Don E.

Barnes, Beth E., jt. auth. see Schulz, Don E.

Barnes, Betsy K. The Pragmatics of the Left Detachment in Spoken Standard French. LC 85-26773. (Pragmatics & Beyond Ser.: VI-3). viii, 123p. (Orig.). 1986. pap. 46.00 (*0-915027-65-8*) J Benjamins Pubng Co.

Barnes, Betty. Diggin' up Bones: Obituaries of Deerfield, Fairview, & Miscellaneous Kearny County Cemetaries, KS. LC 98-140551. 330p. 1998. pap. 25.50 (*0-7884-0790-2*, B067) Heritage Bk.

— Diggin' up Bones: Obituaries of Lakin & Hartland Cemeteries Kearny County, Kansas, 2 vols., Set. 847p. (Orig.). 1996. pap. 54.50 (*0-7884-0370-2*, B066) Heritage Bk.

Barnes, Beverley, ed. see Morgan, Murray.

Barnes, Bill. Building Outdoor Playthings for Kids, with Project Plans. (Illus.). 240p. (Orig.). 1988. 21.95 (*0-8306-0971-7*, 1971); pap. 14.95 (*0-8306-1971-2*) McGraw-Hill Prof.

— Paintball! Strategies & Tactics. LC 93-4012. (Illus.). 176p. 1993. pap. 12.95 (*0-914457-52-7*) Mustang Pub.

Barnes, Bill, et al. The New A to Z on Fuchsias. (Illus.). 1976. 11.95 (*0-686-19065-3*); pap. 9.95 (*0-317-00255-4*) Natl Fuchsia.

***Barnes, Billy E.** 101 Professional Tips to Make Your Photos Sing. 56p. 1999. pap. 12.95 (*0-9676198-9-0*, 101T99) Robuck Pr.

Barnes, Bob. 15 Minutes Alone with God--for Men: Finding Strength for Challenging Times. (Orig.). 1995. pap. 9.99 (*1-56507-325-8*) Harvest Hse.

Barnes, Bob. Minute Meditations for Men. LC 97-44732. 224p. 1998. pap. 9.99 (*1-56507-863-2*) Harvest Hse.

— A Rock Solid Marriage. 2000. pap. 9.99 (*0-8297-1918-0*) Vida Pubs.

— What Makes a Man Feel Loved: Understanding What Your Husband Really Wants. LC 97-29014. 300p. 1998. pap. 9.99 (*1-56507-824-1*) Harvest Hse.

— Who's in Charge Here? Overcoming Power Struggles with Your Kids. LC 97-3343. 1997. pap. 10.99 (*0-310-21743-1*) Zondervan.

— Winning the Heart of Your Stepchild. LC 97-3341. 192p. 1997. pap. 10.99 (*0-310-21804-7*) Zondervan.

Barnes, Bob & Barnes, Emilie. 15-Minute Devotions for Couples. (Orig.). 1995. pap. 9.99 (*1-56507-423-8*) Harvest Hse.

***Barnes, Bob & Barnes, Emilie.** Grateful Hearts Give Thanks: A Treasury of Graces & Blessings. gif. ed. LC 00-28129. 64p. 2000. 14.99 (*0-7369-0129-9*) Harvest Hse.

— A Little Book of Manners for Boys: A Game Plan for Getting along with Others. gif. ed. (Illus.). 32p. (J). 2000. 14.99 (*0-7369-0128-0*) Harvest Hse.

Barnes, Bob, et al. World War II: It Changed Us Forever - Collection of True Experiences. Bigger, Margaret G., ed. LC 94-70744. 140p. 1994. pap. 12.95 (*0-9640606-0-4*) A Borough Bks.

Barnes, Bob, jt. auth. see Barnes, Emilie.

Barnes, Broda & Galton, Lawrence. Hypothyroidism: The Unsuspected Illness. LC 75-29251. 320p. 1976. 26.00 (*0-690-01029-X*) HarperTrade.

Barnes, Brooks M. & Truitt, Barry R. Seashore Chronicles: Three Centuries of the Virginia Barrier Islands. LC 97-2489. 1997. 30.00 (*0-8139-1748-4*) U Pr of Va.

Barnes, Brooks M. & Truitt, Barry R., eds. Seashore Chronicles: Three Centuries of the Virginia Barrier Islands. (Illus.). 282p. 1999. pap. 14.95 (*0-8139-1879-0*) U Pr of Va.

Barnes, Bruce. Introduction to Islam. (Illus.). 192p. (Orig.). 1984. pap. text 7.00 (*0-913811-01-7*) Northeast A S.

— Machine Gun Kelly: To Right a Wrong. 292p. (Orig.). 1992. pap. 12.95 (*0-9632609-0-1*) Tipper Pubns.

— Middle East Perspective. (Illus.). 224p. (Orig.). (C). 1983. pap. text 7.00 (*0-913811-00-9*) Northeast A S.

Barnes, Burton V. & Wagner, Warren H., Jr. Michigan Trees: A Guide to the Trees of Michigan & the Great Lakes. (Biological Science Ser.). (Illus.). 392p. 1981. pap. 18.95 (*0-472-08018-0*, 08018) U of Mich Pr.

Barnes, C. Cabbage Syndrome. 1990. 79.95 (*1-85000-757-8*, Falmer Pr); pap. 37.95 (*1-85000-758-6*, Falmer Pr) Taylor & Francis.

Barnes, C. D. & Pompeiano, O., eds. Neurobiology of the Locus Coeruleus Vol. 88: Progress in Brain Research. 642p. 1991. 323.50 (*0-444-81394-2*) Elsevier.

Barnes, C. H. Shorts Aircraft since 1900. 2nd ed. (Putnam Aviation Ser.). (Illus.). 766p. 1989. 45.00 (*0-87021-662-7*) Naval Inst Pr.

Barnes, Carl F., Jr. Personal Favorites: Fine Prints from the Collection of Carl F. Barnes, Jr. & Anna M. Barnes. (Illus.). 48p. (Orig.). Date not set. pap. text 5.00 (*0-925859-07-9*) Mead Brook Art.

Barnes, Carolyn. A Program for You: A Guide to the Big Book's Design for Living. 183p. (Orig.). pap. 10.00 (*0-89486-741-5*, 5122A) Hazelden.

***Barnes, Carolyn, ed.** Giant Encyclopedia of Art & Craft Activities: Over 500 Activities Created by Teachers for Teachers. LC 00-24529. (Illus.). 500p. 2000. pap. 29.95 (*0-87659-209-4*) Gryphon Hse.

Barnes, Carolyn, ed. The Massachusetts Political Almanac Vol. 2: 1998 Edition, The Executive. rev. ed. 349p. 1998. pap. 45.00 (*0-926766-22-8*) Ctr Leader Stu.

Barnes, Carolyn, et al, eds. Wood, Energy & Households: Perspectives on Rural Kenya. (Energy, Environment & Development in Africa Ser.: No. 6). 213p. 1984. write for info. (*91-7106-235-1*, Pub. by Nordic Africa) Transaction Pubs.

Barnes, Carolyn, jt. auth. see Manning, Marilyn.

Barnes, Carolyn, jt. ed. see Burch, Holly.

***Barnes, Catherine, et al.** Republic of Montenegro: Voter Awareness Assessment & Legal Review, November 1997-February 1998. iv, 270p. 1998. pap. text 29.00 (*1-879720-48-5*) Intl Fndt Elect.

Barnes, Catherine A. Journey of Jim Crow: The Desegregation of Southern Transit. LC 83-7566. (Contemporary American History Ser.). 329p. reprint ed. pap. 102.00 (*0-8357-4585-6*, 203751600008) Bks Demand.

Barnes, Cathy. Echoes from the Arkansas Unit Newspaper, 1926, Published in Morrilton, Arkansas. 240p. 1999. pap. 28.00 (*1-56546-144-4*) Arkansas Res.

— Extracts from the Pilot Newspaper: Morrilton, Conway County, Arkansas, November 14, 1890-May 4, 1894. 105p. (Orig.). 1997. pap. 16.00 (*1-56546-104-5*) Arkansas Res.

***Barnes, Cathy.** Index to the Arkansas Gazette, 1895. 140p. (Orig.). 1999. pap. 28.00 (*1-56546-148-7*) Arkansas Res.

— Index to the Arkansas Gazette, 1896. 221p. 1999. pap. 32.00 (*1-56546-152-5*) Arkansas Res.

Barnes, Cathy. Life & Times from the Clay County Courier Newspaper, Published at Corning, Arkansas, 1902-1903. 154p. 1997. pap. 23.00 (*1-56546-122-3*) Arkansas Res.

— Life & Times from the Clay County Courier Newspaper, 1893-1899, Published in Corning, Arkansas. 138p. 1997. pap. 21.00 (*1-56546-112-6*) Arkansas Res.

— Life & Times from the Clay County Courier Newspaper, 1900-1901, Published in Corning, Arkansas. 135p. 1997. pap. 21.00 (*1-56546-120-7*) Arkansas Res.

— Life & Times from the Clay County Courier Newspaper, 1904-1905, Published in Corning, Arkansas. 139p. 1998. pap. 21.00 (*1-56546-129-0*) Arkansas Res.

— Life & Times from the Clay County Courier Newspaper, 1906-1907 Published in Corning, Arkansas. 133p. 1998. pap. 21.00 (*1-56546-130-4*) Arkansas Res.

— Life & Times from the Clay County Courier Newspaper, 1910, Published in Corning, Arkansas. 199p. 1999. pap. 26.00 (*1-56546-133-9*) Arkansas Res.

— Life & Times from the Clay County Courier Newspaper, 1911, Published in Corning, Arkansas. 190p. 1999. pap. 25.00 (*1-56546-134-7*) Arkansas Res.

— Life & Times from the Clay County Courier Newspaper, 1912, Published in Corning, Arkansas. 172p. 1999. pap. 25.00 (*1-56546-135-5*) Arkansas Res.

***Barnes, Cathy.** Life & Times from the Clay County Courier Newspaper, 1913: Published in Corning, Arkansas. 139p. 2000. pap. 22.00 (*1-56546-163-0*) Arkansas Res.

— Life & Times from the Clay County Courier Newspaper, 1913: Published in Corning, Arkansas. 176p. 2000. pap. 25.00 (*1-56546-170-3*) Arkansas Res.

— Life & Times from the Clay County Courier Newspaper, 1915: Published in Corning, Arkansas. 176p. 2000. pap. 25.00 (*1-56546-173-8*) Arkansas Res.

Barnes, Cathy. Siftings from the Morrilton Democrat Newspaper, 1929: Published in Morrilton, Arkansas. 185p. (Orig.). 1997. pap. 25.00 (*1-56546-106-1*) Arkansas Res.

— Siftings from the Morrilton Democrat Newspaper, 1930, Published in Morrilton, Arkansas. 291p. 1997. pap. 33.00 (*1-56546-111-8*) Arkansas Res.

— Siftings from the Morrilton Democrat Newspaper, 1931, Published in Morrilton, Arkansas. 302p. 1998. pap. 33.00 (*1-56546-125-8*) Arkansas Res.

Barnes, Charles & Kaliuas, Peter W., eds. Sensitization of the Nervous System. (Illus.). 300p. 1988. lib. bdg. 77.00 (*0-936923-12-1*) Telford Pr.

Barnes, Charles B. The Longshoremen. Stein, Leon, ed. LC 77-70482. (Illus.). 1977. reprint ed. lib. bdg. 35.95 (*0-405-10156-2*) Ayer.

Barnes, Charles D. Brain Gut Peptides & Reproductive Peptides. 304p. 1991. lib. bdg. 106.00 (*0-8493-8848-1*, QP552) CRC Pr.

Barnes, Charles D. & Eltherington, Lorne G. Drug Dosage in Laboratory Animals Handbook. 4th ed. Date not set. 100.00 (*0-8493-4499-9*) CRC Pr.

Barnes, Charles D., ed. see Johnston.

Barnes, Charles D., jt. ed. see Kalivas, Peter W.

Barnes, Charles D., jt. ed. see Sarkar, Dipak K.

Barnes, Charles W. Earth, Time, & Life: An Introduction to Physical & Historical Geology. 2nd ed. LC 88-73. 576p. 1988. pap. 84.95 (*0-471-82598-0*) Wiley.

Barnes, Cheryl S. & Barnes, Peter W. Alexander, the Old Town Mouse. (Illus.). 32p. (J). (gr. k-6). 1994. 15.95 (*0-9637688-1-6*) Vacation Spot.

Barnes, Cheryl S., jt. auth. see Barnes, Peter W.

Barnes, Cheryle, jt. auth. see Barnes, David.

Barnes, Christine. Central Oregon: View from the Middle. LC 95-52320. (Illus.). 112p. (Orig.). 1996. pap. 17.95 (*1-56037-087-4*) Am Wrld Geog.

— Color: The Quilter's Guide. Reikes, Ursula G., ed. LC 96-37060. (Illus.). 128p. (Orig.). 1997. pap. 29.95 (*1-56477-164-4*, B275) Martingale & Co.

— Great Lodges of the Canadian Rockies. LC 99-70805. (Illus.). 164p. 1999. 35.00 (*0-9653924-2-2*) WW West.

— Great Lodges of the West. LC 97-60024. (Illus.). 136p. 1997. 34.00 (*0-9653924-1-4*) WW West.

Barnes, Christine, contrib. by. Quilted for Christmas, Bk. II. LC 95-13638. 1995. pap. 22.95 (*1-56477-104-0*, B221) Martingale & Co.

Barnes, Christine, ed. see Edie, Marge.

Barnes, Christine, ed. see McConnell, Donna F.

Barnes, Christopher. Boris Pasternak: Literary Biography, 1890-1928, Vol. 1. (Illus.). 528p. (C). 1989. text 89.95 (*0-521-25957-6*) Cambridge U Pr.

— Boris Pasternak Vol. 2: A Literary Biography, 1928-1960. (Illus.). 520p. (C). 1998. text 80.00 (*0-521-25958-4*) Cambridge U Pr.

B

Barnes, Christopher R., ed. Conodont Paleoecology: The Proceedings of an International Symposium Organized by the Geological Association of Canada & the Pander Society & Held at the University of Waterloo, Waterloo, Ontario, May 15-17, 1975. LC 77-369660. (Geological Association of Canada. Special Paper: No. 15). 330p. reprint ed. pap. 102.30 (*0-608-17204-9*, 202784400056) Bks Demand.

Barnes, Christy & Hutchinson, Janet, eds. The Up-Rising in Dying. 86p. 1990. pap. 10.95 (*0-932776-16-7*) Adonis Pr.

Barnes, Christy M., ed. For the Love of Literature: A Celebration of Language & Imagination. 356p. 1997. pap. 19.95 (*0-88010-416-3*) Anthroposophic.

Barnes, Christy MacKaye. A Wound Awoke Me. 119p. 1994. pap. 12.00 (*0-932776-21-3*) Adonis Pr.

Barnes, Claude, et al. American National & State Government: An African American View. 448p. (C). 1996. pap. text, per. 49.95 (*0-7872-2118-X*) Kendall-Hunt.

Barnes, Claude T. The Natural History of a Mountain Year: Four Seasons in the Wasatch Range. (Illus.). 400p. (C). 1996. reprint ed. pap. 16.95 (*0-87480-474-4*) U of Utah Pr.

Barnes, Clive. Nureyev. limited ed. (Illus.). 240p. 1982. 35.00 (*0-9609736-2-1*) Helene Obolensky Ent.

Barnes, Clive, ed. Best American Plays, 1983-1992. (John Gassner Best Plays Ser.: Ninth Ser.). 1993. 35.00 (*0-685-63464-7*) Random.

Barnes, Clive & Kaye. Nureyev. 1996. 24.50 (*0-02-874114-5*) Free Pr.

Barnes, Clive, jt. ed. see Gassner, John.

Barnes, Colin, et al. Exploring Disability: A Sociological Introduction. LC 99-17508. 224p. 1999. 62.95 (*0-7456-1477-9*); pap. 29.95 (*0-7456-1478-7*) Blackwell Pubs.

Barnes, Colin, jt. auth. see Attard, Gary.

Barnes, Corey. Backstreet Brothers. 1998. pap. 4.99 (*0-375-80193-6*) Random.

Barnes, Cos. A Fuller Stream: Tales of a Modern Woman of the South. 144p. 1996. pap. 14.95 (*0-9651885-0-7*) C Barnes.

Barnes, Craig. Hustling God: Why We Work So Hard for What God Wants to Give. LC 98-51433. 208p. 1999. pap. 16.99 (*0-310-21954-X*) Zondervan.

Barnes, Cynthia, ed. see Reeves, Douglas B.

***Barnes, Cynthia A.** A Manager's Guide - Model Memos: The Classic Compedium of over 800 Indispensible Memos. 464p. 1998. 8.98 (*1-56731-280-2*, MJF Bks) Fine Comms.

Barnes, Cynthia A. Manager's Portfolio of Model Memos for Every Occasion. 2nd ed. LC 96-34632. 352p. (C). 1997. pap. text 16.95 (*0-13-242512-2*) P-H.

— Manager's Portfolio of Model Memos for Every Occasion. 2nd rev. expanded ed. LC 96-34632. 352p. (C). 1997. text 39.95 (*0-13-242520-3*) P-H.

Barnes, Cynthia A., ed. Critical Thinking: Educational Imperative. LC 85-644753. (New Directions for Community Colleges Ser.: No. CC 77). 140p. 1992. pap. 22.00 (*1-55542-749-9*) Jossey-Bass.

***Barnes, Cyril.** Bible Quizzes & Puzzles. 2000. 8.99 (*0-517-16224-5*) Crown Pub Group.

Barnes, Cyril. Bible Wordsearch. 128p. 1995. pap. 6.99 (*0-551-02660-X*) Zondervan.

Barnes, Cyril C. Submarine Telecommunication & Power Cables. LC 78-304105. (IEE Monograph Ser.: Vol. 20). 222p. reprint ed. pap. 68.90 (*0-8357-7041-9*, 203345600086) Bks Demand.

Barnes, Cyrill A. Huntly - Capital of Strathbogie: The Town of the Tower & the Linden Trees. LC 97-130319. xv, 137p. 1998. write for info. (*1-898218-63-3*, Pub. by Scottish Cultural) St Mut.

***Barnes, D.** Object Oriented Programming with Java: A First Programming Text. LC 99-57040. 800p. 2000. write for info. (*0-13-086900-7*) P-H.

Barnes, D. Spectral Sequence Constructors in Algebra & Topology. LC 84-24622. (Memoirs Ser.: No. 53/317). 174p. 1987. reprint ed. pap. 26.00 (*0-8218-2319-1*, MEMO/53/317) Am Math.

Barnes, D. & Wilson, F. Chemistry & Unit Operations in Sewage Treatment. (Illus.). 339p. 1978. 90.00 (*0-85334-783-2*) Elsevier.

Barnes, D. S. The Maybe Stories of Uncle Dan. 93p. (J). 1996. per. 7.95 (*0-614-24784-5*) Tesseract SD.

Barnes, Dallas L. City of Passion. 256p. (Orig.). 1988. pap. 3.95 (*0-380-75504-1*, Avon Bks) Morrow Avon.

Barnes, Dan. Dancing Leaves. 41p. 1987. pap. 2.00 (*0-614-24753-5*) Tesseract SD.

Barnes, Darrell D. AIDS Assault: A Role-Playing Conceptual Game Pitting HIV-I Against the Human Immune System. (Illus.). ii, 49p. (Orig.). (YA). (gr. 6-12). 1994. reprint ed. pap. text 19.95 (*0-9654168-0-1*, 23846) Barnes Publns.

— Aidsassault: A Role Playing Conceptual Game Pitting HIV-1 Against the Human Immune System. 2nd rev. ed. (Illus.). 71p. 1998. pap. text 29.95 (*0-9654168-1-X*, 23846 Frey) Barnes Publns.

Barnes, David & Barnes, Cheryle. Special Educator's Survival Guide: Practical Techniques & Materials for Supervision & Instruction. 210p. 1989. text 32.95 (*0-87628-784-4*) Ctr Appl Res.

Barnes, David & Coles, Caroline. IT for All. 96p. 1995. pap. 17.95 (*1-85346-309-4*, Pub. by David Fulton) Taylor & Francis.

Barnes, David & Mather, Jennie P., eds. Animal Cell Culture Methods. (Methods in Cell Biology Ser.: Vol. 57). (Illus.). 368p. 1998. boxed set 99.95 (*0-12-544159-2*) Acad Pr.

— Animal Cell Culture Methods. 80th ed. (Methods in Cell Biology Ser.: Vol. 57). (Illus.). 368p. 1998. spiral bd. 64.95 (*0-12-480040-8*) Acad Pr.

B

Barnes, David S. The Making of a Social Disease: Tuberculosis in Nineteenth-Century France. LC 94-15230. 1995. 50.00 (*0-520-08772-0*, Pub. by U CA Pr) Cal Prin Full Svc.

Barnes, David W. Statistical Evidence. 1986. 125.00 (*0-316-08148-5*, Aspen Law & Bus) Aspen Pub.

Barnes, David W. & Conley, John M. Statistical Evidence in Litigation: Methodology, Procedure, & Practice. 686p. 1986. 125.00 (*0-316-08145-0*, Aspen Law & Bus) Aspen Pub.

Barnes, David W. & Stout, Lynn A. Cases & Materials on Law & Records. (American Casebook Ser.). 538p. (C). 1992. 57.50 (*0-314-00188-3*) West Pub.

— The Economic Analysis of Tort Law. (American Casebook Ser.). 161p. (C). 1992. pap. 16.50 (*0-314-01089-0*) West Pub.

— Economic Analysis of Tort Law: Teacher's Manual to Accompany The. (American Casebook Ser.). 96p. (C). 1992. pap. text. write for info. (*0-314-01204-4*) West Pub.

— Economic Foundations of Regulation & Antitrust Law. (American Casebook Ser.). 102p. (C). 1992. pap. 14.50 (*0-314-01104-8*) West Pub.

— The Economics of Constitutional Law & Public Choice. (American Casebook Ser.). 127p. (C). 1992. pap. 14.50 (*0-314-01118-8*) West Pub.

— Economics of Constitutional Law & Public Choice, Teacher's Manual to Accompany The. (American Casebook Ser.). 55p. (C). 1992. pap. text. write for info. (*0-314-01305-9*) West Pub.

— Economics of Contract Law. (American Casebook Ser.). 127p. (C). 1992. pap. 16.50 (*0-314-01092-0*) West Pub.

— Economics of Contract Law: Teacher's Manual to Accompany The. (American Casebook Ser.). 80p. (C). 1992. pap. text. write for info. (*0-314-01205-2*) West Pub.

— The Economics of Property Rights & Nuisance Law. LC 92-20399. (American Casebook Ser.). 87p. (C). 1992. pap. 14.50 (*0-314-01088-2*); pap. text, teacher ed. write for info. (*0-314-01202-8*) West Pub.

— The Economics of Regulation & Antitrust: Teacher's Manual to Accompany The. (American Casebook Ser.). 48p. (C). 1992. reprint ed. pap. text. write for info. (*0-314-01203-6*) West Pub.

— Law & Economic, Teacher's Manual to Accompany Cases & Materials On. (American Casebook Ser.). 230p. (C). 1992. pap. text. write for info. (*0-314-01042-4*) West Pub.

Barnes, Demas. From the Atlantic to the Pacific Overland. LC 72-9426. (Far Western Frontier Ser.). (Illus.). 142p. 1978. reprint ed. 21.95 (*0-405-04957-9*) Ayer.

***Barnes, Diane & Barnes, Jack.** Sebago Lake: West Lake. LC 99-69058. (Images of America Ser.). (Illus.). 128p. 2000. pap. 18.99 (*0-7385-0156-5*) Arcadia Publng.

Barnes, Diane, jt. auth. see Barnes, Jack.

Barnes, Dick. Few & Far Between. Burmaster, Orvis C., ed. 60p. (Orig.). 1994. pap., per. 6.95 (*0-916272-61-3*) Ahsahta Pr.

***Barnes, Dick.** What? Me Manage the Soccer Team? Information, How-To, Examples & Checklists for the Team Manager or Coach/Manager. rev. ed. (Illus.). 52p. 1999. pap. 7.95 (*0-9658875-2-9*) Sports Barn.

Barnes, Dick, jt. auth. see Staihar, Janet.

Barnes, Dick, tr. see Richard of St. Victor.

***Barnes, Djuna.** Antiphon, Vol. 54. 2000. pap. 11.95 (*1-892295-56-3*) Green Integer.

Barnes, Djuna. At the Roots of the Stars: The Short Plays. (Sun & Moon Classics/American Theater in Literature Ser.: No. 53). (Illus.). 200p. (Orig.). 1995. pap. 12.95 (*1-55713-160-0*) Sun & Moon CA.

— The Book of Repulsive Women: Eight Rhythms & Fire Drawings. rev. ed. (Sun & Moon Classics Ser.: No. 59). (Illus.). 48p. 1994. pap. 6.95 (*1-55713-173-2*) Sun & Moon CA.

— The Collected Stories. Herring, Philip, ed. & intro. by. (Sun & Moon Classics Ser.: No. 110). 488p. 1996. 24.95 (*1-55713-226-7*) Sun & Moon CA.

— Collected Stories. (Sun & Moon Classics Ser.: Vol. 110). 488p. 1997. pap. text 16.95 (*1-55713-355-7*) Sun & Moon CA.

— Creatures in an Alphabet. LC 82-5086. 1982. 10.95 (*0-385-27797-0*) BDD Bks Young Read.

— Interviews. Barry, Alyce, ed. (Illus.). 406p. 1985. pap. 13.95 (*0-940650-37-1*) Sun & Moon CA.

— Ladies Almanack. (Cutting Edge: Lesbian Life & Literature Ser.). (Illus.). 128p. (C). 1992. pap. text 16.50 (*0-8147-1180-4*) NYU Pr.

— Ladies Almanack. LC 91-14515. (Illus.). 96p. 1992. reprint ed. pap. 9.95 (*0-916583-88-0*) Dalkey Arch.

***Barnes, Djuna.** Nightwood. LC 99-56308. 224p. 2000. 18.95 (*0-679-64024-X*) Modern Lib NY.

Barnes, Djuna. Nightwood. LC 49-1384. 1961. pap. 9.95 (*0-8112-0005-1*, NDP98, Pub. by New Directions) Norton.

— Nightwood: The Original Version & Related Drafts. Plumb, Cheryl J., ed. LC 94-36949. 319p. 1995. 23.95 (*1-56478-080-5*) Dalkey Arch.

— Poe's Mother: Selected Drawings of Djuna Barnes. LC 95-42960. (Illus.). 240p. (Orig.). 1993. 29.95 (*1-55713-143-0*) Sun & Moon CA.

— Ryder. 2nd ed. LC 90-2769. (Illus.). 250p. 1990. reprint ed. pap. 11.95 (*0-916583-55-4*) Dalkey Arch.

— Smoke & Other Early Stories. 2nd rev. ed. Messerli, Douglas, ed. (Sun & Moon Classics Ser.: No. 2). 184p. 1988. pap. 10.95 (*1-55713-014-0*) Sun & Moon CA.

Barnes, Djuna, et al. Unmuzzled Ox Anthology, No. 15. Andre, Michael, ed. (Illus.). pap. 19.95 (*0-934450-08-0*) Unmuzzled Ox.

Barnes, Don. Democratic Classrooms: Theory & Behavior. pap. 4.95 (*0-89741-002-5*) Gila River.

Barnes, Donald. Critical Reading for Proficiency. 1986. pap. text 13.82 (*0-87694-068-8*) Ed Design Inc.

Barnes, Donald R. & Lackey, Richard S., eds. Write It Right: A Manual for Writing Family History & Genealogies. 2nd ed. (C). 1988. pap. 9.95 (*0-9620190-0-3*) Lyon Press.

Barnes, Donna, et al, eds. Writing Process Revisited: Sharing Our Stories. LC 97-25804. (Illus.). 188p. 1997. pap. 21.95 (*0-8141-2815-7*) NCTE.

Barnes, Donna R. Street Scenes: Leonard Bramer's Drawings of 17th-Century Dutch Daily Life. (Illus.). 80p. 1991. pap. 14.95 (*0-8122-1368-8*) U of Pa Pr.

Barnes, Dorothy & Earle, Ralph. Healing Conversations: Therapy & Spiritual Growth. LC 98-13663. 168p. 1998. pap. 10.99 (*0-8308-1948-7*, 1948) InterVarsity.

Barnes, Dorothy L., jt. compiled by see Stevens, Irving F.

Barnes, Douglas. From Communication to Curriculum. 2nd ed. LC 91-31736. 210p. (Orig.). (C). 1992. pap. text 21.00 (*0-86709-298-X*, 0298, Pub. by Boynton Cook Pubs) Heinemann.

Barnes, Douglas & Todd, Frankie. Communication & Learning Revisited: Making Meaning Through Talk. LC 95-3111. 184p. 1995. pap. text 22.00 (*0-86709-356-0*, 0356, Pub. by Boynton Cook Pubs) Heinemann.

Barnes, Douglas, et al. Language, the Learner, & the School. 4th ed. LC 89-22228. 166p. (C). 1989. pap. text 18.50 (*0-86709-251-3*, 0251, Pub. by Boynton Cook Pubs) Heinemann.

Barnes, Douglas, jt. auth. see Sheeran, Yanina.

Barnes, E. H. Atlas & Manual of Plant Pathology. LC 79-10575. (Illus.). 344p. (C). 1979. spiral bd. 65.00 (*0-306-40168-1*, Kluwer Plenum) Kluwer Academic.

Barnes, E. J. & Ramsey, John T. Cicero & Sallust. 1988. pap. text 14.88 (*0-582-36752-2*, 72528) Longman.

Barnes, Elizabeth. Face to Face with Distress: The Professional Use of Self in Psychosocial Care. LC 97-25272. 4p. 1997. pap. text 34.00 (*0-7506-3617-3*) Buttrwrth-Heinemann.

— Last Summer's Girl. (Romance Ser.). 1993. per. 2.99 (*0-373-03278-1*, 1-03278-8) Harlequin Bks.

— Marketing: An Active Learning Approach. 1997. pap. text 50.95 (*0-631-20182-3*) Blackwell Pubs.

— States of Sympathy: Seduction & Democracy in the Early American Novel. LC 96-53284. 152p. 1997. lib. bdg. 52.00 (*0-231-10878-8*) Col U Pr.

Barnes, Elizabeth. States of Sympathy: Seduction & Democracy in the Early American Novel. LC 96-53284. 292p. 1997. pap. 17.50 (*0-231-10879-6*) Col U Pr.

Barnes, Elizabeth, et al. Business Law: An Active Learning Approach. LC 96-6590. (BABS Ser.). 462p. (Orig.). 1997. pap. text 39.95 (*0-631-20183-1*) Blackwell Pubs.

Barnes, Emilie. Christmas Is Coming: Our Family Holiday Organizer. 144p. 1998. spiral bd. 16.99 (*1-56507-912-4*) Harvest Hse.

***Barnes, Emilie.** Cooking Up Fun in the Kitchen: Yummy Ideas for Girls. LC 99-44130. 32p. (J). 2000. 14.99 (*0-7369-0131-0*) Harvest Hse.

Barnes, Emilie. A Cup of God's Love. LC 99-224285. 64p. 1999. pap. 7.99 (*0-7369-0030-6*) Harvest Hse.

***Barnes, Emilie.** A Cup of Hope: Resting in the Promise of God's Faithfulness. 150p. 2000. 12.99 (*0-7369-0271-6*) Harvest Hse.

Barnes, Emilie. Emilie Barnes' 15 Minute Home & Family Organizer. 1998. 9.99 (*0-88486-196-1*, Inspirational Pr) Arrowood Pr.

— Emilie's Creative Home Organizer. rev. ed. 1995. pap. 9.99 (*1-56507-319-3*) Harvest Hse.

— The 15-Minute Organizer. 258p. (Orig.). 1991. pap. 9.99 (*0-89081-857-6*) Harvest Hse.

— Fifteen Minutes Alone with God. LC 94-6869. 1994. pap. 9.99 (*1-56507-228-6*) Harvest Hse.

— 15 Minutes Alone with God. large type ed. LC 96-46017. 440p. 1997. pap. 18.95 (*0-8027-2712-3*) Walker & Co.

— 15 Minutes of Peace with God. 300p. 1997. pap. 9.99 (*1-56507-567-6*) Harvest Hse.

— Fill My Cup, Lord: With the Peace of Your Presence. LC 95-46904. 144p. 1996. 12.99 (*1-56507-358-4*) Harvest Hse.

***Barnes, Emilie.** Help Me Trust You, Lord: Knowing the Healing Touch of God's Love. 144p. 2000. pap. 8.99 (*0-7369-0246-5*) Harvest Hse.

Barnes, Emilie. If Teacups Could Talk: Sharing a Cup of Kindness with Treasured Friends. LC 94-12931. (Illus.). 1994. 15.99 (*1-56507-232-4*) Harvest Hse.

— An Invitation to Tea: Special Celebrations with Treasured Friends. 48p. 1996. pap. 7.99 (*1-56507-462-9*) Harvest Hse.

— Let's Have a Tea Party! LC 97-8362. (Illus.). 32p. (J). (gr. 1-7). 1997. 14.99 (*1-56507-679-6*) Harvest Hse.

— A Little Book of Manners. Buchanan, Anne C., ed. LC 97-36915. (Illus.). 32p. (J). 1998. 14.99 (*1-56507-678-8*) Harvest Hse.

— Making My Room Special: Creative Ways to Decorate Your Room. LC 98-38010. (Illus.). 32p. (YA). 1999. 14.99 (*0-7369-0044-6*) Harvest Hse.

— Minute Meditations for Women. LC 99-21701. 250p. 1999. pap. 9.99 (*0-7369-0101-9*) Harvest Hse.

— More Hours in My Day. rev. ed. LC 94-6866. (Orig.). 1994. pap. 9.99 (*1-56507-233-2*) Harvest Hse.

— My Cup Overflows: With the Comfort of His Love. LC 98-4084. 170p. 1998. 12.99 (*1-56507-907-8*) Harvest Hse.

***Barnes, Emilie.** 101 Ways to Lift Your Spirits. gif. ed. (Illus.). 64p. 2000. pap. 6.99 (*0-7369-0388-7*) Harvest Hse.

Barnes, Emilie. Quiet Moments with God. 560p. 1999. 12.99 (*0-88486-252-6*) Galahad Bks.

— Secrets of the Garden: Creating Beauty from Nature's Gifts. LC 97-143408. (Illus.). 48p. (Orig.). 1997. pap. 7.99 (*1-56507-564-1*) Harvest Hse.

— Simply Dinner: Fabulous Meals in Minutes. LC 98-14701. 96p. 1998. 12.99 (*1-56507-867-5*) Harvest Hse.

— Simply Organized: The Life You Always Searched for...but Were Too Cluttered to Find. LC 96-35336. 96p. (Orig.). 1997. 12.99 (*1-56507-592-7*) Harvest Hse.

— The Spirit of Loveliness: Bringing Beauty, Creativity & Order to Your Life. 160p. 1999. 14.99 (*0-7369-0041-1*) Harvest Hse.

— Survival for Busy Women. exp. ed. 1993. pap. 9.99 (*1-56507-065-8*) Harvest Hse.

— Things Happen When Women Care: Hospitality & Friendship in Today's Busy World. LC 90-35983. (Orig.). 1990. pap. 9.99 (*0-89081-837-1*) Harvest Hse.

— Treasured Christmas Memories. (Illus.). 48p. 1996. 19.99 (*1-56507-519-6*) Harvest Hse.

— The Twelve Teas of Christmas: Sharing the Season with Those You Love. LC 99-14124. (Illus.). 96p. 1999. 16.99 (*0-7369-0052-7*) Harvest Hse.

***Barnes, Emilie.** 2001 Daily Planner: Planning Your Year with Emilie Barnes. 128p. 2000. spiral bd. 8.99 (*0-7369-0418-2*) Harvest Hse.

Barnes, Emilie. The Very Best Christmas Ever! A Season Full of Decorations, Recipes, & Fun Things to Do. LC 98-3111. 32p. (gr. 2-5). 1998. 14.99 (*1-56507-905-1*) Harvest Hse.

— Welcome Home. LC 96-53617. (Illus.). 125p. (Orig.). 1997. 19.99 (*1-56507-586-2*) Harvest Hse.

— Whispers of Prayer. LC 99-224280. 64p. 1999. pap. 7.99 (*0-7369-0031-4*) Harvest Hse.

***Barnes, Emilie & Barnes, Bob.** Abundance of the Heart: Rejoicing in the Fruit of the Spirit. LC 99-37261. 64p. 2000. 15.99 (*0-7369-0260-0*) Harvest Hse.

Barnes, Emilie & Barnes, Bob. The 15-Minute Money Manager. 1993. pap. 9.99 (*1-56507-040-2*) Harvest Hse.

Barnes, Emilie & Brogger, Yoli. Beautiful Home on a Budget. LC 97-36918. (Illus.). 64p. 1998. pap. 12.99 (*1-56507-829-2*) Harvest Hse.

— Decorating Dreams on a Budget. LC 98-31157. 156p. 1999. mass mkt. 5.99 (*0-7369-0037-3*) Harvest Hse.

Barnes, Emilie & Buchanan, Anne. Timeless Treasures: The Charm & Romance of Cherished Memories. (Illus.). 84p. 1996. 15.99 (*1-56507-428-9*) Harvest Hse.

Barnes, Emilie & Buchanan, Anne C. Time Began in a Garden. (Illus.). (Orig.). 1995. 15.99 (*1-56507-368-1*) Harvest Hse.

Barnes, Emilie & Buchanan, Anne Christian. My Best Friends & Me: Fun Things to Do Together. LC 99-17715. (Illus.). 32p. (J). (ps-3). 1999. 14.99 (*0-7369-0121-3*) Harvest Hse.

Barnes, Emilie & Gregg, Sue. The 15-Minute Meal Planner: A Realistic Approach to a Healthy Lifestyle. LC 94-30119. (Illus.). (Orig.). 1995. pap. 9.99 (*1-56507-234-0*) Harvest Hse.

***Barnes, Emilie & Otto, Donna.** Friends Are a Blessing. (Moment Meditation Ser.). 64p. 2000. pap. 7.99 (*0-7369-0192-2*) Harvest Hse.

Barnes, Emilie & Otto, Donna. Friends of the Heart: Friends That Last Forever. LC 99-21979. 144p. 1999. 12.99 (*1-56507-990-6*) Harvest Hse.

Barnes, Emilie, jt. auth. see Barnes, Bob.

Barnes, Emilie, jt. auth. see Gregg, Sue.

Barnes, Emrey, et al. The Traditions Gathered Vol. 3: Swords of Faith. (Mage Ser.). 216p. 1999. pap. 20.00 (*1-56504-447-9*, 4055) White Wolf.

Barnes, Esther A. The Dwarf Dinosaur. (J). 1994. 6.95 (*0-533-11103-X*) Vantage.

Barnes, Eugene B., jt. ed. see Dougherty, David M.

Barnes, F. A. Canyon Country Arches & Bridges. LC 86-50825. (Canyon Country Ser.: No. 15). (Illus.). 416p. (Orig.). 1987. pap. 9.95 (*0-9614586-1-5*) Canyon Country Pubns.

— Canyon Country Camping. rev. ed. (Illus.). 128p. 1991. pap. 6.00 (*0-915272-34-2*) Wasatch Pubs.

— Canyon Country Explorer #1. LC 94-94154. (Canyon Country Ser.: No. 33). (Illus.). 112p. 1994. pap. 12.50 (*0-925685-07-0*) Canyon Country Pubns.

— Canyon Country Explorer #2. LC 95-67290. (Canyon Country Ser.: No. 40). (Illus.). 112p. 1996. pap. 15.00 (*0-925685-18-6*) Canyon Country Pubns.

***Barnes, F. A.** Canyon Country Geology. rev. ed. LC 77-95050. (Canyon Country Ser.: Vol. 11). (Illus.). 160p. 2000. pap. 12.95 (*1-891858-18-1*, 0011) Arch Hunter Bks.

Barnes, F. A. Canyon Country Hiking & Natural History. LC 76-58119. (Canyon Country Ser.). (Illus.). 1977. pap. 7.00 (*0-915272-07-5*) Wasatch Pubs.

— Canyon Country Off-Road Vehicle Trails: Arches & la Sals Areas. LC 77-95043. (Canyon Country Ser.). (Illus.). 1978. pap. 5.00 (*0-915272-13-X*) Wasatch Pubs.

— Canyon Country Off-Road Vehicle Trails: Canyon Rims & Needles Areas. LC 77-95043. (Canyon Country Ser.). (Illus.). 1978. pap. 5.00 (*0-915272-14-8*) Wasatch Pubs.

— Canyon Country Off-Road Vehicle Trails: Island Area. LC 77-95043. (Canyon Country Ser.). (Illus.). 1978. pap. 5.00 (*0-915272-15-6*) Wasatch Pubs.

— Canyon Country Off-Road Vehicle Trails - Arches & La Sals Areas. LC 89-90921. (Canyon Country Ser.: No. 6). (Illus.). 96p. 1989. pap. 6.00 (*0-9614586-0-7*) Canyon Country Pubns.

— Canyon Country Off-Road Vehicle Trails - Canyon Rims & Needles Areas. LC 89-92058. (Canyon Country Ser.: No. 8). (Illus.). 96p. 1990. pap. 6.00 (*0-9614586-7-4*) Canyon Country Pubns.

— Canyon Country Off-Road Vehicle Trails - Island Area. LC 88-70881. (Canyon Country Ser.: No. 4). (Illus.). 80p. (Orig.). 1988. pap. 6.00 (*0-9614586-6-6*) Canyon Country Pubns.

— Canyon Country ORV Trails - Canyon Rims Recreation Area. LC 90-86115. (Canyon Country Ser.: No. 25). (Illus.). 112p. (Orig.). 1991. pap. 6.00 (*0-925685-01-1*) Canyon Country Pubns.

— Canyon Country Prehistoric Life. LC 96-85848. (Canyon Country Ser.: No. 47). (Illus.). 128p. (Orig.). 1998. pap. 14.50 (*0-925685-28-3*) Canyon Country Pubns.

***Barnes, F. A.** Canyon Country Prehistoric Rock Art. rev. ed. LC 82-60129. (Canyon Country Ser.: No. 14). (Illus.). 304p. 2000. pap. 14.95 (*1-891858-24-6*, 0014) Arch Hunter Bks.

Barnes, F. A. Canyon Country Slickrock Hiking & Biking. LC 88-62755. (Canyon Country Ser.: No. 21). (Illus.). 288p. (Orig.). 1990. pap. 12.00 (*0-9614586-4-X*) Canyon Country Pubns.

— Canyonlands National Park: Early History & First Descriptions. LC 87-72287. (Canyon Country Ser.: No. 16). (Illus.). 160p. (Orig.). 1988. pap. 6.00 (*0-9614586-2-3*) Canyon Country Pubns.

— Dinosaur Tracks & Trackers. LC 97-66315. (Canyon Country Ser.: Vol. 54). (Illus.). 176p. 1998. pap. 11.00 (*0-925685-32-1*) Canyon Country Pubns.

— Geology of the Moab Area. LC 92-73225. (Canyon Country Ser.: No. 30). (Illus.). 264p. (Orig.). 1993. pap. 15.00 (*0-925685-04-6*) Canyon Country Pubns.

— Hiking the Historic Route of the 1859 Macomb Expedition. LC 88-62754. (Canyon Country Ser.: No. 20). (Illus.). 48p. (Orig.). 1989. pap. 4.00 (*0-9614586-8-2*) Canyon Country Pubns.

— Hiking the Sand Flats Recreation Area. LC 95-67291. (Canyon Country Ser.: No. 42). (Illus.). 64p. (Orig.). 1995. pap. 6.00 (*0-925685-21-6*) Canyon Country Pubns.

— Navajo Sandstone: A Canyon Country Enigma. (Canyon Country Ser.: No. 55). (Illus.). 96p. 1999. pap. 7.00 (*0-925685-37-2*) Canyon Country Pubns.

— Reisen Auf den Highways Im Canyon Country. LC 92-71599. (Canyon Country Ser.: No. 31). (GER., Illus.). 80p. (Orig.). 1993. pap. 7.00 (*0-925685-06-2*) Canyon Country Pubns.

— Signs of Impact! in Canyon Country. LC 99-474393. (Canyon Country Ser.: Vol. 57). (Illus.). 48p. 1999. pap. 6.00 (*0-925685-39-9*, 0057) Canyon Country Pubns.

— Utah Canyon Country. LC 85-52187. (Utah Geographic Ser.: Vol. 1). (Illus.). 120p. (Orig.). 1986. pap. 9.95 (*0-936331-00-3*) Am Wrld Geog.

Barnes, F. A. & Barnes, M. M. Cameo Cliffs Biking - Hiking - Four-Wheeling. LC 91-76024. (Canyon Country Ser.: No. 28). (Illus.). 160p. (Orig.). 1992. pap. 7.00 (*0-925685-03-8*) Canyon Country Pubns.

— Canyon Country Historic Remnants. LC 96-84260. (Canyon Country Ser.: No. 45). (Illus.). 176p. (Orig.). 1996. pap. 9.50 (*0-925685-26-7*) Canyon Country Pubns.

— Canyon Country's Canyon Rims Recreation Area. LC 89-62344. (Canyon Country Ser.: No. 23). (Illus.). 216p. (Orig.). 1992. pap. 13.50 (*0-925685-00-3*) Canyon Country Pubns.

— Moab Country Day Hikes. LC 95-83944. (Canyon Country Ser.: No. 43). (Illus.). 48p. (Orig.). 1996. pap. 6.00 (*0-925685-25-9*) Canyon Country Pubns.

Barnes, F. A. & Kuehne, Tom. Canyon Country Mountain Biking. LC 87-73014. (Canyon Country Ser.: No. 17). (Illus.). 144p. (Orig.). 1988. pap. 9.00 (*0-9614586-5-8*) Canyon Country Pubns.

Barnes, F. A., jt. auth. see Pendleton, Michalene.

Barnes, F. A., ed. see Bickers, Jack.

Barnes, F. A., ed. see Utesch, Peggy.

Barnes, F. F. Barnes: Ten Generations of the Barnes Family in Bristol, CT. (Illus.). 280p. 1992. reprint ed. pap. 52.00 (*0-8328-2615-4*); reprint ed. lib. bdg. 62.00 (*0-8328-2614-6*) Higginson Bk Co.

Barnes Foundation Staff & Mitchell, Carolyn B. Great French Paintings from the Barnes Foundation. (Illus.). 318p. 1995. pap. 40.00 (*0-679-76221-3*) Knopf.

***Barnes, Fran.** Entrada Sandstone, Canyon Country Dead Zone. (Canyon Country Ser.: Vol. 56). (Illus.). 64p. 1999. pap. 6.00 (*0-925685-38-0*) Canyon Country Pubns.

***Barnes, Fran & Barnes, Terby.** More Moab Country Day Hikes: Forty More One-Day Hikes in the Moab Vicinity. (Canyon Country Ser.: Vol. 59). (Illus.). 48p. 1999. pap. 6.00 (*0-925685-40-2*) Canyon Country Pubns.

Barnes, Frances. Figaro. LC 93-132. (Voyages Ser.). (Illus.). (J). 1994. write for info. (*0-383-03686-0*) SRA McGraw.

Barnes, Frances J., ed. LOVE - From Black Men to Black Women. 78p. 1996. reprint ed. pap. 9.95 (*0-9650742-0-X*) LOVE LINE.

An Asterisk (*) at the beginning of an entry indicates that the title is appearing for the first time.

— LOVE - From Black Women to Black Men. 79p. 1996. pap. 9.95 (*0-9650742-1-8*) LOVE LINE.

Barnes, Francis. The Story of Houlton, from the Public Records & from the Experience of Its Founders, Their Decendants, & Associates to the Present Time (1889) (Illus.). 129p. 1997. reprint ed. pap. 17.50 (*0-8328-5859-5*) Higginson Bk Co.

Barnes, Frank. Fort Sumter. LC 84-600248. (Official National Park Handbook Ser.: No. 127). 1984. pap. 3.50 (*0-912627-24-7*) Natl Park Serv.

Barnes, Frank & Sheth, Jagdish. Worldwide Wireless Communications. (Illus.). 560p. 1996. 150.00 (*0-933217-17-X*) Prof Educ Intl.

Barnes, Frank C. Cartridges of the World. 8th ed. McPherson, M. L., ed. LC 65-16729. (Illus.). 480p. 1997. pap. 24.95 (*0-87349-178-5*, COW8, DBI Bks) Krause Pubns.

— Cartridges of the World. 9th rev. expanded ed. (Illus.). 512p. 2000. pap. 27.95 (*0-87341-909-X*, COW9) Krause Pubns.

Barnes, Frank S., jt. ed. see Wu, Huey-Daw.

Barnes, Frank T. Hooks, Rings & Other Things, an Illustrated Index of New England Iron, 1660-1860 - Wrought & Cast. LC 86-73037. (Illus.). 1988. 40.00 (*0-8158-0440-7*) Chris Mass.

Barnes, Frederick W. The Cellular Cloud. (Illus.). xiii, 221p. 1995. 35.00 (*0-9653311-0-5*); pap. 20.00 (*0-9653311-1-3*) F W Barnes.

Barnes, G. E. Soil Mechanics: Principles & Practice. (Illus.). 365p. (C). 1995. pap. text 39.95 (*0-333-59654-4*) Scholium Intl.

Barnes, Gary & Frey, G. Donald, eds. Screen Film Mammography: Imaging Considerations & Medical Physics Responsibilities. (Illus.). 242p. (C). 1991. reprint ed. pap. text 43.95 (*0-944838-12-X*) Med Physics Pub.

Barnes, George G. Hawkins. Genealogy of the Hawkins Family. 99p. 1997. reprint ed. pap. 17.00 (*0-8328-9056-1*); reprint ed. lib. bdg. 27.00 (*0-8328-9055-3*) Higginson Bk Co.

Barnes, George N. Barnes Genealogies, Including a Collection of Ancestral, Genealogical & Family Records & Biological Sketches of Barnes People. (Illus.). 226p. 1988. reprint ed. pap. 34.00 (*0-8328-0193-3*); reprint ed. lib. bdg. 44.00 (*0-8328-0192-5*) Higginson Bk Co.

Barnes, Gerald P. U. S. Postal Service: Progress Made in Implementing Automated Letter Sequencing, but Some Issues Remain. (Illus.). 66p. (C). 1999. pap. text 20.00 (*0-7881-7777-X*) DIANE Pub.

Barnes, Gerald P., et al. U. S. Postal Service: Information about Restrictions on Mailbox Access. 56p. 1998. pap. text 20.00 (*0-7881-4841-9*) DIANE Pub.

Barnes, Geraldine. Counsel & Strategy in Middle English Romance. LC 92-43903. 175p. (C). 1993. 75.00 (*0-85991-362-7*) Boydell & Brewer.

Barnes, Gerard P. U. S. Postal Service: Development & Inventory of New Products. (Illus.). 61p. (C). 1999. pap. text 20.00 (*0-7881-7833-4*) DIANE Pub.

Barnes, Gilbert. Anti-Slavery Impulse, 1830-1844. 298p. 1993. reprint ed. lib. bdg. 79.00 (*0-7812-5307-1*) Rprt Serv.

Barnes, Gilbert H. & Dumond, Dwight L., eds. Letters of Theodore Dwight Weld, Angelina Grimke & Sarah Grimke, 1822-1844, Vols. 1 & 2. 1934. 33.00 (*0-8446-1055-0*) Peter Smith.

— Letters of Theodore Dwight Weld, Angelina Grimke Weld, & Sarah Grimke. LC 77-121103. (American Public Figures Ser.). 1970. reprint ed. lib. bdg. 95.00 (*0-306-71981-9*) Da Capo.

Barnes, Gill G., et al. Growing Up in Stepfamilies. 346p. 1998. text 85.00 (*0-19-828097-1*) OUP.

Barnes, Gill Gorell. Growing Up in Stepfamilies. 346p. 1998. pap. text (*0-19-828096-3*) OUP.

***Barnes, Gill Gorell, et al.** Systemic Supervision: A Portable Guide for Supervisory Training. LC 99-56653. 240p. 2000. pap. 24.95 (*1-85302-853-3*) Jessica Kingsley.

Barnes, Gina L. Protohistoric Yamato: Archaeology of the First Japanese State. (Anthropological Papers Ser.: No. 78, Vol. 17). (Illus.). xx, 473p. (Orig.). (C). 1988. pap. text 19.95 (*0-915703-11-4*) U Mich Mus Anthro.

— The Rise of Civilization in East Asia: The Archaeology of China, Korea & Japan. 2nd ed. LC 93-60205. Orig. Title: China, Korea & Japan. (Illus.). 288p. 1999. reprint ed. pap. 24.95 (*0-500-27974-8*, Pub. by Thames Hudson) Norton.

Barnes, Ginny Pearson. Successful Negotiating: Letting the Other Person Have Your Way. Career Press Staff, ed. LC 98-5754. 128p. 1998. pap. 10.99 (*1-56414-359-7*) Career Pr Inc.

***Barnes, Gordon E.** The Addiction-Prone Personality. LC 99-53617. (Longitudinal Research in the Social & Behavioral Sciences Ser.). 2000. write for info. (*0-306-46249-4*, Kluwer Plenum) Kluwer Academic.

Barnes, Grace M., compiled by. Alcohol & Youth: A Comprehensive Bibliography. LC 82-15397. 432p. 1982. lib. bdg. 65.00 (*0-313-23136-2*, BAY/, Greenwood Pr) Greenwood.

Barnes, Grace M. & Augustino, Diane K., compiled by. Alcohol & the Family: A Comprehensive Bibliography, 9. LC 86-27112. (Bibliographies & Indexes in Sociology Ser.: No. 9). 474p. 1987. lib. bdg. 75.00 (*0-313-24782-X*, BFA/, Greenwood Pr) Greenwood.

Barnes, Grace M., et al. Alcohol & the Elderly: A Comprehensive Bibliography. LC 80-1786. 138p. 1980. lib. bdg. 49.95 (*0-313-22132-4*, BAE/, Greenwood Pr) Greenwood.

Barnes, Gregory A. English Communication Skills for Professionals: Advanced Intermediate Through Advanced. 192p. 1993. 23.95 (*0-8442-9334-2*, Natl Textbk Co) NTC Contemp Pub Co.

Barnes, Gregory A., jt. auth. see Pica, Teresa.

Barnes, Grenville. A Comperative Evaluation Framework for Cadastrebased Land Information Systems (CLIS) in Developing Countries. (Research Paper Ser.: Vol. 102). (Illus.). xiii, 186p. (C). 1990. pap. 12.00 (*0-934519-12-9*, RP102) U of Wis Land.

Barnes, Grenville, jt. auth. see Lastarria-Cornhiel, Susana.

Barnes, Gwendolyn, jt. ed. see Duplaa, Cristina.

Barnes, H. Oceanography & Marine Biology. 1959. 14.00 (*0-08-026258-9*, Pergamon Pr) Elsevier.

Barnes, H. A. The Birds of India: A Guide to Indian Ornithology, 2 vols. 449p. 1981. text 87.50 (*0-685-14044-X*) Coronet Bks.

Barnes, H. A., et al. An Introduction to Rheology. x,200p. 1989. 142.50 pap. 96.00 (*0-444-87469-0*) Elsevier.

***Barnes, H. Lee.** Gunning for Ho: Vietnam Stories. LC 99-37249. (Western Literature Ser.). 170p. 2000. pap. 15.00 (*0-87417-346-9*) U of Nev Pr.

Barnes, H. N., et al, eds. Alcoholism. (Frontiers of Primary Care Ser.). (Illus.). 225p. 1989. 55.00 (*0-387-96545-9*) Spr-Verlag.

Barnes, H. Verdain, ed. see Wolpert, Samuel M., et al.

Barnes, Harold, jt. ed. see Barnes, Margaret.

Barnes, Harper. Blue Monday. 210p. (Orig.). 1991. pap. 9.95 (*0-935284-92-3*) Patrice Pr.

Barnes, Harriet S. Humphreville, with Collateral Lines Beecher, Bristol, Brown, Bullard, Clark et al: Ancestral Records of Frances Amelia (Smith) Lewis. 56p. 1997. reprint ed. pap. 11.00 (*0-8328-9259-9*); reprint ed. lib. bdg. 21.00 (*0-8328-9258-0*) Higginson Bk Co.

Barnes, Harry E. Barnes Against the Blackout: Essays Against Interventionism. 347p. 1991. pap. 8.95 (*0-939484-36-6*, 0957, Inst Hist Rev) Legion Survival.

— The Barnes Trilogy: Blasting the Historical Blackout, the Court Historians Versus Revisionism, Revisionism & Brainwashing. Brandon, Lewis, ed. 1981. lib. bdg. 600.00 (*0-686-73177-8*) Revisionist Pr.

— Blasting the Historical Blackout. 1971. 250.00 (*0-87700-027-1*) Revisionist Pr.

— The Chickens of the Interventionist Liberals Have Come to Roost. 1971. 250.00 (*0-87700-194-4*) Revisionist Pr.

— The Court Historians Versus Revisionism. 1971. 250.00 (*0-87700-193-6*) Revisionist Pr.

— Crucifying the Savior of France: Petain. 1971. 250.00 (*0-87700-281-9*) Revisionist Pr.

— Evolution of Penology in Pennsylvania, a Study in American Social History. LC 68-55768. (Criminology, Law Enforcement, & Social Problems Ser.: No. 21). (Illus.). 1968. reprint ed. 28.00 (*0-87585-021-9*) Patterson Smith.

— Genesis of the World War, & Introduction to the Problem of War Guilt. 1968. 79.00 (*0-403-00140-4*) Scholarly.

— History & Prospects of the Social Sciences. 1973. 300.00 (*0-87700-029-8*) Revisionist Pr.

— History & Social Intelligence. 1971. 300.00 (*0-87700-030-1*) Revisionist Pr.

— A History of the Penal, Reformatory, & Correctional Institutions of the State of New Jersey: Analytical & Documentary. LC 74-3817. (Criminal Justice in America Ser.). (Illus.). 1974. reprint ed. 54.95 (*0-405-06137-4*) Ayer.

— In Quest of Truth & Justice: De-Bunking the War Guilt Myth. LC 79-172204. (Right Wing Individualist Tradition in America Ser.). 1972. reprint ed. 29.95 (*0-405-00414-1*) Ayer.

— In Quest of Truth & Justice: Debunking the War Guilt Myth. LC 72-78407. 1972. reprint ed. 17.50 (*0-87926-011-4*); reprint ed. pap. 2.95 (*0-87926-012-2*) R Myles.

— The New History & the Social Studies. (Harry Elmer Barnes Ser.). (Illus.). 624p. 1972. reprint ed. lib. bdg. 300.00 (*0-87700-033-6*) Revisionist Pr.

— Pearl Harbor after a Quarter of a Century. LC 75-172203. (Right Wing Individualist Tradition in America Ser.). 1979. reprint ed. 19.95 (*0-405-00413-3*) Ayer.

— Perpetual War for Perpetual Peace. enl. rev. ed. 1982. lib. bdg. 250.00 (*0-87700-454-4*) Revisionist Pr.

— Psychology & History. 1971. 59.95 (*0-87700-034-4*) Revisionist Pr.

— The Public Stake in Revisionism. 1971. 250.00 (*0-87700-282-7*) Revisionist Pr.

— Rauch on Roosevelt. 1971. 59.95 (*0-87700-283-5*) Revisionist Pr.

— Repression of Crime, Studies in Historical Penology. LC 69-14911. (Criminology, Law Enforcement, & Social Problems Ser.: No. 56). 1969. reprint ed. 24.00 (*0-87585-056-1*) Patterson Smith.

— Revisionism: A Key to Peace. 1971. 250.00 (*0-87700-192-8*) Revisionist Pr.

— Revisionism & Brainwashing. 1971. 250.00 (*0-685-26298-7*) Revisionist Pr.

— Revisionism & the Promotion of Peace. 1971. 59.95 (*0-87700-284-3*) Revisionist Pr.

— Select Bibliography of Revisionist Books. rev. ed. 1971. 250.00 (*0-685-26300-2*) Revisionist Pr.

— Selected Revisionist Pamphlets: An Original Arno Press Compilation. LC 72-172205. (Right Wing Individualist Tradition in America Ser.). 1972. reprint ed. 21.95 (*0-405-00415-X*) Ayer.

— Social History of the Western World. 1971. 250.00 (*0-87700-035-2*) Revisionist Pr.

— Social Institutions in an Era of World Upheaval. LC 77-6677. 927p. 1977. reprint ed. lib. bdg. 145.00 (*0-8371-9654-X*, BASO, Greenwood Pr) Greenwood.

— Sociology & Political Theory. LC 74-185842. 1972. reprint ed. lib. bdg. 250.00 (*0-87700-036-0*) Revisionist Pr.

— Sociology Before Comte. 1973. 250.00 (*0-87700-202-9*) Revisionist Pr.

— Story of Punishment: A Record of Man's Inhumanity to Man. 2nd rev. ed. LC 74-108229. (Criminology, Law Enforcement, & Social Problems Ser.: No. 112). (Illus.). (C). 1972. 30.00 (*0-87585-112-6*) Patterson Smith.

— Was Roosevelt Pushed into War? 1971. 200.00 (*0-87700-285-1*) Revisionist Pr.

— Who Started the First World War? 1985. lib. bdg. 79.95 (*0-87700-651-2*) Revisionist Pr.

— World Politics in Modern Civilization, 2 vols. 1973. 750.00 (*0-87700-038-7*) Revisionist Pr.

Barnes, Harry E., jt. auth. see Becker, Howard.

Barnes, Harry E., ed. see Jenks, Leland H.

***Barnes, Harry Lee.** Wallum Pond Estates. fac. ed. (Illus.). 85p. 2000. reprint ed. pap. write for info. (*0-7404-0048-7*) Higginson Bk Co.

Barnes, Hazel E. Existentialist Ethics. LC B 0819.B32. (Midway Reprint Ser.). 479p. reprint ed. pap. 148.50 (*0-608-09376-9*, 205412100004); reprint ed. pap. 148.50 (*0-608-20991-0*, 205451900003) Bks Demand.

— An Existentialist Ethics. LC 78-55038. xii, 468p. 1985. reprint ed. pap. text 19.95 (*0-226-03729-0*) U Ch Pr.

— Humanistic Existentialism: The Literature of Possibility. LC 59-11732. 428p. pap. 132.70 (*0-608-11152-X*, 202261100028) Bks Demand.

— The Meddling Gods: Four Essays on Classical Themes. LC 73-92003. 149p. 1974. reprint ed. pap. 46.20 (*0-608-02687-5*, 206334000004) Bks Demand.

— Sartre & Flaubert. LC 80-26872. 460p. (C). 1981. 30.00 (*0-226-03720-7*) U Ch Pr.

— Sartre & Flaubert. LC 80-26872. 416p. (C). 1982. pap. 10.95 (*0-226-03721-5*) U Ch Pr.

— Sartre & Flaubert. LC 80-26872. 459p. Date not set. reprint ed. pap. 142.30 (*0-608-20992-9*, 205452000003) Bks Demand.

— Sartre & Flaubert. LC 80-26872. 459p. 1981. reprint ed. pap. 142.30 (*0-608-09377-7*, 205412200004) Bks Demand.

— The Story I Tell Myself: A Venture in Existentialist Autobiography. LC 96-29600. 320p. 1997. 29.95 (*0-226-03732-0*) U Ch Pr.

Barnes, Hazel E., ed. see Schopenhauer, Arthur.

Barnes, Hazel E., tr. see Sartre, Jean-Paul.

Barnes, Hazel E., tr. & intro. see Sartre, Jean-Paul.

Barnes, Henry. Life for the Spirit: Rudolf Steiner in the Crosscurrents of Our Time. LC 97-22243. (Vista Ser.: Vol. 1). (Illus.). 320p. 1997. pap. 18.95 (*0-88010-395-7*, 1842) Anthroposophic.

***Barnes, Hermolee Thomas.** Simply Put - Poems, Prose & Sayings. (Illus.). viii, 65p. 1999. pap. 7.95 (*0-9674959-0-3*) CLI-FAN Enter.

Barnes, Homer F. Charles Fenno Hoffman. LC 75-160003. (BCL Ser. I). reprint ed. 34.50 (*0-404-00656-6*) AMS Pr.

Barnes, Howard A. Horace Bushnell & the Virtuous Republic. LC 91-24719. (American Theological Library Association Monograph: No. 27). (Illus.). 215p. 1991. 35.00 (*0-8108-2438-8*) Scarecrow.

Barnes, Hubert L. Geochemistry of Hydrothermal Ore Deposits. 3rd ed. LC 96-34529. 992p. 1997. 140.00 incl. disk (*0-471-57144-X*) Wiley.

Barnes, Hubert L., jt. ed. see Ulmer, Gene C.

Barnes, I. A. Barnes Family in West Virginia, Being a Brief Account of This Branch of the Family in West Virginia. 126p. 1997. reprint ed. pap. 21.00 (*0-8328-7381-0*); reprint ed. lib. bdg. 31.00 (*0-8328-7380-2*) Higginson Bk Co.

***Barnes, Ian.** The Historical Atlas of the American Revolution. Royster, Charles, ed. LC 99-59920. (Illus.). 208p. 2000. 50.00 (*0-415-92243-7*) Routledge.

Barnes, Ian. History Atlas of Asia. (Macmillan Continental History Atlases Ser.). (Illus.). 160p. 1998. 27.95 (*0-02-862581-1*) Macmillan.

— History Atlas of Europe. (Macmillan Continental History Atlases). (Illus.). 160p. 1998. 27.95 (*0-02-862584-6*) Macmillan.

Barnes, Ian & Barnes, Pamela. The Enlarged European Union. 2nd ed. LC 95-14645. 352p. (C). 1995. pap. 40.06 (*0-582-08115-7*) Longman.

Barnes, Ian E., et al. Surgical Endodontics: A Colour Manual. 2nd ed. (Illus.). 128p. 1991. text 95.00 (*0-7236-1571-3*) Buttrwrth-Heinemann.

Barnes, Ian G., jt. auth. see Barnes, Pamela M.

Barnes, Irston R. & Gude, Gilbert. Landscaping for Birds. Briggs, Shirley A., ed. (Illus.). 54p. 1973. 5.00 (*0-318-13602-3*) Audubon Naturalist.

Barnes, Irwin. Truth Is Immortal: The Story of Baptists in Europe. 127p. 1950. reprint ed. 4.50 (*0-87921-015-X*); reprint ed. pap. 2.50 (*0-87921-019-2*) Attic Pr.

Barnes, J. The Treatyse of Fysshinge with an Angle. (English Dialect Society Publications: No. 41a). 1974. reprint ed. pap. 25.00 (*0-8115-0467-0*) Periodicals Srv.

Barnes, J. & Barr, N. Strategies for Higher Education - The Alternative White Paper. (David Hume Papers). 66p. 1988. pap. text 14.00 (*0-08-036589-2*, Pergamon Pr) Elsevier.

Barnes, J. A. The Ethics of Inquiry in Social Science. 1977. text 3.95 (*0-19-560767-8*) OUP.

— Models & Interpretations: Selected Essays. 281p. (C). 1990. text 80.00 (*0-521-36653-4*) Cambridge U Pr.

— A Pack of Lies: Towards a Sociology of Lying. LC 93-23455. (Themes in the Social Sciences Ser.). 214p. (C). 1994. pap. text 19.95 (*0-521-45978-8*) Cambridge U Pr.

Barnes, J. C. Voluntary Isolation of Control in a Natural Muscle Group. (Psychology Monographs General & Applied: Vol. 22). reprint ed. pap. 55.00 (*0-8115-1421-8*) Periodicals Srv.

Barnes, J. H., tr. see Abarbanel, Judah.

Barnes, J. Phillip. Non-Dimensional Characterization of Gear Geometry, Mesh Loss & Windage. (Technical Papers: Vol. 97FTM11). (Illus.). 12p. 1997. pap. text 30.00 (*1-55589-705-3*) AGMA.

Barnes, J. S. Fascism. LC 72-7055. (Select Bibliographies Reprint Ser.). 1977. reprint ed. 20.95 (*0-8369-6922-7*) Ayer.

Barnes, J. Suzanne, jt. auth. see Scrivener, Laurie.

Barnes, J. W. Ores & Minerals: Introducing Economic Geology. 192p. 1991. pap. 80.00 (*0-471-93203-5*) Wiley.

Barnes, J. Wesley. Statistical Analysis for Engineers & Scientists: A Computer-Based Approach, IBM Version. (C). 1994. 96.88 (*0-07-839608-5*) McGraw.

— Statistical Analysis for Engineers & Scientists: A Computer-Based Approach, Macintosh Version. (C). 1994. pap., student ed. 96.88 (*0-07-839605-0*) McGraw.

Barnes, J. Wesley, jt. auth. see Jensen, Paul A.

Barnes, Jack. The Best Barnes. Conley, Susan C. et al, eds. (Illus.). 180p. (Orig.). 1996. pap. 12.95 (*1-879205-57-2*) Nightshade Pr.

— Los Canonazos Iniciales de la Tercera Guerra Mundial: El Ataque de Washington Contra Iraq. (SPA.). 378p. (Orig.). 1991. pap. 13.00 (*0-87348-648-X*) Pathfinder NY.

— Capitalism's World Disorder: Working-Class Politics at the Millennium. (Illus.). 540p. 1999. 60.00 (*0-87348-819-9*); pap. 21.95 (*0-87348-818-0*) Pathfinder NY.

Barnes, Jack. The Changing Face of U. S. Politics. 2nd ed. 510p. pap. text 21.95 (*0-87348-905-5*) Pathfinder NY.

Barnes, Jack. The Changing Face of U. S. Politics: Working-Class Politics & the Trade Unions. 2nd ed. LC 94-66880. 459p. (C). 1994. reprint ed. pap. 19.95 (*0-87348-785-0*); reprint ed. lib. bdg. 55.00 (*0-87348-791-5*) Pathfinder NY.

— The Coming Revolution in South Africa. 198p. 1985. reprint ed. pap. 9.00 (*0-87348-640-4*) Pathfinder NY.

***Barnes, Jack.** El Desorden Mundial del Capitalismo: Politica Obrera al Milenio. (SPA., Illus.). 550p. 2000. pap. 23.95 (*0-87348-889-X*) Pathfinder NY.

Barnes, Jack. For a Workers & Farmers Government in the United States. 61p. pap. 7.00 (*0-87348-680-3*) Pathfinder NY.

— Imperialismens Marsch Mot Fascism Och Krig (Imperialism's March Toward Fascism & War), No. 2. Isacsson, Carl-Erik, ed. (SWE.). 344p. 1995. pap. 19.00 (*91-87860-03-1*) Pathfinder NY.

— Imperialism's March Toward Fascism & War. 333p. 1994. pap. 14.00 (*0-87348-773-7*) Pathfinder NY.

— La Marcha del Imperialismo Hacia el Fascismo y la Guerra (Imperialism's March Toward Fascism & War) Koppel, Martin, ed. (SPA.). 365p. 1995. pap. 15.00 (*0-87348-795-8*) Pathfinder NY.

— La Marche de l'Imperialisme Vers le Fascisme et la Guerre (Imperialism's March Toward Fascism & War) Prairie, Michel, ed. (FRE.). 376p. 1995. pap. 15.00 (*0-87348-803-2*) Pathfinder NY.

***Barnes, Jack.** New International: U. S. Imperialism has Lost the Cold War. 306p. 1998. pap. 14.00 (*0-87348-796-6*) Pathfinder Pubns.

Barnes, Jack. Opening Guns of World War III. (FAR.). 221p. pap. 16.95 (*0-87348-797-4*) Pathfinder NY.

— Les Premieres Salves de la Troisieme Guerre Mondiale: La Guerre Contre l'Irak (Opening Guns of World War III: Washington's Assault on Iraq) (Illus.). 333p. (Orig.). (C). 1991. pap. 13.00 (*0-87348-647-1*) Pathfinder NY.

— La Revolution a Venir en Afrique du Sud. 2nd ed. (FRE.). 196p. 1991. reprint ed. pap. 11.00 (*0-87348-645-5*) Pathfinder NY.

— El Rostro Cambiante de la Politica en Estados Unidos: La Politica Obrera y los Sindicatos. Koppel, Martin, ed.Tr. of Changing Face of U. S. Politics: Working-Class Politics & the Trade Unions. (SPA., Illus.). 510p. 1997. pap. 21.95 (*0-87348-851-2*) Pathfinder NY.

— Sudafrica: La Revolucion en Camino. (SPA., Illus.). 75p. 1986. pap. 6.95 (*0-87348-488-6*) Pathfinder NY.

— Their Trotsky & Ours: Communist Continuity Today. 156p. 1983. reprint ed. pap. 8.00 (*0-87348-636-6*) Pathfinder NY.

Barnes, Jack. U. S. Imperialism Has Lost the Cold War. (Illus.). 339p. pap. text 15.00 (*0-87348-888-1*); pap. text 19.00 (*91-87860-05-8*) Pathfinder NY.

Barnes, Jack. Le Visage Changeant de la Politique aux Etats-Unis (The Changing Face of U. S. Politics) (FRE., Illus.). 524p. 1997. pap. 21.95 (*0-87348-852-0*) Pathfinder NY.

Barnes, Jack & Barnes, Diane. Lake Region. (Images of America Ser.). (Illus.). 128p. 1998. pap. 16.99 (*0-7524-0204-8*) Arcadia Publng.

— Maine Life at the Turn of the Century. LC 95-237757. (Images of America Ser.). 1995. pap. 16.99 (*0-7524-0240-4*) Arcadia Publng.

— The Oxford Hills. (Images of America Ser.). 1995. pap. 16.99 (*0-7524-0060-6*) Arcadia Publng.

— The Sebago Lakes Area. (Images of America Ser.). 1996. pap. 16.99 (*0-7524-0248-X*) Arcadia Publng.

Barnes, Jack & Waters, Mary-Alice. Opening Guns of World War III: Washington's Assault on Iraq. (Illus.). 333p. (Orig.). (C). 1991. pap. 12.00 (*0-87348-642-0*) Pathfinder NY.

Barnes, Jack, jt. auth. see Barnes, Diane.

Barnes, Jack, ed. see Dobbs, Farrell.

Barnes, Jake & Brand, Randall. Microbiology Lab Manual. 132p. (C). 1995. pap. text, spiral bd. 23.04 (*0-7872-0494-3*) Kendall-Hunt.

Barnes, James A. John Carlisle: Financial Statesman. 1990. 18.50 (*0-8446-1056-9*) Peter Smith.

— Law for Business Study Guide. 6th ed. 280p. (C). 1996. text, student ed. 23.12 (*0-256-25479-6*, Irwn McGrw-H) McGrw-H Hghr Educ.

***Barnes, James F. & Reed, Michael C.** Culture Ecology & Polits in Gabons. 360p. 2000. pap. 50.00 (*0-8133-3733-X*) Westview.

B

***Barnes, James G.** Secrets of Customer Relationship Management: A Guide to Getting Much Closer to Your Customers. (Illus.). 288p. 2000. 24.95 (0-07-136253-3) McGraw.

Barnes, James G., et al. The ABC's of the UCC: Article 5, Letters of Credit. LC 97-73345. 75 p. 1998. write for info. (1-57073-378-3) Amer Bar Assn.

Barnes, James G., ed. see Byrne, James E.

Barnes, James J. & Barnes, Patience P. James Vincent Murphy: Translator & Interpreter of Fascist Europe, 1880-1946. LC 86-28172. (Illus.). 314p. (Orig.). 1987. pap. text 26.50 (0-8191-6055-5) U Pr of Amer.

— Private & Confidential: Letters from British Ministers in Washington to Their Foreign Secretaries in London, 1845-67. LC 91-50101. 480p. (C). 1993. 59.50 (0-945636-33-4) Susquehanna U Pr.

Barnes, James N. Promises, Promises! A Review: 6-7 Economic Summit Declarations on Environment & Development. (Illus.). 110p. (Orig.). 1994. pap. 10.00 (0-913890-40-5) Friends of Earth.

Barnes, James N., et al. Bankrolling Successes Vol. II: A Portfolio of Sustainable Development Projects. (Illus.). 109p. (Orig.). 1995. pap. 10.00 (0-913890-94-4) Friends of Earth.

Barnes, James R., et al, eds. Stream Ecology: Application & Testing of General Ecological Theory. LC 83-11145. (Illus.). 412p. (C). 1983. 150.00 (0-306-41460-0, Plenum Trade) Perseus Pubng.

Barnes, Jane. Irish Industrial Schools, 1868-1908. (Illus.). 212p. 1989. 35.00 (0-7165-2426-0, Pub. by Irish Acad Pr) Intl Spec Bk.

Barnes, Jay. Florida's Hurricane History. LC 98-13012. (Illus.). 344p. 1998. 39.95 (0-8078-2443-7); pap. 19.95 (0-8078-4748-8) U of NC Pr.

— North Carolina's Hurricane History. rev. ed. LC 98-16051. 272p. 1998. pap. 19.95 (0-8078-4728-3) U of NC Pr.

— North Carolina's Hurricane History. rev. ed. LC 98-16051. (Illus.). 272p. 1998. 34.95 (0-8078-2416-X) U of NC Pr.

***Barnes, Jeff J.** To Fight or Not to Fight? Should a Pastor Resign under Pressure or Stay. LC 00-90026. 192p. 2000. pap. 16.95 (1-58597-018-2) Leathers Pub.

Barnes, Jeffrey K. Asa Fitch & the Emergence of American Entomology, with an Entomological Bibliography & a Catalog of Taxonomic Names & Type Specimens. (Bulletin Ser.: Bulletin No. 461). (Illus.). 120p. (Orig.). 1988. pap. 12.50 (1-55557-006-2) NYS Museum.

Barnes, Jenny, jt. auth. see Owens, Lee.

Barnes, Jill & Asuka, Ken. Smile for Toto. Rubin, Caroline, ed. Japan Foreign Rights Centre Staff, tr. from JPN. LC 90-37747. (Dragonfly Tales Ser.). (Illus.). 32p. (J). (gr. k-4). 1990. lib. bdg. 14.60 (0-944483-87-9) Garrett Ed Corp.

— Toto in Trouble. Rubin, Caroline, ed. Japan Foreign Rights Centre Staff, tr. from JPN. LC 90-37749. (Dragonfly Tales Ser.). (Illus.). 32p. (J). (gr. k-4). 1990. lib. bdg. 14.60 (0-944483-86-0) Garrett Ed Corp.

Barnes, Jill & Ishinabe, Fusako. Spring Snowman. Rubin, Caroline, ed. Japan Foreign Rights Centre Staff, tr. from JPN. LC 90-37748. (Dragonfly Tales Ser.). (Illus.). 32p. (J). (gr. k-3). 1990. lib. bdg. 14.60 (0-944483-83-6) Garrett Ed Corp.

Barnes, Jill & Kanabe, Junkichi. Road Roller Saves the Day. Rubin, Caroline, ed. Japan Foreign Rights Centre Staff, tr. from JPN. LC 90-3841. (Dragonfly Tales Ser.). (Illus.). 40p. (J). (gr. k-3). 1990. lib. bdg. 15.93 (0-944483-81-X) Garrett Ed Corp.

Barnes, Jill & Tsurmi, Masao. Giant Tree & the Boy. Rubin, Caroline, ed. Japan Foreign Rights Centre Staff, tr. from JPN. LC 90-37751. (Dragonfly Tales Ser.). (Illus.). 40p. (J). (gr. k-4). 1990. lib. bdg. 15.93 (0-944483-80-1) Garrett Ed Corp.

Barnes, Jim. The American Book of the Dead. Poems. LC 81-11458. 120p. 1982. 9.95 (0-252-00938-X); text 14.95 (0-252-00937-1) U of Ill Pr.

— Fiction of Malcolm Lowry & Thomas Mann: Structural Tradition. LC 89-34099. 183p. 1990. lib. bdg. 35.00 (0-943549-03-5) Truman St Univ.

***Barnes, Jim.** Grave Concern. 2000. pap. 16.95 (1-893162-21-4) Erica Hse.

Barnes, Jim. La Plata Cantata. LC 88-17071. (Illus.). 74p. 1989. pap. 12.95 (0-911198-96-2) Purdue U Pr.

— On Native Ground: Memoirs & Impressions. LC 96-36292. (American Indian Literature & Critical Studies Ser.: Vol. 23). 296p. 1997. 27.95 (0-8061-2898-4) U of Okla Pr.

— Paris: Poems. LC 96-45831. 120p. 1997. 16.95 (0-252-06622-7) U of Ill Pr.

— The Sawdust War: Poems by Jim Barnes. 136p. 1992. 12.95 (0-252-06239-6) U of Ill Pr.

— A Season of Loss. LC 85-3634. (Illus.). 84p. 1985. pap. 12.95 (0-911198-75-X) Purdue U Pr.

Barnes, Jim, ed. Five Missouri Poets. LC 79-9319. 124p. 1979. pap. 10.00 (0-933428-01-4) Chariton Review.

Barnes, Jim & Alexander, Keith. Russian Roulette: Nuclear Power Reactors in Eastern Europe & the Former Soviet Union. 76p. (Orig.). 1993. pap. 15.00 (0-913890-97-9) Friends of Earth.

Barnes, Jim, tr. see Nick, Dagmar.

Barnes, Jody, et al, eds. Moss Moon: New Work from the Institute of American Indian Arts. 192p. (C). 1998. pap. text 8.00 (1-881396-14-2) IOA Indian Arts.

Barnes, Joe. Man on a Mountain. LC 68-58686. 1969. 6.95 (0-87651-200-7); pap. 3.50 (0-87651-201-5) Southern U Pr.

— Super Procrastinators. (Illus.). 224p. 1988. 14.95 (0-917732-36-7); pap. text 10.95 (0-917732-37-5) Barnes-Bks.

Barnes, Joe, jt. auth. see Puckett, Christine S.

Barnes, John. Apostrophes & Apocalypses. LC 98-19142. 352p. 1998. text 24.95 (0-312-86147-8) St Martin.

***Barnes, John.** Apostrophes & Apocalypses. 352p. 1999. pap. 14.95 (0-312-85069-7, Pub. by Tor Bks) St Martin.

Barnes, John. Barnes Programming in ADA 95. 2nd ed. LC 98-25179. 720p. (C). 1998. pap. text 49.95 (0-201-34293-6) Addison-Wesley.

— Battlecry. (Time Raider Ser.: No. 605). 1992. per. 3.50 (0-373-63605-9) Harlequin Bks.

— The Beginnings of the Cinema in 1894-1896, Vol. 1. Maltby, Richard, ed. (Illus.). 240p. 1998. text 80.00 (0-85989-564-5, Pub. by Univ Exeter Pr) Northwestern U Pr.

— The Beginnings of the Cinema in England Vol. 2: 1897. 272p. 1997. 60.00 (0-85989-519-X) Univ Exeter Pr.

— The Beginnings of the Cinema in England Vol. 3: 1898. 256p. 1997. 60.00 (0-85989-520-3, Pub. by Univ Exeter Pr) Northwestern U Pr.

— The Beginnings of the Cinema in England Vol. 4: 1899. 340p. 1997. 60.00 (0-85989-521-1, Pub. by Univ Exeter Pr) Northwestern U Pr.

— The Beginnings of the Cinema in England Vol. 5: 1900. Maltby, Richard, ed. & intro. by. 432p. 1997. 70.00 (0-85989-522-X, Pub. by Univ Exeter Pr) Northwestern U Pr.

— Caesar's Bicycle. 304p. 1997. mass mkt. 5.99 (0-06-105661-8, HarperPrism) HarpC.

***Barnes, John.** Candle. LC 99-88631. 240p. 2000. 22.95 (0-312-89077-X, Pub. by Tor Bks) St Martin.

Barnes, John. Earth Made of Glass. LC 98-5246. 416p. 1998. text 25.95 (0-312-85851-5) St Martin.

— Earth Made of Glass. 1999. mass mkt. 5.99 (0-8125-5161-3, Pub. by Tor Bks) St Martin.

— Evita, First Lady: A Biography of Eva Peron. 224p. 1996. reprint ed. pap. 12.00 (0-8021-3479-3, Grove) Grove-Atltic.

— Finity. LC 98-45415. 304p. 1999. text 22.95 (0-312-86118-4) St Martin.

***Barnes, John.** Finity. 304p. 1999. mass mkt. 6.99 (0-8125-7145-2, Pub. by Tor Bks) St Martin.

— Goethe & the Power of Rhythm: A Biographical Essay. (Illus.). 96p. 1999. pap. 10.00 (0-932776-24-8) Adonis Pr.

Barnes, John. High Integrity ADA: The Spark Approach. 384p. 1997. pap. text 54.95 (0-201-17517-7) Addison-Wesley.

— Irish-American Landmarks: A Traveler's Guide. LC 95-17204. 590p. 1995. 39.95 (0-8103-9603-3) Gale.

— Kaleidoscope Century, Vol. 1. 1996. mass mkt. 5.99 (0-8125-3346-1, Pub. by Tor Bks) St Martin.

***Barnes, John.** The Merchants of Souls. 2000. text 25.95 (0-312-89076-1) St Martin.

Barnes, John. A Million Open Doors. 320p. 1993. mass mkt. 4.99 (0-8125-1633-8, Pub. by Tor Bks) St Martin.

— Mother of Storms. 576p. 1995. mass mkt. 5.99 (0-8125-3345-3, Pub. by Tor Bks); mass mkt. write for info. (0-8125-3343-7) Tor Bks.

— One for the Morning Glory. 320p. 1996. 22.95 (0-312-86106-0) Tor Bks.

— One for the Morning Glory. 1996. 22.95 (0-614-32238-3) Tor Bks.

— One for the Morning Glory. 1997. mass mkt. 5.99 (0-8125-5160-5, Pub. by Tor Bks) St Martin.

— One for the Morning Glory. 1997. 11.05 (0-606-11707-5, Pub. by Turtleback) Demco.

— Orbital Resonance. (Illus.). 256p. (YA). (gr. 7 up). pap. 3.99 (0-8125-1623-0, Pub. by Tor Bks) St Martin.

— Orbital Resonance. 256p. 1992. mass mkt. 4.99 (0-8125-3238-4, Pub. by Tor Bks) St Martin.

— The Order of Things: A Life of Joseph Furphy. (Illus.). 472p. 1991. 55.00 (0-19-553187-6) OUP.

— Pioneers of the British Film. (C). 1988. 90.00 (1-85219-012-4, Pub. by Bishopsgate Pr Ltd) St Mut.

— The Rise of the Cinema in Great Britain. 272p. 1987. 29.95 (0-900873-51-5, Pub. by Bishopsgte Pr) Intl Spec Bk.

— Union Fires. 1992. per. 3.50 (0-373-63606-7, 1-63606-7) Harlequin Bks.

— Wartide. (Time Raider Ser.: No. 604). 1992. per. 3.50 (0-373-63604-0, 1-63604-2) Harlequin Bks.

— What Investing Is All About. 4th ed. (C). 1989. mass mkt. 22.95 (0-538-70091-2, HM55DB) S-W Pub.

Barnes, John & O'Cuilleanain, Cormac, eds. Dante & the Middle Ages: Literary & Historical Essays. 1995. 39.50 (0-7165-2527-5, Pub. by Irish Acad Pr) Intl Spec Bk.

Barnes, John & Petrie, Jennifer, eds. Word & Drama in Dante: Essays on the Divina Commedia. (Foundation for Italian Studies at University College Dublin). 208p. (C). 1993. text 39.50 (0-7165-2488-0, Pub. by Irish Acad Pr) Intl Spec Bk.

Barnes, John, jt. auth. see Aldrin, Edwin Eugene, Jr.

Barnes, John, jt. auth. see Aldrin, Edwin Eugene (Buzz), Jr.

Barnes, John, ed. see Furphy, Joseph.

Barnes, John D., ed. see Reeve, Roger N.

Barnes, John E. Cana Revisited: A Personal Pilgrimage. 85p. 1995. pap. 9.95 (1-85311-107-4, 6312, Pub. by Canterbury Press Norwich) Morehouse Pub.

Barnes, John E. & Waring, Alan J. Pocket Programmable Calculators in Biochemistry. LC 79-2547. 385p. reprint ed. pap. 119.40 (0-608-16761-4, 202680900052) Bks Demand.

Barnes, John G. Programming Ada. 3rd ed. (Illus.). (C). 1989. pap. text 39.75 (0-201-17566-5) Addison-Wesley.

— Programming in Ada. 2nd ed. 300p. (Orig.). 1983. pap. 25.95 (0-201-13799-2) Addison-Wesley.

— Programming in Ada 95. LC 95-38017. (International Computer Science Ser.). 702p. (C). 1996. pap. text 44.95 (0-201-87700-7, QA76.73) Addison-Wesley.

— RTL-2 Design & Philosophy. LC 77-363518. (Heyden International Topics in Science Ser.). (Illus.). 176p. reprint ed. pap. 54.60 (0-608-17862-4, 203269200080) Bks Demand.

Barnes, John H. & Sevon, W. D. The Geological Story of Pennsylvania. 2nd ed. (Illus.). 44p. 1999. reprint ed. pap. text 10.00 (0-7881-7416-9) DIANE Pub.

Barnes, John Michael, jt. auth. see Steiner, Rudolf.

Barnes, John S., ed. see Fanning, Nathaniel.

Barnes, John W. Basic Geological Mapping. 3rd ed. LC 95-19760. 144p. 1995. pap. 44.95 (0-471-96031-4) Wiley.

Barnes, Johnny R., Jr., jt. auth. see Engle, Marty M.

Barnes, Jon, jt. auth. see Glover, David.

Barnes, Jon, jt. auth. see Parsons, Alexandra.

Barnes, Jon, jt. auth. see Wyse, Liz.

Barnes, Jon, tr. see Habel, Janette.

Barnes, Jonathan. Aristotle. (Past Masters Ser.). 112p. 1983. pap. text 9.95 (0-19-287581-7) OUP.

***Barnes, Jonathan.** Aristotle. (Very Short Introductions Ser.). (Illus.). 110p. 2000. pap. 8.95 (0-19-285408-9) OUP.

Barnes, Jonathan. Complete Works of Aristotle: The Revised Oxford Translation, Vol. 1. (Bollinger Ser.). 1256p. 1983. text 45.00 (0-691-01650-X, Pub. by Princeton U Pr) Cal Prin Full Svc.

— Greek Philosophers. LC 99-32377. (Past Masters Ser.). 304p. 1999. pap. text 15.95 (0-19-287696-1) OUP.

— Improve Your Eyesight: A Guide to the Bates Method for Better Eyesight Without Glasses. LC 90-6080. 1990. 19.95 (0-941533-93-X, NAB) I R Dee.

***Barnes, Jonathan.** Improve Your Eyesight: A Guide to the Bates Method for Better Eyesight Without Glasses. (Illus.). 120p. 2000. pap. 14.95 (0-285-63508-5, Pub. by Souvenir Pr Ltd) IPG Chicago.

Barnes, Jonathan. Logic & the Imperial Stoa. LC 97-10322. (Philosophia Antiqua Ser.: No. 75). 184p. 1997. 66.00 (90-04-10828-9) Brill Academic Pubs.

— The Presocratic Philosophers. (Arguments of the Philosophers Ser.). 358p. (C). 1983. pap. 32.99 (0-415-05079-0) Routledge.

— The Presocratic Philosophers. rev. ed. (Arguments of the Philosophers Ser.). 680p. 1982. pap. 27.50 (0-7100-9200-8, Routledge Thoemms) Routledge.

Barnes, Jonathan, ed. The Cambridge Companion to Aristotle. (Cambridge Companions to Philosophy Ser.). 432p. (C). 1995. text 64.95 (0-521-41133-5); pap. text 20.95 (0-521-42294-9) Cambridge U Pr.

— Complete Works of Aristotle: The Revised Oxford Translation, Vol. 2. (Bollingen Ser.: Vol. 2). 1256p. 1983. text 45.00 (0-691-01651-8, Pub. by Princeton U Pr) Cal Prin Full Svc.

Barnes, Jonathan, tr. Early Greek Philosophy. 320p. 1987. pap. 12.95 (0-14-044461-0, Penguin Classics) Viking Penguin.

Barnes, Jonathan & Griffin, Miriam D., eds. Philosophia Togata I Vol. 1: Essays on Philosophy & Roman Society, Vol. I. (Illus.). 316p. 1997. reprint ed. pap. text 35.00 (0-19-815085-7) OUP.

***Barnes, Jonathan & Griffin, Miriam D., eds.** Philosophia Togata 2: Plato & Aristotle At Rome. 310p. 1999. pap. text 29.95 (0-19-815222-1) OUP.

Barnes, Jonathan, jt. auth. see Annas, Julia.

Barnes, Jonathan, ed. see Aristotle.

Barnes, Jonathan, ed. see Empiricus, Sextus.

Barnes, Jonathan, jt. ed. see Griffin, Miriam D.

Barnes, Jonathan, ed. see Schofield, Malcolm, et al.

Barnes, Jonathan, ed. see Sextus Empiricus.

Barnes, Jonathan, tr. see Alexander of Aphrodisias.

Barnes, Jonathan, tr. see Patzig, G.

Barnes, Jonathan, tr. & comment see Aristotle.

Barnes, Joseph, ed. Empire in the East. LC 71-128203. (Essay Index Reprint Ser.). 1977. reprint ed. 23.95 (0-8369-1863-0) Ayer.

Barnes, Joseph, tr. see Platonov, Andrei, et al.

Barnes, Joseph E. SuperPro-crastinators. LC 84-71554. 200p. 1985. 14.95 (0-917732-34-0, 767); pap. 10.95 (0-917732-35-9) Barnes-Bks.

— Write for Fun & Money: How to Make Money Writing & Selling Simple Information. 192p. 1995. pap. 15.00 (0-915665-31-X) Premier Publishers.

Barnes, Joyce A. Amistad. LC 98-157772. (Illus.). 144p. (J). 1997. pap. 4.99 (0-14-039063-4, PuffinBks) Peng Put Young Read.

— The Baby Grand, the Moon in July, & Me. 1998. 10.09 (0-606-13157-4, Pub. by Turtleback) Demco.

— The Baby Grand, the Moon in July & Me. LC 93-17984. (J). (gr. 3-7). 1994. 15.99 (0-8037-1586-2, Dial Yng Read) Peng Put Young Read.

— Promise Me the Moon. LC 95-53085. 176p. (YA). 1997. 14.99 (0-8037-1798-9, Dial Yng Read) Peng Put Young Read.

— Promise Me the Moon. LC 95-53085. (YA). 1999. pap. 14.89 (0-8037-1799-7, Dial Yng Read) Peng Put Young Read.

— Promise Me the Moon. 144p. (gr. 3-7). 1999. pap. 4.99 (0-14-038040-X) Viking Penguin.

Barnes, Joyce B. Patches, the Blessed Beast of Burden. (Illus.). 36p. (J). 1990. 15.00 (0-9628493-0-8) J B Barnes.

Barnes, Judy, et al. Coasting: An Expanded Guide to the Northern Gulf Coast. 3rd ed. LC 98-11529. (Illus.). 368p. 1998. pap. text 15.95 (1-56554-343-2) Pelican.

— Coasting Through Mardi Gras: A Guide to Carnival along the Gulf Coast. (Illus.). 117p. 1995. pap. 9.95 (0-9641520-2-9) Coasting.

Barnes, Julia. George Curtis Training Greyhounds. (Illus.). 220p. 1993. 24.95 (0-948955-66-X, Pub. by Ringpr Bks) Seven Hills Bk.

— Why Racism Is Used Against Welfare Programs: Why Workers Should Join Welfare Recipients' Struggles. 1971. pap. 0.10 (0-87898-068-7) New Outlook.

Barnes, Julia, ed. The Complete Book of Greyhounds. (Illus.). 224p. 1994. 29.95 (0-87605-189-1) Howell Bks.

Barnes, Julian. Before She Met Me. LC 92-50091. 1996. pap. 12.00 (0-679-73609-3) Vin Bks.

— Cross Channel. 1997. pap. 12.00 (0-679-76755-X) Random.

— England, England. LC 98-46170. 288p. 1999. 23.00 (0-375-40582-8) Knopf.

— England, England. 1999. pap. 0.00 (0-375-70591-0) Knopf.

***Barnes, Julian.** England, England. 2000. pap. 13.00 (0-375-70550-3) Knopf.

Barnes, Julian. Flaubert's Parrot. LC 90-50162. (Vintage International Ser.). 192p. 1990. pap. 11.00 (0-679-73136-9) Random.

— A History of the World in 10 1/2 Chapters. LC 90-50161. (Vintage International Ser.). 320p. 1990. pap. 13.00 (0-679-73137-7) Random.

— A History of the World in 10 1/2 Chapters. large type ed. 310p. 1990. 22.95 (1-85089-348-9, Pub. by ISIS Lrg Prnt) Transaction Pubs.

— Letters from London. 352p. 1995. pap. 14.00 (0-679-76161-6) Random.

***Barnes, Julian.** Love, Etc. 2001. 24.00 (0-375-41161-5) Knopf.

Barnes, Julian. Metroland. LC 92-50092. 1992. pap. 11.00 (0-679-73608-5) Vin Bks.

— The Porcupine. LC 93-15506. 1993. pap. 10.00 (0-679-74482-7) Vin Bks.

— Staring at the Sun. LC 93-15509. 1993. pap. 12.00 (0-679-74820-2) Vin Bks.

— Talking It Over: A Novel. LC 91-51197. 1992. pap. 13.00 (0-679-73687-5) Vin Bks.

Barnes, Junor A., et al, eds. Signal Transduction Mechanisms, Vol. 15. LC 95-35226. (Developments in Molecular & Cellular Biochemistry Ser.). 928p. (C). 1997. text 302.50 (0-7923-3663-1) Kluwer Academic.

***Barnes, Karen.** Naturopathic First Aid. (Illus.). 96p. 1999. pap. 9.95 (1-55082-248-9) LPC InBook.

Barnes, Kate. Crossing the Field. (Illus.). 48p. 1992. pap. 7.95 (0-942396-67-7) Blackberry ME.

***Barnes, Kate.** Where the Deer Were. (Illus.). 96p. 2000. pap. 15.95 (1-56792-117-5) Godine.

Barnes, Kenneth. From Chaos to Creation. 1999. pap. 21.00 (1-85072-130-0, Pub. by W Sessions) St Mut.

— Nazism, Liberalism, & Christianity: Protestant Social Conscience in Germany & Great Britain, 1925-1937. 216p. 1991. text 28.00 (0-8131-1729-1) U Pr of Ky.

Barnes, Kenneth C. The History of Wennington School Energy Unbound. (C). 1988. 36.00 (0-900657-51-0, Pub. by W Sessions) St Mut.

— Who Killed John Clayton? Political Violence & the Emergence of the New South, 1861-1893. LC 97-37573. 1998. write for info. (0-8223-2058-4); pap. 16.95 (0-8223-2072-X) Duke.

Barnes, Kenneth C., ed. see Strub, Joseph.

Barnes, Kim. Hungry for the World: A Memoir. LC 99-34851. 256p. 2000. 23.00 (0-375-50228-9) Villard Books.

— In the Wilderness: Coming of Age in Unknown Country. 258p. 1997. pap. 12.95 (0-385-47821-6, Anchor NY) Doubleday.

Barnes, Kiser, et al. Law & International Order. LC 96-227044. 212p. 1996. pap. 17.95 (1-870989-73-2) Bahai.

Barnes, Kiser D. Naming of Femi's Brother. (Illus.). 32p. 1987. pap. 4.95 (0-85398-232-5) G Ronald Pub.

Barnes, L. H., jt. auth. see Chalmers, Dalzell.

Barnes, Laura L., et al. Great Lakes Pollution Prevention: Information Resources Catalog. 61p. (Orig.). (C). 1995. pap. text 20.00 (0-7881-2450-1) DIANE Pub.

***Barnes, Laura T.** Twist & Ernest. (Ernest Ser.: Vol. 1). (Illus.). 36p. (J). (ps-4). 1999. 15.95 (0-9674681-0-8) Barnesyard.

Barnes, Lee. Smoky Mountain Hiking & Camping: A Guide to the Great Smoky Mountains National Park. (Illus.). 160p. 1994. pap. 12.95 (0-89732-126-X) Menasha Ridge.

Barnes, Leon. Surgical Pathology of the Head & Neck, Set, Pt. A. (Illus.). 896p. 1985. text 510.00 (0-8247-7216-4) Dekker.

Barnes, Leon, ed. Surgical Pathology of the Head & Neck, Vol. 1. 2nd expanded rev. ed. (Illus.). 1221p. Date not set. write for info. (0-8247-0109-7, 0109-7) Dekker.

— Surgical Pathology of the Head & Neck, Vol. 2. 2nd expanded rev. ed. (Illus.). 1196p. Date not set. write for info. (0-8247-0110-0, 0110-0) Dekker.

Barnes, Lilian. Sweet Bondage. (Rainbow Romances Ser.). 160p. 1993. 14.95 (0-7090-4911-0) Parkwest Pubns.

— Sweet Bondage. large type ed. (Linford Romance Library). 272p. 1998. pap. 17.99 (0-7089-5232-1) Ulverscroft.

***Barnes, Lilly.** Lace Them Up. (Illus.). 64p. (J). (gr. k-3). 1998. pap. 8.95 (0-921051-64-6) Somerville Hse.

— Make It Better. (Life Skills for Little Ones Ser.). (Illus.). 24p. (J). (ps-k). 1998. pap. 12.95 (1-895897-29-7) Somerville Hse.

— Toe Tapper. (Illus.). 32p. (J). 1999. pap. 9.99 (1-58184-027-6) Somerville Hse.

Barnes, Lilly & Quinlan, Patricia. Lace Them Up. (Step by Step Ser.). (Illus.). 32p. (J). (ps-2). 1992. 8.95 (1-56282-282-9, Pub. by Hyprn Child) Little.

Barnes, Linda. The Big Dig, No. 2 352p. 2001. 22.95 (0-7868-6318-8, Pub. by Hyperion) Time Warner.

***Barnes, Linda.** Bitter Finish. large type ed. 275p. 2000. lib. bdg. 28.95 (1-58547-031-7) Ctr Point Pubg.

Barnes, Linda. Cities of the Dead. 272p. 1996. mass mkt. 5.99 (0-440-22095-5) Dell.

— Cold Case. large type ed. LC 97-2926. (Large Print Book Ser.). 1997. 26.56 (1-56895-427-1) Wheeler Pub.

— Coyote. large type ed. (General Ser.). 332p. 1991. lib. bdg. 20.95 (0-8161-5197-0, G K Hall Lrg Type) Mac Lib Ref.

— The Dialectics of Black Humor: Process & Product. (European University Studies: Comparative LIterature: Ser. 18, Vol. 15). 135p. 1978. pap. 26.00 (*3-261-03014-3*) P Lang Pubng.

— Flashpoint. LC 98-56063. 288p. 1999. 22.95 (*0-7868-6317-X*, Pub. by Hyperion) Time Warner.

***Barnes, Linda.** Flashpoint. large type ed. LC 00-22863. 2000. 25.95 (*1-56895-856-0*) Wheeler Pub.

Barnes, Linda. Hardware. large type ed. LC 94-42107. 435p. 1995. lib. bdg. 22.95 (*0-7862-0387-0*) Thorndike Pr.

— Passing the GED. LC 97-19485. 1997. 17.28 (*0-02-803076-1*) Macmillan.

— The Snake Tattoo. 208p. 1990. mass mkt. 5.99 (*0-449-21759-0*, Crest) Fawcett.

— The Snake Tattoo. large type ed. LC 90-32775. (General Ser.). 350p. 1990. lib. bdg. 19.95 (*0-8161-4866-X*, G K Hall Lrg Type) Mac Lib Ref.

— Snapshot. large type ed. LC 93-11280. 543p. 1993. lib. bdg. 21.95 (*1-56054-761-8*) Thorndike Pr.

— Snapshot. large type ed. LC 93-11280. 543p. 1994. lib. bdg. 14.95 (*1-56054-878-9*) Thorndike Pr.

— Snapshot: A Carlotta Carlyle Mystery. 400p. 1994. mass mkt. 5.99 (*0-440-21220-0*) Dell.

— Steel Guitar: A Carlotta Carlyle Mystery. 272p. 1992. mass mkt. 5.99 (*0-440-21268-5*) Dell.

— A Trouble of Fools. LC 98-35286. 224p. 1999. mass mkt. 6.99 (*0-7868-8953-5*, Pub. by Hyperion) Time Warner.

— A Trouble of Fools. large type ed. (General Ser.). 370p. 1989. lib. bdg. 19.95 (*0-8161-4714-0*, G K Hall Lrg Type) Mac Lib Ref.

Barnes, Linda, ed. see Swami Chetanananda.

Barnes, Linda L. Variations on a Teaching/Learning Workshop: Pedagogy & Faculty Development in Religious Studies. LC 99-19774. (Scholars Press Studies in the Humanities). 1p. 1999. pap. 29.95 (*0-7885-0530-0*, 000123) Duke.

Barnes, Linda L., ed. see Chetanananda, Swami.

Barnes, Lisa T. A Passion for Art: Selections from the Berman Collection, the Inaugural Exhibition. LC 89-24821. (Illus.). 72p. 1989. pap. text 12.95 (*0-9624021-0-9*) Ursinus College.

Barnes, Lisa T., et al. James Fuhrman: Marks & Messages. (Illus.). 1992. 10.00 (*0-9624021-5-X*) Ursinus College.

Barnes, Lisa T., jt. auth. see Cobbs, John L.

Barnes, Lisa T., jt. auth. see Lodge, Karen.

Barnes, Lisa T., jt. auth. see Yoakum, Mel.

Barnes, Louis B. Organizational Systems & Engineering Groups: A Comparative Study of Two Technical Groups in Industry. LC 60-13102. 210p. reprint ed. pap. 65.10 (*0-608-11548-7*, 200220800019) Bks Demand.

Barnes, Louis B., et al. Teaching & the Case Method: Text, Cases, & Readings. 3rd ed. LC 94-766. 352p. 1994. 35.00 (*0-87584-403-0*) Harvard Busn.

Barnes, Lucinda & Cooper, Dennis. Charles Ray. LC 90-6359. (Illus.). 44p. (Orig.). 1990. pap. 22.50 (*0-917493-16-8*) Orange Cnty Mus.

Barnes, Lucinda, et al. Tony Cragg: Sculpture, 1975-1990. Schimmel, Paul, ed. & intro. by. LC 90-6394. (Illus.). 178p. (Orig.). 1990. pap. 29.95 (*0-917493-17-6*) Orange Cnty Mus.

— Tony Cragg: Sculpture, 1975-1990. Schimmel, Paul, ed. (Illus.). 178p. (Orig.). 1991. 45.00 (*0-500-09218-4*, Pub. by Thames Hudson) Norton.

Barnes, Lucinda, jt. ed. see Bartman, William S.

Barnes, Lynard. Phobos Lock. 1997. pap. text 9.95 (*0-9668484-0-3*) Trices Co.

Barnes, Lynne, et al. Georgian Baytripper. (Illus.). 1999. pap. 13.95 (*1-55046-296-2*, Pub. by Boston Mills) Genl Dist Srvs.

Barnes, M. C. I. I. Use of Business English, No. 810. (C). 1981. 230.00 (*0-7855-4260-4*, Pub. by Witherby & Co) St Mut.

***Barnes, M. & Ward, A.** Textbook of Rehabilitation Medicine. LC 99-46510. (Illus.). 416p. 2000. pap. text 49.95 (*0-19-262805-4*) OUP.

Barnes, M., jt. auth. see Barnes, Margaret.

Barnes, M. Anderson, jt. auth. see Saith, Ebbie.

Barnes, M. Craig. Thirst For God. 16.99 (*0-310-21955-8*) HarpC.

— When God Interrupts: Finding New Life Through Unwanted Change. LC 95-50979. 160p. (Orig.). 1996. pap. 10.99 (*0-8308-1979-7*, 1979) InterVarsity.

— Yearning: Living Between How It Is & How It Ought to Be. LC 91-30416. 190p. (Orig.). 1992. pap. 10.99 (*0-8308-1378-0*, 1378) InterVarsity.

Barnes, M. J. Politics & Personality. (History Today Ser.). 1967. 14.95 (*0-8023-9074-9*) Dufour.

Barnes, M. M., jt. auth. see Barnes, F. A.

Barnes, Malcolm, tr. see Descola, Jean.

Barnes, Malcolm, tr. see Levaillant, Maurice.

Barnes, Malcolm, tr. see Troyat, Henri.

Barnes, Margaret. Oceanography & Marine Biology: An Annual Review. (Oceanography & Marine Biology Ser.: No. 25). 664p. 1987. 135.00 (*0-08-035065-8*, Pub. by Aberdeen U Pr) Macmillan.

— Oceanography & Marine Biology: An Annual Review, Vol. 20. (Illus.). 778p. 1982. 135.00 (*0-08-028460-4*, Pergamon Pr) Elsevier.

— Oceanography & Marine Biology: An Annual Review, Vol. 26. (Oceanography & Marine Biology Ser.). (Illus.). 650p. 1988. 135.00 (*0-08-036397-0*, Pub. by Aberdeen U Pr) Macmillan.

— Oceanography & Marine Biology: An Annual Review, Vol. 27. (Illus.). 550p. 1989. 135.00 (*0-08-037718-1*, Pub. by Aberdeen U Pr) Macmillan.

Barnes, Margaret, ed. Oceanography & Marine Biology: An Annual Review. LC 64-1930. (Oceanography & Marine Biology Ser.: Vol. 22). (Illus.). 590p. 1984. 135.00 (*0-08-030392-7*, Pergamon Pr) Elsevier.

— Oceanography & Marine Biology: An Annual Review, Vol. 21. (Oceanography & Marine Biology Ser.). (Illus.). 590p. 1983. 135.00 (*0-08-030360-9*, Pergamon Pr) Elsevier.

— Oceanography & Marine Biology: An Annual Review, Vol. 23. (Oceanography & Marine Biology Ser.). (Illus.). 656p. 1985. 135.00 (*0-08-030397-8*, Pub. by Aberdeen U Pr) Macmillan.

— Oceanography & Marine Biology: An Annual Review, Vol. 24. (Oceanography & Marine Biology Ser.). 650p. 1986. 135.00 (*0-08-032458-4*, Pub. by Aberdeen U Pr) Macmillan.

— Oceanography & Marine Biology: An Annual Review, Vol. 28. (Oceanography & Marine Biology Ser.). (Illus.). 1990. 135.00 (*0-08-037981-8*, Pub. by Aberdeen U Pr) Macmillan.

— Oceanography & Marine Biology: An Annual Review, Vol. 29. (Illus.). 560p. 1992. text 135.00 (*0-08-040934-2*, Pub. by Aberdeen U Pr) Macmillan.

Barnes, Margaret, et al, eds. Oceanography & Marine Biology: An Annual Review, Vol. 30. 635p. 1992. 150.00 (*1-85728-071-7*, Pub. by UCL Pr Ltd) Taylor & Francis.

Barnes, Margaret & Barnes, Harold, eds. Oceanography & Marine Biology: An Annual Review, Vol. 18. (Illus.). 528p. 1980. 135.00 (*0-08-025732-1*, Pergamon Pr) Elsevier.

Barnes, Margaret & Barnes, M. Oceanography & Marine Biology, 14 vols., Vol. 3. 1978. 84.00 (*0-08-023643-X*, Pergamon Pr); 84.00 (*0-08-023650-2*, Pergamon Pr) Elsevier.

Barnes, Margaret & Gibson, R. N. Trophic Relationships in the Marine Environment: Proceedings of the 24th European Marine Biology Symposium. (Illus.). 700p. 1990. 130.00 (*0-08-037982-6*, Pub. by Aberdeen U Pr) Macmillan.

Barnes, Margaret A. Biblical Essays: Writings to Touch the Heart String. 100p. Date not set. pap. write for info. (*1-891597-63-9*, SDC Pr) Mleecole.

***Barnes, Margaret A.** A Buzzard in My Best Friend. 2000. 23.95 (*0-86554-713-0*, H532) Mercer Univ Pr.

Barnes, Margaret A. Growing a Spiritual Community. 205p. Date not set. pap. write for info. (*1-891597-53-1*, SDC Pr) Mleecole.

— Keeping Track of the Real You or Checking up on Self: How to Assess Your Spiritual Self. 100p. Date not set. pap. 10.95 (*1-891597-55-8*, SDC Pr) Mleecole.

— Lyrics of Blessings: Love Praises, Vol. I. 50p. Date not set. pap. write for info. (*1-891597-57-4*, SDC Pr) Mleecole.

— Lyrics of Blessings: Love Praises, Vol. II. 50p. Date not set. pap. write for info. (*1-891597-58-2*, SDC Pr) Mleecole.

— Sin & Its Affect. 4p. Date not set. 2.00 (*1-891597-60-4*, SDC Pr) Mleecole.

— The Tragedy & the Triumph of Phenix City, Alabama, 1916-1955. LC 98-27470. (Illus.). 336p. 1998. 24.95 (*0-86554-613-4*, H462) Mercer Univ Pr.

— Years of Grace. 1991. lib. bdg. 21.95 (*1-56849-055-0*) Buccaneer Bks.

Barnes, Margaret C. Brief Gaudy Hour: A Novel of Anne Boleyn. 25.95 (*0-8488-0423-6*) Amereon Ltd.

— The King's Fool. 23.95 (*0-8488-0781-2*) Amereon Ltd.

— The Passionate Brood. 24.95 (*0-8488-0782-0*) Amereon Ltd.

— With All My Heart. 23.95 (*0-8488-0783-9*) Amereon Ltd.

— Years of Grace. 34.95 (*0-89190-658-4*) Amereon Ltd.

Barnes, Margaret G. Twentieth Century Wordsworth. 60p. 1996. pap. 12.95 (*1-85756-236-4*, Pub. by Janus Pubng) Paul & Co Pubs.

Barnes, Marian. Care, Communities & Citizens. LC 96-30249. 1997. write for info. (*0-582-25129-X*) Longman.

Barnes, Marian E. Black Texans: They Overcame. LC 95-30229. 144p. (J). (gr. 6-7). 1996. 15.95 (*1-57168-055-1*, Eakin Pr) Sunbelt Media.

Barnes, Marian E., compiled by. Talk That Talk Some More! On the Cutting Room Floor. LC 92-42419. 320p. 1993. 18.95 (*0-89015-895-9*) Sunbelt Media.

Barnes, Marian E., jt. auth. see Goss, Linda.

Barnes, Marilyn G. Love (And Baby Powder) Covers All. 148p. (Orig.). 1992. pap. 7.95 (*0-939513-88-9*) Joy Pub SJC.

Barnes, Mark & May, Ronald V. Mexican Majolica in Northern New Spain. 1980. reprint ed. pap. 4.95 (*0-686-62076-3*) Acoma Bks.

Barnes, Mark F. Equine Myofascial Release Manual. (Illus.). 48p. 1998. pap. 59.95 (*0-9668183-0-X*) Barky Pubg Inc.

Barnes, Marni, jt. auth. see Marcus, Clare C.

Barnes, Marni, jt. ed. see Marcus, Clare C.

Barnes, Martha J., ed. Reading & Critical Thinking in the Content Areas. 120p. 1988. pap. 10.26 (*0-8092-4478-0*) NTC Contemp Pub Co.

Barnes, Martin. Measurement in Contract Control. 304p. 1977. 23.75 (*0-7277-0040-5*, Pub. by T Telford) RCH.

Barnes, Martin, ed. Financial Control. 117p. 1990. pap. text 28.00 (*0-7277-1522-4*, Pub. by T Telford) RCH.

Barnes, Marvin P. Computer-Assisted Mineral Appraisal & Feasibility. fac. ed. LC 79-52270. (Illus.). 173p. 1980. reprint ed. pap. 53.70 (*0-7837-7846-5*, 204760500007) Bks Demand.

Barnes, Marvin W. Computer Algorithms in Mining Mineral Reserve Estimation. (Illus.). 200p. (C). 1989. write for info. (*0-318-65492-X*) M Barnes & Assocs.

— The Limitations of Popular Techniques for Preproduction Reserve Estimation in Mining. LC 89-92063. (Illus.). 88p. (C). 1989. 15.00 (*0-685-27212-5*); pap. 10.00 (*0-685-27213-3*) M Barnes & Assocs.

Barnes, Mary. The Native Is Restless. unabridged ed. (Illus.). 20p. 1996. spiral bd. 6.00 (*1-92932б-35-1*) Hal Bar Pubg.

Barnes, Mary. The Ultimate Asteroid Book: The Inside Story on the Threat from the Skies. LC 98-28425. (J). 1998. pap. 3.99 (*0-689-82463-7*) Aladdin.

***Barnes, Mary & Duey, Kathleen.** Freaky Facts about Natural Diasters. (J). (gr. 4-6). 2000. per. 3.99 (*0-689-82818-7*) Aladdin.

Barnes, Mary, jt. auth. see Halbert, Bill.

Barnes, Mary, ed. see Clarke, Mickey.

Barnes, Maryke. Setting Wonder Free. (Illus.). 24p. (J). (ps-2). 1993. pap. 4.95 (*1-55037-238-6*, Pub. by Annick); lib. bdg. 14.95 (*1-55037-241-6*, Pub. by Annick) Firefly Bks Ltd.

Barnes, Marylou R., et al. The Neurophysiological Basis of Patient Treatment: Reflexes in Motor Development, Vol. II. LC 72-87895. (Illus.). 1978. pap. 35.00 (*0-936030-01-1*) Stokesville Pub.

Barnes, Marylou R., jt. auth. see Crutchfield, Carolyn.

Barnes, Marylou R., jt. auth. see Crutchfield, Carolyn A.

Barnes, Marylou R., jt. auth. see Scully, Crispian.

Barnes, Maude. Renaissance Vistas. LC 68-55838. (Essay Index Reprint Ser.). 1977. 17.95 (*0-8369-0178-9*) Ayer.

Barnes, Maureen, ed. The Best of Lawrence Green. 400p. (C). 1986. 60.00 (*0-7855-2149-6*) St Mut.

Barnes, Michael. Fortunes in the Ground: Cobalt, Porcupine & Kirkland Lake. (Illus.). 264p. 1995. reprint ed. 28.00 (*0-919783-52-X*) Boston Mills.

— Gold in Ontario. LC 97-135999. (Illus.). 144p. 1995. pap. 28.00 (*1-55046-146-X*) Boston Mills.

***Barnes, Michael.** Ontario. (Hello Canada Ser.). 1999. pap. 7.95 (*1-55041-270-1*) Fitzhenry & W Ltd.

Barnes, Michael. Ontario. LC 94-20253. (Hello Canada Ser.). (Illus.). 76p. (J). (gr. 4-7). 1995. lib. bdg. 19.95 (*0-8225-2754-5*, Lerner Publctns) Lerner Pub.

— Ontario. (Hello Canada Ser.). (Illus.). (J). (gr. 3-6). 1997. pap. 6.95 (*0-8225-9801-9*) Lerner Pub.

— Policing Ontario: The OPP Today. (Illus.). 208p. 29.95 (*1-55046-015-3*, Pub. by Boston Mills) Genl Dist Srvs.

— Temagami. (Illus.). 88p. 1995. pap. 15.95 (*1-55046-031-5*, Pub. by Boston Mills) Genl Dist Srvs.

— Timmins: The Porcupine Country. LC 97-137990. (Illus.). 144p. 1995. 28.00 (*1-55046-050-1*, Pub. by Boston Mills) Genl Dist Srvs.

Barnes, Michael, ed. An Ecology of the Spirit: Religious Reflection & Environmental Consciousness. 248p. (Orig.). (C). 1994. text 5.00 (*0-8191-8959-6*); pap. text 23.50 (*0-8191-8960-X*) U Pr of Amer.

Barnes, Michael, narrated by. Secrets of the Lost Empires: Reconstructing the Glories of Ages Past. 1997. 24.95 (*0-614-27833-3*) Sterling.

Barnes, Michael, et al. Medical Aspects of Personal Injury Litigation. LC 97-23811. 1997. 125.00 (*0-632-04176-5*) Blackwell Sci.

Barnes, Michael, jt. auth. see Ely, Vivian K.

Barnes, Michael, tr. see Vesaas, Tarjei.

Barnes, Michael D. & Fahrenkopf, Frank J., Jr., eds. The Political Truth: A Voter's Guide to the 1996 Presidential Candidates & Elections. (Orig.). Date not set. 14.95 (*0-614-10307-X*) Apolitical Pr.

Barnes, Michael H. In the Presence of Mystery: An Introduction to the Study of Human Religiousness. rev. ed. LC 89-52153. 344p. 1990. pap. 19.95 (*0-89622-425-2*) Twenty-Third.

***Barnes, Michael Horace.** Stages of Thought: The Co-Evolution of Religious Thought & Science. LC 99-23759. 368p. 2000. text 45.00 (*0-19-513389-7*) OUP.

Barnes, Michael J., ed. Politics & Personality, 1760-1827. LC 68-97214. (Selections from History Today Ser.: No. 6). (Illus.). 1967. 10.95 (*0-686-85915-4*) Dufour.

— Politics & Personality, 1760-1827. LC 68-97214. (Selections from History Today Ser.: No. 6). (Illus.). 1967. pap. 9.95 (*0-05-001535-4*) Dufour.

Barnes, Michael L., jt. auth. see Sternberg, Robert J.

Barnes, Michel R. The Power of God: Dunamis in Gregory of Nyssa's Trinitarian Theology. LC 98-20197. 1999. 64.95 (*0-8132-0929-3*) Cath U Pr.

Barnes, Michel R. & Williams, Daniel H., eds. Arianism after Arius: Essays on the Development of the 4th Century Trinitarian Conflicts. 268p. 2000. text 49.95 (*0-567-09641-6*, Pub. by T & T Clark) Bks Intl VA.

Barnes, Michelle. Off to Grandma's House. 2nd ed. (Let Me Read Ser.). 16p. (J). (ps-1). 1995. bds. 2.95 (*0-673-36269-8*, GoodYrBooks) Addson-Wesley Educ.

Barnes, Mike. Calm Jazz Sea. LC 97-104891. 80p. 1996. pap. 12.95 (*0-919626-85-8*, Pub. by Brick Bks) Genl Dist Srvs.

Barnes, Molly. How to Get Hung. LC 94-29432. 224p. 1994. pap. 16.95 (*1-885203-08-X*) Jrny Editions.

Barnes, Molly, et al. Tango Nuevo: Paintings & Sculpture of Herb Alpert. LC 98-61250. (Illus.). 74p. 1999. pap. 40.00 (*0-9666344-0-3*) M Barnes Galleries.

Barnes-Murphy, Rowan. Opposites. (Blackboard Bks.). (Illus.). 16p. (J). (ps). 1993. bds. 3.95 (*0-8249-8611-3*, Ideals Child) Hambleton-Hill.

— Shapes. (Blackboard Bks.). (Illus.). 16p. (J). (ps) 1993. bds. 3.95 (*0-8249-8606-7*, Ideals Child) Hambleton-Hill.

Barnes, Myers. Closing Strong: The Super Sales Handbook. LC 96-95311. (Illus.). 178p. 1997. pap. 14.95 (*0-9654858-1-1*, Pub. by M B A Pubns) Dartnell Corp.

***Barnes, Myers.** Reach the Top: In New Home & Neighborhood Sales. (Illus.). 262p. 2000. pap. 24.95 (*0-9654858-3-8*) M B A Pubns.

Barnes, Myra J. Linguistics & Languages in Science Fiction-Fantasy. LC 74-17864. (Science Fiction Ser.). 208p. 1975. reprint ed. 16.95 (*0-405-06319-9*) Ayer.

***Barnes, N. & Gamble, L.** An Atlas of Chronic Obstructive Pulmonary Disease. (Illus.). 140p. 2001. 85.00 (*1-84214-004-3*) Prthnon Pub.

Barnes, N. Sue, jt. auth. see Curtis, Helena.

Barnes, Nan, et al. A Legal Guide for Connecticut Entrepreneurs. 104p. 1994. pap. text 9.95 (*1-886277-00-1*) CT Small Busn.

Barnes, Nigel. The Beginning of the Never Ending. Barnes, Shakara & Carrington, William C., eds. 96p. (Orig.). 1997. pap. 9.95 (*1-888701-03-X*) Jarrett Pr.

Barnes, Noreen C. & Deutsch, Nicholas, eds. Tough Acts to Follow: One-Act Plays on the Gay-Lesbian Experience. 160p. (Orig.). 1992. pap. 9.95 (*0-9624751-6-5*) Alamo Sq Pr.

Barnes, P. The Gospel: Did Paul & Jesus Agree? 1994. pap. 7.99 (*0-85234-325-6*, Pub. by Evangelical Pr) P & R Pubng.

— Open Your Mouth for the Dumb. 1984. pap. 1.45 (*0-85151-390-5*) Banner of Truth.

Barnes, P., et al, eds. Platelet Activating Factor & Human Disease. (Frontiers in Pharmacology & Therapeutics Ser.). (Illus.). 350p. 1989. 125.00 (*0-632-02684-7*) Blackwell Sci.

Barnes, P., et al. Financial Accounting. 563p. pap. 45.00 (*0-908237-60-X*, Pub. by NSW U Pr) Intl Spec Bk.

Barnes, P. D., et al, eds. Meson-Nuclear Physics, 1976: Carnegie-Mellon Conference. LC 76-26811. (AIP Conference Proceedings Ser.: No. 33). 1976. 24.75 (*0-88318-132-0*) Am Inst Physics.

Barnes, P. D. & Gibson, B. F., eds. Properties & Interactions of Hyperons: Proceedings of the U. S.-Japan Seminar. 328p. 1994. text 99.00 (*981-02-1764-1*) World Scientific Pub.

Barnes, P. T., ed. see Cotter, Kelly & Cotter, Maury.

***Barnes, P. Yvonne.** Spectral Reflectance. 261p. 1998. per. 14.00 (*0-16-060873-2*) USGPO.

Barnes, Pamela, jt. auth. see Barnes, Ian.

***Barnes, Pamela M. & Barnes, Ian G.** Environmental Policy in the European Union. LC 99-15403. 352p. 2000. 95.00 (*1-85898-339-8*) E Elgar.

Barnes, Patience P., jt. auth. see Barnes, James J.

Barnes, Patricia. Spinning Wheels, Spinners & Spinning. 1987. reprint ed. pap. 12.95 (*1-56659-019-1*) Robin & Russ.

Barnes, Patricia G., ed. Domestic Violence: From a Private Matter to a Federal Offense, 3 vols. (Controversies in Constitutional Law Ser.: Vol. 1). 1208p. 1998. reprint ed. 240.00 (*0-8153-3063-4*) Garland.

***Barnes, Patricia G. & Congressional Quarterly Inc. Staff.** Congressional Quarterly's Desk Reference on American Courts: Over 500 Answers to Frequently Asked Questions about Our State & Federal Courts. LC 99-28730. 301p. 1999. 49.95 (*1-56802-435-5*) CQ Pr.

Barnes, Patrick. I Hate Excel. 2nd ed. (Illus.). 368p. 1993. 16.95 (*1-56529-532-3*) Que.

— The Non Orthodox: The Orthodox Teaching on Christians Outside of the Church. 151p. 1999. pap. 19.95 (*0-9649141-6-6*) Regina Orthodox.

Barnes, Patti, jt. auth. see Barnes, Allen.

Barnes, Patty D. The Woman Inside: From Incest Victim to Survivor. LC 88-63769. 152p. (Orig.). 1989. pap. 12.95 (*0-941300-13-7*) Mother Courage.

Barnes, Paul S. How to Win at Fantasy Football: 1991 Fantasy Football Guide. 200p. 1991. pap. 11.50 (*0-9629884-0-5*) BTwo Sports.

Barnes, Paul S., ed. How to Win at Fantasy Football: Fantasy Football Guide, 1992. 200p. 1992. pap. 11.50 (*0-9629884-1-3*) BTwo Sports.

***Barnes, Paula.** Tradition & Innovation: Toni Morrison & the Flight Motif in Fro-American Literature. (Studies in African American History & Culture). 250p. 1999. 45.00 (*0-8153-3539-3*) Garland.

Barnes, Peggy. The Chefs' Healthy Collection. LC 92-30692. (Illus.). 208p. 1993. 17.95 (*0-88289-929-5*) Pelican.

Barnes, Peter. Barnes: Plays One. 2nd ed. (Methuen World Dramatists Ser.). 479p. (C). 1990. pap. 14.95 (*0-413-62180-4*, A0406, Methuen Drama) Methn.

— Barnes: Plays Two, No. Two. 256p. (Orig.). (C). 1993. pap. 15.95 (*0-413-68030-4*, A0682, Methuen Drama) Methn.

— Barnes' People II: Seven Duologues. LC 83-12718. 58p. (Orig.). (C). 1984. pap. 6.50 (*0-435-23065-4*, 23065) Heinemann.

Barnes, Peter. Collected Plays of Peter Barnes. 468p. (Orig.). (C). 1981. pap. 10.00 (*0-435-18281-1*, 18281) Heinemann.

— Dreaming. 2000. pap. 10.95 (*0-413-73560-5*, Methuen Drama) Methn.

Barnes, Peter. Lulu: A Sex Tragedy. Beck, Charlotte, tr. from GER. 82p. (Orig.). (C). 1989. pap. write for info. (*0-413-61390-9*, A0366, Methuen Drama) Methn.

— Milk of the Word. 80p. (Orig.). 1985. pap. 5.99 (*0-85151-434-0*) Banner of Truth.

— Peter Barnes Plays, Vol. 3. (Methuen Contemporary Dramatists). 1996. pap. 17.95 (*0-413-69980-3*, Methuen Drama) Heinemann.

— Revolutionary Witness & Nobody Here but Us Chickens. (Methuen Modern Plays Ser.). 85p. (Orig.). (C). 1989. pap. write for info. (*0-413-62170-7*, A0415, Methuen Drama) Methn.

— The Spirit of Man & More Barnes' People: Seven Monologues. (Methuen Modern Plays Ser.). 104p. (Orig.). (C). 1990. pap. write for info. (*0-413-63130-3*, A0466, Methuen Drama) Methn.

— Sunsets & Glories. LC 91-184655. (Methuen Modern Plays Ser.). 86p. (C). 1990. pap. 10.95 (*0-413-64020-5*, A0491, Methuen Drama) Methn.

***Barnes, Peter.** Woodrow, the White House Mouse. 32p. (J). (gr. k-3). 2000. pap. 5.99 (*0-439-12952-4*) Scholastic Inc.

Barnes, Peter, ed. Lipids in Cereal Technology. (Food Science & Technology Ser.). 1984. text 142.00 (*0-12-079020-3*) Acad Pr.

Barnes, Peter, jt. auth. see Stevens, David.

Barnes, Peter J. Asthma, 2 vols. LC 96-28935. 2100p. 1997. text 260.00 (*0-397-51682-7*, Lippnctt) Lppncott W & W.
— Autonomic Control of the Respiratory System. (Autonomic Nervous System Ser). 352p. 1997. text 63.00 (*3-7186-5140-8*, Harwood Acad Pubs) Gordon & Breach.

Barnes, Peter J., ed. Asthma. 48th ed. (British Medical Bulletin Ser.: Vol. 48, 1). (Illus.). 320p. 1993. text 99.00 (*0-443-04718-9*) Church.

Barnes, Peter J., et al, eds. Asthma: Basic Mechanisms & Clinical Management. 3rd ed. (Illus.). 864p. 1998. boxed set 150.00 (*0-12-079027-0*) Acad Pr.

Barnes, Peter J. & Stockley, Robert A., eds. Molecular Biology of Lung Disease. LC 93-28488. (Illus.). 384p. 1994. 100.00 (*0-632-03344-4*) Blackwell Sci.

Barnes, Peter J., et al. Asthma. 2,368p. 370.00 (*0-7817-1992-5*) Lppncott W & W.
— Asthma: Its Pathogenesis & Treatment. (Lung Biology in Health & Disease Ser.: Vol. 49). (Illus.). 808p. 1990. text 255.00 (*0-8247-8217-8*) Dekker.

Barnes, Peter J., et al. Therapeutics in Respiratory Diseases. 1994. 59.95 (*0-443-04234-9*); text 73.00 (*0-443-04134-2*) Church.

Barnes, Peter J., jt. auth. see Kaliner, Michael A.

Barnes, Peter J., jt. auth. see Newhouse, Michael T.

Barnes, Peter J., jt. ed. see Chung, K. Fan.

Barnes, Peter W. House Mouse, Senate Mouse. LC 96-60354. (Illus.). 32p. (J). (gr. k-3). 1996. 15.95 (*0-9637688-4-0*) Vacation Spot.

***Barnes, Peter W.** Woodrow for President: A Tail of Voting, Campaigns & Elections. LC 99-96765. (Illus.). 32p. (J). (gr. 3-6). 1999. 15.95 (*1-893622-01-0*, Pub. by Vacation Spot) Koen Bk Distributors.

Barnes, Peter W. Woodrow, the White House Mouse. 2nd rev. ed. LC 98-75056. (Illus.). 32p. (J). (gr. 1-3). 1998. 15.95 (*0-9637688-9-1*) Vacation Spot.

Barnes, Peter W. & Barnes, Cheryl S. Cornelius Vandermouse: The Pride of Newport. (Illus.). 32p. (J). 1997. 15.95 (*0-9637688-5-9*) Vacation Spot.
— Marshall, the Courthouse Mouse: A Tail of the U. S. Supreme Court. LC 98-90151. (Illus.). 32p. (J). (gr. 2-5). 1997. 15.95 (*0-9637688-6-7*) Vacation Spot.
— Martha's Vineyard. (Illus.). 32p. (J). (gr. k-6). 1995. 15.95 (*0-9637688-3-2*) Vacation Spot.
— Nat, Nat, the Nantucket Cat. (Illus.). 30p. (J). 1993. 15.95 (*0-9637688-0-8*) Vacation Spot.

Barnes, Peter W., et al. Capital Cooking with Woodrow & Friends. (Illus.). 32p. (J). (gr. 1-6). 1998. pap. 9.95 (*0-9637688-7-5*) Vacation Spot.
— A Mice Way to Learn about Government: A Curriculum Guide. (Illus.). 64p. 1999. pap. text 9.95 (*1-893622-00-2*, VSP Bks) Vacation Spot.

***Barnes, Peter W., et al.** A "Mice" Way to Learn about Voting, Campaigns & Elections: A Curriculum Guide to Woodrow for President. (Illus.). 24p. 1999. pap., teacher ed. 7.95 (*1-893622-02-9*, Pub. by Vacation Spot) Koen Bk Distributors.

Barnes, Peter W., jt. auth. see Barnes, Cheryl S.

Barnes, Philip. A Companion to Post-War British Theatre. 288p. 1986. 58.50 (*0-389-20669-5*, N8233) B&N Imports.

***Barnes, Philip.** A Concise History of the Hawaiian Islands. (Illus.). 86p. 1999. pap. 9.95 (*0-912180-56-0*) Petroglyph.

Barnes, Philip. Indonesia: The Political Economy of Energy. LC 96-118860. (Oxford Institute for Energy Studies). (Illus.). 208p. 1995. text 65.00 (*0-19-730016-2*) OUP.
— The OIES Review of Long-Term Energy Demand. 76p. 1992. 165.95 (*0-948061-69-3*, P7490) PennWell Bks.
— The OIES Review of Long-Term Energy Supply. 75p. 1990. 137.95 (*0-948061-45-6*, P7494) PennWell Bks.

Barnes, R. Eric. Philosophy in Practice: Understanding Value Debate. 261p. (YA). (gr. 9-12). 1996. pap. text 20.00 (*0-931054-41-9*) Clark Pub.

Barnes, R. G. Hydrogen in Metals III: Properties & Applications. Wipf, H., ed. LC 96-38496. (Topics in Applied Physics Ser.: Vol. 73). (Illus.). 320p. 1997. 119.00 (*3-540-61639-X*) Spr-Verlag.

Barnes, R. G., ed. Hydrogen Storage Materials. 350p. 1988. text 120.00 (*0-87849-572-X*, Pub. by Trans T Pub) Enfield Pubs NH.

Barnes, R. H. Sea Hunters of Indonesia: Fishers & Weavers of Lamalera. (Oxford Studies in Social & Cultural Anthropology). (Illus.). 490p. 1997. text 98.00 (*0-19-828070-X*) OUP.
— Two Crows Denies It: A History of Controversy in Omaha Sociology. LC 84-2276. (Illus.). xiv, 272p. 1984. text 50.00 (*0-8032-1182-1*) U of Nebr Pr.

Barnes, R. H., et al, eds. Indigenous Peoples of Asia. LC 93-10487. (Monographs: No. 48). (Illus.). vii, 541p. (Orig.). (C). 1995. 40.00 (*0-924304-14-6*); pap. 22.50 (*0-924304-15-4*) Assn Asian Studies.

Barnes, R. M., ed. Plasma Spectrochemistry: Proceedings of the Winter Conference, Orlando , Florida, January 4-9, 1982. 436p. 1983. pap. 55.00 (*0-08-028745-X*, Pergamon Pr) Elsevier.

Barnes, R. S. The Brackish-Water Fauna of Northwestern Europe: A Guide to Brackish-Water Habitats, Ecology & Macrofauna for Field Workers, Naturalists & Students. (Illus.). 303p. (C). 1994. text 80.00 (*0-521-45529-4*) Cambridge U Pr.
— The Diversity of Living Organisms. 1998. pap. 29.95 (*0-86542-760-7*) Blackwell Sci.

Barnes, R. S. & Mann, K. H., eds. Fundamentals of Aquatic Ecology. 2nd ed. (Illus.). 280p. 1991. pap. 54.95 (*0-632-02983-8*) Blackwell Sci.

Barnes, R. S., et al. Invertebrates: A New Synthesis. 2nd ed. (Illus.). 576p. 1993. pap. 44.95 (*0-632-03127-1*) Blackwell Sci.

***Barnes, R. S. K. & Hughes, R. N.** Introduction to Marine Ecology. 3rd ed. LC 98-38820. (Illus.). 1999. pap. 49.95 (*0-86542-834-4*) Blackwell Sci.

Barnes, R. S.K. The Brackish-water Fauna of Northwestern Europe: A Guide to Brackish-water Habitats, Ecology & Macrofauna for Field Workers, Naturalists & Students. (Illus.). 303p. (C). 1995. pap. text 27.95 (*0-521-45556-1*) Cambridge U Pr.

Barnes, Rachel. The Pre-Raphaelites & Their World. LC 98-158608. (Illus.). 112p. 1997. pap. 25.95 (*1-85437-220-3*, Pub. by Tate Gallery) U of Wash Pr.

Barnes, Ralph M. Motion & Time Study: Design & Measurement of Work. 7th ed. LC 80-173. 704p. 1980. text 103.95 (*0-471-05905-6*) Wiley.

Barnes, Ramon M., ed. Applications of Plasma Emission Spectrochemistry. LC 79-25130. 159p. reprint ed. pap. 49.30 (*0-8357-8804-0*, 203332900085) Bks Demand.

Barnes, Randal J., ed. see Application of Computers & Operations Research in.

Barnes, Reg. American Water Ski Association Official Instructor's Manual: Level I Instructor's Certification. 36p. 1985. pap. 4.50 (*0-318-19111-3*) USA Water Ski.

Barnes, Richard. Mods! 128p. 1994. per. 14.95 (*0-85965-173-8*, Pub. by Plexus) Publishers Group.

***Barnes, Richard.** Who: Maximum R & B. 3rd ed. (Illus.). 168p. 2000. pap. 24.95 (*0-85965-287-4*) Plexus.

Barnes, Richard. The Who: Maximum R&B. 2nd rev. ed. (Illus.). 168p. 1996. pap. 24.95 (*0-85965-186-X*, Pub. by Plexus) Publishers Group.

Barnes, Richard, jt. auth. see Pike, John.

Barnes, Richard S., ed. The Coastline: A Contribution to Our Understanding of Its Ecology & Physiography In Relation to Land-Use & Management & the Pressures to Which It Is Subject. LC 76-51343. (Illus.). 368p. reprint ed. pap. 114.10 (*0-8357-6430-3*, 203580100097) Bks Demand.

Barnes, Richard W., jt. auth. see Wilkinson, Bruce W.

Barnes, Rik. Complete Guide to American Bed & Breakfast. 5th ed. LC 91-659283. (Illus.). 960p. 1997. pap. 19.95 (*1-56554-268-1*) Pelican.

Barnes, Rob. Positive Teaching, Positive Learning. LC 98-49944. 1998. pap. write for info. (*0-415-18139-9*) Routledge.
— Teaching Art to Young Children. LC 86-8032. (Illus.). 215p. (C). 1987. pap. 22.99 (*0-415-07891-1*) Routledge.
— Teaching Art to Young Children Four to Nine. (Illus.). 176p. (C). 1987. pap. text 19.95 (*0-04-371097-2*) Routledge.

Barnes, Robert. Blue Dolphin. Carleton, Nancy, ed. LC 94-1514. 192p. 1994. pap. 9.95 (*0-915811-55-3*) H J Kramer Inc.
— Marriages & Deaths from Baltimore Newspapers, 1796-1816. LC 78-61144. 383p. 2000. reprint ed. pap. 32.50 (*0-8063-0826-5*, Pub. by Clearfield Co) ACCESS Pubs Network.

Barnes, Robert, Jr. Padres Solteros: Una Jornada en el Desierto. Orig. Title: Wilderness Journey. (SPA.). 61p. 1991. pap. 4.99 (*1-56063-094-9*, 498418) Editorial Unilit.

Barnes, Robert & Barnes, Rosemary J. Great Sexpectations. 224p. 1996. pap. 12.99 (*0-310-20137-3*) Zondervan.
— Rock-Solid Marriage: Building a Permanent Relationship in a Throw-Away World. 256p. 1996. pap. 12.99 (*0-310-20804-1*) Zondervan.
— We Need to Talk: Opening Doors of Communication with Your Mate. 224p. 1996. pap. 12.99 (*0-310-20805-X*) Zondervan.

Barnes, Robert, jt. auth. see Blank, Glenn.

Barnes, Robert C. The Complete Encyclopedia of Skiing: The Indispensable Reference for Instructors & All Serious Skiiers. 3rd ed. (Illus.). 336p. 1999. 29.95 (*0-9669131-5-9*) Snowline Pr.

Barnes, Robert C. & Pfeiffer, Judith M. Press, Politics, & Perserverance: Everett C. Johnson & The Press of Kells. LC 98-31420. (Illus.). 320p. 1998. write for info. (*1-884718-82-5*) Oak Knoll.

Barnes, Robert D., jt. auth. see Ruppert, Edward E.

Barnes, Robert G. Single Parenting. 294p. 1992. mass mkt. 5.99 (*0-8423-5920-6*) Tyndale Hse.

Barnes, Robert H. Harry Elmer Barnes: As I Knew Him. LC 94-76342. (Illus.). 160p. 1994. 19.50 (*1-881019-08-X*) High Plns WY.

Barnes, Robert J., ed. see Byron, George Gordon.

Barnes, Robert M. Cutting Edge Futures Trading Methods for the 21st Century: New Concepts for the Next Millennium. 215p. (Orig.). 1996. 24.95 (*0-930233-60-3*) Windsor.
— High-Impact Day Trading: Powerful Techniques for Exploiting Short-Term Market Trends. LC 96-11268. (Illus.). 240p. 1996. 50.00 (*0-7863-0798-6*, Irwn Prfssnl) McGraw-Hill Prof.
— Megaprofit Commodity Methods: Ten New Technical Trading Methods. (Illus.). 151p. 1983. 69.95 (*0-930233-14-X*) Windsor.
— Trading in Choppy Markets: Breakthrough Techniques for Exploiting Non-Trending Markets. 528p. 1996. 50.00 (*0-7863-1007-3*, Irwn Prfssnl) McGraw-Hill Prof.
— Trading System Analysis: Using Trading Simulations to Test, Evaluate & Predict Trading System Performance. LC 96-53447. 192p. 1997. 60.00 (*0-7863-1098-7*, Irwn Prfssnl) McGraw-Hill Prof.

Barnes, Robert T. Strategic Air Command. 208p. 1997. 54.95 (*1-56311-265-5*) Turner Pub KY.

Barnes, Robert W. Baltimore County Families, 1659-1759. 924p. 1998. pap. 65.00 (*0-8063-1234-3*, 353) Clearfield Co.

***Barnes, Robert W.** British Roots of Maryland Families. LC 99-71523. 684p. 1999. 49.50 (*0-8063-1615-2*) Genealog Pub.

Barnes, Robert W. Marriages & Deaths from the "Maryland Gazette," 1727-1839. 243p. 1997. reprint ed. pap. 24.00 (*0-8063-0580-0*, 355, Pub. by Clearfield Co) ACCESS Pubs Network.

Barnes, Robert W. & Cox, Birck, eds. Amputations. LC 99-47747. (Illus.). 250p. 2000. text 39.00 (*1-56053-353-6*) Hanley & Belfus.

Barnes, Robert W., et al. Iowa Doppler Ultrasonic Diagnosis of Peripheral Vascular Disease (Iowa) 1975. write for info. (*0-318-60276-8*) U IA Audiovisual.

Barnes, Robin B., et al, eds. Habent Sua Fata Libelli: or Books Have Their Own Destiny: Essays in Honor of Robert V. Schnucker. LC 98-35348. (Sixteenth Century Essays & Studies: Vol. 50). (Illus.). 167p. 1998. 40.00 (*0-940474-59-X*) Truman St Univ.

Barnes, Roger. Good Buys in IT: A Manager's Guide to Effective Spending. LC 95-8873. 1995. pap. write for info. (*0-07-709097-7*) McGraw.

Barnes, Ron. Fit-Famous. (Orig.). 1994. pap. 14.95 (*0-9641773-1-5*) Colo Cowboy.

Barnes, Ronald. Great Legends of Wales. (Illus.). 156p. 1991. 28.00 (*0-86140-317-7*, Pub. by Smyth) Dufour.

Barnes, Roscoe, III. Discover Your Talent & Find Fulfillment: A Guide to Using Your Skills to Get What You Need & Want Out of Life. 80p. 1994. pap. 6.95 (*0-9626420-0-2*) McKinley & Henson.
— Off to War: Franklin Countians in World War II. LC 95-26626. (Illus.). 98p. (Orig.). 1996. pap. 9.95 (*1-57249-033-0*, Burd St Pr) White Mane Pub.

Barnes, Rosemary J., jt. auth. see Barnes, Robert.

***Barnes-Rothmeier, Vicki.** The Kid Book: Surprising Truths about People We Call Kids. Osborne, Susan Titus, ed. (Illus.). 179p. 1999. 14.95 (*1-929568-05-3*) For Kids Only.

Barnes-Rothmeier, Vicki, jt. auth. see Lotts, Scott J.

Barnes, Rudolph C., Jr. Military Legitimacy: Might & Right in the New Millenium. LC 95-30804. 199p. (C). 1996. 45.00 (*0-7146-4624-5*, Pub. by F Cass Pubs) Intl Spec Bk.

Barnes, Ruth. Indian Block-Printed Cotton Fragments in the Kelsey Museum. (Illus.). 104p. 1993. text 44.50 (*0-472-10293-1*, 10293) U of Mich Pr.
— Indian Block-Printed Textiles in Egypt: The Newberry Collection in the Ashmolean Museum, Oxford, 2 vols., Set. LC 96-30565. (Illus.). 542p. 1997. text 575.00 (*0-19-951364-3*) OUP.

Barnes, Ruth & Eicher, Joanne B., eds. Dress & Gender: Making & Meaning. LC 91-15885. (Cross Cultural Perspectives on Women Ser.). (Illus.). 304p. 1993. 46.00 (*0-85496-720-6*); pap. 19.50 (*0-85496-865-2*, Pub. by Berg Pubs) NYU Pr.

Barnes, S., jt. auth. see Cavanaugh, S. W.

Barnes, S. H., jt. ed. see Blackmore, Stephen.

Barnes, Sam. Humanitarian Aid Coordination During War & Peace in Mozambique, 1985-1995. (Studies on Emergencies & Disaster Relief: Vol. 7). 27p. 1999. pap. 12.95 (*91-7106-433-8*, Pub. by Nordic Africa) Transaction Pubs.

Barnes, Samuel. Identity. (Illus.). 260p. (C). 1981. 9.95 (*0-941192-00-8*) Best West Pr.

Barnes, Samuel H. Representation in Italy: Institutional Tradition & Electrical Choice. LC 76-51819. 198p. Date not set. reprint ed. pap. 61.40 (*0-608-20988-0*, 205451600003) Bks Demand.
— Representation in Italy: Institutionalized Tradition & Electoral Choice. LC 76-51819. (Illus.). 1977. 20.00 (*0-226-03726-6*) U Ch Pr.

Barnes, Samuel H., et al. Political Action: Mass Participation in 5 Western Democracies. LC 78-19649. 607p. 1979. reprint ed. pap. 188.20 (*0-608-01450-8*, 205949400001) Bks Demand.

***Barnes, Sandra J.** Increments. 60p. 2000. pap. 8.50 (*0-9677530-1-5*) Images & Reflec.
— Seeing Clearly. 44p. 1999. pap. 8.50 (*0-9677530-0-7*) Images & Reflec.

Barnes, Sandra T. Africa's Ogun: Old World & New. 2nd ed. LC 96-43166. (African Systems of Thought Ser.). 1997. 45.00 (*0-253-33251-6*); pap. 18.95 (*0-253-21083-6*) Ind U Pr.

Barnes, Sandra T., ed. Africa's Ogun: Old World & New. LC 88-45452. (African Systems of Thought Ser.). (Illus.). 288p. 1989. 45.00 (*0-253-30282-X*); pap. 19.95 (*0-253-20505-0*, MB 505) Ind U Pr.

Barnes, Sandy. Decorative Painting: Flowers & Finishes. (Illus.). 64p. 1998. pap. 12.95 (*0-85532-866-5*, 8665, Pub. by Srch Pr) A Schwartz & Co.

***Barnes, Sandy.** Search Press Book of Decorative Effects for the Home. (Illus.). 2000. 17.95 (*0-85532-905-X*) Srch Pr.

***Barnes, Scottie.** GPS. (Basic Essentials Ser.). (Illus.). 80p. 2000. pap. 7.95 (*0-7627-0635-X*) Globe Pequot.

Barnes, Shakara, ed. see Barnes, Nigel.

Barnes, Sharon A. & VanWormer, Denise A. Who's in Charge? Putting the Pieces Together to Build Confidence, Conquer Fears, & Develop a Successful Classroom. LC 96-94794. (Illus.). 85p. (Orig.). 1996. pap. 19.95 (*0-9653495-0-0*) In Charge Pub.

Barnes, Sondra Anice. Life Is the Way It Is. LC 78-73124. (Illus.). 85p. 1978. pap. 7.50 (*0-9602534-0-8*) Brason-Sargar.
— We Are the Way We Are. LC 86-72759. (Illus.). 85p. (Orig.). 1986. pap. 7.50 (*0-9602534-1-6*) Brason-Sargar.

Barnes, Stanley. All for Jesus. 1997. pap. 9.99 (*1-898787-83-2*) Emerald House Group Inc.

***Barnes, Stanley.** John 3:16. 150p. 1999. pap. 8.99 (*1-84030-066-3*) Emerald House Group Inc.

Barnes, Stephen H., ed. Points of View on American Higher Education: A Selection of Important Contributions Appearing in "The Chronicle of Higher Education", Vol. 1. LC 89-38747. (Studies in Education: Vols. 4-6). 296p. 1990. lib. bdg. 89.95 (*0-88946-939-3*) E Mellen.
— Points of View on American Higher Education: A Selection of Important Contributions Appearing in "The Chronicle of Higher Education", Vol. 2. LC 89-38747. (Studies in Education: Vols. 4-6). 296p. 1990. lib. bdg. 89.95 (*0-88946-940-7*) E Mellen.
— Points of View on American Higher Education: A Selection of Important Contributions Appearing in "The Chronicle of Higher Education", Vol. 3. LC 89-38747. (Studies in Education: Vols. 4-6). 296p. 1990. lib. bdg. 89.95 (*0-88946-941-5*) E Mellen.

Barnes, Steven. Blood Brothers. LC 96-20706. 384p. 1996. 24.95 (*0-312-85707-1*) St Martin.
— Blood Brothers. 1997. mass mkt. 6.99 (*0-8125-4807-8*, Pub. by Tor Bks) St Martin.

***Barnes, Steven.** Charisma. 2000. text 25.95 (*0-312-87004-3*) St Martin.

Barnes, Steven. Firedance. 384p. 1995. mass mkt. 5.99 (*0-8125-1024-0*, Pub. by Tor Bks) St Martin.
— Gorgon Child. 352p. 1989. pap. 3.95 (*0-8125-3152-3*, Pub. by Tor Bks) St Martin.
— Iron Shadows. LC 97-29840. 416p. 1998. text 24.95 (*0-312-85708-X*) St Martin.

***Barnes, Steven.** Iron Shadows. 320p. 2000. mass mkt. 5.99 (*0-8125-4808-6*, Pub. by Tor Bks) St Martin.

Barnes, Steven. The Kundalini Equation. 352p. (Orig.). 1986. mass mkt. 5.99 (*0-8125-3150-7*) Tor Bks.
— Streetlethal. 320p. 1991. mass mkt. 4.99 (*0-8125-1034-8*) Tor Bks.

Barnes, Steven, jt. auth. see Niven, Larry.

***Barnes, Stewart E., et al, eds.** High Temperature Superconductivity. (Conference Proceedings Ser.: Vol. 483). (Illus.). 451p. 1999. 130.00 (*1-56396-880-0*, Pub. by Am Inst Physics) Spr-Verlag.

Barnes, Stuart. Smelling of Roses: A Rugby Life. (Illus.). 206p. 1995. 34.95 (*1-85158-640-7*, Pub. by Mainstream Pubng) Trafalgar.

***Barnes, Stuart & Hunt, Brian.** E-Commerce & V-Business: An International Money Making Machine. 256p. 2000. pap. text 49.95 (*0-7506-4532-6*) Buttrwrth-Heinemann.

Barnes, Stuart & Seabrook, Mike, eds. Nice Tries. 192p. 1996. pap. 13.95 (*0-575-60044-6*, Pub. by V Gollancz) Trafalgar.

Barnes, Sue N., jt. auth. see Curtis, Helena.

Barnes, Susan. Earthquake. deluxe ed. Rabinowitz, Jonathan, ed. (Illus.). 96p. (Orig.). 1990. pap. 55.00 (*0-9627987-0-3*) Turtle Point Pr.

Barnes, Susan J. Rene Magritte Poetic Images. LC 79-89280. (Illus.). 15p. (Orig.). 1979. pap. 4.00 (*0-943526-38-8*) Parrish Art.
— The Rothko Chaptel: An Act of Faith. 2nd ed. (Illus.). 135p. 1996. pap. 23.09 (*0-945472-02-1*) Rothko Chapel.

Barnes, Susan J. & Melion, Walter S., eds. Cultural Differentiation & Cultural Identity in the Visual Arts. (Illus.). 1996. 25.00 (*0-300-07694-0*) Yale U Pr.
— Studies in the History of Art: Cultural Differentiation & Cultural Identity in the Visual Arts. LC 72-600309. (Symposium Papers XII: Vol. 27). (Illus.). 149p. (Orig.). 1989. pap. 18.00 (*0-89468-133-8*) Natl Gallery Art.

Barnes, Susan J. & Wheelock, Arthur K., Jr., eds. Van Dyck 350. (Illus.). 1996. 60.00 (*0-300-07695-9*) Yale U Pr.

Barnes, Suzanne M. Taming the Tongue Thrust. Kobobel, Janet, ed. (Illus.). 62p. 1995. pap. text 79.00 incl. VHS (*0-9676836-0-2*) S M Barnes.

Barnes-Svarney, Patricia L. Asteroid: Earth Destroyer or New Frontier? (Illus.). 278p. (C). 1996. 25.95 (*0-306-45408-4*, Plenum Trade) Perseus Pubng.
— Computer Crunch! (Secret World of Alex Mack Ser.: No. 24). (J). (gr. 3-6). 1998. pap. 3.99 (*0-671-01884-1*) PB.
— High Flyer! (Secret World of Alex Mack Ser.: No. 14). (J). (gr. 3-6). 1997. pap. 3.99 (*0-671-00449-2*, Minstrel Bks) PB.
— Junkyard Jitters! (Secret World of Alex Mack Ser.: No. 11). 144p. (J). (gr. 3-6). 1997. per. 3.99 (*0-671-00367-4*) PB.
— Loyalties. (Starfleet Academy Ser.: No. 10). (J). (gr. 3-6). 1996. pap. 3.99 (*0-671-55280-5*, Minstrel Bks) PB.

Barnes-Svarney, Patricia L. Loyalties. (Starfleet Academy Ser.). 1996. 9.09 (*0-606-09893-3*, Pub. by Turtleback) Demco.

Barnes-Svarney, Patricia L. The New York Public Library Science Desk Reference. (Illus.). 758p. 1995. 39.95 (*0-02-860403-2*) Macmillan.
— Quarantine. (Star Trek: No. 3). (YA). 1997. per. 3.99 (*0-671-00733-5*, Star Trek) PB.

Barnes-Svarney, Patricia L. Quarantine. (Star Trek Voyager Starfleet Academy Ser.). 1997. 9.09 (*0-606-13803-X*, Pub. by Turtleback) Demco.

Barnes-Svarney, Patricia L. Sabrina the Teenage Witch Magic Handbook. 96p. (J). (gr. 7-12). 1998. per. 6.99 (*0-671-02427-2*) S&S Trade.

***Barnes-Svarney, Patricia L.** Sabrina's Guide to the Universe, Vol. 1. 96p. (gr. 4-7). 1999. per. 6.99 (*0-671-03641-6*) PB.
— Secrets of the Sun: A Closer Look at Our Star. (Space Explorer Ser.). (Illus.). (J). 2000. pap. 8.95 (*0-7398-2224-1*) Raintree Steck-V.
— Secrets of the Sun: A Closer Look at the Sun. (Space Explorer Ser.). (Illus.). (J). 2000. 28.54 (*0-7398-2214-4*) Raintree Steck-V.

Barnes-Svarney, Patricia L. Teacher's Pet. (Sabrina, the Teenage Witch Ser.: No. 2). (Illus.). 85p. (J). (gr. 2-5). 1998. pap. 3.99 (*0-671-02381-0*, Minstrel Bks) PB.
— Through the Telescope: A Guide for the Amateur Astronomer. 2nd ed. 309p. 1999. pap. 19.95 (*0-07-134804-2*) McGraw.
— Zimbabwe: Major World Nations. LC 97-18122. (Major World Nations Ser.). (Illus.). 144p. (YA). (gr. 5 up). 1999. lib. bdg. 19.95 (*0-7910-4753-9*) Chelsea Hse.

Barnes-Svarney, Patricia L. & Svarney, Thomas E. Handy Ocean Answer Book. LC 99-49151. 500p. 2000. pap. text 19.95 (*1-57859-063-9*) Visible Ink Pr.

An Asterisk (*) at the beginning of an entry indicates that the title is appearing for the first time.

— The Oryx Guide to Natural History: The Earth & All Its Inhabitants. LC 99-41783. (Illus.). 252p. 1999. 69.95 (*1-57356-159-2*) Oryx Pr.

***Barnes-Svarney, Patricia L. & Svarney, Thomas E.** Skies of Fury: Weather Weirdness Around the World. LC 99-29956. 224p. 1999. pap. 12.00 (*0-684-85000-1*) S&S Trade.

Barnes, Sybil, ed. see Knowlton, Lorna.

Barnes, Sybil, ed. see Stauffer, Ruth.

Barnes, T., et al. Progress in Theoretical Physics: Tenth Annual Montreal-Rochester-Syracuse-Toronto Meeting on HEP. 240p. 1988. text 77.00 (*9971-5-0775-7*) World Scientific Pub.

Barnes, T. D. Early Christianity & the Roman Empire. (Collected Studies: No. CS207). 314p. (C). 1984. reprint ed. lib. bdg. 113.95 (*0-86078-155-0*, Pub. by Variorum) Ashgate Pub Co.

— From Eusebius to Augustine: Selected Papers, 1982-1993. LC 93-48084. 1994. 109.95 (*0-86078-397-9*, Pub. by Variorum) Ashgate Pub Co.

Barnes, T. R. English Verse: Voice & Movement from Wyatt to Yeats. LC 67-29867. 334p. reprint ed. pap. 95.20 (*0-608-17572-2*, 2030579) Bks Demand.

Barnes, T. R., ed. Antipsychotic Drugs & Their Side Effects. (Neuroscience Perspectives Ser.). (Illus.). 287p. 1994. text 78.00 (*0-12-079035-1*) Acad Pr.

Barnes, T. W. & Freeman, Nona. And Jesus Said. . .Through Tom Barnes. Perry, Nell, ed. LC 90-84929. 170p. 1990. 8.50 (*1-878366-03-3*) Nonas Bk Sales.

Barnes, Tag, ed. Commando Diary. 144p. (C). 1991. 95.00 (*0-946771-53-7*, Pub. by Spellmnt Pubs) St Mut.

Barnes, Terby, jt. auth. see Barnes, Fran.

Barnes, Terby, jt. auth. see Newell, Maxine.

Barnes, Teresa A. We Women Worked So Hard: Gender, Urbanization & Social Reproduction in Colonial Harare, Zimbabwe, 1930-1956. LC 99-25010. (Social History of Africa Ser.). 256p. 1999. 24.95 (*0-325-00172-3*); 59.95 (*0-325-00173-1*, E00173) Greenwood.

***Barnes, Teresa Woods.** The Discovery: A Meeting Between the Old World & the New World. 43p. (YA). 2000. spiral bd. 12.00 (*0-932776-25-6*) Adonis Pr.

***Barnes, Thomas A.** Clinical Simulations in Respiratory Care. (C). 1999. cd-rom 52.95 (*0-8036-0246-4*) Davis Co.

Barnes, Thomas C. Gardening for the Birds. LC 98-6128. (Illus.). 280p. 1999. 24.95 (*0-8131-2071-3*) U Pr of Ky.

Barnes, Thomas C., et al. Northern New Spain: A Research Guide. LC 80-24860. 147p. 1981. pap. 18.95 (*0-8165-0709-0*) U of Ariz Pr.

Barnes, Thomas G. Science & Biblical Faith: A Science Documentation. (Illus.). 196p. (Orig.). 1993. pap. 13.00 (*0-9637550-0-5*) T G Barnes.

— Somerset, 1625-1640: A County's Government During the "Personal Rule" LC 82-11012. (Midway Reprint Ser.). 382p. reprint ed. pap. 118.50 (*0-608-09378-5*, 205412300004); reprint ed. pap. 118.50 (*0-608-20993-7*, 205452100003) Bks Demand.

Barnes, Thomas G., ed. The Book of the General Lawes & Libertyes Concerning the Inhabitants of the Massachusetts. LC 75-12004. 88p. 1975. pap. 6.00 (*0-87328-066-0*) Huntington Lib.

Barnes, Thomas G. & Feldman, Gerald D., eds. Breakdown & Rebirth: 1914 to the Present, a Documentary History of Modern Europe, Vol. IV. LC 82-45164. 288p. 1982. reprint ed. pap. text 17.50 (*0-8191-2366-8*) U Pr of Amer.

— Nationalism, Industrialization, & Democracy, 1815-1914: A Documenatary History of Modern Europe, Vol. III. LC 80-5383. 331p. 1980. pap. text 17.00 (*0-8191-1079-5*) U Pr of Amer.

Barnes, Thomas G., ed. see American Bar Foundation Staff.

***Barnes, Thomas J.** Tay Son: Rebellion in Eighteenth Century Vietman. LC 00-190560. 2000. 25.00 (*0-7388-1818-6*) Xlibris Corp.

— Tay Son: Rebellion in Eighteenth Century Vietnam. LC 00-190560. 2000. pap. 18.00 (*0-7388-1819-4*) Xlibris Corp.

Barnes, Thomas R., ed. Along Willona Creek: The Country Correspondence of Kate Loftus Welch to the Waterville Times, 1898-1938. LC 96-90356. (Illus.). xxiv, 262p. 1996. 29.95 (*0-9652804-6-2*) Willona Pr.

Barnes, Thurlow W., ed. see Weed, Thurlow.

Barnes, Tim, ed. see Wood, Charles E., et al.

Barnes, Timothy D. Ammianus Marcellinus & the Representation of Historical Reality. LC 98-19791. (Studies in Classical Philology). 336p. 1998. text 45.00 (*0-8014-3526-9*) Cornell U Pr.

— Athanasius & Constantius: Theology & Politics in the Constantinian Empire. LC 92-33050. 344p. (C). 1993. text 56.00 (*0-674-05067-3*) HUP.

— Constantine & Eusebius. 464p. 1964. pap. 24.95 (*0-674-16531-4*) HUP.

— Constantine & Eusebius. LC 81-4248. (Illus.). 464p. (C). 1981. 47.50 (*0-674-16530-6*) HUP.

— The New Empire of Diocletian & Constantine. LC 81-6569. 324p. reprint ed. pap. 100.50 (*0-7837-2221-4*, 205731100004) Bks Demand.

Barnes, Timothy D., et al. Augustine: From Rhetor to Theologian. McWilliam, Joanne, ed. 247p. (C). 1992. text 35.00 (*0-88920-203-6*) W Laurier U Pr.

Barnes, Timothy J., et al. Electronic CAD Frameworks. LC 92-10976. (International Series in Engineering & Computer Science, VLSI, Computer Architecture, & Digital Screen Processing). 216p. (C). 1992. text 113.00 (*0-7923-9252-3*) Kluwer Academic.

Barnes, Tony. Kaizen Strategies for Successful Leadership. 240p. 1995. 24.95 (*0-273-61709-5*) F T P-H.

— Seneca: The Climber's Guide. 169p. 1995. pap. 19.95 (*0-9643698-1-8*) Earthbnd Spts.

Barnes, Trescott C. Barnes Family Year Book, Vols. I-III. 157p. 1994. reprint ed. pap. 25.00 (*0-8328-4294-X*); reprint ed. lib. bdg. 35.00 (*0-8328-4293-1*) Higginson Bk Co.

***Barnes, Trevor.** The Kingfisher Book of Religions: Festivals, Ceremonies & Beliefs from around the World. LC 98-53303. (Illus.). 160p. (YA). (gr. 4-9). 1999. 22.95 (*0-7534-5199-9*) LKC.

Barnes, Trevor & Gregory, Derek, eds. Reading Human Geography: The Poetics & Politics of Inquiry. LC 95-223591. (Arnold Publications). (Illus.). 528p. 1996. pap. text 35.00 (*0-340-63208-9*) OUP.

Barnes, Trevor & Hayter, Roger, eds. Trouble in the Rainforest: British Columbia's Forest Economy in Transition. LC 98-136789. (Illus.). 250p. 1997. pap. 24.95 (*0-919838-23-5*) U of Wash Pr.

Barnes, Trevor, jt. ed. see Sheppard, Eric.

Barnes, Trevor J. Logics of Dislocation: Models, Metaphors & Meanings of Economic Space. LC 95-42463. (Mappings: Society-Theory-Space Ser.). 292p. 1995. lib. bdg. 44.50 (*1-57230-033-7*, 0033) Guilford Pubns.

— Logics of Dislocation: Models, Metaphors & Meanings of Economic Space. LC 95-42463. (Mappings). (Illus.). 292p. 1995. pap. text 21.95 (*1-57230-039-6*, 0039) Guilford Pubns.

Barnes, Trevor J. & Duncan, James S. Writing Worlds: Discourse, Text & Metaphor in the Representation of Landscape. LC 91-12898. (Illus.). 304p. (C). 1991. pap. 27.99 (*0-415-06983-1*, A6548) Routledge.

***Barnes, Trevor J. & Gertler, Meric S.** The New Industrial Geography: Regions, Regulations & Institutions. LC 99-22501. (Studies in the Modern World Economy). 1999. text. write for info. (*0-415-21802-0*) Routledge.

***Barnes, Tyrone.** Poems & Stories of Reality: Always Believe in Yourself. 24p. 1999. pap. 6.00 (*0-8059-4466-4*) Dorrance.

Barnes, V. E. Englar: Genealogy of the Englar Family, the Descendants of Philip Englar, 1736-1817, Traced down for Five Generations from 1736. 79p. 1997. reprint ed. pap. 16.00 (*0-8328-8482-0*); reprint ed. lib. bdg. 26.00 (*0-8328-8481-2*) Higginson Bk Co.

Barnes, V. E. & Bell, W. C. The Moore Hollow Group of Central Texas. (Reports of Investigations: RI 88). (Illus.). 169p. 1977. pap. 5.00 (*0-318-03228-7*) Bur Econ Geology.

Barnes, V. E. & Schofield, D. A. Potential Low-Grade Iron Ore & Hydraulic-Fracturing Sand in Cambrian Sandstones, Northwestern Llano Region, Texas. (Reports of Investigations: RI 53). (Illus.). 58p. 1964. pap. 2.00 (*0-686-29335-5*) Bur Econ Geology.

Barnes, V. E., et al. Stratigraphy of the Pre-Simpson Paleozoic Subsurface Rocks of Texas & Southeast New Mexico, 2 vols. (Publication Ser.: PUB 5924). (Illus.). 836p. 1959. pap. 7.75 (*0-318-03311-9*) Bur Econ Geology.

Barnes, V. E., jt. auth. see Eifler, G. K., Jr.

Barnes, Verle. Portrait of an Estuary. McKinney, Aubrey R., ed. LC 86-81736. (Adventures in Science Ser.). (Illus.). 220p. 1986. 24.95 (*0-914587-04-8*) Helix Pr.

Barnes, Victoria L. What Every Girl Should Know: A Mother-Daughter Bible Study Designed for Girls. LC 97-75026. 115p. 1997. pap. 3.00 (*0-912375-05-1*) Calvary Miss Pr.

Barnes, Virginia L. & Boddy, Janice. Aman. 336p. (YA). 1995. pap. 14.00 (*0-679-76209-4*) Random.

Barnes, Virginia L., ed. see Teshale, Taddele S.

Barnes, W. & Hodges, G. Aminoglycoside Antibiotics: Guide to Therapy. LC 83-2558. 248p. 1983. 142.00 (*0-8493-5426-9*, CRC Reprint) Franklin.

Barnes, W. E., ed. Basic Physics of Radiotracers, Vol. I. 216p. 1983. 125.00 (*0-8493-6001-3*, QC776, CRC Reprint) Franklin.

— Basic Physics of Radiotracers, Vol. II. 176p. 1983. 104.00 (*0-8493-6002-1*, CRC Reprint) Franklin.

Barnes, W. P. & Gladden, M. H. Feedback & Motor Control in Invertebrates & Vertebrates. LC 85-26895. 350p. 1985. 79.50 (*0-7099-3277-4*, Pub. by C Helm) Routldge.

Barnes, W. W., jt. auth. see Allison, William H.

***Barnes, William.** My Little Black Book. 68p. 1999. pap. write for info. (*0-7392-0428-9*, PO3708) Morris Pubng.

Barnes, William. Thomas Andrews, Voyage into History: Thru the Eyes of Her Builder Titanic Secrets Revealed. LC 99-36297. (Illus.). 208p. 2000. pap. 16.00 (*1-887010-12-2*) Edin Bks.

Barnes, William & Hardy, Thomas. Collected Prose Works of William Barnes, 6 vols. Bradbury, Richard, ed. LC 97-131709. 2860p. (C). 1996. 655.00 (*0-415-14301-2*) Routledge.

Barnes, William C. Apaches & Longhorns: The Reminiscences of Will C. Barnes. Lockwood, Frank C., ed. LC 82-7043. (Illus.). 254p. reprint ed. pap. 78.80 (*0-8357-8584-X*, 203495500091) Bks Demand.

— Arizona Place Names. LC 87-35835. 503p. 1988. reprint ed. pap. 22.50 (*0-8165-1074-1*) U of Ariz Pr.

— Western Grazing Grounds & Forest Ranges. Bruchey, Stuart, ed. LC 78-56685. (Management of Public Lands in the U. S. Ser.). (Illus.). 1979. reprint ed. lib. bdg. 29.95 (*0-405-11317-X*) Ayer.

Barnes, William E., ed. Labor Problem: Plain Questions & Practical Answers. LC 75-156404. (American Labor Ser., No. 2). 1977. reprint ed. 19.95 (*0-405-02914-4*) Ayer.

Barnes, William H. & Morgan, John H. The Foreign Service of the U. S. Origins, Developments & Functions, 96--96. LC 78-13977. (U. S. Dept. of States Publication 7050, Dept. of Foreign Services Ser.: No. 96). (Illus.). 430p. 1979. reprint ed. lib. bdg. 79.50 (*0-313-20675-9*, BAFO) Greenwood.

Barnes, William J. Complex Variables. 130p. 1994. pap. 14.95 (*1-55082-128-8*, Pub. by Quarry Pr) LPC InBook.

Barnes, William L., ed. Earth Observing System, Vol. 2820. 314p. 1996. 66.00 (*0-8194-2208-8*) SPIE.

***Barnes, William L., ed.** Earth Observing Systems IV. 1999. pap. text 120.00 (*0-8194-3236-9*) SPIE.

Barnes, William L., ed. Earth Observing Systems II, Vol. 3117. LC 98-122095. 342p. 1997. 80.00 (*0-8194-2539-7*) SPIE.

— Earth Observing Systems III, Vol. 3439. 1998. 107.00 (*0-8194-2894-9*) SPIE.

Barnes, William R. & Ledebur, Larry C. The New Regional Economies: The U. S. Common Market & the Global Economy. LC 97-4751. (Cities & Planning Ser.: Vol. 2). 192p. 1997. text 42.00 (*0-7619-0938-9*); pap. text 19.95 (*0-7619-0939-7*) Sage.

Barnesa, Lewis. Feeding Your Child: Infant to Toddler. Oski, Frank A., ed. (Pediatrics Ser.). (Illus.). 32p. 1995. pap. 2.95 (*1-885274-13-0*) Health InfoNet Inc.

Barness, Amnon. Partners: The Extraordinary Life of an Ordinary Man. (Illus.). 508p. 1999. 24.95 (*1-58244-010-7*) Rutledge Bks.

Barness, Lewis, jt. auth. see Gilbert-Barness, Enid.

Barness, Lewis A. Advances in Pediatrics, Vol. 28. 1981. 54.50 (*0-8151-0500-2*) Mosby Inc.

— Advances in Pediatrics, Vol.45. (Illus.). 432p. 1998. text 74.95 (*0-8151-8401-8*, 25062) Mosby Inc.

— Advances in Pediatrics, Vol.46. (Illus.). 514p. 1999. text 78.00 (*0-8151-8402-6*, 25063) Mosby Inc.

— Handbook of Pediatric Physical Diagnosis. 7th ed. LC 97-50212. 224p. 1998. pap. text 34.00 (*0-7817-1682-9*) Lppncott W & W.

***Barness, Lewis A., ed.** Advances in Pediatrics, Vol. 48. (Illus.). 500p. 2001. write for info. (*0-323-01526-3*) Mosby Inc.

Barness, Lewis A., ed. see Advances in Pediatrics Staff.

Barnet. Current Issues & End Questions. 5th ed. 1998. pap. text, teacher ed. 5.00 (*0-312-19431-5*); pap. text, teacher ed. 10.00 (*0-312-19719-5*) St Martin.

— Current Issues & Enduring Questions. 1995. pap. text, teacher ed. 5.00 (*0-312-13682-X*); pap. text, teacher ed. 3.44 (*0-312-13681-1*) St Martin.

— Current Issues & Enduring Questions. 5th ed. LC 98-85187. xxxi, 863p. 1998. pap. text 38.95 (*0-312-17154-4*) St Martin.

Barnet. Introduction to Literature. 1997. write for info. (*0-201-33214-0*) Addison-Wesley.

Barnet. Literature for Composition: Essays, Fiction, Poetry & Drama : Includes 1998 MLA Guidelines. 4th ed. (C). 1998. pap. text 53.00 (*0-321-05787-2*) Addison-Wesley Educ.

— Practical Guide to Writing with Readings. 8th ed. LC 99-40170. 588p. (C). 1999. pap. text 49.00 (*0-321-02391-9*) Addison-Wesley Educ.

— Resources for Teaching Criteria. 1992. pap. text, teacher ed. 0.51 (*0-312-09132-X*) St Martin.

— A Short Guide to Writing about Art. 6th ed. LC 99-28221. 280p. (C). 1999. pap. 24.60 (*0-321-04605-6*) Addison-Wesley.

— A Short Guide to Writing about Literature. 8th ed. LC 98-49265. 423p. (C). 1999. pap. 24.20 (*0-321-02650-0*) Addson-Wesley Educ.

Barnet, ed. I'm Introduction Literture Expanded. 1997. text 12.00 (*0-673-54184-3*) P-H.

***Barnet & Berman.** Literature for Composition. 1998. pap. 45.00 (*0-201-45651-6*) Addison-Wesley.

Barnet, A. Barnet Introduction to Literature. 11th ed. (C). 1997. write for info. (*0-201-34602-8*) Addison-Wesley.

***Barnet, Ann B. & Barnet, Richard J.** Youngest Minds: Parenting & Genetic Inheritance in the Development of Intellect & Emotion. 352p. 1999. pap. 14.00 (*0-684-85440-6*, Touchstone) S&S Trade Pap.

Barnet, Ann B., jt. auth. see Barnet, Richard J.

Barnet, Charlie & Dance, Stanley. Those Swinging Years: The Autobiography of Charlie Barnet. (Illus.). 245p. 1992. reprint ed. pap. 12.95 (*0-306-80492-1*, Pub. by Da Capo) HarpC.

Barnet, Diane. Hospitals. LC 98-26924. (Vital Information Ser.). 112p. 1998. pap. 11.95 (*0-89594-908-3*) Crossing Pr.

***Barnet, Marie-Claire.** La Femme Cent Sexes Ou les Genres Communicants. 323p. 1998. 47.95 (*3-906760-26-X*, Pub. by P Lang) P Lang Pubng.

Barnet, Max. Driven, Notes of a Neurotic Entrepreneur: His Trials, Failures & Victories. Feller-Roth, Barbara, ed. LC 93-85983. 465p. (Orig.). 1995. pap. text 15.00 (*1-882521-01-3*) Stones Pt Pr.

— Go West Old Man: A Father's Journey Across America with His Son. Feller-Roth, Barbara, ed. LC 95-73039. 152p. (Orig.). 1996. pap. text 15.00 (*1-882521-03-X*) Stones Pt Pr.

Barnet, Miguel. Biography of a Runaway Slave. Hill, W. Nick, tr. from SPA. LC 94-12832. 217p. 1994. reprint ed. pap. 11.95 (*1-880684-18-7*) Curbstone.

— La Cancion de Rachel (Rachel's Song) (SPA.). 1996. pap. 12.50 (*0-679-76848-3*) Vin Bks.

— Rachel's Song. Hill, W. Nick, tr. from SPA. LC 91-55412. 125p. (Orig.). 1991. pap. 9.95 (*0-915306-87-5*) Curbstone.

Barnet, Peter & Wilkinson, MaryAnn. Decorative Arts, 1900: Highlights from Private Collections in Detroit. LC 93-35718. (Illus.). 158p. 1993. pap. 29.95 (*0-89558-139-6*) Det Inst Arts.

Barnet, Peter, ed. see Detroit Institute of Arts Staff.

Barnet, Richard J. Global Dreams: Imperial Corporations & the New World Order. 480p. 1995. per. 15.00 (*0-684-80027-6*) S&S Trade Pap.

— The Rockets' Red Glare: When America Goes to War: The Presidents & the People. 476p. 1990. 24.95 (*0-685-32960-7*) S&S Trade.

Barnet, Richard J. & Barnet, Ann B. The Youngest Minds: Parenting & Genetic Inheritance in the Development of Intellect & Emotion. LC 98-13450. 352p. 1998. 26.00 (*0-684-81537-0*) S&S Trade.

Barnet, Richard J. & Falk, Richard A., eds. Security in Disarmament. LC 65-12989. 451p. reprint ed. pap. 139.90 (*0-8357-7016-8*, 203340400085) Bks Demand.

Barnet, Richard J. & Jones, Peter D. Main Problems in American History Vol. 6: The United States & the Cold War & the Military-Industrial Complex. abr. ed. (PaperBook Series in History). (Illus.). 128p. (C). 1996. pap. text 2.25 (*1-877891-37-1*) Paperbook Pr Inc.

Barnet, Richard J., jt. auth. see Barnet, Ann B.

Barnet-Sanchez, Holly, ed. see Goldman, Shifra M., et al.

Barnet, Sylvan. Critical Thinking, Reading & Writing: A Brief Guide to Argument. 3rd ed. 1998. pap. 26.95 (*0-312-17153-6*) Bedford Bks.

— Eight Great Tragedies: With Essays. (Mentor Bks.: Md 195). 1957. 11.09 (*0-606-00794-6*, Pub. by Turtleback) Demco.

— The Harper Anthology of Fiction. LC 90-45410. 1300p. (C). 1997. pap. text 59.00 (*0-673-39634-7*) Addson-Wesley Educ.

***Barnet, Sylvan.** An Introduction to Literature: Fiction, Poetry, Drama. 12th ed. LC 00-40551. 2000. pap. write for info. (*0-321-06127-6*) Longman.

Barnet, Sylvan. Literature: Thinking, Reading & Writing Critically. 2nd ed. LC 96-18848. 1800p. (C). 1997. 65.00 (*0-673-52523-6*) Longman.

Barnet, Sylvan. Literature for Composition: Essays, Fiction, Poetry & Drama. 3rd ed. LC 91-16457. xxiii, 1100 p. 1992. teacher ed., student ed. write for info. (*0-673-52180-X*, GoodYrBooks) Addson-Wesley Educ.

Barnet, Sylvan. A Short Guide to Writing about Art. 5th ed. LC 95-51667. (Short Guide Ser.). (C). 1997. pap. text 18.75 (*0-673-52487-6*) Addson-Wesley Educ.

— Types of Drama: Plays & Contexts. 7th ed. LC 96-23983. 1200p. (C). 1997. pap. 60.66 (*0-673-52514-7*) Longman.

Barnet, Sylvan, ed. The Complete Signet Classic Shakespeare. 1776p. (C). 1972. text 76.50 (*0-15-512610-5*, Pub. by Harcourt Coll Pubs) Harcourt.

— 8 Great Comedies. LC 96-8049. 480p. 1996. pap. 13.95 (*0-452-01170-1*, Mer) NAL.

— 8 Great Tragedies. LC 96-8044. 480p. 1996. pap. 13.95 (*0-452-01172-8*, Mer) NAL.

— The Genius of the Early English Theatre. 1996. pap. 14.95 (*0-452-01164-7*, Plume) Dutton Plume.

Barnet, Sylvan, et al, eds. Literature for Composition: Essays, Fiction, Poetry & Drama. 5th ed. LC 99-16379. 1408p. (C). 1999. pap. 53.00 (*0-321-02153-3*) Addson-Wesley Educ.

Barnet, Sylvan, et al. An Introduction to Literature. 11th ed. LC 96-26839. 1500p. (C). 1997. pap. 55.00 (*0-673-52267-9*) Addison-Wesley.

Barnet, Sylvan, et al. Literature for Composition: Essays, Fiction, Poetry & Drama LC 83-11332. xvii, 774p. 1984. write for info. (*0-316-08151-5*) Little.

Barnet, Sylvan, jt. auth. see Stubbs, Marcia.

Barnet, Sylvan, jt. auth. see White, Merry I.

Barnet, Sylvan, ed. see Charney, Maurice.

Barnet, Sylvan, ed. see Shakespeare, William.

Barnett. Atlas of Feline Ophthalmology. 1997. text 150.00 (*0-7020-1662-4*, W B Saunders Co) Harcrt Hlth Sci Grp.

— Becoming a Complete Communicator. 2nd ed. 1996. 15.25 (*0-07-006990-5*) McGraw.

— Bonaparte. (Wordsworth Collection). 224p. 1998. pap. 11.95 (*1-85326-678-7*, Pub. by Wrdsworth Edits) Combined Pub.

— Brief Calculus with Tech. 1997. pap. text, student ed. 29.33 (*0-13-592825-7*) P-H.

— Calculus for Business Economic. 8th ed. 1998. pap. text, student ed. 27.80 (*0-13-961244-0*) P-H.

— College Algebra. 6th ed. 1998. 29.38 (*0-07-365584-8*) McGraw.

— College Algebra. 6th ed. 1999. cd-rom 20.63 (*0-07-013593-2*) McGraw.

— Derive Notebook-analytic Trig W/appl. 6th ed. (Math). 1995. suppl. ed. 25.50 (*0-534-94360-8*) PWS Pubs.

— Directory of Disability Support Services in Community Colleges, 1992. 1992. pap. 10.00 (*0-87117-249-6*, 1342) Comm Coll Pr Am Assn Comm Coll.

Barnett. Environmental Statistics. text. write for info. (*0-471-48971-9*) Wiley.

Barnett. Finite Math Business. 8th ed. 1998. pap. text, student ed. 27.80 (*0-13-932568-9*) P-H.

— Idol Temples & Crafty Priests: The Origins of Enlightenment Anticlericalism. LC 98-17289. 192p. 1999. text 59.95 (*0-312-21590-8*) St Martin.

— Intermediate Algebra. 5th ed. 1994. teacher ed. 61.25 (*0-07-004575-5*) McGraw.

— LBEC Contracts. 1996. 57.00 (*0-316-08072-1*, Aspen Law & Bus) Aspen Pub.

— Lire avec Plaisir. (College French Ser.). (FRE.). (C). 1987. pap., teacher ed. 2.95 (*0-8384-3660-9*) Heinle & Heinle.

— Lire avec Plaisir. 2nd ed. (C). 1992. pap., teacher ed. write for info. (*0-8384-3662-5*) Heinle & Heinle.

— London: The Hub of the Industrial Revolution. 224p. 2000. text 59.50 (*1-86064-196-2*, Pub. by I B T) St Martin.

— Precalculus. 3rd ed. 1993. teacher ed. 26.87 (*0-07-004963-7*) McGraw.

— Rationality: A Study in Behaviour. (Australian National University Press Ser.). 1996. text. write for info. (*0-08-032826-1*, Pergamon Pr) Elsevier.

— Setting Environmental Standards. 1997. lib. bdg. 49.95 (*0-412-82620-8*, Chap & Hall CRC) CRC Pr.

— Sol,odd Pblms - Analytic Trig W/applic. 4th ed. (Math). 1987. student ed. 10.50 (*0-534-08485-0*) Brooks-Cole.

— Stroke: Pathophysiology, Diagnosis & Management. 3rd ed. LC 98-3396. (C). 1998. text 250.00 (*0-443-07551-4*, B1184) Church.

***Barnett.** Student OLC Precalculus. 2000. 12.00 (*0-07-236674-5*, McGrw-H College) McGrw-H Hghr Educ.

Barnett. Syringomyelia MPN. 1998. text 57.00 (*0-7020-2237-3*, W B Saunders Co) Harcrt Hlth Sci Grp.

— El Universo y el Dr. Einstein. (Breviarios Ser.). (SPA.). pap. 4.99 (*968-16-0437-7*, Pub. by Fondo) Continental Bk.

— Veterinary Ophthalmology. 1996. text 62.95 (*0-7234-2956-1*) Wolfe Pubng AZ.

Barnett, et al. Finite Mathematics for Business, Economics, Life Sciences, & Social Sciences. 8th ed. LC 98-27337. 701p. 1998. 96.00 (*0-13-913179-5*) P-H.

Barnett, A. H., ed. Immunogenetics of Insulin-Dependent Diabetes. 1987. text 102.00 (*0-85200-840-6*) Kluwer Academic.

Barnett, Adrian, ed. Small Mammals (Excluding Bats) (C). 1992. 21.00 (*0-907649-51-3*, Pub. by Expedit Advisory Ctr) St Mut.

Barnett, Alan W. Community Murals. LC 79-21552. (Illus.). 520p. 1984. 60.00 (*0-8453-4731-4*, Cornwall Bks) Assoc Univ Prs.

— Murals of Protest. LC 79-21552. (Illus.). 520p. 1984. 60.00 (*0-87982-030-6*) Art Alliance.

***Barnett, Albert, et al.** Que Hacer para la Salud de las Personas de Edad. (SPA., Illus.). 2000. pap. 14.95 (*0-9701245-5-4*) IHA.

— What to Do for Senior Health. (Illus.). 2000. pap. 14.95 (*0-9701245-4-6*) IHA.

Barnett, Albert E. & Mayer, Gloria G., eds. Ambulatory Care Management & Practice. 526p. 1992. 90.00 (*0-8342-0313-8*, 20313) Aspen Pub.

Barnett, Albert E., jt. auth. see Mayer, Thomas A.

Barnett, Alva, jt. auth. see Conyers, James L., Jr.

Barnett, Alva, jt. ed. see Conyers, James L.

Barnett, Andrew, jt. auth. see Hurst, Christopher.

Barnett, Anthony. Anti-Beauty. 64p. 1999. pap. 14.99 (*0-907954-27-8*, Pub. by Allardyce Barnett) SPD-Small Pr Dist.

— Black Gypsy: The Recordings of Eddie South: An Annotated Discography & Itinerary. (Illus.). 128p. 1999. pap. 55.00 incl. audio (*0-907954-26-X*) Allardyce Barnett.

— Capp & Rubato. 62p. 1995. 12.00 (*0-9521256-2-5*, Pub. by Invisible Bks) SPD-Small Pr Dist.

— A Forest Utilization Family: Poems. deluxe limited ed. (Burning Deck Poetry Chapbooks Ser.). 28p. 1982. pap. 15.00 (*0-930901-09-6*) Burning Deck.

***Barnett, Anthony.** Lisa Lisa: Two Prosays. 36p. 2000. pap. 15.00 (*0-907954-28-6*, Pub. by Allardyce Barnett) SPD-Small Pr Dist.

Barnett, Anthony. Little Stars & Straw Breasts. (Illus.). 52p. (Orig.). 1993. pap. write for info. (*0-907954-20-0*, Pub. by Allardyce Barnett) SPD-Small Pr Dist.

— North North, I Said, No, Wait a Minute, South, Oh I Don't Know (148 Political Poems) 64p. (Orig.). 1985. pap. 9.00 (*0-907954-09-X*, Pub. by Allardyce Barnett) SPD-Small Pr Dist.

— Poem about Music. (Burning Deck Poetry Ser.). 1974. 15.00 (*0-930900-00-6*); pap. 4.00 (*0-930900-01-4*) Burning Deck.

— The Resting Bell: Collected Poems. 384p. (Orig.). 1987. 28.00 (*0-907954-06-5*); pap. 16.00 (*0-907954-07-3*) SPD-Small Pr Dist.

— Up Jumped the Devil & Desert Sands, 2 vols. Incl. Desert Sands: The Recordings & Performances & Stuff Smith, an Annotated Discography. LC 95-170462. 348 p. 1995. pap. Not sold separately incl. audio (*0-907954-16-2*, Pub. by Allardyce Barnett); Up Jumped the Devil: The Supplement to Desert Sands, the Recordings & Performances of Stuff Smith. LC 98-164037. (Illus.). 96p. (Orig.). 1998. pap. Not sold separately (*0-907954-24-3*, Pub. by Allardyce Barnett); 75.00 (*0-907954-25-1*, Pub. by Allardyce Barnett) SPD-Small Pr Dist.

Barnett, Anthony, tr. see Albiach, Anne-Marie.

Barnett, Anthony, tr. see Auster, Paul, et al.

Barnett, Anthony, tr. see Berg, Oyvind.

Barnett, Anthony, tr. see Vesaas, Tarjei.

Barnett, Anthony, tr. & illus. see Zanzotto, Andrea.

Barnett, Arthur Doak. China after Mao: With Selected Documents. LC 67-14406. (Walter E. Edge Lectures). 297p. 1967. reprint ed. pap. 92.10 (*0-7837-9295-6*, 206003400004) Bks Demand.

— China & the Major Powers in East Asia. LC 77-21981. 416p. 1978. pap. 18.95 (*0-8157-0823-8*) Brookings.

— China Policy: Old Problems & New Challenges. LC 76-51538. 130p. 1977. 28.95 (*0-8157-0822-X*); pap. 10.95 (*0-8157-0821-1*) Brookings.

— China's Economy in Global Perspective. LC 81-1193. 752p. 1981. 39.95 (*0-8157-0826-2*); pap. 18.95 (*0-8157-0825-4*) Brookings.

— China's Far West. 688p. 1997. reprint ed. 40.00 (*957-638-258-0*) Oriental Bk Store.

— China's Far West: Four Decades of Change. LC 93-4194. 688p. (C). 1994. pap. 40.00 (*0-8133-1774-6*, Pub. by Westview) HarpC.

— The FX Decision: "Another Crucial Moment" in U.S.-China-Taiwan Relations. LC 81-70778. (Studies in Defense Policy). 50p. 1981. pap. 7.95 (*0-8157-0827-0*) Brookings.

— Uncertain Passage: China's Transition to the Post-Mao Era. LC 73-22482. 405p. reprint ed. pap. 125.60 (*0-608-14526-2*, 202536100043) Bks Demand.

— United States Arms Sales: The China-Taiwan Tangle. LC 82-72117. (Studies in Defense Policy). 78p. reprint ed. pap. 30.00 (*0-608-18066-1*, 202797200057) Bks Demand.

Barnett, Arthur Doak, ed. Communist Strategies in Asia. LC 75-32454. 293p. 1976. reprint ed. lib. bdg. 38.50 (*0-8371-8547-5*, BACSA, Greenwood Pr) Greenwood.

Barnett, B. Aspects of Vocal Multiphonics. 7.25 (*0-939044-19-6*) Lingua Pr.

Barnett, B. Lewis, Jr. Between the Lines: (Reflections of a Family Physician) (C). 1989. pap. 18.95 (*0-942295-17-X*) Soc Tchrs Fam Med.

Barnett, B. M., et al, eds. Proceedings of the Symposium on New Sealed Rechargeable Batteries & Supercapacitors. LC 93-70060. (Proceedings Ser.: Vol. 93-23). 532p. 1993. 54.00 (*1-56677-056-4*) Electrochem Soc.

Barnett, Barbara A., jt. auth. see Ellison, Sheila.

Barnett, Beatrice. Urine-Therapy: It May Save Your Life. 7th rev. ed. 56p. 1992. pap. 9.95 (*0-9622182-5-1*) Lifestyle Inst.

Barnett, Betty. Friend Raising: Building a Missionary Support Team That Lasts. 178p. 1991. pap. 8.99 (*0-927545-10-1*) YWAM Pub.

Barnett, Bruce G. & Whitaker, Kathryn S. Restructuring for Student Learning. LC 96-60049. (School Leader's Library). 195p. 1996. pap. 34.95 (*1-56676-382-7*, 764076) Scarecrow.

Barnett, Bruce G., jt. auth. see Sagor, Richard.

Barnett, C. H. Practical Embryology. 124p. 1969. pap. 19.95 (*0-8464-1326-4*) Beekman Pubs.

Barnett, Carellen. Trail Riding Western Montana. LC 96-49969. (Illus.). 160p. 1997. pap. 14.95 (*1-56044-336-7*) Falcon Pub Inc.

Barnett, Carne, et al. Fractions, Decimals, Ratios & Percents: Hard to Teach & Hard to Learn? (Casebook) LC 94-19983. 127p. 1994. pap. text 21.00 (*0-435-08357-0*, 08357) Heinemann.

— Fractions, Decimals, Ratios & Percents: Hard to Teach & Hard to Learn? (Facilitator's Guide) LC 94-19983. 93p. 1994. pap. text, teacher ed. 22.50 (*0-435-08358-9*, 08358) Heinemann.

Barnett, Carol. The Boy & the Donkey. (Illus.). 64p. (J). (ps-3). 1994. 7.95 (*0-8442-9417-9*, Natl Textbk Co) NTC Contemp Pub Co.

— The Boy & the Donkey. (StoryLand Fables Ser.). (Illus.). 48p. (J). (ps-4). 1995. 8.95 incl. audio (*0-8442-9429-2*) NTC Contemp Pub Co.

— Goldilocks & the Three Bears. (Illus.). 64p. (J). (ps-3). 1994. 7.95 (*0-8442-9416-0*, Natl Textbk Co) NTC Contemp Pub Co.

— Goldilocks & the Three Bears. (StoryLand Fables Ser.). (Illus.). 48p. (J). (ps-4). 1995. 8.95 (*0-8442-9428-4*) NTC Contemp Pub Co.

— The Little Red Hen. (Illus.). 64p. (J). (ps-3). 1994. 7.95 (*0-8442-9418-7*, Natl Textbk Co) NTC Contemp Pub Co.

— The Little Red Hen. (StoryLand Fables Ser.). (Illus.). 48p. (J). (ps-4). 1995. pap. 8.95 incl. audio (*0-8442-9430-6*) NTC Contemp Pub Co.

— The Milkmaid & Her Pail. (Illus.). 64p. (J). (ps-3). 1994. 7.95 (*0-8442-9421-7*, Natl Textbk Co) NTC Contemp Pub Co.

— The Milkmaid & Her Pail. (StoryLand Fables Ser.). (Illus.). 48p. (J). (ps-4). 1995. 8.95 (*0-8442-9433-0*) NTC Contemp Pub Co.

Barnett, Carol & Aesop. The Lion & the Mouse. (Illus.). 64p. (J). (ps-3). 1994. 7.95 (*0-8442-9420-9*, Natl Textbk Co) NTC Contemp Pub Co.

— The Lion & the Mouse. (StoryLand Fables Ser.). (Illus.). 48p. (J). (ps-4). 1995. pap. 8.95 incl. audio (*0-8442-9432-2*) NTC Contemp Pub Co.

Barnett, Carole K., jt. ed. see Hirschhorn, Larry.

Barnett, Charles R. Popol Vuh of the Jaguar Priests: Ancient Maya Book of Creation. Devilliers De Knight, Silvia, tr. LC 89-84739. (ENG & SPA., Illus.). 100p. (Orig.). 1994. pap. 9.95 (*0-944482-31-7*) Except Bks NM.

Barnett, Charles R., jt. ed. see Barker, Barry W.

Barnett, Charles W. Battle of Point Pleasant, October 10, 1774. 1998. pap. 15.00 (*0-87012-591-5*) McClain. Battle of Point Pleasant is a captivating in-depth account of the battle of "Tu-Endie-Wei" at Point Pleasant, West Virginia. Lists of battle participants & a biographical index enhance this reprint of historical facts & quoted material. This collection of fascinating information is a must for all history buffs. ***Publisher Paid Annotation.***

Barnett, Cheryl Kay & Olson, Alger James. Sentimental Journey. LC 98-85325. 192p. 1999. pap. 11.95 (*1-56315-195-2*, Pub. by SterlingHse) Natl Bk Netwk.

Barnett, Christopher R., jt. ed. see Barnett, Yvonne A.

Barnett, Claudia, ed. Wendy Wasserstein: A Casebook. LC 98-40418. (Casebooks on Modern Dramatists: Vol. 26). 256p. 1998. 55.00 (*0-8153-2953-9*, H2075) Garland.

Barnett, Clifford R., et al. Poland. LC 58-11469. (Area & Country Surveys Ser.). 479p. 1958. 15.00 (*0-87536-901-4*) HRAFP.

Barnett, Clifford R., jt. auth. see MacGaffey, Wyatt.

Barnett, Colin W. The Impact of Historic Preservation on New Bern, North Carolina: From Tryon Palace to the Coor-Cook House. LC 93-71774. (Illus.). 144p. (Orig.). 1993. pap. 12.95 (*1-878177-04-4*) Bandit Bks.

Barnett, Colleen A. Mystery Women 1980-89: An Encyclopedia of Leading Women Characters in Mystery Fiction, 2. write for info. (*0-938313-41-X*) E B Houchin.

***Barnett, Correlli.** Desert Generals. (Military Classics). (Illus.). 351p. 2000. pap. 10.95 (*0-304-35280-2*) Continuum.

— Swordbearers: Supreme Command in the First World War. (Military Classics). 2000. pap. 9.95 (*0-304-35283-7*) Continuum.

Barnett, Correlli. The Swordbearers: Supreme Command in the First World War. LC 74-19057. (Illus.). 416p. 1975. reprint ed. pap. 15.95 (*0-253-20175-6*, MB 175) Ind U Pr.

Barnett, Correlli, intro. Hitler's Generals. LC 90-63720. (Illus.). 528p. 1991. reprint ed. pap. 14.95 (*0-688-10383-9*, Quil) HarperTrade.

Barnett, Cynthia. Ben's Gift: Reading Level 3. (Sundown Fiction Collection). 64p. 1993. 3.95 (*0-88336-210-4*); audio 9.95 (*0-88336-255-4*) New Readers.

Barnett, D., jt. ed. see Kemp, Nan.

Barnett, Daniel. Avoiding Unfair Dismissal Claims. 284p. 1998. pap. 40.95 (*0-471-96564-2*) Wiley.

***Barnett, Dave.** Electric Power Generation: A Nontechnical Guide. LC 99-56998. 250p. 1999. 64.95 (*0-87814-753-5*) PennWell Bks.

Barnett, David. Literature vs. Theatre: Textual Problems & Theatrical Realization in the Later Plays of Heiner Muller. LC 98-23149. (British & Irish Studies in German Language & Literature: No. 14). 289p. 1998. pap. text 37.95 (*0-8204-4203-8*) P Lang Pubng.

— Plainsong. 75p. 1990. pap. 7.95 (*0-912549-41-6*) Bread & Butter.

Barnett, David. My Listen & Learn Bible. LC 94-23391. 96p. (J). 1994. 5.99 (*0-7814-0092-9*, Chariot Bks) Chariot Victor.

Barnett, David B., et al, eds. Congestive Cardiac Failure: Pathophysiology & Treatment. LC 93-7106. (Fundamental & Clinical Cardiology Ser.: Vol. 14). (Illus.). 408p. 1993. text 175.00 (*0-8247-8821-4*) Dekker.

Barnett, David W. Nondiscriminatory Multifactored Assessment: A Sourcebook. (Illus.). 214p. 1983. pap. 20.95 (*0-89885-082-7*, Kluwer Acad Hman Sci) Kluwer Academic.

Barnett, David W., et al. Designing Preschool Interventions: A Practitioner's Guide. LC 99-33760. (School Practitioner Ser.). 380p. 1999. lib. bdg. 36.00 (*1-57230-491-X*, CO491) Guilford Pubns.

Barnett, Dennis. SAP R-3'S ABAP-4 Command Reference. LC 97-68102. 326p. 1997. 29.99 (*0-7897-1416-7*) Que.

Barnett, Diana. Research It! Write It! A Step-by-Step Guide to Research & Writing. 2nd ed. LC 97-37472. 32p. 1997. pap. 6.95 (*1-57950-016-1*, Alleyside) Highsmith Pr.

Barnett, Dianna L. & Browning, William D. A Primer on Sustainable Building. (Illus.). 138p. (Orig.). 1995. pap. 16.95 (*1-881071-05-7*) Rocky Mtn Inst.

Barnett, Dick. Re-Ignite Your Business: The Secret of Leading with Confidence, Ease & Certainty. LC 97-91544. (Illus.). 126p. (Orig.). 1997. pap. 15.95 (*1-890331-00-7*) Confident Leader.

Barnett, Donald F. & Crandall, Robert W. Up from the Ashes: The Rise of the Steel Minimill in the United States. LC 85-48201. 135p. 1986. 28.95 (*0-8157-0834-3*); pap. 10.95 (*0-8157-0833-5*) Brookings.

Barnett, Donald L. & McGregor, Jeffrey P. Speaking in Other Tongues: A Scholarly Defense. 840p. 1986. 25.00 (*0-934287-23-6*) Comm Chapel Pubns.

— Tongues: The Answer to the Debate. 299p. (Orig.). 1988. pap. 9.95 (*0-934287-24-4*) Comm Chapel Pubns.

Barnett, Donald L. & Njama, Karari. Mau Mau from Within: Autobiography & Analysis of Kenya's Peasant Revolt. LC 65-24519. (Illus.). 510p. reprint ed. pap. 158.10 (*0-7837-3911-7*, 204375900010) Bks Demand.

Barnett, Douglas E. X-Wing Alliance: Official Strategy Guide. LC 99-70164. 1999. pap. 19.99 (*0-7615-2076-7*) Prima Pub.

Barnett, Douglas E., jt. auth. see Vondra, Joan.

Barnett, Doyle. 20 Communication Tips for Couples: A 30-Minute Guide to a Better Relationship. LC 95-2938. 112p. 1995. pap. 8.95 (*1-880032-68-6*) New Wrld Lib.

Barnett, E. & Morley, P. Clinical Diagnostic Ultrasound. (C). (gr. 13). 1986. 350.00 (*0-632-00897-0*, B-0482-6) Mosby Inc.

Barnett, Edgar. Analytical Hypnotherapy: Principles & Practice. 510p. 1989. reprint ed. 32.50 (*0-930298-30-6*) Westwood Pub Co.

— Unlock Your Mind & Be Free! A Practical Approach to Hypnotherapy. 153p. 1984. reprint ed. pap. 9.95 (*0-930298-49-7*) Westwood Pub Co.

***Barnett, Elaine.** Big Book of Presbyterian Stewardship. (Illus.). 176p. 2000. pap. 24.95 (*0-664-50157-5*) Geneva Press.

***Barnett, Elizabeth, et al.** Men & Heart Disease: An Atlas of Racial & Ethnic Disparities in Mortality. (Illus.). 2000. pap. text. write for info. (*0-9665085-2-1*) Prevention Ctr.

Barnett, Ellis & Barnett, Hirst, eds. Debating the Constitution: New Perspectives on Constitutional Reform. 220p. (Orig.). 1993. pap. 24.95 (*0-7456-1081-1*) Blackwell Pubs.

***Barnett, Fiona.** Complete Guide to Flower Arranging. (Illus.). 2000. 14.95 (*0-7548-0466-6*, Lorenz Bks) Anness Pub.

— Flower Arranging. 256p. 2000. pap. 19.95 (*1-84215-097-9*) Anness Pub.

Barnett, Fiona. The New Flower Arranger: Contemporary Approaches to Floral Design. (Illus.). 256p. 1995. 32.50 (*1-85967-080-6*, Lorenz Bks) Anness Pub.

— Wedding Flowers. 1999. pap. text 14.95 (*1-85029-685-5*) Conran Octopus.

— Wedding Flowers. 1991. 24.95 (*0-671-72834-2*) S&S Trade.

Barnett, Frank, ed. see Wilson, Cheryl D.

Barnett, Frank R., jt. ed. see Lord, Carnes.

Barnett, Franklin. Excavation of Main Pueblo at Fitzmaurice Ruin & Fitzmaurice Ruin Booklet. (Illus.). 178p. 1974. pap. 7.50 (*0-89734-017-5*, SP017-5) Mus Northern Ariz.

Barnett, Fred. Shark Stories Vol. 1: Amazing but True. (Illus.). 128p. (Orig.). 1996. pap. 7.95 (*1-887394-00-1*, 1) F Barnett Studios.

***Barnett-Friel, Patricia.** Aspects of Personal Faith: Personality & Religion in Western & Eastern Traditions. 88p. 2000. 49.00 (*1-57309-414-5*); pap. 27.50 (*1-57309-413-7*) U Pr of Amer.

Barnett, Gary H., intro. Proceedings of the Thirty-Second Annual Professional Development Conference. (Illus.). 275p. (Orig.). 1993. pap. 12.95 (*0-939874-92-X*, 431093) ASSE.

Barnett, Gene A. Lanford Wilson. LC 87-5657. (Twayne's United States Authors Ser.: No. 490). 184p. (C). 1987. 28.95 (*0-8057-7498-X*) Macmillan.

Barnett, Gene H., et al, eds. Image-Guided Neurosurgery: Clinical Applications of Surgical Navigation. LC 98-13928. (Illus.). 264p. 1998. 160.00 (*1-57626-083-6*, QMP) Quality Med Pub.

Barnett, George. Progress in Communication Sciences, Vol. 14. Palmer, Mark T., ed. 300p. 1998. 78.50 (*1-56750-347-0*); pap. 39.50 (*1-56750-365-9*) Ablx Pub.

— Whitetail Monarchs: Legends of Autumn. LC 99-38315. (Illus.). 160p. 1999. 29.50 (*1-57223-267-6*) Willow Creek Pr.

Barnett, George & Boster, Franklin J., eds. Progress in Communication Sciences Vol. 13: Advances in Persuasion. (Illus.). 300p. 1997. text 78.50 (*1-56750-277-6*) Ablx Pub.

Barnett, George & Richards, William D., eds. Progress in Communication Sciences, Vol. 12. 304p. 1993. 78.50 (*1-56750-067-6*); pap. 39.50 (*1-56750-068-4*) Ablx Pub.

Barnett, George & Thayer, Lee, eds. Organization - Communication: Emerging Perspectives, Vol. 5. (Illus.). 291p. 1997. text 78.50 (*1-56750-195-8*) Ablx Pub.

Barnett, George, jt. auth. see Thayer, Lee.

Barnett, George, jt. ed. see Saltiel, E. H.

Barnett, George, ed. see Valente, Thomas W.

Barnett, George A., ed. Organization - Communication: Emerging Perspectives, Vol. 6. 300p. 1998. pap. 39.50 (*1-56750-315-2*); text 73.25 (*1-56750-314-4*) Ablx Pub.

Barnett, George A., jt. auth. see Sawhney, Harmeet.

Barnett, George A., ed. see Stone, John F.

Barnett, George E. The Printers: A Study in American Trade Unionism. 1977. lib. bdg. 59.95 (*0-8490-2481-1*) Gordon Pr.

— State Banking in the United States. 1972. 59.95 (*0-8490-1122-1*) Gordon Pr.

— State Banking in the United States Since the Passage of the National Bank Act. LC 78-63887. (Johns Hopkins University. Studies in the Social Sciences. Thirtieth Ser. 1912: Nos. 2-3). reprint ed. 39.50 (*0-404-61141-9*) AMS Pr.

— State Banks & Trust Companies: Since the Passage of the National Bank Act. LC 68-30516. (Reprints of Economic Classics Ser.). 366p. 1969. reprint ed. 45.00 (*0-678-00503-6*) Kelley.

Barnett, George E. & McCabe, David A. Mediation, Investigation & Arbitration in Industrial Disputes. LC 75-156403. (American Labor Ser., No. 2). 1977. reprint ed. 21.95 (*0-405-02913-6*) Ayer.

Barnett, George E., jt. auth. see Hollander, Jacob H.

Barnett, George E., jt. ed. see Hollander, Jacob H.

Barnett, George L. Charles Lamb. (Twayne's English Authors Ser.). (C). 1976. 20.95 (*0-8057-6668-5*) Irvington.

— Charles Lamb: The Evolution of Elia. LC 72-6858. (English Literature Ser.: No. 33). 1972. reprint ed. lib. bdg. 75.00 (*0-8383-1652-2*) M S G Haskell Hse.

Barnett, George L., ed. Eighteenth Century British Novelists on the Novel. LC 68-19045. (Goldentree Books in English Literature). (Orig.). (C). 1968. pap. text 11.95 (*0-89197-136-X*) Irvington.

— Nineteenth-Century British Novelists on the Novel. LC 75-130791. (Goldentree Books in English Literature). (Orig.). (C). 1971. 42.00 (*0-89197-317-6*); pap. text 14.95 (*0-89197-318-4*) Irvington.

Barnett, Glenn. When Jesus Walked: A Story of the Christ. 253p. (Orig.). 1991. pap. 12.00 (*0-9629405-0-X*) Wide Awake Pr.

— Zenobia: Empress of the East. 360p. 1994. pap. 15.00 (*0-9629405-1-8*) Wide Awake Pr.

Barnett, Gordon, et al. The Head: A Legend Is Born. 96p. 1996. pap. 18.00 (*0-671-00104-3*) PB.

Barnett, H. G. Culture Element Distributions No. VII: Oregon Coast. fac. ed. (University of California Publications: No. 1:3). 54p. (C). 1937. reprint ed. pap. 6.56 (*1-55567-115-2*) Coyote Press.

— Culture Element Distributions No. IX: Gulf of Georgia Salish. fac. ed. Lowie, Robert H. et al, eds. (University of California Publications: No. 1:5). 82p. (C). 1939. reprint ed. pap. 9.38 (*1-55567-117-9*) Coyote Press.

Barnett, H. L. & Hunter, Barry B. Illustrated Genera of Imperfect Fungi. 4th ed. LC 98-72362. 240p. 1998. spiral bd. 48.00 (*0-89054-192-2*) Am Phytopathol Soc.

Barnett, H. Villiers, tr. see Massenet, Jules E.

Barnett, Harold C. Toxic Debts & the Superfund Dilemma. LC 93-32059. xviii, 334p. (C). 1994. text 59.95 (*0-8078-2124-1*); pap. text 24.95 (*0-8078-4435-7*) U of NC Pr.

Barnett, Harold J. Atomic Energy in the United States Economy: A Consideration of Certain Industrial, Regional, & Economic Development Aspects. Bruchey, Stuart, ed. LC 78-22658. (Energy in the American Economy Ser.). (Illus.). 1979. lib. bdg. 28.95 (*0-405-11962-3*) Ayer.

Barnett, Harold J & Morse, Chandler. Scarcity & Growth: The Economics of Natural Resource Availability. LC 63-9742. 288p. 1963. pap. 18.95 (*0-8018-0057-9*) Resources Future.

Barnett, Henrietta O., jt. auth. see Barnett, Samuel A.

Barnett, Henry J., et al, eds. Stroke: Pathophysiology, Diagnosis, & Management, Vol. 1. LC 85-19553. (Illus.). 681p. reprint ed. pap. 200.00 (*0-7837-3060-8*, 204275400001) Bks Demand.

An Asterisk (*) at the beginning of an entry indicates that the title is appearing for the first time.

— Stroke: Pathophysiology, Diagnosis, & Management, Vol. 2. LC 85-19553. (Illus.). 671p. reprint ed. pap. 200.00 (*0-7837-3061-6*, 204275400002) Bks Demand.

Barnett, Hilaire. Constitutional & Administrative Law. 836p. 1995. pap. 38.00 (*1-85941-114-2*, Pub. by Cavendish Pubng) Gaunt.

— Constitutional & Administrative Law. 2nd ed. 1101p. 1998. pap. 47.00 (*1-85941-403-6*) Gaunt.

— Introduction to Feminist Jurisprudence. 349p. 1998. pap. 27.00 (*1-85941-237-8*) Gaunt.

— Sourcebook on Feminist Jurisprudence. LC 96-144393. (Sourcebook Ser.). 639p. 1997. pap. 98.00 (*1-85941-113-4*, Pub. by Cavendish Pubng) Gaunt.

Barnett, Hirst, jt. ed. see Barnett, Ellis.

Barnett, Homer G. The Coast Salish of British Columbia, No. 4--4. LC 75-25251. (Univ. of Oregon Monographs, Studies in Anthropology: No. 4). (Illus.). 320p. 1975. reprint ed. lib. bdg. 35.00 (*0-8371-8381-2*, BACSB, Greenwood Pr) Greenwood.

***Barnett, Iris Alphia Blair.** Life Talk. 2000. pap. 8.95 (*0-533-13425-0*) Vantage.

Barnett, J. A., et al. Yeasts: Characteristics & Identification. 2nd ed. (Illus.). 1012p. (C). 1991. text 260.00 (*0-521-35056-5*) Cambridge U Pr.

***Barnett, J. A., et al.** Yeasts: Characteristics & Identification. 3rd ed. (Illus.). 1152p. (C). 2000. 320.00 (*0-521-57396-3*) Cambridge U Pr.

Barnett, James H. The American Christmas: A Study in National Culture. LC 75-22799. (America in Two Centuries Ser.). 1976. reprint ed. 19.95 (*0-405-07671-1*) Ayer.

Barnett, James M. The Diaconate: A Full & Equal Order. rev. ed. LC 94-4923. 256p. (C). 1995. pap. 18.00 (*1-56338-093-5*) TPI PA.

Barnett, Janet & Russell, Randy. The Granny Curse: True Ghost Stories of East Tennessee. LC 99-46957. 112p. 1999. pap. 9.95 (*0-89587-185-8*) Blair.

Barnett, Janet, jt. auth. see Russell, Randy.

Barnett, Jeanie M. Ghana: Major World Nations. LC 97-23012. (Major World Nations Ser.). (Illus.). 144p. (YA). (gr. 5 up). 1999. lib. bdg. 19.95 (*0-7910-4739-3*) Chelsea Hse.

Barnett, Jeanie M., ed. see Wilder, Judith Luther.

Barnett, Jeffery R. Future War: An Assessment of Aerospace Campaigns in 2010. (Illus.). 169p. (C). 1998. pap. text 35.00 (*0-7881-7102-X*) DIANE Pub.

Barnett, Jeffrey R. Future War: An Assessment of Aerospace Campaigns in 2010. (Illus.). 196p. 1996. pap. 12.00 (*1-58566-004-3*) Air Univ.

Barnett, Jill. Bewitching. 464p. 1993. per. 6.50 (*0-671-77863-3*, Pocket Star Bks) PB.

— Bewitching. large type ed. LC 95-17591. 657p. 1995. reprint ed. 22.95 (*0-7862-0500-8*) Thorndike Pr.

— Carried Away. 1996. pap. write for info. (*0-614-98088-7*, Pocket Books) PB.

— Carried Away. 352p. 1996. per. 6.50 (*0-671-52144-6*) PB.

— Dreaming. Marrow, Linda, ed. 336p. (Orig.). 1994. per. 6.50 (*0-671-77868-4*) PB.

— Hearts Haven. Scognamiglio, John, ed. 320p. (Orig.). 1990. mass mkt. 5.99 (*0-671-68412-4*) PB.

— Imagine. 392p. (Orig.). 1995. mass mkt. 6.50 (*0-671-52143-8*, PB Trade Paper) PB.

— Just a Kiss Away. Scognamiglio, John, ed. 352p. 1991. mass mkt. 5.99 (*0-671-72342-1*) PB.

— Just a Kiss Away. 1998. mass mkt. 3.99 (*0-671-02372-1*) S&S Trade.

— A Stockingful of Joy. 400p. 1997. mass mkt. 6.99 (*0-451-40800-4*, Onyx) NAL.

— Surrender a Dream. Marrow, Linda, ed. 384p. (Orig.). 1991. mass mkt. 5.99 (*0-671-72341-3*) PB.

— Wicked. 387p. 1999. mass mkt. 6.99 (*0-671-03412-X*, Pocket Star Bks) PB.

— Wild. 320p. 1998. per. 6.50 (*0-671-00413-1*) S&S Trade.

— Wonderful. 1997. per. 5.99 (*0-671-00412-3*) S&S Trade.

Barnett, Jill, et al. That Summer Place. 1998. mass mkt. 6.99 (*1-55166-449-6*) Harlequin Bks.

Barnett, Jo Ellen. Time's Pendulum. LC 98-49612. 16p. (C). 1999. pap. 14.00 (*0-15-600649-9*) Harcourt.

***Barnett, Jo Ellen.** Time's Pendulum: The Quest to Capture Time - From Sundials to Atomic Clocks. LC 98-4624. (Illus.). 348p. (C). 1998. 27.95 (*0-306-45787-3*, Plenum Trade) Perseus Pubng.

Barnett, John. Barnett's Manual. 3rd ed. (Illus.). 848p. 1996. ring bd. 150.00 (*1-884737-16-1*) VeloPress.

***Barnett, John.** Barnett's Manual, 4 vols. 4th ed. 2000. pap. 99.95 (*1-884737-85-4*); pap. 29.95 (*1-884737-86-2*); pap. 29.95 (*1-884737-87-0*); pap. 29.95 (*1-884737-88-9*); pap. 29.95 (*1-884737-89-7*) VeloPress.

Barnett, John. How to Feel Good As You Age: A Voice of Experience. LC 99-35903. 360p. 1999. 24.95 (*1-889242-07-1*, Pub. by VanderWyk & Burnham); pap. 12.95 (*1-889242-08-X*, Pub. by VanderWyk & Burnham) ACCESS Pubs Network.

Barnett, Jonathan. The Fractured Metropolis: Improving the New City, Restoring the Old City, Reshaping the Region. 256p. 1996. pap. 25.00 (*0-06-430222-9*, Pub. by Westview) HarpC.

***Barnett, Jonathan, ed.** Planning for a New Century: The Regional Agenda. (Illus.). 218p. 2000. pap. 29.95 (*1-55963-806-0*, Shearwater Bks) Island Pr.

Barnett, Judith B. Marine Science Journals & Serials: An Analytical Guide, 7. LC 86-7594. (Annotated Bibliographies of Serials: A Subject Approach Ser.: No. 7). 191p. 1986. lib. bdg. 59.95 (*0-313-24717-X*, BMS/, Greenwood Pr) Greenwood.

Barnett, K. C. Color Atlas & Textbook of Equine Ophthalmology. (C). (gr. 13). 1994. text 110.00 (*0-8151-0420-0*, 23000) Mosby Inc.

Barnett, K. C., et al. Color Atlas & Text of Equine Ophthalmology. 1994. text 135.00 (*0-7234-1925-6*) Wolfe Pub.

Barnett, L. D. Brahma-Knowledge, Philosophy of Vedanta. 1973. 59.95 (*0-87968-780-0*) Gordon Pr.

— Brahman Knowledge: An Outline of the Philosophy of the Vedanta As Set Forth by the Upanishads & by Sankara (1907) 166p. 1998. reprint ed. pap. 12.95 (*0-7661-0608-X*) Kessinger Pub.

— Heart of India (1913) 125p. 1998. reprint ed. pap. 14.95 (*0-7661-0609-8*) Kessinger Pub.

Barnett, L. Margaret. British Food Policy During the First World War. 256p. (C). 1985. text 49.95 (*0-04-942189-1*) Routledge.

Barnett, LaQuela, jt. auth. see Romeo, Joe.

Barnett, Larry D. Legal Construct, Social Concept: A Macrosociological Perspective on Law. LC 92-42409. (Social Institutions & Social Change Ser.). 190p. 1993. lib. bdg. 49.95 (*0-202-30479-5*) Aldine de Gruyter.

— Mutual Funds & Federal Regulation. 458p. 1999. ring bd. 65.00 (*1-879581-64-7*) Lupus Pubns.

Barnett, LaShonda K. Callaloo: And Other Lesbian Love Stories. LC 99-25696. 192p. 1999. pap. 10.95 (*1-892281-08-2*) New Victoria Pubs.

Barnett, LeRoy, compiled by. Shipping Literature of the Great Lakes: A Catalog of Company Publications, 1852-1990. LC 92-53725. 1992. 27.95 (*0-87013-317-9*) Mich St U Pr.

Barnett, LEslie, jt. auth. see Gaddo, Don.

Barnett, Libby, et al. Reiki Energy Medicine: Bringing the Healing Touch into Home, Hospital, & Hospice. LC 96-3962. (Illus.). 192p. 1996. pap. 12.95 (*0-89281-633-3*, Heal Arts VT) Inner Tradit.

Barnett, Lincoln. The Universe & Dr. Einstein. 18.95 (*0-8488-0146-6*); pap. 12.95 (*0-685-73713-6*) Amereon Ltd.

Barnett, Lionel D. Antiquities of India: An Account of the History & Culture of Ancient Hindustan. (C). 1994. 36.00 (*81-206-0530-6*, Pub. by Asian Educ Servs) S Asia.

Barnett, Lisa, et al. The Herbaria of the World. 8th rev. ed. Greuter, W., ed. LC 90-13328. (Regnum Vegetabile Ser.: Vol. 120, Pt. I). x, 693p. 1990. 87.50 (*0-89327-358-9*, 042963, Pub. by Koeltz Sci Bks) Lubrecht & Cramer.

Barnett, Lisa, ed. see Chapman, Gerald.

Barnett, Lisa A., jt. auth. see Scott, Melissa.

Barnett, Lizzie. Memoirs of Lizzie Campbell Doss Barnett. (Wisdom of the Ages Ser.: Vol. 2). 51p. (Orig.). 1996. pap. 20.00 (*0-936390-09-3*) Dialog Pr.

Barnett, Louise. Touched by Fire: The Life, Death & Mythic Afterlife of George Armstrong Custer. 320p. 1995. 30.00 (*0-8050-3720-9*) H Holt & Co.

— Touched by Fire: The Life, Death & Mythic Afterlife of George Armstrong Custer. 1997. pap. 14.95 (*0-8050-5359-X*, Owl) H Holt & Co.

***Barnett, Louise.** Ungentlemanly Acts: The Army's Notorious Incest Trial. LC 99-42881. (Illus.). 224p. 2000. 24.00 (*0-8090-7397-8*) Hill & Wang.

Barnett, Louise K. The Ignoble Savage: American Literary Racism, 1790-1890, 18. LC 75-16964. (Contributions in American Studies: No. 18). (Illus.). 220p. 1976. 55.00 (*0-8371-8281-6*, BIG/, Greenwood Pr) Greenwood.

— Swift's Poetic Worlds. LC 80-54538. 224p. 1982. 32.50 (*0-87413-187-1*) U Delaware Pr.

***Barnett, Louise K. & Thorson, James L., eds.** Leslie Marmon Silko: A Collection of Critical Essays. LC 98-58048. 296p. 1999. 45.00 (*0-8263-2033-3*) U of NM Pr.

Barnett, Louise K., jt. ed. see Jeannet, Angela M.

Barnett, Lynn. A Climate Created: Community Building in the Beacon College Project. 86p. 1995. pap. 15.00 (*0-87117-294-1*, 1389) Comm Coll Pr Am Assn Comm Coll.

— The Nuclear Mentality: A Psychosocial Analysis of the Arms Race. Lee, Ian, ed. 192p. (C). pap. 21.00 (*0-7453-0393-5*, Pub. by Pluto GBR) Stylus Pub VA.

Barnett, Lynn, ed. Directory of Disability Support Services in Community Colleges, 1996. 224p. 1996. pap. 24.00 (*0-87117-305-0*, 1403) Comm Coll Pr Am Assn Comm Coll.

— Rural Workplace Literacy: Community College Partnerships. 1991. pap. 5.00 (*0-87117-247-X*, 1336) Comm Coll Pr Am Assn Comm Coll.

Barnett, Lynn, jt. ed. see Humbert, Pamela.

Barnett, Lynn, jt. ed. see Mahoney, James R.

Barnett, M. E., jt. auth. see Klemperer, Otto.

Barnett, Margaret E. Microbiology Lab Exercises: Complete Version. 2nd ed. 576p. (C). 1992. text. write for info. (*0-697-11308-6*, WCB McGr Hill) McGrw-H Hghr Educ.

— Microbiology Laboratory Exercises. 2nd abr. ed. 368p. (C). 1996. text. write for info. (*0-697-16011-4*, WCB McGr Hill) McGrw-H Hghr Educ.

— Microbiology Laboratory Exercises: Short Version. 368p. (C). 1991. text. write for info. (*0-697-11967-X*, WCB McGr Hill) McGrw-H Hghr Educ.

Barnett, Marguerite, tr. see Domalain, Jean-Yves.

Barnett, Marva T. Writing for Technicians. 3rd ed. LC 86-19843. 358p. (C). 1987. pap. 25.95 (*0-8273-2833-8*) Delmar.

— Writing for Technicians. 3rd ed. LC 86-19843. 358p. (C). 1987. pap., teacher ed. 10.00 (*0-8273-2834-6*) Delmar.

***Barnett, Matthew.** The Church That Never Sleeps: The Amazing Story That Will Change Your View of Church Forever. 228p. 2000. pap. 12.99 (*0-7852-6859-6*) Nelson.

Barnett, Maxine. Where Do I Go from Here. 1998. pap. write for info. (*0-9669484-9-1*) M W Barnett.

***Barnett, Michael.** Dialogues in Arab Politics: Negotiations in Regional Order. LC 98-12600. 376p. 1998. lib. bdg. 40.00 (*0-231-10918-0*) Col U Pr.

Barnett, Michael, jt. ed. see Adler, Emanuel.

Barnett, Michael N. Confronting the Costs of War: Military Power, State, & Society in Egypt & Israel. (Illus.). 336p. 1992. text 65.00 (*0-691-07883-1*, Pub. by Princeton U Pr) Cal Prin Full Svc.

— Dialogues in Arab Politics: Negotiations in Regional Order. LC 98-12600. 376p. 1998. pap. 17.50 (*0-231-10919-9*) Col U Pr.

Barnett, Michael N., ed. Israel in Comparative Perspective: Challenging the Conventional Wisdom. LC 95-15851. (SUNY Series in Israeli Studies). 304p. (C). 1996. text 59.50 (*0-7914-2831-1*); pap. text 19.95 (*0-7914-2832-X*) State U NY Pr.

Barnett, Michael R. & Crewz, David W., eds. Common Coastal Plants in Florida: A Guide to Planting & Maintenance. 2nd ed. LC 97-16535. (Florida Sea Grant College Program Ser.). (Illus.). 124p. 1997. pap. 17.95 (*0-8130-1551-0*) U Press Fla.

Barnett, Michael W., et al, eds. Dynamics & Control of Wastewater Systems. LC 98-85170. (Water Quality Management Library: Vol. 6). 296p. 1998. 104.95 (*1-56676-672-9*) Technomic.

***Barnett, Michelle Noble, et al.** Making Books with Pockets--April. Evans, Marilyn, ed. (Making Books with Pockets : Vol. 4). (Illus.). 96p. (J). (gr. 1-3). 1999. pap., teacher ed. 10.95 (*1-55799-701-2*, 587) Evan-Moor Edu Pubs.

— Making Books with Pockets--August. Evans, Marilyn, ed. (Making Books with Pockets : Vol. 8). (Illus.). 96p. (J). (gr. 1-3). 1999. pap., teacher ed. 10.95 (*1-55799-705-5*, 591) Evan-Moor Edu Pubs.

— Making Books with Pockets--February. Evans, Marilyn, ed. (Making Books with Pockets : Vol. 2). (Illus.). 96p. (J). (gr. 1-3). 1999. pap., teacher ed. 10.95 (*1-55799-699-7*, 585) Evan-Moor Edu Pubs.

— Making Books with Pockets--January. Evans, Marilyn, ed. (Making Books with Pockets : Vol. 1). (Illus.). 96p. (J). (gr. 1-3). 1999. pap., teacher ed. 10.95 (*1-55799-698-9*, 584) Evan-Moor Edu Pubs.

— Making Books with Pockets--July. Evans, Marilyn, ed. (Making Books with Pockets : Vol. 7). (Illus.). 96p. (J). (gr. 1-3). 1999. pap., teacher ed. 10.95 (*1-55799-704-7*, 590) Evan-Moor Edu Pubs.

— Making Books with Pockets--June. Evans, Marilyn, ed. (Making Books with Pockets : Vol. 6). (Illus.). 96p. (J). (gr. 1-3). 1999. pap., teacher ed. 10.95 (*1-55799-703-9*, 589) Evan-Moor Edu Pubs.

— Making Books with Pockets--March. Evans, Marilyn, ed. (Making Books with Pockets : Vol. 3). (Illus.). 96p. (J). (gr. 1-3). 1999. pap., teacher ed. 10.95 (*1-55799-700-4*, 586) Evan-Moor Edu Pubs.

— Making Books with Pockets--May. Evans, Marilyn, ed. (Making Books with Pockets : Vol. 5). (Illus.). 96p. (J). (gr. 1-3). 1999. pap., teacher ed. 10.95 (*1-55799-702-0*, 588) Evan-Moor Edu Pubs.

— Making Books with Pockets--November. Evans, Marilyn, ed. (Making Books with Pockets : Vol. 11). (Illus.). 96p. (J). (gr. 1-3). 1999. pap., teacher ed. 10.95 (*1-55799-708-X*, 594) Evan-Moor Edu Pubs.

— Making Books with Pockets--October. Evans, Marilyn, ed. (Making Books with Pockets : Vol. 10). (Illus.). 96p. (J). (gr. 1-3). 1999. pap., teacher ed. 10.95 (*1-55799-707-1*, 593) Evan-Moor Edu Pubs.

— Making Books with Pockets--September. Evans, Marilyn, ed. (Making Books with Pockets : Vol. 9). (Illus.). 96p. (J). (gr. 1-3). 1999. pap., teacher ed. 10.95 (*1-55799-706-3*, 592) Evan-Moor Edu Pubs.

— Making Books with Pockets-December. Evans, Marilyn, ed. (Making Books with Pockets : Vol. 12). (Illus.). 96p. (J). (gr. 1-3). 1999. pap., teacher ed. 10.95 (*1-55799-709-8*, 595) Evan-Moor Edu Pubs.

***Barnett, Neal & Hoffman, Linda Johnson.** The Reunion Planner 2000: The Step-by-Step Guide Designed to Make Your Reunion a Social & Financial Success! 2nd ed. (Illus.). 230p. 1998. pap. 29.95 incl. cd-rom (*0-9630516-7-9*) Goodman Lauren.

Barnett, Neal, jt. auth. see Hoffman, Linda Johnson.

Barnett, Neil, jt. ed. see Adams, Mike J.

Barnett, Neil, ed. see Cresser, Malcom S.

Barnett, O. W., ed. Potyvirus Taxonomy. LC 92-25228. (Archives of Virology Ser.: Suppl. 5). (Illus.). 400p. 1992. 193.00 (*0-387-82353-0*) Spr-Verlag.

Barnett, Ola W. & LaViolette, Alyce D. It Could Happen to Anyone: Why Battered Women Stay. 200p. 1993. 48.00 (*0-8039-5309-7*); pap. 21.95 (*0-8039-5310-0*) Sage.

Barnett, Ola W., et al. Family Violence Across the Lifespan: An Introduction. LC 96-35666. 466p. 1996. 69.95 (*0-8039-5615-0*); pap. 32.95 (*0-7619-0707-6*) Sage.

Barnett, Ola W., jt. auth. see LaViolette, Alyce D.

Barnett, Patricia J, ed. see Getty Art History Information Program.

Barnett, Paul. Behind the Scenes of the New Testament. LC 90-45492. 247p. (Orig.). 1991. pap. 13.99 (*0-8308-1329-2*, 1329) InterVarsity.

— Bethlehem to Patmos: The New Testament Story. (Biblical Classics Library: Vol. 39). 247p. 1998. reprint ed. mass mkt. 5.99 (*0-85364-874-3*, Pub. by Paternoster Pub) OM Literature.

— Is the New Testament History? (Biblical Classics Library). 173p. (Orig.). 1994. reprint ed. mass mkt. 9.99 (*0-85364-867-0*, Pub. by Paternoster Pub) OM Literature.

— Is the New Testament Reliable? A Look at the Historical Evidence. LC 92-34570. Orig. Title: Is the New Testament History?, (Illus.). 173p. 1992. reprint ed. pap. 11.99 (*0-8308-1834-0*, 1834) InterVarsity.

***Barnett, Paul.** Jesus & the Rise of Early Christianity: A History of the New Testament Times. LC 99-36943. 500p. 1999. 27.99 (*0-8308-1588-0*) InterVarsity.

Barnett, Paul. The Second Epistle to the Corinthians. LC 96-49755. (New International Commentary on the New Testament Ser.). 696p. 1997. 45.00 (*0-8028-2300-9*) Eerdmans.

Barnett, Peter, ed. Facilities Management: Toward Better Practice. LC 95-1293. 1995. 75.00 (*0-632-03941-8*) Blackwell Sci.

Barnett, Peter & Keller, Vaughn F. Improving Patient Adherence in Clinical Practice: A Practical Guide. 350p. 1998. 59.00 (*0-8342-1107-6*, 11076) Aspen Pub.

Barnett, Peter H. Can You Tell Me How What You Are Doing Now Is to Do Something Philosophical? 1980. pap. 5.00 (*0-915066-40-8*) Assembling Pr.

— Time Trap. LC 79-57447. (Illus.). 50p. 1980. pap. 5.00 (*0-915066-37-8*) Assembling Pr.

— Tools of Thought. 287p. 1981. 18.95 (*0-87073-392-3*) Schenkman Bks Inc.

Barnett, Phyllis W., jt. auth. see Mosher-Ashley, Pearl M.

Barnett, R. Higher Education: A Critical Business. LC 96-51029. 1997. pap. 35.95 (*0-335-19703-5*); pap. 114.00 (*0-335-19704-3*) OpUniv Pr.

— Idea of Higher Education. 1990. pap. 34.95 (*0-335-09420-1*) OpUniv Pr.

***Barnett, R. Michael, et al.** The Charm of Strange Quarks: Mysteries & Revolutions of Particle Physics. LC 99-36215. (Illus.). 160p. 2000. 39.95 (*0-387-98897-1*, AIP Pr) Spr-Verlag.

Barnett, Randy E. Contracts. 1360p. 1995. 57.00 (*0-316-08076-4*, Aspen Law & Bus) Aspen Pub.

— Contracts: Cases & Doctrine. 1360p. 1995. teacher ed. write for info. (*0-316-08131-0*, 81310) Aspen Law.

— Contracts: Cases & Doctrine. 2nd ed. LC 99-10393. xxxix, 1283 p. 1999. boxed set 62.00 (*0-7355-0253-6*) Panel Pubs.

— Perspectives on Contract Law. LC 95-76099. (Reader Ser.). 416p. 1995. pap. 18.95 (*0-316-08129-9*, 81299) Aspen Law.

Barnett, Randy E. Perspectives on Contract Law. 416p. 1995. pap. text 25.95 (*0-7355-1277-9*) Panel Pubs.

— The Structure of Liberty: Justice & the Rule of Law. 368p. 1998. text 29.95 (*0-19-829324-0*) OUP.

***Barnett, Randy E.** The Structure of Liberty: Justice & the Rule of Law. 368p. 2000. pap. 15.95 (*0-19-829729-7*) OUP.

Barnett, Randy E., ed. The Rights Retained by the People: The History & Meaning of the Ninth Amendment. 350p. (C). 1989. lib. bdg. 62.00 (*0-913969-22-2*) Univ Pub Assocs.

— The Rights Retained by the People: The History & Meaning of the Ninth Amendment. 350p. (C). 1991. pap. 16.95 (*0-913969-37-0*) Univ Pub Assocs.

— The Rights Retained by the People Vol. II: The History & Meaning of the Ninth Amendment. 350p. (C). 1993. lib. bdg. 64.50 (*0-913969-44-3*) Univ Pub Assocs.

Barnett, Raymond. College Algebra with Trigonometry. 6th ed. 1998. student ed. 29.38 (*0-07-365586-4*) McGraw.

***Barnett, Raymond, et al.** Precalculus: Solutions Manual. 4th ed. (C). 1998. student ed. 29.38 (*0-07-365582-1*) McGrw-H Hghr Educ.

Barnett, Raymond A. Analytic Trigonometry with Applications. (Math). 1976. mass mkt. 15.00 (*0-534-00428-8*) Brooks-Cole.

— Analytic Trigonometry with Applications. 3rd ed. (Math). 295p. (C). 1984. mass mkt. 30.00 (*0-534-02858-6*) Wadsworth Pub.

— Analytic Trigonometry with Applications. 4th ed. (Math). 349p. (C). 1987. mass mkt. 41.25 (*0-534-08484-2*) PWS Pubs.

— Analytic Trigonometry with Applications. 5th ed. (Mathematics Ser.). 1992. pap., student ed. 17.50 (*0-534-16743-8*) PWS Pubs.

— Analytic Trigonometry with Applications. 6th ed. (Mathematics Ser.). 1994. mass mkt., student ed. 18.25 (*0-534-94347-0*) PWS Pubs.

— Calculus for Business, Economics, Life Sciences & Social Sciences. 8th ed. LC 98-27323. 768p. 1998. 93.33 (*0-13-079765-0*) P-H.

— Concepts of Biology Laboratory Manual. 144p. (C). 1996. pap. text, lab manual ed. 19.95 (*0-7872-2520-7*) Kendall-Hunt.

— Finite Mathematics for Management, Life & Social Science. 6th ed. (Illus.). 487p. 1993. text. write for info. (*0-318-72286-0*) Dellen Pub.

— Vectors. LC 75-12664. 140p. (C). 1976. reprint ed. lib. bdg. 14.00 (*0-88275-290-1*) Krieger.

Barnett, Raymond A. & Kearns, Thomas J. Algebra: An Elementary Course. 2nd ed. (C). 1987. pap. text 53.25 (*0-07-003923-2*); pap. text, student ed. 22.50 (*0-07-003770-1*) McGraw.

— Algebra: An Intermediate Course. 2nd ed. (C). 1987. pap. text 57.50 (*0-07-003749-3*) McGraw.

— Elementary Algebra: Structure & Use. 6th ed. LC 93-7179. 474p. (C). 1993. 69.06 (*0-07-004566-6*) McGraw.

— Elementary Algebra: Structure & Use. 6th ed. (C). 1993. pap. text, student ed. 26.88 (*0-07-005105-4*) McGraw.

— Intermediate Algebra: Structure & Use. 5th ed. LC 93-2364. 537p. (C). 1993. 69.69 (*0-07-004573-9*) McGraw.

Barnett, Raymond A. & Kearsn, Thomas J. Algebra for College Students. LC 94-18497. 704p. (C). 1994. 69.06 (*0-07-005001-5*) McGraw.

Barnett, Raymond A. & Ziegler, Michael R. Brief Calculus with Technology. LC 96-45226. 764p. (C). 1996. 96.00 (*0-13-568205-3*) P-H.

Barnett, Raymond A. & Ziegler, Michael R. College Algebra with Trigonometry. 5th ed. LC 92-14680. (Barnett & Ziegler's College Algebra - Precalculus Ser.). (C). 1993. text. write for info. (*0-07-004989-0*); pap. text, student ed. 26.74 (*0-07-005006-6*) McGraw.

Barnett, Raymond A. & Ziegler, Michael R. College Mathematics with Technology Bussiness. LC 96-45225. 1160p. (C). 1997. 98.67 (*0-13-570391-3*) P-H.

B

An Asterisk (*) at the beginning of an entry indicates that the title is appearing for the first time.

B

Barnett, Raymond A. & Ziegler, Michael R. Essentials of College Mathematics for Business, Economics, Life Sciences, & Social Sciences. 3rd ed. LC 94-4707. (College Mathematics Ser.). 745p. (C). 1994. 98.67 (*0-02-305931-1*, Macmillan Coll) P-H.

— Precalculus: Functions & Graphs. 3rd ed. LC 92-15631. (C). 1993. text 61.74 (*0-07-004961-0*) McGraw.

— Precalculus: Functions & Graphs. 3rd ed. LC 92-15631. (C). 1993. pap. text, teacher ed. 26.74 (*0-07-005007-4*) McGraw.

Barnett, Raymond A. & Zielgler, Michael R. College Algebra. 5th ed. LC 92-11134. (C). 1993. text 59.74 (*0-07-004995-5*) McGraw.

— College Algebra. 5th ed. LC 92-11134. (C). 1993. pap. text 26.74 (*0-07-005008-2*) McGraw.

Barnett, Raymond A., et al. Analytic Trigonometry with Applications. 7th ed. LC 98-27338. 1998. pap. 76.95 (*0-534-35838-1*) Brooks-Cole.

***Barnett, Raymond A., et al.** Analytic Trigonometry with Applications. 7th ed. 1998. pap., student ed. 20.50 (*0-534-35839-X*) Brooks-Cole.

Barnett, Raymond A., et al. Applied Calculus for Business, Economics, Life Sciences & Social Sciences. 7th ed. LC 99-23820. (Illus.). 941p. (C). 1999. 93.33 (*0-13-083129-8*) P-H.

— Applied Mathematics for Business, Economics, Life Sciences & Social Sciences. 7th ed. LC 99-23819. (Illus.). 1203p. (C). 1999. 98.67 (*0-13-083120-4*) P-H.

— College Algebra. 6th ed. LC 98-19649. 736p. 1998. 74.06 (*0-07-006321-4*) McGraw.

— College Algebra with Trigonometry. 6th ed. LC 98-19651. 1016p. 1998. 74.06 (*0-07-006336-2*) McGraw.

— College Mathematics for Business, Economics, Life Sciences & Social Sciences. 8th ed. LC 98-24476. 1138p. 1998. 98.67 (*0-13-079768-5*) P-H.

— Precalculus: Functions & Graphs. 4th ed. LC 98-18537. 1016p. 1998. 74.06 (*0-07-006341-9*) McGraw.

Barnett, Raymond A., jt. auth. see Ziegler, Michael R.

***Barnett, Richard.** Deep & Crisp. 48p. 1999. pap. 5.99 (*1-57921-260-3*) WinePress Pub.

Barnett, Richard. Massachusetts, Rhode Island & South New Hampshire Pocket Guide. 7th ed. 192p. 1995. pap. 16.95 (*0-939430-39-8*) Scanner Master.

— Monitor America: Frequencies, Codes, Maps & Descriptions of Public Safety. 3rd ed. (Illus.). 1000p. 1995. pap. 29.95 (*0-939430-31-2*) Scanner Master.

— National Sports & Recreation Frequency Directory. 160p. 1994. pap. 13.95 (*0-939430-30-4*) Scanner Master.

Barnett, Richard, ed. Scanner Master Massachusetts Guide. 4th ed. (Frequency Guide Ser.: No. 10). (Illus.). 520p. 1989. 29.95 (*0-685-34567-X*) Scanner Master.

— Scanner Master Massachusetts Pocket Guide. 3rd ed. (Frequency Guide Ser.: No. 1A). 142p. 1990. 12.95 (*0-685-34568-8*) Scanner Master.

Barnett, Richard & Schwab, Walter, eds. The Western Sephardim: Sephardi Heritage, Vol. 11. (C). 1988. text 150.00 (*0-948466-11-1*, Pub. by Gibraltar Bks) St Mut.

Barnett, Richard & Soomre, Edward. Scanner Master Massachusetts Communications Guide: The Commonwealth's Reference Guide. (Illus.). 692p. 1995. pap. 29.95 (*0-939430-25-8*) Scanner Master.

Barnett, Richard B. North India Between Empires: Awadh, the Mughals & the British, 1720-1801. 1987. reprint ed. 23.50 (*81-85054-24-X*, Pub. by Manohar) S Asia.

Barnett, Richard H. The Eighty Fifty-One Family of Microcontrollers. LC 94-25810. 416p. 1994. pap. text 77.00 (*0-02-306281-9*, Macmillan Coll) P-H.

Barnett, Robert & Akiner, Shirin, eds. Resistance & Reform in Tibet. LC 93-3072. (Illus.). xxx, 314 p. 1994. 39.95 (*0-253-31131-4*) Ind U Pr.

Barnett, Robert, jt. auth. see Rolls, Barbara.

Barnett, Robert A. Food, Family & Fun: A Seasonal Guide to Healthy Eating. (Illus.). 122p. (Orig.). 1997. pap. text 20.00 (*0-7881-3840-5*) DIANE Pub.

— Tonics: 200 Recipes that Improve the Body & the Mind. LC 96-38357. 352p. (Orig.). 1997. pap. 16.00 (*0-06-095111-7*, Perennial) HarperTrade.

Barnett, Robert A., ed. see Hobbs, Christopher.

Barnett, Robert J. Baptism: Who Needs It? 16p. (Orig.). 1991. reprint ed. pap. text 1.79 (*0-87227-171-4*, RBP5203) Reg Baptist.

Barnett, Robert M. Analysis, Computation, Presentation of Engineering Information. 8.50 (*0-89741-000-9*); pap. 7.95 (*0-686-96874-3*) Gila River.

Barnett, Robert W. Economic Shanghai: Hostage to Politics, 1937-1941. LC 75-30094. (Institute of Pacific Relations Ser.). reprint ed. 29.50 (*0-404-59504-9*) AMS Pr.

— Wandering Knights: China Legacies, Lived & Recalled. LC 89-29563. 156p. (gr. 13). 1990. text 57.95 (*0-87332-513-3*, East Gate Bk) M E Sharpe.

Barnett, Robert W. & Blumner, Jacob S., eds. Writing Centers & Writing Across the Curriculum Programs: Building Interdisciplinary Partnerships, 73. LC 98-8236. (Contributions to the Study of Education: Vol. 73). 240p. 1999. 55.00 (*0-313-30699-0*, Greenwood Pr) Greenwood.

Barnett, Roger. What about Jonah? 36p. (Orig.). 1997. pap. 3.00 (*1-880573-33-4*) Bible Search Pubns.

— Why in a Stable? In the Shadow of His Hand. 20p. 1999. pap. 2.50 (*1-880573-47-4*) Bible Search Pubns.

Barnett, Ron & Griffin, Anne, eds. The End of Knowledge in Higher Education. (Institute of Education Ser.). 160p. 1997. 69.50 (*0-304-33705-6*); pap. 26.95 (*0-304-33706-4*) Continuum.

Barnett, Ronald. Improving Higher Education. 224p. 1992. pap. 34.95 (*0-335-09984-X*) OpUniv Pr.

***Barnett, Ronald.** Realizing the University in an Age of Supercomplexity. LC 99-24212. 1999. 36.95 (*0-335-20248-9*) Taylor & Francis.

Barnett, Ronald, ed. Academic Community: Discourse or Discord? (Higher Education Policy Ser.: No. 20). 250p. 1993. 59.95 (*1-85302-534-8*) Taylor & Francis.

Barnett, Rosalind, et al, eds. Gender & Stress. LC 87-12053. 400p. 1987. 50.00 (*0-02-901380-1*) Free Pr.

Barnett, Rosalind & Rivers, Caryl. She Works, He Works. LC 96-10442. 2000. pap. 14.00 (*0-06-251189-0*) Harper SF.

Barnett, Rosalind C. & Baruch, Grace K. Competent Woman: Perspectives on Development. LC 78-8380. (Irvington Social Relations Ser.). 1980. pap. text 12.95 (*0-8290-0092-5*) Irvington.

Barnett, Rosalind C. & Rivers, Caryl. She Works He Works: How Two-Income Families Are Happy, Healthy, & Thriving. LC 98-20217. 272p. 1998. pap. 15.95 (*0-674-80595-X*) HUP.

Barnett, Ruth. People Making People. 168p. (C). 1985. pap. 30.00 (*0-09-154931-0*, Pub. by S Thornes Pubs) St Mut.

Barnett, Ruth A. Stripper in the Mojave. (Demi Livre Selection Ser.). 24p. 1999. 7.00 (*1-884800-25-4*) Four Way Bks.

Barnett, S. Discrete Mathematics: Numbers & Beyond. LC 98-24478. (International Mathematics Series). 456p. (C). 1998. pap. text 50.00 (*0-201-34292-8*) Addison-Wesley.

— Mathematical Formula. 1996. pap. write for info. (*0-582-44758-5*, Pub. by Addison-Wesley) Longman.

Barnett, S. & Cameron, R. G. Introduction to Mathematical Control Theory. 2nd ed. (Oxford Applied Mathematics & Computing Science Ser.). (Illus.). 416p. 1990. pap. text 45.00 (*0-19-859639-1*, 12245) OUP.

Barnett, S., jt. ed. see Gover, M. J.

Barnett, S. A. The Human Species: The Biology of Man. (Illus.). 1990. 16.50 (*0-8446-0477-1*) Peter Smith.

— The Rat: A Study in Behavior. rev. ed. LC 74-33509. xiv, 336p. 1981. pap. text 13.50 (*0-226-03742-8*) U Ch Pr.

***Barnett, S. Anthony.** Science Myth or Magic? A Struggle for Existence. 224p. 2000. pap. 15.95 (*1-86508-122-1*, Pub. by Allen & Unwin Pty) IPG Chicago.

Barnett, S. Anthony. Science of Life: From Cells to Survival. 1999. pap. text 17.95 (*1-86448-610-4*) Allen & Unwn AT.

Barnett, S. J., ed. see Newton, Sir Isaac.

Barnett, Samuel A. The Rat: A Study in Behavior. rev. ed. LC 74-33509. (Illus.). 332p. Date not set. reprint ed. pap. 103.00 (*0-608-20989-9*, 205451700003) Bks Demand.

Barnett, Samuel A., ed. Century of Darwin. LC 71-76891. (Essay Index Reprint Ser.). 1977. 23.95 (*0-8369-1019-2*) Ayer.

Barnett, Samuel A. & Barnett, Henrietta O. Practicable Socialism: Essays on Social Reform. LC 72-3394. (Essay Index Reprint Ser.). 1977. reprint ed. 18.95 (*0-8369-2891-1*) Ayer.

Barnett, Shia, ed. see Miller, Ivan.

Barnett, Shia S. My Soul Sings Acappella: Poetry & Prose. LC 96-94860. (Illus.). xiv, 90p. (Orig.). 1996. pap. 11.95 (*0-9655430-7-2*) Blckberry Bks.

Barnett, Snowdon. Dossiers Secrets. 64p. (C). 1986. pap. 38.00 (*0-947612-18-1*, Pub. by Rivelin Grapheme Pr) St Mut.

— Hiroshima Hypostasis. LC 97-30542. 1997. 14.95 (*0-7734-2811-9*, Mellen Poetry Pr) E Mellen.

Barnett, Stanley B. & Kossoff, George, eds. Safety of Diagnostic Ultrasound. LC 97-38076. (Progress in Obstetric & Gynecological Sonography Ser.). 158p. 1997. 78.00 (*1-85070-646-8*) Prthnon Pub.

Barnett, Stephen. Matrices: Methods & Applications. (Oxford Applied Mathematics & Computing Science Ser.). (Illus.). 466p. 1990. pap. text 45.00 (*0-19-859680-4*) OUP.

— Matrices in Control Theory. rev. ed. LC 82-21321. 206p. (C). 1984. lib. bdg. 24.50 (*0-89874-590-X*) Krieger.

— Polynomials & Linear Control Systems. LC 83-5309. (Monographs & Textbooks in Pure & Applied Mathematics: Vol. 77). 471p. reprint ed. pap. 146.10 (*0-608-08911-7*, 206954600005) Bks Demand.

— Some Modern Applications of Mathematics. 220p. 1995. pap. 48.00 (*0-13-834094-3*) P-H.

Barnett, Stephen M. & Radmore, Paul M. Methods in Theoretical Quantum Optics. LC 97-13764. (Oxford Series on Optical & Imaging Sciences: No. 15). (Illus.). 292p. 1997. text 85.00 (*0-19-856362-0*) OUP.

Barnett, Stephen R., et al. Law of International Telecommunications in the United States. (Law & Economics of International Telecommunications Ser.). 271p. 1988. 89.00 (*3-7890-1308-0*, Pub. by Nomos Verlags) Intl Bk Import.

Barnett, Steve, ed. The Nissan Report: A Bold New Blueprint for Successful Innovation in American Business. 224p. 1994. pap. 11.00 (*0-380-72141-4*, Avon Bks) Morrow Avon.

Barnett, Steven. Games & Sets: The Changing Face of Sport on Television. (Illus.). 224p. 1990. pap. 17.95 (*0-85170-268-6*, Pub. by British Film Inst) Ind U Pr.

Barnett, Steven & International Monetary Fund Staff. The Economy of the West Bank & Gaza Strip: Recent Experience, Prospects & Challenges to Private Sector Development. LC 98-18343. 1998. pap. 15.00 (*1-55775-725-9*) Intl Monetary.

Barnett, Stuart. Hegel after Derrida. LC 97-24518. (Warwick Studies in European Philosophy Ser.). 1998. write for info. (*0-04-151704-0*) Routledge.

— Hegel after Derrida. LC 97-24518. (Warwick Studies in European Philosophy Ser.). 368p. (C). 1998. pap. 25.99 (*0-415-17105-9*) Routledge.

Barnett, Stuart, ed. Hegel after Derrida. (Warwick Studies in European Philosophy Ser.). 368p. (C). 1998. 85.00 (*0-415-17104-0*) Routledge.

Barnett, Susan, jt. auth. see Benson, Barbara.

***Barnett, Suzanne.** Letting the Heart Lead: The King Family Story. 263p. 1999. 19.95 (*0-9630632-4-3*) Abbott-Sterling.

Barnett, Suzanne W. & Fairbank, John K., eds. Christianity in China: Early Protestant Missionary Writings. (Studies in American-East Asian Relations: No. 9). 280p. 1985. 20.00 (*0-674-12881-8*) HUP.

Barnett, Suzanne Wilson, jt. ed. see Symons, Van J.

Barnett, T. Drafting & Negotiating Commercial Leases in Australia. 256p. 1990. boxed set 78.00 (*0-409-49555-7*, Austral, MICHIE) LEXIS Pub.

Barnett, Thomas. Clones & Other Short Stories. 232p. (Orig.). 1997. pap. 6.95 (*1-883228-18-2*) Invictus MI.

Barnett, Thomas P. Romanian & East German Policies in the Third World: Comparing the Strategies of Ceausescu & Honecker. LC 92-3380. 200p. 1992. 57.95 (*0-275-94117-5*, C4117, Praeger Pubs) Greenwood.

Barnett, Timothy J. Legislative Learning: The 104th Republican Freshmen in the House. (Politics & Policy in American Institutions Ser.: Vol. 3). 256p. 1999. 60.00 (*0-8153-3362-5*, SS1414) Garland.

Barnett, Tommy. Adventure Yourself: Discover the Thrill & Excitement of Serving God, Vol. 1. LC 99-58697. 1999. pap. 12.99 (*0-88419-665-8*) Creation House.

— Dream Again: Miraculous True Stories to Restore Your Soul & Give You Hope. LC 98-20156. 256p. 1998. pap. 12.99 (*0-88419-523-6*) Creation House.

— Multiplication: Unlock the Biblical Factors to Multiply Your Effectiveness in Ministry. 1997. 14.99 (*0-88419-450-7*) Creation House.

— There's a Miracle in Your House. 1993. pap. 10.99 (*0-88419-330-6*) Creation House.

Barnett, Tony & Abdelkarim, Abbas. Sudan: The Gezira Scheme & Agricultural Transition. 137p. 1991. text 42.50 (*0-7146-3328-3*, Pub. by F Cass Pubs) Intl Spec Bk.

Barnett, Tony & Blaikie, Piers. AIDS in Africa: Its Present & Future Impact. 200p. 1992. pap. text 20.95 (*0-89862-880-6*) Guilford Pubns.

Barnett, Tony & Karim, Abbas A., eds. Sudan: State, Capital & Transformation. 288p. 1988. lib. bdg. 59.00 (*0-7099-5902-8*, Pub. by C Helm) Routldge.

Barnett, Ursula A. A Vision of Order: A Study of Black South African Literature in English, 1914-1980. LC 83-9296. 336p. 1983. lib. bdg. 35.00 (*0-87023-406-4*) U of Mass Pr.

***Barnett, V.** Comparative Inference. 3rd ed. LC 98-44623. 410p. 1999. 120.00 (*0-471-97643-1*) Wiley.

Barnett, V. Sample Survey Principles & Methods. rev. ed. 192p. 1991. pap. 35.00 (*0-340-54553-4*, Pub. by E A) OUP.

Barnett, Vic. Comparative Statistical Inference. LC 81-14806. (Wiley Series in Probability & Mathematical Statistics). 341p. reprint ed. pap. 105.80 (*0-7837-6366-2*, 204607800010) Bks Demand.

— Elements of Sampling Theory. 152p. 1974. pap. text 9.95 (*0-340-17387-4*, Pub. by E A) Routldge.

Barnett, Vic, ed. Interpreting Multivariate Data. LC 82-121862. (Wiley Series in Probability & Mathematical Statistics). (Illus.). 390p. reprint ed. pap. 120.90 (*0-608-17982-5*, 202788600057) Bks Demand.

Barnett, Vic, et al, eds. Agricultural Sustainability: Economic, Environmental & Statistical Considerations. 278p. 1995. 194.95 (*0-471-95009-2*) Wiley.

Barnett, Vic & Lewis, Toby. Outliers in Statistical Data. 3rd ed. 604p. 1994. 195.00 (*0-471-93094-6*) Wiley.

Barnett, Vic & Turkman, K. Feridun. Statistics for the Environment, Vol. 3, Pollution Assessment & Control, Vol. 3, Pollution Assessment and Control. 3rd ed. LC 97-186332. 358p. 1997. 155.00 (*0-471-96435-2*) Wiley.

Barnett, Vic & Turkman, K. Feridun, eds. Statistics for the Environment: Water Related Issues, Vol. 2, Water Related Issues. 406p. 1994. 180.00 (*0-471-95048-3*) Wiley.

Barnett, Vic, et al. Statistics for the Environment: Statistical Aspects of Health & the Environment. LC 98-7738. 422p. 1999. 180.00 (*0-471-97645-8*) Wiley.

Barnett, Victoria. For the Soul of the People: Protestant Protest Against Hitler. (Illus.). 384p. 1998. reprint ed. pap. 21.00 (*0-19-512118-X*) OUP.

***Barnett, Victoria J.** Bystanders: Conscience & Complicity During the Holocaust. 208p. 2000. pap. 18.50 (*0-275-97045-0*) Greenwood.

Barnett, Victoria J., ed. Bystanders: Conscience & Complicity during the Holocaust, 59. LC 98-51641. (Contributions to the Study of Religion Ser.: 59). 208p. 1999. 57.95 (*0-313-29184-5*) Greenwood.

Barnett, Victoria J., ed. & rev. see Bethge, Eberhard.

Barnett, Victoria J., ed. & tr. see Gerlach, Wolfgang.

Barnett, Vincent. Kondratiev & the Dynamics of Economic Development: Long Cycles & Industrial Growth in Historical Context. LC 97-28137. (Studies in Russian & East European History & Society). 288p. 1998. text 79.95 (*0-312-21048-5*) St Martin.

Barnett, Vincent M., ed. Representation of the United States Abroad. rev. ed. LC 65-15651. 1965. reprint ed. pap. 1.95 (*0-317-04630-6*) Am Assembly.

Barnett, Vivian, et al, eds. Kandinsky: Watercolors & Drawings. (Illus.). 232p. 1992. 75.00 (*3-7913-1184-0*, Pub. by Prestel) te Neues.

Barnett, Vivian E. Guggenheim Museum Thannhauser Collection. (Illus.). 192p. 1994. 40.00 (*0-8109-6867-3*, Pub. by Abrams) Time Warner.

— Handbook: The Guggenheim Museum Collection 1900-1980. 2nd ed. (Illus.). 528p. 1984. reprint ed. pap. 22.00 (*0-89207-046-3*) S R Guggenheim.

— Kandinsky Watercolours Vol. 2: Catalogue Raisonne, 1922-1944. (Illus.). 600p. 1994. text 285.00 (*0-8014-2927-7*) Cornell U Pr.

Barnett, Vivian E., ed. Kandinsky Watercolours Vol. 1: Catalogue Raisonne, 1900-1921. LC 91-27618. (Illus.). 600p. 1992. text 285.00 (*0-8014-2690-1*) Cornell U Pr.

Barnett, Vivian E. & Friedel, Helmut. Vasily Kandinsky: A Colorful Life, the Collection of the Lenbachhaus, Munich. (Illus.). 512p. 1996. 95.00 (*0-8109-6319-1*, Pub. by Abrams) Time Warner.

Barnett, Vivian E., et al. Thannhauser Collection. Orig. Title: Justin K. Thannhauser Collection. (Illus.). 192p. 1991. 45.00 (*0-89207-074-9*) S R Guggenheim.

Barnett, W. Steven. Lives in the Balance: Age-27 Benefit-Cost Analysis of the High Scope Perry Preschool Program. LC 96-21849. (Monographs of the High/Scope Educational Research Foundation). 120p. 1996. 19.95 (*1-57379-007-9*, R1056) High-Scope.

Barnett, W. Steven & Boocock, Sarane S., eds. Early Care & Education for Children in Poverty: Promises, Programs, & Long-Term Results. LC 97-17192. (SUNY Series, Youth Social Services, Schooling, & Public Policy). 341p. (C). 1998. text 65.50 (*0-7914-3619-5*); pap. text 21.95 (*0-7914-3620-9*) State U NY Pr.

Barnett, Walter. Homosexuality & the Bible: An Interpretation. LC 79-84920. 1979. pap. 4.00 (*0-87574-226-2*) Pendle Hill.

Barnett, William A. Nonparametric & Semiparametric Methods in Econometrics & Statistics: Proceedings of the Fifth International Symposium. Powell, James E. et al, eds. (International Symposia in Economic Theory & Econometrics Ser.: No. 5). (Illus.). 507p. (C). 1991. text 85.00 (*0-521-37090-6*) Cambridge U Pr.

Barnett, William A., et al, eds. Dynamic Disequilibrium Modeling: Proceedings of the Ninth International Symposium in Economic Theory & Econometrics. (International Symposia in Economic Theory & Econometrics Ser.: No. 9). (Illus.). 248p. (C). 1996. text 80.00 (*0-521-46275-4*) Cambridge U Pr.

— Dynamic Econometric Modeling: Proceedings of the 3rd International Symposium. (International Symposia in Economic Theory & Econometrics Ser.: No. 3). 392p. 1988. text 89.95 (*0-521-33395-4*) Cambridge U Pr.

— Economic Complexity: Chaos, Sunspots, Bubbles & Nonlinearity. (International Symposia in Economic Theory & Econometrics Ser.). (Illus.). 432p. (C). 1989. text 90.00 (*0-521-35563-X*) Cambridge U Pr.

— Equilibrium Theory & Applications: Proceedings of the 6th International Symposium. (International Symposia in Economic Theory & Econometrics Ser.: No. 6). (Illus.). 492p. (C). 1991. text 85.00 (*0-521-39219-5*) Cambridge U Pr.

— New Approaches to Modeling, Specification Selection & Econometric Inference: Proceedings of the 1st International Symposium. (International Symposia in Economic Theory & Econometrics Ser.: No. 1). (Illus.). 490p. (C). 1990. text 89.95 (*0-521-38465-6*) Cambridge U Pr.

— Nonlinear Dynamics & Economics. (International Symposia in Economic Theory & Econometrics Ser.: No. 10). (Illus.). 417p. (C). 1996. text 64.95 (*0-521-47141-9*) Cambridge U Pr.

***Barnett, William A., et al, eds.** Nonlinear Econometric Modeling in Time Series Analysis: Proceedings of the 11th International Symposium in Economic Theory. (International Symposia in Economic Theory & Econometrics Ser.: No. 11). (Illus.). 240p. (C). 2000. 69.95 (*0-521-59424-3*) Cambridge U Pr.

Barnett, William A., et al, eds. Political Economy: Institutions, Competition & Representation: Proceedings of the 7th International Symposium. LC 92-43595. (International Symposia in Economic Theory & Econometrics Ser.: No. 7). (Illus.). 536p. (C). 1993. text 89.95 (*0-521-41781-3*); pap. text 37.95 (*0-521-42831-9*) Cambridge U Pr.

— Social Choice, Welfare & Ethics: Proceedings of the Eighth International Symposium in Economic Theory & Econometrics. (International Symposia in Economic Theory & Econometrics Ser.: No. 8). (Illus.). 431p. (C). 1995. text 74.95 (*0-521-44340-7*) Cambridge U Pr.

***Barnett, William A. & Serletis, Apostolos.** The Theory of Monetary Aggregation. LC 00-34082. (Contributions to Economic Analysis Ser.). 2000. write for info. (*0-444-50119-3*) Elsevier.

Barnett, William A., ed. see International Symposium in Economic Theory and Econometrics & University of New South Wales.

Barnett, William K. & Hoopes, John W., eds. The Emergence of Pottery: Technology & Innovation in Ancient Societies. LC 94-44464. (Series in Archaeological Inquiry). (Illus.). 304p. 1995. text 55.00 (*1-56098-516-X*); pap. text 34.95 (*1-56098-517-8*) Smithsonian.

***Barnett, Yvonne A. & Barnett, Christopher R., eds.** Aging Methods & Protocols. LC 99-23842. (Methods in Molecular Medicine Ser.: Vol. 38). 400p. 2000. 99.50 (*0-89603-582-4*) Humana.

Barnett, Ziegler. College Algebra:graph Approach. LC 99-49142. 784p. 1999. 77.81 (*0-07-005710-9*) McGraw.

***Barnett, Ziegler.** Precalculus. 708p. 1999. student ed. 25.63 (*0-07-228398-X*) McGraw.

Barnett, Ziegler. Precalculus. LC 99-49637. 1056p. 1999. 77.81 (*0-07-005717-6*) McGraw.

Barnette, Ashley S., ed. see Barnette, David C.

Barnette, Ashley S., ed. see Brill, Gerhard W.

Barnette, Curtis H., et al. Corporate Law Departments & Outside Counsel II. vii, 858p. write for info. (*0-318-58370-4*) Harcourt.

Barnette, David C. How to Be a Mobilian: A Handbook for Newcomers & Old Salts. Barnette, Ashley S., ed. (Illus.). 147p. 1998. pap. 12.95 (*1-888769-37-8*) Pub One Hund One.

— How to Be a Southerner: A Handbook for Newcomers & Old Salts. Barnette, Ashley S., ed. (Illus.). 145p. 1999. pap. 12.95 (*1-888769-38-6*) Pub One Hund One.

— How to Be a Teacher. Barnette, Ashley S., ed. (Illus.). 145p. 1999. pap. 9.95 (*1-888769-39-4*) Pub One Hund One.

An Asterisk (*) at the beginning of an entry indicates that the title is appearing for the first time.

— Men Are from Mars, but the Peanut Man Is from Mobile: 101 Superlative Ways to Know If You're a Mobilian. Barnette, Ashley S., ed. (Illus.). 105p. 1996. pap. 8.95 (*1-888769-11-4*) Pub One Hund One.

— 101 Ways to Know If You're a Teacher. (Illus.). 103p. (Orig.). 1995. pap. 8.95 (*1-888769-10-6*) Pub One Hund One.

Barnette, David C., ed. see Brill, Gerhard W.

Barnette, David W. Map Coloring, Polyhedra & the Four-Color Problem. (Dolciani Mathematical Expositions Ser.: Vol. 8). 1984. text 8.00 (*0-88385-309-4*, DOL-08) Math Assn.

***Barnette, David W.** The Offset Berlin Post Office Stamps of 1920. Manchester, Jason H., ed. (15 G Handbook Ser.: Vol. 2). (Illus.). 26p. 1998. pap. 10.00 (*0-9624796-2-4*) D Manchester.

Barnette, Henlee H. Clarence Jordan: Turning Dreams into Deeds. 120p. 1992. pap. 10.00 (*1-880837-00-5*) Smyth & Helwys.

— Exploring Medical Ethics. LC 82-2116. xiv, 172p. 1982. text 12.95 (*0-86554-031-4*, MUP\H030) Mercer Univ Pr.

— Introducing Christian Ethics. 1998. pap. text 14.99 (*0-8054-1858-X*) Broadman.

Barnette, Jackie, ed. see Pakizer, Debi & Sears, Mary A.

***Barnette, Marcie L., ed.** Handbook for Home Care Aide. 3rd rev. ed. (Illus.). vii, 135p. 1999. pap. write for info. (*1-930304-00-5*) Home Care Univ.

Barnette, Martha. Ladyfingers & Nun's Tummies:From Spare Ribs to Humble Pie: A Lighthearted Look at How Foods Got Their Names. (Illus.). 213p. 1998. pap. 12.00 (*0-375-70298-9*) Vin Bks.

Barnette Pierce, Ruth. Creative Wax Carving: For the Hobbyist, Sculptor & Serious Jewelry Designer. Guymon, Susan, ed. LC 89-50846. (Illus.). 109p. (Orig.). 1989. pap. 19.50 (*0-9624729-0-5*) E R Weaver Inc.

Barnette, W. Douglas. A Study of the Works of Manuel Mantero: A Member of the Spanish Generation of 1950. LC 95-6073. (Hispanic Literature Ser.: Vol. 25). (Illus.). 164p. 1995. text 79.95 (*0-7734-8983-5*) E Mellen.

Barnewall, Marilyn M. Cosmic Canines. LC 98-34098. 1998. pap. 12.00 (*0-345-42459-X*) Ballantine Pub Grp.

Barney, Amy Lou, jt. auth. see Guerin, Renee.

Barney, Anne. Stolen Joy: Healing after Infertility & Infant Loss. LC 93-78192. 48p. (Orig.). 1993. pap. 5.95 (*0-944806-06-6*) Icarus Press.

Barney, D. Paul. Clinical Applications of Herbal Medicine. 1996. 10.95 (*1-885670-23-0*) Woodland UT.

— Physician's Guide to Natural Remedies. 1998. pap. text 19.95 (*1-885670-84-2*) Woodland UT.

Barney, Daniel & Siegel, Kenneth. ICC Termination Act of 1995. Date not set. pap. 69.95 (*0-88711-358-3*) Am Trucking Assns.

***Barney, Darin.** Prometheus Wired. 2000. 29.00 (*0-226-03745-2*) U Ch Pr.

— Prometheus Wired: The Hope for Democracy in the Age of Network Technology. LC 00-23239. 2000. write for info. (*0-226-03746-0*) U Ch Pr.

Barney Design Staff. Barney's Water Fun. (Barney Ser.). 10p. (J). (ps-k). 1997. vinyl bd. 4.99 (*1-57064-199-4*, Barney Publ) Lyrick Pub.

Barney, E. Stevens Genealogy, Embracing Branches of the Family Descending from Puritan Ancestors, 1650 to the Present Time. (Illus.). 319p. 1989. reprint ed. pap. 48.00 (*0-8328-1129-7*); reprint ed. lib. bdg. 56.00 (*0-8328-1128-9*) Higginson Bk Co.

Barney, G. C. Elevator Abstracts: Including Escalators. (Transportation Ser.). 178p. 1987. text 79.95 (*0-470-20835-X*) P-H.

— Elevator Technology. LC 86-15285. (Transportation Ser.). 354p. 1986. text 82.95 (*0-470-20702-7*) P-H.

Barney, G. C. & Ag, Loher. Elevator Electric Drives: Concepts & Principles, Control & Practice. (Illus.). 197p. 1990. spiral bd. 49.95 (*0-13-261462-6*) Elevator Wrld.

Barney, G. Scott, et al, eds. Geochemical Behavior of Disposed Radioactive Waste. LC 83-3106. (ACS Symposium Ser.: No. 246). 424p. 1984. lib. bdg. 87.95 (*0-8412-0827-1*) Am Chemical.

— Geochemical Behavior of Disposed Radioactive Waste. LC 84-3106. (ACS Symposium Ser.: Vol. 246). 421p. 1984. reprint ed. pap. 130.60 (*0-608-03126-7*, 206357900007) Bks Demand.

Barney, Gerald O. The Global Two Thousand Report to the President of the U. S. Entering the 21st Century, 3 vols. Incl. Vl. I. Summary Report. 1981. Vol. II. Technical Supplement. 1981. (Policy Studies on Policy, Planning & Modeling). 800p. 1981. 510.00 (*0-08-025991-X*, Pergamon Pr) Elsevier.

— Global 2000: Report to the President. LC 91-35683. 72p. 1991. pap. 8.95 (*0-932020-96-8*) Seven Locks Pr.

Barney, Gerald O., et al. Global Two Thousand: Implications for Canada. (Illus.). 196p. 1981. 88.00 (*0-08-025390-3*, Pergamon Pr); pap. 25.00 (*0-08-025389-X*, Pergamon Pr) Elsevier.

***Barney, Gerald O., et al.** Threshold 2000: Critical Issues & Spiritual Values for a Global Age. 2nd rev. ed. Orig. Title: Global 2000 Revisited. 176p. 1999. pap. 13.95 (*0-9637897-3-2*) CoNexus Pr.

***Barney, J. Palmer.** Other Side of the Rainbow. 1999. pap. 12.95 (*1-929985-01-0*) Angel Hrt Pub.

***Barney, Jay.** Gaining & Sustaining Competitive Advantage. 2nd ed. 608p. (C). 2000. text. write for info. (*0-201-47158-2*) Addison-Wesley.

Barney, Jay. Gaining & Sustaining Competitive Advantage: Theory & Practice. McEwing, Mary D., ed. LC 96-7024. 570p. (C). 1996. 70.00 (*0-201-51285-8*) Addison-Wesley.

— Gaining & Sustaining Competitive Advantage P-Copy. 592p. (C). 1996. text. write for info. (*0-201-44224-8*) Addison-Wesley.

Barney, Jesse A. Rumney, Then & Now. (Illus.). 244p. 1998. reprint ed. lib. bdg. 31.50 (*0-8328-9726-4*) Higginson Bk Co.

Barney, Kenneth D. Directions, Please. LC 82-82080. (Radiant Life Ser.). 112p. 1983. pap. 3.95 (*0-88243-856-5*, 02-0856); pap., teacher ed. 5.50 (*0-88243-197-8*, 32-0197) Gospel Pub.

— A Faith to Live By. LC 76-27929. (Radiant Life Ser.). 125p. 1977. pap. 3.95 (*0-88243-899-9*, 02-0899); pap., teacher ed. 5.50 (*0-88243-171-4*, 32-0171) Gospel Pub.

— Freedom: A Guarantee for Everybody. LC 75-34644. (Radiant Life Ser.). 126p. 1976. pap. 3.95 (*0-88243-891-3*, 02-0891); pap., teacher ed. 5.50 (*0-88243-165-X*, 32-0165) Gospel Pub.

— If You Love Me. LC 75-22611. (Radiant Life Ser.). 127p. 1977. pap. 3.95 (*0-88243-889-1*, 02-0889) Gospel Pub.

— Win Them Now! LC 90-86362. (Radiant Life Ser.). 128p. 1991. pap. 4.50 (*0-88243-882-4*, 02-0882); pap., teacher ed. 6.95 (*0-88243-203-6*, 32-0203) Gospel Pub.

— You'd Better Believe It! LC 75-22608. (Radiant Life Ser.). 125p. 1976. pap. 3.95 (*0-88243-887-5*, 02-0887) Gospel Pub.

Barney, Laura C., tr. see Abdu'l-Baha.

Barney, Matthew. Cremaster. 5th ed. (Illus.). 100p. 1997. pap. 40.00 (*1-881616-87-8*) Dist Art Pubs.

***Barney, Matthew.** Matthew Barney: Cremaster 2. 160p. 1999. pap. 45.00 (*0-935640-64-9*, Pub. by Walker Art Ctr) Dist Art Pubs.

Barney, Mike. My Day. (World of Discovery Ser.). 1997. text 4.95 (*1-879835-30-4*) Kaeden Corp.

— My Day. large type ed. (Illus.). 16p. (J). (gr. k-2). 1998. pap. 4.95 (*1-879835-26-6*, Kaeden) Kaeden Corp.

Barney, Natalie C. Adventures of the Mind: The Memoirs of Natalie Clifford Barney. Gatton, John S., tr. from FRE. (Cutting Edge: Lesbian Life & Literature Ser.). 304p. (C). 1992. text 47.00 (*0-8147-1177-4*); pap. text 16.00 (*0-8147-1178-2*) NYU Pr.

— Aventures De L'esprit. LC 75-12302. (Homosexuality Ser.). (FRE.). 1975. reprint ed. 23.95 (*0-405-07394-1*) Ayer.

— The One Who Is Legion. 192p. 1987. reprint ed. 28.00 (*0-915032-83-X*); reprint ed. pap. 14.95 (*0-943373-47-6*) Natl Poet Foun.

— A Perilous Advantage: The Best of Natalie Clifford Barney. Livia, Anna, tr. LC 92-13831. (Illus.). 224p. (C). 1992. pap. 10.95 (*0-934678-38-3*); text 19.95 (*0-934678-45-6*) New Victoria Pubs.

— Traits et Portraits. LC 75-12303. (Homosexuality: Lesbians & Gay Men in Society, History & Literature Ser.). (FRE.). 1975. reprint ed. 16.95 (*0-405-07395-X*) Ayer.

Barney, Paul. Clinical Applications of Herbal Medicine, Vol. 2. 1997. pap. text 11.95 (*1-885670-66-4*) Woodland UT.

Barney, Peter. Photography in the West. LC 99-60989. (Illus.). 100p. 1999. 30.00 (*1-888106-91-3*) Agreka Bks.

Barney, Peter, jt. auth. see Boothroyd, Stephen.

Barney Publishing. Barney's Beginnings: Opposites. (Barney's Beginnings Ser.). 32p. (J). (ps-k). 1997. pap. text, wbk. ed. 2.95 (*1-57064-123-4*, Barney Publ) Lyrick Pub.

Barney Publishing Staff. Barney's Finger Puppet & Book Set: A Day with Barney - Barney's Clothes. 9p. 1997. text 9.99 (*1-57064-136-6*, Barney Publ) Lyrick Pub.

— Barney's In, Out & All Around. LC 98-67004. (Barney Ser.). 22p. (J). (ps-k). 1999. bds. 4.95 (*1-57064-445-4*, Barney Publ) Lyrick Pub.

— Matching. 32p. (J). 1997. pap. text, wbk. ed. 2.95 (*1-57064-124-2*, Barney Publ) Lyrick Pub.

***Barney Publishing Staff & Bernthal, Mark S.** Barney & BJ Go to the Zoo. LC 98-655060. (Barney's Go to Ser.). (Illus.). 24p. (J). (ps-k). 1999. pap. 3.25 (*1-57064-446-2*, Barney Publ) Lyrick Pub.

— Barney's Book of Colors. LC 98-67002. (Barney Ser.). (Illus.). 22p. (J). (ps-3). 1999. bds. 5.95 (*1-57064-454-3*, Barney Publ) Lyrick Pub.

Barney Publishing Staff & Bernthal, Mark S. Barney's Outer Space Adventure. LC 98-67844. (Barney Ser.). (Illus.). 24p. (J). (ps-3). 1999. pap. 3.25 (*1-57064-456-X*, Barney Publ) Lyrick Pub.

Barney Publishing Staff & Kearns, Kimberly. Barney & Me on Safari. LC 98-67003. (Barney Ser.). (Illus.). 16p. (J). (ps-k). 1999. bds. 5.95 (*1-57064-448-9*, Barney Publ) Lyrick Pub.

***Barney Publishing Staff & Mody, Monica.** Barney's Mother Goose Hunt. LC 98-65338. (Barney Ser.). (Illus.). 16p. (J). (ps-k). 1999. bds. 5.95 (*1-57064-444-6*, Barney Publ) Lyrick Pub.

Barney, Ralph & Black, Jay, eds. Communitarian Journalism: A Special Issue of "Journal of Mass Media Ethics", Vol. 11, No. 3, 1996. 64p. 1996. pap. 20.00 (*0-8058-9876-X*) L Erlbaum Assocs.

— Where Ethics & Law Converge. (Special Issue of the Journal of Mass Media Ethics Ser.). 64p. 1997. pap. write for info. (*0-8058-9851-4*) L Erlbaum Assocs.

Barney, Ralph, jt. ed. see Black, Jay.

***Barney, Ralph D. & Black, Jay.** Persuasion Ethics: A Special Issue of the Journal of Mass Media Ethics. 64p. 1999. pap. 20.00 (*0-8058-9780-1*) L Erlbaum Assocs.

Barney, Rex. Orioles Memories. 1994. 19.95 (*0-9625427-0-9*) Goodwood Pr.

Barney, Rex & Macht, Norman L. Rex Barney's Thank Youuuu: For 50 Years in Baseball from Brooklyn to Baltimore. LC 92-44664. (Illus.). 279p. 1993. 19.95 (*0-87033-443-3*, Tidewtr Pubs) Cornell Maritime.

***Barney, Richard A.** Plots of Enlightenment: Education & The Novel in Eighteenth-century England. LC 99-21524. 1999. 49.50 (*0-8047-2978-6*) Stanford U Pr.

Barney, Richard W. & Loveless, Robert W. How to Make Knives. 182p. 1994. pap. 13.95 (*0-87341-389-X*) Krause Pubns.

***Barney, Sandra Lee.** Authorized to Heal: Gender, Class & the Transformation of Medicine in Appalachia, 1880-1930. LC 99-30433. 240p. 2000. pap. 17.95 (*0-8078-4834-4*) U of NC Pr.

— Authorized to Heal: Gender, Class & the Transformation of Medicine in Appalachia, 1880-1930. LC 99-30433. (Illus.). 240p. 2000. lib. bdg. 39.95 (*0-8078-2522-0*) U of NC Pr.

Barney, Stephen, jt. ed. see Anderson, Theodore M.

Barney, Stephen A. Studies in Troilus: Chaucer's Text, Meter & Diction. (Medieval Texts & Studies: No. 14). 167p. 1993. 28.00 (*0-937191-45-0*) Mich St U Pr.

— Word-Hoard: An Introduction to Old English Vocabulary. 2nd ed. LC 76-47003. (Yale Language Ser. . 86p. 1985. pap. 12.00 (*0-300-03506-3*) Yale U Pr.

Barney, Stephen A., ed. Chaucer's Troilus: Essays in Criticism. x, 323p. 1980. 89.50 (*0-208-01822-0*) Elliots Bks.

Barney, Tad. Porter Township: or Now When Your Father Was a Boy: Or Now When Your Father Was a Boy. LC 88-61313. 278p. 1989. 15.95 (*0-9620797-0-7*) Rotabar Pub.

Barney, Tina. Everyone Is Afraid of Her Own Life. (Illus.). 256p. 1997. 60.00 (*3-931141-60-8*) Dist Art Pubs.

Barney, William. Battleground for the Union: The Era of The Civil War & Reconstruction 1848. 448p. (C). 1989. pap. text 55.00 (*0-13-069386-3*) P-H.

— The Killdeer Crying: Selected Poems of William Barney. 2nd ed. Oliphant, Dave, ed. (Illus.). 80p. 1983. pap. 7.95 (*0-933384-07-6*); lib. bdg. 11.95 (*0-933384-09-2*) Prickly Pear.

Barney, William, ed. A Companion to Nineteenth-Century America. LC 99-39780. (Companions to American History Ser.). 500p. 1999. 99.95 (*0-631-20985-9*) Blackwell Pubs.

Barney, William D. A Cowtown Chronicle: William D. Barney. Colquitt, Betsy, ed. (American Regional Book Ser.: Vol. 4). 125p. (Orig.). 1999. pap. 12.95 (*0-9651359-3-4*, 1304, Pub. by Browder Springs) Herveys Bklink.

— Listening Back. LC 92-74619. (Illus.). 61p. (Orig.). 1992. pap. 10.00 (*1-878149-16-4*) Counterpoint Pub.

— Words from a Wide Land. LC 93-29508. (Illus.). 194p. 1994. 12.95 (*0-929398-64-5*) UNTX Pr.

Barney, William L. Flawed Victory: A New Perspective on the Civil War. LC 80-68972. 225p. 1980. pap. text 18.50 (*0-8191-1274-7*) U Pr of Amer.

— The Passage of the Republic: An Interdisciplinary History of Nineteenth-Century America. LC 86-80489. 429p. (C). 1987. pap. text 31.56 (*0-669-04758-9*) HM Trade Div.

— The Secessionist Impulse: Alabama & Mississippi in 1860. LC 73-16769. 388p. reprint ed. pap. 20.30 (*0-7837-1411-4*, 204176500023) Bks Demand.

Barnfield, Richard. The Encomion of Lady Pecunia: Or, the Praise of Money. LC 74-80162. (English Experience Ser.: No. 642). 24p. 1974. reprint ed. 15.00 (*90-221-0642-X*) Walter J Johnson.

Barnham, Henry D., ed. Tales of Nasreddin Khoja: 181 Mulla Masreddin Stories. LC 98-42587. 255p. 1999. reprint ed. pap. 16.00 (*0-936347-69-4*) IBEX.

Barnham, Henry D., tr. see Nasar, Al-Din.

***Barnham, Kay.** My Fairy Tale Princess Activity Kit. LC 98-182863. (Illus.). 24p. (J). (ps-3). 1998. 9.98 (*0-7651-0702-3*) Smithmark.

***Barnham, Keith & Vvedensky, Dimitri, eds.** Low Dimensional Semiconductor Structures: Fundamentals & Device Applications. LC QC611.6.S9L67 2000. (Illus.). 410p. (C). 2000. 59.95 (*0-521-59103-1*) Cambridge U Pr.

Barnhardt, David & Barnhardt, Lisa. Flaw & Order. 179p. 1992. pap. 6.95 (*1-56541-001-7*) Chalidze.

Barnhardt, Lisa, jt. auth. see Barnhardt, David.

Barnhardt, Ray, ed. Cross-Cultural Issues in Alaskan Education, Vol. 2, 1982. 206p. 9.95 (*1-877962-10-4*) Univ AK Ctr CCS.

Barnhardt, Ray, jt. auth. see Diamondstone, Judy.

Barnhardt, Tod. A Kick in the Assets: Ten Take-Charge Strategies for Building the Wealth You Want. LC 98-20424. 272p. 1998. 23.95 (*0-399-14430-7*, G P Putnam) Peng Put Young Read.

Barnhardt, Wilton. Emma Who Saved My Life. LC 98-16362. 480p. 1998. pap. 14.00 (*0-312-19118-9*) St Martin.

— Gospel: A Novel. LC 94-46583. 788p. 1995. pap. 16.00 (*0-312-11924-0*, Picador USA) St Martin.

— Show World. LC 98-3035. 311p. 1998. text 24.95 (*0-312-18684-3*) St Martin.

— Show World. 352p. 1999. pap. 14.00 (*0-312-20810-3*, Picador USA) St Martin.

Barnhart. Biographical Notes upon Botanists. 1982. 430.00 (*0-8161-1342-4*, G K Hall & Co) Mac Lib Ref.

— Chambers Dictionaries of Etymology: The Origins & Development of over 25,000 English Words. 1312p. 1999. 45.00 (*0-550-14230-4*, Chambers LKC) LKC.

— Perinatal & Pediatric Respiratory Care. 1995. 450.00 (*0-7216-6742-2*) Harcourt.

Barnhart, Aaron. Barnhart's Guide to TV 2000: The First Complete & Critical Yearbook on Television -- All Shows, New & Returning, Broadcast & Cable. (Illus.). 220p. 1999. pap. 14.95 (*0-9669258-5-8*, TV Barn) Irene.

Barnhart, Anna, jt. auth. see Barnhart, Duane.

Barnhart, B., jt. ed. see Woodhead, Avril D.

Barnhart, Becky. Schwann DVD Advance Vol. 2, No. 6: November/December 2000. (Complete Guide to DVD Movies Ser.). (Illus.). 100p. 2000. pap. 6.95 (*1-57598-063-0*) Schwann Pubns.

***Barnhart, Becky.** Schwann Opus Vol. 11, No. 2: Spring 2000. (Source for Classical Music Information Ser.). (Illus.). 1150p. 2000. pap. 16.95 (*1-57598-074-6*) Schwann Pubns.

— Schwann Opus Vol. 11, No. 3: Summer 2000. (Classical Music Resource Ser.). (Illus.). 1150p. 2000. pap. 16.95 (*1-57598-075-4*) Schwann Pubns.

— Schwann Opus Vol. 11, No. 4: Fall 2000. (Classical Music Resource Ser.). (Illus.). 1150p. 2000. pap. 16.95 (*1-57598-076-2*) Schwann Pubns.

— Schwann Opus Vol. 12, No. 1: Winter 2000. (Classical Music Resource Ser.). (Illus.). 1150p. 2000. pap. 16.95 (*1-57598-077-0*) Schwann Pubns.

— Schwann Spectrum Vol. 9, No. 4: Fall 2000. (Guide to Rock, Jazz, World... & Beyond). (Illus.). 750p. 2000. pap. 16.95 (*1-57598-080-0*) Schwann Pubns.

— Schwann Spectrum Vol. 10, No. 1: Winter 2000. (Guide to Rock, Jazz, World... & Beyond). (Illus.). 750p. 2000. pap. 16.95 (*1-57598-081-9*) Schwann Pubns.

Barnhart, Becky, ed. Schwann Artist 1998: America's Guide to Classical Performers. 20th ed. (Source for Classical Performers Information Ser.). 1200p. 1998. pap. 19.95 (*1-57598-035-5*, Pub. by Schwann Pubns) Valley Media.

***Barnhart, Becky, ed.** Schwann Artist 1999. 21st ed. (Source for Classical Performers Information Ser.). (Illus.). 1200p. 1999. pap. 19.95 (*1-57598-049-5*, Pub. by Schwann Pubns) Valley Media.

Barnhart, Becky, ed. Schwann DVD Advance Vol. 1, No. 1: September/October 1999. (Source for DVD Information Ser.). (Illus.). 100p. 1999. pap. 6.95 (*1-57598-054-1*, Pub. by Schwann Pubns) Valley Media.

— Schwann DVD Advance Vol. 1, No. 2: November/December 2000. (Source for DVD Information Ser.). (Illus.). 100p. 1999. pap. 6.95 (*1-57598-055-X*, Pub. by Schwann Pubns) Valley Media.

— Schwann DVD Advance Vol. 2, No. 1: January/February 2000. (Source for DVD Information Ser.). (Illus.). 100p. 1999. pap. 6.95 (*1-57598-056-8*, Pub. by Schwann Pubns) Valley Media.

— Schwann DVD Advance Vol. 2, No. 2: March/April 2000. (Source for DVD Information Ser.). (Illus.). 100p. 1999. pap. 6.95 (*1-57598-058-4*, Pub. by Schwann Pubns) Valley Media.

— Schwann DVD Advance Vol. 2, No. 3: May/June 2000. (Source for DVD Information Ser.). (Illus.). 100p. 1999. pap. 6.95 (*1-57598-059-2*, Pub. by Schwann Pubns) Valley Media.

— Schwann Opus Vol. 10, No. 2: Spring 1999. (Source for Classical Music Information Ser.). (Illus.). 1100p. 1999. pap. 16.95 (*1-57598-048-7*, Pub. by Schwann Pubns) Valley Media.

— Schwann Opus Vol. 10, No. 3: Summer 1999. (Source for Classical Music Information Ser.). (Illus.). 1100p. 1999. pap. 16.95 (*1-57598-050-9*, Pub. by Schwann Pubns) Valley Media.

— Schwann Opus Vol. 10, No. 4: Fall 1999. (Source for Classical Music Information Ser.). (Illus.). 1100p. 1999. pap. 16.95 (*1-57598-051-7*, Pub. by Schwann Pubns) Valley Media.

— Schwann Opus Vol. 11, No. 1: Winter 1999. (Source for Classical Music Information Ser.). (Illus.). 1100p. 1999. pap. 16.95 (*1-57598-052-5*, Pub. by Schwann Pubns) Valley Media.

— Schwann Spectrum Vol. 8, No. 2: Spring 1999. (Source for Popular Music Information Ser.). (Illus.). 750p. 1999. pap. 16.95 (*1-57598-053-3*, Pub. by Schwann Pubns) Valley Media.

— Schwann Spectrum Vol. 8, No. 3: Summer 1999. (Source for Popular Music Information Ser.). 750p. 1999. pap. 16.95 (*1-57598-057-6*, Pub. by Schwann Pubns) Valley Media.

— Schwann Spectrum Vol. 8, No. 4: Fall 1999. (Source for Popular Music Information Ser.). (Illus.). 750p. 1999. pap. 16.95 (*1-57598-061-4*, Pub. by Schwann Pubns) Valley Media.

— Schwann Spectrum Vol. 9, No. 1: Winter 1999. (Source for Popular Music Information Ser.). (Illus.). 750p. 1999. pap. 16.95 (*1-57598-065-7*, Pub. by Schwann Pubns) Valley Media.

***Barnhart, Becky, ed.** Schwann Spectrum Vol. 9, No. 2: Spring 2000. (Source for Popular Music Information Ser.). (Illus.). 750p. 2000. pap. 16.95 (*1-57598-078-9*) Schwann Pubns.

— Schwann Spectrum Vol. 9, No. 3: Summer 2000. (Guide to Rock, Jazz, World... & Beyond). (Illus.). 750p. 2000. pap. 16.95 (*1-57598-079-7*) Schwann Pubns.

Barnhart, Brent A. Joy in the Journey. 1995. write for info. (*0-9648780-1-1*); pap. write for info. (*0-9648780-0-3*) Tex Hart.

Barnhart, Bruno. The Good Wine: Reading John from the Center. LC 93-23068. 512p. (Orig.). 1993. pap. 19.95 (*0-8091-3416-0*) Paulist Pr.

Barnhart, Clarence L., jt. auth. see Bloomfield, Leonard.

***Barnhart, David K.** Barnhart Dictionary Companion. 2000. pap. 24.50 (*0-87779-704-8*) Merriam-Webster Inc.

Barnhart, David K. The Barnhart Dictionary Companion Index 1982-1985. LC 86-81562. xv, 102p. 1987. 45.00 (*0-936368-05-5*) Lexik Hse.

— The Barnhart New Words Concordance. LC 93-80483. 1995. ring bd., suppl. ed. 80.00 (*0-936368-09-8*) Lexik Hse.

— The Barnhart New-Words Concordance. LC 93-80483. ix, 62p. 1995. ring bd., suppl. ed. 25.00 (*0-936368-08-X*) Lexik Hse.

Barnhart, David K. & Metcalf, Allan A. America in So Many Words: A Year-by-Year Review of Fascinating Words in the History of America. LC 97-14510. 320p. 1997. 18.00 (*0-395-86020-2*) HM.

***Barnhart, David K. & Metcalf, Allan A.** America in So Many Words: Words That Have Shaped America. 320p. 1999. pap. 12.00 (*0-618-00270-7*) HM.

— America in So Many Words: Words That Have Shaped America. (Illus.). 308p. 2000. reprint ed. 18.00 (*0-7881-9254-X*) DIANE Pub.

B

Barnhart, David R. The Church's Desperate Need for Revival. 163p. (Orig.). 1987. 8.95 (*0-9617377-0-0*) Abiding Word Minist.
— Contending for the Faith. LC 94-71879. 213p. (Orig.). 1994. 9.95 (*0-9617377-2-7*) Abiding Word Minist.
— Contending for the Faith Study Guide. 120p. (Orig.). 1994. pap. 5.00 (*0-9617377-3-5*) Abiding Word Minist.
— Israel: Land of Promise & Prophecy. (Illus.). 225p. (Orig.). 1988. 8.95 (*0-9617377-1-9*) Abiding Word Minist.
***Barnhart, Diana & Leon, Vicki.** Tidepools: The Bright World of the Rocky Shoreline. (Illus.). 40p. 1999. reprint ed. pap. 7.95 (*0-945092-49-0*, Pub. by EZ Nature) Cntrl Coast Pr.
Barnhart, Diana & Leon, Vicki. Tidepools: The Bright World of the Rocky Shoreline. rev. ed. LC 94-31822. (Close up: A Focus on Nature Ser.). (Illus.). 48p. (YA). (gr. 5 up). 1994. pap. 7.95 (*0-382-24867-8*) Silver Burdett Pr.
— Tidepools: The Bright World of the Rocky Shoreline. rev. ed. LC 94-31822. (Close up: A Focus on Nature Ser.). (Illus.). 48p. (YA). (gr. 5 up). 1999. lib. bdg. 23.00 (*0-382-24865-1*) Silver Burdett Pr.
Barnhart, Duane & Barnhart, Anna. Duane Barnhart's Cartooning Basics: Creating the Characters. LC 97-91639. (Illus.). 74p. (Orig.). (J). (gr. 2-7). 1997. pap. 12.95 (*0-9657136-0-1*) Cartoon Connect.
Barnhart, Edward N., jt. auth. see Chandler, Albert R.
Barnhart, Gary. The Releasing of the Power. 225p. (Orig.). 1997. pap. 18.99 (*1-57502-410-1*, PO1273) Morris Pubng.
Barnhart, J. E. Religion & the Challenge of Philosophy. (Quality Paperback Ser.: No. 291). 400p. (Orig.). 1975. pap. 9.95 (*0-8226-0291-1*) Littlefield.
— The Study of Religion & Its Meaning. 1977. 51.55 (*90-279-7762-3*) Mouton.
Barnhart, Jack M., ed. see American Society for Testing & Materials Staff.
Barnhart, Janice S. Preventive Discipline: A Roadmap for Good Behavior from Toddler to Teen, Vol. I. LC 96-94978. (Illus.). 148p. (Orig.). 1997. pap. 9.95 (*0-9654940-0-4*) J S Barnhart.
Barnhart, Joe & Kraeger, Linda. Trust & Treachery. (Orig.). 1995. pap. text 52.07 (*1-56870-210-8*) RonJon Pub.
Barnhart, Joe, jt. auth. see Kraeger, Linda.
Barnhart, Joe, jt. auth. see Warren, Thomas B.
Barnhart, Joe E. & Barnhart, Mary A. The New Birth: A Naturalist View of Religious Conversion. LC 81-9557. xiv, 174p. (C). 1981. 15.50 (*0-86554-009-8*, MUP-H011) Mercer Univ Pr.
***Barnhart, Joe E. & Kraeger, Linda T.** In Search of First-Century Christianity. (New Critical Thinking in Theology & Biblical Studies). 224p. 2000. text 69.95 (*0-7546-1238-4*, Pub. by Ashgate Pub) Ashgate Pub Co.
Barnhart, John. Keeping up with the Boys: From St. Edwards to Super Bowl XXX: A Year in a Dynasty. (Illus.). 1996. 36.95 (*0-87833-927-2*); pap. text 19.95 (*0-87833-952-3*) Taylor Pub.
Barnhart, John D., jt. auth. see Riker, Dorothy L.
Barnhart, Judith. Stories to Start With: Interpersonal Relationships, Set. LC 93-81085. (Illus.). 96p. (Orig.). (J). (gr. 4-8). 1993. pap. 15.95 (*1-884063-19-5*) Mar Co Prods.
Barnhart, Margaret P. Journey Unknown: Focusing on the Emotional Aspects of...Cancer,...Mastectomy,...Chemotherapy. rev. ed. (Illus.). 64p. 1994. pap. 14.95 (*0-9625121-1-7*) Journey Pr AZ.
Barnhart, Mary A., jt. auth. see Barnhart, Joe E.
Barnhart, Michael, ed. Congress & United States Foreign Policy: Controlling the Use of Force in the Nuclear Age. LC 86-23057. 196p. (C). 1987. text 19.50 (*0-88706-465-5*) State U NY Pr.
Barnhart, Michael A. Japan & the World since 1868. (International Relations & the Great Powers Ser.). (Illus.). 208p. 1995. text 55.00 (*0-340-52857-5*) OUP.
— Japan & the World since 1868. 3rd ed. (International Relations & the Great Powers Ser.). (Illus.). 208p. 1995. pap. text 18.95 (*0-340-52858-3*, A7004) OUP.
— Japan Prepares for Total War: The Search for Economic Security, 1919-1941. LC 86-16821. (Cornell Studies in Security Affairs). (Illus.). 304p. 1987. pap. text 15.95 (*0-8014-9529-6*) Cornell U Pr.
Barnhart, Norman. Speaking Emotions: Beauty of Thought & Inspiration. (Illus.). 94p. 1997. pap. 7.95 (*1-57502-530-2*, PO1566) Morris Pubng.
Barnhart, Phillip A. Guide to National Professional Certification Programs. 2nd ed. LC 97-219204. 1997. lib. bdg. 99.95 (*0-8493-9960-2*) CRC Pr.
Barnhart, Richard M. Li Kung-Lin's Classic of Filial Piety. (Illus.). 176p. 1994. 50.00 (*0-8109-6462-7*, Pub. by Abrams) Time Warner.
— Painters of the Great Ming: The Imperial Court & the Zhe School. LC 92-43258. 1993. 65.00 (*0-936227-11-7*); pap. 35.00 (*0-936227-12-5*) Dallas Mus.
Barnhart, Richard M., ed. Li Kung-Lin's Classic of Filial Piety. LC 93-17578. (Illus.). 1991. 176p. 1993. 39.95 (*0-87099-679-7*, 0-8109-6462-7) Metro Mus Art.
Barnhart, Richard M., et al. The Jade Studio: Masterpieces of Ming & Qing Painting & Calligraphy from the Wong Nan-P'ing Collection. LC 93-61908. (Illus.). 308p. 1994. pap. 40.00 (*0-89467-066-2*) Yale Art Gallery.
— The Jade Studio: Masterpieces of Ming & Qing Painting & Calligraphy from the Wong Nan-P'ing Collection. LC 93-61908. (Illus.). 308p. 1994. 65.00 (*0-89467-067-0*) Yale Art Gallery.
Barnhart, Richard M., jt. auth. see Fangyu, Wang.
Barnhart, Robert K., ed. The American Heritage Dictionary of Science. (Illus.). 768p. 1988. 32.00 (*0-395-48367-0*) HM.
— The Barnhart Abbreviations Dictionary. LC 96-115251. 464p. 1995. 39.95 (*0-471-57146-6*) Wiley.
— Barnhart Concise Dictionary of Etymology. LC 94-17922. 944p. 1995. 55.00 (*0-06-270084-7*, Harper Ref) HarpC.
— The Barnhart Dictionary of Etymology. 1258p. 1988. 64.00 (*0-8242-0745-9*) Wilson.
Barnhart, Robert K., et al, eds. Third Barnhart Dictionary of New English. 592p. 1990. 52.00 (*0-8242-0796-3*) Wilson.
Barnhart, Robert K. & World Book Editors. The World Book Dictionary. LC 96-25617. (YA). (gr. 4 up). 2000. write for info. (*0-7166-0297-0*) World Bk.
Barnhart, Rochelle, jt. auth. see Anton, Kelly.
Barnhart, Russell T. Beating the Wheel: The System That's Won More Than 6 Million Dollars - From Las Vegas to Monte Carlo. (Illus.). 320p. 1992. pap. 14.95 (*0-8184-0553-8*, L Stuart) Carol Pub Group.
— Dens of Iniquity: A Life among Gamblers, Cheaters & Thieves, Vol. 1. 1999. pap. 14.95 (*0-910575-12-6*) RGE Publishing.
Barnhart, Ruth S. From the Steppes to the Badlands. LC 98-91398. (Illus.). 336p. 1998. pap. 24.95 (*0-9665427-0-3*) NAHSH M.
Barnhart, Shawn. Eberhart/Everhart Ancestry in the United States of America: A Comprehensive Manual, 1727-1995. rev. ed. (Illus.). 148p. (Orig.). 1996. pap. 17.00 (*0-7884-0371-0*, B065) Heritage Bk.
Barnhart, Sherry L. & Czervinske, Michael P. Perinatal & Pediatric Respiratory Care. LC 94-25347. (Pediatric Respiratory Diseases Ser.). (Illus.). 656p. 1995. text 53.00 (*0-7216-6739-2*, W B Saunders Co) Harcrt Hlth Sci Grp.
Barnhart, Sherry L. & Czervinske, Michael P., eds. Clinical Handbook of Perinatal & Pediatric Respiratory Care. (Illus.). 1995. pap. text, spiral bd. 34.95 (*0-7216-6740-6*, W B Saunders Co) Harcrt Hlth Sci Grp.
Barnhart, Sherry L. & Czervinske, Michael P., eds. Perinatal & Pediatric Respiratory Care. (Illus.). 1995. teacher ed. write for info. (*0-7216-5942-X*, W B Saunders Co) Harcrt Hlth Sci Grp.
— Perinatal & Pediatric Respiratory Care. (Illus.). 1995. pap. text, wbk. ed. 16.95 (*0-7216-6741-4*, W B Saunders Co) Harcrt Hlth Sci Grp.
***Barnhart, Stephen L.** Percussionists: A Biographical Dictionary. LC 99-46021. 429p. 2000. lib. bdg. 95.00 (*0-313-29627-8*) Greenwood.
Barnhart, Tod. Five Rituals of Wealth: Barnhart,&Tod. abr. ed. 1995. audio 12.00 (*1-55994-840-X*, CPN 10056) HarperAudio.
Barnhart, Tod. The Five Rituals of Wealth: Proven Strategies for Turning the Little You Have into More Than Enough. 208p. 1996. pap. 13.00 (*0-88730-784-1*, HarpBusn) HarpInfo.
***Barnhart, Tod.** A Kick in the Assets: TenTake-Charge Strategies for Building the Wealth You Want. 1999. reprint ed. pap. 14.95 (*0-399-52531-9*, Perigee Bks) Berkley Pub.
Barnhart, Tom. Front Range Single Tracks: The Best Single-Track Trails Near Denver & Boulder. LC 94-62048. 112p. (Orig.). 1999. pap. 11.95 (*0-9638419-4-7*) Fat Tire Pr.
— Steamboat Single Tracks: The Mountain Biking Guide to Steamboat Springs, Colorado. LC 93-73409. 68p. (Orig.). 1993. pap. 10.95 (*0-9638419-5-5*) Fat Tire Pr.
***Barnhart, Tony.** Southern Fried Football: The History, Passion & Glory of the Great Southern Game. 2000. 24.95 (*1-57243-367-1*) Triumph Bks.
Barnhart, William E. & Schlickman, Eugene P. Kerner: The Conflict of Intangible Rights. LC 99-6065. 504p. 1999. 29.95 (*0-252-02504-0*) U of Ill Pr.
Barnhat, Bruno. Second Simplicity: Toward a Rebirth of Wisdom. LC 98-40942. 320p. 1999. pap. 23.95 (*0-8091-3832-8*) Paulist Pr.
Barnhill, David L. At Home on the Earth: Becoming Native to Our Place: A Multicultural Anthology. LC 98-33876. 341p. 1999. 17.95 (*0-520-21684-9*, Pub. by U CA Pr) Cal Prin Full Svc.
Barnhill, David L., ed. At Home on the Earth: Becoming Native to Our Place: A Multicultural Anthology. LC 98-33876. 344p. 1999. 50.00 (*0-520-21483-8*, Pub. by U CA Pr) Cal Prin Full Svc.
***Barnhill, David Landis & Gottlieb, Roger S., eds.** Deep Ecology & World Religions. LC 00-30081. (C). 2001. pap. text 21.95 (*0-7914-4884-3*) State U NY Pr.
— Deep Ecology & World Religions. LC 00-30081. (C). 2001. text 65.50 (*0-7914-4883-5*) State U NY Pr.
Barnhill, Edward D., et al. Searching Land Titles in South Carolina. 1991. pap. 25.00 (*0-943856-31-0*, 502) SC Bar CLE.
Barnhill, Georgia B. Extracts from the Journals of Ethan Allen Greenwood: Portrait Painter & Museum Proprietor with a List of Portraits Painted by Ethan Allen Greenwood. (Illus.). 109p. (Orig.). 1993. pap. 15.00 (*0-944026-47-8*) Am Antiquarian.
— Wild Impressions: The Adirondacks on Paper. (Illus.). 144p. 1995. pap. 20.00 (*0-910020-45-0*) Adirondack Mus.
Barnhill, Georgia B., ed. Prints of New England. (Illus.). 172p. 1991. 59.95 (*0-912296-92-5*, 39076) Oak Knoll.
Barnhill, Georgia B. & Tatham, David. Wild Impressions: Prints from the Collection of the Adirondack Museum. (Imago Mundi Ser.). (Illus.). 144p. 1955. 40.00 (*1-56792-041-1*) Godine.
Barnhill, Georgia B., et al. Cultivation of Artists in Nineteenth-Century America. LC 97-4458. (Illus.). 212p. 1997. 32.50 (*0-944026-75-3*) Oak Knoll.
Barnhill, Georgia Brady. The Catalogue of American Engravings: A Manual for Users. (Illus.). 1999. pap. write for info. (*0-944026-97-4*) Am Antiquarian.
Barnhill, J. Herschel. From Surplus to Substitution: Energy in Texas. (Texas History Ser.). (Illus.). 45p. 1983. pap. text 9.95 (*0-89641-118-4*) American Pr.
Barnhill, John. Eating Disorders. LC 98-164977. 176p. 1998. mass mkt. 5.50 (*0-440-22538-8*) Doubleday.
Barnhill, Laurence R., jt. ed. see Small, Richard F.
***Barnhill, Linda.** One Precious Soul. 1999. write for info. (*1-58235-451-0*) Watermrk Pr.
Barnhill, Raymond L. Pathology of Melanocytic Nevi & Malignant Melanoma of the Skin. LC 94-33338. (Illus.). 294p. 1994. pap. text 175.00 (*0-7506-9504-8*) Buttrwrth-Heinemann.
— Textbook of Dermatopathology. LC 97-24101. (Illus.). 928p. 1998. text 195.00 (*0-07-005726-5*) McGraw-Hill HPD.
Barnhill, Raymond L., et al. Color Atlas & Synopsis of Pigmented Lesions. (Illus.). 250p. 1995. text 55.00 (*0-07-005110-0*) McGraw-Hill HPD.
Barnhill, Robert E., ed. Geometry Processing for Design & Manufacturing. LC 91-46596. (Miscellaneous Bks.: No. 28). ix, 211p. 1992. pap. 45.00 (*0-89871-280-7*) Soc Indus-Appl Math.
Barnhill, Steve. The Luby's Story: Good Food from Good People. Evett, Alice, ed. LC 88-51273. (Illus.). xvi, 108p. (Orig.). 1989. pap. 6.95 (*0-934955-12-3*) Watercress Pr.
Barnhill, Theodore, et al. High-Yield Bonds: Market Structure, Portfolio Management, & Credit Risk Modeling. LC 98-40324. (Irwin Library of Investment & Finance Series). (Illus.). 574p. 1999. 75.00 (*0-07-006786-4*) McGraw.
Barnhizer, David. The Warrior Lawyer: Powerful Strategies for Winning Legal Battles. LC 96-54272. 1997. 24.95 (*1-57105-050-7*) Transnatl Pubs.
Barnholden, Michael, jt. ed. see Klobucar, Andrew.
Barnholden, Michael, tr. see Dumont, Gabriel.
Barnhoorn, L. A. & Wellens, Karel C., eds. Diversity in Secondary Rules & the Unity of International Law. 1995. lib. bdg. 160.00 (*90-411-0092-X*, Pub. by M Nijhoff) Kluwer Academic.
Barnhouse, Donald G. Expositions of Bible Doctrines, 10 vols. in four, Set. (Bible Study Ser.). 1966. 125.00 (*0-8028-3014-5*) Eerdmans.
— Genesis: Devotional Commentary. 1973. pap. 11.95 (*0-310-20471-2*) Zondervan.
— The Invisible War. 288p. 1980. pap. 15.99 (*0-310-20481-X*) Zondervan.
— Is Anybody up There? LC 76-51734. 1977. 6.95 (*0-9606562-0-0*, BT1102-B26) L Victor Pr.
— Thessalonians: Exposition. 1980. pap. 3.95 (*0-310-20501-8*) Zondervan.
Barnhouse, Donald G., jt. auth. see Ehrenstein, H. H.
Barnhouse, Donald Grey. Bible Truth Illustrated. LC 79-64829. 280p. 1996. pap. 12.99 (*0-8007-5594-4*) Revell.
— Illustrating Great Themes of Scripture. 2nd ed. LC 96-45030. 256p. 1997. reprint ed. pap. 12.99 (*0-8007-5624-X*, Words Fitly Spo) Revell.
— Illustrating the Gospel of John. LC 97-38744. 320p. 1998. reprint ed. pap. 12.99 (*0-8007-5662-2*, The Love Life) Revell.
— Let Me Illustrate: More Than 400 Stories, Anecdotes & Illustrations. (Illus.). 384p. 1994. pap. 12.99 (*0-8007-5508-1*) Revell.
Barnhouse, Meg. The Rock of Ages at the Taj Mahal: Unquiet Meditations. 72p. 1998. pap. 7.00 (*1-55896-377-4*, 5796, Skinner Hse Bks) Unitarian Univ.
Barnhouse, Meg, et al. The Best of Radio Free Bubba. 150p. 1998. pap. 13.00 (*1-891885-03-0*) Hub City Writers.
***Barnhouse, Rebecca.** Recasting the Past: The Middle Ages in Young Adult Literature. (Young Adult Literature Ser.). 110p. 2000. pap. text 15.00 (*0-86709-470-2*, Pub. by Boynton Cook Pubs) Heinemann.
Barnhouse, Rebecca & Withers, Benjamin C., eds. The Old English Hexateuch: Aspects & Approaches. (Publications of the Richard Rawlinson Center). (C). 40.00 (*1-58044-024-X*); pap. 20.00 (*1-58044-050-9*) Medieval Inst.
Barnhouse, Ruth T. A Woman's Identity. LC 93-91042. Orig. Title: Identity. 150p. 1994. reprint ed. pap. 13.95 (*0-9638398-3-7*) Bonne Chance.
Barnhurst, Kevin G. Seeing the Newspaper. LC 92-62727. 1994. pap. 12.00 (*0-685-71199-4*); pap. text 32.95 (*0-312-10800-1*) St Martin.
Barniak, Carl K. The Food of Angels. 96p. (Orig.). 1984. pap. 7.95 (*0-9613803-0-6*) Barniak Pubns.
Barnich, Terrence L., et al. Telecommunications Free Trade Zones: Crafting a Model for Local Exchange Competition. 53p. (Orig.). (C). 1994. pap. text 25.00 (*0-7881-0366-0*) DIANE Pub.
Barnickel. Dictionary of False Friends: German-English. (ENG & GER.). 215p. 1992. 49.95 (*0-7859-7247-1*, 3861170000) Fr & Eur.
Barnickel, Linda A. We Enlisted As Patriots: The Civil War Records of Battery G, 2nd Illinois Light Artillery. 162p. 1998. pap. 18.00 (*0-7884-0915-8*, B068) Heritage Bk.
Barnicle, Frank. Life, Love & Laughter: A Collection of Stories from the Heart...& a Few from the Funny Bone Too! 276p. 1997. 19.95 (*0-941072-29-0*) Southern Herit.
Barnicoat, John. Posters: A Concise History. (World of Art Ser.). (Illus.). 288p. 1985. pap. 14.95 (*0-500-20118-8*, Pub. by Thames Hudson) Norton.
Barnidge. Basic Mathematics. 1994. pap. text, student ed. 29.33 (*0-13-458050-8*) P-H.
Barnie, John. The City. 70p. 1998. pap. 17.95 (*0-8464-4789-4*) Beekman Pubs.
— The Confirmation. 129p. 1998. pap. 23.95 (*0-8464-4790-8*) Beekman Pubs.
— The Confirmation. 129p. 1992. pap. 24.00 (*0-86383-671-2*, Pub. by Gomer Pr) St Mut.
— The Confirmation. 129p. (C). 1992. pap. 40.00 (*0-7855-6762-3*, Pub. by Gomer Pr) St Mut.
— Heroes. 62p. 1994. pap. 12.95 (*0-8464-4778-9*) Beekman Pubs.
— Heroes. 62p. 1996. pap. 14.95 (*0-8464-4622-7*) Beekman Pubs.
— The King of Ashes. 168p. (C). 1989. 33.00 (*0-86383-537-6*, Pub. by Gomer Pr) St Mut.
— The King of Ashes, Vol. XII. 168p. 1989. 32.95 (*0-8464-4656-1*) Beekman Pubs.
— No Hiding Place: Essays on the New Nature & Poetry. 155p. 1997. pap. 18.95 (*0-7083-1342-6*, Pub. by Univ Wales Pr) Paul & Co Pubs.
— War in Medieval Society: Social Values & the Hundred Year War, 1337-99 LC 75-300815. xiii, 204p. 1974. write for info. (*0-297-76643-0*) Weidenfeld & Nicolson.
Barnie, John, ed. The City. 70p. 1993. pap. 35.00 (*0-86383-996-7*, Pub. by Gomer Pr) St Mut.
***Barnier, Carol.** How to Get Your Child off the Refrigerator & on to Learning: Homeschooling Distractible, ADHD, or Just Plain Fidgety Kids. (Illus.). 120p. 2000. pap. 12.99 (*1-883002-70-2*) Emerald WA.
***Barnier, John, ed.** Coming into Focus: A Step-by-Step Guide to Alternative Photographic & Printing Processes. LC 99-88461. (Illus.). 352p. 2000. pap. 35.00 (*0-8118-1894-2*) Chronicle Bks.
Barnier, William J. Discrete Math. Date not set. pap. text, student ed. write for info. (*0-314-52466-5*) West Pub.
Barnier, William J. & Feldman, Norman. Introduction to Advanced Mathematics. 304p. (C). 1990. text 85.00 (*0-13-477084-6*) P-H.
***Barnier, William J. & Feldman, Norman.** Introduction to Advanced Mathematics. 2nd ed. LC 99-52613. 300p. 1999. 84.00 (*0-13-016750-9*) P-H.
Barnish, S. J., tr. from LAT. Cassiodorus: Variae. (Translated Texts for Historians Ser.). 254p. (Orig.). (C). 1992. pap. text 18.50 (*0-85323-436-1*, Pub. by Liverpool Univ Pr) U of Pa Pr.
Barnitz, Albert & Barnitz, Jennie. Life in Custer's Cavalry: Diaries & Letters of Albert & Jennie Barnitz, 1867-1868. Utley, Robert Marshall, ed. LC 86-25104. (Illus.). xiv, 302p. 1987. reprint ed. pap. 13.95 (*0-8032-9553-7*, Bison Books) U of Nebr Pr.
Barnitz, Albert T. Life in Custer's Cavalry: Diaries & Letters of Albert & Jennie Barnitz, 1867-1868. Utley, Robert Marshall, ed. LC 76-52425. (Yale Western Americana Ser.: No. 30). (Illus.). 316p. reprint ed. pap. 98.00 (*0-8357-8209-3*, 203390700087) Bks Demand.
Barnitz, Jacqueline. Latin American Artists in New York since 1970. Nelson, Florencia B. & Carton, Janis B., eds. LC 87-70428. (Illus.). 114p. (Orig.). 1987. pap. 24.00 (*0-935213-10-4*) J S Blanton Mus.
***Barnitz, Jacqueline.** Twentieth-Century Art of Latin America. LC 99-50871. (Illus.). 416p. 2001. 70.00 (*0-292-70857-2*); pap. 34.95 (*0-292-70858-0*) U of Tex Pr.
Barnitz, Jennie, jt. auth. see Barnitz, Albert.
Barnitz, Laura A. Child Soldiers: Youth Who Participate in Armed Conflict. 28p. 1997. pap. 6.00 (*0-9663709-0-2*) Youth Advocate.
— Child Soldiers: Youth Who Participate in Armed Conflicts. 28p. 1997. reprint ed. pap. 6.00 (*0-9663709-4-5*) Youth Advocate.
— Commercial Sexual Exploitation of Children: Youth Involved in Prostitution, Pornography & Sex Trafficking. 44p. 1998. pap. 6.00 (*0-9663709-2-9*) Youth Advocate.
Barnitz, Laura A., ed. see Kilbourne, Susan.
Barnitz, Laura A., ed. see McCauley, Georgia.
Barnitz, Laura A., ed. see McVicker, Carrie.
Barnoski, Michael. Fundamental of Optical Fiber Communications. 1996. 52.00 (*0-614-18455-X*, B01022) Info Gatekeepers.
Barnosky, Anthony D., jt. ed. see Martin, Robert A.
Barnothy, Madeline F., ed. Biological Effects of Magnetic Fields. Incl. Vol. 1. LC 64-13146. 336p. 1964. 59.50 (*0-306-37601-6*, Kluwer Plenum); Vol. 2. LC 64-13146. 328p. 1969. 59.50 (*0-306-37602-4*, Kluwer Plenum); LC 64-13146. write for info. (*0-318-55309-0*, Plenum Trade) Perseus Pubng.
Barnott, Ken. Alternatives Directory: Autumn-Winter 1994. (Services & Products for a Changing World Ser.). 320p. 1994. 7.95 (*0-9643448-0-7*) Alternat Directory.
Barnouin, Barbara. European Labour Movement. 1992. 45.00 (*0-86187-650-4*) St Martin.
Barnouin, Barbara & Changgen, Yu. Ten Years of Turbulence: The Chinese Cultural Revolution. LC 92-2352. (Publication of the Graduate Institute of International Studies, Geneva). 1993. 94.50 (*0-7103-0458-7*, B2340) Routledge.
Barnouin, Barbara & Yu, Changgen. Chinese Foreign Policy During the Cultural Revolution. LC 97-25796. 1997. 127.50 (*0-7103-0580-X*) Col U Pr.
Barnouw. Introduction to Anthropology, 1. 4th ed. (Anthropology Ser.). Date not set. mass mkt. 21.75 (*0-534-10473-8*) Wadsworth Pub.
Barnouw, A. J. & Wohlrabe, Raymond A. The Land & People of Holland. rev. ed. LC 79-37249. (Portraits of the Nations Ser.). (Illus.). (YA). (gr. 6 up). 1972. lib. bdg. 10.89 (*0-397-31254-7*) HarpC Child Bks.
Barnouw, Adriaan Jacob, jt. auth. see Vogel, Jean Philippe.
Barnouw, Dagmar. Critical Realism: History, Photography, & the Work of Siegfried Kracauer. LC 93-42710. 1994. text 65.00 (*0-8018-4753-2*); pap. text 22.95 (*0-8018-4754-0*) Johns Hopkins.
— Germany 1945: Views of War & Violence. LC 96-11185. (Illus.). 256p. (C). 1997. 39.95 (*0-253-33046-7*) Ind U Pr.
— Visible Spaces: Hannah Arendt & the German-Jewish Experience. LC 89-38885. (Jewish Studies). 320p. 1990. text 48.50 (*0-8018-3923-8*) Johns Hopkins.
— Weimar Intellectuals & the Threat of Modernity. LC 87-45246. 352p. 1988. 35.00 (*0-253-36427-2*) Ind U Pr.

An Asterisk (*) at the beginning of an entry indicates that the title is appearing for the first time.

Barnouw, Eric & Miller, Mark C. Conglomerates & the Media. (Illus.). 192p. 1998. pap. 12.95 (*1-56584-472-6*, Pub. by New Press NY) Norton.
Barnouw, Erik. Conglomerates & the Media. 208p. 1997. 23.00 (*1-56584-386-X*, Pub. by New Press NY) Norton.
— Documentary: A History of the Non-Fiction Film. 2nd rev. ed. (Illus.). 416p. 1993. pap. text 15.95 (*0-19-507898-5*) OUP.
— A History of Broadcasting in the United States Vol. 1: A Tower in Babel: 1933. (Illus.). 350p. 1966. text 50.00 (*0-19-500474-4*) OUP.
— House with a Past. LC 92-5318. (Illus.). 106p. (Orig.). 1992. reprint ed. pap. 14.95 (*0-934720-37-1*) VT Hist Soc.
— Media Marathon: A Twentieth-Century Memoir. LC 95-35529. (Illus.). 280p. 1996. text 22.95 (*0-8223-1728-1*) Duke.
— The Sponsor: Notes on a Modern Potentate. (Illus.). 220p. 1979. pap. text 10.95 (*0-19-502614-4*) OUP.
— Tube of Plenty: The Evolution of American Television. 2nd rev. ed. (Illus.). 624p. 1990. pap. 18.95 (*0-19-506484-4*) OUP.
Barnouw, Erik, et al, eds. International Encyclopedia of Communications, 4 vols., Set. (Illus.). 1960p. 1989. text 475.00 (*0-19-504994-2*) OUP.
Barnouw, Erik, jt. auth. see Bannerman, R. LeRoy.
Barnouw, Victor. Acculturation & Personality among the Wisconsin Chippewa. LC 76-43646. (AAA Memoirs: No. 72). reprint ed. 39.50 (*0-404-15481-6*) AMS Pr.
— Culture & Personality. 4th ed. 538p. (C). 1985. 48.00 (*0-534-10479-7*) Wadsworth Pub.
— Wisconsin Chippewa Myths & Tales & Their Relation to Chippewa Life. LC 76-53647. 304p. (C). 1993. reprint ed. pap. 21.95 (*0-299-07314-9*) U of Wis Pr.
***Barnow, Burt S. & King, Christopher T., eds.** Improving the Odds: Increasing the Effectiveness of Publicly Funded Training. LC 99-43470. (Illus.). xvii, 342p. 2000. pap. 24.00 (*0-87766-689-X*) Urban Inst.
***Barnow, Burt S., et al.** Evaluating Comprehensive State Welfare Reform: The Wisconsin Works Program. LC 99-42252. 2000. pap. 18.95 (*0-914341-72-3*) Nelson Rockefeller Inst Govt.
***Barns, Alexander.** The Book Read Backwards: The Deconstruction of Patriarchy & the Wombanization of Being. LC 99-462212. 552p. 2000. 64.50 (*0-7618-1647-X*) U Pr of Amer.
Barns, Cass G. The Sod House. LC 73-100812. 301p. 1970. reprint ed. pap. 93.40 (*0-608-00489-8*, 206130800007) Bks Demand.
Barns, George. Casting the Net: The Unchurched Population in the Mid-Nineties. 47p. (Orig.). 1995. spiral bd. 24.00 (*1-882297-07-5*) Barna Res Grp.
Barns, J. W., jt. ed. see Reymond, E. A.
Barns, John R. Icon Collections in the United States. (Illus.). 30p. 1992. pap. 3.95 (*1-879038-06-4*) Oakwood Pubns.
Barns, R., ed. see Nyks, R. J.
Barnsely, Roland, jt. auth. see Pierce, John.
Barnsley, D. Spon's Building Cost Guide for Educational Premises. 2nd ed. 1998. 70.00 (*0-419-23310-5*, E & FN Spon) Routledge.
Barnsley, D. G. Barnsley's Conveyancing Law & Practice. 3rd ed. 1988. pap. 60.00 (*0-406-55635-0*, U.K., MICHIE); boxed set 106.00 (*0-406-55634-2*, U.K., MICHIE) LEXIS Pub.
Barnsley, Michael F. Fractals Everywhere. 2nd ed. LC 93-15985. (Illus.). 531p. 1993. pap. 54.95 (*0-12-079069-6*) Morgan Kaufmann.
Barnsley, Mike, jt. auth. see Bridgeman, Brian.
Barnstable County Cooperative Extension Staff, jt. auth. see Fornari, C. L.
Barnston, Ginny. Made with Lace: 40 Exquisite Lace Garments & Accessories. 128p. 1997. pap. 19.95 (*0-8019-8939-6*) Krause Pubns.
Barnstone, Aliki. Madly in Love. LC 96-83430. 80p. 1997. pap. 11.95 (*0-88748-248-1*) Carnegie-Mellon.
***Barnstone, Aliki, ed.** Voices of Light: Spiritual & Visionary Poems by Women Around the World, from Ancient Sumeria to Now. LC 99-22397. 284p. 1999. 26.95 (*1-57062-283-3*, Pub. by Shambhala Pubns) Random.
Barnstone, Aliki, et al, eds. The Calvinist Roots of the Modern Era. LC 96-51974. (Illus.). 347p. 1997. pap. 25.00 (*0-87451-808-3*); text 50.00 (*0-87451-807-5*) U Pr of New Eng.
Barnstone, Aliki & Barnstone, Willis, eds. A Book of Women Poets from Antiquity to Now. rev. ed. LC 91-52701. 832p. 1992. reprint ed. pap. 22.00 (*0-8052-0997-2*) Schocken.
Barnstone, Howard. Galveston That Was. 5. 1999. 49.95 (*0-89096-887-X*) Tex A&M Univ Pr.
Barnstone, Tony. Impure. LC 99-14964. (Contemporary Poetry Ser.). 96p. 1999. pap. 10.95 (*0-8130-1690-8*) U Press Fla.
***Barnstone, Tony.** Impure. LC 99-14964. (University of Central Florida Contemporary Poetry Ser.). 1999. 19.95 (*0-8130-1689-4*) U Press Fla.
Barnstone, Tony, ed. Out of the Howling Storm: The New Chinese Poetry. LC 92-56899. (Wesleyan Poetry Ser.). 179p. 1993. pap. 14.95 (*0-8195-1210-9*, Wesleyan Univ Pr); text 30.00 (*0-8195-2207-4*, Wesleyan Univ Pr) U Pr of New Eng.
Barnstone, Tony, jt. auth. see Barnstone, Willis.
Barnstone, Tony, tr. see Wei, Wang.
Barnstone, Willis. Algebra of Night: New & Selected Poems, 1948-1998. LC 98-39888. 407p. (Orig.). 1999. reprint ed. pap. 18.95 (*1-878818-60-0*, Pub. by Sheep Meadow) U Pr of New Eng.
— China Poems. LC 75-43525. (Breakthrough Bks.). 64p. 1976. 18.95 (*0-8262-0194-6*) U of Mo Pr.
— Five A. M. in Beijing: Poems of China. LC 86-43209. 127p. 1987. pap. 13.95 (*0-935296-67-0*, Pub. by Sheep Meadow); text 25.00 (*0-935296-66-2*, Pub. by Sheep Meadow) U Pr of New Eng.
— Funny Ways of Staying Alive. LC 92-38349. (Illus.). 128p. 1993. 12.95 (*0-87451-629-3*) U Pr of New Eng.
— The Poetics of Ecstasy. LC 82-9283. 331p. (C). 1983. pap. 18.95 (*0-8419-0849-4*) Holmes & Meier.
— Poetics of Translation: History, Theory, Practice. 1995. pap. 20.00 (*0-300-06300-8*) Yale U Pr.
— The Secret Reader: 501 Sonnets. LC 95-17105. 440p. (C). 1996. pap. 22.95 (*0-87451-660-9*) U Pr of New Eng.
— Sunday Morning in Fascist Spain: A European Memoir, 1948-1953. LC 93-15493. (Illus.). 312p. (C). 1994. pap. 19.95 (*0-8093-1884-9*) S Ill U Pr.
— Sunday Morning in Fascist Spain: A European Memoir, 1948-1953. LC 93-15493. (Illus.). 312p. (C). 1995. 41.95 (*0-8093-1883-0*) S Ill U Pr.
***Barnstone, Willis.** With Borges on an Ordinary Evening in Buenos Aires. 2000. pap. 14.95 (*0-252-06863-7*) U of Ill Pr.
Barnstone, Willis. With Borges on an Ordinary Evening in Buenos Aires: A Memoir. 208p. (C). 1992. 27.50 (*0-252-01888-5*) U of Ill Pr.
Barnstone, Willis, ed. The Other Bible. LC 83-48416. 768p. 1984. pap. 28.00 (*0-06-250030-9*, CN 4087, Pub. by Harper SF) HarpC.
Barnstone, Willis, ed. Six Masters of the Spanish Sonnet: Francisco de Quevedo, Sor Juana Ines de la Cruz, Antonia Machado, Federico Garcia Lorca, Jorge Luis Borges, Miguel Hernandez. (Illus.). 272p. (C). 1993. 26.95 (*0-8093-1772-9*) S Ill U Pr.
***Barnstone, Willis, tr. from GRE.** The Apocalypse. 2000. pap. 7.00 (*0-8112-1446-X*, Pub. by New Directions) Norton.
Barnstone, Willis, tr. from GRE. Greek Lyric Poetry: Including the Complete Poetry of Sappho. LC 86-31556. 368p. 1988. pap. 12.76 (*0-8052-0831-3*) Schocken.
— Six Masters of the Spanish Sonnet: Francisco De Quevedo, Sor Juana Ines de la Cruz, Antonia Machado, Federico Garcia Lorca, Jorge Luis Borges, Miguel Hernandez. LC 92-12099. (Illus.). 272p. 1997. pap. 19.95 (*0-8093-2127-0*) S Ill U Pr.
— To Touch the Sky: Poems of Mystical, Spiritual & Metaphysical Light. LC 98-43392. 192p. 1999. 13.95 (*0-8112-1396-X*, NDP869, Pub. by New Directions) Norton.
Barnstone, Willis & Barnstone, Tony. Literatures of Asia, Africa & Latin America. LC 95-25423. 2016p. (C). 1998. pap. text 55.00 (*0-02-306065-4*, Macmillan Coll) P-H.
Barnstone, Willis, jt. ed. see Barnstone, Aliki.
Barnstone, Willis, tr. see St. John of the Cross.
Barnstone, Willis, tr. see Volkova, Bronislava, et al.
Barnstone, Willis, tr. see Wei, Wang.
Barnstorff, D. A Key to Shakespeare's Sonnets. LC 70-113549.Tr. of Schussel Zu Shakspeares Sonnetten. reprint ed. 43.50 (*0-404-00657-4*) AMS Pr.
Barnthouse, Lawrence W., et al, eds. Science, Law, & Hudson River Power Plants: A Case Study in Environmental Impact Assessment. LC 88-72144. (AFS Monograph Ser.: No. 4). 347p. 1988. pap. 38.00 (*0-913235-51-2*, 520.04P) Am Fisheries Soc.
— Sustainable Environmental Management: Proceedings of the Pellston Workshop on Sustainability-Based Environmental Management, 25-31 August, 1993, Pellston, Michigan. LC 97-36153. (Special Publications Ser.). (Illus.). 1998. 30.00 (*1-880611-08-2*, SETAC Pr) SETAC.
Barnum. Biotechnology: An Intro with Infotrac. (Environmental Science Ser.). 1997. pap., student ed. 38.25 (*0-534-23441-0*) Wadsworth Pub.
***Barnum, Barbara.** The Haunting of Lila Tilden. Esposito, Lisa, ed. LC 98-61854. 232p. 1999. pap. 14.95 (*1-880254-60-3*) Vista.
Barnum, Barbara J. S. Nursing Theory: Analysis, Application, Evaluation. 5th ed. LC 97-30274. 304p. 1998. pap. text 35.95 (*0-7817-1104-5*) Lppncott W & W.
Barnum, Barbara S. Nursing Theory: Analysis, Application, Evaluation. 3rd ed. (Illus.). 350p. 1990. text 32.50 (*0-673-39920-6*) Lppncott W & W.
— Spirituality in Nursing: From Traditional to New Age. LC 95-25630. 176p. 1996. 29.95 (*0-8261-9180-0*) Springer Pub.
— Writing & Getting Published: A Primer for Nurses. LC 94-43634. 216p. 1995. 28.95 (*0-8261-8690-4*) Springer Pub.
Barnum, Barbara S. & Mallard, Catherine O. Essentials of Nursing Management: Concepts & Context of Practice. Orig. Title: First Line Patient Care Management. 326p. (C). 1989. reprint ed. 50.00 (*0-8342-0018-X*, 20018) Aspen Pub.
Barnum, Barbara S., jt. auth. see Nightingale, Florence.
Barnum, Carol M. The Fiction of John Fowles. 1988. lib. bdg. write for info. (*0-913283-17-7*) Penkevill.
— Prose & Cons: The Do's & Don'ts of Technical & Business Writing. 156p. 1986. pap. text 9.95 (*0-935920-29-3*, Ntl Pubs Blck) P-H.
Barnum, Carol M. & Carliner, Saul. Techniques for Technical Communicators. LC 92-10660. (Illus.). 368p. (Orig.). (C). 1992. pap. text 62.00 (*0-02-306095-6*, Macmillan Coll) P-H.
Barnum, Carol M., jt. auth. see Barnum, Susan.
Barnum, Francis. Grammatical Fundamentals of the Innuit Language As Spoken by the Eskimo of the Western Coast of Alaska. xxv, 384p. 1970. reprint ed. 105.00 (*0-685-66431-7*, 05103140) G Olms Pubs.
Barnum, H. Gardiner. Market Centers & Hinterlands in Baden-Wurttemberg: Marktzentren und Hinterlander in Baden-Wurttemberg. LC 65-28149. (University of Chicago, Department of Geography, Research Paper Ser.: No. 103). 195p. reprint ed. pap. 60.50 (*0-7837-0389-9*, 204071000018) Bks Demand.
Barnum, Howard & Kutzin, Joseph. Public Hospitals in Developing Countries: Resource Use, Cost, Financing. 352p. 1993. 35.95 (*0-8018-4532-7*, 44532) Johns Hopkins.
— Public Hospitals in Developing Countries: Resource Use, Cost, Financing. LC 92-49341. 345p. reprint ed. pap. 107.00 (*0-608-08811-0*, 206945000004) Bks Demand.
Barnum, Howard N. & Squire, Lyn. A Model of an Agricultural Household: Theory & Evidence. LC 78-21397. (World Bank Staff Occasional Papers: No. 27). 119p. reprint ed. pap. 36.90 (*0-7837-4252-5*, 204394200012) Bks Demand.
Barnum, Joel L. OS/2 Warp Presentation Manager API. LC 95-1222. 475p. 1995. pap. 29.95 (*0-471-03873-3*) Wiley.
— Windows 32-Bit Api Programming. 1997. pap. text 59.95 (*0-87930-524-X*) Dobbs Dirs.
***Barnum, P. T.** The Life of P. T. Barnum. LC 99-462094. (Illus.). 2000. pap. write for info. (*0-252-06902-1*) U of Ill Pr.
Barnum, Paul F., ed. see Ellsberg, Bob.
Barnum, Phineas T. Animal Stories. reprint ed. lib. bdg. 22.95 (*0-89190-447-6*, Rivercity Pr) Amereon Ltd.
— Art of Money Getting: Golden Rule for Money Making. LC 99-37683. 128p. 1999. pap. text 14.95 (*1-55709-494-2*, Pub. by Applewood) Consort Bk Sales.
— Barnum's Own Story: Autobiography. Browne, Waldo R., ed. (Illus.). 1962. 33.00 (*0-8446-4001-8*) Peter Smith.
— Struggles & Triumphs. LC 77-125677. (American Journalists Ser.). 1971. reprint ed. 53.95 (*0-405-01651-4*) Ayer.
Barnum, Priscilla H., ed. Dives & Pauper, Vol. I. (OS 275 Ser.: No. 275). (Illus.). (C). 1976. 21.95 (*0-19-722277-3*) OUP.
— Dives & Pauper, Vol. I, Pt. 2. (OS 280 Ser.). (Illus.). (C). 1980. text 32.50 (*0-19-722282-X*) OUP.
Barnum, Susan & Barnum, Carol M. Biotechnology. LC 97-44429. (Biology Ser.). (C). 1997. student ed. 38.25 (*0-534-23436-4*) Wadsworth Pub.
Barnum, Thaddeus. Where Is God in Suffering & Tragedy? LC 97-76055. (Illus.). 266p. 1998. pap. 9.95 (*1-883928-28-1*) Longwood.
Barnum, Thaddeus R. Remember Eve: How the Deceiver Works in the Beleiver's Life. LC 95-76806. 196p. (Orig.). 1995. pap. 8.95 (*1-883928-13-3*) Longwood.
Barnum, William J. Of Rare Design. Cote, Doc & Bonanni, Victoria, eds. 88p. 1999. pap. 10.00 (*0-9636942-6-X*) VB Document.
Barnwell. An Introduction to Critical Reading. 2nd ed. (C). 1993. pap. text, teacher ed. 33.75 (*0-15-501.92-8*) Harcourt Coll Pubs.
— The Pilgrim's Companion. 1993. pap. 13.95 (*1-85230-342-5*, Pub. by Element MA) Penguin Putnam.
***Barnwell, Andrea D.** The Walter O. Evans Collection of African American Art. (Illus.). 168p. 2000. 50.00 (*0-295-97920-8*); pap. 35.00 (*0-295-97922-4*) U of Wash Pr.
Barnwell, David. A History of Language Testing in the United States from Its Beginnings to the Present. LC 96-28087. 1996. pap. 16.00 (*0-927534-59-2*) Biling Rev-Pr.
Barnwell, H. T. The Tragic Drama of Corneille & Racine: An Old Parallel Revisited. 298p. 1982. 70.00 (*0-19-815779-7*) OUP.
Barnwell, H. T., ed. see Racine, Jean.
Barnwell, Janet, ed. Louisiana Voices: Remembering World War II. LC 99-169781. (Williams Center for Oral History Ser.: Vol. 2). (Illus.). 176p. (Orig.). 1998. pap. text 19.95 (*0-8071-2236-X*) La State U Pr.
Barnwell, John. The Arcana of Light on the Path: The Star Wisdom of the Tarot & Light on the Path. (Illus.). 256p. pap. 17.50 (*0-9671503-1-0*, Pub. by Verticordia Pr) Anthroposophic.
Barnwell, John. The Arcana of the Grail Angel: The Spiritual Science of the Holy Blood & of the Holy Grail. unabridged ed. (Illus.). 640p. 1999. pap. 37.50 (*0-9671503-0-2*, 888, Pub. by Verticordia Pr) Anthroposophic.
— Love of Order: South Carolina's First Secession Crisis. LC 81-11441. xv, 256p. 1982. 49.95 (*0-8078-1498-9*) U of NC Pr.
Barnwell, Katharine. Bible Translation: An Introductory Course in Translation Principles. 3rd rev. ed. LC 86-50834. 274p. 1986. pap. text 11.80 (*0-88312-651-6*) S I L Intl.
Barnwell, Katharine. Sisters. LC 97-191714. (Charming Petites Ser.). 80p. 1997. 4.95 (*0-88088-815-6*) Peter Pauper.
Barnwell, Maria. Diabetes. (Outline Ser.). 300p. (Orig.). (C). 1994. per. 23.95 (*1-56930-031-3*) Skidmore Roth Pub.
Barnwell, Marion. A Place Called Mississippi: Mississippi Narratives. LC 96-29607. 1997. 47.50 (*0-87805-963-6*); pap. 18.00 (*0-87805-964-4*) U Pr of Miss.
Barnwell, Marion, et al. On the Way Home. Sareone, Elizabeth & Wynn, Leila, eds. 200p. (Orig.). 1996. pap. 12.95 (*0-9655383-0-3*) Ruby Shoes Pr.
Barnwell, P. S. Emperor, Prefects, & Kings: The Roman West, 395-565. LC 92-16720. (Illus.). viii, 248p. (C). 1993. 59.95 (*0-8078-2071-7*) U of NC Pr.
Barnwell, R. W. & Hussaini, M. Yousuff, eds. Laminar Natural Flow & Laminar Flow Control. (ICASE - NASA LaRC Ser.). (Illus.). vii, 411p. 1991. 98.95 (*0-387-97737-6*) Spr-Verlag.
Barnwell, Thomas & McCraney, Leah. An Introduction to Critical Reading. 416p. (C). 1990. teacher ed. write for info. (*0-03-030373-7*) Harcourt Coll Pubs.
— An Introduction to Critical Reading. 3rd ed. LC 96-76291. 352p. (C). 1996. pap. text 34.00 (*0-15-503441-3*, Pub. by Harcourt Coll Pubs) Harcourt.
Barnwell, Thomas O., Jr., ed. Computing in Civil Engineering: Computers in Engineering Practice. LC 89-37697. 962p. 1989. pap. text 11.00 (*0-87262-722-5*, 722) Am Soc Civil Eng.
Barnwell, Thomas P., et al. Speech Coding: A Computer Laboratory Textbook. LC 95-31853. (Georgia Tech Digital Signal Processing Laboratory Ser.). 208p. 1995. pap., pap. text 46.95 incl. disk (*0-471-51692-9*) Wiley.
Barnwell, William Hazzard. Our Story According to St. Mark. 288p. (Orig.). (C). 1982. 9.95 (*0-86683-634-9*) Harper SF.
— Resource Writer, 3 vols. 3rd ed. LC 94-76472. (C). 1994. pap. text 37.16 (*0-395-68479-X*) HM.
Barnwell, William Hazzard & Dees, Robert. The Resourceful Writer: A Basic Writing Course, 3 vols. 3rd ed. (C). 1995. text, teacher ed. 38.36 (*0-395-68480-3*) HM.
— The Resourceful Writer: A Basic Writing Course. 4th ed. LC 98-71983. 570 p. 1998. pap. text 39.96 (*0-395-90420-X*) HM.
Barnwell, Ysaye M. & Saint James, Synthia. No Mirrors in My Nana's House. LC 97-33356. (Illus.). 32p. (J). (ps-2). 1998. 18.00 (*0-15-201825-5*) Harcourt.
Baro, Ana B., tr. see Marshall, James.
Baro, Gene. 1982 Carnegie International. (Illus.). 128p. 1982. pap. text 7.95 (*0-88039-004-2*) Mus Art Carnegie.
— William Conlon: Paintings, 1969-1981. LC 81-18705. (Illus.). 16p. 1981. pap. text 6.00 (*0-88039-001-8*) Mus Art Carnegie.
Baro, Gene, ed. Famous American Poets. (Pocket Poet Ser.). 1962. pap. 3.95 (*0-8023-9038-2*) Dufour.
Baro, Joan. The Bible: A People Listen to God. Aquinaco, Carmen, tr. from CAT. LC 98-16530. (Illus.). 352p. (J). (gr. 2-8). 1998. 24.95 (*0-8146-2509-6*) Liturgical Pr.
Baro, Jose. Glosario Completo de Los Milagros de Nuestra Senora de Gonzalo de Berceo. LC 86-63037. (SPA.). 249p. 1987. pap. 45.00 (*0-89295-048-X*) Society Sp & Sp-Am.
Baro, M. & Clavaguera, N., eds. Current Topics on Non-Crystalline Solids: Proceedings of the First International Workshop on Non-Crystalline Solids San Feliu De Guixois, Spain May 26-30, 1986. 476p. 1987. pap. 40.00 (*9971-5-0174-0*); text 98.00 (*9971-5-0169-4*) World Scientific Pub.
Baro, M. D. & Surinach, S., eds. Mechanically Alloyed, Metastable & Nanocrystalline Materials: ISMANAM-97. (Materials Science Forum Ser.: Vols. 269-272). (Illus.). 1148p. (C). 1998. text 295.00 (*0-87849-799-4*, Pub. by Trans T Pub) Enfield Pubs NH.
Barocas, David N., tr. see Magriso, Yitzchok.
Barocas, Ira & Williams, Michael. Mastering NAUI Leadership. 1994. pap. 39.95 (*0-916974-58-8*, 12901) NAUI.
***Barocas, Melanie Eve.** Eden: Selected Photographs. 104p. 1998. 45.00 (*0-9676183-0-4*) Eve Editn.
Barocas, Victor. Fairy Tales in Latin: Fabulae Mirabiles. Schearel, Susan, ed. (LAT., Illus.). 80p. (YA). (gr. 6 up). 1999. 12.50 (*0-7818-0787-5*) Hippocrene Bks.
— Planning Benefits Strategically Vol. 38: An Approach to Meeting Organizational Objectives. LC 97-229423. (Building Blocks Ser.). (Illus.). (Orig.). 1997. pap. 24.95 (*1-57963-042-1*, AO238) Am Compensation.
Barocas, Victor S. Benefit Communications: Enhancing the Employer's Investment. (Report: No. 1035). (Illus.). 52p. (Orig.). 1993. pap. text 100.00 (*0-8237-0507-2*) Conference Bd.
Barocci, Thomas A. Non-Profit Hospitals: Their Structure, Human Resources, & Economic Importance. LC 80-22075. 251p. 1980. 59.95 (*0-86569-054-5*, Auburn Hse) Greenwood.
Barocci, Thomas A., jt. auth. see Jerrett, Robert.
Baroche, Christiane. L' Hiver de Beaute. (FRE.). 338p. 1990. pap. 12.95 (*0-7859-2146-X*, 2070382710) Fr & Eur.
Barocio, Ernesto. Bosquejos de Sermones Selectos. 144p. 1981. reprint ed. pap. 6.50 (*0-311-43039-2*) Casa Bautista.
Barocio, Ernesto, tr. see Broadus, J. A.
Barodte, James T., ed. Medical Ultrasound, Vol. 7. 1983. text 30.00 (*0-471-88975-X*) Wiley.
***Baroff, David.** Conatus. LC 98-88531. 192p. 1999. pap. 11.95 (*1-56315-140-5*) SterlingHse.
Baroff, George S. Developmental Disabilities: Psychosocial Aspects. LC 90-43702. (Illus.). 259p. (C). 1991. pap. text 29.00 (*0-89079-412-X*, 1590) PRO-ED.
— Mental Retardation: Nature, Cause & Management. 2nd ed. (Illus.). 400p. (C). 1986. 66.95 (*0-89116-263-1*) Hemisp Pub.
***Baroff, George S.** Mental Retardation: Nature, Cause & Management. 3rd ed. (Illus.). 512p. 1999. 69.95 (*1-58391-000-X*) Brunner-Mazel.
— Mental Retardation: Nature, Cause, & Management, 3rd Ed. 3rd ed. LC 99-24045. 1999. pap. text 39.95 (*1-58391-001-8*) Brunner-Mazel.
Barofsky, I. & Budson, R. D., eds. The Chronic Psychiatric Patient in the Community: Principles of Treatment. LC 82-7338. 570p. 1983. text 57.95 (*0-88331-117-8*) R B Luce.
Barofsky, Ivan, ed. Work & Illness: The Cancer Patient. LC 88-25544. 195p. 1989. 57.95 (*0-275-92390-8*, C2390, Praeger Pubs) Greenwood.
Barofsky, Semour, tr. see Sendak, Philip.
Baroid, Ciaran De, see De Baroid, Ciaran.
Baroin, Catherine. Tubu: The Teda & the Daza. LC 96-32802. (Heritage Library of African Peoples: Set 3). (Illus.). 64p. (YA). (gr. 7-12). 1997. lib. bdg. 16.95 (*0-8239-2000-3*, D2000-3) Rosen Group.
Baroin, M. The Power of Love. 192p. 1989. 73.50 (*0-08-036562-0*, Pergamon Pr) Elsevier.
Baroja. Las Inquietudes de Shanti Andia: Level B. text 8.95 (*0-88436-062-8*) EMC-Paradigm.

B

An Asterisk (*) at the beginning of an entry indicates that the title is appearing for the first time.

Baroja, Julio C. The World of Witches. Glendinning, O. N., tr. LC 64-15829. (Nature of Human Society Ser.). xiv, 314p. 1973. pap. text 14.95 (*0-226-03763-0*, P497) U Ch Pr.

Baroja, Julio Caro, see Caro Baroja, Julio.

Baroja, Y Nessi, Pio. Arbol de la Ciencia. (SPA.). 250p. 1985. pap. 9.85 (*0-8288-8584-2*); pap. 10.95 (*0-8288-8585-0*) Fr & Eur.

— Arbol de la Ciencia. (SPA.). 256p. 1990. 10.95 (*0-7859-5007-9*, S434) Fr & Eur.

— Aventuras, Inventos y Mixtificaciones De Silvestre Paradox. Fox, E. Inman, ed. (Nueva Austral Ser.: No. 116). (SPA.). 1991. pap. text 24.95 (*84-239-1916-1*) Elliots Bks.

— La Casa de Aizgorri. Etxebarria, Maitena, ed. (Nueva Austral Ser.: No. 220). (SPA.). 1991. pap. text 24.95 (*84-239-7220-8*) Elliots Bks.

— Las Inquietudes De Shanti Andia. Villanueva, Dario, ed. (Nueva Austral Ser.: No. 35). (SPA.). 1991. pap. text 17.95 (*84-239-1835-1*) Elliots Bks.

— El Mundo Es Asi. Perez Bowie, Jose A., ed. (Nueva Austral Ser.: No. 142). (SPA.). 1991. pap. text 24.95 (*84-239-1942-0*) Elliots Bks.

— Paradox, Rey. Lasagabaster, Jesus M., ed. (Nueva Austral Ser.: No. 188). (SPA.). 1991. pap. text 24.95 (*84-239-1988-9*) Elliots Bks.

— Zalacain el Aventurero. Senabre, Ricardo, ed. (Nueva Austral Ser.: No. 3). (SPA.). pap. 14.95 (*84-239-1803-3*) Elliots Bks.

— Zalacain the Adventurer. Diendl, James P., tr. from SPA. LC 97-73593. Orig. Title: Zalacain el Aventurero. 234p. 1997. pap. 16.95 (*1-882897-13-7*) Lost Coast.

Barojas, Jorge, ed. Cooperative Networks in Physics Education. LC 88-72091. (AIP Conference Proceedings Ser.: No. 173). 440p. 1988. lib. bdg. 70.00 (*0-88318-373-0*) Am Inst Physics.

Barold, S. Serge & Mugica, Jacques. Recent Advances in Cardiac Pacing: Goals for the 21st Century. LC 97-19572. (Illus.). 464p. 1997. 98.00 (*0-87993-639-8*) Futura Pub.

Barolet, Randall, jt. auth. see Bensky, Dan.

Barolini, Antonio. Croton Elegies. Barolini, Helen, tr. from ITA. (ENG & ITA.). 101p. 1991. pap. 10.00 (*0-920717-39-X*) SPD-Small Pr Dist.

Barolini, Helen. Aldus & His Dream Book: An Illustrated Essay. LC 91-27624. (Illus.). 244p. (Orig.). 1992. pap. 17.50 (*0-934977-22-4*) Italica Pr.

— Chiaroscuro: Essays of Identity. (VIA Folios Ser.: Vol. 11). 170p. 1997. pap. 15.00 (*1-884419-11-9*) Bordighera.

— Chiaroscuro: Essays of Identity. rev. ed. LC 98-48742. 232p. 1999. pap. 19.95 (*0-299-16084-X*) U of Wis Pr.

— Festa. 384p. 1989. pap. 9.95 (*0-15-630515-1*) Harcourt.

— Festa: Recipes & Recollections of Italy. (Illus.). 400p. 1988. 19.95 (*0-15-130630-3*) Harcourt.

— Umbertina. LC 89-6973. 432p. (C). 1989. reprint ed. pap. 12.95 (*0-88143-107-9*) Ayer.

***Barolini, Helen, ed.** The Dream Book: An Anthology of Writing by Italian American Women. 416p. 2000. pap. 19.95 (*0-8156-0662-1*) Syracuse U Pr.

Barolini, Helen, tr. see Barolini, Antonio.

Barolini, Helena. Umbertina. LC 98-44374. 464p. 1998. pap. 18.95 (*1-55861-205-X*) Feminist Pr.

— Umbertina. LC 98-44374. 464p. 1998. 35.00 (*1-55861-204-1*) Feminist Pr.

Barolini, Teodolinda. Dante's Poets: Textuality & Truth in the Comedy. LC 84-42586. 327p. reprint ed. pap. 101.40 (*0-608-06429-7*, 206664200008) Bks Demand.

— The Undivine "Comedy" Detheologizing Dante. LC 92-11859. 360p. 1993. text 65.00 (*0-691-06953-0*, Pub. by Princeton U Pr) Cal Prin Full Svc.

Barolome, Luis. Nueva York. 1998. pap. 59.95 (*84-03-59430-5*) Routledge.

— Nueva York: Guia Completa Para Viajeros. (SPA.). 182p. 1993. pap. 39.95 (*0-7859-7562-4*, 8420749001) Fr & Eur.

Barolsky, Paul. The Faun in the Garden: Michelangelo & the Poetic Origins of Italian Renaissance Art. (Illus.). 198p. (C). 1994. 32.50 (*0-271-01303-6*) Pa St U Pr.

— Giotto's Father & the Family of Vasari's Lives. 160p. 1992. 25.00 (*0-271-00762-1*) Pa St U Pr.

— Michelangelo's Nose: A Myth & Its Maker. LC 90-7506. (Illus.). 190p. 1990. text 35.00 (*0-271-00695-1*) Pa St U Pr.

— Michelangelo's Nose: A Myth & Its Maker. (Illus.). 192p. 1997. pap. 19.95 (*0-271-01684-1*) Pa St U Pr.

— Walter Pater's Renaissance. LC 85-43561. 214p. 1987. 35.00 (*0-271-00436-3*) Pa St U Pr.

— Why Mona Lisa Smiles & Other Tales by Vasari. 128p. 1991. 29.50 (*0-271-00719-2*) Pa St U Pr.

Baromg-Gould, William S., ed. see Doyle, Arthur Conan.

Baron. The Bridge Player's Dictionary. 19.95 (*0-939460-50-5*, 4710) Devyn Pr.

— Business & Its Environment. 3rd ed. LC 99-26984. (Illus.). 785p. 1999. 91.00 (*0-13-081561-6*) P-H.

— Dictionary of Mining Terminology. 3rd ed. (RUS.). 478p. 1981. 15.95 (*0-8288-1919-X*, M8853) Fr & Eur.

— Essentials of Psychology. 2nd ed. 1998. pap. text, student ed. 14.25 (*0-205-28848-0*) Allyn.

— Europe at the Dawn of the Millennium. LC 96-41004. 264p. 1997. text 65.00 (*0-312-16575-7*) St Martin.

— Introspection in Biography: The Biographer's Quest for Self-Awareness. 1985. 45.00 (*0-88163-035-7*) Analytic Pr.

***Baron.** Psychology: Study Guide: Canadian Edition. 3rd ed. 2000. pap. 20.00 (*0-205-32290-5*) Allyn.

Baron. Psychology & Psychology Study Guide, 2 bks. 4th ed. 1997. text, student ed. 77.00 (*0-205-28706-9*) A&B Bks.

***Baron.** Social Psychology. 9th ed. LC 99-18540. 650p. (C). 1999. 82.00 (*0-205-27956-2*, Macmillan Coll) P-H.

Baron. Trans Psychology. 2nd ed. 1992. 177.00 (*0-205-13273-1*, Longwood Div) Allyn.

***Baron & Armstrong.** Performance Management: The New Realities. 480p. 2000. pap. 56.95 (*0-8464-5125-5*) Beekman Pubs.

Baron & Baggett. Record Keeping in the Computer Age. 6th ed. 1986. 21.00 (*0-538-02015-6*) Thomson Learn.

Baron & Byrne. Social Psychology. 9th ed. 1999. pap. text, student ed. 15.00 (*0-205-29804-4*, Longwood Div) Allyn.

***Baron & Byrne.** Social Psychology: Interactive Companion. 9th ed. 2000. 78.67 incl. cd-rom (*0-205-32440-1*) Allyn.

Baron & Kalsher. Psychology. 4th ed. LC 97-214036. 776p. 1997. 80.00 (*0-205-26569-3*) P-H.

— Psychology. 4th ed. 1997. pap. text, student ed. 19.00 (*0-205-27290-8*) P-H.

Baron, et al. Wadsworth Anaerobic Bacteriology Manual. 5th ed. LC 92-49319. 1993. pap. 39.95 (*0-89863-170-X*) Star Pub CA.

Baron, jt. auth. see Armstrong.

Baron, tr. see Mann, Michael.

Baron, Alan. Little Pig's Bouncy Ball. LC 95-35347. (Illus.). 24p. (J). (ps). 1997. reprint ed. pap. 3.29 (*0-7636-0126-8*) Candlewick Pr.

— Red Fox & the Baby Bunnies. LC 96-83533. (Illus.). 24p. (J). (ps up). 1997. 9.99 (*0-7636-0085-7*) Candlewick Pr.

— Red Fox & the Baby Bunnies. LC 96-83533. (Giggle Club Ser.). (Illus.). 24p. (J). (ps-1). 1998. pap. 3.29 (*0-7636-0402-X*) Candlewick Pr.

— Red Fox Dances. (Illus.). 24p. (J). (ps). 1996. 9.99 (*0-614-32380-0*) Candlewick Pr.

— Red Fox Dances. LC 95-71372. (Illus.). 24p. (J). (ps-1). 1997. reprint ed. pap. 3.29 (*0-7636-0127-6*) Candlewick Pr.

— The Red Fox Monster. LC 96-83536. (Illus.). 24p. (J). (ps). 1996. 9.99 (*0-7636-0018-0*) Candlewick Pr.

— Red Fox Monster. LC 96-83536. (Giggle Club Ser.). (Illus.). 24p. (J). (ps-1). 1998. pap. 3.29 (*0-7636-0280-9*) Candlewick Pr.

Baron, Alvin. Bud's Easy Research Paper Computer Manual for Macintosh. 2nd ed. 200p. pap. 9.50 (*1-891707-02-7*) Lawrence Hse.

— Bud's Easy Research Paper Computer Manual for PC. 2nd ed. 200p. pap. 9.50 (*1-891707-01-9*) Lawrence Hse.

Baron, Ana, ed. see Sanchez, Alex H., et al.

Baron, Andy, jt. auth. see Chipman, Mary.

Baron, Angela, jt. auth. see Armstrong, Michael.

Baron, Angela, jt. ed. see Armstrong, Michael.

***Baron, Anthony.** Violence in the Workplace: A Prevention & Management Guide for Businesses. 2nd ed. 185p. 2000. pap. 14.95 (*0-934793-70-0*, Pub. by Pathfinder CA) IPG Chicago.

Baron, Arleen, ed. see Lieberman, Rachel.

Baron, Augustine, Jr., ed. Explorations in Chicano Psychology. LC 81-2639. 222p. 1981. 59.95 (*0-275-90580-2*, C0580, Praeger Pubs) Greenwood.

Baron, Ava, ed. Work Engendered: Toward a New History of American Labor. LC 91-2281. (Illus.). 400p. 1991. text 49.95 (*0-8014-2256-6*); pap. text 18.95 (*0-8014-9543-1*) Cornell U Pr.

Baron Baltimore, jt. auth. see Calvert, Cecil.

Baron, Barnett F., ed. Philanthropy & the Dynamics of Change in East & Southeast Asia. LC 91-71259. (Occasional Papers of the East Asian Institute). 181p. (Orig.). 1991. pap. 12.00 (*0-913418-05-6*) Columbia U E Asian Inst.

Baron, Bat-Ami & Ferguson, Ann. Daring to Be Good: Essays in Feminist Ethico-Politics. LC 97-28333. (Thinking Gender Ser.). 288p. (C). 1998. 75.00 (*0-415-91554-6*); pap. 21.99 (*0-415-91555-4*) Routledge.

Baron, Beth. The Women's Awakening in Egypt: Culture, Society, & the Press. LC 93-27067. 264p. 1994. 35.00 (*0-300-05563-3*) Yale U Pr.

— The Women's Awakening in Egypt: Culture, Society, & the Press. 270p. 1997. pap. text 17.00 (*0-300-07271-6*) Yale U Pr.

Baron, Beth, jt. auth. see Keddie, Nikki R.

Baron, Beth, jt. ed. see Matthee, Rudi.

Baron, Bob, ed. Twentieth Century America: Key Events in History. (Millennium 2000 Ser.). 144p. 1995. 8.95 (*1-55591-279-6*) Fulcrum Pub.

— Twentieth Century America: One-Hundred Influential People. (Millennium 2000 Ser.). 128p. 1995. 8.95 (*1-55591-277-X*) Fulcrum Pub.

Baron, Bob, ed. see Raabe, Tom.

Baron, Carl, ed. see Lawrence, D. H.

Baron, Chris. Drag 'n' Drop CGI: Add Perl CGI Functions to Your Web Site Without Programming. LC 97-16884. 384p. (C). 1997. pap. text 34.95 incl. cd-rom (*0-201-41966-1*) Addison-Wesley.

Baron, Claude, ed. Embedded System Applications. LC 97-24671. 324p. 1997. text 165.00 (*0-7923-9947-1*) Kluwer Academic.

Baron-Cohen. All About Emotions SUPP t/a. 2000. pap. text 2.00 (*0-471-98816-2*) Wiley.

Baron-Cohen, Simon. Mindblindness: An Essay on Autism & Theory of Mind. (Learning, Development & Conceptual Change Ser.). 300p. 1995. 33.00 (*0-262-02384-9*, Bradford Bks) MIT Pr.

— Mindblindness: An Essay on Autism & Theory of Mind. (Learning, Development & Conceptual Change Ser.). (Illus.). 300p. 1997. reprint ed. pap. text 16.50 (*0-262-52225-X*, Bradford Bks) MIT Pr.

— Synaesthesia: Classic & Contemporary Readings. (Illus.). 256p. 1996. 60.95 (*0-631-19763-X*); pap. 26.95 (*0-631-19764-8*) Blackwell Pubs.

Baron-Cohen, Simon, ed. The Maladapted Mind: Classic Readings in Evolutionary Psychopathology. LC 97-199891. 304p. 1997. 69.95 (*0-86377-460-1*) L Erlbaum Assocs.

***Baron-Cohen, Simon, et al, eds.** Understanding Other Minds: Perspectives from Developmental Cognitive Neuroscience. 2nd ed. LC 99-37353. (Illus.). 560p. 2000. text 100.00 (*0-19-852446-3*); pap. text 50.00 (*0-19-852445-5*) OUP.

Baron-Cohen, Simon & Bolton, Patrick. Autism: The Facts. LC 92-49828. (The Facts Ser.). (Illus.). 122p. 1994. pap. text 19.95 (*0-19-262327-3*) OUP.

Baron-Cohen, Simon, jt. auth. see Robertson, Mary M.

***Baron, Cynthia & Peck, Daniel.** Filemaker Advanced Pro 5 Advanced for Windows & Macintosh: Visual Quickpro Guide. 400p. 2000. pap. 24.99 (*0-201-70472-2*) Peachpit Pr.

Baron, Cynthia, jt. auth. see Williams, Robin C.

Baron, Dan. Legacy of Silence: Encounters with Children of the Third Reich. LC 89-7484. 354p. 1989. 37.00 (*0-674-52185-4*) HUP.

— Legacy of Silence: Encounters with Children of the Third Reich. 352p. (C). 1991. pap. text 12.95 (*0-674-52186-2*) HUP.

***Baron, David & Padwa, Lynette.** Moses on Management: 50 Leadership Lessons from the Greatest Manager of All Time. LC 99-26708. 272p. 1999. 23.00 (*0-671-03259-3*) PB.

Baron, David & Padwa, Lynette. Moses on Management: 50 Leadership Lessons from the Greatest Manager of All Time. 320p. 2000. per. 12.95 (*0-671-03260-7*) PB.

Baron, David P. Business & Its Environment. 2nd ed. LC 95-24932. 1995. text 85.00 (*0-13-303314-7*) P-H.

Baron, Denis. Law, Ethics & Pathology. 160p. 1999. pap. 35.00 (*0-7506-0846-3*) Buttrwrth-Heinemann.

Baron, Dennis. De Vere Is Shakespeare: The Evidence of Biography & Wordplay. (Oleander Language & Literature Ser.: No. 19). (Illus.). 160p. (Orig.). 1997. pap. 19.95 (*0-906672-37-6*) Oleander Pr.

— The English-Only Question: An Official Language for Americans? 247p. (C). 1992. reprint ed. pap. 16.00 (*0-300-05660-5*) Yale U Pr.

— Guide to Home Language Repair. LC 93-49855. (Illus.). 165p. 1994. 16.95 (*0-8141-1942-5*) NCTE.

Baron, Dennis E. Grammar & Gender. LC 85-14614. 255p. 1987. pap. 19.00 (*0-300-03883-6*) Yale U Pr.

Baron, Dov, ed. see Dalfin, Chaim.

Baron, Elizabeth. Prophets or Profits? Frazier-Delsignore, Sandra, ed. 187p. (Orig.). 1993. pap. 12.95 (*1-884039-01-4*) Mystic-Art Media.

Baron, Elizabeth & Frazier-Delsignore, Sandra. The Art of Silence: Meditating the Western Way. (Illus.). 187p. (Orig.). 1992. pap. 12.95 (*1-884039-00-6*) Mystic-Art Media.

Baron, Ellen, jt. auth. see Hindler, Janet.

Baron, Enid. Baking Days. Price, Alice L., ed. (Illus.). 56p. (Orig.). 1994. pap. 9.95 (*0-9641148-0-1*) HCE Pubns.

***Baron, Eric R.** Selling is a Team Sport: Turn Your Whole Organization into a Living, Breathing, Selling Machine. 2000. 24.95 (*0-7615-2530-0*) Prima Pub.

Baron-Faust, Rita. Being Female: What Every Woman Should Know about Gynecological Health. LC 97-37162. (Illus.). 384p. 1998. 25.00 (*0-688-12071-7*, Wm Morrow) Morrow Avon.

***Baron-Faust, Rita.** Being Female: What Every Woman Should Know about Gynecological Health. (Illus.). 384p. 1999. reprint ed. pap. 15.00 (*0-688-16976-7*, Wm Morrow) Morrow Avon.

Baron-Faust, Rita. Mental Health: What Every Woman Should Know. (Illus.). 416p. 1997. 23.00 (*0-614-19432-6*, Hearst) Hearst Commns.

***Baron-Faust, Rita.** Mental Wellness for Women. 384p. 1998. reprint ed. pap. 15.00 (*0-688-16113-8*, Quil) HarperTrade.

Baron-Faust, Rita. Mental Wellness for Women: What Every Woman Should Know. 1997. 25.00 (*0-614-20667-7*, Wm Morrow) Morrow Avon.

***Baron-Faust, Rita.** Preventing Heart Disease: What Every Woman Should Know. 280p. 2000. text 20.00 (*0-7881-9141-1*) DIANE Pub.

Baron-Faust, Rita, jt. auth. see Walsleben, Joyce.

Baron Fernandez, Jose. Miguel Servet: Su Vida y Obra. (Nueva Austral Ser.: No. 92). (SPA.). 1991. pap. text 34.95 (*84-239-1892-0*) Elliots Bks.

Baron, Frank, ed. see Liebnitz, Jennifer, et al.

Baron, Frederick M. Handling Occupational Disease Cases. rev. ed. LC 89-678. 1989. 110.00 (*0-318-41452-X*) West Group.

Baron, G. Society, Schools & Progress in England. 1966. 111.00 (*0-08-011594-2*, Pub. by Pergamon Repr) Franklin.

Baron, G., ed. The Politics of School Government. LC 80-40913. (International Studies in Education & Social Change). 304p. 1981. 142.00 (*0-08-025213-3*, CRC Reprint) Franklin.

Baron, G. E. Neutron Physics. (Wykeham Science Ser.: No. 2). 256p. 1970. pap. 18.00 (*0-85109-020-6*) Taylor & Francis.

Baron, Georg, et al. Comparative Neurobiology in Chiroptera, Vol. 1. LC 96-4870. 529p. 1996. 118.00 (*0-8176-5370-8*) Birkhauser.

— Comparative Neurobiology in Chiroptera, Vol. 2. LC 96-4870. 1996. 90.00 (*0-8176-5371-6*) Birkhauser.

— Comparative Neurobiology in Chiroptera, Vol. 3. LC 96-4870. 1996. 118.00 (*0-8176-5372-4*) Birkhauser.

Baron, Gerald R. Friendship Marketing: Growing Your Business by Cultivating Strategic Relationships. LC 97-7808. 187p. (Orig.). 1997. pap. 18.95 (*1-55571-399-8*, Oasis Pr) PSI Resch.

— Friendship Marketing's Salt Principles: Seasoning the Business of Life. LC 97-169117. 1997. pap. text 9.95 (*0-9657071-0-5*) Quest Entrprise.

Baron, Gino V., ed. see Becker, Luc De.

Baron-Hall, Daria. Only at the Children's Table. (J). (gr. 1-6). 1995. lib. bdg. 22.83 incl. audio (*0-8172-2753-9*) Raintree Steck-V.

Baron, Hannelore, ed. Hannelore Baron, 1926-1987. (Illus.). 28p. 1987. pap. 15.00 (*1-880566-08-7*) J Rutberg Fine Arts.

Baron, Hans. Crisis of the Early Italian Renaissance: Civic Humanism & Republican Liberty in an Age of Classicism & Tyranny. rev. ed. 700p. 1966. pap. text 29.95 (*0-691-00752-7*, Pub. by Princeton U Pr) Cal Prin Full Svc.

— In Search of Florentine Civic Humanism: Essays on the Transition from Medieval to Modern Thought, Vol. 1. LC 88-2328. 309p. reprint ed. pap. 95.80 (*0-608-06347-9*, 206670900001) Bks Demand.

— In Search of Florentine Civic Humanism: Essays on the Transition from Medieval to Modern Thought, Vol. 2. LC 88-2328. 224p. reprint ed. pap. 69.50 (*0-608-06348-7*, 206670900002) Bks Demand.

— Petrarch's "Secretum" Its Making & Meaning. LC 84-61721. (Medieval Academy Bks.: No. 94). 254p. 1985. 25.00 (*0-910956-87-1*) Medieval Acad.

Baron, Harold & Steinfeld. Keeping Financial Records for Business, Units 1-15. 7th ed. (BB - Record Keeping I Ser.). 1990. mass mkt., wbk. ed. 27.95 (*0-538-60478-6*) S-W Pub.

— Keeping Financial Records for Business, Units 1-9 - Working Papers, Units 1-9. 7th ed. (BB - Record Keeping I Ser.). 1990. mass mkt., wbk. ed. 15.95 (*0-538-60476-X*) S-W Pub.

— Keeping Financial Records for Business, Units 10-16 - Working Papers. 7th ed. (BB - Record Keeping I Ser.). 1990. mass mkt. 15.95 (*0-538-60477-8*) S-W Pub.

— Perfect Olympic Cyclery Narrative: Keeping Financial Records B. 7th ed. (BB - Record Keeping I Ser.: Vol. 1). 1991. 20.95 (*0-538-60997-4*) S-W Pub.

— Practical Record Keeping & Bookkeeping. 4th ed. (BB - Record Keeping I Ser.). 1988. mass mkt. 36.25 (*0-538-02110-1*) S-W Pub.

— Practical Record Keeping & Bookkeeping. 4th ed. (BB - Record Keeping I Ser.). 1988. mass mkt. 23.95 (*0-538-02112-8*) S-W Pub.

— Practical Record Keeping & Bookkeeping, Units 1-7. 4th ed. (BB - Record Keeping I Ser.). 1987. mass mkt., wbk. ed. 22.95 (*0-538-02111-X*) S-W Pub.

— Practical Record Keeping & Bookkeeping Units 1-5 - Working Papers. 4th ed. (BB - Record Keeping I Ser.). 1988. mass mkt. 34.95 (*0-538-02116-0*) S-W Pub.

— Practical Record Keeping & Bookkeeping Units 1-7, Tests. 4th ed. (BB - Record Keeping I Ser.). 1988. 1.95 (*0-538-02113-6*) S-W Pub.

— Practical Record Keeping & Bookkeeping Units 8-15, Tests. 4th ed. (BB - Record Keeping I Ser.). 1988. 1.95 (*0-538-02114-4*) S-W Pub.

— Product Video Center Narrative: Keeping Financial Records. 7th ed. (BB - Record Keeping I Ser.: Vol. 1). 1991. 26.95 (*0-538-60479-4*) S-W Pub.

— Record Keeping in the Computer Age, Tests. 6th ed. (BB - Record Keeping I Ser.). 1986. 2.95 (*0-538-02013-X*); 2.95 (*0-538-02014-8*) S-W Pub.

Baron, Harry. Magic for Beginners. LC 90-48770. (Illus.). 176p. 1991. pap. 9.95 (*1-55958-089-5*) Prima Pub.

— Magic for Beginners. (Illus.). 154p. 1998. reprint ed. pap. 11.95 (*0-947533-58-3*, Pub. by Breese Bks) Firebird Dist.

— Magic for Beginners No. 2: Card Tricks & Other Close-up Illusions, Vol. 2. LC 95-3352. (Illus.). 160p. 1995. pap. 9.95 (*0-7615-0017-0*) Prima Pub.

— Pick a Card, Any Card: Card Tricks for Beginners. LC 94-6125. (Illus.). 128p. 1994. pap. 9.95 (*1-55958-493-9*) Prima Pub.

Baron, Helen, ed. see Lawrence, D. H.

Baron, Henry J., tr. see Van Der Velde, Rink.

Baron, Henry J., tr. see Van der Velde, Rink.

***Baron, Herman, ed.** Author Index to Esquire, 1933-1973. 289p. 2000. pap. text 20.00 (*0-7881-9218-3*) DIANE Pub.

Baron, Howard C. & Ross, Barbara A. Varicose Veins: A Guide to Prevention & Treatment. LC 95-12535. (Illus.). 160p. 1995. 24.95 (*0-8160-2986-5*) Facts on File.

— Varicose Veins: A Guide to Prevention & Treatment. 160p. 1997. pap. text 14.95 (*0-8160-3652-7*) Facts on File.

Baron, Hyacinthe K., jt. auth. see Everett, Lidia E.

Baron, Ida S., et al. Pediatric Neuropsychology in a Medical Setting. (Illus.). 464p. 1995. text 59.50 (*0-19-506345-7*) OUP.

Baron, J., ed. Biogeochemistry of a Subalpine Ecosystem: Loch Vale Watershed. (Ecological Studies: Vol. 90). (Illus.). 240p. 1991. 131.00 (*0-387-97605-1*) Spr-Verlag.

— Galan: Cuartetos/Quartets. (Gesamtausgaben Collected Works: Vol. XII/5). (ENG & SPA.). lvi, 274p. 1995. lib. bdg. 120.00 (*0-931902-95-9*) Inst Mediaeval Mus.

— Teaching Decision Making to Adolescents. 352p. (C). 1991. text 69.95 (*0-8058-0497-8*) L Erlbaum Assocs.

Baron, J., ed. see Galan, Cristobal.

Baron, J. C., et al, eds. Brain Dopaminergic Imaging with Positron Tomography. (Developments in Nuclear Medicine Ser.). 208p. 1991. text 118.00 (*0-7923-1476-X*) Kluwer Academic.

Baron, J. F. & Treib, J., eds. Volume Replacement. LC 98-18046. (Illus.). x, 143p. 1998. pap. 65.00 (*3-540-64187-4*) Spr-Verlag.

Baron, Jane & Jones, Barbara. The Word Book. 106p. (YA). (gr. 10-12). 1981. pap. text 19.00 (*1-881678-05-9*) CSEE.

Baron, Jean-Francois. Plasma Volume Expansion. (Illus.). 240p. 1992. 115.00 (*2-7184-0584-8*) Blackwell Sci.

Baron, Jeff. Visiting Mr. Green. LC 99-218319. 1998. pap. 5.25 (*0-8222-1681-7*) Dramatists Play.

Baron, Jennette M., jt. auth. see Salo, Baron W.

Baron, Joan B. & Wolf, Dennie P. Performance-Based Student Assessment: Challenges & Possibilities. (Ninety-Fifth Yearbook of the National Society for the Study of Education Ser.: Pt. 1). 350p. 1996. 31.00 (*0-226-03803-3*) U Ch Pr.

Baron, John H. Baroque Music: A Research & Information Guide. LC 92-19620. (Music Research & Information Guides Ser.: Vol. 16). 608p. 1992. text 50.00 (*0-8240-4436-3*, H871) Garland.

— Intimate Music: A History of the Idea of Chamber Music. LC 98-14749. 1998. 64.00 (*1-57647-018-0*) Pendragon NY.

— Intimate Music: A History of the Idea of Chamber Music: Intimate Music. (Illus.). 502p. 1998. pap. text 64.00 (*1-57647-016-4*) Pendragon NY.

Baron, John H., ed. The Brasov Tablature (Brasov Music Manuscript 80) German Keyboard Studies 1608-1684. (Recent Researches in Music of the Baroque Era Ser.: Vol. RRB40). (Illus.). xv, 88p. 1982. pap. 35.00 (*0-89579-162-5*, RRB40) A-R Eds.

Baron, John H., ed. see Galan, Cristobal.

Baron, John H., ed. see Marin, Jose, et al.

Baron, Jonathan. Judgment Misguided: Intuition & Error in Public Decision Making. LC 98-11138. 240p. 1998. text 32.00 (*0-19-511108-7*) OUP.

— Morality & Rational Choice. LC 93-10276. (Theory & Decision Library, Series A, Philosophy & Methodology of the Social Sciences: Vol. 18). 216p. 1993. text 120.50 (*0-7923-2276-2*) Kluwer Academic.

— Thinking & Deciding. 2nd ed. LC 93-46230. (Illus.). 604p. (C). 1994. pap. text 27.95 (*0-521-43732-6*) Cambridge U Pr.

***Baron, Jonathan.** Thinking & Deciding. 3rd ed. (Illus.). 608p. 2001. write for info. (*0-521-65030-5*); pap. write for info. (*0-521-65972-8*) Cambridge U Pr.

Baron, Jonathan, jt. ed. see Mellers, Barbara A.

Baron, Joseph L., ed. A Treasury of Jewish Quotations. LC 85-3857. 648p. 1991. 40.00 (*0-87668-894-6*) Aronson.

— A Treasury of Jewish Quotations. LC 85-3857. 648p. 1996. pap. 40.00 (*1-56821-948-2*) Aronson.

Baron, Julie A., ed. see Marks, Marilyn.

Baron, Karrie A., jt. auth. see Greene, John R.

Baron, Kathy. Tree of Time: A Story of a Special Sequoia. (Illus.). 40p. (J). (gr. 4-7). 1994. pap. 7.95 (*0-939666-73-1*) Yosemite Assn.

Baron, Larry & Straus, Murray A. Four Theories of Rape in American Society: A State-Level Analysis. (Sociology - Women's Studies). 250p. (C). 1993. pap. 18.00 (*0-300-05782-2*) Yale U Pr.

Baron, Lawrence. The Eclectic Anarchism of Eric Muhsam. 1975. lib. bdg. 250.00 (*0-87700-228-2*) Revisionist Pr.

Baron, Linda M. Rhythm & Dues. 2nd ed. 32p. 1981. 6.00 (*0-685-14557-3*) Harlin Jacque.

Baron, Lindamichelle. The Sun Is On. rev. ed. (Illus.). 48p. (J). (gr. 1-6). 1982. pap. 5.95 (*0-940938-02-2*) Harlin Jacque.

Baron, M. Grace. The Origins of the Infinitesimal Calculus. LC 68-21382. 1969. 141.00 (*0-08-012513-1*, Pub. by Pergamon Repr) Franklin.

Baron, M. Grace, jt. auth. see Groden, Gerald.

Baron, Marcia, et al. Ethical Theory: For & Against: Consequences, Maxims, & Virtues. LC 97-10143. (Great Debates in Philosophy Ser.). 300p. (C). 1997. text 57.95 (*0-631-19434-7*); pap. text 26.95 (*0-631-19435-5*) Blackwell Pubs.

Baron, Marcia W. Kantian Ethics Almost Without Apology. 256p. 1995. text 35.00 (*0-8014-2829-7*) Cornell U Pr.

— Kantian Ethics Almost Without Apology. 1999. pap. text 16.95 (*0-8014-8604-1*) Cornell U Pr.

Baron, Marcie. Mom Alphabet a Moi. (FRE., Illus.). 14p. (J). (ps up). 1996. spiral bd., bds. 12.95 (*1-55037-414-1*, Pub. by Annick) Firefly Bks Ltd.

— Your Own ABC. (Illus.). 14p. (YA). (ps up). 1996. bds. 12.95 (*1-55037-497-4*, Pub. by Annick) Firefly Bks Ltd.

Baron, Margaret E. The Origins of the Infinitesimal Calculus. viii, 304p. 1987. reprint ed. pap. 9.95 (*0-486-65371-4*) Dover.

Baron, Mark A. & Boschee, Floyd. Authentic Assessment: The Key to Unlocking Student Success. LC 95-60887. 140p. 1997. pap. 25.95 (*1-56676-351-7*) Scarecrow.

Baron, Mark A., jt. auth. see Boschee, Floyd.

Baron, Mary. Wheat among Bones. LC 79-90839. 104p. 1979. text 25.00 (*0-935296-04-2*, Pub. by Sheep Meadow) U Pr of New Eng.

Baron, Michael. Language & Relationship in Wordsworth's Writing: Elective Affinities (Studies in Eighteenth- & Nineteenth-Century Literature) LC 94-20478. (Studies in Eighteenth & Nineteenth Century Literature). 296p. (C). 1995. 85.00 (*0-582-06195-4*, 77031) Longman.

— Language Relationship Wordsworths Writing. LC 94-20478. (Studies in Eighteenth & Nineteenth Century Literature). 296p. (C). 1995. pap. 41.40 (*0-582-06194-6*, 77030) Addson-Wesley Educ.

Baron, Michael, ed. Alfred, Lord Tennyson. (Everyman's Poetry Ser.). 116p. 1997. pap. 1.95 (*0-460-87802-6*, Everyman's Classic Lib) Tuttle Pubng.

Baron, Michelle. Water Safety with Teddy Ruxpin. (Teddy Ruxpin Safe 'n' Sound Ser.). (Illus.). 34p. (J). (ps). 1988. 9.95 incl. audio (*0-934323-74-7*) Alchemy Comms.

Baron, Mike. Last Command. 1999. pap. text 17.95 (*1-56971-378-2*) Dark Horse Comics.

Baron, Mike & Homan, Jim. The Complete Blankbook. (Illus.). 687p. 1992. pap. text 39.95 (*0-614-04595-9*) Wordbks & Listmats.

Baron, Mike & Rude, Steve. Nexus Collection, Vol. 1. Bennett, Anina, ed. (Nexus Ser.). (Illus.). 144p. 1993. pap. 14.95 (*1-878574-54-X*) Dark Horse Comics.

— Nexus Collection, Vol. 2. (Nexus Ser.). (Illus.). 144p. 1993. pap. 15.95 (*1-878574-80-9*) Dark Horse Comics.

— The Original Nexus, No. 2. Bruning, Richard, ed. (Illus.). 106p. 1986. 29.95 (*0-936211-00-8*); pap. 6.95 (*0-915419-03-3*) Graphitti Designs.

Baron, Mike & Sheppard, Brian. The Complete Wordbook. 300p. 1994. pap. text 27.50 (*0-614-04596-7*) Wordbks & Listmats.

Baron, Nancy. Getting Started in Calligraphy. LC 78-66311. (Illus.). 96p. (YA). (gr. 7 up). 1979. spiral bd. 12.95 (*0-8069-8840-1*) Sterling.

Baron, Nancy & Acorn, John. Birds of Coastal British Columbia. (Illus.). 224p. 1997. pap. 15.95 (*1-55105-098-6*) Lone Pine.

Baron, Nancy, jt. auth. see Acorn, John.

***Baron, Naomi S.** Alphabet to Email: How Written English Evolved & Where It's Headed. LC 99-43735. 296p. 2000. 24.95 (*0-415-18685-4*) Routledge.

Baron, Naomi S. Growing up with Language: How Children Learn to Talk. (Illus.). 288p. 1993. pap. 12.95 (*0-201-62480-X*) Addison-Wesley.

— Speech, Writing, & Sign: A Functional View of Linguistic Representation. LC 79-3626. (Advances in Semiotics Ser.). (Illus.). 319p. 1980. reprint ed. pap. 98.90 (*0-7837-3690-8*, 205786800009) Bks Demand.

Baron, Nick & Nicholas, Michele. Doppelgangers. 224p. 1995. mass mkt. 3.99 (*0-8217-5060-7*, Zebra Kensgtn) Kensgtn Pub Corp.

Baron, Norman, jt. auth. see Baron, Vida C.

Baron of Ravenstone. Scotland Bloody Scotland. 100p. 1996. pap. 9.95 (*0-86241-116-5*, Pub. by Canongate Books) Interlink Pub.

Baron, Pamela Stanton, ed. see State Bar of Texas Guide Committee.

Baron, Paul A., jt. ed. see Willeke, Klaus.

Baron, Paul B. How to Price a Profitable Company: When Privately-Held in the Middle Market in Manufacturing, Distribution & Retail. 2nd ed. 208p. 1996. spiral bd. 79.50 (*0-8144-7910-3*) AMACOM.

— When You Buy or Sell a Company. rev. ed. 396p. 1980. ring bd. 85.00 (*0-936936-50-9*) Ctr Busn Info.

— You're Never Too Old to Laugh. (Orig.). 1994. pap. 19.95 (*0-936936-53-3*) Ctr Busn Info.

Baron, Phil. The Do-Along Songbook. Forse, Ken, ed. (Teddy Ruxpin Adventure Ser.). (Illus.). 26p. (J). (ps). 1986. 9.95 (*0-934323-34-8*); audio. write for info. (*0-318-60970-3*) Alchemy Comms.

— Fire Safety with Teddy Ruxpin. (Teddy Ruxpin Safe 'N' Sound Ser.). (Illus.). 22p. (J). (ps). 1988. write for info. incl. audio (*0-934323-75-5*) Alchemy Comms.

— Gizmos & Gadgets. (Teddy Ruxpin Adventure Ser.). (Illus.). 34p. (J). (ps). 1987. 9.95 incl. audio (*0-934323-45-3*) Alchemy Comms.

— The Mushroom Forest. Forsse, Ken & Becker, Mary, eds. (Teddy Ruxpin Adventure Ser.). (Illus.). 26p. (J). (ps). 1986. 9.95 (*0-934323-36-4*); audio. write for info. (*0-318-60968-1*) Alchemy Comms.

— Quiet Please. (Teddy Ruxpin Adventure Ser.). (Illus.). 34p. (J). (ps). 1987. 9.95 incl. audio (*0-934323-40-2*) Alchemy Comms.

— Wooly & the Giant Snowzos. (Teddy Ruxpin Adventure Ser.). (Illus.). 34p. (J). (ps). 1987. 9.95 incl. audio (*0-934323-42-9*) Alchemy Comms.

Baron, R. B., jt. auth. see Bai, Xinghua.

Baron, Randall, jt. auth. see Benson, John C.

Baron, Randall, jt. auth. see Stewart, Frank.

Baron, Randall, jt. ed. see Benson, John C.

Baron, Renee. What Type Am I? Discover Who You Really Are. LC 97-52023. 208p. 1998. pap. 14.95 (*0-14-026941-X*) Viking Penguin.

Baron, Renee & Wagele, Elizabeth. Are You My Type, Am I Yours: Relationships Made Easy Through the Enneagram. LC 95-14405. 192p. 1995. pap. 15.00 (*0-06-251248-X*, Pub. by Harper SF) HarpC.

— The Enneagram Made Easy: Discover the Nine Types of People. LC 93-31824. 176p. 1994. pap. 17.00 (*0-06-251026-6*, Pub. by Harper SF) HarpC.

Baron, Reuben M. & Graziano, William G. Social Psychology. (Illus.). 540p. (C). 1991. text 48.00 (*0-03-021523-4*) Harcourt Coll Pubs.

***Baron, Richard.** Raid! The Untold Story of Patton's Secret Mission. 288p. 2000. mass mkt. 6.50 (*0-440-23609-6*) Dell.

Baron, Richard. Taxation. 1997. pap., wbk. ed. 90.00 (*0-85297-430-2*, Pub. by Chartered Bank) St Mut.

Baron, Robert. The Cerebral Computer. 552p. 1987. pap. 55.00 (*0-8058-0037-9*) L Erlbaum Assocs.

Baron, Robert, ed. Jefferson the Man: In His Own Words. LC 98-18690. 72p. 1998. pap. 9.95 (*1-55591-426-8*) Fulcrum Pub.

***Baron, Robert & Earhard, Bruce.** Psychology. 3rd ed. 398p. 2000. pap. 26.60 (*0-205-30745-0*) P-H.

Baron, Robert & Schofield, Edmund, eds. Thoreau's World & Ours: A Natural Legacy. LC 93-12848. (Illus.). 429p. 1993. 26.95 (*1-55591-903-0*) Fulcrum Pub.

Baron, Robert A. Copyright & Fair Use: The Great Image Debate. 160p. 1997. pap. text 34.00 (*90-5699-553-7*) Gordon & Breach.

— Psychology: Instructor's Resource Manual. 4th ed. (C). 1997. text, teacher ed. write for info. (*0-205-27288-6*, T7288-8) Allyn.

— Psychology: The Essential Science. 630p. 1989. boxed set 48.00 (*0-205-11432-6*, H14327) Allyn.

***Baron, Robert A.** Psychology with Supersite Pin Code. 5th ed. 768p. 2000. 80.00 (*0-205-32404-5*) Allyn.

***Baron, Robert A. & Byrne, Donn.** Exploring Social Psychology: Study Guide : Canadian Edition. 3rd ed. 2000. pap. 26.60 (*0-205-33095-9*) Allyn.

Baron, Robert A. & Kalsher, Michael J. Essentials of Psychology. 2nd ed. LC 97-47474. 580p. 1998. pap. text 50.00 (*0-205-28146-X*) Allyn.

Baron, Robert A. & Richardson, D. R. Human Aggression. 2nd ed. (Perspectives in Social Psychology Ser.). 440p. 1994. 39.50 (*0-306-44458-5*, Plenum Trade) Perseus Pubng.

Baron, Robert A., et al. Exploring Social Psychology. 4th ed. LC 97-22782. 363p. 1997. pap. text 49.00 (*0-205-27112-X*) Allyn.

— Exploring Social Psychology. 4th ed. 160p. (C). 1998. pap. text, teacher ed. write for info. (*0-205-27534-6*, T7534-5) Allyn.

Baron, Robert A., jt. auth. see Greenberg, Jerald.

Baron, Robert C., ed. Soul of America: Documenting Our Past, Vol. I: 1492-1870. LC 93-21115. 305p. (C). 1994. pap. text 14.95 (*1-55591-921-9*) Fulcrum Pub.

— Soul of America: Documenting Our Past, Vol. II: 1858-1993. LC 93-21115. 212p. (C). 1994. pap. text 14.95 (*1-55591-922-7*) Fulcrum Pub.

Baron, Robert C., et al, eds. Thomas Hornsby Ferril & the American West. 160p. 1996. pap. 17.95 (*1-55591-334-2*) Fulcrum Pub.

— Thomas Hornsby Ferril & the American West. aut. limited num. ed. 160p. 1996. 85.00 (*1-55591-339-3*) Fulcrum Pub.

Baron, Robert C., ed. see Jefferson, Thomas.

Baron, Robert J., jt. auth. see Higbie, Lee.

Baron, Robert Osborne. The Solo Sex: The Ultimate Do It Yourself Handbook for Men. (Illus.). 150p. write for info. (*0-8290-1917-0*) Irvington.

Baron, Robert S., et al. Group Process, Group Decision, Group Action. LC 92-22572. 1992. mass mkt. 20.00 (*0-534-19920-8*) Brooks-Cole.

Baron, Ron, ed. see Peters, Fritz.

Baron, Ron, ed. see Shah, Omar A.

Baron, Ron, ed. see Tam, Bianca.

***Baron, Russell.** Mapping the Journey: Case Studies in Developinng & Implementing Sustainable Development Strategies. 224p. 2000. pap. 30.00 (*1-874719-26-8*) Chelsea Green Pub.

Baron, S. & Leviatan, D., eds. Approximation, Interpolation, & Summability. (Israel Mathematical Conference Proceedings Ser.: Vol. 4). 284p. 1993. pap. 42.00 (*0-685-70695-8*, IMCP/4) Am Math.

Baron, S. Anthony. Violence in the Workplace: Prevention & Management Guide for Business. LC 93-19114. 176p. (Orig.). 1995. 24.95 (*0-934793-48-4*); pap. 14.95 (*0-934793-49-2*) Pathfinder CA.

***Baron, S. Anthony, et al.** When Work Equals Life: The Next Stage of Workplace Violence. 120p. (C). 1999. pap. 17.95 (*0-934793-66-2*) Pathfinder CA.

Baron, S. Anthony, jt. auth. see Wheeler, Eugene D.

Baron, S. R. & Haldane, J. D., eds. Community, Normality & Difference. (Aberdeen University Press Bks.). 224p. 1991. pap. text 22.00 (*0-08-041400-1*, Pub. by Aberdeen U Pr) Macmillan.

Baron, Salo W. The Contemporary Relevance of History: A Study in Approaches & Methods. LC 86-2244. 192p. 1986. text 55.50 (*0-231-06336-9*) Col U Pr.

— Late Middle Ages & Era of European Expansion: Byzantines, Mamelukes & Maghribians, Vol. 17. LC 52-404. 163p. 1980. text 87.50 (*0-231-08854-X*) Col U Pr.

— Modern Nationalism & Religion. LC 79-134050. (Essay Index Reprint Ser). 1977. 22.95 (*0-8369-2142-9*) Ayer.

— A Social & Religious History of the Jews, 18 vols. 2nd enl. rev. ed. Incl. Vol. 1. Ancient Times to the Beginning of the Christian Era. LC 52-404. 1958. text 87.50 (*0-231-08838-8*); Vol. 2. Ancient Times: Christian Era: the First Five Centuries. LC 52-404. 1952. text 87.50 (*0-231-08839-6*); Vol. 3. High Middle Ages: Heirs of Rome & Persia. LC 52-404. 1957. text 87.50 (*0-231-08840-X*); Vol. 4. High Middle Ages: Meeting of the East & West. LC 52-404. 1957. text 87.50 (*0-231-08841-8*); Vol. 5. High Middle Ages: Religious Controls & Dissensions. LC 52-404. 1957. text 87.50 (*0-231-08842-6*); Vol. 6. High Middle Ages: Laws, Homilies & the Bible. LC 52-404. 1958. text 87.50 (*0-231-08843-4*); Vol. 7. High Middle Ages: Hebrew Language & Letters. LC 52-404. 1958. text 87.50 (*0-231-08844-2*); Vol. 8. High Middle Ages: Philosophy & Science. LC 52-404. 1958. text 87.50 (*0-231-08845-0*); Vol. 9. Late Middle Ages & Era of European Expansion, 1200-1650: Under Church & Empire. LC 52-404. 1965. text 87.50 (*0-231-08846-9*); Vol. 10. Late Middle Ages & Era of European Expansion, 1200-1650: On the Empire's Periphery. LC 52-404. 1965. text 87.50 (*0-231-08847-7*); Vol. 11. Late Middle Ages & Era of European Expansion, 1200-1650: Citizen or Alien Conjurer. LC 52-404. 1967. text 87.50 (*0-231-08848-5*); Vol. 12. Late Middle Ages & Era of European Expansion, 1200-1650: Economic Catalyst. LC 52-404. 1967. text 87.50 (*0-231-08849-3*); Vol. 13. Late Middle Ages & Era of European Expansion, 1200-1650: Inquisition, Renaissance & Reformation. LC 52-404. 1970. text 87.50 (*0-231-08850-7*); Vol. 14. Late Middle Ages & Era of European Expansion, 1200-1650: Catholic Restoration & Wars of Religion. LC 52-404. 1970. text 87.50 (*0-231-08851-5*); Vol. 15. Late Middle Ages & Era of European Expansion, 1200-1650: Resettlement & Exploration. LC 52-404. 1973. text 87.50 (*0-231-08852-3*); LC 52-404. write for info. (*0-318-51413-3*) Col U Pr.

— A Social & Religious History of the Jews. 2nd enl. rev. ed. LC 92-25418. (C). 1993. 91.50 (*0-231-08856-6*) Col U Pr.

— Social & Religious History of the Jews, Vol. 16. 1976. text 87.50 (*0-231-08853-1*) Col U Pr.

— Social & Religious History of the Jews, Vols. 5-8. 1960. text 64.50 (*0-231-08877-9*) Col U Pr.

Baron, Salo W., ed. Essays on Maimonides. LC 79-160004. reprint ed. 32.50 (*0-404-00658-2*) AMS Pr.

Baron, Salo W. & Barzilay, Isaac, eds. Jubilee Volume: The American Academy for Jewish Research, 2 vols. LC 74-86233. 710p. 1980. text 127.50 (*0-231-05150-6*) Col U Pr.

Baron, Salo W. & Blau, Joseph L., eds. Judaism: Post Biblical & Talmudic Period. LC 55-1342. 1954. 5.25 (*0-672-60344-6*, LLA135, Bobbs) Macmillan.

Baron, Samual H. & Kollmann, Nancy S., eds. Religion & Culture in Early Modern Russia. LC 96-22921. 240p. 1997. lib. bdg. 35.00 (*0-87580-218-4*) N Ill U Pr.

Baron, Samuel. Medical Microbiology. 2nd ed. 1296p. (C). 1986. text 50.36 (*0-201-10146-7*, Health Sci) Addison-Wesley.

Baron, Samuel, ed. Medical Microbiology. 4th ed. LC 95-50499. (Illus.). (C). 1996. 55.00 (*0-9631172-1-1*) U TX MB Microb.

— Medical Microbiology: General Concepts. LC 96-4860. (Illus.). 1996. pap. 12.00 (*0-9631172-2-X*) U TX MB Microb.

Baron, Samuel, et al, eds. Interferon: Principles & Medical Applications. LC 92-18104. 500p. 1992. pap. text 23.00 (*0-9631172-0-3*) U TX MB Microb.

Baron, Samuel & Jennings, Paula M., eds. Medical Microbiology. 3rd ed. LC 91-10750. (Illus.). 1358p. 1991. reprint ed. pap. 200.00 (*0-7837-9742-7*, 206047000005) Bks Demand.

Baron, Samuel H. Explorations from Muscovite History. (Collected Studies: No. CS 348). 330p. 1991. text 109.95 (*0-86078-302-2*, Pub. by Variorum) Ashgate Pub Co.

— Plekhanov in Russian History & Soviet Historiography. (Pitt Series in Russian & East European). 274p. (C). 1994. text 59.95 (*0-8229-3788-3*) U of Pittsburgh Pr.

Baron, Sandra S., jt. auth. see Sack, Robert D.

Baron, Scott. They Also Served: Military Biographies of Uncommon Americans. LC 97-32343. 1998. pap. 18.95 (*1-877639-37-0*, MIE Pub) Military Information.

Baron, Sheldon, ed. see National Research Council, U. S. Staff.

Baron, Stanley. Digital Imaging & Audio Communication: Telecommunications in the 21st Century. 1996. text 46.95 (*0-442-02106-2*, VNR) Wiley.

Baron, Stanley N. & Krivocheev, Mark I. Digital Image & Audio Communications: Toward a Global Information Infrastructure. (Computer Science Ser.). 288p. 1995. 69.95 (*0-471-28716-4*, VNR) Wiley.

Baron, Stanley W. Brewed in America: A History of Beer & Ale in the United States. LC 72-5030. (Technology & Society Ser.). (Illus.). 424p. 1979. reprint ed. 36.95 (*0-405-04683-9*) Ayer.

Baron, Steven M. Houston Electric: The Street Railways of Houston, Texas. (Illus.). viii, 224p. 1997. 39.00 (*0-9653828-1-8*) S M Baron.

Baron Stockwell, M. Le, see Le Baron Stockwell, M.

Baron, Todd. Outside. 72p. (Orig.). (C). 1994. pap. 9.95 (*0-939691-11-6*) Avenue B.

— Return of the World. 48p. 1988. 6.50 (*0-929022-02-5*) O Bks.

— This... Seasonal Journal. 44p. (Orig.). 1992. pap. 5.00 (*0-945926-25-1*) Paradigm RI.

Baron, Vida C. Wimp Buster: For a Strong & Drug Free America. 149p. 1990. pap. 9.95 (*0-9624701-1-2*) Barez Pub.

Baron, Vida C. & Baron, Norman. Metamedicine: Power & Medicine, the 21st Century Way. (Illus.). 203p. (Orig.). 1990. pap. 14.95 (*0-9624701-0-4*) Barez Pub.

Baron, Virginia, jt. auth. see Michael, Marjorie.

Baron Von Behr, Nicolas. Multinationale Unternehmen & Exportkontrollen: Volkerrechtliche Zulassigkeit & Grenzen Extraterritorialer Ausfuhrbeschrankungen, with an English Summary. (ENG & GER.). 347p. 1996. 57.95 (*3-631-30367-X*) P Lang Pubng.

Baron, W. M. Organisation in Plants. 3rd ed. (Illus.). 272p. 1992. pap. text 35.95 (*0-521-42751-7*) Cambridge U Pr.

Baron, W. R. English Medieval Romance. Carroll, David & Wheeler, Michael, eds. LC 86-15388. (Literature in English Ser.). 304p. (Orig.). (C). 1989. pap. 41.40 (*0-582-49220-3*, 73533) Longman.

— Layamon's Brut. LC 94-48492. 904p. (C). 1995. pap. text 150.00 (*0-582-24651-2*, 77029) Addison-Wesley.

***Baron, Wade & Brown, Ray.** Com+ Software Architecture. 400p. 2001. 49.99 (*0-7356-1127-0*) Microsoft.

Baron, Wendy. The Camden Town Group. 1979. 148.95 (*0-85967-517-3*, Pub. by Scolar Pr) Ashgate Pub Co.

***Baron, Wendy.** Perfect Moderns: A History of the Camden Town Group. LC 99-36706. (Illus.). 180p. 1999. text 78.95 (*1-84014-291-X*, Pub. by Ashgate Pub) Ashgate Pub Co.

Baron, Wendy & Shone, Richard, eds. Walter Sickert, 1860-1942 Paintings. LC 92-31004. (Illus.). 384p. (C). 1993. 70.00 (*0-300-05373-8*) Yale U Pr.

Baron, Wendy, et al. Government Art Collection of the United Kingdom: The Twentieth Century. LC 97-192717. (Illus.). 200p. 1997. pap. 39.95 (*0-9516468-3-4*, Pub. by Merrell Holberton) U of Wash Pr.

Baron, Will. Deceived by New Age. 224p. 1991. pap. 7.99 (*0-8163-1022-X*) Pacific Pr Pub Assn.

Baron, Xavier, ed. London, 1066-1914, 3 vols. (Helm Informationliterary Sources And Documents). 1600p. (C). 1997. 425.00 (*1-873403-43-7*) Routledge.

Barona, Andres & Garcia, Eugene E., eds. Children at Risk: Poverty, Minority Status & Other Issues in Educational Equity. 351p. 1991. 35.00 (*0-932955-16-9*) Natl Assn Schl Psych.

***Barondes, Jessica.** Sweet Sixteen: Lucy, No. 2. LC 99-66682. (Sweet Sixteen Ser.: No. 2). 240p. (YA). (gr. 12 up). 2000. pap. 5.95 (*0-06-440813-2*, HarpTrophy) HarpC Child Bks.

Barondes, Samuel H. Molecules & Mental Illness. 216p. 1999. pap. text 19.95 (*0-7167-6033-9*) W H Freeman.

An Asterisk (*) at the beginning of an entry indicates that the title is appearing for the first time.

B

— Mood Genes: Hunting for Origins of Mania & Depression. LC 99-11427. (Illus.). 256p. 1999. pap. 14.95 (*0-19-513106-1*) OUP.
— Mood Genes: Hunting for Origins of Mania & Depression. LC 98-4678. 237p. 1998. pap. text 24.95 (*0-7167-2943-1*) W H Freeman.
Barondess, Jeremiah A. & Carpenter, Charles C. Differential Diagnosis. (Illus.). 993p. 1994. 75.00 (*0-8121-1446-9*) Lppncott W & W.
Barone. The Almanac of American Politics 2000. LC 70-160417. (Illus.). 1632p. 1999. pap. 54.95 (*0-8129-3194-7*, Times Bks) Crown Pub Group.
— Dermatologic Conditions. LC 99-26966. 407p. 1999. 39.95 (*0-683-30420-8*) Lppncott W & W.
Barone, Andrew, jt. auth. see Anderson, George.
Barone, Antonio. Principles & Applications of Superconducting Quantum Interference Devices. 500p. 1992. text 109.00 (*981-02-0911-8*) World Scientific Pub.
— Superconductive Particle Detectors. (Advances in the Physics of Condensed Matter Ser.: ISI-87). 360p. (C). 1988. text 77.00 (*9971-5-0611-4*) World Scientific Pub.
— Weak Superconductivity: Proceedings of the 2nd Soviet-Italian Symposium, Naples, Italy, 5-7 May 1987. Larkin, A. I., ed. (Progress in High Temperature Superconductivity Ser.: Vol. IV). 420p. (C). 1988. text 121.00 (*9971-5-0504-5*) World Scientific Pub.
Barone, Antonio, ed. Josephson Effect-Achievements & Trends: Advances in the Physics of Condensed Matter, Torino, Italy Sept. 1985. 528p. 1986. pap. 51.00 (*9971-5-0185-6*); text 124.00 (*9971-5-0176-7*) World Scientific Pub.
Barone, Antonio, et al, eds. X-Ray Detection by Superconducting Tunnel Junctions: Proceedings of the International Workshop, Naples, Italy, 12-14 December 1990. 350p. (C). 1991. text 83.00 (*981-02-0649-6*) World Scientific Pub.
Barone, Antonio & Paterno, Gianfranco. Physics & Applications of the Josephson Effect. LC 81-7554. (Wiley-Interscience Publications). 551p. reprint ed. pap. 170.90 (*0-7837-2372-5*, 204005800006) Bks Demand.
Barone, Antonio, et al. Ettias: First School on European Training on Technologies & Industrial Applications of Superconductivity, Naples, Italy, 9-13 September 1991. LC 92-24408. 548p. 1992. text 121.00 (*981-02-1046-9*) World Scientific Pub.
Barone, Arturo. Italians First! An A to Z of Everything Achieved First by Italians. 3rd ed. 256p. 1998. pap. 14.95 (*1-898823-40-5*) Renaissnce Bks Ltd.
Barone, Barbara J., jt. auth. see Clarkson, Sandra P.
Barone, Charles A. Marxist Thought on Imperialism: A Critical Survey. LC 84-23556. 225p. (gr. 13). 1989. pap. text 40.95 (*0-87332-345-9*) M E Sharpe.
— Marxist Thought on Imperialism: Survey & Critique. LC 84-23556. 239p. 1985. reprint ed. pap. 74.10 (*0-7837-9961-6*, 206068800006) Bks Demand.
Barone, D. F., et al. Social Cognitive Psychology: History & Current Domains. LC 97-1614. (Series in Social/Clinical Psychology). (Illus.). 508p. (C). 1997. 102.00 (*0-306-45474-2*, Plenum Trade) Perseus Pubng.
***Barone, David F., et al, eds.** Advanced Personality. LC 98-21499. (Plenum Series in Social-Clinical Psychology). (Illus.). 406p. (C). 1998. 49.50 (*0-306-45745-8*, Plenum Trade) Perseus Pubng.
Barone, David F., et al. Social Cognitive Psychology: History & Current Domains. LC 97-1614. (Series in Social/Clinical Psychology). 508p. (C). 1997. pap. 42.50 (*0-306-45475-0*, Plenum Trade) Perseus Pubng.
Barone, Dennis. Abusing the Telephone. 82p. 1994. 10.00 (*0-9628456-2-0*) Drogue Pr.
— Echoes. LC 98-113352. 172p. (C). 1997. pap. 14.00 (*0-937013-75-7*) Potes Poets.
— A Matter of Habit. (Chapbook Ser.). (Orig.). 1995. pap. 6.00 (*0-945112-21-1*) Generator Pr.
— New-Ark. limited ed. 44p. (Orig.). 1993. pap. 18.00 (*0-937013-48-X*) Potes Poets.
— The Returns. (New American Fiction Ser.: No. 36). 112p. (Orig.). 1996. pap. 10.95 (*1-55713-184-8*) Sun & Moon CA.
— Separate Objects. 83p. 1998. pap. 10.00 (*1-880516-26-8*) Left Hand Bks.
— Tempura Fugit. 22p. 1998. pap. 5.00 (*1-57141-044-9*) Runaway Spoon.
— Wag, Bound. 24p. 1998. pap. 4.00 (*1-893032-06-X*) Jensen Daniels.
Barone, Dennis, ed. Beyond the Red Notebook: Essays on Paul Auster. LC 95-13881. (Penn Studies in Contemporary American Fiction). 225p. 1995. text 37.50 (*0-8122-3317-4*); pap. text 17.95 (*0-8122-1556-7*) U of Pa Pr.
Barone, Dennis & Ganick, Peter, eds. The Art of Practice: Forty-Five Contemporary Poets. 408p. (Orig.). 1994. pap. 18.00 (*0-937013-46-3*) Potes Poets.
Barone, Diane. Resilient Children: Stories of Poverty, Drug Exposure & Literacy Development. LC 98-54836. (Literacy Studies Ser.). 15p. 1999. pap. 24.95 (*0-87207-199-5*, 199) Intl Reading.
Barone, Ermanno. From the Mekong to the Red: The Quest. Giammatteo, Dolores M., ed. 250p. (YA). 1994. pap. 8.95 (*0-918428-46-7*) Sylvan Inst.
Barone, Frank & Foreman, Farrell. Rhythm & Blues. (Does Not Apply Ser.). iv, 48p. 1997. pap. 5.00 (*0-9661978-0-1*) Barone Foreman.
***Barone, Jeanine.** The Travel Authority: Esssential Tips for Hassle-Free Travel. (Illus.). 2000. 4.95 (*0-9678210-0-2*) J Barone.
Barone, Jeanne T. Interviewing: Art & Skill. LC 94-23849. 368p. (C). 1995. pap. text 46.00 (*0-205-14088-2*) Allyn.
Barone, Joe. About a Loving God. 1991. pap. 7.50 (*1-55673-355-0*, 9154, Fairway Pr) CSS OH.
— My Tomb Was Empty: Seven Sermons for Lent & Easter. LC 92-32776. 1992. pap. 6.25 (*1-55673-564-2*, 9311) CSS OH.
Barone, John E. & Webb, Eugene J. Lord, You Must Be Joking! Leader's Guide. 80p. (Orig.). 1994. pap., teacher ed. 7.95 (*0-89390-310-8*) Resource Pubns.
Barone, M. & Selleri, F. Frontiers of Fundamental Physics. (Illus.). 620p. (C). 1994. text 155.00 (*0-306-44825-4*, Kluwer Plenum) Kluwer Academic.
Barone, Michael. The Almanac of American Politics, 1998. 1600p. 1997. 67.95 (*0-89234-081-9*, Times Bks) Crown Pub Group.
— Almanac of American Politics, 1988. Ujifusa, Grant, ed. (Illus.). 1500p. 1987. text 42.95 (*0-89234-037-1*) Natl Journal.
— Almanac of American Politics, 1990. rev. ed. Ujifusa, Grant, ed. (Illus.). 1500p. 1989. 56.95 (*0-89234-043-6*) Natl Journal.
— Almanac of American Politics, 1994. 1993. 59.95 (*0-89234-057-6*); pap. 48.95 (*0-89234-058-4*) Natl Journal.
— Almanac of American Politics, 1996. (Illus.). 1600p. 1995. 64.95 (*0-89234-067-3*); pap. 49.95 (*0-89234-066-5*) Natl Journal.
Barone, Michael. Almanac of American Politics 1998. 1997. 67.95 (*0-8129-2947-0*, Pub. by Crown Pub Group); pap. 52.95 (*0-8129-2948-9*, Pub. by Crown Pub Group) Random House.
Barone, Michael. Our Country: The Shaping of America from Roosevelt to Reagan. 1992. pap. 19.95 (*0-02-901862-5*) Free Pr.
Barone, Michael & Uiifusa, Grant. The Almanac of American Politics 2000. (Illus.). 1696p. 1999. 72.95 (*0-89234-094-0*, Pub. by Natl Journal); pap. 54.95 (*0-89234-093-2*, Pub. by Natl Journal) Times Books.
Barone, Michael & Ujifusa, Grant. The Almanac of American Politics 2000. (Illus.). 1632p. 1999. 72.95 (*0-8129-3193-9*, Times Bks) Crown Pub Group.
Barone, Michael, et al. The Almanac of American Politics, 1998. (Illus.). 1600p. 1997. pap. 52.95 (*0-89234-080-0*) Natl Journal.
— Consumer Behavior. 8th ed. (C). 1995. pap. text, teacher ed. 82.25 incl. trans. (*0-03-010448-3*) Dryden Pr.
— State Legislative Elections: Voting Patterns & Demographics. LC 98-219043. 403p. (C). (gr. 11). 1997. 135.00 (*1-56802-200-X*) Congr Quarterly.
Barone, Michael A., ed. see Johns Hopkins Hospital Staff.
Barone, Michele & Selleri, Franco, eds. Advances in Fundamental Physics: Proceedings of Conference Held in Olympia Greece, Sept. 1993. (Illus.). xii, 474p. (C). 1995. pap. text 85.00 (*0-911767-72-X*) Hadronic Pr Inc.
Barone, Patricia. Handmade Paper: A Collection of Poems. LC 93-83975. (Minnesota Voices Project Ser.: Vol. 60). 80p. (Orig.). 1994. pap. 7.95 (*0-89823-152-3*) New Rivers Pr.
— The Wind. 108p. 1987. pap. 7.95 (*0-89823-085-3*) New Rivers Pr.
Barone, R. Oak Tree & Olive Tree, 2 vols., Set. 1994. pap. 37.50 (*0-7165-2479-1*, Pub. by Irish Acad Pr) Intl Spec Bk.
Barone, Robert G. Just Like Old Times: A One-Act Play. (Illus.). 17p. 1982. pap. 3.00 (*0-88680-102-8*) I E Clark.
Barone, Shirley A. Bugs - Bugs - Bugs, Vol. 10. (Illus.). 44p. (Orig.). (J). (ps-2). 1989. pap. write for info. (*0-318-66620-0*) Toad Hse Bks.
— Easter Parade, Vol. 6. (Illus.). 44p. (Orig.). (J). (ps-2). 1990. pap. write for info. (*0-318-66616-2*) Toad Hse Bks.
— Funny Dinosaurs, Vol. 4. (Illus.). 44p. (Orig.). (J). (ps-2). 1989. pap. write for info. (*0-318-66614-6*) Toad Hse Bks.
— Halloween Fun for Everyone, Vol. 1. (My Give Away Coloring Bk.). (Illus.). 44p. (Orig.). (J). (ps-2). 1989. pap. 1.69 (*0-685-30447-7*) Toad Hse Bks.
— Happy Valentines, Vol. 5. (Illus.). 44p. (Orig.). (J). (ps-2). 1990. pap. text. write for info. (*0-318-66615-4*) Toad Hse Bks.
— I Know My ABC's, Vol. 13. (Illus.). 44p. (Orig.). (J). (ps-2). 1989. pap. write for info. (*0-318-66623-5*) Toad Hse Bks.
— I Know My Numbers, Vol. 14. (Illus.). 44p. (Orig.). (J). (ps-2). 1989. pap. write for info. (*0-318-66624-3*) Toad Hse Bks.
— I Like Monsters, Vol. 9. (Illus.). 44p. (Orig.). (J). (ps-2). 1989. pap. write for info. (*0-318-66619-7*) Toad Hse Bks.
— In My Toy Box, Vol. 8. (Illus.). 44p. (Orig.). (J). (ps-2). 1989. pap. write for info. (*0-318-66618-9*) Toad Hse Bks.
— Kittens & Puppies, Vol. 11. (Illus.). 44p. (Orig.). (J). (ps-2). 1989. pap. write for info. (*0-318-66621-9*) Toad Hse Bks.
— Let's Give Thanks, Vol. 2. (My Give Away Coloring Bk.). (Illus.). 44p. (Orig.). (J). (ps-2). 1989. pap. 1.75 (*0-685-30448-5*) Toad Hse Bks.
— Meet My Friends: Children of the World, Vol. 15. (Illus.). 44p. (Orig.). (J). (ps-2). 1989. pap. write for info. (*0-318-66625-1*) Toad Hse Bks.
— My Teddy Bears, Vol. 12. (Illus.). 44p. (Orig.). (J). (ps-2). 1989. pap. write for info. (*0-318-66622-7*) Toad Hse Bks.
— A Shoe for You, Vol. 7. (Illus.). 44p. (Orig.). (J). (ps-2). 1989. pap. write for info. (*0-318-66617-0*) Toad Hse Bks.
— A Time for Joy (Christmas), Vol. 3. (Illus.). 44p. (Orig.). (J). (ps-2). 1989. pap. write for info. (*0-318-66613-8*) Toad Hse Bks.
***Barone, Stephen B.** General Chemistry. LC 99-89911. (11th Hour Ser.). (Illus.). 225p. 2000. pap. 18.95 (*0-632-04293-1*) Blackwell Sci.
***Barone, Tom.** Aesthetics, Politics, & Educational Inquiry: Essays & Examples. LC 99-15092. (Counterpoints Ser.: No. 117). 288p. (C). 2000. pap. text 29.95 (*0-8204-4520-7*) P Lang Pubng.
Baroni, Allana. Simplify the Holidays: How to Enjoy the Season Without the Stress. LC 98-30974. (Illus.). 144p. 1998. pap. 17.95 (*0-7621-0097-4*, Pub. by RD Assn) Penguin Putnam.
— Your Wedding: Less-Stress Solutions for Your Perfect Day. LC 98-11144. (Simpler Life Ser.). (Illus.). 144p. 1998. 17.95 (*0-7621-0063-X*, Pub. by RD Assn) Penguin Putnam.
Baroni, Geno, ed. see Wenk, Michael G.
***Baroni, Helen J.** The Illustrated Encyclopedia of Zen Buddhism. LC 99-53421. (Illus.). 2000. 89.95 (*0-8239-2240-5*) Rosen Group.
— Obaku Zen: The Emergence of the Third Sect of Zen in Tokugawa, Japan. LC 99-355256. 294p. 2000. text 60.00 (*0-8248-2195-5*); pap. text 32.95 (*0-8248-2243-9*) UH Pr.
Baroni, Mary, jt. ed. see Millonig, Virginia L.
Baroni, Timothy J. A Revision of the Genus Rhodocybe Maire (Agaricales) (Nova Hedwigia Beiheft Ser.: No. 67). (Illus.). 300p. 1981. lib. bdg. 80.00 (*3-7682-5467-4*) Lubrecht & Cramer.
Baroni, Timothy J., jt. auth. see Largent, David L.
Baronio, Giuseppe. On Grafting in Animals: The Degli Innesti Animali. Sax, Joan B., tr. (Illus.). 87p. 1985. bds. 100.00 (*0-318-04638-5*) F A Countway.
***Baronov, David.** The Abolition of Slavery in Brazil: The "Liberation" of Africans Through the Emancipation of Capital, 17. LC 99-58881. (Contributions in Latin American Studies: Vol. 17). 256p. 2000. 62.50 (*0-313-31242-7*, GM1242, Greenwood Pr) Greenwood.
Baronov, David. Feverfew & Migraine Headaches: Everything You Need to Know about. LC 98-50346. (Natural Pharmacist Ser.). (Illus.). 175p. 2000. pap. 6.99 (*0-7615-1753-7*) Prima Pub.
Baron's Educational Series Staff & Mitchell, Carolyn B. Mastering French, Level II, 12 cassettes, Set. (Foreign Service Institute Mastering Series-Level II: Level 2). (FRE & ENG.). 1992. pap., boxed set 79.95 incl. audio (*0-8120-7918-3*) Barron.
Barooah, Jeuti. Single Women in Assamese Hindu Society. (C). 1993. 22.00 (*81-212-0416-X*, Pub. by Gian Publng Hse) S Asia.
Barooah, Pramila P. Handbook on Child: (With Historical Background) (Concepts in Communication Informatics & Librarianship Ser.: No. 32). 1992. 30.00 (*81-7022-415-2*, Pub. by Concept) S Asia.
Baroody, Arthur J. Children's Mathematical Thinking: A Developmental Framework for Pre-School, Primary, & Special Education Teachers. 320p. (C). 1987. pap. text 20.95 (*0-8077-2837-3*) Tchrs Coll.
— Problem Solving, Reasoning & Communicating: Reasoning & Communicating, Grades K to 8. LC 92-27749. (Illus.). 160p. (Orig.). (J). (gr. k-8). 1992. pap. text 16.60 (*0-02-306488-9*, Macmillan Coll) P-H.
Baroody, Arthur J. & Coslick, Ronald T. Fostering Children's Mathematical Power: An Investigative Approach to K-8 Mathematics Instruction. LC 98-24187. 600p. 1998. pap. 49.95 (*0-8058-3105-3*) L Erlbaum Assocs.
Baroody, Judith R. Media Access & the Military: The Case of the Gulf War. LC 97-50220. 248p. (C). 1998. 59.00 (*0-7618-1025-0*); pap. 36.50 (*0-7618-1026-9*) U Pr of Amer.
Baroody, Theodore A. Alkalize or Die. (Illus.). 242p. (Orig.). 1991. pap. 14.95 (*0-9619595-3-3*) Holographic Hlth.
— Ascension - Beginner's Manual. (Illus.). 224p. (Orig.). 1989. pap. text 12.95 (*0-9619595-1-7*) Holographic Hlth.
— Asparagus: Can Do It for You! (Illus.). 56p. (Orig.). 1995. pap. 4.95 (*0-9619595-4-1*) Holographic Hlth.
Baroody, Theodore A., Jr. The Brotherhood of Intuition. 27p. (Orig.). 1987. pap. text 3.00 (*0-9619595-0-9*) Holographic Hlth.
— Hiatal Hernia Syndrome: Insidious Link to Major Illness. (Illus.). 150p. (Orig.). 1987. pap. text 9.95 (*0-9619595-2-5*) Holographic Hlth.
Barooshian, Vahan D. Russian Cubo-Futurism, 1910-1930: A Study in Avant-Gardism. LC 73-81271. (De Proprietatibus Litterarum, Ser. Major: No. 24). 176p. 1974. text 43.85 (*90-279-2659-X*) Mouton.
— V. V. Vereshchagin: Artist at War. LC 92-32515. (Illus.). 216p. (C). 1993. 49.95 (*0-8130-1178-7*) U Press Fla.
Baros, Shirley L., jt. ed. see Morain, Stan.
Barosh, Miyoshi, jt. ed. see Bartman, William S.
Barosh, Miyoshi, ed. see Kelley, Mike & Miller, John.
Barosh, Tom, ed. see Greenly, Ernie.
Barosin, Jacob. A Remnant. LC 88-80085. 1989. 16.95 (*0-89604-093-3*, Holocaust Library); pap. 10.95 (*0-89604-129-8*, Holocaust Library) US Holocaust.
Barot, Rohit, ed. The Racism Problematic: Contemporary Sociological Debates on Race & Ethnicity. LC 96-16101. (Studies in Sociology: Vol. 11). 288p. 1996. 89.95 (*0-7734-8818-9*) E Mellen.
Barot, Rohit & Nichols. Economy Ethnicity & Social Change. 61.95 (*0-7546-1062-4*) Ashgate Pub Co.
***Baroth, Peter.** Mounds of Sounds. iv, 52p. 2000. pap. write for info. (*0-9674900-8-1*) Wordrunner.
Barouch, Dan H. Voyages in Conceptual Chemistry. (Chemistry Ser.). 192p. 1996. pap. 15.00 (*0-7637-0308-7*) Jones & Bartlett.
— Voyages in Conceptual Chemistry: Solutions Manual. (Chemistry Ser.). 64p. 1996. pap. 12.50 (*0-7637-0311-7*) Jones & Bartlett.
Barouche, Crystal. Game of Hearts. write for info. (*0-7860-0570-X*) Kensgtn Pub Corp.
— Midnight Skies. (Arabesque Ser.). 352p. 1997. mass mkt. 4.99 (*0-7860-0465-7*, Pinncle Kensgtn) Kensgtn Pub Corp.
Baroudi, Carol. Mastering COBOL. LC 98-88951. (Mastering Ser.). 1024p. 1999. pap. 49.99 (*0-7821-2321-X*) Sybex.
Baroudi, Carol, jt. auth. see Levine, John.
Barouh, Gail. Support Groups - The Human Face of the HIV-AIDS Epidemic: A Handbook for Health Care Professionals, People with AIDS, Their Loved Ones, & the Community-at-Large. LC 92-81221. x, 94p. 1992. pap. 10.00 (*1-881305-00-7*) LIAAC.
Barouk, L. S. Forefoot Reconstruction. (Illus.). 150p. 1999. 199.00 incl. audio compact disk (*2-287-59656-9*, Pub. by Spl France Editions) Spr-Verlag.
Barovier, Marina. Animals in Glass: A Murano Bestiary. 1997. pap. 35.00 (*88-86502-56-7*, Pub. by Canal & Stamperia) Antique Collect.
— Art of the Barovier. (Illus.). 216p. 1993. 75.00 (*88-7743-127-X*, Pub. by Arsenale Editrice) Antique Collect.
Barovier, Marino, ed. Carlo Scarpa: Glass of an Architect. (Illus.). 304p. 1999. 60.00 (*88-8118-382-X*, Pub. by Skira IT) Abbeville Pr.
Barozzi, A., tr. see Lambros, Paul.
***Barozzi da Vignol, Giacomo.** Canon of the Five Orders of Architecture: Translated into English, with an Introduction & Commentary. LC 99-11820. (Illus.). 9p. 1999. pap. 27.95 (*0-926494-19-8*) Acanthus Pr.
Barozzi, Ronald. Journey with Pain: Creative Strategies for Coping with Chronic Pain. (Illus.). 120p. (Orig.). 1997. pap. 16.95 (*1-56072-327-0*, Nova Kroshka Bks) Nova Sci Pubs.
Barquera Arroyo, Elvia C. Sanchez de la, see Sanchez de la Barquera Arroyo, Elvia C.
Barquero, J. A. Estampas Espanolas. (SPA.). 10.50 (*84-241-5632-3*) E Torres & Sons.
Barquest, G., et al. Shelves, Houses & Feeders for Birds & Mammals. (Illus.). 47p. 1999. pap. text 20.00 (*0-7881-7821-0*) DIANE Pub.
Barquet, A. Traumatic Hip Dislocation in Childhood. (Illus.). 160p. 1987. 93.95 (*0-387-17009-X*) Spr-Verlag.
Barquet, Jesus J., et al. Lo Que No Se Ha Dicho. Monge-Rafuls, Pedro R., ed. & intro. by. LC 94-67316. (Literature/Conversation Ser.: Vol. IV). (ENG & SPA.). 341p. 1994. pap. 20.00 (*0-9625127-3-7*) Ollantay Pr.
Barquet, Ramis, et al. Latin American Masterpieces. (Illus.). 32p. (Orig.). 1997. pap. write for info. (*0-9658637-1-9*) Galeria Ramis.
Barquez, Ruben M., et al. Guide to the Bats of Argentina: Guia de los Murcielagos de Argentina. (ENG & SPA., Illus.). 119p. (Orig.). 1993. pap. 15.00 (*1-883090-00-8*) OK Museum.
— Mammals of Tucuman: Mamiferos de Tucuman. (ENG & SPA., Illus.). 282p. (Orig.). 1991. pap. 15.00 (*1-883090-03-2*) OK Museum.
Barquin, Ramon & Edelstein, Herb. Building, Using & Managing the Data Warehouse. LC 96-53480. 352p. (C). 1997. 41.99 (*0-13-534355-0*) P-H.
— Planning & Designing Data Warehouses. 352p. 1996. pap. text 41.99 (*0-13-255746-0*) P-H.
***Barquist, Barbara & Barquist, David.** Oconomowoc: Barons to Bootleggers. (Illus.). x, 335p. 1999. 40.00 (*0-9675179-0-7*) Barquist.
Barquist, David, jt. auth. see Barquist, Barbara.
Barquist, David L. American & English Pewter at the Yale University Art Gallery: A Supplementary Checklist. LC 85-52296. (Illus.). 80p. (Orig.). 1986. pap. 12.00 (*0-89467-040-9*) Yale Art Gallery.
— American Tables & Looking Glasses in the Mabel Brady Garvan & Other Collections at Yale University. LC 91-50993. (Illus.). 530p. (C). 1992. 80.00 (*0-300-05240-5*) Yale U Pr.
Barquist, David L., et al. American Silver from the Kossack Collection: A Checklist. (Illus.). 23p. (Orig.). 1988. pap. 1.00 (*0-89467-049-2*) Yale Art Gallery.
Barr. Churchill Pocketbook of Oncology. 1997. pap. text 23.95 (*0-443-05102-X*, W B Saunders Co) Harcrt Hlth Sci Grp.
— New Testament Story. 3rd ed. (Religion Ser.). 2001. pap. 50.00 (*0-534-54163-1*) Wadsworth Pub.
— Reading Diagnosis for Teachers: An Instructional Approach. 4th ed. (C). 2000. pap. text. write for info. (*0-8013-3057-2*) Addison-Wesley.
— What's Modern Painting? rev. ed. (Illus.). 48p. 1990. pap. 6.95 (*0-8109-6083-4*, Pub. by Abrams) Time Warner.
***Barr & Edwards, ed.** Multivari Calculas Stanford. 564p. 1998. pap. text 53.00 (*0-536-01809-X*) P-H.
Barr, A. Knowledge Based Systems. (C). 1996. text. write for info. (*0-201-50024-8*) Addison-Wesley.
Barr, A. C., jt. ed. see Garland, T.
Barr, Alan P., ed. The Major Prose of Thomas Henry Huxley. LC 96-13712. (Humanities Center Series on Science & the Humanities). (C). 1997. 50.00 (*0-8203-1864-7*) U of Ga Pr.
— Thomas Henry Huxley's Place in Science & Letters: Centenary Essays. LC 96-13705. 1997. 50.00 (*0-8203-1865-5*) U of Ga Pr.
Barr, Alan R. Wills Styles for Scotland. LC 95-168349. 1994. text. write for info. (*0-406-17940-9*, UK, MICHIE) LEXIS Pub.
Barr, Albert S., III, et al. Maryland Estate Planning, Will Drafting & Estate Administration Forms, Issue 4. 2nd ed. 200p. 1999. ring bd. write for info. (*0-327-01264-1*, 8158715) LEXIS Pub.
Barr, Alfred H., Jr. American Art of the 20's & 30's. 1969. 20.95 (*0-405-01529-1*) Ayer.
— Art in Our Time: Tenth Anniversary Exhibition. LC 79-169294. (Museum of Modern Art Publications in Reprint). (Illus.). 384p. 1972. reprint ed. 35.95 (*0-405-01554-2*) Ayer.
— Cezanne, Gauguin, Seurat, Van Gogh: First Loan Exhibition. LC 72-169295. (Museum of Modern Art Publications in Reprint). (Illus.). 152p. 1972. reprint ed. 26.95 (*0-405-01555-0*) Ayer.
— Cubism & Abstract Art. (Paperbacks in AA History Ser.). (Illus.). 256p. 1986. pap. 26.95 (*0-674-17935-8*) HUP.

An Asterisk (*) at the beginning of an entry indicates that the title is appearing for the first time.

B

— Cubism & Abstract Art. LC 66-26123. (Museum of Modern Art Publications in Reprint). 1967. reprint ed. 32.95 (*0-405-01509-7*) Ayer.

— Matisse: His Art & His Public. LC 66-26118. (Museum of Modern Art Publications in Reprint). 1967. reprint ed. 36.95 (*0-405-01525-9*) Ayer.

— Modern German Painting & Sculpture. LC 76-169296. (Museum of Modern Art Publications in Reprint). (Illus.). 96p. 1972. reprint ed. 21.95 (*0-405-01556-9*) Ayer.

— The New American Painting As Shown in 8 European Countries, 1958-1959. LC 70-169297. (Museum of Modern Art Publications in Reprint). (Illus.). 96p. 1972. reprint ed. 21.95 (*0-405-01557-7*) Ayer.

Barr, Alfred H. Painting & Sculpture in the Museum of Modern Art, 1929-1967. LC 68-54923. (Illus.). 1977. 40.00 (*0-87070-540-7*) Mus of Modern Art.

Barr, Alfred H., Jr. Picasso, 50 Years of His Art. LC 66-26126. (Museum of Modern Art Publications in Reprint). 1967. reprint ed. 28.95 (*0-405-01519-4*) Ayer.

— What Is Modern Painting? (Illus.). 48p. 1975. pap. 6.95 (*0-87070-631-4*, 0-8109-6083-4, Pub. by Mus of Modern Art) Abrams.

Barr, Alfred H., Jr., ed. Fantastic Art, Dada, Surrealism. LC 68-8367. (Museum of Modern Art Publications in Reprint). (Illus.). 1969. reprint ed. 28.95 (*0-405-01510-0*) Ayer.

Barr, Alfred H., Jr. & Brooks, Charles M., Jr. Vincent Van Gogh: A Monograph. LC 66-26121. (Museum of Modern Art Publications in Reprint). 1967. reprint ed. 28.95 (*0-405-01514-3*) Ayer.

Barr, Alfred H., Jr., jt. auth. see Soby, James T.

Barr, Alfred H., Jr., jt. ed. see Cahill, Holger.

Barr, Alfred H., Jr., jt. ed. see Miller, Dorothy C.

Barr, Alfred H., Jr., ed. see Museum of Modern Art Library Staff.

Barr, Allan. A Diagram of Synoptic Relationships. 1998. 29.95 (*0-567-09724-2*, Pub. by T & T Clark) Bks Intl VA.

Barr, Alwyn. Black Texans: A History of African Americans in Texas, 1528-1995. 2nd ed. LC 96-23097. (Illus.). 304p. 1996. pap. 15.95 (*0-8061-2878-X*) U of Okla Pr.

— Polignac's Texas Brigade: With a New Preface. LC 97-51441. (Military History Ser.). (Illus.). 104p. 1998. pap. 12.95 (*0-89096-814-4*) Tex A&M Univ Pr.

— Texans in Revolt: The Battle for San Antonio, 1835. (Illus.). 112p. 1990. reprint ed. 18.95 (*0-292-77042-1*) U of Tex Pr.

Barr, Alwyn & Calvert, Robert A., eds. Black Leaders: Texans for Their Times. (Illus.). x, 237p. 1990. pap. 9.95 (*0-87611-056-1*) Tex St Hist Assn.

***Barr, Amelia.** The Belle of Bowling Green. 252p. 2000. pap. 9.95 (*0-594-00492-6*) Eightn Hundrd.

— Friend Olivia. 252p. 2000. pap. 9.95 (*0-594-00423-3*) Eightn Hundrd.

Barr, Amelia E. All the Days of My Life. Baxter, Annette K., ed. LC 79-8772. (Signal Lives Ser.). (Illus.). 1980. reprint ed. lib. bdg. 63.95 (*0-405-12822-3*) Ayer.

— All the Days of My Life: An Autobiography. 1993. reprint ed. lib. bdg. 75.00 (*0-7812-5863-4*) Rprt Serv.

***Barr, Amelia E.** The Bow of Orange Ribbon. 252p. 2000. pap. 9.95 (*0-594-01489-1*) Eightn Hundrd.

Barr, Amelia E. Christopher, & Other Stories. LC 72-167440. (Short Story Index Reprint Ser.). 1977. reprint ed. 23.95 (*0-8369-3966-2*) Ayer.

***Barr, Amelia E.** The Lion's Whelp. 252p. 2000. pap. 9.95 (*0-594-00426-8*) Eightn Hundrd.

— The Maid of Maiden Lane. 252p. 2000. pap. 9.95 (*0-594-00678-3*) Eightn Hundrd.

Barr, Amelia E. Remember the Alamo. large type ed. (Large Print Heritage Ser.). 385p. (J). (gr. 7-12). 1999. lib. bdg. 34.95 (*1-58118-044-6*, 22513) LRS.

— Remember the Alamo. 329p. 1980. reprint ed. lib. bdg. 11.95 (*0-89968-215-4*, Lghtyr Pr) Buccaneer Bks.

— Scottish Sketches. LC 70-157771. (Short Story Index Reprint Ser.). 1977. reprint ed. 21.95 (*0-8369-3883-6*) Ayer.

***Barr, Amelia E.** Trinity Bells. 252p. 2000. pap. 9.95 (*0-594-00270-2*) Eightn Hundrd.

Barr, Andrew. Drink: A Social History of America. (Illus.). 480p. 1999. 25.95 (*0-7867-0559-0*) Carroll & Graf.

***Barr, Andrew.** Drink: A Social History of America. (Illus.). 480p. 2000. pap. 16.00 (*0-7867-0743-7*, Pub. by Carroll & Graf) Publishers Group.

Barr, Avron. Handbook of Artificial Intelligence, Vol. I. 1989. pap. text 27.95 (*0-201-16885-5*) Addison-Wesley.

— Physically Based Modelling in Graphics & Animation. (C). 1999. 52.95 (*0-201-18366-8*) Addison-Wesley.

Barr, B. I., et al, eds. Bridge Assessment Management & Design: Proceedings of the Centenary Year Bridge Conference, Cardiff, U. K., 26-30 September 1994. LC 94-33283. (Developments in Civil Engineering Ser.: Vol. 45). 522p. 1994. 184.00 (*0-444-82063-9*) Elsevier.

Barr, Barbara. Cottonwood Pass: A Celebration of Flowers in Fabric. Holmes, Sharon, ed. & illus. by. Dumler, Susan, illus. 36p. 1993. pap. 8.95 (*1-880972-07-7*, DreamSpinners) Pssblts Denver.

Barr, Browne. High Flying Geese: Unexpected Reflections on the Church & Its Ministry. (Illus.). 96p. (Orig.). 1984. 5.95 (*0-86683-900-3*) Harper SF.

— Never Too Late to Be Loved: How One Couple under Stress Discovered Intimacy & Joy. LC 96-19410. 220p. 1996. 19.95 (*1-57249-035-7*, Ragged Edge) White Mane Pub.

***Barr, Bruce Charles.** Banishing the Blues of Seasonal Affective Disorder: Using Bright Light Therapy for the Successful Treatment of... (Illus.). 64p. 2000. pap. 8.95 (*0-9677416-0-2*) indoorsun.

Barr, Catherine, ed. From Biography to History: Best Books for Children's Entertainment & Education. LC 98-23147. (Illus.). 523p. (J). (gr. 1-8). 1998. 59.95 (*0-8352-4012-6*) Bowker.

— Reading in Series: A Selection Guide to Books for Children. LC 98-49681. 600p. 1999. 65.00 (*0-8352-4011-8*) Bowker.

Barr, Catherine, ed. see Dinatale, Nancy & Shore, Hennie.

Barr, Charles. Ealing Studios. LC 79-51033. (Illus.). 200p. 1982. 25.00 (*0-87951-101-X*, Pub. by Overlook Pr); pap. 13.95 (*0-87951-147-8*, Pub. by Overlook Pr) Penguin Putnam.

***Barr, Charles.** Ealing Studios: A Movie Book. LC 99-212002. 222p. 1999. pap. 19.95 (*0-520-21554-0*, Pub. by U CA Pr) Cal Prin Full Svc.

— English Hitchcock. (Illus.). 256p. 2000. pap. 24.95 (*0-906506-13-1*, Pub. by Cameron & Hollis) Dist Art Pubs.

Barr, Charles, ed. All Our Yesterdays: Ninety Years of British Cinema. (Illus.). 446p. 1986. 29.95 (*0-85170-179-5*, Pub. by British Film Inst) Ind U Pr.

Barr, Charles, ed. see Selden, Paul H.

Barr, Charlotte. The Bell Buckle Years. LC 92-12352. 1992. pap. 8.95 (*0-918518-93-8*) Iris Pr.

— Sister Woman. 96p. (Orig.). 1990. pap. 11.95 (*0-9624100-0-4*) Bell Buckle.

Barr, Cynthia. Massachusetts Zoning Manual, 1997 Supplement. Healy, Martin R., ed. LC 97-75568. 388p. 1997. ring bd., suppl. ed. 49.50 (*1-57589-072-0*, 97-19.34-SP) Mass CLE.

***Barr, Cynthia M.** Boston Zoning: A Lawyer's Handbook. 2000. pap. write for info. (*1-57589-176-X*) Mass CLE.

Barr, Cyrilla. Elizabeth Sprague Coolidge. LC 97-31635. 436p. 1998. 42.00 (*0-02-864888-9*) Mac Lib Ref.

— The Monophonic Lauda & the Lay Religious Confraternities of Tuscany & Umbria in the Late Middle Ages. (Early Drama, Art & Music Monograph: No. 10). 1988. pap. 15.95 (*0-918720-90-7*); boxed set 25.95 (*0-918720-89-3*) Medieval Inst.

Barr, Cyrilla, jt. ed. see Locke, Ralph P.

Barr, D. G. Exchange Rate Variability: Evidence for the Period 1973-1982. LC HG1582.E53. (Bank of England. Discussion Papers. Technical Ser.: No. 11). 49p. reprint ed. pap. 30.00 (*0-608-15636-1*, 203176800076) Bks Demand.

Barr, D. G. & Cuthbertson, K. An Independent Error Feedback Model of U. K. Company Sector Asset Demands. LC HB0141.B3. (Bank of England, Discussion Papers: Vol. 25). 32p. 1989. reprint ed. pap. 30.00 (*0-608-01651-9*, 206230300002) Bks Demand.

Barr, D. G., jt. auth. see Fleming, J. S.

Barr, D. I. & Wallingford, H. R. Additional Tables for the Hydraulic Design of Pipes, Sewers & Channels. 229p. 79.00 (*0-7277-1667-0*, Pub. by T Telford) RCH.

Barr, D. I., jt. auth. see Wallingford, H. R.

Barr, D. I. H. & Wallingford, HR (Firm) Staff. Tables for the Hydraulic Design of Pipes, Sewers & Channels. 7th ed. LC 98-204432. 1998. write for info. (*0-7277-2638-2*) T Telford.

Barr, David. The Death of the Black Jesus. 82p. 1996. pap. 5.60 (*0-87129-632-2*, D68) Dramatic Pub.

— Making Money at the Races. 1980. pap. 10.00 (*0-87980-268-5*) Wilshire.

Barr, David, et al. Problems with Protease Inhibitor Development Plans. 21p. (Orig.). (C). 1995. pap. text 15.00 (*0-7881-2364-5*) DIANE Pub.

Barr, David F. & Miller, Richard K. Basic Industrial Hearing Conservation. 26.95 (*0-915586-10-X*) Fairmont Pr.

Barr, David L. New Testament Story: An Introduction. 379p. (C). 1987. pap. 42.95 (*0-534-07284-4*) Wadsworth Pub.

— New Testament Story: An Introduction. 2nd ed. LC 94-27204. 574p. 1994. pap. 67.95 (*0-534-16380-7*) Wadsworth Pub.

— Tales of the End: A Narrative Commentary on the Book of Revelation. LC 97-3221. (The Storytellers Bible Ser.). 240p. 1998. pap. 17.95 (*0-944344-66-6*) Polebridge Pr.

Barr, Dean, et al. Blending Quantitative & Traditional Equity Analysis: March 30-31, 1994, Boston, Massachusetts LC 99-208061. (ICFA Continuing Education Ser.). viii, 135 p. 1994. write for info. (*1-879087-41-3*) Assn I M&R.

Barr, Debbie. Carving Caricature Women. LC 98-87123. (Illus.). 64p. (Orig.). 1999. pap. 14.95 (*0-7643-0649-9*) Schiffer.

— Carving Miniature Animals with Debbie Barr. (Illus.). 64p. 1999. pap. 14.95 (*0-7643-0936-6*) Schiffer.

— Caught in the Crossfire. 288p. (Orig.). 1986. pap. 9.95 (*0-310-28561-5*, 12083P) Zondervan.

— Children of Divorce. LC 92-10003. Orig. Title: Caught in the Crossfire. 288p. 1992. pap. 12.99 (*0-310-28741-3*) Zondervan.

Barr, Donald R. & Zehna, Peter W. Probability: Modeling Uncertainty. (Illus.). 480p. 1983. pap. text, teacher ed. 2.00 (*0-201-10799-6*) Addison-Wesley.

***Barr, Donald W.** Wisdom for Sales: A Reference Book to Increase Your Sales & Income. Cockran, Deborah, ed. LC 98-90164. (Illus.). 247p. 1998. 35.00 (*0-9663656-0-7*) Sales-Exec Bks.

***Barr, Donna.** Bosom Enemies: Losing Our Bearings. (Illus.). 64p. 2000. pap. 6.00 (*1-892253-08-9*) Fine Line.

Barr, Donna. Desert Peach: Baby Games. (Illus.). 112p. 1994. pap. 12.95 (*1-883847-05-2*) MU Press.

— The Desert Peach: Beginnings. (Illus.) 104p. (Orig.). 1995. pap. 12.95 (*1-883847-13-3*) MU Press.

— Desert Peach: Belief Systems. (Illus.). 112p. 1994. pap. 12.95 (*1-883847-07-9*) MU Press.

— Desert Peach: Foreign Relations. (Illus.). 112p. 1994. pap. 12.95 (*1-883847-04-4*) MU Press.

— The Desert Peach: Marriage & Mayhem. (Illus.). 120p. 1994. pap. 14.95 (*1-883847-08-7*) MU Press.

— The Desert Peach: Politics, Pilots & Puppies. (Illus.). 120p. 1991. pap. 9.95 (*1-883847-00-1*) MU Press.

— Miki. (Desert Peach Ser.: Vol. 26). (Illus.). 48p. 1996. pap. 4.95 (*1-892253-05-4*, Pub. by Fine Line) Last Gasp.

— New & Different. (Desert Peach Ser.: Vol. 27). (Illus.). 64p. 1997. pap. 5.95 (*1-892253-02-X*, Pub. by Fine Line) Last Gasp.

— Peach Slices. (Illus.). 96p. 1993. pap. 9.95 (*1-883847-01-X*) MU Press.

— "Stinz" "A Dog's Life", Vol. III - 7. (Illus.). 48p. 1998. pap. 4.95 (*1-892253-01-1*) Fine Line.

— Stinz: Charger: The War Stories. (Stinz). (Illus.). 248p. 1999. pap. 20.00 (*1-892253-03-8*) Fine Line.

— Stinz Vol. III 6: A Marvelous Resistance. 1998. pap. 5.50 (*1-892253-00-3*) Fine Line.

***Barr, Donna.** Stinz Vol. 8: Playthings. (Illus.). 1999. pap. 6.00 (*1-892253-06-2*) Fine Line.

Barr, Donna. Tongue Vol. 28: The Desert Peach. (The Desert Peach: Vol. 1). (Illus.). 64p. 1998. pap. 6.00 (*1-892253-04-6*) Fine Line.

Barr, Donna, ed. The Desert Peach: Ersatz Peach. 80p. (Orig.). 1995. pap. 7.95 (*1-883847-14-1*) MU Press.

Barr, Douglas, jt. auth. see Barr, Lynne.

Barr, Dwight L. The Next to the Last Word: Stopping the Cycle of Competition in Human Relationships. LC 98-83084. 208p. 2000. pap. 13.95 (*0-88739-241-5*) Creat Arts Bk.

Barr, Eleanor M., et al. The Women's International League for Peace & Freedom, United States Section, 1919-1959. LC 90-956363. 97 p. 1988. 30.00 (*0-8420-4037-4*) Scholarly Res Inc.

Barr, Euan, ed. see Schaufele, Nancy L. & Kennedy, Donna B.

Barr, George. Fascinating Science Experiments for Young People. LC 93-8111. (Illus.). 158p. (J). (gr. 7-8). 1993. reprint ed. pap. text 3.95 (*0-486-27670-8*) Dover.

— Fun with Science: Forty-Six Entertaining Demonstrations. LC 93-45547. Orig. Title: Show Time for Young Scientists: Entertaining with Science. (Illus.). 160p. (J). 1994. reprint ed. pap. 3.95 (*0-486-28000-4*) Dover.

— Outdoor Science Projects for Young People. Orig. Title: Young Scientist Takes a Walk: Guide to Outdoor Observations. (Illus.). 160p. (J). 1998. reprint ed. pap. 3.95 (*0-486-26855-1*) Dover.

— Science Projects for Young People. 153p. (YA). (gr. 5 up). 1998. reprint ed. pap. 4.95 (*0-486-25235-3*) Dover.

— Science Research Experiments for Young People. (Illus.). 144p. 1989. pap. 3.95 (*0-486-26111-5*) Dover.

— Science Tricks & Magic for Young People. (Illus.). 126p. (J). (gr. 3-11). 1987. reprint ed. pap. 3.95 (*0-486-25453-4*) Dover.

— Sports Science for Young People. 160p. (YA). 1990. pap. 3.95 (*0-486-26527-7*) Dover.

Barr, Geraldine. My Sister Roseanne. LC 93-44653. 1994. 19.95 (*1-55972-230-4*, Birch Ln Pr) Carol Pub Group.

***Barr, Geraldine.** My Sister Roseanne: The True Story of Roseanne Barr Arnold. (Illus.). 293p. 1999. text 25.00 (*0-7881-6789-8*) DIANE Pub.

***Barr, Hank J.** The Jump-Out Boys. LC 98-90735. 1999. pap. 14.95 (*0-533-12903-6*) Vantage.

Barr, Helen. Piers Plowman Tradition. 1993. pap. 12.95 (*0-460-87050-5*) J M Dent & Sons.

— Signes & Sothe: Language in the Piers Plowman Tradition. LC 94-19105. (Piers Plowman Studies: No. X). 202p. (C). 1994. 75.00 (*0-85991-419-4*, DS Brewer) Boydell & Brewer.

Barr, Hilary, tr. see Junger, Ernst.

Barr, Jack, jt. auth. see Barr, Joan.

Barr, James. The Bible in the Modern World. LC 90-31632. 208p. (C). 1990. pap. 15.00 (*0-334-00113-7*) TPI PA.

— Biblical Faith & Natural Theology: The Gifford Lectures for 1991: Delivered in the University of Edinburgh. 256p. 1995. pap. text 21.00 (*0-19-826376-7*) OUP.

— Comparative Philology & the Text of the Old Testament. LC 87-15698. ix, 436p. (C). 1987. reprint ed. text 29.50 (*0-931464-33-1*) Eisenbrauns.

— The Concept of Biblical Theology: An Old Testament Perspective. LC 99-21738. 1999. 48.00 (*0-8006-3191-9*, Fortress Pr) Augsburg Fortress.

***Barr, James.** History & Ideology in the Old Testament: Biblical Studies at the End of a Millennium. LC 99-55615. 216p. 2000. text 39.95 (*0-19-826987-0*) OUP.

Barr, James. The Variable Spellings of the Hebrew Bible: The Schweich Lectures on Biblical Archeology, 1986. (Schweich Lectures on Biblical Archeology, British Academy Ser.). (Illus.). 251p. 1989. text 59.00 (*0-19-726068-3*) OUP.

Barr, James C. Airborne Weather Radar: A User's Guide. LC 93-17077. (Illus.). 142p. 1993. pap. 24.95 (*0-8138-1363-8*) Iowa St U Pr.

Barr, James R., jt. auth. see Schleicher, Robert.

Barr, Jean. Transcendence of Self Is a Way of Life. 119p. 1999. 13.95 (*0-7541-0777-9*, Pub. by Minerva Pr) Unity Dist.

Barr, Jean & Birke, Lynda. Common Science? Women, Science, & Knowledge, Race, Gender & Science. LC 97-47503. (Race, Gender & Science Ser.). 192p. 1998. 29.95 (*0-253-33386-5*); pap. 13.95 (*0-253-21181-6*) Ind U Pr.

Barr, Jennifer N. The Complete Idiot's Guide to Bridal & Baby Showers. (Complete Idiot's Guides (Lifestyle) Ser.). (Illus.). 317p. 1999. pap. 16.95 (*0-02-863183-8*, Pub. by Macmillan Gen Ref) S&S Trade.

Barr, Joan & Barr, Jack. Understanding Deliverance: Workbook & Bible Study. Maranatha Church Staff, ed. (Illus.). 61p. (Orig.). 1987. student ed. 5.00 (*0-9619102-0-8*) New Life Christ.

***Barr, John.** Grace. LC 99-41978. 160p. 1999. 24.95 (*1-885266-85-5*, Pub. by Story Line); pap. 14.95 (*1-885266-81-2*, Pub. by Story Line) Consort Bk Sales.

Barr, John. The Hundred Fathom Curve. LC 96-54884. 88p. 1997. 20.00 (*1-885266-43-X*); pap. 10.00 (*1-885266-38-3*) Story Line.

Barr, John G. Three Paschal Preludes: For Organ. Tucker, Dale, ed. 20p. (C). 1997. pap. text 7.95 (*0-7692-1717-6*, GB9714) Wrner Bros.

Barr, John J. The Dynasty: The Rise & Fall of Social Credit in Alberta. LC 76-374584. 248 p. 1974. write for info. (*0-7710-1015-X*) McCland & Stewart.

Barr, Joseph S., Jr., ed. AAOS Instructional Course Lectures, Vol. 38. LC 43-17054. (Illus.). 502p. 1989. 48.00 (*0-89203-028-3*) Amer Acad Ortho Surg.

Barr, Joseph T., jt. auth. see Zadnik, Karla.

Barr, Josiah H. Early Methodist under Persecution. 1978. pap. 10.99 (*0-88019-020-5*) Schmul Pub Co.

Barr, Judith. A Menstrual Journey: Through the Old & the Dark to the New, the Light, & the Possibility & The Goddess Has Many Faces. LC TX 2807 677. 51p. (Orig.). 1990. pap. text 9.95 (*1-886264-00-7*) Mysteries of Life.

Barr, Judith T., ed. Clinical Effectiveness in Allied Health Practices: Critical Literature Review. 179p. (Orig.). (C). 1996. pap. text 45.00 (*0-7881-2639-3*) DIANE Pub.

Barr, K. S. Operation Blue Star: The True Story. (C). 1993. 16.50 (*81-85944-29-6*, Pub. by UBS Pubs Dist) S Asia.

Barr, Keith, jt. auth. see Holbrook, James E.

Barr, Lee & Barr, Norma. Leadership Development: Maturity & Power. LC 93-39943. 504p. 1994. pap. 19.95 (*0-89015-945-9*) Sunbelt Media.

— The Leadership Equation. Eakin, Edwin M., ed. 192p. 1989. pap. 14.95 (*0-89015-684-0*) Sunbelt Media.

Barr, Leslie. Bob Dylan Anthology. (Illus.). 200p. 1990. pap. 24.95 (*0-8256-1240-3*, AM79757) Music Sales.

Barr, Linda & Gerber, Carole. Creating a Positive School Climate: A Guide for School Climate Committees. Resnik, Hank, ed. (Skills for Growing Ser.). (Illus.). 64p. 1990. pap. text 5.00 (*0-933419-48-1*) Quest Intl.

— The Family Connection: A Guide to Leading Parent Meetings. Resnik, Hank, ed. (Skills for Growing Ser.). (Illus.). 170p. 1990. pap. text 15.00 (*0-933419-46-5*) Quest Intl.

— Positive Leadership in "Skills for Growing" A Guide for Administrators. Resnik, Hank, ed. (Skills for Growing Ser.). (Illus.). 157p. 1990. pap. text 15.00 (*0-933419-47-3*) Quest Intl.

Barr, Linda & Monserrat, Catherine P. Exercise for a Healthy Pregnancy & Birth. rev. ed. (Illus.). 17p. 1992. reprint ed. pap. 2.95 (*0-945886-09-8*) New Futures.

— Teenage Pregnancy: A New Beginning. (Illus.). 112p. (YA). (gr. 6-12). 1996. pap. 15.95 (*0-945886-12-8*) New Futures.

— Teenage Pregnancy: A New Beginning. rev. ed. (Illus.). 60p. (YA). (gr. 6-12). 1996. student ed. 4.95 (*0-945886-13-6*) New Futures.

— Working with Pregnant & Parenting Teens: Resource Guide: Teenage Pregnancy: A New Beginning. (Illus.). 175p. 1996. 27.95 (*0-945886-14-4*) New Futures.

Barr, Linda, jt. auth. see American.

Barr, Linda, jt. auth. see Apacki, Carol.

Barr, Linda, ed. see Apacki, Carol.

Barr, Lockwood. Pelham a Brief, but Most Complete & True Account of the Settlement of the Ancient Town of Pelham, Westchester County, Known One Time...As the Lordshipp & Monnour of Pelham; Also the Story of the Three Modern Villages Called the Pelhams. (Illus.). 190p. 1997. reprint ed. lib. bdg. 27.00 (*0-8328-6202-9*) Higginson Bk Co.

Barr, Lois B. Isaac Unbound: Patriarchal Tradition in the Latin American Jewish Novel. LC 95-44078. 201p. 1995. 35.00 (*0-87918-089-7*); per. 25.00 (*0-87918-082-X*) ASU Lat Am St.

Barr, Lori L., ed. Handbook of Pediatric Imaging. (Handbooks of Diagnostic Imaging Ser.). (Illus.). 492p. 1991. text 155.00 (*0-443-08697-4*) Church.

Barr, Lynne & Barr, Douglas. Sweaterscapes of the American West: A Collection of Designs for Machine or Hand Knitters. LC 94-199899. (Illus.). 80p. 1993. spiral bd. 17.95 (*0-89272-323-8*) Down East.

— Sweaterscapes of the North Country: Unique Intarsia Patterns for Machine or Hand Knitters. LC 91-74034. (Illus.). 72p. 1991. spiral bd. 16.95 (*0-89272-310-6*) Down East.

Barr, M. & Bolland, B. Camelot 3000. Bruning, Richard, ed. (Illus.). 312p. 1997. mass mkt. 14.95 (*0-930289-30-7*, Pub. by Warner Bks) Little.

Barr, M. & Wells, C. H. Toposes, Triples & Theories. (Grundlehren der Mathematischen Wissenschaften Ser.: Vol. 278). (Illus.). xiii, 345p. 1984. 82.95 (*0-387-96115-1*) Spr-Verlag.

Barr, Margaret E. Melanommatales: Loculoascomycetes. LC 90-47767. (North American Flora Ser.: No. 2, Pt. 13). (Illus.). 130p. 1990. pap. 20.50 (*0-89327-360-0*) NY Botanical.

— Prodromus to Class Loculoascomycetes. (Illus.). 168p. 1987. spiral bd. 18.00 (*0-934454-51-5*) Lubrecht & Cramer.

— Some Dictyosporous Genera & Species in the Pleosporales in North America. LC 90-13421. (Memoirs Ser.: No. 62). (Illus.). 92p. 1990. pap. 14.00 (*0-89327-359-7*) NY Botanical.

Barr, Margaret E., et al. An Annotated Catalog of the Pyrenomycetes Described by Charles H. Peck. (Bulletin Ser.: No. 459). (Illus.). 74p. (Orig.). 1986. pap. 7.00 (*1-55557-005-4*) NYS Museum.

— The Pyrenomycetes Described by J. B. Ellis. LC 96-47492. (Memoirs of the New York Botanical Garden Ser.: No. 79). 136p. 1996. text 25.00 (*0-89327-415-1*, MEM 79) NY Botanical.

Barr, Margaret J., ed. Student Affairs & the Law. LC 82-84204. (New Directions for Student Services Ser.: No. SS 22). 105p. 1983. 22.00 (*0-87589-970-6*) Jossey-Bass.

An Asterisk (*) at the beginning of an entry indicates that the title is appearing for the first time.

***Barr, Margaret J. & Mary K. Desler & Associates Staff.** The Handbook of Student Affairs Administration. 2nd rev. ed. LC 99-98002. 640p. 2000. 55.00 (*0-7879-4720-2*, Pfffr & Co) Jossey-Bass.

Barr, Margaret J., et al. New Futures for Student Affairs: Building a Vision for Professional Leadership & Practice. LC 90-41464. (Higher Education Ser.). 335p. 1990. text 36.95 (*1-55542-298-5*) Jossey-Bass.

Barr, Margaret J., jt. auth. see Upcraft, M. Lee.

Barr, Margaret J., & Associates. The Handbook of Student Affairs Administration. LC 92-33894. (Higher Education Ser.). 583p. 1993. text 50.00 (*1-55542-506-2*) Jossey-Bass.

Barr, Margaret S. Medardo Rosso. LC 73-169298. (Museum of Modern Art Publications in Reprint). (Illus.). 94p. 1972. reprint ed. 19.95 (*0-405-01558-5*) Ayer.

Barr, Marilyn. Fearon's Animal Theme Activity Sheets. (J). (ps-1). 1989. pap. 6.99 (*0-8224-0501-6*) Fearon Teacher Aids.

Barr, Marilynn. The Big Book of Animal Patterns. (Illus.). 64p. (J). (ps-2). 1994. pap., teacher ed. 12.95 (*1-878279-67-X*, MM 1988) Monday Morning Bks.

— Cut & Paste: Alphabet. (Illus.). 48p. 1992. pap., teacher ed. 5.95 (*1-878279-34-3*, MM 1951) Monday Morning Bks.

— Cut & Paste: Colors & Shapes. (Illus.). 48p. 1992. pap., teacher ed. 5.95 (*1-878279-36-X*, MM 1953) Monday Morning Bks.

— Cut & Paste: Concepts. (Illus.). 48p. 1992. pap., teacher ed. 6.45 (*1-878279-37-8*, MM 1954) Monday Morning Bks.

— Cut & Paste: Numbers. (Illus.). 48p. (J). (ps-1). 1992. pap., teacher ed. 5.95 (*1-878279-35-1*, MM 1952) Monday Morning Bks.

— International Spring & Summer Festivals. 192p. teacher ed. 15.99 (*0-86653-837-2*, GA1528) Good Apple.

— International Winter Festivals. 192p. teacher ed. 15.99 (*0-86653-712-0*, GA1429) Good Apple.

— Patterns for World Cultures. (Illus.). 128p. (Orig.). 1995. pap., teacher ed. 12.95 (*1-878279-76-9*, MM1997) Monday Morning Bks.

***Barr, Marilynn G.** American Presidents. (Illus.). 128p. (J). 1999. pap. 14.95 (*1-57612-117-8*) Monday Morning Bks.

Barr, Marilynn G. International Fall Festivals: Projects & Patterns for Holiday Gifts, Greetings, Ornaments, Decorations, & Classroom Displays. (Illus.). 192p. (J). (gr. 1-6). 1994. 15.99 (*0-86653-818-6*, GA1510) Good Apple.

— Mother Goose Caboose. 256p. (J). (ps-2). 1991. 14.99 (*0-86653-618-3*, GA1337) Good Apple.

Barr, Marjorie A., jt. auth. see Lerner, William D.

Barr, Marleen, ed. Future Females: A Critical Anthology. LC 81-80215. 1981. 17.95 (*0-87972-174-X*) Bowling Green Univ Popular Press.

Barr, Marleen S. Alien to Femininity: Speculative Fiction & Feminist Theory. (Contributions to the Study of Science Fiction & Fantasy Ser.: No. 27). 214p. 1987. 32.95 (*0-685-33263-2*, BNW/, Greenwood Pr) Greenwood.

— Alien to Femininity: Speculative Fiction & Feminist Theory, 27. LC 86-27093. (Contributions to the Study of Science Fiction & Fantasy Ser.: No. 27). 214p. 1987. 52.95 (*0-313-23634-8*, BNW, Greenwood Pr) Greenwood.

— Feminist Fabulation: Space-Postmodern Fiction. LC 92-20164. (Illus.). 342p. 1992. pap. text 15.95 (*0-87745-377-2*) U of Iowa Pr.

***Barr, Marleen S.** Genre Fission: A New Discourse Practice for Culture Studies. LC 99-58453. (Illus.). 300p. 2000. pap. text 27.95 (*0-87745-703-4*) U of Iowa Pr.

Barr, Marleen S. Lost in Space: Probing Feminist Science Fiction & Beyond. LC 93-12466. xvi, 232p. (C). 1993. pap. 19.95 (*0-8078-4421-7*); text 55.00 (*0-8078-2108-X*) U of NC Pr.

Barr, Marleen S., ed. Future Females, the Next Generation: Feminist Science Fiction's New Voices & Velocities. LC 99-25948. 350p. 2000. 65.00 (*0-8476-9125-X*); pap. 22.95 (*0-8476-9126-8*) Rowman.

Barr, Marleen S. & Feldstein, Richard, eds. Discontented Discourses: Feminism, Textual Intervention, Psychoanalysis. LC 88-11943. 264p. 1989. text 29.95 (*0-252-01562-2*); pap. text 14.95 (*0-252-06023-7*) U of Ill Pr.

Barr, Marleen S., et al. Suzy McKee Charnas, Octavia Butler, Joan Vinge. Schlobin, Roger C., ed. LC 85-2715. (Starmont Reader's Guide Ser.: Vol. 23). (Orig.). 1986. pap. 21.00 (*0-916732-91-6*); lib. bdg. 31.00 (*0-916732-92-4*) Millefleurs.

Barr, Martin W. Mental Defectives: Their History, Treatment & Training. LC 73-2383. (Mental Illness & Social Policy; the American Experience Ser.). 1973. reprint ed. 31.95 (*0-405-05191-3*) Ayer.

Barr, Mary. Assessing Literacy with the Learning Record: Handbook for Teachers Grades K-6. LC 98-45344. 1999. pap. text 15.00 (*0-325-00117-0*) Heinemann.

— Assessing Literacy with the Learning Record: Handbook for Teachers, Grades 6-12. LC 98-43121. 1999. pap. text 15.00 (*0-325-00118-9*) Heinemann.

— Downtown Parking Made Easy. 48p. 1997. pap. 26.95 (*0-915910-44-6*) Downtown Res.

— Funding Downtown Promotions. 48p. 1998. pap. 34.95 (*0-915910-46-2*) Downtown Res.

Barr, Mary, et al, eds. What's Going On? Language Learning Episodes in British & American Classrooms, Grades 4-13. LC 81-18119. (Illus.). 240p. (C). 1982. pap. text 18.50 (*0-86709-013-8*, 0013, Pub. by Boynton Cook Pubs) Heinemann.

Barr, Mary, et al. Honest Appraisal: The Learning Record & Trustworthy Asssessment. pap. text. write for info. (*0-325-00288-6*) Heinemann.

Barr, Mary, jt. auth. see Fernandez, John P.

Barr, Mary A. Sister Woman. Vaughn, Maggi & York, Ron, eds. 94p. (Orig.). 1988. pap. write for info. (*0-318-65749-X*) Bell Buckle.

Barr, Marylin L. Unexpected Light. 64p. 1999. 15.00 (*0-9668972-2-6*) Essex Press.

Barr, Meyer B. Studies in Social & Legal Theories: An Historical Account of the Social, Ethical, Political & Legal Doctrines of the Foremost Ancient & Medievel Philosophers. 148p. 1982. reprint ed. 30.00 (*0-8377-0327-1*, Rothman) W S Hein.

***Barr, Michael, et al.** Programming Embedded System in C & C++ Oram, Andy, ed. (Illus.). 174p. (Orig.). 1999. pap. 29.95 (*1-56592-354-5*) OReilly & Assocs.

***Barr, Michael D.** Lee Kuan Yew: The Beliefs Behind the Man. 288p. 2000. text 39.95 (*0-87840-816-9*) Georgetown U Pr.

Barr, Mike. Batman: Reign of Terror. LC 99-216594. (Illus.). 48p. 1998. pap. 4.95 (*1-56389-229-4*) DC Comics.

***Barr, Mike W.** Batman: Dark Knight Dynasty. LC 98-180628. (Illus.). 128p. 1999. 24.95 (*1-56389-384-3*, Pub. by DC Comics) Time Warner.

Barr, Mike W. Batman: Dark Knight Dynasty. (Illus.). 128p. 1999. 14.95 (*1-56389-390-8*) DC Comics.

— Batman: Full Circle. O'Neil, Dennis, ed. 64p. 1991. pap. 5.95 (*0-930289-98-6*) DC Comics.

— Batman: Son of the Demon. Giordano, Dick, ed. (Illus.). 80p. 1991. mass mkt. 9.95 (*0-930289-25-0*, Pub. by Warner Bks) Little.

— Batman: Year Two. 1990. mass mkt. 9.95 (*0-446-39191-3*, Pub. by Warner Bks) Little.

— The Mirror Universe Saga. Greenberger, Bob, ed. (Illus.). 192p. 1992. mass mkt. 19.95 (*0-930289-96-X*) DC Comics.

Barr, Mike W. & Bolland, Brian. Camelot Three Thousand. 384p. 1988. mass mkt. 12.95 (*0-446-38797-5*, Pub. by Warner Bks) Little.

Barr, Mike W., et al. The Best of Star Trek. Greenberger, Bob et al, eds. (Illus.). 240p. 1992. mass mkt. 19.95 (*1-56389-009-7*) DC Comics.

Barr, Mildred F. Davis. Genealogy of the Davis Family: William Davis of London, England, 1764-1809, & His Descendants. 71p. 1997. reprint ed. pap. 14.00 (*0-8328-8232-1*); reprint ed. lib. bdg. 24.00 (*0-8328-8231-3*) Higginson Bk Co.

Barr, Murray L. Human Nervous System. 6th ed. (Illus.). 480p. 1993. spiral bd. 43.00 (*0-397-51243-0*) Lppncott W & W.

Barr, N. & Mickelson, Belle. Fish & Fisheries: Alaska Sea Week Curriculum Series Grade 5. (Report Ser.: No. 83-07). (Illus.). 172p. 1983. teacher ed., ring bd. 11.50 (*1-56612-017-9*) AK Sea Grant CP.

Barr, N., jt. auth. see Barnes, J.

Barr, N. A. The Economics of the Welfare State 3rd ed. LC 98-60890. xxvi, 471p. 1998. write for info. (*0-8047-3551-4*) Stanford U Pr.

Barr, Nancy. Mrs. Cage. 1993. pap. 5.25 (*0-8222-1313-3*) Dramatists Play.

Barr, Nancy V. We Called It Macaroni: An American Heritage of Southern Italian Cooking. (Illus.). 368p. 1996. pap. 18.00 (*0-679-76577-8*) Random.

***Barr, Nancy Verde.** Simply Italian. 2000. write for info. (*0-375-40226-8*) Knopf.

Barr, Natalie. Honourable Intentions. (Rainbow Romances Ser.: No. 901). 160p. 1994. 14.95 (*0-7090-4982-X*) Parkwest Pubns.

— Honourable Intentions. large type ed. (Linford Romance Library). 1995. pap. 16.99 (*0-7089-7716-2*, Linford) Ulverscroft.

Barr, Nevada. Blind Descent. large type ed. LC 98-3235. 1998. 24.95 (*1-56895-547-2*, Wheeler) Wheeler Pub.

— Blind Descent: An Anna Pigeon Mystery. (Anna Pigeon Mystery Ser.). (Illus.). 384p. 1999. mass mkt. 6.99 (*0-380-72826-5*, Avon Bks) Morrow Avon.

***Barr, Nevada.** Deep South. LC 99-42194. 352p. 2000. 23.95 (*0-399-14586-9*) Putnam Pub Group.

— Deep South. large type ed. LC 00-25381. 2000. 25.95 (*1-56895-867-6*) Wheeler Pub.

Barr, Nevada. Endangered Species. LC 96-42516. (Anna Pigeon Mystery Ser.). 400p. 1998. mass mkt. 6.99 (*0-380-72583-5*, Avon Bks) Morrow Avon.

— Endangered Species. large type ed. LC 97-41811. 1997. 25.95 (*1-57490-108-7*, Beeler LP Bks) T T Beeler.

— Firestorm. large type ed. LC 96-50223. (Large Print Bks.). 1997. 24.95 (*1-56895-399-2*) Wheeler Pub.

— Firestorm Barr. LC 95-38311. 336p. 1997. reprint ed. mass mkt. 6.99 (*0-380-72582-7*, Avon Bks) Morrow Avon.

— Ill Wind. LC 94-33370. (Anna Pigeon Ser.: No. 3). 320p. 1996. mass mkt. 6.99 (*0-380-72363-8*, Avon Bks) Morrow Avon.

— Ill Wind. large type ed. (Large Print Bks.). 1995. pap. 21.95 (*1-56895-252-X*) Wheeler Pub.

***Barr, Nevada.** Liberty Falling. LC 98-37343. (Anna Pigeon Mysteries Ser.). (Illus.). 384p. 2000. mass mkt. 6.99 (*0-380-72827-3*, Avon Bks) Morrow Avon.

Barr, Nevada. Liberty Falling. LC 98-37343. (Anna Pigeon Mystery Ser.). 321p. 1999. 24.95 (*0-399-14459-5*) Putnam Pub Group.

***Barr, Nevada.** Liberty Falling. large type ed. LC 99-18708. (Wheeler Large Print Bks.). 1999. 25.95 (*1-56895-711-4*, Wheeler) Wheeler Pub.

Barr, Nevada. Superior Death. (Anna Pigeon Ser.: No. 2). 320p. 1995. mass mkt. 6.99 (*0-380-72362-X*, Avon Bks) Morrow Avon.

— A Superior Death. large type ed. LC 94-14258. 431p. 1994. lib. bdg. 23.95 (*0-8161-7446-6*, G K Hall Lrg Type) Mac Lib Ref.

— Track of the Cat. LC 98-24019. 1998. 23.95 (*1-56895-572-3*) Wheeler Pub.

— Track of the Cat. (Anna Pigeon Ser.: No. 1). 320p. 1994. reprint ed. mass mkt. 6.99 (*0-380-72164-3*, Avon Bks) Morrow Avon.

Barr, Nicholas. Economics of the Welfare State. 3rd ed. LC 98-60890. 1998. pap. text 24.95 (*0-8047-3552-2*) Stanford U Pr.

— Income Transfers & the Social Safety Net in Russia. LC 92-33406. (Studies of Economics in Transmition: Paper No. 4). 59p. 1992. pap. 22.00 (*0-8213-2268-0*) World Bank.

— Student Loans: The Next Stop. (David Hume Papers). 104p. 1989. pap. text 14.00 (*0-08-037966-4*, Pergamon Pr) Elsevier.

Barr, Nicholas, ed. Labor Markets & Social Policy in Central & Eastern Europe: The Transition & Beyond. (World Bank Publication). (Illus.). 406p. 1994. pap. text 24.95 (*0-19-520998-2*, 60998) OUP.

— Labor Markets & Social Policy in Central & Eastern Europe: The Transition & Beyond - Summary. 48p. 1994. pap. 22.00 (*0-8213-3002-0*, 13002); pap. 22.00 (*0-8213-3003-9*, 13003); pap. 22.00 (*0-8213-3004-7*, 13004); pap. 22.00 (*0-8213-3005-5*, 13005); pap. 22.00 (*0-8213-3006-3*, 13006); pap. 22.00 (*0-8213-3007-1*, 13007); pap. 22.00 (*0-8213-3008-X*, 13008) World Bank.

Barr, Nicholas & Whynes, David K., eds. Current Issues in the Economics of Welfare. LC 92-28596. (Current Issues in Economics Ser.). 256p. 1993. text 49.95 (*0-312-08651-2*) St Martin.

Barr, Norah K., et al, compiled by. M. F. K. Fisher: A Life in Letters: Correspondence, 1929-1991. (Illus.). 520p. 1998. reprint ed. pap. 21.00 (*1-887178-93-7*, Pub. by Counterpt DC) HarpC.

Barr, Norma, jt. auth. see Barr, Lee.

Barr, Pamela T., ed. see Peck, Amelia, et al.

Barr, Pat. Coromandel. large type ed. 1990. 27.99 (*0-7089-2273-2*) Ulverscroft.

— Curious Life for a Lady: The Story of Isabella Bird. LC 77-517952. 347p. 1970. write for info. (*0-333-09647-9*) Macmillan.

Barr, R. C., jt. auth. see Plonsey, R.

Barr, R. J., jt. ed. see Buechler, A. F.

Barr, Randolph W. & Reeves, Anne-Rose. Come & See. 1991. pap. 9.75 (*1-55673-385-2*, 9203) CSS OH.

Barr, Raymond, jt. auth. see Drew, Lucas.

Barr, Rebecca, et al, eds. Handbook of Reading Research, Vol. 2. LC 96-10470. 1104p. 1996. reprint ed. pap. 69.95 (*0-8058-2416-2*) L Erlbaum Assocs.

Barr, Rebecca & Johnson, Barbara. Teaching Reading in Elementary Classrooms: Developing Independent Readers. 500p. (C). 1991. text 55.50 (*0-8013-0173-4*, 75832) Longman.

Barr, Rebecca, et al. How Schools Work. xiv, 205p. 1988. pap. text 14.50 (*0-226-03812-2*) U Ch Pr.

— Reading Diagnosis for Teachers: An Instructional Approach. 3rd rev. ed. LC 94-27768. 368p. (C). 1995. pap. 53.00 (*0-8013-0842-9*) Longman.

Barr, Rebecca, jt. ed. see Bizar, Marilyn.

Barr, Richard L. Rooms with a View: The States of Community in the Modern Theater. LC 98-8995. (Theater--Theory/Text/Performance Ser.). 240p. (C). 1998. text 42.50 (*0-472-10873-5*, 10873) U of Mich Pr.

Barr, Richard S., ed. see Kennington, Jeff L. & Helgason, Richard V.

Barr, Robert. The Dark Island. LC 72-9877. (Black Bat Mystery Ser). 224p. 1973. 5.95 (*0-672-51804-X*, Bobbs) Macmillan.

— Eugene Valmont: His Triumphs. Landes, William-Alan & Wilkes, Ian, eds. 144p. 1998. pap. 20.00 (*0-86025-289-2*) Players Pr.

— In a Steamer Chair, & Other Shipboard Stories. LC 74-116935. (Short Story Index Reprint Ser.). 1977. 20.95 (*0-8369-3437-7*) Ayer.

Barr, Robert, tr. see Comblin, Joseph.

Barr, Robert, tr. see Panikkar, Raimon.

***Barr, Robert D. & Parrett, William.** Hope Fulfilled for At-Risk & Violent Youth: K-12 Programs That Work. 2nd ed. LC 00-42137. 2001. write for info. (*0-205-30886-4*) Allyn.

Barr, Robert D. & Parrett, William H. Hope at Last for at-Risk Youth: A Blueprint for Success in Schools & Communities. LC 94-18807. 320p. 1994. pap. text 48.00 (*0-205-16267-3*) Allyn.

— How to Create Alternative, Magnet, & Charter Schools That Work. LC 97-193228. 235p. (Orig.). 1997. pap. 24.95 (*1-879639-48-3*) Natl Educ Serv.

Barr, Robert D., et al. Defining the Social Studies. LC 77-85192. (National Council for the Social Studies Bulletin: No. 51). 127p. reprint ed. pap. 39.40 (*0-608-16923-4*, 202773100056) Bks Demand.

— The Nature of the Social Studies. LC 77-2014. (C). 1978. pap. 14.95 (*0-88280-049-3*) ETC Pubns.

Barr, Robert E., jt. auth. see Rowan, Richard L.

Barr, Robert R. What Is the Bible? A Nazareth Book. 128p. (J). (gr. 7-12). 1984. 4.95 (*0-86683-727-2*) Harper SF.

Barr, Robert R., ed. see Sobrino, Jon.

Barr, Robert R., tr. see Araya, Victorio.

Barr, Robert R., tr. see Bermudez, Fernando.

Barr, Robert R., tr. see Boff, Clodovis.

Barr, Robert R., tr. see Boff, Clodovis & Boff, Leonardo.

Barr, Robert R., tr. see Boff, Leonardo.

Barr, Robert R., tr. see Cabestrero, Teofilo.

Barr, Robert R., tr. see Carretto, Carlo.

Barr, Robert R., tr. see Comblin, Joseph.

Barr, Robert R., tr. see Croatto, J. Severino.

Barr, Robert R., tr. see Croatto, Jose S.

Barr, Robert R., tr. see Dupuis, S. Jacques.

Barr, Robert R., tr. see Eboussi Boulaga, F.

Barr, Robert R., tr. see Ela, Jean-Marc.

Barr, Robert R., tr. see Ellacuria, Ignacio & Sobrino, Jon.

Barr, Robert R., tr. see Faus Gonzalez, Jose I.

Barr, Robert R., tr. see Galilea, Segundo.

Barr, Robert R., tr. see Gutierrez, Gustavo.

Barr, Robert R., tr. see Hoornaert, Eduardo.

Barr, Robert R., tr. see Lesbaupin, Ivo.

Barr, Robert R., tr. see Maduro, Otto.

Barr, Robert R., tr. see Miranda, Jose P.

Barr, Robert R., tr. see Pallares, Jose C.

Barr, Robert R., tr. see Parker, Cristian.

Barr, Robert R., tr. see Perez Esquivel, Adolfo.

Barr, Robert R., tr. see Preiswerk, Matias.

Barr, Robert R., tr. see Sobrino, Jon.

Barr, Robert R., tr. see Trigo, Pedro.

Barr, Roger. The American Frontier. (World History Ser.). (Illus.). 112p. (YA). (gr. 5-12). 1996. lib. bdg. 22.45 (*1-56006-282-7*, 2827) Lucent Bks.

— Cities. (Lucent Overview Ser.). (Illus.). (J). (gr. 5-8). 1994. lib. bdg. 22.45 (*1-56006-158-8*) Lucent Bks.

— Juvenile Crime. LC 97-27336. (Overview Ser.). (Illus.). (YA). 1998. 22.45 (*1-56006-198-7*) Lucent Bks.

— The Treasure Hunt. 1992. pap. 11.95 (*0-9634408-0-2*) Medallion MN.

— The Vietnam War. LC 91-23067. (America's Wars Ser.). (Illus.). 112p. (J). (gr. 5-8). 1991. lib. bdg. 26.20 (*1-56006-410-2*) Lucent Bks.

Barr, Ronald, jt. ed. see Zelazo, Philip R.

***Barr, Ronald G., et al, eds.** Crying as a Sign, a Symptom & a Signal: Clinical, Emotional & Developmental Aspects of Infant & Toddler Crying. (Clinics in Developmental Medicine Ser.: No. 152). (Illus.). 250p. (C). 2000. write for info. (*1-898683-21-2*, Pub. by Mc Keith Pr) Cambridge U Pr.

Barr, Roseanne. Roseanne. 1990. pap. 5.95 (*0-00-003853-9*, Harp PBks) HarpC.

***Barr, Ruth D.** Don't Say Trivia: It's My Life You're Talking About. 136p. 1999. pap. 13.00 (*0-8059-4811-2*) Dorrance.

Barr, Ruth Davis, ed. see Eppler, William Grant.

Barr, S. Lifegames: Activity-Centered Learning for Early Childhood Education in Economics. 1985. text 18.00 (*0-201-20094-5*) Addison-Wesley.

Barr-Sharrar, Beryl, ed. see National Gallery of Art Staff.

Barr, Sheldon. Venetian Glass: Confections in Glass, 1855-1914. LC 97-32238. (Illus.). 128p. 1998. 39.95 (*0-8109-3939-8*, Pub. by Abrams) Time Warner.

Barr, Stacey, jt. auth. see Barr, Stewart.

Barr, Stacy, jt. auth. see Barr, Stewart.

Barr, Stephen. Experiments in Topology. 210p. 1989. pap. 6.95 (*0-486-25933-1*) Dover.

— Experiments in Topology. LC 64-10866. (Illus.). (J). (gr. 7 up). 1964. 11.95 (*0-690-27862-4*) HarpC Child Bks.

— Intriguing Puzzles in Math & Logic. LC 94-39735. 1994. pap. 5.95 (*0-486-28311-9*) Dover.

— Mathematical Brain-Benders: Second Miscellany of Puzzles. (Illus.). 224p. (YA). (gr. 6 up). 1982. pap. 6.95 (*0-486-24260-9*) Dover.

— New Jersey: The Garden State on the Eve of the 21st Century. LC 98-71768. (Illus.). 414p. 1998. 39.95 (*1-882933-22-2*) Cherbo Pub Grp.

Barr, Steven C. The Almost Complete 78 RPM Record Dating Guide. 177p. 1992. spiral bd. 15.95 (*0-9640687-2-9*) Promar Pubng.

Barr, Stewart. The Colonial Period: U. S. History, 1550-1775. (Learning Packets - Social Studies Ser.). (Illus.). 84p. 1994. ring bd. 18.00 (*1-56976-005-5*, 1424-F3) Zephyr Pr AZ.

— Tapestries: Exploring Identity & Culture in the Classroom. LC 98-199767. 160p. 1997. pap. 30.00 (*1-56976-058-6*, 1080-F3) Zephyr Pr AZ.

Barr, Stewart & Barr, Stacey. American Revolution, 1775-1789: The Struggle for Independence. (Learning Packets - Social Studies Ser.). (Illus.). 59p. 1995. ring bd. 18.00 (*1-56976-023-3*, 1426-F3) Zephyr Pr AZ.

Barr, Stewart & Barr, Stacy. U. S. Constitution: Our Social Contract. (Learning Packets - Social Sciences Ser.). (Illus.). 55p. 1996. ring bd. 18.00 (*1-56976-041-1*, 1430-F3) Zephyr Pr AZ.

Barr, Stringfellow. The Pilgrimage of Western Man. LC 73-21283. 369p. 1974. reprint ed. lib. bdg. 35.00 (*0-8371-6152-5*, BAPI, Greenwood Pr) Greenwood.

***Barr, Susan.** Holiday Guide to New York City. 48p. 1999. pap. 7.95 (*0-9672899-0-4*) Stamford Pr.

Barr Systems, Inc. Staff. BARR - Print. 24p. (Orig.). 1987. pap. 10.00 (*0-938835-06-8*) Barr Syst Inc.

— Barr-Hasp. 2nd ed. (Illus.). 252p. 1988. pap. text 20.00 (*0-938835-07-6*) Barr Syst Inc.

— Barr-Sna Rje. 290p. 1988. pap. text 20.00 (*0-938835-08-4*) Barr Syst Inc.

— BARR-TAPE Release 88. 2nd ed. 108p. (Orig.). 1988. pap. text 10.00 (*0-938835-11-4*) Barr Syst Inc.

— BARR-3 Adapter. 24p. (Orig.). 1988. pap. text 10.00 (*0-938835-09-2*) Barr Syst Inc.

— BARR-6BBB Adapter. 22p. (Orig.). 1988. pap. text 10.00 (*0-938835-10-6*) Barr Syst Inc.

— PC-SYNC Release 88. 84p. (Orig.). 1988. pap. text 10.00 (*0-938835-12-2*) Barr Syst Inc.

Barr, Terri. Lillian: The Librarain. (Illus.). 16p. (J). (ps-2). 1999. pap. 3.75 (*1-880612-86-0*) Seedling Pubns.

Barr, Tery L. Electron Spectroscopy - Chemical Analysis (ESCA) App - Surf - Anal. 384p. 1994. boxed set 147.95 (*0-8493-8653-5*, QD96) CRC Pr.

Barr, Thomas P. The Pottawatomie Baptist Manual Labor Training School. LC 84-80938. (Illus.). 57p. 1984. pap. 3.00 (*0-87726-029-X*) Kansas St Hist.

***Barr, Tim.** Brighter Daze: The Dance Music Revolution. 2000. pap. 19.95 (*1-86074-278-5*) Sanctuary Pubng.

— Kraftwerk: From Dusseldorf to the Future (With Love) (Illus.). 216p. 1999. pap. 17.95 (*0-09-186490-9*, Pub. by Ebury Pr) Trafalgar.

Barr, Tim. The Rough Guide to Techno. (Illus.). 288p. 2000. pap. 9.95 (*1-85828-434-1*) Penguin Putnam.

Barr, Tina. At Dusk on Naskeag Point. LC 84-28621. 1984. pap. 7.00 (*0-9613984-0-X*) Flume Pr.

Barr, Tom. Scenic Driving Oregon. LC 96-33019. (Illus.). 288p. 1996. pap. 14.95 (*1-56044-440-1*) Falcon Pub Inc.

— Unique Georgia: A Guide to the State's Quirks, Charisma, & Character. LC 95-7321. (Illus.). 112p. 1995. pap. 11.95 (*1-56261-240-9*) Avalon Travel.

Barr, Tom. Vector Calculus. LC 96-2759. 449p. (C). 1996. 89.33 (*0-13-400037-4*) P-H.

Barr, Tony. Acting for the Camera: Revised Edition. rev. ed. LC 97-993. 384p. 1997. pap. 14.00 (*0-06-092819-0*, Perennial) HarperTrade.

— A Story Handed Down: Introducing the Dutch School. 88p. (Orig.). 1995. pap. 2.00 (*0-915531-45-3*) OR Catholic.

Barr, V. Promotion Strategies for Design & Construction. 1995. pap. 39.95 (*0-442-01439-2*, VNR) Wiley.

Barr, Vickie M., ed. Heath National Resource Directory on Postsecondary Education & Disability. 64p. (C). 1997. pap. text 25.00 (*0-7881-4604-1*) DIANE Pub.

Barr, Vilma. The Best of Neon. (Illus.). 256p. 1991. 49.99 (*0-935603-60-3*, 30385) Rockport Pubs.

Barr, Vilma. Promotion Strategies. (Architecture Ser.). 182p. 1995. 39.95 (*0-471-28559-5*, VNR) Wiley.

Barr, Vilma & Antman, Dani. The Illustrated Room: A Century of Interior Design Rendering. LC 97-10379. (Illus.). 272p. 1997. 69.95 (*0-07-006131-9*) McGraw.

Barr, Vilma & Field, Katherine. Stores. LC 96-20790. 184p. 1997. 47.50 (*0-86636-339-4*) PBC Intl Inc.

— Stores: Retail Display & Design. LC 96-20790. 184p. 1999. pap. 42.50 (*0-86636-530-3*) PBC Intl Inc.

Barr, Vilma, et al. High Performance Entrepreneurship. 400p. 1996. pap. 19.95 (*0-471-12613-6*); text 39.95 (*0-471-12612-8*) Wiley.

Barr, Vilma, ed. see Bernstein, Louis & Garibaldi, Louis E.

Barr, William, ed. see Starokadomskiy, Leonid M.

Barr, William, ed. & tr. see De Bray, Emile F.

Barr, William, ed. & tr. see Klutschak, Heinrich.

Barr, William, tr. see Boas, Franz.

Barr, William, tr. & intro. see Filchner, Wilhelm.

Barr, William A. Christmas, Christmas, Christmas. Mesko, Annah, ed. (Illus.). 336p. 1999. pap. 16.95 (*0-89896-552-7*) Larksdale.

Barr, William B. History of the Barr Family, Beginning with Great Grandfather Robert Barr, & Mary Wills: Their Decendants down to the Latest Child. (Illus.). 216p. 1988. reprint ed. pap. 32.00 (*0-8328-0195-X*); reprint ed. lib. bdg. 40.00 (*0-8328-0194-1*) Higginson Bk Co.

Barr, William R. Constructive Christian Theology in the Worldwide Church. LC 96-53630. 576p. 1997. pap. 39.00 (*0-8028-4143-0*) Eerdmans.

Barr, William R. & Yocom, Rena M., eds. The Church in the Movement of the Spirit. LC 94-5572. 1994. pap. 13.00 (*0-8028-0554-X*) Eerdmans.

Barr, Willie D. From Slavery to Prison. (Illus.). 250p. 1998. pap. 15.95 (*0-9663147-0-0*) W D Barr.

Barr, Wilma & Frey, Lucille. Living in Alaska. 100p. (J). 1995. pap. 12.95 (*1-878051-44-X*) Circumpolar Pr.

— Living in Alaska. (Illus.). 100p. (J). (gr. 2-5). 1995. pap. 9.95 (*1-878051-43-1*) Circumpolar Pr.

Barra, Allen. Inventing Wyatt Earp: His Life & Many Legends. (Illus.). 432p. 1998. 27.00 (*0-7867-0562-0*) Carroll & Graf.

***Barra, Allen.** Inventing Wyatt Earp: His Life & Many Legends. (Illus.). 432p. 1999. pap. text 14.95 (*0-7867-0685-6*) Carroll & Graf.

Barra, Eilis De. Bless 'Em All: The Lanes of Cork. LC 98-202369. 144p. 1997. pap. 11.95 (*1-85635-175-0*, Pub. by Mercier Pr) Irish Amer Bk.

***Barra, Ernest R.** Biretta. 1999. pap. 7.95 (*0-533-13038-7*) Vantage.

Barra, Paul A. Crimson Ring. Coy, Stanley C., ed. 170p. (Orig.). 1994. pap. 11.95 (*1-881459-12-8*) Eagle Pr SC.

Barra, Tomas De La, see De la Barra, Tomas.

Barracato, Jay. Toxics Release Inventory: Teachers Guide. LC 98-84913. (Teach with Databases Ser.: No. 1). (Illus.). 1998. teacher ed. 35.00 incl. cd-rom (*0-87355-171-0*, PB143X01) Natl Sci Tchrs.

Barracato, Jay, jt. auth. see Spooner, Barbara.

***Barracca, Debra.** Adventures of Taxi Dog. (J). 2000. pap. 5.99 (*0-14-056665-1*, PuffinBks) Peng Put Young Read.

— Adventures of Taxi Dog. (Illus.). (J). 2000. 11.44 (*0-606-18386-8*) Turtleback.

Barracca, Debra. Maxi, the Hero. 32p. (J). (ps-3). 1994. pap. 5.99 (*0-14-055497-1*, PuffinBks) Peng Put Young Read.

— Maxi, the Hero. (J). 1994. 11.19 (*0-606-07850-9*) Turtleback.

— Maxi, the Star. 32p. 1999. pap. 5.99 (*0-14-056557-4*, PuffinBks) Peng Put Young Read.

Barracca, Debra & Barracca, Sal. Maxi, the Hero. LC 90-38329. (Illus.). 30p. (J). (ps-3). 1991. 14.99 (*0-8037-0939-0*, Dial Yng Read) Peng Put Young Read.

Barracca, Debra, jt. auth. see Barracca, Sal.

Barracca, Sal & Barracca, Debra. The Adventures of Taxi Dog. Fogelman, Phyllis J., ed. LC 89-1056. (Illus.). 32p. (J). (ps-3). 1990. 15.99 (*0-8037-0671-5*, Dial Yng Read) Peng Put Young Read.

Barracca, Sal, jt. auth. see Barracca, Debra.

Barrack. Mosaik. 3rd ed. 1992. teacher ed. 29.37 (*0-07-004048-6*) McGraw.

Barrack, Charles. Sievers' Law in Germanic. LC 95-44271. (Berkeley Insights in Linguistics & Semiotics Ser.: Vol. 22). XII, 288p. (C). 1998. text 52.95 (*0-8204-3042-0*) P Lang Pubng.

Barrack, Charles M. & Rabura, Horst M. Mosaik: Deutsche Grammatik. 3rd ed. 416p. (C). 1992. pap. 49.69 (*0-07-003964-X*) McGraw.

— Mosaik: Deutsche Grammatik. 3rd ed. (C). 1992. pap. text 22.18 (*0-07-004049-4*) McGraw.

Barrack, Charles Michael. A Diachronic Phonology from Proto-Germanic to Old English Stressing West-Saxon Conditions. LC 72-94519. (Janua Linguarum, Series Practica: No. 144). (Illus.). 134p. (Orig.). 1975. pap. text 53.85 (*90-279-3216-6*) Mouton.

Barrack, John B. & Edwards, James D. The New Income Tax Inventory Capitalization Rules: A Case Study. Barth, Claire, ed. 57p. (Orig.). 1989. pap. 20.00 (*0-86641-176-3*, 89238) Inst Mgmt Account.

Barrack, Martin K. How We Communicate: The Most Vital Skill. LC 88-81231. 203p. 1988. 18.95 (*0-944435-02-5*) Glenbridge Pub.

***Barrack, Martin K.** Second Exodus. 388p. 1999. 14.95 (*0-9657125-2-4*) Magnificat Inst.

Barracliffe, Ron. The New Hampshire Insider's Guide. LC 83-60054. (Illus.). 160p. (Orig.). 1983. pap. 2.95 (*0-9611606-0-8*) New Impressions.

***Barraclough.** Cancer & Emotion. 3rd ed. LC 98-37039. 236p. (C). 1999. pap. 49.95 (*0-471-98597-X*) Wiley.

Barraclough, Brian. Suicide: Clinical & Epidemiological Studies. 200p. 1987. lib. bdg. 32.50 (*0-7099-5009-8*, Pub. by C Helm) Routldge.

Barraclough, Brian, jt. ed. see Silverstone, Trevor.

Barraclough, David. Movie Record Breakers. 1992. 12.98 (*1-55521-771-0*) Bk Sales Inc.

— Myths & Legends. 1992. 19.98 (*1-55521-812-1*) Bk Sales Inc.

Barraclough, Frances H., tr. see Arguedas, Jose M.

Barraclough, Frances Horning, tr. see Arguedas, Jose Maria.

Barraclough, Geoffrey. Challenging Artstraws. rev. ed. Doyle, Connie, ed. (Design & Make Ser.). (Illus.). 29p. (J). (gr. 3-6). 1996. reprint ed. 6.99 (*1-884461-07-7*) NES Arnold.

— History in a Changing World. LC 84-12976. 246p. 1984. reprint ed. lib. bdg. 59.75 (*0-313-24369-7*, BAHC, Greenwood Pr) Greenwood.

— Main Trends in History. rev. ed. 1991. 45.00 (*0-8419-1287-4*); pap. 19.95 (*0-8419-1062-6*) Holmes & Meier.

— The Medieval Papacy. (Library of World Civilization Ser.). (Illus.). (C). 1979. pap. text 13.25 (*0-393-95100-6*) Norton.

— The Origins of Modern Germany. 504p. 1984. reprint ed. pap. 15.95 (*0-393-30153-2*) Norton.

Barraclough, Geoffrey, ed. Hammand Concise Atlas of World History. 5th rev. ed. (Illus.). 192p. 1998. pap. 34.95 (*0-8437-1121-3*, 1121-3) Hammond World.

Barraclough, Geoffrey, tr. Mediaeval Germany, 911-1250: Essays by German Historians, 2 vols., Set. LC 75-41019. (BCL Ser. II). reprint ed. 49.50 (*0-404-14800-X*) AMS Pr.

Barraclough, Geoffrey, ed. see Historical Association, London Staff.

Barraclough, Hugh. Cawthorn & Barraclough: The Sale & Management of Flats - Practice & Precedents. 2nd ed. 1996. write for info. (*0-406-02282-8*, CBSM2, MICHIE) LEXIS Pub.

Barraclough, Hugh & Matthews, Paul. A Practitioner's Guide to the Trusts of Land & Appointment of Trustees Act, 1996. 234p. 1996. pap. 46.50 (*1-85811-115-3*, Pub. by CLT Prof) Gaunt.

Barraclough, Hugh G. Sale & Management of Flats. 2nd ed. 516p. 1994. boxed set 121.00 (*0-406-02281-X*, UK, MICHIE) LEXIS Pub.

Barraclough, Jennifer, et al, eds. The Psychoimmunology of Human Cancer: Mind & Body in the Fight for Survival? LC 94-8027. (Illus.). 452p. 1995. text 89.50 (*0-19-262365-6*) OUP.

Barraclough, Jennifer & Gill, David. Hughes' Outline of Modern Psychiatry. 4th rev. ed. LC 95-50016. 312p. 1996. pap. 55.00 (*0-471-96358-5*) Wiley.

Barraclough, John. Mohandas Gandhi. LC 97-19301. (Lives & Times Ser.). (J). 1998. 19.92 (*1-57572-561-4*) Heinemann Lib.

— Mother Teresa. LC 97-16133. (Lives & Times Ser.). (J). 1998. 19.92 (*1-57572-562-2*) Heinemann Lib.

Barraclough, John & Sayer, Geoff. South Africa. LC 95-25035. (Worldforum Ser.). (J). 1998. 18.50 (*1-57572-025-6*) Heinemann Lib.

Barraclough, June. Daughter of Haworth. large type ed. (Magna Large Print Ser.). 518p. 1997. 27.50 (*0-7505-1145-1*) Thorndike Pr.

— Familiar Acts. large type ed. LC 94-34501. 415p. 1994. lib. bdg. 22.95 (*0-7838-1125-X*, G K Hall Lrg Type) Mac Lib Ref.

— Family Snapshots. large type ed. (Large Print Ser.). 480p. 1997. 27.99 (*0-7089-3696-2*) Ulverscroft.

***Barraclough, June.** First Finds: A Yorkshire Childhood. large type unabridged ed. 1999. 25.95 (*0-7531-5083-2*, 150832, Pub. by ISIS Lrg Prnt) ISIS Pub.

Barraclough, June. Swifter Wings Than Time. large type ed. (Magna Large Print Ser.). 439p. 1997. 27.99 (*0-7505-1144-3*, Pub. by Mgna Lrg Print) Ulverscroft.

— Time Will Tell. large type ed. (General Ser.). 592p. 1993. 27.99 (*0-7089-2871-4*) Ulverscroft.

Barraclough, K. C. Steelmaking, 1850 to 1900. 320p. 1990. text 64.00 (*0-901462-71-3*, Pub. by Inst Materials) Ashgate Pub Co.

***Barraclough, Maureen & Kralik, Milan J., Jr.** Sovereigns & Soldiers on Horseback: Bronze Equestrian Monuments from Ancient Rome to Our Times. (Illus.). 262p. 1999. pap. 14.95 (*0-938864-23-8*) Ipswich Pr.

Barraclough, Oswald. The Future of Man. 161p. (C). 1989. 65.00 (*1-85200-006-6*, Pub. by United Writers Pubns) St Mut.

Barraclugh, K. G. Steelmaking Before Bessemer, 2 vols. 681p. 1984. 59.00 (*0-904357-64-3*) Ashgate Pub Co.

Barraco, Robin A., ed. Nucleus of the Solitary Tract. LC 93-26818. 448p. 1993. lib. bdg. 212.50 (*0-8493-4707-6*, QP377) CRC Pr.

Barrada, Amr, jt. auth. see Bemis, Judith.

Barradas, R. G., ed. see Electrochemical Society Staff.

Barraford, Andrew E. The Golden Sphere: A Cosmology of the Dialectic. 90p. 1990. 29.95 (*0-9627758-0-0*) Silverfox Bks.

Barraford, Nora M. Barraford-Jenne Vol. 1: A Multilineal Genealogy. Jenne, Francis R. et al, eds. 345p. (C). 1986. 50.00 (*0-9627758-6-X*) Silverfox Bks.

Barraga, Natalie C. Increased Visual Behavior in Low Vision Children. LC 64-5969. (American Foundation for the Blind Research Ser.: No. 13). 188p. reprint ed. pap. 58.30 (*0-7837-2758-5*, 204314100006) Bks Demand.

Barraga, Natalie C. & Erin, Jane N. Visual Handicaps & Learning. 3rd ed. LC 91-27820. 213p. (Orig.). 1992. pap. text 28.00 (*0-89079-515-0*, 0387) PRO-ED.

Barraga, Natalie C., jt. auth. see Dorward, Barbara.

Barragan, Shannon, ed. see Walker, Jeff E.

Barragato, F., jt. ed. see Mottana, A.

Barragato, Stefano. Zen Light: Unconventional Commentaries on the Denkoroku. LC 97-5244. 1997. pap. text 14.95 (*0-8048-3106-8*) Tuttle Pubng.

Barrager, Raymond P. & Salvador, Jesusa V. Pilipino-English - English-Pilipino Dictionary & Phrasebook. (ENG & TAG.). 120p. 1996. pap. 11.95 (*0-7818-0451-5*) Hippocrene Bks.

Barragry, Thomas B. Veterinary Clinical Pharmacology & Therapeutics. Cann, Carroll C., ed. (Illus.). 1076p. 1994. 79.50 (*0-8121-1447-7*) Lppncott W & W.

Barragy, Terrence J. & Huebel, Harry R., eds. From Colony to Republic: Readings in American History to 1877. 279p. (C). 1983. pap. text 10.75 (*0-9611604-1-1*) C Del Grullo.

— From Republic to Empire: Readings in American History Since 1877. 283p. (Orig.). (C). 1982. pap. 0.75 (*0-918464-51-X*) Texas A&M Univ.

— From Republic to Empire: Readings in American History since 1877. 283p. (C). 1982. pap. text 10.75 (*0-9611604-0-3*) C Del Grullo.

Barraine, Raymond. Nouveau Dictionnaire de Droit et de Sciences Economiques. (FRE.). 540p. 1974. 59.95 (*0-8288-6203-6*, M6023) Fr & Eur.

— Nouveau Dictionnaire de Droit et de Sciences Economiques. 4th ed. (FRE.). 540p. 1974. pap. 32.95 (*0-7859-0937-0*, M6023) Fr & Eur.

Barral i Altet, Xavier. The Romanesque. Stierlin, Henri, ed. & photos by by. Huber, Claude et al, photos by. (World Architecture Ser.). (Illus.). 240p. 1998. 29.99 (*3-8228-7201-6*) Taschen Amer.

Barral, Jean-Pierre. Manual Thermal Diagnosis. (Illus.). 130p. (C). 1996. text 35.00 (*0-939616-24-0*) Eastland.

— The Thorax. LC 90-85570. (Illus.). 186p. (C). 1991. text 44.00 (*0-939616-12-2*) Eastland.

— Urogenital Manipulation. LC 93-72643. (Illus.). 249p. (C). 1993. text 48.00 (*0-939616-18-1*) Eastland.

— Visceral Manipulation II, Vol. 2. LC 87-82743. (Illus.). 264p. (C). 1989. text 48.00 (*0-939616-09-2*) Eastland.

Barral, Jean-Pierre & Croibier, Alain. Trauma: An Osteopathic Approach. (Illus.). (C). 2000. 60.00 (*0-939616-32-7*) Eastland.

Barral, Jean-Pierre & Mercier, Pierre. Visceral Manipulation. LC 87-82743.Tr. of Manipulations Viscerales. (Illus.). 278p. 1988. text 50.00 (*0-939616-06-8*) Eastland.

Barral, Mary-Rose. Life-Sharing for a Creative Tomorrow. LC 91-18281. (American University Studies: Philosophy: Ser. V, Vol. 119). 175p. (C). 1992. text 39.95 (*0-8204-1541-3*) P Lang Pubng.

Barral, R. M. Progressive Neutralism: A Philosophical Aspect of American Education. Matczak, Sebastian A., ed. LC 72-80678. (Philosophical Questions Ser.: No. 6). 1970. 35.00 (*0-912116-03-X*) Learned Pubns.

Barral, Xavier & Mostert, Marco, eds. Image Text & Script: Studies on the Transformations of Visual Literacy (400 AD-800 AD) (Transformation of the Roman World Ser.). (Illus.). 301p. 1999. 97.50 (*90-04-11113-1*) Brill Academic Pubs.

***Barram, David J., ed.** Annual Report of the President on Federal Advisory Committees: Fiscal Year 1999. 28th ed. (Illus.). 116p. 2000. pap. text 30.00 (*0-7881-8876-3*) DIANE Pub.

Barramundi, Schellberg. Didgeridoo Package. 158p. pap. 29.95 incl. audio compact disk (*90-74597-08-4*, Pub. by Binkey Kok) Weiser.

Barran, Alicia C. De, see Finch, Henry & De Barran, Alicia C., eds.

Barran, Jordis. Zwischen Ethik und Interesse. (Illus.). 204p. 1997. 42.95 (*3-631-30557-5*) P Lang Pubng.

Barranco, David, tr. see Clark, I. E.

Barranco, Manuel. Mexico - Its Educational Problems: Suggestions for Their Solution. LC 79-176518. (Columbia University, Teachers College, Contributions to Education Ser.: No. 73). reprint ed. 37.50 (*0-404-55073-8*) AMS Pr.

Barrand, F., jt. auth. see Fontaine, A. B.

Barranger, John A., jt. ed. see Strauss, Michael.

Barranger, Milly S. Jessica Tandy: A Bio-Bibliography, 22. LC 91-25094. (Bio-Bibliographies in the Performing Arts Ser.: No. 22). (GER.). 168p. 1991. lib. bdg. 49.95 (*0-313-27716-8*, BJT/, Greenwood Pr) Greenwood.

— Margaret Webster: A Bio-Bibliography, 47. LC 93-37191. (Bio-Bibliographies in the Performing Arts Ser.: No. 47). 256p. 1994. lib. bdg. 75.00 (*0-313-28439-3*, Greenwood Pr) Greenwood.

— Theatre: A Way of Seeing. 2nd ed. 380p. (C). 1985. pap. write for info. (*0-534-05646-6*) Wadsworth Pub.

— Theatre: A Way of Seeing. 3rd ed. 393p. (C). 1990. pap. 35.95 (*0-534-14418-7*) Wadsworth Pub.

Barranger, Milly S. Theatre: A Way of Seeing. 4th ed. 416p. 1994. 60.95 (*0-534-24024-0*) Wadsworth Pub.

Barranger, Milly S. Understanding Plays. 2nd ed. LC 93-36946. 768p. 1993. pap. text 59.00 (*0-205-15096-9*) Allyn.

Barrante, James R. Applied Mathematics for Physical Chemistry. 2nd ed. LC 97-17387. 227p. (C). 1997. pap. text 24.00 (*0-13-741737-3*) P-H.

Barrantes, Francisco J. Nicotinic Acetylcholine Receptors. 208p. 1998. 159.00 (*1-57059-514-3*) Landes Bioscience.

Barrantes, Francisco J. & Blanca, Bahia, eds. Nicotinic Acetylcholine Receptors. (Biotechnology Intelligence Unit Ser.). 208p. 1998. 159.00 (*3-540-64258-7*) Spr-Verlag.

Barrantes, Kanier, tr. see Ruth, Merle.

Barrantes, R., jt. auth. see Sierra, R.

Barrantes, Susan. Polo. LC 98-172791. (Illus.). 208p. 1998. 60.00 (*0-8478-5778-6*, Pub. by Rizzoli Intl) St Martin.

***Barranti, Laurie.** Pet Pocketbook: A Record-Keeping Journal for Your Pet. 2nd ed. 20p. 2000. pap. 8.00 (*0-9675257-1-3*) Bananknotcom.

Barranti-Teague, Laurie. Pet Health Journal. 105p. 1997. pap. write for info. (*0-9675257-0-5*) Bananknotcom.

Barraquer, Joaquin. Microsurgery of the Cornea: An Atlas & Textbook. 400p. 1984. text 231.00 (*84-85835-03-4*) Gordon & Breach.

***Barras, Jacqueline.** Light in Watercolour No. 18: Step-by-Step Leisure Arts. Vol. 18. 48p. 2001. pap. 10.95 (*0-85532-906-8*, Pub. by Srch Pr) Midpt Trade.

Barras, Jonetta R. The Corner Is No Place for Hiding. Comitz, Cindy & Cavalieri, Grace, eds. 67p. (Orig.). 1995. pap. write for info. (*0-938572-13-X*) Bunny Crocodile.

— The Last of the Black Emperors: The Hollow Comeback of Marion Barry in the New Age Black Leaders. 287p. (Orig.). 1998. pap. 24.00 (*0-9631246-6-8*) Bancroft MD.

***Barras, Jonetta Rose.** Whatever Happened to Daddy's Little Girl? The Impact of Fatherlessness on Black Women. 272p. 2000. 25.00 (*0-345-42246-5*, Ballantine) Ballantine Pub Grp.

Barras, Margaret W. Texas Criminal Codes & Rules: Annotated. LC 99-202234. 1133 p. 1997. write for info. (*1-57625-042-3*) Amer Law Media.

Barras, R. C., jt. ed. see Morris, A. L.

Barrass, B., jt. auth. see Derrett, D. R.

***Barrass, C. B.** Ship Stability Sketches & Notes. 128p. 2001. pap. 28.95 (*0-7506-4850-3*) Buttrwrth-Heinemann.

Barrass, Robert. Scientists Must Write: A Guide to Better Writing for Scientists, Engineers & Students. (Illus.). 176p. (gr. 13). 1978. pap. 20.99 (*0-412-15430-7*, NO. 6385) Chapman & Hall.

— Students Must Write: A Guide to Better Coursework & Examinations. 2nd ed. LC 95-14275. (Illus.). 208p. (C). 1995. pap. 16.99 (*0-415-13222-3*) Routledge.

— Study: A Guide to Effective Study, Revision & Examination Techniques. (Illus.). 192p. (C). (gr. 13). 1984. pap. 24.99 (*0-412-25690-8*, NO. 9186) Routledge.

Barrass, Robert & Madhavan, Shobhana. European Economic Integration: Institutions, Issues, & Policies. LC 95-47472. 1996. pap. write for info. (*0-07-707836-5*) McGraw-H Intl.

Barrasso, R., jt. ed. see Luesley, David.

Barrat-Brown, Michael. Fair Trade: Reform & Realities in the International Trading System. LC 92-33430. 192p. (C). 1993. text 22.50 (*1-85649-074-2*, Pub. by Zed Books) St Martin.

Barrat, Pamela. M. Annei Lucani Belli Civilis Liber V: A Commentary. xvi, 284p. 1979. pap. 82.00 (*90-256-0806-X*, Pub. by AM Hakkert) BookLink Distributors.

Barrat, Rodford. Elements of Numerology. LC 97-173123. (Elements of...Ser.). 1997. pap. 9.95 (*1-86204-071-0*, Pub. by Element MA) Penguin Putnam.

***Barrat, Rodford.** Numerology: Intro Guide to the Power of Numbers as a Guide for Life. (New Perspectives Ser.). 2000. pap. 9.95 (*1-86204-625-5*, Pub. by Element MA) Penguin Putnam.

Barratt. Short Changed: Africa in World Trade. LC 92-34001. (Transnational Institute Ser.). 220p. (C). pap. 18.95 (*0-7453-0699-3*, Pub. by Pluto GBR) Stylus Pub VA.

Barratt, A. Gorky's Lower Depths: Critical Study. (Critical Studies in Russian Literature Ser.). 1996. pap. 14.95 (*1-85399-436-7*, Pub. by Brist Class Pr) Focus Pub-R Pullins.

Barratt, A., ed. Zamyatin: We (My) (Bristol Russian Texts Ser.). (RUS.). 166p. 1994. pap. 18.95 (*1-85399-378-6*, Pub. by Brist Class Pr) Focus Pub-R Pullins.

Barratt, Alan M. & Georges, D. Patrick. The Synolic Manager: Getting It All Together. LC 98-89873. 365p. 1999. 25.00 (*0-7388-0303-0*); pap. 15.00 (*0-7388-0304-9*) Xlibris Corp.

Barratt, Alexander, ed. Pentinent Psalm: A Commentary on the Penitential Psalms. Hull, Dame Eleanor, tr. (Early English Text Society-Original Ser.: Vol. 307). (FRE & ENG., Illus.). 368p. (C). 1996. text 75.00 (*0-19-722309-5*) OUP.

Barratt, Alexander, jt. ed. see Ayto, John.

Barratt, Alexandra, ed. Women's Writing in Middle English. (Annotated Texts Ser.). (C). 1992. pap. text 38.44 (*0-582-06192-X*, 79198) Longman.

— Women's Writing in Middle English. (Annotated Texts Ser.). 296p. (C). 1995. text. write for info. (*0-582-06193-8*) Longman.

Barratt, Alexandra, tr. see Gertrude the Great of Helfta.

Barratt, Andrew. Between Two Worlds: A Critical Introduction to the Master & Margarita. 302p. 1987. 75.00 (*0-19-815664-2*) OUP.

Barratt, Andrew, ed. & tr. see Gorky, Maksim.

B

An Asterisk (*) at the beginning of an entry indicates that the title is appearing for the first time.

Barratt, Barnaby B. Psychic Reality & Psychoanalytic Knowing. LC 84-6353. (Advances in Psychoanalysis: Theory, Research, & Practice Ser.: No. 3). 316p. reprint ed. pap. 98.00 (*0-7837-4501-X*, 204427800001) Bks Demand.
— Psychoanalysis & the Postmodern Impulse: Knowing & Being since Freud's Psychology. LC 92-36941. 272p. (C). 1993. text 47.00 (*0-8018-4547-5*) Johns Hopkins.
Barratt-Boyes, Brian G., jt. auth. see Kirklin, John W.
Barratt-Brown, Michael. Europe, Time to Leave & How to Go , No. 34. LC 75-318866. (Spokesman Pamphlet Ser. No. 34). 14p. 1973. write for info. (*0-85124-064-X*) Spkesman.
— From Labourism to Socialism: The Political Economy of Labour in the 1970's. LC 73-159780. (Spokesman Bks.). 252p. 1972. write for info. (*0-85124-045-3*) Spkesman.
— The Yugoslav Tragedy: Lessons for Socialists LC 97-115501. (Socialist Renewal Ser.). 81 p. 1996. write for info. (*0-85124-588-9*) Spkesman.
Barratt, C. L., jt. ed. see Glover, T. D.
***Barratt, Carol.** All the Tunes You've Ever Wanted to Play. 303p. 1999. pap. text 15.95 (*0-7119-7662-7*, OP48140) Music Sales.
Barratt, Carol. The Mother Goose Songbook. (J). (gr. k up). 1986. 4.98 (*0-685-16882-4*, 615754) Random Hse Value.
Barratt, Carrie R. John Singleton Copley & Margaret Kemble Gage: Turkish Fashion in Eighteenth Century America LC 98-68034. 45p. 1998. write for info. (*1-879067-04-8*) Putnam Found.
***Barratt, Carrie Rebora.** Queen Victoria & Thomas Sully. (Illus.). 224p. 2000. 35.00 (*0-691-07034-2*) Princeton U Pr.
Barratt, Christopher L. & Cooke, I. D., eds. Advances in Clinical Andrology. (C). 1988. text 95.50 (*0-7462-0034-X*) Kluwer Academic.
Barratt, Christopher L. & Cooke, Ian, eds. Donor Insemination. (Illus.). 241p. (C). 1993. text 59.95 (*0-521-40433-9*) Cambridge U Pr.
Barratt, Daniel. Pictures of Jesus. (C). 1989. 45.00 (*0-907839-45-2*, Pub. by Brynmill Pr Ltd) St Mut.
Barratt, Dorothy, et al. Becoming Friends, What Friends Believe. (Illus.). 78p. (J). (gr. 5-6). 1990. student ed. 3.50 (*0-943701-17-1*); teacher ed., ring bd. 19.95 (*0-943701-16-3*) George Fox Pr.
***Barratt, Glen C.** A Different Land. LC 99-97537. 2000. pap. 11.95 (*0-533-13418-8*) Vantage.
Barratt, Glynn R. The Russian Discovery of Hawaii. (Illus.). 259p. 1987. text 27.50 (*0-915013-08-8*) Editions Ltd.
— The Russian View of Honolulu. (Illus.). 424p. (C). 1988. 27.50 (*0-88629-060-0*) Editions Ltd.
— Voices in Exile: The Decembrist Memoirs. LC 75-310670. 403p. reprint ed. pap. 125.00 (*0-608-12524-5*, 202385200034) Bks Demand.
Barratt, Glynn R., tr. see Ivashintsov, Nikolai A.
Barratt, Iris K. Divination Workbook: An Experts Guide to Awakening the Power & Wisdom of Your Soul. (Illus.). 119p. 1998. spiral bd. 24.95 (*1-893087-02-6*) Linden Pubs.
— Divination Workbook: An Expert's Guide to Awakening the Power & Wisdom of Your Soul. 2nd rev. ed. Austin, Leah, ed. 1999. reprint ed. pap. text 24.95 (*1-893087-03-4*) Awaken Vis.
Barratt, Krome. Logic & Design: The Syntax of Art, Art & Mathematics. (Illus.). 328p. 1980. 25.00 (*0-89860-033-2*) Eastview.
— Logic & Design in Art, Science, & Mathematics. 326p. 1993. pap. 21.95 (*1-55821-268-X*) Lyons Pr.
Barratt, Neil. State of Cybernation: Cultural, Political & Economic Implications of the Internet. (Business & Management Ser.). 1996. pap. 19.95 (*0-7494-2053-7*) Kogan Page Ltd.
Barratt, Olivia E. Basket Making: How to Use Classic Basket-Making Techniques with Modern Materials to Create 10 Unusual Baskets. (Illus.). 96p. (Orig.). 1995. pap. 14.95 (*0-8050-2617-7*, Owl) H Holt & Co.
Barratt, Olivia Elton. Basket Making. 1999. pap. 14.95 (*1-85974-211-4*) New5 Holland.
Barratt, Robert S., jt. auth. see Wilson, Otto.
Barratt, Rod, jt. auth. see Feates, Frank S.
Barratt, T. Martin, et al. Pediatric Nephrology. 4th ed. LC 97-48546. 1998. 189.00 (*0-683-30055-5*) Lppncott W & W.
Barrau, Jacques. Les Plantes Potageres. (FRE., Illus.). 96p. 1996. pap. 19.95 (*2-909808-27-0*, Pub. by Art Bks Intl) Partners Pubs Grp.
— Subsistence Agriculture in Melanesia, 2 vols., 1. (BMB Ser.). 1974. reprint ed. 25.00 (*0-527-02327-2*) Periodicals Srv.
— Subsistence Agriculture in Melanesia, 2 vols., 2. (BMB Ser.). 1974. reprint ed. 25.00 (*0-527-02331-0*) Periodicals Srv.
Barraud, Cecile, et al, eds. Of Relations & the Dead: Four Societies Viewed from the Angle of Their Exchanges. Suffern, Stephen J., tr. from FRE. (Explorations in Anthropology Ser.). 132p. 1994. 37.50 (*0-85496-953-5*, Pub. by Berg Pubs); pap. 16.50 (*1-85973-046-9*, Pub. by Berg Pubs) NYU Pr.
Barraud, P. J. Diptera: Family Calcidae, Tribe Megarhinini & Cuiicini, Vol. 5. (Fauna of British India Ser.). (Illus.). xxviii, 484p. 1977. reprint ed. 30.00 (*0-685-04534-X*) Scholarly Pubns.
Barrax, Gerald. An Audience of One. LC 79-3050. (Contemporary Poetry Ser.). 94p. 1980. pap. 14.95 (*0-8203-0502-2*) U of Ga Pr.
— The Deaths of Animals & Lesser Gods. Rowell, Charles H., ed. (Callaloo Poetry Ser.: No. 4). (Illus.). 73p. (Orig.). 1984. pap. 9.95 (*0-912759-02-X*) U Pr of Va.
— From a Person Sitting in Darkness: New & Selected Poems. LC 98-37901. (Southern Messenger Poets Ser.). 201p. 1998. pap. 17.95 (*0-8071-2314-5*); text 24.95 (*0-8071-2313-7*) La State U Pr.
Barraza, Ruth A. & Lier, Aida W. Sendas Literarias, Level 1. LC 94-11182. (SPA.). 1994. mass mkt. 55.95 (*0-8384-5126-8*) Heinle & Heinle.
Barre, Frances La, see La Barre, Frances.
Barre, Harold. Managing 12 Volts: How to Upgrade, Operate & Troubleshoot 12 Volt Systems. LC 95-92383. (Illus.). 213p. (Orig.). 1996. pap. 19.95 (*0-9647386-1-9*) Summer Breeze Pub.
***Barre Historical Society Staff.** Barre. (Images of America Ser.). 1999. pap. 18.99 (*0-7385-0001-1*) Arcadia Publng.
Barre, Lloyd M. The Rhetoric of Political Persuasion: The Narrative Artistry & Political Intentions of 2 Kings 9-11. Karris, Robert J., ed. LC 87-15878. (Catholic Biblical Quarterly Monographs: No. 20). ix, 161p. 1988. pap. 5.00 (*0-915170-19-1*) Catholic Bibl Assn.
Barre, Michael L. The God-List in the Treaty Between Hannibal & Philip V of Macedonia: A Study in Light of the Ancient Near Eastern Treaty Tradition. LC 82-13961. (Near Eastern Studies). 208p. (C). 1983. text 38.00 (*0-8018-2787-6*) Johns Hopkins.
Barre, Michael L., ed. see Murphy, Roland E.
Barre, Richard. Bearing Secrets: A Wil Hardesty Mystery. 312p. 1996. 22.95 (*0-8027-3280-1*) Walker & Co.
— Bearing Secrets: A Wil Hardesty Mystery, Vol. 2. Vol. 2. 288p. 1998. reprint ed. pap. 5.99 (*0-425-16641-4*) Ace Bks.
— Blackheart Highway. LC 98-52048. 336p. 1999. pap. 21.95 (*0-425-16903-0*, Prime Crime) Berkley Pub.
***Barre, Richard.** Blackheart Highway. (Wil Hardesty Ser.: Vol. 4). 326p. 2000. mass mkt. 6.99 (*0-425-17467-0*) Berkley Pub.
Barre, Richard. The Ghosts of Morning: A Will Hardesty Mystery. LC 97-34963. 336p. 1998. 21.95 (*0-425-16300-8*) Berkley Pub.
— The Ghosts of Morning: A Will Hardesty Mystery. 1999. reprint ed. mass mkt. 5.99 (*0-425-16931-6*, Prime Crime) Berkley Pub.
— The Innocents. 1997. mass mkt. 5.99 (*0-425-16109-9*, Prime Crime) Berkley Pub.
— The Innocents. 332p. 1995. 19.95 (*0-8027-3261-5*) Walker & Co.
Barrea-Marlys, Mirta, jt. ed. see Cortes, Eladio.
Barreaud, M. Dictionnaire des Footballeurs Etranger Championat Prof. Francaise (1939-97) (FRE.). 1998. 79.95 (*0-320-00268-3*) Fr & Eur.
***Barreca, Regina.** American Humor Anthology. 416p. 1999. mass mkt. 6.95 (*0-451-52751-8*, Sig) NAL.
Barreca, Regina. Last Laughs: Perspectives on Women & Comedy. 322, vip. 1988. pap. text 26.00 (*0-677-22030-8*) Gordon & Breach.
— Last Laughs: Perspectives on Women & Comedy, Vol. 2. vi, 322p. 1988. text 52.00 (*0-677-22020-0*) Gordon & Breach.
— Perfect Husbands & Other Fairy Tales: Demystifying Marriage, Men & Romance. LC 94-32826. 288p. 1994. pap. 15.95 (*0-385-47538-1*, Anchor NY) Doubleday.
— Sweet Revenge: The Wicked Delights of Getting Even. 304p. 1997. reprint ed. mass mkt. 6.99 (*0-425-15766-0*) Berkley Pub.
— They Used to Call Me Snow White... But I Drifted: Women's Strategic Use of Humor. LC 90-50511. 240p. 1992. pap. 12.95 (*0-14-016835-4*, Penguin Bks) Viking Penguin.
***Barreca, Regina.** Too Much of a Good Thing Is Wonderful. 250p. 2000. pap. 16.95 (*0-939883-06-6*, Pub. by Bibliopola Pr) U Pr of New Eng.
Barreca, Regina. Untamed & Unabashed: Essays on Women & Humor in British Literature. LC 93-30645. (Humor in Life & Letters Ser.). 192p. 1994. text 32.50 (*0-8143-2136-4*) Wayne St U Pr.
— Women of the Century: Thirty Modern Short Stories. 3rd ed. LC 92-50040. 376p. (C). 1993. pap. text 23.95 (*0-312-07523-5*) St Martin.
Barreca, Regina, ed. Fay Weldon's Wicked Fictions. LC 94-20493. 248p. 1994. 35.00 (*0-87451-642-0*) U Pr of New Eng.
— New Perspectives on Women & Comedy. (Studies in Gender & Culture). xii, 244p. 1992. text 52.00 (*2-88124-533-1*); pap. text 24.00 (*2-88124-534-X*) Gordon & Breach.
— The Penguin Book of Women's Humor. 658p. 1996. pap. 16.95 (*0-14-017294-7*, Penguin Bks) Viking Penguin.
— Sex & Death in Victorian Literature. LC 89-11020. 272p. 1990. 10.00 (*0-253-31015-6*) Ind U Pr.
Barreca, Regina & Jacobus, Lee A., eds. Helene Cixous: Critical Impressions. (LIT Book Ser.: Vol. 1). 352p. 1999. text 25.00 (*90-5700-500-X*, ECU33); pap. text 13.00 (*90-5700-501-8*, ECU17) Gordon & Breach.
Barreca, Regina & Morse, Deborah D., eds. The Erotics of Instruction. LC 96-44614. 198p. 1997. pap. 17.95 (*0-87451-806-7*); text 40.00 (*0-87451-805-9*) U Pr of New Eng.
***Barreca, Stephen L.** Comparison of Economic Life Techniques. 74p. 1999. pap. 495.00 (*1-884154-12-3*) Tech Futures.
Barreda, Pedro. The Black Protagonist in the Cuban Novel. Bancroft, Page, tr. from SPA. LC 78-19689. 192p. 1979. lib. bdg. 27.50 (*0-87023-262-2*) U of Mass Pr.
Barreda, Pedro & Bejar, Eduardo. Poetica de la Nacion. Poesia Romantica en Hispanoamerica (Critica y Antologia) LC 98-60877. (SPA., Illus.). 707p. 1998. pap. 45.00 (*0-89295-090-0*) Society Sp & Sp-Am.
Barreda Tarrazona, I., jt. ed. see Georgantzis, N.
***Barreintos, Armando.** Pension Reform in Latin America. LC 98-72852. (Illus.). 266p. 1998. text 67.95 (*1-85972-699-2*) Ashgate Pub Co.
***Barreira, G., et al, eds.** Calorimetry in High Energy Physics. 880p. 2000. 148.00 (*981-02-4304-9*) World Scientific Pub.
Barreira, Joseph & Moreira, Raymond. Horses in the Killing. LC 97-182560. (Illus.). 122p. (Orig.). 1996. pap. 10.95 (*0-9652266-0-3*) Amer Against Equine.
Barreiro. Young Witches: London Babylon. Vol. 2. (Illus.). 100p. 1997. pap. 16.95 (*1-56097-241-6*) Fantagraph Bks.
Barreiro & Lopez, F. Solano. Young Witches. (Eros Graphic Novel Ser.: No. 3). 104p. 1992. pap. 16.95 (*1-56097-202-5*, Pub. by Fantagraph Bks) Seven Hills Bk.
Barreiro, jt. auth. see Noe.
Barreiro, Elias. Guitar Music of Cuba. 184p. 1996. 24.95 incl. audio compact disk (*0-7866-2303-9*, MB96178BCD) Mel Bay.
Barreiro, Elias. Vivaldi Quartet for Guitar. 76p. 1996. pap. 9.95 (*0-7866-0829-3*, 95546) Mel Bay.
Barreiro, F. Low x Physics: Proceedings of the 5th Workshop Madrid, Spain 1997. 1998. 58.00 (*981-02-3514-3*) World Scientific Pub.
Barreiro, F. & Sanchez-Gomez, J. L., eds. Lepton Nucleon Interactions at High Energies: Proceedings of the XVth Winter Meeting on Fundamental Physics. 384p. (C). 1988. text 100.00 (*9971-5-0469-3*) World Scientific Pub.
Barreiro, Jose. The Indian Chronicles. LC 93-12810. 304p. (C). 1993. 9.95 (*1-55885-067-8*) Arte Publico.
Barreiro, Jose, ed. Chiapas: Challenging History. 92p. 1994. pap. 12.00 (*0-614-29682-X*) Akwe Kon Pr.
— Indian Roots of American Democracy. 195p. 1992. pap. 12.00 (*1-881178-00-5*) Akwe Kon Pr.
— Indigenous Economics: Toward a Natural World Order. (Illus.). 112p. (Orig.). 1992. pap. 10.00 (*0-614-29681-1*) Akwe Kon Pr.
— Native American Expressive Culture. 176p. (Orig.). Date not set. pap. 12.00 (*0-614-29683-8*) Akwe Kon Pr.
— Native Americans: Akwe: Icon's Journal of Indigenous Issues. (Illus.). 64p. (Orig.). Date not set. mass mkt. 20.00 (*0-614-29686-2*) Akwe Kon Pr.
— Unbroken Circles: Traditional Arts of Contemporary Woodland Peoples. (Illus.). 96p. (Orig.). 1990. pap. 10.00 (*0-614-29680-3*) Akwe Kon Pr.
Barreiro, Richardo. Moving Fortress. (Illus.). 64p. (Orig.). 1988. pap. 8.98 (*0-922173-00-1*) Four Winds Pub Group.
Barrel, John. The Dark Side of the Landscape: The Rural Poor in English Painting 1730-1840. LC 78-72334. 192p. 1983. pap. text 24.95 (*0-521-27655-1*) Cambridge U Pr.
Barrel, Ray, et al. Job Creation in the U. S. 124p. 1997. pap. 55.00 (*0-11-270995-8*, HM09958, Pub. by Statnry Office) Bernan Associates.
Barrell. Problem Based Learning: An Inquiry Approach. 168p. 1998. pap. text 30.95 (*0-205-29410-3*, Longwood Div) Allyn.
Barrell, A. D. The Papacy, Scotland & Northern England, 1342-1378. (Cambridge Studies in Medieval Life & Thought: No. 30). (Illus.). 317p. (C). 1995. text 59.95 (*0-521-44182-X*) Cambridge U Pr.
***Barrell, A. D. M.** Medieval Scotland. LC 99-86098. (Cambridge Medieval Textbooks Ser.). (Illus.). 280p. 2000. write for info. (*0-521-58443-4*); pap. write for info. (*0-521-58602-X*) Cambridge U Pr.
Barrell, Brigitte & Filson, Brent. Another Bridge. 128p. 1992. 14.95 (*0-9631422-7-5*) Far Hills Pubns.
***Barrell, Doris.** Ethics & Real Estate. LC 00-32330. 2000. write for info. (*0-7931-3847-7*, Real Estate Ed) Dearborn.
Barrell, Doris, jt. auth. see Sirota, David.
***Barrell, Harry F.** An Outline of Anglo-Saxon Law. 84p. 1999. reprint ed. 30.00 (*1-56169-545-9*) Gaunt.
Barrell, John. The Birth of Pandora: And the Division of Knowledge. LC 91-35864. (New Cultural Studies). (Illus.). 288p. (C). 1992. text 39.95 (*0-8122-3153-8*) U of Pa Pr.
Barrell, John. Book of English Pastoral Verse. 1975. 22.50 (*0-19-519798-4*) OUP.
— Imagining the King's Death: Figurative Treason, Fantasies of Regicide, 1793-1796. (Illus.). 820p. 2000. text 115.00 (*0-19-811292-0*) OUP.
Barrell, John. The Infection of Thomas De Quincey: The Psychopathology of Imperialism. LC 90-49489. (Illus.). 288p. (C). 1991. 42.50 (*0-300-04932-3*) Yale U Pr.
Barrell, John, ed. Painting & the Politics of Culture: New Essays on British Art, 1700-1850. (Illus.). 320p. 1992. 85.00 (*0-19-817392-X*) OUP.
Barrell, Kay. The Technical Production Handbook: A Guide for Performing Arts Presenting Organizations & Touring Companies. rev. ed. McKell, Mimi, ed. LC 90-50991. (Illus.). 56p. 1991. pap. 7.50 (*0-9611710-6-5*) Western States.
Barrell, Ray, ed. Economic Convergence & Monetary Union in Europe. (Illus.). 288p. (C). 1992. 65.00 (*0-8039-8720-X*); pap. 24.00 (*0-8039-8721-8*) Sage.
— The U. K. Labour Market: Comparative Aspects & Institutional Developments. LC 93-36552. (Illus.). 282p. (C). 1994. pap. text 22.95 (*0-521-46825-6*) Cambridge U Pr.
***Barrell, Ray, et al, eds.** Productivity, Innovation & Economic Performance. LC 99-87220. (National Institute of Economic & Social Research Economic & Social Studies). (Illus.). 304p. 2000. text 74.95 (*0-521-78031-4*) Cambridge U Pr.
Barrell, Ray & Pain, Nigel, eds. Innovation, Investment & the Difference of Technology in Europe: German Direct Investment & Economic Growth in Postwar Europe. (National Institute of Economic & Social Research Economic & Social Studies: No. 39). (Illus.). 194p. (C). 1999. text 54.95 (*0-521-62087-2*) Cambridge U Pr.
Barrell, Ray & Whitley, John. Macroeconomic Policy Coordination in Europe: The ERM & Monetary Union. 288p. 1993. pap. 24.95 (*0-8039-8765-X*) Sage.
Barrell, Ray & Whitley, John, eds. Macroeconomic Policy Coordination in Europe: The ERM & Monetary Union. 304p. (C). 1993. text 69.95 (*0-8039-8764-1*) Sage.
Barrell, Rex A. Anthony Ashley Cooper, Earl of Shaftesbury & 'Le Refuge Francais' Correspondence. LC 88-13823. (Studies in British History: Vol. 15). (Illus.). 264p. 1989. lib. bdg. 89.95 (*0-88946-466-9*) E Mellen.
— Bolingbroke & France. LC 88-19852. (Illus.). 152p. (C). 1988. lib. bdg. 38.00 (*0-8191-7127-1*) U Pr of Amer.
— The Correspondence of Abel Boyer, Huguenot Refugee. LC 92-3521. 240p. 1992. lib. bdg. 89.95 (*0-7734-9488-X*) E Mellen.
— Francis Atterbury (Sixteen Sixty-Two - Seventeen Thirty-Two), Bishop of Rochester, & His French Correspondents. LC 89-48245. (Studies in British History: Vol. 19). (Illus.). 104p. 1990. lib. bdg. 59.95 (*0-88946-451-0*) E Mellen.
— George Augustus Selwyn (1719-1791) & France: Unpublished Correspondence. (Studies in British History: Vol. 24). 219p. 1991. write for info. (*0-88946-585-1*) E Mellen.
— Horace Walpole (1717-1797) & France. LC 91-21106. (Studies in British History: Vol. 26). (Illus.). 648p. 1991. lib. bdg. 129.95 (*0-7734-9737-4*) E Mellen.
Barrell, Rex A., ed. The French Correspondence of James, 1st Earl Waldegrave (1684-1741) LC 95-19654. (Studies in British History: Vol. 38). 176p. 1996. text 79.95 (*0-7734-9073-6*) E Mellen.
Barrell, Rex A., jt. auth. see O'Cleirigh, Padraig M.
Barrell, Rex A., ed. see Malthus, Cecil.
Barrell, Tony & Tanaka, Rick. Okinawa Dreams OK. 220p. Date not set. pap. 25.00 (*3-931126-11-0*, Pub. by Die Gestalten) Consort Bk Sales.
Barrell, Tony, jt. auth. see Tanaka, Rick.
Barreneche, Raul. At Spillis Candela. Costa, Eduardo, tr. (Illus.). Price not set. (*0-9662230-4-7*) Edizioni Pr.
Barrenechea, Teresa & Goodbody, Mary. The Basque Table: Passionate Home Cooking from One of Europe's Great Regional Cuisines. LC 98-29295. (Illus.). 224p. 1998. 22.95 (*1-55832-140-3*, Pub. by Harvard Common Pr) Natl Bk Netwk.
— The Basque Table: Passionate Home Cooking from One of Europe's Great Regional Cuisines. LC 98-29295. (Illus.). 240p. 2000. pap. 14.95 (*1-55832-141-1*, Pub. by Harvard Common Pr) Natl Bk Netwk.
Barreno, Maria I. New Portuguese Letters. 326p. 1994. pap. 11.95 (*0-930523-98-9*) Readers Intl.
Barreno, Maria I., et al. New Portuguese Letters. Lane, Helen R. & Gillespie, Faith, trs. 326p. 1994. 19.95 (*0-930523-97-0*) Readers Intl.
Barrentine, Larry B. Concepts for R & R Studies. 48p. 1991. pap. 23.00 (*0-87389-107-4*, H0634) ASQ Qual Pr.
— A Simplified Approach to Design of Experiments. LC 98-42759. 160p. 1999. pap. 24.00 (*0-87389-444-8*, H1016) ASQ Qual Pr.
Barrentine, Pat, ed. When the Canary Stops Singing: Women's Perspectives on Transforming Business. LC 93-27145. (Illus.). 290p. 1994. 24.95 (*1-881052-41-9*) Berrett-Koehler.
Barrentine, Shelby J. & International Reading Association Staff. Reading Assessment: Principles & Practices for Elementary Teachers : a Collection of Articles from the Reading Teacher. LC 99-21205. 14p. 1999. 26.95 (*0-87207-250-9*) Intl Reading.
Barrera. Harcourt Brace Lectura: Level 9. 1987. 35.25 (*0-15-331029-4*) Harcourt Schl Pubs.
— HBJ Lectura 1987 Level 1. 1987. pap., student ed. 13.00 (*0-15-331021-9*) Harcourt Schl Pubs.
— HBJ Lectura 1987 Level 2. (SPA.). 1987. pap., student ed. 13.00 (*0-15-331022-7*) Harcourt Schl Pubs.
— HBJ Lectura 1987 Level 3. (SPA.). 1987. pap., student ed. 13.00 (*0-15-331023-5*) Harcourt Schl Pubs.
— HBJ Lectura 1987 Level R. (SPA.). 1987. pap., student ed. 16.00 (*0-15-331020-0*) Harcourt Schl Pubs.
— Lectura, 1987, Level 4. 1987. 52.50 (*0-15-331024-3*) Harcourt Schl Pubs.
— Lectura, 1987, Level 5. 1987. 30.25 (*0-15-331025-1*) Harcourt Schl Pubs.
— Lectura, 1987, Level 6. 1987. 32.25 (*0-15-331027-8*) Harcourt Schl Pubs.
— Lectura, 1987, Level 7. 1987. 32.25 (*0-15-331028-6*) Harcourt Schl Pubs.
— Mathematics Today, 1987, Level 4. 1987. 43.25 (*0-15-331030-8*); 40.00 (*0-15-350035-2*) Harcourt Schl Pubs.
Barrera, A. & Huchim, J. Architectural Restoration at Uxmal, 1986-1987. (University of Pittsburgh Latin American Archaeology Reports: No. 1). (ENG & SPA., Illus.). 1990. pap. 13.00 (*1-877812-02-1*, R001) UPLAAP.
Barrera-Benitez, Heriberto, jt. ed. see Teranishi, Roy.
***Barrera, Brenda & Wineberg, Eliot.** Chicago Running Guide. LC 99-56797. (City Running Guide Ser.). (Illus.). 160p. 2000. pap. 16.95 (*0-7360-0132-8*) Human Kinetics.
Barrera, E. V. & Marquis, F., eds. In Situ Reactions for Synthesis of Composites, Ceramics, & Intermetallics: Proceedings: Symposium Sponsored by the Joint: ASM-MSD-SMD Composites Committee & MDMD Powder Materials Committee (124th: 1995: Las Vegas) Proceedings. LC 94-73758. (Illus.). 217p. 1995. 20.00 (*0-87339-283-3*, 2833) Minerals Metals.
***Barrera, Enriqueta.** Evolution of the Cretaceous Ocean-Climate System. LC 99-23143. (Special Paper Ser.). 445p. 1999. write for info. (*0-8137-2332-9*) Geol Soc.

*__Barrera, Frankie M.__ The Diary of Baby Chulo: A Memoir in the Form of a Novel. 200p. 1999. pap. 15.95 (*0-9670848-0-6*) Popol Vuh.

Barrera, Heather. Tax Incidence: A Selected Bibliography. (CPL Bibliographies Ser.: No. 109). 67p. 1983. 10.00 (*0-86602-109-4*, Sage Prdcls Pr) Sage.

Barrera, Jeronimo, jt. auth. see DeMaria, Rusel.

Barrera, Julio T. The Jewish Bible & the Christian Bible: An Introduction to the History of the Bible. Watson, Wilfred G., tr. from SPA. LC 97-23769. (Illus.). 650p. 1997. 140.75 (*90-04-10888-2*); pap. 59.50 (*90-04-10889-0*) Brill Academic Pubs.

Barrera, Julio T., jt. auth. see Martinez, Florentino G.

Barrera, Julio Trebolle. Jewish Bible & the Christian Bible: An Introduction to the History of the Bible. Watson, Wilfred G., tr. from SPA. LC 97-23769. 576p. 1997. pap. text 49.00 (*0-8028-4473-1*) Eerdmans.

— Jewish Bible & the Christian Bible: An Introduction to the History of the Bible. Watson, Wilfred G., tr. from SPA. LC 97-23769. 576p. 1998. 119.00 (*0-8028-3830-8*) Eerdmans.

Barrera, Mario. Beyond Aztlan: Ethnic Autonomy in Comparative Perspective. LC 88-5432. 221p. 1988. 55.00 (*0-275-92923-X*, C2923, Praeger Pubs) Greenwood.

— Beyond Aztlan: Ethnic Autonomy in Comparative Perspective. LC 88-5432. 212p. (C). 1990. reprint ed. pap. text 13.00 (*0-268-00688-1*) U of Notre Dame Pr.

— Race & Class in the Southwest: A Theory of Racial Inequality. LC 78-62970. 261p. (C). 1980. pap. text 14.00 (*0-268-01601-1*) U of Notre Dame Pr.

Barrera, Mario, ed. Work Family Sex Roles Language. LC 80-53691. 1980. pap. 5.95 (*0-89229-007-2*) TQS Pubns.

Barrera, Mario & Vialpando, Geraldo. Action Research: In Defense of the Barrio. (Monographs: Pamphlet No. 1). 36p. 1974. pap. 20.00 (*0-89551-017-0*) UCLA Chicano Studies.

Barrera, R. G. & Mochan, W. L., eds. Electrodynamics of Interfaces & Composite Systems: Proceedings of the International Workshop on Electrodynamics of Interfaces & Composite Systems, Taxco, Mexico, 10-14 Aug. 1987. (Advanced Series in Surfact Science: Vol. 4). 592p. 1988. text 137.00 (*9971-5-0632-7*, ZB0632PP) World Scientific Pub.

Barrera, Rick, jt. auth. see Alessandra, Anthony J.

Barrera, Rosaura, ed. International Human Resource Management Reference Guide. rev. ed. 216p. pap. 75.00 (*0-939900-73-4*) Soc Human Resc Mgmt.

Barrera, Sandra A., tr. see Fermin, Alice.

Barrera y Leirado, Cayetano A. De La, see De la Barrera Y Leirado, Cayetano A.

Barreras, Rosalinda B., et al, eds. Kaleidoscope: A Multicultural Booklist for Grades K-8. 2nd ed. LC 98-132446. (Illus.). 232p. (J). 1997. pap. 16.95 (*0-8141-2541-7*) NCTE.

Barrere, Dorothy B. Tracing the Past at Honaunau. (Illus.). 28p. (Orig.). 1994. pap. text 4.75 (*0-940295-15-6*) HI Natural Hist.

Barrere, Dorothy B., et al. Hula: Historical Perspectives. LC 79-56806. (Pacific Anthropological Records Ser.: No. 30). 160p. 1980. pap. 15.00 (*0-910240-49-3*) Bishop Mus.

Barrere, Dorothy B., ed. see Kamakau, S. M.

Barrere, Dorothy B., ed. see Li, John Papa.

Barrere, Jean B., ed. see Hugo, Victor.

Barrero, Olga V., tr. see Ni, Hua-Ching.

Barres, Maurice. Deracines. (Folio Ser.: No. 1983). (FRE.). pap. 15.95 (*2-07-038071-8*) Schoenhof.

— Les Deracines. (FRE.). 536p. 1988. pap. 16.95 (*0-7859-2100-1*, 2070380718) Fr & Eur.

— Un Jardin sur l'Oronte. (FRE.). 218p. 1990. pap. 11.95 (*0-7859-2149-4*, 2070382923) Fr & Eur.

— La Mort de Venise. Germain, Marie-Odile, ed. & pref. by. (FRE., Illus.). 160p. 1995. pap. 64.95 (*2-86808-045-6*) Intl Scholars.

Barres, Mavora, ed. see Rachilde.

Barrese, Pauline N. Italian Cooking, Home Style. 1977. pap. 5.95 (*0-912656-19-0*) Berkley Pub.

Barresi, Anthony L., jt. auth. see Taylor, Fannie.

Barresi, Charles M. & Stull, Donald E., eds. Ethnic Elderly & Long-Term Care. LC 92-6066. 312p. 1992. 39.95 (*0-8261-7370-5*) Springer Pub.

Barresi, Dorothy. All of the Above. LC 90-20532. (Barnard New Women Poets Ser.). 75p. 1991. pap. 12.00 (*0-8070-6815-2*) Beacon Pr.

— The Post-Rapture Diner. (Poetry Ser.). 86p. (C). 1996. pap. 10.95 (*0-8229-5581-4*) U of Pittsburgh Pr.

— The Post-Rapture Diner. (Poetry Ser.). 86p. (C). 1996. text 24.95 (*0-8229-3896-0*) U of Pittsburgh Pr.

Barresi, John, jt. auth. see Martin, Raymond.

Barret. Methode de Prononciation de Francais. 29.95 (*0-685-36698-7*) Fr & Eur.

Barret & Logan. Lesbian & Gay Counseling: A Practice Primer. (Counseling Ser.). 2001. pap. text 27.00 (*0-534-55084-3*) Wadsworth Pub.

*__Barret, David.__ Scales, Patterns & Exercises for Harmonica. 48p. 1998. pap. 7.95 (*0-7866-2591-0*, 96458) Mel Bay.

Barret-Ducrocq, Francoise. Love in the Time of Victoria: Sexuality, Class & Gender in Nineteenth-Century London. Howe, John, tr. 304p. 1991. 29.95 (*0-685-50118-3*, A5362) Verso.

Barret-Hamilton, Gerald E. & Hinton, Martin A. A History of British Mammals, 2 vols., Set. Sterling, Keir B., ed. LC 77-81081. (Biologists & Their World Ser.). (Illus.). 1978. reprint ed. lib. bdg. 101.95 (*0-405-10648-3*) Ayer.

— A History of British Mammals, 2 vols., Vol. 1. Sterling, Keir B., ed. LC 77-81081. (Biologists & Their World Ser.). (Illus.). 1978. reprint ed. lib. bdg. 50.95 (*0-405-10649-1*) Ayer.

— A History of British Mammals, 2 vols., Vol. 2. Sterling, Keir B., ed. LC 77-81081. (Biologists & Their World Ser.). (Illus.). 1978. reprint ed. lib. bdg. 50.95 (*0-405-10650-5*) Ayer.

Barret, M. J. Wit & Wisdom of Gene Roddenberry. 96p. 1995. 6.99 (*0-06-105316-3*) HarpC.

Barret, Richard C. Man Behind Magic. 1999. pap. 4.99 (*0-14-032738-X*, Viking) Viking Penguin.

Barret, Robert. The Theorike & Practike of Moderne Warres. LC 74-26523. (English Experience Ser.: No. 155). (Illus.). 247p. 1969. reprint ed. 65.00 (*90-221-0155-X*) Walter J Johnson.

*__Barret, Robert L.__ Gay Fathers: Encouraging the Hearts of Gay Dads & Their Families. rev. ed. 224p. 2000. 23.00 (*0-7879-5075-0*) Jossey-Bass.

Barret, Robert L., jt. auth. see Robinson, Bryan E.

Barret, Sharon Kebschull. Desserts from an Herb Garden. LC 99-20258. (Illus.). 141p. 1999. 24.95 (*0-312-20581-3*) St Martin.

Barreto, Amilcar A. Language, Elites & the State: Nationalism in Puerto Rico & Quebec. LC 97-38541. 176p. 1998. 55.00 (*0-275-96183-4*, Praeger Pubs) Greenwood.

Barreto de Oliveira, Francisco E., ed. Social Security Systems in Latin America. (Inter-American Development Bank Ser.). 160p. 1994. 18.50 (*0-940602-91-1*) IADB.

Barreto, Delia. Muscles: A Study Aid for Students of the Allied Health Professions. (Illus.). 48p. (C). 1974. pap. 3.00 (*0-87936-005-4*) Scholium Intl.

Barreto, Eduardo, jt. auth. see Dematteis, J. M.

Barreto, M. Lopes, jt. auth. see Kreidl, N.

Barreto, Martha S., jt. auth. see Jiminez, Adriana.

Barrett. Consumer Health. 7th ed. 2000. 42.25 (*0-07-232366-3*) McGraw.

— Count 'Em: A Counting & Rhyming Book. LC 99-31892. (J). 2000. 16.00 (*0-689-82104-2*) S&S Childrens.

— Death Bed Visions. 1988. 12.95 (*0-85030-520-9*, Pub. by Aqrn Pr) HarpC.

— Dragsters. (J). 1991. pap. text 4.95 (*0-516-95176-9*) Childrens.

— Editing Series, Vol. 1. Date not set. pap. text, teacher ed. 21.95 (*0-314-06227-0*) West Pub.

— Editing Series, Vol. 2. Date not set. pap. text, teacher ed. 21.95 (*0-314-06228-9*) West Pub.

— Editing Series, Vol. 2. 1996. mass mkt. 37.95 (*0-314-04946-0*) West Pub.

— Five Centuries of Spanish Literature. (C). 1996. pap. 37.95 (*0-8384-3754-0*) Heinle & Heinle.

— Flower Arrangers Garden. (Country Wisdom Bulletins Ser.: Vol. A-103). 1988. pap. 2.95 (*0-88266-513-8*) Storey Bks.

*__Barrett.__ Leaf Baby. LC 96-75965. (Illus.). 12p. (J). (ps). 1998. pap. 5.95 (*0-15-201057-2*) Harcourt.

Barrett. Looking in on Music Teaching. 1998. 22.00 (*0-697-38695-3*, WCB McGr Hill) McGrw-H Hghr Educ.

— Los Angeles Radio People, 1957-1997. 1997. 4.95 (*0-9658907-0-8*) db Mkting.

— Mechanics of Environmental Carcinogenesis, Vol. I. 160p. 1987. 182.00 (*0-8493-4671-1*) CRC Pr.

— Office Skills. Date not set. text, teacher ed. 45.95 (*0-314-82302-6*) West Pub.

— Office Skills. 2nd ed. (Kf - Office Education Ser.). (C). 1997. mass mkt. 58.95 (*0-314-20550-0*) West Pub.

— Population Geography. (J). 1992. pap. text. write for info. (*0-05-004507-5*) Addison-Wesley.

— Practical Use of Speech Communication. 6th ed. (C). 1995. pap. write for info. (*0-03-017068-0*) Harcourt Coll Pubs.

— Quality Management for the Construction Professional: What a Mess! 1995. pap. 24.00 (*0-85406-677-2*, Pub. by R-I-C-S Bks) St Mut.

*__Barrett.__ Rudy. (Illus.). 320p. 2000. text 26.00 (*0-465-00523-3*, Pub. by Basic) HarpC.

Barrett. Snow Baby. LC 96-75966. (Illus.). 12p. (J). 1998. pap. 5.95 (*0-15-201054-8*) Harcourt.

— Speaking in America. 7th ed. (C). 1993. pap. text, teacher ed. 9.75 (*0-03-094052-4*) Harcourt Coll Pubs.

— Trucks. (J). 1991. pap. text 4.95 (*0-516-95146-7*) Childrens.

Barrett & Green. Day to Day English, Bk. 1. Date not set. pap. text. write for info. (*0-582-22325-3*, Pub. by Addison-Wesley) Longman.

— Day to Day English, Bk. 2. Date not set. pap. text. write for info. (*0-582-22326-1*, Pub. by Addison-Wesley) Longman.

Barrett & Kimbrell. Office Skills for the 90s: General Office Procedures. (Finishing Touches Ser.). 1992. pap., student ed. 18.00 (*0-314-86851-8*) Thomson Learn.

— Office Skills Workbook: Office Procedures-Microcomputer. 2nd ed. (Finishing Touches Ser.). 1998. pap., student ed. 17.00 (*0-314-12988-X*) Thomson Learn.

Barrett, jt. auth. see Arnaudet, Martin C.

Barrett, Kathleen Anne. Measure Once, Kill Twice. LC 99-475199. (Thumbprint Mysteries Ser.). 128p. (gr. 1). 1999. pap. 5.95 (*0-8092-0644-7*, 064470) NTC Contemp Pub Co.

Barrett, A. J. Quiz Me! Query Me! 39p. (YA). (gr. 3-6). 1997. pap. 5.00 (*0-89824-350-5*, 3505) Trillium Pr.

Barrett, A. J. & Gordon, M. Y. Bone Marrow Disorders: The Biological Basis of Treatment. 2nd ed. LC 92-22052. (Illus.). 432p. 1993. 165.00 (*0-632-03353-3*) Blackwell Sci.

Barrett, A. J., jt ed. see Bond, J. S.

Barrett, A. John, jt. auth. see Treleaven, Jennifer G.

Barrett, A. N. & Mackay, A. L. Spatial Structure & the Microcomputer: Selected Mathematical Techniques. (Computer Science Ser.). 218p. (C). 1987. pap. 30.00 (*0-333-39284-1*) Scholium Intl.

*__Barrett, Alan & European Centre for the Development of Vocational Training Staff.__ Exploring the Returns to Continuing Vocational Training in Enterprises: A Review of Research Within & Outside of the European Union. LC 98-234481. (Cedefop Panorama Ser.). 53p. 1998. write for info. (*92-828-4450-1*, Pub. by Comm Europ Commun) Bernan Associates.

Barrett, Alan, et al. The Economics of Solid Waste Management in Ireland LC 96-173435. (Policy Research Ser.). x, 130 p. 1995. write for info. (*0-7070-0161-7*) Econ & Soc Res.

— The Fiscal System & the Polluter Pays Principle: A Case Study of Ireland. LC 97-70345. 240p. 1997. 69.95 (*1-85972-638-0*, Pub. by Ashgate Pub) Ashgate Pub Co.

Barrett, Alan A. Non-Contentious Costs. (Practice Notes Ser.). 88p. 1992. pap. write for info. (*0-85121-530-0*, Pub. by Cavendish Pubng) Gaunt.

Barrett, Alan H., ed. see Bekefi, George.

Barrett, Alan J. Handbook of Proteolytic Enzymes, Vols. 1-2. LC 98-23079. (C). 1998. text 250.00 (*0-12-079370-9*) Acad Pr.

— Mammalian Proteases Vol. 2: A Glossary & Bibliography: Exopeptidases. McDonald, J. K., ed. 377p. 1986. text 104.00 (*0-12-079502-7*) Acad Pr.

Barrett, Alan J., et al, eds. Proteolytic Enzymes: Serine & Cysteine Peptidases. (Methods in Enzymology Ser.: Vol. 244). (Illus.). 765p. 1994. text 125.00 (*0-12-182145-5*) Acad Pr.

*__Barrett, Alan J. & Donowitz, Mark, eds.__ Current Topics in Membranes Vol. 50: Gastrointestinal Transport. 400p. 1999. 95.00 (*0-12-153350-6*) Acad Pr.

Barrett, Alan J. & McDonald, J. Ken. Mammalian Proteases Vol. 1: A Glossary & Bibliography: Endopeptidases. 1980. text 104.00 (*0-12-079501-9*) Acad Pr.

Barrett, Albert M. People under Pressure. 1960. 16.95 (*0-685-01131-3*) NCUP.

Barrett, Andrea. The Forms of Water. LC 06-44. 304p. 1994. pap. 12.00 (*0-671-79522-8*) PB.

— Lucid Stars. 336p. 1997. pap. 12.95 (*0-385-31943-6*, Delta Trade) Dell.

— The Middle Kingdom. Rosenman, Jane, ed. 288p. 1992. reprint ed. pap. 12.00 (*0-671-72961-6*, WSP) PB.

— Secret Harmonies. Rosenman, Jane, ed. 256p. 1991. reprint ed. 12.00 (*0-671-73137-8*, WSP) PB.

— Ship Fever & Other Stories. LC 95-14562. 224p. 1996. 21.00 (*0-393-03853-X*) Norton.

— Ship Fever & Other Stories. 256p. 1996. pap. 12.00 (*0-393-31600-9*) Norton.

— The Voyage of the Narwhal: A Novel. LC 98-11246. (Illus.). 416p. 1998. 24.95 (*0-393-04632-X*) Norton.

— The Voyage of the Narwhal: A Novel. 400p. 1999. pap. 14.00 (*0-393-31950-4*) Norton.

— The Voyage of the Narwhal: A Novel. 2000. pap. write for info. (*0-393-10269-6*) Norton.

— The Voyage of the Narwhal: A Novel. large type ed. 1950. pap. 30.00 (*0-7862-1752-9*, G K Hall Lrg Type) Mac Lib Ref.

— The Voyage of the Narwhal: A Novel. large type ed. LC 98-48562. 1999. 30.00 (*0-7862-1751-0*, G K Hall Lrg Type) Mac Lib Ref.

Barrett, Angela. The Random House Book of Stories from the Ballet. LC 94-22640. 112p. (J). (gr. 3-7). 1995. 20.00 (*0-679-87125-X*) Random.

*__Barrett, Ann.__ High Altitude Planting: A Practical Guide to Landscaping, Gardening & Planting above 6000' White, Dana et al, eds. (Illus.). 132p. 1999. pap. 21.95 (*0-9673331-0-5*) Barrett Enterp.

Barrett, Ann & Moro, Wendy. The Funny Bride Guide: A Very Humorous but Practical Guide for the Bride. (Illus.). 80p. 1999. pap. 15.00 (*0-9671323-0-4*) A Barrett & W Moro.

Barrett, Ann, jt. auth. see Dobbs, Jane.

Barrett, Anna P. Juneteenth: Celebrating Freedom in Texas. LC 97-50513. (Illus.). 88p. 1999. 12.95 (*1-57168-180-9*, Eakin Pr) Sunbelt Media.

— The Middlebatchers: Throw a Party for the Marriage of Hetty Wish & Lester Leg, Vol. 1. Darst, Shelia S., ed. (Illus.). 118p. (Orig.). (J). (gr. 3-7). 1984. pap. 7.95 (*0-89896-105-X*) Larksdale.

— Neecie & the Swarming Germs. Carmical, Phillip, ed. (Illus.). 50p. (J). (gr. 2-4). 1998. pap. 9.95 (*0-9661330-0-5*) ORP.

— Neecie Celebrates Juneteenth. Edwards, Lana C., ed. (Neecie Books). (Illus.). 49p. (J). (gr. 2-5). 1999. 9.95 (*0-9661330-2-1*) ORP.

— Neecie Loves Trouble, Vol. II. Edwards, Lana C., ed. (Neecie Ser.: Vol. 2). (Illus.). 48p. (J). (gr. 2-5). 1999. 9.95 (*0-9661330-1-3*) ORP.

Barrett, Anthony A. Agrippina: Sex, Power, & Politics in the Early Empire. LC 96-60318. (Illus.). 320p. 1996. 37.50 (*0-300-06598-1*) Yale U Pr.

— Agrippina: Sex, Power, & Politics in the Early Empire. (Illus.). 320p. 1999. pap. text 18.00 (*0-300-07856-0*) Yale U Pr.

— Caligula: The Corruption of Power. (Illus.). 360p. 1998. pap. 18.00 (*0-300-07429-8*) Yale U Pr.

Barrett, Anthony N., jt. auth. see Graham, Deryn.

Barrett, Arthur, jt. auth. see Magnani, Duane.

Barrett, Barbara, jt. auth. see Nickels, William G.

Barrett, Bernard M., Jr., ed. Patient Care in Plastic Surgery. 2nd ed. LC 95-44090. (Illus.). 528p. (C). (gr. 13). 1995. pap. text 54.00 (*0-8151-0563-0*, 25685) Mosby Inc.

Barrett, Bettina T. Bear-Star My Name. LC 89-32680. 76p. (Orig.). 1989. pap. 7.50 (*0-931832-32-2*) Fithian Pr.

— Heartscape. 48p. 1999. pap. 6.00 (*1-890887-10-2*) Mille Grazie.

Barrett, Betty. Rays of Hope: Words of Comfort for the Body of Christ. LC 99-231402. 126p. (Orig.). 1997. pap. 8.99 (*1-884369-70-7*, EBED Pubns) McDougal Pubng.

Barrett, Bill. Brown Water Cafe: An Illustrate Novel. (Illus.). 111p. (Orig.). 1998. pap. 6.95 (*0-9654849-0-4*) Owlseeall Pub.

*__Barrett, Bill, ed.__ Current Agricultural Trade Issues with Canada: Congressional Hearing. 90p. 2000. reprint ed. pap. text 20.00 (*0-7881-8687-6*) DIANE Pub.

Barrett, Bonnie. Cantus Cunarum: English Nursery Rhymes in Latin. (LAT., Illus.). 30p. (YA). (gr. 6-12). 1991. spiral bd. 4.15 (*0-939507-00-5*, B707) Amer Classical.

— Love in Atlantis. LC 90-53327. 182p. 1991. 22.00 (*0-933256-77-9*) Second Chance.

Barrett, Brad & Pezman, Steve, eds. Photo: Grannis-Surfing's Golden Age, 1960-1969. (Illus.). 223p. 1998. 60.00 (*0-9663771-0-9*) Surfer Jour CA.

*__Barrett, Brenda.__ Principles of Business Law. 2000. pap. write for info. (*1-86152-575-3*) Thomson Learn.

Barrett, Brenda & Howells, Richard. Cases & Materials on Occupational Health & Safety Law. 436p. 1995. pap. 44.00 (*1-85941-135-5*, Pub. by Cavendish Pubng) Gaunt.

Barrett, Brenda, jt. auth. see Howells, Richard.

Barrett, Bruce A. Managing Insect Pests in the Home Vegetable Garden. (Illus.). 59p. 1998. pap. text 20.00 (*0-7881-4845-1*) DIANE Pub.

Barrett, Bruce A. & Woodruff, Ginger S. Brigham Young University Housing Through the Years. 1994. 24.00 (*0-8425-2321-9*, Friends of the Library); pap. 14.00 (*0-8425-2322-7*, Friends of the Library) Brigham.

*__Barrett, Bryant.__ The Code Napoleon Vol. 2: Verbally Translated from the French, to Which is Prefixed an Introductory Course, Containing a Succinct Account of the Civil Regulations, Comprised in the Jewish Law, the Ordinances of Menu, the Ta Tsing Leu Lee, the Zend Avesta, the Laws of Solon, the Twelve Tables of Rome, the Laws of the Barbarians, the Assises of Jerusalem & the Koran. 575p. 2000. reprint ed. 175.00 (*1-56169-586-6*, 18657) Gaunt.

Barrett, Buckley B. World War I: A Cataloging Reference Guide. LC 93-19745. (Cataloging Guide Ser.: No. 4). iv, 380p. 1995. pap. 33.00 (*0-89370-924-7*) Millefleurs.

Barrett, Buckley B., jt. auth. see Bloomberg, Marty.

*__Barrett, Buckley Barry.__ Churchill: A Concise Bibliography. Vol. 50. 2000. lib. bdg. write for info. (*0-313-31450-0*) Greenwood.

*__Barrett, Burke, Wilson, Castle, Daffin & Frappier, LLP Staff.__ Handbook of Bankruptcy. (Mortgage Lending Handbook Ser.). 313p. (C). 1999. 85.00 (*1-57599-056-3*, PB4-110134-HH-P, Real Est Fin Pr) Mortgage Bankers.

Barrett, C., et al. The Principles of Engineering Materials. (C). 1973. text 63.75 (*0-13-709394-2*) P-H.

Barrett, C., ed. see Tatarkiewicz, Wladyslaw.

Barrett, C. B., jt. ed. see Lees, D. R.

Barrett, C. Daniel. North Carolina Employment Law. 90.00 (*0-327-12386-9*) LEXIS Pub.

Barrett, C. Daniel. North Carolina Employment Law. LC 98-85224. 1998. text. write for info. (*0-327-00136-4*, 68493-10) LEXIS Pub.

— North Carolina Employment Law, 1999 Supplement. 75p. 1999. pap. write for info. (*0-327-01328-1*, 6849311) LEXIS Pub.

*__Barrett, C. K.__ The Acts of the Apostles. (International Critical Commentary Ser.: Vol. 2). 720p. 1999. 69.95 (*0-567-08542-2*, Pub. by T & T Clark) Bks Intl VA.

Barrett, C. K. Acts One-Fourteen Vol. 1. (International Critical Commentary Ser.). 720p. 1994. text 69.95 (*0-567-09653-X*, Pub. by T & T Clark) Bks Intl VA.

— A Commentary on the Epistle of the Romans. 2nd ed. (Black's New Testament Commentaries Ser.). 270p. 1991. pap. text 37.50 (*0-7136-3358-1*, Pub. by A & C Blk) Lubrecht & Cramer.

— The Epistle to the Romans. rev. ed. (Black's New Testament Commentary Ser.: No. 6). 278p. 1991. 24.95 (*1-56563-055-6*) Hendrickson MA.

— The First Epistle to the Corinthians. (Black's New Testament Commentary Ser.: No. 7). 420p. 1993. 24.95 (*1-56563-020-3*) Hendrickson MA.

— Jesus & the Word & Other Essays, Vol. 41. LC 95-35047. (Princeton Theological Monographs). 1995. 20.00 (*1-55635-029-5*) Pickwick.

— New Testament Background: Selected Documents:Revised & Expanded Edition. expanded rev. ed. LC 95-16264. 400p. 1995. pap. 18.00 (*0-06-060881-1*, Pub. by Harper SF) HarpC.

— Paul: An Introduction to His Thought. LC 94-1153. 160p. (Orig.). 1994. pap. 14.95 (*0-664-25541-8*) Westminster John Knox.

— The Second Epistle to the Corinthians. (Black's New Testament Commentary Ser.: No. 8). 366p. 1993. 24.95 (*1-56563-021-1*) Hendrickson MA.

— Signs of an Apostle. (Biblical Classics Library: Vol. 19). 144p. 1996. reprint ed. mass mkt. 2.99 (*0-85364-743-7*, Pub. by Paternoster Pub) OM Literature.

Barrett, Carol. As It Was: Stories from the History of Southern Oregon & Northern California. Baxter, John, ed. LC 98-87804. (Illus.). 256p. 1998. pap. 19.95 (*0-9667741-0-8*) JPR Foundation.

Barrett, Carolyn M. The Magic of Matsumoto: The Suzuki Method of Education. LC 94-39778. vii, 156p. 1995. 19.95 (*0-88280-126-0*) ETC Pubns.

Barrett, Cece. The Dangers of Diet Drugs & Other Weight-Loss Products. LC 98-29712. (Teen Health Library of Eating Disorder Prevention). (Illus.). 64p. (YA). (gr. 7-12). 1999. lib. bdg. 17.95 (*0-8239-2768-7*, EDDIDR) Rosen Group.

Barrett, Charles F., et al. Modern Office Procedures. 2nd ed. LC 93-9868. 1993. mass mkt. 31.00 (*0-314-01899-9*) West Pub.

Barrett, Charles F., jt. auth. see Kimbrell, Grady.

Barrett, Charles Francis. Office Skills, 1990. 1991. mass mkt. 40.25 (*0-314-77273-1*) West Pub.

B

An Asterisk (*) at the beginning of an entry indicates that the title is appearing for the first time.

Barrett, Charles K. The Gospel of John & Judaism. Smith, D. Moody, tr. LC 75-15435. 111p. reprint ed. pap. 34.50 (*0-608-16400-3*, 202689700053) Bks Demand.

Barrett, Charles P., et al. Primer of Sectional Anatomy with MRI & CT Correlation. 2nd ed. (Illus.). 160p. 1994. pap. 25.00 (*0-683-00472-7*) Lppncott W & W.

Barrett, Charles R. The History of the Society of Apothecaries of London. LC 75-23680. (Illus.). reprint ed. 49.50 (*0-404-13233-2*) AMS Pr.

Barrett, Charles S., et al, eds. Advances in X-Ray Analysis, Vol. 28. LC 58-35928. 408p. 1985. 95.00 (*0-306-41939-4*, Plenum Trade) Perseus Pubng.

— Advances in X-Ray Analysis, Vol. 29. LC 58-35928. 618p. 1986. 110.00 (*0-306-42287-5*, Plenum Trade) Perseus Pubng.

— Advances in X-Ray Analysis, Vol. 30. LC 58-35928. (Illus.). 620p. 1987. 110.00 (*0-306-42690-0*, Plenum Trade) Perseus Pubng.

— Advances in X-Ray Analysis, Vol. 33. (Illus.). 724p. 1990. 125.00 (*0-306-43615-9*, Plenum Trade) Perseus Pubng.

— Advances in X-Ray Analysis, Vol. 34. (Illus.). 764p. (C). 1991. text 162.00 (*0-306-44003-2*, Kluwer Plenum) Kluwer Academic.

— Advances in X-Ray Analysis, Vol. 35. (Illus.). 1334p. (C). 1992. text 234.00 (*0-306-44249-3*, Kluwer Plenum) Kluwer Academic.

B

Barrett, Charles S., et al. Advances in X-Ray Analysis, Vol. 31. LC 58-35928. (Illus.). 542p. 1988. 110.00 (*0-306-42932-2*, Plenum Trade) Perseus Pubng.

Barrett, Charles S., et al. Advances in X-Ray Analysis, Vol. 32. (Illus.). 708p. 1989. 125.00 (*0-306-43236-6*, Plenum Trade) Perseus Pubng.

Barrett, Christopher B. & Cason, Jeffrey W. Overseas Research: A Practical Guide. LC 96-48307. 168p. 1997. text 35.00 (*0-8018-5513-6*); pap. text 12.95 (*0-8018-5514-4*) Johns Hopkins.

Barrett, Christopher B. & Dorosh, Paul A. Rice Prices & Farmers' Welfare in Madagascar: A Non-Parametric Analysis. (Working Papers: No. 73). 31p. (C). 1996. pap. 7.00 (*1-56401-173-9*) Cornell Food.

Barrett, Cleveland S. Can You Hear My Echo - The Ghetto Poet Hulk. (Orig.). 1997. pap. write for info. (*1-57553-524-6*) Watermrk Pr.

Barrett, Clive. The Egyptian Gods & Goddesses: The Mythology & Beliefs of Ancient Egypt. (Illus.). 174p. 1998. pap. text 19.00 (*0-7881-5533-4*) DIANE Pub.

— Viking Gods. 1989. 22.95 (*0-85030-775-9*, Pub. by Aqm Pr) Harper SF.

Barrett, Colin. Manager's Guide to Freight Loss & Damage Claims. Hunter, Ann A., ed. (Illus.). 232p. (C). 1989. text 37.50 (*0-87408-048-7*) Loft Pr.

***Barrett, Colin.** Manager's Guide to Freight Loss & Damage Claims. 2nd ed. (Illus.). 300p. 2000. write for info. (*1-893846-52-0*) Loft Pr.

Barrett, Colin. Transportation Questions & Answers, Vol. 30. 400p. 1991. 59.95 (*0-9630797-0-0*) Loft Pr.

Barrett, Cook-Fuller. Nutrition 94 & 95. 6th ed. 1993. 12.74 (*1-56134-256-4*) McGraw.

Barrett, Cyril, ed. see Wittgenstein, Ludwig Josef Johann.

Barrett, D. Listen to the Silence. 1990. pap. 10.75 (*0-89084-749-5*, 047662) Bob Jones Univ.

Barrett, D., ed. see Gordon, Douglas H.

Barrett, Dan. Essential Java Script for Web Professionals. LC 99-16801. (Essential Series for Web Professionals Ser.). 208p. 1999. pap. text 29.99 (*0-13-013056-7*) P-H.

Barrett, Daniel. T. W. Robertson & the Prince of Wales's Theatre. LC 93-21442. (AUS XXVI: Vol. 23). XXI, 279p. (C). 1995. text 49.95 (*0-8204-2369-6*) P Lang Pubng.

Barrett, Daniel, Jr. & Barrett, Marcella L. I Got Your Fax Covered! LC 90-84166. (Illus.). 58p. 1990. 10.95 (*0-9627855-0-4*) Barrett OH.

Barrett, Daniel & Peel, Val. Business Journals at SRIS. (Key to British Library Holdings Ser.). 264p. 1996. pap. 59.95 (*0-7123-0827-X*, Pub. by SRIS) L Erlbaum Assocs.

Barrett, Daniel J. NetResearch: Finding Information Online. 200p. 1997. pap. 24.95 (*1-56592-245-X*) Thomson Learn.

***Barrett, David.** Basic Harmonica Method. 24p. 1998. pap. 9.95 incl. audio compact disk (*0-7866-2888-X*, 96699BCD) Mel Bay.

— Blues Harp. 32p. 1997. pap. 0.95 (*0-7866-2455-8*, 96290) Mel Bay.

— Blues Harp Classics: Beginning Level. 32p. 1997. pap. 0.95 (*0-7866-2501-5*, 96319) Mel Bay.

Barrett, David. Building Harmonica Technique. 80p. 1997. 17.95 incl. audio compact disk (*0-7866-2779-4*, 95167BCD) Mel Bay.

Barrett, David. Complete Classic Chicago Blues Harp CD Package. 144p. 1995. pap. 29.95 incl. cd-rom (*0-7866-0900-1*, 95452COP); pap. 17.95 (*0-7866-0531-6*, 95452) Mel Bay.

— Masters of the Chicago Blues Harp. 88p. 1997. pap. 14.95 (*0-7866-2884-7*, 96476) Mel Bay.

Barrett, David. Secret Societies: From the Ancient & Arcane to the Modern & Clandestine. LC 98-111022. (Illus.). 264p. 1998. 27.95 (*0-7137-2647-4*, Pub. by Blandford Pr) Sterling.

Barrett, David, jt. auth. see Barkow, Al.

Barrett, David, tr. see Aristophanes.

Barrett, David, tr. see Horton, Walter & Bell, Carey.

Barrett, David B. Application of Pharmaceutical Cgmps. LC 98-206164. x, 198p. 1997. 149.00 (*1-885259-50-6*) Food & Drug Law.

***Barrett, David B., et al.** World Christian Encyclopedia: A Comparative Survey of Churches & Religions AD 30-AD 2200. 2nd ed. LC 99-57323. 2000. write for info. (*0-19-510318-1*); write for info. (*0-19-510319-X*); write for info. (*0-19-510320-3*) OUP.

Barrett, David B., et al, eds. World Christian Encyclopedia: A Comparative Survey of Churches & Religions, AD 30 - AD 2200, 3 vols. 2nd ed. LC 99-57323. (Illus.). 2384p. 2000. text 395.00 (*0-19-507963-9*) OUP.

Barrett, David D. Dixie Mission: The United States Army Observer Group in Yenan, 1944. (China Research Monographs: No. 6). (Illus.). 92p. 1970. pap. 4.00 (*0-912966-07-6*) IEAS.

Barrett, David E. & Frank, Deborah A. The Effects of Undernutrition on Children's Behavior. (Food & Nutrition in History & Anthropology Ser.: Vol. 6). xxvi, 348p. 1987. text 157.00 (*2-88124-190-5*) Gordon & Breach.

***Barrett, David M.** Mayo Clinic on Prostate Health. (Mayo Clinic on Health Ser.). 188p. 2000. pap. 14.95 (*1-893005-03-8*) Mayo Fndtn Med Ed & Res.

Barrett, David M. Uncertain Warriors: Lyndon Johnson & His Vietnam Advisers. LC 93-15654. 284p. 1994. pap. 15.95 (*0-7006-0631-9*) U Pr of KS.

Barrett, David M., ed. Lyndon B. Johnson's Vietnam Papers: A Documentary Collection. LC 96-37250. 896p. (C). 1997. text 99.95 (*0-89096-741-5*) Tex A&M Univ Pr.

***Barrett, David M., ed.** Mayo Clinic on Prostate Disease. 2000. pap. 14.95 (*1-57566-541-7*, Knsington) Kensgtn Pub Corp.

***Barrett, David P. & Shyu, Lawrence N.** Chinese Collaboration with Japan, 1932-1945: The Limits of Accomodation. LC 00-39486. 2000. write for info. (*0-8047-3768-1*) Stanford U Pr.

Barrett, David P., jt. auth. see Comfort, Philip W.

Barrett, David S., jt. auth. see Lavy, Christopher.

Barrett, David V. The Dream Record Book. (Illus.). 64p. 1998. 17.95 (*0-7894-2075-9*) DK Pub Inc.

— Dreams. LC 95-11678. (Predictions Library). (Illus.). 56p. 1995. 8.95 (*0-7894-0309-9*, 6-70515) DK Pub Inc.

— Graphology. LC 95-11681. (Predictions Library). (Illus.). 56p. 1995. 8.95 (*0-7894-0308-0*, 6-70514) DK Pub Inc.

— Numerology. LC 95-11680. (Predictions Library). (Illus.). 56p. 1995. 8.95 (*0-7894-0307-2*, 6-70513) DK Pub Inc.

— Palmistry. LC 95-11682. (Predictions Library). (Illus.). 56p. 1995. 8.95 (*0-7894-0311-0*, 6-70517) DK Pub Inc.

— Runes. LC 95-11679. (The Predictions Library). (Illus.). 56p. 1995. 8.95 (*0-7894-0310-2*, 6-70516) DK Pub Inc.

— Secret Societies. 1999. pap. 14.95 (*0-7137-2772-1*, Pub. by Blandford Pr) Sterling.

— Sects, 'Cults' & Alternative Religions: A World Survey & Sourcebook. (Illus.). 272p. pap. 19.95 (*0-7137-2756-X*, Pub. by Blandford Pr) Sterling.

— Sects, 'Cults' & Alternative Religions: A World Survey & Sourcebook. LC 97-124907. (Illus.). 272p. 1997. 27.95 (*0-7137-2567-2*, Pub. by Blandford Pr) Sterling.

— Tarot. LC 95-11682. (Predictions Library). (Illus.). 56p. 1995. 8.95 (*0-7894-0306-4*, 6-70512) DK Pub Inc.

Barrett, Dean. Hangman's Point. LC 97-97142. 544p. 1998. 24.95 (*0-9661899-1-4*) Village East.

— Kingdom of Make-Believe. LC 98-87830. 344p. 1999. pap. 11.95 (*0-9661899-0-6*) Village East.

— Memoirs of a Bangkok Warrior: Thailand Only Yesterday. LC 98-87832. 320p. 1999. pap. 11.95 (*0-9661899-2-2*) Village East.

***Barrett, Deidere.** The Committee of Sleep: Dreams & Creative Problem-Solving. 2001. 24.00 (*0-8129-3241-2*, Times Bks) Crown Pub Group.

Barrett, Deirdre. The Pregnant Man. 2nd ed. 256p. 1999. pap. 13.00 (*0-8129-2906-3*, Times Bks) Crown Pub Group.

— The Pregnant Man: Cases from a Hypnotherapist's Couch. LC 97-46345. 256p. 1998. 23.00 (*0-8129-2905-5*, Times Bks) Crown Pub Group.

Barrett, Deirdre, ed. Trauma & Dreams. LC 96-13023. 288p. 1996. 37.95 (*0-674-90552-0*) HUP.

Barrett, Derm. Claves de la TQM: Una Guia Concisa Para Directivos. (ENG & SPA.). 199p. 1995. pap. 20.00 (*84-87022-19-7*) Productivity Inc.

— Fast Focus on TQM: A Concise Guide to Companywide Learning. LC 93-50864. (Illus.). 200p. 1994. reprint ed. 20.00 (*1-56327-049-8*) Productivity Inc.

Barrett, Don, et al. A Map History of the Ancient World. 1988. pap. text 19.44 (*0-582-66350-4*, 74671) Longman.

Barrett, Donald N., ed. Values in America. LC 61-14877. 192p. 1967. reprint ed. pap. 59.60 (*0-608-00893-1*, 206168700010) Bks Demand.

Barrett, Dorothea. Vocation & Desire: George Eliot's Heroines. 208p. 1989. 35.00 (*0-415-00979-0*, A3453) Routledge.

Barrett, Dorothea, ed. & intro. see Eliot, George, pseud.

Barrett, E. C., ed. The First WetNet Precipitation Intercomparison Project, PIP-1, Vol. 11. 374p. 1994. pap. text 85.00 (*3-7186-5690-6*, Harwood Acad Pubs) Gordon & Breach.

— Remote Sensing for Hazard Monitoring & Disaster Assessment: Marine & Coastal Applications, Vol. 2. (Current Topics in Remote Sensing Ser.). xii, 240p. 1991. text 160.00 (*2-88124-809-8*) Gordon & Breach.

Barrett, E. C., et al, eds. Satellite Remote Sensing for Hydrology & Water Management: The Mediterranean Coasts & Islands, Vol. 1. xiv, 322p. 1990. text 283.00 (*2-88124-732-6*) Gordon & Breach.

Barrett, E. Thorpe. Write Your Own Business Contracts: What Your Attorney Won't Tell You. 2nd ed. (Illus.). 340p. 1994. pap. 24.95 (*1-55571-170-7*) PSI Resch.

***Barrett, E. Thorpe.** Write Your Own Business Contracts: What Your Attorney Won't Tell You. 3rd ed. 315p. 2000. pap. 24.95 (*1-55571-487-0*, Pub. by PSI Resch) Midpt Trade.

Barrett, Eaton S. The Heroine: or Adventures of a Fair Romance Reader, 3 vols., 1 bk. LC 79-8233. reprint ed. 44.50 (*0-404-61775-1*) AMS Pr.

Barrett, Ed, jt. auth. see Terra, Joseph.

Barrett, Edith J., jt. auth. see Cook, Fay L.

Barrett, Edna L. Who's Who in California. 24th ed. 1995. lib. bdg. 195.00 (*1-880142-03-1*) Gibralter Pub.

— Who's Who in California. 25th ed. 1995. lib. bdg. 205.00 (*1-880142-04-X*) Gibralter Pub.

— Who's Who in California. 26th ed. 503p. 1996. lib. bdg. 205.00 (*1-880142-05-8*) Gibralter Pub.

— Who's Who in California, 1998-1999. 550p. 1998. text 215.00 (*1-880142-06-6*) Gibralter Pub.

Barrett, Edna L., ed. Who's Who in California. 23rd ed. 1994. lib. bdg. 195.00 (*1-880142-02-3*) Gibralter Pub.

Barrett, Edward. Common Preludes. 72p. (Orig.). 1994. pap. 10.00 (*0-922792-67-4*) GP Hudson NY.

Barrett, Edward, ed. The Society of Text: Hypertext, Hypermedia, & the Social Construction of Information. (Illus.). 479p. 1991. reprint ed. pap. text 29.00 (*0-262-52161-X*) MIT Pr.

— Sociomedia: Multimedia, Hypermedia & the Social Construction of Knowledge. 600p. 1994. pap. text 30.00 (*0-262-52193-8*) MIT Pr.

— Text, Context, & Hypertext: Writing with & for the Computer. (Information Systems Ser.). 250p. 1988. 55.00 (*0-262-02275-3*) MIT Pr.

Barrett, Edward & Redmond, Marie, eds. Contextual Media: Multimedia & Interpretation. (Technical Communication, Multimedia & Information Systems Ser.). 300p. 1995. 38.50 (*0-262-02383-0*) MIT Pr.

— Contextual Media, Multimedia & Interpretation. (Technical Communication, Multimedia & Information Systems Ser.). (Illus.). 280p. 1997. reprint ed. pap. text 18.00 (*0-262-52239-X*) MIT Pr.

Barrett, Eileen & Cramer, Patricia. Virginia Woolf: Lesbian Readings. LC 97-4667. (Cutting Edge Ser.). 1997. text 55.00 (*0-8147-1263-0*); pap. text 19.50 (*0-8147-1264-9*) NYU Pr.

Barrett, Eileen & Cramer, Patricia, eds. Reading, Re: Writing, Re: Teaching Virginia Woolf Vol. 4: Selected Papers from the Fourth Annual Conference on Virginia Woolf. (Illus.). 320p. (C). 1995. pap. 39.50 (*0-944473-23-7*) Pace Univ Pr.

Barrett, Eileen & Cullinan, Mary. American Women Writers: Diverse Voices in Prose since 1845. LC 90-71610. 776p. (Orig.). (C). 1992. pap. text 36.95 (*0-312-04121-7*) St Martin.

Barrett, Eileen & Cullinan, Mary, eds. American Women Writers. LC 90-71610. 1280p. 1992. text 49.95 (*0-312-06556-6*) St Martin.

Barrett, Eileen, jt. ed. see Daugherty, Beth R.

Barrett, Elizabeth, jt. auth. see Bovard, Victoria.

Barrett, Elizabeth A., ed. Visions of Rogers's Science-Based Nursing. 432p. 1990. 30.95 (*0-88737-447-6*) Natl League Nurse.

Barrett, Elizabeth A., jt. ed. see Malinski, Violet M.

Barrett, Elizabeth A. Manhart, see Madrid, Mary & Manhart Barrett, Elizabeth A., eds.

Barrett, Elizabeth B. & Haydon, Benjamin R. Invisible Friends: The Correspondence of Elizabeth Barrett Barrett & Benjamin Robert Haydon, 1842-1845. Pope, Willard B., ed. LC 72-80659. (Illus.). 220p. 1972. 20.00 (*0-674-46586-5*) HUP.

Barrett, Elizabeth K., jt. auth. see Haskell, Simon H.

***Barrett, Ellen.** Baja California, 1535-1956. xx, 285p. 1999. reprint ed. 65.00 (*1-57898-150-6*) Martino Pubng.

Barrett, Eric, ed. Storm: Using RS for Improved Monitoring & Prediction of Heavy Rainfall & Related Events. (Remote Sensing Reviews Ser.). 284p. 1996. pap. text 34.00 (*90-5702-101-3*, Harwood Acad Pubs) Gordon & Breach.

***Barrett, Eric & Barrett, Gillian.** Ruth Petrovna - Reaching Russians: The Inspiring Story of Lifelong Missionary Ruth Deyneka Shala. (Illus.). 272p. 1998. pap. write for info. (*1-56773-002-7*) Slavic Gospel.

***Barrett, Eric C. & Curtis, Leonard F.** Introduction to Environmental Remote Sensing. 4th ed. (Illus.). 432p. 1999. pap. 44.95 (*0-7487-4006-6*) Standard Pub.

Barrett, Eric C. & Fisher, David. Scientists Who Believe. mass mkt. 5.99 (*0-8024-7634-1*, 279) Moody.

Barrett, Erin, jt. auth. see Mingo, Jack.

Barrett, Ethel. Storytelling, It's Easy. 1965. pap. 7.99 (*0-310-20561-1*, 6832P) Zondervan.

***Barrett, Ethel, as told by.** The War for Mansoul. rev. ed. Orig. Title: Chronicles of Mansoul. 196p. 1998. 6.95 (*0-87813-961-3*) Christian Light.

Barrett, Everard. Mathematics Power Learning for Children, 3 vols., Bk. I. 1993. pap. text, teacher ed. write for info. (*1-883324-01-7*) Prof B Ent.

— Mathematics Power Learning for Children, 3 vols., Bk. II. 1993. pap. text, teacher ed. write for info. (*1-883324-02-5*) Prof B Ent.

— Mathematics Power Learning for Children, 3 vols., Bk. III. 1993. pap. text, teacher ed. write for info. (*1-883324-03-3*) Prof B Ent.

— Mathematics Power Learning for Children, 3 vols., Set. 1993. pap. text, teacher ed. write for info. (*1-883324-00-9*) Prof B Ent.

Barrett, Fran, et al. Management Without Precedent: Readings to Strengthen Community-Based Organizations. 2nd rev. ed. Community Resource Exchange Staff, ed. (Illus.). 286p. 1995. pap. 29.95 (*0-9655305-0-7*) Commun Res Exchange.

***Barrett, Francis.** The Magus: A Complete System of Occult Philosophy. fac. ed. LC 99-49429. (Illus.). 432p. 2000. pap. 19.95 (*0-87728-942-5*) Weiser.

— The Magus: A Complete System of Occult Philosophy. limited ed. LC 99-49429. 432p. 2000. 85.00 (*0-87728-943-3*) Weiser.

Barrett, Francis. The Magus: A Complete System of Occult Philosophy. 228p. 1975. reprint ed. pap. 18.95 (*0-8065-0462-5*, Citadel Pr) Carol Pub Group.

Barrett, Francis, ed. The Secret Book of Artephius. 1984. reprint ed. pap. 4.95 (*0-916411-28-1*) Holmes Pub.

Barrett, Francis, ed. see Freher, Dionysius.

Barrett, Frank. Illustrated Buyers Guide: Mercedes. 2nd ed. LC 98-14353. (Illustrated Buyer's Guide Ser.). (Illus.). 208p. 1998. pap. 17.95 (*0-7603-0451-3*) MBI Pubg.

— Illustrated Mercedes-Benz Buyer's Guide. 2nd ed. (Illustrated Buyer's Guide Ser.). (Illus.). 192p. 1994. pap. text 17.95 (*0-87938-902-8*) MBI Pubg.

Barrett, Frank J., Jr. Hanover. LC 97-199065. (Images of America Ser.). 1997. pap. 16.99 (*0-7524-0571-3*) Arcadia Publng.

— Hanover, Vol. II. (Images of America Ser.). (Illus.). 128p. 1998. pap. 16.99 (*0-7524-1272-8*) Arcadia Publng.

Barrett, Fred. Names That Sell: How to Create Great Names for Your Company, Product, or Service. LC 94-79374. 224p. (Orig.). 1995. pap. 14.95 (*0-9636614-7-7*) Alder Pr OR.

— Sea-Mountain: Cascade Head-Salmon River Anthology. The Oregon Coast. LC 93-71456. (Illus.). 108p. 1993. pap. 19.95 (*0-9636614-8-5*) Alder Pr OR.

Barrett, G. C. & Elmore, D. T. Amino Acids & Peptides. LC 97-31093. (Illus.). 250p. (C). 1998. 80.00 (*0-521-46292-4*); pap. 34.95 (*0-521-46827-2*) Cambridge U Pr.

Barrett, G. Vincent & Blair, John P. How to Conduct & Analyze Real Estate Market & Feasability Studies. 3rd ed. (C). 2001. 56.00 (*0-13-231028-7*, Macmillan Coll) P-H.

Barrett, Gary W. & Peles, John D., eds. Landscape Ecology of Small Mammals. LC 98-37571. (Illus.). 304p. 1999. 74.95 (*0-387-98646-4*) Spr-Verlag.

Barrett, Gary W. & Rosenberg, Rutger, eds. Stress Effects on Natural Ecosystems. LC 80-40851. (Environmental Monographs & Symposia). 323p. reprint ed. pap. 100.20 (*0-7837-3222-8*, 204323900007) Bks Demand.

Barrett, Gene, jt. auth. see Apostle, Richard.

Barrett, Gillian, jt. auth. see Barrett, Eric.

Barrett, Glen, ed. see Anderson, John C.

Barrett, Gloria. Statistics with the TI-83. Nichols, Steve, ed. (Illus.). 202p. (J). (gr. 11 up). 1997. pap. text 25.00 (*1-887050-31-0*) Meridian Creative.

***Barrett, Graham C., ed.** Amino Acid Derivatives. LC 99-39045. (The Practical Approach in Chemistry Ser.). (Illus.). 288p. 2000. text 130.00 (*0-19-855853-8*) OUP.

Barrett, Gregory. Archetypes in Japanese Film: The Sociopolitical & Religious Significance of the Principal Heroes & Heroines. LC 87-43126. (Illus.). 256p. 1989. 50.00 (*0-941664-93-7*) Susquehanna U Pr.

***Barrett, Gregory.** Tutu. (Illus.). 160p. 2000. 34.95 (*1-86508-083-7*, Pub. by Allen & Unwin Pty) IPG Chicago.

Barrett, H. H. & Gmitro, A. F., eds. Information Processing in Medical Imaging: Proceedings of the 13th International Conference, IPMI '93, Flagstaff, Arizona, USA, June 14-18, 1993. (Lecture Notes in Computer Science Ser.: Vol. 687). xvi, 567p. 1993. 79.95 (*0-387-56800-X*) Spr-Verlag.

Barrett, H. H. & Swindell, William. Radiological Imaging: The Theory of Formation & Detection & Processing, Vol. 2. LC 80-69416. (Biophysics & Bioengineering Ser.). 1981. text 135.00 (*0-12-079602-3*) Acad Pr.

Barrett, Harold. Maintaining the Self in Communication: Concept & Guidebook. LC 97-72960. xiii, 305p. (Orig.). 1998. pap. text 19.95 (*0-9658440-5-6*) Alpha & Omega.

— Practical Uses of Speech Communication. 6th ed. 320p. (C). 1987. pap. text 23.50 (*0-03-003272-5*) Harcourt Coll Pubs.

— Rhetoric & Civility: Human Development, Narcissism, & the Good Audience. LC 90-32467. (SUNY Series in Speech Communication). 202p. (C). 1991. pap. text 21.95 (*0-7914-0484-6*) State U NY Pr.

— The Sophists: Rhetoric, Democracy, & Plato's Idea of Sophistry. LC 87-21051. 96p. (Orig.). (C). 1987. pap. text 7.95 (*0-88316-557-0*) Chandler & Sharp.

Barrett, Henry. The Viola: Complete Guide for Teachers & Students. 2nd ed. LC 70-169498. 232p. 1996. pap. text 29.95 (*0-8173-0885-7*) U of Ala Pr.

Barrett-Hirschhaut, Jaclyn. 1000 Questions about Your Wedding. LC 97-33878. 470p. 1997. pap. 16.99 (*1-56530-266-4*, Pub. by Summit TX) BookWorld.

Barrett, Hugh. Early to Rise. 168p. 1994. pap. 12.95 (*0-85236-273-0*, Pub. by Farming Pr) Diamond Farm Bk.

***Barrett, Hugh.** Early to Rise. large type unabridged ed. 164p. 1999. 23.95 (*0-7531-5078-6*, 150786, Pub. by ISIS Lrg Prnt) ISIS Pub.

Barrett, Irwin. Wilderness Nova Scotia: A Photographer's Journal. LC 99-159132. (Illus.). 1998. 29.95 (*1-55109-141-0*) Nimbus Publ.

Barrett, Ivan J. Heroic Mormon Women. 1991. 11.95 (*1-55503-323-7*, 01924) Covenant Comms.

— Joseph Smith & the Restoration: A History of the LDS Church to 1846. 2nd rev. ed. LC 70-167990. (Illus.). ix, 677p. 1973. pap. text 16.95 (*0-8425-0672-1*, Friends of the Library) Brigham.

Barrett, J. Economic Issues in Trypanosomiasis Control. 183p. 1997. pap. 90.00 (*0-85954-483-4*, Pub. by Nat Res Inst) St Mut.

Barrett, J., jt. auth. see Golding, D. N.

Barrett, J. Carl, ed. Mechanisms of Environmental Carcinogenesis, 2 vols., Set. 352p. 1987. 274.00 (*0-8493-4670-3*, RC268) CRC Pr.

Barrett, J. Carl & Tennant, Raymond W., eds. Mammalian Cell Transformation: Mechanisms of Carcinogenesis & Assays for Carcinogens. LC 85-14616. (Carcinogenesis - A Comprehensive Survey Ser.: No. 9). (Illus.). 479p. 1985. reprint ed. pap. 148.50 (*0-608-00674-2*, 206126100007) Bks Demand.

Barrett, J. E., et al, eds. Advances in Behavioral Pharmacology, Vol. 7. 216p. (C). 1989. text 59.95 (*0-8058-0351-3*) L Erlbaum Assocs.

An Asterisk (*) at the beginning of an entry indicates that the title is appearing for the first time.

Barrett, J. Edward. Faith in Focus: A Compact Introduction to Christian Theology - Intermediate Level. 2nd enl. rev. ed. LC 89-36107. 150p. (C). 1989. pap. text 19.50 (*0-8191-7548-X*) U Pr of Amer.

Barrett, J. Lee. Speedboat Kings. (Michigan Heritage Library: Vol. 4). 145p. 1986. reprint ed. 20.00 (*0-915056-21-6*) Hardscrabble Bks.

Barrett, J. May, jt. auth. see Fang, Jing P.

Barrett, J. May, ed. see Addiss, Stephen, et al.

Barrett, J. May Lee, ed. see Krahl, Regina.

Barrett, J. O. The Book of Revelation: Missionary Message of the New Testament. 123p. 1947. reprint ed. 4.50 (*0-87921-005-2*) Attic Pr.

Barrett, Jack. Introduction to Atomic & Molecular Structure. LC 74-93558. 343p. reprint ed. pap. 106.40 (*0-608-15891-7*, 203078600074) Bks Demand.

Barrett, Jack & Malati, Mournir A. Fundamentals of Inorganic Chemistry: An Introductory Text for Degree Course Studies. 320p. 1997. pap. 29.95 (*1-85816-638-1*, Pub. by Horwood Pub); pap. 29.95 (*0-85816-338-1*, Pub. by Horwood Pub) Paul & Co Pubs.

Barrett, Jalma. Bobcat. LC 98-9878. (Wildcats of North America Ser.). (Illus.). 24p. (J). (gr. 3-5). 1998. lib. bdg. 16.95 (*1-56711-257-9*) Blackbirch.

— Cougar. LC 98-9876. (Wildcats of North America Ser.). (Illus.). 24p. (J). (gr. 3-5). 1998. lib. bdg. 16.95 (*1-56711-258-7*) Blackbirch.

***Barrett, Jalma.** Coyote. LC 99-40287. (Wild Canines! Ser.). (Illus.). 24p. (J). (gr. 3-5). 2000. lib. bdg. 16.95 (*1-56711-261-7*) Blackbirch.

Barrett, Jalma. Feral Cats. LC 98-3429. (Wildcats of North America Ser.). (Illus.). 24p. (J). (gr. 3-5). 1998. lib. bdg. 16.95 (*1-56711-260-9*) Blackbirch.

***Barrett, Jalma.** Foxes. LC 99-32641. (Wild Canines! Ser.). 24p. (J). (gr. 3-5). 2000. lib. bdg. 16.95 (*1-56711-263-3*) Blackbirch.

Barrett, Jalma. Lynx. LC 98-9881. (Wildcats of North America Ser.). (Illus.). 24p. (J). (gr. 3-5). 1998. lib. bdg. 16.95 (*1-56711-259-5*) Blackbirch.

***Barrett, Jalma.** Wolf. LC 99-32649. (Wild Canines! Ser.). 24p. (J). (gr. 3-5). 2000. lib. bdg. 16.95 (*1-56711-262-5*) Blackbirch.

Barrett, James E. The Hymnary II: A Table For Service Planning. 2nd ed. 96p. 1987. ring bd. 14.50 (*0-942466-11-X*); ring bd. 18.00 (*0-942466-12-8*) Hymnary Pr.

— The Psalmnary: Gradual Psalms for Cantor & Congregation. 196p. 1982. ring bd. 26.00 (*0-942466-04-7*); ring bd. 23.00 (*0-942466-03-9*) Hymnary Pr.

Barrett, James E., ed. The Daily Lectionary. 70p. 1982. pap. 2.45 (*0-942466-02-0*) Hymnary Pr.

— The Hymnary: A Table for Service Planning. 95p. 1979. ring bd. 17.00 (*0-942466-01-2*); ring bd. 13.50 (*0-942466-00-4*) Hymnary Pr.

Barrett, James E., ed. see American Psychopathological Association Staff.

Barrett, James E., jt. ed. see Carroll, Bernard J.

Barrett, James E., jt. ed. see Clayton, Paula J.

Barrett, James E., jt. ed. see Robins, Lee N.

Barrett, James E., jt. ed. see Rose, Robert M.

Barrett, James E., ed. & intro. see Hall, Linda B.

Barrett, James P. The Endangered Forests. 160p. (C). 1996. 26.95 (*0-7872-2434-0*) Kendall-Hunt.

Barrett, James R. William Z. Foster & the Tragedy of American Radicalism. LC 99-6192. (Working Class in American History Ser.). (Illus.). 392p. 1999. 34.95 (*0-252-02046-4*) U of Ill Pr.

— Work & Community in the Jungle: Chicago's Packinghouse Workers, 1894-1922. LC 86-19127. (Working Class in American History Ser.). (Illus.). 328p. 1987. text 29.95 (*0-252-01378-6*); pap. text 15.95 (*0-252-06136-5*) U of Ill Pr.

Barrett, James T. Microbiology & Immunology Casebook. LC 95-13078. 272p. 1995. pap. text 19.95 (*0-316-08132-9*) Lppncott W & W.

— Textbook of Immunology: International Edition. 5th ed. (Illus.). 496p. (C). (gr. 13). 1987. text 23.00 (*0-8016-0406-0*, 00406) Mosby Inc.

Barrett, James W., ed. End of 'The World' LC 72-117866. (Select Bibliographies Reprint Ser.). 1977. 26.95 (*0-8369-5319-3*) Ayer.

Barrett, Jane. Human Anatomy & Physics II (Bio 1414) (C). 1997. pap. text 7.95 (*1-56870-257-4*) RonJon Pub.

Barrett, Janet R., et al. Sound Ways of Knowing: Enhancing the Curriculum Through Music. LC 97-19813. 375p. (C). 1997. 35.00 (*0-02-864530-8*, Schirmer Books) Mac Lib Ref.

Barrett, Jay A. Evolution of the Ordinance of Seventeen Eighty-Seven with an Account of the Earlier Plans for the Government of the Northwest Territory. LC 79-146372. (First American Frontier Ser.). (Illus.). 1975. reprint ed. 23.95 (*0-405-02823-7*) Ayer.

Barrett, Jean. Archer's Crossing. 400p. 1999. mass mkt. 5.99 (*0-8439-4502-8*) Dorchester Pub Co.

— Fugitive Father. (Intrigue Ser.: Vol. 475). 1998. per. 3.99 (*0-373-22475-3*, 1-22475-7) Harlequin Bks.

— Man of the Midnight Sun. (Intrigue Ser.). 1996. per. 3.75 (*0-373-22384-6*, 1-22384-1) Harlequin Bks.

— My Lover's Secret. 1999. per. 3.99 (*0-373-22528-8*, 1-22528-3) Harlequin Bks.

— Rehenes de un Amor: Held Hostage. (Harlequin Deseo Ser.: No. 214).Tr. of Love Hostage. (SPA.). 1997. per. 3.50 (*0-373-35214-X*, 1-35214-5) Harlequin Bks.

— The Shelter of Her Arms. (Intrigue Ser.). 1995. per. 2.99 (*0-373-22308-0*, 1-22308-0) Harlequin Bks.

— Ward Management & Teaching. 423p. (C). 1989. 75.00 (*81-7002-032-8*, Pub. by Himalayan Bks) St Mut.

Barrett, Jean A. Archery. 3rd ed. (Illus.). 132p. (C). 1991. reprint ed. pap. text 10.50 (*0-88133-537-1*) Waveland Pr.

***Barrett, Jeffrey A.** The Quantum Mechanics of Minds & Worlds. LC 99-28680. 288p. 2000. text 45.00 (*0-19-823838-X*) OUP.

Barrett, Jeffrey W. Impulse to Revolution in Latin America. LC 84-26297. 368p. 1985. 65.00 (*0-275-90058-4*, C0058, Praeger Pubs) Greenwood.

Barrett, Jim. Careers, Aptitude & Selection Tests: Match Your IQ, Personality & Abilities to Your Ideal Career. 160p. 1998. pap. 17.95 (*0-7494-2557-1*) Kogan Page Ltd.

— Quick Guide: Ponds & Fountains. 2nd ed. Tringali, Laura, ed. LC 93-73997. (Quick Guide Ser.). (Illus.). 80p. 1998. pap. 7.95 (*1-880029-29-4*) Creative Homeowner.

— Quick Guide: Storage Sheds. LC 93-71658. (Quick Guide Ser.). (Illus.). 80p. 1996. pap. 7.95 (*1-880029-20-0*) Creative Homeowner.

— Total Leadership. 1998. pap. text 30.00 (*0-7494-2577-6*) Kogan Page Ltd.

— Working with Tile. Kerrigone, Kimberly, ed. LC 92-74900. (Illus.). 176p. 1994. pap. 14.95 (*1-880029-15-4*) Creative Homeowner.

Barrett, Jim & Williams, Geoff. Test Your Own Job Aptitude: Exploring Your Career Potential. rev. ed. 224p. 1992. pap. 12.95 (*0-14-016834-6*, Penguin Bks) Viking Penguin.

Barrett, Jim, ed. see Creative Homeowner Press Editors.

Barrett, Joan & Thompson, Linda. Playing Together, Learning Together. 128p. (Orig.). 1995. pap., teacher ed. 8.95 (*0-673-36160-8*, GoodYrBooks) Addson-Wesley Educ.

Barrett, Joan, ed. see Dionisi, David.

Barrett, Joanne. Cooking with Honey. 1983. pap. 2.95 (*0-88266-276-7*, Garden Way Pub) Storey Bks.

Barrett, Joanne, jt. auth. see Long, Ron.

Barrett, John. Bible Stories. (Illus.). 32p. (J). (gr. k-4). 1992. pap. 19.95 (*1-882954-04-1*) Aspen Press.

— Daniel Discovers Daniel. LC 79-17897. (Illus.). 32p. (J). (gr. k-5). 1980. 16.95 (*0-87705-423-1*, Kluwer Acad Hman Sci) Kluwer Academic.

— The Day the Toys Came to Silver Dollar City. (City Stories Ser.). (Illus.). (J). (gr. k-10). 1978. 1.99 (*0-686-22891-X*) Silver Dollar.

— Fecal Seeds in Space Plus Two Bonus Tracks: A Collection of Three Novellas by John Danielle Barrett II. (Illus.). 246p. 1999. pap. 10.00 (*0-9669255-0-5*) Fist Full.

— The Littlest Mule. Silver Dollar City, Inc. Staff, ed. (City Stories Ser.). (Illus.). (J). (ps-5). 1977. 2.99 (*0-686-19125-0*) Silver Dollar.

***Barrett, John.** World of Tennis 2000. 2000. pap. 22.95 (*0-00-218946-1*, Pub. by HarpC) Trafalgar.

Barrett, John. Zeke Hatfield & a Ghost Named Rocky. (City Stories Ser.). (Illus.). (J). (gr. k-10). 1978. 1.99 (*0-686-22892-8*) Silver Dollar.

Barrett, John, ed. Connecticut Walk Book: 18th Edition. 18th ed. (Illus.). 1997. 18.00 (*0-9619052-4-7*) CT Forest & Pk Assn.

Barrett, John, et al, eds. Papers on the Prehistoric Archaeology of Cranborne Chase. (Oxbow Monographs in Archaeology: No. 11). (Illus.). 251p. 1991. pap. 42.00 (*0-946897-31-X*, Pub. by Oxbow Bks) David Brown.

Barrett, John & Iredale, David. Discovering Old Handwriting. (Handbook Ser.: No. 285). (Illus.). 184p. 1995. pap. 12.50 (*0-7478-0268-8*, Pub. by Shire Pubns) Parkwest Pubns.

Barrett, John & Nyhus, Lloyd M. Treatment of Shock: Principles & Practice. 2nd ed. LC 85-18170. 254p. reprint ed. pap. 78.80 (*0-7837-2690-2*, 204306800006) Bks Demand.

Barrett, John, jt. auth. see Iredale, David.

Barrett, John, jt. auth. see MacLiammoir, Michael.

Barrett, John, tr. see Weil, Grete.

Barrett, John A., ed. Environmental Issues in Insolvency Proceedings. LC 97-49419. xv, 211p. 1998. pap. text 79.00 (*90-411-0722-3*) Kluwer Law Intl.

Barrett, John A., jt. auth. see Klotz, James M.

Barrett, John C. Some Challenges in Contemporary Archaeology. (Oxbow Lectures: No. 2). 12p. 1995. pap. 5.30 (*0-946897-98-0*, Pub. by Oxbow Bks) David Brown.

***Barrett, John E.** Babies! (CTW Sesame Street Elmo's World Ser.). (Illus.). 12p. (J). (ps). 2000. bds. 4.99 (*0-375-80572-9*, Pub. by Random Bks Yng Read) Random.

— Balls! (Sesame Street Elmo's World Ser.). (Illus.). 12p. (J). (ps). 2000. bds. 4.99 (*0-375-80574-5*, Pub. by Random Bks Yng Read) Random.

— Food! (Sesame Street Elmo's World Ser.). 12p. (J). 2000. bds. 4.99 (*0-375-80573-7*, Pub. by Random Bks Yng Read) Random.

— Puppies! (Sesame Street Elmo's World Ser.). (Illus.). 12p. (J). (ps). 2000. bds. 4.99 (*0-375-80575-3*, Pub. by Random Bks Yng Read) Random.

— Too Big for Bottles. (Illus.). 12p. (J). (ps-k). 2000. 3.99 (*0-375-81044-7*) Random.

— Too Big for Diapers. (Illus.). 12p. (J). (ps-k). 2000. 3.99 (*0-375-81045-5*) Random.

Barrett, John E., photos by. Big Bird Is Yellow: A Sesame Street Book of Colors. LC 89-63996. (Board Bks.). (Illus.). 14p. (J). (ps). 1990. 4.99 (*0-679-80752-7*, Pub. by Random Bks Yng Read) Random.

Barrett, John E. & View-Master International Staff, photos by. Big Bird's Mother Goose. LC 83-63404. (Chunky Bks. Ser.). (Illus.). 28p. (J). (ps). 1984. 3.99 (*0-394-86745-9*, Pub. by Random Bks Yng Read) Random.

Barrett, John G. The Civil War in North Carolina. LC 63-22810. xi, 484p. 1963. 39.95 (*0-8078-0874-1*) U of NC Pr.

— The Civil War in North Carolina. LC 63-22810. 484p. 1995. pap. 19.95 (*0-8078-4520-5*) U of NC Pr.

— North Carolina As a Civil War Battleground, 1861-1865. (Illus.). 1998. reprint ed. pap. 8.00 (*0-86526-088-5*) NC Archives.

— Sherman's March Through the Carolinas. LC 56-14242. x, 325p. 1996. 34.95 (*0-8078-0701-X*) U of NC Pr.

— Sherman's March Through the Carolinas. LC 56-14242. 335p. (C). 1996. pap. 18.95 (*0-8078-4566-3*) U of NC Pr.

Barrett, John G. & Yearns, W. Buck, eds. North Carolina Civil War Documentary. LC 79-17604. (Illus.). xvi, 365p. 1980. 32.50 (*0-8078-1407-5*) U of NC Pr.

Barrett, John M. It's Hard Not to Worry: Stories for Children about Poverty. (Illus.). (Orig.). (J). (gr. 1-6). 1988. pap. 4.75 (*0-377-00178-3*) Friendship Pr.

— No Time for Me: Learning to Live with Busy Parents. LC 78-21257. (Illus.). 32p. (J). (ps-3). 1985. 16.95 (*0-87705-385-5*, Kluwer Acad Hman Sci) Kluwer Academic.

Barrett, John P. Crow: A Wild Creature. (Illus.). 160p. 1997. 20.00 (*0-9619629-7-6*) Gaff Pr.

— How to Make a Book: An Illustrated Guide to Making Books by Hand. Butterfield, Nancy & Boswell, James, eds. LC 93-26724. (Illus.). 180p. 1993. 17.50 (*0-9619629-3-3*) Gaff Pr.

— I'll Be Home in Half-an-Hour. Butterfield, Nancy & Boswell, James, eds. LC 95-21013. 144p. (Orig.). 1995. pap. 12.50 (*0-9619629-6-8*) Gaff Pr.

— Sea Stories Bk. 2: Seagods & Soundogs. LC 87-82430. (Illus.). 160p. 1991. 15.00 (*0-9619629-1-7*) Gaff Pr.

Barrett, John P. & Wolleson, Fred. Sea Stories: Of Dolphins & Dead Sailors. LC 87-82430. (Illus.). 128p. 1988. 15.00 (*0-9619629-0-9*) Gaff Pr.

Barrett, John S., tr. & afterword by see Von Doderer, Heimito.

Barrett, John W. Regional Silviculture of the United States. 3rd ed. 656p. 1994. 140.00 (*0-471-59817-8*) Wiley.

Barrett, Jon H. Individual Goals & Organizational Objectives: A Study of Integration Mechanisms. LC 77-632403. 123p. reprint ed. pap. 38.20 (*0-7837-5259-8*, 204499600005) Bks Demand.

Barrett, Joyce D. Willie's Not the Hugging Kind. LC 89-1868. (Illus.). 32p. (J). (gr. k-3). 1989. 16.00 (*0-06-020416-8*); lib. bdg. 15.89 (*0-06-020417-6*) HarpC Child Bks.

— Willie's Not the Hugging Kind. LC 89-1868. (Trophy Picture Bk.). (Illus.). 32p. (J). (ps-3). 1991. pap. 5.95 (*0-06-443264-5*, HarpTrophy) HarpC Child Bks.

Barrett, Judi. Animals Should Definitely Not Act Like People. 2nd ed. (J). 1989. 9.15 (*0-606-03712-8*, Pub. by Turtleback) Demco.

Barrett, Judi. Animals Should Definitely Not Wear Clothing. 2nd ed. (J). 1989. 11.19 (*0-606-03713-6*, Pub. by Turtleback) Demco.

Barrett, Judi. Old MacDonald Had an Apartment House. LC 97-17349. (Illus.). 32p. (J). (ps-2). 1998. 16.00 (*0-689-81757-6*) Atheneum Yung Read.

***Barrett, Judi.** Pickles to Pittsburgh. (J). (gr. k-6). 1999. 24.95 incl. audio (*0-87499-538-8*) Live Oak Media.

Barrett, Judi. The Things That Are Most in the World. LC 97-5155. (Illus.). 32p. (J). (ps-3). 1998. lib. bdg. 16.00 (*0-689-81333-3*) Atheneum Yung Read.

***Barrett, Judi.** Which Witch Is Which? LC 99-11710. (Illus.). 2001. 20.01 (*0-689-82940-X*) Atheneum Yung Read.

Barrett, Judi, ed. Animals Should Definitely Not Wear Clothing. (J). (ps-4). 1990. pap. 15.95 incl. audio (*0-87499-146-3*) Live Oak Media.

Barrett, Judith. Los Animales No Se Visten. unabridged ed.Tr. of Animals Should Definely Not Wear Clothes. (SPA., Illus.). (J). (gr. k-3). 1991. pap. 15.95 incl. audio (*0-87499-227-3*) Live Oak Media.

— Los Animales No Se Visten, 4 bks., Set. unabridged ed.Tr. of Animals Should Definely Not Wear Clothes. (SPA., Illus.). (J). (gr. k-3). 1991. teacher ed. 49.95 incl. audio (*0-87499-229-X*) Live Oak Media.

— Animals Should Definitely Not Act Like People. (Illus.). (J). (gr. k-3). 1991. pap. 15.95 incl. audio (*0-87499-230-3*) Live Oak Media.

— Animals Should Definitely Not Act Like People. 2nd ed. (Illus.). 32p. (J). (ps-2). 1988. reprint ed. mass mkt. 3.95 (*0-689-71287-1*) Aladdin.

Barrett, Judith. Animals Should Definitely Not Act Like People, 4 bks., Set. (Illus.). (J). (gr. k-3). pap. 33.95 incl. audio (*0-87499-232-X*) Live Oak Media.

Barrett, Judith. Animals Should Definitely Not Wear Clothing. LC 70-115078. (Illus.). 32p. (J). (ps-2). 1970. text, lib. bdg. 13.95 (*0-689-20592-9*) Atheneum Yung Read.

— Animals Should Definitely Not Wear Clothing. (Illus.). 32p. (J). (gr. k-3). 1990. reprint ed. 24.95 incl. audio (*0-87499-147-1*); reprint ed. pap. 15.95 incl. audio (*0-87488-146-3*) Live Oak Media.

— Animals Should Definitely Not Wear Clothing. 2nd ed. LC 88-7825. (Illus.). 32p. (J). (ps-3). 1988. reprint ed. mass mkt. 5.99 (*0-689-70807-6*) Aladdin.

— Animals Should Definitely Not Wear Clothing, 4 vols., Set. (Illus.). 32p. (J). (gr. k-3). 1990. reprint ed. pap. 33.95 incl. audio (*0-87499-148-X*) Live Oak Media.

— Benjamin's Three Hundred Sixty-Five Birthdays. 2nd ed. LC 92-2497. (Illus.). 40p. (J). (ps-1). 1992. 13.95 (*0-689-31791-3*) Atheneum Yung Read.

— Benjamin's 365 Birthdays. 2nd ed. LC 92-2497. (Illus.). 40p. (J). (ps-1). 1992. reprint ed. pap. 4.95 (*0-689-71635-4*) Aladdin.

— Cloudy with a Chance of Meatballs. LC 87-29643. (Illus.). 32p. (J). (ps-3). 1982. mass mkt. 4.99 (*0-689-70749-5*) Aladdin.

— Cloudy with a Chance of Meatballs. LC 78-2945. (Illus.). 32p. (J). (ps-3). 1978. 16.00 (*0-689-30647-4*) Atheneum Yung Read.

— Cloudy with a Chance of Meatballs. (J). 1982. 10.19 (*0-606-00417-3*, Pub. by Turtleback) Demco.

— Cloudy with a Chance of Meatballs. unabridged ed. (Illus.). (J). (ps-4). 1985. 24.95 incl. audio (*0-941078-93-0*); pap. 15.95 incl. audio (*0-941078-91-4*) Live Oak Media.

— Cloudy with a Chance of Meatballs, 4 bks., Set. unabridged ed. (Illus.). (J). (ps-4). 1985. pap. 33.95 incl. audio (*0-941078-92-2*) Live Oak Media.

— Pasta Verde. 288p. 1998. 16.95 (*0-02-862286-3*) Macmillan.

— Pickles to Pittsburgh: The Sequel to Cloudy with a Chance of Meatballs. LC 95-40510. (Illus.). 32p. (J). (ps-3). 1997. 16.00 (*0-689-80104-1*) Atheneum Yung Read.

— Risotto Risotti. 1996. 25.00 (*0-614-19371-0*) Macmillan.

— Saved By Soup: More Than 100 Delicious Low-Fat Soups To Eat And Enjoy Every Day. LC 98-6421. (Illus.). 192p. 1999. 24.00 (*0-688-15300-3*, Wm Morrow) Morrow Avon.

Barrett, Judith & Wasserman, Norma. Risotto. 336p. 1989. pap. 16.95 (*0-02-030395-5*) Macmillan.

Barrett, Julia, pseud. Presumption: An Entertainment: A Sequel to Pride & Prejudice. large type ed. LC 93-43082. 409p. 1994. lib. bdg. 21.95 (*0-7862-0153-3*) Thorndike Pr.

— The Third Sister: A Continuation of Jane Austen's Sense & Sensibility. (Mira Bks.). 1998. mass mkt. 5.99 (*1-55166-446-1*, 1-66446-5, Mira Bks) Harlequin Bks.

***Barrett, Julia, pseud & Austen, Jane.** Jane Austen's Charlotte: Her Fragment of a Last Novel Completed by Julia Barrett. LC 99-47961. 240p. 2000. 21.95 (*0-87131-908-X*) M Evans.

Barrett, Julia, pseud & Austen, Jane. Presumption: An Entertainment: A Sequel to Pride & Prejudice. LC 93-5778. 240p. 1993. 19.95 (*0-87131-736-2*) M Evans.

— Presumption: An Entertainment: A Sequel to Pride & Prejudice. LC 95-4686. 238p. 1995. reprint ed. pap. 11.95 (*0-226-03813-0*) U Ch Pr.

Barrett, Julie. Quantum Leap: A to Z. 288p. (Orig.). 1995. mass mkt. 5.99 (*1-57297-044-8*) Blvd Books.

Barrett Justis, Suzanne. Dragons Out My Window. LC 98-90072. 264p. 1998. pap. 12.95 (*0-9662936-0-6*, 16412) Weatherly Hall.

Barrett, K. Nightbrood First Contact: Silent Death Races Book. (Silent Death - The Next Millennium Ser.). (Illus.). 60p. 1996. pap. 16.00 (*1-55806-264-5*, 7213) Iron Crown Ent Inc.

Barrett, Karen, et al. Child Development. annot. ed. teacher ed. 58.83 (*0-02-801361-1*) Glencoe.

Barrett, Karen C., et al. Child Development. LC 93-27325. 1993. 53.95 (*0-02-801359-X*) Glencoe.

***Barrett, Karen Lawton.** Hers to Remember. (Intrigue Ser.: Vol. 560). 2000. per. 4.25 (*0-373-22560-1*) Harlequin Bks.

Barrett, Karen Lawton. Promise of Paradise. large type ed. (Black Satin Romance Ser.). 255p. 1997. 27.99 (*1-86110-035-3*) Ulverscroft.

Barrett, Kate R., jt. auth. see Allison, Pamela C.

Barrett, Kate W. Some Practical Suggestions on the Conduct of a Rescue Home: Including Life of Dr. Kate Waller Barrett. LC 74-3928. (Women in America Ser.). Orig. Title: Fifty Years Work with Girls. 186p. 1974. reprint ed. 23.95 (*0-405-06075-0*) Ayer.

Barrett, Katharine. Animals in Action. rev. ed. Bergman, Lincoln & Fairwell, Kay, eds. (Great Explorations in Math & Science (GEMS) Ser.). (Illus.). 64p. (YA). (gr. 5-8). 1991. reprint ed. pap. 10.50 (*0-912511-10-9*, GEMS) Lawrence Science.

***Barrett, Katharine & Willard, Carolyn.** Schoolyard Ecology. Bergman, Lincoln et al, eds. (Great Explorations in Math & Science (GEMS) Ser.). (Illus.). 120p. (J). (gr. 3-6). 1999. pap., teacher ed. 16.00 (*0-924886-35-8*, GEMS) Lawrence Science.

Barrett, Katharine, et al. Aquatic Habitats: Exploring Desktop Ponds. Bergman, Lincoln et al, eds. (Great Explorations in Math & Science (GEMS) Ser.). (Illus.). 136p. (J). (gr. 2-6). 1998. pap. text 16.00 (*0-924886-01-3*, GEMS) Lawrence Science.

— Investigating Artifacts: Making Masks, Creating Myths, Exploring Middens. Bergman, Lincoln et al, eds. (Great Explorations in Math & Science (GEMS) Ser.). (Illus.). 120p. (J). (gr. k-6). 1992. pap. 13.50 (*0-912511-82-6*, GEMS) Lawrence Science.

***Barrett, Katherine.** Investigating Artifacts: Making Masks, Creating Myths, Exploring Middens. 2000. pap. 13.50 (*0-924886-49-8*, GEMS) Lawrence Science.

— Mapping Animal Movements. rev. ed. Bergman, Lincoln & Fairwell, Kay, eds. (Great Explorations in Math & Science (GEMS) Ser.). (Illus.). 56p. (J). 1999. pap. 10.50 (*0-924886-24-2*, GEMS) Lawrence Science.

***Barrett, Katherine & Sneider, Cary I.** Mapping Fish Habitats. rev. ed. Bergman, Lincoln & Fairwell, Kay, eds. (Great Explorations in Math & Science (GEMS) Ser.). (Illus.). 60p. 1999. pap. 10.50 (*0-924886-25-0*, GEMS) Lawrence Science.

***Barrett, Katherine, et al.** Science & Math Explorations for Young Children: A GEMS/PEACHES Handbook for Early Childhood Educators, Childcare Providers & Parents. Bergman, Lincoln et al, eds. (Great Explorations in Math & Science (GEMS) Ser.). (Illus.). 80p. 1999. pap., teacher ed. 15.00 (*0-924886-30-7*, GEMS) Lawrence Science.

Barrett, Kathleen A. A Corpse in the Basement. LC 99-189211. (Thumbprint Mysteries Ser.). 128p. 1999. pap. 5.95 (*0-8092-0643-9*, 064390) NTC Contemp Pub Co.

***Barrett, Kathleen A.** Lethal Delivery, Postage Prepaid. (Thumbprint Mysteries Ser.). 128p. 1999. pap. 5.95 (*0-8092-0645-5*, 064550) NTC Contemp Pub Co.

An Asterisk (*) at the beginning of an entry indicates that the title is appearing for the first time.

Barrett, Kathleen A. Milwaukee Autumns Can Be Lethal. LC 98-96230. (Milwaukee Mystery Ser.: Bk. 3). 192p. 1998. 18.95 (*0-8034-9308-8*, Avalon Bks) Bouregy.

— Milwaukee Summers Can Be Deadly. LC 97-93461. (Milwaukee Mystery Ser.: Bk. 2). 192p. 1997. 17.95 (*0-8034-9239-1*, Avalon Bks) Bouregy.

— Milwaukee Winters Can Be Murder. LC 96-96756. (Milwaukee Mystery Ser.: Bk. 1). 192p. 1996. 18.95 (*0-8034-9224-3*, Avalon Bks) Bouregy.

Barrett, Kay, ed. see Watson, Beverly H.

Barrett, Kay L., ed. see Watson, Beverly H.

Barrett, Kevin & Forbeck, Matt. Silent Death: The Next Millennium Rulebook. Dennis, Don, ed. (Silent Death - The Next Millennium Ser.). (Illus.). 176p. 1995. pap. 18.00 (*1-55806-235-1*, 7201) Iron Crown Ent Inc.

Barrett, Kevin, jt. auth. see Forbeck, Matt.

Barrett, Kirt K. The Flight of Fancy. LC 89-60346. (Illus.). 38p. (J). (gr. 3-9). 1989. lib. bdg. 12.95 (*0-9622496-0-2*) Roanoke Park.

Barrett, L. L., tr. see Verissimo, Erico.

Barrett, Lady. Personality Survives Death. 1972. 59.95 (*0-8490-0819-0*) Gordon Pr.

Barrett, Lawrence. Edwin Forrest. LC 71-91894. 1972. 20.95 (*0-405-08238-X*, Pub. by Blom Pubns) Ayer.

— Edwin Forrest. 1881. 9.00 (*0-403-00242-7*) Scholarly.

Barrett-Lennard, Godfrey T. Carl Rogers' Helping System: Journey & Substance. LC 98-61269. xi, 415 p. 1998. pap. write for info. (*0-7619-5676-X*) Sage.

Barrett-Lennard, R. J. Christian Healing after the New Testament: Some Approaches to Illness in the Second, Third, & Fourth Centuries. LC 93-3835. 1994. 46.50 (*0-8191-9129-9*) U Pr of Amer.

Barrett-Lennard, Thomas. Position in Law of Women: A Concise & Comprehensive Treatise on the Position of Women at Common Law As Modified by the Doctrines of Equity & by Recent Legislation; Together with the Married Women's Property Acts, 1870, 1874, 1882: The Rules of the Supreme Court, 1883, Relating to Taking Acknowledgements & the Postal Regulations, 1883, Affecting Married Women. xxviii, 181p. 1983. reprint ed. 32.50 (*0-8377-0336-0*, Rothman) W S Hein.

Barrett, Leonard E., Sr. The Rastafarians. rev. ed. LC 97-10974. 328p. 1997. pap. 16.00 (*0-8070-1039-1*) Beacon Pr.

Barrett, Lesley. Blackwork. (Illus.). 48p. (Orig.). 1996. pap. 11.95 (*0-85532-806-1*, 8061, Pub. by Srch Pr) A Schwartz & Co.

Barrett, Linda, ed. see Ahern, Matt.

Barrett, Linda, ed. see Anderson, Al.

Barrett, Linda, ed. see Barrett, Pete.

Barrett, Linda, ed. see Caputi, Gary.

Barrett, Linda, ed. see Davis, Bill.

Barrett, Linda, ed. see Gennaro, Andy.

Barrett, Linda, ed. see Kamienski, Don.

Barrett, Linda, ed. see Kumiski, John A.

Barrett, Linda, ed. see LaBonte, George.

Barrett, Linda, ed. see Rasuso, John N.

Barrett, Linda, ed. see Ristori, Al.

Barrett, Lindon. Blackness & Value: Seeing Double. LC 97-52757. (Cambridge Studies in American Literature & Culture Ser.: No. 117). 272p. (C). 1998. text 54.95 (*0-521-62103-8*) Cambridge U Pr.

Barrett, Liz. Frommer's Irreverent Guide to San Francisco. 2nd ed. 228p. 1998. 12.95 (*0-02-862239-1*) Macmillan.

Barrett, Liz, jt. auth. see Scott, Dave.

Barrett, Liz, jt. ed. see King, Jo L.

Barrett, Lois. All about Weddings: We Do Everything but Choose Your Spouse. 50p. (Orig.). 1996. pap. write for info. (*0-9655628-0-8*) L Barrett.

— Doing What Is Right: What the Bible Says about Covenant & Justice. LC 88-22595. 96p. 1989. pap. 6.99 (*0-8361-3490-7*) Herald Pr.

— A Mennonite Statement & Study on Violence. 68p. 1998. pap. 8.95 (*0-87303-339-6*) Faith & Life.

— The Way God Fights: War & Peace in the Old Testament. LC 87-11936. (Peace & Justice Ser.: Vol. 1). 96p. 1987. pap. 6.99 (*0-8361-3447-8*) Herald Pr.

Barrett, Lynne. The James M. Cain Cookbook. Hoopes, Roy, ed. LC 86-72296. 144p. (C). 1988. pap. 11.95 (*0-88748-047-0*) Carnegie-Mellon.

— The Land of Go. LC 87-71458. (Fiction Ser.). 1988. 11.95 (*0-88748-044-6*) Carnegie-Mellon.

***Barrett, Lynne.** The Secret Names of Women: Stories. LC 98-71951. (Series in Short Fiction). 152p. 1999. pap. 15.95 (*0-88748-287-2*, Pub. by Carnegie-Mellon) Cornell U Pr.

Barrett, M. D., jt. ed. see Kuczaj, Stan A., II.

Barrett, M. Edgar & Cormick, Mary P. Management Strategy in the Oil & Gas Industries: Cases & Readings. fac. ed. LC 82-15524. 605p. pap. 187.60 (*0-7837-7417-6*, 204721200006) Bks Demand.

Barrett, Marcella L., jt. auth. see Barrett, Daniel, Jr.

Barrett, Margaret & Dennis, Charles. Given the Evidence. LC 99-217717. 320p. 1998. 23.00 (*0-671-00153-1*) S&S Trade.

— Given the Evidence. 1999. reprint ed. mass mkt. 7.99 (*0-671-00154-X*, Pocket Star Bks) PB.

Barrett, Margaret M., ed. Corn Lovers Cook Book. (Illus.). 86p. 1999. pap. 6.95 (*1-885590-46-6*) Golden West Pub.

Barrett, Margreth. Cases & Materials on Intellectual Property. LC 95-18565. (American Casebook Ser.). 976p. (C). 1995. 60.00 (*0-314-06126-6*) West Pub.

— Intellectual Property. 2nd rev. ed. LC 98-113756. (Professor Ser.). 327p. (Orig.). 1996. pap. text 17.95 (*1-56542-190-6*) E Pub Corp.

— Intellectual Property, Cases & Materials, Teacher's Manual to Accompany. (American Casebook Ser.). 590p. (C). 1996. pap. text. write for info. (*0-314-21355-4*) West Pub.

Barrett, Maria. Dishonored. 416p. 1998. mass mkt. 6.50 (*0-446-60628-6*, Pub. by Warner Bks) Little.

Barrett, Marie. The Education Guide. 192p. (C). 1994. pap. 21.00 (*0-907151-86-8*, Pub. by IMMEL Pubng) St Mut.

Barrett, Marilyn. Aggies, Immies, Shooters, & Swirls: The Magical World of Marbles. LC 93-32150. (Illus.). 96p. 1994. 24.95 (*0-8212-2001-2*, Pub. by Bulfinch Pr) Little.

Barrett, Mark. The Art of Bartending. 208p. 1997. mass mkt. 5.99 (*0-425-16089-0*) Berkley Pub.

Barrett, Mark, et al. ASSET Test (Assessing Semantic Skills Through Everyday Themes) 1988. teacher ed., spiral bd. 89.95 (*1-55999-017-1*); teacher ed., spiral bd. 42.00 (*1-55999-018-X*) LinguiSystems.

— Word Test - R, Elementary Test Kit: A Test of Expressive Vocabulary & Semantics. rev. ed. 80p. (J). 1990. spiral bd. 89.95 (*1-55999-140-2*) LinguiSystems.

— Word Test - R, Elementary Test Manual: A Test of Expressive Vocabulary & Semantics. rev. ed. 80p. (J). 1990. spiral bd. 66.00 (*1-55999-133-X*) LinguiSystems.

— The Word Test--Adolescent - Complete Kit: A Test of Expressive Vocabulary & Semantics. (YA). (gr. 7-12). 1989. spiral bd. 89.95 (*1-55999-096-1*) LinguiSystems.

— The Word Test--Adolescent - Examiner's Manual: A Test of Expressive Vocabulary & Semantics. (YA). (gr. 7-12). 1989. spiral bd. 66.00 (*1-55999-097-X*) LinguiSystems.

Barrett, Martin L. & Wagner, Clifford H. C & UNIX: Tools for Software Design. LC 95-1816. 464p. 1995. pap. 58.95 (*0-471-30927-3*) Wiley.

Barrett, Martyn D. The Development of Language. LC 99-226239. 464p. 1999. 59.95 (*0-86377-846-1*, Pub. by Psychol Pr) Taylor & Francis.

Barrett, Martyn D., ed. Children's Single-Word Speech. LC 84-29101. (Wiley Series in Developmental Psychology & Its Applications). 339p. pap. 105.10 (*0-7837-8491-0*, 204929800010) Bks Demand.

***Barrett, Marvin.** Meet Thomas Jefferson. (Illus.). 1999. pap. text 11.10 (*0-8335-3937-X*) Econo-Clad Bks.

Barrett, Marvin. Meet Thomas Jefferson. LC 88-19069. (Set-up Biographies Ser.). (Illus.). 72p. (J). (gr. 2-4). 1989. reprint ed. pap. 3.99 (*0-394-81964-0*, Pub. by Random Bks Yng Read) Random.

— Second Chance: A Life after Death. LC 98-44020. 224p. 1999. 24.95 (*0-930407-42-3*) Parabola Bks.

Barrett, Mary. When God Comes to Visit. 1998. pap. 9.99 (*1-873796-66-8*) Review & Herald.

Barrett, Mary B. Beach Baby. LC 96-75964. (Illus.). 12p. 1997. 5.95 (*0-15-201056-4*, Red Wagon Bks) Harcourt.

— The Man of the House at Huffington Row: A Christmas Story. LC 97-2212. (Illus.). 32p. (C). (gr. 1-3). 1998. 16.00 (*0-15-201580-9*) Harcourt.

Barrett, Mary Brigid. Day Care Days. LC 97-52105. 32p. (J). (ps-1). 1999. 12.95 (*0-316-08456-5*) Little.

Barrett, Mary Ellin. Irving Berlin. (Illus.). 320p. 1994. 23.00 (*0-671-72533-5*) S&S Trade.

— Irving Berlin: A Daughter's Memoir. (Illus.). 320p. 1996. reprint ed. pap. 14.95 (*0-87910-078-8*) Limelight Edns.

Barrett, Mary Ellin, jt. auth. see Arnaudet, Martin L.

Barrett, Mary H., jt. auth. see Barrett, Paul W.

Barrett, Mary J., jt. auth. see Trepper, Terry S.

Barrett, Mary Jo, jt. ed. see Trepper, Terry S.

Barrett, Matthew J., jt. auth. see Herwitz, David R.

Barrett, Matthew J., jt. auth. see Nerwitz, David R.

***Barrett, Michael.** Beginning at Moses: A Guide to Finding Christ in the Old Testament. 348p. 1999. pap. 14.99 (*1-889893-39-0*) Emerald House Group Inc.

Barrett, Michael E., et al. A Review & Evaluation of Literature Pertaining to the Quantity & Control of Pollution from Highway Runoff & Construction. (Illus.). 140p. (Orig.). (C). 1995. pap. text 35.00 (*0-7881-1949-4*) DIANE Pub.

Barrett, Michael L. & Beerel, Annabel C. Expert Systems in Business: A Practical Approach. (Information Technology Ser.). 232p. 1988. text 38.95 (*0-470-21083-4*) P-H.

Barrett, Michele. Imagination in Theory: Culture, Writing, Words & Things. LC 98-46639. 1999. pap. 17.95 (*0-8147-1344-0*) NYU Pr.

— Imagination in Theory: Culture, Writing, Words & Things. LC 98-46639. (Illus.). 232p. 1999. text 55.00 (*0-8147-1343-2*) NYU Pr.

— The Politics of Truth: From Marx to Foucault. LC 91-66613. 208p. (C). 1992. 39.50 (*0-8047-2004-5*); pap. 13.95 (*0-8047-2005-3*) Stanford U Pr.

— Women's Oppression Today: The Marxist Feminist Encounter. rev. ed. 304p. (C). 1989. pap. 19.00 (*0-86091-931-5*, Pub. by Verso) Norton.

Barrett, Michele & Phillips, Anne, eds. Destabilizing Theory: Contemporary Feminist Debates. LC 91-67234. 240p. (C). 1992. 39.50 (*0-8047-2030-4*); pap. 14.95 (*0-8047-2031-2*) Stanford U Pr.

Barrett, Michele, ed. see Kaplan, Cora.

Barrett, Mike, ed. see Sheehan, John.

***Barrett, Neal, Jr** Bad Eye Blues, Vol. 1. 1999. mass mkt. 5.99 (*1-57566-484-4*) Kens Hse.

Barrett, Neal, Jr Bad Eye Blues. LC 96-79077. 288p. 1997. 21.95 (*1-57566-173-X*, Knsington) Kensgtn Pub Corp.

***Barrett, Neal, Jr** The Day the Decorators Came. unabridged ed. 64p. 2000. 40.00 (*1-892284-70-7*); pap. 12.00 (*1-892284-69-3*) Subtrmean Pr.

Barrett, Neal, Jr Dead Dog Blues. 352p. 1997. mass mkt. 5.50 (*1-57566-179-9*, Knsington) Kensgtn Pub Corp.

***Barrett, Neal.** Dungeons & Dragons: The Movie. (Illus.). (J). 2000. mass mkt. 6.99 (*0-7869-1439-4*) Wizards Coast.

***Barrett, Neal, Jr** The Lizard Shoppe. 2000. mass mkt. 6.50 (*0-553-58195-3*) Bantam.

Barrett, Neal. Lizard's Rage. (Spider-Man Super-Thriller Ser.: No.8). 144p. 1997. per. 4.99 (*0-671-00798-X*) PB.

— Perpetuity Blues & Other Stories. 2000. 21.95 (*0-9655901-4-3*, Pub. by Golden Gryphon) IPG Chicago.

Barrett, Neal, Jr Pink Vodka Blues. 304p. 1997. mass mkt. 5.99 (*1-57566-237-X*, Knsington) Kensgtn Pub Corp.

— Pink Vodka Blues. 320p. 1992. text 18.95 (*0-312-07766-1*) St Martin.

— Skinny Annie Blues. 256p. 1996. 21.95 (*1-57566-058-X*, Knsington) Kensgtn Pub Corp.

— Skinny Annie Blues. 304p. 1997. mass mkt. 5.50 (*1-57566-134-9*, Knsington) Kensgtn Pub Corp.

— Slightly off Center. (Illus.). 160p. (Orig.). 1992. pap. 9.50 (*1-883722-00-4*) Swan Pr TX.

— Warrior's Revenge. (Spider-Man Super-Thriller Ser.: No. 8). (Illus.). 1984. pap. 1.50 (*0-671-00800-5*) PB.

Barrett, Neil. Advertising on the Internet: Getting Your Message Across on the World-Wide Web. 127p. 1997. pap. text 14.95 (*0-7494-2166-5*) Kogan Page Ltd.

— Digital Crime: Policing the Cybernation. 224p. 1998. pap. 19.95 (*0-7494-2098-7*) Kogan Page Ltd.

***Barrett, Niall.** Bookcases: Eleven Outstanding Projects from America's Best Craftsmen. LC 99-15008. 192p. 1999. pap. 24.95 (*1-56158-303-0*) Taunton.

— Classic Kitchen Projects: 18 Distinctive Projects from an American Craftsman. (Illus.). 2000. pap. 19.95 (*1-56158-386-3*) Taunton.

Barrett, Nina. Girls: A True Story of Lifelong Friendship. LC 98-19420. 288p. 1998. 22.50 (*0-684-81370-X*) S&S Trade.

— I Wish Someone Had Told Me: A Realistic Guide to Early Motherhood. LC 97-7795. 1997. pap. text 14.00 (*0-89733-442-6*) Academy Chi Pubs.

— The Playgroup: Motherhood in 3 Variations. 1994. 21.00 (*0-671-74710-X*) S&S Trade.

Barrett, Noel J. Martin B. Hellriegel: Pastoral Liturgist. (Illus.). 209p. (Orig.). 1990. pap. 10.00 (*0-9626257-1-X*) CBCCU Amer.

Barrett, Norman S. Bicicross. LC 90-70885. (Picture Library). (SPA., Illus.). 32p. (J). (gr. 3-5). 1990. lib. bdg. 20.00 (*0-531-07904-X*) Watts.

— Canoeing. Franklin Watts Ltd., ed. LC 86-51222. (Picture Library). (Illus.). 32p. (J). (ps-3). 1988. lib. bdg. 20.00 (*0-531-10349-8*) Watts.

— Carros de Carrera. LC 90-70887. (Picture Library). (SPA., Illus.). 32p. (J). (gr. 3-5). 1990. lib. bdg. 20.00 (*0-531-07905-8*) Watts.

— Cocodrilos y Caimanes. LC 90-71415. (Picture Library). (SPA., Illus.). 32p. (J). (gr. 3-5). 1991. lib. bdg. 20.00 (*0-531-07919-8*) Watts.

— Coral Reef. LC 90-42931. (Picture Library). (Illus.). 32p. (J). (gr. 3-5). 1991. lib. bdg. 20.00 (*0-531-14110-1*) Watts.

— Expedition. 1998. 84.00 (*0-531-19438-8*) Watts.

— Flying Machines. LC 93-33238. (Visual Guides Ser.). (Illus.). 48p. (J). (gr. 5-7). 1994. lib. bdg. 20.00 (*0-531-14301-5*) Watts.

— Hang Gliding. Franklin Watts Ltd., ed. LC 86-51223. (Picture Library). (Illus.). 32p. (J). (gr. 3-5). 1988. lib. bdg. 20.00 (*0-531-10350-1*) Watts.

— Ice Sports. LC 88-50382. (Picture Library). (Illus.). 32p. (J). (gr. 3-5). 1989. lib. bdg. 20.00 (*0-531-10627-6*) Watts.

— Mountains. (Picture Library). 32p. 1990. lib. bdg. 20.00 (*0-531-10838-4*) Watts.

— Scuba Diving. LC 88-50372. (Picture Library). (Illus.). 32p. (J). (gr. k-6). 1990. lib. bdg. 20.00 (*0-531-10631-4*) Watts.

— Serpientes. LC 90-70891. (Picture Library). (SPA., Illus.). 32p. (J). (gr. k-4). 1990. lib. bdg. 20.00 (*0-531-07909-0*) Watts.

— Sport Machines. LC 93-33236. (Visual Guides Ser.). (Illus.). 48p. (J). (gr. 5-7). 1994. lib. bdg. 20.00 (*0-531-14299-X*) Watts.

— Sports Facts. LC 94-24740. (Pocket Guides Ser.: No. 24). (Illus.). 128p. (J). 1996. pap. 6.95 (*0-7894-1021-4*) DK Pub Inc.

— Transport Machines. LC 93-33235. (Visual Guides Ser.). (Illus.). 48p. (J). (gr. 5-7). 1994. lib. bdg. 20.00 (*0-531-14298-1*) Watts.

Barrett, Nuriel & Varma, Ved P. Educational Therapy in the Clinic & the Classroom. (Illus.). 206p. (Orig.). 1996. pap. 45.00 (*1-56593-781-3*, 1524) Singular Publishing.

Barrett, P. Barchester England: Catholic Life in the Nineteen Century. pap. 49.95 (*0-687-85094-0*) Abingdon.

Barrett, P., jt. auth. see Macdonald, D.

Barrett, P. J., et al. Geology of the Central Transantarctic Mountains, Papers 14-15. (Antarctic Research Ser.: Vol. 36). 90p. 1986. 33.00 (*0-87590-157-3*) Am Geophysical.

***Barrett, Pamela, ed.** Insight Guide Tenerife. 4th rev. ed. (Insight Guides Ser.). (Illus.). 302p. 2000. pap. 22.95 (*1-58573-060-2*, Insight Guides) Langenscheidt.

Barrett, Patricia R. Flowering Shrubs. Foster, Kim & Oxley, Connie, eds. (Country Wisdom Bulletin Ser.). (Illus.). 32p. 1992. pap. 2.95 (*0-88266-757-2*, Garden Way Pub) Storey Bks.

***Barrett, Patricia R.** The Sacred Garden: Soil for the Growing Soul. LC 99-57683. 144p. 2000. pap. 9.95 (*0-8192-1831-6*) Morehouse Pub.

Barrett, Patti. Container Gardening. LC 96-3200. (Bulletin Ser.: No. A-151). 1996. pap. 2.95 (*0-88266-344-5*) Storey Bks.

— Growing & Using Lavender. LC 96-2877. (Bulletin Ser.: Vol. A-155). 1996. pap. 2.95 (*0-88266-475-1*) Storey Bks.

— Growing & Using Sage. LC 96-53549. (Storey Publishing Bulletin Ser.: Vol. A-166). 1997. pap. 2.95 (*0-88266-712-2*) Storey Bks.

— Too Busy to Clean. 2nd ed. LC 97-50340. 1998. pap. text 12.95 (*1-58017-029-3*, Storey Pub) Storey Bks.

— Too Busy to Clean? Over 500 Tips & Techniques to Make Housecleaning Easier. Watson, Ben, ed. LC 89-46015. (Illus.). 128p. (Orig.). 1990. pap. 9.95 (*0-88266-598-7*) Storey Bks.

***Barrett, Paul.** Dinosaurus. LC 98-60616. (Illus.). 256p. (J). (gr. 4-7). 1998. 14.98 (*0-7651-0891-7*) Smithmark.

Barrett, Paul, et al. A Year in the Life of the Supreme Court. Smolla, Rodney A., ed. LC 95-4130. (Constitutional Conflicts Ser.). 312p. 1995. pap. 14.95 (*0-8223-1665-X*) Duke.

— A Year in the Life of the Supreme Court. Smolla, Rodney A. & Devins, Neal, eds. LC 95-4130. (Constitutional Conflicts Ser.). 312p. 1995. text 49.95 (*0-8223-1653-6*) Duke.

Barrett, Paul H. & Freeman, R. B., eds. The Works of Charles Darwin: Geological Observations on South America, Vol. IX. (Illus.). 360p. (C). 1987. lib. bdg. 95.00 (*0-8147-1794-2*) NYU Pr.

— The Works of Charles Darwin: Geological Observations on the Volcanic Island Visited During the Voyage of H. M. S. Beagle (1844), Vol. VIII. (Illus.). 168p. (C). 1987. lib. bdg. 95.00 (*0-8147-1793-4*) NYU Pr.

— The Works of Charles Darwin: The Zoology of the Voyage of H. M. S. Beagle, under the Command of Captain Fitzroy, During the Years 1832-1836, Vol. IV, Pts. I & II. (Illus.). 264p. (C). 1987. lib. bdg. 95.00 (*0-8147-1789-6*) NYU Pr.

— The Works of Charles Darwin: The Zoology of the Voyage of H. M. S. Beagle, under the Command of Captain Fitzroy, During the Years 1832-1836, Vol. VI, Pt. IV & V. (Illus.). 376p. (C). 1987. lib. bdg. 95.00 (*0-8147-1791-8*) NYU Pr.

Barrett, Paul H., ed. see Darwin, Charles.

Barrett, Paul M. The Good Black: A True Story of Race in America. 368p. 2000. pap. 13.95 (*0-452-27859-7*, Plume) Dutton Plume.

— The Good Black: A True Story of Race in America. LC 98-24517. 304p. 1999. 23.95 (*0-525-94344-7*) NAL.

***Barrett, Paul W., Sr.** The Toilet Paper Strategy: Ordinary People Can Do Extraordinary Things! 128p. 1999. pap. 12.95 (*0-932045-31-6*, Pub. by Dace Pub) ACCESS Pubs Network.

Barrett, Paul W. & Barrett, Mary H. Young Brothers Massacre. LC 87-19156. (Illus.). 160p. (Orig.). 1988. pap. 14.95 (*0-8262-0650-6*) U of Mo Pr.

Barrett, Penny. Getting Two-gether: Looking for Love in All the Right Places. (Illus.). 150p. (Orig.). 1989. 14.95 (*0-317-93338-8*); pap. text 5.95 (*0-317-93339-6*) Single Assn.

Barrett, Pete. Fishing for Sharks. 4th rev. ed. Barrett, Linda, ed. (Fisherman Library). (Illus.). 136p. 1988. 19.95 (*0-923155-05-8*) Fisherman Lib.

— Fishing for Tuna & Marlin. Barrett, Linda, ed. (Illus.). 304p. (Orig.). 1993. pap. 19.95 (*0-923155-16-3*) Fisherman Lib.

— Saltwater Fishing Guide. Barrett, Linda, ed. (Fisherman Library). (Illus.). 256p. (C). 1994. pap. text 19.95 (*0-923155-14-7*) Fisherman Lib.

Barrett, Peter. Profitable Practice Management. LC 92-38837. 1993. mass mkt. 49.95 (*0-419-15590-2*, E & FN Spon) Routledge.

Barrett, Peter, ed. Facilities Management Research Directions. 226p. 1993. pap. 99.00 (*0-85406-592-X*, Pub. by R-I-C-S Bks) St Mut.

Barrett, Peter & Barrett, Susan. The Circle Sarah Drew. Incl. Line Sophie Drew. LC 72-89449. (Illus.). 1973. 15.95 (*0-87592-029-2*); Square Ben Drew. LC 72-89449. (Illus.). 1973. 15.95 (*0-87592-049-7*); LC 72-89449. (Illus.). 32p. (J). (ps-2). 1973. 15.95 (*0-87592-012-8*) Scroll Pr.

Barrett, Peter & Males, R., eds. Practice Management: New Perspectives for the Construction Professional. (Illus.). 366p. (C). 1991. 85.00 (*0-419-17150-9*, E & FN Spon) Routledge.

Barrett, Peter & Stanley, Catherine. Better Construction Briefing. LC 98-51418. 1999. write for info. (*0-632-05102-7*) Blackwell Sci.

Barrett, Peter, ed. see Ayling, Robert I.

Barrett, Peter A. Doubts & Certainties: Working Together to Restructure Schools. 208p. 1991. pap. 18.95 (*0-8106-1843-5*) NEA.

Barrett, R. & McCloud, Mac. Ruth Weisberg - Mid-Life, 1961-1990. (Artists & Their Work Ser.). (Illus.). 134p. (Orig.). 1990. pap. 29.95 (*1-877675-10-5*) Midmarch Arts.

Barrett, R., et al. June Wayne - The Djuna Set. (Artists & Their Work Ser.). (Illus.). 70p. (Orig.). 1989. pap. 29.95 (*0-932325-23-8*) Midmarch Arts.

***Barrett, Rebecca & Haines, Carolyn.** Moments with Eugene: A Collection of Memories. LC 00-35711. 2000. write for info. (*0-9663954-1-7*) KaliOka Pr.

Barrett, Richard. Business Foundation: The GNVQ Resource Pack. (Illus.). 412p. 1998. pap. 600.00 (*0-7487-2013-8*) St Mut.

— The Commission. LC 82-72373. (Illus.). 438p. 1982. 25.00 (*0-9609396-0-1*) Barrett.

— A Guide to Liberating Your Soul. (Illus.). 160p. 1995. pap. 13.95 (*0-9643226-3-3*) Fulfilling Bks.

— The Illustrated Encyclopedia of Railroad Lighting Vol. 1: The Railroad Lantern. LC 93-87267. (Illus.). 390p. 1994. 62.95 (*1-884650-00-7*) Railroad Res.

— Liberating the Corporate Soul: A Values-Driven Approach to Building a Visionary Organization. LC 98-29208. 248p. 1998. pap. text 18.95 (*0-7506-7071-1*) Buttrwrth-Heinemann.

— Spiritual Unfoldment: A Guide to Liberating Your Soul. LC 94-90699. (Illus.). 160p. (Orig.). 1995. 24.95 (*0-9643226-0-9*) Fulfilling Bks.

Barrett, Richard, et al. Templates for the Solution of Linear Systems: Building Blocks for Iterative Methods. LC 94-127058. (Miscellaneous Titles in Applied Mathematics Ser.: No. 43). xvii, 124p. 1993. pap. 23.00 (*0-89871-328-5*) Soc Indus-Appl Math.

Barrett, Richard, jt. ed. see Serageldin, Ismail.

An Asterisk (*) at the beginning of an entry indicates that the title is appearing for the first time.

Barrett, Richard A. Culture & Conduct: An Excursion in Anthropology. 240p. (C). 1984. pap. write for info. (*0-534-03034-3*) Wadsworth Pub.

— Culture & Conduct: An Excursion in Anthropology. 2nd ed. 238p. (C). 1990. 12.00 (*0-534-14724-0*) Wadsworth Pub.

Barrett, Richard C. Boston's Depots & Terminals: A History of Boston's 32 Railroad Stations. LC 95-92696. (Illus.). 240p. 1996. 54.95 (*1-884650-03-1*) Railroad Res.

— The Illustrated Encyclopedia of Railroad Lighting Vol. 2: The Railroad Signal Lamp. LC 93-87267. 380p. 1999. 69.95 (*1-884650-01-5*) Railroad Res.

Barrett, Richard D. & Ware, Molly E. Planned Giving Essentials: A Step by Step Guide to Success. LC 96-48718. 165p. 1997. pap. 59.00 (*0-8342-0900-4*) Aspen Pub.

Barrett, Richard E. Using the 1990 U.S. Census for Research. LC 94-17655. (Guides to Major Social Science Data Bases Ser.: Vol. 3). 104p. 1994. 28.95 (*0-8039-5389-5*); pap. 11.50 (*0-8039-5390-9*) Sage.

Barrett, Richard E., ed. Slagging & Fouling Due to Impurities in Combustion Gases. LC 89-84355. 869p. 1990. 50.00 (*0-939204-36-3*) Eng Found.

Barrett, Richard H., ed. Barrett. Leaves from Familiy Trees (Biographical & Genealogical Sketches of Barrett & Related Families) (Illus.). 249p. 1996. reprint ed. pap. 39.00 (*0-8328-5298-8*); reprint ed. lib. bdg. 49.00 (*0-8328-5297-X*) Higginson Bk Co.

Barrett, Richard H., jt. auth. see Hanson, Marvin L.

Barrett, Richard S. Fair Employment Myths & Methods. LC 98-4929. 208p. 1998. 59.95 (*1-56720-141-5*, Quorum Bks) Greenwood.

Barrett, Richard S., ed. Fair Employment Strategies in Human Resource Management. LC 95-50464. 336p. 1996. 65.00 (*0-89930-986-0*, Quorum Bks) Greenwood.

Barrett, Rob. The Psychiatric Team & the Social Definition of Schizophrenia: An Anthropological Study of Person & Illness. (Studies in Social & Community Psychiatry). (Illus.). 359p. (C). 1996. text 80.00 (*0-521-41653-1*) Cambridge U Pr.

***Barrett, Robert.** Ashen Knight: The Bloody Order. (Vampire Ser.). 2000. pap. text 17.95 (*1-56504-241-7*) White Wolf.

***Barrett, Robert Assheton.** The Barretts of Jamaica: The Family of Elizabeth Barrett Browning. LC 99-40058. (Illus.). xii, 212p. 1999. lib. bdg. 40.00 (*0-911459-28-6*) Wedgestone Pr.

Barrett, Robert B. & Gibson, Roger F., eds. Perspectives on Quine. (Philosophers & Their Critics Ser.: No. 6). 358p. 1993. pap. text 31.95 (*0-631-19178-X*) Blackwell Pubs.

Barrett, Robert K., jt. ed. see Wu, Jonathan T.

Barrett-Rodenberry, Majel, compiled by. The Star Trek Cookbook. 1997. pap. 12.00 (*0-614-19378-8*) PB.

Barrett, Roger K., jt. auth. see Herbert, David L.

Barrett, Ron & Brown, Patty. Bah! Humbug! One Hundred One Reasons to Hate the Holidays. Rubenstein, Julie, ed. (Illus.). 96p. 1992. pap. 7.00 (*0-671-79600-3*) PB.

Barrett, Rosalind, jt. auth. see Ramsey, Allan.

Barrett, Rowland P., ed. Severe Behavior Disorders in the Mentally Retarded: Nondrug Approaches to Treatment. (Applied Clinical Psychology Ser.). (Illus.). 426p. (C). 1986. 102.00 (*0-306-42162-3*, Plenum Trade) Perseus Pubng.

Barrett, Rowland P. & Matson, Johnny L., eds. Advances in Developmental Disorders, Vol. 2. 320p. 1993. 85.00 (*1-85302-093-1*) Taylor & Francis.

Barrett, S. Challenging Behaviors: A Practical Guide to Assessment & Intervention. 288p. (C). 1998. pap. text 44.75 (*1-56593-180-7*, 0495) Singular Publishing.

Barrett, S., ed. The 1991 International Directory of Noise & Vibration Manufacturers & Suppliers. 92p. 1991. pap. 54.00 (*1-85617-071-3*, Pub. by Elsvr Adv Tech) Elsevier.

Barrett, S. A. Material Aspects of Pomo Culture. (Public Museum of the City of Milwaukee, Bulletins Ser.: Vol. 20, Pt. 1). (Illus.). 194p. 1952. pap. text 20.63 (*1-55567-880-7*) Coyote Press.

— Material Aspects of Pomo Culture. (Public Museum of the City of Milwaukee, Bulletins Ser.: Vol. 20, Pt. 2). (Illus.). 281p. 1952. pap. text 29.38 (*1-55567-881-5*) Coyote Press.

Barrett, S. C., et al, eds. Evolution & Function of Heterostyly. (Monographs on Theoretical & Applied Genetics: Vol. 15). (Illus.). 288p. 1992. 158.95 (*0-387-52110-0*) Spr-Verlag.

Barrett, S. D. & Dhesi, S S. The Structure of Rare-Earth Metal Surfaces. 250p. 1999. 48.00 (*1-86094-165-6*, Pub. by Imperial College) World Scientific Pub.

Barrett, S. M. Geronimo's Story of His Life. (Native American Voices Ser.). 216p. 1991. reprint ed. 170.95 (*0-7835-1762-9*) Time-Life.

Barrett, S. M., told to. Geronimo: His Own Story. rev. ed. (Illus.). 208p. 1996. pap. 12.95 (*0-452-01155-8*, Mer) NAL.

Barrett, S. M., jt. auth. see Geronimo.

Barrett, S. M., ed. see Geronimo.

Barrett, Sally. The Sound of the Week. 144p. (J). (gr. k-4). 1980. 13.99 (*0-916456-63-3*, GA 184) Good Apple.

Barrett, Samuel A. Ancient Aztalan. LC 70-11394. 1970. reprint ed. lib. bdg. 89.50 (*0-8371-4624-0*, BAAA, Greenwood Pr) Greenwood.

— Ceremonies of the Pomo Indians. fac. ed. (University of California Publications in American Archaeology & Ethnology: Vol. 12: 10). 44p. (C). 1917. reprint ed. pap. text 5.00 (*1-55567-207-8*) Coyote Press.

— The Dream Dance of the Chippewa & Menominee Indians of Northern Wisconsin. LC 76-43647. (Bulletin of the Public Museum of the City of Milwaukee Ser.: Vol. 1). reprint ed. 44.50 (*0-404-15482-4*) AMS Pr.

— The Ethno-Geography of the Pomo & Neighboring Indians. fac. ed. (University of California Publications in American Archaeology & Ethnology: Vol. 6: 1). 338p. (C). 1908. reprint ed. pap. text 35.63 (*1-55567-174-8*) Coyote Press.

— The Geography & Dialects of the Miwok Indians. fac. ed. (University of California Publications in American Archaeology & Ethnology: Vol. 6: 2). 36p. (C). 1908. reprint ed. pap. text 4.06 (*1-55567-175-6*) Coyote Press.

— Material Aspects of Pomo Culture, 2 pts. in 1 vol. LC 76-43649. (Bulletin of the Public Museum of the City of Milwaukee Ser.: Vol. 20). reprint ed. 67.50 (*0-404-15483-2*) AMS Pr.

— The Material Culture of the Klamath Lake & Modoc Indians of Northeastern California & Southern Oregon. fac. ed. (University of California Publications in American Archaeology & Ethnology: Vol. 5: 4). (Illus.). 55p. (C). 1910. reprint ed. pap. text 6.56 (*1-55567-172-1*) Coyote Press.

— Myths of the Southern Sierra Miwok. fac. ed. (University of California Publications in American Archaeology & Ethnology: Vol. 16: 1). 28p. (C). 1919. reprint ed. pap. text 3.13 (*1-55567-221-3*) Coyote Press.

— Pomo Bear Doctors. fac. ed. (University of California Publications in American Archaeology & Ethnology: Vol. 12: 11). 22p. (C). 1917. reprint ed. pap. text 2.81 (*1-55567-208-6*) Coyote Press.

— Pomo Myths. fac. ed. Edwards, Ira, ed. (Public Museum of the City of Milwaukee Ser.: Bulletin 15). 702p. (C). 1933. reprint ed. pap. text 62.50 (*1-55567-661-8*) Coyote Press.

Barrett, Samuel A. The Washo Indians. fac. ed. (Public Museum of the City of Milwaukee, Bulletins Ser.: Vol. 2:1). (Illus.). 53p. (C). 1917. reprint ed. pap. text 6.88 (*1-55567-793-2*) Coyote Press.

Barrett, Samuel A. The Washo Indians. LC 76-43651. (Bulletin of the Public Museum of the City of Milwaukee Ser.: Vol. 2, No. 1). reprint ed. 29.50 (*0-404-15485-9*) AMS Pr.

— The Wintun Hesi Ceremony. fac. ed. (University of California Publications in American Archaeology & Ethnology: Vol. 14: 4). 54p. (C). 1919. reprint ed. pap. text 6.56 (*1-55567-219-1*) Coyote Press.

Barrett, Samuel A. & Gifford, E. W. Miwok Material Culture. (Public Museum of the City of Milwaukee, Bulletins Ser.: No. 2). (Illus.). 260p. (C). 1933. pap. text 27.50 (*1-55567-740-1*) Coyote Press.

Barrett, Samuel A. & Gifford, Edward W. Miwok Material Culture: Indian Life of the Yosemite Region. LC 76-43652. (Illus.). 261p. 1982. reprint ed. pap. 7.95 (*0-939666-12-X*) Yosemite Assn.

Barrett, Samuel A. & Smith-Ferri, Sherrie. Pomo Indian Basketry. LC 96-41513. 1996. write for info. (*0-936127-07-4*) P A Hearst Mus.

Barrett, Samuel A., jt. auth. see Kroeber, A. L.

Barrett, Sean, ed. see Cambias, James.

Barrett, Sean, ed. see Ross, S. John.

Barrett, Sean D., contrib. by. Flying High: Airline Prices & European Regulation. 104p. 1987. text 55.95 (*0-566-05541-4*, Pub. by Avebry) Ashgate Pub Co.

***Barrett, Sharon Kebschull.** Morning Glories: Breakfast, Brunch, & Light Fare from an Herb Garden. LC 00-23030. (Illus.). 156p. 2000. text 24.95 (*0-312-25224-2*) St Martin.

Barrett, Sheila. A View to Die For. write for info. (*1-85371-689-8*, Pub. by Poolbeg Pr) Dufour.

Barrett, Sherry. Keep Them Calling! Superior Service on the Telephone. LC 95-78189. (How-To Book Ser.). 95p. (Orig.). 1996. pap. 12.95 (*1-884926-47-9*, COURT) Amer Media.

Barrett, Shirley. Love Serenade: Screenplay. 1997. pap. 17.95 (*0-86819-529-4*, Pub. by Currency Pr) Accents Pubns.

Barrett, Shirley L. Parties with a Purpose: A Handbook for Activity Directors. 128p. 1980. pap., spiral bd. 33.95 (*0-398-03986-0*) C C Thomas.

Barrett, Singer Alesia. Coping with Your Child's Chronic Illness. LC 98-36373. 95p. 1999. 9.95 (*1-885003-14-5*) R D Reed Pubs.

Barrett, Stanley R. Anthropology: A Student's Guide to Theory & Method. 272p. 1996. text, student ed. 50.00 (*0-8020-0848-8*) U of Toronto Pr.

— Anthropology: A Student's Guide to Theory & Method. 272p. 1996. pap. text, student ed. 18.95 (*0-8020-7833-8*) U of Toronto Pr.

— Is God a Racist? The Right Wing in Canada. (Illus.). 416p. 1987. text 40.00 (*0-8020-5758-6*); pap. text 20.95 (*0-8020-6673-9*) U of Toronto Pr.

— Paradise: Class, Commuters, & Ethnicity in Rural Ontario. (Anthropological Horizons Ser.: No. 5). 304p. (C). 1994. text 50.00 (*0-8020-0442-3*); pap. text 18.95 (*0-8020-7232-1*) U of Toronto Pr.

— The Rebirth of Anthropological Theory. 288p. 1988. pap. text 17.95 (*0-8020-6718-2*) U of Toronto Pr.

Barrett, Stephanie. Moving Right Along: The Complete Handbook to Survive Packing & Moving. (Illus.). 128p. 1986. pap. 9.95 (*0-9615962-0-1*) Signals Pub.

Barrett, Stephen, jt. auth. see Cook-Fuller, Charlotte.

Barrett, Stephen, jt. auth. see Raso, Jack.

Barrett, Stephen, jt. auth. see Reynolds, Linda.

Barrett, Stephen, ed. see Cook-Fuller, Charlotte.

Barrett, Stephen, ed. see Homola, Samuel.

Barrett, Stephen, ed. see Magner, George.

Barrett, Stephen J. Chemical Sensitivity: The Truth about Environmental Illness. LC 97-53181. 220p. 1998. 26.95 (*1-57392-195-5*) Prometheus Bks.

Barrett, Stephen J. & Herbert, Victor. The Vitamin Pushers: How the "Health Food" Industry Is Selling America a Bill of Goods. LC 94-21714. (Illus.). 548p. (C). 1994. 28.95 (*0-87975-909-7*) Prometheus Bks.

***Barrett, Stephen M.** Sociology of the American Indians. (LC History-America-E). 142p. 1999. reprint ed. lib. bdg. 69.00 (*0-7812-4285-1*) Rprt Serv.

Barrett, Stephen W., et al. Fire Episodes in the Inland Northwest (1540-1940) Based on Fire History Data. (Illus.). 24p. 1997. reprint ed. pap. 3.40 (*0-89904-944-3*, Ecosytems Resrch) Crumb Elbow Pub.

Barrett, Steven & Jarvis, William. The Health Robbers: A Close Look at Quackery in America. rev. ed. LC 93-25357. (Illus.). 544p. 1993. 28.95 (*0-87975-855-4*) Prometheus Bks.

Barrett, Susan. Day in the Life of a Kitten. LC 97-200933. (Illus.). (J). 1997. pap. 3.50 (*0-8167-4284-7*) Troll Communs.

— A Day in the Life of a Puppy. LC 97-171528. (Illus.). (J). 1997. pap. 3.50 (*0-8167-4201-4*) Troll Communs.

— Stephen & Violet. large type ed. 1990. 27.99 (*0-7089-2116-7*) Ulverscroft.

Barrett, Susan, jt. auth. see Barrett, Peter.

Barrett, Susan L. It's All in Your Head: A Guide to Understanding Your Brain & Boosting Your Brain Power. rev. ed. Espeland, Pamela, ed. LC 92-18090. (Illus.). 160p. (Orig.). (J). (gr. 4-9). 1992. pap. 9.95 (*0-915793-45-8*) Free Spirit Pub.

Barrett, Susan L. A Teacher's Guide to It's All in Your Head: A Guide to Understanding Your Brain & Boosting Your Brain Power. Espeland, Pamela, ed. 52p. 1992. pap., teacher ed. 10.95 (*0-915793-46-6*) Free Spirit Pub.

Barrett, Susie M., jt. ed. see Walsh, Elizabeth.

***Barrett, Suzanne.** A Christmas Bouquet. (Bouquet Ser.). 1999. mass mkt. 3.99 (*0-8217-6412-8*, Zebra Kensgtn) Kensgtn Pub Corp.

Barrett, Suzanne. Taming Rowan, 1, 9. 256p. 1999. mass mkt. 3.99 (*0-8217-6297-4*) Kensgtn Pub Corp.

***Barrett, Suzanne.** Wild Irish Rogue. (Bouquet Ser.: Vol. 53). 2000. mass mkt. 3.99 (*0-8217-6649-X*, Zebra Kensgtn) Kensgtn Pub Corp.

Barrett, Sylvia. The Arsenic Milkshake: And Other Mysteries Solved by Forensic Science. LC 95-128044. 224p. 1995. pap. 16.95 (*0-385-25523-3*) Doubleday.

***Barrett, Sylvia E., et al, eds.** Natural Organic Matter & Disinfection By-Products: Characterization & Control in Drinking Water. (ACS Symposium Ser.). (Illus.). 416p. 2000. text 135.00 (*0-8412-3676-3*, Pub. by Am Chemical) OUP.

***Barrett, Ted, ed.** Chronicle of Golf. 304p. 2000. 29.95 (*1-85868-976-7*, Pub. by Carlton Bks Ltd) Natl Bk Netwk.

Barrett, Terence. Life after Suicide: The Survivor's Grief Experience. 149p. 1989. pap. 10.95 (*0-9664758-0-1*) Aftermath Res.

Barrett, Terence W. & Grimes, Dale M. Advanced Electromagnetism: Foundations, Theory & Applications. 650p. 1995. text 124.00 (*981-02-2095-2*) World Scientific Pub.

***Barrett, Terry.** Criticizing Art: Understanding the Contemporary. 2nd ed. xii, 208p. 2000. pap. text 23.95 (*0-7674-1165-X*, 1165-X) Mayfield Pub.

— Criticizing Photographs: An Introduction to Understanding Images. 3rd ed. LC 99-26895. xiii, 222p. 1999. pap. text 22.95 (*0-7674-1186-2*) Mayfield Pub.

Barrett, Terry. Talking about Student Art. LC 97-69073. (Art Education in Practice Ser.). 120p. 1997. pap. 15.55 (*0-87192-361-0*) Davis Mass.

Barrett, Terry L., jt. ed. see Greenway, Hubert T., Jr.

***Barrett, Thomas.** China, Marxism & Democracy: Selections from October Review LC 99-10401. (Revolutionary Studies). 1999. 59.95 (*1-57392-367-2*, Humanity Bks) Prometheus Bks.

Barrett, Thomas. Great Hanging at Gainesville. 1961. pap. 7.50 (*0-87611-004-9*) Tex St Hist Assn.

Barrett, Thomas, ed. China, Marxism, & Democracy: Selections from "October Review" LC 95-30166. (Revolutionary Studies). 276p. (C). 1996. text 60.00 (*0-391-03923-7*) Humanities.

Barrett, Thomas J. Harnessing the Earthworm. (Illus.). 1947. pap. 10.00 (*0-914116-08-8*) Shields.

— Harnessing the Earthworm. (Illus.). 192p. 1976. reprint ed. 7.95 (*0-916302-14-8*); reprint ed. pap. 5.95 (*0-916302-09-1*) Bookworm Pub.

Barrett, Thomas M. At the Edge of Empire: The Terek Cossacks & the North Caucasus Frontier, 1700-1860. LC 99-28671. 336p. 1999. 55.00 (*0-8133-3671-6*, Pub. by Westview) HarpC.

Barrett, Thomas S. & Livermore, Putnam. The Conservation Easement in California. LC 83-4329. 173p. 1983. 40.00 (*0-933280-20-3*) Island Pr.

Barrett, Thomas S., jt. auth. see Diehl, Janet.

Barrett, Timothy H. Zen: The Reason of Unreason; Eastern Wisdom. 64p. 1993. 9.95 (*0-8118-0403-8*) Chronicle Bks.

Barrett, Tracy. Anna of Byzantium. LC 98-47457. 224p. 1999. 14.95 (*0-385-32626-2*) BDD Bks Young Read.

***Barrett, Tracy.** Anna of Byzantium. 2000. mass mkt. 4.50 (*0-440-41536-5*, LE) Dell.

Barrett, Tracy. Growing up in Colonial America. LC 94-39224. (Illus.). 96p. (J). (gr. 4-6). 1995. lib. bdg. 23.40 (*1-56294-578-5*) Millbrook Pr.

— Harpers Ferry: The Story of John Brown's Raid. LC 92-39810. (Spotlight on American History Ser.). 1994. 11.15 (*0-606-06450-8*, Pub. by Turtleback) Demco.

— Kidding Around Nashville: What to Do, Where to Go & How to Have Fun in Nashville. LC 00-503371. (Kidding Around Ser.). (Illus.). 144p. (J). (gr. 1-5). 1998. pap. 7.95 (*1-56261-373-1*) Avalon Travel.

— Nat Turner & the Slave Revolt. LC 92-12086. (Gateway Civil Rights Ser.). (Illus.). 32p. (J). (gr. 2-4). 1993. pap. 4.95 (*1-56294-792-3*) Millbrook Pr.

— Nat Turner & the Slave Revolt. LC 92-12086. (Gateway Civil Rights Ser.). 1993. 10.15 (*0-606-06609-8*, Pub. by Turtleback) Demco.

Barrett, Tracy, tr. & contrib. by see Angiolieri, Cecco.

Barrett, Valerie, jt. auth. see Wolf-Cohen, Elizabeth.

Barrett, Victoria. Beyond the Misty Shore. (Seascape Ser.: Vol. 1). 1996. mass mkt. 5.99 (*0-312-95761-0*, Pub. by Tor Bks) St Martin.

— Festival. 448p. 1997. mass mkt. 5.50 (*0-7860-0421-5*, Pinncle Kensgtn) Kensgtn Pub Corp.

— Maybe This Time. 480p. 1996. mass mkt. 4.99 (*0-7860-0291-3*, Pinncle Kensgtn) Kensgtn Pub Corp.

— Message from Cupid. 1998. mass mkt. 5.99 (*0-312-96483-8*) St Martin.

— Upon a Mystic Tide. (Seascape Ser.). 1996. mass mkt. 5.99 (*0-312-96038-7*) St Martin.

Barrett, Virginia. Jessica's Dress-Ups. LC 92-31909. (Voyages Ser.). (Illus.). (J). 1994. write for info. (*0-383-03579-1*) SRA McGraw.

Barrett, W. A., jt. auth. see Stainer, John.

Barrett, W. F. Psychical Research. 255p. 1996. reprint ed. spiral bd. 20.00 (*0-7873-0073-X*) Hlth Research.

— Psychical Research. 255p. 1996. reprint ed. pap. 17.95 (*1-56459-658-3*) Kessinger Pub.

Barrett, Ward J. The Sugar Hacienda of the Marqueses del Valle. LC 74-110146. (Illus.). 155p. reprint ed. pap. 48.10 (*0-8357-7042-7*, 203320500085) Bks Demand.

Barrett, Warrick L. & Michaels, Scott. Johnny Bright, Champion. 176p. mass mkt. 4.99 (*1-55197-038-4*) Picasso Publ.

Barrett, Wayne C. The Church Finance Idea Book: Hundreds of Proven Ideas for Funding Your Ministry. LC 88-72382. 160p. 1989. pap. 9.95 (*0-88177-065-5*, DR065) Discipleship Res.

— Get Well! Stay Well! Prescriptions for a Financially Healthy Congregation. LC 96-72436. 96p. 1997. pap. 14.95 (*0-88177-213-5*, DR123) Discipleship Res.

— More Money, New Money, Big Money: Creative Strategies for Funding Today's Church. LC 92-76039. 168p. 1993. pap. 14.95 (*0-88177-120-1*, DR120) Discipleship Res.

Barrett, Wayne W., et al. The Real Positive Definite Completion Problem: Cycle Completability, No. 584. LC 96-12848. (Memoirs of the American Mathematical Society Ser.). 69p. 1996. pap. 32.00 (*0-8218-0473-1*, MEMO/122/584) Am Math.

Barrett, Wilbert F., ed. Selections from the Poems of John Greenleaf Whittier: Fifty-Four of His Poems with Notes & Biographical Sketch. 142p. 1983. reprint ed. pap. 6.00 (*1-878651-04-8*) HPL Pr.

Barrett, William. Barrett: Genealogy of Some of the Descendants of Thomas Barrett, Sr. of Braintree, Ma. 1635. (Illus.). 295p. 1992. reprint ed. pap. 46.00 (*0-8328-2481-X*); reprint ed. lib. bdg. 56.00 (*0-8328-2480-1*) Higginson Bk Co.

Barrett, William, ed. Zen Buddhism: Selected Writings of D. T. Suzuki. 320p. 1996. pap. 11.95 (*0-385-48349-X*, Image Bks) Doubleday.

Barrett, William A. Balfe: His Life & Work. 312p. 1991. reprint ed. lib. bdg. 89.00 (*0-7812-9331-6*) Rprt Serv.

— English Church Composers: The Great Musicians. LC 70-102224. (Select Bibliographies Reprint Ser.). 1977. 21.95 (*0-8369-5109-3*) Ayer.

Barrett, William E. The Edge of Things. 336p. lib. bdg. 25.95 (*0-88411-067-2*) Amereon Ltd.

— Irrational Man. LC 58-8081. 320p. 1962. reprint ed. pap. 12.95 (*0-385-03138-6*, Anchor NY) Doubleday.

— The Left Hand of God. 23.95 (*0-685-10845-7*, Queens House) Amereon Ltd.

— The Left Hand of God. 1990. reprint ed. lib. bdg. 19.95 (*0-89968-475-0*) Buccaneer Bks.

— The Lilies of the Field. 17.95 (*0-8488-0424-4*) Amereon Ltd.

— The Lilies of the Field. 128p. 1988. mass mkt. 5.99 (*0-446-31500-1*, Pub. by Warner Bks) Little.

— The Lilies of the Field. adapted ed. 1967. pap. 5.25 (*0-8222-0665-X*) Dramatists Play.

— The Lilies of the Field. 1993. reprint ed. lib. bdg. 21.95 (*1-56849-166-2*) Buccaneer Bks.

— Shape of Illusion. 22.95 (*0-8488-0426-0*) Amereon Ltd.

Barrett, William Edmund. Lilies of the Field. 1962. 10.60 (*0-606-00966-3*, Pub. by Turtleback) Demco.

Barrett, William F. On the Threshold of the Unseen (1917) 354p. 1998. reprint ed. pap. 27.95 (*0-7661-0561-X*) Kessinger Pub.

***Barrett, William L. & Practising Law Institute Staff.** What the Business Lawyer Needs to Know about ADR. LC 98-137295. (Litigation Course Handbook Ser.). 776 p. 1998. 129.00 (*0-87224-408-3*) PLI.

Barrett, William T., II, ed. The Overland Journal of Amos Piatt Josselyn. 129p. 1978. 12.50 (*0-685-02326-5*) Holmes.

Barrett, Yvette, et al, eds. The Environmental Education Reference Collection. 200p. 1994. ring bd. 20.00 (*0-614-00510-8*) Natl Consort EET.

Barretta-Herman, Angela. Welfare State to Welfare Society: Restructuring New Zealand's Social Services. LC 93-32456. (Children of Poverty Ser.). 376p. 1993. text 20.00 (*0-8153-1545-7*) Garland.

Barrette, Bill. Eva Hesse Sculpture. (Illus.). 274p. 1992. reprint ed. pap. 65.00 (*0-943221-14-5*) Timken Pubs.

Barrette, Bill & Yau, John. Berlin Diptychon. (Illus.). 96p. (Orig.). 1995. pap. 19.95 (*0-943221-23-4*) Timken Pubs.

Barrette, Doris, jt. auth. see Dube, Jasmine.

Barrette, Elizabeth, et al. Hadrosaur Tales Vol. II: A Review of Literary Science Fiction. Summers, David L., ed. 120p. (Orig.). 1997. pap. 5.95 (*1-885093-09-8*) Hadrosaur Pr.

Barrette, Gary T., ed. see Adelphi-AIESEP 85 World Sport Conference (1985: Ad.

Barrette, Judith, jt. auth. see Nicolay, Carol.

Barrette, Paul, jt. auth. see Fol, Monique.

Barrette, Paul, tr. see Latini, Brunetto.

B

Barretto. Batman: Scar of the Bat. O'Neil, Dennis, ed. (Illus.). 48p. 1996. pap. 4.95 (*1-56389-231-6*) DC Comics.

Barriault, Anne B. Spalliera Paintings of Renaissance Tuscany: Fables of Poets for Patrician Homes. LC 92-19920. (Illus.). 240p. (C). 1994. 65.00 (*0-271-00897-0*) Pa St U Pr.

Barriault, Anne B., et al. Selections: Virginia Museum of Fine Arts. West, Rosalie A., ed. LC 97-24981. (Illus.). 132p. 1997. pap. 22.00 (*0-917046-47-1*) Va Mus Arts.

Barriault, Anne B., ed. see Brandt, Frederick R. & Hight, Eleanor M.

Barriault, Anne B., ed. see Egerton, Judy.

Barricade Books Staff. O. J. Jokes Book: How Many O. J. Jokes Does It Take to Turn a Stomach. 1994. pap. 4.95 (*1-56980-026-X*) Barricade Bks.

Barricelli, Gian P. Alessandro Manzoni. LC 76-16481. (Twayne's World Authors Ser.). 194p. (C). 1976. text 17.95 (*0-8057-6251-5*) Irvington.

Barricelli, Jean-Pierre. Dante's Vision of the Artist: Four Modern Illustrators of the Commedia. LC 92-10820. (Illus.). XIV, 154p. (C). 1993. text 68.95 (*0-8204-1558-8*) P Lang Pubng.

— Fireplaces of Civilizations: Literary Portraits of Florence, Paris, Sicily, Seville & Granada. LC 93-7946. (FRE, GER, ITA & SPA.). x, 176p. 1993. pap. 13.00 (*1-879378-07-8*) Xenos Riverside.

Barricelli, Jean-Pierre, et al, eds. Teaching Literature & Other Arts. LC 89-13829. (Options for Teaching Ser.: No. 10). vi, 183p. 1990. lib. bdg. 19.75 (*0-87352-364-4*, J210C) Modern Lang.

Barricelli, Jean-Pierre & Gibaldi, Joseph, eds. Interrelations of Literature. LC 82-7956. vi, 329p. (C). 1982. pap. 18.00 (*0-87352-091-2*, T160P); lib. bdg. 32.00 (*0-87352-090-4*, T160C) Modern Lang.

Barricelli, Jean-Pierre & Weinstein, Leo. Ernest Chausson: The Composer's Life & Works. LC 73-7192. (Illus.). 241p. 1973. reprint ed. lib. bdg. 59.50 (*0-8371-6915-1*, BAEC, Greenwood Pr) Greenwood.

Barricelli, Peter. Create a Co-Op City: A Cooperative Adventure Using Architecture & Design. LC 97-74023. (Illus.). 78p. 1997. teacher ed. 9.95 (*0-9659692-0-7*) JLB Enterprises.

Barrick, Augusta I. The Power of Effective Speech. (Orig.). 1959. pap. 14.95 (*0-8084-0251-X*) NCUP.

Barrick-Hickey, Beth. 1001 Beauty Solutions: The Ultimate One-Step Adviser for Your Everyday Beauty Questions. LC 95-24937. (Illus.). 160p. 1995. pap. 12.95 (*1-57071-049-X*) Sourcebks.

Barrick, J. Robin. Mechanical Systems for Health Care Facilities. (Management & Compliance Ser.: Vol. 8). (Illus.). 308p. 1993. ring bd. 110.00 (*0-87258-654-5*, 055216) Am Hospital.

Barrick, Marilyn C. Sacred Psychology of Love: The Quest from Relationships that Unite Heart & Soul. LC 99-60189. 1999. pap. text 12.95 (*0-922729-49-2*) Summit Univ.

Barrick, Nolan E. The Unobserved Heritage of Texas Tech. LC 84-51938. (Illus.). 64p. 1985. pap. 5.00 (*0-89672-125-6*) Tex Tech Univ Pr.

Barrick, R. K. & Harmon, H. Animal Production & Management. 416p. 1988. text 19.96 (*0-07-003852-X*) McGraw.

Barrick, W. Boyd & Spencer, John R., eds. In the Shelter of Elyon: Essays in Honor of G. W. Ahlstrom. (Journal for the Study of the Old Testament Supplement Ser.: Vol. 31). 330p. 1984. 85.00 (*0-905774-65-5*, Pub. by Sheffield Acad) CUP Services.

Barrickman, John, jt. auth. see McKinley, John.

***Barrie.** Peter Pan. LC 99-35540. (Illus.). 176p. 1999. pap. text 2.00 (*0-486-40783-7*) Dover.

Barrie & Jenkins. Bible: Old Testament. LC 95-120656. 352p. 1995. 27.95 (*0-8050-3169-3*) H Holt & Co.

***Barrie, Alexander.** War Underground: The Tunnellers of the Great War. 272p. 2000. text 68.00 (*1-86227-081-3*, Pub. by Spellmnt Pubs) St Mut.

Barrie, Anmarie. Amazon Parrots As a New Pet. 64p. 1995. pap. text 6.95 (*0-7938-0184-2*, TU-030) TFH Pubns.

— A Beginner's Guide to Budgerigars. (Beginner's Guide Ser.). (Illus.). 64p. 1986. 4.95 (*0-86622-300-2*, T-101) TFH Pubns.

— A Beginner's Guide to Cockatiels. (Beginner's Guide Ser.). (Illus.). 64p. 1986. 4.95 (*0-86622-302-9*, T-103) TFH Pubns.

— A Beginner's Guide to Lovebirds. (Illus.). 64p. 1986. 4.95 (*0-86622-315-0*, T-116) TFH Pubns.

— Cats & the Law. (Illus.). 160p. 1990. 17.95 (*0-86622-079-8*, TS-136) TFH Pubns.

— Cats & the Law. (Illus.). 160p. 1999. reprint ed. pap. text 22.00 (*0-7881-6324-8*) DIANE Pub.

— Conures As a New Pet. (Illus.). 64p. 1995. pap. 6.95 (*0-7938-1997-0*, TU028) TFH Pubns.

— Dogs & the Law. (Illus.). 160p. 1989. lib. bdg. 17.95 (*0-86622-088-7*, TS-130) TFH Pubns.

— Gerbils As a New Pet. (Illus.). 64p. (Orig.). 1990. pap. 6.95 (*0-86622-608-7*, TU-002) TFH Pubns.

— Goldfish As a New Pet. (Illus.). 64p. (Orig.). 1990. pap. 6.95 (*0-86622-606-0*, TU-001) TFH Pubns.

— Guide to Owning a Chinchilla. (Illus.). 64p. 1997. pap. 6.95 (*0-7938-2161-4*, RE-512) TFH Pubns.

— Guide to Owning a Cockatiel. (Illus.). 64p. 1997. pap. 6.95 (*0-7938-2002-2*, RE-202) TFH Pubns.

— Guide to Owning a Hamster. (Illus.). 64p. 1996. pap. 6.95 (*0-7938-2154-1*, RE505) TFH Pubns.

— Guinea Pigs As a Hobby. (Save Our Planet Ser.). (Illus.). 98p. 1991. pap. 8.95 (*0-86622-420-3*, TT008) TFH Pubns.

— Hamsters As a New Pet. (Illus.). 64p. (Orig.). 1990. pap. 6.95 (*0-86622-610-9*, TU-003) TFH Pubns.

— Hamsters for Those Who Care. (Illus.). 32p. 1994. pap. 4.95 (*0-7938-1376-X*, B105) TFH Pubns.

— The Professional's Book of Koi. (Illus.). 160p. 1998. text 17.95 (*0-86622-528-5*, TS-158) TFH Pubns.

— Rabbits for Those Who Care. (Illus.). 32p. 1994. pap. 4.95 (*0-7938-1377-8*, B117) TFH Pubns.

— Snakes for Those Who Care. (Illus.). 32p. 1994. pap. 4.95 (*0-7938-1389-1*, B111) TFH Pubns.

— A Step by Step Book about Canaries. (Step-by-Step Ser.). (Illus.). 64p. 1987. pap. 5.95 (*0-86622-461-0*, SK-004) TFH Pubns.

— A Step by Step Book about Cockatiels. (Step-by-Step Ser.). (Illus.). 64p. (Orig.). 1987. pap. 5.95 (*0-86622-453-X*, SK-007) TFH Pubns.

— A Step by Step Book about Guinea Pigs. (Step-by-Step Ser.). (Illus.). 64p. (Orig.). 1987. pap. 5.95 (*0-86622-450-5*, SK-013) TFH Pubns.

— A Step by Step Book about Hamsters. (Step-by-Step Ser.). (Illus.). 64p. 1987. pap. 5.95 (*0-86622-458-0*, SK-014) TFH Pubns.

— A Step-by-Step Book about Our First Aquarium. (Step-by-Step Ser.). (Illus.). 64p. (J). 1987. pap. 5.95 (*0-86622-454-8*, SK003); lib. bdg. 9.95 (*0-86622-923-X*, SK003X) TFH Pubns.

— A Step-by-Step Book about Rabbits. (Step-by-Step Ser.). (Illus.). 64p. 1987. pap. 5.95 (*0-86622-475-0*, SK-001); lib. bdg. 9.95 (*0-86622-924-8*, SK-001) TFH Pubns.

— Your New Garden Pond. (Illus.). 64p. 1991. pap. 6.95 (*0-86622-533-1*, TU-021) TFH Pubns.

***Barrie, Anna.** The Linden Tree. large type ed. 432p. 1999. 31.99 (*0-7505-1364-0*, Pub. by Mgna Lrg Print) Ulverscroft.

Barrie, Barbara. Adam Zigzag. 192p. (YA). (gr. 5-9). 1995. mass mkt. 3.99 (*0-440-21964-7*, LLL BDD) BDD Bks Young Read.

Barrie, Barbara. Adam Zigzag. LC 93-8735. 1996. 9.09 (*0-606-08968-3*, Pub. by Turtleback) Demco.

Barrie, Barbara. Don't Die of Embarrassment: Life after Colostomy & Other Adventures. LC 98-52468. 256p. 1999. pap. 11.00 (*0-684-84624-1*, Fireside) S&S Trade Pap.

— Second Act: Life after Colostomy & Other Adventures. LC 97-11993. 224p. 1997. 22.50 (*0-684-83587-8*) S&S Trade.

Barrie, Brooke. Contemporary Outdoor Sculpture. (Illus.). 192p. 1999. 50.00 (*1-56496-421-3*) Rockport Pubs.

Barrie, Bruner F. Mold Making, Casting & Patina. LC 91-92469. 175p. 1992. pap. text 20.00 (*0-9631867-0-1*) A B F & S.

— A Sculptor's Guide to Tools & Materials. 134p. 1997. pap. text 19.95 (*0-9631867-1-X*) A B F & S.

Barrie, Dennis. Artists in Michigan, 1900-1976: A Biographical Dictionary. LC 88-14832. (Great Lakes Bks.: No. 5). (Illus.). 240p. reprint ed. pap. 74.40 (*0-608-10535-X*, 207115500009) Bks Demand.

Barrie, Donald S. Dundalk, Newry & Greenore Railway. (C). 1985. 39.00 (*0-85361-260-9*) St Mut.

— Taff Vale Railway. (C). 1985. 50.00 (*0-85361-027-4*) St Mut.

Barrie, Donald S., ed. Derwent Valley Railway. (C). 1985. 39.00 (*0-85361-233-1*) St Mut.

Barrie, Donald S. & Paulson, Boyd C. Professional Construction Management. 3rd ed. 672p. (C). 1991. 79.38 (*0-07-003889-9*) McGraw.

Barrie, Giles, jt. auth. see Coleman, Ron.

Barrie, J. M. Auld Licht Idylls & Better Dead. LC 76-106246. (Short Story Index Reprint Ser.). 1977. 20.95 (*0-8369-3282-X*) Ayer.

— Auld Licht Manse, - Other Sketches. LC 78-116936. (Short Story Index Reprint Ser.). 1977. 19.95 (*0-8369-3438-5*) Ayer.

— Courage. 15.95 (*0-89190-519-7*) Amereon Ltd.

— Farewell Miss Julie Logan. 16.95 (*0-88411-599-2*) Amereon Ltd.

— Holiday in Bed, & Other Sketches: With a Short Biographical Sketch of the Author. LC 70-160930. (Short Story Index Reprint Ser.). 1977. reprint ed. 17.95 (*0-8369-3909-3*) Ayer.

— The Little Minister. 381p. Date not set. 26.95 (*0-8488-2205-6*) Amereon Ltd.

— The Little Minister. 300p. (J). 1980. reprint ed. lib. bdg. 18.95 (*0-89967-007-5*, Harmony Rain) Buccaneer Bks.

— The Little Minister. 232p. (J). 1981. reprint ed. lib. bdg. 18.95 (*0-89966-329-X*) Buccaneer Bks.

— The Little White Bird: or Adventures in Kensington Gardens. 1991. reprint ed. lib. bdg. 21.95 (*1-56849-045-3*) Buccaneer Bks.

— Margaret Ogilvy. 1980. 29.00 (*0-403-00243-5*) Scholarly.

— M'Connachie & J. M. B. Speeches. LC 78-156611. (Essay Index Reprint Ser.). 1977. reprint ed. 23.95 (*0-8369-2343-X*) Ayer.

— Pantaloon. Landes, William-Alan, ed. LC 93-19587. 1993. pap. 6.00 (*0-88734-316-3*) Players Pr.

— Peter Pan. (Illus.). 160p. (J). 1998. 24.95 (*1-85149-702-1*) Antique Collect.

— Peter Pan. 176p. (J). 1985. mass mkt. 4.95 (*0-553-21178-1*, Bantam Classics) Bantam.

— Peter Pan. LC 87-403. (Illus.). 144p. (J). (gr. 2 up). 1995. 19.95 (*0-8050-0276-6*, Bks Young Read) H Holt & Co.

Barrie, J. M. Peter Pan. (Illus.). (J). 1995. mass mkt. 8.95 (*0-340-62664-X*, Pub. by Hodder & Stought Ltd) Trafalgar.

Barrie, J. M. Peter Pan. (Illustrated Classics Ser.). (Illus.). 128p. (J). 1991. pap. 2.95 (*1-56156-029-4*) Kidsbks.

— Peter Pan. LC 92-53172. (Illus.). 224p. (J). (ps-3). 1992. 12.95 (*0-679-41792-3*, Evrymans Lib Childs) Knopf.

Barrie, J. M. Peter Pan. 1988. 2.98 (*0-671-10162-5*) PB.

Barrie, J. M. Peter Pan. LC 94-76734. (Illus.). 256p. (YA). (gr. 5-9). 1996. pap. 3.99 (*0-14-036674-1*, PuffinBks) Peng Put Young Read.

— Peter Pan. Hanft, Joshua, ed. (Great Illustrated Classics Ser.: Vol. 46). (Illus.). 240p. (J). (gr. 3-6). 1995. 9.95 (*0-86611-997-3*) Playmore Inc.

— Peter Pan. (Folio - Junior Ser.: No. 411). (FRE., Illus.). 239p. (J). (gr. 5-10). 1988. pap. 9.95 (*2-07-033411-2*) Schoenhof.

— Peter Pan. (J). 1978. pap. 1.95 (*0-590-30054-7*) Scholastic Inc.

— Peter Pan. 208p. (J). (gr. 4-7). 1993. pap. 3.25 (*0-590-46735-2*, Apple Classics) Scholastic Inc.

***Barrie, J. M.** Peter Pan. (Illus.). (J). 2001. 24.95 (*1-58479-029-6*) Stewart Tabori & Chang.

Barrie, J. M. Peter Pan. Shebar, Susan, ed. LC 87-15480. (Illus.). 48p. (J). (gr. 2-6). 1988. lib. bdg. 19.95 (*0-8167-1199-2*) Troll Communs.

— Peter Pan. Shebar, Susan, ed. LC 87-15480. (Illus.). 48p. (J). (gr. 4-7). 1997. pap. 5.95 (*0-8167-1200-X*) Troll Communs.

— Peter Pan. (Deluxe Watermill Classic Ser.). 176p. (YA). 1998. pap. 2.95 (*0-8167-2555-1*) Troll Communs.

— Peter Pan. 1985. 9.05 (*0-606-02465-4*, Pub. by Turtleback) Demco.

— Peter Pan. (J). 1990. 15.15 (*0-606-00686-9*, Pub. by Turtleback) Demco.

— Peter Pan. (Children's Library). (gr. 4-7). 1998. pap. 3.95 (*1-85326-120-3*, 1203WW, Pub. by Wrdsworth Edits) NTC Contemp Pub Co.

— Peter Pan. LC 90-23077. (Step into Classics Ser.). (Illus.). 96p. (J). (gr. 2-7). 1991. pap. 3.99 (*0-679-81044-7*, Pub. by Random Bks Yng Read) Random.

— Peter Pan. abr. ed. (Children's Classics Ser.). (J). 1998. pap. 16.95 incl. audio (*1-85998-588-2*) Trafalgar.

— Peter Pan & Other Plays: The Admirable Crichton; Peter Pan; When Wendy Grew Up; What Ever. Hollindale, Peter, ed. (Oxford Drama Library). 374p. 1995. text 65.00 (*0-19-812162-8*) OUP.

— Peter Pan & Other Plays: The Admirable Crichton; Peter Pan; When Wendy Grew Up; What Every Woman Knows; Mary Rose. Hollindale, Peter, ed. & intro. by. (Oxford World's Classics Ser.). 374p. 1999. pap. 13.95 (*0-19-283919-5*) OUP.

— Peter Pan & Wendy. LC 98-31003. (Abbeville Classics Ser.). (Illus.). 176p. (J). 1999. 12.95 (*0-7892-0560-2*, Abbeville Kids); pap. 7.95 (*0-7892-0550-5*, Abbeville Kids) Abbeville Pr.

— Peter Pan & Wendy. (Illus.). 160p. (J). (gr. 3-6). 1992. pap. 17.95 (*1-85145-449-7*, Pub. by Pavilion Bks Ltd) Trafalgar.

***Barrie, J. M.** Peter Pan & Wendy. Carruth, Jane, ed. (Illus.). 92p. (J). (gr. 4-6). 2000. reprint ed. 25.00 (*0-7881-9230-2*) DIANE Pub.

Barrie, J. M. Peter Pan Book & Charm. LC 99-33256. (Charming Classic Bks.). 256p. (J). (gr. 4-7). 2000. 5.95 (*0-694-01318-8*) HarpC Child Bks.

— Peter Pan in Kensington Gardens. (J). 18.95 (*0-8488-0427-9*) Amereon Ltd.

— Peter Pan in Kensington Gardens. 150p. (J). 1980. reprint ed. lib. bdg. 16.95 (*0-89967-006-7*, Harmony Rain) Buccaneer Bks.

— Peter Pan in Kensington Gardens. 175p. (J). 1981. reprint ed. lib. bdg. 16.95 (*0-89966-328-1*) Buccaneer Bks.

— Peter Pan in Kensington Gardens & Peter & Wendy. Hollingdale, Peter, ed. (Oxford World's Classics Ser.). (Illus.). 288p. 1999. pap. 7.95 (*0-19-283929-2*) OUP.

— Peter Pan in Neverland: A Musical Fantasy in 2 Acts. (Illus.). 58p. 1995. pap. 4.50 (*0-88680-414-0*) I E Clark.

— Peter Pan: or The Boy Who Would Not Grow Up. adapted ed. 1994. pap. 5.25 (*0-8222-1345-1*) Dramatists Play.

— Rosalind. Landes, William-Alan, ed. LC 93-15725. 1993. pap. 6.00 (*0-88734-331-7*) Players Pr.

— Sentimental Tommy. 21.95 (*0-8488-0192-X*) Amereon Ltd.

— Sentimental Tommy. (BCL1-PR English Literature Ser.). 503p. 1992. reprint ed. lib. bdg. 99.00 (*0-7812-7430-3*) Rprt Serv.

— The Story of Peter Pan. unabridged ed. LC 92-18641. (Children's Thrift Classics Ser.). (Illus.). 96p. (J). 1998. reprint ed. 1.00 (*0-486-27294-X*) Dover.

— A Tillyloss Scandal. LC 77-98560. (Short Story Index Reprint Ser.). 1977. 19.95 (*0-8369-3134-3*) Ayer.

— The Twelve Pound Look (Playscript) LC 93-13403. 1993. pap. 5.00 (*0-88734-330-9*) Players Pr.

— What Every Woman Knows. LC 97-6902. (Dover Thrift Editions Ser.). 80p. 1997. reprint ed. pap. text 1.50 (*0-486-29578-8*) Dover.

Barrie, J. M. Wild in the Country. mass mkt. 6.95 (*0-7472-5200-9*, Pub. by Headline Bk Pub) Trafalgar.

Barrie, J. M. The Will (Playscript) LC 93-17547. 1993. pap. 5.00 (*0-88734-329-5*) Players Pr.

— A Window in Thrums. 1996. 59.00 (*0-403-00118-8*) Scholarly.

— A Window in Thrums. (BCL1-PR English Literature Ser.). 272p. 1992. reprint ed. lib. bdg. 79.00 (*0-7812-7431-1*) Rprt Serv.

— Works of J. M. Barrie: Peter Pan Edition, 18 vols. Incl. Vol. 1. Auld Licht Idylls, etc. LC 79-146660. reprint ed. 57.50 (*0-404-08781-7*); Vol. 2. My Lady Nicotine, Etc. LC 79-146660. reprint ed. 57.50 (*0-404-08782-5*); Vol. 3. When a Man's Single. LC 79-146660. reprint ed. 57.50 (*0-404-08783-3*); Vol. 4. Little Minister. LC 79-146660. reprint ed. 57.50 (*0-404-08784-1*); Vol. 5. Sentimental Tommy. LC 79-146660. reprint ed. 57.50 (*0-404-08785-X*); Vol. 6. Tommy & Grizel. LC 79-146660. reprint ed. 57.50 (*0-404-08786-8*); Vol. 7. Little White Bird. LC 79-146660. reprint ed. 57.50 (*0-404-08787-6*); Vol. 8. Margaret Ogilvy & Others. LC 79-146660. 263p. 1975. reprint ed. 57.50 (*0-404-08788-4*); Vol. 9. Courage, etc. LC 79-146660. reprint ed. 57.50 (*0-404-08789-2*); Vol. 10. Peter Pan & Other Plays. LC 79-146660. reprint ed. 57.50 (*0-404-08790-6*); Vol. 11. Admirable Crichton: And Other Plays. LC 79-146660. reprint ed. 57.50 (*0-404-08791-4*); Vol. 12. What Every Woman Knows & Other Plays. LC 79-146660. reprint ed. 57.50 (*0-404-08792-2*); Vol. 13. Dear Brutus & Other Plays. LC 79-146660. reprint ed. 57.50 (*0-404-08793-0*); Vol. 14. Mary Rose & Other Plays. LC 79-146660. reprint ed. 57.50 (*0-404-08794-9*); Vol. 15. M'Connachie & J. M. B., Etc. LC 79-146660. reprint ed. 57.50 (*0-404-08795-7*); Vol. 16. Greenwood Hat, etc. LC 79-146660. reprint ed. 57.50 (*0-404-08796-5*); Vol. 17. Boy David. LC 79-146660. reprint ed. 57.50 (*0-404-08797-3*); Vol. 18. Professor's Love-Story, Etc. LC 79-146660. reprint ed. 57.50 (*0-404-08798-1*); LC 79-146660. write for info. (*0-404-08780-9*) AMS Pr.

Barrie, J. M., jt. auth. see Johnstone, Michael.

Barrie, Joan. Reading English. (Illus.). 132p. (Orig.). (J). (gr. k-3). 1995. ring bd. 18.95 (*0-614-29815-6*) Evrst Cultural.

— Tiggy Primary Academics: A Reproducible Social Studies Through Literature Mini Program & Reproducible Student Storybook: Tiggy & Me & Butterfly, Too! Blanco, T. et al, trs. LC 92-23008. (ENG, JPN & SPA., Illus.). 330p. (J). (ps-12). 1993. teacher ed., ring bd. 19.95 (*0-936788-14-3*) Evrst Cultural.

Barrie, Ron & Macpherson, Ken. Cadillac of Destroyers: HMCS St. Laurent & Her Successors. LC 97-121923. (Illus.). 104p. 1998. 29.95 (*1-55125-036-5*, Pub. by Vanwell Publ) Howell Pr VA.

Barrie, Shirely, et al. Wanna Play: Thin Ice; Carring the Calf. 216p. (Orig.). 1997. pap. 14.95 (*0-88754-495-9*) Theatre Comm.

Barrie, Steven, jt. auth. see Bennett, Peter.

Barrie, Thomas. Spiritual Path, Sacred Place: Myth, Ritual, & Meaning in Architecture. (Illus.). 240p. (Orig.). 1996. pap. 30.00 (*1-57062-005-9*, Pub. by Shambhala Pubns) Random.

Barrielle, Ludovic-Marie. Rules for Discerning the Spirits: In the "Spiritual Exercises" of St. Ignatius of Loyola. 60p. 1992. reprint ed. pap. 4.25 (*0-935952-77-2*) Angelus Pr.

Barrientos. Women & Agribusiness: Working Miracles in the Chilean Fruit Export Sector. LC 98-30662. 256p. 1999. text 72.00 (*0-312-21998-9*) St Martin.

Barrientos, A. La Iglesia en Que Sirvo.Tr. of Church in Which I Serve. (SPA.). pap. 10.99 (*0-7899-0255-9*, 491047) Editorial Unilit.

Barrientos, Alberto. Teologia de la Liberacion: Respuesta Pastoral.Tr. of Liberation Theology. (SPA.). 1991. 2.99 (*1-56063-093-0*, 497709) Editorial Unilit.

Barrientos, Carlos H. A Guitarist's Practical Guide to the Modes. (Illus.). i, 35p. 1996. 16.95 (*0-9679569-0-0*) Carma Prod.

Barrientos, Guido. Reaching Out/Dame la Mano: Utilization of Mental Resources in El Paso & Mexico. 184p. 1997. pap. 15.00 (*0-87404-240-2*) Tex Western.

Barrientos, Jane. Art of Deception, Vol. 1. 2nd ed. (Illus.). 50p. 1997. pap. 9.95 (*1-57377-011-6*) Easl Pubns.

— Art of Deception, Vol. 2. (Illus.). 36p. 1998. pap. 9.95 (*1-57377-043-4*, 019884-2230) Easl Pubns.

Barrientos, M. R. Spanish-English - English-Spanish Maritime Dictionary. (ENG & SPA.). 230p. 1986. pap. 28.50 (*84-283-1514-0*, Pub. by Paraninfo) IBD Ltd.

Barrientos, Parra O. Revision der Gattung Pediastrum Meyen (Chlorophyta) (Bibliotheca Phycologica Ser.: No. 48). (Illus.). 1979. 48.00 (*3-7682-1254-8*) Lubrecht & Cramer.

***Barrientos, Stephanie.** Women & Agribusiness: Working Miracles in the Chilean Fruit Export Sector. LC 98-30662. (Women's Studies at York.). xvii, 231 p. 1999. write for info. (*0-333-68293-9*, Pub. by Macmillan) Macmillan.

Barrier, jt. auth. see Daniel.

Barrier Free Environments, Inc. Staff. The Accessible Housing Design File. 213p. 1991. pap. 64.95 (*0-471-28436-X*, VNR) Wiley.

Barrier Free Environments, Inc. Staff. The Accessible Housing Design File. (Illus.). 320p. 1991. pap. 54.95 (*0-442-00775-2*, VNR) Wiley.

Barrier Free Environments, Inc. Staff. UFAS Retrofit Guide: Accessibility Modifications for Existing Buildings. (Architecture Ser.). 358p. 1993. pap. 64.95 (*0-471-28574-9*, VNR) Wiley.

Barrier Free Environments, Inc. Staff, des. UFAS Retrofitting Guide: Accessibility Modifications for Existing Buildings: Designed to be Used in Conjunction with the Uniform Federal Accessibility Standards for Compliance with Title II of the Americans with Disabilities Act, Section 50-4 of the Rehabilitation Act of 1973, the Architectural Barriers Acts of 1968. LC 92-42361. 1993. text 54.95 (*0-442-01567-4*, VNR) Wiley.

Barrier, Gerald N., ed. The Census in British India: New Perspectives. 1982. 18.00 (*0-8364-0847-0*, Pub. by Manohar) S Asia.

Barrier, Jean & Kennedy, Alice. English Is Fun I. (Illus.). 96p. (J). (gr. k-8). 1981. pap. 6.00 (*0-911743-01-4*) Barrier & Kennedy.

— English Is Fun II. Catoe, Kaye et al, eds. (Illus.). 96p. (J). (gr. 2-8). 1985. pap. text 6.00 (*0-911743-04-9*); pap. text, teacher ed. 8.00 (*0-911743-06-5*) Barrier & Kennedy.

— Expanded Ideas for English Is Fun 1. (English Is Fun Ser.). (Illus.). 115p. 1982. pap., teacher ed. 12.00 (*0-911743-02-2*) Barrier & Kennedy.

Barrier, Michael. Carl Barks & the Art of the Comic Book. LC 81-20899. (Illus.). 228p. 1982. 70.00 (*0-9607652-0-4*); pap. 20.00 (*0-9607652-1-2*) M Lilien.

— Hollywood Cartoons: American Animation in Its Golden Age. LC 98-7471. (Illus.). 672p. 1999. 39.95 (*0-19-503759-6*) OUP.

Barrier, N. Gerald. India & America: American Publishing on India 1930-1985. 1986. 44.00 (*81-85054-09-6*, Pub. by Manohar) S Asia.

Barrier, N. Gerald, ed. The Roots of Communal Politics: The Cawnpur Riot Commission Report. LC 76-6253. 1976. reprint ed. 16.00 (*0-88386-609-9*) S Asia.

B

An Asterisk (*) at the beginning of an entry indicates that the title is appearing for the first time.

— The Sikh Diaspora. (C). 1989. 44.00 (*0-685-35370-2*) S Asia.

Barrier, N. Gerald, jt. ed. see Case, Margret H.

Barrier, N. Gerald, jt. ed. see Singh, P.

Barrier, Rusty & Seymour, Tricia. Rise to the Stars: A Daily Focus Book for Network Marketing Entrepreneurs. 384p. 1998. pap. 12.95 (*1-892670-00-3*) Entelechea Pr.

Barrier, Rusty, jt. auth. see Seymour, Tricia.

Barrierio, et al. Fundamental Physics - Physics at Hera: Proceedings of XXIst International Meeting. 484p. 1994. text 97.00 (*981-02-1707-2*) World Scientific Pub.

Barriero, Enrique & Alcatena, Quique. Subterra Bk. 2: Moving Fortress. Villagran, Enrique & Dixon, Charles, trs. from SPA. (Illus.). 56p. (Orig.). 1989. pap. 8.98 (*0-922173-02-8*) Four Winds Pub Group.

***Barriga, Angel.** Microelectronics Design of Fuzzy Logic-Based Systems. (Illus.). 2000. 89.95 (*0-8493-0091-6*) CRC Pr.

Barriga, Marian, tr. see Zunkel, C. Wayne.

Barriga, Omar. Veterinary Parasitology. (Illus.). 316p. (C). 1995. pap. text 16.00 (*1-57074-242-1*) Greyden Pr.

Barriga, Patricio, et al. The Facilitator Model. (Technical Notes Ser.: No. 11). 32p. (Orig.). 1975. pap. 2.00 (*0-932288-24-3*); pap. 2.00 (*0-932288-25-1*) Ctr Intl Ed U of MA.

— Fotonovella. (Technical Notes Ser.: No. 13). 12p. (Orig.). 1975. pap. 2.00 (*0-932288-28-6*); pap. 2.00 (*0-932288-29-4*) Ctr Intl Ed U of MA.

***Barrigan, Barbara & Kovaleski, Lisa, eds.** Syllogism 2. 150p. 1999. pap. 9.00 (*0-9673885-0-3*, 001-99) Manfst Pr.

Barril, Joan. Barcelona: Conquest of Space: Architecture (1982-1992) (Illus.). 96p. 1993. 75.00 (*84-343-0702-2*) Elliots Bks.

Barrile, Anna R., jt. ed. see Cavazza, Albertina.

***Barrilleaux, Jon.** 3D User Interfaces with Java 3D. 520p. 2000. pap. 49.95 (*1-884777-90-2*) Manning Pubns.

***Barrineau, Frances.** Grab a Bag Cookbook: Recipes That Begin in a Bag with the Dry Ingredients & Are Completed Later with the Liquid Ingredients. 203p. 2000. 15.95 (*0-942407-51-2*) Father & Son.

Barrineau, H. E., III. Civil Liability in Criminal Justice. 2nd rev. ed. LC 93-74613. 150p. (C). 1994. pap. 17.95 (*0-87084-095-9*) Anderson Pub Co.

Barrineau, Nancy W., ed. see Dreiser, Theodore.

Barring, Torsten. Confessions of a Naked Piano Player. 1998. mass mkt. 6.95 (*1-56333-626-X*, Badboy) Masquerade.

— Guy Traynor. (Orig.). 1996. mass mkt. 5.95 (*1-56333-414-3*, Badboy) Masquerade.

— Peter Thornwell. (Orig.). 1993. mass mkt. 4.95 (*1-56333-149-7*, Badboy) Masquerade.

— Shadowman. (Orig.). 1994. mass mkt. 4.95 (*1-56333-178-0*, Badboy) Masquerade.

— The Switch. (Orig.). 1992. mass mkt. 4.95 (*1-56333-061-X*, Badboy) Masquerade.

Barringer, Bernie. Complete Guide to Farmland Fur Trapping. (Illus.). 280p. (Orig.). 1997. pap. 14.95 (*1-885149-04-2*) Moving Mtn.

— Iowa Fishing Atlas: Iowa's Top Fifty-Five Fishing Lakes. 2nd rev. ed. (Illus.). 140p. 19.95 (*1-885149-00-X*) Moving Mtn.

***Barringer, Bernie.** Iowa Fishing Atlas No. I: 68 Lakes. 2nd rev. ed. (Illus.). 168p. 1998. spiral bd. 19.95 (*1-885149-07-7*) Moving Mtn.

Barringer, Bernie. Iowa Rivers & Streams Vol. 2: Iowa Fishing Atlas. (Illus.). 222p. 1996. spiral bd. 19.95 (*1-885149-03-4*) Moving Mtn.

Barringer, Bernie & Miranda, Tom. Corn Fed Giants: Step by Step Guide to Locating & Harvesting Whitetails in Farmland. (Illus.). 192p. (Orig.). 1993. pap. 14.95 (*1-885149-01-8*) Moving Mtn.

Barringer, Bernie, ed. see Christensen, Daryl.

Barringer, Bernie R., ed. & pref. see Burns, M. Doug.

Barringer, Carol E. Thresholds No. 6: Viewing Culture. Cella, Edward et al, eds. (Illus.). 96p. 1992. pap. 10.00 (*1-892751-00-3*) Thresholds.

***Barringer, Daniel Moreau & Adams, John Stokes.** The Law of Mines & Mining in the United States, 2 vols. 1676p. 2000. reprint ed. 370.00 (*1-56169-587-4*) Gaunt.

Barringer, E. E. Alone on a Wide, Wide Sea: The Story of 835 Naval Air Squadron in WW II. (Illus.). 209p. 1995. 31.95 (*0-85052-278-1*, Pub. by Leo Cooper) Trans-Atl Phila.

Barringer, Herbert R., et al. Asians & Pacific Islanders in the United States. LC 92-4867. (Population of the United States in the 1980s: A Census Monograph Ser.). (Illus.). 384p. 1992. 42.50 (*0-87154-095-9*) Russell Sage.

— Asians & Pacific Islanders in the United States. 384p. (C). 1995. reprint ed. pap. text 18.50 (*0-87154-096-7*) Russell Sage.

Barringer, Howard. The Imperative Future: Principles of Executable Temporal Logic. LC 96-13638. (Advanced Software Development Ser.). xv, 239p. 1996. write for info. (*0-86380-190-0*) Research Studies Pr Ltd.

Barringer, Janice & Schlesinger, Sarah. The Pointe Book: Shoes, Training & Technique. rev. ed. LC 96-43844. 208p. 1998. pap. 18.95 (*0-87127-204-0*) Princeton Bk Co.

Barringer, Judith. Divine Escorts: Nereids in Archaic & Classical Greek Art. (Illus.). 360p. 1995. text 54.50 (*0-472-10418-7*, 10418); pap. text 27.95 (*0-472-08275-2*, 08275) U of Mich Pr.

Barringer, Mary R. & Womack, Cindy L. Home Care Helper: A Guide to Personal & Medical Information. 1995. pap. 6.50 (*0-9641671-0-7*) MarCin Enter.

Barringer, Richard, ed. Changing Maine. (Illus.). (Orig.). 1990. pap. text 11.95 (*0-939561-07-7*) Univ South ME.

— Toward a Sustainable Maine: The Politics, Economics, & Ethics of Sustainability. (Orig.). 1993. pap. 10.00 (*0-939561-18-2*) Univ South ME.

Barringer, Robert, ed. Rome & Constantinople: Essays in the Dialogue of Love. 86p. (Orig.). 1985. pap. 2.00 (*0-917651-05-7*) Holy Cross Orthodox.

Barringer, Robert, tr. see Staniloae, Dumitru.

Barringer, Tim. Frederic Leighton: Antiquity, Renaissance, Modernity. LC 98-88584. Vol. 5. (Illus.). 384p. 1999. 60.00 (*0-300-07937-0*) Yale U Pr.

— Reading the Pre-Raphaelites. LC 98-60960. (Illus.). 176p. 1999. pap. text 19.95 (*0-300-07787-4*) Yale U Pr.

Barringer, Tim & Flynn, Tom. Colonialism & the Object. LC 97-3320. (Illus.). 240p. (C). 1998. pap. 25.99 (*0-415-15776-5*) Routledge.

Barringer, Tim & Flynn, Tom, eds. Colonialism & the Object. LC 97-3320. (Illus.). 240p. (C). 1998. 85.00 (*0-415-15775-7*) Routledge.

Barrington. Math Foundations in Computer Science. 2000. 60.50 (*0-07-006276-5*) McGraw.

Barrington, jt. auth. see Reid.

Barrington, Alan. Here Am I Send Me: The Essential Handbook for Every Christian Who Has Sensed the Calling of God. 192p. 1999. pap. 11.95 (*1-58169-033-9*) Genesis Comm Inc.

— The Truth about Santa Claus: When Your Child Is Ready to Hear . . . (Illus.). 32p. (J). (ps-3). 1997. pap. 5.99 (*1-56043-242-X*, CP201, Third Stry Window) Genesis Comm Inc.

Barrington, Boyd C. Magna Carta & Other Great Charters of England: With an Historical Treatise & Copious Explanatory Notes. 342p. 1993. reprint ed. 45.00 (*0-8377-1955-0*, Rothman) W S Hein.

***Barrington, Carol.** Shifra Stein's Day Trips from Houston: Getaways Less Than Two Hours Away. 8th ed. LC 99-18089. (Day Trips Ser.). (Illus.). 240p. 1999. pap. text 13.95 (*0-7627-0546-9*) Globe Pequot.

Barrington, Daines. The Probability of Reaching the North Pole Discussed. 96p. 1987. 12.95 (*0-87770-424-4*) Ye Galleon.

Barrington, Emilie I. Life, Letters & Work of Frederic Baron Leighton, 2 vols. LC 70-140032. (Illus.). reprint ed. 127.50 (*0-404-00659-0*) AMS Pr.

***Barrington, Harold P.** The Great Adventure: A World I Soldier's Diary. (Illus.). 194p. 2000. pap. 13.95 (*1-890676-62-4*, Pub. by Beavers Pond) Bookman Bks.

Barrington, Harry, jt. auth. see Reid, Margaret A.

Barrington, Hermester. Death Trap at La Puente: Fisico Nuclear. Walsh, Phillip, Jr. & Brown, Kurt, eds. 18p. (Orig.). 1995. pap. 4.95 (*0-9649280-0-0*) Viva La Lucha.

Barrington Hofer, Grace & Day, Rachel. Oigan Ninos (Listen Children) (ENG & SPA., Illus.). 96p. (J). 1997. 12.95 (*1-57168-015-2*, Eakin Pr) Sunbelt Media.

— Oigan Ninos, Listen Children: A Book of Nursery Rhymes, Poems, Songs & Riddles in Spanish & in English. (ENG & SPA., Illus.). 96p. (J). (ps-7). 1995. pap. 12.95 (*0-89015-865-7*, Eakin Pr) Sunbelt Media.

Barrington, Jacky, ed. One Hundred Years of Frontier Living. 2nd ed. 184p. (Orig.). 1994. pap. 10.00 (*0-9617036-2-8*) Bandar Log.

Barrington, John. Kouros: Photographs. 1995. per. 24.95 (*0-85449-129-5*, Pub. by Gay Mens Pr) LPC InBook.

***Barrington, John.** On the Trail of Rob Roy McGregor. (Illus.). 192p. 2000. pap. 14.95 (*0-946487-59-6*) Luath Pr Ltd.

— Red Sky at Night. (Illus.). 256p. 2000. pap. 16.95 (*0-946487-60-X*) Luath Pr Ltd.

Barrington, Jonah. Ireland of Sir Jonah Barrington: Selections from His Personal Sketches. Staples, Hugh B., ed. LC 67-21201. 1967. 19.50 (*0-317-61239-5*) Dufour.

Barrington Jones, Barbara & Thomas, Janet. Dear Barbara: Answers to the Most-Asked Questions from Teenage Girls. LC 98-10392. (YA). 1998. pap. write for info. (*1-57345-369-2*) Deseret Bk.

Barrington, Judith. History & Geography. LC 88-33478. 112p. 1989. 15.95 (*0-933377-03-7*, Pub. by Eighth Mount Pr); pap. 7.95 (*0-933377-02-9*, Pub. by Eighth Mount Pr) Consort Bk Sales.

***Barrington, Judith.** Lifesaving: A Memoir. LC 99-46447. 192p. 2000. 22.95 (*0-933377-45-2*); pap. 13.95 (*0-933377-44-4*, Pub. by Eighth Mount Pr) Consort Bk Sales.

Barrington, Judith. Trying to Be an Honest Woman. LC 85-80278. 80p. 1985. pap. 6.95 (*0-933377-00-2*, Pub. by Eighth Mount Pr) Consort Bk Sales.

— Writing the Memoir: From Truth to Art. LC 96-43065. 200p. (Orig.). 1997. pap. 13.95 (*0-933377-40-1*); lib. bdg. 22.95 (*0-933377-41-X*) Eighth Mount Pr.

Barrington, Judith, ed. An Intimate Wilderness: Lesbian Writers on Sexuality. LC 91-13022. 320p. 1991. pap. 14.95 (*0-933377-09-6*) Eighth Mount Pr.

***Barrington, Lara.** Boucles d'or et les Trois Ours. adapted ed. LC 95-941621. (Best-Sellers Ser.).Tr. of Goldilocks & the Three Bears. (FRE.). (J). 2000. pap. 9.95 incl. audio (*2-921997-01-0*, Pub. by Coffragants) Penton Overseas.

Barrington, Linda, ed. The Other Side of the Frontier: Economic Explorations into Native American History. LC 98-27900. (American & European Economic History Ser.). 320p. (C). 1998. pap. 28.00 (*0-8133-3396-2*, Pub. by Westview) HarpC.

***Barrington, Linda, ed.** The Other Side of the Frontier: Economic Explorations into Native American History. LC 98-27900. (American & European Economic History Ser.). 320p. (C). 1998. 75.00 (*0-8133-3395-4*, Pub. by Westview) HarpC.

Barrington, Lynn, jt. auth. see Berry, Carmen Renee.

Barrington, Margaret. My Cousin Justin. Orig. Title: Turn Ever Northward. 288p. (Orig.). (YA). (gr. 10-12). 1990. pap. 11.95 (*0-85640-456-X*, Pub. by Blackstaff Pr) Dufour.

Barrington, Porter. The Christian Life - Master Outlines & Notes - Chinese Edition. Hsu, Wesley, tr. (CHI.). 129p. 1993. pap. 5.50 (*1-56582-044-4*) Christ Renew Min.

Barrington, Rex. Everybody's Wedding Workbook: A Complete Illustrated Guide Step-by-Step Engagement Through... 1978. pap. 17.95 (*0-933095-00-7*) Gazebo I.

Barrington, T. J., jt. auth. see Needle, Barry.

Barrinuevo, German, jt. auth. see Kozikowski, Alan P.

Barrio-Garay, Jose L. Jose Guitierrez Solana: Paintings & Writings. LC 72-3524. (Illus.). 426p. 1976. 90.00 (*0-8387-1228-2*) Bucknell U Pr.

Barrio, Raymond. The Plum Plum Pickers. 2nd ed. LC 84-70568. 232p. 1984. pap. 16.00 (*0-916950-51-4*) Biling Rev-Pr.

Barrion, A. T. & Litsinger, J. A. Riceland Spiders of South & Southeast Asia. (Illus.). 736p. 1996. text 240.00 (*0-85198-967-5*) OUP.

Barrios, Alfred A. The Habit Buster. 1987. pap. 4.95 (*0-9601926-4-6*) Self-Prog Control.

— Stress Test Biofeedback Card & Booklet. 1985. pap. 3.95 (*0-9601926-3-8*) Self-Prog Control.

— Towards Greater Freedom & Happiness. 3rd ed. LC 78-63152. 1985. 15.95 (*0-9601926-1-1*) Self-Prog Control.

***Barrios De Chamorro, Violeta, et al.** Dreams of the Heart: The Autobiography of President Violeta Barrios De Chamorro of Nicaragua. (Illus.). 352p. 1999. reprint ed. text 25.00 (*0-7881-6602-6*) DIANE Pub.

Barrios, Eduardo. El Hermano Asno. (SPA.). 5.95 (*0-8288-2552-1*) Fr & Eur.

Barrios, Ervin, tr. see Buehrens, John A. & Church, Forrest.

Barrios, Flor F. Blessed by Thunder: Memoir of a Cuban Girlhood. LC 99-20902. (Illus.). 250p. 1999. 22.95 (*1-58005-021-2*) Seal Pr WA.

Barrios, Isabella, ed. see Clifford, Ann.

Barrios, Isabella, ed. see Smith, Dennis S.

Barrios, John. Salmon. (Took Modern Poetry in English Ser.: Vol. 50). (Illus.). 32p. 1999. pap. 5.00 (*1-879457-59-8*) Norton Coker Pr.

***Barrios, John.** The Stilling at Bylot Island. (Illus.). 32p. 2000. pap. 4.00 (*1-879457-66-0*, Pritchard) Norton Coker Pr.

Barrios, Pilar E. The Poetic Works of Pilar E. Barrios: Piel Negra, Mis Cantos, Campo Afuera. (B. E. Ser.: No. 25). 1959. 50.00 (*0-8115-2976-2*) Periodicals Srv.

Barrios, Richard. A Song in the Dark: The Birth of the Musical Film. (Illus.). 512p. 1995. pap. 21.95 (*0-19-508811-5*) OUP.

Barrios, Roberto, jt. auth. see Selman, Moises.

Barrios, Rosalito. 50 Areas de Interes Especial para la Conservacion en Guatemala. (America Verde Publications). (SPA., Illus.). 171p. (Orig.). 1996. pap. 10.00 (*1-886765-05-7*) Nature VA.

Barris, Chuck. The F. A. R. R. Theory: The World's Simplest Formula for Making up Your Mind! (Illus.). 80p. (Orig.). 1997. 9.95 (*0-9651731-2-7*) Chuck Barris.

Barris, George. Barris Kustom Tech of the 50s Vol. 2: Grilles, Scoops, Fins & Fre, Vol. 2. Thacker, Tony, ed. LC 96-60751. (Illus.). 128p. (Orig.). 1997. pap. 19.95 (*0-9652005-1-5*, 102) Thaxton Pr.

— Barris Kustom Techniques of the 50's Vol. 1: Top Chops, Sectioning, Dechroming & Fadeaways. Thacker, Tony, ed. LC 96-60751. (Illus.). 128p. (Orig.). 1996. pap. 19.95 (*0-9652005-0-7*, 101) Thaxton Pr.

— Barris Kustom Techniques of the 50's Vol. 3: Lights, Skirts, Engines & Interiors. Thacker, Tony, ed. (Illus.). 128p. (Orig.). 1997. pap. text 19.95 (*0-9652005-2-3*, 103) Thaxton Pr.

— Barris Kustom Techniques of the 50's Vol. 4: Flames, Scallops, Paneling & Striping. Thacker, Tony, ed. (Illus.). 128p. (Orig.). 1997. pap. text 19.95 (*0-9652005-3-1*, 104) Thaxton Pr.

Barris, George, photos by. Marilyn - Her Life in Her Own Words: Marilyn Monroe's Revealing Last Words & Photographs. LC 95-19254. (Illus.). 192p. 1995. 24.95 (*1-55972-306-8*, Birch Ln Pr) Carol Pub Group.

Barris, George & Fetherston, David. Barris Kustoms of the 60's. (Illus.). 128p. 1998. pap. 19.95 (*0-9652005-8-2*, 109) Thaxton Pr.

— Barris Kustoms of the 1950's. (Illus.). 128p. 1994. pap. 21.95 (*0-87938-943-5*) MBI Pubg.

Barris, George, jt. auth. see Fetherston, David.

Barris, Jeremy. God & Plastic Surgery: Marx, Nietzsche, Freud & the Obvious. 256p. (Orig.). (C). 1990. pap. text 10.00 (*0-936756-41-1*) Autonomedia.

Barris, Roann, et al. Bodies of Knowledge in Psychosocial Practice. LC 88-43098. 172p. 1988. pap. 24.00 (*1-55642-071-4*) SLACK Inc.

— Occupational Therapy in Psychosocial Practice. LC 88-43104. 150p. 1988. pap. 24.00 (*1-55642-072-2*) SLACK Inc.

Barris, Sara L. & Seltzer, Doryle P. Together Forever: An Adoption Story Coloring Book. (Illus.). 32p. (J). 1992. pap. 3.95 (*0-9632023-0-8*) Shoot Star Pr.

Barrisford, J. Jackie Bind Up, Nos. 3 & 4. (Illus.). (J). mass mkt. 11.95 (*0-340-68735-5*, Pub. by Hodder & Stought Ltd) Trafalgar.

Barrish, Cris. Fatal Embrace: A Tale of Love, Obsession & Murder in the Thomas Capano/Anne Fahey Case. 2nd ed. 304p. 1999. pap. 6.99 (*0-312-97031-5*, St Martins Paperbacks) St Martin.

Barrish, Harriet H. & Barrish, I. J. Managing & Understanding Parental Anger. rev. ed. LC 89-22503. (Coping Parent Ser.). 64p. 1989. pap. 6.95 (*0-933701-41-1*) Westport Pubs.

Barrish, Harriet H., jt. auth. see Barrish, I. J.

Barrish, I. J. & Barrish, Harriet H. Surviving & Enjoying Your Adolescent. LC 89-38432. (Coping Parent Ser.). 96p. 1989. pap. 7.95 (*0-933701-42-X*) Westport Pubs.

Barrish, I. J., jt. auth. see Barrish, Harriet H.

***Barrish, Seth.** An Actor's Companion: 99 Bits of Craft. Brock, Lee, ed. 150p. 2000. 12.95 (*0-9676058-2-2*) TBG Pubng.

Barriskill, Janet. Visiting the Mino Kilns: With a Translation of Arakawa Toyozo's "The Traditions & Techniques of Mino Pottery" (University of Sydney East Asian Ser.: No. 9). (Illus.). 156p. (C). 1995. text 48.00 (*0-646-20424-6*, Pub. by Wild Peony Pty) UH Pr.

Barritt, C. Building Construction, Vol. 2. Date not set. pap. text. write for info. (*0-582-41352-4*, Pub. by Addison-Wesley) Longman.

Barritt, C. M. The Building Acts & Regulations Applied: Buildings for Public Assembly & Residential Use. xviii, 366p. 1997. pap. 32.50 (*0-582-30201-3*, 15717) Gaunt.

— The Building Acts & Regulations Applied: Houses & Flats. 2nd ed. xiv, 253p. (C). 1995. pap. 28.00 (*0-582-27449-4*, 15713) Gaunt.

— The Building Acts & Regulations Applied: Shops, Offices & Factories. 3rd ed. xvi, 303p. (C). 1996. pap. 28.00 (*0-582-25630-5*, 15705, Pub. by Addison-Wesley) Gaunt.

Barritt, Denis P. & Carter, Charles F. The Northern Ireland Problem: A Study in Group Relations. LC 82-15568. 163p. 1982. reprint ed. lib. bdg. 55.00 (*0-313-23262-8*, BANI, Greenwood Pr) Greenwood.

Barritt, Greg J. Communication Within Animal Cells. (Illus.). 358p. 1992. pap. text 57.50 (*0-19-854726-9*) OUP.

Barritt, Loren S. An Elementary School in Holland: Experiment in Practice. LC 96-123932. 256p. (Orig.). 1996. pap. 29.00 (*90-6224-879-9*, Pub. by Uitgeverij Arkel) LPC InBook.

Barriuso, Jose. I, in Christ Arisen. Elmo, Francis, tr. from SPA. LC 81-85745. Orig. Title: Yo, en Cristo Resucitado. 100p. 1982. pap. 6.99 (*0-9607590-0-X*) Action Life Pubns.

— Pilgrimage of the People of God, 3 vols., Set. Gonzales, Bertha et al, trs. LC 98-93444. 2000. pap. 30.00 (*0-936707-10-0*) Action Life Pubns.

— Pilgrimage of the People of God, Vol. I. Gonzales, Bertha et al, trs. from SPA. LC 98-93444. (Illus.). 2000. pap. 10.00 (*0-936707-02-X*) Action Life Pubns.

— Pilgrimage of the People of God, Vol. II. Gonzales, Bertha et al, trs. from SPA. LC 98-93444. 2000. pap. 10.00 (*0-936707-03-8*) Action Life Pubns.

— Pilgrimage of the People of God, Vol. III. Gonzales, Bertha et al, trs. 2000. pap. 10.00 (*0-936707-09-7*) Action Life Pubns.

Barriuso, Jose & Angelisanti, Raffaele. Man's Pilgrimage Towards the "New Earth" 42p. 1979. 2.00 (*0-9607590-4-2*) Action Life Pubns.

Barro, Robert & Martin, Xavier Sala I. Economic Growth. 1998. 65.00 (*0-262-02459-4*) MIT Pr.

Barro, Robert J. Determinants of Economic Growth: A Cross-Country Empirical Study. LC 96-50235. (Lionel Robbins Memorial Lectures). (Illus.). 128p. 1997. 24.00 (*0-262-02421-7*) MIT Pr.

— Determinants of Economic Growth: A Cross-Country Empirical Study. (Lionel Robbins Memorial Lectures). (Illus.). 160p. 1998. reprint ed. pap. text 12.50 (*0-262-52254-3*) MIT Pr.

— Economic Growth & Convergence. LC 93-31955. (Occasional Papers: No. 46). 1993. pap. 9.95 (*1-55815-283-0*) ICS Pr.

— Getting It Right: Markets & Choices in a Free Society. (Illus.). 208p. 1996. 24.00 (*0-262-02408-X*) MIT Pr.

— Getting It Right: Markets & Choices in a Free Society. (Illus.). 208p. 1997. reprint ed. pap. text 12.00 (*0-262-52226-8*) MIT Pr.

— The Impact of Social Security on Private Saving: Evidence from the U. S. Time Series. LC 78-16945. (AEI Studies: No. 199). 56p. reprint ed. pap. 30.00 (*0-8357-4491-4*, 203734400008) Bks Demand.

— Macroeconomic Policy. (Illus.). 384p. 1990. 55.50 (*0-674-54080-8*) HUP.

— Macroeconomics. 5th ed. LC 97-26136. 150p. 1997. 65.00 (*0-262-02436-5*) MIT Pr.

Barro, Robert J., ed. Modern Business Cycle Theory. LC 88-28303. (Illus.). 400p. 1989. 49.95 (*0-674-57860-0*) HUP.

Barro, Susan C. & Conrad, Susan G. Use of Ryegrass Seeding As an Emergency Revegetation Measure in Chaparal Systems. 24p. 1998. reprint ed. pap. 3.50 (*0-89904-521-9*, Ecosytems Resrch) Crumb Elbow Pub.

***Barroca, Leonor, et al, eds.** Software Architecture: Advances & Applications. LC 99-36697. (Illus.). 255p. 1999. pap. 69.95 (*1-85233-636-6*, Pub. by Spr-Verlag) Spr-Verlag.

Barrocas, Salvador. Sentir: Poemas. LC 99-62941. (Coleccion Espejo de Paciencia). (SPA., Illus.). 169p. 2000. pap. 16.00 (*0-89729-898-5*) Ediciones.

Barrois, Georges A. The Face of Christ in the Old Testament. 172p. 1974. pap. 11.95 (*0-913836-22-2*) St Vladimirs.

— The Fathers Speak: St. Basil the Great, St. Gregory Nazianzus, St. Gregory of Nyssa. LC 83-31958. 235p. (Orig.). 1985. pap. 11.95 (*0-88141-037-3*) St Vladimirs.

— Jesus Christ & the Temple. LC 80-19700. 163p. (Orig.). 1980. pap. 5.95 (*0-685-04737-7*, BS680 T4837) St Martin.

— Jesus Christ & the Temple. LC 80-19700. 164p. (Orig.). 1980. pap. 9.95 (*0-913836-73-7*) St Vladimirs.

— Scripture Readings in Orthodox Worship. 197p. 1977. pap. 10.95 (*0-913836-41-9*) St Vladimirs.

Barroll, Hope H. Barroll in Great Britain & America, 1554-1910. 124p. 1997. reprint ed. pap. 18.00 (*0-8328-7385-3*); reprint ed. lib. bdg. 28.00 (*0-8328-7384-5*) Higginson Bk Co.

Barroll, J. Leeds. Politics, Plague & Shakespeare's Theater: The Stuart Years. 264p. 1995. pap. text 15.95 (*0-8014-8275-5*) Cornell U Pr.

B

— Shakespearean Tragedy. LC 82-49309. 312p. 1984. 35.00 (0-918016-18-5) Folger Bks.

— Shakespearean Tragedy: Genre, Tradition, & Change in Antony & Cleopatra. 312p. 1984. 45.00 (0-918016-68-1) Folger Bks.

Barroll, J. Leeds, ed. Medieval & Renaissance Drama in England, Vol. 7. (Illus.). 448p. 1995. 72.50 (0-8386-3570-9) Fairleigh Dickinson.

— Medieval & Renaissance Drama in England: An Annual Gathering of Research, Criticism, & Reviews, 6 vols. LC 83-45280. (Illus.). 1991. write for info. (0-404-62300-X) AMS Pr.

— Medieval & Renaissance Drama in England: An Annual Gathering of Research, Criticism, & Reviews, 6 vols., Vol. 1. (Illus.). 1984. 57.50 (0-404-62305-0) AMS Pr.

— Medieval & Renaissance Drama in England: An Annual Gathering of Research, Criticism, & Reviews, 6 vols., Vol. 2. 1985. 57.50 (0-404-62301-8) AMS Pr.

— Medieval & Renaissance Drama in England: An Annual Gathering of Research, Criticism, & Reviews, 6 vols., Vol. 3. (Illus.). 1986. 57.50 (0-404-62302-6) AMS Pr.

— Medieval & Renaissance Drama in England: An Annual Gathering of Research, Criticism, & Reviews, 6 vols., Vol. 4. (Illus.). 1989. 57.50 (0-404-62303-4) AMS Pr.

— Medieval & Renaissance Drama in England: An Annual Gathering of Research, Criticism & Reviews, 6 vols., Vol. 5. (Illus.). 1991. 57.50 (0-404-62304-2) AMS Pr.

— Shakespeare Studies, Vol. 21. 320p. 1993. 52.50 (0-8386-3520-2) Fairleigh Dickinson.

— Shakespeare Studies, Vol. XXII. (Illus.). 400p. 1994. 52.50 (0-8386-3580-6) Fairleigh Dickinson.

— Shakespeare Studies, Vol. XXIII. (Illus.). 296p. 1995. 52.50 (0-8386-3640-3) Fairleigh Dickinson.

Barroll, J. Leeds & Cerasano, Susan P., eds. Medieval & Renaissance Drama in England, Vol. 8. (Illus.). 288p. 1996. write for info. (0-8386-3641-1) Fairleigh Dickinson.

Barroll, Leeds, ed. Shakespeare Studies, Vol. XXV. 320p. 1997. 55.00 (0-8386-3757-4) Fairleigh Dickinson.

— Shakespeare Studies, Vol. XXVI. (Illus.). 432p. 1998. 60.00 (0-8386-3782-5) Fairleigh Dickinson.

*Barroll, Leeds, ed. Shakespeare Studies, Vol. XXVII. 296p. 1999. 60.00 (0-8386-3835-X) Fairleigh Dickinson.

Barromi, Joel, jt. auth. see Shapira, Yoram.

Barron. Medical Disorders During Pregnancy. 3rd ed. 2000. 89.95 (0-323-00772-4) Mosby Inc.

— Understanding Visual Basic. Date not set. pap. text, teacher ed. write for info. (0-314-09375-3) West Pub.

Barron & Dienes. Constitutional Law: 1991 Cumulative Supplement. 312p. 1991. pap. text. write for info. (0-87473-404-5, 10615-10, MICHIE) LEXIS Pub.

Barron & Lyskawa. MS Win NT 4.0 WorkStation. (Illustrated Ser.). (Illus.). (C). 1997. pap. 10.95 (0-7600-5180-1) Course Tech.

Barron, et al. Constitutional Law: 1997 Supplement. 5th ed. 363p. 1996. pap. text, suppl. ed. 56.00 (1-55834-402-0, 10601-13, MICHIE) LEXIS Pub.

— The Internet Unleashed, 1996. LC 95-74793. (Illus.). 1456p. 1995. 49.99 incl. cd-rom (1-57521-041-X) Sams.

— Microsoft Internet Explorer 3.0: Illustrated Brief Edition. (Illustrated Ser.). (Illus.). 96p. (C). 1997. pap. 12.95 (0-7600-4687-5) Course Tech.

Barron, jt. auth. see Mitchell.

Barron, jt. auth. see Salkind.

Barron, jt. auth. see Swanson.

Barron, A. R., et al, eds. Covalent Ceramics II - Non-Oxides Vol. 327: Materials Research Society Symposium Proceedings. LC 94-26124. 389p. 1994. text 17.50 (1-55899-226-X) Materials Res.

Barron, Alfred, ed. see Noyes, John H.

Barron, Almen L., ed. Microbiology of Chlamydia, Vol. I. 256p. 1988. 149.00 (0-8493-6877-4, QR201, CRC Reprint) Franklin.

Barron, Ann & Lyskawa, Chet. Microsoft Front Page 98: Illustrated Standard Edition. 10th ed. (Illustrated Ser.). 216p. (C). 1998. pap. 21.95 (0-7600-5947-0) Course Tech.

Barron, Ann & Lyskawa, Chet. Microsoft Frontpage 2000 - Illustrated Introductory. (Illus.). 216p. per. 21.95 (0-7600-6346-X, Pub. by Course Tech) Thomson Learn.

Barron, Ann E. & Ivers, Karen S. The Internet & Instruction: Activities & Ideas. 2nd ed. LC 98-15021. 1998. 28.50 (1-56308-613-1) Libs Unl.

Barron, Ann E. & Orwig, Gary W. Multimedia Technologies for Training: An Introduction. LC 94-36876. (Illus.). xv, 211p. 1994. pap. text 29.00 (1-56308-262-4) Libs Unl.

— New Technologies for Education: A Beginner's Guide. 3rd ed. LC 96-39108. 265p. 1997. pap. 40.00 (1-56308-477-5) Libs Unl.

Barron, Ann E., jt. auth. see Ivers, Karen S.

Barron, Ann E., jt. ed. see Tennyson, Robert D.

Barron, Barbara M., jt. auth. see Newburger, Manuel H.

Barron, Bruce. Heaven on Earth? The Social & Political Agendas of Dominion Theology. 192p. 1992. pap. 12.99 (0-310-53611-1) Zondervan.

— Politics for the People. LC 95-49665. 167p. (Orig.). 1996. pap. 9.99 (0-8308-1984-3, 1984) InterVarsity.

Barron, Bruce A. Outsmarting Managed Care: A Doctor Shares His Insider's Secret to Getting What You Want. LC 99-31033. 304p. 1999. pap. 15.00 (0-8129-2981-0, Times Bks) Crown Pub Group.

Barron, Caroline M. & Saul, Nigel. England & the Low Countries in the Late Middle Ages. LC 99-200479. (Illus.). 192p. 1998. pap. 25.95 (0-7509-1834-9, Pub. by Sutton Pub Ltd) Intl Pubs Mktg.

Barron, Caroline M. & Saul, Nigel, eds. England & the Low Countries in the Late Middle Ages. 192p. 1995. text 59.95 (0-312-12589-5) St Martin.

Barron, Caroline M. & Sutton, Anne F., eds. Medieval London Widows, 1300-1500. LC 94-19301. 1994. 60.00 (1-85285-085-X) Hambledon Press.

Barron, Charles. As the Bat at Noon. LC 96-20550. 55p. (Orig.). 1996. pap. 5.00 (0-88734-385-6) Players Pr.

*Barron, Charles. The Old Adam. unabridged ed. 32p. 2000. pap. 5.00 (0-88734-844-0) Players Pr.

Barron, Cheryl C. & Scherzer, Cathy C. Great Parties for Young Children. LC 81-50232. (Illus.). 155p. 1981. pap. 8.95 (0-8027-7175-0) Walker & Co.

Barron, Cheryll A. Dreamers of the Valley of Plenty: A Portrait of the Napa Valley. 1995. 25.00 (0-684-81295-9) S&S Trade.

Barron, Clarence W. More They Told Barron. Pound, Arthur & Moore, Samuel T., eds. LC 73-1991. (Big Business; Economic Power in a Free Society Ser.). 1973. reprint ed. 23.95 (0-405-05075-5) Ayer.

Barron, Colin M. Running Your Own Private Residential or Nursing Home. 148p. 1990. 29.95 (1-85302-062-1) Taylor & Francis.

Barron, D. W. & Bishop, J. M. Advanced Programming: A Practical Course LC 83-17060. (Wiley Series in Computing). xii, 277p. 1984. write for info. (0-471-90521-6) Wiley.

*Barron, David. The Adventures of Bob & Red. Thatch, Nancy R., ed. LC 99-13494. (Books for Students by Students). (Illus.). 29p. (J). (gr. 2-4). 1999. lib. bdg. 15.95 (0-933849-71-0) Landmark Edns.

Barron, David. Computer Operating Systems 3e -ppr. 3rd ed. (ITCP-UK Computer Science). (C). 1995. mass mkt. 23.10 (0-412-30450-3) Chapman & Hall.

*Barron, David. The World of Scripting Languages. LC 99-89450. (Worldwide Series in Computer Science: Vol. 2). 500p. 2000. pap. 49.99 (0-471-99886-9) Wiley.

Barron, David M., tr. see Crupi, Susan R.

Barron, David N., et al. Competition, Deregulation, & the Fortunes of Credit Unions. 89p. 1995. pap. 100.00 (1-880572-18-4) Filene Res.

Barron, David W., ed. Pascal: The Language & Its Implementation. LC 78-1010. (Wiley Series in Computing). 311p. reprint ed. pap. 96.50 (0-8357-2767-X, 203989200014) Bks Demand.

Barron, David William. Computer Operating Systems. 3rd ed. (ITCP-UK Computer Science Ser.). 2000. pap. 23.95 (1-85032-228-7) Thomson Learn.

Barron, Don. Creativity, Vol. 22. LC 74-168254. (Illus.). 364p. 1993. text 59.95 (0-88108-111-6) Art Dir.

Barron, Don, ed. Creativity. LC 59-14827. (Creativity Ser.: Vol. 7). (Illus.). 1978. 20.00 (0-910158-35-5) Art Dir.

— Creativity, Eleven. LC 74-168254. (Creativity Annuals Ser.). (Illus.). 368p. 1982. 25.00 (0-910158-93-2) Art Dir.

— Creativity, No. 15. LC 74-168254. 450p. 1986. 37.50 (0-88108-025-X) Art Dir.

— Creativity, No. 16. LC 87-71252. 472p. 1987. 49.50 (0-88108-040-3) Art Dir.

— Creativity, Ten. LC 74-168254. (Illus.). 368p. 1982. 25.00 (0-910158-77-0) Art Dir.

— Creativity, Vol. 24. LC 74-168254. 364p. 1995. text 62.95 (0-88108-152-3) Art Dir.

— Creativity, Vol. 27. (Illus.). 320p. 1998. 62.95 (0-88108-213-9) Art Dir.

— Creativity Eighteen. LC 74-168254. (Illus.). 412p. 1989. text 55.00 (0-88108-064-0) Art Dir.

— Creativity Fourteen. LC 74-168254. (Illus.). 1985. 34.50 (0-88108-022-5) Art Dir.

— Creativity Nine. LC 74-168254. (Illus.). 370p. 1980. text 20.00 (0-910158-55-X) Art Dir.

— Creativity Seventeen. LC 74-168254. (Illus.). 428p. 1988. text 55.00 (0-88108-057-8) Art Dir.

— Creativity Thirteen, Vol. 13. LC 74-168254. (Illus.). 1984. 25.00 (0-88108-008-X) Art Dir.

— Creativity Twelve. LC 74-168254. (Illus.). 1983. 25.00 (0-910158-99-1) Art Dir.

— Creativity Twenty-One. LC 74-168254. 370p. 1992. text 59.95 (0-88108-101-9) Art Dir.

— Creativity Twenty-Three No. 23. LC 74-168254. 370p. 1994. text 59.95 (0-88108-133-7) Art Dir.

— Creativity 26. LC 97-70358. (Illus.). 320p. 1997. 62.95 (0-88108-200-7) Art Dir.

— Letterheads, No. 8. LC 78-640636. (Illus.). 274p. 1992. text 59.95 (0-88108-104-3) Art Dir.

Barron, Don & Art Direction Staff, eds. Creativity, Eight. LC 59-14827. (Creativity Ser.: No. 8). (Illus.). 1979. 20.00 (0-910158-54-1) Art Dir.

Barron, Don, jt. auth. see Baker, Arthur.

Barron, Earle P. Ewell's March Home: The Civil War & Early Times in & Around Geenwich, Virginia. LC 99-94379. 140p. 1999. pap. 10.00 (0-7392-0219-7, PO3246) Morris Pubng.

*Barron, Earle P. Presence Lingers: Face to Face with Nature in the Southern Appalachians. 114p. 1999. pap. 9.00 (0-7392-0465-3, 3777) Morris Pubng.

Barron, Elizabeth. Miss Drayton's Crusade. 240p. (Orig.). 1986. mass mkt. 2.95 (0-446-30172-8, Pub. by Warner Bks) Little.

Barron, Ellen, et al. Medical Microbiology: A Short Course. LC 93-16481. (Illus.). 1072p. (Orig.). 1994. pap. 74.50 (0-471-56728-0, Wiley-Liss) Wiley.

Barron, Enid M. & Nielsen, Ilga, eds. Agriculture & Sustainable Land Use in Europe: Papers from Conferences of European Environmental Advisory Councils. LC 99-171755. (NIJHOFF Law Specials Ser.: Vol. 38). 208p. 1998. pap. 80.00 (90-411-9691-9) Kluwer Law Intl.

Barron, Eric J. Climatic Variation in Earth History. LC 95-61063. (Illus.). 40p. (Orig.). (C). 1996. pap. text 18.50 (0-935702-82-2) Univ Sci Bks.

Barron, Eric J. & Moore, George T. Climate Model Applications in Paleoenvironmental Analysis. (SEPM Short Course Notes Ser.: No. 33). (Illus.). 344p. 1994. pap. text 59.00 (1-56576-012-3) SEPM.

Barron, F. Laurie. Walking in Indian Moccasins: The Native Policies of Tommy Douglas & the CCF. LC 98-111154. (Illus.). 252p. 1997. text 65.00 (0-7748-0609-5, E78) U of Wash Pr.

Barron, Frank. No Rootless Flower: An Ecology of Creativity. Runco, Mark A., ed. LC 95-13623. (Perspectives on Creativity Ser.). 416p. 1995. text 75.00 (1-881303-02-0); pap. text 26.50 (1-881303-03-9) Hampton Pr NJ.

Barron, Frank, et al, eds. Creators on Creating. LC 96-38805. (New Consciousness Reader Ser.). 288p. (Orig.). 1997. pap. 14.95 (0-87477-854-9, Tarcher Putnam) Putnam Pub Group.

Barron, Gene. Invited into His Presence: Praying Effectively. LC 97-26455. 1997. pap. 9.99 (0-89900-756-2) College Pr Pub.

Barron, George. Mushrooms of Northeast North America: Midwest to New England. (Illus.). 336p. 1999. pap. 19.95 (1-55105-201-6) Lone Pine.

— Mushrooms of Ontario & Eastern Canada. 3rd ed. (Illus.). 336p. (Orig.). 1999. pap. 19.95 (1-55105-199-0) Lone Pine.

Barron, George L. The Genera of Hyphomycetes from Soil. LC 68-14275. 378p. 1977. reprint ed. 44.50 (0-88275-004-6) Krieger.

Barron, Hal S. Mixed Harvest: The Second Great Transformation in the Rural North, 1870-1930. LC 96-51451. (Studies in Rural Culture). 320p. (gr. 13). 1997. 19.95 (0-8078-4659-7); lib. bdg. 55.00 (0-8078-2354-6) U of NC Pr.

Barron, Harold. Essentials of Microsoft Visual Basic 4.0. 2nd ed. (Df - Computer Applications Ser.). 1996. mass mkt. 9.00 (0-314-20500-4) S-W Pub.

Barron, Iann & Curnow, Ray. The Future of Microelectronics. 256p. 1979. pap. 29.00 (0-335-00268-4) OpUniv Pr.

Barron, Irene, ed. see Kahaner, David K.

Barron, J. Patrick, tr. see Kato, Harubumi, ed.

Barron, James, ed. Humor & Psyche: Psychoanalytic Perspectives. LC 98-33349. 248p. 1999. 45.00 (0-88163-257-0) Analytic Pr.

*Barron, James Douglas. She's Had a Baby: And I'm Having a Meltdown. LC 99-11070. 176p. 1999. pap. 10.00 (0-688-16823-X, Quil) HarperTrade.

Barron, James Douglas. She's Having a Baby: --and I'm Having a Breakdown. LC 97-48802. (Illus.). 128p. 1998. pap. 10.00 (0-688-15825-0, Wm Morrow) Morrow Avon.

Barron, James W., ed. Making Diagnosis Meaningful: Enhancing Evaluation & Treatment of Psychological Disorders. LC 98-12803. 363p. 1998. 39.95 (1-55798-496-4) Am Psychol.

— Self-Analysis: Critical Inquiries, Personal Visions. LC 93-15733. 320p. 1993. text 45.00 (0-88163-143-4) Analytic Pr.

Barron, James W., et al, eds. Interface of Psychoanalysis & Psychology. 666p. 1992. 69.95 (1-55798-156-6) Am Psychol.

Barron, James W. & Sands, Harry. Impact of Managed Care on Psychodynamic Treatment. LC 96-9118. 320p. 1996. 47.50 (0-8236-2542-7) Intl Univs Pr.

Barron, Janet J. The Writer's Bible: Everything You Need to Know about Writing & How to Get Your Work Published. 2nd ed. v, 305p. 1997. pap. 19.95 (0-9674674-0-3) B E S T ME.

Barron, Jeannette M. & Graham, Jorie. Jeannette Montgomery Barron & Jorie Graham. LC 98-204812. (Illus.). 128p. 1997. 34.95 (3-931141-62-4) Dist Art Pubs.

Barron, Jerome A. Constitutional Law. 5th ed. LC 99-184963. 1999. pap. 24.50 incl. disk (0-314-22666-4) West Pub.

— Freedom of the Press for Whom? The Right of Access to Mass Media. LC 72-75387. 383p. reprint ed. pap. 118.80 (0-608-17137-9, 205621600056) Bks Demand.

Barron, Jerome A. & Dienes, C. Thomas. Constitutional Law. 3rd ed. (Black Letter Ser.). 440p. 1991. reprint ed. pap. text 24.50 (0-314-80211-8) West Pub.

— Constitutional Law. 4th ed. LC 95-4800. (Black Letter Ser.). 430p. (C). 1995. pap. text 24.50 (0-314-06209-2) West Pub.

— Constitutional Law in a Nutshell. 2nd ed. (Nutshell Ser.). 483p. 1993. reprint ed. pap. text 17.00 (0-314-80710-1) West Pub.

— Constitutional Law in a Nutshell. 3rd ed. LC 95-4798. (Nutshell Ser.). 529p. (C). 1995. 19.00 (0-314-06379-X) West Pub.

— Constitutional Law in a Nutshell. 4th ed. LC 99-175554. (Nutshell Ser.). 595 p. 1999. 20.50 (0-314-22661-3) West Pub.

— First Amendment Law in a Nutshell. (Nutshell Ser.). 531p. (C). 1993. pap. 23.50 (0-314-02581-2) West Pub.

Barron, Jerome A., et al. Constitutional Law: Principles & Policy, Cases & Materials. 4th ed. (Contemporary Legal Education Ser.). 1495p. 1992. 47.00 (0-685-62352-1, MICHIE) LEXIS Pub.

— Constitutional Law: Principles & Policy, Cases & Materials, 1999 Cumulative Supplement. 5th ed. 250p. 1999. pap. write for info. (0-327-01311-7, 1060116) LEXIS Pub.

Barron, Jerome A., jt. auth. see Gillmor, Donald M.

Barron, Jerone A., et al. Constitutional Law: Principles & Policy (Cases & Materials) 1998 Cumulative Supplement. 5th ed. (Michie Contemporary Legal Education Ser.). 250p. 1998. pap. 11.00 (0-327-00314-6, 1060115) LEXIS Pub.

Barron, John. Breaking the Ring: The Bizarre Case of the Walker Family Spy Ring. 240p. 1988. pap. 3.95 (0-380-70520-6, Avon Bks) Morrow Avon.

— KGB - Rabota Sovetskikh Sekretnykh Agentov. (RUS., Illus.). 544p. 1988. reprint ed. 22.00 (0-911971-29-7) Effect Pub.

— KGB Today: The Hidden Hand. LC 83-4645. 496p. 1983. 19.95 (0-88349-164-8) Readrs Digest Pr.

— Mig Pilot. 1980. 10.95 (0-685-04285-5) Readrs Digest Pr.

— Mig Pilot: The Final Escape of Lieutenant Belenko. 232p. 1981. mass mkt. 4.50 (0-380-53868-7, Avon Bks) Morrow Avon.

— Operation Solo: The FBI's Man in the Kremlin. (Illus.). 368p. 1997. pap. 12.95 (0-89526-429-3) Regnery Pub.

*Barron, John. The Parent's Guide to Science Fairs. LC 99-38907. 160p. 1999. pap. 15.95 (0-7373-0269-0, 02690W) NTC Contemp Pub Co.

Barron, John. Pilot MIGa: Poslednii Polet Leitinanta Belenko.Tr. of MIG Pilot - the Final Escape of Lieutenant Belenko. (RUS., Illus.). 172p. 1987. 15.00 (0-911971-04-1) Effect Pub.

Barron, John & Lynch, Gerald J. Economics. 3rd ed. 208p. (C). 1993. text, student ed. 24.68 (0-256-09228-1, Irwn McGrw-H) McGrw-H Hghr Educ.

Barron, John M. & Lindheimer, Marshall D. Medical Disorders During Pregnancy, No. 2. 2nd ed. (Illus.). 576p. (C). (gr. 13). 1994. text 92.00 (0-8016-8002-6, 08002) Mosby Inc.

Barron, John M. & Lynch, Gerald J. Economics. 3rd ed. LC 92-17017. 768p. (C). 1992. text 55.50 (0-256-09227-3, Irwn McGrw-H) McGrw-H Hghr Educ.

Barron, John M. & Staten, Michael E. Consumer Attitudes Toward Credit Insurance. LC 95-39294. (Innovations in Financial Markets & Institutions Ser.). 160p. (C). 1995. lib. bdg. 84.50 (0-7923-9671-5) Kluwer Academic.

Barron, John M., et al. Macroeconomics. (Illus.). 715p. (C). 1989. 77.00 (0-201-13623-6) Addison-Wesley.

Barron, John M., et al. On the Job Training. LC 97-10295. 210p. (C). 1997. text 35.00 (0-88099-178-X) W E Upjohn.

Barron, John M., et al. On the Job Training. LC 97-10295. 210p. (C). 1997. pap. text 17.00 (0-88099-175-5) W E Upjohn.

Barron, Jonathan C. Understanding & Using Microsoft Visual BASIC. LC 95-38007. 450p. (C). 1996. mass mkt. 33.95 (0-314-07155-5) West Pub.

— Understanding & Using Microsoft Visual BASIC Version 4.0. LC 96-17876. (Microcomputing Ser.). 450p. 1996. mass mkt. 36.95 (0-314-20078-9) West Pub.

— West's Essentials of Microsoft Visual Basic. LC 94-49431. (Microcomputing Ser.). 1995. mass mkt. 23.95 (0-314-05531-2) West Pub.

*Barron, Jonathan N. & Selinger, Eric Murphy, eds. Jewish American Poetry: Poems, Commentary, & Reflections. LC 00-25283. (Brandeis Series in American Jewish History, Culture & Life). 416p. 2000. pap. 22.95 (1-58465-043-5); text 60.00 (1-58465-042-7) U Pr of New Eng.

Barron, Jonathan N., jt. ed. see Wilcox, Earl J.

Barron, Judy. I Want to Learn to Fly. (J). 1995. 7.95 incl. audio (0-590-22971-0) Scholastic Inc.

— I Want to Learn to Fly. 32p. (J). (ps-3). 1995. pap. 4.95 (0-590-22329-1) Scholastic Inc.

— I Want to Learn to Fly. (J). 1995. 10.15 (0-606-07689-1, Pub. by Turtleback) Demco.

Barron, Judy & Barron, Sean. There's a Boy in Here. 272p. 1994. mass mkt. 4.99 (0-380-72292-5, Avon Bks) Morrow Avon.

Barron, Kathryn. Critter Crackers: The ABC Book of Limericks. Thatch, Nancy R., ed. LC 95-8700. (Books for Students by Students). (Illus.). 29p. (J). (gr. k-3). 1995. lib. bdg. 15.95 (0-933849-58-3) Landmark Edns.

Barron, Kimberly, jt. auth. see Evans, Robert C.

*Barron, Kirk W. Johnny Tractor & Friends: A New Kind of Job. Torgerson, Dell & Reyner, Mark, eds. (John Deere Storybook for Little Folks Ser.). (Illus.). 14p. (J). (gr. 3 up). 1999. 6.95 (1-887327-26-6) Ertl Co.

— Johnny Tractor & Friends: Afraid of Nothing. Torgerson, Dell & Reyner, Mark, eds. (John Deere Storybook for Little Folks Ser.). (Illus.). 14p. (J). (gr. 3 up). 1999. 6.95 (1-887372-25-3) Ertl Co.

*Barron, Leanna. The Harmony Kingdom Reference Guide: The Millennium Edition. 2nd ed. Perry, Corinna et al, eds. 164p. 1999. pap. 15.00 (0-9676908-0-3) Harmony Ball Co.

Barron, Marietta. Two Worlds. 94p. (Orig.). 1999. pap. 9.99 (0-88092-120-X, 120-X) Royal Fireworks.

Barron, Marlene. Aprendo a Leer y a Escribir de la Manera en Que Aprendo a Hablar. LC 90-18302.Tr. of I Learn to Read & Write the Way I Learn to Talk. (SPA.). 32p. 1993. pap. text 7.95 (1-878450-53-0, 505) R Owen Pubs.

— I Learn to Read & Write the Way I Learn to Talk: A Very First Book about Whole Language. LC 90-34286. 32p. (Orig.). (C). 1990. pap. text 7.95 (1-878450-07-7, 32) R Owen Pubs.

— Ready, Set, Count. LC 95-1306. (Ready, Set, Learn Ser.). 160p. (J). 1995. pap. 12.95 (0-471-10282-2) Wiley.

— Ready, Set, Explore. LC 96-151538. (Ready, Set, Learn Ser.). 148p. 1996. pap. 12.95 (0-471-10273-3) Wiley.

— Ready, Set, Read & Write. LC 96-118339. 150p. (J). 1995. pap. 12.95 (0-471-10283-0) Wiley.

Barron, Marlene & Young, Karen R. Ready, Set, Cooperate. LC 95-36111. (Ready, Set, Learn Ser.). 160p. 1996. pap. 12.95 (0-471-10275-X) Wiley.

*Barron, Mary Kemper & Lyskawa, Chet. Microsoft Windows 98 Illustrated. (C). 1998. pap. 10.95 (0-7600-5959-4) Thomson Learn.

B

An Asterisk (*) at the beginning of an entry indicates that the title is appearing for the first time.

Barron, Mary L., et al. Nursing Assessment of the Pregnant Woman: Antepartal Screening & Laboratory Evaluation. LC 98-20272. 1998. 15.00 (*0-86525-081-2*) March of Dimes.

***Barron, Matthew.** The Gateworld Chronicles. 2001. pap. 8.00 (*0-8059-4986-0*) Dorrance.

Barron, Michael. Auditorium Accoustics & Architectural Design. LC 92-38096. (Illus.). 464p. (C). 1993. 140.00 (*0-419-17710-8*, E & FN Spon) Routledge.

— Auditorium Acoustics & Architectural Design. LC 92-38096. 1992. write for info. (*0-442-31623-2*, E & FN Spon) Routledge.

Barron, Milton L. The Aging American: An Introduction to Social Gerontology & Geriatrics. LC 74-8874. (Illus.). 269p. 1974. reprint ed. lib. bdg. 55.00 (*0-8371-7595-X*, BAAG, Greenwood Pr) Greenwood.

Barron, Mitch & Abell, Susan, eds. Facing Independence: Your Guide to Living on Your Own. (Illus.). 59p. (YA). (gr. 7-12). 1995. pap. 6.00 (*1-878848-53-4*, 243) Natl Res Ctr.

***Barron, Nancy.** Return to Sender: Getting a Refund or Replacement for Your Lemon Car. 208p. 2000. pap. 16.00 (*1-881793-81-8*) Nat Consumer Law.

Barron, Neil, ed. Anatomy of Wonder: A Critical Guide to Science Fiction. 4th ed. 912p. 1995. pap. 39.00 (*0-8352-3684-6*) Bowker.

— Fantasy & Horror: A Critical & Historical Guide to Literature, Illustration, Film, T. V., Radio & the Internet. LC 98-46564. 816p. 1999. 85.00 (*0-8108-3596-7*) Scarecrow.

— Fantasy Literature: A Reader's Guide. LC 89-23693. 613p. 1990. text 20.00 (*0-8240-3148-2*, H874) Garland.

— Horror Literature: A Reader's Guide. LC 89-27456. 623p. 1990. text 20.00 (*0-8240-4347-2*, H1220) Garland.

Barron, Neil, et al, eds. What Do I Read Next? 600p. 1990. 110.00 (*0-8103-7555-9*) Gale.

Barron, Pamela, jt. ed. see Feehan, Patricia E.

Barron, Pamela P., jt. ed. see Doll, Carol A.

Barron, Pattie. Creating a Mediterranean Garden: Plant a Low-Mainenance, Drought-Proof Paradise--Anywhere. 1999. 35.00 (*1-85967-891-2*) Anness Pub.

Barron, Paul. Federal Regulation of Real Estate & Mortgage Lending. 3rd ed. 1992. pap. 135.00 (*0-685-69648-0*, FRRE) Warren Gorham & Lamont.

Barron, Paul & Berenson, Michael A. Federal Regulation of Real Estate & Mortgage Lending. 4th ed. LC 98-14800. 1998. 165.00 (*0-8366-1225-6*) West Group.

Barron, Paul A. God & the Universe - Life & Death: A Search for Meaning. LC 96-86265. 1997. 42.00 (*0-9654266-1-0*, 510); pap. 30.00 (*0-9654266-0-2*, 510) Suburban Print.

***Barron, Rachel.** Lise Meitner: Discoverer of Nuclear Fission. LC 99-49724. (Great Scientists Ser.). (Illus.). 112p. (YA). (gr. 5 up). 1999. lib. bdg. 19.95 (*1-883846-52-8*) M Reynolds.

Barron, Rachel. Richard Nixon: American Politician. LC 98-29836. (Notable Americans Ser.). (Illus.). 112p. (YA). (gr. 5 up). 1998. lib. bdg. 18.95 (*1-883846-33-1*) M Reynolds.

***Barron, Randall F.** Cryogenic Heat Transfer. LC 98-54423. 750p. 1999. 79.95 (*1-56032-551-8*); write for info. (*1-56032-552-6*) Hemisp Pub.

Barron, Randall F. Cryogenic Systems. 2nd ed. (Monographs on Cryogenics). (Illus.). 512p. 1985. text 89.95 (*0-19-503567-4*) OUP.

Barron, Ray. The Forties - When We Were Dreamers of Dreams. 1987. 14.95 (*0-8283-1915-4*) Branden Bks.

***Barron, Rex.** Fed Up! LC 00-23138. (Illus.). 32p. (J). (ps up). 2000. 15.99 (*0-399-23450-0*, G P Putnam) Peng Put Young Read.

Barron, Richard, tr. see Drolma, Delog D.

Barron, Richard, tr. see Lingpa, Dudjom.

***Barron, Robert.** Heaven in Stone & GLass: Experiencing the Spirituality of the Great Cathedrals. (Illus.). 128p. 2000. pap. 16.95 (*0-8245-1863-2*, Pub. by Crossroad NY) Natl Bk Netwk.

Barron, Robert. Thomas Aquinas: Spiritual Master. LC 95-34303. (Spiritual Legacy Ser.). 180p. 1996. pap. 14.95 (*0-8245-2507-8*) Crossroad NY.

***Barron, Robert & Senior, Donald.** Opening Hearts, Minds & Doors: Embodying the Inclusive & Vulnerable Love of God. Stratman, Bernard F., ed. 37p. 1999. pap. text 3.00 (*1-893060-02-0*) NFPC.

Barron, Robert, et al. Understanding People: Children, Youth, Adults. LC 75-172116. 96p. 1989. pap. text 9.95 (*0-910566-15-1*) Evang Trg Assn.

Barron, Robert E. And Now I See: A Theology of Transformation. LC 98-13578. 168p. 1998. pap. text 13.95 (*0-8245-1753-9*, Crsrd) Crossroad NY.

— A Study of the De Potentia of Thomas Aquinas in Light of the Dogmatik of Paul Tillich: Creation As Discipleship. LC 93-1354. 516p. 1993. text 119.95 (*0-7734-2238-2*) E Mellen.

Barron, Ron, ed. Engineering Condition Monitoring: Practice, Methods, & Applications. 245p. 1997. 105.00 (*0-582-24656-3*) Addison-Wesley.

Barron, S. Leonard & Roberts, D. F., eds. Issues in Fetal Medicine: Proceedings of the 29th Annual Symposium of the Galton Institute, London, 1992. LC 94-233. 1995. text 69.95 (*0-312-12161-X*) St Martin.

Barron, Samuel B. Lone Star Defenders: A Chronicle of the Third Texas Cavalry Regiment in the Civil War. 1983. reprint ed. 27.95 (*0-89201-103-3*) Zenger Pub.

Barron, Sarah, et al. A Bibliography on Computational Molecular Biology & Genetics. 115p. (Orig.). (C). 1992. pap. text 40.00 (*0-941375-91-9*) DIANE Pub.

Barron, Sean, jt. auth. see Barron, Judy.

Barron, Shiela T., jt. auth. see Koretz, Daniel M.

***Barron Staff.** American Indians. 2000. pap. text 5.95 (*0-7641-1071-3*) Barron.

— Animal Olympics. (Illus.). 20p. (ps-3). 2000. 2.95 (*0-7641-1616-9*) Barron.

— Aztecs. 2000. pap. text 5.95 (*0-7641-1083-7*) Barron.

— Blood & Bones. (Illus.). 20p. (ps-3). 2000. 2.95 (*0-7641-1617-7*) Barron.

— Deadly Dinosaurs. (Illus.). 20p. (ps-3). 2000. 2.95 (*0-7641-1618-5*) Barron.

— Spooky Bat. (Illus.). (J). 2000. 5.95 (*0-7641-5292-0*) Barron.

— Spooky Spider. (Illus.). 2000. 5.95 (*0-7641-5293-9*) Barron.

— Tickly Monster. (Illus.). 2000. 15.95 (*0-7641-5290-4*) Barron.

— Tu Cuerpo de la Cabeza a los Pies. 2000. pap. text 5.95 (*0-7641-1519-7*) Barron.

— Wacky Planets. (Illus.). 20p. (ps-3). 2000. 2.95 (*0-7641-1619-3*) Barron.

— Your Body, from Head to Toe. 24p. (ps-3). 2000. pap. text 5.95 (*0-7641-1518-9*) Barron.

Barron, Stephanie. Degenerate Art: The Fate of the Avant-Garde in Nazi Germany. (Illus.). 424p. 1991. 75.00 (*0-8109-3653-4*, Pub. by Abrams) Time Warner.

— Exiles & Emigres: The Flight of European Artists from Hitler. LC 96-78500. (Illus.). 384p. 1997. 75.00 (*0-8109-3271-7*, Pub. by Abrams) Time Warner.

— German Expressionist Sculpture. (Illus.). 224p. 1985. pap. 27.95 (*0-226-03821-1*) U Ch Pr.

***Barron, Stephanie.** Jane & the Genius of the Place. (Jane Austen Mystery Ser.: Vol. 4). 384p. 2000. mass mkt. 5.99 (*0-553-57839-1*) Bantam.

Barron, Stephanie. Jane & the Genius of the Place. LC 99-27636. (Jane Austen Mystery Ser.). 551p. 1999. 28.95 (*0-7862-2017-1*) Thorndike Pr.

— Jane & the Man of the Cloth. large type ed. LC 97-5828. (Cloak & Dagger Ser.). 530p. 1997. 25.95 (*0-7862-1087-7*) Thorndike Pr.

— Jane & the Man of the Cloth. (Jane Austen Mystery Ser.: No. 2). 368p. 1997. reprint ed. mass mkt. 5.99 (*0-553-57489-2*) Bantam.

***Barron, Stephanie.** Jane & the Stillroom Maid. (Jane Austen Mystery Ser.). 304p. 2000. 22.95 (*0-553-10734-8*, Spectra) Bantam.

Barron, Stephanie. Jane & the Unpleasantness at Scargrave Manor. LC 95-36743. (Jane Austen Mystery Ser.: No. 1). 352p. 1996. mass mkt. 5.99 (*0-553-57593-7*, Crimeline) Bantam.

— Jane & the Unpleasantness at Scargrave Manor. large type ed. LC 96-50226. (Jane Austen Mystery Ser.: No. 1). 1997. 24.95 (*1-56895-400-X*, Compass) Wheeler Pub.

— Jane & the Wandering Eye. (Jane Austen Mystery Ser.: No. 3). 336p. 1998. mass mkt. 5.99 (*0-553-57817-0*) Bantam.

— Jane & the Wandering Eye. large type ed. LC 97-47416. (Cloak & Dagger Ser.). 1998. 27.95 (*0-7862-1353-1*) Thorndike Pr.

***Barron, Stephanie, et al, eds.** Reading California: Art, Image, & Identity, 1900-2000. (Illus.). 400p. 2000. 50.00 (*0-520-22766-2*); pap. 24.95 (*0-520-22767-0*, Pub. by U CA Pr) Cal Prin Full Svc.

Barron, Stephanie & Dube, Wolf-Dieter. German Expressionism 1909-1923. LC 97-76622. 399p. 1997. 60.00 (*0-8478-2078-5*, Pub. by Rizzoli Intl) St Martin.

Barron, Stephanie, et al. Exiles & Emigres: The Flight of European Artists from Hitler. LC 96-78500. 432 P. :p. 1997. write for info. (*0-87587-178-X*) LA Co Art Mus.

***Barron, Stephanie, et al.** Made in California: Art, Image, & Identity, 1900-2000. (Illus.). 344p. 2000. 65.00 (*0-520-22764-6*); pap. 34.95 (*0-520-22765-4*) U CA Pr.

Barron, T. A. The Ancient One. LC 91-45862. (Illus.). 368p. (YA). (gr. 6 up). 1992. 17.95 (*0-399-21899-8*, Philomel) Peng Put Young Read.

— The Ancient One. 352p. (J). 1994. mass mkt. 4.99 (*0-8125-3654-1*, Pub. by Tor Bks) St Martin.

Barron, T. A. The Ancient One. (J). 1994. 11.09 (*0-606-11042-9*, Pub. by Turtleback) Demco.

Barron, T. A. The Fires of Merlin. LC 97-49561. (Illus.). 320p. (YA). (gr. 5 up). 1998. 19.99 (*0-399-23020-3*, Philomel) Peng Put Young Read.

***Barron, T. A.** Fires of Merlin, (Lost Years of Merlin Ser.: Vol. 3). (Illus.). (J). 2000. mass mkt. 5.99 (*0-441-00713-9*) Ace Bks.

Barron, T. A. Heartlight. LC 89-70947. 272p. (J). (gr. 5-9). 1990. 15.95 (*0-399-22180-8*, Philomel) Peng Put Young Read.

— Heartlight. 272p. (J). 1995. mass mkt. 4.99 (*0-8125-5170-2*, Pub. by Tor Bks) St Martin.

Barron, T. A. Heartlight. 1995. 10.09 (*0-606-11451-3*, Pub. by Turtleback) Demco.

Barron, T. A. The Lost Years of Merlin. LC 96-33920. (Lost Years of Merlin Ser.: No. 1). 336p. (J). (gr. 4-7). 1996. pap. 19.99 (*0-399-23018-1*, Philomel) Peng Put Young Read.

***Barron, T. A.** The Lost Years of Merlin. (J). (gr. 4-7). 1998. mass mkt. 4.99 (*0-8125-7777-9*) Tor Bks.

Barron, T. A. The Lost Years of Merlin. (Lost Years of Merlin Ser.: No. 1). 270p. (J). (gr. 4-7). 1999. reprint ed. mass mkt. 5.99 (*0-441-00668-X*) ACE.

— The Merlin Effect. LC 93-36234. 280p. (J). (gr. 5-9). 1994. 19.95 (*0-399-22689-3*, Philomel) Peng Put Young Read.

— The Merlin Effect. (J). 1996. mass mkt. 5.99 (*0-8125-5169-9*, Pub. by Tor Bks) St Martin.

— The Merlin Effect. 1996. 11.09 (*0-606-11618-4*, Pub. by Turtleback) Demco.

***Barron, T. A.** Mirror of Merlin. LC 99-13043. 245p. (J). (gr. 5). 1999. 19.99 (*0-399-23455-1*) Peng Put Young Read.

Barron, T. A. Rocky Mountain National Park: A 100 Year Perspective. (Illus.). 216p. 1995. 70.00 (*1-56579-123-1*) Westcliffe Pubs.

— The Seven Songs of Merlin. LC 97-9619. (Lost Years of Merlin Ser.: Bk. 2). 320p. (J). (gr. 5 up). 1997. 19.99 (*0-399-23019-X*, Philomel) Peng Put Young Read.

***Barron, T. A.** The Seven Songs of Merlin. (YA). 2000. reprint ed. mass mkt. 5.99 (*0-441-00701-5*) Ace Bks.

Barron, T. A. Where is Grandpa? LC 97-30997. (Illus.). 32p. (J). (ps-3). 2000. 15.99 (*0-399-23037-8*, Philomel) Peng Put Young Read.

***Barron, T. A.** Wings of Merlin. (Lost Years of Merlin Ser.: Vol. 5). (Illus.). 256p. (J). (gr. 5 up). 2000. 19.99 (*0-399-23456-X*, Philomel) Peng Put Young Read.

Barron, T. A., jt. auth. see Fielder, John.

Barron, T. J. Constitutions & National Identity. 332p. 1989. pap. 80.00 (*1-85933-003-7*, Pub. by Mercat Pr Bks) St Mut.

Barron, Taghrid, ed. Who's Wealthy in America, 1996, Vol. 2. 96th ed. 1995. 425.00 (*0-930807-57-X*) Taft Group.

Barron, Taghrid, ed. see Clough, Len C., et al.

Barron, Taghrid, ed. see Tueller, A. B.

Barron, Terry. Terry Barron's No Nonsense Guide to Fly-Fishing Pyramid Lake: A Quick, Clear Understanding of the Nation's Top Lahontan Cutthroat Trout Fishery. LC 99-187485. (Illus.). 54p. 1998. pap. 15.95 (*0-9637256-3-7*) D Comm.

Barron-Tieger, Barbara, jt. auth. see Tieger, Paul.

Barron-Tieger, Barbara, jt. auth. see Tieger, Paul D.

Barron, W. R. Sir Gawain & the Green Knight. LC 98-35048. 1998. pap. write for info. (*0-389-21018-8*) Barnes & Noble Inc.

***Barron, W. R., ed.** The Arthur of the English: The Arthurian Legend in English Life & Literature. LC 99-494974. 290p. 1999. 65.00 (*0-7083-1477-5*, Pub. by Univ Wales Pr) Paul & Co Pubs.

Barron, W. R. & Weinberg, S., eds. Layamon's Arthur: The Arthurian Section of Layamon's Brut. (Illus.). 320p. (Orig.). (C). 1989. pap. text 69.95 (*0-582-03464-1*) Longman.

Barron, W. R., ed. see Henryson, Robert.

Barron, William. Old Whaling Days. LC 97-106459. (Conway Classics Ser.). 1998. 19.95 (*0-85177-695-7*) Brasseys.

Barron, William F., et al. Fundamentals of Economics for Environmental Managers. LC 97-41001. 240p. 1998. 65.00 (*1-56720-159-8*, Quorum Bks) Greenwood.

Barron's Educational Editors. Acrylics. (Art Handbooks). (Illus.). 1997. 9.95 (*0-7641-5011-1*) Barron.

— Amazing Nature. (Megascope Ser.). (Illus.). 64p. (J). (gr. 5). 1998. 6.95 (*0-7641-5090-1*) Barron.

***Barron's Educational Editors.** Animal Behavior. (Illus.). 128p. (gr. 6-12). 1999. pap. text 8.95 (*0-7641-0952-9*) Barron.

Barron's Educational Editors. Arabic. LC 98-7812. (TravelWise Ser.). (ARA & ENG., Illus.). 290p. 1998. pap. 16.95 incl. audio (*0-7641-7118-6*); pap. 8.95 (*0-7641-0394-6*) Barron.

***Barron's Educational Editors.** Away in a Manger. 8p. 1999. 12.95 (*0-7641-5200-9*) Barron.

— Baby Bear: Cubs. (Animal Babies Ser.). (Illus.). 32p. (J). (gr. k-2). 2000. pap. 5.95 (*0-7641-1480-8*) Barron.

— Barron's Book of Cartoons. LC 99-37447. (Illus.). 112p. 1999. 22.00 (*0-7352-0142-0*, Pub. by PH Pr) S&S Trade.

Barron's Educational Editors. Barron's Compact Guide to Colleges. 11th rev. ed. 760p. 1998. pap. 8.95 (*0-7641-0505-1*) Barron.

***Barron's Educational Editors.** Barron's Guide to Law Schools. 14th ed. 440p. 2000. pap. text 16.95 (*0-7641-1396-8*) Barron.

Barron's Educational Editors. Barron's Guide to the Most Competitive Colleges. LC 98-16763. 768p. 1998. pap. 14.95 (*0-7641-0029-7*) Barron.

— Barron's Profiles of American Colleges. 23rd rev ed. LC 87-640099. (Barron's Profiles of American Colleges Ser.). (Illus.). 1591p. 1998. pap. 25.00 incl. disk (*0-7641-7134-8*) Barron.

— Barron's Profiles of American Colleges Northeast. 13th rev. ed. 440p. 1998. pap. 14.95 (*0-7641-0504-3*) Barron.

— Barron's Regents Exams & Answers: Spanish Level 3 (Comprehensive Spanish) (SPA.). 1996. pap. text 13.95 (*0-8120-8317-2*) Barron.

— Barron's Regents Power Pack: Sequential Mathematics I. 2nd ed. 1995. pap. 13.95 (*0-8120-8374-1*) Barron.

— Biology. (Barron's Regents Passware Computer Study Program Ser.). 1997. pap. 19.95 incl. disk (*0-7641-7002-3*) Barron.

— Biology. 2nd ed. (Barron's Power Packs Ser.). 1996. pap. 14.95 (*0-8120-8367-9*) Barron.

— Captain Cook & His Exploration of the Pacific. (Great Explorers Ser.). (Illus.). 32p. (J). (gr. 5). 1998. pap. 5.95 (*0-7641-0533-7*) Barron.

— Chinese. LC 98-7810. (TravelWise Language Learning Ser.). (CHI & ENG., Illus.). 290p. 1998. pap. 8.95 (*0-7641-0373-3*) Barron.

***Barron's Educational Editors.** Chinese. LC 98-7810. (TravelWise Ser.). (CHI & ENG., Illus.). 290p. 1998. pap. 16.95 incl. audio (*0-7641-7098-8*) Barron.

Barron's Educational Editors. Columbus & the Renaissance Explorers. (Great Explorers Ser.). (Illus.). 32p. (J). (gr. 5). 1998. pap. 5.95 (*0-7641-0530-2*) Barron.

***Barron's Educational Editors.** Compact Guide to Colleges. 12th ed. 2000. pap. text 8.95 (*0-7641-1320-8*) Barron.

— Computer Age. (Modern Media Ser.). 32p. 2000. pap. 5.95 (*0-7641-1066-7*) Barron.

Barron's Educational Editors. Croatian. Luft, Kathleen, tr. LC 97-48407. (TravelWise Language Learning Ser.). (CRO & ENG.). 290p. 1998. pap. 8.95 (*0-7641-0369-5*); pap. 16.95 incl. audio (*0-7641-7093-7*) Barron.

— Drake & 16th Century Explorers. (Great Explorers Ser.). (Illus.). 32p. (J). (gr. 5). 1998. pap. 5.95 (*0-7641-0532-9*) Barron.

— Earth Science. (Barron's Regents Passware Computer Study Program Ser.). 1997. pap. 19.95 incl. disk (*0-7641-7001-5*) Barron.

— Egyptian Life. (Early Civilizations Ser.). 32p. (J). 1998. pap. 5.95 (*0-7641-0628-7*) Barron.

— Exploration of Africa. (Great Explorers Ser.). (Illus.). 32p. (YA). (gr. 5 up). 1998. pap. 5.95 (*0-7641-0632-5*) Barron.

— Exploration of North America. LC 98-73627. (Great Explorers Ser.). (Illus.). 32p. (YA). (gr. 5 up). 1998. pap. 5.95 (*0-7641-0634-1*) Barron.

— Exploration of Space. LC 98-73625. (Great Explorers Ser.). (Illus.). 32p. (YA). (gr. 5 up). 1998. pap. 5.95 (*0-7641-0636-8*) Barron.

***Barron's Educational Editors.** Film & Television. (Modern Media Ser.). (Illus.). 32p. 2000. pap. 5.95 (*0-7641-1065-9*) Barron.

— 500 Popular Annuals & Perennials for American Gardeners. 288p. 1999. pap. text 12.95 (*0-7641-1177-9*) Barron.

— 500 Popular Shrubs & Trees for American Gardeners. 288p. 1999. pap. text 12.95 (*0-7641-1178-7*) Barron.

Barron's Educational Editors. Flowers. (Art Handbooks). (Illus.). 96p. 1997. 9.95 (*0-7641-5014-6*) Barron.

— French. Brodkey, Florence, tr. LC 97-47438. (TravelWise Language Learning Ser.). (ENG & FRE.). 290p. 1998. pap. 8.95 (*0-7641-0380-6*); pap. 16.95 incl. audio (*0-7641-7105-4*) Barron.

— German. (TravelWise Ser.). (ENG & GER.). 290p. 1998. pap. 16.95 incl. audio (*0-7641-7115-1*) Barron.

— German. LC 97-48406. (TravelWise Language Learning Ser.). (ENG & GER.). 290p. 1998. pap. 8.95 (*0-7641-0386-5*) Barron.

***Barron's Educational Editors.** German Shepherd. (All about Your Pet Ser.). 32p. (J). 2000. pap. 3.50 (*0-7641-1490-5*) Barron.

Barron's Educational Editors. Global Studies. (Barron's Regents Passware Computer Study Program Ser.). 1997. pap. text 19.95 incl. disk (*0-7641-7006-6*) Barron.

— Greek Life. (Early Civilizations Ser.). 32p. (J). 1998. pap. 5.95 (*0-7641-0630-9*) Barron.

***Barron's Educational Editors.** Hen. (My Little Animals Ser.). 8p. (J). 2000. 3.50 (*0-7641-5241-6*) Barron.

Barron's Educational Editors. Horses & Ponies. (Pocket Gems Ser.). (Illus.). 64p. (J). (gr. 1 up). 1996. 3.95 (*0-8120-6588-3*) Barron.

***Barron's Educational Editors.** Human Body in Action. 128p. 1999. pap. text 8.95 (*0-7641-0950-2*) Barron.

— Iguanas. (All about Your Pet Ser.). (Illus.). 32p. (J). 2000. pap. 3.50 (*0-7641-1492-1*) Barron.

Barron's Educational Editors. Italian. Root Taucher, Mary, tr. LC 97-49402. (TravelWise Language Learning Ser.). (ENG & ITA.). 290p. 1998. pap. 8.95 (*0-7641-0378-4*); pap. 16.95 incl. audio (*0-7641-7104-6*) Barron.

— Japanese. LC 98-7807. (TravelWise Language Learning Ser.). (ENG & JPN., Illus.). 290p. 1998. pap. 8.95 (*0-7641-0371-7*); pap. 16.95 incl. audio (*0-7641-7095-3*) Barron.

***Barron's Educational Editors.** Keeping Creepy Crawlies. (Unusual Pets Ser.). (Illus.). 64p. (J). (gr. 3-7). 2000. pap. 5.95 (*0-7641-1280-5*) Barron.

— Keeping Lizards. (Unusual Pets Ser.). (Illus.). 64p. (J). (gr. 3). 2000. pap. 5.95 (*0-7641-1281-3*) Barron.

— Kittens. (Animal Babies Ser.). (Illus.). 32p. (J). (gr. k-2). 2000. pap. 5.95 (*0-7641-1481-6*) Barron.

Barron's Educational Editors. Landscapes. LC 96-85273. (Art Handbooks). (Illus.). 96p. 1996. 9.95 (*0-8120-6616-2*) Barron.

— Life in the Middle Ages. (Megascope Ser.). (Illus.). 64p. (J). (gr. 5). 1998. 6.95 (*0-7641-5094-4*) Barron.

— Magellan & the Exploration of South America. (Great Explorers Ser.). (Illus.). 32p. (J). (gr. 5). 1998. pap. 5.95 (*0-7641-0531-0*) Barron.

— Manet: A New Realism. (Great Artists Ser.). (Illus.). 32p. 1997. pap. text 5.95 (*0-7641-0295-8*) Barron.

— Masters of Music Series Assortment. 1999. 14.95 (*0-7641-7314-6*) Barron.

***Barron's Educational Editors.** Middle Ages. 128p. 1999. pap. text 8.95 (*0-7641-0948-0*) Barron.

Barron's Educational Editors. Mix & Match Assortment. 1999. 24.95 (*0-7641-7313-8*) Barron.

***Barron's Educational Editors.** Music & Sound. (Modern Media Ser.). (Illus.). 32p. 2000. pap. 5.95 (*0-7641-1067-5*) Barron.

Barron's Educational Editors. My Journey Through Art: Create Your Own Masterpieces. (Illus.). 48p. (J). (gr. 2 up). 1994. pap. 6.95 (*0-8120-1924-5*) Barron.

— Mysteries, True & False. (Megascope Ser.). (Illus.). 64p. (J). (gr. 5). 1998. 6.95 (*0-7641-5095-2*) Barron.

— Oils. LC 96-85325. (Art Handbooks). (Illus.). 96p. 1996. 9.95 (*0-8120-6615-4*) Barron.

***Barron's Educational Editors.** On the Trail of Monkeys. (On the Trail Ser.). 128p. 1999. pap. text 11.95 (*0-7641-1163-9*) Barron.

— On the Trail of Sea Turtles. (On the Trail Ser.). 128p. 1999. pap. text 11.95 (*0-7641-1164-7*) Barron.

Barron's Educational Editors. Pass Key to the ASVAB: Armed Services Vocational Aptitude Battery. 2nd ed. LC 96-48239. (Barron's Educational Ser.). 288p. 1997. 7.95 (*0-8120-9741-6*) Barron.

— Petsitter's Mix. 1999. pap. text 11.85 (*0-7641-7316-2*) Barron.

— The Pharaohs of Ancient Egypt. (Megascope Ser.). (Illus.). 64p. (J). (gr. 5). 1998. 6.95 (*0-7641-5096-0*) Barron.

— Physics Power Pack. 1996. pap. text 15.95 (*0-8120-8471-3*) Barron.

— Pioneers of the Air. LC 98-73626. (Great Explorers Ser.). (Illus.). 32p. (YA). (gr. 5 up). 1998. pap. 5.95 (*0-7641-0633-3*) Barron.

***Barron's Educational Editors.** Pond & River Life. (Natural World Ser.). 32p. (J). (gr. 5). 2000. mass mkt. 5.95 (*0-7641-1075-6*) Barron.

Barron's Educational Editors. Portuguese. LC 97-48406. (TravelWise Ser.). (ENG & POR.). 292p. 1998. pap. 16.95 incl. audio (*0-7641-7111-9*) Barron.

— Portuguese. Luft, Kathleen, tr. LC 97-48408. (TravelWise Language Learning Ser.). (ENG & POR.). 290p. 1998. pap. 8.95 (*0-7641-0391-1*) Barron.

— Power Pack: Chemistry, 2 vols. 2nd ed. 1998. pap. 14.95 (*0-7641-7162-3*) Barron.

***Barron's Educational Editors.** Profiles of American Colleges, Northeast. 14th ed. (Profiles of American Colleges Ser.). 2000. pap. text 14.95 (*0-7641-1319-4*) Barron.

— Puppies. (Animal Babies Ser.). (Illus.). 32p. (J). (gr. k-2). 2000. pap. 5.95 (*0-7641-1482-4*) Barron.

— Rabbit. (My Little Animals Ser.). 8p. (J). 2000. 3.50 (*0-7641-5238-6*) Barron.

Barron's Educational Editors. Railways. (History Ser.). (Illus.). 32p. (J). (gr. 5). 1998. pap. 5.95 (*0-7641-0538-8*) Barron.

— Roman Life. (Early Civilizations Ser.). (Illus.). 32p. (J). 1998. pap. 5.95 (*0-7641-0629-5*) Barron.

***Barron's Educational Editors.** Romans: History Society Religion. 128p. 1999. pap. text 8.95 (*0-7641-0949-9*) Barron.

Barron's Educational Editors. Russian Now! LC 96-83956. 1996. 18.95 (*0-8120-6633-2*); pap. text, teacher ed. 9.95 (*0-8120-9454-9*); pap. text, wbk. ed. 6.95 (*0-8120-9453-0*) Barron.

— Russian Now! Grammar Book. 1996. pap. text 5.95 (*0-8120-9633-9*) Barron.

***Barron's Educational Editors.** Sea Lion. (My Little Animals Ser.). 8p. (J). 2000. 3.50 (*0-7641-5239-4*) Barron.

Barron's Educational Editors. Searching for Human Origins. (Megascope Ser.). (Illus.). 64p. (J). (gr. 5). 1998. 6.95 (*0-7641-5092-8*) Barron.

***Barron's Educational Editors.** Seashore Life. (Natural World Ser.). 32p. (J). (gr. 5). 2000. pap. 5.95 (*0-7641-1076-4*) Barron.

Barron's Educational Editors. Sequential Mathematics Course 1, Vol. 1. (Barron's Regents Passware Computer Study Program Ser.). 1997. pap. 19.95 incl. disk (*0-7641-7003-1*) Barron.

— Sequential Mathematics Course 2 11, Vol. 2. (Barron's Regents Passware Computer Study Program Ser.). 1997. pap. 19.95 incl. disk (*0-7641-7005-8*) Barron.

***Barron's Educational Editors.** Snakes. (All about Your Pet Ser.). 32p. (J). 2000. pap. 3.50 (*0-7641-1491-3*) Barron.

Barron's Educational Editors. Spanish. Simo, Ana, tr. LC 97-47437. (TravelWise Language Learning Ser.). (ENG & SPA.). 290p. 1998. pap. 8.95 (*0-7641-0376-8*) Barron.

***Barron's Educational Editors.** Spanish. Simo, Ana, tr. LC 97-47437. (TravelWise Ser.). (ENG & SPA.). 379p. 1998. pap. 16.95 incl. audio (*0-7641-7100-3*) Barron.

Barron's Educational Editors. Still Life. LC 96-85335. (Art Handbooks). (Illus.). 96p. 1996. 9.95 (*0-8120-6618-9*) Barron.

— Submarines. (History Ser.). (Illus.). 32p. (J). (gr. 5). 1998. pap. 5.95 (*0-7641-0536-1*) Barron.

***Barron's Educational Editors.** Telecommunications. (Modern Media Ser.). 32p. 2000. pap. 5.95 (*0-7641-1068-3*) Barron.

Barron's Educational Editors. Telephone French: Allo J'Ecoute! (Telephone Language Teacher Ser.). (ENG & FRE.). 96p. 1998. pap. 13.95 incl. audio (*0-7641-7157-7*) Barron.

— Telephone German: Ruf Mal An! (Telephone Language Teacher Ser.). (ENG & GER.). 96p. 1998. pap. 13.95 incl. audio (*0-7641-7153-4*) Barron.

— Telephone Italian: Pronto! (Telephone Language Teacher Ser.). (ENG & ITA.). 96p. 1998. pap. 13.95 incl. audio (*0-7641-7151-8*) Barron.

***Barron's Educational Editors.** Telephone Spanish: Digame! (Telephone Language Teacher Ser.). (ENG & SPA.). 96p. 1998. pap. 13.95 incl. audio (*0-7641-7155-0*) Barron.

— Tiger. (My Little Animals Ser.). 8p. (J). 2000. 3.50 (*0-7641-5240-8*) Barron.

— Tropical Fish Keeping. (All about Your Pet Ser.). (Illus.). 32p. (J). 2000. pap. 3.50 (*0-7641-1494-8*) Barron.

Barron's Educational Editors. Understanding the Human Body. (Megascope Ser.). (Illus.). 64p. (J). (gr. 5). 1998. 6.95 (*0-7641-5093-6*) Barron.

***Barron's Educational Editors.** Urban Animal. (Natural World Ser.). (Illus.). 32p. (J). (gr. 5). 2000. pap. 5.95 (*0-7641-1077-2*) Barron.

Barron's Educational Editors. Viking Life. (Early Civilizations Ser.). 32p. (J). 1998. pap. 5.95 (*0-7641-0631-7*) Barron.

— Warships. (History Ser.). (Illus.). 32p. (J). (gr. 5). 1998. pap. 5.95 (*0-7641-0535-3*) Barron.

— Watercolor: Barron's Art Handbook. LC 96-85330. (Illus.). 96p. 1996. 9.95 (*0-8120-6617-0*) Barron.

— Weapons & Warfare. (History Ser.). (Illus.). 32p. (J). (gr. 5). 1998. pap. 5.95 (*0-7641-0534-5*) Barron.

***Barron's Educational Editors.** Winning Women in Baseball & Softball. (Sport Success Ser.). 112p. (J). (gr. 5). 2000. pap. 6.95 (*0-7641-1231-7*) Barron.

— Woodland Life. (Natural World Ser.). 32p. (J). (gr. 5). 2000. mass mkt. 5.95 (*0-7641-1074-8*) Barron.

Barron's Educational Editors, ed. Anna Karenina. LC 84-21646. (Barron's Book Notes Ser.). 1985. pap. 2.50 (*0-8120-3501-1*) Barron.

— Barron's Guide to Law Schools. 13th rev. ed. 420p. 1998. pap. 14.95 (*0-7641-0431-4*) Barron.

Barron's Educational Editors, tr. Painting Pets with Watercolors. LC 94-46432. (Easy Painting & Drawing Ser.).Tr. of Animales Domesticos a la Acuarela. (ENG & SPA., Illus.). 64p. 1995. 12.95 (*0-8120-9293-7*) Barron.

***Barron's Educational Editors & Perez, Eulalia.** 100 Best Games. 136p. (J). 2000. pap. 12.95 (*0-7641-1343-7*) Barron.

Barron's Educational Editors, jt. auth. see Griffith, Francis J.

Barron's Educational Editors, tr. see Parramon Ediciones Team Staff, ed.

***Barron's Educational Series, Inc. Staff.** How to Prepare for the ASVAB: Armed Services Vocational Aptitude Battery. 6th ed. LC 00-22013. 580p. 2000. pap. 14.95 (*0-7641-0780-1*) Barron.

— How to Prepare for the ASVAB: Armed Services Vocational Aptitude Battery. 6th ed. 580p. 2000. pap. 29.95 incl. cd-rom (*0-7641-7380-4*) Barron.

— Pass Key to the ASVAB: Armed Services Vocational Aptitude Battery. 3rd ed. LC 99-87334. 290p. 2000. pap. 8.95 (*0-7641-0783-6*) Barron.

***Barron's Educational Staff.** Chinese Life. (Ticktock Bks.). (Illus.). (J). 2000. pap. 5.95 (*0-7641-1070-5*) Barron.

— Inca Life. (Ticktock Bks.). (Illus.). (J). 2000. pap. 5.95 (*0-7641-1069-1*) Barron.

— Profiles of American Colleges. 24th abr. ed. (Profiles of American Colleges Ser.). 2000. pap. 24.95 (*0-7641-7294-8*) Barron.

***Barron's Educational Staff, ed.** Cats. (Cuddle Up Bks.). (Illus.). (J). 2000. 4.95 (*0-7641-5296-3*) Barron.

— Dogs. (Cuddle Up Bks.). (Illus.). (J). 2000. 4.95 (*0-7641-5295-5*) Barron.

— Lambs. (Cuddle Up Bks.). (Illus.). (J). 2000. 4.95 (*0-7641-5299-8*) Barron.

Barron's Educational Staff, ed. Native Son. (Barron's Book Notes Ser.). 134p. 1986. pap. 2.95 (*0-8120-3529-1*) Barron.

***Barron's Educational Staff, ed.** Rabbits. (Cuddle Up Bks.). (Illus.). (J). 2000. 4.95 (*0-7641-5297-1*) Barron.

Barrons, Keith C. A Catastrophe in the Making: With Letters to the Pope. 320p. 1992. 19.95 (*0-931541-21-2*) Mancorp Pub.

Barron's Technical Staff, compiled by. Metric Converter. 1977. pap. text 2.50 (*0-8120-0707-7*) Barron.

Barron's Test Preparation Staff. How to Prepare for GRE Computer ST. 1995. 29.95 (*0-8120-8216-8*) Baron Bks.

— How to Prepare for the ACT. 11th rev. ed. 1998. pap. 29.95 incl. 3.5 hd (*0-7641-7138-0*) Barron.

— How to Prepare for the GED. 10th rev. ed. LC 98-27424. 1999. reprint ed. pap. 29.95 incl. disk (*0-7641-7205-0*) Barron.

— How to Prepare for the SAT I with Safari CD-Rom. 792p. 1998. pap. text 29.95 incl. cd-rom (*0-7641-7120-8*) Barron.

— How to Recognize Styles. (Art Handbooks). (Illus.). 96p. 1997. 9.95 (*0-7641-5015-4*) Barron.

Barros, Ana I. Discrete & Fractional Programming Techniques for Location Models. LC 98-11766. (Combinatorial Optimization Ser.). 178p. 1998. 97.00 (*0-7923-5002-2*) Kluwer Academic.

Barros, Anne. Ornament & Object: Canadian Jewellery & Metal Art, 1946-1996. LC 98-118747. 176p. 1997. 28.00 (*1-55046-218-0*, Pub. by Boston Mills) Genl Dist Srvs.

Barros-Bailey, Mary & Boyd, Dawn. Internet Disability Resources '98. (Illus.). 600p. 1997. per. 59.95 incl. cd-rom (*1-887515-04-6*) AHAB Press.

Barros, Carolyn. Autobiography: Narratives of Transformation. LC 97-23875. 264p. (C). 1997. text 44.50 (*0-472-10786-0*, 10786) U of Mich Pr.

***Barros, Carolyn A. & Smith, Johanna M., eds.** Life-Writings by British Women, 1660-1815: An Anthology. LC 99-86617. (Illus.). 416p. 2000. text 50.00 (*1-55553-432-5*); pap. text 20.00 (*1-55553-431-7*) NE U Pr.

Barros, Cristina. Las Once y Sereno: Tipo Mexicanos Del Siglo XIX. (SPA., Illus.). 130p. 1994. 23.99 (*968-16-4531-6*, Pub. by Fondo) Continental Bk.

Barros, James. Betrayal from Within: Joseph Avenol, Secretary-General of the League of Nations, 1933-1940. LC 75-81413. 301p. reprint ed. pap. 93.40 (*0-8357-7147-4*, 202197800024) Bks Demand.

— Britain, Greece & the Politics of Sanctions: Ethiopia, 1935-1936. (Royal Historical Society Ser.: No. 33). 260p. 1982. 75.00 (*0-901050-86-5*) Boydell & Brewer.

— Trygve Lie & the Cold War: The UN Secretary-General Pursues Peace, 1946-1953. 444p. 1989. text 37.00 (*0-87580-148-X*) N Ill U Pr.

Barros, James & Gregor, James. Double Deception: Stalin, Hitler & the Invasion of Russia. LC 94-11771. (Illus.). 270p. 1995. lib. bdg. 32.00 (*0-87580-191-9*) N Ill U Pr.

Barros, Maria D., tr. see Larsson, Goran.

Barros-Neto, Jose. College Algebra. 2nd ed. Date not set. pap. text, student ed. 23.25 (*0-314-65235-3*) West Pub.

— Introduction to the Theory of Distributions. LC 80-11323. 236p. 1981. reprint ed. lib. bdg. 23.50 (*0-89874-128-9*) Krieger.

Barros-Neto, Jose & Artino, Ralph A. Hypoelliptic Boundary-Value Problems. LC 79-29732. (Lecture Notes in Pure & Applied Mathematics Ser.: Vol. 53). 104p. reprint ed. pap. 32.30 (*0-608-08912-5*, 206954700005) Bks Demand.

Barros, Paul De, see De Barros, Paul.

Barros, Ricardo, et al. Hacia un Crecimiento Moderno: Ensayos en Honor de Carlos Diaz-Alejandro. Ranis, Gustav, ed. & pref. by. (SPA.). 186p. (C). 1996. pap. text 18.50 (*0-940602-99-7*) IADB.

Barrosa Du Bocacho, Manuel M. De, see De Barrosa Du Bocacho, Manuel M.

Barroso. Lambada Bk. 2: Venus with a Hot Crotch. (Eros Graphic Novel Ser.). 104p. 1996. pap. 12.95 (*1-56097-226-2*) Fantagraph Bks.

Barroso & Helga. Lambada Bk. 1: Buttfuque U. (Eros Graphic Novel Ser.). 168p. 1996. pap. 14.95 (*1-56097-221-1*) Fantagraph Bks.

Barrots, W. & Ripley, E. Fatigue of Aircraft Structures: Proceedings of Symposium, Paris, May, 1961. LC 63-10105. (International Series of Monographs in Aeronautics & Astronautics: Vol. 12). 1963. 170.00 (*0-08-009895-9*, Pub. by Pergamon Repr) Franklin.

Barrow. Aging: The Individual & Society. 7th ed. (Sociology-Upper Level Ser.). 1998. pap. 76.95 (*0-534-55242-0*) Wadsworth Pub.

— The Aging Individual & Society. 5th ed. Date not set. pap. text, teacher ed. write for info. (*0-314-01019-X*) West Pub.

— Aging Individual & Society, Vol. 6. Date not set. pap. text, teacher ed. write for info. (*0-314-06245-9*) West Pub.

— Physical Chemistry & SG. 6th ed. 1997. 88.00 (*0-07-561219-4*) McGraw.

— Physical Chemistry/Life Science. 2nd ed. 1981. student ed. 23.12 (*0-07-003859-7*) McGraw.

— Solving Differential Equations With Maple V Release 4. LC 97-205220. (Mathematics Ser.). 1997. pap. 33.95 (*0-534-34555-7*) Brooks-Cole.

Barrow, et al. Gender, Race & Identity. (Conference Proceedings Ser.). 265p. 1993. pap. text. write for info. (*0-931559-01-4*) Southern Humanities.

Barrow, jt. auth. see Brown, Robert.

Barrow, Ann, jt. illus. see Stanley, George Edward.

Barrow, Bennet H. Plantation Life in the Florida Parishes of Louisiana, 1836-1846, As Reflected in the Diary of Bennet H. Barrow. Davis, Edwin A., ed. LC 74-163680. reprint ed. 34.50 (*0-404-01989-7*) AMS Pr.

Barrow, C. J. Developing Environment. (C). 1996. pap. text 56.00 (*0-582-08700-7*) Addison-Wesley.

— Environmental & Social Impact Assessment: An Introduction. (Arnold Publications). (Illus.). 320p. 1997. text 75.00 (*0-340-66272-7*); pap. text 29.95 (*0-340-66271-9*) OUP.

— Land Degradation: Development & Breakdown of Terrestrial Environments. (Illus.). 313p. (C). 1991. text 90.00 (*0-521-35333-5*) Cambridge U Pr.

— Water Resources & Agricultural Development in the Tropics. 1987. pap. 24.95 (*0-582-30137-8*, Pub. by Addison-Wesley) Longman.

Barrow, Charles A. Industrial Relations Law. LC 97-192689. 370p. 1997. pap. 48.00 (*1-85941-115-0*, Pub. by Cavendish Pubng) Gaunt.

Barrow, Charles K. & Segars, J. H., eds. The Forgotten Confederates: A Collection of Historical Accounts about Black Confederates. (Journal of Confederate History Ser.: Vol. 14). (Illus.). 200p. 1995. pap. 16.95 (*1-889332-12-7*); text 21.00 (*1-889332-10-0*) So Herit Pr.

Barrow, Christine. Family in the Caribbean: Themes & Perspectives. LC 98-43653. 400p. (C). 1999. reprint ed. text 44.95 (*1-55876-207-8*); reprint ed. pap. text 22.95 (*1-55876-208-6*) Wiener Pubs Inc.

Barrow, Christopher J. Environmental Management: Principles & Practice LC 99-17744. 1999. pap. write for info. (*0-415-18561-0*) Routledge.

***Barrow, Christopher J.** Environmental Management: Principles & Practice. LC 99-17744. (Environmental Management Ser.). 326p. (C). 1999. pap. write for info. (*0-415-18560-2*) Routledge.

Barrow, Christopher J., jt. ed. see Saha, Suranjit K.

Barrow, Clyde W. Critical Theories of the State: Marxist, Neo-Marxist, Post-Marxist. LC 92-34761. (Illus.). 256p. (C). 1993. pap. 19.95 (*0-299-13714-7*) U of Wis Pr.

— Critical Theories of the State: Marxist, Neo-Marxist, Post-Marxist. LC 92-34761. 236p. reprint ed. pap. 73.20 (*0-608-07462-4*, 206768900009) Bks Demand.

***Barrow, Clyde W.** More Than a Historian: The Political & Economic Thought of Charles A. Beard. LC 00-37391. 378p. 2000. 39.95 (*0-7658-0027-6*) Transaction Pubs.

Barrow, Clyde W. Universities & the Capitalist State: Corporate Liberalism & the Reconstruction of American Higher Education, 1894-1928. (History of American Thought & Culture Ser.). 350p. (Orig.). (C). 1990. pap. text 21.95 (*0-299-12404-5*) U of Wis Pr.

Barrow, Colin. The Essence of Small Business. 2nd ed. LC 97-38534. (Essence of Management Ser.). 1998. write for info. (*0-13-748641-3*) P-H.

Barrow, Connie V. Poems of Pearls & Praise. 1998. pap. write for info. (*1-57553-692-7*) Watermrk Pr.

Barrow, Daniel L., jt. auth. see Alleyne, Cargill H., Jr.

Barrow, Daniel L., jt. ed. see Hadley, Mark N.

Barrow, David & Chang, Glen. The Life & Sculpture of Wah Ming Chang. (Illus.). 90p. 1990. write for info. (*0-9625293-0-3*); pap. write for info. (*0-9625293-1-1*) W M Chang.

Barrow, David, et al. Solving Ode's with Maple V. (Brooks/Cole Symbolic Computation Ser.). 264p. (C). 1996. pap. 18.25 (*0-534-34402-X*) Brooks-Cole.

Barrow, Deborah J., et al. The Federal Judiciary & Institutional Change. LC 96-5994. (Illus.). 160p. (C). 1996. text 42.50 (*0-472-10634-1*, 10634) U of Mich Pr.

Barrow, Elaine, jt. auth. see Hulme, M.

Barrow, G. I. & Feltham, R. K., eds. Cowan & Steel's Manual for the Identification of Medical Bacteria. 3rd ed. (Illus.). 351p. (C). 1993. text 80.00 (*0-521-32611-7*) Cambridge U Pr.

Barrow, G. W. The Kingdom of the Scots: Government, Church & Society from the Eleventh to the Fourteenth Century. LC 74-171374. (Illus.). xvii, 404p. 1973. write for info. (*0-7131-5682-1*) OUP.

***Barrow, G. W., ed.** The Charters of David I: The Written Acts of David I King of Scots, 1124-53 & of His Son Henry, Earl of Northumberland, 1139-52. LC 99-10218. (Illus.). 180p. 1999. 110.00 (*0-85115-731-9*) Boydell & Brewer.

***Barrow, Gaylon.** The Hanging at Stinking Creek. 146p. 2000. pap. 13.95 (*0-7414-0365-X*) Buy Books.

Barrow, Geoffrey R. The Satiric Vision of Blas de Otero. LC 88-4877. 168p. 1989. text 26.00 (*0-8262-0687-5*) U of Mo Pr.

Barrow, Geoffrey W. Kingship & Unity: Scotland, 1000 to 1306, A. D. 185p. 1989. pap. 16.50 (*0-7486-0104-X*, Pub. by Edinburgh U Pr) Col U Pr.

— Kingship & Unity: Scotland, 1000-1306. LC 81-182606. (New History of Scotland Ser.: No. 2). 191p. reprint ed. pap. 59.30 (*0-608-16554-9*, 202635800049) Bks Demand.

— Robert Bruce & the Community of the Realm of Scotland. rev. ed. (Illus.). 448p. 1988. pap. 30.00 (*0-85224-604-8*, Pub. by Edinburgh U Pr) Col U Pr.

— Scotland & Its Neighbours in the Middle Ages. LC 92-21984. 228p. 1992. 60.00 (*1-85285-052-3*) Hambledon Press.

Barrow, George. Ceylon: Past & Present. (C). 1995. reprint ed. 17.00 (*81-206-1073-3*, Pub. by Asian Educ Servs) S Asia.

Barrow, George L. The Round Towers of Ireland. (Illus.). 232p. 1979. 35.00 (*0-8159-6726-8*) Devin.

Barrow, Georgia M. Aging, the Individual & Society. 6th ed. LC 95-30482. 427p. (C). 1996. 49.00 (*0-314-04444-2*) West Pub.

Barrow, Georgia M. & Shuttlesworth, Guy. Aging, the Individual, & Society. 5th ed. LaMarre, ed. 380p. (C). 1993. pap. text 47.25 (*0-314-93332-8*) West Pub.

Barrow, Gordon M. Physical Chemistry. 6th ed. (Illus.). 910p. (C). 1996. 102.19 (*0-07-005111-9*) McGraw.

— Physical Chemistry. 6th ed. (C). 1996. student ed. 33.75 (*0-07-005113-5*) McGraw.

— Physical Chemistry for the Life Sciences. 2nd ed. (Illus.). 448p. (C). 1981. text 65.00 (*0-07-003858-9*) McGraw.

Barrow-Green, June. Poincare & the Three Body Problem. LC 96-11112. (History of Mathematics Ser.: Vol. 11). 272p. 1996. 49.00 (*0-8218-0367-0*, HMATH/11) Am Math.

Barrow, Harold M., et al. Practical Measurement in Physical Education & Sport. 4th ed. LC 88-34035. (Illus.). 364p. 1989. text 39.95 (*0-8121-1216-4*) Lppncott W & W.

Barrow, Isaac. Lectiones Geometricae. 149p. 1976. reprint ed. 65.00 (*3-487-06089-2*) G Olms Pubs.

— The Mathematical Works, 2 vols. in 1. Whevell, W., ed. (Illus.). xix, 734p. 1973. reprint ed. 225.00 (*3-487-04788-8*) G Olms Pubs.

— Theological Works of Isaac Barrow, 9 vols. Napier, Alexander, ed. LC 72-161751. reprint ed. lib. bdg. 215.00 (*0-404-00670-1*) AMS Pr.

Barrow, Jan. Flood Find. (J). (gr. 4-5). 1996. pap. 9.95 (*0-8464-4630-8*) Beekman Pubs.

Barrow, Jan. The Flood Find. 69p. (J). 1996. pap. 9.75 (*0-8464-4832-7*) Beekman Pubs.

***Barrow, Jerry R., ed.** Shrubland Ecosystem Dynamics in a Changing Environment: Proceedings (1995) (Illus.). 275p. (C). 2000. reprint ed. pap. text 35.00 (*0-7881-8528-4*) DIANE Pub.

Barrow, Joe Louis, Jr. & Munder, Barbara. Joe Louis: 50 Years an American Hero. large type ed. (General Ser.). 357p. 1990. lib. bdg. 18.95 (*0-8161-4851-1*, G K Hall Lrg Type) Mac Lib Ref.

Barrow, John C. Fostering Cognitive Development of Students. LC 85-46005. (Jossey-Bass Higher Education Ser.). 414p. reprint ed. pap. 128.40 (*0-7837-6504-5*, 204561600007) Bks Demand.

Barrow, John D. The Artful Universe. (Illus.). 300p. 1995. 35.00 (*0-19-853996-7*) OUP.

***Barrow, John D.** Between Inner Space & Outer Space: Essays on Science Art & Philosophy. LC 98-44106. (Illus.). 288p. 1999. 30.00 (*0-19-850254-0*) OUP.

— Between Inner Space & Outer Space: Essays on Science, Art, & Philosophy. (Illus.). 288p. 2000. pap. 13.95 (*0-19-288041-1*) OUP.

Barrow, John D. Impossibility: The Limits of Science & the Science of Limits. LC 97-35202. (Illus.). 292p. (C). 1998. 27.50 (*0-19-851890-0*) OUP.

***Barrow, John D.** Impossibility: The Limits of Science & the Science of Limits. (Illus.). 304p. 1999. pap. 15.95 (*0-19-513082-0*) OUP.

Barrow, John D. Sketches of the Royal Society & Royal Society Club. 216p. 1971. reprint ed. 30.00 (*0-7146-2405-5*, Pub. by F Cass Pubs) Intl Spec Bk.

***Barrow, John D.** Universe That Discovered Itself. (Illus.). 432p. 2000. pap. 16.95 (*0-19-286200-6*) OUP.

Barrow, John D. The World Within the World. (Illus.). 416p. 1988. reprint ed. 35.00 (*0-19-851979-6*) OUP.

Barrow, John D., et al, eds. The Physical Universe: The Interface Between Cosmology, Astrophysics & Particle Physics: Proceedings of the XII Autumn School of Physics, Lisbon, Portugal, October 1-5, 1990 Particle Physics. (Lecture Notes in Physics Ser.: Vol. 383). viii, 312p. 1991. 50.95 (*0-387-54293-0*) Spr-Verlag.

Barrow, John D. & Tipler, Frank J. The Anthropic Cosmological Principle. (Illus.). 726p. 1988. pap. 18.95 (*0-19-282147-4*) OUP.

Barrow, Julia, ed. English Episcopal Acta: Hereford, 1079-1234, Vol. 7. (English Episcopal Acta Ser.: No. VII). (Illus.). 484p. 1993. text 89.00 (*0-19-726109-4*) OUP.

Barrow, Julia, tr. see Le Goff, Jacques.

Barrow, Lee G. Early Court Records of Pulaski County, Georgia, 1809-1825. LC 98-209286. vii, 292 p. 1994. write for info. (*0-89308-502-2*) Southern Hist Pr.

***Barrow, Lloyd H.** Science Fair Projects Investigating Earthworms. LC 99-36381. (Science Fair Success Ser.). (Illus.). 104p. (gr. 6 up). 2000. lib. bdg. 20.95 (*0-7660-1291-3*) Enslow Pubs.

Barrow, Logie & Bullock, Ian. Democratic Ideas in the British Labour Movement, 1880-1914. 336p. (C). 1996. text 69.95 (*0-521-56042-X*) Cambridge U Pr.

An Asterisk (*) at the beginning of an entry indicates that the title is appearing for the first time.

Barrow, Loyd M. The Negro Kingdom - Three Generations: The Vanished Colony. (Illus.). 86p. (Orig.). 1996. pap. 8.95 (*0-9646054-7-3*) Moosehead Communs.

Barrow, M. G., jt. ed. see Mayes, M. A.

Barrow, M. H., jt. auth. see Rase, Howard F.

Barrow, Madeline H. To Air Is Human: A Manual for People with Chronic Lung Disease. large type ed. (Illus.). 72p. 1999. pap. 7.95 (*0-939838-51-6*) Pritchett & Hull.

Barrow, Mark V. Heart Talk: Understanding Cardiovascular Diseases. (Illus.). 500p. (Orig.). 1992. pap. 30.00 (*0-9630510-0-8*) Cor-Ed Pub.

— A Passion for Birds: American Ornithology after Audubon. LC 97-18600. 336p. 1998. text 39.50 (*0-691-04402-3*, Pub. by Princeton U Pr) Cal Prin Full Svc.

***Barrow, Mark V.** Passion for Birds: American Ornithology after Audubon. 2000. pap. text 19.95 (*0-691-04954-8*, Pub. by Princeton U Pr) Cal Prin Full Svc.

Barrow, Mark V., et al. Health & Disease of American Indians North of Mexico: A Bibliography, 1800-1969. LC 70-161004. 161p. reprint ed. pap. 50.00 (*0-8357-6713-2*, 203534500095) Bks Demand.

Barrow, Michael. Statistics for Economics, Accountancy & Business Studies. 1996. pap. text. write for info. (*0-582-23953-2*, Pub. by Addison-Wesley) Longman.

Barrow, N. J. Plant Nutrition, From Genetic Engineering to Field Practice: Proceedings of the Twelfth International Plant Nutrition Colloquium, 21-26 September 1993, Perth, Western Australia. LC 93-32992. (Developments in Plant & Soil Sciences Ser.). 830p. (C). 1994. text 509.50 (*0-7923-2540-0*) Kluwer Academic.

— Reactions with Variable-Change Soils. (Developments in Plant & Soil Sciences Ser.). (C). 1987. text 122.00 (*90-247-3589-0*) Kluwer Academic.

Barrow, O. J. The Criminal Procedure Act 51 of 1977. 9th ed. LC 98-102365. 272p. 1997. pap. 30.00 (*0-7021-4030-9*, Pub. by Juta & Co) Gaunt.

***Barrow, O. J.** The Criminal Procedure Act 51 of 1977. 11th ed. 1999. pap. 34.00 (*0-7021-4984-5*, Pub. by Juta & Co) Gaunt.

***Barrow, O. J. & Erasmus, H. J., eds.** The Supreme Court Act 59 of 1959 & the Magistrates' Court Act 32 of 1944. 1999. pap. 40.00 (*0-7021-4983-7*, Pub. by Juta & Co) Gaunt.

Barrow, Owen J. The Criminal Procedure Act Fifty-One of 1977. 6th ed. 306p. 1994. pap. 28.00 (*0-7021-3091-5*, Pub. by Juta & Co) Gaunt.

— The Criminal Procedure Act 51 of 1977. 8th ed. 280p. 1996. pap. 38.00 (*0-7021-3573-9*, Pub. by Juta & Co) Gaunt.

— Die Strafproseswet 51 van 1977. 5th ed. 315p. 1993. pap. write for info. (*0-7021-2958-5*, Pub. by Juta & Co) Gaunt.

Barrow, Owen J., jt. auth. see Erasmus, H. J.

***Barrow, Peter.** Stet's legacy: Circles of Prophecy - Book I. LC 00-191043. 2000. 25.00 (*0-7388-2215-9*); pap. 18.00 (*0-7388-2216-7*) Xlibris Corp.

Barrow, R. H. Los Romanos. (Breviarios Ser.). (SPA.). pap. 7.99 (*968-16-0004-5*, Pub. by Fondo) Continental Bk.

Barrow, Reginald H. Athenian Democracy. 1993. pap. 18.95 (*1-85399-576-2*, Pub. by Brist Class Pr) Focus Pub-R Pullins.

Barrow, Reginald H. Greek & Roman Education. 1996. pap. 18.95 (*0-17-438501-3*) Focus Pub-R Pullins.

— Greek & Roman Education. (Inside the Ancient World Ser.). 88p. 2001. reprint ed. pap. text 16.95 (*1-85399-511-8*, Pub. by Brist Class Pr) Focus Pub-R Pullins.

— Plutarch & His Times. LC 76-6599. (BCL Ser. II). 1979. reprint ed. 39.50 (*0-404-15276-7*) AMS Pr.

— The Romans. (History of Britain Ser.: No. F895-1). (Illus.). (Orig.). (YA). (gr. 5 up). 1990. pap. 3.95 (*1-85543-006-1*, Ladybrd) Penguin Putnam.

Barrow, Robin. Language, Intelligence, & Thought. 144p. 1993. 70.00 (*1-85278-094-0*) E Elgar.

— Utilitarianism: A Contemporary Statement. 208p. 1991. text 80.00 (*1-85278-097-5*) E Elgar.

Barrow, Robin & Milburn, Geoffrey. A Critical Dictionary of Educational Concepts: An Appraisal of Selected Ideas & Issues in Educational Theory & Practice. 2nd ed. 384p. (C). 1990. text 45.00 (*0-8077-3058-0*) Tchrs Coll.

Barrow, Robin & Woods, Ronald N. An Introduction to Philosophy of Education. 3rd ed. 224p. (C). 1989. pap. 24.99 (*0-415-01285-6*) Routledge.

***Barrow, S.** A Revision of Phoenix. 61p. 1998. reprint ed. pap. 15.00 (*1-900347-63-6*, Pub. by Royal Botnic Grdns) Balogh.

Barrow, Steve. Rough Reggae, No. 1. LC 97-223840. (Illus.). 384p. 1997. pap. 19.95 (*1-85828-247-0*) Viking Penguin.

Barrow, T. Inside the Music Business. 1995. pap. text 19.95 (*1-85713-012-X*) Chapman & Hall.

Barrow, Terence. An Illustrated Guide to Maori Art. (Illus.). 104p. 1984. pap. 16.95 (*0-8248-0979-3*) UH Pr.

Barrow, Terence & Lanterman, Ray. More Incredible Hawaii. LC 85-5112. (Illus.). 120p. (Orig.). 1986. pap. 6.95 (*0-8048-1427-9*) Tuttle Pubng.

Barrow, Thomas, jt. auth. see Coke, Van D.

Barrow, Thomas C. Trade & Empire: The British Customs Service in Colonial America, 1660-1775. LC 67-11666. 348p. 1967. 34.50 (*0-674-89925-3*) HUP.

***Barrow, Tony.** Beatles: Magical Mystery Tour. (Illus.). 56p. 1999. pap. 15.95 (*0-7119-7575-2*) Music Sales.

Barrow, Tony & Newby, Julian. Inside the Music Business. (Blueprint Ser.). 256p. (C). 1994. pap. 24.99 (*0-415-13660-1*) Routledge.

Barrow, William. An Essay on Education: 1804 Edition, 2 vols., Set. 18th ed. Stern, Jeffrey, ed. & intro. by. (Classics in Education Ser.). 784p. 1996. reprint ed. 185.00 (*1-85506-268-2*) Bks Intl VA.

Barrow, William, ed. see APLIC International Staff.

Barrow, William J. Manuscripts & Documents: Their Deterioration & Restoration. 2nd ed. LC 72-89855. (Illus.). 112p. reprint ed. pap. 34.80 (*0-8357-3144-8*, 203940700012) Bks Demand.

Barrow-Zimm, Gilda & Hill, Chuck. Food & Wine Northwest Style. (Illus.). 136p. 1991. pap. 12.95 (*0-9617699-3-9*) Speed Graphics.

Barrowclough, Christine & Tarrier, Nicholas. Families of Schizophrenic Patients: Cognitive Behavioral Intervention. LC 92-32395. 276p. 1992. pap. 51.00 (*1-56593-021-5*, 0264) Thomson Learn.

Barrowe, John. A Description of Pitcairn's Island & Its Inhabitants. LC 72-302. (World History Ser.: No. 48). 1972. reprint ed. lib. bdg. 75.00 (*0-8383-1409-0*) M S G Haskell Hse.

Barrowman. Science & Math. (Techknowledge Reference Ser.). (J). (gr. k-12). 1997. pap. 21.95 (*0-538-64484-2*) S-W Pub.

Barrowman, J. A. Physiology of the Gastro-Intestinal Lymphatic System. LC 77-22823. (Monographs of the Physiological Society: No. 33). 340p. reprint ed. pap. 96.90 (*0-608-17040-2*, 2027280) Bks Demand.

Barrowman, Rachel. The Turnbull: A Library & Its World. 240p. 1996. pap. 29.95 (*1-86940-137-9*, Pub. by Auckland Univ) Paul & Co Pubs.

Barrowman, Tom, et al. Apple Technic Control One Technology Pack. Helgoe, Cathy & Lough, Tom, eds. (Illus.). 416p. (YA). (gr. 6-12). 1991. 575.00 (*0-914831-75-5*, 958) Lego Dacta.

— MS-DOS Technic Control One Technology Pack. Helgoe, Cathy & Lough, Tom, eds. (Illus.). 416p. (YA). (gr. 6-12). 1991. 595.00 (*0-914831-78-X*, 968) Lego Dacta.

— Technic Control One Resource Guide. Helgoe, Cathy & Lough, Tom, eds. (Illus.). 416p. (YA). (gr. 6-12). 1991. text 75.00 (*0-914831-74-7*, 959) Lego Dacta.

Barrows & Case. Speech Drills for Children in Form of Play. 1973. text 2.00 (*0-686-09392-5*) Expression.

Barrows & Hall. Jack in the Box. 1973. text 1.25 (*0-686-09391-7*) Expression.

Barrows, jt. auth. see Burns, Patrick J.

Barrows, jt. auth. see Hart.

Barrows, Alison. Access 97 for Windows for Dummies Quick Reference. LC 96-79263. (For Dummies Ser.). (Illus.). 224p. 1997. spiral bd. 12.99 (*0-7645-0056-2*) IDG Bks.

***Barrows, Alison.** Access 2000 for Windows for Dummies. LC 99-61123. (For Dummies: Quick Reference (Computers) Ser.). (Illus.). 240p. 1999. spiral bd. 12.99 (*0-7645-0445-2*) IDG Bks.

Barrows, Alison. Dummies 101: WordPerfect 8 for Windows. 4th ed. LC 97-72403. (Dummies 101 Ser.). 288p. 1997. pap. 24.99 incl. cd-rom (*0-7645-0189-5*) IDG Bks.

Barrows, Allison. The Artist's Friends. LC 96-43533. (Illus.). 32p. (J). (ps-4). 1997. 14.95 (*1-57505-054-4*, Carolrhoda) Lerner Pub.

— The Artist's Model. LC 95-33326. (Illus.). 32p. (J). (ps-3). 1996. lib. bdg. 19.93 (*0-87614-948-4*, Carolrhoda) Lerner Pub.

Barrows, Anita. A Record. 48p. 1998. 5.00 (*1-890044-08-3*) Riverstone PA.

— The Road Past the View. LC 96-20463. (QRL Poetry Bks.: Vol. XXXI). (Illus.). vii, 142p. 1992. 20.00 (*0-614-06446-5*) Quarterly Rev.

Barrows, Anita, tr. see Kristeva, Julia.

Barrows, Anita, tr. see Rilke, Rainer Maria.

Barrows, Clayton W. & Bosselman, Robert H. Hospitality Management Education. LC 98-38132. xvi, 286 p. 1999. 49.95 (*0-7890-0441-0*) Haworth Pr.

— Hospitality Management Education. 1999. write for info. (*0-07-890044-1*) McGraw.

Barrows, Clayton W., jt. auth. see Powers, Tom.

Barrows, Clifford. The Fall Guy. Barenbaum, Ruth, ed. (Opening Doors Ser.: No. 1). (Illus.). 32p. 1989. pap. 4.00 (*1-877829-03-X*) Homegrown Bks.

Barrows, David P. The Ethno-Botany of the Coahuilla Indians of Southern California. LC 76-43653. reprint ed. 34.50 (*0-404-15487-5*) AMS Pr.

— Ethnobotany of the Coahuilla Indians of Southern California. 1977. pap. 12.00 (*0-939046-16-4*) Malki Mus Pr.

— History of the Philippines. 1977. 36.95 (*0-8369-7152-3*, 7984) Ayer.

Barrows, Edward M. The Great Commodore: The Exploits of Matthew Calbraith. LC 72-23. (Select Bibliographies Reprint Ser.). 1977. reprint ed. 26.95 (*0-8369-9952-5*) Ayer.

— Handbook of Ethological, Ecological, & Evolutionary Terminology. 688p. 1994. boxed set 257.95 (*0-8493-3238-9*, QL750) CRC Pr.

Barrows, Gordon H. World Petroleum Arrangements, 1993. Jeune, D. & Guerra, M., eds. (Basic Oil Laws & Concession Contracts Ser.). 589p. 1989. 695.00 (*0-89069-027-8*) Barrows Co.

Barrows, Howard S. How to Design a Problem-Based Curriculum for the Preclinical Years, Pt. 8. (Medical Education Ser.: Vol. 8). 160p. 1985. 32.95 (*0-8261-4900-6*) Springer Pub.

— Practice-Based Learning. 145p. 1994. pap. 19.95 (*0-931369-27-4*) Southern IL Univ Sch.

Barrows, Howard S. Problem-Based Learning Applied to Medical Education. 35.00 (*0-931369-34-7*) Southern IL Univ Sch.

Barrows, Howard S. Training Standardized Patients to Have Physical Findings. 50p. 1999. pap. 20.00 (*0-931369-33-9*) Southern IL Univ Sch.

— The Tutorial Process. rev. ed. 75p. (C). 1992. pap. 12.95 (*0-931369-25-8*) Southern IL Univ Sch.

— What Your Tutor May Never Tell You. 45p. (Orig.). 1996. pap. 9.95 (*0-931369-29-0*) Southern IL Univ Sch.

Barrows, Howard S. & Pickell, Garfield C. Developing Clinical Problem-Solving Skills: A Guide to More Effective Diagnosis & Treatment. (Illus.). 264p. (C). 1991. pap. 19.95 (*0-393-71010-6*) Norton.

Barrows, Howard S., et al. The Clinical Practice Examination. (Illus.). 192p. (Orig.). (C). 1992. pap. 20.95 (*0-931369-24-X*) Southern IL Univ Sch.

Barrows, John R., ed. U-Bet: A Greenhorn in Old Montana. LC 89-24970. 292p. 1990. reprint ed. pap. 90.60 (*0-608-03466-5*, 206417300008) Bks Demand.

***Barrows, John Stuart.** Fryeburg, Maine: An Historical Sketch. (Illus.). 325p. 2000. reprint ed. pap. 28.50 (*0-7884-1509-3*, 1509) Heritage Bk.

Barrows, Laurie. Job Jungle. (Illus.). 72p. (J). (gr. k-4). 1998. pap. 6.32 (*0-934783-48-9*) CFKR Career.

Barrows, Marjorie. Treasures of Love & Inspiration. LC 85-70378. 1993. 8.98 (*0-88365-698-1*) Galahad Bks.

Barrows, R. C. The Electric Man. 216p. 1995. pap. 10.95 (*0-9644497-1-4*) Sandstar Pr.

— Island Masters: With Other Stories & Autobiography. Frick, Carol, ed. (Illus.). 216p. 1995. pap. 10.95 (*0-9644497-0-6*) Sandstar Pr.

Barrows, Richard & Roth, Michael. Land Tenure & Investment in African Agriculture: Theory & Evidence. (LTC Paper Ser.: Vol. 136). 29p. (C). 1989. pap. 4.00 (*0-934519-52-8*, LTC136) U of Wis Land.

***Barrows, Robert G.** Albion Fellows Bacon: Indiana's Municipal Housekeeper. LC 00-25134. (Midwestern History & Culture Ser.). 2000. write for info. (*0-253-33774-7*) Ind U Pr.

Barrows, Robert G., jt. ed. see Bodenhamer, David J.

Barrows, Robert M., ed. The Barrows Popularity Factor. 1996. pap. 29.95 (*0-9653108-0-9*, BPF-1) R M Barrows.

Barrows, Rosemary. Sir Lawrence Alma Tadema. LC 96-30853. (Illus.). 256p. 1997. 65.00 (*0-8478-2001-7*, Pub. by Rizzoli Intl) St Martin.

Barrows, Roxane, jt. auth. see Hart, Jerome.

Barrows, Sydney B. Getting a Little Work Done. 24.95 (*0-06-019435-9*); pap. 14.00 (*0-06-093239-2*) HarpC.

Barrows, Sydney B. Just Between Us Girls: Secrets about Men from the Mayflower Madam. 1997. mass mkt. 6.50 (*0-312-96047-6*) St Martin.

Barrows, Sydney B. & Novak, William. Mayflower Madam: The Secret Life of Sydney Biddle Barrows. large type ed. 457p. 1987. reprint ed. lib. bdg. 19.95 (*1-55736-007-3*) BDD LT Grp.

Barrows, Walter. Grassroots Politics in an African State: Integration & Development in Sierra Leone. LC 74-84655. 250p. 1976. 45.00 (*0-8419-0183-X*, Africana) Holmes & Meier.

Barrows, William. The Indian's Side of the Indian Question. LC 72-5517. (Select Bibliographies Reprint Ser.). 1977. reprint ed. 16.95 (*0-8369-6895-6*) Ayer.

— Oregon: The Struggle for Possession. LC 72-3766. (American Commonwealths Ser.: No. 2). reprint ed. 39.50 (*0-404-57202-2*) AMS Pr.

Barrows, William, ed. The General: Twelve Nights in the Hunters' Camp. LC 70-179504. (Select Bibliographies Reprint Ser.). (Illus.). 1977. reprint ed. 23.95 (*0-8369-6633-3*) Ayer.

Barrows, William, jt. ed. see Leadbetter, Laurie.

Barrows, William, jt. ed. see Vanderlin, Jane.

Barrs, Jerram, jt. auth. see Macaulay, Ranald.

Barrs, Myra & Pidgeon, Sue, eds. Reading the Difference: Gender & Reading in Elementary Classrooms. (Illus.). 144p. (C). 1994. pap. text 17.00 (*1-57110-005-9*) Stenhse Pubs.

Barrs, Myra, et al. The Primary Language Record: Handbook for Teachers. 64p. 1989. pap. text 30.00 (*0-435-08521-2*, 08521) Heinemann.

Barrs, Myra, ed. see CLPE Staff.

Barrucand, M. Arquitectura Islamica. 1996. pap. 24.95 (*3-8228-0679-X*) Taschen Amer.

Barrucand, Marianne & Bednorz, Achim. Moorish Architecture: In Andalusia. LC 00-500343. (Architecture & Design Ser.). (Illus.). 250p. 1999. reprint ed. 24.99 (*3-8228-7634-8*) Taschen Amer.

Barrum, James A., et al. Community Based Corrections. 19p. 1983. 2.00 (*0-318-02514-0*) S Houston Employ.

Barrus, Ben M., et al. A People Called Cumberland Presbyterians: A History of the Cumberland Presbyterian Church, 2. 650p. 1998. pap. 45.00 (*1-57910-100-3*) Wipf & Stock.

Barrus, Clara. The Life & Letters of John Burroughs, 2 vols., Set. (BCL1-PS American Literature Ser.). 1992. reprint ed. lib. bdg. 150.00 (*0-7812-6682-3*) Rprt Serv.

— The Life & Letters of John Burroughs, 2 vols., Set. 1993. reprint ed. lib. bdg. 150.00 (*0-7812-5267-9*) Rprt Serv.

— Our Friend, John Burroughs. LC 76-130262. (American Biography Ser.: No. 32). 1970. reprint ed. lib. bdg. 75.00 (*0-8383-1169-5*) M S G Haskell Hse.

Barrus, Emery. Legacy of a Hunter: A Novel. 256p. (Orig.). 1995. pap. 10.95 (*0-931832-88-8*) Fithian Pr.

— The Other Wife: A Novel. LC 91-10871. 288p. 1991. text 22.95 (*0-931832-87-X*) Fithian Pr.

Barrus, Nancy W. & Evans, James A. A Handbook for Must & Wine Analysis. LC 91-65481. (Illus.). 128p. (Orig.). (C). 1991. pap. 24.95 (*1-879819-00-7*) U TX Lands Surface.

Barrus, Pamela L. Dream Sleeps: Castle & Palace Hotels of Europe. 2nd rev. ed. Meyers, Carole T., ed. LC 97-43138. Orig. Title: Guide to the Recommeded Castle & Palace Hotels of Europe. (Illus.). 304p. 1998. pap. 17.95 (*0-917120-16-7*) Carousel Pr.

Barrus, Roger M. & Eastby, John, eds. America Through the Looking Glass: A Conservative Constitutionalist Critique of the 1992 Election. 296p. 1994. pap. text 27.95 (*0-8476-7968-3*); lib. bdg. 69.50 (*0-8476-7967-5*) Rowman.

***Barrutia.** Fonetica. 2nd ed. 464p. 1998. text. write for info. incl. audio (*0-471-33007-8*) Wiley.

Barrutia, Richard & Schwegler, Armin. Fonacetica y Fonologia Espanolas: Teoria y Practica. 2nd ed. 464p. 1994. text 73.95 (*0-471-30946-X*) Wiley.

Barry. Applied English. 1995. pap. text, teacher ed. write for info. (*0-13-606476-0*) Allyn.

— Critical Edge: Critical Thinking & Reading. (C). 1992. pap. text, teacher ed. 3.75 (*0-03-078951-6*) Harcourt Coll Pubs.

Barry. The Healthy Heart Formula: The Powerful, New Commonsense Approach to Preventing & Reversing Heart Disease. 320p. 1996. pap. 14.95 (*0-471-34732-9*) Wiley.

Barry. Moral Issues in Business. (Philosophy Ser.). 1979. pap. 16.00 (*0-534-00709-0*) Wadsworth Pub.

— Philosophy: A Text with Readings. (Philosophy Ser.). 1980. pap. 17.75 (*0-534-00767-8*) Wadsworth Pub.

— The Seventeen Guide to Guys & Dating. (J). 1998. 17.00 (*0-689-81087-3*); per. 4.50 (*0-689-81086-5*) S&S Childrens.

Barry & Melling, D. J., eds. Culture in History: Production, Consumption, & Values in Historical Perspective. 248p. 1992. pap. text 25.95 (*0-85989-380-4*, Pub. by Univ Exeter Pr) Northwestern U Pr.

Barry, jt. auth. see Olen.

Barry, Maxx. Syrup. LC 98-53485. 294p. 1999. 23.95 (*0-670-88640-8*) Viking Penguin.

***Barry, Maxx.** Syrup. 2000. pap. 11.95 (*0-14-029187-3*) Viking Penguin.

Barry, A. L. To the Ends of the Earth: A Journey Through Acts. LC 97-6400. 1997. 12.99 (*0-570-04985-7*, 12-3335) Concordia.

Barry, Ada L. Yunini's Story of the Trail of Tears. LC 74-7924. (Illus.). reprint ed. 49.50 (*0-404-11810-0*) AMS Pr.

Barry, Alfred. The Life & Works of Sir Charles Barry. LC 72-83088. (Illus.). 420p. 1977. reprint ed. 31.95 (*0-405-08239-8*, Pub. by Blom Pubns) Ayer.

Barry, Alyce, ed. see Barnes, Djuna.

Barry, Amy J. & Deppenschmidt, Kurt. A Child's Grief Journey: Help Children Process Their Grief & Begin to Heal. LC 97-81417. (Illus.). 36p. 1997. pap. text 8.95 (*1-57543-058-4*) Mar Co Prods.

Barry, Andrew, et al, eds. Foucault & Political Reason: Liberalism, Neo-Liberalism & Rationalities of Government. 256p. 1996. pap. text 17.95 (*0-226-03826-2*); lib. bdg. 45.00 (*0-226-03825-4*) U Ch Pr.

Barry, Anita K. English Grammar: Language as Human Behavior. LC 97-10061. 303p. 1997. 63.00 (*0-13-835281-X*) P-H.

Barry, Ann. At Home in France. 1997. pap. 12.00 (*0-345-40787-3*) Ballantine Pub Grp.

Barry, Ann M. The Advertising Portfolio. (Illus.). 128p. 1991. pap. 14.95 (*0-8442-3126-6*, NTC Business Bks) NTC Contemp Pub Co.

Barry, Anne M. Visual Intelligence: Perception, Image, & Manipulation in Visual Communication. LC 96-42465. 425p. (C). 1997. text 59.50 (*0-7914-3435-4*); pap. text 20.95 (*0-7914-3436-2*) State U NY Pr.

Barry, Arthur L. The Antimicrobic Susceptibility Test: Principles & Practices. LC 76-18846. 248p. reprint ed. pap. 76.90 (*0-8357-5633-5*, 205599600043) Bks Demand.

Barry, B. Austin. Construction Measurements. 2nd ed. (Practical Construction Guides Ser.). 368p. 1988. 130.00 (*0-471-83663-X*) Wiley.

— Errors in Practical Measurement in Surveying, Engineering, & Technology. 183p. (C). reprint ed. text 65.00 (*0-910845-47-6*, 433) Landmark Ent.

Barry, B. T. & Thwaites, C. G. Tin & Its Alloys & Compounds. LC 83-12760. (Ellis Horwood Series in Industrial Metals). 268p. 1983. text 91.95 (*0-470-27480-8*) P-H.

Barry, Barbara R. Musical Time: The Sense of Order. LC 89-71132. (Harmonologia Ser.: No. 5). (Illus.). 325p. 1990. lib. bdg. 56.00 (*0-945193-01-7*) Pendragon NY.

Barry, Bernard, jt. auth. see Sadler, Philip J.

Barry, Bill. How to Copyright & Trademark Your Own Comic Book! Bennett, S. A., ed. (World of Cartooning Ser.). (Illus.). 64p. 1992. 16.95 (*0-944099-21-1*) Comic Art.

— How to Draw a Comic Book. Harryman, O. J., ed. (World of Cartooning Ser.). (Illus.). 128p. (Orig.). 1996. pap. 15.00 (*0-944099-09-2*) Comic Art.

— How to Draw a Comic Strip. abr. ed. Harryman, O. J. & Bennett, S. A., eds. (World of Cartooning Ser.). (Illus.). 128p. 1996. pap. 15.00 (*0-944099-10-6*) Comic Art.

— Top Secret: A Graphic Novel. Harryman, Joan, ed. (Illus.). 80p. (Orig.). 1988. pap. 9.95 (*0-944099-04-1*) Comic Art.

— The World of Cartooning . . . A Complete Guide: How to Draw & Sell Cartoons. (Illus.). 176p. 1989. pap. 19.95 (*0-944099-02-5*) Comic Art.

Barry, Bob, ed. see Lynch, Lonnie T.

Barry, Boubacar. Senegambia & the Atlantic Slave Trade. LC 97-6026. (African Studies Ser.: Vol. 92). (Illus.). 384p. (C). 1998. text 59.95 (*0-521-59226-7*); pap. text 18.95 (*0-521-59760-9*) Cambridge U Pr.

Barry, Brian. Justice & Liberty Vol. 2: Essays in Political Theory. (Illus.). 312p. 1991. pap. 32.00 (*0-19-827299-5*, 9755) OUP.

— Justice As Impartiality, Vol. II. (Oxford Political Theory Ser.). (Illus.). 332p. 1996. reprint ed. pap. text 26.00 (*0-19-829092-6*) OUP.

— Political Argument: A Reissue with a New Introduction. (California Series on Social Choice & Political Economy: No. 20). 335p. 1990. pap. 18.95 (*0-520-07051-8*, Pub. by U CA Pr) Cal Prin Full Svc.

— Power & Democracy Vol. 1: Essays in Political Theory. (Illus.). 344p. 1991. pap. 32.00 (*0-19-827297-9*, 9272) OUP.

B

An Asterisk (*) at the beginning of an entry indicates that the title is appearing for the first time.

— Sociologists, Economists, & Democracy. LC 78-55039. (Illus.). vi, 202p. 1978. pap. text 8.00 (0-226-03823-8) U Ch Pr.

— Sociologists, Economists, & Democracy. 208p. 1988. pap. text 19.00 (0-226-03824-6, Midway Reprint) U Ch Pr.

— A Treatise on Social Justice: Theories of Justice, 1989, Vol. 1. (California Series on Social Choice & Political Economy: Vol. 16). 443p. 1989. reprint ed. pap. 19.95 (0-520-07649-4, Pub. by U CA Pr) Cal Prin Full Svc.

Barry, Brian, ed. Power & Political Theory: Some European Perspectives. LC 75-25556. 312p. reprint ed. pap. 96.80 (0-608-17684-2, 203040300069) Bks Demand.

Barry, Brian & Goodin, Robert E., eds. Free Movement: Ethical Issues in the Transnational Migration of People & Money. 320p. 1992. 50.00 (0-271-00887-3); pap. 19.95 (0-271-00888-1) Pa St U Pr.

Barry, Brian & Hardin, Russell, eds. Rational Man & Irrational Society? An Introduction & Sourcebook. LC 81-21508. 415p. 1982. reprint ed. pap. 128.70 (0-608-02989-0, 205962900006) Bks Demand.

Barry, Brian, jt. ed. see Sikora, R. I.

Barry, Brian W. Dermatological Formulations: Percutaneous Absorption. (Drugs & the Pharmaceutical Sciences Ser.: Vol. 18). (Illus.). 496p. 1983. text 199.00 (0-8247-1729-5) Dekker.

Barry, Bryan W. Strategic Planning Workbook for Nonprofit Organizations. 2nd rev. ed. Hyman, Vincent, ed. LC 97-8103. (Illus.). 130p. (Orig.). 1997. pap. text 28.00 (0-940069-07-5) A H Wilder.

Barry, Caroline. The Rocket Girl. LC 97-186149. (J). 1996. pap. 7.95 (1-85594-143-0, Pub. by Attic Press) Intl Spec Bk.

Barry, Catherine. Christmas Ornaments. (Illus.). 64p. 1998. 9.95 (1-85967-747-9) Anness Pub.

***Barry, Charles & Rashish, Peter S., eds.** NATO Looking Ahead: Report of the European Institute on Defense Industry Cooperation & the Economics of Enlargement. LC 99-61100. 70p. 1999. pap. 15.00 (1-886607-13-3) European Inst.

Barry, Charles L., ed. Reforging . . . Transatlantic Relations. 1997. pap. text 15.00 (1-57906-027-7) NYU Pr.

Barry, Charles L. & Johnson, Kenneth G. Accelerating on the Run: In-Stream Business Improvement from the War Room to the Boardroom. Maris, Judy, ed. 159p. (Orig.). 1998. pap. 15.00 (0-9667804-9-3) BJG Pubns.

***Barry, Chris.** Portland Undercover: How to Visit New England's Hippest City Without Looking Like a Tourist. (Illus.). 96p. 2000. pap. 9.95 (0-9700303-0-4) Maine Pubng.

Barry, Chris. Sneathen & Gonne. (Orig.). 1994. lib. bdg. 15.00 (0-88092-190-0) Royal Fireworks.

Barry, Christopher. Mosquito Point. (Joe Bass Ser.). (Illus.). 115p. (YA). (gr. 8 up). 1996. pap. 9.99 (0-88092-318-0) Royal Fireworks.

— Mystery Creek. 1992. pap. 9.99 (0-88092-187-0) Royal Fireworks.

— Sneathen & Gonne. (Orig.). 1992. pap. 9.99 (0-88092-189-7) Royal Fireworks.

— The White Wing: A Joe Bass Adventure. (Illus.). 94p. (YA). (gr. 8 up). 1994. pap. 9.99 (0-88092-087-4) Royal Fireworks.

***Barry, Christopher B.** Alternative Investing: Proceedings of the AIMR Seminar "Alternative Assets", March 4-5, 1998, Boston, Massachusetts. LC 99-208083. (Illus.). 1998. write for info. (0-935015-24-8) Inst Charter Finan Analysts.

— Emerging Stock Markets: Risk, Return & Performance. (Finance Ser.). 1997. pap. 27.95 (0-943205-45-X) RFICFA.

Barry, Colman J. Worship & Work. 3rd rev. ed. LC 80-10753. (Illus.). 606p. 1994. pap. 24.95 (0-8146-1123-0) Liturgical Pr.

Barry, Cooper, ed. Beethoven Compendium: A Guide to Beethoven's Life & Music. (Illus.). 350p. 1996. pap. 24.95 (0-500-27871-7, Pub. by Thames Hudson) Norton.

Barry, D., jt. ed. see Alexander-Mott, LeeAnn.

Barry, Dana. Easy Chemistry. (Illus.). 96p. 1994. pap., teacher ed. 11.95 (1-55734-648-8) Tchr Create Mat.

Barry, Dave. Babies & Other Hazards of Sex. LC 84-11526. (Illus.). 96p. 2000. pap. 8.95 (0-87857-510-3, 10-105-1) Rodale Pr Inc.

— Big Trouble. LC 99-25489. 320p. 1999. 23.95 (0-399-14567-2, G P Putnam) Penguin Putnam Young Read.

— Claw Your Way to the Top. LC 86-13013. (Illus.). 96p. 2000. pap. 12.95 (0-87857-652-5, 20-564-1) Rodale Pr Inc.

— Dave Barry Does Japan. 224p. 1993. pap. 11.00 (0-449-90810-0, Columbine) Fawcett.

— Dave Barry in Cyberspace. 224p. 1997. pap. 11.00 (0-449-91230-2) Fawcett.

— Dave Barry is from Mars & Venus. 1998. pap. 11.95 (0-345-42578-2) Ballantine Pub Grp.

— Dave Barry Is Not Making This Up. 256p. 1995. pap. 11.00 (0-449-90973-5) Fawcett.

***Barry, Dave.** Dave Barry Is Not Taking This Sitting Down! LC 00-31415. (Illus.). 224p. 2000. 23.00 (0-609-60067-2) Crown Pub Group.

Barry, Dave. Dave Barry Slept Here: A Sort of History of the United States. 1998. mass mkt. 5.99 (0-345-41660-0) Ballantine Pub Grp.

— Dave Barry Slept Here: A Sort of History of the United States. 192p. 1990. pap. 10.00 (0-449-90462-8, Columbine) Fawcett.

— Dave Barry Talks Back. (Illus.). 1992. pap. 11.00 (0-517-58868-4, Crown) Crown Pub Group.

***Barry, Dave.** Dave Barry Turns 50. 1999. pap. 12.95 (0-345-43169-3) Ballantine Pub Grp.

Barry, Dave. Dave Barry Turns 50. LC 98-18978. 224p. 1998. 22.00 (0-609-60327-2, Crown) Crown Pub Group.

— Dave Barry Turns 50. large type ed. 1999. pap. 22.00 (0-7838-0260-9, G K Hall & Co) Mac Lib Ref.

— Dave Barry Turns 50. large type ed. LC 98-27431. 1998. pap. 22.00 (0-375-70418-3) Random.

Barry, Dave. Dave Barry Turns 40. 1991. pap. 10.00 (0-449-90587-X) Fawcett.

Barry, Dave. Dave Barry's Bad Habits: A One Hundred Percent Fact-Free Book. 304p. 1995. pap. 8.95 (0-8050-2964-8) H Holt & Co.

— Dave Barry's Book of Bad Songs. LC 96-36790. 112p. 1997. 12.95 (0-8362-1443-9) Andrews & McMeel.

***Barry, Dave.** Dave Barry's Book of Bad Songs. (Illus.). 2000. pap. 9.95 (0-7407-0600-4) Andrews & McMeel.

Barry, Dave. Dave Barry's Complete Guide to Guys. 224p. 1996. pap. 11.00 (0-449-91026-1) Fawcett.

— Dave Barry's Greatest Hits. 1997. mass mkt. 5.99 (0-345-41999-5) Ballantine Pub Grp.

— Dave Barry's Greatest Hits. 1989. pap. 10.00 (0-449-90406-7, Columbine) Fawcett.

— Dave Barry's Guide to Guys. 1996. pap. 10.00 (0-614-97889-0, Columbine) Fawcett.

— Dave Barry's Guide to Life. 1998. 9.99 (0-517-20355-3) Random Hse Value.

— Dave Barry's Guide to Marriage & or Sex. LC 87-18461. (Illus.). 96p. 2000. pap. 12.95 (0-87857-725-4, 20-718-1) Rodale Pr Inc.

— Dave Barry's Only Travel Guide You'll Ever Need. 1999. mass mkt. 5.99 (0-345-43113-8) Ballantine Pub Grp.

— Dave Barry's Only Travel Guide You'll Ever Need. (Illus.). 192p. 1992. pap. 11.00 (0-449-90759-7, Columbine) Fawcett.

***Barry, Dave.** Dave Berry's Complete Guide to Guys. 272p. 2000. mass mkt. 6.99 (0-345-44063-3, Ballantine) Ballantine Pub Grp.

Barry, Dave. Homes & Other Black Holes. 1995. mass mkt. 5.99 (0-345-39440-2) Ballantine Pub Grp.

— Homes & Other Black Holes: The Happy Homeowner's Guide. (Illus.). 96p. 1988. pap. 10.00 (0-449-90274-9, Columbine) Fawcett.

— Stay Fit & Healthy until You're Dead. Yepsen, Roger B., ed. LC 85-11931. (Illus.). 96p. 1985. pap. 8.95 (0-87857-570-7, 10-136-1) Rodale Pr Inc.

— Taming of the Screw: Several Million Homeowner's Problems. LC 83-11205. (Illus.). 96p. (Orig.). 1983. pap. 8.95 (0-87857-484-0, 10-197-1) Rodale Pr Inc.

Barry, Dave, et al. Naked Came the Manatee: A Novel. Hiaasen, Carl, ed. 208p. 1998. pap. 11.95 (0-449-00124-5, Columbine) Fawcett.

— Together: How We Belong. (Target Ser.). 160p. (Orig.). (J). (gr. 2-4). 1997. pap. text 11.95 (0-8167-4277-4) Troll Communs.

Barry, David. Women & Political Insurgency: France in the Mid-Nineteenth Century. 208p. 1996. text 59.95 (0-312-12947-5) St Martin.

***Barry, David G., et al, eds.** The Corporate Venturing Directory & Yearbook: 2000 Edition. 352p. 1999. pap. 495.00 (1-893648-08-7) Asset Alternatives.

Barry, Desmond. The Chivalry of Crime: A Novel. LC 99-21443. 480p. 2000. 24.95 (0-316-12038-3, Back Bay) Little.

***Barry, Desmond.** The Chivalry of Crime: A Novel. 480p. 2001. pap. 14.95 (0-316-12084-7, Back Bay) Little.

Barry, Desmond T. Litigating the Aviation Case from Pre-Trial to Closing Argument. 2nd ed. LC 98-27113. xii, 349p. 1998. 84.95 (1-57073-595-6) Amer Bar Assn.

Barry, Diana, tr. see Dedieu, Maurice.

Barry, Dianne P. Human Resources in Patient Financial Services. 160p. 1993. text 40.00 (1-882198-13-1) Hlthcare Fin Mgmt.

Barry, Don, tr. see Lyotard, Jean F.

Barry, Donald. European History. 220p. (C). 1995. pap. text, spiral bd. 19.95 (0-7872-1326-8) Kendall-Hunt.

— European History: An Outline & Synthesis. 2nd ed. 260p. (C). 1997. spiral bd. 23.95 (0-7872-4252-7) Kendall-Hunt.

***Barry, Donald & Keith, Ronald C., eds.** Regionalism, Multilateralism, & the Politics of Global Trade. (Canada & International Relations Ser.). 302p. 1999. 85.00 (0-7748-0737-2) UBC Pr.

Barry, Donald, jt. auth. see Hilliker, John F.

Barry, Donald B & Whitcomb, Howard R. Legal Foundations Public Administration. 2nd ed. (Paralegal). 384p. (C). 1986. mass mkt. 53.50 (0-314-30387-1) West Pub.

Barry, Donald D., ed. Toward the "Rule of Law" in Russia? Political & Legal Reform in the Transition Period. LC 92-9677. 430p. (gr. 13). 1992. text 137.95 (1-56324-063-3) M E Sharpe.

Barry, Donald D., et al, eds. Law & the Gorbachev Era: Essays in Honor of Dietrich Andre Loeber. (C). 1988. lib. bdg. 174.50 (90-247-3678-1) Kluwer Academic.

Barry, Donald D., jt. auth. see Feofanov, Yuri.

Barry, Donald K. Forms of Life & Following Rules: A Wittgensteinian Defence of Relativism. (Philosophy of History & Culture Ser.: No. 18). xiv, 192p. 1996. 77.00 (90-04-10540-9) Brill Academic Pubs.

Barry, Douglas K. The Object Database Handbook: How to Select, Implement, & Use Object-Oriented Databases. LC 96-10800. 352p. 1996. pap. 49.99 (0-471-14718-4) Wiley.

— Object Database Implementations: Comlex Data. 34p. Date not set. pap. 85.00 (1-884842-41-0) SIGS Bks & Multimedia.

Barry, E. Barry - Barrymore: Records of the Barrys of County Cork, from the Earliest to the Present Time, with Pedigrees. 214p. 1995. reprint ed. pap. 35.00 (0-8328-4572-8); reprint ed. lib. bdg. 45.00 (0-8328-4571-X) Higginson Bk Co.

Barry, Eileen. Give Me Your Love. large type ed. (Linford Romance Library). 271p. 1984. pap. 16.99 (0-7089-6043-X) Ulverscroft.

— The Month of Gladness. large type ed. (Linford Romance Library). 304p. 1985. pap. 16.99 (0-7089-6061-8, Linford) Ulverscroft.

— The Redundant Heart. large type ed. (Linford Romance Library). 320p. 1995. pap. 16.99 (0-7089-7772-3, Linford) Ulverscroft.

— Television Sweetheart. large type ed. (Linford Romance Library). 327p. 1984. pap. 16.99 (0-7089-6012-X) Ulverscroft.

Barry, Elaine. Fabricating the Self: The Fictions of Jessica Anderson. 2nd ed. 232p. 1996. pap. 24.95 (0-7022-2814-1, Pub. by Univ Queensland Pr) Intl Spec Bk.

Barry, Elizabeth, jt. auth. see Fabricant, Florence.

Barry, Esther S. Barry. William & Esther Barry & Their Descendants: A Memorial Record. 84p. 1997. reprint ed. pap. 16.00 (0-8328-7389-6); reprint ed. lib. bdg. 26.00 (0-8328-7388-8) Higginson Bk Co.

Barry, Frank D., jt. ed. see Melton, Gary B.

Barry, Frederick. Scientific Habit of Thought. reprint ed. 31.50 (0-404-00666-3) AMS Pr.

Barry, Freedom. I Do: Spiritual Awakening Through Individual Endeavor. 61p. 1992. 12.00 (0-9634250-3-X) J & L Pubns.

— Passkey. LC 92-27550. 80p. 1993. 15.00 (0-9634250-4-8) J & L Pubns.

***Barry, Gerald.** Reflections from a Small Town: Newspaper Columns from the 1950s. Barry, Margaret, ed. (Illus.). 200p. 2000. pap. 15.00 (0-9654447-8-3) One Big Pr.

— The Story of Sailor's Snug Harbor. 2000. 27.95 (0-8232-2072-9) Fordham.

— The Story of Sailor's Snug Harbor. 2000. pap. 19.95 (0-8232-2073-7) Fordham.

Barry, Gerald D., jt. auth. see National Medical School Review (R) Staff.

Barry, H. Localizability & Space in Quantum Physics. (Lecture Notes in Physics Ser.: Vol. 308). vii, 81p. 1988. 29.95 (0-387-50052-9) Spr-Verlag.

Barry, Helen B. Imagine Yourself: Using Imagery to Get Well. Costa, Gwen, ed. LC 91-4450. 1990. pap. 13.95 (0-87949-336-4) Ashley Bks.

Barry, Herbert, III & Schlegel, Alice, eds. Cross-Cultural Samples & Codes. LC 79-3878. 468p. 1980. reprint ed. pap. 145.10 (0-608-00897-4, 206169100010) Bks Demand.

Barry, Herbert, III, jt. auth. see Schlegel, Alice.

Barry, Iris. Let's Go to the Movies. LC 79-169357. (Arno Press Cinema Program Ser.). (Illus.). 318p. 1978. reprint ed. 20.95 (0-405-03911-5) Ayer.

Barry, J. Out of Africa Piano Selections. 24p. 1986. pap. 7.95 (0-7935-2385-0, 00123603) H Leonard.

Barry, J., jt. auth. see Hall, M.

***Barry, Jackson G.** Art, Culture & the Semiotics of Meaning - Culture's Changing Signs of Life in Poetry, Drama, Painting & Sculpture. LC 98-46252. (Semaphores & Signs Ser.). 192p. 1999. text 49.95 (0-312-21967-9) St Martin.

Barry, James. Georgian Bay: An Illustrated History. Hudson, Noel, ed. (Illus.). 240p. 1992. 45.00 (1-55046-062-5, Pub. by Boston Mills) Genl Dist Srvs.

— Georgian Bay: The Sixth Great Lake. LC 97-188915. (Illus.). 208p. 1995. pap. 15.95 (1-55046-172-9, Pub. by Boston Mills) Genl Dist Srvs.

— Measures of Science: Theological & Technological Impulses in Early Modern Thought. LC 96-26448. (Northwestern University Studies in Phenomenology & Existential Philosophy). 236p. 1996. 69.95 (0-8101-1424-0); pap. 19.95 (0-8101-1425-9) Northwestern U Pr.

— Prairie Relics in California: A Guidebook Based on Dr. James Barry's 1971 Survey & Maps. Dremann, Craig C., ed. (Illus.). 1989. pap. 5.50 (0-933421-31-1) Redwood Seed.

Barry, James, Jr., ed. see Merleau-Ponty, Maurice.

Barry, James A. The Sword of Justice: Ethics & Coercion in International Politics. LC 98-24559. 232p. 1998. 57.95 (0-275-96092-7, Praeger Pubs) Greenwood.

Barry, James D. Ball Lightning & Bead Lightning: Extreme Forms of Atmospheric Electricity. LC 79-19017. (Illus.). 308p. 1980. 85.00 (0-306-40272-6, Plenum Trade) Perseus Pubng.

Barry, James P. Old Forts of the Great Lakes: Sentinels of the Wilderness. LC 95-109263. (Illus.). (Orig.). 1994. pap. 19.95 (1-882376-05-6) Thunder Bay Pr.

— Ships of the Great Lakes: 300 Years of Navigation. 3rd rev. ed. (Illus.). 274p. 1996. reprint ed. 40.00 (1-882376-27-7); reprint ed. pap. 24.95 (1-882376-26-9) Thunder Bay Pr.

— Wrecks & Rescues of the Great Lakes; A Photographic History. (Illus.). 1994. reprint ed. pap. 18.95 (1-882376-01-3) Thunder Bay Pr.

***Barry, Jan.** A Citizen's Guide to Grassroots Campaigns. LC 99-56790. 180p. 2000. text 48.00 (0-8135-2800-3) Rutgers U Pr.

— A Citizen's Guide to Grassroots Campaigns. LC 99-56790. 180p. (C). 2000. pap. 19.00 (0-8135-2801-1) Rutgers U Pr.

Barry, Jan. Draw, Design & Paint. (Illus.). 144p. (J). (gr. 2-6). 1990. 13.99 (0-86653-536-5, GA1142) Good Apple.

Barry, Jane. Grand Illusions. 448p. 1988. mass mkt. 4.50 (0-380-70491-9, Avon Bks) Morrow Avon.

Barry, Jennifer, jt. auth. see Johns, Pamela Sheldon.

Barry, Jim, et al. Critical Issues in Organizational Behavior. 352p. 1999. pap. 21.99 (1-86152-193-6) Thomson Learn.

Barry, Jimi, ed. see Cahill, Robert B. & Hrebic, Herbert J.

***Barry, John.** Environment & Social Theory. LC 99-10360. (Introductions to Environment Ser.). 208p. (C). 1999. pap. write for info. (0-415-17270-5); text. write for info. (0-415-17269-1) Routledge.

— Rethinking Green Politics: Nature, Virtue, & Progress. LC 98-61591. 304p. 1999. 82.00 (0-7619-5605-0); pap. 25.95 (0-7619-5606-9) Sage.

Barry, John. Rock Climbing. (Illus.). 128p. 1989. pap. 18.95 (0-8117-2231-7) Stackpole.

— Yorkshire Sonnets. (C). 1988. 35.00 (0-904524-46-9, Pub. by Rivelin Grapheme Pr) St Mut.

***Barry, John & Proops, John L. R.** Citizenship, Sustainability & Enviromental Research: Q Methodology & Local Exchange Trading Systems. LC 00-34826. 2000. write for info. (1-84064-253-X) E Elgar.

Barry, John A. Technobabble. (Illus.). 288p. (C). 1993. pap. text 15.00 (0-262-52182-2) MIT Pr.

Barry, John A., jt. auth. see Stevens, Susan G.

Barry, John F. One Faith, One Lord: A Study of Basic Catholic Belief. 128p. 1994. text. write for info. (0-8215-2197-7) Sadlier.

Barry, John F., et al. With You Always: Confirmation. 112p. 1991. 13.26 (0-8215-1603-5) Sadlier.

— With You Always: Confirmation: Catechist Edition. 112p. 1991. 16.77 (0-8215-1613-2) Sadlier.

— With You Always: Confirmation Journal. 112p. 1991. 5.37 (0-8215-1634-5) Sadlier.

Barry, John M. Rising Tide: The Great Mississippi Flood of 1927 & How It Changed America. LC 96-40077. 528p. 1997. 27.00 (0-684-81046-8) S&S Trade.

— Rising Tide: The Great Mississippi Flood of 1927 & How It Changed America. 528p. 1998. per. 15.00 (0-684-84002-2, Touchstone) S&S Trade Pap.

Barry, John M., compiled by. Nautical Research Journal Index, Vols. 1-40. LC 96-71037. 216p. (Orig.). 1996. pap. 19.95 (0-9603456-6-3) Nautical Res.

Barry, John M., jt. auth. see Rosenberg, Steven.

Barry, John M., jt. auth. see Rosenberg, Steven A.

Barry, John R. Wireless Infrared Communications. LC 94-19272. (International Series in Engineering & Computer Science). 192p. (C). 1994. text 102.50 (0-7923-9476-3) Kluwer Academic.

Barry, John R. & Wingrove, C. Ray, eds. Let's Learn about Aging: A Book of Readings. 350p. 1977. text 18.95 (0-87073-673-6) Schenkman Bks Inc.

Barry, John S. A Historical Sketch of Hanover, Ma. (Illus.). 448p. 1993. reprint ed. lib. bdg. 47.50 (0-8328-3072-0) Higginson Bk Co.

Barry, John W. Masonry & the Flag. 109p. 1992. reprint ed. pap. 12.95 (1-56459-049-6) Kessinger Pub.

Barry, John W., jt. ed. see Hall, Franklin R.

Barry, Jonathan. Middling Sort of People Vol. 1: Culture, Society, & Politics in England, 1550-1800. 1994. text 55.00 (0-312-12356-6) St Martin.

— Tudor Stuart Town. (C). 1990. pap. text 28.50 (0-582-05130-4, Pub. by Addison-Wesley) Longman.

Barry, Jonathan, ed. The Tudor & Stuart Town: A Reader in English Urban History, 1530-1688. (Readers in Urban History Ser.). 272p. (C). 1990. pap. text 22.75 (0-685-72459-X, 78601) Longman.

Barry, Jonathan, et al, eds. Witchcraft in Early Modern Europe: Studies in Culture & Belief. LC 95-22865. (Past & Present Publications). 382p. (C). 1996. text 64.95 (0-521-55224-9) Cambridge U Pr.

— Witchcraft in Early Modern Europe: Studies in Culture & Belief. (Past & Present Publications). (Illus.). 384p. (C). 1998. reprint ed. pap. text 19.95 (0-521-63875-5) Cambridge U Pr.

Barry, Jonna, ed. see Hafer, Todd.

Barry, Joseph & Derevlany, John, eds. Yuppies Invade My House at Dinnertime: A Tale of Brunch, Bombs, & Gentrification in an American City. LC 87-82140. (Illus.). 208p. (Orig.). 1987. pap. 7.95 (0-944421-01-6) Big River NJ.

Barry, Joseph A., ed. see Zevi, Bruno.

Barry, Kathleen. The Prostitution of Sexuality. (C). 1996. pap. text 19.00 (0-8147-1277-0) NYU Pr.

Barry, Kathleen C., jt. auth. see Burhan-Stipanov, Linda.

Barry, Kathleen L. Female Sexual Slavery. 336p. (C). 1984. pap. text 18.50 (0-8147-1069-7) NYU Pr.

— The Prostitution of Sexuality. 381p. (C). 1994. text 45.00 (0-8147-1217-7) NYU Pr.

Barry, Kieren. The Greek Qabalah: Alphabetical Mysticism & Numerology in the Ancient World. LC 99-22783. 304p. 1999. pap. 16.95 (1-57863-110-6) Weiser.

***Barry, Kristen Lawton & Clunies, Sandra, eds.** Brief Interventions & Therapies for Substance Abuse. (Illus.). 234p. (C). 2000. pap. text 35.00 (0-7567-0167-8) DIANE Pub.

Barry, Laura Pass, jt. auth. see Weekley, Carolyn J.

Barry, Lording. Ram Alley. LC 75-133679. (Tudor Facsimile Texts. Old English Plays Ser.: No. 129). reprint ed. 59.50 (0-404-53429-5) AMS Pr.

Barry, Louise. Comprehensive Index to Publications, 1875-1930. 515p. 1959. 9.95 (0-87726-011-7) Kansas St Hist.

Barry, Louise M. A Price Beyond Rubies: A Novel of the Civil War. (Illus.). 492p. 1996. pap. 25.95 (0-89745-201-1) Sunflower U Pr.

Barry, Lynda. Cruddy: A Novel. LC 99-26418. (Illus.). 288p. 1999. 21.50 (0-684-82974-6) S&S Trade.

***Barry, Lynda.** Cruddy: An Illustrated Novel. (Illus.). 2000. pap. 12.00 (0-684-83846-X, Scribner Pap Fic) S&S Trade Pap.

— Cruddy: An Illustrated Novel. aut. ed. (Illus.). 288p. 1999. pap. 22.50 (0-684-86530-0) S&S Trade.

Barry, Lynda. The Freddie Stories. LC 96-30006. (Illus.). 128p. 1999. pap. 12.95 (1-57061-106-8) Sasquatch Bks.

An Asterisk (*) at the beginning of an entry indicates that the title is appearing for the first time.

— The Good Times Are Killing Me. LC 96-38098. (Illus.). 128p. (Orig.). 1999. reprint ed. pap. 12.95 (*1-57061-105-X*) Sasquatch Bks.

*Barry, Lynda.** The Greatest of Marlys. LC 99-86069. (Illus.). 224p. 2000. pap. 15.95 (*1-57061-260-9*) Sasquatch Bks.

Barry, M. A. Credit Strategy: The Key to Profitable Trading. LC 96-47157. 296p. 1997. 120.50 (*0-471-96661-4*) Wiley.

Barry, M. D., jt. auth. see Mustoe, L.

Barry, M. D., jt. auth. see Mustoe, L. R.

Barry, Marc, jt. auth. see Penenberg, Adam L.

Barry, Margaret, ed. see Barry, Gerald.

Barry, Margaret, jt. ed. see Crosby, Charles.

*Barry, Margaret S.** The Witch & the Holiday Club. large type ed. (Illus.). (J). 1998. pap. 16.95 (*0-7540-6035-7*, Galaxy Child Lrg Print) Chivers N Amer.

Barry, Mary J. Alaska's Ghosts, Enigmas, Outlaws & Things That Go Bump! LC 94-94498. (Illus.). 136p. (Orig.). 1994. pap. 12.00 (*0-9617009-3-9*) M J P Barry.

— Around the Yukon Stove: A Collection of Alaskan Tales. (Illus.). 140p. 1988. pap. 6.95 (*0-9617009-1-2*) M J P Barry.

— A History of Mining on the Kenai Peninsula, Alaska. rev. ed. LC 96-95346. (Illus.). 304p. 1997. pap. 30.00 (*0-9617009-5-5*) M J P Barry.

*Barry, Mary J.** Jack & Nellie Brown: Pioneer Settlers of Anchorage, Alaska. (Illus.). 150p. 2000. pap. write for info. (*0-9617009-7-1*) M J P Barry.

Barry, Mary J. Seward, Alaska - A History of the Gateway City Vol. 1: Prehistory to 1914. LC 86-71202. (Illus.). 182p. (Orig.). 1987. pap. 25.00 (*0-9617009-0-4*) M J P Barry.

— Seward, Alaska - A History of the Gateway City Vol. 2: 1914-1923. LC 86-71202. (Illus.). 225p. (YA). (gr. 8 up). 1993. pap. 25.00 (*0-9617009-2-0*) M J P Barry.

— Seward, Alaska - A History of the Gateway City Vol. 3: Growth, Tragedy, Recovery, Adaptation, 1924-1993. LC 86-71202. (Illus.). 408p. (YA). (gr. 8 up). 1995. reprint ed. pap. 37.50 (*0-9617009-4-7*) M J P Barry.

Barry, Mary M. An Analysis of the Prosodic Structure of Selected Poems of T. S. Eliot. rev. ed. LC 69-19281. 162p. reprint ed. pap. 50.30 (*0-8357-5439-1*, 202952000061) Bks Demand.

Barry, Maxine. Caribbean Flame. large type ed. 437p. 1997. 27.99 (*1-86110-048-5*) Ulverscroft.

— Dark Desire. (Scarlet Ser.). 1998. mass mkt. 3.99 (*1-85487-566-3*, Pub. by Scarlet Bks) London Brdge.

— Dark Desire. 1998. text 19.95 (*1-85487-547-7*, Pub. by Scarlet Bks) London Brdge.

— Dear Enemy. (Scarlet Ser.). (Orig.). 1997. mass mkt. 3.99 (*1-85487-947-2*, Pub. by Scarlet Bks) London Brdge.

— Destinies. 400p. (Orig.). 1997. mass mkt. 3.99 (*1-85487-722-4*, Pub. by Scarlet Bks) London Brdge.

— Fire & Ice. large type ed. (Black Satin Romance Ser.). 435p. 1997. 27.99 (*1-86110-040-X*) Ulverscroft.

— Resolutions. 400p. (Orig.). 1997. mass mkt. 3.99 (*1-85487-903-0*, Pub. by Scarlet Bks) London Brdge.

Barry, Michael. Chicken Recipes the Crafty Way. 1998. pap. 8.95 (*0-7117-0964-5*, Pub. by JARR UK) Seven Hills Bk.

— Crafty French Cooking. (Illus.). 176p. 1997. pap. 24.95 (*1-85793-936-0*, Pub. by Pavilion Bks Ltd) Trafalgar.

— Exotic Food the Crafty Way. (Illus.). 240p. (Orig.). 1997. pap. 19.95 (*0-7117-0855-X*, Pub. by JARR UK) Seven Hills Bk.

— Great Aviation Stories, Vol. 1. 160p. 1993. pap. 40.00 (*0-9515387-4-8*, Pub. by Saturn Bks-AerRianta) St Mut.

— International Aviation Quiz Book, Vol. 1. 136p. 1989. pap. 40.00 (*0-9515387-0-5*, Pub. by Saturn Bks-AerRianta) St Mut.

— Michael Barry's Christmas Recipes the Crafty Way. 64p. 1998. 8.95 (*0-7117-0963-7*, Pub. by JARR UK) Seven Hills Bk.

Barry, Michael. The Mystery of Robert Emmet's Grave: A Fascinating Story of Deception, Intrigue & Misunderstanding LC 91-151802. 77p. 1991. write for info. (*0-9515387-2-1*, Pub. by Saturn Bks-AerRianta) St Mut.

Barry, Michael. Old English Recipes. (Illus.). 144p. 1996. pap. 16.95 (*0-7117-0811-8*, Pub. by JARR UK) Seven Hills Bk.

Barry, Michael, compiled by. Crafty Italian Cookery. 1998. pap. 19.95 (*0-7117-0962-9*, Pub. by JARR UK) Seven Hills Bk.

*Barry, Michael, et al.** The Fallacy of Flexibility: Workplace Reform in the Queensland Open Cut Coal Industry. 256p. 1999. pap. 35.00 (*1-86448-782-8*, Pub. by Allen & Unwin Pty) Paul & Co Pubs.

Barry, Michael, et al. MCSE Test Prep: Networking Essentials. LC 98-136920. 1997. 29.99 (*1-56205-826-6*) New Riders Pub.

Barry, Michelle, ed. see Frattalone, Sam.

Barry, Miranda. Chocolate Bar Bust. (Ghostwriter Ser.). 1995. 8.60 (*0-606-07577-1*, Pub. by Turtleback) Demco.

Barry, Norman. Classical Liberalism in the Age of Post Communism. LC 95-40188. (Shaftesbury Papers: No. 6). 96p. 1996. pap. 13.00 (*1-85898-256-1*) E Elgar.

— Welfare. (Concepts in Social Thought Ser.). 160p. (C). 1990. pap. 13.95 (*0-8166-1883-6*) U of Minn Pr.

— Welfare. 2nd ed. 1998. 69.95 (*0-335-20143-1*) OpUniv Pr.

— Welfare. 2nd ed. 1998. pap. text 19.95 (*0-335-20142-3*) Taylor & Francis.

*Barry, Norman P.** Business Ethics. (ICHOR Business Bks.). 1999. pap. 21.95 (*1-55753-162-5*) Purdue U Pr.

Barry, Norman P. An Introduction to Modern Political Theory. 3rd ed. LC 95-8225. 344p. 1995. pap. 19.95 (*0-312-12750-2*) St Martin.

— An Introduction to Modern Political Theory. 4th ed. 1996. pap. 17.95 (*0-333-61682-0*) St Martin.

*Barry, Norman P.** An Introduction to Modern Political Theory. 4th ed. LC 00-35265. 2000. pap. write for info. (*0-312-23516-X*) St Martin.

Barry, Norman P. The Morality of Business Enterprise. (David Hume Papers: No. 13). 120p. (C). 1991. pap. text 11.85 (*0-08-037964-8*, Pub. by Aberdeen U Pr) Macmillan.

— Welfare. 160p. 1990. pap. 9.99 (*0-335-15595-2*) OpUniv Pr.

— Welfare. LC 98-17007. (Concepts in Social Thought Ser.). 144p. 1998. 37.95 (*0-8166-3224-3*); pap. 14.95 (*0-8166-3225-1*) U of Minn Pr.

Barry, Norman P., jt. auth. see Shenfield, Arthur A.

Barry, Ona, jt. auth. see Stanley, John.

Barry, P. J. Reasonable Circulation. 1989. pap. 3.25 (*0-8222-0947-0*) Dramatists Play.

Barry, Patricia, jt. auth. see Robertson, Debbie.

Barry, Patricia A. In Search of Captain Warner: 1849. rev. ed. (Riders of the Western Great Basin Ser.: Vol. 1). (Illus.). 72p. pap. 10.00 (*0-9645403-0-4*) P Barry.

Barry, Patricia D. Mental Health & Mental Illness. 6th ed. LC 97-16220. 464p. 1997. pap. text 28.95 (*0-397-55473-7*) Lppncott W & W.

— Psychosocial Nursing: Care of Physically Ill Patients & Their Families. 3rd ed. LC 95-40125. 624p. 1996. pap. text 31.95 (*0-397-55146-0*) Lppncott W & W.

Barry, Patrick. St. Benedict & Christianity in England. 40p. 1996. pap. 4.95 (*0-85244-338-2*, 966, Pub. by Gracewing) Morehouse Pub.

— St. Benedict's Rule: A New Translation for Today. 128p. 1998. pap. 16.95 (*0-85244-435-4*, 4917, Pub. by Gracewing) Morehouse Pub.

*Barry, Patrick D.** Geometry & Trigonometry. 250p. 2000. 75.00 (*1-898563-69-1*, Pub. by Horwood Pub) Paul & Co Pubs.

Barry, Peter. Beginning Theory: An Introduction to Literary & Cultural Theory. LC 94-43136. 320p. 1995. text 69.95 (*0-7190-4325-5*, Pub. by Manchester Univ Pr); text 19.95 (*0-7190-4326-3*, Pub. by Manchester Univ Pr) St Martin.

Barry, Peter J. The Effects of Credit Policies on U. S. Agriculture. (Studies in Agricultural Policy). 124p. (Orig.). 1995. pap. 10.00 (*0-8447-3905-7*) Am Enterprise.

*Barry, Peter J., et al.** Financial Management in Agriculture. 6th ed. xvi, 678p. 2000. 66.25 (*0-8134-3176-X*) Interstate.

Barry, Peter J., et al. Financial Management in Agriculture, Includ. Casebook. 5th ed. 1998. student ed. 22.95 (*0-8134-2979-X*, 2979) Interstate.

Barry, Peter J., jt. auth. see Robison, Lindon J.

Barry, Philip. The Philadelphia Story: A Comedy in Three Acts. LC 83-45700. reprint ed. 42.50 (*0-404-20018-4*) AMS Pr.

Barry, Philip, et al. British Ballads from Maine. LC 81-5548. (Music Ser.). (Illus.). 535p. 1982. reprint ed. lib. bdg. 49.50 (*0-306-76135-1*) Da Capo.

Barry, R. Construction of Buildings, 5 vols. (Illus.). 508p. 1971. pap. 189.95 (*0-8464-0276-9*) Beekman Pubs.

*Barry, R.** The Construction of Buildings 7th ed. LC 99-32090. 1999. write for info. (*0-632-05261-9*) Blackwell Sci.

Barry, R. Construction of Buildings, Vol. 1. 6th ed. 208p. 1996. pap. text 27.95 (*0-632-04107-2*) Blackwell Sci.

— Construction of Buildings, Vol. 4. 4th ed. 192p. 1996. pap. text 24.95 (*0-632-03911-6*) Blackwell Sci.

Barry, Raymond J. Mother Son & Other Plays. (Illus.). 276p. (Orig.). 1997. pap. 13.95 (*0-9657588-0-X*) R J Barry.

Barry, Rebecca B. Voyageurettes: Their Legends & Stories. 1998. pap. text 12.95 (*1-885061-52-8*) Adventure Pubns.

*Barry, Richard, Jr.** Cruise Ship Passengers Ask the Wackiest Questions! Questions, Comments, Jokes & Stories That Will Keep You Laughing. 2000. pap. 13.95 (*0-9662857-1-9*) Portofino Pubns.

Barry, Richard, Sr. The Management of International Oil Operations. LC 93-14287. 600p. 1993. 74.95 (*0-87814-400-5*) PennWell Bks.

— Mr. Rutledge of South Carolina. LC 71-146851. (Select Bibliographies Reprint Ser.). 1980. reprint ed. 26.95 (*0-8369-5618-4*) Ayer.

Barry, Richard, jt. auth. see Burggraf, Virginia.

*Barry, Richard A., ed.** Optical Networks & Their Applications. LC 98-86314. (Trends in Optics & Photonics Ser.: Vol. 20). (Illus.). 380p. 1998. pap. 55.00 (*1-55752-545-5*) Optical Soc.

Barry, Richard M. Built on Solid Principles. LC 99-177421. 121 p. 1998. pap. 9.95 (*0-9665924-0-9*, SP-18) RM Barry.

Barry, Rick & Cohn, Jordan. Rick Barry's Pro Basketball Bible, 1996-97 Edition. 8th ed. (Illus.). 400p. 1996. pap. 19.95 (*0-9636385-5-6*) Basketball Bks.

— Rick Barry's Pro Basketball Bible, 1995-96 Edition. (Illus.). 450p. (Orig.). 1995. pap. 18.95 (*0-9636385-7-2*) Basketball Bks.

Barry, Robert. Breaking the Thread of Life: On Rational Suicide. LC 93-36053. 370p. (C). 1994. 44.95 (*1-56000-142-9*) Transaction Pubs.

— Breaking the Thread of Life: On Rational Suicide. 353p. 1996. pap. text 24.95 (*1-56000-923-3*) Transaction Pubs.

— Mr. Willowby's Christmas Tree. 32p. Date not set. 16.95 (*0-8488-2206-4*) Amereon Ltd.

— Mr. Willowby's Christmas Tree. (Illus.). 32p. (J). (ps-2). 1992. pap. 6.99 (*0-440-40726-5*, YB BDD) BDD Bks Young Read.

*Barry, Robert.** Mr. Willowby's Christmas Tree. (Illus.). (J). 2000. 17.99 (*0-385-90006-6*) Doubleday.

— Mr. Willowby's Christmas Tree. (Illus.). (J). 2000. 15.95 (*0-385-32721-8*) Random Bks Yng Read.

Barry, Robert. Mr. Willowby's Christmas Tree. (Illus.). 32p. (J). 1992. reprint ed. lib. bdg. 18.95 (*0-89966-935-2*) Buccaneer Bks.

— A Theory of Almost Everything: A Scientific & Religious Quest for Ultimate Answers. 208p. (Orig.). 1996. pap. 13.95 (*1-85168-123-X*, Pub. by Onewrld Pubns) Penguin Putnam.

*Barry, Robert, et al.** Recording Conceptual Art: Early Interviews with Barry, Huebler, Kaltenbach, Lewitt, Morris, Oppenheim, Siegelaub, Smithson & Weiner. LC 00-32583. (Illus.). 2001. write for info. (*0-520-22010-2*) U CA Pr.

Barry, Robert E. Applied English Language Business Skills for Everyday. LC 94-37186. 447p. 1994. pap. text 68.00 (*0-13-606047-1*) P-H.

— Basic Business English. 2nd ed. (Illus.). 384p. 1986. pap. text 85.00 (*0-13-057225-X*) P-H.

— Mr. Willowby's Christmas Tree. (J). 1991. 11.19 (*0-606-05483-9*, Pub. by Turtleback) Demco.

Barry, Robert E., jt. ed. see Webb, Ralph L.

Barry, Robert L. Medical Ethics: Essays on Abortion & Euthanasia. (American University Studies: Theology & Religion: Ser. VII, Vol. 45). XI, 308p. (C). 1989. text 41.95 (*0-8204-0925-1*) P Lang Pubng.

Barry, Robert L. & Bradley, Gerard V., eds. Set No Limits: A Rebuttal to Daniel Callahan's Proposal to Limit Health Care for the Elderly. 160p. 1991. text 22.95 (*0-252-01860-5*) U of Ill Pr.

Barry, Robert L., jt. auth. see Seebauer, Edmund G.

Barry, Roberta, ed. see King, Lucie.

Barry, Roger B. & Chorley, Richard J. Atmosphere, Weather & Climate 5. (Illus.). 448p. 1988. text 99.50 (*0-415-04585-1*, A1130); pap. text 29.95 (*0-416-07152-X*, A1134) Routledge.

Barry, Roger D. Basic Chemistry. LC 74-79831. (Health Occupations Ser.). 1975. 3.71 (*0-672-61432-4*, Bobbs); student ed. 7.50 (*0-672-61377-8*, Bobbs); pap. text 13.92 (*0-672-61376-X*, Bobbs) Macmillan.

— Organic Chemistry. LC 74-79834. (Allied Health Ser.). 1975. student ed. 5.10 (*0-672-61379-4*, Bobbs) pap. text 8.35 (*0-672-61378-6*, Bobbs) Macmillan.

Barry, Roger G. Mountain Weather & Climate. LC 80-42348. (Illus.). 313p. 1981. 57.50 (*0-416-73730-7*, NO. 3464) Routledge.

— Mountain Weather & Climate. 2nd ed. (Physical Environment Ser.). (Illus.). 432p. (C). 1992. pap. 34.99 (*0-415-07113-5*, A6547) Routledge.

Barry, Roger G. & Chorley, Richard J. Atmosphere, Weather & Climate. 7th ed. LC 97-22866. (Illus.). 464p. (C). 1998. 100.00 (*0-415-16019-7*); pap. 40.00 (*0-415-16020-0*) Routledge.

Barry, Ruth & Wolf, Beverly. An Epitaph for Vocational Guidance: Myths, Actualities, Implications. LC 62-13478. 256p. reprint ed. pap. 79.40 (*0-608-14892-X*, 202599000048) Bks Demand.

Barry, S. L., et al. Amazing Animals of Australia. Crump, Donald J., ed. LC 84-29558. (Books for World Explorers Series 6: No. 2). (Illus.). 104p. (J). (gr. 3-8). 1985. 8.95 (*0-87044-515-4*); lib. bdg. 12.50 (*0-87044-520-0*) Natl Geog.

Barry, Scott I. The Streeter. 288p. (Orig.). 1994. mass mkt. 4.99 (*0-8125-0000-8*, Pub. by Tor Bks) St Martin.

Barry, Sebastian. Elsewhere. 128p. (J). (gr. 1-12). 1985. 15.95 (*0-85105-903-1*, Pub. by Smyth) Dufour.

— Fanny Hawke Goes to the Mainland Forever. 64p. 1990. pap. 9.95 (*1-85186-060-6*) Dufour.

— Our Lady of Sligo. 1998. pap. 5.25 (*0-8222-1690-6*) Dramatists Play.

Barry, Sebastian. Plays, No. 1. LC 97-223096. (Contemporary Dramatists Ser.). 1997. pap. 14.95 (*0-413-71120-X*) Methn.

Barry, Sebastian. Rhetorical Town. 68p. 1985. pap. 11.95 (*0-85105-426-9*, Pub. by Smyth) Dufour.

— The Steward of Christendom. 1998. pap. 5.25 (*0-8222-1609-4*) Dramatists Play.

— The Steward of Christendom. 1996. pap. 11.95 (*0-413-70260-X*, Methuen Drama) Methn.

— Three Plays. LC 96-146616. 1996. pap. 15.95 (*0-413-69890-4*, Methuen Drama) Methn.

— Water-Colourist. 56p. 1983. pap. 10.95 (*0-85105-412-9*, Pub. by Smyth) Dufour.

— The Whereabouts of Eneas McNulty. 320p. 1999. pap. 12.95 (*0-14-028018-9*) Viking Penguin.

— The Whereabouts of Eneas McNulty. large type ed. LC 98-44511. 1999. 30.00 (*0-7862-1709-X*) Thorndike Pr.

Barry, Sebastian, ed. Inherited Boundaries: The Younger Poets of the Republic of Ireland. 192p. 1985. pap. 15.95 (*0-85105-439-0*, Pub. by Smyth) Dufour.

Barry, Sheila, ed. see International Biodeterioration Symposium Staff.

Barry, Sheila A. 58 Ways to Play Solitare. Date not set. 2.95 (*0-8069-1358-4*) Sterling.

— Giant Book of Puzzles & Games. (Illus.). 640p. 1997. pap. 17.95 (*0-8069-9761-3*) Sterling.

*Barry, Sheila A.** Little Giant Book of after School Fun. Sloane, Paul et al, eds. LC 99-45913. (Illus.). 352p. (J). 1999. 6.95 (*0-8069-7122-3*) Sterling.

Barry, Sheila A. Super-Colossal Book of Puzzles, Tricks & Games. (Illus.). 640p. (YA). 1992. reprint ed. 9.99 (*0-517-07769-8*) Random Hse Value.

— World's Best Card Games for One. (Illus.). 128p. 1993. pap. 4.95 (*0-8069-8637-9*) Sterling.

— The World's Best Party Games. LC 86-30038. (Illus.). 128p. (J). (gr. 6-10). 1987. pap. 5.95 (*0-8069-6424-7*) Sterling.

— World's Best Travel Games. LC 87-7065. (Illus.). 128p. (J). (gr. 5 up). 1988. pap. 4.95 (*0-8069-6776-5*) Sterling.

Barry, Sheila A., ed. Kids' Funniest Jokes. LC 93-23045. (Illus.). 96p. (J). (gr. 2-10). 1994. pap. 4.95 (*0-8069-0448-8*) Sterling.

Barry, Siuban, et al. Worthy Foundation: The Cathedral Church of St. Canice, Kilkenny. 104p. 1985. pap. 14.95 (*0-85105-435-8*, Pub. by Smyth) Dufour.

Barry, Stephen P. Royal Service. 288p. 1984. pap. 3.95 (*0-380-67397-5*, Avon Bks) Morrow Avon.

*Barry, Stephen T.** Selling More Through Creative Financing. 160p. 2000. pap. 14.95 (*1-58099-022-3*, Pub. by Velocity Busn) IPG Chicago.

Barry, T. & Reynard, K. W., eds. Computerization & Networking of Materials Database, Vol. 3. (Special Technical Publication Ser.: No. STP 1140). (Illus.). 500p. 1992. text 77.00 (*0-8031-1437-0*, STP1140) ASTM.

Barry, T. B., et al, eds. Colony & Frontier in Medieval Ireland: Essays Presented to J. F. Lydon. LC 95-47678. 1995. 60.00 (*1-85285-122-8*) Hambledon Press.

*Barry, Terry.** A History of Settlement in Ireland. LC 99-31496. 376p. 1999. write for info. (*0-415-18208-5*) Routledge.

Barry, Thomas E., et al, eds. Marketing & the Black Consumer: An Annotated Bibliography. LC 76-3722. (American Marketing Association Bibliography Ser.: No. 22). 52p. reprint ed. pap. 30.00 (*0-608-11537-1*, 201462200093) Bks Demand.

Barry, Tim. The Totally Unauthorized Microsoft Joke Book. 96p. 1999. pap. 10.00 (*0-9667417-0-6*, IT Pr) Intelligent Technologies.

Barry, Tom. Central America Inside Out: The Essential Guide to Its Societies, Politics & Economies. LC 90-29050. 512p. 1991. pap. 16.95 (*0-8021-3260-X*, Grove) Grove-Atltic.

— The Challenge of Cross-Border Environmentalism: The U. S.-Mexico Case. 121p. 1994. pap. 9.95 (*0-911213-45-7*) Interhemisp Res Ctr.

— El Conflicto de Baja Intensidad. (SPA.). 60p. 1987. 5.95 (*0-911213-13-9*) Interhemisp Res Ctr.

— Crossing the Line: Immigrants, Economic Integration, & Drug Enforcement on the U. S.-Mexico Border. 146p. 1994. pap. 9.95 (*0-911213-46-5*) Interhemisp Res Ctr.

— Destabilization of Nicaragua. 39p. 1986. pap. 5.95 (*0-911213-09-0*) Interhemisp Res Ctr.

— El Salvador: A Country Guide. 2nd ed. 193p. 1991. pap. 9.95 (*0-911213-30-9*) Interhemisp Res Ctr.

— Guerrilla Days in Ireland: A Personal Account of the Anglo-Irish War. 4th ed. LC 95-69274. (Illus.). 254p. 1995. pap. 12.95 (*1-57098-047-0*) Roberts Rinehart.

— Inside Belize. 2nd ed. 180p. 1995. pap. text 11.95 (*0-911213-54-6*) Interhemisp Res Ctr.

— Inside Guatemala. 307p. 1992. pap. text 11.95 (*0-911213-40-6*) Interhemisp Res Ctr.

— Low Intensity Conflict: The New Battlefield in Central America. 70p. (Orig.). 1986. pap. 5.95 (*0-911213-05-8*) Interhemisp Res Ctr.

— Mexico: A Country Guide. 401p. (Orig.). (C). 1992. pap. text 14.95 (*0-911213-35-X*) Interhemisp Res Ctr.

— Public & Private Humanitarian Aid: Legal & Ethical Issues. 21p. 1988. 5.95 (*0-911213-17-1*) Interhemisp Res Ctr.

— Rain of Dollars: U. S. Economic Intervention in Central America. 38p. 1986. 5.95 (*0-911213-08-2*) Interhemisp Res Ctr.

— Roots of Rebellion: Land & Hunger in Central America. LC 87-4519. 220p. (Orig.). 1987. 25.00 (*0-89608-288-1*) South End Pr.

— Roots of Rebellion: Land & Hunger in Central America. LC 87-4519. (Illus.). 234p. (Orig.). 1987. reprint ed. pap. 72.60 (*0-7837-9239-5*, 204999000004) Bks Demand.

— Zapata's Revenge: Free Trade & the Farm Crisis in Mexico. 318p. 1995. 40.00 (*0-89608-500-7*); pap. 16.00 (*0-89608-499-X*) South End Pr.

Barry, Tom & Leaver, Erik. The Next Fifty Years: The United Nations & the United States. LC 96-14989. 202p. (Orig.). 1996. pap. 11.95 (*0-911213-61-9*) Interhemisp Res Ctr.

Barry, Tom & Lindsay-Poland, John. Inside Panama. 200p. 1995. pap. text 11.95 (*0-911213-50-3*) Interhemisp Res Ctr.

Barry, Tom & Preusch, Deb. AIFLD: Agents As Organizers. rev. ed. 76p. 1990. 5.95 (*0-911213-11-2*) Interhemisp Res Ctr.

— El Salvador: The Other War. 54p. 1986. 5.95 (*0-911213-10-4*) Interhemisp Res Ctr.

— The Soft War: The Uses & Abuses of U. S. Economic Aid in Central America. LC 87-13238. 320p. 1988. reprint ed. pap. 99.20 (*0-7837-9240-9*, 204999100004) Bks Demand.

Barry, Tom, et al. Bananas, Bucks, & Boots: Focus on the Eastern Caribbean. 68p. (Orig.). 1984. pap. 5.00 (*0-911213-03-1*) Interhemisp Res Ctr.

— Guatemala: The Politics of Counterinsurgency. 101p. (Orig.). 1986. pap. 5.95 (*0-911213-06-6*) Interhemisp Res Ctr.

— Humanitarios de la Neuva Derecha. (SPA.). 32p. 1988. 5.95 (*0-911213-12-0*) Interhemisp Res Ctr.

— Jamaica: Open for Business. 48p. (Orig.). 1984. pap. 5.00 (*0-911213-02-3*) Interhemisp Res Ctr.

— The New Right Humanitarians. 66p. (Orig.). 1986. pap. 5.95 (*0-911213-07-4*) Interhemisp Res Ctr.

— Strangers in Paradise: Transnational Corporations in the Caribbean. 44p. (Orig.). 1984. pap. 5.00 (*0-911213-04-X*) Interhemisp Res Ctr.

Barry, Tom, jt. auth. see Garst, Rachel.

Barry, Tom, jt. auth. see Honey, Martha.

Barry, Tom, jt. auth. see Norsworthy, Kent.

Barry, Tom F. & Honey, Martha. Global Focus: A New Foreign Policy Agenda 1997-98. LC 96-54281. 282p. (Orig.). 1997. pap. 15.95 (*0-911213-62-7*) Interhemisp Res Ctr.

Barry, Ursula. Lifting the Lid. (C). 1990. 40.00 (*0-946211-25-6*) St Mut.

B

An Asterisk (*) at the beginning of an entry indicates that the title is appearing for the first time.

Barry, Vincent. Dog Ate My Homework: Personal Responsibility--How We Avoid It & What to Do about It. 224p. (J). 1998. pap. 10.95 (*0-8362-5281-0*) Andrews & McMeel.

Barry, Vincent, jt. auth. see Shaw, William H.

Barry, Vincent E. Applying Ethics: A Text with Readings. 2nd ed. 421p. (C). 1984. pap. write for info. (*0-534-03687-2*) Wadsworth Pub.

— Moral Issues in Business. 3rd ed. 502p. (C). 1985. pap. write for info. (*0-534-05484-6*) Wadsworth Pub.

— Philosophy: A Text with Readings. 2nd ed. 544p. (C). 1983. pap. write for info. (*0-534-01216-7*) Wadsworth Pub.

Barry, Vincent E. & Soccio, Douglas J. Practical Logic: An Antidote for Uncritical Thinking. 4th ed. Weaver, JoAnn, ed. (Illus.). 512p. (C). 1992. text 50.25 (*0-03-073907-1*, Pub. by Harcourt Coll Pubs) Harcourt.

Barry, Vincent E., jt. auth. see Olen, Jeffrey.

Barry, Vincent E., jt. auth. see Shaw, William H.

Barry, Vincent E., jt. auth. see Velasquez, Manuel.

Barry, W., et al, eds. Accelerator Instrumentation: Third Annual Workshop. (AIP Conference Proceedings Ser.: No. 252). 304p. 1992. 90.00 (*0-88318-934-8*) Am Inst Physics.

Barry, W. & Zindler, H. Fehler ABC: English-German. (GER.). 87p. (C). 1975. pap. text 18.25 (*3-12-551100-3*, Pub. by Klett Edition) Intl Bk Import.

Barry, W. J., et al, eds. Prosody & Information Structure. (Journal: Phonetica: Vol. 50, No. 3, 1993). (Illus.). 72p. 1993. pap. 21.75 (*3-8055-5878-3*) S Karger.

Barry, W. J., ed. see Simpson, A.

Barry, William. A History of Framingham, Mass. iv, 456p. 1983. reprint ed. 35.00 (*0-917890-28-0*) Heritage Bk.

— A History of Framingham, Mass., Including the Plantation, from 1640 to 1846: Also, a Register of Inhabitants Before 1800 with Genealogical Sketches. 456p. 1989. reprint ed. lib. bdg. 45.50 (*0-8328-0825-3*, MA0048) Higginson Bk Co.

Barry, William, jt. auth. see Doyle, Arthur Conan.

Barry, William A. Finding God in All Things: A Companion to the Spiritual Exercises of St. Ignatius. LC 91-72115. 144p. (Orig.). 1991. pap. 9.95 (*0-87793-460-6*) Ave Maria.

— God & You: Praying As a Personal Relationship. 88p. 1988. pap. 4.95 (*0-8091-2935-3*) Paulist Pr.

— Our Way of Proceeding. LC 97-73844. (Series IV: Vol. 19). vii, 190p. 1997. pap. 12.95 (*1-880810-30-1*) Inst Jesuit.

— Paying Attention to God: Discernment in Prayer. LC 89-85963. 128p. (Orig.). 1990. pap. 7.95 (*0-87793-413-4*) Ave Maria.

— Spiritual Direction & the Encounter with God: A Theological Inquiry. LC 91-43159. 132p. 1992. pap. 8.95 (*0-8091-3305-9*) Paulist Pr.

— What Do I Want in Prayer? LC 94-17578. 144p. 1994. pap. 8.95 (*0-8091-3482-9*) Paulist Pr.

— Who Do You Say I Am? Meeting the Historical Jesus in Prayer. LC 95-48160. 152p. 1996. pap. 9.95 (*0-87793-575-0*) Ave Maria.

— With an Everlasting Love: Developing an Intimate Relationship with God. LC 99-37973. 176p. 1999. pap. 8.95 (*0-8091-3892-1*) Paulist Pr.

Barry, William A. & Connolly, William G. The Practice of Spiritual Direction. 224p. (Orig.). 1986. pap. 17.00 (*0-86683-951-8*, Pub. by Harper SF) HarpC.

Barry, William A. & Maloney, Kerry A., eds. A Hunger for God: Ten Approaches to Prayer. LC 91-61107. 160p. (Orig.). (C). 1991. pap. 10.95 (*1-55612-452-X*, LL1452) Sheed & Ward WI.

Barry, William E. & Butler, Joyce. William E. Barry's "Sketch of an Old River" LC 93-24163. (Illus.). 88p. 1993. 25.00 (*0-914659-64-2*) Phoenix Pub.

Barry, William F. Roma Sacra: Essays on Christian Rome. LC 68-14896. (Essay Index Reprint Ser.). 1977. 20.95 (*0-8369-0174-6*) Ayer.

Barry, William J. The Information Engineering Method. 520p. 1990. pap. text 69.95 (*0-9629801-0-2*) B Four Grp.

— The Information Engineering Methode Process Modeling Workbook. 155p. 1990. student ed. 69.95 (*0-9629801-1-0*) B Four Grp.

Barrymore, D., jt. auth. see Barrymore, Frank.

Barrymore, Dick. Breaking Even. LC 97-75732. (Illus.). 340p. 1997. pap. 15.95 (*1-57510-037-1*) Pictorial Hist.

Barrymore, Drew. Sammy Sosa. LC 99-34135. (Overcoming Adversity Ser.). (Illus.). 128p. (gr. 5-9). 1999. pap. 9.95 (*0-7910-5301-6*) Chelsea Hse.

Barrymore, Drew & Gold, Todd. Little Girl Lost. Chelius, Jane, ed. 303p. 1991. reprint ed. per. 6.99 (*0-671-68923-1*, Pocket Star Bks) PB.

Barrymore, Frank & Barrymore, D. Too Much, Too Soon. 1981. reprint ed. lib. bdg. 21.95 (*0-89966-425-3*) Buccaneer Bks.

Barrymore, John. Confessions of an Actor. LC 70-84506. (Illus.). 1980. 20.95 (*0-405-08240-1*, Pub. by Blom Pubns) Ayer.

— The Life & Times of John Barrymore. 1978. reprint ed. 15.85 (*0-89966-250-1*) Buccaneer Bks.

Bars, Henry, et al, eds. The Story of Two Souls: The Correspondence of Jacques Maritain & Julien Green. Doering, Bernard, tr. LC 88-80056. (Illus.). 276p. 1988. 50.00 (*0-8232-1190-8*) Fordham.

Bars, Itzhak, et al, eds. Future Perspectives in String Theory: Strings '95, University of Southern California, Los Angeles 13 - 18 March 1995. 700p. 1996. text 148.00 (*981-02-2472-9*, Phm-P2943) World Scientific Pub.

Barsa, Betty R. The Independence of Urban Hispanic Elderly: The Growing Need for Social Support Networks. LC 98-42314. (Studies on the Elderly in America). 232p. 1998. 56.00 (*0-8153-3245-9*) Garland.

Barsa International Publishers, Inc. Staff. Claves para la Vida: Libro de la Salud. (SPA., Illus.). 512p. 1999. write for info. (*1-56409-032-9*) EBP Latin Am.

Barsacchi, Marco & Gatto, Vincenzo. L' Italiano Si Impara in Due. (Italian Studies). 112p. 1994. pap. text 22.95 (*0-8020-7212-7*) U of Toronto Pr.

Barsacq, Andre, ed. see Labiche, Eugene.

Barsalou, Lawrence W. Cognitive Psychology: An Overview for Cognitive Scientists. 424p. 1992. pap. 39.95 (*0-89859-966-0*); text 89.95 (*0-8058-0691-1*) L Erlbaum Assocs.

***Barsam, Richard.** The Movies:Format & Content. 1999. pap. 19.95 (*0-393-97436-7*) Norton.

Barsam, Richard M. Nonfiction Film: A Critical History. rev. ed. LC 91-26985. (Illus.). 504p. 1992. text 72.50 (*0-253-31124-1*); pap. text 24.95 (*0-253-20706-1*, MB 706) Ind U Pr.

— The Vision of Robert Flaherty: The Artist As Myth & Filmmaker. LC 87-45245. (Illus.). 160p. 1988. pap. 11.95 (*0-253-20460-7*, MB 460) Ind U Pr.

— The Vision of Robert Flaherty: The Artist As Myth & Mythmaker. LC 87-45488. (Illus.). 156p. reprint ed. pap. 48.40 (*0-608-09268-1*, 205407000002) Bks Demand.

Barsamian, David, jt. auth. see Chomsky, Noam.

Barsamian, David, ed. see Ahmad, Eqbal.

Barsamian, Michael & Gizelbach, Richard. Machine Trades Print Reading. LC 92-32497. (Illus.). 240p. 1996. 27.60 (*1-56637-269-0*) Goodheart.

***Barsamian, Michael A. & Gizelbach, Richard.** Machine Trades Print Reading. LC 00-34076. (Illus.). 2000. write for info. (*1-56637-594-0*) Goodheart.

Barsan. Acute Drug Therapy. 1999. text 59.00 (*0-7216-6517-9*, W B Saunders Co) Harcrt Hlth Sci Grp.

Barsan, et al. Emergency Drug Therapy. (Illus.). 672p. 1990. text 105.00 (*0-7216-2584-3*, W B Saunders Co) Harcrt Hlth Sci Grp.

Barsan, Uasile C., tr. see Ronnett, Alexander .

Barsanti, Chris, jt. auth. see Langer, Adam.

Barsanti, Michael J., ed. see Good, Wendy V.

Barsby, J., ed. Ovid: Amores I. (Bristol Latin Texts Ser.). (LAT.). 192p. 1991. reprint ed. 20.95 (*0-906515-45-9*, Pub. by Brist Class Pr) Focus Pub-R Pullins.

Barsby, J., ed. see Plautus.

Barsby, J., ed. see Plautus, J. A.

Barsby, John, ed. see Terence.

Barsch. Ready-to-Use Printer's Ornaments & Dingbats: 1,611 Different Copyright-Free Designs Printed One Side. (Clip Art Ser.). (Illus.). 64p. pap. 5.95 (*0-486-28498-0*) Dover.

Barsch, D. & Maeusbacher, R., eds. Some Contributions to the Study of Landforms & Geomorphic Processes. (Zeitschrift fuer Geomorphologie - Annals of Geomorphology Ser.: Supplementband 92). (Illus.). viii, 239p. 1993. pap. 88.00 (*3-443-21092-9*, Pub. by Gebruder Borntraeger) Balogh.

Barsch, Dietrich. Rockglaciers: Indicators for the Present & Former Geoecology in High Mountain Environments. LC 96-13769. (Physical Environment Ser.: Vol. 16). 352p. 1996. 179.95 (*3-540-60742-0*) Spr-Verlag.

Barsch, Dietrich, ed. see Douglas, Ian.

Barsch, Dietrich, ed. see Douglas, Ian & Lorrain, R. D.

Barsch, Dietrich, ed. see Sweeting, M. M.

Barsch, Dietrich, ed. see Young, R. & Young, A.

Barsch, Jeffrey. Barsch Learning Style Inventory. 1991. 14.00 (*0-87879-905-2*) Acad Therapy.

Barsch, Jim. Daddy, Where Is God? large type ed. (Illus.). 20p. (J). (ps-1). 1999. 12.95 (*0-9662781-8-6*) TrueLove Pub.

Barsch, Lynne. Radio Rescue. LC 99-22384. (Illus.). 40p. (gr. k-3). 2000. 16.00 (*0-374-36166-5*, Frances Foster) FS&G.

Barsch, Ray. The Magic of Vowels. Kratoville, Betty Lou, ed. (Orig.). (J). (gr. 1-4). 1997. pap. text, wbk. ed. 14.00 (*1-57128-079-0*, 8079-0) High Noon Bks.

Barsch, Ray H. Fine Tuning: An Auditory-Visual Training Program: Intermediate - Advanced Level. Kratoville, Betty Lou, ed. 224p. (Orig.). 1995. student ed. 15.00 (*1-57128-001-4*, 001-4) Acad Therapy.

— Fine Tuning: An Auditory-Visual Training Program: Primary - Intermediate Level. Kratoville, Betty Lou, ed. (Illus.). 176p. (Orig.). 1995. student ed. 15.00 (*1-57128-000-6*, 000-6) Acad Therapy.

Barschall, Henry H., ed. see International Symposium on Polarization Phenomena.

Barsh, Russel L. & Henderson, James Y. The Road: Indian Tribes & Political Liberty. LC 77-91777. 1979. pap. 15.95 (*0-520-04636-6*, Pub. by U CA Pr) Cal Prin Full Svc.

Barsha, Tony, jt. auth. see Mednick, Murray.

***Barsham.** Sir Arthur Conan Doyle. (Nineteenth Century Ser.). 2000. 68.95 (*1-85928-264-4*) Ashgate Pub Co.

Barshay, Andrew E. State & Intellectual in Imperial Japan: The Public Man in Crisis. 335p. 1991. pap. 18.95 (*0-520-07393-2*, Pub. by U CA Pr) Cal Prin Full Svc.

***Barshefsky, Charlene.** 1998 Trade Policy Agenda & 1997 Annual Report of the President of the U. S. on the Trade Agreement Program. 273p. 1999. pap. text 35.00 (*0-7881-8133-5*) DIANE Pub.

Barshi, Immanuel, jt. ed. see Payne, Doris L.

Barshick, Christopher M., ed. see Duckworth, Douglas C., et al.

Barsi, Agi. What Will You Do? (Illus.). xvi, 176p. 1999. pap. 15.95 (*0-9671693-9-9*) A Better Life.

Barsi, James C. The Basic Researcher's Guide to Homesteads & Other Federal Land Records. (Basic Researcher's Guide Ser.). 80p. 1994. pap. 12.95 (*0-9643192-0-9*) Nuthatch Grove.

Barskaya, Anna. French Painting: The Hermitage Museum, Leningrad. (Second Half of the 19th to Early 20th Century Ser.). 1975. 125.00 (*0-7855-0700-0*) St Mut.

— French Painting from the Hermitage: Mid-19th to Early 20th Century. (C). 1987. 410.00 (*0-7855-3316-8*) St Mut.

Barskaya, Anna, compiled by. Monet. (Illus.). 50p. 1982. pap. 16.95 (*0-8109-2265-7*, 2219-3) Abrams.

Barskaya, Anna & Georgiyevskaya, E. Paul Cezanne. 200p. 1982. 50.00 (*0-7855-0704-3*, Pub. by Collets) St Mut.

Barskett, James. History of the Island of Saint Domingo from Its First Discovery by Columbus. 446p. 1972. reprint ed. 45.00 (*0-7146-2703-8*, Pub. by F Cass Pubs) Intl Spec Bk.

***Barsky, Allan Edward.** Conflict Resolution for the Helping Professions. (Social Work Ser.). 1999. pap. 40.95 (*0-534-35923-X*) Brooks-Cole.

Barsky, Arthur J., III. Worried Sick: Our Troubled Quest for Wellness. LC 87-32508. 1988. 17.95 (*0-316-08255-4*, Little Brwn Med Div) Lppncott W & W.

Barsky, Brian A. Computer Graphics & Computer-Aided Geometric Design Using Beta-Splines. (Computer Science Workbench Ser.). (Illus.). 200p. 1988. 71.95 (*0-387-70006-4*) Spr-Verlag.

Barsky, Brian A., ed. see Apodaca, Anthony A. & Gritz, Larry.

Barsky, Brian A., ed. see Gallier, Jean H.

Barsky, Brian A., ed. see Glassner, Andrew S.

Barsky, Brian A., ed. see Magnenat-Thalmann, Nadia & Volino, Pascal.

Barsky, Hannah K. Guillaume Dupuytren: A Surgeon in His Place & Time. LC 82-99963. 295p. 1984. 14.95 (*0-533-05600-4*) Vantage.

Barsky, Ivy & Murphy, Patrick. Conversation Pieces. (Illus.). 48p. 1994. 30.00 (*0-88454-076-6*) U of Pa Contemp Art.

Barsky, Jonathan. Finding the Profit in Customer Satisfaction. LC 98-16209. 176p. 1998. pap. 14.95 (*0-8092-2843-2*, 284320, Contemporary Bks) NTC Contemp Pub Co.

— World Class Customer Satisfaction. 252p. 1996. text 25.00 (*0-7863-0128-7*, Irwn Prfssnl) McGraw-Hill Prof.

***Barsky, Noah P.** Organizational Determinants of Budgetary Influence & Involvement LC 99-36250. 1999. write for info. (*0-8153-3550-4*) Garland.

Barsky, Noah P., jt. auth. see Jablonsky, Stephen F.

Barsky, Robert Franklin. Constructing a Productive Other: Discourse Theory & the Convention Refugee Hearing. LC 94-33456. (Pragmatics & Beyond New Ser.: No. 29). x, 272p. 1994. lib. bdg. 64.00 (*1-55619-297-5*) J Benjamins Pubng Co.

— Noam Chomsky: A Life of Dissent. LC 96-29013. (Illus.). 256p. 1998. pap. text 16.50 (*0-262-52255-1*) MIT Pr.

— Noam Chomsky: A Life Of Dissent. LC P85.C47B37 1997. (Illus.). 250p. 1997. text 32.95 (*1-55022-282-1*, Pub. by ECW) Genl Dist Srvs.

— Noam Chomsky: A Life of Dissent, Vol. 1. LC P85.C47B37 1997. 248p. 1997. 33.00 (*0-262-02418-7*) MIT Pr.

Barsky, Robert Franklin & Brauer, Richard. Noam Chomsky: A Life of Dissent, 3 vols., 2. Wong, Warren J. et al, eds. (Illus.). 400p. 1980. 80.00 (*0-262-02148-X*) MIT Pr.

***Barsky, Steve.** The Simple Guide to Snorkeling Fun. LC 98-89488. (Illus.). 160p. 1999. pap. 19.95 (*0-941332-71-3*, B0947) Best Pub Co.

Barsky, Steve, et al. The Simple Guide to Rebreather Diving. LC 97-77520. 280p. 1998. pap. 26.95 (*0-941332-65-9*, D972) Best Pub Co.

***Barsky, Steven M.** Diving in High Risk Environments. 3rd rev. ed. LC 99-91639. (Illus.). 197p. 1999. pap. 31.95 (*0-9674305-1-8*) Hammerhead Pr.

Barsky, Steven M. Dry Suit Diving. (Specialty Diver Ser.). 93p. 1990. pap. text 10.95 (*0-943717-87-6*) Concept Sys.

— Small Boat Diving. LC 94-79808. (Illus.). 208p. (Orig.). 1994. 14.95 (*0-941332-43-8*, D727) Best Pub Co.

— Spearfishing for Skin & Scuba Divers. LC 97-71104. (Illus.). 224p. (Orig.). 1997. pap. 14.95 (*0-941332-59-4*, D927) Best Pub Co.

***Barsky, Steven M., et al.** Dry Suit Diving. 3rd ed. LC 99-65785. (Illus.). 185p. 1999. pap. 16.50 (*0-9674305-0-X*) Hammerhead Pr.

Barsky, Steven M., et al. Dry Suit Diving: A Guide to Diving Dry. 1992. pap. 12.95 (*0-922769-36-2*) Watersport Pub.

Barsky, Vladimir. Chromaticism. 211p. 1996. text 53.00 (*3-7186-5704-X*, ECU22, Harwood Acad Pubs); pap. text 17.00 (*3-7186-5705-8*, ECU68, Harwood Acad Pubs) Gordon & Breach.

Barskya, Anna. Paul Gauguin: Mysterious Affinities. (Great Painters Ser.). (Illus.). 176p. 1996. 40.00 (*1-85995-141-4*) Parkstone Pr.

Barsness, Jim. The Monster's Progress. 48p. 1999. pap. text 19.95 (*1-889097-31-4*, Pub. by Hard Pr MA) Consort Bk Sales.

Barsness, John. The Life of the Hunt. LC 95-60555. (Illus.). 192p. 1995. 29.00 (*1-885106-17-3*) Wild Adven Pr.

— Montana Time: The Seasons of a Trout Fisherman. 144p. 1996. pap. text 14.95 (*1-55821-492-5*) Lyons Pr.

— Optics for the Hunter: An Evaluation of Binoculars, Scopes, Range Finders & Spotting Scopes. (Illus.). 225p. 1999. 24.95 (*1-57157-156-6*, Pub. by Safari Pr) Natl Bk Netwk.

— Shotguns for Wingshooting. LC 99-61455. 208p. 1999. 49.95 (*0-87341-671-6*) Krause Pubns.

***Barsness, John.** Western Skies: Bird Hunting in the Rockies & on the Plains, 1. 160p. 1999. pap. text 18.95 (*1-55821-923-4*) Lyons Pr.

Barsness, John C. Western Skies: Bird Hunting in the Rockies & on the Plains. LC 94-11159. 160p. 1994. 18.95 (*1-55821-307-4*) Lyons Pr.

Barsness, Larry. Heads, Hides & Horns: The Compleat Buffalo Book. LC 85-2606. (Illus.). 249p. 1985. reprint ed. pap. 77.20 (*0-7837-9184-4*, 204988300003) Bks Demand.

Barsocchini, Peter. Mission: Impossible. 1996. mass mkt. 5.99 (*0-671-54921-9*) PB.

Barsom, John M., ed. Flaw Growth & Fracture: 10th Conference - STP 631. 531p. 1977. 49.75 (*0-8031-0356-5*, STP631) ASTM.

— Fracture Mechanics: Retrospective Early Classic Papers (1913-1965), Vol. RPS 1. 392p. 1987. 29.00 (*0-8031-0483-9*, RPS1) ASTM.

***Barsom, John M. & Rolfe, Stanley T.** Fracture & Fatigue Control in Structures. LC 99-45439. 516p. 2000. 89.95 (*0-7506-7315-X*) Buttrwrth-Heinemann.

***Barsom, John M. & Rolfe, Stanley T., eds.** Fracture & Fatigue Control in Structures: Applications of Fracture Mechanics. 3rd ed. LC 99-45439. 525p. 1999. 90.00 (*0-8031-2082-6*, MNL41) ASTM.

Barsom, John M. & Vecchio, Robert S. Fatigue of Welded Components. 1997. pap. 75.00 (*0-9656164-6-0*, 422) Welding Res Coun.

Barson, A. J. Fetal & Neonatal Pathology. 1982. 69.50 (*0-275-91359-7*, C1359, Praeger Pubs) Greenwood.

Barson, Alan. Math Games for Fun & Practice. 1993. pap. 16.75 (*0-201-29106-1*) Addison-Wesley.

Barson, John. Cass la Grammaire a l'Oeuvre. 5th ed. (C). 1996. text 40.25 (*0-03-072397-3*) Harcourt.

— La Grammaire a l'Oeuvre. 5th ed. (FRE.). (C). 1995. pap. text 50.00 (*0-03-072394-9*) Harcourt Coll Pubs.

— Tapescript La Gram A L'Oev. 5th ed. 108p. (C). 1996. pap. text 33.50 (*0-03-072396-5*) Holt R&W.

***Barson, Kalman A.** Accounting: 1999 Supplement. 89p. 1999. pap., suppl. ed. 70.00 (*0-471-35180-6*) Wiley.

— The Complete Book of Income Reconstruction. LC 99-29189. 1999. write for info. (*0-87051-256-0*) Am Inst CPA.

Barson, Kalman A. Investigative Accounting in Divorce. LC 95-49276. (Family Law Library). 522p. 1996. 170.00 (*0-471-13513-5*) Wiley.

— Investigative Accounting in Matrimonial Proceedings. 632p. 1993. 106.00 (*0-13-109166-2*) Aspen Law.

Barson, Michael. The Illustrated Who's Who of Hollywood Directors Vol. 1: The Sound Era. LC 94-40212. (Illus.). 530p. 1995. pap. 27.50 (*0-374-52428-9*, Noonday) FS&G.

— The Illustrated Who's Who of Hollywood Directors Vol. 1: The Sound Era. LC 94-40212. (Illus.). 480p. 1995. text 50.00 (*0-374-17452-0*) FS&G.

— Teenage Confidential: An Illustrated History of the American Teen. LC 97-8171. (Illus.). 132p. 1997. pap. text 16.95 (*0-8118-1584-6*) Chronicle Bks.

***Barson, Michael & Heller, Steven.** Wedding Bell Blues: 100 Years of Our Great Romance with Marriage. LC 99-43437. (Illus.). 132p. 2000. pap. 18.95 (*0-8118-2154-4*) Chronicle Bks.

Barsony, Mary. Star Formation. (C). 1998. write for info. (*0-201-57697-X*) Addison-Wesley.

— Star Formation. (C). 1999. pap. write for info. (*0-201-57696-1*) Addison-Wesley.

Barsotti, Joan B. Christopher & Grandma on Safari. (Apple Hill Ser.). (Illus.). 32p. (Orig.). (J). (ps-2). 1996. pap. 6.95 (*0-9642112-2-X*) Barsotti Bks.

— Grandmother's Bell & the Wagon Train/1849. LC 96-85163. (Illus.). 32p. (J). (gr. 2-4). 1997. 14.95 (*0-9642112-4-6*); pap. 6.95 (*0-9642112-3-8*) Barsotti Bks.

— The Little Green Frog & Other Poems. LC 98-93135. (Illus.). 32p. (J). (ps-4). 1999. 14.95 (*0-9642112-6-2*); pap. 6.95 (*0-9642112-5-4*) Barsotti Bks.

— Mike & Nick & the Pumpkin Patch. (Apple Hill Ser.: No. 1). (Illus.). 24p. (Orig.). (J). (ps-2). 1993. pap. 5.99 (*0-9642112-0-3*) Barsotti Bks.

— Nana Gets a Cat. (Apple Hill Ser.: No. 2). (Illus.). 24p. (Orig.). (J). (ps-2). 1994. pap. 5.99 (*0-9642112-1-1*) Barsotti Bks.

Barsoum, Michael W. Fundamentals of Ceramics. LC 96-24295. (Mcgraw-Hill Series in Materials Science & Engineering). 1996. write for info. (*0-07-005522-X*) McGraw.

— Fundamentals of Ceramics. LC 96-24295. (Mcgraw-Hill Series in Materials Science & Engineering). (Illus.). 568p. (C). 1996. 84.38 (*0-07-005521-1*) McGraw.

Barsoum, R. S., ed. Simplified Methods in Pressure Vessel Analysis: Presented at 1978 ASME-CSME Montreal Pressure Vessel & Piping Conference, Montreal , Quebec, Canada, June 25-29, 1978. LC 78-51570. (PVP Ser.: Vol. 29). (Illus.). 133p. reprint ed. pap. 41.30 (*0-608-17870-5*, 203270100080) Bks Demand.

***Barsoux, Jean-Louis.** Insead: From Institution to Institution. 2000. text 69.95 (*0-312-23385-X*) St Martin.

Barsoux, Jean-Louis & Lawrence, Peter. French Management: Elitism in Action. LC 90-77629. 195p. 1997. pap. 35.95 (*0-304-70238-2*, HB3711, Pub. by Cassell) LPC InBook.

Barsoux, Jean-Louis, jt. auth. see Schneider, Susan.

***Barss, Andrew & Langendoen, D. Terence, eds.** Anaphora, Binding & Control: An Overview. 288p. 1999. 59.95 (*0-631-21117-9*); pap. text 29.95 (*0-631-21118-7*) Blackwell Pubs.

Barss, Beulah M. The Pioneer Cook: A Historical View of Canadian Prairie Food, Vol. 1. 134p. (Orig.). 1980. pap. 7.95 (*0-920490-11-5*) Temeron Bks.

Barss, Karen J. Clean Water. (Earth at Risk Ser.). (Illus.). 128p. (YA). (gr. 5 up). 1992. lib. bdg. 19.95 (*0-7910-1583-1*) Chelsea Hse.

Barss, Peter, et al. Injury Prevention: An International Perspective: Epidemiology, Surveillance, & Policy. (Illus.). 398p. 1998. text 59.50 (*0-19-511982-7*) OUP.

An Asterisk (*) at the beginning of an entry indicates that the title is appearing for the first time.

***Barstad, Fred.** Best Easy Day Hikes Mount St. Helens. LC 98-56520. (Illus.). 80p. 1999. pap. 6.95 (*1-56044-697-8*) Falcon Pub Inc.

Barstad, Fred. Hiking Mount St. Helens. LC 98-50261. (Illus.). 240p. 1999. pap. 14.95 (*1-56044-696-X*) Falcon Pub Inc.

— Hiking Oregon's Mount Hood & Badger Creek Wilderness. LC 98-19015. (Illus.). 242p. 1998. pap. 16.95 (*1-56044-643-9*) Falcon Pub Inc.

Barstad, Jan. Guide to Hohokam Pottery. LC 99-32412. (Illus.). 48p. 1999. pap. 4.95 (*1-877856-95-9*) SW Pks Mnmts.

Barstad, Malfred I. Hiking Oregon's Eagle Cap Wilderness. LC 96-988. (Illus.). 302p. 1996. pap. 16.95 (*1-56044-399-5*) Falcon Pub Inc.

Barstad, Noel, tr. see Gebser, Jean.

Barston, R. P. International Politics since 1945: Key Issues in the Making of the Modern World. 336p. 1991. text 95.00 (*1-85278-063-0*) E Elgar.

— Modern Diplomacy. MacLennan, Andres, ed. LC 87-3943. 264p. 1988. text 36.95 (*0-582-01403-4*, 73620) Longman.

— Modern Diplomacy. MacLennan, Andres, ed. LC 87-3943. 264p. (C). 1988. pap. text 28.50 (*0-582-49441-9*, 73620) Longman.

— Modern Diplomacy. 2nd ed. (C). 1997. pap. text 21.75 (*0-582-09953-6*, Pub. by Addison-Wesley) Longman.

Barstone, Willis, tr. see Sappho.

Barstow. Human Element & Other Stories. Date not set. pap. text. write for info. (*0-582-23369-0*, Pub. by Addison-Wesley) Longman.

Barstow, A. E. Sikhs: An Ethnology. (Illus.). (C). 1994. reprint ed. 10.00 (*0-614-04745-5*, Pub. by Low Price) S Asia.

Barstow, Anne L. Joan of Arc: Heretic, Mystic, Shaman. LC 86-12756. (Studies in Women & Religion: Vol. 17). (Illus.). 156p. 1986. lib. bdg. 69.95 (*0-88946-532-0*) E Mellen.

— Married Priests & the Reforming Papacy: The 11th Century Debates. LC 82-7914. (Texts & Studies in Religion: Vol. 12). 288p. 1982. lib. bdg. 89.95 (*0-88946-987-3*) E Mellen.

— Witchcraze: A New History of the European Witch Hunts. LC 92-56410. 272p. 1995. pap. 14.00 (*0-06-251036-3*, Pub. by Harper SF) HarpC.

Barstow, Anne L., jt. ed. see Gillikin, Jo.

Barstow, Barbara & Riggle, Judith. Beyond Picture Books. 2nd ed. LC 94-49731. (Illus.). 501p. 1995. 49.95 (*0-8352-3519-X*) Bowker.
This indispensable companion to A to Zoo identifies & profiles more that 2,500 superior first readers that present themes of interest to young children & feature lively interaction of text & illustration. It includes a core list of 200 outstanding titles that helps simplify collection development. *Publisher Paid Annotation.*

— Beyond Picture Books: A Guide to First Readers. 354p. 1989. 43.00 (*0-8352-2515-1*) Bowker.

Barstow, Frank. Beat the Casino. 1990. per. 5.99 (*0-671-70959-3*) S&S Trade.

Barstow, Jack. Nightmare on Elm Street V: The Dream Child. New Line Cinema Staff, ed. LC 92-499. 1992. lib. bdg. 13.95 (*1-56239-160-7*) ABDO Pub Co.

Barstow, Jane M. One Hundred Years of American Women Writing, 1848-1948: An Annotated Bio-Bibliography. LC 97-4001. (Magill Bibliographies Ser.). 1997. 42.00 (*0-8108-3314-X*) Scarecrow.

***Barstow, Kurt.** The Gualenghi d'Este Hours: Art & Devotion in Renaissance Ferrara. LC 00-21320. (Monographs on Illuminated Manuscripts). (Illus.). 272p. 2000. 95.00 (*0-89236-370-3*) J P Getty Trust.

Barstow, Martin A., ed. White Dwarfs: Proceedings of the NATO Advanced Research Workshop Eight European Workshop on White Dwarfs, Leicester, United Kingdom, July 20-24, 1992. LC 93-1727. (NATO Advanced Study Institutes Series C, Mathematical & Physical Sciences: Vol. 403). 588p. (C). 1993. text 343.00 (*0-7923-2332-7*) Kluwer Academic.

Barstow, Phillida. The English Country House Party. LC 99-167423. (History Paperbacks Ser.). (Illus.). 224p. 1998. pap. 19.95 (*0-7509-1849-7*, Pub. by Sutton Pub Ltd) Intl Pubs Mktg.

Barstow, Phyllida. The Nabob's Wife. large type ed. 1991. 27.99 (*0-7089-2401-8*) Ulverscroft.

— Shadows on the Snow. large type ed. (Historical Romance Ser.). 752p. 1993. 27.99 (*0-7089-2981-8*) Ulverscroft.

Barstow, Stan. B-Movie. large type ed. 240p. 1988. 11.50 (*0-7089-1815-8*) Ulverscroft.

— Give Us This Day. large type ed. 1991. 27.99 (*0-7089-2439-5*) Ulverscroft.

— Next of Kin. large type ed. (General Ser.). 448p. 1993. 11.50 (*0-7089-2907-9*) Ulverscroft.

Barsuhn, Rochelle. Growing Sophia: The Story of a Premature Birth. 154p. (Orig.). 1996. pap. 11.95 (*0-9650848-2-5*, GS0151) deRuyter-Nelson.

Barsukov, V. & Beck, F., eds. New Promising Electrochemical Systems for Rechargeable Batteries: Proceedings of the NATO Advanced Research Workshop, Puscha Voditsa Near Kiev, Ukraine, May 14 - 17, 1995. LC 96-1342. (NATO Advanced Science Institutes Ser.: No. 3). 536p. (C). 1996. text 291.00 (*0-7923-3948-7*) Kluwer Academic.

Barsukov, V. L., et al, eds. Venus Geology, Geochemistry, & Geophysics: Research Results from the Soviet Union. LC 91-25232. (Illus.). 421p. 1992. 85.00 (*0-8165-1222-1*) U of Ariz Pr.

Barsy, Carlotta De, see De Barsy, Carlotta.

Barsy, Kalman. Del Nacimiento de la Isla de Boriken. LC 82-83288. (Coleccion Sur). (SPA., Illus.). 76p. (J). (gr. 6). 1982. pap. 8.75 (*0-940238-01-2*) Ediciones Huracan.

— La Estructura Dialectica del "El Otono del Patriarca" LC 88-14338. 202p. 1989. pap. 10.95 (*0-8477-3611-3*) U of PR Pr.

Barszcz, James, jt. auth. see Vesterman, William.

Bart, Benjamin F. Flaubert. LC 67-27410. 807p. reprint ed. pap. 200.00 (*0-608-13993-9*, 202223000025) Bks Demand.

Bart, Elizabeth. Rights of the Elderly: Who Decides If You Live or Die. large type ed. 130p. 2000. spiral bd. 17.97 (*1-891829-03-3*) Peaceful Angel.

Bart, Frederick J. The Comprehensive Catalog of U. S. Paper Money Errors. (Illus.). 192p. 1994. 35.00 (*0-931960-39-8*) BNR Pr.

Bart, H., et al, eds. Topics in Matrix & Operator Theory: Workshop on, Rotterdam, Netherlands, June 26-29, 1989. (Operator Theory Ser.: Vol. 50). 388p. 1991. 129.00 (*0-8176-2570-4*) Birkhauser.

Bart, Herbert M. History of Dumfries & Galloway. xvi, 411p. 1997. reprint ed. pap. 30.50 (*0-7884-0756-2*, M100) Heritage Bk.

Bart, Istvan. The Kiss: 20th Century Hungarian Short Stories. 428p. 1989. pap. 60.00 (*963-13-4099-6*, Pub. by Corvina Bks) St Mut.

***Bart, Istvan.** The Kiss: 20th Century Hungarian Short Stories. LC 98-136132. 1999. pap. 23.00 (*963-13-4250-6*, Pub. by Corvina Bks) St Mut.

Bart, Jill. The Naked & the Nude. (Illus.). 32p. (Orig.). (C). 1993. pap. text 5.00 (*1-878173-31-6*) Birnham Wood.

Bart, Jody. Women Succeeding in the Sciences: Theories & Practices Across Disciplines. LC 99-26055. 2000. pap. 24.95 (*1-55753-122-6*) Purdue U Pr.

Bart, Jonathan, et al. Sampling & Statistical Methods for Behavioral Ecologists. LC 97-35086. (Illus.). 352p. (C). 1998. text 74.95 (*0-521-45095-0*); pap. text 29.95 (*0-521-45705-X*) Cambridge U Pr.

***Bart, Judy.** Women Succeeding in the Sciences: Theories & Practices Across Disciplines. 2000. 49.95 (*1-55753-121-8*) Purdue U Pr.

***Bart, Muriel.** Sisters - Strangers. Wise, Noreen, ed. (Lemonade Collection). 208p. (J). (gr. k up). 2000. pap. 9.95 (*1-58584-281-8*) Huckleberry CT.

Bart, Pauline B. & Moran, Eileen G., eds. Violence Against Women. (Gender & Society Readers Ser.: Vol. 1). (Illus.). 320p. (C). 1993. text 56.00 (*0-8039-5044-6*); pap. text 26.00 (*0-8039-5045-4*) Sage.

Bart, Pauline B. & O'Brian, Patricia. Stopping Rape: Successful Survival Strategies. LC 93-16306. (Athene Ser.). 216p. (C). 1985. pap. text 17.95 (*0-8077-6212-1*) Tchrs Coll.

Bart, Pauline B. & O'Brien, Patricia H. Stopping Rape: Successful Survival Strategies. LC 85-6589. (Athene Ser.). 200p. 1985. 39.50 (*0-08-032814-8*, Pergamon Pr); pap. 15.95 (*0-08-032813-X*, Pergamon Pr) Elsevier.

Bart, Peter. The Gross: The Hits, the Flops: The Summer That Ate Hollywood. LC 98-53853. 304p. 1999. text 24.95 (*0-312-19894-9*) St Martin.

***Bart, Peter.** The Gross: The Hits, the Flops: The Summer That Ate Hollywood. 336p. 2000. pap. 14.95 (*0-312-25391-5*) St Martin.

— Who Killed Hollywood? How Tinseltown Let Its Golden Era Get Tarnished. 352p. 2000. 24.95 (*1-58063-116-9*) Renaissance.

Bart, Phil. Working Class Unity: The Role of Communists in the Chicago Federation of Labor, 1919-1923. 1975. pap. 0.40 (*0-87898-114-4*) New Outlook.

Bart, Philip, et al, eds. Highlights of a Fighting History: Sixty Years of the Communist Party, U. S. A. LC 79-14009. (Illus.). 540p. 1979. 15.00 (*0-7178-0559-X*); pap. 5.25 (*0-7178-0502-6*) Intl Pubs Co.

Bart, Sirl E. The History of a False Religion. 129p. 1971. reprint ed. spiral bd. 14.00 (*0-7873-0074-8*) Hlth Research.

Bart, Stuart, ed. see Charest-Papagno, Noella.

***Bart, Tanya.** The Fabrics of Fairytale: Stories Spun from Far & Wide. (Illus.). 80p. (J). (gr. 1-6). 2000. 19.99 (*1-84148-061-4*) Barefoot Bks NY.

Bart, William M. & Wong, Martin R., eds. Psychology of School Learning, 2 vols. Incl. Vol. 1. Environmentalism. 249p. 1974. text 1974. pap. write for info. (*0-318-53724-9*) Irvington.

Barta, B., et al. Fertility, Female Employment & Policy Measures in Hungary. (Women, Work & Development Ser.: No. 6). viii, 88p. (Orig.). 1984. pap. 13.50 (*92-2-103624-3*) Intl Labour Office.

Barta, Carolyn. Bill Clements: Texian to His Toenails. LC 96-2707. (Illus.). 480p. 1996. 29.95 (*1-57168-090-X*, Eakin Pr) Sunbelt Media.

— Perot & His People: Disrupting the Balance of Political Power. Towle, Mike, ed. 500p. 1993. 22.95 (*1-56530-065-3*) Summit TX.

Barta, Dale, et al. Czechoslovakian Glass & Collectibles, Vol. 2. (Illus.). 144p. 1996. pap. 16.95 (*0-89145-721-6*, 4714) Collector Bks.

Barta, J., jt. auth. see Vogt, A.

Barta, Louis W. The Three Days of Darkness, Vol. 1. rev. ed. (Illus.). 24p. (Orig.). 1989. pap. 2.95 (*0-9655050-7-3*) L W Barta Pubns.

***Barta, Pavel, et al.** Kings of the Ice: Hockey - 20th Century. (Illus.). 568p. 2000. 148.95 (*1-55321-101-4*, Pub. by NDE Pub) IPG Chicago.

Barta, Peter I. Bely, Joyce, & Doblin: Peripatetics in the City Novel. LC 96-142. (Florida James Joyce Ser.). 152p. 1996. 34.95 (*0-8130-1450-6*) U Press Fla.

***Barta, Peter I., ed.** Metamorphosis in Russian Modernism. 300p. (C). 2000. 44.95 (*963-9116-90-4*); pap. 21.95 (*963-9116-91-2*) Ctrl Europ Univ.

Barta, Peter I., et al, eds. Russian Literature & the Classics. (Studies in Russian & European Literature: Vol. 1). 248p. 1996. text 36.00 (*3-7186-0605-4*); pap. text 15.00 (*3-7186-0606-2*) Gordon & Breach.

Barta, Peter I. & Goebel, Ulrich. The Contexts of Aleksandr Sergeevich Pushkin. (Studies in Slavic Language & Literature: Vol. 1). 150p. 1989. write for info. (*0-88946-291-7*) E Mellen.

Barta, Peter I. & Goebel, Ulrich, eds. The European Foundations of Russian Modernism. LC 91-32518. (Studies in Slavic Language & Literature: Vol. 7). 344p. 1991. lib. bdg. 99.95 (*0-7734-9660-2*) E Mellen.

Barta, Steve. The Source, Vol. 1. 96p. 1987. pap. 12.95 (*0-937589-00-4*, 00240885) H Leonard.

Barta, Tony, ed. Screening the Past: Film & the Representation of History. LC 97-37811. 296p. 1998. 59.95 (*0-275-95402-1*, Praeger Pubs) Greenwood.

Bartail, Patrice, jt. auth. see Barbe, Philippe.

Bartal, Antonius, ed. Glossarium Mediae Et Infimae Latinitatis Regni Hungariae. xxviii, 723p. 1971. reprint ed. 200.00 (*0-318-70749-7*) G Olms Pubs.

Bartal, Arie H. & Hirshaut, Yashar, eds. Methods of Hybridoma Formation. LC 87-3588. (Contemporary Biomedicine Ser.: Vol. 7). 504p. 1987. 125.00 (*0-89603-100-4*) Humana.

Bartal, Israel & Polonsky, Antony, eds. Polin: Focusing on Galicia: Jews, Poles & Ukrainians, 1772-1918. (Studies in Polish Jewry: Vol. 12). (Illus.). 416p. 1999. 55.00 (*1-874774-59-5*, Pub. by Littman Lib); pap. 29.50 (*1-874774-40-4*, Pub. by Littman Lib) Intl Spec Bk.

Bartal, Israel, jt. auth. see Opalski, Magdalena.

***Bartali, El Houssine, et al, eds.** CIGR Handbook of Agricultural Engineering Vol. II: Animal Production & Aquacultural Engineering. LC 98-93767. (Illus.). 395p. 1999. text 45.00 (*0-929355-98-9*, M0798) Am Soc Ag Eng.

Bartalini, Gualtiero. The Opera According to Bartalini: A Book of Doggerel Libretti & Comical Illustrati. LC 94-12809. (Illus.). 128p. 1994. pap. 24.00 (*1-56640-994-2*) Pomegranate Calif.

Bartalsky, Kathy. Soaring on Broken Wings: A Story of Triumph in Tragedy. pap. 9.99 (*0-8024-2316-7*, 287) Moody.

Bartanen. Teaching & Directing Forensics. 186p. 1993. pap. text 44.00 (*0-13-777269-6*) P-H.

Bartanen, Michael D. Lincoln-Douglas Debate. LC 92-80478. 200p. 1994. pap. 23.99 (*0-8442-5014-7*) NTC Contemp Pub Co.

Bartanen, Michael D. & Frank, David A. Nonpolicy Debate. 2nd ed. Orig. Title: Debating Values. 220p. (C). 1994. pap. text 40.00 (*0-13-776717-X*) P-H.

Bartanus, Joseph. Golf for All Golfers: Super Golf Swing Techniques. LC 95-61460. 118p. 1996. pap. 7.95 (*0-7880-0630-4*, Fairway Pr) CSS OH.

Bartas, Guillaume D. Du, see Du Bartas, Guillaume D.

Bartch, Marian R. Math & Stories. (J). (gr. k-3). 1996. 13.95 (*0-614-09791-6*, GoodYrBooks) Addson-Wesley Educ.

— Math & Stories. 184p. (gr. k-3). 1996. pap. 13.95 (*0-673-36317-1*, GoodYrBooks) Addson-Wesley Educ.

— Math & Stories. 1997. pap. text 13.95 (*0-673-36321-X*) Addson-Wesley Educ.

Bartch, Marian R., jt. auth. see Mallett, Jerry J.

Barteau, Harry C. Historical Dictionary of Luxembourg. LC 95-26325. (European Historical Dictionaries Ser.: No. 14). 392p. 1996. 56.00 (*0-8108-3106-6*) Scarecrow.

Bartecchi, Carl E. Emergency Cardiac Maneuvers: A Rescuer's Handbook. 2nd ed. 1990. pap. 7.95 (*0-929240-15-4*) EMIS.

Bartecchi, Carl E. & Schrier, Robert W. The Science & Art of Living a Longer & Healthier Life. LC 97-214604. (Illus.). 207p. (Orig.). 1997. pap. 14.95 (*0-929240-80-4*) EMIS.

— The Science & Art of Living a Longer & Healthier Life: Charting a Course for the New Millennium. 2nd rev. ed. LC 99-58003. (Illus.). 271p. 2000. pap. 14.95 (*0-917634-04-7*) EMIS.

Barteck, Lynn & Mullin, Karen, eds. Enduring Issues in Sociology. (Enduring Issues Ser.). 312p. (C). 1995. pap. text 17.45 (*1-56510-257-6*, 2576); lib. bdg. 27.45 (*1-56510-258-4*, 2584) Greenhaven.

***Bartecki, Adam & Burgess, John.** The Colour of Metal Compounds. (Illus.). 209p. 2000. 85.00 (*90-5699-250-3*, G & B Science) Gordon & Breach.

***Barteczko, K. J. & Jacob, M. I.** The Testicular Descent in Human: Origin, Development & Fate of the Gubernaculum Hunteri, Processus Vaginalis Peritonei & Gonadal Ligaments. LC 00-38801. (Advances in Anatomy, Embryology & Cell Biology Ser.: Vol. 156). (Illus.). vi, 90p. 2000. pap. 65.00 (*3-540-67315-6*) Spr-Verlag.

Bartee. Architect Logid Design. 1991. student ed. 27.50 (*0-07-003919-4*) McGraw.

Bartee, Alice F. & Bartee, Wayne C. Litigating Morality: American Legal Thought & Its English Roots. LC 91-27816. 168p. 1992. 55.00 (*0-275-94127-2*, C4127, Praeger Pubs) Greenwood.

Bartee, Edwin M. America's Mount Olympus: What's Really Gone Wrong in Corporate America & How Its Shareholders Can Fix It. (Illus.). 256p. (Orig.). 1993. pap. 16.00 (*0-9635771-0-7*) Henderson Grp.

Bartee, Thomas C. Computer Architecture & Logic Design. 640p. (C). 1990. text 69.00 (*0-07-003909-7*) McGraw.

***Bartee, Wayne C.** A Time to Speak Out: The Leipzig Citizen Protests & the Fall of East Germany. LC 00-38560. 2000. write for info. (*0-275-96982-7*) Greenwood.

Bartee, Wayne C., jt. auth. see Bartee, Alice F.

Bartek, Ann S. I Want to Play Tennis. large type ed. LC 96-94780. (Illus.). 24p. (Orig.). (J). (ps-3). 1996. pap. 4.99 (*0-9654655-0-0*) Jaad Pub.

Bartek, Marian. Selective Epitaxial Growth for Smart Silicon Sensor Applications. (Illus.). x, 147p. (Orig.). 1995. pap. 59.50 (*90-407-1178-X*, Pub. by Delft U Pr) Coronet Bks.

Bartekt. Industrial Electronics. 64p. 1997. pap. text 14.95 (*0-7668-0021-0*) Delmar.

Bartel. Metro Daily News. (C). 1994. pap. text, teacher ed. 9.27 (*0-13-043852-9*) P-H.

Bartel, An, ed. see Ramsey, Mason L.

***Bartel, Barry C.** Let's Talk: Communication Skills & Conflict Transformation. 80p. 1999. pap. 8.95 (*0-87303-340-X*) Faith & Life.

Bartel, Carl R. Instructional Analysis & Materials Development. 232p. 1976. pap. 32.96 (*0-8269-4273-3*) Am Technical.

Bartel, Constance. A Woman Like That. large type ed. 624p. (Orig.). 1987. 27.99 (*0-7089-8426-6*) Ulverscroft.

Bartel, Dietrich. Musica Poetica: Musical-Rhetorical Figures in German Baroque Music. LC 97-2450. (Illus.). xv, 471p. 1997. text 60.00 (*0-8032-1276-3*) U of Nebr Pr.

Bartel, Donald L., ed. see American Society of Mechanical Engineers Staff.

Bartel, Janice R. & Belt, Sage C. A Guide to Botanical Resources of Southern California. (Illus.). 88p. 1977. 4.00 (*0-938644-13-0*) Nat Hist Mus.

Bartel, Joan. The Metropolitan Daily News: Understanding American Newspapers. 272p. 1993. pap. text 26.33 (*0-13-043258-X*) P-H.

***Bartel, Mimi.** Oh, No! Not Another Ruin: Wickedly Funny Travel Tales of an American Adventuress. LC 99-75764. (Illus.). 360p. 2000. pap. 16.95 (*0-9671636-1-7*, Pub. by Floating Gallery) ACCESS Pubs Network.

Bartel, Nettie R., jt. auth. see Hammill, Donald D.

Bartel, Nettie R., jt. auth. see Kendall, Philip C.

Bartel, Neva A. A Celebration of Progress: A History of Kellogg Community College. 86p. 1992. pap. write for info. (*0-318-69525-1*) Kellogg Comm Coll.

Bartel, Paul L. & Fields, Stanley, eds. The Yeast Two-Hybrid System. LC 96-39040. (Advances in Molecular Biology Ser.). (Illus.). 360p. 1997. pap. text 49.95 (*0-19-510938-4*) OUP.

Bartel, Pauline. Amazing Animal Actors. LC 97-25460. (Illus.). 184p. (Orig.). 1997. pap. 16.95 (*0-87833-974-4*) Taylor Pub.

— Complete Gone with the Wind Trivia Book. LC 89-30442. 208p. 1989. pap. 9.95 (*0-87833-619-2*) Taylor Pub.

— Reel Elvis! The Ultimate Trivia Guide to the King's Movies. LC 93-48746. 192p. 1994. pap. 10.95 (*0-87833-852-7*) Taylor Pub.

***Bartel, Pauline.** Spellcasters: Witches & Witchcraft in History, Folklore, & Popular Culture. 2000. 24.95 (*0-87833-183-2*) Taylor Pub.

Bartel, Rainer. Excel 5.0 for Beginners. 1994. pap. 22.95 incl. disk (*1-55755-257-6*) Abacus MI.

Bartel, Richard D. The Challenge of Economics: Readings from Challenge, the Magazine of Economic Affairs. LC 83-27108. 352p. 1984. reprint ed. pap. 109.20 (*0-8357-2585-5*, 204029000015) Bks Demand.

Bartela, Robert. Credit Management. LC 67-11256. (Illus.). 496p. reprint ed. pap. 153.80 (*0-608-10971-1*, 201239100081) Bks Demand.

Bartelds, M., jt. auth. see Wijnolst, N.

***Bartelik, Marek.** To Invent a Garden: The Life & Art of Adja Yunkers. LC 99-54000. (Illus.). 140p. 2000. 45.00 (*1-55595-185-6*) Hudson Hills.

Bartell, jt. auth. see Nash.

Bartell, Angela B., et al, eds. Wisconsin Civil Litigation Forms Manual. LC 95-44419. 600p. 1995. ring bd. 179.00 incl. disk (*0-945574-77-0*) State Bar WI.

Bartell, D. P., jt. auth. see Neice, K. C.

Bartell, Dick & Macht, Norman. Rowdy Richard: A Firsthand Account of the National League Baseball Wars of the 1930's & the Men Who Fought Them. 2nd ed. (Illus.). 388p. 1987. 18.95 (*0-938190-97-0*) North Atlantic.

Bartell, Ernest & Payne, Leigh A., eds. Business & Democracy in Latin America. (Latin American Ser.). 292p. (C). 1995. pap. 19.95 (*0-8229-5537-7*); text 49.95 (*0-8229-3853-7*) U of Pittsburgh Pr.

***Bartell, Ernest J. & O'Donnell, Alejandro, eds.** The Child in Latin America: Health, Development, & Rights. (From the Helen Kellogg Institute of International Studies). 371p. 2000. 50.00 (*0-268-02257-7*, Pub. by U of Notre Dame Pr) Chicago Distribution Ctr.

Bartell, H. Robert & Simpson, Elizabeth T. Pension Funds of Multiemployer Industrial Groups, Unions, & Nonprofit Organizations. (Occasional Papers: No. 105). 64p. 1968. reprint ed. 20.00 (*0-87014-491-X*) Natl Bur Econ Res.

Bartell, Joyce J., ed. see Center for Study of the American Experience Staff.

Bartell, Karen H. American Business English. LC 95-61196. 248p. (Orig.). (C). 1995. pap. text 16.95 (*0-472-06608-0*, 06608) U of Mich Pr.

— Sovereignty of the Dragons LC 99-13671. (Five Star Original Romance Ser.). 1999. 24.95 (*0-7862-1887-8*, Five Star MI) Mac Lib Ref.

Bartell, Linda L. Alyssa. (Avon Romance Ser.). 368p. 1987. pap. 3.95 (*0-380-75157-7*, Avon Bks) Morrow Avon.

— Brittany. 384p. 1989. pap. 3.95 (*0-380-75545-9*, Avon Bks) Morrow Avon.

— Marisa. 384p. (Orig.). 1988. pap. 3.95 (*0-380-75380-4*, Avon Bks) Morrow Avon.

— Tender Crusader. 384p. 1997. mass mkt. 4.99 (*0-8217-5751-2*, Zebra Kensgtn) Kensgtn Pub Corp.

— Tender Scoundrel. 384p. 1996. mass mkt. 4.99 (*0-8217-5192-1*, Zebra Kensgtn) Kensgtn Pub Corp.

Bartell, Steven M. Ecological Risk Estimation. (Illus.). 272p. 1992. lib. bdg. 99.95 (*0-87371-163-7*, L163) Lewis Pubs.

Bartello, Jack. We the People Are the Messiah. 236p. 1999. pap. 14.95 (*0-9668252-1-7*, Pub. by Project Enlightmnt) ACCESS Pubs Network.

Bartelme, Elizabeth, jt. ed. see Rosenbaum, Herbert D.

***Bartelme, Nicole & Bingel, Christina.** 2000 TriBeCa Guide. 280p. 1999. spiral bd. 15.00 (*1-886016-50-X*, TriBeCa) SoHo Prtnship.

Bartelme, Tony & Hicks, Brian. Into the Wind: Around Alone - The Story of the World's Longest Race. Mullins, Steve, ed. LC 99-71145. (Illus.). 136p. 1999. 35.85 (*0-934870-94-2*) Evening Post.

***Bartelme, Tony & Hicks, Brian.** Into the Wind: Around Alone - The Story of the World's Longest Race. Mullins, Steve, ed. LC 99-71145. (Illus.). 136p. 1999. 35.85 (*1-929647-00-X*) Evening Post.

Bartelmus, Peter, jt. ed. see Uno, Kimio.

Bartelmus, Peter L. Environment, Growth & Development: The Concepts & Strategies of Sustainability. LC 93-34234. (Illus.). 192p. (C). 1994. pap. 22.99 (*0-415-08484-9*) Routledge.

Bartelmus, Rudiger, et al, eds. Konsequente Traditionsgeschichte: Festschrift fur Klaus Baltzer Zum 65. Geburtstag. (Orbis Biblicus et Orientalis Ser.: Vol. 126). (GER.). 401p. 1993. text 75.75 (*3-7278-0871-3*, Pub. by Presses Univ Fribourg) Eisenbrauns.

Bartels, A. Farbatlas Mediterrane Pflanzen (Color Atlas of Mediterranean Plants) (GER., Illus.). 400p. 1997. 24.00 (*3-8001-3488-8*, Pub. by Eugen Ulmer) Balogh.

— Farbatlas Tropenpflanzen (Color Atlas of Tropical Plants) 3rd rev. ed. (GER., Illus.). 384p. 1993. 26.00 (*3-8001-3468-3*, Pub. by Eugen Ulmer) Balogh.

— Gartengehoelze.Baeume und Straeucher fuer Mitteleuropaeischer und Mediterrane Gaerten (Garden Trees & Shrubs of Central European & Mediterranean Gardens) 3rd rev. ed. (GAA & GER., Illus.). 606p. 1991. 194.00 (*3-8001-6399-3*, Pub. by Eugen Ulmer) Balogh.

— Das Grosse Buch der Ziergehoelze (The Big Book of Ornamental Trees) (GER., Illus.). 320p. 1997. 40.00 (*3-8001-6593-7*, Pub. by Eugen Ulmer) Balogh.

Bartels, A., jt. auth. see Roloff, A.

Bartels, Alice. The Beast. (Illus.). 32p. (J). (ps-2). 1990. 14.95 (*1-55037-101-0*, Pub. by Annick); pap. 5.95 (*1-55037-102-9*, Pub. by Annick) Firefly Bks Ltd.

— The Grandmother Doll. (Illus.). 24p. (J). (ps-2). 1993. pap. 4.95 (*1-55037-336-6*, Pub. by Annick) Firefly Bks Ltd.

Bartels, Alice L., jt. auth. see Bartels, Dennis A.

Bartels, C. Bruce. Advertising for the Non-Advertising Executive. (Illus.). 77p. (Orig.). 1993. pap. text 19.00 (*0-9651843-9-0*) Good Thinking.

Bartels, Carolyn M. The Civil War in Missouri Day by Day, 1861-1865. (Illus.). 180p. text 32.95 (*0-9636780-2-7*) Two Trails Pubg.

— The Civil War in Missouri Day by Day, 1861-1865. (Illus.). 1992. spiral bd. 19.50 (*0-9636780-0-0*) Two Trails Pubg.

— The Civil War in Missouri Day by Day, 1861-1865. (Illus.). 1994. per. 19.50 (*0-9636780-1-9*) Two Trails Pubg.

— Civil War Stories of Missouri. 300p. 1995. pap. 14.95 (*0-9636780-3-5*) Two Trails Pubg.

— MSG Missouri State Guard. 1994. pap. 32.95 (*0-9636780-5-1*); text 42.95 (*0-9636780-4-3*) Two Trails Pubg.

Bartels, Christine. The Intonation of English Statements & Questions: A Compositional Interpretation. rev. ed. LC 99-21401. (Outstanding Dissertations in Linguistics Ser.). 320p. 1999. 69.00 (*0-8153-3356-0*) Garland.

Bartels, Christoph, et al. The Fossils of the Hunsruck Slate: Marine Life in the Devonian. LC 97-11979. (Paleobiology Ser.: No. 3). (Illus.). 324p. (C). 1998. text 85.00 (*0-521-44190-0*) Cambridge U Pr.

Bartels, Cornelius P. & Ketellapper, Ronald H. Exploratory & Explanatory Statistical Analysis of Spatial Data. 1979. lib. bdg. 133.00 (*0-89838-004-9*) Kluwer Academic.

Bartels, Dennis A. & Bartels, Alice L. When the North Was Red: Aboriginal Education in Soviet Siberia. (McGill-Queen's Native & Northern Ser.: No. 11). (Illus.). 160p. 1995. 55.00 (*0-7735-1336-1*, LA1391, Pub. by McG-Queens Univ Pr) CUP Services.

Bartels, Diane R. Sharpie: The Life Story of Evelyn Sharp Nebraska's Aviatrix. Dageforde, Linda J., ed. LC 96-85189. 344p. (Orig.). 1996. pap. 14.95 (*1-886225-16-8*, 2000) Bartels Pubg.

Bartels, Dianne M., et al, eds. Beyond Baby M: Ethical Issues in New Reproductive Techniques. LC 89-49394. (Contemporary Issues in Biomedicine, Ethics, & Society Ser.). 296p. 1990. 49.50 (*0-89603-166-7*) Humana.

— Prescribing Our Future: Ethical Challenges in Genetic Counseling. LC 92-21469. 208p. 1993. pap. text 23.95 (*0-202-30453-1*); lib. bdg. 47.95 (*0-202-30452-3*) Aldine de Gruyter.

Bartels, Eckhart. German Trucks & Cars in WW II Vol. III: Opelat War. LC 91-60856. (Illus.). 48p. 1991. pap. 9.95 (*0-88740-309-3*) Schiffer.

— Opel Military Vehicles, 1906-1956. Force, Edward, tr. from GER. LC 97-65444. 176p. 1997. 29.95 (*0-7643-0267-1*) Schiffer.

Bartels, Emily C. Spectacles of Strangeness: Imperialism, Alienation, & Marlowe. LC 92-45865. 240p. (C). 1993. text 32.50 (*0-8122-3193-7*) U of Pa Pr.

Bartels, Emily Carroll, ed. Critical Essays on Christopher Marlowe. LC 96-38626. 1997. 49.00 (*0-7838-0017-7*, G K Hall & Co) Mac Lib Ref.

Bartels, Francis L. The Roots of Ghana Methodism. LC 64-21525. 382p. reprint ed. pap. 108.90 (*0-608-30391-7*, 2050799) Bks Demand.

Bartels, J. Instructions to Jurors on Identification Testimony: U. S. vs. Busic. (Monographs: No. CR-46). 1976. 3.00 (*1-55524-047-X*) Ctr Respon Psych.

Bartels, Joanie. Dancin' Magic. (Magic Ser.). (J). (gr. k-4). 1991. pap. 9.95 incl. audio (*1-881225-08-9*) Discov Music.

Bartels, Kay-Uwe. Katholische Soziallehre und Ordoliberale Ordnungskonzeption: Eine Ordnungspolitische Analyse der Enzyklika Centesimus Annus (Papst Johannes Paul II, Mai 1991) (Europaische Hochschulschriften: Reihe 5: Bd. 2129). (GER.). XII, 161p. 1997. 42.95 (*3-631-31597-X*) P Lang Pubng.

Bartels, Kerstin. Musik in Deutschen Texten des Mittelalters. (Europaische Hochschulschriften Ser.: Reihe 1, Bd. 1601). (GER.). 518p. 1996. 82.95 (*3-631-31106-0*) P Lang Pubng.

Bartels, Larry M. Presidential Primaries & the Dynamics of Public Choice. LC 87-38187. (Illus.). 397p. reprint ed. pap. 123.10 (*0-608-06384-3*, 206674500008) Bks Demand.

***Bartels, Larry M. & Vavreck, Lynn, eds.** Campaign Reform: Insights & Evidence. (Illus.). 320p. (C). 2000. text 69.50 (*0-472-09731-8*, 09731); pap. text 25.95 (*0-472-06731-1*, 06731) U of Mich Pr.

Bartels, M. Contractual Adaptation & Conflict Resolution. 188p. 1985. 116.00 (*90-6544-186-7*) Kluwer Academic.

Bartels, Martin. A Native's Guide to Chicago's Northwest Suburbs. LC 99-62508. (Illus.). 1999. pap. 12.95 (*1-893121-00-3*) Lake Claremont.

— Selbstbewusstsein und Unbewusstes: Studien Zu Freud und Heidegger. (Quellen und Studien zur Philosophie: Vol. 10). (C). 1976. 92.30 (*3-11-005778-6*) De Gruyter.

Bartels, Michael M. Missouri Pacific River & Prairie Rails: The MoPac in Nebraska. (Illus.). 204p. 1997. 56.95 (*0-942035-39-9*) South Platte.

***Bartels, Michael M.** Rock Island Town: Fairbury, Nebraska - Western Division. (Illus.). 80p. 1999. pap. 18.95 (*0-942035-52-6*) South Platte.

Bartels, Mike, et al. The Chicago & North Western Cowboy Line: A History of the Longest Hail-to-Trail Project in America. (Illus.). 64p. 1998. pap. 18.95 (*0-942035-44-5*) South Platte.

Bartels, Peter, jt. auth. see Marchevsky, Alberto.

Bartels, R., tr. see Stoer, J. & Bulirsch, R.

Bartels-Rabb, Lisa M., jt. auth. see Van Gulden, Holly.

Bartels, Richard H., et al. An Introduction to Splines for Use in Computer Graphics & Geometric Modeling. LC 86-27650. (Illus.). 476p. 1998. text 59.95 (*0-934613-27-3*) Morgan Kaufmann.

— An Introduction to Splines for Use in Computer Graphics & Geometric Modelling. 476p. 1987. reprint ed. pap. text 48.95 (*1-55860-400-6*) Morgan Kaufmann.

Bartels, Robert. Marketing Literature. Assael, Henry, ed. LC 78-228. (Century of Marketing Ser.). 1979. lib. bdg. 47.95 (*0-405-11165-7*) Ayer.

— Marketing Theory & Metatheory. LC 72-105536. 310p. reprint ed. 96.10 (*0-8357-9035-5*, 201778900008) Bks Demand.

Bartels, Robert, ed. Comparative Marketing: Wholesaling in Fifteen Countries. LC 82-25149. (Illus.). 317p. 1983. lib. bdg. 75.00 (*0-313-23838-3*, BARC, Greenwood Pr) Greenwood.

Bartels, Sabine. Harley Davidson. 1994. 12.98 (*0-7858-0081-6*) Bk Sales Inc.

Bartels, Sabine. Jukebox. 1994. 12.98 (*0-7858-0080-8*) Bk Sales Inc.

Bartels, Sabine. Pinball. 1994. 12.98 (*0-7858-0071-9*) Bk Sales Inc.

Bartelski, Konrad & Neillands, Robin. Learn Downhill Skiing in a Weekend. 1992. 16.00 (*0-679-40952-1*) Knopf.

Bartelson, Jens. A Genealogy of Sovereignty. (Cambridge Studies in International Relations: 39). 329p. (C). 1995. text 59.95 (*0-521-47308-X*); pap. text 22.95 (*0-521-47888-X*) Cambridge U Pr.

Bartelt, Andrew H. The Book Around Immanuel: Style & Structure in Isaiah 2-12. LC 96-8275. (Biblical & Judaic Studies from the University of California, San Diego: Vol. 4). xi, 287p. 1996. text 32.50 (*1-57506-006-X*) Eisenbrauns.

Bartelt, Dana, et al. Both Sides of Peace: Israeli & Palestinian Political Posters. LC 97-66258. (Illus.). 160p. 1998. pap. 29.95 (*1-885449-04-6*) City Gallery Cntmprry Art.

Bartelt, Margaret. Diagnostic Microbiology. LC 99-32887. (Illus.). 476p. (C). 1999. pap. text, student ed. 29.95 (*0-8036-0301-0*) Davis Co.

Bartelt, Terry L. Digital Electronics: Concepts & Applications. 480p. (C). 1991. text 26.85 (*0-13-209990-X*) P-H.

— Industrial Electronics. LC 96-35775. (Electronics Technology Ser.). 608p. 1997. mass mkt. 98.95 (*0-8273-6104-1*) Delmar.

***Bartelt, Terry L.** Industrial Instrumentation & Process Control. 2nd ed. (Student Material TV). (C). 2001. pap. 68.25 (*0-7668-1974-4*) Delmar.

Barteluk, Wendy D. Library Displays on a Shoestring: 3-Dimensional Techniques for Promoting Library Services. LC 93-4813. (Illus.). 128p. 1993. 29.00 (*0-8108-2662-3*) Scarecrow.

Barten, Harvey H., jt. ed. see Bellak, Leopold.

***Barten, Peter G. J.** Contrast Sensitivity of the Human Eye & Its Effects on Image Quality. LC 99-40877. 208p. 1999. 65.00 (*0-8194-3496-5*) SPIE.

Barten, Sybil S. & Franklin, Margery B., eds. Developmental Processes Vol. I: Heinz Werner's Selected Writings, 2 vols. LC 77-92187. 562p. (Orig.). 1978. 50.00 (*0-8236-1250-3*) Intl Univs Pr.

— Developmental Processes Vol. II: Heinz Werner's Selected Writings, 2 vols. LC 77-92187. 562p. (Orig.). 1978. 50.00 (*0-8236-1251-1*) Intl Univs Pr.

Barten, Sybil S., jt. ed. see Franklin, Margery B.

Bartenev, G. M. & Lavrentev, V. V. Friction & Wear of Polymers. (Tribology Ser.: Vol. 6). xviii, 320p. 1981. 181.50 (*0-444-42000-2*) Elsevier.

Bartenieff, Irmgard & Lewis, D. Body Movement: Coping with the Environment. xiv, 290p. 1980. text 39.00 (*0-677-05500-5*) Gordon & Breach.

Bartenieff, Irmgard, et al. Four Adaptations of Effort Theory in Research & Teaching. LC 73-47570. (Illus.). viii, 72p. (C). 1970. pap. text 14.95 (*0-932582-06-0*) Dance Notation.

Bartens, Angela. Die Iberoromanisch-Basierten Kreolsprachen. vii, 345p. 1995. 61.95 (*3-631-48682-0*) P Lang Pubng.

Bartenstein, Fred & Bartenstein, Isabel. New Jersey's Revolutionary War Powder Mill. (Illus.). 194p. 1975. 5.50 (*0-614-29776-1*) M C H S.

Bartenstein, Isabel, jt. auth. see Bartenstein, Fred.

Barter. HIV & AIDS: Your Questions. 1994. pap. text 25.00 (*0-443-04752-9*, W B Saunders Co) Harcrt Hlth Sci Grp.

— Nursing Management. (Nursing Education Ser.). 1998. 24.95 (*0-8273-7853-X*) Delmar.

Barter, Alice. Theaters of the Heart & Mind. LC 97-65993. 124p. 1998. pap. 13.50 (*0-88739-124-9*) Creat Arts Bk.

Barter, Catherine. Alone among the Zulus: The Narrative of a Journey Through the Zulu Country. 1995. pap. 25.50 (*0-86980-914-8*, Pub. by Univ Natal Pr) Intl Spec Bk.

***Barter, James.** Alcatraz. LC 99-30280. (Building History Ser.). (Illus.). 128p. (YA). (gr. 6-9). 2000. lib. bdg. 23.70 (*1-56006-596-6*) Lucent Bks.

Barter, James. Artists of the Renaissance. LC 98-29497. (History Makers Ser.). (Illus.). 144p. (YA). (gr. 4-12). 1998. lib. bdg. 23.70 (*1-56006-439-0*) Lucent Bks.

— The Palace of Versailles. LC 98-15262. (Building History Ser.). (YA). (gr. 7 up). 1998. 23.70 (*1-56006-433-1*) Lucent Bks.

Barter, Judith A. American Drawings & Watercolors from the Wadsworth Atheneum. LC 87-72426. (Illus.). 96p. 1988. pap. 19.95 (*0-917418-85-9*) Am Fed Arts.

— American Drawings & Watercolors from the Wadsworth Atheneum. LC 87-72426. (Illus.). 96p. 1988. 35.00 (*0-933920-99-7*) Hudson Hills.

Barter, Judith A., et al, eds. Mary Cassatt: Modern Woman. LC 98-7306. (Illus.). 376p. 1998. 65.00 (*0-8109-4089-2*, Pub. by Abrams) Time Warner.

Barter, Judith A. & Mochon, Anne. Porkopolis: Sue Coe's Jungle. (Illus.). 40p. (Orig.). 1993. pap. text 5.00 (*0-914337-16-5*) Mead Art Mus.

Barter, Judith A. & Trapp, Frank A. Nineteenth Century American Art. (Mead Art Museum Monographs: Vol. 5). (Illus.). 18p. 1985. pap. 3.00 (*0-914337-04-1*) Mead Art Mus.

Barter, Judith A., et al. American Arts in the Art Institute of Chicago: From Colonial Times to World War I. (Illus.). 356p. 1998. 75.00 (*0-86559-172-5*) Art Inst Chi.

— Decorative Arts at Amherst College. Trapp, Frank A., ed. (Mead Art Museum Monographs: Vol. 3). 27p. 1982. pap. 3.00 (*0-914337-03-3*) Mead Art Mus.

— French Art. (Mead Art Museum Monographs: Vols. 8 & 9). (Illus.). 64p. 1987. pap. 5.00 (*0-914337-10-6*) Mead Art Mus.

— Mary Cassatt: Modern Woman. LC 98-7306. (Illus.). 376p. 1998. pap. 29.95 (*0-86559-167-9*) Art Inst Chi.

Barter, Karin, tr. see Ogundijo, Bayo, ed.

***Barter, Philip J. & Rye, Kerry-Anne, eds.** Plasma Lipids & Their Role in Disease. (Advances in Vascular Biology Ser.: Vol. 5). 368p. 1999. text 120.00 (*90-5702-466-7*, Harwood Acad Pubs) Gordon & Breach.

Barter Publishing Staff. Barter Referral Directory: Black Business Edition. 300p. 1997. ring bd. 29.95 (*0-911617-62-0*) Prosperity & Profits.

— Barter Telemarketing Script Presentations. 78p. (Orig.). 1992. ring bd. 29.95 (*0-911617-42-6*) Prosperity & Profits.

— Recipe Greetings for Barter. 53p. 1989. ring bd. 25.95 (*0-911617-87-6*) Prosperity & Profits.

— Recycling Commodity Exchange Encyclopaedia: World Mapping Edition. rev. ed. 102p. 1991. ring bd. 95.00 (*0-911617-77-9*) Prosperity & Profits.

Barter Publishing Staff, ed. Barter Education, Schools, Workshops, Centers, Etc. A How to Find or Locate Workbook. 80p. 1985. ring bd. 29.95 (*0-911617-10-8*) Prosperity & Profits.

— Barter Referral Directory: Craftperson's Edition. rev. ed. 300p. 1997. ring bd. 29.95 (*0-911617-60-4*) Prosperity & Profits.

— Barter Referral Directory: International Business Edition. rev. ed. 300p. 1997. ring bd. 39.95 (*0-911617-61-2*) Prosperity & Profits.

— Barter Referral Directory: Manufacturing Edition. rev. ed. 300p. 1997. ring bd. 29.95 (*0-911617-59-0*) Prosperity & Profits.

— Barter Referral Directory: Small Business Edition. rev. ed. 300p. 1997. 29.95 (*0-911617-64-7*) Prosperity & Profits.

— Barter Referral Directory: Vacation Time Exchanges, Share-a-Transportation Edition. rev. ed. 300p. 1997. ring bd. 29.95 (*0-911617-58-2*) Prosperity & Profits.

— Barter Referral Directory: Women's Edition. rev. ed. 300p. 1997. ring bd. 29.95 (*0-911617-63-9*) Prosperity & Profits.

— Popcorn Commodity Exchange Encyclopaedia. 1984. ring bd. 49.95 (*0-911617-06-X*) Prosperity & Profits.

Barter, Stephen L. Barter: Real Estate Finance. 2nd ed. 1997. write for info. (*0-406-02481-2*, BREF2, MICHIE) LEXIS Pub.

Barter, Tanya, et al. Bentwood. LC 84-60339. (Illus.). 48p. (Orig.). 1984. pap. 10.00 (*0-911517-02-2*) Mus of Art RI.

— Ceramics & Glass at the Essex Institute. LC 85-71260. (E.I. Museum Booklet Ser.). (Illus.). 64p. 1985. pap. 5.95 (*0-88389-088-7*, PEMP197, Essx Institute) Peabody Essex Mus.

Barter, V. C. & Brooks, M., eds. AI, 1988. (Lecture Notes in Computer Science Ser.: Vol. 406). viii, 463p. 1990. 49.95 (*0-387-52062-7*) Spr-Verlag.

Barterian, jt. auth. see Evans.

Barteve, Reine. Nowhere & a Man with Women. Alexander, Lorraine et al, trs. from FRE. 90p. (Orig.). (C). 1987. pap. text 8.95 (*0-913745-27-8*) Ubu Repertory.

Bartfai, Tamas & Ottoson, David, eds. Neuro-Immunology of Fever. LC 92-48954. (Wenner-Gren International Ser.). 300p. 1992. 178.50 (*0-08-042001-X*, Pergamon Pr) Elsevier.

Bartfay, S. A. Wild Things. 24p. (Orig.). 1997. 4.00 (*0-9656161-1-8*) Quale Pr.

Bartfeld, Fernande, ed. see De Vigny, Alfred.

Bartfeld, Martha. Magic Mandala Coloring Book: Sacred Geometry for Awakening & Healing. (Illus.). 216p. 1998. spiral bd. 19.95 (*0-9662285-0-2*) Mandalart Creations.

***Bartfeld, Martha.** Mandala Designs. 2000. pap. 2.95 (*0-486-41034-X*) Dover.

Bartges, Dan. Spectator Sports Made Simple: How to Watch, Understand & Enjoy Baseball, Football & Basketball. LC 98-47087. (Illus.). 320p. 1999. pap. 12.95 (*1-57028-204-8*, 82048H, Mstrs Pr) NTC Contemp Pub Co.

Barth. Feminine & Masculine Gender Identity: A Special Issue of Psychoanalytic Inquiry, Vol. 15, No. 1, 1995. 1995. pap. 19.95 (*0-88163-996-6*) L Erlbaum Assocs.

— Harbrace College Workbook. 12th ed. (C). 1994. pap. text 29.00 (*0-15-501465-X*, Pub. by Harcourt Coll Pubs) Harcourt.

— Lewis & Clark Expedition, Vol. 1. 240p. 1998. pap. text 11.95 (*0-312-11118-5*) St Martin.

— Neutral Zone Campaign. 1999. per. 15.00 (*0-671-04002-2*) PB.

Barth, A. The Religions of India. 332p. 1989. 25.00 (*0-7855-1200-4*) St Mut.

— The Religions of India. 1990. reprint ed. 11.00 (*81-85418-02-0*, Pub. by Low Price) S Asia.

— The Religions of India. 6th ed. Wood, J., tr. from FRE. 309p. 1990. reprint ed. 24.95 (*0-940500-64-7*) Asia Bk Corp.

Barth, A., jt. auth. see Schowen, R. L.

Barth, A. D. & Oko, R. J. Abnormal Morphology of Bovine Spermatozoa. LC 89-1770. (Illus.). 294p. (C). 1989. text 74.95 (*0-8138-0112-5*) Iowa St U Pr.

Barth, Alan. Government by Investigation. LC 71-122068. 231p. 1973. reprint ed. 35.00 (*0-678-03150-9*) Kelley.

— The Price of Liberty. LC 74-176486. (Civil Liberties in American History Ser.). 1972. reprint ed. lib. bdg. 29.50 (*0-306-70416-1*) Da Capo.

Barth, Andreas, et al, eds. Digital Libraries in Computer Science: The MeDoc Approach, Vol. 139. LC 98-18913. (Lecture Notes in Computer Science Ser.: Vol. 1392). viii, 239p. 1998. pap. 43.00 (*3-540-64493-8*) Spr-Verlag.

***Barth, Bob.** Sea Dwellers: The Humor, Drama & Tragedy of the U. S. Navy Sealab Programs. LC 99-32021. (Illus.). 184p. 1999. pap. 16.95 (*0-9653359-3-3*) Doyle Pub.

Barth, C. A. & Schlimme, E., eds. Milk Proteins. 240p. 1989. 54.00 (*0-387-91349-1*) Spr-Verlag.

Barth, Claire, ed. see Akresh, Murray S., et al.

Barth, Claire, ed. see Atkinson, John H., et al.

Barth, Claire, ed. see Barrack, John B. & Edwards, James D.

Barth, Claire, ed. see Blochet, Edward.

Barth, Claire, ed. see Boer, Germain.

Barth, Claire, ed. see Brown, Carol E. & Philips, Mary E.

Barth, Claire, ed. see Dhavale, Dileep.

Barth, Claire, ed. see Enthoven, Adolf, et al.

Barth, Claire, ed. see Epstein, Marc.

Barth, Claire, ed. see Hales, H. Lee & Cole, Raymond C., Jr.

Barth, Claire, ed. see Harr, David J. & Godfrey, James T.

Barth, Claire, ed. see Jenson, Richard L., et al.

Barth, Claire, ed. see Kovalev, Valery V., et al.

Barth, Claire, ed. see Landekich, Stephen.

Barth, Claire, ed. see Madden, Donald L. & Holmes, James R.

Barth, Claire, ed. see Martinson, Otto B.

Barth, Claire, ed. see Rittenberg, Larry & Nair, R. D.

Barth, Claire, jt. ed. see Romano, Patrick L.

Barth, Claire, ed. see Sadhwani, Arjan T. & Tyson, Thomas.

Barth, Claire, ed. see Sandretto, Michael J.

Barth, Claire, ed. see Schiff, Michael & Schiff, Jonathan B.

Barth, Claire, ed. see Schiff, Michael, et al.

Barth, Claire, ed. see Steedle, Lamont F.

Barth, Claire, ed. see Vangermeersch, Richard.

Barth, Clarence. History of the Twentieth Aero Squadron. 8th ed. (Great War Ser.: No. 8). (Illus.). 116p. 1990. reprint ed. 29.95 (*0-89839-153-9*) Battery Pr.

Barth, Diana, ed. see International Conference London Staff.

Barth, Dominic, tr. see Bassede, Francine.

Barth, Dominic, tr. see Davenier, Christine.

Barth, Dominic, tr. see Verboven, Agnes.

Barth, Dorlous. My Appalachian Heritage: Yes, I'm a Hillbilly. LC 96-69807. 1996. pap. 12.95 (*1-881908-16-X*) PanPress.

Barth, E. M. The Logic of the Articles in Traditional Philosophy: A Contribution to the Study of Conceptual Structures. Potts, P., tr. from DUT. LC 73-94452. (Synthese Historical Library: No. 10).Tr. of De Logica Van De Lidwoorden in De Traditionele Filosophy. 560p. 1974. lib. bdg. 211.50 (*90-277-0350-7*) Kluwer Academic.

— The Logic of the Articles in Traditional Philosophy: A Contribution to the Study of Conceptual Structures.

An Asterisk (*) at the beginning of an entry indicates that the title is appearing for the first time.

B

— The Theology of Schleiermacher. 1996. 49.95 (*0-567-09339-5*) Bks Intl VA.

— The Theology of Schleiermacher: Lectures at Gottingen, Winter Semester of 1923-24. Ritschl, Dietrich, ed. Bromiley, Geoffrey W., tr. LC 82-2330. 307p. reprint ed. pap. 95.20 (*0-8357-4353-5*, 203718000007) Bks Demand.

— Witness to the Word: A Commentary on First John: Lectures at Munster in 1925 & at Bonn in 1933. Furst, Walther, ed. Bromiley, Geoffrey W., tr. LC 86-4391. 173p. reprint ed. pap. 53.70 (*0-8357-4354-3*, 203718100007) Bks Demand.

— Wolfgang Amadeus Mozart. 48p. 1986. reprint ed. pap. 5.00 (*0-8028-0007-6*) Eerdmans.

— The Word of God & the Word of Man. Horton, Douglas, tr. 1958. 19.00 (*0-8446-1599-4*) Peter Smith.

***Barth, Kelly L.** Birds of Prey. LC 99-38326. (Overview Ser.). (Illus.). 128p. (YA). (gr. 6-9). 2000. lib. bdg. 23.70 (*1-56006-493-5*) Lucent Bks.

Barth, Lewis M. An Analysis of Vatican 30. LC 72-8353. (Monographs of the Hebrew Union College: Vol. 1). 360p. 1973. reprint ed. pap. 111.60 (*0-608-02087-7*, 206274000004) Bks Demand.

Barth, Lewis M., ed. Berit Mila in the Reform Context. 246p. 1990. 30.00 (*0-8216-5082-3*, 381631) UAHC.

Barth, Linda. The Distinctive Book of Redneck Baby Names. LC 96-54005. 96p. (Orig.). 1997. pap. 6.95 (*0-8362-2578-3*) Andrews & McMeel.

Barth, M. A. Bulletin of Religion, ISPP Vol. 1, No. 4. 60p. 1974. reprint ed. 2.00 (*0-88065-050-8*) Scholarly Pubns.

Barth, Margaret. Freeport Journal: History of a Decade, 1876-1886. 228p. 1987. per. 16.95 (*0-933227-61-2*, 198) Closson Pr.

Barth, Margaret M., jt. ed. see Murphy, William E.

Barth, Marge, jt. auth. see Barth, Jeff.

Barth, Marge, ed. see Barth, Jeff.

***Barth, Markus.** The Letter to Philemon: A New Translation with Notes & Commentary. LC 00-28776. (Critical Commentary Ser.). 2000. write for info. (*0-8028-3829-4*) Eerdmans.

Barth, Markus. The People of God. (JSNT Supplement Ser.: No. 5). 103p. 1983. pap. 12.25 (*0-905774-55-8*, Pub. by Sheffield Acad) CUP Services.

— The People of God. (JSNT Supplement Ser.: No. 5). 103p. 1983. 28.50 (*0-905774-54-X*, Pub. by Sheffield Acad) CUP Services.

— Rediscovering the Lord's Supper: Communion with Israel, with Christ & among the Guests. LC 87-46294. 117p. reprint ed. pap. 36.30 (*0-7837-2635-X*, 204298500006) Bks Demand.

Barth, Markus & Blanke, Helmut. Colossians: A New Translation with Introduction & Commentary. Beck, Astrid B., tr. LC 93-35736. (Anchor Bible Ser.: Vol. 34B). 504p. 1995. 39.95 (*0-385-11068-5*) Doubleday.

Barth, Melissa E., et al. Reading for Difference: Texts on Gender, Race & Class. LC 92-71247. 608p. (Orig.). (C). 1993. pap. text 37.00 (*0-15-500216-3*, Pub. by Harcourt Coll Pubs); teacher ed. write for info. (*0-15-500151-5*) Harcourt Coll Pubs.

Barth, Michael, ed. Research Quarterly. rev. ed. (Illus.). 66p. (Orig.). 1996. pap. 100.00 (*0-89382-387-2*) Nat Assn Insurance.

— Research Quarterly, Vol. II, No. 3. rev. ed. 58p. (Orig.). (C). 1996. pap. 100.00 (*0-89382-418-6*, RSH-2S) Nat Assn Insurance.

— Research Quarterly, April 1996. rev. ed. 62p. (Orig.). (C). 1996. pap. write for info. (*0-89382-406-2*) Nat Assn Insurance.

Barth, Michael C. & Titus, James G. Greenhouse Effect & Sea Level Rise. 384p. (C). 1984. text 44.95 (*0-442-20991-6*) Chapman & Hall.

Barth, Mike, ed. Research Quarterly, Vol. II, Issue 4. 60p. (Orig.). (C). 1997. pap. 100.00 (*0-89382-440-2*, RSH-ZS) Nat Assn Insurance.

— Research Quarterly, Vol. III, Issue 1. 52p. (Orig.). (C). 1997. pap. 50.00 (*0-89382-459-3*, RSH-ZS) Nat Assn Insurance.

— Research Quarterly, Vol. III, Issue 2. 50p. (Orig.). (C). 1997. pap. 50.00 (*0-89382-460-7*, RSH-ZS) Nat Assn Insurance.

Barth, Miles. Ruth Orkin: A Retrospective. 40p. (Orig.). 1995. pap. 15.00 (*0-9646247-0-2*) Est R Orkin.

Barth, Miles. Weegee's World. LC 97-11990. (Illus.). 256p. 1997. 75.00 (*0-8212-2375-5*, Pub. by Bulfinch Pr) Little.

***Barth, Miles.** Weegee's World. (Illus.). 256p. 2000. pap. 29.95 (*0-8212-2649-5*, Pub. by Bulfinch Pr) Little.

***Barth, Miles & Merritt, Ray, eds.** A Thousand Hounds. 2000. 29.99 (*3-8228-6223-1*) Taschen Amer.

Barth, Paul. Die Philosophie der Geschichte Als Soziologie, Band 1. (GER.). xi, 870p. 1971. reprint ed. write for info. (*3-487-04069-7*) G Olms Pubs.

Barth, Peter. Logic-Based O-1 Constraint Programming. (Operations Research - Computer Science Interface Ser.: Vol. 5). 272p. (C). 1995. lib. bdg. 119.50 (*0-7923-9663-4*) Kluwer Academic.

— Worker's Compensation in Florida: Administrative Inventory. LC 99-31174. 145p. 1999. 35.00 (*0-935149-80-5*, WC-99-3) Workers Comp Res Inst.

Barth, Peter, jt. auth. see Niss, Michael.

Barth, Peter, jt. auth. see Steiniger, Birte.

Barth, Peter F. Piercing the Autumn Sky: A Guide to Discovering the Natural Freedom of Mind. LC 93-77066. 128p. (Orig.). 1993. pap. 9.95 (*0-9635796-3-0*) Lame Turtle.

Barth, Peter S. The Tragedy of Black Lung: Federal Compensation for Occupational Disease. LC 87-8332. 292p. 1987. 24.00 (*0-88099-045-7*); pap. 14.00 (*0-88099-044-9*) W E Upjohn.

— Workers' Compensation in Connecticut: Administrative Inventory. LC 87-29445. 1987. 35.00 (*0-935149-08-2*, WC-87-3) Workers Comp Res Inst.

Barth, Peter S. & Eccleston, Stacey M. Revisiting Workers' Compensation in Texas: Administrative Inventory. LC 95-1658. 1995. 35.00 (*0-935149-51-1*, WC-95-1) Workers Comp Res Inst.

Barth, Peter S. & Telles, Carol A. Workers' Compensation in California: Administrative Inventory. LC 92-33150. 1992. 35.00 (*0-935149-38-4*, WC-92-8) Workers Comp Res Inst.

Barth, Peter S., et al. Workers' Compensation in Texas: Administrative Inventory. LC 89-5285. 1989. 35.00 (*0-935149-18-X*, WC-89-1) Workers Comp Res Inst.

Barth, R. Osha Handbook. (C). 1995. pap. text 29.50 (*0-07-005374-X*) McGraw.

— Site Assessment: Preliminary Edition. (C). 1993. pap. text 28.00 (*0-07-005146-1*) McGraw.

Barth, R. & Topper, Andrew. Sampling & Monitoring of Environmental Contaminants. (C). 1993. pap. text 18.74 (*0-07-005153-4*) McGraw.

Barth, R. Carl, ed. Journal of the Johannes Schwalm Historical Association, Inc., Vol. 2, No. 4. (Illus.). 94p. (Orig.). 1984. pap. 9.00 (*0-939016-09-5*) Johannes Schwalm Hist.

— Journal of the Johannes Schwalm Historical Association, Inc., Vol. 3, No. 2. Burgoyne, Bruce E., tr. (Illus.). 104p. (Orig.). 1986. pap. 9.00 (*0-939016-11-7*) Johannes Schwalm Hist.

— Journal of the Johannes Schwalm Historical Association, Inc., Vol. 3, No. 3. Burgoyne, Bruce E., tr. from GER. (Illus.). 132p. (Orig.). 1987. pap. 9.50 (*0-939016-12-5*) Johannes Schwalm Hist.

— Journal of the Johannes Schwalm Historical Association, Inc., Vol. 3, No. 4. Burgoyne, Bruce E., tr. from GER. (Illus.). 96p. (Orig.). 1988. pap. 9.00 (*0-939016-13-3*) Johannes Schwalm Hist.

— Journal of the Johannes Schwalm Historical Association, Inc., Vol. 4, No. 1. Burgoyne, Bruce E., tr. from GER. (Illus.). (Orig.). (C). 1989. 10.00 (*0-939016-15-X*) Johannes Schwalm Hist.

— Journal of the Johannes Schwalm Historical Association, Inc., Vol. 4, No. 2. Burgoyne, Bruce E. & Jones, George F., trs. from GER. (Illus.). (Orig.). (C). 1990. pap. 11.00 (*0-939016-16-8*) Johannes Schwalm Hist.

— Journal of the Johannes Schwalm Historical Association, Inc., Vol. 4, No. 3. Burgoyne, Bruce E., tr. from GER. (Illus.). 96p. (Orig.). (C). 1991. 11.00 (*0-939016-18-4*) Johannes Schwalm Hist.

— Journal of the Johannes Schwalm Historical Association, Inc., Vol. 5, No. 1. Burgoyne, Bruce E. & Retzer, Henry, trs. 96p. (Orig.). (C). 1993. 15.00 (*0-939016-22-2*) Johannes Schwalm Hist.

— Journal of the Johannes Schwalm Historical Association, Inc., 1992, Vol. 4, No. 4. Burgoyne, Bruce E. & Retzer, Henry, trs. 96p. (Orig.). (C). 1992. 11.00 (*0-939016-19-2*) Johannes Schwalm Hist.

— Journal of the Johannes Schwalm Historical Association, Inc., 1994, Vol. 5, No. 2. Burgoyne, Bruce E. et al, trs. from FRE. (Illus.). 96p. (Orig.). 1994. 15.00 (*0-939016-23-0*) Johannes Schwalm Hist.

Barth, R. Carl, ed. see Schwalm, Theo R.

Barth, R. L., ed. see Lewis, Janet.

Barth, R. L., ed. see Winters, Yvor.

Barth, Rachel, et al. The Spirit Ways. (Mage Ser.). (Illus.). 136p. 1999. pap. 15.95 (*1-56504-453-3*, 4043) White Wolf.

Barth, Richard. Deathics: A Margaret Binton Mystery. large type ed. LC 93-17003. 1993. lib. bdg. 17.95 (*1-56054-741-3*) Thorndike Pr.

— The Final Shot. large type ed. LC 92-29410. 343p. 1992. reprint ed. lib. bdg. 17.95 (*1-56054-554-2*) Thorndike Pr.

***Barth, Richard.** Jumper. 2000. 22.95 (*0-312-26608-1*) St Martin.

Barth, Richard, et al, eds. Child Welfare Research Review. LC 94-1252. 392p. 1994. 64.50 (*0-231-08074-3*); pap. 29.50 (*0-231-08075-1*) Col U Pr.

Barth, Richard, ed. see IMF Institute Staff.

Barth, Richard, ed. see Schwalm, Mark A., et al.

Barth, Richard C. Pioneers of the Colorado Parks: North, Middle & South Parks: From 1850 to 1900. Cornell, Wayne, ed. LC 97-36878. (Illus.). 288p. 1997. pap. 17.95 (*0-87004-381-1*, 038110) Caxton.

Barth, Richard C., et al, eds. Coordinating Stabilization & Structural Reform: Proceedings of the Seminar Coordination of Structural Reform & Macroeconomic Stabilization, Washington, D. C., June 17-26, 1993. 1995. 22.00 (*1-55775-430-6*) Intl Monetary.

Barth, Richard C., ed. see Fisher, Robert, et al.

Barth, Richard C., ed. see Schwalm, Mark A., et al.

Barth, Richard P. Reducing the Risk. 2nd ed. (SPA.). 60p. 1995. pap. 18.95 (*1-56071-453-0*) ETR Assocs.

— Reducing the Risk: Building Skills to Prevent Pregnancy, STD & HIV. 2nd ed. LC 92-39092. 1993. 34.95 (*1-56071-147-7*) ETR Assocs.

— Reducing the Risk: Building Skills to Prevent Pregnancy, STD & HIV. 3rd ed. LC 95-30962. 1995. write for info. (*1-56071-398-4*) ETR Assocs.

***Barth, Richard P., et al, eds.** Adoption & Prenatal Alcohol & Drug Exposure: Research, Policy & Practice. LC 99-45583. 2000. 28.95 (*0-87868-720-3*, CWLA Pr) Child Welfare.

Barth, Richard P., et al, eds. Families Living with Drugs & HIV: Intervention & Treatment Strategies. LC 92-1693. 384p. 1993. pap. text 24.95 (*0-89862-150-X*) Guilford Pubns.

Barth, Richard P. & Berry, Marianne. Adoption & Disruption: Rates, Risks, & Responses. (Modern Applications of Social Work Ser.). 261p. 1988. pap. text 26.95 (*0-202-36054-7*); lib. bdg. 49.95 (*0-202-36049-0*) Aldine de Gruyter.

Barth, Richard P., et al. From Child Abuse to Permanency Planning: Child Welfare Services Pathways & Placements. LC 93-37377. (Modern Applications of Social Work Ser.). 310p. 1994. pap. text 23.95 (*0-202-36086-5*); lib. bdg. 47.95 (*0-202-36085-7*) Aldine de Gruyter.

Barth, Robert L., ed. see Winters, Yuor.

Barth, Rochelle, ed. Win Knowlton: New Sculpture. (Illus.). 24p. 1990. pap. 15.00 (*0-924008-07-5*) Blum Helman.

Barth, Rochelle, ed. see Blau, Douglas.

Barth, Roland. Ephesians, Vol. 34. 464p. 1974. 40.00 (*0-385-04412-7*); 34.00 (*0-385-08037-9*) Doubleday.

Barth, Roland S. Cruising Rules: Relationships at Sea. LC 96-80123. (Illus.). 110p. (Orig.). 1997. pap. 12.95 (*0-9654467-0-0*) Head Tide Pr.

— Improving Schools from Within: Teachers, Parents, & Principals Can Make the Difference. LC 89-43460. (Education-Higher Education Ser.). 18p. 1991. reprint ed. pap. text 19.00 (*1-55542-368-X*) Jossey-Bass.

— Run School Run. LC 79-25686. (Illus.). 304p. 1980. 36.50 (*0-674-78036-1*) HUP.

— Run School Run. 304p. 1985. pap. 17.00 (*0-674-78037-X*) HUP.

Barth, Samuel & Codor, Dick. All You Want to Know about Sabbath Services. LC 95-19972. 1995. pap. 1.95 (*0-87441-590-X*) Behrman.

Barth, Shannon. Show! Don't Tell! How to Personalize College Essays. Berescik, Susan, ed. (Illus.). 175p. 1993. spiral bd. 19.95 (*0-9638297-0-X*) Intl Editing.

Barth, Steve & Heacox, Kim. The Pacific: Hawaii & Alaska. LC 94-29730. (Guides to Natural America Ser.). (Illus.). 1995. 19.95 (*0-89599-044-X*) Smithsonian Bks.

— The Smithsonian Guide to Natural America: The Pacific. (Illus.). 304p. 1995. pap. 19.95 (*0-679-76155-1*) Random.

***Barth, T. J., et al, eds.** High-Order Methods for Computational Physics. LC 99-30074. (Lecture Notes in Computational Science & Engineering Ser.: Vol. 9). viii, 582p. 1999. 93.00 (*3-540-65893-9*) Spr-Verlag.

Barth, Ulrich. Die Christologie Emanuel Hirschs: Eine Systematische und Problemgeschichtliche Darstellung Ihrer Geschichtsmethodologischen, Erkenntniskritischen und Subjektivitatstheoretischen Grundlagen. xvi, 669p. (C). 1992. lib. bdg. 163.10 (*3-11-012894-2*, 238-91) De Gruyter.

***Barth, Uta, photos by.** Uta Barth: At the Edge of the Decipherable. rev. ed. (Illus.). 56p. 1999. pap. 24.95 (*1-58418-005-6*) FotoFolio.

Barth, Valerie. Time One-Thousand Action Words. (Illus.). 110p. (Orig.). (J). (gr. 2-6). 1992. pap. 11.95 (*981-01-0383-2*, Pub. by Europ Lang Inst) Midwest European Pubns.

Barth, W. P. & Lange, H., eds. Arithmetic of Complex Manifolds. (Lecture Notes in Mathematics Ser.: Vol. 1399). v, 171p. 1989. 32.95 (*0-387-51729-4*, 3568) Spr-Verlag.

Barth, W. P., et al. Compact Complex Surfaces. (Series of Modern Surveys in Mathematics, Band 4: Vol. 4). 320p. 1984. 158.95 (*0-387-12172-2*) Spr-Verlag.

Barth, William. Money Management Using Lotus 1-2-3. Murray, Toni, ed. LC 94-70484. (Crisp Computer Ser.). (Illus.). 119p. (Orig.). 1994. pap. 11.95 (*1-56052-276-3*) Crisp Pubns.

— What Happened to the Church? LC 98-233992. 464p. 1997. pap. 21.00 (*0-8059-4169-X*) Dorrance.

Barth, Wolfgang, et al, eds. Abelian Varieties: Proceedings: International Conference on Abelian Varieties (1993: Egloffstein, Germany) LC 94-47103. 344p. (C). 1995. 135.95 (*3-11-014411-5*) De Gruyter.

Bartha, Christina, jt. auth. see McDonough, Hanna.

Bartha, Georges De, see Duncan, Alastair & De Bartha, Georges.

Bartha, L., et al, eds. The Chemistry of Non-Sag Tungsten. 170p. 1995. 87.50 (*0-08-042676-X*, Pergamon Pr) Elsevier.

Barthakuria, Apurba C. India in the Age of the Pancatantra. (C). 1992. text 24.00 (*0-685-66322-1*, Pub. by Punthi Pus) S Asia.

Barthal, Lea, jt. auth. see Ne'eman, Nira.

Barthe, Joe De, see De Barthe, Joe.

Barthe, R. Lexique Occitan-Francais: Occitan-French Lexicon. 3rd ed. (FRE.). 238p. 1984. pap. 35.00 (*0-8288-1038-9*, F45930) Fr & Eur.

Barthel, Diane. Historic Preservation: Collective Memory & Historical Identity. LC 95-53795. (Illus.). 220p. (C). 1996. pap. 16.95 (*0-8135-2293-5*); text 48.00 (*0-8135-2292-7*) Rutgers U Pr.

— Putting on Appearances: Gender & Advertising. (Women in the Political Economy Ser.). 232p. 1989. pap. 19.95 (*0-87722-661-X*) Temple U Pr.

Barthel, Diane L. Amana: From Pietist Sect to American Community. LC 83-14624. 238p. reprint ed. pap. 73.80 (*0-7837-1900-0*, 204210400001) Bks Demand.

Barthel, J., ed. Materials Science for High Technologies - MASHTEC '90. 880p. 1990. text 283.00 (*0-87849-612-2*, Pub. by Trans T Pub) Enfield Pubs NH.

Barthel, J., et al, eds. Electrolyte Data Collection: Viscosity of Nonaqueous Solutions II: Aprotic & Protic Non-Alcohol Solutions C1-C3. (Dechema Chemistry Data Ser.: Vol. 12, Pt. 3A). (Illus.). 440p. 1997. lib. bdg. 250.00 (*3-926959-84-3*, Pub. by Dechema) Scholium Intl.

— Electrolyte Data Collection: Viscosity of Nonaqueous Solutions II: Aprotic & Protic Non-Alcohol Solutions C4-C8. (Dechema Chemistry Data Ser.: Vol. 12, Pt. 3B). (Illus.). 387p. 1997. lib. bdg. 230.00 (*3-926959-85-1*, Pub. by Dechema) Scholium Intl.

— Electrolyte Data Collection: Viscosity of Nonaqueous Solutions 1: Alcohol Solutions. (Dechema Chemistry Data Ser.: Vol. 12, Pt. 3). (Illus.). 355p. 1997. lib. bdg. 235.00 (*3-926959-79-7*, Pub. by Dechema) Scholium Intl.

Barthel, J. & Beueder, R. Electrolyte Data Collection: Conductivities, Transfer Numbers & Limiting Ionic Conductivities. Eckermann, Reiner & Kreysa, Gerhard, eds. (Dechema Chemistry Data Ser.: Vol. 12, Pt. 1). (Illus.). 416p. 1992. text 225.00 (*3-926959-33-9*, Pub. by Dechema) Scholium Intl.

Barthel, J. & Neueder, R. Electrolyte Data Collection: Conductivities, Transference Numbers & Limiting Ionic Conductivities of Ethanol Solutions. Eckermann, Reiner, ed. (Dechema Chemistry Data Ser.: Vol. 12 - Pt. 1A). (Illus.). 268p. 1993. 250.00 (*3-926959-39-8*, Pub. by Dechema) Scholium Intl.

Barthel, J., et al. Electrolyte Data Collection: Conductivities, Transference Numbers & Limiting Ionic Conductivities of Solutions of Aproptic, Protophobic Solvents. Kreysa, Gerhard, ed. (Dechema Chemistry Data Ser.: Vol. 12, Pt, 1C). 546p. 1995. lib. bdg. 270.00 (*3-926959-69-X*, Pub. by Dechema) Scholium Intl.

— Electrolyte Data Collection: Dielectric Properties of Nonaqueous Electrolyte Solutions. Kreysa, Gerhard, ed. (Dechema Chemistry Data Ser.: Vol. 12, Pt. 2A). (Illus.). 414p. 1996. text 270.00 (*3-926959-75-4*, Pub. by Dechema) Scholium Intl.

— Electrolyte Data Collection: Dielectric Properties of Water & Aqueous Electrolyte Solutions. Kreysa, Gerhard, ed. (Dechema Chemistry Data Ser.: Vol. 12, Part 2). 395p. 1995. text, lib. bdg. 295.00 (*3-926959-62-2*, Pub. by Dechema) Scholium Intl.

Barthel, J. M., et al. Physical Chemistry of Electrolyte Solutions: Modern Aspects. Baumgartel, Hellmut et al, eds. LC 98-188809. (Topics in Physical Chemistry Ser.: Vol. 5). 440p. 1998. 109.00 (*3-7985-1076-8*, Pub. by D Steinkopff) Spr-Verlag.

Barthel, Joan. Love or Honor. 1990. mass mkt. 4.95 (*0-380-71105-2*, Avon Bks) Morrow Avon.

Barthel, Joan, jt. auth. see Clooney, Rosemary.

Barthel, Josef & Neueder, R. Electrolyte Data Collection: Tables, Diagrams, Correlations & Literature Survey LC 96-100991. (Chemistry Data Ser.). 1992. write for info. (*3-926959-94-0*, Pub. by Dechema) Scholium Intl.

Barthel, Manfred. What Bible Really Sa. Howson, Mark, tr. from GER. LC 83-3001. (Illus.). 416p. 1983. pap. 15.00 (*0-688-01979-X*, Quil) HarperTrade.

— What the Bible Really Says. 416p. 1992. reprint ed. 9.99 (*0-517-46002-5*) Random Hse Value.

Barthel, Thomas. Poems & Short Stories for Study. 245p. (C). 1999. pap. text 25.00 (*1-891877-02-X*) Sheron Ent.

Barthelemy, jt. auth. see Curtus.

Barthelemy, Adrien. Arabic-French Dictionary: Dictionnaire Arabe-Francais, Dialectes de Syrie: Alep, Damas, Liban, Jerusalem. (ARA & FRE.). 1100p. 1983. 225.00 (*0-8288-0438-9*, F369) Fr & Eur.

Barthelemy, Anthony. Critical Essays on Shakespeare's Othello. (Critical Essays on British Literature Ser.). 256p. 1994. 49.00 (*0-8161-8866-1*, Twyne) Mac Lib Ref.

Barthelemy, Anthony G. Black Face, Maligned Race: The Representation of Blacks in English Drama from Shakespeare to Southerne. fac. ed. LC 86-27716. 229p. 1987. reprint ed. pap. 71.00 (*0-7837-7934-8*, 204769000008) Bks Demand.

Barthelemy, Anthony G., intro. Collected Black Women's Narratives. (Schomburg Library of Nineteenth-Century Black Women Writers). (Illus.). 343p. 1990. reprint ed. pap. 13.95 (*0-19-506669-3*) OUP.

Barthelemy, D. Critique Textuelle de l'Ancien Testament Vol. 1: Josue, Juges, Ruth, Samuel, Rois, Chroniques, Esdras, Nehemie, Esther Rapport Final du Comite pour l'Analyse Textuelle de l'Ancien Testament Hebreu Institue par l'Alliance Biblique Universelle, Etabli en Cooperation avec A. R. Hulst, N. Lohfink, W. D. Ruger, H. P. & Sanders, J. A., eds. (Orbis Biblicus et Orientalis Ser.). (FRE.). 1982. text 157.00 (*2-8271-0245-5*, 50/1, Pub. by Ed Univ Fri) Eisenbrauns.

— Critique Textuelle de l'Ancien Testament Vol. 2: Isaie, Jeremie, Lamentations. (Orbis Biblicus et Orientalis Ser.). (FRE.). 1986. text 231.00 (*2-8271-0322-2*, 50/2, Pub. by Ed Univ Fri) Eisenbrauns.

— Critique Textuelle de l'Ancien Testament Vol. 3: Ezechiel, Daniel et les 12 Prophetes. (Orbis Biblicus et Orientalis Ser.). (FRE.). 1992. text 245.00 (*2-8271-0574-8*, 50/3, Pub. by Ed Univ Fri) Eisenbrauns.

Barthelemy, D., jt. ed. see Milik, Jozef T.

Barthelemy-Madaule, Madeleine. Bergson et Teilhard de Chardin. (FRE.). 1963. pap. write for info. (*0-7859-4884-8*) Fr & Eur.

— Lamarck the Mythical Precursor: A Study of the Relations Between Science & Ideology. Shank, Michael, tr. from FRE. 176p. 1982. 25.00 (*0-262-02179-X*) MIT Pr.

Barthelemy, Paul. Experiencing World Religions. 1982. teacher ed. 18.00 (*1-881678-24-5*) CSEE.

Barthelemy, Robert. The Sky Is Not the Limit: Breakthrough Leadership. 208p. (Orig.). 1997. per. 29.95 (*1-57444-106-X*) St Lucie Pr.

Barthelenghi, Carolyn J. The Architecture of Transformation: Transcending the Paralysis of Power. 200p. 1991. 35.00 (*0-9629235-0-8*) Stonecrest Ent.

Barthell, Edward E., Jr. Gods & Goddesses of Ancient Greece. LC 72-129664. 1981. 49.95 (*0-87024-165-6*) U of Miami Pr.

Barthelmas, Della G. The Signers of the Declaration of Independence: A Biographical & Genealogical Reference. LC 97-11663. (Illus.). 340p. 1997. boxed set 55.00 (*0-7864-0318-7*) McFarland & Co.

Barthelme, Donald. Forty Stories. 256p. 1989. pap. 12.95 (*0-14-011245-6*, Penguin Bks) Viking Penguin.

— Not-Knowing. 2100p. 1999. pap. 15.00 (*0-679-74120-8*) Discovery.

Barthelme, Donald. Sadness. LC 74-196317. 183p. 1973. write for info. (*0-224-00897-8*) Jonathan Cape.

Barthelme, Donald. 60 Stories. 1993. pap. 14.95 (*0-14-015300-4*, Viking) Viking Penguin.

An Asterisk (*) at the beginning of an entry indicates that the title is appearing for the first time.

— Snow White. LC 67-14324. 192p. 1996. per. 10.00 (*0-684-82479-5*) S&S Trade.
— Teachings of Don Barthelme. 1998. pap. 15.00 (*0-679-74119-4*) Vin Bks.

Barthelme, Donald, jt. auth. see Frank, Peter.

Barthelme, Frederick. Bob the Gambler. 224p. 1998. pap. 12.00 (*0-395-92474-X*) HM.
— Chroma. 176p. 1996. reprint ed. pap. 11.00 (*0-8021-3461-0*, Grove) Grove-Atltic.

***Barthelme, Frederick.** The Law of Averages: New & Selected Stories. 352p. 2000. 25.00 (*1-58243-115-9*, Pub. by Counterpt DC) HarpC.

Barthelme, Frederick. Moon Deluxe: Stories. LC 95-22804. 240p. 1995. pap. 12.00 (*0-8021-3437-8*, Grove) Grove-Atltic.
— Natural Selection. 212p. 1990. 18.95 (*0-685-46943-3*, Viking) Viking Penguin.
— Painted Desert: A Novel. 1997. pap. 11.95 (*0-14-024214-7*) Viking Penguin.
— Painted Desert: A Novel. 288p. 1999. pap. 20.95 (*0-670-85840-4*) Viking Penguin.
— Second Marriage. LC 95-22802. 224p. 1995. pap. 11.00 (*0-8021-3436-X*, Grove) Grove-Atltic.
— Two Against One. 272p. 1996. reprint ed. pap. 12.00 (*0-8021-3460-2*, Grove) Grove-Atltic.

***Barthelme, Frederick & Barthelme, Steven.** Double Down: Reflections on Gambling & Loss. LC 99-23957. (Illus.). 224p. 1999. 24.00 (*0-395-95429-0*) HM.

Barthelme, Marion K., ed. Women in the Texas Populist Movement: Letters to the Southern Mercury. LC 96-53089. (Centennial Series of the Association of Former Students: Vol. 67). (Illus.). 256p. (C). 1997. pap. 16.95 (*0-89096-775-X*); text 39.95 (*0-89096-742-3*) Tex A&M Univ Pr.

Barthelme, Steve. And He Tells the Little Horse the Whole Story. LC 87-45477. (Poetry & Fiction Ser.). 160p. 1987. 16.95 (*0-8018-3543-7*) Johns Hopkins.

Barthelme, Steven, jt. auth. see Barthelme, Frederick.

Barthelmess, Casey E., jt. auth. see Frink, Maurice.

Barthels, Katharine, jt. auth. see Kreighbaum, Ellen.

Barthels, Katharine M., jt. auth. see Kreighbaum, Ellen.

Barthem, Ronaldo & Goulding, Michael. The Catfish Connection: Ecology, Migration, & Conservation of Amazon Predators. LC 96-47920. (Biology & Resource Management in the Tropics Ser.). 1997. 45.00 (*0-231-10832-X*) Col U Pr.

Barthes, M. & Leon, J. Mustrede, eds. Nonlinear Coherent Structures. (Lecture Notes in Physics Ser.: Vol. 353). x, 280p. 1990. 44.95 (*0-387-52240-9*) Spr-Verlag.

Barthes, Roland. L' Aventure Semiologique. (FRE.). 1991. pap. 19.95 (*0-7859-2720-4*) Fr & Eur.
— Barthes. 192p. 1975. 12.95 (*0-7859-0660-6*, M3043) Fr & Eur.
— A Barthes' Reader. 496p. 1983. pap. 17.00 (*0-374-52144-1*) FS&G.
— Camera Lucida. 119p. 1982. pap. 10.00 (*0-374-52134-4*) FS&G.
— Critical Essays. Howard, Richard, tr. xxi, 279p. 1972. pap. 15.95 (*0-8101-0589-6*) Northwestern U Pr.
— Criticism & Truth. Keunemen, Katrine P., ed. & tr. by. from FRE. LC 86-27264.Tr. of Critique et Veite. 119p. (Orig.). 1987. pap. 12.95 (*0-8166-1609-4*) U of Minn Pr.
— Critique et Verite. (FRE.). 80p. 1966. pap. 24.95 (*0-7859-0929-X*, F80540) Fr & Eur.
— Le Degre Zero de l'Ecriture. (FRE.). 1953. 29.95 (*0-686-53930-3*, F1870); pap. 10.95 (*0-8288-9059-5*) Fr & Eur.
— The Eiffel Tower & Other Mythologies. Howard, Richard, tr. from FRE. LC 96-39164. 152p. 1997. pap. 12.95 (*0-520-20982-6*, Pub. by U CA Pr) Cal Prin Full Svc.
— Elements of Semiology. 111p. 1977. pap. 10.00 (*0-374-52146-8*) FS&G.
— L' Empire des Signes. (FRE.). 152p. 1991. reprint ed. pap. 19.95 (*0-7859-0661-4*, M12736) Fr & Eur.
— Empire of Signs. 109p. 1983. pap. 9.00 (*0-374-52207-3*) FS&G.
— Essais Critiques: L'Obvie et l'Obtus. (FRE.). 239p. 1992. pap. 17.95 (*0-7859-0662-2*, F80560) Fr & Eur.
— Essais Critiques Vol. 3: L'Obvie et l'Obtus. (FRE.). 1992. pap. 18.95 (*0-7859-2727-1*) Fr & Eur.
— Essais Critiques Vol. 4: Le Bruissement de la Langue. (FRE.). 1993. pap. 20.95 (*0-7859-2733-6*) Fr & Eur.
— The Fashion System. Ward, Matthew & Howard, Richard, trs. 351p. 1990. pap. 16.95 (*0-520-07177-8*, Pub. by U CA Pr) Cal Prin Full Svc.
— Fragments d'un Discours Amoureux. (FRE.). 280p. 1977. pap. 45.00 (*0-7859-0663-0*, M4831) Fr & Eur.
— The Grain of the Voice, 1962-1980: Interviews. Coverdale, Linda, tr. from FRE. (Illus.). 378p. 1991. pap. 17.95 (*0-520-07237-5*, Pub. by U CA Pr) Cal Prin Full Svc.
— Image Music Text. 220p. 1978. pap. 13.95 (*0-374-52136-0*) FS&G.
— Incidents. 1992. pap. 15.95 (*0-520-07104-2*, Pub. by U CA Pr) Cal Prin Full Svc.
— Lecon. (FRE.). 1989. pap. 10.95 (*0-7859-2713-1*) Fr & Eur.
— Lover's Discourse. LC 78-7794. 224p. 1979. pap. text 11.00 (*0-374-52161-1*) FS&G.
— Michelet. Howard, Richard, tr. 1992. pap. 14.95 (*0-520-07826-8*, Pub. by U CA Pr) Cal Prin Full Svc.
— Michelet. rev. ed. (FRE., Illus.). 187p. 1988. pap. 18.95 (*0-7859-0664-9*, F68560) Fr & Eur.
— Mythologies. Lavers, Annette, tr. 159p. 1972. pap. 10.00 (*0-374-52150-6*) FS&G.
— Mythologies. (FRE.). 256p. 1970. 34.95 (*0-686-53938-9*, F80570); pap. 14.95 (*0-7859-0665-7*, F80570) Fr & Eur.
— Mythologies. 1983. 22.50 (*0-8446-5982-7*) Peter Smith.
— On Racine. Howard, Richard, tr. 1992. pap. 13.95 (*0-520-07824-1*, Pub. by U CA Pr) Cal Prin Full Svc.
— Le Plaisir du Texte. (FRE.). 1982. pap. 19.95 (*0-7859-3561-4*, F80575) Fr & Eur.
— Pleasures of the Text. 80p. 1975. pap. 9.00 (*0-374-52160-3*) FS&G.
— The Responsibility of Forms. Howard, Richard, tr. (Illus.). 320p. 1984. 22.95 (*0-8090-8075-3*) Hill & Wang.
— The Responsibility of Forms: Critical Essays on Music, Art, & Representation. Howard, Richard, tr. from FRE. (Illus.). 320p. 1991. pap. 16.95 (*0-520-07238-3*, Pub. by U CA Pr) Cal Prin Full Svc.
— Roland Barthes. LC 94-7545. 1994. pap. 14.95 (*0-520-08783-6*, Pub. by U CA Pr) Cal Prin Full Svc.
— The Rustle of Language. Howard, Richard, tr. 1989. pap. 17.95 (*0-520-06629-4*, Pub. by U CA Pr) Cal Prin Full Svc.
— S-Z. (FRE.). 288p. 1976. 29.95 (*0-686-53944-3*, F56510); pap. 16.95 (*0-7859-0670-3*, F56510) Fr & Eur.
— Sade, Fourier, Loyola. (FRE.). 1980. pap. 14.95 (*0-7859-0667-3*, M5801) Fr & Eur.
— Sade-Fourier-Loyola. LC 96-42538. 184p. 1997. reprint ed. pap. 14.95 (*0-8018-5526-8*) Johns Hopkins.

***Barthes, Roland.** Selections from Oevres Completes. 2000. text. write for info. (*0-8090-8528-3*) Hill & Wang.

Barthes, Roland. The Semiotic Challenge. Howard, Richard, tr. from FRE. LC 94-7124. 1994. pap. 16.95 (*0-520-08784-4*, Pub. by U CA Pr) Cal Prin Full Svc.
— Sur Racine. (FRE.). 1979. pap. 11.95 (*0-7859-0668-1*, F13010) Fr & Eur.
— Systemes de la Mode. (FRE.). 1983. pap. 18.95 (*0-7859-0669-X*, F13020) Fr & Eur.
— S/Z. Miller, Richard, tr. 576p. 1975. pap. 12.00 (*0-374-52167-0*) FS&G.
— Writing Degree Zero. 94p. 1977. pap. 10.00 (*0-374-52139-5*) FS&G.

Barthes, Roland & Miller, D. A. Incidents Bringing Out Roland Barthes, 2 vols., Vol. Set. 1992. pap. 30.00 (*0-520-08102-1*, Pub. by U CA Pr) Cal Prin Full Svc.

Barthle, Jeanette. Cowboys, Kids & Critters. LC 94-227585. 132p. 1994. pap. 7.95 (*1-879894-04-1*) Saratoga Pub.

Barthle, Leona W. Wycinanki: Polish Paper Cuts. LC 94-71641. 120p. 1994. pap. 35.00 (*0-9641189-0-4*) L W Barthle.

Barthlet, John. The Pedegrewe of Heretiques. LC 79-76432. (English Experience Ser.: No. 76). 180p. 1969. reprint ed. 30.00 (*90-221-0076-6*) Walter J Johnson.

Barthlott, Wilhelm, et al, eds. Biodiversity: A Challenge for Development Research & Policy. LC 97-51324. (Illus.). 464p. 1998. 109.00 (*3-540-63949-7*) Spr-Verlag.

Bartholdi, Carol. Greatest Ski Resorts in North America. 6th rev. ed. (Illus.). 286p. 1993. pap. 18.95 (*0-929498-05-4*) GuideBook Pub.

Bartholdi, Carol, jt. auth. see Weber, Robert E.

Bartholdi, P., ed. see Burton, W. Butler, et al.

Bartholemew, Jack, jt. auth. see Willie, Randall R.

Bartholet, E. J., jt. auth. see Cadish, J.

Bartholet, Elizabeth. Family Bonds: Adoption, Infertility & the New World of Child Production. LC 99-26320. 288p. 1999. pap. 18.00 (*0-8070-2803-7*) Beacon Pr.

Bartholet, Elizabeth. Nobody's Children: Abuse & Neglect, Foster Drift & the Adoption Alternative. LC 99-22976. 320p. 1999. 28.50 (*0-8070-2318-3*) Beacon Pr.

***Bartholet, Elizabeth.** Nobody's Children: Abuse & Neglect, Foster Drift & the Adoption Alternative. 2000. pap. 17.50 (*0-8070-2319-1*) Beacon Pr.

Bartholine, Guiseppe, et al, eds. Imidazopyridines in Anxiety Disorders: A Novel Experimental & Therapeutic Approach. LC 93-11076. (L. E. R. S. Monograph Ser.: No. 8). (Illus.). 271p. 1993. reprint ed. pap. 77.30 (*0-608-05833-5*, 2059798) Bks Demand.

Bartholini, Giuseppe, et al, eds. Epilepsy & GABA Receptor Agonists: Basic & Therapeutic Research. LC 85-1944. (L. E. R. S. Monograph Ser.: Vol. 3). 496p. 1985. reprint ed. pap. 153.80 (*0-608-00313-1*, 206103000007) Bks Demand.
— GABA & Mood Disorders: Experimental & Clinical Research. LC 85-19634. (L. E. R. S. Monograph Ser.: No. 4). (Illus.). 240p. 1986. reprint ed. pap. 74.40 (*0-608-00582-7*, 206116900007) Bks Demand.

Bartholm. Scandinavian Folk Designs. (Design Library). (Illus.). 48p. (Orig.). pap. 4.95 (*0-486-25578-6*) Dover.

Bartholmew, David J. The Statistical Approach to Social Measurement. (Illus.). 239p. 1996. text 54.95 (*0-12-079860-3*) Acad Pr.

Bartholo, Long. I Can Keyboard. 1986. 14.64 (*0-02-819240-0*) Macmillan.

Bartholoma, A., jt. ed. see Flemming, B. W.

Bartholomae. Brief Rhetoric. 1995. pap. write for info. (*0-312-01553-4*) St Martin.

***Bartholomae.** Literature As Writing. 2001. pap. write for info. (*0-312-18352-6*) St Martin.

Bartholomae. Responding to Student. Date not set. pap. text. write for info. (*0-312-10083-3*) St Martin.
— Ways of Reading. 4th ed. 1998. pap. text 28.80 (*0-312-20250-4*) St Martin.
— Ways of Reading. 5th ed. LC 98-87520. xxi, 903p. 1998. pap. 35.95 (*0-312-17893-X*); pap. text, teacher ed. 10.00 (*0-312-17894-8*) St Martin.
— Ways of Reading & Everyday Writing. 1997. pap. text 37.80 (*0-312-18846-3*) St Martin.
— Work with Past, Vol. 1. 2001. pap. write for info. (*0-312-13816-4*) St Martin.

Bartholomae, Barbara, ed. see Abatecola, John A.

Bartholomae, David. Reading the Lives of Others. LC 94-71844. 257p. 1994. pap. 28.95 (*0-312-11511-3*) St Martin.
— Ways of Reading. 3rd ed. 1993. pap. text, teacher ed. 1.06 (*0-312-06643-0*) St Martin.
— Ways of Reading. 4th ed. 1996. pap. text, teacher ed. 10.00 (*0-312-11707-8*) St Martin.

Bartholomae, David & Petrosky, Anthony R. Facts, Artifacts & Counterfacts: Theory & Method for a Reading & Writing Course. LC 86-4235. 226p. (Orig.). (C). (gr. 13). 1986. pap. text 22.50 (*0-86709-155-5*, 0135, Pub. by Boynton Cook Pubs) Heinemann.

Bartholomae, David, jt. ed. see Petrosky, Anthony R.

Bartholomai, A., ed. Food Factories: Processes, Equipment & Costs. 290p. 1987. 205.00 (*3-527-26490-6*, Wiley-VCH) Wiley.

Bartholomaus, Brett. Moments Beautiful Moments Bright. 28p. 1993. pap. 4.95 (*1-886028-09-5*) Savage Pr.

Bartholomay, Julia A. The Shield of Perseus: The Vision & Imagination of Howard Nemerov. LC 70-137851. 176p. reprint ed. pap. 54.60 (*0-8357-6714-0*, 203534600095) Bks Demand.

Bartholomees, James B., Jr. Buff Facings & Gilt Buttons: Staff & Headquarters Operations in the Army of Northern Virginia, 1861-1865. LC 98-19676. (Illus.). 256p. 1998. 29.95 (*1-57003-220-3*) U of SC Pr.

Bartholomeusz, Tessa J. Women under the Bo Tree: Buddhist Nuns in Sri Lanka. LC 93-33586. (Studies in Religious Traditions: No. 5). 304p. (C). 1994. text 69.95 (*0-521-46129-4*) Cambridge U Pr.

Bartholomeusz, Tessa J. & De Silva, Chandra R., eds. Buddhist Fundamentalism & Minority Identities in Sri Lanka. LC 97-35501. 212p. (C). 1998. text 59.50 (*0-7914-3833-3*); pap. text 19.95 (*0-7914-3834-1*) State U NY Pr.

Bartholomew. Essential Anatomy & Physiology. 1997. pap. text, student ed. 34.10 (*0-13-359936-1*) P-H.
— From the Heart of a Gentle Brother. LC 97-42126. 176p. 1998. pap. text 12.95 (*1-56170-386-9*) Hay House.
— I Come As a Brother: A Remembrance of Illusions. 2nd rev. ed. LC 97-21711. 192p. 1997. pap. 12.95 (*1-56170-385-0*, 813) Hay House.
— I Come As a Brother: Bartholomew. Moore, M., ed. 175p. 1986. pap. 10.95 (*0-9614010-1-X*) High Mesa Pr.
— Journeys with a Brother: Japan to India. Moore, Mary M. & Franklin, Joy, eds. 290p. (Orig.). 1995. pap. 12.95 (*0-9614010-7-9*) High Mesa Pr.
— Journeys with a Brother: Japan to India. 2nd rev. ed. LC 99-34632. 304p. (Orig.). 1999. reprint ed. pap. 12.95 (*1-56170-389-3*, 871) Hay House.
— Love in Bloom. 1998. mass mkt. 12.95 (*0-373-80515-2*, 1-80515-9) Harlequin Bks.
— Mastering Keyboarding & Word Processing: An Applied Approach to Letters & Memos. 3rd ed. (TA - Typing/Keyboarding Ser.). 1994. mass mkt. 11.00 (*0-538-62000-5*) S-W Pub.
— Mastering Keyboarding & Word Processing: Applied Approach - Center & Table. 3rd ed. (TA - Typing/Keyboarding Ser.). 1995. mass mkt. 11.00 (*0-538-62004-8*); mass mkt. 11.00 (*0-538-62006-4*) S-W Pub.
— Mastering Keyboarding & Word Processing, Reports/Forms: An Applications Approach. 3rd ed. (TA - Typing/Keyboarding Ser.). 1994. mass mkt. 11.00 (*0-538-62002-1*) S-W Pub.
— Planetary Brother. 2nd rev. ed. LC 98-55705. 176p. 1999. pap. 12.95 (*1-56170-388-5*, 870) Hay House.
— Transportation Engineering. (C). 1997. pap. text, teacher ed. write for info. (*0-321-40044-5*) Addison-Wesley.
— Transportation Engineering. (C). 1998. text. write for info. (*0-321-01060-4*) Addson-Wesley Educ.

Bartholomew, jt. auth. see Martini.

Bartholomew, A. T., ed. see Butler, Samuel.

Bartholomew, Alan. Electric Gadgets & Gizmos: Battery-Powered Buildable Gadgets That Go! (Kids Can Do It Ser.). (Illus.). 48p. (J). (gr. 4 up). 1998. pap. 5.95 (*1-55074-439-9*, Pub. by Kids Can Pr) Genl Dist Srvs.

Bartholomew, Ann, ed. see Bartholomew, Craig L. & Metz, Lance E.

Bartholomew, Ann, ed. see Hansell, Norris.

Bartholomew, Ann, ed. see Winpenny, Thomas R.

Bartholomew-Began, Sharon E. A Morphogenetic Re-Evaluation of Haplomitrium Nees (Hepatophyta) Gradstein, S. R., ed. (Bryophytorum Bibliotheca: Vol. 41). (GER., Illus.). 484p. 1991. pap. 130.00 (*3-443-62013-2*, Pub. by Gebruder Borntraeger) Balogh.

Bartholomew, Calvin H. & Fuentes, G. A. Catalyst Deactivation, 1997: Proceedings of the International Symposium, Cancun, Mexico, October 5-8, 1997, Vol. 111. LC 97-33988. (Studies in Surface Science & Catalysis: 111). 704p. 1997. 330.50 (*0-444-82603-3*) Elsevier.

Bartholomew, Carl. Granmax: The Saving of a Steam Train. LC 97-26946. (J). 1997. write for info. (*1-56763-356-0*); pap. write for info. (*1-56763-357-9*) Ozark Pub.

Bartholomew, Charles A., ed. Mud, Muscle, & Miracles: Marine Salvage in the United States Navy. (Illus.). 505p. (C). 1990. 32.00 (*0-945274-03-3*) Naval Hist Ctr.

Bartholomew, Courtenay. A Scientist Researches Mary: Mother & Coredemptrix. (Illus.). 301p. 1998. pap. 18.95 (*1-890137-10-3*) One Hund-One Fnd.
— A Scientist Researches Mary: The Art of the Covenant. 337p. 1995. pap. 12.95 (*1-890137-08-1*) One Hund-One Fnd.
— A Scientist Researches Mary Ark of the Covenant. vi 338p. 1995. 21.00 (*1-890137-13-8*) One Hund-One Fnd.

***Bartholomew, Courtnay.** A Scientist Researches Mary: Mother of All Nations. (Illus.). 208p. 1999. pap. 14.95 (*1-57918-123-6*, 3801) Queenship Pub.

Bartholomew, Craig L. & Metz, Lance E. The Anthracite Iron Industry of the Lehigh Valley. Bartholomew, Ann, ed. LC 88-25719. 1988. pap. 17.95 (*0-930973-08-9*) H M Historical.

Bartholomew, David J. Mathematical Methods in Social Science. LC 80-41593. (Handbook of Applicable Mathematics, Guidebook Ser.: No. 1). 163p. reprint ed. pap. 50.60 (*0-7837-6367-0*, 204607900010) Bks Demand.
— Stochastic Models for Social Processes. 3rd ed. LC 82-117228. (Wiley Series in Probability & Mathematical Statistics). 377p. reprint ed. pap. 116.90 (*0-8357-3392-0*, 203964900013) Bks Demand.

Bartholomew, David J. Uncertain Belief: Is It Rational to Be a Christian? LC 95-24826. 300p. 1996. text 35.00 (*0-19-826378-3*, Clarendon Pr) OUP.

***Bartholomew, David J.** Uncertain Belief: Is It Rational to Be a Christian? 304p. 2000. pap. text 19.95 (*0-19-827014-3*) OUP.

Bartholomew, David J. & Knott, Martin. Latent Variable Models & Factor Analysis. 2nd ed. LC 99-461933. (Kendall's Library of Statistics: No. 7). (Illus.). 240p. 1999. text 45.00 (*0-340-69243-X*, Pub. by E A) OUP.

Bartholomew, David J., et al. Statistical Techniques for Manpower Planning, 2E. 2nd ed. LC 90-28589. (Probability & Mathematical Statistics: Applied Probability & Statistics Section Ser.). 364p. 1991. 235.00 (*0-471-92879-8*) Wiley.

Bartholomew, David M. Pioneer Naturalist on the Plains: The Diary of Elam Bartholomew, 1871-1934. LC 98-199500. (Illus.). 350p. 1998. pap. 24.95 (*0-89745-221-6*) Sunflower U Pr.

Bartholomew, Dorothy. Collection of Short Stories. 88p. 1996. pap. 19.95 (*0-8059-4054-5*) Dorrance.

Bartholomew, Douglas R., jt. auth. see Bennett, Peggy D.

Bartholomew, E. Early Armoured Cars. (Album Ser.: No. 209). (Illus.). 32p. (C). 1989. pap. 6.25 (*0-85263-908-2*, Pub. by Shire Pubns) Parkwest Pubns.
— First World War Tanks. 1989. pap. 25.00 (*0-85263-799-3*, Pub. by Shire Pubns) St Mut.

Bartholomew, Edwin, jt. auth. see Martini, Frederic H.

Bartholomew, Fletcher. Hideous Idiocy: Forty Years of Psychiatric Slander by the U. S. Government. LC 96-94052. 212p. (Orig.). 1996. pap. 13.95 (*0-939823-03-9*) Info Inst.
— Iconoclasm: The Way Out of the High Technology Dark Age. LC 86-82910. 376p. 1987. 14.95 (*0-939823-00-4*) Info Inst.
— Iconoclasm: The Way Out of the High Technology Dark Age. 2nd ed. LC 86-82910. 440p. 1989. write for info. (*0-939823-01-2*) Info Inst.
— Iconoclasm: The Way Out of the High Technology Dark Age. 3rd ed. 440p. 1995. 24.00 (*0-939823-02-0*) Info Inst.
— Iconoclasm: The Way Out of the High Technology Parkage. LC 96-94067. 440p. (Orig.). (C). 1996. reprint ed. pap. 15.00 (*0-939823-04-7*) Info Inst.

Bartholomew, G. E. Re-Incarnation, the Only Mode of Propagation & a Romance of Fifteen Thousand Years. 140p. 1993. spiral bd. 14.00 (*0-7873-0076-4*) Hlth Research.

Bartholomew, G. W., et al. Sesquicentennial Chronological Tables of the Written Laws of the Republic of Singapore, 1834-1984. cxii, 350p. 1987. 117.00 (*9971-70-053-0*, MICHIE) LEXIS Pub.

Bartholomew, Gail & Bailey, Bren. Maui Remembers: A Local History. (Illus.). 178p. 1994. pap. 22.95 (*1-56647-070-6*) Mutual Pub HI.

Bartholomew, Gail, jt. auth. see Bartlett, Patricia M.

Bartholomew, George A., jt. auth. see Peterson, Richard S.

Bartholomew, George W., Jr. Record of the Bartholomew Family: Historical, Genealogical, & Biographical. (Illus.). 769p. 1988. reprint ed. pap. 115.00 (*0-8328-0197-6*); reprint ed. lib. bdg. 123.00 (*0-8328-0196-8*) Higginson Bk Co.

Bartholomew, Gilbert L., jt. auth. see Allen, Ronald J.

Bartholomew, Harland. Land Uses in American Cities. LC 55-5059. (Harvard City Planning Studies: No. 15). 208p. reprint ed. pap. 64.50 (*0-7837-4098-0*, 205792100011) Bks Demand.

Bartholomew, Henry S. Pioneer History of Elkhart County: With Sketches & Stories. (Illus.). 337p. 1997. reprint ed. lib. bdg. 39.50 (*0-8328-6647-4*) Higginson Bk Co.

Bartholomew, James. The City of London. (Illus.). 128p. (C). 1989. 25.00 (*0-941533-66-2*, NAB) I R Dee.
— Inside the Tower. (Illus.). 128p. (Orig.). (C). 1990. pap. 18.95 (*1-56131-006-9*, NAB) I R Dee.
— Yew & Non-Yew: Gardening for Horticultural Climbers. 160p. 1998. 17.95 (*0-7126-7705-4*, Pub. by CEN3) Trafalgar.

***Bartholomew, James.** Yew & Non-Yew: Gardening for Horticultural Climbers. (Illus.). 160p. 1999. reprint ed. pap. 13.95 (*0-09-927206-7*, Pub. by Arrow Bks) Trafalgar.

Bartholomew, James, photos by. The Magic of Kew. LC 88-5296. (Illus.). 128p. (C). 1988. 25.00 (*0-941533-23-9*, NAB); pap. 18.95 (*0-941533-24-7*, NAB) I R Dee.

Bartholomew, Jane, ed. see Hassler, Jill K.

Bartholomew, John. Mini Atlas, Britain: Britain in Your Pocket, 1991. 91st rev. ed. (Illus.). 1987. pap. 15.95 (*0-7028-0789-3*) Brtholomew.

Bartholomew, John. The Steel Band. (Topics in Music Ser.). (Illus.). 48p. 1985. pap. text 10.95 (*0-19-321329-X*) OUP.

Bartholomew, John. World Travel Kenya & Tanzania. (Illus.). pap. 12.95 (*0-7028-2584-0*) Brtholomew.

Bartholomew, John, & Son Staff. Bartholomew Mini World Atlas, 1996. 1996. 17.95 (*0-7028-2965-X*, Pub. by Brtholomew) Hammond World.
— Bartholomew Mini World Atlas, 1996. deluxe ed. 1996. 17.95 (*0-7028-3352-5*, Pub. by Brtholomew) Hammond World.

Bartholomew, Keith & McCarthy, Samantha, eds. Update One - Federal Fisheries Management: A Guidebook to the Magnuson Fishery Conservation & Management Act. rev. ed. 1987. reprint ed. pap. 2.00 (*0-945216-01-7*) U OR Ocean & Law Ctr.

B

Bartholomew, Kenneth A. Doctor, Please Close the Door: A Book on Living Wills, Powers of Attorney, Terminal Care & the Right to Die with Dignity! LC 93-39045. 96p. 1994. pap. 9.95 (*0-942963-45-8*) Distinctive Pub.

Bartholomew, Leland, ed. see Banchieri, Adriano.

***Bartholomew, Lois Thompson.** The White Dove. LC 99-33517. (Illus.). 208p. (YA). 2000. 15.00 (*0-618-00464-5*) HM.

Bartholomew, Martin F. Successful Business Strategies Using Telecommunications Services. LC 97-19473. 304p. 1997. 69.00 (*0-89006-904-2*) Artech Hse.

Bartholomew, Marty. Flyfisher's Guide to Colorado. LC 97-43890. (Illus.). 300p. (Orig.). 1998. pap. 26.95 (*1-885106-56-4*) Wild Adven Pr.

Bartholomew, Mel. Cash from Square Foot Gardening. LC 85-50122. 256p. 1985. pap. 9.95 (*0-88266-395-X*, Storey Pub) Storey Bks.

— Square Foot Gardening. 1981. pap. 16.95 (*0-87857-341-0*) Rodale Pr Inc.

Bartholomew, Mervin J., et al, eds. Basement Tectonics Eight: Characterization & Comparison of Ancient & Mesozoic Continental Margins, Proceedings of the Eighth International Conference, Butte, Montana, August 8-12, 1988. LC 92-41537. (Proceedings of the International Conferences on Basement Tectonics Ser.: Vol. 2). 768p. (C). 1993. lib. bdg. 306.00 (*0-7923-2088-3*) Kluwer Academic.

— The Grenville Event in the Appalachians & Related Topics. LC 83-25503. (Geological Society of America Ser.: Vol. 194). (Illus.). 295p. reprint ed. pap. 91.50 (*0-608-07723-2*, 206781100010) Bks Demand.

Bartholomew, Nancy. Drag Strip. LC 99-22205. 272p. 1999. text 23.95 (*0-312-20295-4*) St Martin.

***Bartholomew, Nancy.** Drag Strip. 288p. 2000. mass mkt. 5.99 (*0-312-97579-1*, St Martins Paperbacks) St Martin.

— Film Strip. 272p. 2000. 23.95 (*0-312-26161-6*) St Martin.

Bartholomew, Nancy. The Miracle Strip. LC 98-7330. 256p. 1998. text 22.95 (*0-312-19299-1*) St Martin.

— The Miracle Strip: A Sierra Lavotini Mystery. 256p. 1999. pap. 5.99 (*0-312-97095-1*, Minotaur) St Martin.

— Your Cheatin' Heart: A Novel. 326p. 2000. mass mkt. 5.99 (*0-06-101409-5*) HarpC.

Bartholomew of Lucca. On the Government of Rulers: De Regimine Principum. Blythe, James M., tr. from LAT. LC 97-2015. (Middle Ages Ser.). 320p. 1997. text 55.00 (*0-8122-3370-0*) U of Pa Pr.

Bartholomew, Paul, et al. Monsters of the Northwoods. LC 92-23460. 1992. pap. 12.95 (*0-925168-00-9*) North Country.

Bartholomew, Paul C. American Constitutional Law: Governmental Organization, Powers & Procedure, No. 1. 2nd ed. (Quality Paperback Ser.: No. 240). 350p. 1978. pap. 16.00 (*0-8226-0240-7*) Littlefield.

— Summaries of Leading Cases on the Constitution. 13th rev. ed. (Orig.). (C). 1991. pap. text 21.95 (*0-8226-3008-7*) Littlefield.

Bartholomew, Paul C., jt. auth. see Pettengill, Samuel B.

Bartholomew, Pauline. Growing to Show: How to Grow Prize-Winning African Violets. rev. ed. LC 85-72283. (Illus.). 112p. (Orig.). 1986. pap. 12.95 (*0-9615715-1-9*) D M Prestia.

Bartholomew, Ralph, Jr., photos by. Retail Fictions: The Commercial Photography of Ralph Bartholomew Jr. LC 97-76008. (Illus.). 160p. 1998. pap. 24.95 (*0-87587-183-6*, 810051) LA Co Art Mus.

Bartholomew, Rebecca. Audacious Women: Early British Mormon Immigrants. LC 94-23624. 304p. (Orig.). 1998. 18.95 (*1-56085-066-3*) Signature Bks.

— Lost Heroines: Little-Known Women Who Changed Their World. iv, 161p. 1997. pap. 10.95 (*0-9656117-0-1*) Uintah Springs.

Bartholomew, Rebecca & Arrington, Leonard J. Rescue of the 1856 Handcart Companies. LC 92-42327. (Charles Redd Monographs in Western History: No. 11). (Illus.). 72p. 1993. reprint ed. pap. 6.95 (*0-941214-04-4*, C Redd Ctr Wstrn Studies) Signature Bks.

***Bartholomew, Robert E.** Exotic Deviance: Medicalizing Cultural Idioms. 288p. 2000. 59.95 (*0-87081-597-0*); pap. 29.95 (*0-87081-598-9*) Univ Pr Colo.

Bartholomew, Robert E. Mass Hysteria: A Social History of the Strange. 250p. 1995. text 37.50 (*0-89341-751-3*) Hollowbrook.

Bartholomew, Robert E. & Howard, George S. UFOs & Alien Contact: Two Centuries of Mystery. LC 97-48845. 345p. 1998. 26.95 (*1-57392-200-5*) Prometheus Bks.

Bartholomew, Roy A. & Orr, John. Learning to Read & Make Mechanical Drawings. (gr. 7-9). 1982. pap. text 7.96 (*0-02-664820-2*); 2.00 (*0-02-664830-X*) Glencoe.

Bartholomew Staff. Glencoe Keyboarding. 1985. text 25.05 (*0-02-819230-3*) Glencoe.

Bartholomew Staff. Mini Atlas of Britain. deluxe ed. (Illus.). pap. 15.95 (*0-7028-1203-X*) Brtholomew.

Bartholomew, Stuart H. Construction Contracting: Business & Legal Principles. LC 96-40846. 330p. 1997. 73.00 (*0-13-264441-X*) P-H.

— Estimating for Heavy Construction. LC 99-29570. 404p. 1999. pap. text 81.00 (*0-13-598327-4*) P-H.

Bartholomew, Terese T. & Kao, Mayching. The Charming Cicada Studio: Masterworks by Chao Shao-an. Morrison, Michael, ed. LC 96-79222. (CHI & ENG., Illus.). 192p. 1997. 40.00 (*0-939117-11-8*) Asian Art Mus.

Bartholomew, Terese T., et al. A Matter of Taste: Selected Chinese Art from California Collections. (Illus.). 52p. 1986. pap. 7.50 (*0-9609784-5-3*) CCF San Francisco.

Bartholomew, Terese T., jt. auth. see Berger, Patricia.

Bartholomew, Therese T., ed. Mongolia: The Legacy of Chinggis Khan. LC 95-60283. (Illus.). 339p. 1995. 60.00 (*0-500-23705-0*, Pub. by Thames Hudson) Norton.

Bartholomew, Therese Tse, jt. ed. see Suk-Yee, Lai.

Bartholomew, W. E. Ed McClanahan, Bibliography of a Voice: A Descriptive Bibliography, 1954-1999. LC 99-71230. (Illus.). xiv, 78p. 1999. pap. 15.00 (*0-9673004-1-X*) Sylph Pubns.

— Ed McClanahan, Bibliography of a Voice: A Descriptive Bibliography, 1954-1999. deluxe ed. LC 99-71230. (Illus.). xiv, 78p. 1999. 75.00 (*0-9673004-0-1*) Sylph Pubns.

Bartholomew, Wilmer T. Acoustics of Music. LC 79-17650. (Illus.). 242p. 1980. reprint ed. lib. bdg. 38.50 (*0-313-22087-5*, BAAC, Greenwood Pr) Greenwood.

— Acoustics of Music. (Music Book Index Ser.). 242p. 1992. reprint ed. lib. bdg. 79.00 (*0-7812-9513-0*) Rprt Serv.

Bartholow, Cora H., ed. The Report, Vol. 18. 1978. 5.00 (*0-935057-33-1*) OH Genealogical.

— The Report, Vol. 19. 1979. 5.00 (*0-935057-34-X*) OH Genealogical.

— The Report, Vol. 20. 1980. 5.00 (*0-935057-35-8*) OH Genealogical.

— The Report, Vol. 21. 1981. 2.50 (*0-935057-36-6*) OH Genealogical.

— The Report, Vol. 22. 1982. 3.75 (*0-935057-37-4*) OH Genealogical.

Bartholow, Gerald. Peace Soup: The Recipe for a Peaceful Life in the New Millennium. 288p. mass mkt. 19.95 (*0-9679005-0-6*) P S I Pubng AL.

Bartholow, Roberts S. A Manual of Instructions for Enlisting & Discharging Soldiers. (American Civil War Medical Ser.: No. 6). 276p. 1991. reprint ed. 45.00 (*0-930405-37-4*) Norman SF.

Barthomeu, D., et al. Guidelines for Mastering the Properties of Molecular Sieves: Relationship Between the Physiocochemical Properties of Zeolitic Systems & Their Low Dimensionality. (NATO ASI Ser.: Vol. 221). (Illus.). 438p. (C). 1990. text 125.00 (*0-306-43599-3*, Kluwer Plenum) Kluwer Academic.

Barthorp, Michael. British Army on Campaign, 1816-1902 Vol. 2: The Crimea 1854-56. (Men-at-Arms Ser.: No. 196). (Illus.). 48p. pap. 12.95 (*0-85045-827-7*, 9129, Pub. by Osprey) Stackpole.

— British Army on Campaign, 1816-1902, Vol. 4. (Men-at-Arms Ser.: No. 201). (Illus.). 48p. pap. 11.95 (*0-85045-849-8*, 9134, Pub. by Osprey) Stackpole.

— British Army on Campaign, 1816-1902 Vol. 1: 1816-53. (Men-at-Arms Ser.: No. 193). (Illus.). 48p. pap. 11.95 (*0-85045-793-9*, 9126, Pub. by Osprey) Stackpole.

— British Army on Campaign, 1816-1907, Vol. 3. (Men-at-Arms Ser.: No. 198). (Illus.). 48p. pap. 11.95 (*0-85045-835-8*, 9131, Pub. by Osprey) Stackpole.

— Indian Infantry Regiments 1860-1914. LC 99-174976. (Men-at-Arms Ser.: No. 92). (Illus.). 48p. 1979. pap. 11.95 (*0-85045-307-0*, 9214, Pub. by Osprey) Stackpole.

— The Indian Mutiny 1857-59. (Men-at-Arms Ser.). (Illus.). 48p. 1994. pap. 11.95 (*1-85532-369-9*, 9239, Pub. by Osprey) Stackpole.

— The Jacobite Rebellions, 1689-1745. (Men-at-Arms Ser.: No. 118). (Illus.). 48p. pap. 12.95 (*0-85045-432-8*, 9051, Pub. by Osprey) Stackpole.

— Napoleon's Egyptian Empire. (Men-at-Arms Ser.: No. 79). (Illus.). 48p. pap. 11.95 (*0-85045-126-4*, 9207, Pub. by Osprey) Stackpole.

— The Old Contemptibles: BEF, 1914. (Elite Ser.: No. 24). (Illus.). 64p. pap. 12.95 (*0-85045-898-6*, 9424, Pub. by Osprey) Stackpole.

— Russian Army, 1798-1814 Vol. 2: Cavalry, 1799-1814. (Men-at-Arms Ser.: No. 189). (Illus.). 48p. pap. 11.95 (*0-85045-746-7*, 9122, Pub. by Osprey) Stackpole.

— Wellington's Generals. (Men-at-Arms Ser.: No. 84). (Illus.). 48p. 1990. pap. 11.95 (*0-85045-299-6*, 9212, Pub. by Osprey) Stackpole.

Barthorpe, Michael. Frontier Ablaze: The North-West Frontier Rising, 1897-98. deluxe ed. 1996. 100.00 (*1-85915-033-0*) Combined Pub.

Barthou, Louis. Mirabeau. LC 72-7091. (Select Bibliographies Reprint Ser.). 1977. reprint ed. 26.95 (*0-8369-6923-5*) Ayer.

Barthrop, Michael. Marlborough's Army, 1702-11. (Men-at-Arms Ser.: No. 97). (Illus.). 48p. pap. 11.95 (*0-85045-346-1*, 9007, Pub. by Osprey) Stackpole.

Barticus, R., ed. New Jersey Federal Civil Practice Manual. 900p. 1993. suppl. ed. 99.00 (*0-685-65980-1*) NJ Inst CLE.

Bartik, Timothy J. Who Benefits from State & Local Economic Development Policies? LC 91-27375. 354p. 1991. pap. 21.00 (*0-88099-113-5*); text 39.00 (*0-88099-114-3*) W E Upjohn.

Bartimeus, Paula. Eating with the Seasons: How to Achieve Health & Vitality by Eating in Harmony with Nature. LC 97-48331. 160p. 1998. pap. 14.95 (*1-86204-201-2*, Pub. by Element MA) Penguin Putnam.

Bartimus, Tad & McCartney, Scott. Trinity's Children: Living along America's Nuclear Highway. (Illus.). 326p. 1992. 21.95 (*0-15-167719-0*) Harcourt.

— Trinity's Children: Living along America's Nuclear Highway. LC 92-39101. (Illus.). 326p. (C). 1993. pap. 11.95 (*0-8263-1433-3*) U of NM Pr.

Bartinique, A. Patricia. Gustav Stickley - His Craft. (Illus.). 120p. (Orig.). 1992. pap. text 22.95 (*0-9634994-0-8*) Craftsman Farms.

— Kindred Styles: The Arts & Crafts Furniture of Charles P. Limbert. (Illus.). 128p. (Orig.). 1995. pap. write for info. (*0-9648116-0-X*) Gall Fivethirtytwo.

Bartinique, Patricia. Gustav Stickley His Craft. 2nd ed. (Illus.). 120p. 1998. reprint ed. pap. 22.50 (*0-940326-21-3*) Turn of Cent.

Bartiromo, Sandra. Positively Pasta. Keenan, Mackie, ed. LC 83-51536. (Illus.). 54p. (Orig.). 1983. spiral bd. 4.95 (*0-916005-00-3*) Silver Sea.

Bartiromo, Sandra & Weir, Debbie. Try It! Simple Vegetarian Recipes for the Non-Vegetarian. (Illus.). (Orig.). 1984. spiral bd. 4.95 (*0-916005-02-X*) Silver Sea.

Bartis, Peter T. Folklife Sourcebook: A Directory of Folklife Resources in the United States. 165p. 1994. pap. text 12.00 (*0-16-043069-0*, Library of Cong) USGPO.

Bartis, Peter T. & Fertig, Barbara C. Folklife Sourcebook: A Directory of Folklife Resources in the United States & Canada. LC 85-600334. 152p. 1986. 10.00 (*0-8444-0521-3*) Lib Congress.

***Bartisch, George.** Theriac. Blanchard, Donald, tr. from GER.Tr. of Warhafftige. (Illus.). 44p. 2000. pap. 25.00 (*0-9700529-0-1*) Blanchards Bks.

Bartke, Andrei, ed. Marihuana - Cannaboids: Neurobiology & Neurophysiology. 608p. 1992. boxed set 198.95 (*0-8493-7931-8*, QP801) CRC Pr.

Bartke, Andrzej, ed. Function of Somatic Cells in the Testis. LC 93-39374. 1994. write for info. (*0-387-94196-7*) Spr-Verlag.

Bartke, J. Relativistic Heavy Ion Physics. 400p. 1998. text 67.00 (*981-02-1231-3*) World Scientific Pub.

Bartke, Wolfgang. Biographical Dictionary & Analysis of China's Party Leadership, 1922-1988. 530p. 1990. 215.00 (*3-598-10876-1*) K G Saur Verlag.

— China's Economic Aid. LC 74-78315. 206p. 1975. 30.00 (*0-8419-0179-1*) Holmes & Meier.

— Who Was Who in the People's Republic of China, 2 vols. LC 98-112370. 850p. 1997. 350.00 (*3-598-11331-5*) K G Saur Verlag.

— Who's Who in the People's Republic of China. Verellen, Franciscus, tr. LC 80-27599. 743p. 1981. reprint ed. pap. 200.00 (*0-7837-9933-0*, 206066000006) Bks Demand.

— Who's Who in the People's Republic of China, 2 vols., Set. 3rd ed. (Illus.). 900p. 1991. lib. bdg. 325.00 (*3-598-10771-4*) K G Saur Verlag.

Bartke, Wolfgang & Schier, Peter. China's New Party Leadership: Biographies & Analysis of the Twelfth Central Committee of the Chinese Communist Party. LC 84-14130. 289p. 1985. reprint ed. pap. 89.60 (*0-7837-9949-7*, 206067600006) Bks Demand.

Bartknecht, W. Dust Explosions. (Illus.). 250p. 1989. 141.95 (*0-387-50100-2*) Spr-Verlag.

***Bartko & King.** The Two Regular Guys Cookbook: Menus & Other Tidbits. 96p. 2000. spiral bd. 9.95 (*1-56530-308-3*, 674-050, Pub. by Summit TX) BookWorld.

Bartko, D., et al. New Trends in Clinical Pharmacology. (Current Problems in Neurology Ser.: Vol. 7). 320p. 1988. 74.95 (*0-86196-146-3*, Pub. by J Libbey Med) Bks Intl VA.

Bartko, Janine, ed. see Stix, Andi.

Bartkovich, Kevin G., et al. Contemporary Calculus Through Applications. LC 95-36878. 1995. write for info. (*0-939765-87-X*) Janson Pubns.

Bartkowiak, Julia, jt. ed. see Narayan, Uma.

Bartkowiak, Robert A. Electric Circuit Analysis. 704p. (C). 1982. text 100.95 (*0-471-60355-4*) Wiley.

Bartkowski, Frances. Feminist Utopias. LC 88-37399. x, 198p. 1989. reprint ed. pap. 9.95 (*0-8032-6091-1*, Bison Books); reprint ed. text 45.00 (*0-8032-1205-4*) U of Nebr Pr.

— Travelers, Immigrants, Inmates. LC 94-32674. 1995. pap. 17.95 (*0-8166-2362-7*); text 44.95 (*0-8166-2361-9*) U of Minn Pr.

Bartkowski, Frances, jt. auth. see Kolmar, Wendy K.

Bartkowski, Joseph. Sanctuary. 48p. 1998. pap. write for info. (*1-886094-76-4*) Chicago Spectrum.

Bartkowski, Renee. Prayers for Married Couples. LC 89-80027. 96p. (Orig.). 1989. pap. 4.95 (*0-89243-301-9*) Liguori Pubns.

— With This Ring: A Practical Guide for Newlyweds. LC 91-77984. 112p. (Orig.). 1992. pap. text 5.95 (*0-89243-430-9*) Liguori Pubns.

Bartkus, Viva O. The Dynamic of Secession: An Analytical Framework. LC 98-35138. (Studies in International Relations: No. 64). 240p. (C). 1999. pap. text 19.95 (*0-521-65970-1*) Cambridge U Pr.

***Bartkus, Viva O.** The Dynamic of Secession: An Analytical Framework. LC 98-35138. (Studies in International Relations: No. 64). 240p. (C). 1999. text 59.95 (*0-521-65032-1*) Cambridge U Pr.

***Bartky, Ian R.** Selling the True Time: Nineteenth Century Timekeeping in America. LC 99-86739. 327p. 2000. 45.00 (*0-8047-3874-2*) Stanford U Pr.

Bartky, Sandra L. Femininity & Domination: Studies in the Phenomenology of Oppression. 176p. (C). (gr. 13). 1990. pap. 17.99 (*0-415-90186-3*, A3598) Routledge.

Bartky, Sandra L., jt. ed. see Fraser, Nancy.

Bartky, Walter. Highlights of Astronomy. (Illus.). 1961. pap. text 2.95 (*0-226-03840-8*, P509) U Ch Pr.

***Bartl, Almuth.** Animals. (Eddie's Finger Quiz Bks.). (Illus.). (J). 2000. pap. 4.95 (*0-7641-1602-9*) Barron.

— Comparisons. (Eddie's Finger Quiz Bks.). (Illus.). (J). 2000. pap. 4.95 (*0-7641-1613-4*) Barron.

— Concentration. (Eddie's Finger Quiz Bks.). (Illus.). (J). 2000. pap. 4.95 (*0-7641-1611-8*) Barron.

— Connections. (Eddie's Finger Quiz Bks.). (Illus.). (J). 2000. pap. 4.95 (*0-7641-1612-6*) Barron.

— Nature. (Eddie's Finger Quiz Bks.). (Illus.). (J). 2000. pap. 4.95 (*0-7641-1609-6*) Barron.

— Opposites. (Eddie's Finger Quiz Bks.). (Illus.). (J). 2000. pap. 4.95 (*0-7641-1603-7*) Barron.

Bartl, R. & Frisch, B. Biopsy of Bone in Internal Medicine: An Atlas & Sourcebook. LC 93-20357. (Current Histopathology Ser.: Vol. 21). 240p. (C). 1993. text 241.50 (*0-7923-8802-X*) Kluwer Academic.

Bartl, R., et al. Bone Marrow Biopsies Revisited. (Illus.). xiv, 138p. 1984. 50.50 (*3-8055-3937-1*) S Karger.

— Knochenmarkbiopsie. (Illus.). xvi, 140p. 1984. 50.50 (*3-8055-3875-8*) S Karger.

Bartl, R., jt. auth. see Frisch, B.

Bartl, R., jt. ed. see Frisch, Bertha.

Bartl, Timothy J. America Wants Flexible Work. 120p. 1998. pap. 19.95 (*0-9667568-3-5*) LPA Inc.

Bartle, Barton K. Computer Software in Music & Music Education: A Guide. LC 87-16532. 266p. 1987. 31.00 (*0-8108-2056-0*) Scarecrow.

Bartle, Beth & Carroll, Mary C. A Walking Tour of Independence National Historical Park. (Illus.). 45p. 1997. reprint ed. pap. text 15.00 (*0-7881-4613-0*) DIANE Pub.

Bartle, Brian. Here Comes Tow Truck. LC 91-77448. (Pop-up Trucks at Work Ser.). (Illus.). 12p. (J). (ps-1). 1992. 4.95 (*0-448-40593-8*, G & D) Peng Put Young Read.

Bartle, Dorothy B., ed. see Wait, George W.

Bartle, George. An Old Radical & His Brood: A Portrait of Sir John Bowring & His Family. (Illus.). 148p. 1995. pap. 12.95 (*1-85756-132-5*, Pub. by Janus Pubng) Paul & Co Pubs.

***Bartle, Keith D.** Capillary Electrochromatograph. (Illus.). 2000. pap. 72.00 (*0-85404-530-9*) Royal Soc Chem.

Bartle, Nathalie & Lieberman, Susan. Venus in Blue Jeans: Why Mothers & Daughters Need to Talk About Sex. 272p. 1999. pap. 12.95 (*0-440-50880-0*, Dell Trade Pbks) Dell.

Bartle, Nathalie A. & Liberman, Susan A. Venus in Blue Jeans: Encouraging Candid Talk Between Mothers & Daughters on Sex. LC 98-9619. 288p. 1998. 24.00 (*0-395-84172-0*) HM.

Bartle, Nicole, tr. see Burger, Udo.

Bartle, Nicole, tr. see Knopfhart, Alfred.

Bartle, Pat. As We Teach & Learn Module 5: Recognizing Our Catholic Identity: Prayer & Liturgy, 10 modules. Ristau, Karen & Haney, Regina, eds. 54p. 1997. pap. 64.00 (*1-55833-156-5*) Natl Cath Educ.

Bartle, Robert G. The Elements of Integration & Lebesgue Measure. 192p. 1995. pap. 54.95 (*0-471-04222-6*) Wiley.

— The Elements of Real Analysis. 2nd ed. 496p. (C). 1976. text 100.95 (*0-471-05464-X*) Wiley.

Bartle, Robert G., et al, eds. Geometry of Normed Linear Spaces. LC 86-3305. (Contemporary Mathematics Ser.: Vol. 52). 171p. 1986. pap. 25.00 (*0-8218-5057-1*, CONM/52) Am Math.

Bartle, Robert G. & Sherbert, Donald R. Introduction to Real Analysis. 2nd ed. LC 91-25482. 416p. (C). 1991. text 95.95 (*0-471-51000-9*) Wiley.

— Introduction to Real Analysis. 3rd ed. LC 99-13829. 400p. 1999. text 98.95 (*0-471-32148-6*) Wiley.

Bartle, Wilmot T., ed. see Spencer, Anne M.

Bartle, Wilmot T., jt. ed. see Sweeney, Mary S.

Bartleman, Frank. Azusa Street: The Roots of Modern-Day Pentecost. 2nd ed. LC 80-82806. 188p. 1993. pap. 8.99 (*0-88270-439-7*) Bridge-Logos.

Bartles, James, jt. auth. see Bittar, E. Edward.

Bartles, Kirsten, intro. Asyst 88 International Conference Proceedings: Connecting Users & Applications. (Illus.). 300p. (Orig.). 1989. pap. 25.00 (*0-924729-00-7*) Keithley Instruments.

Bartleson, John. Survive Alive. (Illus.). 16p. (J). (gr. k-3). 1996. pap. 2.50 (*1-883697-47-6*) Hara Pub.

— Survive Alive Life Safety Kit. (J). (gr. k-3). 1996. pap. 27.00 (*1-883697-48-4*) Hara Pub.

***Bartlet & Muir.** Talking the Walk: 32 Sessions for New Small Groups. (Youth Specialties Ser.). 2000. pap. 15.99 (*0-310-23313-5*) Zondervan.

Bartlet, Clive. The English Longbowman. (Warrior Ser.). (Illus.). 64p. 1995. pap. 12.95 (*1-85532-491-1*, Pub. by Osprey) Stackpole.

Bartlet, Edward. Stratonice. (Fropse Ser.: No. 11, Vol. LXX11B). 1997. 92.00 (*0-918728-95-9*) Pendragon NY.

Bartlet, Elizabeth, ed. see Mehul, Etienne N.

Bartlet, John. Familiar Quotations. (Works of John Bartlett). 1989. reprint ed. lib. bdg. 79.00 (*0-7812-1902-7*) Rprt Serv.

Bartlet, M. Elizabeth, ed. see Rossini, Gioachino.

Bartlet, Paul B., jt. auth. see Pohl, Amelia E.

Bartlett. America: What Went Wrong? 22.95 (*0-8488-1530-0*) Amereon Ltd.

— Bartlett's Book of Love Quotations. LC 93-27519. 272p. (gr. 8). 1994. 15.95 (*0-316-08292-9*) Little.

— Bartlett's Roget's Thesaurus. LC 96-18343. 1456p. (gr. 8). 1996. 20.95 (*0-316-10138-9*) Little.

— Everything You Wanted to Know. 1995. 25.00 (*0-226-03841-6*) U Ch Pr.

— Management of Respiratory Tract Infections. 2nd ed. LC 99-13107. 1999. 15.00 (*0-683-30633-2*) Lppncott W & W.

— Peace, War & European Powers. LC 96-6785. 224p. 1996. text 49.95 (*0-312-16137-9*) St Martin.

— Sports Biomechanics. LC 98-21961. (Illus.). 304p. (Orig.). (C). 1999. pap. 37.99 (*0-419-18440-6*, E & FN Spon) Routledge.

***Bartlett & Willis.** Motor Boat & Yachting Logbook for Cruising under Power. 96p. 2000. pap. 14.95 (*1-898660-36-0*, Pub. by Fernhurst Bks) Motorbooks Intl.

Bartlett, A. Bob the Dog. (Illus.). (J). 1996. pap. text 11.95 (*0-340-65672-7*, Pub. by Hodder & Stought Ltd) Trafalgar.

Bartlett, A. Erice the Reindeer. (Illus.). (J). pap. text 11.95 (*0-340-65598-4*, Pub. by Hodder & Stought Ltd) Trafalgar.

Bartlett, Adeline C. Larger Rhetorical Patterns in Anglo-Saxon Poetry. LC 72-159999. reprint ed. 24.50 (*0-404-00667-1*) AMS Pr.

Bartlett, Albert L. Story of Haverhill in Massachusetts: With a Chronological Record of Historical Events with Notes. 550p. Date not set. text 35.00 (*1-878651-12-9*) HPL Pr.

Bartlett, Alison, jt. auth. see Lawrence, Michael.

Bartlett, Amy. Afterwards. (National Poetry Ser.). 66p. (Orig.). 1985. 13.95 (*0-89255-090-2*); pap. 7.95 (*0-89255-091-0*) Persea Bks.

An Asterisk (*) at the beginning of an entry indicates that the title is appearing for the first time.

Bartlett, Ann C. Cultures of Piety: Medieval English Devotional Literature in Translation. LC 98-46130. 1999. (*0-8014-3443-2*) Cornell U Pr.

Bartlett, Anne C. Cultures of Piety: Medieval English Devotional Literature in Translation. LC 98-46130. 1999. pap. 17.95 (*0-8014-8455-3*) Cornell U Pr.

— Male Authors, Female Readers: Representation & Subjectivity in Middle English Devotional Literature. 208p. 1995. text 35.00 (*0-8014-3038-0*) Cornell U Pr.

Bartlett, Anne C., et al, eds. Vox Mystica: Essays on Medieval Mysticism in Honor of Professor Valerie M. Lagorio. (Illus.). 250p. 1995. 75.00 (*0-85991-439-9*) Boydell & Brewer.

***Bartlett, Apple Parish, et al.** Sister. LC 00-27968. (Illus.). 384p. 2000. text 35.00 (*0-312-24240-9*) St Martin.

Bartlett, Barbara B. & Haynie, Willaim S., eds. To God with Love. 140p. (J). (ps-7). 1995. spiral bd. 12.00 (*0-9622553-6-X*, 125-110) Selah Pub Co.

Bartlett, Barrie E. Beauzee's Grammaire Generale: Theory & Methodology. LC 74-81133. (Janua Linguarum, Series Major: No. 82). 202p. 1975. text 80.00 (*90-279-3433-9*) Mouton.

Bartlett, Beatrice S. Monarchs & Ministers: The Grand Council in Mid-Ch'ing China, 1723-1820. (Illus.). 417p. 1990. 60.00 (*0-520-06591-3*, Pub. by U CA Pr) Cal Prin Full Svc.

— Monarchs & Ministers: The Grand Council in Mid-Ch'ing China, 1723-1820. (Illus.). 417p. (C). 1994. pap. 22.50 (*0-520-08645-7*, Pub. by U CA Pr) Cal Prin Full Svc.

Bartlett, Bob. Growing Toward Intimacy. 128p. 1997. 7.50 (*1-885996-05-5*) Good Grnd Pr.

Bartlett, Brett R. Bible Baffles: Twenty-Four Mazes Based on Favorite Bible Stories. (Illus.). 40p. (Orig.). 1990. pap. 4.98 (*0-88290-371-3*) Horizon Utah.

— Mormon Mazes: Twenty-Four Mazes Based on Familiar Church Events. 26p. 1985. 4.98 (*0-88290-301-2*, 1340) Horizon Utah.

Bartlett, Brian. Planet Harbor. 95p. 1989. pap. 7.95 (*0-86492-102-0*, Pub. by Goose Ln Edits) Genl Dist Srvs.

— Underwater Carpentry. 115p. 1993. pap. 12.95 (*0-86492-133-0*, Pub. by Goose Ln Edits) Genl Dist Srvs.

Bartlett, Bruce. Stereo Microphone Techniques. 192p. 1991. pap. text 43.95 (*0-240-80076-1*, Focal) Buttrwrth-Heinemann.

Bartlett, Bruce & Bartlett, Jenny. On-Location Recording Techniques. LC 99-10574. 304p. 1999. pap. text 29.95 (*0-240-80379-5*, Focal) Buttrwrth-Heinemann.

— Practical Recording Techniques: The Step-by-Step Approach to Professional Audio Recording. 2nd ed. LC 97-41861. 488p. 1998. pap. text 29.95 (*0-240-80306-X*, Focal) Buttrwrth-Heinemann.

Bartlett, Bruce & Roth, Timothy P., eds. The Supply Side Solution. LC 83-7619. (Illus.). 304p. reprint ed. pap. 94.30 (*0-8357-4829-4*, 203776600009) Bks Demand.

Bartlett, C. J. Global Conflict. 408p. (C). 1984. text 35.95 (*0-582-49069-3*, 73468) Longman.

— GLOBAL CONFLICT1880 1970. 408p. (C). 1989. pap. text 30.80 (*0-582-49070-7*, 73468) Longman.

— Great Britain & Sea Power, 1815-1853. (Modern Revivals in Military History Ser.). 368p. 1993. 69.95 (*0-7512-0141-3*, Pub. by Gregg Pub) Ashgate Pub Co.

— SPEC RELATNSHP:SINCE1945. (Post War World Ser.). 196p. (C). 1992. pap. text 28.50 (*0-582-02395-5*, 79340) Longman.

Bartlett, Charlene & Bickford, Jayne E. Cemetery Inscriptions, & Revolutionary War of 1812, & Civil War Veterans of Bowdoin, Maine. x, 182p. (Orig.). 1993. pap. text 18.50 (*1-55613-771-0*) Heritage Bk.

Bartlett, Charles H. Tales of Kankakee Land. (Illus.). 1977. reprint ed. 17.50 (*0-915056-07-0*) Hardscrabble Bks.

Bartlett, Christopher A., et al, eds. Managing the Global Firm. 368p. 1996. pap. 22.95 (*0-415-13518-4*) Routledge.

— Managing the Global Firm. 336p. (C). (gr. 13). 1989. pap. 35.95 (*0-415-03711-5*, A4199) Thomson Learn.

***Bartlett, Christopher A. & Ghoshal, Sumantra.** The Individualized Corporation: A Fundamentally New Approach to Management. 368p. 1999. pap. 16.00 (*0-88730-831-7*, HarpBusn) HarpInfo.

Bartlett, Christopher A. & Ghoshal, Sumantra. Managing Across Borders: The Transnational Solution. 288p. 1991. pap. 16.95 (*0-87584-303-4*) Harvard Busn.

— Managing Across Borders: The Transnational Solution. 1989. text 35.00 (*0-07-103208-8*) McGraw.

— Managing Across Borders: The Transnational Solution. 2nd ed. LC 98-26004. 416p. 1998. 29.95 (*0-87584-849-4*) Harvard Busn.

— Transnational Management: Text Cases & Readings in Cross Border Management. 2nd ed. 1995. write for info. (*0-256-16553-X*, Irwn Prfssnl) McGraw-Hill Prof.

***Bartlett, Christopher A. & Ghoshal, Sumantra.** Transnational Management: Text, Cases, & Readings in Cross-Border Management. 3rd ed. LC 99-34641. (McGraw-Hill Advanced Topics in Global Management Ser.). 2000. write for info. (*0-256-24781-1*, Irwn McGrw-H) McGrw-H Hghr Educ.

Bartlett, Christopher A. & Ghoshal, Sumantra. Transnational Management, International: Text Cases & Readings in Cross Border Management. (C). 1991. text, student ed. 31.50 (*0-256-11746-2*, Irwn McGrw-H) McGrw-H Hghr Educ.

Bartlett, Christopher A., jt. auth. see Ghoshal, Sumantra.

Bartlett, Clifford, ed. see Keyte, Hugh.

Bartlett, Clifford, jt. ed. see Rutter, John.

Bartlett, Cynthia Chalmers. Beacon Hill. LC 96-209883. (Images of America Ser.). 128p. 1996. pap. 16.99 (*0-7524-0296-X*) Arcadia Publng.

Bartlett, Darius J., jt. auth. see Wright, Dawn J.

Bartlett, David F., ed. The Metric Debate. LC 79-53270. (Illus.). 150p. reprint ed. pap. 46.50 (*0-8357-5501-0*, 203511600093) Bks Demand.

Bartlett, David L. Between the Bible & the Church: New Methods for Biblical Preaching. LC 98-31140. 192p. 1999. pap. 17.00 (*0-687-02825-6*) Abingdon.

— Ministry in the New Testament. LC 93-19849. (Overtures to Biblical Theology Ser.). 224p. 1993. pap. 19.00 (*0-8006-1565-4*, 1-1565) Augsburg Fortress.

— The Political Economy of Dual Transformations: Market Reforms & Democratization in Hungary. LC 96-36553. 320p. (C). 1997. text 54.50 (*0-472-10794-1*, 10794) U of Mich Pr.

— Romans. Miller, Patrick D., ed. LC 95-10453. (Westminster Bible Companion Ser.). 160p. 1995. pap. 15.00 (*0-664-25254-0*) Westminster John Knox.

Bartlett, David L., ed. see Craddock, Fred B.

Bartlett, David L., ed. see Mann, Thomas W.

Bartlett, David L., ed. see Ringe, Sharon H.

Bartlett, David M. Modern Agitators. LC 70-133146. (Black Heritage Library Collection). 1977. 28.95 (*0-8369-8702-0*) Ayer.

Bartlett, David W. Life & Public Services of Hon. Abraham Lincoln, with a Portrait on Steel, to Which Is Added a Biographical Sketch of Hon. Hannibal Hamlin. LC 78-95064. (Select Bibliographies Reprint Ser.). 1977. 33.95 (*0-8369-5066-6*) Ayer.

Bartlett, Dean. Stress: Perspectives & Processes. LC 98-14536. (Health Psychology Ser.). 1998. 85.00 (*0-335-19928-3*); pap. 27.95 (*0-335-19927-5*) OpUniv Pr.

***Bartlett, Deborah.** Power Lines to Productivity & Profit. 1999. 4.99 (*1-56229-484-9*) Pneuma Life Pub.

Bartlett, Donald A. Plant Engineering Management. LC 74-144106. (Manufacturing Management Ser.: Vol. 5). 233p. reprint ed. pap. 72.30 (*0-608-16167-5*, 205573700034) Bks Demand.

Bartlett, Donald L., jt. auth. see Steele, James B.

***Bartlett, Douglas H., ed.** Molecular Marine Microbiology. 220p. 2000. 119.99 (*1-898486-20-4*, Pub. by Horizon Sci) Intl Spec Bk.

Bartlett, Dwight K., ed. Corporate Book Reserving for Postretirement Healthcare Benefits. (Pension Research Council Publications). 128p. (C). 1991. text 30.95 (*0-256-09142-0*) U of Pa Pr.

***Bartlett, E. G.** Jungle Nurse. 280p. 2000. 18.99 (*0-7089-5695-5*) Ulverscroft.

— Mysterious Stranger. large type ed. 264p. 2000. pap. 18.99 (*0-7089-5646-7*, Linford) Ulverscroft.

Bartlett, E. G. Strangers in Eden. large type ed. (Linford Romance Library). 1991. pap. 16.99 (*0-7089-7109-1*) Ulverscroft.

Bartlett, Ed, jt. auth. see RiskCare Staff.

Bartlett, Edward E., et al. Medical Practice Management Skills. iv, 288p. 1995. pap. 54.00 (*1-930548-17-6*) Tennenhouse Prof Pubns.

Bartlett, Elizabeth. Address in Time. LC 78-75102. 1979. 15.95 (*0-8023-1271-3*) Dufour.

— The Czar Is Dead. 64p. (C). 1986. pap. 38.00 (*0-947612-22-X*, Pub. by Rivelin Grapheme Pr) St Mut.

— Two Women Dancing: New & Selected Poems. Rumens, Carol, ed. 224p. 1996. pap. 19.95 (*1-85224-297-3*, Pub. by Bloodaxe Bks) Dufour.

Bartlett, Elizabeth Ann. Journey of the Heart: Spiritual Insights on the Road to a Transplant. 192p. 1996. pap. 12.95 (*1-57025-128-2*) Pfeifer-Hamilton.

***Bartlett, Esther & Field, Marion.** Working as a Nurse: How to Make Your Career in a Fulfilling Profession. (Illus.). 144p. 2000. pap. 19.95 (*1-85703-443-0*, Pub. by How To Bks) Midpt Trade.

Bartlett, Eugene R. Cable Communications: Building the Information Infrastructure. 319p. 1995. 50.00 (*0-07-005355-3*) McGraw.

Bartlett, Eugene R. Cable Television Handbook: Systems & Operations. LC 99-43784. 384p. 1999. 69.95 (*0-07-006891-7*) McGraw.

— Cable Television Technology & Operations. 421p. 1990. 65.00 (*0-07-003957-7*) McGraw.

Bartlett, F. C. Remembering. (Illus.). 337p. (C). 1995. text 59.95 (*0-521-48278-X*); pap. text 19.95 (*0-521-48356-5*) Cambridge U Pr.

Bartlett, Frances & Lai, Ivan. Hong Kong on a Plate. (Illus.). 238p. 1997. pap. 19.95 (*962-7992-06-2*, Pub. by Saqi) Intl Spec Bk.

Bartlett, Frederic C. Thinking: An Experimental & Social Study. LC 82-983. 203p. 1982. reprint ed. lib. bdg. 59.50 (*0-313-23412-4*, BART, Greenwood Pr) Greenwood.

Bartlett, G. M. Recent Developments in High Speed Chain Drives. (Technical Papers: Vol. P83). (Illus.). 10p. 1926. pap. text 30.00 (*1-55589-440-2*) AGMA.

Bartlett, G. W. The Bartlett: Forefathers & Descendants of Willard & Genevieve Wilson Bartlett, & Allied Families Moulton - McGehee - Endress. (Illus.). 270p. 1993. reprint ed. pap. 42.00 (*0-8328-3259-6*); reprint ed. lib. bdg. 52.00 (*0-8328-3258-8*) Higginson Bk Co.

Bartlett, George. Fuchsias: A Colour Guide. (Illus.). 320p. 1996. 45.00 (*1-85223-927-1*, Pub. by Crolwood) Trafalgar.

— Fuchsias: Step by Step for Growing Success. (Illus.). 128p. 1996. pap. 16.95 (*1-85223-971-9*, Pub. by Crolwood) Trafalgar.

— Fuchsias: The Complete Guide. (Illus.). 192p. 1993. pap. 22.95 (*1-85223-745-7*, Pub. by Crolwood) Trafalgar.

Bartlett, Georgia. Floral Medley. 63p. 1996. pap. 10.50 (*1-56770-344-5*) S Scheewe Pubns.

— Flower Show. (Illus.). 64p. 1997. pap. 10.50 (*1-56770-415-8*) S Scheewe Pubns.

— Painting Fantasy Flowers. 100p. 1989. pap. text 7.50 (*1-56770-215-5*) S Scheewe Pubns.

— Petals. 62p. 1995. pap. 10.50 (*1-56770-317-8*) S Scheewe Pubns.

— Soft Petals. 48p. 1987. pap. text 6.50 (*1-56770-171-X*) S Scheewe Pubns.

Bartlett, Gillian. Great Careers for People Interested in Art & Design, Vol. 6. 3rd ed. LC 95-62268. (Career Connections Ser.: Series 3). 48p. 1995. text 23.00 (*0-7876-0863-7*, GML00597-110113, UXL) Gale.

Bartlett, Grace. From the Wallowas. (Illus.). 144p. (Orig.). 1992. pap. text 16.00 (*0-918957-08-7*) Pika Oregon.

Bartlett, Hall. The Rest of Our Lives. 1989. mass mkt. 4.95 (*0-8217-2674-9*, Zebra Kensgtn) Kensgtn Pub Corp.

Bartlett, Harriet T. An Esoteric Reading of Biblical Symbolism. 1669p. 1996. spiral bd. 174.50 (*0-7873-0077-2*) Hlth Research.

— An Esoteric Reading of Biblical Symbolism (1916) 227p. 1996. reprint ed. pap. 17.00 (*1-56459-601-X*) Kessinger Pub.

— Jesus & Krishnamurti: Their Lives & Teachings (1928) 50p. 1998. reprint ed. pap. 7.95 (*0-7661-0153-3*) Kessinger Pub.

Bartlett, Harriett M. Analyzing Social Work Practice by Fields. rev. ed. LC 88-29152. 68p. 1988. reprint ed. 8.95 (*0-87101-167-0*) Natl Assn Soc Wkrs.

— Social Work Practice in the Health Field. LC 61-17630. 285p. 1961. 12.95 (*0-87101-035-6*) Natl Assn Soc Wkrs.

Bartlett, Hazel & Gregory, Julia. Catalogue of Early Books on Music (Before 1800) LC 69-12684. (Music Ser.). 1969. reprint ed. lib. bdg. 45.00 (*0-306-71223-7*) Da Capo.

Bartlett, Helen. Nursing Homes for the Elderly: Questions of Quality & Policy. LC 92-27857. 225p. 1993. text 61.00 (*3-7186-5331-1*) Gordon & Breach.

Bartlett, Helen, jt. ed. see Challis, Linda.

Bartlett, Henrietta & Pollard, Alfred. A Census of Shakespeare's Plays in Quarto, 1594-1709. LC 70-135724. reprint ed. 47.50 (*0-404-00669-8*) AMS Pr.

Bartlett, Irving H. The American Mind in the Mid-Nineteenth Century. 2nd ed. Eisenstadt, A. S. & Franklin, John H., eds. LC 81-14988. (American History Ser.). 160p. (C). 1982. pap. text 11.95 (*0-88295-809-7*) Harlan Davidson.

***Bartlett, J. D. & Bartlett, Patricia.** Bearded Dragons. LC 99-26239. (Reptile Keepers Ser.). 48p. 1999. pap. text 5.95 (*0-7641-1125-6*) Barron.

— Green Iguanas. LC 99-29656. (Reptile Keepers Ser.). 48p. 1999. pap. text 5.95 (*0-7641-1126-4*) Barron.

Bartlett, J. G. The Gregory Stone Genealogy Ancestry & Descendants of Deacon Gregory Stone of Cambridge, Massachusetts, 1320-1917. (Illus.). 913p. 1993. reprint ed. pap. 107.00 (*0-8328-3062-3*); reprint ed. lib. bdg. 117.00 (*0-8328-3061-5*) Higginson Bk Co.

— Robert Coe, Puritan, His Ancestry & Descendants, 1340-1910. (Illus.). 664p. 1989. reprint ed. pap. 94.50 (*0-8328-0409-6*); reprint ed. lib. bdg. 102.50 (*0-8328-0408-8*) Higginson Bk Co.

Bartlett, J. L., jt. auth. see Helmrath, M. O.

Bartlett, J. Neville. Davidsons of Mugiemoss: A History of C. Davidson & Sons. LC 97-1025. (Illus.). 200p. 1997. 65.00 (*0-485-11514-X*, Pub. by Athlone Pr) Humanities.

***Bartlett, James D. & Jaanus, Siret D.** Clinical Ocular Pharmacology. (Illus.). 1120p. 2000. 125.00 (*0-7506-7039-8*) Buttrwrth-Heinemann.

Bartlett, James Y. Golf Gurus: The Wisdom of the Game's Greatest Instructors. LC 95-53052. x, 214p. 1996. 19.95 (*0-87833-912-4*) Taylor Pub.

— Learn Golf the Lazy Way. (Lazy Way Ser.). 288p. 1920. pap. 12.95 (*0-02-863164-1*) Free Pr.

Bartlett, Jane. Ms. B's F. Quotations. LC 91-66093. 112p. (Orig.). 1991. pap. 6.95 (*0-9610330-4-5*) J Tabler-Bks.

— Will You Be Mother? Women Who Choose to Say No. 233p. (C). 1995. text 45.00 (*0-8147-1244-4*); pap. text 17.50 (*0-8147-1245-2*) NYU Pr.

Bartlett, Janet & McHale, Barbara. Labor of Love: The Perfect Pregnancy Planner. 65p. 1993. spiral bd. 7.95 (*0-9629092-0-3*) Heart-Bound Bks.

Bartlett, Jaye. Caterpillar Had a Dream: A Poetic Story about Dreams Coming True. (Illus.). (J). 1991. 8.95 (*1-878064-02-9*) TLC Books.

— Caterpillar Had a Dream: A Story about Dreams Coming True. (Illus.). 38p. (Orig.). (J). (ps up). 1990. lib. bdg. 11.95 incl. audio (*1-878064-00-2*) New Age CT.

Bartlett, Jeffrey. Little Trip to Heaven: Ireland, 1994. 206p. 1997. pap. 10.95 (*1-889883-02-6*) Provine Pr.

— One Vast Page: Essays on the Beat Writers, Their Books, & My Life, 1950-1980. 165p. 1991. pap. 8.95 (*1-889883-00-X*) Provine Pr.

Bartlett, Jennifer. Jennifer Bartlett: Rhapsody. LC 85-3952. (Contemporary Artists Ser.). (Illus.). 96p. 1985. 35.00 (*0-8109-1577-4*, Pub. by Abrams) Time Warner.

Bartlett, Jenny, jt. auth. see Bartlett, Bruce.

Bartlett, Jimmy, ed. see Facts & Comparisons Staff.

***Bartlett, Jimmy D.** Ophthalmic Drug Facts. (Illus.). 1999. pap. 54.95 (*1-57439-060-0*) Facts & Comparisons.

Bartlett, Jimmy D. & Jaanus, Siret D. Clinical Ocular Pharmacology. 3rd ed. LC 95-19146. (Illus.). 1057p. 1995. text 85.00 (*0-7506-9448-3*) Buttrwrth-Heinemann.

— Clinical Ocular Pharmacology: Pocket Handbook. 3rd ed. LC 96-42981. 512p. 1996. pap. text 42.00 (*0-7506-9641-9*) Buttrwrth-Heinemann.

Bartlett, Joe. Satan Tried to Kill Me: "But God" Had a Better Plan. (Illus.). 91p. 1998. pap. 10.00 (*0-9664311-0-3*) One Day.

Bartlett, John. Bartlett's Familiar Quotations. 16th ed. 16p. 1992. write for info. (*0-316-08287-2*) Little.

— Bartlett's Familiar Quotations. 16th ed. Kaplan, Justin, ed. 1472p. (gr. 8). 1992. 47.50 (*0-316-08277-5*) Little.

— Bartlett's Familiar Quotations. 17th ed. 2000. write for info. (*0-316-08460-3*) Little.

— Bartletts Quote-A-Day. 368p. 1998. pap. text 9.95 (*0-316-08715-7*) Little Brown Yemanja Sings.

— Bartlett's Quote-a-Day 2000. 316p. 1999. pap. 10.95 (*0-316-08746-7*) Little.

***Bartlett, John.** Familiar Shakespearean Quotations. (Big Works Collection). (Illus.). 1p. 1999. 29.95 (*1-929142-19-6*) One Page Bk.

Bartlett, John. Medical Management of HIV Infection: 1995 Edition. 260p. 1995. 17.95 (*0-924428-09-0*) Phys Sci Pub.

— Medical Management of HIV Infection: 1995 Edition. 1996. spiral bd. write for info. (*0-614-05153-3*) Phys Sci Pub.

— New & Complete Concordance of Shakespeare. (Works of John Bartlett). 1989. reprint ed. lib. bdg. 198.00 (*0-7812-1905-1*) Rprt Serv.

— New Method of Chess Notation. (Works of John Bartlett). 1989. reprint ed. lib. bdg. 79.00 (*0-7812-1903-5*) Rprt Serv.

— A Shakespeare Phrase Book. (Works of John Bartlett). 1989. reprint ed. lib. bdg. 79.00 (*0-7812-1904-3*) Rprt Serv.

— The Works of John Bartlett. 1989. reprint ed. lib. bdg. 79.00 (*0-685-27839-5*) Rprt Serv.

Bartlett, John, ed. Complete Concordance to Shakespeare. 1910p. 1969. reprint ed. text 95.00 (*0-312-15645-6*) St Martin.

Bartlett, John, jt. auth. see Megaw, T. M.

Bartlett, John A. British Ceramic Art, 1870-1940. LC 92-82036. (Illus.). 240p. 1993. 69.95 (*0-88740-456-1*) Schiffer.

Bartlett, John C. Management of Respiratory Tract Infections. LC 97-13539. 120p. 1997. pap. 15.00 (*0-683-30236-1*) Lppncott W & W.

Bartlett, John G. The Johns Hopkins Hospital Guide to Medical Care of Patients with HIV Infection. 4th ed. LC 93-41024. 1993. 10.00 (*0-683-00448-4*) Lppncott W & W.

— The Johns Hopkins Hospital Guide to Medical Care of Patients with HIV Infection. 5th ed. LC 95-10374. 1995. 13.95 (*0-683-00449-2*) Lppncott W & W.

— The Johns Hopkins Hospital 1996 Guide to Medical Care of Patients with HIV Infection. 6th ed. LC 96-14175. 172p. 1996. pap. 12.00 (*0-683-30004-0*) Lppncott W & W.

Bartlett, John G. The Johns Hopkins Hospital 2000 Guide to Medical Care of Patients with Hiv Infection. 9th ed. 200p. pap. text. write for info. (*0-7817-2342-6*) Lppncott W & W.

Bartlett, John G. 1998 Pocket Book of Infectious Disease Therapy. 9th ed. LC 98-194526. 357p. 1998. pap. 14.95 (*0-683-30632-4*) Lppncott W & W.

— 1995 Pocket Book of Infectious Disease Therapy. 6th ed. 282p. 1995. pap. 13.95 (*0-683-00445-X*) Lppncott W & W.

— Pocket Book Infectious Disease Therapy, 1997. 8th ed. 379p. 1997. pap. 14.95 (*0-683-30357-0*) Lppncott W & W.

— Pocketbook of Infectious Disease Therapy, 1994. (Illus.). 272p. 1994. 13.95 (*0-683-00444-1*) Lppncott W & W.

Bartlett, John G. 2000 Pocket Book of Infectious Disease Therapy. 10th ed. 350p. pap. text 14.95 (*0-7817-2341-8*) Lppncott W & W.

Bartlett, John G., ed. 1996 Pocket Book of Infectious Disease Therapy. (Illus.). 350p. 1997. pap. 14.95 (*0-683-18238-2*) Lppncott W & W.

Bartlett, John G. & Johns Hopkins Hospital Staff. The Johns Hopkins Hospital 1998-1999 Guide to Medical Care of Patients with HIV Infection. 8th ed. LC 98-8416. 191p. 1998. pap. 12.00 (*0-683-30631-6*) Lppncott W & W.

Bartlett, John G., et al. The Guide to Living with HIV Infection: Developed at the Johns Hopkins AIDS Clinic. 4th rev. ed. LC 97-36903. 400p. 1998. pap. 15.95 (*0-8018-5854-2*); text 42.00 (*0-8018-5853-4*) Johns Hopkins.

***Bartlett, John M. & Stirling, David, eds.** PCR Protocols. 2nd ed. 450p. 2000. 79.50 (*0-89603-627-8*); 119.50 (*0-89603-642-1*) Humana.

Bartlett, John M. S., ed. Ovarian Cancer: Methods & Protocols. (Methods in Molecular Medicine Ser.: Vol. 39). (Illus.). 839p. 2000. 149.50 (*0-89603-583-2*) Humana.

Bartlett, John R. Census of the Inhabitants of the Colony of Rhode Island & Providence Plantations: 1774. 246p. 1984. reprint ed. pap. 12.50 (*0-912606-20-7*) Hunterdon Hse.

***Bartlett, John R.** Census of the Inhabitants of the Colony of Rhode Island & Providence Plantations, 1774. 359p. 1999. reprint ed. pap. 30.00 (*0-8063-4805-4*) Clearfield Co.

Bartlett, John R. Dictionary of Americanism: A Glossary of Words & Phrases, Usually Regarded As Peculiar to the United States. 1976. reprint ed. 79.00 (*0-403-06365-5*, Regency) Scholarly.

— Dictionary of Americanisms: A Glossary of Words & Phrases, Usually Regarded As Peculiar. 1988. reprint ed. lib. bdg. 89.00 (*0-7812-0500-X*) Rprt Serv.

***Bartlett, John R.** 1 Maccabees. (Guides to the Apocrypha & Pseudepigrapha Ser.: No. 5). 111p. 1998. pap. 14.95 (*1-85075-763-1*, Pub. by Sheffield Acad) CUP Services.

Bartlett, John R. Literature of the Rebellion. LC 77-109311. 477p. 1970. reprint ed. lib. bdg. 69.50 (*0-8371-3568-0*, BLR&) Greenwood.

— Shakespeare Concordance, 4 vols., Set. 1976. 1500.00 (*0-87968-266-3*) Gordon Pr.

Bartlett, John R., ed. Archaeology & Biblical Interpretation. 192p. (C). 1997. pap. 22.99 (*0-415-14114-1*) Routledge.

— Archaeology & Biblical Interpretation. LC 96-13808. (Illus.). 192p. (C). 1997. 60.00 (*0-415-14113-3*) Routledge.

— Records of the Colony of Rhode Island & Providence Plantations in New England, 10 vols., Set. reprint ed. lib. bdg. 900.00 (*0-404-00680-9*) AMS Pr.

B

***Bartlett, John Russell.** Catalogue of Books & Pamphlets Relating to the Civil War in the United States. fac. ed. 477p. 2000. 65.00 (1-57898-222-7) Martino Pubng.

Bartlett, John W. The Future Is Ours: A Handbook for Students Activists in the 21St Century. LC 96-22616. (Illus.). 224p. 1996. pap. 14.95 (0-8050-4787-5) H Holt & Co.

Bartlett, Jonathan. Cook's Dictionary. 1999. pap. 22.00 (0-525-93618-1) NAL.

— The Cooks Dictionary. 1996. pap. write for info. (0-8092-3027-5) NTC Contemp Pub Co.

— The Cook's Dictionary & Culinary Reference. 448p. 1996. 35.00 (0-8092-3120-4, 312040, Contemporary Bks) NTC Contemp Pub Co.

— The Cook's Dictionary & Culinary Reference, 1. 448p. 1999. pap. 25.00 (0-8092-2794-0, 279400, Contemporary Bks) NTC Contemp Pub Co.

Bartlett, Joseph W. Equity Finance: Venture Capital, Buyouts, Restructurings & Reorganizations, 3. 1784p. 1997. boxed set 370.00 (0-7355-0644-2) Panel Pubs.

Bartlett, Joseph W. Fundamentals of Venture Capital. LC 99-47550. 120p. 1999. 24.95 (1-56833-126-6) Madison Bks UPA.

— Law Business: A Tired Monopoly. vii, 198p. 1982. reprint ed. 32.50 (0-8377-0324-7, Rothman) W S Hein.

Bartlett, Joseph W. & Steinglass, David E. Standard Documents for Community Development Venture Capital Transactions. LC 97-41244. 168p. (C). 1997. 37.50 (0-7618-0953-8) U Pr of Amer.

Bartlett, K. Towards Still Greater Professionalism. (Tolley Medal Ser.). 1971. 1.50 (0-686-52206-0, WPT 4) Syracuse U Cont Ed.

Bartlett, Kasyan, jt. photos by see Bartlett, Magnus.

Bartlett, Katharine T. Gender & Law: Theory, Doctrine, Commentary. 1056p. 1993. teacher ed. write for info. (0-316-08293-7, 82937) Aspen Law.

— Gender & Law: Theory, Doctrine, Commentary. 1056p. 1993. 54.00 (0-316-08290-2, Aspen Law & Bus) Aspen Pub.

Bartlett, Katharine T. & Harris, Angela P. Gender & Law: Theory, Doctrine, Commentary. 2nd ed. LC 97-32502. 1998. boxed set 62.00 (1-56706-740-9) Panel Pubs.

Bartlett, Katharine T. & Kennedy, Rosanne, eds. Feminist Legal Theory: Readings in Law & Gender. (New Perspectives on Law, Culture, & Society Ser.). 446p. (C). 1991. pap. text 37.00 (0-8133-1248-5, Pub. by Westview) HarpC.

Bartlett, Katharine T. & Wegner, Judith W., eds. Children with Special Needs. 512p. 1987. 44.95 (0-88738-690-3) Transaction Pubs.

Bartlett, Kenneth, ed. The Civilization of the Italian Renaissance: A Sourcebook. (Sources in Modern History Ser.). 441p. (C). 1992. pap. text 32.76 (0-669-20900-7) HM Trade Div.

Bartlett, Kenneth, ed. see Schutz, Albert L.

Bartlett, Kenneth G., jt. ed. see Dominguez, George S.

Bartlett, Kenneth R., ed. see Piccolomini, Anneas Sylvis.

Bartlett, Lanier, ed. see Bell, Horace.

Bartlett, Larry D. & Helms, Lelia B. Recent Developments in Public Education Law. 17p. 1993. reprint ed. text 10.00 (1-56534-086-8) Ed Law Assn.

Bartlett, Laurence. William Congreve: An Annotated Bibliography, 1978-1994. annot. ed. LC 96-11672. (Author Bibliographies Ser.: No. 97). 1996. 29.00 (0-8108-3166-X) Scarecrow.

Bartlett, Lee. Kenneth Rexroth. LC 87-73497. (Western Writers Ser.: No. 84). (Illus.). 50p. (Orig.). 1988. pap. 4.95 (0-88430-083-8) Boise St U W Writ Ser.

— Kenneth Rexroth & James Laughlin: Selected Letters. 1991. 27.50 (0-393-02939-5) Norton.

— William Everson. LC 85-70127. (Western Writers Ser.: No. 67). (Illus.). 50p. (Orig.). 1985. pap. 4.95 (0-88430-041-2) Boise St U W Writ Ser.

— William Everson: The Life of Brother Antoninus. LC 87-11034. (Illus.). 288p. 1988. 25.95 (0-8112-1060-X, Pub. by New Directions) Norton.

Bartlett, Lee, ed. Benchmark & Blaze: The Emergence of William Everson. LC 78-27137. 292p. 1979. lib. bdg. 24.00 (0-8108-1198-7) Scarecrow.

— William Everson - On Writing the Waterbirds & Other Presentations: Collected Forewords & Afterwords 1935-1981. LC 83-3123. 288p. 1983. 24.00 (0-8108-1617-2) Scarecrow.

Bartlett, Lee & Campo, Allan. William Everson: A Descriptive Bibliography, 1934-1976. LC 77-5397. (Author Bibliographies Ser.: No. 33). 119p. 1977. 21.00 (0-8108-1037-9) Scarecrow.

Bartlett, Lee, ed. see Everson, William.

Bartlett, Lesley, jt. auth. see Lutz, Catherine.

Bartlett, Levi. Genealogical & Biographical Sketches of the Bartlett Family in England & America. 114p. 1988. reprint ed. pap. 19.50 (0-8328-0199-2); reprint ed. lib. bdg. 27.50 (0-8328-0198-4) Higginson Bk Co.

***Bartlett, Linda P. & Jordan, Gretchen S.** Feast for Life: A Benefit Cookbook - Over 100 Celebrities & Chefs Share Their Favorite Recipes. (Illus.). 192p. 2000. reprint ed. 35.00 (0-7881-9263-9) DIANE Pub.

Bartlett, Lu, jt. auth. see Elder, William V., III.

Bartlett, Lynn. Defy the Eagle. 1986. pap. 6.95 (0-373-97021-8) Harlequin Bks.

— Defy the Eagle. 640p. 1987. mass mkt. 4.95 (0-373-97050-1) Harlequin Bks.

— Defy the Eagle. (Historical Ser.). 1994. per. 3.99 (0-373-28807-7, 1-28807-5) Harlequin Bks.

Bartlett, Magnus & Bartlett, Kasyan, photos by. Over Hong Kong. (Illus.). 160p. 1998. 34.95 (962-217-506-6) Tuttle Pubng.

Bartlett, Margaret F. Clean Brook. LC 60-8257. (Let's-Read-&-Find-Out Science Bks.). (Illus.). (J). (gr. k-3). 1960. lib. bdg. 11.89 (0-690-19556-7) HarpC Child Bks.

Bartlett, Maria C. Married Widows: The Wives of Men in Long-Term Care. LC 93-22707. (Studies on the Elderly in America). 136p. 1993. text 15.00 (0-8153-1535-X) Garland.

Bartlett, Marie. Trooper Down! 288p. 1990. mass mkt. 4.50 (0-671-67610-5) PB.

— Trooper Down! Life & Death on the Highway Patrol. LC 88-5896. (Illus.). 258p. 1988. 16.95 (0-912697-81-4) Algonquin Bks.

Bartlett, Melissa, jt. auth. see Volhard, Jack.

Bartlett, Merrill L. Assault from the Sea: Essays on the History of Amphibious Warfare. LC 83-2178. (Illus.). 453p. 1993. pap. 26.95 (0-87021-076-9) Naval Inst Pr.

— Lejeune, 1867-1942: A Marine's Life. LC 96-17123. (Bluejacket Bks.). (Illus.). 256p. 1996. pap. 16.95 (1-55750-063-0) Naval Inst Pr.

Bartlett, Merrill L. & Ballendorf, Dirk A. Pete Ellis: An Amphibious Warfare Prophet, 1880-1923. LC 96-43522. (Illus.). 200p. 1996. 27.95 (1-55750-060-6) Naval Inst Pr.

Bartlett, Merrill L., jt. auth. see Alexander, Joseph H.

Bartlett, Michael, ed. Winning Foodservice Ideas: The Best of "Restaurants & Institutions" LC 93-11409. (Restaurants & Institutions Ser.). 288p. 1993. 54.95 (0-471-30820-X) Wiley.

Bartlett, Michael H., et al. Archaeology in the City: A Hohokam Village in Phoenix, Arizona. LC 86-918. 80p. (Orig.). 1986. pap. 10.95 (0-8165-0970-0) U of Ariz Pr.

Bartlett, Napier. Military Record of Louisiana: Including Biographical & Historical Papers Relating to the Military Organizations of the State. LC 64-11967. 260p. 1996. pap. 17.95 (0-8071-2078-2) La State U Pr.

Bartlett, Neil. The House on Brooke Street. LC 97-40839. 224p. 1998. pap. 12.95 (0-452-27781-7, Plume) Dutton Plume.

— Who Was That Man? A Present for Mr. Oscar Wilde. 256p. 1992. pap. 14.95 (1-85242-123-1) Serpents Tail.

Bartlett, Neil, tr. The Game of Love & Chance. 80p. 1992. pap. 11.95 (0-948230-58-4, Pub. by Absolute Classics) Theatre Comm.

Bartlett, Nellie A. Bartlett. Aaron Bartlett of Brookfield, Mass., with Some of His Descendants. (Illus.). 107p. 1997. reprint ed. pap. 17.00 (0-8328-7395-0); reprint ed. lib. bdg. 27.00 (0-8328-7394-2) Higginson Bk Co.

Bartlett, Nick. In the Teeth of the Wind: Memoir of the Royal Naval Air Service in the First World War. LC 94-66595. (Illus.). 159p. 1994. 24.95 (1-55750-393-1) Naval Inst Pr.

Bartlett, Patricia, jt. auth. see Bartlett, J. D.

Bartlett, Patricia, jt. auth. see Bartlett, R. D.

Bartlett, Patricia, jt. auth. see Bartlett, R.D.

***Bartlett, Patricia M. & Bartholomew, Gail.** Driftwood Sculpture: From Finding to Fine Finishing. (Illus.). 144p. 2000. 34.95 (0-9676197-0-X) Waterfront Pubns.

Bartlett, Patricia P., jt. auth. see Bartlett, R. D.

Bartlett, Patricia P., jt. auth. see Bartlett, Richard D.

Bartlett, Pauline & Knauber, Jeanne. Damage Control for Women: Overcoming Hard Times. 110p. (Orig.). 1996. pap. 12.95 (0-9648418-0-0) Nouveau Vent Unltd.

Bartlett, Peter. The Poor Law of Lunacy: The Administration of Pauper Lunatics in Mid-Nineteenth-Century England. LC 98-51388. 310p. 1999. 85.00 (0-7185-0104-7) Bks Intl VA.

***Bartlett, Peter & Sandland, Ralph.** Mental Health Law: Policy & Practice. 494p. 2000. pap. 50.00 (1-85431-941-8, 18660, Pub. by Blackstone Pr) Gaunt.

Bartlett, Peter & Wright, David. Outside the Walls of the Asylum: On Care in the Community in Modern Britain & Ireland. LC 98-54264. 260p. 1999. 90.00 (0-485-11541-7, Pub. by Athlone Pr); pap. 33.95 (0-485-12147-6, Pub. by Athlone Pr) Transaction Pubs.

Bartlett, Peter, jt. auth. see Anthony, Martin.

Bartlett, Philip N., jt. auth. see Gardner, Julian W.

Bartlett, Phyllis B., ed. see Meredith, George.

Bartlett, R., jt. auth. see Clendenning, P. H.

Bartlett, R. D. Anoles, Basilisks & Water Dragons. LC 96-46980. 1997. pap. 6.95 (0-8120-9789-0) Barron.

***Bartlett, R. D.** Iguana Handbook. LC 99-89614. (Pet Handbks.). (Illus.). 144p. 2000. pap. 9.95 (0-7641-1234-1) Barron.

Bartlett, R. D. Lizard Care from A-To-Z. LC 96-44418. 1997. pap. text 9.95 (0-8120-9810-2) Barron.

***Bartlett, R. D. & Bartlett, Patricia.** Corn Snakes. LC 99-14654. (Reptile Guidebook Ser.). (Illus.). 48p. 1999. pap. 4.95 (0-7641-1120-5) Barron.

— Leopard & Fat-Tailed Geckos. LC 99-14653. (Illus.). 48p. 1999. pap. write for info. (0-7641-1119-1) Barron.

Bartlett, R. D. & Bartlett, Patricia P. Chameleons: A Complete Pet Owner's Manual. (Illus.). 112p. 1995. pap. 6.95 (0-8120-9157-4) Barron.

***Bartlett, R. D. & Bartlett, Patricia P.** A Field Guide to Texas Reptiles & Amphibians. LC 99-39015. (Field Guide Ser.). 1999. pap. 21.95 (0-87719-337-1, 9337) Gulf Pub.

Bartlett, R. D. & Bartlett, Patricia P. Frogs, Toads, & Tree Frogs: Everything About Selection, Care, Nutrition, Breeding, & Behavior. LC 95-40896. (Barron's Educational Ser.). (Illus.). 1996. pap. 6.95 (0-8120-9156-6) Barron.

— Turtles & Tortoises. LC 96-11156. (Complete Pet Owner's Manual Ser.). (Illus.). 112p. 1996. pap. 6.95 (0-8120-9712-2) Barron.

Bartlett, R. D., jt. auth. see Tennant, Alan.

Bartlett, R. E. Wastewater Treatment. (Illus.). xii, 326p. 1971. 61.00 (0-685-43725-6) Elsevier.

Bartlett, R. H., ed. see Symposium, Boston Staff.

Bartlett, R. R., ed. Leflunomide: Proceedings of the Vienna Symposium, 12 October 1993. LC 94-43800. 1994. write for info. (3-7643-5150-0); write for info. (0-8176-5150-0) Birkhauser.

Bartlett, Randall. The Crisis of America's Cities. LC 98-23185. 304p. (C). 1998. text 64.95 (0-7656-0301-2) M E Sharpe.

— The Crisis of America's Cities. LC 98-23185. 304p. (C). (gr. 13). 1998. pap. text 26.95 (0-7656-0302-0) M E Sharpe.

— Economics & Power: An Inquiry into Human Relations & Markets. (Illus.). 224p. (C). 1989. text 49.95 (0-521-35562-1) Cambridge U Pr.

Bartlett, Raymond C. Medical Microbiology: Quality & Clinical Relevance. LC 73-18482. (Wiley Biomedical-Health Publication Ser.). (Illus.). 269p. reprint ed. pap. 83.40 (0-608-30312-7, 205516800011) Bks Demand.

Bartlett, R.D. & Bartlett, Patricia. Snakes. LC 97-29243. (Complete Pet Owner's Manual Ser.). (Illus.). 1998. pap. 6.95 (0-7641-0055-6) Barron.

Bartlett, Rebecca A., ed. Choices Outstanding Academic Books, 1992-1997: Reviews of Scholarly Titles That Every Library Should Own. LC 98-19856. 628p. (Orig.). (C). 1998. pap. 80.00 (0-8389-7929-7) Assn Coll & Res Libs.

Bartlett, Richard. Digest for the Successful Terrarium. (Illus.). 80p. Date not set. 6.95 (1-56465-172-X, 16040) Tetra Pr.

— Direct Option. 1992. pap. 11.95 (0-13-218090-1) P-H.

— Iguanas. (Barron's Pet Owner's Manuals Ser.). 1995. pap. 6.95 (0-8120-1876-1) Barron.

Bartlett, Richard & Goetzmann, William H. Exploring the American West. LC 82-12483. (Official National Park Handbook Ser.: No. 116). 1982. pap. 7.50 (0-912627-13-1) Natl Park Serv.

***Bartlett, Richard D., et al.** Terrarium & Cage Construction & Care. LC 98-38742. (Illus.). 244p. 1999. pap. 14.95 (0-7641-0673-2) Barron.

Bartlett, Richard A. Great Surveys of the American West. LC 62-16475. (American Exploration & Travel Ser.: Vol. 38). (Illus.). 464p. 1980. pap. 19.95 (0-8061-1653-6) U of Okla Pr.

— Nature's Yellowstone. LC 89-31748. 250p. 1989. reprint ed. pap. 9.95 (0-8165-1109-8) U of Ariz Pr.

— Troubled Waters: Champion International & the Pigeon River Controversy. LC 94-18741. (Outdoor Tennessee Ser.). (Illus.). 376p. 1995. pap. 18.95 (0-87049-888-6); text 35.00 (0-87049-887-8) U of Tenn Pr.

— Yellowstone: A Wilderness Besieged. LC 85-988. 437p. 1989. reprint ed. pap. 19.95 (0-8165-1098-9) U of Ariz Pr.

— Yellowstone Holiday. (Illus.). 296p. 1998. pap. 19.95 (1-86106-595-7, Pub. by Minerva Pr) Unity Dist.

Bartlett, Richard C. The Direct Option. LC 93-19819. 304p. 1994. 19.95 (0-89096-583-8); pap. 9.95 (0-89096-584-6) Tex A&M Univ Pr.

— Saving the Best of Texas: A Partnership Approach to Conservation. LC 94-43734. (Illus.). 240p. (Orig.). 1995. 40.00 (0-292-70834-3); pap. 19.95 (0-292-70835-1) U of Tex Pr.

***Bartlett, Richard D.** Ball Pythons. LC 99-48389. (Reptile Keepers Ser.). 48p. 2000. pap. 5.95 (0-7641-1124-8) Barron.

— Horned Frog Family & African Bullfrogs. LC 99-42834. (Reptile Keepers Ser.). 48p. 2000. pap. write for info. (0-7641-1127-2) Barron.

— Red-Eyed Tree Frogs & Other Leaf Frogs. LC 99-43597. (Reptile Keepers Ser.). 48p. 2000. pap. write for info. (0-7641-1122-1) Barron.

Bartlett, Richard D. & Bartlett, Patricia P. Corn Snakes & Other Rat Snakes. LC 95-50351. (Complete Pet Owner's Manual Ser.). (Illus.). 112p. 1996. pap. 6.95 (0-8120-9622-3) Barron.

— A Field Guide to Florida Reptiles & Amphibians. LC 98-34749. (Illus.). 288p. 1998. pap. 18.95 (0-88415-277-4, 5277) Gulf Pub.

— Geckos. LC 95-3640. (Illus.). 1995. pap. 6.95 (0-8120-9082-9) Barron.

***Bartlett, Richard D. & Bartlett, Patricia P.** Milksnakes & Tricolored Kingsnakes. LC 99-42835. (Reptile Keepers Ser.). 48p. 2000. pap. 5.95 (0-7641-1128-0) Barron.

Bartlett, Richard D. & Bartlett, Patricia P. Monitors, Tegus, & Related Lizards: A Complete Pet Owner's Manual. LC 96-19488. (Illus.). 112p. 1996. pap. 6.95 (0-8120-9696-7) Barron.

***Bartlett, Robert.** England under the Norman & Angevin Kings, 1075-1225. LC 99-16108. (Illus.). 600p. 2000. 45.00 (0-19-822741-8) OUP.

Bartlett, Robert. The Making of Europe: Conquest, Colonization, & Cultural Change, 950-1350. 447p. 1993. text 55.00 (0-691-03298-X, Pub. by Princeton U Pr) Cal Prin Full Svc.

— The Making of Europe: Conquest, Colonization & Cultural Change, 950-1350. LC 93-195830. 432p. 1993. write for info. (0-7139-9074-0, A Lane) Viking Penguin.

— The Making of Europe: Conquest, Colonization, & Cultural Change, 9500-1350. 447p. 1993. pap. text 19.95 (0-691-03780-9, Pub. by Princeton U Pr) Cal Prin Full Svc.

***Bartlett, Robert.** The Story of Thanksgiving. LC 99-41337. 40p. 2000. 14.95 (0-06-028778-0); lib. bdg. 14.89 (0-06-028779-9) HarpC Child Bks.

Bartlett, Robert, ed. Policy & Impact Assessment. (Orig.). 1988. pap. 15.00 (0-944285-06-6) Pol Studies.

Bartlett, Robert & MacKay, Angus, eds. Medieval Frontier Societies. (Illus.). 400p. 1990. text 89.00 (0-19-822881-3) OUP.

Bartlett, Robert B., et al. A Cultural Resource Assessment of Promontories in Western Oklahoma. (Archeological Resource Survey Report: No. 38). (Illus.). 42p. (C). 1993. pap. text 3.00 (1-881346-30-7) Univ OK Archeol.

Bartlett, Robert B., jt. ed. see Zwischenberger, Joseph B.

Bartlett, Robert C. & Collins, Susan D., eds. Action & Contemplation: Studies in the Moral & Political Thought of Aristotle. LC 98-31974. (SUNY Series in Ancient Greek Philosophy). 352p. (C). 1999. text 73.50 (0-7914-4251-9, Suny Pr); pap. text 24.95 (0-7914-4252-7, Suny Pr) State U NY Pr.

Bartlett, Robert C., ed. see Xenophon.

Bartlett, Robert C., tr. see Bayle, Pierre.

Bartlett, Robert H. Critical Care Physiology. 304p. 1995. 72.95 (0-316-08264-3); text 65.00 (0-316-08269-4) Lppncott W & W.

— The Michigan Critical Care Handbook: Physiology, Pharmacology, Treatment Algorithms, Scoring Systems: 1,000 Indispensable Facts, Figures, & Graphs for the Adult ICU. 13th ed. 40p. 1995. spiral bd. 29.00 (0-316-08268-6) Lppncott W & W.

Bartlett, Robert H., et al, eds. Life Support Systems in Intensive Care. LC 84-5054. (Illus.). 629p. reprint ed. pap. 195.00 (0-8357-7607-7, 205693000096) Bks Demand.

Bartlett, Robert H., jt. auth. see Zwischenberger, Joseph B.

Bartlett, Robert M. They Dared to Live. LC 76-90606. (Essay Index Reprint Ser.). 1977. 23.95 (0-8369-1273-X) Ayer.

— They Did Something about It. LC 70-90607. (Essay Index Reprint Ser.). 1977. 19.95 (0-8369-1243-8) Ayer.

— They Work for Tomorrow. LC 70-111813. (Essay Index Reprint Ser.). 1977. 19.95 (0-8369-1592-5) Ayer.

Bartlett, Robert Merrill. The Story of Thanksgiving. (Illus.). 40p. (J). (gr. 2-5). 5.95 (0-06-446238-2) HarpC.

Bartlett, Robert R. Preparing International Proposals. LC 97-217878. 256p. 1997. 68.00 (0-7277-2582-3, 2582, Pub. by T Telford) RCH.

Bartlett, Robert V. The Reserve Mining Controversy: Science, Technology, & Environmental Quality. LC 79-48019. 307p. 1980. reprint ed. pap. 95.20 (0-608-01046-4, 205935400001) Bks Demand.

Bartlett, Robert V., ed. Policy Through Impact Assessment: Institutionalized Analysis As a Policy Strategy, 235. LC 89-2122. (Contributions in Political Science Ser.: No. 235). 212p. 1989. 62.95 (0-313-26775-8, BPZ, Greenwood Pr) Greenwood.

Bartlett, Robert V., et al, eds. International Organizations & Environmental Policy, 355. LC 94-47417. (Contributions in Political Science Ser.: No. 355). 296p. 1995. 69.50 (0-313-29623-5, Greenwood Pr) Greenwood.

Bartlett, Robert V., jt. auth. see Caldwell, Lynton K.

Bartlett, Robert V., ed. see Caldwell, Lynton K.

Bartlett, Robert W. Solution Mining: Leaching & Fluid Recovery of Methods. LC 92-4419. xxxii, 276p. 1992. text 96.00 (2-88124-546-3) Gordon & Breach.

***Bartlett, Robert W.** Solution Mining: Leaching & Recovery of Materials. 2nd ed. 472p. 1998. text 69.00 (90-5699-633-9, Harwood Acad Pubs) Gordon & Breach.

Bartlett, Robin L. Introducing Race & Gender into Economics. LC 97-210000. 224p. (C). 1997. 75.00 (0-415-16282-3) Routledge.

Bartlett, Robin L., ed. Introducing Race & Gender into Economics. LC 97-210000. 210p. (C). 1997. pap. 23.95 (0-415-16283-1) Routledge.

Bartlett, Rodney J. Recent Advances in Coupled-Cluster Methods. LC 97-6030. (Recent Advances in Computational Chemistry Ser.). 1997. write for info. (981-02-3112-1) World Scientific Pub.

Bartlett, Rodney J., ed. Comparison of AB INITIO Quantum Chemistry with Experiment for Small Molecules: The State of the Art. 1985. text 249.00 (90-277-2129-7) Kluwer Academic.

Bartlett, Roger. Introduction to Sports Biomechanics. LC 96-67515. (Illus.). 304p. (C). 1996. pap. 39.99 (0-419-20840-2, E & FN Spon) Routledge.

***Bartlett, Roger.** Sports Biomechanics: Preventing Injury & Improving Performance. (Illus.). 304p. (Orig.). (C). 1999. text 100.00 (0-419-24810-2, E & FN Spon) Routledge.

Bartlett, Roger, jt. auth. see Partnership, Derek L.

Bartlett, Roger A., jt. ed. see Goldberg, Daniel J.

Bartlett, Roger W. Power Base Attribution & the Perceived Legitimacy of Managerial Accounting. LC 82-23697. (Research for Business Decisions Ser.: No. 57). (Illus.). 145p. reprint ed. pap. 45.00 (0-8357-1393-8, 207035800088) Bks Demand.

Bartlett, Roland W. The Fans Vote! One Hundred Baseball Superstars. LC 82-5118. (Illus.). 256p. 1983. 19.95 (0-88280-088-4); pap. 14.95 (0-88280-089-2) ETC Pubns.

Bartlett, Ronald W. & Wolfson, Marty. Galbraiths Garbled Economics. LC 74-79430. (Illus.). 1974. pap. 2.95 (0-916114-03-1) Wolfson.

Bartlett, Rosamund. Wagner & Russia. (Studies in Russian Literature). (Illus.). 427p. (C). 1995. text 69.95 (0-521-44071-8) Cambridge U Pr.

Bartlett, Rosamund, jt. auth. see Benn, Anna.

Bartlett, Roxana. Slip-Stitch Knitting: Color Patterns the Easy Way. LC 97-43187. (Illus.). 96p. 1998. pap. 21.95 (1-883010-32-2) Interweave.

Bartlett, Ruhl J. John C. Fremont & the Republican Party. LC 73-87663. (American Scene Ser.). 1970. reprint ed. lib. bdg. 24.50 (0-306-71763-8) Da Capo.

Bartlett, Samuel C. From Egypt to Palestine: Through Sinai, the Wilderness & the South Country: History of the Israelites. Davis, Moshe, ed. LC 77-70668. (America & the Holy Land Ser.). (Illus.). 1977. reprint ed. lib. bdg. 47.95 (0-405-10227-5) Ayer.

— Historical Sketches of the Missions of the American Board. LC 78-38436. (Religion in America, Ser. 2). 210p. 1979. reprint ed. 23.95 (0-405-04057-1) Ayer.

***Bartlett, Sarah.** Auras & How to See Them. (Illus.). 128p. 2000. pap. 14.95 (1-85585-746-4, Pub. by Collins & Br) Sterling.

— Feng Shui for Entertaining. 2000. pap. 12.00 (0-575-60337-2, Pub. by Vista) Trafalgar.

Bartlett, Sarah. Feng Shui for Lovers: How to Create Harmony & Energy in the Spaces of Your Heart & Home. LC 98-12416. 256p. 1999. pap. 14.00 (*1-56836-271-4*) Kodansha.

— The Love Tarot: Uses the Powers of the Mystic Deck to Guide You in Love, Romance & Sex. 96p. 1995. 17.95 (*0-8212-2223-6*, Pub. by Bulfinch Pr) Little.

— The Money Machine: How KKR Manufactured Power & Profits. 368p. 1999. reprint ed. 35.95 (*0-7351-0067-5*) Replica Bks.

— The Money Machine: How KKR Manufactured Power & Profits. 1992. reprint ed. mass mkt. 12.99 (*0-446-39401-7*, Pub. by Warner Bks) Little.

— Mythical Lovers, Divine Desires The World's Great Love Legends. 1999. 24.95 (*0-7137-2718-7*) Blandford Pr.

***Bartlett, Sarah.** Sensual Woman: An Exploration of the True Meaning & Value of Sensuality. 2000. 24.95 (*1-902809-00-9*, London House) Allison & Busby.

Bartlett, Sarah. World of Myths & Mythology: A Source Book. LC 99-179999. 320p. 1998. pap. 24.95 (*0-7137-2673-3*, Pub. by Blandford Pr) Sterling.

Bartlett, Susan. Not Necessarily Christmas. 98p. 1991. 19.95 (*0-9630473-0-2*) Quilted Cot.

— Seal Island School. LC 98-26865. (Illus.). 80p. (J). (gr. 2-5). 1999. 13.99 (*0-670-88349-2*) Viking Penguin.

Bartlett, Sy & Lay. Twelve O'Clock High. (Illus.). 274p. 1989. pap. 16.95 (*0-942397-16-9*) Buckeye Aviat Bk.

Bartlett, Sy, jt. auth. see Lay, Beirne, Jr.

Bartlett, T. E. The Bartletts: Ancestral, Genealogical, Biographical, Historical. (Illus.). 112p. 1988. reprint ed. pap. 19.50 (*0-8328-0201-8*); reprint ed. lib. bdg. 29.50 (*0-8328-0200-X*) Higginson Bk Co.

Bartlett, Thomas. Fall & Rise of the Irish Nation. (C). 1992. text 85.00 (*0-389-20974-0*) B&N Imports.

— A Military History of Ireland. Jeffrey, Keith, ed. (Illus.). 592p. 1997. pap. text 27.95 (*0-521-62989-6*) Cambridge U Pr.

Bartlett, Thomas, et al, eds. Irish Studies: A General Introduction. 1988. 45.00 (*0-389-20805-1*, N8363) B&N Imports.

Bartlett, Thomas & Jeffery, Keith, eds. A Military History of Ireland. (Illus.). 591p. (C). 1996. text 69.95 (*0-521-41599-3*) Cambridge U Pr.

***Bartlett, Thomas, et al.** The 1798 Rebellion: A Bicentennial Perspective. Whelan, Kevin, ed. 480p. 2000. 55.00 (*1-85182-430-8*, Pub. by Four Cts Pr); pap. 29.95 (*1-85182-431-6*, Pub. by Four Cts Pr) Intl Spec Bk.

— The 1798 Rebellion: A Bicentennial Perspective. limited ed. Whelan, Kevin, ed. 480p. 2000. 150.00 (*1-85182-429-4*, Pub. by Four Cts Pr) Intl Spec Bk.

Bartlett, Thomas, et al. The 1798 Rebellion: An Illustrated History. (Illus.). 192p. 1998. pap. text 18.95 (*1-57098-255-4*) Roberts Rinehart.

Bartlett, Thomas, jt. auth. see Whiteman, Thomas A.

Bartlett, Thomas, ed. see Tone, Theobald W.

***Bartlett, Tim.** GPS Afloat. (Illus.). 96p. 2000. pap. 18.95 (*1-898660-69-7*, 130668AE, Pub. by Fernhurst Bks) Motorbooks Intl.

Bartlett, Tim. Navigation at Speed. 64p. (C). 1990. text 65.00 (*0-906754-76-3*, Pub. by Fernhurst Bks) St Mut.

***Bartlett, Tim.** Radar Afloat. (Illus.). 96p. 2000. pap. 16.95 (*1-898660-71-9*, 130669AE, Pub. by Fernhurst Bks) Motorbooks Intl.

Bartlett, Tim. Radar for Small Craft. (Illus.). 95p. 1998. pap. 16.95 (*1-898660-48-4*) Motorbooks Intl.

— A Small Boat Guide to Electronics Afloat. (Illus.). 91p. (C). 1998. pap. 16.95 (*0-906754-72-0*, Pub. by Fernhurst Bks) Motorbooks Intl.

— A Small Boat Guide to Radar. 96p. (C). 1990. text 65.00 (*0-906754-58-5*, Pub. by Fernhurst Bks) St Mut.

***Bartlett, Tim.** Understanding Navigation. (Illus.). 64p. 2000. pap. 12.95 (*1-898660-70-0*, 130670AE, Pub. by Fernhurst Bks) Motorbooks Intl.

Bartlett, Tim. Weather Companion. (Illus.). 24p. 1999. pap. 11.95 (*1-898660-59-X*) Fernhurst Bks.

Bartlett, Tim, jt. auth. see Willis, Tom.

Bartlett, Vernon. Topsy-Turvy. LC 77-110179. (Short Story Index Reprint Ser.). 1977. 20.95 (*0-8369-3330-3*) Ayer.

Bartlett, Virginia K. Keeping House: Women's Lives in Western Pennsylvania, 1790-1850. (Illus.). 200p. (C). 1994. text 39.95 (*0-8229-3854-5*) U of Pittsburgh Pr.

Bartlett, W. A. & Gallatin, D. B. B & G Cartridge Manual. 1956. 5.00 (*0-913150-12-6*) Pioneer Pr.

***Bartlett, W. H.** Bartlett's Classic Illustrations of America: All 121 Engravings from American Scenery, 1840. (Illus.). 2000. pap. 14.95 (*0-486-41221-0*) Dover.

***Bartlett, Wayne.** God Wills It! An Illustrated History of the Crusades. 288p. 1999. 39.95 (*0-7509-1880-2*, Pub. by Sutton Publng) Intl Pubs Mktg.

— God Wills It! An Illustrated History of the Crusades. (Illus.). 2000. reprint ed. pap. 19.95 (*0-7509-2558-2*, Pub. by Sutton Publng) Intl Pubs Mktg.

— An Ungodly War: The Sack of Constantinople & the Fourth Crusade. (Illus.). 256p. 2000. 29.95 (*0-7509-2378-4*) Sutton Publng.

Bartlett, Webster. Getting down to Business: How-to Start Any Business Today. 2nd ed. 120p. (C). 1995. pap. text 24.95 (*1-57555-000-8*); disk 14.95 (*1-57555-001-6*) Cedar Bay Pr.

Bartlett, William W. Mortgage-Backed Securities: Products, Analysis, Training. 1988. 49.95 (*0-317-03944-X*) NY Inst Finance.

— The Valuation of Mortgage-Backed Securities. 516p. 1993. text 80.00 (*1-55623-973-4*, Irwn Prfssnl) McGraw-Hill Prof.

Bartlette, Reginald J. Off the Record: Motown by Master Number, 1959-1989. LC 89-92326. (Rock & Roll Reference Ser.: No. 34). (Illus.). 544p. 1991. 60.00 (*1-56075-003-0*) Popular Culture.

Bartley, Abel A. Keeping the Faith 1940-1970: Race, Politics & Social Development In Jacksonville, Florida, 184. LC 99-16140. Vol. 184. 208p. 2000. 59.95 (*0-313-31035-1*) Greenwood.

Bartley, Azimi, ed. Experiments & Exercise General & Biology. 206p. 1999. pap. text 18.75 (*0-536-02633-5*) P-H.

Bartley, Betty, jt. auth. see Balough, Linda.

Bartley, Bronwyn, jt. auth. see Bartley, Bruce.

Bartley, Bruce & Bartley, Bronwyn. Obedience Training. (Illus.). 112p. 1995. 35.00 (*1-85223-799-6*, Pub. by Crolwood) Trafalgar.

Bartley, David, ed. see Cassady, David.

Bartley, Ernest R. The Tidelands Oil Controversy. Bruchey, Stuart, ed. LC 78-53555. (Development of Public Land Law in the U. S. Ser.). 1979. reprint ed. lib. bdg. 25.95 (*0-405-11368-4*) Ayer.

Bartley, James, et al. Mateo. Carro, Daniel et al, eds. (Comentario Biblico Mundo Hispano Ser.: Vol. 14). (SPA., Illus.). 379p. 1993. pap. 9.99 (*0-311-03114-5*, Edit Mundo) Casa Bautista.

Bartley, James, ed. see Douglas, J. D. & Tenney, Merril C.

***Bartley, James W.** La Adoracion Que Agrada al Altisimo.Tr. of Worship That Pleases the Most High. (SPA.). 200p. 1999. pap. text 8.95 (*0-311-32444-4*) Casa Bautista.

Bartley, Jim. Stephen & Mr. Wilde. LC 94-159071. 1999. pap. 10.95 (*0-921368-36-4*) Genl Dist Srvs.

Bartley, Mary. St. Louis Lost: Uncovering the City's Architectural Treasures. (Illus.). 200p. 1994. 44.95 (*0-9631448-4-7*) VA Pub Corp.

— St. Louis Lost: Rediscovering the City's Lost Architectural Treasures. 3rd ed. (Illus.). 204p. 1998. reprint ed. pap. 29.95 (*1-891442-01-5*) VA Pub Corp.

Bartley, Mel, et al. The Sociology of Health Inequalities. (Sociology of Health & Illness Ser.). 256p. 1998. pap. 24.95 (*0-631-20929-8*) Blackwell Pubs.

Bartley, Numan V. The Creation of Modern Georgia. 2nd ed. LC 90-30699. (Brown Thrasher Bks.). 312p. 1990. pap. 16.95 (*0-8203-1178-2*) U of Ga Pr.

— From Thurmond to Wallace: Political Tendencies in Georgia, 1948-1968. LC 75-117253. 127p. reprint ed. pap. 39.40 (*0-608-14639-0*, 202582700046) Bks Demand.

— New South, 1945-1980. LC 95-19542. (A/History of the South Ser.: Vol. XI). 1995. 39.95 (*0-8071-1944-X*) La State U Pr.

— New South, 1945-1980. (A/History of the South Ser.: Vol. XI). (Illus.). 545p. 1995. 39.95 (*0-8071-2038-3*) La State U Pr.

— New South, 1945-1980. LC 95-19542. (History of the South Ser.: Vol. XII). 548p. 1996. pap. text 19.95 (*0-8071-2122-3*) La State U Pr.

— Rise of Massive Resistance: Race & Politics in the South During the 1950s. (Illus.). 416p. 1999. pap. text 17.95 (*0-8071-2419-2*) La State U Pr.

Bartley, Numan V., ed. The Evolution of Southern Culture. LC 87-19162. 168p. 1988. pap. 18.00 (*0-8203-1032-8*) U of Ga Pr.

Bartley, Numan V. & Graham, Hugh D. Southern Politics & the Second Reconstruction. 1976. pap. 4.95 (*0-8018-1897-4*) Johns Hopkins.

— Southern Politics & the Second Reconstruction. LC 74-24377. (Illus.). 252p. reprint ed. pap. 78.20 (*0-608-06038-0*, 206637000008) Bks Demand.

***Bartley, Paula.** Prostitution: Prevention & Reform in England, 1860-1914. (Illus.). 224p. 2000. pap. 25.99 (*0-415-21457-2*) Routledge.

Bartley, Paula. Votes for Women, 1860-1928: Access to History - In Depth. (Access to History Ser.). (Illus.). 120p. 1998. pap. text 17.00 (*0-340-69724-5*, Pub. by Hodder & Stought Ltd) Lubrecht & Cramer.

Bartley, Paula & Loxton, Cathy. Plains Women: Women in the American West. (Women in History Ser.). (Illus.). 48p. (C). 1991. pap. 13.95 (*0-521-38616-0*) Cambridge U Pr.

Bartley, Peter. The Gospel Jesus: Fact or Fiction? 110p. 1996. pap. text 10.95 (*1-85390-335-3*) Ignatius Pr.

— Mormonism: The Prophet, the Book & the Cult. 102p. (Orig.). 1989. pap. 8.95 (*1-85390-063-X*, Pub. by Veritas Pubns) St Mut.

Bartley, Peter, ed. Mormonism: The Prophet, the Book & the Cult: A Critique of Mormonism from the Origins to the Present Day. 130p. 1989. pap. 22.00 (*0-7855-6977-4*, Pub. by Veritas Pubns) St Mut.

Bartley, R. & Brahe, C. The ABC of Evidence. 4th ed. 846p. 1988. boxed set 64.00 (*0-908508-03-4*, Austral, MICHIE) LEXIS Pub.

Bartley, Rashida. The Writings of Just One Negro Woman. write for info. (*0-9678817-0-6*) SopeBox.

Bartley, Reg. Crawford's Proof in Criminal Cases. 5th ed. 300p. 1996. pap. 80.00 (*0-455-21402-6*, Pub. by Cavendish Pubng) Gaunt.

Bartley, Regina. The Joy of Machine Embroidery. LC 76-6259. (Illus.). 160p. 1976. 12.95 (*0-8092-8346-8*) NTC Contemp Pub Co.

***Bartley, Richard & Coffey, Paul.** Management of Low Back Pain in Primary Care. (Illus.). 176p. 2000. pap. text 32.00 (*0-7506-4787-6*) Buttrwrth-Heinemann.

Bartley, Robert L. The Seven Fat Years: And How to Do It Again. 352p. 1992. 22.95 (*0-02-901915-X*) Free Pr.

— The Seven Fat Years: And How to Do It Again. 256p. 1994. pap. 12.95 (*0-02-901695-9*) Free Pr.

— The Seven Fat Years: And How to Do It Again. 1995. pap. 12.00 (*0-02-874022-X*) Free Pr.

***Bartley, Robert L.** Whitewater From the Editorial Pages of the Wall Street Journal: A Journal Briefing. 1999. pap. text 16.95 (*1-881944-18-2*) Dow Jones & Co.

Bartley, Robert L., ed. Whitewater Vol. 1: From the Editorial Pages of the Wall Street Journal (A Journal Briefing) LC 94-79762. 586p. 1994. pap. 14.95 (*1-881944-02-6*) Dow Jones & Co.

— Whitewater Vol. 4: Including Monica, China, the Starr Report. 350p. 1998. pap. 16.95 (*1-881944-10-7*) Dow Jones & Co.

Bartley, Robert L., et al, eds. Whitewater Vol. 2: From the Editorial Pages of the Wall Street Journal. LC 94-79762. 500p. (Orig.). 1997. pap. 14.95 (*1-881944-04-2*) Dow Jones & Co.

— Whitewater Vol. 3: From the Editorial Pages of the Wall Street Journal. 350p. 1998. pap. 16.95 (*1-881944-06-9*) Dow Jones & Co.

Bartley, Russell, tr. see Borge, Tomas.

Bartley, Scott A., ed. Vermont Families in 1791, Vol. 1. LC 92-64323. 311p. 1992. 30.00 (*0-89725-086-9*, 1395) Picton Pr.

Bartley, W. W., III. The Retreat to Commitment. LC 84-14862. 285p. 1984. pap. 22.95 (*0-8126-9127-X*) Open Court.

— Wittgenstein. 2nd ed. LC 85-8962. 218p. (C). 1985. pap. 15.95 (*0-87548-441-7*) Open Court.

Bartley, W. W., III, et al. The Political Economy of Freedom: Essays in Honor of F. A. Hayek. Leube, Kurt R. & Zlabinger, Albert H., eds. (International Car. Menger Library). 320p. 1985. 52.00 (*3-88405-057-5*) Philosophia Pr.

Bartley, W. W., III, ed. see Hayek, Friedrich A.

Bartley, W. W., III, ed. see Popper, Karl R.

Bartley, Whitman S. Iwo Jima: Amphibious Epic. (Elite Unit Ser.). (Illus.). 253p. 1988. reprint ed. 39.95 (*0-89839-108-3*) Battery Pr.

Bartling, Charles E. Managing Association Turnarounds. LC 98-232659. xvi, 139 p. 1997. pap. 41.95 (*0-88034-131-9*) Am Soc Assn Execs.

Bartling, Charles E. Strategic Alliances for Nonprofit Organizations. LC 98-22608. xvii, 89p. 1998. pap. 29.95 (*0-88034-143-2*) Am Soc Assn Execs.

Bartman, Frank. Azusa Street. 175p. 1997. mass mkt. 5.99 (*0-88368-486-1*) Whitaker Hse.

***Bartlow, Bruce G.** Medical Care of the Soul: A Practical & Healing Guide to End-of-Life Issues for Families, Patients, & Healthcare Providers. 304p. 2000. 32.50 (*1-55566-253-6*); pap. 18.00 (*1-55566-254-4*) Johnson Bks.

Bartlow, Evelyn A. Emily & the Santa Fe Trail. unabridged ed. LC 97-75944. (Illus.). 64p. (J). (gr. 4-7). 1998. pap. 8.00 (*1-890826-04-9*) Rock Creek Pr.

Bartman, Elizabeth. Ancient Sculptural Copies in Miniature. LC 91-28195. (Columbia Studies in the Classical Tradition: Vol. 19). (Illus.). xiv, 222p. 1992. 105.50 (*90-04-09532-2*) Brill Academic Pubs.

— Portraits of Livia: Imaging the Imperial Woman in Augustan Rome. LC 97-46126. (Texts in the History of Philosophy Ser.). (Illus.). 288p. (C). 1998. text 95.00 (*0-521-58394-2*) Cambridge U Pr.

Bartman, Joeffrey, tr. see Aleixandre, Vicente.

Bartman, William S., ed. Andrew Spence. (Illus.). 46p. (Orig.). 1992. pap. text 20.00 (*0-923183-07-8*) ART Pr NY.

— Anne Scott Plummer. (Exploring the Work of Artists in Mid-Career Ser.). (Illus.). 32p. (Orig.). 1989. pap. text 14.95 (*0-923183-02-7*) ART Pr NY.

— Jimmy DeSana. (Exploring the Work of Artists in Mid-Career Ser.). (Illus.). 48p. (Orig.). 1990. pap. text 20.00 (*0-923183-03-5*) ART Pr NY.

— Judy Fiskin. (Exploring the Work of Artists in Mid-Career Ser.). (Illus.). 40p. (Orig.). 1988. pap. text 14.95 (*0-923183-00-0*) ART Pr NY.

— Pat Sparkuhl. (Exploring the Work of Artists in Mid-Career Ser.). (Illus.). 32p. (Orig.). 1991. pap. text 20.00 (*0-923183-05-1*) ART Pr NY.

Bartman, William S. & Barnes, Lucinda, eds. Kim Abeles. (Exploring the Work of Artists in Mid-Career Ser.). (Illus.). 32p. (Orig.). 1988. pap. text 14.95 (*0-923183-01-9*) ART Pr NY.

— Three California Artists: Kim Abeles, Judy Fiskin, Anne Scott Plummer, 3 bks., Set. (Illus.). 102p. 1992. boxed set 34.95 (*0-923183-10-8*) ART Pr NY.

Bartman, William S. & Barosh, Miyoshi, eds. Allan McCollum. (Explores the Work of Artists in Mid-Career Ser.). (Illus.). 80p. 1996. pap. text 25.00 (*0-923183-14-0*) ART Pr NY.

— Felix Gonzalez-Torres. (Explores the Work of Artists in Mid-Career Ser.). (Illus.). 96p. 1994. pap. text 35.00 (*0-923183-12-4*) ART Pr NY.

Bartman, William S., ed. see Clemins, Vija & Close, Chuck.

Bartman, William S., ed. see Kelley, Mike & Miller, John.

Bartman, William S., jt. ed. see Sappington, Rodney.

Bartmann, Dieter & Beckmann, Martin J. Inventory Control: Models & Methods. LC 92-23268. (Lecture Notes in Economics & Mathematical Systems Ser.: Vol. 388). xv, 252p. 1992. 65.95 (*0-387-55820-9*); pap. 52.00 (*3-540-55820-9*) Spr-Verlag.

Bartnett, Beatrice. Auricular Therapy: Theory & Practice. (Illus.). 146p. (Orig.). 1992. pap. 34.95 (*0-9622182-1-9*) Lifestyle Inst.

— The Key to the Ear. 1992. 7.95 (*0-9622182-4-3*) Lifestyle Inst.

— Peace Labyrinth: Sacred Geometry. (Illus.). 52p. (Orig.). 1995. pap. 9.95 (*0-9622182-7-8*) Lifestyle Inst.

— Urine - Therapy - It May Save Your Life. 52p. (Orig.). 1992. pap. 5.90 (*0-9622182-3-5*) Lifestyle Inst.

***Bartnett, Joy & Madden, Deborah, eds.** The Complete Directory for Pediatric Disorders. (Illus.). 800p. (J). 1999. 190.00 (*1-891482-61-0*) Grey Hse Pub.

— The Complete Directory for Pediatric Disorders. (Illus.). 1000p. 2000. pap. 165.00 (*1-891482-60-2*) Grey Hse Pub.

Bartnick, Laura L. Every Day Bride: A Woman's Daily Devotional. 1997. pap. text 16.95 (*1-885831-00-5*) Proclaim Pubng.

Bartnicki-Garcia, S. & Bracker, C., eds. Cell Structure & Function, No. 8. (Mycota: Vol. VIII). Date not set. write for info. (*3-540-60186-4*) Spr-Verlag.

Bartnicki, Jerzy, jt. ed. see Alcamo, Joseph.

***Bartnikas, R.** Power & Communication Cables Handbook. (Professional Engineering Ser.). 900p. 1999. 129.95 (*0-07-135385-2*) McGraw.

Bartnikas, R., ed. Electrical Insulating Liquids. LC 93-27813. (Engineering Dielectrics Ser.: Vol. 3). 1993. 83.00 (*0-8031-2055-9*, \) ASTM.

— Engineering Dielectrics: Electrical Insulating Liquids. LC 93-27813. (MGH, Monograph: No. 2). (Illus.). 452p. 1993. pap. text 83.00 (*0-614-13312-2*, MONO2) ASTM.

— Engineering Dielectrics, Volume IIB: Electrical Properties of Solid Insulating Materials: Measurement Techniques. LC 78-72477. (Special Technical Publication Ser.: No. 926). (Illus.). 557p. 1987. 64.00 (*0-8031-0491-X*, STP926) ASTM.

Bartnikas, R. & Eichhorn, R. M., eds. Engineering Dielectrics, Volume IIA, Electrical Properties of Solid Insulating Materials: Molecular Structure & Electrical Behavior - STP 783. LC 82-70637. 695p. 1983. text 60.00 (*0-8031-0228-3*, STP783) ASTM.

Bartnikas, R. & McMahon, E. J., eds. Engineering Dielectrics: Volume 1: Corona Measurement & Interpretation - STP 669. 520p. 1984. 49.00 (*0-8031-0332-8*, STP669) ASTM.

***Bartnikas, R. & Srivastava, K. D., eds.** Power & Communication Cables: Theory & Applications. LC 99-18442. 896p. 1999. 129.95 (*0-7803-1196-5*, PC5665-QOE) Inst Electrical.

Bartnikowski, Mary. Everyday Naked: Sacred & Profane Morsels of Truth. LC 98-18810. 272p. 1998. pap. 12.95 (*0-89087-876-5*) Celestial Arts.

Bartnitzke, S., jt. ed. see Bullerdiek, J.

Barto, Andrew G., jt. auth. see Sutton, Richard S.

Barto, Renzo. How to Draw Cartoon Characters. LC 92-23057. (How to Draw Ser.). (Illus.). 32p. (J). (gr. k-6). 1997. pap. 2.95 (*0-8167-3218-3*) Troll Communs.

— How to Draw Cartoon Characters. LC 92-23057. (How to Draw Ser.). (Illus.). 32p. (J). (gr. k-6). 1997. lib. bdg. 17.25 (*0-8167-3265-5*) Troll Communs.

Barto, Renzo. How to Draw Cartoon Characters. LC 93-23057. 1994. 7.70 (*0-606-06479-6*, Pub. by Turtleback) Demco.

Barto, Renzo. How to Draw Monster, Weirdoes, & Aliens. LC 92-23056. (How to Draw Ser.). (Illus.). 32p. (J). (gr. k-6). 1993. pap. 2.95 (*0-8167-3217-5*); lib. bdg. 17.25 (*0-8167-3245-0*) Troll Communs.

— How to Draw Monsters, Weirdoes & Aliens. 1994. 7.70 (*0-606-06480-X*, Pub. by Turtleback) Demco.

***Barto, Renzo.** Ht Draw Cartoon Characters. (Illus.). 1999. pap. text 9.90 (*0-7857-6347-3*) Econo-Clad Bks.

Bartocci, Barbara. Midlife Awakenings: Discovering the Gifts Life Has Given Us. LC 98-18814. 120p. 1998. pap. 8.95 (*0-87793-659-5*) Ave Maria.

***Bartocci, Barbara.** Nobody's Child Anymore: Grieving, Caring & Comforting When Parents Die. LC 00-102081. 128p. 2000. pap. 11.95 (*1-893732-21-5*) SORIN BKS.

Bartocci, Barbara. Unexpected Answers. LC 93-87104. 168p. (Orig.). 1994. pap. 7.95 (*0-87973-742-5*, 742) Our Sunday Visitor.

Bartocci, Claudio, et al, eds. Differential Geometric Methods in Theoretical Physics: Proceedings of the 19th International Conference Held at Rapallo, Italy, 19-24 June 1990. (Lecture Notes in Physics Ser.: Vol. 375). xx, 401p. 1991. 56.95 (*0-387-53763-5*) Spr-Verlag.

Bartocci, Claudio, et al. The Geometry of Supermanifolds. (C). 1991. text 137.50 (*0-7923-1440-9*) Kluwer Academic.

Bartok. Romanian Folk Music Texts. (Rumanian Folk Music Ser: Vol. 3). 1967. lib. bdg. 223.00 (*90-247-0625-4*) Kluwer Academic.

— Rumanian Folk Music, 5 vols., Set. 1987. lib. bdg. 94.00 (*90-247-0622-X*) Kluwer Academic.

Bartok, Bela. Album for the Young: Centennial Edition. 144p. 1994. otabind 10.95 (*0-7935-3222-1*, 50482124) H Leonard.

***Bartok, Bela.** Allegro Barbaro & Other Short Works for Solo Piano. 1998. pap. text 9.95 (*0-486-40110-3*) Dover.

Bartok, Bela. Bartok's Stage Works: Includes: Bluebeard's Castle; analysis of The Wooden Prince & The Miraculous Mandarin. John, Nicholas, ed. (English National Opera Guide Series: Bilingual Libretto, Articles: Bilingual Libretto, Articles, No. 44). (Illus.). 112p. (Orig.). 1992. pap. 9.95 (*0-7145-4194-X*) Riverrun NY.

— Bela Bartok Essays. Suchoff, Benjamin, ed. LC 92-20719. (Illus.). xvi, 567p. 1992. reprint ed. pap. text 35.00 (*0-8032-6108-X*, Bison Books) U of Nebr Pr.

— Bela Bartok Studies in Ethnomusicology. Suchoff, Benjamin, ed. LC 96-26380. (Illus.). xxiii, 295p. 1997. text 50.00 (*0-8032-4247-6*) U of Nebr Pr.

***Bartok, Bela.** Cadenzas: W. A. Mozart, Concerto for Two Pianos & Orchestra in E Major, K. 365. (Illus.). 20p. 2000. pap. 12.00 (*0-9641961-1-5*) Bartok Recs.

Bartok, Bela. Carols & Christmas Songs: Colinde, Vol. 4. (Rumanian Folk Music Ser.). 1975. lib. bdg. 223.00 (*90-247-1737-X*) Kluwer Academic.

— Hungarian Folk Music. Calvocoressi, M. D., tr. LC 77-87537. 320p. reprint ed. 55.00 (*0-404-16600-8*) AMS Pr.

— Instrumental Melodies. (Rumanian Folk Music Ser: Vol. 1). 1967. lib. bdg. 223.00 (*90-247-0623-8*) Kluwer Academic.

— Maramures County, Vol. 5. (Rumanian Folk Music Ser). 1975. lib. bdg. 185.00 (*90-247-1738-8*) Kluwer Academic.

B

— Piano Music of Bela Bartok, Series I. 167p. 1982. pap. 11.95 (*0-486-24108-4*) Dover.

— Piano Music of Bella Bartok, Series II. 192p. 1982. pap. 11.95 (*0-486-24109-2*) Dover.

— Ten Pieces for Five Viols. Goldstein, David, ed. (Contemporary Consort Ser.: No. 21). 32p. 1992. pap. text 12.00 (*1-56571-066-5*, CC021) PRB Prods.

— Vocal Melodies. (Rumanian Folk Music Ser: Vol. 2). 1967. lib. bdg. 223.00 (*90-247-0624-6*) Kluwer Academic.

— Yugoslav Folk Music, 4 vols., Set. Suchoff, Benjamin, ed. LC 78-8188. 1981p. (C). 1979. text 395.00 (*0-87395-383-5*) State U NY Pr.

Bartok, Bela, et al. Bartok Letters: The Musical Mind. Gillies, Malcolm & Gombocz, Adrienne, eds. (Illus.). 656p. 2000. text 115.00 (*0-19-816144-1*) OUP.

***Bartok, John W.** Greenhouses for Homeowners & Gardeners. LC 00-30485. (NRAES Ser.: Vol. 137). (Illus.). 214p. 2000. pap. text 25.00 (*0-935817-51-4*, NRAES-137) NRAES.

Bartok, John W., Jr., jt. auth. see Aldrich, Robert A.

Bartok, M., et al. Stereochemistry of Heterogeneous Metal Catalysis. LC 84-13085. (Illus.). 656p. reprint ed. pap. 200.00 (*0-7837-4393-9*, 204413300012) Bks Demand.

Bartok, Mira & Ronan, Christine. Alaskan Eskimos & Aleuts. (Ancient & Living Cultures Ser.). (Illus.). 32p. (J). (gr. 3). 1994. pap. 9.95 (*0-673-36157-8*, GoodYrBooks) Addson-Wesley Educ.

— Alaskan Eskimos & Aleuts. (Big World Read Along Ser.). (Illus.). 20p. (J). (gr. k-2). 1995. bds. 4.95 (*0-673-36259-0*, GoodYrBooks) Addson-Wesley Educ.

— Ancient Celts: Stencils. (Ancient & Living Cultures Ser.). (Illus.). 32p. (Orig.). (J). (gr. 3 up). 1993. pap. 9.95 (*0-673-36101-2*, GoodYrBooks) Addson-Wesley Educ.

— Ancient China. (Ancient & Living Cultures Ser.). (Illus.). 32p. (J). (gr. 3 up). 1994. pap. 9.95 (*0-673-36180-2*, GoodYrBooks) Addson-Wesley Educ.

— Ancient Egypt & Nubia. (Ancient & Living Cultures Ser.). (Illus.). 32p. (J). (gr. 3 up). 1994. pap. 9.95 (*0-673-36179-9*, GoodYrBooks) Addson-Wesley Educ.

— Ancient Greece. (Ancient & Living Cultures Ser.). 28p. (Orig.). (J). (gr. 3 up). 1995. pap. 9.95 (*0-673-36255-8*, GoodYrBooks) Addson-Wesley Educ.

— Ancient Japan: Stencils. (Ancient & Living Cultures Ser.). (Illus.). 32p. (Orig.). (J). (gr. 3 up). 1992. pap. 9.95 (*0-673-36054-7*, GoodYrBooks) Addson-Wesley Educ.

— Ancient Mexico: Stencils. (Ancient & Living Cultures Ser.). (Illus.). 32p. (Orig.). (J). (gr. 3 up). 1992. pap. 9.95 (*0-673-36055-5*, GoodYrBooks) Addson-Wesley Educ.

— Ancient Rome. (Ancient & Living Cultures Ser.). 32p. (Orig.). (J). (gr. 3 up). 1995. pap. 9.95 (*0-673-36304-X*, GoodYrBooks) Addson-Wesley Educ.

— The Incas & Their Ancestors: Ages 8 Plus. Dempsey, Roberta, ed. (Illus.). 24p. (Orig.). (YA). 1994. pap. 9.95 (*0-673-36156-X*, GoodYrBooks) Addson-Wesley Educ.

— Indians of the Great Plains. (Big World Read Along Ser.). (Illus.). 20p. (J). (gr. k-2). 1995. bds. 4.95 (*0-673-36260-4*, GoodYrBooks) Addson-Wesley Educ.

— Indians of the Great Plains: Stencils. (Ancient & Living Cultures Ser.). (Illus.). 32p. (Orig.). (J). 1993. pap. 9.95 (*0-673-36138-1*, GoodYrBooks) Addson-Wesley Educ.

— Indonesia, Thailand & Cambodia. (Ancient & Living Cultures Ser.). 32p. (J). (gr. 3 up). 1996. pap. 9.95 (*0-673-36313-9*, GoodYrBooks) Addson-Wesley Educ.

— The Navajo. (Ancient & Living Cultures Ser.). 32p. (J). (gr. 3 up). 1996. pap. 9.95 (*0-673-36314-7*, GoodYrBooks) Addson-Wesley Educ.

— Northern Woodland Indians. (Ancient & Living Cultures Ser.). 28p. (Orig.). (J). (gr. 3 up). 1995. pap. 9.95 (*0-673-36256-6*, GoodYrBooks) Addson-Wesley Educ.

— Northwest Coast Indians. LC 96-100915. (Big World Read Along Ser.). (Illus.). 20p. (J). (gr. k-2). 1995. bds. 4.95 (*0-673-36257-4*, GoodYrBooks) Addson-Wesley Educ.

— Northwest Coast Indians: Stencils. (Ancient & Living Cultures Ser.). (Illus.). 32p. (Orig.). (J). (gr. 3 up). 1992. pap. 9.95 (*0-673-36056-3*, GoodYrBooks) Addson-Wesley Educ.

— Pueblo Indians of the Southwest. (Big World Read Along Ser.). (Illus.). 20p. (J). (gr. k-2). 1995. bds. 4.95 (*0-673-36258-2*, GoodYrBooks) Addson-Wesley Educ.

— Pueblo Indians of the Southwest: Stencils. (Ancient & Living Cultures Ser.). (Illus.). 32p. (J). (gr. 3 up). 1993. pap. 9.95 (*0-673-36102-0*, GoodYrBooks) Addson-Wesley Educ.

— Southeastern Indians. (Ancient & Living Cultures Ser.). 32p. (Orig.). (J). (gr. 3 up). 1995. pap. 9.95 (*0-673-36305-8*, GoodYrBooks) Addson-Wesley Educ.

— West Africa: Ghana, Stencils. (Ancient & Living Cultures Ser.). (Illus.). 32p. (Orig.). (J). (gr. 3 up). 1992. pap. 9.95 (*0-673-36053-9*, GoodYrBooks) Addson-Wesley Educ.

— West Africa: Nigeria: Stencils. (Ancient & Living Cultures Ser.). (Illus.). 32p. (Orig.). (J). 1993. pap. 9.95 (*0-673-36137-3*, GoodYrBooks) Addson-Wesley Educ.

Bartok, William, ed. Combustion of Synthetic Fuels. LC 83-2822. (ACS Symposium Ser.: No. 217). 246p. 1983. lib. bdg. 38.95 (*0-8412-0773-9*) Am Chemical.

— Combustion of Synthetic Fuels. LC 83-2822. (ACS Symposium Ser.: No. 217). (Illus.). 255p. 1983. reprint ed. pap. 79.10 (*0-608-03201-8*, 206372000007) Bks Demand.

Bartol. Criminal Behavior: A Psychological Approach. 5th ed. LC 98-41092. 504p. 1998. 60.00 (*0-13-787649-1*) P-H.

— Management Study Guide. 3rd ed. 1997. pap. 25.31 (*0-07-006984-0*) McGraw.

— Psychology & Law. 2nd ed. 1994. write for info. (*0-534-16321-1*) Thomson Learn.

Bartol, Anne M., jt. auth. see Bartol, Curt R.

Bartol, Curt R. Psychology & American Law. 373p. (C). 1983. mass mkt. 44.00 (*0-534-01217-5*) Brooks-Cole.

Bartol, Curt R. & Bartol, Anne M. Delinquency & Justice. 2nd ed. LC 97-23352. 387p. 1997. 63.00 (*0-13-841883-7*) P-H.

— Psychology & Law: Research & Application. 2nd ed. LC 93-39459. 1993. mass mkt. 48.00 (*0-534-16320-3*) Brooks-Cole.

Bartol, Cyrus A. Discourses on the Christian Spirit & Life: With an Introduction. 2nd ed. LC 72-4951. (Romantic Tradition in American Literature Ser.). 418p. 1972. reprint ed. 33.95 (*0-405-04622-7*) Ayer.

Bartol, Frank R. I Thought You'd Never Ask! (Illus.). vii, 232p. 1997. pap. 8.95 (*0-9661412-0-2*) Bartol Pub.

Bartol, Kathryn M. & Martin, David C. Management. 2nd ed. LC 93-26387. (Series in Management). (C). 1993. text 71.00 (*0-07-005078-3*) McGraw.

— Management. 2nd ed. (C). 1993. pap. text, student ed. 22.50 (*0-07-005116-X*) McGraw.

— Management. 3rd ed. LC 96-46735. 848p. (C). 1997. 81.88 (*0-07-005722-2*) McGraw.

Bartola, Carla, et al. Yefief 6 Vol. 3: Severance: The Constitution of Mercy. (Illus.). 190p. 2000. pap. 24.95 (*1-884434-11-8*, Pub. by Images For Media) SPD-Small Pr Dist.

Bartold, P. Mark & Narayanan, A. Sampath. Biology of the Periodontal Connective Tissues. LC 98-17716. (Illus.). 278p. 1998. text 86.00 (*0-86715-340-7*) Quint Pub Co.

Bartold, Thomas, jt. auth. see Siembieda, Kevin.

Bartold, Thomas, ed. see Siembieda, Kevin.

Bartold, Thomas, ed. see Siembieda, Kevin & Long, Kevin.

Bartold, Thomas, ed. see Wallis, James & Siembieda, Kevin.

Bartold, V. V. Histoire des Turcs D'Asie Centrale. Donskis, M., tr. from TUR. LC 77-10594. (Studies in Islamic History: No. 2). (Illus.). 197p. 1977. reprint ed. lib. bdg. 35.00 (*0-87991-451-3*) Porcupine Pr.

— An Historical Geography of Iran. LC 83-24548. (Modern Classics in Near Eastern Studies). 308p. 1984. reprint ed. pap. 95.50 (*0-608-03316-2*, 206402800008) Bks Demand.

***Bartoldus, Candy.** A Comprehensive Review of Wetland Assessment Procedures: A Guide for Wetland Practioners. 1999. pap. text. write for info. (*1-883226-04-X*) Environ Concern.

Bartoletti, Susan & Lisandrelli, Elaine. Easy Writer: Student Worksheets, Level G. (Illus.). 38p. (Orig.). (J). (gr. 7-9). 1986. pap. text 14.95 (*0-913935-37-9*) ERA-CCR.

— Easy Writer: Student Worksheets, Level H. (Illus.). 38p. (Orig.). (J). (gr. 8-10). 1986. pap. text 14.95 (*0-913935-38-7*) ERA-CCR.

***Bartoletti, Susan C.** A Coal Miner's Bride: The Diary of Annetka Kaminski, Lattimer, Pennsylvania, 1896. LC 99-29864. (Dear America Ser.). (Illus.). 208p. (J). (gr. 4-7). 2000. 10.95 (*0-439-05386-2*, Dear America) Scholastic Inc.

Bartoletti, Susan C. Dancing with Dziadziu. LC 95-47964. (Illus.). 40p. (J). 1997. 15.00 (*0-15-200675-3*) Harcourt.

— No Man's Land. LC 98-24714. 176p. (J). (gr. 5-9). 1999. 15.95 (*0-590-38371-X*, Blue Sky Press) Scholastic Inc.

Bartoletti, Susan C., et al. Study Skills Workout. (Illus.). 90p. (Orig.). (J). (gr. 5-8). 1987. pap. 9.95 (*0-673-18995-3*, GoodYrBooks) Addson-Wesley Educ.

Bartoletti, Susan Campbell. Growing Up in Coal Country. LC 96-3142. (Illus.). 112p. (YA). (gr. 4-7). 1996. 16.95 (*0-395-77847-6*) HM.

***Bartoletti, Susan Campbell.** Growing Up in Coal Country. LC 96-3142. (Illus.). 128p. (YA). (gr. 4-7). 1999. pap. 7.95 (*0-395-97914-5*) HM.

— Kids on Strike! LC 98-50575. (Illus.). 208p. (J). (gr. 4-7). 1999. 20.00 (*0-395-88892-1*) HM.

Bartoli, Adrian. Components of Fire. Sigmond, Aaron, ed. (Illus.). 176p. 1999. 44.95 (*0-9647874-6-6*) Mako Pubng.

Bartoli, Cosimo. Measurement & Perspective: Del Modo Di Misurare, 1564. (Printed Sources of Western Art Ser.). (ITA.). 294p. 1981. reprint ed. pap., boxed set 50.00 (*0-915346-67-2*) A Wofsy Fine Arts.

Bartoli, Eleonara, tr. see Inghilleri, Paolo.

Bartoli, Jill. Unequal Opportunity: Learning to Read in the U. S. A. (Language & Literacy Ser.). 256p. (C). 1994. text 40.00 (*0-8077-3385-7*); pap. text 19.95 (*0-8077-3384-9*) Tchrs Coll.

Bartoli, Jill & Botel, Morton. Reading - Learning Disability: An Ecological Approach. 280p. (C). 1988. pap. text 19.95 (*0-8077-2904-3*) Tchrs Coll.

Bartoli, Marco. Clare of Assisi. Teresa, Frances, tr. LC 93-10669. 244p. 1993. pap. 21.95 (*0-8199-0963-7*) Franciscan Pr.

Bartoli, Pietro S. & Bellori, Giovanni P. Ancient Funerary Lamps: Le Antiche Lucerne, 1691, 3 vols. (Printed Sources of Western Art Ser.). (ITA., Illus.). 324p. 1972. reprint ed. pap. 60.00 (*0-915346-70-2*) A Wofsy Fine Arts.

Bartolic, L. Croatian-English - English-Croatian Dictionary of Naval Architecture, Mechanical & Nuclear Engineering Terms. 4th ed. (CRO & ENG.). 275p. 1991. 39.50 (*86-03-99995-3*, Pub. by Skolska Knjiga) IBD Ltd.

— Croatian-English--English-Croatian Dictionary of Mechanical Engineering: Power Engineering with Basic Mechanical Terms. (CRO & ENG.). 250p. 1991. 20.00 (*0-7859-8925-0*) Fr & Eur.

— Croatian-English--English-Croatian Dictionary of Naval Architecture Mechanical & Nuclear Engineering Terms. 4th ed. (CRO & ENG.). 275p. 1991. 20.00 (*0-7859-8926-9*) Fr & Eur.

Bartolic, Ljerka. English-Serbocroatian Technical Dictionary. (ENG & SER.). 274p. 1987. pap. 49.95 (*0-8288-0654-3*, F70680) Fr & Eur.

***Bartolini, Claudio, et al.** Mesozoic Sedimentary & Tectonic History of North-Central Mexico. LC 99-38981. (Special Paper Ser.). 1999. write for info. (*0-8137-2340-X*) Geol Soc.

***Bartolini, Stefano.** The Class Cleavage: The Political Mobilization of the European Left, 1860-1980. (Cambridge Studies in Comparative Politics). (Illus.). 608p. 2000. 64.95 (*0-521-65021-6*) Cambridge U Pr.

Bartolini, Stefano & Mair, Peter, eds. Party Politics in Contemporary Western Europe. 192p. 1985. 35.00 (*0-7146-3271-6*, Pub. by F Cass Pubs) Intl Spec Bk.

***Bartollas.** Introduction to Law Enforcement. LC 98-22355. 372p. 1998. pap. text 50.00 (*0-205-27454-4*) Allyn.

Bartollas, Clemens. Introduction to Corrections. 2nd ed. (C). 1990. text 31.20 (*0-685-46020-7*) Addson-Wesley Educ.

***Bartollas, Clemens.** Juvenile Delinquency. 5th ed. LC 98-35647. 606p. 1999. 70.00 (*0-205-29342-5*) Allyn.

Bartollas, Clemens & Braswell, Michael. American Criminal Justice: An Introduction. 2nd ed. LC 96-86414. (Illus.). 650p. 1996. pap. 49.95 (*0-87084-099-1*) Anderson Pub Co.

Bartollas, Clemens & Conrad, Joseph. Introduction to Corrections. 2nd ed. (C). 1997. pap. 74.00 (*0-06-040527-9*) Addson-Wesley Educ.

Bartollas, Clemens & Miller, Stuart J. Juvenile Justice in America. 2nd ed. LC 97-5900. 432p. 1997. 78.00 (*0-13-857616-5*) P-H.

***Bartollas, Clemens & Miller, Stuart J.** Juvenile Justice in America. 3rd ed. LC 00-32642. 480p. 2000. 68.00 (*0-13-014423-1*) P-H.

Bartollas, Clemens, jt. auth. see van Wormer, Katherine Stuart.

Bartolo, B. D., ed. Disordered Solids: Structures & Processes. LC 89-49260. (Ettore Majorana International Science Series, Life Sciences: Vol. 46). (Illus.). 449p. 1989. 115.00 (*0-306-42820-2*, Plenum Trade) Perseus Pubng.

Bartolo, David C., et al. Restorative Proctocolectomy. LC 92-48681. (Illus.). 176p. 1993. 95.00 (*0-632-03333-9*) Blackwell Sci.

Bartolo, Joel Di, see Di Bartolo, Joel.

Bartolo, Michael, jt. auth. see De Marco, Guido.

Bartolo, Michael, jt. auth. see Idris, Kamil.

Bartolome. Articulate Executive. 304p. 1993. 29.95 (*0-07-103425-0*) McGraw.

Bartolome, Fernando, pref. The Articulate Executive: Orchestrating Effective Communication. LC 93-23956. (Harvard Business Review Book Ser.). 304p. 1993. 29.95 (*0-87584-433-2*) Harvard Busn.

Bartolome, Leopoldo J. The Colonos of Apostoles: Adaptive Strategy & Ethnicity in a Polish-Ukrainian. LC 89-6617. (Studies in Anthropology: No. 9). 1990. 59.50 (*0-404-62609-2*) AMS Pr.

Bartolome, Lilia I. Misteaching of Academic Discourse: The Politics of Language in the Classroom. LC 98-9693. (C). 1998. text 60.00 (*0-8133-3144-7*, Pub. by Westview) HarpC.

Bartolome, Lilia I., jt. ed. see Trueba, Enrique T.

Bartolomei, Sonja & Reifsnyder, Constance A. Patient Care in Interventional Radiology: A Resource Manual. LC 97-18581. 1998. 135.00 (*0-8342-0816-4*, S306) Aspen Pub.

Bartolomeis, P. De, see De Bartolomeis, P.

Bartolomeo, Christina. Cupid & Diana. LC 97-38388. 224p. 1998. 22.00 (*0-684-83977-6*, Scribner Pap Fic) S&S Trade Pap.

***Bartolomeo, Christina.** Cupid & Diana. large type ed. LC 98-48559. 1999. 30.00 (*0-7862-1750-2*, G K Hall Lrg Type) Mac Lib Ref.

Bartolomeo, Christina. Cupid & Diana: A Novel. 240p. 1999. pap. 11.00 (*0-684-85622-0*, Scribner Pap Fic) S&S Trade Pap.

Bartolomeo, Joseph F. A New Species of Criticism: Eighteenth-Century Discourse on the Novel. LC 93-29770. 1994. 36.50 (*0-87413-488-9*) U Delaware Pr.

Bartolomeo, Matteo. Eco-Management Accounting LC 99-15362. (Eco-Efficiency in Industry & Science Bks.). 1999. write for info. (*0-7923-5562-8*) Kluwer Academic.

Bartolozzi, C. & Lencioni, R., eds. Liver Malignancies: Diagnostic & Interventional Radiology. LC 99-23562. (Medical Radiology Ser.). (Illus.). 450p. 1999. 299.00 (*3-540-64756-2*) Spr-Verlag.

Bartolozzi, P., et al, eds. Adult Scoliosis. (Progress in Spinal Pathology Ser.). (Illus.). 170p. 1990. 54.95 (*0-387-82201-1*) Spr-Verlag.

***Bartolucci.** Museum & Metamorphosis. 2000. 25.00 (*1-58243-090-X*, Pub. by Counterpt DC) HarpC.

***Bartolucci, Marisa.** Architecture & Design New York. (Architecture & Design Ser.). (Illus.). 96p. 1999. pap. 14.00 (*0-9641863-5-7*) Understand Busn.

***Bartolucci, Marisa, et al.** American Contemporary Furniture. LC 00-28675. (Illus.). 208p. 2000. pap. 35.00 (*0-7893-0492-9*) Universe.

Barton. Contemporary Handbook of Literary Terms. LC 96-76860. (C). Date not set. pap. text 10.76 (*0-395-74205-6*) HM.

— Crisis in Organizations: Managing & Communicating in the Heat of Chaos. 2nd ed. (SWC-General Business Ser.). 2000. pap. 34.95 (*0-324-02429-0*) Thomson Learn.

— Introduction to the Relativity. LC 99-17294. 240p. 1999. pap. 30.00 (*0-471-99896-6*) Wiley.

— Lyndon B. Johnson: Young Texan. 2nd ed. (J). 1995. pap. 3.95 (*0-689-71654-0*) Aladdin.

***Barton.** The Three Bears. LC 90-43151. 32p. (J). (ps-1). 1999. pap. 4.95 (*0-06-443365-X*) HarpC Child Bks.

Barton. Upper Limb & Hand. (C). 1998. text 57.00 (*0-7020-2236-5*, W B Saunders Co) Harcrt Hlth Sci Grp.

— Using Childern's Literature. (C). 1999. pap. text. write for info. (*0-15-508049-0*) Harcourt Coll Pubs.

— Voice Onstage & Off. (C). 1994. 53.50 incl. audio (*0-15-502975-4*) Harcourt.

***Barton & Williams.** Fairchilds Passage. 1998. mass mkt. 5.99 (*0-8125-4422-6*) Tor Bks.

Barton, et al. What Do I Read Next? A Reader's Guide to Current Genre Fiction 1996. 7th ed. 656p. 1996. 110.00 (*0-7876-1048-8*) Gale.

— What Do I Read Next? 1995. 6th ed. 1995. 110.00 (*0-8103-9146-5*) Gale.

Barton, jt. auth. see Lewis.

Barton, ed. see Deslongchamps, Pierre.

Barton, ed. see Paquette, Leo A.

Barton, A. States of Matter, States of Mind. (Illus.). 320p. 1997. 98.00 (*0-7503-0417-0*) IOP Pub.

Barton, A. D. Anatomy of Accounting. 3rd ed. LC 83-7015. 1984. pap. text 49.95 (*0-7022-2009-4*, Pub. by Univ Queensland Pr) Intl Spec Bk.

Barton, Albert. Story of Primrose, 1831-1895. (Illus.). 112p. 1997. reprint ed. pap. 17.50 (*0-8328-6981-3*); reprint ed. lib. bdg. 25.00 (*0-8328-6980-5*) Higginson Bk Co.

Barton, Allan & Slocombe, Andrew. States of Matter, States of Mind. LC 97-30212. (Illus.). 320p. 1997. pap. 32.00 (*0-7503-0418-9*) IOP Pub.

Barton, Allan F. Alcohols with Water. (Solubility Data Ser.). 1984. 130.00 (*0-08-025277-X*, Pergamon Pr) Elsevier.

— Handbook of Solubility Parameters & Other Cohesion Parameters. 608p. 1983. 152.95 (*0-8493-3295-8*, QD543) CRC Pr.

— Handbook of Solubility Parameters & Other Cohesion Parameters. 2nd ed. (Illus.). 768p. 1991. boxed set 271.95 (*0-8493-0176-9*, QD543) CRC Pr.

— Resource Recovery & Recycling. LC 78-13601. (Environmental Science & Technology Ser.). (Illus.). 432p. reprint ed. pap. 134.00 (*0-7837-3520-0*, 205785400008) Bks Demand.

Barton, Allen H., ed. see Weiss, Carol H.

Barton, Andrew & Adler, Samuel. Andrew Barton: The Disappointment or the Force of Credulity (1767) Graue, Jerald C. & Layng, Judith, eds. (Recent Researches in American Music Ser.: No. RRAM 3-4). (Illus.). 169, xvip. 1976. pap. 55.00 (*0-89579-078-5*) A-R Eds.

Barton, Angela C. Feminist Science Education. LC 97-49819. (Athena Ser.). 1998. 44.00 (*0-8077-6294-6*); pap. 19.95 (*0-8077-6293-8*) Tchrs Coll.

Barton, Anna. The Natural Pharmacist: Saw Palmetto & the Prostrate. LC 98-49607. 208p. 2000. pap. 6.99 (*0-7615-1559-3*) Prima Pub.

Barton, Anne. Byron: "Don Juan" (Landmarks of World Literature Ser.). (Illus.). 124p. (C). 1992. text 29.95 (*0-521-32933-7*) Cambridge U Pr.

— Essays, Mainly Shakespearean. (Illus.). 406p. (C). 1994. text 80.00 (*0-521-40444-4*) Cambridge U Pr.

Barton, Anne. The Evil That We Do. 264p. mass mkt. 4.99 (*1-55197-086-4*) Picasso Publ.

Barton, Anne. The Names of Comedy. 239p. 1990. text 37.50 (*0-8020-5657-1*) U of Toronto Pr.

— Shakespeare & the Idea of the Play. LC 76-58419. 223p. 1977. reprint ed. lib. bdg. 69.50 (*0-8371-9446-6*, BASI, Greenwood Pr) Greenwood.

Barton-Aschman Associates Inc. Staff. Shared Parking. LC 83-51648. 86p. (Orig.). 1983. pap. 57.95 (*0-87420-652-9*, S-22) Urban Land.

Barton, B. J., ed. see Beckett, Cheryl.

Barton, Babette B., et al, eds. Taxation of Business Enterprises, Cases & Materials. LC 98-9478. (American Casebook Ser.). 900p. 1998. 62.50 (*0-314-21120-9*) West Pub.

Barton, Barbara. Gardening by Mail. 5th ed. LC 98-115874. 440p. 1997. pap. 24.00 (*0-395-87770-9*) HM.

— Ruckus along the Rivers. (Illus.). 110p. 1996. pap. 4.95 (*0-943639-28-X*) Anchor Pub Co.

Barton, Benjamin S. New Views of the Origin of the Tribes & Nations of America. (LC History-America-E). 133p. 1999. reprint ed. lib. bdg. 69.00 (*0-7812-4306-8*) Rprt Serv.

— Notes on the Animals of North America, 1793. Sterling, Keir B., ed. & intro. by. LC 73-17801. (Natural Sciences in America Ser.). 150p. 1974. 15.95 (*0-405-05719-9*) Ayer.

Barton, Beverly. Blackwood's Woman (The Protectors) (Intimate Moments Ser.). 1996. per. 3.99 (*0-373-07707-6*, 1-07707-2) Silhouette.

— Camaron. (Desire Ser.). 1993. mass mkt. 2.99 (*0-373-05796-2*, 5-05796-3) Silhouette.

— A Child of Her Own. (Desire Ser.: No. 1077). 1997. per. 3.50 (*0-373-76077-9*, 1-76077-6) Silhouette.

— Defending His Own. 1995. per. 3.75 (*0-373-07670-3*, 1-07670-2) Silhouette.

***Barton, Beverly.** Egan Cassidy's Kid. (Intimate Moments Ser.: Bk. 1015). 2000. mass mkt. 4.50 (*0-373-27085-2*, 1-27085-9) Silhouette.

Barton, Beverly. Emily & the Stranger. (Intimate Moments Ser.). 1998. per. 4.25 (*0-373-07860-9*, 1-07860-9) Silhouette.

— Une Femme en Peril. (Amours d'Aujourd'Hui Ser.: Bk. 316). 1999. mass mkt. 4.99 (*0-373-38316-9*, 1-38316-5) Harlequin Bks.

— Gabriel Hawk's Lady: The Protectors. (Intimate Moments Ser.: No. 830). 1998. per. 3.99 (*0-373-07830-7*, 1-07830-2) Silhouette.

— Guarding Jeannie. (Intimate Moments Ser.). 1996. per. 3.75 (*0-373-07688-6*, 1-07688-4) Silhouette.

— Having His Baby: 3 Babies for 3 Brothers. (Desire Ser.: No. 1216). 1999. per. 3.75 (*0-373-76216-X*, 1-76216-0) Silhouette.

***Barton, Beverly.** Her Secret Weapon. (Intimate Moments Ser.: Bk. 1034). 2000. mass mkt. 4.50 (*0-373-27104-2*, 1-27104-8) Silhouette.

An Asterisk (*) at the beginning of an entry indicates that the title is appearing for the first time.

Barton, Beverly. His Secret Child (3 Babies for 3 Brothers) (Desire Ser.: No. 1203). 1999. per. 3.75 (*0-373-76203-8*, 1-76203-8) Harlequin Bks.

— His Woman, His Child: 3 Babies for 3 Brothers. 1999. per. 3.75 (*0-373-76209-7*, 1-76209-5) Silhouette.

— Un Hombre Inocente. Orig. Title: Cameron. (SPA.). 1996. per. 3.50 (*0-373-35132-1*) Harlequin Bks.

***Barton, Beverly.** Imposible de Resistir (Impossible to Resist) (Deseo Ser.). (SPA.). 2000. mass mkt. 3.50 (*0-373-35359-6*, 1-35359-8) Harlequin Bks.

— In the Arms of a Hero. Vol. 10. 256p. 2000. per. 4.50 (*0-373-65039-6*) Harlequin Bks.

Barton, Beverly. Keeping Annie Safe: The Protectors. (Intimate Moments Ser.: Bk. 937). 1999. per. 4.25 (*0-373-07937-0*, 1-07937-5) Silhouette.

— Lone Wolf's Lady. (Intimate Moments Ser.). 1998. per. 4.25 (*0-373-07877-3*, 1-07877-3) Silhouette.

— Lover & Deceiver. (Intimate Moments Ser.). 1994. per. 3.50 (*0-373-07557-X*, 5-07557-7) Silhouette.

— A Man Like Morgan Kane. 1997. per. 3.99 (*0-373-07819-6*, 1-07819-5) Silhouette.

***Barton, Beverly.** El Mayor Regalo (The Greatest Gift) His Woman, His Child. (Deseo Ser.: No. 193). (SPA.). 2000. per. 3.50 (*0-373-35323-5*, 1-35323-4) Silhouette.

Barton, Beverly. Milliardaire Sans Bagages. (Rouge Passion Ser.: Vol. 472). 1998. mass mkt. 3.50 (*0-373-37472-0*, 1-37472-7) Harlequin Bks.

— The Mother of My Child. (Desire Ser.). 1994. per. 2.99 (*0-373-05831-4*, 5-05831-8) Silhouette.

***Barton, Beverly.** Murdock's Last Stand: (The Protectors) (Intimate Moments Ser.: No. 979). 2000. per. 4.50 (*0-373-07979-6*, 1-07979-7) Harlequin Bks.

Barton, Beverly. Nine Months: 36 Hours. (Thirty-Six Hours Ser.: Vol. 10). 1998. per. 4.50 (*0-373-65015-9*, 1-65015-9) Harlequin Bks.

— Nothing but Trouble. (Desire Ser.). 1994. per. 2.99 (*0-373-05881-0*, 1-05881-7) Silhouette.

***Barton, Beverly.** Out of Danger. 2000. mass mkt. 4.50 (*0-373-82240-5*, 1-82240-2) Harlequin Bks.

Barton, Beverly. The Outcast. 1995. per. 3.50 (*0-373-07614-2*, 1-07614-0) Silhouette.

— Paladin's Woman. (Intimate Moments Ser.). 1993. mass mkt. 3.50 (*0-373-07515-4*, 5-07515-5) Silhouette.

— Por Caminos Extranos. (Deseo Ser.: No. 218).Tr. of Along Strange Roads. (SPA.). 1997. per. 3.50 (*0-373-35218-2*, 1-35218-6) Harlequin Bks.

— Roarke's Wife. 1997. per. 3.99 (*0-373-07807-2*, 1-07807-0) Silhouette.

— Sans Passe, Sans Amour. (Rouge Passion Ser.: Bk. 495). 1999. mass mkt. 3.50 (*0-373-37495-X*, 1-37495-8) Harlequin Bks.

— Talk of the Town. (Desire Ser.: No. 711). 1992. pap. 2.89 (*0-373-05711-3*, 5-05711-2) Harlequin Bks.

— The Tender Trap. 1997. per. 3.50 (*0-373-76047-7*, 1-76047-9) Silhouette.

— Tierna Pasion - Tender Passion, Vol. 201. (Silhouette Deseo).Tr. of Tender Passion. (SPA.). 1997. per. 3.50 (*0-373-35201-8*, 1-35201-2) Harlequin Bks.

Barton, Bill. Iris. 448p. 1999. mass mkt. 6.99 (*0-380-73038-3*, Avon Bks) Morrow Avon.

Barton, Blair L. Best Bike Routes on Cape Cod: Martha's Vineyard & Nantucket. (Illus.). 1994. 29.95 (*1-884526-01-2*) Barton Dame.

— Best Bike Routes on Long Island: Including Block Island, R. I. (Illus.). 1993. spiral bd. 29.95 (*1-884526-00-4*) Barton Dame.

Barton, Blanche. The Church of Satan. (Illus.). 200p. (Orig.). 1990. pap. 8.95 (*0-9623286-2-6*) Hells Kitchen.

— The Secret Life of a Satanist: The Authorized Biography of Anton LaVey. LC 98-169959. 262p. 1992. pap. 14.95 (*0-922915-12-1*) Feral Hse.

Barton, Bob. The Best & Dearest Chick of All. (Northern Lights Books for Children Ser.). (Illus.). 24p. (J). (ps-3). 1994. pap. 7.95 (*0-88995-117-9*, Pub. by Red Deer) Genl Dist Srvs.

— Tell Me Another: Storytelling & Reading Aloud at Home, at School, & in the Community. LC 86-18406. 160p. (Orig.). (C). 1986. pap. 12.95 (*0-435-08231-0*, 08231) Heinemann.

Barton, Bob & Booth, David. Stories in the Classroom: Storytelling, Reading Aloud, & Roleplaying with Children. LC 89-77379. 194p. (C). 1990. pap. text 20.00 (*0-435-08527-1*, 08527) Heinemann.

Barton, Bob & Yudin. The Storm Wife. (Illus.). 32p. (J). (gr. 1-5). Date not set. 12.95 (*1-55082-060-5*) LPC InBook.

Barton, Bob & Yudin, Georgi. The Storm Wife. (Illus.). 32p. 1993. per. 8.95 (*1-55082-061-3*, Pub. by Quarry Pr) LPC InBook.

Barton, Brian. The Blitz: Belfast in the War Years. LC 89-81778. (Illus.). 335p. 2000. pap. 29.95 (*0-85640-426-8*, Pub. by Blackstaff Pr) Dufour.

— Northern Ireland in the Second World War. (Illus.). 164p. (Orig.). 1996. pap. 16.95 (*0-901905-69-0*, Pub. by Ulster Hist Fnd) Irish Bks Media.

— A Pocket History of Ulster. (Illus.). 224p. 1997. pap. 8.95 (*0-86278-428-X*, Pub. by OBrien Pr) Irish Amer Bk.

***Barton, Brian & Foy, Michael A.** Easter Rising: Day-by-Day. 2000. 29.95 (*0-7509-1706-7*, Pub. by Sutton Publng) Intl Pubs Mktg.

Barton, Brian & Roche, Patrick J., eds. The Northern Ireland Question: Perspectives & Policies. 224p. 1994. 61.95 (*1-85628-881-1*, Pub. by Avebry) Ashgate Pub Co.

Barton, Brian, jt. auth. see Roche, Patrick J.

Barton, Brian, jt. ed. see Roche, Patrick J.

Barton, Bruce. Acts. LC 99-21515. (Life Application Bible Commentary Ser.). 1999. pap. text 14.99 (*0-8423-2861-0*) Tyndale Hse.

— The Book Nobody Knows. 306p. 1992. reprint ed. lib. bdg. 23.95 (*0-89966-950-6*) Buccaneer Bks.

— Man Nobody Knows. 1998. pap. 7.95 (*0-9652894-1-9*) GA Publng.

***Barton, Bruce.** Man Nobody Knows. 128p. 2000. pap. text 12.95 (*1-56663-294-3*, Pub. by I R Dee) Natl Bk Netwk.

Barton, Bruce. The Man Nobody Knows. 240p. 1992. reprint ed. lib. bdg. 29.95 (*0-89966-949-2*) Buccaneer Bks.

— The Man Nobody Knows - His Method. Fonseca, Raul G., ed. 48p. (Orig.). 1987. pap. 1.00 (*0-940999-28-5*, C-2134) Star Bible.

— Nest. 1987. 2.50 (*0-941127-00-1*) Dacotah Terr Pr.

— Scripture Kit: Scripture Study at Its Best. 11th ed. (Illus.). 200p. 1996. 29.95 (*0-9645314-0-2*) B Barton.

Barton, Bruce, et al. A Path Through Stone. 2nd ed. 79p. (C). 1996. pap. 8.95 (*0-9647066-0-1*) Wellstone Pr.

Barton, Bruce A., jt. auth. see Pennell, William.

Barton, Bruce B. Galatians. LC 94-2246. (Life Application Bible Commentary Ser.). 14.99p. 1994. pap. 14.99 (*0-8423-3026-7*) Tyndale Hse.

Barton, Bruce B. & Veerman, David R. James. (Life Application Bible Commentary Ser.). 192p. 1992. pap. 14.99 (*0-8423-2891-2*, 75-2891-2) Tyndale Hse.

— Romans. (Life Application Bible Commentary Ser.). 320p. 1992. pap. 14.99 (*0-8423-2890-4*) Tyndale Hse.

***Barton, Bruce B., et al.** 1 & 2 Thessalonians: Life Application Commentary. LC 98-45169. 1999. pap. 14.99 (*0-8423-2862-9*) Tyndale Hse.

Barton, Bruce B., et al. 1 & 2 Timothy, Titus. LC 93-4926. (Life Application Bible Commentary Ser.). 304p. 1993. pap. 10.99 (*0-8423-2832-7*) Tyndale Hse.

— I Peter, II Peter & Jude. LC 95-37612. (Life Application Bible Commentary Ser.). 1996. pap. 14.99 (*0-8423-3031-3*) Tyndale Hse.

— Hebrews. LC 96-53647. (Life Application Bible Commentary Ser.). 288p. 1997. pap. 14.99 (*0-8423-2856-4*) Tyndale Hse.

— John. LC 93-22472. (Life Application Bible Commentary Ser.). 1993. pap. 14.99 (*0-8423-2893-9*) Tyndale Hse.

— Lab Commentary: Matthew. LC 96-15075. 640p. 1996. pap. 14.99 (*0-8423-3034-8*) Tyndale Hse.

— Luke. LC 97-27767. (Life Application Bible Commentary Ser.). 1998. 16.99 (*0-8423-2852-1*) Tyndale Hse.

— Mark. LC 94-3689. (Life Application Bible Commentary Ser.). 507p. 1994. pap. 14.99 (*0-8423-3028-3*, 75-3028-3) Tyndale Hse.

— Philippians, Colossians, & Philemon. LC 95-6670. (Life Application Bible Commentary Ser.). 275p. 1995. pap. 14.99 (*0-8423-2974-9*) Tyndale Hse.

Barton-Burke, Margaret. Cancer Chemotherapy. 480p. 1991. 50.00 (*0-86720-434-6*) Jones & Bartlett.

— Chemotherapy Care Plans. (Nursing-Health Science Ser.). 432p. (C). 1992. spiral bd. 34.95 (*0-86720-339-0*) Jones & Bartlett.

Barton Burke, Margaret. Oncology Nursing Homecare Handbook. 285p. 1993. pap. text 39.95 (*0-86720-643-8*) Jones & Bartlett.

Barton, Byron. Airplanes. LC 85-47899. (Illus.). 32p. (J). (ps). 1986. 6.95 (*0-694-00060-4*); lib. bdg. 15.89 (*0-690-04532-8*) HarpC Child Bks.

— Airport. LC 79-7816. (Illus.). 32p. (J). (ps). 1982. lib. bdg. 15.89 (*0-690-04169-1*) HarpC Child Bks.

— Airport. LC 79-7816. (Trophy Picture Bk.). (Illus.). 32p. (J). (ps-3). 1987. pap. 5.95 (*0-06-443145-2*, HarpTrophy) HarpC Child Bks.

— Airport. 1987. 11.15 (*0-606-03542-7*, Pub. by Turtleback) Demco.

— Big Machines Board Book. (Illus.). 12p. (J). (ps up). 1996. 3.95 (*0-694-00622-X*, HarpFestival) HarpC Child Bks.

— Boats. LC 85-47900. (Illus.). 32p. (J). (ps). 1986. 4.95 (*0-694-00059-0*) HarpC Child Bks.

— Boats. LC 85-47900. (Illus.). 32p. (J). (ps-3). 1986. lib. bdg. 14.89 (*0-690-04536-0*) HarpC Child Bks.

— Boats Board Book. (Illus.). 16p. (J). (ps-k). 1998. 6.95 (*0-694-01165-7*) HarpC Child Bks.

— Bones, Bones, Dinosaur Bones. LC 89-71306. (Illus.). 32p. (J). (ps-1). 1990. 15.95 (*0-690-04825-4*); lib. bdg. 15.89 (*0-690-04827-0*) HarpC Child Bks.

Barton, Byron. Building a House. 1981. 10.15 (*0-606-03140-5*, Pub. by Turtleback) Demco.

Barton, Byron. Building a House: Big Book. LC 80-22674. (ESL Theme Links Ser.). (Illus.). 32p. 1992. pap. text 24.00 (*1-56334-182-4*) Hampton-Brown.

— Building a House: Small Book. LC 80-22674. (Illus.). 32p. (J). (gr. k-3). 1992. pap. text 6.00 (*1-56334-185-9*) Hampton-Brown.

— Buzz, Buzz, Buzz. LC 93-46931. (Illus.). 32p. (J). (ps-2). 1995. mass mkt. 4.95 (*0-689-71873-X*) Aladdin.

Barton, Byron. Buzz, Buzz, Buzz. 1995. 10.15 (*0-606-07331-0*, Pub. by Turtleback) Demco.

Barton, Byron. Dinosaurs Board Book. (Illus.). 12p. (J). (ps up). 1996. 3.95 (*0-694-00621-1*, HarpFestival) HarpC Child Bks.

— Dinosaurs, Dinosaurs. LC 88-22938. (Illus.). 40p. (J). (ps-1). 1989. lib. bdg. 15.89 (*0-690-04768-1*) HarpC Child Bks.

— Dinosaurs, Dinosaurs. LC 88-22938. (Illus.). 40p. (J). (ps-3). 1989. 15.95 (*0-694-00269-0*) HarpC Child Bks.

— Dinosaurs, Dinosaurs. LC 88-22938. (Trophy Picture Bk.). (Illus.). 40p. (J). (ps-1). 1993. pap. 5.95 (*0-06-443298-X*, HarpTrophy) HarpC Child Bks.

— Dinosaurs, Dinosaurs. (J). 1993. 11.15 (*0-606-02593-6*, Pub. by Turtleback) Demco.

— Dinosaurs, Dinosaurs Big Book. LC 88-22938. (Big Bk.). (Illus.). 40p. (J). (ps-1). 1991. 22.95 (*0-06-020410-9*) HarpC Child Bks.

— Dinosaurs, Dinosaurs Board Book. (Illus.). 32p. (J). (ps up). 1994. 7.95 (*0-694-00625-4*, HarpFestival) HarpC Child Bks.

— I Want to Be an Astronaut. LC 87-24311. (Illus.). 32p. (J). (ps-1). 1988. 14.00 (*0-694-00261-5*) HarpC Child Bks.

— I Want to Be an Astronaut. LC 87-24311. (Illus.). 32p. (J). (ps-1). 1988. lib. bdg. 15.89 (*0-690-04744-4*) HarpC Child Bks.

— I Want to Be an Astronaut. LC 87-24311. (Trophy Picture Bk.). (Illus.). 32p. (J). (ps-3). 1992. pap. 6.95 (*0-06-443280-7*, HarpTrophy) HarpC Child Bks.

— I Want to Be an Astronaut. (J). 1992. 11.15 (*0-606-00516-1*, Pub. by Turtleback) Demco.

— I Want to Be an Astronaut Board Book. (Illus.). 32p. (J). (ps-k). 1997. 6.95 (*0-694-01106-1*, HarpFestival) HarpC Child Bks.

— The Little Red Hen Board Book. (Illus.). 32p. (J). (ps up). 1997. 7.95 (*0-694-00999-7*, HarpFestival) HarpC Child Bks.

— Machines at Work. LC 86-24221. (Illus.). 32p. (J). (ps-1). 1987. lib. bdg. 15.89 (*0-690-04573-5*) HarpC Child Bks.

— Machines at Work. LC 86-24221. (Illus.). 32p. (J). (ps-3). 1987. 15.95 (*0-694-00190-2*) HarpC Child Bks.

— Machines at Work Board Book. (Illus.). 32p. (J). (ps up). 1997. 6.95 (*0-694-01107-X*, HarpFestival) HarpC Child Bks.

— Planes Board Book. (Illus.). 16p. (J). (ps-k). 1998. 6.95 (*0-694-01166-5*) HarpC Child Bks.

— The Three Bears Board Book. (Illus.). 32p. (J). (ps up). 1997. 7.95 (*0-694-00998-9*, HarpFestival) HarpC Child Bks.

— Tools Board Book. (Illus.). 12p. (J). (ps up). 1996. 3.95 (*0-694-00623-8*, HarpFestival) HarpC Child Bks.

— Trains. LC 85-47898. (Illus.). 32p. (J). (ps). 1986. 13.95 (*0-694-00061-2*); lib. bdg. 14.89 (*0-690-04534-4*) HarpC Child Bks.

— Trains Board Book. (Illus.). 16p. (J). (ps-k). 1998. 6.95 (*0-694-01167-3*) HarpC Child Bks.

— Trucks. LC 85-47901. (Illus.). 32p. (J). (ps). 1986. 5.95 (*0-694-00062-0*) HarpC Child Bks.

— Trucks. LC 85-47901. (Illus.). 32p. (J). (ps-k). 1986. lib. bdg. 15.89 (*0-690-04530-1*) HarpC Child Bks.

— Trucks & Trains Board Book Set, 2 vols. (Illus.). 32p. (J). (ps-k). 1999. 14.95 (*0-694-01255-6*, HarpFestival HarpC Child Bks.

— Trucks Board Book. (Illus.). 16p. (J). (ps-k). 1998. 5.95 (*0-694-01164-9*) HarpC Child Bks.

— The Wee Little Woman. LC 94-18683. (Illus.). 32p. (J). (ps-1). 1995. lib. bdg. 14.89 (*0-06-023388-5*) HarpC Child Bks.

— The Wee Little Woman. LC 94-18683. (Illus.). 32p. (J). (ps-3). 1995. 14.95 (*0-06-023387-7*) HarpC Child Bks.

— Where's Al? LC 78-171866. (Illus.). 32p. (J). (ps-3). 1989. pap. 6.95 (*0-395-51582-3*, Clarion Bks) HM.

— Where's Al? (J). 1972. 12.15 (*0-606-04420-5*, Pub. by Turtleback) Demco.

Barton, Byron. The Little Red Hen. LC 91-4051. 32p. (J). (ps-1). 1993. 15.95 (*0-06-021675-1*); lib. bdg. 15.89 (*0-06-021676-X*) HarpC Child Bks.

— Little Red Hen Big Book. LC 91-4051. (Trophy Picture Bk.). 32p. (J). (ps-1). 1994. pap. 21.95 (*0-06-443379-X*, HarpTrophy) HarpC Child Bks.

— The Three Bears. LC 90-43151. 32p. (J). (ps-3). 1991. 15.95 (*0-06-020423-0*) HarpC Child Bks.

— The Three Bears. LC 90-43151. 32p. (J). (ps-3). 1991. lib. bdg. 15.89 (*0-06-020424-9*) HarpC Child Bks.

Barton, C. C. & La Pointe, P. R. Fractals in Petroleum Geology & Earth Processes. (Illus.). 342p. (C). 1995. text 95.00 (*0-306-44868-8*, Kluwer Plenum) Kluwer Academic.

— Fractals in the Earth Sciences. (Illus.). 284p. (C). 1995. text 65.00 (*0-306-44865-3*, Kluwer Plenum) Kluwer Academic.

***Barton, Carlin A.** Roman Honor: The Fire in the Bones. LC 00-37409. 2001. write for info. (*0-520-22525-2*) U CA Pr.

Barton, Carlin A. Sorrows of the Ancient Romans: The Gladiator & the Monster. 224p. (C). 1992. pap. text 15.95 (*0-691-01091-9*, Pub. by Princeton U Pr) Cal Prin Full Svc.

Barton, Carol. Instructions for Assembly. 1993. pap. 25.00 (*0-932526-46-2*) Nexus Pr.

***Barton, Carol.** The Pocket Paper Engineer Vol. I: How to Make Pop-Ups. (Illus.). 50p. 2000. pap. 40.00 (*0-9627752-0-7*) Pop Kinetics.

Barton, Charles. Howard Hughes & His Flying Boat. 2nd rev. ed. LC 98-90157. (Illus.). 288p. 1998. pap. 19.95 (*0-9663175-0-5*) C Barton Inc.

Barton, Charles, jt. auth. see Johnston, A. M.

Barton, Charles D. America: To Pray or Not to Pray. rev. ed. LC 88-194216. (Illus.). 216p. 1994. pap. 6.95 (*0-925279-42-0*) Wallbuilders.

— America's Godly Heritage. (Orig.). 1993. pap. 3.95 (*0-925279-29-3*) Wallbuilders.

Barton, Charles K. B. Getting Even: Revenge as a Form of Justice. LC 99-22765. 256p. 1999. 39.95 (*0-8126-9401-5*); pap. 21.95 (*0-8126-9402-3*) Open Court.

Barton, Chris. Management of Office Emergencies. LC 98-35485. (Illus.). 398p. 1999. pap. text 32.00 (*0-07-006303-6*) McGraw-Hill HPD.

Barton, Chris & Douglas, Gillian. Law & Parenthood. 272p. 1995. pap. text 50.00 (*0-406-04499-6*, MICHIE) LEXIS Pub.

Barton, Chris & Hibbs, Mary. Q & A Family Law. 2nd ed. 251p. 1998. pap. 24.00 (*1-85431-809-8*, Pub. by Blackstone Pr) Gaunt.

Barton, Chris, et al. Q & A Family Law. 1994. 8.95 (*1-85431-307-X*, Pub. by Blackstone Pr) Gaunt.

Barton, Christopher. Cohabitation Contracts. LC 84-6102. 115p. 1985. text 87.95 (*0-566-00711-8*, Pub. by Dartmth Pub) Ashgate Pub Co.

Barton, Clara. The Story of My Childhood. Baxter, Annette K., ed. LC 79-8773. (Signal Lives Ser.). (Illus.). 1980. reprint ed. lib. bdg. 18.95 (*0-405-12823-1*) Ayer.

***Barton, Craig Evan, ed.** Sites of Memory: Perspectives on Architecture & Race. LC 00-8110. (Illus.). 208p. 2001. pap. 24.95 (*1-56898-233-X*) Princeton Arch.

Barton, Cynthia H. Transcendental Wife: The Life of Abigail May Alcott. LC 96-16217. 196p. 1996. pap. text 29.50 (*0-7618-0387-4*); lib. bdg. 52.50 (*0-7618-0386-6*) U Pr of Amer.

Barton, Cyril. As the Tree Grows: So Grows the Tree. LC 84-90901. (Illus.). 223p. (Orig.). 1983. 14.00 (*0-9613277-0-7*); pap. 8.00 (*0-9613277-1-5*) C Barton.

Barton, D. Indigenous Agroforestry in Latin America: A Blueprint for Sustainable Agriculture? 1994. pap. 25.00 (*0-85954-373-0*, Pub. by Nat Res Inst) St Mut.

Barton, D. B. Engine Houses. (C). 1990. pap. 35.00 (*0-85025-312-8*, Pub. by Tor Mark Pr) St Mut.

Barton, D. H., ed. see Simonsen, John.

Barton, D. Plunket. History of Our Inns of Court. LC 87-81958. 320p. 1987. reprint ed. lib. bdg. 45.00 (*0-89941-581-4*, 305330) W S Hein.

***Barton, D. Plunket, et al, as told by.** The Story of Our Inns of Court. 320p. 2000. reprint ed. 80.00 (*1-56169-617-X*) Gaunt.

Barton, D. Plunket, et al. Story of the Inns of Court. (Illus.). 320p. 1986. reprint ed. 45.00 (*0-8377-1936-4*, Rothman) W S Hein.

Barton, D. S., ed. see McCorkle, John.

***Barton, Dan.** Killer Material. 304p. 2000. 24.95 (*0-312-25222-6*, Minotaur) St Martin.

***Barton, David.** Benjamin Rush: Signer of the Declaration of Independence. (Illus.). 312p. 1999. pap. 9.95 (*0-925279-73-0*, Pub. by Wallbuilders) Spring Arbor Dist.

— Benjamin Rush: Signer of the Declaration of Independence. (Illus.). 312p. 1999. 15.95 (*0-925279-74-9*, Pub. by Wallbuilders) Spring Arbor Dist.

Barton, David. The Bulletproof George Washington. (Illus.). 59p. (Orig.). (YA). (gr. 8-12). 1990. pap. 5.95 (*0-925279-14-5*) Wallbuilders.

— Education & the Founding Fathers. unabridged ed. 26p. (Orig.). 1993. pap. 3.95 (*0-925279-30-7*) Wallbuilders.

— The Foundations of American Government. unabridged ed. 16p. (Orig.). 1993. pap. 2.95 (*0-925279-32-3*) Wallbuilders.

— Impeachment: Restraining an Overactive Judiciary. (Illus.). 62p. (Orig.). 1996. pap. 6.95 (*0-925279-55-2*) Wallbuilders.

— Keys to Good Government. unabridged ed. 30p. (Orig.). 1994. pap. 3.95 (*0-925279-36-6*) Wallbuilders.

— Literacy: An Introduction to the Ecology of Language. 232p. 1994. pap. 28.95 (*0-631-19091-0*) Blackwell Pubs.

— Notes from the Exile. LC 82-84118. 70p. (Orig.). 1983. pap. 3.95 (*0-941692-05-1*) Elysian Pr.

— Original Intent: The Courts, the Constitution & Religion. 2nd large type ed. 550p. (Orig.). 1997. pap. 12.95 (*0-925279-57-9*) Wallbuilders.

— Spirit of the American Revolution. unabridged ed. 23p. (Orig.). 1994. pap. 3.95 (*0-925279-43-9*) Wallbuilders.

— Surviving the Cold. (QRL Poetry Bks.: XXII). 1981. 20.00 (*0-614-06388-4*) Quarterly Rev.

Barton, David, ed. Sustaining Local Literacies. LC 93-50655. 108p. 1994. 39.95 (*1-85359-227-7*, Pub. by Multilingual Matters) Taylor & Francis.

Barton, David, intro. The New England Primer. LC 98-119773. (Illus.). 1991. reprint ed. text 6.95 (*0-925279-17-X*) Wallbuilders.

***Barton, David & Hall, Nigel.** Letter Writing as a Social Practice. LC 99-39098. (Studies in Written Language & Literacy: Vol. 9). vi, 262p. 2000. pap. 29.95 (*1-55619-208-8*) J Benjamins Pubng.

Barton, David & Hall, Nigel, eds. Letter Writing As a Social Practice. Date not set. write for info. (*1-85359-413-X*, Pub. by Multilingual Matters); pap. write for info. (*1-85359-412-1*, Pub. by Multilingual Matters) Taylor & Francis.

***Barton, David & Hall, Nigel, eds.** Letter Writing as a Social Practice. LC 99-39098. (Studies in Written Language & Literacy: Vol. 9). vi, 262p. 2000. text 70.00 (*1-55619-207-X*) J Benjamins Pubng.

Barton, David & Hamilton, Mary. Local Literacies: Reading & Writing in One Community. LC 97-39774. (Illus.). 320p. (C). 1998. 90.00 (*0-415-17149-0*); pap. 27.99 (*0-415-17150-4*) Routledge.

Barton, David & Ivanic, Roz, eds. Writing in the Community. (Written Communication Annual Ser.: Vol. 6). (Illus.). 320p. 1991. 62.00 (*0-8039-3632-X*); pap. 26.00 (*0-8039-3633-8*) Sage.

***Barton, David, et al.** Situated Literacies. LC 99-12658. (Literacies Ser.). 224p. (C). 1999. text. write for info. (*0-415-20670-7*) Routledge.

Barton, David, et al. Situated Literacies: Reading & Writing in Context. LC 99-12658. 1999. pap. 29.99 (*0-415-20671-5*) Routledge.

Barton, David A. Discovering Chapels & Meeting Houses. 1989. pap. 25.00 (*0-7478-0097-9*, Pub. by Shire Pubns) St Mut.

Barton, David K. CW & Doppler Radar. LC 78-24055. (Radars Ser.: Vol. 7). (Illus.). 420p. 1978. reprint ed. pap. 130.20 (*0-608-17718-0*, 203012500067) Bks Demand.

— Frequency Agility & Diversity. LC 74-82597. (Radars Ser.: Vol. 6). 430p. reprint ed. pap. 133.30 (*0-608-14983-7*, 202596000047) Bks Demand.

— Modern Radar System Analysis. (Radar Library). 590p. 1988. text 83.00 (*0-89006-170-X*) Artech Hse.

— Monopulse Radar. LC 74-82597. (Radars Ser.: Vol. 1). 343p. reprint ed. pap. 106.40 (*0-608-13080-X*, 202505900041) Bks Demand.

— Pulse Compression. LC 74-82597. (Radars Ser.: Vol. 3). 237p. 1975. reprint ed. pap. 73.50 (*0-608-10467-1*, 202506000041) Bks Demand.

B

— Radar Clutter. LC 82-215301. (Radars Ser.: No. 5). 430p. reprint ed. pap. 133.30 (*0-608-15931-X*, 203092100071) Bks Demand.

— The Radar Equation. LC 74-82597. (Radars Ser.: No. 2). 248p. reprint ed. pap. 76.90 (*0-608-15932-8*, 203092300072) Bks Demand.

— Radar Resolution & Multipath Effects. LC 74-82597. (Radars Ser.: Vol. 4). 376p. reprint ed. pap. 116.60 (*0-608-13073-7*, 202506100041) Bks Demand.

— Radar System Analysis. LC 76-45811. (Artech Radar Library). (Illus.). 620p. reprint ed. pap. 192.20 (*0-608-16030-X*, 203312900083) Bks Demand.

Barton, David K. & Barton, William F. Modern Radar System Analysis Software: Version 2.0. (Radar Software Library). 100p. 1992. 425.00 incl. disk (*0-89006-673-6*) Artech Hse.

Barton, David K. & Ward, Harold R. Handbook of Radar Measurement. LC 84-45414. (Illus.). 442p. reprint ed. pap. 137.10 (*0-7837-1800-4*, 204200100001) Bks Demand.

Barton, David K., et al. Radar Technology Encyclopedia. LC 96-52026. (Radar Technology Ser.). 536p. 1997. 115.00 (*0-89006-893-3*) Artech Hse.

Barton, David R. United States Foreign Trade Highlights, 1995. 169p. 1996. per. 15.00 (*0-16-048761-7*) USGPO.

— United States Foreign Trade Highlights, 1996. 176p. 1997. per. 16.00 (*0-16-054693-1*) USGPO.

B

Barton, Derek, et al. Comprehensive Natural Products Chemistry. LC 98-15249. 1999. write for info. (*0-08-043153-4*) Elsevier.

Barton, Derek H. Some Recollections of Gap Jumping. Seeman, Jeffrey I., ed. LC 90-872. (Profiles, Pathways, & Dreams Ser.). (Illus.). 143p. 1991. text 36.00 (*0-8412-1770-X*, Pub. by Am Chemical) OUP.

Barton, Derek H., ed. New Principles in Organic Chemistry: The Discovery & Invention of Chemical Reactions. 400p. 1996. text 99.00 (*981-02-1361-1*) World Scientific Pub.

— Reason & Imagination: Reflections on Research in Organic Chemistry. 892p. 1996. 55.00 (*981-02-2596-2*) World Scientific Pub.

Barton, Derek H. & Nakanishi, Koji, eds. Comprehensive Natural Products Chemistry, 9 vols. LC 98-15249. (Illus.). 8500p. 1997. text 3744.00 (*0-08-042709-X*, Pergamon Pr) Elsevier.

Barton, Derek H. & Ollis, W. D., eds. Comprehensive Organic Chemistry, 6 vols. 8034p. 1979. 2659.25 (*0-08-030732-9*, Pergamon Pr); pap. 800.00 (*0-08-022066-5*, Pergamon Pr) Elsevier.

Barton, Derek H. & Parekh, S. I. Half a Century of Free Radical Chemistry. LC 92-24681. (Lezioni Lincee Lectures). (Illus.). 176p. (C). 1993. text 59.95 (*0-521-44005-X*); pap. text 22.95 (*0-521-44580-9*) Cambridge U Pr.

Barton, Derek H., et al. The Activation of Dioxygen & Homogenous Catalytic Oxidation. (Illus.). 514p. (C). 1993. text 135.00 (*0-306-44591-3*, Kluwer Plenum) Kluwer Academic.

— Comprehensive Organic Chemistry, 1-3. Incl. Vol. 1. Stereochemistry, Hydrocarbons, Halo Compounds & Oxygen Compounds. 1242p. 1979. 453.25 (*0-08-021313-8*); Vol. 2. Nitrogen Compounds, Carboxylic Acids & Phosphorous Compounds. 1344p. 1979. 495.00 (*0-08-021314-6*); Vol. 3. Sulphur, Selenium, Boron, & Organometallic Compounds. 1338p. 1979. 495.00 (*0-08-021315-4*); Vol. 4. Heterocyclic Compounds. 1220p. 1979. 453.25 (*0-08-021316-2*); Vol. 5. Biological Compounds. 1642p. 1979. 453.25 (*0-08-021317-0*); Vol. 6. Formula, Subject, Author, Reaction & Reagent Indexes. 1642p. 1979. 453.25 (*0-08-022931-X*); Vols. 1-3. 1979. 687.50 Vols. 4-6. 1979. 687.50 1979. 3488.00 (*0-08-021319-7*) Elsevier.

— Comprehensive Organic Chemistry, Half Set. 1979. 687.50 (*0-08-023815-7*) Elsevier.

Barton, Derek H., ed. see Ivanov, V. T. & Ovchinnikov, Yu A.

Barton, Derek H., ed. see Jung, M.

Barton, Donna V., ed. see Huang, Jianshi & Lafferty, Carolyn K.

Barton, Doran L. Fozziliny George Moo's Guide to VMS & the Internet. 160p. 1995. pap. 12.00 (*0-9647608-1-9*) Blessed Victim.

Barton, Dunbar P. Shakespeare & the Law, 1929. LC 99-26602. 1999. 60.00 (*1-58477-000-7*) Lawbk Exchange.

Barton, Dwight L. The Way I Saw It. LC 94-231082. (Illus.). 152p. (Orig.). Date not set. pap. 9.00 (*0-944996-12-4*) Carlsons.

***Barton, Edward Read, ed.** Mythopoetic Perspectives of Men's Healing Work: An Anthology for Therapists & Others. LC 99-54739. 300p. 2000. 64.00 (*0-89789-646-7*, H646, Bergin & Garvey) Greenwood.

Barton, Elisa M. Confessions of a Lost Mother: By ElisaMB@aol.com. LC 96-1419. xvii, 157p. (Orig.). 1996. pap. 14.95 (*0-9650795-0-3*) E M Barton.

Barton, Ellen L. Nonsentential Constituents: A Theory of Grammatical Structure & Pragmatic Interpretation. LC 90-31712. (Pragmatics & Beyond New Ser.: Vol. 2). xviii, 247p. 1990. 65.00 (*1-55619-045-X*) J Benjamins Pubng Co.

***Barton, Emily.** The Testament of Yves Gundron. LC 99-32035. 336p. 2000. text 25.00 (*0-374-22179-0*) FS&G.

Barton, F. R., ed. R. B. Woodward Remembered: A Collection of Papers in Honour of Robert Burns Woodward 1917-1979. 542p. 1982. 120.00 (*0-08-029238-0*, Pergamon Pr) Elsevier.

Barton, Freeman, ed. Our Destiny We Know: Essays in Honor of Edwin K. Gedney. 269p. (Orig.). 1996. pap. 9.99 (*1-881909-24-7*) Advent Christ Gen Conf.

Barton, G. Edward, et al. Computational Complexity & Natural Language. (Computational Models of Cognition & Perception Ser.). 320p. 1987. 40.00 (*0-262-02266-4*, Bradford Bks) MIT Pr.

Barton, G. Michael. Self-Insuring Benefits Programs Vol. 40: An Approach to Controlling Costs & Maintaining Quality. LC 97-194649. (Building Blocks Ser.). (Illus.). (Orig.). 1997. pap. 24.95 (*1-57963-045-6*, AO240) Am Compensation.

Barton, Gabriel. Elements of Green's Functions & Propagation: Potentials, Diffusion, & Waves. (Illus.). 478p. 1989. pap. text 45.00 (*0-19-851998-2*) OUP.

***Barton, Gabriel.** Introduction to the Relativity Principle. LC 99-17294. 240p. 1999. 84.95 (*0-471-99895-8*) Wiley.

Barton, Gabriel, tr. see Le Bellac, Michel.

Barton, Gabriel, tr. see Ruhia, Charles.

Barton, Gail & Friedman, Rohn, eds. Handbook of Emergency Psychiatry for Clinical Administrators. LC 86-12090. (Emergency Health Services Review Ser.: Vol. 3, Nos. 2-3). 390p. 1986. 59.95 (*0-86656-532-9*) Haworth Pr.

Barton, Gail M., jt. auth. see Barton, Walter E.

Barton, Gaynor, jt. auth. see Beidler, Peter G.

Barton, George A. Ecclesiastes: Critical & Exegetical Commentary. Driver, Samuel R. et al, eds. LC 08-15777. (International Critical Commentary Ser.). 236p. 1994. 39.95 (*0-567-05014-9*, Pub. by T & T Clark) Bks Intl VA.

Barton, George E. Ordered Pluralism: A Philosophical Plan of Action for Teaching. 2.50 (*0-8156-7022-2*, NES 42) Syracuse U Cont Ed.

— Teaching the Sick: A Manual of Occupational Therapy & Re-Education. Phillips, William R. & Rosenberg, Janet, eds. LC 79-6895. (Physically Handicapped in Society Ser.). (Illus.). 1980. reprint ed. lib. bdg. 19.95 (*0-405-13106-2*) Ayer.

Barton, Greg, jt. ed. see Kingsbury, Damien.

Barton, H. Arnold. A Folk Divided: Homeland Swedes & Swedish Americans, 1840-1940. LC 95-152978. (Studia Multiethnica Upsaliensia: No. 10). 403p. 1994. pap. 57.50 (*91-554-3338-3*) Coronet Bks.

— A Folk Divided: Homeland Swedes & Swedish Americans, 1840-1940. LC 93-32345. (Illus.). 448p. (C). 1994. pap. 26.95 (*0-8093-1944-6*) S Ill U Pr.

— A Folk Divided: Homeland Swedes & Swedish Americans, 1840-1940. LC 93-32345. (Illus.). 448p. (C). 1994. 41.95 (*0-8093-1943-8*) S Ill U Pr.

— Letters from the Promised Land: Swedes in America, 1840-1914. LC 74-22843. (Illus.). 256p. 1980. pap. 16.95 (*0-8166-1009-6*) U of Minn Pr.

— Northern Arcadia: Foreign Travelers in Scandinavia, 1765-1815. LC 98-15892. (Illus.). 224p. 1999. 39.95 (*0-8093-2203-X*) S Ill U Pr.

— The Search for Ancestors: A Swedish-American Family Saga. LC 78-15537. (Illus.). 189p. 1979. 21.95 (*0-8093-0893-2*) S Ill U Pr.

— The Search for Ancestors: A Swedish-American Family Saga. 178p. 1979. pap. 11.95 (*0-318-16621-6*) Swedish-Am.

Barton, H. Arnold, ed. Scandinavians & America. 1974. pap. 1.50 (*0-318-03682-7*) Swedish-Am.

Barton, H. Arnold, jt. auth. see Firman, Axel.

Barton, H. Arnold, ed. see Hoflund, Charles J.

Barton, Hana J. With a Nugget in My Shoe. LC 94-96552. (Illus.). 184p. (Orig.). 1997. pap. 16.95 (*0-9646326-0-8*) Jeffry & Spencer Pub.

Barton, Harlan N. Peak to Peak: Colorado Front Range Ski Trails Guidebook & Map. rev. ed. (Illus.). 232p. 1995. pap. 18.95 (*0-9624606-1-3*) Frnt Range Pub.

Barton, Hildor A. Clipper Ship & Covered Wagon: Essays from the Swedish Pioneer Historical Quarterly. Scott, Franklyn D., ed. LC 78-14619. (Scandinavians in America Ser.). (Illus.). 1979. 31.95 (*0-405-11666-7*) Ayer.

Barton, Hugh & Bruder, Noel. Guide to Local Environmental Auditing. 386p. 1995. pap. 38.00 (*1-85383-234-0*, Pub. by Escan Pubns) Island Pr.

Barton, Hugh M. Transitions: Legal Considerations in Selling of Closing a Medical Practice. LC 98-180733. 91p. 1998. pap. 29.00 (*0-9640262-9-5*) TX Med Assn.

Barton, Humphrey. Vertue XXXV. 180p. 1985. 18.95 (*0-916025-05-5*) Armchair Sail Pub.

Barton, Ian M., ed. Roman Domestic Buildings. LC 94-192593. (Exeter Studies in History). (Illus.). 176p. 1995. pap. text 19.95 (*0-85989-415-0*, Pub. by Univ Exeter Pr) Northwestern U Pr.

— Roman Public Buildings. 190p. 1989. pap. text 17.95 (*0-85989-239-5*, Pub. by Univ Exeter Pr) Northwestern U Pr.

Barton, J. Isaiah 1-39. (Old Testament Guides Ser.: No. 19). 126p. 1995. pap. 12.50 (*1-85075-541-8*, Pub. by Sheffield Acad) CUP Services.

Barton, J. G. Ultimate Word Challenges. LC 93-74243. (Illus.). 176p. 1994. pap. 7.95 (*0-940685-48-5*) Cardoza Pub.

Barton, J. H., jt. auth. see Howard, V. A.

Barton, J. L., ed. see Novotny, Frantisek.

Barton, Jacqueline K., jt. ed. see Good, Mary L.

Barton, James, et al, eds. Portfolio Assessment: A Handbook for Educators. (Assessment Bookshelf Ser.). 113p. (Orig.). 1996. teacher ed. 16.50 (*0-201-49387-X*) Addison-Wesley.

Barton, James C. & Edwards, Corwin Q., eds. Hemochromatosis: Genetics, Pathophysiology, Diagnosis & Treatment. (Illus.). 588p. (C). 2000. 215.00 (*0-521-59380-8*) Cambridge U Pr.

Barton, James H., et al. Science & Our Global Heritage: Multidisciplinary Perspectives on Sustainable Development. (Illus.). 400p. (C). 1996. pap. text 49.95 (*1-884687-04-0*) N Horzns Pub.

Barton, Jane Hughes. Remarriage after 50: What Women, Men & Adult Children Need to Know. 3rd ed. 90p. 2000. reprint ed. pap. 11.95 (*0-9639891-0-3*) Roger-Thomas.

Barton-Jay, David. The Enema As an Erotic Art & Its History. (Illus.). 336p. (Orig.). (C). 1984. pap. 54.95 (*0-910409-00-5*) Barton-Jay Proj.

Barton, Jerome, ed. Barton's Comic Recitations & Humorous Dialogues... LC 79-167474. (Granger Index Reprint Ser.). 1977. reprint ed. 15.95 (*0-8369-6279-6*) Ayer.

Barton, Jill, jt. auth. see Root, Phyllis.

Barton, Jim. Greater Swiss Mountain Dog: AKC Rank #116. (Rare Breed Ser.). (Illus.). 96p. 1997. 19.95 (*0-7938-0752-2*, RX-102) TFH Pubns.

Barton, Joe, ed. Medicare Home Health: Congressional Hearings. 130p. (C). 1999. reprint ed. pap. text 25.00 (*0-7881-8096-7*) DIANE Pub.

Barton, Joel R., III & Grice, William A. Tennis. 5th ed. (Illus.). 176p. 2000. pap. text 12.95 (*0-89641-334-9*) American Pr.

Barton, John. Condition of the Labouring Classes of Society. 1979. 15.95 (*0-405-10579-7*) Ayer.

***Barton, John.** Ethics & the Old Testament. LC 97-45168. 112p. 1998. pap. 12.00 (*1-56338-234-2*) TPI PA.

Barton, John. Holy Writings, Sacred Text: The Canon in Early Christianity. LC 97-41413. 224p. (Orig.). 1998. pap. 19.95 (*0-664-25778-X*) Westminster John Knox.

— How the Bible Came to Be. LC 97-41412. 96p. 1998. pap. 10.00 (*0-664-25785-2*) Westminster John Knox.

— Notes Toward a Family Tree. 112p. 1994. pap. 10.95 (*1-55082-066-4*, Pub. by Quarry Pr) LPC InBook.

— Playing Shakespeare. 211p. (C). 1988. pap. 13.95 (*0-413-54790-6*, A0216, Methuen Drama) Methn.

— Reading the Old Testament: Method in Biblical Study. enl. rev. ed. 294p. 1997. pap. 26.95 (*0-664-25724-0*) Westminster John Knox.

— West of Darkness. 128p. 1987. 9.95 (*0-920806-90-2*, Pub. by Penumbra Pr) U of Toronto Pr.

Barton, John, ed. The Cambridge Companion to Biblical Interpretation. LC 97-27945. (Companions to Religion Ser.). (Illus.). 320p. (C). 1998. pap. 18.95 (*0-521-48593-2*) Cambridge U Pr.

Barton, John & Balentine, Samuel F., eds. Language, Theology, & the Bible: Essays in Honor of James Barr. LC 93-32123. 432p. 1994. 68.00 (*0-19-826191-8*, Clarendon Pr) OUP.

Barton, John & Fisher, Bart. International Trade & Investment: Regulating International Business. 976p. 1986. teacher ed. write for info. (*0-316-08282-1*, 82821) Aspen Law.

Barton, John & Fisher, Bart S. International Trade & Investment: Regulating International Business. 976p. (C). 1986. boxed set 57.00 (*0-316-08280-5*, Aspen Law & Bus) Aspen Pub.

— International Trade & Investment: Selected Documents. (C). 1986. 15.95 (*0-316-08281-3*, Aspen Law & Bus) Aspen Pub.

Barton, John & Reimer, David, eds. After the Exile: Essays in Honor of Rex Mason. LC 96-41586. 1996. text 40.00 (*0-86554-524-3*, MUP/H404) Mercer Univ Pr.

Barton, John & Rogers, Richard, eds. Chemical Reaction Hazards. 2nd ed. LC 96-77740. 220p. 1997. 80.00 (*0-88415-274-X*, 5274) Gulf Pub.

Barton, John & Yun, Hunki. Golf on the Web. LC 97-13578. 384p. 1997. pap. text 16.95 (*1-55828-556-3*, MIS Pr) IDG Bks.

Barton, John, jt. auth. see Morgan, Robert P.

Barton, John, jt. auth. see Sauter, Gerhard.

Barton, John A. Book of Snakes. 1998. 12.99 (*0-7858-0952-X*) Bk Sales Inc.

Barton, John C., ed. Sports Encyclopedia Vol. 1-10: Index & Reference Book of New Information, Set. 1500p. (YA). 1996. 335.00 (*0-7883-1075-5*); pap. 275.00 (*0-7883-1076-3*) ABBE Pubs Assn.

Barton, John H. Supplement to Investing '89. 640p. 1989. 30.00 (*0-316-08284-8*) Little.

Barton, John H., et al. Law in Radically Different Cultures. LC 82-24802. (American Casebook Ser.). 960p. (C). 1983. 65.00 (*0-314-70396-9*) West Pub.

Barton, John J. & Nackman, Lee R. Scientific & Engineering Programming in C++ (Illus.). 688p. (C). 1994. 55.95 (*0-201-53393-6*) Addison-Wesley.

Barton, John P., ed. Neutron Radiography, Including Radioscopy & Complementary Inspection Methods Using Neutrons: Proceedings of the 4th World Conference, San Francisco, California, U. S. A., May 10-16, 1992. LC 93-25896. 896p. 1993. text 288.00 (*2-88124-624-9*) Gordon & Breach.

Barton, John P., et al, eds. Neutron Radiography: Proceedings of the 2nd World Conference Paris, France, June 16-20, 1986. (C). 1987. text 357.00 (*90-277-2495-4*) Kluwer Academic.

Barton, John P. & Von Der Hardt, Peter. Neutron Radiography. 1983. text 411.50 (*90-277-1528-9*) Kluwer Academic.

Barton, Jonathan R. A Political Geography of Latin America. LC 96-47376. (Illus.). 264p. (C). 1997. 85.00 (*0-415-12189-2*); pap. 25.99 (*0-415-12190-6*) Routledge.

Barton, Josef J. Peasants & Strangers: Italians, Rumanians, & Slovaks in an American City, 1890-1950. LC 74-14085. (Harvard Studies in Urban History). 231p. reprint ed. pap. 71.70 (*0-7837-4136-7*, 205795900011) Bks Demand.

Barton, Judi & Rosenblatt, Nate. Only Personal Letter Book You'll Ever Need. 1994. pap. 19.95 (*0-929543-43-2*) Round Lake Pub.

Barton, Judy S. Little Feelings. LC 97-41720. (Illus.). 67p. (J). 1998. pap. text 9.95 (*1-57392-183-1*) Prometheus Bks.

Barton, Karel. Protection Against Atmospheric Corrosion: Theories & Methods. Duncan, John R., tr. LC 75-26570. 204p. reprint ed. pap. 63.30 (*0-608-18827-1*, 203048200069) Bks Demand.

Barton, Kathleen. Semiconductors Explained. Gorham, Kelly, ed. (Electricity & Electronics Ser.). 28p. (YA). (gr. 10 up). 1994. student ed. 7.00 (*0-8064-0015-3*, E30) Bergwall.

Barton, Keith C., jt. auth. see Dielman, Ted.

Barton, Keith C., jt. auth. see Levstik, Linda S.

Barton-Kriese, Paul. The Politics of Diversity in the United States: Positive Dreams & Pyrrhic Victories. 88p. (Orig.). (C). 1993. pap. text 18.50 (*0-8191-9222-8*); lib. bdg. 32.00 (*0-8191-9221-X*) U Pr of Amer.

Barton-Kriese, Paul & Ives, Kenneth. Truth-Speaking & Power among Friends (Quakers) Ethical Alternatives & Consequences. (Studies in Quakerism: No. 15). 52p. 1987. pap. 5.00 (*0-89670-018-6*) Progresiv Pub.

Barton, L. V. Seed Preservation & Longevity. 216p. 1992. pap. 200.00 (*0-7855-0390-0*, Pub. by Intl Bks & Periodicals) St Mut.

Barton, L. V., jt. auth. see Crocker, W.

Barton, Larry L., ed. Sulfate-Reducing Bacteria. (Biotechnology Handbooks Ser.: Vol. 8). (Illus.). 352p. (C). 1995. text 89.50 (*0-306-44857-2*, Kluwer Plenum) Kluwer Academic.

Barton, Larry L. & Hemming, Bruce C., eds. Iron Chelation in Plants & Soil Microorganisms. (Illus.). 490p. 1993. text 104.00 (*0-12-079870-0*) Acad Pr.

Barton, Larry L., jt. ed. see Shively, Jessup M.

Barton, Laurence. Ethics: The Enemy in the Workplace. (Illus.). 368p. (C). 1998. pap. text 20.00 (*0-7881-5677-2*) DIANE Pub.

— Ethics: The Enemy in the Workplace. LC 94-31478. (C). 1994. mass mkt. 52.95 (*0-538-83873-6*) S-W Pub.

Barton, Lela V., ed. Bibliography of Seeds. LC 66-20492. 858p. 1967. text 164.00 (*0-231-02937-3*) Col U Pr.

Barton, Len. Disability & Dependency. 1989. 69.95 (*1-85000-616-4*); pap. 34.95 (*1-85000-617-2*) Taylor & Francis.

— The Politics of Special Educational Needs. 200p. 1988. 75.00 (*1-85000-370-X*, Falmer Pr); pap. 37.95 (*1-85000-371-8*, Falmer Pr) Taylor & Francis.

Barton, Len, ed. Integration: Myth or Reality? 250p. 1989. pap. 33.00 (*1-85000-615-6*, Falmer Pr) Taylor & Francis.

Barton, Len & Walker, Stephen, eds. Gender, Class & Education. 210p. (C). 1983. 30.00 (*0-905273-42-7*, Falmer Pr); pap. 16.00 (*0-905273-41-9*, Falmer Pr) Taylor & Francis.

— Social Crisis & Educational Research. 347p. 1984. 28.00 (*0-7099-3235-9*, Pub. by C Helm); pap. 14.50 (*0-7099-3248-0*, Pub. by C Helm) Routldge.

Barton, Len, jt. ed. see Armstrong, Felicity.

Barton, Len, jt. ed. see Clough, Peter.

Barton, Len, jt. ed. see Walker, Stephen.

Barton, Leonard S. The American Library Compendium & Index of World Art. LC 97-78095. xxii, 537p. 1998. text 40.00 (*0-910046-98-0*); pap. text 25.00 (*0-910046-99-9*) Amer Libr Color Slide.

Barton, Leslie M. A Study of Eighty-One Principal American Markets. LC 75-22800. (America in Two Centuries Ser.). (Illus.). 1976. reprint ed. 37.95 (*0-405-07672-X*) Ayer.

Barton, Lisa S., jt. auth. see Taylor, Eric H.

Barton, Lois. A Quaker Promise Kept: Philadelphia Friends' Work with the Allegany Senecas, 1795-1965. (Illus.). 128p. (Orig.). 1990. pap. 14.95 (*0-9609420-3-3*) S Butte Pr.

— Spencer Butte Pioneers: One Hundred Years on the Sunny Side of the Butte 1850-1950. Northwest Matrix Staff & Mills, Charlotte, eds. LC 82-61837. (Illus.). 144p. 1982. pap. 11.95 (*0-9609420-0-9*) S Butte Pr.

— Through My Window: More Autobiographical Sketches. (Illus.). 72p. 1997. pap. 8.50 (*0-9609420-5-X*) S Butte Pr.

Barton, Lois, ed. see Masterson, Martha G.

Barton, Louis L. Check Processing Operations: A Hands-on-Guide to Developing & Managing a State-of-the-Art Check Processing Operation. 250p. (C). 1994. text 60.00 (*1-55738-735-4*, Irwn Prfssnl) McGraw-Hill Prof.

Barton, Lucy. Appreciating Costume. 1969. pap. 8.95 (*0-87440-001-5*) Bakers Plays.

— Historic Costume for the Stage. rev. ed. (Illus.). 1961. 33.95 (*0-87440-002-3*) Bakers Plays.

Barton, Lucy & Edson, Doris. Period Patterns. (Illus.). 1942. pap. 11.95 (*0-87440-003-1*) Bakers Plays.

Barton, Lyndon O. Mechanism Analysis: Simplified Graphical & Analytical Techniques. 2nd rev. ed. LC 92-37563. (Mechanical Engineering Ser.: Vol. 81). (Illus.). 752p. 1993. text 189.00 (*0-8247-8794-3*) Dekker.

Barton, M., tr. see Lowndes, Florin.

Barton, M., tr. see Steiner, Rudolf.

***Barton, M. Laverne & Hill, Robert C.** In the Bishop's Shadow: A Kaleidoscopic Look at the Self-Annihilating World to Which the Brave-Hearted Bishop Ralph Henry Houston Was Sent to Minister. LC 98-83117. 272 p. 1999. 15.00 (*0-89989-233-7*) Cross Rds Atlta.

Barton, Malgorzata, ed. see Wasilewski, Marian.

Barton, Malgorzata, ed. & illus. see Wasilewski, Marian.

***Barton, Marcella Biro, ed.** Welsh-Americans: The Manuscript Collection - The Historical Society of Pennsylvania. LC 99-52245. (Madog Canter for Welch Studies Ser.). 504p. 1999. 64.50 (*0-7618-1580-5*) U Pr of Amer.

Barton, Marcus. Sams Teach Yourself MCSE Windows 98 in 14 Days. LC 98-87205. 550p. 1998. pap. 35.00 (*0-672-31339-1*, Sams Sftwre) MCP SW Interactive.

An Asterisk (*) at the beginning of an entry indicates that the title is appearing for the first time.

— Teach Yourself MCSE Windows 95 in 14 Days: MCSE Exam Preparation Guide. LC 97-67993. 500p. 1997. pap. 35.00 (*0-672-31183-6*) Mac USA.

Barton, Margaret. Garrick. LC 78-612. (Illus.). 312p. 1978. reprint ed. lib. bdg. 38.50 (*0-313-20270-2*, BAGAR, Greenwood Pr) Greenwood.

Barton, Maritza. Cocine Saludablemente. 224p. 1998. per. 11.00 (*0-684-84486-9*) S&S Trade.

— Cure a Su Nino Naturalmente (Heal Your Child Naturally) (SPA.). 224p. 1998. pap. 11.00 (*0-684-85465-1*, Fireside) S&S Trade Pap.

— Curese Naturalmente. 1996. per. 11.00 (*0-684-83301-8*) S&S Trade.

— Gotitias de Amor para Mis Hijo. (SPA.). 160p. 1998. per. 9.00 (*0-684-84500-8*) S&S Trade.

***Barton, Marlin.** The Dry Well. 2001. 24.95 (*1-929490-07-0*) Beil.

Barton, Matthew, tr. see Archiati, Pietro.

Barton, Matthew, tr. see Kast, Verena.

Barton, Matthew, tr. see Steiner, Rudolf.

Barton, Matthew, tr. see Thun, Maria.

Barton, Michael. Harrisburg: Life by the Moving Road. LC 98-73005. (Illus.). 224p. 1998. 29.95 (*0-9654754-4-1*) Am Historical Pr.

Barton, Michael C., et al. Rediscovering Darwin: Evolutionary Theory & Archeological Explanation. LC 97-47355. (Archeological Papers of the American Anthropological Association). 322p. 1998. write for info. (*0-913167-87-8*) Am Anthro Assn.

Barton, Michael X. Weeping Angel Prediction. 30p. 1985. reprint ed. spiral bd. 7.00 (*0-7873-1279-7*) Hlth Research.

Barton, N. R. & Stephansson, O., eds. Rock Joints: Proceedings of a Regional Conference of the International Society of Rock Mechanics, Loen, Norway, 4 - 6 June 1990. (Illus.). 820p. (C). 1990. text 181.00 (*90-6191-109-5*, Pub. by A A Balkema) Ashgate Pub Co.

Barton, Nina, jt. auth. see Keith, Bill.

Barton, O. S., jt. auth. see McCorkle, John.

Barton, Pat. A Week Is a Long Time. (Illus.). 28p. (J). (gr. k-5). 6.95 (*0-200-72464-9*) Academy Chi Pubs.

Barton, Paul. Susuism & Susueconomics - What Susu Is: An Economic System that Stresses Collective Savings & Independence. unabridged ed. (Orig.). 1997. pap. 12.00 (*1-56411-138-5*, 4BBG0142) Untd Bros & Sis.

Barton, Paul & Maldonado, David, eds. Hispanic Christianity Within Mainline Protestant Traditions: A Bibliography. LC 98-235124. 318p. 1998. 40.00 (*0-9657839-3-6*) AETH Bks.

Barton, Paul, et al. The Molecular Biology of Cardiac Development & Growth. LC 95-31277. (Molecular Biology Intelligence Unit Ser.). 268p. 1995. 99.00 (*1-57059-302-7*) Landes Bioscience.

Barton, Paul E., jt. auth. see Kazis, Richard.

Barton, Peggy & Quinn, John. Murder at Mill Hollow, Vol. 1. (Illus.). 70p. (J). (gr. 3-8). 1997. pap. 2.95 (*0-9660703-0-5*) Barton Bks.

Barton, Peter & Dempster, Dan. Dan Dempster: Waterworks. (Illus.). 20p. (C). 1997. pap. 4.50 (*1-886845-03-4*) Penin Fine Arts.

***Barton, Philip.** Dick Barton. 140p. 2000. pap. 13.95 (*1-84002-149-7*) Theatre Comm.

Barton, Phoebe L. Understanding the U. S. Health Services System. LC 98-3742. 473p. 1998. 65.00 (*1-56793-081-6*) Health Admin Pr.

Barton, Phyllis S. William Frederick Foster, A. N. A. Portrait of a Painter. (Illus.). 472p. (C). 1988. 155.00 (*0-9619161-0-9*) Richlaine Pub.

Barton, R. Texas Search & Seizure. LC 99-201889. 500p. 1997. 125.00 (*0-07-172489-3*) Juris Pubng.

Barton, R. M. A History of the Cornish China-Clay Industry. 1966. 39.95 (*0-685-53310-7*) Ars Ceramica.

Barton, R. N. Hengistbury Head, Dorset Vol. 2: The Late Upper Palaeolithic & Early Mesolithic Sites. (Illus.). 299p. 1992. 68.00 (*0-947816-34-8*, Pub. by Oxford Univ Comm Arch) David Brown.

Barton, R. N., ed. Trauma & Its Metabolic Problems. (British Medical Bulletin Ser.: Vol. 41, No. 3). (Illus.). 104p. 1985. 56.00 (*0-443-03250-5*) Church.

Barton, R. Ruth. Becoming a Woman of Strength: 14 Life Challenges for Women & the Men Who Love Them. LC 94-12458. 280p. 1994. pap. 9.99 (*0-87788-063-8*, H Shaw Pubs) Waterbrook Pr.

— Becoming Women of Purpose. (Fisherman Bible Studyguide Ser.). 64p. (Orig.). 1992. pap. 4.99 (*0-87788-061-1*, H Shaw Pubs) Waterbrook Pr.

— Women Like Us: Wisdom for Today's Issues. (Fisherman Bible Studyguide Ser.). 96p. 1989. pap. text 4.99 (*0-87788-943-0*, H Shaw Pubs) Waterbrook Pr.

Barton, Ralph. Science in Rhyme Without Reason. 1972. 59.95 (*0-8490-1000-4*) Gordon Pr.

Barton, Ray & Diehl, John. TI-83 Enhanced Statistics. 140p. (YA). (gr. 9-12). 1997. spiral bd. 25.00 (*1-886018-10-3*) Venture Pubng.

Barton, Rebecca C. Black Voices in American Fiction Nineteen Hundred to Nineteen Thirty. LC 76-10511. 1976. pap. 5.50 (*0-917428-00-5*, Dowling College) Global Pubns.

— Witnesses for Freedom: Negro Americans in Autobiography. LC 76-29575. 1977. pap. 6.50 (*0-917428-02-1*, Dowling College) Global Pubns.

Barton, Richard. Acting Onstage & Off. 2nd ed. (C). 1993. text 47.00 (*0-03-072192-X*, Pub. by Harcourt Coll Pubs) Harcourt.

Barton, Richard L., ed. Ties That Blind in Canadian-American Relations: The Politics of News Discourse. (Communication Ser.). 240p. (C). 1990. text 69.95 (*0-8058-0743-8*) L Erlbaum Assocs.

Barton, Robert. Acting: Onstage & Off. (Illus.). 320p. (C). 1989. teacher ed. write for info. (*0-318-64062-7*) Harcourt Coll Pubs.

— Acting: Onstage & Off. 2nd ed. (Illus.). 320p. (C). 1992. pap. text. write for info. (*0-318-69241-4*) Harcourt Coll Pubs.

— Style for Actors. LC 92-16227. 340p. 1993. text 54.95 (*0-87484-958-6*, 958) Mayfield Pub.

***Barton, Robert.** Voice Onstage & Off. (Illus.). 1999. pap. text 51.50 (*0-15-513354-3*) Harcourt.

Barton, Robert & DalVera, Rocco. Voice: Onstage & Off. 350p. (Orig.). (C). 1994. text 52.00 (*0-15-500120-5*, Pub. by Harcourt Coll Pubs) Harcourt.

Barton, Roger E., et al, eds. The Dental Assistant. 6th ed. LC 87-31199. (Illus.). 655p. 1988. text 31.50 (*0-8121-1141-9*) Lppncott W & W.

Barton, Roger E., ed. see Murray, Henry V. & Sluder, Troy B.

Barton, Roger E., ed. see Sowter, John B.

Barton, Ronald, jt. auth. see Lebacqz, Karen.

Barton, Roy F. The Half-Way Sun: Life among the Headhunters of the Philippines. LC 76-44685. reprint ed. 45.00 (*0-404-15902-8*) AMS Pr.

— Kalingas, Their Institutions & Custom Law. LC 72-161778. reprint ed. 44.50 (*0-404-09015-X*) AMS Pr.

— Philippine Pagans: The Autobiographies of Three Ifugaos. LC 76-44686. reprint ed. 49.50 (*0-404-15903-6*) AMS Pr.

Barton, Russell N. Webs & Arrows. (YA). 1995. 19.95 (*0-9650434-0-1*, 0010); pap. write for info. (*0-9650434-1-X*, 0010) Ridgewood MN.

***Barton, Russell R.** Graphical Methods for the Design of Experiments. LC 99-34026. (Lecture Notes in Statistics Ser.: Vol. 143). 208p. 1999. pap. 45.00 (*0-387-94750-7*) Spr-Verlag.

Barton, Ruth H. Equal to the Task: Men & Women in Partnership at Work, at Church & at Home. LC 98-11313. 224p. 1998. pap. 11.99 (*0-8308-1357-8*, 1357) InterVarsity.

***Barton, Ruth Haley.** Becoming a Woman of Strength: 14 Life Challenges for Women & the Men Who Love Them. rev. ed. LC 99-41585. 1999. pap. text 11.99 (*0-87788-068-9*, H Shaw Pubs) Waterbrook Pr.

Barton, S., jt. auth. see Goldmeier, D.

Barton, S. E. Current Practice in Genitourinary Medicine. LC 99-213410. (Illus.). 448p. 1999. text 98.50 (*0-340-74084-1*, Pub. by E A) OUP.

Barton, Sheila J. Survey of State Criminal History Information Systems (1995) (Illus.). 57p. (C). 1997. pap. text 20.00 (*0-7881-4560-6*) DIANE Pub.

***Barton, Sheila J.** Survey of State Criminal History Information Systems, 1997: A Criminal Justice Information Policy Report. (Illus.). 56p. (C). 1999. pap. text 20.00 (*0-7881-8358-3*) DIANE Pub.

***Barton, Sheila J., ed.** National Conference on Sex Offender Registries Proceedings. 118p. 2000. reprint ed. pap. text 30.00 (*0-7881-8832-1*) DIANE Pub.

Barton, Simon. The Aristocracy in Twelfth-Century Leon & Castile. LC 96-44325. (Cambridge Studies in Medieval Life & Thought: Fourth Series, No. 34). 384p. (C). 1997. text 69.95 (*0-521-49727-2*) Cambridge U Pr.

Barton, Stephen C. Discipleship & Family Ties in Mark & Matthew. LC 93-46383. (Society for New Testament Studies Monographs: No. 80). 275p. (C). 1995. text 69.95 (*0-521-46530-3*) Cambridge U Pr.

— The Family in Theological Perspective. 352p. pap. 34.95 (*0-567-08522-8*, Pub. by T & T Clark) Bks Intl VA.

— The Spirituality of the Gospels. 162p. 1994. pap. 9.95 (*1-56563-147-1*) Hendrickson MA.

***Barton, Stephen C.** Where Shall Wisdom Be Found? Wisdom in the Bible, the Church & the Contemporary World. 544p. 1999. pap. 37.95 (*0-567-08642-9*, Pub. by T & T Clark) Bks Intl VA.

Barton, Stephen E. & Silverman, Carol J., eds. Common Interest Communities: Private Governments & the Public Interest. LC 94-20963. 318p. (Orig.). 1994. pap. 23.95 (*0-87772-359-1*) UCB IGS.

Barton, Tamsyn. Ancient Astrology. LC 93-32441. (Sciences of Antiquity Ser.). (Illus.). 264p. (C). (gr. 13). 1994. pap. 24.99 (*0-415-11029-7*, B3718) Routledge.

Barton, Tamsyn S. Power & Knowledge: Astrology, Physiognomics, & Medicine in the Roman Empire. (Body in Theory: Histories of Cultural Materialism Ser.). (Illus.). 272p. (C). 1995. text 49.50 (*0-472-10425-X*, 10425) U of Mich Pr.

Barton, Thomas F. & Saran, P. P., eds. Leaders in American Geography. (Illus.). 1993. text 40.00 (*81-85218-73-0*, Pub. by Prestige) Advent Bks Div.

Barton, Thomas George & International Union of Conservation of Nature & Natural Resources Staff. Our People, Our Resources: Supporting Rural Communities in Participatory Action Research on Population Dynamics & the Local Environment. LC 98-121789. xv, 259 p. 1997. write for info. (*2-8317-0389-1*) IEEE Standards.

Barton, Thomas H. Rectifiers, Cycloconverters, & AC Controllers. LC 93-46642. (Monographs in Electrical & Electronic Engineering: No. 33). (Illus.). 712p. 1994. text 65.00 (*0-19-856163-6*, Clarendon Pr) OUP.

Barton, Thomas K. Appleton & Lange's Review for the USMLE Step 1. 2nd rev. ed. 331p. (C). 1997. pap. 36.95 (*0-8385-0265-2*, A0265-7, Apple Lange Med) McGraw.

— Appleton & Lange's Review for the USMLE Step 1. 3rd ed. LC 99-462606. 331p. 1999. pap. 36.95 (*0-8385-0375-6*, Apple Lange Med) McGraw.

Barton, Thomas L., et al. Open-Book Management: Creating an Ownership Culture. LC 97-77705. (Illus.). 246p. 1998. pap. 38.50 (*1-885065-12-4*, 098-02) Finan Exec.

Barton, Thomas R. & Pillai, Vijayan K. Welfare As We Know It: A Family-Level Analysis of AFDC Receipt. LC 97-1987. (Studies in Health & Human Services: Vol. 27). 180p. 1997. text 79.95 (*0-7734-8670-4*) E Mellen.

Barton, V. K. Meniere's Disease: An Information Book for People with Meniere's Disease. 136p. 1991. pap. 60.00 (*0-646-05022-2*, Pub. by Menieres Aust) St Mut.

Barton, W. S., compiled by. Epitaphs from Cemetery on Worcester Massachusetts Common. 36p. (Orig.). 1996. reprint ed. pap. 8.00 (*1-878545-25-6*) ACETO Bookmen.

Barton, Walter E. Fifty Years of Tax Law Practice. LC 71-103240. vi, 304p. 1969. lib. bdg. 32.50 (*0-89941-455-9*, 500220) W S Hein.

— The History & Influence of the American Psychiatric Association. LC 86-17250. 400p. 1987. text 29.95 (*0-88048-231-1*, 8231) Am Psychiatric.

Barton, Walter E. & Barton, Gail M. Ethics & Law in Mental Health Administration. LC 84-4610. xxi, 378p. 1984. 55.00 (*0-8236-1765-3*) Intl Univs Pr.

— Mental Health Administration: Principles & Practice, 2 vols., I. LC 81-7064. 845p. 1982. 56.95 (*0-89885-061-4*, Kluwer Acad Hman Sci) Kluwer Academic.

— Mental Health Administration: Principles & Practice, 2 vols., II. LC 81-7064. 845p. 1982. 56.95 (*0-89885-062-2*, Kluwer Acad Hman Sci) Kluwer Academic.

— Shrinking Time for Health Administrators: Father - Daughter Psychiatrists Discuss Time Management. (Illus.). 104p. 1998. pap. 9.00 (*0-8059-4509-1*) Dorrance.

Barton, Walter E. & Sanborn, Charlotte J., eds. Law & the Mental Health Professions: Friction at the Interface. LC 77-90226. xviii, 330p. (Orig.). 1978. 50.00 (*0-8236-2950-3*) Intl Univs Pr.

Barton, Wayne. Art of Chip Carving. LC 97-51570. (Illus.). 128p. 1998. 17.95 (*0-8069-4894-9*) Sterling.

— Chip Carving: Techniques & Patterns. LC 84-8779. (Illus.). 128p. (Orig.). 1984. pap. 12.95 (*0-8069-7924-0*) Sterling.

— Chip Carving Patterns. LC 89-26174. (Illus.). 128p. (Orig.). 1990. pap. 12.95 (*0-8069-5782-4*) Sterling.

— Fairchild's Passage. LC 96-54798. 384p. 1997. text 24.95 (*0-312-86141-9*) St Martin.

— High Country. LC 98-52522. 1999. 22.95 (*0-7838-8525-3*) Thorndike Pr.

***Barton, Wayne.** Lockhart's Nightmare. 352p. 2000. mass mkt. 6.99 (*0-8125-7196-7*) Forge NYC.

— Manhunt. (Orig.). 2000. mass mkt. 5.99 (*0-425-17339-9*) Berkley Pub.

Barton, Wayne. New & Traditional Styles of Chip Carving: From Classic to Positive Imaging. LC 93-43377. (Illus.). 128p. 1994. pap. 12.95 (*0-8069-8574-7*) Sterling.

— Ride down the Wind. large type ed. LC 92-27527. (Nightingale Ser.). 320p. 1993. lib. bdg. 14.95 (*0-8161-5626-3*, G K Hall Lrg Type) Mac Lib Ref.

— Wildcat. 1995. mass mkt. 4.99 (*0-671-74579-4*) PB.

Barton, Wayne & Williams, Stan. High Country. Grad Doug, ed. 256p. 1993. mass mkt. 3.99 (*0-671-74577-8*) PB.

— Live by the Gun. large type ed. 331p. 1992. pap. 14.95 (*0-8161-5465-1*, G K Hall Lrg Type) Mac Lib Ref.

— Lockharts Nightmare. LC 98-2878. 384p. 1998. text 24.95 (*0-312-86142-7*) St Martin.

— Manhunt. Grad, Doug, ed. 224p. (Orig.). 1992. pap. 3.50 (*0-671-74576-X*) PB.

— Shadow of Doubt. Grad, Doug, ed. 256p. (Orig.). 1994. mass mkt. 4.50 (*0-671-74578-6*) PB.

***Barton Wilderman, Marjorie.** Winning in the Second Half. LC 99-64525. 161p. 2000. pap. 17.95 (*1-58501-016-2*, Pub. by CeShore Pubg) Natl Bk Netwk.

Barton, William. Acts of Conscience. LC 96-3004. 416p. (Orig.). 1997. mass mkt. 12.99 (*0-446-67251-3*, Pub. by Warner Bks) Little.

— Acts of Conscience. 400p. (Orig.). 1998. mass mkt. 5.99 (*0-446-60511-5*, Pub. by Warner Bks) Little.

— Alpha Centauri. LC 96-45325. 438p. 1998. mass mkt. 6.99 (*0-380-78205-7*, Eos) Morrow Avon.

— When We Were Real. 337p. 1999. mass mkt. 6.99 (*0-446-60706-1*, Pub. by Warner Bks) Little.

Barton, William & Capobianco, Michael. Alpha Centauri. LC 96-45325. 448p. 1997. pap. 13.00 (*0-380-79282-6*, Avon Bks); mass mkt. 23.00 (*0-380-97511-4*, Avon Bks) Morrow Avon.

— White Light. LC 98-17586. 368p. 1998. pap. 13.00 (*0-380-79515-9*, Eos) Morrow Avon.

— White Light. 352p. 1999. mass mkt. 6.99 (*0-380-79516-7*, Avon Bks) Morrow Avon.

***Barton, William A.** GURPS Space: Roleplaying in the World of Tomorrow. 3rd ed. Punch, Sean, ed. (Illus.). 176p. 1999. pap. 22.95 (*1-55634-390-6*, Pub. by S Jackson Games) BookWorld.

Barton, William A. Recovering for Psychological Injuries. 2nd ed. Griffith, Christine M. & Holloway, Arnett ..., eds. LC 90-30974. 417p. 1990. 80.00 (*0-941916-5?-0*) West Group.

— Winning Trial Techniques: A Roadmap for Effective Advocacy. 175p. 1992. pap. 165.00 incl. audio (*0-943380-37-5*) PEG MN.

Barton, William A., intro. Barry Slotnick's Summation in State of New York vs. Bernhard H. Goetz. (Classics of the Courtroom: Vol. XVII). 90p. 1991. pap. 15.00 (*0-943380-23-5*) PEG MN.

— Cruzan vs. Director, Missouri Department of Health - An Overview & Analysis. (Classics of the Courtroom: Vol. XXI). 156p. 1992. pap. 15.00 (*0-943380-27-8*) PEG MN.

— Thurgood Marshall's Arguments Before the U. S. Supreme Court in Brown vs. the Board of Education: The School Desegration Cases. (Classics of the Courtroom: Vol. XX). 48p. 1992. pap. 10.00 (*0-943380-26-X*) PEG MN.

Barton, William E. Lieutenant William Barton of Morris County, New Jersey, & His Descendants. (Illus.). 148p. 1988. reprint ed. pap. 22.00 (*0-8328-0203-4*); reprint ed. lib. bdg. 30.00 (*0-8328-0202-6*) Higginson Bk Co.

— Life of Clara Barton, 2 vols. LC 71-86171. reprint ed. 78.50 (*0-404-00730-9*) AMS Pr.

— Lincoln at Gettysburg. (History - United States Ser.). 263p. 1992. reprint ed. lib. bdg. 79.00 (*0-7812-6168-6*) Rprt Serv.

— Old Plantation Hymns. LC 72-38499. reprint ed. 27.50 (*0-404-09918-1*) AMS Pr.

— Parables of a Country Parson: Heartwarming Stories of Christian Faith & Life. Rosell, Garth & Flewelling, Stan, eds. 194p. 1998. pap. 12.95 (*1-56563-419-5*) Hendrickson MA.

Barton, William F., jt. auth. see Barton, David K.

Barton, William F., jt. auth. see Leonov, Sergey A.

Barton, William H., jt. auth. see Gottfredson, Denise C.

Barton, William H., jt. ed. see Schwartz, Ira M.

Barton, Winifred W. John P. Williamson: A Brother to the Sioux. LC 80-53176. (Illus.). 308p. 1980. reprint ed. 10.00 (*0-9610012-0-8*) Sunnycrest Pub.

Bartone, Carl, et al. Toward Environmental Strategies for Cities: Policy Considerations for Urban Environmental Management in Developing Countries. LC 94-13583. (Urban Management Program Ser.: No. 18). 128p. 1994. pap. 22.00 (*0-8213-2827-1*, 12827) World Bank.

Bartone, Edee M., jt. auth. see Bartone, Michael A.

Bartone, Elisa. American Too. LC 96-75917. (Illus.). 40p. (J). (gr. k up). 1996. 16.00 (*0-688-13278-2*); lib. bdg. 15.93 (*0-688-13279-0*) Lothrop.

— Peppe the Lamplighter. LC 92-1397. (Illus.). (J). (ps-3). 1993. 16.00 (*0-688-10268-9*); lib. bdg. 15.93 (*0-688-10269-7*) Lothrop.

— Peppe the Lamplighter. LC 92-1397. (Illus.). 32p. (J). (gr. k-3). 1997. mass mkt. 4.95 (*0-688-15469-7*, Wm Morrow) Morrow Avon.

Bartone, Elisa. Peppe the Lamplighter. LC 92-1397. 1997. 10.15 (*0-606-11737-7*, Pub. by Turtleback) Demco.

Bartone, Jay. Humor Agnostica: Bible One-Line Selections Tuned Hilarious & Jolly for the Hell & Heavenly Bound Humanoids. Date not set. pap. 29.50 (*0-7883-1785-7*) ABBE Pubs Assn.

— Humor Agnostica: Bible One-Line Selections Turned Hilarious & Jolly for the Hell & Heavenly Bound Humanoids. Date not set. 39.50 (*0-7883-1784-9*) ABBE Pubs Assn.

Bartone, John C. Adipose Tissues--For Clinical & Scientific Research: Index of New Information. 160p. 1998. 47.50 (*0-7883-1716-4*); pap. 44.50 (*0-7883-1717-2*) ABBE Pubs Assn.

— Anti-Cancer Substances in Therapeutic Use in Health & Disease: Index of New Information, 4 vols. Incl. Vol. 1, A-F. (Illus.). 160p. 1997. 47.50 (*0-7883-1684-2*); Vol. 2, G-L. (Illus.). 160p. 1997. 47.50 (*0-7883-1686-9*); Vol. 3, M-R. (Illus.). 160p. 1997. 47.50 (*0-7883-1688-5*); Vol. 4, S-Z. (Illus.). 160p. 1997. 47.50 (*0-7883-1690-7*); 190.00 (*0-7883-1682-6*) ABBE Pubs Assn.

— AntiCancer Substances in Therapeutic Use in Health & Disease: Index of New Information, 4 vols. Incl. Vol. 1, A-F. (Illus.). 160p. 1997. pap. 44.50 (*0-7883-1685-0*); Vol. 2, G-L. (Illus.). 160p. 1997. pap. 44.50 (*0-7883-1687-7*); Vol. 3, M-R. (Illus.). 160p. 1997. pap. 44.50 (*0-7883-1689-3*); Vol. 4, S-Z. (Illus.). 160p. 1997. pap. 44.50 (*0-7883-1691-5*); 178.00 (*0-7883-1683-4*) ABBE Pubs Assn.

— Bartone's Guidebook to Biological Warfare: Index of Modern Information. LC 89-80338. 175p. 1990. 47.50 (*1-55914-100-X*); pap. 44.50 (*1-55914-101-8*) ABBE Pubs Assn.

— Biological Warfare & Chemical Gases: Index of New Information & Research Reference Book. 150p. 1996. 47.50 (*0-7883-1138-7*); pap. 44.50 (*0-7883-1139-5*) ABBE Pubs Assn.

— Biological Warfare & Chemical Gases: Index of New Information & Research Reference Book. rev. ed. 151p. 1998. 47.50 (*0-7883-2084-X*); pap. 44.50 (*0-7883-2085-8*) ABBE Pubs Assn.

— Biology of Crime: Index of New Information. 160p. 1998. 47.50 (*0-7883-1748-2*); pap. 44.50 (*0-7883-1749-0*) ABBE Pubs Assn.

***Bartone, John C.** Biology of Crime: Index of New Information for Reference & Research. rev. ed. 143p. 1999. pap. 44.50 (*0-7883-2145-5*) ABBE Pubs Assn.

— Biology of Crime: Index of New Information for Reference & Research. 2nd rev. ed. 143p. 1999. 47.50 (*0-7883-2144-7*) ABBE Pubs Assn.

Bartone, John C. Biology of Elephantiasis, Lymphatic Filariasis & Albendazole: Index of New Information. 150p. 1998. 47.50 (*0-7883-2036-X*); pap. 44.50 (*0-7883-2037-8*) ABBE Pubs Assn.

***Bartone, John C.** Biology of Elephantiasis, Lymphatic Filariasis & Albendazole: Index of New Information. rev. ed. 143p. 1999. pap. 44.50 (*0-7883-2201-X*) ABBE Pubs Assn.

— Biology of Elephantiasis, Lymphatic Filariasis & Albendazole: Index of New Information. 2nd rev. ed. 143p. 1999. 47.50 (*0-7883-2200-1*) ABBE Pubs Assn.

Bartone, John C. Biology of Infections: Index of New Information. 160p. 1998. 47.50 (*0-7883-1766-0*); pap. 44.50 (*0-7883-1767-9*) ABBE Pubs Assn.

— Biology of War & Its Variations: Index of New Information with References. 160p. 1997. 47.50 (*0-7883-1408-4*); pap. 44.50 (*0-7883-1409-2*) ABBE Pubs Assn.

— Biology of Warfare: Index of New Information & Research Reference Book. 150p. 1996. 47.50 (*0-7883-1136-0*); pap. 44.50 (*0-7883-1137-9*) ABBE Pubs Assn.

Bartone, John C., II. Biomedical Engineering: Index of Modern Information. LC 88-48000. 150p. 1990. 47.50 (*1-55914-076-3*); pap. 44.50 (*1-55914-077-1*) ABBE Pubs Assn.

B

Bartone, John C. Breast Cancer, Fat & Adipose Tissue with Toxic & Non-Toxic Chemicals & Residues: Index of New Information. 160p. 1997. 47.50 (*0-7883-1714-8*); pap. 44.50 (*0-7883-1715-6*) ABBE Pubs Assn.

Bartone, John C., Sr. Breast Cancers: Index of New Information - Chemically Induced. (Illus.). 160p. 1995. 47.50 (*0-7883-0698-7*); pap. 44.50 (*0-7883-0699-5*) ABBE Pubs Assn.

Bartone, John C. Cancer & Its Causes: Index of Modern Authors & Subjects with Guide for Rapid Research. LC 90-56234. (Illus.). 205p. 1991. 47.50 (*1-55914-244-8*); pap. 44.50 (*1-55914-245-6*) ABBE Pubs Assn.

— Cancer & Its Psychological Influences: Index of Modern Authors & Subjects with Guide for Rapid Research. 180p. 1991. 47.50 (*1-55914-246-4*); pap. 44.50 (*1-55914-247-2*) ABBE Pubs Assn.

— Cancer Disease & Patients: Emotional Feelings, Fears & Future: Index of New Information. 160p. 1997. 47.50 (*0-7883-1756-3*); pap. 44.50 (*0-7883-1757-1*) ABBE Pubs Assn.

— Cancer Vaccines: Index of New Information for Reference & Research. 160p. 1997. 47.50 (*0-7883-1668-0*); pap. 44.50 (*0-7883-1669-9*) ABBE Pubs Assn.

Bartone, John C., Sr. Cancers - by Diverse Experiments & Chemically Produced: Index of New Information Including Authors, Methods & Results. (Illus.). 210p. 1995. 47.50 (*0-7883-0440-2*); pap. 44.50 (*0-7883-0441-0*) ABBE Pubs Assn.

— Cancers - Research on Causes of the Disease: Index of New Information Including Theories & Sources in Life, Work, Hobbies & Environmental Types of Recreation. LC 95-15408. (Illus.). 185p. 1995. 47.50 (*0-7883-0436-4*); pap. 44.50 (*0-7883-0437-2*) ABBE Pubs Assn.

— Cancers Produced by Radiation: Index of New Information Including Human Risks & Results. rev. ed. LC 96-187. 135p. 1996. pap. 44.50 (*0-7883-1017-8*) ABBE Pubs Assn.

Bartone, John C. Cancers Produced by Radiation: Index of New Information Including Human Risks & Results. rev. ed. LC 96-187. 135p. 1996. 47.50 (*0-7883-1016-X*) ABBE Pubs Assn.

Bartone, John C., Sr. Chemical Induction of New Tumors & Cancers: Index of New Information Including Human Risks & Results. (Illus.). 190p. 1995. 47.50 (*0-7883-0482-8*); pap. 44.50 (*0-7883-0483-6*) ABBE Pubs Assn.

Bartone, John C. Chemical Warfare--Military & Civilian Considerations: Index of New Information with Bibliography. (Illus.). 150p. 1999. 47.50 (*0-7883-2256-7*); pap. 44.50 (*0-7883-2257-5*) ABBE Pubs Assn.

— Chemical Warfare Agents & Substances: Index of New Information with References. (Illus.). 150p. 1999. pap. 44.50 (*0-7883-2227-3*) ABBE Pubs Assn.

***Bartone, John C.** Chemoprevention of Disease, Anti-Cancer Attempts, Strategy for Health Protection & Chemical Therapies: Index of New Information. rev. ed. 147p. 1999. pap. 44.50 (*0-7883-2153-6*) ABBE Pubs Assn.

— Chemoprevention of Disease, Anti-Cancer Attempts, Strategy for Health Protection & Chemical Therapies: Index of New Information. 2nd rev. ed. 147p. 1999. 47.50 (*0-7883-2152-8*) ABBE Pubs Assn.

Bartone, John C. Chemoprevention of Disease, Anti-Cancer Attempts, Strategy for Health Protection & Clinical Therapies: Index of New Information. 150p. 1998. 47.50 (*0-7883-1368-1*); pap. 44.50 (*0-7883-1369-X*) ABBE Pubs Assn.

— Consumer Car Care for the Wise, the Poor & the Helpless. LC 95-15996. 1995. 37.50 (*0-7883-0722-3*); pap. write for info. (*0-7883-0723-1*) ABBE Pubs Assn.

— Consumer Reference Book & Index about Cocaine & Its Dangerous Influences. 90p. 1994. pap. 29.95 (*0-7883-0281-7*) ABBE Pubs Assn.

— Consumer Reference Book & Index about Hazardous Substances in Your Life. 90p. 1994. pap. 29.95 (*0-7883-0283-3*) ABBE Pubs Assn.

— Consumer Reference Book & Index about HIV, AIDS, & Treatments. rev. ed. LC 96-188. 125p. 1996. pap. 29.95 (*0-7883-1025-9*) ABBE Pubs Assn.

— Consumer Reference Book & Index about Informed Consent. 90p. 1994. pap. 29.95 (*0-7883-0285-X*) ABBE Pubs Assn.

— Consumers' Reference Book & Index about Abortion in Today's World. rev. ed. 147p. 1997. pap. 29.95 (*0-7883-1508-0*) ABBE Pubs Assn.

— Consumers' Reference Book & Index about Adolescent Behavior. 90p. 1994. pap. 29.95 (*0-7883-0341-4*) ABBE Pubs Assn.

— Consumers' Reference Book & Index about Automobile Accidents. 90p. 1994. pap. 29.95 (*0-7883-0333-3*) ABBE Pubs Assn.

— Consumers' Reference Book & Index about Civil Rights. 90p. 1994. pap. 29.95 (*0-7883-0337-6*) ABBE Pubs Assn.

— Consumers' Reference Book & Index about Cosmetics Good & Bad. 90p. 1994. pap. 29.95 (*0-7883-0326-0*) ABBE Pubs Assn.

— Consumers' Reference Book & Index about Crime Prevention. 90p. 1994. pap. 29.95 (*0-7883-0323-6*) ABBE Pubs Assn.

— Consumers' Reference Book & Index about Crime Today in the U. S. A. 90p. 1994. pap. 29.95 (*0-7883-0321-X*) ABBE Pubs Assn.

— Consumers' Reference Book & Index about Exercise. 90p. 1994. pap. 29.95 (*0-7883-0319-8*) ABBE Pubs Assn.

— Consumers' Reference Book & Index about Food, Diet & Cancer. 90p. 1994. pap. 29.95 (*0-7883-0279-5*) ABBE Pubs Assn.

— Consumers' Reference Book & Index about Hazardous Substance in Your Life. rev. ed. 133p. 1997. pap. 29.95 (*0-7883-1398-3*) ABBE Pubs Assn.

— Consumers' Reference Book & Index about Human Rights. 90p. 1994. pap. 29.95 (*0-7883-0335-X*) ABBE Pubs Assn.

— Consumers' Reference Book & Index about Hypnosis. rev. ed. 111p. 1997. pap. 29.95 (*0-7883-1399-1*) ABBE Pubs Assn.

— Consumers' Reference Book & Index about Illness & Diseases Caused by Jobs & Occupations. 90p. 1994. pap. 29.95 (*0-7883-0297-3*) ABBE Pubs Assn.

— Consumers' Reference Book & Index about Juvenile Delinquency. 90p. 1994. pap. 29.95 (*0-7883-0287-6*) ABBE Pubs Assn.

— Consumers' Reference Book & Index about Love & Libido. 90p. 1994. pap. 29.95 (*0-7883-0305-8*) ABBE Pubs Assn.

— Consumers' Reference Book & Index about Magic & Superstitions. 90p. 1994. pap. 29.95 (*0-7883-0291-4*) ABBE Pubs Assn.

— Consumers' Reference Book & Index about Marriage. 90p. 1994. pap. 29.95 (*0-7883-0307-4*) ABBE Pubs Assn.

— Consumers' Reference Book & Index about Massage. 90p. 1994. pap. 29.95 (*0-7883-0293-0*) ABBE Pubs Assn.

— Consumers' Reference Book & Index about Nutrition. 90p. 1994. pap. 29.95 (*0-7883-0329-5*) ABBE Pubs Assn.

— Consumers' Reference Book & Index about Relaxation & Its Methods. rev. ed. 149p. 1997. pap. 29.95 (*0-7883-1472-6*) ABBE Pubs Assn.

— Consumers' Reference Book & Index about Rights to Medical Treatment. 90p. 1994. pap. 29.95 (*0-7883-0311-2*) ABBE Pubs Assn.

— Consumers' Reference Book & Index about Sex & Bisexuality. 90p. 1994. pap. 29.95 (*0-7883-0331-7*) ABBE Pubs Assn.

— Consumers' Reference Book & Index about Sex Counseling & Diseases. 90p. 1994. pap. 29.95 (*0-7883-0339-2*) ABBE Pubs Assn.

— Consumer's Reference Book & Index about Sex Counseling & Diseases. LC 96-12666. 1996. pap. 29.95 (*0-7883-0833-5*) ABBE Pubs Assn.

— Consumer's Reference Book & Index about Sports. 90p. 1996. pap. 29.95 (*0-7883-1024-0*) ABBE Pubs Assn.

— Consumers' Reference Book & Index about Stress & Distress Including Treatments. rev. ed. LC 96-3126. 125p. 1996. pap. 29.95 (*0-7883-1148-4*) ABBE Pubs Assn.

— Consumers' Reference Book & Index about the Health Benefits of Garlic. 90p. 1994. pap. 29.95 (*0-7883-0315-5*) ABBE Pubs Assn.

— Consumers' Reference Book & Index about...Death. 90p. 1994. pap. 29.95 (*0-7883-0327-9*) ABBE Pubs Assn.

— Consumer's Reference Book & Index Concerning Diagnostic Errors in Medicine. 90p. 1994. pap. 29.95 (*0-7883-0303-1*) ABBE Pubs Assn.

— Consumer's Reference Book & Index Concerning Medical Malpractice. rev. ed. 143p. 1996. pap. 29.95 (*0-7883-1156-5*) ABBE Pubs Assn.

— Electric Injuries Including Lightning: Index of New Information with Authors & Subjects. LC 96-12481. 1996. 47.50 (*0-7883-0778-9*); pap. 44.50 (*0-7883-0779-7*) ABBE Pubs Assn.

Bartone, John C., II. Electronics in Health Sciences: Index of Modern Information. LC 88-47951. 150p. 1988. 47.50 (*0-88164-992-9*) ABBE Pubs Assn.

— Fiber Optics: Index of New Information with Authors & Subjects. rev. ed. LC 95-16709. 155p. 1995. 47.50 (*0-7883-0714-2*); pap. 44.50 (*0-7883-0715-0*) ABBE Pubs Assn.

— Firearms & Gunshot Wounds: Index of Modern Information. LC 88-47970. 150p. 1990. 47.50 (*1-55914-198-0*); pap. 44.50 (*1-55914-199-9*) ABBE Pubs Assn.

Bartone, John C. Guns, Firearms, Crime, & Controversy: Index of New Information with References. (Illus.). 150p. 1996. 47.50 (*0-7883-0780-0*); pap. 44.50 (*0-7883-0781-9*) ABBE Pubs Assn.

— Health - Personal Influences, Attitudes, Behavior & Self-Care: Index of New Information. (Illus.). 150p. 1998. 47.50 (*0-7883-2034-3*); pap. 44.50 (*0-7883-2035-1*) ABBE Pubs Assn.

— Health - The World's Most Important & Valuable Venture & Its Blatant Neglect: Index of New Information for Homo Sapiens on Planet Earth. (Illus.). 180p. 1998. 47.50 (*0-7883-2012-2*); pap. 44.50 (*0-7883-2013-0*) ABBE Pubs Assn.

— Health, Life & Disease - Or Why Research Should Be of Great Importance to All Governments, Consumers, Community Leaders, Military Chiefs, Civic & Civilian Pioneers, Cosmopolitans & Librarians: A Philosophy of Progress Made Simple. 120p. 1997. 39.95 (*0-7883-1424-6*); pap. 34.95 (*0-7883-1425-4*) ABBE Pubs Assn.

— Human Body Encyclopedia of Exposures to Environmental Conditions for Ill Health, Sickness & Disease Including Various Cancers: Cumulative Index of New Information with Authors, Subjects, Research Categories & Bibliography, 5 vols. Incl. Vol. 1 (A to E). (Illus.). 160p. 1997. 49.95 (*0-7883-1412-2*); Vol. 2 (F to J). (Illus.). 160p. 1997. 49.95 (*0-7883-1414-9*); Vol. 3 (K to O). (Illus.). 160p. 1997. 49.95 (*0-7883-1416-5*); Vol. 4 (P to T). (Illus.). 160p. 1997. 49.95 (*0-7883-1418-1*); Vol. 5 (V to Z). (Illus.). 160p. 1997. 49.95 (*0-7883-1420-3*); 1997. 199.00 (*0-7883-1410-6*) ABBE Pubs Assn.

— Human Body Encyclopedia of Exposures to Environmental Conditions for Ill Health, Sickness, & Disease Including Various Cancers: Cumulative Index of New Information with Authors, Subjects, Research Categories, & Bibliography. Incl. Vol. 1 (A to E). (Illus.). 160p. 1997. pap. 44.95 (*0-7883-1413-0*); Vol. 2 (F to J). (Illus.). 160p. 1997. pap. 44.95 (*0-7883-1415-7*); Vol. 3 (K to O). (Illus.). 160p. 1997. pap. 44.95 (*0-7883-1417-3*); Vol. 4 (P to T). (Illus.). 160p. 1997. pap. 44.95 (*0-7883-1419-X*); Vol. 5 (V to Z). (Illus.). 160p. 1997. pap. 44.95 (*0-7883-1421-1*); 1997. Set pap. 175.00 (*0-7883-1411-4*) ABBE Pubs Assn.

— Human Carcinogens: Index of New Information with Authors, Subjects & References. 150p. 1997. 47.50 (*0-7883-1358-4*); pap. 44.50 (*0-7883-1359-2*) ABBE Pubs Assn.

— Hypnosis: Guidebook for Medicine, Reference & Research. LC 83-46102. 150p. 1985. 47.50 (*0-88164-136-7*); pap. 44.50 (*0-88164-137-5*) ABBE Pubs Assn.

— Information Services for the World: Index of Progress. LC 88-47952. 150p. 1990. 44.50 (*1-55914-010-0*); pap. 39.50 (*1-55914-011-9*) ABBE Pubs Assn.

— Intelligence Tests: General Survey with Research Subject Index & Bibliography. LC 82-72024. 155p. 1984. 37.50 (*0-941864-64-2*); pap. 34.50 (*0-941864-65-0*) ABBE Pubs Assn.

— Medical Analysis of the Neck: The "Choke-Hold" As Practiced by Cops Is Attempted Murder & Pre-Mediated Homicide: Citizens Beware! (Neck Anatomy Made Simple for Consumers & Lawyers) (Illus.). 149p. 1997. 47.50 (*0-7883-1394-0*); pap. 44.50 (*0-7883-1395-9*) ABBE Pubs Assn.

— Medical Anatomy & Clinical Research: Index of Modern Authors & Subjects with Guide for Rapid Research. LC 90-56294. 160p. 1991. 47.50 (*1-55914-372-X*); pap. 44.50 (*1-55914-373-8*) ABBE Pubs Assn.

— Medical Research & the Jungle of Science: A New System for Universal Organization of All Subjects with Permanent Listing of All Publications, Authors & Contributors. rev. ed. (Illus.). 170p. 1996. 59.95 (*0-7883-1022-4*); pap. 49.50 (*0-7883-1023-2*) ABBE Pubs Assn.

— Medical Research of Combat Disorders - Diagnosis, Psychology & Therapy: Index of New Information with Authors, Subjects & Bibliographical References. 150p. 1996. 47.50 (*0-7883-0678-2*); pap. 44.50 (*0-7883-0679-0*) ABBE Pubs Assn.

— Medical Uses of Television As a Media for Health, Dangers, News, Advertising & Brain-Washing: Index of New Information for World Review. (Illus.). 160p. 1997. 47.50 (*0-7883-1396-7*); pap. 44.50 (*0-7883-1397-5*) ABBE Pubs Assn.

— Medical Uses of Television As a Media for Health, Dangers, News, Advertising & Brain-Washington: Index of New Information for World Review. rev. ed. 167p. 1998. 47.50 (*0-7883-1858-6*); pap. 44.50 (*0-7883-1859-4*) ABBE Pubs Assn.

— Methods in Hypnosis: Guidebook for Medicine, Reference & Research. LC 83-46103. 150p. 1985. 47.50 (*0-88164-138-3*); pap. 44.50 (*0-88164-139-1*) ABBE Pubs Assn.

Bartone, John C., II. Muscles & Drug Effects: Medical Subject Analysis with Research Bibliography. LC 84-45657. 150p. 1987. 47.50 (*0-88164-216-9*); pap. 44.50 (*0-88164-217-7*) ABBE Pubs Assn.

Bartone, John C. Neoplasms--Prevention, Control & Results: Index of New Information for Reference & Research. 160p. 1997. 47.50 (*0-7883-1666-4*); pap. 44.50 (*0-7883-1667-2*) ABBE Pubs Assn.

— Pesticide Residues in Food & Human Bodies: Index of New Information. 160p. 1997. 47.50 (*0-7883-1670-2*); pap. 44.50 (*0-7883-1671-0*) ABBE Pubs Assn.

— Pesticides & Human Cancer Involvement: Index of New Information. 160p. 1997. 47.50 (*0-7883-1650-8*); pap. 44.50 (*0-7883-1651-6*) ABBE Pubs Assn.

— Publishing, Promoting & Selling Your Book for Self-Publishers & Impatient Writers. LC 88-47598. (Illus.). 150p. 1988. 39.50 (*0-88164-624-5*); pap. 34.50 (*0-88164-643-1*) ABBE Pubs Assn.

— Research: Developments & Progress in Science, Life & Medicine Including Concerns & World-Wide Criticisms. 185p. 1997. 47.50 (*0-7883-1020-8*); pap. 44.50 (*0-7883-1021-6*) ABBE Pubs Assn.

— Rice - The Crop That Feeds the World: Index of New Information for Health, Business & Industry. (Illus.). 170p. 1997. 47.50 (*0-7883-1736-9*); pap. 44.50 (*0-7883-1737-7*) ABBE Pubs Assn.

Bartone, John C., II. Ultraviolet Rays, Factors & Adverse Effects: Medical Analysis Index with Research Bibliography. LC 85-47862. 150p. 1987. 47.50 (*0-88164-398-X*); pap. 44.50 (*0-88164-399-8*) ABBE Pubs Assn.

Bartone, John C. War: A Medical, Psychological & Scientific Subject Analysis with Research Index & Bibliography. LC 83-71661. 160p. 1984. 47.50 (*0-941864-91-X*); pap. 44.50 (*0-941864-90-1*) ABBE Pubs Assn.

— War Syndromes of the Persian Gulf Battles: Index of New Information with References. 165p. 1997. 47.50 (*0-7883-1528-5*); pap. 44.50 (*0-7883-1529-3*) ABBE Pubs Assn.

— War with Military & Civil Aspects: Subject Analysis with Bibliography. LC 87-47631. 160p. 1987. 47.50 (*0-88164-542-7*); pap. 44.50 (*0-88164-543-5*) ABBE Pubs Assn.

Bartone, John C., ed. Sexology Encyclopedia: Index & Reference Books of New Information, 25 vols., Set. (Illus.). 3750p. 1996. 1200.00 (*0-7883-1050-X*); pap. 950.00 (*0-7883-1051-8*) ABBE Pubs Assn.

— Sexology Encyclopedia Vol. 19: Vasectomy & Medicine: Index & Reference Books of New Information. (Illus.). 145p. 1996. 49.95 (*0-7883-0886-6*); pap. 39.95 (*0-7883-0887-4*) ABBE Pubs Assn.

Bartone, John C., jt. auth. see Markle, Helen M.

Bartone, John C., ed. see American Health Research Institute Staff.

Bartone, John C., ed. see Bronsen, Hugo H.

Bartone, John C., ed. see Buckner, Allen Z.

Bartone, John C., ed. see Clygout, Sanivar H.

Bartone, John C., ed. see Drummond, Harold P.

Bartone, John C., ed. see Farrell, Alexander D.

Bartone, John C., ed. see Hallcrest, Judy J.

Bartone, John C., ed. see Holibrook, Vicky W.

Bartone, John C., ed. see Holtz, Jerry B.

Bartone, John C., ed. see Hurley, Patricia S.

Bartone, John C., ed. see Irving, Alfred H.

Bartone, John C., ed. see Jensen, Virginia L.

Bartone, John C., ed. see Lydeen, Lottie F.

Bartone, John C., ed. see Markle, Helen M.

Bartone, John C., ed. see Mikker, Max L.

Bartone, John C., ed. see Mordune, Ruby Q.

Bartone, John C., ed. see Parkenham, Bette M.

Bartone, John C., ed. see Rice, Marian L.

Bartone, John C., ed. see Rockford, Doris E.

Bartone, John C., ed. see Shank, Arlene S.

Bartone, John C., ed. see Valpone, Estee V.

Bartone, John C., ed. see Van Wertz, Sandy M.

Bartone, John C., ed. see Zoltano, Rosalie F.

Bartone, Mary R. Cancer Prevention & Control: Index of Modern Information. LC 88-47856. 150p. 1990. 47.50 (*1-55914-176-X*); pap. 44.50 (*1-55914-177-8*) ABBE Pubs Assn.

— Computer Assisted Instruction in the Health Sciences: Index of New Information with Authors & Subjects. LC 92-54230. 180p. 1992. 47.50 (*1-55914-608-7*); pap. 44.50 (*1-55914-609-5*) ABBE Pubs Assn.

— Computer-Assisted Instruction in the Health Sciences: Index of New Information with Authors & Subjects. 159p. 1997. 47.50 (*0-7883-1566-8*); pap. 44.50 (*0-7883-1567-6*) ABBE Pubs Assn.

— Food & Its Dangerous Ingredients for Health & Safety in America: Index of New Information with Authors & Subjects. LC 95-15405. 1995. 47.50 (*0-7883-0756-8*); pap. write for info. (*0-7883-0757-6*) ABBE Pubs Assn.

— Medical Wit & Humor: Index of Modern Writings. LC 95-16708. 1995. write for info. (*0-7883-0480-1*); pap. 44.50 (*0-7883-0481-X*) ABBE Pubs Assn.

— Research on Health: A Medical Subject Analysis with Bibliography. LC 84-45738. 150p. 1987. 47.50 (*0-88164-254-1*); pap. 44.50 (*0-88164-255-X*) ABBE Pubs Assn.

Bartone, Michael A. & Bartone, Edee M. Construction & Building Materials: Research of Harmful Health Aspects & Disease-Causing Influences. (Illus.). 185p. 1997. 47.50 (*0-7883-1600-1*); pap. 44.50 (*0-7883-1601-X*) ABBE Pubs Assn.

Bartonek, Antonin. Classification of the West Greek Dialects at the Time about 350 B.C. 230p. (Orig.). 1972. pap. 68.00 (*0-685-33038-9*, Pub. by AM Hakkert) BookLink Distributors.

Bartoo, Glenn. Decisions by Consensus: A Study of the Quaker Method. (Studies in Quakerism: No. 4). 48p. (Orig.). 1978. pap. 3.00 (*0-89670-003-8*) Progresiv Pub.

Bartos. Marketing Women around the World. 338p. 1989. 29.95 (*0-07-103209-6*) McGraw.

Bartos, ed. Production Methods & Workability of Concrete. LC 96-209718. (Illus.). 560p. (C). 1996. 150.00 (*0-419-22070-4*, E & FN Spon) Routledge.

— Special Concretes Workability & Mixing. LC 94-181863. (Rilem Proceedings Ser.). (Illus.). 288p. (C). 1994. 130.00 (*0-419-18870-3*, E & FN Spon) Routledge.

Bartos, Adam, photos by. Willem de Kooning: Sculpture. (Illus.). 76p. 1996. 29.95 (*1-880146-15-0*) M Marks.

Bartos, Aniko J., jt. auth. see Baird, Alan C.

Bartos, Anthony L., et al, eds. Nondestructive Characterization of Materials. (Materials Science Forum Ser.: Vols. 210-213). 924p. 1996. 333.00 (*0-87849-708-0*, Pub. by Trans T Pub) Enfield Pubs NH.

Bartos, Eileen, ed. see Weber, Irving.

Bartos, F. M. The Hussite Revolution: 1424-1437. 204p. 1986. text 48.50 (*0-88033-097-X*, Pub. by East Eur Monographs) Col U Pr.

Bartos-Hoppner, Barbara. The Pied Piper of Hamelin. LC 87-45150.Tr. of Der/Rattenfanger von Hameln. (Illus.). 32p. (J). (gr. k-3). 1987. 9.95 (*0-397-32239-9*) HarpC Child Bks.

— The Pied Piper of Hamelin. LC 87-45150.Tr. of Der/Rattenfanger von Hameln. (Illus.). 32p. (J). (gr. k-3). 1987. lib. bdg. 11.89 (*0-397-32240-2*) HarpC Child Bks.

Bartos, J., jt. auth. see Pesez, Maurice.

Bartosch, Bob & Bartosch, Pauline. Overcomers Outreach: A Bridge to Recovery. 276p. 1994. 16.00 (*0-9643136-0-X*) Meister Pr.

Bartosch, Janet, et al. God's Gift of Sexuality - Leader's Guide. rev. ed. LC 99-217853. 248p. 1998. pap. 17.95 (*1-57895-059-7*, Witherspoon Pr) Curriculm Presbytrn KY.

Bartosch, Pauline, jt. auth. see Bartosch, Bob.

Bartosek, Ivan, et al, eds. Animals in Toxicological Research. LC 82-12285. (Monographs of the Mario Negri Institute for Pharmacological Research). 224p. 1982. reprint ed. pap. 69.50 (*0-608-00378-6*, 206109200007) Bks Demand.

Bartosek, Miroslav, et al, eds. SOFSEM '95 Theory & Practice of Informatics: Proceedings of the 22nd Seminar on Current Trends in Theory & Practice of Informatics, Milovy, Czech Republic, November 23-December 1, 1995. LC 95-46102. (Lecture Notes in Computer Science Ser.: Vol. 1012). 499p. 1995. 81.00 (*3-540-60609-2*) Spr-Verlag.

Bartosova, Ludmila, et al. Diseases of the Hair & the Scalp. (Current Problems in Dermatology Ser.: Vol. 12). (Illus.). x, 252p. 1984. 71.50 (*3-8055-3783-2*) S Karger.

Bartoszcze, Michael A., jt. auth. see Stopa, Peter J.

Bartoszewski, Wladyslaw. The Warsaw Ghetto: A Christian's Testimony. LC 87-42842. (Illus.). 160p. (C). 1988. 16.50 (*0-8070-5602-2*) Beacon Pr.

Bartoszewski, Wladyslaw T. The Convent at Auschwitz. 169p. 1991. 17.95 (*0-8076-1267-7*) Braziller.

Bartoszynski, Robert & Niewiadomska-Bugaj, Magdalena. Probability & Statistical Inference. LC 96-4105. (Series in Probability & Statistics). 848p. 1996. 84.95 (*0-471-31073-5*) Wiley.

Bartoszynski, Tomek & Judah, Haim. Set Theory: On the Structure of the Real Line. LC 95-34063. (Illus.). 560p. 1995. text 78.00 (*1-56881-044-X*) AK Peters.

Bartoszynski, Tomek & Scheepers, Marion, eds. Set Theory. LC 95-34595. (Contemporary Mathematics Ser.: Vol. 192). 184p. 1995. pap. 45.00 (*0-8218-0306-9*, CONM/192) Am Math.

Bartov, Omer. Hitler's Army: Soldiers, Nazis & War in the Third Reich. 256p. 1992. reprint ed. pap. text 13.95 (*0-19-507903-5*) OUP.

***Bartov, Omer.** Holocaust: Origins, Implementation & Aftermath. LC 99-44232. (Rewriting Histories Ser.). 312p. 2000. pap. 24.99 (*0-415-15036-1*) Routledge.

— Mirrors of Destruction: War, Genocide & Modern Identity. LC 99-39974. 304p. 2000. 35.00 (*0-19-507723-7*) OUP.

***Bartov, Omer, ed.** Holocaust: Origins, Implementation & Aftermath. LC 99-44232. (Rewriting Histories Ser.). 312p. (C). 2000. text 85.00 (*0-415-15035-3*) Routledge.

***Bartov, Omer & Mack, Phyllis, eds.** In God's Name: Genocide & Religion in the 20th Century, 4. LC 99-45111. (Studies on War & Genocide: Vol. 4). 400p. 2000. 69.95 (*1-57181-214-8*) Berghahn Bks.

Bartow, Arthur, contrib. by. The Director's Voice. LC 88-4937. 360p. 1988. reprint ed. pap. 16.95 (*0-930452-74-7*) Theatre Comm.

Bartow, Charles. The Preaching Moment. 2nd ed. 128p. (C). 1995. pap. text 19.95 (*0-7872-1252-0*) Kendall-Hunt.

Bartow, Charles L. God's Human Speech: A Practical Theology of Proclamation. LC 97-10577. 203p. 1997. pap. 20.00 (*0-8028-4335-2*) Eerdmans.

Bartow, Donald W. Bartow's Healing Handbook, No. 1: A Biblical Guide to Healing & Wholeness. 472p. 1992. 14.95 (*0-938736-28-0*) Life Enrich.

Bartow, Evelyn. Bartow Genealogy, Pts. 1 & 2. (Illus.). 318p. 1988. reprint ed. pap. 49.50 (*0-8328-0205-0*); reprint ed. lib. bdg. 59.50 (*0-8328-0204-2*) Higginson Bk Co.

— Bartow Genealogy, Containing Every One of the Name of Bartow, Descended from Dr. Thomas Bartow. 60p. 1997. reprint ed. pap. 12.00 (*0-8328-7401-9*); reprint ed. lib. bdg. 22.00 (*0-8328-7400-0*) Higginson Bk Co.

Bartow, Gary & Aronson. Implementing a Database API: An Object Oriented Approach. 275p. (C). 2001. pap. text 35.00 (*0-13-186198-0*) P-H.

Bartow, Stuart. The Stats Belong to No One. 24p. 1994. pap. 7.00 (*0-937669-50-4*) Owl Creek Pr.

Bartra, Roger. Agrarian Structure & Political Power in Mexico. Ault, Stephen K., tr. from SPA. LC 92-11605. 256p. 1993. pap. text 16.95 (*0-8018-4542-4*) Johns Hopkins.

— The Artificial Savage: Modern Myths of the Wild Man. Follett, Christopher J., tr. LC 96-36753. 336p. (C). 1997. text 49.50 (*0-472-10757-7*, 10757) U of Mich Pr.

— The Imaginary Networks of Political Power. Joysmith, Claire, tr. from SPA. LC 91-23147. (Illus.). 225p. (C). 1992. text 40.00 (*0-8135-1741-9*); pap. text 17.00 (*0-8135-1742-7*) Rutgers U Pr.

— Wild Men in the Looking-Glass: The Mythic Origins of European Otherness. Berrisford, Carl T., tr. from SPA. (Illus.). 240p. (C). 1994. text 49.50 (*0-472-10477-2*, 10477) U of Mich Pr.

***Bartram, Alan.** Making Books: Designs in British Publishing since 1945. LC 99-29885. (Illus.). 160p. 1999. 39.95 (*1-884718-93-0*, 55471) Oak Knoll.

Bartram, Alan, jt. auth. see Sutton, James.

Bartram, Clive & Frudinger, Andrea. Handbook of Anal Endosonography. LC 97-9522. 128p. 1997. pap. 55.00 (*1-871816-35-1*, Pub. by Wrightson Biomed) Taylor & Francis.

Bartram, Clive I., et al. Radiology in Inflammatory Bowel Disease. LC 83-7518. (Diagnostic Radiology Ser.: No. 2). (Illus.). 327p. reprint ed. pap. 101.40 (*0-7837-4302-5*, 204399300012) Bks Demand.

Bartram, E. B. Manual of Hawaiian Mosses. (BMB Ser.: No. 101). 1969. reprint ed. 45.00 (*0-527-02207-1*) Periodicals Srv.

Bartram, George. A Job Abroad. LC 74-30372. viii, 192 p. (J). 1975. write for info. (*0-02-521030-0*) Mac Bks.

Bartram, Graham & Waine, Anthony, eds. Brecht in Perspective. LC 81-13755. 247p. 1982. pap. 76.60 (*0-608-05245-0*, 206578200001) Bks Demand.

Bartram, Greg & Belavich-Ivac, Lois. Simple Hands-On Science. LC 99-90368. (Illus.). 71p. 1999. 12.95 (*0-9671431-0-1*) New Directns Teachers.

Bartram, J. & Bartram, W. John & William Bartram's America. Cruickshank, Helen G., ed. (American Naturalists Ser.). (Illus.). 1990. pap. 12.95 (*0-8159-5118-3*) Devin.

Bartram, Jamie & Ballance, Richard, eds. Water Quality Monitoring: Practical Guide to the Design & Implementation of Freshwater Quality Studies & Monitoring Program (Illus.). 388p. (C). (gr. 13). 1996. pap. 39.99 (*0-419-21730-4*, E & FN Spon) Routledge.

***Bartram, Jamie & Rees, Gareth.** Monitoring Bathing Waters: A Practical Guide to the Design & Implementation of Assessments & Monitoring Programmes. LC 99-40950. 1999. pap. text. write for info. (*0-419-24380-1*, E & FN Spon) Routledge.

***Bartram, Jamie & Rees, Gareth, eds.** Monitoring Bathing Waters: Practical Guide to Design & Implementation of Assessments & Monitoring Programmes. LC 99-40950. 352p. (C). 2000. text. write for info. (*0-419-24370-4*, E & FN Spon) Routledge.

Bartram, Jamie, jt. ed. see Khorus, Ingrid.

Bartram, John. Observations on the Inhabitants, Climate, Soil, River Productions, Animals & Other Matters Worthy of Notice. 1993. reprint ed. lib. bdg. 89.00 (*0-7812-5425-6*) Rprt Serv.

***Bartram, Peter.** The Perfect Project Manager. 1999. pap. 15.95 (*0-09-940506-7*, Pub. by Random) Trafalgar.

— Writing a Press Release: How to Get the Right Kind of Publicity & News Coverage. 3rd ed. (Illus.). 144p. (Orig.). 1999. pap. 19.95 (*1-85703-485-6*, Pub. by How To Bks) Trans-Atl Phila.

Bartram, Ralph H., jt. auth. see Henderson, Brian.

***Bartram, Sharon.** Evaluating Training: A Resource for Measuring the Results & Impact of Training on People, Departments & Organizations. LC 98-32253. 1999. write for info. (*0-566-07805-8*); write for info. (*0-566-08196-2*) Ashgate Pub Co.

Bartram, Sharon & Gibson, Brenda. Training Needs Analysis: A Resource for Identifying Training Needs, Selecting Training Strategies, & Developing Training Plans. 2nd ed. LC 96-40148. 209p. 1997. text 93.95 (*0-566-07916-X*, Pub. by Gower); ring bd. 144.95 (*0-566-07917-8*, Pub. by Gower) Ashgate Pub Co.

Bartram, W., jt. auth. see Bartram, J.

Bartram, William. Travels. 1955. pap. 8.95 (*0-486-20013-2*) Dover.

— Travels. (Illus.). 432p. 1988. pap. 13.95 (*0-14-025300-9*, Penguin Bks) Viking Penguin.

— Travels & Other Writings. Slaughter, Thomas P., ed. LC 95-49282. (Illus.). 701p. 1996. 40.00 (*1-883011-11-6*, Pub. by Library of America) Penguin Putnam.

— The Travels of William Bartram. (American Biography Ser.). 414p. 1991. reprint ed. lib. bdg. 89.00 (*0-7812-8013-3*) Rprt Serv.

— William Bartram on the Southeastern Indians. Waselkov, Gregory A. & Braund, Kathryn E., eds. LC 94-29756. (Indians of the Southeast Ser.). (Illus.). xvi, 343p. 1995. text 65.00 (*0-8032-4772-9*) U of Nebr Pr.

Bartram, William & Harper, Francis. The Travels of William Bartram. LC 97-52702. 1998. pap. 24.95 (*0-8203-2027-7*) U of Ga Pr.

Bartrip, P. W. Workmen's Compensation in Twentieth Century Britain: Law, History & Social Policy. 180p. 1987. text 82.95 (*0-566-05485-X*, Pub. by Dartmth Pub) Ashgate Pub Co.

Bartron, Harry. Drummer Boy: A Novel of the American Civil War. 1997. 24.95 (*0-533-12275-9*) Vantage.

***Bartrop, Paul R.** Surviving the Camps Vol. XXIII: Unity in Adversity During the Holocaust. (Studies in the Shoah). 232p. 2000. 57.00 (*0-7618-1629-1*); pap. 32.50 (*0-7618-1630-5*) U Pr of Amer.

Bartrop, Paul R., ed. False Havens: The British Empire & the Holocaust. (Studies in the Shoah: Vol. X). 308p. (Orig.). (C). 1995. lib. bdg. 49.00 (*0-8191-9771-8*) U Pr of Amer.

Bartruff, B. Duane. Here Am I Send Me: The Recruitment, Management, & Training of Volunteers. (Orig.). 1993. pap. 9.99 (*0-89900-606-X*) College Pr Pub.

Bartruff, B.Duane. Become the Person You're Meant To Be. 9.99 (*1-85792-064-3*, Pub. by Christian Focus) Spring Arbor Dist.

Bartrum, P. C., ed. Early Welsh Genealogical Tracts. LC 66-66362. 242p. reprint ed. pap. 75.10 (*0-608-14979-9*, 202569800046) Bks Demand.

Bartrum, P. C. & University of Wales Press Staff. Welsh Genealogies, A.D. 300-1400 LC 77-353402. 8 p. 1974. 25.00 (*0-7083-0561-X*) Univ Wales Pr.

Bartrum, Royal J., Jr. & Crow, Harte C. Real-Time Ultrasound: A Manual for Physician & Technical Personnel. 2nd ed. LC 77-72802. (Illus.). 1983. text 65.00 (*0-7216-1552-X*, W B Saunders Co) Harcrt Hlth Sci Grp.

Bartrum, Royal J., jt. auth. see Young, Stuart W.

Bartsch, jt. auth. see O'Neill.

Bartsch, Adam Von, see Koch, Robert A. & Von Bartsch, Adam.

Bartsch, Anna. The Hidden Hand. Bartsch, Arthur, tr. from GER. 234p. 1988. pap. 9.95 (*0-919797-90-3*) Kindred Prods.

Bartsch, Arthur, tr. see Bartsch, Anna.

Bartsch, Charles. Coming Clean for Economic Development: A Resource Book on Environmental Cleanup & Economic Development Opportunities. 170p. 1996. pap. 36.00 (*1-882061-59-4*) Northeast-Midwest.

— Customized Job Training & Economic Development. Murphy, Jenny & Kailo, Andrea, eds. 24p. (Orig.). 1985. pap. 16.00 (*0-317-04859-7*) Natl Coun Econ Dev.

— Job Training Partnership Act. Murphy, Jenny & Kailo, Andrea, eds. 30p. (Orig.). 1984. pap. 16.00 (*0-317-04919-4*) Natl Coun Econ Dev.

Bartsch, Charles, ed. Financing Manufacturing Efficiency & Growth: A Manufacturers Guide to State & Federal Resources. 4th ed. (Illus.). 334p. (C). 1996. pap. text 36.00 (*1-882061-60-8*) Northeast-Midwest.

Bartsch, Charles & Collaton, Elizabeth. Brownfields: Cleaning & Reusing Contaminated Properties. LC 96-20685. 144p. 1997. 55.00 (*0-275-95656-3*, Praeger Pubs) Greenwood.

Bartsch, Charles, et al. Advancing Manufacturing Competitiveness: A Practitioners Guide to Federal Programs. 180p. 1995. pap. text 36.00 (*1-882061-58-6*) Northeast-Midwest.

***Bartsch, Christian.** The Pineal Gland & Cancer: Neuro-Imuno-Endocrine Interactions. LC 00-35760. 2000. write for info. (*3-540-64051-7*) Spr-Verlag.

Bartsch, E. English-German Economic Dictionary: Oekonomisches Worterbuch Englisch-Deutsch. 2nd ed. (ENG & GER.). 784p. 1986. 125.00 (*0-8288-0087-1*, M7753) Fr & Eur.

***Bartsch, Elga.** Liability for Environmental Damages: Incentives for Precaution & Risk Allocation. LC 99-197950. (Illus.). 220p. (C). 1999. text 69.50 (*3-16-146999-2*) JCB Mohr.

Bartsch, Elmar, jt. ed. see Purschel, Heiner.

Bartsch, G. Approaches in Urologic Surgery. LC 94-30311.Tr. of Operative Zugangeswege in der Urologie. (Illus.). 1994. 299.00 (*0-86577-543-5*) Thieme Med Pubs.

Bartsch, H. N-Nitroso Compounds in Carcinogenesis: Occurrence & Biological Effects. (IARC Scientific Publications: No. 41). (Illus.). 672p. 1986. 75.00 (*0-19-723041-5*) OUP.

Bartsch, H., et al, eds. Methods for Detecting DNA Damaging Agents in Humans: Applications in Cancer Epidemiology & Prevention. (IARC Scientific Publications: No. 89). (Illus.). 544p. 1988. pap. 115.00 (*92-832-1189-8*) OUP.

Bartsch, Hans H. & Bengel, Juergen, eds. Salutogenese in der Onkologie Symposium, Freiburg, February, 1995. (Illus.). viii, 126p. 1996. pap. 41.75 (*3-8055-6396-5*) S Karger.

Bartsch, Hans H. & Mertelsmann, R., eds. Knochenmark - und Periphere Stammzelltransplantation: Medizinische Probleme der Posttransplantations - Phase und Rehabilitationsstrategien. (Tumortherapie und Rehabilitation Ser.: Vol. 1). (Illus.). viii, 136p. 1996. pap. 71.50 (*3-8055-6262-4*) S Karger.

Bartsch, Hans H. & Von Hornstein, Wilhelm F., eds. Interdisziplinare Schmerztherapie Bei Tumorpatienten: Strolegen der Akut-Langzeibehandlung. (Band Der). (Illus.). viii, 140p. 1998. pap. 56.50 (*3-8055-6594-1*) S Karger.

Bartsch, Helmut & Singer, Bea, eds. Exocyclic DNA Adducts in Mutagenesis & Carcinogenesis. (IARC Scientific Publications). 400p. 2000. pap. text 69.00 (*92-832-2150-8*) OUP.

Bartsch, Ilse. A Synopsis of the Antarctic Halacaroidea Vol. 4: Synopsis of the Antarctic Benthos. (Theses Zoologicae Ser.: Vol. 21). (Illus.). 176p. 1993. 68.60 (*3-87429-344-0*, Pub. by Koeltz Sci Bks) Lubrecht & Cramer.

Bartsch, Ilse & Schwank, Peter. Gastrotricha und Nemertini. (Suesswasserfauna von Mitteleuropa Ser.: Band 3, 2 parts). (GER., Illus.). 261p. 1989. pap. text 133.00 (*3-437-30606-5*) Balogh.

Bartsch, James A. & Kline, Roger. Produce Handling for Direct Marketing, Vol. 51. (Illus.). 26p. 1992. pap. text 7.00 (*0-935817-31-X*, NRAES-51) NRAES.

***Bartsch, Joel A.** Kremlin Gold: 1000 Years of Russian Gems & Jewels. (Illus.). 192p. 2000. 49.50 (*0-8109-6695-6*, Pub. by Abrams) Time Warner.

Bartsch, John H. School Materials Safety Manual: A Collection of Material Safety Data Sheets (Plus Updating Service) LC 87-14889. 439p. 1987. 129.00 (*0-931690-22-6*) Genium Pub.

Bartsch, Karen & Wellman, Henry M. Children Talk about the Mind. (Illus.). 248p. 1995. text 50.00 (*0-19-508005-X*) OUP.

— Children Talk about the Mind. (Illus.). 248p. 1997. reprint ed. pap. text 24.95 (*0-19-511566-X*) OUP.

Bartsch, Karl F. Chrestomathie Provencale. 6th ed. LC 72-38500. (FRE.). reprint ed. 55.00 (*0-404-08346-3*) AMS Pr.

— Die Lateinischen Sequenzen des Mittelalters in Musikalischer und Rhythmischer Beziehung. 245p. 1967. reprint ed. 65.00 (*0-318-71254-7*) G Olms Pubs.

Bartsch, Karl F. & Koschwitz, Eduard. Chrestomathie Provencale (Tenth-Fifteenth Siecles) xi, 661p. 1971. reprint ed. 115.00 incl. 3.5 hd (*0-318-71315-2*) G Olms Pubs.

Bartsch, Norbert, jt. auth. see Rohrig, Ernst.

***Bartsch-Parker, Elizabeth, et al.** Lonely Planet British Phrasebook. 320p. 1999. pap. 5.95 (*0-86442-484-1*) Lonely Planet.

Bartsch, R., et al. Semantics & Contextual Expression. (Groningen-Amsterdam Studies in Semantics). 336p. (Orig.). (C). 1990. pap. 75.40 (*90-6765-443-4*) Mouton.

Bartsch, Ranate. Situations, Tense, & Aspect: Dynamic Discourse Ontology & the Semantic Flexibility of Temporal System in German & English. (Groningen-Amsterdam Studies in Semantics: No. 13). 1995. 113.85 (*0-614-08071-1*) Mouton.

Bartsch, Renate. Dynamic Conceptual Semantics: A Logico-Philosophical Investigation into Concept Formation & Understanding. (Studies in Logic, Language & Information: No. 15). 296p. (C). 1998. 64.95 (*1-57586-125-9*); pap. 24.95 (*1-57586-124-0*) CSLI.

— Norms of Language. (Linguistics Library). (Illus.). 348p. (C). 1987. pap. text 29.95 (*0-582-00419-5*, 70403) Longman.

— Norms of Language: Theoretical & Practical Aspects. LC 86-27515. (Longman Linguistics Library). (Illus.). 364p. 1987. pap. 112.90 (*0-608-05250-7*, 206578800001) Bks Demand.

— Norms of Language Theoretical & Practical Aspects. Anderson, Mark, ed. (Linguistics Library). 368p. (Orig.). 1988. pap. 18.95 (*0-685-18890-6*) Longman.

— Situations, Tense, & Aspect: Dynamic Discourse Ontology & the Semantic Flexibility of Temporal System in German & English. (Groningen-Amsterdam Studies in Semantics: No. 13). x, 289p. (C). 1995. lib. bdg. 113.85 (*3-11-014584-7*) Mouton.

Bartsch, Richard A. & Maeda, Mizuo, eds. Molecular & Ionic Recognition with Imprinted Polymers, Vol. 703. LC 98-6979. (ACS Symposium Ser.: No. 703). (Illus.). 352p. 1998. text 110.00 (*0-8412-3574-0*) OUP.

Bartsch, Richard A. & Way, J. Douglas, eds. Chemical Separations with Liquid Membranes. LC 96-27197. (ACS Symposium Ser.: No. 642). (Illus.). 432p. 1996. text 125.00 (*0-8412-3447-7*, Pub. by Am Chemical) OUP.

Bartsch, Ron. Aviation Law in Australia. 327p. 1996. pap. 49.00 (*0-455-21376-3*, Pub. by Cavendish Pubng) Gaunt.

Bartsch, Shadi. Actors in the Audience: Theatricality & Doublespeak from Nero to Hadrian. LC 93-48739. (Revealing Antiquity Ser.: No. 6). 320p. 1994. text 43.50 (*0-674-00357-8*, BARACT) HUP.

— Decoding the Ancient Novel: The Reader & the Role of Description in Heliodorus & Achilles Tatius. 360p. (C). 1989. text 39.50 (*0-691-04238-1*, Pub. by Princeton U Pr) Cal Prin Full Svc.

— Decoding the Ancient Novel: The Reader & the Role of Description in Heliodorus & Achilles Tatius. LC 88-37474. 211p. reprint ed. pap. 65.50 (*0-608-20147-2*, 207141900011) Bks Demand.

— Ideology in Cold Blood: A Reading of Lucan's Civil War. LC 97-18200. 240p. 1999. 45.00 (*0-674-44291-1*) HUP.

Bartsch, T., et al. Scriptural & Topical Indices LBW. 1971. 4.50 (*0-89536-727-0*) CSS OH.

Bartsch, Thomas. Topological Methds for Variational Problems with Symmetries. LC 93-41151. (Lecture Notes in Mathematics Ser.: Vol. 1560). x, 152p. 1993. write for info. (*3-540-57378-X*) Spr-Verlag.

***Bartsch, Ulrich & Muller, Benito.** Fossil Fuels in a Changing Climate: Impacts of the Kyoto Protocol & Developing Country Participation. 300p. 2000. text 60.00 (*0-19-730024-3*) OUP.

Bartsch, Uta. Alan Ayckbourns Dramenfiguren. (Anglistische und Amerikanistische Texte und Studien Ser.: Vol. 1). x, 296p. 1986. 45.00 (*3-487-07746-9*) G Olms Pubs.

Bartsch, William H. Doomed at the Start: American Pursuit Pilots in the Philippines, 1941-1942. LC 91-34307. (Military History Ser.: No. 24). (Illus.). 528p. (C). 1995. pap. 18.95 (*0-89096-679-6*) Tex A&M Univ Pr.

Bartsch-Winkler, Susan & Reed, Katherine M., eds. Geologic Studies in Alaska by the U. S. Geological Survey During 1985. (Illus.). 188p. 1998. reprint ed. 26.00 (*0-89904-547-2*, Ecosytems Resrch); reprint ed. pap. 20.00 (*0-89904-548-0*, Ecosytems Resrch) Crumb Elbow Pub.

Bartschat, Klaus, ed. Computational Atomic Physics: Electron & Positron Collisions with Atoms & Ions. (Illus.). 244p. 1996. 74.95 (*3-540-60179-1*) Spr-Verlag.

***Bartschi, Willy.** Foundations/Business Organizations for Paralegals. (C). 2000. pap. 29.75 (*0-7668-1652-4*) Delmar.

Bartscht, Waltraud E. Computer Analysis of Multiple Translations: An Alternative Method for Literary Interpretation. LC 93-9989. (History & Language Ser.: No. 3). 1994. write for info. (*0-8204-2125-1*) P Lang Pubng.

Bartsocas, Christos S. & Loukopoulos, Dimitris, eds. Genetics of Hematological Disorders. 256p. 1991. 140.00 (*1-56032-205-5*) Hemisp Pub.

Bartson, Lester, ed. see Hammond, Mason.

Bartson, Ronald J. & Rabboh, Bob. Principles of Macroeconomics. 4th ed. LC 96-144247. 508p. (C). 1996. pap. text 48.00 (*0-536-59284-5*, HB172) Pearson Custom.

Bartson, Ronald J., jt. auth. see Rabboh, Bob.

Bartson, Ronald J., jt. auth. see Rabboh, Bob A.

Bartstra, G. J., ed. Bird's Head Approaches - Modern Quaternary Research Southeast Asia Vol. 15: Papers Collected for JISR, Irian Jaya Studies - A Programme for Interdisciplinary Research. (Illus.). 275p. (C). 1998. text 76.00 (*90-5410-683-2*, Pub. by A A Balkema) Ashgate Pub Co.

Bartstra, G. J., et al, eds. Modern Quaternary Research in Southeast Asia, Vol. 3. 171p. (C). 1977. text 76.00 (*90-6191-016-1*, Pub. by A A Balkema) Ashgate Pub Co.

Bartstra, G. J. & Casparie, W. A., eds. Modern Quaternary Research in Southeast Asia, Vol. 1. 108p. (C). 1975. text 76.00 (*90-6191-006-4*, Pub. by A A Balkema) Ashgate Pub Co.

— Modern Quaternary Research in Southeast Asia, Vol. 2. 82p. (C). 1976. text 76.00 (*90-6191-013-7*, Pub. by A A Balkema) Ashgate Pub Co.

— Modern Quaternary Research in Southeast Asia, Vol. 4. 80p. (C). 1978. text 76.00 (*90-6191-031-5*, Pub. by A A Balkema) Ashgate Pub Co.

— Modern Quaternary Research in Southeast Asia, Vol. 5. 110p. (C). 1979. text 76.00 (*90-6191-083-8*, Pub. by A A Balkema) Ashgate Pub Co.

— Modern Quaternary Research in Southeast Asia, Vol. 6. 128p. (C). 1981. text 76.00 (*90-6191-219-9*, Pub. by A A Balkema) Ashgate Pub Co.

— Modern Quaternary Research in Southeast Asia, Vol. 7. 246p. (C). 1982. text 76.00 (*90-6191-200-8*, Pub. by A A Balkema) Ashgate Pub Co.

— Modern Quaternary Research in Southeast Asia, Vol. 8. 188p. (C). 1984. text 76.00 (*90-6191-540-6*, Pub. by A A Balkema) Ashgate Pub Co.

— Modern Quaternary Research in Southeast Asia, Vol. 11. 173p. (C). 1990. text 76.00 (*90-6191-883-9*, Pub. by A A Balkema) Ashgate Pub Co.

— Modern Quaternary Research in Southeast Asia Vol. 9: Papers Read at Symposium I, 12th Congress of the Indo-Pacific Prehistory Association, Philippines, 26th Jan.-2nd Feb. 1985. 166p. (C). 1985. text 76.00 (*90-6191-605-4*, Pub. by A A Balkema) Ashgate Pub Co.

Bartstra, G. J., ed. see Buening, K. R.

Bartstra, G. J., ed. see Kempers, A. J.

Bartstra, Gert-Jan, ed. see Stuyts, Inge-Lise M.

B

B

Bartter, Martha A. The Way to Ground Zero: The Atomic Bomb in American Science Fiction, 33. LC 88-15461. (Contributions to the Study of Science Fiction & Fantasy Ser.: No. 33). 290p. 1988. 59.95 (*0-313-25892-9*, BBT/, Greenwood Pr) Greenwood.

Bartunek, Carol. Introduction to World Religions: An Outline & Resource Guide. 92p. (C). 1996. spiral bd. 19.95 (*0-7872-2095-7*) Kendall-Hunt.

Bartunek, Jean M. & Louis, Meryl R. Insider/Outsider Team Research. (Qualitative Research Methods Ser.: Vol. 40). 96p. 1996. 24.00 (*0-8039-7158-3*); pap. 10.50 (*0-8039-7159-1*) Sage.

Bartunek, Jean M., jt. auth. see Kolb, Deborah M.

Bartusch, Nancy. Sign Numbers. (Illus.). 54p. (Orig.). (J). (ps-3). 1988. pap. 5.00 (*0-916708-17-9*) Modern Signs.

***Bartusiak, Marcia.** Einstein's Unfinished Symphony: Listening to the Sounds of Space-Time. 2000. 24.95 (*0-309-06987-4*, Joseph Henry Pr) Natl Acad Pr.

Bartusiak, Marcia. Through a Universe Darkly. 400p. 1995. pap. 12.50 (*0-380-72420-0*, Avon Bks) Morrow Avon.

Bartusiak, Marcia, ed. see National Academy of Sciences Staff.

Bartusis, Mark C. The Late Byzantine Army: Arms & Society, 1204-1453. (Middle Ages Ser.). 464p. 1997. pap. text 18.50 (*0-8122-1620-2*) U of Pa Pr.

Bartuska, George E. Career Fastrax: Your Personal Roadmap for Success. 12p. 1993. 19.95 (*1-57005-000-7*) Tech Res Grp.

— Establishing & Maintaining Major Accounts. (Illus.). 60p. 1993. ring bd. 75.00 (*1-57005-001-5*) Tech Res Grp.

— Fast Priority: Featuring Instant Priority Management. (Illus.). 1993. 49.95 (*1-57005-003-1*) Tech Res Grp.

— Fast Reference: Set of Twenty Business Task Reference Guides. (Illus.). 1993. 75.00 (*1-57005-002-3*) Tech Res Grp.

Bartuska, Tom & Young, Gerald, eds. The Built Environment: A Creative Inquiry into Design & Planning. LC 92-54360. (Illus.). 340p. (C). 1994. pap. text 27.95 (*1-56052-187-2*) Crisp Pubns.

Barty-King, Hugh. Maples Fine Furnishers. 1992. 29.95 (*1-870948-67-X*, Pub. by Quiller Pr) St Mut.

Bartz, Albert E. Basic Statistical Concepts. 4th ed. LC 98-11398. (Illus.). 456p. 1998. 75.00 (*0-13-737180-2*, Merrill Coll) P-H.

— Descriptive Statistics of Education & Behavior. 5th ed. 144p. (C). 1986. pap. text 27.00 (*0-02-306444-7*, Pub. by P-H) S&S Trade.

Bartz, Christine E., ed. see Case, Frederick W., Jr.

Bartz, D., ed. Visualization in Scientific Computing '98: Proceedings of the Eurographics Workshop in Blaubeuren, Germany, April 20-22, 1998. (Illus.). vii, 151p. 1998. pap. 59.95 (*3-211-83209-2*) Spr-Verlag.

Bartz, David & Miller, Laura. Twelve Teaching Methods to Enhance Student Learning. (What Research Says to the Teacher Ser.). 32p. 1991. pap. 3.95 (*0-8106-1093-0*) NEA.

Bartz, Gabriele. Fra Angelico. (Masters Of Italian Art Ser.). (Illus.). 140p. 1998. 19.95 (*3-8290-0246-7*, 520539) Konemann.

Bartz, James L. Company Property: Of Wells Fargo & Co's. Express, 1852-1918. LC 92-75535. 176p. 1993. 54.95 (*1-882824-04-0*); pap. 29.95 (*1-882824-06-7*) Graphic Pubs.

— Company Property: Of Wells Fargo & Co's. Express, 1852-1918. deluxe ed. LC 92-75535. 176p. 1993. lthr. 125.00 (*1-882824-05-9*) Graphic Pubs.

***Bartz, James Lynn.** Messenger Twelve: Gold Dust, Slaves & a Sing-Song Girl. LC 00-90248. 256p. 2000. 24.00 (*0-9678756-0-9*) Westbound.

Bartz, Paul A. Letting God Create Your Day Vol. 1, No. 1: Scripts from the International Broadcast Creation Moments. 84p. (Orig.). (YA). 1989. pap. write for info. (*0-318-65237-4*) Colorsong Prodns.

Bartz, Paul A. & Bible Science Association Editors. Our Miraculous World. LC 86-82927. v, 97 p. 1987. write for info. (*0-8403-4236-5*) Kendall-Hunt.

Bartz-Schmidt, K. U., jt. auth. see Severin, M.

Bartz, Thorsten. Allgegenwartige Fronte - Sozialistische und Linke Kriegsromane in der Weimarer Republik, 1918-1933: Motive, Funktionen und Positionen im Vergleich Mit Nationalistischen Romanen und Aufzeichnungen im Kontext Einer Kriegsliterarischen Debatte. (GER.). 315p. 1997. 57.95 (*3-631-31643-7*) P Lang Pubng.

Bartz, Wayne R., jt. auth. see Vogler, Roger E.

Bartz, Wilfried J., ed. Engine Oils & Automotive Lubrication. LC 92-24358. (Mechanical Engineering Ser.: Vol. 80). (Illus.). 832p. 1992. text 215.00 (*0-8247-8807-9*) Dekker.

Bartzokas, C. A., et al. A Psychological Approach to Hospital-Acquired Infections. LC 94-27126. 164p. 1995. text 79.95 (*0-7734-9030-2*) E Mellen.

Baru, David. The Amnesia Club. 380p. 1996. pap. write for info. (*1-85863-913-1*, Pub. by Minerva Pr) Unity Dist.

Baru, Rama V. Private Health Care in India: A Sociological Inquiry. LC 98-28220. 1998. write for info. (*0-7619-9286-3*) Sage.

Baru, Sanjaya. The Political Economy of Indian Sugar: State Intervention & Structural Change. 240p. 1990. 21.00 (*0-19-562423-8*) OUP.

Barua, Amol K. Mind & Mental Factors in Early Buddhist Psychology. (C). 1990. text 21.00 (*81-85119-54-6*, Pub. by Northern Bk Ctr) S Asia.

Barua, B. P. Eminent Thinkers in India & Pakistan. (C). 1991. text 14.00 (*81-7095-025-2*) S Asia.

***Barua, Benimadhab.** A History of Pre-Buddhistic Indian Philosophy. 1998. 36.00 (*81-208-0796-0*) Motilal Bnarsidass.

Barua, Bharati. A Study of the Socio-Religious Ceremony of Upanayana: Investiture with Sacred Thread in the Sutras & the Dharmasastra. (C). 1995. 16.00 (*81-85094-77-2*, Pub. by Punthi Pus) S Asia.

Barua, D. & Greenough, W. B. Cholera. (Current Topics in Infectious Disease Ser.). (Illus.). 392p. (C). 1992. text 69.50 (*0-306-44077-6*, Kluwer Plenum) Kluwer Academic.

Barua, Deepali. Urban History of India (A Case Study) LC 94-902288. (C). 1995. 22.50 (*81-7099-538-8*, Pub. by Motilal Bnarsidass) S Asia.

Barua, Pradeep. Race, Politics & Military Modernization in Later Colonial India. 212p. 1998. pap. 25.00 (*0-85958-668-5*, Pub. by Univ of Hull Pr) Paul & Co Pubs.

Barua, S. N. Tribes of Indo-Burma Border. (C). 1991. 36.00 (*81-7099-308-3*, Pub. by Mittal Pubs Dist) S Asia.

Baruah, A. K. Systems Analysis in Political Science: A Marxist Critique of David Easton. 208p. (C). 1987. 37.95 (*81-85024-25-1*, Pub. by Uppal Pub Hse) Asia Bk Corp.

Baruah, Hrishikesh, jt. auth. see Das, Pradip K.

Baruah, S. L. Comprehensive History of Assam. (C). 1995. 36.00 (*81-215-0015-X*, Pub. by M Manoharial) Coronet Bks.

Baruah, Sangita, jt. auth. see Gunda, Kavita.

Barucci, Valentina, et al. Maximality Properties in Numerical Semigroups & Applications to One-Dimensional Analytically Irreducible Local Domains. LC 96-44757. (Memoirs of the American Mathematical Society Ser.: Vol. 125/598). 78p. 1997. pap. 36.00 (*0-8218-0544-4*, MEMO/125/598) Am Math.

Baruch & Kennedy, Robert F., Jr. Alternative Conventional Defense, Vol. 2. 1991. 75.00 (*0-8448-1600-0*, Crane Russak) Taylor & Francis.

Baruch, Bernard. Baruch: My Own Story. 1993. reprint ed. lib. bdg. 41.95 (*1-56849-095-X*) Buccaneer Bks.

— The Public Years. 1993. reprint ed. lib. bdg. 24.95 (*1-56849-096-8*) Buccaneer Bks.

— Short Sales & Manipulation of Securities. 67p. 1997. pap. 19.95 (*1-883272-19-X*) Traders Lib.

Baruch, Elaine H. Embryos, Ethics, & Woman's Rights: Exploring the New Reproductive Technologies. D'Adamo, Amadeo F. et al, eds. LC 87-38148. (Women & Health Ser.: Vol. 13, Nos. 1-2). 259p. 1988. pap. 19.95 (*0-918393-45-0*, Harrington Park) Haworth Pr.

— Women Analyze Women: In France, England, & the United States. 424p. (C). 1991. pap. text 18.50 (*0-8147-1170-7*) NYU Pr.

— Women, Love, & Power: Literary & Psychoanalytic Perspectives. 288p. (C). 1992. pap. text 18.50 (*0-8147-1199-5*) NYU Pr.

Baruch, Elaine H. & Serrano, Lucienne J. She Speaks, He Listens: Women on the French Analysts' Couch. 207p. (C). 1995. pap. 17.99 (*0-415-91127-3*) Routledge.

Baruch, Elaine Hoffman, et al, eds. Embryos, Ethics, & Women's Rights Exploring the New Reproductive Technologies. LC 87-38147. (Women & Health Ser.: Vol. 13, Nos. 1-2). (Illus.). 259p. 1988. text 49.95 (*0-86656-707-0*) Haworth Pr.

Baruch, Grace K., jt. auth. see Barnett, Rosalind C.

Baruch, Jacques-Olivier. Incredibly Fast. LC 93-462. (Frontiers of the Invisible Ser.). (Illus.). 48p. (YA). (gr. 6 up). 1993. lib. bdg. 14.95 (*0-02-708435-3*, New Dscvry Bks) Silver Burdett Pr.

Baruch, L., jt. auth. see Whitehead, A. K.

Baruch, Maurice. Russian Portraits in Watercolour: 1825-1855. 1997. 98.00 (*2-909838-07-2*) A Gourcuff.

Baruch, Miriam S. Diary of the "Y" 120p. 1978. write for info. (*0-8187-0049-1*) Harlo Press.

Baruchel, J., et al, eds. Neutron & Synchrotron Radiation for Condensed Matter Studies Vol. I: Theory, Instruments & Methods. 468p. 1993. pap. 59.00 (*0-387-56561-2*) Spr-Verlag.

— Neutron & Synchrotron Radiation for Condensed Matter Studies Vol. II: Applications to Soft Condensed Matter & Biology. 310p. 1994. 61.95 (*0-387-57693-2*) Spr-Verlag.

— Neutron & Synchrotron Radiation for Condensed Matter Studies Vol. II: Applications to Solid State Physics & Chemistry, Vol. 2. 321p. 1994. 61.95 (*0-387-57691-6*) Spr-Verlag.

Baruchello, Gianfranco & Martin, Henry. How to Imagine: A Narrative on Art & Agriculture. LC 83-14954. 160p. 1984. 20.00 (*0-914232-51-7*, Documentext) McPherson & Co.

— How to Imagine: A Narrative on Art & Agriculture. limited ed. LC 83-14954. 160p. 1984. 200.00 (*0-914232-53-3*, Documentext) McPherson & Co.

— The Imagination of Art, Set. (Illus.). 320p. 1986. reprint ed. 18.00 (*0-914232-81-9*) McPherson & Co.

— Why Duchamp: An Essay on Aesthetic Impact. LC 85-11544. 160p. 1985. 20.00 (*0-914232-71-1*); pap. 10.00 (*0-914232-73-8*) McPherson & Co.

— Why Duchamp: An Essay on Aesthetic Impact. deluxe ed. LC 85-11544. 160p. 1985. 400.00 (*0-914232-72-X*) McPherson & Co.

Baruchovitch, Schneur Z. Likkutei Amarim Tanya: Bi-Lingual Edition. Schochet, J. Immanuel et al, trs. LC 84-82007. 1006p. 1993. reprint ed. 25.00 (*0-8266-0400-5*) Kehot Pubn Soc.

— Maamorei Admur Hazoken. 460p. reprint ed. 17.00 (*0-8266-5566-1*, 5566); reprint ed. 17.00 (*0-8266-5569-6*, 5569); reprint ed. 17.00 (*0-8266-5570-X*, 5570) Kehot Pubn Soc.

— Maamorei Admur Hazoken: Bereishes Ushemos. 574p. reprint ed. 17.00 (*0-8266-5472-X*) Kehot Pubn Soc.

— Maamorei Admur Hazoken: Hanochos. 238p. reprint ed. 17.00 (*0-8266-5559-9*) Kehot Pubn Soc.

— Maamorei Admur Hazoken: 5565, Vol. 1. 592p. reprint ed. 17.00 (*0-8266-5465-7*, 5565) Kehot Pubn Soc.

— Maamorei Admur Hazoken: 5565, Vol. 2. 556p. reprint ed. 17.00 (*0-8266-5466-5*, 5565) Kehot Pubn Soc.

— Maamorei Admur Hazoken Vol. 2: 5562. (HEB.). 426p. reprint ed. 17.00 (*0-8266-5462-2*, 5562); reprint ed. 17.00 (*0-8266-5469-X*, 5568) Kehot Pubn Soc.

— Maamorei Admur Hazoken Ha'ktzorim: Hakzorim. (HEB.). 653p. reprint ed. 17.00 (*0-8266-5561-0*) Kehot Pubn Soc.

— Shulchon Oruch, Vol. 1. (HEB.). reprint ed. 11.25 (*0-8266-5502-5*) Kehot Pubn Soc.

— Shulchon Oruch, Vol. 2. (HEB.). reprint ed. 11.25 (*0-8266-5503-3*) Kehot Pubn Soc.

— Shulchon Oruch, Vol. 3. (HEB.). reprint ed. 11.25 (*0-8266-5504-1*) Kehot Pubn Soc.

— Shulchon Oruch, Vol. 4. (HEB.). reprint ed. 11.25 (*0-8266-5505-X*) Kehot Pubn Soc.

Baruchovitch, Schneur Zalman. Lessons in Tanya. Kaploun, Uri, ed. Wineberg, Sholom B., tr. (Lessons in Tanya Ser.: Vol. 3). 320p. 1991. 17.00 (*0-8266-0543-5*) Kehot Pubn Soc.

Baruchovitsh, Shneur Z. Maamorei Admur Hazoken: Inyonim. 608p. reprint ed. 17.00 (*0-8266-5476-2*) Kehot Pubn Soc.

— Maamorei Admur Hazoken: Nevi'im. 376p. reprint ed. 17.00 (*0-8266-5474-6*) Kehot Pubn Soc.

— Maamorei Admur Hazoken: Vayikro Devorim. 606p. reprint ed. 17.00 (*0-8266-5473-8*) Kehot Pubn Soc.

— Maamorei Admur Hazoken Vol. 2: Ketubim. 602p. reprint ed. 17.00 (*0-8266-5475-4*) Kehot Pubn Soc.

Baruchson-Arbib, Shifra. Social Information Science: Love, Health & the Information Society the Challenge of the 21st Century. LC 97-29574. 124p. 1996. pap. 22.95 (*1-898723-36-2*, Pub. by Sussex Acad Pr) Intl Spec Bk.

Barucki. Architecture Is Elementary: Visual Thinking Through Architectural Concepts. pap. text. write for info. (*0-471-48946-8*) Wiley.

Barugel, Alberto. The Sacrifice of Isaac in the Spanish & Sephardic Balladry. (American University Studies: Romance Languages & Literature: Ser. II, Vol. 116). XII, 242p. (C). 1991. text 49.95 (*0-8204-0954-5*) P Lang Pubng.

Baruh, Haim. Analytical Dynamics. LC 98-34940. 744p. 1998. 106.56 (*0-07-365977-0*) McGraw.

Barui, Balai. The Salt Industry of Bengal, 1757-1800. 1985. 17.50 (*0-8364-1478-0*, Pub. by KP Bagchi) S Asia.

Baruk, Stella. Dictionnaire de Mathematiques. (FRE.). 1360p. 1995. 225.00 (*0-7859-9943-4*) Fr & Eur.

Barus, Carl. Experiments with the Displacement Interferometer. LC 15-26885. (Carnegie Institution of Washington Publication Ser.: No. 229). 119p. reprint ed. pap. 36.90 (*0-608-30470-0*, 200312900020) Bks Demand.

Barusch, Amanda S. Elder Care: Family Training & Support. (Sourcebooks for the Human Services Ser.: Vol. 18). (Illus.). 200p. 1991. text 56.00 (*0-8039-4227-3*); pap. text 26.00 (*0-8039-4185-4*) Sage.

— Elder Care: Family Training & Support. LC 91-11225. (Sage Sourcebooks for the Human Services Ser.: No. 18). (Illus.). 213p. 1991. reprint ed. pap. 66.10 (*0-608-04299-4*, 206507800012) Bks Demand.

— Older Women in Poverty: Private Lives & Public Policies. LC 94-12588. (Illus.). 272p. (C). 1994. 34.95 (*0-8261-7960-6*) Springer Pub.

Baruss, Imants. Authentic Knowing: The Convergence of Science & Spiritual Aspiration. LC 95-20709. (Illus.). 240p. 1996. 37.95 (*1-55753-084-X*); pap. 18.95 (*1-55753-085-8*) Purdue U Pr.

— The Personal Nature of Notions of Consciousness: A Theoretical & Empirical Examination of the Role of the Personal in the Understanding of Consciousness. 228p. (C). 1990. lib. bdg. 42.00 (*0-8191-7707-5*) U Pr of Amer.

Barut. Nonlinear Equations. 1978. text 126.50 (*90-277-0936-X*) Kluwer Academic.

Barut, Asim O. Electrodynamics & Classical Theory of Fields & Particles. (Illus.). 256p. 1980. pap. text 7.95 (*0-486-64038-8*) Dover.

— Selected Popular Writings of E. U. Condon. Van Der Merwe, Alwyn, ed. (Illus.). 304p. 1991. 59.95 (*0-387-97421-0*) Spr-Verlag.

Barut, Asim O., ed. Foundations of Radiation Theory & Quantum Electrodynamics. LC 79-25715. (Illus.). 230p. 1980. 69.50 (*0-306-40277-7*, Plenum Trade) Perseus Pubng.

— New Frontiers in Quantum Electrodynamics & Quantum Optics. LC 90-7932. (NATO ASI Ser.: Vol. 232). (Illus.). 620p. (C). 1990. text 191.00 (*0-306-43669-8*, Kluwer Plenum) Kluwer Academic.

— Quantum Theory, Groups, Fields & Particles. 1983. text 180.50 (*90-277-1552-1*) Kluwer Academic.

Barut, Asim O., et al, eds. Selected Scientific Papers of E. U. Condon. (Illus.). 632p. 1991. 145.95 (*0-387-97420-2*) Spr-Verlag.

— Spin & Polarization Dynamics in Nuclear & Particle Physics. 372p. (C). 1990. text 141.00 (*981-02-0018-8*) World Scientific Pub.

Barut, Asim O. & Brittin, Wesley E., eds. Boulder Lectures in Theoretical Physics, 1967 Vol. 10a: Quantum Theory & Statistical Physics, Vol. 10. x, 572p. 1968. text 323.00 (*0-677-12890-8*) Gordon & Breach.

— Topics in Strong Interactions. LC 72-197924. (Lectures in Theoretical Physics: No. 14A). (Illus.). 479p. reprint ed. pap. 148.50 (*0-8357-5512-6*, 203512700093) Bks Demand.

Barut, Asim O. & Doebner, H. D., eds. Conformal Groups & Related Symmetries - Physical Results & Mathematical Background. (Lecture Notes in Physics Ser.: Vol. 261). vi, 443p. 1986. 64.95 (*0-387-17163-0*) Spr-Verlag.

Barut, Asim O. & Raczka, R. Theory of Group Representations & Applications. 740p. 1986. text 99.00 (*9971-5-0216-X*); pap. text 54.00 (*9971-5-0217-8*) World Scientific Pub.

Barut, Asim O. & Van Der Merwe, Alwyn, eds. Selected Scientific Papers of Alfred Lande. (C). 1987. text 267.50 (*90-277-2594-2*) Kluwer Academic.

Barut, Asim O., et al. Dynamical Groups & Spectrum Generating Algebra, 2 vols. 1168p. (C). 1988. pap. text 106.00 (*9971-5-0147-3*) World Scientific Pub.

— Dynamical Groups & Spectrum Generating Algebra, 2 vols., Vol. I. 1168p. (C). 1988. text 240.00 (*9971-5-0146-5*) World Scientific Pub.

— Polarization Dynamics in Nuclear & Particle Physics. 450p. 1993. text 121.00 (*981-02-1423-5*) World Scientific Pub.

— Quantum Systems: New Trends & Methods. 420p. 1995. text 122.00 (*981-02-2099-5*) World Scientific Pub.

Barut, Asim O., ed. see Conference on De Sitter & Conformal Groups & Their.

Barut, Asim O., ed. see NATO Advanced Study Institute Staff.

Baruth, Leroy G. & Huber, Charles H. An Introduction to Marital Theory & Therapy. LC 83-14275. (Psychology Ser.). 300p. 1984. text 28.50 (*0-534-02820-9*) Brooks-Cole.

— An Introduction to Marital Theory & Therapy. 332p. (C). 1991. reprint ed. pap. text 22.95 (*0-88133-608-4*) Waveland Pr.

Baruth, Leroy G. & Manning, Lee M. Multicultural Counseling & Psychotherapy: A Lifespan Perspective. 2nd ed. LC 98-7606. 426p. 1998. pap. text 67.00 (*0-13-271925-8*, Merrill Coll) P-H.

Baruth, Leroy G. & Manning, M. Lee. Support Services Renewal in Education. Bailey, William J., ed. (Educational Leadership for the 21st Century Ser.: Vol. 1). 274p. 1995. 39.95 (*1-56676-203-0*, 762030) Scarecrow.

Baruth, Leroy G., jt. auth. see Huber, Charles H.

Baruth, Leroy G., jt. auth. see Manning, M. Lee.

Baruth, Philip E. The Dream of the White Village: A Novel in Stories. LC 98-65692. 333p. 1998. 24.00 (*0-9657144-1-1*) Onion River Pr.

— The Dream of the White Village: A Novel in Stories. LC 98-65692. 333p. 1999. pap. 14.00 (*0-9657144-2-X*) Onion River Pr.

— Introducing Charlotte Charke: Actress, Author, Enigma. LC 98-8907. 1998. 47.50 (*0-252-02415-X*); pap. 19.95 (*0-252-06723-1*) U of Ill Pr.

— The Millennium Shows. 160p. (Orig.). 1994. pap. 12.95 (*0-9637025-5-6*) Albion Bks.

Baruzzi, A., et al, eds. From Luigi Galvani to Contemporary Neurobiology: Contributions to the Celebration of the IX Centenary of the University of Bologna, Bologna, 27-28 September, 1988. (FIDIA Research Ser.: Vol. 22). vii, 193p. 1990. 90.00 (*0-387-97229-3*) Spr-Verlag.

Barve, Betty. Alaskan Dog Mushers Trail Food & Old Fashion Recipe Book. (ENG.). 100p. 1989. pap. text 9.00 (*1-57833-055-6*) Todd Commns.

Barve, Lavon. Preserving Alaskan Style. (ENG.). 127p. 1992. pap. text 8.00 (*1-57833-056-4*) Todd Commns.

Barwald, Werner. Office & Data Communication French-German, German-French. (FRE & GER.). 197p. 1993. 125.00 (*0-8288-7384-4*, 3861170183) Fr & Eur.

Barwell, Anna, tr. see Von Hanstein, Otfrid.

Barwell, F. T. Bearing Systems: Principles & Practice. (Illus.). 1980. 98.00 (*0-19-856319-1*) OUP.

Barwell, Ian. Transport & the Village: Findings from African Village-Level Travel & Transport. LC 96-34972. 77p. 1996. pap. 22.00 (*0-8213-3747-5*, 13747) World Bank.

— Le Transport et le Village: Conclusions d'Une Serie d'Eniquetes-Villages et d'Etudes de Cas Realisees en Afrique. (Discussion Paper Ser.: No. 344F). 83p. 1998. pap. 22.00 (*0-8213-4225-8*, 14225) World Bank.

Barwell, Ian & Hathway, George. The Design & Manufacture of Animal Drawn Carts. (Illus.). 122p. 1986. pap. 21.00 (*0-946688-52-4*, Pub. by Intermed Tech) Stylus Pub VA.

Barwell, Ian, jt. auth. see Dawson, Jonathan.

***Barwell, Keith.** Hitler Youth: The Hitlerjugend in Peace & War, 1933-1945. (Illus.). 192p. 2000. 24.95 (*0-7603-0946-9*, 130679AP, Pub. by MBI Pubg) Motorbooks Intl.

Barwick, D., et al. Metaphors of Interpretation: Essays in Honour of W. E. H. Stanner. LC 84-71361. (Illus.). 318p. 1987. pap. text 38.00 (*0-08-029875-3*, Pergamon Pr) Elsevier.

Barwick, Daniel. Intentional Implications: The Impact of a Reduction of Mind on Philosophy. 172p. (Orig.). 1994. pap. text 26.50 (*0-8191-9515-4*); lib. bdg. 49.50 (*0-8191-9514-6*) U Pr of Amer.

***Barwick, Dee D. & Fertig, Judith, eds.** This Place Called Home - A Kansas City Cookbook. 192p. 1998. pap. 17.95 (*1-892431-19-X*) KCPT.

Barwick, Frances. Pictures from the Douglas M. Duncan Collection. LC 74-75587. 160p. reprint ed. pap. 49.60 (*0-608-12795-7*, 202349100033) Bks Demand.

Barwick, Garfield, ed. Australian Commentary to Halsbury's Laws of England, 8 vols. ring bd. 787.00 (*0-409-30938-9*, MICHIE) LEXIS Pub.

Barwick, Gary, jt. auth. see Kay, Betty Carlson.

Barwick, Humphrey. Concerning the Force & Effect of Manual Weapons of Fire. LC 74-80163. (English Experience Ser.: No. 643). 86p. 1974. reprint ed. 20.00 (*90-221-0643-8*) Walter J Johnson.

Barwick, Jo Ann, ed. see House Beautiful Magazine Editors.

Barwick, Kathryn. Pollution Prevention in California: An Overview of California's Pollution Prevention Programs & Technologies. (Illus.). 108p. (Orig.). (C). 1995. pap. text 30.00 (*0-7881-2398-X*) DIANE Pub.

Barwick-Kuhnert, ed. Charisii. (LAT.). 1997. 89.50 (*3-8154-1137-8*, T1137, Pub. by B G Teubner) U of Mich Pr.

Barwick, Mary. The Alabama Angels. (Illus.). 64p. 1993. 15.00 (*0-345-38574-8*) Ballantine Pub Grp.
— The Alabama Angels in Anywhere, L. A. (Lower Alabama) (Illus.). 32p. (Orig.). (J). 1991. pap. 8.95 (*0-9622815-6-5*, Black Belt) Black Belt Communs.
— Alabama Angels Join H. E. M. A. (Illus.). 32p. 1995. pap. 8.95 (*1-881320-63-4*, Black Belt) Black Belt Communs.
Barwick, Nancie M. Beyond Disability: Toward Self-Acceptance & Peace. large type ed. Hansgen, K. C., ed. 105p. 1997. pap. 15.00 (*0-9663488-0-X*) Hypnotherapy Wrks.
***Barwick, Nick.** Clinical Counselling in Schools. LC 99-58558. (Clinical Counselling in Context Ser.). 2000. pap. write for info. (*0-415-20517-4*) Routledge.
Barwick, Samuel O. Barwick Family of the U. S. Concise History of Barwicks from the Time of Their Coming to This Country In . . . 1652 & 1664 up to (1907), the Lost Links of Their Genealogy Found & the Barwicks of the East, West & South. 78p. 1997. reprint ed. pap. 16.00 (*0-8328-7403-5*); reprint ed. lib. bdg. 26.00 (*0-8328-7402-7*) Higginson Bk Co.
Barwick, Sandra. Diana Remembered, 1961-1997. (Illus.). 120p. 1998. text 25.00 (*0-7881-5887-2*) DIANE Pub.
Barwig, Susan & Hilliard, Stewart. Schutzhund: Theory & Training Methods. (Illus.). 256p. 1991. 24.95 (*0-87605-731-8*) Howell Bks.
***Barwin, Gary.** Grandpa's Snowman. (Illus.). 24p. (J). (ps-1). 2000. lib. bdg. 17.95 (*1-55037-635-7*, Pub. by Annick Pr); per. 5.95 (*1-55037-634-9*, Pub. by Annick Pr) Firefly Bks Ltd.
— The Magic Mustache. (Illus.). 32p. (J). (gr. k-3). 1999. text 17.95 (*1-55037-607-1*, Pub. by Annick Pr) Firefly Bks Ltd.
Barwin, Gary. Outside the Hat. 114p. 1998. pap. 19.95 (*1-55245-030-9*, Pub. by Coach Hse Bks) SPD-Small Pr Dist.
— The Racing Worm Brothers. (Illus.). 32p. (YA). (ps up). 1998. pap. 5.95 (*1-55037-540-7*, Pub. by Annick Pr); lib. bdg. 15.95 (*1-55037-541-5*, Pub. by Annick Pr) Firefly Bks Ltd.
Barwin, Gary & Jorisch, Stephane. The Magic Mustache. (Illus.). 32p. (J). (gr. k-3). 1999. pap. 6.95 (*1-55037-606-3*, Pub. by Annick Pr) Firefly Bks Ltd.
Barwin, Steven & Tick, Gabriel D. Slam Dunk. LC 98-930371. (Sports Stories Ser.). 88p. (J). (gr. 3-8). 1998. text 5.50 (*1-55028-598-X*, Pub. by J Lorimer) Formac Dist Ltd.
Barwis, J. H., et al, eds. Sandstone Petroleum Reservoirs. (Casebooks in Earth Sciences Ser.). (Illus.). xv, 583p. 1990. 175.00 (*0-387-97217-X*) Spr-Verlag.
Barwise. Health: Health & Wellbeing. LC 94-33850. (Environmental Agenda Ser.). (C). pap. 8.95 (*0-7453-0929-1*, Pub. by Pluto GBR) Stylus Pub VA.
Barwise, J. Handbook of Mathematical Logic. (Studies in Logic & the Foundations of Mathematics: No. 90). xii,1166p. 1982. pap. 50.00 (*0-444-86388-5*, North Holland) Elsevier.
Barwise, J. & Feferman, Solomon, eds. Model-Theoretic Logics. (Perspectives in Mathematical Logic Ser.). (Illus.). 750p. 1985. 318.95 (*0-387-90936-2*) Spr-Verlag.
Barwise, Joanne. Animal Tracks of Western Canada. (Illus.). 128p. 1989. pap. 5.95 (*0-919433-20-0*) Lone Pine.
Barwise, Jon. The Situation in Logic. LC 88-38961. (CSLI Lecture Notes Ser.: No. 17). 337p. 1988. 64.95 (*0-937073-33-4*); pap. 19.95 (*0-937073-32-6*) CSLI.
Barwise, Jon, et al, eds. Situation Theory & Applications, Vol. 2. (Center for the Study of Language & Information-Lecture Notes Ser.). xii, 625p. 1991. 74.95 (*0-937073-71-7*); pap. 29.95 (*0-937073-70-9*) CSLI.
Barwise, Jon & Etchemendy, John. Hyperproof. LC 93-30747. (CSLI Lecture Notes Ser.: No. 42). 1995. pap. 31.95 incl. disk (*1-881526-11-9*) CSLI.
— The Language of First-Order Logic: Including the Macintosh (TM) Program Tarski's World 4.0. 3rd rev. ed. LC 93-419. (CSLI Lecture Notes Ser.: No. 23). 322p. 1993. pap. 37.50 incl. disk (*0-937073-99-7*) CSLI.
— Language, Proof & Logic. LC 99-41113. (Illus.). 530p. (C). 1999. pap. text 43.95 (*1-889119-08-3*) Seven Bridges.
— Tarski's World 4.0: IBM-Compatible Windows Version 4.0. LC 93-30042. (CSLI Lecture Notes Ser.: No. 45). 142p. (C). 1993. pap. 23.95 incl. disk (*1-881526-28-3*) CSLI.
— Tarski's World 4.0: Version 4.0 for the Macintosh. LC 93-30034. (CSLI Lecture Notes Ser.: No. 25). 144p. (C). 1993. pap. 23.95 incl. disk (*1-881526-27-5*) CSLI.
Barwise, Jon & Moss, Lawrence S. Vicious Circles: On the Mathematics of Non-Wellfounded Phenomena. (Lecture Notes Ser.). 350p. (C). 1996. 69.95 (*1-57586-009-0*); pap. 24.95 (*1-57586-008-2*) CSLI.
Barwise, Jon & Perry, John. Situations & Attitudes. LC 99-14053. (David Hume Ser.). 376p. (C). 1999. reprint ed. pap. text 22.95 (*1-57586-193-3*) CSLI.
Barwise, Jon & Seligman, Jerry. Information Flow: The Logic of Distribued Systems. (Cambridge Tracts in Theoretical Computer Science Ser.: No. 44). 290p. (C). 1997. text 39.95 (*0-521-58386-1*) Cambridge U Pr.
Barwise, Jon, jt. ed. see Allwein, Gerard.
Barwise, K. J. Admissible Sets & Structures: An Approach to Definability Theory. (Perspectives in Mathematical Logic Ser.). (Illus.). 400p. 1976. 123.95 (*0-387-07451-1*) Spr-Verlag.
Barwise, Patrick & Ehrenberg, Andrew. Television & It's Audience. 224p. (C). 1989. text 39.95 (*0-8039-8154-6*); pap. text 16.95 (*0-8039-8155-4*) Sage.
***Barwise, Patrick & Hammond, Kathy.** The Future of Media. (Predictions Ser.). 58p. 1999. pap. 3.95 (*0-297-81988-7*, Pub. by Weidenfeld & Nicolson) Trafalgar.
Barwise, Patrick, jt. ed. see Papadakis, Vassilis.
Barwold, Johannes. Paleocology of Volcanic Soils in the Columbian Central Cordillera (Parque Nacional Natural de los Nevados) (Dissertationes Botanicae Ser.: Band 95). (Illus.). 212p. 1986. pap. 53.00 (*3-443-64007-9*, Pub. by Gebruder Borntraeger) Balogh.
Bary, Brett de, see Karatani, Kojin.
Bary, David, tr. from SPA. A Tooth for a Tooth: Selected Poems of Juan Larrea (1925-1932) LC 86-28093. 142p. 1987. lib. bdg. 34.50 (*0-8191-5753-8*) U Pr of Amer.
Bary, N. & Mullins, M. Treatise on Trigonometric Series, Vol. 1. LC 63-12682. 1964. 246.00 (*0-08-010002-3*, Pub. by Pergamon Repr) Franklin.
— Treatise on Trigonometric Series, Vol. 2. LC 63-12682. 1964. 240.00 (*0-08-011307-9*, Pub. by Pergamon Repr) Franklin.
Bary Nee, Brett De, see Nee, Victor G. & De Bary Nee, Brett.
Bary, Valeska, jt. auth. see Cahn, Frances.
Bary, William T. de. East Asian Civilizations: A Dialogue in Five Stages. LC 87-14928. (Edwin O. Reischauer Lectures). 176p. 1988. 27.50 (*0-674-22405-1*) HUP.
Bary, William T. De, see De Bary, William T.
Bary, William T. De, see Saikaku, Ihara & De Bary, William T.
Bary, William T. De, see De Bary, William T.
Bar'yakhtar, V. Physics Reviews Vol. 16, Pt. 3: Solitons & Thermodynamics of Low-Dimensions Magnets, Vol. 16. (Soviet Scientific Reviews Ser.: Section A). 253p. 1992. pap. text 319.00 (*3-7186-5383-4*, Harwood Acad Pubs) Gordon & Breach.
Baryakhtar, V. G., et al, eds. Plasma Theory & Nonlinear & Turbulent Processes in Physics: Proceedings of the 3rd International Workshop on Nonlinear & Turbulent Processes in Physics, 2 vols., I. 1000p. (C). 1988. text 239.00 (*9971-5-0546-0*) World Scientific Pub.
Baryakhtar, V. G., et al. Dynamics of Topological Magnetic Solitons: Experiment & Theory. LC 94-12048. (Springer Tracts in Modern Physics Ser.: Vol. 129). 1994. 96.95 (*0-387-56935-9*) Spr-Verlag.
Bar'Yakhtar, V. G., et al. Nonlinear World - Fourth International Workshop on Nonlinear & Turbulent Processes in Physics, 2 vols., 1. 1540p. 1990. text 298.00 (*981-02-0271-7*) World Scientific Pub.
— Nonlinear World - Fourth International Workshop on Nonlinear & Turbulent Processes in Physics, 2 vols., Set. 1540p. 1990. text. write for info. (*981-02-0272-5*) World Scientific Pub.
***Baryakhtar, V. G., et al.** Theory of Adiabatic Potential & Atomic Properties of Simple Metals. 336p. 1999. text 125.00 (*90-5699-088-8*, Harwood Acad Pubs) Gordon & Breach.
Baryakhtar, V. G., ed. see Krivoglaz, Mikhail A.
Baryla, Michael. Building Intranets with IBM Internet Connection Server & Lotus Domino. LC 97-34129. (ITCP-US Computer Science Ser.). 350p. 1997. pap. 49.99 (*1-85032-897-8*) ITCP.
Barylski, Robert V. The Soldier in Russian Politics, 1985-1996. LC 97-51704. 624p. 1997. text 59.95 (*1-56000-335-9*) Transaction Pubs.
Baryshnik, Jeff. Fee Free Investing: How To Buy Stocks & Bonds & Never Pay A Broker'S Fee. 272p. 1999. pap. 13.95 (*0-385-25899-2*) Bantam.
Barz, Brigitte. Festivals with Children. (J). 1988. pap. 10.50 (*0-86315-055-1*, 20241, Pub. by Floris Bks) Gryphon Hse.
Barz, Ellynor. Gods & Planets: The Archetypes of Astrology. Matthews, Boris, tr. from GER. LC 93-17281. (Illus.). 216p. (Orig.). 1993. pap. 16.95 (*0-933029-71-3*) Chiron Pubns.
Barz, Gregory F. & Cooley, Timothy J., eds. Shadows in the Field: New Perspective for Fieldwork in Ethnomusicology. (Illus.). 256p. 1996. pap. 19.95 (*0-19-510911-2*) OUP.
Barz, Helmut. For Men, Too: A Grateful Critique of Feminism. Ziegler, Katherine, tr. from GER. LC 90-25651. 144p. (Orig.). 1991. pap. 3.95 (*0-933029-42-X*) Chiron Pubns.
Barz, Irmhild & Schroder, Marianne, eds. Nominationsforschung Im Deutschen. (Illus.). 499p. 1997. 73.95 (*3-631-31366-7*) P Lang Pubng.
Barz, Patrick Le, see Dias, Danielle & Le Barz, Patrick.
Barz, Richard C. Bhakti Sect of Vallabhacarya. (C). 1992. reprint ed. 24.00 (*81-215-0576-3*, Pub. by M Manoharial) Coronet Bks.
Barz, Richard C. & Yadav, Yogendra. An Introduction to Hindi & Urdu. 342p. (C). 1993. 37.50 (*81-215-0605-0*, Pub. by M Manoharial) Coronet Bks.
Barz, Sandra B., ed. Inuit Artists Print Workbook, Vol. I. (Illus.). 324p. 1981. pap. 30.00 (*0-9605898-0-5*) Arts & Culture.
— Inuit Artists Print Workbook, Vol. II. 324p. 1990. pap. 50.00 (*0-9605898-1-3*) Arts & Culture.
Barzan, Robert. Sacred Sex: How to Live an Erotic Life. 20p. 1998. pap. 4.95 (*0-9645384-5-8*) White Crane.
Barzan, Robert, ed. Sex & Spirit: Exploring Gay Men's Spirituality. LC 95-60287. 144p. (Orig.). 1995. pap. 10.95 (*0-9645384-0-7*) White Crane.
Barzan, Robert, jt. auth. see Gilson, James.
Barzansky, Barbara M. & Gevitz, Norman, eds. Beyond Flexner: Medical Education in the Twentieth Century, 34. LC 91-24333. (Contributions in Medical Studies: No. 34). 264p. 1992. 59.95 (*0-313-25984-4*, BMU, Greenwood Pr) Greenwood.
Barzansky, Barbara M., jt. ed. see Garg, Mohan L.
Barzanti, Sergio. The Underdeveloped Areas Within the Common Market. LC 65-10822. 447p. reprint ed. pap. 138.60 (*0-8357-7064-8*, 205228900085) Bks Demand.
Barzdins, J. & Bjorner, D., eds. Baltic Computer Science: Selected Papers. (Lecture Notes in Computer Science Ser.: Vol. 502). x, 619p. 1991. 63.95 (*0-387-54131-4*) Spr-Verlag.
Barzdukas, Audrius. Goldminds: Gold Medal Mental Strategies for Everyday Life. LC 92-53279. (Illus.). 120p. (Orig.). 1995. pap. 14.00 (*1-884125-21-2*) Cooper Pubng.
Barzel, Ronen. Physically-Based Modeling for Computer Graphics: A Structured Approach. (Illus.). 334p. 1992. text 48.00 (*0-12-079880-8*) Acad Pr.
Barzel, Yoram. Economic Analysis of Property Rights. 2nd ed. LC HB701.B37 1997. (Political Economy of Institutions & Decisions Ser.). (Illus.). 175p. (C). 1997. text 54.95 (*0-521-59275-5*); pap. text 17.95 (*0-521-59713-7*) Cambridge U Pr.
— Productivity Change, Public Goods & Transaction Costs: Essays at the Boundaries of Microeconomics. (Economists of the Twentieth Century Ser.). 512p. 1995. 110.00 (*1-85898-076-3*) E Elgar.
Barzelay, Martin E. & Lacy, George W. Scientific Automobile Accident Reconstruction, 6 vols., Set. 1964. ring bd. 1070.00 (*0-8205-1343-1*) Bender.
Barzelay, Michael. Breaking Through Bureaucracy: A New Vision for Managing in Government. 1992. pap. 17.95 (*0-520-07801-2*, Pub. by U CA Pr) Cal Prin Full Svc.
***Barzelay, Michael.** The New Public Management: Improving Research & Policy Dialogue. LC 00-55168. 2001. write for info. (*0-520-22443-4*) U CA Pr.
Barzelay, Michael & Amajani, Babak J. Breaking Through Bureaucracy: A New Vision for Managing in Government. (C). 1992. 48.00 (*0-520-07800-4*, Pub. by U CA Pr) Cal Prin Full Svc.
Barzetti, Valerie & Rovinski, Yanina, eds. Toward a Green Central America: Integrating Conservation & Development. LC 92-9644. (Illus.). 128p. (Orig.). reprint ed. pap. 39.70 (*0-608-20809-4*, 207190800003) Bks Demand.
Barzilai, Gad. Wars, Internal Conflicts, & Political Order: A Jewish Democracy in the Middle East. LC 92-37349. (SUNY Series in Israeli Studies). 311p. (C). 1996. text 71.50 (*0-7914-2943-1*); pap. text 23.95 (*0-7914-2944-X*) State U NY Pr.
***Barzilai, Shuli.** Lacan & the Matter of Origins. LC 99-39702. 1999. pap. text 19.95 (*0-8047-3382-1*) Stanford U Pr.
Barzilay, Isaac, jt. ed. see Baron, Salo W.
Barzilay, Joshua. Water We Drink: Water Quality & Its Effects on Health. 1999. write for info. (*0-8135-2657-3*) Rutgers U Pr.
Barzilay, Joshua, et al. The Water We Drink: Water Quality & Its Effects on Health. LC 98-55318. 1999. 40.00 (*0-8135-2698-1*); pap. 17.00 (*0-8135-2673-6*) Rutgers U Pr.
Barzini, Luigi. The Italians. LC 63-17858. 352p. (C). 1977. pap. 13.00 (*0-689-70540-9*, 225) Macmillan.
— The Italians. 1990. 24.50 (*0-8446-6146-5*) Peter Smith.
— The Italians. 384p. 1996. per. 13.00 (*0-684-82500-7*) S&S Trade.
Barzman, John, tr. see Debeir, Jean-Claude, et al.
Barzman, Karen E., jt. contrib. by see Feinberg, Larry J.
***Barzman, Karen-Edis.** The Florentine Academy & the Early Modern State: The Discipline of "Disegno" LC 99-37545. (Illus.). 400p. (C). 2000. 75.00 (*0-521-64162-4*) Cambridge U Pr.
Barzotti, Dominique, jt. auth. see Le Hellaye, Catherine.
Barzun, Isabel, tr. see Fabre, Michel J.
Barzun, Jacques. The American University: How It Runs, Where It Is Going. LC 92-28479. xxxvi, 356p. (C). 1992. pap. text 15.95 (*0-226-03845-9*) U Ch Pr.
— Begin Here: The Forgotten Conditions of Teaching & Learning. Philipson, Morris, ed. 234p. 1991. 24.95 (*0-226-03846-7*) U Ch Pr.
— Begin Here: The Forgotten Conditions of Teaching & Learning. Philipson, Morris, ed. LC 90-25877. 234p. 1992. pap. 12.95 (*0-226-03847-5*) U Ch Pr.
— Berlioz & His Century: An Introduction to the Age of Romanticism. LC 81-16072. 448p. (C). 1982. reprint ed. pap. 18.95 (*0-226-03861-0*) U Ch Pr.
— The Bibliophile of the Future: His Complaints About the Twentieth Century. 1976. 3.00 (*0-89073-048-2*, 174) Boston Public Lib.
— Classic, Romantic & Modern. xvi, 272p. 1975. pap. text 12.95 (*0-226-03852-1*, P643) U Ch Pr.
— Clio & the Doctors: History, Psycho-History, & Quanto-History. LC 74-5723. (Midway Reprint Ser.). xii, 186p. 1989. reprint ed. pap. text 18.00 (*0-226-03857-3*) U Ch Pr.
— Critical Questions: On Music & Letters, Culture & Biography, 1940-1980. Friedland, Bea, ed. LC 81-22023. 288p. 1982. lib. bdg. 27.00 (*0-226-03863-7*) U Ch Pr.
— Critical Questions: On Music & Letters, Culture & Biography, 1940-1980. Friedland, Bea, ed. LC 81-22023. 288p. 1984. pap. 10.95 (*0-226-03864-5*) U Ch Pr.
— The Culture We Deserve. Krystal, Arthur, ed. LC 88-33927. 197p. 1990. pap. 15.95 (*0-8195-6237-8*, Wesleyan Univ Pr) U Pr of New Eng.
— Darwin, Marx, Wagner: Critique of a Heritage. 2nd ed. LC 80-27274. xxii, 396p. 1981. pap. text 21.00 (*0-226-03859-9*) U Ch Pr.
— An Essay on French Verse - for Readers of English Poetry. LC 90-48759. 192p. 1991. 12.95 (*0-8112-1157-6*, Pub. by New Directions) Norton.
— From Dawn to Decadence: 500 Years of Western Cultural Life - 1500 to the Present. LC 99-16194. 816p. 2000. 36.00 (*0-06-017586-9*, HarpCollins) HarperTrade.
— God's Country & Mine. LC 73-3919. 344p. 1973. reprint ed. lib. bdg. 35.00 (*0-8371-6860-0*, BAGC, Greenwood Pr) Greenwood.
— The House of Intellect. (Midway Reprint Ser.). viii, 274p. 1975. pap. text 15.00 (*0-226-03855-6*) U Ch Pr.
— The House of Intellect. LC 77-28070. 276p. 1978. reprint ed. lib. bdg. 59.50 (*0-313-20071-8*, BAHI, Greenwood Pr) Greenwood.
— Is Democratic Theory for Export? Sixth Morgenthau Memorial Lecture on Ethics & Foreign Policy. 30p. (Orig.). 1986. pap. text 4.00 (*0-87641-227-4*) Carnegie Ethics & Intl Affairs.
— The Modern Researcher. 5th ed. (C). 1992. pap. text 33.50 (*0-15-562513-6*, Pub. by Harcourt Coll Pubs) Harcourt.
— The Modern Researcher. 6th ed. (C). 2002. pap. text 31.00 (*0-15-505529-1*) Harcourt Coll Pubs.
— Of Human Freedom. 2nd rev. ed. LC 76-47651. 212p. 1977. reprint ed. lib. bdg. 38.50 (*0-8371-9321-4*, BAOH, Greenwood Pr) Greenwood.
— On Writing, Editing, & Publishing: Essays Explicative & Hortatory. LC 85-16562. (Chicago Guides to Writing, Editing & Publishing Ser.). 160p. (C). 1986. pap. 8.95 (*0-226-03858-0*) U Ch Pr.
— Race: A Study in Superstition. rev. ed. LC 78-63649. (Studies in Fascism: Ideology & Practice). 288p. reprint ed. 34.50 (*0-404-16899-X*) AMS Pr.
— Simple & Direct: A Rhetoric for Writers. rev. ed. LC 93-47049. 314p. (C). 1994. pap. 15.00 (*0-226-03868-8*) U Ch Pr.
— A Stroll with William James. LC 84-2612. viii, 352p. 1983. reprint ed. lib. bdg. 30.00 (*0-226-03865-3*) U Ch Pr.
— A Stroll with William James. LC 84-2612. 352p. 1984. reprint ed. pap. 14.95 (*0-226-03866-1*) U Ch Pr.
— Teacher in America. LC 80-82370. 496p. 1981. reprint ed. 14.00 (*0-913966-78-9*); reprint ed. pap. 6.00 (*0-913966-79-7*) Liberty Fund.
— Teacher in America. 328p. (C). 1986. reprint ed. pap. text 28.50 (*0-8191-5447-4*) U Pr of Amer.
Barzun, Jacques, ed. Pleasures of Music: An Anthology of Writings about Music & Musicians from Cellini to Bernard Shaw. abr. ed. 382p. 1977. pap. text 13.50 (*0-226-03854-8*, P727) U Ch Pr.
Barzun, Jacques & Graff, Henry F. The Modern Researcher. 5th ed. LC 91-74063. (Illus.). 416p. 1992. 24.95 (*0-395-64494-1*) HM.
— The Modern Researcher. 5th ed. 400p. (C). 1992. pap. text. write for info. (*0-318-69122-1*) Harcourt Coll Pubs.
Barzun, Jacques & Taylor, Wendell H. A Catalogue of Crime: A Reader's Guide to the Literature of Mystery, Detection, & Related Genres. LC 88-45884. 864p. (YA). (gr. 7 up). 1989. 50.00 (*0-06-010263-2*) HarperTrade.
Barzun, Jacques, et al. Research Philosophy & Techniques: Selected Readings. 2nd ed. Lewis, Christine L., ed. LC 92-71748. 172p. 1992. pap. text 32.00 (*0-89462-070-3*, ARP101) IIA.
Barzun, Jacques, ed. see Metzger, Walter P. & Reece, J. McGee.
Barzun, Jacques, tr. see Diderot, Denis.
Barzun, Jacques, tr. see Flaubert, Gustave.
Barzun, Jacques, tr. & intro. see Berlioz, Hector.
Bas, C., et al, eds. Flora Agaricina Neerlandica, Vol. 1. (Illus.). 1500p. (C). 1988. text 70.00 (*90-6191-859-6*, Pub. by A A Balkema) Ashgate Pub Co.
Bas, C., et al. Flora Agaricina Neerlandica, Vol. 2. 160p. 1990. 70.00 (*90-6191-971-1*, Pub. by A A Balkema) Ashgate Pub Co.
— Flora Agaricina Neerlandica, Vol. 3. (Illus.). 190p. (C). 1995. pap. 43.00 (*90-5410-617-4*, Pub. by A A Balkema); text 70.00 (*90-5410-616-6*, Pub. by A A Balkema) Ashgate Pub Co.
***Bas, C., et al.** Flora Agaricina Neerlandica, Vol. 6. (Illus.). 190p. 2001. write for info. (*90-5410-496-1*, Pub. by A A Balkema) Ashgate Pub Co.
— Flora Agaricina Neerlandica, Vol. 7. (Illus.). 190p. 2002. text. write for info. (*90-5410-499-6*, Pub. by A A Balkema) Ashgate Pub Co.
— Flora Agaricina Neerlandica: Critical Monographs on Families of Agarics & Boleti Occuring in the Netherlands, Vol. 5. (Illus.). 190p. 2000. text. write for info. (*90-5410-494-5*, Pub. by A A Balkema) Ashgate Pub Co.
— Flora Agaricina Neerlandica Vol. 4: Critical Monographs on Families of Agarics & Boleti Occurring in the Netherlands. (Illus.). 190p. (C). 1999. text 75.00 (*90-5410-492-9*, Pub. by A A Balkema); pap. text 45.00 (*90-5410-493-7*, Pub. by A A Balkema) Ashgate Pub Co.
Bas, Ed. Indoor Air Quality in the Building Environment. LC 93-7908. 1993. 17.95 (*0-912524-82-0*) Busn News.
Bas, Joe, jt. ed. see Carter, E. Dale, Jr.
Bas, Tom Le, see Le Bas, Tom, ed.
Basa, Eniko M. Hungarian Literature. (Review of National Literatures Ser.: Vol. 17). 192p. 1993. pap. 14.95 (*0-918680-35-2*) Griffon House.
Basadur, Min. Power of Innovation: How to Make Innovation a Way of Life & How to Put Creative Solutions... LC 95-19365. (Illus.). 330p. 1994. 28.95 (*0-273-61362-6*) F T P-H.
Basadur, Min & Pitts, Barbara. Applications in Organizational Behaviour. 162p. (C). 1991. 29.60 (*0-536-58012-X*) Pearson Custom.
Basagni, Fabio & Uri, Pierre, eds. Monetary Relations & World Development. LC 77-15650. 137p. 1977. 47.95 (*0-275-90254-4*, C0254, Praeger Pubs) Greenwood.
Basak, Amitava. Analogue Electronic Circuits & Systems. (Electronics Texts for Engineers & Scientists Ser.). (Illus.). 375p. (C). 1991. text 115.00 (*0-521-36046-3*); pap. text 49.95 (*0-521-36913-4*) Cambridge U Pr.
— Permanent-Magnet DC Linear Motors. LC 96-204958. (Monographs in Electrical & Electronic Engineering). (Illus.). 200p. (C). 1996. text 80.00 (*0-19-859392-9*) OUP.
Basak, Amitava, jt. ed. see Moses, A. J.
Basak, Sudeshna. Socio-Cultural Study of a Minority Linguistic Group. (C). 1990. text 28.00 (*81-7018-627-7*, Pub. by BR Pub) S Asia.

B

Basakat, Ibtisam, tr. from ENG. How to Begin in Re-Evaluation Counseling. (ARA.). 16p. 1999. pap. 1.00 (*1-58429-050-1*) Rational Isl.

Basal Mission Staff. Grammar of the Modern Kannada Language. (ENG & KAN.). 176p. 1988. 29.95 (*0-8288-8419-6*, M14133) Fr & Eur.

— A Kannada Vocabulary of Some Homonyms & Technical Words. 1984. 29.95 (*0-8288-1766-9*, M14133) Fr & Eur.

Basaldua, Emilio, et al. The Journal of Decorative & Propaganda Arts No. 18/1992: Argentine Theme Issue. (SPA.). 119p. (Orig.). 1992. pap. 6.00 (*0-9631601-1-7*) Wolfson Fnd D&P Arts.

— The Journal of Decorative & Propaganda Arts No. 18/1992: Argentine Theme Issue. (Illus.). 250p. (Orig.). 1992. pap. 25.00 (*0-9631601-0-9*) Wolfson Fnd D&P Arts.

Basalla, George. The Evolution of Technology. (Cambridge History of Science Ser.). (Illus.). 256p. 1989. pap. text 17.95 (*0-521-29681-1*) Cambridge U Pr.

Basalla, George & Palter, Robert. The Annus Mirabilis of Sir Isaac Newton: An Exhibit of Books & Manuscripts from the History of Science Collection. (Illus.). 32p. 1966. 5.00 (*0-87959-121-8*) U of Tex H Ransom Ctr.

***Basalla, Susan & Debelius, Maggie.** So What Are You Going to Do with That? The Complete Guide to Post-Academic Careers. 256p. 2001. pap. 15.00 (*0-374-52621-4*) FS&G.

Basaly, Nadia A., jt. ed. see Billatos, Samir B.

Basan, Ghillie. Classic Turkish Cooking. LC 96-39854. (Illus.). 1997. text 29.95 (*0-312-15617-0*) St Martin.

Basan, Paul B., ed. Trace Fossil Concepts. LC QE0719.B3. (Society of Economic Paleontologists & Mineralogists, Special Publication Ser.: No. 5). (Illus.). 185p. reprint ed. pap. 57.40 (*0-608-15487-3*, 202967500062) Bks Demand.

Basanes, Federico, et al, eds. Can Privatization Deliver? Infrastructure for Latin America. LC 99-71691. (Illus.). 347p. 1999. pap. text 19.95 (*1-886938-38-5*) IADB.

Basansky, Bea. The Ultimate Woman. rev. ed. 160p. 1992. reprint ed. pap. 8.95 (*0-9632190-8-1*) Longwood.

— The Ultimate Woman Study Guide. pap. 4.00 (*0-9632190-2-2*) Longwood.

Basansky, Bill. How to Know the Father's Voice. 112p. 1992. pap. 5.99 (*0-89274-888-5*, HH-888) Harrison Hse.

— How to Live Above Fear & Anxiety. 32p. 1991. pap. 3.00 (*0-89274-058-2*, HH-058) Harrison Hse.

— The Life & Power of the Blood Covenant. 96p. 1993. pap. 7.00 (*0-89274-824-9*, HH-824) Harrison Hse.

— The Miracle of New Life: Minibook. 48p. 1992. pap. 1.00 (*0-89274-896-6*, HH-896) Harrison Hse.

— Power of the Renewed Mind. 48p. 1991. pap. 3.00 (*0-89274-021-3*, HH-021) Harrison Hse.

— Renewing the Mind Through the Word. 48p. 1991. pap. 3.00 (*0-89274-023-X*, HH-023) Harrison Hse.

Basansky, William. Hereditary Traits: Breaking the Destructive Cycle of Hereditary Influence. 240p. (Orig.). 1992. pap. 9.95 (*0-9632190-1-4*) Longwood.

Basant, Rakesh, jt. auth. see Visaria, Pravin.

Basar, E. Brain Function & Oscillations: Integrative Brain Function. Neurophysiology & Cognitive Processes. Haken, H., ed. (Springer Series in Synergetics). (Illus.). xiv, 350p. 1998. 89.95 (*3-540-64345-1*) Spr-Verlag.

— Brain Oscillations: Principles & Approaches. LC 98-3612. (Series in Synergetics). (Illus.). 250p. 1998. 89.95 (*3-540-64338-9*) Spr-Verlag.

Basar, E. & Bullock, Theodore H., eds. Induced Rhythms in the Brain. (Brain Dynamics Ser.). (Illus.). 480p. 1992. 193.00 (*0-8176-3537-8*) Birkhauser.

Basar, T. & Olsder, G. J. Dynamic Noncooperative Game Theory. LC 98-46719. (Classics in Applied Mathematics: Vol. 23). (Illus.). xv, 519p. 1998. reprint ed. pap. text 49.50 (*0-89871-429-X*, BKCL0023) Soc Indus-Appl Math.

Basar, Tamer S., ed. Dynamic Games & Applications in Economics. (Lecture Notes in Economics & Mathematical Systems Ser.: Vol. 265). ix, 288p. 1986. 41.70 (*0-387-16435-9*) Spr-Verlag.

Basar, Tamer S. & Bernard, P., eds. Differential Games & Applications. (Lecture Notes in Control & Information Sciences: Vol. 119). (Illus.). 201p. 1989. 45.95 (*0-387-50758-2*) Spr-Verlag.

Basar, Tamer S. & Bernhard, P. Hs-Optimal Control & Related Minimax Design Problems: A Dynamic Game Approach. (Systems & Control: Foundations & Applications Ser.). 240p. 1991. 49.50 (*0-8176-3554-8*) Birkhauser.

Basar, Tamer S. & Bernhard, Pierre. H-Optimal Control & Related Minimax Design Problems: A Dynamic Game Approach. 2nd ed. LC 95-34333. (Systems & Control Ser.). 411p. 1995. 71.00 (*0-8176-3814-8*); write for info. (*3-7643-3814-8*) Birkhauser.

Basar, Tamer S. & Haurie, Alain, eds. Advances in Dynamic Games & Applications. LC 94-937. (Annals of the International Society of Dynamic Games Ser.: Vol. 1). 418p. 1994. 87.50 (*0-8176-3691-9*) Birkhauser.

Basara, Lisa R. & Montagne, Michael. Searching for Magic Bullets: Orphan Drugs, Consumer Activism, & Pharmaceutical Development. LC 93-35534. (Illus.). 276p. 1994. pap. 14.95 (*1-56024-859-9*) Haworth Pr.

— Searching for Magic Bullets: Orphan Drugs, Consumer Activism, & Pharmaceutical Development. LC 93-35534. (Illus.). 276p. 1994. lib. bdg. 39.95 (*1-56024-858-0*) Haworth Pr.

Basarab, David J., Sr. & Root, Darrell K. The Training Evaluation Process: A Practical Approach to Evaluating Corporate Training Programs. LC 92-25675. (Evaluation in Education & Human Services Ser.). 288p. (C). 1992. lib. bdg. 90.00 (*0-7923-9266-3*) Kluwer Academic.

Basarich, Joel V., ed. Initiation a la Science de la Gestion, Edition 1995: FLMI 340. (FLMI Insurance Education Program Ser.). (FRE.). 93p. pap. 20.00 (*0-939921-65-0*, Pub. by Life Office) PBD Inc.

Basarich, Joel V., ed. see Desouttes, Nicholas, et al.

Basarich, Joel V., ed. see Goodwin, Dennis W.

Basarich, Joel V., ed. see Huggins, Kenneth.

Basarich, Joel V., ed. see Huggins, Kenneth, et al.

Basarich, Joel V., ed. see Jones, Harriett E.

Basarich, Joel V., ed. see Polk, Dean L.

Basaroff, F. The Sacrament of Matrimony According to the Doctrine & Ritual of the Eastern Orthodox Church. Bjerring, N., tr. from RUS. 1977. pap. 1.95 (*0-89981-081-0*) Eastern Orthodox.

Basart, Ann P. Serial Music: A Classified Bibliography of Writings on 12 Tone & Electronic Music. LC 75-45460. 151p. 1976. reprint ed. lib. bdg. 49.75 (*0-8371-8753-2*, BASM, Greenwood Pr) Greenwood.

Basava, C. & Anantharamaiah, G. M. Peptides: Design, Synthesis, & Biological Activity. 352p. 1994. 76.50 (*0-8176-3703-6*) Birkhauser.

Basavaraj, B. H. & Williams, B., eds. Pipeline Engineering, 1993. LC 82-77407. 77p. 1993. pap. 30.00 (*0-7918-0952-8*, H00784) ASME.

Basawa, I. V. & Taylor, R. L., eds. Selected Proceedings of the Sheffield Symposium on Applied Probability. LC 91-77908. (IMS Lecture Notes - Monographs: Vol. 18). x, 278p. 1992. pap. 15.00 (*0-940600-25-0*) Inst Math.

Basawa, I. V., jt. ed. see Prabhu, N. U.

Basawa, Ishwar V., et al, eds. Selected Proceedings of the Symposium on Estimating Equations. LC 97-77203. (Lecture Notes-Monograph Ser.: Vol. 32). 1998. pap. 69.00 (*0-940600-44-7*) Inst Math.

Basawa, Ishwar V & Rao, Prakasa, eds. Statistical Inference for Stochastic Processes. LC 79-50533. (Probability & Mathematical Statistics Ser.). 1980. text 100.00 (*0-12-080250-3*) Acad Pr.

Basawa, Ishwar V & Scott, D. J. Asymptotic Optimal Inference for Non-Ergodic Models. (Lecture Notes in Statistics Ser.: Vol. 17). 170p. 1983. 54.95 (*0-387-90810-2*) Spr-Verlag.

Basawa, Ishwarasa V., jt. ed. see Bhat, Ramdas B.

Basayne, Henry S. & Janowitz, Linda R. Let Us Make a Wedding! A Guidebook for Creating Your Own Ceremony. (Illus.). 200p. (Orig.). 1993. pap. 15.95 (*0-9637071-0-8*) Basayne-Janowitz.

— Weddings: The Magic of Creating Your Own Ceremony. LC 99-23465. 220p. 1999. pap. 19.95 (*1-885221-92-4*) BookPartners.

Basbanes, Nicholas. A Gentle Madness. Date not set. pap. 17.95 (*0-8050-4826-X*) H Holt & Co.

— Lives Beyond Life. Date not set. write for info. (*0-8050-5015-9*) H Holt & Co.

Basbanes, Nicholas A. A Gentle Madness: Bibliophiles, Bibliomane & the Eternal Passion for Books. LC 94-33931. (Illus.). 638p. 1995. 35.00 (*0-8050-3653-9*) H Holt & Co.

— A Gentle Madness: Bibliophiles, Bibliomanes, & the Eternal Passion for Books. LC 99-226880. (Illus.). 656p. 1999. pap. 18.95 (*0-8050-6176-2*, Pub. by H Holt & Co) VHPS.

Basbaum, A. I. & Besson, Jean-Marie, eds. Towards a New Pharmacotherapy of Pain. LC 90-42921. (Dahlem Workshop Reports - Life Sciences). 468p. 1991. 369.95 (*0-471-92854-2*) Wiley.

Bascand, Geoffrey M., jt. auth. see Browne, Christopher.

Bascetta, Cynthia A. Social Security Disability: SSA Must Hold Itself Accountable for Continued Improvement in Decision-Making. (Illus.). 75p. (C). 1998. pap. text 20.00 (*0-7881-7546-7*) DIANE Pub.

Basch, E. E. Optical Fiber Transmission. 1996. 79.95 (*0-614-18453-3*, B11021) Info Gatekeepers.

Basch, Ernst. The Fascist: His State & His Mind. LC 72-180386. (Studies in Fascism: Ideology & Practice). reprint ed. 41.50 (*0-404-56101-2*) AMS Pr.

Basch, Harry, jt. auth. see Slater, Shirley.

Basch, Hary, jt. auth. see Slater, Shirley.

Basch, Lester D. & Finkelstein, Milton. Spelling Made Easy. 1974. pap. 3.00 (*0-87980-288-X*) Wilshire.

Basch, Linda, et al. Nations Unbound: Transnational Projects, Postcolonial Predicaments, & Deterritorialized Nation-States. LC 93-28765. 344p. 1993. text 55.00 (*2-88124-607-9*); pap. text 27.00 (*2-88124-630-3*) Gordon & Breach.

***Basch, Linda G. & Craven, Roberta Jill.** Transforming Academia: Challenges & Opportunities for An Engaged Anthropology LC 99-30178. (American Ethnological Society Monograph Ser.). 1999. write for info. (*0-913167-92-4*) Am Anthro Assn.

***Basch, Margaret.** Every Woman Should Go to Law School or Read This Book. LC 99-55366. 256p. 2000. pap. 14.00 (*0-06-095360-8*, HarpRes) HarpInfo.

Basch, Marty. Above the Circle. LC 97-90363. 170p. (Orig.). 1997. pap. text 14.95 (*0-9646510-1-7*) Top of the Wrld.

— Against the Wind: A Maine to Alaska Bicycling Adventure. (Illus.). 152p. 1995. pap. 12.95 (*0-9646510-0-9*) Top of the Wrld.

— The White Mountain Ride Guide. LC 98-60319. (Illus.). 168p. 1998. pap. 12.95 (*0-9646510-2-5*) Top of the Wrld.

— Winter Trails of Maine: The Best Cross-Country Ski & Snowshoe Trails. LC 99-37535. (Illus.). 224p. 1999. pap. text 14.95 (*0-7627-0556-6*) Globe Pequot.

— Winter Trails of Vermont & New Hampshire: The Best Cross Country & Snowshoe Trails. LC 98-36049. (Winter Trails Ser.: Vol. 1). (Illus.). 24p. 1998. pap. 11.95 (*0-7627-0305-9*) Globe Pequot.

Basch, Michael, tr. see Rektorys, Karel.

Basch, Michael F. Doing Psychotherapy. LC 79-3084. 188p. 1980. pap. 40.00 (*0-465-01684-7*, Pub. by Basic) HarpC.

— Practicing Psychotherapy: A Casebook. LC 91-55601. 224p. 1992. 42.00 (*0-465-06175-3*, Pub. by Basic) HarpC.

— Understanding Psychotherapy: The Science Behind the Art. LC 88-47763. (Illus.). 352p. 1990. pap. 17.00 (*0-465-08860-0*, Pub. by Basic) HarpC.

Basch, Michal, tr. see Bunke, Helga & Bunke, Olaf, eds.

Basch, Miguel & Morales, Camilo, eds. Expanding Access to Financial Services in Latin America. LC 96-75386. (Inter-American Development Bank Ser.). 284p. (Orig.). (C). 1995. pap. text 18.50 (*1-886938-02-4*) IADB.

Basch, N. Bernard & McQueen, Judy. Buying Serials: A How-to-Do-It Manual for Librarians. (How-to-Do-It Ser.). 188p. 1990. pap. text 49.95 (*1-55570-058-6*) Neal-Schuman.

***Basch, Norma.** Framing American Divorce: From the Revolutionary Generation to the Victorians. LC 98-33947. 258p. 1999. 29.95 (*0-520-21490-0*, Pub. by U CA Pr) Cal Prin Full Svc.

Basch, Norma. In the Eyes of the Law: Women, Marriage, & Property in Nineteenth-Century New York. fac. ed. LC 82-2454. 256p. 1982. reprint ed. pap. 79.40 (*0-608-01008-1*, 206186600012) Bks Demand.

Basch, Paul F. International Health. (Illus.). 392p. 1978. text 29.95 (*0-19-502328-5*) OUP.

— Textbook of International Health. 2nd ed. LC 98-50118. (Illus.). 576p. 1999. text 59.50 (*0-19-513204-1*) OUP.

— Vaccines & World Health: Science, Policy & Practice. LC 93-23283. (Illus.). 288p. 1994. text 49.95 (*0-19-508532-9*) OUP.

Basch, Peter, jt. auth. see Gwynne, Fred.

***Basch, Rachel.** Degrees of Love. LC 98-30754. 368p. 1999. mass mkt. 6.50 (*0-06-101404-4*) HarpC.

Basch, Rachel. Degrees of Love: A Novel. LC 97-40319. 256p. 1998. 23.95 (*0-393-04625-7*) Norton.

Basch, Reva. Electronic Information Delivery: Ensuring Quality & Value. LC 94-12967. 272p. 1995. 96.95 (*0-566-07567-9*, Pub. by Gower) Ashgate Pub Co.

— Researching Online for Dummies. LC ZA4201.B36 1998. (For Dummies Ser.). 384p. 1998. pap. 24.99 incl. cd-rom (*0-7645-0382-0*) IDG Bks.

***Basch, Reva.** Researching Online for Dummies. 2nd ed. 408p. 2000. pap. 24.99 incl. cd-rom (*0-7645-0546-7*) IDG Bks.

Basch, Reva. Secrets of the Super Net Searchers: The Reflections, Revelations & Hard-Won Wisdom of 35 of the World's Top Internet Researchers. LC 97-106242. (Cyber Age Bks.). 340p. (Orig.). 1996. pap. 29.95 (*0-910965-22-6*) Info Today Inc.

— Secrets of the Super Searchers: The Accumulated Wisdom of 23 of the World's Top Online Searchers. 238p. 1993. pap. 39.95 (*0-910965-12-9*) Info Today Inc.

Basch, Reva, ed. see Bates, MaryEllen.

Basch, Reva, ed. see Detwiler, Susan.

Basch, Reva, ed. see Hane, Paula J.

Basch, Reva, ed. see Tudor, Jan.

Basch, Shari. Best of Internet Activities. LC 99-226251. (Illus.). 1999. pap., teacher ed. 24.95 (*1-57690-449-0*, TCM2449) Tchr Create Mat.

Basch, Victor. Schumann, a Life of Suffering. Phillips, Catherine A., tr. LC 76-107791. (Select Bibliographies Reprint Ser.). 1977. 24.95 (*0-8369-5175-1*) Ayer.

— Schumann, a Life of Suffering. (Music Book Index Ser.). 243p. 1992. reprint ed. lib. bdg. 79.00 (*0-7812-9468-1*) Rprt Serv.

Basche, T., ed. Optical Probing of Single Molecules. 250p. 1996. 305.00 (*3-527-29316-7*) Wiley.

Baschek, B., et al, eds. New Aspects of Magellanic Cloud Research: Proceedings of the European Meeting on the Magellanic Clouds, 2nd, Heidelberg, Germany, 1992. LC 92-45282. (Lecture Notes in Physics Ser.: Vol. 416). 1993. 96.95 (*0-387-56432-2*) Spr-Verlag.

Baschek, B., jt. auth. see Unsold, A.

Baschiera, Dino, et al. Genesis Lunar Outpost: Criteria & Design. Hansmann, Timothy & Moore, Gary T., eds. (Publications in Architecture & Urban Planning: No. R90-1). (Illus.). xii, 107p. (C). 1990. 13.00 (*0-938744-69-0*) U of Wis Ctr Arch-Urban.

Baschnagel, Jhorg, jt. auth. see Paul, Wolfgang.

Baschwitz Institute for Public Opinion & Mass Psyc, jt. auth. see Institute for Political Science Staff.

Bascia, Nina. Unions in Teachers' Professional Lives: Social, Intellectual, & Practical Concerns. LC 93-45998. (Series on School Reform). 128p. (C). 1994. text 34.00 (*0-8077-3339-3*); pap. text 15.95 (*0-8077-3338-5*) Tchrs Coll.

Bascietto. Ecosystem Toxicology for Environmental Management. 1997. write for info. (*0-87371-471-7*, L471) Lewis Pubs.

Bascio, Patrick. The Failure of White Theology: A Black Theological Perspective. LC 93-24030. (Martin Luther King, Jr., Memorial Studies in Religion, Culture, & Social Development: Vol. 3). 168p. (C). 1994. text 37.95 (*0-8204-2257-6*) P Lang Pubng.

Bascio, Patrick, jt. auth. see Novikov, Euvgeny.

Basco, Monica R. & Rush, A. John. Cognitive-Behavioral Therapy for Bipolar Disorder. LC 96-13739. 291p. 1996. lib. bdg. 36.00 (*1-57230-090-6*) Guilford Pubns.

Basco, Monica Ramirez. Never Good Enough: Freeing Yourself from the Chains of Perfectionism. LC 98-31575. (Illus.). 273p. 1999. 23.00 (*0-684-84963-1*) Free Pr.

— Never Good Enough: How to Use Perfectionism to Your Advantage Without Letting It Ruin Your Life. 288p. 2000. per. 12.00 (*0-684-86293-X*) S&S Trade.

Bascom. Science of Composite Materials. 2001. write for info. (*0-471-60915-3*) Wiley.

Bascom, Arlene, jt. auth. see Johnson, Lucile.

Bascom, Barbara B. & McKelvey, Carole A. The Complete Guide to Foreign Adoption: What to Expect & How to Prepare for Your New Child. LC 96-48425. 384p. 1997. per. 14.00 (*0-671-54646-5*) PB.

Bascom, George S. Faint Echoes. (Orig.). 1991. pap. 12.95 (*0-89745-141-4*) Sunflower U Pr.

— Medicine Circle. 118p. 1993. pap. 15.95 (*0-89745-169-4*) Sunflower U Pr.

Bascom, Harold. Apata. (Caribbean Writers Ser.). 279p. (Orig.). (C). 1986. pap. 8.95 (*0-435-98828-X*) Heinemann.

Bascom, John. Aesthetics: Or the Science of Beauty. rev. ed. LC 75-3030. (Philosophy in America Ser.). reprint ed. 42.00 (*0-404-59029-2*) AMS Pr.

— Philosophy of English Literature. xiii, 318p. 1985. reprint ed. lib. bdg. 49.00 (*0-932051-94-4*) Rprt Serv.

— A Philosophy of Religion: Or, the Rational Grounds of Religious Belief. LC 75-3037. reprint ed. 57.50 (*0-404-59035-7*) AMS Pr.

— The Philosophy of Rhetoric. LC 98-12972. 312p. 1998. write for info. (*0-8201-1508-8*) Schol Facsimiles.

— Science, Philosophy & Religion. LC 75-3041. reprint ed. 42.50 (*0-404-59039-X*) AMS Pr.

Bascom, Johnathan. Losing Place: Refugee Populations & Rural Transformations in East Africa. LC 97-45095. (Refugee & Forced Migration Studies). 224p. 1998. 39.95 (*1-57181-083-8*) Berghahn Bks.

Bascom, Lionel, jt. auth. see DeSoto, Richard J.

Bascom, Lionel, jt. auth. see Monaco, Richard.

***Bascom, Lionel C.** A Renaissance in Harlem. 2001. write for info. (*0-380-79902-2*, Perennial) HarperTrade.

***Bascom, Lionel C., ed.** A Renaissance in Harlem: Lost Voices of an American Community. LC 99-33449. 320p. 1999. 24.00 (*0-380-97664-1*, Avon Bks) Morrow Avon.

Bascom, Lionel C. & Loecher, Barbara. By the Light. LC 95-94151. 224p. (Orig.). 1995. mass mkt. 4.99 (*0-380-77801-7*, Avon Bks) Morrow Avon.

Bascom, Robert O. The Fort Edward Book, Containing Some Historical Sketches, with Illustrations & Family Records. (Illus.). 274p. 1997. reprint ed. lib. bdg. 35.00 (*0-8328-6142-1*) Higginson Bk Co.

Bascom, Wilbert O. The Economics of Financial Reform in Developing Countries. LC 93-39172. 1994. text 75.00 (*0-312-12069-9*) St Martin.

Bascom, William. Ponape: A Pacific Economy in Transition. LC 65-64597. (University of California, Anthropological Records: Vol. 22). 166p. reprint ed. pap. 51.50 (*0-608-13953-X*, 202132200021) Bks Demand.

— The Yoruba of Southwestern Nigeria. (Illus.). 118p. 1984. reprint ed. pap. text 10.50 (*0-88133-038-8*) Waveland Pr.

Bascom, William R. African Art in Cultural Perspective: An Introduction. (Illus.). 192p. (C). 1973. pap. text 14.00 (*0-393-09375-1*) Norton.

— African Folktales in the New World. LC 91-46789. (Folkloristics Ser.). (Illus.). 282p. 1992. pap. 18.95 (*0-253-20736-3*) Ind U Pr.

— Ifa Divination: Communication Between Gods & Men in West Africa. LC 69-10349. (Illus.). 604p. 1991. reprint ed. pap. 27.95 (*0-253-20638-3*) Ind U Pr.

— Sixteen Cowries: Yoruba Divination from Africa to the New World. LC 78-3239. (Illus.). 800p. 1980. 49.95 (*0-253-35280-0*) Ind U Pr.

— Sixteen Cowries: Yoruba Divination from Africa to the New World. LC 78-3239. (Illus.). 800p. 1993. pap. 24.95 (*0-253-20847-5*) Ind U Pr.

Bascom, William R., ed. African Dilemma Tales. (World Anthropology Ser.). xiv, 162p. 1975. 26.95 (*90-279-7509-4*) Mouton.

Bascom, William R. & Herskovits, Melville Jean, eds. Continuity & Change in African Cultures. LC 58-13135. 1962. pap. text 4.25 (*0-226-03880-7*, P85) U Ch Pr.

— Continuity & Change in African Cultures. LC 58-13135. (Illus.). 320p. reprint ed. pap. 99.20 (*0-608-09380-7*, 205412500004) Bks Demand.

Bascom, William R. & Herskovits, Melville Jean, eds. Continuity & Change in African Cultures. LC 58-13135. (Illus.). 316p. Date not set. reprint ed. pap. 98.00 (*0-608-20994-5*, 205452200003) Bks Demand.

Bascomb, Lionel C., jt. auth. see Harris, Barbara.

Bascombe, K. N. Waltham Abbey. (Best of Britain in Old Photographs Ser.). (Illus.). 128p. 1998. pap. 14.50 (*0-7509-1029-1*, Pub. by Sutton Pub Ltd) Intl Pubs Mktg.

Bascombe, Mike. The Butterflies of Hong Kong. LC 98-88101. 664p. (C). 1999. text 142.50 (*0-12-080290-2*) Acad Pr.

Bascompte, Jordi & Sole, Ricard V. Modeling Spatiotemporal Dynamics in Ecology. LC 97-26698. (Environmental Intelligence Unit (SV) Ser.). 216p. 1998. 112.00 (*1-57059-505-4*) Landes Bioscience.

Bascompte, Jordi & Sole, Ricard V., eds. Modeling Spatiotemporal Dynamics in Ecology. LC 97-26698. (Environmental Intelligence Unit (SV) Ser.). (Illus.). 216p. 1998. 112.00 (*3-540-63449-5*) Spr-Verlag.

Bascove. Stone & Steel: Paintings & Writings Celebrating the Bridges of New York City. LC 97-17832. (Illus.). 96p. 1998. 30.00 (*1-56792-081-0*) Godine.

Bascur, Osvalde A., ed. Latin American Perspectives: Exploration, Mining, & Processing. LC 99-162967. (Illus.). 412p. 1998. pap. 82.00 (*0-87335-155-X*, 155-X) SMM&E Inc.

***Bascuti, Ellen.** Luis Palau: Evangelist to the World. (Heroes of the Faith Ser.). 208p. 2000. pap. 3.97 (*1-57748-803-2*) Barbour Pub.

Basdekis, Demetrios. Miguel de Unamuno. LC 74-92029. (Columbia Essays on Modern Writers Ser.: No. 44). 48p. (Orig.). 1970. pap. text 12.00 (*0-231-03259-5*) Col U Pr.

Basden, Barbara & Jones Staff. Laboratory Experiences in Introductory Psychology. 160p. (C). 1996. pap. text, per. 14.95 (*0-7872-2590-8*) Kendall-Hunt.

Basden, G. T. Niger Ibos. (Illus.). 456p. 1966. reprint ed. 45.00 (*0-7146-1632-X*, Pub. by F Cass Pubs) Intl Spec Bk.

Basden, Paul. The Worship Maze: Finding a Style to Fit Your Church. LC 99-21812. 168p. 1999. pap. 10.99 (*0-8308-2204-6*, 2204) InterVarsity.

An Asterisk (*) at the beginning of an entry indicates that the title is appearing for the first time.

Basdeo. Spanish 201: Exercises. 1998. 14.25 (*0-07-228247-9*) McGraw.
— Spanish 202: Exercises. 1998. 12.74 (*0-07-228244-4*) McGraw.
***Basdevant, Jean-Louis & Dalibard, J.** Quantum Mechanics Solver: How to Apply Quantum Theory to Modern Physics. LC 99-58086. (Advanced Texts in Physics Ser.). (Illus.). xii, 239p. 1999. pap. 48.00 (*3-540-63409-6*) Spr-Verlag.
Base, Graeme. Animalia. (Illus.). 32p. (J). (ps up). 1987. 18.95 (*0-8109-1868-4*, Pub. by Abrams) Time Warner.
— Animalia. (Illus.). 32p. (J). 1993. 11.95 (*0-8109-1939-7*, Pub. by Abrams) Time Warner.
— Animalia. (Illus.). 32p. (J). (gr. 1 up). 1996. pap. 6.99 (*0-14-055996-5*) Viking Penguin.
— Animalia. anniversary ed. (Illus.). 32p. (J). 1997. 29.95 (*0-8109-1999-0*, Pub. by Abrams) Time Warner.
— Animalia Coloring Book. (Illus.). 32p. (J). 1995. pap. 12.95 (*0-8109-2633-4*, Pub. by Abrams) Time Warner.
— Animalia Wall Frieze. (Illus.). 26p. 1991. pap. 24.95 (*0-8109-2475-7*, Pub. by Abrams) Time Warner.
— Animalia/Eleventh Hour Gift Pack. (Illus.). 32p. 1994. 21.95 (*0-8109-3137-0*) Abrams.
— The Discovery of Dragons. LC 97-104979. (Illus.). 36p. 1996. 16.95 (*0-8109-3237-7*, Pub. by Abrams) Time Warner.
— The Eleventh Hour: A Curious Mystery. (Illus.). 32p. (J). 1989. 18.95 (*0-8109-0851-4*, Pub. by Abrams) Time Warner.
— The Eleventh Hour: A Curious Mystery. (Illus.). 32p. (J). 1993. 11.95 (*0-8109-3265-2*, Pub. by Abrams) Time Warner.
— The Eleventh Hour: A Curious Mystery. LC 97-13621. (Illus.). 32p. (YA). (gr. 1-4). 1997. pap. 6.99 (*0-14-056160-9*) Viking Penguin.
— Jabberwocky: A Book of Brillig Dioramas. LC 96-138445. (Illus.). 14p. (J). (ps-3). 1996. 19.95 (*0-8109-3520-1*, Pub. by Abrams) Time Warner.
— My Grandma Lived in Gooligulch. (Illus.). 42p. 1990. 16.95 (*0-8109-1547-2*, Pub. by Abrams) Time Warner.
— My Grandma Lived in Gooligulch. LC 96-102798. (Illus.). 18p. (J). 1995. 19.95 (*0-8109-4288-7*, Pub. by Abrams) Time Warner.
— Sign of the Sea Horse. 1998. 11.98 (*0-8109-8154-8*, Pub. by Abrams) Time Warner.
— The Sign of the Seahorse: A Tale of Greed & High Adventure in Two Acts. (Illus.). 44p. 1992. 19.95 (*0-8109-3825-1*) Abrams.
— The Sign of the Seahorse: A Tale of Greed & High Adventure in Two Acts. LC 97-50096. (Picture Puffin Ser.). 48p. (J). 1998. pap. 7.99 (*0-14-056387-3*, PuffinBks) Peng Put Young Read.
— The Sign of the Seahorse: A Tale of Greed & High Adventure in Two Acts. (Picture Puffin Ser.). 1998. 13.19 (*0-606-13774-2*, Pub. by Turtleback) Demco.
***Base, Graeme.** The Worst Band in the Universe: A Totally Cosmic Musical Adventure. LC 99-20968. (Illus.). 48p. (J). (gr. 3-6). 1999. 19.95 (*0-8109-3998-3*, Pub. by Abrams) Time Warner.
Baseball America Staff. Baseball America's Dictionary 1996. 1996. pap. 10.95 (*0-671-56110-3*) S&S Trade.
— Baseball America's Directory: The Complete Pocket Baseball Guide, 1999 ed. (Baseball America's Ser.). 1999. pap. text 12.95 (*0-945164-09-2*) Baseball Amer.
— Baseball America's Directory 1998: The Complete Pocket Baseball Guide. 1998. mass mkt. 12.95 (*0-945164-00-9*) Baseball Amer.
— Baseball America's 1999 Almanac. (Baseball America's Ser.). 1999. pap. text 12.95 (*0-945164-08-4*) Baseball Amer.
— Baseball America's 1995 Almanac. 1995. 12.95 (*0-671-88440-9*) Baseball Amer.
— Baseball America's 1995 Directory. 1995. 9.95 (*0-671-88441-7*) Baseball Amer.
— Baseball America's 1995 Directory. 1995. pap. 10.95 (*0-671-52503-4*) S&S Trade.
— Baseball America's 1996 Almanac. 400p. 1996. pap. 12.95 (*0-671-56111-1*) S&S Trade.
Baseball Encyclopedia Editors, jt. auth. see Major League Baseball Properties, Inc. Staff.
Baseball Weekly Staff, jt. ed. see White, Paul.
Basedow, David. Developments In the Management of Chemotherapy-Induced Nausea & Vomiting: A Workshop Held At Lake Tahoe Nevada, April 11, 1987. (Illus.). 24p. (Orig.). 1987. write for info. (*0-944036-00-7*) Medicine Grp USA.
Basedow, Herbert. The Australian Aboriginal. LC 76-44687. (Illus.). reprint ed. 55.00 (*0-404-15904-4*) AMS Pr.
Basedow, Johann B. Elementarwerk. (GER.). lxxi, 1154p. 1972. reprint ed. write for info. (*3-487-04323-8*) G Olms Pubs.
Basedow, Johann B. Methodischer Unterricht in der Ueberzeugenden Erkenntniss der Biblischen Religion: Zur Fortgesetzten Ausfuehrung des in der Philalethie Angegebenen Plans. (GER.). xxxii, 368p. 1985. reprint ed. write for info. (*3-487-07576-8*) G Olms Pubs.
***Basedow, Jurgen & Kono, Toshiyuki, eds.** Legal Aspects of Globalisation: Conflicts of Laws, Internet, Capital Markets & Insolvency in a Global Economy. 244p. 2000. text 66.25 (*90-411-1332-0*) Kluwer Law Intl.
Basehart, Harry, jt. auth. see Saffell, David C.
Basehart, Harry, jt. ed. see Saffell, David C.
Baseheart, Mary C. Person in the World: Introduction to the Philosophy of Edith Stein. LC 97-2846. 216p. 1997. text 107.00 (*0-7923-4490-1*) Kluwer Academic.
Baseheart, Mary C., intro. see Stein, Edith.
***Basel Art Staff.** Art 31 Basel. (Illus.). 2000. pap. 40.00 (*3-921669-24-3*) Weltkunst Verlag.
Basel, Gene I. The River Rat: Odyssey of a Fallen Warrior. 227p. 1998. pap. 8.95 (*1-57502-753-4*, PO2087) Morris Pubng.
Basel, H. Fritz & Basel, K. Giese. Evaluation of the Teratogenic Potential of Chemicals in the Rat. (Journal: Pharmacology: Vol. 40, Suppl. 1, 1990). (Illus.). iv, 28p. 1990. pap. 11.50 (*3-8055-5177-0*) S Karger.
Basel, Jean-Paul P. Development of Mathematics 1900-1950. LC 94-25339. (FRE.). 1994. 85.50 (*0-8176-2821-5*) Birkhauser.
Basel, K. Giese, jt. auth. see Basel, H. Fritz.
Baseler, Marilyn C. Asylum for Mankind: America, 1607-1800. LC 97-53079. (Illus.). 320p. 1998. text 42.50 (*0-8014-3481-5*) Cornell U Pr.
Baseley, Joel, tr. see Luther, Martin.
Baseline Editors & Monaco, James. Encyclopedia of Film. 1991. pap. 18.95 (*0-399-51606-9*, Perigee Bks) Berkley Pub.
Baseline Editors, jt. auth. see Monaco, James.
***Baselis-Bitoun, Lison.** La Guerre de Troie: Advanced Placement French Literature. (FRE.). 63p. (YA). (gr. 9-12). 1999. student ed., wbk. ed. 6.67 (*1-877653-69-1*) Wayside Pub.
— Le Mariage de Figaro: Advanced Placement French Literature. (FRE.). 95p. (YA). (gr. 9-12). 1999. student ed., wbk. ed. 7.33 (*1-877653-68-3*) Wayside Pub.
Baselis-Bitoun, Lison. Study Guide: Une Si Longue Lettre - Advanced Placement French Literature. (FRE.). 71p. (YA). (gr. 11-12). 1997. pap. text 7.33 (*1-877653-39-X*) Wayside Pub.
Baselitz, Georg. Contemporary Art: The Collection of the ZKM, Center for Art & Media Karlsruhe. Klotz, Heinrich, ed. (Illus.). 340p. 1997. 65.00 (*3-7913-1869-1*, Pub. by Prestel) te Neues.
— Georg Baselitz. (Illus.). 220p. 1998. pap. 45.00 (*88-8158-118-3*, 720013, Pub. by Charta) Dist Art Pubs.
— Georg Baselitz. (Illus.). 48p. 1994. pap. 30.00 (*1-885013-01-9*) M Werner.
***Baselitz, Georg.** Georg Baselitz: Holzschnitte 1966,1991. (Illus.). 128p. 2000. 60.00 (*3-87909-403-9*, Pub. by Wienand) Nazraeli Press.
Baselitz, Georg. George Baselitz: Pastels, Watercolors, Drawings. (Illus.). 54p. 1992. 9.95 (*1-880146-04-5*) M Marks.
Baselitz, Georg, text. Georg Baselitz: Recent Paintings. (Illus.). 64p. 1990. 40.00 (*0-947564-30-6*, Pub. by A D'Offay Gallery) Dist Art Pubs.
Baselitz, Georg, jt. auth. see Power, Kevin.
Baselt, Bernd, ed. see Knupfer, Sebastian.
Baselt, Bernd, ed. see Telemann, Georg P.
Baselt, Fonda D. The Sunny Side of Genealogy. 102p. 1999. reprint ed. pap. 9.95 (*0-8063-1205-X*, 385) Genealog Pub.
Baselt, Randall C. Biological Monitoring Methods for Industrial Chemicals. LC 79-56927. 313p. reprint ed. pap. 97.10 (*0-8357-7866-5*, 203628300002) Bks Demand.
— Biological Monitoring Methods for Industrial Chemicals. 3rd ed. LC 95-71023. 400p. 1997. 129.00 (*0-9626523-2-6*) Chem Toxicol Inst.
— Disposition of Toxic Drugs & Chemicals in Man. (Illus.). 900p. 1999. text 119.00 (*0-9626523-3-4*, Pub. by Chem Toxicol Inst) BookMasters.
— Ferrari: Brochures & Sales Literature - A Source Book 1968-1989, Vol. 2. (Illus.). 350p. (Orig.). 1992. pap. 75.00 (*0-9626523-0-X*) Chem Toxicol Inst.
Baselt, Randall C. & Cravey, Robert H. Disposition of Toxic Drugs & Chemicals in Man. 4th ed. (Illus.). 1000p. 1994. text 99.50 (*0-9626523-1-8*) Chem Toxicol Inst.
Baselt, Randall C., jt. auth. see Houts, Marshall.
Baseman, Diana. The Pennsylvania Home Education Handbook: Using Your Educational Style in Complying with the Law. 4th rev. ed. (Illus.). 1997. pap. 14.95 (*0-9624505-0-2*) Tall Oaks Bks.
Baseman, Sharon R., ed. see Cohen, Cindy Klein & Heiney, John T.
Basenko, S. V., jt. auth. see Voronkov, M. G.
Baser, E, ed. Dynamics of Sensory & Cognitive Processing by the Brain. (Brain Dynamics Ser.). (Illus.). 420p. 1988. 121.00 (*0-387-16994-6*) Spr-Verlag.
Baser, Heather. Technology, Women, & Farming Systems. (Studies in Technology & Social Change: No. 5). 26p. (Orig.). (C). 1988. pap. 4.00 (*0-945271-08-5*) ISU-CIKARD.
Baserga, Renato. The Biology of Cell Reproduction. LC 84-12902. (Illus.). 256p. 1985. 40.50 (*0-674-07406-8*) HUP.
— Multiplication & Division in Mammalian Cells. LC 75-25166. (Biochemistry of Disease Ser.: No. 6). (Illus.). 255p. reprint ed. pap. 79.10 (*0-7837-0864-5*, 204117200019) Bks Demand.
Baserga, Renato, ed. The Cell Cycle & Cancer. LC 73-134779. (Biochemistry of Disease Ser.: No. 1). (Illus.). 495p. reprint ed. pap. 153.50 (*0-7837-0660-X*, 204099600019) Bks Demand.
— Tissue Growth Factors. (Handbook of Experimental Pharmacology Ser.: Vol. 57). (Illus.). 500p. 1981. 272.00 (*0-387-10623-5*) Spr-Verlag.
Baserga, Renato, jt. ed. see Clarkson, Bayard.
Basett, Lucinda. From Panic to Power: Bassett,&Lucinda. abr. ed. 1995. audio 18.00 (*0-694-51595-7*, CPN 2511) HarperAudio.
Basetti-Sani, Giulio. Louis Massignon: Christian Ecumenist. 262p. 1974. 6.95 (*0-8199-0496-1*, Frncscn Herld) Franciscan Pr.
Basevski, Dimitar & Brownjohn, Alan. Temporal Stay: Poems. LC 96-61885. 68p. 1998. pap. 14.95 (*1-85610-043-X*, Pub. by Forest Bks) Dufour.
Basey, Harold E. Discovering Sierra Reptiles & Amphibians. (Discovering Sierra Ser.). (Illus.). 56p. (Orig.). 1976. pap. 4.95 (*0-939666-03-0*) Yosemite Assn.
Basey, Marty. Flour Power: Your Guide to Whole Grain Milling. (Illus.). 192p. 1999. pap. 9.95 (*0-89529-919-3*, Avery) Penguin Putnam.
Basford, K. E. & Tukey, J. W. Graphical Analysis of Multiresponse Data Illustrated with a Plant Breeding Trial: Interdisciplinary Statistics. 592p. 1998. boxed set 81.95 (*0-8493-0384-2*) CRC Pr.
Basford, Kathleen. The Green Man. LC 97-50143. (Illus.). 128p. 1998. pap. 35.00 (*0-85991-497-6*, DS Brewer) Boydell & Brewer.
Basford, Terry K. The Near-Death Experience: An Annotated Bibliography. LC 89-78521. 192p. 1990. text 10.00 (*0-8240-6349-X*, SS481) Garland.
Basgall, M. E., jt. auth. see Bouey, P. D.
Basgall, Mark E. & Giambastiani, Mark A. Prehistoric Use of a Marginal Environment: Continuity & Change in Occupation of the Volcanic Tablelands, Mono & Inyo Counties, California. (Center for Archaeological Research at Davis Ser.). (Illus.). 351p. (Orig.). 1995. pap. 22.50 (*1-883019-13-3*) U CA Dept Anthrop.
Basgelen, Nezih, jt. auth. see Ousterhout, Robert G.
Basgoz, Ilhan & Furniss, Norman, eds. Turkish Workers in Europe: An Interdisciplinary Study. (Turkish Studies: Vol. 5). 191p. (C). 1985. 11.95 (*0-685-29323-8*) IN Univ Turkish.
Basgoz, Ilhan & Glazer, Mark, eds. Studies in Turkish Folklore. (Turkish Studies: Vol. 1). 232p. (C). 1978. 12.95 (*0-685-29320-3*) IN Univ Turkish.
Basgoz, Ilhan & Kagitcibasi, Cigdem, eds. Sex Roles, Family & Community in Turkey. (Turkish Studies: Vol. 3). 414p. (C). 1982. 14.95 (*0-685-29321-1*) IN Univ Turkish.
Basgoz, Ilhan & Wilson, H. E. Educational Problems in Turkey, 1920-1940. LC 67-65317. (Uralic & Altaic Ser.: Vol. 86). 268p. 1968. pap. text. write for info. (*0-87750-077-0*) Curzon Pr Ltd.
Basgoz, Ilhan, jt. ed. see Akural, Sabri M.
Basgoz, Ilhan, ed. see Emre, Yunus.
Basgoz, Ilhan, ed. see Faik, Sait.
Bash, Anita, et al. Treating the Earth as If We Plan to Stay: A Resource Guide to Individual Action. (Illus.). 28p. (Orig.). 1990. pap. 3.00 (*0-9626493-0-9*) Beyond War Fndtn.
Bash, Anthony. Ambassadors for Christ: An Exploration of Ambassadorial Language in the New Testament. LC 97-139964. (WissUnt Zum Neuen Testament 2/92 Ser.: Vol. 2/92). 339p. 1997. pap. 79.50 (*3-16-146718-3*, Pub. by JCB Mohr) Coronet Bks.
Bash, Barbara. Ancient Ones: The World of the Old-Growth Douglas Fir. (Tree Tales Ser.). (Illus.). 32p. (J). (gr. k-3). 1994. 16.95 (*0-87156-561-7*, Pub. by Sierra Club Childrens) Little.
— Desert Giant, Vol. 1. (J). (gr. 4-7). 1990. pap. 6.95 (*0-316-08307-0*) Little.
— Desert Giant; The World of the Saguaro Cactus. (Tree Tales Ser.). (J). 1989. 12.15 (*0-606-02746-7*, Pub. by Turtleback) Demco.
— Desert Giant Vol. 1: The World of the Saguaro Cactus. 1990. pap. 5.95 (*0-685-33583-6*) Little.
— In the Heart of the Village: The World of the Indian Banyan Tree. (Tree Tales Ser.). (Illus.). 32p. (J). (gr. k-3). 1996. 16.95 (*0-87156-575-7*, Pub. by Sierra Club Childrens) Little.
— Shadows of Night: The Hidden World of the Little Brown Bat. LC 92-22713. (Illus.). 32p. (J). (gr. k-3). 1993. 16.95 (*0-87156-562-5*, Pub. by Sierra Club Childrens) Little.
— Shadows of Night: The Hidden World of the Little Brown Bat. (Illus.). 32p. (J). (gr. k-3). 1995. pap. 6.95 (*0-87156-440-8*, Pub. by Sierra Club Childrens) Little.
Bash, Barbara. Tree of Life: The World of the African Baobab. (Tree Tales Ser.). 1989. 11.15 (*0-606-06827-9*, Pub. by Turtleback) Demco.
Bash, Barbara. Urban Roosts: Where Birds Nest in the City. (Illus.). 32p. (J). (gr. 4-7). 1992. pap. 6.95 (*0-316-08312-7*) Little.
Bash, Barbara. Urban Roosts: Where Birds Nest in the City. (J). 1990. 12.15 (*0-606-02226-0*, Pub. by Turtleback) Demco.
Bash, Deborah. Jerusalem's Best Buys. 188p. 1990. pap. 11.95 (*0-9626234-0-7*) First Street Pr.
Bash, Evelyn. Cracker Town. (Illus.). 121p. (Orig.). 1995. pap. 8.95 (*0-937866-52-0*) Atlantic Pub Co.
Bash, Harry H. Social Problems & Social Movements: An Exploration into the Sociological Construction of Alternative Realities. LC 93-28775. 280p. (C). 1995. text 49.95 (*0-391-03844-3*) Humanities.
— Sociology, Race & Ethnicity: A Critique of American Ideological Intrusions Upon Sociological Theory. (Monographs in Sociology). xii, 292p. 1979. text 110.00 (*0-677-05390-8*) Gordon & Breach.
Bash, Kent, jt. auth. see Witzel, Michael K.
Bash, Lee, jt. ed. see Runfola, Maria.
Bash, Leslie, jt. auth. see Coulby, David.
Bash, Leslie, jt. auth. see Griffin, Jon.
Basha, Angela R., et al, eds. Gracious Goodness Christmas in Charleston. LC 96-79114. (Illus.). 126p. 1996. 16.95 (*0-9629477-1-7*) Bishop England.
Basha, Angela R., et al. Gracious Goodness, Charleston! LC 91-65567. 386p. 1991. 16.95 (*0-9629477-0-9*) Bishop England.
Basha, Anwer, jt. auth. see Ahmad, Viqar U.
Basha, Anwer, jt. auth. see Ahmad, Viqar Uddin.
Basha, Anwer, jt. ed. see Atta-Ur-Rahman.
Basha, F. Z., jt. auth. see Rahman, A. U.
Basha, Genc. Controlled Killing of Exfoliated Colorectal Cancer Cells. (Acta Biomedica Lovaniensia Ser.). (Illus.). 122p. 1998. pap. 45.00 (*90-6186-887-4*, Pub. by Leuven Univ) Coronet Bks.
Basha, Y. & Dheri, V. English-Albanian Dictionary. (ALB & ENG.). 362p. (C). 1987. 130.00 (*0-569-09271-X*, Pub. by Collets) St Mut.
Basham. Successful Parenting Guide: Get Ready for School. Date not set. pap. text. write for info. (*0-582-02621-0*, Pub. by Addison-Wesley) Longman.
Basham, A. L. The Civilizations of Monsoon Asia. 1975. text 22.95 (*0-685-14062-8*) Coronet Bks.
— History & Doctrines of the Ajivikas. (C). 1981. reprint ed. 15.00 (*0-8364-2195-7*, Pub. by Motilal Bnarsidass) S Asia.
— The Origins & Development of Classical Hinduism. Zysk, Kenneth G., ed. (Illus.). 208p. 1991. pap. text 13.95 (*0-19-507349-5*) OUP.
— Wonder That Was India. (C). 1995. reprint ed. 24.00 (*0-8364-2913-3*, Pub. by Rupa) S Asia.
— Wonder That Was India. (C). 1997. reprint ed. 26.00 (*0-283-99257-3*, Pub. by Rupa) S Asia.
Basham, A. L., ed. A Cultural History of Inida. (Oxford India Paperbacks Ser.). 640p. 1998. reprint ed. pap. text 19.95 (*0-19-563921-9*) OUP.
Basham, A. L. & Bhattacharjee, Arun. The Father of the Nation. (C). 1988. 27.00 (*81-7024-172-3*, Pub. by Ashish Pub Hse) S Asia.
***Basham, Allan, et al.** Team Building in Education. 224p. (C). 1999. pap. text 34.95 (*0-89108-267-0*, 9905) Love Pub Co.
Basham, Beth, ed. Women of Faith of the Presbyterian Church (U. S. A.), Vol. 1. unabridged ed. LC 97-176969. (Illus.). 200p. (Orig.). 1997. pap. 14.00 (*1-57153-011-8*) Bridge Resources.
Basham, Beth & Lisherness, Sara, eds. Striking Terror No More Vol. 1: The Church Responds to Domestic Violence. unabridged ed. LC 97-10417. 131p. 1997. pap. 4.99 (*1-57895-014-7*, Bridge Res) Curriculm Presbytrn KY.
Basham, Beth, ed. see Chisholm, Cathy C.
Basham, Beth, ed. see Davison, James E.
Basham, Beth, ed. see Johnson, Martha.
Basham, Beth, ed. see Kulp, Ann Z.
Basham, Beth, ed. see Ribal, Lizzy.
Basham, Beth, ed. see Sharp Herold, Betty.
Basham, Beth, ed. see Wilmore, Gayraud S.
Basham, Diana. The Trial of Woman. (Women's Classics Ser.). (Illus.). 246p. (C). 1992. text 42.50 (*0-8147-1174-X*) NYU Pr.
Basham, Don. Can a Christian Have a Demon. 128p. 1991. pap. 5.95 (*0-89228-015-8*) Impact Christian.
— Deliver Us from Evil. LC 72-81891. 228p. (gr. 10). 1995. pap. 9.99 (*0-8007-9069-3*) Chosen Bks.
— A Handbook on Holy Spirit Baptism. 118p. 1971. pap. 6.99 (*0-88368-003-3*) Whitaker Hse.
— Libranos del Mal. 2nd ed.Tr. of Deliver us from Evil. (SPA.). 240p. 1991. pap. text 7.99 (*0-88113-313-2*) Caribe Betania.
Basham, Frances & Ughetti, Bob. Car Culture. 144p. 1994. per. 14.95 (*0-85965-032-4*, Pub. by Plexus) Publishers Group.
Basham, Kim D., jt. auth. see Suprenant, Bruce A.
Basham, Kim D., ed. see American Society of Civil Engineers, Materials Eng.
Basham, Kimberley A. & Miracle, Vickie A. Critical Care Multidisciplinary Outcome Pathways. Carter, Robin, ed. LC 98-5490. 512p. (C). 1998. pap. text 49.95 (*0-7216-7373-2*, W B Saunders Co) Harcrt Hlth Sci Grp.

Basham, Mary A. & Hailey, Mark R. Body Mechanics: Fitness Journal & Guide. (Illus.). 228p. 1999. spiral bd. 24.00 (*0-9664957-0-5*) Visionary Magic.
Body Mechanics is a colorful 6 month fitness journal & guide designed to educate, motivate & chart the progress of those interested in health & fitness. The information allows a person to design the right exercise program for their individual needs: taking in account medical history, individual background, personal goals & time management. BODY MECHANICS is comprised of 4 sections. Getting Started, Measuring Up, Working Out & Charting Your Progress. Each section provides information, tips & suggestions for a successful workout. Charting Your Progress is the heart of BODY MECHANICS & is broken into 5 color coded sections: LEGS, BACK & SHOULDERS, CHEST & ABS, ARMS & CARDIO allowing the reader to record their workout routines for any given day. BODY MECHANICS is perfect for anyone currently or wishing to workout. Due to the abundance of people joining fitness clubs the demand for BODY MECHANICS is high. Also, since the book is a 6 month journal, the consumer will desire to purchase a new BODY MECHANICS allowing for repeat business. To order contact Turning Point Marketing & Management, Inc., 410-295-7800 or Access Publishers Network 213-276-5196. *Publisher Paid Annotation.*

Basham, Peter W., jt. ed. see Gregersen, Soren.
Basham, Richard. Crisis in Blanc & White. LC 78-16950. (Illus.). 304p. 1978. pap. 15.95 (*0-87073-571-3*) Schenkman Bks Inc.
Basham, Tom. Renegade: Battle for Jacob's Star: The Official Strategy Guide. 1995. pap. text 19.95 (*0-7615-0181-9*) Prima Pub.
— Su-27 Flanker. 1996. pap. text 12.95 (*0-7615-0546-6*) Prima Pub.

B

An Asterisk (*) at the beginning of an entry indicates that the title is appearing for the first time.

— Werewolf vs. Comanche: The Official Strategy Guide. LC 95-68598. 1995. pap. text 19.95 (*0-7615-0053-7*) Prima Pub.

Bashara, N. M., jt. auth. see Azzam, R. M.

Basharov, A. M., jt. auth. see Maimistov, A. I.

***Bashaw, Carolyn Terry.** "Stalwart Women" A Historical Analysis of Deans of Women in the South. LC 99-31310. (Athene Series in Women's Studies). 192p. 1999. write for info. (*0-8077-6300-4*); pap. text. write for info. (*0-8077-6299-7*) Tchrs Coll.

Bashaw, Carolyn Terry, jt. ed. see Nidiffer, Jana.

Bashaw, Donna R., et al. California Durable Powers of Attorney. Gerber, Mary, ed. LC 96-83298. 494p. 1996. ring bd. 109.00 (*0-88124-956-4*, ES-32660) Cont Ed Bar-CA.

Bashaw, W. L. Mathematics for Statistics. LC 84-11228. 344p. (C). 1984. reprint ed. lib. bdg. 40.50 (*0-89874-761-9*) Krieger.

***Bashe, Gilbert G., et al.** Branding Health Services: Defining Yourself in the Marketplace. LC 99-88085. 304p. 2000. 49.00 (*0-8342-1175-0*) Aspen Pub.

Bashe, Philip, jt. auth. see Teeley, Peter.

Bashe, Phillip, jt. auth. see McFarlane, Rodger.

Bashear, Suliman. Arabs & Others in Early Islam, Vol. 8. LC 97-41871. (Studies in Late Antiquity & Early Islam). 161p. 1998. lib. bdg. 24.95 (*0-87850-126-6*) Darwin Pr.

Basheer, Anisa. Environmental Epidemiology. (C). 1995. 22.00 (*0-614-13266-5*, Pub. by Rawat Pubns) S Asia.

***Basheer, Jafar A.** Unholy Doublecross: The Tampering of the "Good Book", Vol. 1. 1999. pap. text 20.00 (*0-9666279-0-3*) JAF Pubg.

***Bashein, Barbara J.** Data Warehouses: More Than Just Mining. 125p. 1999. pap. 39.75 (*1-885065-19-1*, Pub. by Finan Exec) E Elgar.

Bashein, Barbara J., et al. Safety Nets: Secrets of Effective Information Technology Controls. LC 96-61916. 150p. (Orig.). 1997. pap. 38.00 (*1-885065-08-6*, 097-03) Finan Exec.

Bashevkin, Sylvia. Women on the Defensive: Living Through Conservative TImes. LC 97-35168. 328p. 1998. pap. text 18.00 (*0-226-03885-8*); lib. bdg. 47.50 (*0-226-03883-1*) U Ch Pr.

— Women on the Defensive: Living Through Conservative Times. 288p. 1998. pap. text 19.95 (*0-8020-8187-8*) U of Toronto Pr.

Bashevkin, Sylvia B. Toeing the Lines: Women & Party Politics in English Canada. LC 86-145327. (Illus.). 240p. reprint ed. pap. 74.40 (*0-7837-0534-4*, 204086200019) Bks Demand.

— Toeing the Lines: Women & Party Politics in English Canada. 2nd ed. 182p. (C). 1993. pap. text 26.00 (*0-19-540850-0*, 14483) OUP.

— True Patriot Love: The Politics of Canadian Nationalism. (Studies in Canadian Politics). (Illus.). 288p. 1991. pap. text 15.95 (*0-19-540810-1*) OUP.

Bashford. Purity & Pollution: Gender, Embodiment & Victorian Medicine. LC 97-28323. 250p. 1998. text 59.95 (*0-312-21038-8*) St Martin.

Bashford, A. S. Cable Laying: Guidelines to Exposures & Insurance. 2nd ed. 1999. pap. 80.00 (*1-85609-015-9*, Pub. by Witherby & Co) St Mut.

— Guidelines to Charter Parties, Towage Contracts & Their Insurances. 1997. pap. 60.00 (*1-85609-136-8*, Pub. by Witherby & Co) St Mut.

— Marine Liabilities Guidelines to Exposures & Insurance of Port Authorities & Other Port Related Industries or Activities. 41p. 1989. 75.00 (*0-948691-82-4*, Pub. by Witherby & Co) St Mut.

— Marine Liabilities Guidelines to Exposures & Insurance of Port Authorities & Other Port Related Industries or Activities. (C). 1989. 90.00 (*0-948691-29-8*, Pub. by Witherby & Co) St Mut.

***Bashford, Bruce.** Oscar Wilde: The Critic As Humanist. LC 98-54801. 200p. 1999. 36.00 (*0-8386-3769-8*) Fairleigh Dickinson.

Bashford, C. L., jt. ed. see Harris, D. A.

***Bashford, Christina & Langley, Leanne, eds.** Music & British Culture, 1785-1914: Essays in Honour of Cyril Ehrlich. (Illus.). 448p. 2001. text 105.00 (*0-19-816730-X*) OUP.

Bashford, Howard H. Understanding the Construction Industry. 150p. (C). 2001. pap. 29.33 (*0-13-642430-9*, Macmillan Coll) P-H.

Bashford, Ralph. A New Guide to Better Fishing. (Illus.). 252p. 1987. pap. 6.00 (*0-9617953-0-1*) Otha Bk.

***Bashian, Kathleen Ryniker.** Once upon a Carpet. LC 99-90654. (Illus.). 96p. 1999. 34.95 (*0-9672698-0-6*) Cultl Conn VA.

Bashier, Zakaria. Muslim Women in the Midst of Change. 32p. 1996. pap. 3.75 (*0-614-21391-6*, 855) Kazi Pubns.

Bashir, Askia H. How to Manage Your Parents: How to Supervise Your Parents. unabridged ed. Monsho, K. Anoa et al. eds. 136p. (Orig.). 1995. pap. text 10.00 (*0-9650628-0-5*) Bilalian Prod.

Bashir, Elena & Israr-Ud-Din, eds. Proceedings of the Second International Hindukush Cultural Conference. (Hindukush & Karakoram Studies: No. 1). (Illus.). 534p. 1997. text 65.00 (*0-19-577571-0*) OUP.

***Bashir, Imran & Goel, Amrit L.** Testing Object-Oriented Software: Life-Cycle Solutions. LC 99-16553. 304p. 1999. 46.95 (*0-387-98896-3*) Spr-Verlag.

Bashir, Iskandar. Civil Service Reform in Lebanon. 1977. 19.95 (*0-8156-6050-2*, Pub. by Am U Beirut) Syracuse U Pr.

Bashir, Kai. Mind Control Within the United States. unabridged ed. 325p. (Orig.). 1997. write for info. (*0-9658174-1-5*); pap. 18.00 (*0-9658174-0-7*) Kai Bashir.

Bashir, Mir. The Art of Hand Analysis. 1997. pap. text 15.95 (*1-85398-102-8*, Pub. by Ashgrove Pr) Words Distrib.

Bashiri, Iraj, tr. see Hidayat, Sadiq.

Bashkin, V., jt. auth. see Radojevic, M.

Bashkin, V. N. & Park, Soon-Ung. Acid Deposition & Ecosystem Sensitivity in East Asia. LC 98-38394. 1998. 95.00 (*1-56072-611-3*) Nova Sci Pubs.

Bashkina, Nina H. & Trask, David F., eds. The United States & Russia: The Beginning of Relations, U. S. Department of State. LC 80-607939. 1982. reprint ed. lib. bdg. 80.00 (*0-89941-229-7*, 201510) W S Hein.

Bashkirov, Andrei G. Nonequilibrium Statistical Mechanics of Heterogeneous Fluid Systems. LC 94-23470. 176p. 1995. boxed set 149.95 (*0-8493-2860-8*) CRC Pr.

Bashkirtseff, Marie, et al. I Am the Most Interesting Book of All: The Diary of Marie Bashkirtseff. LC 96-39815. 1997. 35.00 (*0-8118-0224-8*) Chronicle Bks.

Bashkoff, Tracey. Miriam Shapiro: The Politics of the Decorative. (Illus.). 15p. 1992. pap. 5.00 (*0-933793-21-9*) Guild Hall.

***Bashkoff, Tracey, et al.** Sugimoto Portraits. (Illus.). 170p. 2000. 60.00 (*0-8109-6928-9*, Pub. by Abrams) Time Warner.

Bashkoff, Tracey R. Relative Truths: East End Photography. (Illus.). 5p. 1992. pap. 5.00 (*0-614-14070-6*) Guild Hall.

Bashline, L. James. The Fly Fisherman's Bible. LC 92-29445. (Outdoor Bible Ser.). 208p. 1993. pap. 12.95 (*0-385-42242-3*) Doubleday.

Bashline, L. James, ed. The Eastern Trail. (Illus.). 320p. 1972. 8.95 (*0-88395-014-6*) Freshet Pr.

***Bashline, Sylvia.** The New Cleaning & Cooking Fish. LC 99-18297. (The Freshwater Angler Ser.). (Illus.). 160p. 1999. 19.95 (*0-86573-096-2*) Creat Pub Intl.

Bashline, Sylvia G. The Bounty of the Earth Cookbook. LC 93-43372. 280p. 1994. pap. 14.95 (*1-55821-302-3*) Lyons Pr.

— Cleaning & Cooking Fish. LC 82-80889. (Hunting & Fishing Library). (Illus.). 160p. 1982. 19.95 (*0-86573-011-3*) Creat Pub Intl.

***Bashline, Sylvia G.** The Fish & Game Cookbook: Over 200 Time-Honored Recipes. LC 99-86263. (Illus.). 2000. 14.95 (*1-58574-011-X*) Lyons Pr.

— Fixm' Fish: The Complete Guide to Cleaning & Cooking Freshwater Fish. LC 99-58002. (Freshwater Angler Ser.). (Illus.). 192p. 2000. pap. 12.95 (*0-86573-116-0*) Creat Pub Intl.

Bashline, Sylvia G. Sylvia Bashline's Savory Game Cookbook. 176p. 1989. pap. write for info. (*0-9622756-0-3*) Iron Blue.

Bashmakov, I. A. Energy Reviews Vol. 5, Pt. 4: Forecasting Long-Term Worldwide Energy Developments - Modelling As a Tool for Energy Systems Research, Vol. 5. (Soviet Technology Reviews Ser.: Section A). 87p. 1992. pap. text 92.00 (*3-7186-5275-7*, Harwood Acad Pubs) Gordon & Breach.

Bashmakova, I. Nine Papers from the International Congress of Mathematicians, 1986. LC 90-22430. (Translations Ser.: Series 2, Vol. 147). 100p. 1990. 56.00 (*0-8218-3133-X*, TRANS2/147) Am Math.

Bashmakova, Isabella. Diophantus & Diophantine Equations. Shenitzer, Abe, tr. from RUS. LC 97-74342. (Dolciani Mathematical Expositions Ser.: No. 20). 104p. 1997. pap. text 21.95 (*0-88385-526-7*) Math Assn.

***Bashmakova, Isabella & Smirnova, Galina.** The Beginnings & Evolution of Algebra. LC 99-68950. 196p. 2000. pap. text 24.95 (*0-88385-329-9*) Math Assn.

Basho, Matsu. Back Roads to Far Towns. Corman, Cid & Susumu, Kamaike, trs. from JPN. (Illus.). 176p. 1996. reprint ed. pap. 18.00 (*0-88001-467-9*) HarpC.

— Back Roads to Far Towns: Basho's Oku-no-Hosomichi. Corman, Cid & Susumu, Kamaike, trs. from JPN. Orig. Title: Oku-no-Hosomichi. (Illus.). 175p. (C). 1998. pap. text 18.00 (*0-7881-5450-8*) DIANE Pub.

— Basho's "Narrow Road" Spring & Autumn Passages. Sato, Hiroaki, tr. from JPN. LC 96-4392. (Illus.). 186p. (Orig.). 1998. pap. 15.00 (*1-880656-20-5*, Rock Spring Collect) Stone Bridge Pr.

— The Essential Basho: Narrow Road to the Interior & Other Writings. Hamill, Sam, tr. LC 98-4309. 240p. 1999. 20.00 (*1-57062-282-5*, Pub. by Shambhala Pubns) Random.

— A Haiku Journey: Basho's "The Narrow Road to the Far North" & Selected Haiku. Britton, Dorothy, tr. from JPN. LC 74-24903. (Illus.). 128p. 1980. pap. 9.00 (*0-87011-423-9*) Kodansha.

Basho, Matsu. Narrow Road to Oku. 1997. pap. 25.00 (*4-7700-2028-7*, Pub. by Kodansha Int) OUP.

Basho, Matsu. The Narrow Road to the Deep North & Other Travel Sketches. Yuasa, Nobuyuki, tr. from JPN. (Classics Ser.). 176p. 1966. pap. 16.99 (*0-14-044185-9*, Penguin Classics) Viking Penguin.

— Narrow Road to the Interior. Hamill, Sam, tr. from JPN. LC 91-8574. (Centaur Editions Ser.). (Illus.). 120p. (Orig.). 1991. pap. 10.00 (*0-87773-644-8*, Pub. by Shambhala Pubns) Random.

— On Love & Barley: Haiku of Basho. Stryk, Lucien, tr. & intro. by. (Classics Ser.). 96p. 1986. pap. 9.95 (*0-14-044459-9*, Penguin Classics) Viking Penguin.

Basho, Matsu, et al. Little Enough: Forty-Nine Haiku. Corman, Cid, tr. & pref. by. LC 91-72695. 80p. (Orig.). 1991. pap. 10.00 (*0-917788-48-6*) Gnomon Pr.

— Monkey's Raincoat (Sarumino) Linked Poetry of the Basho School with Haiku Selections. Mayhew, Lenore, tr. from JPN. LC 85-51629. (Illus.). 151p. 1985. 9.95 (*0-8048-1500-3*) Tuttle Pubng.

— One Man's Moon: Fifty Haiku by Basho, Buson, Issa, Hakuin, Shiki, Santoka. Corman, Cid, tr. from JPN. LC 84-80472. 72p. (Orig.). 1984. pap. 10.00 (*0-917788-26-5*) Gnomon Pr.

Bashook, Philip G. & Dockery, J. Lee, eds. The ABMS Handbook on Board Certification & the Americans with Disabilities Act. LC 92-73098. 68p. 1992. pap. 20.00 (*0-934277-16-8*) Am Bd Med Spec.

Bashook, Philip G., jt. ed. see Mancall, Elliott L.

Bashore, Theodore R., jt. ed. see Allen, Philip A.

Bashow, David L. All the Fine Young Eagles. LC 97-119859. (Illus.). 360p. 1996. 27.95 (*0-7737-2976-3*) Stoddart Publ.

— All the Fine Young Eagles. (Illus.). 360p. 1997. pap. 18.95 (*0-7737-5913-1*) Stoddart Publ.

Bashshur, Rashid L., et al, eds. Arabic Essays, 2 pts., Set. (Contemporary Arabic Readers Ser.: Vol. II). 1976. 19.95 (*0-916798-12-7*) Intl Bk Ctr.

— Telemedicine: Theory & Practice. LC 96-36746. (Illus.). 454p. 1996. text 89.95 (*0-398-06731-7*); pap. text 69.95 (*0-398-06732-5*) C C Thomas.

Basi, Raghbir S. Contextual Management: A Global Perspective. LC 97-45066. (Illus.). 308p. 1998. 49.95 (*0-7890-0419-4*, Intl Busn Pr) Haworth Pr.

Basiaco, Noemi, tr. see Galt, Graham.

Basic Accounting Theory Committee. A Statement of Basic Accounting Theory. 100p. 1966. 12.00 (*0-86539-008-8*) Am Accounting.

Basic Aspects of Blood Trauma in Extracorporeal Ox. Basic Aspects of Blood Trauma: A Workshop, Proceedings of the Symposium, Stolberg Near Aachen, Federal Rep. of Germany, Nov. 21-23, 1978. Schonbein, H. Schmid & Teitel, P., eds. 1979. pap. text 191.50 (*90-247-2279-9*) Kluwer Academic.

Basic Auditing Concepts Committee. A Statement of Basic Auditing Concepts, Vol. 6. (Studies in Accounting Research). 58p. 1973. 12.00 (*0-86539-018-5*) Am Accounting.

Basic Environmental Problems of Man in Space II, I & Klein, K. E. Proceedings: Proceedings of the Basic Environmental Problems of Man in Space II, International Symposium, 6th, Bonn, Germany, November 3-6, 1980. Hordinsky, J. R., ed. 250p. 1982. pap. 77.00 (*0-08-028697-6*, A140, Pergamon Pr) Elsevier.

Basic Mechanisms in Two-phase Flow & Heat Transfer. Basic Mechanisms in Two-Phase Flow & Heat Transfer: Proceedings of the Symposium, Chicago, 1980. Rothe, P. H. & Lahey, R. T., eds. LC 80-69186. 135p. reprint ed. pap. 41.90 (*0-8357-5982-2*, 202418100035) Bks Demand.

Basichis, Gordon. Beautiful Bad Girl: The Vicki Morgan Story. (Illus.). 400p. 1985. 17.95 (*0-915643-14-6*) Santa Barb Pr.

Basics Design Staff. Homes of Prominence: Gold Seal Home Plans. 1997. pap. 19.95 (*1-892150-09-3*) Design Basics.

Basie, Count. Good Morning Heartache. 19.95 (*0-317-45950-3*) Random.

Basiev, T. T. & Mirov, S. B. Room Temperature Tunable Color Center Lasers. LC 92-41423. (Laser Science & Technology Ser.). 160p. 1994. pap. text 104.00 (*3-7186-5349-4*) Gordon & Breach.

Basil, Caesarea. Letters, 4 Vols, 3. LC 65-18318. (Loeb Classical Library: No. 190, 215, 243, 270). 504p. 1930. 19.95 (*0-674-99268-7*) HUP.

— Letters, Vol. 1, Nos. 1-185. Way, Agnes C., tr. LC 65-18318. (Fathers of the Church Ser.: Vol. 13). 345p. 1951. 20.95 (*0-8132-0013-X*) Cath U Pr.

— Letters, Vol. 2, Nos. 186-368. Way, Agnes C., tr. LC 65-18318. (Fathers of the Church Ser.: Vol. 28). 369p. 1955. 21.95 (*0-8132-0028-8*) Cath U Pr.

— Paradise. 1994. pap. text 1.95 (*0-89981-068-3*) Eastern Orthodox.

— St. Basil the Great on The Forty Martyrs of Sebaste, Paradise, & the Catholic Faith. 1979. pap. 3.95 (*0-89981-083-7*) Eastern Orthodox.

***Basil, Copper.** Turn down an Empty Glass. large type ed. 272p. 1999. pap. 18.99 (*0-7089-5481-2*, Linford) Ulverscroft.

Basil, Douglas C., et al. Women in Management. 140p. 1972. 14.50 (*0-8290-1568-X*) Irvington.

Basil, Duncan. Eyes on the Lord: View of a Contemplative. 96p. 1996. pap. 10.95 (*0-85439-476-1*, Pub. by St Paul Pubns) St Mut.

— Year of Mystery. 96p. 1994. pap. 35.00 (*0-85439-505-9*, Pub. by St Paul Pubns) St Mut.

Basil, John D. The Mensheviks in the Revolution of 1917. 220p. 1984. 24.95 (*0-89357-109-1*) Slavica.

Basil, Lupi. Journey of Dreams & Illusions. (Illus.). 60p. (Orig.). 1996. pap. 7.95 (*0-9655816-2-4*) Wings of Dawn.

Basil, Malin. Saudi Arabia Through the Eyes of an Artist. (Illus.). 84p. (C). 1995. 75.00 (*0-907151-17-5*, Pub. by IMMEL Pubng) St Mut.

Basil, Miller. Ann Judson: Heroine of Burma. 2000. pap. write for info. (*0-310-22845-X*) Zondervan.

Basil, Robert, ed. Not Necessarily the New Age: Critical Essays. LC 88-12635. 395p. 1988. 28.95 (*0-87975-490-7*) Prometheus Bks.

Basil, Robert, et al, eds. On the Barricades: Religion & Free Inquiry in Conflict. LC 89-63454. 384p. (Orig.). 1989. pap. 23.95 (*0-87975-563-6*) Prometheus Bks.

***Basil, Saint.** Ascetical Works. Wagner, M. Monica, tr. LC 50-10735. (Fathers of the Church Ser.: Vol. 9). 2000. pap. 48.95 (*0-8132-0966-8*) Cath U Pr.

***Basile, Carole G., et al.** Awareness to Citizenship: Environmental Literacy for the Elementary Child. LC 00-41752. 160p. 2000. pap. 24.50 (*0-7618-1771-9*) U Pr of Amer.

Basile, Carole G., et al. Nature at Your Doorstep: Real World Investigations for Primary Students. LC 96-39312. (Illus.). 190p. 1997. pap. text, student ed. 22.00 (*1-56308-455-4*) Teacher Ideas Pr.

Basile, Deana, tr. see Battistella, Bruna.

Basile, Francis R. Buffalo's Best: The Indispensable Guide to Buffalo's Best Restaurants, Cafes, Nightlife, Arts & More. LC 99-72513. (Illus.). 155p. 1999. pap. 16.95 (*0-9656691-1-4*) Backhouse Pr.

***Basile, Francis R.** Rochester's Best: The Indispensable Guide to Rochester's Best Restaurants, Nightlife, Arts & More. 2nd rev. ed. LC 00-90418. Orig. Title: Rochester's Best Places. (Illus.). 180p. 2000. pap. 14.95 (*0-9656691-3-0*) Backhouse Pr.

Basile, Francis R. Rochester's Best Places: The Indispensable Guide to Rochester's Best Restaurants, Nightlife, Museums & Shopping. (Illus.). 160p. 1997. pap. 12.95 (*0-9656691-0-6*) Backhouse Pr.

Basile, Frank. Personal & Professional Effectiveness. 150p. (Orig.). 1995. pap. 16.95 (*1-878208-59-4*) Guild Pr IN.

— Scheduling Multifamily Maintenance. LC 88-62050. 96p. 1988. pap. 20.00 (*0-86718-322-5*) Home Builder.

Basile, Frank & Caruso, George C. Multihousing Management One. Tennyson, Dorris, ed. LC 94-15085. 385p. 1994. 45.00 (*0-86718-396-9*) Home Builder.

Basile, Frank, et al. Multihousing Management: Advanced Principles & Practices. LC 85-63079. 286p. 1986. pap. 34.00 (*0-86718-252-0*) Home Builder.

Basile, Frank M. Come Fly with Me. 18th ed. Holliday, Carol, ed. (Illus.). 52p. (Orig.). 1978. pap. 5.00 (*0-937008-00-1*) Charisma Pubns.

— Flying to Your Success. 108p. 1987. 6.00 (*0-937008-05-2*) Charisma Pubns.

Basile, Giambattista. Der Pentamerone Oder das Marchen Aller Marchen. (Volkskundliche Quellen Ser.: No. III). xxiv, 749p. 1973. reprint ed. 80.00 (*3-487-04921-X*) G Olms Pubs.

— Two Stories. Stefanile, Felix, tr. from ITA. & intro. by. (Poverty Pamphlets Ser.: No. 50). 28p. (Orig.). 1986. pap. text 2.50 (*0-935552-21-9*) Sparrow Pr.

Basile, Joseph J., jt. auth. see Bamberger, Michael A.

Basile, Leonard J. Learning Center Activities: Math. (Illus.). 80p. (J). (gr. k-2). 1997. pap., teacher ed. 9.95 (*1-57690-071-1*, TCM2071) Tchr Create Mat.

— Learning Center Activities: Reading Skills. (Illus.). 80p. (J). (gr. k-2). 1997. pap., teacher ed. 9.95 (*1-57690-070-3*, TCM2070) Tchr Create Mat.

Basile, Louis J., jt. ed. see Ferraro, John R.

Basile, Mary E., et al. Lex Mercatoria & Legal Pluralism: A Late Thirteenth-Century Treatise & Its Afterlife. (Ames Foundation Publications). (Illus.). 212,42,118p. 1998. 60.00 (*1-893606-12-0*) W S Hein.

Basile, Michael L., jt. ed. see Stromquist, Nelly P.

Basile, Ralph J., et al. Downtown Development Handbook. LC 80-50928. (Community Builders Handbook Ser.). (Illus.). 278p. 1980. reprint ed. pap. 86.20 (*0-7837-8935-1*, 204964500002) Bks Demand.

Basile, Teresa, jt. auth. see Gulik, Stanley J.

Basile, Teresa, ed. see Petit, Marianne.

Basile, Teresa, ed. see Rose, Elizabeth.

Basile, Tony. Rebellious Recipes. (Illus.). 116p. 1997. pap. 6.95 (*0-9646605-1-2*) Panther Mtn.

Basilevsky, Alexander. Statistical Factor Analysis & Related Methods: Theory & Applications. (Probability & Mathematical Statistics Ser.). 737p. 1994. 139.95 (*0-471-57082-6*) Wiley.

Basili, Victor R., jt. auth. see Abd-El-Hafiz, Salwa K.

Basilicato, Tony. Skip's & Wiggles Play it Safe ! Big Electronic Game Book. (Preschool Playlights Ser.). 12p. (J). (gr. k-3). 1999. bds. 15.99 (*1-57584-300-5*) Rdrs Digest.

Basilicato, Tony, et al. Buzz & Flutter's Electronic Game Book: Includes Toy. (Preschool Playlights Ser.). (Illus.). 12p. (J). (gr. k-3). 1997. bds. 15.99 (*0-88705-979-1*) Rdrs Digest.

Basilico, Gabriele. Gabriele Basilico: Italy. LC 98-204210. 160p. 1997. 34.95 (*3-931141-58-6*) Dist Art Pubs.

***Basilico, Gabriele.** I Tempi Di Roma. (FRE., Illus.). 2000. pap. 30.00 (*2-84576-023-X*) Vilo Intl.

Basilico, Gabriele. Interrupted City. 132p. 1999. 29.00 (*84-89698-53-8*, Pub. by Actar) Dist Art Pubs.

Basilious, Sam B. Fluid Therapy, Electrolytes, & Acid-Base Balance in Veterinary Practice. (Veterinary Medicine Ser.). (Illus.). 350p. (Orig.). (C). 1993. text 99.99 (*0-9630843-9-9*); text 399.99 incl. disk (*0-9630843-8-0*); text, student ed. 49.99 (*0-9630843-6-4*) Infoconnect.

— My Cat: Companion Animals. (My Companion Ser.). (Illus.). 100p. (Orig.). 1993. pap. write for info. incl. disk (*0-9630843-5-6*) Infoconnect.

Basilious, Sam H. Doctor Veterinarian Board Review, Bk. II. (Illus.). 504p. (Orig.). (C). 1991. pap. 75.00 (*0-9630843-1-3*) Infoconnect.

— Doctor Veterinarian Quick Review, Bk. I. (Illus.). 232p. (Orig.). (C). 1991. pap. 42.50 (*0-9630843-0-5*) Infoconnect.

Basilius. The Ascetic Works of Saint Basil. Clarke, W. K., tr. & intro. by. LC 80-2352. reprint ed. 57.50 (*0-404-18902-4*) AMS Pr.

Basilius, Harold A., ed. Contemporary Problems in Religion. 128p. 1977. 18.95 (*0-8369-1545-3*) Ayer.

Basill, Claire D. & Ennes, Lynn W. Voice Technology--Developments & Applications: Index of New Information for Reference & Research. 160p. 1997. 47.50 (*0-7883-1674-5*); pap. 44.50 (*0-7883-1675-3*) ABBE Pubs Assn.

Basill, Claire D., jt. auth. see Ennes, Lynn W.

Basils, Frederik. Der Asil Araber Im Lichte Neuer Genetischer Erkenntnisse: The Asil Arabian in the Light of New Genetic Knowledge. (Documenta Hippologica Ser.). (Illus.). 51p. 1981. write for info. (*3-487-08224-1*) G Olms Pubs.

Basily, Lascelle De, see De Basily, Lascelle.

Basily, Nicolas De, see De Basily, Nicolas.

Basin & Range Province Seismic-Hazards Summit Staff & Western States Seismic Policy Council Staff, eds. Proceedings Volume, Basin & Range Province Seismic-Hazards Summit. LC 99-167786. (Miscellaneous Publication / Utah Geological Survey Ser.: 98-2). (Illus.). 204p. 1998. pap. 15.00 (*1-55791-623-3*) Utah Geological Survey.

An Asterisk (*) at the beginning of an entry indicates that the title is appearing for the first time.

Basin Research Associates Staff. Excavations at John Dryden Cave (26WA3051), Smoke Creek Desert, Washoe County, Nevada. fac. ed. (Illus.). 344p. 1986. reprint ed. pap. text 36.25 (*1-55567-564-6*) Coyote Press.

Basing, Patricia. Trades & Crafts in Medieval Manuscripts. (Illus.). 123p. (C). 1990. 30.00 (*1-56131-002-6*, NAB) I R Dee.

Basinger. Computing Today. Date not set. pap. text, teacher ed. 21.95 (*0-314-75058-4*) West Pub.

— Computing Today. 1990. mass mkt., wbk. ed. 21.75 (*0-314-75057-6*) West Pub.

Basinger, David. The Case for Freewill Theism: A Philosophical Assessment. LC 96-19420. 204p. (Orig.). 1996. pap. 14.99 (*0-8308-1876-6*, 1876) InterVarsity.

— Divine Power in Process Theism: A Philosophical Critique. LC 87-24080. (SUNY Series in Philosophy). 135p. (C). 1988. pap. text 24.95 (*0-88706-709-3*) State U NY Pr.

*__Basinger, David.__ Labelled Deduction. LC 00-28202. (Applied Logic Ser.). 2000. write for info. (*0-7923-6237-3*) Kluwer Academic.

Basinger, David & Basinger, Randall. Philosophy & Miracle: The Contemporary Debate. LC 86-12766. (Problems in Contemporary Philosophy Ser.: Vol. 2). 130p. 1986. lib. bdg. 69.95 (*0-88946-327-1*) E Mellen.

— Predestination & Free Will. LC 85-23887. 180p. (Orig.). 1986. pap. 13.99 (*0-87784-567-0*, 567) InterVarsity.

Basinger, J. Martin & Miller, Ben. Artistry in Silver & Steel: The Adolph Bayers Legend. (Illus.). 360p. 1996. 49.95 (*0-9655103-0-1*) oTo Cos.

— Artistry in Silver & Steel: The Adolph Bayers Legend, Vol. 2. Wilson, Laura L., ed. LC 97-69361. (Illus.). 1997. 49.95 (*0-9655103-1-X*) oTo Cos.

Basinger, J. Martin, et al. Artistry in Silver & Steel No. III: The Adolph Bayers Legend. (Illus.). 1999. 49.95 (*0-9655103-2-8*) oTo Cos.

Basinger, Jeanine. The It's a Wonderful Life Book. LC 86-45307. 384p. 1986. pap. 29.95 (*0-394-74719-4*) Knopf.

— Silent Stars. LC 98-48060. 496p. 1999. 35.00 (*0-679-43840-8*) Knopf.

*__Basinger, Jeanine.__ Silent Stars. 2000. 24.95 (*0-8195-6451-6*) U Pr of New Eng.

Basinger, Jeanine. A Woman's View: How Hollywood Spoke to Women, 1930-1960. LC 95-17136. (Illus.). 542p. 1995. pap. 22.95 (*0-8195-6291-2*, Wesleyan Univ Pr) U Pr of New Eng.

Basinger, Louis F. The Techniques of Observation & Learning Retention: A Handbook for the Policeman & the Lawyer. (Illus.). 88p. 1973. pap., spiral bd. 20.95 (*0-398-02935-0*) C C Thomas.

Basinger, Missy, jt. auth. see Basinger, Sherry.

Basinger, Randall, jt. auth. see Basinger, David.

Basinger, Rebekah Burch, jt. auth. see Jeavons, Thomas H.

Basinger, Sherry & Basinger, Missy. Wizzer Rabbit Wants You to Be Drug Free. (Illus.). 17p. (Orig.). (J). 1988. pap. write for info. (*0-9620945-0-1*) S & M Basinger.

Basinski, Michael. The Flight to the Moon. (Illus.). 12p. (Orig.). 1993. pap. 3.00 (*0-926935-81-X*) Runaway Spoon.

— Red Rain Too. 17p. (Orig.). 1992. pap. 3.00 (*0-926935-64-X*) Runaway Spoon.

— Unnome. 26p. 1997. pap. 3.00 (*1-57141-039-2*) Runaway Spoon.

Basirico, Laurence A. Marriages & Families in a Diverse Society. 368p. (C). 1997. pap., student ed. 25.00 (*0-06-502013-8*) Addson-Wesley Educ.

Basista. Problem Solving 2nd ed. 1999. pap. text 18.00 (*0-471-37227-7*) Wiley.

Basit, Abdul. Essence of the Quran. 96p. (C). 1997. pap. 7.95 (*1-871031-55-9*) Kazi Pubns.

Basit, Tehmina N. Eastern Values; Western Milieu: Identities & Aspirations of Adolescent British Muslim Girls. LC 97-72267. 208p. 1997. text 69.95 (*1-85972-503-1*, Pub. by Avebry) Ashgate Pub Co.

Basiuk, Victor. Technology, World Politics, & American Policy. LC 76-51841. (Institute of War & Peace Studies). 409p. 1977. 64.00 (*0-231-04154-3*) Col U Pr.

Baskakova, M. A. Legal Dictionary for Businessmen: Russian-English, English-Russian. 6th rev. ed. 640p. (C). 1995. 35.00 (*0-8285-5199-5*) Firebird NY.

Baskara Rao, N. Determinants of Fertility Decline: A Study of Rural Karnataka. 1986. 17.50 (*81-7003-060-9*, Pub. by S Asia Pubs) S Asia.

Baskaran, G., et al. Strongly Correlated Electron Systems: Proceedings of Adriatico Research Conference & Workshop. (Progress in High Temperature Superconductivity Ser.: Vol. 23). 506p. 1990. text 151.00 (*981-02-0066-8*) World Scientific Pub.

— Strongly Correlated Electron Systems II: Prog in Hts, Vol. 29, Vol. 29. 444p. 1991. pap. 38.00 (*981-02-0510-4*); text 118.00 (*981-02-0509-0*) World Scientific Pub.

— Strongly Correlated Electron Systems III: Proceedings of the Adriatico Research Conference & Miniworkshop. (Series on Progress in High Temperature Superconductivity: No. 33). 400p. 1992. text 95.00 (*981-02-0903-7*) World Scientific Pub.

*__Baskaran, S. Theodore.__ The Dance of the Sarus: Essays of a Wandering Naturalist. 144p. 2000. text 9.95 (*0-19-564966-4*) OUP.

Baskas, Harriet. Museums of the Northwest: The Best Collections in Washington, Oregon & Lower British Columbia. LC 98-51573. (Illus.). 320p. 1999. pap. 18.95 (*1-57061-152-1*) Sasquatch Bks.

Baskas, Harriet & Woog, Adam. Atomic Marbles & Branding Irons: A Guide to Museums, Collections, & Roadside Curiosities in Washington & Oregon. (Illus.). 272p. (Orig.). 1993. pap. 12.95 (*0-912365-79-X*) Sasquatch Bks.

Baskauskas, Liucija. An Urban Enclave: Lithuanian Refugees in Los Angeles. LC 83-45348. (Immigrant Communities & Ethnic Minorities in the U. S. & Canada Ser.: No. 7). 1985. 39.50 (*0-404-19402-8*) AMS Pr.

Basker, David. Uwe Timm. Williams, Rhys, ed. (Contemporary German Writers Ser.). 128p. 1998. pap. write for info. (*0-7083-1447-3*, Pub. by Univ Wales Pr) Paul & Co Pubs.

Basker, David, jt. ed. see Hopwood, Mererid.

Basker, James G., jt. auth. see Ribeiro, Alvaro.

Baskervil, P. H. Skelton: The Skeltons of Paxton, Pawhatan County, Va., Including Sketches of the Families of Skelton, Gifford & Crane. (Illus.). 119p. 1992. reprint ed. pap. 22.00 (*0-8328-2727-4*); reprint ed. lib. bdg. 32.00 (*0-8328-2726-6*) Higginson Bk Co.

Baskervill, Charles R. English Elements in Johnson's Early Comedy. LC 67-21711. 338p. 1967. reprint ed. 75.00 (*0-87752-004-6*) Gordian.

Baskervill, P. Hamilton. Andrew Meade of Ireland & Virginin: His Ancestors & Descendants. (Illus.). 228p. 1998. pap. 21.00 (*0-7884-1025-3*, B074) Heritage Bk.

Baskervill, Patrick H. Baskerville. Genealogy of the Baskerville Family & Some Allied Families, Including English Descent, from 1266 A.D. (Illus.). 214p. 1997. reprint ed. pap. 34.00 (*0-8328-7405-1*); reprint ed. lib. bdg. 44.00 (*0-8328-7404-3*) Higginson Bk Co.

— Hamilton. The Hamiltons of Burnside, North Carolina & Their Ancestors & Descendants. (Illus.). 158p. 1997. reprint ed. pap. 23.00 (*0-8328-8926-1*); reprint ed. lib. bdg. 33.00 (*0-8328-8925-3*) Higginson Bk Co.

Baskerville. New Baby. (J). pap. 4.95 (*0-7136-4111-8*, 93347, Pub. by A & C Blk) Talman.

Baskerville, ed. Geology & Engineering Geology of the New York Metropolitan Area, No. T361. (IGC Field Trip Guidebooks Ser.). 72p. 1989. 21.00 (*0-87590-601-X*) Am Geophysical.

Baskerville, Barnet. The People's Voice: The Orator in American Society. LC 79-4001. 269p. reprint ed. pap. 83.40 (*0-608-17704-0*, 203004800067) Bks Demand.

Baskerville, David. Music Business Handbook & Career Guide. 6th ed. LC 95-764. (Illus.). 588p. 1995. 32.00 (*0-8039-7153-2*) Sage.

Baskerville, Elizabeth. David's Kiss. LC 98-92840. (Illus.). 24p. (J). (ps-3). 1999. 14.95 (*1-890493-75-9*, Binnacle Kids) Binnacle.

— Dr. Baskerville's Baby Basics: Your Child's First Year. LC 98-71208. (Illus.). 158p. 2000. pap. 9.95 (*1-890493-52-X*, Pub. by Binnacle) Midpt Trade.

Baskerville, Patricia E. & Palmer, Patricia. Words for the Soul: Soul Searching Spiritual Enlightement & Identity Discovery. rev. ed. (Illus.). 1998. pap. 18.97 (*0-9661777-0-3*) Brenuth.

Baskerville, Peter. Unwilling Idlers: The Urban Unemployed & Their Families in Late Victorian Canada. LC 99-164249. (Illus.). 304p. 1998. text 55.00 (*0-8020-4320-8*); pap. text 24.95 (*0-8020-8144-4*) U of Toronto Pr.

Baskerville, Richard. Designing Information Systems Security. LC 87-31959. (John Wiley Information Systems Ser.). 263p. reprint ed. pap. 81.60 (*0-7837-4512-5*, 204429100001) Bks Demand.

Baskerville, Richard, ed. see IFIP WG8.2 Working Conference on Information Techn.

Baskerville, Rosetta G. The King of the Snakes & Other Folk-Lore Stories from Uganda. LC 78-67685. (Folktale Ser.). reprint ed. 29.50 (*0-404-16054-9*) AMS Pr.

Baskerville, Stephen W. Of Laws & Limitations: An Intellectual Portrait of Louis Dembitz Brandeis. LC 92-58957. 1994. 48.50 (*0-8386-3478-8*) Fairleigh Dickinson.

*__Baskes, Jeremy.__ Indians, Merchants & Markets: Trade & Repartimiento Production of Cochineal Dye in Late Colonial Oaxaca, 1750-1821. LC 00-39489. (Illus.). 2000. write for info. (*0-8047-3512-3*) Stanford U Pr.

Baskes Litwin, Laura. Benjamin Banneker: Astronomer & Mathematician. LC 98-34913. (African-American Biographies Ser.). 112p. (YA). (gr. 6 up). 1999. lib. bdg. 20.95 (*0-7660-1208-5*) Enslow Pubs.

Baskett, Franz K. The Accident Prone Man. LC 93-18469. 80p. (Orig.). 1994. pap. 12.95 (*0-914061-40-2*) Orchises Pr.

Baskett, Geoffrey. Daily Light. (Collins Gem Ser.). 1993. pap. 8.00 (*0-00-470279-4*) Collins.

Baskett, Kathryn, jt. auth. see Adams, Pamela W.

Baskett, Kathryn K., jt. auth. see Adams, Pamela W.

Baskett, Kathryn K., ed. see Adams, Pamela W.

*__Baskett, Mary W.__ John Henry Twachtman, American Impressionist Painter as Printmaker: A Catalogue Raisonne of His Prints. LC 99-71680. (Illus.). 160p. 1999. 90.00 (*0-9628234-3-0*) M Hausberg.

*__Baskett, Mickey.__ Decorating Your Garden: A Bouquet of Beautiful & Useful Craft Projects to Make & Enjoy. (Illus.). 128p. 1999. pap. 14.95 (*0-8069-9470-3*) Sterling.

Baskett, Mickey. Fantastic Furniture: Intriguing Paint Techniques & Projects. LC 98-40850. (Illus.). 1999. 24.95 (*0-8069-6263-1*) Sterling.

*__Baskett, Mickey.__ Fantastic Furniture: Intriguing Paint Techniques & Projects. (Illus.). 2000. pap. 14.95 (*0-8069-6425-1*) Sterling.

— Glass Painting in an Afternoon. LC 99-18588. (Illus.). 112p. 1999. 22.95 (*0-8069-3949-4*) Sterling.

Baskett, Mickey. Great Paper Quilling. LC 99-37112. (Illus.). 128p. 1999. 24.95 (*0-8069-3936-2*) Sterling.

*__Baskett, Mickey.__ Making Beautiful Hemp & Bead Jewelry. (Illus.). 96p. 1999. pap. 12.95 (*0-8069-6275-5*) Sterling.

Baskett, Mickey. Wonderful Wire Works. LC 99-18589. 128p. 1999. 24.95 (*0-8069-3943-5*) Sterling.

Baskett, Peter J. & Weller, R. O. Medicine for Disasters. (Illus.). 494p. 1988. text 185.00 (*0-7236-0949-7*, Pub. by John Wright) Buttrwrth-Heinemann.

Baskett, Peter J. F., et al. Practical Procedures in Anesthesia & Critical Care. (Illus.). 298p. (C). (gr. 13). 1994. 71.00 (*1-56375-606-4*) Gower-Mosby.

Baskett, Peter J. F., ed. see International Congress on Immediate Care Staff.

Baskett, Simon. The Mini Rough Guide to Madrid. (Illus.). 256p. 1998. pap. 9.95 (*1-85828-353-1*) Viking Penguin.

Baskett, Thomas F. Essential Management of Obstetric Emergencies. LC 84-15390. (Wiley-Medical Publication). (Illus.). 233p. reprint ed. pap. 72.30 (*0-8357-8632-3*, 203505600092) Bks Demand.

Baskett, Tom, Jr., jt. auth. see Sanders, Jerry.

Baskett, William D. Parts of the Body in the Later Germanic Dialects. LC 75-161725. (Chicago. University. Linguistic Studies in Germanic: No. 5). reprint ed. 29.50 (*0-404-50285-7*) AMS Pr.

Baskette, Floyd K. & Sissors, Jack Z. The Art of Editing. 6th ed. LC 96-29201. 462p. 1996. 63.00 (*0-205-26219-8*) Allyn.

Baskette, Michael. Chef Manager. 192p. (C). 2000. pap. 29.33 (*0-13-754912-1*, Macmillan Coll) P-H.

Baskette, Michael & Mainella, Eleanor M. The Art of Nutritional Cooking. 2nd ed. LC 98-18834. 405p. (C). 1998. pap. text 64.00 (*0-13-754417-0*) P-H.

Basketter. Toxicology of Contact Dermatitis. LC 98-48821. 188p. 1999. 135.00 (*0-471-97201-0*) Wiley.

Baskey, Teresa. Lifepac Gold History Grade 8 Boxed Set. (Illus.). (J). (gr. 8). 1999. teacher ed., student ed., boxed set 45.95 (*0-7403-0040-7*, HIS0815) Alpha AZ.

Baskey, Terry. Lifepac Gold History Grade 5 Boxed Set. (Illus.). (J). (gr. 5). 2000. teacher ed., student ed., boxed set 45.95 (*0-86717-034-4*, HIS0515) Alpha AZ.

Baskfield, Lynn, jt. auth. see Shaw, Shirley J.

Baskin. Fanciful Beasts. (J). 16.00 (*0-689-80251-X*) Aladdin.

— The Invitation. 176p. (J). 1993. per. write for info. (*0-920813-54-2*) Sister Vis Pr.

— Public Relations. 4th ed. 1996. 20.00 (*0-697-20123-5*, WCB McGr Hill) McGrw-H Hghr Educ.

— Public Relations. 5th ed. 2000. 50.74 (*0-07-231456-7*) McGraw.

Baskin & Aronoff. Public Relations. 3rd ed. 1992. 13.75 (*0-697-08631-3*, WCB McGr Hill) McGrw-H Hghr Educ.

Baskin, Alex. John Reed: The Early Years in Greenwich Village. 1990. 35.95 (*0-914924-03-6*) Archives Soc Hist.

Baskin, Alex, ed. The American Civil Liberties Union Papers: A Guide to the Records of the A. C. L. U. Cases 1912-1946. LC 70-28011. 1972. pap. 12.95 (*0-914924-00-1*) Archives Soc Hist.

— Studies in the Social Aspects of the Depression: Social Science Research Council, 13 vols., Set. 1972. reprint ed. 219.00 (*0-405-00840-6*) Ayer.

— The Unemployed. LC 74-20094. 1975. 35.95 (*0-914924-01-X*) Archives Soc Hist.

Baskin, Alex, jt. ed. see Sanger, Margaret.

Baskin, Arthur B. Principles of Organization in Organisms. (C). 1992. pap. 40.00 (*0-201-58789-0*) Addison-Wesley.

*__Baskin, Arthur B., ed.__ Cooperative Knowledge Processing for Engineering Design. LC 98-49600. 11p. 1998. 175.00 (*0-412-83750-1*) Kluwer Academic.

Baskin, Barbara H. & Harris, Karen H. Books for the Gifted Child, Vol. 1. LC 79-27431. (Serving Special Populations). 263p. 1980. 34.95 (*0-8352-1161-4*) Bowker.

Baskin, Barbara H. & Harris, Karen H., eds. The Special Child in the Library. LC 76-21268. 207p. reprint ed. pap. 64.20 (*0-608-12593-8*, 202395500034) Bks Demand.

Baskin, Carols C. & Baskin, Jerry M. Seeds: Ecology, Biogeography, & Evolution of Dormancy & Germination. LC 97-80574. (Illus.). 666p. 1998. boxed set 99.95 (*0-12-080260-0*) Acad Pr.

Baskin, Deborah R. & Sommers, Ira B. Casualties of Community Disorder: Women's Careers in Violent Crime. LC 97-30633. (Crime & Society Ser.). (C). 1997. pap. text 24.00 (*0-8133-2994-9*, Pub. by Westview) HarpC.

Baskin, Diana. Divine Memories of Sathya Sai Baba. 304p. (Orig.). 1990. pap. 9.00 (*1-878599-00-3*) Birth Day.

Baskin, Ellen. Serials on British Television. 346p. 1996. 86.95 (*1-85928-015-3*, Pub. by Scolar Pr) Ashgate Pub Co.

Baskin, Ellen, jt. auth. see Hicken, Mandy.

Baskin, Jerry M., jt. auth. see Baskin, Carols C.

*__Baskin, John.__ New Burlington: The Life & Death of an American Village. 2000. pap. 14.95 (*0-393-32020-0*) Norton.

Baskin, Jonathan & Miranti, Paul J., Jr. A History of Corporate Finance. (Historical Perspectives on Modern Economics Ser.). 362p. (C). 1999. pap. text 18.95 (*0-521-65536-6*) Cambridge U Pr.

Baskin, Judith. Jewish Women in Historical Perspective. 2nd ed. LC 98-26374. 1999. pap. text 19.95 (*0-8143-2713-3*) Wayne St U Pr.

Baskin, Judith R., ed. Jewish Women in Historical Perspective. LC 91-10491. 300p. reprint ed. pap. 93.00 (*0-608-10575-9*, 207119500009) Bks Demand.

— Women of the Word: Jewish Women & Jewish Writing. (Illus.). 382p. 1994. 39.95 (*0-8143-2422-3*); pap. text 19.95 (*0-8143-2423-1*) Wayne St U Pr.

Baskin, Judith R. & Tenenbaum, Shelly, eds. Gender & Jewish Studies: A Curriculum Guide. LC 93-74870. 200p. (Orig.). (C). 1994. pap. text 13.95 (*0-930395-19-0*) Biblio NY.

Baskin, Ken. Corporate DNA: Learning from Life. LC 98-5770. 224p. 1998. pap. text 18.95 (*0-7506-9844-6*) Buttrwrth-Heinemann.

Baskin, Larry, et al. Handbook of Pediatric Urology. LC 97-5381. (Illus.). 208p. 1997. pap. text 34.95 (*0-316-08352-6*) Lppncott W & W.

*__Baskin, Laurence S. & Hayward, Simon W.__ Advances in Bladder Research. LC 99-31871. (Advances in Experimental Medicine & Biology Ser.). 1999. write for info. (*0-306-46112-9*, Kluwer Plenum) Kluwer Academic.

Baskin, Leonard. Haggadah: With an Original Signed Lithograph. deluxe ed. 128p. 1974. boxed set 500.00 (*1-55660-240-5*) A Wofsy Fine Arts.

— Leonard Baskin's Miniature Natural History. (Illus.). 28p. (J). (gr. k up). 1993. reprint ed. 14.95 (*0-88708-265-3*, Picture Book Studio) S&S Childrens.

Baskin, Maria M. & Morton, Lois W. Working World: Language & Culture of the Job Market. 236p. (C). 1986. pap. text 20.50 (*0-15-596710-X*) Harcourt Coll Pubs.

*__Baskin, Maurice, intro.__ Association Law Compendium. LC 99-175037. (Legal Section Ser.). ix, 628p. 1998. ring bd. 115.00 (*0-88034-133-5*) Am Soc Assn Execs.

Baskin, Otis W. & Aronoff, Craig. Public Relations: The Profession & the Practice. 4th ed. 528p. (C). 1997. text, student ed. write for info. (*0-07-114032-8*) Brown & Benchmark.

Baskin, Otis W., et al. Public Relations: The Profession & the Practice. 4th ed. LC 96-83186. 528p. (C). 1996. text. write for info. (*0-697-20122-8*) Brown & Benchmark.

Baskin, Ronald J. & Yeh, Yin, eds. Optical Studies of Muscle Cross-Bridges. 256p. 1987. 120.00 (*0-8493-6157-5*, QP321, CRC Reprint) Franklin.

Baskin-Salzberg, Anita. Turtles. (First Bks.). 1998. pap. 6.95 (*0-531-15898-5*) Watts.

Baskin, Steven I. Principles of Cardiac Toxicology. (Illus.). 576p. 1991. lib. bdg. 159.00 (*0-8493-8809-0*, RC682) CRC Pr.

Baskin, Steven I., ed. Principles of Cardiac Toxicology. 500p. 1990. 62.50 (*0-936923-48-2*) Telford Pr.

Baskin, Steven I. & Salem, Harry. Oxidants, Antioxidants & Free Radicals. LC 97-13108. 450p. 1997. boxed set 135.00 (*1-56032-644-1*) Hemisp Pub.

Baskin, Steven I., jt. auth. see Salem, Harry.

Baskin, Wade, tr. from FRE. History of Philosophy. Incl. Hellenistic & Roman Age. 1965. pap. text 7.00 (*0-226-07221-5*, P199); pap. write for info. (*0-318-56051-8*) U Ch Pr.

Baskin, Wade, ed. see Sartre, Jean-Paul.

Baskin, Wade, tr. see Brehier, Emile.

Baskin, Wade, tr. see De Saussure, Ferdinand.

Baskin, Wade, tr. see Einstein, Albert.

Baskin, Wade, tr. see Sartre, Jean-Paul.

Baskin, Yvonne. The Work of Nature: How Diversity of Life Sustains Us. (Illus.). 288p. 1998. pap. 17.95 (*1-55963-520-7*) Island Pr.

— Work of Nature: How the Diversity of Life Sustains Us. LC 96-52051. (Illus.). 288p. 1997. text 25.00 (*1-55963-519-3*, Shearwater Bks) Island Pr.

Baskins, Cristelle L. Cassone Painting, Humanism & Gender in Early Modern Italy. LC 97-32147. (Cambridge Studies in New Art History & Criticism). (Illus.). 300p. (C). 1998. 70.00 (*0-521-58393-4*) Cambridge U Pr.

Baskins, Don. Well-Shod: A Horseshoeing Guide for Owners & Farriers. Witte, Randy, ed. LC 97-224659. (Illus.). 159p. 1997. pap. 15.95 (*0-911647-42-2*) Western Horseman.

Baskoff, Florence. New Worlds: A Course in Guided Composition, with Readings & Conversation, 3 vols. (C). 1992. 25.16 (*0-395-52632-9*) HM.

— New Worlds: A Course in Guided Composition, with Readings & Conversation, 3 vols. 3rd ed. (C). 1992. text 23.96 (*0-395-43196-4*) HM.

Baskov, E. A. The Fundamentals of Paleohydrogeology of Ore Deposits. (Illus.). 225p. 1987. 118.95 (*0-387-17234-3*) Spr-Verlag.

Baskwewill, Jane. Langage Integre Et L'Evalua... Whole Language Checklists.Tr. of Le Langage Integre et l'Evaluation de l'Enfant: Guide Pratique. (FRE.). mass mkt. 7.99 (*0-590-71981-5*) Scholastic Inc.

Baskwill. Every Child Can Read. 96p. 1997. pap. 10.95 (*0-590-10389-X*) Scholastic Inc.

Baskwill, Jane. Big Interactive Literacy Builders: Complete How-To's for Making Manipulative Reading Tools. 1998. pap. text 7.95 (*0-590-12877-9*) Scholastic Inc.

— Connections: A Child's. 1993. pap. 7.95 (*0-590-73458-X*) Scholastic Inc.

— Parents & Teachers. 1993. pap. 8.95 (*0-590-73187-4*) Scholastic Inc.

— Somewhere. LC 95-31866. (Illus.). (J). (ps-2). 1996. 13.95 (*1-57255-131-3*) Mondo Pubng.

— Touch the Earth. LC 97-3944. (Illus.). 32p. (J). (gr. 1-5). 1999. pap. 4.95 (*1-57255-428-2*) Mondo Pubng.

Baskwill, Jane & Whitman, P. Whole Language Source, Nos. 1 & 2. 1993. pap., teacher ed. 52.50 (*0-590-71637-9*) Scholastic Inc.

Baskwill, Jane & Whitman, Paulette. Evaluation: Whole Language. 1993. pap. 8.95 (*0-590-71858-4*) Scholastic Inc.

— Guide to Classroom. 24p. (J). (gr. k-4). 1993. pap. 7.95 (*0-590-71369-8*) Scholastic Inc.

Baskys, Andrius & Remington, Gary, eds. Brain Mechanisms & Psychotropic Drugs. LC 95-47545. 288p. 1996. boxed set 139.95 (*0-8493-8386-2*) CRC Pr.

Baslar, Kemal. The Concept of the Common Heritage of Mankind in International Law. LC 97-44703. (Developments in International Law Ser.: No. 30). 464p. 1997. 183.00 (*90-411-0505-0*) Kluwer Academic.

Basle, Herve. Le Fils du Cordonnier. large type ed. 1996. pap. 25.99 (*2-84011-141-1*) Ulverscroft.

Basler, A., jt. ed. see Obe, G.

Basler, Christian O., jt. ed. see Basler, Roy P.

Basler, K., jt. auth. see Kollbrunner, C. F.

An Asterisk (*) at the beginning of an entry indicates that the title is appearing for the first time.

Basler, Konrad. The Dorlikon Emigrants: Swiss Settlers & Cultural Founders in the United States. Villager, Laura, tr. from GER. (Swiss American Historical Society Publications: Vol. 10). (Illus.). 74p. (C). 1997. text 19.95 (*0-8204-2675-X*) P Lang Pubng.

Basler, Lucille. District of Ste. Genevieve: 1725-1980. Kellogg, Dennis & Palmer, Kathleen, eds. LC 80-70736. (Illus.). 360p. 1980. 22.50 (*0-686-32932-5*) Vedette Print.

Basler, Otto, jt. auth. see Schulz, Hans.

Basler, Otto, jt. contrib. by see Schulz, Hans.

Basler, Robert, ed. see Reuters America Staff.

Basler, Roy P. Abraham Lincoln: His Speeches & Writings. (Quality Paperbacks Ser.). (Illus.). 888p. 1990. reprint ed. pap. 19.95 (*0-306-80404-2*) Da Capo.

— The Collected Works of Abraham Lincoln, Vol. 10, 1st Supplement. 320p. (C). 1990. reprint ed. text 50.00 (*0-8135-1552-1*) Rutgers U Pr.

— The Muse & the Librarian, 10. LC 72-780. (Contributions in American Studies: No. 10). 207p. 1974. 49.95 (*0-8371-6134-7*, BML/, Greenwood Pr) Greenwood.

— A Touchstone for Greatness: Essays, Addresses & Occasional Pieces about Abraham Lincoln, 4. LC 72-781. (Contributions in American Studies: No. 4). 257p. 1973. 55.00 (*0-8371-6135-5*, BTG/, Greenwood Pr) Greenwood.

B

Basler, Roy P. & Basler, Christian O., eds. The Collected Works on Abraham Lincoln, 1848-1865, Vol. II, 2nd Supplement. 130p. (C). 1990. text 40.00 (*0-8135-1532-7*) Rutgers U Pr.

Basler, Roy P., ed. see Scripps, John L.

Basmadjian, Diran. Art of Modeling in Science & Engineering. 450p. 1999. 89.95 (*0-8493-0248-X*) CRC Pr.

***Basmadjian, Diran.** Art of Modeling in Science & Engineering. 688p. 1999. boxed set 89.95 (*1-58488-012-0*, Chap & Hall CRC) CRC Pr.

Basmadjian, Diran. The Little Adsorption Book: A Practical Guide for Engineers & Scientists. LC 96-32834. (Illus.). 160p. 1996. per. 44.95 (*0-8493-2692-3*) CRC Pr.

Basmaji, Jacques, et al. On Artin's Conjecture for Odd 2-Dimensional Representations. Frey, Gerhard, ed. LC 94-23241. (Lecture Notes in Mathematics Ser.: Vol. 1585). 1994. text. write for info. (*0-387-58387-4*) Spr-Verlag.

— On Artin's Conjecture for Odd 2-Dimensional Representations. Frey, Gerhard, ed. LC 94-23241. (Lecture Notes in Mathematics Ser.: Vol. 1585). 1994. 35.95 (*3-540-58387-4*) Spr-Verlag.

Basmajian, John V. Biofeedback: Principles & Practice for Clinicians. 3rd ed. (Illus.). 396p. 1989. 65.00 (*0-683-00357-7*) Lppncott W & W.

— Primary Anatomy. (Illus.). 404p. (C). 1998. pap. text 19.80 (*0-87563-806-6*) Stipes.

Basmajian, John V. & Banerjee, Sikhar N., eds. Clinical Decision Making in Rehabilitation: Efficacy & Outcomes. LC 96-2745. 240p. 1996. text 41.95 (*0-443-08993-0*) Church.

Basmajian, John V. & DeLuca, Carlo J. Muscles Alive: Their Functions Revealed by Electromyography. 5th ed. (Illus.). 562p. 1985. 65.00 (*0-683-00414-X*) Lppncott W & W.

Basmajian, John V. & MacConaill, M. A. Muscles & Movements: A Basis for Human Kinesiology. rev. ed. LC 76-6883. 412p. 1977. 42.50 (*0-88275-398-3*) Krieger.

Basmajian, John V. & Wolf, Steven. Therapeutic Exercise. 5th ed. (Illus.). 460p. 1990. 49.00 (*0-683-00433-6*) Lppncott W & W.

Basmajian, John V., et al. Through the Molecular Maze. 3rd ed. (Illus.). (C). 1991. pap. text 7.95 (*1-879336-00-6*) Bio-Venture.

Basmajian, John V., jt. auth. see Kumbhare, Dinesh.

Basman, Michael. The Killer Grob. (PECH Pergamon Chess Ser.). 128p. 1991. write for info. (*0-08-037130-2*, 6201, Pub. by CHES) Macmillan.

— Play the St. George. (Illus.). 132p. 1982. 19.95 (*0-08-029718-8*, Pergamon Pr); pap. 13.90 (*0-08-029717-X*, Pergamon Pr) Elsevier.

Basman, Mike. Chess Openings. (Crowood Chess Library). 256p. 1989. pap. 19.95 (*0-946284-74-1*, Pub. by Cro1wood) Trafalgar.

Basmann, R. L. Advances in Econometrics: Economic Inequality Measurement & Policy, Vol. 3. Rhodes, George F., Jr. et al, eds. 282p. 1984. 78.50 (*0-89232-443-0*) Jai Pr.

Basmann, R. L., et al. The Generalized Fechner-Thurstons Direct Utility Function & Some of Its Uses. (Lecture Notes in Economics & Mathematical Systems Ser.: Vol. 316). viii, 159p. 1988. 43.95 (*0-387-96853-9*) Spr-Verlag.

— Some New Methods for Measuring & Describing Economic Inequality. LC 93-40398. (Contemporary Studies in Economic & Financial Analysis: Vol. 71). 1994. 78.50 (*1-55938-385-2*) Jai Pr.

Basmossy, Gary & Van Raaij, Fred, eds. European Advances in Consumer Research: Proceedings of the 1992 Conference, Vol. 1. 574p. 1993. 49.00 (*0-915552-31-0*) Assn Consumer Res.

Basner, Austin E. Tales from the Jaffa Gate. 200p. 1998. pap. 15.00 (*0-9666017-4-2*) Arden Intl.

Basner, Ruth H. Yesteryears: A Pictorial History of Stark County, Ohio. LC 96-28363. 1996. write for info. (*0-89865-973-6*) Donning Co.

Basnight, Bob. What Ship Is That? (Illus.). 160p. (Orig.). 1996. pap. 15.95 (*1-55821-433-X*, 1433X) Lyons Pr.

Basoglu, Metin, ed. Torture & Its Consequences: Current Treatment Approaches. (Illus.). 552p. (C). 1998. pap. text 54.95 (*0-521-65954-X*) Cambridge U Pr.

Basok, Tanya. Keeping Heads above Water: Salvadorean Refugees in Costa Rica. 184p. 1993. 60.00 (*0-7735-0977-1*, Pub. by McG-Queens Univ Pr) CUP Services.

Basoli, Antonio. Collezione Di Varie Scene Teatrali. LC 68-21205. (ITA., Illus.). 1972. reprint ed. 26.95 (*0-405-08241-X*, Pub. by Blom Pubns) Ayer.

Basolo, F., ed. Chemtracts Vol. 10: Organic Chemistry, Inorganic Chemistry, Biochemistry & Molecular Biology, 14 issues. 1997. 420.00 (*0-614-30188-2*, 10001) Spr-Verlag.

Basolo, Fred, et al, eds. Transition Metal Chemistry, Vols. 1-2. LC 72-95642. (ACS Reprint Collection). reprint ed. pap. 12.95 (*0-8412-0356-3*) Am Chemical.

Basolo, Fred & Pearson, Ralph G. Mechanisms of Inorganic Reactions: A Study of Metal Complexes in Solution. 2nd ed. LC 66-28755. (Illus.). 715p. reprint ed. pap. 200.00 (*0-608-18195-1*, 205659700078) Bks Demand.

Basolo, Fred, ed. see NATO Science Committee Conference on Catalysis Sta.

Basom, Kit. Magic Child. 272p. (C). 1992. pap. write for info. (*1-874640-15-7*, Pub. by Argyll Pubng) St Mut.

Bason, F. T. A Bibliography of the Writings of William Somerset Maugham. LC 74-6376. (Bibliography Ser.: No. 59). 1974. lib. bdg. 75.00 (*0-8383-1880-0*) M S G Haskell Hse.

Basor, E. I. & Gohberg, I., eds. Toeplitz Operators & Related Topics: The Harold Widom Anniversary Volume. LC 94-13097. (Operator Theory, Advances & Applications Ser.: Vol. 71). 208p. 1994. 77.00 (*0-8176-5068-7*) Birkhauser.

Basov, N. G., ed. Coherent Cooperative Phenomena. McNeill, Donald H., tr. from RUS. LC 78-2008. (Proceedings of the P. N. Lebedev Physics Institute Ser.: No. 87). (Illus.). 162p. 1978. reprint ed. pap. 50.30 (*0-608-05545-X*, 206601300006) Bks Demand.

— Cosmic Rays in the Stratosphere & in near Space. Wood, James S., tr. from RUS. LC 78-2007. (Proceedings of the P. N. Lebedev Physics Institute Ser.: No. 88). (Illus.). 187p. 1978. reprint ed. pap. 58.00 (*0-608-05546-8*, 206601400006) Bks Demand.

— Electronic Characteristics & Electron-Phonon Interaction in Superconducting Metals & Alloys. Burdick, David L., tr. from RUS. LC 77-16799. (Proceedings of the P. N. Lebedev Physics Institute Ser.: No. 82). (Illus.). 104p. 1977. reprint ed. pap. 32.30 (*0-608-05541-7*, 206600900006) Bks Demand.

— Exciton & Domain Luminescence of Semiconductors. Hutchison, R. C., tr. from RUS. LC 79-14567. (Proceedings of the P. N. Lebedev Physics Institute Ser.: No. 97). (Illus.). 119p. 1979. reprint ed. pap. 36.90 (*0-608-05553-0*, 206602100006) Bks Demand.

— High-Power Lasers & Laser Plasmas. Adashko, J. George, tr. from RUS. LC 78-794. (Proceedings of the P. N. Lebedev Physics Institute Ser.: No. 85). (Illus.). 249p. 1978. reprint ed. pap. 77.20 (*0-608-05544-1*, 206601200006) Bks Demand.

— The Kinetics of Simple Models in the Theory of Oscillations. McNeill, Donald H., tr. from RUS. LC 78-5936. (Proceedings of the P. N. Lebedev Physics Institute Ser.: No. 90). (Illus.). 216p. 1978. reprint ed. pap. 67.00 (*0-608-05548-4*, 206601600006) Bks Demand.

— Lasers & Their Applications. Tybulewicz, Albin, tr. from RUS. LC 76-26590. (Proceedings of the P. N. Lebedev Physics Institute Ser.: No. 76). (Illus.). 231p. 1976. reprint ed. pap. 71.70 (*0-608-05535-2*, 206600300006) Bks Demand.

— Lasers & Their Applications in Physical Research. McNeill, Donald H., tr. from RUS. LC 78-13582. (Proceedings of the P. N. Lebedev Physics Institute Ser.: No. 91). (Illus.). 234p. 1979. reprint ed. pap. 72.60 (*0-608-05549-2*, 206601700006) Bks Demand.

— Luminescence Centers in Crystals. Tybulewicz, Albin, tr. from RUS. LC 76-41167. (Proceedings of the P. N. Lebedev Physics Institute Ser.: No. 79). (Illus.). 182p. 1976. reprint ed. pap. 56.50 (*0-608-05538-7*, 206600600006) Bks Demand.

— Microwave Studies of Exciton Condensation in Germanium. Burdick, David L., tr. from RUS. LC 78-10160. (Proceedings of the P. N. Lebedev Physics Institute Ser.: No. 100). (Illus.). 97p. 1979. reprint ed. pap. 30.10 (*0-608-05554-9*, 206602200006) Bks Demand.

— Neutral Current Sheets in Plasmas. Parsons, Dave, tr. from RUS. LC 76-17087. (Proceedings of the P. N. Lebedev Physics Institute Ser.: No. 74). (Illus.). 171p. 1976. reprint ed. pap. 53.10 (*0-608-05533-6*, 206600100006) Bks Demand.

— Nonlinear Optics of Semiconductor Lasers. (Proceedings of the Lebedev Physics Institute Ser.: Vol. 166). 281p. (C). 1987. text 165.00 (*0-941743-01-2*) Nova Sci Pubs.

— Optical Properties of Semiconductors. Tybulewicz, Albin, tr. from RUS. LC 75-37609. (Proceedings of the P. N. Lebedev Physics Institute Ser.: No. 75). (Illus.). 189p. 1976. reprint ed. pap. 58.60 (*0-608-05534-4*, 206600200006) Bks Demand.

— Phase Conjugation of Laser Emission. (Proceedings of the Lebedev Physics Institute Ser.: Vol. 172). 240p. (C). 1987. text 165.00 (*0-941743-07-1*) Nova Sci Pubs.

— Problems in the General Theory of Relativity & Theory of Group Representations. Mason, Alan, tr. from RUS. LC 78-12612. (Proceedings of the P. N. Lebedev Physics Institute Ser.: No. 96). (Illus.). 193p. 1978. reprint ed. pap. 59.90 (*0-608-05552-2*, 206602000006) Bks Demand.

— Pulse Gas-Discharge Atomic & Molecular Lasers. Tybulewicz, Albin, tr. from RUS. LC 76-57191. (Proceedings of the P. N. Lebedev Physics Institute Ser.: No. 81). (Illus.). 196p. 1976. reprint ed. pap. 60.80 (*0-608-05540-9*, 206600800006) Bks Demand.

— Pulsed Neutron Research. LC 78-12997. (Proceedings of the P. N. Lebedev Physics Institute Ser.: No. 94). (Illus.). 112p. 1979. reprint ed. pap. 34.80 (*0-608-05551-4*, 206601900006) Bks Demand.

— Radio, Submillimeter, & X-Ray Telescopes. Oldham, Edward U., tr. from RUS. LC 76-48290. (Proceedings of the P. N. Lebedev Physics Institute Ser.: No. 77). (Illus.). 229p. 1976. reprint ed. pap. 71.00 (*0-608-05536-0*, 206600400006) Bks Demand.

— Research in Molecular Laser Plasmas. Tybulewicz, Albin, tr. from RUS. LC 76-25553. (Proceedings of the P. N. Lebedev Physics Institute Ser.: No. 78). (Illus.). 123p. 1976. reprint ed. pap. 38.20 (*0-608-05537-9*, 206600500006) Bks Demand.

— Superconductivity. Archard, G. D., tr. from RUS. LC 77-17959. (Proceedings of the P. N. Lebedev Physics Institute Ser.: No. 86). (Illus.). 178p. 1977. reprint ed. pap. 55.20 (*0-608-05543-3*, 206601100006) Bks Demand.

— Synchrotron Radiation. LC 76-54915. (Proceedings of the P. N. Lebedev Physics Institute Ser.: No. 80). (Illus.). 232p. 1976. reprint ed. pap. 72.00 (*0-608-05539-5*, 206600700006) Bks Demand.

— Techniques & Methods of Radio-Astronomic Reception. LC 78-26720. (Proceedings of the P. N. Lebedev Physics Institute Ser.: No. 93). (Illus.). 156p. 1979. reprint ed. pap. 48.40 (*0-608-05550-6*, 206601800006) Bks Demand.

— Theoretical Problems in the Spectroscopy & Gas Dynamics of Lasers. McNeill, Donald H., tr. from RUS. LC 77-17616. (Proceedings of the P. N. Lebedev Physics Institute Ser.: No. 83). (Illus.). 232p. 1977. reprint ed. pap. 72.00 (*0-608-05542-5*, 206601000006) Bks Demand.

Basov, N. G. & Ochkin, V. N., eds. Control of Spectra of Molecular Lasers. 180p. 1995. pap. 89.00 (*1-898326-14-2*, Pub. by CISP) Balogh.

Basov, N. G. & Tybulewicz, Albin, eds. Electrical & Optical Properties of III-V Semiconductors. LC 77-26132. (Proceedings of the P. N. Lebedev Physics Institute Ser.: No. 89). (Illus.). 126p. 1978. reprint ed. pap. 39.10 (*0-608-05547-6*, 206601500006) Bks Demand.

***Basow.** Gender: Stereotypes & Roles. 4th ed. (Psychology Ser.). (C). 2002. text 40.75 (*0-534-56448-8*) Wadsworth Pub.

Basow. Sex-Role Stereotypes. (Psychology Ser.). 1980. mass mkt. 20.00 (*0-8185-0394-7*) Brooks-Cole.

Basow, Susan. Gender: Stereotypes & Roles. 3rd ed. LC 91-38410. 399p. (C). 1992. mass mkt. 34.75 (*0-534-12120-9*) Brooks-Cole.

— Gender Stereotypes: Traditions & Alternatives. 2nd ed. LC 85-30145. 320p. (Orig.). (C). 1986. mass mkt. 25.00 (*0-534-06474-4*) Brooks-Cole.

Basque. Methods of Placer Mining. rev. ed. (Illus.). 88p. 1996. pap. 6.95 (*0-919531-40-7*, Pub. by Sunfire Pubns) Gem Guides Bk.

***Basque, Garnet.** Ghost Towns & Mining Camps of the Boundary Country. 1999. pap. 22.95 (*1-895811-82-1*) Heritage Hse.

Basque, Garnet. The Gold Panner's Manual: A Complete Guide for the Novice. rev. ed. LC 98-45011. 108p. 1999. pap. 12.95 (*1-55821-873-4*) Lyons Pr.

***Basque, Garnet.** Methods of Placer Mining. 1999. pap. 9.95 (*1-895811-84-8*) Heritage Hse.

Basque, Guy. The Electronic Superhighway: The Shape of Technology & Law to Come. Mackaay, Ejan et al, eds. LC 95-40066. (Computer-Law Ser.: Vol. 18). 1995. 95.00 (*90-411-0135-7*) Kluwer Law Intl.

Basquez, Juan J., jt. ed. see Puncel, Maria.

***Basquiat, Jean Michel.** Jean-Michel Bisquiat. 1999. 85.00 (*1-891475-14-2*) T Shafrazi.

Basquiat, Jean Michel. King for a Decade. 1998. pap. text 22.00 (*4-7713-0275-8*) Dist Art Pubs.

***Basquin, Susan.** Goat Song. (Illus.). 176p. 2000. pap. 15.00 (*1-880158-28-0*, Pub. by J N Townsend) A C Hood.

Basra, Amarjit S. Cotton Fibers: Developmental Biology, Quality Improvement & Textile Processing. LC 99-20218. 388p. 1999. 89.98 (*1-56022-867-9*, Food Products) Haworth Pr.

***Basra, Amarjit S., ed.** Crop Responses & Adaptations to Temperature Stress: New Insights & Approaches. LC 00-39305. 296p. 2000. pap. text 49.95 (*1-56022-906-3*, Food Products) Haworth Pr.

— Crop Responses & Adaptations to Temperature Stress: New Insights & Approaches. LC 00-39305. (Illus.). 296p. 2000. lib. bdg. 94.95 (*1-56022-890-3*, Food Products) Haworth Pr.

Basra, Amarjit S., ed. Crop Sciences: Recent Advances. LC 97-18156. 312p. 1997. 79.95 (*1-56022-059-7*, Food Products); pap. 29.95 (*1-56022-060-0*, Food Products) Haworth Pr.

***Basra, Amarjit S., ed.** Heterosis & Hybrid Seed Production in Agronomic Crops. LC 99-30844. (Illus.). 272p. 1999. lib. bdg. 79.95 (*1-56022-876-8*) Haworth Pr.

— Hybrid Seed Production in Vegetables: Rationale & Methods in Selected Crops. LC 00-22367. 170p. 2000. 39.95 (*1-56022-074-0*, Food Products); pap. text 24.95 (*1-56022-075-9*, Food Products) Haworth Pr.

— Mechanisms of Plant Growth & Improved Productivity: Modern Approaches. LC 94-12080. (Books in Soils, Plants & the Environment: Vol. 33). (Illus.). 496p. 1994. text 195.00 (*0-8247-9192-4*) Dekker.

— Plant Growth Regulators in Agriculture & Horticulture: Their Role & Commercial Uses. LC 00-39357. (Illus.). 272p. (C). 2000. pap. text 39.95 (*1-56022-896-2*, Food Products); lib. bdg. 94.95 (*1-56022-891-1*, Food Products) Haworth Pr.

Basra, Amarjit S., ed. Seed Quality: Basic Mechanisms & Agricultural Implications. LC 93-6092. 440p. 1995. 89.95 (*1-56022-850-4*) Haworth Jrnl Co-Edits.

Basra, Amarjit S., ed. Stress-Induced Gene Expression in Plants. LC 93-6159. xiii, 287p. 1994. text 152.00 (*3-7186-5466-0*) Gordon & Breach.

Basra, Amarjit S. & Basra, Ranjit K., eds. Mechanisms of Environmental Stress Resistance in Plants. 432p. 1997. text 81.00 (*90-5702-036-X*, ECU121, Harwood Acad Pubs) Gordon & Breach.

Basra, Ranjit K., jt. ed. see Basra, Amarjit S.

Basrani, Enrique. Fractures of the Teeth: Prevention & Treatment of the Vital & Non-Vital Pulp. Rappaport, Harold M., tr. LC 84-27783. 172p. reprint ed. pap. 53.40 (*0-7837-1479-3*, 205717400023) Bks Demand.

***Basri, Carole L.** Advanced Corporate Compliance Workshop 1999. LC 99-189447. (Corporate Law & Practice Course Handbook Ser.). 360p. 1999. 129.00 (*0-87224-568-3*) PLI.

Bass. Booker T. Washington. 1996. 24.95 (*0-8057-3977-7*, Twyne) Mac Lib Ref.

— Education in Tibet. LC 98-36349. 1998. text 65.00 (*1-85649-673-2*, Pub. by Zed Books) St Martin.

***Bass.** Education in Tibet. LC 98-36349. 1998. pap. text 25.00 (*1-85649-674-0*, Pub. by Zed Books) St Martin.

Bass. National Park Geology. (Earth Science Ser.). 2001. 37.00 (*0-534-51702-1*) Wadsworth Pub.

— Pathology. 1996. pap. text 27.00 (*0-443-05003-1*, W B Saunders Co) Harcrt Hlth Sci Grp.

Bass, Alan, tr. see Derrida, Jacques.

***Bass, Alice.** Anticipation: Dramas for Advent. LC 99-44224. (Intermission Scripts Ser.). 1999. 12.99 (*0-570-05386-2*) Concordia.

— Celebration: Dramas for Christmas. LC 99-44223. (Intermission Scripts Ser.). 1999. 12.99 (*0-570-05387-0*) Concordia.

— Jubilation: Dramas for Easter. LC 99-37049. (Intermission Scripts Ser.). 80p. 1999. 12.99 (*0-570-05390-0*) Concordia.

— Preparation: Dramas for Lent. LC 99-38521. (Intermission Scripts Ser.). 80p. 1999. 13.00 (*0-570-05391-9*) Concordia.

Bass, Althea. Cherokee Messenger. LC 96-8056. (Civilization of the American Indian Ser.: Vol. 12). (Illus.). 360p. 1996. pap. 17.95 (*0-8061-2879-8*) U of Okla Pr.

— Nightwalker & the Buffalo. (Indian Culture Ser.). 32p. (J). (gr. 5-9). 1972. pap. 4.95 (*0-89992-032-2*) Coun India Ed.

***Bass, B. R.** Application of NCSA Habanero Tool for Collaboration on Structural Integrity Assessments. 53p. 1998. pap. 4.50 (*0-16-062972-1*) USGPO.

— International Comparative Assessment Study of Pressurized Thermal Shock in Reactor Pressure Vessels. 135p. 1999. per. 14.00 (*0-16-059023-X*) USGPO.

Bass, Bernard M. Leadership & Performance Beyond Expectations. LC 84-24724. 224p. 1985. 32.95 (*0-02-901810-2*) Free Pr.

— A New Paradigm of Leadership: An Inquiry into Transformational Leadership. LC 97-18769. 258p. 1997. write for info. (*0-8058-2696-3*); pap. write for info. (*0-8058-2697-1*) L Erlbaum Assocs.

Bass, Bernard M., et al, eds. Advances in Organizational Psychology: An International Review. LC 87-9484. 314p. 1987. reprint ed. pap. 97.40 (*0-608-01081-2*, 205939000001) Bks Demand.

Bass, Bernard M. & Avolio, Bruce J., eds. Improving Organizational Effectiveness Through Transformational Leadership. (Illus.). 236p. (C). 1993. text 49.95 (*0-8039-5235-X*); pap. text 23.95 (*0-8039-5236-8*) Sage.

Bass, Bernard M. & Stogdill, Ralph M. Bass & Stogdill's Handbook of Leadership: Theory, Research, & Managerial Applications. 3rd ed. 1216p. 1990. 90.00 (*0-02-901500-6*) Free Pr.

Bass, Beverly. The Hotel del Coronado Cookbook. LC 92-43542. (Illus.). 288p. 1993. 29.95 (*0-88289-912-0*) Pelican.

Bass, Charissa T. & Walton, Emma L. Bass. Descendants of Dea. Samuel & Ann Bass. (Illus.). 223p. 1997. reprint ed. pap. 34.00 (*0-8328-7413-2*); reprint ed. lib. bdg. 44.00 (*0-8328-7412-4*) Higginson Bk Co.

Bass, Charlotte C. Quilting & Applique with Southwest Indian Designs. LC 98-7403. (Illus.). 48p. 1998. pap. 15.95 (*0-87961-251-7*) Naturegraph.

Bass, Clarence. Challenge Yourself: Leanness, Fitness & Health at Any Age. LC 99-90116. (Illus.). 224p. 1999. pap. 19.95 (*0-9609714-7-5*) Clarence Bass.

— The Lean Advantage. LC 84-71083. (Illus.). 251p. 1984. pap. 14.95 (*0-9609714-2-4*) Clarence Bass.

— The Lean Advantage 3: Four More Years. LC 94-133928. 216p. 1994. pap. 15.95 (*0-9609714-6-7*) Clarence Bass.

— The Lean Advantage 2: The Second Four Years. LC 84-71083. (Illus.). 231p. (Orig.). 1989. pap. 14.95 (*0-9609714-4-0*) Clarence Bass.

— Lean for Life. (Illus.). 247p. (Orig.). 1992. pap. 15.95 (*0-9609714-5-9*) Clarence Bass.

— Ripped: The Sensible Way to Achieve Ultimate Muscularity. LC 80-81446. (Illus.). 88p. 1980. pap. 11.95 (*0-9609714-0-8*) Clarence Bass.

— Ripped Three: The Recipes, the Routines & the Reasons. LC 80-81446. (Illus.). 195p. 1986. pap. 14.95 (*0-9609714-3-2*) Clarence Bass.

— Ripped Two. LC 80-81446. (Illus.). 179p. 1982. pap. 14.95 (*0-9609714-1-6*) Clarence Bass.

Bass, Cynthia. Maiden Voyage. 304p. 1998. mass mkt. 5.99 (*0-553-58063-9*) Bantam.

Bass, David. Your Personal Fitness Trainer. 1995. 29.95 (*0-7897-0771-3*) Que.

Bass De Martinez, Bernice B., jt. auth. see Sims, William E.

***Bass, Deborah.** Inside Incarceration Institutions. 52p. 1999. pap. 7.00 (*0-9671417-3-7*) BibleScope.

An Asterisk (*) at the beginning of an entry indicates that the title is appearing for the first time.

Bass, Deborah. Magnificent Man: Created in God's Image. Bass, Samuel, ed. 64p. 1999. pap. 6.00 (*0-9671417-0-2*) BibleScope.
— Tragedy to Triumph. (Illus.). 58p. 1999. pap. 5.00 (*0-9671417-1-0*) BibleScope.
Bass, Deborah, jt. auth. see Bass, Samuel.
Bass, Deborah S. Caring Families: Supports & Interventions. LC 90-6277. 281p. 1990. pap. text 23.95 (*0-87101-185-9*) Natl Assn Soc Wkrs.
— Helping Vulnerable Youths: Runaway & Homeless Adolescents in the United States. LC 92-21848. 187p. 1992. 18.95 (*0-87101-221-9*) Natl Assn Soc Wkrs.
Bass, Dick & Wells, Frank. Seven Summits. 384p. 1988. mass mkt. 15.99 (*0-446-38516-6*, Pub. by Warner Bks) Little.
Bass, Dorothy C. Practicing Our Faith: A Guide for Conversation, Learning & Growing. LC 96-80241. 56p. 1998. pap., student ed. 6.00 (*0-7879-0365-5*) Jossey-Bass.
— Receiving the Day: Christian Practices for Opening the Gift of Time. LC 99-6444. 172p. 1999. 20.00 (*0-7879-4287-1*) Jossey-Bass.
Bass, Dorothy C., ed. Practicing Our Faith: A Way of Life for a Searching People. LC 96-45782. (Religion in Practice Ser.). 1997. mass mkt. 22.50 (*0-7879-0336-1*) Jossey-Bass.
— Practicing Our Faith: A Way of Life for a Searching People. (Religion in Practice Ser.). 256p. 1998. pap. 14.00 (*0-7879-3883-1*) Jossey-Bass.
Bass, Dorothy C. & Smith, Kenneth B., eds. The United Church of Christ: Studies in Identity & Polity. LC 86-83022. (Studies in Ministry & Parish Life). 107p. (C). 1987. text 22.95 (*0-913552-37-2*) Exploration Pr.
Bass, Eben E. Dante Gabriel Rossetti: Poet & Painter. X, 363p. (C). 1990. text 64.95 (*0-8204-1028-4*) P Lang Pubng.
Bass, Ellen. I Like You to Make Jokes with Me, But I Don't Want You to Touch Me. 2nd ed. Salgado, Maria A., tr. (ENG & SPA., Illus.). 28p. (J). 1993. pap. 6.95 (*0-914996-27-4*) Lollipop Power.
— I'm Not Your Laughing Daughter. LC 73-79503. 96p. 1973. 17.50 (*0-87023-128-6*) U of Mass Pr.
Bass, Ellen & Davis, Laura. Beginning to Heal: The First Book for Survivors of Child Sexual Abuse. LC 92-54425. 128p. 1993. pap. 10.00 (*0-06-096927-X*, Perennial) HarperTrade.
***Bass, Ellen & Davis, Laura.** The Courage to Heal. abr. ed. 1999. pap. 40.50 incl. audio Courage-to-Change.
— The Courage to Heal: Bass,&Ellen, Set. abr. ed. 1992. audio 18.00 (*0-89845-833-1*, CPN 2116) HarperAudio.
Bass, Ellen & Davis, Laura. The Courage to Heal - Third Edition - Revised & Expanded: A Guide for Women Survivors of Child Sexual Abuse. 3rd rev. ed. LC 93-48353. 608p. 1994. pap. 22.50 (*0-06-095066-8*, Perennial) HarperTrade.
Bass, Ellen & Kaufman, Kate. Free Your Mind: The Book for Gay, Lesbian & Bisexual Youth - And Their Allies. LC 96-4157. 448p. 1996. pap. 14.00 (*0-06-095104-4*, Perennial) HarperTrade.
Bass, Ellen & Thornton, Louise. I Never Told Anyone: Writing by Women Survivors of Sexual Abuse. LC 90-55489. 288p. 1991. reprint ed. pap. 13.00 (*0-06-096573-8*, Perennial) HarperTrade.
Bass, Eric. In My Grandmother's Purse: Playscript. (J). 1995. 6.00 (*0-87602-331-6*) Anchorage.
Bass, F. G. & Bulgakov, A. A. Kinetic & Electrodynamic Phenomena in Classical & Quantum Semiconductor Superlattices. LC 97-158467. 490p. (C). 1997. lib. bdg. 145.00 (*1-56072-425-0*) Nova Sci Pubs.
Bass, F. G. & Fuchs, Marjorie. Wave Scattering from Statistically Rough Surfaces. LC 77-23113. 1979. 241.00 (*0-08-019896-1*, Pub. by Pergamon Repr) Franklin.
Bass, Fayne & Sherman, Stanley. Because of the Cross. 64p. 1993. pap. 1.25 (*0-940999-79-X*, B0019) Star Bible.
Bass, Florence. Christian Liberty Nature Reader, Bk. 1. Kramer, Wendy, ed. (Illus.). 162p. (J). (gr. 1-2). 1996. pap. text 6.00 (*1-930092-51-2*, CLP29950) Christian Liberty.
Bass-Foster, Cheryl. Broken to Be Made Whole. 170p. 1993. pap. 8.95 (*1-884687-01-6*) N Horzns Pub.
— Broken to Be Made Whole. 2nd ed. (Illus.). 156p. 1996. pap. 9.95 (*0-936369-64-7*) Son-Rise Pubns.
— How to Live Happy & Healthy: When Your World Is Falling Apart. Libb, Melva, ed. (Illus.). 96p. 1996. pap. write for info. (*0-936369-71-X*) Son-Rise Pubns.
Bass, Gary J. A Practical & Simple Guide to a Home Mortgage: A Step-by-Step Guide to Finding & Financing Your Next House. LC 87-82025. 66p. (Orig.). 1987. pap. text 6.95 (*0-944319-00-9*) G & P Pub.
***Bass, Gary Jonathan.** Stay the Hand of Vengeance: The Politics of War Crimes Tribunals. LC 00-36692. (Studies in International History & Politics). 368p. 2000. pap. 29.95 (*0-691-04922-X*, Pub. by Princeton U Pr) Cal Prin Full Svc.
Bass, Gene & Portice, Jack. Carving Weathered Wood: Tips & Techniques for Award-Winning Carvings. LC 91-37969. (Illus.). 72p. (Orig.). 1991. pap. 10.95 (*1-879511-00-2*, Vestal Pr) Madison Bks UPA.
Bass, George. Here Comes the King. 1992. pap. 7.75 (*1-55673-440-9*, 9243) CSS OH.
Bass, George F., ed. Ships & Shipwrecks of the Americas: A History Based on Underwater Archaeology. LC 88-50246. (Illus.). 272p. 1996. pap. 24.95 (*0-500-27892-X*, Pub. by Thames Hudson) Norton.
Bass, George F., et al. Yassi Ada: Vol. I, A Seventh-Century Byzantine Shipwreck. LC 81-40401. (Nautical Archaeology Ser.: No. 1). (Illus.). 368p. 1982. 89.50 (*0-89096-063-1*) Tex A&M Univ Pr.
Bass, George Houston, ed. see Hughes, Langston & Hurston, Zora Neale.
Bass, George M. The Cradle, the Cross & the Crown. Sherer, Michael L., ed. (Orig.). 1986. pap. 7.75 (*0-89536-817-X*, 6866) CSS OH.
— Great Stories of the Faith. 1989. pap. 8.50 (*1-55673-134-5*, 9859) CSS OH.
— Is the Cross Still There? 1991. pap. 7.75 (*1-55673-279-1*, 9112) CSS OH.
— Lectionary Preaching Workbook, Vol. III, Pt. A. 1989. pap., wbk. ed. 39.50 (*1-55673-135-3*, 9860) CSS OH.
— Lectionary Preaching Workbook: Small Version, Vol. I. 1996. wbk. ed. 23.95 (*1-55673-243-0*) CSS OH.
Bass, Gloria J. The Seafood Lovers Cookbook. LC 93-73153. 194p. (Orig.). 1993. pap. 15.95 (*0-935132-22-8*) C H Fairfax.
Bass, H., et al, eds. Algebraic K-Theory & Its Applications: Proceedings of the School ICTP, Trieste, Italy 1-19 September 1997. LC 98-49298. 607p. 1998. 78.00 (*981-02-3491-0*) World Scientific Pub.
Bass, H., ed. see Di Biase, F.
Bass, H. Royce. History of Braintree: Including a Memorial of Families That Have Resided in Town. (Illus.). 208p. 1997. reprint ed. lib. bdg. 29.50 (*0-8328-6502-8*) Higginson Bk Co.
Bass, Hans H., ed. Algebraic K-Theory 1: Higher K-Theories. LC 73-13419. (Lecture Notes in Mathematics Ser.: Vol. 341). xv, 335p. 1986. pap. 49.30 (*0-387-06434-6*) Spr-Verlag.
— Algebraic K-Theory 2: Classical Algebraic K-Theory, & Connections with Arithmetic. LC 73-13420. (Lecture Notes in Mathematics Ser.: Vol. 342). xv, 527p. 1986. 74.95 (*0-387-06435-4*) Spr-Verlag.
Bass, Hans H., et al, eds. Analytic Number Theory: Proceedings of a Conference in Honor of Heini Halberstam. LC 96-19918. (Progress in Mathematics Ser.: Vol. 138). xiv, 449p. 1996. 96.00 (*0-8176-3824-5*) Birkhauser.
***Bass, Harold Franklin, Jr.** Historical Dictionary of United States Political Parties. Woronoff, Jon, ed. LC 99-53752. (Historical Dictionaries of Religions, Philosophies & Movements Ser.: No. 29). 448p. (C). 2000. 69.50 (*0-8108-3736-6*) Scarecrow.
Bass, Helen G., jt. auth. see Gulati, Bodh R.
Bass, Hyman. Cyclic Renormalization & Automorphism Groups of Rooted Trees. LC 95-46524. (Lecture Notes in Mathematics Ser.: No. 1621). 163p. 1995. 38.95 (*3-540-60595-9*) Spr-Verlag.
— Introduction to Some Methods of Algebraic K-Theory. LC 73-19925. (CBMS Regional Conference Series in Mathematics: No. 20). 68p. 1974. reprint ed. pap. 24.00 (*0-8218-1670-5*, CBMS/20) Am Math.
Bass, Hyman & Lubotzky, A. Tree Lattices. (Progress in Mathematics Ser.: Vol. 176). 232p. 1999. 49.50 (*0-8176-4120-3*) Birkhauser.
***Bass, Hyman, et al.** Algebra, K-Theory, Groups & Education: On the Occasion of Hyman Bass's 65th Birthday. LC 99-44937. (Contemporary Mathematics Ser.). 238p. 1999. write for info. (*0-8218-1087-1*) Am Math.
Bass, I. Scott & Young, Anthony. Dietary Supplement Health & Education Act: A Legislative History & Analysis. 320p. (Orig.). 1996. pap. 99.00 (*1-885259-37-9*) Food & Drug Law.
Bass, Ian, tr. see Meyer, T. H.
Bass, Iris. What's Your Opera I. Q.? A Quiz Book for Opera Lovers. 1991. pap. 7.95 (*0-8065-1211-3*, Citadel Pr) Carol Pub Group.
— What's Your Opera I. Q.? A Quiz Book for Opera Lovers. LC 96-50272. 208p. 1997. pap. 12.00 (*0-8065-1862-6*, Citadel Pr) Carol Pub Group.
Bass, Ivan E. Bass Family History: Esau Bass (Revolutionary Soldier), His Brother Jonathan Bass, & Their Descendants. (Illus.). 449p. 1997. reprint ed. pap. 67.00 (*0-8328-7411-6*); reprint ed. lib. bdg. 77.00 (*0-8328-7410-8*) Higginson Bk Co.
Bass, J. D., jt. ed. see Shankland, T. J.
Bass, Jack. Unlikely Heroes. LC 89-78036. 360p. 1990. pap. 22.95 (*0-8173-0491-6*) U of Ala Pr.
Bass, Jack & DeVries, Walter. The Transformation of Southern Politics: Social Change & Political Consequence since 1945. LC 95-2855. 544p. 1995. pap. 25.00 (*0-8203-1728-4*) U of Ga Pr.
Bass, Jack & Nelson, Jack. The Orangeburg Massacre. rev. ed. LC 84-9092. xviii, 248p. 1996. pap. 17.95 (*0-86554-552-9*) Mercer Univ Pr.
Bass, Jack & Thompson, Marilyn W. Ol' Strom: An Unauthorized Biography of Strom Thurmond. LC 98-66360. (Illus.). 272p. 1998. 24.00 (*1-56352-523-2*) Longstreet.
Bass, Jack, et al. The American South Comes of Age: Study Guide. 54p. (C). 1986. pap. text, student ed. 6.50 (*0-685-14207-8*) McGraw.
Bass, James & Briggs, Homer. Fait Accompli: An Historical Account of the 457th Bomb Group. LC 96-114470. 400p. 1995. write for info. (*0-9648925-0-2*) J Bass Pubns.
Bass, Jan, jt. auth. see Houts, Tim.
***Bass, Jo Ann & Sax, Richard.** Eat at Joe's: The Joe's Stone Crab Restaurant Cookbook. LC 00-27901. (Illus.). 128p. 2000. reprint ed. 19.95 (*1-57959-511-1*, Pub. by BB&T Inc) Publishers Group.
Bass, Joe R., jt. auth. see Lewis, Kenneth H.
Bass, Joel E., jt. auth. see Carin, Arthur A.
Bass, John A. Almanzo & Laura Ingalls Wilder's Old Home Town: 63 Years on Rocky Ridge Farm in Mansfield, Wright County, Missouri. (Ingalls-Wilder-Lane Signature Ser.: Bk. 12). (Illus.). 100p. 1998. pap. 10.00 (*1-891453-12-2*) Ingalls-Wilder.
— The Connection I: The Complete Story of the Ingalls & Quiner Families in Jefferson County, Wisconsin. (Ingalls-Wilder-Lane Signature Ser.: Bk. 3). (Illus.). 100p. 1997. pap. 10.00 (*1-891453-03-3*) Ingalls-Wilder.
— The Connection II: The Complete Story of the Ingalls & Wilder Families in Dakota Territory (South Dakota) (Ingalls-Wilder-Lane Signature Ser.: Bk. 10). (Illus.). 100p. 1998. pap. 10.00 (*1-891453-10-6*) Ingalls-Wilder.
— The Deepest Roots I: The Complete Story of the Ingalls & Colby Families of the Early Years. (Ingalls-Wilder-Lane Signature Ser.: Bk. 1). (Illus.). 100p. 1997. pap. 10.00 (*1-891453-01-7*) Ingalls-Wilder.
— The Deepest Roots II: The Complete Story of the Tucker/Quiner/Doer Families of the Early Years. (Ingalls-Wilder-Lane Signature Ser.: Bk. 2). (Illus.). 100p. 1997. 10.00 (*1-891453-02-5*) Ingalls-Wilder.
— The Deepest Roots III: The Complete Story of the Wilder Family of the Early Years. (Ingalls-Wilder-Lane Signature Ser.: Bk. 9). (Illus.). 100p. 1998. pap. 10.00 (*1-891453-09-2*) Ingalls-Wilder.
— The Ingalls Pepin County-Pierce County-Burnett County, Wisconsin Story. (Ingalls-Wilder-Lane Signature Ser.: Bk. 4). (Illus.). 100p. 1997. pap. 10.00 (*1-891453-04-1*) Ingalls-Wilder.
— The Ingalls Redwood County-Wabasha County, Minnesota Story. (Ingalls-Wilder-Lane Signature Ser.: Bk. 7). (Illus.). 100p. 1998. pap. 10.00 (*1-891453-07-6*) Ingalls-Wilder.
— Ingalls-Wilder-Lane Signature Series, 15 vols., Vols. 1-15. (Illus.). 1500p. 1998. pap. 150.00 (*1-891453-00-9*) Ingalls-Wilder.
— Laura Ingalls Wilder: Her Writing, Her Award, Her Libraries, Her Historic Highway. (Ingalls-Wilder-Lane Signature Ser.: Bk. 15). (Illus.). 100p. 1998. pap. 10.00 (*1-891453-15-7*) Ingalls-Wilder.
— Little Hotel on the Prairie: The "Missing Link" Years: a Story of the Charles Ingalls Family in Burr Oak, Winneshick County, Iowa. (Ingalls-Wilder-Lane Signature Ser.: Bk. 8). (Illus.). 100p. 1998. pap. 10.00 (*1-891453-08-4*) Ingalls-Wilder.
— Little House: A Story of the Charles Ingalls Family in Rutland Township, Montgomery County, Kansas. (Ingalls-Wilder-Lane Signature Ser.: Bk. 6). (Illus.). 100p. 1998. pap. 10.00 (*1-891453-06-8*) Ingalls-Wilder.
— Little House in Louisiana: The Complete Story of the Wilder Family in Louisiana. (Ingalls-Wilder-Lane Signature Ser.: Bk. 13). (Illus.). 100p. 1998. pap. 10.00 (*1-891453-13-0*) Ingalls-Wilder.
— Little House in Rothville: A Story of the Charles Ingalls Family in Rothville, Chariton County, Missouri: Little House: the Untold Story-the Other "Missing Link" (Ingalls-Wilder-Lane Signature Ser.: Bk. 5). (Illus.). 100p. 1997. pap. 10.00 (*1-891453-05-X*) Ingalls-Wilder.
— Little House in Westville: A Story of the Ingalls & Wilder Families in Westville, Holmes County, Florida. (Ingalls-Wilder-Lane Signature Ser.: Bk. 11). (Illus.). 100p. 1998. pap. 10.00 (*1-891453-11-4*) Ingalls-Wilder.
— Rose Wilder Lane Her Way: An Inspiring Biography of the Life of Laura Ingalls Wilder's Daughter Rose Wilder Lane. (Ingalls-Wilder-Lane Signature Ser.: Bk. 14). (Illus.). 100p. 1998. pap. 10.00 (*1-891453-14-9*) Ingalls-Wilder.
***Bass, Jon.** Last-instar Larvae & Pupae of the Simuliidae of Britain & Ireland: A Key with Brief Ecological Notes. LC 99-184282. (Illus.). 1998. write for info. (*0-900386-58-4*) St Mut.
Bass, Jules. Cooking with Herb, the Vegetarian Dragon: A Cookbook for Kids. (Illus.). 40p. (J). (gr. 1 up). 1999. 16.95 (*1-84148-041-X*) Barefoot Bks NY.
— Herb, the Vegetarian Dragon. (Illus.). 32p. (J). (gr. 1-5). 1999. 15.95 (*1-902283-36-8*) Barefoot Bks NY.
***Bass, Jules.** Herb, the Vegetarian Dragon. (Illus.). 32p. (J). (gr. 1-5). 2000. reprint ed. pap. 5.99 (*1-84148-127-0*) Barefoot Bks NY.
Bass, Kelley, jt. auth. see Worthen, William B.
Bass, Kelly, et al. Educationally Interpretive Exhibition: Rethinking the Display of Student Art. (Illus.). 20p. (Orig.). 1997. pap. 15.00 (*0-937652-99-7*, 207) Natl Art Ed.
Bass, Larry J., et al. Professional Conduct & Discipline in Psychology. LC 96-8182. 330p. 1996. pap. text 24.95 (*1-55798-372-0*) Am Psychol.
Bass, Lawrence W. Management by Task Forces: A Manual on the Operation of Interdisciplinary Teams. LC 74-82702. 197p. 1975. 22.50 (*0-912338-09-1*); fiche 9.50 (*0-912338-10-5*) Lomond.
Bass, Len, et al. Software Architecture in Practice. LC 97-13979. 480p. (C). 1997. 47.95 (*0-201-19930-0*) Addison-Wesley.
Bass, Leonard J., et al, eds. Human-Computer Interaction: Proceedings, Third International Conference, EWHCI '93, Moscow, Russia, August 3-7, 1993. LC 93-38412. (Lecture Notes in Computer Science Ser.: Vol. 753). 1993. 54.00 (*0-387-57433-6*) Spr-Verlag.
Bass, Lewis. Products Liability: Design & Manufacturing Defects. 587p. 1986. text 50.00 (*0-07-004036-2*) Shepards.
Bass, M. & Stitch, M. L., eds. Laser Handbook, Vol. 5. xvi, 692p. 1985. 291.50 (*0-444-86934-4*, North Holland) Elsevier.
Bass, M., jt. ed. see Stitch, M. L.
Bass, Mabry. Mabry Bass's Tarboro: From 1950 to 1990. Taylor, Roland, ed. 480p. 1997. pap. 19.95 (*1-884570-77-1*) Research Triangle.
Bass, Maia S. Black Redemption. 2nd rev. ed. LC 96-68849. 90p. (Orig.). 1996. pap. 10.00 (*1-889088-11-0*) Shango Prodn Co.
— Time Travels: A Collection of Poetry & Essays. (Illus.). (Orig.). 1997. pap. write for info. (*0-614-29839-3*) Shango Prodn Co.
Bass, Maureen. Soul Food: Spiritual Staples for the Journey of Life. Garrett, Jennifer & Altman, Linda, eds. (Illus.). 134p. (Orig.). (C). 1990. pap. text 9.95 (*0-964551C-0-4*) Valhalla Press.
Bass, Mike, jt. auth. see Huggins, Bob.
Bass, Milton. The Broken-Hearted Detective. Isaacson, Dana, ed. 256p. (Orig.). 1994. mass mkt. 4.99 (*0-671-74243-4*) PB.
— The Half-Hearted Detective. Isaacson, Dana, ed. 256p. (Orig.). 1993. mass mkt. 4.99 (*0-671-74242-6*) PB.
Bass, Nelson E. Curfew. Richards, Henry J., tr. from SPA.Tr. of Toque de Queda. 115p. 1991. pap. 9.00 (*0-939423-02-2*) Afro Hispanic Inst.
— When the Guayacans Were in Bloom. Richards, Henry J., tr. from SPA. LC 87-72081.Tr. of Cuando los Guayacanes Florecian. 230p. (Orig.). (C). 1987. pap. 15.00 (*0-939423-01-4*) Afro Hispanic Inst.
Bass, Phyllis. Across the Curriculum Super Value Blackline Workbooks Series, 3 vols., Set. Knoblock, Kathy, ed. (Illus.). 192p. 1998. teacher ed., wbk. ed. 14.85 (*1-58232-004-7*, BH 8895153) Bryan Hse.
— Phonics Super Value Blackline Workbooks Series, 5 vols., Set. Knoblock, Kathy, ed. (Illus.). 320p. 1998. teacher ed., wbk. ed. 24.75 (*1-58232-002-0*, BH 8899555) Bryan Hse.
Bass, Phyllis & Knoblock, Kathy. Across the Curriculum Super Value Blackline Workbooks Series, 3 vols., Set. (Illus.). 192p. 1998. teacher ed., wbk. ed. 14.85 (*1-58232-001-2*, BH 8895453); teacher ed., wbk. ed. 24.75 (*1-58232-003-9*, BH 8895255) Bryan Hse.
Bass, Phyllis, jt. auth. see Knoblock, Kathy.
Bass, R. F. Cutting Brownain Paths. LC 98-46548. (Memoirs of the American Mathematical Society Ser.). 1999. 40.00 (*0-8218-0968-7*) Am Math.
— Diffusions & Elliptic Operators. Gani, J. et al, eds. LC 97-26428. (Probability & Its Applications Ser.). 248p. 1997. 64.95 (*0-387-98315-5*) Spr-Verlag.
Bass, R. M. Credit Management. 3rd rev. ed. 302p. (C). 1999. pap. 47.50 (*0-7487-1374-3*, Pub. by S Thornes Pubs) Trans-Atl Phila.
***Bass, Ralph E., Jr.** What about Baptism: A Discussion on the Mode, Candidate & Purpose of Christian Baptism. 81p. 1999. 25.00 (*0-9656853-1-4*) Nicene Pr.
Bass, Richard. Probabilistic Techniques in Analysis. LC 94-34721. (Probability & its Applications Ser.). (Illus.). 350p. 1994. 67.95 (*0-387-94387-0*) Spr-Verlag.
Bass, Richard, ed. see Rashid, Muhammad Ho.
Bass, Rick. Book of Yaak. 224p. 1996. 21.95 (*0-395-77014-9*) HM.
— Book of Yaak. 208p. 1997. pap. 12.00 (*0-395-87746-6*) HM.
— Brown Dog of the Yaak: Essays on Art & Activism. LC 98-50947. (Credo Ser.: Vol. 1). 192p. 1999. 20.00 (*1-57131-227-7*); pap. 12.00 (*1-57131-224-2*) Milkweed Ed.
***Bass, Rick.** Colter: The True Story of the Best Hunting Dog I Ever Had. LC 00-20524. 160p. 2000. 22.00 (*0-395-92618-1*) HM.
— The Deer Pasture. LC 84-40556. (Wardlaw Book Ser.). (Illus.). 144p. 2000. 19.95 (*0-89096-228-6*) Tex A&M Univ Pr.
Bass, Rick. The Deer Pasture: Essays. rev. ed. (Illus.). 240p. 1996. pap. 12.00 (*0-393-31435-9*, Norton Paperbks) Norton.
— Fiber. LC 98-15556. (Illus.). 64p. 1998. 15.95 (*0-8203-2063-3*) U of Ga Pr.
— Fiber. aut. limited num. ed. (Illus.). 57p. 1998. text 100.00 (*0-8203-2086-2*) U of Ga Pr.
— In the Loyal Mountains. 224p. 1997. pap. 12.00 (*0-395-87747-4*, Mariner Bks) HM.
— The Lost Grizzlies: A Search for Survivors in the Wilderness of Colorado. (Illus.). 220p. 1995. 22.95 (*0-395-71759-0*) HM.
— The Lost Grizzlies: A Search for Survivors in the Wilderness of Colorado. 288p. 1997. pap. 13.00 (*0-395-85700-7*) HM.
— The New Wolves. LC 98-36557. 128p. 1998. 18.95 (*1-55821-697-9*) Lyons Pr.
— The New Wolves. LC 98-36557. 1998. lib. bdg. 18.95 (*1-55821-773-8*) Lyons Pr.
— The Ninemile Wolves. 170p. 1993. pap. 10.00 (*0-345-38251-X*) Ballantine Pub Grp.
— Oil Notes. LC 95-14871. (Illus.). 192p. 1995. pap. 10.95 (*0-87074-383-X*) SMU Press.
— Platte River. 160p. 1995. pap. 10.00 (*0-345-39249-3*) Ballantine Pub Grp.
— The Sky, the Stars, the Wilderness. LC 97-24379. 189p. 1997. 23.00 (*0-395-71758-2*) HM.
— The Sky, the Stars, the Wilderness. 192p. 1998. pap. 12.00 (*0-395-92475-8*) HM.
— The Watch. 1998. 23.50 (*0-8446-6931-8*) Peter Smith.
— The Watch: Stories. 1994. pap. 12.00 (*0-393-31135-X*) Norton.
— Where the Sea Used to Be. LC 98-12842. 320p. 1998. 25.00 (*0-395-77015-7*) HM.
— Where the Sea Used to Be. 496p. 1999. pap. 14.00 (*0-395-95781-8*) HM.
— Wild to the Heart. rev. ed. (Illus.). 176p. 1997. pap. 12.00 (*0-393-31487-1*, Norton Paperbks) Norton.
— Winter: Notes from Montana. 160p. 1992. pap. 12.00 (*0-395-61150-4*) HM.
***Bass, Rick.** Winter: Notes from Montana. 1999. 24.50 (*0-8446-7015-4*) Peter Smith.
Bass, Rick, et al. On Nature's Terms: Contemporary Voices. Stine, Peter & Lyon, Thomas J., eds. LC 92-5239. (Louise Lindsey Merrick Natural Environment Ser.: No. 13). 224p. 1992. 35.00 (*0-89096-511-0*); pap. 15.95 (*0-89096-522-6*) Tex A&M Univ Pr.
***Bass, Rick, et al.** The Return of the Wolf: Reflections on the Future of Wolves in the Northeast. Elder, John, ed. 2000. 24.95 (*0-87451-967-5*) U Pr of New Eng.
Bass Riff, Riff. Metallica Riff. 80p. 1997. otabind 17.95 (*1-57560-048-X*, Pub. by Cherry Lane) H Leonard.
Bass, Robert D. Swamp Fox. LC 59-5368. (Illus.). 1982. pap. 11.95 (*0-87844-051-8*) Sandlapper Pub Co.

B

Bass, Robert E. Some Features of Organization in Nature: A Contribution to Unified Science. 2nd rev. ed. 1991. pap. 14.00 (*0-686-29224-3*) Adamson Print.

Bass, Ron & Hicks, Scott. Snow Falling on Cedars: The Shooting Script. LC 99-48497. (Shooting Script Ser.). (Illus.). 192p. 2000. pap. 16.95 (*1-55704-372-8*, Pub. by Newmarket) Norton.

Bass, Ronald E., et al. CEQA Deskbook: A Step-by-Step Guide. 3rd rev. ed. (Illus.). 432p. 1999. pap. 50.00 (*0-923956-58-1*) Solano Pr.

***Bass, Ronald E., et al.** The NEPA Book: A Step-by-Step Guide to the National Environmental Policy Act. 2000. pap., wbk. ed. 50.00 (*0-923956-67-0*) Solano Pr.

Bass, Ronald R. History of the Thirty-First Arkansas Confederate Infantry. (Illus.). 142p. (Orig.). 1996. pap. 22.50 (*1-56546-096-0*) Arkansas Res.

Bass, Ruth. Beans Love Herbs: A Fresh from the Garden Cookbook. LC 96-47466. (Fresh from the Garden Cookbook Ser.). (Illus.). 64p. 1997. 9.95 (*0-88266-964-8*, Storey Pub) Storey Bks.

— Herbal Breads. Lappies, Pamela, ed. (Fresh from the Garden Cookbook Ser.). (Illus.). 64p. 1996. 9.95 (*0-88266-923-0*, 923-0, Storey Pub) Storey Bks.

— Herbal Salads. Lappies, Pamela, ed. (Fresh from the Garden Cookbook Ser.). (Illus.). 64p. 1996. 9.95 (*0-88266-925-7*, 925-7, Storey Pub) Storey Bks.

— Herbal Soups. Lappies, Pamela, ed. (Fresh from the Garden Cookbook Ser.). (Illus.). 64p. 1996. 9.95 (*0-88266-924-9*, 924-9, Storey Pub) Storey Bks.

***Bass, Ruth.** Herbal Soups, Salads, Breads & Sweets: A Fresh from the Garden Cookbook. LC 00-29142. 2000. write for info. (*1-58017-289-X*) Storey Bks.

Bass, Ruth. Herbal Sweets. Lappies, Pamela, ed. (Fresh from the Garden Cookbook Ser.). (Illus.). 64p. 1996. 9.95 (*0-88266-922-2*, 922-2, Storey Pub) Storey Bks.

***Bass, Ruth.** Herbs Love Tomatoes, Peppers, Onions & Zucchini: A Fresh from the Garden Cookbook. LC 00-28514. (Illus.). 2000. write for info. (*1-58017-290-3*) Storey Bks.

Bass, Ruth. Mushrooms Love Herbs. LC 96-14312. (Illus.). 64p. 1996. 9.95 (*0-88266-933-8*, Storey Pub) Storey Bks.

— Onions Love Herbs. LC 96-14311. (Illus.). 64p. 1996. 9.95 (*0-88266-934-6*, Storey Pub) Storey Bks.

— Peppers Love Herbs. LC 96-15283. (Illus.). 64p. 1996. 9.95 (*0-88266-932-X*, Storey Pub) Storey Bks.

— Potatoes Love Herbs. LC 96-36505. (Fresh from the Garden Cookbook Ser.). (Illus.). 64p. 1997. 9.95 (*0-88266-963-X*) Storey Bks.

— Rice Loves Herbs. LC 96-38028. (Fresh from the Garden Cookbook Ser.). (Illus.). 64p. 1997. 9.95 (*0-88266-961-3*) Storey Bks.

— Tomatoes Love Herbs. LC 96-10636. (Illus.). 64p. 1996. 9.95 (*0-88266-931-1*) Storey Bks.

— Zucchini (& Other Squash) Love Herbs. LC 96-39969. (Fresh from the Garden Cookbook Ser.). (Illus.). 64p. 1997. 9.95 (*0-88266-962-1*) Storey Bks.

***Bass, Samuel.** The Church in Metaphase: A Process for a Pure Church. VII, 52p. 1999. pap. write for info. (*0-9671417-2-9*) BibleScope.

— The Power of Youth: Understanding the Power of Youth God's Way. 80p. (YA). 2000. pap. write for info. (*0-9671417-5-3*) BibleScope.

***Bass, Samuel & Bass, Deborah.** Balaam's Back: False Spirituality & Artificial Truth. 98p. (C). 2000. pap. 10.00 (*0-9671417-4-5*) BibleScope.

Bass, Samuel, ed. see Bass, Deborah.

Bass, Scott A., ed. Aging & Active: Dimensions of Productive Engagement among Older Americans. LC 95-4262. 301p. 1995. 32.50 (*0-300-06326-1*) Yale U Pr.

Bass, Scott A., et al, eds. Achieving a Productive Aging Society. LC 92-22757. 328p. 1993. 75.00 (*0-86569-032-4*, T032, Auburn Hse); pap. 35.00 (*0-86569-033-2*, R033, Auburn Hse) Greenwood.

— International Perspectives on State & Family Support for the Elderly. LC 93-32907. (Journal of Aging & Social Policy: Vol. 5, Nos. 1-2). (Illus.). 232p. 1993. lib. bdg. 49.95 (*1-56024-480-1*) Haworth Pr.

— Public Policy & the Old Age Revolution in Japan. LC 96-38930. (Journal of Aging & Social Policy: Vol. 8, Nos. 2/3). 203p. (C). 1996. 34.95 (*0-7890-0012-1*) Haworth Pr.

Bass, Sharon P. This Is the Maine Coon Cat. (Illus.). 128p. 1983. 23.95 (*0-86622-096-8*, H-1057) TFH Pubns.

Bass, Sophie F. Pig-Tail Days in Old Seattle. LC 72-77591. (Illus.). 200p. (J). (gr. 4-6). 1973. 12.50 (*0-8323-0206-6*) Binford Mort.

Bass, Stanley S. & Day, Chet. Ideal Health Through Sequential Eating: Perfection in Food Combining. 26p. 1993. pap. 8.50 (*1-885194-03-X*) Hlth & Beyond.

Bass, Stephen, jt. auth. see Sargent, Caroline.

Bass, Stephen, jt. auth. see Upton, Christopher.

***Bass, Susan Perkoff & Muller, Manuel Ruiz, eds.** Protecting Biodiversity: National Laws Regulating Access to Genetic Resources in the Americas. 100p. 2000. pap. 17.95 (*0-88936-900-3*, Pub. by IDRC Bks) Stylus Pub VA.

Bass, Ted. Adventures with Charlie the Chipmunk: Christian Stories for Children. (Illus.). 132p. (Orig.). (J). (gr. 4-6). 1997. pap. 10.00 (*1-57502-605-8*, PO1748) Morris Pubng.

Bass, Thomas A. Camping with the Prince & Other Tales of Science in Africa. 1990. 19.95 (*0-395-03954-1*) HM.

— Camping with the Prince & Other Tales of Science in Africa. LC 97-6252. 282p. 1997. pap. 13.95 (*1-55921-206-3*) Moyer Bell.

— The Eudaemonic Pie. 1986. pap. 5.95 (*0-394-74310-5*) Vin Bks.

— The Predictors. 1998. write for info. (*0-201-62473-7*) Addison-Wesley.

***Bass, Thomas A.** The Predictors. LC 98-41820. 336p. 1999. 25.00 (*0-8050-5756-0*) H Holt & Co.

Bass, Thomas A. The Predictors: How a Band of Maverick Physicists Used Chaos Theory to Trade Their Way to a Fortune on Wall Street. 320p. 2000. pap. 15.00 (*0-8050-5757-9*, Owl) H Holt & Co.

— Reinventing the Future: Conversations with the World's Leading Scientists. 272p. (C). 1995. pap. 14.00 (*0-201-40795-7*) Addison-Wesley.

— Vietnamerica: The War Comes Home. LC 95-49994. 278p. 1996. 25.00 (*1-56947-050-2*) Soho Press.

— Vietnamerica: The War Comes Home. 278p. 1997. pap. 14.00 (*1-56947-088-X*) Soho Press.

Bass, Tom. Play Football the NFL Way. 6th ed. 1991. pap. 16.95 (*0-312-05947-7*) St Martin.

Bass, William M. Human Osteology: A Laboratory & Field Manual. 4th rev. ed. (Special Publications: No.2). (Illus.). 361p. (C). 1995. spiral bd. 25.00 (*0-943414-81-4*, 140240) MO Arch Soc.

Bass, William M., III, et al. Fay Tolten & the Initial Middle Missouri Variant. Wood, W. Raymond, ed. LC 76-620007. (Research Ser.: No. 13). (Illus.). 43p. (Orig.). 1976. pap. 5.00 (*0-943414-14-8*) MO Arch Soc.

Bassachs, Anna G., et al. Tiny Hands: Autumn. (Illus.). 48p. (J). 1998. pap. 7.95 (*0-7641-0740-2*) Barron.

— Tiny Hands: Celebrations. (Illus.). 48p. (J). 1998. pap. 7.95 (*0-7641-0742-9*) Barron.

— Tiny Hands: Winter. (Illus.). 48p. (J). (ps-3). 1998. pap. 7.95 (*0-7641-0741-0*) Barron.

***Bassaede, Francine.** A Day with the Bellyflops. LC 99-27171. (Illus.). 32p. (J). (ps-2). 2000. lib. bdg. 15.99 (*0-531-33242-X*) Orchard Bks Watts.

Bassam, M., ed. General Relativity & Gravitational Physics. LC 98-195196. 500p. 1997. text 65.00 (*981-02-3152-0*) World Scientific Pub.

Bassam, N. E., et al. Genetic Aspects of Plant Mineral Nutrition: Proceedings of the Third International Symposium on Genetic Aspects of Plant Mineral Nutrition, 19-24 June 1988, Braunschweig FRG. (Developments in Plant & Soil Sciences Ser.). (C). 1990. lib. bdg. 342.00 (*0-7923-0785-2*) Kluwer Academic.

Bassam Omari, jt. auth. see Baumgartner, Fritz.

Bassan, Fernande, et al. French Language & Literature: An Annotated Bibliography. LC 89-1186. 380p. 1989. text 20.00 (*0-8240-4798-2*, H954) Garland.

Bassan, Fernande, jt. auth. see Dumas, Alexandre.

Bassan, M., ed. Stephen Crane: A Collection of Critical Essays. 1967. 12.95 (*0-13-188888-9*, Spectrum IN) Macmillan Gen Ref.

Bassanese, Fiora A. Understanding Luigi Pirandello. Hardin, James N., ed. LC 96-25198. (Understanding Modern European & Latin American Literature Ser.). 200p. 1997. text 29.95 (*1-57003-081-2*) U of SC Pr.

Bassani, Antonella & Zartman, I. William. Algerian Gas Negotiations. (Pew Case Studies in International Affairs). 50p. (C). 1993. pap. text 3.50 (*1-56927-103-8*) Geo U Inst Dplmcy.

Bassani, F. & Parravicini, G. Pastori. Electron States & Optical Transitions in Solids. 312p. 1975. 138.00 (*0-08-016846-9*, Pub. by Pergamon Repr) Franklin.

Bassani, Giorgio. Behind the Door. Weaver, William, tr. from ITA. LC 75-29308. (Helen & Kurt Wolff Bk.). 150p. 1976. reprint ed. pap. 3.95 (*0-15-611685-5*, Harvest Bks) Harcourt.

— The Garden of the Finzi-Continis. Weaver, William, tr. LC 77-77261. (Helen & Kurt Wolff Bk.). 204p. (C). 1977. pap. 11.00 (*0-15-634570-6*, Harvest Bks) Harcourt.

— The Garden of the Finzi-Continis. LC 96-76468. (Library of the Holocaust). 200p. 1996. reprint ed. 8.98 (*1-56731-099-0*, MJF Bks) Fine Comms.

— Le Jardin des Finzi-Contini. (FRE.). 384p. 1975. pap. 11.95 (*0-7859-1795-0*, 2070366340) Fr & Eur.

— Les Lunnettes d'Or et Autres Histoires de Ferrare. (FRE.). 448p. 1982. pap. 11.95 (*0-7859-1959-7*, 2070373940) Fr & Eur.

Bassani, Giovanni B., jt. auth. see Antoni, Pietro D.

Bassani, L., et al, eds. Recent Results & Perspective Instrumental Developments in X- & Gamma-Ray Astronomy: Proceedings of the Topical Meeting of the COSPAR Interdisciplinary Scientific Commission E (Meetings E4 & E8) of the COSPAR 28th Plenary Meeting Held in The Hague, The Netherlands, 25 June-6 July, 1990. (Advances in Space Research Ser.: Vol. 11, No. 8). 434p. 1991. pap. 156.50 (*0-08-041162-2*, Pergamon Pr) Elsevier.

Bassani, L. & Di Cocco, G., eds. Imaging in High Energy Astronomy: Proceedings of the International Workshop Held in Anacapri (Capri-Italy) 26-30 September, 1994. 388p. (C). 1996. text 169.00 (*0-7923-3788-3*) Kluwer Academic.

Bassani, R. & Piccigallo, B. Hydrostatic Lubrication. LC 92-21007. (Tribology Ser.: Vol. 22). (Illus.). xvi, 542p. 1992. 231.00 (*0-444-88498-X*) Elsevier.

Bassanini, P. & Elcrat, A. R. Theory & Applications of Partial Differential Equations. LC 97-38643. (Mathematical Concepts & Methods in Science & Engineering Ser.: VOL. 46). (Illus.). 438p. (C). 1997. text 138.00 (*0-306-45640-0*, Kluwer Plenum) Kluwer Academic.

Bassano. Earth Physical Science. 1991. teacher ed. 17.98 (*0-8013-0986-7*) S&S Trade.

— Life Science T/e. 128p. 1989. 17.98 (*0-8013-0985-9*) S&S Trade.

— Social Studies. 160p. 1993. pap. 16.35 (*0-8013-0349-4*) Addison-Wesley.

— Social Studies T/e. 176p. 1993. 17.98 (*0-8013-0989-1*) S&S Trade.

Bassano, Giovanni. Motet, "Ave Regina Coelorum" for Twelve Voices or Voices & Instruments. Charteris, Richard, ed. (Baroque Ser.: No. 11). i, 30p. 1994. pap. text 10.00 (*1-56571-110-6*) PRB Prods.

Bassano, Mary. Healing with Music & Color: A Beginner's Guide. LC 92-16857. 112p. (Orig.). 1992. pap. 9.95 (*0-87728-760-0*) Weiser.

— The Light of the Spirit: An Introductory Guide. LC 96-13474. 128p. (Orig.). 1996. pap. 9.95 (*0-87728-871-2*) Weiser.

Bassano, Sharron. First Class Reader! Integrated Skills Lessons for Beginners. Duffy, John, ed. (Illus.). vi, 129p. 1994. pap. text 8.75 (*1-882483-29-4*) Alta Bk Ctr.

— Sounds Easy! (Sounds Easy Ser.). (Illus.). 57p. 1980. audio 10.95 (*0-88084-041-2*) Alemany Pr.

Bassano, Sharron & Christison, Mary A. Community Spirit: A Practical Guide to Collaborative Language Learning. (Illus.). 124p. 1995. pap. text 19.95 (*1-882483-30-8*) Alta Bk Ctr.

— Drawing Out: Creative, Personalized Whole Language Activities. (Illus.). xiii, 130p. 1995. pap. text 16.95 (*1-882483-32-4*) Alta Bk Ctr.

Bassano, Sharron, jt. auth. see Christison, M.

Bassano, Sharron, jt. auth. see Christison, Mary A.

Bassard, Katherine C. Spiritual Interrogations. LC 98-23197. (Princeton Studies in Culture, Power & History). 192p. 1998. pap. text 15.95 (*0-691-01647-X*, Pub. by Princeton U Pr) Cal Prin Full Svc.

— Spiritual Interrogations: Culture, Gender, & Community in Early African American Women's Writing. LC 98-23197. (Studies in Culture - Power - History). 192p. 1998. text 42.50 (*0-691-01639-9*, Pub. by Princeton U Pr) Cal Prin Full Svc.

Bassarear, Tom. Mathematics for Elementary Teachers. (C). 1997. text, teacher ed. 11.96 (*0-395-66961-8*) HM.

— Mathematics for Elementary Teachers: Explorations Manual. 256p. (C). 1997. pap. text 23.96 (*0-395-66960-X*) HM.

***Basse, Ellen Margrethe.** Environmental Law in Denmark. 232p. 2000. pap. text 64.00 (*90-411-1340-1*) Kluwer Law Intl.

Basse, J. H., tr. see Faust, Bernhard C.

Basseches, Joshua T. The Scrimshaw of Manuel Cunha: Late Work from Madeira Revealed. Frank, Stuart M., ed. (Kendall Whaling Museum Monograph: No. 2). (Illus.). 19p. 1988. pap. text 8.50 (*0-937854-26-3*) Kendall Whaling.

Basseches, Joshua T. & Frank, Stuart M. Edward Burdett, 1805 to 1833, America's First Master Scrimshaw Artist. (Museum Monographs: No. 5). (Illus.). 1991. pap. text 8.50 (*0-937854-29-8*) Kendall Whaling.

Basseches, Michael. Dialectical Thinking & Adult Development. LC 84-2935. (Publications for the Advancement of Theory & History in Psychology, the PATH Ser.). 440p. (C). 1984. text 78.50 (*0-89391-017-1*) Ablx Pub.

***Bassede, Francine.** A Day with the Bellyflops. LC 99-27171. (Illus.). 32p. (J). (ps-2). 2000. 14.95 (*0-531-30242-3*) Orchard Bks Watts.

Bass'ede, Francine. George Paints His House. LC 98-30531. (Illus.). 32p. (J). (ps-1). 1999. 14.95 (*0-531-30150-8*) Orchard Bks Watts.

Bassede, Francine. George's Store at the Shore. Barth, Dominic, tr. from FRE. LC 97-38282. (Illus.). 32p. (J). (ps-1). 1998. pap. 14.95 (*0-531-30083-8*); lib. bdg. 15.99 (*0-531-33083-4*) Orchard Bks Watts.

Bassee, Nicolas. German Renaissance Patterns for Embroidery: A Facsimile Copy of Nicolas Bassee's New Modelbuch of 1568. Epstein, Kathleen A., ed. & tr. by. from GER. LC 94-71881. (Illus.). 124p. (Orig.). 1995. pap. 20.00 (*0-9633331-4-3*) Curious Works.

Bassegoda Muste, Buenaventura. Nuevo Glosario, Diccionario Poliglota de la Arquitectura. (CAT, ENG, FRE, GER & ITA.). 366p. 1976. pap. 75.00 (*0-8288-5745-8*, S50134) Fr & Eur.

Bassein, Beth A. The Matriarch's Power: A Cross Cultural Literary Study. LC 93-17015. (American University Studies: Feminist Studies: Ser. XXVII, Vol. 4). XII, 168p. (C). 1993. text 39.95 (*0-8204-2205-3*) P Lang Pubng.

— Slopes to the River. 72p. 1996. pap. 14.95 (*0-7734-2753-8*, Mellen Poetry Pr) E Mellen.

— Women & Death: Linkages in Western Thought & Literature, 44. LC 83-8544. (Contributions in Women's Studies: No. 44). 236p. 1984. 59.95 (*0-313-23924-X*, BWD/, Greenwood Pr) Greenwood.

Bassein, Susan. An Infinite Series Approach to Calculus. (Illus.). xvi, 361p. (C). 1993. text 35.00 (*0-914098-27-6*) Publish or Perish.

— Mathematics Electrified! (Illus.). 93p. (Orig.). (YA). (gr. 12 up). 1996. wbk. ed. 15.00 (*0-9654724-0-X*) Grant Pub.

***Basser, Herbert W.** Studies in Exegesis: Christian Critiques of Jewish Law & Rabbinic Responses, 70-300 C. E. LC 00-39802. (Reference Library of Ancient Judaism). 2000. write for info. (*90-04-11848-9*) Brill Academic Pubs.

Basset, Brian. Bless This Home Office, with Tax Credits: An Adam Collection. LC 97-71623. 128p. 1997. pap. text 9.95 (*0-8362-3689-0*) Andrews & McMeel.

***Basset, Brian.** Cafe Adam: An Adam Home Collection. 128p. 1999. pap. 9.95 (*0-7407-0005-7*) Andrews & McMeel.

Basset, Brian. Life Begins at Six-Forty: An Adam Collection. (Illus.). 128p. (Orig.). 1993. pap. 8.95 (*0-8362-1721-7*) Andrews & McMeel.

— Life in the Fast-Food Lane. (Illus.). 128p. (Orig.). 1991. pap. 8.95 (*0-8362-1873-6*) Andrews & McMeel.

— Minivanity: An Adam Collection. (Illus.). 128p. 1995. pap. 8.95 (*0-8362-0417-4*) Andrews & McMeel.

Basset, Delfin C. Dictionary of Proverbs: Spanish/English & English/Spanish. (ENG & SPA.). 400p. 1998. pap. 13.95 (*0-7641-0251-6*) Barron.

Basset, Delfin C. Dictionary of Proverbs: Spanish/English & English/Spanish. (SPA & ENG.). 441p. 1996. 69.95 (*0-320-01241-7*) Fr & Eur.

— Phraseological Dictionary. (ENG & SPA.). 383p. 1995. 49.95 (*0-320-02839-9*) Fr & Eur.

Basset, Edward, jt. ed. see Beers, Roland F.

Basset, F., ed. see International Symposium on Pulmonary Interstitium.

Basset, Jean-Marie, et al, eds. Surface Organometallic Chemistry: Molecular Approaches to Surface Catalysis. (C). 1988. text 191.00 (*90-277-2724-4*) Kluwer Academic.

Basset, Mary T., jt. auth. see Bijlmakers, Leon A.

Bassett. Clays Handbook of Environmental Health. (Mechanical Engineering Ser.). 1991. text 121.95 (*0-412-39480-4*) Chapman & Hall.

— Environmental Health Procedures. 3rd ed. (Architecture Ser.). 1992. text 69.50 (*0-412-39490-1*) Chapman & Hall.

— The Professional Nanny. (Early Childhood Education Ser.). 1997. teacher ed. 10.50 (*0-8273-7385-6*) Delmar.

***Bassett.** Sherwood Anderson Revisited. 2000. 28.95 (*0-8057-1611-4*) Thorndike Pr.

Bassett, Abbe. The Planets Through the Signs: Astrology for Living. 152p. 1987. pap. 12.50 (*0-89540-170-3*, SB-170, Sun Bks) Sun Pub.

Bassett, Anna. The Gray Raincoat. 116p. (Orig.). 1993. pap. 11.95 (*0-916147-38-X*) Regent Pr.

Bassett, Brian. Adam. (Illus.). 128p. (Orig.). 1989. pap. 7.95 (*0-8362-1841-8*) Andrews & McMeel.

Bassett, Britt, jt. auth. see Aboba, Bernard.

Bassett, Caroline. Mac Tips & Tricks: Essential Book for the Mac User. LC 94-221889. 1994. pap. 14.95 (*1-55958-537-4*) Prima Pub.

Bassett, D. R. & Hamielac, Alvin E., eds. Emulsion Polymers & Emulsion Polymerization. LC 81-10823. (ACS Symposium Ser.: No. 165). 1981. 65.95 (*0-8412-0642-2*) Am Chemical.

Bassett, David R. & Hamielec, Alvin E., eds. Emulsion Polymers & Emulsion Polymerization: Based on a Symposium. LC 81-10823. (ACS Symposium Ser.: Vol. 165). 617p. 1981. reprint ed. pap. 191.30 (*0-608-03045-7*, 206349800007) Bks Demand.

***Bassett, E. E., et al.** Statistics: Problems & Solutions. 230p. 2000. 58.00 (*981-02-4293-X*); 24.00 (*981-02-4321-9*) World Scientific Pub.

Bassett, Edward G., jt. ed. see Beers, Roland F., Jr.

Bassett, Edward M. Zoning: The Laws, Administration, & Court Decisions During the First Twenty-Five Years. LC 73-11916. (Metropolitan America Ser.). 280p. 1974. reprint ed. 19.95 (*0-405-05385-1*) Ayer.

Bassett, Elizabeth. Beyond the Blue Mountains: Wisdom & Compassion in Living & Dying. 224p. 1999. 19.95 (*0-9666941-3-9*, Pub. by Medio Media) Continuum.

— Nature Walks in Northern Vermont & the Champlain Valley: More Than 40 Scenic Nature Walks. LC 98-3375. 1998. pap. text 12.95 (*1-878239-58-9*) AMC Books.

Bassett, Frank H., III, ed. AAOS Instructional Course Lectures, Vol. 37. LC 43-17054. (Illus.). 299p. 1988. 42.00 (*0-89203-022-4*) Amer Acad Ortho Surg.

Bassett, Fred. Awake My Heart: Psalms for Life. 96p. (Orig.). 1998. pap., boxed set 16.95 (*1-55725-209-2*) Paraclete MA.

Bassett, Frederick W., ed. Awake My Heart: Psalms for Life. LC 98-4971. 110p. 1998. pap. 14.95 (*1-55725-199-1*, 930-046, Pub. by Paraclete MA) BookWorld.

Bassett, Glenn. Tennis Today. 1989. pap. 19.25 (*0-314-68952-4*) West Pub.

Bassett, Glenn A. The Evolution & Future of High Performance Management Systems. LC 93-12992. 232p. 1993. 62.95 (*0-89930-813-9*, Q813, Quorum Bks) Greenwood.

— Management Strategies for Today's Project Shop Economy. LC 90-20712. 264p. 1991. 65.00 (*0-89930-574-1*, BMQ/, Quorum Bks) Greenwood.

— Operations Management for Service Industries: Competing in the Service Era. LC 92-19835. 272p. 1992. 57.95 (*0-89930-746-9*, BOB, Quorum Bks) Greenwood.

Bassett, Helen W., et al, eds. International Folk-Lore Congress of the World's Columbian Exposition, July, 1893. LC 80-788. (Folklore of the World Ser.). (Illus.). 1981. reprint ed. lib. bdg. 35.95 (*0-405-13327-8*) Ayer.

Bassett, Isaac N. Past & Present of Mercer County, 2 vols. (Illus.). 1117p. 1997. reprint ed. lib. bdg. 118.00 (*0-8328-5771-8*) Higginson Bk Co.

Bassett, J. C. Wisdom's Children. 143p. 1993. pap. 4.95 (*0-88172-202-2*) Believers Bkshelf.

Bassett, Jan. Guns & Brooches: Australian Army Nursing from the Boer War to the Gulf War. (Illus.). 262p. 1997. pap. text 38.00 (*0-19-554084-0*) OUP.

— The Oxford Illustrated Dictionary of Australian History. (Illus.). 316p. (C). 1993. 49.95 (*0-19-553243-0*) OUP.

— The Oxford Illustrated Dictionary of Australian History. (Illus.). 310p. 1998. reprint ed. pap. text 24.00 (*0-19-554083-2*) OUP.

Bassett, Jan, ed. The Concise Oxford Dictionary of Australian History. 2nd ed. (Oxford Paperback Reference Ser.). 348p. 1995. pap. text 29.95 (*0-19-553664-9*) OUP.

— Great Southern Landings: An Anthology of Antipodean Travel. 344p. 1995. 35.00 (*0-19-553582-0*) OUP.

Bassett, Jane & Fogelman, Peggy. Looking at European Sculpture: A Guide to Technical Terms. LC 96-39855. (Looking at . . . Ser.). (Illus.). 104p. (Orig.). 1997. pap. 12.95 (*0-89236-291-X*) OUP.

Bassett, Jeni, jt. auth. see Kroll, Steven.

Bassett, Jennifer. Milo. (Illus.). 32p. 1998. pap. text 4.95 (*0-19-421963-1*) OUP.

— The Phantom of the Opera. (Illus.). 48p. 1993. pap. text 5.95 (*0-19-422707-3*) OUP.

An Asterisk (*) at the beginning of an entry indicates that the title is appearing for the first time.

— The Watchers. (Illus.). 24p. 1996. pap. text 4.95 (*0-19-421932-1*) OUP.

Bassett, Jennifer, ed. Alice's Adventures in Wonderland. (Illus.). 48p. 1995. pap. text 5.95 (*0-19-422723-5*) OUP.

— Black Beauty. (Illus.). 80p. 1995. pap. text 5.95 (*0-19-422754-5*) OUP.

— The Children of the New Forest. (Illus.). 48p. 1996. pap. text 5.95 (*0-19-422748-0*) OUP.

— A Christmas Carol. (Illus.). 64p. 1996. pap. text 5.95 (*0-19-422752-9*) OUP.

— Five Children & It. (Illus.). 48p. 1996. pap. text 5.95 (*0-19-422747-2*) OUP.

— Gulliver's Travels. (Illus.). 80p. 1995. pap. text 5.95 (*0-19-422730-8*) OUP.

— The Jungle Book. (Illus.). 48p. 1997. pap. text 5.95 (*0-19-422746-4*) OUP.

— Lorna Doone. (Illus.). 80p. 1997. pap. text 5.95 (*0-19-422755-3*) OUP.

— The Prisoner of Zenda. (Illus.). 64p. 1995. pap. text 5.95 (*0-19-422726-X*) OUP.

— Robinson Crusoe. (Illus.). 48p. 1993. pap. text 5.95 (*0-19-422720-0*) OUP.

— The Secret Garden. (Illus.). 60p. 1993. pap. text 5.95 (*0-19-422721-9*) OUP.

— A Tale of Two Cities. (Illus.). 80p. 1995. pap. text 5.95 (*0-19-422727-8*) OUP.

— Through the Looking Glass. (Illus.). 64p. 1995. pap. text 5.95 (*0-19-422749-9*) OUP.

— The Wind in the Willows. (Illus.). 64p. 1995. pap. text 5.95 (*0-19-422753-7*) OUP.

Bassett, Jennifer, ed. see Alcott, Louisa May.

Bassett, Jennifer, ed. see London, Jack.

Bassett, Jennifer, ed. see Montgomery, L. M.

Bassett, Jennifer, ed. see Twain, Mark, pseud.

***Bassett, Jerry F., contrib. by.** Facts from Jesus. 2000. pap. 12.95 (*1-56794-205-9*) Star Bible.

***Bassett, John.** The Millennium Virus. (Illus.). 183p. 1999. pap. 9.95 (*1-891899-50-3*) Derivations.

Bassett, John E. Faulkner, an Annotated Checklist of Recent Criticism. LC 83-11277. (Serif Series: Bibliographies & Checklists: No. 42). 284p. reprint ed. pap. 88.10 (*0-7837-1354-1*, 204150200020) Bks Demand.

— Faulkner in the Eighties: An Annotated Critical Bibliography. LC 91-31218. (Author Bibliographies Ser.: No. 88). 334p. 1991. 40.00 (*0-8108-2485-X*) Scarecrow.

— Harlem in Review: Critical Reactions to Black American Writers, 1917-1939. LC 90-51013. 232p. 1992. 36.50 (*0-945636-28-8*) Susquehanna U Pr.

— A Heart of Ideality in My Realism & Other Essays on Howells & Twain. LC 90-46908. (Locust Hill Literary Studies: No. 9). 164p. 1991. lib. bdg. 30.00 (*0-933951-36-1*) Locust Hill Pr.

— Thomas Wolfe: An Annotated Critical Bibliography. (Scarecrow Author Bibliographies Ser.: Vol. 96). 456p. 1996. 54.50 (*0-8108-3146-5*) Scarecrow.

— Vision & Revisions: Essays on Faulkner. LC 89-14046. (Locust Hill Literary Studies: No. 4). 255p. (C). 1989. lib. bdg. 30.00 (*0-933951-32-9*) Locust Hill Pr.

Bassett, John E., ed. Defining Southern Literature: Perspectives & Assessments, 1831-1952. LC 96-1453. 456p. 1997. 57.50 (*0-8386-3642-X*) Fairleigh Dickinson.

— William Faulkner. (Critical Heritage Ser.). 438p. (C). 1997. 140.00 (*0-415-15933-4*) Routledge.

Bassett, John S. Anti-Slavery Leaders of North Carolina. LC 78-63864. (Johns Hopkins University. Studies in the Social Sciences. Thirtieth Ser. 1912: 6). reprint ed. 37.50 (*0-404-61120-6*) AMS Pr.

— The Constitutional Beginnings of North Carolina (1653-1729) LC 78-63829. (Johns Hopkins University. Studies in the Social Sciences. Thirtieth Ser. 1912: 3). reprint ed. 37.50 (*0-404-61089-7*) AMS Pr.

— The Federalist System, 1789-1801. (BCL1 - U. S. History Ser.). 327p. 1992. reprint ed. lib. bdg. 89.00 (*0-7812-6135-X*) Rprt Serv.

— Makers of a New Nation. 1928. 100.00 (*0-686-83612-X*) Elliots Bks.

— Makers of a New Nation. (BCL1 - U. S. History Ser.). 344p. 1991. reprint ed. lib. bdg. 89.00 (*0-7812-6035-3*) Rprt Serv.

— Middle Group of American Historians. LC 67-22070. (Essay Index Reprint Ser.). 1977. 23.95 (*0-8369-0175-4*) Ayer.

— Slavery & Servitude in the Colonies of North Carolina. LC 78-63849. (Johns Hopkins University. Studies in the Social Sciences. Thirtieth Ser. 1912: 4-5). reprint ed. 37.50 (*0-404-61106-0*) AMS Pr.

— Slavery in the State of North Carolina. LC 79-161726. (Johns Hopkins University. Studies in the Social Sciences. Thirtieth Ser. 1912: No. 1899: 7-8). reprint ed. 37.50 (*0-404-00246-3*) AMS Pr.

— Southern Plantation Overseer As Revealed in His Letters. (History - United States Ser.). 280p. 1992. reprint ed. lib. bdg. 79.00 (*0-7812-6152-X*) Rprt Serv.

Bassett, John T. War Journal of an Innocent Soldier. 160p. 1991. mass mkt. 4.50 (*0-380-71130-3*, Avon Bks) Morrow Avon.

— War Journal of an Innocent Soldier. LC 89-14973. 128p. (C). 1989. lib. bdg. 22.50 (*0-208-02260-0*, Archon Bks) Shoe String.

Bassett, Joseph A. Theology for Pew & Pulpit: The Everlasting Song. LC 95-46836. 184p. 1996. pap. 24.95 (*0-942597-90-7*, Ragged Edge) White Mane Pub.

Bassett, Judith, et al. The People & the Land: Te Tangata Me Te Whenua an Illustrated History of New Zealand 1820-1920. 352p. 1996. pap. 39.95 (*0-04-614013-1*) Paul & Co Pubs.

***Bassett, K. Douglas.** Latter-Day Commentary on the Book of Mormon. 1999. 25.95 (*1-57734-534-7*, 01114298) Covenant Comms.

Bassett, Karey L. Mechanics of Design: A Comprehensive Guide to Professional Floral Design. 64p. 1994. pap. text 12.50 (*0-9648962-1-4*) FTD Assn.

Bassett, Katie. Don't Give Up. LC 96-92448. (Illus.). 20p. (Orig.). (J). (gr. k-5). 1996. pap. 7.00 (*0-9654492-0-3*) Numbers Unltd.

Bassett, Lawrence & Metzger, Norman. Achieving Excellence: A Prescription for Health Care Managers. 205p. (C). 1986. 65.00 (*0-87189-277-4*) Aspen Pub.

Bassett, Lawrence, et al. MRI Atlas of the Musculoskeletal System. 1988. 153.00 (*0-8493-2751-2*) CRC Pr.

Bassett, Lawrence W. High-Quality Mammography: Information for Referring Providers, Quick Reference Guide for Clinicians, No. 13. 20p. 1994. pap. 19.00 (*0-16-045315-1*) USGPO.

— Quality Determinants of Mammography, Clinical Practice Guideline, No. 13. 184p. 1994. per. 7.00 (*0-16-045303-8*) USGPO.

Bassett, Lawrence W. & Hendrick, R. Edward. Quality Determinants of Mammography: Clinical Practice Guideline. (Illus.). 170p. (Orig.). (C). 1995. pap. text 45.00 (*0-7881-0782-8*) DIANE Pub.

Bassett, Lawrence W., et al. Diagnosis of Diseases of the Breast. Bralow, Lisette, ed. LC 95-51372. 448p. 1996. text 152.00 (*0-7216-3796-5*, W B Saunders Co) Harcrt Hlth Sci Grp.

— Film-Screen Mammography: An Atlas of Instructional Cases. 320p. 1991. text 155.00 (*0-88167-756-6*, 2235) Lppncott W & W.

— Film-Screen Mammography: An Atlas of Instructional Cases. LC 90-9169. 320p. reprint ed. pap. 99.20 (*0-608-09753-5*, 206992600007) Bks Demand.

Bassett, Lee. The Lonesome Beauty of the Moment. 1996. pap. text 10.00 (*0-911287-14-0*) Blue Begonia.

— News from the Past-Mistakes Hermitage. (Illus.). 24p. 1983. 5.00 (*0-911287-01-9*) Blue Begonia.

— Poems of Lee Bassett, 1973-2000. (Illus.). 190p. 1999. 40.00 (*0-911287-37-X*, Pub. by Blue Begonia); pap. 15.00 (*0-911287-34-5*, Pub. by Blue Begonia) Partners Pubs Grp.

Bassett, Lucinda. From Panic to Power: Proven Techniques to Calm Your Anxieties, Conquer Your Fears, & Put You in Control of Your Life. LC 95-21052. 288p. 1997. pap. 13.00 (*0-06-092758-5*, Perennial) HarperTrade.

Bassett, Lynne Z., jt. auth. see Larkin, Jack.

***Bassett, Mark.** Bassett's Roseville Prices. (Illus.). 160p. 2000. pap. 9.95 (*0-7643-1143-3*) Schiffer.

— Introducing Roseville Pottery. LC 99-15193. (Illus.). 288p. 1999. pap. 39.95 (*0-7643-0921-8*) Schiffer.

Bassett, Mark & Naumann, Victoria. Cowan Pottery & the Cleveland School. LC 96-51919. (Illus.). 272p. 1997. 69.95 (*0-7643-0238-8*) Schiffer.

Bassett, Mark T., ed. Blues of a Lifetime: The Autobiography of Cornell Woolrich. LC 91-73287. 152p. (C). 1991. 39.95 (*0-87972-535-4*); pap. 15.95 (*0-87972-536-2*) Bowling Green Univ Popular Press.

Bassett, Marnie. The Governor's Lady: Mrs. Philip Gidley King. 148p. 1992. pap. 14.95 (*0-522-84499-5*, Pub. by Melbourne Univ Pr) Paul & Co Pubs.

Bassett, Michael. The Mother of All Departments: The History of the Department of Internal Affairs. LC 97-221697. (Illus.). 256p. 1997. pap. 29.95 (*1-86940-175-1*, Pub. by Auckland Univ) Paul & Co Pubs.

— Sir Joseph Ward: A Political Biography. (Auckland University Press Book). (Illus.). 340p. (C). 1993. 39.95 (*1-86940-079-8*, 14466) OUP.

— The State in New Zealand, 1840-1984: Socialism Without Doctrines. (Illus.). 300p. 1998. pap. 27.50 (*1-86940-193-X*, Pub. by Auckland Univ) Paul & Co Pubs.

Bassett, Monica. Infant & Child Care Skills. 32p. 1996. teacher ed. 10.95 (*0-8273-5508-4*) Delmar.

Bassett, Monica M. Infant & Child Care Skills. LC 94-23165. (Illus.). 292p. (C). 1995. mass mkt. 25.75 (*0-8273-5507-6*) Delmar.

Bassett, Monica M. The Professional Nanny. LC 97-7422. (Early Childhood Education Ser.). 380p. (C). 1997. pap. 49.95 (*0-8273-7384-8*) Delmar.

***Bassett, Otta.** Tennis Today. 2nd ed. LC 99-16332. (Health Sciences Ser.). 1999. 29.95 (*0-534-35835-7*) Wadsworth Pub.

Bassett, Pamela. Blood Substitutes, Selected Growth Factors, Stem Cells & Hemoglobin Modifiers: Products, Markets & Opportunities. (Illus.). 500p. 1995. spiral bd. 2950.00 (*1-57936-052-1*, 907) IBC USA.

— Delivery Systems for Cosmetic Ingredients: Technologies, Trends & Market Opportunities. DiClemente, Susan C., ed. LC 99-167076. (Illus.). 420p. 1997. spiral bd. 4950.00 (*1-57936-095-5*, 965) IBC USA.

— Drug Delivery Systems. (Illus.). 370p. 1995. spiral bd. 3950.00 (*1-57936-055-6*, 904) IBC USA.

— Drug Delivery Systems: Trends, Technologies & Market Opportunities. 2nd rev. ed. DiClemente, Susan C., ed. (Illus.). 600p. 1996. spiral bd. 3950.00 (*1-57936-051-3*, 935) IBC USA.

— Oxygen Therapeutics - Current Technologies, Trends & Market Opportunities. 2nd rev. ed. DiClemente, Susan C., ed. (Illus.). 775p. 1997. spiral bd. 3950.00 (*1-57936-050-5*, 939) IBC USA.

— Tissue Engineering: Technologies, Trends & Market Opportunities. DiClemente, Susan C., ed. LC 99-164426. (Illus.). 585p. 1998. spiral bd. 4950.00 (*1-57936-100-5*, 968, Drug & Market Dev) IBC USA.

Bassett, Patricia M., jt. auth. see Waddell, Karen L.

Bassett, Patrick F. & Crosier, Louis M., eds. Looking Ahead: Independent School Issues & Answers. LC 94-70106. 219p. (Orig.). 1994. pap. 19.95 (*0-9627671-6-6*) Avocus Pub.

Bassett, Patrick F. & Moore, Malcolm. The English Companion. (Illus.). 144p. (YA). (gr. 9-12). 1989. reprint ed. pap. text 10.67 (*1-877653-04-7*) Wayside Pub.

Bassett, Paul. God's Way: Evangelism Explained. 198 . pap. 8.99 (*0-85234-147-4*, Pub. by Evangelical Pr) P & R Pubng.

— Help I Don't Understand Computers. 1999. pap. tex 6.95 (*1-84024-061-X*) Summers.

Bassett, Paul, jt. auth. see Ferris, Stewart.

Bassett, Paul G. Framing Software Reuse: Lessons from the Real World. LC 96-15821. 384p. (C). 1996. 55.00 (*0-13-327859-X*) P-H.

Bassett, Paul M., ed. Great Holiness Classics Vol. 1: Holiness Teaching: New Testament Times to Wesley. LC 96-44597. 344p. 1996. 34.99 (*0-8341-1575-1*) Beacon Hill.

Bassett, Paul M. & Greathouse, William M. The Historical Development. (Exploring Christian Holiness Ser.: Vol. 2). 328p. 1985. 21.99 (*0-8341-0926-3*) Beacon Hill.

***Bassett, Peter.** Parsifal. 2000. pap. 14.95 (*1-86254-512-X*, Pub. by Wakefield Pr) BHB Intl.

***Bassett, Peter, contrib. by.** A Ring for the Millennium: A Guide to Wagner's Der Ring Des Nibelungen. LC 99-181144. (Illus.). 140p. 1998. pap. 12.95 (*1-86254-471-9*, Pub. by Wakefield Pr) BHB Intl.

Bassett, R. H. Romantic Ceylon: Its History, Legend & Story. LC 98-904950. 324 p. 1997. write for info. (*81-206-1274-4*) Asian Educ Servs.

Bassett, R. L. Data Collection & Field Experiments at the Apache Leap Research Site: May 1995 - 1996. 146p. 1997. per. 14.00 (*0-16-054697-4*) USGPO.

— Field Studies at the Apache Leap Research Site in Support of Alternative Conceptual Models. 216p. 1997. per. 19.00 (*0-16-054696-6*) USGPO.

Bassett, R. L. & Bentley, M. E. Deep Brine Aquifers in the Palo Duro Basin: Regional Flow & Geochemical Constraints. (Reports of Investigations: RI 130). (Illus.). 59p. 1983. pap. 2.50 (*0-318-03280-5*) Bur Econ Geology.

Bassett, R. L., jt. auth. see Gustavson, T. C.

Bassett, R. L., jt. ed. see Melchior, Daniel C.

Bassett, R. L., jt. ed. see Melchoir, Daniel C.

***Bassett, Randall K.** Border Texts: Cultural Readings for Contemporary Writers. LC 98-71984. xiv, 690p. 1999. write for info. (*0-395-67728-9*) HM.

Bassett, Reginald G. Democracy & Foreign Policy: Case History of the Sino-Japanese Dispute, 1931-33. 680p. 1968. reprint ed. 35.00 (*0-7146-2209-5*, Pub. by F Cass Pubs) Intl Spec Bk.

— Essentials of Parliamentary Democracy. 2nd ed. 1964. reprint ed. 29.50 (*0-7146-1547-1*, Pub. by F Cass Pubs) Intl Spec Bk.

— 1931 Political Crisis. 478p. 1986. 91.95 (*0-566-05178-9*, Pub. by Dartmth Pub) Ashgate Pub Co.

Bassett, Ronald. HMS Sheffield: The Life & Times of Old Shiny. LC 88-61703. (Illus.). 288p. 1988. 31.95 (*0-87021-434-9*) Naval Inst Pr.

Bassett, Scott & Bassett, Tammy. Artemus & the Alphabet. (Illus.). 32p. (J). (ps). 1980. 6.95 (*0-9605548-0-7*); lib. bdg. 6.95 (*0-9605548-1-5*) Bassett & Brush.

Bassett, Steve. The Battered Rich. Ashton, Sylvia, ed. LC 79-15043. 1980. 22.95 (*0-87949-159-0*) Ashley Bks.

Bassett, Steven. The Origins of Anglo Saxon Kingdoms. 300p. 1989. text 59.00 (*0-7185-1317-7*, Pub. by Leicester U Pr) Cassell & Continuum.

Bassett, Steven, ed. Death in Towns: Urban Responses to the Dying & the Dead, 100-1600. (Illus.). 258p. 1995. pap. 19.95 (*0-7185-2280-X*) St Martin.

— Death in Towns, 100-1600. 256p. 1993. text 69.00 (*0-7185-1418-1*) St Martin.

Bassett, Steven & Brooks, Nicholas, eds. The Origins of Anglo-Saxon Kingdoms. (Studies in the Early History of Britain). (Illus.). 312p. 1994. pap. text 25.00 (*0-7185-1367-3*) St Martin.

***Bassett, T. D. Seymour.** The Gods of the Hills: Piety & Society in Nineteenth-Century Vermont. LC 00-33037. (Illus.). 2000. write for info. (*0-934720-43-6*) VT Hist Soc.

Bassett, T. D. Seymour. The Growing Edge: Vermont Villages, 1840-1880. LC 92-14661. (Illus.). 1992. pap. 18.95 (*0-934720-36-3*) VT Hist Soc.

Bassett, Tammy, jt. auth. see Bassett, Scott.

Bassett, Thomas J. & Crummey, Donald E., eds. Land in African Agrarian Systems. LC 92-27696. (Illus.). 430p. (Orig.). (C). 1993. 50.00 (*0-299-13610-8*) U of Wis Pr.

Bassett, Thomas J. & Crummey, Donald E., eds. Land in African Agrarian Systems. LC 92-27696. (Illus.). 430p. (Orig.). 1993. reprint ed. 133.30 (*0-608-07457-8*, 206768400009) Bks Demand.

Bassett-VanKirk, Parney, jt. auth. see VanKirk, Jacques.

Bassett-VanKirk, Parney, jt. auth. see Vankirk, Jacques.

Bassett, W. H. Clay's Handbook of Environmental Health. 16th ed. 752p. 1992. 99.95 (*0-442-31488-4*) Chapman & Hall.

— Clay's Handbook of Environmental Health. 17th ed. (Illus.). 912p. (C). 1995. 160.00 (*0-412-54870-4*, Chap & Hall NY) Chapman & Hall.

— Environmental Health Procedures. 3rd ed. LC 91-45976. 464p. 1991. pap. 59.95 (*0-442-31530-9*) Chapman & Hall.

— Environmental Health Procedures. 4th ed. LC 95-67915. 512p. 1995. text 72.00 (*0-412-56190-5*, Chap & Hall NY) Chapman & Hall.

— Environmental Health Procedures. 5th ed. LC 98-206472. (Illus.). 560p. (C). 1998. 75.00 (*0-419-22970-1*, E & FN Spon) Routledge.

Bassett, W. H., jt. auth. see Clay, Henry H.

Bassett, William. History of the Town of Richmond, Cheshire Co., from Its First Settlement to 1882. (Illus.). 578p. 1998. reprint ed. lib. bdg. 62.00 (*0-8328-7032-3*) Higginson Bk Co.

— Religious Organizations & the Law, 2 vols. (Civil Rights Ser.). 1996. ring bd. write for info. (*0-614-06273-X*) West Group.

Bassett, William T. Counseling the Childless Couple. LC 63-14722. (Successful Pastoral Counseling Ser.). 139p. reprint ed. pap. 43.10 (*0-608-16812-2*, 202693800053) Bks Demand.

Bassett, William W. California Community Property Handbook. 3rd ed. LC 91-75064. 540p. 1991. pap. 25.00 (*1-55943-124-5*, 80205-10, MICHIE) LEXIS Pub.

— Religious Organizations & the Law. LC 97-4503. 1997. write for info. (*0-8366-1119-5*) West Group.

Bassette & Chapman. Plants & Flowers, 1786 Illustrations for Artists & Designers. (Illus.). 288p. (Orig.). pap. 14.95 (*0-486-26957-4*) Dover.

Bassette, E. J. Silent Cry (Ray, Deke & Me) The Key to Stopping the Violence. Baker, Derrick K., ed. 272p. 1994. 21.95 (*0-9642800-0-0*) ThreeB Pubng.

Bassette, Suzanne. Talkeetna Twines: An Alaska Novel of Mystery, Survival, & Romance. LC 98-65164. 260p. 1998. pap. 14.95 (*1-888125-27-6*) Publ Consult.

Bassetti, Gwenyth & Galton, Jean. Cooking with Artisan Breads: Using Rustic Loaves for Perfect Crostini, Panini, Bruschetta, Flavorful Stuffings & Inventive Main Courses. LC 98-10123. 144p. 1998. pap. 22.95 (*1-57061-135-1*) Sasquatch Bks.

Bassetto, A., et al. Yang-Mills Theories in Algebraic Non-Covariant Gauges. 240p. (C). 1991. text 41.00 (*981-02-0578-3*) World Scientific Pub.

Bassey, Linus A. African Fables: Bedtime Stories by the Son of an African Chief. 3rd ed. Orig. Title: African Bedtime Stories. (Illus.). 52p. 1990. reprint ed. pap. text 6.95 (*1-56411-113-X*, 4BBG0118) Untd Bros & Sis.

Bassey, Magnus O. Missionary Rivalry & Educational Expansion in Nigeria, 1885-1945. LC 99-12629. (Studies in the History of Missions: Vol. 15). 204p. 1999. text 89.95 (*0-7734-8153-2*) E Mellen.

Bassey, Magnus O., ed. Western Education & Political Domination in Africa: A Study in Critical & Dialogical Pedagogy. LC 99-12712. 184p. 1999. 59.95 (*0-89789-622-X*, Bergin & Garvey) Greenwood.

Bassey, Michael. Case Study Research in Educational Settings. LC 98-30734. (Doing Qualitative Research in Educational Settings Ser.). 1999. 85.00 (*0-335-19985-2*); pap. 24.95 (*0-335-19984-4*) OpUniv Pr.

Bassey, Shirley. Never, Never, Never. 1979. pap. 9.95 (*0-686-09062-4*, A0038OPX) Wrner Bros.

Bassford, Christopher. Clausewitz in English: The Reception of Clausewitz in Britain & America, 1815-1945. 293p. (C). 1998. pap. text 35.00 (*0-7881-5444-3*) DIANE Pub.

— Clausweitz in English: The Reception of Clausewitz in Britain & America, 1815-1945. 304p. 1994. text 65.00 (*0-19-508383-0*) OUP.

— On Waterloo. 260p. 1999. 24.95 (*0-8133-1737-1*) Westview.

— The Spit-Shine Syndrome: Organizational Irrationality in the American Field Army, 76. LC 87-37551. (Contributions in Military Studies Ser.: No. 76). 188p. 1988. 52.95 (*0-313-26215-2*, BFP/, Greenwood Pr) Greenwood.

Bassham, Ben. Conrad Wise Chapman: Artist & Soldier of the Confederacy. LC 97-36355. (Illus.). 348p. 1998. 60.00 (*0-87338-593-4*) Kent St U Pr.

Bassham, Ben & Cordova, Ruben C. Conrad Wise Chapman: The Valley of Mexico. Dunham, Judith, ed. Sumar, Rosario, tr. (ENG & SPA., Illus.). 48p. (Orig.). 1996. pap. 5.00 (*1-879067-02-1*) Putnam Found.

Bassham, Ben L. The Lithographs of Robert Riggs with a Catalogue Raisonne. (Illus.). 104p. 1987. 40.00 (*0-87982-514-6*) Art Alliance.

Bassham, Ben L., jt. auth. see Chapman, Conrad W.

Bassham, Ben L., ed. & intro. see Warshawsky, Abel G.

Bassham, Gregory. Original Intent & the Constitution: A Philosophical Study. LC 91-44467. 256p. (C). 1992. text 55.00 (*0-8476-7737-0*) Rowman.

Bassham, Hugh. The Search for Total Health. 96p. (Orig.). 1993. pap. 8.99 (*1-56043-752-9*, Treasure Hse) Destiny Image.

Bassham, Lanny. With Winning in Mind: The Mental Management System. LC 96-84757. (Illus.). 162p. 1996. pap. 12.95 (*1-885221-47-9*) BookPartners.

Bassham, Lawrence E., III, jt. auth. see Polk, W. Timothy.

Bassham, Olan, jt. auth. see Edwards.

Basshart, Renate. Fashion Jewelry to Make Yourself: With Directions. Force, Edward, tr. from GER. LC 95-34075. (Illus.). 128p. (Orig.). 1995. pap. 24.95 (*0-88740-874-5*) Schiffer.

Basshe, Emanuel J. The Centuries: Portrait of a Tenement House. LC 71-168508. (Black Heritage Library Collection). 227p. 1977. reprint ed. 18.95 (*0-8369-8878-7*, Pub. by Blom Pubns) Ayer.

Basshuysen, Richard Van, see Schafer, Fred & Van Basshuysen, Richard.

Bassi, Domenicus, jt. auth. see Martini, Aemidius.

Bassi, Karen. Acting Like Men: Gender, Drama, & Nostalgia in Ancient Greece. LC 98-36063. 296p. (C). 1999. text 44.50 (*0-472-10625-2*, 10625) U of Mich Pr.

***Bassi, Laurie J. & Woodbury, Stephen A.** Long-Term Unemployment & Reemployment Policies. LC 00-30199. (Research in Employment Policy Ser.). 2000. write for info. (*0-7623-0577-0*) Jai Pr.

Bassi, Laurie J., et al. Assessment, Development & Measurement. LC 97-77500. (What Works Ser.). 186 p. 1997. write for info. (*1-56286-049-6*) Am Soc Train & Devel.

Bassi, Laurie Jo, et al. Training & Development Practices: Leadership Development, Conflict Management, Diversity Training, Technology Training, Behavioral Modeling. LC 97-77497. (What Works). 1997. write for info. (*1-56286-075-5*) Am Soc Train & Devel.

Bassichis, William H. Don't Panic: A Guide to Introductory Physics for Students of Science & Engineering, 2 vols., Vols. I & II. (Illus.). (C). 1988. write for info. (*0-318-65816-X*) OR Pub NY.

B

Bassie-Sweet, Karen. At the Edge of the World: Caves & Late Classic Mava World View. LC 95-45428. (Illus.). 272p. (C). 1996. 32.95 (0-8061-2829-1) U of Okla Pr.
— From the Mouth of the Dark Cave: Commemorative Sculpture of the Late Classic Maya. LC 90-50680. 304p. 1991. 34.95 (0-8061-2323-0) U of Okla Pr.
Bassili, John N., ed. On-Line Cognition in Person Perception. 240p. (C). 1989. 49.95 (0-8058-0423-4) L Erlbaum Assocs.
Bassiliades, Nick, jt. ed. see Vlahavas, Ioannis.
Bassin, Donna. Representations of Motherhood. (Illus.). 304p. 1996. pap. 18.00 (0-300-06863-8) Yale U Pr.
Bassin, Donna, ed. see Applegarth, Adrienne.
Bassin, Joan. Architectural Competitions in Nineteenth-Century England. Foster, Stephen, ed. LC 84-2599. (Architecture & Urban Design Ser.: No. 6). 259p. 1984. reprint ed. pap. 80.30 (0-8357-1565-5, 207046400095) Bks Demand.
Bassin, Mark. Imperial Visions: Nationalism & Geographical Imagination in The Russian Far East, 1840-1865. LC 98-30355. (Cambridge Studies in Historical Geography: No.29). (Illus.). 336p. (C). 1999. text 69.95 (0-521-39174-1) Cambridge U Pr.
Bassin, Milton G. Statics & Strength of Materials. 4th ed. 496p. 1987. text 57.63 (0-07-004023-0) McGraw.
Bassin, William M. Quantitative Business Analysis. LC 80-21090. 256p. (YA). (gr. 11-12). 1981. teacher ed. write for info. (0-672-97697-8); text. write for info. (0-672-97696-X) Macmillan.
Bassindale, Alan. The Third Dimension in Organic Chemistry. LC 84-166041. 256p. reprint ed. pap. 79.40 (0-7837-3216-3, 204323400007) Bks Demand.
Bassindale, Alan & Gaspar, P. P. Frontiers of Organosilicon Chemistry. 1991. 154.00 (0-85186-097-4) CRC Pr.
Bassinger, Todd F. Software Law: A User Friendly Legal Guide for Software Developers. LC 97-8433. (Legal Survival Guides Ser.). 256p. (Orig.). 1997. pap. 29.95 incl. disk (1-57071-163-1, Sphinx Pubng) Sourcebks.
Bassingthwaighte, James B., et al. Fractal Physiology. (American Physiological Society Book: No. 2). (Illus.). 384p. 1994. text 59.95 (0-19-508013-0) OUP.
***Bassingthwaite, Don.** If Whispers Call. (Dark Matter Ser.). 2000. mass mkt. 6.99 (0-7869-1679-6) Wizards Coast.
Bassini, Giorgio. The Garden of the Finzi-Continis. 1994. reprint ed. lib. bdg. 27.95 (1-56849-255-3) Buccaneer Bks.
Bassiouni, M. Cherif. Crimes Against Humanity in International Criminal Law. LC 92-13220. 872p. (C). 1992. lib. bdg. 252.50 (0-7923-1737-8) Kluwer Academic.
***Bassiouni, M. Cherif.** Crimes Against Humanity in International Criminal Law. 2nd rev. ed. LC 99-31739. 1999. 225.00 (90-411-1222-7) Kluwer Law Intl.
Bassiouni, M. Cherif. A Draft International Criminal Code & Draft Statute for An International Criminal Tribunal. 1987. lib. bdg. 217.50 (0-89838-918-6) Kluwer Academic.
— International Criminal Law Conventions & Their Penal Provisions. LC 97-25965. x, 1250 p. 1997. 185.00 (1-57105-065-5) Transnatl Pubs.
— International Extradition: U. S. Law & Practice. 3rd rev. ed. LC 95-36695. 967p. 1996. lib. bdg. 150.00 (0-379-10178-5) Oceana.
— The Law of the International Criminal Tribunal for the Former Yugoslavia: A Documentary History & Analysis. LC 95-50417. 1094p. 1996. 135.00 (1-57105-004-3) Transnatl Pubs.
— The Protection of Human Rights in the Administration of Criminal Justice: A Compendium of United Nations Norms & Standards. 529p. (C). 1994. lib. bdg. 105.00 (0-941320-87-1) Transnatl Pubs.
Bassiouni, M. Cherif, ed. The Contributions of Specialized Institutes & Non-Governmental Organizations to the United Nations Criminal Justice Program: In Honor of Adolfo Beria di Argentine. LC 95-45767. 1995. lib. bdg. 136.00 (90-411-0139-X, Pub. by M Nijhoff) Kluwer Academic.
— International Criminal Law, Vol. 3. 1200p. 1987. lib. bdg. 55.00 (0-941320-32-4) Transnatl Pubs.
***Bassiouni, M. Cherif, ed.** The Statute of the International Criminal Court: A Documentary History. LC 98-61370. 824p. 1999. text 95.00 (1-57105-095-7) Transnatl Pubs.
Bassiouni, M. Cherif, et al, eds. International Criminal Law: Cases & Materials. LC 95-83057. 1454p. (C). 1996. text 80.00 (0-89089-862-6) Carolina Acad Pr.
Bassiouni, M. Cherif & Paust, Jordan L., eds. International Criminal Law: Cases & Materials. (C). 1996. lib. bdg. 80.00 (0-89089-894-4) Carolina Acad Pr.
Bassiouni, M. Cherif & Vetere, Eduardo, eds. Organized Crime: A Compilation of U. N. Documents, 1975-1998. LC 98-39562. 664p. 1998. lib. bdg. 125.00 (1-57105-084-1) Transnatl Pubs.
Bassiouni, M. Cherif & Ziyad, Motala, eds. The Protection of Human Rights in African Criminal Proceedings. LC 94-16406. 1995. lib. bdg. 151.00 (0-7923-2888-4) Kluwer Academic.
Bassiri, Kaveh. Programming Applications for Netscape Servers. LC 98-23135. 1008p. (C). 1998. pap. text 49.95 (0-201-41970-X) Addison-Wesley.
Bassiry, Reza. Power vs. Profit: Multinational Corporation-Nation State Interaction. Bruchey, Stuart, ed. LC 80-566. (Multinational Corporations Ser.). 1981. lib. bdg. 31.95 (0-405-13363-4) Ayer.
Bassis, Michael S. & Gelles, Richard J. Sociology: An Introduction. 4th ed. (C). 1991. text, student ed. 36.50 (0-07-911031-2) McGraw.
Bassis, William L. Arc Welding Questions & Answers. 30p. 1997. pap. 10.00 (1-57074-401-7) Greyden Pr.
— Arc Welding Theories: Techniques. (Illus.). 131p. 1997. pap. 39.00 (1-57074-400-9) Greyden Pr.
Bassiti, K. Optimum Separation Design for Subsea & Floating Production Systems. 1989. 150.00 (90-6314-568-3, Pub. by Lorne & MacLean Marine) St Mut.
Bassler, Jouette M. 1 Timothy, 2 Timothy, Titus. LC 96-3018. (Abingdon New Testament Commentaries Ser.). 240p. 1996. pap. 20.95 (0-687-00157-9) Abingdon.
Bassler, Jouette M., ed. Pauline Theology, Vol. 1. 304p. 1994. pap. 22.00 (0-8006-2860-8, Fortress Pr) Augsburg Fortress.
Bassler, Karl-Heinz. Vitamin-Lexikon: Fur Artze, Apotheker und Ernahrungswissenschaftler. (GER.). 432p. 1992. 105.00 (0-7859-8360-0, 3437006606) Fr & Eur.
Bassler, R. & Hubner. Pathology of Neoplastic & Endocrine Induced Diseases of the Breast. 484p. 1987. 220.00 (0-89574-232-2, Pub. by Gustav Fischer) Balogh.
Bassler, Thomas J. & Burger, Robert E. The Whole Life Diet: An Integrated Program of Nutrition & Exercise for a Lifestyle of Total Health. LC 79-19375. 204p. 1979. 9.95 (0-87131-305-7) M Evans.
Bassler, U. Neural Basis of Elementary Behavior in Stick Insects. Strausfeld, C., tr. (Studies of Brain Function: Vol.10). (Illus.). 180p. 1983. 86.95 (0-387-11918-3) Spr-Verlag.
Bassman, Emily S. Abuse in the Workplace: Management Remedies & Bottom Line Impact. LC 92-7505. 224p. 1992. 49.95 (0-89930-673-X, BGJ, Quorum Bks) Greenwood.
Bassman, Lillian. Lillian Bassman. 108p. 1997. 50.00 (0-8212-2376-3, Pub. by Bulfinch Pr) Little.
Bassman, Lynette, ed. The Whole Mind: The Definitive Guide to Complementary Treatments for Mind, Mood, & Emotion. LC 97-31585. 574p. 1998. pap. 22.95 (1-57731-050-0) New Wrld Lib.
Bassman, Michael, jt. auth. see Bassman, Theda.
Bassman, Stuart W. & Wester, William C. Hypnosis, Headache, & Pain Control: An Intergative Approach. LC 96-40515. 1997. write for info. (1-886610-02-9) Am Soc Clin Hyp Pr.
Bassman, Theda. The Beauty of Hopi Jewelry. 2nd ed. (Illus.). 64p. (Orig.). 1993. reprint ed. pap. 14.95 (1-885772-01-7) Kiva Pubng.
— The Beauty of Navajo Jewelry. LC 97-70356. (Illus.). 80p. (Orig.). 1997. pap. 16.95 (1-885772-02-5) Kiva Pubng.
— Hopi Kachina Dolls & Their Carvers. LC 91-65658. (Illus.). 192p. 1991. 59.95 (0-88740-373-5) Schiffer.
— The Kachina Dolls of Cecil Calnimptewa: Their Power - Their Splendor. LC 94-209501. (Illus.). 102p. 1995. 70.00 (0-918080-85-1) Treas Chest Bks.
— Treasures of the Hopi. LC 96-53291. (Illus.). 116p. 1997. pap. 12.95 (0-87358-672-7) Northland AZ.
— Treasures of the Navajo. LC 96-53299. (Illus.). 124p. 1997. pap. 12.95 (0-87358-673-5) Northland AZ.
— Treasures of the Zuni. LC 96-36125. (Illus.). 116p. 1997. pap. 12.95 (0-87358-674-3) Northland AZ.
— Zuni Jewelry. 2nd rev. ed. (Illus.). 64p. 1999. pap. 12.95 (0-7643-0875-0) Schiffer.
Bassman, Theda & Bassman, Michael. Zuni Jewelry. LC 92-60622. (Illus.). 64p. 1992. pap. 12.95 (0-88740-413-8) Schiffer.
Bassnet, Susan. Sylvia Plath. LC 86-22293. (Women Writers Ser.). 176p. 41.00 (0-389-20687-3, N8245); pap. 14.00 (0-389-20688-1, N8246) B&N Imports.
Bassnett, Susan. Comparative Literature: A Critical Introduction. LC 92-45856. 192p. 1993. pap. 22.95 (0-631-16705-6) Blackwell Pubs.
— Elizabeth the First. LC 87-37398. (Women's Ser.). 139p. 1989. pap. 16.50 (0-907582-98-2) Berg Pubs.
— Feminist Experiences: The Women's Movement in Four Cultures. 168p. (C). 1986. pap. text 15.95 (0-04-301274-4) Routledge.
— Studying British Cultures: Introduction. LC 97-204890. (New Accents Ser.). 240p. (C). 1997. pap. 18.99 (0-415-11440-3) Routledge.
***Bassnett, Susan.** Translating Literature. LC 97-229475. (English Association). 152p. 1998. reprint ed. 60.00 (0-85991-522-0, DS Brewer) Boydell & Brewer.
Bassnett, Susan. Translation Studies. rev. ed. (New Accents Ser.). 192p. (C). 1991. pap. 18.99 (0-415-06528-3, A6321) Routledge.
Bassnett, Susan, compiled by. Magdalena: International Women's Experimental Theatre. LC 89-31863. (Illus.). 136p. 1990. 19.95 (0-85496-016-3) Berg Pubs.
Bassnett, Susan, ed. Shakespeare: The Elizabethan Plays. LC 93-9838. (English Dramatists Ser.). 1993. text 39.95 (0-312-09663-1) St Martin.
— Studying British Cultures: Introduction. LC 97-204890. (New Accents Ser.). 240p. (C). 1997. 65.00 (0-415-16581-4) Routledge.
Bassnett, Susan & Kuhiwczak, Piotr, eds. Ariadne's Thread: Polish Women Poets. LC 88-80462. 74p. 1988. pap. 16.95 (0-948259-40-X, Pub. by Forest Bks) Dufour.
Bassnett, Susan & Lefevere, Andre. Constructing Cultures: Essays on Literary Translation. LC 97-47653. (Topics in Translation Ser.). 1998. 79.00 (1-85359-353-2); pap. 24.95 (1-85359-352-4) Multilingual.
Bassnett, Susan & Lefevre, Andre, eds. Translation, History & Culture. 224p. 1995. pap. 24.95 (0-304-33622-X) Continuum.
— Translation, History & Culture. 256p. 1990. text 49.00 (0-86187-100-6) St Martin.
Bassnett, Susan & Lorch, Jennifer, eds. Luigi Pirandello in the Theatre: A Documentary Record. LC 92-41548. (Contemporary Theatre Studies: Vol. 3). 224p. 1993. text 30.00 (3-7186-5375-3); pap. text 14.00 (3-7186-5376-1) Gordon & Breach.
Bassnett, Susan & Trivedi, Harish. Post-Colonial Translation: Theory & Practice. LC 98-12969. (Translation Studies). 240p. (C). 1999. 75.00 (0-415-14744-1); pap. 25.99 (0-415-14745-X) Routledge.
Bassnett, Susan, jt. auth. see Grundy, P.
Bassnett, Susan, tr. see Glantz, Margo.
Basso, Adrienne. His Wicked Embrace, 1. 352p. 1999. mass mkt. 5.99 (0-8217-6284-2) Kensgtn Pub Corp.
***Basso, Adrienne.** Sweet Sensations. 1999. mass mkt. 3.99 (0-8217-6409-8, Zebra Kensgtn) Kensgtn Pub Corp.
Basso, Bill, jt. auth. see Lewison, Wendy Cheyette.
Basso, Bob. Confessions of an American Speaker: If B. S. Were Concrete, I'd be Route 66. LC 98-55528. 280p. 1999. pap. 15.00 (0-9651213-0-5) Sligo Pr.
— Fruitpunch. LC 97-69742. 212p. 1997. pap. 15.95 (0-9617166-2-2) New Breed Pr.
— I Never Wanted to Set the World on Fire: But Now that I'm Fifty, Maybe It's a Good Idea! LC 94-48651. 200p. 1995. pap. 12.95 (1-55622-387-0, Seaside Pr) Wordware Pub.
Basso, Ellen. In Favor of Deceit: A Study of Tricksters in an Amazonian Society. LC 87-18784. 376p. 1987. 52.00 (0-8165-1022-9) U of Ariz Pr.
Basso, Ellen, jt. ed. see Saul, Lynn.
Basso, Ellen B. The Last Cannibals: A South American Oral History. LC 94-25376. (Illus.). 352p. (C). 1995. pap. 19.95 (0-292-70819-X); text 40.00 (0-292-70818-1) U of Tex Pr.
Basso, Ellen B., ed. see Hendricks, Janet W., et al.
Basso, Eric. Accidental Monsters: Poems & Texts, 1976. 176p. 1998. pap. 14.00 (1-878580-81-7) Asylum Arts.
***Basso, Eric.** Bartholomew Fair. 134p. 1999. pap. 13.00 (1-878580-24-8, Pub. by Asylum Arts) SPD-Small Pr Dist.
Basso, Eric. Bartholomew Fair. 1998. pap. 13.00 (1-57650-099-3) Hi Jinx Pr.
— The Beak Doctor: Short Fiction 1972-1976. 232p. 1999. pap. 13.00 (1-878580-35-3) Asylum Arts.
— Catafalques: Poems, 1987-1989. 182p. 1999. pap. 13.00 (1-878580-09-4) Asylum Arts.
— The Catwalk Watch: Poems, 1977-1979. 232p. 1999. pap. 15.00 (1-878580-03-5) Asylum Arts.
— Enigmas: Short Plays, 1979-1982. 275p. 1999. pap. 16.00 (1-878580-60-4) Asylum Arts.
— Ghost Light: Poems, 1990-1994. 169p. 1999. pap. 14.00 (1-878580-96-5) Asylum Arts.
— The Golem Triptych. LC 93-70300. 380p. (Orig.). 1994. 22.00 (1-878580-15-9); pap. 12.95 (1-878580-16-7) Asylum Arts.
***Basso, Eric.** The Sabattier Effect. 82p. 2000. pap. 12.00 (1-878580-55-8) Asylum Arts.
Basso, Eric. The Smoking Mirror: Poems, 1980-1986. 128p. 1999. pap. 12.00 (1-878580-66-3) Asylum Arts.
Basso, Etolia S. & Basso, Hamilton, eds. World from Jackson Square. LC 72-8579. (Essay Index Reprint Ser.). 1977. reprint ed. 24.95 (0-8369-7306-2) Ayer.
Basso, Hamilton. Mainstream. LC 73-106406. (Essay Index Reprint Ser.). 1977. 21.95 (0-8369-1444-9) Ayer.
***Basso, Hamilton.** The View from Pompey's Head. LC 99-51822. 600p. 1999. 32.95 (1-56000-472-X) Transaction Pubs.
Basso, Hamilton. View from Pompey's Head. LC 98-23624. (Voices of the South Ser.). 416p. 1998. pap. 16.95 (0-8071-2334-X) La State U Pr.
— The View from Pompey's Head. 1994. reprint ed. lib. bdg. 24.95 (1-56849-557-9) Buccaneer Bks.
Basso, Hamilton, jt. ed. see Basso, Etolia S.
Basso, Keith. Wisdom Sits in Places: Landscape & Language among the Western Apache. LC 95-39272. 171p. 1996. 40.00 (0-8263-1723-5); pap. 14.95 (0-8263-1724-3) U of NM Pr.
Basso, Keith H. The Cibecue Apache. (Illus.). 106p. (C). 1986. reprint ed. pap. text 9.95 (0-88133-214-3) Waveland Pr.
— Portraits of the Whiteman. LC 78-31535. 144p. 1979. pap. text 16.95 (0-521-29593-9) Cambridge U Pr.
Basso, Keith H. & Selby, Henry A., eds. Meaning in Anthropology. LC 75-21189. (School of American Research Advanced Seminar Ser.). 267p. reprint ed. pap. 82.80 (0-608-15775-9, 203099500073) Bks Demand.
Basso, Keith H., jt. ed. see Feld, Steven.
Basso, Keith H., ed. see Goodwin, Grenville.
Basso, Lawrence V., jt. auth. see Gosling, James P.
***Basso, Matthew.** Across the Great Divide: Cultures of Masculinity in the American West. (Illus.). 320p. 2000. 75.00 (0-415-92470-7); pap. 22.99 (0-415-92471-5) Routledge.
Basso, Michael J. The Underground Guide to Teenage Sexuality. 2nd rev. ed. LC 96-48166. (Illus.). 256p. (Orig.). (YA). 1997. reprint ed. pap. 14.95 (1-57749-034-7) Fairview Press.
Basso, Thomas. The Panic-Proof Investor: Lessons in Profitable Investing from a Market Wizard. 5th ed. 151p. 1994. pap. 14.95 (0-471-03024-4) Wiley.
Bassoff, Bruce. The Secret Sharers: Studies in Contemporary Fictions. LC 82-20766. (Ars Poetica Ser.: No. 1). (Illus.). 152p. 1983. 34.50 (0-404-62501-0) AMS Pr.
Bassoff, Evelyn. Cherishing Our Daughters: How Parents Can Raise Girls to Become Strong & Loving Women. LC 97-25115. 278p. 1999. pap. 13.95 (0-452-27472-9, Plume) Dutton Plume.
Bassoff, Evelyn S. Between Mothers & Sons: The Making of Vital & Loving Men. 275p. (C). 1998. text 21.00 (0-7881-5365-X) DIANE Pub.
— Between Mothers & Sons: The Making of Vital & Loving Men. 288p. 1995. pap. 13.95 (0-452-27462-1, Plume) Dutton Plume.
— Mothering Ourselves: Help & Healing for Adult Daughters. 240p. 1992. reprint ed. pap. 12.95 (0-452-26788-9, Plume) Dutton Plume.
— Mothers & Daughters: Loving & Letting Go. 306p. 1989. pap. 13.95 (0-452-26319-0, Dutt) Dutton Plume.
Bassoff, Lawrence. Crime Scenes - Movie Poster Art of the Film Noir. LC 97-93804. (Illus.). 160p. (Orig.). 1997. pap. 35.00 (1-886310-11-4) Bassoff Collect.
— Errol Flynn: The Movie Posters. LC 94-96622. (Illus.). 168p. (Orig.). 1995. pap. 35.00 (1-886310-10-6) Bassoff Collect.
***Bassoff, Lawrence.** Mighty Movies: Movie Poster Art from Hollywood's Greatest Adventure Epics & Spectaculars. LC 99-95159. (Illus.). 152p. 1999. pap. 35.00 (1-886310-14-9, Pub. by Bassoff Collect) SCB Distributors.
Bassoli, F., jt. auth. see Gareff, G.
Bassom, David. Creating Babylon Five. LC 97-93924. 144p. 1997. pap. 18.00 (0-345-41452-7) Ballantine Pub Grp.
— Ewan McGregor: An Illustrated Story. (Illus.). 80p. 1999. pap. 9.95 (0-600-59653-2, Pub. by Hamlyn Publishing Group Ltd) Sterling.
***Bassom, David.** George Clooney: An Illustrated Story. (Illustrated Story Ser.). (Illus.). 80p. 2000. pap. 9.95 (0-600-59271-5, Pub. by P HM) Trafalgar.
Bassompierre, Guy De, see De Bassompierre, Guy.
Basson, A. H. David Hume. LC 78-26704. 183p. 1981. reprint ed. lib. bdg. 49.75 (0-313-20668-6, BADH, Greenwood Pr) Greenwood.
Basson, Dion. South Africa's Interim Constitution: Text & Notes. 369p. 1994. pap. 40.00 (0-7021-3286-1, Pub. by Juta & Co) Gaunt.
— South Africa's Interim Constitution: Text & Notes. rev. ed. 374p. 1995. pap. 33.00 (0-7021-3403-1, Pub. by Juta & Co) Gaunt.
Basson, Dion & Viljoen, H. South African Constitutional Law. 450p. 1988. pap. 40.00 (0-7021-2015-4, Pub. by Juta & Co) Gaunt.
— Suid-Afrikaanse Staatsreg. 450p. 1988. pap. write for info. (0-7021-2011-1, Pub. by Juta & Co) Gaunt.
Basson, M., et al. Probabilistic Management of Water Resource & Hydropower Systems. 1994. 65.00 (0-918334-89-6) WRP.
Basson, Philip W. Pivotal Catalogues in the Aeneid. xii, 208p. (Orig.). 1975. pap. 54.00 (90-256-0767-5, Pub. by AM Hakkert); pap. text 40.00 (0-317-57962-2, Pub. by AM Hakkert) Coronet Bks.
Bassoul, Pierre, jt. auth. see Simon, J.
Basstaire, Jean, jt. auth. see Peguy, Charles.
Basstein, G. & Sijtstra, A. New Developments in Design, Manufacturing & Applications of Cylkro-(Face) Gears. (Nineteen Ninety-Four Fall Technical Meeting Ser.: Vol. 93FTM7). (Illus.). 12p. 1993. pap. text 30.00 (1-55589-641-3) AGMA.
Bassuk. Practioners Get Psychoactive Drive. 1977. 19.95 (0-306-30953-X) Da Capo.
Bassuk, Daniel. Abraham Lincoln & the Quakers. LC 87-60763. (Orig.). 1987. pap. 4.00 (0-87574-273-4) Pendle Hill.
Bassuk, Daniel, ed. see Zielinski, Stanislaw.
Bassuk, Ellen L., ed. The Doctor-Activist: Physicians Fighting for Social Change. (Illus.). 276p. (C). 1996. 27.95 (0-306-45176-X, Kluwer Plenum) Kluwer Academic.
Bassuk, Ellen L., et al, eds. Lifelines: Clinical Perspectives on Suicide. LC 82-9105. 250p. 1982. 45.00 (0-306-40971-2, Plenum Trade) Perseus Pubng.
Bassuk, Ellen L. & Birk, Ann W., eds. Emergency Psychiatry: Concepts, Methods, & Practices. LC 84-11709. (Critical Issues in Psychiatry Ser.). 468p. 1984. 69.50 (0-306-41655-7, Plenum Trade) Perseus Pubng.
Bassuk, Ellen L. & Carman, Rebecca W., eds. The Doctor-Activist: Physicians Fighting for Social Change. 276p. (C). 1996. 27.95 (0-306-45267-7, Plenum Trade) Perseus Pubng.
Bassuk, Ellen L., et al. Behavioral Emergencies: A Field Guide for EMT's & Paramedics. 1983. teacher ed. write for info. (0-316-08331-3, Little Brwn Med Div); pap. text 16.00 (0-316-08330-5) Lppncott W & W.
Bassuk, Ellen L., jt. auth. see Melnick, Sharon M.
Bassuk, Ellen L., jt. ed. see Gelenberg, Alan J.
Bast. Legal Research & Writing. (Paralegal Ser.). 80p. 1995. text, teacher ed. 12.50 (0-8273-7186-1) Delmar.
Bast, Carol M. Florida Courts. 2nd ed. 86p. (C). 1998. per. 15.50 (0-929563-47-6) Pearson Pubns.
— Legal Research & Writing. LC 94-29908. 400p. (C). 1995. mass mkt. 49.95 (0-8273-6215-3) Delmar.
Bast, Felicity. The Poetical Cat. rev. ed. 1996. 15.00 (0-374-23540-6) FS&G.
Bast, Henry. El Problema Que Unicamente Dios Pudo Resolver. (SPA., Illus.). 86p. 1995. mass mkt. 3.99 (0-8254-1054-1, Edit Portavoz) Kregel.
Bast, Herbert. Upholstery Made Easy. 200p. 1997. reprint ed. pap. 14.95 (1-57002-059-0) Univ Publng Hse.
Bast, Joseph L., et al. Eco-Sanity: A Common Sense Guide to Environmentalism. LC 94-10687. (Illus.). 332p. (C). 1995. text 22.95 (1-56833-028-6) Madison Bks UPA.
— Health Care in Oklahoma: Prescription for Reform: A Common Sense Alternative to National Health Insurance. Tanner, Terry, ed. 172p. (Orig.). 1993. pap. 12.95 (0-913507-47-4) New Forums.
— Why We Spend Too Much on Health Care. 10p. 1992. pap. 8.95 (0-9632027-0-7) Heartland Inst.
— Why We Spend Too Much on Health Care...& What We Can Do about It. (Illus.). 176p. (C). 1993. 41.00 (0-9632027-1-5); pap. text 8.95 (0-9632027-2-3) Heartland Inst.
***Bast, Robert C., Jr., et al.** Cancer Medicine - 5. (ACS Atlas of Clinical Oncology Ser.). 2900p. 2000. boxed set 225.00 incl. cd-rom (1-55009-113-1) DEKR.
Bast, Robert J. Honor Your Fathers: Catechisms & the Emergence of a Patriarchal Ideology in Germany, c. 1400-1600. LC 97-28706. (Studies in Medieval & Reformation Thought: No. 63). xx, 272p. 1997. 103.00 (90-04-10856-4) Brill Academic Pubs.

***Bast, Robert James, et al.** Community & Change: The Harvest of Late Medieval & Reformation History: Essays Presented to Heiko A. Oberman on His 70th Birthday. LC 00-41359. 2000. write for info. (*90-04-11633-8*) Brill Academic Pubs.

Bast, Rochelle, ed. Handbook for Senior Adult Camping. 68p. 1977. pap. 4.00 (*0-943272-11-4*) Inst Recreation Res.

Bast, S. L. Loos Family Genealogy, 1535-1958. 245p. 1991. reprint ed. pap. 37.00 (*0-8328-2040-7*); reprint ed. lib. bdg. 47.00 (*0-8328-2039-3*) Higginson Bk Co.

Bast, William. James Dean. (Illus.). 250p. 1992. reprint ed. lib. bdg. 27.95 (*0-89966-929-8*) Buccaneer Bks.

Basta, Daniel J. & Bower, Blair T., eds. Analyzing Natural Systems: Analysis for Regional Residuals-Environmental Quality Management. LC 81-48248. 546p. 1982. pap. text 30.00 (*0-8018-2820-1*) Resources Future.

Basta, Daniel J., et al. Analysis for Residuals-Environmental Quality Management: Case Study of the Ljubljana Area of Yugoslavia. LC 77-17250. (Resources for the Future Ser.). 258p. reprint ed. pap. 80.00 (*0-8357-5424-3*, 2052112) Bks Demand.

Basta, Lofty L. & Post, Carole. Graceful Exit: Life & Death on Your Own Terms. (Illus.). 368p. (C). 1996. 27.95 (*0-306-45270-7*, Plen Insight) Perseus Pubng.

Basta, Margo M., jt. auth. see Siegel, Alice.

Basta, Nicholas. Careers in High Tech. (Illus.). 112p. 1994. 17.95 (*0-8442-4180-6*, VGM Career) NTC Contemp Pub Co.

— The Environmental Career Guide: Job Opportunities with the Earth in Mind. 208p. 1991. pap. 16.95 (*0-471-53413-7*) Wiley.

— Opportunities in Energy Careers. (Illus.). 160p. 1993. pap. 10.95 (*0-8442-8584-6*, VGM Career) NTC Contemp Pub Co.

— Opportunities in Energy Careers. (Illus.). 160p. 1995. 13.95 (*0-8442-8583-8*, VGM Career) NTC Contemp Pub Co.

— Opportunities in Engineering Careers. rev. ed. LC 95-31373. (Opportunities in... Ser.). (Illus.). 160p. 1995. 14.95 (*0-8442-4591-7*, Natl Textbk Co) NTC Contemp Pub Co.

— Top Professions: The 100 Most Popular, Dynamic, & Profitable Careers in America Today. LC 89-22898. 228p. (Orig.). 1989. pap. 10.95 (*0-87866-866-7*) Petersons.

Basta, Nick. Careers in High Tech. 2nd ed. LC 98-30398. (Professional Careers Ser.). 104p. 1998. 17.95 (*0-8442-6405-9*, 64059, VGM Career); pap. 13.95 (*0-8442-6406-7*, 64067, VGM Career) NTC Contemp Pub Co.

— Opportunities in Engineering Careers. rev. ed. LC 95-31373. (Opportunities In . . . Ser.). 160p. pap. 11.95 (*0-8442-4592-5*, 45925, Natl Textbk Co) NTC Contemp Pub Co.

***Basta, Samir Sanad.** Culture, Conflict & Children: Transmission of Violence to Children. 272p. 2000. 47.50 (*0-7618-1741-7*) U Pr of Amer.

Bastable, Bernard. A Mansion & Its Murder. LC 98-16788. 192p. 1998. 22.00 (*0-7867-0515-9*) Carroll & Graf.

— To Die Like a Gentleman. large type ed. LC 93-45725. 261p. 1994. lib. bdg. 18.95 (*0-7862-0165-7*) Thorndike Pr.

Bastable, Susan B. Nurse As Educator: Principle of Teaching & Learning. LC 97-7066. (Nursing Ser.). 432p. 1997. pap. 40.00 (*0-7637-0310-9*) Jones & Bartlett.

Bastani-Parizi, Mohammad E., jt. auth. see Atabai, Badri.

Bastard, Gerald. Wave Mechanics Applied to Semiconductor Heterostructures. LC 90-47219. (Monographs of Physics). 357p. 1991. pap. text 84.95 (*0-470-21708-1*) Halsted Pr.

Bastasch, Rick. Waters of Oregon: A Source Book on Oregon's Water & Water Management. LC 97-32127. (Illus.). 288p. 1998. pap. 22.95 (*0-87071-427-9*) Oreg St U Pr.

Bastea, Eleni. The Creation of Modern Athens: Planning the Myth. LC 99-10717. (Illus.). 300p. (C). 1999. 80.00 (*0-521-64120-9*) Cambridge U Pr.

***Bastedo & Kemnitz.** Canine Care & Cuisine. 279p. 1999. text 28.95 (*1-86105-118-2*) Robson.

— Healthy Cat Book: Feline Care & Cuisine. 186p. 1999. text 25.95 (*1-86105-178-6*) Robson.

Bastedo, Alexandra. Beware Dobermanns, Donkeys & Ducks. LC 95-73119. (Illus.). 190p. 1996. 23.95 (*0-86051-973-2*, Robson-Parkwest) Parkwest Pubns.

— Beware Dobermanns, Donkeys & Ducks. 190p. 1997. pap. 12.95 (*1-86105-019-4*, Robson-Parkwest) Parkwest Pubns.

Bastedo, Jamie. Reaching North: A Celebration Of The Subarctic. 256p. 1998. pap. 15.95 (*0-88995-170-5*, Pub. by Red Deer) Genl Dist Srvs.

— Shield Country: The Life & Times Of The Oldest Piece Of The Planet. 276p. 1999. pap. 18.95 (*0-88995-191-8*, Pub. by Red Deer) Genl Dist Srvs.

***Bastedo, Jaya.** A Winter Walk with Haley. (Illus.). 24p. (J). (ps-5). 1999. pap. 7.95 (*1-894303-06-7*) RRP.

Bastedo, Suzanne, ed. see Burns, Roberts.

Bastedo, Suzanne, ed. see Stanley, Jacqueline Vickery.

Bastel, Heribert. Die Zielfrage in der Kirchlichen Jugendarbeit Im Schnittpunkt Padagogischer und Theologischer Reflexionen: Eine Untersuchung des Kirchlichen Jugendverbandes der Jugend-Germeinschaften Christlichen Lebens. (Europaische Hochschulschriften Ser.: Reihe 11, Bd. 499). (GER.). 175p. 1992. 31.80 (*3-631-44141-X*) P Lang Pubng.

Basten, Fred, jt. auth. see Miller, Robert.

Basten, Fred E. Glorious Technicolor: The Movies' Magic Rainbow. (80th Anniversary Edition Ser.). 256p. 1995. 50.00 (*0-9647065-3-9*) Technicolor.

— Lost Artwork of Hollywood: Classic Images from Cinema's Golden Age. (Illus.). 192p. 1996. 40.00 (*0-8230-8345-4*) Watsn-Guptill.

Basten, Fred E. & Phoenix, Charles. Fabulous Las Vegas in the 50s: Glitz, Glamour & Games. LC 99-6676. (Illus.). 128p. 1999. 26.95 (*1-883318-05-X*) Angel City Pr.

Basten, Fred E., jt. auth. see Calistro, Paddy.

Basten, Fred E., jt. auth. see Segal, Fred.

Baster, A. S. The Imperial Banks. Wilkins, Mira, ed. LC 76-29994. (European Business Ser.). 1977. reprint ed. lib. bdg. 25.95 (*0-405-09752-2*) Ayer.

— The International Banks. Wilkins, Mira, ed. LC 76-29995. (European Business Ser.). 1977. reprint ed. lib. bdg. 23.95 (*0-405-09753-0*) Ayer.

Bastero, J. & San Miguel, M., eds. Probability & Banach Spaces. (Lecture Notes in Mathematics Ser.: Vol. 1221). ix, 222p. 1986. 35.30 (*0-387-17186-X*) Spr-Verlag.

Bastero, Juan L. Mary, Mother of the Redeemer. 272p. 1999. pap. 39.50 (*1-85182-263-1*, Pub. by Four Cts Pr) Intl Spec Bk.

Basterra, Francisco J. Bioethics. (Theology & Life Ser.). 352p. 1994. pap. 19.95 (*0-8146-5503-3*) Liturgical Pr.

— Bioethics. 352p. 1994. 75.00 (*0-85439-458-3*, Pub. by St Paul Pubns) St Mut.

Bastert, G. & Wallwiener, D., eds. Lasers in Gynecology: Possibilities & Limitations. (Illus.). 528p. 1992. 250.00 (*0-387-53409-1*) Spr-Verlag.

Bastiaanse, Roelien, jt. ed. see Visch-Brink, Evy.

Bastiaenen, J. A. Moral Tone of Jacobean & Caroline Drama. LC 68-951. (Studies in Drama: No. 39). 1969. reprint ed. lib. bdg. 75.00 (*0-8383-0507-5*) M S G Haskell Hse.

Bastiaensen, A. A., et al, eds. Fructus Centesimus. (C). 1989. pap. text 410.50 (*0-7923-0463-2*) Kluwer Academic.

Bastiaensen, Johan. Rural Development Central America. LC 99-33853. 2000. text 65.00 (*0-312-22659-4*) St Martin.

***Bastian, Misty L. & Parpart, Jane L.** Great Ideas for Teaching about Africa. LC 98-49639. 244p. 1999. 55.00 (*1-55587-815-6*) L Rienner.

Bastian, Ann, et al. Choosing Equality: The Case for Democratic Schooling. 240p. 1986. pap. 22.95 (*0-87722-454-4*) Temple U Pr.

Bastian, Anthony S. Parent's Guide to Washington Public Schools. 104p. (Orig.). 1991. pap. 5.95 (*0-9630022-3-6*) Bastian Bks.

Bastian, David F. Grant's Canal. LC 95-23875. 96p. 1996. pap. 6.95 (*0-942597-93-1*) White Mane Pub.

Bastian, Frank O. Creutzfeldt-Jakob Disease & Other Transmissible Diseases. 272p. 1991. 63.00 (*0-685-65367-6*) Mosby Inc.

Bastian, Geoff, jt. auth. see Crean, David.

Bastian, Glenn F. Basic Concept of Respiratory System: The Respiratory System. LC 94-4204. (Illustrated Review of Anatomy of Physiology: Systems Ser.). 112p. (C). 1997. pap. text, wbk. ed. 13.60 (*0-06-501709-9*) Addson-Wesley Educ.

Bastian, Glenn F. Basic Concepts of Chemistry, the Cell & Tissues. (Illustrated Review of Anatomy of Physiology: Systems Ser.). 144p. (C). 1997. pap., wbk. ed. 10.20 (*0-06-501703-X*) Addson-Wesley Educ.

— Basic Concepts of the Cardiovascular System: The Cardiovascular System. (Illustrated Review of Anatomy of Physiology: Systems Ser.). 208p. (C). 1997. pap. text, wbk. ed. 13.60 (*0-06-501707-2*) Addson-Wesley Educ.

— Basic Concepts of the Digestive System. LC 94-1897. (Illustrated Review of Anatomy of Physiology: Systems Ser.). 160p. (C). 1997. pap. text, wbk. ed. 13.60 (*0-06-501710-2*) Addson-Wesley Educ.

Bastian, Glenn F. Basic Concepts of the Muscular & Skeletal Systems: The Muscular/Skeletal Systems. LC 93-25475. (Illustrated Review of Anatomy of Physiology: Systems Ser.). (Illus.). 208p. (C). 1997. pap. text, wbk. ed. 13.60 (*0-06-501704-8*) Addson-Wesley Educ.

— Basic Concepts of the Nervous System: The Nervous System. (Illustrated Review of Anatomy of Physiology: Systems Ser.). 352p. (C). 1997. pap. text, wbk. ed. 13.60 (*0-06-501705-6*) Addson-Wesley Educ.

— Basic Concepts of the Reproductive System: The Reproductive System. (Illustrated Review of Anatomy of Physiology: Systems Ser.). (Illus.). 160p. (C). 1997. pap. text, wbk. ed. 13.60 (*0-06-501712-9*) Addson-Wesley Educ.

— Basic Concepts of the Urinary System: The Urinary System. (Illustrated Review of Anatomy of Physiology: Systems Ser.). 144p. (C). 1997. pap. text, wbk. ed. 13.60 (*0-06-501711-0*) Addson-Wesley Educ.

Bastian, Glenn F. Illustrated Review of Anatomy & Physiology (Endocrine) The Endocrine System. 128p. (C). 1997. pap. text, wbk. ed. 13.60 (*0-06-501706-4*) Addson-Wesley Educ.

Bastian, Glenn F. Illustrated Review of Anatomy & Physiology (Lymphatric/Immune) The Lymphatic/Immune System. 128p. (C). 1997. pap. text, wbk. ed. 13.60 (*0-06-501708-0*) Addson-Wesley Educ.

Bastian, Hans-Werner. Making Designer Furniture for Children, the Home & Garden. (Illus.). 80p. (Orig.). 1994. pap. 23.50 (*1-85486-111-5*, Pub. by Nexus Special Interests) Trans-Atl Phila.

Bastian, Hartmut. Ullstein Lexikon der Pflanzenwelt: Ullstein Lexicon of the Plant World. (GER.). 1973. 49.95 (*0-8288-6333-4*, M7675) Fr & Eur.

— Ullstein Lexikon der Tierwelt. (GER.). 1967. 49.95 (*0-8288-6694-5*, M7676) Fr & Eur.

Bastian, Heiner. Anselm Kiefer: Dein und Mein Alter und das Alter der Welt: Your Age & Mine & the Age of the World. (Illus.). 68p. 1998. 40.00 (*1-880154-17-X*) Gagosian Gallery.

Bastian, Heiner & Beuys, Joseph. Joseph Beuys: Zeichnungen. (FRE & GER., Illus.). 180p. 1983. pap. 40.00 (*3-7165-0465-3*, Pub. by Benteli Verlag) Dist Art Pubs.

Bastian, Henry C. A Treatise on Aphasia & Other Speech Defects. LC 78-72786. (Brainedness, Handedness & Mental Abilities Ser.). reprint ed. 49.50 (*0-404-60851-5*) AMS Pr.

Bastian, Jean. Laramie County, Wyoming. (Illus.). 47p. 1987. 60.00 (*0-88107-076-9*) Curtis Media.

Bastian, Jens. A Matter of Time: From Work Sharing to Temporal Flexibility in Belgium, France & Britain. 304p. 1994. 79.95 (*1-85628-911-7*, Pub. by Avebury) Ashgate Pub Co.

Bastian, Jens, ed. The Political Economy of Transition in Central & Eastern Europe: The Light(s) at the End of the Tunnel. LC 98-73760. 5p. 1998. text 59.95 (*1-85972-661-5*) Ashgate Pub Co.

***Bastian, Lois B.** Chipmunk Family. LC 99-38206. 2000. 22.50 (*0-531-11683-2*) Watts.

Bastian, Misty L. & Parpart, Jane L. Great Ideas for Teaching about Africa. LC 98-49639. x, 244p. 1999. pap. 29.95 (*1-55587-816-4*) L Rienner.

Bastian, Ralph J., tr. see Portalie, Eugene.

***Bastian, Robert K., ed.** Constructed Wetlands for Wastewater Treatment & Wildlife Habitat: 17 Case Studies. (Illus.). 174p. (C). 2000. reprint ed. pap. text 30.00 (*0-7881-8609-4*) DIANE Pub.

Bastian, Sonia, ed. Claudius Quadrigarius - Lexicon in Q. Claudium Quadrigarium. (Alpha-Omega, Reihe A Ser.: Bd. LXI). viii, 73p. 1983. 25.00 incl. 3.5 hd (*3-487-07378-1*) G Olms Pubs.

Bastian, Sunil, ed. Devolution & Development in Sri Lanka. (C). 1994. text 22.00 (*81-220-0349-4*, Pub. by Konark Pubs) S Asia.

Bastian, Thomas A. Tenacity of the Spirit: Biography of Dionisio Q. Quimosing. (Illus.). 169p. (Orig.). (C). 1991. pap. 10.75 (*971-10-0450-X*, Pub. by New Day Pub) Cellar.

Bastianel, Sergio. Prayer & Christian Ethics. (C). 1988. 39.00 (*0-7855-3218-8*, Pub. by St Paul Pubns) St Mut.

— Prayer in Christian Moral Life. 128p. (C). 1990. 60.00 (*0-85439-283-1*, Pub. by St Paul Pubns) St Mut.

Bastianel, Sergio, ed. Prayer in Christian Moral Life. 112p. (C). 1988. 49.00 (*0-7855-2322-7*, Pub. by St Paul Pubns) St Mut.

Bastiani, John, ed. Home-School Work in Multicultural Settings. (Home & School - A Working Alliance Ser.). 160p. 1997. pap. 24.95 (*1-85346-428-7*, Pub. by David Fulton) Taylor & Francis.

Bastiani, John & Wolfendale, Sheila, eds. Home-School Work in Britain: Review, Reflection, & Development. LC 96-131678. (Home & School - A Working Alliance Ser.). 160p. 1996. pap. 24.95 (*1-85346-395-7*, Pub. by David Fulton) Taylor & Francis.

Bastianich, Lidia. La Cucina di Lidia. 288p. 1990. 36.50 (*0-385-24511-4*) Doubleday.

Bastianich, Lidia M. Lidia's Italian Table: More than 200 Recipes from the First Lady of Italian Cooking. Styler, Christopher & Hoenig, Pam, eds. LC 98-2949. (Illus.). 320p. 1998. 26.00 (*0-688-15410-7*, Wm Morrow) Morrow Avon.

***Bastianse, Roelien.** Grammatical Disorders in Aphasia. 1999. pap. text 65.00 (*1-86156-135-0*) Whurr Pub

Bastias, John C., jt. ed. see Christopoulos, George A.

Bastiat, Frederic. Economic Harmonies. De Huszar, George B., ed. Boyers, W. Hayden, tr. from FRE. LC 96-85212. 596p. 1996. reprint ed. pap. 14.95 (*0-910614-13-X*) Foun Econ Ed.

— Economic Sophisms. LC 95-83126. 291p. 1996. reprint ed. pap. 11.95 (*0-910614-14-8*) Foun Econ Ed.

— The Law. 78p. 1996. reprint ed. pap. 2.95 (*0-910614-01-6*) Foun Econ Ed.

— The Law. 2nd ed. LC 95-83091. 100p. 1996. 12.95 (*1-57246-020-2*) Foun Econ Ed.

— The Law. 2nd ed. 1998. 2.95 (*1-57246-074-1*) Foun Econ Ed.

— The Law. 2nd ed. LC 98-73568. 1998. 12.95 (*1-57246-073-3*) Foun Econ Ed.

— Paix et Liberte, ou le Budget Republicain. LC 72-147492. (Library of War & Peace; the Political Economy of War). 1972. lib. bdg. 46.00 (*0-8240-0286-5*) Garland.

— Providence & Liberty, Vol. I. Audouin, Raoul, ed. & tr. by. 91p. (C). 1991. pap. text 6.00 (*1-880595-00-1*) Acton Inst Stu Rel.

Bastible, James C., ed. see Ott, Ludwig.

Basticci, Vespasiano Da, see Da Basticci, Vespasiano

Bastick, Tony. Intuition, How We Think & Act. LC 82-186835. (Illus.). 518p. reprint ed. pap. 160.60 (*0-8357-3047-6*, 203930300012) Bks Demand.

Bastid, Marianne. Educational Reform in Early Twentieth Century China. Bailey, Paul J., tr. from FRE. LC 85-15201. (Michigan Monographs in Chinese Studies: No. 53). 331p. 1989. text 50.00 (*0-89264-061-8*); pap. text 25.00 (*0-89264-062-6*) Ctr Chinese Studies.

Bastid, Marianne, jt. ed. see Hayhoe, Ruth.

Bastida, Julio R. Field Extensions & Galois Theory. (Encyclopedia of Mathematics & Its Applications Ser.: No. 22). 384p. 1984. text 100.00 (*0-521-30242-0*) Cambridge U Pr.

Bastide, Derek. The Primary RE Coordinator's Handbook. 159p. 1997. pap. 23.95 (*0-7507-0613-9*, Falmer Pr) Taylor & Francis.

— Religious Education Five-Twelve. 1987. 60.00 (*1-85000-149-9*, Falmer Pr) Taylor & Francis.

Bastide, Derek, ed. Good Practice in Primary Religious Education. 224p. 1992. 79.95 (*1-85000-634-2*, Falmer Pr); pap. 29.95 (*1-85000-639-3*, Falmer Pr) Taylor & Francis.

Bastide, Francois-Regis. Les Adieux. (FRE.). 320p. 1980. pap. 11.95 (*0-7859-1923-6*, 2070372219) Fr & Eur.

— L' Enchanteur et Nous. (FRE.). 512p. 1982. pap. 13.95 (*0-7859-1961-9*, 2070374025) Fr & Eur.

— La Vie Revee. (FRE.). 1982. pap. 12.95 (*0-7859-1945-7*, 2070373428) Fr & Eur.

Bastide, Francois-Regis & Palanque, Philippe, eds. Design, Specification & Verification of Interactive Systems '95: Proceedings of the Eurographics Workshop in Toulouse, France, June 7-9, 1995. (Eurographics Ser.). (Illus.). x, 370p. 1995. pap. 95.00 (*3-211-82739-0*) Spr-Verlag.

Bastide, Francois-Regis, et al. Les Haitiens en France. (Publications de l'Institut d'Etudes et de Recherches Interethniques et Interculturelles Ser.: No. 4). (FRE., Illus.). 229p. 1975. pap. text 49.25 (*90-279-7515-9*) Mouton.

Bastide, Madeleine, ed. Signals & Images: Proceedings, GIRI Meeting on Signals & Images (7th/8th, 1993-1994, Montepellier, France/Israel, December) LC 97-868. 300p. 1997. text 167.00 (*0-7923-4466-9*) Kluwer Academic.

Bastien, Charles. QC Sources. 420p. (Orig.). (C). 1984. 17.95 (*0-916429-00-8*) IAQC Pr.

Bastien, James W. How to Teach Piano Successfully. 3rd ed. LC 88-80602. (Illus.). 1989. pap. text 29.95 (*0-8497-6109-3*, GP40) Kjos.

— A Parent's Guide to Piano Lessons. LC 76-21927. (Illus.). 1976. pap. 3.75 (*0-910842-05-1*, WP29) Kjos.

Bastien, James W. & Bastien, Jane S. Beginning Piano for Adults. LC 68-25633. (Illus.). 1968. 13.95 (*0-910842-02-7*, GP23) Kjos.

Bastien, Jane S., jt. auth. see Bastien, James W.

Bastien, Joseph. The Kiss of Death: Chagas Disease in the Americas. LC 98-18279. xxiv, 301p. 1998. 39.95 (*0-87480-559-7*) U of Utah Pr.

Bastien, Joseph W. Drum & Stethoscope: Integrating Ethnomedicine & Biomedicine in Bolivia. LC 92-53602. (Illus.). 320p. 1992. 34.95 (*0-87480-386-1*) U of Utah Pr.

— Healers of the Andes: Kallawaya Herbalists & Their Medicinal Plants. LC 87-13351. (Illus.). 207p. reprint ed. pap. 64.20 (*0-7837-3967-2*, 204379600011) Bks Demand.

— Mountain of the Condor: Metaphor & Ritual in an Andean Ayllu. (Illus.). 227p. (C). 1985. reprint ed. pap. text 12.50 (*0-88133-143-0*) Waveland Pr.

Bastien, Norma J., ed. Franklin the Flea. 32p. (Orig.). (J). (gr. k). 1994. 2.95 (*1-883196-01-9*) Royal Unicorn.

Bastien, Peter E. Praying with Martin Luther. Koch, Carl, ed. (Companions for the Journey Ser.). (Illus.). 128p. 1999. pap. 8.95 (*0-88489-580-7*) St Marys.

Bastien, Pierre C., jt. auth. see Levy, Brooks E.

***Bastille, E. Richard.** The Thirtieth Annual Bastille Family Reunion: A Short Memoir on Family Values. 163p. (C). 2000. pap. 11.95 (*0-9702707-0-4*) Hart West.

Bastin, Bruce. Red River Blues: The Blues Tradition in the Southeast. (Music in American Life Ser.). 432p. (C). 1995. 17.95 (*0-252-06521-2*) U of Ill Pr.

Bastin, Edson S. Interpretation of Ore Textures. LC 51-3907. (Geological Society of America, Memoir Ser.: No. 45). 129p. reprint ed. pap. 40.00 (*0-608-11120-1*, 200794700066) Bks Demand.

Bastin, G. & Dochain, D., eds. On-Line Estimation & Adaptive Control of Bioreactors: Process Measurement & Control. 394p. 1990. 231.00 (*0-444-88430-0*) Elsevier.

Bastin, Georges. Diccionario de Psicologia Sexual. 2nd ed. (SPA.). 412p. 1978. pap. 39.95 (*0-7859-5086-9*, S13099) Fr & Eur.

Bastin, J. M., jt. ed. see Frennet, A.

Bastin, Marcel, et al. God Day by Day Vol. 1: Lent & the Easter Season. 320p. (Orig.). 1984. pap. 10.95 (*0-8091-2642-7*) Paulist Pr.

— God Day by Day Vol. 3: Ordinary Time-Luke. 1989. pap. 14.95 (*0-8091-3056-4*) Paulist Pr.

— God Day by Day Vol. 5: Ordinary Time-Mark. 1989. pap. 12.95 (*0-8091-3057-2*) Paulist Pr.

***Bastin, Marjolein.** Nature Diary. (Illus.). 128p. 1999. spiral bd. 14.95 (*1-55670-958-7*) Stewart Tabori & Chang.

Bastin, Marjolein. Vera's Special Hobbies. (Illus.). 28p. (J). (ps-2). 1985. 2.95 (*0-8120-5692-2*) Barron.

Bastin, Marjolein. Nature Diary. 128p. 1997. 12.95 (*1-55670-101-2*) Stewart Tabori & Chang.

Bastin, T. & Kilmister, C. W. Combinatorial Physics, Vol. 9. LC 95-34079. (K & E Series on Knots & Everything). 200p. 1995. 38.00 (*981-02-2212-2*) World Scientific Pub.

Basting, Anne D. The Stages of Age: Performing Age in Contemporary American Culture. LC 98-9015. (Illus.). 232p. (C). 1998. text 39.50 (*0-472-10939-1*, 10939) U of Mich Pr.

***Bastis, Madeline K.** Peaceful Dwelling: Meditations for Healing & Living. LC 00-32594. 2001. pap. write for info. (*0-8048-3234-X*) Tuttle Pubng.

Bastl, Elaine. The Marketing of Cooperative Advertising. (Illus.). 110p. 1983. 15.95 (*0-912875-00-3*) Basbery Pub.

Bastock, T. W., jt. ed. see Martin, K.

Bastola, S. N. Water Resources Development of the Mighty Himalayan Rivers: Indus, Ganga-Yamuna, Brahamaputra Rivers. 1994. pap. 75.00 (*0-7855-0423-0*, Pub. by Ratna Pustak Bhandar) St Mut.

Baston, Robert J. Delegation Skills, Vols. 1 & 2. 122p. 1991. ring bd. 299.00 (*0-7494-0458-2*, Kogan Pg Educ) Stylus Pub VA.

— Delegation Skills: Participant Guide. 60p. 1991. ring bd. 59.95 (*0-7494-0486-8*, Kogan Pg Educ) Stylus Pub VA.

Baston, Robert J. & Eastwood, Michael G. The Penrose Transform: Its Interaction with Representation Theory. (Oxford Mathematical Monographs). (Illus.). 228p. 1990. text 65.00 (*0-19-853565-1*) OUP.

B

***Bastos, Augusto Roa.** I the Supreme. Lane, Helen, tr. from SPA. LC 00-20980. 433p. 2000. reprint ed. pap. 13.95 (*1-56478-247-6*, Pub. by Dalkey Arch) Chicago Distribution Ctr.

***Bastos, Cristiana.** Global Responses to Aids: Science in Emergency. LC 99-32161. 1999. write for info. (*0-253-21335-5*) Ind U Pr.

— Global Responses to AIDS: Science in Emergency. LC 99-32161. 1999. 27.95 (*0-253-33590-6*) Ind U Pr.

Bastos, Hugo, jt. auth. see Zarate, Armando.

Bastos, J., et al, eds. Realising CIM's Industrial Potential: Proceedings of CIM Europe 9th Annual Conference, 12-14 May, 1993, Amsterdam, Netherlands. LC 93-78139. (Design & Manufacturing Ser.: Vol. 2). 397p. (gr. 12). 1993. 117.00 (*90-5199-130-4*, Pub. by IOS Pr) IOS Press.

Bastos, Joao, jt. auth. see Ida, Nathan.

Bastos, Maria-Ines. Winning the Battle to Lose the War: Brazilian Electronics Policy Under U. S. Threat of Sanction. LC 94-3384. 198p. (C). 1994. pap. 35.00 (*0-7146-4111-1*, Pub. by F Cass Pubs) Intl Spec Bk.

***Bastos, Maria-Ines & Mitter, Swasti, eds.** Europe & Developing Countries in the Globalised Information Economy: Employment & Distance Education. LC 98-44184. (UNU/Intech Studies in New Technology & Development). 245p. 1999. 90.00 (*0-415-19704-X*) Routledge.

Bastow, Donald & Howard, Geoffrey. Car Suspension & Handling. 3rd ed. LC 93-8678. 378p. 1993. 69.00 (*1-56091-404-1*, R-133) Soc Auto Engineers.

Bastow, Tania & Jones, Ceri. Making Headway: Talking in Pairs Intermediate. (Illus.). 80p. 1999. pap. text 9.95 (*0-19-435555-1*) OUP.

— Making Headway: Talking in Pairs Pre-Intermediate. (Illus.). 80p. 1999. pap. text 9.95 (*0-19-435548-9*) OUP.

Bastraw, Mike, ed. 50 Extremely Short Fiction Stories. viii, 50p. 1982. pap. 3.95 (*0-910619-01-8*) Niekas Pubns.

Bastress. Interviewing, Counseling, & Negotiating: Skills for Effective Representation. 576p. 1990. pap. text 32.50 (*0-316-34571-7*, Aspen Law & Bus) Aspen Pub.

Bastress, E. Karl, ed. see American Society of Mechanical Engineers Staff.

Bastress, Frances. The Relocating Spouse's Guide to Employment: Options & Strategies in the U. S. & Abroad. LC 86-19230. (Illus.). 265p. (Orig.). 1986. pap. 12.95 (*0-937623-00-8*) Woodley Pubns.

— The Relocating Spouse's Guide to Employment: Options & Strategies in the U. S. & Abroad. rev. ed. LC 87-16045. 265p. (Orig.). 1987. pap. 12.95 (*0-937623-01-6*) Woodley Pubns.

— The Relocating Spouse's Guide to Employment: Options & Strategies in the U. S. & Abroad. 3rd rev. ed. LC 88-33772. 265p. (Orig.). 1989. pap. 12.95 (*0-937623-02-4*) Woodley Pubns.

— Teachers in New Careers: Stories for Successful Transitions. LC 84-12647. 240p. 1984. 13.50 (*0-910328-40-4*) Sulzburger & Graham Pub.

Bastress, Francis. The New Relocating Spouse's Guide to Employment: Options & Strategies in the U. S. & Abroad. 4th ed. 352p. 1993. 32.95 (*0-942710-57-6*) Impact VA.

Bastress, Robert M. The West Virginia State Constitution: A Reference Guide, 22. LC 95-10220. (Reference Guides to the State Constitutions of the United States: No. 22). 352p. 1995. lib. bdg. 99.50 (*0-313-27409-6*, Greenwood Pr) Greenwood.

Bastros, Augusto R. El Fiscal (The Prosecutor) 368p. 1995. pap. 16.95 (*0-679-76092-X*) Vin Bks.

Bastrup, Harold A. One Police Officer's Experiences: Deputy Sheriff to Chief of Police. (Illus.). 415p. 1998. reprint ed. pap. 13.95 (*0-9649226-0-6*) Depol Pubn.

Bastwick, John. The Letany of J. Bastwick. LC 76-57354. (English Experience Ser.: No. 773). 1977. reprint ed. lib. bdg. 9.50 (*90-221-0773-6*) Walter J Johnson.

Bastyra, Judy. Cookie Fun. LC 96-36382. (Illus.). 24p. (J). (ps-2). 1997. 11.95 (*0-7534-5062-3*) LKC.

Bastyra, Judy. Fun Food. LC 96-37362. (Illus.). 24p. (J). (gr. 1-4). 1997. lib. bdg. 17.27 (*1-57505-204-0*, Carolrhoda) Lerner Pub.

— Hanukkah Fun: Great Things to Make & Do. (Illus.). 32p. (J). pap. 7.95 (*0-7534-5011-9*) LKC.

— Homeless. 1996. write for info. (*0-237-51532-6*) EVN1 UK.

Bastyra, Judy. Parties for Kids. LC 97-31788. (Illus.). 80p. (YA). (gr. 5 up). 1998. 10.95 (*0-7534-5092-5*) LKC.

— Pizza Fun. LC 96-30161. (Illus.). 24p. (J). (ps-2). 1997. 11.95 (*0-7534-5061-5*, Kingfisher) LKC.

***Basu.** Devata - Gods & Goddesses of the Hindus. 1999. reprint ed. 12.00 (*81-7536-177-8*, Pub. by Low Price) S Asia.

— This Land is Ours. 2000. 18.50 (*81-7017-391-4*, Pub. by Abhinav Pubns) S Asia.

***Basu & Miroshnik, Victoria.** Japanese Foreign Investments & the Management of Japanese Multinational Companies. (International Business & Economics Ser.). 2000. 75.00 (*0-08-043629-3*, Pergamon Pr) Elsevier.

***Basu, A.** Education in Modern India. 1999. 20.00 (*81-7020-463-1*, Pub. by Cosmo Pubn) S Asia.

Basu, A. & Li, X. B. Computer Vision: Systems, Theory, & Applications. (Computer Science Ser.). 268p. 1993. text 109.00 (*981-02-1392-1*) World Scientific Pub.

Basu, A., jt. ed. see Johnsson, M. J.

Basu, A. K. Ecological & Resource Study of the Ganga Delta in India. (C). 1992. 18.50 (*81-7024-112-X*, Pub. by KP Bagchi) S Asia.

— Rabindranth Tagore: The Poet of India. (C). 1993. 14.00 (*81-85182-92-2*, Pub. by Indus Pub) S Asia.

Basu, A. N. Bemisia Tabaci (Gennadius) A Crop Pest & the Principal Whitefly Vector of Plant Viruses. LC 94-24699. 192p. (C). 1995. pap. 68.00 (*0-8133-8895-3*, Pub. by Westview) HarpC.

— Essentials of Viruses, Vectors & Plant Diseases. (C). 1993. 26.00 (*81-224-0431-6*) S Asia.

Basu, Alaka & Aaby, Peter, eds. The Methods & Uses of Anthropological Demography. (International Studies in Demography). (Illus.). 340p. 1998. text 85.00 (*0-19-829337-2*) OUP.

Basu, Alaka M. Culture, the Status of Women, & Demographic Behaviour: Illustrated with the Case of India. (Illus.). 288p. 1993. 55.00 (*0-19-828360-1*) OUP.

Basu, Alaka M., jt. auth. see Jeffery, Roger.

Basu, Amrita. Two Faces of Protest: Contrasting Modes of Women's Activism in India. 1992. pap. 16.95 (*0-520-08919-7*, Pub. by U CA Pr) Cal Prin Full Svc.

Basu, Amrita, ed. The Challenge of Local Feminisms: Women's Movements in Global Perspective. (Social Change in Global Perspective Ser.). (Illus.). 512p. (C). 1995. pap. text 34.00 (*0-8133-2628-1*, Pub. by Westview) HarpC.

Basu, Amrita & Jeffery, Patricia. Appropriating Gender: Women's Agency the State & Politicized Religion in South Asia. LC 97-11336. (Zones of Religion Ser.). 276p. (C). 1997. pap. 20.99 (*0-415-91866-9*) Routledge.

— Appropriating Gender: Women's Agency the State & Politicized Religion in South Asia. LC 97-11336. (Zones of Religion Ser.). 276p. (C). 1997. 75.00 (*0-415-91865-0*) Routledge.

Basu, Amrita & Kohli, Atul, eds. Community Conflicts & the State in India. LC 98-902939. 300p. 1998. text 29.95 (*0-19-564236-8*) OUP.

***Basu, Amrita & Kohli, Atul, eds.** Community Conflicts & the State in India. (Illus.). 300p. 2000. pap. 11.95 (*0-19-565249-5*) OUP.

Basu, Anuradha. Public Expenditure Decision Making: The Indian Experience. 244p. 1995. 32.00 (*0-8039-9250-5*) Sage.

Basu, Aparna. Mridula Sarabhai: Rebel with a Cause. (Illus.). 290p. (C). 1996. text 24.95 (*0-19-563110-2*) OUP.

Basu, Aparna, ed. Imperialism, Nationalism & Regionalism in Canadian & Modern Indian History. (C). 1989. 19.50 (*81-85054-73-8*, Pub. by Manohar) S Asia.

Basu, Aparna & Ray, Bharati. Women's Struggles: A History of the All India Women's Conference 1927-1990. (C). 1990. 27.00 (*81-85425-42-6*, Pub. by Manohar) S Asia.

Basu, Asish & Hart, Stanley R., eds. Earth Processes: Reading the Isotopic Code. LC 96-1381. (Geophysical Monographs: Vol. 95). 1996. 65.00 (*0-87590-077-1*) Am Geophysical.

***Basu, Asit P. & Rigdon, Steve E.** Statistical Models for the Reliability of Repairable Systems. LC 99-57532. 224p. 2000. 84.95 (*0-471-34941-0*) Wiley.

Basu, Asit P., et al. Frontiers in Reliability. LC 97-44020. (Series on Quality, Reliability, & Engineering Statistics). 435p. 1998. 64.00 (*981-02-3360-4*) World Scientific Pub.

Basu, Asit P., jt. ed. see Balakrishnan, N.

Basu, Asok. The Himalayas: A Classified Social Scientific Bibliography. 1987. 48.50 (*81-7074-013-4*, Pub. by KP Bagchi) S Asia.

Basu, Asoke, jt. auth. see Segalman, Ralph.

***Basu, B. D.** History of Education in India. 1999. 20.00 (*81-7020-494-1*, Pub. by Cosmo Pubn) S Asia.

Basu, B. N. Electromagnetic Theory & Applications in Beam-Wave Electronics: Electromagnetics & Beam-Wave Electronics. LC 95-46596. (Series on Quality, Reliability & Engineering Statistics). 450p. 1996. text 86.00 (*981-02-2320-X*) World Scientific Pub.

Basu, Badal K. The Onge. (C). 1990. text 10.00 (*81-7046-074-3*, Pub. by Seagull Bks) S Asia.

Basu, Bikash C. Handbook of Gynaecology. 490p. 1981. 69.00 (*0-7855-0734-5*, Pub. by Current Dist) St Mut.

— Handbook of Obstetrics. (C). 1986. 60.00 (*0-07-100135-2*, Pub. by Current Dist) St Mut.

— Practical Obstetrics & Gynecology. (C). 1983. 150.00 (*0-89771-340-0*, Pub. by Current Dist) St Mut.

— Practical Obstetrics & Gynecology. 2nd ed. (C). 1982. 75.00 (*0-7855-6114-5*, Pub. by Current Dist) St Mut.

— Practical Obstetrics & Gynecology. 3rd ed. 1982. 59.00 (*0-7855-0824-4*, Pub. by Current Dist) St Mut.

Basu, Bikash C., ed. Handbook of Obstetrics. (C). 1986. 60.00 (*0-89771-338-9*, Pub. by Current Dist) St Mut.

Basu, D. D. Commentary on the Constitution of India, Vol. P: Silver Jubilee Edition. (C). 1990. 110.00 (*0-7855-6556-6*) St Mut.

***Basu, D. N.** Agro-Climatic Regional Planning in India, Vols. 1 & 2. 670p. 1998. pap. 600.00 (*81-7022-583-3*, Pub. by Print Hse) St Mut.

Basu, Debashish. Scam, Who Won, Who Lost, Who Got Away. (C). 1993. 24.00 (*81-85944-10-5*, Pub. by UBS Pubs Dist) S Asia.

Basu, Deepika. Working Class in Bengal: Formative Years. (C). 1993. 18.00 (*81-7074-129-7*) S Asia.

Basu, Dilip K., ed. The Rise & Growth of the Colonial Port Cities in Asia. LC 85-11095. (Monographs: No. 25). (Illus.). 332p. (Orig.). 1985. lib. bdg. 56.00 (*0-8191-4761-3*) U Pr of Amer.

Basu, Dilip K & Sisson, Richard, eds. Economic & Social Development in India. 244p. (C). 1986. pap. 14.95 (*0-8039-9510-5*, Pub. by Sage India Pvt) Sage.

Basu, Dipak R. Monetary & Financial Planning for a Transitory Economy: An Adaptive Control Model for India. 160p. 1995. 61.95 (*1-85972-021-8*, Pub. by Avebry) Ashgate Pub Co.

Basu, Dipak R. & Miroshnik, Victoria. Japanese Foreign Investments, 1970-1998: Perspectives & Analyses. LC 99-23674. (Illus.). 216p. 2000. text 69.95 (*0-7656-0502-3*) M E Sharpe.

Basu, Dulal K. Handbook of Ear, Nose & Throat. 300p. 1985. 75.00 (*0-7855-0733-7*, Pub. by Current Dist) St Mut.

Basu, Durga D. Commentaries the Constitution of India, Vol. N. (C). 1988. 160.00 (*0-7855-3715-5*) St Mut.

— Commentary on the Constitution of India, Vol. A-M. 6th ed. (C). 1988. 1290.00 (*0-7855-3714-7*) St Mut.

Basu, Helene, jt. auth. see Werbner, Pnina.

Basu, Julie & Shome, Probal. Essential SQLJ Programming: The Complete Guide to the ANSI Standard for Embedded SQL in Java. 320p. 1999. pap. 44.99 incl. cd-rom (*0-471-34920-8*) Wiley.

Basu, K. Agrarian Structure & Economic Underdevelopment. (Fundamentals of Pure & Applied Economics Ser.: Vol. 37). x, 102p. 1990. pap. text 44.00 (*3-7186-4993-4*) Gordon & Breach.

Basu, K. S. Management Similarities & Differences under Different Culture. 56p. 1970. pap. text 68.00 (*0-677-61505-1*) Gordon & Breach.

Basu, Kalipada. West Bengal Economy: Past, Present & Future. (C). 1989. 34.00 (*0-8364-2480-8*, Pub. by Firma KLM) S Asia.

Basu, Kaushik. Analytical Development Economics. LC 96-40312. (Illus.). 312p. 1997. 45.00 (*0-262-02423-3*) MIT Pr.

— The International Debt Problem, Credit Rationing & Loan Pushing: Theory & Experience. LC 91-39784. (Studies in International Finance: No. 70). 44p. 1991. pap. text 13.50 (*0-88165-242-3*) Princeton U Int Finan Econ.

— Of People, of Places: Sketches from an Economist's Diary. LC 94-907468. (Oxford India Paperbacks Ser.). 180p. 1995. pap. text 6.95 (*0-19-563473-X*) OUP.

***Basu, Kaushik.** Prelude to Political Economy: A Study of the Social & Political Foundations of Economics. 336p. 2000. text 39.95 (*0-19-829671-1*) OUP.

Basu, Kaushik. Revealed Preference of Government. LC 78-67300. 127p. reprint ed. pap. 36.20 (*0-608-15692-2*, 2031619) Bks Demand.

Basu, Kaushik, ed. Agrarian Questions. (Oxford in India Readings: Themes in Economics Ser.). 256p. 1994. 24.00 (*0-685-69207-8*) OUP.

Basu, Kaushik, ed. Agrarian Questions. (Oxford in India Readings). 260p. 1994. text 24.00 (*0-19-563101-3*) OUP.

Basu, Kaushik, ed. Agrarian Questions. (Oxford in India Readings: Themes in Economics). 260p. 1997. pap. 10.95 (*0-19-564192-2*) OUP.

Basu, Kaushik, et al, eds. Capital, Investment & Development: Essays in Memory of Sukhamoy Chakravarty. (Illus.). 288p. 1999. pap. text 14.95 (*0-19-564758-0*) OUP.

Basu, Nirban. Political Parties & the Labour Politics, 1937-47: With Special Reference to Bengal. (C). 1992. 14.00 (*81-85195-48-X*, Pub. by Minerva) S Asia.

— Working Class Movement: Study of Jute Mills of Bengal 1937-1947. LC 94-902185. (C). 1994. 20.00 (*81-7074-148-3*, Pub. by KP Bagchi) S Asia.

Basu, P. K. & Nagar, A., eds. Recent Developments in Computational Mechanics. LC 93-73611. 139p. pap. 47.50 (*0-7918-1254-5*) ASME.

Basu, Prabir, ed. Circulating Fluidized Bed Technology: Proceedings of the First International Conference on Circulating Fluidized Beds, Halifax, Canada, 18-20 November 1985. (Illus.). 464p. 1986. 60.00 (*0-08-031868-1*, E135, B125, A115, C130, A125, Pergamon Pr) Elsevier.

Basu, Prabir, et al. Boilers & Burners: Design & Theory. LC 99-17360. (Mechanical Engineering Ser.). (Illus.). 584p. 1999. 99.50 (*0-387-98703-7*) Spr-Verlag.

— Circulating Fluidized Bed Technology, III: Proceedings of the Third International Conference on Circulating Fluidized Beds, Nagoya, Japan, 14-18 October 1990. (Illus.). 660p. 1991. 48.00 (*0-08-040509-6*, Pergamon Pr) Elsevier.

— Circulating Fluidized Bed Technology, III: Proceedings of the Third International Conference on Circulating Fluidized Beds, Nagoya, Japan, 14-18 October 1990. LC 91-8239. (Illus.). 660p. 1991. 296.00 (*0-08-040508-8*, TP156, Pub. by Pergamon Repr) Franklin.

Basu, Prabir, jt. auth. see Faddeyev, D.

Basu, Prabir, jt. auth. see Nosova, L.

Basu, Prasanta K. Dental Materials. 1985. 59.00 (*0-7855-0814-7*, Pub. by Current Dist) St Mut.

— Theory of Optical Processes in Semiconductors: Bulk & Microstructures. LC 97-15618. (Series on Seminconductor Science & Technology: No. 4). (Illus.). 464p. 1998. text 150.00 (*0-19-851788-2*) OUP.

Basu, R. & Jezek, Z. The Eradication of Smallpox from India. (WHO Regional Publications, South-East Asia Ser.: No. 5). 346p. 1979. text 30.00 (*92-9022-105-4*) World Health.

Basu, Romen. Canvas & the Brush. 116p. 1970. 5.95 (*0-317-00320-8*, Pub. by Filma K L Mukhopadhyay) Motorbooks Intl.

— Committed Footprints. 71p. 1998. 9.95 (*81-207-2095-4*) Facet Bks.

— A Gift of Love. 176p. 1974. 7.95 (*0-317-00323-2*, Pub. by Writers Wksp) Taylor & Francis.

— Gliding on Silent Water. 198p. 1996. write for info. (*81-7017-343-4*) R Basu.

— A House Full of People. 186p. 1968. 6.95 (*0-317-00322-4*, Pub. by Navana Publishers) S Asia.

— In Silence. 268p. 1995. mass mkt. write for info. (*0-932377-64-5*) Facet Bks.

— The Street Corner Boys. Hauge, Veronica, tr. 154p. (YA). (gr. 9-10). 1992. 14.95 (*0-932377-40-8*) Facet Bks.

— The Tamarind Tree. 227p. 1976. 7.95 (*0-317-00324-0*, Pub. by Writers Wksp) Taylor & Francis.

— Torn Apart. 198p. 1997. write for info. (*0-932377-67-X*) R Basu.

— The Unquiet Waves. 120p. 1996. mass mkt. write for info. (*0-932377-53-X*) Facet Bks.

— Your Life to Live. 180p. 1972. 7.95 (*0-317-00321-6*, Pub. by Filma K L Mukhopadhyay) Motorbooks Intl.

Basu, Ron. Total Manufacturing Solutions. 288p. 1998. pap. text 41.95 (*0-7506-4041-3*) Buttrwrth-Heinemann.

Basu, Rumki. The United Nations: Structure & Functions of an International Organisation. (C). 1993. reprint ed. write for info. (*81-207-1494-6*) Sterling Pubs.

***Basu, S.** The Can't Go Wrong Book of Cocktails. 1998. pap. 250.00 (*81-86982-30-2*, Pub. by Business Pubns) St Mut.

— It Happened That Year. 1998. pap. 30.00 (*81-86982-54-X*, Pub. by Business Pubns) St Mut.

Basu, S. C. Handbook of Jurisprudence Representation. (C). 1990. 80.00 (*0-89771-337-0*, Pub. by Current Dist) St Mut.

Basu, S. C. Handbook of Preventive & Social Medicine. 480p. 1991. pap. (*81-86793-27-5*) Current Bks Intl.

Basu, S. C. Handbook of Preventive & Social Medicine. 420p. 1977. 100.00 (*0-7855-0817-1*, Pub. by Current Dist) St Mut.

— Handbook of Surgery Rep. (C). 1990. 100.00 (*0-89771-336-2*, Pub. by Current Dist) St Mut.

Basu, S. C. & Choudhury, A. K. R. Handbook of Surgery Including Instruments, Bandaging Surgical Problems, Specimens & Operative Surgery. 816p. 1995. pap. (*81-86793-28-3*) Current Bks Intl.

Basu, Sajal. Factions Ideology & Politics, India. 1990. 20.00 (*81-85195-26-9*, Pub. by Minerva) S Asia.

— In Quest of Freedom: Shibnath Banerjee & His Times. 1990. 22.00 (*81-85195-30-7*, Pub. by Minerva) S Asia.

Basu, Sam N. & Rolfes, Harold L. Strategic Credit Management: Strategic Approach. LC 95-19597. 239p. 1995. 99.95 (*0-471-58343-X*) Wiley.

Basu, Samarendra & Millette, James R., eds. Electron Microscopy in Forensic, Occupational & Environmental Health Sciences. LC 86-25290. 294p. 1986. 75.00 (*0-306-42466-5*, Plenum Trade) Perseus Pubng.

Basu, Sankar, ed. see Levy, Bernard.

Basu, Sankar, ed. see Levy, Bernard, et al.

Basu, Santanu, ed. High-Power Lasers. LC 99-170359. (Proceedings of SPIE Ser.: Vol. 3264). 184p. 1998. 80.00 (*0-8194-2703-9*) SPIE.

Basu, Shankar. Corporate Purpose: Why It Matters More Than Strategy. LC 99-36245. 250p. 1999. 60.00 (*0-8153-3374-9*) Garland.

Basu, Sreelekha. Bengali Patriotic Songs & Brahmo Samaj: A Pilot Documentation. (C). 1996. 24.00 (*81-207-1745-7*, Pub. by Manohar) S Asia.

Basu, Srimati. She Comes to Take Her Rights: Indian Women, Property, & Propriety. LC 98-25982. (Illus.). 288p. (C). 1999. text 65.50 (*0-7914-4095-8*); pap. text 21.95 (*0-7914-4096-6*) State U NY Pr.

Basu, T. K. Clinical Implications of Drug Use, 2 vols., Vol. 1. 160p. 1980. 46.95 (*0-8493-5391-2*, RM300) CRC Pr.

— Clinical Implications of Drug Use, 2 vols., Vol. 2. 144p. 1980. 86.00 (*0-8493-5392-0*, RM300, CRC Reprint) Franklin.

— Drug-Nutrient Interactions. 180p. 1988. lib. bdg. 55.00 (*0-7099-3203-0*) Routledge.

— Financial Accounting Theory. (C). 1989. 30.00 (*0-89771-433-4*, Pub. by Current Dist) St Mut.

Basu, Tapan K., ed. T. S. Eliot: An Anthology of Recent Criticism. 1993. 27.95 (*81-85753-01-6*, Pub. by Pencraft International) Advent Bks Div.

Basu, Tapan K. & Dikerson, John W. Vitamins in Human Health & Disease. LC 97-122527. (A CAB International Publication). 368p. 1996. pap. text 50.00 (*0-85198-986-1*) OUP.

Basu, Tapan K., et al. Antioxidants in Human Health & Disease. LC 98-33114. (CABI Publishing Ser.). 480p. 1999. text 110.00 (*0-85199-334-6*) OUP.

***Basualdo, Carlos & Tepfer, Ellen.** Painting Zero Degree. (Illus.). 84p. 2000. pap. 19.95 (*0-916365-57-3*, Pub. by Ind Curators) Dist Art Pubs.

Basualdo, Carlos, jt. auth. see Reed, David.

Basuraychaudhuri, N. C. Welfare State of Britain & India. (C). 1989. 29.00 (*81-85195-20-X*) S Asia.

Basurto, Carmen G. & Basurto, Jose Luis Castillo. Mis Primeras Letras: Libro de Lectura y Escritura Para Primer Ano, Letra Script y Ligada. 2nd ed. (SPA., Illus.). 127p. 1997. pap. 12.98 (*968-24-5347-X*) Trillas.

Basurto, Jose Luis Castillo, jt. auth. see Basurto, Carmen G.

Baswell, Christopher. Virgil in Medieval England: Figuring the Aeneid from the Twelfth Century to Chaucer. (Cambridge Studies in Medieval Literature: No. 24). (Illus.). 456p. (C). 1995. text 69.95 (*0-521-46294-0*) Cambridge U Pr.

Basworth, Velma H. Approaching Footsteps: Puget Sound Indians - Bainbridge Island Sawmills. 113p. 1998. pap. text 19.95 (*1-881908-21-6*) PanPress.

Basye. Clearing Land Titles: Second Edition. write for info. (*0-318-57509-4*) West Pub.

Basye, Ann. Kids in the Loop: Chicago Adventures for Kids & Their Grown-Ups. LC 94-49523. 244p. (Orig.). 1995. pap. 11.95 (*1-55652-236-3*) Chicago Review.

Basye, Anne. Business Letters Ready to Go. LC 98-9247. (. . . Ready to Go! Ser.). (Illus.). 160p. 1998. pap. 12.95 incl. disk (*0-8442-3571-7*, NTC Business Bks) NTC Contemp Pub Co.

— Opportunities in Direct Marketing Careers. LC 92-25827. (Opportunities In . . . Ser.). (Illus.). 160p. pap. 12.95 (*0-8442-4037-0*, 297OIDM, VGM Career) NTC Contemp Pub Co.

— Opportunities in Direct Marketing Careers. LC 92-25827. (Opportunities in...Ser.). (Illus.). 160p. 1994. 14.95 (*0-8442-4036-2*, VGM Career) NTC Contemp Pub Co.

***Basye, Anne.** Opportunities in Direct Marketing Careers. LC 99-57941. (Opportunities in... Ser.). 160p. 2000. 14.95 (*0-658-00209-0*, 002090) NTC Contemp Pub Co.

— Opportunities in Direct Marketing Careers. rev. ed. LC 99-57941. (Opportunities in... Ser.). 160p. 2000. pap. 11.95 (*0-658-00210-4*, 002104) NTC Contemp Pub Co.

An Asterisk (*) at the beginning of an entry indicates that the title is appearing for the first time.

Basye, Anne. Opportunities in Telemarketing Careers. LC 93-48712. (Opportunities In . . . Ser.). (Illus.). 160p. 1994. pap. 11.95 (*0-8442-4134-2*, 41342, VGM Career) NTC Contemp Pub Co.
— Opportunities in Telemarketing Careers. LC 93-48712. (Illus.). 160p. 1995. 14.95 (*0-8442-4133-4*, 41334, VGM Career) NTC Contemp Pub Co.
Basye, Jennifer. The Air Courier's Handbook: Travel the World on a Shoestring... 4th rev. ed. 48p. 1994. pap. 10.00 (*1-885050-00-3*) Big City Bks.
— How to Become a Successful Weekend Entrepreneur: Secrets of Making an Extra 100 Dollars or More Each Week Using Your Spare Time. LC 92-40478. 208p. (Orig.). 1993. pap. 10.95 (*1-55958-288-X*) Prima Pub.
— 101 Best Extra-Income Opportunities for Women. LC 97-23634. 192p. 1997. per. 14.00 (*0-7615-0916-X*) Prima Pub.
Basye, Jennifer, et al. 101 Uses for the Royal Family: New Uses for Old Royals. LC 93-32302. (Illus.). 96p. 1993. pap. 5.95 (*1-55958-475-0*) Prima Pub.
***Basye, Melvin, ed.** Dealing with Workplace Violence: A Guide for Agency Planners. 149p. 1999. pap. text 25.00 (*0-7881-8086-X*) DIANE Pub.
Basye, O. Basye Family in the U. S. (Illus.). 987p. 1991. reprint ed. pap. 135.00 (*0-8328-1768-6*); reprint ed. lib. bdg. 145.00 (*0-8328-1767-8*) Higginson Bk Co.
Basye, Paul E., jt. auth. see Simes, Lewis M.
Basyouny, Iman F. Just a Gaze: Female Clientele of Diet Clinics in Cairo: An Ethnomedical Study. (Cairo Papers in Social Science: Vol. 21, No. 1). 158p. 1999. pap. 10.00 (*977-424-479-6*, Pub. by Am Univ Cairo Pr) Col U Pr.
Baszan. Development in France. (Social Science & Medicine). 1985. pap. 28.00 (*0-08-032655-2*, Pergamon Pr) Elsevier.
Baszanger, Isabelle. Inventing Pain Medicine: From the Laboratory to the Clinic. LC 97-30922. 352p. (C). 1998. text 50.00 (*0-8135-2501-2*); pap. text 22.00 (*0-8135-2502-0*) Rutgers U Pr.
Bat-Ami, Miriam. Dear Elijah: A Passover Story. LC 96-42386. (J). 1997. pap. 9.95 (*0-8276-0592-7*) JPS Phila.
— Two Suns in the Sky. LC 98-88522. 224p. (YA). (gr. 7-12). 1999. 15.95 (*0-8126-2900-0*, Pub. by Front St-Cricket Bks) Publishers Group.
Bat Conservation International Staff. The Vacationer's Guide to Bat Watching. 97p. 1999. pap. 10.95 (*0-292-70875-0*) U of Tex Pr.
Bat-Ireedui, J. & Sanders, Alan J. Mongolian Phrasebook. (MON., Illus.). 208p. 1995. pap. 5.95 (*0-86442-308-X*) Lonely Planet.
Bat-Ireedui, Jantsangiyn, jt. auth. see Sanders, Alan J.
Bat-ireedui, Jantsangiyn, jt. auth. see Sanders, Alan J. K.
Bat-Ireedui, Jantsangiyn, jt. auth. see Sanders, Alan Jk.
***Bat-Ochir, Bold.** Mongolian Nomadic Society A Reconstruction of the Medieval History of Mongolia. LC 99-37870. 1999. text 59.95 (*0-312-22827-9*, St Martin Griffin) St Martin.
Bat-or, Sunny. Who Cares for the Caregiver? Learning to Take Care of Yourself While Caring for Others. (In-Service Sourcebook Ser.). 64p. 1995. pap. text 29.95 (*1-888343-03-6*) Hartman Pub.
Bata, Reda M., ed. Alternate Fuels: A Decade of Success & Promise. LC 94-74714. 1995. pap. 29.00 (*1-56091-593-5*, PT48) Soc Auto Engineers.
Bata, Thomas. Knowledge in Action: The Bata System of Management. 350p. (gr. 12). 1992. 49.00 (*90-5199-059-6*, Pub. by IOS Pr) IOS Press.
***Batabyal, Amitrajeet A., ed.** The Economics of International Environmental Agreements. LC 99-42545. (International Library of Environmental Economics & Policy). 300p. 1999. text 74.95 (*1-84014-894-2*, Pub. by Ashgate Pub) Ashgate Pub Co.
Bataglini, R., Sr. The Corvette Coloring Book: Official Coloring Book of the National Corvette Museum. (Illus.). 24p. (Orig.). (J). 1995. pap. text 5.00 (*0-9647030-0-9*) Tin Type.
Bataille, Christophe. Absinthe. Howard, Richard, tr. from FRE. LC 98-51925. 96p. 1999. 22.95 (*0-8101-6042-0*, Marlboro) Northwestern U Pr.
— Annam. Howard, Richard, tr. from FRE. LC 96-24528. 112p. 1996. 15.95 (*0-8112-1330-7*, Pub. by New Directions) Norton.
— The Hourmaster. Howard, Richard, tr. from FRE. LC 97-42141. 208p. 1998. reprint ed. 17.95 (*0-8112-1357-9*, Pub. by New Directions) Norton.
Bataille, F. Les Reactions Macrochimiques Chez les Champignons Suives D'Indications sur la Morphologie des Spores. 1969. reprint ed. 32.00 (*3-7682-0654-8*) Lubrecht & Cramer.
Bataille, Georges. Abbe C. (Folio Ser.: No. 106). (FRE.). 1972. pap. 9.95 (*2-07-036106-3*) Schoenhof.
— L' Abbe C. (FRE.). 1972. pap. 11.95 (*0-7859-1697-0*, 2070361063) Fr & Eur.
— L' Abbe C. Facey, Philip A., tr. from FRE. LC 82-17704. 160p. 1983. 13.95 (*0-7145-2709-2*) M Boyars Pubs.
— L' Abbe C. Facey, Philip A., tr. from FRE. 158p. 1994. reprint ed. pap. 11.95 (*0-7145-2848-X*) M Boyars Pubs.
— The Absence of Myth: Writings on Surrealism. Richardson, Michael, ed. & tr. by. LC 94-964. 200p. (gr. 13). 1994. 30.00 (*0-86091-419-4*, Pub. by Verso) Norton.
— The Accursed Share, Vol. 1. Hurley, Robert, tr. from FRE. LC 87-34072. 197p. 1988. pap. 12.95 (*0-942299-11-6*) Zone Bks.
— The Accursed Share, Vols. II & III. Hurley, Robert, tr. from FRE. LC 87-34072. 460p. 1991. 32.95 (*0-942299-20-5*) Zone Bks.
— The Accursed Share, Vols. II & III. Hurley, Robert, tr. from FRE. LC 87-34072. 460p. 1993. pap. 18.95 (*0-942299-21-3*) Zone Bks.
— Bleu du Ciel. (Imaginaire Ser.). (FRE.). 1991. pap. 12.95 (*2-07-072328-3*) Schoenhof.
— Blue of Noon. Matthews, Harry, tr. from FRE.Tr. of Le/Bleu du Ciel. 155p. 1986. reprint ed. pap. 12.95 (*0-7145-2850-1*) M Boyars Pubs.
— The Collected Poetry. Spitzer, Mark, tr. from FRE. & intro. by. LC 98-14172. 130p. 1998. pap. 15.95 (*0-8023-1325-6*) Dufour.
— The Collected Poetry of Georges Bataille. Spitzer, Mark, tr. from ENG. LC 98-14172. 156p. 1998. 29.95 (*0-8023-1324-8*) Dufour.
— The Dead Man. Austen, Jayne, tr. 80p. 1989. pap. 8.00 (*0-9642284-0-8*) Ediciones La Calavera.
— Death & Sensuality: A Study of Eroticism & the Taboo. Kastenbaum, Robert J., ed. LC 76-19560. (Death & Dying Ser.). 1979. reprint ed. lib. bdg. 31.95 (*0-405-09556-2*) Ayer.
— Erotism: Death & Sensuality. Dalwood, Mary, tr. from FRE. 288p. (Orig.). 1986. reprint ed. pap. 14.95 (*0-87286-190-2*) City Lights.
— Experience Interieure. (Tel Ser.). (FRE.). 180p. 1986. pap. 13.95 (*2-07-029786-1*) Schoenhof.
— The Impossible. Hurley, Robert, tr. from FRE. 188p. (Orig.). 1991. pap. 11.95 (*0-87286-262-3*) City Lights.
— Inner Experience. Boldt, Leslie A., tr. from FRE. & intro. by. LC 87-10154. (SUNY Series, Intersections). 209p. (C). 1988. text 59.50 (*0-88706-634-8*); pap. text 19.95 (*0-88706-635-6*) State U NY Pr.
— Literature & Evil. Hamilton, Alastair, tr. from FRE. LC 83-25872. 208p. 1986. pap. 14.95 (*0-7145-0346-0*) M Boyars Pubs.
— Litterature et le Mal. (Folio Essais Ser.: No. 148). (FRE.). 1990. pap. 9.95 (*2-07-032607-1*) Schoenhof.
— On Nietzsche. 1993. pap. 14.95 (*1-55778-644-5*) Paragon Hse.
— Story of the Eye. Neugroschel, Joachim, tr. from FRE. 72p. (Orig.). 1987. reprint ed. pap. 9.95 (*0-87286-209-7*) City Lights.
— The Tears of Eros. Connor, Peter, tr. from FRE.Tr. of Les/Larmes d'Eros. (Illus.). 208p. (Orig.). 1989. pap. 15.95 (*0-87286-222-4*) City Lights.
— Theorie de la Religion. (Tel Ser.). (FRE.). 159p. 1973. pap. 14.95 (*2-07-070577-3*) Schoenhof.
— Theory of Religion. Hurley, Robert, tr. from FRE. LC 88-20591. 126p. 1989. pap. 11.95 (*0-942299-09-4*) Zone Bks.
— Theory of Religion. Hurley, Robert, tr. from FRE. LC 88-20591. 126p. 1989. 23.95 (*0-942299-08-6*) Zone Bks.
— The Trial of Gilles De Rais. Robinson, Richard, tr. from FRE. 285p. (Orig.). (C). 1991. pap. 12.95 (*1-878923-02-1*) Amok Bks.
Bataille, Georges, et al, eds. Encyclopedia Acephalica. White, Iain, tr. from FRE. (Atlas Arkhive Ser.: Vol. 3). (Illus.). 160p. (Orig.). 1998. pap. 19.99 (*0-947757-87-2*, Pub. by Atlas Pr) Serpents Tail.
Bataille, Georges, et al. My Mother, Madame Edwarda & the Dead Man. Wainhouse, Austryn, tr. from FRE. 224p. 1994. pap. 14.95 (*0-7145-3004-2*) M Boyars Pubs.
Bataille, Gretchen M., ed. Native American Women: A Biographical Dictionary. LC 92-19990. (Biographical Directories of Minority Women Ser.: Vol. 1). (Illus.). 360p. 1993. text 20.00 (*0-8240-5267-6*, SS649) Garland.
***Bataille, Gretchen M., et al, eds.** The Worlds between Two Rivers: Perspectives on American Indians in Iowa. (Illus.). 232p. 2000. pap. text 17.95 (*0-87745-700-X*) U of Iowa Pr.
Bataille, Gretchen M. & Sands, Kathleen M. American Indian Women: Telling Their Lives. LC 83-10234. ix, 211p. 1984. pap. 11.95 (*0-8032-6082-2*, Bison Books) U of Nebr Pr.
Bataille, Gretchen M. & Silet, Charles L., eds. The Pretend Indians: Images of Native Americans in the Movies. LC 79-27432. 232p. reprint ed. pap. 72.00 (*0-608-18795-X*, 203031700068) Bks Demand.
Bataille, Gretchen M., et al. Ethnic Studies in the United States: A Guide to Research. LC 95-44834. 312p. 1996. text 61.00 (*0-8153-1476-0*, SS923) Garland.
— Ethnic Studies in the United States: A Guide to Research. LC 95-44834. (Reference Library of Social Science: Vol. 923). 295p. 1996. 45.00 (*0-08-153476-0*) Garland.
***Bataille, Robert R.** The Writing Life of Hugh Kelly: Politics, Journalism & Theater in Late 18th Century London. LC 99-45455. (Illus.). 2000. 44.95 (*0-8093-2288-9*) S Ill U Pr.
Bataillon, Louis-Jacques. La Prediction au XIIIe Siecle en France & Italie: Etudes & Documents. (Collected Studies: No. CS 402). (ENG, FRE & ITA.). 352p. 1993. 119.95 (*0-86078-375-8*, Pub. by Variorum) Ashgate Pub Co.
Batalden, Sandra L., jt. auth. see Batalden, Stephen K.
Batalden, Stephen K. Catherine II's Greek Prelate: Eugenios Voulgaris in Russia, 1771-1806. (East European Monographs: No. 115). 197p. 1983. text 48.00 (*0-88033-006-6*, Pub. by East Eur Monographs) Col U Pr.
Batalden, Stephen K., ed. Seeking God: The Recovery of Religious Identity in Orthodox Russia, Ukraine, & Georgia. LC 93-16553. 295p. (C). 1993. lib. bdg. 35.00 (*0-87580-178-1*) N Ill U Pr.
Batalden, Stephen K. & Batalden, Sandra L. The Newly Independent States of Eurasia: Handbook of Former Soviet Republics. 2nd ed. LC 97-3893. (Illus.). 248p. (J). (gr. 7). 1997. pap. 39.50 (*0-89774-940-5*) Oryx Pr.
Batalden, Steven K. & Noonan, Thomas, eds. Russian & East European Studies, Vol. 1: Econ. Reform in Poland: The Aftermath of M. 278p. 1991. 73.25 (*1-55938-288-0*) Jai Pr.
— Russian & East European Studies, Vol. 2: On the Heights of Creation: Lyrics by Fedo. 330p. 1993. 73.25 (*0-614-09950-1*) Jai Pr.
— Russian & East European Studies, Vol. 3: Playing Politics: Soviet Sport Diplomacy t. 184p. 1993. 73.25 (*1-55938-472-7*) Jai Pr.
— Russian & East European Studies, Vol. 4. Date not set. 73.25 (*1-55938-899-4*) Jai Pr.
— Russian & East European Studies Vol. 2: On the Heights of Creation: Lyrics by Fedo. LC 92-34415. (Russian & East European Studies: Vol. 2). 330p. 1993. 73.25 (*1-55938-525-1*) Jai Pr.
***Batali, Mario.** Holiday Food: Family Recipes for the Most Festive. 2000. write for info. (*0-609-60774-X*) C Potter.
Batali, Mario. Simple Italian Food: Recipes from My Two Villages. LC 98-35508. (Illus.). 287p. 1998. 32.50 (*0-609-60300-0*) C Potter.
Batalla, Guillermo B. Identidad y Pluralismo Cultural en America Latina. 210p. 1992. pap. 12.50 (*0-8477-0792-1*) U of PR Pr.
— Simbiosis de Culturas (Simbiosis of Cultures) (SPA.). 572p. 1993. pap. 20.99 (*968-16-4293-7*, Pub. by Fondo) Continental Bk.
Batalla, T. E., ed. Reform of the Venezuelan Fiscal System. LC 88-37957. 441p. 1989. reprint ed. pap. 136.80 (*0-608-00144-9*, 206092500006) Bks Demand.
Batalle, Diane. The Whip Angels: New Edition. (Velvet Ser.). pap. 12.95 (*1-84068-014-8*, Velvet Pub) Creation Books.
Batalov, Andrei & Lidov, Aleksei, eds. Jerusalem in Russian Culture. LC 94-2068. (Illus.). 284p. (C). 1993. text 65.00 (*0-89241-524-X*) Caratzas.
Batarec, Evelyn. Lexique des Terme de Prothese Dentaire (Lexicon of Dental Prosthetics Terminology) 2nd ed. (FRE.). 90p. 1980. pap. 29.95 (*0-7859-4805-8*, M6024) Fr & Eur.
Batastini & Davidson. Pharmacological Calculus for Nursing. 3rd ed. LC 98-46290. (C). 1999. 21.95 (*0-7668-0166-7*) Delmar.
Batastini, Peggy H. Pharmacological Calculations for Nurses. 2nd ed. 187p. (C). 1991. pap. 26.50 (*0-8273-4727-8*) Delmar.
Batastini, Peggy H. & Davidson, Judy K. Pharmacological Calculations for Nurses: A Worktext. 202p. 1989. pap. text 24.95 (*0-8273-4202-0*) Delmar.
Batastini, Robert J., ed. The Passion of Our Lord Jesus Christ. 118p. 1999. 45.00 (*1-57999-043-6*, G-4998) GIA Pubns.
***Batastini, Robert J., ed.** Worship Week Calendar 2000. 200p. 1999. spiral bd. 9.95 (*1-57999-052-5*, G-4984) GIA Pubns.
Batastini, Robert J., et al, eds. Hymnal for Catholic Students. 233p. 1988. 8.50 (*0-941050-16-5*) GIA Pubns.
— Ritual Song: Instrumental Edition - B Flat Instruments. 800p. 1997. spiral bd. 85.00 (*1-57999-001-0*, G-4500IB) GIA Pubns.
— Ritual Song: Instrumental Edition - C Instruments. 800p. 1997. spiral bd. 85.00 (*1-57999-000-2*, G-4500IC) GIA Pubns.
***Batastini, Robert J. & Cymbala, Michael A., eds.** Catholic Community Hymnal: Accompaniment Book. 450p. 1999. 49.00 (*1-57999-045-2*, G-5000K) GIA Pubns.
— Catholic Community Hymnal: Choir Book. 825p. 1999. 20.50 (*1-57999-046-0*, G-5000C) GIA Pubns.
Batastini, Robert J. & Cymbala, Michael A., eds. The Catholic Community Hymnal: Pew Edition. 950p. 1999. 9.75 (*1-57999-044-4*, G-5000H) GIA Pubns.
— Gather Comprehensive. 500p. 1994. text 12.50 (*0-941050-62-9*, G-4200H) GIA Pubns.
Batastini, Robert J. & Cymbula, Michael A., eds. Gather Comprehensive with Sunday Readings. rev. ed. 500p. 1998. 13.75 (*1-57999-037-1*, G-4200R) GIA Pubns.
Batastini, Robert J. & Rawlings Sydnor, James, eds. Our Growing Years - Pew Edition: A Hymnal. 377p. 1998. text 24.00 (*1-57999-017-7*, G-4750) GIA Pubns.
Batastini, Robert J. & Sydnor, James R., eds. Our Growing Years - Accompaniment, 2 vols. 624p. 1998. spiral bd. 49.50 (*1-57999-018-5*, G-4750A) GIA Pubns.
— Our Growing Years - Full Music Edition: A Hymnal. 400p. 1998. 16.00 (*1-57999-032-0*, G-4750C) GIA Pubns.
Batastini, Robert J., ed. see Haugen, Marty & Proulx Richard.
Batatu, Hanna. The Egyptian, Syrian, & Iraqi Revolutions: Some Observations on Their Underlying Causes & Social Character. 29p. (Orig.). 1984. text 6.95 (*0-932568-10-6*) GU Ctr CAS.
— The Old Social Classes & the Revolutionary Movements of Iraq: A Study of Iraq's Old Landed & Commercial Classes & of Its Communists, Bathists, & Free Officers. LC 78-51157. (Princeton Studies on the Near East). (Illus.). 1310p. reprint ed. pap. 200.00 (*0-608-06415-0*, 206662600008) Bks Demand.
— Syria's Peasantry, the Descendants of Its Lesser Rural Notables & Their Politics. LC 98-21289. 1999. 49.50 (*0-691-00254-1*, Pub. by Princeton U Pr) Cal Prin Full Svc.
***Batavia, Mitch.** Understanding Clinical Research: A Non-Technical Guide. (Illus.). 120p. 2000. pap. text 16.95 (*0-7506-7193-9*) Buttrwrth-Heinemann.
Batavia, Mitch. The Wheelchair Evaluation: A Practical Guide. LC 98-2710. 360p. 1998. pap. text 29.95 (*0-7506-7037-1*) Buttrwrth-Heinemann.
Batawi, M. A. El, see Kaloyanova, Fina P. & El Batawi, M. A.
Batch, Donald L., jt. auth. see Branson, Branley A.
Batch, Nicholas, jt. ed. see Steel, Matthew.
Batchelder, Alan B. Economics of Poverty. LC 78-14017 5. (Illus.). 256p. reprint ed. 79.40 (*0-8357-9876-3*, 201115300074) Bks Demand.
Batchelder, Ann & Orban, Nancy, eds. Fiberarts Design Book, Bk. V. LC 95-6604. (Fiberarts Design Book Ser.). (Illus.). 240p. 1995. 34.95 (*0-937274-86-0*) Lark Books.
Batchelder, Ann G. The Seal of Orestes: Self-Reference & Authority in Sophocles' Electra. 180p. (C). 1994. pap. text 25.95 (*0-8476-7991-8*); lib. bdg. 58.50 (*0-8476-7990-X*) Rowman.
***Batchelder, David.** All Through the Day All Through the Year: Family Prayers & Celebrations. 2000. pap. 12.99 (*0-8066-4039-1*, Augsburg) Augsburg Fortress.
Batchelder, Donald & Warner, Elizabeth G., eds. Beyond Experience: The Experiential Approach to Cross-Cultural Education. LC 77-82854. (Intercultural Exchange Ser.). 196p. 1977. reprint ed. pap. text 9.00 (*0-936141-00-X*) Experiment Pr.
Batchelder, Dorothy. The Fishmonger Cookbook: An Expert's Guide to Selecting, Preparing, Cooking & Serving the Very Best Fish & Seafood. (Illus.). 320p. 1992. pap. 14.95 (*0-89909-359-0*, 80-151-1) Yankee Bks.
Batchelder, H. M., jt. auth. see Osgood, Chas S.
Batchelder, Helen. PMS: Everything You Need to Know about. LC 98-49608. (Natural Pharmacist Ser.). (Illus.). 177p. 2000. pap. 6.99 (*0-7615-1615-8*) Prima Pub.
Batchelder, J. W. Metric Madness. (Illus.). 256p. 1981. 12.95 (*0-8159-6220-7*); pap. 5.95 (*0-8159-6219-3*) Devin.
Batchelder, Jean. History & Heroes of N. H. Aviation. Harrison, Kay D., ed. LC 95-80558. (Illus.). 300p. (Orig.). 1995. pap. text 16.00 (*0-9648993-0-2*) Arrow Publ.
***Batchelder, Jon C., ed.** Proton Emitting Nuclei: PROCON '99 - First International Symposium. LC 00-102142. (AIP Conference Proceedings Ser.: Vol. 518). (Illus.). xv, 351p. 2000. 110.00 (*1-56396-937-8*, Pub. by Am Inst Physics) Spr-Verlag.
Batchelder, Samuel. Introduction & Early Progress of the Cotton Manufacture in the U. S. LC 68-55476. (Library of Early American Business & Industry: No. 27). iv, 108p. 1972. reprint ed. 35.00 (*0-678-00903-1*) Kelley.
Batchelder, Susan, jt. ed. see Bridwell-Bowles, Lillian.
Batchelder, Susan, jt. ed. see Evans, Carolyn & Miller, Carol.
Batchelder, Susan, ed. see McNaron, Toni A. & Olano, Pamela J.
Batchelder, Susan, ed. see Miller, Carol.
Batcheller, Birney C. People of Wallingford. (Illus.). 317p. 1995. reprint ed. lib. bdg. 39.50 (*0-8328-5130-2*) Higginson Bk Co.
Batchelor. Journey of the Spirit. 1997. 14.95 (*0-7459-3392-0*, Pub. by Lion Pubng) Trafalgar.
Batchelor, A. W., jt. auth. see Stachowiak, G. W.
Batchelor, A. W., jt. auth. see Stachowiak, Gwidon.
Batchelor, Andrew, Jr., jt. auth. see Batchelor, Andrew J., Sr.
Batchelor, Andrew J., Sr. & Batchelor, Andrew, Jr. Computer Applications for Business Planning: A Practical Hands-On Text. 3rd ed. (Illus.). 380p. (C). 1997. 89.00 incl. disk (*0-9623374-5-5*) Tangent Pub.
Batchelor, Andrew J., Sr. & Batchelor, Andrew J., Jr. Computer Applications for Business Planning: A Practical Hands-On Text. 3rd ed. (Illus.). 380p. (C). 1997. pap. text 55.00 (*0-9623374-4-7*) Tangent Pub.
— The Process of Business Planning: A Practical Hands-On Text. 3rd ed. (Illus.). 261p. (C). 1997. pap. text 55.00 (*0-9623374-6-3*) Tangent Pub.
Batchelor, Andrew J., Jr. & Nesmith, Timothy E. VentureTrac (r) Complete Business Development Program. (Illus.). 480p. (Orig.). 1997. 129.00 incl. disk (*0-9623374-3-9*) Tangent Pub.
Batchelor, Andrew J., Jr., jt. auth. see Batchelor, Andrew J., Sr.
Batchelor, Andrew W., jt. auth. see Lam, Loh N.
Batchelor, Anne. Batchelor. A Batchelor's Delight, the Adventures of a Family Historian. (Illus.). 78p. 1997. reprint ed. pap. 15.50 (*0-8328-7415-9*); reprint ed. lib. bdg. 25.50 (*0-8328-7414-0*) Higginson Bk Co.
— A Batchelor's Delight. (C). 1989. text 55.00 (*0-948929-40-5*) St Mut.
Batchelor, Bruce G. Intelligent Image Processing in Prolog. (Illus.). 392p. 1991. 149.00 (*0-387-19647-1*) Spr-Verlag.
Batchelor, Bruce G., ed. Selected Papers on Industrial Machine Vision Systems. LC 94-7899. (Milestone Ser.: Vol. MS 97). 1994. pap. 45.00 (*0-8194-1579-0*) SPIE.
— Selected Papers on Industrial Machine Vision Systems. LC 94-7899. (Milestone Ser.: Vol. MS 97/HC). 1994. 55.00 (*0-8194-1580-4*) SPIE.
Batchelor, Bruce G., et al, eds. Machine Vision Systems for Inspection & Metrology VII, Vol. 3521. LC 99-159849. 1998. 89.00 (*0-8194-2982-1*) SPIE.
Batchelor, Bruce G. & Waltz, Frederick. Interactive Image Processing for Machine Vision. LC 92-44424. 1993. 163.95 (*0-387-19814-8*) Spr-Verlag.
Batchelor, Bruce G. & Whelan, Paul F. Intelligent Vision Systems for Industry. LC 96-37943. xxii, 458p. 1997. 129.00 (*3-540-19969-1*) Spr-Verlag.
Batchelor, Bruce G., et al. Machine Vision Applications, Architectures & Systems Integration III: 31 October-2 November, 1994, Boston, Massachusetts LC 94-67544. (Proceedings Ser.). x, 446p. 1994. pap. write for info. (*0-8194-1682-7*) SPIE.
— Machine Vision Applications, Architectures & Systems Integration IV: 23-24 October, 1995, Philadelphia, Pennsylvania. LC 95-69915. x, 326 p. 1995. write for info. (*0-8194-1961-3*) SPIE.
Batchelor, Bruce T. Authors Guide: Book Publishing for the Rest of Us! 54p. 1996. spiral bd. 4.00 (*1-55212-206-9*, No. 96-0101) Trafford Pub.
Batchelor, Bruce T., jt. auth. see Bates, Albert K.
Batchelor, D. M. Stinky Socks & Chicken Pox. (Illus.). 36p. (J). 1997. pap. 4.95 (*0-9664683-1-7*) Batchelor Dean.
— Through the Eyes of a Child. (Illus.). 38p. (J). (ps up). 1996. pap. 4.95 (*0-9664683-0-9*) Batchelor Dean.

B

Batchelor, David. Minimalism. (Movements in Modern Art Ser.). (Illus.). 80p. (C). 1998. pap. 15.00 (*0-521-62759-1*) Cambridge U Pr.

Batchelor, David, et al, photos by. Lewitt Sol: Structures, 1962-1993. (GER., Illus.). 128p. 1993. pap. 68.00 (*0-905836-78-2*, Pub. by Museum Modern Art) St Mut.

Batchelor, David, et al. Realism, Rationalism, Surrealism: Art Between the Wars. LC 92-50987. (Illus.). 371p. (C). 1993. reprint ed. pap. 27.50 (*0-300-05519-6*) Yale U Pr.

Batchelor De Garcia, Karen & Slaughter, Randi. In Plain English: An Integrated Skills Approach. (Illus.). 1986. pap. text 12.95 (*0-201-10961-1*) Addison-Wesley.

Batchelor, Dean. The American Hot Rod. (Illus.). 192p. 1995. 29.95 (*0-87938-982-6*) MBI Pubg.

— Illustrated Ferrari Buyer's Guide. 4th rev. ed. LC 96-35799. (Illustrated Buyer's Guide Ser.). (Illus.). 192p. 1996. pap. 17.95 (*0-7603-0243-X*) MBI Pubg.

— Illustrated Porsche Buyers Guide. 4th ed. LC 97-44433. (Illustrated Buyer's Guide Ser.). (Illus.). 192p. 1997. pap. 17.95 (*0-7603-0227-8*) MBI Pubg.

Batchelor, Donald B., ed. Radio Frequency Power in Plasmas. LC 91-77853. (AIP Conference Proceedings Ser.: No. 244). (Illus.). 416p. 1992. lib. bdg. 99.00 (*0-88318-937-2*) Am Inst Physics.

Batchelor, Ervin S., Jr. & Dean, Raymond S., eds. Pediatric Neuropsychology: Interfacing Assessment & Treatment for Rehabilitation. 384p. 1995. pap. text 39.80 (*0-205-16486-2*, Longwood Div) Allyn.

B

***Batchelor, G. K.** An Introduction to Fluid Dynamics. (Cambridge Mathematical Library). 634p. (C). 2000. pap. 39.95 (*0-521-66396-2*) Cambridge U Pr.

Batchelor, George K. The Life & Legacy of G. I. Taylor. (Illus.). 300p. (C). 1996. text 80.00 (*0-521-46121-9*) Cambridge U Pr.

Batchelor, J. Renaissance Armor. 1998. pap. text 4.95 (*0-486-40157-X*) Dover.

Batchelor, James Q. Industrial Hygiene: Index of New Information. 160p. 1998. 47.50 (*0-7883-1660-5*); pap. 44.50 (*0-7883-1661-3*) ABBE Pubs Assn.

***Batchelor, John.** Ainu of Japan: The Religion, Superstitions & General History of the Hair. limited ed. (Illus.). 336p. 2000. reprint ed. 75.00 (*1-57898-241-3*) Martino Pubng.

Batchelor, John. The Ainu of Japan: The Religion, Superstitions, & General History of the Hairy Aborigines of Japan. 1977. 28.95 (*0-8369-7153-1*, 7985) Ayer.

***Batchelor, John.** Classic Motorcycles Book: 24 Full-Color Cards. (Illus.). (J). 1999. pap. 4.95 (*0-486-40822-1*) Dover.

Batchelor, John. Jet Fighters Coloring Book. (Illus.). 48p. (J). 1998. pap. 2.95 (*0-486-40357-2*) Dover.

***Batchelor, John.** John Ruskin: A Life. (Illus.). 384p. 2000. 30.00 (*0-7867-0814-X*, Pub. by Carroll & Graf) Publishers Group.

Batchelor, John, ed. see Conrad, Joseph.

Batchelor, John, ed. & intro. see Conrad, Joseph.

Batchelor, John Calvin. Ain't You Glad You Joined the Republicans? A Short History of the GOP. 88p. 1995. 25.00 (*0-8050-3267-3*) H Holt & Co.

— American Falls: A Novel. 88p. 1995. pap. 15.00 (*0-8050-3787-X*, Owl) H Holt & Co.

— Father's Day. 1995. 23.00 (*0-8050-3266-5*) H Holt & Co.

— Father's Day. 1996. mass mkt. 6.99 (*0-312-95858-7*) St Martin.

— The Further Adventures of Halley's Comet: A Novel. LC 94-49338. 88p. 1995. pap. 14.00 (*0-8050-3788-8*, Owl) H Holt & Co.

— Gordon Liddy Is My Muse, by Tommy "Tip" Paine: A Novel. LC 95-14540. 88p. 1995. pap. 12.00 (*0-8050-3790-X*, Owl) H Holt & Co.

— Joseph Conrad: A Critical Biography. (Critical Biographies Ser.). (Illus.). 368p. 1993. 58.95 (*0-631-16416-2*) Blackwell Pubs.

— The Life of Joseph Conrad: A Critical Biography. Rawson, Claude, ed. (Critical Biographies Ser.). (Illus.). 336p. 1996. pap. 25.95 (*0-631-19912-8*) Blackwell Pubs.

— Peter Nevsky & the True Story of the Russian Moon Landing: A Novel. 88p. 1995. pap. 15.00 (*0-8050-4667-4*, Owl) H Holt & Co.

— Walking the Cat, by Tommy "Tip" Paine: Gordon Liddy Is My Muse, II. LC 95-14537. 89p. 1995. pap. 12.00 (*0-8050-3789-6*, Owl) H Holt & Co.

— Wall Street. Date not set. 25.00 (*0-8050-5072-8*) H Holt & Co.

***Batchelor, John H.** 100 Historic Airplanes in Full Color. LC 00-31775. (Pictorial Archive Ser.). (Illus.). 2000. write for info. (*0-486-41246-6*) Dover.

Batchelor, John J., ed. The Art of Literary Biography. (Illus.). 300p. 1995. 34.00 (*0-19-818289-9*) OUP.

***Batchelor, Louise.** Whoops! LC 98-60355. 24p. (J). (ps-1). 2000. 9.95 (*1-84089-024-X*, Pub. by Zero to Ten) IPG Chicago.

— Whoops! (Illus.). 24p. (J). 2000. pap. 6.95 (*1-84089-125-4*, Pub. by Zero to Ten) IPG Chicago.

Batchelor, Margaret A., jt. auth. see Connor, Anthony C.

Batchelor, Martine. Principles of Zen: The Only Introduction You'll Ever Need. 160p. 1999. pap. 11.00 (*0-7225-3672-0*) Thorsons PA.

Batchelor, Mary. Children's Prayers from Around the World. LC 95-8518. 94p. (J). (gr. 4-7). 1995. 13.99 (*0-8066-2830-8*, 9-2830, Augsburg) Augsburg Fortress.

***Batchelor, Mary.** Jesus Story. 1999. pap. 14.95 (*0-7459-4270-9*, Pub. by Lion Pubng) Trafalgar.

Batchelor, Mary. The Lion Christian Poetry Collection. LC 98-195121. 576 p. 1995. write for info. (*0-7459-2746-7*) Lion USA.

— Mooring's Book of Prayers. 1996. 24.99 (*0-345-40520-X*) Ballantine Pub Grp.

— My Own Book of Prayers. (Illus.). 64p. (J). (gr. k-3). 1996. 11.95 (*0-687-01879-X*) Abingdon.

— Poetry for the Soul: 700 Best Loved Christian Poems. large type ed. 1996. 20.00 (*0-7838-1683-9*, G K Hall Lrg Type) Mac Lib Ref.

— La Vida de Jesus.Tr. of Story of Jesus. (SPA.). 191p. (J). 1992. 1.89 (*1-56063-544-4*, 490475) Editorial Unilit.

— Windows of the Bible. LC 99-164710. 1997. 24.99 (*0-7459-3769-1*) Lion USA.

Batchelor, Mary, compiled by. The Doubleday Prayer Collection. LC 97-12714. (Illus.). 528p. 1997. 22.00 (*0-385-48847-5*) Doubleday.

Batchelor, Murray T. & Wille, Luc T., eds. Statistical Physics on the Eve of the 21st Century: In Honour of J. B. McGuire on the Occasion of His 65th Birthday Florida Atlantic University May 1999. 400p. 1998. 84.00 (*981-02-3678-6*) World Scientific Pub.

Batchelor, Peter. People in Rural Development: The Religious Radicals of the 16th & 17th Centuries. 2nd rev. ed. xii, 228p. 1993. pap. 16.99 (*0-85364-541-8*, Pub. by Paternoster Pub) OM Literature.

Batchelor, Peter & Willett, Susan. Disarmament & Defence Industrial Adjustment in South Africa. (A SIPRI Publication). (Illus.). 264p. 1998. text 65.00 (*0-19-829413-1*) OUP.

Batchelor, Peter F. & Matson, Christopher. The Western Front, 1915: VCs of the First World War. (Illus.). 224p. 1996. 31.95 (*0-7509-1106-9*, Pub. by Sutton Pub Ltd) Intl Pubs Mktg.

Batchelor, R., tr. see Bernanos, Georges.

Batchelor, R. E. Using Spanish Synonyms. 729p. (C). 1994. pap. 27.95 (*0-521-44694-5*) Cambridge U Pr.

— Using Spanish Synonyms. 729p. (C). 1995. text 85.00 (*0-521-44160-9*) Cambridge U Pr.

Batchelor, R. E. & Chebli-Saadi, M. French for Marketing: Using French in Media & Communications. LC 96-51789. (Illus.). 368p. (C). 1998. text 64.95 (*0-521-58500-7*); pap. text 25.95 (*0-521-58535-X*) Cambridge U Pr.

***Batchelor, R. E. & Offord, M. H.** Using French: A Guide to Contemporary Usage. 3rd ed. 320p. 2000. 64.95 (*0-521-64177-2*); pap. 23.95 (*0-521-64593-X*) Cambridge U Pr.

Batchelor, R. E. & Offord, Malcolm H. Using French: A Guide to Contemporary Usage. 288p. (C). 1993. pap. 22.95 (*0-521-44821-2*); text 59.95 (*0-521-44361-X*) Cambridge U Pr.

— Using French Synonyms. 603p. (C). 1993. pap. 27.95 (*0-521-37878-8*); text 80.00 (*0-521-37277-1*) Cambridge U Pr.

Batchelor, R. E. & Pountain, Christopher J. Using Spanish: A Guide to Contemporary Usage. 334p. (C). 1992. pap. 22.95 (*0-521-26987-3*); text 69.95 (*0-521-42123-3*) Cambridge U Pr.

Batchelor, Ray. Henry Ford, Mass Production & Design. LC 94-22346. 1995. text 74.95 (*0-7190-4173-2*, Pub. by Manchester Univ Pr) St Martin.

***Batchelor, Reg.** The Murder Game. large type ed. 296p. 1999. pap. 18.99 (*0-7089-5557-6*, Linford) Ulverscroft.

Batchelor, Rhonda. Bearings. 1986. pap. 7.50 (*0-919626-27-0*, Pub. by Brick Bks) Genl Dist Srvs.

Batchelor, Stephen. Alone with Others: An Existential Approach to Buddhism. LC 82-21054. 144p. 1983. pap. 10.00 (*0-8021-5127-2*, Grove) Grove-Atltic.

— The Awakening of the West: The Encounter of Buddhism & Western Culture. 416p. 1994. 30.00 (*0-938077-68-6*); pap. 18.00 (*0-938077-69-4*) Parallax Pr.

— Buddhism Without Beliefs. 144p. 1998. pap. 12.00 (*1-57322-656-4*, Riverhd Trade) Berkley Pub.

— The Faith to Doubt: Glimpses of Buddhist Uncertainty. LC 89-28008. 138p. (Orig.). 1989. pap. 10.00 (*0-938077-22-8*) Parallax Pr.

— Tibet Guide: Central & Western Tibet. 2nd rev. ed. LC 97-40033. (Illus.). 424p. 1998. pap. 24.95 (*0-86171-134-3*) Wisdom MA.

***Batchelor, Stephen.** Verses from the Center: A Buddhist Vision of the Sublime. 208p. 2000. 22.95 (*1-57322-162-7*, Riverhead Books) Putnam Pub Group.

Batchelor, Stephen, ed. & tr. see Rabten, Geshe.

Batchelor, Stephen, tr. see Rabten, Geshe.

***Batchelor, Tracy & Cudkowicz, Merit E.** Principles of Neuroepidemiology. (Illus.). 400p. 2000. text 90.00 (*0-7506-7042-8*) Buttrwrth-Heinemann.

Batchen, Geoffrey. Burning with Desire: The Conception of Photography. LC 97-4022. (Illus.). 304p. 1997. 40.00 (*0-262-02427-6*) MIT Pr.

— Burning with Desire: The Conception of Photography. (Illus.). 288p. 1999. pap. text 20.00 (*0-262-52259-4*) MIT Pr.

***Batchen, Geoffrey.** Each Wild Idea: Writing, Photography, History. LC 00-42355. (Illus.). 2001. write for info. (*0-262-02486-1*) MIT Pr.

Batcher, Joyce. Microwaving with a Gourmet Flair. Hamernik, Arlene, ed. (Illus.). 67p. 1983. reprint ed. pap. 2.50 (*0-9602930-1-9*) Microwave Helps.

Batchlor, B. G. & Waltz, F. M., eds. Machine Vision Systems Integration: Critical Reviews. 1991. pap. 20.00 (*0-8194-0471-3*, VOL. CR36) SPIE.

***Batchlor, Larry G.** Juneteenth Story Activity & Coloring Book: From African Slaves to African Americans. large type ed. Goings, Kenneth & La Rue, Linda, eds. (Illus.). 60p. (J). 2000. pap. 10.00 (*0-9701357-0-X*) Jubilee Day June.

Batchvarov, Velislav, jt. auth. see Malik, Marek.

Batchvarova, Ekaterina, jt. auth. see Gryning, Sven-Erik.

Batdorf, Carol. Clancy & Tidepool Friends. 76p. 1987. pap. 3.95 (*0-88839-336-9*) Hancock House.

Batdorf, Carol. Love Quest. 224p. 1994. pap. 14.95 (*0-88839-337-7*) Hancock House.

— Northwest Native Harvest. 96p. (Orig.). 1990. pap. 7.95 (*0-88839-245-1*) Hancock House.

— Power Quest. LC 90-91108. (Illus.). 224p. 1990. pap. 12.95 (*0-88839-240-0*) Hancock House.

— Spirit Quest: The Initiation of an Indian Boy. LC 89-91010. (Illus.). 160p. (Orig.). 1990. reprint ed. pap. 12.95 (*0-88839-210-9*) Hancock House.

— Tinka: A Day in a Little Girl's Life. (Illus.). 32p. (Orig.). (J). (gr. 1-6). 1990. pap. 5.95 (*0-88839-249-4*) Hancock House.

— Totem Poles: An Ancient Art. (Illus.). 24p. (Orig.). (J). (gr. 1-6). 1990. pap. 6.95 (*0-88839-248-6*) Hancock House.

Batdorf, Lynn R. Boxwood Handbook: A Practical Guide to Knowing & Growing Boxwood. LC 95-75228. (Illus.). 99p. (Orig.). 1995. pap. 15.00 (*1-886833-00-1*) Am Boxwood Soc.

Batdorff, Donna, jt. auth. see Roemmele, Jacqueline A.

Bate, A. K., ed. Joseph of Exeter No. I-III: The Trojan War. (Classical Texts Ser.). 1986. pap. 22.00 (*0-85668-295-0*, Pub. by Aris & Phillips) David Brown.

Bate, A. K, ed. Joseph of Exeter Nos. I-III: The Trojan War. (Classical Texts Ser.). 1986. 59.99 (*0-85668-294-2*, Pub. by Aris & Phillips) David Brown.

Bate, Barbara. Lay Speakers Preach: Sharing God's Story in the Pulpit. 16p. 1997. pap. 5.95 (*0-88177-196-1*, DR196) Discipleship Res.

— Leading in the Spirit: A Guidebook for Learning Leaders in the Church. 32p. 1997. pap. 12.95 (*0-88177-234-8*, DR234) Discipleship Res.

— Libertad en la Predicacion: A Los Cuatro Rincones Del Mundo. Lopez, Hugo L., tr. 116p. 1999. pap. 8.95 (*0-88177-294-1*) Discipleship Res.

Bate, Barbara & Bowker, Judy. Communication & the Sexes. 2nd rev. ed. (Illus.). 415p. (C). 1997. pap. text 23.95 (*0-88133-933-4*) Waveland Pr.

Bate, Barbara A. Freedom in the Pulpit: A Vision for Growth in Preaching. LC 95-83447. 102p. 1996. pap. 14.95 (*0-88177-152-X*, DR152) Discipleship Res.

Bate, Barbara A., et al, eds. Women Communicating: Studies of Women's Talk. LC 88-1582. (Communication & Information Science Ser.). 336p. 1988. pap. 39.50 (*0-89391-476-2*); text 73.25 (*0-89391-475-4*) Ablx Pub.

Bate Cabal Assocs. Staff. Cincinnati Journal of Ceremonial Magick, Issue 1, Vol. 1. Lindenschmidt, Louis, ed. (Illus.). 88p. (Orig.). 1976. pap. 10.00 (*1-890399-00-0*, 010) Blck Moon.

— Cincinnati Journal of Magick, Issue 6, Vol. 2. Lindenschmidt, Louis, ed. (Illus.). 64p. (Orig.). 1988. pap. 5.00 (*1-890399-05-1*, 015) Blck Moon.

Bate, David & Leperlier, Francois. Mise en Scene: Photographs by Claude Cahun, Tacita Dean, & Virginia Nimarkoh. (Illus.). 64p. 1995. 14.95 (*0-905263-59-6*) Dist Art Pubs.

***Bate, Dick.** Coaching the Advanced Player: 40 Advanced Training Games & Exercises. (Illus.). 83p. 1999. pap. 12.95 (*1-890946-33-8*) Reedswain.

— Soccer: The Sweeper. (Illus.). 30p. 1999. pap. 9.95 (*1-890946-30-3*) Reedswain.

Bate, George L. Public Schools vs. American Political Liberty: Restoring Freedom of Education in a Nation Imperiled by Public Schools. LC 87-82986. 91p. (Orig.). 1987. pap. 7.00 (*0-944776-00-0*) Freesponse Pr.

Bate, John. The Mysterys of Nature & Art: In Foure Tretises. LC 77-6850. (English Experience Ser.: No. 845). 1977. reprint ed. lib. bdg. 45.00 (*90-221-0845-7*) Walter J Johnson.

Bate, John P., tr. De Jure Naturae et Gentium Dissertationes: Washington, D. C. - Carnegie Institution 1916. LC 95-77195. (Classics in International Law Reprint Ser.: No.5, Vol.2). (LAT.). 16, iv, 233p. 1995. reprint ed. 95.00 (*0-89941-946-1*) W S Hein.

— Dissertations on the Law of Nature & of Nations, Vol. 2. LC 95-77195. (Classics in International Law Reprint Ser.: No. 5). 1995. 95.00 (*1-57588-253-1*, 310120) W S Hein.

— Synopsis of the Law of Nations, Vol. 2. LC 95-77196. (Classics in International Law Reprint Ser.: No. 6). 1995. reprint ed. 100.00 (*1-57588-267-1*, 310140) W S Hein.

Bate, John P., tr. see Nys, Ernest, ed.

Bate, Jonathan. The Genius of Shakespeare. (Illus.). 412p. 1998. pap. 17.95 (*0-19-512823-0*) OUP.

— Shakespeare & Ovid. 308p. 1994. reprint ed. pap. text 22.00 (*0-19-818324-0*) OUP.

— Shakespeare & the English Romantic Imagination. (Illus.). 296p. 1989. pap. 22.00 (*0-19-812994-7*) OUP.

— Shakespearean Constitutions: Politics, Theater, Criticism, 1730-1830. (Illus.). 250p. 1989. 65.00 (*0-19-811749-3*) OUP.

***Bate, Jonathan.** The Song of the Earth. LC 99-44113. 248p. 2000. 29.95 (*0-674-00168-0*) HUP.

Bate, Jonathan & Jackson, Russell, eds. Shakespeare: An Illustrated Stage History. (Illus.). 266p. (C). 1996. 45.00 (*0-19-812372-8*) OUP.

Bate, Jonathan, ed. see International Shakespeare Association Staff.

Bate, Jonathan, ed. see Shakespeare, William.

Bate, Keith, ed. Three Latin Comedies. (LAT.). viii, 96p. pap. text 7.43 (*0-88844-455-9*) Brill Academic Pubs.

Bate, Kerry W. & Bryson, Maureen S. The Joseph Sylvester Family Letters, 1882-1989. (Illus.). ix, 592p. 1998. 50.00 (*0-9664088-3-7*) M S Bryson.

Bate, Kerry W., jt. auth. see Bryson, Maureen S.

Bate, Lucy. Little Rabbit's Loose Tooth. LC 75-6833. (Illus.). 32p. (J). (gr. k-3). 1988. pap. 5.99 (*0-517-55122-5*, Pub. by Crown Bks Yng Read) Random.

— Little Rabbit's Loose Tooth. (J). 1975. 11.19 (*0-606-02965-6*, Pub. by Turtleback) Demco.

Bate, Marjorie D. & Casey, Mary C. Legal Office Procedures. 2nd ed. (Illus.). 544p. 1980. text 56.76 (*0-07-004058-3*) McGraw.

Bate, Michael & Arias, Alfonso M., eds. The Development of Drosophila Melanogaster. LC 92-46185. 1536p. 1993. 125.00 (*0-87969-423-8*) Cold Spring Harbor.

Bate, Michele & Miller, Arthur. Accelerated Learning: French. Rose, Diana, ed. (Illus.). 391p. (Orig.). 1986. pap., student ed. 229.00 (*0-905553-23-3*, Pub. by Accel Lrn Sys) McClelland & Stewart.

Bate, Paul. Strategies for Cultural Change. (Illus.). 320p. 1996. pap. text 39.95 (*0-7506-2328-4*) Buttrwrth-Heinemann.

Bate, Paul & Mangham, Iain L. Exploring Participation. LC 80-41415. (Illus.). 302p. reprint ed. pap. 93.70 (*0-8357-4599-6*, 203753100008) Bks Demand.

Bate, Paul, jt. ed. see Child, John.

Bate, Percy H. English Pre-Raphaelite Painters. LC 71-140350. (Select Bibliographies Reprint Ser.). 1977. 33.95 (*0-8369-5593-5*) Ayer.

— The English Pre-Raphaelite Painters: Their Associates & Successors. enl. rev. ed. LC 79-129383. reprint ed. 48.00 (*0-404-00691-4*) AMS Pr.

Bate, Roger. Environmental Health: Problems & Preoccupations. LC 98-55393. 1999. write for info. (*0-7506-4223-8*) Buttrwrth-Heinemann.

***Bate, Roger.** Food, Health & Environment. 302p. 1999. 59.95 (*0-7506-4222-X*, Newnes) Buttrwrth-Heinemann.

— Life's Adventure: Virtual Risk in a Real World. 192p. 2000. pap. 29.95 (*0-7506-4679-9*) Buttrwrth-Heinemann.

Bate, Roger, ed. What Risk? LC 97-24157. 320p. 1997. text 59.95 (*0-7506-3810-9*) Buttrwrth-Heinemann.

Bate, Roger & Morris, Julian. Global Warming: Apocalypse or Hot Air? (IEA Studies on the Environment). 54p. 1994. pap. 14.95 (*0-255-36331-1*, Pub. by Inst Economic Affairs) Coronet Bks.

Bate, Roger R., et al. Fundamentals of Astrodynamics. (Illus.). 455p. (C). 1971. pap. 10.95 (*0-486-60061-0*) Dover.

Bate, Stuart C. Inculturation of the Christian Mission to Heal in the South African Context. LC 99-21901. (Studies in the History of Missions: Vol. 17). 384p. 1999. reprint ed. lib. bdg. 99.95 (*0-7734-8023-4*) E Mellen.

Bate, Walter J. The Achievement of Samuel Johnson. LC 78-56308. (Illus.). 259p. reprint ed. pap. 80.30 (*0-608-09381-5*, 205412600004); reprint ed. pap. 80.30 (*0-608-20995-3*, 205452300003) Bks Demand.

Bate, Walter Jackson. The Burden of the Past & the English Poet. 160p. 1991. pap. 15.00 (*0-674-08587-6*, BATBUX) HUP.

— John Keats. LC 63-17194. (Harvard Paperbacks Ser.: No. 142). (Illus.). 784p. 1979. pap. text 25.95 (*0-674-47825-8*) Belknap Pr.

— Negative Capability: The Intuitive Approach in Keats. LC 75-28991. reprint ed. 27.00 (*0-404-14002-5*) AMS Pr.

— Samuel Johnson. LC 97-47734. 672p. Date not set. pap. 25.00 (*1-887178-76-7*, Pub. by Counterpt DC) HarpC.

— The Stylistic Development of Keats. LC 83-48836. reprint ed. 23.00 (*0-404-20019-2*) AMS Pr.

Bate, Walter Jackson & Perkins, David, eds. British & American Poets: Chaucer to the Present. 1048p. (C). 1986. pap. text 43.00 (*0-15-505588-7*, Pub. by Harcourt Coll Pubs) Harcourt.

Bate, Walter Jackson, ed. see Burke, Edmund.

Bate, Walter Jackson, ed. see Johnson, Samuel.

Bate, Weston. A History of Brighton. 2nd ed. (Illus.). 466p. 1989. reprint ed. 29.95 (*0-522-84270-4*, Pub. by Melbourne Univ Pr) Paul & Co Pubs.

Bateille, Andre. Caste, Class & Power: Changing Patterns of Stratification in a Tanjore Village. 2nd ed. LC 96-902098. (Illus.). 310p. 1996. text 22.95 (*0-19-563847-6*) OUP.

Batelle Columbus Labs. Staff & Duffy, A. R. Study of Feasibility of Basing Natural Gas Pipeline Operating Pressure on Hydrostatic Test Pressure. 100p. 1968. pap. 10.00 (*0-318-12706-7*, L30050) Am Gas Assn.

Batelman, Kenneth. Adobe Illustrator 3 Paths & Curves. LC 95-14989. (Illus.). 324p. 1995. pap. 24.95 (*0-471-12027-8*) Wiley.

Bately, Janet, ed. Anglo-Saxon Chronicle 3 MS A. Vol. 3. 304p. 1986. 75.00 (*0-85991-103-9*) Boydell & Brewer.

— Old English Orosius. (SS 6 Ser.). (Illus.). 1981. text 69.00 (*0-19-722406-7*) OUP.

***Bately, Nicholas.** World's Futures & Options Markets: The Classified Directory of the World's Exchanges & Contracts. (Illus.). 1434p. 2000. 149.95 (*0-471-86345-9*) Wiley.

Bateman, et al, eds. Historical Encyclopedia of Illinois. (Illus.). 635p. 1997. reprint ed. lib. bdg. 65.00 (*0-8328-5708-4*) Higginson Bk Co.

— Historical Encyclopedia of Illinois & History of Henderson County, 2 vols. (Illus.). 905p. 1997. reprint ed. lib. bdg. 99.00 (*0-8328-5747-5*) Higginson Bk Co.

Bateman, jt. auth. see Sigband.

Bateman, Andy. Digital Communications: Design for the Real World. LC 98-25172. 250p. 1998. pap. 77.00 incl. cd-rom (*0-201-34301-0*) Addison-Wesley.

— Digital Signal Processing Design. (C). 2000. text. write for info. (*0-201-39851-6*) Addison-Wesley.

Bateman, Ann. Who Gets to Go? 25p. 1996. pap. 5.75 (*1-57438-005-2*, 2564) Ed Ministries.

Bateman, Anthony & Holmes, Jeremy. Introduction to Psychoanalysis: Contemporary Theory & Practice. LC 95-7617. 304p. (C). 1995. 80.00 (*0-415-10738-5*); pap. 22.99 (*0-415-10739-3*) Routledge.

***Bateman, Anthony, et al.** Introduction to Psychotherapy: An Outline of Psychodynamic Principles & Practice. 3rd ed. LC 99-86481. 2000. pap. write for info. (*0-415-20569-7*) Routledge.

Bateman, Audray. An Austin Album. (Illus.). 1979. 25.00 (*0-88426-056-9*) Encino Pr.

Bateman, B. Identifying Coca-Cola Collectibles. 80p. 1997. 7.98 (*0-7858-0773-X*) Bk Sales Inc.

Bateman, Barbara D. Better IEPs: Doing It the Right Way. 108p. (C). 1992. pap. text 15.95 (*1-882679-15-6*) Otter Ink.

An Asterisk (*) at the beginning of an entry indicates that the title is appearing for the first time.

— The Essentials of Teaching. 93p. (C). reprint ed. pap. text 19.95 (*1-882679-44-X*) Otter Ink.

Bateman, Barbara D. & Linden, Mary A. Better IEP's: How to Develop Legally Correct & Educationally Useful Programs. 3rd ed. LC 98-228588. (Illus.). 248p. 1998. pap. 22.50 (*1-57035-164-3*, 63IEP) Sopris.

Bateman, Bill, jt. auth. see Schaeffer, Randy.

Bateman, Bradley W. Keynes's Uncertain Revolution. LC 96-14662. 200p. (C). 1996. text 47.50 (*0-472-10708-9*, 10708) U of Mich Pr.

Bateman, Bradley W. & Davis, John B., eds. Keynes & Philosophy: Essays on the Origins of Keyne's Thought. 176p. 1991. text 85.00 (*1-85278-306-0*) E Elgar.

— Keynes & Philosophy: Essays on the Origins of Keynes's Thought. 176p. 1993. pap. 30.00 (*1-85278-845-3*) E Elgar.

Bateman, Brenda G., jt. auth. see Williams, Susan.

Bateman, Charles. Beethovan - The Easy Way: Easy Piano. 9.95 (*1-56922-132-4*, 07-2058) Creat Cncpts.

— Choice Easy Piano Classics. 80p. (Orig.). 1995. pap. 11.95 (*1-56922-095-6*, 07-2037) Creat Cncpts.

***Bateman, Charles.** Easy Classical Themes for Piano. (Illus.). 144p. 1998. pap. 14.95 (*1-56922-190-1*, 07-2064) Creat Cncpts.

Bateman, Charles. Exciting Easy Classics for Piano. 1997. pap. text 14.95 (*1-56922-161-8*) Creat Cncpts.

— Exquisite Waltz Themes for Piano. 192p. (Orig.). 1994. pap. 14.95 (*1-56922-034-4*, 07-2022) Creat Cncpts.

— More Exciting Easy Classics for Piano. (Illus.). 144p. 1996. pap. text 14.95 (*1-56922-162-6*, 07-2054) Creat Cncpts.

— Mozart - The Easy Way: Easy Piano. 11.95 (*1-56922-111-1*, 07-2043) Creat Cncpts.

— Prime Easy Piano Classics. 80p. (Orig.). 1996. pap. 11.95 (*1-56922-103-0*, 07-2039) Creat Cncpts.

— Select Easy Piano Classics. 80p. (Orig.). 1995. pap. 11.95 (*1-56922-098-0*, 07-2038) Creat Cncpts.

Bateman, Claire. The Bicycle Slow Race. LC 90-28734. (Wesleyan New Poets Ser.). 66p. 1991. 14.95 (*0-8195-2196-5*, Wesleyan Univ Pr) U Pr of New Eng.

— Friction. LC 98-42513. 140p. 1998. pap. 13.95 (*0-933377-48-7*) Eighth Mount Pr.

***Bateman, Claire.** Friction. LC 98-42513. 140p. 1998. lib. bdg. 22.95 (*0-933377-49-5*, Pub. by Eighth Mount Pr) Consort Bk Sales.

Bateman, Colin. Cycle of Violence. 256p. 1996. 21.45 (*1-55970-349-0*, Pub. by Arcade Pub Inc) Time Warner.

— Cycle of Violence. 1997. pap. 12.45 (*1-55970-378-4*, Pub. by Arcade Pub Inc) Time Warner.

— Divorcing Jack. LC 95-17773. 272p. 1995. 19.45 (*1-55970-310-5*, Pub. by Arcade Pub Inc) Time Warner.

— Divorcing Jack. 288p. 1996. pap. 11.45 (*1-55970-359-8*, Pub. by Arcade Pub Inc) Time Warner.

— Of Wee Sweetie Mice & Men. LC 96-29456. 1997. 23.45 (*1-55970-376-8*, Pub. by Arcade Pub Inc) Time Warner.

Bateman, Don. The Complete Trumpet Player, Bk. 1. Vol. 1. (Illus.). 48p. 1986. pap. 12.95 (*0-7119-0648-3*, AM39207) Music Sales.

— The Complete Trumpet Player, Bk. 2. Vol. 2. (Illus.). 48p. 1986. pap. 12.95 (*0-7119-0649-1*, AM39215) Music Sales.

— The Complete Trumpet Player, Bk. 3. Vol. 3. (Illus.). 48p. 1986. pap. 12.95 (*0-7119-0650-5*, AM39223) Music Sales.

Bateman, Edward A. Development of the County-Unit School District in Utah: A Study in Adaptability. LC 75-176541. (Columbia University. Teachers College. Contributions to Education Ser.: No. 790). reprint ed. 37.50 (*0-404-55790-2*) AMS Pr.

***Bateman, Eric.** The Prophets Have Spoken LC 99-23282. 1999. write for info. (*1-57345-503-2*) Deseret Bk.

Bateman, Fred & Weiss, Thomas. A Deplorable Scarcity: The Failure of Industrialization in the Slave Economy. LC 80-13238. 251p. reprint ed. pap. 77.90 (*0-7837-0305-8*, 204062700018) Bks Demand.

Bateman, Fred, jt. auth. see Atack, Jeremy.

Bateman, Fred, ed. see Maskus, Keith E.

Bateman, Fred, ed. see Schahill, Edward M.

Bateman, Fred, ed. see Switzer, Lorne.

Bateman, Fred, ed. see Williams, Mansfield W.

***Bateman, H. Paul.** Agricultural Engineering on the Prairie: Illinois Style : A History of the University of Illinois Department of Agricultural Engineering, 1921-1997. LC 97-62103. xiv, 337 p. 1998. write for info. (*0-9647738-2-1*) Scherer Communs.

Bateman, Hal, ed. American Athletics Annual, 1985. 1985. 12.00 (*0-317-41102-0*) Athletics Cong.

— American Athletics Annual 1986. 1986. 10.00 (*0-317-41105-5*) Athletics Cong.

— American Athletics Annual 1987. 1987. write for info. (*0-318-63172-5*) Athletics Cong.

— American Athletics Annual 1988. 1988. write for info. (*0-318-63173-3*) Athletics Cong.

— American Athletics Annual 1989. 1990. 10.00 (*0-685-33562-3*) Athletics Cong.

— American Athletics Annual 1990. 1991. 10.00 (*0-685-41037-4*) Athletics Cong.

Bateman, Helen, jt. auth. see Time-Life Books Editors.

Bateman, Herbert. Early Jewish Hermeneutics & Hebrews 1: 5-13: The Impact of Early Jewish Exegesis on the Interpretation of a Significant New Testament Passage. LC 96-41935. (American University Studies VII: Vol. 193). XIV, 438p. (C). 1997. text 61.95 (*0-8204-3324-1*) P Lang Pubng.

***Bateman, Herbert W.** Three Central Issues in Contemporary Dispensationalism: A Comparison of Traditional & Progressive Views. LC 99-43085. 352p. 2000. pap. 15.99 (*0-8254-2062-8*) Kregel.

Bateman, Ian J. & Willis, Ken G., eds. Contingent Valuation of Environmental Preferences: Assessing Theory & Practice in the USA, Europe & Developing Countries. (Illus.). 668p. 1999. text 125.00 (*0-19-828853-0*) OUP.

Bateman, J. J. Erasmi Opera Omnia Erasmus, Vol. VII-6. 340p. 1996. 187.00 (*0-444-82395-6*, North Holland) Elsevier.

Bateman, Jack. Harbor of Refuge. LC 96-61944. (Illus.). 64p. (Orig.). 1997. 14.99 (*1-883893-95-X*) WinePress Pub.

Bateman, James A. Animal Traps & Trapping. rev. ed. LC SK0283.B3. 288p. reprint ed. pap. 89.30 (*0-608-00478-2*, 206129700007) Bks Demand.

Bateman, John J., ed. see Erasmus, Desiderius.

Bateman, John J., tr. & anno. see Erasmus, Desiderius.

Bateman, John M. Loch Ness Conspiracy. 240p. 1988. 14.95 (*0-8315-0192-8*) Speller.

Bateman, Keith T. & Veldman, Cynthia J. 24-Hour Coverage: An Analysis & Report about Current Developments. 57p. 1991. pap. text 15.00 (*1-887271-07-4*) Alliance Am Insurers.

Bateman, Kitty, et al. The New York Times Reading Experience. 40p. 1979. pap. text. write for info. (*0-912853-02-6*) NY Times.

Bateman, Kristine. Cooking Lite for Life. (Illus.). 296p. 1997. pap. 23.99 (*0-9649109-1-8*) Mrs Batemans.

— Mrs. Bateman's Low Fat Baking Butter Cookbook. (Illus.). 198p. 1995. pap. text 21.95 (*0-9649109-0-X*) Mrs Batemans.

Bateman, L. Gods Crippled Children. 1993. pap. text 10.00 (*0-00-548287-9*) Collins SF.

Bateman, Mark, jt. ed. see Fossey, Richard.

Bateman, Michael. Cafe Brazil. LC 99-46364. (Cafe Cookbook Ser.). 128p. 1999. pap. 19.95 (*0-8092-2594-8*, 259480, Contemporary Bks) NTC Contemp Pub Co.

Bateman, Milford. Business Cultures in Central & Eastern Europe. LC 97-136228. (Illus.). 224p. 1996. pap. text 34.95 (*0-7506-2480-9*) Buttrwrth-Heinemann.

Bateman, Neil. Advocacy Skills: A Handbook for Human Service Professionals. 176p. 1995. pap. 33.95 (*1-85742-200-7*, Pub. by Arena) Ashgate Pub Co.

Bateman, Newton & Selby, Paul, eds. Historical Encyclopedia of Illinois, 2 vols. (Illus.). 1030p. 1994. lib. bdg. 105.00 (*0-8328-4364-4*) Higginson Bk Co.

— Illinois Historical & Effingham County Biographical. (Illus.). 893p. 1993. reprint ed. lib. bdg. 89.50 (*0-8328-3234-0*) Higginson Bk Co.

Bateman, Paul. Deepest Valley: Guide to Owens Valley. 6th rev. ed. Putnam, Jeff & Smith, Genny, eds. LC 95-10973. (Illus.). 280p. 1995. pap. 15.95 (*0-931378-14-1*) Live Oak.

Bateman, Penny. The Aztecs Activity Book. (British Museum Activity Bks.). (Illus.). 16p. (J). 1994. pap. 5.95 (*0-500-27764-8*, Pub. by Thames Hudson) Norton.

***Bateman, R.** The Controlled Droplet Application of Pesticides. (CABI Publishing Ser.). 280p. 2000. text 90.00 (*0-85199-352-4*) OUP.

Bateman, R. J. Basic Draughtsmanship. 44p. 1985. 9.00 (*0-7277-0233-5*, Pub. by T Telford) RCH.

Bateman, Robert. Natural Worlds. (Illus.). 192p. 1996. 60.00 (*0-684-82986-X*) S&S Trade.

— Pinelands. LC 98-106192. 248p. 1994. 21.95 (*0-937548-27-8*); pap. 12.95 (*0-937548-28-6*) Plexus Pub.

— Whitman's Tomb: Stories from the Pines. LC 97-177101. 215p. 1997. 21.95 (*0-937548-32-4*) Plexus Pub.

Bateman, Robert & Archbold, Rick. Safari. LC 98-6139. 32p. (J). (gr. k-3). 1998. 17.95 (*0-316-08265-1*) Little.

Bateman, Robert, tr. see Hummel, Monte, et al.

Bateman, Robert L., III, ed. Digital War: A View from the Front Lines. LC 99-31044. 256p. 1999. 29.95 (*0-89141-685-4*) Presidio Pr.

Bateman, Ronald S. & Mounts, Harry C., Jr. The Promotional Edge: The Complete Guide to the Successful Oral Interview. 3rd rev. ed. LC 98-91379. ii, 167p. 1998. pap. text 12.95 (*0-9663652-0-8*) Promot Edge Pub.

Bateman, Sam, jt. ed. see Sherwood, Dick.

Bateman, Selby. SimIsle: The Official Strategy Guide. 1995. pap. text 19.95 (*0-7615-0085-5*) Prima Pub.

— Unlock the Secrets of Total Annihilation: The Official Game Guide. 1997. pap. text 19.95 (*1-56893-903-5*) GT Interactive Software.

Bateman, Sherry. Gluten Free...& Eating Can Still be Fun. (Orig.). 1991. pap. 7.95 (*0-943487-33-1*) Sevgo Pr.

Bateman-Snell. Management. 4th ed. 720p. 1998. 81.88 (*0-256-26142-3*) McGraw.

Bateman, Suzanne E., jt. auth. see Bateman, William R.

***Bateman, Teresa.** Farm Flu. LC 00-8158. (Illus.). (J). 2000. write for info. (*0-8075-2274-0*) A Whitman.

Bateman, Teresa. Harp O' Gold. LC 99-18821. (J). 2001. write for info. (*0-8234-1523-6*) Holiday.

— Leprechaun Gold. LC 97-19111. (Illus.). 32p. (J). (gr. k-2). 1998. lib. bdg. 16.95 (*0-8234-1344-6*) Holiday.

***Bateman, Teresa.** Leprechaun Gold. (Illus.). (J). 1998. pap. 6.95 (*0-8234-1514-7*) Holiday.

Bateman, Teresa. The Ring of Truth. LC 96-5336. (Illus.). 32p. (J). (gr. k-3). 1997. 16.95 (*0-8234-1255-5*) Holiday.

***Bateman, Teresa.** The Ring of Truth. (Illus.). (J). 1999. pap. 6.95 (*0-8234-1518-X*) Holiday.

***Bateman, Teresa & Brewster, Patience.** The Mer-Baby. LC 00-35097. (Illus.). (J). 2001. write for info. (*0-8234-1531-7*) Holiday.

Bateman, Thomas H. Carter, Fisher & Allied Famillies: Genealogical Study with Biographical Notes. (Illus.). 241p. 1997. reprint ed. pap. 36.50 (*0-8328-7867-7*); reprint ed. lib. bdg. 46.50 (*0-8328-7866-9*) Higginson Bk Co.

— Houston & Allied Families: Genealogical Study with Biographical Notes. (Illus.). 683p. 1997. reprint ed. pap. 99.50 (*0-8328-9221-1*); reprint ed. lib. bdg. 109.50 (*0-8328-9220-3*) Higginson Bk Co.

Bateman, Thomas P. & Zeithaml, Carl P. Management: Function & Strategy. 796p. (C). 1989. text 64.95 (*0-256-05733-8*, Irwn McGrw-H) McGrw-H Hghr Educ.

Bateman, Thomas S. & Snell, Scott. Management: Building Competitive Advantage. 4th ed. LC 98-8256. 1998 96.59 (*0-07-304025-8*) McGraw.

Bateman, Thomas S. & Snell, Scott A. Management. 3rd ed. 264p. (C). 1995. text, student ed. 24.37 (*0-256-19717-2*, Irwn McGrw-H) McGrw-H Hghr Educ.

— Management: Building Competitive Advantage. 3rd ed. 704p. (C). 1995. text 68.95 (*0-256-14053-7*, Irwn Prfssnl) McGraw-Hill Prof.

Bateman, Thomas S. & Zeithaml, Carl P. Management: Function & Strategy. 2nd annot. ed. LC 92-22184. 752p. (C). 1992. teacher ed. write for info. (*0-256-11780-2*, Irwn McGrw-H) McGrw-H Hghr Educ.

Bateman, Thomas S., jt. auth. see Organ, Dennis W.

Bateman, Walter L. Open to Question: The Art of Teaching & Learning by Inquiry. LC 90-53089. (Higher Education Ser.). 245p. 1990. 32.95 (*1-55542-268-3*) Jossey-Bass.

Bateman, Wes. Dragons & Chariots. 65p. (Orig.). 1991 pap. 9.95 (*0-929385-45-4*) Light Tech Pubng.

— Knowledge from the Stars. 171p. (Orig.). 1993. pap. 11.95 (*0-929385-39-X*) Light Tech Pubng.

Bateman, William B., et al, eds. Patient & Family Education in Managed Care: Seizing the Teachable Moment. LC 99-37810. (Illus.). 264p. 1999. text 36.95 (*0-8261-1295-1*) Springer Pub.

Bateman, William G. & Harvey, Virginia I. Extended Manifold Twill Weaves. (Illus.). 63p. (Orig.). 1989. pap. 14.95 (*0-916658-49-X*) Shuttle Craft.

Bateman, William O. Political & Constitutional Law of the United States of America. xiv, 386p. 1993. reprint ed. 47.50 (*0-8377-1919-4*, Rothman) W S Hein.

Bateman, William R. & Bateman, Suzanne E. Hy-Tek Saves Christmas. LC 95-78745. (My Little Happy Book Ser.: Vol. 1, No. 1). (Illus.). 24p. (Orig.). (J). (ps-4). 1995. pap. 6.95 (*0-9649159-0-1*) Hy-Tek Intl.

Baten, Lea. Japanese Animal Art. 1995. 39.95 (*4-07-974943-0*) Shufu No.

— Japanese Dolls: The Image & the Motif. (Illus.). 152p. 1986. 24.95 (*4-07-974386-6*, Pub. by Shufunomoto Co Ltd) Tuttle Pubng.

— Japanese Folk Toys: The Playful Art. (Illus.). 176p. 1992. 39.95 (*4-07-975612-7*, Pub. by Shufunomoto Co Ltd) Tuttle Pubng.

— Playthings & Pastimes in Japanese Prints. LC 94-43737. (Illus.). 160p. 1995. 39.95 (*0-8348-0344-5*) Weatherhill.

Bateni, Mohammad R. Farhang Moaser: English-Persian Dictionary. (Illus.). xv, 982p. 1992. lib. bdg. 45.00 (*1-56859-009-1*, Pub. by Farhang Moaser Pubs) Mazda Pubs.

***Batens, Diderik.** Frontiers of Paraconsistent Logic. LC 99-54624. (Studies in Logic & Computation Ser.). 2000. write for info. (*0-86380-253-2*) Taylor & Francis.

Batens, Diderik & Van Dendegem, Jean P., eds. Theory & Experiment: Recent Insights & New Perspectives on Their Relation. 296p. (C). 1988. text 140.50 (*90-277-2645-0*, D Reidel) Kluwer Academic.

Bater & French. Studies in Russian Historical Geography, 2 vols. 1983. 237.00 (*0-12-081200-2*) Acad Pr.

Bater, James H. Russia & the Post Soviet Scene: A Geographical Perspective. LC 96-221604. (Arnold Publications). 368p. 1996. pap. text 39.95 (*0-340-60149-3*) OUP.

— The Soviet Scene: A Geographical Perspective. (Illus.). 256p. 1989. 49.50 (*0-7131-6613-4*, Pub. by E A); pap. text 16.95 (*0-7131-6420-4*, Pub. by E A) Routldge.

Bates. Becoming an Art Teacher. (Education Ser.). 2000. pap. text 72.95 (*0-534-52239-4*) Brooks-Cole.

***Bates.** Broadband Telecommunications Handbook. 656p. 1999. 65.00 (*0-07-134648-1*) McGraw.

Bates. Genetics Module. 1998. pap. 10.50 (*0-07-233501-7*) McGraw.

Bates. Normandy Before 1066. 2nd ed. 1996. pap. text. write for info. (*0-582-08410-5*) Longman.

Bates. People & Culture of the Middle East. 2nd ed. 352p. 2000. pap. 36.00 (*0-13-656489-5*) P-H.

— Resources for Teaching Ideas. 1996. pap. text, teacher ed. 23.00 (*0-312-13805-9*) St Martin.

— Whats in a Name. 1998. pap. text 14.00 (*0-205-28388-8*, Longwood Div) Allyn.

Bates & Fratkin. Cultural Anthropology. 2nd ed. 493p. 1998. pap. text 59.00 (*0-205-28062-5*) P-H.

Bates, et al. Lushootseed Dictionary. rev. ed. LC 94-5716. Orig. Title: Dictionary of Puget Salish. 381p. 1994. reprint ed. pap. 35.00 (*0-295-97323-4*) U of Wash Pr.

Bates, J. Leonard. Senator T. J. Walsh of Montana: Law & Public Affairs, from Truman to FDR. LC 98-58022. (Illus.). 410p. 1999. 39.95 (*0-252-02470-2*) U of Ill Pr.

Bates & Wacker SC Staff & European Commission. Tourism & the European Union: A Practical Guide: EU Funding, Other Support, EU Policy & Tourism. LC 97-168125. 1996. 30.00 (*92-827-5734-X*, Pub. by Comm Europ Commun) Bernan Associates.

Bates, A. Dead Game. 176p. (J). (gr. 7-9). 1993. pap. 3.99 (*0-590-45829-9*) Scholastic Inc.

— Final Exam. 208p. (YA). (gr. 7-9). 1990. pap. 3.25 (*0-590-43291-5*, Point) Scholastic Inc.

— Krazy 4 U. (J). 1996. mass mkt. 3.99 (*0-590-50951-9*) Scholastic Inc.

— More Chiller Thriller. (J). 1992. pap., boxed set 12.70 (*0-590-66251-1*) Scholastic Inc.

— Mother's Helper. 176p. (YA). (gr. 7-9). 1991. 3.25 (*0-590-44582-0*, Point) Scholastic Inc.

— Party Line. 176p. (J). (gr. 7 up). 1989. pap. 3.99 (*0-590-44238-4*) Scholastic Inc.

— What's the Opposite of a Best Friend? 160p. (J). (gr. 4-7). 1993. pap. 2.95 (*0-590-44145-0*) Scholastic Inc.

Bates, A. P., et al. The System of Criminal Law: Cases & Materials - New South Wales. 1040p. 1979. pap. 98.00 (*0-409-30441-7*, A.T., MICHIE) LEXIS Pub.

Bates, A. Tony. Technology, Open Learning, & Distance Education. LC 94-44835. (Studies in Distance Education). 240p. (C). 1995. pap. 25.99 (*0-415-12799-8*) Routledge.

Bates, A. W., jt. auth. see Epper, Rhonda M.

Bates, Adams. Dover: A Family Portrait. (Images of America Ser.). 1995. pap. 12.99 (*0-7524-0201-3*) Arcadia Publng.

Bates, Albert. Climate in Crisis: The Greenhouse Effect & What We Can Do. LC 89-17890. (Illus.). 228p. (Orig.). 1990. pap. 11.95 (*0-913990-67-1*) Book Pub Co.

Bates, Albert C. Bates. Ancestral Lines for Eight Generations of Capt. Lemuel Bates, 1729-1820, with Some Records of His Descendants. 68p. 1997. reprint ed. pap. 14.00 (*0-8328-7421-3*); reprint ed. lib. bdg. 24.00 (*0-8328-7420-5*) Higginson Bk Co.

— East Granby Records of the Congregational Church in Turkey Hills, Now the Town of East Granby, 1776-1858. (Illus.). 158p. 1997. reprint ed. pap. 19.50 (*0-8328-5638-X*) Higginson Bk Co.

— East Granby Records of the Society or Parish of Turkey Hills, Now the Town of East Granby, 1737-1791. 78p. 1997. reprint ed. pap. 15.50 (*0-8328-5637-1*) Higginson Bk Co.

— The Work of Hartford's First Printer. 16p. 1925. pap. 1.00 (*0-940748-47-9*) Conn Hist Soc.

Bates, Albert K. & Batchelor, Bruce T. Yukon Channel Charts: Sternwheeler-Style Strip Maps of the Historic Yukon River. 3rd ed. LC 96-910403. (Illus.). 68p. 1997. spiral bd. 12.64 (*1-55212-000-7*, No. 96-0003) Trafford Pub.

Bates, Albert K., jt. auth. see Bates, Dorothy R.

Bates, Alfred, et al, eds. The Drama, Its History, Literature & Influence on Civilization, 22 vols. (Illus.). reprint ed. write for info. (*0-404-02190-5*) AMS Pr.

Bates, Alfred C., ed. Rolls of Connecticut Men in the French & Indian War, 1755-1762 Vols. IX & X: Collections of the Connecticut Historical Society, 2 vols. 852p. 1997. reprint ed. pap. 70.00 (*0-8063-4679-5*) Clearfield Co.

Bates, Alice. For All Time: The Story of Ann Judson. 48p. (J). (gr. 1-6). 1998. pap. text 6.95 (*1-56309-257-3*, N987102) Womans Mission Union.

— Missions Day Camp: Biovocational Missionaries. Gross, Karen, ed. 23p. (J). (gr. 1-6). 1992. pap. text 2.95 (*1-56309-058-9*, W927106) Womans Mission Union.

Bates, Andrea & Hanson, Norm. Aquatic Exercise Therapy. Biblis, Margaret, ed. LC 95-19485. 240p. 1996. pap. text 37.00 (*0-7216-5681-1*, W B Saunders Co) Harcrt Hlth Sci Grp.

Bates, Andrew. Trinity. 1997. 29.95 (*1-56504-750-8*) White Wolf.

Bates, Andrew, jt. auth. see Radner, Ronni.

Bates, Anna L. Weeder in the Garden of the Lord: Anthony Comstock's Life & Career. 226p. (C). Date not set. lib. bdg. 39.50 (*0-7618-0076-X*) U Pr of Amer.

Bates, Anthony W. Managing Technological Change: Strategies for College & University Leaders. LC 99-44483. 320p. 1999. 34.95 (*0-7879-4681-8*) Jossey-Bass.

***Bates, Ara, ed.** Cuba: Issues & Bibliography. 245p. 2000. lib. bdg. 59.00 (*1-56072-832-9*) Nova Sci Pubs.

Bates, Arlo. In the Bundle of Time. LC 71-116937. (Short Story Index Reprint Ser.). 1977. 23.95 (*0-8369-3439-3*) Ayer.

— The Intoxicated Ghost & Other Stories, Vol 1. LC 72-4419. (Short Story Index Reprint Ser.). 1977. reprint ed. 23.95 (*0-8369-4170-5*) Ayer.

— The Pagans. LC 70-104411. 275p. reprint ed. lib. bdg. 32.00 (*0-8398-0153-X*) Irvington.

— The Pagans. (C). 1986. reprint ed. pap. text 7.95 (*0-8290-1860-3*) Irvington.

— The Philistines. LC 74-104412. 442p. reprint ed. lib. bdg. 32.00 (*0-8398-0154-8*) Irvington.

— The Philistines. 442p. (C). 1986. reprint ed. pap. text 8.95 (*0-8290-1880-8*) Irvington.

— The Puritans. LC 68-20005. (Americans in Fiction Ser.). 424p. reprint ed. pap. text 5.95 (*0-89197-911-5*); reprint ed. lib. bdg. 29.00 (*0-8398-0155-6*) Irvington.

Bates, Arthenia J. Seeds Beneath the Snow: Vignettes from the South. LC 69-18851. 146p. 1975. 14.95 (*0-88258-046-9*) Howard U Pr.

Bates, Austin A., ed. Schenectady County: Its History to the Close of the Nineteenth Century. With Biographical Sketches. (Illus.). 721p. 1997. reprint ed. lib. bdg. 75.00 (*0-8328-6231-2*) Higginson Bk Co.

Bates, Barbara. Bargaining for Life: A Social History of Tuberculosis, 1876-1938. LC 91-40040. (Studies in Health, Illness, & Caregiving). (Illus.). 456p. (Orig.). (C). 1992. pap. text 20.95 (*0-8122-1367-X*) U of Pa Pr.

Bates, Barbara, et al. A Guide to Physical Examination & History Taking. 6th ed. LC 94-11970. (Illus.). 736p. 1994. text 57.95 (*0-397-55053-7*, Lippnctt) Lppncott W & W.

Bates, Barclay. The Last of the White Guys. LC 98-74017. 240p. 1999. 18.95 (*0-9667039-9-5*, 1) Bloomsbury.

***Bates, Barry T.** Biology 1470. 1999. pap. text 13.70 (*1-56870-363-5*) RonJon Pub.

— Biology 1472. (C). 1999. pap. text 12.64 (*1-56870-362-7*) RonJon Pub.

Bates, Benjamin J., ed. Economic Impacts of the 1996 Telecommunications Act: A Special Issue of "The Journal of Media Economics" 63p. 1998. pap. 20.00 (*0-8058-9828-X*) L Erlbaum Assocs.

Bates, Beverly. Divorce Hits Home: Christian Living - Encouragement. Nelson, Becky, ed. 20p. (YA). (gr. 7-12). 1994. pap. text 1.95 (*1-56309-087-2*, C946106, Wrld Changers Res) Womans Mission Union.

Bates, Bill. Shoot for the Star. 272p. 1996. mass mkt. 5.99 (*0-8499-3986-0*) Word Pub.

Bates, Bill & Butterworth, Bill. Shoot for the Star. LC 94-30584. 1994. 19.99 (*0-8499-1170-2*) Word Pub.

Bates, Bob. Adventures in Acrylics & Oils, No. 1. (How to Draw & Paint Ser.). (Illus.). 32p. (Orig.). 1989. pap. 6.95 (*0-929261-42-9*, HT186) W Foster Pub.

— Adventures in Acrylics & Oils, No. 2. (How to Draw & Paint Ser.). (Illus.). 32p. (Orig.). 1989. pap. 6.95 (*0-929261-45-3*, HT200) W Foster Pub.

— Expressive Drawing: Mastering the Art of Sketching. (Illus.). (Orig.). 1985. pap. 10.95 (*0-917121-02-3*, 40-100) M F Weber Co.

Bates, Bradford, jt. ed. see Simms, Ronald.

***Bates, Brian & McHorney, Chris.** Developing a Theoretical Model of Counterproliferation for the 21st Century. LC 00-36438. 248p. 2000. text 89.95 (*0-7734-7767-5*) E Mellen.

Bates, Bud. Client/Server Internetworking. LC 97-37414. (Illus.). 352p. 1997. pap. text 50.00 (*0-07-005442-8*) McGraw.

— Wireless Networked Communications Concepts, Technology & Implementation. 304p. 1994. 55.00 (*0-07-004674-3*) McGraw.

Bates, Bud & Gregory, Donald. Voice & Data Communications Handbook. LC 95-22058. (Illus.). 660p. 1996. text 65.00 (*0-07-005147-X*) McGraw.

B

Bates, C. C., et al. Geophysics in the Affairs of Man: A Personalized History of Exploration Geophysics & Its Allied Sciences of Seismology & Oceanography. (Illus.). 536p. 1982. 225.00 (*0-08-024026-7*, Pub. by Pergamon Repr) Franklin.

Bates, Carolyn M. & Brodsky, Annette M. Sex in the Therapy Hour: A Case of Professional Incest. LC 88-19032. 236p. 1993. pap. text 18.95 (*0-89862-098-8*) Guilford Pubns.

Bates, Carson & Wigtil, James. Skill Building for Drug Education. 100p. 1994. pap. text 35.00 (*0-86720-757-4*) Jones & Bartlett.

Bates, Channing, ed. see Shane, Victor.

Bates, Charles. Ransoming the Mind: An Integration of Yoga & Modern Therapy. LC 86-50084. (Illus.). 329p. (Orig.). 1986. pap. 11.95 (*0-936663-00-6*) Yes Intl.

Bates, Charles C. & Fuller, John F. America's Weather Warriors, 1814-1985. LC 85-40746. (Illus.). 384p. 1986. 34.95 (*0-89096-240-5*) Tex A&M Univ Pr.

Bates, Charles F. Central Information File: Conversion & Implementation. LC 76-55780. (Bank Study Ser.). 191p. reprint ed. pap. 59.30 (*0-608-16775-4*, 205218200053) Bks Demand.

Bates, Charlotte F. Cambridge Book of Poetry. LC 72-80371. (Granger Index Reprint Ser.). 1977. 31.95 (*0-8369-6052-1*) Ayer.

Bates, Christopher. Culture Shock! Taiwan. (Illus.). 280p. 1994. pap. 12.95 (*1-55868-175-2*) Gr Arts Ctr Pub.

Bates, Christopher J., jt. auth. see Williams, Anthony N.

Bates, Clement. Law of Limited Partnership. xxii, 275p. 1996. reprint ed. 42.50 (*0-8377-1982-8*, Rothman) W S Hein.

Bates, Colleen D. The Eclectic Gourmet Guide to Los Angeles. 2nd rev. ed. LC 98-53671. 320p. 1999. pap. 11.95 (*0-89732-297-5*) Menasha Ridge.

Bates, Cornelia F., tr. see Becquer, Gustavo A.

Bates, Craig D. & Lee, Martha J. Tradition & Innovation: A Basket History of the Indians of the Yosemite- Mono Lake Area. (Illus.). 225p. (C). 1994. 49.95 (*0-939666-54-5*) Yosemite Assn.

Bates, Craig D. & Medley, Steven P., eds. Legends of the Yosemite Miwok. 2nd rev. ed. (Illus.). 1993. reprint ed. pap. 11.95 (*0-939666-57-X*) Yosemite Assn.

***Bates, Crispin.** South Asians Ii Diaspora: Community, Empire & Migration. LC 00-33318. (Illus.). 2000. write for info. (*0-312-23595-X*) St Martin.

***Bates, Cynthia.** Courage on the Line. (Sports Stories Ser.). 117p. (J). (gr. 3-7). 1999. pap. 5.50 (*1-55028-648-X*, Pub. by J Lorimer) Orca Bk Pubs.

Bates, Cynthia. Mikayla's Victory, Vol. 29. 100p. (J). (gr. 3-8). 1999. text 5.50 (*1-55028-638-2*, Pub. by J Lorimer) Orca Bk Pubs.

Bates, D. B. Incidents on Land & Water: or Four Years on the Pacific Coast: Being a Narrative of the Burning of the Ships Nonantum, Humayoon, & Fanchon. LC 74-3930. (Women in America Ser.). (Illus.). 344p. 1974. reprint ed. 29.95 (*0-405-06076-9*) Ayer.

Bates, D. E. B. Field Geology in Color. (Color Ser.). 1977. 7.95 (*0-668-04208-7*, ARCO) Macmillan.

Bates, D. V., et al, eds. Assessment of Inhalation Hazards. (Illus.). 382p. 1989. 73.00 (*3-540-50952-6*, 509526) Spr-Verlag.

Bates, Daisy. The Long Shadow of Little Rock. LC 86-19129. 260p. 1987. reprint ed. pap. 16.00 (*0-938626-75-2*) U of Ark Pr.

Bates, Daniel & Plog, Fred. Cultural Anthropology. 3rd ed. (C). 1990. text 52.25 (*0-07-004066-4*) McGraw.

— Cultural Anthropology. 3rd ed. (C). 1990. text 19.06 (*0-07-004067-2*) McGraw.

Bates, Daniel & Rassam, Amal. Peoples & Cultures of the Middle East. (Illus.). 288p. 1996. pap. text 47.33 (*0-13-656793-2*) P-H.

Bates, Daniel G. Human Adaptive Strategies: Culture, Ecology, & Politics. LC 97-36032. 198p. 1997. pap. text 29.00 (*0-205-26998-2*) P-H.

Bates, Daniel G. & Lees, Susan H., eds. Case Studies in Human Ecology. LC 96-9676. (Illus.). 391p. (C). 1996. pap. 41.00 (*0-306-45246-4*, Plenum Trade) Perseus Pubng.

Bates, Daniel G. & Lees, Susan H., eds. Case Studies in Human Ecology. LC 96-9676. (Illus.). 391p. (C). 1996. 69.50 (*0-306-45245-6*, Plenum Trade) Perseus Pubng.

Bates, Daniel G. & Plog, Fred. Human Adaptive Strategies. (C). 1991. text 24.50 (*0-07-004071-0*) McGraw.

Bates, Daryl, jt. ed. see Ables, Hildred Hughes.

Bates, David. Breaking Trail in the Central Appalachians: A Narrative. LC 87-72050. 194p. 1987. 12.50 (*0-915746-35-2*) Potomac Appalach.

Bates, David, ed. Regesta Regum Anglo-Normannorum: The Acta of William I, 1066-1087. 1,192p. 1999. text 175.00 (*0-19-820674-7*) OUP.

Bates, David & Curry, Anne, eds. England & Normandy in the Middle Ages. LC 94-26433. xiv, 336 p. 1994. 65.00 (*1-85285-083-3*) Hambledon Press.

Bates, David & Maxwell, T. G. Luxford's Police Law in New Zealand. 4th ed. 675p. 1991. boxed set 144.00 (*0-409-78728-0*, NZ, MICHIE) LEXIS Pub.

Bates, David H. Lincoln in the Telegraph Office: Recollections of the United States Military Telegraph Corps During the Civil War. LC 95-10908. (Illus.). xxi, 432p. 1995. pap. 14.95 (*0-8032-6125-X*, Bison Books) U of Nebr Pr.

— Lincoln in the Telegraph Office: Recollections of the United States Military Telegraph Corps During the Civil War. large type unabridged ed. (Illus.). viii, 432p. (C). 1996. reprint ed. 33.95 (*1-889881-09-0*) Old Bks Pub.

***Bates, David J.** Angel Flight to New Jerusalem: The End of Time. 172p. 1999. pap. 9.95 (*0-7392-0467-X*, PO3780) Morris Pubng.

Bates, David M., et al, eds. Biology & Utilization of the Curcurbitaceae. LC 89-42885. (Illus.). 503p. reprint ed. pap. 156.00 (*0-608-20872-8*, 207197100003) Bks Demand.

Bates, David V. A Citizen's Guide to Air Pollution. LC 72-75504. (Environmental Damage & Control in Canada Ser.: No. 2). (Illus.). 160p. reprint ed. pap. 49.60 (*0-7837-1162-X*, 204169100022) Bks Demand.

— Environmental Health Risks & Public Policy: Decision Making in Free Societies. LC 94-2410. (Jessie & John Danz Lectures). 1994. 30.00 (*0-295-97336-6*) U of Wash Pr.

— Environmental Health Risks & Public Policy: Decision Making in Free Societies. LC 94-2410. (Jessie & John Danz Lectures). (Illus.). 117p. 1994. pap. 12.95 (*0-295-97337-4*) U of Wash Pr.

— Respiratory Function in Disease. 3rd ed. 560p. 1989. text 77.00 (*0-7216-1592-9*, W B Saunders Co) Harcrt Hlth Sci Grp.

Bates, Don, ed. Knowledge & the Scholarly Medical Traditions. LC 96-7762. (Illus.). 383p. (C). 1995. text 64.95 (*0-521-48071-X*); pap. text 24.95 (*0-521-49975-5*) Cambridge U Pr.

Bates, Donald. Architecture after Geometry. 112p. 1997. pap. 39.95 (*0-471-97686-5*) Wiley.

Bates, Donald L., jt. auth. see Krell, David F.

Bates, Dorothy R. Eat Cheaply: Simple, Easy & Delicious Meals for 4 for Under $10. 160p. (Orig.). 1996. pap. write for info. (*1-882330-06-4*) Magni Co.

— The George Bernard Shaw Vegetarian Cookbook in Six Acts: Based on George Bernard Shaw's Favorite Recipes. rev. ed. Minney, R. J., ed. & adapted by by. LC 86-73060. (Illus.). 144p. 1987. pap. 8.95 (*0-913990-51-5*) Book Pub Co.

— Holiday Diet Cookbook: How to Survive the Holidays (& Never Break Your Diet) rev. ed. Barnard, Neal D., ed. (Illus.). 96p. 1994. pap. write for info. (*1-882330-04-8*) Magni Co.

— Holiday Diet Cookbook: How to Survive the Holidays, & Never Break Your Diet. 3rd ed. Barnard, Neal D., ed. (Illus.). 64p. 1994. reprint ed. pap. 9.95 (*1-882330-43-9*) Magni Co.

— Holiday Diet Cookbook: Survive the Holidays & Never Break Your Diet. 96p. 1993. pap. 9.95 (*1-882330-18-8*) Magni Co.

— Kids Can Cook: Vegetarian Recipes Kitchen-Tested by Kids for Kids. LC 99-35930. (Illus.). 128p. 1999. reprint ed. pap. 12.95 (*1-57067-086-2*) Book Pub Co.

— The Tempeh Cookbook. LC 89-35499. (Illus.). 96p. (Orig.). 1989. pap. 10.95 (*0-913990-65-5*) Book Pub Co.

— TVP Cookbook: Using the Quick-Cooking Meat Substitute. LC 91-27400. (Illus.). 96p. 1991. pap. 7.95 (*0-913990-79-5*) Book Pub Co.

Bates, Dorothy R. & Bates, Albert K. The Y2K Survival Guide & Cookbook. LC 99-179450. (Illus.). 128p. 1999. pap. 12.95 (*0-9669317-0-X*) Global Vill Inst.

Bates, Dorothy R. & Wingate, Colby. Cooking with Gluten & Seitan. LC 92-44423. 128p. 1993. pap. 7.95 (*0-913990-95-7*) Book Pub Co.

Bates, Dorothy R., jt. auth. see Hagler, Louise.

Bates, Douglas. Pulitzer Prize: The Inside Story of America's Most Prestigious Award. 1991. 19.95 (*1-55972-070-0*, Birch Ln Pr) Carol Pub Group.

Bates, Douglas M. & Watts, Donald G. Nonlinear Regression Analysis & Its Applications. LC 88-6065. (Probability & Mathematical Statistics Ser.). 384p. 1988. 114.95 (*0-471-81643-4*) Wiley.

Bates, Douglas M., jt. auth. see Pinheiro, Jose C.

Bates, Edw. C., jt. auth. see DeForest, Heman P.

Bates, Edward. The Diary of Edward Bates, 1859-1866. (American Biography Ser.). 685p. 1991. reprint ed. lib. bdg. 109.00 (*0-7812-8014-1*) Rprt Serv.

Bates, Edward E., Jr. Georgia Domestic Relations Forms. 590p. 1994. spiral bd. 159.00 (*0-87189-061-5*, 80940-10, MICHIE); ring bd., suppl. ed. 85.00 (*0-685-74610-0*, MICHIE) LEXIS Pub.

— Georgia Domestic Relations Forms, Issue 9. 150p. 1998. ring bd. write for info. (*0-327-00546-7*, 8094214) LEXIS Pub.

Bates, Edward F. History & Reminiscences of Denton County. (Illus.). 412p. 1997. reprint ed. lib. bdg. 44.50 (*0-8328-6927-9*) Higginson Bk Co.

Bates, Elizabeth, ed. Language Development: The Essential Readings. (Illus.). 156p. 1999. 59.95 (*0-631-21744-4*); pap. 24.95 (*0-631-21745-2*) Blackwell Pubs.

Bates, Elizabeth, et al. From First Words to Grammar: Individual Differences & Dissociable Mechanisms. (Illus.). 352p. 1988. text 59.95 (*0-521-34142-6*) Cambridge U Pr.

— From First Words to Grammar: Individual Differences & Dissociable Mechanisms. (Illus.). 338p. (C). 1991. pap. text 21.95 (*0-521-42500-X*) Cambridge U Pr.

Bates, Eric, jt. ed. see Hall, Bob.

Bates, Eric R., ed. Black, White & Brown: The Hard Lessons Learned Forty Years after Brown Vs. Board of Education. (Southern Exposure Ser.). (Illus.). 64p. (Orig.). (C). 1994. pap. 5.00 (*0-943810-60-4*) Inst Southern Studies.

— Fishy Business. (Illus.). 64p. (Orig.). 1991. pap. 5.00 (*0-943810-50-7*) Inst Southern Studies.

— Law & Disorder. (Illus.). 64p. (Orig.). 1990. pap. 5.00 (*0-943810-47-7*) Inst Southern Studies.

— Meltdown on Main Street. (Illus.). 64p. (Orig.). 1989. pap. 5.00 (*0-943810-40-X*) Southern Exposure.

— Proud Threads: Twenty Years after Beating J. P. Stevens, What Have Textile Workers Won? (Southern Exposure Ser.). (Illus.). 64p. (Orig.). (C). 1994. pap. 5.00 (*0-943810-59-0*) Inst Southern Studies.

— Southern Exposure Turns Twenty: A Special Anniversary Edition. (Southern Exposure Ser.). (Illus.). 127p. (Orig.). (C). 1993. pap. 8.95 (*0-943810-56-6*) Inst Southern Studies.

— Thrombolysis & Adjunctive Therapy for Acute Myocardial Infarction. LC 92-49831. (Fundamental & Clinical Cardiology Ser.: Vol. 10). (Illus.). 528p. 1992. text 140.00 (*0-8247-8664-5*) Dekker.

Bates, Eric R., ed. No Place Like Home: As Nursing Homes Profit from Pain, Communities Fight to Reform Them. (Southern Exposure Ser.). (Illus.). 64p. (Orig.). (C). 1992. pap. 5.00 (*0-943819-54-7*) Inst Southern Studies.

Bates, Eric R. & Arnow, Pat, eds. Beyond Black & White: As the South Becomes More Diverse, How Will We Face Our Multiracial Future? (Southern Exposure Ser.). (Illus.). 64p. (Orig.). (C). 1994. pap. 5.00 (*0-943810-61-2*) Inst Southern Studies.

Bates, Eric R. & Holmes, David R. Saphenous Vein Bypass Graft Disease. LC 98-5321. (Fundamental & Clinical Cardiology Ser.). (Illus.). 352p. 1998. text 150.00 (*0-8247-9902-X*) Dekker.

Bates, Eric R., ed. see Wood, Peter.

Bates, Erica & Linder-Peiz, Susie. Health Care Issues. 2nd ed. 248p. 1990. pap. 27.95 (*0-04-442108-7*, Pub. by Allen & Unwin Pty) Paul & Co Pubs.

Bates, Ernest S. Story of the Supreme Court. 377p. 1982. reprint ed. 48.50 (*0-8377-0322-0*, Rothman) W S Hein.

Bates, Ernest S. & Allison. Bible. 1993. 25.00 (*0-671-87959-6*) S&S Trade.

Bates, Ernest S., jt. auth. see Carlson, Oliver.

Bates, Evelyn, ed. see Fischer, Lee & Fischer, Bruce.

Bates, F., et al. The Australian Social Worker & the Law. 3rd ed. vii, 349p. 1991. pap. 49.00 (*0-455-21032-2*, Pub. by LawBk Co) Gaunt.

Bates, F. L. Sociopolitical Ecology: Human Systems & Ecological Fields. LC 97-29385. (Contemporary Systems Thinking Ser.). 294p. (C). 1997. 59.50 (*0-306-45653-2*, Plenum Trade) Perseus Pubng.

Bates, F. W. Pacific Odyssey: History of the U. S. S. Steele During WWII. 2nd ed. Swank, Walbrook, ed. LC 98-44055. 92p. 1998. reprint ed. pap. 9.95 (*1-57249-145-0*, Burd St Pr) White Mane Pub.

Bates, Finis L. The Escape & Suicide of John Wilkes Booth: The First True Account of Lincoln's Assassination. 1988. reprint ed. lib. bdg. 65.00 (*0-7812-0171-3*) Rprt Serv.

— The Escape & Suicide of John Wilkes Booth: The First True Account of Lincoln's Assassination, Containing a Complete Confession of Booth Many Years after His Crime. 1979. reprint ed. 59.00 (*0-403-06413-9*, Regency) Scholarly.

Bates, Frank, et al. The Australian Social Worker & the Law. 4th ed. 377p. 1996. pap. 59.00 (*0-455-21382-8*, Pub. by Cavendish Pubng) Gaunt.

Bates, Frank G. Rhode Island & the Formation of the Union. LC 68-1297. (Columbia University. Studies in the Social Sciences: No. 27). reprint ed. 35.00 (*0-404-51027-2*) AMS Pr.

Bates, Fredra, et al. Evalworks: A Template for Speech-Language Evaluations. (Illus.). 60p. (Orig.). (C). 1988. pap. write for info. (*0-318-63775-8*) SW Linguistic.

Bates, G. M. Environmental Law in Australia. 3rd ed. 1991. pap. 76.00 (*0-409-30309-7*, AT, MICHIE) LEXIS Pub.

Bates, G. W. Natural History Museums Vol. 1: An Illustrated Guide to Over 350 Museums in the Eastern United States. 1992. pap. 12.95 (*0-9629759-5-8*) Batax Mus.

— Your Fortune in Real Estate Photography. 1996. pap. 19.95 (*0-9629759-7-4*) Batax Mus.

Bates, G. W., ed. Museum Jobs from A-Z. LC 94-153083. 1994. pap. text 9.95 (*0-9629759-4-X*) Batax Mus.

Bates, Gale. Tales of Tutu Nene & Nele. (Illus.). 36p. (J). (ps-4). 1991. 10.95 (*0-89610-193-2*) Island Heritage.

Bates, Gary D., jt. auth. see Tirella, Russ.

Bates, Gary L. Refrigeration Systems & Accessories. (Illus.). 342p. 1991. teacher ed., ring bd. 100.00 (*1-928594-28-X*); student ed., ring bd. 100.00 (*1-928594-27-1*) BOMI Inst.

Bates, Georgia, jt. auth. see Bardi, Carol A.

Bates, Grace F., ed. Mason's Basic Medical-Surgical Nursing. 6th ed. LC 96-9332. (Illus.). 835p. 1996. text 45.00 (*0-07-105428-6*) McGraw-Hill HPD.

Bates, Grace F., et al. Basic Drug Therapy & Arithmetic Review. 5th ed. 419p. 1991. text 21.95 (*0-07-105244-5*) McGraw-Hill HPD.

Bates, Grace F., jt. auth. see Mason, Mildred A.

Bates, Graham & Bowles, Jane. Money & the Markets: An Astrological Guide. 240p. 1994. pap. 16.00 (*1-85538-370-5*, Pub. by Aqrn Pr) Harper SF.

Bates, Greg, ed. see Novick, Michael.

***Bates, Guy.** Leper & Other Strangers. (Illus.). vi, 136p. 2000. 24.95 (*0-9679472-0-0*) Wysiwyg Pubng.

Bates, H. E. The Best of H. E. Bates. LC 76-167441. (Short Story Index Reprint Ser.). 1977. reprint ed. 37.95 (*0-8369-3967-0*) Ayer.

— Black Boxer: Tales. LC 73-178437. (Short Story Index Reprint Ser.). 1977. reprint ed. 20.95 (*0-8369-4037-7*) Ayer.

— A Crown of Wild Myrtle. 144p. 1995. 18.95 (*1-85695-346-7*, Pub. by ISIS Lrg Prnt) Transaction Pubs.

— The Darling Buds of May: The Pop Larkin Chronicles. large type ed. LC 93-15035. 644p. 1993. lib. bdg. 22.95 (*1-56054-730-8*) Thorndike Pr.

— Day's End & Other Stories. 1971. reprint ed. 39.00 (*0-403-00504-3*) Scholarly.

— Elephant's Nest in a Rhubarb Tree & Other Stories. LC 88-38040. (New Directions Classics Ser.). 216p. 1989. 17.95 (*0-8112-1087-1*, Pub. by New Directions); pap. 9.95 (*0-8112-1088-X*, NDP669, Pub. by New Directions) Norton.

— The Fallow Land. LC 79-144867. (Literature Ser.). 328p. 1972. reprint ed. 39.00 (*0-403-00854-9*) Scholarly.

— The Flying Goat. large type ed. 336p. 1995. 27.99 (*0-7089-3423-4*) Ulverscroft.

— A House of Women. large type ed. 1991. 11.50 (*0-7089-2402-6*) Ulverscroft.

— The Jacaranda Tree. 21.95 (*0-8488-0911-4*) Amereon Ltd.

— A Month by the Lake & Other Stories. LC 87-5680. (New Directions Classics Ser.). 224p. 1987. 17.95 (*0-8112-1035-9*, Pub. by New Directions); pap. 9.95 (*0-8112-1036-7*, NDP645, Pub. by New Directions) Norton.

— A Party for the Girls: Six Stories. LC 87-26874. (New Directions Classics Ser.). 224p. 1988. 21.95 (*0-8112-1050-2*, Pub. by New Directions); pap. 10.95 (*0-8112-1051-0*, NDP653, Pub. by New Directions) Norton.

— Spella-Ho. large type ed. 1991. 27.99 (*0-7089-2474-3*) Ulverscroft.

— Through the Woods: The English Woodland - April to April. (Illus.). 144p. 1995. 30.00 (*0-7112-0992-8*, Pub. by F Lincoln) Trafalgar.

— The Two Sisters. large type ed. (General Fiction Ser.). 416p. 1993. 27.99 (*0-7089-2963-X*) Ulverscroft.

— Woman Who Had Imagination & Other Stories. LC 77-103239. (Short Story Index Reprint Ser.). 1977. 20.95 (*0-8369-3276-5*) Ayer.

Bates, Harry E., ed. Connecting Time & Space. (Illus.). 136p. (Orig.). (C). 1992. reprint ed. per. 26.00 (*0-917853-47-4*) Am Assn Physics.

Bates, Henry & Busenbark, R. Finches & Softbilled Birds. 735p. 1970. 29.95 (*0-86622-654-0*, H-908) TFH Pubns.

Bates, Henry J. & Busenbark, Robert I. Parrots & Related Birds. (Illus.). 494p. 1978. 29.95 (*0-87666-967-4*, H-912) TFH Pubns.

Bates, Inge & Riseborough, George. Youth & Inequality. LC 92-43088. 1993. pap. 34.95 (*0-335-15695-9*) OpUniv Pr.

Bates, Ira J., ed. see National Hospice Organization Staff.

Bates, Irene & Smith, E. Gary. Lost Legacy: The Mormon Office of Presiding Patriarch. LC 95-5370. (Illus.). 368p. 1995. text 32.50 (*0-252-02163-0*) U of Ill Pr.

***Bates, Ivan.** All by Myself. LC 99-71483. (Illus.). 32p. (J). (ps-2). 2000. 14.95 (*0-06-028585-0*) HarpC.

— All By Myself. LC 99-71483. 32p. (J). (ps-2). pap. 4.95 (*0-06-443608-X*) HarpC Child Bks.

Bates, J., jt. auth. see Jones, P. C.

Bates, J. B., ed. Thin-Film Solid Ionic Devices & Materials. LC 95-61595. (Proceedings Ser.: Vol. 95-22). (Illus.). 232p. 1996. 47.00 (*1-56677-117-X*) Electrochem Soc.

***Bates, J. Douglas.** The Pulitzer Prize: The Inside Story of America's Most Prestigious Award. (Illus.). 291p. 2000. reprint ed. text 20.00 (*0-7881-9053-9*) DIANE Pub.

Bates, J. K. & Seefeldt, W. B., eds. Scientific Basis for Nuclear Waste Management X. (MRS Symposium Proceedings Ser.: Vol. 84). 1987. text 17.50 (*0-931837-49-9*) Materials Res.

Bates, J. M. & Weber, C. I., eds. Ecological Assessments of Effluent Impacts on Communities of Indigenous Aquatic Organisms - STP 730. 328p. 1981. 32.50 (*0-8031-0801-X*, STP730) ASTM.

Bates, J. R., et al, eds. Understanding Climate: Selected Works of Yale Mintz. LC 93-33951. (Illus.). 336p. 1993. 62.00 (*0-937194-30-1*) A Deepak Pub.

Bates, J. Regis & Gregory, Donald. Voice & Data Communications Handbook: Signature Edition. 2nd ed. LC 97-41786. (Series on Computer Communications). (Illus.). 902p. 1997. pap. 65.00 (*0-07-006396-6*) McGraw.

Bates, James D. Minnesota Legal Forms, 1981-1993: Probate. 180p. ring bd. 69.95 incl. disk (*0-917126-97-1*, MICHIE) LEXIS Pub.

— Minnesota Legal Forms, 1981-1993: Probate. 180p. 1993. ring bd., suppl. ed. 25.00 (*0-685-49511-6*, MICHIE) LEXIS Pub.

Bates, James L. The Origins of Teapot Dome: Progressive Parties & Petroleum. LC 78-5265. (Illus.). 278p. 1978. reprint ed. lib. bdg. 65.00 (*0-313-20383-0*, BAOT, Greenwood Pr) Greenwood.

***Bates, Jared L., ed.** Special Inspection of "Initial Entry Training Equal Opportunity/Sexual Harassment Policies & Procedures" 80p. (C). 2000. pap. text 20.00 (*0-7881-8734-1*) DIANE Pub.

Bates, Jeff, ed. see Blehert, Dean.

An Asterisk (*) at the beginning of an entry indicates that the title is appearing for the first time.

Bates, Jefferson D. Jazzbo Brown from Reston Town: Poems for Moldy Figs: A Jazz Reminiscence. (Poetry Ser.: No. 5). (Illus.). (Orig.). 1993. pap. 4.95 (*0-938823-06-X*) Pogment Pr.

— Poems for Old Geezers & Young Whippersnappers. (Poetry Ser.: No. 4). (Illus.). 96p. (Orig.). 1990. pap. 6.95 (*0-938823-04-3*) Pogment Pr.

***Bates, Jefferson D.** Writing with Precision: How to Write So That You Cannot Possibly Be Misunderstood. LC 99-46544. 288p. 2000. pap. 13.95 (*0-14-028853-8*) Penguin Putnam.

Bates, Jeffrey D. & Hucek, Jeffrey M. Minnesota Legal Forms: Probate. Date not set. ring bd. 95.00 (*0-327-01031-2*, 81804, MICHIE) LEXIS Pub.

Bates, Jem. The Canadian Writer's Market. 13th rev. ed. 336p. 1998. pap. 19.99 (*0-7710-8770-5*) McCland & Stewart.

— Canadian Writer's Market: An Extensive Guide for Freelance Writers. 11th ed. 1994. pap. 14.95 (*0-7710-8795-0*) McCland & Stewart.

Bates, Jennifer. The First Night Out of Eden. LC 97-46987. (University of Central Florida Contemporary Poetry Ser.). 80p. 1998. 19.95 (*0-8130-1596-0*); pap. 10.95 (*0-8130-1597-9*) U Press Fla.

Bates-Jensen, Barbara & Sussman, Carrie. Wound Care: A Collaborative Practice Manual for Physical Therapists & Nurses. LC 97-40496. 608p. 1998. 58.00 (*0-8342-0748-6*) Aspen Pub.

Bates, John. A Northwoods Companion: Fall & Winter. (Illus.). 240p. (Orig.). 1997. pap. 14.95 (*0-9656763-1-5*) Manitowish River.

— A Northwoods Companion: Spring & Summer. LC 97-70781. (Illus.). 240p. (Orig.). 1997. pap. 14.95 (*0-9656763-0-7*) Manitowish River.

***Bates, John.** Quirky Quiz Questions. (Illus.). 224p. 2001. pap. 9.95 (*0-7160-2094-7*, Pub. by Elliot RW Bks) Midpt Trade.

Bates, John. Trailside Botany: 101 Favorite Trees, Ferns, & Wildflowers of the Upper Midwest. LC 95-14380. (Illus.). 240p. (Orig.). 1995. pap. 12.95 (*1-57025-070-7*) Pfeifer-Hamilton.

Bates, John, et al, eds. Protecting Children: Challenges & Change. LC 96-80033. 288p. 1997. text 64.95 (*1-85742-323-2*, Pub. by Arena) Ashgate Pub Co.

***Bates, John, et al, eds.** Protecting Children: Challenges & Change. 263p. 1999. pap. 34.95 (*0-7546-1129-9*) Ashgate Pub Co.

Bates, John & Bates, Nina. Abingdon Christmas Drama Collection for Children. 40p. (Orig.). 1993. pap. 5.95 (*0-687-07774-5*) Abingdon.

Bates, John E. & Wachs, Theodore D., eds. Temperament: Individual Differences at the Interface of Biology & Behavior. LC 93-47187. (Illus.). 362p. 1994. text 29.95 (*1-55798-222-8*) Am Psychol.

Bates, John H. & Benson, Charles J. Marine Environment Law. (Lloyd's Shipping Law Library). ring bd. 395.00 (*1-85044-452-8*) LLP.

Bates, Jonathan B. Creating Lightweight Components with ATL. LC 98-88516. (Orig.). 1999. pap. text 49.99 (*0-672-31535-1*) Sams.

Bates, Jonathan B. & Tompkins, Timothy J. Practical Visual C++ 6. 1999. pap. 29.99 (*0-7897-2142-2*) Que.

Bates, Jonathan B., jt. auth. see Jones, P.

Bates, Jonathan G. Managing Value for Money in the Public Sector. LC 92-38464. 264p. 1993. mass mkt. 79.95 (*0-412-46360-1*) Chapman & Hall.

Bates, Joseph D. Atlantic Salmon Flies & Fishing. LC 96-33186. (Illus.). 400p. 1995. 34.95 (*0-8117-0181-6*) Stackpole.

— Streamer Fly Tying & Fishing. LC 94-44618. (Illus.). 384p. 1995. 34.95 (*0-8117-1702-X*) Stackpole.

Bates, Joseph D. & Richards, Pamela B. Fishing Atlantic Salmon: The Flies & the Patterns. LC 95-49549. (Illus.). 416p. 1996. 75.00 (*0-8117-0636-2*) Stackpole.

Bates, Joseph D., Jr. & Strand, Mark. Find Fish Anywhere, Anytime. LC 81-61686. (Complete Angler's Library). 233p. 1991. write for info. (*0-914697-39-0*) N Amer Outdoor Grp.

Bates, Judy F. China Dog: And Other Tales from a Chinese Laundry. LC 98-114712. 152p. 1998. pap. write for info. (*1-896705-30-8*) Sister Vis Pr.

Bates, Julia. One Road down from the Wilderness. LC 89-32035. (Illus.). 80p. (Orig.). 1989. pap. 7.50 (*0-931832-30-6*) Fithian Pr.

— Vernissage: Poems. LC 98-14176. (Illus.). 72p. 1998. pap. 10.00 (*1-56474-266-0*) Fithian Pr.

Bates, Karen & Hudson, Karen E. Basic Black: Home Training for Modern Times. 1997. 24.95 (*0-614-25352-7*) Doubleday.

Bates, Karen, ed. see Stocking, Jerry.

Bates, Karen Grigsby & Hudson, Karen E. Basic Black: Home Training for Modern Times. 496p. 1996. 26.00 (*0-385-48434-8*) Doubleday.

Bates, Katharine L. America the Beautiful. LC 92-46199. (Illus.). 32p. (J). 1993. text, lib. bdg. 16.00 (*0-689-31861-8*) Atheneum Yung Read.

Bates, Katharine L., ed. Ballad Book. LC 78-103081. (Granger Index Reprint Ser.). 1977. 20.95 (*0-8369-6096-3*) Ayer.

Bates, Katharine L. & Coman, Katharine, eds. English History As Told by English Poets. LC 71-103082. (Granger Index Reprint Ser.). 1977. 25.95 (*0-8369-6097-1*) Ayer.

Bates, Katharine L., tr. see Becquer, Gustavo A.

Bates, Katherine. Do the Dead Depart (1908) 266p. 1998. reprint ed. pap. 18.95 (*0-7661-0596-2*) Kessinger Pub.

Bates, Katherine L. The English Religious Drama. (Works of Katherine Lee Bates). 254p. 1985. reprint ed. lib. bdg. 59.00 (*0-7812-0903-X*) Rprt Serv.

Bates, Katherine L. & Coman, Katherine, eds. English History Told by English Poets. LC 71-103082. (Granger Index Reprint Ser.). 452p. reprint ed. lib. bdg. 23.00 (*0-8290-0506-4*) Irvington.

Bates, Keith, jt. auth. see Heck, Jim.

Bates, Kenneth. The Enamelist. (Illus.). (Orig.). 1991. reprint ed. pap. 25.00 (*0-933847-08-4*) Wooden Porch Bks.

Bates, L. M. The Spirit of London's River. 200p. 1984. 60.00 (*0-905418-43-3*, Pub. by Gresham Bks) St Mut.

— Thames Cavalcade. 208p. 1994. 65.00 (*0-86138-090-8*, Pub. by T Dalton) St Mut.

— The Thames on Fire: The Battle of London River, 1939-1945. 200p. 1990. 39.00 (*0-86138-037-1*, Pub. by T Dalton) St Mut.

Bates, L. M., jt. auth. see Cushman, R. H.

Bates, Larry. The New Economic Disorder. 1994. pap. text 9.99 (*0-88419-383-7*) Creation House.

Bates, Larry M. & Rod, David L., eds. Conservative Systems & Quantum Chaos. LC 96-1821. (Fields Institute Communications Ser.: Vol. 8). 176p. 1996. text 75.00 (*0-8218-0254-2*, FIC/8) Am Math.

Bates, Larry M., jt. auth. see Cushman, Richard H.

Bates, Lincoln S. Two Hours Beyond Atlanta: Day Trips from the Capital of the South, 3. (Adventure Roads Travel Ser.). (Illus.). 144p. 1996. pap. 12.95 (*0-943734-27-4*) Ocean Tree Bks.

Bates, Linda. Transitions: An Interactive Reading, Writing & Grammar Text. 2nd ed. 400p. (C). 1997. pap. text 23.95 (*0-521-65782-2*) Cambridge U Pr.

— Transitions: An Interactive Reading, Writing & Grammar Text: Instructor's Manual. 2nd ed. 60p. (C). 1997. pap., teacher ed. 6.00 (*0-521-65781-4*) Cambridge U Pr.

Bates, Louise. In My Neighborhood: Paint Box Fun. (J). (ps-3). 1993. pap. 1.95 (*0-590-46289-X*) Scholastic Inc.

Bates, Louise A., et al. Your Ten to Fourteen Year Old. 368p. 1989. pap. 11.95 (*0-440-50678-6*) Dell.

Bates, M., ed. Bronchial Carcinoma: An Integrated Approach to Diagnosis & Management. (Illus.). 240p. 1985. 125.00 (*0-387-13234-1*) Spr-Verlag.

Bates, M., jt. auth. see Bates, N.

Bates, M. Searle. Religious Liberty: An Inquiry. LC 77-166096. (Civil Liberties in American History Ser.). 1972. reprint ed. lib. bdg. 59.50 (*0-306-70235-5*) Da Capo.

Bates, Madeleine & Weischedel, Ralph M., eds. Challenges in Natural Language Processing. (Studies in Natural Language Processing). (Illus.). 308p. (C). 1993. text 59.95 (*0-521-41015-0*) Cambridge U Pr.

Bates, Madison C. Bates. Brief History & Genealogy of Joseph Harrison Bates. 52p. 1997. reprint ed. pap. 10.00 (*0-8328-7419-1*); reprint ed. lib. bdg. 20.00 (*0-8328-7418-3*) Higginson Bk Co.

Bates, Malcolm S. Cascade Voices: Conversations with Washington Mountaineers. (Illus.). 224p. 1992. pap. 16.95 (*0-938567-34-9*) Mountaineers.

— Three Fingers: The Mountain, the Men & a Lookout. (Illus.). 160p. 1987. pap. 12.95 (*0-938567-03-9*) Mountaineers.

Bates, Margaret. The Belfast Cookery Book. (Illus.). 230p. 1993. pap. 19.95 (*0-85640-516-7*, Pub. by Blackstaff Pr) Dufour.

— Lake City. 1973. pap. 3.95 (*0-936564-08-3*) Little London.

Bates, Marilyn. Mixed Blood. 36p. 1998. pap. 6.00 (*0-9663293-4-1*) Main St Rag.

Bates, Marilyn, jt. auth. see Keirsey, David West.

Bates, Marston. The Nature of Natural History. 336p. 1950. pap. text 16.95 (*0-691-02446-4*, Pub. by Princeton U Pr) Cal Prin Full Svc.

Bates, Martin. Between Desert & Sea. (C). 1988. 25.00 (*0-904524-50-7*, Pub. by Rivelin Grapheme Pr) St Mut.

Bates, Martine. Prism Moon. (Northern Lights Young Novels Ser.). 165p. (J). (gr. 3-9). 1993. pap. 8.95 (*0-88995-095-4*, Pub. by Red Deer) Genl Dist Srvs.

— The Taker's Key. 208p. 1998. pap. 8.95 (*0-88995-184-5*, Pub. by Red Deer) Genl Dist Srvs.

Bates, Mary E. The Online Deskbook: Online Magazine's Essential Desk Reference for Online & Internet Searchers. (Illus.). 450p. (Orig.). 1995. pap. 29.95 (*0-910965-19-6*) Info Today Inc.

Bates, Mary Ellen. Mining for Gold on the Internet: How to Find Investment & Financial Information on the Internet. 300p. 2000. pap. 24.95 (*0-07-134981-2*) McGraw.

Bates, Mary W. Ellis: Genealogical Data Regarding the Descendants of John Ellis of Sandwich, Massachusetts. (Illus.). 118p. 1997. reprint ed. pap. 19.00 (*0-8328-8468-5*); reprint ed. lib. bdg. 29.00 (*0-8328-8467-7*) Higginson Bk Co.

Bates, Maryann S. Biocultural Dimensions of Chronic Pain: Implications for Treatment of Multi-Ethnic Populations. LC 95-15487. (SUNY Series in Medical Anthropology). 205p. (C). 1995. text 49.50 (*0-7914-2735-8*); pap. text 16.95 (*0-7914-2736-6*) State U NY Pr.

***Bates, MaryEllen.** Super Searchers Do Business: The Online Secrets of Top Business Researchers. Basch, Reva, ed. LC 99-21689. (Super Searchers Ser.). 206p. (C). 1999. pap. 24.95 (*0-910965-33-1*) Info Today Inc.

Bates, Michael. Ultimate. (Bloodlust Ser.). 1995. 9.09 (*0-606-07300-0*, Pub. by Turtleback) Demco.

Bates, Michael & Savage, Elizabeth. Dinars & Dirhams: Coins of the Islamic Lands: The Early Period. (Nasser D. Khalili Collection of Islamic Art: Vol. XIX). (Illus.). 432p. (C). 2000. text 280.00 (*0-19-727617-2*) OUP.

Bates, Michael L. Islamic Coins, 2. 52p. 1982. 8.00 (*0-685-55384-1*) Am Numismatic.

— Islamic Coins, Set. 52p. 1982. boxed set 39.00 (*0-685-55385-X*) Am Numismatic.

***Bates, Michell.** Perfect Pony. (Sandy Lane Stables Ser.). (Illus.). 112p. (J). (gr. 4-9). 1999. pap. text 3.95 (*0-7460-3329-X*, Usborne) EDC.

Bates, Michelle. A Horse for the Summer. (Sandy Lane Stables Ser.). 128p. (J). (gr. 4-8). 1996. pap. 3.95 (*0-7460-2484-3*, Usborne); lib. bdg. 11.95 (*0-88110-842-1*, Usborne) EDC.

— Horse in Danger. (Sandy Lane Stables Ser.). 96p. (J) (gr. 4-8). 1998. pap. 3.95 (*0-7460-3327-3*, Usborne); lib. bdg. 11.95 (*1-58086-148-2*, Usborne) EDC.

— Midnight Horse. (gr. 4-8). 1997. pap. text 3.95 (*0-7460-2486-X*, Usborne) EDC.

— Midnight Horse. 112p. (J). (gr. 4-8). 1998. lib. bdg. 11.95 (*0-88110-907-X*) EDC.

— Perfect Pony. (Sandy Lane Stables Ser.). (Illus.). 112p. (gr. 4-8). 1999. 11.95 (*1-58086-175-X*) EDC.

***Bates, Michelle.** Racing Vacation. (Sandy Lane Stables Ser.). 130p. (J). (gr. 4-8). 2000. pap. 3.95 (*0-7460-3460-1*, Usborne) EDC.

Bates, Michelle. Ride by Moonlight. (Sandy Lane Stables Ser.). 96p. (J). (gr. 4-8). 1998. pap. 3.95 (*0-7460-2480-0*, Usborne); lib. bdg. 11.95 (*1-58086-116-4*, Usborne) EDC.

— Strangers at the Stables. (Sandy Lane Stables Ser.). (Illus.). 96p. (Orig.). (J). (gr. 4-8). 1997. pap. 3.95 (*0-7460-2488-6*, Usborne); lib. bdg. 11.95 (*0-88110-944-4*, Usborne) EDC.

Bates, Michelle & Leigh, Susannah. Sandy Lane Stables Omnibus. (Sandy Lane Stables Ser.). 337p. (J). (gr. 4-8). 1998. pap. 9.95 (*0-7460-3153-X*, Usborne) EDC.

— Sandy Lane Stables Omnibus. (Sandy Lane Stables Ser.). (Illus.). 337p. (J). (gr. 4-8). 1998. lib. bdg. 17.95 (*0-88110-965-7*, Usborne) EDC.

Bates, Michelle, ed. see Dolby, Karen.

Bates, Michelle, ed. see Leigh, Susannah.

Bates, Milton J. The Wars We Took to Vietnam: Cultural Conflict & Storytelling. LC 95-46772. 325p. (C). 1996. pap. 19.95 (*0-520-20433-6*, Pub. by U CA Pr) Cal Prin Full Svc.

Bates, Milton J., ed. see Stevens, Wallace.

Bates, N. Introduction to Legal Studies. 4th ed. 456p. 1984. pap. 30.00 (*0-409-49403-8*, Austral, MICHIE) LEXIS Pub.

Bates, N. & Bates, M. Legal Studies for Victoria, Vol. 1. 2nd ed. pap. 40.00 (*0-409-31047-6*, Austral, MICHIE) LEXIS Pub.

— Legal Studies for Victoria, Vol. 2. 2nd ed. 1995. pap. 41.00 (*0-409-31048-4*, Austral, MICHIE) LEXIS Pub.

Bates, Natica I., jt. ed. see Hooton, Earnest A.

Bates, Natica I., ed. see Reisner, G. A.

Bates, Nina, jt. auth. see Bates, John.

Bates, Norman. Employee Background Investigation Guide. 1998. pap. 34.95 (*0-7506-7045-2*, Newnes) Buttrwrth-Heinemann.

— Employee Background Investigations Guide. 208p. 1998. pap. text 34.95 (*0-7506-7056-8*) Buttrwrth-Heinemann.

***Bates, Norman & Laszlo, Christopher.** Large Scale Organizational Change: An Executive's Guide. LC 99-40495. 264p. 1999. pap. text 19.95 (*0-7506-7230-7*) Buttrwrth-Heinemann.

Bates, O. Bates of Virginia & Missouri. 160p. 1997. reprint ed. pap. 24.00 (*0-8328-7417-5*); reprint ed. lib. bdg. 34.00 (*0-8328-7416-7*) Higginson Bk Co.

Bates, Oric, ed. Varia Africana Two. LC 33-6339. (Harvard African Studies: Vol. 2). 1976. reprint ed. 35.00 (*0-527-01025-1*) Periodicals Srv.

Bates, Oric & Sterns, F. H., eds. Varia Africana One. LC 33-6339. (Harvard African Studies: Vol. 1). 1976. reprint ed. 35.00 (*0-527-01024-3*) Periodicals Srv.

Bates, Owen. Mail Order Dealer's Advertising Rate Manual. 110p. 1994. pap. 15.00 (*0-915665-30-1*) Premier Publishers.

Bates, Owen & Michaels, Neal. How to Make Your Fortune with Books. 2nd ed. 1991. pap. write for info. (*0-915665-23-9*) Premier Publishers.

— How to Prepare Your Own Mail Order Catalog Without Merchandise...for Pennies. 3rd ed. 96p. 1994. pap. 19.95 (*0-915665-28-X*) Premier Publishers.

Bates, P., ed. Bats of the Indian Subcontinent: Macintosh-Windows Version. 2000. text 149.00 (*3-540-14642-3*) Spr-Verlag.

***Bates, P. W., et al, eds.** Differential Equations & Computational Simulations. 520p. 2000. 96.00 (*981-02-4268-9*) World Scientific Pub.

Bates, Paul. Practical Digital Data & Data Communication with LSI Applications. (Illus.). (C). 1987. write for info. (*0-318-61640-8*) P-H.

— Price Guide to Pepsi Cans. (Illus.). 83p. (Orig.). 1992. pap. 5.00 (*1-56046-131-4*) Interact Pubs.

Bates, Paul, et al. Enjoy Coca-Cola. (Illus.). 274p. (Orig.). 1992. reprint ed. pap. 19.95 (*1-56046-132-2*) Interact Pubs.

— Handbook of Coca-Cola Hobbleskirt Bottles. (Illus.). 49p. (Orig.). 1987. pap. 8.00 (*1-56046-104-7*) Interact Pubs.

— Handbook of Commemorative & Offer Soda Cans. (Illus.). 192p. (Orig.). 1988. pap. 12.00 (*1-56046-154-3*) Interact Pubs.

— Handbook of Commemorative Soda Bottles. (Illus.). 74p. (Orig.). 1992. reprint ed. pap. 12.00 (*1-56046-114-4*) Interact Pubs.

— Handbook of Embossed Soda Bottles. (Illus.). 208p. (Orig.). 1992. reprint ed. pap. 12.00 (*1-56046-115-2*) Interact Pubs.

— Handbook of International Coca-Cola Bottles. (Illus.). 50p. (Orig.). 1988. pap. 8.00 (*1-56046-105-5*) Interact Pubs.

— Handbook of International Commemorative Soda Cans. (Illus.). 83p. (Orig.). 1988. pap. 9.00 (*1-56046-155-1*) Interact Pubs.

— Handbook of Miniature Soda Bottles. (Illus.). 54p. (Orig.). 1992. reprint ed. pap. 12.00 (*1-56046-112-8*) Interact Pubs.

— Handbook of Painted Label Soda Bottles. LC 89-84892. (Illus.). 350p. (Orig.). 1992. reprint ed. pap. 24.95 (*1-56046-113-6*) Interact Pubs.

— Handbook of Soda Bottle Caps. (Illus.). 88p. (Orig.). 1988. pap. 6.00 (*1-56046-108-X*) Interact Pubs.

— Handbook of Soda Bottles from Alabama. 70p. (Orig.). 1989. pap. 9.00 (*1-56046-200-0*) Interact Pubs.

— Handbook of Soda Bottles from Alaska. 52p. (Orig.). 1989. pap. 5.00 (*1-56046-201-9*) Interact Pubs.

— Handbook of Soda Bottles from Arizona. 52p. (Orig.). 1989. pap. 5.00 (*1-56046-202-7*) Interact Pubs.

— Handbook of Soda Bottles from Arkansas. 50p. (Orig.). 1989. pap. 7.00 (*1-56046-203-5*) Interact Pubs.

— Handbook of Soda Bottles from California. 70p. (Orig.). 1989. pap. 9.00 (*1-56046-204-3*) Interact Pubs.

— Handbook of Soda Bottles from Colorado. 52p. (Orig.). 1989. pap. 5.00 (*1-56046-205-1*) Interact Pubs.

— Handbook of Soda Bottles from Connecticut. 52p. (Orig.). 1989. pap. 5.00 (*1-56046-206-X*) Interact Pubs.

— Handbook of Soda Bottles from Delaware. 52p. (Orig.). 1989. pap. 5.00 (*1-56046-207-8*) Interact Pubs.

— Handbook of Soda Bottles from District of Columbia. 60p. (Orig.). 1989. pap. 7.00 (*1-56046-208-6*) Interact Pubs.

— Handbook of Soda Bottles from Florida. 70p. (Orig.). 1989. pap. 9.00 (*1-56046-209-4*) Interact Pubs.

— Handbook of Soda Bottles from Georgia. 70p. (Orig.). 1989. pap. 9.00 (*1-56046-210-8*) Interact Pubs.

— Handbook of Soda Bottles from Idaho. 30p. (Orig.). 1989. pap. 5.00 (*1-56046-212-4*) Interact Pubs.

— Handbook of Soda Bottles from Illinois. 80p. (Orig.). 1989. pap. 11.00 (*1-56046-213-2*) Interact Pubs.

— Handbook of Soda Bottles from Indiana. 70p. (Orig.). 1989. pap. 9.00 (*1-56046-214-0*) Interact Pubs.

— Handbook of Soda Bottles from Iowa. 60p. (Orig.). 1989. pap. 7.00 (*1-56046-215-9*) Interact Pubs.

— Handbook of Soda Bottles from Kansas. 70p. (Orig.). 1989. pap. 9.00 (*1-56046-216-7*) Interact Pubs.

— Handbook of Soda Bottles from Kentucky. 50p. (Orig.). 1989. pap. 7.00 (*1-56046-217-5*) Interact Pubs.

— Handbook of Soda Bottles from Louisiana. 55p. (Orig.). 1989. pap. 7.00 (*1-56046-218-3*) Interact Pubs.

— Handbook of Soda Bottles from Maine. 52p. (Orig.). 1989. pap. 5.00 (*1-56046-219-1*) Interact Pubs.

— Handbook of Soda Bottles from Maryland. 70p. (Orig.). 1989. pap. 11.00 (*1-56046-220-5*) Interact Pubs.

— Handbook of Soda Bottles from Massachusetts. 52p. (Orig.). 1989. pap. 5.00 (*1-56046-221-3*) Interact Pubs.

— Handbook of Soda Bottles from Michigan. 70p. (Orig.). 1989. pap. 9.00 (*1-56046-222-1*) Interact Pubs.

— Handbook of Soda Bottles from Minnesota. 50p. (Orig.). 1989. pap. 7.00 (*1-56046-223-X*) Interact Pubs.

— Handbook of Soda Bottles from Mississippi. (Illus.). 70p. (Orig.). 1989. pap. 9.00 (*1-56046-224-8*) Interact Pubs.

— Handbook of Soda Bottles from Missouri. 85p. (Orig.). 1989. pap. 11.00 (*1-56046-250-7*) Interact Pubs.

— Handbook of Soda Bottles from Montana. 52p. (Orig.). 1989. pap. 5.00 (*1-56046-251-5*) Interact Pubs.

— Handbook of Soda Bottles from Nebraska. 52p. (Orig.). 1989. pap. 5.00 (*1-56046-252-3*) Interact Pubs.

— Handbook of Soda Bottles from Nevada. 52p. (Orig.). 1989. pap. 5.00 (*1-56046-253-1*) Interact Pubs.

— Handbook of Soda Bottles from New Hampshire. 50p. (Orig.). 1989. pap. 5.00 (*1-56046-254-X*) Interact Pubs.

— Handbook of Soda Bottles from New Jersey. 80p. (Orig.). 1989. pap. 11.00 (*1-56046-255-8*) Interact Pubs.

— Handbook of Soda Bottles from New Mexico. 55p. (Orig.). 1989. pap. 5.00 (*1-56046-256-6*) Interact Pubs.

— Handbook of Soda Bottles from New York. 70p. (Orig.). 1989. pap. 11.00 (*1-56046-257-4*) Interact Pubs.

— Handbook of Soda Bottles from North Carolina. 75p. (Orig.). 1989. pap. 9.00 (*1-56046-258-2*) Interact Pubs.

— Handbook of Soda Bottles from North Dakota. 55p. (Orig.). 1989. pap. 5.00 (*1-56046-259-0*) Interact Pubs.

— Handbook of Soda Bottles from Ohio. 60p. (Orig.). 1989. pap. 9.00 (*1-56046-260-4*) Interact Pubs.

— Handbook of Soda Bottles from Oklahoma. 50p. (Orig.). 1989. pap. 7.00 (*1-56046-261-2*) Interact Pubs.

— Handbook of Soda Bottles from Oregon. 52p. (Orig.). 1989. pap. 5.00 (*1-56046-262-0*) Interact Pubs.

— Handbook of Soda Bottles from Pennsylvania. 85p. (Orig.). 1989. pap. 11.00 (*1-56046-263-9*) Interact Pubs.

— Handbook of Soda Bottles from Rhode Island. 50p. (Orig.). 1989. pap. 5.00 (*1-56046-264-7*) Interact Pubs.

— Handbook of Soda Bottles from South Carolina. 60p. (Orig.). 1989. pap. 7.00 (*1-56046-265-5*) Interact Pubs.

— Handbook of Soda Bottles from South Dakota. 52p. (Orig.). 1989. pap. 5.00 (*1-56046-266-3*) Interact Pubs.

— Handbook of Soda Bottles from Tennessee. 70p. (Orig.). 1989. pap. 9.00 (*1-56046-267-1*) Interact Pubs.

— Handbook of Soda Bottles from Texas. 70p. (Orig.). 1989. pap. 9.00 (*1-56046-268-X*) Interact Pubs.

— Handbook of Soda Bottles from Utah. 54p. (Orig.). 1989. pap. 5.00 (*1-56046-269-8*) Interact Pubs.

— Handbook of Soda Bottles from Vermont. 50p. (Orig.). 1989. pap. 5.00 (*1-56046-270-1*) Interact Pubs.

— Handbook of Soda Bottles from Virginia. 50p. (Orig.). 1989. pap. 9.00 (*1-56046-271-X*) Interact Pubs.

— Handbook of Soda Bottles from Washington. 54p. (Orig.). 1989. pap. 5.00 (*1-56046-272-8*) Interact Pubs.

— Handbook of Soda Bottles from West Virginia. 70p. (Orig.). 1989. pap. 9.00 (*1-56046-273-6*) Interact Pubs.

— Handbook of Soda Bottles from Wisconsin. 75p. (Orig.). 1989. pap. 9.00 (*1-56046-274-4*) Interact Pubs.

— Handbook of Soda Bottles from Wyoming. 52p. (Orig.). 1989. pap. 5.00 (*1-56046-225-6*) Interact Pubs.

— Handbook of Soda Drinking Glasses. (Illus.). 61p. (Orig.). 1988. pap. 8.00 (*1-56046-107-1*) Interact Pubs.

— Handbook of Soda Match Covers. (Illus.). 59p. (Orig.). 1987. pap. 6.00 (*1-56046-109-8*) Interact Pubs.

B

An Asterisk (*) at the beginning of an entry indicates that the title is appearing for the first time.

— Handbook of Soda Patches. (Illus.). 54p. (Orig.). 1987. pap. 3.00 (*1-56046-106-3*) Interact Pubs.
— Handbook of Soda Playing Cards. (Illus.). 56p. (Orig.). 1987. pap. 5.00 (*1-56046-110-1*) Interact Pubs.
— Handbook of United States Soda Canners. (Illus.). 52p. (Orig.). 1987. pap. 8.00 (*1-56046-156-X*) Interact Pubs.
— Me & My RC. (Illus.). 84p. (Orig.). 1989. pap. 8.00 (*1-56046-128-4*) Interact Pubs.
— The Pepper-Upper. (Illus.). 100p. (Orig.). 1989. pap. 12.00 (*1-56046-127-6*) Interact Pubs.
— Pepsi Generations. (Illus.). 164p. (Orig.). 1992. reprint ed. pap. 14.00 (*1-56046-130-6*) Interact Pubs.
— Soda Can Collectors Guide, 3 vols., Set. (Illus.). 502p. (Orig.). 1992. reprint ed. pap. 29.95 (*1-56046-157-8*) Interact Pubs.
— Soda Can Collectors Guide (A&P to Fyne Taste), Vol. 1. (Illus.). 179p. (Orig.). 1992. pap. 10.00 (*1-56046-151-9*) Interact Pubs.
— Soda Can Collectors Guide (Galaxy to Pussypop), Vol. 2. (Illus.). 161p. (Orig.). 1987. pap. 10.00 (*1-56046-152-7*) Interact Pubs.
— Soda Can Collectors Guide (Q-Tonic to Zippy), Vol. 3. (Illus.). 162p. (Orig.). 1987. pap. 10.00 (*1-56046-153-5*) Interact Pubs.
— The Uncola. (Illus.). 99p. (Orig.). 1989. pap. 8.00 (*1-56046-129-2*) Interact Pubs.

Bates, Paul E. Vicarious Thrills: Reflections on a Championship Season of High School Basketball. LC 94-22660. (Illus.). 225p. (C). 1995. 36.95 (*0-8093-1978-0*); pap. 16.95 (*0-8093-1979-9*) S Ill U Pr.
Bates, Paul W. Monthly Chronicles - April. (Illus.). 24p. (Orig.). 1992. pap. 4.95 (*1-56046-004-0*) Interact Pubs.
— Monthly Chronicles - August. (Illus.). 24p. (Orig.). 1992. pap. 4.95 (*1-56046-008-3*) Interact Pubs.
— Monthly Chronicles - December. (Illus.). 24p. (Orig.). 1992. pap. 4.95 (*1-56046-012-1*) Interact Pubs.
— Monthly Chronicles - February. (Illus.). 24p. (Orig.). 1992. pap. 4.95 (*1-56046-002-4*) Interact Pubs.
— Monthly Chronicles - January. (Illus.). 24p. (Orig.). 1992. pap. 4.95 (*1-56046-001-6*) Interact Pubs.
— Monthly Chronicles - July. (Illus.). 24p. (Orig.). 1992. pap. 4.95 (*1-56046-007-5*) Interact Pubs.
— Monthly Chronicles - June. (Illus.). 24p. (Orig.). 1992. pap. 4.95 (*1-56046-006-7*) Interact Pubs.
— Monthly Chronicles - March. (Illus.). 24p. (Orig.). 1992. pap. 4.95 (*1-56046-003-2*) Interact Pubs.
— Monthly Chronicles - May. (Illus.). 24p. (Orig.). 1992. pap. 4.95 (*1-56046-005-9*) Interact Pubs.
— Monthly Chronicles - November. (Illus.). 24p. (Orig.). 1992. pap. 4.95 (*1-56046-011-3*) Interact Pubs.
— Monthly Chronicles - October. (Illus.). 24p. (Orig.). 1992. pap. 4.95 (*1-56046-010-5*) Interact Pubs.
— Monthly Chronicles - September. (Illus.). 24p. (Orig.). 1992. pap. 4.95 (*1-56046-009-1*) Interact Pubs.
— Pages of Time, 1984. (Illus.). 24p. (Orig.). 1993. pap. 4.95 (*1-56046-084-9*) Interact Pubs.
— Pages of Time, 1918. (Illus.). 24p. (Orig.). 1993. pap. 4.95 (*1-56046-018-0*) Interact Pubs.
— Pages of Time, 1980. (Illus.). 24p. (Orig.). 1993. pap. 4.95 (*1-56046-080-6*) Interact Pubs.
— Pages of Time, 1988. (Illus.). 24p. (Orig.). 1993. pap. 4.95 (*1-56046-088-1*) Interact Pubs.
— Pages of Time, 1985. (Illus.). 24p. (Orig.). 1993. pap. 4.95 (*1-56046-085-7*) Interact Pubs.
— Pages of Time, 1989. (Illus.). 24p. (Orig.). 1993. pap. 4.95 (*1-56046-089-X*) Interact Pubs.
— Pages of Time, 1981. (Illus.). 24p. (Orig.). 1993. pap. 4.95 (*1-56046-081-4*) Interact Pubs.
— Pages of Time, 1987. (Illus.). 24p. (Orig.). 1993. pap. 4.95 (*1-56046-087-3*) Interact Pubs.
— Pages of Time, 1986. (Illus.). 24p. (Orig.). 1993. pap. 4.95 (*1-56046-086-5*) Interact Pubs.
— Pages of Time, 1983. (Illus.). 24p. (Orig.). 1993. pap. 4.95 (*1-56046-083-0*) Interact Pubs.
— Pages of Time, 1982. (Illus.). 24p. (Orig.). 1993. pap. 4.95 (*1-56046-082-2*) Interact Pubs.
— Pages of Time, 1911. (Illus.). 24p. (Orig.). 1993. pap. 4.95 (*1-56046-311-2*) Interact Pubs.
— Pages of Time, 1915. (Illus.). 24p. (Orig.). 1993. pap. 4.95 (*1-56046-015-6*) Interact Pubs.
— Pages of Time, 1950. (Illus.). 24p. (Orig.). 1989. pap. 4.95 (*1-56046-050-4*) Interact Pubs.
— Pages of Time, 1958. (Illus.). 24p. (Orig.). 1989. pap. 4.95 (*1-56046-058-X*) Interact Pubs.
— Pages of Time, 1955. (Illus.). 24p. (Orig.). 1989. pap. 4.95 (*1-56046-055-5*) Interact Pubs.
— Pages of Time, 1954. (Illus.). 24p. (Orig.). 1989. pap. 4.95 (*1-56046-054-7*) Interact Pubs.
— Pages of Time, 1959. (Illus.). 24p. (Orig.). 1989. pap. 4.95 (*1-56046-059-8*) Interact Pubs.
— Pages of Time, 1951. (Illus.). 24p. (Orig.). 1989. pap. 4.95 (*1-56046-051-2*) Interact Pubs.
— Pages of Time, 1957. (Illus.). 24p. (Orig.). 1989. pap. 4.95 (*1-56046-057-1*) Interact Pubs.
— Pages of Time, 1956. (Illus.). 24p. (Orig.). 1989. pap. 4.95 (*1-56046-056-3*) Interact Pubs.
— Pages of Time, 1953. (Illus.). 24p. (Orig.). 1989. pap. 4.95 (*1-56046-053-9*) Interact Pubs.
— Pages of Time, 1952. (Illus.). 24p. (Orig.). 1989. pap. 4.95 (*1-56046-052-0*) Interact Pubs.
— Pages of Time, 1940. (Illus.). 24p. (Orig.). 1989. pap. 4.95 (*1-56046-040-7*) Interact Pubs.
— Pages of Time, 1948. (Illus.). 24p. (Orig.). 1989. pap. 4.95 (*1-56046-048-2*) Interact Pubs.
— Pages of Time, 1945. (Illus.). 24p. (Orig.). 1989. pap. 4.95 (*1-56046-045-8*) Interact Pubs.
— Pages of Time, 1944. (Illus.). 24p. (Orig.). 1989. pap. 4.95 (*1-56046-044-X*) Interact Pubs.
— Pages of Time, 1949. (Illus.). 24p. (Orig.). 1989. pap. 4.95 (*1-56046-049-0*) Interact Pubs.
— Pages of Time, 1941. (Illus.). 24p. (Orig.). 1989. pap. 4.95 (*1-56046-041-5*) Interact Pubs.
— Pages of Time, 1947. (Illus.). 24p. (Orig.). 1989. pap. 4.95 (*1-56046-047-4*) Interact Pubs.
— Pages of Time, 1946. (Illus.). 24p. (Orig.). 1989. pap. 4.95 (*1-56046-046-6*) Interact Pubs.
— Pages of Time, 1943. (Illus.). 24p. (Orig.). 1989. pap. 4.95 (*1-56046-043-1*) Interact Pubs.
— Pages of Time, 1942. (Illus.). 24p. (Orig.). 1989. pap. 4.95 (*1-56046-042-3*) Interact Pubs.
— Pages of Time, 1914. (Illus.). 24p. (Orig.). 1993. pap. 4.95 (*1-56046-014-8*) Interact Pubs.
— Pages of Time, 1919. (Illus.). 24p. (Orig.). 1993. pap. 4.95 (*1-56046-019-9*) Interact Pubs.
— Pages of Time, 1990. (Illus.). 24p. (Orig.). 1993. pap. 4.95 (*1-56046-090-3*) Interact Pubs.
— Pages of Time, 1991. (Illus.). 24p. (Orig.). 1993. pap. 4.95 (*1-56046-091-1*) Interact Pubs.
— Pages of Time, 1992. (Illus.). 24p. (Orig.). 1993. pap. 4.95 (*1-56046-092-X*) Interact Pubs.
— Pages of Time, 1917. (Illus.). 24p. (Orig.). 1993. pap. 4.95 (*1-56046-017-2*) Interact Pubs.
— Pages of Time, 1970. (Illus.). 24p. (Orig.). 1993. pap. 4.95 (*1-56046-070-9*) Interact Pubs.
— Pages of Time, 1978. (Illus.). 24p. (Orig.). 1993. pap. 4.95 (*1-56046-078-4*) Interact Pubs.
— Pages of Time, 1975. (Illus.). 24p. (Orig.). 1993. pap. 4.95 (*1-56046-075-X*) Interact Pubs.
— Pages of Time, 1974. (Illus.). 24p. (Orig.). 1993. pap. 4.95 (*1-56046-074-1*) Interact Pubs.
— Pages of Time, 1979. (Illus.). 24p. (Orig.). 1993. pap. 4.95 (*1-56046-079-2*) Interact Pubs.
— Pages of Time, 1971. (Illus.). 24p. (Orig.). 1993. pap. 4.95 (*1-56046-071-7*) Interact Pubs.
— Pages of Time, 1977. (Illus.). 24p. (Orig.). 1993. pap. 4.95 (*1-56046-077-6*) Interact Pubs.
— Pages of Time, 1976. (Illus.). 24p. (Orig.). 1993. pap. 4.95 (*1-56046-076-8*) Interact Pubs.
— Pages of Time, 1973. (Illus.). 24p. (Orig.). 1993. pap. 4.95 (*1-56046-073-3*) Interact Pubs.
— Pages of Time, 1972. (Illus.). 24p. (Orig.). 1993. pap. 4.95 (*1-56046-072-5*) Interact Pubs.
— Pages of Time, 1916. (Illus.). 24p. (Orig.). 1993. pap. 4.95 (*1-56046-016-4*) Interact Pubs.
— Pages of Time, 1960. (Illus.). 24p. (Orig.). 1989. pap. 4.95 (*1-56046-060-1*) Interact Pubs.
— Pages of Time, 1968. (Illus.). 24p. (Orig.). 1989. pap. 4.95 (*1-56046-068-7*) Interact Pubs.
— Pages of Time, 1965. (Illus.). 24p. (Orig.). 1989. pap. 4.95 (*1-56046-065-2*) Interact Pubs.
— Pages of Time, 1964. (Illus.). 24p. (Orig.). 1989. pap. 4.95 (*1-56046-064-4*) Interact Pubs.
— Pages of Time, 1969. (Illus.). 24p. (Orig.). 1989. pap. 4.95 (*1-56046-069-5*) Interact Pubs.
— Pages of Time, 1961. (Illus.). 24p. (Orig.). 1989. pap. 4.95 (*1-56046-061-X*) Interact Pubs.
— Pages of Time, 1967. (Illus.). 24p. (Orig.). 1989. pap. 4.95 (*1-56046-067-9*) Interact Pubs.
— Pages of Time, 1966. (Illus.). 24p. (Orig.). 1989. pap. 4.95 (*1-56046-066-0*) Interact Pubs.
— Pages of Time, 1963. (Illus.). 24p. (Orig.). 1989. pap. 4.95 (*1-56046-063-6*) Interact Pubs.
— Pages of Time, 1962. (Illus.). 24p. (Orig.). 1989. pap. 4.95 (*1-56046-062-8*) Interact Pubs.
— Pages of Time, 1910. (Illus.). 24p. (Orig.). 1993. pap. 4.95 (*1-56046-310-4*) Interact Pubs.
— Pages of Time, 1913. (Illus.). 24p. (Orig.). 1993. pap. 4.95 (*1-56046-013-X*) Interact Pubs.
— Pages of Time, 1930. (Illus.). 24p. (Orig.). 1989. pap. 4.95 (*1-56046-030-X*) Interact Pubs.
— Pages of Time, 1938. (Illus.). 24p. (Orig.). 1989. pap. 4.95 (*1-56046-038-5*) Interact Pubs.
— Pages of Time, 1935. (Illus.). 24p. (Orig.). 1989. pap. 4.95 (*1-56046-035-0*) Interact Pubs.
— Pages of Time, 1934. (Illus.). 24p. (Orig.). 1989. pap. 4.95 (*1-56046-034-2*) Interact Pubs.
— Pages of Time, 1939. (Illus.). 24p. (Orig.). 1989. pap. 4.95 (*1-56046-039-3*) Interact Pubs.
— Pages of Time, 1931. (Illus.). 24p. (Orig.). 1989. pap. 4.95 (*1-56046-031-8*) Interact Pubs.
— Pages of Time, 1937. (Illus.). 24p. (Orig.). 1989. pap. 4.95 (*1-56046-037-7*) Interact Pubs.
— Pages of Time, 1936. (Illus.). 24p. (Orig.). 1989. pap. 4.95 (*1-56046-036-9*) Interact Pubs.
— Pages of Time, 1933. (Illus.). 24p. (Orig.). 1989. pap. 4.95 (*1-56046-033-4*) Interact Pubs.
— Pages of Time, 1932. (Illus.). 24p. (Orig.). 1989. pap. 4.95 (*1-56046-032-6*) Interact Pubs.
— Pages of Time, 1912. (Illus.). 24p. (Orig.). 1993. pap. 4.95 (*1-56046-312-0*) Interact Pubs.
— Pages of Time, 1920. (Illus.). 24p. (Orig.). 1989. pap. 4.95 (*1-56046-020-2*) Interact Pubs.
— Pages of Time, 1928. (Illus.). 24p. (Orig.). 1989. pap. 4.95 (*1-56046-028-8*) Interact Pubs.
— Pages of Time, 1925. (Illus.). 24p. (Orig.). 1989. pap. 4.95 (*1-56046-025-3*) Interact Pubs.
— Pages of Time, 1924. (Illus.). 24p. (Orig.). 1989. pap. 4.95 (*1-56046-024-5*) Interact Pubs.
— Pages of Time, 1929. (Illus.). 24p. (Orig.). 1989. pap. 4.95 (*1-56046-029-6*) Interact Pubs.
— Pages of Time, 1921. (Illus.). 24p. (Orig.). 1989. pap. 4.95 (*1-56046-021-0*) Interact Pubs.
— Pages of Time, 1927. (Illus.). 24p. (Orig.). 1989. pap. 4.95 (*1-56046-027-X*) Interact Pubs.
— Pages of Time, 1926. (Illus.). 24p. (Orig.). 1989. pap. 4.95 (*1-56046-026-1*) Interact Pubs.
— Pages of Time, 1923. (Illus.). 24p. (Orig.). 1989. pap. 4.95 (*1-56046-023-7*) Interact Pubs.
— Pages of Time, 1922. (Illus.). 24p. (Orig.). 1989. pap. 4.95 (*1-56046-022-9*) Interact Pubs.

Bates, Peter. Japan & the British Commonwealth Occupation Force, 1946-52. 288p. 1993. 49.00 (*1-85753-000-4*, Pub. by Brasseys) Brasseys.
Bates, Peter, ed. U. S. Chinese Conference on Differential Equations & Applications. (Illus.). 368p. (C). 1998. 42.00 (*1-57146-048-9*) Intl Pr Boston.
Bates, Peter W., et al. Existence & Persistence of Invariant Manifolds for Semiflows in Banach Space. LC 98-25200. (Memoirs of the American Mathematical Society Ser.: Vol. 135, No. 645). 129p. 1998. pap. 41.00 (*0-8218-0868-0*) Am Math.
Bates, R. L. & Jackson, J. A. Glossary of Geology. 754p. 1990. reprint ed. 225.00 (*0-8288-9245-8*, M15561) Fr & Eur.
Bates, R. S. & Lowther, E. H. The Breeding Birds of Kashmir. (Illus.). 390p. 1991. text 39.95 (*0-19-562562-5*) OUP.
Bates, Regis J. Introduction to T1-T3 Networking. LC 92-18448. (Telecommunications Ser.). 240p. 1992. text 93.00 (*0-89006-624-8*) Artech Hse.
***Bates, Regis J.** Nortel Networks Layer 3 Switching. (Networking Ser.). 352p. 2000. pap. text. write for info. (*0-07-212426-1*) Osborne-McGraw.
— Voice & Data Communications Handbook. 3rd ed. (Networking Ser.). 1999. pap. 65.00 (*0-07-212276-5*) McGraw-Hill Prof.
Bates, Richard. The Management of Culture & Knowledge. 122p. (C). 1986. 60.00 (*0-7300-0376-0*, Pub. by Deakin Univ) St Mut.
— Public Administration & the Crisis of the State. 117p. (C). 1985. 48.00 (*0-7300-0212-8*, Pub. by Deakin Univ) St Mut.
Bates, Richard, ed. Educational Administration & the Management of Knowledge. 139p. (C). 1983. 50.00 (*0-7300-0012-5*, Pub. by Deakin Univ) St Mut.
— Evaluating Schools: A Critical Approach. 121p. (C). 1988. 65.00 (*0-7300-0588-7*, Pub. by Deakin Univ) St Mut.
— Liberalism, Marxism & the Struggle for the State: Prolegomena to the Study of Public Administration. 152p. (C). 1985. 60.00 (*0-7300-0301-9*, Pub. by Deakin Univ) St Mut.
Bates, Richard & Kynaston, Edward. Thinking Aloud. 444p. (C). 1983. 45.00 (*0-7300-0015-X*, Pub. by Deakin Univ) St Mut.
Bates, Richard D. & Nahata, Milap C. Children's Medications: A Guide to Schools & Day Care Centers. LC 95-8554. viii, 360p. 1995. pap. text 29.95 (*0-929375-15-7*) H W Bks.
— Children's Medications: A Parent's Guide. LC 95-8561. (Illus.). viii, 360p. (Orig.). 1995. pap. 19.95 (*0-929375-16-5*) H W Bks.
Bates, Richard R., jt. ed. see Kennedy, Donald.
Bates, Robert. Prosperity & Violence. 22.95 (*0-393-05038-6*) Norton.
Bates, Robert & Jackson, Julia A. Glossary of Geology. 4th ed. LC 87-3579. 800p. 1997. text 110.00 (*0-922152-34-9*) Am Geol.
Bates, Robert B. & Beavers, William A. Carbon-13 NMR Spectral Problems. LC 79-92216. (Organic Chemistry Ser.). 259p. 1981. text 89.50 (*0-89603-010-5*) Humana.
Bates, Robert H. Analytic Narratives. LC 98-9624. 296p. 1998. text 50.00 (*0-691-00128-6*, Pub. by Princeton U Pr); pap. text 19.95 (*0-691-00129-4*, Pub. by Princeton U Pr) Cal Prin Full Svc.
— Essays on the Political Economy of Rural Africa. (California Series on Social Choice & Political Economy: Vol. 8). 178p. 1987. pap. 18.95 (*0-520-06014-8*, Pub. by U CA Pr) Cal Prin Full Svc.
— Markets & States in Tropical Africa: The Political Basis of Agricultural Policies. LC 80-39732. (California Series on Social Choice & Political Economy: Vol. 1). 176p. 1981. pap. 19.95 (*0-520-05229-3*, Pub. by U CA Pr) Cal Prin Full Svc.
Bates, Robert H. Open Economy Politics: The Political Economy of the World Coffee Trade. LC 96-20694. 240p. 1997. text 35.00 (*0-691-02655-6*, Pub. by Princeton U Pr) Cal Prin Full Svc.
Bates, Robert H. Open Economy Politics: The Political Economy of the World Coffee Trade. 1999. pap. text 17.95 (*0-691-00519-2*, Pub. by Princeton U Pr) Cal Prin Full Svc.
— Unions, Parties, & Political Development: A Study of Mineworkers in Zambia. LC 78-158135. 303p. reprint ed. pap. 94.00 (*0-608-14191-7*, 202198000024) Bks Demand.
Bates, Robert H., ed. Toward a Political Economy of Development: A Rational Choice Perspective. (California Series on Social Choice & Political Economy: Vol. 14). 1988. pap. 19.95 (*0-520-06052-0*, Pub. by U CA Pr) Cal Prin Full Svc.
— Toward a Political Economy of Development: A Rational Choice Perspective. LC 87-10870. (California Series on Social Choice & Political Economy: No. 14). 403p. reprint ed. pap. 125.00 (*0-7837-4763-2*, 204451000003) Bks Demand.
Bates, Robert H., et al, eds. Africa & the Disciplines: The Contributions of Research in Africa to the Social Sciences & Humanities. LC 93-3770. 272p. 1993. pap. text 12.95 (*0-226-03901-3*); lib. bdg. 24.95 (*0-226-03900-5*) U Ch Pr.
Bates, Robert H., jt. auth. see Houston, Charles S.
Bates, Robert L. Mineral Resources A-Z. LC 90-34301. 128p. (YA). (gr. 6 up). 1991. lib. bdg. 20.95 (*0-89490-244-X*) Enslow Pubs.
Bates, Robert L., et al, eds. Geowriting, a Guide to Writing, Editing, & Printing in Earth Science. 5th ed. 138p. Date not set. pap. 13.75 (*0-922152-14-4*) Am Geol.
Bates, Robin & Fraser, Neil. Investment Decisions in the Nationalized Fuel Industries. LC 74-76575. 202p. reprint ed. pap. 57.60 (*0-608-17022-4*, 2027275) Bks Demand.

Bates, Robin, et al. Alternative Policies for the Control of Air Pollution in Poland. LC 94-45657. (Environment Papers: No. 7). 84p. 1994. pap. 22.00 (*0-8213-2753-4*) World Bank.
— Images, 23 bks. (Illus.). (J). 550.85 (*0-88682-399-4*, Creat Educ) Creative Co.
Bates, Roger. How to Be Funnier: Happier, Healthier & More Successful Too! Schneider, Peter et al, eds. (Illus.). 256p. 1995. pap. 19.95 (*0-9642324-4-8*); text 24.95 (*0-9642324-3-X*) Trafton Pubng.
— What Risk? (Illus.). 352p. 1999. pap. text 29.95 (*0-7506-4228-9*) Buttrwrth-Heinemann.
Bates, Roger G. Determination of PH: Theory & Practice. 2nd ed. LC 72-8779. (Illus.). 495p. reprint ed. pap. 153.50 (*0-608-10223-7*, 201929300011) Bks Demand.
Bates, S. M., tr. see Gromov, Mikhael.
Bates, S. R. & Gangloff, E., eds. Atherogenesis & Aging. (Illus.). 240p. 1987. 155.00 (*0-387-96393-6*) Spr-Verlag.
Bates, Samuel A., compiled by. Arnold Family, As Entered upon the Records of the Towns of Braintree, 1640 to 1853. (Illus.). 48p. 1997. reprint ed. pap. 10.00 (*0-8328-7293-8*); reprint ed. lib. bdg. 20.00 (*0-8328-7292-X*) Higginson Bk Co.
Bates, Samuel A., ed. Records of the Town of Braintree, Massachusetts, 1640-1793. 939p. 1989. reprint ed. lib. bdg. 94.00 (*0-8328-0810-5*, MA0218) Higginson Bk Co.
Bates, Samuel E. Genealogy of the Descendants of Edward Bates of Weymouth, Massachusettes. 145p. 1988. reprint ed. pap. 24.00 (*0-8328-0209-3*); reprint ed. lib. bdg. 32.00 (*0-8328-0208-5*) Higginson Bk Co.
Bates, Samuel P. History of Pennsylvania Volunteers, 1861-5, 14 vols. (Illus.). 1995. reprint ed. 700.00 (*1-56837-226-4*) Broadfoot.
— Our County & Its People: Historical & Memorial Record of Crawford Co. (Illus.). 972p. 1997. reprint ed. lib. bdg. 97.50 (*0-8328-6404-8*) Higginson Bk Co.
Bates, Sanford. Prisons & Beyond. LC 72-157324. (Select Bibliographies Reprint Ser.). 1977. reprint ed. 26.95 (*0-8369-5784-9*) Ayer.
Bates, Sarah F., et al. Searching Out the Headwaters: Change & Rediscovery in Western Water Policy. LC 93-4637. 230p. 1993. pap. 19.95 (*1-55963-218-6*); text 40.00 (*1-55963-217-8*) Island Pr.
Bates, Sarah F., jt. auth. see Reisner, Marc P.
Bates, Sarah F., jt. ed. see Knight, Richard L.
Bates, Sarah F., jt. ed. see MacDonnell, Lawrence J.
Bates, Schyuler B. To Bridesmaids with Love: A Guide to Being in Your Friend's Wedding & Remaining Friends Afterward. 90p. 1998. pap. 8.50 (*0-9662382-0-6*) Doubletake Pr.
Bates, Scott. Guillaume Apollinaire. rev. ed. (World Authors Ser.). 200p. (C). 1989. 26.95 (*0-8057-8246-X*, TWAS 14) Macmillan.
— Songs for the Queen of the Animals: A Book of Animal Poems. (ENG & FRE., Illus.). 96p. (Orig.). 1993. pap. 7.00 (*0-9627687-5-8*) Proctors Hall Pr.
Bates, Sean & Weinstein, Alan. Lectures on the Geometry of Quantization. (Berkeley Mathematical Lecture Notes Ser.: Vol. 8). 137p. 1997. pap. 25.00 (*0-8218-0798-6*) Am Math.
Bates, Stephen. Battleground: One Mother's Crusade, the Religious Right, & the Struggle for Our Schools. rev. ed. LC 94-17764. 1995. pap. 15.95 (*0-8050-3516-8*) H Holt & Co.
Bates, Stephen, jt. auth. see Diamond, Edwin.
Bates, Timothy. An Analysis of Income Differentials among Self-Employed Minorities. (Minority Economic Development Ser.: No. 1). 57p. 1988. pap. 5.95 (*0-318-39975-X*) CAAS Pubns.
— Race, Self-Employment, & Upward Mobility: An Illusive American Dream. LC 97-17782. (Woodrow Wilson Center Press Ser.). 300p. pap. text 16.95 (*0-8018-5799-6*) Johns Hopkins.
Bates, Timothy, jt. auth. see Fusfeld, Daniel R.
Bates, Timothy M. Race, Self-Employment & Upward Mobility: An Illusive American Dream. LC 97-17782. (Woodrow Wilson Center Press Ser.). 300p. text 47.95 (*0-8018-5798-8*) Johns Hopkins.
Bates, Tom H. The General's Mess. 1981. 30.00 (*0-7223-1396-9*, Pub. by A H S Ltd) St Mut.
Bates, Ulku, et al. Brocade of the Pen: The Art of Islamic Writing. Fisher, Carol G., ed. (Illus.). (Orig.). 1991. pap. 13.00 (*1-879147-10-6*) Kresge Art Mus.
Bates, Ulku U. Women's Realities, Women's Choices: An Introduction to Women's Studies. 2nd ed. (Hunter College Women's Studies Collective Ser.). (Illus.). 616p. (C). 1995. pap. text 43.95 (*0-19-505883-6*) OUP.
Bates, Virginia T. & Chamberlain, Beverly. Antique Bottle Finds in New England. LC 68-9146. 80p. reprint ed. pap. 30.00 (*0-8357-5636-X*, 202094100020) Bks Demand.
Bates, W. H. The Cure of Imperfect Sight by Treatment Without Glasses. 313p. 1996. reprint ed. pap. 20.00 (*0-7873-0078-0*) Hlth Research.
— Reprints. 100p. 1993. reprint ed. pap. 12.00 (*0-7873-0079-9*) Hlth Research.
Bates, Wesley W. The Point of the Graver. 160p. 1994. pap. write for info. (*0-88984-182-9*) Porcup Quill.
Bates, William. The Complete Works of William Bates, 4 vols. 1992. 106.99 (*0-87377-930-4*) GAM Pubns.
Bates, William & Crowther, Betty. Toward a Typology of Opiate Users. 160p. 1974. pap. text 13.95 (*0-87073-960-3*) Schenkman Bks Inc.
Bates, William H. The Bates Method for Better Eyesight Without Glasses. LC 80-39877. 200 p. 1981. write for info. (*0-03-026630-0*) H Holt & Co.
— The Bates Method for Better Eyesight Without Glasses. LC 80-39878. 208p. 1995. pap. 8.95 (*0-8050-0241-3*, Owl) H Holt & Co.
Bates, Woody. Power-Zoning. (Illus.). 30p. 1999. spiral bd. 14.95 (*0-9671118-1-1*) Woodys Ways.

Bates-Yakobson, Helen, jt. auth. see Von Gronicka, Andre.

Bateson, Ann L. Process of Legal Research. 4th ed. 1996. pap. text 34.95 (*0-7355-0633-7*) Panel Pubs.

***Bateson, Catherine.** A Dangerous Girl. 2000. pap. 16.95 (*0-7022-3168-1*, Pub. by Univ Queensland Pr) Intl Spec Bk.

Bateson, Catherine. The Vigilant Heart. LC 98-193904. ix, 88p. 1998. pap. 19.95 (*0-7022-3048-0*, Pub. by Univ Queensland Pr) Intl Spec Bk.

Bateson, Charles. The Convict Ships of Australia 1787-1868. (C). 1987. 114.00 (*0-85174-195-9*) St Mut.

Bateson, Donald. Scottish Coins. (Album Ser.: Vol. 189). (Illus.). 32p. pap. 6.95 (*0-85263-847-7*, Pub. by Shire Pubns) Parkwest Pubns.

Bateson, Frederick W. English Poetry: A Critical Introduction. LC 78-6657. 205p. 1978. reprint ed. lib. bdg. 35.00 (*0-313-20461-6*, BAEN, Greenwood Pr) Greenwood.

— Wordsworth: A Re-Interpretation. LC 83-45410. reprint ed. 27.50 (*0-404-20020-6*) AMS Pr.

Bateson, Frederick W. & Meserole, Harrison T. A Guide to English & American Literature. 3rd ed. LC 76-19083. 352p. 1977. 50.00 (*0-87752-186-7*) Gordian.

Bateson, Frederick W., ed. see Sheridan, Richard Brinsley.

Bateson, Gregory. Naven: A Survey of the Problems Suggested by a Composite Picture of the Culture of a New Guinea Tribe Drawn from Three Points of View. 2nd ed. (Illus.). xix, 312p. 1958. 45.00 (*0-8047-0519-4*); pap. 16.95 (*0-8047-0520-8*) Stanford U Pr.

— Steps to an Ecology of Mind: Collected Essays in Anthropology, Psychiatry, Evolution & Epistemology. LC 99-45031. 542p. 2000. pap. 18.00 (*0-226-03905-6*); lib. bdg. 43.00 (*0-226-03906-4*) U Ch Pr.

Bateson, Gregory. Steps to Ecology Mind. 1980. mass mkt. 3.50 (*0-345-29351-7*) Ballantine Pub Grp.

Bateson, Gregory & Mead, Margaret. Balinese Character: A Photographic Analysis. (Illus.). 277p. 1942. pap. 60.00 (*0-89072-780-5*) NY Acad Sci.

Bateson, Gregory, ed. see Perceval, John.

Bateson-Hill, Margaret. Lao Lao of Dragon Mountain. (Illus.). (J). 1998. 14.95 (*1-84089-035-5*); pap. 7.95 (*1-84089-011-8*) Zero to Ten.

***Bateson-Hill, Margaret.** Masha & the Firebird. (Illus.). 32p. (J). 2000. 17.95 (*1-84089-134-3*, Pub. by Zero to Ten) IPG Chicago.

Bateson-Hill, Margaret. Shota & the Star Quilt. LC 98-26678. (J). (gr. 1-5). 1998. 14.95 (*1-84089-021-5*) Zero to Ten.

Bateson, J. D. Sylloge of Coins of the British Isles Vol. 35: Scottish Coins in the Ashmolean Museum, Oxford & the Hunterian Museum, Glasgow: Scottish Coins. (Illus.). 286p. 1987. text 112.00 (*0-19-726047-0*) OUP.

Bateson, J. S. Coinage of Scotland. (Illus.). 1997. lib. bdg. 55.00 (*0-907605-74-5*) S J Durst.

Bateson, John E. Managing Services Marketing. 3rd ed. 704p. (C). 1995. text 81.00 (*0-03-098666-4*) Dryden Pr.

Bateson, John E. & Hoffman, K. Douglas. Instructor's Manual & Transparency Masters to Accompany Managing Services Marketing. 3rd ed. 320p. (C). 1995. pap. text, teacher ed. 79.00 (*0-03-098708-3*) Dryden Pr.

Bateson, John E. & Mitchell, M. B., eds. Organometallic Reagents in Organic Synthesis. (Smith Kline Beecham Symposium Ser.). (Illus.). 304p. 1994. text 83.00 (*0-12-499150-5*) Acad Pr.

Bateson, John E., jt. auth. see Hoffman, K. Douglas.

Bateson, John E., ed. see Comnes, Leslie & Sly, Carolie.

Bateson, John E.G., et al. Managing Services Marketing: Text & Readings. 4th ed. LC 98-73895. (Dryden Press Marketing Ser.). 471p. (C). 1998. text 81.00 (*0-03-022519-1*, Pub. by Harcourt Coll Pubs) Harcourt.

Bateson, M., ed. George Ashby's Poems. (EETS Extra Ser.: Vol. 76). 1965. reprint ed. 20.00 (*0-19-722526-8*, Pub. by EETS) Boydell & Brewer.

Bateson, M. C. Clinical Investigation in Gastroenterology. (C). 1988. text 88.00 (*0-7462-0103-6*) Kluwer Academic.

Bateson, M. C., ed. Gallstone Disease & Its Management. 1986. text 167.00 (*0-85200-979-8*) Kluwer Academic.

Bateson, Malcolm C. & Bouchier, Ian A. Clinical Investigations in Gastroenterology. 2nd ed. LC 96-6551. 256p. 1997. text 110.50 (*0-7923-4391-3*) Kluwer Academic.

Bateson, Margaret & Lelie, Herman. A Victorian Village. LC 95-5315. (Illus.). 4p. (J). 1995. text 19.95 (*0-312-11485-0*) St Martin.

Bateson, Margaret, jt. auth. see Lellie, Herman.

Bateson, Mary. Mediaeval England, 1066-1350. LC 70-152973. (Select Bibliographies Reprint Ser.). 1977. reprint ed. 35.95 (*0-8369-5725-3*) Ayer.

Bateson, Mary C. Change, Adaptation & Learning: A Science Masters Series Book. 176p. 1997. 25.00 (*0-465-00914-X*, Pub. by Basic) HarpC.

— Change, Adaptation & Learning: A Science Masters Series Book. 176p. 1998. pap. write for info. (*0-465-00915-8*) Basic.

— Composing a Life. 256p. 1990. pap. 12.95 (*0-452-26505-3*, Plume) Dutton Plume.

— Our Own Metaphor: A Personal Account of a Conference on the Effects of Conscious Purpose on Human Adaptation. LC 91-561. (Illus.). 366p. (C). 1991. pap. text 16.95 (*1-56098-070-2*) Smithsonian.

— Peripheral Visions: Learning along the Way. 256p. 1995. pap. 15.00 (*0-06-092630-9*, Perennial) HarperTrade.

Bateson, Mary C. & Goldsby, Richard A. Thinking AIDS: The Social Response to the Biological Threat. 1989. 12.95 (*0-685-22769-3*); pap. 7.95 (*0-685-22770-7*) Addison-Wesley.

***Bateson, Mary Catherine.** Full Circles, Overlapping Lives: Culture & Generation in Transition. 288p. 2000. 25.00 (*0-375-50101-0*) Random.

Bateson, P. P. & Klopfer, P. H. Perspectives in Ethology Vol. 8: Whither Ethology? (Illus.). 292p. (C). 1988. text 85.00 (*0-306-42948-9*, Kluwer Plenum) Kluwer Academic.

— Perspectives in Ethology Vol. 9: Human Understanding & Animal Awareness. LC 86-649219. (Illus.). 330p. (C). 1990. text 85.00 (*0-306-43651-5*, Kluwer Plenum) Kluwer Academic.

Bateson, P. P. & Klopfer, Peter H., eds. Perspectives in Ethology Vol. 4: Advantages of Diversity. LC 73-79427. 276p. 1980. 65.00 (*0-306-40511-3*, Plenum Trade) Perseus Pubng.

— Perspectives in Ethology Vol. 5: Ontogeny. LC 73-79427. 536p. 1982. 79.50 (*0-306-41063-X*, Plenum Trade) Perseus Pubng.

— Perspectives in Ethology Vol. 6: Mechanisms. LC 73-79427. 324p. 1985. 69.50 (*0-306-41846-0*, Plenum Trade) Perseus Pubng.

— Perspectives in Ethology Vol. 7: Alternatives. LC 86-649219. 298p. 1987. 65.00 (*0-306-42429-0*, Plenum Trade) Perseus Pubng.

Bateson, P. P., et al. Perspectives in Ethology Vol. 10: Behavior & Evolution, Vol. 10. LC 86-649219. (Illus.). 302p. (C). 1993. text 85.00 (*0-306-44398-8*, Kluwer Plenum) Kluwer Academic.

Bateson, P. P. G., jt. ed. see Turner, Dennis.

Bateson, Patrick, ed. The Development & Integration of Behaviour: Essays in Honor of Robert Hinde. (Illus.). 516p. (C). 1991. text 105.00 (*0-521-40356-1*); pap. text 36.95 (*0-521-40709-5*) Cambridge U Pr.

Bateson, Patrick, jt. auth. see Martin, Paul.

Bateson, Robert. Introduction to Control System Technology. 6th ed. LC 98-17541. 736p. (C). 1998. 100.00 (*0-13-895483-6*) P-H.

Bateson, Robert N. & Raygor, Robin D. BASIC Programming for the Apple Computer. (Illus.). 278p. 1985. pap. text, teacher ed. write for info. (*0-314-87247-7*) West Pub.

Bateson, Robert N., jt. auth. see Raygor, Robin D.

Bateson, Vaughan. Masonry & Magic of Frater Rudyard Kipling. (Orig.). 1993. pap. 6.95 (*1-55818-238-1*) Holmes Pub.

Bateson, W. Mendell's Principles of Heredity. 228p. Date not set. 21.95 (*0-8488-2207-2*) Amereon Ltd.

Bateson, William. Materials for the Study of Variation: Treated with Especial Regard to Discontinuity in the Origin of Species. (Foundations of Natural History Ser.). (Illus.). 652p. 1992. reprint ed. pap. text 32.50 (*0-8018-4420-7*) Johns Hopkins.

— Mendel's Principles of Heredity: A Defence. fac. ed. (Illus.). 212p. 1996. 39.50 (*0-9653362-0-4*) Genetics Heritage.

— Problems of Genetics. LC 79-15467. 1979. 17.00 (*0-300-02435-5*); pap. 15.00 (*0-300-02436-3*, Y-350) Yale U Pr.

Batey, Angus. Beastie Boys. (Illus.). 208p. 1998. pap. text 17.95 (*1-897783-14-0*) Music Sales.

Batey, Carol. This Train Is Bound for Glory: Moving Beyond Our Family Crisis. LC 97-77574. 75p. 1997. pap. 9.95 (*0-9653019-7-4*) Carney-Miller.

Batey, Carol S. Parents Are Lifesavers: A Handbook for Parent Involvement in Schools. LC 95-32513. 120p. 1996. 43.95 (*0-8039-6240-1*); pap. 18.95 (*0-8039-6241-X*) Corwin Pr.

Batey, Colleen E., et al, eds. The Viking Age in Caithness, Orkney, & the North Atlantic. (Illus.). 560p. 1995. pap. 26.00 (*0-7486-0632-7*, Pub. by Edinburgh U Pr) Col U Pr.

***Batey, Colleen E. & Morris, Christopher D.** Vikings in the West. (Illus.). 176p. 2000. 32.50 (*0-7524-1439-9*, Pub. by Tempus Pubng) Arcadia Publng.

Batey, Colleen E., ed. see Graham-Campbell, James.

Batey, J., et al, eds. Flat-Panel Display Materials Vol. 345: Materials Research Society Symposium Proceedings. LC 94-37470. 339p. 1994. text 30.00 (*1-55899-245-6*) Materials Res.

***Batey, Mavis.** Alexander Pope: Poetry & Landscape. (Illus.). 140p. 2000. 45.00 (*1-899531-05-X*) Barn Elms.

Batey, Mavis. Regency Gardens: A New Garden History. (Garden History Ser.: No. 7). (Illus.). 96p. 1995. pap. 12.50 (*0-7478-0289-0*, Pub. by Shire Pubns) Parkwest Pubns.

Batey, Peter, jt. auth. see Congdon, Peter.

Batey, Richard A. The Letter of Paul to the Romans. LC 68-58865. 1984. 12.95 (*0-915547-26-0*) Abilene Christ U.

Batey, Robert, jt. ed. see Garcia, Sandra A.

Bath, Alan H. Tracking the Axis Enemy: The Triumph of Anglo-American Naval Intelligence. LC 98-18726. (Modern War Studies). 312p. 1998. 34.95 (*0-7006-0917-2*) U Pr of KS.

Bath, Amanda, ed. see Calders, Pere.

Bath-Balogh, Mary. Oral Biology for Dental Hygienist. 1997. pap. text, wbk. ed. 20.95 (*0-7216-6903-4*, W B Saunders Co) Harcrt Hlth Sci Grp.

Bath-Balogh, Mary & Fehrenbach, Margaret J. Illustrated Dental Embryology, Histology, & Anatomy. (Illus.). 415p. 1997. pap., teacher ed. write for info. (*0-7216-6688-4*, W B Saunders Co) Harcrt Hlth Sci Grp.

— Oral Biology for Dental Hygienists. Kaszczuk, Selma, ed. LC 96-16729. (Illus.). 416p. 1996. pap. text 44.00 (*0-7216-6687-6*, W B Saunders Co) Harcrt Hlth Sci Grp.

Bath, C. Richard, jt. auth. see Tanski, Janet.

Bath, G. M. Central Asia & Western Himalaya: A Forgotten Link. 76p. 1986. 75.00 (*81-85046-34-4*, Pub. by Scientific) St Mut.

***Bath International Fluid Power Workshop.** Fluid Power Engineering: Challenge & Solutions, Vol. 10. Burrows, Clifford Robert & Edge, Kevin A., eds. LC 98-30566. 1998. 199.00 (*0-86380-227-3*) Research Studies Pr Ltd.

Bath, Markus. Modern Spectral Analysis with Geophysical Applications. Cooper, Michael R., ed. (Open File Publications: No. 2). 530p. 1995. pap. 65.00 (*1-56080-031-3*, 758) Soc Expl Geophys.

Bath, Michael. Speaking Pictures: English Emblem Books & Renaissance Culture. LC 93-10073. (Medieval & Renaissance Library). 1993. write for info. (*0-582-06197-0*) Longman.

— Speaking Pictures: English Emblem Books & Renaissance Culture. LC 93-10073. (Medieval & Renaissance Library). 1994. pap. text. write for info. (*0-582-06196-2*) Longman.

Bath, Michael, et al, eds. The Art of the Emblem: Essays in Honor of Karl Josef Hoeltgen. LC 92-8701. (Studies in the Emblem: No. 10). (Illus.). 280p. 1993. 62.50 (*0-404-63710-8*) AMS Pr.

Bath, Michael & Russell, Daniel S. Deviceful Settings: The English Renaissance Emblem & Its Contexts : Selected Papers from the Third International Emblem Conference, Pittsburgh, 1993. LC 96-51673. (Occasional Studies Ser.). 1997. write for info. (*0-404-63713-2*) AMS Pr.

Bath, Trevor & Jones, Joy. The Gardener's Guide to Growing Hardy Geraniums. (Gardener's Guide Ser.). (Illus.). 160p. 1994. 29.95 (*0-88192-278-1*) Timber

Bath, William P., et al. A Proper Reply to a Late Scurrilous Libel Intitled Sedition & Defamation Display'd (1731) No. 2: British Ideas & Issues, 1660-1820. LC 97-42766. 1998. 24.50 (*0-404-59652-5*) AMS Pr.

***Batha, Thomas D. U. S. Martial .22RF Rifles. (Illus.). 104p. 2000. pap. 13.95 (*1-880677-16-4*) Excalibur AZ. US Martial .22RF Rifles is a detailed review of the firearms used as martial .22RF training rifles by the US services. Beginning with the Model 1889 Rolling Block conversion, the book traces the use of the Krag, Hoffer-Thompson, Winder Musket, Winchester Model 1903, Model 1922 Springfield Gallery Practice Rifles, Remington Model 513T, Winchester Model 75, Stevens Model 416T, Mossberg Models 42MB & 44US & the H&R Model 65 & MC-58. Postwar rifles covered include the Mossberg Model, 144US, the Winchester Model 52 series, the Remington Models 511-P, 40-X, 521 & 541-X, M16 Conversions, the H&R Model 5200, the Kimber Model 82 Government & miscellaneous rifles. A comprehensive appendix of rifle data is included in the book. Contact Excalibur Publications, PO Box 35369, Tucson, AZ 85740-5369. Voice: (520) 575-9057. Fax: (520) 575-9068.**
Publisher Paid Annotation.

Bathanti, Joseph. This Metal. 136p. (Orig.). 1996. pap. 10.95 (*1-879934-30-2*) St Andrews NC.

Bathe, Dorothy, jt. auth. see Bathe, Greville.

Bathe, Greville & Bathe, Dorothy. Oliver Evans: A Chronicle of Early American Engineering. LC 72-5031. (Technology & Society Ser.). (Illus.). 380p. 1978. reprint ed. 46.95 (*0-405-04684-7*) Ayer.

Bathe, John R., ed. Leading Sector Fund Trader-Past Issues, January 1987 to December 1988. 160p. (Orig.). 1989. pap. 50.00 (*0-317-93448-1*) Alphanational.

Bathe, Klaus-Jurgen. Finite Element Procedures. rev. ed. LC 95-1231. 1037p. (C). 1995. 105.00 (*0-13-301458-4*) P-H.

Bathe, Klaus-Jurgen, ed. Nonlinear Finite Element Analysis & Adina: Proceedings of the 3rd Adina Conference, Massachusetts, U. S. A., 10-12 June 1981. 206p. 1981. 125.00 (*0-08-027594-X*, Pergamon Pr) Elsevier.

— Nonlinear Finite Elements Analysis & Adina. (Computers & Structures Ser.: No. 17). 311p. 1983. 136.00 (*0-08-030566-0*, Pub. by Pergamon Repr) Franklin.

Bathe, Klaus-Jurgen, et al, eds. Finite Element Methods for Nonlinear Problems. (Illus.). 800p. 1986. 248.95 (*0-387-16226-7*) Spr-Verlag.

Bathelter, Dean. The Other Side of a Memory. (Illus.). viii, 228p. 1996. write for info. (*0-9654636-0-5*) Kenlex Pub.

***Bather, John.** Decision Theory: An Introduction to Dynamic Programming & Sequential Decisions. LC 00-29620. 2000. pap. write for info. (*0-471-97649-0*) Wiley.

Batherman, Muriel. Before Columbus. (Illus.). 32p. (J). (gr. k-3). 1990. pap. 6.95 (*0-395-54954-X*) HM.

— Before Columbus. (J). 1981. 11.15 (*0-606-03062-X*, Pub. by Turtleback) Demco.

Bathersfield, Arnold. I Me You. (Illus.). 164p. 1995. 15.50 (*0-9613919-2-8*) Evergreen Prods.

— In Being: The Name of the Game by Arnold Bathersfield. LC 84-90392. (Illus.). 90p. 1994. pap. 10.00 (*0-9613919-0-1*) Evergreen Prods.

— Stay Up: I Within. LC 90-84864. 140p. 1991. 12.50 (*0-9613919-1-X*) Evergreen Prods.

Bathersfield, Arnold, et al. Gurus & Griots. Gibbs, C. Jeanean, ed. LC 87-90523. (Illus.). 108p. (YA). (gr. 7 up). 1987. pap. 6.00 (*0-9618755-0-X*) Palm Tree Ent

Bathgate, T. So, What's Next? 6.99 (*1-871676-84-3*, Pub. by Christian Focus) Spring Arbor Dist.

Bathias, Claude & Bailon, Jean-Paul, eds. La Fatigue Des Materiaux et Des Structures. LC 80-143443. (Collection Universite de Compiegne). (FRE., Illus.). 564p. reprint ed. pap. 174.90 (*0-7837-6946-6*, 204677500003) Bks Demand.

Bathie, George. Baking for Profit: Starting a Small Bakery. 128p. 2000. pap. 17.50 (*1-85339-407-6*, Pub. by Intermed Tech) Stylus Pub VA.

Bathie, H. Perrier De La, see De La Bathie, H. Perrier

Bathie, William W. Fundamentals of Gas Turbines. 2nd ed. LC 95-32998. 480p. 1995. text 99.95 (*0-471-31122-7*) Wiley.

Bathke, W. L. & Haney, W. A., eds. Land Management in the 70's: Concepts & Models. (Illus.). 1972. 10.00 (*0-911302-19-0*) San Francisco Pr.

Bathla, Sonia. Women, Democrac & the Media: Cultural & Political Representations in the Indian Press. LC 98-27693. 1998. write for info. (*0-7619-9288-X*) Sage.

— Women, Democracy & the Media: Cultural & Political Representations in the Indian Press. LC 98-27693. 1998. write for info. (*0-7619-9287-1*) Sage.

— Women, Democracy & the Media: Cultural & Political Representations in the Indian Press LC 98-27693. 209 p. 1998. write for info. (*81-7036-749-2*) Sage.

Batho, Edith C. The Ettrick Shepherd. (BCL1-PR English Literature Ser.). 233p. 1992. reprint ed. lib. bdg. 79.00 (*0-7812-7561-X*) Rprt Serv.

Batho, Rosemary. Beginners Guide to Flower Arranging. 1997. 24.95 (*1-85391-575-0*) Merehurst Ltd.

Batho, Rosemary, et al. The Advanced Guide to Floristry. (Illus.). 160p. 1999. 29.95 (*1-85391-517-3*) Merehurst Ltd.

Bathory, Peter D., ed. Leadership in America: Consensus, Corruption, & Charisma. LC 77-17714. 1978. pap. text 7.95 (*0-582-28039-7*) Longman.

Bathrick, David. The Powers of Speech: The Politics of Culture in the GDR. LC 95-2354. (Modern German Culture & Literature Ser.). x, 303p. 1995. text 50.00 (*0-8032-1258-5*) U of Nebr Pr.

Bathrick, David, jt. ed. see Huyssen, Andreas.

Bathrick, Michael. John Herrick Ledger, Pine Plains, New York. 86p. 1988. pap. 15.50 (*1-56012-085-1*, 85) Kinship Rhinebeck.

Bathrick, S., et al. From Receiver to Remote Control: The TV Set. Geller, Matthew & Williams, Reese, eds. (Illus.). 144p. 1990. pap. text 20.00 (*0-915557-70-3*) New Mus Contemp Art.

Bathroom Readers' Institute Staff. The Best of Uncle John's Bathroom Reader. (Uncle John's Bathroom Reader Ser.). 600p. 1995. pap. 16.95 (*1-879682-62-1*) Bathroom Reader.

Bathroom Reader's Institute Staff. Uncle John's Absolutely Absorbing Bathroom Reader, Vol. 12. 522p. 1999. pap. 16.95 (*1-879682-73-7*) Bathroom Reader.

— Uncle John's Bathroom Reader. 224p. (Orig.). 1988. pap. 9.95 (*0-312-02663-3*) St Martin.

— Uncle John's Fifth Bathroom Reader. 224p. 1992. pap. 9.95 (*1-879682-28-1*) Bathroom Reader.

— Uncle John's Fourth Bathroom Reader. 224p. (Orig.). 1991. pap. 9.95 (*0-312-06484-5*) St Martin.

— Uncle John's Giant 10th Anniversary Bathroom Reader. 522p. 1997. pap. text 16.95 (*1-879682-68-0*) Bathroom Reader.

— Uncle John's Great Big Bathroom Reader, Vol. 11. 468p. 1998. pap. 16.95 (*1-879682-69-9*) Bathroom Reader.

— Uncle John's Indispensable Guide to the Year 2000. 230p. 1998. pap. 5.95 (*1-879682-70-2*) Bathroom Reader.

***Bathroom Reader's Institute Staff.** Uncle John's Legendary Lost Bathroom Reader. 682p. 1999. pap. 18.95 (*1-879682-74-5*) Bathroom Reader.

Bathroom Reader's Institute Staff. Uncle John's Second Bathroom Reader. 224p. (Orig.). 1989. pap. 9.95 (*0-312-03446-6*) St Martin.

— Uncle John's Seventh Bathroom Reader. 228p. 1994. pap. 9.95 (*1-879682-58-3*) Bathroom Reader.

— Uncle John's Sixth Bathroom Reader. 6th ed. 228p. 1993. pap. 9.95 (*1-879682-45-1*) Bathroom Reader.

— Uncle John's Ultimate Bathroom Reader. 8th ed. (Uncle John's Bathroom Readers Ser.: Vol. 8). 324p. 1996. pap. 12.95 (*1-879682-65-6*) Bathroom Reader.

Bathroom Reader's Institute Staff & Vedral, Joyce L. Uncle John's Third Bathroom Reader: The Bathroom Readers' Institute. 224p. (Orig.). 1990. pap. 9.95 (*0-312-04586-7*) St Martin.

Bathsua, Makin. An Essay to Revive the Ancient Education of Gentlewomen, in Religion, Manners, Arts & Tongues. (Augustan Reprints Ser.: No. 202). 1980. reprint ed. 14.50 (*0-404-70202-3*) AMS Pr.

Bathum, Mike. Four-Step Color Projects. (Portfolio of Illustrated Four-Step Art Projects Ser.). (Illus.). 72p. 1983. pap. text 12.95 (*0-87628-321-0*) Ctr Appl Res.

— Four-Step Crafts Projects. (Portfolio of Illustrated Four-Step Art Projects Ser.). (Illus.). 72p. 1984. pap. text 12.95 (*0-87628-322-9*) Ctr Appl Res.

— Four-Step Design Projects. (Portfolio of Illustrated Four-Step Art Projects Ser.). (Illus.). 72p. 1983. pap. text 12.95 (*0-87628-323-7*) Ctr Appl Res.

— Four-Step Drawing & Composition Projects. (Portfolio of Illustrated Four-Step Art Projects Ser.). (Illus.). 72p. 1983. pap. text 12.95 (*0-87628-324-5*) Ctr Appl Res.

— Four-Step Illustration Projects. (Portfolio of Illustrated Four-Step Art Projects Ser.). (Illus.). 72p. 1984. pap. 12.95 (*0-87628-325-3*) Ctr Appl Res.

— Four-Step Printmaking Projects. (Portfolio of Illustrated Four-Step Art Projects Ser.). (Illus.). 72p. 1983. pap. 12.95 (*0-87628-327-X*) Ctr Appl Res.

— Painting. (Portfolio of Illustrated Four-Step Art Projects Ser.). (Illus.). 72p. 1983. pap. text 12.95 (*0-87628-326-1*) Ctr Appl Res.

Bathurst, A. B. Apsley & Bathurst Families. 136p. 1996. reprint ed. pap. 22.00 (*0-8328-5380-1*); reprint ed. lib. bdg. 32.00 (*0-8328-5379-8*) Higginson Bk Co.

Bathurst, Bella. The Lighthouse Stevensons: The Extraordinary Story of the Building of the Scottish Lighthouses by the Ancestors of Robert Louis Stevenson. LC 99-26174. 304p. 1999. 24.00 (*0-06-019427-8*) HarpC.

— The Lighthouse Stevensons: The Extraordinary Story of the Building of the Scottish Lighthouses by the Ancestors of Robert Louis Stevenson. 304p. 2000. pap. 14.00 (*0-06-093226-0*, Perennial) HarperTrade.

***Bathurst, Bella.** The Lighthouse Stevensons: The Extraordinary Story of the Building of the Scottish Lighthouses by the Ancestors of Robert Louis Stevenson. large type ed. LC 99-88111. (Nonfiction Ser.). 2000. 28.95 (*0-7838-8964-X*, G K Hall Lrg Type) Mac Lib Ref.

Bathurst, Charles. Remarks on the Differences in Shakespeare's Versification in Different Periods of His Life. LC 75-113550. 1970. reprint ed. 34.50 (*0-404-00692-2*) AMS Pr.

Bathurst, Effie G. A Teachers College Follow-Up Service: Its Factors & Development in an Unsupervised Service Area. LC 79-176542. (Columbia University. Teachers College. Contributions to Education Ser.: No. 478). reprint ed. 37.50 (*0-404-55478-4*) AMS Pr.

Bathurst, R. G. Carbonate Sediments & Their Diagenesis. 2nd ed. (Developments in Sedimentology Ser.: Vol. 12). xx,660p. 1975. pap. 132.00 (*0-444-41353-7*) Elsevier.

Bathurst, Robert B. Intelligence & the Mirror. 144p. (C). 1993. text 55.00 (*0-8039-8948-2*) Sage.

***Bati, Anwer.** Essential Cigar: A Book for Connoisseurs. (Illus.). 1999. 9.98 (*1-84038-285-6*) Hermes Hse.

Bati, Anwer & Chase, Simon. The Cigar Companion. 3rd ed. (Illus.). 224p. 1997. 24.95 (*0-7624-0142-7*) Running Pr.

Batia, Shobha K. & Blaney, Geoffrey W., eds. Recent Advances in Instrumentation, Data Acquisition & Testing in Soil Dynamics. LC 91-30336. 144p. 1991. pap. text 20.00 (*0-87262-854-X*) Am Soc Civil Eng.

Baticle, Jeannine. Goya: Painter of Terrible Splendor. (Discoveries Ser.). (Illus.). 176p. 1994. pap. 12.95 (*0-8109-2818-3*, Pub. by Abrams) Time Warner.

***Batie, Howard.** Awakening the Healer Within. 2000. pap. 12.95 (*1-56718-055-8*) Llewellyn Pubns.

Batie, Sandra S., et al. Managing Agriculture Contamination of Ground Water: State Strategies. Feinstein, Gerry R., ed. 50p. (Orig.). 1989. pap. text 10.00 (*1-55877-057-7*) Natl Governor.

Batie, Steve, ed. Business As Usual: Nebraska Cornhuskers 1995 National Football Championship. pap. 14.95 (*0-9638025-6-9*, Pub. by Lincoln Jrnl Star) Booksource.

Batienon, Albert. I'll Plant My Ear to the Ground: Poems. LC 96-11662. 64p. 1997. pap. 14.95 (*0-7734-2690-6*, Mellen Poetry Pr) E Mellen.

Batiffol, Louis. Century of the Renaissance. (National History of France Ser.: No. 3). reprint ed. 45.00 (*0-404-50793-X*) AMS Pr.

— Marie de Medicis & the French Court in the Seventeenth Century. Davis, H. W., ed. King, Mary, tr. from FRE. LC 72-137368. (Select Bibliographies Reprint Ser.). 1977. reprint ed. 19.95 (*0-8369-5569-2*) Ayer.

Batik, Albert L. The Engineering Standard, a Most Useful Tool. 350p. 1992. 40.00 (*0-9622523-0-1*) El Rancho CO.

— Guide to Standards. Llyne, Jennifer, ed. 140p. (Orig.). 1989. 12.00 (*0-317-93671-9*) El Rancho CO.

Batin, Adela W. & Batin, Christopher M. Best Recipes of Alaska's Fishing Lodges. 320p. (Orig.). 1995. pap. 24.95 (*0-916771-10-5*) Alaska Angler.

Batin, Adela W., jt. auth. see Batin, Christopher M.

Batin, Adela W., ed. & photos by see Batin, Christopher M. & Rudnick, Terry.

Batin, Christopher M. Chris Batin's Twenty Great Alaska Fishing Adventures: A Travel - Planning Guide for Those Who Want the Best in Alaska Sportfishing Adventures. (Illus.). 224p. (Orig.). 1991. 24.95 (*0-916771-09-1*) Alaska Angler.

— How to Catch Alaska's Trophy Sportfish. LC 84-70673. (Illus.). 368p. (Orig.). 1994. 60.00 (*0-916771-01-6*); pap. 25.95 (*0-916771-11-3*) Alaska Angler.

— Hunting in Alaska: A Comprehensive Guide. rev. ed. (Illus.). 416p. 1994. reprint ed. pap. 29.95 (*0-916771-12-1*) Alaska Angler.

Batin, Christopher M. & Batin, Adela W. Fishing Alaska on Dollars a Day. rev. ed. (Fishing Alaska on Fifteen Dollars a Day Ser.). (Illus.). 352p. 1994. pap. 24.95 (*0-916771-14-8*) Alaska Angler.

Batin, Christopher M. & Rudnick, Terry. How to Catch Trophy Halibut: Proven Tips, Techniques & Strategies of the Experts. Batin, Adela W., ed. & photos by by. (Illus.). 369p. (Orig.). 1996. pap. 25.95 (*0-916771-15-6*) Alaska Angler.

Batin, Christopher M., jt. auth. see Batin, Adela W.

Batin, Christopher M., ed. see Liere, Alan.

Batina, Loreli A. Immunology Investigations: A Laboratory Manual. (Illus.). 210p. (C). 1997. pap. text, lab manual ed. 32.95 (*0-89863-176-9*) Star Pub CA.

***Batina, Raymond G. & Ihori, Toshihiro.** Consumption Tax Policy & the Taxation of Capital Income. (Illus.). 400p. 2000. text 74.00 (*0-19-829790-4*) OUP.

Batini, Carol, et al. Conceptual Database Design. 470p. (C). 1991. 47.00 (*0-8053-0244-1*) Benjamin-Cummings.

Batinski, Michael C. Jonathan Belcher, Colonial Governor. LC 95-32666. 232p. 1996. text 29.95 (*0-8131-1946-4*) U Pr of Ky.

***Bationo, Emmanuel.** Die Afrikanische Rezeption Von Brecht Im Lichte der Literaturtheorien: Aufgezeigt Am Beispiel Von Wole Soyinkas Opera Wonyosi. (GER.). iv, 157p. 1999. 32.00 (*3-631-34366-3*) P Lang Pubng.

Batioukova, Z. I. & Shaposhnikova, T. D. Innovation in Russian Schools. Korolov, Maria, tr. from RUS. LC 97-65264. 86p. 1997. pap. 9.50 (*0-87367-496-0*) Phi Delta Kappa.

Batisch, George. Ophthalmodouleia: That Is the Service of the Eyes. Blanchard, Donald, tr. from GER. (Hirschberg History of Ophthalmology Ser.: Vol. III). Orig. Title: Ophthalmodouleia, Das ist Augendienst. (Illus.). 600p. 1996. lthr. write for info. (*0-614-30296-X*) Blanchards Brook.

Batish, Ashwin. First Ten Thaat Raga Chalans: Chalan Notations. (First Ten Thaat Raga Chalans Ser.). 56p. 1993. text 11.95 (*1-882319-35-4*) Batish Pubns.

Batish, Ashwin. First Ten Thaat Raga Chalans: Chalan Practice Tapes. (First Ten Thaat Raga Chalans Ser.). 56p. 1993. text Price not set. incl. audio (*1-882319-09-5*) Batish Pubns.

Batish, Ashwin, jt. auth. see Batish, Shiv D.

Batish, Shiv D. & Batish, Ashwin. Ragopedia Vol. 1: Exotic Scales of North India, 2 vols. 1989. spiral bd. 35.00 (*1-882319-00-1*) Batish Pubns.

Batisse, M., jt. auth. see Grenon, M.

Batist, M. De, see De Batist, M., ed.

Batista, Fulgencio. Growth & Decline of the Cuban Republic. 1964. 10.00 (*0-8159-5614-2*) Devin.

Batista, Jaoa, ed. see Getz, Gene A.

Batista, Manuel G. Inner Sightings on "Who Am I" Secrets about Who, How, Why, When & Where. Van Ronk, Ruth, ed. 15p. 1994. 3.95 (*0-9644989-0-1*) Insight Publ.

Batista, Robert. Ooh Baby Baby. 301p. 2000. pap. write for info. (*1-888097-02-7*) Wrd Is Bond.

— Street Angel. 90p. (Orig.). (YA). (gr. 8 up). 1998. pap. write for info. (*1-888097-01-9*) Wrd Is Bond.

Batiste, Enric, tr. see Ros, Roser.

Batiste, Sarah, jt. illus. see James, Philip.

***Batiuk, Tom.** Funky Winkerbean: Could Be a Book Deal Here! 2000. pap. 9.95 (*1-56163-266-X*) NBM.

— Lisa's Story. 2000. pap. 12.95 (*0-399-52666-8*, Perigee Bks) Berkley Pub.

Batiuk, Tom & Ayers, Chuck. And One Slice with Anchovies! (Crankshaft Collection). (Illus.). 128p. 1993. pap. 8.95 (*0-8362-1707-1*) Andrews & McMeel.

— Crankshaft. (Illus.). 128p. 1992. pap. 8.95 (*0-8362-1889-2*) Andrews & McMeel.

— I've Still Got It! A Crankshaft Collection. (Illus.). 128p. 1995. pap. 9.95 (*0-8362-0419-0*) Andrews & McMeel.

— Safe Return Home: An Inspirational Book for Caregivers of Alzheimer's Patients. LC 98-3785. 112p. 1998. 12.95 (*0-8362-6913-6*) Andrews & McMeel.

Batizy, Levente G., jt. auth. see Terezhalmy, G. T.

Batjer, H. Hunt, et al, eds. Cerebrovascular Disease. LC 96-13565. 1,104p. 1996. text 275.00 (*0-397-51661-4*) Lppncott W & W.

Batkay, William M. Authoritarian Politics in Transitional States. 1982. text 49.00 (*0-914710-96-6*, 102) Col U Pr.

***Batker, Carol J.** Reforming Fictions: Native, African & Jewish American Women's Literature & Journalism in the Progressive Era. LC 99-89025. 2000. pap., boxed set 17.50 (*0-231-11851-1*) Col U Pr.

— Reforming Fictions: Native, African & Jewish American Women's Literature & Journalism in the Progressive Era. LC 99-89025. 2000. 49.50 (*0-231-11850-3*) Col U Pr.

Batki, John, tr. see Forgacs, Eva.

Batki, John, tr. see Jozsef, Attila.

Batki, John, tr. see Krudy, Gyula.

Batki, John, tr. see Lengyel, Peter.

Batki, John, tr. see Szep, Erno.

Batkin, Leonid M. Political Mirages: Russia at the Crossroads. 1995. 115.00 (*1-56072-265-7*) Nova Sci Pubs.

Batkin, Maureen. Gifts for Good Children Pt. II: The History of Children's China 1890-1990. (Illus.). 310p. 1996. 60.00 (*0-903685-30-2*, Pub. by R Dennis) Antique Collect.

— Wedgwood Ceramics, 1846-1959. (Illus.). 1982. 95.00 (*0-903685-11-6*, Pub. by R Dennis) Antique Collect.

Batkin, Maureen, jt. auth. see Atterbury, Paul.

Batkin, Ruth B. Educational Measurement: Subject, Reference & Research Guide. LC 87-47613. 160p. 1987. pap. 34.50 (*0-88164-535-4*) ABBE Pubs Assn.

Batko, Marc, tr. see Soelle, Dorothee.

Batley, Edward M. Catalyst of Enlightenment: Gotthold Ephraim Lessing: Productive Criticism of Eighteenth-Century Germany. (Illus.). 436p. 1990. 64.00 (*3-261-04193-5*) P Lang Pubng.

Batley, Graeme E., ed. Trace Element Speciation: Analytical Methods & Problems. 360p. 1989. lib. bdg. 249.00 (*0-8493-4712-2*) CRC Pr.

Batley, Richard & Campbell, Adrian, eds. The Political Executive: Politicians & Management in European Local Government. 85p. 1992. text 25.00 (*0-7146-3480-8*, Pub. by F Cass Pubs) Intl Spec Bk.

Batley, Richard, jt. ed. see Gibson, John.

Batlle, Beth. Sparks in the Night. LC 87-5563. 158p. 1987. 13.75 (*0-930950-11-9*); pap. 8.75 (*0-930950-12-7*) Nopoly Pr.

Batman, Nancy Jo. It's Not Polite to Play Dead at the Supper Table. (Illus.). 104p. (Orig.). 1994. pap. 9.99 (*0-8272-1612-2*) Chalice Pr.

— Yeah, But How Would She Look Beside the Go-Kart Trophy. LC 92-19199. (Illus.). 104p. (Orig.). 1992. pap. 9.99 (*0-8272-4403-7*) Chalice Pr.

Batman, Richard. The Outer Coast. LC 85-7613. (Illus.). 400p. 1985. 18.95 (*0-15-170450-3*) Harcourt.

Batman, Richard, ed. see Pattie, James O.

Batman, Stephen. Doome Warning All Men to the Judgement. LC 84-1441. 472p. 1984. reprint ed. 75.00 (*0-8201-1394-8*) Schol Facsimiles.

— The Golden Booke of the Leaden Gods, Repr. Of 1577 Ed. LC 75-27856. (Renaissance & the Gods Ser.: Vol. 13). (Illus.). 1976. lib. bdg. 88.00 (*0-8240-2062-6*) Garland.

***Batmanghelidj, F.** ABC of Asthma Allergies & Lupus: Eradicate Asthma - Now! (Illus.). 240p. 2000. pap. 17.00 (*0-9629942-6-X*) Global Hlth.

— How to Deal with Back Pain & Rheumatoid Joint Pain. (Illus.). 100p. 1991. pap. 14.95 (*0-9629942-0-0*) Global Hlth.

Batmanghelidj, F. Your Body's Many Cries for Water: You Are Not Sick, You Are Thirsty! 2nd rev. ed. (Illus.). 180p. 1997. 27.00 (*0-9629942-5-1*) Global Hlth.

— Your Body's Many Cries for Water: You Are Not Sick, You Are Thirsty! Don't Treat Thirst with... 2nd ed. (Illus.). 180p. 1995. pap. 14.95 (*0-9629942-3-5*) Global Hlth.

Batmanglij, M., ed. see Hafez.

Batmanglij, Najmieh. A Taste of Persia: An Introduction to Persian Cooking. LC 98-31208. (Illus.). 176p. 1999. pap. 17.95 (*0-934211-54-X*) Mage Pubs Inc.

Batmanglij, Najmieh Khalili. New Food of Life: Ancient Persian & Modern Iranian Cooking & Ceremonies. LC TX725.I7 B373 1992. (Illus.). 440p. 1993. 44.95 (*0-934211-34-5*) Mage Pubs Inc.

— Persian Cooking for a Healthy Kitchen. LC 94-907. (Illus.). 190p. 1994. 29.95 (*0-934211-40-X*) Mage Pubs Inc.

Batnitzky, Solomon, jt. ed. see Sarwar, Mohammed.

Baton Rouge Advocate Staff, ed. Greatest Moments in LSU Football History. (Illus.). 250p. 1998. 29.95 (*1-58261-018-5*) Sprts Pubng.

***Batonyi, Gabor.** Britain & Central Europe, 1918-1933. LC 98-55138. 248p. 1999. text 60.00 (*0-19-820748-4*) OUP.

Bator, Joseph. International Airline Phrase Book in Six Languages: English, French, German, Italian, Portuguese, Spanish. LC 67-25870. 204p. (Orig.). 1968. pap. 6.95 (*0-486-22017-6*) Dover.

Bator, Paul M. The International Trade in Art. LC 82-17405. viii, 108p. (C). 1983. pap. text 6.95 (*0-226-03910-2*) U Ch Pr.

Bator, Paul M., et al. Hart & Wechsler's - The Federal Courts & the Federal System. 3rd ed. (University Casebook Ser.). 1898p. 1990. reprint ed. text 48.50 (*0-88277-647-9*) Foundation Pr.

Bator, Robert. Daily Life in Ancient & Modern Istanbul. LC 98-53959. (Cities Through Time Ser.). (Illus.). 64p. (J). (gr. 4-7). 2000. lib. bdg. 23.93 (*0-8225-3217-4*, Runestone Pr) Lerner Pub.

Batori, Istvan S., et al, eds. Computational Linguistics - Computerlinguistik: An International Handbook on Computer Oriented Language Research - Ein Internationales Handbuch zur Computergestutzten Sprachforschung und Ihrer Anwendungen. (Handbooks of Linguistics & Communication Science: Vol. - Band 4). xxxiv, 933p. (C). 1989. lib. bdg. 588.50 (*3-11-009792-3*) De Gruyter.

Batory, Dana M. & Pollak, David E. Vintage Woodworking Machinery: An Illustrated Guide to Four Manufacturers. LC 97-70454. (Illus.). 148p. 1997. pap. 21.95 (*1-879335-75-1*) Astragal Pr.

***Batory, Joseph P.** Yo! Joey! The Unique Memoirs of an Unusual School Superintendent. 150p. 2000. pap. 11.95 (*0-9679216-0-0*) Leadrshp Pr PA.

Batouka, Niaz, jt. auth. see Paris, Catherine.

Batoutah, Ibn. Voyages d'Ibn Batoutah, 4 vols. Defremery, G. & Sanguimetti, B. R., trs. (FRE.). 2047p. reprint ed. lib. bdg. 325.00 (*0-89241-177-5*) Caratzas.

***Batoz, Jean-Louis.** Integrated Design & Manufacturing in Mechanical Engineering '98: Proceedings of the 2nd IDMME Conference Held in Compiaegne, France, 27-29 May 1998. LC 99-50112. 1999. write for info. (*0-7923-6024-9*) Kluwer Academic.

Batra. The Future of the World. 1995. 25.00 (*0-02-507673-6*) Macmillan.

Batra, Sumita & Wilde, Liz. The Art of Mehndi. LC 99-17704. (Illus.). 144p. 1999. pap. 19.95 (*0-14-028401-X*) Viking Penguin.

Batra, I. P., ed. Metallization & Metal - Semiconductor Interfaces. (Illus.). 522p. (C). 1989. text 174.00 (*0-306-43159-9*, Kluwer Plenum) Kluwer Academic.

Batra, Lekh R. Monilinia Fungi of the World: Their Ecology, Biosystematics & Control. (Mycologia Memoirs Ser.: No. 16). (Illus.). 500p. 1991. lib. bdg. 120.00 (*0-945345-34-8*, Pub. by Gebruder Borntraeger) Balogh.

— World Species of Monilinia (Fungi) (Mycologia Memoir Ser.: No. 16). (Illus.). x, 246p. 1991. 88.00 (*3-443-76006-6*, Pub. by Gebruder Borntraeger) Balogh.

Batra, Manjula. Protection of Human Rights in Criminal Justice Administration: A Study of the Rights of Accused. (C). 1989. 250.00 (*0-7855-4774-6*) St Mut.

— Protection of Human Rights in Criminal Justice Administration: A Study of the Rights of the Accused - Indian & Soviet Legal Systems. (C). 1990. 110.00 (*0-89771-186-6*) St Mut.

Batra, Mukesh. Homoeopathy. 212p. 1989. 16.95 (*0-318-36362-3*) Asia Bk Corp.

Batra, N. D. The Hour of Television: Critical Approaches. LC 87-4315. (Illus.). 301p. 1987. 31.00 (*0-8108-1989-9*) Scarecrow.

— A Self-Renewing Society: The Role of Television & Communications Technology. 194p. (Orig.). (C). 1990. pap. text 23.00 (*0-8191-7949-3*); lib. bdg. 43.50 (*0-8191-7948-5*) U Pr of Amer.

Batra, Neelam. The Healing Powers of India. 2001. write for info. (*0-688-16554-0*, Hearst) Hearst Commns.

***Batra, Neelam.** Indian Cooking. LC 97-24366. 320p. 1998. 25.00 (*0-688-15690-8*, Wm Morrow) Morrow Avon.

Batra, Neelam. The Indian Vegetarian. 400p. 1998. pap. 18.95 (*0-02-862285-5*) Macmillan.

— New Indian Cookbook. 1997. 25.00 (*0-02-861004-0*) Macmillan.

— TK (Indian Cooking) Hoenig, Pam, ed. 320p. 1998. write for info. (*0-614-30564-0*, Wm Morrow) Morrow Avon.

Batra, Neelam & Rothschild-Sherwin, Shelley. The Indian Vegetarian. LC 93-41193. 432p. 1994. 25.00 (*0-02-507675-2*, Maxwell Macmillan) Macmillan.

Batra, R. C., et al, eds. Impact, Waves, & Fracture Vol. 205: Impact, Waves, & Fracture. LC 95-77179. (1995 Joint ASME Applied Mechanics & Materials Summer Meeting Ser.: Vol. 205). 488p. 1995. 160.00 (*0-7918-1320-7*, H00952) ASME.

Batra, R. C. & Zbib, Hussein M., eds. Material Instabilities, Theory & Application: Proceedings: International Mechanical Engineering Congress & Exposition (1994: Chicago, IL) LC 94-78972. (AMD - MD Ser.: Vol. 183, Vol. 50). 369p. 1995. pap. 100.00 (*0-7918-1400-9*, G00895) ASME Pr.

Batra, Rajeev & Glazer, Rashi, eds. Cable TV Advertising: In Search of the Right Formula. LC 88-37395. 199p. 1989. 59.95 (*0-89930-406-0*, BTA, Quorum Bks) Greenwood.

***Batra, Rajeev & William Davidson Institute Staff.** Marketing Issues in Transitional Economies LC 99-35795. (Series on Transitional & Emerging Economies). 1999. write for info. (*0-7923-8498-9*) Kluwer Academic.

Batra, Rajeev, et al. Advertising Management. 5th ed. LC 95-25901. 754p. 1995. 99.00 (*0-13-305715-1*) P-H.

***Batra, Ravi.** The Crash of the Millenium: Surviving the Coming Inflationary Depression. LC 99-29467. 288p. 1999. 24.00 (*0-609-60512-7*, Crown) Crown Pub Group.

Batra, Ravi. The Downfall of Capitalism & Communism: Can Capitalism be Saved? 2nd ed. (Illus.). 350p. 1990. 25.00 (*0-939352-09-5*) Liberty Pr TX.

— Muslim Civilization & the Crisis in Iran. 218p. (Orig.). 1980. pap. 3.95 (*0-686-95468-8*) Ananda Marga.

— Prout: An Economic Solution to Poverty in the Third World. (Illus.). 220p. (Orig.). (C). 1989. pap. 9.95 (*0-88476-075-8*) Ananda Marga.

— Regular Cycles of Money, Inflation, Regulation & Depression. LC 85-50598. (Illus.). 192p. (C). 1985. 20.00 (*0-939352-04-4*) Liberty Pr TX.

— Stock Market Crashes of 1998 & 1999: The Asian Crisis & Your Future. LC 98-65087. (Illus.). 219p. 1998. 24.00 (*0-939352-76-1*); pap. 18.00 (*0-939352-78-8*) Liberty Pr TX.

Batra, Romesh C., ed. Contemporary Research in Engineering Science. LC 95-25403. 685p. 1995. 196.95 (*3-540-60384-0*) Spr-Verlag.

Batra, S. K., ed. see Symposium on Cotton Dust: Sampling, Monitoring, &.

Batra, S. L., jt. auth. see Singh, Bhupinder.

Batra, Satish K. Public Accountability of State Enterprise in India. 1992. text 25.00 (*81-7045-050-0*, Pub. by Assoc Pub Hse) Advent Bks Div.

Batra, Vijay K., jt. auth. see Narang, V. P.

***Batrae, Margot.** Switcheroo. (Sabrina, the Teenage Witch Ser.: Vol. 30). 160p. (YA). (gr. 3-6). 2000. per. 4.50 (*0-671-04067-7*, Archway) PB.

Batrae, Margot. While the Cat's Away. (Sabrina, the Teenage Witch Ser.: No. 25). 160p. (YA). (gr. 7-12). 1999. per. 4.50 (*0-671-02821-9*, Archway) PB.

Batran, Aziz A. Islam & Revolution in Africa. LC 84-72246. 51p. 1985. reprint ed. pap. 4.95 (*0-915597-17-9*) Amana Bks.

Batsakis, John G. Tumors of the Head & Neck. 3rd ed. (Illus.). 776p. 1996. write for info. (*0-683-00477-8*) Lppncott W & W.

***Batsakis, John G. & Rice, Dale H.** Surgical Pathology of the Head & Neck LC 99-35712. 1999. write for info. (*0-7817-2354-X*) Lppncott W & W.

Batsanov, S. S. Chemistry Reviews Vol. 15, Pt. 4: The Concept of Electronegativity & Structural Chemistry, Vol. 15. (Soviet Scientific Reviews Ser.: Section B). 79p. 1990. text 76.00 (*3-7186-5052-5*, Harwood Acad Pubs) Gordon & Breach.

— Effects of Explosions of Materials: Modifications & Synthesis under High-Pressure Shock Compression & Mechanical Properties. LC 93-6197. (High Pressure Shock Compression of Condensed Matter Ser.). (Illus.). 208p. 1994. 98.95 (*0-387-94123-1*) Spr-Verlag.

Batschelet, Edward. Introduction to Mathematics for Life Scientists. 3rd ed. (Illus.). 643p. 1992. reprint ed. 39.50 (*0-387-09648-5*) Spr-Verlag.

Batschelet, Margaret W. Early American Scientific & Technical Literature: An Annotated Bibliography of Books, Pamphlets, & Broadsides. LC 90-8095. 148p. 1990. 25.00 (*0-8108-2318-7*) Scarecrow.

***Batschelet, Margaret W.** Web Writing/Web Designing. LC 00-32276. (Illus.). 2001. write for info. (*0-205-31742-1*) Allyn.

Batschelet, Margaret W., jt. auth. see Woodson, Linda.

Batschelet, Margaret W., jt. auth. see Woodson, Linda T.

Batschiet, Margaret. Writing for the Technical Professions. Trzyna, Thomas N., ed. LC 98-3485. 560p. (C). 1998. spiral bd. 59.00 (*0-321-01122-8*) Addson-Wesley Educ.

Batschmann, Oskar. Artist in the Modern World: The Conflict Between Market & Self-Expression. LC 97-38047. (Illus.). 270p. 1997. 40.00 (*0-300-07323-2*) Yale U Pr.

— Hans Holbein. Hurley, Cecilia & Griener, Pascal, trs. from GER. LC 97-65592. 256p. 1997. text 55.00 (*0-691-01743-3*, Pub. by Princeton U Pr) Cal Prin Full Svc.

— Nicolas Poussin: Dialectics of Painting. 228p. 1997. 50.00 (*0-948462-10-8*, Pub. by Reaktion Bks) Consort Bk Sales.

— Nicolas Poussin: Dialectics of Painting. (Illus.). 174p. 1999. pap. 29.95 (*0-948462-43-4*, Pub. by Reaktion Bks) Consort Bk Sales.

***Batschmann, Oskar.** Tadashi Kawamata: Work in Progress in Zug. 164p. 2000. pap. 45.00 (*3-7757-9001-2*) Gerd Hatje.

***Batschmann, Oskar & Griener, Pascal.** Hans Holbein. (Illus.). 1999. pap. 24.95 (*0-691-00516-8*, Pub. by Princeton U Pr) Cal Prin Full Svc.

Batschmann, Oskar, ed. see Hoffmann, Volker & Autenrieth, Hans P.

Batshaw, Mark L. Children with Disabilities. 4th ed. LC 97-6941. 1997. 58.00 (*1-55766-293-2*) P H Brookes.

An Asterisk (*) at the beginning of an entry indicates that the title is appearing for the first time.

***Batshaw, Mark L.** Your Child Has a Disability: A Complete Sourcebook of Daily & Medical Care. 368p. 1998. pap. text. write for info. (*1-55766-374-2*) P H Brookes.

Batshaw, Mark L. Your Child Has a Handicap: A Practical Guide to Daily Care. 1993. 33.95 (*0-316-08369-0*) Little.

Batsie, John. Readings Introductory Socilgy: Sociolgy Cultura Insights. 224p. (C). 1996. 20.00 (*0-536-59588-7*) Pearson Custom.

Batsis, Thomas M. Crisis Management in Catholic Schools. 279p. 1994. pap. 8.00 (*1-55833-140-9*) Natl Cath Educ.

Batsleer, Janet. Working with Girls & Young Women in Community Settings. 240p. 1996. text 64.95 (*1-85742-303-8*, Pub. by Arena) Ashgate Pub Co.

Batsleer, Janet, et al. Rewriting English: The Politics of Gender & Class. (New Accents Ser.). 160p. (C). 1986. text 27.50 (*0-416-38930-9*, 9473); pap. text 12.95 (*0-416-38940-6*, 9474) Routledge.

Batsleer, Janet, jt. ed. see Humphries, Beth.

Batson, Ann B. Having It Y'All: An Insider's Guide to Life Southern Style. rev. ed. LC 93-15829. 1993. pap. 7.95 (*1-55853-234-X*) Rutledge Hill Pr.

Batson, Beatrice. John Bunyan's Grace Abounding & the Pilgrim's Progress: An Overview of Literary Studies, 1690-1987. LC 87-35684. 266p. 1988. text 15.00 (*0-8240-6630-8*) Garland.

Batson, C. Daniel. The Altruism Question: Toward a Social-Psychological Answer. 272p. 1991. text 59.95 (*0-8058-0245-2*) L Erlbaum Assocs.

Batson, C. Daniel, et al. Religion & the Individual: A Social-Psychological Perspective. 2nd ed. LC 92-28606. (Illus.). 440p. (C). 1993. pap. text 33.95 (*0-19-506209-4*) OUP.

***Batson, Denzil.** We Called It War! The Untold Story of the Combat Infantry in Korea. LC 99-71599. 153p. 1999. pap. 11.95 (*1-890622-68-0*) Leathers Pub.

Batson, E. Beatrice, ed. The Christian Dimension of Shakespearean Drama. LC 93-46262. 200p. 1994. 79.95 (*0-7734-9425-1*) E Mellen.

Batson, G. B., jt. ed. see Shah, S. P.

Batson, Gary, jt. ed. see Batson, Horace W.

Batson, George. Gift of Murder! 1974. pap. 5.25 (*0-8222-0443-6*) Dramatists Play.

— Ramshackle Inn. 1944. pap. 5.25 (*0-8222-0929-2*) Dramatists Play.

Batson, George & Harman, Donn. Her Majesty, Miss Jones. 1959. pap. 5.25 (*0-8222-0513-0*) Dramatists Play.

Batson, George & Kirkland, Jack. Strange Boarders. 1947. pap. 5.25 (*0-8222-1087-8*) Dramatists Play.

Batson, H. E., tr. see Von Mises, Ludwig.

Batson, Horace W. & Batson, Gary, eds. Overcoming Stress: Everything You Ever Need to Know! 100p. (Orig.). 1987. pap. 9.95 (*0-938503-00-6*) Welstar Pubns.

Batson, Howard K. Common-Sense Church Growth. LC 99-14809. 144p. 1999. pap. 14.00 (*1-57312-179-7*) Smyth & Helwys.

***Batson, Juanita L.** A Quotian Dilemma. 2000. mass mkt. 7.95 (*1-55279-000-2*) Picasso Publ.

Batson, Judy. Oxford in Fiction: An Annotated Bibliography. LC 88-34700. 219p. 1989. text 10.00 (*0-8240-7036-4*) Garland.

Batson, Mary M. Quest for the Holy Trail. 170p. 1999. pap. write for info. (*0-7392-0289-8*, PO3396) Morris Pubng.

Batson, Raymond, jt. auth. see Greeley, Ronald.

Batson, Raymond, jt. ed. see Greeley, Ronald.

Batson, Robert G., tr. see Masaryk, Thomas G.

Batson, Ronald, jt. auth. see Roth, Susan.

Batson, Sallie L. Great Hair! Your Complete Hair Care & Styling Guide. 144p. (Orig.). 1995. pap. 4.99 (*0-425-15022-4*) Berkley Pub.

— Great Hair! Your Complete Hair Care Guide & Styling Guide. 1995. mass mkt. 4.99 (*0-425-15023-2*) Berkley Pub.

Batson, Sallie L., jt. auth. see Hofstein, Riquette.

Batson, Sallie L., jt. auth. see Wiener, Hattie.

Batson, Steve. Country Store Counter Jars & Tins. LC 96-72028. (Illus.). 160p. 1997. pap. 29.95 (*0-7643-0240-X*) Schiffer.

Batson, Trent & Bergman, Eugene, eds. Angels & Outcasts: An Anthology of Deaf Characters in Literature. 3rd ed. LC 85-20669. 368p. 1984. pap. 19.95 (*0-930323-17-3*) Gallaudet Univ Pr.

Batson, Trenton W. & Bergman, Eugene, eds. The Deaf Experience: An Anthology of Literature by & about the Deaf. 2nd ed. LC 76-27476. 384p. (C). 1976. pap. 9.00 (*0-914562-03-7*) Merriam-Eddy.

Batsto, Karena, jt. auth. see Alexander, Rosemary.

Batstone, David. From Conquest to Struggle: Jesus of Nazareth in Latin America. LC 89-49227. 238p. (C). 1991. text 59.50 (*0-7914-0421-8*); pap. text 19.95 (*0-7914-0422-6*) State U NY Pr.

Batstone, David, ed. New Visions for the Americas: Religious Engagement & Social Transformation. LC 93-28257. 280p. 1993. 18.00 (*0-8006-2690-7*) Augsburg Fortress.

Batstone, David & Mendieta, Eduardo, eds. The Good Citizen. LC 98-37926. 163p. 1999. 21.00 (*0-415-92093-0*, D5703) Routledge.

***Batstone, David & Mendieta, Eduardo, eds.** The Good Citizen. 2000. reprint ed. pap. 16.95 (*0-415-92908-3*) Routledge.

Batstone, David & Mendieta, Eduardo, eds. Liberation Theologies, Postmodernity & the Americas. LC 96-54817. 320p. (C). 1997. pap. 22.99 (*0-415-91659-3*) Routledge.

— Liberation Theologies, Postmodernity & the Americas. LC 96-54817. 320p. (C). 1997. 75.00 (*0-415-91658-5*) Routledge.

Batstone, Eric. The Reform of Workplace Industrial Relations: Theory, Myth & Evidence. rev. ed. (Illus.). 272p. 1988. 59.00 (*0-19-827585-4*); pap. 24.95 (*0-19-827282-0*) OUP.

Batstone, Eric, et al. New Technology & the Process of Labour Regulation. 272p. 1987. 65.00 (*0-19-827274-X*) OUP.

Batstone, Rob. Grammar. Widdowson, H. G. & Candlin, C. N., eds. (Illus.). 158p. 1994. pap. text 14.95 (*0-19-437132-8*) OUP.

Batstone, Roger, et al, eds. The Safe Disposal of Hazardous Wastes: The Special Needs & Problems of Developing Countries, 3 vols. (Technical Papers: No. 93). 854p. 1989. 26.00 (*0-8213-1144-1*, 11144) World Bank.

Batstone, William W., jt. ed. see Rayor, Diane J.

Batt, Alan, ed. see Sadar, Albin.

Batt, Bruce. Snow Geese: Grandeur & Calamity on An Artic Landscape. LC 98-13037. (Illus.). 82p. 1998. pap. 17.95 (*1-57223-182-3*) Willow Creek Pr.

Batt, Bruce D., et al, eds. The Ecology & Management of Breeding Waterfowl. 696p. (C). 1992. text 49.95 (*0-8166-2001-6*) U of Minn Pr.

Batt, Chris. Information Technology in Public Libraries. 6th ed. 159p. 1998. pap. 55.00 (*1-85604-253-7*, LAP2537, Pub. by Library Association) Bernan Associates.

Batt, Chris, jt. auth. see Clayton, Marlene.

Batt, Deleece. Hiragana Gambatte! (Illus.). 112p. (J). 1994. pap. 13.00 (*4-7700-1797-9*) Kodansha.

— Katakana Gambatte! Adachi Office Staff, ed. (Illus.). 112p. 1994. pap., wbk. ed. 10.00 (*4-7700-1881-9*) Kodansha.

Batt, John & James, William. The Family Law Decision-Making Process: An Annotated Law, Psychology & Policy Science Bibliography. LC 79-63673. 262p. 1979. lib. bdg. 38.00 (*0-930342-93-3*, 300050) W S Hein.

Batt, John, jt. auth. see Abbott, Walter F.

Batt, Miles G. The Complete Guide to Creative Watercolor. LC 87-71439. (Illus.). (C). 1988. 35.00 (*0-9619386-5-X*) Crtive Art Pubns.

***Batt, Phil.** The Compleat Phil Batt: A Kaleidoscope. LC 99-96227. 296p. 1999. 29.95 (*0-9677135-5-2*); pap. 18.95 (*0-9677135-0-1*) P Batt.

Batt, Ronald E., et al. A Pictorial History, 1846-1966: School of Medicine & Biomedical Sciences, University at Buffalo. LC 95-47775. 1996. write for info. (*0-89865-963-9*) Donning Co.

Batt, Rosemary, jt. auth. see Appelbaum, Eileen.

Batt, Sharon. Patient No More: The Politics of Breast Cancer. 432p. 1994. pap. 16.95 (*0-921881-30-4*, Pub. by Gynergy-Ragweed) U of Toronto Pr.

Batt, Vivienne, jt. auth. see Underwood, Geoffrey.

Batta, Gy, et al. Methods for Structure Elucidation by High-Resolution NMR: Applications to Organic Molecules of Moderate Molecular Weight, Vol. 8. LC 97-40556. (Analytical Spectroscopy Library: 8). 368p. 1997. 244.00 (*0-444-82157-0*) Elsevier.

***Battafarano, Italo Michele.** Die Im Chaos Bluhenden Zitronen. 262p. 1999. 41.95 (*3-906762-79-3*) P Lang Pubng.

Battaglia, Anthony J., Jr. Protect It Now. 16p. 1992. pap., student ed. 15.00 incl. audio (*1-880254-04-2*) Vista.

Battaglia, Aurelius, ed. Mother Goose. (J). (ps-1). 1973. pap. 3.25 (*0-394-82661-2*, Pub. by Random Bks Yng Read) Random.

Battaglia, Aurelius. Animal Sounds. (Sturdy Board Bks.). 22p. (J). (ps). 1981. bds. 4.99 (*0-307-12122-4*, 12122, Goldn Books) Gldn Bks Pub Co.

Battaglia, B., et al, eds. Antarctic Communities: Species, Structure & Survival. LC 96-37973. (Illus.). 490p. (C). 1997. text 155.00 (*0-521-48033-7*) Cambridge U Pr.

Battaglia, Carmelo L. Breeding Better Dogs. rev. ed. (Illus.). 192p. 1990. reprint ed. pap., wbk. ed. 59.95 incl. VHS (*0-9614063-0-5*) BEI Pubns.

— Breeding Better Dogs. 4th rev. ed. (Illus.). 192p. 1987. reprint ed. pap. text 17.00 (*0-932419-06-2*) BEI Pubns.

— Proper Care of German Shepherds. 256p. 1998. 16.95 (*0-7938-0495-7*, TW144) TFH Pubns.

***Battaglia, Carol.** Drifting among the Whales. Zagury, Carolyn, ed. LC 99-72875. 128p. 1999. pap. 14.95 (*1-880254-64-6*) Vista.

Battaglia, Carol. Jagged Rhythms. Zagury, Carolyn S., ed. LC 97-60581. 108p. 1997. pap. 12.95 (*1-880254-45-X*) Vista.

— Murmurs. Zagury, Carolyn, ed. LC 96-60060. (Illus.). 96p. 1996. pap. 12.95 (*1-880254-36-0*) Vista.

Battaglia, Concetta. Of You & Other Paths: Third Collection of Poetry. LC 96-96886. 108p. (Orig.). 1996. pap. 11.95 (*0-9654032-0-3*) Arts in Media.

Battaglia, Debbora. On the Bones of the Serpent: Person, Memory & Mortality in Sabarl Island Society. (Illus.). 264p. 1990. pap. text 17.95 (*0-226-03889-0*) U Ch Pr.

— On the Bones of the Serpent: Person, Memory & Mortality in Sabarl Island Society. (Illus.). 264p. 1996. lib. bdg. 49.50 (*0-226-03888-2*) U Ch Pr.

Battaglia, Debbora, ed. Rhetorics of Self Making. LC 94-398. 1995. 40.00 (*0-520-08798-4*, Pub. by U CA Pr); pap. 16.95 (*0-520-08799-2*, Pub. by U CA Pr) Cal Prin Full Svc.

Battaglia, Franco & George, Thomas F. Fundamentals in Chemical Physics. LC 98-29282. 8p. 1998. write for info. (*0-7923-5214-9*) Kluwer Academic.

Battaglia, Frederick C. Placental Function & Fetal Nutrition. LC 97-11147. 288p. 1997. text 74.00 (*0-7817-1406-0*) Lppncott W & W.

Battaglia, Laura, et al, eds. Communication: Means & Technologies for Exchanging Information. (Illus.). 64p. (J). (gr. 4-6). 1998. text 17.00 (*0-7881-5264-5*) DIANE Pub.

Battaglia, Pat. So You Think You're Smart: One Hundred Fifty Fun & Challenging Brain Teasers. 96p. 1988. pap. 9.95 (*0-07-155543-9*) McGraw.

— So You Think You're Smart - One Hundred Fifty Fun & Challenging Brain Teasers. (Illus.). 114p. 1988. 14.95 (*0-8306-9406-4*, 3106H); pap. 8.95 (*0-8306-3106-2*, 3106) McGraw-Hill Prof.

Battaglia, Richard A. Handbook of Livestock Management. 2nd ed. LC 96-2751. 589p. 1997. 105.00 (*0-13-256413-0*) P-H.

***Battaglia, Richard A.** Handbook of Livestock Management. 3rd ed. LC 99-45217. (Illus.). 640p. 2000. 95.00 (*0-13-010491-4*) P-H.

Battaglia, Richard A., et al. Who's Who in Food Chemistry-Europe. 256p. 1996. 74.95 (*3-540-60239-9*) Spr-Verlag.

Battaglia, S. Prostate Accessory Male Sex Gland. (Journal: Applied Pathology: Vol. 3, No. 4). (Illus.). iv, 72p. 1986. pap. 52.25 (*3-8055-4464-2*) S Karger.

Battaglia, S., ed. Amyloids, Part II. (Journal: Applied Pathology: Vol. 3, Nos. 1-2). (Illus.). 116p. 1986. pap. 55.75 (*3-8055-4458-8*) S Karger.

— Amyloids, Pt. 1. (Journal: Applied Pathology: Vol. 2, No. 6, 1984). (Illus.). vi, 86p. 1986. pap. 41.75 (*3-8055-4351-4*) S Karger.

Battaglini, Marina, ed. see Jesuit Historical Institute Inc. Staff, et al.

Battaglini, Miele C., ed. Treasured Italian Recipes, Bk. II. (Illus.). 146p. (Orig.). 1996. pap. 11.95 (*0-9627629-1-6*) ERRC.

Battaglini, Miele C., ed. see East Rochester Rotary Club Staff.

Battail, J.-F. L' Avocat Philosophe Geraud de Cordemoy (1626-1684) (International Archives of the History of Ideas Ser.: No. 60). 276p. 1973. lib. bdg. 99.50 (*90-247-1542-3*) Kluwer Academic.

Battaile. Computers. 1993. wbk. ed. 19.95 (*0-316-08375-5*, Aspen Law & Bus) Aspen Pub.

Battaile, Connie. Circulation Services in a Small Academic Library. LC 91-42733. (Library Management Collection). 224p. 1992. lib. bdg. 55.00 (*0-313-28126-2*, BTL/, Greenwood Pr) Greenwood.

Battaile, Connie H. The Oregon Book: Information A to Z. LC 98-90263. xi, 677p. 1998. pap. 24.95 (*0-9657638-2-X*) Saddle Mtn.

Battaile, Kristen L. An Introduction to Computers for Paralegals. 2nd ed. 288p. 1997. pap. text 40.00 (*1-56706-483-3*, 64833) Panel Pubs.

— An Introduction to Computers for Paralegals, Incl. instr's. manual. 2nd ed. LC 97-194629. 400p. 1997. pap. text, wbk. ed. 25.00 (*1-56706-461-2*, 64612) Panel Pubs.

Battaile, William G., Jr., jt. auth. see Evans, Alison.

Battaille, Charles A., jt. auth. see Joiner, James R.

Battaini, F., jt. ed. see Govoni, S.

Battalio, John T. ATTW Contemporary Studies in Technical Communication Vol. 8: The Rhetoric of Science in the Evolution of American Ornithological Discourse. LC 98-7685. 1998. 73.25 (*1-56750-395-0*); pap. 24.95 (*1-56750-396-9*) Ablx Pub.

— Essays in the Study of Scientific Discourse: Methods, Practice & Pedagogy. LC 98-5848. (Attw Contemporary Studies In Technical Communication ;). 1998. 73.25 (*1-56750-384-5*); pap. 24.95 (*1-56750-385-3*) Ablx Pub.

Battan, David. Handwriting Analysis: A Guide to Personality. LC 83-19287. (Illus.). 272p. 1984. 12.95 (*0-914598-88-0*) Intl Resources.

— Handwriting Analysis: A Guide to Personality. LC 83-19287. (Illus.). 272p. 1990. pap. 10.95 (*0-937480-15-0*) Intl Resources.

Battan, Louis J. Cloud Physics & Cloud Seeding. LC 78-25711. (Illus.). 144p. 1979. reprint ed. lib. bdg. 55.00 (*0-313-20770-4*, BACL, Greenwood Pr) Greenwood.

— The Nature of Violent Storms, 19. LC 80-24986. (Science Study Ser.: No. S19). (Illus.). 158p. 1981. reprint ed. lib. bdg. 35.00 (*0-313-22582-6*, BANV, Greenwood Pr) Greenwood.

— Radar Observation of the Atmosphere. LC 72-84405. (Illus.). 334p. Date not set. reprint ed. pap. 103.60 (*0-608-20996-1*, 205452400003) Bks Demand.

— Radar Observation of the Atmosphere. rev. ed. LC 72-84405. (Illus.). 334p. reprint ed. pap. 103.60 (*0-608-09382-3*, 205412700004) Bks Demand.

— Radar Observation of the Atmosphere. rev. ed. (Illus.). 334p. (C). 1991. reprint ed. 81.00 (*1-878907-27-1*) TechBooks.

Battaner, Eduardo. Astrophysical Fluid Dynamics. (Illus.). 256p. (C). 1996. pap. text 30.95 (*0-521-43747-4*) Cambridge U Pr.

— Astrophysical Fluid Dynamics. (Illus.). 256p. (C). 1996. text 80.00 (*0-521-43166-2*) Cambridge U Pr.

Battani, Mohammed I. Opus Astronomicum, 3 vols. in 1. cxvii, 1028p. 1977. reprint ed. 400.00 (*3-487-06262-3*) G Olms Pubs.

Battarbee, R. W., et al, eds. Diatoms & Lake Acidity. (Developments in Hydrobiology Ser.). 1986. text 292.50 (*90-6193-536-9*) Kluwer Academic.

Battat, Eileen, jt. auth. see Helzel, Florence B.

Battat, Joseph, et al. Suppliers to Multinationals: Linkage Programs to Strengthen Local Companies in Developing Countries. (FIAS Occasional Paper Ser.: No. 6). 45p. 1996. pap. 22.00 (*0-8213-3746-7*, 13746) World Bank.

Battat, Joseph Y. Management in Post-Mao China: An Insider's View. LC 86-6957. (Research for Business Decisions Ser.: No. 76). (Illus.). 198p. reprint ed. pap. 61.40 (*0-8357-1663-5*, 207036200088) Bks Demand.

Battcock, Gregory, ed. Minimal Art: A Critical Anthology. LC 94-32628. 1995. 22.50 (*0-520-20147-7*, Pub. by U CA Pr) Cal Prin Full Svc.

***Batte, Gary.** Carving Crazy Critters. (Illus.). 64p. (Orig.). 1999. pap. 14.95 (*1-56523-114-7*, Pub. by Fox Chapel Pub) IPG Chicago.

Batteau, Allen W. The Invention of Appalachia. LC 90-10881. (Anthropology of Form & Meaning Ser.). 239p. 1990. 40.00 (*0-8165-1172-1*) U of Ariz Pr.

Battegay, Raymond. Diccionario de Psiquiatria. (SPA.). 680p. 1989. 150.00 (*0-7859-5827-4*, 8425415802) Fr & Eur.

— Hunger Diseases. (Illus.). 160p. 1991. text 34.50 (*0-88937-054-0*) Hogrefe & Huber Pubs.

Battelle, Arthur. Early Years on the Tractor Seat. (Illus.). 144p. 1994. pap. 12.95 (*0-85236-276-5*, Pub. by Farming Pr) Diamond Farm Bk.

— More Years on the Tractor Seat. (Illus.). 145p. 1995. pap. 12.95 (*0-85236-315-X*, Pub. by Farming Pr) Diamond Farm Bk.

Battelle Columbus Laboratories Staff, et al. Evaluation of the Influence of Absorbed & Absorbed Hydrogen on the Mechanical Properties & Fracture Behavior of Materials to Be Used in a Hydrogen-Gas Transmission System. 185p. 1974. pap. 10.00 (*0-318-12610-9*, L21177) Am Gas Assn.

— Indoor Epidemiology Study. 51p. 1974. pap. 4.00 (*0-318-12641-9*, M50677) Am Gas Assn.

— Measuring the Yield Strength of Pipe in the Mill Expander. 62p. 1973. pap. 4.00 (*0-318-12654-0*, L22273) Am Gas Assn.

— Report on an Analysis of the Office of Pipeline Safety Annual Report Data for the Natural Gas Distribution Companies 1970-1975. 83p. 1977. pap. 2.00 (*0-318-12690-7*, X50577) Am Gas Assn.

— Superturbulent Combustion Noise. 136p. 1976. 5.25 (*0-318-12713-X*, M40077) Am Gas Assn.

Battelle Institute Materials Science Colloquia Sta. Interatomic Potentials & Simulation of Lattice Defects. Gehlen, Pierre C. et al, eds. LC 72-77229. (Illus.). 802p. 1972. reprint ed. pap. 200.00 (*0-608-05502-6*, 206597100006) Bks Demand.

Battelle Memorial Institute Staff. Agriculture 2000: A Look at the Future. Bucher, Mary, ed. LC 82-25308. (Illus.). 199p. 1983. 16.00 (*0-935470-18-2*); pap. 8.95 (*0-935470-15-8*) Battelle.

— Development of Increased Use of Copper as an Alloy in Cast Iron. 61p. 1964. 9.15 (*0-317-34506-0*, 13) Intl Copper.

— Life-Cycle Assessment: Inventory Guideline & Principles. 144p. 1994. lib. bdg. 54.95 (*1-56670-015-9*) Lewis Pubs.

— Strength & Water Resistance of Adhesive-Bonded Copper Metals. 96p. 1970. 14.40 (*0-317-34548-6*, 108) Intl Copper.

— A Survey of Corrosion Inhibitors & Related Additives to Improve the Corrosion Resistance & Heat Transfer of Copper & Its Alloys. 59p. 1969. 8.85 (*0-317-34552-4*, 148) Intl Copper.

Battelle Memorial Institute Staff, et al. Plastic Piping Systems Development for Natural Gas Applications. 50p. 1970. pap. 4.00 (*0-318-12668-0*, X10180) Am Gas Assn.

Batten. Encyclopedia of Government Advisory Organizations. 11th ed. 1996. 550.00 (*0-7876-0090-3*) Taft Group.

Batten, Aimee C., ed. see Stiffler, Robert.

Batten, Alam H., jt. auth. see International Astronomical Union Staff.

Batten, Alan H. Resolute & Undertaking Characters: The Lives of Wilhelm & Otto Struve. (C). 1988. text 140.50 (*90-277-2652-3*) Kluwer Academic.

Batten, Alan H., ed. Algols. (C). 1989. text 199.00 (*0-7923-0319-9*) Kluwer Academic.

Batten, Alan H., jt. auth. see International Astronomical Union Staff.

Batten, Charles, Jr., intro. Pamela Censured: In a Letter to the Editor. LC 92-23719. (Augustan Reprints Ser.: No. 175). 1976. reprint ed. 14.50 (*0-404-70175-2*, PR3664) AMS Pr.

Batten, Chris. Ambulances. (Album Ser.: No. 328). (Illus.). 32p. 1997. pap. 4.75 (*0-7478-0329-3*, Pub. by Shire Pubns) Parkwest Pubns.

Batten, D. F., ed. see Emmerink, R. H.

Batten, Dallas, et al. The Conduct of Monetary Policy in the Major Industrial Countries: Instruments & Operating Procedures. (Occasional Papers: No. 70). v, 34p. 1990. pap. 10.00 (*1-55775-143-9*) Intl Monetary.

Batten, David. Introduction to River Fishing. (Illus.). 128p. pap. 15.95 (*1-85223-760-0*, Pub. by Crolwood) Trafalgar.

Batten, David, et al, eds. Networks in Action: Communication, Economics & Human Knowledge. LC 95-1430. (Illus.). 327p. 1995. 107.00 (*3-540-58944-9*) Spr-Verlag.

***Batten, David F.** Discovering Artificial Economics: How Agents Learn & Economies Evolve. 304p. 2000. pap. 39.00 (*0-8133-9770-7*) Westview.

— Learning, Innovation & Urban Evolution. LC 00-40546. 2000. write for info. (*0-7923-8577-2*) Kluwer Academic.

Batten, David F. Spatial Analysis of Interacting Economies. 1982. lib. bdg. 64.00 (*0-89838-109-6*) Kluwer Academic.

Batten, David F., et al, eds. Overcoming Isolation: Information & Transportation Networks in Development Strategies for Peripheral Areas. LC 95-30839. (Advances in Spatial Science Ser.). (Illus.). viii, 272p. 1995. 112.00 (*3-540-59423-X*) Spr-Verlag.

— Recent Advances in Spatial Equilibrium Modelling: Methodology & Applications. (Advances in Spatial Science Ser.). (Illus.). viii, 392p. 1996. 117.00 (*3-540-60708-0*) Spr-Verlag.

Batten, David F. & Karlsson, Charlie. Infrastructure & the Complexity of Economic Development. LC 96-28733. (Advances in Spatial Science Ser.). 298p. 1996. 109.50 (*3-540-61333-1*) Spr-Verlag.

Batten, David F., et al. The Cosmo-Creative Society: Logistical Networks in a Dynamic Economy. Kobayashi, K. & Yoshikawa, Kojiro, eds. LC 93-34383. (Advances in Spatial & Network Economics Ser.). (Illus.). viii, 296p. 1993. 119.95 (*0-387-57158-2*) Spr-Verlag.

B

Batten, David F., ed. see Reynolds-Feighn, A. J.

Batten, David J. & Keen, Michael C., eds. Northwest European Micorpaleontology & Palymology. 1989. text 153.00 (0-470-21487-2) P-H.

Batten, George J. Programmable Controllers: Hardware, Software & Applications. 2nd ed. LC 93-48744. (Illus.). 281p. 1994. 39.00 (0-07-004214-4) McGraw.

Batten, George L. Programmable Controllers: Hardware, Software & Applications. 2nd ed. 1994. 39.00 (0-07-442144-1) McGraw.

Batten, Guinn. The Orphaned Imagination: Melancholy & Commodity Culture in English Romanticism. LC 97-49691. 1998. 59.95 (0-8223-2205-6); pap. 19.95 (0-8223-2221-8) Duke.

Batten, J. International Finance in Australia. 480p. 1993. pap. 82.00 (0-409-30730-0, Austral, MICHIE) LEXIS Pub.

Batten, Jack. Mind over Murder: DNA & Other Forensic Adventures. (Illus.). xvi, 260p. 1996. 27.99 (0-7710-1066-4) McCland & Stewart.

— Mind over Murder: DNA & Other Forensic Adventures. (Illus.). 280p. 1997. pap. text 14.95 (0-7710-1069-9) McCland & Stewart.

Batten, Joe, et al. Dare to Live Workbook: Your Daily Guide to Expanding Personal Possibilities. 130p. 1999. 24.95 (1-928858-00-7) Edgemont Inc.

Batten, Joe, jt. auth. see Hansen, Mark Victor.

Batten, Joe D. Beyond Management by Objectives. LC 66-29660. 112p. reprint ed. pap. 34.80 (0-8357-7159-8, 202358000033) Bks Demand.

— Building a Total Quality Culture. Gerould, Philip, ed. LC 92-54371. (Fifty-Minute Ser.). 88p. (Orig.). 1992. pap. 10.95 (1-56052-176-7) Crisp Pubns.

— Tough-Minded Leadership. 240p. 1991. pap. 15.95 (0-8144-7761-5) AMACOM.

Batten, Joe D., et al. Leadership Principles of Jesus: Modern Parables of Achievement & Motivation. LC 97-11019. 350p. (Orig.). 1997. pap. 15.99 (0-89900-782-1) College Pr Pub.

Batten, John R., ed. Proceedings of the 1980 National Literacy Forum. limited ed. 182p. 1980. pap. text 3.00 (0-942717-13-9) Intl Inst Rural.

Batten, L. A., et al. Red Data Birds in Britain: Action for Rare, Threatened & Important Species. 349p. (C). 1991. text (0-85661-056-9, 784656) Poyser.

Batten, Loring W. Ezra & Nehemiah: Critical & Exegetical Commentary. Driver, Samuel R. et al, eds. LC 13-12806. (International Critical Commentary Ser.). 400p. 1913. 39.95 (0-567-05008-4, Pub. by T & T Clark) Bks Intl VA.

Batten, Lynn M. Combinatorics of Finite Geometries. 2nd ed. 207p. (C). 1997. text 64.95 (0-521-59014-0); pap. text 25.95 (0-521-59993-8) Cambridge U Pr.

Batten, Lynn M. & Beutelspacher, Albrecht. The Theory of Finite Linear Spaces: Combinatorics of Points & Lines. 224p. (C). 1993. text 52.95 (0-521-33317-2) Cambridge U Pr.

Batten, Lynn Margord, jt. auth. see Baker, Catherine Anne.

Batten, Margaret. Year Twelve: Students Expectations & Experiences. (C). 1989. pap. text 60.00 (0-86431-044-7, Pub. by Aust Council Educ Res) St Mut.

***Batten, Margaret & Frigo, Tracey.** Enhancing English Literacy Development Skills in Aboriginal & Torres Strait Islander Students. 228p. 1998. pap. 27.95 (0-86431-260-1, Pub. by Aust Council Educ Res) Stylus Pub VA.

Batten, Margaret & Russell, Jean, eds. Programs for At-Risk Youth: A Review of the American, Canadian & British Literature since 1984. 1995. pap. 75.00 (0-86431-179-6, Pub. by Aust Council Educ Res) St Mut.

Batten, Margaret, jt. ed. see Withers, Graeme.

Batten, Mary. Baby Wolf, Level 2. LC 97-29413. (All Aboard Reading Ser.). (Illus.). 48p. (J). (gr. 1-3). 1998. pap. 3.99 (0-448-41645-X, G & D) Peng Put Young Read.

— Baby Wolf, Level 2. LC 97-29413. (All Aboard Reading Ser.). (Illus.). 48p. (J). (gr. 1-3). 1998. lib. bdg. 13.89 (0-448-41833-9, G & D) Peng Put Young Read.

***Batten, Mary.** Extinct! Strange Animals from the Past. (Road to Reading Mile 4 Ser.). (Illus.). (J). 2000. 10.99 (0-307-46405-9); pap. write for info. (0-307-26405-X) Gldn Bks Pub Co.

— Hungry Plants. LC 99-34416. (Road to Reading Ser.). (Illus.). 48p. (ps-3). 2000. pap. text 3.99 (0-307-26401-7) Gldn Bks Pub Co.

— Shark Attack Almanac. (Kidbacks Ser.). (J). 1997. 11.19 (0-606-11836-5, Pub. by Turtleback) Demco.

— Winking, Blinking Sea. LC 99-48391. 32p. (J). (gr. 2-4). 2000. lib. bdg. 20.90 (0-7613-1550-0) Millbrook Pr.

***Batten, Mary & Mirocha, Paul.** Hungry Plants. LC 99-34416. (Road to Reading Ser.). 48p. 2000. pap. 10.99 (0-307-46401-6) Gldn Bks Pub Co.

Batten, R. L., tr. see Heim, U. & Pfeiffer, K. M.

Batten, Thomas R. Communities & Their Development: An Introductory Study with Special Reference to the Tropics. LC 80-14699. (Illus.). 248p. 1980. reprint ed. lib. bdg. 35.00 (0-313-22447-1, BACD, Greenwood Pr) Greenwood.

***Battenburg, John & Martinez, William, Jr.** Communicative Activities for the Second Language Classroom. 88p. (C). 1999. per. 16.95 (0-7872-6432-6) Kendall-Hunt.

Battenfeld, Robert L., jt. auth. see Roberson, William H.

Battenfield, Betty L. Designing Clinical Evaluation Tools. 43p. (Orig.). 1986. pap. 15.95 (0-88737-290-2, 23-2160) Natl League Nurse.

Battenhouse, Roy, ed. Shakespeare's Christian Dimension: An Anthology of Commentary. LC 93-31520. 1994. 35.00 (0-253-31122-5) Ind U Pr.

Batterberry, Arian, jt. auth. see Batterberry, Michael.

Batterberry, Ariane, jt. auth. see Batterberry, Michael.

Batterberry, Michael & Batterberry, Arian. Fashion: A Mirror of History. (Illus.). 400p. 1977. 22.95 (0-318-41012-5) Random Hse Value.

— Fashion Mirror of History. (Illus.). 400p. 1979. reprint ed. 22.95 (0-685-43882-1) Random Hse Value.

Batterberry, Michael & Batterberry, Ariane. On the Town in New York. 2nd anniversary ed. LC 98-23443. (Illus.). 354p. (Orig.). (C). (gr. 13). 1998. 30.00 (0-415-92020-5) Routledge.

Batterbury, Mark. Ophthalmology: An Illustration. LC 99-27851. (Illus.). 1999. text 31.00 (0-443-05537-8) Harcourt.

Batterham, T. J. NMR Spectra of Simple Heterocycles. LC 80-11724. 560p. 1982. reprint ed. lib. bdg. 69.50 (0-89874-140-8) Krieger.

Batterman, Charles A. The Techniques of Springboard Diving. (Illus.). 1977. pap. text 4.95 (0-262-52043-5) MIT Pr.

Batterman, Deborah. Manager's Desk Book on Employment Law. 1984. pap. 29.95 (0-88057-196-9) Exec Ent Pubns.

Batterman, Lee C. Two Cents & a Milk Bottle. LC 97-12092. (Illus.). 272p. (J). (gr. 3-5). 1997. 15.95 (1-881283-17-8) Alef Design.

Batters, Elmer. Batters. 1996. pap. 5.99 (3-8228-8679-3) Taschen Amer.

— Legs That Dance to Elmer's Tune. (Photo & Sexy Bks.). (Illus.). 216p. 1997. 69.69 (3-8228-8188-0) Taschen Amer.

Battersby, Alan R., jt. ed. see Taylor, William I.

***Battersby, Christin.** Gender & Genius. 1999. pap. 17.95 (0-7043-4300-2, Pub. by Womens Press) Trafalgar.

Battersby, Christine. Gender & Genius: Towards a Feminist Aesthetics. LC 89-46346. 200p. 1990. 27.50 (0-253-31126-8); pap. 10.95 (0-253-20578-6, MB 578) Ind U Pr.

— The Phenomenal Woman: Feminist Transitions & Metaphysical Traditions. LC 97-32058. 256p. (C). 1998. 75.00 (0-415-92035-3); pap. 18.99 (0-415-92036-1) Routledge.

Battersby, Gregory J. Primer on Technology Licensing. 200p. 1996. 34.95 (1-888206-06-3) Kent Communs.

Battersby, Gregory J. & Grimes, Charles W. Multimedia & Technology Licensing Agreements: Forms with Commentary. 752p. 1995. 160.00 incl. disk (0-7913-2377-3) Warren Gorham & Lamont.

***Battersby, Gregory J. & Grimes, Charles W.** 1999 Licensing Update. LC 99-26304. 1999. write for info. (0-7355-0552-7) Panel Pubs.

Battersby, Gregory J. & Grimes, Charles W. The Toy & Game Inventor's Guide. 2nd ed. LC 96-181662. 240p. 1996. pap. 15.95 (1-888206-01-2) Kent Communs.

Battersby, Gregory J., jt. auth. see Grimes, Charles W.

Battersby, H. F. Prevost. Psychic Certainties. 230p. 1998. reprint ed. pap. 18.95 (0-7661-0301-3) Kessinger Pub.

Battersby, James L. Paradigms Regained: Pluralism & the Practice of Criticism. LC 91-18260. 328p. (C). 1991. text 37.50 (0-8122-3127-9) U of Pa Pr.

— Rational Praise & Natural Lamentation: Johnson, Lycidas, & Principles of Criticism. LC 77-89774. 288p. 1980. 38.50 (0-8386-2148-1) Fairleigh Dickinson.

— Reason & the Nature of Texts. LC 96-21300. 224p. 1996. text 34.95 (0-8122-3359-X) U of Pa Pr.

Battersby, Mark E. Empty Nester's Financial Handbook. LC 97-71170. 256p. 1998. 17.95 (0-02-861754-1) Macmillan.

— Salonovitan's Tax & Financial Primer. LC 94-39613. (Illus.). 192p. 1996. pap. 27.95 (1-56253-215-4) Thomson Learn.

Battersby, S. B. Dictionary Environmental Scien. LC 97-1638. 1997. text 174.95 (0-471-96918-4) Wiley.

Battersby, William. Brother Solomon: Martyr of the French Revolution. (Illus.). 181p. 1991. reprint ed. pap. 5.00 (0-9623279-6-4) Christian Brothers.

Battersby, William J., tr. see De La Salle, John B.

Battershall, Fletcher. Book-Binding for Bibliophiles. Thompson, Jack C., ed. & intro. by. LC 95-71504. v, 53p. (C). 1995. reprint ed. pap. 8.95 (1-887719-02-4) Caber Pr.

Battershaw, Brian, tr. see Gorlitz, Walter.

Battershaw, Brian, tr. see Schucking, Levin L.

Battershill, Chris, jt. auth. see Kingsford, Michael.

Battershill, Christopher, jt. auth. see Kingsford, Michael.

Battershill, Norman. Draw Seascapes. 2nd ed. 48p. 1998. pap. 7.95 (0-7136-4857-0) A & C Blk.

— Painting Gardens. LC 94-27793. (Illus.). 128p. 1995. pap. text 12.95 (0-486-28401-8) Dover.

— Painting Landscapes in Oils. (Leisure Arts Ser.: No. 3). (Illus.). 32p. pap. 4.95 (0-85532-402-3, 402-3, Pub. by Srch Pr) A Schwartz & Co.

— Working with Oils. (Leisure Arts Ser.: No. 1). (Illus.). 32p. pap. 4.95 (0-85532-400-7, 400-7, Pub. by Srch Pr) A Schwartz & Co.

Batterson. Biography of Stephen Smale. (C). 1998. write for info. (0-201-40760-4) Addison-Wesley.

Batterson, Jack A. Blind Boone: Missouri's Ragtime Pioneer. LC 98-34157. (Missouri Heritage Readers Ser.). (Illus.). 136p. 1998. pap. 9.95 (0-8262-1198-4) U of Mo Pr.

Batterson, Robert, ed. see Chilton, Kenneth.

***Batterson, Steve.** Stephen Smale: A Mathematician Who Broke the Dimension Barrier LC 99-38205. 1999. write for info. (0-8218-2045-1) Am Math.

Battery Conference on Applications & Advances Staf. Proceedings of the Second Annual Battery Conference on Applications & Advances, January 14-16, 1986: California State University - Long Beach, Long Beach, California. Das, R. L. et al, eds. LC 87-83054. (Electrochemical Society Proceedings Ser.: No. 87-16). (Illus.). 286p. reprint ed. pap. 88.70 (0-7837-4422-6, 205248200012) Bks Demand.

Battery Design & Optimization Symposium Staff. Battery Design & Optimization: Proceedings of the Symposium, Pittsburgh, Pa, 1978. Gross, Sidney, ed. LC 79-51500. (Electrochemical Society Proceedings Ser.: Vol. 79-1). 493p. reprint ed. pap. 152.90 (0-8357-5995-4, 205205900032) Bks Demand.

***Battery, Lee, et al.** Your Gift: An Eductional, Spiritual & Personal Resource for Hospice Volunteers. Olson, Sharon L., ed. LC 99-91643. (Illus.). 176p. 2000. pap. 12.95 (0-9638984-4-2) Seasons.

Battery Press, Inc. Staff, ed. see British Gen. Staff.

Battestin, Martin C. A Henry Fielding Companion. LC 99-32531. 360p. 2000. lib. bdg. 79.95 (0-313-29707-X) Greenwood.

— The Providence of Wit: Aspects of Form in Augustan Literature & the Arts. x, 331p. (C). 1974. pap. text 16.50 (0-8139-1235-0) U Pr of Va.

Battestin, Martin C., ed. British Novelists, 1660-1800, 2 vols. 39th ed. (Dictionary of Literary Biography Ser.: Vol. 39). 1577p. 1985. text 296.00 (0-8103-1717-6) Gale.

Battestin, Martin C., ed. see Fielding, Henry.

Battestin, Martin C., ed. see Fielding, Henry & Fielding, Sarah.

Battestini, Simon P., ed. see Georgetown University Round Table Meeting on Lingu.

Batteux, Charles. Einschrankung der Schonen Kunste Auf Einen Einzigen Grundsatz (Les Beaux Arts Reduits en un Meme Principe, Deutsch) xxxvi, 1010p. 1976. reprint ed. write for info. (3-487-06045-0) G Olms Pubs.

Batteux, S. Dictionary, Grammaire Sioux-Francais. (FRE.). 1997. 95.00 (0-320-00818-5) Fr & Eur.

Battey, George M., Jr. History of Rome & Floyd County Vol. I: Including Numerous Incidents of More Than Local Interest, 1540-1922. (Illus.). 640p. 1997. reprint ed. lib. bdg. 66.00 (0-8328-6628-8) Higginson Bk Co.

Battey, George Magruder, Jr. A History of Rome & Floyd County, Georgia 1540-1922. LC 74-76719. (Illus.). 728p. 2000. reprint ed. 45.00 (0-87797-003-3) Cherokee.

Battey, H. V. Battey: Samson Battey of Rhode Island, the Immigrant Ancestor & His Descendants. 400p. 1993. reprint ed. pap. 59.50 (0-8328-2817-3); reprint ed. lib. bdg. 69.50 (0-8328-2816-5) Higginson Bk Co.

Battey, Maurice Hugh. Mineralogy Students. 2nd ed. 1996. text 42.00 (0-582-44005-X) Addison-Wesley.

Battey, N. H., et al, eds. Post-Translational Modifications in Plants. LC 92-28694. (Society for Experimental Biology Seminar Ser.: No. 53). (Illus.). 330p. (C). 1993. text 100.00 (0-521-41181-5) Cambridge U Pr.

Battey, Thomas C. The Life & Adventures of a Quaker among the Indians. 339p. 1972. reprint ed. 26.95 (0-87928-025-5) Corner Hse.

Battie, David. David Battie's Guide to Understanding 19th & 20th Century British Porcelain. LC 95-142915. (Illus.). 320p. 1994. 59.50 (1-85149-123-6) Antique Collect.

Battie, David, ed. Sotheby's Concise Encyclopedia of Porcelain. (Illus.). 208p. 1995. pap. 29.95 (1-85029-648-0, Pub. by Conran Octopus) Antique Collect.

Battie, David & Cottle, Simon. Sotheby's Concise Encyclopedia of Glass. (Illus.). 208p. 1995. pap. 29.95 (1-85029-654-5, Pub. by Conran Octopus) Antique Collect.

Battie, David & Turner, Michael. The Price Guide to Nineteenth & Twentieth Century British Pottery. 2nd ed. (Price Guide Ser.). (Illus.). 244p. 1987. 49.50 (1-85149-109-0) Antique Collect.

Battien, Pauline. The Gold Seekers: A 200 Year History of Mining in Washington, Idaho, Montana & Lower British Columbia. (Illus.). 265p. (Orig.). 1989. pap. 19.95 (0-940151-16-2) Statesman-Exam.

Battien, Pauline, jt. auth. see Morgenroth, Chris.

***Battier, Marc, ed.** Aesthetics of Live Electronic Music. (Illus.). 88p. 1999. pap. text 21.00 (90-5755-114-4, Harwood Acad Pubs) Gordon & Breach.

Battifarano, A. J. & Richardson, Alan. The Four Seasons of Italian Cooking: Harvest Recipes from the Farms & Vineyards of the Italian Countryside. LC 98-2731. (Illus.). 192p. (gr. 11). 1998. 27.50 (0-7835-5328-5) Time-Life.

Battifora & McCaughey. Tumors of the Serosal Membranes. (AFIP Atlas of Tumor Pathology Ser.: Vol. 15). (Illus.). 128p. 1995. pap. text 45.00 (1-881041-19-0) Am Registry Path.

Battig, Franziska Bitter. Die Entwicklung der Schriftlichen Erzahlfahigkeit Vom. 4, Bis. 6: Primarschuljahr. (GER.). 187p. 1999. 30.95 (3-906761-80-0, Pub. by P Lang) P Lang Pubng.

Battigalli, Pierpaolo, ed. Decisions, Games & Markets. (Studies in Risk & Uncertainty). 384p. (C). 1996. lib. bdg. 157.50 (0-7923-9841-6) Kluwer Academic.

Battigelli. John Dryden Revisited. 2000. 28.95 (0-8057-7809-8, Twyne) Mac Lib Ref.

Battigelli, Anna. Margaret Cavendish & the Exiles of the Mind. LC 97-47261. (Studies in the English Renaissance). 192p. 1998. 32.00 (0-8131-2068-3) U Pr of Ky.

Battikha, Jihad. Director Power Solutions. LC 96-49658. 475p. 1996. pap. text 39.99 (1-56205-665-4) New Riders Pub.

Battikha, N. E. The Condensed Handbook of Measurement & Control. LC 97-4212. 1997. pap. 45.00 (1-55617-582-5) ISA.

— Developing Guidelines for Instrumentation & Control: Implementing Standards & Verifying Work Performed. LC 94-29633. 267p. 1994. 48.00 (1-55617-525-6) ISA.

— The Management of Control Systems: Justification & Technical Auditing. 256p. 1992. 55.00 (1-55617-199-4) ISA.

Battilotti, Stefano. Noninteracting Control with Stability for Nonlinear System. LC 94-11384. (Lecture Notes in Control & Information Sciences: Vol. 196). 1994. write for info. (0-387-19891-1) Spr-Verlag.

Battimelli, G. & Paoloni, G. Essays & Recollections on 20th Century Physics - A Selection of Historical Writings. LC 96-1976. 800p. 1997. text 112.00 (981-02-2369-2) World Scientific Pub.

Battin. Puzzles about Art. 2nd ed. 2001. pap. text. write for info. (0-312-15759-2) St Martin.

Battin, Barbara, jt. ed. see Bell, Richard H.

Battin, George W. & Moscrip, F. A. Past & Present of Marshall County, Iowa, Vol. 1 & 2. (Illus.). 1168p. 1993. reprint ed. lib. bdg. 115.00 (0-8328-3517-X) Higginson Bk Co.

Battin, M. Pabst, et al. Physician Assisted Suicide: Expanding the Debate. LC 97-52070. 320p. (C). 1998. 75.00 (0-415-92002-7) Routledge.

Battin, Margaret, et al. Praying for a Cure: Medical Ethics in Conflict with Religious Freedom. (Point/Counterpoint Ser.). 224p. 1998. 57.00 (0-8476-8773-2) Rowman.

Battin, Margaret P. The Death Debate: Ethical Issues in Suicide. 242p. (C). 1995. pap. text 18.80 (0-13-524307-6) P-H.

— Ethical Issues in Suicide. 2nd ed. LC 94-38363. (Illus.). 240p. (C). 1994. pap. text 20.40 (0-13-304668-0) P-H.

— The Least Worst Death: Essays in Bioethics on the End of Life. (Illus.). 320p. (C). 1994. pap. text 26.95 (0-19-508265-6) OUP.

Battin, Margaret P., et al, eds. Physician Assisted Suicide: Expanding the Debate. 320p. 1998. pap. 21.99 (0-415-92003-5) Routledge.

Battin, Margaret P. & Lipman, Arthur G., eds. Drug Use in Assisted Suicide & Euthanasia. LC 95-49632. (Journal of Pharmaceutical Care in Plan & Symptom Control Ser.: Vol. 3, Nos. 3/4 & Vol. 4, Nos 1/2). 360p. 1996. 59.95 (1-56024-814-9, Pharmctl Prods) Haworth Pr.

— Drug Use in Assisted Suicide & Euthanasia. LC 95-49632. (Journal of Pharmaceutical Care in Plan & Symptom Control Ser.: Vol. 3, Nos. 3/4 & Vol. 4, Nos. 1/2). 360p. 1996. pap. 29.95 (1-56024-843-2, Pharmctl Prods) Haworth Pr.

Battin, Margaret P. & Maris, Ronald W., eds. Suicide & Ethics. (Special Issues Ser.: Vol. 13, No. 3). 112p. 1984. pap. 9.95 (0-89862-577-7) Guilford Pubns.

Battin, Margaret P., et al. Puzzles about Art: An Aesthetics Casebook. LC 87-60519. 226p. (Orig.). (C). 1989. pap. text 26.95 (0-312-00307-2) St Martin.

Battin, Patricia, ed. see Council on Library & Information Resources Staff, et al.

Battin, R. H. An Introduction to the Mathematics & Methods of Astrodynamics. (Educ Ser.). 796p. 1987. 62.95 (0-930403-25-8, 25-8) AIAA.

Battin, Richard H. An Introduction to the Mathematics & Methods of Astrodynamics. LC 99-13266. (Education Ser.). 13p. 1999. write for info. (1-56347-342-9) AIAA.

Battin, Wendy. Little Apocalypse. LC 97-71487. (Richard Snyder Publication Award Ser.). 83p. (Orig.). 1997. pap. 10.00 (0-912592-40-0) Ashland Poetry.

***Battinelli, Thomas.** Physique, Fitness & Performance. (Calvin P. Horn Lectures). 2000. 99.95 (0-8493-0231-5) CRC Pr.

Battino. Nitrogen & Air. (Solubility Data Ser.). 1982. 130.00 (0-08-023961-7, Pergamon Pr) Elsevier.

— Oxygen & Ozone. (Solubility Data Ser.). 1981. 130.00 (0-08-023952-8, Pergamon Pr) Elsevier.

Battino, Rubin, jt. auth. see Wood, Scott E.

Battiscombe, Georgina. Shaftesbury: The Great Reformer, 1801-1885. LC 74-32370. 1975. 15.00 (0-395-19953-0) HM.

***Battison, Brian.** The Christmas Bow Murder. 2000. pap. 9.95 (0-7490-0475-4, Pub. by Allison & Busby) Intl Pubs Mktg.

Battison, Brian. The Christmas Bow Murder. large type ed. 480p. 1995. 27.99 (0-7089-3407-2) Ulverscroft.

— Flying Pigs. 224p. 1998. 27.00 (0-09-478550-3, Pub. by Constable & Co) Trafalgar.

***Battison, Brian.** Flying Pigs. large type ed. 408p. 2000. 31.99 (0-7089-4178-8) Ulverscroft.

— Jeopardy's Child: A DCI Jim Ashworth Investigation. 1999. mass mkt. 9.95 (0-7490-0304-9) Allison & Busby.

Battison, Brian. Jeopardy's Child: A DCI Jim Ashworth Investigation. 224p. 1998. 27.00 (0-09-477530-3, Pub. by Constable & Co) Trafalgar.

***Battison, Brian.** Mirror Image. large type ed. 408p. 1999. 31.99 (0-7089-4129-X) Ulverscroft.

— Poetic Justice: A DCI Jim Ashworth Investigation. mass mkt. 9.95 (0-7490-0419-3) Allison & Busby.

Battison, Brian. Truths Not Told. large type ed. (Linford Mystery Large Print Ser.). 512p. 1998. pap. 17.99 (0-7089-5293-3, Linford) Ulverscroft.

Battison, Robbin M. Lexical Borrowing in American Sign Language. LC 78-59164. (Illus.). 240p. 1978. pap. text 18.95 (0-932130-02-X) Linstok Pr.

Battison, Robbin M., jt. auth. see Baker, Charlotte.

Battista, Garth, ed. The Runner's Literary Companion. 336p. 1996. pap. 13.95 (0-14-025353-X) Viking Penguin.

— The Runner's Literary Companion: Great Stories & Poems about Running. LC 94-71686. 336p. 1994. 23.00 (1-55821-335-X, Pub. by Breakaway Bks) Consort Bk Sales.

Battista, Kathy. Art New York. pap. 15.00 (1-84166-021-3, Pub. by Ellipsis) Norton.

Battista, Lloyd M. The Nose Knows: A Sensualist Guide to Great Joints. LC 96-44558. (Illus.). 256p. (Orig.). 1996. pap. 13.00 (1-879415-23-2) Mtn n Air Bks.

B

An Asterisk (*) at the beginning of an entry indicates that the title is appearing for the first time.

Battista, Michael T. Shape Makers: Developing Geometric Reasoning with the Geometer's Sketchpad LC 98-232545. 224p. 1998. write for info. (*1-55953-291-2*) Key Curr Pr.

Battista, Michael T. & Berle-Carman, Mary. Containers & Cubes: 3-D Geometry: Volume. Anderson, Catherine et al, eds. (Investigations in Number, Data, & Space Ser.). (Illus.). 158p. (Orig.). (J). (gr. 5-6). 1995. pap., teacher ed. 22.95 (*0-86651-993-9*, DS21429) Seymour Pubns.

— Containers & Cubes: 3-D Geometry: Volume. rev. ed. Anderson, Catherine & Cory, Beverly, eds. (Investigations in Number, Data, & Space Ser.). (Illus.). 171p. (Orig.). (YA). (gr. 5 up). 1997. pap. text 22.95 (*1-57232-803-7*, 47050) Seymour Pubns.

Battista, Michael T. & Clements, Douglas H. Exploring Solids & Boxes: 3-D Geometry. Samii, Priscilla C. et al, eds. (Investigations in Number, Data, & Space Ser.). (Illus.). 112p. (Orig.). 1994. pap., teacher ed. 22.95 (*0-86651-808-8*, DS21246) Seymour Pubns.

— Exploring Solids & Boxes: 3-D Geometry. rev. ed. Anderson, Catherine & Cory, Beverly, eds. (Investigations in Number, Data, & Space Ser.). (Illus.). 111p. (Orig.). (YA). (gr. 3 up). 1997. pap. text 22.95 (*1-57232-703-0*, 43850) Seymour Pubns.

— Seeing Solids & Silhouettes: 3-D Geometry. Samii, Priscilla C. & Cory, Beverly, eds. LC 94-214856. (Investigations in Number, Data, & Space Ser.). (Illus.). 112p. (Orig.). 1994. pap., teacher ed. 22.95 (*0-86651-797-9*, DS21237) Seymour Pubns.

— Seeing Solids & Silhouettes: 3-D Geometry. rev. ed. Anderson, Catherine & Cory, Beverly, eds. (Investigations in Number, Data, & Space Ser.). (Illus.). 116p. (Orig.). (YA). (gr. 4 up). 1997. pap. text 22.95 (*1-57232-745-6*, 43892) Seymour Pubns.

***Battiste, Marie.** Reclaiming Indigenous Voice & Vision. 256p. 2000. pap. 24.95 (*0-7748-0746-6*) UBC Pr.

Battistella, B. The Gospel for Young Children. (Illus.). (J). (ps-4). 1988. 39.00 (*0-85439-193-2*, Pub. by St Paul Pubns) St Mut.

Battistella, Bruna. Mary from Nazareth. Basile, Deana, tr. from ITA. LC 94-2694. (Illus.). 128p. (Orig.). (J). (gr. 2-4). 1996. 12.95 (*0-8198-4772-0*) Pauline Bks.

Battistella, Edwin L. The Logic of Markedness. 192p. 1996. text 49.95 (*0-19-510394-7*) OUP.

— Markedness: The Evaluative Superstructure of Language. LC 89-29453. (SUNY Series in Linguistics). 265p. (C). 1990. text 89.50 (*0-7914-0369-6*); pap. text 29.95 (*0-7914-0370-X*) State U NY Pr.

Battistella, Graziano, ed. Italian Americans in the 'Eighties: A Sociodemographic Profile. LC 88-29932. 225p. 1989. pap. 14.50 (*0-934733-41-4*) CMS.

Battistelli, Ellen S. Making Managed Health Care Work for Kids in Foster Care: A Guide to Purchasing Services. 80p. 1996. pap. 7.95 (*0-87868-683-5*) Child Welfare.

— Managed Health Care Guide for Caseworkers & Foster Parents. LC 97-19976. 1997. pap. 9.95 (*0-87868-682-7*, CWLA Pr) Child Welfare.

Battistelli, Ellen S. & Child Welfare League of America Staff. The Health Care of Children in Out-of-House Care: A Survey of State Child Welfare Commissioners. LC 98-3391. 32p. 1998. pap. 9.95 (*0-87868-706-8*, 7068, CWLA Pr) Child Welfare.

***Battisti-Cole, Teresa.** Silent One: The Adventure of a Hearing Impaired Heroine. LC 98-75000. (Illus.). 38p. (J). (gr. 1 up). 1998. reprint ed. pap. 12.00 (*0-9667227-1-X*) Lonely Blue.

Battisti-Cole, Teresa. Silent One: The Adventure of a Hearing Impaired Heroine. LC 98-75000. (Illus.). 38p. (YA). (gr. 1 up). 1998. reprint ed. pap. 12.00 (*0-9667227-0-1*) Lonely Blue.

Battistin, Leontino, et al, eds. Parkinson's Disease, Pt. 69. (Advances in Neurology Ser.: Vol. 69). (Illus.). 752p. 1995. text 173.00 (*0-7817-0341-7*) Lppncott W & W.

Battistini, Lawrence H. Japan & America from Earliest Times to the Present. LC 76-98210. 198p. 1970. reprint ed. lib. bdg. 38.50 (*0-8371-3245-2*, BAJA, Greenwood Pr) Greenwood.

— Rise of American Influence in Asia & the Pacific. LC 74-12576. 241p. 1974. reprint ed. lib. bdg. 65.00 (*0-8371-7728-6*, BAAI, Greenwood Pr) Greenwood.

***Battistini, Matilde.** Picasso. LC 00-27067. (Illus.). (J). 2000. write for info. (*0-7894-6123-4*) DK Pub Inc.

***Battiston-Zuliani, Regine.** Max Frisch Romancier: Son Evolution de Mein Name Sei Gantenbein a Der Mensch Erscheint Im Holozan. (Publications Universitaires Europeennes: Vol. 1732). xii, 300p. 1999. 46.95 (*3-906763-54-4*, Pub. by P Lang) P Lang Pubng.

Battistone, Catherine. Malory's Morte D'Arthur: Remarking Arthurian Tradition. text. write for info. (*0-312-22998-4*) St Martin.

Battistoni, Richard M. Public Schooling & the Education of Democratic Citizens. LC 85-9133. 200p. 1985. text 35.00 (*0-87805-280-1*) U Pr of Miss.

Battistoni, Richard M., et al, eds. Experiencing Citizenship: Concepts & Models for Service-Learning in Political Science. (Service-Learning in the Disciplines Ser.). 256p. 1997. pap. 28.50 (*1-56377-007-5*, SL13DS) Am Assn Higher Ed.

Battistoni, Richard M., ed. see Barber, Benjamin R.

Battle, Bernard, jt. auth. see Kemp, Fred.

Battle, Carl. The Retirement Handbook: How to Maximize Your Assets & Protect Your Quality of Life. 2nd rev. ed. LC 98-70407. Orig. Title: Senior Counsel: Legal & Financial Strategies for Age 50 & Beyond. 256p. 1998. pap. 18.95 (*1-880559-96-X*) Allworth Pr.

Battle, Carl W. Legal-Wise: Self-Help Legal Guide for Everyone. 3rd rev. ed. LC 96-84661. 208p. 1996. pap. 18.95 (*1-880559-52-8*) Allworth Pr.

— The Patent Guide: A Friendly Handbook for Protecting & Profiting from Patents. LC 96-79670. (Illus.). 224p. (Orig.). 1997. pap. 18.95 (*1-880559-72-2*) Allworth Pr.

Battle, Cecelia. Caboose Cat. (Illus.). 24p. (J). (ps-3). 1998. pap. 4.99 (*0-941072-32-0*) Southern Herit.

Battle, Charles, ed. see West, Gordon.

Battle, Charles W., ed. see Fulton, Stanley R. & Rawlins, John C.

Battle, Dee & Lesser, Alayne. The Best of Bakelite & Other Plastic Jewelry. (Illus.). 160p. (YA). (gr. 10-13). 1996. 39.95 (*0-88740-901-6*) Schiffer.

Battle, Dolores E. Communication Disorders in Multi-Cultural Populations. 2nd ed. LC 97-26065. 504p. 1997. text 49.50 (*0-7506-9825-X*) Buttrwrth-Heinemann.

Battle, Effie T., et al. Six Poets of Racial Uplift. LC 96-48714. 1996. 30.00 (*0-7838-1431-3*, Hall Reference) Macmillan.

Battle, Eliot F. A Letter to Young Black Men: You Won't Find Role Models on Street Corners. LC 97-61435. (YA). 1997. write for info. (*0-923950-18-4*) Tucker IL.

Battle, Herbert B. & Yelverton, Lois. Battle Book: Genealogy of the Battle Family in America. 768p. 1993. reprint ed. pap. 99.50 (*0-8328-3607-9*); reprint ed. lib. bdg. 109.50 (*0-8328-3606-0*) Higginson Bk Co.

Battle, J. H., ed. History of Bucks County, Pa. (Illus.). 1176p. 1993. reprint ed. lib. bdg. 115.00 (*0-8328-2882-3*) Higginson Bk Co.

Battle, J. H., ed. see Perrin, William H.

Battle, J. M. & Sherlock, J. D., eds. Gorbachev Reforms - Annotated Bibliography of Soviet Writings, July 1987-1989. 13.50 (*0-685-47908-0*) Academic Intl.

— Gorbachev Reforms - Annotated Bibliography of Soviet Writings, 1985-June 1987. 1988. 20.00 (*0-685-24297-8*) Academic Intl.

— Gorbachev Reforms - Annotated Bibliography of Soviet Writings, 1985-June 1987, Pt. 1. 1988. pap. 13.50 (*0-87569-102-1*) Academic Intl.

Battle, Jackie, ed. see Bishop, Twyla D.

Battle, Jackie, ed. see Lang-Marshall, Mary.

Battle, Jackie, ed. see Sellers, Cikethia.

Battle, Jackson B. & Lipeles, Maxine I. Water Pollution, 4 vols., Vol. 2. 3rd ed. (Environmental Law Ser.). 744p. 1998. pap. text 39.95 (*0-87084-243-9*) Anderson Pub Co.

Battle, Jacqueline M., ed. see Rich, Diane.

Battle, James. Culture-Free Self-Esteem Inventories for Children & Adults Complete Battery. 2nd ed. Preston, J. B., ed. 1981. pap. 115.00 (*0-87562-067-1*) PRO-ED.

Battle, Kemp. Hearts of Fire. LC 97-50043. 464p. 1998. pap. 14.00 (*0-609-80183-X*, Crown) Crown Pub Group.

Battle, Kemp P. History of the University of North Carolina, 2 vols., 1. LC 74-13351. (Illus.). 1974. reprint ed. 30.00 (*0-87152-187-3*) Reprint.

— History of the University of North Carolina, 2 vols., 2. LC 74-13351. (Illus.). 1974. reprint ed. 30.00 (*0-87152-188-1*) Reprint.

— History of the University of North Carolina, 2 vols., Set. LC 74-13351. (Illus.). 1974. reprint ed. 60.00 (*0-87152-308-6*) Reprint.

Battle, L. C. Langenscheidts Handworterbucher: Katalanisch. Haensch, G., ed. 1997. pap. write for info. (*3-468-04350-3*) Langenscheidt.

Battle, Laurie C., et al, eds. The Descendants of Mathew Battle, England to Virginia, 1647: A Collection of Family Records, Genealogical & Historical. LC 92-31939. 1992. 44.95 (*0-87152-459-7*) Reprint.

Battle-Lavert, Gwendolyn. The Music in Derrick's Heart. LC 97-34115. (Illus.). 32p. (J). (ps-3). 2000. 16.95 (*0-8234-1353-5*) Holiday.

— Off to School. LC 94-43094. (Illus.). 32p. (J). (gr. k-3). 1995. lib. bdg. 15.95 (*0-8234-1185-0*) Holiday.

***Battle-Lavert, Gwendolyn.** The Shaking Bag. LC 99-16974. (Illus.). 32p. (J). (gr. 1-3). 2000. lib. bdg. 15.95 (*0-8075-7328-0*) A Whitman.

Battle, Leroy A. Easier Said. (Illus.). 208p. 1995. pap. 18.50 (*1-884878-04-0*) Annapol Pubng.

Battle, Lois. Bed & Breakfast. 1997. pap. 12.95 (*0-14-025911-2*) Viking Penguin.

— Bed & Breakfast. large type ed. LC 96-37676. 554p. 1997. 26.95 (*0-7862-0972-0*) Thorndike Pr.

— A Habit of the Blood. 1988. pap. 4.50 (*0-317-62241-2*) St Martin.

— Storyville. 1997. pap. 12.95 (*0-14-026769-7*) Viking Penguin.

— Storyville. large type ed. LC 93-12037. (Basic Ser.). 654p. 1993. reprint ed. lib. bdg. 23.95 (*1-56054-659-X*) Thorndike Pr.

— War Brides. 368p. 1998. pap. 12.95 (*0-14-027643-2*) Viking Penguin.

Battle, Michael. Reconciliation: The Ubuntu Theology of Desmond Tutu. LC 97-8407. 272p. (Orig.). 1997. pap. 19.95 (*0-8298-1158-3*) Pilgrim OH.

***Battle, Michael, ed.** The Wisdom of Desmond Tutu. (Wisdom of Ser.). (Illus.). 48p. 2000. 6.95 (*0-664-22210-2*, Pub. by Westminster John Knox) Presbyterian Pub.

Battle, Richard V. The Volunteer Handbook: How to Organize & Manage a Successful Organization. LC 88-50078. 204p. 1992. pap. 12.95 (*0-929174-01-1*) Vol Concepts.

Battle, Schar, ed. see Battle, Tom.

Battle, Stafford L. Cold War Poems. 50p. 1985. pap. 5.95 (*0-943454-03-4*) Jotarian.

Battle, Stafford L., ed. see Mills, Joseph A.

Battle, Stanley F., ed. The Black Adolescent Parent. LC 87-332. (Child & Youth Services Ser.: Vol. 9, No. 1). 142p. 1987. text 39.95 (*0-86656-554-X*) Haworth Pr.

Battle, Stanley F., jt. auth. see Feit, Marvin D.

Battle, T. P. & Henein, H., eds. Processing & Handling of Powders & Dusts. LC 96-79954. (Illus.). 296p. 1997. 64.00 (*0-87339-359-7*, 3597) Minerals Metals.

Battle, Thomas C., ed. see Robinson, Harry G., III & Edwards, Hazel R.

Battle, Tom. Face the Solution: It Only Takes a Moment. Battle, Schar, ed. 61p. (Orig.). 1990. pap. 3.00 (*0-9627066-1-2*) Battle Minist.

— The Heartbeat of God. Battle, Schar, ed. LC 92-282486. 57p. (Orig.). 1992. pap. 3.00 (*0-9627066-2-0*) Battle Minist.

— Love Power. Battle, Schar, ed. 124p. 1994. pap. 4.00 (*0-9627066-4-7*) Battle Minist.

Battles, Curtis, ed. see Khiwa-Kiwuwa, Edward.

Battles, Edith. The Witch in Room Six. LC 86-45785. 144p. (J). (gr. 3-7). 1987. 11.95 (*0-06-020412-5*) HarpC Child Bks.

Battles, F. Analysis of the Institutes of Religion. 421p. 1993. reprint ed. ring bd. 24.95 (*1-57383-013-5*) Regent College.

Battles, Ford L. The Apologists: Study Outlines. (Study Outline Ser.: No. 1). 1991. pap. 8.00 (*1-55635-013-9*) Pickwick.

— Interpreting John Calvin. Benedetto, Robert, ed. LC 96-3394. 384p. 1996. 29.99 (*0-8010-2097-2*) Baker Bks.

— Irenaeus, Against Heresies: Clement of Alexandria, the Exhortation to the Greeks, &, Quis Dives Salvetur? (Study Outlines) LC 93-22092. 1993. pap. 12.50 (*1-55635-019-8*) Pickwick.

Battles, Ford L., ed. The Formation of the United Church of Christ (U. S. A.) LC 79-25049. (Bibliographia Tripotamopolitana Ser.: No. 2). 1970. 7.00 (*0-931222-01-X*) Pitts Theolog.

Battles, Ford L., jt. auth. see Rosenstock-Huessy, Eugen.

Battles, Ford L., ed. see Calvin, John.

Battles, Louise P. From the Mouths of Babes: Wee Wisdom from Little Ones. (Illus.). 95p. Date not set. pap. 5.95 (*1-885055-00-5*) Aiken-Argo.

Battles, Marion D., ed. The Fruit of Lips: Of Why Four Gospels? LC 78-8524. (Pittsburgh Theological Monographs: No. 19). 144p. 1978. reprint ed. pap. 6.25 (*0-915138-31-X*) Pickwick.

***Battles, Ralph & Thompson, Robert.** Fundamentals of Agribusiness Finance. (Illus.). 2000. 39.95 (*0-8138-2069-3*) Iowa St U Pr.

Battley, Nick. An Introduction to Commodity Futures & Options. 2nd ed. 1997. text 32.50 (*1-55738-920-9*, Irwn Prfssnl) McGraw-Hill Prof.

— World Futures & Options Directory, 1991-1992. 1990. 95.00 (*0-07-707343-6*) McGraw.

— Worlds Futures & Options Markets: A Country by Country Directory of the Exchanges Contracts. 1993. text 95.00 (*1-55738-513-0*, Irwn Prfssnl) McGraw-Hill Prof.

Battley, Nick, ed. Fitzroy Dearborn Directory of the World's Futures & Options Markets. 1050p. 1994. lib. bdg. 95.00 (*1-884964-08-7*) Fitzroy Dearborn.

— The St. James World Directory of Futures & Options. 91st ed. 700p. 1991. 95.00 (*1-55862-143-1*) St James Pr.

Battley, Nick, et al. The European Bond Markets: An Overview & Analysis for Money Managers & Traders. 6th ed. LC 97-20370. 1997. write for info. (*0-07-709407-7*) McGraw.

Battlin, Margaret P. & David, J. Suicide: The Philosophical Issues. 292p. 1981. 27.00 (*0-7206-0579-2*, Pub. by P Owen Ltd) Dufour.

Battlo, Jean. Appalachian Gothic Tales. LC 97-93246. 1997. pap. 12.00 (*0-87012-577-X*) McClain.

A unique look into the gothic world in Appalachia through short stories & histories. The author, a writer of plays, short stories & histories, explores the mysteries of this tradition-rich culture through her tales. *Publisher Paid Annotation.*

— Behold the Man. Burns, Rebecca, ed. LC 94-72916. 119p. (Orig.). 1996. pap. 10.95 (*0-941092-28-3*) Mtn St Pr.

—McDowell County, in West Virginia & America. 550p. 1998. 45.00 (*0-87012-579-6*) McClain.

An in-depth look into the history of McDowell County, West Virginia. Approximately 550 pages with impressive historical photo display. *Publisher Paid Annotation.*

Battmann, Wolfgang. Stabilitat und Wandel Im Unternehmen: Das Management Zwischen Tradition und Innovation. (Wirtschaftspsychologie Ser.: Bd. 6). (GER., Illus.). VIII, 157p. 1997. 35.95 (*3-631-32430-8*) P Lang Pubng.

Batto, Bernard F. Slaying the Dragon: Mythmaking in the Biblical Tradition. 176p. (Orig.). 1992. pap. 18.95 (*0-664-25353-9*) Westminster John Knox.

Batto, Bernard F., et al. The Biblical Canon in Comparative Perspective: Scripture in Context IV. (Ancient Near Eastern Texts & Studies: Vol. 11). 352p. 1991. 99.95 (*0-7734-9648-3*) E Mellen.

***Battram, Arthur.** Navigating Complexity: The Essential Guide to Complexity Theory in Business & Management. (Illus.). 267p. 1999. pap. 19.95 (*1-85835-870-1*, Pub. by Stylus Pub VA) LPC InBook.

Battram, Arthur, ed. Navigating Complexity: The Essential Guide to Complexity Theory in Business & Management. 280p. 1998. pap. 18.95 (*1-85835-899-X*, Indust Soc) Stylus Pub VA.

Battrick, Bruce, ed. see Astrophysics & Space Science Staff.

Battrick, Craig J., ed. see Roberts-Dominguez, Jan.

Battrick, Craig J., ed. see Sherk, Warren.

Battrick, Elizabeth. Beatrix Potter's Tale. large type ed. (Ulverscroft Large Print Ser.). 432p. 1998. 29.99 (*0-7089-3891-4*) Ulverscroft.

Batts, H. Lewis, Jr., et al, eds. Proceedings: Great Lakes Solar Greenhouse Conference IV. Kalamazoo, Michigan, Nov. 6-7, 1981. 177p. 1982. pap. 10.00 (*0-939294-05-2*, SB-416-G7-1981) Beech Leaf.

Batts, H. Lewis, Jr. & Tenenbaum, Michael, eds. Proceedings: Great Lakes Solar Greenhouse Conference II Kalamazoo, Michigan, June, 8-9, 1979. (Illus.). xiii, 137p. (Orig.). 1980. pap. 10.00 (*0-939294-02-8*, SB-416-G7-1979) Beech Leaf.

Batts, H. Lewis, Jr., ed. & illus. see Bystrom, Robert.

Batts, John S., ed. see Newton, Eric.

Batts, Kenneth P., jt. auth. see Ludwig, Jurgen.

Batts, Michael S. A Brief Survey of Germanic Studies at Canadian Universities from the Beginnings to 1995. (Canadian Studies in German Language & Literature: Vol. 44). 191p. 1998. 32.95 (*3-906760-57-X*, Pub. by P Lang) P Lang Pubng.

— A Brief Survey of Germanic Studies at Canadian Universities from the Beginnings to 1995. LC 98-27967. (Canadian Studies in German Language & Literature: Vol. 44). 191p. 1998. pap. text 32.95 (*0-8204-4204-6*) P Lang Pubng.

— A History of Histories of German Literature, 1835-1914. 320p. 1993. 70.00 (*0-7735-1140-7*, Pub. by McG-Queens Univ Pr) CUP Services.

Batts, Michael S., et al, eds. Essays on German Literature, in Honour of G. Joyce Hallamore. LC 68-117292. (Illus.). 267p. reprint ed. pap. 82.80 (*0-608-10227-X*, 201412600094) Bks Demand.

Batts, Miriam M. Passing of the Summer. 1998. pap. write for info. (*1-57553-710-9*) Watermrk Pr.

Batts, Sidney F. The Protestant Wedding Sourcebook: A Complete Guide for Developing Your Own Service. LC 92-19807. 192p. (Orig.). 1993. pap. 25.00 (*0-664-25303-2*) Westminster John Knox.

Battson, Jill. Hard Candy. LC 97-170041. 112p. 1997. pap. 9.99 (*1-895837-01-4*) Insomniac.

Battuta, Ibn. The Adventures of Ibn Battuta. Dunn, Ross E., tr. 373p. 1996. pap. 15.95 (*0-614-21691-5*, 10) Kazi Pubns.

Batty, Beatrice. Forty Two Years Amongst the Indians & Eskimo. 1996. reprint ed. 36.00 (*81-206-1151-9*, Pub. by Asian Educ Servs) S Asia.

Batty, C. David. An Introduciton to the Twentieth Edition of the Dewey Decimal Classification. LC 92-37286. 218p. reprint ed. pap. 67.60 (*0-608-20964-3*, 207183600002) Bks Demand.

Batty, D. Sexually Abused Children: Making Their Placement Work. (C). 1989. 39.00 (*0-903534-94-0*, Pub. by Brit Ag for Adopt & Fost) St Mut.

— Working with Children. (C). 1989. 50.00 (*0-903534-65-7*, Pub. by Brit Ag for Adopt & Fost) St Mut.

Batty, D., ed. The Implications of AIDS for Children in Care. (C). 1989. 39.00 (*0-903534-72-X*, Pub. by Brit Ag for Adopt & Fost) St Mut.

Batty, Daphne & Wrighton, Pete, eds. Your Child & Foster Care: A Guide for Bith Parents Considering Private Fostering. 1996. pap. 22.00 (*1-873868-31-6*) BAAF.

Batty, Daphne, jt. auth. see Meerstadt, P. W.

Batty, Daphne, jt. compiled by see Private Fostering Special Interest Group Staff.

Batty, Joseph Clair. Designing & Presenting Financial Information. 268p. 1988. text 96.95 (*0-566-02715-1*, Pub. by Gower) Ashgate Pub Co.

Batty, Joseph Clair & Folkman, Steven L. Food Engineering Fundamentals. LC 83-6808. 316p. reprint ed. pap. 98.00 (*0-7837-2839-5*, 205763300006) Bks Demand.

***Batty, Joyce S.** Pure Mathematics Bk. 1, Pt. 1: The Core Syllabus for A Level. 1999. pap. 39.95 (*0-7217-2356-X*, Pub. by Schofield) St Mut.

Batty, Michael & Longley, Paul. Fractal Cities: A Geometry of Form & Function. (Illus.). 394p. 1994. text 56.00 (*0-12-455570-5*) Acad Pr.

Batty, Michael, et al. Optimization & Discrete Choice in Urban Systems. Nijkamp, Peter, ed. (Lecture Notes in Economics & Mathematical Systems Ser.: Vol. 247). vi, 371p. 1985. 47.50 (*0-387-15660-7*) Spr-Verlag.

Batty, Michael, jt. ed. see Longley, Paul.

***Batty, Peter.** The Divided Union. (Illus.). 224p. 1999. pap. 18.99 (*0-7524-1771-1*, Pub. by Tempus Pubng) Arcadia Publng.

Battye, Adrian. Clause Structure & Language Change. Roberts, Ian, ed. (Oxford Studies in Comparative Syntax). (Illus.). 384p. 1995. text 75.00 (*0-19-508632-5*) OUP.

***Battye, Adrian.** French Language Today: Linguistic Introduction. 2nd ed. (FRE & ENG.). 384p. 2000. pap. 25.99 (*0-415-19838-0*) Routledge.

Battye, Adrian & Hintz, Marie-Anne. French Language Today. LC 91-39192. 392p. (C). 1992. pap. 24.99 (*0-415-07814-8*) Routledge.

Battye, Adrian & Hintze, Marie-Anne. The French Language Today. 320p. 1992. 39.95 (*0-04-445717-0*, A8170); pap. 19.95 (*0-04-445716-2*, A8171) Routledge.

***Battye, Adrian & Hintze, Marie-Anne.** The French Language Today. 2nd ed. LC 99-87392. 384p. 2000. write for info. (*0-415-19837-2*) Routledge.

Battye, Adrian & Roberts, Ian, eds. Clause Structure & Language Change. (Oxford Studies in Comparative Syntax). (Illus.). 384p. 1995. pap. text 45.00 (*0-19-508633-3*) OUP.

Batu, Vedat. Aquifer Hydraulics: A Comprehensive Guide to Hydrogeologic Data Analysis. LC 97-17107. 752p. 1998. text 120.00 incl. disk, 3.5 hd (*0-471-18502-7*) Wiley.

***Batuca, Dan G. & Jordaan, J. M., Jr.** Silting & Desilting of Reservoirs. (Illus.). 330p. (C). 2000. text 99.00 (*90-5410-477-5*, Pub. by A A Balkema) Ashgate Pub Co.

Batuev, A. S. Higher Integrative Systems of the Brain. xvi, 296p. 1987. text 220.00 (*2-88124-143-3*) Gordon & Breach.

B

Batuev, A. S., jt. auth. see Storozhuk, V. M.

Batugina, I. M. & Petukhov, I. M. Geodynamic Zoning of Mineral Deposits for Planning & Exploitation of Mines. (Russian Translation Ser.: No. 77). 169p. (C). 1990. text 110.00 (*90-6191-948-7*, Pub. by A A Balkema) Ashgate Pub Co.

Batugina, I. M., jt. auth. see Petukhov, I. M.

Batukhtin, V. D. Nonsmooth & Discontinuous Problems of Control & Optimization: A Proceedings Volume from the IFAC Workshop, Chelyabinsk, Russia, June 17-20, 1998. LC 98-49283. 244p. 1999. 65.00 (*0-08-043237-9*, Pergamon Pr) Elsevier.

Batulukisi, Niangi, jt. auth. see Maurer, Evan M.

Baturin, V. V. & Billington, N. S. Fundamentals of Industrial Ventilation. 3rd ed. LC 73-160513. (International Series of Monographs in Heating Ventilation & Refrigeration: Vol. 8). 1972. 218.00 (*0-08-015828-5*, Pub. by Pergamon Repr) Franklin.

Baturinsky, V., jt. auth. see Karpov, Anatoly.

***Baturone, I.** Microelectric Design of Fuzzy Logic-Based Systems. LC 00-29235. 2000. write for info. (*0-8493-0633-7*) CRC Pr.

Batusic, Nikola. Zagreb Croatian National Theatre. 189p. 1985. 25.00 (*0-918660-84-X*) Ragusan Pr.

Baty, G. & Chavance, R. El Arte Teatral (Theatrical Art) (SPA.). 295p. 1996. reprint ed. pap. 12.99 (*968-16-3808-5*, Pub. by Fondo) Continental Bk.

Baty, Gordon B. Entrepreneurship for the Nineties. 256p. (C). 1990. pap. text 24.80 (*0-13-282294-6*) P-H.

Baty, Keith, jt. auth. see Graham, Robert.

Baty, Laurie A., et al, eds. The Daguerreian Annual, 1994. (Illus.). (Orig.). 1994. pap. 45.00 (*1-881186-00-8*) Daguerreian.

— The Daguerreian Annual, 1995. (Illus.). (Orig.). 1995. pap. 45.00 (*1-881186-01-6*) Daguerreian.

Baty, Paige. E-Mail Trouble: Love & Addiction @ the Matrix. LC 98-8963. 169p. 1999. 29.95 (*0-292-70863-7*) U of Tex Pr.

Baty, Roberta M. Rambling of a Wide-Eyed Wanderer. Spears-Stewart, Reta, ed. 1998. pap. 15.00 (*1-892477-05-X*) Barnabs Pub.

Baty, S. Paige. American Monroe: The Making of a Body Politic. LC 94-10258. 1995. 50.00 (*0-520-08805-0*, Pub. by U CA Pr) Cal Prin Full Svc.

— American Monroe: The Making of a Body Politic. LC 94-10258. 1996. pap. 17.95 (*0-520-08806-9*, Pub. by U CA Pr) Cal Prin Full Svc.

— E-Mail Trouble: Love & Addiction @ the Matrix. LC 98-8963. 169p. 1999. pap. 14.95 (*0-292-70864-5*) U of Tex Pr.

Baty, T. Polarized Law (With an English Translation of the Hague Conventions on Private International Law) Three Lectures on Conflicts of Law, Delivered at the University of London. (Legal Reprint Ser.). xv, 210p. 1986. reprint ed. 35.00 (*0-421-35520-4*) W S Hein.

Baty, Wayne, ed. see Cooper, William B.

Baty, Wayne M., jt. auth. see Himstreet, William C.

Batygin, Yun K. Space Charge Dominated Beam Physics for Heary Ion Fusion. (AIP Conference Proceeding Ser.: No. 480). (Illus.). 232p. 1999. 78.00 (*1-56396-860-6*) Am Inst Physics.

***Batygin, Yuri.** Theory of High Brightness Beam Transport & Acceleration. 1999. 44.00 (*981-02-4027-9*) World Scientific Pub.

Batyshev, A. I., jt. auth. see Ryabov, V. R.

Batz Cooperman, Jeannette. The Broom Closet: Secret Meanings of Domesticity in Postfeminist Novels by Louise Erdrich, Mary Gordon, Toni Morrison, Marge Piercy, Jane Smiley & Amy Tan. LC 97-51352. (Writing about Women: Vol. 25). 239p. (C). 1999. pap. text 29.95 (*0-8204-3953-3*) P Lang Pubng.

Batz, Jeannette. Half Life: What We Give up to Work. 160p. (Orig.). 1993. pap. 9.95 (*0-9631448-3-9*) VA Pub Corp.

Batz, Julie, jt. auth. see New Ways to Work Staff.

Batzdorf, Ulrich. Syringomyelia Vol. 4: Current Concepts in Diagnosis & Treatment. (Illus.). 228p. 1991. 78.00 (*0-683-00475-1*) Lppncott W & W.

Batzdorff, Susanne. Aunt Edith: The Jewish Heritage of a Catholic Saint. LC 98-60893. (Illus.). 240p. 1998. pap. 14.95 (*0-87243-240-8*) Templegate.

Batzdorff, Susanne, tr. see Herbstrith, Waltraud, ed.

Batzdorff, Susanne M., ed. see Stein, Edith.

Batzel, Alice M. Who Shot the Sheriff? . . . A Legend of Utah Territory. 1998. 4.00 (*1-57514-308-9*, 1175) Encore Perform Pub.

Batzer. Invertebrates Freshwater Wetlands North. (General Science Ser.). 1997. text 64.95 (*0-442-02575-0*, VNR) Wiley.

Batzer, Darold P., et al, eds. Freshwater Wetlands. LC 98-39322. 1120p. 1999. 195.00 (*0-471-29258-3*) Wiley.

Batzer, Frances R. Contemporary Issues in Perimenopause & Menopause. LC 97-71114. (Illus.). 260p. (C). 1999. pap. text 29.95 (*1-884065-16-3*) Assocs in Med.

Batzer, Hans & Lohse, Friedrich. Introduction to Macromolecular Chemistry. 2nd ed. LC 78-6175. 311p. reprint ed. pap. 96.50 (*0-608-18839-5*, 203049300069) Bks Demand.

Batzing. Microbiology. (Biology Ser.). 2001. text, wbk. ed. 15.00 (*0-534-37566-9*); text, lab manual ed. 28.00 (*0-534-37564-2*); pap. text 48.00 (*0-534-55620-5*) Brooks-Cole.

Batzler, L. Richard. Journeys on Your Spiritual Path. LC 82-82069. 1982. 9.95 (*0-935710-04-3*) Hid Valley MD.

— The Rising Tide of Suicide: A Guide to Prevention, Intervention & Postvention. LC 85-82029. 200p. (Orig.). 1988. pap. 10.00 (*0-935710-08-6*) Hid Valley MD.

— Sunlight & Shadows: Portraits of Priorities for Living & Dying. LC 85-82029. (Illus.). 60p. (Orig.). 1986. pap. 4.95 (*0-935710-09-4*) Hid Valley MD.

— Through the Valley of the Shadow: A Guide for the Care of the Dying & Their Loved Ones. LC 83-11282. 1983. 11.95 (*0-935710-05-1*) Hid Valley MD.

Batzler, L. Richard, jt. auth. see Tauraso, Nicola M.

Batzner, Nike. Arte Povera, Manifeste, Statements, Kritiken. (GER., Illus.). 288p. 1995. text 11.00 (*3-364-00314-9*) Gordon & Breach.

— Mantegna. (Masters of Italian Art Ser.). (Illus.). 140p. 1998. 19.95 (*3-8290-0252-1*, 520532) Konemann.

Bau, David, III, jt. auth. see Trefethen, Lloyd N.

Bau, H. H., et al, eds. Bifurcation Phenomena & Chaos in Thermal Convection. (HTD Series, Vol. 214: AMD: Vol. 138). 120p. 1992. 37.50 (*0-7918-1055-0*, G00699) ASME.

Bau, Joseph. Dear God, Have You Ever Gone Hungry? Yurman, Sam, tr. from HEB. LC 98-17133. (Illus.). 240p. 1998. 24.45 (*1-55970-431-4*, Pub. by Arcade Pub Inc) Time Warner.

***Bau, Joseph.** Dear God, Have You Ever Gone Hungry? (Illus.). 2000. pap. 13.95 (*1-55970-540-X*, Pub. by Arcade Pub Inc) Time Warner.

Bau, Robert, ed. Transition Metal Hybrides: A Symposium Sponsored by the ACS Division of Inorganic Chemistry at the 2nd Joint Conference of the Chemical Institute of Canada & the American Chemical Society, Montreal, May 30-June 2, 1977. LC 78-7327. (Advances in Chemistry Ser.: No. 167). (Illus.). 440p. 1978. reprint ed. pap. 136.40 (*0-608-06751-2*, 206694800009) Bks Demand.

Baubeta, Pat O. De, see Coulthard, Malcolm & De Baubeta, Pat O., eds.

Baubeta, Patricia A. Odber de, see Odber de Baubeta, Patricia A.

Baubeta, Patricia A. Odber de, see Coulthard, Malcolm & Odber de Baubeta, Patricia A., eds.

Baublitz, Millard, jt. auth. see Busher, Peter.

Baublitz, Jacinth I. Relationshift. 216p. (Orig.). 1983. pap. 15.95 (*0-9610316-0-3*) J I Baublitz.

Baublitz, Millard, jt. auth. see Busher, Peter.

Baubock, Rainer. From Aliens to Citizens. 250p. 1994. pap. 41.95 (*1-85972-059-5*) Ashgate Pub Co.

Baubock, Rainer. Transnational Citizenship: Membership & Rights in International Migration. 360p. 1994. 95.00 (*1-85278-942-5*) E Elgar.

Baubock, Rainer, et al, eds. The Challenge of Diversity: Integration & Pluralism in Societies of Immigration. 280p. 1996. pap. 39.95 (*1-85972-401-9*, Pub. by Avebry) Ashgate Pub Co.

Baubock, Rainer & Rundell, John. Blurred Boundaries: Migration, Ethnicity, Citizenship. 356p. 1998. pap. 41.95 (*1-84014-893-4*, Pub. by Ashgate Pub) Ashgate Pub Co.

Bauby, Cathrina. Understanding Each Other: Improving Communication Through Effective Dialogue. LC 76-43576. (Illus.). 59p. 1976. pap. text 9.95 (*0-317-65121-8*) Intl Gen Semantics.

Bauby, Jean-Dominique. The Diving Bell & the Butterfly: A Memoir of Life in Death. Leggatt, Jeremy, tr. from FRE. 144p. 1997. 20.00 (*0-375-40115-6*) Knopf.

— The Diving Bell & the Butterfly: A Memoir of Life in Death. Leggatt, Jeremy, tr. 132p. 1998. pap. 11.00 (*0-375-70121-4*) Vin Bks.

— The Diving Bell & the Butterfly: A Memoir of Life in Death. LC 97-34582. (Wheeler Large Print Book Ser.). 1997. 24.95 (*1-56895-496-4*) Wheeler Pub.

— Le Scaphandre Et le Papillon. 1999. pap. 11.95 (*2-266-08059-8*) Midwest European Pubns.

Bauby, Jean-Dominique & Harrington, Mona. Care & Equality: Inventing a New Family Politics. LC 98-43233. 208p. 1999. 24.00 (*0-375-40015-X*) Knopf.

Bauccio, Michael L., ed. ASM Engineered Materials Reference Book. 2nd ed. 580p. 1994. 139.00 (*0-87170-502-8*, 6418) ASM.

— ASM Metals Reference Book. 3rd ed. LC 93-28716. 614p. 1993. 144.00 (*0-87170-478-1*, 6118) ASM.

Bauch, Hope, ed. see Walker, Faith.

Bauch, Jerold P., ed. Early Childhood Education in the Schools. 352p. 1988. pap. 24.95 (*0-8106-1464-2*) NEA.

Bauch, Kurt. Das Mittelalterliche Grabbild: Figuerliche Grabbilder des 11.bis 15. (Illus.). 376p. (C). 1976. 415.40 (*3-11-004482-X*) De Gruyter.

Bauchau, Henry. Oedipus on the Road. Glasheen, Anne-Marie, tr. LC 97-72130. 1997. 24.45 (*1-55970-382-2*, Pub. by Arcade Pub Inc) Time Warner.

Baucher, Francois. Methode der Reitkunst nach neuen Grundsatzen. (Illus.). 124p. 1978. write for info. (*3-487-08160-1*) G Olms Pubs.

Bauchot, Roland. Snakes: A Natural History. (Illus.). 220p. 1997. 21.95 (*0-8069-0653-7*) Sterling.

Bauchot, Roland, ed. Snakes: A Natural History. LC 93-43892. (Illus.). 220p. 1994. 39.95 (*0-8069-0654-5*) Sterling.

Bauchum, Rosalind. African-American Organizations: A Selective Bibliography. (Organizations & Interest Groups Ser.). 150p. 1997. text 23.00 (*0-8153-1130-3*) Garland.

Bauck, Paul B. Stand Out in the Crowd: Inspire Your Boss to Be Loyal to You. 95p. 1998. pap. 12.95 (*0-9666643-0-2*) Bauck & Assocs.

Bauckham, Richard. The Climax of Prophecy: Studies on the Book of Revelation. 568p. 1998. pap. 44.95 (*0-567-08625-9*, Pub. by T & T Clark) Bks Intl VA.

***Bauckham, Richard.** God Crucified: Monotheism & Christology in the New Testament. (New Studies in Biblical Theology). 79p. 1999. pap. 12.00 (*0-8028-4642-4*) Eerdmans.

— God Crucified: Monotheism & Christology in the New Testament. (Didsbury Lectures). 79p. 1998. reprint ed. pap. 11.99 (*0-85364-944-8*, Pub. by Paternoster Pub) OM Literature.

Bauckham, Richard. Gospels for All Christians: Rethinking the Gospel Audiences. LC 97-30621. 226p. 1997. pap. text 22.00 (*0-8028-4444-8*) Eerdmans.

— James. LC 98-30604. (New Testament Readings Ser.). 1999. write for info. (*0-415-10369-X*); pap. 29.99 (*0-415-10370-3*) Routledge.

— Scripture, Tradition & Reason: A Study of the Criteria of Christian Doctrine. Drewery, Benjamin, ed. 306p. pap. 29.95 (*0-567-08557-0*, Pub. by T & T Clark) Bks Intl VA.

— Scripture, Tradition & Reason: A Study of the Criteria of Christian Doctrine. Drewery, Benjamin, ed. 306p. (C). 47.95 (*0-567-09482-0*, Pub. by T & T Clark) Bks Intl VA.

Bauckham, Richard, ed. God Will Be All In All: Eschatology of Jurgen Moltmann. 320p. pap. 29.95 (*0-567-08663-1*) T&T Clark Pubs.

Bauckham, Richard & Hart, Trevor. At the Cross: Meditations on People Who Were There. LC 98-54080. (Illus.). 128p. 1999. pap. 9.99 (*0-8308-2202-X*, 2202) InterVarsity.

— Hope Against Hope: Christian Eschatology at the Turn of the Millennium. LC 99-49158. 240p. 1999. pap. 16.00 (*0-8028-4391-3*) Eerdmans.

Bauckham, Richard J. Jude & the Relatives of Jesus in the Early Church. 432p. 1994. 59.95 (*0-567-09573-8*) Bks Intl VA.

— II Peter, Jude. (Biblical Commentary Ser.: Vol. 50). 29.99 (*0-8499-0249-5*) Word Pub.

— The Theology of Jurgen Moltmann. 288p. pap. 29.95 (*0-567-29277-0*) Bks Intl VA.

— The Theology of the Book of Revelation. LC 92-15805. (New Testament Theology Ser.). 185p. (C). 1993. pap. text 16.95 (*0-521-35691-1*) Cambridge U Pr.

Bauco, Luigi. Diccionario del Pendulo de Foucault. (SPA.). 320p. 1989. pap. 39.95 (*0-7859-6314-6*, 8478170081) Fr & Eur.

Baucom, Alfred H. Hospitality Design for the Gray Generation: Meeting the Needs of a Growing Market. LC 95-54177. (Healthcare & Senior Living Design Ser.). 280p. 1996. 80.00 (*0-471-13789-8*) Wiley.

Baucom, Donald H. & Epstein, Norman B. Cognitive-Behavioral Marital Therapy. LC 89-7279. 448p. 1990. text 54.95 (*0-87630-558-3*) Brunner-Mazel.

Baucom, Ian. Out of Place: Englishness, Empire & the Locations of Identity. LC 98-25219. 1999. pap. 18.95 (*0-691-00403-X*, Pub. by Princeton U Pr) Cal Prin Full Svc.

— Out of Place: Englishness, Empire & the Locations of Identity. LC 98-25219. 1999. 55.00 (*0-691-01666-6*, Pub. by Princeton U Pr) Cal Prin Full Svc.

Baucom, John. Bonding & Breaking Free: What Good Parents Should Know. 224p. (Orig.). 1988. pap. 7.95 (*0-310-20521-2*, 6335P) Zondervan.

— The Zelda Complex: How to Avoid Toxic Relationships. LC 95-23635. 224p. 1996. 19.95 (*0-925190-75-6*) Fairview Press.

Baucom, John Q. Baby Steps to Happiness: 52 Inspiring Ways to Make Your Life Happy. LC 96-68842. 304p. 1996. pap. 12.95 (*0-914984-86-1*) Starburst.

— Elvis Syndrome: How to Avoid Death by Success. 224p. 1995. 19.95 (*0-925190-38-1*) Fairview Press.

— Help Your Children Say No to Drugs. 176p. 1987. pap. 8.95 (*0-310-20901-3*, 6336P) Zondervan.

— Little Baby Steps to Happiness. LC 96-68841. 160p. 1996. pap. 6.95 (*0-914984-87-X*) Starburst.

— Simple Secrets of Parenting: Easy As ABC. LC 97-2301. (Illus.). 64p. (Orig.). 1997. pap. 9.95 (*0-87868-638-X*) Child Welfare.

Baucom, John Q., jt. auth. see Lombardi, Vince, Jr.

Baucum, Don. Psychology. LC 95-43647. (Barron's EZ-101 Study Keys Ser.). 1996. pap. 6.95 (*0-8120-9580-4*) Barron.

***Baucum, Don.** Psychology. LC 98-54394. (Barron's College Review Ser.). 400p. 1999. pap. 14.95 (*0-7641-0674-0*) Barron.

Baucus, Jean & Paladin, Vivian. Helena: An Illustrated History. (Illus.). 239p. 1996. reprint ed. pap. 22.95 (*0-917298-40-3*) MT Hist Soc.

Baucus, Max, et al. Developing a Consensus for the Future: A Report of the China Policy Task Force. Gong, Gerrit W., ed. LC 96-5514. (CSIS Panel Reports). 70p. (C). 1996. pap. text 19.95 (*0-89206-285-1*) CSIS.

Baud-Bovy, Manuel & Lawson, Fred. Tourism & Recreation Development: Handbook for Planning & Design. 2nd ed. LC 98-19816. (Illus.). 304p. 2000. pap. text 79.95 (*0-7506-3086-8*) Buttrwrth-Heinemann.

Baud, Charles A. Harmonie der Gesichtszuege.Tr. of Harmonie du Visage. (Illus.). xx, 150p. 1982. pap. 42.75 (*3-8055-0067-X*) S Karger.

Baud, I. S. Forms of Production & Women's Labour: Gender Aspects of Industrialisation in India & Mexico. (Illus.). 321p. (C). 1992. 36.00 (*0-8039-9418-4*) Sage.

Baud, I. S. A. & De Bruijne, G. A., eds. Gender, Small-Scale Industry & Development Policy. 214p. 1992. text 55.00 (*1-85339-152-2*, Pub. by Intermed Tech) Stylus Pub VA.

Baud, I. S. A. & DeBruijne, G. A., eds. Gender, Small-Scale Industry & Development Policy. 214p. 1992. pap. 29.50 (*1-85339-156-5*, Pub. by Intermed Tech) Stylus Pub VA.

Baud, Isa & Smyth, Ines. Searching for Security: Women's Responses to Economic Transformations. LC 96-21815. (Studies in Development & Society). 176p. (C). 1996. 75.00 (*0-415-14227-X*) Routledge.

Baud, Michiel. Peasants & Tobacco in the Dominican Republic, 1870-1930. LC 94-18760. (Illus.). 336p. (C). 1995. text 35.00 (*0-87049-891-6*) U of Tenn Pr.

Baud, R. V. Photoelastic Study of Contact Stresses in Gears. (Technical Papers: Vol. P76). (Illus.). 19p. 1931. pap. text 30.00 (*1-55589-235-3*) AGMA.

Baud, R. V., jt. auth. see Timoshenko, S.

Baudard, Gerard-Henry. Dictionnaire des Correspondents de Teilhard de Chardin. (FRE.). 200p. 1974. pap. 18.95 (*0-7859-8204-3*, 2900588030) Fr & Eur.

Baudeau, Nicolas. Idees d'un Citoyen sur les Besoins, les Droits et les Devoirs des Vrais Pauvres. (Economistes Francais du XVIIIe Siecle Ser.). 1990. reprint ed. 52.00 (*3-601-00143-8*) Periodicals Srv.

Baudel, J. Dictionary of Agricultural Equipment & Machinery: French, English, German, Spanish, Italian & Portuguese. (ENG, FRE, GER, ITA & SPA.). 1400p. 1989. 150.00 (*0-7859-7458-X*, 2856080340) Fr & Eur.

— Technical Dictionary of Agricultural Machinery & Equipment. (ENG, FRE, GER, ITA & POR.). 1400p. 1989. 165.00 (*2-85608-034-0*) IBD Ltd.

Baudelaire, Charles. Baudelaire: Les Fleurs du Mal. (Coll. Prestige). 1961. 49.95 (*0-685-11190-3*) Fr & Eur.

— Baudelaire: Les Fleurs du Mal. Chesters, Graham, ed. (Bristol French Texts Ser.). (FRE.). 248p. 1995. reprint ed. pap. 20.95 (*1-85399-344-1*, Pub. by Brist Class Pr) Focus Pub-R Pullins.

— Baudelaire in English. Clark, Carol & Sykes, Robert, eds. LC 98-165931. lv, 267p. (Orig.). 1997. pap. 14.95 (*0-14-044644-3*) Viking Penguin.

— Baudelaire Revisited: Forty-One Poems. Lappin, Kendall E., tr. LC 81-90014. (Illus.). 196p. 1981. pap. 7.95 (*0-9605710-0-0*) KEL Pubns.

— Baudelaire's Paris. 26p. 1990. pap. 9.95 (*0-948259-97-3*) Dufour.

— Charles Baudelaire, un Poete Maudit: Choix de Poemes Traduits en Vers Anglais avec une Biographie et des Notes. LC 77-10245. reprint ed. 34.00 (*0-404-16301-7*) AMS Pr.

— Complete Poems. Martin, Walter, tr. 220p. 1997. pap. 27.95 (*1-85754-049-2*, Pub. by Carcanet Pr) Paul & Co Pubs.

— The Complete Verse. Scarfe, Francis, ed. & tr. by. 396p. 1994. pap. 16.95 (*0-85646-152-0*, Pub. by Anvil Press) Dufour.

— Correspondance: Janvier 1832-Fevrier 1860, Vol. 1. deluxe ed. (Pleiade Ser.). (FRE.). 1973. 63.95 (*2-07-010782-5*) Schoenhof.

— Correspondance: Mars 1860-Mars 1866, Vol. 2. deluxe ed. (Pleiade Ser.). (FRE.). 1973. 63.95 (*2-07-010783-3*) Schoenhof.

— Correspondance Vol. 2: Mars 1860-Mars 1866. deluxe ed. Pichois, Claude, ed. (FRE.). 1160p. 1973. lib. bdg. 95.00 (*0-7859-3825-7*) Fr & Eur.

— Correspondance Vol. 3: Janvier 1832-Fevrier 1860. deluxe ed. Pichois, Raymond, ed. (FRE.). 1208p. 1973. lib. bdg. 95.00 (*0-7859-3824-9*) Fr & Eur.

— Curiosites Esthetiques, l'Art Romantique et Autres Oeuvres Esthetiques. Lemaitre, Henri, ed. (Coll. Prestige). 49.95 (*0-685-34099-6*) Fr & Eur.

— Curiosites Esthetiques, l'Art Romantique et Autres Oeuvres Esthetiques. Lemaitre, Henri, ed. (Class. Garnier Ser.). (FRE.). 1144p. 1963. pap. 55.00 (*0-8288-9060-9*, F57191) Fr & Eur.

— Echoes of Baudelaire: Selected Poems. Lappin, Kendall, tr. from FRE. LC 91-73680. 200p. 1992. 17.95 (*1-878580-28-0*) Asylum Arts.

— Les Ecrits Esthetiques. (FRE.). 1986. pap. 18.95 (*0-7859-3188-0*, 2264007508) Fr & Eur.

— Fatal Destinies: The Edgar Allen Poe Essays. Mele, Joan F., tr. from FRE. 1981. pap. 4.95 (*0-916696-17-0*) Cross Country.

— Les Fleurs du Mal. (Coll. GF). pap. 8.95 (*0-7859-0617-7*, F53870) Fr & Eur.

— Les Fleurs du Mal. Adam, ed. (Class. Garnier Ser.). pap. 29.95 (*0-685-34100-3*) Fr & Eur.

— Les Fleurs du Mal. Howard, Richard, tr. from FRE. LC 81-13283. (Illus.). 400p. 1983. pap. 18.95 (*0-87923-462-8*) Godine.

— Les Fleurs du Mal. 1999. pap. 9.95 (*2-266-08326-0*) Midwest European Pubns.

— Les Fleurs du Mal. (FRE.). (C). 1972. pap. 14.95 (*0-8442-1854-5*, VF1854-5) NTC Contemp Pub Co.

— Les Fleurs du Mal. (Poesie Ser.). (FRE.). 320p. 1972. pap. 11.95 (*2-07-031952-0*) Schoenhof.

— Les Fleurs du Mal. unabridged ed. (FRE.). pap. 5.95 (*2-87714-125-X*, Pub. by Bookking Intl) Distribks Inc.

— The Flowers of Evil. McGowan, James, tr. & notes by. (Oxford World's Classics Ser.). 458p. 1998. pap. 9.95 (*0-19-283545-9*) OUP.

— The Flowers of Evil. rev. ed. Mathews, Marthiel & Mathews, Jackson, eds. LC 89-9430. Vol. 688. 480p. 1989. pap. 16.95 (*0-8112-1117-7*, NDP684, Pub. by New Directions) Norton.

— The Flowers of Evil & Other Works - Les Fleurs Du Mal Et Oeuvres Choisies: A Dual-Language Book. Fowlie, Wallace, ed. (ENG & FRE.). 304p. 1992. reprint ed. pap. 8.95 (*0-486-27092-0*) Dover.

— The Flowers of Evil & Paris Spleen. Crosby, William H., tr. (ENG & FRE.). 489p. 1991. 30.00 (*0-918526-86-8*) BOA Edns.

— The Flowers of Evil & Paris Spleen. Crosby, William H., tr. (ENG & FRE.). 489p. 1998. pap. 17.00 (*0-918526-87-6*, Pub. by BOA Edns) Consort Bk Sales.

— Fusees-Mon Coeur Mis a Nu-la Belgique Deshabilee. (FRE.). 738p. 1986. pap. 10.95 (*0-7859-2231-8*, 207037727X) Fr & Eur.

Baudelaire, Charles. Invitation to the Voyage. Prince, Pamela & Handel, Jane, eds. Wilbur, Richard & Cosman, Carol, trs. LC 97-72023. (Illus.). 48p. 1997. 19.95 (*0-8212-2398-4*, Pub. by Bulfinch Pr) Little.

Baudelaire, Charles. Letters of Charles Baudelaire to His Mother, 1833-1866. Symons, Arthur, tr. LC 70-173184. 1972. reprint ed. 24.95 (*0-405-08242-8*, Pub. by Blom Pubns) Ayer.

— Letters of Charles Baudelaire to His Mother, 1833-1866: Eighteen Thirty-Three - Eighteen Sixty-Six. Symons,

An Asterisk (*) at the beginning of an entry indicates that the title is appearing for the first time.

Arthur, ed. LC 73-153490. (Studies in French Literature: No. 45). 1971. reprint ed. lib. bdg. 75.00 (0-8383-1241-1) M S G Haskell Hse.

— Little Poems in Prose. rev. ed. Starr, Martin P., ed. Crowley, Aleister, tr. from FRE. & illus. by. LC 93-34882. 144p. 1995. 29.95 (0-933429-08-8) Teitan Pr.

— The Mirror of Art, Critical Studies. Mayne, Jonathan, ed. LC 77-10247. (Illus.). reprint ed. 32.50 (0-404-16303-3) AMS Pr.

— My Heart Laid Bare & Other Prose Writings. Quennell, Peter, ed. LC 75-34313. (Studies in French Literature: No. 45). 1974. lib. bdg. 75.00 (0-8383-1870-3) M S G Haskell Hse.

— My Heart Laid Bare & Other Prose Writings. Quennell, Peter, ed. Cameron, Norman, tr. from FRE. 225p. 1986. reprint ed. pap. 13.95 (0-948166-07-X, Pub. by Soho Bk Co) Dufour.

— Oeuvres Completes. (FRE.). 1980. pap. 48.95 (0-7859-3034-5) Fr & Eur.

— Oeuvres Completes, 1. Le Dantec, ed. (Pleiade Ser.). 72.95 (2-07-010167-3) Schoenhof.

— Oeuvres Completes, 2. Le Dantec, ed. (Pleiade Ser.). 65.95 (2-07-010853-8) Schoenhof.

— Oeuvres Completes, Tome 1. deluxe ed. (Pleiade Ser.). (FRE.). 1604p. 1975. 85.95 (2-07-010829-5) Schoenhof.

— Oeuvres Completes, Vol. 1. Pichois, Claude, ed. (FRE.). 1664p. 1975. lib. bdg. 115.00 (0-7859-3830-3) Fr & Eur.

— The Painter of Modern Life & Other Essays. Mayne, Jonathan, ed. (Illus.). 298p. 1988. 13.95 (0-306-80279-1) Da Capo.

— The Painter of Modern Life & Other Essays. rev. ed. Mayne, Jonathan, ed. & tr. by. (Arts & Letters Ser.). (Illus.). 264p. (C). 1995. pap. 14.95 (0-7148-3365-7) Chronicle Bks.

— Paradis Artificiels. 1964. pap. 10.95 (0-8288-9063-3, LIV160) Fr & Eur.

— Paradis Artificiels. (Folio Ser.: No. 964). (FRE.). pap. 8.95 (2-07-036964-1) Schoenhof.

— Les Paradises Artificiels. (FRE.). 1977. pap. 10.95 (0-7859-1857-4, 2070369641) Fr & Eur.

— Paris Spleen. Varese, Louise, tr. from FRE. LC 48-5012. 1970. pap. 8.95 (0-8112-0007-8, NDP294, Pub. by New Directions) Norton.

— The Parisian Prowler: Le Spleen de Paris, Petits Poemes en Prose. 2nd ed. Kaplan, Edward K., tr. LC 96-32135. 1997. pap. text 14.95 (0-8203-1879-5) U of Ga Pr.

— Petits Poemes en Prose: Le Spleen de Paris. Lemaitre, Henri, ed. (Coll. Prestige). 49.95 (0-685-34103-8); pap. 29.95 (0-685-34102-X) Fr & Eur.

— Petits Poemes en Prose: Le Spleen de Paris. Ruff, Doris, ed. (Coll. GF). (FRE.). 1962. pap. 10.95 (0-8288-9064-1) Fr & Eur.

— Petits Poemes en Prose: Le Spleen de Paris. (Poesie Ser.). (FRE.). pap. 9.95 (2-07-031999-7) Schoenhof.

— Poemes d'Amour de Baudelaire: Avec des Documents Nouveaux. LC 77-10249. (Illus.). reprint ed. 20.50 (0-404-16305-X) AMS Pr.

— Poems: Baudelaire. LC 93-14363. (Pocket Poets Ser.). (ENG & FRE.). 256p. 1993. 12.50 (0-679-42910-7) Everymns Lib.

— The Poems in Prose & la Fanfarlo. 270p. 1989. pap. 16.95 (0-85646-170-9, Pub. by Anvil Press) Dufour.

— The Poems of Charles Baudelaire. Sturm, F. P., tr. LC 77-10250. 192p. reprint ed. 49.50 (0-404-16306-8) AMS Pr.

— Selected Critical Studies of Baudelaire. Parmee, D., ed. LC 76-29452. reprint ed. 45.00 (0-404-15300-3) AMS Pr.

— Selected Flowers of Evil. rev. ed. Mathews, Marthiel & Mathews, Jackson, eds. LC 58-9276. 1955. pap. 9.95 (0-8112-0006-X, NDP71, Pub. by New Directions) Norton.

— Selected Letters of Charles Baudelaire: The Conquest of Solitude. Lloyd, Rosemary, ed. & tr. by. from FRE. LC 85-16461. xxxii, 296p. 1986. 29.95 (0-226-03928-5) U Ch Pr.

— Selected Poems. Clark, Carol, tr. 1995. pap. 12.95 (0-14-044624-9) Viking Penguin.

— Selected Poems from "Flowers of Evil" unabridged ed. Fowlie, Wallace, tr. (Thrift Editions Ser.). 64p. 1995. pap. text 1.00 (0-486-28450-6) Dover.

— Selected Poems from Les Fleurs du Mal: A Bilingual Edition. LC 97-38283. (ENG & FRE.). 248p. 1998. 24.95 (0-226-03925-0) U Ch Pr.

— Selected Poems from Les Fleurs du Mal: A Bilingual Edition. Shapiro, Norman R., tr. (ENG & FRE., Illus.). 209p. 2000. pap. 16.00 (0-226-03926-9) U Ch Pr.

— Le Spleen de Paris. (FRE.). 1973. pap. 10.95 (0-8288-9061-7, F57314) Fr & Eur.

— Le Spleen de Paris - Les Paradis Artificiels. unabridged ed. (FRE.). pap. 7.95 (2-87714-226-4, Pub. by Bookking Intl) Distribks Inc.

— Twenty Prose Poems. rev. ed. Hamburger, Michael, tr. from FRE. & intro. by. 64p. 1988. reprint ed. pap. 6.95 (0-87286-216-X) City Lights.

— Le Voyage. (C). 1990. pap. 50.00 (0-906887-47-X, Pub. by Greville Pr) St Mut.

Baudelaire, Charles & Mallarme, Stephane. Poison & Vision: Poems & Prose of Baudelaire, Mallarme & Rimbaud. 350p. 1996. pap. 24.95 (3-7052-0640-0, Pub. by Poetry Salzburg) Intl Spec Bk.

Baudelaire, Charles & Pichois, Claude. Oeuvres Completes, Vol. 2. (FRE.). 1712p. 1976. lib. bdg. 115.00 (0-7859-3831-1) Fr & Eur.

Baudelaire, Charles, tr. see Poe, Edgar Allan.

Baudenbacher, Carl. A Brief Guide to European State Aid Law. large type ed. LC 98-114556. (European Business Law & Practice Ser.: No. 13). 86p. 1997. 46.00 (90-411-0939-0) Kluwer Academic.

Baudendistel, Robert F. Horticulture: A Basic Awareness. 2nd ed. 368p. (C). 1982. pap. text 98.00 (0-8359-2895-0) P-H.

Bauder, Thomas. Write English, Bk. 3. (Illus.). 72p. (Orig.). (C). 1994. pap. text 7.95 (0-8325-0513-7, Natl Textbk Co) NTC Contemp Pub Co.

Baudet, Henri. Paradise on Earth: Some Thoughts on European Images of Non-European Man. Wentholt, Elizabeth, tr. LC 76-21632. 87p. 1977. reprint ed. lib. bdg. 55.00 (0-8371-8973-X, BAPOE, Greenwood Pr) Greenwood.

Baudez, Claude-Francois. Maya Sculpture of Copan: The Iconography. LC 93-43681. (Illus.). 320p. 1994. 65.00 (0-8061-2594-2) U of Okla Pr.

Baudez, Claude-Francois & Picasso, Sydney. Lost Cities of the Maya. (Discoveries Ser.). (Illus.). 176p. 1992. pap. 12.95 (0-8109-2841-8, Pub. by Abrams) Time Warner.

Baudhuin, John. What Is Chemical Dependency? 20p. 1998. pap., wbk. ed. 4.25 (0-89486-564-1, 5568B) Hazelden.

Baudin, Antoine. Le Realisme Socialiste Sovietique de la Periode Jdanovienne (1947-1953) Vol. 1: Les Arts Plastiques et Leurs Institutions. (FRE., Illus.). 434p. 1997. 53.95 (3-906758-08-7, Pub. by P Lang) P Lang Pubng.

***Baudin, Antoine & Heller, Leonid.** Usages a l'Interieur, Image a Exporter. xvii, 394p. 1998. 50.95 (3-906758-09-5, Pub. by P Lang) P Lang Pubng.

Baudin, Emile. La Philosophie de Pascal, 3 vols. Incl. Pascal et Descartes. 358p. 1976. pap. 45.00 (0-7859-5233-0, F40735); Pascal et la Casuistique. 246p. 1947. pap. 45.00 (0-7859-5235-7, F40737); Vol. 2. Pascal, les Libertins et les Jansenites. 412p. 1947. pap. 45.00 (0-7859-5234-9, F40736); (Coll. Etre et Penser). (FRE.). pap. write for info. (0-318-52002-8) Fr & Eur.

Baudin, Jeff & Bradley, John. Mac Anatomy: A Graphical Guide. 1995. pap. 32.95 incl. cd-rom (1-55828-438-9, MIS Pr) IDG Bks.

Baudin, Maurice, Jr., ed. Contemporary Short Stories & Representive Selections, Vol. 2. 1954. pap. 4.35 (0-672-60017-X, AHS13, Bobbs) Macmillan.

Baudino, Gael. Dragon Death. (Dragonsword Ser.: No. 3). 384p. (Orig.). 1992. mass mkt. 4.99 (0-451-45147-3, ROC) NAL.

— The Duel of Dragons. (Dragonsword Ser.: No. 2). 384p. (Orig.). 1991. mass mkt. 4.99 (0-451-45097-3, ROC) NAL.

— Shroud of Shadow. 352p. 1993. mass mkt. 4.99 (0-451-45294-1, ROC) NAL.

Baudler, Georg. God & Violence. LC 91-68344. (Illus.). 368p. 1992. pap. 19.95 (0-87243-193-2) Templegate.

Baudo, R., et al, eds. Top of the World Environmental Research: Mount Everest-Himalayan Ecosystem. (Illus.). 303p. 1998. 92.00 (90-5782-004-8, Pub. by Backhuys Pubs) Balogh.

Baudoin, A. B., et al, eds. Laboratory Exercises in Plant Pathology: An Instructional Kit. 1993. 139.00 (0-89054-086-1) Am Phytopathol Soc.

Baudoin, A. B. A. M. & American Phytopathological Society Staff. Laboratory Exercises in Plant Pathology: An Instructional Kit - (Student's Exercises) (C). 1990. pap., student ed. 150.00 (81-85046-86-7, Pub. by Scientific Pubs) St Mut.

Baudoin, Anne-Marie. Vocabulary of the Automobile Vol. 1: The MotorEnglish Vocabulary of the Automobile: The Motor. (ENG & FRE.). 106p. 1992. pap. 24.95 (0-8288-6337-7, M-6025) Fr & Eur.

— Vocabulary of the Automobile Vol. 2: Maintenance & Repairs. (ENG & FRE.). 90p. 1990. pap. 24.95 (0-8288-9378-0) Fr & Eur.

— Vocabulary of the Automobile Vol. 4: The Chassis & Body. (ENG & FRE.). 101p. 1980. pap. 24.95 (0-8288-9377-2) Fr & Eur.

Baudoin, Anne-Marie, et al. Vocabulary of the Automobile Vol. 3: The Transmission. (ENG & FRE.). 87p. 1992. pap. 24.95 (0-8288-0763-9, M9036) Fr & Eur.

Baudoin, E. Margaret, et al. Reader's Choice. 3rd ed. 352p. 1994. pap. text 16.95 (0-472-08265-5, 08265) U of Mich Pr.

— Reader's Choice Bk. 1: International Editions. 184p. 1993. pap. text 10.95 (0-472-08185-3, 08185) U of Mich Pr.

— Reader's Choice Bk. 2: International Editions. 224p. 1993. pap. text 10.95 (0-472-08186-1, 08186) U of Mich Pr.

Baudoin, Jean. Recueil d'Emblemes Divers, 2 vols. 1296p. 1977. reprint ed. 240.00 (3-487-06299-2) G Olms Pubs.

Baudoin, Patricia, tr. see Laidi, Zaki.

Baudot, Alain. Musiciens Romains de l'Antiquite. LC 74-183208. (FRE., Illus.). 167p. reprint ed. pap. 51.80 (0-7837-6950-4, 204677900003) Bks Demand.

Baudot, Alain, et al. Dictionnaire Officiel des Mots de Tete. (FRE.). 1984. 19.95 (0-7859-8596-4, 0919762719) Fr & Eur.

Baudot, Barbara S. & Moomaw, William. People & Their Planet: Searching for Balance. LC 98-23533. 336p. 1999. text 75.00 (0-312-21715-3) St Martin.

Baudot, Francois. Alaia. (Fashion Memoir Ser.). (Illus.). 1996. 24.00 (0-500-01719-0) Thames Hudson.

— Alaia. 1997. 18.95 (0-7893-0089-3, Pub. by Universe) St Martin.

— Chanel. (Illus.). 80p. 1996. text 18.95 (0-7893-0064-8) St Martin.

— Chanel. (Fashion Memoir Ser.). (Illus.). 400p. 1996. 24.00 (0-500-01720-4) Thames Hudson.

***Baudot, Francois.** Chanel Jewelry. (Illus.). 80p. 2000. text 18.95 (0-7893-0468-6) Universe.

Baudot, Francois. Christian Lacroix. (Illus.). 80p. 1997. text 18.95 (0-7893-0121-0) St Martin.

— Fashion: 20th Century. 400p. 1999. pap. 29.95 (0-7893-0376-0) Universe.

***Baudot, Francois.** Ferragamo. (Fashion Ser.). (Illus.). 80p. 2000. 25.00 (0-7893-0469-4) Universe.

Baudot, Francois. Poiret LC 98-160735. (Fashion Memoir Ser.). 79 p. 1997. write for info. (0-500-01814-6) Thames Hudson.

— Schiaparelli. LC 97-61196. (Illus.). 80p. 1997. text 18.95 (0-7893-0116-4) St Martin.

— Thiery Mugler. (Illus.). 80p. 1998. 18.95 (0-7893-0205-5, Pub. by Universe) St Martin.

— Yohji Yamamoto. LC 98-160733. (Fashion Memoir Ser.). 79 p. 1997. write for info. (0-500-01815-4) Thames Hudson.

Baudot, Francois & Rival, Pierre. Savoir-Faire: Great Traditions in French Elegance. (Illus.). 240p. 1995. 65.00 (2-08-013552-X, Pub. by Flammarion) Abbeville Pr.

Baudot, Francois, jt. auth. see Universe Publishing Incorporated Staff.

Baudot, Georges. Utopia & History in Mexico: The First Chronicles of Mexican Civilization, 1520-1569. Ortiz De Montellano, Bernard R. & Ortiz De Montellano, Thelma, trs. 730p. 1995. 49.95 (0-87081-401-X) Univ Pr Colo.

— La Vida Cotidiana en la America Espanola en Tiempos de Felipe II (Daily Life in Spanish America During the Reign of Felipe II) (SPA.). 344p. 1983. pap. 8.99 (968-16-1463-1, Pub. by Fondo) Continental Bk.

Baudot, Jacques & Bergquist, Gilbert T., eds. Ethical & Spiritual Dimensions of Social Progress: World Summit for Social Development. 115p. (C). 1998. pap. text 35.00 (0-7881-7401-0) DIANE Pub.

Baudot, Marcel, et al, eds. The Historical Encyclopedia of World War II. (Illus.). 550p. 1996. 14.98 (1-56731-094-X, MJF Bks) Fine Comms.

Baudouin, Charles. Contemporary Studies. LC 75-76892. (Essay Index Reprint Ser.). 1977. 20.95 (0-8369-0002-2) Ayer.

— Power Within Us. LC 68-16905. (Essay Index Reprint Ser.). 1977. 18.95 (0-8369-0176-2) Ayer.

— Suggestion & Autosuggestion. 349p. 1993. pap. 27.00 (0-89540-243-2, SB-243) Sun Pub.

Baudouin-Croix, Marie. Leonie Martin: A Difficult Life. Mooney, Mary F., tr. 120p. 1993. pap. text 29.95 (1-85390-281-0, Pub. by Veritas Pubns) St Mut.

***Baudouin-Croix, Marie.** Saint Anthony of Padua: Proclaimer of the Good News. Keefe, Maryellen, tr. from FRE. (Along the Paths of the Gospel Ser.). (Illus.). 72p. (gr. 2-5). 1999. 9.95 (0-8198-7016-1) Pauline Bks.

— Saint Therese of Lisieux: And the "Little Way" of Love. Keefe, Maryellen, tr. from FRE. (Along the Paths of the Gospel Ser.). (Illus.). 72p. (gr. 2-5). 1999. 9.95 (0-8198-7021-8) Pauline Bks.

Baudrillar. Revenge of the Crystal: Selected Writings by Jean Baudrillard on the Modern Object & Its Destiny, 1968-1983. 198p. (C). 49.95 (0-7453-0298-X, Pub. by Pluto GBR); pap. 17.95 (0-7453-0305-6) Pluto GBR.

Baudrillard, Jean. America. Turner, Chris, tr. 200p. (C). (gr. 13). 1989. pap. 19.00 (0-86091-978-1, Pub. by Verso) Norton.

— Andy Warhol Paintings, 1960-1986. 184p. 1996. pap. 50.00 (3-7757-0570-8, Pub. by Gerd Hatje) Dist Art Pubs.

— The Consumer Society: Myths & Structures. 224p. 1997. 75.00 (0-7619-5691-3); pap. 26.95 (0-7619-5692-1) Sage.

— Cool Memories II: 1987-1990. Turner, Chris, tr. LC 95-25070. (Post-Contemporary Interventions Ser.) 104p. 1996. pap. text 15.95 (0-8223-1793-1) Duke.

— Cool Memories II: 1987-1990. Turner, Chris, tr. LC 95-25070. (Post-Contemporary Interventions Ser.) 104p. (C). 1996. text 39.95 (0-8223-1785-0) Duke.

— De La Seduction. (Folio Essais Ser.: No. 81). (FRE.). pap. 9.95 (2-07-032465-6) Schoenhof.

— The Ecstasy of Communication. 107p. Date not set. 7.00 (0-936756-36-5) Autonomedia.

— Fatal Strategies. Fleming, Jim, ed. Beitchman, Philip, tr. from FRE. 192p. (C). 1990. 24.95 (0-936756-51-9); pap. 10.00 (0-936756-50-0) Autonomedia.

— For a Critique of the Political Economy of the Sign. Levin, Charles, tr. from FRE. 1981. pap. 16.00 (0-914386-24-7); lib. bdg. 26.00 (0-914386-23-9) Telos Pr.

— Forget Foucault. 137p. Date not set. 7.00 (0-936756-10-1) Autonomedia.

— Fragments: Cool Memories III, 1991-95. 1997. pap. 19.00 (1-85984-123-6, Pub. by Verso) Norton.

— Fragments: Cool Memories III, 1991-95. (C). 1997. 65.00 (1-85984-891-5, Pub. by Verso) Norton.

— The Gulf War Did Not Take Place. Patton, Paul, tr. & intro. by. LC 95-19574. 96p. 1995. 25.00 (0-253-32946-9); pap. 11.95 (0-253-21003-8) Ind U Pr.

— The Illusion of the End. Turner, Chris, tr. from FRE. 125p. 1994. 35.00 (0-8047-2500-4); pap. 12.95 (0-8047-2501-2) Stanford U Pr.

— In the Shadow of the Silent Majorities. 123p. Date not set. 7.00 (0-936756-00-4) Autonomedia.

***Baudrillard, Jean.** Jean Baudrillard: Photographies, 1985-1998. (Illus.). 2000. pap. 39.95 (3-89322-982-1) Dr Cantz sche Druckerei GmbH.

Baudrillard, Jean. Jean Baudrillard: Selected Writings. Poster, Mark, ed. Mourrain, Jacques, tr. LC 87-63008. 238p. 1988. 37.50 (0-8047-1478-9); pap. 13.95 (0-8047-1480-0) Stanford U Pr.

— L'Autre. LC 99-495143. (Contemporary Artists Ser.). 1999. pap. 29.95 (0-7148-3842-X) Phaidon Press.

— The Mirror of Production. Poster, Mark, tr. LC 74-82994. (C). 1975. pap. 14.00 (0-914386-06-9) Telos Pr.

— Paroxysm. Turner, Chris, tr. LC 98-39610. 120p. 1998. 60.00 (1-85984-844-3, Pub. by Verso); pap. 18.00 (1-85984-241-0, Pub. by Verso) Norton.

— The Perfect Crime. Turner, Chris, tr. LC 96-15755. (FRE.). 224p. 1996. 45.00 (1-85984-919-9, Pub. by Verso) Norton.

— Pour une Critique de l'Economie Politique du Signe. (Tel Ser.). (FRE.). 268p. 1972. pap. 14.95 (2-07-029614-8) Schoenhof.

***Baudrillard, Jean.** Revenge of the Crystal: Selected Writings on Modern Object & Its Destiny, 1968-1983. (Classics Ser.). 198p. 1999. pap. 17.95 (0-7453-1443-0) Pluto GBR.

Baudrillard, Jean. Seduction. Kroker, Arthur & Kroker, Marilouise, eds. Singer, Brian, tr. from FRE. (Culture Texts Ser.). 187p. 1991. pap. 13.95 (0-312-05294-4) St Martin.

— Simulacra & Simulation. Glaser, Sheila, tr. (Body in Theory: Histories of Cultural Materialism Ser.). 176p. 1994. pap. 15.95 (0-472-06521-1, 06521) U of Mich Pr.

— Simulacra & Simulation. Glaser, Sheila, tr. (Body in Theory: Histories of Cultural Materialism Ser.). 176p. 1995. text 39.50 (0-472-09521-8, 09521) U of Mich Pr.

— Simulations. 159p. Date not set. 7.00 (0-936756-02-0) Autonomedia.

— Societe de Consommation, Ses Mythes, Ses Structures. (Folio Essais Ser.: No. 35). (FRE.). 318p. 1970. pap. 11.95 (2-07-032349-8) Schoenhof.

— Les Strategies Fatales. (FRE.). 1986. pap. 16.95 (0-7859-3129-5) Fr & Eur.

— Symbolic Exchange & Death. Grant, Ian, tr. (Theory, Culture & Society Ser.: Vol. 25). 288p. (C). 1993. text 59.95 (0-8039-8398-0); pap. 22.95 (0-8039-8399-9) Sage.

— The System of Objects. 200p. (C). 1996. pap. 20.00 (1-85984-068-X, Pub. by Verso) Norton.

— The System of Objects. 208p. (C). (gr. 13 up). 1996. 65.00 (1-85984-943-1, Pub. by Verso) Norton.

— The Transparency of Evil: Essays in Extreme Phenomena. Baddeley, J. St. John, tr. 200p. (C). (gr. 13). 1993. 60.00 (0-86091-387-2, A9737, Pub. by Verso) Norton.

— The Transparency of Evil: Essays on Extreme Phenomena. Baddeley, J. St. John, tr. 200p. (C). (gr. 13). 1993. pap. 20.00 (0-86091-588-3, A9741, Pub. by Verso) Norton.

***Baudrillard, Jean.** The Vital Illusion. 2001. 17.95 (0-231-12100-8) Col U Pr.

Baudrillard, Jean, jt. auth. see Calle, Sophie.

Baudrillart, Henri J. Publicistes Modernes. Mayer, J. P., ed. LC 78-67330. (European Political Thought Ser.). 1979. reprint ed. lib. bdg. 42.95 (0-405-11676-4) Ayer.

Baudry, M., et al. Advances in Synaptic Plasticity. LC 98-51887. 312p. 1999. 65.00 (0-262-02460-8) MIT Pr.

Baudry, Leon. The Quarrel over Future Contingents (Louvain, 1465-1475) 468p. (C). 1989. lib. bdg. 245.00 (0-7923-0454-3, Pub. by Kluwer Academic) Kluwer Academic.

Baudry, Michel, et al, eds. Synaptic Plasticity: Molecular, Cellular, & Functional Aspects. LC 93-19699. (Illus.). 1993. 50.00 (0-262-02359-8, Bradford Bks) MIT Pr.

Baudry, Michel & Davis, Joel L., eds. Long-Term Potentiation: A Debate of Current Issues. (Bradford Series in Complex Adaptive Systems). 464p. 1991. 70.00 (0-262-02330-X, Bradford Bks) MIT Pr.

— Long Term Potentiation: A Debate of Current Issues, Vol. 2. (Illus.). 440p. 1994. 85.00 (0-262-02370-9, Bradford Bks) MIT Pr.

— Long-Term Potentiation: A Debate of Current Issues, Vol. 3. LC 91-11092. Vol. 3. (Illus.). 448p. 1996. 75.00 (0-262-02409-8, Bradford Bks) MIT Pr.

Bauduin, C., jt. auth. see De Munter, M.

Baudy, Gerhard J. Die Brande Roms: Ein Apokalyptisches Motiv in der Antiken Historiographie. (Spudasmata Ser.: Bd. 50). (GER.). 75p. 1991. 25.00 (3-487-09480-0) G Olms Pubs.

Baudy, Robert & Thompson, Sandra. Baudy, the Animal Man: The Biography of Robert Baudy. LC 95-41123. (Illus.). 560p. 1996. 39.95 (1-56825-033-9); pap. 29.95 (1-56825-032-0) Rainbow Books.

Baue, A. E., et al, eds. Sepsis & Organ Dysfunction: A Tribute to Roger Bone. 200p. 1999. pap. 95.00 (88-470-0052-1, Pub. by Spr-Verlag) Spr-Verlag.

— Sepsis & Organ Dysfunction: Epidemiology & Scoring Systems, Pathophysiology & Therapy. LC 98-15825. (Illus.). 198p. 1998. 89.00 (88-470-0297-4) Spr-Verlag.

***Baue, A. E., et al, eds.** Sepsis & Organ Dysfunction: The Challenge Continues. 2000. pap. text (88-470-0096-3) Spr-Verlag.

Baue, Arthur. Glenn's Thoracic & Cardiovascular Surgery, 2 vols., Set, Vols. 1 & 2. 6th ed. (Illus.). 3276p. (C). 1996. pap. text 350.00 (0-8385-3134-2, A3134-2, Apple Lange Med) McGraw.

***Baue, Arthur, et al, eds.** Multiple Organ Failure: Pathophysiology, Prevention & Therapy. LC 99-39600. (Illus.). 600p. 2000. 135.00 (0-387-98733-9) Spr-Verlag.

Baueer, Hans-Gunther, tr. see Gerthold, Peter.

Bauek, Helen, jt. auth. see Rayson, Ann.

Bauemkind, R. H., et al. Standardized Tests: A Practical Handbook. LC 91-65016. 1991. pap. text 28.50 (0-317-05384-1) EDITS Pubs.

Bauer. Alison's Wings. (J). 1997. lib. bdg. 14.49 (0-7868-2349-6, Pub. by Hyperion) Little.

— Bibeltheologisches Woerterbuch, 2 vols. (GER.). 660p. 1994. 250.00 (0-7859-7248-X, 3222122563) Fr & Eur.

— Charlotte Gil Yellow Wallpaper. LC 97-74959. 350p. 1998. pap. text 11.95 (0-312-13292-1) St Martin.

— Readings & Responses in American Government. 2000. 26.00 (0-534-52804-X) Wadsworth Pub.

Bauer. Thanksgiving Stories & Poems. LC 93-18631. 96p. 1997. pap. write for info. (0-06-446173-4, HarpTrophy) HarpC Child Bks.

Bauer, jt. auth. see Kaye.

Bauer, Billy. Sideman: The Autobiography of Billy Bauer. Luba, Thea, ed. LC 97-93133. (Illus.). 215p. 1997. reprint ed. pap. 19.95 (0-9657237-0-4) W H Bauer.

Bauer, A., et al. Shop Floor Control Systems: From Design to Implementation. (Illus.). 364p. 1991. 67.95 (0-442-31329-2) Chapman & Hall.

B

Bauer, Aaron M. & Henle, Klaus. Familia Gekkonidae (Reptilia, Sauria) Australia & Oceania, Pt. I. LC 93-46710. (Das Tierreich - The Animal Kingdom Ser.: Pt. 109). xiii, 306p. (C). 1994. lib. bdg. 460.00 (*3-11-014114-0*) De Gruyter.

Bauer, Adolf. Die Entstehung Des Herodoteischen Geschichtswerkes. (GER.). 173p. 1976. reprint ed. 40.00 (*3-487-06143-0*) G Olms Pubs.

Bauer, Agi L. Black Becomes a Rainbow. 1991. 18.95 (*0-87306-572-7*); pap. 16.95 (*0-87306-573-5*) Feldheim.

Bauer, Alan D. The End: A Reader's Guide to Revelation. LC 97-91783. (Illus.). 240p. (Orig.). 1997. pap. write for info. (*0-9658798-0-1*) Square Halo Bks.

Bauer, Angela M. Gender in the Book of Jeremiah: A Feminist-Literary Reading. Gossai, Hemchand, ed. LC 98-17378. (Studies in Biblical Literature: Vol. 5). XII, 203p. 1998. 47.95 (*0-8204-3899-5*) P Lang Pubng.

Bauer, Angela M., jt. auth. see McCarney, Stephen B.

Bauer, Anna E. Rosenzweigs Sprachdenken Im "Stern der Erlosung" und in Seiner Korrespondenz Mit Martin Buber Zur Verdeutschung der Schrift. (Europaische Hochschulschriften Ser.: Reihe 23, Bd. 466). (GER.). 471p. 1992. 67.80 (*3-631-45219-5*) P Lang Pubng.

Bauer, Anne M. Learners with Emotional & Behavioral Disorders: An Introduction. LC 98-16495. 305p. 1998. pap. text 51.00 (*0-13-241373-6*) P-H.

Bauer, Anne M., et al, eds. Children Who Challenge the System. LC 92-15714. (Social & Policy Issues in Education Ser.). 264p. (C). 1993. pap. 24.95 (*0-89391-772-9*); text 73.25 (*0-89391-718-4*) Ablx Pub.

Bauer, Anne M. & Shea, Thomas M. Inclusion 101: How to Teach All Learners. LC 98-30328. 352p. 1999. 35.00 (*1-55766-372-6*) P H Brookes.

Bauer, Anne M., jt. auth. see Johnson, Lawrence J.

Bauer, Anne M., jt. auth. see Shea, Thomas M.

Bauer, Armin, et al. A Generation at Risk: The Situation of Children in the Central Asian Republics. LC 98-224240. 250p. 1998. pap. 10.00 (*971-561-097-8*, Pub. by Asian Devel Bank) Paul & Co Pubs.

— Women & Gender Relations: The Kyrgyz Republic in Transition. 138p. 1998. pap. 10.00 (*971-561-099-4*, Pub. by Asian Devel Bank) Paul & Co Pubs.

— Women & Gender Relations in Kazakstan: The Social Cost. LC 99-184420. 134p. 1998. pap. 10.00 (*971-561-098-6*, Pub. by Asian Devel Bank) Paul & Co Pubs.

Bauer, Arnold J. Chilean Rural Society from the Spanish Conquest to 1930. LC 75-2724. (Cambridge Latin American Studies: No. 21). 287p. reprint ed. pap. 81.80 (*0-608-12273-4*, 2024421) Bks Demand.

Bauer, Arthur O. Being in Mission: A Resource for the Local Church & Community. LC 86-29445. 114p. 1987. reprint ed. pap. 35.40 (*0-608-00243-7*, 206074500006) Bks Demand.

Bauer, Arthur R. Legal & Ethical Aspects of Fetal Tissue Transplantation. LC 93-42908. (Medical Intelligence Unit Ser.). 128p. 1993. 99.00 (*1-57059-021-4*) Landes Bioscience.

Bauer, B. L., et al, eds. Cerebellar Infarct: Minimal Invasive Endoscopy Neurosurgery - Midline Tumors. 1994. 79.00 (*0-387-57668-1*) Spr-Verlag.

Bauer, B. L. & Hellwig, D., eds. Minimally Invasive Neurosurgery I. (Acta Neurochirugica - Supplementum Ser.: Vol. 54). 200p. 1992. 108.00 (*0-387-82321-2*) Spr-Verlag.

— Minimally Invasive Neurosurgery II. (Acta Neurochirugica - Supplementum Ser.: Vol. 61). 115p. 1995. 88.00 (*0-387-82593-2*) Spr-Verlag.

Bauer, B. L. & Kuhn, T. J. Severe Head Injuries: Pathology, Diagnosis & Treatment. LC 97-16897. 260p. 1997. text. write for info. (*3-540-62701-4*) Spr-Verlag.

Bauer, B. L., jt. ed. see Hellwig, D.

Bauer, Barbara B. & Hill, Signe S. Essentials of Mental Health Care: Planning & Interventions. (Illus.). 203p. 1986. pap. text 25.00 (*0-7216-1367-5*, W B Saunders Co) Harcrt Hlth Sci Grp.

— Mental Health Nursing: An Introductory Text. 2nd ed. LC 99-29020. (Illus.). 430p. (C). 2000. pap. text. write for info. (*0-7216-7753-3*, W B Saunders Co) Harcrt Hlth Sci Grp.

Bauer, Bernhard. Ullstein Synonymen-Lexikon. (GER.). 19.95 (*0-7859-8424-0*, 3548346332) Fr & Eur.

Bauer, Beth C. Beth Bauer's Enjoy China More. abr. ed. (Beth Bauer's Ser.). (Illus.). 232p. (C). 1988. reprint ed. pap. 14.95 (*0-937133-01-9*) Cain Lockhart.

— Enjoy China More, Excerpts. 50p. 1985. pap., student ed. 4.95 (*0-937133-00-0*) Cain Lockhart.

Bauer, Bill. Last Lambs: Poems from the Vietnam War. LC 97-7510. 72p. (Orig.). 1997. pap. 11.95 (*1-886157-12-X*) BkMk.

— Promises in the Dust. LC 94-43704. 64p. (Orig.). 1995. pap. 10.00 (*1-886157-01-4*) BkMk.

Bauer, Bob, jt. ed. see Sher, Chuck.

Bauer, Brent A., jt. auth. see Lillie, John H.

Bauer, Brian, ed. see Maranjian, Selena.

Bauer, Brian S. The Development of the Inca State. (Illus.). 203p. (Orig.). 1996. pap. 12.95 (*0-292-70848-3*) U of Tex Pr.

— The Sacred Landscape of the Inca: The Cusco Ceque System. LC 97-49914. (Illus.). 272p. 1998. 50.00 (*0-292-70865-3*) U of Tex Pr.

Bauer, Brian S. & Dearborn, David S. Astronomy & Empire in the Ancient Andes: The Cultural Origins of Inca Sky Watching. LC 95-3565. (Illus.). 208p. 1995. 37.50 (*0-292-70829-7*) U of Tex Pr.

***Bauer, Brigitte L.** Archaic Syntax in Indo-European: The Spread of Transitivity in Latin & French. LC 00-24833. (Trends in Linguistics Ser.). 2000. write for info. (*3-11-016723-9*) De Gruyter.

Bauer, Brigitte L. The Emergence & Development of SVO Patterning in Latin & French: Diachronic & Psycholinguistic Perspectives. (Illus.). 272p. 1995. text 60.00 (*0-19-509103-5*) OUP.

Bauer, Bruce. Sextant Handbook: Adjustment, Repair, Use & History. 2nd ed. 1995. pap. 15.95 (*0-07-005219-0*) Intl Marine.

Bauer, Bruno. Christ & the Caesars: The Origin of Christianity from Romanized Greek Culture. LC 98-73628. Orig. Title: Christus und die Caesaren. 370p. 1999. 50.00 (*0-9669977-0-0*) Charles Hse.

— Christus und die Caesaren. iv, 387p. 1968. reprint ed. 95.00 incl. 3.5 hd (*0-318-70704-7*) G Olms Pubs.

— The Trumpet of the Last Judgement Against the Athiest & Antichrist: An Ultimatum. Stepelevich, Lawrence, tr. from GER. LC 88-1785. (Studies in German Thought & History: Vol. 5). 224p. 1989. lib. bdg. 89.95 (*0-88946-356-5*) E Mellen.

Bauer, C., et al, eds. Biophysics & Physiology of Carbon Dioxide. (Proceedings in Life Sciences Ser.). (Illus.). 480p. 1980. 71.95 (*0-387-09892-5*) Spr-Verlag.

— Erythropoietin: Molecular Physiology & Clinical Applications. LC 93-30025. (Illus.). 488p. 1993. text 145.00 (*0-8247-9139-8*) Dekker.

Bauer, C. A. White Horses. 384p. 1999. mass mkt. 5.99 (*0-7860-0663-3*) Kensgtn Pub Corp.

Bauer, C. F. Latin Perfect Endings -ere & -erunt. (LD Ser.: Vol. 13). 1933. pap. 25.00 (*0-527-00759-5*) Periodicals Srv.

Bauer, Cameron. Algebra for Athletes. LC 98-35903. 264p. 2000. 28.00 (*1-56072-528-1*) Nova Sci Pubs.

Bauer, Camille. Graded French Reader: Deuxieme Etape. 4th ed. (ENG & FRE.). 323p. (C). 1992. pap. text 29.96 (*0-669-20463-3*) HM Trade Div.

— Graded French Reader: Premiere Etape. 4th ed. LC 86-81281. 322p. (C). 1987. pap. text 15.00 (*0-685-19358-6*) HM Trade Div.

— Graded French Reader: Premiere Etape. 5th ed. (ENG & FRE.). 307p. (C). 1992. pap. text 29.96 (*0-669-20462-5*) HM Trade Div.

Bauer, Camille, jt. auth. see Campbell, Hugh D.

Bauer, Carl J. Against the Current: Privatization, Water Markets & the State in Chile. LC 98-28298. (Natural Resources Management & Policy Ser.). 1998. 97.50 (*0-7923-8227-7*) Kluwer Academic.

***Bauer, Carlos.** The All-Time Japanese Baseball Register. 320p. 2000. spiral bd. 23.95 (*1-893392-04-X*) Baseball Pr Bks.

Bauer, Carlos, jt. auth. see Hoie, Bob.

Bauer, Carlos, tr. see Garcia Lorca, Federico.

***Bauer, Caroline F.** Leading Kids to Books Through Crafts. LC 99-41387. (Mighty Easy Motivator Ser.). 160p. (J). 1999. 30.00 (*0-8389-0769-5*) ALA.

Bauer, Caroline F. Leading Kids to Books Through Puppets. LC 97-1357. (Mighty Easy Motivators Ser.). (Illus.). 144p. 1997. 22.00 (*0-8389-0706-7*) ALA.

— Read for the Fun of It: Active Programming with Books for Children. (Illus.). 372p. 1992. 45.00 (*0-8242-0824-2*) Wilson.

Bauer, Caroline Feller. Caroline Feller Bauer's New Handbook for Storytellers. (Illus.). 550p. 1995. reprint ed. pap. text 30.00 (*0-8389-0664-8*) ALA.

— Celebrations: Read-Aloud Holiday & Theme Book Programs. LC 85-714. (Illus.). 301p. 1985. 45.00 (*0-8242-0708-4*) Wilson.

— Halloween: Stories & Poems. LC 88-2675. (Trophy Nonfiction Bk.). (Illus.). 96p. (J). (gr. 2-5). 1992. pap. 4.95 (*0-06-446111-4*, HarpTrophy) HarpC Child Bks.

— Handbook for Storytellers. LC 76-56385. (Illus.). 399p. reprint ed. pap. 123.70 (*0-7837-6153-8*, 204587500009) Bks Demand.

— Leading Kids to Books Through MAGIC. LC 95-53049. (Mighty Easy Motivators Ser.). (Illus.). 125p. 1996. 29.00 (*0-8389-0684-2*, 0684-2-2045) ALA.

— My Mom Travels a Lot. (Illus.). (J). (gr. k-3). 1983. flmstrp 32.95 (*0-941078-24-8*) Live Oak Media.

— The Poetry Break: An Annotated Anthology with Ideas for Introducing Children to Poetry. LC 93-42069. 372p. 1994. 45.00 (*0-8242-0852-8*) Wilson.

— Presenting Reader's Theater: Plays & Poems to Read Aloud. (Illus.). 254p. 1987. 45.00 (*0-8242-0748-3*) Wilson.

— Thanksgiving: Stories & Poems. LC 93-18631. (Illus.). 96p. (J). (gr. 2-5). 1994. 14.00 (*0-06-023326-5*) HarpC Child Bks.

— This Way to Books. LC 82-19985. 378p. 1983. 45.00 (*0-8242-0678-9*) Wilson.

Bauer, Caroline Feller, ed. Halloween: Stories & Poems. LC 88-2675. (Illus.). 96p. (J). (gr. 2-5). 1989. lib. bdg. 14.89 (*0-397-32301-8*) HarpC Child Bks.

— Rainy Day: Stories & Poems. LC 85-45170. (Illus.). 96p. (J). (gr. 2-5). 1986. 13.95 (*0-397-32104-X*); lib. bdg. 15.89 (*0-397-32105-8*) HarpC Child Bks.

— Snowy Day: Stories & Poems. LC 85-45858. (Illus.). 80p. (J). (gr. 2-5). 1986. lib. bdg. 15.89 (*0-397-32177-5*) HarpC Child Bks.

— Valentine's Day: Stories & Poems. LC 91-37641. (Illus.). 96p. (J). (gr. 2-5). 1993. 16.95 (*0-06-020823-6*) HarpC Child Bks.

— Windy Day: Stories & Poems. LC 86-42994. (Illus.). 96p. (J). (gr. 2-5). 1988. 12.95 (*0-397-32207-0*) HarpC Child Bks.

Bauer, Caroline Feller, ed. see Tomes, Margot.

Bauer, Carolyn. Arizona Traveler: Ghost Towns of Arizona - Remnants of the Mining Days. (American Traveler Ser.: Vol. 8). (Illus.). 48p. 1988. pap. 5.95 (*1-55838-095-7*) R H Pub.

— Colorado Traveler: Colorado Ghost Towns - Remnants of the Mining Days. (American Traveler Ser.: Vol. 1). (Illus.). 48p. 1987. pap. 6.95 (*1-55838-067-1*) R H Pub.

***Bauer, Cat.** Harley, Like a Person. LC 99-46814. 250p. (YA). (gr. 7-12). 2000. 16.95 (*1-890817-48-1*, Pub. by Winslow Pr); pap. 6.95 (*1-890817-49-X*, Pub. by Winslow Pr) Publishers Group.

Bauer, Catherine K. Modern Housing. LC 73-11908. (Metropolitan America Ser.). (Illus.). 380p. 1974. reprint ed. 25.95 (*0-405-05386-X*) Ayer.

Bauer, Catherine K., jt. auth. see Hitchcock, Henry-Russell, Jr.

Bauer, Catherine Lazers. One Day on Earth: A Third Eye View. LC 99-27397. 318p. 1999. 15.95 (*0-9620507-8-4*, Pub. by Cosmic Concepts Pr) New Leaf Dist.

Bauer, Cathryn. Acupressure for Everybody: Gentle, Effective Techniques for Healing & Relaxing. 160p. (Orig.). 1995. pap. 11.95 (*0-8050-1579-5*, Owl) H Holt & Co.

— Pocket Guide to Acupressure Points for Women. LC 97-11570. (Crossing Press Pocket Ser.). (Illus.). 102p. (Orig.). 1997. pap. 6.95 (*0-89594-879-6*) Crossing Pr.

Bauer, Cecile. Caregiver's Gethsemane: When a Loved One Longs to Die. LC 95-831. 144p. (Orig.). 1995. pap. 8.95 (*0-8091-3572-8*) Paulist Pr.

— Stepping Stones: Meditations & Prayers for Spiritual Renewal. LC 99-40902. 144p. 2000. pap. 8.95 (*0-8091-3916-2*) Paulist Pr.

Bauer, Dale M. Edith Wharton's Brave New Politics. LC 94-13432. 1995. 55.00 (*0-299-14420-8*); pap. 18.95 (*0-299-14424-0*) U of Wis Pr.

— Feminist Dialogics: A Theory of Failed Community. LC 87-10172. 204p. (C). 1988. text 24.50 (*0-88706-651-8*) State U NY Pr.

Bauer, Dale M. & McKinstry, Susan J., eds. Feminism, Bakhtin, & the Dialogic. LC 90-47263. 259p. (C). 1992. text 64.50 (*0-7914-0769-1*); pap. text 21.95 (*0-7914-0770-5*) State U NY Pr.

Bauer, David. Winning Grants: Leader's Guide. 86p. (Orig.). 1985. pap. text 9.95 (*0-9614949-4-8*) GPN.

Bauer, David G. Administering Grants, Contracts & Funds: Evaluating & Improving Your Grants System. LC 94-38180. 248p. 1989. pap. 36.95 (*1-57356-215-7*) Oryx Pr.

Bauer, David G. The Complete Grants Sourcebook for Higher Education. 3rd ed. (Ace/Oryx Series on Higher Education). (Illus.). 352p. 1995. reprint ed. pap. text 65.00 (*1-57356-416-8*) Oryx Pr.

Bauer, David G. The Fundraising Primer. 1995. 24.95 (*0-590-49374-4*, 241B38 1993) Scholastic Inc.

***Bauer, David G.** How to Evaluate & Improve Your Grants Effort. (Ace/Oryx Press Series on Higher Education). 232p. 2001. text 36.95 (*1-57356-363-3*) Oryx Pr.

Bauer, David G. The How to Grants Manual: Successful Grantseeking Techniques for Obtaining Public & Private Grants. 4th rev. ed. LC 99-31057. (Illus.). 264p. 1999. boxed set 34.95 (*1-57356-326-9*) Oryx Pr.

— The How To Grants Manual: Successful Techniques for Obtaining Private & Public Grants. 1984. 20.00 (*0-02-902430-7*, 2012) Free Pr.

— The Principal's Guide to Winning Grants. (Education Ser.). 144p. 1998. pap. 24.95 (*0-7879-4494-7*) Jossey-Bass.

***Bauer, David G.** Successful Grants Program Management. LC 99-44129. 208p. 1999. pap. text 29.95 (*0-7879-5039-4*) New Lexington.

Bauer, David G. The Teacher's Guide to Winning Grants. (Education Ser.). 128p. 1998. pap. 24.95 (*0-7879-4493-9*) Jossey-Bass.

***Bauer, David G.** Technology Funding for Schools. LC 99-49004. 256p. 2000. pap. 29.95 (*0-7879-5040-8*, Pfffr & Co) Jossey-Bass.

Bauer, David G., jt. auth. see American Council on Education Staff.

Bauer, David R. Biblical Resources for Ministry: A Bibliography of Works in Biblical Studies. 2nd enl. rev. ed. 144p. 1995. pap. 9.00 (*0-916035-62-X*) Evangel Indiana.

— Matthew. (NIV Application Commentary Ser.). 464p. 24.99 (*0-310-49310-2*) Zondervan.

Bauer, David R. The Structure of Matthew's Gospel: A Study in Literary Design. (JSNT Supplement Ser.: No. 31). 182p. 1988. 57.50 (*1-85075-105-6*, Pub. by Sheffield Acad) CUP Services.

Bauer, David R. The Structure of Matthew's Gospel: A Study in Literary Design. (JSNT Supplement Ser.: No. 31). 182p. 1988. reprint ed. pap. 18.95 (*1-85075-104-8*, Pub. by Sheffield Acad) CUP Services.

***Bauer, David R. & Martin, Jonathan W., eds.** Service Life Prediction; Methodology & Metrologies. (ACS Symposium Ser.). (Illus.). 418p. 2000. text 135.00 (*0-8412-3693-3*) Am Chemical.

Bauer, David R. & Martin, Jonathan W., eds. Service Life Prediction of Organic Coatings: A Systemic Approach, Vol. 722. LC 98-32089. (Illus.). 480p. 1999. 125.00 (*0-8412-3597-X*) OUP.

Bauer, David R., jt. ed. see Powell, Mark Allan.

Bauer, David S. UNIX(R) Security Handbook. (Illus.). 117p. (C). 1991. 49.00 (*1-878108-12-3*) Telcordia Technologies.

Bauer, Dee K. & MESD School Health Services Staff. School Emergencies Manual. rev. ed. 1994. ring bd. 37.50 (*1-880118-05-X*, 245-01) MESD Pr.

Bauer, Dee K., jt. auth. see Sanderson, Jan.

Bauer, Doreen. Foundations of Physical Rehabilitation. (Illus.). 238p. 1989. pap. text 22.95 (*0-443-03716-7*) Church.

Bauer, Douglas. The Book of Famous Iowans: A Novel. LC 97-2228. 288p. 1995. 25.00 (*0-8050-4300-4*) H Holt & Co.

— The Book of Famous Iowans: A Novel. 288p. 1998. pap. 13.00 (*0-8050-6002-2*, Owl) H Holt & Co.

— Dexterity: A Novel. 320p. 1998. pap. 23.00 (*0-8050-4302-0*, Pub. by H Holt & Co) VHPS.

— Prairie City, Iowa: Three Seasons at Home. LC 88-13121. (Iowa Heritage Collection). 330p. 1988. reprint ed. pap. 10.95 (*0-8138-1328-X*) Iowa St U Pr.

***Bauer, Douglas.** The Stuff of Fiction: Advice on Craft. (Illus.). 128p. 2000. pap. 15.95 (*0-472-06733-8*, 06733) U of Mich Pr.

— The Stuff of Fiction: Advice on Craft. (Illus.). 128p. (C). 2000. text 39.50 (*0-472-09733-4*, 09733) U of Mich Pr.

Bauer, Douglas. The Very Air. LC 97-22106. 384p. 1997. pap. 14.00 (*0-8050-4301-2*) St Martin.

Bauer, E. S. Theoretical Biology: Reprint of the 1935 Edition with a Preface, a Biographical & Critical Essay. Tigyi, J. et al, eds. (ENG & RUS.). 294p. (C). 1982. reprint ed. 42.00 (*963-05-3014-7*, Pub. by Akade Kiado) St Mut.

Bauer, Eddy. The Illustrated World War Two Encyclopedia, 28 vols., Set. 1980. 335.44 (*0-87475-520-4*) Websters Unified.

***Bauer, Elizabeth K.** Commentaries on the Constitution, 1790-1860, 1952. LC 98-45409. 400p. 1999. reprint ed. 75.00 (*1-886363-66-8*) Lawbk Exchange.

Bauer, Ernest, tr. see Cormier-Boudreau, Marielle & Gallant, Melvin.

Bauer, Erwin & Bauer, Peggy. Baja to Borrow: A Pacific Coast Wildlife Odyssey. (Illus.). 160p. 1999. reprint ed. text 29.00 (*0-7881-6434-1*) DIANE Pub.

— Denali: The Wild Beauty of Denali National Park. LC 99-40083. (Illus.). 80p. 2000. pap. 14.95 (*1-57061-209-9*) Sasquatch Bks.

Bauer, Erwin, jt. auth. see Bauer, Peggy.

Bauer, Erwin A. Bass Fisherman's Bible. 3rd ed. 224p. 1989. pap. 12.95 (*0-385-24690-0*) Doubleday.

— Bears: Behavior, Ecology, Conservation. LC 96-2185. (Illus.). 160p. 1997. 35.00 (*0-89658-282-5*) Voyageur Pr.

— Bears: Behavior, Ecology, Conservation. (Illus.). 160p. 1999. pap. 19.95 (*0-89658-428-3*) Voyageur Pr.

— Elk: Behavior, Ecology, Conservation. (Illus.). 160p. 1999. pap. 19.95 (*0-89658-377-5*) Voyageur Pr.

— Mule Deer: Behavior, Ecology, Conservation. LC 94-39531. (Illus.). 160p. 1995. 35.00 (*0-89658-263-9*) Voyageur Pr.

— The Saltwater Fisherman's Bible. 3rd ed. 176p. 1991. pap. 12.95 (*0-385-26444-5*) Doubleday.

— Whitetails: Behavior, Ecology, & Conservation. LC 93-17728. (Illus.). 160p. 1995. pap. text 19.95 (*0-89658-308-2*) Voyageur Pr.

— Whitetails: Behavior, Ecology, Conservation. LC 93-17728. (Illus.). 160p. 1993. 14.95 (*0-89658-196-9*) Voyageur Pr.

— Yellowstone. LC 92-38044. (Illus.). 128p. 1993. 29.95 (*0-89658-177-2*) Voyageur Pr.

— Yellowstone. rev. ed. LC 98-31497. (Pictorial Discovery Guide Ser.). (Illus.). 144p. 1999. pap. 19.95 (*0-89658-423-2*) Voyageur Pr.

Bauer, Erwin A. & Bauer, Peggy. Antlers: Nature's Majestic Crown. LC 94-9033. (Illus.). 160p. 1995. 14.95 (*0-89658-253-1*) Voyageur Pr.

— Big Game of North America. LC 96-35224. (Illus.). 160p. 1998. 35.00 (*0-89658-336-8*) Voyageur Pr.

— Photographing Wild Texas. (Illus.). 112p. 1985. pap. 16.95 (*0-292-76497-9*) U of Tex Pr.

***Bauer, Erwin A. & Bauer, Peggy, photos by.** Antlers: Nature's Majestic Crown. (Illus.). 160p. 2000. reprint ed. pap. 19.95 (*0-89658-374-0*) Voyageur Pr.

— Big Game of North America: Behavior, Ecology, Conservation. LC 00-38182. (Illus.). 160p. 2000. reprint ed. pap. 19.95 (*0-89658-480-1*) Voyageur Pr.

Bauer, Erwin A. & Bauer, Peggy, photos by. Elk: Behavior, Ecology, Conservation. LC 95-24582. (Illus.). 160p. 1996. 35.00 (*0-89658-275-2*) Voyageur Pr.

***Bauer, Erwin A. & Bauer, Peggy, photos by.** Mule Deer: Behavior, Ecology, Conservation. (Illus.). 160p. 2000. reprint ed. pap. 19.95 (*0-89658-376-7*) Voyageur Pr.

Bauer, Erwin A. & Bauer, Peggy, photos by. Wild Dogs: The Wolves, Coyotes, & Foxes of North America. LC 93-29205. (Illus.). 120p. 1994. 27.50 (*0-8118-0690-1*); pap. 16.95 (*0-8118-0405-4*) Chronicle Bks.

Bauer, Erwin A., jt. photos by see Bauer, Peggy.

Bauer, Eugene E. Boeing: The First Century. LC 99-94012. (Illus.). 405p. 2000. 24.50 (*1-879242-08-7*) Taba Pub.

Follow Bill Boeing as he gathered men of like vision around him in a remote, primitive corner of the United States in 1916 passing a legacy of dedication to excellence to eight subsequent presidents who in spite of crisis after crisis, molded the largest & most respected aircraft manufacturing enterprise in the world, pleasing customers & confounding competitors with innovative products. At the end of World War II, four companies were manufacturing commercial airplanes in the U.S. Convair dropped out in 1961, Lockheed withdrew in 1981 & Boeing acquired McDonnell Douglas in 1997. At the millennium, Boeing stood alone at the top. The company had reached the pinnacle by consistently out-thinking, out-performing & out-working the competition. This book reveals the details product by product & decision by decision for the entire history of the company & includes 57 photos. Taba Publishing, Inc., 24103 SE 384th, Enumclaw, WA 98022. Phone (360) 825-9709, Fax (360) 825-7371. Distributed by the Ingram Book Co., Phone (615) 793-5000; Baker & Taylor Books, (815) 472-2444; &

An Asterisk (*) at the beginning of an entry indicates that the title is appearing for the first time.

Partners West, (800) 563-2385 or purchase directly from Taba Publishing. *Publisher Paid Annotation.*

— BOEING in Peace & War. LC 91-61446. (Illus.). 375p. 1991. 21.95 (*1-879242-06-0*) Taba Pub.
— Boeing in Peace & War. LC 90-92124. (Illus.). 365p. 1991. pap. 14.95 (*1-879242-04-4*) Taba Pub.
— Contrails: Reminisces of a Boeing Salesman. LC 96-90165. (Illus.). 377p. (Orig.). 1996. pap. 12.95 (*1-879242-07-9*) Taba Pub.
Bauer, F. L. Decrypted Secrets: Methods & Maxims of Cryptology. LC 96-37583. 472p. 1997. 39.95 (*3-540-60418-9*) Spr-Verlag.
Bauer, F. L., ed. Logic, Algebra, & Computation. (NATO ASI Series F: Computer & Systems Sciences, Special Programme AET: Vol. 79). vii, 485p. 1991. 130.95 (*0-387-54315-5*) Spr-Verlag.
Bauer, F. L., et al, eds. Logic & Algebra of Specification. (NATO ASI Series F: Computer & Systems Sciences, Special Programme AET: Vol. 94). vii, 444p. 1993. 119.95 (*0-387-55813-6*) Spr-Verlag.
Bauer, F. L. & Broy, Manfred, eds. Program Construction: International Summer School. (Lecture Notes in Computer Science Ser.: Vol. 69). 1982. 47.00 (*0-387-09251-X*) Spr-Verlag.
Bauer, F. L. & Samelson, K., eds. Language Hierarchies & Interfaces. (Lecture Notes in Computer Science Ser.: Vol. 46). 1977. 35.00 (*0-387-07994-7*) Spr-Verlag.
Bauer, F. L. & Woessner, H. Algorithmic Language & Program Development. (Texts & Monographs in Computer Science). (Illus.). 520p. 1982. 59.00 (*0-387-11148-4*) Spr-Verlag.
Bauer, F. L., et al. Magnetohydrodynamic Equilibrium & Stability of Stellarators. (Illus.). x, 196p. 1984. 79.95 (*0-387-90966-4*) Spr-Verlag.
— The Munich Project CIP. (Lecture Notes in Computer Science Ser.: Vol. 292). 522p. 1988. 53.00 (*0-387-18779-0*) Spr-Verlag.
Bauer, Frantisek & Marek, Jindrich. Isentropic Gas Flow: Tables & Correction Nomograms. LC 62-28534. 667p. reprint ed. pap. 200.00 (*0-608-30076-4*, 201938800011) Bks Demand.
Bauer, Franz. Lexikon der Reproduktionstechnik. 2nd ed. (GER.). 634p. 1986. 75.00 (*0-7859-8533-6*, 3880133387) Fr & Eur.
Bauer, Fred. Daily Living, Daily Giving. 1982. 10.95 (*0-89952-084-7*) Littlebrook.
— For Rainy Mondays & Other Dry Spells. 1982. 8.95 (*0-89952-024-3*) Littlebrook.
Bauer, Fred, ed. Norman Rockwell's Faith of America. (Illus.). 160p. 1996. 14.98 (*0-89660-066-1*, Artabras) Abbeville Pr.
Bauer, Fred & Reufenacht, Peter. Chilp. LC 72-89351. (Illus.). 24p. (J). (gr. k-4). 1973. 13.95 (*0-87592-011-X*) Scroll Pr.
***Bauer-Freitag, L.** Healing: The Emerging Holistic Paradigm. (Illus.). 148p. 1999. per. 16.00 (*0-615-11458-X*) HARKEN!.
Bauer-Freitag, Lilo. Healing the Emerging Holistic Paradigm. 160p. 1998. pap. 16.00 (*1-880710-30-7*) Monterey Pacific.
***Bauer, Friedrich L.** Decrypted Secrets: Methods & Maxims of Cryptology. 2nd rev. expanded ed. LC 99-89580. (Illus.). xii, 487p. 2000. 39.95 (*3-540-66871-3*) Spr-Verlag.
Bauer, G., et al, eds. Low-Dimensional Electronic Systems: New Concepts, Proceedings of the Seventh International Winter School, Austria, Mauterndorf, February 24-28, 1992. LC 92-36489. (Solid-State Sciences Ser.: Vol. 111). 1993. 119.95 (*0-387-55998-1*) Spr-Verlag.
— Narrow Gap Semiconductors: Proceedings of the 8th International Conference Shanghai, China 21-24 April, 1997. LC 98-199778. 480p. 1998. 110.00 (*981-02-3344-2*) World Scientific Pub.
— Two-Dimensional Systems: Physics & New Devices. (Solid-State Sciences Ser.: Vol. 67). (Illus.). 335p. 1986. 78.95 (*0-387-16748-X*) Spr-Verlag.
***Bauer, G. & Whachtler, K.** Ecology & Evolution of the Freshwater Mussels Unionoida. LC 00-44062. (Ecological Studies). (Illus.). 2000. write for info. (*3-540-67268-0*) Spr-Verlag.
Bauer, Gary. Our Hopes - Our Dreams: A Vision for America. (Orig.). 1996. mass mkt. 3.99 (*1-56179-433-3*) Focus Family.
Bauer, Gary L., jt. auth. see Knight, Robert H.
Bauer, George H. Sartre & the Artist. LC 76-88232. 246p. reprint ed. pap. 76.30 (*0-608-12641-1*, 202408200035) Bks Demand.
Bauer, George R. Fairfax Ghosts: The "Bomber Builders" & Others Who Made a Difference. LC 95-92246. 146p. 1995. 29.95 (*0-9647176-0-3*) NBTPG.
— The New Czech Republic: Year of Turmoil. LC 97-93901. 1997. pap. 9.95 (*0-9658761-0-1*) G R Bauer.
***Bauer, Gerald.** Paris. 1998. pap. text 12.95 (*2-86656-117-1*) Scala Edit.
Bauer, Gerald J., et al, eds. Emerging Trends in Sales Thought & Practice. LC 97-48619. 264p. 1998. 65.00 (*1-56720-036-2*, Quorum Bks) Greenwood.
Bauer, Gerald W. Congregational Endowment Funds: Empowering the Vision of God's Coming Kingdom. pap. 7.50 (*1-56699-161-7*) Alban Inst.
— Invited to Serve: How to Discern God's Calling in Your Life. LC 97-92606. 96p. 1998. pap. 8.95 (*0-9659912-0-2*) Proclam OH.
Bauer, Gerhard. Soccer Techniques, Tactics & Teamwork. (Illus.). 160p. 1993. pap. 14.95 (*0-8069-8730-8*) Sterling.
Bauer, Gerhard, ed. Geiler von Kayserberg Saemtliche Werke Vol. 3: Part 1: Die Deutschen Schriften Section 1: Die Zu Geilers Lebzeiten Erschienenen Schriften. (Ausgaben Deutschen Literatur des XV bis XVIII Jahrhunderts Ser.). (GER.). xxx, 975p. (C). 1995. lib. bdg. 676.95 (*3-11-013995-2*) De Gruyter.
— Johannes Geiler von Kayserberg (1445-1510) Samtliche Werke, 9 vols. (Ausgaben Deutscher Literatur des XV bis XVIII Jahrhunderts Ser.). (GER.). xx, 808p. (C). 1991. lib. bdg. 500.00 (*3-11-012364-9*) De Gruyter.
Bauer, Gerhard, jt. auth. see Breitmaier, Eberhard.
***Bauer, Gerie.** Numerology for Beginners: Easy Guide to Love, Money, Destiny. 2000. pap. 9.95 (*1-56718-057-4*) Llewellyn Pubns.
Bauer, Glen, jt. ed. see Beckerman, Michael.
Bauer, Grace. Where You've Seen Her. (Green Ser.). 1993. pap. 6.00 (*0-938631-11-X*) Pennywhistle Pr.
— The Women at the Well. LC 97-66182. (Illus.). 104p. (Orig.). (C). 1997. pap. 15.00 (*0-916620-33-6*) Portals Pr.
Bauer, Gregory P. The Analysis of the Transference in the Here & Now. LC 92-49521. 248p. 1993. 50.00 (*0-87668-143-7*) Aronson.
Bauer, Gregory P., ed. Essential Papers on Transference Analysis. LC 93-8962. 240p. 1993. pap. 45.00 (*0-87668-529-7*) Aronson.
— Wit & Wisdom in Dynamic Psychotherapy. LC 90-40191. 320p. 1990. 50.00 (*0-87668-768-0*) Aronson.
Bauer, Gregory P. & Kobos, Joseph C. Brief Therapy: Short-Term Psychodynamic Intervention. LC 87-1487. 312p. 1987. 50.00 (*0-87668-940-3*) Aronson.
Bauer, Gretchen. Labor & Democracy in Namibia, 1971-1996. LC 97-49202. 180p. 1998. text 34.95 (*0-8214-1216-7*); pap. text 17.95 (*0-8214-1217-5*) Ohio U Pr.
Bauer, Gunther & Richter, Wolfgang, eds. Optical Characterization of Epitaxial Semiconductor Layers. LC 95-44724. 436p. 1995. 82.95 (*3-540-59129-X*) Spr-Verlag.
Bauer, H. J., ed. Progress in Multiple Sclerosis Research. (Illus.). 630p. 1980. 68.95 (*0-387-09867-4*) Spr-Verlag.
Bauer, H. W., et al, eds. Forum 1982 Fuer Experimentelle und Klinische Urologie. (Beitraege zur Urologie Ser.: Band 3). (Illus.). x, 324p. 1983. pap. 87.00 (*3-8055-3718-2*) S Karger.
Bauer, Hans, ed. In the Beginning: Great First Lines from Your Favorite Books. (Illus.). 204p. 1998. pap. text 9.00 (*0-7881-5386-2*) DIANE Pub.
Bauer, Hans & Leander, Pontus. Grammatik des Biblisch-Aramaischen. (GER.). xv, 381p. 1995. reprint ed. write for info. (*3-487-00258-2*) G Olms Pubs.
— Historische Grammatik der Hebraischen Sprache des Alten Testaments. (Olms Paperbacks Ser.: Vol. 19). (GER.). iv, 91p. 1995. reprint ed. pap. write for info. (*3-487-05479-5*) G Olms Pubs.
— Historische Grammatik der Hebraischen Spraches des Alten Testaments. (GER.). iv, 91p. 1995. reprint ed. write for info. (*3-487-00207-8*) G Olms Pubs.
Bauer, Hans, jt. auth. see Bernard, Franz.
Bauer, Heidi, ed. The Privilege for Which We Struggle: Woman Suffrage Leaders of Minnesota. unabridged ed. (Illus.). 190p. 1999. pap. 12.95 (*0-914227-10-6*, 5500) Minn Hist.
Bauer, Heinrich. Vollstaendige Grammatik der neuhochdeutschen Sprache, 5 vols. (C). 1967. reprint ed. 615.40 (*3-11-000365-1*) De Gruyter.
Bauer, Heinz. Probability Theory. Burckel, Robert B., tr. from GER. (De Gruyter Studies in Mathematics: Vol. 23). (GER.). xv, 523p. (C). 1995. lib. bdg. 79.95 (*3-11-013935-9*) De Gruyter.
Bauer, Heinz, ed. see Herve, Michel.
Bauer, Helen, jt. auth. see Rayson, Ann.
Bauer, Helen P. Rudyard Kipling: A Study in Short Fiction. LC 94-6829. (Twayne's Studies in Short Fiction: No. 58). 192p. 1994. 25.95 (*0-8057-8345-8*, Twyne) Mac Lib Ref.
Bauer, Helmut, ed. Design Guide Europe. 208p. 1996. pap. 29.00 (*3-923922-46-9*, 620601, Pub. by Nazraeli Pr) Dist Art Pubs.
Bauer, Henry H. Beyond Velikovsky: The History of a Public Controversy. LC 83-17935. 368p. 1984. text 29.95 (*0-252-01104-X*) U of Ill Pr.
***Bauer, Henry H.** Beyond Velikovsky: The History of a Public Controversy. 368p. 1999. pap. text 19.95 (*0-252-06845-9*) U of Ill Pr.
Bauer, Henry H. The Enigma of Loch Ness: Making Sense of a Mystery. LC 85-24554. 264p. 1986. pap. text 17.95 (*0-252-06031-8*) U of Ill Pr.
***Bauer, Henry H.** Science or Pseudoscience: Magnetic Healing, Psychic Phenomena & Other Heterodoxies. LC 00-8332. (Illus.). 2001. write for info. (*0-252-02601-2*) U of Ill Pr.
Bauer, Henry H. Scientific Literacy & the Myth of the Scientific Method. 192p. 1992. 24.95 (*0-252-01856-7*) U of Ill Pr.
— Scientific Literacy & the Myth of the Scientific Method. 192p. 1994. 13.95 (*0-252-06436-4*) U of Ill Pr.
Bauer, Hermann, jt. auth. see Prater, Andreas.
Bauer, Hilaria, et al. Coca-Cola Valued Youth Program: Tutor Workbook. (Illus.). 185p. (Orig.). (YA). 1996. pap. text, wbk. ed. write for info. (*1-878550-64-0*) Inter Dev Res Assn.
Bauer, Irmgard L. Patients' Privacy: An Explanatory Study of Patients' Perception of Their Privacy in a German Acute Care Hospital. LC 94-16735. (Developments in Nursing & Health Care Ser.). 184p. 1994. 66.95 (*1-85628-918-4*, Pub. by Avebry) Ashgate Pub Co.
Bauer, Jacek, jt. auth. see Gutkowski, Witold.
Bauer, James J. The Runaway Learning Machine: Growing up Dyslexic. LC 92-71009. 96p. (Orig.). (C). 1992. pap. text 6.95 (*0-932796-43-5*) Ed Media Corp.
— Too Much Time on Sycamore Street: A Self-Help Resource for Adolescents & Adults with Learning Disabilities. LC 99-60704. 144p. 1999. pap. 10.95 (*0-932796-90-7*) Ed Media Corp.
Bauer, Jan. Alcoholism & Women. 144p. 1995. pap. 6.00 (*0-919123-10-4*, Pub. by Inner City Bks) BookWorld.
— Impossible Love: Why the Heart Must Go Wrong. LC 93-35881. 208p. (Orig.). 1993. pap. 19.00 (*0-88214-359-X*) Spring Pubns.
Bauer, Jaroslav. Field Guide in Color to Minerals, Rocks & Precious Stones. 1992. 9.98 (*1-55521-091-0*) Bk Sales Inc.
— Guide in Color to Precious & Semiprecious Stones. 1992. 9.98 (*1-55521-362-6*) Bk Sales Inc.
Bauer, Jeffrey C. Not What the Doctor Ordered: How to End the Medical Monopoly in Pursuit of Managed Care. 2nd rev. ed. LC 97-43100. (Illus.). 240p. 1997. 24.95 (*0-07-006721-X*) McGraw.
— Statistical Analysis for Decision-Makers in Healthcare: Understanding & Evaluating Critical Information in a Competitive Market. 225p. (C). 1995. text 55.00 (*1-55738-633-1*, Irwn Prfssnl) McGraw-Hill Prof.
Bauer, Jennifer B. Kids First! Family Education Program. 1997. pap. text 12.95 (*0-933025-59-9*) Blue Bird Pub.
Bauer, Jerome L., ed. see International SAMPE Symposium & Exhibition Staff.
Bauer, Jessica K., et al. Visions of Long Dark Highways. 24p. 1998. pap. 6.95 (*0-9664146-9-1*) Gemini-Libra.
***Bauer, Joan.** Backwater. (Illus.). 240p. (J). (gr. 5 up). 2000. pap. 5.99 (*0-698-11865-0*) Peng Put Young Read.
Bauer, Joan. Backwater. LC 98-50729. (gr. 7 up). 1999. 16.99 (*0-399-23141-2*) Putnam Pub Group.
***Bauer, Joan.** Hope Was Here. (Illus.). 192p. (J). (gr. 7 up). 2000. 16.99 (*0-399-23142-0*) Putnam Pub Group.
Bauer, Joan. Rules of the Road. LC 97-32198. 208p. (YA). (gr. 7 up). 1998. 15.99 (*0-399-23140-4*) Putnam Pub Group.
***Bauer, Joan.** Rules of the Road. LC 97-32198. (Illus.). 208p. (YA). (gr. 7-12). 2000. reprint ed. pap. 4.99 (*0-698-11828-6*, PuffinBks) Peng Put Young Read.
Bauer, Joan. Squashed. 208p. (YA). 1994. mass mkt. 4.50 (*0-440-21912-4*) Dell.
Bauer, Joan. Squashed. 1992. 9.09 (*0-606-07094-X*, Pub. by Turtleback) Demco.
Bauer, Joan. Squashed. large type ed. LC 93-6722. 243p. 1993. pap. 15.95 (*1-56054-685-9*) Thorndike Pr.
— Sticks. (Illus.). 192p. (J). (gr. 3-7). 1997. pap. 3.99 (*0-440-41387-7*) Dell.
— Sticks. (J). 1997. 9.09 (*0-606-11912-4*, Pub. by Turtleback) Demco.
— Thwonk. 224p. (YA). (gr. 7 up). 1996. mass mkt. 4.50 (*0-440-21980-9*, LLL BDD) BDD Bks Young Read.
— Thwonk. 1996. 9.60 (*0-606-09967-0*, Pub. by Turtleback) Demco.
Bauer, Joan. Thwonk, Set. unabridged ed. (J). (gr. 6). 1997. pap. 46.24 incl. audio (*0-7887-1552-6*, 40424) Recorded Bks.
Bauer, JoAnn, ed. Celebration of Humboldt County Authors Speakers Directory. 71p. 1993. pap. 6.00 (*0-9638036-0-3*) Frnds Redwood.
Bauer, Joanne R. & Bell, Daniel A., eds. The East Asian Challenge for Human Rights. LC 98-11653. (Illus.). 400p. (C). 1999. text 57.95 (*0-521-64230-2*); pap. text 21.95 (*0-521-64536-0*) Cambridge U Pr.
Bauer, Joel J. & Mount Sinai Hospital (New York, N. Y.) Staff. Mt. Sinai Clinical Handbook of Surgery: A Case-Oriented Approach. LC 98-6114. 706p. 1998. spiral bd. 33.95 (*0-683-18001-0*) Lppncott W & W.
Bauer, Johann. Cell Electrophoresis. 336p. 1994. boxed set 136.95 (*0-8493-8918-6*) CRC Pr.
— Der Leittext Als (Fach-)Textlinguistisches Phanomen: Analyse und Optimierungsmoglichkeiten Einer Betriebsinternen Textsorte. (Forum Linguisticum Ser.: No. 34). (Illus.). 418p. 1997. 63.95 (*3-631-31709-3*) P Lang Pubng.
Bauer, Johann J. Bibliotheca Librorum Rariorum Universalis. 2543p. 1982. reprint ed. 600.00 (*3-487-07122-3*) G Olms Pubs.
Bauer, Johannes B. Diccionario de Teologia Biblica. 2nd ed. (SPA.). 582p. 1985. 69.95 (*0-7859-5087-7*, S50203) Fr & Eur.
Bauer, John. Effective Regulation of Public Utilities. LC 75-39230. (Getting & Spending: The Consumer's Dilemma Ser.). 1976. reprint ed. 33.95 (*0-405-08007-7*) Ayer.
***Bauer, John.** Progressive Scale Studies for Cello: Intermediate Level. 100p. 1998. spiral bd. 14.95 (*0-7866-2969-X*, 96746) Mel Bay.
— Progressive Scale Studies for Viola: Intermediate Level. 104p. 1998. spiral bd. 14.95 (*0-7866-2970-3*, 96745) Mel Bay.
— Progressive Scale Studies for Violin: Intermediate Level. 104p. 1998. spiral bd. 14.95 (*0-7866-2971-1*, 96744) Mel Bay.
Bauer, Joseph P. Federal Antitrust Law: 1997 Supplement, 12 vols. 1996. pap. 275.00 (*0-614-30944-1*) Anderson Pub Co.
Bauer, Joseph P., jt. auth. see Kintner, Earl W.
Bauer, Joy. The Complete Idiot's Guide to Eating Smart. 1997. write for info. (*0-614-25231-8*) Macmillan.
— The Complete Idiot's Guide to Eating Smart. LC 96-79347. 1996. 16.95 (*0-02-861276-0*) Macmillan Gen Ref.
***Bauer, Joy.** The Complete Idiot's Guide to Total Nutrition. 2nd ed. LC 99-64168. (Illus.). 374p. 1999. pap. 16.95 (*0-02-862956-6*) Macmillan Gen Ref.
Bauer, Judith. What's It Like to Be a Doctor. LC 89-34398. (What's It Like to Be a...Ser.). (Illus.). 32p. (J). (gr. k-3). 1996. pap. 2.95 (*0-8167-1802-4*) Troll Communs.
Bauer, Judith A., ed. & compiled by see Redemptorist Pastoral Publication Staff.
Bauer, Judith A., ed. & compiled by see Tickle, Phyllis.
Bauer, K. Jack. The Mexican War, 1846-1848. LC 92-13927. (Illus.). xxviii, 486p. (C). 1992. pap. 22.00 (*0-8032-6107-1*, Bison Books) U of Nebr Pr.
— Zachary Taylor: Soldier, Planter, Statesman of the Old Southwest. LC 85-11028. (Southern Biography Ser.). (Illus.). 348p. (C). 1993. pap. 19.95 (*0-8071-1851-6*) La State U Pr.
— Zachary Taylor: Soldier, Planter, Statesman of the Old Southwest. Speirs, Katherine E., ed. LC 94-71615. (Signature Ser.). (Illus.). 347p. 1994. reprint ed. 32.50 (*0-945707-08-8*) Amer Political.
Bauer, K. Jack, ed. The New American State Papers: Naval Affairs, 1789 to 1860, 10 vols., Set. LC 80-53884. 3000p. 1981. lib. bdg. 650.00 (*0-8420-2173-6*) Scholarly Res Inc.
Bauer, K. Jack & Roberts, Stephen S. Register of Ships of the U. S. Navy, 1775-1990: Major Combatants. LC 91-25241. 376p. 1991. lib. bdg. 99.50 (*0-313-26202-0*, BRK, Greenwood Pr) Greenwood.
Bauer, K. Jack, jt. ed. see Coletta, Paolo E.
Bauer, K. Jack, jt. ed. see Gilbert, Benjamin F.
Bauer, Karen & Drew, Rosa. First Grade Homework, No. 3348. Shiotsu, Vicky, ed. (Illus.). 96p. (J). 1998. pap. 9.98 (*1-57471-348-5*) Creat Teach Pr.
***Bauer, Karen, et al.** Instant Math Centers K-1. Simon, Ruth B., ed. (Illus.). 128p. 2000. pap. text, teacher ed. 12.98 (*1-57471-689-1*) Creat Teach Pr.
Bauer, Karen W. Psychology of Women: Selected Readings. 172p. 1993. spiral bd. 26.95 (*0-8403-8409-2*) Kendall-Hunt.
Bauer, Karin. Adorno's Nietzschean Narratives: Critiques of Ideology, Readings of Wagner. LC 98-17953. 328p. (C). 1999. text 73.50 (*0-7914-4279-9*, Suny Pr); pap. text 24.95 (*0-7914-4280-2*, Suny Pr) State U NY Pr.
Bauer, Karl M. Cystoscopic Diagnosis: Technique & Typical Findings. Mukherjee, K. K., tr. LC 69-15642. (Illus.). 167p. reprint ed. pap. 51.80 (*0-608-30255-4*, 201452400093) Bks Demand.
Bauer, Kathleen & Dent, Julianne. College Class Piano. 78p. (C). 1993. pap. text 27.00 (*1-881986-08-X*) Demibach Eds.
Bauer, Kathleen, et al. College Class Piano: Teacher Edition. 78p. (C). 1993. teacher ed. 35.00 (*1-881986-09-8*) Demibach Eds.
Bauer, Kathleen, jt. auth. see Dent, Julianne.
Bauer, Kenneth D., et al, eds. Clinical Flow Cytometry: Principles & Applications. LC 92-13746. (Illus.). 660p. 1992. 125.00 (*0-683-00480-8*) Lppncott W & W.
Bauer-King, Nancy. The Word from the Wise Old Woman: Sermons from a Feminine Perspective. LC 98-9665. 112p. 1998. pap. 9.95 (*0-7880-1293-2*) CSS OH.
Bauer, Klaus-Jurgen. Adolf Krischanitz, Architect: Buildings & Projects, 1986-1998. LC 98-38514. (Illus.). 192p. 1998. 70.00 (*3-7643-5824-6*) Birkhauser.
Bauer, Kurt, et al. Common Fragrance & Flavor Materials: Preparation, Properties & Uses. LC 97-22233. 290p. 1997. 155.00 (*3-527-28850-3*, Wiley-VCH) Wiley.
Bauer, Kurt H. Coated Pharmaceutical Dosage Forms: Fundamentals, Manufacturing Techniques, Biopharmaceutical Aspects, Test Methods, & Raw Materials. Stanienda, Erdmute, tr. from GER. LC 97-52405. 1998. 119.95 (*0-8493-7518-5*) CRC Pr.
Bauer, Larry. Figure Skating: Easy Olympic Sports Readers. Coan, Sharon, ed. (U. S. Olympic Committee Easy Olympic Sports Readers Ser.). (Illus.). 16p. (J). (gr. k-3). 1998. pap. 2.99 (*1-58000-012-6*) Griffin CA.
— Figure Skating: Olympic Easy Reader. (Easy Readers Ser.). 16p. (J). (ps-1). 1997. pap. 2.99 (*1-57690-451-2*) Tchr Create Mat.
— Ice Hockey. (Olympic Easy Readers Ser.). 16p. (J). (gr. k-1). 1997. pap. 2.99 (*1-57690-453-9*) Tchr Create Mat.
— Ice Hockey: Easy Olympic Sports Readers. Coan, Sharon, ed. (U. S. Olympic Committee Easy Olympic Sports Readers Ser.). (Illus.). 16p. (J). (gr. k-3). 1998. pap. 2.99 (*1-58000-010-X*) Griffin CA.
— Skiing. (Olympic Easy Readers Ser.). 16p. (J). (ps-1). 1997. pap. 2.99 (*1-57690-450-4*) Tchr Create Mat.
— Skiing: Easy Olympic Sports Readers. Coan, Sharon, ed. (U. S. Olympic Committee Easy Olympic Sports Readers Ser.). (Illus.). 16p. (J). (gr. k-3). 1998. pap. 2.99 (*1-58000-009-6*) Griffin CA.
— Sledding. (Olympic Easy Readers Ser.). 16p. (J). (ps-1). 1997. pap. 2.99 (*1-57690-454-7*) Tchr Create Mat.
— Sledding: Easy Olympic Sports Readers. Coan, Sharon, ed. (U. S. Olympic Committee Easy Olympic Sports Readers Ser.). (Illus.). 16p. (J). (gr. k-3). 1998. pap. 2.99 (*1-58000-008-8*) Griffin CA.
— Snowboarding. (Olympic Easy Readers Ser.). 16p. (J). (ps-1). 1997. pap. 2.99 (*1-57690-455-5*) Tchr Create Mat.
— Snowboarding: Easy Olympic Sports Readers. Coan, Sharon, ed. (U. S. Olympic Committee Easy Olympic Sports Readers Ser.). (Illus.). 16p. (J). (gr. k-3). 1998. pap. 2.99 (*1-58000-013-4*) Griffin CA.
— Speed Skating. (Olympic Easy Readers Ser.). 16p. (J). (ps-1). 1997. pap. 2.99 (*1-57690-452-0*) Tchr Create Mat.
— Speed Skating: Easy Olympic Sports Readers. Coan, Sharon, ed. (U. S. Olympic Committee Easy Olympic Sports Readers Ser.). (Illus.). 16p. (J). (gr. k-3). 1998. pap. 2.99 (*1-58000-011-8*) Griffin CA.
Bauer, Laurie. English Word-Formation. LC 82-14693. (Cambridge Textbooks in Linguistics Ser.). 326p. 1983. pap. text 26.95 (*0-521-28492-9*) Cambridge U Pr.
— Introducing Linguistic Morphology. 300p. 1990. pap. 23.50 (*0-85224-582-3*, Pub. by Edinburgh U Pr) Col U Pr.
Bauer, Laurie K., jt. auth. see Shelton, Maria M.
Bauer, Lawrence, jt. ed. see Cotliar, William.

B

Bauer, Lawrence M., III. How to Publish a Card Pack. Marcus, Ruth E., ed. (Illus.). 72p. (Orig.). 1988. pap. 9.95 (*0-317-91170-8*) Solar Pr.

Bauer, Lawrence M., ed. see Bodian, Nat G. & Luedtke, Robert.

Bauer, Leonard. The Impact of Consumer Activism on the Insurance Industry. 164p. 1991. pap. 25.00 (*0-614-05734-5*) CPCU Society.

Bauer, Linda, ed. The New American Sampler Cookbook. LC 90-47480. (Illus.). 303p. 1991. reprint ed. pap. 94.00 (*0-608-07345-8*, 2067573) Bks Demand.

Bauer, Linda J. Career Gear. 1995. pap. 8.95 (*1-886158-07-X*) Macalester.

Bauer, Louise & Smith, Gary. Community Living for the Developmentally Disabled. (State Legislative Reports: Vol. 18, No. 12). 6p. 1993. 15.00 (*1-55516-339-4*, 7302-1812) Natl Conf State Legis.

Bauer, Lutz. Zeit des Zweiten Tempels - Ziet der Gerechtigkeit: Zur Sozio-Okonomischen Konzeption Im Haggai-Sacharja-Maleachi-Korpus. (Beitraege zur Erforschung des Alten Testaments & Antiken Judentums Ser.: Bd. 31). (GER., Illus.). 324p. 1992. 58.80 (*3-631-45230-6*) P Lang Pubng.

Bauer, Margaret D. The Fiction of Ellen Gilchrist. LC 98-50943. 1999. 49.95 (*0-8130-1699-1*) U Press Fla.

Bauer, Maria. Beyond the Chestnut Trees. LC 83-42917. (Illus.). 224p. 1984. 21.95 (*0-87951-190-7*, Pub. by Overlook Pr) Penguin Putnam.

— Beyond the Chestnut Trees. LC 83-42917. (Illus.). 224p. 1986. pap. 12.95 (*0-87951-244-X*, Pub. by Overlook Pr) Penguin Putnam.

Bauer, Maria, et al. Woodstock Originals: From the Byrdcliffe Writers, Vol. IV. 142p. (Orig.). 1995. pap. 8.95 (*0-9625244-1-7*) Byrdcliffe Writers.

Bauer, Marion. Sonata for Viola (Or Clarinet) & Piano. (Women Composers Ser.: No. 18). 50p. 1986. reprint ed. lib. bdg. 23.50 (*0-306-76249-8*) Da Capo.

— Twentieth Century Music: How It Developed, How to Listen to It. (Music Ser.). 354p. 1978. reprint ed. lib. bdg. 37.50 (*0-306-79503-5*) Da Capo.

— Twentieth Century Music: How It Developed, How to Listen to It: Music Book Index. 463p. 1993. reprint ed. lib. bdg. 99.00 (*0-7812-9563-7*) Rprt Serv.

Bauer, Marion D. Alison's Fierce & Ugly Halloween. LC 96-38547. (Hyperion Chapters Ser.). (Illus.). 48p. (J). (gr. 1-3). 1997. pap. 3.95 (*0-7868-1211-7*, Pub. by Hyprn Ppbks) Little.

— Bear's Hiccups: A Holiday House Reader. LC 97-10881. (Illus.). 48p. (J). (gr. k-2). 1998. lib. bdg. 14.95 (*0-8234-1339-X*) Holiday.

— Christmas in the Forest. LC 97-41952. (Illus.). (J). (gr. k-3). 1998. lib. bdg. 15.95 (*0-8234-1371-3*) Holiday.

Bauer, Marion D. Face to Face: A Novel. 1991. 9.09 (*0-606-05274-7*, Pub. by Turtleback) Demco.

— On My Honor. unabridged ed. (J). (gr. 5-6). 1992. pap. 21.98 incl. audio (*0-8072-7370-8*, YA 839 SP) Listening Lib.

— Sleep, Little One, Sleep! LC 98-19567. (Illus.). 32p. (J). (ps). 1999. 16.00 (*0-689-82250-2*) S&S Bks Yung.

Bauer, Marion D. A Taste of Smoke. (J). 1995. pap. 4.99 (*0-440-91045-5*) BDD Bks Young Read.

— Turtle Dreams. LC 97-2213. (Holiday House Reader Ser.). (Illus.). 48p. (J). (gr. k-3). 1997. lib. bdg. 14.95 (*0-8234-1322-5*) Holiday.

Bauer, Marion Dane. Alison's Fierce & Ugly Halloween. (Hyperion Chapters Ser.). (J). 1997. 9.15 (*0-606-13116-7*, Pub. by Turtleback) Demco.

— Alison's Puppy. LC 96-7464. (Illus.). 48p. (J). (gr. 1-3). 1997. lib. bdg. 14.49 (*0-7868-2237-6*, Pub. by Hyprn Child) Little.

— Alison's Puppy. LC 96-7464. (Illus.). 48p. (J). (gr. 1-3). 1997. pap. 3.99 (*0-7868-1140-4*, Pub. by Hyprn Ppbks) Little.

— Alison's Wings. LC 95-38772. (Illus.). 48p. (J). (gr. 1-3). 1996. 13.45 (*0-7868-0105-0*, Pub. by Hyprn Child) Little.

— Alison's Wings. (Hyperion Chapters Ser.). 1996. 9.15 (*0-606-08978-0*, Pub. by Turtleback) Demco.

— Am I Blue? Coming Out from the Silence. 1995. 11.05 (*0-606-07184-9*, Pub. by Turtleback) Demco.

— A Dream of Queens & Castles. 128p. (J). (gr. 3-7). 1990. 13.95 (*0-395-51330-8*, Clarion Bks) HM.

***Bauer, Marion Dane.** An Early Winter. 2001. pap. 4.50 (*0-440-41694-9*) BDD Bks Young Read.

Bauer, Marion Dane. An Early Winter. LC 98-54975. 128p. (J). (gr. 5-9). 1999. 15.00 (*0-395-90372-6*, Clarion Bks) HM.

***Bauer, Marion Dane.** A Frog's Best Friend. LC 00-36986. (Illus.). (J). 2002. write for info. (*0-8234-1501-5*) Holiday.

Bauer, Marion Dane. Ghost Eye. 112p. (J). (gr. 2-6). 1992. 13.95 (*0-590-45298-3*, Scholastic Hardcover) Scholastic Inc.

— Ghost Eye. (J). 1992. 8.09 (*0-606-07561-5*, Pub. by Turtleback) Demco.

— Ghost Eye. abr. ed. 96p. (J). (gr. 2-6). 1995. pap. 3.50 (*0-590-45299-1*) Scholastic Inc.

— If You Were Born a Kitten. LC 96-7408. (Illus.). 32p. (J). (ps up). 1997. per. 16.00 (*0-689-80111-4*) S&S Bks Yung.

— Jason's Bears. LC 98-52968. (Illus.). 32p. (J). (ps-3). 2000. 14.99 (*0-7868-0356-8*, Pub. by Hyperion) Time Warner.

— Jason's Bears. LC 98-52968. (Illus.). 32p. (J). (ps-3). 2000. lib. bdg. 15.49 (*0-7868-2303-8*, Pub. by Hyprn Child) Time Warner.

— On My Honor. 96p. (J). (gr. k-6). 1987. pap. 4.99 (*0-440-46633-4*, YB BDD) BDD Bks Young Read.

— On My Honor. LC 86-2679. 96p. (J). (gr. 4-7). 1986. 15.00 (*0-89919-439-7*, Clarion Bks) HM.

Bauer, Marion Dane. On My Honor. 90p. (J). (gr. 5-6). pap. 4.50 (*0-8072-1455-8*) Listening Lib.

— On My Honor. (J). 1986. 9.60 (*0-606-03630-X*, Pub. by Turtleback) Demco.

Bauer, Marion Dane. Our Stories: A Fiction Workshop for Young Authors. 208p. (YA). 1996. 14.95 (*0-395-81598-3*, Pub. by Ticknor & Fields) HM.

***Bauer, Marion Dane.** Palabra de Honor. (SPA.). 1998. pap. 8.50 (*84-279-3234-0*) Noguer Edit.

Bauer, Marion Dane. A Question of Trust. 128p. (YA). (gr. 4 up). 1994. 14.95 (*0-590-47915-6*, Scholastic Hardcover) Scholastic Inc.

— A Question of Trust. (YA). (gr. 4 up). 1994. 8.09 (*0-606-08591-2*, Pub. by Turtleback) Demco.

— A Taste of Smoke. 112p. (J). (gr. 4-7). 1995. pap. 3.99 (*0-440-41034-7*) Dell.

— A Taste of Smoke. LC 92-32585. 112p. (YA). (gr. 5 up). 1993. 14.95 (*0-395-64341-4*, Clarion Bks) HM.

— A Taste of Smoke. (J). 1995. 9.09 (*0-606-08269-7*, Pub. by Turtleback) Demco.

— Te Lo Prometo (On My Honor) (SPA.). (J). 1996. pap. text 7.95 (*84-279-3190-5*) Lectorum Pubns.

— Te Lo Prometo (On My Honor) (J). 1994. 13.15 (*0-606-10514-X*, Pub. by Turtleback) Demco.

— Touch the Moon. LC 87-663. (Illus.). 96p. (J). (gr. 4-7). 1987. 15.00 (*0-89919-526-1*, Clarion Bks) HM.

— What's Your Story? A Young Person's Guide to Writing Fiction. 144p. (YA). (gr. 5 up). 1992. 15.00 (*0-395-57781-0*, Clarion Bks); pap. 6.95 (*0-395-57780-2*, Clarion Bks) HM.

— When I Go Camping with Grandma. LC 93-33809. (Illus.). 32p. (J). (ps-3). 1997. 15.95 (*0-8167-3448-8*) BrdgeWater.

— When I Go Camping with Grandma. LC 93-33809. (Illus.). 32p. (J). (ps-3). 1996. pap. 4.95 (*0-8167-3449-6*) Troll Communs.

— When I Go Camping with Grandma. LC 93-33809. 1996. 10.15 (*0-606-10057-1*, Pub. by Turtleback) Demco.

— A Writer's Story: From Life to Fiction. LC 94-48800. 160p. (YA). (gr. 5 up). 1995. 14.95 (*0-395-72094-X*, Clarion Bks); pap. 6.95 (*0-395-75053-9*, Clarion Bks) HM.

Bauer, Marion Dane, compiled by. Our Stories: A Fiction Workshop for Young Authors. 208p. (J). (gr. 5). 1996. pap. 6.95 (*0-395-81599-1*) HM.

Bauer, Marion Dane, ed. Am I Blue: Coming Out from the Silence. LC 93-29574. (Trophy Bk.). 288p. (J). (gr. 12 up). 1995. pap. 5.95 (*0-06-440587-7*, HarpTrophy) HarpC Child Bks.

Bauer, Mark S. & McBride, Linda. Structured Group Psychotherapy for Bipolar Disorder: The Life Goals Program. (Illus.). 280p. (Orig.). 1996. 43.95 (*0-8261-9300-5*) Springer Pub.

Bauer, Mary Anne. Back to School: A Survival Guide for Parents. 40p. 1987. pap. 3.95 (*0-317-61668-4*) M A Bauer.

— Simply Entertaining. 180p. 1985. pap. 8.95 (*0-9613619-1-3*); spiral bd. 10.95 (*0-9613619-2-1*) M A Bauer.

Bauer, Max. Precious Stones Vol. 1: A Popular Account of Their Characters, Occurrence & Applications. Spencer, L. J., tr. (Illus.). (C). 1968. pap. 10.95 (*0-486-21910-0*) Dover.

— Precious Stones Vol. 2: A Popular Account of Their Characters, Occurrence & Applications. Spencer, L. J., tr. (Illus.). (C). 1968. pap. 12.95 (*0-486-21911-9*) Dover.

***Bauer, Michael.** The Secrets of Success Cookbook: Signature Dishes & Insider Tips from San Francisco's Best Restaurants. 2000. pap. 18.95 (*0-8118-2723-2*) Chronicle Bks.

— The Secrets of Success Cookbook: Signature Recipes & Insider Tips from San Francisco's Best Restaurants. LC 99-53772. 429p. 2000. pap. 19.95 (*0-8118-2502-7*) Chronicle Bks.

Bauer, Michael & Irwin, Fran, eds. The San Francisco Chronicle Cookbook. LC 96-26460. (Illus.). 448p. 1997. pap. 18.95 (*0-8118-1445-9*) Chronicle Bks.

Bauer, Nancy. The Irrational Doorways of Mr. Gerard. LC 94-214721. 321p. 1994. pap. 14.95 (*0-86492-174-8*) Goose Ln Eds.

— Samara the Wholehearted. 163p. 1991. pap. 12.95 (*0-86492-103-9*, Pub. by Goose Ln Edits) Genl Dist Srvs.

Bauer, Nona K. The Proper Care of Golden Retrievers. AKC Rank No. 4. (Illus.). 256p. 1996. 16.95 (*0-7938-2082-0*, TW143) TFH Pubns.

— World of Golden Retriever. (Illus.). 480p. 1993. 79.95 (*0-86622-694-X*, TS197) TFH Pubns.

***Bauer, Nona Kilgore.** Golden Retrievers for Dummies. (For Dummies (Lifestyles) Ser.). (Illus.). 334p. 2000. pap. 15.99 (*0-7645-5267-8*) IDG Bks.

Bauer, Nona Kilgore, see Kilgore Bauer, Nona.

Bauer, Norma T. The Housewife Dilemma: Positive Perspectives for Reluctant Homemakers. (Illus.). 100p. (Orig.). 1988. pap. 5.00 (*0-9624340-0-0*) N T Bauer.

***Bauer, Otto.** Question of Nationalities & Social Democracy. Nimni, Ephraim J., ed. 2000. 60.00 (*0-8166-3265-0*) U of Minn Pr.

Bauer, Otto F. Fundamentals of Debate: Theory & Practice. 2nd rev. ed. xli, 203p. 1999. pap. text 18.95 (*0-9659052-1-7*) Rockbrook Pr.

— Lower Moments in Higher Education. (Illus.). x, 155p. (Orig.). 1997. pap. 11.95 (*0-9659052-0-9*) Rockbrook Pr.

Bauer, P., et al, eds. Mathematical Statistics & Probability Theory: Statistical Inference & Methods, Vol. B. (C). 1987. text 166.50 (*90-277-2581-0*) Kluwer Academic.

Bauer, P. W., et al, eds. Geology of the Santa Fe Region. (Guidebook Ser.: No. 46). (Illus.). 338p. 1995. pap. 60.00 (*1-58546-081-8*) NMex Geol Soc.

— Tectonic Development of the Southern Sangre de Cristo Mountains, New Mexico. (Guidebook Ser.: No. 41). (Illus.). 450p. 1990. 55.00 (*1-58546-076-1*) NMex Geol Soc.

Bauer, Pamela. Babe in the Woods. (Superromance Ser.: No. 792). 1998. per. 4.25 (*0-373-70792-4*, 1-70792-6) Harlequin Bks.

***Bauer, Pamela.** Corporate Cowboy. (American Romance Ser.: Vol. 814). 2000. per. 4.25 (*0-373-16814-4*) Harlequin Bks.

Bauer, Pamela. Daddy's Home. (Superromance Ser.). 1999. mass mkt. 4.25 (*0-373-70863-7*, 1-70863-5) Harlequin Bks.

— Fancy's Baby. 1997. per. 4.50 (*0-373-82556-0*, 1-82556-1) Harlequin Bks.

— I Do, I Do. 1994. per. 3.50 (*0-373-70605-7*, 1-70605-0) Harlequin Bks.

— Mail Order Cowboy. (American Romance Ser.). 1998. per. 3.99 (*0-373-16718-0*, 1-16718-8) Harlequin Bks.

— Merry's Christmas. LC 95-22605. 299p. 1995. per. 3.75 (*0-373-70670-7*, 1-70670-4) Harlequin Bks.

— The Model Bride. (Superromance Ser.). 1993. mass mkt. 3.39 (*0-373-70548-4*, 1-70548-2) Harlequin Bks.

— The Pick-Up Man. (American Romance Ser.). 1997. per. 3.75 (*0-373-16668-0*, 1-16668-5) Harlequin Bks.

***Bauer, Pamela.** Saving Christmas, 803. (American Romance Ser.). 1999. mass mkt. 3.99 (*0-373-16803-9*) Harlequin Bks.

— Taming the Boss. (Romance Ser.: Vol. 359). 2000. per. 3.50 (*0-373-03598-5*) Harlequin Bks.

— That Summer Thing. (Superromance Ser.). 2000. mass mkt. 4.50 (*0-373-70930-7*, 1-70930-2) Harlequin Bks.

Bauer, Pamela & Kaye, Judy. Almost a Father. (Romance Ser.). 1998. per. 3.50 (*0-373-03506-3*, 1-03506-2) Harlequin Bks.

— Almost a Father (Kids & Kisses) large type ed. (Large Print Ser.). 1998. per. 3.50 (*0-373-15752-5*, Harlequin) Harlequin Bks.

— Make-Believe Mother. large type ed. Vol. 432. 250p. 1999. per. 3.50 (*0-373-15832-7*, 1-15832-8, Mira Bks) Harlequin Bks.

— Make-Believe Mother: Kids & Kisses. (Kids & Kisses Ser.). 1998. per. 3.50 (*0-373-03538-1*, 1-03538-5, Mira Bks) Harlequin Bks.

— Make-Believe Mother: Kids & Kisses. large type ed. (Larger Print Ser.). 1999. per. 3.50 (*0-373-15784-3*, 1-15784-1) Harlequin Bks.

Bauer, Pamela, jt. auth. see Kaye, Judy.

Bauer, Parker, jt. auth. see Sternberg, Dick.

Bauer, Patricia M. So That's Who You Used to Be! A Reunion Planning Guide. LC 95-94014. (Illus.). 169p. (Orig.). 1995. pap. 18.95 (*0-9646152-0-7*) P M Bauer.

Bauer, Paul, jt. auth. see Robinson, Frazier.

Bauer, Paul D. & Robinson, Frazier. Catching Dreams: My Life in the Negro Baseball Leagues. LC 98-51650. 256p. 1999. 27.95 (*0-8156-0563-3*) Syracuse U Pr.

Bauer, Paul E. & Collicott, Howard E., eds. Entry Vehicle Heating & Thermal Protection System. LC 83-9219. (PAAS Ser.: Vol. 85). 556p. 1983. 65.95 (*0-915928-74-4*, V-85) AIAA.

***Bauer, Peggy & Bauer, Erwin.** Glacier Bay: The Wild Beauty of Glacier Bay National Park. 75p. 2001. pap. 14.95 (*1-57061-210-2*) Sasquatch Bks.

Bauer, Peggy & Bauer, Erwin A., photos by. Wild Kittens. (Illus.). 80p. 1995. pap. 10.95 (*0-8118-1012-7*) Chronicle Bks.

— Wild Puppies. (Illus.). 80p. 1995. pap. 10.95 (*0-8118-1039-9*) Chronicle Bks.

Bauer, Peggy, jt. auth. see Bauer, Erwin.

Bauer, Peggy, jt. auth. see Bauer, Erwin A.

Bauer, Peggy, jt. photos by see Bauer, Erwin A.

Bauer, Peter T. Development Aid: End it or Mend It. LC 93-8145. (Occasional Papers - International Center for Economic Growth: No. 43). 1993. pap. 9.95 (*1-55815-276-8*) ICS Pr.

— The Development Frontier: Essays in Applied Economics. LC 90-5124. (Illus.). 248p. 1991. 37.95 (*0-674-20033-0*, BAUDEV) HUP.

— Economic Analysis & Policy in Underdeveloped Countries, 4. LC 81-13361. (Duke University Commonwealth-Studies Center Publication Ser.: No. 4). 145p. 1981. reprint ed. lib. bdg. 49.75 (*0-313-23272-5*, BACA, Greenwood Pr) Greenwood.

— Equality, the Third World & Economic Delusion. 303p. 1983. pap. 17.95 (*0-674-25986-6*) HUP.

— Reality & Rhetoric. 192p. 1986. pap. 15.00 (*0-674-74947-2*) HUP.

— Reality & Rhetoric: Studies in the Economics of Development. 192p. 1984. 27.50 (*0-674-74946-4*) HUP.

— West African Trade: A Study of Competition, Oligopoly & Monopoly in a Changing Economy. LC 67-19585. (Reprints of Economic Classics Ser.). xix, 450p. 1967. reprint ed. 49.50 (*0-678-06510-1*) Kelley.

Bauer, R., et al, eds. Atlas of Hip Surgery. LC 96-130091. (Illus.). 334p. 1996. 225.00 (*0-86577-601-6*) Thieme Med Pubs.

— Atlas of Spinal Operations. LC 93-37755. (Illus.). 1993. 225.00 (*0-86577-496-X*) Thieme Med Pubs.

Bauer, R. & Koslowski, H. J. Chemiefaser-Lexikon. 10th ed. (GER.). 300p. 1993. 150.00 (*0-8288-5296-0*, M7318) Fr & Eur.

Bauer, Raymond A. The New Man in Soviet Psychology. LC 52-5385. (Harvard University, Russian Research Center Studies: No. 7). 255p. reprint ed. pap. 79.10 (*0-608-30588-X*, 201768300007) Bks Demand.

Bauer, Raymond A. & Fenn, Dan H., Jr. The Corporate Social Audit. LC 72-83832. (Social Science Frontiers Ser.). 109p. 1977. pap. 16.95 (*0-87154-103-3*) Russell Sage.

Bauer, Raymond A. & Loeschen, R. Chemistry for the Allied Health Sciences. 1980. 28.95 (*0-685-03784-3*); student ed. 16.95 (*0-685-03785-1*); student ed. 10.95 (*0-685-03786-X*) P-H.

Bauer, Raymond A. & Wasiolek, Edward. Nine Soviet Portraits. LC 79-4609. (Illus.). 190p. 1979. reprint ed. lib. bdg. 55.00 (*0-313-20929-4*, BANS, Greenwood Pr) Greenwood.

Bauer, Raymond A., et al. How the Soviet System Works: Cultural, Psychological, & Social Themes. LC 56-8549. (Russian Research Center Studies: Vol. 24, No. 1). 288p. reprint ed. pap. 89.30 (*0-7837-2222-2*, 205731200004) Bks Demand.

Bauer, Raymond B., jt. ed. see Berguer, Ramon.

Bauer, Raymond T. & Martin, Joel W. Crustacean Sexual Biology. 1991. text 95.50 (*0-231-06880-8*) Col U Pr.

Bauer, Rebecca H. Seasons of Praise. LC 96-226283. 239p. 1996. 18.99 (*1-56476-582-2*, 6-3582, Victor Bks) Chariot Victor.

— The 25 Days of Christmas. (Illus.). 144p. 1994. 17.99 (*1-56476-417-6*, 6-3417, Victor Bks) Chariot Victor.

Bauer, Richard E. The Spirit of the Guard. 122p. 1981. pap. 7.95 (*0-89279-071-7*) R E Bauer.

Bauer, Richard J., Jr. Genetic Algorithms & Investment Strategies: An Alternative Approach to Neural Networks & Chaos Theory. (Finance Editions Ser.). 320p. 1994. 65.00 (*0-471-57679-4*) Wiley.

Bauer, Richard J. & Dahlquist, Julie R. Technical Markets Indicators: Analysis & Performance. LC 98-23564. (Trading Advantage Ser.). 426p. 1998. 69.95 (*0-471-19721-1*) Wiley.

Bauer, Robert. The New Catalogue of Historical Records, 1898 to 1908-09. 494p. 1993. reprint ed. lib. bdg. 99.00 (*0-7812-9702-8*) Rprt Serv.

Bauer, Robert A., ed. The Austrian Solution: International Conflict & Cooperation. LC 81-21916. 238p. reprint ed. pap. 73.80 (*0-8357-2704-1*, 203981700013) Bks Demand.

— The Interaction of Economics & Foreign Policy. LC 75-2243. 166p. reprint ed. pap. 51.50 (*0-608-17031-3*, 202772300056) Bks Demand.

— The United States in World Affairs: Leadership, Partnership, or Disengagement. LC 74-14990. (Essays on Alternatives of U. S. Foreign Policy Ser.). 144p. reprint ed. pap. 44.70 (*0-608-17019-4*, 202772400056) Bks Demand.

Bauer, Robert F. Paying the Political Price: A Handbook on Political Reform. (Orig.). 1996. pap. write for info. (*1-879650-02-9*) Perkins Coie.

Bauer, Robert S., jt. auth. see Benedict, Paul K.

Bauer, Robert T. & Barber, Maryann. Exploring Microsoft Word 7.0 for Windows 95. LC 96-128076. 384p. 1995. spiral bd. 37.33 (*0-13-504044-2*) P-H.

Bauer, Roger. Inevitabilis Vis Fatorum: Der Triumph des Schicksalsdramas Auf der Europaischen Buhne um 1800 Herausgegeben von Roger Bauer in Verbindung Mit Michael de Graat und Johannes von Schlebrugge. (GER.). 269p. 1990. 22.95 (*3-261-04112-9*) P Lang Pubng.

Bauer, Ron. Easy DOS It! 4th rev. ed. (Illus.). 78p. 1988. pap. 7.50 (*0-942019-04-0*) Easy Way Pr.

— The Easy Modem Book. (Illus.). (Orig.). 1987. pap. 5.00 (*0-942019-02-4*) Easy Way Pr.

— Hard DOS It! 2nd rev. ed. (Illus.). 104p. 1988. pap. 7.50 (*0-942019-05-9*) Easy Way Pr.

— Ron Bauer's Easy DOS It! 5th rev. ed. Trottier, Ann, ed. (Easy Way Ser.: Vol. 1). (Illus.). 160p. 1992. pap. 14.95 (*0-942019-10-5*) Easy Way Pr.

Bauer, Ronald S., ed. Epoxy Resin Chemistry II. LC 83-6385. (ACS Symposium Ser.: No. 221). 300p. 1983. lib. bdg. 43.95 (*0-8412-0777-1*) Am Chemical.

— Epoxy Resin Chemistry II: Based on a Symposium. LC 83-6385. (ACS Symposium Ser.: No. 221). 320p. 1983. reprint ed. pap. 99.20 (*0-608-04335-4*, 206511500001) Bks Demand.

Bauer, Roy, jt. auth. see Tang, Victor.

Bauer, Roy A., et al. The Silverlake Project: Transformation at IBM. (Illus.). 240p. 1992. 30.00 (*0-19-506754-1*) OUP.

Bauer, Rudloph, jt. ed. see Lawson, Larry D.

Bauer, Rudolf. Operative Approaches in Orthopedic Surgery & Traumatology. Sharon, Gerhard S., tr. from GRE. 334p. 1988. 205.00 (*0-86577-265-7*) Thieme Med Pubs.

***Bauer, Russell.** Bear Tracks: The Story of the Rushin' Bear as Told by the Bear Himself. deluxe ed. 218p. 1999. pap. 14.95 (*0-935680-62-4*) Kentucke Imprints.

Bauer, S. Wise. The Revolt. 425p. 1996. pap. 12.99 (*0-8499-3935-6*) Word Pub.

Bauer, Seth. Walking to Fitness. (Illus.). 128p. (Orig.). 1991. pap. 8.95 (*0-9630398-0-6*) Walking.

Bauer, Sharon A. & Bauer, William E., eds. Life Capsule: Preserving the Past for the Future. (Illus.). vi, 182p. 1999. pap. 29.50 (*0-9659729-0-9*) K & J Pub.

Bauer Staff, ed. How to Skip Stones: 43 More of Life's Forgotten Pleasures. (Illus.). 96p. (J). 1998. pap. 9.70 (*0-7868-8376-6*, Pub. by Hyperion) Time Warner.

Bauer, Stanley, contrib. by. Protection of Laboratory Workers from Infectious Disease Transmitted by Blood, Body Fluids, & Tissue: Tentative Guideline (1991) 3rd ed. 1991. 95.00 (*0-614-20212-4*, M29-T2) NCCLS.

Bauer, Stephen M. At Ease in the White House: The Uninhibited Memoirs of a Presidential Social Aide. 1991. 19.95 (*1-55972-061-1*, Birch Ln Pr) Carol Pub Group.

— How to Sell to the United States Government: Marketing Goods & Services to America's Greatest Customers. LC 93-40571. 1994. pap. 12.95 (*0-8065-1489-2*, Citadel Pr) Carol Pub Group.

Bauer, Steven. Steven Spielberg's Amazing Stories. 21.95 (*0-8488-0732-4*) Amereon Ltd.

An Asterisk (*) at the beginning of an entry indicates that the title is appearing for the first time.

— The Strange & Wonderful Tale of Robert McDoodle: The Boy Who Wanted to Be a Dog. LC 96-35360. (Illus.). 32p. (J). (gr. k-3). 1999. 16.00 (*0-689-80619-1*) S&S Bks Yung.

Bauer, Stuart B., jt. auth. see Gonzales, Edmond T.

Bauer, Susan W. Though the Darkness Hide Thee. LC 98-10258. 400p. 1998. pap. 11.99 (*1-57673-237-1*, Multnomah Fiction) Multnomah Pubs.

Bauer, Susan Wise & Wise, Jessie. The Well Trained Mind: A Guide to Classical Education at Home. LC 99-18915. 736p. 1999. text 35.00 (*0-393-04752-0*) Norton.

Bauer, Tammy L., ed. UNIX System Price Performance Guide: Winter 1996. (Illus.). 175p. (Orig.). 1995. pap. 39.95 (*1-881351-18-1*) AIM Tech.

Bauer-Tornack, Gunther. Sozialgestalt und Recht in der Kirche: Eine Untersuchung Zum Verhaltnis von Karl Barth und Erik Wolf. (Europaische Hochschulschriften Ser.: Reihe 23, Bd. 542). (GER.). 478p. 1996. 76.95 (*3-631-48531-X*) P Lang Pubng.

Bauer, Tricia. Boondocking. LC 98-50897. 1999. pap. 11.95 (*0-312-19839-6*) St Martin.

— Boondocking: A Novel. LC 97-13325. 227p. 1997. 21.95 (*1-882593-19-7*) Bridge Wrks.

***Bauer, Tricia.** Hollywood & Hardwood. 192p. 2000. pap. 11.95 (*0-312-26337-6*) St Martin.

Bauer, Tricia. Hollywood & Hardwood: A Novel. LC 98-43998. 182p. 1999. 22.95 (*1-882593-26-X*) Bridge Wrks.

***Bauer, Tricia.** Shelterbelt. 2000. 24.95 (*0-312-26647-2*) St Martin.

Bauer, Tricia. Working Women: And Other Stories. LC 95-14083. 204p. 1995. 19.95 (*1-882593-11-1*) Bridge Wrks.

Bauer, Vera, tr. see Gildemeister, Heide.

Bauer, W. & Mignerey, A. Advances in Nuclear Dynamics: Proceedings of the 11th Winter Workshop on Nuclear Dynamics Held in Key West, Florida, February 1-3, 1995, Vol. 1. LC 96-18856. (Illus.). 245p. (C). 1996. text 107.00 (*0-306-45296-0*, Kluwer Plenum) Kluwer Academic.

— Advances in Nuclear Dynamics: Proceedings of the 13th Winter Workshop Held in Marathon, Florida, February 1-8, 1997, Vol. 3. LC 97-40605. 280p. (C). 1998. text 95.00 (*0-306-45719-9*, Kluwer Plenum) Kluwer Academic.

Bauer, W. & Ritter, H.-G., eds. Advances in Nuclear Dynamics 4. LC 98-40689. (Illus.). 388p. (C). 1998. text 148.00 (*0-306-46036-X*, Kluwer Plenum) Kluwer Academic.

Bauer, Walter. Griechisch-Deutsches Woerterbuch zu den Schriften des Neuen Testaments und der Uebrigen Urchristlichen Literatur. 6th rev. ed. (GER & GRE.). 1988. 121.55 (*3-11-010647-7*) De Gruyter.

— Orthodoxy & Heresy in Earliest Christianity. LC 71-141252. 352p. reprint ed. pap. 109.20 (*0-608-17174-3*, 202787600056) Bks Demand.

— Orthodoxy & Heresy in Earliest Christianity. Kraft, Robert & Krodel, Gerhard A., eds. Philadelphia Seminar on Christian Origins Staff, tr. from GEH. 352p. 1996. reprint ed. pap. 24.00 (*0-9623642-7-4*) Sigler Pr.

Bauer, Walter, et al, eds. A Greek-English Lexicon of the New Testament & Other Early Christian Literature. 2nd rev. ed. Arndt, William F., tr. from GER. LC 78-14293. (ENG & GRE.). 944p. 1979. 55.00 (*0-226-03932-3*) U Ch Pr.

Bauer, Walter K. A Century of Musical Humor & Show Business Wit. Levine, Norman, ed. LC 88-90883. (Illus.). iv, 52p. (Orig.). 1988. pap. text 6.00 (*0-9614120-9-7*) Plucked.

Bauer, Wilhelm. Der Altere Pythagoreismus. (Berner Studien Zur Philosophie und Ihrer Geschichte Ser.: Bd. VIII). viii, 232p. 1976. reprint ed. 40.00 (*3-487-05553-8*) G Olms Pubs.

Bauer, William B. Brethen of the Brule. rev. ed. LC 95-94071. (Illus.). 208p. 1995. pap. 14.95 (*0-9640154-0-4*) Brother Bills.

— Out of Dr. Bill's Black Bag: From Northern Wisconsin . . . a Country Doctor Looks Back (1941-1991) LC 94-94225. 315p. (Orig.). 1994. pap. text 19.95 (*0-9640154-1-2*) Brother Bills.

Bauer, William E., jt. ed. see Bauer, Sharon A.

Bauer, William H., ed. Manual of Philatelic Judging: How Exhibits Are Judged. 4th rev. ed. (Illus.). 88p. 1999. pap. text 12.00 (*0-933580-21-5*) Am Philatelic Society.

Bauer, William H., et al. Colorado Post Offices, 1859-1989. LC 90-34759. (Illus.). 280p. 1990. 19.95 (*0-918654-42-4*) CO RR Mus.

Bauer, William H., jt. ed. see APS Judges Accreditation Committee Staff.

***Bauer, Wolfgang.** Dark Matter. 256p. 1999. 29.95 (*0-7869-1433-5*) Random Bks Yng Read.

Bauer, Wolfgang. The Feverhead. 112p. 1993. reprint ed. pap. 12.99 (*0-947757-65-1*, Pub. by Atlas Pr) Serpents Tail.

— German Economic Policy. 1982. lib. bdg. 250.00 (*0-87700-348-3*) Revisionist Pr.

— The Golden Caskets: Chinese Novellas of Two Millennia. Levenson, Christopher & Franke, Herbert, trs. from GER. LC 77-26034. Orig. Title: Die Goldeme Truhe. (Illus.). 391p. 1978. reprint ed. lib. bdg. 35.00 (*0-313-20091-2*, BAGO, Greenwood Pr) Greenwood.

— Griechisch-Deutsch Woerterbuch der Neuen Testament. 6th ed. (GER & GRE.). 1888p. 1988. 250.00 (*0-614-00395-4*) Fr & Eur.

— Lexikon der Symbole. 14th ed. (GER.). 580p. 1993. 39.95 (*0-7859-8551-4*, 3921695546) Fr & Eur.

Bauer, Wolfgang, ed. Advances in Nuclear Dynamics. 300p. (C). 1991. text 89.00 (*981-02-0696-8*) World Scientific Pub.

Bauer, Wolfgang & Back, B. B. Advances in Nuclear Dynamics: Proceedings of the 8th Winter Workshop on Nuclear Dynamics. 300p. 1992. text 95.00 (*981-02-1036-1*) World Scientific Pub.

Bauer, Wolfgang & Westfall, Gary D., eds. Advances in Nuclear Dynamics, Vol. 2. LC 96-28266. (Illus.). 417p. (C). 1996. text 150.00 (*0-306-45396-7*, Kluwer Plenum) Kluwer Academic.

Bauer, Wolfgang, et al. Meyers Enzyklopaedisches Lexikon Vol. 5: Bud-Con. 9th ed. (GER.). 872p. 1971. 275.00 (*0-7859-6896-2*, 3411012552) Fr & Eur.

Bauer, Yehuda. American Jewry & the Holocaust: The American Jewish Joint Distribution Committee, 1939-1945. LC 80-26035. 524p. 1981. 42.95 (*0-8143-1672-7*) Wayne St U Pr.

— A History of the Holocaust. (Adult Titles Ser.). 398p. 1982. pap. 16.95 (*0-531-05641-4*) Watts.

— The Jewish Emergence from Powerlessness. LC 78-25830. 103p. reprint ed. pap. 32.00 (*0-608-12851-1*, 202359200033) Bks Demand.

— Jewish Reactions to the Holocaust. 226p. 1989. pap. 12.00 (*965-05-0482-6*, Pub. by Israel Ministry Def) Gefen Bks.

— Jews for Sale? Nazi-Jewish Negotiations, 1933-1945. 328p. 1996. pap. 17.00 (*0-300-06852-2*) Yale U Pr.

— Jews for Sale? Nazi-Jewish Negotiations, 1939-1945. LC 94-27780. 328p. 1995. 37.50 (*0-300-05913-2*) Yale U Pr.

***Bauer, Yehuda.** Rethinking the Holocaust. 320p. 2000. 29.95 (*0-300-08256-8*) Yale U Pr.

Bauer, Yehuda. They Chose Life: Jewish Resistance in the Holocaust. LC 73-89085. (Illus.). 64p. (Orig.). 1973. pap. 2.00 (*0-87495-000-7*) Am Jewish Comm.

Bauer, Yehuda, et al. Remembering for the Future: Working Papers & Addenda, 3 vols., Set. (Illus.). 3250p. 1989. 609.25 (*0-08-036754-2*, Pergamon Pr) Elsevier.

Bauerfeind, Jack C., ed. Carotenoid As Colorants & Vitamin A Precursors: Technological & Nutritional Applications. LC 80-984. (Food Science & Technology Ser.). 1981. text 194.00 (*0-12-082850-2*) Acad Pr.

Bauerfeld, Wulf, et al, eds. Broadband Islands '94: Connecting with the End User: Proceedings of the Third International Conference on Broadband Islands, Hamburg, Germany, 7-9 June 1994. LC 94-13848. 494p. 1994. 190.00 (*0-444-81905-3*, North Holland) Elsevier.

Bauerie, R., et al, eds. Semantics from Different Points of View. (Language & Communication Ser.: Vol. 6). (Illus.). 1979. 54.95 (*0-387-09676-0*) Spr-Verlag.

Bauerlain, Mark, ed. see Riddel, Joseph N.

***Bauerle, D.** Laser Processing & Chemistry. 3rd enl. rev. ed. (Advanced Texts in Physics Ser.). 800p. 2000. (*3-540-66891-8*) Spr-Verlag.

Bauerle, Dieter. Chemical Processing with Lasers. (Materials Science Ser.: Vol. 1). (Illus.). 255p. 1986. 71.95 (*0-387-17147-9*) Spr-Verlag.

— Laser Processing & Chemistry. LC 96-5. (Illus.). 600p. 1996. 99.50 (*3-540-60541-X*) Spr-Verlag.

Bauerle, E. G. & Ten Kroode, F. Lie Algebras Pt. 2: Finite & Infinite Dimensional Lie Algebras & Applications in Physics. LC 98-163919. 564p. 1997. 152.50 (*0-444-82836-2*, North Holland) Elsevier.

Bauerle, G. G. & De Kerf, E. A. Lie Algebras Pt. 1: Finite & Infinite Dimensional Lie Algebras & Applications in Physics. (Studies in Mathematical Physics: Vol. 1). xvi, 394p. 1990. 135.50 (*0-444-88776-8*, North Holland) Elsevier.

Bauerle, P. A., ed. Inducible Gene Expression, 2, Set. LC 94-27957. (Progress in Gene Expression Ser.). 500p. 1994. 154.00 (*0-8176-3800-8*) Birkhauser.

— Inducible Gene Expression Vol. 1: Environmental Stresses & Nutrients, 2, 1. LC 94-27957. xii, 284p. 1994. 93.50 (*0-8176-3728-1*) Birkhauser.

— Inducible Gene Expression Vol. 2: Hormonal Signals, 2, 2. LC 94-27957. xii, 284p. 1994. 93.50 (*0-8176-3734-6*) Birkhauser.

Bauerle, Patrick & Landa, Norbert. The Cell Works. (Microexplorers Ser.). (Illus.). 42p. (J). (gr. 3-7). 1997. 11.95 (*0-7641-5052-9*) Barron.

— Your Body's Heroes & Villains. (Microexplorers Ser.). (Illus.). 42p. (J). (gr. 3-7). 1997. 11.95 (*0-7641-5051-0*) Barron.

Bauerle, Rainer, et al, eds. Meaning, Use, & Interpretation of Language. 1983. 150.00 (*3-11-008901-7*) De Gruyter.

Bauerle, Ruth H., ed. Picking up Airs: Hearing the Music in Joyce's Text. LC 92-23294. 216p. (C). 1993. text 34.95 (*0-252-01984-9*) U of Ill Pr.

Bauerle, Ruth H., jt. auth. see Hodgart, Matthew J.

Bauerlein, Mark. Literary Criticism: An Autopsy. (Critical Authors & Issues Ser.). 176p. (C). 1997. pap. 16.50 (*0-8122-1625-3*) U of Pa Pr.

— Literary Criticism: An Autopsy. LC 97-14199. (C). (gr. 13). 1997. text 36.50 (*0-8122-3411-1*) U of Pa Pr.

— The Pragmatic Mind: Emerson, James, Peirce, & the Psychology of Belief. LC 97-6289. 176p. 1997. lib. bdg. 45.95 (*0-8223-2004-5*) Duke.

— The Pragmatic Mind: Emerson, James, Peirce, & the Psychology of Belief. LC 97-6289. xix, 136p. 1997. pap. text 15.95 (*0-8223-2013-4*) Duke.

— Whitman & the American Idiom. LC 91-10929. 191p. 1991. text 27.50 (*0-8071-1681-5*) La State U Pr.

Bauermeister, Erica & Smith, Holly. Let's Hear It for the Girls: 375 Great Books for Readers 2-14. LC 96-9791. 240p. (C). 1999. pap. 10.95 (*0-14-025732-2*) Viking Penguin.

Bauermeister, Erica, et al. 500 Great Books by Women: A Reader's Guide. LC 94-15989. 400p. 1994. pap. 12.95 (*0-14-017590-3*, Viking) Viking Penguin.

Bauernfeind, A., et al, eds. Cystic Fibrosis Pulmonary Infections: Lessons from Around the World. (Respiratory Pharmacology & Pharmacotherapy Ser.). 333p. 1996. 190.00 (*0-8176-5027-X*) Birkhauser.

Bauernfeind, George. Income Taxation: Accounting Methods & Periods, 2 vols. (Tax & Estate Planning Ser.). 2496p. 1983. text 235.00 (*0-07-004096-6*) Shepards.

Bauernfeind, J. Christopher. The Safe Use of Vitamin A. Arroyave, G. et al, eds. (Illus.). 44p. (Orig.). 1980. pap. text 3.50 (*0-935368-24-8*) ILSI.

— L' Usage Prudent de la Vitamine A. Arroyave, G. et al, eds. Vincent, Marc, tr. (FRE., Illus.). 77p. (Orig.). 1984. pap. text 3.50 (*0-935368-39-6*) ILSI.

Bauernfeind, J. Christopher & Lachance, Paul A., eds. Nutrient Additions to Food: Nutritional, Technological & Regulatory Aspects. 622p. 1991. 135.00 (*0-917678-29-X*) Food & Nut Pr.

Bauers, F. William, Jr. Where There's a Will ... A Guide for the Executor or Administrator of an Estate. 268p. 1998. per. 29.95 (*0-9660611-1-X*) Edgewood Pub.

Bauers, Mary, ed. see Sverge, Rijk.

***Bauerschmidt, Frederick C.** Julian of Norwich & the Mystical Body Politic of Christ. LC 98-41339. (Studies in Spirituality & Theology). 312p. 1999. 35.00 (*0-268-01194-X*, Pub. by U of Notre Dame Pr) Chicago Distribution Ctr.

Bauersfeld, Heinrich, jt. ed. see Cobb, Paul.

Baues, Hans J. Combinatorial Homotopy & Four-Dimensional Complexes. (Expositions in Mathematics Ser.: Vol. 2). xxvii, 380p. (C). 1991. lib. bdg. 99.95 (*3-11-012488-2*) De Gruyter.

— Geometry of Loop Spaces & the Cobar Construction. LC 80-12430. (Memoirs Ser.: Vol. 25/230). 171p. 1980. pap. 17.00 (*0-8218-2230-6*, MEMO/25/230) Am Math.

***Baues, Hans J.** New Combinatorial Foundation of Homology & Homotopy: Applications to Spaces, Diagrams, Transformation Groups, Compactifications, Differential Algebras, Algebraic Theories, Simplicial Objects & Resolutions: Applications to Spaces, Diagrams, Transformation Groups, Compactifications, Differential Algebras, Algebraic Theories, Simplicial Objects & Resolutions LC 98-45574. (Springer Monographs In Mathematics). xv, 362 p. 1998. 99.00 (*3-540-64984-0*) Spr-Verlag.

Baues, Hans J., et al. Homotopy Theory & Models: Based on Lectures Held at a DMV Seminar in Blaubeuren Aubry, Marc, ed. LC 95-3636. (DMV Seminar Ser.: Bk. 24). 1995. 33.00 (*0-8176-5185-3*) Birkhauser.

Baugardner, D., jt. auth. see Elseth, Gerald D.

Baugh. United States Foreign Policymaking. (C). 1999. pap. text. write for info. (*0-15-508134-9*) Harcourt Coll Pubs.

Baugh, Albert C., ed. Chaucer's Major Poetry. (C). 1963. text 48.60 (*0-13-128223-9*) P-H.

Baugh, Albert C., et al, eds. Literary History of England. 2nd ed. (C). 1967. text, student ed. 105.00 (*0-13-537605-X*) P-H.

Baugh, Albert C. & Cable, Thomas. A History of the English Language. 4th ed. LC 92-25294. 464p. (C). 1992. 81.00 (*0-13-395708-X*) P-H.

Baugh, Alexander L. A Call to Arms: The 1838 Mormon Defense of Northern Missouri. (Dissertations in Latter-Day Saint History Ser.). 125p. Date not set. pap. 17.95 (*0-8425-2470-3*, BYU Studies) Brigham.

Baugh, Beth, ed. see Hobbs, Christopher.

Baugh, Bob. Changing Work: A Union Guide to Workplace Change. (Illus.). 112p. 1994. pap. 8.00 (*1-892075-07-5*, HRDI 006) AFL CIO.

Baugh, Bruce. America Offline: PSI Order Orgotek. (Trinity Ser.). (Illus.). 1998. pap. 17.95 (*1-56504-762-1*, 9003) White Wolf.

***Baugh, Bruce.** Blood & Silk. (World of Darkness Ser.). 2000. pap. 21.95 (*1-56504-242-5*) White Wolf.

Baugh, Bruce. Darkness Revealed: Descent into Darkness, Vol. 1. 1998. pap. text 15.95 (*1-56504-751-6*) White Wolf.

Baugh, Bruce & Cenrzyk, Mark. World of Darkness: Tokyo. (Wruith Ser.). (Illus.). 1998. pap. 18.00 (*1-56504-633-1*, 6103) White Wolf.

Baugh, Bruce & Dansky, Richard. Darkness Revealed: Ascent into Light. (Trinity Ser.: Vol. 3). (Illus.). 1998. pap. 15.95 (*1-56504-753-2*, 9103) White Wolf.

— Darkness Revealed: Passage Through Shadow. (Trinity Ser.: Vol. 2). (Illus.). 1998. pap. 15.95 (*1-56504-752-4*, 9102) White Wolf.

Baugh, Bruce & Grabowski, Geoff. Doomslayers: Into the Labyrinth. (Wruith Ser.). (Illus.). 1998. pap. 18.00 (*1-56504-635-8*, 6064) White Wolf.

Baugh, Bruce, et al. Ends of Empire. (Wruith Ser.). (Illus.). 160p. 1999. pap. 19.95 (*1-56504-618-8*, 6014) White Wolf.

***Baugh, Bruce, et al.** Hunter: The Reckoning. (Illus.). 272p. 1999. 29.95 (*1-56504-735-4*, 8100) White Wolf.

Baugh, Bruce, et al. The Thousand Hells. (Vampire Ser.). (Illus.). 128p. 1999. pap. 17.95 (*1-56504-226-3*, 2902) White Wolf.

Baugh, Bryan. Draw Future Worlds. LC 98-66657. (Illus.). 64p. (J). (gr. 3-7). 1998. pap. 7.95 (*1-56565-925-2*, 09252W, Pub. by Lowell Hse Juvenile) NTC Contemp Pub Co.

— 50 Nifty Dinosaurs to Draw. LC 99-73113. (50 Nifty Ser.). (Illus.). 80p. (J). (gr. 1-4). 1999. pap. 6.95 (*0-7373-0198-8*, 01988W) NTC Contemp Pub Co.

Baugh, Carl E. Panorama of Creation. (Illus.). 91p. 1992. pap. 7.95 (*1-879366-01-0*) Hearthstone OK.

***Baugh, Carl E.** Why Do Men Believe Evolution Against All Odds? 1999. 21.95 (*1-57558-049-7*) Hearthstone OK.

Baugh, Carl E. & Wilson, Clifford. Footprints & the Stones of Time. (Illus.). 161p. 1992. pap. 14.50 (*1-879366-17-7*) Hearthstone OK.

Baugh, Carl E. & Wilson, Clifford A. Dinosaur. 2nd ed. (Illus.). 184p. 1991. reprint ed. pap. 12.95 (*0-939497-01-8*) Promise Pub.

Baugh, Carl E., jt. auth. see Uselton, Bill.

Baugh, Carolyn, ed. see Abdallah, Fadel I.

Baugh, Carolyn, ed. see Ghazi, Abidullah & Ghazi, Tasneema.

Baugh, Carolyn, ed. see Ghazi, Suhaib.

Baugh, Carolyn, ed. see Kiswani, Sabrine.

Baugh, Christopher. Garrick & Loutherbourg. (Theatre in Focus Ser.). 1990. pap. write for info. incl. sl. (*0-85964-198-8*) Chadwyck-Healey.

Baugh, Daniel A. Naval Administration, 1715-1750. (C). 1987. 160.00 (*0-7855-3931-X*) St Mut.

Baugh, Edward, ed. see Carberry, H. D.

Baugh, G. C., ed. A History of Shropshire, Vol. IV: Agriculture, Vol. IV. (Victoria History of the Counties of England Ser.). (Illus.). 326p. 1990. 145.00 (*0-19-722775-9*) OUP.

— A History of the County of Shropshire Vol. X: Munslow Hundred & Wenlock Borough & Liberty. (Victoria History of the Counties of England Ser.). (Illus.). 542p. (C). 1999. text 120.00 (*0-19-722789-9*) OUP.

— Shropshire, Vol. III. (Victoria History of the Counties of England Ser.). (Illus.). 1979. 145.00 (*0-19-722730-9*) OUP.

Baugh, H. Dean. The McArdel Diary: Saga of an Irish American. 308p. mass mkt. 4.99 (*1-55197-035-X*) Picasso Publ.

Baugh, Jim R., jt. auth. see Neill, Robert H.

***Baugh, John.** Beyond Ebonics: Linguistic Pride & Racial Prejudice. LC 99-16833. (Illus.). 176p. 2000. 29.95 (*0-19-512046-9*) OUP.

Baugh, John. Black Street Speech: Its History, Structure, & Survival. (Texas Linguistics Ser.). 160p. (C). 1983. pap. 10.95 (*0-292-70745-2*) U of Tex Pr.

— Out of the Mouths of Slaves: African-American Language & Educational Malpractice. LC 98-28384. 200p. 1999. 25.00 (*0-292-70872-6*); pap. 12.95 (*0-292-70873-4*) U of Tex Pr.

***Baugh, Ken & Hurst, Rich.** Getting Real. LC 99-49433. 2000. pap. 13.00 (*1-57683-179-5*) NavPress.

Baugh, Kenneth, Jr. The Methodology of Herbert Blumer. (American Sociological Assn. Rose Monographs). 118p. (C). 1990. text 42.50 (*0-521-38246-7*) Cambridge U Pr.

Baugh, L. Sue. Write First-Class Memos. (Here's How Ser.). 224p. 1999. pap. 12.95 (*0-8442-2912-1*) NTC Contemp Pub Co.

Baugh, L. Sue. Essentials of English Grammar. 160p. 1992. 14.95 (*0-8442-5444-4*, Natl Textbk Co) NTC Contemp Pub Co.

— Essentials of English Grammar. 144p. 1993. pap. 6.95 (*0-8442-5445-2*, Natl Textbk Co) NTC Contemp Pub Co.

— Essentials of English Grammar: Practical Guide to the Mastery of English. 2nd ed. 160p. 1995. pap. 8.13 (*0-8442-5821-0*, 58210) NTC Contemp Pub Co.

— Everyday American English Dictionary. 406p. 1996. pap. text 5.95 (*0-8442-0337-8*) NTC Contemp Pub Co.

— Handbook for Business Writing. 2nd ed. (Handbook for...Ser.). (Illus.). 304p. 1993. 24.95 (*0-8442-3277-7*, NTC Business Bks) NTC Contemp Pub Co.

— Handbook for Business Writing. 2nd ed. (Handbook for...Ser.). 304p. 1995. pap. 14.95 (*0-8442-3278-5*, NTC Business Bks) NTC Contemp Pub Co.

— Handbook for Memo Writing. (Handbook for...Ser.). (Illus.). 224p. 1995. pap. 12.95 (*0-8442-3272-6*, NTC Business Bks) NTC Contemp Pub Co.

— Handbook for Memo Writing. (Illus.). 224p. 1995. 32.95 (*0-8442-3271-8*, 32718, NTC Business Bks) NTC Contemp Pub Co.

— Handbook for Practical Letter Writing. LC 89-64423. (Illus.). 272p. 1993. 29.95 (*0-8442-3268-8*, 32688, Natl Textbk Co) NTC Contemp Pub Co.

— Handbook for Practical Letter Writing. (Illus.). 272p. 1994. pap. 12.95 (*0-8442-3269-6*, Natl Textbk Co) NTC Contemp Pub Co.

— How to Write First-Class Letters: The Handbook for Practical Letter Writing. LC 98-19080. (Illus.). 272p. 1994. pap. 12.95 (*0-8442-4099-0*, 40990) NTC Contemp Pub Co.

— How to Write First-Class Memos: The Handbook for Practical Memo Writing. (How to Write...Ser.). (Illus.). 224p. 1995. pap. 12.95 (*0-8442-3406-0*, NTC Business Bks) NTC Contemp Pub Co.

— How to Write Term Papers & Reports. LC 89-64424. 304p. 1994. pap. 9.95 (*0-8442-5645-5*, Natl Textbk Co) NTC Contemp Pub Co.

Baugh, L. Sue. How to Write Term Papers & Reports. 2nd rev. ed. LC 96-18720. (Illus.). 304p. (C). 1996. pap. 13.69 (*0-8442-5899-7*, 58997) NTC Contemp Pub Co.

Baugh, L. Sue. Write First-Class Letters. LC 98-8252. (Here's How Ser.). 320p. 1998. pap. 16.95 (*0-8442-2487-1*) NTC Contemp Pub Co.

— Write Term Papers & Reports. (Here's How Ser.). 256p. 1999. pap. 14.95 (*0-8442-2608-4*) NTC Contemp Pub Co.

Baugh, L. Sue & Hamper, Robert J. Handbook for Writing Proposals. (Handbook for...Ser.). (Illus.). 224p. 1996. pap. 18.95 (*0-8442-3274-2*, NTC Business Bks) NTC Contemp Pub Co.

Baugh, L. Sue, et al. Handbook for Business Writing. 288p. 1992. text 19.95 (*0-8442-3148-7*, NTC Business Bks) NTC Contemp Pub Co.

— Handbook for Business Writing. 288p. 1994. pap. 12.95 (*0-8442-3149-5*, NTC Business Bks) NTC Contemp Pub Co.

— How to Write First-Class Business Correspondence: The Handbook for Business Writing. LC 97-43999. (How to Write...Ser.). 304p. 1995. pap. 14.95 (*0-8442-3405-2*, NTC Business Bks) NTC Contemp Pub Co.

— Write First-Class Business Correspondence. LC 99-13610. (Here's How Ser.). 320p. 1999. pap. 14.95 (*0-8442-2074-4*, 20744, Natl Textbk Co) NTC Contemp Pub Co.

Baugh, L. Sue, jt. auth. see Hamper, Robert J.

B

Baugh, Laura. Out of the Rough: An Intimate Portrait of Laura Baugh & Her Sobering Journey. LC 99-28337. 256p. 1999. 22.95 (*1-55853-755-4*) Rutledge Hill Pr.

Baugh, Lloyd. Imaging the Divine: Jesus & Christ Figures in Film. LC 97-2903. (Illus.). 350p. (Orig.). 1997. pap. 24.95 (*1-55612-863-0*, LL1863) Sheed & Ward WI.

*__Baugh, Mark A.__ Sports Nutrition: The Awful Truth. LC 99-35634. 174p. 2000. pap. 14.95 (*1-56825-042-8*, 042-8) Rainbow Books.

Baugh, P. J., ed. Gas Chromatography: A Practical Approach. (Practical Approach Ser.: Vol. 133). (Illus.). 448p. 1994. pap. text 55.00 (*0-19-963271-5*) OUP.

Baugh, Patricia, jt. auth. see Davis, Candace Sten.

Baugh, Phil, jt. auth. see Gillies, Alan C.

Baugh, Ruth E. Geographic Regions of California. (Illus.). 76p. (C). 1955. pap. text 7.95 (*0-87015-057-X*) Pacific Bks.

*__Baugh, S. M.__ First John Reader: Intermediate Greek Reading Notes & Grammar. LC 99-28120. 160p. 1999. pap. 18.99 (*0-87552-095-2*) P & R Pubng.

Baugh, S. M. A New Testament Greek Primer. 248p. 1995. pap. text 29.99 (*0-87552-099-5*) P & R Pubng.

Baugh, Sue. Essentials of English Grammar: A Practical Guide to Mastery of English. 2nd ed. 160p. 1994. pap. 17.44 (*0-8442-5820-2*, 58202) NTC Contemp Pub Co.

Baugh, T. G. & Ericson, J. E. Prehistoric Exchange Systems in North America. (Interdisciplinary Contributions to Archaeology Ser.). (Illus.). 476p. (C). 1994. 64.50 (*0-306-44756-8*, Plenum Trade) Perseus Pubng.

Baugh, T. G., jt. auth. see Ericson, J. E.

Baugh, Timothy G., ed. see Berta, Susan M., et al.

Baugh, Virgil E. Rendezvous at the Alamo: Highlights in the Lives of Bowie, Crockett, & Travis. LC 85-8570. (Illus.). ix, 251p. 1985. reprint ed. pap. 13.95 (*0-8032-6074-1*, Bison Books) U of Nebr Pr.

Baughan, Annabelle S., et al. Manual of Haematology. LC 85-11286. (Illus.). 274p. 1986. pap. text 19.95 (*0-443-02564-9*) Church.

Baughan, Barbara C. & Pilson, Betty A. Patrick County, Virginia Deed Index Abstracts, 1791-1850. 411p. 1997. pap. 30.00 (*1-888265-14-0*) Willow Bend.

Baughan, Brook McClintic, jt. auth. see Baughan, Kalon.

*__Baughan, Kalon & Baughan, Brook McClintic.__ Painting the Faces of Wildlife Step-by-Step. LC 99-56287. (Illus.). 128p. 2000. 28.99 (*0-89134-962-6*, North Lght Bks) F & W Pubns Inc.

Baughan, Raymond J. If the Shoe Fits: Selected Sermons. 177p. (Orig.). 1992. pap. text 10.95 (*0-9626716-2-2*) UUF Huntington.

Baughan, Rosa. Character Indicated by Handwriting. 140p. 1996. reprint ed. spiral bd. 12.00 (*0-7873-1143-X*) Hlth Research.

— The Handbook of Palmistry. 3rd rev. ed. 68p. 1996. reprint ed. spiral bd. 11.00 (*0-7873-0081-0*) Hlth Research.

— The Influence of the Stars: A Book of Old World Lore. 4th ed. 252p. 1996. reprint ed. spiral bd. 14.00 (*0-7873-0080-2*) Hlth Research.

Baughen, Michael. Breaking the Prayer Barrier: Getting Through to God. 144p. 1996. 14.99 (*0-87788-384-X*, H Shaw Pubs) Waterbrook Pr.

Baughen, Simon. Shipping Law. lxix, 396p. 1998. pap. 63.00 (*1-85941-313-7*, Pub. by Cavendish Pubng) Gaunt.

Baugher, Jacob I. Organization & Administration of Practice-Teaching in Privately Endowed Colleges of Liberal Arts. LC 72-176543. (Columbia University. Teachers College. Contributions to Education Ser.: No. 487). reprint ed. 37.50 (*0-404-55487-3*) AMS Pr.

Baugher, Joseph F. The Space-Age Solar System. LC 87-6255. 464p. 1987. pap. 86.95 (*0-471-85034-9*) Wiley.

Baugher, Robert. A Guide to Understanding Guilt During Bereavement. unabridged ed. 38p. (Orig.). 1997. pap. 5.00 (*0-9635975-1-5*) Caring People.

Baugher, Robert & Calija, Marc. A Guide for the Bereaved Survivor. rev. ed. 59p. 1991. pap. 5.00 (*0-9635975-0-7*) Caring People.

Baughman, A. J. History of Huron County: Its Progress & Development, with Biographical Sketches of Prominent Citizens of the County, 2 vols. (Illus.). 1062p. 1997. reprint ed. lib. bdg. 115.00 (*0-8328-6326-2*) Higginson Bk Co.

Baughman, A. J., ed. Centennial Biographical History of Ruhland & Ashland County, Ohio. (Illus.). 831p. 1993. reprint ed. lib. bdg. 83.00 (*0-8328-3004-6*) Higginson Bk Co.

Baughman, Cynthia, ed. Woldman's Engineering Alloys, Mat.DB. 320p. 1994. disk 369.00 (*0-614-03550-3*, 7440U) ASM Intl.

— Women on Ice: Feminist Essays on the Tonya Harding/Nancy Kerrigan Spectacle. LC 95-24887. (Illus.). 304p. (C). 1995. pap. 19.99 (*0-415-91151-6*, B7157) Routledge.

— Women on Ice: Feminist Essays on the Tonya Harding/Nancy Kerrigan Spectacle. LC 95-24887. (Illus.). 304p. (C). (gr. 13). 1995. 85.00 (*0-415-91150-8*, B7153) Routledge.

Baughman, D. Richard & Liu, Y. A. Neural Networks in Bioprocessing & Chemical Engineering. LC 95-34841. (Illus.). 488p. 1996. text, boxed set 69.95 incl. disk (*0-12-083030-2*) Acad Pr.

Baughman, Dennis D., et al. A Mile in Their Shoes. Harr, Cindy et al, eds. LC 95-4582. (Joe & Penny Heisel Ser.: United States of America Armed Forces Veterans Ser.: Vol. 2). 1995. 30.00 (*1-885851-08-1*) St Vincent Coll.

Baughman, Diane C. & Hackley, JoAnn C. Handbook for Brunner & Suddarth's Textbook of Medical-Surgical Nursing. LC 95-25922. 688p. 1995. pap. text 21.00 (*0-397-55162-2*) Lppncott W & W.

Baughman, J. Ross. Some Ancestors of the Baughman Family in America: Tracing Back Twelve Generations from Switzerland Through Virginia. LC 89-61454. (Illus.). 171p. 1994. pap. 25.00 (*0-917968-17-4*) Shenandoah Hist.

Baughman, James C. Trustees, Trusteeship, & the Public Good: Issues of Accountability for Hospitals, Museums, Universities, & Libraries. LC 86-25574. 205p. 1987. 57.95 (*0-89930-195-9*, BLT/, Quorum Bks) Greenwood.

Baughman, James L. Henry R. Luce & the Rise of the American News Media. (Twayne's 20th Century American Biography Ser.). 272p. 1987. pap. 14.95 (*0-8057-7755-5*) Macmillan.

— The Republic of Mass Culture: Journalism, Filmmaking, & Broadcasting in America since 1941. (American Moment Ser.). 256p. 1992. text 40.00 (*0-8018-4276-X*); pap. text 13.95 (*0-8018-4277-8*) Johns Hopkins.

— The Republic of Mass Culture: Journalism, Filmmaking, & Broadcasting in America since 1941. 2nd ed. LC 96-26395. (American Moment Ser.). 304p. 1997. text 40.00 (*0-8018-5520-9*); pap. text 14.95 (*0-8018-5521-7*) Johns Hopkins.

— Television's Guardians: The FCC & the Politics of Programming, 1958-1967. LC 84-13178. (Illus.). 328p. 1985. pap. 101.70 (*0-608-05199-3*, 206573600001) Bks Demand.

Baughman, James P. Charles Morgan & the Development of Southern Transportation. LC 68-17281. (Illus.). 342p. reprint ed. pap. 106.10 (*0-8357-3201-0*, 203947200012) Bks Demand.

— The Mallorys of Mystic: Six Generations in American Maritime Enterprise. LC 70-184363. (American Maritime Library: No. 4). (Illus.). 549p. reprint ed. pap. 170.20 (*0-7837-6147-3*, 204454800009) Bks Demand.

Baughman, Janet. Soaring with the Spirit. 100p. (Orig.). 1997. pap. 5.50 (*1-57502-377-6*, P01199) Morris Pubng.

Baughman, John J., ed. DePauw: A Pictorial History. (Illus.). 234p. 1987. 30.00 (*0-936631-12-0*) DePauw Univ.

Baughman, John L. Fourteen Keys to Great Truth Puzzles. LC 87-72924. 272p. 1988. pap. 12.95 (*0-87516-597-4*) DeVorss.

Baughman, John W. & McCabe, Alice S. Gwinnett County, Georgia, Deaths 1923. (Illus.). 108p. 1991. 20.00 (*0-914923-09-9*) Gwinnett Hist.

Baughman, Judith S. Facts on File Bibliography of American Fiction, 1588-1865. Bruccoli, Matthew J., ed. LC 94-26621. (Bibliography Ser.). 336p. 1992. lib. bdg. 95.00 (*0-8160-2115-5*) Facts on File.

Baughman, Judith S., jt. auth. see Bruccoli, Matthew J.

Baughman, Judith S., ed. see Bruccoli, Matthew J.

Baughman, Judith S., jt. ed. see Bruccoli, Matthew J.

Baughman, Judith S., ed. see Dickey, James.

Baughman, Judith S., ed. see Fitzgerald, F. Scott.

Baughman, Kerrie, jt. auth. see Bullough, Robert V.

*__Baughman, Lynette.__ A Spy Within. 311p. 1999. pap. 14.00 (*0-9666366-4-3*) Top Pubns.

Baughman, M. Dale. Baughman's Handbook of Humor in Education. 1974. 16.50 (*0-13-072504-8*) P-H.

Baughman, Martin L., et al. Electric Power in the United States: Models & Policy Analysis. 1979. 50.00 (*0-262-02130-7*) MIT Pr.

Baughman, Mel M. The Birder's Journal. (Illus.). 416p. 1993. pap. 14.95 (*0-8117-2514-6*) Stackpole.

*__Baughman, Mel M.__ The Birder's Journal. 2nd ed. LC 00-34428. (Illus.). 2001. pap. write for info. (*0-8117-2697-5*) Stackpole.

Baughman, Mel M., ed. see Reiger, George W.

Baughman, Melvin J., et al. Woodland Stewardship: A Practical Guide for Midwestern Landowners. 1993. pap. 14.95 (*0-9623116-6-9*) U MN Ext Serv.

Baughman, Michael. Mohawk Blood: A Native American Quest. 128p. 1995. 19.95 (*1-55821-376-7*) Lyons Pr.

— A River Seen Right: A Fly Fisherman's North Umpqua. (Illus.). 144p. 1995. 25.00 (*1-55821-421-6*) Lyons Pr.

*__Baughman, Michael & Hadella, Charlotte.__ Warm Springs Millennium: Voices from the Reservation. LC 00-21339. (Illus.). 216p. 2000. 35.00 (*0-292-70885-8*); pap. 16.95 (*0-292-70886-6*) U of Tex Pr.

*__Baughman, Michelle.__ Inspirations. 1999. pap. write for info. (*1-58235-194-5*) Watermrk Pr.

Baughman, Ray E. The Abundant Life. mass mkt. 4.99 (*0-8024-0047-7*, 73) Moody.

*__Baughman, Ray E.__ Abundant Life - Chinese Edition: Simplified Scripts. 141p. 1999. pap. 9.50 (*1-56582-111-4*) Christ Renew Min.

— Abundant Life - CRM Chinese Edition. (CHI.). 141p. 1999. pap. 9.50 (*1-56582-124-6*) Christ Renew Min.

Baughman, Ray E. La Vida Abundante. Orig. Title: The Abundant Life. (SPA.). 192p. 1981. pap. 5.99 (*0-8254-1056-8*, Edit Portavoz) Kregel.

*__Baughman, Rhonda.__ Carnal Capers in Canton, Ohio: A Bitter Harvest. 1999. pap. write for info. (*1-58235-048-5*) Watermrk Pr.

Baughman, Robert W. Kansas Post Offices. 2nd ed. LC 62-34174. (Illus.). 256p. 1977. reprint ed. pap. 6.50 (*0-87726-004-4*) Kansas St Hist.

Baughman, Rowland. Collective Bargaining Simulation. 22p. (C). 1994. 13.26 (*1-56870-155-1*) RonJon Pub.

— Organizational Behavior Lecture Notes. 64p. (C). 1993. student ed. 15.63 (*1-56870-059-8*) RonJon Pub.

*__Baughman, Steven A.__ Steve Baughman - Celtic Fingerstyle Guitar Solos. 56p. 1998. pap. 17.95 incl. audio compact disk (*0-7866-3851-6*, 97259BCD) Mel Bay.

— Steve Baughman's Celtic Guitar. 96p. 1998. pap. 22.95 incl. audio compact disk (*0-7866-2955-X*) Mel Bay.

Baughman, Steven A. & Curry, Elizabeth A., eds. Strategic Planning for Library Multitype Cooperatives: Samples & Examples, 1997. (ASCLA Changing Horizons Ser.: Vol. 1). 200p. (Orig.). 1997. pap. 30.00 (*0-8389-7914-9*) ALA.

Baughman, T. H. Before the Heroes Came: Antarctica in the 1890s. LC 93-1056. (Illus.). 160p. 1999. 40.00 (*0-8032-1228-3*, Bison Books) U of Nebr Pr.

*__Baughman, T. H.__ Before the Heroes Came: Antarctica in the 1890s. LC 93-1056. (Illus.). 160p. 1999. pap. 12.00 (*0-8032-6163-2*, Bison Books) U of Nebr Pr.

Baughman, T. H. Pilgrims on the Ice: Robert Falcon Scott's First Antarctic Expedition. LC 99-20685. (Illus.). 360p. 1999. text 45.00 (*0-8032-1289-5*) U of Nebr Pr.

Baughman, T. H., ed. & intro. see Passel, Charles F.

Baughman, W. Henry & Niva, George D. First Aid for Injury & Illness: Textbook & Workbook. 256p. (C). 1996. pap. text, spiral bd. 38.95 (*0-8403-9621-X*) Kendall-Hunt.

Baughman, Wayne. Wrestling on & off the Mat. (Illus.). 300p. 1992. text. write for info. (*0-9618446-0-4*) R W Baughman.

Baughman, Willis S., jt. auth. see Blumberg, Stephen M.

Baughn, Paula. Connections. Orig. Title: Connections: Building a Bridge to Your Future. (Illus.). 44p. (YA). (gr. 9). 1998. pap. text 4.95 (*1-892766-02-7*) ICPAC.

— Directions. 4th rev. ed. Orig. Title: Directions: For the Road to Life after High School. (Illus.). 32p. (YA). (gr. 11). 1998. pap. text 4.95 (*1-892766-03-5*) ICPAC.

Baughn, Paula, ed. see Koss, Jan.

Baugus, Clara. Poems to Treasure. 1997. pap. write for info. (*1-57553-550-5*) Watermrk Pr.

Bauhaus & Droste, M. Bauhaus. 1998. 24.99 (*3-8228-7672-0*, Pub. by Benedikt Taschen) Bks Nippan.

Bauhman, Judith S., jt. ed. see Bruccoli, Matthew J.

Baukal, Charles E. Computational Fluid Dynamics in Industrial Combustion. 760p. ring bd. 99.95 (*0-8493-2000-3*) CRC Pr.

Baukal, Charles E. Heat Transfer in Industrial Combustion. LC 99-88045. (Industrial Combustion Ser.). 568p. 2000. 89.95 (*0-8493-1699-5*) CRC Pr.

— Oxygen-Enhanced Combustion. LC 97-46803. 384p. 1998. boxed set 79.95 (*0-8493-1695-2*) CRC Pr.

Bauke-Ruegg, Jan. Die Allmacht Gottes: Systematisch-Theologische Erwagungen Zwischen Metaphysik, Postmoderne und Poesie. 400p. 1998. 118.00 (*3-11-015905-8*) De Gruyter.

Bauknight, Brain K. Of Gardens & Grandchildren: Reflections on Love & Life. LC 92-33158. 96p. 1993. 9.00 (*0-687-28423-6*) Dimen for Liv.

Bauknight, Brian K. Body Building: Creating a Ministry Team Through Spiritual Gifts. Miller, Herb, ed. (Leadership Insight Ser.). 176p. (Orig.). 1996. pap. 12.95 (*0-687-01710-6*) Abingdon.

— Gracious Imperatives: Discipleship Toward the 21st Century. 1992. pap. 7.95 (*0-687-15677-7*) Abingdon.

— Of Gardens & Grandchildren: Reflections on Love & Life. large type ed. 96p. 1993. pap. 1.88 (*0-687-28424-4*) Dimen for Liv.

— On a Wing & a Prayer: Devotions for Busy Christians. LC 97-44055. 208p. 1998. pap. 10.00 (*0-687-05211-4*) Dimen for Liv.

Bauknight, Suzanne H., jt. auth. see Thames, Jon P.

Baul, Lee K. Derisive Laughter from a Bad Poet: Excerpts from the Teachings of an American Baul. 2nd rev. ed. Bompois, Michelle & Wenzlaff, Helma, trs. from ENG. LC 93-77422. 80p. 1993. pap. text 8.95 (*0-934252-36-X*, Pub. by Hohm Pr) SCB Distributors.

— In the Mood of, in the Style of, the Eccentricities, Idiosyncrasies, & Sacred Utterances of a Contemporary Western Baul. LC 94-75701. 176p. 1994. 35.00 (*0-934252-43-2*, Pub. by Hohm Pr) SCB Distributors.

— In the Style of the Eccentricities, Idiosyncrasies & Sacred Utterances of a Contemporary Western Baul. LC 92-56587. 212p. 1993. 35.00 (*0-934252-34-3*, Pub. by Hohm Pr) SCB Distributors.

Baulac & Bellemain. Geometry: Cabri Interactive. (Mathematics Ser.). 1992. pap. 17.95 (*0-534-17060-9*) Brooks-Cole.

— Geometry: Cabri Interactive. (Mathematics Ser.). 1992. 104.95 (*0-534-17058-7*) Brooks-Cole.

Bauland, Peter. Hooded Eagle: Modern German Drama on the New York Stage. LC 67-31564. 1968. 39.95 (*0-8156-2119-1*) Syracuse U Pr.

— The Hooded Eagle: Modern German Drama on the New York Stage. LC 67-31564. 308p. 1968. reprint ed. pap. 95.50 (*0-608-07589-2*, 205990400010) Bks Demand.

Baulch, D. L., et al. Evaluated Kinetic Data for High Temperature Reactions, 3 vols., 1. LC 76-371748. 444p. 1976. reprint ed. pap. 137.70 (*0-608-04793-7*, 202575000001) Bks Demand.

— Evaluated Kinetic Data for High Temperature Reactions, 3 vols., 2. LC 76-371748. 573p. 1976. reprint ed. pap. 177.70 (*0-608-04794-5*, 202575000002) Bks Demand.

— Evaluated Kinetic Data for High Temperature Reactions, 3 vols., 3. LC 76-371748. 607p. 1976. reprint ed. pap. 188.20 (*0-608-04795-3*, 202575000003) Bks Demand.

Bauld, Harry. On Writing the College Application Essay: The Key to Acceptance at the College of Your Choice. LC 86-46043. 160p. 1987. pap. 12.00 (*0-06-463722-0*, EH 722) HarpC.

Bauld, Jane S. The Gift of the Gold Coin. Carpenter, Christina D., ed. (Illus.). 32p. (J). (ps-5). Date not set. 15.95 (*1-886440-03-4*) Portunus Pubng.

Bauld, Jane S. Hector's Escapades: The First Night Out. LC 97-32037. (Illus.). 39p. (J). 1997. 13.95 (*1-57168-185-X*) Sunbelt Media.

— Hector's Escapades: The First Night Out. LC 97-32037. (Illus.). 39p. (J). 1998. pap. 7.95 (*1-57168-244-9*, Eakin Pr) Sunbelt Media.

— Parables for Children. (J). (ps-2). 1998. 8.95 (*1-880384-16-7*) Coldwater Pr.

Bauld, Jane S. & Petrick, Thomas W. The Story of Mother Tree. LC 97-68119. (Illus.). 16p. (Orig.). (J). (gr. k-2). 1996. pap. 8.95 (*1-880384-12-4*) Coldwater Pr.

*__Bauld, Jane Scoggins.__ We Need Librarians. LC 99-46868. (Helpers in Our School Ser.). 24p. (J). (ps-2). 2000. lib. bdg. 13.25 (*0-7368-0531-1*, Pebble Bks) Capstone Pr.

Bauld, Jane Scoggins. Helpers in Our School. (Illus.). 24p. 39.80 (*0-7368-0560-5*, Pebble Bks) Capstone Pr.

— Never, Ever Shake a Baby. large type ed. (Illus.). 32p. (J). (gr. k-6). 1999. pap. write for info. (*0-9651123-1-4*, Pub. by E W Allen) Any Baby Can.

— Voyage of the Third Seed. large type ed. (Illus.). 32p. (J). 2000. 17.95 (*1-929701-02-0*) Under Green.

— We Need Custodians. LC 99-47365. (Helpers in Our School Ser.). 24p. (J). (ps-2). 2000. lib. bdg. 13.25 (*0-7368-0530-3*, Pebble Bks) Capstone Pr.

— We Need Principals. LC 99-46801. (Helpers in Our School Ser.). 24p. (J). (ps-2). 2000. lib. bdg. 13.25 (*0-7368-0532-X*, Pebble Bks) Capstone Pr.

— We Need Teachers. LC 99-46802. (Helpers in Our School Ser.). 24p. (J). (ps-2). 2000. lib. bdg. 13.25 (*0-7368-0533-8*, Pebble Bks) Capstone Pr.

*__Bauld, Jane Scoggins & Hefner, Kim.__ 101 Things to Cook. large type ed. 125p. (J). (ps-3). 1999. pap. 8.95 (*1-929701-01-2*) Under Green.

Bauld, Jane Scoggins, et al. Come to the Gathering. unabridged ed. (Illus.). v, 85p. (J). (gr. k-4). 1998. per. 12.95 (*0-9651123-2-2*, PyroWriters) E W Allen.

Bauld, Nathan L. Radicals, Ion Radicals & Triplets: The Spin-Bearing Intermediates of Organic Chemistry. LC 96-37072. 1997. write for info. (*1-56081-962-6*, Wiley-VCH) Wiley.

— Radicals, Ion Radicals & Triplets: The Spin Bearing Intermediates of Organic Chemistry. LC 96-37072. 240p. 1997. 98.95 (*0-471-19035-7*, Wiley-VCH) Wiley.

Bauldock, Gerald. Reaching for the Moon. LC 88-92848. 303p. (Orig.). (YA). (gr. 7-12). 1989. pap. text 14.95 (*0-9621728-0-4*) B-Dock Pr.

Bauldry, William. Calculus: Mathematics & Modeling Updated Preliminary Edition. 2nd ed. 656p. (C). 1999. pap. text 66.00 (*0-201-33860-2*) Addison-Wesley.

Bauldry, William C. & Fielder, Joseph R. Calculus Projects with Maple. 2nd ed. 144p. 1996. mass mkt. 30.95 (*0-534-23748-7*) Brooks-Cole.

Bauldry, William C., et al. Maple. LC 95-127133. 296p. 1994. pap. 31.95 (*0-471-06368-1*) Wiley.

Bauldry, William C., jt. auth. see Ellis, Wade.

Baule, Steve. Technology Planning. LC 96-33499. (Professional Growth Ser.). 107p. 1996. pap. 29.95 (*0-938865-55-2*) Linworth Pub.

*__Baule, Steven M.__ Facilities Planning for School Library Media & Technology Centers. 100p. 1999. pap. 36.95 (*0-938865-74-9*) Linworth Pub.

Bauleke, Ann. Kirby Puckett: Fan Favorite. LC 92-15271. (Achievers Ser.). (J). 1993. lib. bdg. 18.60 (*0-8225-0490-1*, Lerner Publctns) Lerner Pub.

— Kirby Puckett: Fan Favorite. (Illus.). 64p. (J). (gr. 4-9). 1993. pap. 4.95 (*0-8225-9633-4*, Lerner Publctns) Lerner Pub.

Baulieu, Etienne-Emile, et al, eds. Neurosteroids: A New Regulatory Function in the Nervous System. LC 99-10461. (Contemporary Endocrinology Ser.: Vol. 16). (Illus.). 396p. 1999. 135.00 (*0-89603-545-X*) Humana.

Baulieu, Etienne-Emile & Segal, Sheldon J., eds. The Antiprogestin Steroid RU 486 & Human Fertility Control. LC 85-19815. (Reproductive Biology Ser.). 364p. 1985. 95.00 (*0-306-42103-8*, Plenum Trade) Perseus Pubng.

Baulieu, J. L., et al. Nuclear Medicine & Lung Disease. (Illus.). xii, 124p. 1993. 167.00 (*0-387-59605-4*) Spr-Verlag.

Baulieu, L., et al. Quantum Field Theory & String Theory. (NATO ASI Ser.: 328). (Illus.). 430p. (C). 1995. text 144.00 (*0-306-44886-6*, Kluwer Plenum) Kluwer Academic.

Baulieu, Laurent. Strings, Branes & Dualities LC 98-44431. (NATO Advanced Study Institutes Ser.). 493p. 1998. write for info. (*0-7923-5344-7*) Kluwer Academic.

Baulieu, Laurent, et al, eds. Low-Dimensional Applications of Quantum Field Theory: Proceedings of a NATO ASI Held in Cargese, France, July 11-29, 1995. LC 97-17158. (NATO ASI Ser.: Vol. 362). 384p. (C). 1997. text 129.50 (*0-306-45686-9*) Plenum.

Baultrish, Libby, ed. see Johnston, John P.

Baultrish, Tim, ed. see Johnston, John P.

Baum. American Courts, 4 vols. 4th ed. (C). 1997. pap. text 40.76 (*0-395-87105-0*) HM.

— Applications & Topics. (Barnett Math Ser.). 192p. (C). 1991. pap. text, suppl. ed. 15.80 (*0-02-306770-5*, Macmillan Coll) P-H.

— Aquarobics: The Training Manual. (C). 1998. pap. text. write for info. (*0-7020-2234-9*, Pub. by W B Saunders) Saunders.

— Atlas of Nuclear Medicine Imaging. 3rd ed. (C). Date not set. 225.00 (*0-8385-0276-8*) Appleton & Lange.

— Consumer Law. 2nd ed. (LA - Business Law Ser.). 1988. pap., wbk. ed. 16.95 (*0-538-12520-9*) S-W Pub.

— Family Law. 2nd ed. (LA - Business Law Ser.). 1988. mass mkt., wbk. ed. 16.95 (*0-538-12530-6*) S-W Pub.

— An Introduction to Law. 2nd ed. (LA - Business Law Ser.). 1988. mass mkt., wbk. ed. 16.95 (*0-538-12510-1*) S-W Pub.

Baum. An Introduction to Organic Chemistry. 5th ed. 320p. 1994. pap. text, student ed., lab manual ed. 45.00 (*0-02-306771-3*, Pub. by P-H) S&S Trade.

Baum. Logic. 4th ed. (C). 1995. 110.50 (*0-15-503404-9*) Harcourt.

— Logic. 4th ed. (C). 1995. pap. text, teacher ed. 42.00 (*0-15-503399-9*) Harcourt Coll Pubs.

— Logic. 4th ed. (C). 1996. pap. text, student ed. 22.50 (*0-15-503400-6*, Pub. by Harcourt Coll Pubs) Harcourt.

— Mindstorms. write for info. (*0-07-135252-X*) McGraw.

— Property Investment Appraisal. 2nd ed. (ITBP Textbooks Ser.). 1998. pap. 19.99 (*1-86152-396-3*) Thomson Learn.

— Tort Law. 2nd ed. (LA - Business Law Ser.). 1988. mass mkt., wbk. ed. 16.95 (*0-538-12550-0*) S-W Pub.

Baum, ed. Cilia, Mucus, & Mucociliary Interactions. LC 97-44126. (Illus.). 616p. 1998. text 225.00 (*0-8247-0138-0*) Dekker.

Baum & Sams. Statutory Valuations. 3rd ed. 1997. pap. 20.99 (*1-86152-195-2*) Thomson Learn.

Baum, Abe, jt. ed. see Aiello, J. R.

Baum, Andrew, et al, eds. Cambridge Handbook of Psychology, Health & Medicine. (Illus.). 1250p. (C). 1997. pap. text 69.95 (*0-521-43686-9*) Cambridge U Pr.

— Stress & Disease Processes: Perspectives in Behavioral Medicine. (Advances in Behavioral Medicine Ser.). 328p. 1992. text 69.95 (*0-8058-1161-3*) L Erlbaum Assocs.

Baum, Andrew & Crosby, Neil. Property Investment Appraisal. 2nd ed. 304p. (C). 1995. pap. 31.95 (*0-415-09328-7*, C0136) Thomson Learn.

Baum, Andrew & Mackmin, David. The Income Approach to Property Valuation. 3rd ed. 272p. (Orig.). (C). 1989. pap. 25.95 (*0-415-04389-1*, A6256) Thomson Learn.

— The Income Approach to Property Valuation. 3rd ed. 272p. (Orig.). (C). (gr. 13). 1989. pap. 28.95 (*0-415-04388-3*, A6252) Thomson Learn.

Baum, Andrew & Mackmin, David. Income Approach to Property Valuation. 4th ed. 1997. pap. write for info. (*1-86152-501-X*, Pub. by ITBP) Thomson Learn.

Baum, Andrew & Sams, Gary. Statutory Valuations. 3rd ed. 288p. 1997. mass mkt. 27.95 (*0-415-13762-4*) Routledge.

Baum, Andrew & Shapiro, Alvin P., eds. Behavioral Aspects of Cardiovascular Disease. 368p. 1991. text 59.95 (*0-8058-0771-3*) L Erlbaum Assocs.

Baum, Andrew & Singer, J. E., eds. Issues in Child Health & Adolescent Health: Handbook of Psychology & Health, Vol. 2. 304p. 1982. 69.95 (*0-89859-184-8*) L Erlbaum Assocs.

Baum, Andrew & Singer, Jerome E., eds. Advances in Environmental Psychology Vol. 2: Applications of Personal Control. 208p. 1980. 49.95 (*0-89859-018-3*) L Erlbaum Assocs.

— Advances in Environmental Psychology Vol. 3: Energy Conservation, Psychological Perspectives. LC 81-2820. 224p. 1981. text 59.95 (*0-89859-063-9*) L Erlbaum Assocs.

— Advances in Environmental Psychology Vol. 5: Methods & Environmental Psychology. 232p. (C). 1985. text 49.95 (*0-89859-680-7*) L Erlbaum Assocs.

— Stress: Handbook of Psychology & Health, Vol. 5. 352p. 1987. text 79.95 (*0-89859-209-7*) L Erlbaum Assocs.

Baum, Andrew, et al. The Income Approach to Property Valuation. 4th ed. 288p. (Orig.). 1997. pap. 28.95 (*0-415-11709-7*) Thomson Learn.

— An Introduction to Health Psychology. 3rd ed. LC 96-35210. 448p. (C). 1997. pap. 48.13 (*0-07-022961-9*) McGraw.

Baum, Andrew, jt. ed. see Stunkard, Albert J.

Baum, Andrew, jt. ed. see Temoshok, Lydia.

Baum, Andrew, jt. ed. see Weiner, Herbert.

Baum, Andrew S., ed. Behavior, Health & Aging. LC 99-88820. (Perspectives in Behavioral Medicine Ser.). 264p. 1999. write for info. (*0-8058-3404-4*) L Erlbaum Assocs.

Baum, Andrew S., jt. ed. see Dimsdale, Joel E.

Baum, Andrew S., jt. ed. see Krantz, David S.

Baum, Andrew S., jt. ed. see Stein, Marvin.

Baum, Andrew W., et al, eds. Handbook of Health Psychology. Date not set. 225.00 (*0-8058-1495-7*) L Erlbaum Assocs.

Baum, Arline & Baum, Joseph. Opt: An Illusionary Tale. (Illus.). 32p. (J). (ps-3). 1989. pap. 5.99 (*0-14-050573-3*, PuffinBks) Peng Put Young Read.

Baum, B., jt. ed. see Cohen, M.

***Baum, Brian.** Ask Ernie. 2000. write for info. (*0-8129-3282-X*) Random.

Baum, C. E., et al. Ultra-Wideband, Short-Pulse Electromagnetics No. 3: Proceedings of the Third International Conference Held in Albuquerque, New Mexico, May 27-31, 1996, Vol. 3. LC 97-11193. (Illus.). 520p. (C). 1997. text 129.50 (*0-306-45593-5*, Kluwer Plenum) Kluwer Academic.

Baum, Carl E. Detection & Identification of Visually Obscured Targets. LC 98-24454. 1998. 85.00 (*1-56032-533-X*) Taylor & Francis.

Baum, Carl E. & Kritikos, Haralambos N., eds. Electromagnetic Symmetry. (Electromagnetics Library). 376p. 1995. 75.00 (*1-56032-321-3*) Taylor & Francis.

Baum, Carl E. & Stone, Alexander P. Transient Lens Synthesis. 1990. 85.00 (*0-89116-986-5*) Hemisp Pub.

Baum, Carolyn M., jt. auth. see Christiansen, Charles.

Baum, Dale. The Civil War Party System: The Case of Massachusetts, 1848-1876. LC 83-19687. xviii, 289p. 1984. 45.00 (*0-8078-1588-8*) U of NC Pr.

— Shattering of Texas Unionism: Politics in the Lone Star State During the Civil War Era. LC 98-10534. (Illus.). 336p. 1998. text 37.50 (*0-8071-2245-9*) La State U Pr.

Baum, Dan. Citizen Coors: An American Dynasty. LC 99-16830. (Illus.). 352p. 2000. 27.00 (*0-688-15448-4*, Wm Morrow) Morrow Avon.

— Smoke & Mirrors: The War on Drugs & the Politics of Failure. 416p. 1997. pap. 13.95 (*0-316-08446-8*) Little.

***Baum, Dave.** Dave Baum's Definitive Guide to Lego Mindstorms. (Technology in Action Ser.). 300p. 1999. pap. 24.95 incl. cd-rom (*1-893115-09-7*, Pub. by APress L P) Spr-Verlag.

***Baum, David.** Lightning in a Bottle. LC 99-88245. 2000. pap. 18.95 (*0-7931-3595-8*) Dearborn.

Baum, David B. Preparation of the Case. (Art of Advocacy Ser.). 1981. 160.00 (*0-8205-1038-6*) Bender.

Baum, Ed. Maine Atlantic Salmon: A National Treasure. LC 97-94393. (Illus.). 240p. 1997. 49.95 (*0-9660496-9-1*) Atlan Salmon.

Baum, Edward J. Estimating Chemical Properties of Environmental Contaminants. LC 97-33124. 1997. lib. bdg. 75.00 (*0-87371-938-7*) Lewis Pubs.

Baum, Eric, jt. ed. see Landweber, Laura.

Baum, Eric B., ed. Computational Learning & Cognition: Proceedings of the 3rd NEC Research Symposium. LC 92-46134. (Proceedings in Applied Mathematics Ser.: No. 64). xi, 276p. 1993. 53.00 (*0-89871-311-0*) Soc Indus-Appl Math.

Baum, Frank, et al. Dorothy & the Wizard of Oz. 39p. 1978. pap. 3.75 (*0-87129-802-3*) Dramatic Pub.

Baum, Frank, jt. auth. see Perry, Ruth F.

Baum, Gerald L., ed. Textbook of Pulmonary Diseases. 3rd ed. 1983. 99.00 (*0-316-08386-0*, Little Brwn Med Div) Lppncott W & W.

Baum, Gerald L. & Wolinsky, Emanuel, eds. Textbook of Pulmonary Diseases, 2 vols. 6th ed. LC 97-27989. (Illus.). 2040p. 1997. text 210.00 (*0-316-08434-4*) Lppncott W & W.

Baum, Gerald L., jt. auth. see Segal.

Baum, Gregory. Essays in Critical Theology. LC 94-19427. 256p. (Orig.). 1994. pap. 16.95 (*1-55612-710-3*) Sheed & Ward WI.

— Journeys: The Impact of Personal Experience on Religious Thought. LC 75-31401. 278p. reprint ed. pap. 86.20 (*0-8357-9486-5*, 201352500086) Bks Demand.

— Karl Polanyi on Ethics & Economics: Foreword by Marguerite Mendell. LC 97-156913. 112p. 1996. 49.95 (*0-7735-1395-7*, Pub. by McG-Queens Univ Pr); pap. 14.95 (*0-7735-1396-5*, Pub. by McG-Queens Univ Pr) CUP Services.

— Truth Beyond Relativism: Karl Mannheim's Sociology of Knowledge. LC 77-76605. (Pere Marquette Lectures). 1977. 15.00 (*0-87462-509-2*) Marquette.

Baum, Gregory, ed. The Twentieth Century: A Theological Overview. LC 99-23295. 250p. 1999. pap. 20.00 (*1-57075-282-6*) Orbis Bks.

Baum, Gregory & Ellsberg, Robert, eds. The Logic of Solidarity: Commentaries on Pope John Paul II's Encyclical on Social Concern. LC 89-27941. 248p. 1989. reprint ed. pap. 76.90 (*0-7837-9836-9*, 206056500005) Bks Demand.

Baum, Gregory & Wells, Harold, eds. The Reconciliation of Peoples: Challenge to the Churches. LC 96-45029. 200p. (Orig.). 1997. pap. 18.00 (*1-57075-107-2*) Orbis Bks.

Baum, Gregory, et al. The Earth Shelter Handbook. (Illus.). 252p. (Orig.). 1980. 15.95 (*0-937816-13-2*); pap. 12.95 (*0-937816-05-1*) Tech Data.

Baum, Gregory B., ed. Sociology & Human Destiny: Studies in Sociology, Religion & Society. 224p. 1982. 17.50 (*0-8164-0110-1*) Harper SF.

— Work & Religion. (Concilium Ser.: Vol. 131). 128p. (Orig.). 1980. 6.95 (*0-8164-2273-7*) Harper SF.

Baum, Gregory B. & Coleman, John, eds. The Church & Racism. (Concilium Ser.: Vol. 151). 128p. (Orig.). 1982. 6.95 (*0-8164-2382-2*) Harper SF.

— Neo-Conservatism: Social & Religious Phenomenon. (Concilium Ser.: Vol. 141). 128p. (Orig.). 1981. 6.95 (*0-8164-2308-3*) Harper SF.

— New Religious Movements. (Concilium Ser.: Vol. 161). 128p. (Orig.). 1983. 6.95 (*0-8164-2441-1*) Harper SF.

Baum, H. Molecular Aspects of Medicine, ser. vol. 2. (Molecular Aspects of Medicine Ser.). 1979. pap. 18.25 (*0-08-025888-3*, no. 6, Pergamon Pr) Elsevier.

Baum, H., et al, eds. Molecular Aspects of Medicine, Vol. 4. (Illus.). 452p. 1982. 180.00 (*0-08-030007-3*, Pergamon Pr) Elsevier.

— Molecular Aspects of Medicine, Vol. 5. (Illus.). 470p. 1983. 180.00 (*0-08-030429-X*, Pergamon Pr) Elsevier.

— Molecular Aspects of Medicine, Vol. 6. (Illus.). 584p. 1984. 180.00 (*0-08-031724-3*, Pergamon Pr) Elsevier.

— Molecular Aspects of Medicine, Vol. 7. (Illus.). 554p. 1985. 205.00 (*0-08-033239-0*, H210, H125, Pub. by PPL) Elsevier.

Baum, H. & Gergely, J., eds. Molecular Aspects of Medicine, 4 pts., Vol. 1. Incl. Pt. 1. Radioimmunoassay & Reproductive Endocrinology. 1977. pap. 12.75 (*0-08-021518-1*); Pt. 2. Haemoglobin Structure & Functions: Its Relevance in Biochemistry & Medicine. 1977. Pt. 3. Oedema in the Newborn. Barnes, ed. 1977. pap. 14.50 (*0-08-021538-6*); Pt. 4. Enzymic Regulation & Its Clinical Significance. 1977. pap. 14.50 (*0-08-022642-6*); pap. write for info. (*0-318-55183-7*) Elsevier.

— Molecular Aspects of Medicine, Vol. 2. LC 80-40473. (Illus.). 453p. 1980. 85.00 (*0-08-026355-0*, Pergamon Pr) Elsevier.

— Molecular Aspects of Medicine Vol. 1: Complete. 600p. 1978. 85.00 (*0-08-020277-2*, Pergamon Pr) Elsevier.

Baum, H. & Roman, I. Modern Aspects of Medicine, Vol. 3, No. 5. (Illus.). 133p. 1980. pap. 14.50 (*0-08-027378-5*, Pergamon Pr) Elsevier.

Baum, Harald, ed. Japan: Economic Success & the Legal System. LC 96-45041. xxii, 401p. (C). 1996. lib. bdg. 99.95 (*3-11-015160-X*) De Gruyter.

Baum, Harald & Nottage, Luke R. Japanese Business Law in Western Languages: An Annotated Selective Bibliography. LC 97-32088. x, 223p. 1998. 67.50 (*0-8377-0366-2*, Rothman) W S Hein.

Baum, Harold. The Biochemists' Song Book. 2nd ed. 96p. 1995. pap. 17.95 (*0-7484-0416-3*) Taylor & Francis.

Baum, Henry. Oscar Caliber Gun. 189p. 1997. pap. 9.95 (*1-887128-21-2*) Soft Skull Pr.

Baum, Hilary S., jt. auth. see Spitzer, Theodore M.

Baum, Howell S. The Organization of Hope. LC 96-5109. (SUNY Series in Urban Public Policy). 336p. (C). 1997. text 75.50 (*0-7914-3193-2*); pap. text 25.95 (*0-7914-3194-0*) State U NY Pr.

— Organizational Membership: Personal Development in the Workplace. LC 89-29799. (SUNY Series in the Sociology of Work). 290p. 1990. text 29.50 (*0-7914-0385-8*) State U NY Pr.

— Planners & Public Expectations. LC 82-16961. 325p. 1983. reprint ed. pap. 100.80 (*0-608-05351-1*, 206505700012) Bks Demand.

Baum, J. David, ed. Birth Risks. LC 92-48554. (Nestle Nutrition Workshop Ser.: Vol. 31). 254p. 1993. reprint ed. pap. 78.80 (*0-608-04702-3*, 206542300004) Bks Demand.

Baum, J. David, jt. ed. see Williams, A. F.

***Baum, Jan A.** Low Flow Anaesthesia. 2nd ed. (Illus.). 256p. 2000. text 80.00 (*0-7506-4672-1*) Buttrwrth-Heinemann.

Baum, Jan A. & Nunn, Geoffrey. Low-Flow Anaesthesia: The Theory & Practice of Low Flow, Minimum Flow & Closed System Anaesthesia. LC 96-167207. 192p. 1996. text 80.00 (*0-7506-2127-3*) Buttrwrth-Heinemann.

Baum, Joan. The Calculating Passion of Ada Byron. LC 86-14103. xix, 133p. (C). 1986. 25.00 (*0-208-02119-1*, Archon Bks) Shoe String.

— Mind-Forg'd Manacles: Slavery & the English Romantic Poets. LC 93-45722. xiv, 253p. (C). 1994. lib. bdg 29.50 (*0-208-02187-6*, Archon Bks) Shoe String.

Baum, Joanne. It's Time to Know: Ten Marijuana Users Share Their Personal Stories. Nielson, Nancy, ed. 208p. (Orig.). 1996. pap. 13.95 (*1-56246-124-9*, 3130, HazeldenJohnson Inst) Hazelden.

Baum, Joel A. Advances in Strategic Management Vol. 15: Disciplinary Roots of Strategic Management Research, Vol. 15. 1998. 78.50 (*0-7623-0462-6*) Jai Pr.

Baum, Joel A. & Singh, Jitendra V., eds. The Evolutionary Dynamics of Organizations. (Illus.). 528p. (C). 1994. pap. text 49.95 (*0-19-508584-1*) OUP.

Baum, John D. Elements of Point-Set Topology. (Illus.). 160p. 1991. reprint ed. pap. 6.95 (*0-486-66826-6*) Dover.

***Baum, Jonathan D., et al.** Drug Charts in Basic Pharmacology. 310p. 2000. pap. text 18.95 (*0-942447-37-9*) Med Surveill.

Baum, Joseph, jt. auth. see Baum, Arline.

Baum, K. C., et al. Grand Junction Rock: Rock Climbs of Unaweep Canyon & Adjacent Areas. 2nd ed. LC 97-226548. (Illus.). 1997. write for info. (*0-939860-08-2*) Tremaine Graph & Pub.

Baum, Kenneth & Trubo, Richard. The Mental Edge: Maximize Your Sports Potential with the Mind-Body Connection. LC 98-49937. 182p. 1999. pap. 13.95 (*0-399-52481-9*, Perigee Bks) Berkley Pub.

***Baum, Kenneth & Trubo, Richard.** Metabolize: The Personalized Program for Weight Loss. LC 99-43243. 304p. 2000. 23.95 (*0-399-14590-7*) Putnam Pub Group.

Baum, L. Frank. Adventures of the Magical Monarch of Mo & His People. (J). (gr. 5-6). Date not set. lib. bdg. 20.95 (*0-88411-771-5*) Amereon Ltd.

— American Fairy Tales. (Illus.). xxi, 224p. 1978. pap. 6.95 (*0-486-23643-9*) Dover.

***Baum, L. Frank.** Annotated Wizard of Oz: Centennial Edition. annot. ed. (Illus.). 432p. 2000. 39.95 (*0-393-04992-2*) Norton.

Baum, L. Frank. Baum's American Fairy Tales. 1997. pap. 12.95 (*0-929605-75-6*) Books of Wonder.

— The Book of the Hamburgs: A Brief Treatise upon the Mating, Rearing & Management of the Different Varieties of Hamburgs. (Illus.). 71p. (J). (gr. 3 up). 1991. pap. 8.95 (*0-929605-14-4*) Books of Wonder.

— By the Candelabra's Glare. LC 80-28443. 136p. 1981. reprint ed. 50.00 (*0-8201-1361-1*) Schol Facsimiles.

— Dorothy & the Wizard in Oz. (J). (gr. 4 up). 1990. 22.50 (*0-8446-6141-4*) Peter Smith.

— Dorothy & the Wizard in Oz. (J). 1997. pap. 4.95 (*0-8167-2885-2*) Troll Communs.

— Dorothy & the Wizard in Oz. (Illus.). 256p. (J). (gr. 5-10). 1984. reprint ed. pap. 6.95 (*0-486-24714-7*) Dover.

— Dorothy & the Wizard in Oz. LC 90-592. (Books of Wonder). (Illus.). 272p. (J). (gr. 2 up). 1990. reprint ed. 22.00 (*0-688-09826-6*, Wm Morrow) Morrow Avon.

— Dorothy & the Wizard of Oz. 20.95 (*0-8488-0704-9*) Amereon Ltd.

— Dot & Tot of Merryland. (Illus.). 154p. (J). (gr. 2 up). 1995. 44.95 (*0-929605-38-1*); pap. 11.95 (*0-929605-37-3*) Books of Wonder.

— The Emerald City of Oz. (J). 21.95 (*0-8488-0733-2*) Amereon Ltd.

— The Emerald City of Oz. LC 92-61765. (Books of Wonder). (Illus.). 304p. (YA). (gr. 2 up). 1993. 20.00 (*0-688-11558-6*, Wm Morrow) Morrow Avon.

— The Emerald City of Oz. (J). (gr. 4 up). 1990. 22.50 (*0-8446-6399-9*) Peter Smith.

— The Emerald City of Oz. (Illus.). 336p. (J). 1988. reprint ed. pap. 7.95 (*0-486-25681-2*) Dover.

— The Emerald City of Oz No. 6. LC 52-2380. 320p. (J). 1985. mass mkt. 5.99 (*0-345-33464-7*, Del Rey) Ballantine Pub Grp.

— The Enchanted Island of Yew. (Illus.). 192p. (J). (gr. 3 up). 1996. pap. 12.95 (*0-929605-52-7*) Books of Wonder.

— The Enchanted Island of Yew. (Illus.). 192p. (J). (gr. 3 up). 1996. reprint ed. 34.95 (*0-929605-55-1*) Books of Wonder.

— The Flying Girl & Her Chum. 2nd ed. LC 98-119515. (Illus.). 160p. (YA). 1997. reprint ed. pap. 12.95 (*0-9644988-5-5*) Hungry Tiger.

— Glinda of Oz. (J). 21.95 (*0-8488-0784-7*) Amereon Ltd.

***Baum, L. Frank.** Glinda of Oz. LC 99-88614. (Illus.). 288p. (J). 2000. pap. 8.95 (*0-486-41018-8*) Dover.

Baum, L. Frank. Glinda of Oz No. 14. 272p. (J). 1985. mass mkt. 4.99 (*0-345-33394-2*, Del Rey) Ballantine Pub Grp.

— The Land of Oz. 21.95 (*0-8488-0785-5*) Amereon Ltd.

— The Land of Oz. (J). 1997. pap. 2.95 (*0-89375-992-9*) NAL.

— The Land of Oz. (Illus.). 320p. (YA). (gr. 3 up). 1999. reprint ed. 12.95 (*1-56852-226-6*, Konecky & Konecky) W S Konecky Assocs.

— The Land of Oz No. 2, 2. LC 79-52645. 288p. (J). 1985. mass mkt. 5.99 (*0-345-33568-6*) Ballantine Pub Grp.

— The Life & Adventures of Santa Claus. (J). 1988. 16.95 (*0-8488-0428-7*) Amereon Ltd.

— The Life & Adventures of Santa Claus. Baisden, Greg S., ed. (Illus.). 96p. (J). 1992. text 24.95 (*1-879450-76-3*) Kitchen Sink.

— The Life & Adventures of Santa Claus. LC 83-11529. 160p. (J). (gr. 7-12). 1986. mass mkt. 3.95 (*0-451-52064-5*, Sig Classics) NAL.

— The Life & Adventures of Santa Claus. (Illus.). (J). (gr. 3-8). 1990. 21.75 (*0-8446-5450-7*) Peter Smith.

— The Life & Adventures of Santa Claus. (J). 1999. 6.99 (*0-517-20579-3*) Random Hse Value.

— The Life & Adventures of Santa Claus. (Illus.). (J). 1993. reprint ed. lib. bdg. 18.95 (*1-56849-175-1*) Buccaneer Bks.

— The Life & Adventures of Santa Claus. (Illus.). 208p. 1976. reprint ed. pap. 6.95 (*0-486-23297-2*) Dover.

— Little Wizard Stories of Oz. LC 93-77316. (Books of Wonder). (Illus.). 192p. (J). (gr. 2 up). 1994. 20.00 (*0-688-12126-8*, Wm Morrow) Morrow Avon.

— The Lost Princess of Oz. (J). 22.95 (*0-8488-0786-3*) Amereon Ltd.

— The Lost Princess of Oz. unabridged ed. LC 98-46178. (Illus.). 336p. (J). 1999. pap. 8.95 (*0-486-40344-0*) Dover.

— The Magic of Oz. (J). 20.95 (*0-8488-0787-1*) Amereon Ltd.

— The Magic of Oz. (Illus.). 256p. (J). 1985. mass mkt. 4.95 (*0-345-33288-1*, Del Rey) Ballantine Pub Grp.

— The Magic of Oz. LC 97-48701. (Illus.). 288p. (J). 1998. pap. 7.95 (*0-486-40019-0*) Dover.

— The Magical Monarch of Mo. (Illus.). (J). (gr. 4-8). 1982. 22.50 (*0-8446-1609-5*) Peter Smith.

— El Mago de Oz. 1987. 15.05 (*0-606-10414-3*, Pub. by Turtleback) Demco.

— El Maravilloso Mago de Oz (Wizard of Oz) (SPA., Illus.). 160p. (Orig.). (J). 1996. pap. 2.95 (*0-486-28968-0*) Dover.

— The Marvelous Land of Oz. 22.95 (*0-88411-773-1*) Amereon Ltd.

— The Marvelous Land of Oz. (Illus.). 287p. (J). (gr. 4-6). 1985. pap. 7.95 (*0-486-20692-0*) Dover.

— The Marvelous Land of Oz. LC 85-4856. (Books of Wonder). (Illus.). 294p. (J). (gr. 2 up). 1985. 22.95 (*0-688-05439-0*, Wm Morrow) Morrow Avon.

— The Marvelous Land of Oz. 1990. 22.50 (*0-8446-6231-3*) Peter Smith.

— The Marvelous Land of Oz. large type ed. (Large Print Heritage Ser.). 231p. (YA). 1998. lib. bdg. 28.95 (*1-58118-022-5*, 21999) LRS.

— The Marvelous Land of Oz. LC 96-40055. (Illus.). 144p. (J). 1997. reprint ed. pap. text 1.50 (*0-486-29686-5*) Dover.

— The Master Key. 22.95 (*0-8488-0734-0*) Amereon Ltd.

Baum, L. Frank. The Master Key. (Illus.). 160p. (YA). (gr. 3 up). 1997. 34.95 (*0-929605-68-3*) Books of Wonder.

Baum, L. Frank. Mother Goose in Prose. (J). (gr. k up). 1986. 4.98 (*0-685-16878-6*, 519046) Random Hse Value.

— Our Landlady. Koupal, Nancy T., ed. & anno. by. LC 95-32094. (Illus.). xii, 287p. 1996. pap. 16.95 (*0-8032-6156-X*, Bison Books) U of Nebr Pr.

— Our Landlady. annot. ed. Koupal, Nancy T., ed. & anno. by. LC 95-32094. (Illus.). xii, 287p. 1996. text 45.00 (*0-8032-1221-6*) U of Nebr Pr.

— Oz No. 4: Dorothy & Wizard in Oz. 240p. 1986. mass mkt. 4.99 (*0-345-34168-6*, Del Rey) Ballantine Pub Grp.

— Oz No. 8: Tik Tok of Oz. 272p. 1985. mass mkt. 4.99 (*0-345-33435-3*, Del Rey) Ballantine Pub Grp.

— Oz No. 10: Rinkitink in Oz. 304p. 1985. mass mkt. 5.99 (*0-345-33317-9*, Del Rey) Ballantine Pub Grp.

— Oz No. 11: Lost Princess of Oz. 304p. 1985. mass mkt. 4.99 (*0-345-33367-5*, Del Rey) Ballantine Pub Grp.

***Baum, L. Frank.** Oz Box Set. 272p. (J). 2000. pap., boxed set 19.50 (*0-06-440947-3*, HarpTrophy) HarpC Child Bks.

Baum, L. Frank. Oz-Story, No. 1. Maxine, David, ed. (Illus.). 128p. (Orig.). (J). (gr. 2-5). 1995. pap. 14.95 (*0-9644988-1-2*) Hungry Tiger.

— Ozma of Oz. 1996. 22.95 (*0-8488-0706-5*) Amereon Ltd.

— Ozma of Oz. LC 88-63291. (Books of Wonder). (Illus.). 288p. (J). (gr. 2 up). 1989. 21.95 (*0-688-06632-1*, Wm Morrow) Morrow Avon.

— Ozma of Oz. (Juveniles Ser.). (Illus.). 288p. (J). (gr. 2 up). 1985. reprint ed. pap. 6.95 (*0-486-24779-1*) Dover.

— Ozma of Oz No. 3. LC 77-89301. 264p. (Orig.). (J). 1986. mass mkt. 4.99 (*0-345-33589-9*, Del Rey) Ballantine Pub Grp.

— The Patchwork Girl of Oz. (J). 25.95 (*0-8488-0705-7*) Amereon Ltd.

— The Patchwork Girl of Oz. (Illus.). 336p. (J). 1990. pap. 7.95 (*0-486-26514-5*) Dover.

— The Patchwork Girl of Oz. LC 94-77238. (Books of Wonder). (Illus.). 352p. (J). (gr. 4-7). 1995. 20.00 (*0-688-13354-1*, Wm Morrow) Morrow Avon.

— The Patchwork Girl of Oz. LC 94-77238. (J). 1992. 22.50 (*0-8446-6495-2*) Peter Smith.

— The Patchwork Girl of Oz. (J). 1997. pap. 2.95 (*0-8167-1469-X*) Troll Communs.

— The Patchwork Girl of Oz No. 7. LC 79-88483. 384p. (J). 1985. mass mkt. 4.99 (*0-345-33290-3*) Ballantine Pub Grp.

— Policeman Bluejay. LC 81-9044. 152p. (J). (gr. 1-6). 1981. reprint ed. 50.00 (*0-8201-1367-0*) Schol Facsimiles.

B

— Queen Zixi of Ix: The Story of the Magic Cloak. (Illus.). 231p. (J). (gr. 1-3). 1971. reprint ed. pap. 5.95 (0-486-22691-3) Dover.

— Rinkitink in Oz. (J). 22.95 (0-8488-0735-9) Amereon Ltd.

— Rinkitink in Oz. (Illus.). 336p. (J). (gr. 4 up). 1993. reprint ed. pap. text 6.95 (0-486-27756-9) Dover.

— The Road to Oz. 20.95 (0-8488-0788-X) Amereon Ltd.

— The Road to Oz. (Illus.). 1990. 21.75 (0-8446-6250-X) Peter Smith.

— The Road to Oz. 272p. 1986. reprint ed. pap. 6.95 (0-486-25208-6) Dover.

— The Road to Oz. LC 90-48349. (Books of Wonder). (Illus.). 272p. (J). (gr. 4-7). 1991. reprint ed. 16.95 (0-688-09997-1, Wm Morrow) Morrow Avon.

Baum, L. Frank. The Road to Oz, Set. unabridged ed. (J). (gr. 1-3). 1982. pap. 24.95 incl. audio (1-55685-545-1) Audio Bk Con.

Baum, L. Frank. The Road to Oz No. 5. LC 79-88480. 272p. (J). 1986. mass mkt. 4.95 (0-345-33467-1, Del Rey) Ballantine Pub Grp.

— The Scarecrow of Oz. (J). 20.95 (0-8488-0707-3) Amereon Ltd.

— The Scarecrow of Oz. LC 98-41017. 1999. pap. text 8.95 (0-486-40548-6) Dover.

— The Scarecrow of Oz. LC 96-76266. (Illus.). 304p. (gr. 5-7). 1997. 22.00 (0-688-14719-4, Wm Morrow) Morrow Avon.

— The Scarecrow of Oz. (J). 1997. pap. 2.95 (0-8167-2897-6) Troll Communs.

— The Sea Fairies. (Illus.). 240p. (J). (gr. 3 up). 1987. 24.95 (0-929605-03-9); pap. 12.95 (0-929605-00-4) Books of Wonder.

— The Sea Fairies. LC 98-14331. (Illus.). (J). 1998. pap. 6.95 (0-486-40182-0) Dover.

— Sky Island. (Illus.). 288p. (J). (gr. 3 up). 1988. pap. 12.95 (0-929605-02-0) Books of Wonder.

Baum, L. Frank. Sky Island. (Illus.). 288p. (J). (gr. 4-10). 1988. 24.95 (0-929605-01-2) Books of Wonder.

Baum, L. Frank. Surprising Adventures of the Magical Monarch of Mo & His People. (Illus.). 237p. (J). (ps-4). 1968. pap. 7.95 (0-486-21892-9) Dover.

— Tick Tock of Oz. 20.95 (0-8488-0708-1) Amereon Ltd.

— Tik-Tok of Oz. LC 95-79594. (Illus.). 304p. (J). (gr. 4-7). 1996. 22.00 (0-688-13355-X, Wm Morrow) Morrow Avon.

— Tik-Tok of Oz. (J). 1997. pap. 2.95 (0-8167-2895-X) Troll Communs.

— Tik-Tok of Oz. LC 93-37906. (Illus.). 304p. (J). 1994. reprint ed. pap. 6.95 (0-486-28002-0) Dover.

***Baum, L. Frank.** The Tin Woodman of Oz. LC 98-72950. (Illus.). 336p. (J). 1998. 22.00 (0-688-14976-6, Wm Morrow) Morrow Avon.

Baum, L. Frank. The Tin Woodman of Oz No. 12. (Illus.). 272p. (J). 1985. mass mkt. 4.99 (0-345-33436-1, Del Rey) Ballantine Pub Grp.

— The Tin Woodsman of Oz. 20.95 (0-8488-0709-X) Amereon Ltd.

— The Wizard of Oz. (Illus.). 30p. (J). 1995. pap. 7.95 (1-55859-820-0) Abbeville Pr.

— The Wizard of Oz. LC 79-52644. 240p. (J). 1986. mass mkt. 5.99 (0-345-33590-2, Del Rey) Ballantine Pub Grp.

— The Wizard of Oz. LC 95-9772. (Children's Thrift Classics Ser.). (Illus.). 96p. (J). 1995. pap. text 1.00 (0-486-28585-5) Dover.

— The Wizard of Oz. 1963. 4.25 (0-87129-402-8, W39) Dramatic Pub.

— The Wizard of Oz. LC 82-1109. (Illus.). 232p. (J). (gr. 4-6). 1995. 19.95 (0-8050-0221-9, Bks Young Read) H Holt & Co.

— The Wizard of Oz. pap. write for info. (0-688-16677-6, Wm Morrow) Morrow Avon.

— The Wizard of Oz. 256p. (YA). 1984. mass mkt. 3.95 (0-451-51864-0, Sig Classics) NAL.

— The Wizard of Oz. LC 96-21733. (Illus.). 105p. (J). (gr. 2-6). 1996. 19.95 (1-55858-638-5, Pub. by North-South Bks NYC) Chronicle Bks.

— The Wizard of Oz. Denslow, W. W., ed. LC 93-50738. (Illustrated Junior Library). (Illus.). 224p. (J). 1994. 14.99 (0-448-40561-X, G & D) Peng Put Young Read.

— The Wizard of Oz. LC 79-52644. (Puffin Classics Ser.). (Illus.). 189p. (YA). (gr. 5 up). 1995. pap. 3.99 (0-14-036693-8, PuffinBks) Peng Put Young Read.

***Baum, L. Frank.** The Wizard of Oz. 1999. pap. 2.99 (0-14-130546-0, PuffinBks) Peng Put Young Read.

Baum, L. Frank. The Wizard of Oz. Vogel, Malvina, ed. (Great Illustrated Classics Ser.: Vol. 8). (Illus.). 240p. (J). (gr. 3-6). 1989. 9.95 (0-86611-959-0) Playmore Inc.

— The Wizard of Oz. LC 97-4980. (J). 1997. 18.00 (0-679-88758-X, Pub. by Random Bks Yng Read) Random.

— The Wizard of Oz. 160p. (J). (gr. 4-7). 1989. pap. 3.50 (0-590-44089-6, Apple Classics) Scholastic Inc.

— The Wizard of Oz. 196p. 1993. pap. 2.50 (0-8125-2335-0, Pub. by Tor Bks) St Martin.

— The Wizard of Oz. (J). 1982. 10.09 (0-606-04376-4, Pub. by Turtleback) Demco.

— Wizard of Oz. (Children's Library). 1998. pap. 3.95 (1-85326-112-2, 1122WW, Pub. by Wrdsworth Edits) NTC Contemp Pub Co.

— The Wizard of Oz. abr. ed. Escott, John, ed. (Classics for Young Readers Ser.). (Illus.). 64p. (J). (gr. 1-4). 1996. 5.98 (1-85854-286-3) Brimax Bks.

— The Wizard of Oz. adapted ed. (Living Classics Ser.). (Illus.). 32p. (J). (gr. 3-7). 1997. 14.95 (0-7641-7046-5) Barron.

***Baum, L. Frank.** The Wizard of Oz. anniversary ed. (Illus.). 96p. (J). (ps up). 2000. 21.95 (0-375-81137-0, Pub. by Random Bks Yng Read) Random.

Baum, L. Frank. The Wizard of Oz. limited ed. (Illus.). 105p. (J). (gr. 2-6). 1996. 200.00 (1-55858-657-1, Pub. by North-South Bks NYC) Chronicle Bks.

— The Wizard of Oz. (Illus.). 272p. (YA). (gr. 3 up). 1999. reprint ed. 12.95 (1-56852-225-8, Konecky & Konecky) W S Konecky Assocs.

***Baum, L. Frank.** The Wizard of Oz: Centennial Edition. 100th anniversary ed. (Illus.). 240p. (J). (gr. 4-7). 2000. 29.95 (0-8050-6430-3) H Holt & Co.

Baum, L. Frank. The Wizard of Oz: Collectors Edition. 1992. 6.98 (0-88365-797-X) Galahad Bks.

— Wizard of Oz - Color Book. (J). 1978. pap. 2.95 (0-486-20452-9) Dover.

— The Wizard of Oz Book & Charm. LC 99-22562. (Charming Classic Bks.). (Illus.). 208p. (J). (gr. 3-7). 1999. 5.95 (0-694-01319-6) HarpC Child Bks.

— The Wizard of Oz (El Mago de Oz) (SPA.). (J). 9.95 (84-204-3509-0) Santillana.

— The Wizard of Oz Waddle Book. LC 93-10069. (Illus.). 160p. (J). 1993. reprint ed. 24.95 (1-55709-205-2); reprint ed. 85.00 (1-55709-203-6) Applewood.

— The Woggle-Bug Book. LC 78-6887. 72p. (J). (gr. 1-6). 1978. reprint ed. 50.00 (0-8201-1308-5) Schol Facsimiles.

— Wonderful Wizard of Oz. (Illus.). (J). (gr. 4 up). 1990. 23.00 (0-8446-1610-9) Peter Smith.

— Wonderful Wizard of Oz. (Deluxe Watermill Classic Ser.). 176p. (YA). 1998. pap. 4.95 (0-8167-2565-9) Troll Communs.

— The Wonderful Wizard of Oz. (J). (gr. 5-6). 20.95 (0-88411-772-3) Amereon Ltd.

— The Wonderful Wizard of Oz. LC 92-53173. (Everyman's Library of Children's Classics). (Illus.). 192p. (J). 1992. 12.95 (0-679-41794-X, Evrymans Lib Childs) Knopf.

— The Wonderful Wizard of Oz. LC 86-62556. (Books of Wonder). (Illus.). 316p. (J). (ps up). 1987. 22.00 (0-688-06944-4; Wm Morrow) Morrow Avon.

— The Wonderful Wizard of Oz. Wolstenholme, Susan & Denslow, W. W., eds. (Oxford World's Classics Ser.). (Illus.). 336p. (J). 2000. pap. 10.95 (0-19-283930-6) OUP.

***Baum, L. Frank.** The Wonderful Wizard of Oz. (Illus.). 176p. (YA). 2000. 24.95 (1-86205-343-X, Pub. by Pavilion Bks Ltd) Trafalgar.

Baum, L. Frank. The Wonderful Wizard of Oz. (YA). 1991. pap. 2.95 (0-89375-991-0) Troll Communs.

— The Wonderful Wizard of Oz. Mabie, Grace, ed. LC 92-12704. (Illustrated Classics Ser.). (Illus.). 48p. (J). (gr. 3-6). 1992. pap. 5.95 (0-8167-2865-8) Troll Communs.

— The Wonderful Wizard of Oz. Mabie, Grace, ed. & adapted by by. LC 92-12704. (Illustrated Classics Ser.). (Illus.). 48p. (J). (gr. 3-6). 1992. lib. bdg. 19.95 (0-8167-2864-X, BW219) Troll Communs.

— The Wonderful Wizard of Oz. large type ed. (Large Print Heritage Ser.). 198p. (YA). (gr. 7-12). 1997. lib. bdg. 26.95 (1-58118-011-X, 21511) LRS.

— Wonderful Wizard of Oz. (Illus.). 267p. (J). (gr. k-6). 1960. reprint ed. pap. 8.95 (0-486-20691-2) Dover.

— The Wonderful Wizard of Oz. 139p. (J). 1981. reprint ed. lib. bdg. 15.95 (0-89966-347-8); reprint ed. lib. bdg. 11.95 (0-89967-021-0, Harmony Rain) Buccaneer Bks.

— The Wonderful Wizard of Oz. unabridged ed. LC 95-47924. (Illus.). 128p. 1996. reprint ed. pap. text 1.50 (0-486-29116-2) Dover.

— The Wonderful Wizard of Oz: The Kansas Centennial Edition. LC 99-22379. (Illus.). 216p. 1999. 24.95 (0-7006-0985-7) U Pr of KS.

***Baum, L. Frank.** The Wonderful Wizard of Oz: The Kansas Centennial Edition. LC 99-22379. (Illus.). 216p. 1999. 100.00 (0-7006-0986-5) U Pr of KS.

— The Wonderful Wizard of Oz: 100th Anniversary Edition. 272p. (J). 2000. 24.95 (0-06-029323-3) HarpC Child Bks.

Baum, L. Frank. The Wonderful World of Oz. Zipes, Jack D., ed. & intro. by. LC 97-50449. (Twentieth-Century Classics Ser.). (J). 1998. pap. 13.95 (0-14-118085-4) Viking Penguin.

***Baum, L. Frank & Denslow, W. W.** Oz-Story 5. Maxine, David, ed. (Oz Ser.: No. 5). (Illus.). 128p. (J). (gr. 3-7). 1999. pap. 14.95 (1-929527-00-4) Hungry Tiger.

Baum, L. Frank & Glassman, Peter. The Lost Princess of Oz. LC 97-78415. (Illus.). 352p. (J). (gr. 4-7). 1998. 24.00 (0-688-14975-8, Wm Morrow) Morrow Avon.

***Baum, L. Frank & McGraw, Eloise.** The Wizard of Oz. (Classics Ser.). 208p. (J). 1999. per. 3.99 (0-689-83142-0) S&S Childrens.

Baum, L. Frank & McGraw, Eloise J. Oz-Story, No. 2. Maxine, David, ed. (Illus.). 128p. (Orig.). (J). (gr. 2-6). 1996. pap. 14.95 (0-9644988-2-0) Hungry Tiger.

Baum, L. Frank & Mitchell, Kathy. The Wizard of Oz. LC 84-82589. 174p. (J). 1986. write for info. (0-307-67115-1, Whitman Coin) St Martin.

Baum, L. Frank & Payes, Rachel C. Oz-Story, Vol. 3. Maxine, David, ed. & illus. by. Shanower, Eric, illus. 128p. (Orig.). (J). (gr. 2-6). 1997. pap. 14.95 (0-9644988-4-7) Hungry Tiger.

Baum, L. Frank & Shanahan, Patrick. Oz. 53p. 1996. pap. 5.50 (0-87129-713-2, O55) Dramatic Pub.

***Baum, L. Frank, et al.** Oz-Story, Vol. 4. Maxine, David, ed. (Illus.). 128p. (Orig.). (J). (gr. 3-7). 1998. pap. 14.95 (0-9644988-7-1) Hungry Tiger.

Baum, L. Frank, jt. auth. see Carr, M. J.

Baum, L. Frank, jt. auth. see Gardner, Martin.

Baum, L. Frank, jt. auth. see Glassman, Peter.

Baum, L. Frank, jt. auth. see Koste, V. Glasgow.

Baum, L. Frank, jt. auth. see Morris, Kimberly.

Baum, L. Frank, jt. auth. see Neill, John R.

Baum, L. Frank, jt. auth. see Stewart, Jesse.

Baum, L. Frank, ed. see Baum, Maud G.

Baum, Laurie. Astrological Secrets of the New Millenium: How to Create the Future You Want. LC 97-29948. 408p. 1997. per. 16.00 (0-7615-1024-9) Prima Pub.

***Baum, Laurie A.** Astrological Secrets for the New Millennium. LC 99-26090. 1999. 9.99 (0-517-20655-2) Random Hse Value.

— Insomnia Journal: Between Dusk & Dawn. (Illus.). 144p. 1997. pap. 19.95 (1-55670-664-2) Stewart Tabori & Chang.

Baum, Laurie A. & Pounds, Bette G., eds. The National Directory of Psychotherapy Training Institutes. LC 93-574. 224p. 1993. pap. 21.95 (0-87630-720-9) Brunner-Mazel.

Baum, Lawrence. American Courts, 3 vols. 3rd ed. LC 93-78688. (C). 1993. pap. text 37.16 (0-395-67539-1) HM.

— The Puzzle of Judicial Behavior. LC 97-4870. (Analytical Perspectives on Politics Ser.). 232p. (C). 1997. text 44.50 (0-472-10670-8, 10670); pap. text 19.95 (0-472-08335-X, 08335) U of Mich Pr.

— The Supreme Court. 6th ed. LC 97-38477. 301p. (YA). (gr. 11). 1998. text 23.97 (1-56802-321-9); pap. text 16.77 (1-56802-320-0) Congr Quarterly.

***Baum, Lenore Y.** Lenore's Natural Cuisine: Your Essential Guide to Wholesome, Vegetarian Cooking. LC 99-90885. (Illus.). 256p. 2000. pap. 17.95 (0-9674627-3-8) Culinary Pubns.

***Baum, Linda B.** Daughters of the Dying . . . And Sons of the Same: Help for Christian Caregivers. Jenkins, Pam, ed. (Illus.). 118p. 1999. pap. write for info. (0-7392-0334-7, PO3503) Morris Pubng.

Baum, Lloyd, et al. Textbook of Operative Dentistry. 3rd ed. LC 94-8371. (Illus.). 688p. 1994. text 72.00 (0-7216-3484-2, W B Saunders Co) Harcrt Hlth Sci Grp.

Baum, M, jt. auth. see Ray, C.

Baum, Markus. Against the Wind: Eberhard Arnold & the Bruderhof. Plough Publishing House Staff, ed. & tr. by. from GER. LC 98-5665. Orig. Title: Stein des Anstosses. (Illus.). 317p. 1998. pap. 14.00 (0-87486-953-6) Plough.

Baum, Martha & Twiss, Pamela. Social Work Intervention in an Economic Crisis: The River Communities Project. LC 96-357. 220p. 1996. 39.95 (0-7890-6036-1) Haworth Pr.

Baum, Mary, ed. see Merrin, Leona M.

Baum, Maud G. In Other Lands Than Ours. Baum, L. Frank, ed. LC 82-10254. 240p. 1983. 50.00 (0-8201-1385-9) Schol Facsimiles.

Baum, Michael A., jt. auth. see Bello, Mark.

Baum, Michael S. Federal Certification Authority Liability & Policy: Law & Policy of Certificate-Based Public Key & Digital Signatures. (Government Contract Report GCR-94-654). 421p. (Orig.). 1994. pap. write for info. (1-886843-00-7, PB#94191202) Ntl Inst Stndrds.

— Verisign Certification Practice Statement. (Certification Practice Statement Ser.). 80p. (Orig.). 1996. ring bd. write for info. (0-9653555-0-0) VeriSign.

Baum, Michael S., jt. auth. see Ford, Warwick.

Baum, Nathan, jt. auth. see Douglas, Nancy E.

***Baum, Neil.** Marketing Your Clinical Practice: Ethically, Effectively, Economically. 2nd ed. 2000. 75.00 (0-8342-1745-7) Aspen Pub.

Baum, Neil & Henkel, Gretchen. Marketing Your Clinical Practice: Ethically, Effectively, Economically. 316p. 1991. 80.00 (0-8342-0233-6) Aspen Pub.

Baum, Neil & Zablocki, Elaine. Take Charge of Your Medical Practice...Before Someone Else Does It for You: Practical Practice Managment for the Managed Care Market. LC 96-6738. 224p. 1996. 63.00 (0-8342-0799-0, 20799) Aspen Pub.

Baum, Neil, jt. auth. see Wilson, Steven K.

Baum, Neil H. The Urology Office Manual. (Office Manual Ser.). 200p. 1994. 145.00 (1-890018-04-X) Anadem Pubng.

Baum, Paull F. Chaucer: A Critical Appreciation. LC 58-12587. 244p. reprint ed. pap. 75.70 (0-608-14813-X, 202618500048) Bks Demand.

Baum, Paull F., ed. see Duke University Library Staff.

Baum, R. F. Doctors of Modernity: Darwin, Marx, & Freud. 200p. (Orig.). 1986. pap. 8.95 (0-89385-215-5) Sugden.

Baum, R. P., et al, eds. Clinical Use of Antibodies: Tumors, Infection, Infarction, Rejection in the Diagnosis of AIDS. (C). 1991. text 122.00 (0-7923-1424-7) Kluwer Academic.

***Baum, Rachel R.** Funeral & Memorial Service Readings, Poems & Tributes. LC 99-29046. 183p. 1999. lib. bdg. 29.95 (0-7864-0699-2) McFarland & Co.

Baum, Richard. Burying Mao: Chinese Politics in the Age of Deng Xiaoping. LC 94-9892. 500p. 1994. text 55.00 (0-691-03639-X, Pub. by Princeton U Pr) Cal Prin Full Svc.

— Prelude to Revolution. 1975. text 52.50 (0-231-03900-X) Col U Pr.

— Reform & Reaction in Post-Mao China: The Road Through Tiananmen. 208p. (C). 1991. pap. 20.99 (0-415-90318-1, A4598) Routledge.

Baum, Richard & Bennett, Louise B. China in Ferment: Perspectives on the Cultural Revolution. LC 70-153433. (A Spectrum Book Ser.). viii, 246 p. 1971. write for info. (0-13-132688-0) Prentice ESL.

Baum, Richard & Sheehan, William. In Search of Planet Vulcan: The Ghost in Newton's Clockwork Universe. LC 96-45674. (Illus.). 326p. (C). 1997. 28.95 (0-306-45567-6, Plenum Trade) Perseus Pubng.

Baum, Robert. Logic. 4th ed. LC 95-77198. 708p. (C). 1995. text 65.00 (0-15-501617-2, Pub. by Harcourt Coll Pubs) Harcourt.

Baum, Robert J. Ethics & Engineering Curricula. LC 80-10099. (Teaching of Ethics Ser.). 79p. 1980. pap. 4.00 (0-916558-12-6) Hastings Ctr.

Baum, Robert M. Shrines of the Slave Trade: Diola Religion & Society in Precolonial Senegambia. LC 98-19659. (Illus.). 304p. 1999. text 55.00 (0-19-512392-1) OUP.

Baum, Roberta. Parashat Hashavua: Genesis. (ENG & HEB.). 80p. Date not set. pap. text 5.95 (0-87441-680-9) Behrman.

Baum, Roberta O. Shabbat Morning Service Bk. 1: The Shema & Its Blessings. 86p. 1985. pap., teacher ed. 16.95 (0-87441-430-X) Behrman.

— Shabbat Morning Service Bk. 2: The Shabbat Amidah. 109p. 1986. pap., teacher ed. 16.95 (0-87441-437-7); pap. text 7.95 (0-87441-432-6) Behrman.

— Shabbat Morning Service Bk. 3: Torah Service & Selected Concluding Prayers. 7.95 (0-87441-449-0); pap., teacher ed. 16.95 (0-87441-468-7) Behrman.

— Shabbat Shalom. (Illus.). (J). 1995. pap. 4.95 (0-87441-520-9) Behrman.

Baum, Roberta O. & Winter, Magda. Derech Chochmah. 96p. (J). 1995. pap. text 5.95 (0-87441-471-7) Behrman.

Baum, Roberta O., jt. contrib. by see Stern, Chaim.

Baum, Roger S. Dorothy of Oz. LC 89-6918. (Books of Wonder). (Illus.). 176p. (J). 1989. 17.00 (0-688-07848-6, Wm Morrow) Morrow Avon.

Baum, S. J., ed. Current Methodology in Experimental Hematology. (Bibliotheca Haemotologica Ser.: No. 48). (Illus.). vi, 418p. 1985. 215.75 (3-8055-3722-0) S Karger.

Baum, S. J., et al, eds. Experimental Hematology Today, 1980. (Illus.). xiv, 342p. 1981. 142.25 (3-8055-1705-X) S Karger.

— Experimental Hematology Today, 1981. (Illus.). xiv, 250p. 1981. 142.25 (3-8055-2255-X) S Karger.

— Experimental Hematology Today, 1982. (Illus.). xx, 270p. 1982. 172.25 (3-8055-3486-8) S Karger.

— Experimental Hematology Today, 1988. (Illus.). 192p. 1989. 126.00 (0-387-96932-2) Spr-Verlag.

— Recent Advances & Future Directions in Bone Marrow Transplantation. (Experimental Hematology Today 1987 Ser.). (Illus.). xxiii, 200p. 1987. 108.00 (0-387-96582-3) Spr-Verlag.

Baum, S. J. & Ledney, G. D., eds. Experimental Hematology Today. (Illus.). 1977. 142.00 (0-387-90208-2) Spr-Verlag.

— Experimental Hematology Today 1978. LC 78-8054. (Illus.). 1978. 142.00 (0-387-90323-2) Spr-Verlag.

— Experimental Hematology Today, 1979. (Illus.). 1979. 211.00 (0-387-90380-1) Spr-Verlag.

***Baum, Seth J.** Total Guide to a Healthy Heart. 320p. 2000. pap. text 14.00 (1-57566-562-X) Kensgtn Pub Corp.

Baum, Seth J. Total Guide to a Healthy Heart: Integrative Strategies for Reversing Heart Disease. 1999. 25.00 (1-57566-448-8) Kensgtn Pub Corp.

Baum, Sheldon. Atlas of Nuclear Medicine Imaging. 2nd ed. (Illus.). 232p. (C). 1994. 235.00 (0-8385-0449-3, A0449-7, Apple Lange Med) McGraw.

Baum, Sheldon, jt. auth. see Van Nostrand, Douglas.

Baum, Stanley, ed. Abrams' Angiography, 3 vols., Vols. I, II & III. 4th ed. 3000p. 1996. text 495.00 (0-316-08226-0) Lppncott W & W.

Baum, Stanley & Pentecost, Michael J., eds. Abrams' Angiography Vol. III: Interventional Radiology, 3. 4th ed. LC 96-24525. 1000p. 1996. text 225.00 (0-316-08432-8) Lppncott W & W.

Baum, Stanley, jt. auth. see Abrams, Herbert L.

Baum, Stanley A. Abrams' Angiography, Vols. 1-3. 4th ed. 3000p. 650.00 (0-7817-2902-5) Lppncott W & W.

Baum, Stuart J. & Hill, John W. Introduction to Organic & Biological Chemistry. (Illus.). 528p. (C). 1993. write for info. (0-318-69794-7) Macmillan.

Baum, Susan, et al. Chi Square, Pie Square & Me. 120p. (Orig.). 1987. pap. 14.99 (0-89824-171-5) Trillium Pr.

Baum, Susan E. & Cray-Andrews, Martha. Creativity One, Two, Three: Fostering the Creative Potential of Young Children. 1992. pap. 14.99 (0-89824-076-X) Trillium Pr.

***Baum, Susan M., et al, eds.** Nurturing the Gifts & Talents of Primary Grade Students. 370p. 1998. pap. 32.95 (0-936386-71-1) Creative Learning.

Baum, Susan M., et al. To Be Gifted & Learning Disabled: From Definitions to Practical Intervention Strategies. 149p. (Orig.). 1991. pap. 16.95 (0-936386-59-2) Creative Learning.

Baum, T. Managing Human Resources in the European Tourism & Hospitality Industry: A Strategic Approach. (Illus.). 296p. 1995. mass mkt. 19.99 (0-412-55630-8) Chapman & Hall.

***Baum, Thomas & Mudambi, Ram.** Economic & Managemnt Methods for Tourism & Hospitality Research. LC 98-24166. 296p. 1999. 85.00 (0-471-98392-6) Wiley.

Baum, Timothy. Man Ray's Paris Portraits, 1921-39. rev. ed. (Illus.). 132p. 1997. 19.95 (0-9660353-0-5) S Dali Mus.

Baum, Tom. Out of Body. LC 96-52646. 1997. text 22.95 (0-312-15620-0) St Martin.

— Out of Body. 256p. 1998. mass mkt. 5.99 (0-312-96735-7, Pub. by Tor Bks) St Martin.

Baum, Tom, ed. Human Resource Issues in International Tourism. LC 93-190823. (Illus.). 271p. reprint ed. pap. 84.10 (0-608-06254-5, 206658300008) Bks Demand.

— Human Resources Issues International Tourism. 256p. 1993. pap. 46.95 (0-7506-0091-8) Buttrwrth-Heinemann.

Baum, Tom, jt. ed. see Conlin, Michael V.

Baum, Urban, ed. see Twesten, Gary.

Baum, Vicki. Grand Hotel. 22.95 (0-89190-431-X) Amereon Ltd.

— Grand Hotel. 1990. reprint ed. lib. bdg. 25.95 (0-89968-476-9) Buccaneer Bks.

***Baum, Vicki.** A Tale from Bali. 2000. pap. 19.95 (962-593-502-9, Pub. by Periplus) Tuttle Pubng.

Baum, Vicki, jt. auth. see Ogilvie, Elizabeth.

Baum, Victor C. & O'Flaherty, Jennifer E. Anesthesia for Genetic, Metabolic, & Dysmorphic Syndromes of Childhood. LC 98-41895. 1999. 110.00 (0-7817-1552-0) Lppncott W & W.

An Asterisk (*) at the beginning of an entry indicates that the title is appearing for the first time.

Baum, Warren C. The Project Cycle. rev. ed. 16p. 1978. pap. write for info. (*0-8213-0022-9*, 10022) World Bank.
— The Project Cycle. rev. ed. (FRE.). 25p. 1982. pap. write for info. (*0-8213-0134-9*, 10134); pap. write for info. (*0-8213-0135-7*, 10135) World Bank.
Baum, Warren C., jt. auth. see Kirmani, Syed S.
Baum, Willa K. Oral History for the Local Historical Society. 3rd rev. ed. LC 95-42556. (American Association for State & Local History Book Ser.). 80p. 1987. reprint ed. pap. 13.95 (*0-7619-9133-6*) AltaMira Pr.
— Transcribing & Editing Oral History. LC 77-3340. (American Association for State & Local History Book Ser.). (Illus.). 128p. 1991. reprint ed. pap. 15.95 (*0-910050-26-0*) AltaMira Pr.
Baum, Willa K. & Riess, Suzanne B. Catalogue of the Regional Oral History Office II: 1980-1996. (Orig.). 1997. pap. write for info. (*0-614-13304-1*) U CA Region Oral Hist.
Baum, Willa K., jt. ed. see Dunaway, David K.
Baum, Willa K., jt. ed. see Riess, Suzanne B.
Baum, William M. Understanding Behaviorism. 320p. (C). 1997. pap. 36.00 (*0-06-500286-5*) Addson-Wesley Educ.
Bauman. Gilbert Remedies. 10th ed. 1995. pap. text 20.95 (*0-15-900325-3*) Harcourt Legal.
— Ideas & Details. 2nd ed. (C). 1994. pap. text, teacher ed. 33.75 (*0-15-502149-4*) Harcourt Coll Pubs.
— The Shape of Ideas. (C). 1994. pap. text, teacher ed. 32.00 (*0-15-502183-4*) Harcourt Coll Pubs.
— The Shape of Ideas. 12th ed. LC 94-78467. (C). 1994. pap. text 33.00 (*0-15-501460-9*, Pub. by Harcourt Coll Pubs) Harcourt.
Bauman, Alisa & Kaufman, Brian. Symptom Solver: Understanding-&-Treating-the Most Common Male Health Concerns. Men's Health Books Staff, ed. LC 96-22076. (Illus.). 176p. 1996. pap. 14.95 (*0-87596-357-9*) Rodale Pr Inc.
Bauman, Alisa & Prevention Health Books. Fight Fat: Secrets to Successful Weight Loss. LC 97-35553. (Women's Edge Health Enhancement Guides). 1998. write for info. (*0-87596-480-X*) Rodale Pr Inc.
Bauman, Alisa, et al. Fat to Firm at Any Age: How You Can Have a Slimmer, Well-Toned Body at Age 30, 40 & Beyond. LC 97-22062. (Illus.). 512p. 1999. pap. 15.95 (*1-57954-128-3*) Rodale Pr Inc.
Bauman, Beau. The Most Important Thing I've Learned in Life. 192p. 1994. pap. 7.95 (*0-671-89228-2*, Fireside) S&S Trade Pap.
Bauman, Bill. Oneness: Our Heritage, Our Path, Our Destiny. LC 92-85431. 192p. (Orig.). (C). 1992. pap. text 13.00 (*0-9631696-0-2*) Wrld Peace Inst.
Bauman, Chris & Fishman, Sylvia E. Childhood Inventory of Language & Development Chart (CHILD) (J). (ps-1). 1991. 8.50 (*0-937857-27-0*, 1592) Speech Bin.
Bauman, Clarence. The Spiritual Legacy of Hans Denck: Interpretation & Translation of Key Texts. LC 90-20241. (Studies in Medieval & Reformation Thought: Vol. 47). (ENG & GER.). ix, 287p. 1990. 110.50 (*90-04-09291-9*) Brill Academic Pubs.
Bauman, Dean. Whispers of His Word: Food for the Soul. 210p. (Orig.). 1997. pap. 17.77 (*1-57502-277-X*, PO977) Morris Pubng.
Bauman, Diane, et al. Beyond Basic Dog Training Workbook. (Illus.). 216p. 1994. pap. 14.95 (*0-931866-74-X*) Alpine Pubns.
Bauman, Diane L. Beyond Basic Dog Training. 2nd ed. (Illus.). 256p. 1991. 24.95 (*0-87605-410-6*) Howell Bks.
— Life with People: A Story. LC 89-90777. (Illus.). 64p. (Orig.). 1989. pap. 6.95 (*0-9622356-0-1*) Paw Prints Pr.
Bauman, Donna J. Seeing Through the Heart. (Illus.). 100p. 1994. pap. text 18.00 (*0-9631696-1-0*) Wrld Peace Inst.
Bauman, Edward J., ed. Guidance & Control 1981, Jan. 31-Feb. 4, 1981, Keystone CO. LC 57-43769. (Advances in the Astronautical Sciences Ser.: Vol. 45). (Illus.). 506p. 1981. 60.00 (*0-87703-150-9*, Am Astronaut Soc); pap. 50.00 (*0-87703-151-7*, Am Astronaut Soc) Univelt Inc.
Bauman, Edward J. & Emsley, Zubin W., eds. Guidance & Control 1983, Feb. 5-9, 1983, Keystone, CO: 1983. LC 57-43769. (Advances in the Astronautical Sciences Ser.: Vol. 51). (Illus.). 494p. 1983. 60.00 (*0-87703-182-7*, Am Astronaut Soc); pap. 50.00 (*0-87703-183-5*, Am Astronaut Soc) Univelt Inc.
Bauman, Elizabeth, ed. see Kozen, Frances.
Bauman, Elizabeth H. Coals of Fire. LC 53-12197. (Christian Peace Shelf Ser.). (Illus.). 128p. (J). (gr. 5-9). 1954. pap. 6.99 (*0-8361-1957-6*) Herald Pr.
***Bauman, G. Duncan.** Behind the Headlines. LC 99-38421. (Illus.). 272p. 1999. pap. 17.95 (*1-880397-31-5*) Patrice Pr.
Bauman, Hans. Thank You, Brother Bear. (J). 1995. pap. 4.95 (*0-590-25487-1*) Scholastic Inc.
Bauman, Harold. Grief's Slow Work. (Visitation Pamphlet Ser.). 16p. 1986. pap. 2.99 (*0-8361-1711-5*) Herald Pr.
***Bauman, Harold.** How Do I Live Through Grief? Strength & Hope in Times of Loss. (Bible Answers Library). 48p. 2000. pap. 1.99 (*1-57748-819-9*) Barbour Pub.
Bauman, Harold E. Presence & Power: Releasing the Holy Spirit. LC 88-34747. 128p. (Orig.). 1989. pap. 8.99 (*0-8361-3493-1*) Herald Pr.
Bauman, James J. A Guide to Issues in Indian Language Retention. LC 80-25194. 76p. reprint ed. pap. 30.00 (*0-8357-3381-5*, 203963100013) Bks Demand.
Bauman, Janina. Winter in the Morning: A Young Girl's Life in the Warsaw Ghetto, 1939-1945. 256p. 1986. 27.95 (*0-02-902530-3*) Free Pr.
***Bauman, John F., et al, eds.** From the Tenement to the Taylor Home: In Search of an Urban Housing Policy in Twentieth-Century America. LC 99-55272. 2000. 55.00 (*0-271-02013-X*); pap. 17.95 (*0-271-02012-1*) Pa St U Pr.
Bauman, John F. & Coode, Thomas H. In the Eye of the Great Depression: New Deal Reporters & the Agony of the American People. (Illus.). 240p. 1988. pap. 12.50 (*0-87580-541-8*) N Ill U Pr.
Bauman, John F., jt. auth. see Coode, Thomas H.
***Bauman, John W.** Road Hazards: Being a Guide for New Car Buyers, Owners & Drivers. LC 99-91158. 100p. 1999. 25.00 (*0-7388-0650-1*); pap. 18.00 (*0-7388-0651-X*) Xlibris Corp.
***Bauman, Jon.** Pioneering a Global Vision: The Story of Baker & McKenzie. 1999. 24.95 (*0-15-900433-0*) Harcourt.
Bauman, Jon. The Sovereignes & the Admiral. (Illus.). 1992. 24.95 (*1-878096-23-0*, Epigram Pr) Best E TX Pubs.
Bauman, Karl E. Research Methods for Community Health & Welfare: An Introduction. 160p. 1980. pap. text 19.95 (*0-19-502699-3*) OUP.
Bauman, Kay. Solomon Island: Folktales from Malaita. LC 97-69557. 96p. 1998. pap. 15.95 (*1-887750-77-0*) Rutledge Bks.
Bauman, Lawrence. The Ten Most Troublesome Teen-Age Problems: And How to Solve Them. 240p. 1998. pap. 12.95 (*0-8065-2014-0*) Carol Pub Group.
Bauman, Lawrence & Riche, Robert. The Nine Most Troublesome Teenage Problems & How to Solve Them. 186p. 1986. 15.95 (*0-8184-0392-6*) Carol Pub Group.
— The Ten Most Troublesome Teenage Problems: And How to Solve Them. LC 96-51713. 240p. 1997. pap. 19.95 (*1-55972-396-3*, Birch Ln Pr) Carol Pub Group.
Bauman, Lester. The True Christian. 237p. 1994. 9.00 (*0-7399-0204-0*, 2446) Rod & Staff.
Bauman, Lewis. The Tongues Movement. 1979. pap. 1.00 (*0-88469-047-4*) BMH Bks.
Bauman, M. Garrett. Ideas & Details: A Guide to College Writing. 300p. (C). 1992. teacher ed. write for info. (*0-318-69136-1*) Harcourt Coll Pubs.
— Ideas & Details: A Guide to College Writing. 3rd ed. LC 96-79900. 240p. (C). 1997. pap. text 29.50 (*0-15-503875-3*, Pub. by Harcourt Coll Pubs) Harcourt.
Bauman, Margaret L. The Neurobiology of Autism. Kemper, Thomas L., ed. LC 93-5358. (Johns Hopkins Series in Psychiatry & Neuroscience). 272p. 1997. pap. text 35.00 (*0-8018-5680-9*) Johns Hopkins.
Bauman, Marilyn. Edward L. Loper Sr. The Prophet of Color. (Illus.). 136p. 1999. 39.95 (*1-878647-56-3*) APU Pub Grp.
Bauman, Mark B., jt. auth. see Delmar Staff.
Bauman, Mark K. Harry H. Epstein & the Rabbinate As Conduit for Change. LC 92-55112. 1994. 32.50 (*0-8386-3541-5*) Fairleigh Dickinson.
Bauman, Mark K. & Kalin, Berkley, eds. The Quiet Voices: Southern Rabbis & Black Civil Rights, 1880 to 1990. LC 97-19187. (Judaic Studies). 444p. 1997. text 34.95 (*0-8173-0892-X*) U of Ala Pr.
Bauman, Michael. Historians of the Christian Tradition: Their Methodologies & Influence on Western Thought. 1998. pap. 49.99 (*0-8054-1862-8*) Broadman.
— Pilgrim Theology: Taking the Path of Theological Discovery. LC 92-13328. 1992. pap. 14.99 (*0-310-58531-7*) Zondervan.
Bauman, Michael, ed. The Christian Vision: Man & Marxism: Religion & the Communist Retreat. LC 91-71376. 200p. 1991. 9.95 (*0-916308-81-2*) Hillsdale Coll Pr.
— The Christian Vision Vol. 7: Man & the Marketplace. LC 94-77458. 164p. 1994. pap. 9.95 (*0-916308-70-7*) Hillsdale Coll Pr.
— A Scripture Index to John Milton's "De Doctrina Christiana" (Medieval & Renaissance Texts & Studies: Vol. 67). 184p. 1989. 18.00 (*0-86698-076-8*, MR67) MRTS.
Bauman, Michael, et al, eds. Evangelical Apologetics. LC 97-163125. 1996. pap. 14.99 (*0-87509-685-9*) Chr Pubns.
Bauman, Michael & Beckwith, Francis J., eds. Are You Politically Correct? Debating America's Cultural Standards. LC 92-33259. (Contemporary Issues Ser.). 266p. (Orig.). (C). 1992. pap. 16.95 (*0-87975-769-8*) Prometheus Bks.
Bauman, Michael & Hall, David. God & Caesar: Essays from the 1993 Evangelical Theological Society Convention. LC 94-72351. 370p. 1994. pap. 14.99 (*0-87509-574-7*) Chr Pubns.
Bauman, Michael E. The Best of the Manion Forum: A Conservative & Free Market Sourcebook. LC 90-28855. 600p. 1991. lib. bdg. 119.95 (*0-7734-9935-0*) E Mellen.
Bauman, Paul. Agassi & Ecstasy: The Turbulent Life of Andre Agassi. LC 97-30844. (Illus.). 313p. 1997. 24.95 (*1-56625-085-4*) Bonus Books.
Bauman, Paul & Crampton, Faith E. When School Districts Become Entrepreneurs: Opportunity or Danger? 8p. 1995. 15.00 (*1-55516-396-3*, 7302-2011) Natl Conf State Legis.
Bauman, Paul C. Governing Education: Public Sector Reform or Privatization. LC 95-35765. 192p. 1995. pap. text 42.00 (*0-205-16220-7*) Allyn.
Bauman, R. H., jt. ed. see Weiselberg, M.
Bauman, Richard. Verbal Art as Performance. 150p. (C). 1984. reprint ed. pap. text 11.95 (*0-88133-048-5*) Waveland Pr.
Bauman, Richard, ed. Folklore, Cultural Performances & Popular Entertainments: A Communications-Centered Handbook. (Illus.). 336p. (C). 1992. pap. text 23.95 (*0-19-506920-X*) OUP.
Bauman, Richard & Sherzer, Joel, eds. Explorations in the Ethnography of Speaking. 2nd ed. (Studies in the Social & Cultural Foundations of Language: No. 8). (Illus.). 536p. (C). 1989. pap. text 36.95 (*0-521-37933-4*) Cambridge U Pr.
Bauman, Richard, et al. Reflections on the Folklife Festival: An Ethnography of Participant Experience. (Special Publications: No. 2). (Illus.). 70p. (C). 1992. text 22.50 (*1-879407-03-5*); pap. text 9.95 (*1-879407-02-7*) IN Univ Folk Inst.
Bauman, Richard, ed. see Paredes, Americo.
Bauman, Richard A. Crime & Punishment in Ancient Rome. LC 96-21587. 240p. (C). 1996. 80.00 (*0-415-11375-X*) Routledge.
— Human Rights in Ancient Rome LC 99-24401. 1999. text. write for info. (*0-415-17320-5*) Routledge.
— Women & Politics in Ancient Rome. 304p. (C). 1994. pap. 25.99 (*0-415-11522-1*, B4828) Routledge.
Bauman, Robert P., et al. From Promise to Performance: A Journey of Transformation at SmithKline Beecham. LC 96-10892. 320p. 1997. 27.50 (*0-87584-634-3*) Harvard Busn.
Bauman, Susan. In Search of the Japanese Spirit in Talent Education. 56p. 1994. pap. text 7.95 (*0-87487-767-9*) Summy-Birchard.
Bauman, Thomas, ed. German Opera, Seventeen Seventy to Eighteen Hundred. 400p. 1986. lib. bdg. 15.00 (*0-8240-8870-0*) Garland.
Bauman, Thomas & McClymonds, Marita P., eds. Opera & the Enlightenment. LC 94-11009. (Illus.). 331p. (C). 1995. text 64.95 (*0-521-46172-3*) Cambridge U Pr.
Bauman, Thomas, ed. see Andre, Johann.
Bauman, Thomas, ed. see Benda, Georg A.
Bauman, Thomas, ed. see Gotter, Friedrich W.
Bauman, Thomas, ed. see Heermann, Gottlob E.
Bauman, Thomas, ed. see Wieland, Christoph M.
Bauman, Thomas, ed. see Winter, Peter.
Bauman, Tim, et al. Issues & Technology in the Management of Impacted Western Wildlife: Proceedings of a National Symposium (1985) 309p. 1986. pap. 35.00 (*0-916055-02-7*) Thorne Eco Inst.
Bauman, Toni & Zinkgraf, June. Fall Fantasies, Winter Wonders, Spring Surprises, 3 bks., Set. teacher ed. 39.99 (*1-56417-123-X*, GA1100) Good Apple.
— Spring Surprises, Set. 240p. (J). (gr. k-6). 1979. 13.99 (*0-916456-54-4*, GA109) Good Apple.
— Winter Wonders. 240p. (J). (gr. k-6). 1978. 13.99 (*0-916456-29-3*, GA89) Good Apple.
Bauman, Toni, jt. auth. see Zinkgraf, June.
***Bauman-Waengler, Jacqueline.** Articulation & Phonological Disorders: A Clinical Focus. LC 99-44138. 400p. (C). 1999. 58.00 (*0-205-28064-1*, Macmillan Coll) P-H.
Bauman, William. Smart Handicapping Made Easy. 1979. pap. 5.00 (*0-87980-270-7*) Wilshire.
Bauman, Yoram, jt. auth. see Thein Durning, Alan.
Bauman, Zugmunt. Work, Consumerism & the New Poor. LC 97-47455. (Issues in Society Ser.). 160p. 1998. 85.00 (*0-335-20156-3*) OpUniv Pr.
Bauman, Zygmont. Postmodernity & Its Discontents. LC 96-47838. 1997. text 50.00 (*0-8147-1303-3*) NYU Pr.
***Bauman, Zygmunt.** Culture as Praxis. LC 98-75101. (Theory, Culture & Society Ser.). 148 p. 1999. write for info. (*0-7619-5988-2*) Sage.
Bauman, Zygmunt. Freedom. Parkin, Frank, ed. (Concepts in the Social Sciences Ser.). 128p. (Orig.). 1988. 32.50 (*0-335-15592-8*); pap. 9.99 (*0-335-15591-X*) OpUniv Pr.
— Freedom. LC 88-27716. (Concepts in Social Thought Ser.). 120p. (Orig.). 1989. pap. 13.95 (*0-8166-1757-0*) U of Minn Pr.
***Bauman, Zygmunt.** Globalization. 2000. reprint ed. pap. 14.50 (*0-231-11429-X*) Col U Pr.
Bauman, Zygmunt. Globalization: The Human Consequences. LC 98-18508. (European Perspectives Ser.). 161p. 1998. 24.50 (*0-231-11428-1*) Col U Pr.
— Hermeneutics & Social Science: Approaches to Understanding. (Modern Revivals in Sociology Ser.). 263p. 1992. 71.95 (*0-7512-0045-X*, Pub. by Gregg Pub) Ashgate Pub Co.
***Bauman, Zygmunt.** In Search of Politics. LC 99-71005. 212p. 1999. 49.50 (*0-8047-3833-5*) Stanford U Pr.
— In Search of Politics. 1999. pap. text 17.95 (*0-8047-3834-3*) Stanford U Pr.
— The Individualized Society. 270p. 2000. 59.95 (*0-7456-2506-1*, Pub. by Polity Pr); 24.95 (*0-7456-2507-X*, Pub. by Polity Pr) Blackwell Pubs.
Bauman, Zygmunt. Intimations of Postmodernity. 272p. (C). 1991. pap. 22.99 (*0-415-06750-2*, A5876) Routledge.
— Legislators & Interpreters: On Modernity, Post-Modernity, & Intellectuals. LC 87-47721. 226p. (C). 1987. 45.00 (*0-8014-2104-7*) Cornell U Pr.
— Life in Fragments: Essays in Postmodern Morality. 256p. (Orig.). 1995. pap. text 28.95 (*0-631-19267-0*) Blackwell Pubs.
***Bauman, Zygmunt.** Liquid Modernity. 240p. 2000. text 59.95 (*0-7456-2409-X*, Pub. by Polity Pr); pap. text 24.95 (*0-7456-2410-3*, Pub. by Polity Pr) Blackwell Pubs.
Bauman, Zygmunt. Modernity & Ambivalence. LC 90-46479. 300p. 1991. text 47.50 (*0-8014-2603-0*) Cornell U Pr.
— Modernity & the Holocaust. LC 89-7274. 250p. 1989. text 47.50 (*0-8014-2397-X*) Cornell U Pr.
— Modernity & the Holocaust. LC 89-7274. 280p. 1992. pap. text 17.95 (*0-8014-8032-9*) Cornell U Pr.
— Mortality, Immortality, & Other Life Strategies. iv, 215p. (C). 1992. 42.50 (*0-8047-2163-7*); pap. 15.95 (*0-8047-2164-5*) Stanford U Pr.
— Postmodern Ethics. LC 93-16048. 264p. 1993. pap. 28.95 (*0-631-18693-X*) Blackwell Pubs.
— Postmodernity & Its Discontents. LC 96-47838. 1997. pap. text 18.00 (*0-8147-1304-1*) NYU Pr.
— Socialism: The Active Utopia. LC 75-28243. (Controversies in Sociology Ser.: No. 3). 148p. 1976. 19.75 (*0-8419-0240-2*) Holmes & Meier.
— Thinking Sociologically: An Introduction for Everyone. 240p. (C). 1989. pap. text 27.95 (*0-631-16362-X*) Blackwell Pubs.
— Work, Consumerism & the New Poor. LC 97-47455. (Issues in Society Ser.). 106p. 1998. pap. 24.95 (*0-335-20155-5*) OpUniv Pr.
***Bauman, Zygmunt.** Community. 2001. 54.95 (*0-7456-2634-3*, Pub. by Polity Pr); pap. 19.95 (*0-7456-2635-1*, Pub. by Polity Pr) Blackwell Pubs.
Baumann. Buisness Applications: Microcomputer & Information Technology. 1997. mass mkt. 54.95 (*0-314-22318-5*) West Pub.
Baumann. Microsoft Word 6.0 for Windows, Microcomputer & Information Technology. (Data Processing & Information System Ser.). 1996. pap. 26.50 (*0-314-07124-5*) West Pub.
Baumann & Flynn. MS Excel 5.0 for Windows, Microcomputer & Information Technology. (Data Processing & Information System Ser.). 1996. pap. 26.50 (*0-314-07122-9*) West Pub.
Baumann, jt. auth. see Arendt.
Baumann, jt. auth. see Mandell.
Baumann, Alex, jt. auth. see Tihanyi, Jeno.
Baumann, Arthur A. Last Victorians. LC 70-104991. (Essay Index Reprint Ser.). 1977. 23.95 (*0-8369-1445-7*) Ayer.
— Personalities. LC 68-54323. (Essay Index Reprint Ser.). 1977. 20.95 (*0-8369-0177-0*) Ayer.
Baumann, B. Imaginative Participation: The Career of an Organizing Concept in a Multidisciplinary Context. 214p. 1975. pap. text 78.50 (*90-247-1693-4*, Pub. by M Nijhoff) Kluwer Academic.
Baumann, Bommi. How It All Began: A Personal Account of a West German Urban Guerrilla. Ellenbogen, Hellene & Parker, Wayne, trs. from GER. Orig. Title: Wie Alles Anfing. 136p. 1977. reprint ed. pap. 5.95 (*0-88978-045-5*) Left Bank.
Baumann, Carl L., tr. see Baegert, Johann J.
Baumann, Carole E. Eugene N. Marais & the Problem of the Animal Psyche. 1985. 10.00 (*0-7855-1875-4*) St Mut.
— Program Planning about World Affairs. 70p. 1991. pap. 10.00 (*0-944675-47-6*) Amer Forum.
Baumann, Carole E., ed. Europe in NATO: Deterrence, Defense, & Arms Control. LC 87-22892. 388p. 1987. 65.00 (*0-275-92490-4*, C2490, Praeger Pubs) Greenwood.
***Baumann, Catherine C., contrib. by.** The Challenge of Land Use Planning after Urban Earthquakes: Observations from the Great Hanshin Earthquake of 1995. (Illus.). 42p. (C). 1999. reprint ed. pap. text 20.00 (*0-7881-8378-8*) DIANE Pub.
Baumann, Catherine C., et al. Schriftbilder. Thorson, Helga M. et al, eds. (GER., Illus.). 147p. (Orig.). (C). 1988. pap. text 10.00 (*0-317-93404-X*) IP Inc MN.
Baumann, Duane D. The Recreational Use of Domestic Water Supply Reservoirs: Perception & Choice. LC 69-318025. (University of Chicago, Department of Geography, Research Paper Ser.: No. 121). 139p. reprint ed. pap. 43.10 (*0-7837-0398-8*, 204071900018) Bks Demand.
Baumann, Duane D. & Haimes, Yacov Y., eds. The Role of Social & Behavioral Sciences in Water Resources, Planning & Management: Conference Proceedings. 424p. 1988. 6.00 (*0-87262-668-7*) Am Soc Civil Eng.
Baumann, Duane D., et al. Urban Water Demand Management & Planning. LC 97-30667. (Illus.). 350p. 1997. 60.00 (*0-07-050301-X*) McGraw.
Baumann, Ed, jt. auth. see Heise, Kenan.
Baumann, Ernst F. & Bloom, Norman. Toward a New World: Powerful Proof of the Existence of God; a Personal God Who Knows You. abr. rev. ed. (Illus.). 300p. 1995. text 20.00 (*0-9648440-2-8*) Coll of The Canons.
Baumann, Felix, jt. ed. see Karabelnik, Marianne.
Baumann, Fred & Cuhaj, George, eds. 1999 Krause-Minkus Standard Catalog of U. S. Stamps. 2nd ed. LC 98-84632. (Illus.). 602p. 1999. pap. 19.95 (*0-87341-682-1*, SCM02) Krause Pubns.
Baumann, Fred E. Fraternity & Politics: Choosing One's Brothers. LC 98-15649. 160p. 1998. 55.00 (*0-275-96292-X*, Praeger Pubs) Greenwood.
Baumann, Fred E., ed. Democratic Capitalism? Essays in Search of a Concept. LC 86-7755. 222p. (Orig.). reprint ed. pap. 68.90 (*0-7837-3560-X*, 204341600009) Bks Demand.
Baumann, Fred E. & Jensen, Kenneth M., eds. American Defense Policy & Liberal Democracy. LC 88-34899. 170p. reprint ed. pap. 52.70 (*0-7837-3562-6*, 204341800009) Bks Demand.
— Crime & Punishment Issues in Criminal Justice. LC 88-25854. 144p. reprint ed. pap. 44.70 (*0-7837-3561-8*, 204341700009) Bks Demand.
— Religion & Politics. LC 88-34438. 124p. reprint ed. pap. 38.50 (*0-7837-3563-4*, 204341900009) Bks Demand.
Baumann, G. Symmetry Analysis of Differential Equations with Mathematica. LC 98-26975. (Illus.). 464p. 1998. 69.95 incl. cd-rom (*0-387-98552-2*) Spr-Verlag.
Baumann, Gerd. Contesting Culture: Discourses of Identity in Multi-Ethnic London. (Studies in Social & Cultural Anthropology: Vol. 100). (Illus.). 228p. (C). 1996. pap. text 19.95 (*0-521-55554-X*) Cambridge U Pr.
— Contesting Culture: Discourses of Identity in Multi-Ethnic London. (Studies in Social & Cultural Anthropology: No. 100). (Illus.). 228p. (C). 1996. text 59.95 (*0-521-55482-9*) Cambridge U Pr.
— Mathematica in Theoretical Physics. (Electronic Library of Science). (Illus.). 348p. 1996. 59.00 incl. disk (*0-387-94424-9*) Spr-Verlag.
— The Multicultural Riddle: Rethinking National, Ethnic & Religious Identities LC 98-49911. (Zones of Religion Ser.). 1999. pap. 19.99 (*0-415-92213-5*) Routledge.

B

An Asterisk (*) at the beginning of an entry indicates that the title is appearing for the first time.

*Baumann, Gerd.** The Multicultural Riddle: Rethinking National, Ethnic & Religious Identities. LC 98-49911. 1999. write for info. (*0-415-92212-7*) Routledge.

Baumann, Gerd. National Integration & Local Integrity: The Miri of the Nuba Mountains in the Sudan. (Illus.). 232p. 1988. text 62.00 (*0-19-823401-5*) OUP.

Baumann, Gerd, ed. The Written Word: Literacy in Transition. (Wolfson College Lectures). (Illus.). 224p. 1986. 49.95 (*0-19-875068-4*) OUP.

Baumann, Hans. Thank You, Brother Bear. 1995. 10.15 (*0-606-09960-3*, Pub. by Turtleback) Demco.

— What Time Is It Around the World? LC 75-24710. (Illus.). (J). (gr. k-5). 1979. 14.95 (*0-87592-061-6*) Scroll Pr.

Baumann, Hans D. Control Valve Primer: A User's Guide. fac. ed. LC 91-28927. (Illus.). 145p. pap. 45.00 (*0-7837-7634-9*, 204738700007) Bks Demand.

— Control Valve Primer: A User's Guide. 2nd ed. LC 94-6002. (Illus.). 184p. reprint ed. pap. 57.10 (*0-608-08590-1*, 206911300003) Bks Demand.

— Control Valve Primer: A User's Guide. 3rd ed. LC 98-214487. viii, 169 p. 1998. 76.00 (*1-55617-640-6*) ISA.

Baumann, J. Bruce, ed. Cincinnati Then & Now: Cincinnati & Northern Kentucky. LC 95-74934. (Illus.). 112p. 1995. 29.95 (*1-884850-08-1*) Scripps Howard.

— Six.Six: The 1994 Killer Quake. (Illus.). 80p. (Orig.). 1994. pap. 12.95 (*1-884850-01-4*) Scripps Howard.

B

Baumann, J. Bruce, ed. see Blair, Seabury, Jr.

Baumann, J. Bruce, ed. see Creekmore, Betsey B.

Baumann, J. Bruce, ed. see Krakel, Dean.

Baumann, J. Bruce, ed. see Mellon, Steve & Baker, Don.

Baumann, J. Bruce, ed. see Mellon, Steve & Noyes, Charlene.

Baumann, J. Bruce, ed. see Rumbach, John.

Baumann, James. Ohio Cum Laude: The Whole Ohio College Catalogue. LC 97-16302. (Illus.). 384p. 1997. pap. text 29.95 (*1-882203-11-9*) Orange Frazer.

Baumann, James, jt. auth. see Mitchell, Cameron.

Baumann, James F. Reading Assessment: An Instructional Decision Making Perspective. 416p. (C). 1990. pap. text 39.00 (*0-675-20840-8*, Merrill Coll) P-H.

Baumann, James F., ed. Teaching Main Idea Comprehension. LC 85-23185. 286p. reprint ed. pap. 88.70 (*0-7837-1237-5*, 204137400020) Bks Demand.

Baumann, James F. & Johnson, Dale O., eds. Writing for Publication in Reading & Language Arts. LC 91-13333. 250p. 1991. reprint ed. pap. 77.50 (*0-608-03471-1*, 206418100008) Bks Demand.

Baumann, Jurgen, et al. Meyers Enzyklopaedisches Lexikon Vol. 22: Sn-Sud & Nachtrag 7. 9th ed. (GER.). 872p. 1978. 275.00 (*0-7859-6912-8*, 3411012722) Fr & Eur.

Baumann, K. Ring Out, Wild Bells. LC 89-20061. 80p. (J). (gr. 3-7). 1992. 17.95 (*0-15-267100-5*, Harcourt Child Bks) Harcourt.

Baumann, Kathy & Conners, Erin. Through Tara's Eyes: Helping Children Cope with Alzheimer's Disease. (Illus.). 36p. 1995. pap. 5.00 (*1-930181-01-9*) A H A F.

Baumann, Ken. Arming the Suckers: Illinois Troops. 237p. 1989. 29.95 (*0-89029-529-8*) Morningside Bkshop.

Baumann, Lotte, tr. see Ranke, Kurt.

Baumann, Mandell. Q Basic. (Computer Programming Ser.). 1996. spiral bd. 48.25 incl. disk (*0-314-00822-5*, Pub. by West Pub) Thomson Learn.

— Qbasic. 2nd ed. (Computer Applications). (C). 1997. text 30.25 (*0-314-22026-7*) West Pub.

Baumann, Mary A. & Bahntge, Mary A. Legal Keyboarding: Typewriters, Electric Typewriters, Word Processors. 286p. 1985. pap. text 21.95 (*0-471-88590-8*) P-H.

— Legal Terminology & Transcription: Word Processing. 176p. (C). 1986. pap. text 26.25 (*0-471-82042-3*) P-H.

Baumann, Michele, jt. auth. see Isacoff, Stuart.

Baumann, Miges, et al, eds. The Life Industry: Biodiversity, People & Profits. 206p. 1996. pap. 18.95 (*1-85339-341-X*, Pub. by Intermed Tech) Stylus Pub VA.

Baumann, N., et al, eds. Late Onset Neurometabolic Genetic Disorders: From Clinical to Molecular Aspects of Lysosomal & Peroxisomal Disease - Journal: Developmental Neuroscience, Vol. 13, Nos. 4-5. (Illus.). 196p. 1991. pap. 106.25 (*3-8055-5524-5*) S Karger.

*Baumann, P. H. & von Berlepsch, K.** Komplementarmedizin Aus der Sicht der Wissenschaft: Bericht der Expertengruppe Zum Nationalen Forschungsprogramm 34, Komplementarmedizin, 1992-1998, Schweizerischer Nationalfonds NFP34. (Forschende Komplementarmedizin/Research in Complementary Medicine Ser.). vi, 66p. 1999. 36.50 (*3-8055-6837-1*) S Karger.

Baumann, Paul. Collecting Antique Marbles. 3rd ed. LC 99-61446. 176p. 1999. pap. 23.95 (*0-87341-724-0*) Krause Pubns.

Baumann, Paul, et al, eds. Up Close from Afar: Using Remote Sensing to Teach the American Landscape. LC 95-154084. (Pathways in Geography Ser.: No. 8). (Illus.). 83p. (Orig.). 1994. pap. text 17.50 (*0-9627379-9-2*) NCFGE.

Baumann-Reynolds, Sally. Francois Mitterand: The Making of a Socialist Prince in Republican France. LC 94-37201. 224p. 1995. 57.95 (*0-275-94887-0*, Praeger Pubs) Greenwood.

Baumann, Richard. Foods That Made Wisconsin Famous: 150 Great Recipes. Stoga, Stan, ed. LC 99-70831. (Illus.). 224p. 1999. pap. 16.95 (*0-915024-70-5*) Trails Media.

Baumann, Richard G. Retrospective: Lawrence McKinin. (Illus.). 48p. (Orig.). 1983. pap. 5.00 (*0-910501-01-7*) U of Missouri Mus Art Arch.

Baumann, Roland, ed. A Manual of Archival Techniques. rev. ed. LC 82-623264. 150p. 1982. pap. 5.95 (*0-89271-020-9*) Pa Hist & Mus.

Baumann, Roland M., compiled by. Guide to the Microfilm of the Records of Pennsylvania's Revolutionary Governments, 1775-1790. LC 79-624725. 1978. 13.95 (*0-911124-96-9*) Pa Hist & Mus.

Baumann, Ruediger. BASIC Game Plans: Computer Games & Puzzles Programmed in BASIC. 350p. 1988. 32.00 (*0-8176-3366-9*) Birkhauser.

Baumann, Sandra C. The Economics Institute Guide to Graduate Study in Economics & Agricultural Economics in the United States of America & Canada. 9th ed. LC 95-61170. (Illus.). 376p. (Orig.). (C). 1995. pap. text 24.00 (*0-88024-158-6*) Econ Inst.

Baumann, Sean E. Psychiatry & Primary Health Care. 525p. 1999. pap. 35.00 (*0-7021-4207-7*, Pub. by Juta & Co) Intl Spec Bk.

Baumann, Susan K. Computer Science. 1992. mass mkt. 46.50 (*0-314-91838-8*) West Pub.

— Computer Science. annot. ed. Date not set. text, teacher ed. 45.95 (*0-314-92765-4*) West Pub.

— Hypercard. Date not set. wbk. ed., lab manual ed. write for info. (*0-314-04924-X*) West Pub.

— Microcomputer & Information Processing. 11th ed. (DF - Computer Applications Ser.). (C). 1997. pap. write for info. (*0-314-20548-9*) West Pub.

— Programming & Q Basic. Date not set. pap. text, teacher ed. 16.95 (*0-314-02538-3*) West Pub.

— Programming Basic Apple. Date not set. pap. text, teacher ed. 21.95 (*0-314-72072-3*) West Pub.

— Q Basic: Test Bank. Date not set. pap. text, teacher ed. 15.95 (*0-314-00884-5*) West Pub.

— Qbasic. (DG - Computer Programming Ser.). (C). 1992. mass mkt. 39.00 (*0-314-00071-2*) West Pub.

— Qbasic. 2nd ed. LC 97-123321. (DF - Computer Applications Ser.). (C). 1996. mass mkt. 61.95 (*0-314-20547-0*) West Pub.

— Technology. annot. ed. Date not set. text, teacher ed. write for info. (*0-314-09713-9*) West Pub.

— Understanding Pascal: Turbo Version. (DF - Computer Applications Ser.). 1990. mass mkt. 45.50 (*0-314-49897-4*) West Pub.

— Understanding Structured Programming in BASIC. (DG - Computer Programming Ser.). 1989. mass mkt. 43.00 (*0-314-67029-7*) West Pub.

Baumann, Susan K. & Flynn, Meredith. Microcomputers & Information Technology. 10th ed. 400p. 1996. mass mkt. 41.00 (*0-314-04945-2*); mass mkt. 46.25 (*0-314-04944-4*) West Pub.

Baumann, Susan K. & Mandell, Steven L. Programming in HyperCard. LC 93-25651. 1994. mass mkt. 34.25 (*0-314-02735-1*) West Pub.

— Qbasic. Perlee, Clyde, ed. 450p. (YA). 1992. mass mkt. 43.50 (*0-314-78351-2*) West Pub.

— Qbasic. 2nd ed. 550p. (C). 1996. mass mkt. 36.75 (*0-314-20659-0*) West Pub.

— Understanding Structured Programming in BASIC, Apple Version. large type ed. 1991. 128.00 (*0-614-09878-5*, L-95703-00) Am Printing Hse.

Baumann, Thomas H. Kensington-Talmadge, 1910-1997. 2nd rev. ed. Wilson, David, ed. (Illus.). 216p. 1997. 29.95 (*1-880663-68-6*) Ellipsys Intl.

Baumann, Urs, jt. ed. see Veiel, Hans O.

Baumann, Uwe, ed. Henry the Eighth in History, Historiography, & Literature. LC 92-40944. 327p. 1993. 56.00 (*3-631-44143-6*) P Lang Pubng.

Baumann, Uwe, jt. ed. see Boventer, Hermann.

Baumann, Uwe, ed. see Zangen, Britta.

Baumann, Walter. Roses from the Steel Dust: Collected Essays on Ezra Pound. LC 99-40588. 280p. 1999. 49.95 (*0-943373-61-1*); pap. 17.95 (*0-943373-62-X*) Natl Poet Foun.

Baumann, Wolf-Rudiger. The Merchants Adventurers & the Continental Cloth-Trade, 1560s-1620s. (European University Institute, Series B (History): No. 2). xiv, 425p. (C). 1990. lib. bdg. 135.40 (*3-11-012582-X*) De Gruyter.

Baumann, Wolfgang J., ed. Platelet-Activating Factor & Structurally Related Alkyl Ether Lipids. 524p. (C). 1991. 60.00 (*0-935315-40-3*) Am Oil Chemists.

Baumbach, Charles R., jt. auth. see Gimmy, Arthur E.

*Baumbach, Cheryl.** 15 Seconds with God: Quick Devotions to Ponder All Day. 128p. 1999. pap. 7.95 (*0-9673747-0-7*) L G I Pr.

Baumbach, Emily J. Celebrities: The Complete Michael Database. 64p. (Orig.). 1996. pap. 9.95 (*0-9650668-1-9*) Causalworks.

Baumbach, G. Air Quality Control. 496p. 1996. 99.95 (*0-387-57992-3*) Spr-Verlag.

— Air Quality Control. 1996. 59.00 (*3-540-57992-3*) Spr-Verlag.

Baumbach, Gerard F. Experienceing Mystagogy: The Sacred Pause of Easter. LC 95-31453. 288p. (Orig.). 1996. pap. 14.95 (*0-8091-3615-5*) Paulist Pr.

*Baumbach, Gerard F.** Letters from a Wounded Heart: Reflections to Stregthen & Comfort the Soul. 96p. 2000. pap. 8.95 (*0-8091-3988-X*) Paulist Pr.

Baumbach, Gerard F. Spirituality for Lent & Easter: A Guide for Bridging the Mysteries. LC 98-34868. 160p. 1999. pap. 8.95 (*0-8091-3837-9*) Paulist Pr.

Baumbach, Jonathan. Babble. LC 76-2876. 117p. 1976. 15.95 (*0-914590-26-X*); pap. 6.95 (*0-914590-27-8*) Fiction Coll.

— Chez Charlotte & Emily. LC 79-52033. 1979. 15.95 (*0-914590-56-1*); pap. 7.95 (*0-914590-57-X*) Fiction Coll.

— D-Tours. LC 98-13870. 175p. 1998. pap. 12.95 (*1-57366-037-X*) Fiction Coll.

— The Life & Times of Major Fiction. LC 86-29215. 208p. 1987. 15.95 (*0-932511-08-2*) Fiction Coll.

— My Father More or Less. LC 81-71644. 152p. 1982. 15.95 (*0-914590-66-9*); pap. 6.95 (*0-914590-67-7*) Fiction Coll.

— Reruns. LC 74-77780. 170p. 1974. pap. 5.95 (*0-914590-01-4*) Fiction Coll.

— The Return of Service. Stories. LC 79-18102. (Illinois Short Fiction Ser.). 140p. 1979. text 14.95 (*0-252-00784-0*) U of Ill Pr.

— Separate Hours. White, Curtis, ed. 204p. 1990. text 18.95 (*0-932511-27-9*); pap. text 8.95 (*0-932511-28-7*) Fiction Coll.

— Seven Wives: A Novel. 128p. 1994. 18.95 (*0-932511-86-4*); pap. 8.95 (*0-932511-87-2*) Fiction Coll.

Baumbach, Jonathan & Spielberg, Peter, eds. Statements Two. LC 76-56053. 1977. 10.95 (*0-914590-36-7*); pap. 6.95 (*0-914590-37-5*) Fiction Coll.

Baumbach, Lisa. Mutation Detection Protocols. (Methods in Molecular Biology Ser.). (Illus.). 1998. 69.50 (*0-89603-496-8*) Humana.

Baumbach, Werner. The Life & Death of the Luftwaffe. (War & Warriors Ser.). (Illus.). 224p. 1991. 12.95 (*0-939482-37-1*, 0166, Noontide Pr) Legion Survival.

Baumback, Clifford M. Baumback's Guide to Entrepreneurship. 1981. 27.95 (*0-13-066761-7*) P-H.

Baumberg, S., et al, eds. Genetics & Product Formation in Streptomyces. (FEMS Symposium Ser.: No. 55). (Illus.). 340p. (C). 1991. text 138.00 (*0-306-43885-2*, Kluwer Plenum) Kluwer Academic.

— Population Genetics of Bacteria. (Society for General Microbiology Symposium Ser.: No. 52). (Illus.). 360p. (C). 1995. text 115.00 (*0-521-48052-3*) Cambridge U Pr.

Baumberg, Simon, ed. Prokaryotic Gene Expression. LC 98-52907. (Frontiers in Molecular Biology Ser.). (Illus.). 346p. 1999. text 125.00 (*0-19-963604-4*) OUP.

— Prokaryotic Gene Expression. LC 98-52907. (Frontiers in Molecular Biology Ser.: No. 21). (Illus.). 346p. 1999. pap. text 55.00 (*0-19-963603-6*) OUP.

Baumberger, Julie P. & Harper, Ruth E. Assisting Students with Disabilities: What School Counselors Can & Must Do. (Practical Skills for Counselors (PSFC) Ser.). 120p. 1999. pap. 16.95 (*0-8039-6648-2*); lib. bdg. 39.95 (*0-8039-6647-4*) Corwin Pr.

*Baumbich, Charlene.** 365 Ways to Connect with Your Kids: No Matter What Their Age (or Yours) 224p. 2001. pap. 14.99 (*1-56414-480-1*, New Page Bks) Career Pr Inc.

Baumbich, Charlene A. Book of Duh: Celebrating Those Less-Than-Magic Moments. LC 97-20096. 1997. pap. text 5.99 (*0-87788-060-3*, H Shaw Pubs) Waterbrook Pr.

— Don't Miss Your Kids! LC 90-27667. 160p. 1994. pap. 9.99 (*0-8308-1641-0*, 1641, Saltshaker Bk) InterVarsity.

— How to Eat Humble Pie: And Not Get Indigestion. 2nd ed. 175p. (Orig.). 1997. reprint ed. pap. 12.00 (*1-890156-00-0*) Arbor Hill Pr.

— The Twelve Dazes of Christmas: And One Holy Night. LC 96-16489. 141p. (Orig.). 1996. pap. 9.99 (*0-8308-1961-4*, 1961, Saltshaker Bk) InterVarsity.

*Baumbich, Charlene Ann.** The Book of Duh: Celebrating Those Less-Than-Magic Moments. 2nd ed. (Illus.). 94p. 2000. reprint ed. pap. 6.00 (*1-890156-03-5*) Arbor Hill Pr.

Baumbick, Robert J., jt. ed. see Thompson, Daniel B.

Baumbusch, Brigitte. Animals Observed. Paoli, Erika, tr. from ITA. LC 99-29620. (Art for Children Ser). (Illus.). 29p. (J). (ps-3). 1999. 9.95 (*1-55670-970-6*) STC Pubns.

*Baumbusch, Brigitte.** Looking at Nature. Paoli, Erika, tr. from ITA. LC 99-29621. (Art for Children Ser). (Illus.). 29p. (J). (ps-3). 1999. 9.95 (*1-55670-971-4*) STC Pubns.

— Many Faces of the Face. LC 99-15470. (Art for Children Ser.). (Illus.). 29p. (J). (ps-3). 1999. pap. 9.95 (*1-55670-968-4*) Stewart Tabori & Chang.

*Baumbusch, Brigitte, ed.** Figuring Figures. LC 99-29622. (Art for Children Ser). (Illus.). 29p. (J). (ps-3). 1999. 9.95 (*1-55670-969-2*) STC Pubns.

Baumbusch, Steve, tr. see Zambon, Mariagarzia.

Baumchen, Franz. German Economic Terms for Foreigners: Deutsche Wirtschaftssprache fuer Auslaender. (GER.). 260p. 1982. pap. 45.00 (*0-8288-1274-8*, M14262) Fr & Eur.

Baumchen, Hal, jt. auth. see Anderson, Neil T.

Baume, Cecile De La, see De La Baume, Cecile.

Baume, L. J. FDI Lexicon of English Dental Terms. (ENG, FRE, GER & SPA.). 400p. 1985. 75.00 (*0-8288-7607-X*) Fr & Eur.

Baume, Nicholas, et al. About Face: Andy Warhol Portraits. (Illus.). 140p. 1999. pap. 25.00 (*0-918333-14-8*) Wadsworth Atheneum.

Baumeister. Drugs & Behavior. (Psychology Ser.). 1919. mass mkt. 53.95 (*0-534-34484-4*) Wadsworth Pub.

*Baumeister, Andrea.** Liberalism & the Politics of Difference. 224p. 2000. pap. text 25.00 (*0-7486-0909-1*) Col U Pr.

Baumeister, Andrea, jt. ed. see Horton, John.

Baumeister, Friedrich C. Gesammelte Werke Abteilung: Ergaenzungsreihe, Vol. 24. (Materialien und Dokumente Ser.). (GER.). 400p. 1989. write for info. (*3-487-09057-0*) G Olms Pubs.

— Gesammelte Werke Abteilung: Ergaenzungsreihe, Vol. 25. (GER.). 656p. 1988. write for info. (*3-487-09058-9*) G Olms Pubs.

Baumeister, R. F. Self-Esteem: The Puzzle of Low Self-Regard. LC 93-7043. (Social - Clinical Psychology Ser.). (Illus.). 286p. (C). 1993. 45.00 (*0-306-44373-2*, Plenum Trade) Perseus Pubng.

Baumeister, Roy F. Breaking Hearts: The Two Sides of Unrequited Love. 241p. 1994. pap. text 18.95 (*0-89862-152-6*) Guilford Pubns.

— Evil: Inside Human Violence & Cruelty. LC 96-41940. 400p. 1996. pap. text 24.95 (*0-7167-2902-4*) W H Freeman.

— Evil: Inside Human Violence & Cruelty. 431p. 1999. pap. text 15.95 (*0-7167-3567-9*) W H Freeman.

— Masochism & the Self. 256p. (C). 1989. text 59.95 (*0-8058-0486-2*) L Erlbaum Assocs.

— Meanings of Life. LC 91-17859. 426p. 1991. lib. bdg. 45.00 (*0-89862-763-X*) Guilford Pubns.

— Meanings of Life. LC 91-17859. 426p. 1992. reprint ed. pap. text 25.00 (*0-89862-531-9*) Guilford Pubns.

*Baumeister, Roy F.** The Self in Social Psychology: Essential Readings. LC 99-16279. 464p. 1999. write for info. (*0-86377-572-1*) L Erlbaum Assocs.

Baumeister, Roy F., ed. Public Self & Private Self. (Social Psychology Ser.). (Illus.). 270p. 1986. 63.00 (*0-387-96303-0*) Spr-Verlag.

*Baumeister, Roy F., ed.** The Self in Social Psychology. LC 99-16279. (Key Readings in Social Psychology Ser.). 492p. 1999. pap. text 34.95 (*0-86377-573-X*) L Erlbaum Assocs.

*Baumeister, Roy F. & Tice, Dianne M.** The Social Dimension of Sex. 272p. 2000. pap. 24.00 (*0-205-32442-8*) Allyn.

Baumeister, Roy F. & Wotman, Sara R. Breaking Hearts: The Two Sides of Unrequited Love. LC 92-2418. 241p. 1992. lib. bdg. 39.95 (*0-89862-543-2*) Guilford Pubns.

Baumeister, Roy F., jt. auth. see Berglas, Steven.

Baumeister, Theodore, III, jt. ed. see Avalione, E. A.

Baumeister, Theodore, jt. ed. see Avallone, E. A.

Baumeister, W. Pflanzenlexikon: Plant Lexicon, 5 vols. (GER.). 1280p. 1969. pap. 99.95 (*0-8288-6611-2*, M7580) Fr & Eur.

Baumel, H. & Deixonne, B., eds. Exocrine Pancreatic Cancer. (Illus.). 250p. 1986. 146.00 (*0-387-16530-4*) Spr-Verlag.

Baumel, Judith. Now. 1996. 16.95 (*1-881163-14-8*); pap. 10.95 (*1-881163-15-6*) Miami Univ Pr.

Baumel, Judith T. Double Jeopardy: Gender & the Holocaust. LC 98-35764. 300p. 1998. 49.50 (*0-85303-346-3*, Pub. by M Vallentine & Co); pap. 25.00 (*0-85303-345-5*, Pub. by M Vallentine & Co) Intl Spec Bk.

— Kibbutz Buchenwald: Survivors & Pioneers. LC 96-18311. (Illus.). 224p. (C). 1997. text 48.00 (*0-8135-2336-2*); pap. text 17.95 (*0-8135-2337-0*) Rutgers U Pr.

— Unfulfilled Promise: Rescue & Resettlement of Jewish Refugee Children in the United States, 1934-1945. LC 90-32118. (Illus.). 227p. (Orig.). (C). 1990. pap. 27.50 (*0-938737-21-X*) Denali Press.

Baumel, Judith T., ed. Israel State Archives, Jerusalem. LC 89-16915. (Archives in the Holocaust Ser.: Vol. 13). 400p. 1991. text 121.00 (*0-8153-0143-X*) Garland.

Baumel, Julian J., ed. Handbook of Avian Anatomy: Nomina Anatomica Avium. 2nd ed. (Publications of the Nuttall Ornithological Club: No. 23). (Illus.). 779p. 1993. 65.00 (*1-877973-34-3*) Nuttall Ornith.

Baumel, Syd. Dealing with Depression Naturally. 240p. (Orig.). 1995. pap. 19.95 (*0-87983-645-8*, Keats Publng) NTC Contemp Pub Co.

*Baumel, Syd.** Dealing with Depression Naturally: Alternative & Complementary Therapies for Restoring Emotional Health. 2nd ed. LC 00-29587. (Illus.). 304p. 2000. pap. 19.95 (*0-658-00291-0*, 002910, Keats Publng) NTC Contemp Pub Co.

Baumel, Syd. Natural Antidepressants. (Good Health Guides Ser.). 48p. 1998. pap. 3.95 (*0-87983-900-7*, 39007K, Keats Publng) NTC Contemp Pub Co.

— Serotonin. (Good Health Guides Ser.). 48p. 1998. pap. 3.95 (*0-87983-823-X*, 3823XK, Keats Publng) NTC Contemp Pub Co.

Baumer, Anne. Bibliography of the History of Biology (Bibliographie zur Geschichte der Biologie) LC 97-43596. xi, 307p. 1997. 63.95 (*0-8204-3513-9*) P Lang Pubng.

— Bibliography of the History of Biology (Bibliographie zur Geschichte der Biologie) (GER., Illus.). 1997. 63.95 (*3-631-32261-5*) P Lang Pubng.

Baumer, Bernice H. How to Teach Your Dyslexic Child to Read: A Proven Method for Parents. (Illus.). 160p. 1996. 15.95 (*1-55972-334-3*, Birch Ln Pr) Carol Pub Group.

— How to Teach Your Dyslexic Child to Read: A Proven Method for Parents & Teachers. LC 98-9399. (Illus.). 176p. 1998. pap. text 12.95 (*0-8065-1981-9*, Citadel Pr) Carol Pub Group.

Baumer, Bettina. Kalatattvakosa Vol. II: A Lexicon of Fundamental Concepts of the Indian Arts: Concepts of Space & Time. (C). 1992. text 44.00 (*81-208-1044-9*, Pub. by Motilal Bnarsidass) S Asia.

*Baumer, Bettina.** Kalatattvakosa Vol. III: A Lexicon of Fundamental Concepts of the Indian Art (Primal Elements, Mahabhuta) 446p. 1998. pap. 225.00 (*81-208-1402-9*, Pub. by Motilal Bnarsidass) St Mut.

Baumer, Bettina, ed. see Abhinavagupta.

Baumer, Bettina, jt. ed. see Vatsyayan, Kapila.

Baumer, Franklin L. Main Currents of Western Thought: Readings in Western European Intellectual History from the Middle Ages to the Present. 4th ed. LC 77-90945. 806p. 1978. reprint ed. pap. 25.00 (*0-300-02233-6*) Yale U Pr.

*Baumer, Fred A. & Hvass, Debra.** Selling Is Everyone's Job: The Guidebook for Designing & Running a Referral Program. (Business Improvement Ser.). 45p. 2000. pap. 10.95 (*0-9677723-0-3*) BI Business.

Baumer-Schleinkofer, Anne. Nazi Biology & Schools. LC 95-30154. 252p. 1995. 51.95 (*3-631-48798-3*) P Lang Pubng.

Baumer, William. Not All Warriors. (Essay Index Reprint Ser.). 325p. 1982. reprint ed. lib. bdg. 18.00 (*0-8290-0790-3*) Irvington.

Baumer, William H. Not All Warriors. LC 70-152156. (Essay Index Reprint Ser.). 1977. 21.95 (*0-8369-2180-1*) Ayer.

Baumert, Gerhard, et al. German Election Studies, 1961. Hildebrandt, Kai, tr. from GER. LC 75-40620. 1975. write for info. (*0-89138-122-8*) ICPSR.

Baumert, John H., ed. see Alksne, Z. K. & Ikaunieks, Ya Y.

Baumert, Norbert & Madigan, Patrick. Woman & Man in Paul: Overcoming a Misunderstanding. (Good News Studies: No. 40). 560p. (Orig.). 1996. pap. 34.95 (*0-8146-5055-4*, M Glazier) Liturgical Pr.

Baumgaarten, J. Alan, jt. auth. see Barksdale, Karl.

Baumgaertner, Jill. Flannery O'Connor: A Proper Scaring. rev. ed. LC 98-37131. 1998. pap. 10.95 (*0-940895-38-2*) Cornerstone IL.

Baumgardner, Barbara. A Passage Through Divorce. LC 99-201110. 1999. 14.99 (*0-8054-1117-8*) Broadman.

— A Passage Through Grief: An Interactive Journal. LC 96-42206. 1999. 12.99 (*0-8054-6072-1*) Broadman.

Baumgardner, Barbara, jt. compiled by see Gray, Alice.

Baumgardner, Gerald D. Implementing the Internet into Higher Education. LC 97-170377. 142p. (Orig.). (C). 1997. pap. text 14.95 (*0-943025-94-X*) Cummngs & Hath.

Baumgardner, James. Medicare & Graduate Medical Education. (Illus.). 49p. (Orig.). (C). 1995. pap. text 25.00 (*0-7881-2559-1*) DIANE Pub.

***Baumgardner, Jennifer & Richards, Amy.** Manifesta: Young Women, Feminism & the Future. 240p. 2000. pap. 13.00 (*0-374-52622-2*) FS&G.

Baumgardner, Kandy, jt. auth. see Elseth, Gerald.

Baumgardner, Mary A. Alexandra, Keeper of Dreams. Wheeler, Penny & Wilson, Miriam W., eds. LC 93-83250. (Illus.). 37p. (J). (gr. k-4). 1993. reprint ed. 16.95 (*0-944576-08-7*) Rocky River Pubs.

Baumgardner, R. W., Jr. Landsat-Based Lineament Analysis, East Texas Basin & Sabine Uplift Area. (Reports of Investigations: RI 167). (Illus.). 26p. 1987. 2.50 (*0-318-23676-1*) U of Tex Econ Geology.

— Morphometric Studies of Subhumid & Semiarid Drainage Basins, Texas Panhandle & Northeastern New Mexico. (Reports of Investigations: RI 163). (Illus.). 68p. 1987. pap. 3.00 (*0-318-23672-9*) Bur Econ Geology.

Baumgardner, R. W., Jr. & Scanlon, B. R. Surface Fissures in the Hueco Bolson & Adjacent Basins, West Texas, GC92-2. (Illus.). 44p. 1992. pap. 3.50 (*0-317-05171-7*, GC92-2) Bur Econ Geology.

Baumgardner, Robert E., ed. Local Government Infrastructure Management. (Sessions Proceedings Ser.). 33p. 1986. 3.00 (*0-87262-533-8*) Am Soc Civil Eng.

Baumgardner, Robert J. The English Language in Pakistan. (Illus.). 342p. 1998. text 29.95 (*0-19-577444-2*) OUP.

Baumgardner, Robert J., ed. South Asian English: Structure, Use, & Users. LC 95-8057. (English in the Global Context Ser.). 312p. 1995. text 44.95 (*0-252-02196-7*); pap. text 16.95 (*0-252-06493-3*) U of Ill Pr.

Baumgardner, Steve R. College & Jobs: Conservations with Recent Graduates. LC 87-25374. (Insight Bk.). 196p. 1988. 30.95 (*0-89885-413-X*, Kluwer Acad Hman Sci); pap. 14.95 (*0-89885-416-4*, Kluwer Acad Hman Sci) Kluwer Academic.

Baumgardner, Tracy. Prayers & Meditations from Around the World. (Illus.). 80p. 1997. 6.95 (*0-87573-065-5*) Jain Pub Co.

Baumgardt, John P. How to Identify Flowering Plant Families. LC 82-10592. (Illus.). 269p. 1982. pap. 22.95 (*0-917304-21-7*) Timber.

Baumgardt, M. Creative Multimedia Design: Tips & Tricks Step by Step. 96p. 1999. 35.75 incl. cd-rom (*3-540-62707-3*) Spr-Verlag.

— Creative Web Design: Tips & Tricks Step by Step. LC 98-5476. (Illus.). 160p. 1998. pap. 39.00 incl. cd-rom (*3-540-62662-X*) Spr-Verlag.

***Baumgardt, Michael.** Adobe Photoshop 5.5 Web Design: With ImageReady 2 & GoLive 4.0. 311p. 1999. pap. 40.00 (*0-201-70012-3*) Adobe Pr.

Baumgartl. Transition & Sustainability: Actors & Interests in Eastern European Environmental Policies, Vol. IELP. LC 97-10312. (International Environmental Law & Policy Ser.). 1997. 121.50 (*90-411-0681-2*) Kluwer Law Intl.

Baumgart, Alice J. & Larson, Jenniece. Canadian Nursing Faces the Future: Development & Change. 2nd ed. (Illus.). 680p. (C). (gr. 13). 1992. pap. text 30.00 (*0-8016-6330-X*, 06330) Mosby Inc.

Baumgart, Hildegard. Jealousy: Experiences & Solutions. Jacobson, Manfred & Jacobson, Evelyn, trs. LC 89-37321. 368p. 1990. 41.95 (*0-226-03935-8*) U Ch Pr.

— Jealousy: Experiences & Solutions. Jacobson, Manfred & Jacobson, Evelyn, trs. 356p. 1999. reprint ed. text 25.00 (*0-7881-6376-0*) DIANE Pub.

Baumgart, Howard D. Over Fifty Years of Caring: A History of Rainier School & Mental Retardation. LC 96-95407. (Illus.). vi, 432p. 1997. pap. 25.00 (*0-9629616-3-9*) Magden Assocs.

Baumgart, Klaus. Anna & the Little Green Dragon. 1992. 10.15 (*0-606-07198-9*, Pub. by Turtleback) Demco.

Baumgart, Klaus. Don't Be Afraid, Tommy. LC 97-51155. (Illus.). 28p. (J). (ps-2). 1998. 14.95 (*1-888444-32-0*, 21150) Little Tiger.

— Laura's Christmas Star. LC 99-27986. (Illus.). 32p. (J). (ps-2). 1999. 16.95 (*1-888444-59-2*, Pub. by Little Tiger) Futech Educ Prods.

— Laura's Star. LC 97-26739. (Illus.). 32p. (J). (ps-2). 1997. 16.95 (*1-888444-24-X*, 21022) Little Tiger.

— The Little Green Dragon Steps Out. LC 92-5120. (Little Green Dragon Ser.). (Illus.). 32p. (J). (ps-3). 1992. 12.95 (*1-56282-254-3*, Pub. by Hyprn Child) Little.

— Where Are You, Little Green Dragon? LC 92-72026. (Little Green Dragon Ser.). (Illus.). 32p. (J). (ps-3). 1993. lib. bdg. 12.89 (*1-56282-345-0*, Pub. by Hyprn Child) Little.

— Where Are You, Little Green Dragon? LC 92-72026. (Little Green Dragon Ser.). (Illus.). 32p. (J). (ps-3). 1993. 12.95 (*1-56282-344-2*, Pub. by Hyprn Child) Little.

— Where Are You, Little Green Dragon? LC 92-72026. (Little Green Dragon Ser.). (Illus.). 32p. (J). (ps-3). 1995. pap. 4.95 (*0-7868-1073-4*, Pub. by Hyprn Ppbks) Little.

— Where Are You, Little Green Dragon? (J). 1993. 10.15 (*0-606-08903-9*, Pub. by Turtleback) Demco.

***Baumgart, Rainer, ed.** Secure Networking - CQRE (Secure) '99: International Exhibition & Congress Dusseldorf, Germany, November 30 - December 2, 1999, Proceedings. LC 99-58804. (Lecture Notes in Computer Science Ser.: ol. 1740). ix, 258p. 1999. pap. 52.00 (*3-540-66800-4*) Spr-Verlag.

Baumgart, Susan. Rainforest Animals Dot-to-Dot. (Illus.). 64p. (J). 1995. pap. 5.95 (*0-8069-0896-3*) Sterling.

Baumgart, Winfried. The Crimean War, 1853-1856. (Modern Wars Ser.). (Illus.). 256p. 1999. text 75.00 (*0-340-75960-7*, Pub. by E A) OUP.

***Baumgart, Winfried.** The Crimean War, 1853-1856. (Modern Wars Ser.). (Illus.). 256p. 1999. pap. 24.95 (*0-340-61465-X*, Pub. by E A) OUP.

Baumgartel, Elise J. The Cultures of Prehistoric Egypt, 2 vols. in 1. LC 80-24186. (Illus.). 164p. 1981. reprint ed. lib. bdg. 72.50 (*0-313-22524-9*, BACU, Greenwood Pr) Greenwood.

— Cultures of Prehistoric Egypt Two: Petrie's Naqada Excavation. fiche 8.00 (*0-900416-50-5*, Pub. by Aris & Phillips) David Brown.

Baumgartel, Elise J. & Koenigsberg, D. Phil. Petrie's Naqada Excavation: A Supplement. 1970. 60.00 (*0-85388-005-0*, Pub. by Aris & Phillips) David Brown.

Baumgartel, Hellmut. Analytic Perturbation: Theory for Matrices & Operators. (Operator Theory, Advances & Applications Ser.). 400p. 1985. 149.00 (*0-8176-1664-0*) Birkhauser.

— Operator Algebraic Methods in Quantum Field Theory. LC 95-37753. (Series of Lectures). 228p. 1995. text 52.50 (*3-05-501655-6*, Pub. by Akademie Verlag) Wiley.

Baumgartel, Hellmut & Wollenberg, Manfred. Mathematical Scattering Theory. (Operator Theory, Advances & Applications Ser.: Vol. 9). 1983. text 68.95 (*3-7643-1519-9*) Birkhauser.

Baumgartel, Hellmut, ed. see Barthel, J. M., et al.

Baumgartel, Hellmut, ed. see Illenberger, E. & Momigny, J.

Baumgartel, K. & Sauer, Kenneth H. Topics on Nonlinear Wave Plasma Interaction. 224p. 1988. 58.00 (*0-8176-1864-3*) Birkhauser.

Baumgarten, jt. auth. see Spies.

Baumgarten, Alan, jt. auth. see Davis, Glenn.

***Baumgarten, Albert I.** Apocalyptic Time. LC 00-29731. (Numen Book Series Studies in the History of Religions). 2000. write for info. (*90-04-11879-9*) Brill Academic Pubs.

Baumgarten, Albert I. The Flourishing of Jewish Sects in the Maccabean Era: An Interpretation. LC 97-5232. (Journal for the Study of Judaism Ser.: Vol. 55). 240p. 1997. text 84.00 (*90-04-10751-7*) Brill Academic Pubs.

Baumgarten, Albert I., et al. Self, Soul & Body in Religious Experience. LC 98-21200. (Studies in the History of Religions). 1998. write for info. (*90-04-10943-9*) Brill Academic Pubs.

Baumgarten, Alexander & Richards, Frank F. Clinical Laboratory Science Series, CRC: Section F, Immunology, 2 pts., Pt. 1, Vol 1. 1978. 251.00 (*0-8493-7021-3*, RB37, CRC Reprint) Franklin.

— Clinical Laboratory Science Series, CRC: Section F, Immunology, 2 pts., Pt. 2, Vol. 1. 480p. 1979. 257.00 (*0-8493-7022-1*, CRC Reprint) Franklin.

Baumgarten, Alexander G. Aesthetica. 1986. write for info. (*3-487-00167-5*) G Olms Pubs.

— Metaphysica. 2nd ed. (GER.). 432p. 1982. reprint ed. write for info. (*3-487-00377-5*) G Olms Pubs.

***Baumgarten, Barbara D.** Teach Us to Number Our Days: A Liturgical Advent Calendar. LC 99-30559. 160p. 1999. pap. 16.95 (*0-8192-1765-4*, 2508) Morehouse Pub.

Baumgarten, Barbara D. Visual Art As Theology. LC 93-46854. (New Studies in Aesthetics: Vol. 21). (Illus.). XVI, 272p. (C). 1995. text 57.95 (*0-8204-2462-5*) P Lang Pubng.

***Baumgarten, Barbara Dee.** A Vestment for All Seasons. 160p. 2002. pap. 17.95 (*0-8192-1866-9*) Morehouse Pub.

Baumgarten, Bernd & Giessler, Alfred. OSI Conformance Testing Methodology & TTCN. LC 94-36819. 340p. 1994. 194.50 (*0-444-89712-7*) Elsevier.

***Baumgarten, Bernd, et al.** Dragon Naturally Speaking Quicktorial. 144p. (C). 1999. pap. 18.95 (*0-538-68950-1*) Thomson Learn.

Baumgarten, David, jt. auth. see Haynes-Seman, Clare.

Baumgarten, E. Lee. Price Guide & Bibliographic Checklist for Children's & Illustrated Books 1880-1960. LC 95-96231. 382p. 1995. 95.00 (*0-9647285-0-8*); pap. 68.00 (*0-9647285-1-6*) E L Baumgarten.

Baumgarten, H., jt. ed. see Peters, J. H.

Baumgarten, H. G., et al, eds. Serotoninergic Neurons & 5-HT Receptors in the CNS. LC 97-23528. (Handbook of Experimental Pharmacology Ser.: No. 129). (Illus.). 680p. 1997. 379.00 (*3-540-62666-2*) Spr-Verlag.

***Baumgarten, H. G. & Ghothert, M., eds.** Serotoninergic Neurons & 5-HT Receptors in the CNS. LC 99-52203. (Handbook of Experimental Pharmacology Ser.). (Illus.). xxx, 767p. 2000. 109.00 (*3-540-66715-6*) Spr-Verlag.

Baumgarten, Henry E. Organic Syntheses Collective Volumes, Vol. 5, Vols. 40-49, Vol. 5, Vols. 40-49. 1248p. 1973. 149.00 (*0-471-05707-X*) Wiley.

Baumgarten, Henry E., jt. auth. see Linstromberg, Walter W.

***Baumgarten, J. Alan.** Dragon Naturally Speaking. 1999. pap. write for info. (*0-538-69455-6*) Thomson Learn.

Baumgarten, J. Alan, jt. auth. see Rutter, Michael.

Baumgarten, Jon A. & Latman, Alan. Corporate Copyright & Information Practices. (Illus.). iv, 200p. write for info. (*0-318-58174-4*) Harcourt.

Baumgarten, Joseph M., ed. Qumran Cave 4 Vol. XIII: The Damascus Document. (Discoveries in the Judaean Desert Ser.: No. XVIII). (Illus.). 256p. 1997. text 140.00 (*0-19-826396-1*) OUP.

Baumgarten, Joseph M., et al, eds. Qumran Cave 4 XXXV: Halakhic Texts. (Discoveries in the Judaean Desert Ser.: Xxxv). (Illus.). 192p. 2000. 85.00 (*0-19-827006-2*) OUP.

Baumgarten, Linda. Eighteenth-Century Clothing at Williamsburg. LC 86-20726. (Wallace Gallery Decorative Arts Publications). (Illus.). 79p. 1986. pap. 10.95 (*0-87935-109-8*) Colonial Williamsburg.

***Baumgarten, Linda, et al.** Costume Close-Up: Clothing Construction & Pattern, 1750-1790. LC 99-33258. (Illus.). 128p. 1999. pap. 24.95 (*0-87935-188-8*) Colonial Williamsburg.

— Costume Close-Up: Clothing Construction & Pattern, 1750-1790. LC 99-33258. 1999. pap. 24.95 (*0-89676-226-2*) QSMG Ltd.

Baumgarten, Lothar, et al. Parkett: Distance, Nos. 44-45. 200p. pap. 29.50 (*3-907509-94-3*) Dist Art Pubs.

Baumgarten, Murray. City Scriptures: Modern Jewish Writing. LC 81-6879. 293p. 1982. 35.95 (*0-674-13278-5*) HUP.

Baumgarten, Murray & Daleski, William, eds. Home & Homelessness in the Victorian Imagination. LC 95-43227. (Studies in Nineteenth-Century Literature & Culture: No. 2). xx, 355p. 1993. 55.00 (*0-404-64352-3*) AMS Pr.

Baumgarten, Otto, et al. Geistige Und Sittliche Wirkungen des Krieges in Deutschland. (Wirtschafts-Und Sozialgeschichte des Weltkrieges (Osterreichische Und Ungarische Serie)). (GER.). 1927. 125.00 (*0-317-27472-4*) Elliots Bks.

Baumgarten, P. M. Henry Charles Lea's Historical Writings. 1975. 250.00 (*0-87968-262-0*) Gordon Pr.

Baumgarten, Paul A., et al. Producing, Financing & Distributing Film: A Comprehensive Legal & Business Guide. rev. ed. LC 91-43708. 240p. 1992. reprint ed. pap. 17.95 (*0-87910-107-5*) Limelight Edns.

Baumgarth, William P., ed. see Aquinas, Thomas, Saint.

Baumgarth, William P., tr. see Aquinas, Thomas, Saint.

Baumgartl, Bernd & Favell, Adrian, eds. New Xenophobia in Europe. 416p. (C). 1995. lib. bdg. 91.00 (*90-411-0865-3*) Kluwer Academic.

Baumgartmer, Thomas, et al. The Shaping of the Socio-Economic Systems. (Studies in Cybernetics: Vol. 11). xiv, 360p. 1986. text 106.00 (*2-88124-003-8*) Gordon & Breach.

— The Shaping of the Socio-Economic Systems. (Studies in Cybernetics: Vol. 2). xiv, 360p. 1986. pap. text 59.00 (*2-88124-027-5*) Gordon & Breach.

Baumgartner. Measurement Evaluation in P. E. 5th ed. 1994. teacher ed. 9.68 (*0-697-15219-7*) McGraw.

— Praying for End. LC 99-14214. 1999. text 26.95 (*0-312-21092-2*) St Martin.

— Rheumatoid Arthritis. 119.00 (*0-86577-602-4*) Thieme Med Pubs.

Baumgartner & Jack. Measurement Evaluation. 6th ed. LC 98-23747. 1998. 42.50 (*0-697-29484-6*, WCB McGr Hill) McGrw-H Hghr Educ.

Baumgartner & Strong. Conduct/Read Resource Health. 1996. pap. 37.25 (*0-697-41747-6*, WCB McGr Hill) McGrw-H Hghr Educ.

Baumgartner, jt. auth. see Burns, Tom R.

Baumgartner, A. & Liebscher, J. J. Allgemeine Hydrologie. Quantitative Hydrologie. 1990. (Lehrbuch der Hydrogeologie Ser.: Vol. 1). (GER., Illus.). 673p. 1990. text 120.00 (*3-443-30001-4*, Pub. by Gebruder Borntraeger) Balogh.

Baumgartner, A. & Picot, C. E., eds. Molecular Basis of Polymer Networks. (Proceedings in Physics Ser.: Vol. 42). (Illus.). ix, 223p. 1989. 67.95 (*0-387-51649-2*) Spr-Verlag.

Baumgartner, Albert & Liebscher, Hans-Juergen. Lehrbuch der Hydrologie Band 1: Allgemeine Hydrologie. Quantitative Hydrologie. (GER.). xl, 694p. 1996. 93.00 (*3-443-30002-2*, Pub. by Gebruder Borntraeger) Balogh.

Baumgartner, Angela L. Escape the Expense: How to Make Your Wedding a Big Success Without a Big Budget. Stephens, Lori, ed. (Illus.). 63p. 1991. pap. 10.98 (*1-892498-00-6*) Rinky Dink Pr.

Baumgartner, Anne S. A Comprehensive Dictionary of the Gods. 1989. pap. 9.95 (*0-8065-1123-0*, Citadel Pr) Carol Pub Group.

Baumgartner, Apollinaris W. Catholic Journalism. LC 75-159997. (BCL Ser. I). reprint ed. 21.50 (*0-404-00693-0*) AMS Pr.

***Baumgartner, Barbara.** All My Shining Silver: Stories of Values from Around the World. LC 00-22671. (Illus.). (J). 2000. write for info. (*0-7894-6663-5*) DK Pub Inc.

Baumgartner, Barbara. The Gingerbread Man. LC 97-33386. (Nursery Classics Ser.). (Illus.). (J). 1998. 8.95 (*0-7894-2963-2*) DK Pub Inc.

— Good As Gold. LC 98-12899. (J). 1998. write for info. (*0-7894-3482-2*) DK Pub Inc.

Baumgartner, C. Clinical Electrophysiology of the Somatosensory Cortex: A Combined Study Using Electrocortigraphy, Scalp-EEG, & Magnetoencephalography. (Illus.). 220p. 1993. 103.00 (*0-387-82391-3*) Spr-Verlag.

Baumgartner, C., et al, eds. Biomagnetism: Fundamental Research & Clinical Applications. LC 95-7844. (Studies in Applied Electromagnetics & Mechanics: Vol. 7). 874p. (YA). (gr. 12). 1995. 156.00 (*90-5199-233-5*, 233-5) IOS Press.

Baumgartner, Christine, jt. ed. see Schneider, Jochem.

Baumgartner, D. J. & Duedall, Iver W., eds. Physical & Chemical Processes: Transport & Transformation: Oceanic Processes in Marine Pollution, Vol. 6. LC 89-2526. 262p. (C). 1990. 64.50 (*0-89874-964-6*) Krieger.

Baumgartner, Elzbieta. Ameryka Dla Kazdego: Czyli Poradnik Dla Polakow W U. S. A. 360p. 1992. pap. text 25.00 (*0-9633932-0-0*) Polpress Servs.

— Ameryka Dla Kazdego: Czyli Poradnik Dla Polakow W U. S. A. Minakowska, Malgorzata, ed. (POL., Illus.). 442p. 1995. pap. text 25.00 (*0-9633932-2-7*) Polpress Servs.

— Ameryka Dla Kazdego: Czyli Poradnik Dlo Polakow w Ujn, Vol. 2. (POL.). 420p. (Orig.). 1993. pap. text 25.00 (*0-9633932-1-9*) Polpress Servs.

— Jak Inwestowac W Fundusze Powiernicze. (POL.). 140p. 1997. pap. text 20.00 (*0-9633932-4-3*) Polpress Servs.

Baumgartner, Emmanuelle. Dictionnaire Etymologique et Historique de la Langue Francais. (FRE.). 848p. 1996. pap. 59.95 (*0-7859-9492-0*) Fr & Eur.

Baumgartner, Erich W., ed. Re-Visioning Adventist Mission in Europe. LC 97-74990. (Illus.). 280p. 1998. pap. 11.95 (*1-883925-18-5*) Andrews Univ Pr.

Baumgartner, Frank R. Conflict & Rhetoric in French Policymaking. LC 89-4742. (Series in Policy & Institutional Studies). 303p. 1989. text 49.95 (*0-8229-3616-X*) U of Pittsburgh Pr.

Baumgartner, Frank R. & Jones, Bryan D. Agendas & Instability in American Politics. LC 92-20106. (American Politics & Political Economy Ser.). (Illus.). 312p. (C). 1993. pap. text 15.00 (*0-226-03939-0*); lib. bdg. 52.50 (*0-226-03938-2*) U Ch Pr.

Baumgartner, Frank R. & Leech, Beth L. Basic Interests: The Importance of Groups in Politics & in Political Science. LC 97-42952. 248p. 1998. text 55.00 (*0-691-05914-4*, Pub. by Princeton U Pr); pap. text 15.95 (*0-691-05915-2*, Pub. by Princeton U Pr) Cal Prin Full Svc.

Baumgartner, Frederic J. Change & Continuity in the French Episcopate: The Bishops & the Wars of Religion, 1547-1610. LC 86-13495. (Duke Monographs in Medieval & Renaissance Studies: No. 7). (Illus.). xv, 340p. 1986. text 41.00 (*0-8223-0675-1*) Duke.

— France in the Sixteenth Century. 334p. 1995. pap. 19.95 (*0-312-15856-4*); text 49.95 (*0-312-09965-7*) St Martin.

— France in the Sixteenth Century. 368p. 1995. pap. 18.95 (*0-312-09964-9*) St Martin.

— From Spear to Flintlock: A History of War in Europe & the Middle East to the French Revolution. LC 91-10421. 368p. 1991. 59.95 (*0-275-93955-3*, C3955, Praeger Pubs) Greenwood.

— Henry II: King of France 1547-1559. 358p. (C). 1996. pap. text, per. 53.95 (*0-7872-2174-0*, 41217401) Kendall-Hunt.

— Louis XII. 319p. 1996. pap. 18.95 (*0-312-16173-5*) St Martin.

Baumgartner, Frederick & Baumgartner, Marguerite. Oklahoma Bird Life. (Illus.). 548p. (C). 1992. 49.95 (*0-8061-1792-3*) U of Okla Pr.

Baumgartner, Fritz. Heart & Heart-Lung Transplant. 2nd ed. Date not set. text. write for info. (*0-7216-7363-5*, W B Saunders Co) Harcrt Hlth Sci Grp.

Baumgartner, Fritz & Bassam Omari. Cardiothoracic Surgery. 2nd ed. LC 99-31800. (Vademecum Ser.). 1999. spiral bd. 45.00 (*1-57059-559-3*) Landes Bioscience.

Baumgartner, Fritz & Reitz. Heart & Heart-Lung Transplantation. (Illus.). 442p. 1989. text 210.00 (*0-7216-2101-5*, W B Saunders Co) Harcrt Hlth Sci Grp.

Baumgartner, J., et al, eds. Population & Community Ecology for Insect Management & Conservation: Proceedings of the Ecology & Population Dynamics Section, 20th International Congress Florence, 25-31 August, 1996. (Illus.). 253p. (C). 1998. text 85.00 (*90-5410-930-0*, Pub. by A A Balkema) Ashgate Pub Co.

Baumgartner, James E., et al, eds. Axiomatic Set Theory. LC 84-18457. (Contemporary Mathematics Ser.: Vol. 31). 259p. 1985. reprint ed. pap. 36.00 (*0-8218-5026-1*, CONM/31) Am Math.

Baumgartner, Jerome W. Rancho Santa Margarita Remembered. 2nd rev. ed. (Illus.). 192p. (Orig.). 1996. pap. 12.95 (*1-56474-182-6*) Fithian Pr.

***Baumgartner, Jody C.** Modern Presidential Electioneering: An Organizational & Comparative Approach. LC 99-55884. 248p. 2000. 65.00 (*0-275-96760-3*, Praeger Pubs) Greenwood.

Baumgartner, John S. Systems Management. LC 79-11634. 521p. reprint ed. pap. 161.60 (*0-608-16711-8*, 202679900052) Bks Demand.

Baumgartner, Ken. Controlled Substances Handbook, Vol. 5. 5th rev. ed. 550p. 1996. ring bd. 248.00 (*0-933544-90-1*) Gov Info Srvs.

Baumgartner, Lisa, jt. ed. see Merriam, Sharan B.

Baumgartner, M. On Dryden's Relation to Germany. (Studies in Dryden: No. 10). 1979. pap. 29.95 (*0-8383-0084-7*) M S G Haskell Hse.

Baumgartner, M. P. The Moral Order of a Suburb. 192p. 1989. text 60.00 (*0-19-505413-X*) OUP.

— The Moral Order of a Suburb. 192p. (C). 1991. reprint ed. pap. text 20.95 (*0-19-506995-1*, 5317) OUP.

Baumgartner, Marguerite, jt. auth. see Baumgartner, Frederick.

Baumgartner, Mary A. Buzzy Newton's Terrible Discovery. (Illus.). 40p. (J). (ps-5). 1999. pap. write for info. (*0-944576-10-9*) Rocky River Pubs.

Baumgartner, Mary P., ed. The Social Organization of Law. 2nd ed. LC 98-86588. (Illus.). 435p. (C). 1998. pap. text 49.95 (*0-12-083170-8*) Acad Pr.

Baumgartner, P. Theory Reasoning in Connection Calculi. LC 99-10004. (Lecture Notes in Artificial Intelligence Ser.: Vol. 1527). ix, 283p. 1999. pap. 49.00 (*3-540-65509-3*) Spr-Verlag.

B

An Asterisk (*) at the beginning of an entry indicates that the title is appearing for the first time.

Baumgartner, P., ed. see Fourth International Workshop on Theorem Proving w.

Baumgartner, Peter. How to Make Books & Boxes: Portfolios, Photograph Albums & Decorative Papers. (Illus.). 96p. (Orig.). 1996. 18.95 (*0-85532-812-6*, 8126, Pub. by Srch Pr) A Schwartz & Co.

— Speaking Minds: Interviews with Twenty Eminent Cognitive Scientists. 350p. 1995. pap. text 17.95 (*0-691-02901-6*, Pub. by Princeton U Pr) Cal Prin Full Svc.

Baumgartner, Peter & Payr, Sabine, eds. Speaking Minds: Cognitive Science Past, Present & Future. LC 94-24797. 376p. 1995. text 39.50 (*0-691-03678-0*, Pub. by Princeton U Pr) Cal Prin Full Svc.

Baumgartner, Richard A. Blue Lightning: Wilder's Mounted Infantry Brigade in the Battle of Chickamauga. (Illus.). 248p. 1997. 30.00 (*1-885033-17-6*) Blue Acorn Pr.

— Kennesaw Mountain June, 1864. (Illus.). 208p. 1998. 27.50 (*1-885033-20-6*) Blue Acorn Pr.

*__Baumgartner, Richard A.__ Kennesaw Mountain June 1864. (Illus.). 208p. 2000. pap. 20.00 (*1-885033-25-7*) Blue Acorn Pr.

Baumgartner, Richard A. & Strayer, Larry M. Echoes of Battle: The Struggle for Chattanooga. (Illus.). 484p. 1997. 40.00 (*1-885033-16-8*) Blue Acorn Pr.

Baumgartner, Richard A., ed. see Nagel, Fritz.

*__Baumgartner, S.__ Ambivalent Joint Production & the Natural Environment: An Economic & Thermodynamic Analysis. (Contributions to Economics Ser.). (Illus.). xiii, 323p. 2000. pap. text 73.00 (*3-7908-1290-0*, Pub. by Physica-Verlag) Spr-Verlag.

Baumgartner, Susan. Brains for Breakfast: Growing up German in America. 160p. 1994. pap. 15.95 (*0-9631258-7-7*) Historic Idaho.

Baumgartner, Ted A. & Jackson, Andrew S. Measurement for Evaluation in Physical Education & Exercise Science. 2nd ed. 480p. (C). 1995. text, per. write for info. incl. 3.5 ld (*0-697-27971-5*) Brown & Benchmark.

— Measurement for Evaluation in Physical Education & Exercise Science. 5th ed. 465p. (C). 1994. text 49.80 (*0-697-15218-9*); text. write for info. (*0-697-24971-9*) Brown & Benchmark.

Baumgartner, Ted A. & Strong, Clinton H. Conducting & Reading Research in Health. 2nd ed. LC 97-8348. 384p. (C). 1997. text. write for info. (*0-697-29509-5*, WCB McGr Hill) McGrw-H Hghr Educ.

— Conducting & Reading Research in Health & Human Performance. 352p. (C). 1994. text. write for info. (*0-697-11169-5*) Brown & Benchmark.

Baumgartner, Thomas & Midttun, Atle. The Politics of Energy Forecasting: A Comparative Study of Energy Forecasting in Western Europe & North America. LC 86-23885. 328p. 1987. 74.00 (*0-19-828547-7*) OUP.

Baumgartner, Ulrich, et al, eds. Saving Behavior & the Asset Price "Bubble" in Japan: Analytical Studies. LC 95-10141. (Occasional Papers: No. 124). 86p. 1995. pap. 15.00 (*1-55775-462-4*) Intl Monetary.

Baumgartner, Walter. Jeremiah's Poems of Lament. pap. 8.95 (*1-85075-115-3*, Pub. by Sheffield Acad) CUP Services.

Baumgartner, Walter, jt. auth. see Koehler, Ludwig.

Baumgartner, Walter, jt. auth. see Pond, Dale.

Baumgartner, Walter, jt. ed. see Koehler, Ludwig.

Baumgartner, William, et al, eds. Atlas of Cardiac Surgery. (Illus.). 300p. 2000. text 195.00 (*1-56053-310-2*) Hanley & Belfus.

Baumgartner, William S., et al. The Johns Hopkins Cardiac Surgical Manual. (Illus.). 560p. (C). (gr. 13). 1994. spiral bd. 54.95 (*0-8016-2248-4*, 02248) Mosby Inc.

Baumgartnerq, Gabriele & Hebig, Dieter. Biographisches Handbuch der SB2, 2. 1057p. 1996. 390.00 (*3-598-11130-4*) K G Saur Verlag.

Baumgerten, Rutter. Power Business Reading. 1999. 13.95 (*0-538-69222-7*) Thomson Learn.

*__Baumgold, Sharon & Reardon, Timothy A.__ Handling Civil Writs in the Courts of Appeal: Action Guide - Fall 1998. Waxman, Robert N., ed. 88p. 1998. ring bd. 58.00 (*0-7626-0271-6*, CP-11196) Cont Ed Bar-CA.

Baumheckel, Ralph & Borghoff, Kent. International Harvester Farm Equipment Product History, 1831-1985. LC 97-75110. (Illus.). 408p. 1997. 39.95 (*0-929355-86-5*, H0497) Am Soc Ag Eng.

Baumhoff, Martin A. California Athabascan Groups. fac. ed. Rowe, J. H. et al, eds. (University of California Publications: No. 16:5). 86p. (C). 1958. reprint ed. pap. 9.69 (*1-55567-146-2*) Coyote Press.

— Ecological Determinants of Aboriginal California Populations. (University of California Publication in American Archaeology & Ethnology Ser.: No. 49(2)). (Illus.). 89p. (C). 1963. pap. text 10.00 (*1-55567-698-7*) Coyote Press.

— An Introduction to Yana Archaeology. fac. ed. (Reports of the University of California Archaeological Survey: No. 40). (Illus.). 80p. 1957. reprint ed. pap. 9.06 (*1-55567-357-0*) Coyote Press.

Baumhoff, Martin A., et al. Papers on California Archaeology, Nos. 37-43. fac. ed. (Reports of the University of California Archaeological Survey: No. 33). (Illus.). 80p. 1956. reprint ed. pap. 9.06 (*1-55567-351-1*) Coyote Press.

Baumhoff, Martin A., jt. auth. see Meighan, Clement W.

Baumhover, Lorin A. & Beall, S. Colleen, eds. Abuse, Neglect, & Exploitation of Older Persons: Strategies for Assessment & Intervention. LC 95-42646. (Illus.). 288p. (Orig.). 1996. pap. 29.00 (*1-878812-29-7*) Hlth Prof Pr.

— Abuse, Neglect & Exploitation of Older Persons: Strategies for Assessment & Intervention. 272p. 1996. pap. write for info. (*1-85302-405-8*, Pub. by Jessica Kingsley) Taylor & Francis.

Baumhover, Lorin S. & Jones, Joan D., eds. Handbook of American Aging Programs. LC 76-28641. 188p. 1977. lib. bdg. 55.00 (*0-8371-9287-0*, BAA/, Greenwood Pr) Greenwood.

Baumjohann, W. & Treumann, R. A. Basic Space Plasma Physics. LC 97-102954. 400p. 1996. 58.00 (*1-86094-017-X*) World Scientific Pub.

Baumjohann, W., jt. auth. see Kamide, Y.

Baumjohann, W., jt. auth. see Treumann, R. A.

Baumker, Wilhelm. Das Katholische Deutsche Kirchenlied in Seinen Singweisen, 4 vols., Set. (GER.). lvi, 2372p. 1997. reprint ed. 780.00 (*3-487-00269-8*) G Olms Pubs.

Bauml, Betty J. & Bauml, Franz H. A Dictionary of Gestures. 2nd ed. LC 96-17616. (Illus.). 604p. 1997. 79.50 (*0-8108-3189-9*) Scarecrow.

Bauml, Franz H., ed. Kudrun: Die Handschrift. (C). 1969. 146.15 (*3-11-000376-7*) De Gruyter.

Bauml, Franz H., jt. auth. see Bauml, Betty J.

Bauml, H. & Franz-Birnbaum, D. Attila: The Man & His Image. (Illus.). 132p. 1999. pap. 25.00 (*963-13-3595-X*, Pub. by Corvina Bks) St Mut.

Bauml, James, ed. Poisonous Plants of Southern California. LC 98-201697. (Illus.). 36p. 1998. pap. 4.00 (*0-9660222-2-X*) Arboretum LA Cty.

Baumler, Gary P. John. LC 97-65974. (People's Bible Ser.). 281p. 1998. pap. 11.99 (*0-8100-0719-3*, 15N0578) Northwest Pub.

Baumli, Francis, ed. Men Freeing Men: Exploding the Myth of the Traditional Male. LC 85-21487. 352p. (Orig.). 1985. pap. 16.95 (*0-9615480-0-2*) New Atlantis.

Baumli, George R., ed. Legal, Institutional, Financial, & Environmental Aspects of Water Issues. 232p. 1989. pap. text 5.00 (*0-87262-715-2*, 715) Am Soc Civil Eng.

— Principles of Project Formulation for Irrigation & Drainage Projects. LC 82-73505. 144p. 1982. pap. 18.00 (*0-87262-345-9*) Am Soc Civil Eng.

Baumlin, James S. & Baumlin, Tita F., eds. Ethos: New Essays in Rhetorical & Critical Theory. LC 93-34318. (SMU Studies in Composition & Rhetoric). 408p. 1994. text 34.95 (*0-87074-344-9*); pap. text 16.95 (*0-87074-345-7*) SMU Press.

Baumlin, Tita F., jt. ed. see Baumlin, James S.

Baumohl, Jim, ed. see National Coalition for the Homeless Staff.

Baumol. Economic Principles & Policies. 7th rev. ed. (C). 1997. pap. text 5.75 (*0-03-021132-8*) Harcourt Coll Pubs.

*__Baumol.__ Economics: Principles & Policy. 8th ed. (C). 1999. text 65.00 (*0-03-025948-7*, Pub. by Harcourt Coll Pubs) Harcourt.

Baumol. Economique Macro. 2nd ed. (C). 1991. pap. write for info. (*0-03-998298-X*) Harcourt Coll Pubs.

— Economique Micro. 2nd ed. (C). 1991. pap. write for info. (*0-03-998290-4*) Harcourt Coll Pubs.

— Macroeconomics. 7th ed. (C). 1997. pap. 66.50 (*0-03-023163-9*) Harcourt.

— Macroeconomics. 7th ed. 1997. 256.00 (*0-03-011728-3*, Pub. by Harcourt Coll Pubs) Harcourt.

— Macroeconomics. 7th ed. (C). 1997. pap. text, student ed. 29.50 (*0-03-011724-0*, Pub. by Harcourt Coll Pubs) Harcourt.

*__Baumol.__ Microecon: Principles & Policy. 8th ed. (C). 1999. pap. text 47.00 (*0-03-026847-8*, Pub. by Harcourt Coll Pubs) Harcourt.

Baumol. Microeconomics. 7th ed. (C). 1997. pap. 66.50 (*0-03-023164-7*) Dryden Pr.

— Microeconomics. 7th ed. 1997. 256.00 (*0-03-011738-0*) Harcourt Coll Pubs.

— Microeconomics. 7th ed. (C). 1997. pap. text, student ed. 29.50 (*0-03-011734-8*, Pub. by Harcourt Coll Pubs) Harcourt.

— Wsj Edition:micro:prin & Policy 7e Updte. (C). 1997. pap. text 72.50 (*0-03-023536-7*) Harcourt Coll Pubs.

Baumol, William J. Economics: Principles & Policy. 7th ed. 1997. 90.00 (*0-03-023162-0*) Harcourt Coll Pubs.

— Entrepreneurship, Management, & the Structure of Payoffs. LC 93-4456. (Illus.). 280p. 1994. 40.00 (*0-262-02360-1*) MIT Pr.

— Macro: Priciples & Policies. 7th ed. 1997. pap. text 73.00 (*0-03-025049-8*, Pub. by Harcourt Coll Pubs) Harcourt.

— Microtheory: Applications & Origins. 336p. 1986. 45.00 (*0-262-02245-1*) MIT Pr.

— The Stock Market & Economic Efficiency. LC 65-24469. (Moorhouse I.X. Millar Lecture Ser.: No. 6). 109p. reprint ed. pap. 33.80 (*0-7837-5881-2*, 204560100006) Bks Demand.

— Superfairness: Applications & Theory. (Illus.). 280p. 1988. pap. text 16.50 (*0-262-52131-8*) MIT Pr.

— Transmission Pricing & Stranded Costs in the Electric Power Industry. LC 95-14087. 200p. 1995. 49.95 (*0-8447-3922-7*) Am Enterprise.

Baumol, William J. What Price? Knorr, Klaus E., ed. LC 77-781. (Illus.). 1977. reprint ed. lib. bdg. 65.00 (*0-8371-9356-7*, KNWP, Greenwood Pr) Greenwood.

Baumol, William J., et al, eds. Convergence of Productivity: Cross-National Studies & Historical Evidence. LC 93-11494. (Illus.). 360p. 1994. pap. text 35.00 (*0-19-508390-3*) OUP.

— Productivity & American Leadership: The Long View. (Illus.). 408p. 1991. pap. text 21.50 (*0-262-52163-6*) MIT Pr.

Baumol, William J. & Blinder, Alan S. Economics: Principles & Policy. 4th ed. 926p. (C). 1989. student ed. 11.50 (*0-685-19763-8*); 0.75 (*0-15-518861-5*); disk. write for info. (*0-15-518775-9*) Harcourt Coll Pubs.

— Economics Principles & Policy. 7th ed. 992p. (C). 1997. pap. text 100.50 (*0-03-025052-8*) Dryden Pr.

— Microeconomics: Principles of Policy. 7th ed. 624p. (C). 1997. pap. text 73.00 (*0-03-025051-X*) Dryden Pr.

Baumol, William J. & Bowen, William G. The Performing Arts: The Economic Dilemma. (Modern Revivals in Economics Ser.). 600p. 1993. 82.95 (*0-7512-0106-5*, Pub. by Gregg Revivals) Ashgate Pub Co.

Baumol, William J. & McLennan, Kenneth, eds. Productivity, Growth & U. S. Competitiveness. (CED Supplementary Paper). 228p. 1985. lib. bdg. 19.95 (*0-87186-245-X*) Comm Econ Dev.

Baumol, William J. & Oates, Wallace E. The Theory of Environmental Policy. 312p. 1988. pap. text 26.95 (*0-521-31112-8*) Cambridge U Pr.

*__Baumol, William J. & Ordover, Janusz A., eds.__ Welfare Economics, 3 Vols. Set. 1869p. 2000. write for info. (*1-85278-200-5*) E Elgar.

Baumol, William J. & Wolff, Edward N. Side Effects of Progress. (Public Policy Brief Highlights Ser.: No. 41A). (Illus.). 6p. 1998. pap. write for info. (*0-941276-44-9*) J Levy.

— Side Effects of Progress: How Technological Change Increases the Duration of Unemployment. (Public Policy Brief Ser.: No. 41). (Illus.). 36p. 1998. pap. 3.00 (*0-941276-43-0*) J Levy.

Baumol, William J., et al. The Economics of Mutual Fund Markets: Competition Versus Regulation. (C). 1989. lib. bdg. 142.00 (*0-7923-9043-1*) Kluwer Academic.

Baumol, William J., jt. auth. see Gomory, Ralph E.

Baumol, William J., jt. ed. see Becker, William E.

Baumol, William J., jt. ed. see Darnell, Adrian.

Baumol, Yehoshva. Blaze in the Darkening Gloom: The Life of Rav Meir Shapiro. Wengrov, Charles, tr. from HEB. 1994. 19.95 (*0-87306-675-8*) Feldheim.

Baumont, Maurice. The Origins of the Second World War. Ferguson, Simone D., tr. LC 77-16652. 327p. 1978. 45.00 (*0-300-02215-8*) Yale U Pr.

Baumrin, Bernard & Freedman, Benjamin. Moral Responsibility & the Professions. LC 83-83296. (Professional Ethics Ser.). 400p. (Orig.). 1983. pap. text 20.50 (*0-930586-10-7*) Haven Pubns.

Baumrind, Diana. Child Maltreatment & Optimal Caregiving in Social Contexts. LC 95-17454. (Michigan State University Series on Children, Youth, & Families: Vol. 1). 200p. 1995. text 44.00 (*0-8153-1918-5*, SS1007) Garland.

Baumrucker, Steven J. Love at First Byte: Surviving Cyberspace. (Illus.). 224p. (Orig.). 1995. pap. 14.95 (*0-9646312-1-0*) LMAO Pub Co.

Baums, Roosevelt. In Search of the Dove That Brings Love. Yancey, Jacquelyn G. & Williamson, Dorothy, eds. 67p. (Orig.). (YA). (gr. 3 up). 1995. pap. 7.50 (*0-934138-03-6*) Rosey-Royce.

— A Minority View of How to Campaign for Political Office. Augst, Nancy & Mathews, Michelle, eds. (Illus.). 76p. (Orig.). 1982. pap. 4.95 (*0-934138-00-1*) Rosey-Royce.

— My Children's Struggles. Ellis, Edwin A. & Michels, Joanne, eds. LC 82-60222. (Illus.). 126p. 1983. pap. 2.25 (*0-934138-02-8*) Rosey-Royce.

Baums, Theodor, et al, eds. Institutional Investors & Corporate Governance. LC 93-21087. xxviii, 696p. (C). 1993. lib. bdg. 190.80 (*3-11-013643-0*) De Gruyter.

Baums, Theodor & Wymeersch, E. Asset-Backed Securitization in Europe. LC 96-22278. 262p. 1996. 195.00 (*90-411-0916-1*) Kluwer Law Intl.

Baums, Theodor, jt. auth. see Wymeersch, E.

Baumslag, C. B. & Chandler, B. Group Theory. LC 68-6033. (Schaum's Outline Ser.). (Illus.). 288p. (C). 1968. pap. 14.95 (*0-07-004124-5*) McGraw.

Baumslag, Gilbert. Lecture Notes on Nilpotent Groups. LC 78-145636. (CBMS Regional Conference Series in Mathematics: No. 2). 73p. 1971. pap. 17.00 (*0-8218-1651-9*, CBMS/2) Am Math.

— Lecture Notes on Nilpotent Groups. LC 78-145636. (Regional Conference Series in Mathematics: No. 2). 80p. 1971. pap. 30.00 (*0-608-05175-6*, 205259600001) Bks Demand.

— Topics in Combinatorial Group Theory. LC 93-8950. (Lectures in Mathematics ETH Zurich). 164p. 1993. 34.50 (*0-8176-2921-1*) Birkhauser.

Baumslag, Gilbert, ed. Reviews on Infinite Groups, 1940-1970. LC 73-21521. 548p. 1974. pap. 201.00 (*0-8218-0201-1*, REVINFINC) Am Math.

Baumslag, Gilbert, et al, eds. Geometric & Computational Perspectives on Infinite Groups: Proceedings, Joint DIMACS/Geometry Center Workshop, U. of Minnesota, 1994. LC 95-43529. (DIMACS Series in Discrete Mathematics & Theoretical Computer Science: Vol. 25). 212p. 1995. text 59.00 (*0-8218-0449-9*, DIMACS/25) Am Math.

Baumslag, Gilbert, ed. see Magnus, Wilhelm.

Baumslag, Naomi, ed. Primary Health Care Pioneer: The Selected Works of Dr. Cicely D. Williams. 1986. 12.00 (*0-87553-140-7*) Am Pub Health.

Baumslag, Naomi & Michels, Dia L. Milk, Money, & Madness: The Culture & Politics of Breastfeeding. LC 95-14975. (Illus.). 288p. 1995. 26.95 (*0-89789-407-3*, Bergin & Garvey) Greenwood.

Baumstark, Alfons L., ed. Advances in Oxygenated Processes, Vol. 1. 208p. 1988. 109.50 (*0-89232-866-5*); 109.50 (*0-89121-940-4*) Jai Pr.

— Advances in Oxygenated Processes, Vol. 2. 236p. 1990. 109.50 (*0-89232-950-5*) Jai Pr.

— Advances in Oxygenated Processes, Vol. 3. 179p. 1991. 109.50 (*1-55938-328-3*) Jai Pr.

— Advances in Oxygenated Processes, Vol. 4. 1995. 109.50 (*1-55938-451-4*) Jai Pr.

— Advances in Oxygenated Processes, Vol. 5. Date not set. 109.50 (*0-7623-0066-3*) Jai Pr.

Baumstark-Khan, C., et al. Fundamentals for the Assessment of Risks from Environmental Radiation. LC 99-14202. (NATO Science Ser.). xiv, 537p. 1999. write for info. (*0-7923-5667-5*) Kluwer Academic.

Baumstark, Reinhold, et al. Liechtenstein: The Princely Collections. (Illus.). 400p. 1985. pap. 50.00 (*0-87099-386-0*, 0-8109-6481-3) Metro Mus Art.

Baumstein, Paschal. A Carolina Basillica. (Illus.). iv, 16p. 1999. pap. 15.00 (*0-9614976-9-6*) Archives Belmont.

Baumstein, Paschal M. The Art of Michael McInerney. (Illus.). 1997. 15.00 (*0-9614976-6-1*) Archives Belmont.

— A Carolina Cathedral. (Illus.). (Orig.). 1992. pap. 15.00 (*0-9614976-3-7*) Archives Belmont.

— Historical Research in the Archives of Belmont Abbey. rev. ed. (Illus.). 1993. pap. 15.00 (*0-9614976-4-5*) Archives Belmont.

— My Lord of Belmont: A Biography of Leo Haid. (Illus.). xxii, 396p. 1995. reprint ed. pap. 18.00 (*0-9614976-5-3*) Archives Belmont.

— My Lord of Belmont: A Biography of Leo Haid. (Illus.). xxii, 396p. 1985. reprint ed. 21.00 (*0-9614976-0-2*) Archives Belmont.

Baumstein, Paschal M. & Estes, Debra G. Blessing the Years to Come. (Illus.). 128p. 1997. 29.95 (*0-9614976-7-X*) Archives Belmont.

*__Baumstein, Paschal Michael.__ The Legacy of Felix Hintemeyer. (Illus.). 20p. 2000. pap. 15.00 (*1-890763-26-8*) Archives Belmont.

Baun, Garry. Blue Creek, by Cracky. 118p. (Orig.). 1990. pap. 9.95 (*0-940151-18-9*) Statesman-Exam.

Baun, Michael J. Imperfect Union: The Maastricht Treaty & the New Politics of European Integration. Hoffman, Stanley, ed. (New Europe: Interdisciplinary Perspectives Ser.). 176p. (C). 1996. pap. 24.00 (*0-8133-2711-3*, Pub. by Westview) HarpC.

*__Baun, Michael J.__ A Wider Europe: The Process & Politics of European Union Enlargement. 304p. 2000. 69.00 (*0-8476-9036-9*); pap. 22.95 (*0-8476-9037-7*) Rowman.

Baun, Michael J., jt. ed. see Franklin, Daniel P.

*__Baunach, Ecomae.__ Island of Oahu. LC 99-90857. (Travel Book for Kids Ser.: No. 1). (Illus.). 32p. (J). (ps-3). 2000. pap. 8.95 (*0-9651202-9-5*) Park Publishing.

— Islands of Kauai & Niiha. LC 99-90857. (Travel Book for Kids Ser.: No. 2). (Illus.). 28p. (J). (ps-3). 2000. pap. 8.95 (*0-9651202-8-7*) Park Publishing.

— Maui & Hawaii Islands. LC 99-90857. (Travel Book for Kids Ser.: No. 3). (Illus.). 32p. (J). (ps-3). 2000. pap. 8.95 (*0-9651202-7-9*) Park Publishing.

Baunach, Ecomae. Notes to Nancy. LC 96-92445. (Illus.). 144p. (J). (ps-6). 1996. 9.95 (*0-9651202-4-4*) Park Publishing.

Baunach, Phyllis J. Mothers in Prison. 2nd ed. 150p. (C). 1985. pap. 21.95 (*0-88738-741-1*) Transaction Pubs.

Baunan, Tore. Classification of Floating Production Systems: A Cost Effective Verification System. 1989. 150.00 (*90-6314-569-1*, Pub. by Lorne & MacLean Marine) St Mut.

Bauner, Patricia B., ed. see Rossini, Gioachino.

Baur, et al. International Symposium on Vector Boson Self-Interactions: Conference Proceeding. (AIP Conference Proceedings Ser.: No. 350). (Illus.). 432p. 1995. 145.00 (*1-56396-520-8*) Am Inst Physics.

Baur, jt. auth. see Crooks.

Baur, Alfred. Healing Sounds: Fundamentals of Chirophonetics. 1993. 42.95 (*0-945803-24-9*) R Steiner Col.

Baur, Benedict. Frequent Confession. 272p. 1999. pap. 9.95 (*1-889334-16-2*) Scepter Pubs.

— In Silence with God. 220p. 1997. pap. 9.95 (*0-933932-93-6*) Scepter Pubs.

Baur, Brian C. Franklin D. Roosevelt: The Stamp Collecting President. LC 99-12216. (Illus.). 1999. 30.00 (*0-940403-79-X*); pap. 14.95 (*0-940403-80-3*) Linns Stamp News.

— Franklin D. Roosevelt & the Stamps of the United States, 1933-45. (Illus.). 376p. (Orig.). 1993. pap. 14.95 (*0-940403-58-7*) Linns Stamp News.

Baur, Donald C., et al. Natural Resources Law Handbook. 363p. 1991. pap. text 79.00 (*0-86587-243-0*) Gov Insts.

Baur, Ferdinand C. Das Manichaeische Religionssystem, Nach den Quellen Neu Untersucht. (GER.). xi, 500p. 1973. reprint ed. write for info. (*3-487-04736-5*) G Olms Pubs.

Baur, Gregory R., jt. auth. see Pigford.

Baur, H. Thermophysics of Polymers I: Theory. LC 98-53819. (Illus.). 79p. 1999. 139.00 (*3-540-65046-6*) Spr-Verlag.

Baur, Hans. Hitler at My Side. unabridged ed. Butler, Lyndel, tr. from GER. LC 85-80773. (Illus.). 228p. 1986. 28.00 (*1-930571-00-3*) WW Two Bks.

Baur-Heinhold, Margarete. Decorative Ironwork: Wrought Iron Gratings, Gates & Railings. (Illus.). 176p. 1996. 49.95 (*0-7643-0153-5*) Schiffer.

Baur, John. The Inlander: The Life & Work of Charles Burchfield, 1893-1967. LC 80-51780. (Illus.). 288p. 1982. 50.00 (*0-8453-4734-9*, Cornwall Bks) Assoc Univ Prs.

Baur, John E. Christmas on the American Frontier, 1800-1900. LC 93-8918. (Illus.). 320p. 1993. reprint ed. lib. bdg. 44.00 (*1-55888-171-9*) Omnigraphics Inc.

Baur, John I. American Painting Nineteen Hundred to Nineteen Seventy-Six. LC 75-27361. (Illus.). 96p. 1975. pap. 2.00 (*0-89062-022-9*) Katonah Gal.

— The Inlander: Life & Work of Charles Burchfield, 1893-1967. LC 80-51780. (Illus.). 208p. 1982. 50.00 (*0-87413-186-3*) U Delaware Pr.

Baur, John I. & Conrads, Margaret C. Meditations on Nature: The Drawings of David Johnson. LC 87-32370. (Illus.). 92p. (Orig.). 1988. pap. 6.25 (*0-943651-04-2*) Hudson Riv.

Baur, John I. & Fleischman, Lawrence A. Burchfield's Seasons. (Illus.). 48p. 1982. pap. 15.00 (*0-87920-013-8*) Kennedy Gall.

— Charles E. Burchfield: The Late Years & Selected Earlier Works. (Illus.). 48p. 1979. pap. 15.00 (*0-87920-014-6*) Kennedy Gall.
— Charles E. Burchfield at Kennedy Galleries: The Early Years, 1915-1929. (Illus.). 88p. 1977. pap. 15.00 (*0-87920-015-4*) Kennedy Gall.
— John Marin & the Sea. (Illus.). 80p. 1982. pap. 15.00 (*0-87920-021-9*) Kennedy Gall.
— John Marin Watercolors, 1929-1939. (Illus.). 34p. 1987. pap. 15.00 (*0-87920-022-7*) Kennedy Gall.
— John Marin's Mountains. (Illus.). 64p. 1983. pap. 15.00 (*0-87920-020-0*) Kennedy Gall.
— John Marin's New York. (Illus.). 88p. 1981. 20.00 (*0-87920-019-7*) Kennedy Gall.
Baur, John I., ed. see Whittredge, Worthington.
Baur, Karla, jt. auth. see Crooks, Robert.
Baur, Marianne. Transforming Universities: Changing Patterns of Governance, Structure & Learning in Swedish Higher Education, 48. 1999. pap. text 44.95 (*1-85302-675-1*) Taylor & Francis.
Baur, Michael. Hegel & the Tradition: Essays in Honour of H. S. Harris. LC 98-139410. 416p. 1997. text 60.00 (*0-8020-0927-1*) U of Toronto Pr.
Baur, Michael, ed. The Importance of Truth, Vol. 67: Annual ACPA Proceedings, 1993. 1994. pap. 20.00 (*0-918090-27-X*) Am Cath Philo.
***Baur, Michael, ed.** Texts & Their Interpretation Vol. 72: ACPA Proceedings, 1998. 364p. 1999. pap. 30.00 (*0-918090-32-6*, Pub. by Am Cath Philo) Philos Document.
Baur, Michael, ed. Virtues & Virtue Theories: Proceedings of the American Catholic Philosophical Association, 1997. (Proceedings of the ACPA Ser.: Vol. 71). 300p. 1998. pap. 20.00 (*0-918090-31-8*) Am Cath Philo.
Baur, Michael & Dahlstrom, Daniel O. The Emergence of German Idealism. LC 98-30101. (Studies in Philosophy & the History of Philosophy). 1999. 59.95 (*0-8132-0928-5*) Cath U Pr.
Baur, Michael, tr. see Fichte, Johann Gottlieb.
Baur, P. V. Catalogue of the Rebecca Darlington Stoddard Collection of Greek & Roman Vases. LC 78-63552. (Yale Oriental Series: Researches: No. 8). reprint ed. 74.50 (*0-404-60278-9*) AMS Pr.
Baur, Rupprecht S., et al. Resumierende Auswahlbibliographie Zur Neueren Sowjetischen Sprachlehrforschung (Gesteuerter Fremdsprachenerwerb) (Linguistic & Literary Studies in Eastern Europe: No. 3). lxviii, 318p. 1980. 84.00 (*90-272-1504-9*) J Benjamins Pubng Co.
Baur, Susan. Hypochondria: Woeful Imaginings. LC 87-19144. 260p. 1988. pap. 14.95 (*0-520-06751-7*, Pub. by U CA Pr) Cal Prin Full Svc.
Baur, Veronika. Metal Candlesticks: History, Styles & Techniques. (Illus.). 184p. 1996. 49.95 (*0-7643-0156-X*) Schiffer.
Baur, Werner. Gewaessergüete - Bestimmen und Beurteilen (Limnology - Recognition & Understanding) 3rd rev. ed. (Illus.). 160p. 1997. pap. 20.00 (*3-8263-8483-0*, Pub. by Blckwell Wissenschafts) Balogh.
Baur, Wolfgang. Dataware. 1998. 16.95 (*0-7869-1215-4*, Pub. by TSR Inc) Random.
— In the Cage: A Guide to Sigils. (Advanced Dungeons & Dragons, 2nd Edition Ser.). 1995. 15.00 (*0-7869-0111-X*, Pub. by TSR Inc) Random.
Baur, Wolfgang & Smith, L. W. Planes of Chaos. 1994. 30.00 (*1-56076-874-6*, Pub. by TSR Inc) Random.
Baur, Wolfgang-Dieter. Johann Georg Hamann Als Publizist: Zum Verhaltnis von Verkundigung Unf Offentlichkeit. (Theologische Bibliothek Toepelmann Ser.: Vol. 49). (GER.). xi, 393p. 1991. lib. bdg. 98.50 (*3-11-012247-2*) De Gruyter.
Baures, Mary. Undaunted Spirits: Portraits of Recovery from Trauma. LC 93-37931. 232p. 1994. pap. 16.95 (*0-914783-71-8*) Charles.
***Baurov, A.** On the Structure of Physical Vacuum & a New Interaction in Nature Vol. 235: Theory, Experiment, Applications. LC 00-25277. (Horizons in World Physics Ser.). 217p. 2000. lib. bdg. 89.00 (*1-56072-805-1*) Nova Sci Pubs.
***Baurys, Florence.** The Coyote Calf. LC 99-34282. (Illus.). 32p. (J). 2000. 16.95 (*0-88415-236-7*) Gulf Pub.
— Spur for Christmas. LC 99-31005. 1999. 16.95 (*0-88415-300-2*, 5300) Gulf Pub.
Baurys, Florence. A Time for Alzheimers. LC 98-19749. 196p. 1998. pap. 16.95 (*1-885373-13-9*) Emerald Ink.
Baus, Marc, et al, eds. Observation, Prediction & Simulation of Phase Transitions in Complex Fluids: Proceedings of the NATO ASI, Varenna, Italy, July 25 - August 5, 1994. LC 95-9887. (NATO Advanced Science Institutes Ser.: No. 460). 684p. (C). 1995. text 327.50 (*0-7923-3439-6*) Kluwer Academic.
***Bausani, Alessandro.** Religion in Iran: From Zoroaster to Baha'ullah. LC 00-36102. 2000. write for info. (*0-933273-26-6*) Bibliotheca Persica.
Bausano, William, compiled by. Sacred Latin Texts & English Translations for the Choral Conductor & Church Musician: Propers of the Mass, 68. LC 97-42485. (Music Reference Collection: Vol. 68). 304p. 1998. lib. bdg. 69.50 (*0-313-30636-2*, Greenwood Pr) Greenwood.
Bausbacher, Ed & Hunt, Roger. Process Plant Layout & Piping Design. LC 93-9725. (Illus.). 464p. (C). 1993. text 67.60 (*0-13-138629-8*) P-H.
Bausch, jt. auth. see Cassill.
Bausch, Bill. The Parish of the Next Millennium. LC 97-60028. 304p. 1997. pap. 14.95 (*0-89622-719-7*) Twenty-Third.
Bausch, David K. The Official Price Guide to Automobilia. (Illus.). 192p. 1996. pap. 19.95 (*0-676-60030-1*) Hse Collectbls.
Bausch, Richard. The Fireman's Wife & Other Stories. 224p. 1991. pap. 10.00 (*0-393-30790-5*) Norton.
— Good Evening, Mr. & Mrs. America & All the Ships at Sea: A Novel. large type ed. LC 96-37397. 602p. 1997. 24.95 (*0-7862-0968-2*) Thorndike Pr.
— Good Evening Mr. & Mrs. America, & All the Ships at Sea: Novel, A. 352p. 1997. pap. 14.00 (*0-06-092857-3*, Perennial) HarperTrade.
— Hello to the Cannibals. Date not set. 25.00 (*0-06-019295-X*) HarpC.
— Hello to the Cannibals. 2002. pap. 13.00 (*0-06-093080-2*, Perennial) HarperTrade.
— In the Night Season: A Novel. LC 97-43690. 336p. 1998. 24.00 (*0-06-018735-2*) HarpC.
— In the Night Season: A Novel. 336p. 1999. pap. 13.00 (*0-06-093030-6*) HarpC.
— Real Presence. LC 99-15679. (Voices of the South Ser.). 296p. 1999. pap. 15.95 (*0-8071-2477-X*) La State U Pr.
Bausch, Richard. Real Presence: A Novel. LC 79-27136. 279 p. 1980. 9.95 (*0-8037-7779-5*, Dial Yng Read) Peng Put Young Read.
— Someone to Watch over Me: Stories. Date not set. pap. 14.00 HarpC.
— Someone to Watch over Me: Stories. 224p. 2000. pap. 13.00 (*0-06-093070-5*, Perennial) HarperTrade.
Bausch, Richard. Someone to Watch Over Me: Stories by. LC 98-50193. 224p. 1999. 24.00 (*0-06-017333-5*, HarperFlamingo) HarpC.
— Take Me Back: A Novel. LC 98-23623. (Voices of the South Ser.). 376p. 1998. pap. 15.95 (*0-8071-2331-5*) La State U Pr.
— Take Me Back: A Novel. LC 80-25762. 362p. 1981. 11.95 (*0-8037-8487-2*, Dial Yng Read) Peng Put Young Read.
Bausch, Richard, jt. auth. see Cassill, R. V.
***Bausch, Robert.** A Hole in the Earth. LC 99-46042. 368p. 2000. 24.00 (*0-15-100529-X*) Harcourt.
— On the Way Home. (Voices of the South Ser.). 240p. 2000. pap. 15.95 (*0-8071-2638-1*) La State U Pr.
Bausch, Robert. On the Way Home. 240p. 1983. pap. 3.50 (*0-380-63131-8*, 63131-8, Avon Bks) Morrow Avon.
— The White Rooster: And Other Stories. 168p. 1995. 19.95 (*0-87905-721-1*) Gibbs Smith Pub.
Bausch, William J. Becoming a Man: Basic Information, Guidance, & Attitudes on Sex for Boys. LC 87-51569. 324p. (J). (gr. 5-12). 1988. pap. 12.95 (*0-89622-357-4*) Twenty-Third.
— Catholics in Crisis? The Church Confronts Contemporary Challenges. LC 98-61592. 240p. 1999. pap. 14.95 (*0-89622-965-3*) Twenty-Third.
— More Telling Stories, Compelling Stories. LC 92-60889. 200p. (Orig.). 1993. pap. 9.95 (*0-89622-534-8*) Twenty-Third.
— A New Look at the Sacraments. 2nd ed. LC 82-74313. 300p. 1983. pap. 12.95 (*0-89622-174-1*) Twenty-Third.
— Pilgrim Church: A Popular History of Catholic Christianity. LC 89-50938. 480p. 1989. 19.95 (*0-89622-395-7*) Twenty-Third.
— Storytelling the Word: Homilies & How to Write Them. LC 95-62067. 304p. (Orig.). 1996. pap. 14.95 (*0-89622-687-5*) Twenty-Third.
— Telling Stories, Compelling Stories. LC 90-71137. 200p. (Orig.). 1991. pap. 9.95 (*0-89622-456-2*) Twenty-Third.
— Timely Homilies: The Wit & Wisdom of an Ordinary Pastor. LC 89-52152. 176p. (Orig.). 1990. pap. text 9.95 (*0-89622-426-0*) Twenty-Third.
— The Total Parish Manual: Everything You Need to Empower Your Faith Community. LC 94-60340. 328p. (Orig.). 1994. pap. 29.95 (*0-89622-607-7*) Twenty-Third.
— While You Were Gone: A Handbook for Returning Catholics, & Those Thinking about It. LC 93-60817. 112p. (Orig.). 1994. pap. 5.95 (*0-89622-575-5*) Twenty-Third.
***Bausch, William J.** The Word in & Out of Season: Homilies for Preachers & Seekers. 304p. 2000. pap. 14.95 (*1-58595-003-3*) Twenty-Third.
Bausch, William J. A World of Stories for Preachers & Teachers: And All Who Love Stories That Move & Challenge. LC 97-62564. 544p. 1998. pap. 29.95 (*0-89622-919-X*) Twenty-Third.
***Bausch, William J.** The Yellow Brick Road: A Storyteller's Approach to the Spiritual Journey. 320p. 1999. pap. 14.95 (*0-89622-991-2*) Twenty-Third.
Bauschatz, Paul C. The Well & the Tree: World & Time in Early Germanic Culture. LC 81-14766. (Illus.). 280p. 1982. reprint ed. pap. 86.80 (*0-7837-9206-9*, 204995600004) Bks Demand.
Bauschinger, J. & Peters, J. Logarithmic Trigonometrical Tables to 8 Decimal Places or Numbers 1-200,000 & Trigon: Functions for Sexagesmil Second of the Quadrant, 2vols. 3rd ed. 1971. 175.00 (*0-934454-57-4*) Lubrecht & Cramer.
Bauschinger, Sigrid. The Trumpet of Reform: German Literature in New England of the Nineteenth Century. Hansen, Thomas, tr. from GER. LC 98-37817. (Studies in German Literature & Culture). 190p. 1999. 55.00 (*1-57113-176-0*) Camden Hse.
Bause, Dave. The Best Season: Spring, Vol. I. LC 86-90814. 88p. 1986. pap. 10.95 (*0-9612032-3-4*) Copy Fast.
— How to Promote More Wedding Business Without Headaches. (Illus.). 1985. 11.95 (*0-685-10678-0*) Copy Fast.
Bause, Dave, et al. Create Your Own Newsletter Handbook. LC 83-91092. (Illus.). 80p. 1983. 24.95 (*0-9612032-0-X*) Copy Fast.
Bause, Dawn, et al. Romance Begins in the Kitchen: Romantic Italian Recipes & Their Complementary Wines. LC 97-70185. (Illus.). 176p. 1997. pap. 14.95 (*0-9656889-0-9*) Bause Hse.
***Bause, Jens.** Literaturdidaktik Und Asthetik: Eine Didaktik der Asthetischen Umorientierung, Dargestellt an Untersuchungen Zur Dramatischen Form. 256p. 1999. 45.95 (*3-631-34030-3*) P Lang Pubng.
***Bausell, Charles W., Jr., ed.** Indian Issues: Cheyenne River Sioux Tribe's Additional Compensation for the Oahe Dam. (Illus.). 54p. (C). 1999. pap. text 20.00 (*0-7881-8383-4*) DIANE Pub.
Bausell, R. Barker. Advanced Research Methodology: An Annotated Guide to Sources. LC 91-16135. 911p. 1991. 92.00 (*0-8108-2355-1*) Scarecrow.
— Conducting Meaningful Experiments: 40 Steps to Becoming a Scientist. 160p. (C). 1994. text 48.00 (*0-8039-5530-8*); pap. text 21.95 (*0-8039-5531-6*) Sage.
Bausenhart, Werner. German Immigration & Assimilation in Ontario, 1783-1918. 128p. (Orig.). (C). 1989. pap. 15.00 (*0-921252-10-2*) LEGAS.
Bauserman, Joseph M. & Rule, Warren R. A Brief History of Systems Approaches in Counseling & Psychotherapy. 74p. (Orig.). (C). 1995. pap. text 17.50 (*0-8191-9997-4*); lib. bdg. 29.00 (*0-8191-9996-6*) U Pr of Amer.
Bausiere, R., et al. Power Electronic Converters: DC-DC Conversion. Kassakian, John G. & Naunin, D. H., eds. LC 92-10524. (Electric Energy Systems & Engineering Ser.).Tr. of Les/Convertisseurs de l'Electronique de Puissance. (Illus.). 360p. 1993. 158.95 (*0-387-54760-6*) Spr-Verlag.
Bausinger, Hermann. Folk Culture in a World of Technology. Dettmer, Elke, tr. from GER. LC 89-15492. (Folklore Studies in Translation). (Illus.). 208p. 1990. 10.00 (*0-253-31127-6*) Ind U Pr.
Bauske, Gloria. Pebbles on the Prairie. 108p. 1999. pap. 12.95 (*1-57579-144-7*) Pine Hill Pr.
— Petals on the Prairie. 108p. 1999. pap. 12.95 (*1-57579-145-5*) Pine Hill Pr.
— Puddles on the Prairie. 108p. 1999. pap. 12.95 (*1-57579-146-3*) Pine Hill Pr.
***Bauske, Gloria K.** Diamond in the Rough. 108p. 1999. pap. write for info. (*1-57579-175-7*, Pub. by Pine Hill Pr) Penmarch Pub.
— When Heart & Soul Collide. 108p. 1999. pap. write for info. (*1-57579-171-4*, Pub. by Pine Hill Pr) Penmarch Pub.
Bauslaugh, Robert A. The Concept of Neutrality in Classical Greece. LC 90-10880. 316p. 1990. 58.00 (*0-520-06687-1*, Pub. by U CA Pr) Cal Prin Full Svc.
Bausman, Joseph H. History of Beaver County, Pennsylvania, 2 vols., Vol. I. (Illus.). 612p. 1992. reprint ed. lib. bdg. 67.00 (*0-8328-1412-1*) Higginson Bk Co.
— History of Beaver County, Pennsylvania, 2 vols., Vol. II. (Illus.). 703p. 1992. reprint ed. lib. bdg. 72.00 (*0-8328-1413-X*) Higginson Bk Co.
Bausmith, John C. Maplewood. LC 98-86896. (Images of America Ser.). (Illus.). 128p. 1998. pap. 16.99 (*0-7524-1279-5*) Arcadia Publng.
Baussan, Olivier, jt. auth. see Chibois, Jacques.
Baustert, Raymond. L' Univers Moral de Malherbe: Etude de la Pensee dans l'Oeuvre Poetique, 2 vols. (Publications Universitaires Europeennes Ser.: Series 13, Vol. 222). (FRE.). 957p. 1997. 75.95 (*3-906758-07-9*, Pub. by P Lang) P Lang Pubng.
***Bauston, Gene & Bauston, Lorri, eds.** Our Companion Animals: Tales of Transformation from Farm Sanctuary. 2001. pap. 14.00 (*1-930051-23-9*) Lantern Books.
Bauston, Lorri, jt. ed. see Bauston, Gene.
***Bausum, Ann.** Dragon Bones & Dinosaur Eggs: A Photo-Biography of Roy Chapman Andrews. LC 99-38363. (Illus.). 64p. (J). (gr. 4-6). 2000. 17.95 (*0-7922-7123-8*, Pub. by Natl Geog) S&S Trade.
Bausum, Henry S., et al, eds. The Journal of Military History Cumulative Index, 1937-1994, Vols. 1-58. LC 95-16161. 1995. write for info. (*0-935524-02-9*) Soc Military Hist.
Bauswein, Jean-Jacques & Vischer, Lukas, eds. The Reformed Family Worldwide: A Survey of Reformed Churches, Theological Schools, & International Organizations. 688p. 1998. pap. 35.00 (*0-8028-4496-0*) Eerdmans.
Baute, Mike. Always Jukin Official Guide to Collectible Jukeboxes. 3rd rev. ed. (Illus.). 132p. 1996. pap. 19.95 (*0-929953-01-0*) Always Jukin.
Bautier, Robert-Henri. Commerce Mediterranean et Banquiers Italiens au Moyen Age. Lalou, Elizabeth, ec. (Collected Studies: No. CS362). (FRE.). 237p. 1992. text 119.95 (*0-86078-311-1*, Pub. by Variorum) Ashgate Pub Co.
— Etudes Sur la France Capetienne: De Louis VI aux de Philippe le Bel. Lalou, Elizabeth, ed. (Collected Studies: No. CS359). (FRE.). 352p. 1992. text 119.95 (*0-86078-306-5*, Pub. by Variorum) Ashgate Pub Co.
— Recherches sur l'Histoire de la France Medievale: Des Merovingiens aux Premiers Capetians. Dufour, J., ed. (Collected Studies: No. CS 351). 350p. 1991. text 119.95 (*0-86078-300-6*, Pub. by Variorum) Ashgate Pub Co.
— Sur l'Histoire Economique de la France Medievale: La Route, le Fleuve, la Foire. Guyotjeannin, O., ed. (Collected Studies: No. CS 340). 360p. 1991. text 119.95 (*0-86078-293-X*, Pub. by Variorum) Ashgate Pub Co.
Bautisa, Felix B., tr. see Fernandez, Pablo, ed.
***Bautista, Albert.** Stage Cut-Outs: Jimi Hendrix & His Concert Set. 2nd ed. (Illus.). 53p. 1999. pap. 27.95 (*1-930436-02-5*) Graser One.
— Stage Cut-Outs: Jimi Hendrix & His Gig Set. 2nd ed. (Illus.). 43p. 1999. pap. 28.95 (*1-930436-01-7*) Graser One.
— Stage Cut-Outs: Jimi Hendrix & His Jam Set. 2nd ed. (Illus.). 31p. 1999. pap. 19.95 (*1-930436-00-9*) Graser One.
***Bautista, Edna R.** Viva el Amor: A Latino Wedding Planner in English & Spanish. LC 98-83092.Tr. of Viva el Amor: Agenda de una Boda Latina. (Illus.). 240p. 2000. pap. 15.95 (*0-86541-051-8*) Filter.
Bautista, Gloria, ed. Voces Femeninas de Hispanoamerica. (Latin American Ser.). (SPA.). 321p. (C). 1996. text 55.00 (*0-8229-3877-4*) U of Pittsburgh Pr.
— Voces Femeninas de Hispanoamerica. (Latin American Ser.). (SPA.). 321p. (C). 1996. pap. 22.95 (*0-8229-5558-X*) U of Pittsburgh Pr.
Bautista Gutierrez, Gloria. Pinceladas Literarias Hispanoamericanas. 352p. 1999. pap. text 52.95 (*0-471-29747-X*) Wiley.
Bautista, Joyce. Bags, Boxes & Tags: The Best of Graphic Design for Shopping Bags & More. (Illus.). 192p. 1999. pap. 50.00 incl. cd-rom (*1-56496-471-X*); pap. 40.00 (*1-56496-557-0*) Rockport Pubs.
Bautista, Maria, jt. auth. see Ramos, Teresita V.
Bautista, R. G., et al, eds. Rare Earths. LC 96-80049. (Illus.). 768p. 1997. 60.00 (*0-87339-363-5*, 3635) Minerals Metals.
Bautista, Raymundo, et al, eds. Representation Theory of Algebras: Proceedings of the 7th International Conference on Representations of Algebras, Held August 22-26, 1994. LC 96-307. (Conference Proceedings, Canadian Mathematical Society Ser.: Vol. 18). 749p. 1996. pap. 129.00 (*0-8218-0395-6*, CMSAMS/18) Am Math.
— Representation Theory of Algebras & Related Topics: Proceedings of the Workshop on Representation Theory of Algebras & Related Topics. LC 96-4255. (Conference Proceedings - Canadian Mathematical Society Ser.: Vol. 19). 406p. 1996. pap. 95.00 (*0-8218-0396-4*, CMSAMS/19) Am Math.
Bautista, Rehato G. & Mishra, Brajendra, eds. Rare Earths & Actinides: Science, Technology, & Applications IV. (Illus.). 172p. pap. 48.00 (*0-87339-470-4*) Minerals Metals.
Bautista, Renato G., ed. Emerging Separation Technologies for Metals II. (Illus.). 679p. 1996. 110.00 (*0-87339-340-6*) Minerals Metals.
Bautista, Renato G. & Jackson, Norton, eds. Rare Earths: Resources, Science, Technology & Applications: Proceedings of an International Symposium Held Jointly by TMS & AusIMM During the TMS Annual Meeting, San Diego, CA, March 1-5, 1992. LC 91-51131. (Illus.). 480p. 1991. pap. 148.80 (*0-608-04893-3*, 206558500004) Bks Demand.
Bautista, Renato G., ed. see Metallurgical Society of AIME Staff.
Bautista, Renato G., ed. see Minerals, Metals & Materials Society Staff.
Bautista, Romeo M. Impediments to Trade Liberalization in the Philippines. 120p. 1989. pap. 19.95 (*0-566-05782-4*, Pub. by Avebry) Ashgate Pub Co.
Bautista, Romeo M. & Valdes, Alberto. The Bias Against Agriculture: Trade & Macroeconomic Policies in Developing Countries. 340p. 1993. pap. 24.95 (*1-55815-245-8*) ICS Pr.
Bautista, Sara, tr. see Collingwood, Guillermo.
Bautista, Sara, tr. see Cutting, Jorge.
Bautista, Sara, tr. see Mackintosh, Carlos H.
Bautista, Sara, tr. see Marshall, Alejandro & Bennett, Gordon H.
Bautista, SAra, tr. see Pollock, Algernon J.
Bautista, Sara, tr. see Pollock, Algernon J. & Bennett, Gordon H.
Bautista, Sara, tr. see Rossier, H.
Bautista, Sara, tr. see Voorehoeve, H. C. & Bennett, Gordon H.
Bautista, Veltisezar. The Filipino Americans: Their History, Culture, & Traditions (From 1763 to the Present) LC 98-72131. (Illus.). 256p. 1998. 24.95 (*0-931613-14-0*) Bkhaus.
Bautista, Veltisezar B. The Book of U. S. Postal Exams: How to Score 95-100& Get a Job! 5th expanded rev. ed. (Illus.). 376p. 1997. pap. 19.95 (*0-931613-13-2*) Bkhaus.
***Bautista, Veltisezar B.** The Book of U. S. Postal Exams: How to Score 95-100 Percent & Get a Job! 6th rev. ed. LC 99-73131. (Illus.). 416p. 1999. pap. 21.95 (*0-931613-15-9*, Pub. by Bkhaus) Publishers Group.
Bautista, Veltisezar B. How to Build a Successful One-Person Business: A Common-Sense Guide to Starting & Growing a Company. 2nd expanded rev. ed. (Illus.). 352p. 1995. pap. 24.95 (*0-931613-12-4*) Bkhaus.
— How to Teach Your Child: Things to Know from Kindergarten Through Grade 6. 2nd rev. ed. LC 92-71512. (Illus.). 320p. 1992. pap. 12.95 (*0-931613-08-6*) Bkhaus.
— Improve Your Grades: A Practical Guide to Academic Excellence. 2nd enl. rev. ed. LC 90-81542. (Illus.). 192p. 1990. pap. 9.95 (*0-931613-06-X*) Bkhaus.
***Bautista, Veltisezar B.** Improve Your Grades: How to Become an Honor Student. 3rd ed. (Illus.). 256p. (YA). 2000. pap. 16.95 (*0-931613-16-7*, Pub. by Bkhaus) Publishers Group.
Bautze, J. & Art Services International Staff. Interaction of Cultures: Indian & Western Painting, 1780-1910: From the Ehrenfeld Collection. LC 97-36749. 1998. 50.00 (*0-88397-117-8*); pap. 29.95 (*0-88397-124-0*) Art Srvc Intl.
Bautze, Joachim K. Early Indian Terracottas. LC 94-4594. (Iconography of Religions Ser.: No. 17). 96p. 1995. pap. 49.50 (*90-04-09924-7*) Brill Academic Pubs.
Bauval, Gilbert. The Orion Mystery. 352p. 1994. mass mkt. 29.95 (*0-385-25483-0*) Doubleday.
Bauval, R., jt. auth. see Hancock, G.
Bauval, Robert & Gilbert, Adrian. The Orion Mystery. (Illus.). 336p. 1996. pap. write for info. (*0-385-25542-X*) Doubleday.
Bauval, Robert, jt. auth. see Gilbert, Adrian.
Bauval, Robert, jt. auth. see Hancock, Graham.
Bauval, Robert, jt. auth. see Hanscock, Graham.
Bauvel, jt. auth. see Hancock.

B

An Asterisk (*) at the beginning of an entry indicates that the title is appearing for the first time.

Bauvel, Hancock. Message of Sphinx. 1997. mass mkt. 18.95 (0-385-25675-2) Doubleday.

Bauw, Robert De, see Dore, Julia & De Bauw, Robert.

Bauwens, Jeanne & Hourcade, Jack J. Cooperative Teaching: Rebuilding the Schoolhouse for All Students. (Illus.). 237p. (C). 1995. pap. text 31.00 (0-89079-607-6, 6769) PRO-ED.

Bauwens, L. Bayesian Full Information Analysis of Simultaneous Equation Models Using Integration by Monte Carlo. (Lecture Notes in Economics & Mathematical Systems Ser.: Vol. 232). vi, 114p. 1984. 30.00 (0-387-13384-4) Spr-Verlag.

Bauwens, Luc, et al. Bayesian Inference in Dynamic Econometric Models. 376p. 2000. text 74.00 (0-19-877312-9); pap. text 35.00 (0-19-877313-7) OUP.

Bauz, Luis, tr. see Warren, Patricia N.

Bauza, Carmen M., ed. see Antonsanti, Hector M.

Bauza, Carmen M., ed. see Bonilla, Antulio P.

Bauza, Carmen M., ed. see Luiggi, Sadi O.

Bauza, Carmen M., ed. see Martinez, Felix J. & Rosario, Benjamin.

Bauza, Juan L. La Sustituta y Otros Cuentos. (Aqui y Ahora Ser.). 64p. 1997. pap. 6.95 (0-8477-0284-7) U of PR Pr.

Bauzen, Peter & Bauzen, Susanne. Flower Pressing. Kuttner, Paul, tr. from GER. LC 77-167661. (Little Craft Bks.). (YA). (gr. 7 up). 1982. pap. 4.95 (0-8069-7674-8) Sterling.

Bauzen, Susanne, jt. auth. see Bauzen, Peter.

Bauzet, JoAnn. Reading for Today, Bk. 4. 1997. pap., student ed. 10.00 (0-8114-9222-2) Raintree Steck-V.

Bauzon, Kenneth E. Liberalism & the Quest for Islamic Identity in the Philippines. LC 89-82249. xx, 219p. (Orig.). (C). 1991. pap. text 25.95 (0-89386-028-X) Acorn NC.

Bauzon, Kenneth E., ed. Development & Democratization in the Third World: Myths, Hopes, & Realities. 250p. 1992. 75.00 (0-8448-1722-8, Crane Russak); pap. 37.95 (0-8448-1723-6, Crane Russak) Taylor & Francis.

***BaVa, JaNa'.** Building New Relationships: Once You Understand Who You've Become. LC 99-73253. 120p. 1999. pap. 12.95 (1-890622-79-6) Leathers Pub.

Bavarel, Michel. New Communities, New Ministries: The Church Resurgent in Africa, Asia, & Latin America. Martin, Francis, tr. from FRE. LC 82-22318. Orig. Title: Chretienes Du Bout Du Monde. 128p. (Orig.). reprint ed. pap. 39.70 (0-7837-5506-6, 204527600005) Bks Demand.

Bavaro, Joseph J. & Mossman, Thomas L. The Furniture of Gustav Stickley: History, Techniques, Projects. LC 95-47410. (Illus.). 175p. 1996. reprint ed. pap. 19.95 (0-941936-35-X) Linden Pub Fresno.

Bavel, Zamir. Introduction to the Theory of AUTOMATA, 2 vols. 2nd ed. Incl. Vol. 1. Structure. 2nd ed. (Illus.). 295p. (C). 1989. text 44.00 (0-9623885-0-5); Vol. 2. Transition Preserving Functions & Infinite Automata. 2nd ed. (Illus.). 367p. (C). 1989. text 55.00 (0-9623885-1-3); 88.00 (0-9623885-2-1) ZB Pub Indus.

— A Math Companion for Computer Science. (Illus.). 1992. pap. 35.00 (0-9623885-4-8) ZB Pub Indus.

Bavelas, Janet B., et al. Equivocal Communication. LC 96-21136. (Series in Interpersonal Communication: Vol. 11). (Illus.). 320p. (C). 1990. 52.00 (0-8039-2942-0); pap. 24.50 (0-8039-2943-9) Sage.

— Equivocal Communication. LC 90-8205. (Sage Series in Interpersonal Communication: No. 11). (Illus.). 338p. 1990. reprint ed. pap. 104.80 (0-608-04300-1, 206507900012) Bks Demand.

Bavendam, Fred, jt. illus. see Zuchora-Walske, Christine.

Baver, Mary & Kellar, Elizabeth J. Managing Your Hazardous Waste: A Step-by-Step Guide. 214p. 1992. pap. text 79.00 (0-86587-311-9) Gov Insts.

Baver, Sherrie L. The Political Economy of Colonialism: The State & Industrialization in Puerto Rico. LC 92-46553. 176p. 1993. 55.00 (0-275-94503-0, C4503, Praeger Pubs) Greenwood.

Baverman, Jordan. To Hasten the Homecoming: How Americans Fought World War II Through the Media. 260p. 1996. 22.95 (1-56833-047-2) Madison Bks UPA.

Bavernfeind, Robert H., et al. Standardized Tests: A Practical Handbook. LC 91-65016. x, 150p. (C). 1991. pap. text 28.50 (0-9632550-0-2) DMore Pubs.

Baverstam, Jennifer, ed. see Fogelstorm, Per Anders.

Baverstock, S., jt. auth. see Thomson, David.

Baveye, P., et al. Fractals in Soil Science. LC 97-35156. (Advances in Soil Science Ser.). (Illus.). 400p. 1997. lib. bdg. 79.95 (1-56670-105-8) Lewis Pubs.

Baveye, Philippe, et al, eds. Soil Science Education: Philosophy & Perspectives. LC 94-17681. (SSSA Special Publications: No. 37). 174p. 1994. 18.00 (0-89118-809-6) Soil Sci Soc Am.

Bavid, Maria Elean, jt. auth. see Lembey, Stephen H.

Baviello, Mary A., et al. The Scrubber Strategy. Allen, Richard C., ed. LC 82-81547. 188p. reprint ed. pap. 58.30 (0-7837-0336-8, 204065500017) Bks Demand.

Bavier, Michael, jt. auth. see Witteveen, Gordon.

Bavier, Robert N., Jr. Keys to Racing Success. 1982. 19.95 (0-396-08064-2, G P Putnam) Peng Put Young Read.

Bavin, E. L. & Wales, M. L. Language Programs in Primary Schools, Some Australian Experiences. 83p. (C). 1988. 65.00 (0-7300-0552-6, Pub. by Deakin Univ) St Mut.

Bavin-Mizzi, Jill. Ravished: Sexual Violence in Victorian Australia. 1995. pap. 25.95 (0-86840-111-0, Pub. by New South Wales Univ Pr) Intl Spec Bk.

Bavinck, Herman. The Doctrine of God. (Student's Reformed Theological Library). 407p. 1997. reprint ed. 36.99 (0-85151-255-0) Banner of Truth.

— In the Beginning: Foundations of Creation Theology. Bolt, John, ed. Vriend, John, tr. from DUT. LC 99-28133. 296p. (C). (gr. 13). 1999. pap. 15.99 (0-8010-2190-1) Baker Bks.

— The Last Things: Hope for This World & the Next. Bolt, John, ed. Vriend, John, tr. from DUT. LC 96-1438. 208p. (C). (gr. 12). 1996. pap. 19.99 (0-8010-2088-3, Gereformeerds D) Baker Bks.

Bavinck, Johan H. The Church Between Temple & Mosque: A Study of the Relationship Between the Christian Faith & Other Religions. LC 66-22946. 206p. reprint ed. pap. 63.90 (0-608-14486-X, 202531600043) Bks Demand.

Bavinck, John H. An Introduction to the Science of Missions. Freeman, David H., tr. LC 60-13405. Orig. Title: Inleiding in de Zendingswetenschap. 323p. 1993. pap. 14.99 (0-87552-124-X) P & R Pubng.

Bavink, Bernhard. The Natural Sciences. LC 74-26248. (History, Philosophy & Sociology of Science Ser.). 1975. reprint ed. 58.95 (0-405-06578-7) Ayer.

Bavishi, Vinod B. Global Directory of Accounting & Auditing Research: Year in Review, 1994-95. 900p. 1996. pap. 195.00 (1-877587-28-1) CIFA & Res Inc.

— Global Directory of Financial Research: Year in Review, 1994-95. 900p. 1996. pap. 195.00 (1-877587-29-X) CIFA & Res Inc.

— Global Register of the Leading International Accounting Firms. 1000p. 1995. pap. 195.00 (1-877587-07-9) CIFA & Res Inc.

Bavishi, Vinod B., ed. Global Company Handbook 1993: An Analysis of the Financial Performance of the World's Leading 12,000 Companies, Vols. 1-4. 2nd ed. 3500p. (Orig.). 1993. pap. 495.00 (1-877587-06-0) CIFA & Res Inc.

— Global Company Handbook 1995: Analysis of Financial Performance of the World's Leading 12,000 Companies. 3rd ed. 5000p. (Orig.). 1996. pap. 495.00 (1-877587-09-5) CIFA & Res Inc.

— Global Company Handbook 1995: Analysis of the World's 50 Capital Markets. 3rd ed. (Orig.). 1996. pap. 195.00 (1-877587-12-5) CIFA & Res Inc.

— Global Company Handbook 1995: Asia-Pacific. 3rd ed. (Orig.). 1996. pap. 145.00 (1-877587-14-1) CIFA & Res Inc.

— Global Company Handbook 1995: Europe-Africa-Middle East. 3rd ed. (Orig.). 1996. pap. 145.00 (1-877587-13-3) CIFA & Res Inc.

— Global Company Handbook 1995: The Americas. 3rd ed. (Orig.). 1996. pap. 145.00 (1-877587-15-X) CIFA & Res Inc.

— International Accounting & Auditing Trends, 1993, I & II. 3rd ed. 1225p. (Orig.). 1993. pap. 345.00 (1-877587-05-2) CIFA & Res Inc.

— International Accounting & Auditing Trends, 1995, Vol. I & II. 4th ed. 988p. (Orig.). 1995. pap. 345.00 (1-877587-08-7) CIFA & Res Inc.

— International Accounting & Auditing Trends, 1995 Vol. I: International Accounting Trends. 4th ed. (Orig.). 1995. pap. 195.00 (1-877587-10-9) CIFA & Res Inc.

— International Accounting & Auditing Trends, 1995 Vol. II: International Auditing Trends. 4th ed. (Orig.). 1995. pap. 195.00 (1-877587-11-7) CIFA & Res Inc.

Bavishi, Vinod B. & Wyman, Harold E. Who Audits the World? Trends in the Worldwide Accounting Profession. 900p. 1983. pap. 75.00 (0-913795-01-1) Ctr Trans Acct Fin.

Baviskar, Amita. In the Belly of the River: Tribal Conflicts over Development in the Narmada Valley. (Studies in Social Ecology & Environmental History). (Illus.). 302p. 1998. reprint ed. pap. text 11.95 (0-19-564392-5) OUP.

Baviskar, B. S., jt. ed. see Attwood, Donald W.

Baviskar, B. S., jt. ed. see Shah, A. M.

Bavister, Barry D., ed. The Mammalian Preimplantation Embryo: Regulation of Growth & Differentiation In Vitro. LC 87-13986. (Illus.). 398p. (C). 1987. text 132.00 (0-306-42595-5, Kluwer Plenum) Kluwer Academic.

— Preimplantation Embryo Development. LC 92-49441. 352p. 1993. 129.00 (0-387-97934-4); write for info. (3-540-97934-4) Spr-Verlag.

Bavister, Barry D., et al, eds. Fertilization in Mammals. (Serono Symposia, USA Ser.). (Illus.). 492p. (C). 1990. text 80.00 (1-878601-03-2) Serono Symposia USA.

***Bavister, Steve.** Digital Photography: A No-Nonsense, Jargon-Free Guide for Beginners. 2000. pap. 19.95 (1-85585-781-2, Pub. by Collins & Br) Sterling.

Bavly, Dan A. Corporate Governance & Accountability: What Role for the Regulator, Director & Auditor? LC 98-38314. 232p. 1999. 59.95 (1-56720-280-2, Quorum Bks) Greenwood.

Bavly, Sarah. Family Food Consumption in Palestine. LC 76-176544. (Columbia University. Teachers College. Contributions to Education Ser.: No. 946). reprint ed. 37.50 (0-404-55946-8) AMS Pr.

Bavoil, Patrik M., jt. ed. see Clark, Virginia L.

Bavolek, Juliana D., jt. auth. see Bavolek, Stephen J.

Bavolek, Stephen J. A Handbook for Understanding Child Abuse & Neglect. 2nd ed. 256p. 1985. pap. text 21.95 (0-934309-07-8) Family Dev Res.

Bavolek, Stephen J. & Bavolek, Juliana D. Nurturing Program for Parents & Young Children (Birth to Five Years Old) Activities Manual for Home-Based Family Parenting Curriculum. 533p. 1985. ring bd. 45.00 (0-934309-08-6) Family Dev Res.

— Nurturing Program for Parents & Young Children (Birth to Five Years Old) Family Resource Handbook. (Illus.). 189p. 1985. ring bd. 10.00 (0-934309-09-4) Family Dev Res.

Bavolek, Stephen J. & Comstock, Christine M. Nurturing Program for Parents & Children: Activities Manual for Children 4 to 7 Years. 2nd ed. 195p. 1985. pap. text 23.00 (0-934309-05-1) Family Dev Res.

— Nurturing Program for Parents & Children: Activities Manual for Children 8 to 12 Years. 2nd ed. 195p. 1985. pap. text 23.00 (0-934309-06-X) Family Dev Res.

— Nurturing Program for Parents & Children: Activities Manual for Parents. 2nd ed. 174p. 1985. pap. text 23.00 (0-934309-01-9) Family Dev Res.

— Nurturing Program for Parents & Children: Parent Handbook. (Illus.). 173p. (Orig.). 1985. pap. text 11.00 (0-934309-00-0) Family Dev Res.

— Nurturing Program for Parents & Children: Program Implementation Manual. 74p. 1985. pap. text 11.00 (0-934309-04-3) Family Dev Res.

Bavor & Mitchell. Wetland Systems in Water Pollution Control. (Water Science & Technology Ser.). 336p. 1994. pap. 190.00 (0-08-042532-1, Pergamon Pr) Elsevier.

Bavota, Michael. Seafood Lover's Bible. LC 99-18051. (Illus.). 192p. 1999. 14.95 (1-57416-027-3) Clear Light.

Bavousett, Glenn B. More World War II Aircraft in Combat: 47 Famous Warplanes Depicted in Raging Conflict. LC 80-12082. (Illus.). 15.00 (0-668-04550-7, ARCO) Macmillan.

Bawa, Joanna. Computers & Your Health: Problems, Prevention & Cures. 192p. 1996. pap. 12.95 (0-89087-809-9) Celestial Arts.

Bawa, Joanna, jt. ed. see Trenner, Lesley.

Bawa, K. S. & Hadley, M., eds. Reproductive Ecology of Tropical Forest Plants. (Man & the Biosphere Ser.: Vol. 7). (Illus.). 422p. 1991. 65.00 (1-85070-268-3) Prthnon Pub.

Bawa Muhaiyaddeen, M. R. The Asma'ul-Husna: The 99 Beautiful Names of Allah. LC 79-19619. (Illus.). 211p. 1979. 16.00 (0-914390-31-7); pap. 11.00 (0-914390-13-9) Fellowship Pr PA.

— A Book of God's Love. LC 81-4503. (Illus.). 126p. 1981. 12.00 (0-914390-19-8) Fellowship Pr PA.

— A Book of God's Love. LC 81-4503. (Illus.). 126p. 1994. pap. 7.00 (0-914390-42-2) Fellowship Pr PA.

— Come to the Secret Garden: Sufi Tales of Wisdom. LC 83-49210. (Illus.). 450p. (J). 1994. pap. 17.00 (0-914390-46-5) Fellowship Pr PA.

— The Divine Luminous Wisdom That Dispels the Darkness. rev. ed. (Illus.). 288p. 1997. pap. 11.00 (0-914390-11-2) Fellowship Pr PA.

— Four Steps to Pure Iman. LC 81-1429. (Illus.). 70p. 1979. pap. 8.00 (0-914390-17-1) Fellowship Pr PA.

— God, His Prophets & His Children. LC 78-12891. (Illus.). 256p. 1978. pap. 11.00 (0-914390-09-0) Fellowship Pr PA.

— Golden Words of a Sufi Sheikh. LC 82-11854. 472p. 1994. pap. 15.00 (0-914390-47-3) Fellowship Pr PA.

— The Guidebook to the True Secret of the Heart, Vol. 2. LC 75-44557. (Illus.). 232p. 1976. pap. 11.00 (0-914390-08-2) Fellowship Pr PA.

— My Love You, My Children: One Hundred & One Stories for Children of All Ages. LC 81-9847. (Illus.). 425p. 1981. 23.00 (0-914390-20-1) Fellowship Pr PA.

— Question of Life - Answers of Wisdom, Vol. 1. 350p. 1995. pap. 15.00 (0-914390-43-0) Fellowship Pr PA.

— Songs of God's Grace. LC 73-91016. (Illus.). 154p. 1974. pap. 7.00 (0-914390-02-3) Fellowship Pr PA.

— Truth & Light: Brief Explanations. LC 74-76219. (Illus.). 144p. 1974. pap. 6.00 (0-914390-04-X) Fellowship Pr PA.

— Wisdom of Man: Selected Discourses. LC 80-20541. (Illus.). 168p. 1980. 12.00 (0-914390-16-3) Fellowship Pr PA.

— Wisdom of Man: Selected Discourses. LC 80-20541. (Illus.). 168p. 1994. pap. 7.00 (0-914390-45-7) Fellowship Pr PA.

Bawa, P. S. Managing Mobility. 1991. text 17.95 (0-7069-5452-1, Pub. by Vikas) S Asia.

Bawa, Seema. Religion & Art of the Chamba Valley (A. D. 700-1300) LC 98-907084. xii, 183p. 1998. 68.00 (81-7320-038-6, Pub. by Agam Kala Prakashan) S Asia.

Bawa, Ujagar S. Aasaa Di Vaar: A Part of Sikh Scriptures. LC 92-61607. (Books on Sikhism Ser.). 184p. (YA). (gr. 8-12). 1993. 12.50 (0-942245-08-3) Wash Sikh Ctr.

— Bichitra Naatik: A Part of Sikh Scriptures. LC 90-71341. (Books on Sikhism Ser.). 172p. 1991. pap. 16.00 (0-942245-06-7) Wash Sikh Ctr.

— Dukhbhanjanee Sahib: A Part of Sikh Scriptures. LC 91-65479. (Books on Sikhism Ser.). (PAN.). 107p. (YA). (gr. 8-12). 1993. 7.50 (0-942245-07-5) Wash Sikh Ctr.

— Jaap Sahib & Sawayay: A Part of Sikh Scriptures. LC 92-62362. (Books on Sikhism Ser.). (PAN.). 133p. (YA). (gr. 8-12). 1993. 10.00 (0-942245-91-1) Wash Sikh Ctr.

— Japuji Sahib, Reharas Sahib, Anand Sahib, Kirtan Sohila: A Part of Sikh Scriptures. (PAN.). 416p. (YA). (gr. 8-12). 1999. 20.00 (0-942245-10-5) Wash Sikh Ctr.

— Sikhism: A Short Expose. (Books on Sikhism Ser.). 30p. (J). 1988. pap. 2.00 (0-942245-02-4) Wash Sikh Ctr.

— Sri Sukhmani Sahib: A Part of Sikh Scriptures. LC 89-51589. (Books on Sikhism Ser.). 304p. (J). 1997. reprint ed. pap. 15.00 (0-942245-05-9) Wash Sikh Ctr.

Bawa, Ujagar S., jt. auth. see Singh, Vir.

Bawa, Ujagar S., jt. auth. see Singh, Vir S.

Bawcutt, N. W., ed. The Control & Censorship of Caroline Drama: The Records of Sir Henry Herbert, Master of the Revels, 1623-73. 360p. (C). 1996. text 80.00 (0-19-812246-2) OUP.

Bawcutt, N. W., ed. see Ford, John.

Bawcutt, N. W., ed. see Marlowe, Christopher.

Bawcutt, N. W., ed. see Middleton, Thomas & Rowley, Wm.

Bawcutt, N. W., ed. see Shakespeare, William.

Bawcutt, Nigel, ed. Collections, XV. (Malone Society Reprints Ser.: No. 154). (Illus.). 210p. 1994. text 45.00 (0-19-729031-0) OUP.

Bawcutt, Paul A. Captive Insurance Companies. (C). 1987. 550.00 (0-7855-4309-0, Pub. by Witherby & Co) St Mut.

Bawcutt, Paul A., jt. auth. see Banninster, Jim E.

Bawcutt, Priscilla. Dunbar the Makar. 410p. (C). 1992. text 110.00 (0-19-812963-7) OUP.

— William Dunbar. 464p. (C). 1996. pap. 45.00 (0-582-06187-3) Addison-Wesley.

— William Dunbar. (C). 1996. text 74.00 (0-582-06188-1) Addison-Wesley.

***Bawden, Bill & Sullivan, Tim.** Signposts: How to Be a Catholic Man in the World Today. (Illus.). 128p. 2000. pap. 13.95 (0-932085-38-5) Word Among Us.

Bawden, C. R. Tales of an Old Lama. (Buddhica Britannica Ser.: Vol. VIII). (C). 1997. text 48.00 (0-9515424-7-8, Pub. by Inst Buddhist Stud) S Asia.

***Bawden, Charles R.** An Anthology of Mongolian Traditional Literature. 450p. 1999. 110.00 (0-7103-0654-7, Pub. by Kegan Paul Intl) Col U Pr.

Bawden, Charles R. The Modern History of Mongolia. 256p. 1989. pap. 19.95 (0-7103-0326-2) Routledge.

— Mongolian-English Dictionary. 900p. 1992. 169.95 (0-7103-0439-0, A9512) Routledge.

Bawden, David. User-Oriented Evaluation of Information Resources. 200p. 1990. text 74.95 (0-566-05209-1, Pub. by Gower) Ashgate Pub Co.

Bawden, Frederick C. Plant Viruses & Virus Diseases. LC 64-11825. 368p. reprint ed. pap. 114.10 (0-7837-3427-1, 205774800008) Bks Demand.

Bawden, Garth. The Moche. (Peoples of America Ser.). (Illus.). 288p. 1997. 44.95 (1-55786-520-5) Blackwell Pubs.

***Bawden, Garth.** The Moche. (Peoples of America Ser.). (Illus.). 384p. 1999. pap. 27.95 (0-631-21863-7) Blackwell Pubs.

Bawden, Garth & Conrad, Geoffrey W. The Andean Heritage: Masterpieces of Peruvian Art from the Collections of the Peabody Museum. LC 82-80550. (Peabody Museum Press Ser.). (Illus.). 112p. 1982. pap. 12.00 (0-87365-805-1) Peabody Harvard.

Bawden, Henry H. The Principles of Pragmatism: A Philosophical Interpretation of Experience. LC 75-3034. (Philosophy in America Ser.). 1976. reprint ed. 37.50 (0-404-59042-X) AMS Pr.

***Bawden, Jennifer.** Get a Life, Then Get a Man. LC 99-45729. 244p. 2000. pap. 12.95 (0-452-28135-0, Plume) Dutton Plume.

Bawden, Juliet. Applique Style: The Best of Contemporary Design - Plus Stylish Projects to Make at Home. LC 97-157294. (Illus.). 128p. 1997. 29.95 (0-304-34769-8, Pub. by Cassell) Sterling.

— Applique Style: The Best of Contemporary Design - Plus Stylish Projects to Make at Home. (Illus.). 128p. 1999. pap. 21.95 (0-304-34920-8, Pub. by Cassell) Sterling.

— The Art & Craft of Papier Mache. LC 94-22237. (Illus.). 144p. 1995. pap. 17.95 (0-8118-0805-X) Chronicle Bks.

Bawden, Juliet. Cross Stitch Kit: 25 Elegant & Easy-to-Make Projects for Every Room in the House, with Fabric. (Illus.). 1997. 24.95 (0-8230-1127-5) Watsn-Guptill.

Bawden, Juliet. The Cushion Book: Creating Pillows, Bolsters & Decorative Accents. (Illus.). 128p. 1995. 24.95 (0-7892-0098-8) Abbeville Pr.

— The Decorative Stamping Sourcebook. (Illus.). 128p. 1997. 24.99 (0-89134-790-9, North Lght Bks) F & W Pubns Inc.

— Fanciful Frames. (Illus.). 160p. 1995. pap. 19.95 (0-8019-8659-1) Krause Pubns.

— The Hat Book: Creating Hats for Every Occasion. LC 93-37114. (Illus.). 144p. 1994. pap. 14.95 (0-937274-73-9) Lark Books.

— Hearts: The Art of Making Gifts of Love & Affection. LC 92-17873. (Illus.). 128p. 1993. 23.00 (0-671-78960-0) S&S Trade.

— Jewelry & Accessories: Beautiful Designs to Make & Wear. (Illus.). 128p. 1995. pap. 17.99 (0-89134-654-6, North Lght Bks) F & W Pubns Inc.

— Lamps & Shades: Beautiful Ideas to Make & Decorate. LC 97-183698. (Illus.). 128p. 1997. 27.95 (1-85368-733-2, Pub. by New5 Holland) Sterling.

— Lamps & Shades: Beautiful Ideas to Make & Decorate. LC 97-183698. (Illus.). 128p. 1999. pap. text 17.95 (1-85368-761-8) New5 Holland.

***Bawden, Juliet.** No-Sew Soft Furnishings: Quick & Easy Techniques for Effective Home Furnishings. LC 99-190256. (Illus.). 128p. 1999. 24.95 (0-7063-7770-2, Pub. by WrLock) Sterling.

Bawden, Juliet. Papier Mache: Projects, Techniques, Pull-Out Designs. (Illus.). 96p. 1998. 27.50 (1-85029-682-0, Pub. by Conran Octopus) Trafalgar.

— Papier Mache: Projects, Techniques, Pull-Out Designs. (Illus.). 96p. 1998. reprint ed. pap. 19.95 (1-85029-973-0) Conran Octopus.

— Pretty Gifts That Say I Love You: Over 35 Projects with Step-by-Step Instructions. (Illus.). 112p. 1998. 24.95 (1-85028-408-3, Pub. by Collins & Br) Trafalgar.

— Rag Rug Inspirations: New Designs for Traditional Techniques. (Illus.). 144p. 1998. pap. text 19.95 (0-304-34909-7) Continuum.

— To Dye For: 25 Great Dyeing Ideas in the Home. LC 96-39666. (Illus.). 112p. (Orig.). 1997. pap. 15.95 (0-87951-785-9, Pub. by Overlook Pr) Penguin Putnam.

— The Weekend Crafter - Decoupage: Original Ideas for More Than 50 Quick & Easy Designs. LC 97-28542. (Weekend Crafter Ser.). Orig. Title: Decoupage in a Weekend. (Illus.). 80p. 1998. pap. 14.95 (1-57990-005-4, Pub. by Lark Books) Random.

— The Weekend Crafter - Stamping: Beautiful Ways to Decorate Paper, Fabric, Wood & Ceramics in a Weekend. LC 97-29966. (Weekend Crafter Ser.). Orig. Title: Stamping in a Weekend. (Illus.). 80p. 1998. pap. 14.95 (1-57990-004-6, Pub. by Lark Books) Random.

***Bawden, Nina.** Afternoon of a Good Woman. large type unabridged ed. 1999. pap. 19.95 (0-7531-5878-7, 158787, Pub. by ISIS Lrg Prnt) ISIS Pub.

Bawden, Nina. Afternoon of a Good Woman. large type unabridged ed. 280p. 1998. 24.95 (0-7531-5587-7, 155877) ISIS Pub.

***Bawden, Nina.** Anna Apparent. large type unabridged ed. 249p. 1999. 26.95 (*0-7531-5586-9*, 155869, Pub. by ISIS Lrg Prnt); pap. 19.95 (*0-7531-5811-6*, 158116, Pub. by ISIS Lrg Prnt) ISIS Pub.

Bawden, Nina. The Birds on the Trees. large type ed. LC 94-48848. 304p. 1995. pap. 20.95 (*0-7862-0412-5*) Thorndike Pr.

— Carrie's War. LC 72-13253. 160p. (J). (gr. 4-7). 1973. lib. bdg. 14.89 (*0-397-31450-7*) HarpC Child Bks.

— Devil by the Sea. LC 76-13177. (YA). (gr. 7-12). 1976. 12.95 (*0-397-31683-6*) HarpC Child Bks.

— The Grain of Truth. 20.95 (*0-88411-121-0*) Amereon Ltd.

— Granny the Pag. LC 95-38191. 192p. (J). (gr. 4-7). 1996. 15.00 (*0-395-77604-X*, Clarion Bks) HM.

— Granny the Pag. LC 97-38408. 192p. (J). 1998. pap. 4.99 (*0-14-038447-2*, PuffinBks) Peng Put Young Read.

— Granny the Pag. (J). 1998. 10.09 (*0-606-12955-3*, Pub. by Turtleback) Demco.

— Henry. large type ed. (Illus.). 1995. pap. 33.50 (*0-614-09586-7*, L-34862-00) Am Printing Hse.

— Humbug. 144p. (J). (gr. 4-7). 1992. 13.95 (*0-395-62149-6*, Clarion Bks) HM.

— Humbug. 144p. (J). (gr. 5 up). 1994. pap. 4.99 (*0-14-036586-9*, PuffinBks) Peng Put Young Read.

— Humbug. (J). 1994. 9.09 (*0-606-05882-6*, Pub. by Turtleback) Demco.

— In My Own Time: Almost an Autobiography. LC 95-13092. 176p. 1995. 25.95 (*0-395-74429-6*, Clarion Bks) HM.

— In My Own Time: Almost an Autobiography. large type ed. 22.95 (*1-85695-138-3*, Pub. by ISIS Lrg Prnt) Transaction Pubs.

— A Little Love, a Little Learning. 21.95 (*0-88411-122-9*) Amereon Ltd.

***Bawden, Nina.** A Little Love, a Little Learning. large type unabridged ed. 296p. 1999. 26.95 (*0-7531-5584-2*, 155842, Pub. by ISIS Lrg Prnt); pap. 19.95 (*0-7531-5863-9*, 158639, Pub. by ISIS Lrg Prnt) ISIS Pub.

Bawden, Nina. The Odd Flamingo. 22.95 (*0-88411-126-1*) Amereon Ltd.

— Off the Road. LC 97-42576. 192p. (J). (gr. 4 up). 1998. 16.00 (*0-395-91321-7*, Clarion Bks) HM.

— The Outside Child. 1994. 9.09 (*0-606-05968-7*, Pub. by Turtleback) Demco.

— The Peppermint Pig. LC 74-26922. 192p. (J). (gr. 3-6). 1975. lib. bdg. 13.89 (*0-397-31618-6*) HarpC Child Bks.

— The Real Plato Jones. LC 92-43873. 176p. (J). 1993. 13.95 (*0-395-66972-3*, Clarion Bks) HM.

— The Real Plato Jones. 1996. 10.09 (*0-606-10907-2*, Pub. by Turtleback) Demco.

— Rebel on a Rock. LC 77-10686. 160p. (J). (gr. 7 up). 1978. lib. bdg. 13.89 (*0-397-32140-6*) HarpC Child Bks.

— Tortoise by Candlelight. 21.95 (*0-88411-123-7*) Amereon Ltd.

— Under the Skin. 22.95 (*0-88411-124-5*) Amereon Ltd.

— A Woman of My Age. 159p. 1976. reprint ed. lib. bdg. 18.95 (*0-88411-125-3*, Queens House) Amereon Ltd.

Bawden, W. F. & Archibald, J. F. Innovative Mine Design for the 21st Century. 1046p. 1993. 168.00 (*90-5410-325-6*, Pub. by A A Balkema) Ashgate Pub Co.

Bawdwin, John W. The Language of Sex: Five Voices from Northern France Around 1200. LC 93-6040. (Chicago Series on Sexuality, History, & Society). 360p. 1994. 37.50 (*0-226-03613-8*) U Ch Pr.

Bawer, Bruce. Beyond Queer. 304p. 1996. 25.00 (*0-684-82766-2*); pap. 24.00 (*0-02-874117-X*) Free Pr.

— Coast to Coast. 64p. (Orig.). 1993. pap. 11.95 (*0-934257-51-5*) Story Line.

— The Contemporary Stylist. 304p. (C). 1987. teacher ed. write for info. (*0-15-513717-4*) Harcourt Coll Pubs.

— Place at the Table: The Gay Individual in American Society. 1993. 21.00 (*0-671-79533-3*) S&S Trade.

— Place at the Table: The Gay Individual in American Society. 272p. 1994. per. 12.00 (*0-671-89439-0*) S&S Trade Pap.

— Prophets & Professors: Essays on the Lives & Works of Modern Poets. 352p. 1995. 26.95 (*1-885266-05-7*); pap. 15.95 (*1-885266-04-9*) Story Line.

— The Screenplay's the Thing: Movie Criticism, 1986-1990. LC 92-7219. 298p. (C). 1992. lib. bdg. 32.50 (*0-208-02332-1*, Archon Bks) Shoe String.

— Stealing Jesus: How Fundamentalism Betrays Christianity. 352p. 1998. pap. 14.00 (*0-609-80222-4*, Crown) Crown Pub Group.

Bawkoff, S. G., jt. ed. see Chew, J. C.

Bawtree, Michael. The New Singing Theatre. (Illus.). 270p. 1991. pap. text 22.95 (*0-19-385867-3*) OUP.

Bawtree, Victoria, jt. compiled by see Rahnema, Majid.

Bax, jt. auth. see Short, David.

Bax, Ad. Two-Dimensional Nuclear Magnetic Resonance in Liquids. 1982. reprint ed. text 140.50 (*90-277-1412-6*) Kluwer Academic.

Bax, Arnold E. Farewell, My Youth. (Music Book Index Ser.). 112p. 1992. reprint ed. lib. bdg. 69.00 (*0-7812-9461-4*) Rprt Serv.

Bax, Clifford. Polite Satires. LC 76-40385. (One-Act Plays in Reprint Ser.). 1976. reprint ed. 20.00 (*0-8486-2001-1*) Roth Pub Inc.

— Pretty Witty Nell: An Account of Nell Gwyn & Her Environment. LC 76-83871. (Illus.). 306p. 1972. reprint ed. 24.95 (*0-405-08243-6*, Pub. by Blom Pubns) Ayer.

Bax, Clifford, tr. see Goldoni, Carlo.

Bax, Clifford, tr. see Steiner, Rudolf.

Bax, D. Hieronymus Bosch & Lucas Cranach: Two Last Judgement Triptychs. (Verhandelingen der Koninklijke Nederlandse Akademie van Wetenschappen, Afd. Letterkunde, Nieuwe Reeks Ser.: No. 117). 472p. pap. 62.00 (*0-444-85545-9*) Elsevier.

Bax, Douglas S., tr. see Bonhoeffer, Dietrich.

Bax, Ernest Belfort. German Society at the Close of the Middle Ages. LC 83-45653. reprint ed. 32.50 (*0-404-19803-1*) AMS Pr.

— Last Episodes of the French Revolution. LC 74-159489. (World History Ser.: No. 48). 1971. lib. bdg. 75.00 (*0-8383-1282-9*) M S G Haskell Hse.

— Outlooks from the New Standpoint. (Essay Index Reprint Ser.). 1977. 20.95 (*0-8369-2742-7*) Ayer.

— Religion of Socialism: Being Essays in Modern Socialist Criticism. LC 74-39668. (Essay Index Reprint Ser.). 1977. reprint ed. 20.95 (*0-8369-2743-5*) Ayer.

— Reminiscences & Reflexions of a Mid & Late Victorian. LC 67-27466. 283p. 1967. reprint ed. 45.00 (*0-678-00313-0*) Kelley.

— The Social Side of the Reformation in Germany, 3 vols. Incl. Peasants' War in Germany, 1525-1526. LC 68-57371. xi, 367p. 1968. reprint ed. lib. bdg. 39.50 (*0-678-00445-5*); Set lib. bdg. 100.00 (*0-678-00772-1*) Kelley.

Bax, Mart. Medjugorje: Religion, Politics, & Violence in Rural Bosnia. 180p. 1995. pap. 25.00 (*90-5383-384-6*) Paul & Co Pubs.

Bax, Mart, et al, eds. Faith & Polity: Essays on Religion & Politics. 200p. 1993. pap. 37.50 (*90-5383-080-4*, Pub. by VU Univ Pr) Paul & Co Pubs.

Bax, Mart & Koster, Adrianus, eds. Power & Prayer: Anthropological Essays on Politics & Religion. 200p. 1993. pap. 35.00 (*90-5383-209-2*, Pub. by VU Univ Pr) Paul & Co Pubs.

Bax, Martin. Edmond Went Far Away. LC 88-16324. (Illus.). 48p. (J). (ps-3). 1989. 12.95 (*0-15-225105-7*, Harcourt Child Bks) Harcourt.

— The Hospital Ship. LC 76-16033. 1976. 7.95 (*0-8112-0584-3*, Pub. by New Directions); pap. 3.95 (*0-8112-0585-1*, NDP402, Pub. by New Directions) Norton.

Bax, Peter. Stage Management. 1977. 24.95 (*0-405-09118-4*, 1700) Ayer.

Baxandall & Fraad, Rosalyn. Words on Fire: The Life & Writing of Elizabeth Gurley Flynn. (Douglass Series on Women's Lives & the Meaning of Gender). (Illus.). 320p. 1987. text 45.00 (*0-8135-1240-9*); pap. text 17.95 (*0-8135-1241-7*) Rutgers U Pr.

Baxandall, Elizabeth & Ilingworth, Doris. Out of the Blue. 64p. (C). 1988. pap. 35.00 (*0-7212-0703-0*, Pub. by Regency Pr GBR) St Mut.

Baxandall, Lee. World Guide to Nude Beaches & Resorts. (Illus.). 274p. 1995. pap. 28.00 (*0-934106-20-7*) Naturists.

— World Guide to Nude Beaches & Resorts. 1997. 16.80 (*0-934106-21-5*) Naturists.

Baxandall, Lee, ed. see Marx, Karl & Engels, Friedrich.

Baxandall, Lee, tr. see Brecht, Bertolt.

Baxandall, Michael. Giotto & Orators: Humanist Observers of Painting in Italy & Discovery of Pictorial Composition. (Illus.). 196p. 1986. pap. text 29.95 (*0-19-817387-3*) OUP.

— The Limewood Sculptors of Renaissance Germany, 1475-1525. LC 79-23258. (Illus.). 1982. pap. 32.50 (*0-300-02829-6*, Y-414) Yale U Pr.

— Painting & Experience in Fifteenth-Century Italy: A Primer in the Social History of Pictorial Style. 2nd ed. (Illus.). 190p. 1988. pap. text 13.95 (*0-19-282144-X*) OUP.

— Patterns of Intention. LC 85-6049. 180p. 1987. pap. 16.00 (*0-300-03763-5*, Y-699) Yale U Pr.

— Shadows & Enlightenment. LC 94-40132. 192p. 1995. 30.00 (*0-300-05979-5*) Yale U Pr.

— Shadows & Enlightenment. 222p. 1997. pap. 20.00 (*0-300-07272-4*) Yale U Pr.

Baxandall, Michael, jt. auth. see Alpers, Svetlana.

Baxandall, Rosalyn. America's Working Women. 2nd ed. (Illus.). 430p. 1995. pap. 14.95 (*0-393-31262-3*) Norton.

***Baxandall, Rosalyn & Gordon, Linda, eds.** Dear Sisters: Dispatches from the Women's Liberation Movement. 320p. 2000. text 30.00 (*0-465-01706-1*, Pub. by Basic) HarpC.

Baxandall, Rosalyn F., jt. auth. see Ewen, Elizabeth.

Baxendale, J. & Busi, F. The Study of Fast Processes & Transient Species by Electron Pulse Radiolysis. 1982. text 249.00 (*90-277-1431-2*) Kluwer Academic.

Baxendale, John & Pawling, Christopher. Narrating the Thirties: A Decade in the Making, 1930 to the Present. 256p. 1996. text 59.95 (*0-312-12898-3*) St Martin.

Baxendale, Martin. Plop! (Illus.). 64p. 1998. pap. 6.95 (*1-889647-36-5*) Boston Am.

— The Very Small Garden. 128p. 1987. 25.95 (*0-285-62736-8*) Intl Spec Bk.

***Baxendale, Trevor.** Coldheart. (Doctor Who Ser.). 288p. 2000. mass mkt. 6.95 (*0-563-55595-5*, Pub. by BBC Bks) Genl Dist Srvs.

Baxendale, Trevor. Janus Conjunction. 1998. pap. 5.95 (*0-563-40599-6*) BBC.

Baxes, Gregory A. Digital Image Processing: Principles & Applications. 480p. 1994. pap. 59.99 incl. disk (*0-471-00949-0*) Wiley.

Baxevanis, Andreas & Ouellette, B. F. Bioinformatics: A Practical Guide to the Analysis of Genes & Proteins. LC 97-39019. 384p. 1998. pap. 64.95 (*0-471-19196-5*) Wiley.

— Bioinformatics: A Practical Guide to the Analysis of Genes & Proteins. 39. 370p. (C). 1998. 164.95 (*0-471-32441-8*) Wiley.

Baxevanis, John J. The Wine Regions of America: Geographical Reflections & Appraisals. LC 92-60540. (Illus.). 400p. (Orig.). (C). 1992. pap. 55.00 (*0-922983-51-8*) Vinifera Wine.

— The Wines of Bordeaux & Western France. 288p. 1987. 53.50 (*0-8476-7490-8*, R7490) Rowman.

— The Wines of Champagne, Burgundy, & Eastern & Southern France. 224p. 1987. 53.50 (*0-8476-7534-3*, R7534) Rowman.

***Baxi, Upendra.** The Future of Human Rights. 160p. 2000. text 14.95 (*0-19-565289-4*) OUP.

Baxi Upendra. Law & Property-Critical Essays. (C). 1988. 140.00 (*0-7855-3675-2*) St Mut.

Baxi, Upendra. Liberty & Corruption - The Antulay Case & Beyond. (C). 1989. 100.00 (*0-89771-757-0*, Pub. by Eastern Book) St Mut.

— The Right to Be Human. (C). 1987. 32.00 (*81-7062-021-X*, Pub. by Lancer India) S Asia.

***Baxi, Upendra, et al, eds.** Reconstructing the Republic. LC 99-939101. 431p. 1999. 34.00 (*81-241-0495-6*, Pub. by Har-Anand Pubns) Nataraj Bks.

Baxi Upendra & Parekh, Bhikhu. Crisis & Change in Contemporary India. LC 94-21922. 448p. 1995. text 32.00 (*0-8039-9182-7*) Sage.

Baxley, Gladys B., jt. auth. see Kumpeer, Karol L.

Baxley, Wayne. Jungo File: The Carden. 1996. pap. text 29.95 (*0-7935-6730-0*) H Leonard.

Baxstrom, Jerri L. Von Vereiningung zu Vereiningung: A Survey of German Culture from 1871 to the Present. (GER., Illus.). 80p. 1997. pap. text 26.00 (*0-942017-54-4*, 04-6433) Amer Assn Teach German.

Baxt, George. The Clark Gable & Carole Lombard Murder Case. large type ed. LC 98-26426. 1998. 27.95 (*0-7862-1543-7*) Thorndike Pr.

— Homosexuality Ain't What It Used to Be. Date not set. pap. 12.95 (*1-55583-447-7*, Alyson Bks) Alyson Pubns.

— The Humphrey Bogart Murder Case. large type ed. (Niagara Large Print Ser.). 299p. 1996. 29.50 (*0-7089-5843-5*) Ulverscroft.

— A Queer Kind of Death. LC 98-15555. 300p. 1998. pap. 10.00 (*1-55583-448-5*) Alyson Pubns.

— A Queer Kind of Love: A Pharoah Love Mystery. 288p. 1994. 20.00 (*1-883402-01-8*) S&S Trade.

— A Queer Kind of Umbrella: A Pharoah Love Mystery. 1995. 21.00 (*1-883402-35-2*) S&S Trade.

— A Queer Kind of Umbrella: A Pharoah Love Mystery. LC 95-17055. 240p. 1995. 20.50 (*0-684-81496-X*) Simon & Schuster.

— The Tallulah Bankhead Murder Case. large type ed. (General Ser.). 363p. 1989. lib. bdg. 17.95 (*0-8161-4707-8*, G K Hall Lrg Type) Mac Lib Ref.

Baxt, R. & Fletcher, Keith L. Afterman & Baxt's Cases & Materials on Corporations & Associations. 6th ed. 1016p. 1992. pap. 96.00 (*0-409-30329-1*, Austral, MICHIE) LEXIS Pub.

Baxt, R., et al. Afterman & Baxt's Cases & Materials on Corporations & Associations. 7th ed. 1000p. 1996. pap. write for info. (*0-409-31092-1*, MICHIE) LEXIS Pub.

— Securities Industry Law. 5th ed. LC 96-150604. 408p. 1996. pap. write for info. (*0-409-31142-1*, MICHIE) LEXIS Pub.

— Stock Markets & the Securities Industry: Law & Practice. 3rd ed. 1988. pap. 61.00 (*0-409-49467-4*, A.T., MICHIE) LEXIS Pub.

Baxt, R., jt. auth. see Hardingham, I. J.

Baxter. Ice Bones. 2000. 23.00 (*0-06-105134-9*); mass mkt. 5.99 (*0-06-102021-4*) HarpC.

— Long Tusk. 2000. 23.00 (*0-06-105133-0*); mass mkt. 5.99 (*0-06-105135-7*) HarpC.

— Martin Amis. 1998. 23.95 (*0-8057-7804-7*, Twyne) Mac Lib Ref.

— Race Equality in Health Care. 1997. pap. text 36.00 (*0-7020-2031-1*) Bailliere Tindall.

— Working with the Families of Our Children: Kinko's Quickprint Advance Pages. (C). 1996. spiral bd. write for info. (*0-201-89245-6*) Addison-Wesley.

Baxter, jt. auth. see Juarez de Ku.

Baxter, ed. see Atkinson, Rhonda H. & Longman, Debbie G.

Baxter, ed. see Best, John B.

Baxter, ed. see Brownell, Gregg, et al.

Baxter, ed. see Dempsey, John S.

Baxter, ed. see Duiker, William J. & Spielvogel, Jackson J.

Baxter, ed. see Exoo, Calvin F.

Baxter, ed. see Goldberg, Raymond.

Baxter, ed. see Gravetter, Frederick J. & Wallnau, Larry B.

Baxter, ed. see Hauss, Charles.

Baxter, ed. see Hilley, Martha & Olson, Lynn F.

Baxter, ed. see Horowitz, David, et al.

Baxter, ed. see Matthews, Warren.

Baxter, ed. see Spielvogel, Jackson J.

Baxter, ed. see Tarr, G. Alan.

Baxter, ed. see Upshur, Jiu-Hwa & Holoka, Jim.

Baxter, ed. see Upshur, Jiu-Hwa, et al.

Baxter, ed. see Warren, Bruce.

Baxter, ed. see Welch, Susan, et al.

Baxter, jt. ed. see White, James E.

Baxter, ed. see Wright, Craig.

***Baxter & Babbie.** Communication Research Methods. (Speech & Theater Ser.). 2002. pap. 43.00 (*0-534-50778-6*) Wadsworth Pub.

***Baxter, Alan.** German Warfare: Breakthroughs in Immunology. 240p. 2000. pap. 14.95 (*1-86508-070-5*, Pub. by Allen & Unwin Pty) IPG Chicago.

Baxter, Albert. History of the City of Grand Rapids, Michigan. (Illus.). 854p. 1993. reprint ed. lib. bdg. 86.00 (*0-8328-3491-2*) Higginson Bk Co.

Baxter, Albert T. Motorcycle Accident Investigation. 2nd ed. 261p. (C). 1997. pap. text 44.50 (*1-884566-09-X*) Inst Police Tech.

Baxter, Albert T. Motorcycle Accident Investigation. 2nd rev. ed. LC 97-183937. (Illus.). 348p. 1997. pap. text 44.50 (*1-884566-21-9*) Inst Police Tech.

Baxter, Alison. Equity & Trusts. 208p. (C). 1990. pap. 45.00 (*1-85352-770-X*, Pub. by HLT Pubns) St Mut.

— Wills, Probate & Administration. 200p. (C). 1990. pap. 60.00 (*1-85352-898-6*, Pub. by HLT Pubns) St Mut.

Baxter, Angus. In Search of Your British & Irish Roots: A Complete Guide to Tracing Your English, Welsh, Scottish, & Irish Ancestors. 4th ed. LC 99-71442. 1994. reprint ed. pap. 18.95 (*0-8063-1611-X*) Genealog Pub.

— In Search of Your Canadian Roots. 3rd ed. 400p. 2000. pap. 19.95 (*0-8063-1626-8*) Genealog Pub.

Baxter, Angus. In Search of Your European Roots. 2nd ed. 304p. 1999. reprint ed. pap. 16.95 (*0-8063-1446-X*) Genealog Pub.

— In Search of Your German Roots: A Complete Guide to Tracing Your Ancestors in the Germanic Areas of Europe. 3rd ed. LC 94-76790. 122p. 1999. reprint ed. pap. 11.95 (*0-8063-1447-8*) Genealog Pub.

Baxter, Anne & Lozano-Diaz, Nora O., eds. Woman's Work: A Guide to Growth & Self-Discovery. LC 94-34353. 120p. (Orig.). 1994. pap. 9.99 (*0-8361-3695-0*) Herald Pr.

Baxter, Annette K., ed. Madeleine. LC 79-8767. (Signal Lives Ser.). 1980. reprint ed. lib. bdg. 37.95 (*0-405-12817-7*) Ayer.

— Sex & Equality: An Original Anthology. LC 74-3972. (Women in America Ser.). 220p. 1977. reprint ed. 23.95 (*0-405-06121-8*) Ayer.

— Signal Lives Series, 51 bks., Set. 1980. lib. bdg. 1889.50 (*0-405-12815-0*) Ayer.

Baxter, Annette K. & Stein, Leon, eds. American Women: Images & Realities, 44 bks., Set. 17788p. 1972. reprint ed. 1088.00 (*0-405-04445-3*) Ayer.

Baxter, Annette K., ed. see Antin, Mary.

Baxter, Annette K., ed. see Atherton, Gertrude F.

Baxter, Annette K., ed. see Bacon, Albion F.

Baxter, Annette K., ed. see Bailey, Abigail.

Baxter, Annette K., ed. see Barr, Amelia E.

Baxter, Annette K., ed. see Barton, Clara.

Baxter, Annette K., ed. see Belmont, Eleanor R.

Baxter, Annette K., ed. see Boyle, Sarah P.

Baxter, Annette K., ed. see Brown, Harriet C.

Baxter, Annette K., ed. see Carson, Ann.

Baxter, Annette K., ed. see Churchill, Caroline N.

Baxter, Annette K., ed. see Cleghorn, Sarah N.

Baxter, Annette K., ed. see Dall, Caroline W.

Baxter, Annette K., ed. see Daviess, Maria T.

Baxter, Annette K., ed. see Dorr, Rheta C.

Baxter, Annette K., ed. see Dumond, Annie H.

Baxter, Annette K., ed. see Eaton, Margaret O.

Baxter, Annette K., ed. see Farrar, Elizabeth R.

Baxter, Annette K., ed. see Felton, Rebeca L.

Baxter, Annette K., ed. see Garden, Mary & Biancolli, Louis L.

Baxter, Annette K., ed. see Gilson, Mary B.

Baxter, Annette K., ed. see Hurst, Fannie.

Baxter, Annette K., ed. see Jacobs-Bond, Carrie.

Baxter, Annette K., ed. see Jelliffe, Belinda D.

Baxter, Annette K., ed. see Jones, Amanda T.

Baxter, Annette K., ed. see Logan, Kate V.

Baxter, Annette K., ed. see Longworth, Alice R.

Baxter, Annette K., ed. see MacDougall, Alice F.

Baxter, Annette K., ed. see Meyer, Agnes E.

Baxter, Annette K., ed. see Mowatt, Anna C.

Baxter, Annette K., ed. see Odlum, Hortense.

Baxter, Annette K., ed. see Phelps, Elizabeth S.

Baxter, Annette K., ed. see Potter, Elizabeth.

Baxter, Annette K., ed. see Rinehart, Mary Roberts.

Baxter, Annette K., ed. see Robinson, Josephine D.

Baxter, Annette K., ed. see Roe, Elizabeth A.

Baxter, Annette K., ed. see Sanders, Sue.

Baxter, Annette K., ed. see Sangster, Margaret E.

Baxter, Annette K., ed. see Sherwood, Mary E.

Baxter, Annette K., ed. see Sigourney, Lydia H.

Baxter, Annette K., ed. see Smith, Elizabeth O.

Baxter, Annette K., jt. ed. see Stein, Leon.

Baxter, Annette K., ed. see Terhune, Mary V.

Baxter, Annette K., ed. see Terrell, Mary C.

Baxter, Annette K., ed. see Ueland, Brenda.

Baxter, Annette K., ed. see Van Hoosen, Bertha.

Baxter, Annette K., ed. see Vorse, Mary H.

Baxter, Annette K., ed. see Wilcox, Ella W.

Baxter, Annette K., ed. see Wilson, Edith B.

Baxter, Archibald. We Will Not Cease. 216p. Date not set. pap. 12.95 (*0-9605388-7-9*) Tern Pr.

Baxter, Ardeth, ed. see Kelly, Matt & Interviewees of From the Plaza.

Baxter, Arthur B. Men, Martyrs & Mountebanks. LC 73-104992. (Essay Index Reprint Ser.). 1977. 23.95 (*0-8369-1446-5*) Ayer.

Baxter, Barbara A. The Beaux-Arts Medal in America: Catalogue of the Exhibition Held at the American Numismatic Society, September 26, 1987-April 16, 1988. (Illus.). 92p. 1987. 25.00 (*0-89722-221-0*) Am Numismatic.

***Baxter, Bart.** The Man with St. Vitus' Dance. 44p. 2000. pap. 10.00 (*0-9647199-9-1*) Floating Bridge Pr.

Baxter, Bart. Peace for the Arsonist. 68p. (Orig.). 1995. pap. 7.00 (*0-9637849-7-8*) Bacchae Pr.

***Baxter, Bart E.** Sonnets from the Mare Imbrium. 36p. 1999. pap. 8.00 (*0-9647199-7-5*) Floating Bridge Pr.

Baxter, Batsell B. Family of God: A Study of the New Testament Church. 2nd rev. ed. (Classics Ser.). 169p. 1998. reprint ed. pap. 9.99 (*0-89225-208-1*, G52081) Gospel Advocate.

Baxter, Beth, ed. see Burnett, Frances Hodgson.

Baxter, Beth, ed. see Cleland, John.

Baxter, Beth, ed. see Hudson, William Henry.

Baxter, Beth, ed. see Lovecraft, H. P., et al.

Baxter, Beth, ed. see Maupassant, Guy de, et al.

Baxter, Betty & Blaxter, David. The Complete Mastiff. (Illus.). 160p. 1993. 27.95 (*0-87605-234-0*) Howell Bks.

Baxter, Brandon, jt. see Crowther, Terence G.

***Baxter, Brian.** Ecologism: An Introduction. LC 99-53928. 256p. 2000. pap. 22.95 (*0-87840-781-2*) Georgetown U Pr.

Baxter, Bruce. The Montana History Calendar. (Illus.). (Orig.). 1993. pap. 6.95 (*0-9625849-1-6*) Montana Hist.

***Baxter, Carol & Whelan, Ruth, eds.** Toleration & Religious Identity: The Implications of the Edict of Nantes for France, Britain & Ireland. 192p. 2000. 55.00 (*1-85182-481-2*, Pub. by Four Cts Pr) Intl Spec Bk.

Baxter, Carolyn. Prison Solitary. LC 79-54299. 1979. 2.00 (*0-912678-41-0*, Greenfld Rev Pr) Greenfld Rev Lit.

Baxter, Catherine S., ed. Stedman's Medical & Surgical Equipment Words. 2nd ed. LC 96-5666. 861p. 1996. 35.95 (*0-683-18144-0*) Lppncott W & W.

— Stedman's Radiology & Oncology Words: Including HIV-AIDS, Hematology. 2nd rev. ed. LC 95-24138. (Stedman's Word Bks.). 673p. 1995. 34.95 (*0-683-07966-2*) Lppncott W & W.

Baxter, Charles. Believers: A Novella & Stories. LC 96-31640. 272p. 1997. 23.00 (*0-679-44267-7*) Pantheon.

— Believers: A Novella & Stories. 288p. 1998. pap. 13.00 (*0-679-77653-2*) Vin Bks.

— Burning down the House: Essays on Fiction. LC 96-78742. 246p. 1997. 22.95 (*1-55597-256-X*) Graywolf.

— Burning Down the House: Essays on Fiction. 246p. 1998. pap. text 15.00 (*1-55597-270-5*) Graywolf.

***Baxter, Charles.** The Feast of Love: A Novel. LC 99-53088. 320p. 2000. 24.00 (*0-375-41019-8*) Pantheon.

Baxter, Charles. First Light. LC 88-9871. 288p. 1988. pap. 12.95 (*0-14-010091-1*, Penguin Bks) Viking Penguin.

— The Harmony of the World. LC 96-31639. 1997. pap. 11.00 (*0-679-77651-6*) Vin Bks.

— A Relative Stranger. (Contemporary American Fiction Ser.). 240p. 1991. reprint ed. pap. 12.95 (*0-14-015628-3*, Penguin Bks) Viking Penguin.

— Shadow Play. 400p. 1994. pap. 12.95 (*0-14-023510-8*, Penguin Bks) Viking Penguin.

— Through the Safety Net. LC 98-26445. 256p. pap. 13.00 (*0-679-77649-4*) Vin Bks.

***Baxter, Charles, ed.** The Business of Memory: The Art of Remembering in an Age of Forgetting. LC 98-88485. 186p. 1999. pap. 16.00 (*1-55597-287-X*, Pub. by Graywolf) Consort Bk Sales.

— Ploughshares, Fall 1999 Vol. 25: Fiction Issue. 233p. 1999. pap. 9.95 (*0-933277-26-1*) Ploughshares.

Baxter, Charles, jt. auth. see Connor, Judith.

Baxter, Christie I. Program-Related Investments: A Technical Manual for Foundations. LC 96-46710. (Nonprofit Law, Finance, & Management Ser.). (Illus.). 475p. 1997. 140.00 (*0-471-17833-0*) Wiley.

Baxter, Christine, jt. auth. see Darling, Rosalyn B.

Baxter, Clark, ed. see Austin, Murray & Honey, Rex.

Baxter, Claude F. & Melnechuk, Theodore, eds. Perspectives in Schizophrenia Research. fac. ed. LC 80-5052. (Illus.). 463p. pap. 143.60 (*0-7837-7168-1*, 204712900005) Bks Demand.

Baxter, Colin. Edinburgh. (Illus.). 96p. 1994. pap. 18.95 (*0-948661-33-X*, Pub. by Colin Baxter Ltd) Voyageur Pr.

— France. (Illus.). 112p. 1999. 29.95 (*1-900455-50-1*, Pub. by Colin Baxter Ltd) Voyageur Pr.

— Hares. (Illus.). 48p. (Orig.). 1995. pap. 11.95 (*0-948661-28-3*, Pub. by Colin Baxter Ltd) Voyageur Pr.

— The Lake District. (Illus.). 112p. 1998. 32.95 (*1-900455-29-3*, Pub. by Colin Baxter Ltd) Voyageur Pr.

— Portrait of Scotland. LC 97-1885. (Illus.). 96p. 1997. 19.95 (*0-89658-360-0*) Voyageur Pr.

***Baxter, Colin.** Portrait of Scotland. (Illus.). 96p. 2000. pap. 16.95 (*0-89658-515-8*) Voyageur Pr.

Baxter, Colin. Scotland. 1994. pap. 18.95 (*1-900455-77-3*, Pub. by Colin Baxter Ltd) Voyageur Pr.

***Baxter, Colin.** Scotland. (Illus.). 112p. 2000. 29.95 (*1-84107-032-7*, Pub. by Colin Baxter Ltd) Voyageur Pr.

Baxter, Colin. Scotland from the Air. LC 98-6415. (Illus.). 96p. 1998. 19.95 (*0-89658-405-4*) Voyageur Pr.

Baxter, Colin, jt. auth. see Walton, Kenneth.

***Baxter, Colin F.** Field Marshall Bernard Law Montgomery, 1887-1976: A Selected Bibliography, Vol. 23. LC 99-33434. (Bibliographies of Battles & Leaders Ser.). 184p. 1999. lib. bdg. 59.95 (*0-313-29119-5*) Greenwood.

Baxter, Colin F. The Normandy Campaign, 1944: A Selected Bibliography, 9. LC 91-46970. (Bibliographies of Battles & Leaders Ser.: No. 9). 184p. 1992. lib. bdg. 55.00 (*0-313-28301-X*, BXN, Greenwood Pr) Greenwood.

— The War in North Africa, 1940-1943: A Selected Bibliography, 16. LC 95-39494. (Bibliographies of Battles & Leaders Ser.: No. 16). 136p. 1996. lib. bdg. 55.00 (*0-313-29120-9*, Greenwood Pr) Greenwood.

Baxter, Colin F., ed. The American Military Tradition: From Colonial Times to the Present. (Illus.). 260p. 1993. 45.00 (*0-8420-2381-X*) Scholarly Res Inc.

Baxter, Craig & Kennedy, Charles H. Pakistan, 1997. LC 97-50622. 200p. 1998. 65.00 (*0-8133-2975-2*, Pub. by Westview) HarpC.

Baxter, Craig & Rahman, Syedur. Historical Dictionary of Bangladesh. 2nd ed. LC 96-15454. (Asian Historical Dictionaries Ser.: No. 21). 1996. 49.50 (*0-8108-3187-2*) Scarecrow.

***Baxter, Craig, et al.** Government & Politics in South Asia. 4th ed. LC 98-23781. 448p. 1998. pap. text 35.00 (*0-8133-3413-6*, Pub. by Westview) HarpC.

Baxter, Craig, jt. ed. see Kennedy, Charles H.

***Baxter, D.** Beer: Quality, Safety & Nutritional Aspects. (Illus.). 2000. pap. text 34.00 (*0-85404-588-0*) Royal Soc Chem.

Baxter, D. British Locomotive Catalogue, 1825-1923, Vol. 1. 1977. 35.00 (*0-7855-7143-4*) St Mut.

Baxter, D., jt. auth. see Olszewsky, J.

Baxter, Daniel J. The Least of These My Brethren. LC 98-4555. 272p. (C). 1998. pap. 13.00 (*0-15-600588-3*) Harcourt.

Baxter, David, et al, intros. Texas Wildlife: Photographs from Texas Parks & Wildlife Magazine. LC 77-99281. (Louise Lindsey Merrick Natural Environment Ser.: No. 1). (Illus.). 192p. 1993. reprint ed. 24.95 (*0-89096-047-X*) Tex A&M Univ Pr.

Baxter, Donald E. The Foot & Ankle in Sport. (Illus.). 400p. (C). (gr. 13). 1994. text 155.00 (*0-8016-6890-5*, 06890) Mosby Inc.

Baxter, Dottie. You, Had a Great Life. Theobald, Jen, ed. (Orig.). 1988. pap. 2.99 (*0-9621988-0-3*) D Baxter.

Baxter, Edmund. De Quincey's Art of Autobiography. 224p. 1990. 59.00 (*0-389-20919-8*) B&N Imports.

Baxter, Edward, tr. see Meunier-Tardif, Ghislaine.

Baxter, Edward, tr. see Verne, Jules.

Baxter, Elaine D., jt. auth. see Seitz, Laura S.

Baxter, Ellen. The Heights: A Community Housing Strategy. Harris, Angela & Muir, Theda, eds. LC 87-401534. 73p. (Orig.). 1986. pap. text 7.50 (*0-88156-048-0*) Comm Serv Soc NY.

Baxter, Ellen & Hopper, Kim. Private Lives - Public Spaces: Homeless Adults on the Streets of New York City. LC 82-234971. 129p. (Orig.). 1981. pap. 7.50 (*0-88156-002-2*) Comm Serv Soc NY.

***Baxter, Freddie Mae.** The Seventh Child. 240p. 2000. pap. 12.00 (*0-375-70593-7*) Vin Bks.

Baxter, Freddie Mae. The Seventh Child: A Lucky Life. Miller, Gloria Bley, ed. LC F128.68.H3B39 1999. 240p. 1999. 21.00 (*0-375-40620-4*) Knopf.

Baxter, G. David & Diamantopolous, Costas. Therapeutic Lasers: Theory & Practice. LC 93-14226. (Illus.). 192p. 1995. text 39.00 (*0-443-04393-0*) Church.

Baxter, G. F. & Yellon, Derek M. Delayed Preconditioning & Adaptive Cardioprotection. LC 98-38542. (Developments in Cardiovascular Medicine Ser.). 228p. 1998. 98.00 (*0-7923-5259-9*) Kluwer Academic.

Baxter, George. Baxter on Magic: A Guide to Proper Techniques for Magic the Gathering. LC 96-39507. 180p. 1996. pap. 12.95 (*1-55622-523-7*) Wordware Pub.

— Mastering Portal. LC 97-51726. 1997. pap. 14.95 (*1-55622-583-0*) Wordware Pub.

— Pro Magic: The Art of Professional Deck Construction. LC 98-101145. 180p. 1997. pap. 12.95 (*1-55622-524-5*) Wordware Pub.

— Tables of Magic. 160p. 1996. pap. 9.95 (*1-55622-486-9*) Wordware Pub.

Baxter, George & Stultz, Russell A. Magic Cards Simplified: For Player Parents & Beginning Players of Magic, the Gathering. LC 96-41000. viii, 125 p. 1997. pap. 7.95 (*1-55622-522-9*) Wordware Pub.

Baxter, George, jt. auth. see Wolfe, C.

Baxter, George H. Alliances Revealed: A Review of the Alliances Edition of Magic: The Gathering. LC 96-34122. 1996. pap. 9.95 (*1-55622-521-0*) Wordware.

— Dominating Dominia: A Type II Tournament Player's Guide for Magic, the Gathering. LC 96-2014. 1996. pap. 12.95 (*1-55622-491-5*) Wordware Pub.

***Baxter, George H.** Dominating Dominia II. 1998. pap. text 15.95 (*1-55622-630-6*) Wordware Pub.

— Mastering Legends of the Five Rings. LC 98-11887. 1998. pap. 16.95 (*1-55622-626-8*) Wordware Pub.

Baxter, George H. Mastering Overpower. 1997. pap. text 14.95 (*1-55622-576-8*) Wordware Pub.

Baxter, Gillian. Bargain Horses. 138p. (C). 1990. pap. 35.00 (*0-85131-561-5*, Pub. by J A Allen) St Mut.

Baxter, Glen. The Billiard Table Murders. 256p. 1991. pap. 10.00 (*0-380-76668-X*, Avon Bks) Morrow Avon.

— Blizzard of Tweed. 1999. 19.95 (*1-58234-056-0*) Bloomsbury Pubg.

Baxter, Gordon. More BAX Seat: New Logs of a Pasture Pilot. 196p. 1988. 17.95 (*0-8306-9029-8*, 2429H); pap. 11.95 (*0-8306-9429-3*) McGraw-Hill Prof.

— Village Creek. 328p. 1981. reprint ed. pap. 7.95 (*0-940672-03-0*) Shearer Pub.

Baxter, Grant M., et al. Clinical Diagnostic Ultrasound. 2nd ed. LC 98-25578. (Illus.). 687p. 1999. 299.95 (*0-632-03744-X*) Blackwell Sci.

Baxter, Grant W. & Stuart, Wendy J. Death & the Adolescent: A Resource Handbook for Bereavement Support Groups in Schools. (Illus.). 192p. 1998. text 30.00 (*0-8020-0820-8*); pap. text 19.95 (*0-8020-7812-5*) U of Toronto Pr.

***Baxter, Harry & Baxter, Michael.** The Right Way to Read Music. (Illus.). 192p. 2001. pap. 8.95 (*0-7160-2008-4*, Pub. by Elliot RW Bks) Midpt Trade.

Baxter-Hastings, N. & Laws, P. Workshop Calculus Vol. 2: Guided Exploration with Review. (Texts in Mathematical Science Ser.). (Illus.). 416p. 1998. pap. text 39.95 (*0-387-98349-X*) Spr-Verlag.

***Baxter, Hazel.** Doctor in Doubt. large type ed. 2000. pap. 20.99 (*1-85389-993-3*, Dales) Ulverscroft.

Baxter Healthcare Corporation Staff. Baxter's Environmental Compliance Manual: Procedures, Checklists, & Forms for Effective Compliance, 3 vols., Set with forms on disk. Blackburn, William R. & Sandborg, Verie, eds. (Environmental Law Ser.). (Illus.). 1993. ring bd. 475.00 incl. disk (*0-614-07302-2*) West Group.

Baxter Healthcare Corporation Staff, et al. Baxter's Environmental Compliance Manual: Procedures, Checklists, & Forms for Effective Compliance, 3 vols. Blackburn, William R. & Sandborg, Verie, eds. LC 93-12596. (Environmental Law Ser.). 1993. ring bd. 425.00 (*0-87632-907-5*) West Group.

Baxter, Ian. Essays on Private Law: Foreign Law & Foreign Judgments. LC 66-9312. 218p. reprint ed. pap. 67.60 (*0-608-13074-5*, 201412700093) Bks Demand.

Baxter, Irvin, Jr. A Message for the President. rev. ed. LC 94-66846. 165p. (Orig.). 1994. reprint ed. pap. 12.50 (*0-941559-02-5*) Endtime Pub.

— Mideast Treaty: Greatest Prophetic Fulfillment in 2,000 Years. LC 94-70128. 160p. (Orig.). (C). 1994. pap. 12.50 (*0-941559-01-7*) Endtime Pub.

Baxter, J. & Harvey, L. Sonnets for Ethiopians. LC 74-38009. (Black Heritage Library Collection). 1977. reprint ed. 21.95 (*0-8369-8977-5*) Ayer.

— That Which Concerneth Me. LC 79-178468. (Black Heritage Library Collection). 1977. reprint ed. 19.95 (*0-8369-8911-2*) Ayer.

Baxter, J. Edward, tr. see Verne, Jules.

Baxter, J. L. Behavioural Foundations of Economics. LC 92-37142. 288p. 1993. write for info. (*0-333-55239-3*) St Martin.

Baxter, J. N. Baxter. Memorial of the Baxter Family. 114p. 1991. reprint ed. pap. 19.00 (*0-8328-1988-3*); reprint ed. lib. bdg. 29.00 (*0-8328-1987-5*) Higginson Bk Co.

Baxter, J. O. Dividing New Mexico's Waters, 1700-1912. LC 95-50235. (Illus.). 135p. 1997. pap. 24.95 (*0-8263-1747-2*) U of NM Pr.

Baxter, J. Sidlow. Awake, My Heart. LC 93-37840. 384p. 1994. pap. 13.99 (*0-8254-2175-6*) Kregel.

— Explore the Book. 2320p. 1986. 79.99 (*0-310-20620-0*, 6728) Zondervan.

— For God So Loved: An Exposition of John 3:16. 192p. 1995. pap. 9.99 (*0-8254-2173-X*, 95-005) Kregel.

— His Deeper Work in Us. 256p. 1993. pap. 11.99 (*0-8254-2172-1*) Kregel.

— Mark These Men. LC 91-41881. 168p. 1992. pap. 9.99 (*0-8254-2197-7*) Kregel.

— The Master Theme of the Bible: A Comprehensive Study of the Lamb of God. LC 96-46397. 208p. 1997. pap. 10.99 (*0-8254-2147-0*) Kregel.

— A New Call to Holiness. LC 93-13809. 256p. 1993. pap. 11.99 (*0-8254-2170-5*) Kregel.

— The Other Side of Death: What the Bible Teaches about Heaven & Hell. LC 96-46396. 256p. 1997. pap. 12.99 (*0-8254-2158-6*) Kregel.

— Our High Calling. LC 93-13810. 208p. 1993. pap. 10.99 (*0-8254-2171-3*) Kregel.

Baxter, J. W. & Sinnott, John P. World Patent Law & Practice, 3 vols. (Patent Law & Practice Ser.). 1968. ring bd. 710.00 (*0-8205-1055-6*) Bender.

Baxter, James C. The Meiji Unification Through the Lens of Ishikawa Prefecture. LC 94-38297. (Harvard East Asian Monographs: No. 165). 353p. 1995. 38.00 (*0-674-56466-9*, BAXMEI) HUP.

Baxter, James H. An Old St. Andrews Music Book. LC 70-178515. (Medieval Studies). reprint ed. 52.50 (*0-404-56525-5*) AMS Pr.

— Printing Postage Stamps by Line Engraving. LC 81-50924. 1982. reprint ed. lib. bdg. 30.00 (*0-88000-129-1*) Quarterman.

Baxter, James H., tr. see Aurelius, Augustinus.

Baxter, James K. Collected Poems. Weir, J. E., ed. 688p. (C). 1996. text 75.00 (*0-19-558337-X*) OUP.

— The Essential Baxter. Weir, John E., ed. (Illus.). 160p. 1994. 35.00 (*0-19-558285-3*) OUP.

Baxter, James K. & Millar, Paul. Autumn Testament. LC 98-140448. 1997. write for info. (*0-19-558386-8*) OUP.

Baxter, James P. The Greatest of Literary Problems: The Authorship of the Shakespeare Works. LC 79-161734. reprint ed. lib. bdg. 57.50 (*0-404-00694-9*) AMS Pr.

— The Pioneers of New France in New England. 450p. 1980. reprint ed. 25.00 (*0-917890-20-5*) Heritage Bk.

— Pioneers of New France in New England (Mostly Maine), with Contemporary Letters & Documents. 450p. 1995. reprint ed. lib. bdg. 45.00 (*0-8328-4667-8*) Higginson Bk Co.

Baxter, James P., ed. The British Invasion from the North: The Campaigns of Generals Carleton & Burgoyne from Canada, 1776-1777. LC 74-114756. (Era of the American Revolution Ser.). 1970. reprint ed. 49.50 (*0-306-71926-6*) Da Capo.

***Baxter, James Phinney.** Documentary History of the Stae of Maine: Containing the Baxter Manuscripts, IX. 511p. 2000. pap. 34.37 (*0-7884-1483-6*, 1483) Heritage Bk.

Baxter, James Phinney. Scientists Against Time. 1968. pap. text 6.95 (*0-262-52012-5*) MIT Pr.

Baxter, Janeen. Work at Home: The Domestic Division of Labor. pap. 19.95 (*0-7022-2504-5*, Pub. by Univ Queensland Pr) Intl Spec Bk.

Baxter, Jeanne, jt. auth. see Koehler, Mike.

Baxter, Jeremy & Logan, Brian, eds. Software Tools for Developing Agents: Papers from the AAAI Workshop. (Technical Reports: Vol. WS-98-10). (Illus.). 152p. 1998. spiral bd. 25.00 (*1-57735-063-4*) AAAI Pr.

Baxter, Jim, ed. Mint Juleps, Wisteria, & Queers: Gay & Lesbian Culture in the South. (Illus.). 64p. (Orig.). 1988. pap. 5.00 (*0-943810-38-8*) Southern Exposure.

Baxter, Joan. Sword of No Blade. LC 92-1773. (Illus.). 160p. (Orig.). 1992. pap. 11.95 (*0-87728-748-1*) Weiser.

— Television Musicals: Plots Critiques, Casts & Credits for 222 Shows Written for & Presented on Television, 1944-1996. LC 97-13655. (Illus.). 216p. 1997. lib. bdg. 48.50 (*0-7864-0286-5*) McFarland & Co.

Baxter, John. Bunuel. LC 98-6807. (Illus.). 324p. 1998. 24.00 (*0-7867-0506-X*) Carroll & Graf.

— Bunuel. 1999. pap. 12.95 (*0-7867-0619-8*) Carroll & Graf.

***Baxter, John.** Deluxe Encyclopedia of Mandolin Chords. 72p. 2000. pap. 9.95 (*0-7866-4797-3*, 98354) Mel Bay.

— Making of Dungeons & Dragons: The Movie. 2000. pap. 19.95 (*0-7869-1751-2*) Wizards Coast.

— Mythmaker: The Life & Work of George Lucas. 464p. 2000. pap. 14.00 (*0-380-81188-X*, HarpEntertain) Morrow Avon.

— Mythmaker: The Life & Work of George Lucas, Vol. 1. LC 99-37051. (Illus.). 496p. 1999. 27.50 (*0-380-97833-4*, Avon Bks) Morrow Avon.

Baxter, John. Stanley Kubrick: A Biography. LC 97-19738. (Illus.). 400p. 1997. pap. 13.95 (*0-7867-0485-3*) Carroll & Graf.

— Steven Spielberg: The Unauthorized Biography. LC 98-127824. (Illus.). 460p. 1998. pap. 15.95 (*0-00-638444-7*, Pub. by HarpC) Trafalgar.

— Taking the Pain Out of Window Cleaning. Bruton, Lynn, ed. (Illus.). 96p. 1992. 14.95 (*0-9632123-0-3*) Crystal Pr CA.

— Taking the Pane Out of Window Cleaning. Bruton, Lynn, ed. (Illus.). 96p. 1992. pap. 9.95 (*0-9632123-1-1*) Crystal Pr CA.

— Woody Allen: A Biography. 512p. 1999. 27.00 (*0-7867-0666-X*) Carroll & Graf.

***Baxter, John.** Woody Allen: A Biography. (Illus.). 512p. 2000. reprint ed. pap. 14.00 (*0-7867-0807-7*, Pub. by Carroll & Graf) Publishers Group.

Baxter, John & Koffman, Laurence, eds. Baxter & Koffman: Police, the Constitution & the Community. 1985. 54.00 (*0-86205-105-3*, MICHIE); pap. 27.00 (*0-86205-106-1*, MICHIE) LEXIS Pub.

Baxter, John & Koffman, Lawrence, eds. Police: The Constitution & the Community. 274p. 1985. 25.00 (*0-7855-1462-7*, Pub. by NCCL) St Mut.

***Baxter, John & Ray, Carlton.** Salmon. LC 99-89958. (WorldLife Library). (Illus.). 72p. 2000. pap. 16.95 (*0-89658-466-6*) Voyageur Pr.

Baxter, John, et al. Scottish Highlands & Islands. LC 95-72836. (Passport's Regional Guides of Great Britain Ser.). (Illus.). 128p. 1996. pap. 12.95 (*0-8442-4880-0*, 48800, Passprt Bks) NTC Contemp Pub Co.

Baxter, John, jt. auth. see Reder, Alan.

Baxter, John, ed. see Aristotle.

Baxter, John, ed. see Barrett, Carol.

Baxter, John, jt. ed. see Usher, Michael.

Baxter, John W. William Dunbar: A Biographical Study. LC 71-148872. (Select Bibliographies Reprint Ser.). 1977. reprint ed. 23.95 (*0-8369-5672-9*) Ayer.

Baxter, Judith & Quigley, Beth, eds. Life & Times: Recollections of Eliza Cox Carter. (Mercury Ser.: History No. 48). (Illus.). 144p. 1997. pap. 19.95 (*0-660-15970-8*, Pub. by CN Mus Civilization) U of Wash Pr.

Baxter, Judith, ed. see Chopin, Kate.

Baxter, Kathleen A. & Agness, Marcia. Gotcha! Nonfiction Book Talks to Get Kids Excited about Reading. LC 99-34279. (Illus.). 183p. (J). 1999. pap. 24.50 (*1-56308-683-2*) Libs Unl.

Baxter, Kathleen M. Come & Get It: A Natural Foods Cookbook for Children. rev. ed. LC 81-70782. (Illus.). 128p. (J). (ps-6). 1989. lib. bdg. 13.95 (*0-9603696-4-3*); spiral bd. 8.95 (*0-9603696-3-5*) Children First.

***Baxter, Keith.** My Sentiments Exactly. 1999. pap. 35.00 (*1-84002-053-9*, Pub. by Theatre Comm) Consort Bk Sales.

Baxter, L. & DeSollar, R., eds. Applications of Advanced Technology to Ash-Related Problems in Boilers. (Illus.). 676p. (C). 1996. 179.00 (*0-306-45376-2*, Kluwer Plenum) Kluwer Academic.

Baxter, Larry K. Capacitive Sensors: Design & Applications. LC 96-15907. 1996. write for info. (*0-7803-1130-2*) IEEE Standards.

Baxter, Lawrence G. & Hoexter, Cora. Administrative Law. rev. ed. 857p. 1984. reprint ed. pap. 67.50 (*0-7021-2224-6*, Pub. by Juta & Co) Gaunt.

— Administrative Law Pt. III: 1991 Supplement. 141p. 1991. pap., suppl. ed. 17.50 (*0-7021-2766-3*, Pub. by Juta & Co) Gaunt.

Baxter, Leon. The Drawing Book. LC 90-4476. (Illus.). 64p. (J). (gr. 1-7). 1993. reprint ed. pap., per. 7.95 (*0-8249-8633-4*, Ideals Child) Hambleton-Hill.

— The Drawing Book. rev. ed. (Illus.). 62p. (J). (gr. k-6). 1991. reprint ed. lib. bdg. 16.95 (*1-878363-38-7*) Forest Hse.

Baxter, Leon. Let's Pray! 128p. (J). (ps-1). 1998. 9.99 (*0-8054-1684-6*) Broadman.

Baxter, Les, jt. auth. see Sterling, Donald J.

Baxter, Leslie A. & Montgomery, Barbara M. Relating: Dialogues & Dialectics. LC 96-18281. (Communication Ser.). 285p. 1996. pap. text 23.00 (*1-57230-101-5*, 0101); lib. bdg. 42.00 (*1-57230-099-X*) Guilford Pubns.

Baxter, Leslie A., jt. ed. see Montgomery, Barbara M.

Baxter, Lewis R. & Friedel, Robert O. Current Psychiatric Diagnosis & Treatment. LC 98-39106. 1998. 39.95 (*1-57340-121-8*) Current Med.

***Baxter, Linda.** The Winter of the Stone Woman. (Illus.). 75p. 1999. pap. 5.60 (*0-7891-2926-4*) Perfection Learn.

— The Winter of the Stone Woman. (Illus.). 75p. (J). (gr. 4-8). 1999. 10.60 (*0-7807-8965-2*, Covercraft) Perfection Learn.

Baxter, Lucy E. The Life of William Barnes, Poet & Philologist, by His Daughter. (BCL1-PR English Literature Ser.). 358p. 1992. reprint ed. lib. bdg. 89.00 (*0-7812-7429-X*) Rprt Serv.

Baxter, M. L. Exact Determination of Tooth Surfaces for Spiral Bevel & Hypoid Gears. (Technical Papers: Vol. P139.02). (Illus.). 9p. 1966. pap. text 30.00 (*1-55589-186-1*) AGMA.

— The Unitool Method. (Technical Papers: P129.11). (Illus.). 8p. 1954. pap. text 30.00 (*1-55589-158-6*) AGMA.

Baxter Magolda, Marcia B. Creating Contexts for Learning & Self-Authorship: Constructive-Developmental Pedagogy. LC 99-6496. (Issues in Higher Education Ser.). 320p. (C). 1999. pap. 24.95 (*0-8265-1346-8*) Vanderbilt U Pr.

Baxter, Mark. The Rock-n-Roll Singer's Survival Manual. (Illus.). 248p. 17.95 (*0-614-20088-1*, 00660176) H Leonard.

— The Singer's Toolbox Featuring Mark Baxter. (Star Licks Beginning Video Ser.). 121p. 1996. VHS 14.95 (*0-7935-6870-6*) H Leonard.

An Asterisk (*) at the beginning of an entry indicates that the title is appearing for the first time.

Baxter, Martin & Rennie, Andrew. Financial Calculus: An Introduction to Derivative Pricing. (Illus.). 242p. (C). 1996. text 44.95 (0-521-55289-3) Cambridge U Pr.

Baxter, Mary K. A Divine Revelation of Heaven. LC 98-24168. 205p. 1998. pap. 12.99 (0-88368-524-8) Whitaker Hse.

— A Divine Revelation of Hell. LC 96-49171. 216p. 1993. pap. 12.99 (0-88368-279-6) Whitaker Hse.

— Una Revelacion Divina del Cielo. Lamigueiro, Fernando, tr. LC 99-12722. (SPA.). 208p. 1999. pap. 10.99 (0-88368-572-8) Whitaker Hse.

— Una Revelacion Divina del Infierno.Tr. of Divine Revelation of Hell. 1993. write for info. (0-614-28320-5) Anchor Distributors.

— Una Revelacion Divina del Infierno. LC 97-131 Tr. of Divine Revelation of Hell. (SPA.). 141p. 1993. pap. 9.99 (0-88368-288-5) Whitaker Hse.

Baxter, Mary L. All Our Tomorrows. LC 97-31795. 1997. 22.95 (0-7862-1258-6) Five Star.

— And Baby Makes Perfect. (Desire Ser.: No. 727). 1992. per. 2.89 (0-373-05727-X) Silhouette.

— Another Kind of Love. (Men Made in America Ser.). 1993. mass mkt. 3.59 (0-373-45154-7, 1-45154-1) Silhouette.

— Autumn Awakening. 1997. per. 5.50 (1-55166-300-7, 1-66300-4, Mira Bks) Harlequin Bks.

— Corazon Desbocado (Wild Heart) (Deseo Ser.). (SPA.). 1998. per. 3.50 (0-373-35232-8, 1-35232-7) Harlequin Bks.

— Dancler's Woman. (Desire Ser.). 1993. per. 2.99 (0-373-05822-5, 5-05822-7) Silhouette.

— A Day in April. 1996. per. 5.99 (1-55166-165-9, 1-66165-1, Mira Bks) Harlequin Bks.

— A Day in April. (Silhouette Ser.: No. 244). 1992. per. 4.99 (0-373-48244-2) Silhouette.

— Un Defi pour Dixon. (Rouge Passion Ser.: Vol. 466). (FRE.). 1998. mass mkt. 3.50 (0-373-37466-6, 1-37466-9) Harlequin Bks.

— Hard Candy. 1998. per. 5.99 (1-55166-440-2) Harlequin Bks.

— Heart of Texas: Man of the Month. (Desire Ser.: No. 1249). 1999. per. 3.75 (0-373-76249-6, 1-76249-1) Silhouette.

— Hot Texas Nights. 368p. (Orig.). 1996. mass mkt. 5.99 (0-446-60203-5, Pub. by Warner Bks) Little.

— Joni's Magic. 1992. mass mkt. 4.99 (0-373-48236-1, 5-48236-9) Harlequin Bks.

— Lightning Strikes. (Thirty-Six Hours Ser.: No. 1). 1997. per. 4.50 (0-373-65006-X, 1-65006-8) Harlequin Bks.

— Lone Star Heat. 1999. mass mkt. 5.99 (1-55166-289-2, 0-66289-0, Mira Bks) Harlequin Bks.

— Mike's Baby. (Desire Ser.). 1993. per. 2.89 (0-373-05781-4, 5-05781-5) Silhouette.

— Moonbeams Aplenty. LC 96-533. (Western Lovers Ser.). 248p. 1995. per. 3.99 (0-373-88519-9, 1-88519-3) Harlequin Bks.

***Baxter, Mary L.** One Summer Evening. 384p. 1999. per. 5.99 (1-55166-523-9, Mira Bks) Harlequin Bks.

Baxter, Mary L. Priceless. 368p. (Orig.). 1995. mass mkt. 5.99 (0-446-36495-9, Pub. by Warner Bks) Little.

— Saddle Up (Man of the Month) (Desire Ser.). 1996. per. 3.50 (0-373-05991-4, 1-05991-4) Silhouette.

— Slow Talkin' Texan: Man of the Month. (Desire Ser.: No. 1177). 1999. mass mkt. 3.75 (0-373-76177-5, 0-76177-5) Silhouette.

— Sweet Justice. LC 94-136599. 384p. (Orig.). 1994. mass mkt. 5.50 (0-446-36494-0, Pub. by Warner Bks) Little.

— Tall in the Saddle. (Desire Ser.: No. 660). 1991. per. 2.75 (0-373-05660-5) Harlequin Bks.

— Tears of Yesterday. (Mira Bks.). 1998. per. 5.50 (1-55166-417-8, 1-66417-6, Mira Bks) Harlequin Bks.

— Tight-Fittin' Jeans. (Desire Ser.). 1997. per. 3.50 (0-373-76057-4, 1-76057-8) Silhouette.

Baxter, Mary L., et al. Getting Hitched Vol. 8, No. 5: Marriage, Diamond Style; Married to the Enemy; The Perfect Husband; I Thee Wed. (Romance Digest Ser.: No. 82747). 1999. mass mkt. 3.50 (0-373-82747-4, 1-82747-6) Harlequin Bks.

— Texas Heat: Slow Burn, & Baby Makes Perfect, Everything but Time, 3 bks. in 1. (By Request Ser.). 1999. per. 6.99 (0-373-20168-0, 1-20168-0) Harlequin Bks.

***Baxter, Mary Lynn.** Her Perfect Man. (Desire Ser.: Bk. 1328). 2000. mass mkt. 3.99 (0-373-76328-X, 1-76328-3) Silhouette.

Baxter, Mary Lynn. Knight Sparks. (Men at Work Ser.). 1998. per. 4.50 (0-373-81033-4) Harlequin Bks.

***Baxter, Mary Lynn.** Sultry. 2000. mass mkt. 5.99 (1-55166-588-3, 1-66588-4, Mira Bks) Harlequin Bks.

— 36 Hours: The Christmas That Changed Everything. 2000. mass mkt. 6.50 (0-373-48412-7) Harlequin Bks.

Baxter, Maurice G. Daniel Webster & the Supreme Court. LC 66-28116. 280p. 1966. 32.50 (0-87023-008-5) U of Mass Pr.

— Henry Clay & the American System. LC 94-48090. (Illus.). 272p. 1995. 34.95 (0-8131-1919-7) U Pr of Ky.

***Baxter, Maurice G.** Henry Clay the Lawyer. LC 99-32612. 160p. 2000. 24.95 (0-8131-2147-7) U Pr of Ky.

Baxter, Maurice G. One & Inseparable: Daniel Webster & the Union. LC 83-26597. (Illus.). 664p. 1984. 42.50 (0-674-63821-2) HUP.

Baxter Mendrinos, Roxanne. Building Information Literacy Using Technology: A Practical Guide for Schools & Libraries. 2nd ed. 250p. 1999. pap. 32.00 (1-56308-690-5) Libs Unl.

Baxter, Meriwether L. Multiple Iteration - Respectable Trial-&-Error. (Nineteen Ninety Fall Technical Meeting Ser.: Vol. 90FTM11). (Illus.). 12p. 1990. pap. text 30.00 (1-55589-563-8) AGMA.

Baxter, Michael, jt. auth. see Baxter, Harry.

Baxter, Michael, jt. auth. see White, David A.

Baxter, Michelle, ed. see Huhtala, Jon & Novotny, George.

Baxter, Mike. Exploratory Multivariate Analysis in Archaeology. (Illus.). 296p. 1994. pap. 60.00 (0-7486-0423-5, Pub. by Edinburgh U Pr) Col U Pr.

Baxter, N., et al. Learning Discrete Mathematics with ISETL. (Illus.). xvii, 416p. 1988. 53.95 (0-387-96898-9) Spr-Verlag.

Baxter, Nancy N. All the Bright Sons of Morning. 454p. 1992. pap. 14.95 (1-878208-14-4) Guild Pr IN.

— Charmed Circle-Indianapolis, 1895: A Mystery. 350p. 1994. pap. 15.95 (1-878208-52-7) Guild Pr IN.

— Gallant Fourteenth: The Story of an Indiana Civil War Regiment. 205p. (J). 1980. reprint ed. 24.95 (0-9617367-8-X) Guild Pr IN.

— Lords of the Rivers. LC 88-82312. (Heartland Chronicles Ser.: Bk. II). (Illus.). 500p. 1988. pap. 14.95 (0-9617367-7-1) Guild Pr IN.

— The Miamis! 100p. (J). (gr. 4-6). 1987. 16.95 (0-9617367-3-9) Guild Pr IN.

— The Movers: A Saga of the Scotch-Irish. LC 86-22859. (Heartland Chronicles Ser.). (Illus.). 515p. 1986. pap. 14.95 (0-9617367-1-2) Guild Pr IN.

Baxter, Nancy N., ed. see Hale, Janet.

Baxter, Neale J. Is there Another Degree in Your Future? Choosing Among Professional & Graduate Schools. 13p. 1994. per. 1.25 (0-16-045323-2) USGPO.

Baxter, Neale J. Opportunities in Counseling & Development. (Illus.). 146p. 1988. 13.95 (0-8442-6182-3, VGM Career); pap. 10.95 (0-8442-6183-1, VGM Career) NTC Contemp Pub Co.

— Opportunities in Federal Government Careers. 2nd ed. (Opportunities in...Ser.). (Illus.). 160p. 1994. 14.95 (0-8442-4000-1, VGM Career) NTC Contemp Pub Co.

— Opportunities in Government Service. (Illus.). 153p. 1980. pap. 10.95 (0-8442-6619-1, VGM Career) NTC Contemp Pub Co.

— Opportunities in Government Service. (Illus.). 160p. 1995. 13.95 (0-8442-6618-3, VGM Career) NTC Contemp Pub Co.

— Opportunities in State & Local Government Careers. (Illus.). 160p. 1987. 13.95 (0-8442-6193-9, VGM Career); pap. 10.95 (0-8442-6194-7, VGM Career) NTC Contemp Pub Co.

— Opportunities in State & Local Government Careers. LC 92-14629. (Opportunities in...Ser.). (Illus.). 160p. 1994. 14.95 (0-8442-4040-0, VGM Career) NTC Contemp Pub Co.

Baxter, Neale J. & Toch, Mark U. Opportunities in Counseling & Development Careers. LC 93-46078. 160p. 1994. pap. 11.95 (0-8442-4098-2, VGM Career) NTC Contemp Pub Co.

Baxter, Neale J., et al. Opportunities in Counseling & Development Careers. LC 96-52397. (Opportunities In . . . Ser.). (Illus.). 160p. pap. 11.95 (0-8442-4689-1, 46891, VGM Career) NTC Contemp Pub Co.

Baxter, Nevins D. Commercial Paper Market. LC 65-29170. 169p. reprint ed. pap. 52.40 (0-8357-9038-X, 205172700005) Bks Demand.

Baxter, Nicola. Autumn. (Toppers Ser.). 24p. (J). 1997. pap. 4.95 (0-516-26085-5) Childrens.

***Baxter, Nicola.** Baby Chick's Day. (Illus.). 12p. (J). (ps). 2000. 4.99 (0-689-82963-9) Litle Simon.

— Baby Duck's Day. (J). 2000. 4.99 (0-689-82962-0) Litle Simon.

— Best Loved Magical Tales for Bedtime. (Illus.). 480p. (J). (gr. 3-4). 2000. pap. text 20.00 (0-7881-6893-2) DIANE Pub.

— Castle under Attack. LC 99-55202. (Dorling Kindersley Readers). 32p. (J). (gr. 1-3). 2000. 12.95 (0-7894-6094-7, D K Ink); pap. text 3.95 (0-7894-5460-2, D K Ink) DK Pub Inc.

Baxter, Nicola. Chick & Bunny's Easter Basket, 1 vol. (Illus.). 6p. (ps). 1999. bds. 14.99 (0-448-41955-6, G & D) Peng Put Young Read.

***Baxter, Nicola.** Mission to the Arctic. (Dorling Kindersley Readers). 48p. (J). (gr. 2-3). 2000. 12.95 (0-7894-6095-5, D K Ink); pap. text 3.95 (0-7894-5459-9, D K Ink) DK Pub Inc.

Baxter, Nicola. My Book of Friendship. LC 97-62148. (Illus.). 32p. 1998. 7.98 (0-7651-9147-4) Smithmark.

— My Pretty Princess, Set. LC 95-13701. (Illus.). 19p. (J). 1995. pap. 14.95 (0-8120-8393-8) Barron.

— Nuestra Fantastica Tierra. (Biblioteca de Descubrimientos Ser.).Tr. of Our Wonderful Earth. (SPA., Illus.). (J). (gr. 3-6). 1997. 11.95 (0-915741-84-9, SY7075) C D Stampley Ent.

Baxter, Nicola. Our Wonderful Earth. (Launch Pad Library). (Illus.). 32p. (J). (gr. k-4). 1997. 11.95 (0-915741-77-6) C D Stampley Ent.

Baxter, Nicola. Parallel Universe. LC 97-3613. (J). (gr. 4-6). 1997. lib. bdg. 24.00 (0-531-14465-8) Watts.

— Parallel Universe. (J). (gr. 7). 1997. pap. text 12.95 (0-531-15867-5) Watts.

— Puss in Boots. (Favorite Tales Ser.). (Illus.). 28p. (J). 1994. 2.99 (0-7214-5455-0, Ladybrd) Penguin Putnam.

— Rain, Wind, & Storm. LC 97-8063. (Living with the Weather Ser.). (J). 1998. 25.69 (0-8172-5050-6) Raintree Steck-V.

— Rapunzel. (Favorite Tales Ser.). (Illus.). 28p. (J). 1994. 2.99 (0-7214-5451-8, Ladybrd) Penguin Putnam.

— Rumpelstiltskin. (Favorite Tales Ser.). (Illus.). 28p. (J). 1994. 2.99 (0-7214-5456-9, Ladybrd) Penguin Putnam.

— Spring. (Toppers Ser.). 24p. (J). (gr. 1-2). 1997. pap. 4.95 (0-516-26086-3) Childrens.

— Summer. (Toppers Ser.). 24p. (J). (gr. 1-2). 1997. pap. 4.95 (0-516-26087-1) Childrens.

— Time to Sleep, Little Lamb. (J). 1996. pap. 14.95 (0-689-80782-1) Atheneum Yung Read.

— Two Minute Bunny Tales. (Illus.). 32p. (J). 1994. 2.99 (0-7214-5444-5, Ladybrd) Penguin Putnam.

— Winter. (Toppers Ser.). 24p. (J). (gr. 3-4). 1997. pap. 4.95 (0-516-26088-X) Childrens.

— Yes, You Can, Little Duck! (Illus.). 14p. (J). 1996. 14.95 (0-689-80781-3) Atheneum Yung Read.

Baxter, Nicola, ed. Children's Classic Poetry Collection. (Illus.). 96p. (J). (gr. 4-7). 1996. 9.98 (0-7651-9745-6) Smithmark.

— Children's Classic Poetry Collection. (Illus.). 96p. 2000. reprint ed. text 20.00 (0-7881-9044-X) DIANE Pub.

Baxter, Nicola, jt. auth. see Eibl, Martha M.

Baxter, Nicola, ed. see Grimm, Wilhelm K. & Grimm, Jacob W.

***Baxter, Nicole.** 5 Minute Bedtime Stories. (Illus.). 80p. (J). 1999. pap. 12.98 (1-58048-062-4) Sandvik Pub.

Baxter, P. T., ed. When the Grass Is Gone: Development Intervention in African Arid Lands. (Scandinavian Institute of African Studies). 214p. 1991. 52.00 (91-7106-318-8) Coronet Bks.

Baxter, P. T., et al, eds. Being & Becoming Oromo: Historical & Anthropological Enquiries. 311p. 1995. 79.95 (1-56902-025-6) Red Sea Pr.

— Being & Becoming Oromo: Historical & Anthropolcgical Enquiries. 311p. 1996. pap. 24.95 (1-56902-034-5) Red Sea Pr.

Baxter, Pam, ed. Social Science Reference Services. (The Reference Librarian: Vol. 48). 253p. 1995. 39.95 (1-56024-718-5) Haworth Pr.

Baxter, Pam M. Psychology: A Guide to Reference & Information Sources. (Reference Sources in the Social Sciences Ser.). xxi, 219p. 1993. lib. bdg. 36.50 (0-87287-708-6) Libs Unl.

Baxter, Pam M., jt. auth. see Reed, Jeffrey G.

Baxter, Pat J. & Naff, Cynthia D. An Owner's Guide to Parenting Teenagers: A Step-by-Step, Solution-Focused Approach to Raising Adolescents Without Losing Your Mind. LC 96-136286. 212p. (Orig.). 1996. pap. 14.95 (0-9650651-0-3) Real Life Pr.

Baxter, Paul W., ed. Contributions to the Archaeology of Oregon: 1989-1994. (Occasional Papers). (Illus.). 188p. (Orig.). (C). 1994. pap. text 12.00 (0-929553-04-7) Assn Oregon Arch.

Baxter, Paula A. & Bird-Romero, Allison. Encyclopedia of Native American Jewelry: A Guide to History, People & Terms. (Illus.). 296p. 2000. boxed set 65.00 (1-57356-128-2) Oryx Pr.

Baxter, Percival P. Greatest Mountain: Katahdin's Wilderness. LC 99-14277. 112p. 1999. pap. 20.00 (0-88448-213-8) Tilbury Hse.

Baxter, Peter. Just Watch! Sternberg, Paramount & America in 1932. (Illus.). 224p. 1994. 47.95 (0-85170-386-C, Pub. by British Film Inst); pap. 19.95 (0-85170-387-9, Pub. by British Film Inst) Ind U Pr.

Baxter, Peter, et al. A Quest for Chilean Plants. (Illus.). 32p. 1998. pap. 15.00 (1-872291-67-8) Balogh.

***Baxter, Peter J., et al, eds.** Hunter's Diseases of Occupations. 9th ed. (An Arnold Publication Ser.). 1,000p. 2000. text 198.50 (0-340-67750-3) OUP.

Baxter-Petralia, Patricia, jt. auth. see Smith, Susan L.

Baxter, Philip. P. R. O. B. E., No. 3. pap. write for info (0-06-100519-3, Harp PBks) HarpC.

Baxter, P.T.W., et al. Being & Becoming Oromo: Historical & Anthropological Enquiries. 312p. 1996. text 39.95 (91-7106-379-X) Transaction Pubs.

***Baxter, R.** Ministry We Need. 1998. pap. text 6.99 (0-946462-51-8) Grace Pubns Trust.

Baxter, R. & Williams, I. Population Forecasting & Uncertainty at the National & Local Scale. 1978. pap. 13.25 (0-08-023112-8, Pergamon Pr) Elsevier.

Baxter, R. C., et al, eds. The Insulin-Like Growth Factors & Their Regulatory Proteins: Proceedings of the Third International Symposium on Insulin-Like Growth Factors, Sydney, February 1994. LC 94-15908. (International Congress Ser.: No. 1056). 484p. 1994. 278.50 (0-444-81756-5, Excerpta Medica) Elsevier.

Baxter, R. E. & Phillips, C. Ports, Inland Waterways & Civil Aviation. Maunder, W. F., ed. 1979. 143.00 (0-08-022460-1, Pub. by Pergamon Repr) Franklin.

Baxter, Raymond J., jt. auth. see Adams, Arthur G.

Baxter, Reed. Country Heartworks, No. 2. 65p. 1996. pap. 10.50 (1-56770-365-8) S Scheewe Pubns.

Baxter, Richard. Historymakers. rev. ed. 1999. pap. text 11.99 (1-85792-380-4) Christian Focus.

— A Holy Commonwealth. Lamont, William, ed. (Cambridge Texts in the History of Political Thought Ser.). 288p. (C). 1994. text 59.95 (0-521-40518-1); pap. text 21.95 (0-521-40580-7) Cambridge U Pr.

— Pocket Guide to Musculoskeletal Assessment. Biblis, Margaret, ed. LC 97-18626. (Illus.). 208p. 1998. pap. text 24.95 (0-7216-3337-4, W B Saunders Co) Harcrt Hlth Sci Grp.

— The Practical Works of Richard Baxter, 23 vols. Orme, William, ed. LC 72-161735. reprint ed. lib. bdg. write for info. (0-404-00700-7) AMS Pr.

— The Practical Works of Richard Baxter. (Giant Summit Bks.). 1000p. 1981. reprint ed. pap. 14.95 (0-8010-0804-2) Baker Bks.

— The Practical Works of Richard Baxter, 4 vols. 2nd ed. Incl. . Call to the Unconverted: Volume 2 of the Practical Works. 2nd ed. 1063p. 2000. reprint ed. text 60.00 (1-877611-15-8); . Christian Directory: Volume 1 of the Practical Works. 2nd ed. Packer, J. I., frwd. 1023p. 2000. reprint ed. text 60.00 (1-877611-13-1) No. 3. Saints' Everlasting Rest: Volume 3 of the Practical Works. 2nd ed. 1068p. 2000. reprint ed. text 60.00 (1-877611-28-X); No. 4. Reformed Pastor: Volume 4 of the Practical Works. 2nd ed. 1047p. 2000. reprint ed. text 60.00 (1-877611-36-0); 4201p. 2000. reprint ed. Set text 240.00 (1-877611-37-9) Soli Deo Gloria.

— The Reformed Pastor. 1979. pap. 6.99 (0-85151-191-0) Banner of Truth.

— The Saints' Everlasting Rest. Beougher, Timothy K., ed. & pref. by. (Collection of Classics Ser.). 71p. 1994. pap. text 2.95 (1-879089-18-1) B Graham Ctr.

***Baxter, Richard.** Saint's Everlasting Rest. 704p. 2000. 29.99 (1-85792-389-8) Christian Focus.

Baxter, Richard, et al, eds. Urban Development Models. LC 79-301020. (Cambridge University Centre for Land Use & Built Form Studies Conference Proceedings: No. 3). 343p. reprint ed. pap. 106.40 (0-608-13089-3, 202521600043) Bks Demand.

Baxter, Richard, jt. ed. see Perraton, Jean.

Baxter, Richard C. Christmas Three: A Trilogy of Christmas Tales. LC 93-20585. (Illus.). 52p. 1993. pap. 7.95 (0-912526-63-7) Lib Res.

— Prisms: A Collection of Short Stories. LC 92-2413. 368p. 1992. 18.95 (0-912526-57-2) Lib Res.

Baxter, Robert. Baxter's Alaska. 1987. 9.95 (0-913384-47-X) Rail-Europe-Baxter.

— Baxter's Britrail Guide. LC 72-83184. 1987. 9.95 (0-913384-06-2) Rail-Europe-Baxter.

— Baxter's East Coast Weekend Guide (Williamsburg-Quebec) 1987. 9.95 (0-913384-85-2) Rail-Europe-Baxter.

— Baxter's Eurailpass Travel Guide Vol. 1: Southern & Central Europe. 1987. 9.75 (0-913384-80-1) Rail-Europe-Baxter.

— Baxter's Eurailpass Travel Guide Vol. 2: Central & Northern Europe. 1987. 9.95 (0-913384-81-X) Rail-Europe-Baxter.

— Baxter's Eurailpass Travel Guide (All 16 European Countries) 1987. 14.95 (0-913384-82-8) Rail-Europe-Baxter.

— Baxter's Europe (Europe City Guide) 1987. 14.95 (0-913384-83-6) Rail-Europe-Baxter.

— Baxter's U. S. A. (The U. S. A. by Car, Bus, Train & Plane) LC 77-92700. 1981. per. 12.95 (0-913384-44-5) Rail-Europe-Baxter.

— Baxter's West Coast Weekend Guide (San Diego-Vancouver) 1987. 9.95 (0-913384-84-4) Rail-Europe-Baxter.

— Bicentennial Images. 1976. per. 14.95 (0-913384-19-4) Rail-Europe-Baxter.

Baxter, Robert. Jason & the Golden Fleece. LC 80-50068. 32p. (J). (gr. 4-8). 1980. lib. bdg. 18.60 (0-89375-360-2) Troll Communs.

— Perseus & Medusa. LC 80-50083. 32p. (J). (gr. 4-8). 1980. pap. 3.95 (0-89375-366-1); lib. bdg. 18.60 (0-89375-362-9) Troll Communs.

— Theseus & the Minotaur. LC 80-50067. 32p. (J). (gr. 4-8). 1980. lib. bdg. 18.60 (0-89375-363-7) Troll Communs.

— Theseus & the Minotaur. LC 80-50067. 32p. (J). (gr. 4-8). 1997. pap. 3.95 (0-89375-367-X) Troll Communs.

***Baxter, Roberta.** Horse Injuries: Their Prevention & Treatment. 1999. 35.00 (1-86126-260-4, Pub. by Cro1wood) Trafalgar.

Baxter, Ron. Bestiaries & Their Users in the Middle Ages. LC 98-211645. (Illus.). 256p. 1998. 35.95 (0-7509-1853-5, Pub. by Sutton Pub Ltd) Intl Pubs Mktg.

Baxter, S. The Role of IT/IS Manager. 1996. pap. 129.00 (1-85953-056-7, Pub. by Tech Comm) St Mut.

Baxter, Sandra L. Safe & Drug-Free Schools: Balancing Accountability with State & Local Flexibility. 57p. (C). 1998. pap. text 20.00 (0-7881-7337-5) DIANE Pub.

Baxter, Sheila. A Child Is Not a Toy: Voices of Children in Poverty. 246p. 1993. pap. 12.00 (0-921586-26-4, Pub. by New Star Bks) Genl Dist Srvs.

Baxter, Sheila. No Way to Live: Poor Women Speak Out. 2nd rev. ed. (Illus.). 234p. 1995. pap. 14.00 (0-921586-43-4, Pub. by New Star Bks) Genl Dist Srvs.

— Still Raising Hell: Poverty, Activism & Community Change. (Illus.). 164p. 1997. pap. 12.95 (0-88974-076-3, Pub. by Press Gang Pubs) LPC InBook.

Baxter, Stanley. The Parliamo Glasgow Omnibus. 92p. pap. 9.95 (1-874744-00-9, Pub. by Birlinn Ltd) Dufour.

Baxter, Stephen. Anti-Ice. 304p. 1994. mass mkt. 5.99 (0-06-105421-6, HarperPrism) HarpC.

***Baxter, Stephen.** Manifold: Time. LC 99-42045. 528p. 2000. 24.00 (0-345-43075-1, Del Rey) Ballantine Pub Grp.

— Manifold: Time. 2000. mass mkt. 6.99 (0-345-43076-X) Ballantine Pub Grp.

— Moonseed. 672p. 1999. mass mkt. 6.99 (0-06-105903-X) HarpC.

— The Role of the IT/IS Manager. (Financial Times Management Briefings Ser.). 1997. pap. 89.50 (0-273-63217-5) F T P-H.

Baxter, Stephen. Silverhair. LC 99-12666. (Mammoths Trilogy Ser.: Vol. 1). 224p. 1999. 24.00 (0-06-105132-2) HarpC.

— Silverhair. 304p. 2000. mass mkt. 5.99 (0-06-102020-6, Avon Bks) Morrow Avon.

— Titan. 688p. 1998. mass mkt. 6.99 (0-06-105713-4, HarperPrism) HarpC.

— Vacuum Diagrams. LC 98-7785. 384p. 1999. pap. 15.00 (0-06-105395-3, HarperPrism) HarpC.

— Voyage MM. 784p. 1997. mass mkt. 6.99 (0-06-105708-8, HarperPrism) HarpC.

Baxter, Stephen, jt. auth. see Clarke, Arthur C.

Baxter, Stephen B. William Third & the Defense of European Liberty, 1650-1702. LC 75-8476. (Illus.). 462p. 1976. reprint ed. lib. bdg. 35.00 (0-8371-8161-5, BAWI, Greenwood Pr) Greenwood.

Baxter, Stephen M. Ring. 512p. 1996. mass mkt. 6.50 (0-06-105694-4, HarperPrism) HarpC.

— The Time Ships. 544p. 1996. mass mkt. 6.50 (0-06-105648-0, HarperPrism) HarpC.

Baxter, Sylvester, jt. auth. see Cushing, Frank H.

B

An Asterisk (*) at the beginning of an entry indicates that the title is appearing for the first time.

Baxter, Timothy M. The Cratylus: Plato's Critique of Naming. LC 92-25897. (Philosophia Antiqua Ser.: Vol. 58). x, 206p. 1992. 78.00 (*90-04-09597-7*) Brill Academic Pubs.

Baxter, V. K. Labor & Politics in the U. S. Postal Service. (Studies in Work & Industry). (Illus.). 388p. (C). 1994. 45.00 (*0-306-44753-3*, Plenum Trade) Perseus Pubng.

Baxter, W. P. & Williams, McRae, eds. Two & Company. rev. ed. (Illus.). 410p. reprint ed. 16.95 (*0-9627326-0-5*) St Thomas Garrison.

Baxter, W. T. Accounting Theory. LC 95-45924. (New Works in Accounting History). 376p. 1996. reprint ed. text 94.00 (*0-8153-2246-1*) Garland.

Baxter, W. T., ed. see Staubus, George J.

Baxter, William. Pea Ridge & Prairie Grove. Sperry, Phillip A., ed. 270p. 1993. reprint ed. 32.95 (*1-56869-038-X*); reprint ed. pap. 19.95 (*1-56869-039-8*) Oldbuck Pr.

Baxter, William, ed. see Kelly, Matt & Interviewees of From the Plaza.

Baxter, William E. & Hathcox, David W., III. America's Care of the Mentally Ill: A Photographic History. LC 93-48732. (Illus.). 176p. 1994. text 31.95 (*0-88048-539-6*, 8539) Am Psychiatric.

Baxter, William H. A Handbook of Old Chinese Phonology. LC 92-12353. (Trends in Linguistics, Studies & Monographs: Vol. 64). xiii, 922p. (C). 1992. lib. bdg. 260.00 (*3-11-012324-X*) Mouton.

Baxter, William T. Collected Papers on Accounting: Original Anthology. Brief, Richard P., ed. LC 77-87311. (Contemporary Accounting Thought Ser.). 1978. lib. bdg. 37.95 (*0-405-10924-5*) Ayer.

***Baxter, Williams.** Pea Ridge & Prairie Grove. LC 99-59554. 136p. 2000. pap. 16.00 (*1-55728-591-8*) U of Ark Pr.

Bay, Mia. The White Image in the Black Mind: African-American Ideas about White People, 1830-1925. LC 98-48935. 296p. 2000. text 45.00 (*0-19-510045-X*) OUP.

***Bay, Mia.** The White Image in the Black Mind: African-American Ideas about White People, 1830-1925. LC 98-48935. 296p. 2000. pap. 19.95 (*0-19-513279-3*) OUP.

Bay, Ann P. A Kid's Guide to the Smithsonian. (Illus.). 160p. (J). 1996. pap. 15.95 (*1-56098-693-X*) Smithsonian.

— A Kid's Guide to the Smithsonian. (Illus.). 1p. (J). (gr. 1-5). 1996. 26.95 (*1-56098-734-0*) Smithsonian.

Bay Area Consumer's Checklist Editors Staff, jt. auth. see Remick, Sue.

Bay Area Hospital Staff. Quick Reference Handbook of Oncology. (Illus.). 181p. 1996. pap. text 23.00 (*0-7216-6894-1*, W B Saunders Co) Harcrt Hlth Sci Grp.

***Bay, Austin.** Prism. 2000. pap. 21.00 (*0-06-095565-1*) HarpC.

Bay, Austin, jt. auth. see Dunnigan, James F.

Bay, Bill. Fun with the Cello. (Fun Bks.). 32p. 1978. pap. 5.95 (*0-87166-438-0*, 93482) Mel Bay.

— Fun with the Clarinet. (Fun Bks.). 32p. 1970. pap. 5.95 (*0-87166-439-9*, 93272) Mel Bay.

— Fun with the Harmonica. (Fun Bks.). 32p. 1972. pap. 4.95 (*0-87166-448-8*, 93305) Mel Bay.

— Fun with the Saxophone. (Fun Bks.). 32p. 1983. pap. 5.95 (*0-87166-458-5*, 93273) Mel Bay.

— Fun with the String Bass. (Fun Bks.). 32p. 1978. pap. 5.95 (*0-87166-459-3*, 93483) Mel Bay.

— Fun with the Viola. (Fun Bks.). 32p. 1978. pap. 5.95 (*0-87166-468-2*, 93615) Mel Bay.

— Mel Bay's Deluxe Guitar Praise Book. 64p. (Orig.). 1973. pap. 4.95 (*0-89228-007-7*) Impact Christian.

— Mel Bay's Guitar Hymnal. 80p. (Orig.). 1972. pap. 4.95 (*0-89228-009-3*) Impact Christian.

— Trumpet Pocketbook. 32p. 1981. pap. 0.95 (*0-87166-559-X*, 93743) Mel Bay.

Bay, Christian. The Structure of Freedom. rev. ed. LC 58-10475. xii, 419p. 1970. reprint ed. pap. 17.95 (*0-8047-0540-2*) Stanford U Pr.

Bay, Christian & Walker, Charles C. Civil Disobedience: Theory & Practice. 50p. 1975. 39.99 (*0-919618-55-3*, Pub. by Black Rose); pap. 4.99 (*0-919618-56-1*, Pub. by Black Rose) Consort Bk Sales.

Bay, D. E. & Harris, R. L. Introduction to Veterinary Entomology. 2nd ed. (Illus.). 111p. (C). 1989. pap. text 25.00 (*0-9624083-0-1*) Stonefly Pub.

Bay, Darlene, jt. auth. see Douglas, Patricia.

Bay, Edna G. Wives of the Leopard: Gender, Politics, & Culture in the Kingdom of Dahomey. LC 97-45943. 392p. 1998. pap. 19.50 (*0-8139-1792-1*); text 55.00 (*0-8139-1791-3*) U Pr of Va.

Bay, Edna G., jt. ed. see Hafkin, Nancy J.

Bay, Elaine N. Abstracts of Selected Rains County Texas Newspapers, 1890-1939. 126p. 1999. pap. 15.50 (*0-7884-1148-9*, B092) Heritage Bk.

— Rains County (Texas) Leader, 1912. 321p. 1999. pap. 28.00 (*0-7884-1081-4*, B091) Heritage Bk.

Bay, Elaine N. & Welch, Henrietta. Rains County, Texas School Census, 1936-1939. 233p. 1998. pap. 21.00 (*0-7884-0846-1*, B090) Heritage Bk.

***Bay, Elaine Nall.** Rains County (Texas) Leader - 1917. 337p. 1999. pap. 28.50 (*0-7884-1403-8*, B093) Heritage Bk.

Bay-Hansen, C. D. Fisheries of the Pacific Northwest Coast. 1991. 17.95 (*0-533-09470-4*) Vantage.

— Fisheries of the Pacific Northwest Coast, Vol. 2: Sport & Nontraditional Fisheries. 1994. 17.95 (*0-533-10744-X*) Vantage.

Bay, Jane. Precious Jewels of Tibet: A Journey to the Roof of the World. LC 98-12269. 208p. 1998. pap. 14.95 (*1-57416-004-4*) Clear Light.

Bay, Jean. I Got So Mad. (Barbie Ser.). 24p. 1999. 3.29 (*0-307-13322-2*) Gldn Bks Pub Co.

Bay, Jeanette G. A Treasury of Flannelboard Stories. (Illus.). 200p. 1995. pap., student ed. 19.95 (*0-917846-51-6*, 34021, Alleyside) Highsmith Pr.

Bay, John S. Fundamentals of Linear State Space Systems. LC 98-25177. (McGraw-Hill Series in Electrical Engineering). 571p. 1999. 67.50 (*0-256-24639-4*) Dorsey.

Bay, Mel. Classic Guitar Method. 1996. audio compact disk 15.98 (*0-7866-1699-7*, 93207CD) Mel Bay.

— Classic Guitar Method, Vol. 1. 48p. 1960. pap. 6.95 (*0-87166-332-5*, 93207); pap. 14.95 incl. audio (*0-87166-334-1*, 93207P); audio 9.98 (*0-87166-333-3*, 93207C) Mel Bay.

— Classic Guitar Method, Vol. 2. 48p. 1960. pap. 6.95 (*0-87166-335-X*, 93208) Mel Bay.

— Classic Guitar Method, Vol. 3. 48p. 1960. pap. 6.95 (*1-56222-202-3*, 93209) Mel Bay.

— Complete Tenor Banjo Method. (Complete Book). 104p. 1986. spiral bd. 10.95 (*1-56222-018-7*, 93236) Mel Bay.

— Deluxe Encyclopedia of Banjo Chords: For Five String or Plactrum Banjo G & C Tuning. (For Five String or Plactrum Banjo G & C Tuning Ser.). 128p. 1973. spiral bd. 11.95 (*0-87166-919-6*, 93299) Mel Bay.

— Deluxe Encyclopedia of Tenor Banjo Chords. 64p. 1973. pap. 8.95 (*0-87166-877-7*, 93327) Mel Bay.

— Deluxe Guitar Scale Book. 72p. 1973. pap. 9.95 (*0-87166-918-8*, 93282) Mel Bay.

— Easy Way Christmas Guitar Folio. 20p. 1966. pap. 4.95 (*0-87166-737-1*, 93224) Mel Bay.

— Easy Way to Guitar A. (Illus.). 48p. 1965. pap. 6.95 (*0-87166-875-0*, 93194) Mel Bay.

— Easy Way to Guitar B. 48p. 1965. pap. 6.95 (*0-87166-642-1*, 93195) Mel Bay.

— Easy Way to Guitar C. 48p. 1965. pap. 6.95 (*0-87166-767-3*, 93196) Mel Bay.

— Fun with the Baritone Uke. (Fun Bks.). 40p. 1961. pap. 4.95 (*0-87166-435-6*, 93266) Mel Bay.

***Bay, Mel.** Fun with the Baritone Uke. 40p. 1998. pap. 19.95 incl. audio compact disk (*0-7866-4512-1*, 93266CDP) Mel Bay.

— Fun with the Guitar. (Fun Bks.). 40p. 1958. pap. 4.95 (*0-87166-445-3*, 93262) Mel Bay.

Bay, Mel. Fun with the Mandolin. (Fun Bks.). 40p. 1963. pap. 4.95 (*0-87166-450-X*, 93258) Mel Bay.

— Fun with the Tenor Banjo. (Fun Bks.). 40p. 1962. pap. 4.95 (*0-87166-460-7*, 93260) Mel Bay.

***Bay, Mel.** Fun with the Tenor Banjo. 40p. 1998. pap. 19.95 incl. audio compact disk (*0-7866-4510-5*, 93260CDP) Mel Bay.

Bay, Mel. Fun with the Ukulele. (Fun Bks.). 40p. 1961. pap. 4.95 (*0-87166-465-8*, 93270) Mel Bay.

— Mel Bay Presents Spanish Chris. 40p. 1997. pap. 9.95 (*0-7866-3258-5*) Mel Bay.

— Modern Guitar Method: Grade 5. 48p. 1951. pap. 6.95 (*0-87166-364-3*, 93204) Mel Bay.

Bay, Mel & Bay, William. Fun with the Guitar. (Fun Bks.). 1998. pap. 13.95 incl. audio (*0-87166-447-X*, 93262P) Mel Bay.

Bay, Mel & Bay, William. Modern Guitar Method: Grade 1. 48p. 1948. pap. 19.95 incl. audio compact disk (*0-7866-0906-0*, 93200CDP) Mel Bay.

— Modern Guitar Method Grade 2. 48p. 1949. pap. 29.95 incl. audio compact disk (*0-7866-1385-8*, 93201CDP) Mel Bay.

Bay, Mel & Carr, Joe. Fun with the Mandolin. (Fun Bks.). 1994. vdisk 19.95 (*0-7866-0143-4*, 93258VX) Mel Bay.

Bay, Mel & Castle, Joseph. The Complete Carcassi Guitar Method. (ENG & SPA.). 112p. 1974. spiral bd. 9.95 (*0-87166-378-3*, 93611EN/SP) Mel Bay.

Bay, Mel, Publications, Inc. Staff. Banjo Chords. 32p. 1961. pap. 4.95 (*0-87166-367-8*, 93267) Mel Bay.

— Baritone Uke Chords. 32p. 1961. pap. 4.95 (*0-87166-864-5*, 93265) Mel Bay.

— Complete Mandolin Method. (Complete Book). 1968. pap. 10.95 (*0-87166-763-0*, 93221) Mel Bay.

— Complete Method for Classic Guitar. 144p. 1991. pap. 14.95 (*0-87166-961-7*, 93400) Mel Bay.

— Complete Method for Modern Guitar. (Complete Book). 320p. 1993. pap. 29.95 (*0-87166-665-0*, 93396) Mel Bay.

— Complete Method for Modern Guitar. (Complete Book). (SPA.). 320p. 1996. spiral bd. 29.95 (*0-7866-0905-2*, 93396SP) Mel Bay.

— Fun with Folk Songs. 40p. 1963. pap. 4.95 (*0-87166-444-5*, 93288) Mel Bay.

— Fun with the Banjo. (Fun Bks.). 40p. 1962. pap. 4.95 (*0-87166-432-1*, 93268) Mel Bay.

— Fun with the Banjo. (Fun Bks.). 1986. audio 9.98 (*0-87166-433-X*, 93268C) Mel Bay.

— Fun with the Banjo. (Fun Bks.). 1993. pap. 13.95 incl. audio (*0-87166-434-8*, 93268P) Mel Bay.

— Fun with the Guitar. (Fun Bks.). 1986. audio 9.98 (*0-87166-446-1*, 93262C) Mel Bay.

— Fun with the Mandolin. (Fun Bks.). 1986. audio 9.98 (*0-87166-451-8*, 93258C) Mel Bay.

— Fun with the Mandolin. (Fun Bks.). 1993. pap. 13.95 incl. audio (*0-87166-452-6*, 93258P) Mel Bay.

— Graded Guitar Solos. 24p. 1957. pap. 5.95 (*0-87166-886-6*, 93217) Mel Bay.

— Guitar Chords. 48p. 1959. pap. 4.95 (*0-87166-090-3*, 93261) Mel Bay.

— Guitar Melody Chord Playing System. 96p. 1966. spiral bd. 11.95 (*0-87166-494-1*, 93215) Mel Bay.

— Guitar Primer. 48p. 1957. pap. 5.95 (*0-87166-822-X*, 93197) Mel Bay.

— Mandolin Chords: In Picture & Diagram Form. (Illus.). 32p. 1963. pap. 4.95 (*0-87166-863-7*, 93257) Mel Bay.

— Modern Guitar Method: Grade 1. 48p. 1948. pap. 6.95 (*0-87166-354-6*, 93200) Mel Bay.

— Modern Guitar Method: Grade 1. 1980. audio 9.98 (*0-87166-355-4*, 93200C) Mel Bay.

— Modern Guitar Method: Grade 1. (SPA.). 48p. 1986. pap. 6.95 (*1-56222-011-X*, 93210SP) Mel Bay.

— Modern Guitar Method: Grade 1. 1993. 14.95 incl. audio (*0-87166-356-2*, 93200P); audio compact disk 14.95 (*0-7866-0450-6*, 93200CD) Mel Bay.

— Modern Guitar Method: Grade 2. 48p. 1949. pap. 6.95 (*0-87166-357-0*, 93201) Mel Bay.

— Modern Guitar Method: Grade 2. 1989. pap. 22.95 incl. audio (*0-87166-358-9*, 93201C) Mel Bay.

— Modern Guitar Method: Grade 2. 1993. 22.95 incl. audio (*0-87166-359-7*, 93201P) Mel Bay.

— Modern Guitar Method: Grade 3. 48p. 1949. pap. 6.95 (*0-87166-360-0*, 93202) Mel Bay.

— Modern Guitar Method: Grade 3. 1992. audio 9.98 (*0-87166-361-9*, 93202C) Mel Bay.

— Modern Guitar Method: Grade 3. 1993. 14.95 incl. audio (*0-87166-362-7*, 93202P) Mel Bay.

— Modern Guitar Method: Grade 4. 48p. 1950. pap. 6.95 (*0-87166-363-5*, 93203) Mel Bay.

— Modern Guitar Method: Grade 6. 40p. 1952. pap. 6.95 (*0-87166-365-1*, 93205) Mel Bay.

— Modern Guitar Method: Grade 7. 40p. 1953. pap. 6.95 (*0-87166-366-X*, 93206) Mel Bay.

— Old Time Fiddle Solos. 24p. 1977. pap. 6.95 (*0-87166-880-7*, 93449) Mel Bay.

— Rhythm Guitar Chord System. 48p. 1973. pap. 5.95 (*0-87166-515-8*, 93214) Mel Bay.

— Tenor Banjo Chords. 32p. 1961. pap. 5.95 (*0-87166-013-X*, 93259) Mel Bay.

— Tenor Banjo Melody Chord Playing System. 116p. 1979. spiral bd. 11.95 (*1-56222-076-4*, 93629) Mel Bay.

— Ukulele Chords: In Picture & Diagram Form. (Illus.). 32p. 1961. pap. 4.95 (*0-87166-865-3*, 93269) Mel Bay.

Bay, Mel, Publications, Inc. Staff & Bay, William. Modern Guitar Method: Grade 1. 48p. 1996. pap. 14.95 incl. audio compact disk (*0-7866-2784-0*, 93200BCD) Mel Bay.

Bay, Mel, Publications, Inc. Staff & Castle, Joseph. Folio of Easy Classic Guitar Solos. 32p. 1962. pap. 5.95 (*0-87166-914-5*, 93212) Mel Bay.

Bay, Patricia L. Therapy in a Nutshell: 10 Simple Lessons That Will Change Your Life. LC 98-175855. (Illus.). 236p. 1998. pap. 14.95 (*1-883952-07-7*) Hse of Steno.

Bay, Philip de, see de Bay, Philip.

Bay, Roger R., jt. ed. see Raynor, Bill.

Bay, Taco. We & Our Relationship to the Three Worlds Around Us. LC 79-27423. 28p. (Orig.). 1996. pap. 2.95 (*0-935690-00-X*) Schaumburg Pubns.

Bay, Timothy. First to the Moon. LC 92-75989. (Famous Firsts Ser.). (J). 1993. 9.95 (*0-383-03818-9*) SRA McGraw.

***Bay, Tom.** Look Within or Do Without: The 13 Qualities Winners All Share. 224p. 2000. pap. 14.99 (*1-56414-490-9*) Career Pr Inc.

Bay, Tom & Macpherson, David. Change Your Attitude: Creating Success One Thought at a Time. LC 98-26005. 224p. 1998. pap. 15.99 (*1-56414-378-3*) Career Pr Inc.

Bay, Tom, jt. auth. see Macpherson, David.

Bay, Vera. Distant Thunder. 175p. 1995. write for info. (*0-9643212-0-3*) Ragga Inshallah.

Bay Village Women's Club Foundation Staff. Bay Traditions. Popp, Gwelda, ed. (Illus.). 238p. 1986. 10.00 (*0-9616678-0-X*) BV Wom Club & Fnd.

Bay, William. Banjo Chord Chart. 4p. 1973. pap. 3.95 (*0-87166-876-9*, 93321) Mel Bay.

— Baritone Uke Pocket Book. 32p. 1981. pap. 0.95 (*0-87166-537-9*, 93757) Mel Bay.

***Bay, William.** Barre Chords: Rock Power Chords Pocketbook. 32p. 2000. pap. 0.95 (*0-7866-5368-X*, 98649) Mel Bay.

Bay, William. Basic Rock & Blues Guitar. 1996. vdisk 29.95 (*0-7866-2058-7*, 95045VX) Mel Bay.

— Basic Rock & Blues Guitar Method. 72p. 1997. 17.95 incl. audio compact disk (*0-7866-2774-3*, 95045BCD) Mel Bay.

***Bay, William.** Bass Chords. (QwikGuide Ser.). 64p. 2000. pap. 5.95 (*0-7866-5086-9*, 98593) Mel Bay.

— Bass Chords PB. 32p. 2000. pap. write for info. (*0-7866-5367-1*, 98648) Mel Bay.

Bay, William. Bass Guitar Chord Chart. 4p. 1971. pap. 3.95 (*0-87166-778-9*, 93297) Mel Bay.

— Blues Guitar Styles. 24p. 1971. pap. 5.95 (*0-87166-368-6*, 93291) Mel Bay.

— Building Right Hand Technique. 132p. 1982. pap. 10.95 (*1-56222-211-2*, 93780) Mel Bay.

— Children's Classic Guitar Method. 56p. 1985. pap. 6.95 (*0-87166-871-8*, 94067) Mel Bay.

Bay, William. Children's Guitar Method, Vol. 1. 48p. 1982. pap. 21.95 incl. audio compact disk (*0-7866-0810-2*, 93833CDP) Mel Bay.

Bay, William. Children's Guitar Method, Vol. 1. (Illus.). 48p. (J). 1982. pap. 6.95 (*0-87166-386-4*, 93833) Mel Bay.

— Children's Guitar Method, Vol. 1. 1986. audio compact disk 15.98 (*0-7866-0809-9*, 93833CD) Mel Bay.

— Children's Guitar Method, Vol. 1. (Illus.). (J). 1986. audio 9.98 (*0-87166-387-2*, 93833C) Mel Bay.

— Children's Guitar Method, Vol. 1. (Illus.). (J). 1993. 14.95 incl. audio (*0-87166-388-0*, 93833P) Mel Bay.

— Children's Guitar Method, Vol. 1. 1994. vdisk 24.95 (*0-7866-0170-1*, 93833VX) Mel Bay.

***Bay, William.** Children's Guitar Method, Vol. I. 48p. 1998. pap. 17.95 incl. audio compact disk (*0-7866-4664-0*, 93833BCD) Mel Bay.

Bay, William. Children's Guitar Method, Vol. 2. (Illus.). 48p. (J). 1982. pap. 6.95 (*0-87166-389-9*, 93834) Mel Bay.

— Children's Guitar Method, Vol. 3. 48p. (J). 1982. pap. 6.95 (*0-87166-392-9*, 93835) Mel Bay.

— Children's Harmonica Method. 40p. 1985. pap. 5.95 (*0-87166-917-X*, 94068) Mel Bay.

— Chord Diagram Book. 48p. 1978. pap. 3.95 (*0-87166-780-0*, 93457) Mel Bay.

***Bay, William.** Chord Writing-Chord Diagram Book. 64p. 2000. pap. 5.95 (*0-7866-5767-7*, 99241) Mel Bay.

— Clarinet Fingering Chart. 4p. 1983. pap. 3.95 (*0-87166-501-8*, 93894) Mel Bay.

Bay, William. Clarinet Pocket Book. 32p. 1981. pap. 0.95 (*0-87166-539-5*, 93744) Mel Bay.

***Bay, William.** Classics for Flatpicking. 32p. 2000. pap. 9.95 incl. audio compact disk (*0-7866-5329-9*, 98056BCD) Mel Bay.

Bay, William. Complete Book of Guitar Chords, Scales & Arpeggios. (Complete Book). 296p. 1992. pap. 19.95 (*1-56222-526-X*, 94792) Mel Bay.

— Complete Jazz Clarinet Book. (Complete Bks.). 144p. 1995. spiral bd. 10.95 (*0-7866-0282-1*, MB95302) Mel Bay.

— Complete Jazz Flute Book. (Complete Bks.). 144p. 1980. spiral bd. 10.95 (*0-7866-0281-3*, MB95301) Mel Bay.

— Complete Jazz Sax Book. (Complete Bks.). 144p. 1994. spiral bd. 10.95 (*0-7866-0229-5*, MB95300) Mel Bay.

— Complete Jazz Trumpet Book. (Complete Bks.). 144p. 1996. pap. 10.95 (*0-7866-0280-5*, MB95299) Mel Bay.

— Deluxe Encyclopedia of Guitar Chords. 144p. 1971. pap. 11.95 (*0-87166-664-2*, 93283) Mel Bay.

***Bay, William.** Deluxe Encyclopedia of Guitar Chords. 144p. 2000. pap. 11.95 (*0-7866-5250-0*, 932835) Mel Bay.

Bay, William. Deluxe Gospel Guitar Method, Vol. 1. 104p. 1983. spiral bd. 9.95 (*0-87166-685-5*, 93921) Mel Bay.

— Deluxe Gospel Guitar Method, Vol. 2. 112p. 1984. spiral bd. 10.95 (*0-87166-690-1*, 93922) Mel Bay.

— Deluxe Guitar Praise Book. 68p. 1973. pap. 4.95 (*0-87166-724-X*, 93338) Mel Bay.

— Easiest Electric Bass Book. 24p. 1992. pap. 3.95 (*1-56222-302-X*, 94685) Mel Bay.

— Easiest Electronic Keyboard Songbook. 32p. 1990. pap. 3.95 (*1-56222-021-7*, 94431) Mel Bay.

— Easiest Guitar Chord Book. 20p. 1990. pap. 3.95 (*0-87166-984-6*, 94413) Mel Bay.

— The Easiest Guitar Song Book. 24p. 1990. pap. 3.95 (*0-87166-986-2*, 94415) Mel Bay.

— The Easiest Harmonica Book. 20p. 1990. pap. 3.95 (*0-87166-982-X*, 94411) Mel Bay.

— The Easiest Mandolin Book. 32p. 1993. pap. 3.95 (*1-56222-563-4*, 94833) Mel Bay.

— The Easiest Piano Chord Book. 32p. 1990. pap. 3.95 (*0-87166-983-8*, 94412) Mel Bay.

— The Easiest Rock Guitar Book. 20p. 1990. pap. 3.95 (*0-87166-987-0*, 94416) Mel Bay.

— Easy Solos for Beginning Trumpet. (Building Excellence Ser.). 36p. 1992. pap. 5.95 (*1-56222-307-0*, 94707) Mel Bay.

— Easy Way Christmas Song Folio - B Flat Instrument. 20p. 1971. pap. 4.95 (*1-56222-136-1*, 93286) Mel Bay.

— Easy Way Christmas Songs Folio - C Instrument. 20p. 1971. pap. 4.95 (*1-56222-074-8*, 93287) Mel Bay.

— Easy Way X-mas Song Folio - E Flat Instrument. 20p. 1985. pap. 4.95 (*1-56222-138-8*, 93285) Mel Bay.

— Electric Bass Pocket Book. 32p. 1981. pap. 0.95 (*0-87166-541-7*, 93751) Mel Bay.

— Electric Blues Guitar Method. 1996. vdisk 29.95 (*0-7866-2059-5*, 94522VX) Mel Bay.

— Electric Blues Guitar Method. 64p. 1997. pap. 17.95 incl. audio compact disk (*0-7866-2958-4*) Mel Bay.

***Bay, William.** Essential Guitar Chords/Barre Chords - Best Bet Jazz. 64p. 2000. pap. 5.95 (*0-7866-5711-1*, 99096) Mel Bay.

— Famous Gospel Favorites for Flatpicking Guitar. 32p. 2000. pap. 5.95 incl. audio compact disk (*0-7866-5081-8*, 98587BCD) Mel Bay.

Bay, William. Favorite Carols Made Easy. 24p. 1990. pap. 3.95 (*1-56222-022-5*, 94485) Mel Bay.

***Bay, William.** Favorite Guitar Pickin Tunes. 32p. 2000. pap. 5.95 incl. audio compact disk (*0-7866-5084-2*, 98591BCD) Mel Bay.

Bay, William. Favorite Student Flute Classics. 24p. 1978. pap. 5.95 (*1-56222-079-9*, 93441) Mel Bay.

— Favourite English Carols. 32p. 1993. pap. 4.95 (*1-56222-876-5*, 95039) Mel Bay.

***Bay, William.** Fingerpicking Blues Solos. 32p. 2000. pap. 9.95 incl. audio compact disk (*0-7866-5070-2*, 98634BCD) Mel Bay.

— Flute Fingering Chart. 4p. 1983. pap. 3.95 (*0-87166-502-6*, 93896) Mel Bay.

Bay, William. Flute Pocket Book. 32p. 1981. pap. 0.95 (*0-87166-543-3*, 93745) Mel Bay.

***Bay, William.** Full-Page Fingerboard Pad. 96p. 1998. pap. 4.95 (*0-7866-3361-1*, 97187) Mel Bay.

— Full Page Mandolin Tab Pad. 96p. 1999. pap. 4.95 (*0-7866-3398-0*, 97185) Mel Bay.

— Full-Page Tab Pad. 96p. 1997. 4.95 (*0-7866-3225-9*, 96981) Mel Bay.

Bay, William. Fun with the Flute. (Fun Bks.). 32p. 1970. pap. 5.95 (*0-87166-443-7*, 93274) Mel Bay.

— Fun with the Ocarina. 32p. 1986. pap. 3.95 (*0-87166-453-4*, 94147) Mel Bay.

— Fun with the Ocarina, Incl. instrument. 32p. pap. 8.95 (*0-87166-454-2*, 94147PIX) Mel Bay.

— Fun with the Strums - Baritone Uke. (Fun Bks.). 40p. 1965. pap. 5.95 (*0-87166-471-2*, 93356) Mel Bay.

— Fun with the Strums - Five-String Banjo. (Fun Bks.). 40p. 1974. pap. 5.95 (*0-87166-470-4*, 93352) Mel Bay.

— Fun with the Strums - Guitar. (Fun Bks.). 40p. 1974. pap. 5.95 (*0-87166-472-0*, 93353) Mel Bay.

— Fun with the Strums - Mandolin. (Fun Bks.). 40p. 1975. pap. 5.95 (*0-87166-473-9*, 93357) Mel Bay.

An Asterisk (*) at the beginning of an entry indicates that the title is appearing for the first time.

— Fun with the Strums - Ukulele. (Fun Bks.). 40p. 1975. pap. 5.95 (*0-87166-475-5*, 93355) Mel Bay.
— Fun with the Tin Whistle. (Fun Bks.). 40p. 1990. 13.95 incl. audio (*0-7866-1054-9*, 94526P); pap. 4.95 (*1-56222-061-6*, 94526); audio 9.98 (*1-56222-073-X*, 94526C) Mel Bay.
— Fun with the Trombone. (Fun Bks.). 32p. 1971. pap. 5.95 (*0-87166-463-1*, 93275) Mel Bay.
— Fun with the Trumpet. (Fun Bks.). 32p. 1970. pap. 6.95 (*0-87166-464-X*, 93271) Mel Bay.
— Fun with the Violin. (Fun Bks.). 32p. 1971. 5.95 (*0-87166-469-0*, 93276) Mel Bay.
***Bay, William.** Great Guitar Picking Tunes. 32p. 2000. pap. 9.95 incl. audio compact disk (*0-7866-5317-5*, 98054BCD) Mel Bay.
Bay, William. Great Hymns for Guitar. 112p. 1983. spiral bd. 9.95 (*0-87166-696-0*, 93981) Mel Bay.
— Guitar Chord Chart. 1973. pap. 3.95 (*0-87166-841-6*, 93322) Mel Bay.
— Guitar Christmas Carols. 40p. 1974. pap. 4.95 (*0-87166-726-6*, 93361) Mel Bay.
— Guitar Class Method, Vol. 1. 146p. 1972. spiral bd. 9.95 (*0-87166-530-1*, 93300) Mel Bay.
Bay, William. Guitar Class Method, Vol. 1. 146p. 1972. 22.95 (*0-7866-2493-0*, 93300CDP); spiral bd. 17.95 incl. audio (*0-7866-0912-5*, 93300P) Mel Bay.
Bay, William. Guitar Class Method, Vol. 1. 1976. audio 9.98 (*0-87166-531-X*, 93300C) Mel Bay.
— Guitar Class Method, Vol. 1. 1996. audio compact disk 13.98 (*0-7866-2350-0*, 93300CD) Mel Bay.
— Guitar Class Method, Vol. 2. 200p. 1980. spiral bd. 12.95 (*0-87166-532-8*, 93726) Mel Bay.
— Guitar Daily Studies Pocket Book. 32p. 1981. pap. 0.95 (*0-87166-545-X*, 93755) Mel Bay.
— Guitar Handbook. 32p. 1997. 9.95 incl. audio compact disk (*0-7866-2707-7*, 94135BCD) Mel Bay.
— Guitar Hymnal. 80p. 1972. pap. 5.95 (*0-87166-697-9*, 93311) Mel Bay.
— Guitar Manuscript Book. 64p. 1993. spiral bd. 4.95 (*1-56222-840-4*, 95006) Mel Bay.
— Guitar Scales in Tablature. 80p. 1992. pap. 9.95 (*1-56222-415-8*, 94760) Mel Bay.
— Guitar Studies: Grade 1. 48p. 1985. pap. 6.95 (*0-87166-396-1*, 94051) Mel Bay.
— Guitar Studies: Grade 2. 32p. 1986. pap. 5.95 (*0-87166-397-X*, 94052) Mel Bay.
***Bay, William.** Guitar Tab Book. (QwikGuide Ser.). 64p. 2000. pap. 5.95 (*0-7866-5717-0*, 99161) Mel Bay.
— Guitar Warm-Up Studies & Solos. 32p. 2000. pap. 5.95 incl. audio compact disk (*0-7866-5085-0*, 98592BCD) Mel Bay.
Bay, William. Harmonica Handbook. 32p. 1997. 9.95 incl. audio compact disk (*0-7866-2706-9*, 94174BCD) Mel Bay.
— Harmonica Pocket Companion. 128p. 1983. spiral bd. 7.95 (*0-87166-967-6*, 93884) Mel Bay.
— Harmonica Pocketbook. 32p. 1980. pap. 0.95 (*0-87166-546-8*, 93706) Mel Bay.
— Harmonica Songbook. 80p. 1982. pap. 8.95 (*0-87166-500-X*, 93882) Mel Bay.
— Instant Guitar Chord Finder. 96p. 1992. pap. 9.95 (*1-56222-545-6*, 094794) Mel Bay.
— Instant Guitar Chord Finder: Guitar-Chord. 1992. pap. 6.95 (*1-56222-546-4*, 94824) Mel Bay.
***Bay, William.** Jazz Lines. 32p. 2000. pap. 9.95 incl. audio compact disk (*0-7866-5318-3*, 98055BCD) Mel Bay.
— Jazz Manuscript Pad. 96p. 1997. pap. 8.95 (*0-7866-3252-6*, 97015) Mel Bay.
— Jazz Tunes. (QwikGuide Ser.). 32p. 2000. pap. 5.95 incl. audio compact disk (*0-7866-5297-7*, 98628BCD) Mel Bay.
Bay, William. Kid's Electronic Keyboard Method. 80p. 1990. pap. 7.95 (*0-87166-773-8*, 94322) Mel Bay.
***Bay, William.** Mandolin Tablature Pad. 48p. 1999. pap. 4.95 (*0-7866-3397-2*) Mel Bay.
— Manuscript Book. (QwikGuide Ser.). 64p. 2000. pap. 5.95 (*0-7866-5718-9*, 99162) Mel Bay.
— Mastering the Guitar Book, No. 2C. 144p. 1999. 14.95 (*0-7866-3510-X*, 97197) Mel Bay.
— Mastering the Guitar Book IA CD Package. 144p. 1997. 28.95 (*0-7866-2806-5*) Mel Bay.
— Masters of the Plectrum Guitar. 280p. 1995. pap. 29.95 (*0-7866-0267-8*, 95293) Mel Bay.
— Mel Bay's Chord Diagram Pad. 80p. 1997. pap. 4.95 (*0-7866-3101-5*, 96875) Mel Bay.
— Mel Bays Guitar Chord Solo Manuscript Book. 32p. 2000. pap. 3.95 (*0-7866-5769-3*, 99242) Mel Bay.
— Mel Bay's Guitar Tab Pad. 80p. 1997. pap. 4.95 (*0-7866-3100-7*, 96874) Mel Bay.
Bay, William. Mel Bay's Mandolin Chord Chart. LC 99-168487. 4p. 1998. pap. 3.95 (*0-7866-2554-6*) Mel Bay.
— More Fun with the Clarinet. (Fun Bks.). 32p. 1976. pap. 5.95 (*0-87166-476-3*, 93385) Mel Bay.
— More Fun with the Flute. (Fun Bks.). 32p. 1976. pap. 5.95 (*0-87166-477-1*, 93386) Mel Bay.
— More Fun with the Saxophone. (Fun Bks.). 32p. 1981. 5.95 (*0-87166-478-X*, 93493) Mel Bay.
— More Fun with the Trombone. (Fun Bks.). 32p. 1976. pap. 5.95 (*0-87166-479-8*, 93387) Mel Bay.
— More Fun with the Trumpet. (Fun Bks.). 32p. 1976. pap. 5.95 (*0-87166-480-1*, 93384) Mel Bay.
— More Fun with the Violin. (Fun Bks.). 32p. 1976. pap. 5.95 (*0-87166-481-X*, 93388) Mel Bay.
— More Songs for Harmonica. 32p. 1990. pap. 5.95 (*1-56222-000-4*, 94426) Mel Bay.
***Bay, William.** Musical Ideas Manuscript Book. 112p. 1998. pap. 7.95 (*0-7866-4113-4*, 98170) Mel Bay.
Bay, William. One Hundred Gospel Favorites for Gt. 112p. 1983. pap. 11.95 (*0-87166-694-4*, 93977) Mel Bay.

Bay, William. Saxophone Fingering Chart. 4p. 1983. pap. 3.95 (*0-87166-503-4*) Mel Bay.
Bay, William. Saxophone Pocket Book, Bk. 2. 32p. 1981. pap. 0.95 (*0-87166-555-7*, 93748) Mel Bay.
***Bay, William.** 7 Festive Trumpet Solos. 52p. 1998. pap. write for info. incl. audio compact disk (*0-7866-4438-9*, 94023CDP) Mel Bay.
— Sing-Along Christmas Carols. 24p. 1998. pap. 9.95 incl. audio compact disk (*0-7866-4414-1*, 94117BCD) Mel Bay.
Bay, William. Student Bass Method. 48p. 1986. pap. 5.95 (*0-87166-883-1*, 94097) Mel Bay.
— Student Bass Method (Metodado para el Estudiante de Bajo) (SPA.). 48p. 1991. pap. 6.95 (*1-56222-184-1*, 94563SP) Mel Bay.
— Tenor Banjo Pocketbook. 32p. 1981. pap. 0.95 (*0-87166-557-3*, 93756) Mel Bay.
Bay, William. Trombone Position Chart. 4p. 1983. pap. 3.95 (*0-87166-504-2*, 93897) Mel Bay.
— Trumpet Fingering Chart. 4p. 1983. pap. 3.95 (*0-87166-505-0*, 93893) Mel Bay.
Bay, William. Trumpet Handbook. (Building Excellence Ser.). 40p. 1998. pap. 14.95 incl. audio compact disk (*0-7866-3311-5*) Mel Bay.
— Trumpet Method. 88p. 1978. spiral bd. 8.95 (*0-87166-915-3*, 93448) Mel Bay.
***Bay, William.** Trumpet Praise. 44p. 1998. pap. 22.95 incl. audio (*0-7866-4114-2*, 94054CDP) Mel Bay.
Bay, William. Trumpet Primer. 24p. 1977. 4.95 (*0-87166-376-7*, 93405) Mel Bay.
***Bay, William.** Tunes for Guitar Technique. 32p. 2000. pap. 5.95 incl. audio compact disk (*0-7866-5083-4*, 98590BCD) Mel Bay.
Bay, William. You Can Teach Yourself Classic Guitar. 112p. 1994. pap. 9.95 (*0-7866-0015-2*, 95119); audio 9.98 (*0-7866-0016-0*, 95119C); audio compact disk 15.98 (*0-7866-0390-9*, 95119CD) Mel Bay.
Bay, William. You Can Teach Yourself Classic Guitar. 112p. 1994. pap. 18.95 incl. audio (*0-7866-1217-7*, 95119P) Mel Bay.
Bay, William. You Can Teach Yourself Classic Guitar. 1995. VHS 29.95 (*0-7866-0427-1*, 95119VX) Mel Bay.
Bay, William. You Can Teach Yourself Classic Guitar. 1996. pap. 11.95 (*0-7866-0874-9*) Mel Bay.
— You Can Teach Yourself Classic Guitar. 112p. 1999. pap. 17.95 incl. audio compact disk (*0-7866-4409-5*, 95119BCD) Mel Bay.
Bay, William. You Can Teach Yourself Guitar. 112p. 1989. pap. 9.95 (*0-87166-262-0*, 94301) Mel Bay.
— You Can Teach Yourself Guitar. 1990. audio 9.98 (*0-87166-749-5*, 94301C); audio compact disk 15.98 (*0-7866-0347-X*, 94301CD) Mel Bay.
— You Can Teach Yourself Guitar. 1993. 18.95 incl. audio (*0-87166-750-9*, 94301P) Mel Bay.
— You Can Teach Yourself Guitar. 1994. VHS 29.95 (*0-7866-0171-X*, 94301VX) Mel Bay.
— You Can Teach Yourself Guitar. 1996. cd-rom 49.95 (*0-7866-2457-4*, 94301CDR) Mel Bay.
***Bay, William.** You Can Teach Yourself Guitar. 112p. 1999. pap. 17.95 incl. audio compact disk (*0-7866-4410-9*, 94301BCD) Mel Bay.
Bay, William. You Can Teach Yourself Guitar Chords. 112p. 1997. pap. 9.95 (*0-7866-0055-1*, 95120) Mel Bay.
— You Can Teach Yourself Recorder. LC 91-759561. 80p. 1989. pap. 9.95 (*0-87166-742-8*, 94337) Mel Bay.
Bay, William. You Can Teach Yourself Recorder. 80p. 1989. pap. 24.95 incl. audio compact disk (*0-7866-0993-1*, 94337CDP); pap. 17.95 incl. audio compact disk (*0-7866-5011-7*, 94337BCD) Mel Bay.
Bay, William. You Can Teach Yourself Recorder. 1990. pap. 18.95 incl. audio (*0-87166-754-1*, 94337) Mel Bay.
— You Can Teach Yourself Recorder. 1990. audio 9.98 (*0-87166-753-3*, 94337C); audio compact disk 15.98 (*0-7866-0379-8*, 94337CD) Mel Bay.
— You Can Teach Yourself Recorder. 80p. 1993. 13.95 (*0-7866-0800-5*, 94337PIX) Mel Bay.
— You Can Teach Yourself Uke. 96p. 1993. 24.95 incl. audio compact disk (*0-7866-1114-6*, 94809CDP); 18.95 incl. audio (*0-7866-1115-4*, 94809P); pap. 9.95 (*1-56222-454-9*, 94809); audio 9.98 (*1-56222-455-7*, 94809C); audio compact disk 15.98 (*0-7866-0386-0*, 94809CD) Mel Bay.
— You Can Teach Yourself Uke. 96p. 1996. 38.95 incl. VHS (*0-7866-2491-4*, 94809VPX); VHS 29.95 (*0-7866-2056-0*, 94809VX) Mel Bay.
***Bay, William, compiled by.** Best of Acoustic Guitar Solos - 1999 Edition. 92p. 1999. pap. 24.95 incl. audio compact disk (*0-7866-4727-2*, 98363BCD) Mel Bay.
***Bay, William & Christiansen, Mike.** Mastering the Guitar, Bk. 2A. 184p. 1998. pap. 31.95 incl. audio compact disk (*0-7866-3651-3*, 97195CDP) Mel Bay.
— Mastering the Guitar, Bk. 2B. 152p. 1999. pap. 29.95 incl. audio compact disk (*0-7866-3813-3*, 97196CDP); pap. 24.95 incl. audio compact disk (*0-7866-4448-6*, 97196BCD) Mel Bay.
— Mastering the Guitar, Bk. 2C. 144p. 1999. pap. 24.95 incl. audio compact disk (*0-7866-4449-4*, 97197BCD); pap. 33.95 incl. audio compact disk (*0-7866-3815-X*, 97197CDP) Mel Bay.
Bay, William & Christiansen, Mike. Mastering the Guitar, Level 2A. 184p. 1998. pap. 14.95 (*0-7866-3507-X*, 97195); pap. 24.95 incl. audio compact disk (*0-7866-3650-5*, 97195BCD) Mel Bay.
— Mastering the Guitar: A Comprehensive Method for Today's Guitarist!, Bk. 1A. 144p. 1996. pap. 9.95 (*0-7866-2804-9*, 96620) Mel Bay.
— Mastering the Guitar: A Comprehensive Method for Today's Guitarist!, Bk. 1B. 144p. 1997. pap. 9.95 (*0-7866-2801-4*, 96621) Mel Bay.

Bay, William & Christiansen, Mike. Mastering the Guitar Bk. 1A: Beginning Level. 144p. 1997. spiral bd. 22.95 incl. audio compact disk (*0-7866-2927-4*, 96620BCD) Mel Bay.
— Mastering the Guitar Bk. 1B: Beginning-Intermediate Level. 144p. 1997. spiral bd. 22.95 incl. audio compact disk (*0-7866-2928-2*, 96621BCD) Mel Bay.
— Mastering the Guitar - Class Method. 136p. 2000. spiral bd. write for info. (*0-7866-5700-6*, 97121) Mel Bay.
Bay, William & Christiansen, Mike. Mastering the Guitar - Technique Studies. 152p. 1997. pap. 9.95 (*0-7866-2817-0*, 96622) Mel Bay.
***Bay, William & Christiansen, Mike.** Mastering the Guitar Book, Vol. 2B. 152p. 1999. 14.95 (*0-7866-3509-6*, 97196) Mel Bay.
— Mastering the Guitar Book IB CD Package. 144p. 1997. 9.95 (*0-7866-2803-0*, 96621CDP) Mel Bay.
Bay, William & Flint, Tommy. Easiest Fingerpicking Guitar Book. 24p. 1990. pap. 3.95 (*0-87166-990-0*, 94423) Mel Bay.
Bay, William & Griffin, Neil. Easiest Banjo Book. 24p. 1990. 3.95 (*0-87166-981-1*, 94406) Mel Bay.
Bay, William & Lonergan, Mark. You Can Teach Yourself Rock Guitar. 1989. 18.95 incl. audio (*0-87166-308-2*, 94305P); pap. 9.95 (*0-87166-267-1*, 94305); audio 9.98 (*0-87166-321-X*, 94305C) Mel Bay.
— You Can Teach Yourself Rock Guitar. 1993. audio compact disk 15.98 (*0-7866-0377-1*, 94305CD) Mel Bay.
— You Can Teach Yourself Rock Guitar. 1996. VHS 29.95 (*0-7866-2055-2*, 94305VX) Mel Bay.
***Bay, William & Lonergan, Mark.** You Can Teach Yourself Rock Guitar. 108p. 1998. pap. 17.95 incl. audio compact disk (*0-7866-4402-8*, 94305BCD) Mel Bay.
Bay, William & Zucco, Frank. Beginning Mandolin Solos. 44p. 1997. pap. 14.95 incl. audio compact disk (*0-7866-2935-5*, 94884BCD) Mel Bay.
Bay, William, et al. Easiest Country Guitar Book. 24p. 1990. pap. 3.95 (*0-87166-989-7*, 94422) Mel Bay.
Bay, William, jt. auth. see Banks, Sue.
Bay, William, jt. auth. see Bay, Mel.
Bay, William, jt. auth. see Bay, Mel, Publications, Inc. Staff.
Bay, William, jt. auth. see Christiansen, Mike.
Bay, William, jt. auth. see Mel Bay Staff.
Bay, William B. Mere Creatures of the State? Education, Religion & the Courts. (Illus.). 142p. (Orig.). 1994. pap. 13.95 (*1-883357-99-3*, Crisis Bks) Dumb Ox Bks.
Baya, C. Advances in Medical Biology: Results of the 4th EC Medical & Health Research Program. LC 93-80284. (Studies in Biomedical & Health Research). 380p. (gr. 12). 1994. 117.00 (*90-5199-146-0*, Pub. by IOS Pr) IOS Press.
***Bayan, Matthew J.** Eat Fat, Be Healthy: Understanding the Heart-Stopper Gene & When a Low-Fat Diet Can Kill You. LC 99-45721. 224p. 2000. 22.50 (*0-684-86527-0*) Scribner.
Bayan, Rich. The Cynic's Dictionary. 192p. 1997. reprint ed. pap. 8.95 (*0-688-15125-6*, Quil) HarperTrade.
Bayan, Richard. Words That Sell. LC 84-71532. (Orig.). 1989. pap. 26.95 (*0-87280-150-0*, 3354, Asher-Gallant) Caddylak Systs.
— Words That Sell. 144p. (Orig.). 1987. pap. 14.95 (*0-8092-4799-2*, 479920, Contemporary Bks) NTC Contemp Pub Co.
Bayani, Manijeh & Contadini, Anna. The Decorated Word Pt. I: Qua'rans of the 17th to 19th Centuries. (Nasser D. Khalili Collection of Islamic Art: Vol. IV). (Illus.). 324p. 1999. text 235.00 (*0-19-727603-2*) OUP.
Bayar, Steven & Hirschman, Francine. Teens & Trust: Building Bridges in Jewish Education. LC 93-18138. 1993. 12.95 (*0-933873-76-X*) Torah Aura.
Bayard, Ann C., jt. auth. see Krause, Wolfgang.
Bayard, Caroline. The New Poetics in Canada & Quebec From Concretism to Post-Modernism. 374p. 1989. text 45.00 (*0-8020-5726-8*) U of Toronto Pr.
Bayard, Caroline, ed. One Hundred Years of Critical Solitudes. 356p. (C). 1992. text 25.00 (*1-55022-117-5*, Pub. by ECW) Genl Dist Srvs.
Bayard, Charles J. The Development of the Public Land Policy, 1783-1820, with Special Reference to Indiana. Bruchey, Stuart, ed. LC 78-53556. (Development of Public Land Law in the U. S. Ser.). 1979. lib. bdg. 30.95 (*0-405-11364-1*) Ayer.
Bayard, James. Brief Exposition of the Constitution of the United States: With an Appendix Containing the Declaration of Independence & the Articles of Confederation, & a Copious Index. 178p. 1993. reprint ed. 37.50 (*0-8377-1953-4*, Rothman) W S Hein.
Bayard, Jane. Works of Splendor & Imagination: The Exhibition Watercolor, 1770-1870. LC 81-52432. (Illus.). 83p. (Orig.). 1981. pap. 15.00 (*0-930606-32-9*) Yale Ctr Brit Art.
Bayard, Jean, jt. auth. see Bayard, Robert T.
Bayard, Louis. Fool's Errand: A Novel. LC 98-55139. 470p. 1999. pap. 12.95 (*1-55583-494-9*, Pub. by Alyson Pubns) Consort Bk Sales.
***Bayard, Pierre.** Who Killed Roger Ackroyd? The Mystery Behind the Agatha Christie Mystery. Cosman, Carol, tr. from FRE. LC 99-54834. 176p. 2000. 22.95 (*1-56584-579-X*, Pub. by New Press NY) Norton.
Bayard, Robert T. Socorrol Tengo un Hijo Adolescente. 1999. pap. text 14.95 (*84-7880-926-0*) E Temas de Hoy.
Bayard, Robert T. & Bayard, Jean. How to Deal with Your Acting-Up Teenager: Practical Help for Desperate Parents. LC 83-1414. 224p. 1986. pap. 11.95 (*0-87131-479-7*) M Evans.
Bayard, Tania, ed. Gardening for Fragrance, No. 121. (Plants & Gardens Ser.). (Illus.). 1989. per. 7.95 (*0-945352-54-9*) Bklyn Botanic.

Bayard, Thomas O. & Elliott, Kimberly A. Reciprocity & Retaliation in U. S. Trade Policy. LC 94-22348. 503p. 1994. pap. 25.00 (*0-88132-084-6*) Inst Intl Eco.
Bayard, Thomas O. & Young, Soo-Gil, eds. Economic Relations Between the United States & Korea: Conflict or Cooperation? LC 88-8257. (Institute for International Economics. Special Report Ser.: No. 8). 190p. (Orig.). reprint ed. pap. 58.90 (*0-7837-4220-7*, 204390900012) Bks Demand.
Bayart, Jean-Francois. The State in Africa: The Politics of the Belly. Harrison, Chris et al, trs. LC 92-28666. 400p. (C). 1992. text 69.95 (*0-582-06422-8*, 79465) Longman.
Bayart, Jean-Francois, et al. The Criminalization of the State in Africa. LC 98-38856. (African Issues Ser.). 192p. 1999. 39.95 (*0-253-33524-8*); pap. 18.95 (*0-253-21286-3*) Ind U Pr.
Bayat, Asef. Street Politics: Poor People's Movements in Iran. LC 97-18986. 256p. 1997. pap. 18.50 (*0-231-10859-1*); lib. bdg. 50.00 (*0-231-10858-3*) Col U Pr.
Bayat, Assef. Work, Politics, & Power: An International Perspective on Workers' Control & Self-Management. 244p. 35.00 (*0-85345-833-2*, Pub. by Monthly Rev); pap. 22.00 (*0-85345-834-0*, Pub. by Monthly Rev) NYU Pr.
***Bayat, Mangol.** Mysticism & Dissent: Socioreligious Thought in Qajar Iran. LC 99-48925. 224p. 1999. pap. text 22.95 (*0-8156-2853-6*) Syracuse U Pr.
Bayat, Mangol. Mysticism & Dissent: Socioreligious Thought in Qajar Iran. 228p. (C). 1997. reprint ed. pap. text 25.00 (*0-7881-3967-3*) DIANE Pub.
Bayat, Mojdeh & Jamnia, Mohammad A. Tales from the Land of the Sufis. 180p. 1996. pap. 12.00 (*0-614-21368-1*, 1211) Kazi Pubns.
Bayat, Mojdeh, jt. auth. see Jamnia, Mohammad A.
Bayazitoglu. Elements of Heat Transfer. 1988. student ed. 35.93 (*0-07-004155-5*) McGraw.
Bayazitoglu, Y., et al, eds. Proceedings of the 1995 National Heat Transfer Conference: August 6-9, 1995, Portland, Oregon, Vol. 1. 96p. 1995. 72.00 (*0-7918-1714-8*, H00996) ASME.
Bayazitoglu, Y. & Arpaci, V. S., eds. Fundamentals of Heat Transfer in Electromagnetic, Electrostatic & Acoustic Fields. (HTD Ser.: Vol. 248). 92p. 1993. 35.00 (*0-7918-1161-1*, G00805) ASME.
Bayazitoglu, Y. & Peterson, G. P., eds. Fundamental Issues in Small Scale Heat Transfer. (HTD Ser.: Vol. 227). 84p. 1992. 30.00 (*0-7918-1072-0*, G00716) ASME.
Bayazitoglu, Y. & Sathuvalli, U. B., eds. Heat Transfer in Porous Media & Two-Pulse Flow; The Energy & Environmental Expo '95 - The Energy-Sources Technology Conference & Exhibition, Houston, Texas - January 29-February 1, 1995. (HTD Ser.: Vol. 302). 180p. 1995. 84.00 (*0-7918-1296-0*, H00928) ASME.
Bayazitoglu, Y., jt. ed. see Kroeger, P. G.
Bayazitoglu, Yildiz & Ozisik, M. Necati. Elements of Heat Transfer. 433p. (C). 1988. 99.38 (*0-07-004154-7*) McGraw.
***Baybes de Luna, Antonio.** Arrhythmias & Sudden Death in Athletes. LC 00-41099. (Developments in Cardiovascular Medicine Ser.). 2000. write for info. (*0-7923-6337-X*, Kluwer Acad) Kluwer Academic.
Baybes de Luna, Antonio, see Baybes de Luna, Antonio.
Baybrook, Gar. The Spurious Books of the Bible. 224p. 1994. per. 9.95 (*0-945383-61-4*) Teach Servs.
Baycrest Terrace Memoirs Group Staff. From Our Lives: Memoirs. 240p. 1991. 15.95 (*0-88962-097-0*); pap. 8.95 (*0-88962-098-9*) Mosaic.
Baycroft, Timothy. Nationalism in Europe, 1789-1945. LC 99-174434. (Perspectives in History Ser.). 104p. 1999. pap. 11.95 (*0-521-59871-0*) Cambridge U Pr.
Baycura, John F., jt. auth. see Baycura, Peter.
Baycura, Peter & Baycura, John F. Lyndora Chronicles, the Legendary Decades, 1902-1921. LC 99-185532. (Illus.). 286p. 1998. pap. 25.00 (*0-9665813-0-X*) J Baycura.
Baydack, Richard K., et al, eds. Practical Approaches to the Conservation of Biological Diversity. LC 98-25753. 320p. 1998. text 65.00 (*1-55963-543-6*); pap. text 35.00 (*1-55963-544-4*) Island Pr.
Baydo. A Topical History of the United States. 16.95 (*0-88295-008-8*) Forum Pr IL.
Baydo, Gerald R. A Topical History of the United States. LC 86-26949. (Illus.). 1978. pap. text 16.95 (*0-88273-008-8*) Forum Pr IL.
Baydo, Jerry R. History of the American Indian. 173p. 1992. pap. 15.00 (*0-911541-20-9*) Gregory Pub.
— History of the U. S. with Topics, Vol. 1. 439p. pap. 30.00 (*0-911541-44-6*) Gregory Pub.
Baydo, Jerry R., et al, contrib. by. Readings in United States History with Topics, Vol. II. (Illus.). 553p. 1995. 28.00 (*0-911541-37-3*) Gregory Pub.
— A Student Workbook for History of the United States with Topics, Vol. II. 206p. 1995. 12.00 (*0-911541-38-1*) Gregory Pub.
Baydo, Jerry R., ed. Readings in American History. 128p. 1992. 12.00 (*0-911541-21-7*) Gregory Pub.
Baydo, Jerry R. & Zimmerman. History of the U. S. with Topics, Vol. II. 551p. 1994. pap. 30.00 (*0-911541-30-6*) Gregory Pub.
Baydoun, Nabil, et al. Accounting in the Asia-Pacific Region. LC 97-15854. 440p. 1997. text 39.95 (*0-471-24866-5*) Wiley.
Baydun, M., ed. Holy Quran. (ARA., Illus.). 600p. 1984. 125.00 (*0-86685-133-X*, LDL1340) Intl Bk Ctr.
Baydush, Lisa, ed. see Green Acres School Staff.
Baye. Managerial Economics. 3rd ed. LC 99-26274. 1999. 64.74 (*0-07-228917-1*) McGraw.
— Managerial Economics Workbook. 3rd ed. 256p. 1999. pap., wbk. ed. 26.88 (*0-07-228918-X*) McGraw.

B

An Asterisk (*) at the beginning of an entry indicates that the title is appearing for the first time.

B

Baye, Michael. Advances in Applied Microeconomics, Vol. 7. 1998. 73.25 (*0-7623-0302-6*) Jai Pr.

— Managerial Economics & Business Strategy. 232p. (C). 1994. text 24.37 (*0-256-13730-7*, Irwn McGrw-H) McGrw-H Hghr Educ.

— Managerial Economics & Business Strategy. 2nd ed. LC 96-17337. 576p. (C). 1996. text 69.75 (*0-256-17955-7*, Irwn McGrw-H) McGrw-H Hghr Educ.

— Managerial Economics & Business Strategy: Student Workbook Package. 2nd ed. (C). 1996. text 74.75 (*0-256-21623-1*, Irwn McGrw-H) McGrw-H Hghr Educ.

***Baye, Michael R.** Managerial Economics & Business Strategy. 3rd ed. LC 99-26274. (Illus.). 2000. write for info. (*0-07-116933-4*, Irwn Prfssnl) McGraw-Hill Prof.

Baye, Michael R. Money & Banking. LC 94-76473. (C). Date not set. text 68.76 (*0-395-64395-3*) HM.

— Money & Banking. (C). 1995. pap., teacher ed. 11.96 (*0-395-72566-6*); pap. text, student ed. 20.36 (*0-395-72567-4*) HM.

Baye, Michael R. & Black, D. A. Consumer Behavior, Cost of Living Measures, & the Income Tax. (Lecture Notes in Economics & Mathematical Systems Ser.: Vol. 276). vii, 119p. 1986. 29.60 (*0-387-16797-8*) Spr-Verlag.

***Bayefsky, Anne F.** Enforcing International Human Rights Law: The UN Treaty System in the 21st Century. LC 00-42421. 2000. write for info. (*90-411-1415-7*) Kluwer Law Intl.

— Self-determination in International Law: Quebec & Lessons : Legal Opinions. LC 99-17099. 528p. 2000. write for info. (*90-411-1154-9*) Kluwer Law Intl.

***Bayens, Geralo J. & Roberson, Cliff.** Criminal Justice Research Methods: Theory & Practice. LC 99-69690. (Illus.). 348p. (C). 2000. pap. text 37.95 (*1-928916-06-6*) Copperhouse.

***Bayer.** Take Care of Yourself: French Edition. 2000. 18.00 (*0-7382-0126-X*, Pub. by Perseus Pubng) HarpC.

Bayer, jt. auth. see Rigney.

Bayer, Robert C. & Bayer, Juanita. Lobsters Inside Out: A Lobster Workbook / 3rd ed. LC 98-66215. 32p. 1998. write for info. (*0-7872-3273-4*) Kendall-Hunt.

Bayer, A. Clinicians Guide to Aspirin. (Illus.). 192p. 1999. text 39.95 (*0-412-81900-7*, Pub. by E A) OUP.

Bayer, Ada-Helen, et al, eds. Advanced Methodological Issues in Culturally Competent Evaluation for Substance Abuse Prevention. (Illus.). 266p. (C). 1998. pap. text 45.00 (*0-7881-4781-1*) DIANE Pub.

Bayer, Alan E. The Assimilation of American Family Patterns by European Immigrants & Their Children. Cordasco, Francesco, ed. LC 80-839. (American Ethnic Groups Ser.). 1981. lib. bdg. 19.95 (*0-405-13403-7*) Ayer.

Bayer, Alan E., jt. auth. see Braxton, John M.

Bayer, Andrea, et al. Jusepe de Ribera, 1591-1652. LC 92-21779. (Illus.). 304p. 1992. 45.00 (*0-87099-647-9*, 0-8109-6416-3); pap. 19.95 (*0-87099-648-7*) Metro Mus Art.

***Bayer-Berenbaum, Linda.** Ruth Bader Ginsburg: Supreme Court Justice. LC 99-55998. (Women of Achievement Ser.). 112p. 1999. 19.95 (*0-7910-5287-7*) Chelsea Hse.

Bayer, C. W. The Celtic Harp at Stonehenge: The Structure of Ancient British & Celtic Learning. LC 94-92038. 100p. 1994. pap. 20.00 (*0-9628890-1-6*) Purple Mntn.

— The Historical Method of the Celtic Harp: For Dancing, Singing & Divisions. LC 91-90035. 60p. 1991. pap. 30.00 (*0-9628890-0-8*) Purple Mntn.

— Profit, Plots & Lynching: The Creation of Nevada Territory. LC 95-67579. 200p. 1995. pap. 30.00 (*0-9628890-3-2*) Purple Mntn.

Bayer, Cary. The Prosperity Aerobics. 80p. 7.95 (*0-9644224-0-9*, Pub. by Bayer Commun) New Leaf Dist.

Bayer, Charles H. The Babylonian Captivity of the Mainline Church. 176p. (Orig.). 1996. pap. 15.99 (*0-8272-0221-0*) Chalice Pr.

— Building a Biblical Faith: A Guide to Christian Theology. LC 94-32750. 128p. (Orig.). 1995. pap. 12.99 (*0-8272-0220-2*) Chalice Pr.

— Hope for the Mainline Church. 128p. (Orig.). 1991. pap. 10.99 (*0-8272-1424-3*) Chalice Pr.

— When It Is Dark Enough: Sermons for Advent, Christmas & Epiphany - Gospel. LC 93-51080. (Orig.). 1994. pap. 11.25 (*0-7880-0000-4*) CSS OH.

Bayer, Charles H. & Hausman, Robert A. Homiletic Meditations: Advent Through the Transfiguration of Our Lord, First Reading & Gospel, Cycle C, Vol. 1. LC 94-207. (Orig.). 1994. pap. 18.50 (*0-7880-0050-0*) CSS OH.

Bayer, Cherie L., jt. auth. see Stafford, Laura.

Bayer, Chris. Elephant Tracks: On the Trail of Gold Rush Song & Dance. (Illus.). 1998. pap. 25.00 (*0-9628890-8-3*) Purple Mntn.

Bayer, Clemens. Zur Infloreszenzmorphologie der Malvales. (Dissertationes Botanicae Ser.: Band 212). (GER., Illus.). vi, 285p. 1994. pap. 65.00 (*3-443-64124-5*, Pub. by Gebruder Borntraeger) Balogh.

Bayer, Deborah. Jailer's Inn. Bixby, Robert, ed. 40p. 1996. pap. 6.00 (*1-882983-33-5*) March Street Pr.

Bayer, Edward J. Rape Within Marriage: A Moral Analysis Delayed. LC 85-5289. 160p. (Orig.). 1985. lib. bdg. 47.50 (*0-8191-4613-7*) U Pr of Amer.

Bayer, Edward J., et al, eds. Handbook on Critical Sexual Issues. rev. ed. LC 89-16252. 220p. 1989. pap. 9.95 (*0-935372-25-3*) NCBC.

Bayer, Eleanor & Bayer, Leo. Third Best Sport. 1959. pap. 5.25 (*0-8222-1134-3*) Dramatists Play.

Bayer, Erich. Woerterbuch Zur Geschichte: Dictionary of History. 4th ed. (GER.). 1980. pap. 39.95 (*0-8288-1492-9*, M6905) Fr & Eur.

Bayer, Frederick M. & Voss, Gilbert L., eds. Studies in Tropical American Mollusks. LC 70-170142. 1971. 22.95 (*0-87024-230-X*) U of Miami Pr.

***Bayer, George.** George Wollsten: Expert Stock Trader. (Investment Greats Ser.). 240p. 2000. 30.00 (*0-273-64314-2*) F T P H.

Bayer, Gregory W., ed. see Niemeyer, Juanita.

Bayer, Gregory W., ed. see Taber, David.

Bayer, Hanna, ed. see Thielemann, Hans B.

Bayer, Hans. A Dog's Life. Miller, Ray, Jr., ed. & tr. by. from GER. LC 93-17843. (Illus.). 180p. (C). 1993. pap. text 29.50 (*0-8191-9141-8*); lib. bdg. 49.50 (*0-8191-9140-X*) U Pr of Amer.

— Gottfried von Straburg und der "Archipoeta" (Spolia Berolinensia Ser.: Bd. 8). (GER.). 1996. write for info. (*3-615-00177-X*) G Olms Pubs.

Bayer, Hans F. Jesus' Predictions of Vindication & Resurrection: The Provenance, Meaning, & Correlation of the Synoptic Predictions. 290p. 1986. pap. 62.50 (*3-16-145014-0*, Pub. by JCB Mohr) Coronet Bks.

Bayer, Henry G. The Belgians: First Settlers in New York & in the Middle States, with a Review of the Events Which Led to Their Immigration. (Illus.). 373p. 1997. reprint ed. lib. bdg. 39.50 (*0-8328-6886-8*) Higginson Bk Co.

Bayer, Herbert, et al, eds. Bauhaus 1919-1928. LC 77-169299. (Museum of Modern Art Publications in Reprint). (Illus.). 224p. 1972. reprint ed. 36.95 (*0-405-01559-3*) Ayer.

Bayer, Jane. A My Name Is Alice. (ps-3). 1992. pap. 5.99 (*0-14-054668-5*) NAL.

— A My Name Is Alice. 1987. 11.19 (*0-606-00278-2*, Pub. by Turtleback) Demco.

Bayer, Jessica. Objects of Desire. 24p. (Orig.). 1991. pap. 4.00 (*0-945926-26-X*) Paradigm RI.

Bayer, Joannes. Uranometria. (Mapping of the Stars Ser.). (GRE & LAT., Illus.). 216p. 1998. reprint ed. pap. 780.00 (*1-85297-021-9*, Pub. by Archival Facs) St Mut.

Bayer, John. The Lazarus Project. LC 98-49223. 320p. 1999. pap. 12.99 (*0-8054-0172-5*) Broadman.

Bayer, John F. Necessary Risk. LC 97-43159. 324p. 1998. pap. 12.99 (*0-8054-4016-X*) Broadman.

***Bayer, John F.** The Omega Deception. LC 99-46480. 320p. 2000. pap. 12.99 (*0-8054-1966-7*) Broadman.

Bayer, Josef. Directionality & Logical Form: On the Scope of Focusing Particles & Wh-in-Situ. (Studies in Natural Language & Linguistic Theory: Vol. 34). 344p. (C). 1995. text 140.50 (*0-7923-3752-2*) Kluwer Academic.

Bayer, Juanita, jt. auth. see Bayer, Robert C.

Bayer, Konrad. The Head of Vitus Bering. 1994. pap. 11.95 (*0-947757-83-X*, Pub. by Atlas Pr) Serpents Tail.

— Selected Works. 1986. pap. 13.99 (*0-947757-06-6*, Pub. by Atlas Pr) Serpents Tail.

Bayer, Leo, jt. auth. see Bayer, Eleanor.

Bayer, Leona & Bayley, Nancy. Growth Diagnosis: Selected Methods for Interpreting & Predicting Physical Development from One Year to Maturity. 2nd ed. LC 75-19240. 255p. reprint ed. pap. 79.10 (*0-608-15103-3*, 202578300046) Bks Demand.

***Bayer, Les.** Devotions for the Chronologically Gifted. LC 99-32402. 224p. 1999. 15.00 (*0-570-05358-7*) Concordia.

***Bayer, Linda.** Quincy Jones. LC 00-20605. (Black Americans of Achievement Ser.). (Illus.). 128p. (YA). (gr. 4-7). 2000. write for info. (*0-7910-5304-0*) Chelsea Hse.

Bayer, Linda. Ruth Bader Ginsburg: Supreme Court Justice. LC 99-55998. (Illus.). 112p. 1999. pap. 9.95 (*0-7910-5288-5*) Chelsea Hse.

***Bayer, Linda N.** Elie Wiesel: Portrait for Remembrance. LC 00-8567. (Holocaust Biographies Ser.). 2000. lib. bdg. 19.95 (*0-8239-3306-7*) Rosen Group.

— Out of Control: Gambling & Other Impulse Control Disorders. (Encyclopedia of Psychological Disorders Ser.). 2000. write for info. (*0-7910-5313-X*) Chelsea Hse.

— Personality Disorders. LC 99-28888. (Encyclopedia of Psychological Disorders Ser.). 144p. 2000. 24.95 (*0-7910-5317-2*) Chelsea Hse.

— Quincy Jones. (Overcoming Adversity Ser.). (Illus.). 128p. 2000. pap. text 9.95 (*0-7910-5305-9*) Chelsea Hse.

Bayer, Linda N. Sleep Disorders. LC 99-28882. (Encyclopedia of Psychological Disorders Ser.). 144p. (YA). (gr. 7 up). 2000. write for info. (*0-7910-5314-8*) Chelsea Hse.

***Bayer, Linda N.** Strange Visions: Hallucinogen-Related Disorder. (Encyclopedia of Psychological Disorders Ser.). 144p. 2000. 24.95 (*0-7910-5315-6*) Chelsea Hse.

— Uneasy Lives: Understanding Anxiety Disorder. (Encyclopedia of Psychological Disorders Ser.). 144p. 2000. 24.95 (*0-7910-5316-4*) Chelsea Hse.

Bayer, M. Jamaica in Focus. 1993. pap. 12.00 (*0-85345-885-5*) Monthly Rev.

Bayer, Marcel. Jamaica in Focus. (In Focus Ser.). 100p. 2000. pap. 12.95 (*1-56656-285-6*) Interlink Pub.

Bayer, Margaret Canfield. Wyoming Pioneer Woman, Pauline Krueger Bayer. LC 98-67661. vi, 274p. 1998. write for info. (*0-9666502-0-4*) Kolman WoodKrft.

***Bayer, Michael T.** Computer Telephony Demystified: Putting CTI, Media Services & IP Telephony to Work. (Demystified Ser.). (Illus.). 700p. 2000. pap. text 49.95 (*0-07-135987-7*) McGraw-Hill Prof.

Bayer, Michael T. CTI Business Solutions: How to Put Computer Telephony Integration to Work. LC 96-29858. (Illus.). 352p. 1997. pap. 49.95 (*0-07-006153-X*) McGraw.

Bayer, Osvaldo, et al, texts. Represion y Reconstruccion de una Cultura: El Caso Argentino. (SPA.). 1988. 12.00 (*950-23-0406-3*) Edins Hispanoamer.

Bayer, Oswald & Suggate, Alan M., eds. Worship & Ethics: Lutherans & Anglicans in Dialogue. LC 95-42323. (Theologische Bibliothek Toepelmann Ser.: Vol. 70). xv, 295p. (C). 1996. lib. bdg. 152.30 (*3-11-014377-1*) De Gruyter.

Bayer, Patricia. Art Deco Architecture: Design, Decoration, & Detail from the Twenties & Thirties. (Illus.). 224p. 1992. 65.00 (*0-8109-1923-0*) Abrams.

— Art Deco Architecture: Design, Decoration, & Detail from the Twenties & Thirties. LC 99-70862. (Illus.). 224p. 1999. pap. 29.95 (*0-500-28149-1*, Pub. by Thames Hudson) Norton.

— Art Deco Interiors: Decoration & Design Classics of the 1920s & 1930s. LC 97-61367. (Illus.). 1998. pap. 27.50 (*0-500-28020-7*, Pub. by Thames Hudson) Norton.

Bayer, Patricia, ed. see Castle, Wendell & Hunter-Stiebel, Penelope.

Bayer, R. G. Aspects of an Engineering Model for Sliding Wear. (Technical Papers: Vol. P109.22). (Illus.). 21p. 1970. pap. text 30.00 (*1-55589-444-5*) AGMA.

Bayer, R. G., jt. ed. see Rigney, D.

Bayer, Range D. Cormorant-Fisherman Conflict in Tillamook County, Oregon. LC 89-80373. (Studies in Oregon Ornithology: No. 6). (Illus.). 99p. 1989. pap. 9.50 (*0-939819-05-8*) Gahmken Pr.

***Bayer, Range D.** Cormorant Harassment to Protect Juvenile Salmonids in Tillamook County, Oregon. LC 00-23174. (Studies in Oregon Ornithology). 2000. pap. write for info. (*0-939819-09-0*) Gahmken Pr.

Bayer, Range D. Oiled Birds: How to Search for & Capture Oiled Birds at Oregon Intertidal Areas. (Studies in Oregon Ornithology: No. 5). (Illus.). 29p. 1988. pap. 7.00 (*0-939819-04-X*) Gahmken Pr.

— Records of Bird Skins Collected along the Oregon Coast. LC 89-16883. (Studies in Oregon Ornithology: No. 7). 246p. 1989. pap. 20.00 (*0-939819-06-6*) Gahmken Pr.

Bayer, Range D. & Ferris, Reed W. Reed Ferris' 1930-1943 Bird Banding Records & Birds Observations for Tillamook County, Oregon. LC 87-81812. (Studies in Oregon Ornithology: No. 3). (Illus.). ix, 131p. (Orig.). 1987. pap. 17.00 (*0-939819-02-3*) Gahmken Pr.

Bayer, Range D. & Lowe, Roy W. Waterbird & Mammal Censuses at Siuslaw Estuary, Lane County, Oregon. LC 87-83287. (Studies in Oregon Ornithology: No. 4). (Illus.). x, 101p. 1988. pap. 10.00 (*0-939819-03-1*) Gahmken Pr.

Bayer, Raymond G. Mechanical Wear Prediction & Prevention. LC 94-6941. (Mechanical Engineering Ser.: Vol. 91). (Illus.). 672p. 1994. text 199.00 (*0-8247-9027-8*) Dekker.

Bayer, Raymond G., ed. Effects of Mechanical Stiffness & Vibration on Wear. LC 95-13958. (STP Ser.: No. 1211). 1995. 71.00 (*0-8031-1991-7*, STP1211) ASTM.

— Selection & Use of Wear Tests for Coatings - STP 769. 179p. 1982. 21.00 (*0-8031-0710-2*, STP769) ASTM.

— Selection & Use of Wear Tests for Metals - STP 615. 111p. 1977. pap. 10.75 (*0-8031-0563-0*, STP615) ASTM.

— Wear Tests for Plastics: Selection & Use - STP 701. 106p. 1981. pap. 18.00 (*0-8031-0599-1*, STP701) ASTM.

Bayer, Raymond G., jt. ed. see Ludema, Kenneth C.

Bayer, Raymond G., jt. ed. see Ruff, A. W.

Bayer, Raymond G., jt. ed. see Yust, C. S.

Bayer, Richard C. Capitalism & Christianity: The Possibility of Christian Personalism. LC 99-18210. 176p. 1999. pap. 19.95 (*0-87840-731-6*); pap. 19.95 (*0-87840-730-8*) Georgetown U Pr.

***Bayer-Roach, Dawn.** Creative Birth: Nurturing the Miracle Inside You. (Illus.). 300p. 2000. Price not set. (*0-9677504-0-7*) Perk Pr.

Bayer, Robert F. Paying the Political Price: (Summer 1996 Supplement) 1996. pap. 14.00 (*1-879650-03-7*) Perkins Coie.

Bayer, Ronald. Private Acts, Social Consequences: AIDS & the Politics of Public Health. 280p. 1989. 35.00 (*0-02-901961-3*) Free Pr.

— Private Acts, Social Consequences: AIDS & the Politics of Public Health. LC 90-42039. 282p. 1991. pap. 17.95 (*0-8135-1624-2*) Rutgers U Pr.

Bayer, Ronald, ed. The Health & Safety of Workers: Case Studies in the Politics of Professional Responsibility. 318p. 1988. text 45.00 (*0-19-505365-6*) OUP.

Bayer, Ronald, et al, eds. In Search of Equity: Health Needs & the Health Care System. LC 83-4095. (Hastings Center Series in Ethics). 266p. 1983. 45.00 (*0-306-41212-8*, Plenum Trade) Perseus Pubng.

***Bayer, Ronald & Oppenheimer, Gerald M.** AIDS Doctors: Voices from the Epidemic - An Oral History. 320p. 2000. 25.00 (*0-19-512681-5*) OUP.

Bayer, Ronald, jt. ed. see Kirp, David L.

Bayer, S., jt. auth. see Altman, J.

Bayer, Samuel L. Confessions of a Lapsed Neo-Davidsonian: Events & Arguments in Compositional Semantics. rev. ed. LC 97-12385. (Outstanding Dissertations in Linguistics Ser.). 312p. 1997. text 74.00 (*0-8153-2846-X*) Garland.

Bayer, Shirley, jt. auth. see Altman, Joseph.

Bayer, Shirley A. & Altman, Joseph. Neocortical Development. 272p. 1991. text 150.00 (*0-88167-778-7*) Lppncott W & W.

Bayer, Shirley A., jt. auth. see Altman, Joseph.

Bayer, Thomas, ed. see Weiss, Herbert, et al.

***Bayer, Thora I. & Cassirer, Ernst.** Cassirer's Metaphysics of Symbolic Forms: A Philosophical Commentary. LC 00-33412. 2000. write for info. (*0-300-08331-9*) Yale U Pr.

Bayer, William. Breaking Through, Selling out, Dropping Dead & Other Notes on Filmmaking. rev. ed. LC 89-2779. 272p. 1989. reprint ed. pap. 13.95 (*0-87910-123-7*) Limelight Edns.

— Mirror Maze. 400p. 1995. mass mkt. 5.99 (*0-515-11523-1*, Jove) Berkley Pub.

— Wallflower. 1992. mass mkt. 5.99 (*0-515-10843-X*, Jove) Berkley Pub.

Bayer, William, see Hunt, David, pseud.

Bayerische Staatsbibliothek Staff, ed. Bayerische Staatsbibliothek Katalog der Geschichtszeitschriften (BSB-Gez) Bavarian State Library Catalogue of Histo Periodical, 2 vols., Set. (Zeitschriften der Bayerischen Staatsbibliothek Ser.: Pt. 2). (ENG & GER.). 450p. 1991. lib. bdg. 200.00 (*3-598-22242-4*) K G Saur Verlag.

— Bayerische Staatsbibliothek Katalog der Musikzeitschriften (BSB-MuZ) TeilI-Bd: Bavarian State Library Catalogue of Music Periodicals. (Zeitschriften der Bayerischen Staatsbibliothek Ser.). (GER.). 252p. 1990. lib. bdg. write for info. (*3-598-22241-6*) K G Saur Verlag.

Bayerle, G. The Hungarian Letters of Ali Pasha of Buda 1604-1616. (Bibliotheca Orientalis Hungarica Ser.: No. 36). 295p. (C). 1991. 120.00 (*963-05-5928-5*, Pub. by Akade Kiado) St Mut.

Bayerle, Gustav. Ottoman Diplomacy in Hungary: Letter from the Pashas of Buda, 1590-1593. LC 74-188493. (Uralic & Altaic Ser.: Vol. 101). 196p. (Orig.). 1972. pap. text 16.00 (*0-87750-169-6*) Res Inst Inner Asian Studies.

— Ottoman Tributes in Hungary According to Sixteenth Century Tapu Registers of Novigrad. (Near & Middle East Monographs: No. 8). 1973. text 76.95 (*90-279-2437-6*) Mouton.

Bayern, Cynthia D. & Kramer, Diane E. The Creativity Game. LC 98-177411. 99p. (Orig.). 1986. pap. 14.95 (*0-943456-17-7*) Bearly Ltd.

Bayers & Calter. Intro to Algebra & Trigonometry with Applications. 222p. 1998. pap. text 30.75 (*0-536-01513-9*) Pearson Custom.

Bayerschmidt, Carl F. & Hollander, Lee M., eds. Njal's Saga. LC 79-10657. (Illus.). 389p. 1980. reprint ed. lib. bdg. 79.50 (*0-313-20814-X*, NJSA, Greenwood Pr) Greenwood.

Bayerschmidt, Carl F., tr. see Reuter, Fritz.

Bayertz, Kurt. GenEthics: Technological Intervention in Human Reproduction As a Philosophical Problem. 362p. (C). 1995. text 74.95 (*0-521-41693-0*) Cambridge U Pr.

— Solidarity. LC 98-47221. (Philosophical Studies in Contemporary Culture). 7p. 1998. 140.00 (*0-7923-5475-3*) Kluwer Academic.

Bayertz, Kurt, ed. The Concept of Moral Consensus: The Case of Technological Interventions into Human Reproduction. LC 93-40700. (Philosophy & Medicine Ser.: Vol. 46). 256p. (C). 1994. lib. bdg. 139.00 (*0-7923-2615-6*, Pub. by Kluwer Academic) Kluwer Academic.

— Sanctity of Life & Human Dignity. (Philosophy & Medicine Ser.: Vol. 52). 328p. (C). 1996. text 161.50 (*0-7923-3739-5*) Kluwer Academic.

Bayes de Luna, Antonio. Clinical Electrocardiography: A Textbook. 2nd ed. LC 97-22254. (Illus.). 416p. 1998. 125.00 (*0-87993-682-7*) Futura Pub.

Bayes, Jane. Globalization Religion & Gender. text. write for info. (*0-312-22812-0*) St Martin.

Bayes, Jane, jt ed. see Kelly, Rita M.

Bayes, Jane H. Minority Politics & Ideologies in the United States. Jones, Victor, ed. LC 82-17698. (Chandler & Sharp Publications in Political Science Ser.). 144p. (Orig.). (C). 1982. pap. text 9.95 (*0-88316-551-1*) Chandler & Sharp.

Bayes, Jane H., ed. Women & Public Administration: International Perspectives. LC 91-36589. (Women & Politics Ser.: Vol. 11, No. 4). 165p. 1992. pap. text 24.95 (*1-56023-014-2*, Harrington Park) Haworth Pr.

— Women & Public Administration: International Perspectives. LC 91-38143. (Women & Politics Ser.: Vol. 11, No. 4). (Illus.). 165p. 1992. text 39.95 (*1-56024-233-7*) Haworth Pr.

Bayes, Kenneth. Living Architecture. (Rudolf Steiner's Ideas in Practice Ser.). (Illus.). 128p. (Orig.). 1994. pap. 9.95 (*0-88010-380-9*) Anthroposophic.

Bayes, Ron, ed. see D'Ambrosi, Sybil, et al.

Bayes, Ronald. X-Ing Warm. 34p. (Orig.). 1968. pap. 2.00 (*0-932264-06-9*) Trask Hse Bks.

Bayes, Ronald H. Guises: A Chainsong for the Muse. 1993. pap. 12.95 (*1-880811-10-3*) North Lights.

Bayes, Ronald H., ed. see Flanagan, Roy K.

Bayes, Ronald H., ed. see Gurkin, Kathryn B.

Bayes, Ronald H., ed. see Land, E. Waverly.

Bayes, Ronald H., ed. see Miller, Rob H.

Bayes, Stephen. Avid Handbook: Basic & Intermediate Techniques for the Media Composer & MC Express. LC 98-2566. 232p. 1998. pap. text 34.95 (*0-240-80347-7*) Buttrwrth-Heinemann.

***Bayes, Steve.** The Avid Handbook: Techniques for the Avid Media Composer & Avid Xpress. 3rd ed. (Illus.). 248p. 2000. pap. 34.95 (*0-240-80404-X*, Focal) Buttrwrth-Heinemann.

Bayes, Steve. The Avid Handbook Techniques for the Avid Media Composer & Avid Xpress. LC 99-11774. 235p. 1999. pap. 34.95 (*0-240-80391-4*, Focal) Buttrwrth-Heinemann.

Bayet, Albert. Le Suicide et la Morale: Suicide & Morality. LC 74-25739. (European Sociology Ser.). 830p. 1975. reprint ed. 66.95 (*0-405-06495-0*) Ayer.

Bayevsky, David. Parapushkinistika. 3rd expanded ed. LC 98-38469. (RUS., Illus.). (Orig.). 1999. pap. 15.00 (*0-916201-23-6*) M I P Co.

***Bayfield, James E.** Quantum Evolution: An Introduction to Time-Dependent Quantum Mechanics. LC 98-53673. 386p. 1999. 99.95 (*0-471-18174-9*) Wiley.

Bayfield, M. A. A Study of Shakespeare's Versification. LC 77-130616. reprint ed. 39.50 (*0-404-00695-7*) AMS Pr.

Baygan, Lee. Makeup for Theatre, Film & Television: A Step by Step Photographic Guide. LC 81-1911. (Illus.). 208p. 1982. spiral bd. 29.95 (*0-89676-093-6*, Drama Pubs) QSMG Ltd.

Bayh, Birch. One Heartbeat Away: Presidential Disability & Succession. LC 68-28241. 1968. pap. 5.80 (*0-672-51385-4*, Bobbs) Macmillan.

Bayha, Franklin H., jt. auth. see Karger, Delmar W.

Bayhaqi, Al-Imam. The Seventy-Seven Branches of Faith. 66p. 1996. pap. 8.95 (*0-614-21344-4*, 1122) Kazi Pubns.

Bayhi, F. J. Then Comes the Morning. 1986. pap. 20.00 (*0-614-30819-4*, BTHENC) Claitors.

Bayindir-Upmann, Thorsten. Fiscal Policy & Enviromental Welfare: Modelling Interjurisdictional Competition. LC 97-44512. (New Horizons in Environmental Economics Ser.). 160p. 1998. 70.00 (*1-85898-738-5*) E Elgar.

Bayizian, Elise A. Mesrob Mashtotz: A Fifth Century Life. (Armenian Church Classics Ser.). (Illus.). 39p. (Orig.). 1984. pap. 4.00 (*0-934728-14-3*) D O A C.

Bayizian, Elise A., tr. see Verneuil, Henri.

***Baykut, D. & Krian, A.** Current Perspectives of the Extracorporeal Circulation. viii, 136p. 2000. pap. (*3-7985-1214-0*) D Steinkopff.

Bayle, Antoine L. Traite des Maladies du Cerveau et de Ses Membranes: Maladies Mentales. LC 75-16682. (Classics in Psychiatry Ser.). (FRE.). 1976. reprint ed. 51.95 (*0-405-07414-X*) Ayer.

Bayle, Francis & Rohden, Peter R. Les Idees Politiques de Joseph de Maistre & Joseph de Maistre als Politischer Theoretiker, 2 vols. Mayer, J. P., ed. LC 78-67331. (European Political Thought Ser.). (FRE & GER.). 1979. reprint ed. lib. bdg. 35.95 (*0-405-11677-2*) Ayer.

Bayle, Pierre. Bayle: Political Writings. Jenkinson, Sally L., ed. LC 98-43279. (Cambridge Texts in the History of Political Thought Ser.). 410p. (C). 1999. 64.95 (*0-521-47094-3*) Cambridge U Pr.

— Bayle: Political Writings. Jenkinson, Sally L., ed. (Cambridge Texts in the History of Political Thought Ser.). 410p. (C). 1999. pap. 24.95 (*0-521-47677-1*) Cambridge U Pr.

— Dictionnaire Historique et Critique: Amsterdam Edition of 1740. (FRE.). 3720p. 1995. reprint ed. 2995.00 (*0-7859-9942-6*) Fr & Eur.

— Historical & Critical Dictionary: Selections. Popkin, Richard H., tr. LC 64-16703. (Orig.). 1965. pap. 11.50 (*0-672-60406-X*, LLA175, Bobbs) Macmillan.

— Historical & Critical Dictionary: Selections. Popkin, Richard H., tr. from FRE. & intro. by. LC 90-5246. 512p. (Orig.). 1991. reprint ed. pap. text 16.95 (*0-87220-103-1*); reprint ed. lib. bdg. 37.95 (*0-87220-104-X*) Hackett Pub.

— Historisches und Critisches Worterbuch, 4 vols., Set. cxxviii, 3459p. 1978. reprint ed. 1265.00 (*3-487-04790-X*) G Olms Pubs.

— Oeuvres Diverses, 5 vols., Set. 1990. reprint ed. 2225.00 (*3-487-05456-6*) G Olms Pubs.

— Oeuvres Diverses Nos. 1-4: DenHaag 1727-1731: Volumes Supplementaires aux Oeuvres Diverses: Choix d'Articles du Dictionnaire Historique et Critique. cxxii, 5103p. 1982. reprint ed. 915.00 (*3-487-07223-8*) G Olms Pubs.

***Bayle, Pierre.** Various Thoughts on the Occasion of a Comet. Bartlett, Robert C., tr. LC 00-22910. (C). 2000. text 78.50 (*0-7914-4547-X*); pap. text 26.95 (*0-7914-4548-8*) State U NY Pr.

Baylen, Joseph O. & Conway, Alan, eds. Soldier-Surgeon: The Crimean War Letters of Dr. Douglas A. Reid, 1855-1856. LC 67-21109. (Illus.). 168p. reprint ed. 52.10 (*0-8357-9765-1*, 201617100098) Bks Demand.

Bayler, Bob, jt. auth. see Bayler, Lavon.

Bayler, Bob, jt. ed. see Bayler, Lavon.

Bayler, Lavon. Fresh Winds of the Spirit Bk. 2: Liturgical Resources for Year A. LC 86-21191. 120p. (Orig.). 1992. pap. 15.95 (*0-8298-0927-9*) Pilgrim OH.

— Gathered by Love: Worship Resources for Year C. LC 94-35081. 344p. (Orig.). 1994. pap. 16.95 (*0-8298-1008-0*) Pilgrim OH.

— Led by Love: Worship Resources for Year B. LC 95-51672. 344p. (Orig.). 1996. pap. 16.95 (*0-8298-1124-9*) Pilgrim OH.

Bayler, Lavon & Bayler, Bob. When We Pray: A Prayer Journal for Pastors & Worship Leaders Year A. LC 94-39950. 136p. (Orig.). 1995. pap. 16.95 (*0-8298-1103-6*) Pilgrim OH.

— When We Pray: A Prayer Journal for Pastors & Worship Leaders Year B. LC 94-39950. 120p. (Orig.). 1995. pap. 16.95 (*0-8298-1028-5*) Pilgrim OH.

Bayler, Lavon & Bayler, Bob, eds. When We Pray: A Prayer Journal for Pastors & Worship Leaders Year C, Year C. 120p. (Orig.). 1997. pap. 16.95 (*0-8298-1159-1*) Pilgrim OH.

Bayles, Allison L. Essence of Religion. LC 93-1611. 80p. (Orig.). 1993. pap. 5.95 (*1-880090-08-2*) Galde Pr.

Bayles, David & Orland, Ted. Art & Fear: Observations on the Perils (And Rewards) of Artmaking. LC 93-27573. 122p. (Orig.). 1994. pap. 12.95 (*0-88496-379-9*) Capra Pr.

Bayles, Debora L. Extranets: Building the Business to Business Web. LC 97-39018. 368p. (C). 1997. pap. 39.95 incl. cd-rom (*0-13-650912-6*) P-H.

***Bayles, Deborah L. & Bhatia, Hamir.** E-Commerce Logistics & E-Fulfillment. 300p. 2000. pap. 44.99 (*0-13-030328-3*) P-H.

Bayles, Deborah L., jt. auth. see Borich, Gary D.

Bayles, Doris J. The Sea Maiden. 410p. mass mkt. 5.99 (*1-896329-08-X*) Picasso Publ.

Bayles, Ernest E., et al. Education for a Learning Society. (NSCTE Monographs). 1969. 10.00 (*0-933669-02-X*) Soc Profs Ed.

Bayles, F. P., jt. auth. see Bayles, H. G.

Bayles, H. G. & Bayles, F. P. Bayles Families of Long Island & N. J., & Their Descendants: Also Ancestors of James Bayles & Julia Halsey Day. 270p. 1994. reprint ed. lib. bdg. 52.00 (*0-8328-4295-8*) Higginson Bk Co.

Bayles, Kathryn A. & Tomoeda, Cheryl K. The ABCs of Dementia. (Orig.). 1993. pap. text 35.00 (*0-9639381-1-8*) Canyonlnds Pubng.

— The Functional Linguistic Communication Inventory. (Illus.). (C). 1994. teacher ed. 125.00 (*0-9639381-0-X*) Canyonlnds Pubng.

— Improving Function in Dementia & Other Cognitive-Linguistic Disorders: A Guide & Resource Book. (Illus.). (C). 1997. pap. text 79.00 (*0-9639381-3-4*) Canyonlnds Pubng.

Bayles, Kathryn A., et al. Communication & Cognition in Normal Aging & Dementia. LC 90-21692. 400p. (Orig.). (C). 1987. pap. text 36.00 (*0-89079-330-1*, 1606) PRO-ED.

Bayles, M. D. Contemporary Utilitarianism. 1990. 16.50 (*0-8446-5627-5*) Peter Smith.

Bayles, Martha. Hole in Our Soul: The Loss of Beauty & Meaning in American Popular Music. 452p. 1994. 24.95 (*0-02-901962-1*) Free Pr.

Bayles, Martha, ed. Hole in Our Soul: The Loss of Beauty & Meaning in American Popular Music. 461p. 1996. reprint ed. pap. 16.95 (*0-226-03959-5*) U Ch Pr.

Bayles, Michael D. Morality & Population Policy. LC 79-23965. 158p. 1980. pap. 49.00 (*0-608-05127-6*, 206568600005) Bks Demand.

— Principles of Law. 388p. 1989. pap. text 65.50 (*90-277-2413-X*, D Reidel) Kluwer Academic.

— Principles of Law: A Normative Analysis. LC 87-4542. (Law & Philosophy Library). 388p. 1987. lib. bdg. 159.50 (*90-277-2412-1*, D Reidel) Kluwer Academic.

— Principles of Legislation: The Uses of Political Authority. LC 78-3220. 237p. reprint ed. pap. 73.50 (*0-608-16056-3*, 203318600084) Bks Demand.

— Procedural Justice. 276p. (C). 1990. lib. bdg. 148.50 (*0-7923-0567-1*, Pub. by Kluwer Academic) Kluwer Academic.

Bayles, Michael D., ed. Ethics & Population. 190p. 1976. 29.95 (*0-87073-405-9*) Transaction Pubs.

Bayles, Michael D. & Chapman, Bruce. Justice, Rights & Tort Law. 280p. 1983. text 120.50 (*90-277-1639-0*, D Reidel) Kluwer Academic.

Bayles, Michael D. & Henley, Kenneth. Right Conduct: Theories & Applications. 2nd ed. 432p. (C). 1988. pap. 43.44 (*0-07-553966-7*) McGraw.

Bayles, Patricia & Parks-Doyle, Jodi, eds. The Web of Inclusion: Faculty Helping Faculty. 153p. 1995. pap. 25.95 (*0-88737-642-8*) Natl League Nurse.

Bayles, Richard M. History of Windham County Connecticut. (Illus.). 1204p. 1998. reprint ed. lib. bdg. 119.00 (*0-8328-7054-4*) Higginson Bk Co.

Bayles, Richard M., ed. History of Newport County, Rhode Island. (Illus.). 1060p. 1992. reprint ed. lib. bdg. 100.00 (*0-8328-2254-X*) Higginson Bk Co.

— History of Richmond County (Staten Island) from Its Discovery to the Present Time (1887) (Illus.). 741p. 1997. reprint ed. lib. bdg. 76.00 (*0-8328-6213-4*) Higginson Bk Co.

Bayles, W. H. Old Taverns of New York. 1977. lib. bdg. 59.95 (*0-8490-2373-4*) Gordon Pr.

Bayless, jt. auth. see Johnson.

Bayless, A. Arleen, jt. compiled by see Herzog, Jill A.

Bayless, Allan E. Compact Sight Reduction Table: Modified H. O. 211, Ageton's Table. 2nd ed. LC 89-22126. (Illus.). 32p. 1989. pap. 6.00 (*0-87033-403-4*) Cornell Maritime.

Bayless, Arleen & Herzog, Jill, compiled by. Osage County Kansas Cemeteries & Old Soldiers & Obituaries. LC 96-105263. 669p. (Orig.). 1996. 76.00 (*0-943259-15-0*) Topeka Geneal Soc.

Bayless Behnken, Patricia A., see Behnken, Patricia A. Bayless.

Bayless, Deann G., jt. auth. see Bayless, Rick.

Bayless, Eileen. The Old Testament Condensed: From the Authorized King James Version. LC 96-79928. 288p. (Orig.). 1997. pap. 11.95 (*1-56167-345-5*) Am Literary Pr.

Bayless, George A. Marine Atlas Vol. I: Olympia to Malcolm Island. 12th rev. ed. (Illus.). 50p. 1997. write for info. (*0-9674750-0-7*, Pub. by Bayless Enter Inc) Fish Supply.

— Marine Atlas Vol. II: Port Hardy to Skagway. 12th rev. ed. (Illus.). 50p. 1997. write for info. (*0-9674750-1-5*, Pub. by Bayless Enter Inc) Fish Supply.

Bayless, Kathleen. Music: A Way of Life for the Young Child. 4th ed. 288p. (C). 1990. pap. text 45.00 (*0-675-21372-X*, Merrill Coll) P-H.

Bayless, Laura. The Edge of the Nest. (Illus.). 64p. (Orig.). 1992. pap. 8.00 (*0-9633978-0-X*) Fledgling Pr.

— White Streams & Touchstones. 76p. (Orig.). 1997. pap. 10.00 (*0-9633978-1-8*) Fledgling Pr.

Bayless, Martha. Parody in the Middle Ages: The Latin Tradition. LC 96-19030. 440p. (C). 1996. text 54.50 (*0-472-10649-X*, 10649) U of Mich Pr.

Bayless, Maureen. Howard's House Is Haunted. (J). 1993. pap. 4.50 (*0-590-74559-X*) Scholastic Inc.

— Strike! (Illus.). 24p. (J). (ps-3). 1994. pap. 5.95 (*0-921556-41-1*, Pub. by Gynergy-Ragweed) U of Toronto Pr.

Bayless, Raymond, jt. auth. see McAdams, Elizabeth.

***Bayless, Rick.** Mexico One Plate at a Time. 2000. 30.00 (*0-684-84186-X*) Scribner.

Bayless, Rick. Salsas That Cook: Using Classic Salsas to Enliven Our Favorite Dishes. (Illus.). 128p. 1998. pap. 18.00 (*0-684-85694-8*) S&S Trade.

Bayless, Rick & Bayless, Deann G. Authentic Mexican: Regional Cooking from the Heart of Mexico. Guarnaschelli, Maria D., ed. LC 86-12706. (Cookbook Library). (Illus.). 448p. 1987. 30.00 (*0-688-04394-1*, Wm Morrow) Morrow Avon.

— Rick Bayless's Mexican Kitchen: Recipes & Techniques of A World-Class Cuisine. LC 96-218444. (Illus.). 448p. 1996. 35.00 (*0-684-80006-3*) S&S Trade.

Bayless, Rose, ed. see Ezzex, E. Duke.

Bayless, Sharon, jt. auth. see Solomon, Ronni P.

Bayless, Sharon, jt. ed. see Solomon, Ronni P.

Bayless, Skip, intro. Sammy's Season. LC 98-47738. 112p. 1998. pap. 14.95 (*0-8092-2591-3*, 259130, Contemporary Bks) NTC Contemp Pub Co.

***Bayless, Theodore M. & Hanauer, Stephen B.** Advanced Therapy of Inflammatory Bowel Disease. 400p. 2000. 79.95 (*1-55009-122-0*) DEKR.

Bayless, Theodore M., jt. ed. see Paige, David M.

Bayless, Warren, ed. see Costa, Tom.

***Bayley, Barrington J.** Eye of Terror. 288p. 2000. per. 5.95 (*0-671-78390-4*) PB.

Bayley, C. A. Imperial Meridian: The British Empire & the World, 1780-1830. LC 88-8435. (Illus.). 312p. (Orig.). (C). 1989. pap. 40.06 (*0-582-49438-9*, 78189) Longman.

Bayley, C. S. Chiefs & Leading Families in Rajputana. (C). 1992. 16.00 (*81-85326-58-4*, Pub. by Vintage) S Asia.

Bayley, Charles C. Mercenaries for the Crimea: The German, Swiss, & Italian Legions in British Service, 1854-1856. LC 77-357169. 205p. reprint ed. pap. 63.60 (*0-608-12531-8*, 202385900034) Bks Demand.

Bayley, David H. Forces of Order: Police Behavior in Japan & the United States. LC 75-17304. 217p. reprint ed. pap. 67.30 (*0-608-17952-3*, 202903800058) Bks Demand.

— Forces of Order: Policing Modern Japan. rev. ed. LC 90-41028. 240p. 1991. pap. 16.95 (*0-520-07262-6*, Pub. by U CA Pr) Cal Prin Full Svc.

— A Model of Community Policing: The Singapore Story. (Illus.). 35p. 1996. reprint ed. pap. text 15.00 (*0-7881-2669-5*) DIANE Pub.

— Police for the Future. (Studies in Crime & Public Policy). 208p. 1996. pap. text 17.95 (*0-19-510458-7*) OUP.

— Social Control & Political Change. LC 86-201513. (Center for International Studies, Woodrow Wilson School of Public & International Affairs: Vol. 49). (Illus.). 139p. pap. 43.10 (*0-8357-7025-7*, 203337200085) Bks Demand.

— Social Control & Political Change. LC 86-201513. (Research Monograph: No. 49). 134p. 1985. 8.00 (*0-685-17694-0*) Princeton CIS.

Bayley, David H., ed. What Works in Policing? LC 97-16779. (Readings in Crime & Punishment Ser.). (Illus.). 256p. (C). 1997. text 50.00 (*0-19-510820-5*); pap. text 22.95 (*0-19-510821-3*) OUP.

Bayley, David H., et al. The Challenge of Community Policying: Testing the Promises. Rosenbaum, Dennis P., ed. LC 94-811. 1994. 54.00 (*0-8039-5443-3*); pap. 24.50 (*0-8039-5444-1*) Sage.

Bayley, David H., jt. auth. see Skolnick, Jerome H.

Bayley, Edwin R. & Former Members of the Milwaukee Journal Staff. Ask Harvey, Pls. LC 94-13249. 1994. pap. 9.95 (*1-879483-20-3*) Prairie Oak Pr.

Bayley, Elizabeth W. Trauma Nursing: Comprehensive Curriculum. 1992. 52.50 (*0-86720-628-4*) Jones & Bartlett.

Bayley, Elizabeth W. & Turcke. Trauma Nursing: Comprehensive Curriculum. (Nursing Ser.). 1992. pap. 47.50 (*0-86720-331-5*) Jones & Bartlett.

Bayley, Elizabeth W. & Turcke, Susan A. A Comprehensive Curriculum for Trauma Nursing. 2nd rev. ed. (Illus.). 696p. Date not set. pap. text 55.00 (*0-935890-19-X*) Emerg Nurses IL.

Bayley, Elizabeth W., et al. Teaching Trauma Nursing. 2nd rev. ed. Date not set. ring bd. 45.00 (*0-935890-24-6*) Emerg Nurses IL.

Bayley, F. Bayley: The Bailleuls of Flanders & Bayleys of Willow Hall. 272p. 1992. reprint ed. pap. 43.00 (*0-8328-2630-8*); reprint ed. lib. bdg. 53.00 (*0-8328-2629-4*) Higginson Bk Co.

Bayley, Frank W., ed. see Dunlap, William.

Bayley, Gordon. Local Government: Is It Manageable? 1979. 58.00 (*0-08-024279-0*, Pub. by Pergamon Repr) Franklin.

Bayley, H., et al, eds. Biomolecular Materials by Design Vol. 330: Materials Research Society Symposium Proceedings. LC 94-26494. 341p. 1994. text 30.00 (*1-55899-229-4*) Materials Res.

Bayley, Harold. The Hidden Symbols of the Rosicrucians. 1989. reprint ed. pap. 6.95 (*1-55818-118-0*, Sure Fire) Holmes Pub.

— The Lost Language of Symbolism, Vol. 1. (Illus.). 388p. 1988. reprint ed. pap. 10.95 (*0-8065-1100-1*, Citadel Pr) Carol Pub Group.

— The Lost Language of Symbolism, Vol. 2. 1990. pap. 10.95 (*0-8065-1163-X*, Citadel Pr) Carol Pub Group.

— A New Light on the Renaissance Displayed in Contemporary Emblems. LC 67-23851. (Illus.). 288p. 1972. reprint ed. 24.95 (*0-405-08244-4*, Pub. by Blom Pubns) Ayer.

— Tragedy of Sir Francis Bacon. LC 70-133281. (English Biography Ser.: No. 31). 1970. reprint ed. lib. bdg. 75.00 (*0-8383-1180-6*) M S G Haskell Hse.

Bayley, James E. Aspects of Relativism: Moral, Cognitive & Literary. 178p. (Orig.). (C). 1992. lib. bdg. 44.50 (*0-8191-8597-3*) U Pr of Amer.

Bayley, John. Elegy for Iris. LC 98-40895. 288p. 1998. text 22.95 (*0-312-19864-7*) St Martin.

— Elegy for Iris. LC 99-48446. 288p. 2000. pap. 13.00 (*0-312-25382-6*, Picador USA) St Martin.

— Elegy for Iris. 1999. 28.95 (*0-7838-8564-4*) Thorndike Pr.

— Housman's Poems. 208p. 1992. text 60.00 (*0-19-811763-9*) OUP.

***Bayley, John.** Iris & Her Friends: A Memoir of Memory & Desire. LC 99-33124. 256p. 1999. 22.95 (*0-393-04856-X*) Norton.

— Iris & Her Friends: A Memoir of Memory & Desire. large type ed. LC 00-20354. (Biography Ser.). 2000. 26.95 (*0-7862-2473-8*, MML06500-171753) Thorndike Pr.

— Iris & Her Friends: A Memoir of Memory & Desire. 288p. 2000. reprint ed. pap. 13.95 (*0-393-32079-0*) Norton.

Bayley, John. Leo Tolstoy. (Writers & Their Work Ser.). 95p. (Orig.). 1996. pap. text 17.00 (*0-7463-0744-6*, Pub. by Northcote House) U Pr of Miss.

— The Red Hat. LC 98-10249. 224p. 1998. text 21.95 (*0-312-18658-4*) St Martin.

Bayley, John, ed. see Hardy, Thomas.

Bayley, John, ed. see Tolstoy, Leo.

Bayley, John, ed. & intro. see James, Henry.

Bayley, John B., ed. see Letarouilly, Paul.

Bayley, John O. Tolstoy & the Novel. iv, 320p. 1999. pap. 16.95 (*0-226-03960-9*) U Ch Pr.

Bayley, Lesley. Competitors Handbook. LC 97-177064. (Illus.). 176p. 1997. 29.95 (*0-7063-7393-6*, Pub. by WrLock) Sterling.

Bayley, Lesley & Davis, Caroline. The Less Than Perfect Rider: Overcoming Common Riding Problems. LC 93-33471. (Illus.). 160p. 1994. per. 29.95 (*0-87605-976-0*) Howell Bks.

Bayley, Lesley & Maxwell, Richard. Understanding Your Horse: How to Overcome Common Behaviour Problems. (Illus.). 160p. 1997. 27.50 (*1-57076-073-X*, Trafalgar Sq Pub) Trafalgar.

Bayley, Marianne. For Better, for Worse. large type ed. (Linford Romance Library). 288p. 1997. pap. 16.99 (*0-7089-5028-0*, Linford) Ulverscroft.

Bayley, Michael. Caer Sidhe Vol. I: The Celtic Night Sky. 22.95 (*1-86163-014-X*) Holmes Pub.

Bayley, Michael. Caer Sidhe Vol. II: The Celtic Night Sky. (Orig.). 1999. pap. 22.95 (*1-86163-020-4*, Pub. by Capall Bann Pubng) Holmes Pub.

— Celtic Astrology & Astronomy Vol. I: Caer Sidhe. (Orig.). 1997. pap. 22.95 (*1-898307-74-1*, Pub. by Capall Bann Pubng) Holmes Pub.

Bayley, Michael. Kecks, Keddles & Kesh: Celtic Language & the Cog Almanac. 1997. pap. 22.95 (*1-898307-62-8*, Pub. by Capall Bann Pubng) Holmes Pub.

Bayley, Monica. Black Africa Cookbook. (Illus.). 1977. reprint ed. pap. 2.50 (*0-915696-04-5*) Determined Prods.

— Pacific Islands Cook Book. (Illus.). (Orig.). 1977. pap. 2.50 (*0-915696-05-3*) Determined Prods.

Bayley, Monica, text. The Snoopy Omnibus of Fun Facts from the Snoopy Fun Fact Calendars. LC 82-71285. (Illus.). (J). 1983. 6.95 (*0-915696-54-1*); pap. 4.95 (*0-915696-81-9*) Determined Prods.

Bayley, Monica & Perl, Susan. Susan Perl's Park Peepl. LC 81-67306. (Illus.). 7.95 (*0-915696-25-8*) Determined Prods.

Bayley, Nancy. Development of Motor Abilities During the First Three Years. (SRCD M Ser.: Vol. 1, No. 1). 1935. pap. 25.00 (*0-527-01486-9*) Periodicals Srv.

Bayley, Nancy, jt. auth. see Bayer, Leona.

***Bayley, Nicola.** Canciones Tontas. 1998. pap. text 11.00 (*84-264-3566-1*) Editorial Lumen.

Bayley, Nicola. Copycats. LC 91-58722. (Illus.). 96p. (J). (ps up). 1992. 14.95 (*1-56402-114-9*) Candlewick Pr.

— The Necessary Cat: A Celebration of Cats in Picture & Word. LC 97-46491. (Illus.). 80p. (J). (gr. 3-7). 1998. 17.99 (*0-7636-0571-9*) Candlewick Press.

Bayley, P. York Notes: ABC of Shakespeare. (C). 1988. pap. text 9.95 (*0-582-02250-9*) Moonbeam Pubns.

Bayley, Peter M., jt. ed. see Taylor, W. R.

Bayley, Robert & Preston, Dennis R., eds. Second Language Acquisition & Linguistic Variation. (Studies in Bilingualism: No. 10). xix, 317p. 1996. pap. 29.95 (*1-55619-734-9*) J Benjamins Pubng Co.

Bayley, Roberta, jt. auth. see Bockris, Victor.

Bayley, Ruth. Jesus the Counselor. 1993. pap. 6.95 (*1-55673-584-7*, 7983) CSS OH.

Bayley, S. C. & Sheeler, Willard D. Foundations for Reading & Writing, Bk. 3 & 4. Evans, A. R., ed. (Welcome to English Ser.). (Illus.). 1978. student ed. 3.45 (*0-89285-035-3*) ELS Educ Servs.

— Foundations for Reading & Writing, Bk. 4. Evans, A. R., ed. (Welcome to English Ser.). (Illus.). 1978. 3.45 (*0-89285-036-1*) ELS Educ Servs.

***Bayley, Stephen.** General Knowledge. 288p. 2000. pap. 29.95 (*1-86154-068-X*, Pub. by Booth-Clibborn) Dist Art Pubs.

Bayley, Stephen. Harley Earl. (Design Heroes Ser.). (Illus.). 160p. 1991. 24.95 (*0-8008-3802-5*) Taplinger.

— In Good Shape. 256p. (C). 1979. pap. text 50.00 (*0-85072-096-6*) St Mut.

Bayley, Susan C. Our Man Sam: Making the Most Out of Life with Muscular Dystrophy. 112p. 1998. pap. 9.95 (*0-9667440-0-4*) S Bayle.

Bayley, Thomas, et al. Sailing Ships: A Lift-the-Flap Discovery. LC 97-12373. 18p. (J). 1998. 16.95 (*0-531-30065-X*) Orchard Bks Watts.

Bayley, Victor. Adventure Through Khyber. (C). 1988. 39.00 (*81-212-0142-X*, Pub. by Gian Publng Hse) S Asia.

Baylies, Francis. An Historical Memoir of the Colony of New Plymouth... 1608 to 1692, 2 vols. LC 75-31110. reprint ed. 195.00 (*0-404-13630-3*) AMS Pr.

— History of the Northwest Coast. 170p. 1986. pap. 11.95 (*0-87770-384-1*) Ye Galleon.

Baylin, DeFrank, et al. The MMDS (Wireless Cable) Installation Manual. (Illus.). 326p. 1996. pap. 40.00 (*0-917893-28-X*) Baylin Pubns.

Baylin, E. N. Functional Modeling of Systems. xxviii, 438p. 1990. pap. text 176.00 (*2-88124-731-8*) Gordon & Breach.

Baylin, Eric. The Guru Gita: An Introduction. LC 97-67959. 62p. 1997. pap. 4.75 (*0-911307-58-3*) SYDA Found.

Baylin, Frank. Digital Satellite Television: Theory, Installation & Repair. 5th ed. (Illus.). 480p. (Orig.). 1997. pap. 50.00 (*0-917893-22-0*) Baylin Pubns.

— Install, Aim & Repair Your Satellite TV System. 2nd ed. (Illus.). 64p. 1992. pap. 10.00 (*0-917893-16-6*) Baylin Pubns.

B

An Asterisk (*) at the beginning of an entry indicates that the title is appearing for the first time.

— Miniature Satellite Dishes: The New Digital Television. 2nd ed. (Illus.). 128p. 1995. pap. text 20.00 (*0-917893-24-7*) Baylin Pubns.

— 1997 World Satellite Yearly Update. (Illus.). 160p. (Orig.). 1997. pap. 60.00 (*0-917893-30-1*) Baylin Pubns.

— 1996/97 World Satellite Yearly. (Illus.). 1996. 90.00 (*0-917893-26-3*) Baylin Pubns.

Baylin, Frank. World Satellite Yearly, 1998/2000. 864p. 1999. pap. 90.00 (*0-917893-32-8*) Baylin Pubns.

Baylin, Frank & Borkoff, Steve. Wireless Cable & SMATV. (Illus.). 386p. 1992. 50.00 (*0-917893-17-4*) Baylin Pubns.

Baylin, Frank & Gale, Brent. Home Satellite TV Installation & Troubleshooting Manual. 5th rev. ed. 326p. 1993. pap. 30.00 (*0-917893-31-X*) Baylin Pubns.

— Satellite & Cable TV: Scrambling & Descrambling. 2nd rev. ed. (Illus.). 272p. (Orig.). 1988. pap. text 20.00 (*0-917893-07-7*) Baylin Pubns.

Baylin, Frank, et al. World Satellite TV & Scrambling Methods: The Technicians' Handbook. 3rd ed. (Illus.). 362p. (Orig.). 1993. pap. 40.00 (*0-917893-19-0*) Baylin Pubns.

Baylin, Frank, jt. auth. see Dye, Steve.

Baylis, Albert H. From Creation to the Cross: Understanding the First Half of the Bible. 288p. 1996. boxed set 24.99 (*0-310-49080-4*) Zondervan.

B

Baylis, Bayard, et al. Elementary Statistics: A Conceptual Approach Using a Spreadsheet. 200p. (C). 1998. pap. text, mass mkt. 25.00 (*0-9666708-0-9*) Barge Canal.

Baylis, Bayard, jt. auth. see Pereira, Carlos.

Baylis, Bill. Tall Tales: Reading Level 2-3. LC 93-16084. (Timeless Tales Ser.). 1993. 4.95 (*0-88336-463-8*); audio 9.95 (*0-88336-544-8*) New Readers.

Baylis, Francoise, ed. see Freedman, Benjamin.

Baylis, Francoise C., ed. The Health Care Ethics Consultant. LC 94-13467. (Contemporary Issues in Biomedicine, Ethics, & Society Ser.). 224p. 1994. text 49.50 (*0-89603-278-7*) Humana.

Baylis, H. A. Nematoda: Ascaroidea & Strongyloidea. (Fauna of British India Ser.). xxxvi, 416p. 1978. reprint ed. 30.00 (*0-88065-051-6*) Scholarly Pubns.

— Nematoda: Filaricidea, Dictophymoidea & Trichinelloidea, Vol. 2. (Fauna of British India Ser.). xxviii, 280p. 1978. reprint ed. 30.00 (*0-88065-052-4*) Scholarly Pubns.

Baylis, Janice. Sleep on It! The Practical Side of Dreaming. LC 77-74164. 254p. 1977. pap. 10.00 (*0-917738-04-7*) Sun Man Moon.

Baylis, Janice F. Personal Dream Journal. (Illus.). 1977. student ed. 4.00 (*0-917738-01-2*) Sun Man Moon.

Baylis, Janice H. Sex, Symbols & Dreams. LC 96-93018. (Illus.). 242p. (Orig.). 1997. pap. 17.00 (*0-917738-05-5*) Sun Man Moon.

Baylis, John. Ambiguity & Deterrence: British Nuclear Strategy, 1945-1964. LC 95-30526. (Nuclear History Program Ser.). 508p. 1996. text 89.00 (*0-19-828012-2*, Clarendon Pr) OUP.

— Anglo-American Relations since 1939. LC 96-44100. 224p. 1997. text 24.95 (*0-7190-4779-X*, Pub. by Manchester Univ Pr) St Martin.

— The Diplomacy of Pragmatism: Britain & the Formation of NATO, 1942-1949. LC 92-5602. (American Diplomatic History Ser.: No. 5). 208p. 1993. 35.00 (*0-87338-471-7*) Kent St U Pr.

***Baylis, John & O'Neill, Robert John, eds.** Alternative Nuclear Futures: The Role of Nuclear Weapons in the Post-cold War World. LC 99-45061. 272p. 2000. 60.00 (*0-19-829624-X*) OUP.

Baylis, John & Rengger, N. J., eds. Dilemmas of World Politics: International Issues in a Changing World. 456p. 1992. 75.00 (*0-19-827351-7*); pap. text 24.95 (*0-19-827350-9*) OUP.

Baylis, John & Smith, Steve, eds. The Globalization of World Politics: An Introduction to International Relations. LC 96-24110. (Illus.). 554p. 1997. pap. text 31.95 (*0-19-878109-1*) OUP.

— The Globalization of World Politics: An Introduction to International Relations. LC 96-24110. (Illus.). 554p. (C). 1997. text 92.00 (*0-19-878108-3*) OUP.

Baylis, John, et al. Contemporary Strategy No. II. 2nd rev. ed. LC 86-22872. 250p. (C). 1987. 34.00 (*0-8419-1019-7*); pap. 17.95 (*0-8419-1020-0*) Holmes & Meier.

Baylis, Maggie & Castle, Coralie. Real Bread: A Fearless Guide to Making It. 2nd ed. LC 92-30790. (One Hundred One Productions Ser.). (Illus.). 240p. 1993. reprint ed. pap. 11.95 (*1-56426-554-4*, One Hund One Prods) Cole Group.

Baylis, Peter H. & Padfield, Paul L., eds. The Posterior Pituitary: Hormone Secretion in Health & Disease. LC 85-16315. (Basic & Clinical Endocrinology Ser.: No. 6). (Illus.). 411p. reprint ed. pap. 127.50 (*0-7837-0865-3*, 204117300019) Bks Demand.

Baylis, Robert. Ephesians: Living in God's Household. LC 76-43523. (Fisherman Bible Studyguide Ser.). 45p. 1976. pap. 4.99 (*0-87788-223-1*, H Shaw Pubs) Waterbrook Pr.

Baylis, Robert H. My People: The Story of Those Christians Sometimes Called Plymouth Brethren. LC 95-41247. 336p. 1995. pap. 24.99 (*0-87788-577-X*, H Shaw Pubs) Waterbrook Pr.

Baylis, Thomas A. The West & Eastern Europe: Economic Statecraft & Political Change. LC 93-14139. 256p. 1993. 59.95 (*0-275-94676-2*, C4676, Praeger Pubs); pap. 22.95 (*0-275-94734-3*, Praeger Pubs) Greenwood.

Baylis, W. E. Electrodynamics a Modern Geometric Approach. LC 98-31155. 350p. 1998. 49.50 (*0-8176-4025-8*) Birkhauser.

Baylis, W. E. & Drake, G. W., eds. Atomic Physics 16: Sixteenth International Conference on Atomic Physics. (Conference Proceedings Ser.: Vol. 477). 432p. 1999. 120.00 (*1-56396-752-9*) Am Inst Physics.

Baylis, William E. Clifford (Geometric) Algebras with Applications to Physics, Mathematics & Engineering. LC 96-25142. 1996. write for info. (*3-7643-3868-7*) Birkhauser.

***Baylis, William E.** Electrodynamics: A Modern Geometric Approach LC 98-31155. (Progress in Physics Ser.). xv, 380p. 1999. write for info. (*3-7643-4025-8*) Birkhauser.

Baylis, William E. Theoretical Methods in the Physical Sciences: An Introduction to Problem Solving Using Maple V. (Illus.). xvii, 286p. 1994. 42.50 (*0-8176-3715-X*) Birkhauser.

Baylis, William E., ed. Clifford (Geometric) Algebras with Applications to Physics, Mathematics & Engineering. LC 96-25142. 517p. 1996. 59.50 (*0-8176-3868-7*) Birkhauser.

Bayliss. Anglo-American Relations since 1939. LC 96-44100. 224p. 1997. text 69.95 (*0-7190-4778-1*, Pub. by Manchester Univ Pr) St Martin.

— Electrical Transmission & Distribution. 2nd ed. 978p. 1999. text 155.00 (*0-7506-4059-6*, Newnes) Buttrwrth-Heinemann.

Bayliss, A. E., ed. Invitation to Verse: An Anthology. LC 72-167475. (Granger Index Reprint Ser.). 1977. reprint ed. 18.95 (*0-8369-6280-X*) Ayer.

Bayliss, Brian. The Measurement of Supply & Demand in Freight Transport. 140p. 1988. text 78.95 (*0-566-05526-0*, Pub. by Avebry) Ashgate Pub Co.

Bayliss, Brian T. Transport Policy & Planning: An Integrated Analytical Approach. (EDI Technical Materials Ser.). 79p. 1992. pap. 22.00 (*0-8213-1944-2*, 11944) World Bank.

Bayliss, Colin. Transmission & Distribution Electrical Engineering. LC 97-105442. (Illus.). 672p. 1999. text 155.00 (*0-7506-2287-3*) Buttrwrth-Heinemann.

Bayliss, Colin, ed. The Music of Sir Peter Maxwell Davies: An Annotated Catalogue. 304p. (C). 1991. text 80.00 (*0-948929-46-4*) St Mut.

Bayliss, D. A. & Chandler, K. A. Steelwork Corrosion Control. 458p. 1991. mass mkt. 178.50 (*1-85166-575-7*) Elsevier.

Bayliss, D. A., jt. auth. see Chandler, K. A.

Bayliss, J. S. Introduction to Coding Theory. LC 97-75115. 304p. 1997. ring bd. 39.95 (*0-412-78690-7*, Chap & Hall CRC) CRC Pr.

— Marketing for Engineers. (Management of Technology Ser.: No. 4). 391p. 1984. 45.00 (*0-86341-035-9*, MTO04Z) INSPEC Inc.

Bayliss, Jonathan. Gloucesterbook. 624p. 1992. 27.50 (*0-9625780-1-0*) Protean Pr.

— Gloucestertide. LC 95-72786. 665p. (Orig.). 1996. pap. 19.95 (*0-9625780-2-9*) Protean Pr.

— Prologos. unabridged ed. LC 98-74560. (Gloucesterman Ser.). 1091p. 1999. pap. 24.95 (*0-9667807-0-1*) Basilicum Pr.

Bayliss, P. F. Law Relating to Health Care Professions. (C). 1987. 135.00 (*0-901812-63-3*); pap. 100.00 (*0-7855-3753-8*) St Mut.

Bayliss, Paul W., ed. Intelligent Networks: The Path to Global Networking. LC 92-9945. xiv, 605p. 1992. 95.00 (*90-5199-091-X*, Pub. by IOS Pr) IOS Press.

***Bayliss, Peg.** Mom... Dad... This Is What I've Been Trying To Tell You: A Book for Kids to Read to Their Parents. (Illus.). 24p. (J). 1999. pap. 6.95 (*1-57543-078-9*) Mar Co Prods.

Bayliss, Peter, jt. see Ackland, Joss.

Bayliss, R. I. & Tunbridge, W. M. Thyroid Disease: The Facts. 3rd ed. LC 98-3834. (The Facts Ser.). (Illus.). 206p. 1998. pap. 19.95 (*0-19-262946-8*) OUP.

Bayliss-Smith, Timothy P. The Ecology of Agricultural Systems. 2nd ed. LC 82-1132. (Cambridge Topics in Geography Ser.: No. 2). (Illus.). 112p. 1982. pap. text 22.95 (*0-521-29829-6*) Cambridge U Pr.

Bayliss-Smith, Timothy P. & Feachem, Richard G., eds. Subsistence & Survival: Rural Ecology in the Pacific. 1978. text 220.00 (*0-12-083250-X*) Acad Pr.

Bayliss-Smith, Timothy P., et al. Islands, Islanders & the World: The Colonial & Post-Colonial Experience of Eastern Fiji. (Cambridge Human Geography Ser.). (Illus.). 352p. 1989. text 74.95 (*0-521-26877-X*) Cambridge U Pr.

Bayliss, Wyke. Five Great Painters of the Victorian Era: Leighton, Millais, Burne-Jones, Watts, Holman Hunt. LC 72-129384. (Illus.). reprint ed. 39.50 (*0-404-00696-5*) AMS Pr.

Baylon, Anne D. & Garlitski, Ania, eds. 1995 Timeline of Events: Central & Eastern Europe. (Timeline of Events Ser.). 62p. (Orig.). (C). Date not set. pap. 15.00 (*0-9631515-8-4*) Strategic Decisions.

Baylon, David, jt. auth. see Eklund, Ken.

Baylor. Math for Business. 632p. 1998. pap. text 45.71 (*0-536-01386-1*) Pearson Custom.

Baylor, Betty, ed. Rachmaninoff/Preludes, Op. 23. 64p. 1987. pap. 8.95 (*0-7390-0283-X*, 515) Alfred Pub.

Baylor, Byrd. Amigo. (J). 1963. 11.19 (*0-606-03982-1*, Pub. by Turtleback) Demco.

— Amigo. 2nd ed. (Illus.). 48p. (J). (ps-3). 1989. reprint ed. mass mkt. 5.99 (*0-689-71299-5*) Aladdin.

— And It Is Still That Way: Legends Told by Arizona Indian Children. (J). 1976. 13.05 (*0-606-04405-1*, Pub. by Turtleback) Demco.

— And It Is Still That Way: Legends Told by Arizona Indian Children. (J). (gr. k-6). 1998. reprint ed. pap. 8.95 (*0-938317-36-9*) Cinco Puntos.

— The Best Town in the World. LC 83-9033. (Illus.). 32p. (J). (gr. 1-3). 1983. 14.95 (*0-684-18035-9*) Scribner.

Baylor, Byrd. Best Town in the World. (J). 1986. 9.15 (*0-606-03181-2*, Pub. by Turtleback) Demco.

Baylor, Byrd. The Best Town in the World. LC 86-3381. (Illus.). 32p. (J). (gr. 1-3). 1986. reprint ed. mass mkt. 3.95 (*0-689-71086-0*) Aladdin.

— The Desert Is Theirs. LC 74-24417. (Illus.). 32p. (J). (ps-3). 1975. 15.00 (*0-684-14266-X*) Atheneum Yung Read.

— The Desert Is Theirs. 1981. 11.15 (*0-606-02085-3*, Pub. by Turtleback) Demco.

— The Desert Is Theirs. LC 86-17323. (Illus.). 32p. (J). (gr. 1-5). 1987. reprint ed. mass mkt. 5.95 (*0-689-71105-0*) Aladdin.

— Desert Voices. LC 80-17061. (Illus.). 32p. (J). (ps-3). 1981. 14.95 (*0-684-16712-3*) Scribner.

— Desert Voices. 1993. 11.15 (*0-606-02592-8*, Pub. by Turtleback) Demco.

— Desert Voices. LC 92-24475. (Illus.). 32p. (J). (gr. 1-5). 1993. reprint ed. mass mkt. 5.95 (*0-689-71691-5*) Aladdin.

— Everybody Needs a Rock. LC 74-9163. (Illus.). 32p. (J). (gr. k-3). 1985. pap. 5.99 (*0-689-71051-8*) Aladdin.

— Everybody Needs a Rock. LC 74-9163. (Illus.). 32p. (J). (ps-3). 1974. 16.00 (*0-684-13899-9*) Scribner.

— Everybody Needs a Rock. (J). 1985. 11.19 (*0-606-03333-5*, Pub. by Turtleback) Demco.

— Guess Who My Favorite Person Is. 2nd ed. LC 77-7151. (Illus.). 32p. (J). (gr. 1-4). 1992. text 14.95 (*0-684-19514-3*) Scribner.

— Halcon, Soy Tu Hermano. Mills, Tedi L., tr.Tr. of Hawk, I'm Your Brother. (SPA.). 48p. Date not set. 12.99 (*968-16-3652-X*, Pub. by Fondo) Continental Bk.

— Hawk, I'm Your Brother. LC 75-39296. (Illus.). 48p. (J). (ps-3). 1976. 16.00 (*0-684-14571-5*) Scribner.

— Hawk, I'm Your Brother. 1986. 10.15 (*0-606-03304-1*, Pub. by Turtleback) Demco.

— Hawk, I'm Your Brother. LC 86-10742. (Illus.). 48p. (J). (gr. 1-5). 1986. reprint ed. pap. 4.95 (*0-689-71102-6*) Aladdin.

— If You Are a Hunter of Fossils. LC 79-17926. (Illus.). 32p. (J). (gr. 3-6). 1984. mass mkt. 5.99 (*0-689-70773-8*) Aladdin.

— I'm in Charge of Celebrations. LC 85-19633. (Illus.). 32p. (J). (ps-3). 1986. 14.95 (*0-684-18579-2*) Scribner.

Baylor, Byrd. I'm in Charge of Celebrations. 1995. 11.19 (*0-606-07693-X*, Pub. by Turtleback) Demco.

Baylor, Byrd. Moon Song. LC 81-18427. (Illus.). 24p. (J). (gr. 3-6). 1982. lib. bdg. 13.95 (*0-684-17463-4*) Scribner.

— One Small Blue Bead. 2nd ed. LC 90-28160. (Illus.). 32p. (J). (gr. 2-5). 1992. 16.00 (*0-684-19334-5*) Scribner.

— The Other Way to Listen. 32p. 1997. per. 5.99 (*0-689-81053-9*) S&S Childrens.

— The Other Way to Listen. LC 78-23430. (Illus.). 32p. (J). (ps-3). 1978. 15.00 (*0-684-16017-X*) Scribner.

— Other Way to Listen. 1997. 11.19 (*0-606-13683-5*, Pub. by Turtleback) Demco.

— The Table Where Rich People Sit. (Illus.). 32p. (J). (gr. 1-4). 1998. per. 5.99 (*0-689-82008-9*) S&S Childrens.

— The Table Where Rich People Sit. 1998. 11.19 (*0-606-13832-3*, Pub. by Turtleback) Demco.

— The Way to Start a Day. LC 78-113. (Illus.). 32p. (J). (ps-3). 1978. 14.95 (*0-684-15651-2*) Scribner.

— Way to Start a Day. 1986. 10.15 (*0-606-00991-4*, Pub. by Turtleback) Demco.

— The Way to Start a Day. LC 85-28802. (Illus.). 32p. (J). (gr. 1-4). 1986. reprint ed. mass mkt. 4.95 (*0-689-71054-2*) Aladdin.

— When Clay Sings. (J). 1972. 11.19 (*0-606-02308-9*, Pub. by Turtleback) Demco.

— When Clay Sings. LC 86-20587. (Illus.). 32p. (J). (gr. 1-4). 1987. reprint ed. mass mkt. 5.99 (*0-689-71106-9*) Aladdin.

— When Clay Sings. LC 70-180758. (Illus.). 32p. (J). (ps-3). 1987. reprint ed. 16.00 (*0-684-18829-5*) Scribner.

— Yes Is Better Than No. (Illus.). 242p. 1991. reprint ed. pap. 9.95 (*0-918080-53-3*) Treas Chest Bks.

Baylor, George. Bull Run to Bull Run: Four Years in the Army of Northern Virginia. 1983. reprint ed. 35.00 (*0-89201-106-8*) Zenger Pub.

Baylor, George W. Into the Far Wild Country: True Tales of the Old Southwest. LC 96-60102. (Illus.). 450p. 1996. 35.00 (*0-87404-237-2*) Tex Western.

Baylor, Henry B., jt. auth. see Baylor, O. W.

Baylor, Lavon. Taught by Love: Worship Resources for Year A. LC 97-44052. 368p. (Orig.). 1998. pap. 16.95 (*0-8298-1235-0*) Pilgrim OH.

Baylor, Michael G., ed. The Radical Reformation. (Cambridge Texts in the History of Political Thought Ser.). 334p. (C). 1991. pap. text 19.95 (*0-521-37948-2*) Cambridge U Pr.

Baylor, Michael G., ed. Revelation & Revolution: Basic Writings of Thomas Muntzer. LC 91-58965. 1993. 39.50 (*0-934223-16-5*) Lehigh Univ Pr.

Baylor, Murray, ed. Satie - 3 Gymnopedies & 3 Gnossiennes. (Alfred Masterwork Edition Ser.). 24p. 1985. pap. 6.95 (*0-7390-0692-4*, 2501) Alfred Pub.

Baylor, O. W. & Baylor, Henry B. Baylor. History of the Baylors: Collection of Records & Important Family Data. 48p. 1997. reprint ed. pap. 12.00 (*0-8328-7431-0*); reprint ed. lib. bdg. 22.00 (*0-8328-7430-2*) Higginson Bk Co.

Baylor, Robert & Moore, James, eds. In the Presence of This Continent: American Themes & Ideas. LC 75-130653. 1971. pap. text 16.95 (*0-03-084397-9*) Irvington.

Baylor, Ronald G. Governmental Immunity in Michigan. LC 91-73441. 250p. 1991. ring bd. 95.00 (*0-685-51911-2*, 91-020) U MI Law CLE.

— Governmental Immunity in Michigan. LC 91-73441. 250p. 1992. suppl. ed. 45.00 (*0-685-59116-6*, 92-026) U MI Law CLE.

Baylor University Staff. Homecoming: Special Foods, Special Memories. LC 94-71086. 1994. 16.95 (*0-9640969-0-0*) Baylor U Alumni.

Bayly, A. C. Origins of Nationality in South Asia: Patriotism & Ethical Government in the Making of Modern India. LC 99-932096. 350p. 1999. text 35.00 (*0-19-564457-3*) OUP.

Bayly, Anselm. The Alliance of Musick, Poetry & Oratory. (Anglistica & Americana Ser.: Vol. 108). vi, 384p. 1989. reprint ed. 80.00 (*3-487-09068-6*) G Olms Pubs.

— An Introduction to Languages: Literary & Philosophical. (Works of Anselm Bayly). 188p. 1985. reprint ed. lib. bdg. 59.00 (*0-932051-65-0*) Rprt Serv.

Bayly, Brian. Chemical Change in Deforming Material. (Oxford Monographs on Geology & Geophysics: No. 21). (Illus.). 256p. 1993. text 90.00 (*0-19-506764-9*) OUP.

Bayly, C. A. Empire & Information: Intelligence Gathering & Social Communication in India, 1780-1870. LC 96-13146. (Cambridge Studies in Indian History & Society: No. 1). 426p. (C). 1997. text 69.95 (*0-521-57085-9*) Cambridge U Pr.

***Bayly, C. A.** Empire & Information: Intelligence Gathering & Social Communication in India, 1780-1870. (Cambridge Studies in Indian History & Society: No. 1). (Illus.). 426p. (C). 1999. pap. 27.95 (*0-521-66360-1*) Cambridge U Pr.

Bayly, C. A. Indian Society & the Making of the British Empire. (New Cambridge History of India Ser.: II: 1). (Illus.). 248p. 1988. text 59.95 (*0-521-25092-7*) Cambridge U Pr.

— Indian Society & the Making of the British Empire. (New Cambridge History of India Ser.: II: 1). (Illus.). 241p. (C). 1990. pap. text 22.95 (*0-521-38650-0*) Cambridge U Pr.

— The Raj: India & the British, 1600-1947. (Illus.). 432p. 1994. 95.00 (*1-55859-848-0*) Abbeville Pr.

Bayly, C. A. Ruler, Townsmen & Bazaars: North Indian Society in the Age of British Expansion 1770-1870. (Oxford India Paperbacks Ser.). (Illus.). 530p. 1994. pap. text 14.95 (*0-19-562876-4*) OUP.

Bayly, C. A. & Kolff, Dirk H., eds. Two Colonial Empires. 1986. lib. bdg. 139.00 (*90-247-3274-3*) Kluwer Academic.

Bayly, C.A. Rulers, Townsmen & Bazaars: North Indian Society in the Age of British Expansion 1770-1870. (Illus.). 530p. 1998. pap. text (*0-19-564398-4*) OUP.

Bayly, Clifford. Basic Drawing Techniques. (Understand How to Draw Ser.: No. 1). (Illus.). 32p. pap. 4.95 (*0-85532-570-4*, Pub. by Srch Pr) A Schwartz & Co.

Bayly, Doreen E. Reflexology Today: The Stimulation of the Body's Healing Forces Through Foot Massage. 64p. 1984. pap. 9.95 (*0-89281-284-2*) Inner Tradit.

Bayly, I. A. Guides to the Identification of Microinvertebrates of the Continental Waters of the World Vol. 2: The Non-Marine Centropagidae (Copepoda: Calanoida) of the World. Dumont, H. J., ed. (Illus.). iv, 30p. 1992. pap. 25.00 (*90-5103-075-4*, Pub. by SPB Acad Pub) Balogh.

***Bayly, Ian.** Rock of Ages: Human Use & Natural History of Australian Granites. (Illus.). 144p. 1999. 45.00 (*1-876268-19-0*, Pub. by Univ of West Aust Pr); pap. 34.95 (*1-876268-29-8*, Pub. by Univ of West Aust Pr) Intl Spec Bk.

Bayly, Jaime. No Se lo Digas a Nadie (Don't Say Anything) 1997. pap. 12.95 (*84-322-1503-1*, Pub. by E Seix Barral) Continental Bk.

— Ultimos Dias de La Prensa.Tr. of Last Days of the Press. (SPA.). 1997. pap. 20.95 (*84-322-4757-X*, Pub. by E Seix Barral) Continental Bk.

Bayly, Joseph. The Gospel Blimp...& Other Modern Parables. LC 83-70533. 128p. 1992. pap. 6.99 (*0-7814-0935-7*, LifeJourney) Chariot Victor.

— Heaven: What Would It Be Like to Talk to God about Heaven. 24p. 1993. pap. 5.99 (*1-55513-325-8*, LifeJourney) Chariot Victor.

— The Last Thing We Talk About: Help & Hope for Those Who Grieve. LC 92-12678. 128p. 1992. pap. text 6.99 (*0-7814-0048-1*, LifeJourney) Chariot Victor.

— Psalms of My Life. LC 59-93301. 128p. 1992. pap. 6.99 (*0-7814-0933-0*, LifeJourney) Chariot Victor.

***Bayly, Joseph.** Psalms of My Life. LC 99-41106. 80p. 2000. 12.99 (*1-56476-785-X*) SP Pubns.

— A Voice in the Wilderness. LC 99-39738. 360p. 2000. pap. 12.99 (*1-56476-787-6*) SP Pubns.

Bayly, Lewis. The Practice of Piety. 343p. 1994. reprint ed. 24.95 (*1-877611-66-2*) Soli Deo Gloria.

Bayly, M. Brian. Mechanics in Structural Geology. (Illus.). 224p. 1991. 87.95 (*0-387-97615-9*); 52.95 (*0-387-97652-3*) Spr-Verlag.

Bayly, Rich, jt. ed. see Larue, Gerald A.

***Bayly, Susan.** Caste, Society & Politics in India from the 18th Century to the Modern Age. LC 98-38434. (History of India Ser.: Vol. IV:3). (Illus.). 378p. (C). 1999. 54.95 (*0-521-26434-0*) Cambridge U Pr.

Bayly, Susan. Saints, Goddesses & Kings: Muslims & Christians in South Indian Society, 1700-1900. (Cambridge South Asian Studies: No. 43). (Illus.). 520p. (C). 1990. text 100.00 (*0-521-37201-1*) Cambridge U Pr.

Baym, Gordon & McLerran. Ultrarelativistic Heavy Ion Collisions. LC 89-141. 352p. 1989. 43.25 (*0-201-15670-9*) Addison-Wesley.

Baym, Gordon & Pethick, Christopher. Landau Fermi Liquid Theory: Concepts & Applications. LC 91-16606. 216p. 1991. 105.00 (*0-471-82418-6*) Wiley.

Baym, Gordon, jt. auth. see Kadanoff, Leo P.

Baym, Nina. American Women Writers & the Work of History, 1790-1860. LC 94-11283. 325p. (C). 1995. pap. text 17.95 (*0-8135-2143-2*) Rutgers U Pr.

— Feminism & American Literary History. LC 92-2854. 260p. (C). 1992. text 45.00 (*0-8135-1854-7*); pap. text 16.95 (*0-8135-1855-5*) Rutgers U Pr.

— New Age American Literature, 2. 5th ed. 1999. pap. text. write for info. (*0-393-99017-6*) Norton.

An Asterisk (*) at the beginning of an entry indicates that the title is appearing for the first time.

***Baym, Nina.** Norton Anthology of American Literature. 5th ed. LC 98-26885. 2700p. 1999. pap. 52.25 (0-393-97291-7) Norton.

Baym, Nina. Novels, Readers, & Reviewers: Responses to Fiction in Antebellum America. LC 84-5033. 288p. 1984. pap. text 17.95 (0-8014-9466-4) Cornell U Pr.

— The Scarlet Letter: A Reading. (Twayne's Masterwork Studies: No. 1). 20.95 (0-685-40583-4, 500, Twyne) Mac Lib Ref.

— The Scarlet Letter: A Reading. 152p. 1986. 17.95 (0-685-19706-9, Twayne) Mac Lib Ref.

— The Scarlet Letter: A Reading. (Masterwork Studies). 152p. 1986. 29.00 (0-8057-7957-4, 1); mass mkt. 13.95 (0-8057-8001-7) Macmillan.

— Woman's Fiction: A Guide to Novels by & about Women in America, 1820-70. 2nd ed. LC 92-25929. 360p. (C). 1993. pap. text 16.95 (0-252-06285-X) U of Ill Pr.

Baym, Nina, ed. The Lamplighter. (American Women Writers Ser.). 480p. (Orig.). (C). 1988. pap. text 17.00 (0-8135-1333-2) Rutgers U Pr.

Baym, Nina, et al, eds. The Norton Anthology of American Literature Vol. 1: 1620-1865, Vol. 1. 5th ed. LC 97-45578. 2600p. (C). 1998. pap. text 52.25 (0-393-95871-X) Norton.

— The Norton Anthology of American Literature Vol. 2: 1865 to the Present, Vol. 2. 5th ed. LC 97-45578. 2950p. (C). 1998. pap. text 52.25 (0-393-95872-8) Norton.

Baym, Nina, et al. History of the Book in American Culture Vol. 2: James Russell Wiggins Lectures, 1991-97. (Illus.). 1998. pap. 34.95 (0-944026-93-1) Am Antiquarian.

Baym, Nina, ed. see Chopin, Kate.

***Bayman, James M.** Norton Anthology of American Literature With Walden Norton Critical: Shorter Edition. 5th ed. 1999. pap. text, boxed set 44.50 (0-393-99019-2) Norton.

Bayman, James M. & Stark, Miriam T. Exploring the Past: Readings in Archaeology. LC 98-52051. 584p. 1999. pap. 35.00 (0-89089-699-2) Carolina Acad Pr.

Bayman, Benjamin F. & Hamermesh, Morton. A Review of Undergraduate Physics. LC 85-26577. 336p. 1986. pap. 73.95 (0-471-81684-1) Wiley.

Bayme, Steven. Understanding Jewish History: Text & Commentaries. Date not set. 39.50 (0-614-27519-9) Ktav.

— Understanding Jewish History: Text & Commentaries. 1997. pap. 24.95 (0-88125-554-8) Ktav.

Bayme, Steven & Biale, David. Spotlight on the Family: Public Policy & Private Responsibility. LC 88-70021. 60p. (Orig.). 1988. pap. 7.00 (0-87495-098-8) Am Jewish Comm.

Bayme, Steven & Rosen, Gladys, eds. The Jewish Family & Jewish Continuity. LC 94-29158. 1994. 24.95 (0-88125-495-9) Ktav.

Baynac, Jacques. The Story of Tatiana. 1994. pap. 6.00 (0-934868-31-X) Black & Red.

Baynard, Caroline & David, Jack. Out-Posts - Avant-Postes. 254p. (C). 1978. pap. text 12.00 (1-55022-039-X, Pub. by ECW) Genl Dist Srvs.

— Out-Posts/Avant-Postes. 254p. (C). 1978. text 20.00 (1-55022-040-3, Pub. by ECW) Genl Dist Srvs.

Baynard, Catherine L. Miracles & Messengers. 287p. 1998. pap. 12.95 (0-9667971-0-8) Linkpoint.

— Strangers & Synchronicity. 290p. 1998. pap. 12.95 (0-9667971-1-6) Linkpoint.

Baynard, Ed. Ed Baynard: Woodblock Prints & Watercolored Lithographs, 1980. (Illus.). 40p. 1980. pap. 8.00 (0-614-13067-0) Tyler Graphics Ltd.

Bayne. Counseling & Psychology for Health Professionals. 250p. 1992. pap. 41.50 (1-56593-117-3, 0420) Singular Publishing.

Bayne. Hanging in There. 66.95 (0-7546-1185-X) Ashgate Pub Co.

Bayne. Statistical Analysis. 2nd ed. 2000. text. write for info. (0-201-89214-6) Addison-Wesley.

***Bayne, Allan P. & Platford, Gary.** Bugs, Sweat & Fears: Beginner's Guide to Wilderness Canoe Camping. (Illus.). 208p. 1999. pap. 14.95 (0-88801-234-9, Pub. by Turnstone Pr) Genl Dist Srvs.

Bayne, Bijan C. Sky Kings: Black Pioneers of Professional Basketball. LC 96-38708. (African-American Experience Ser.). (J). (gr. 6-9). 1997. lib. bdg. 24.00 (0-531-11308-6) Watts.

— Sky Kings: Black Pioneers of Professional Basketball. (African-American Experience Ser.). (J). (gr. 6-9). 1998. pap. 9.95 (0-531-15900-0) Watts.

Bayne, Bradford, ed. see Tinkham, Michael.

Bayne, Brian L., ed. Cellular Toxicology & Marine Pollution. 44p. 1985. pap. 8.25 (0-08-032621-8, Pub. by PPL) Elsevier.

— The Effects of Stress & Pollution on Marine Animals. LC 84-18145. 400p. 1984. 55.00 (0-275-91125-X, C1125, Praeger Pubs) Greenwood.

Bayne, C. K. & Rubin, I. B. Practical Experimental Design & Optimization Methods for Chemists. (Illus.). 205p. 1987. 60.00 (0-89573-136-3, Wiley-VCH) Wiley.

Bayne, Charles J. The Fall of Utopia. LC 76-42718. (Communal Societies in America Ser.). reprint ed. 34.00 (0-404-60053-0) AMS Pr.

***Bayne, Clair A.** Applied Electricity & Electronics. LC 99-42167. (Illus.). 688p. (YA). (gr. 9-12). 2000. text 47.96 (1-56637-707-2) Goodheart.

Bayne, Clarence, et al. Statistics Applied to Canadian Issues. (C). 1991. pap. text 31.40 (0-536-58107-X) Pearson Custom.

Bayne, Coy. I Gave My Life for My Country: The Only Soldier in U. S. History to Be Pronounced Dead - but Lives. (Illus.). 170p. (Orig.). 1993. pap. 9.95 (1-883180-00-7) Bayne Pub.

Bayne, James W., jt. auth. see Konzo, Seichi.

Bayne-Jardine, Colin & Holly, Peter, eds. Developing Quality Schools. 224p. 1994. 85.00 (0-7507-0242-7, Falmer Pr); pap. 29.95 (0-7507-0243-5, Falmer Pr) Taylor & Francis.

Bayne-Jones, Stanhope. The Evolution of Preventive Medicine in the United States Army, 1607-1939. Anderson, Robert S., ed. LC 68-60098. 268p. reprint ed. pap. 83.10 (0-7837-1464-5, 205715900016) Bks Demand.

Bayne, Joycelyn. Australia: Year by Year. (Illus.). 87p. (C). 1989. 110.00 (0-7316-3343-1) St Mut.

***Bayne, Kaitlyn.** Little Book of Knock Knock Jokes. (Illus.). 120p. 2000. 4.95 (1-930408-04-8) Lawrnce Teach.

***Bayne, Kim M.** Internet Marketing Plan: The Complete Guide to Instant Web Presence. 2nd ed. LC 99-55598. 411p. (C). 2000. pap. text 39.99 incl. cd-rom (0-471-35598-4) Wiley.

Bayne, Nicholas, jt. auth. see Putnam, Robert D.

Bayne, Peter. Essay in Biography & Criticism. LC 73-39681. (Essay Index Reprint Ser.). 1977. reprint ed. 28.95 (0-8369-2744-3) Ayer.

Bayne-Powell, Rosamond. Travellers in Eighteenth-Century England. LC 74-174875. (Illus.). 241p. 1972. reprint ed. 23.95 (0-405-08245-2, Pub. by Blom Pubns) Ayer.

Bayne, R. The Myers-Briggs Type Indicator: A Critical Review & Practical Guide. 186p. 1996. pap. text 55.00 (1-56593-353-2, 0677) Singular Publishing.

Bayne, R., et al. Counselor's Handbook: A Practical A-Z Guide to Professional & Clinical Practice. 196p. 1994. 37.95 (1-56593-293-5, 0617) Singular Publishing.

***Bayne, R., et al.** The Counselor's Handbook: A Practical A-Z Guide to Professional & Clinical Practice. 2nd ed. 207p. 1999. pap. 29.95 (0-7487-3309-4) Standard Pub.

***Bayne, Robin.** A Matter of Life. 278p. 2000. pap. 18.99 (1-58365-031-8, Indigo Publicatns) BT Pub.

Bayne, Rowan, et al, eds. New Directions in Counselling. 336p. (C). 1996. pap. 29.99 (0-415-13143-X) Routledge.

Bayne-Smith, Marcia. Race, Gender, & Health. LC 95-35483. (Series on Race & Ethnic Relations: Vol. 15). (Illus.). 240p. 1995. 52.00 (0-8039-5504-9) Sage.

Baynes, C. F. & Wilhelm, R., trs. I Ching or Book of Changes. 3rd ed. LC 67-24740. (Bollingen Ser.: No. 19). 806p. 1967. 22.50 (0-691-09750-X, Pub. by Princeton U Pr) Cal Prin Full Svc.

Baynes, C. F., tr. see Wilhelm, Hellmut & Wilhelm, Richard.

Baynes, C. F., tr. see Wilhelm, R., ed.

Baynes, Cary F., tr. see Jung, Emma.

Baynes-Cope, A. D. Caring for Books & Documents. 2nd ed. 48p. (C). 1989. pap. 12.95 (0-941533-68-9, NAB) I R Dee.

Baynes, H. G., tr. see Jung, C. G., et al.

Baynes, Helton G. Germany Possessed. LC 73-180389. (Studies in Fascism). reprint ed. 42.00 (0-404-56106-3) AMS Pr.

Baynes, John. Far from a Donkey: The Life of General Sir Ivor Maxse. (Illus.). 256p. 1995. 29.95 (1-85753-185-X, Pub. by Brasseys) Brasseys.

— How Maps Are Made. fac. ed. LC 86-29342. (How It Is Made Ser.). (Illus.). 32p. 1987. reprint ed. pap. 30.00 (0-7837-8150-4, 204785500008) Bks Demand.

— Urquhart of Arnhem: The Life & Times of Major General R. E. Urquhart, CB DSO. (Illus.). 285p. 1993. 41.00 (0-08-041318-8, Pub. by Brasseys) Brasseys.

Baynes, Joseph. Letters . . . Regarding the Absence of Consideration in Our Present Form of Government for Our Coloured Population (1906) (Colin Webb Natal & Zululand Ser.: No. 2). 44p. 1992. pap. 11.95 (0-86980-878-8, Pub. by Univ Natal Pr) Intl Spec Bk.

Baynes, Ken & Pugh, Francis. The Art of the Engineer. LC 97-66457. 1997. 75.00 (0-7188-2506-3, Lutterworth-Parkwest) Parkwest Pubns.

Baynes, Kenneth, et al, eds. After Philosophy: End or Transformation? 300p. (Orig.). (C). 1986. pap. text 22.00 (0-262-52113-X) MIT Pr.

— After Philosophy: End or Transformation? 300p. (Orig.). (C). 1986. 47.50 (0-262-02254-0) MIT Pr.

Baynes, Kenneth, tr. see Honneth, Axel.

Baynes, Norman H. The Byzantine Empire. LC 75-41020. reprint ed. 37.50 (0-404-14641-4) AMS Pr.

— Byzantine Studies & Other Essays. LC 74-11586. (Illus.). 392p. 1974. reprint ed. lib. bdg. 69.50 (0-8371-7673-5, BABYS, Greenwood Pr) Greenwood.

— Constantine the Great & the Christian Church. 1974. lib. bdg. 59.95 (0-87968-934-X) Gordon Pr.

— Constantine the Great & the Christian Church. LC 74-34500. (World History Ser.: No. 48). (C). 1972. reprint ed. lib. bdg. 75.00 (0-8383-0131-2) M S G Haskell Hse.

Baynes, Norman H., jt. tr. see Dawes, Elizabeth.

Baynes, Pauline. Thanks Be to God: Prayers from Around the World. LC 89-28622. 32p. (J). (ps up). 1990. mass mkt. 13.95 (0-02-708541-4, Mac Bks Young Read) S&S Childrens.

Baynes, Richard C. The Life & Ancestry of John Thistlewaite Baynes (1833-1891) LC 87-73152. 144p. 1988. 16.00 (0-9619743-0-3) R C Baynes.

Baynes, Thomas S. Shakespeare Studies & an Essay on English Dictionaries. reprint ed. 49.50 (0-404-00697-3) AMS Pr.

Baynham, Elizabeth. Alexander the Great: The Unique History of Quintus Curtius. LC 98-19713. 256p. (C). 1999. text 39.50 (0-472-10858-1, 10858) U of Mich Pr.

Baynham, Elizabeth, jt. see Bosworth, A. B.

Baynham, John. 101 Signs You're Spending Too Much Time with Your Cat. Carle, Cliff, ed. (Illus.). 96p. 1999. pap. 6.95 (1-57644-097-4) CCC Pubns.

Baynham, Mike. Literacy Practices. LC 93-39308. 1999. text. write for info. (0-582-08709-0, Pub. by Addison-Wesley) Longman.

Baynham, Simon. Zimbabwe in Transition. 284p. (Orig.). 1992. pap. 53.00 (91-22-01508-6) Coronet Bks.

Baynton, Barbara. Barbara Baynton. Krimmer, Sally & Lawson, Alan, eds. (UQP Australian Authors Ser.). 340p. (C). 1981. pap. 18.95 (0-7022-1469-8) Intl Spec Bk.

Baynton, Douglas C. Forbidden Signs: American Culture & the Campaign Against Sign Language, 1847-1920. LC 96-12889. 256p. 1998. pap. 15.00 (0-226-03964-1) U Ch Pr.

— Forbidden Signs: American Culture & the Campaign Against Sign Language, 1847-1920. LC 96-12889. (Illus.). 236p. 1999. 27.50 (0-226-03963-3) U Ch Pr.

Baynton, Martin. Why Do You Love Me. LC 89-1861. (Illus.). 32p. (J). (ps-3). 1990. 15.93 (0-688-09157-., Grenwillow Bks) HarpC Child Bks.

Baynton, Martin, jt. auth. see Carmine, Mary.

Baynton-Power, Henry. How to Compose Music: A Simple Guide for the Amateur to the Composition of Melodies & to Their Effective Harmonization. 2nd ed. LC 79-23654. (Illus.). 90p. 1980. reprint ed. lib. bdg. 35.00 (0-313-22214-2, BPHC) Greenwood.

— How to Compose Music: Music Book Index. 90p. 1993. reprint ed. lib. bdg. 69.00 (0-7812-9659-5) Rprt Serv.

Bayo, Alberto. One Hundred Fifty Questions for a Guerrilla. Brown, Robert K., ed. Hartenstein, Hugo & Harber, Dennis, trs. from SPA. LC 63-2215. (Illus.). 96p. 1963. pap. 15.00 (0-87364-022-5) Paladin Pr.

Bayo, Eduardo, jt. auth. see Garcia de Jalon, Javier.

Bayo, Edwin A. Introduccion al Gobierno y Leyes de Florida. (SPA.). 233p. 1995. pap. 19.95 (0-9648368-0-7) Danzon FL.

Bayod, Jose M., et al, eds. P-Adic Functional Analysis. (Lecture Notes in Pure & Applied Mathematics Ser. Vol. 137). (Illus.). 236p. 1991. pap. text 135.00 (0-8247-8660-2) Dekker.

Bayod Serrat, Ramon. Diccionario Laboral. (SPA.). 546p. 1969. pap. 14.95 (0-8288-6576-0, S50139) Fr & Eur.

Bayon, D. Aventura Plastica de Hispanoamerica. (Breviarios Ser.). (SPA.). pap. 11.99 (968-16-4821-8, Pub. by Fondo) Continental Bk.

Bayon, Damian. Hacia Tamayo (A Look at Tamayo) (SPA., Illus.). 67p. (J). 1995. 45.99 (968-16-4355-0, Pub. by Fondo) Continental Bk.

Bayon, Damian C. & Fresan, Juan. Construccion de Lo Visual. LC 76-10371. (SPA., Illus.). 221p. 1981. reprint ed. pap. 4.00 (0-8477-2108-6) U of PR Pr.

Bayon, Mlle., jt. auth. see Lebrun, Francesca.

Bayona, Ricardo T., jt. auth. see Stendal, Russell M.

Bayone, Jeff & Beesley, Amanda. It's Bridge, Baby. LC 98-11424. 240p. 1998. pap. 12.95 (1-57322-678-5, Riverhd Trade) Berkley Pub.

Bayor, Ronald H. Fiorello la Guardia: Ethnicity & Reform. Kraut, Alan M. & Wakelyn, Jon L., eds. LC 92-32970. (American Biographical History Ser.). (Illus.). 224p. (C). 1993. pap. text 12.95 (0-88295-894-1) Harlan Davidson.

— Neighbors in Conflict: The Irish, Germans, Jews & Italians. LC 77-14260. (Johns Hopkins University Studies in Historical & Political Science: Ser. 96, No. 1). 249p. reprint ed. pap. 77.20 (0-608-15313-3, 202923900059) Bks Demand.

— Neighbors in Conflict: The Irish, Germans, Jews & Italians of New York City, 1929-41. LC 87-19064. 248p. 1988. pap. text 11.95 (0-252-01437-5) U of Ill Pr.

— Race & the Shaping of Twentieth-Century Atlanta. LC 95-39552. (Fred W. Morrison Series in Southern Studies). (Illus.). 350p. (C). 1997. 39.95 (0-8078-2270-1) U of NC Pr.

***Bayor, Ronald H.** Race & the Shaping of Twentieth-Century Atlanta. LC 95-39552. (Fred W. Morrison Series in Southern Studies). (Illus.). 350p. 2000. reprint ed. pap. 19.95 (0-8078-4898-0) U of NC Pr.

Bayor, Ronald H. & Meagher, Timothy J., eds. The New York Irish. LC 95-20319. (Illus.). 720p. 1996. 50.00 (0-8018-5199-8) Johns Hopkins.

— The New York Irish. LC 95-20319. 758p. 1997. reprint ed. pap. text 25.95 (0-8018-5764-3) Johns Hopkins.

Bayou Civic Club, Inc. Staff. Down the Bayou: A Collection of Favorite Cajun Recipes. Landry, Margie & Boulet, Ann, eds. (Illus.). 254p. 1989. reprint ed. 16.95 (0-9613375-0-8) Larose Civic.

Bayoumi, Magdy A., ed. VLSI Signal Processing Technology. 248p. (C). 1994. text 125.00 (0-7923-9490-9) Kluwer Academic.

Bayoumi, Magdy A., jt. auth. see Cauwenberghs, Gert.

***Bayoumi, Moustafa & Rubin, Andrew, eds.** The Edward Said Reader. 320p. 2000. pap. 15.00 (0-375-70936-3) Vin Bks.

Bayoumi, Salah E., jt. auth. see Ragab, Abdel-Rahman A.

Bayoumi, Tamim. Financial Deregulation & Household Saving. fac. ed. LC HG1588.. (Bank of England, Economics Division, Working Paper Ser.: No. 5). 22p. 1992. reprint ed. pap. 30.00 (0-7837-8336-1, 204912300010) Bks Demand.

— Financial Integration & Real Activity. LC 97-18822. (Studies in International Trade Policy). 176p. (C). 1997. text 52.50 (0-472-10870-0, 10870) U of Mich Pr.

***Bayoumi, Tamim.** Financial Integraty & Real Activity. 1999. text. write for info. (0-7190-4700-5) Manchester Univ Pr.

Bayoumi, Tamim. Regional Trading Blocs, Mobile Capital & Exchange Rate Co-Ordination. (Bank of England, Working Paper Ser.: No. 12). (Illus.). 48p. 1993. pap 30.00 (0-608-04965-4, 206554400004) Bks Demand.

Bayoumi, Tamim, jt. auth. see Eichengreen, Barry J.

Bayoumi, Tamim, jt. auth. see Sterne, Gabriel.

***Bayoumi, Tamim A. & Collyns, Charles.** Post-Bubble Blues: How Japan Responded to Asset Price Collapse. LC 99-58930. 1999. write for info. (1-55775-872-7) Intl Monetary.

Bayport Heritage Association Staff. Bayport Heritage. (Images of America Ser.). 1997. pap. 16.99 (0-7524-0810-0) Arcadia Publng.

Bayrak, Tosun, jt. auth. see Yahyaal-Suhrawardi, Hazrat S.

Bayrak, Tosun, tr. see Badruddin, Shaikh.

Bayrak, Tosun, tr. & intro. see Al-Jilani, Hadrat'Abd A.

Bayraktaroglu, Arin, jt. auth. see Bayraktaroglu, Sinan.

Bayraktaroglu, Sinan & Bayraktaroglu, Arin. Colloquial Turkish. LC 91-37807. (Colloquials Ser.). 240p. (C). (gr. 13). 1992. audio 24.99 (0-415-04074-4, A6949) Routledge.

— Colloquial Turkish, Set. LC 91-37807. (Colloquials Ser.). 240p. (gr. 13). 1992. pap. 34.99 incl. audio (0-415-04075-2, A6953) Routledge.

Bayram, Ali. English-Turkish Dictionary of Technical Terms. (ENG & TUR.). 583p. 1989. pap. 195.00 (0-7859-7140-8) Fr & Eur.

— Turkish-English Comprehensive Dictionary. (ENG & TUR.). 650p. 1996. 60.00 (0-7818-0468-X) Hippocrene Bks.

Bayrataroglu, Arin. Culture Shock! Turkey. LC 96-75617. (Illus.). 1996. pap. text 12.95 (1-55868-253-8) Gr Arts Ctr Pub.

Bayreuth, O. Hutzinger, ed. The Handbook of Environmental Chemistry, Vol. 2. (Illus.). 256p. 1989. 118.00 (0-387-51126-1) Spr-Verlag.

Bayreuther, Rainer. Richard Strauss' Alpensinfonie. (Musikwissenschaftliche Publikationen: Bd. 6). 517p. Date not set. 90.00 (3-487-10261-7) G Olms Pubs.

Bayrle, Thomas. Thomas Bayrle: Big Book. (Illus.). 432p. 1991. pap. 40.00 (3-88375-170-7, Pub. by Walther Konig) Dist Art Pubs.

***Bayroll, Andrew I.** The Stuff Type Is Made Of. LC 99-31987. 77p. 1999. spiral bd. 22.00 (0-13-022004-3) P-H.

Bays. Enlightenment Is Not the Tooth Fairy: Put Your Ego. LC 98-125131. 304p. 1997. per., boxed set 22.50 (0-7872-3793-0) Kendall-Hunt.

Bays, Brad A. Townsite Settlement & Dispossession in the Cherokee Nation, 1866-1907. LC 97-17753. (Native Americans). (Illus.). 288p. 1998. text 67.00 (0-8153-2912-1) Garland.

Bays, Carter. The Encyclopedia of Early American Sewing Machines. 2nd ed. LC 93-90700. (Illus.). 305p. 1994. write for info. (0-9637916-0-5) C Bays.

Bays, Daniel, jt. auth. see Suleski, Ronald.

Bays, Daniel H. Christianity in China: From the 18th Century to the Present. 1999. pap. text 24.95 (0-8047-3651-0) Stanford U Pr.

Bays, Daniel H., ed. Christianity in China from the Eighteenth Century to the Present. LC 95-53046. (C). 1996. 65.00 (0-8047-2609-4) Stanford U Pr.

Bays, Daniel H., jt. auth. see Stanley, Margaret.

Bays, Gary. From Composition to Professional Communication. 400p. (C). 2001. pap. 37.33 (0-13-887381-X, Macmillan Coll) P-H.

Bays, Gwendolyn, tr. see Sutra, Lalitavistara.

Bays, Harold. The Prespective, Libel, & the Ten Rules of 90's Journalism: Medicine, Music, Stand-up Comedy, Janitor Work, & the Systematic Dismantling of Individual Liberties by an Irresponsible Press. LC 95-78352. (Orig.). 1995. 29.95 (0-9647944-0-3); pap. 19.95 (0-9647944-1-1) Blue Shoes Pubng.

Bays, Harold & Nilsson, Mike. What to Know When She's Expecting. large type ed. LC 97-93295. 213p. 1997. pap. 9.95 (0-9647944-3-8) Blue Shoes Pubng.

Bays, Jamie M. Once upon a Wishing Tree. 318p. (Orig.). 1988. pap. 4.95 (0-9620341-0-X) J M Bays.

Bays, Jill. Drawing Workbook. LC 99-202839. 1999. wbk. ed. 24.95 (0-7153-0719-3, Pub. by D & C Pub) Sterling.

— Flowers in the Landscape. (Illus.). 128p. 1996. 24.95 (0-7153-0267-1, Pub. by D & C Pub) Sterling.

— The Watercolorist's Garden. (Illus.). 128p. 1997. pap. 19.95 (0-7153-0620-0, Pub. by D & C Pub) Sterling.

Bays, Kathryn, jt. ed. see Mohn, Caroline.

Bays, L. R., jt. ed. see Urbistondo, R.

Bays, Michael. Product Release Engineering for Software Engineering. LC 99-16017. 256p. (C). 1999. 48.00 (0-13-636564-7) P-H.

Bays, Patricia. The Great Adventure: Exploring Christian Faith. 128p. 1997. pap. 11.95 (1-55126-176-6) Forward Movement.

Bays, Peter, jt. auth. see Twyning, John P.

Baysal, O., ed. CFD for Design & Optimization, Vol. 232. LC 95-81280. (1995 ASME International Mechanical Engineering Congress & Exposition Ser.: FED-Vol. 232). 100p. 1995. 48.00 (0-7918-1743-1, H01029) ASME.

Baysal, O. & Saxena, V., eds. CFD Algorithms & Applications for Parallel Processors. LC 93-71640. (FED Ser.: Vol. 156). 83p. 1993. pap. 30.00 (0-7918-0964-1, H00796) ASME.

Bayse, Daniel J. As Free as an Eagle: The Inmate's Family Survival Guide. 235p. (Orig.). 1991. pap. 17.50 (0-929310-63-2) Am Correctional.

— Helping Hands: A Handbook for Volunteers in Prisons & Jails. 78p. (Orig.). 1993. pap. 9.50 (0-929310-85-3) Am Correctional.

— Working in Jails & Prisons: Becoming Part of the Team. LC 95-8358. 87p. 1995. pap. 15.00 (1-56991-021-9, 534) Am Correctional.

Bayse, Daniel J., jt. auth. see Castillo, George R.

Bayse, David D., contrib. by. A Candidate Reference Method for Serum Digoxin: A Model for Radioimmunoassay Reference Methods; Tentative Guideline (1996) 1996. 75.00 (1-56238-298-5, I/LA9-T) NCCLS.

Baysinger, M. Ali & Ulmer, Louise. Electrolysis & You. (Illus.). 68p. (Orig.). 1987. pap. 15.00 (0-941367-00-2) Peach Blossom Pubns.

B

An Asterisk (*) at the beginning of an entry indicates that the title is appearing for the first time.

Baysting, Arthur, et al, eds. Making Policy Not Tea: Women in Parliament. (Illus.). 212p. 1994. 32.00 (*0-19-558275-6*) OUP.

Bayt, Phyllis T. Administering Medications. (Health Occupations Ser.). 1982. write for info. (*0-672-61538-X*); pap. write for info. (*0-672-61522-3*) Macmillan.

— Administering Medications: A Competency-Based Program for Health Occupations. 3rd ed. LC 93-16412. 1993. text. write for info. (*0-02-800886-3*); teacher ed. write for info. (*0-02-800887-1*) Glencoe.

***Bayt, Phyllis Theiss.** Administering Medications: Pharmacology for Health Careers. 4th ed. LC 99-15303. 496p. 1999. pap. text 42.80 (*0-02-804876-8*) Glencoe.

Bayton, Mavis. Frock Rock: Women Performing Popular Music. (Illus.). 260p. 1999. 35.00 (*0-19-816615-X*) OUP.

Baytop, Adrianne. Black Aesthetics. LC 98-90304. 1998. pap. 8.95 (*0-533-12754-8*) Vantage.

Baytos, Larry. Dante's Dilemma: MBAs from Hell. LC 97-94730. (Illus.). ix, 325p. 1998. pap. 14.00 (*0-9661019-0-1*) Cheshire Bks.

Baytos, Lawrence M. Designing & Implementing Successful Diversity Programs. LC 94-34051. 352p. (C). 1994. text 69.95 (*0-13-128034-1*) P-H.

Bayuel, Leopold. Ocean Optics Research in the U. S. S. R. Gallant, Jonathan, ed. Sargent, Peter, tr. from RUS. iv, 141p. (Orig.). 1989. pap. text 75.00 (*1-55831-095-9*) Delphic Associates.

***Bayuk, J. L.** Stepping Through the IS Audit: What to Expect - How to Prepare. (Illus.). 124p. 2000. pap. 45.00 (*1-893209-05-9*) Info Systs Audit.

Bayuk, Shelah S., ed. see Carlen, Daniel D.

Bayuk, Shelah S., ed. see Etheridge, Dell W.

Bayvel, L. P. & Orzechowski, Z., eds. Liquid Atomization. (Combustion: An International Ser.). 420p. 1993. 124.00 (*0-89116-959-8*, Pub. by Tay Francis Ltd) Taylor & Francis.

Baza, Larry T. & Davies, Hugh M. La Frontera - the Border: Art about the Mexico - United States Border Experience. LC 92-62591. (Illus.). 199p. 1993. pap. 29.00 (*0-934418-41-1*) Mus Contemp Art.

Bazaldua, Barbara. Barbie, Television Reporter: The Jewel Thief. LC 97-76907. (Little Golden Storybks.). (Illus.). 24p. (J). (ps-3). 1998. 2.29 (*0-307-98864-3*, 98864, Goldn Books) Gldn Bks Pub Co.

— Hercules: A Race to the Rescue. LC 97-70003. (Little Golden Bks.). (Illus.). 24p. (J). (ps-k). 1997. 2.29 (*0-307-98801-5*, 98801, Goldn Books) Gldn Bks Pub Co.

— Let's Go to the Airport. LC 97-70005. (Little Golden Bks.). 24p. (J). (ps-k). 1998. 2.29 (*0-307-98833-3*, 98833, Goldn Books) Gldn Bks Pub Co.

— Let's Go to the Dairy Farm. LC 97-76886. (Little Golden Bks.). (Illus.). 24p. (J). 1998. 2.29 (*0-307-98224-6*, 98224, Goldn Books) Gldn Bks Pub Co.

— Rainbow Puppies. (Little Golden Bks.). 24p. (J). (ps-k). 1998. 2.29 (*0-307-98858-9*, 98858, Goldn Books) Gldn Bks Pub Co.

— Snow Puppies. LC 96-75807. (Little Golden Bks.). (J). 1996. 2.29 (*0-307-98786-8*, 98786, Goldn Books) Gldn Bks Pub Co.

***Bazaldua, Charles.** 102 Dalmatians. (Illus.). (J). 2000. pap. 3.99 (*0-307-20006-X*, Goldn Books) Gldn Bks Pub Co.

Bazalgette, Cary. In Front of the Children: Screen Entertainment & Young Audiences. 1995. pap. text 19.95 (*0-85170-453-0*, Pub. by British Film Inst) Ind U Pr.

— Media Education: Teaching English in the National Curriculum. (Illus.). 61p. (C). 1991. pap. text 15.00 (*0-340-53695-0*, Pub. by Hodder & Stought Ltd) Lubrecht & Cramer.

Bazalgette, Cary, et al, eds. New Directions: Media Education Worldwide. (Illus.). 256p. (C). 1993. pap. 21.95 (*0-85170-350-X*, Pub. by British Film Inst) Ind U Pr.

Bazalgette, Leon. Henry Thoreau, Bachelor of Nature. (BCL1-PS American Literature Ser.). 357p. 1992. reprint ed. lib. bdg. 89.00 (*0-7812-6882-6*) Rprt Serv.

— Walt Whitman: The Man & His Work. Fitzgerald, Ellen, tr. LC 72-128770. 1971. reprint ed. lib. bdg. 60.50 (*0-8154-0352-6*) Cooper Sq.

Bazalgette, Peter, jt. auth. see Edwards, David.

***Bazan, Bill J.** Medicine in Search of Meaning: A Spiritual Journey for Physicians. 176p. 1999. pap. 15.95 (*0-9668228-2-X*) Caritas Commns.

Bazan, Emilia P. Emilia Pardo Bazan: "The White Horse" & Other Stories. Fedorchek, Robert M., tr. from SPA. LC 92-54944. (Illus.). 168p. (C). 1993. 29.50 (*0-8387-5258-6*) Bucknell U Pr.

— Poesias Ineditas U Olvidadas. Hemingway, Maurice, ed. (Exeter Hispanic Text Ser.: No. 51). (SPA.). 200p. 1996. pap. text 17.95 (*0-85989-339-1*, Pub. by Univ Exeter Pr) Northwestern U Pr.

— The Tribune of the People. Borenstein, Walter, tr. from SPA. LC 98-43482. 264p. 1999. 42.50 (*0-8387-5390-6*) Bucknell U Pr.

Bazan-Figueras, Patricia. Eugenio Cambaceres Vol. 19: Precursor de la Novela Argentina Contemporanea. (American University Studies: No. XXII). X, 215p. (C). 1995. text 48.95 (*0-8204-2057-3*) P Lang Pubng.

Bazan, Kathryn Lee, jt. auth. see Vincoli, Jeffrey Wayne.

Bazan, N., ed. New Targets in Inflammation: Inhibitors of COX-2 or Adhesion Molecules. 160p. (C). 1996. lib. bdg. 74.00 (*0-614-24339-4*) Kluwer Academic.

Bazan, N. G., et al. Neurobiology of Essential Fatty Acids. LC 92-16989. (Advances in Experimental Medicine & Biology Ser.: Vol. 318). (Illus.). 454p. (C). 1992. text 135.00 (*0-306-44233-7*, Kluwer Plenum) Kluwer Academic.

— Neurochemical Correlates of Cerebral Ischemia Vol. 7: Advances in Neurochemistry. (Illus.). 392p. (C). 1992. text 110.00 (*0-306-43944-1*, 441, Kluwer Plenum) Kluwer Academic.

Bazan, Nicolas G., ed. Lipid Mediators in Eye Inflammation. (New Trends in Lipid Mediators Research Ser.: Vol. 5). (Illus.). x, 192p. 1990. 155.00 (*3-8055-5067-7*) S Karger.

— Lipid Mediators in Ischemic Brain Damage & Experimental Epilepsy. (New Trends in Lipid Mediators Research Ser.: Vol. 4). (Illus.). viii, 262p. 1990. 207.00 (*3-8055-5068-5*) S Karger.

Bazan, Nicolas G., et al, eds. Phospholipids in the Nervous System. (FIDIA Research Ser.: Vol. 17). (Illus.). 300p. 1989. 118.00 (*0-387-96994-2*) Spr-Verlag.

Bazan, Nicolas G. & U'Prichard, David C., eds. Molecular Neurobiology, 1987. (Illus.). 416p. 1988. 95.00 (*0-89603-152-7*) Humana.

— Molecular Neurobiology, 1988. (Illus.). 332p. 1989. 95.00 (*0-89603-176-4*) Humana.

Bazan, Walter G. Healing Hands: The Natural Healing Arts. 104p. 1998. reprint ed. pap. 11.00 (*0-7873-0082-9*) Hlth Research.

Bazanna, Gualtiero, jt. auth. see Bache, Richard.

Bazant. Concrete at High Temperatures. 544p. (C). 1996. 89.95 (*0-582-08626-4*) Addison-Wesley.

— Inelastic Analysis of Structures. (C). 2000. pap. text. write for info. (*0-471-98772-7*) Wiley.

Bazant, Vladimir. Handbook of Organosilicon Compounds Advances since 1961, 3 vols., Vol. 1. Hetflejs, J. et al, trs. LC 74-21879. 765p. reprint ed. pap. 200.00 (*0-7837-0716-9*, 204104400001) Bks Demand.

— Handbook of Organosilicon Compounds Advances since 1961, 3 vols., Vol. 2. Hetflejs, J. et al, trs. LC 74-21879. 627p. reprint ed. pap. 194.40 (*0-7837-0717-7*, 204104400002) Bks Demand.

— Handbook of Organosilicon Compounds Advances since 1961, 3 vols., Vol. 3. Hetflejs, J. et al, trs. LC 74-21879. 734p. reprint ed. pap. 200.00 (*0-7837-0718-5*, 204104400003) Bks Demand.

Bazant, Zdenek & Carol, Ignacio, eds. Creep & Shrinkage of Concrete: Proceedings of the Fifth International Rilem Symposium. (Illus.). 960p. 1993. pap. 232.50 (*0-419-18630-1*) Thomson Learn.

Bazant, Zdenek P. English - Czech Technical Dictionary. 4th ed. (CZE & ENG.). 1026p. 1985. 39.95 (*0-8288-9068-4*, F119080) Fr & Eur.

— Fracture & Size Effect in Concrete & Other Quasibrittle Materials. LC 97-26399. 640p. 1997. boxed set 99.95 (*0-8493-8284-X*) CRC Pr.

Bazant, Zdenek P., ed. Current Trends in Concrete Fracture Research. (C). 1991. text 171.00 (*0-7923-1366-6*) Kluwer Academic.

— Fracture Mechanics of Concrete Structures. LC 92-12904. 1992. mass mkt. 402.95 (*1-85166-869-1*) Elsevier.

— Mathematical Modeling of Creep & Shrinkage of Concrete. fac. ed. LC 88-17422. (Wiley Series in Numerical Methods in Engineering). (Illus.). 485p. 1988. reprint ed. pap. 150.40 (*0-608-00985-7*, 206184100012) Bks Demand.

— Mechanics of Geomaterials: Rocks, Concretes & Soils. LC 84-10448. (Wiley Series in Numerical Methods in Engineering). 631p. reprint ed. pap. 195.70 (*0-8357-8948-9*, 203360900086) Bks Demand.

Bazant, Zdenek P., et al, eds. Fracture & Damage in Quasibrittle Structures: Experiment, Modelling & Computer Analysis; Proceedings of the U. S.-Europe Workshop, Prague, Czech Republic, 1994. (Illus.). 664p. (C). 1994. 180.00 (*0-419-19280-8*, E & FN Spon) Routledge.

Bazant, Zdenek P. & Cedolin, Luigi. Stability of Structures: Elastic, Inelastic & Damage Theories. (Oxford Engineering Science Ser.: No. 26). (Illus.). 1014p. (C). 1991. text 99.00 (*0-19-505529-2*) OUP.

Bazant, Zdenek P. & Wittmann, F. H., eds. Creep & Shrinkage in Concrete Structures. LC 82-4766. (Wiley Series in Numerical Methods in Engineering). 373p. reprint ed. pap. 115.70 (*0-608-16349-X*, 202668600051) Bks Demand.

Bazaraa, Mokhtar S., et al. Linear Programming & Network Flows. 2nd ed. LC 89-32063. 704p. 1990. text 108.95 (*0-471-63681-9*) Wiley.

— Nonlinear Programming: Theory & Algorithms. 2nd ed. LC 92-30957. 656p. 1993. text 103.95 (*0-471-55793-5*) Wiley.

Bazargan, Mehdi. The Inevitable Victory. Yousefi, Mohammad, tr. from PER. 35p. 1979. pap. 2.00 (*0-941722-03-1*) Book Dist Ctr.

— Work & Islam. Yousefi, Mohammack, tr. from PER. 62p. 1979. 6.95 (*0-941722-04-X*) Book Dist Ctr.

Bazargan, Susan, jt. ed. see Downing, David B.

Bazarini, Ronald. Boys: A Schoolmaster's Journal. 1988. 12.95 (*0-8027-1053-0*) Walker & Co.

Bazarov, I. P. Theory of Many-Particle Systems. Adashko, J. George, tr. (AIP Translation Ser.). (Illus.). 312p. 1989. 89.95 (*0-88318-601-2*) Spr-Verlag.

Bazarte, Melanie. Discipline 101: Because Kids Don't Come with Instructions. (Illus.). 40p. 1998. 11.95 (*0-9664365-1-2*) Dr Melanie.

— Dr. Melanie's 115 Fingerplays & Action Songs. 55p. 1997. 13.95 (*0-9664365-2-0*) Dr Melanie.

***Bazarte, Melanie.** Let's Pretend! The Why & How of Dramatic Play. (Illus.). 32p. 1998. pap. 9.95 (*0-9664365-3-9*) Dr Melanie.

Bazarte, Melanie. Parenting 101: Because Kids Don't Come with Instructions. (Illus.). 438p. 1998. 27.95 (*0-9664365-0-4*) Dr Melanie.

Bazbera, Henry. Medieval Sicily: The First Absolute State. Cipolla, Gaetano, ed. LC 94-27273. (Sicilian Studies: Vol. II). (Illus.). 152p. (C). 1994. pap. text 12.00 (*1-881901-05-X*) LEGAS.

Bazeley, W. J., ed. Tertiary Tectonics & Sedimentation in the Cuyama Basin, San Luis Obispo, Santa Barbara & Ventura Counties, California. (Illus.). 173p. (Orig.). 1988. pap. 14.00 (*1-878861-10-7*) Pac Section SEPM.

Bazeli, Marilyn J. & Heintz, James L. Technology Across the Curriculum: Activities & Ideas. LC 96-45459. 190p. 1997. lib. bdg., teacher ed. 24.50 (*1-56308-444-9*) Libs Unl.

***Bazell, Chris & Gibson, Bryan.** Domestic Violence: And Occupation of the Family Home. 190p. 1999. pap. 39.00 (*1-872870-60-0*, 18471, Pub. by Waterside Pr) Gaunt.

Bazell, Chris & Lomax, Ian S., eds. Unit Fines. 60p. 1992. 45.00 (*1-85190-177-9*, Pub. by Tolley Pubng) St Mut.

Bazell, Chris, et al. Child Maintenance: A Guide to the Child Support Act 1991. 111p. (C). 1993. 110.00 (*1-85190-193-0*, Pub. by Tolley Pubng) St Mut.

Bazell, Christopher, jt. auth. see Baker, Stuart.

Bazellan, Eduard M. & Raizer, I. U. Spark Discharge. Smirnova, L. N., tr. LC 97-14858. 320p. 1997. boxed set 119.95 (*0-8493-2868-3*) CRC Pr.

Bazelmans, Joe. By Weapons Made Worry: Lords, Retainers & Their Relationship in Beowulf. (Amsterdam Archaeological Studies). (Illus.). 300p. 1999. 46.50 (*90-5356-325-3*, Pub. by Amsterdam U Pr) U of Mich Pr.

Bazelon, Bruce & McGuinn, William. Directory of American Military Goods Dealers & Makers, 1785-1915: Supplement to Directory of American Military Goods Dealers & Makers. 2nd rev. ed. (Illus.). 371p. 1995. text 32.50 (*1-888578-03-3*) R E F Typesetting Pub.

Bazelon, Bruce S. Horstmanns: The Enterprise of Military Equipage. (Illus.). 213p. 1997. text 25.00 (*1-888578-04-1*) R E F Typesetting Pub.

— Horstmann's The Enterprise of Military Equipage. (Illus.). 199p. 1997. 25.00 (*0-917218-80-9*) A Mowbray.

Bazelon, Bruce S., ed. Swords from Public Collections in the Commonwealth of Pennsylvania. (Illus.). 127p. 1987. pap. 12.00 (*0-917218-26-4*) A Mowbray.

***Bazelon, Bruce S. & McGuinn, William F.** A Directory of American Military Goods Dealers & Makers, 1785-1915: Combined Edition. (Illus.). 419p. 1999. 35.00 (*0-917218-88-4*) A Mowbray.

Bazelon, Coleman. Where Do We Go from Here? The FCC Auctions & the Future of Radio Spectrum Management. LC 97-152459. 100p. 1997. per. 8.50 (*0-16-049057-X*, Congress) USGPO.

Bazelon, Coleman, et al. Where Do We Go from Here? FCC Auctions & the Future of Radio-Spectrum Management. (Illus.). 80p. (Orig.). 1997. pap. text 30.00 (*0-7881-4508-8*) DIANE Pub.

Bazelon, David T. The Paper Economy. LC 78-11587. 467p. 1979. reprint ed. lib. bdg. 79.50 (*0-313-21001-2*, BATP, Greenwood Pr) Greenwood.

Bazemore, Gordon, jt. ed. see Walgrave, Lode.

***Bazemore, S. Gordon & Schiff, Mara.** Restorative Community Justice: Repairing Harm & Transforming Communities. LC 00-40577. 2000. pap. write for info. (*1-58360-506-1*) Anderson Pub Co.

Bazen, Stephen, et al, eds. Low-Wage Employment in Europe. LC 98-27888. 240p. 1999. 80.00 (*1-85898-932-9*) E Elgar.

Bazer, Fuller W. The Endocrinology of Pregnancy. LC 98-3059. (Contemporary Endocrinology Ser.: Vol. 9). (Illus.). 592p. 1998. 149.50 (*0-89603-462-3*) Humana.

Bazergui, Andre, jt. auth. see Payne, James R.

Bazerman. Writing Skills Handbook. 4th ed. LC 97-72440. (C). 1997. pap. text 14.76 (*0-395-86811-4*) HM.

Bazerman, Charles. A Constructive Experience. LC 93-22839. 267p. (C). 1994. 36.95 (*0-8093-1906-3*) S Ill U Pr.

— The Informed Reader: Contemporary Issues in the Disciplines. LC 88-81322. 1988. teacher ed. 2.36 (*0-318-36884-6*) HM.

— Informed Reader & Dictionary. (C). 1997. 45.56 (*0-395-68217-7*) HM.

— The Informed Writer. 3rd ed. LC 88-81321. 1988. teacher ed. 2.36 (*0-318-36885-4*) HM.

— The Informed Writer, 4 vols. 4th ed. (C). 1991. pap. text, teacher ed. 3.16 (*0-395-60131-2*) HM.

— The Informed Writer, 5 vols. 5th ed. LC 94-76474. (C). 1994. pap. text 33.56 (*0-395-68723-3*) HM.

— Involved: Writing for College, Writing for Your Self. 400p. (C). 1996. pap. text 29.16 (*0-395-67182-5*) HM.

— Involved: Writing for College, Writing for Your Self. (C). 1996. text, teacher ed. 11.96 (*0-395-67184-1*) HM.

— The Languages of Edison's Electric Light. LC 98-51881. (Inside Technology Ser.). 400p. 1999. 39.50 (*0-262-02456-X*) MIT Pr.

— Shaping Written Knowledge: The Genre & Activity of the Experimental Article in Science. LC 88-40187. (Rhetoric of the Human Sciences Ser.). 400p. (C). 1988. pap. text 24.95 (*0-299-11694-8*) U of Wis Pr.

— Shaping Written Knowledge: The Genre & Activity of the Experimental Article in Science. LC 88-40187. (Rhetoric of the Human Sciences Ser.). 368p. 1988. reprint ed. pap. 114.10 (*0-7837-9775-3*, 206050400005) Bks Demand.

— Students Being Disciplined: Getting Confused, Getting by, Getting Rewarded, Getting Smart, Getting Real. Bridwell-Bowles, Lillian & Donethower, Kim, eds. (Technical Reports: Vol. 12). 9p. (Orig.). 1996. pap. 2.00 (*1-881221-20-2*) U Minn Ctr Interdis.

— Writing Skills Handbook, 3 vols. 3rd ed. (C). 1992. pap. text 4.36 (*0-395-61456-2*) HM.

Bazerman, Charles & Paradis, James, eds. Textual Dynamics of the Professions: Historical & Contemporary Studies of Writing in Professional Communities. LC 90-50079. (Rhetoric of the Human Sciences Ser.). 416p. (Orig.). (C). 1991. text 45.00 (*0-299-12590-4*); pap. text 19.95 (*0-299-12594-7*) U of Wis Pr.

Bazerman, Charles & Russell, David R., eds. Landmark Essays on Writing Across the Curriculum, Vol. 6. (Landmark Essays Ser.). 272p. (C). 1994. pap. text 22.50 (*1-880393-09-3*, Hermagoras) L Erlbaum Assocs.

Bazerman, Charles & Wiener, Harvey S. Writing Skills Handbook, 3 vols. 3rd ed. 160p. (C). 1992. pap. text 14.76 (*0-395-61455-4*) HM.

Bazerman, Charles, jt. auth. see Wiener, Harvey S.

Bazerman, Charles, jt. ed. see Russell, David.

Bazerman, Max. Judgment in Managerial Decision Making. 4th ed. LC 97-14096. 208p. 1997. pap. 40.95 (*0-471-17807-1*) Wiley.

Bazerman, Max H. Environment, Ethics & Behavior: The Psychology of Environmental Valuation & Degradation. LC 96-50093. (New Lexington Press Social & Behavioral Science Ser.). 1997. 58.00 (*0-7879-0809-6*) Jossey-Bass.

— Environment, Ethics & Behavior: The Psychology of Environmental Valuation & Degradation. LC 96-50093. (New Lexington Press Social & Behavioral Science Ser.). 1997. pap. 28.00 (*0-7879-0818-5*) Lxngtn Bks.

— Smart Money Decisions: Why You Do What You Do with Money & How to Change for the Better. LC 98-40652. 256p. 1999. 24.95 (*0-471-29611-2*) Wiley.

Bazerman, Max H. & Lewicki, Roy J., eds. Negotiating in Organizations. LC 83-10156. 392p. 1983. reprint ed. pap. 121.60 (*0-608-01184-3*, 205948200001) Bks Demand.

Bazerman, Max H. & Neale, Margaret A. Negotiating Rationally. (Illus.). 288p. 1992. 29.95 (*0-02-901985-0*) Free Pr.

— Negotiating Rationally. (Illus.). 288p. 1994. per. 16.95 (*0-02-901986-9*) Free Pr.

Bazerman, Steven H. & Drangel, Jason M. Guide to Registering Trademarks. LC 98-41819. 1998. ring bd. 172.00 (*1-56706-683-6*) Aspen Law.

Bazes, Terry R. Goldsmith's Return. 287p. (Orig.). 1995. pap. 14.00 (*1-877727-54-7*) White Pine.

Bazhanov, Boris. Bazhanov & the Damnation of Stalin. Doyle, David M., tr. from RUS. LC 89-35310. (Illus.). 303p. 1990. 30.00 (*0-8214-0948-4*) Ohio U Pr.

Bazhanov, V. V. & Burden, C. J. Statistical Mechanics & Field Theory: Proceedings of the 7th Physics Summer School. LC 96-135642. 450p. 1995. text 86.00 (*981-02-2397-8*) World Scientific Pub.

Bazhaw, W. O. My Fifty-One Years in Oil Exploration. (Illus.). 135p. 1990. 23.95 (*0-929566-05-X*) Post Point Pr.

— The Search for Cheops & His Treasure. (Illus.). 158p. 1988. pap. 12.95 (*0-929566-01-7*) Post Point Pr.

Bazian, Menachem. Using Visual FoxPro 6: Special Edition. LC 98-86968. (Using ... / Que Ser.). 1999. pap. 49.99 (*0-7897-1808-1*) Que.

Bazil, Michelle K., jt. auth. see Kirschenbaum, Harold L.

Bazilchuk, Nancy & Strimbeck, G. Richard. Longstreet Highroad Guide to the Vermont Mountains. LC 98-89178. (Illus.). 320p. 1999. pap. 18.95 (*1-56352-504-6*) Longstreet.

Bazilevic, I. E., et al. Thirteen Papers on Algebra, Topology, Complex Variables, & Linear Programming. (Translations Ser.: Series 2, Vol. 71). 236p. 1968. 44.00 (*0-8218-1771-X*, TRANS2/71) Am Math.

Bazilian, Barbara, jt. auth. see Fine, Judith.

Bazillion, Richard. Modernizing Germany: Karl Bidermann's Career in the Kingdom of Saxony, 1835-1901. LC 89-27468. (American University Studies: History: Ser. IX, Vol. 84). XXI, 450p. 1989. text 66.95 (*0-8204-1185-X*) P Lang Pubng.

Bazillion, Richard J. & Braun, Connie. Academic Libraries as High-Tech Gateways: A Guide to Design & Space Decisions. LC 95-14035. (Illus.). 180p. (Orig.). 1995. pap. 40.00 (*0-8389-0656-7*, 0656-7-2045) ALA.

Bazin, Andre. Bazin at Work: Major Essays & Reviews from the Forties & Fifties. Cardullo, Bert, ed. & tr. by. from FRE. Piette, Alain, tr. from FRE. (Illus.). 256p. (C). 1997. pap. 19.99 (*0-415-90018-2*) Routledge.

— Bazin at Work: Major Essays & Reviews from the Forties & Fifties. Cardullo, Bert, ed. & tr. by. from FRE. Piette, Alain, tr. from FRE. (Illus.). 256p. (C). 1997. 75.00 (*0-415-90017-4*) Routledge.

— Jean Renoir. Truffaut, Francois, ed. Halsey, W. W., II & Simon, William H., trs. from FRE. (Illus.). 320p. 1992. reprint ed. pap. 14.95 (*0-306-80465-4*) Da Capo.

— Orson Welles: A Critical View. Rosenbaum, Jonathan, tr. (Illus.). 138p. 1991. reprint ed. pap. 13.95 (*0-918226-28-7*) Acrobat.

— What Is Cinema?, Vol. 1. Gray, Hugh, tr. & compiled by by. LC 67-18899. 1968. pap. 16.95 (*0-520-00092-7*, Pub. by U CA Pr) Cal Prin Full Svc.

— What Is Cinema?, Vol. 2. Gray, Hugh, tr. & compiled by by. 1972. pap. 16.95 (*0-520-02255-6*, Pub. by U CA Pr) Cal Prin Full Svc.

Bazin, Germain. Baroque & Rococo. LC 84-51843. (World of Art Ser.). (Illus.). 288p. 1985. pap. 14.95 (*0-500-20018-1*, Pub. by Thames Hudson) Norton.

Bazin, Germain, jt. ed. see Huyghe, Rene.

Bazin, Herve. Au Nom du Fils. (FRE.). 1979. pap. 12.95 (*0-7859-3055-8*) Fr & Eur.

— Les Bienheureux de la Desolation. (FRE.). 1980. pap. 15.95 (*0-7859-2680-1*) Fr & Eur.

— Cri de la Chouette. (FRE.). 1974. pap. 10.95 (*0-7859-3053-1*) Fr & Eur.

— Le Demon de Minuit. (FRE.). 1990. pap. 12.95 (*0-7859-3158-9*, 2253054798) Fr & Eur.

— L' Ecole des Peres. (FRE.). 1993. pap. 12.95 (*0-7859-3177-5*, 2253062588) Fr & Eur.

— L' Ecole des Peres. large type ed. (FRE.). 49.95 (*0-7859-6521-1*) Fr & Eur.

An Asterisk (*) at the beginning of an entry indicates that the title is appearing for the first time.

***Bazin, Herve.** Eradication of Smallpox: Edward Jenner & the First & Only Eradication of a Human Infectious Disease. (Illus.). 233p. 2000. 49.95 (*0-12-083475-8*) Acad Pr.

Bazin, Herve. Un Feu Devore un Autre Feu. (FRE.). 1980. pap. 10.95 (*0-7859-3101-5*) Fr & Eur.
— L' Huile sur le Feu. (FRE.). 1981. pap. 12.95 (*0-7859-3065-5*) Fr & Eur.
— Leve-Toi et Marche. (FRE.). 1958. pap. 12.95 (*0-7859-3408-1*) Fr & Eur.
— Madame Ex. (FRE.). 1977. pap. 12.95 (*0-7859-3081-7*) Fr & Eur.
— Le Matrimonie. (FRE.). 1984. pap. 12.95 (*0-7859-3062-0*) Fr & Eur.
— La Mort du Petit Cheval. (FRE.). 1955. pap. 10.95 (*0-7859-3073-6*) Fr & Eur.
— Qui J'Ose Aimer. (FRE.). 1979. pap. 10.95 (*0-7859-3074-4*) Fr & Eur.
— La Terre Qui Meurt. (FRE.). 1988. pap. 10.95 (*0-7859-3217-8*, 2266022679) Fr & Eur.
— La Tete Contre les Murs. (FRE.). 1956. pap. 12.95 (*0-7859-3069-8*) Fr & Eur.
— Vipere au Poing. (FRE.). 1972. pap. 10.95 (*0-7859-3056-6*) Fr & Eur.

Bazin, Herve, ed. Rat Hybrodimas & Rat Monoclonal Antibodies. 480p. 1990. lib. bdg. 299.00 (*0-8493-5438-2*, QR185) CRC Pr.

Bazin, J. & Terray, E., eds. Guerres de Lignages et Guerres D'Etats en Afrique. (FRE.). 534p. 1982. pap. text 40.00 (*2-903928-00-2*) Gordon & Breach.

Bazin, Michael J., ed. Mathematical Models in Microbial Population Dynamics, Vol. I. 216p. 1982. 122.00 (*0-8493-5951-1*, QR86, CRC Reprint) Franklin.

Bazin, Michael J. & Prosser, James I. Physiological Models in Microbiology, 2 vols., Set. LC 87-18330. 1988. reprint ed. 184.00 (*0-8493-5953-8*, CRC Reprint) Franklin.

Bazin, Michael J. & Prosser, James I., eds. Physiological Models in Microbiology, 2 vols., Vol. I. 160p. 1988. 90.00 (*0-8493-5954-6*, QR84, CRC Reprint) Franklin.
— Physiological Models in Microbiology, 2 vols., Vol. II. 160p. 1988. 95.00 (*0-8493-5955-4*, QR84, CRC Reprint) Franklin.

Bazin, Michael J. & Smith, O. L. Soil Microbiology: A Model of Decomposition. 272p. 1982. 161.00 (*0-8493-5952-X*, QR111, CRC Reprint) Franklin.

Bazin, Michael J., jt. auth. see Menell, A.

Bazin, Nancy T. & Seymour, Marilyn D., eds. Conversations with Nadine Gordimer. LC 90-12556. (Literary Conversations Ser.). xxiv, 321 p. 1990. pap. 15.95 (*0-87805-445-6*); text 39.50 (*0-87805-444-8*) U Pr of Miss.

Bazin, Rene. Marriage of Mademoiselle Gimel, & Other Stories. Hoyt, Edna K., tr. LC 71-128719. (Short Story Index Reprint Ser.). 1977. 19.95 (*0-8369-3610-8*) Ayer.
— The Nun (L'Isolee) 243p. 1995. pap. 10.95 (*1-887548-02-5*) St Michael NC.

Bazire, Joyce, ed. The Metrical Life of St. Robert of Knaresborough: Together with the Other Middle English Pieces in British Museum MS. Egerton 3143. (EETS Original Ser.: No. 228). 1968. reprint ed. 30.00 (*0-19-722228-5*, Pub. by EETS) Boydell & Brewer.

Bazire, Joyce & Cross, James E., eds. Eleven Old English Rogationtide Homilies. LC 83-107819. (Toronto Old English Ser.: No. 7). 175p. reprint ed. pap. 54.30 (*0-608-16737-1*, 205612700050) Bks Demand.

Bazirjian, Rosann, ed. New Automation Technology for Acquisitions & Collection Development. LC 95-35322. 207p. 1995. 39.95 (*1-56024-732-0*, Z689) Haworth Pr.

***Bazler, Judith A., ed.** Science Experiments on File, 2 Vols. rev. ed. (Illus.). 580p. (YA). (gr. 4-12). 2000. ring bd. write for info. (*0-8160-3998-4*) Facts on File.

Bazley & Nikolai. Financial Accounting: Concepts & Uses. 2nd ed. (SWC-Accounting Ser.). 1992. mass mkt. 62.50 (*0-538-82228-7*) S-W Pub.

Bazley, John D., jt. auth. see Nikolai, Loren A.

Bazoge, Benoit & Paquet, Gilles, eds. Administration: Unity & Diversity: L'Administration: Unite & Diversite. LC 87-140121. (ENG & FRE.). 353p. 1986. reprint ed. pap. 109.50 (*0-608-02200-4*, 206287000004) Bks Demand.

Bazrod, Sondra Farrell. Hunt for Amazing Treasures. LC 99-23462. 256p. 1999. pap. 12.95 (*0-440-50888-6*) Dell.

Bazu, M. I., jt. auth. see Bajenescu, T. I.

Bazykin, A. D. & Zarkhin, Yu G., eds. Mathematics & Modelling. 310p. 1993. lib. bdg. 165.00 (*1-56072-104-9*) Nova Sci Pubs.

Bazykin, Alexander. Nonlinear Dynamics of Interacting Populations. LC 98-11768. (Neural Systems Ser.). 193p. 1997. text 76.00 (*981-02-1685-8*) World Scientific Pub.

Bazzana, Kevin. Glenn Gould: The Performer in the Work: A Study in Performance Practice. (Illus.). 320p. (C). 1997. 35.00 incl. cd-rom (*0-19-816656-7*) OUP.

Bazzaz, F. A. Plants in Changing Environments: Linking Physiological, Population, & Community Ecology. (Illus.). 329p. (C). 1996. text 74.95 (*0-521-39190-3*); pap. text 30.95 (*0-521-39843-6*) Cambridge U Pr.

Bazzaz, Fakhri, jt. ed. see Korner, Christian.

Bazzaz, Fakhri A. & Grace, John, eds. Plant Resource Allocation. LC 97-12027. (Physiological Ecology Ser.). (Illus.). 303p. 1997. text 84.95 (*0-12-083490-1*) Morgan Kaufmann.

Bazzell, Margaret. Throw Like a Girl. unabridged ed. (Illus.). 28p. 1996. pap. 4.50 (*1-891408-02-X*, GBP-3) Green Bean.

Bazzett, Mary, ed. see Doherty, Catherine D.

Bazzi, Kamal. Concerning Love. LC 99-64514. 64p. 2000. pap. 9.95 (*1-56315-218-5*, Pub. by SterlingHse) Natl Bk Netwk.

Bazzi, Michael, jt. auth. see Errico, Rocco A.

Bazzle, Glennon E. Anatomy of the Perfect Golf Swing: The Surest Way to Better Golf. (Illus.). 1998. pap. 9.95 (*0-9667079-0-7*) Lobdell & Potter.

Bazzoni, Jana O., jt. auth. see Da Vinci Nichols, Nina.

Bazzucchi, Donatella. My Day. (Illus.). 14p. (J). (ps). 1994. pap. 3.99 (*1-881445-35-6*) Sandvik Pub.
— My First Activity Book. (J). 1995. pap. text 26.95 (*1-884832-06-7*) JTG Nashville.

Bazzy, Connie F., compiled by. La Guia de Unity para Curacion. LC 93-61531. (SPA.). 1994. pap. 7.95 (*0-87159-079-4*) Unity Bks.
— La Guia de Unity Para Vivir Prosperamente. LC 93-61520. (SPA.). 123p. 1994. pap. 7.95 (*0-87159-091-3*) Unity Bks.

BBA, Inc. Staff. Cape Sable to Clearwater, FL. 3rd ed. 44p. 1997. spiral bd. 59.95 (*1-885595-19-0*) Better Boating.
— Chart Kit Region 8: Florida West Coast & the Keys. 10th ed. 88p. 1997. spiral bd. 109.99 (*1-885595-17-4*) Better Boating.
— Chart Kit Region 7: Florida East Coast & the Keys. 10th ed. 76p. 1997. spiral bd. 109.95 (*1-885595-18-2*) Better Boating.
— Chart Kit Region 10: Virgin Islands. 5th ed. 1994. ring bd. 44.95 (*1-885595-01-8*) Better Boating.
— Chart Kit Region 4: Chesapeake & Delaware Bays. 7th ed. 78p. 1994. ring bd. 99.95 (*1-885595-00-X*) Better Boating.
— Florida Keys. 6th ed. 30p. 1997. spiral bd. 59.95 (*1-885595-20-4*) Better Boating.
— Jacksonville to Miami. 5th ed. 38p. 1997. 59.95 (*1-885595-21-2*) Better Boating.

BBC Radio 4 Staff. More Poetry Please. (Everyman's Poetry Ser.). 128p. 1998. 3.50 (*0-460-87899-9*, Everyman's Classic Lib) Tuttle Pubng.

BBC Radio 4 Staff, jt. auth. see Hall, Lee.

BBC Staff. Buzz Two. 96p. 1993. pap., student ed. 8.95 (*0-88432-815-5*, BEN410); pap., student ed. 7.95 (*0-88432-816-3*, BEN411); teacher ed. 59.95 incl. audio (*0-88432-814-7*, SEN410) Audio-Forum.
— Choosing Your English for French Speakers. unabridged ed. 346p. 1994. 44.50 incl. audio (*0-88432-672-1*, S32592) Audio-Forum.
— English, "Follow Me to America", 8 bks. (YA). 1991. pap., student ed. 595.00 incl. audio, VHS (*0-88432-991-7*, SV7350) Audio-Forum.
— English, "Follow Me to America", 2 bks., Set. (YA). 1991. pap. 95.00 incl. audio, VHS (*0-614-01474-3*, SV7351) Audio-Forum.
— English from Portuguese: Calling All Beginners. 394p. 1956. pap. 65.00 incl. audio (*0-88432-663-2*, S32579) Audio-Forum.
— English from South & Southeast Asia: Tiger's Eye Series, 3 cass. (URD.). 200p. 1993. pap. 59.50 incl. audio (*0-88432-783-3*, SEN380) Audio-Forum.
— English, "On We Go", 3 cass. pap., teacher ed. 395.00 incl. VHS (*0-88432-654-3*, SV7238) Audio-Forum.
— English Pronunciation: Learning the Sounds of American English. unabridged ed. 128p. (YA). pap. 49.50 incl. audio (*0-88432-674-8*, S32560) Audio-Forum.
— ESL, One Potato. unabridged ed. (Illus.). 34p. (J). 1992. pap. text 19.95 incl. audio (*0-88432-763-9*, 504070) Audio-Forum.
— Financial English. unabridged ed. pap. 44.50 incl. audio (*0-88432-679-9*, SEN225) Audio-Forum.
— France: The All-in-One Travel & Language Guide. LC 97-32219. (Get Around in . . . Ser.). (FRE., Illus.). 128p. 1998. pap. 8.95 (*0-8442-0151-0*, 01510) NTC Contemp Pub Co.
— Germany, Austria, & Switzerland: The All-in-One Travel & Language Guide. LC 98-51066. (Get Around in . . . Ser.). (GER., Illus.). 128p. 1998. pap. 8.95 (*0-8442-0152-9*, 01529) NTC Contemp Pub Co.

BBC Staff. Getting on In Arabic. unabridged ed. (ARA.). 44.50 incl. audio (*0-88432-666-7*, S325AR) Audio-Forum.

BBC Staff. How to Listen. unabridged ed. 109p. pap. 19.95 incl. audio (*0-88432-657-8*, SEN220) Audio-Forum.
— Italy: The All-in-One Travel & Language Guide. (Get Around in . . . Ser.). (ITA., Illus.). 128p. 1998. pap. 8.95 (*0-8442-0154-5*, 01545) NTC Contemp Pub Co.
— Mexico & Central America: The All-in-One Travel & Language Guide. (Get Around in . . . Ser.). (SPA., Illus.). 128p. 1998. pap. 8.95 (*0-8442-0150-2*, 01502) NTC Contemp Pub Co.
— Muzzy Readers, 6 bks., Set, Series I. (J). 1990. 59.95 incl. audio (*1-85497-327-4*) Audio-Forum.
— Muzzy Readers, 6 bks., Set, Series II. (Illus.). (J). 1990. 59.95 incl. audio (*1-85497-262-6*) Audio-Forum.

BBC Staff & BBC Staff. English for Bengali Speakers, 3 cass., Set. unabridged ed. (English: Tiger's Eye Ser.). (BEN.). 200p. 1993. pap. 59.50 incl. audio (*0-88432-778-7*, SEN330) Audio-Forum.
— English for Hindi Speakers, 3 cass., Set. unabridged ed. (English: Tiger's Eye Ser.). (HIN.). 200p. 1993. pap. 59.50 incl. audio (*0-88432-779-5*, SEN340) Audio-Forum.
— English for Marathi Speakers, 3 cass., Set. unabridged ed. (English: Tiger's Eye Ser.). (MAR.). 200p. 1993. pap. 59.50 incl. audio (*0-88432-780-9*, SEN350) Audio-Forum.
— English for Tamil Speakers, 3 cass., Set. (English: Tiger's Eye Ser.). (TAM.). 200p. 1993. pap. 59.50 incl. audio (*0-88432-781-7*, SEN360) Audio-Forum.
— English for Teluga Speakers, 3 cass., Set. (English: Tiger's Eye Ser.). (TEL.). 200p. 1993. pap. 59.50 incl. audio (*0-88432-782-5*, SEN370) Audio-Forum.

BBC Staff & Newman, Penny. Getting by in Portuguese. 2nd ed. LC 96-17357. 1996. pap. 18.95 incl. audio (*0-8120-8447-0*) Barron.

BBC Staff, jt. auth. see Audley, R. J.

BBC Staff, jt. auth. see BBC Staff.

BBC Worldwide Publishing Staff. Short Trips. (Doctor Who Ser.). 1998. pap. 5.95 (*0-563-40560-0*) BBC.

BBC1 Staff. English for French Speakers. pap. 64.50 incl. audio (*0-88432-658-6*, SEN310) Audio-Forum.

Bberanger, Gberard, et al. The Book of Steel. LC 98-199433. xxvii, 1390 p. 1996. write for info. (*2-7430-0022-8*) Technique et Documentation.

BBN. Big Dig. 1997. pap. 10.50 (*0-538-67010-X*) Thomson Learn.
— Rock Band. 1997. pap., student ed. 10.50 (*0-538-66578-0*) Thomson Learn.

BBN Staff. Orca. (MS - Middle School Science Ser.). 1998. teacher ed. 70.00 (*0-538-66312-X*) S-W Pub.
— Orca. (MS - Middle School Science Ser.). 1998. pap., student ed. 13.95 (*0-538-66313-8*) S-W Pub.
— Shipwreck. (MS - Middle School Science Ser.). 1998. teacher ed. 70.00 (*0-538-66304-9*) S-W Pub.
— Shipwreck. (MS - Middle School Science Ser.). 1998. pap., student ed. 13.95 (*0-538-66305-7*) S-W Pub.

BBQ Digest Staff. Heart of Dixie: Glovebox Guide to BBQ. 192p. (Orig.). 1997. pap. 12.95 (*1-56352-374-4*) Longstreet.
— Palmetto State Glovebox Guide to BBQ: South Carolina. LC 96-79806. 192p. (Orig.). 1997. pap. 12.95 (*1-56352-408-2*) Longstreet.
— The Peach State Glovebox Guide to BBQ: Georgia. 192p. (Orig.). 1997. pap. 12.95 (*1-56352-375-2*) Longstreet.

BCA Rules Committee Staff, ed. Billiards - The Official Rules & Record Book, 1992. rev. ed. 160p. (C). 1991. pap. text 5.95 (*1-878493-02-7*) Billiard Congress of Amer.

BCC Staff. Advanced Novel Separations. 196p. 1994. 2450.00 (*0-89336-604-8*, C107R) BCC.
— Chemical Vapor Deposition. 144p. 1990. 2450.00 (*0-89336-693-5*, GB-130) BCC.
— Electrically Driven Separations. 171p. 1992. 1950.00 (*0-89336-889-X*, C111) BCC.
— Mass Merchandised Healthy Foods. 241p. 1991. 2350.00 (*0-89336-733-8*, GA 047N) BCC.
— Membranes for the Nineties: Surface Modification. LC 97-120759. 174p. 1990. 2850.00 (*0-89336-739-7*, C112) BCC.
— Microseusors Fabrication & Applications. 154p. 1990. 1850.00 (*0-89336-734-6*, G124) BCC.
— Neural Networks, Neurocomputers & Beyond. 346p. 1990. 1950.00 (*0-89336-719-2*, G117) BCC.
— New Trends in Antivirals: Highlighting Antisense Oligonucleotides. 156p. 1990. 2450.00 (*0-89336-619-6*, C109) BCC.
— Plastics in Non-Packaging Medical Applications. 224p. 1990. 2350.00 (*0-89336-725-7*, P121) BCC.
— Private Networks: Growth Markets. 117p. 1990. 1950.00 (*0-89336-735-4*, G126) BCC.
— Stereoselective Chemical Technology. 199p. 1990. 2850.00 (*0-89336-724-9*, C079) BCC.
— U. S. Chromatography Reagents Markets. 338p. 1993. 2250.00 (*0-89336-738-9*, C114) BCC.
— The Value Added in Plastics Compounding. 275p. 1990. 3150.00 (*0-89336-727-3*, P-070R) BCC.

BCS & Associates Staff. Banking Smarter: How to Save Money in Your Business Banking Relationship. 1995. text 39.95 (*0-9645966-0-1*, Irwn Prfssnl) McGraw-Hill Prof.

BCSP Staff, jt. auth. see Williams, Lut.

Bdit. Casinos: The International Guide. 4th ed. 1995. pap. 25.00 (*0-9618612-6-6*) Bain Dror.

BDO Consulting Team Staff, jt. ed. see Crossgrove, David.

BDO Seidman, LLP Staff, compiled by. BDO Seidman, LLP Comprehensive Guide to Manufacturing Software. rev. ed. 1050p. 1999. 597.00 incl. cd-rom (*0-9629217-9-3*) Lionheart Pub.
— BDO Seidman, LLP Comprehensive Guide to Manufacturing Software. 14th rev. ed. 1050p. 1999. ring bd. 497.00 (*0-9629217-4-2*) Lionheart Pub.

BDO Seidman, LLP Staff, ed. BDO Seidman, LLP Comprehensive Guide to Manufacturing & Distribution Software. 13th rev. ed. 1050p. 1997. ring bd. 495.00 (*0-9629217-8-5*) Lionheart Pub.

BDO Seidman's Manufacturing Services Staff. BDO Seidman's Comprehensive Guide to Manufacturing Software. 1995. 395.00 (*0-614-32376-2*) Lionheart Pub.

Bdolak, Levanah S. The Aura Coloring Book. Wolff, Arita, ed. (Illus.). 120p. (Orig.). 1991. pap. 11.95 (*0-944278-01-9*) Voyant.
— Eco-Spirit: A Spiritual Guide to Healing the Planet. Wolff, Anita & Moscowitz, Harold, eds. (Illus.). 400p. (Orig.). 1992. pap. 9.95 (*0-944278-02-7*) Voyant.

Bdsa, jt. auth. see Weaver.

Be, Be. The "Be" Attitudes: Positive Approaches to Become a Better You. Caton, Patrick, ed. LC 97-77652. (Illus.). 168p. 1998. pap. 5.95 (*1-56245-336-X*) Great Quotations.

Be Development Team Staff. Be Advanced Topics. 372p. 1998. pap. 39.95 incl. cd-rom (*1-56592-396-0*) OReilly & Assocs.
— Be Developer's Guide. 970p. 1997. pap. 49.95 (*1-56592-287-5*) OReilly & Assocs.

Be, Priscilla, et al. Land of Extremes: A Collection from the San Francisco Women Writers Workshop. (Illus.). 72p. (Orig.). 1991. pap. 5.00 (*1-880306-02-6*) SF Women Writs.

Bea, Holly. Good Night, God. LC 99-11014. (Illus.). 32p. (J). (ps-k). 2000. 14.00 (*0-915811-84-7*, Pub. by H J Kramer Inc) New Wrld Lib.
— My Spiritual Alphabet Book. LC 98-32194. (Illus.). 32p. (J). (ps-2). 2000. 14.00 (*0-915811-83-9*) H J Kramer Inc.
— Where Does God Live? LC 96-30382. (Illus.). 32p. (J). (gr. k-2). 1997. 14.00 (*0-915811-73-1*, Starseed) H J Kramer Inc.

Bea, Louise de, jt. auth. see Sandahl, Pierre.

Bea, Robert G., ed. see Moore, William.

Beabout, Gregory R. Freedom & Its Misuses: Kierkegaard on Anxiety & Despair. LC 95-50161. (Studies in Philosophy: Vol. 12). 1996. pap. 20.00 (*0-87462-612-9*) Marquette.

Beabout, Gregory R. & Wennemann, Daryl J. Applied Professional Ethics: A Developmental Approach for Use with Case Studies. LC 93-39775. 188p. (Orig.). (C). 1994. pap. text 25.50 (*0-8191-9374-7*); lib. bdg. 49.50 (*0-8191-9373-9*) U Pr of Amer.

Beach. When I Hear a Tale. (C). 1996. 48.00 (*0-02-307081-1*, Macmillan Coll) P-H.

***Beach & Reinhartz.** Supervisory Leadership: Focus on Instruction. LC 99-26285. 324p. 1999. 58.67 (*0-205-30601-2*) Allyn.

Beach, Abigail, jt. auth. see Davies, Celia.

Beach, Abigail, jt. ed. see Weight, Richard.

Beach, Allen P. Lake Champlain As Centuries Pass. 128p. 1994. pap. 9.95 (*0-9641856-0-1*) LCMM.

***Beach, Amy.** Amy Beach: The Sea-Fairies, Opus 59. Kuster, Andrew, ed. (Recent Researches in American Music Ser.: Vol. RRA32). (Illus.). xiii, 73p. 1999. pap. 40.00 (*0-89579-435-7*) A-R Eds.

Beach, Amy. Twenty-Three Songs. (Women Composers Ser.). 102p. 1992. reprint ed. 29.50 (*0-306-79717-8*) Da Capo.

Beach Associates Consultants Staff, Consultants, jt. auth. see Hoard, Samuel L.

B

Beach-Balthis, Judy. Ano Nuevo: A Children's Guide. rev. ed. Balthis, Frank S., ed. (Children's Guides on the National Parks Ser.). (Illus.). 24p. (Orig.). (J). (gr. k-8). 1994. pap. 3.95 (*0-918355-02-8*) Firehole Pr.
— Point Reyes: A Children's Guide. Balthis, Frank S., ed. (Children's Guides on the National Parks Ser.). (Illus.). 24p. (Orig.). (J). (gr. k-8). 1993. pap. 3.95 (*0-918355-03-6*) Firehole Pr.
— Yellowstone: A Children's Guide. Balthis, Frank, ed. (Children's Guides on the National Parks Ser.). (Illus.). 36p. (Orig.). (J). (gr. k-8). 1994. pap. 3.95 (*0-918355-01-X*) Firehole Pr.

Beach, Barbara. Children's Book Review Index 1991 Cumulation. 91st ed. 1992. 138.00 (*0-8103-7492-7*) Gale.

Beach, Barbara, ed. Book Review Index Annual Cumulation, 1987. 87th ed. 1988. 260.00 (*0-8103-0579-8*) Gale.
— Book Review Index Cumulation 1985. 85th ed. 1986. 260.00 (*0-8103-0576-3*) Gale.
— Book Review Index, 1986: Annual Cumulation. 86th ed. 1203p. 1987. 260.00 (*0-8103-0578-X*) Gale.
— Book Review Index 1988 Cumulation. 88th ed. 1989. 260.00 (*0-8103-0580-1*) Gale.
— Children's Book Review Index: 1987 Cumulation. 87th ed. 580p. 1988. 138.00 (*0-8103-0647-6*) Gale.
— Children's Book Review Index, 1988 Cumulation. 88th ed. 1989. 138.00 (*0-8103-0648-4*) Gale.

Beach, Barbara, jt. ed. see Tarbert, Gary C.

Beach, Barbara A., jt. auth. see Howley, Lara E.

Beach, Beatrice, jt. auth. see Hu, C. T.

***Beach, Bert Beverly, et al.** 101 Questions Adventists Ask. Lale, Tim, ed. LC 00-23565. 138p. 2000. 14.99 (*0-8163-1790-9*) Pacific Pr Pub Assn.

Beach, Cecilia, compiled by. French Women Playwrights of the Twentieth Century: A Checklist, 24. LC 95-39490. (Bibliographies & Indexes in Women's Studies: No. 24). 536p. 1996. lib. bdg. 85.00 (*0-313-29175-6*, Greenwood Pr) Greenwood.

Beach, Cecilia, ed. French Women Playwrights Before the Twentieth Century: A Checklist, 22. LC 94-28703. (Bibliographies & Indexes in Women's Studies: No. 22). 272p. 1994. lib. bdg. 69.50 (*0-313-29174-8*) Greenwood.

Beach, Chandler B. The Reference Work: A Cyclopaedia for Teachers, Students & Families, 4 Vols. 1112p. 1996. 1250.00 (*81-7044-286-9*, Pub. by Print Hse) St Mut.

Beach, Charles, ed. The Scenery of the Catskills. 50p. pap. 8.95 (*0-941567-36-2*) J C & A L Fawcett.

Beach, Charles & Fordyce, Edward, eds. A Solar World: Proceedings of the Annual Meeting of the International Solar Energy Society, 3 vols., Set. 1977. pap. text 115.00 (*0-89553-004-X*) Am Solar Energy.

***Beach, Charles Fisk.** Commentaries on the Law of Trusts & Trustees Vols. 1 & 2: As Administered in England & in the United States of America. 1999. reprint ed. 385.00 (*1-56169-564-5*) Gaunt.

Beach, Charles M., et al. Distribution of Income & Wealth in Ontario: Theory & Evidence. (Ontario Economic Council Research Studies). 1981. pap. 10.95 (*0-8020-3369-5*) U of Toronto Pr.

Beach, Christopher. ABC of Influence: Ezra Pound & the Remaking of American Poetic Tradition. LC 91-3972. (C). 1992. 48.00 (*0-520-07527-7*, Pub. by U CA Pr) Cal Prin Full Svc.
— Artifice & Indeterminacy: An Anthology of New Poetics. LC 98-21775. (Modern & Contemporary Poetics Ser.). 392p. 1998. text 44.95 (*0-8173-0946-2*) U of Ala Pr.
— Poetic Culture: Contemporary American Poetry Between Community & Institution. LC 99-27504. (Avant-Garde & Modernism Studies). 248p. 1999. pap. 17.95 (*0-8101-1678-2*) Northwestern U Pr.
— Poetic Culture: Contemporary American Poetry Between Community & Institution. LC 99-27504. 248p. 1999. 59.95 (*0-8101-1677-4*) Northwestern U Pr.

Beach, Christopher, ed. Artifice & Indeterminacy: An Anthology of New Poetics. LC 98-21775. 392p. 1998. pap. text 19.95 (*0-8173-0954-3*) U of Ala Pr.

Beach, Clara M. Our Highland Heritage. (Illus.). 391p. 29.00 (*0-9617450-0-2*) Highland Twnship.

Beach, D. N. The Shona & Zimbabwe, 900-1850: An Outline of Shona History. LC 80-14116. 424p. 1980. 54.50 (*0-8419-0624-6*, Africana) Holmes & Meier.

Beach, Dan, jt. auth. see Moore, Ralph E.

Beach, David. The Greater Cleveland Environment Book: Caring for Home & Bioregion. LC 98-96206. (Illus.). 337p. 1998. pap. 14.95 (0-9663999-0-0) EcoCity Clvlnd.

Beach, David, et al, eds. Cell Cycle Control in Eukaryotes (Current Communications in Molecular Biology) Current Communications in Molecular Biology. (Illus.). 211p. 1988. pap. 20.00 (0-87969-317-7) Cold Spring Harbor.

Beach, David P. & Alvager, Torsten K. Handbook for Scientific & Technical Research. 224p. (C). 1991. text 50.27 (0-13-431040-3) P-H.

Beach, David P. & Bridges, Roy G. Industrial Control Electronics. 304p. (C). 1990. pap. text 49.60 (0-13-459256-5) P-H.

Beach, David P. & Foraker, William J. Electronics: Fundamentals & Everyday Applications. 272p. 1991. pap., teacher ed. 16.00 (0-8273-4644-1) Delmar.

***Beach, David R.** Homegrown Hops: An Illustrated How-to Do-It Manual. 2nd ed. LC 97-93552. (Illus.). 110p. 2000. write for info. (0-9621195-2-0) D R Beach.

Beach, David R. Let's Grow Raspberries! LC 90-93433. (Illus.). 90p. (Orig.). 1991. pap. 8.00 (0-9621195-1-2) D R Beach.

Beach, Daytona, et al. Dirt: A Collection from the San Francisco Women Writers Workshop. (Illus.). 64p. (Orig.). 1990. pap. 5.00 (1-880306-01-8) SF Women Writs.

Beach, Dick, jt. auth. see Ford, Bob.

***Beach, Don M.** Sydney Kangaroo's Christmas. LC 99-93251. 22p. (J). 1999. 14.95 incl. audio (0-9671485-0-2) Dot E Pubs.

Beach, Don M., jt. auth. see Reinhartz, Judy.

Beach, Dore. The Responsible Conduct of Research. (Illus.). 162p. 1996. pap. 64.95 (3-527-29333-7, Wiley-VCH) Wiley.

Beach, Earl. Progress & Prosperity. LC 99-10. 202p. 1999. 13.00 (1-55212-242-5) Trafford Pub.

Beach, Edward A. The Potencies of God(s) Schelling's Philosophy of Mythology. LC 91-15128. (SUNY Series in Philosophy). 317p. (C). 1994. text 59.50 (0-7914-0973-2); pap. text 19.95 (0-7914-0974-0) State U NY Pr.

Beach, Edward L. Dust on the Sea. 448p. 1989. mass mkt. 3.95 (0-8217-2580-7, Zebra Kensgtn) Kensgtn Pub Corp.

— Run Silent, Run Deep. 378p. Date not set. 26.95 (0-8488-2627-2) Amereon Ltd.

— Run Silent, Run Deep. LC 85-21801. (Classics of Naval Literature Ser.). 343p. 1986. reprint ed. 32.95 (0-87021-557-4) Naval Inst Pr.

— Salt & Steel: Reflections of a Submariner. LC 98-47175. 27p. 1999. 26.95 (1-55750-054-1) Naval Inst Pr.

— Scapegoats: A Defense of Kimmel & Short at Pearl Harbor. (Illus.). 240p. 1995. 26.95 (1-55750-059-2) Naval Inst Pr.

— The Wreck of the Memphis. 24.95 (0-88411-774-X) Amereon Ltd.

— The Wreck of the Memphis. LC 98-14334. (Classics of Naval Literature Ser.). 328p. 1998. 32.95 (1-55750-070-3) Naval Inst Pr.

Beach, Edward L. & Maroon, Fred J. Keepers of the Sea: A Profile. deluxe ed. LC 82-61291. (Illus.). 256p. 1983. 85.00 (0-87021-736-4) Naval Inst Pr.

Beach, Edward L., jt. auth. see Noel, John V., Jr.

Beach, Elmer T. Beach in America, Containing General Information Regarding the Brother Richard, John & Thomas Beach, Planters in the Original Settlements of New Haven Col., Wallingford Col. & Milford Col., Conn, 1638-1641, & Genealogical Record on a Portion of the Descendants of Richard Beach . . . 149p. 1997. reprint ed. pap. 24.00 (0-8328-7433-7); reprint ed. lib. bdg. 34.00 (0-8328-7432-9) Higginson Bk Co.

Beach, Frank A. Human Sexuality in Four Perspectives. Diamond, Milton et al, eds. LC 76-17235. 336p. reprint ed. pap. 104.20 (0-608-10736-0, 201911400010) Bks Demand.

Beach, Fred F. The Custody of School Funds: An Appraisal of Systems of School Fund Custody with Particular Reference to New York State. LC 73-176546. (Columbia University. Teachers College. Contributions to Education Ser.: No. 577). reprint ed. 37.50 (0-404-55577-2) AMS Pr.

Beach, George K. If Yes Is the Answer, What Is the Question? 1995. pap. 15.00 (1-55896-295-6, Skinner Hse Bks) Unitarian Univ.

— James Luther Adams in Dialogue: A Study Guide to Prophethood of All Believers. (All Souls Resources for Adult Religious Education Ser.). 30p. 1988. pap. text 6.00 (0-9622111-0-9) Unitarian Ch All Souls.

Beach, George K., ed. The Essential James Luther Adams: Selected Essays & Addresses. 248p. 1998. pap. 15.00 (1-55896-352-9, Skinner Hse Bks) Unitarian Univ.

Beach, George K., ed. & intro. see Adams, James L.

***Beach, Heather L.** Transboundary Freshwater Dispute Resolution: Theory, Practice & Annotated References. LC 00-8341. 2000. write for info. (92-808-1038-3, Pub. by UN Univ Pr) Brookings.

Beach, Hugh. Contributions to Circumpolar Studies. (Uppsala Research Reports in Cultural Anthropology: No. 7). 182p. (Orig.). 1986. pap. text 41.50 (91-506-0530-5, Pub. by Uppsala Universitet) Coronet Bks.

— A Year in Lapland: Guest of the Reindeer Herders. LC 92-30436. (Illus.). 280p. 1993. 24.95 (1-56098-230-6) Smithsonian.

Beach, Hugh & Gurr, Nadin. Flattering the Passions: Or, the Bomb & Britain's Bid for a World Role. 279p. 1999. text 49.50 (1-86064-168-7) St Martin.

Beach, J. Mark, tr. see Westerink, H.

Beach, Jeremy, ed. see Noszlopy, George.

Beach, John M., tr. see Gary, Romain.

Beach, Joseph W. The Comic Spirit in George Meredith: An Interpretation. (BCL1-PR English Literature Ser.). 230p. 1992. reprint ed. lib. bdg. 79.00 (0-7812-7595-4) Rprt Serv.

— Method of Henry James. rev. ed. 1954. 20.00 (0-87556-020-2) Saifer.

— Obsessive Images. O'Connor, William V., ed. LC 73-11620. 396p. 1973. reprint ed. lib. bdg. 69.50 (0-8371-7079-6, BEOI, Greenwood Pr) Greenwood.

— The Outlook for American Prose. LC 68-22901. (Essay Index Reprint Ser.). 1977. 20.95 (0-8369-0179-7) Ayer.

— The Outlook for American Prose. (BCL1-PS American Literature Ser.). 284p. 1992. reprint ed. lib. bdg. 79.00 (0-7812-6635-1); reprint ed. lib. bdg. 79.00 (0-7812-6639-4) Rprt Serv.

— A Romantic View of Poetry. 1990. 16.50 (0-8446-1061-5) Peter Smith.

— Romantic View of Poetry. 1988. reprint ed. lib. bdg. 29.00 (0-7812-0048-2) Rprt Serv.

— Romantic View of Poetry. reprint ed. 39.00 (0-403-03886-3) Somerset Pub.

Beach, Judy & Spencer, Kathleen. Big Fearon Book of Teachers' Holiday Helpers. 1987. pap. 20.99 (0-8224-6776-3) Fearon Teacher Aids.

— Christmas. (Teachers' Holiday Helpers Ser.). 1987. pap. 6.99 (0-8224-6773-9) Fearon Teacher Aids.

— Halloween. (Teachers' Holiday Helpers Ser.). 1987. pap. 6.99 (0-8224-6771-2) Fearon Teacher Aids.

— Minds-On Fun for Fall. (J). (gr. k-4). 1991. pap. 10.99 (0-86653-948-4) Fearon Teacher Aids.

— Minds-On Fun for Spring. (J). (gr. k-4). 1991. pap. 10.99 (0-86653-946-8) Fearon Teacher Aids.

— Minds-On Fun for Summer. (J). (gr. k-4). 1991. pap. 10.99 (0-86653-945-X) Fearon Teacher Aids.

— Minds-On Fun for Winter. (J). (gr. k-4). 1991. pap. 10.99 (0-86653-947-6) Fearon Teacher Aids.

— Springtime. (Teachers' Holiday Helpers Ser.). (J). (gr. 1-3). 1987. pap. 6.99 (0-8224-6775-5) Fearon Teacher Aids.

— Thanksgiving. (Teachers' Holiday Helpers Ser.). (J). (gr. 1-3). 1987. pap. 6.99 (0-8224-6772-0) Fearon Teacher Aids.

— Valentine's Day. (Teachers' Holiday Helpers Ser.). (J). (gr. 1-3). 1987. pap. 6.99 (0-8224-6774-7) Fearon Teacher Aids.

Beach, Kenneth, Jr., jt. auth. see Mager, Robert F.

Beach, Lee R. The Psychology of Decision Making: People in Organizations. LC 96-51267. (Foundations for Organizational Science Ser.: Vol. 6). 240p. (C). 1997. 30.00 (0-7619-0079-9, 00799); pap. 13.99 (0-7619-0080-2, 00802) Sage.

Beach, Lee R., ed. Decision Making in the Workplace: A Unified Perspective. 224p. 1996. text 49.95 (0-8058-1992-4) L Erlbaum Assocs.

Beach, Lee R., ed. Decision Making in the Workplace: A Unified Perspective. 224p. 1996. pap. text 24.50 (0-8058-1993-2) L Erlbaum Assocs.

Beach, Lee R., ed. Image Theory: Theoretical & Empirical Foundations. LC 97-27902. (Management Ser.). 250p. 1997. pap. write for info. (0-8058-2646-7) L Erlbaum Assocs.

Beach, Lewis. Cornwall, Connecticut. (Illus.). 200p. 1997. reprint ed. lib. bdg. 29.00 (0-8328-5629-0) Higginson Bk Co.

Beach, Lynn. Curse of the Claw. MacDonald, Pat, ed. (Phantom Valley Ser.: 9). 128p. (J). 1993. pap. 3.50 (0-671-75927-2, Minstrel Bks) PB.

— Curse of the Claw. (Phantom Valley Ser.: 9). (J). 1993. 8.60 (0-606-02832-3, Pub. by Turtleback) Demco.

— The Dark. MacDonald, Patricia, ed. (Phantom Valley Ser.). 128p. (Orig.). (J). 1991. pap. 3.50 (0-671-74089-X, Minstrel Bks) PB.

— Dark. (Phantom Valley Ser.). (J). 1991. 8.60 (0-606-02071-3, Pub. by Turtleback) Demco.

— The Evil One. (Phantom Valley Ser.). 128p. (Orig.). (J). 1991. pap. 3.50 (0-671-74088-1, Minstrel Bks) PB.

— Evil One. (Phantom Valley Ser.). (J). 1991. 8.60 (0-606-05001-9, Pub. by Turtleback) Demco.

— Headless Ghost. (Phantom Valley Ser.). (J). 1992. 8.09 (0-606-02834-X, Pub. by Turtleback) Demco.

— Phantom Valley: The Headless Ghost. McDonald, Patricia, ed. 128p. (Orig.). (J). (gr. 3-6). 1992. pap. 2.99 (0-671-75926-4, Minstrel Bks) PB.

— The Spell. MacDonald, Patricia, ed. (Phantom Valley Ser.: No. 5). 128p. (Orig.). (YA). 1992. pap. 2.99 (0-671-75923-X, Minstrel Bks) PB.

— Spell. (Phantom Valley Ser.). (J). 1992. 8.09 (0-606-02076-4, Pub. by Turtleback) Demco.

Beach, M. S., et al. The Ely Ancestry: Lineage of Richard Ely of Plymouth, England Who Came to Boston about 1655 & Settled at Lyme, Connecticut in 1660. (Illus.). 639p. 1989. reprint ed. pap. 80.00 (0-8328-0519-X); reprint ed. lib. bdg. 90.00 (0-8328-0518-1) Higginson Bk Co.

Beach, Mark. A Bibliographic Guide to American Colleges & Universities: From Colonial Times to the Present. LC 74-11704. 314p. 1975. lib. bdg. 55.00 (0-8371-7690-5, BCU/, Greenwood Pr) Greenwood.

— Desegregated Housing & Interracial Neighborhoods: A Bibliographic Guide. 91p. 1975. 1.00 (0-318-15821-3, N-5) Natl Neighbors.

— Editing Your Newsletter: How to Produce an Effective Publication Using Traditional Tools & Computers. 4th ed. LC 94-29802. (Illus.). 160p. 1995. pap. 22.99 (0-89879-641-5, Wrtrs Digest Bks) F & W Pubns Inc.

— Graphically Speaking: An Illustrated Guide to the Working Language of Design & Printing. (Illus.). 312p. (Orig.). 1992. pap. 29.50 (0-943381-07-X, 30445, Elk Ridge Pub) Coast to Coast.

— Papers for Printing: How to Choose the Right Paper at the Right Price for Any Printing Job. 2nd ed. (Illus.). 108p. (Orig.). (C). 1991. pap. 39.50 (0-943381-06-1, 30280) Coast to Coast.

Beach, Mark, compiled by. A Subject Bibliography of the History of American Higher Education. LC 83-22565. 165p. 1984. lib. bdg. 42.95 (0-313-23276-8, BEH/, Greenwood Pr) Greenwood.

Beach, Mark & Floyd, Elaine. Newsletter Sourcebook. 2nd ed. LC 97-42969. (Illus.). 144p. 1998. pap. 27.99 (0-89879-869-8, Wrtrs Digest Bks) F & W Pubns Inc.

Beach, Mark & Kenly, Eric. Getting It Printed. 3rd ed. LC 98-35378. (Illus.). 208p. 1998. pap. 32.99 (0-89134-858-1, North Lght Bks) F & W Pubns Inc.

Beach, Mary A., jt. auth. see Stetson, Daniel E.

Beach, Milo C. The Adventures of Rama. LC 83-1473. (Illus.). 64p. (Orig.). 1983. 15.00 (0-934686-51-3) Freer.

— Early Mughal Painting (The Polsky Lecture in India & Southeast Asian Art & Archaeology) LC 87-197. (Illus.). 176p. 1987. 44.50 (0-674-22185-0) HUP.

— The Imperial Image: Paintings for the Mughal Court. LC 81-8762. (Illus.). 240p. 1982. 45.00 (0-934686-37-8); pap. 22.50 (0-934686-38-6) Freer.

— Mughal & Rajput Painting. (New Cambridge History of India Ser.: I: 3). (Illus.). 285p. (C). 1992. text 100.00 (0-521-40027-9) Cambridge U Pr.

Beach, Milo C., et al. The King of the World: An Imperial Mughal Manuscript from the Royal Library, Windsor Castle. LC 96-61424. (Illus.). 232p. 1997. 85.00 (0-500-97448-9, Pub. by Thames Hudson) Norton.

Beach, Milo C., jt. auth. see Welch, Stuart C.

Beach, Moses Y. The Wealthy Citizens of New York. LC 73-1992. (Big Business; Economic Power in a Free Society Ser.). 1980. reprint ed. 17.95 (0-405-05117-4) Ayer.

Beach, Nancy, jt. auth. see Dyer, Scott.

Beach, Neva, et al. The Ghirardelli Chocolate Cookbook. LC 95-16335. (Illus.). 144p. (Orig.). 1995. pap. 16.95 (0-89815-769-2) Ten Speed Pr.

Beach, Neva, jt. auth. see Benzola, Edward J.

Beach, Paul Wayne. How to Read & Write Music, Vol. 1. 2nd rev. ed. (Illus.). 150p. (Orig.). 1999. pap. 29.95 (0-9653116-1-9) Aesthetic Artist.

Beach Printing Advertising, Inc. Staff, ed. see Wilcox, Phyllis A.

Beach, R. D. & Gibbons, R. D. Beach: The Rev. John Beach & His Descendants. 397p. 1991. reprint ed. pap. 61.00 (0-8328-2093-8); reprint ed. lib. bdg. 71.00 (0-8328-2092-X) Higginson Bk Co.

***Beach, Rachel Trout.** The Journals of Rachel Trout Beach. Rinaldo, Peter M. & Rinaldo, Dorothy W., eds. LC 99-74750. (Illus.). 250p. 1999. 14.95 (1-890849-02-2) DorPete Pr.

Beach, Rex Ellingwood. The Auction Block. (Collected Works of Rex Ellingwood Beach). 440p. 1998. reprint ed. lib. bdg. 108.00 (1-58201-540-6) Classic Bks.

— The Barrier. (Collected Works of Rex Ellingwood Beach). 309p. 1998. reprint ed. lib. bdg. 98.00 (1-58201-541-4) Classic Bks.

— Big Brother. (Collected Works of Rex Ellingwood Beach). 367p. 1998. reprint ed. lib. bdg. 98.00 (1-58201-532-5) Classic Bks.

— The Crimson Gardenia. (Collected Works of Rex Ellingwood Beach). 250p. 1998. reprint ed. lib. bdg. 88.00 (1-58201-542-2) Classic Bks.

— Flowing Gold. (Collected Works of Rex Ellingwood Beach). 377p. 1998. reprint ed. lib. bdg. 98.00 (1-58201-533-3) Classic Bks.

— Going Some. (Collected Works of Rex Ellingwood Beach). 293p. 1998. reprint ed. lib. bdg. 88.00 (1-58201-534-1) Classic Bks.

— The Goose Woman. (Collected Works of Rex Ellingwood Beach). 266p. 1998. reprint ed. lib. bdg. 88.00 (1-58201-543-0) Classic Bks.

— Heart of the Sunset. 1975. lib. bdg. 16.30 (0-89966-016-9) Buccaneer Bks.

— Heart of the Sunset. (Collected Works of Rex Ellingwood Beach). 365p. 1998. reprint ed. lib. bdg. 98.00 (1-58201-535-X) Classic Bks.

— The Iron Trail. (Collected Works of Rex Ellingwood Beach). 390p. 1998. reprint ed. lib. bdg. 98.00 (1-58201-544-9) Classic Bks.

— Laughing Bill Hyde. (Collected Works of Rex Ellingwood Beach). 392p. 1998. reprint ed. lib. bdg. 98.00 (1-58201-536-8) Classic Bks.

— The Ne'er-Do-Well. (Collected Works of Rex Ellingwood Beach). 401p. 1998. reprint ed. lib. bdg. 108.00 (1-58201-545-7) Classic Bks.

— The Net. (Collected Works of Rex Ellingwood Beach). 332p. 1998. reprint ed. lib. bdg. 98.00 (1-58201-546-5) Classic Bks.

— Oh, Shoot! Confessions of an Agitated Sportsman. (Collected Works of Rex Ellingwood Beach). 280p. 1998. reprint ed. lib. bdg. 88.00 (1-58201-537-6) Classic Bks.

— Pardners. LC 74-101792. (Short Story Index Reprint Ser.). 1977. 20.95 (0-8369-3180-7) Ayer.

— Pardners. (Collected Works of Rex Ellingwood Beach). 278p. 1998. reprint ed. lib. bdg. 88.00 (1-58201-538-4) Classic Bks.

— Rainbow's End. (Collected Works of Rex Ellingwood Beach). 375p. 1998. reprint ed. lib. bdg. 98.00 (1-58201-539-2) Classic Bks.

— The Silver Horde. (Collected Works of Rex Ellingwood Beach). 389p. 1998. reprint ed. lib. bdg. 98.00 (1-58201-547-3) Classic Bks.

— The Spoilers. (Collected Works of Rex Ellingwood Beach). 313p. 1998. reprint ed. lib. bdg. 98.00 (1-58201-548-1) Classic Bks.

— The Spoilers. LC 71-96874. (Illus.). 324p. reprint ed. lib. bdg. 9.25 (0-8398-0157-2) Irvington.

— The Winds of Chance. (Collected Works of Rex Ellingwood Beach). 521p. 1998. reprint ed. lib. bdg. 118.00 (1-58201-549-X) Classic Bks.

Beach, Richard. A Teacher's Introduction to Reader-Response Theories. LC 92-38891. (Teacher's Introduction Ser.). 209p. 1993. pap. 12.95 (0-8141-5018-7) NCTE.

Beach, Richard, et al, eds. Developing Discourse Practices in Adolescence & Adulthood. LC 90-428. (Advances in Discourse Processes Ser.: Vol. 39). 448p. (C). 1990. pap. 42.50 (0-89391-662-5); text 78.50 (0-89391-602-1) Ablx Pub.

Beach, Richard & Bridwell, Lillian S., eds. New Directions in Composition Research. LC 83-5716. (Perspectives in Writing Research Ser.). (Illus.). 432p. 1984. reprint ed. pap. 134.00 (0-608-07581-7, 205989600010) Bks Demand.

Beach, Richard, jt. auth. see Anson, Chris M.

Beach, Richard, jt. auth. see Joyce, William W.

Beach, Richard J. SIGGRAPH 89 Conference Proceedings Vol. 23, No. 3: Computer Graphics. 408p. (C). 1989. pap. text 53.95 (0-201-50434-0) Addison-Wesley.

— SIGGRAPH 90 Conference Proceedings Vol. 24, No. 4: Computer Graphics. 1990. pap. text 39.95 (0-201-50933-4) Addison-Wesley.

Beach, Richard W. & Marshall, James D. Teaching Literature in the Secondary School. 571p. (C). 1990. text 54.50 (0-15-589104-9, Pub. by Harcourt Coll Pubs) Harcourt.

Beach, S. A. Apples of New York, 2 vols., Set. 1993. reprint ed. lib. bdg. 150.00 (0-7812-5229-6) Rprt Serv.

Beach, Sandra, ed. see Connolly, John J.

***Beach, Sean C.** Tyler Hicks' Encyclopedia of Wealth Building Secrets. 5th rev. ed. 450p. 2000. pap. 20.00 (1-56150-360-6) Intl Wealth.

Beach, Sean C., ed. Tyler Hicks' Encyclopedia of Wealth Building Secrets. 3rd rev. ed. 450p. 1998. pap. 20.00 (1-56150-249-9) Intl Wealth.

— Tyler Hicks' Encyclopedia of Wealth Building Secrets. 4th rev. ed. 450p. 1999. pap. 20.00 (1-56150-300-2) Intl Wealth.

Beach, Seth C. Daughters of the Puritans: A Group of Brief Biographies. LC 67-22054. (Essay Index Reprint Ser.). 1977. 21.95 (0-8369-0180-0) Ayer.

Beach, Sharon S. High-End Expert Systems Tools. 1989. 500.00 (0-471-50887-X) Wiley.

Beach, Steven R., et al. Depression in Marriage: A Model for Etiology & Treatment. LC 90-2775. (Treatment Manuals for Practitioners Ser.). 242p. 1990. pap. text 24.00 (0-89862-216-6) Guilford Pubns.

***Beach, Steven R. H.** Marital & Family Processes in Depression: A Scientific Foundation for Clinical Practice. LC 00-29321. 2000. write for info. (1-55798-695-9) Am Psychol.

Beach, Stewart. Good Morning-Sun's Up. LC 79-108178. (Illus.). 32p. (J). (ps-3). 13.95 (0-87592-021-7) Scroll Pr.

Beach, Sylvia. Shakespeare & Company. LC 91-15230. (Illus.). 246p. 1991. reprint ed. pap. 10.95 (0-8032-6097-0, Bison Books) U of Nebr Pr.

Beach, Sylvia, tr. see Michaux, Henri.

Beach, Thomas. Creepy, Crawly Halloween Fright. (Illus.). 12p. (J). (ps-3). 1996. pap. 9.95 (0-8167-3395-3) Troll Communs.

Beach, Vincent W., Jr. George Chapman: An Annotated Bibliography of Commentary & Criticism. LC 95-11696. (Reference Publications in Literature). 1995. 50.00 (0-8161-9077-1, G K Hall & Co) Mac Lib Ref.

Beach, Virginia C. Medway. LC 99-10585. (Illus.). 136p. 1999. 35.00 (0-941711-38-2) Wyrick & Co.

Beach, Waldo. Christian Ethics in the Protestant Tradition. LC 88-8213. 132p. 1989. pap. 24.95 (0-8042-0793-3) Westminster John Knox.

— Christmas Wonder: An Anthology of Verse & Song. LC 73-79038. 96p. reprint ed. pap. 30.00 (0-608-16794-0, 202692400053) Bks Demand.

— Ethical Education in American Public Schools. 64p. 1992. pap. 9.95 (0-8106-1540-1) NEA.

Beach, Wayne A. Conversations About Illness: Family Preoccupations with Bulimia. (Everyday Communication Ser.). 160p. 1996. text 36.00 (0-8058-1756-5); pap. text 17.50 (0-8058-1757-3) L Erlbaum Assocs.

***Beach, William N.** In the Shadow of Mount McKinley. (Illus.). 289p. 2000. pap. 22.95 (1-56833-155-X) Madison Bks UPA.

Beach, William R., et al. Atlas of Arthroscopic Surgery. 352p. 1997. text 175.00 (0-397-51507-3) Lppncott W & W.

Beach York, Carol, see York, Carol Beach.

Beacham, A. D., Jr. A Brief History of the Pentecostal Holiness Church. 1983. pap. 5.95 (0-911866-21-3) LifeSprings Res.

***Beacham, A. D., Jr.** Light for the Journey: A Fresh Focus on Doctrine. 124p. 1998. pap. 5.95 (0-911866-41-8) LifeSprings Res.

Beacham, Billy, jt. auth. see Hanks, Billie.

Beacham, Doug & Kendall, R. T. Tithing: A Call to Serious, Biblical Giving. 1991. pap., teacher ed. 12.95 (0-911866-16-7) LifeSprings Res.

Beacham, Frank, et al. American Cinematographer Video Manual. (Illus.). 420p. 1992. 34.95 (0-935578-10-2) ASC Holding.

— American Cinematographer Video Manual. 2nd ed. (Illus.). 408p. 1994. write for info. (0-935578-12-9) ASC Holding.

Beacham, Richard C. Adolphe Appia: Artist & Visionary of the Modern Theatre. LC 94-133. (Contemporary Theatre Studies: Vol. 6). 320p. 1994. text 45.00 (3-7186-5507-1); pap. text 20.00 (3-7186-5508-X) Gordon & Breach.

— Power into Pageantry: Spectacle Entertainments of Early Imperial Rome. LC 99-11449. (Illus.). 288p. 1999. 35.00 (0-300-07382-8) Yale U Pr.

An Asterisk (*) at the beginning of an entry indicates that the title is appearing for the first time.

— The Roman Theatre & Its Audience. (Illus.). 276p. (C). 1992. 41.00 (*0-674-77913-4*) HUP.

— The Roman Theatre & Its Audience. (Illus.). 288p. 1996. pap. 18.00 (*0-674-77914-2*) HUP.

***Beacham, Stephanie.** The Bible - Old Testament: King James Version. unabridged ed. 1998. audio Price not set. (*0-7871-1804-4*, Dove Audio) NewStar Media.

Beacham, Walton, ed. Research Guide to Biography & Criticism, Set, Vols. 1 & 2. LC 85-2188. (Literature Ser.). 1386p. (C). 1985. lib. bdg. 169.00 (*0-933833-00-8*) Beacham Pub Corp.

— Research Guide to Biography & Criticism, Vols. 5-6. 1150p. 1992. lib. bdg. 169.00 (*0-933833-27-X*) Beacham Pub Corp.

— Research Guide to Biography & Criticism: World Drama. 752p. 1986. lib. bdg. 79.00 (*0-933833-06-7*) Beacham Pub Corp.

Beacham, Walton, et al, eds. New Virginia Review Anthology 2. LC 79-644281. (Illus.). 336p. 1981. 13.50 (*0-318-20431-2*) New VA.

Beacham, Walton & Lowe, David, eds. Research Guide to Biography & Criticism, 1990 Update. 650p. 1990. lib. bdg. 79.00 (*0-933833-23-7*) Beacham Pub Corp.

Beacham, Walton, ed. see Mott, Michael.

Beachamp, Virginia W., ed. A Private War: The Letters & Diaries of Madge Preston, 1862-1867. 374p. 1991. reprint ed. pap. 17.95 (*0-8135-1728-1*) Rutgers U Pr.

Beachcroft, Thomas O. You Must Break Out Sometimes & Other Stories. LC 75-113648. (Short Story Index Reprint Ser.). 1977. 20.95 (*0-8369-3377-X*) Ayer.

Beachem, Cedric D. & Warke, W. R., eds. Fractography-Microscopic Cracking Process - STP 600. 272p. 1976. 27.50 (*0-8031-0360-3*, STP600) ASTM.

Beachem, Cedric D., ed. see American Society for Metals Staff.

Beachey. Anatomy & Physiology in Respiratory Care. LC 97-1309. (Illus.). 409p. (gr. 13). 1997. pap. text, wbk. ed. 40.00 (*0-8151-1198-3*, 27684) Mosby Inc.

Beachey, Ray. The Warrior Mullah: The Horn Aflame, 1892-1920. (Illus.). 173p. 1998. text 25.00 (*0-7881-5471-0*) DIANE Pub.

Beachey, Will. Respiratory Care Anatomy & Physiology: Foundations for Clinical Practice. 1997. wbk. ed. write for info. (*0-8151-2582-8*) Mosby Inc.

Beachley, O. T., Jr., jt. auth. see Scaife, Charles W.

Beachum, Millie. Millie's Fimo Notebook. Bernardino, Valerie, ed. (Illus.). 16p. (Orig.). 1991. pap. 3.95 (*0-938685-07-4*) Dees Delights.

Beachy, Alvin J. The Concept of Grace in the Radical Reformation. 253p. 1977. 77.50 (*90-6004-383-9*, Pub. by B De Graaf) Coronet Bks.

Beachy, E. R. Just Plain People: Tales & Truths of Amish Life. (Illus.). 144p. 1993. reprint ed. pap. 9.95 (*0-8117-3003-4*) Stackpole.

Beachy, Eli R. Trivia of the Un-Civil War. LC 98-207582. 37 p. 1998. 7.00 (*1-55856-284-2*, 167) Closson Pr.

Beachy, J. Wayne. A Bird of Peace Is Born in Petersburg. (Illus.). (Orig.). (J). (gr. 5). 1981. pap. 2.50 (*0-9608084-0-X*) B Hawkins Studio.

— The Extraordinary Ordinary Christmas Matoaca, 1870. (Illus.). 20p. (Orig.). (J). (gr. 5). 1984. pap. 2.50 (*0-9608084-2-6*) B Hawkins Studio.

— The Ghost of Rat Castle: A Story of Old Petersburg. (Illus.). 24p. (J). (gr. 5). 1983. pap. 2.50 (*0-9608084-1-8*) B Hawkins Studio.

— Of Growing up in War. 40p. 1988. 9.99 (*0-9608084-4-2*); pap. 3.99 (*0-685-17363-1*) B Hawkins Studio.

— Richmond Theater Fire, 1862. (Illus.). 24p. (Orig.). (YA). (gr. 5 up). 1987. pap. 3.00 (*0-9608084-3-4*) B Hawkins Studio.

***Beachy, John A.** Introductory Lectures on Rings & Modules. LC 98-54417. (London Mathematical Society Student Texts Ser.: No. 47). (Illus.). 256p. (C). 1999. 64.95 (*0-521-64340-6*); pap. 24.95 (*0-521-64407-0*) Cambridge U Pr.

Beachy, John A. & Blair, William D. Abstract Algebra. 2nd rev. ed. 427p. (C). 1996. text 42.95 (*0-88133-866-4*) Waveland Pr.

Beachy, Mary D. & Wolferman, Kristie. When Peanut Butter Is Not Enough. (Illus.). 100p. (J). (gr. 2-7). 1986. pap. 7.95 (*0-9616883-0-0*) Petit Appetit.

***Beachy, Mary Ellen.** Light on Your Path: True Stories & Scriptures. 237p. (YA). (gr. 2-12). 1999. pap. 10.95 (*1-890050-35-0*) Carlisle Press.

Beachy, Patricia O., ed. see Organization for Obstetric, Gynecologic & Neonatal.

***Beachy, Stephen.** Distortions. 2000. 49.95 (*1-56023-998-0*); pap. 22.95 (*1-56023-999-9*) Haworth Pr.

Beachy, Stephen. The Whistling Song. LC 92-31579. 416p. 1992. pap. 9.95 (*0-393-30949-5*) Norton.

***Beachy, Thomas.** Pennsylvania Deitsh Dictionary: Deitsh to English - English to Deitsh. 164p. 1999. 9.95 (*1-890050-37-7*) Carlisle Press.

Beachy, Walter, et al. Living in the Light of the Lords Return: Pass on the Torch of Truth to Each Generation until the Lord Jesus Christ Appears Again. (Biblical Heritage Ser.: No. 6). 72p. (Orig.). 1995. pap. 3.99 (*0-940883-06-6*) Calvary Pubns.

Beacom, Brian. Wet Wet Wet. (Illus.). 192p. 1996. 29.95 (*1-85158-739-X*, Pub. by Mainstream Pubng) Trafalgar.

***Beacon Books Staff.** Connoisseur's Guide to Golf Courses in England & Wales. 2000. pap. 14.95 (*1-901839-10-9*) Globe Pequot.

— Connoisseur's Guide to Golf Courses in Florida. 2000. pap. 14.95 (*1-901839-15-X*) Globe Pequot.

— Connoisseur's Guide to Golf Courses in the Carolinas. 2000. pap. 14.95 (*1-901839-17-6*) Globe Pequot.

Beacon Books Staff. England & Wales. (Golfing Gems Ser.). 1999. pap. text 14.95 (*1-901839-07-9*) Beacon Bay Pr.

***Beacon Books Staff.** Golfing Breaks: The Complete Guide to Hotels with Courses in Great Britain & Ireland. 2000. pap. text 14.95 (*1-901839-13-3*) Globe Pequot.

Beacon Books Staff. Ireland. (Golfing Gems Ser.). (Orig.). 1999. pap. text 14.95 (*1-901839-09-5*) Beacon Bks.

— Scotland. (Golfing Gems Ser.). 1999. pap. text 14.95 (*1-901839-08-7*) Beacon Bks.

***Beacon Books Staff, ed.** England & Wales 2001. (Golfing Gems Ser.). (Illus.). 2000. pap. 14.95 (*1-901839-22-2*) Beacon Bks.

— Ireland 2001. (Golfing Gems Ser.). (Illus.). 2000. pap. 14.95 (*1-901839-26-5*) Beacon Bks.

— Scotland 2001. (Golfing Gems Ser.). (Illus.). 2000. pap. 14.95 (*1-901839-24-9*) Beacon Bks.

***Beacon Books Staff, BOOKS.** Connoisseur's Guide to Golf Courses in Ireland. 1999. pap. 14.95 (*1-901839-12-5*) Beacon Pub.

— Connoisseur's Guide to Golf Courses in Scotland. 1999. pap. text 14.95 (*1-901839-11-7*) Beacon Pub.

***Beacon Hill Institute Staff.** Just Services: Balancing the Scales of Legal Services Funding in Massachusetts. 78p. 2000. pap. write for info. (*1-886320-06-3*) BHIFPPR.

— Ray Shamie: Innovator, Entrepreneur, Humanitarian, Visionary. 20p. 1999. pap. write for info. (*1-886320-05-5*) BHIFPPR.

Beacon Hill Press Staff. Beacon Small-Group Bible Studies, I Corinthians, Living As a Responsible Christian. 60p. 1982. pap. 4.99 (*0-8341-0755-4*) Beacon Hill.

— Discover the Word. 136p. 1998. pap. text 6.50 (*0-8341-1700-2*) Beacon Hill.

— Discover The Word: Leaders Guide. 52p. 1998. pap. text 5.50 (*0-8341-1701-0*) Beacon Hill.

— Great Passages of the Bible. 1998. pap. text 6.50 (*0-8341-1687-1*) Beacon Hill.

— Great Passages of the Bible: Leaders Guide. 44p. 1998. pap. text 5.50 (*0-8341-1688-X*) Beacon Hill.

— Liberating Law. (Dialog Ser.). 144p. 1999. pap. text, student ed. 6.50 (*0-8341-1708-8*) Beacon Hill.

— Mirror Image: 12 Ways to Becoming More Christlike. 44p. 1999. pap. text, teacher ed. 5.50 (*0-8341-1723-1*) Beacon Hill.

— Mirror Image: 12 Ways to Becoming More Christlike. 128p. 1999. pap. text, student ed. 6.50 (*0-8341-1722-3*) Beacon Hill.

— Stewardship Strategies: Sermons, Letters & Strategies for Promoting Biblical Stewardship. 168p. 1998. 79.99 (*0-8341-1743-6*) Beacon Hill.

***Beacon Hill Press Staff.** Unseen Powers: Realities of Our Relation to the Spiritual Realm. 2000. pap. 6.50 (*0-8341-1805-X*); pap., teacher ed. 5.50 (*0-8341-1804-1*) Beacon Hill.

***Beacon Press Staff.** Drawing Us In: Essays on How We Experience Visual Art. LC 99-86940. 2000. pap. 20.00 (*0-8070-6606-0*) Beacon Pr.

Beacon Press Staff, et al, eds. Here Lies My Heart: Why We Marry, Why We Don't & What We Find There. LC 98-39975. 208p. 1999. pap. 15.00 (*0-8070-6217-0*) Beacon Pr.

Beacon, Ursula, ed. see Oliver, Eric.

Beaconsfield, Benjamin D. First Earl of Lothair. (BCL1-PR English Literature Ser.). 485p. 1992. reprint ed. lib. bdg. 99.00 (*0-7812-7433-8*) Rprt Serv.

— First Earl of Lothair. 1981. reprint ed. lib. bdg. 16.00 (*0-403-00458-6*) Scholarly.

— First Earl of Tancred, or the New Crusade. 1981. reprint ed. lib. bdg. 17.00 (*0-403-00457-8*) Scholarly.

— Popanilla & Other Tales. fac. ed. LC 79-113649. (Short Story Index Reprint Ser.). 1977. 23.95 (*0-8369-3378-8*) Ayer.

Beaconsfield, Hannah. Welcome to Planet Earth: A Guide for Walk-Ins, Starseeds & Lightworkers of All Varieties. 1998. pap. 14.95 (*0-929385-98-5*) Light Tech Pubng.

Beacroft, Bernard. The Voyages of Christopher Columbus. Reeves, Marjorie, ed. (Then & There Ser.). (Illus.). 96p. (Orig.). (gr. 7-12). 1978. pap. text 4.95 (*0-582-21727-X*) Longman.

***Beade, Lisa Roseman, et al.** Rhode Island: The Wealth of Nations - A Peoples History. LC 99-41082. (History Ser.). (Illus.). 1999. 39.00 (*1-58192-004-0*) Community Comm.

Beadle, C. L., et al. Photosynthesis in Relation to Plant Production in Terrestrial Environments. (Illus.). 162p. 1985. text 105.00 (*1-85148-003-X*, Tycooly Pub) Weidner & Sons.

Beadle, Cosette & Hampshire, Joan. Star Track Reading & Spelling: A Training Manual for Low Flyers. 250p. 1997. pap. 95.00 (*1-56593-606-X*, 1258) Singular Publishing.

***Beadle, D., ed.** Progress in Neuropharmacology & Neurotoxicology of Pesticides & Drugs. 217p. 1999. 160.00 (*0-85404-729-8*, Pub. by Royal Soc Chem) Spr-Verlag.

Beadle, Edward R. & Castillo, Vincent J., eds. Accelerator Instrumentation. LC 90-55838. (AIP Conference Proceedings Ser.: No. 212). 232p. 1990. lib. bdg. 80.00 (*0-88318-645-4*) Am Inst Physics.

Beadle, Eugene H., Jr. Fishing the Eastern Sierras in Snowy Waters. LC 95-90993. 130p. (Orig.). 1996. pap. 9.95 (*0-533-11814-X*) Vantage.

Beadle, George W. Genetics & Modern Biology. LC 63-21535. (American Philosophical Society, Memoirs Ser.: Vol. 57). 83p. reprint ed. pap. 30.00 (*0-608-13256-X*, 202513400042) Bks Demand.

Beadle, Harold E., Jr. Fishing the Eastern Sierras in Snowy Water. LC 97-90004. (Illus.). 1997. pap. 14.95 (*0-533-12265-1*) Vantage.

Beadle, Jeremy. Doing Business. 1995. per. 10.95 (*0-85449-110-4*, Pub. by Gay Mens Pr) LPC InBook.

Beadle, Jeremy J. The Virgin Guide to Classical Music. 320p. 1995. pap. 12.95 (*0-86369-658-9*, Pub. by Virgin Bks) London Brdge.

Beadle, John H. The Undeveloped West: or Five Years in Territories. LC 72-9427. (Far Western Frontier Ser.). (Illus.). 828p. 1973. reprint ed. 56.95 (*0-405-04958-7*) Ayer.

Beadle, Muriel. These Ruins are Inhabited. LC 77-83865. (Midway Reprint Ser.). 359p. Date not set. reprint ed. pap. 111.30 (*0-608-20997-X*, 205452500003) Bks Demand.

— Where Has All the Ivy Gone? A Memoir of University Life With a New Epilogue. LC 77-89292. (Midway Reprint Ser.). 414p. Date not set. reprint ed. pap. 128.40 (*0-608-20998-8*, 205452600003) Bks Demand.

Beadle, Richard. New Science out of Old Books: Studies in Manuscripts & Early Printed Books in Honour of A. I. Doyle. Piper, A. J., ed. (Illus.). 467p. 1995. 121.95 (*1-85928-003-X*, Pub. by Scolar Pr) Ashgate Pub Co.

Beadle, Richard, ed. The Cambridge Companion to Medieval English Theatre. (Cambridge Companions to Literature Ser.). (Illus.). 394p. (C). 1994. pap. text 19.95 (*0-521-45916-8*) Cambridge U Pr.

***Beadle, Richard & King, Pamela M., eds.** York Mystery Plays: A Selection in Modern Spelling. (Oxford World's Classics Ser.). (Illus.). 320p. 1999. pap. 11.95 (*0-19-283710-9*) OUP.

Beadle, Richard, jt. compiled by see McKitterick, Rosamond.

Beadle, Richard, jt. ed. see Takamiya, Toshiyuki.

Beadle, Robert W., jt. ed. see Semonin, Richard W.

Beadle, Tony. Chevrolets of the 1950s. LC 97-21736. (Illus.). 128p. 1997. pap. 19.95 (*0-7603-0395-9*) MBI Pubg.

Beadles, Gloria. Middle School Media Magic. Britt, Leslie & Keeling, Jan, eds. LC 96-75149. (Illus.). 64p. (Orig.). (J). (gr. 5-8). 1995. pap. text 8.95 (*0-86530-339-8*, IP 310-2) Incentive Pubns.

Beadles, Patricia, jt. auth. see Harlowe, Diane.

Beadles, William T., jt. auth. see Crawford, Muriel L.

***Beadwork Magazine Staff & Dairy Barn Cultural Arts Center Staff, prods.** The Best in Contemporary Beadwork: Bead International 2000. (Illus.). 2000. 29.95 (*1-883010-77-2*) Interweave.

Beafield, Marion W., Jr., jt. auth. see Alces, Peter A.

Beagan, Glenda. The Medlar Tree. 148p. (Orig.). 1992. pap. 18.95 (*1-85411-068-3*, Pub. by Seren Bks) Dufour.

Beagle, Abbey, ed. see Bradley, Susan.

Beagle, M. J. The New Hampshire Primer: An Almost Fool-Proof Guide for Winning the New Hampshire Presidential Primary. (Illus.). 64p. (Orig.). 1995. pap. text 9.95 (*0-9642213-4-9*) Moose Cntry.

Beagle, M. J., ed. Sit Free or Die: John Stark, Clear Thinking, Daniel Webster, & New Hampshire's Outhouse Heritage. (Illus.). 50p. (Orig.). 1994. pap. text 4.95 (*0-9642213-0-6*) Moose Cntry.

***Beagle, Peter S.** Dance for Emilia. 2000. 14.95 (*0-451-45800-1*, ROC) NAL.

Beagle, Peter S. A Fine & Private Place. (Illus.). 304p. 1992. mass mkt. 14.95 (*0-451-45096-5*, ROC) NAL.

— A Fine & Private Place. 1993. reprint ed. lib. bdg. 18.95 (*0-89968-419-X*, Lghtyr Pr) Buccaneer Bks.

— Giant Bones. LC 96-29872. 224p. 1997. mass mkt. 4.95 (*0-451-45651-3*) NAL.

— The Innkeeper's Song: A Novel. 352p. 1994. mass mkt. 14.95 (*0-451-45414-6*, ROC) NAL.

— The Last Unicorn. 224p. 1991. mass mkt. 13.95 (*0-451-45052-3*, ROC) NAL.

— The Last Unicorn. large type ed. LC 98-41762. 1998. 23.95 (*0-7838-0395-8*, G K Hall Lrg Type) Mac Lib Ref.

— The Rhinoceros Who Quoted Nietzsche & Other, Odd Acquaintances. 183p. 1997. pap. 14.00 (*0-9648320-7-0*) Tachyon Pubns.

— Tamsin. LC 99-30695. 275p. 1999. 21.95 (*0-451-45763-3*, ROC) NAL.

Beagle, Peter S. & Berliner, Janet, eds. Peter S. Beagle's Immortal Unicorn. 416p. 1998. mass mkt. 6.50 (*0-06-105480-1*, HarperPrism) HarpC.

***Beagle, Peter S. & Berliner, Janet, eds.** Peter S. Beagle's Immortal Unicorn, Vol. II. (Immortal Unicorn Ser.). 464p. 1999. mass mkt. 5.99 (*0-06-105929-3*, HarperPrism) HarpC.

Beagle, Rebecca S., tr. see Soyer, Abraham.

Beaglehole, Ernest. Notes on Hopi Economic Life. LC 76-43655. (Yale Univ. Publications in Anthropology: No. 15). reprint ed. 24.50 (*0-404-15489-1*) AMS Pr.

— Property: A Study in Social Psychology. LC 73-14147. (Perspectives in Social Inquiry Ser.). 332p. 1974. reprint ed. 20.95 (*0-405-05493-9*) Ayer.

Beaglehole, Ernest & Beaglehole, Pearl. Ethnology of Pukapuka. (BMB Ser.: No. 150). 1972. reprint ed. 50.00 (*0-527-02258-6*) Periodicals Srv.

Beaglehole, John C. The Life of Captain James Cook. LC 73-87124. (Illus.). xiv, 804p. 1974. pap. 24.95 (*0-8047-2009-6*) Stanford U Pr.

Beaglehole, John C., ed. The Journals of Captain Cook on His Voyages of Discovery: Edited from Original Manuscripts: Four Volumes & a Portfolio, 5 vols. LC 99-18458. (Illus.). 2720p. 1999. 1070.00 (*0-85115-744-0*) Boydell & Brewer.

Beaglehole, Pearl, jt. auth. see Beaglehole, Ernest.

Beaglehole, R., et al. Basic Epidemiology. (CHI, ENG, FRE & SPA.). viii, 174p. 1993. pap. text 18.00 (*92-4-154446-5*, 1150395) World Health.

— Basic Epidemiology. (ENG & FRE.). xv, 216p. 1994. pap. text, teacher ed. 27.00 (*0-614-08032-0*, 1930060) World Health.

Beaglehole, Robert & Bonita, Ruth. Public Health at the Crossroads: Achievements & Prospects. (Illus.). 260p. (C). 1997. text 74.95 (*0-521-58373-X*); pap. text 32.95 (*0-521-58665-8*) Cambridge U Pr.

Beaglehole, T. H. Thomas Munro & the Development of Administrative Policy in Madras, 1792-1818: The Origins of the Munro System. LC 65-17209. 193p. reprint ed. pap. 55.10 (*0-608-12267-X*, 2024419) Bks Demand.

Beagley, Joyce & Shore, Delia. Alva Community, Oklahoma. (Illus.). 567p. 1987. 60.00 (*0-88107-075-0*) Curtis Media.

Beagon, Mary. Roman Nature: The Thought of Pliny the Elder. (Classical Monographs). 270p. 1992. text 65.00 (*0-19-814726-0*) OUP.

Beahan. Hard Target. 1990. pap. text 14.95 (*0-920911-91-9*, Pub. by Breakwater Bks) BookWorld.

Beahan, Laurence T. My Grampa's Woods: The Adirondacks. 2000. pap. write for info. (*0-925168-75-0*) North Country.

Beahan, Virginia & McPhee, Laura. No Ordinary Land: Encounters in a Changing Environment. (Illus.). 112p. 1998. 53.00 (*0-89381-733-3*) Aperture.

***Beahm, E. C.** Technical Assistance in Review of Source Term- Related Issues of Advanced Reactors. 28p. 1998. pap. 2.75 (*0-16-062961-6*) USGPO.

Beahm, George. Kirk's Works. (Fantasy Artists Ser.: No. 2). (Illus.). (Orig.). 1980. pap. 10.00 (*0-9603276-1-4*) Heresy Pr.

— Stephen King: America's Best-Loved Boogeyman. LC 98-5322. 304p. 1998. pap. 12.95 (*0-8362-5427-9*) Andrews & McMeel.

— Stephen King Country. LC 98-66652. (Illus.). 144p. 1999. 14.95 (*0-7624-0456-6*) Running Pr.

Beahm, George W. The Stephen King Companion. 32.95 (*0-8488-1550-5*) Amereon Ltd.

— The Stephen King Companion. rev. ed. LC 95-23170. 332p. 1995. pap. 12.95 (*0-8362-0455-7*) Andrews & McMeel.

— Stephen King from A to Z: An Encyclopedia of His Life & Work. LC 98-22006. 272p. 1998. pap. 14.95 (*0-8362-6914-4*) Andrews & McMeel.

Beahrs, John O. Limits of Scientific Psychiatry: The Role of Uncertainty in Mental Health. LC 86-11692. 250p. 1986. text 39.95 (*0-87630-420-X*) Brunner-Mazel.

Beahrs, Oliver, et al. Surgical Consultations: Update 2. 512p. 1994. 75.00 (*0-8151-0553-3*) Mosby Inc.

— Surgical Consultations: Update 3. 512p. 1995. 75.00 (*0-8151-0554-1*) Mosby Inc.

— Surgical Consultations: Update 4. 1996. 75.00 (*0-8151-0555-X*) Mosby Inc.

Beahrs, Oliver H., et al. An Atlas of the Surgical Techniques of Oliver H. Beahrs. LC 84-1231. (Illus.). 332p. 1985. text 110.00 (*0-7216-1602-X*, W B Saunders Co) Harcrt Hlth Sci Grp.

— Colorectal Tumors. LC 65-8436. (Illus.). 334p. 1986. text 69.50 (*0-397-50677-5*, Lippnctt) Lppncott W & W.

Beahrs, Oliver H., ed. see American Joint Committee on Cancer.

Beai, Steve. Censoring the Censors. LC 97-77922. 1998. pap. 12.95 (*1-886094-81-0*) Chicago Spectrum.

Beaird, Richard F. Sweet Revenge. 416p. (Orig.). 1986. mass mkt. 3.50 (*0-8217-1904-1*, Zebra Kensgtn) Kensgtn Pub Corp.

***Beaird, Steven & Hayes, William E.** Building an Endowment. 81p. 1999. pap. 8.00 (*1-55833-222-7*) Natl Cath Educ.

Beak, Barbara. Octavia Warms Up. LC 91-31644. (Illus.). 24p. (J). 1992. 1.99 (*0-85953-786-2*) Childs Play.

— Walter Worm's Good Turn. LC 91-33548. (Illus.). 24p. (J). 1992. 1.99 (*0-85953-785-4*) Childs Play.

Beake, Fred. Imaginations of Mr. Shelley. 68p. pap. write for info. (*3-7052-0930-2*, Pub. by Poetry Salzburg) Intl Spec Bk.

Beake, Fred. Places & Elegies: Poems & Translations. LC 98-213925. 1998. pap. 14.95 (*3-7052-0118-2*, Pub. by Poetry Salzburg) Intl Spec Bk.

Beake, Fred. Towards the West & Other Poems. 68p. pap. write for info. (*3-7052-0648-6*, Pub. by Poetry Salzburg) Intl Spec Bk.

— The Whiteness of Her Becoming. 235p. write for info. (*3-7052-0220-0*, Pub. by Poetry Salzburg) Intl Spec Bk.

Beake, Fred, ed. A Mingling of Streams Vols. 1-9: An Anthology of Poems Selected from "The Poet's Voice" 243p. pap. write for info. (*3-7052-0912-4*, Pub. by Poetry Salzburg) Intl Spec Bk.

Beake, Fred, et al, eds. The Poet's Voice. 1997. pap. 8.95 (*3-7052-0084-4*, Pub. by Poetry Salzburg) Intl Spec Bk.

Beake, Lesley. Song of Be. (J). 1995. 9.09 (*0-606-08183-6*, Pub. by Turtleback) Demco.

Beaken, Mike. The Making of Language. 208p. 1996. pap. 19.50 (*0-7486-0717-X*, Pub. by Edinburgh U Pr) Col U Pr.

Beakes, N., et al. Our Wonderful World: Solutions for Math & Science. (J). (gr. 5-9). 1987. 16.95 (*1-881431-08-8*, 1308) AIMS Educ Fnd.

Beakley, Brian & Ludlow, Peter, eds. The Philosophy of Mind: Classical Problems - Contemporary Issues. (Illus.). 648p. 1992. 42.50 (*0-262-02340-7*, Bradford Bks); pap. text 28.50 (*0-262-52167-9*, Bradford Bks) MIT Pr.

Beakley, Brian, tr. see Lyotard, Jean-Francois.

Beakley, Clyde A. Laugh Quickly. 136p. 1992. pap. write for info. (*0-9636782-0-5*) C Beakley.

— Mild & Bitter. 44p. 1949. text 9.45 (*0-9636782-2-1*) C Beakley.

— Mild & Bitter, Vol. 2. 94p. 1966. text 12.45 (*0-9636782-9-9*) C Beakley.

— Summer Snow & Other Words. (Orig.). pap. write for info. (*0-9636782-1-3*) C Beakley.

Beakley, George C. Freehand Drawing & Visualization. LC 81-3803. (gr. 12). 1982. pap. text. write for info. (*0-672-97972-1*) Macmillan.

B

Beakman, Claudia & Dougherty, Karla. Playing the Personals: Dating in the '90s. LC 97-122164. 1996. mass mkt. 5.99 (*0-671-88826-9*, Pocket Books) PB.

Beaky. Harvest Reader. 2nd ed. (C). 1991. pap. text, teacher ed. 5.00 (*0-15-535253-9*) Harcourt Coll Pubs.

Beal. The Fantasy Book. 1997. 22.00 (*0-684-80409-3*) S&S Trade.

Beal, Anthony. D. H. Lawrence. LC 72-81101. (Writers & Critics Ser.). 128 p. 1972. write for info. (*0-399-50264-5*) Capricrn Books.

Beal, Anthony. A Short Apprehensive History of the World. 189p. 20.99 (*0-9635524-1-4*); pap. 10.99 (*0-9635524-0-6*) Brainerd Bks.

Beal, Bob & Macleod, Rod. Prairie Fire: The 1885 North-West Rebellion. (Illus.). 384p. (Orig.). 1994. pap. 19.99 (*0-7710-1109-1*) McCland & Stewart.

Beal, Carole R. Boys & Girls: The Development of Gender Roles. LC 93-6422. 416p. (C). 1993. pap. 45.94 (*0-07-004533-X*) McGraw.

Beal, Chandra M. Splash Across Texas! The Definitive Guide to Swimming in Central Texas. (Illus.). 400p. 1999. (*0-9671604-0-5*) La Luna Pubg.

Beal, Christine. Masonry: Concrete, Brick & Stone. 2nd ed. Samuelson, Alexander & Schiff, David, eds. LC 96-84686. (Illus.). 176p. 1998. pap. 14.95 (*1-880029-86-3*) Creative Homeowner.

Beal, D. F., ed. Advances in Computer Chess: Proceedings of the International Conference, Brunel University, U. K., 1984, No. 4. (Chess Ser.). (Illus.). 200p. 1986. 39.95 (*0-08-029763-3*, P115, D135, Pub. by PPL) Elsevier.

Beal, Daniel E. Dances from Norway. (Illus.). 192p. (Orig.). 1988. pap. text 14.95 (*0-317-91222-4*) D E Beal.

Beal, Diana J., jt. auth. see Ward, Frank A.

Beal, Don, jt. ed. see Levy, David N.

Beal, Doug. Sports Illustrated Volleyball: The Keys to Excellence. (Orig.). 1993. pap. 12.95 (*1-56800-009-X*, Pub. by Sports Illus Bks) Natl Bk Netwk.

***Beal, Edward W.** Cardinal Rules of Legal Interpretation. LC 00-39624. 2000. write for info. (*1-57588-642-1*) W S Hein.

***Beal, Eileen.** Choosing a Career in the Restaurant Industry. rev. ed. (World of Work Ser.). (Illus.). 64p. (YA). (gr. 7-12). 1999. 16.95 (*0-8239-3002-5*) Rosen Group.

Beal, Eileen. Ritalin. (Drug Abuse Prevention Library). 64p. (J). (gr. 7-12). 1998. pap. 6.95 (*1-56838-248-0*) Hazelden.

Beal, Ellen, ed. Peterson's Study Abroad, 1998. 5th ed. 1000p. 1997. pap. 26.95 (*1-56079-861-0*) Petersons.

— Peterson's Summer Opportunities for Kids & Teenagers, 1998. 15th ed. 1248p. 1997. pap. 26.95 (*1-56079-852-1*) Petersons.

Beal, Ellen, jt. ed. see Greenberg, Peter.

Beal, Ernest O. & Thieret, John W. Aquatic & Wetland Plants of Kentucky. (Kentucky Nature Preserves Commission Scientific & Technical Ser.: Vol. 5). (Illus.). vii, 315p. 1986. reprint ed. pap. 26.00 (*0-9673646-4-7*) KY State Nature.

Beal, Fred E. Proletarian Journey: New England, Gastonia, Moscow. LC 73-179505. (Select Bibliographies Reprint Ser.). 1977. reprint ed. 26.95 (*0-8369-6634-1*) Ayer.

Beal, George. The Julian Messner Young Reader's Thesaurus. (J). 1984. pap. 6.95 (*0-685-09676-9*) S&S Trade.

— The Kingfisher Illustrated Pocket Thesaurus. LC 96-64. (Illus.). 160p. (J). (gr. 4-8). 1996. pap. 10.95 (*1-85697-673-4*) LKC.

— The Kingfisher Illustrated Thesaurus. rev. ed. LC 95-40613. (Illus.). 144p. (YA). (gr. 5 up). 1996. 16.95 (*1-85697-680-7*, Kingfisher) LKC.

— Playing Cards & Tarots. 1989. pap. 25.00 (*0-85263-924-4*, Pub. by Shire Pubns) St Mut.

— The Simon & Schuster Young Readers' Thesaurus. Barish, Wendy, ed. (Illus.). 192p. (J). (gr. 3-7). 1984. pap. 6.95 (*0-685-09127-9*) Litle Simon.

— The Simon & Schuster Young Readers' Thesaurus. (Illus.). 192p. (YA). (gr. 4 up). 1984. pap. 8.99 (*0-671-50816-4*) S&S Bks Yung.

— Simon & Schuster Young Readers' Thesaurus. LC 84-226920. (J). 1984. 13.05 (*0-606-03467-6*, Pub. by Turtleback) Demco.

***Beal, George.** Whitaker's Obituary Almanack: The Essential Guide to the Obituaries of 1999. 300p. 2000. pap. 40.00 (*0-11-702266-7*, Pub. by Statnry Office) Balogh.

Beal, George & Chatterton, Martin. The Kingfisher First Thesaurus. LC 92-45572. (Illus.). 144p. (J). (gr. 2-6). 1993. 16.95 (*1-85697-914-8*, Kingfisher) LKC.

Beal, Graham J. Joe Goode. LC 76-39803. 12p. 1976. pap. 2.00 (*0-685-64996-2*) Wash U Gallery.

Beal, Graham W. The Charles Parsons Collection of Paintings. LC 77-3962. (Illus.). 80p. 1977. pap. 5.00 (*0-936316-08-X*) Wash U Gallery.

— David Nash: Voyages & Vessels. LC 94-14907. (Illus.). 83p. (Orig.). 1994. pap. 19.95 (*0-936364-23-8*) Joslyn Art.

Beal, Graham W. & Farber, Janet L. Midlands Invitational, 1992: Installation. LC 92-46761. 1993. pap. 12.00 (*0-936364-22-X*) Joslyn Art.

Beal, Graham W., et al. Fifty Favorites from the Joslyn Art Museum. LC 94-3684. (Illus.). 110p. (Orig.). 1994. pap. 19.95 (*0-936364-24-6*) Joslyn Art.

Beal, Granville. Beal. John Beal of Hingham & One Line of His Descendants. 42p. 1997. reprint ed. pap. 9.00 (*0-8328-7441-8*); reprint ed. lib. bdg. 19.00 (*0-8328-7440-X*) Higginson Bk Co.

Beal, James, jt. auth. see Ahrari, M. E.

Beal, James A., et al. Forest Insects of the Southeast: With Special Reference to Species Occurring in the Piedmont Plateau of North Carolina. LC 52-3620. (Duke University, School of Forestry Bulletin Ser.: No. 14). 218p. reprint ed. pap. 67.60 (*0-7837-6043-4*, 204585600008) Bks Demand.

Beal, James P. Employee Productivity System: Job Descriptions - Performance Evaluations for AG & IND. EQ Dealerships. Beal, Lenore A., ed. 1994. disk 200.00 (*0-9634476-2-9*) Taking Care Of Busn.

— Employee Productivity System: Job Descriptions - Performance Evaluations for AG & IND. EQ Dealerships. Beal, Lenore A., ed. 300p. 1992. reprint ed. wbk. ed. 500.00 (*0-9634476-0-2*) Taking Care Of Busn.

— Packaged Repair Guides for Service Departments in Equipment Dealerships: Parts & Labor Are Included with Detailed Breakdowns. Beal, Lenore A., ed. 65p. 1988. wbk. ed. 500.00 (*0-9634476-5-3*) Taking Care Of Busn.

— Pre-Delivery & Set-Up Guides for Sales & Service Departments in Case-IH & John Deere: Equipment Dealerships. Beal, Lenore A., ed. (Managed Approach to time & Costs Ser.). 6p. 1987. wbk. ed. 150.00 (*0-9634476-4-5*) Taking Care Of Busn.

— Sales Department Gross Margin Profit Based Compensation System: A Blue Print to Profit Base, an AG & IND. Equipment Dealership Sales Team. Beal, Lenore A., ed. 50p. 1996. wbk. ed. 200.00 (*0-9634476-3-7*) Taking Care Of Upper Busn.

***Beal, John.** The Runner from Upper Boon Docks. (Illus.). 181p. 1999. write for info. (*0-7541-0775-2*, Pub. by Minerva Pr) Unity Dist.

Beal, John M. & Raffensperger, John G. Diagnosis of Acute Abdominal Disease. LC 79-811. 177p. reprint ed. pap. 54.90 (*0-608-30233-3*, 205541500022) Bks Demand.

Beal, John M., jt. auth. see Preston, Frederick W.

Beal, John P., et al, eds. New Commentary on the Code of Canon Law. LC 98-49546. 1984p. 2000. 89.95 (*0-8091-0502-0*) Paulist Pr.

Beal, John P., ed. see John Paul, II, pseud.

Beal, John R. Reflections: The Beal Family: As I Remember. Bixby, Robert & Bixby, Kathleen, eds. (Illus.). 245p. 1990. 25.00 (*0-9624453-0-4*) March Street Pr.

Beal, John W. Joslyn Art Museum: A Building History. LC 94-34536. (Illus.). 100p. (Orig.). 1998. pap. 24.95 (*0-936364-25-4*) Joslyn Art.

Beal, K. Big Book Package, 4 vols., Set. (Multicultural Sing-Along Big Book Program Ser.). (Illus.). 16p. (J). (gr. 1-3). 1994. pap. text 93.20 (*0-201-52205-5*) Addison-Wesley.

— Here It's Winter Big Book. (Multicultural Sing-Along Big Book Program Ser.). (Illus.). 16p. (J). (gr. 1-3). 1991. pap. text 23.30 (*0-201-52203-9*) Addison-Wesley.

— I Like You Big Book. (Multicultural Sing-Along Big Book Program Ser.). (Illus.). 16p. (J). (gr. 1-3). 1991. pap. text 23.30 (*0-201-52204-7*) Addison-Wesley.

— I Like You Little Book. (Multicultural Sing-Along Big Book Program Ser.). (Illus.). 16p. (J). (gr. 1-3). 1991. pap. text 4.78 (*0-201-52209-8*) Addison-Wesley.

— I Like You Little Books Four-Pack, Set. (Multicultural Sing-Along Big Book Program Ser.). (Illus.). 16p. (J). (gr. 1-3). 1994. pap. text 17.64 (*0-201-52213-6*) Addison-Wesley.

— I Love My Family Big Book. (Multicultural Sing-Along Big Book Program Ser.). (Illus.). 16p. (J). (gr. 1-3). 1991. pap. text 23.30 (*0-201-52202-0*) Addison-Wesley.

— I Love My Family Little Books Four-Pack, Set. (Multicultural Sing-Along Big Book Program Ser.). (Illus.). 16p. (J). (gr. 1-3). 1994. pap. text 17.64 (*0-201-52211-X*) Addison-Wesley.

Beal, Kathleen. It's Pink I Think. 1994. pap. text 17.64 (*0-201-52210-1*) Addison-Wesley.

— It's Pink I Think Big Book. (Multicultural Sing-Along Big Book Program Ser.). (Illus.). 16p. (J). (gr. 1-3). 1991. pap. text 23.30 (*0-201-52201-2*) Addison-Wesley.

— It's Pink I Think Little Book. (Multicultural Sing-Along Big Book Program Ser.). (Illus.). 16p. (J). (gr. 1-3). 1991. pap. text 4.78 (*0-201-52206-3*) Addison-Wesley.

— It's Winter: Little Book. (Multicultural Sing-Along Big Book Program Ser.). (Illus.). 16p. (J). (gr. 1-3). 1991. pap. text 4.78 (*0-201-52208-X*) Addison-Wesley.

— It's Winter: Little Book, Set. (Multicultural Sing-Along Big Book Program Ser.). (Illus.). 16p. (J). (gr. 1-3). 1994. pap. text 17.64 (*0-201-52212-8*) Addison-Wesley.

— Multicultural Sing-Along Big Books Complete Program. 1994. pap. 212.59 (*0-201-52214-4*) Addison-Wesley.

— Teacher's Guide. (C). 1992. text 20.40 (*0-201-52216-0*) Addison-Wesley.

Beal, Laura, ed. see Hulbert, Elizabeth M.

Beal, Lenore A., ed. see Beal, James P.

Beal, M. Flint, jt. ed. see Bar, Peter Rudolf.

Beal, Mary P., compiled by. Grotto Stories Vol. 1: From the Heart of Notre Dame. (Illus.). 80p. (Orig.). 1996. pap. 10.95 (*0-9652337-0-7*) M Sunshine.

Beal, Mary R. & Gilbert, Janet P. Music Curriculum Guidelines for Moderately Retarded Adolescents. 122p. (C). 1982. pap., spiral bd. 27.95 (*0-398-04757-X*) C C Thomas.

Beal, Merri. I Will Fight No More Forever: Chief Joseph & the Nez Perce War. LC 62-13278. (Illus.). 384p. 1963. pap. 16.95 (*0-295-74009-4*) U of Wash Pr.

Beal, Myron C., ed. 1998 Yearbook: Scientific Contributions of William L. Johnston, DO, FAAO. (Illus.). 370p. 1998. pap. 50.00 (*0-940668-09-2*) Am Acad Osteopathy.

— 1995-1996 AAO Yearbook: Osteopathic Vision. (Illus.). 205p. (Orig.). (C). 1996. pap. 40.00 (*0-940668-04-1*) Am Acad Osteopathy.

Beal, Peter. In Praise of Scribes: Manuscripts & Their Makers in Seventeenth-Century England. (Lyell Lectures in Bibliography). (Illus.). 339p. 1998. text 130.00 (*0-19-818471-9*) OUP.

— Index of English Literary Manuscripts, 1625-1700, Vol. II, Pt. 1, A-K. (Illus.). 616p. 1987. text 400.00 (*0-7201-1855-7*) Continuum.

Beal, Peter, ed. The Harmony of the Muses. (English Verse Miscellanies of the Seventeenth Century Ser.). 256p. 1990. 56.95 (*0-85967-784-2*, Pub. by Scolar Pr) Ashgate Pub Co.

— J. Cleaveland Revived. (English Verse Miscellanies of the Seventeenth Century Ser.). 220p. 1990. 65.95 (*0-85967-785-0*, Pub. by Scolar Pr) Ashgate Pub Co.

— The Stoughton Manuscript. (English Verse Miscellanies of the Seventeenth Century Ser.). 296p. 1991. 69.95 (*0-85967-787-7*, Pub. by Scolar Pr) Ashgate Pub Co.

Beal, Peter & Griffiths, Jeremy. English Manuscript Studies, 1100-1700, Vol. 3. 340p. 1992. text 90.00 (*0-8020-2822-5*) U of Toronto Pr.

— English Manuscript Studies, 1100-1700, Vol. 4. 340p. 1993. text 90.00 (*0-8020-0571-3*) U of Toronto Pr.

Beal, Peter & Griffiths, Jeremy, eds. English Manuscript Studies, Vol. 7. (Illus.). 256p. 1998. text 90.00 (*0-7123-0659-5*) U of Toronto Pr.

Beal, Peter, jt. ed. see Griffiths, Jeremy.

Beal, Rayma K. & Berryman-Miller, Sherrill, eds. Dance for the Older Adult. (Illus.). 165p. 1988. pap. text 15.95 (*0-88314-385-2*) Princeton Bk Co.

Beal, Rebecca J. Jacob Eichholtz, 1776-1842, Portrait Painter of Pennsylvania. 1969. 12.00 (*0-910732-07-8*) Pa Hist Soc.

Beal, Richard A. Highway Seventeen. (Illus.). (Orig.). 1991. pap. 12.95 (*0-9629974-0-4*) Pacific Grp.

Beal, Robert C., ed. Directional Ocean Wave Spectra. LC 91-16779. (Studies in Earth & Space Sciences). (Illus.). 240p. 1991. text 65.00 (*0-8018-4261-1*) Johns Hopkins.

Beal, Ronald L. Texas Administrative Practice & Procedure. 95.00 (*0-327-01939-5*) LEXIS Pub.

Beal, Ronald L. Texas Administrative Practice & Procedure First Edition, Issue 1. 151p. 1999. ring bd. 35.00 (*0-327-01187-4*, 6054411) LEXIS Pub.

— Texas Administrative Practive & Procedure. LC 98-179703. 1997. ring bd. 95.00 (*1-55834-367-9*, 60541-10, MICHIE) LEXIS Pub.

Beal, Ronald L., jt. auth. see Bocchina, Anthony J.

Beal, Ronald L., jt. auth. see Bocchino, Anthony J.

Beal, Roy E., ed. Engine Coolant Testing. (STP Ser.: Vol. 1335). (Illus.). 450p. 1999. 175.00 (*0-8031-2610-7*, STP1335) ASTM.

— Engine Coolant Testing: Second Symposium, STP 887. LC 85-30710. (Illus.). 287p. text 58.00 (*0-8031-0432-4*, STP887) ASTM.

— Engine Coolant Testing Vol. 3: STP 1192. (Special Technical Publication Ser.). (Illus.). 310p. 1993. text 83.00 (*0-8031-1851-1*, STP1192) ASTM.

Beal, Samuel. Buddhism in China. 1977. 19.95 (*0-8369-7129-9*, 7963) Ayer.

— A Catena of Buddhist Scriptures from the Chinese. 2nd ed. (Bibliotheca Indo-Buddhica Ser.: No. 62). 436p. (C). 1989. reprint ed. 35.00 (*81-7030-183-1*) S Asia.

— Si-Yu-Ki: Buddhist Records of the Western World. (C). 1994. text 44.00 (*81-208-1107-0*, Pub. by Motilal Bnarsidass) S Asia.

Beal, Samuel, tr. Travels of Fah-Hian & Sung Yun: Buddhist Pilgrims, from China to India, 400 A. D. & 518 A. D. (C). 1993. reprint ed. 17.50 (*81-206-0824-0*, Pub. by Asian Educ Servs) S Asia.

Beal, Samuel, jt. auth. see Hui Lin.

Beal, Samuel, tr. see Dhammapada.

Beal, Samuel, tr. see Fa-Hsien.

Beal, Stephen. The Very Stuff: Poems on Color, Thread, & the Habits of Women. 120p. (Orig.). 1996. pap. 14.95 (*1-883010-16-0*) Interweave.

Beal, Stephen, ed. Stepping Stones to Recovery for Men. LC 92-20195. 240p. (Orig.). pap. 7.95 (*0-934125-28-7*) Hazelden.

Beal, Steven. The Complete Idiot's Guide to Home Movies. (Complete Idiot's Guides (Lifestyle)). 400p. 1999. pap. text 16.95 (*0-02-863606-6*) Macmillan.

Beal, Suzy. The Autobiography of... 2nd large type ed. 273p. 1995. ring bd., wbk. ed. 29.95 (*0-9656204-0-9*) Paper Trails.

— The Autobiography of...a Teacher's Guide. large type ed. 40p. 1997. ring bd. 29.95 (*0-9656204-1-7*) Paper Trails.

Beal, Timothy K. The Book of Hiding: Gender, Ethnicity, Annihilation, & Esther. LC 97-2288. (Biblical Limits Ser.). 168p. (C). 1997. 70.00 (*0-415-16779-5*); pap. 24.99 (*0-415-16780-9*) Routledge.

Beal, Timothy K. & Gunn, David M., eds. Reading Bibles, Writing Bodies: Identity & the Book. LC 96-1112. (Biblical Limits Ser.). 312p. (C). 1996. 85.00 (*0-415-12664-9*); pap. 24.99 (*0-415-12665-7*) Routledge.

Beal, Timothy K., jt. ed. see Linafelt, Tod.

Beal, Virginia A., jt. auth. see Martin, Ethel A.

Beal, William J., ed. Beal. Joseph Beal & His Wife Elizabeth (Cleghorn) Beal of Perinton, Monroe County, NY, & Rollin, Lenawee County, MI. (Illus.). 114p. 1997. reprint ed. pap. 19.00 (*0-8328-7443-4*); reprint ed. lib. bdg. 29.00 (*0-8328-7442-6*) Higginson Bk Co.

Beal, Willis. National Air Quality & Emissions Trends Report, 1995. (Illus.). 168p. (C). 1998. pap. text 35.00 (*0-7881-4554-1*) DIANE Pub.

Bealby, J. T., tr. see Hoffmann, E. T. A.

Bealby, Jonny. Running with the Moon. 320p. pap. 16.95 (*0-7493-2098-2*, Pub. by Random) Trafalgar.

Beale. Fuzzy Systems Toolbox-Book Only. (Electrical Engineering Ser.). 1995. pap. 30.00 (*0-534-94513-9*) PWS Pubs.

***Beale.** Small Animal Arthroscopy. 2002. text. write for info. (*0-7216-8969-8*, W B Saunders Co) Harcrt Hlth Sci Grp.

Beale & Demuth. Neural Network Design. (Electrical Engineering Ser.). 1996. pap. 37.95 (*0-534-95259-3*) PWS Pubs.

Beale, Andrew. Essential Constitutional & Administrative Law. Bourne, Nicholas, ed. (Essential Law Ser.). 164p. 1995. pap. write for info. (*1-85941-123-1*, Pub. by Cavendish Pubng) Gaunt.

— Solving Problems in Constitutional & Administrative Law. 230p. 1995. pap. 20.00 (*1-85941-001-4*, Pub. by Cavendish Pubng) Gaunt.

Beale, Anne, jt. auth. see Sheavyn, Phoebe.

Beale, Arthur C., jt. auth. see Wasserman, Jeanne L.

Beale, Betty. Power at Play: A Memoir of Parties, Politicians, & the Presidents in My Bedroom. LC 92-41187. (Illus.). 355p. 1993. 20.00 (*0-89526-503-6*) Regnery Pub.

***Beale, Brian & Adderly, Brenda.** The Arthritis Cure for Pets. (Illus.). 224p. (gr. 8). 2000. 19.95 (*0-316-08590-1*) Little.

Beale, C., jt. auth. see Collins, P.

Beale, Calvin L. Taste of the Country: A Collection of Calvin Beale's Writings. Morrison, Peter A., ed. LC 87-43183. 320p. 1990. lib. bdg. 32.50 (*0-271-00631-5*) Pa St U Pr.

Beale, Charles W. The Secret of the Earth. LC 74-15950. (Science Fiction Ser.). 256p. 1975. reprint ed. 23.95 (*0-405-06276-1*) Ayer.

Beale, David. Driven by Nissan? A Critical Guide to New Management Techniques. 200p. (C). 1994. pap. 19.50 (*0-85315-799-5*, Pub. by Lawrence & Wishart) NYU Pr.

— A Pictorial History of Our English Bible. (Illus.). 79p. (Orig.). 1982. pap. 7.00 (*0-89084-149-7*, 018044) Bob Jones Univ.

Beale, David O. In Pursuit of Purity: A History of American Fundamentalism since 1850. 475p. 1986. pap. 15.95 (*0-89084-350-3*, 030304) Bob Jones Univ.

— In Pursuit of Purity: American Fundamentalism since 1850. 475p. 1986. 18.95 (*0-89084-351-1*, 030296) Bob Jones Univ.

— S. B. C. House on the Sand? 246p. (Orig.). 1985. pap. 8.25 (*0-89084-281-7*, 025106) Bob Jones Univ.

Beale, Elaine. Murder in the Castro. LC 97-14674. 192p. 1997. pap. 10.95 (*0-934678-87-1*) New Victoria Pubs.

Beale, Erica, ed. see Kyasht, Lydia.

Beale, Evelyn M. Mathematical Programming in Practice. LC 68-95780. (Illus.). 207p. reprint ed. pap. 64.20 (*0-608-11447-2*, 205189800013) Bks Demand.

Beale, G. The Building Services Thesaurus. 1993. 100.00 (*0-86022-341-8*, Pub. by Build Servs Info Assn) St Mut.

Beale, G. K. The Book of Revelation: A Commentary on the Greek Text. LC 97-51674. (New International Greek Testament Commentary Ser.). 1408p. 1998. 75.00 (*0-8028-2174-X*) Eerdmans.

— John's Use of the Old Testament in Revelation. LC 99-169584. (JSNTS Ser.: Vol. 166). 443p. 1999. 85.00 (*1-85075-894-8*, Pub. by Sheffield Acad) CUP Services.

Beale, Galen & Boswell, Mary Rose. The Earth Shall Blossom: Shaker Herbs & Gardening. (Illus.). 263p. 1991. pap. 18.95 (*0-88150-183-2*, Pub. by Countryman) Norton.

Beale, George W. A Lieutenant of Cavalry in Lee's Army. 231p. 1994. 25.00 (*0-935523-43-X*) Butternut & Blue.

Beale, H. G., et al. Beale, Bishop & Furmston: Contract - Cases & Materials. 3rd ed. 1995. pap. write for info. (*0-406-04997-1*, BBFC3, MICHIE) LEXIS Pub.

— Contract - Cases & Materials. 2nd ed. 750p. 1990. pap. 56.00 (*0-406-51751-7*, UK, MICHIE) LEXIS Pub.

Beale, Harriet B., jt. auth. see Lane, Anne W.

Beale, Helen P., ed. Bibliography of Plant Viruses & Index to Research. LC 73-3200. 1495p. 1976. text 221.50 (*0-231-03763-5*) Col U Pr.

Beale, Hugh, jt. ed. see Guy, John.

Beale, Hugh, jt. ed. see Lando, Ole.

Beale, Irene A. Genesee Country Senecas. LC 91-77008. (Illus.). 143p. (Orig.). 1992. pap. 10.00 (*0-9608132-4-1*) Chestnut Hill Pr.

— Genesee Valley Events, 1668-1986. LC 86-71531. (Illus.). 198p. (Orig.). 1986. pap. 9.00 (*0-9608132-3-3*) Chestnut Hill Pr.

— Genesee Valley People, 1743-1962. LC 83-71772. (Illus.). 224p. (Orig.). 1983. pap. 9.00 (*0-9608132-1-7*) Chestnut Hill Pr.

— Genesee Valley Women, 1743-1985. LC 84-73387. 223p. (Orig.). 1985. pap. 9.00 (*0-9608132-2-5*) Chestnut Hill Pr.

— William P. Letchworth: A Man for Others. LC 01-90673. 214p. (Orig.). 1982. pap. 9.00 (*0-9608132-0-9*) Chestnut Hill Pr.

Beale, Ivan L., jt. auth. see Corballis, Michael C.

Beale, Jane G. Keyboard Arithmetic. 29p. (Orig.). (J). (gr. 1-8). 1986. pap. 3.50 (*0-937781-09-6*) G Beale Pr.

Beale, Jenny. Women in Ireland: Voices of Change. LC 86-45747. 224p. 1987. 31.50 (*0-253-36461-2*) Ind U Pr.

Beale, John T., et al, eds. Vortex Flows & Related Numerical Methods: Proceedings of the NATO Advanced Research Workshop, Grenoble, France, June 15-19, 1992. LC 93-7414. (NATO Advanced Study Institutes Series C, Mathematical & Physical Sciences: Vol. 395). 396p. 1993. text 236.00 (*0-7923-2250-9*) Kluwer Academic.

Beale, Joseph H. A Bibliography of Early English Law Books. LC 26-16217. Bk. 2 & Bk. 6. viii, 304p. 1993. reprint ed. lib. bdg. 75.00 (*0-89941-351-X*, 502180) W S Hein.

Beale, Lionel S. Our Morality & the Moral Question: From the Medical Side. LC 73-20615. (Sex, Marriage & Society Ser.). 208p. 1974. reprint ed. 21.95 (*0-405-05793-8*) Ayer.

Beale, Lucy. Beyond Limits: Discovering the Spiritual Through Day-to-Day Living. 3rd ed. 59p. 1988. pap. 6.95 (*0-945153-16-3*) Sound Pub CO.

Beale, Lucy & Fields, Rick. The Win-Win Way: The New Approach Transforming American Business & Life. 176p. 1988. pap. 6.95 (*0-15-696795-2*) Harcourt.

— The Win-Win Way: The Ultimate Strategy for Personal & Professional Success. 1987. 14.95 (*0-15-197280-X*) Harcourt.

***Beale, Marjorie A.** Modernist Enterprise: French Elites & The Threat of Modernity, 1900-1940. LC 99-16483. 1999. 49.50 (*0-8047-3511-5*) Stanford U Pr.

Beale, Mark. Secrets of Enjoyable Pipe Smoking. 50p. 1998. pap. 9.95 (*1-57502-819-0*, P02255) Morris Pubng.

Beale, Nicole. Key to Friendship. LC 99-220263. (Charming Petites Ser.). 1998. 4.95 (*0-88088-831-8*) Peter Pauper.

Beale, O. C. Racial Decay: A Compilation of Evidence from World Sources. 1976. lib. bdg. 59.95 (*0-8490-2498-6*) Gordon Pr.

Beale, Paul, jt. auth. see Partridge, Eric.

Beale, Paul, ed. see Partridge, Eric.

Beale, Pax. Pyruvate Phenomenon: Discovering the Remarkable Strength, Stamina & Weight-Loss Supplement. 1997. pap. text 12.00 (*1-885670-79-6*) Woodland UT.

***Beale, Peter.** Death by Design: The Fate of British Tank Crews in the Second World War. LC 99-163549. 214p. 1998. 39.95 (*0-7509-0802-5*, Pub. by Sutton Pub Ltd) Bks Intl VA.

Beale, Peter. Death by Design: The Fate of British Tank Crews in WWII. (Illus.). 39.95p. 1998. 39.95 (*0-7509-1059-3*, Pub. by Sutton Pub Ltd) Intl Pubs Mktg.

— Tank Tracks: The 9th Battalion Royal Tank Regiment at War 1940-1945. (Illus.). 256p. (Orig.). 1997. pap. 19.95 (*0-7509-1519-6*, Pub. by Sutton Pub Ltd) Intl Pubs Mktg.

— Tank Tracks: The 9th Battalion Royal Tank Regiment at War, 1940-1945. 1997. 33.95 (*0-7509-0880-7*, Pub. by Sutton Pub Ltd) Intl Pubs Mktg.

***Beale, Philip O.** A History of the Post in England from the Romans to the Stuarts. LC 97-38528. (Illus.). 288p. 1998. 61.95 (*1-85928-404-3*, HE6945.B4, Pub. by Ashgate Pub) Ashgate Pub Co.

Beale, R. L. History of the Ninth Virginia Calvary. 34.50 (*0-8488-0912-2*) Amereon Ltd.

Beale, Richard. Endrhymes for the Soul. (Illus.). 73p. 100.00 (*0-9639832-1-0*) Chstnut Hill.

— Silence & the Gift: Prayers & Drawings. LC 94-11027. (Illus.). 1994. pap. 7.50 (*0-939485-08-7*) St Andrew Pr.

Beale, Richard A. Codex Genome: The Mystery of the Name. 24p. 1994. pap. 10.00 (*0-9639832-0-2*) Chstnut Hill.

Beale, Ruby L., jt. auth. see Cox, Taylor, Jr.

***Beale, Russell.** Executive Coaching: From Boardroom to Locker Room. 224p. 2000. pap. 16.95 (*1-58151-041-1*, Pub. by BookPartners) Midpt Trade.

Beale, Russell & Jackson, T. Neural Computing: An Introduction. (Illus.). 256p. 1990. pap. 41.00 (*0-85274-262-2*) IOP Pub.

Beale, Russell, jt. auth. see Fiesler, Emile.

Beale, Russell, jt. ed. see Dix, Alan J.

Beale, Sara S. Grand Jury Law & Practice. 2nd ed. LC 97-41499. 1997. write for info. (*0-8366-1151-9*) West Group.

Beale, Sara S. & Bryson, William C. Grand Jury Law & Practice, 2 vols. LC 85-29164. (Criminal Law Ser.). 1992. ring bd. 230.00 (*0-685-14575-1*) West Group.

Beale, Sara S., jt. auth. see Abrams, Norman.

Beale, Sara S., ed. see Abrams, Norman.

Beale, Stephen. Color Image Editing with Photo Finish. 224p. 1993. pap. 27.95 (*0-941845-10-9*) Micro Pub Pr.

— Plug-in Power: Energize Your Graphics Software with Add-in Utilities. LC 96-194091. (Illus.). 240p. 1995. pap. 27.95 (*0-941845-15-X*) Micro Pub Pr.

Beale, Stephen & Cavuoto, James. The Scanner Book: A Complete Guide to the Use & Applications of Desktop Scanners. 224p. 1989. pap. 22.95 (*0-941845-02-8*) Micro Pub Pr.

Beale, Stephen, jt. auth. see Cavuoto, James.

Beale, T., jt. auth. see Stanford, J.

***Beale, Theodore.** The War in Heaven. (Eternal Warriors Ser.: Vol. 1). 416p. 2000. per. 6.50 (*0-671-01893-0*, Pocket Books) PB.

Beale, Thomas W. Excavations at Tepe Yahya: The Early Periods. Lamberg-Karlovsky, C. C., ed. LC 84-62628. (American School of Prehistoric Research Bulletins Ser.: No. 38). (Illus.). 346p. 1986. pap. 32.00 (*0-87365-541-9*) Peabody Harvard.

Beale, Walter H. A Pragmatic Theory of Rhetoric. LC 86-11807. 186p. 1987. text 21.95 (*0-8093-1300-6*) S Ill U Pr.

— Real Writing: Argumentation, Reflection, Information. LC 85-14512. 398p. reprint ed. pap. 123.40 (*0-7837-5208-3*, 204493600005) Bks Demand.

Bealer, Alex W. Art of Blacksmithing. 440p. 1995. 9.98 (*0-7858-0395-5*) Bk Sales Inc.

— Old Ways of Working Wood. 256p. 1996. 9.98 (*0-7858-0710-1*) Bk Sales Inc.

— Only the Names Remain: The Cherokees & the Trail of Tears. (Illus.). 80p. (J). (gr. 4-6). 1996. pap. 4.95 (*0-316-08519-7*) Little.

— Only the Names Remain: The Cherokees & the Trail of Tears. 1996. 10.05 (*0-606-08839-3*, Pub. by Turtleback) Demco.

Bealer, Bonnie K., jt. auth. see Weinberg, Bennett Alan.

***Beales, Amanda.** Rose Basics: A Step-by-Step Guide to Growing, Training & General Care. (Illus.). 128p. 1999. pap. text 11.95 (*0-8069-1965-5*) Sterling.

Beales, Amanda. Roses: A Care Manual. LC 99-57593. (Plant Care Manual Ser.). (Illus.). 128p. 1999. 22.00 (*1-57145-644-9*, Laurel Glen Pub) Advantage Pubs.

Beales, David, et al. Community Care of Older People. LC 97-42034. 1997. write for info. (*1-85775-032-2*, Radcliffe Med Pr) Scovill Paterson.

Beales, Derek. Joseph II: In the Shadow of Maria Theresa, 1741-1780, Vol. I. (Illus.). 546p. 1987. text 100.00 (*0-521-24240-1*) Cambridge U Pr.

Beales, J. Howard & Muris, Timothy J. State & Federal Regulation of National Advertising. LC 92-38187. (Studies in Regulation & Federalism). 150p. (Orig.). 1993. pap. 9.75 (*0-8447-3824-7*, AEI Pr) Am Enterprise.

Beales, Janet R. Teacher, Inc. A Private-Practice Option for Educators. (Illus.). 24p. (Orig.). 1995. pap. 5.00 (*0-9647703-0-X*, S95-05) Mackinac Ctr Public Pol.

Beales, Joan. English Pronunciation in the Eighteenth Century: Thomas Spence's Grand Repository of the English Language. LC 98-51328. (Illus.). 252p. 1999. text 105.00 (*0-19-823781-2*) OUP.

Beales, Peter. Classic Roses. rev. ed. LC 97-23619. (Illus.). 454p. 1997. 65.00 (*0-8050-5584-3*) H Holt & Co.

— Modern Roses. 1989. write for info. (*0-8050-0963-9*) H Holt & Co.

— Roses: An Illustrated Encyclopaedia & Grower's Handbook of Species Roses, Old Roses & Modern Roses, Shrub Roses & Climbers. (Illus.). 480p. 1995. 60.00 (*0-8050-2053-5*, J Macrae Bks) H Holt & Co.

Beales, Peter & Balfour, R. C., frwds. Classic Roses: An Illustrated Encyclopedia of Old Roses, Shrub Roses & Climbers. LC 85-14159. 432p. 1995. 60.00 (*0-8050-1002-5*) H Holt & Co.

Beales, Valerie. Emma & Freckles. LC 91-20751. (Illus.). 208p. (J). (gr. 5-9). 1992. pap. 13.00 (*0-671-74686-3*) S&S Bks Yung.

***Bealey, Frank, et al.** Elements in Political Science. LC 99-487857. 356p. 1999. 90.00 (*0-7486-1197-5*, Pub. by Edinburgh U Pr) Col U Pr.

Bealey, Frank W. Democracy in the Contemporary State. 302p. 1988. text 69.00 (*0-19-827573-0*) OUP.

Bealey, Frank W., ed. The Blackwell Dictionary of Political Science: A User's Guide to Its Terms. LC 98-33143. 384p. 1999. pap. 29.95 (*0-631-20695-7*) Blackwell Pubs.

Bealey, Frank W. & Pelling, Henry. Labour & Politics, 1900-1906: A History of the Labour Representation Committee. LC 82-15828. 313p. (C). 1982. lib. bdg. 75.00 (*0-313-23693-3*, BELAP, Greenwood Pr) Greenwood.

Bealey, Frank W. & Sewel, John. The Politics of Independence: A Study of a Scottish Town. 280p. 1981. 36.00 (*0-08-025736-4*, Pergamon Pr) Elsevier.

Beall, jt. auth. see Seiler.

Beall, Anne E. & Sternberg, Robert J., eds. The Psychology of Gender. LC 93-11508. 278p. 1993. lib. bdg. 42.00 (*0-89862-286-7*) Guilford Pubns.

— The Psychology of Gender. 278p. 1995. pap. text 21.00 (*0-89862-283-2*) Guilford Pubns.

Beall, Babs, et al. It's a Guy Thing: A Woman's Guide to Universal Guy Behavior. 108p. 1996. pap. 7.95 (*1-888500-11-5*) Catalpa Press.

***Beall, Charla.** Group Officer's Handbook: A Group Officer's Guide to Effectively Managing a Successful Term in Office. LC 99-73175. 195p. 1999. pap. 24.95 (*1-890622-76-1*) Leathers Pub.

Beall, Christine. Building Moisture Control Manual. LC 98-16859. (Illus.). 380p. 1998. 74.95 (*0-07-005155-0*) McGraw.

***Beall, Christine.** Masonry & Concrete. (Complete Construction Ser.). (Illus.). 464p. 2000. pap. text 39.95 (*0-07-006706-6*) McGraw.

Beall, Christine. Masonry Design & Detailing. 4th rev. ed. LC 97-1066. (Illus.). 613p. 1997. 94.95 (*0-07-005844-X*) McGraw.

Beall, Christine & Creative Homeowner Press Editors. Quick Guide: Masonry Walls. Samuelson, Alexander, ed. LC 97-66870. (Quick Guide Ser.). (Illus.). 80p. 1997. pap. 7.95 (*1-880029-92-8*) Creative Homeowner.

Beall, Cynthia M., jt. auth. see Goldstein, Melvyn C.

Beall, Glenn. Rotational Molding: Design, Materials, Tooling & Processing. LC 98-33646. 1998. 68.00 (*1-56990-260-7*) Hanser-Gardner.

Beall, Helen. Pass the Word: The Art of Oral Communication. 68p. 1993. pap. 11.95 (*0-89745-162-7*) Sunflower U Pr.

Beall, Herbert & Trimbur, John. A Short Guide to Writing about Chemistry. 182p. (C). 1997. pap. 24.60 (*0-673-46882-8*) Addson-Wesley Educ.

Beall, Herbert, jt. auth. see Fine, Leonard W.

Beall, J. H. Hickey, the Days. LC 79-65655. (Illus.). 72p. 1981. per. 10.00 (*0-915380-09-9*) Word Works.

Beall, James L. How to Achieve Security, Confidence & Peace. 417p. 1994. pap. 10.99 (*0-88270-268-8*) Bridge-Logos.

— Laying the Foundation: Achieving Christian Maturity. LC 76-42084. 389p. 1976. pap. 12.99 (*0-88270-198-3*) Bridge-Logos.

— Your Pastor, Your Shepherd. LC 77-77579. 208p. (Orig.). 1994. pap. 8.99 (*0-88270-216-5*) Bridge-Logos.

Beall, Jo, ed. A City for All: Valuing Difference & Working with Diversity. LC 97-3813. 256p. 1997. pap. 25.00 (*1-85649-470-8*, Pub. by Zed Books) St Martin.

Beall, John N., III. The Fighter's Edge, Levels 1 & 2: Tsun Jo Wing Chun Kung Fu, Vol. 2. (Illus.). 200p. (Orig.). 1993. pap. text 22.95 (*0-9636521-1-7*) Lux Et Veritas.

Beall, Julianne. Dewey for Windows Guide. LC 99-164250. 212p. 1998. pap. text 35.00 (*0-910608-65-2*) OCLC Forest Pr.

***Beall, Julianne & Couture-Lafleur, Raymonde.** Dewey Decimal Classification--Francophone Perspectives: Papers from a Workshop Presented at the General Conference of the International Federation of Library Associations & Institutions (IFLA) Amsterdam, Netherlands, August 20, 1998. LC 99-35669. 1999. 20.00 (*0-910608-67-9*) OCLC Forest Pr.

Beall, Karen F. & Kiehl, David W. Graphic Excursions: American Prints in Black & White, 1900-1950 - Selections from the Collection of Reba & Dave Williams. (Illus.). 155p. 1991. pap. 25.00 (*0-87923-909-3*) Am Fed Arts.

Beall, Karen F. & Library of Congress Prints Division Staff. American Prints in the Library of Congress: A Catalogue of the Collection. (Illus.). 592p. 1991. reprint ed. 125.00 (*1-55660-088-7*) A Wofsy Fine Arts.

Beall, Karen F., jt. auth. see Kiehl, David.

Beall, Kenneth F. C. I. A. Confidential. 24p. 1999. pap. 7.00 (*0-8059-4584-9*) Dorrance.

Beall, M. M. Beall-Bell, & Bell Families: Colonial Families of the U. S. Descended from the Immigrants Who Arrived Before 1700, Mostly from England & Scotland . . . Of the Names Bell, Beal, Bale, Beale, Beall. 296p. 1997. reprint ed. pap. 46.00 (*0-8328-7449-3*); reprint ed. lib. bdg. 56.00 (*0-8328-7448-5*) Higginson Bk Co.

Beall, Mary K. Singing in the Spirit. 144p. 1998. pap. 12.95 (*0-916642-65-8*, 8007) Hope Pub.

Beall, Mary K. & Carter, John. The Magnificent 7, Teacher's Handbook. 48p. 1995. pap. 19.95 (*0-7390-0097-7*, 11695) Alfred Pub.

Beall, Mary K., jt. auth. see Carter, John.

Beall, Mary Kay, jt. auth. see Carter, John.

Beall, Melissa L. Guide to Oral Communication. 2nd ed. 144p. 1996. per. 17.95 (*0-8403-8758-X*) Kendall-Hunt.

Beall, Michael. AutoCAD 14 Fundamentals. LC 97-222723. 1997. 39.99 (*1-56205-767-7*) New Riders Pub.

— AutoCAD 13 for Professionals: Level 1. 1996. student ed. 30.00 (*1-56205-540-2*) New Riders Pub.

Beall, Otho T. & Shryock, Richard H. Cotton Mather. 1979. 23.95 (*0-405-10580-0*) Ayer.

Beall, Pamela Conn. Wee Sing America. (Wee Sing Ser.). (Illus.). 64p. (J). (ps-3). 1998. pap. 12.99 incl. audio (*0-8431-7437-4*, Wee Sing Bks) Putnam Pub Group.

***Beall, Pamela Conn.** Wee Sing & Learn ABC. (Wee Sing & Learn Bks.). (Illus.). 32p. (J). (ps-k). 2000. pap. 7.99 (*0-8431-7596-6*, Price Stern) Peng Put Young Read.

— Wee Sing & Learn Colors. (Wee Sing & Learn Bks.). (Illus.). 32p. (J). (ps-k). 2000. pap. 7.99 (*0-8431-7598-2*, Price Stern) Peng Put Young Read.

— Wee Sing & Learn 123. (Illus.). 32p. (J). (ps-k). 2000. pap. 7.99 (*0-8431-7597-4*, Price Stern) Peng Put Young Read.

Beall, Pamela Conn. Wee Sing Around the World. (Wee Sing Ser.). (Illus.). 64p. (J). (ps-3). 1998. pap. 12.99 incl. audio, cd-rom (*0-8431-7438-2*, Wee Sing Bks) Putnam Pub Group.

— Wee Sing Dinosaurs. (Wee Sing Ser.). (Illus.). 64p. (J). (ps-3). 1998. pap. 12.99 incl. audio, cd-rom (*0-8431-7439-0*, Wee Sing Bks) Putnam Pub Group.

— Wee Sing Fun 'n' Folk. (Wee Sing Ser.). (Illus.). 64p. (J). (ps-3). 1998. pap. 12.99 incl. audio, cd-rom (*0-8431-7440-4*, Wee Sing Bks) Putnam Pub Group.

Beall, Pamela Conn & Nipp, Hagen S. Wee Sing for Christmas. (Wee Sing Ser.). (Illus.). 64p. (J). (ps-3). 1998. pap. 12.99 incl. audio (*0-8431-7436-6*, Wee Sing Bks) Putnam Pub Group.

Beall, Pamela Conn & Nipp, Susan. Wee Sing & Pretend. pap. 9.99 incl. audio (*0-8431-7621-0*, Price Stern); pap. 2.99 (*0-8431-7634-2*, Price Stern) Peng Put Young Read.

— Wee Sing & Pretend. (Illus.). 64p. (ps-3). 2000. pap. 12.99 incl. audio compact disk (*0-8431-7636-9*, Price Stern) Peng Put Young Read.

— Wee Sing Animals, Animals, Animals. (Illus.). 64p. (ps-3). 2000. pap. 12.99 incl. audio compact disk (*0-8431-7635-0*, Price Stern) Peng Put Young Read.

— Wee Sing in the Car. (Illus.). 64p. (ps-3). 2000. pap. 12.99 incl. audio (*0-8431-7637-7*, Price Stern) Peng Put Young Read.

Beall, Pamela Conn & Nipp, Susan H. Wee Sing America. (Wee Sing Ser.). (Illus.). 64p. (J). (ps-2). 1994. 9.95 incl. audio (*0-8431-3799-1*, Price Stern) Peng Put Young Read.

— Wee Sing & Play. (Wee Sing Ser.). (Illus.). 64p. (J). (ps-2). 1983. pap. 9.99 incl. audio (*0-8431-3796-7*, Price Stern) Peng Put Young Read.

— Wee Sing & Play. 64p. (J). (ps-3). 1997. 12.95 incl. audio (*0-8431-7879-5*, Wee Sing Bks) Putnam Pub Group.

— Wee Sing Around the World. (Wee Sing Ser.). (Illus.). 65p. (J). (ps-6). 1994. 9.95 incl. audio (*0-8431-3729-0*, Price Stern) Peng Put Young Read.

— Wee Sing Bible Songs. LC 95-71286. (Wee Sing Ser.) (Illus.). 64p. (J). (ps-2). 1986. 9.99 incl. audio (*0-8431-3795-9*) Peng Put Young Read.

Beall, Pamela Conn & Nipp, Susan H. Wee Sing Children's Songs & Fingerplays. (J). (ps-3). 1994. 12.95 incl. audio compact disk Peng Put Young Read.

— Wee Sing Children's Songs & Fingerplays. LC 95-71288. (Wee Sing Ser.). (Illus.). 64p. (J). (ps-2). 1994. 9.99 incl. audio (*0-8431-3793-2*) Peng Put Young Read.

Beall, Pamela Conn & Nipp, Susan H. Wee Sing for Baby, Set. (Wee Sing Ser.). (Illus.). 64p. (J). (ps-3). 1996. pap. 12.95 incl. audio (*0-8431-7949-X*, Wee Sing Bks) Putnam Pub Group.

— Wee Sing for Christmas. (Wee Sing Ser.). (Illus.). 64p. (J). (ps-3). 1984. pap. 9.99 incl. audio (*0-8431-3800-9*, Price Stern) Peng Put Young Read.

— Wee Sing Fun 'n' Folk. (Illus.). 64p. (J). (ps-3). 1994. pap. 9.95 incl. audio (*0-8431-3802-5*, Price Stern) Peng Put Young Read.

— Wee Sing Fun 'n' Folk. rev. ed. (Illus.). 64p. (J). (ps-3). 1994. pap. 2.99 (*0-8431-3810-6*, Price Stern) Peng Put Young Read.

— Wee Sing Games, Games, Games. (Wee Sing Ser.). (Illus.). 64p. (J). (ps-3). 1998. mass mkt. 12.99 incl. audio compact disk (*0-8431-7402-1*, Price Stern) Peng Put Young Read.

— Wee Sing Games, Games, Games: More Than 60 Favorites to Play & Sing. LC 97-76637. (Wee Sing Ser.). (Illus.). 64p. (J). (ps-3). 1998. pap. 2.99 (*0-8431-7400-5*, Price Stern) Peng Put Young Read.

— Wee Sing Games, Games, Games: More Than 60 Favorites to Play & Sing. (Wee Sing Ser.). (Illus.). 64p. (J). (ps-3). 1998. 9.99 (*0-8431-7404-8*, Wee Sing Bks) Putnam Pub Group.

— Wee Sing More Bible Songs. (Illus.). 64p. (J). (ps-3). 1997. 12.95 incl. audio (*0-8431-7881-7*, Wee Sing Bks) Putnam Pub Group.

— Wee Sing Nursery Rhymes & Lullabies. (Wee Sing Ser.). (Illus.). 64p. (J). (ps-2). 1985. pap. 9.99 incl. audio (*0-8431-3794-0*, Price Stern) Peng Put Young Read.

— Wee Sing Silly Songs. (Wee Sing Ser.). (Illus.). 64p. (J). (ps-2). pap. 9.95 incl. audio (*0-8431-3803-3*, Price Stern) Peng Put Young Read.

— Wee Sing Silly Songs. (Illus.). 64p. (J). 1996. pap. 9.99 incl. audio (*0-8431-7981-3*, Wee Sing Bks) Putnam Pub Group.

— Wee Sing Silly Songs. (Illus.). 64p. (J). (ps-3). 1997. 12.95 incl. audio (*0-8431-7878-7*, Wee Sing Bks) Putnam Pub Group.

— Wee Sing Sing-Alongs. (Wee Sing Ser.). Orig. Title: Wee Sing Around the Campfire. (Illus.). 64p. (J). (ps-2). 1983. pap. 9.99 incl. audio (*0-8431-3804-1*, Price Stern) Peng Put Young Read.

— Wee Sing Sing-Alongs. Orig. Title: Wee Sing Around the Campfire. (Illus.). 64p. (J). (ps-3). 1997. 12.95 incl. audio (*0-8431-7880-9*, Wee Sing Bks) Putnam Pub Group.

***Beall, Pamela Conn & Nipp, Susan Hagen.** Wee Sing Animals, Animals, Animals. (Illus.). 64p. 1999. bds. 9.99 (*0-8431-7553-2*, Price Stern) Peng Put Young Read.

Beall, Pamela Conn, et al. Wee Sing Bible Songs. (Wee Sing Ser.). (Illus.). 64p. (J). (ps-3). 1996. pap. 12.95 incl. audio, audio compact disk (*0-8431-7938-4*, Price Stern) Peng Put Young Read.

— Wee Sing Children's Songs & Fingerplays. (Wee Sing Ser.). (Illus.). 64p. (J). (ps-3). 1996. pap. 12.95 incl. audio, audio compact disk (*0-8431-7940-6*, Price Stern) Peng Put Young Read.

— Wee Sing Dinosaurs. (Wee Sing Ser.). (Illus.). 64p. (J). (ps-2). 1991. pap. 9.95 incl. audio (*0-8431-3801-7*, Price Stern) Peng Put Young Read.

— Wee Sing for Baby. (Illus.). 64p. (J). (ps). 1996. pap. 9.99 incl. audio (*0-8431-7990-2*, Wee Sing Bks) Putnam Pub Group.

Beall, Patricia C. Teaching Your Child to Read for the Fun of It. LC 88-82067. (Illus.). 105p. (Orig.). 1989. pap. 10.95 (*0-9621138-0-8*) Hand Pub.

***Beall, Ron.** Introduction to Market Research: A Project Approach. 3rd ed. LC 98-223145. viii, 333 p. 1998. 81.95 (*0-7872-4780-4*) Kendall-Hunt.

Beall, Ron. Introduction to Market Research: A Project Approach. 3rd ed. 490p. (C). 1998. pap. text 81.95 (*0-7872-4779-0*, 41477901) Kendall-Hunt.

Beall, S. Colleen, jt. ed. see Baumhover, Lorin A.

Beall, Sylvia, ed. see Wright, Barbara J.

Beall, Todd S., et al. Old Testament Parsing Guide. rev. ed. 688p. 2000. 32.99 (*0-8054-2032-0*) Broadman.

Beall, William R., jt. auth. see Weis, Frederick L.

Beall, Wilma. Horse Farms & Horse Tales of the Bluegrass. (Illus.). 104p. 1992. pap. 12.95 (*0-9634179-0-8*) Sunshine KY.

Bealle, John. Public Worship, Private Faith: Sacred Harp & American Folksong. LC 97-19852. 320p. 1997. 50.00 (*0-8203-1921-X*); pap. 20.00 (*0-8203-1988-0*) U of Ga Pr.

Beals. Marriages & Related Items Abstracted from Clayton Enterprise Newspaper of Clayton, Adams County, IL, 1879-1900. 206p. 1997. pap. 18.00 (*0-7884-0766-X*, B107) Heritage Bk.

— Mysteries from the Finger Lakes. 1989. pap. 12.50 (*0-9624738-0-4*) Six Lakes Arts.

Beals & Kirchner, Sandra. Marriages (1895-1905) & Deaths (1895-1900) & Related Items Abstracted from the Golden New Era of Golden Adams County, IL. LC 98-117876. 98p. 1998. pap. 17.00 (*0-7884-0792-9*, B109) Heritage Bk.

***Beals & Kirchner, Sandy.** Deaths Abstracted from the Camp Point Journal, 1883-1892, Camp Point, Adams County, Illinois. 392p. 1999. pap. 33.00 (*0-7884-1275-2*) Heritage Bk.

— Deaths Abstracted from the Camp Point Journal, 1893-1903: Camp Point, Adams County, Illinois. 377p. 1999. pap. 31.50 (*0-7884-0908-5*, B111) Heritage Bk.

Beals & Kirchner, Sandy. Obituaries & Death Related Items Abstracted from the Hendon Dispatch of Mendon, Adams County, Illinois, 1877-1905. LC 97-222196. vi, 465p. 1997. pap. 25.50 (*0-7884-0748-1*, B104) Heritage Bk.

Beals, et al. Archaeological Studies in Northeast Arizona: A Report on the Archaeological Work of the Rainbow Bridge - Monument Valley Expedition. fac. ed. (University of California Publications in American Archaeology & Ethnology: No. 44:1). (Illus.). 247p. (C). 1945. reprint ed. pap. 26.25 (*1-55567-321-X*) Coyote Press.

Beals, ed. see Goldschmidt, Walter.

Beals, ed. see Heizer, R. F.

Beals, ed. see Heizer, R. F. & Lemert, E. M.

Beals, ed. see Wilson, H. Clyde.

Beals, Alan R. Gopalpur: A South Indian Village. LC 79-20364. 125p. (C). 1980. pap. text 23.50 (*0-03-045371-2*) Harcourt Coll Pubs.

Beals, Ann. Crisis in the Christian Science Church. 145p. 1978. pap. 6.95 (*0-930227-08-5*) Bookmark CA.

Beals, Carleton. Banana Gold. LC 72-111708. (American Imperialism: Viewpoints of United States Foreign Policy, 1898-1941 Ser.). 1977. reprint ed. 26.95 (*0-405-02002-3*) Ayer.

— Crime of Cuba. LC 76-111709. (American Imperialism: Viewpoints of United States Foreign Policy, 1898-1941 Ser.). 1970. reprint ed. 29.95 (0-405-02003-1) Ayer.

— Latin America: World in Revolution. LC 74-9631. (Illus.). 352p. 1974. reprint ed. lib. bdg. 38.50 (0-8371-7598-4, BELAW, Greenwood Pr) Greenwood.

— Our Yankee Heritage. LC 73-111814. (Essay Index Reprint Ser.). 1977. 23.95 (0-8369-1593-3) Ayer.

Beals, Carol W. Cheerful Giving & Kingdom Living. 64p. 1998. pap. 7.95 (1-884570-86-0) Research Triangle.

Beals, G. Numismatic Terms of Spain & Spanish America. (Illus.). 1966. pap. 15.00 (0-932106-05-6) S J Durst.

Beals, George F. How Implication Binds & Silence Forbids: Studies in Biblical Hermeneutics. LC 98-96828. xiv, 259p. 1999. pap. 12.99 (0-9669247-0-3) PC Pubs.

Beals, Herbert K. & Weatherford, Marion T. For Honor & Country: The Diary of Bruno de Hezeta. (North Pacific Studies: No. 7). (Illus.). 194p. (Orig.). 1985. 19.95 (0-87595-120-1) Oregon Hist.

B

Beals, Ivan A. Beacon Small-Group Bible Studies: Psalms: Keeping the Heart Aglow. 96p. (Orig.). 1984. pap. 4.99 (0-8341-0885-2) Beacon Hill.

— Beacon Small Group Bible Studies, Nahum-Habakkuk. 80p. (Orig.). 1988. pap. 4.99 (0-8341-1214-0) Beacon Hill.

— Heralding Scriptural Holiness. 136p. 1987. 9.99 (0-8341-1202-7) Nazarene.

— Our Racist Legacy: Will the Church Resolve the Conflict? LC 96-85046. (Church & the World Ser.: Vol. 9). 350p. (Orig.). 1996. pap. 21.95 (0-940121-36-0, P307) Cross Cultural Pubns.

— A Theology of Forgiveness: Towards a Paradigm of Racial Justice. LC 98-3064. 314p. 1998. 74.95 (1-57309-227-4); pap. 54.95 (1-57309-226-6) Intl Scholars.

— What It Means to Forgive. (Christian Living Ser.). 48p. (Orig.). 1987. pap. 3.50 (0-8341-1185-3) Beacon Hill.

*Beals, Joseph J., Sr. Death Abstracted from the Camp Point Journal, 1873-1882, Camp Point, Adams County, Illinois. 194p. 1999. (0-7884-1229-9, B109) Heritage Bk.

*Beals, Joseph J. & Kirchner, Sandy. Births & Related Items Abstracted from the Camp Point Journal, 1873-1903. 128p. 1999. pap. 16.50 (0-7884-1214-0, B102) Heritage Bk.

Beals, Joseph J. & Kirchner, Sandy. Marriages & Related Items Abstracted from the Mendon Dispatch of Mendon, Adams County Illinois, 1877-1905. LC 98-104804. vi, 231p. 1997. pap. 16.00 (0-7884-0749-X, B103) Heritage Bk.

Beals, Judy. How to Build Miniature Furniture & Room Settings. Stern, Marcia, ed. (Illus.). 72p. (Orig.). 1992. pap. 9.95 (0-89024-044-2, 10-7780, Greenberg Pubs) Kalmbach.

Beals, Katharine, et al, eds. Papers from the 30th Regional Meeting of CLS, Vol. 1. 457p. 1994. pap. 16.00 (0-914203-45-2) Chicago Ling.

— Papers from the 29th Regional Meeting of CLS, Vol. 1. 499p. 1993. pap. 16.00 (0-914203-42-8) Chicago Ling.

— Parasession on the Correspondence of Conceptual, Semantic & Grammatical Representations, Vol. 2. 391p. 1993. pap. 16.00 (0-914203-43-6) Chicago Ling.

— Parasession on Variation in Linguistic Theory, Vol. 2. 349p. 1994. pap. 16.00 (0-914203-46-0) Chicago Ling.

*Beals, Kevin. Environmental Detectives: Grades 5-8. (Illus.). (YA). (gr. 5-8). 2000. pap. 25.50 (0-924886-23-4) Lawrence Science.

Beals, Kevin & Willard, Carolyn. Mystery Festival. rev. ed. Bergman, Lincoln et al, eds. (Great Explorations in Math & Science (GEMS) Ser.). (Illus.). 268p. (J). (gr. 2-8). 1998. pap. 25.50 (0-924886-10-2, GEMS) Lawrence Science.

Beals, M., et al, eds. Microlocal Analysis & Nonlinear Waves. (IMA Volumes in Mathematics & Its Applications Ser.: Vol. 30). (Illus.). xiii, 199p. 1991. 42.95 (0-387-97591-8) Spr-Verlag.

Beals, Melba Pettillo. Warriors Don't Cry: A Searing Memoir of the Battle to Integrate Little Rock's Central High. Rubenstein, Julie, ed. 336p. 1995. per. 14.00 (0-671-86639-7, WSP) PB.

— Warriors Don't Cry: A Searing Memoir of the Battle to Integrate Little Rock's Central High. 1995. 9.60 (0-606-08350-2, Pub. by Turtleback) Demco.

— Warriors Don't Cry: A Searing Memoir of the Battle to Integrate Little Rock's Central High. abr. ed. Greenberg, Anne, ed. (Illus.). 240p. (J). (gr. 4-7). 1995. per. 4.50 (0-671-89900-7, Archway) PB.

— White Is a State of Mind: A Memoir. LC 98-40768. 352p. 1999. 23.95 (0-399-14464-1) Putnam Pub Group.

*Beals, Melba Pettillo. White Is a State of Mind: A Memoir. 2000. reprint ed. pap. 12.95 (0-425-17269-4) Berkley Pub.

Beals, Michael. Propagation & Interaction of Singularities in Nonlinear Hyperbolic Problems. (Progress in Nonlinear Differential Equations & Their Applications Ser.: No. 3). 150p. 1989. 42.50 (0-8176-3449-5) Birkhauser.

Beals, Paul A. A People for His Name: A Church-Based Missions Strategy. 2nd rev. ed. LC 95-34891. (Illus.). 260p. 1995. pap. text 11.95 (0-87808-764-8, WCL764-8) William Carey Lib.

Beals, R. Advanced Mathematical Analysis. LC 73-6884. (Graduate Texts in Mathematics Ser.: Vol. 12). 288p. (C). 1988. 48.95 (0-387-90065-9) Spr-Verlag.

Beals, R. Michael. LP Boundedness of Fourier Integral Operators. LC 82-8754. (Memoirs of the American Mathematical Society Ser.: Vol. 38/264). 57p. 1982. pap. 16.00 (0-8218-2264-0, MEMO/38/264) Am Math.

Beals, Ralph. Cheran: A Sierra Tarascan Village. LC 97-34631. (Illus.). 256p. (Orig.). 1998. pap. 17.95 (0-8061-3024-5) U of Okla Pr.

Beals, Ralph L. The Aboriginal Culture of the Cahita Indians. LC 76-43657. (Ibero-Americana Ser.: No. 19). reprint ed. 34.50 (0-404-15490-5) AMS Pr.

— Cheran: A Sierra Tarascan Village, No. 2--2. LC 69-13812. (Illus.). 225p. 1971. reprint ed. lib. bdg. 65.00 (0-8371-3166-9, BECH, Greenwood Pr) Greenwood.

— Contemporary Culture of the Cahita Indians. (Bureau of American Ethnology Bulletins Ser.). 244p. 1995. lib. bdg. 89.00 (0-7812-4142-1) Rprt Serv.

Beals, Ralph L. The Contemporary Culture of the Cahita Indians. fac. ed. (Smithsonian Institution, Bureau of American Ethnology, Bulletins Ser.: No. 142). (Illus.). 277p. (C). 1945. reprint ed. pap. text 29.38 (1-55567-758-4) Coyote Press.

Beals, Ralph L. Ethnology of the Nisenan. fac. ed. (University of California Publications in American Archaeology & Ethnology: Vol. 31: 6). 82p. (C). 1933. reprint ed. pap. text 9.38 (1-55567-286-8) Coyote Press.

Beals, Richard. Fundamentals of Real Estate Principles & Practices for Salespersons & Brokers. (Illus.). 275p. 1983. student ed. 8.50 (0-89764-001-2) Prof Real Estate.

— Fundamentals of Real Estate Principles & Practices for Salespersons & Brokers. (Illus.). 275p. 1983. reprint ed. pap. text 12.95 (0-89764-000-4) Prof Real Estate.

— National Real Estate Examination Study Guide. 1982. pap. text 10.95 (0-89764-002-0) Lincolns Leadership.

Beals, Richard, et al, eds. Conference on Modern Analysis & Probability. LC 84-484. (Contemporary Mathematics Ser.: No. 26). 432p. 1984. pap. 47.00 (0-8218-5030-X, CONM/26) Am Math.

Beals, Richard & Greiner, Peter. Calculus on Heisenberg Manifolds. LC 88-9939. (Annals of Mathematics Studies: No. 119). 204p. reprint ed. pap. 63.30 (0-608-06433-5, 206664600008) Bks Demand.

Beals, Richard, et al. Direct & Inverse Scattering on the Line. LC 88-14487. (Mathematical Surveys & Monographs: Vol. 28). 209p. 1988. text 66.00 (0-8218-1530-X, SURV/28) Am Math.

Beals, Richard L. Think Big. (Orig.). 1992. pap. 9.00 (0-9632343-0-7) R L Beals.

Beals, Richards, ed. see Baoudndi, M. Salah, et al.

Beals, Scott. The Private School Guide Los Angeles County. Hopkins, David, ed. 340p. (Orig.). pap. 19.95 (0-929950-19-4) ME Pubns.

Beals, Sharon, photos by. What Cats Are. LC 96-38609. (Illus.). 1997. 8.95 (0-8118-1660-5) Chronicle Bks.

— What Dogs Do. LC 94-44120. (Illus.). 64p. 1995. 7.95 (0-8118-1023-2) Chronicle Bks.

*Beals, Sharon, photos by. What Kittens Are. LC 98-40398. (Illus.). 64p. 1999. 8.95 (0-8118-2077-7) Chronicle Bks.

Beals, Sharon, photos by. What Puppies Do. (Illus.). 64p. 1998. 8.95 (0-8118-2074-2) Chronicle Bks.

Beals, Theodore F., jt. auth. see McDowell, Elizabeth M.

Bealu, Marcel. The Experience of the Night. Donougher, Christine, tr. from FRE. LC 97-176254. (Europe 1992-97 Ser.).Tr. of L'Experience de la Nuit. 226p. 1997. pap. 13.99 (1-873982-67-4, Pub. by Dedalus) Hippocrene Bks.

Bealy, Frank, ed. The Blackwell Dictionary of Political Science: A User's Guide to Its Terms. LC 98-33143. 352p. 1999. 69.95 (0-631-20694-9) Blackwell Pubs.

Beam, Bill. A Collection of Southwestern Cowboy Poetry: A Working Cowboy's Poetry. LC 93-90945. (Illus.). 80p. (Orig.). 1994. pap. 24.95 (0-9639786-3-2) Shadow Rider.

— Cowboy Up! A Collection of Cowboy Poetry. LC 95-69758. (Illus.). 60p. (Orig.). 1995. pap. 19.95 (0-9639786-8-3) Shadow Rider.

Beam, Burton T., Jr. Group Benefits: Basic Concepts & Alternatives. 7th ed. LC 97-70994. 500p. (C). 1997. text 56.00 (0-943590-93-0) Amer College.

*Beam, Burton T., Jr. Group Benefits: Basic Concepts & Alternatives. 8th ed. 550p. (C). 2000. text 56.00 (1-57996-027-8, Pub. by Amer College) Maple-Vail Bk.

Beam, Burton T., Jr. Group Health Insurance. 2nd ed. LC 97-70988. 400p. (C). 1997. text 55.00 (0-943590-94-9) Amer College.

Beam, Burton T. & McFadden, John J. Employee Benefits. 5th ed. LC 97-30576. 1997. 62.95 (0-7931-2782-3, 4106-4605) Dearborn.

*Beam, Burton T., Jr., et al. Fundamentals of Insurance for Financial Planning. LC 99-73663. 750p. (C). 1999. text 77.00 (1-57996-018-9) Amer College.

Beam, C. Richard, ed. see Brendle, Thomas R.

Beam, Charles R. The Power of Mastering Your Primal Sense. LC 97-92221. (Illus.). 308p. 1997. 19.95 (0-9653985-1-X, 9702) StarSide Pr.

— Pretending Dreams - The Ladies. 2nd rev. ed. LC 97-91245. (Illus.). 72p. 1997. 14.95 (0-9653985-7-9) StarSide Pr.

— Pretending Dreams - The Men. LC 97-91246. (Illus.). 73p. 1997. 14.95 (0-9653985-2-8) StarSide Pr.

— Songs of Eros: Twelve Erotic Tales from the Arc of the Zodiac. LC 98-88590. (Illus.). 312p. 1999. 24.95 (1-891490-01-X, 04-9904) StarSide Pr.

Beam, David. The Broken Wing. 305p. 1998. pap. 10.00 (0-9660594-0-9) MCK.

Beam, Gary. Advanced Clipper dBASE. 1991. 29.95 (0-8306-6652-4) McGraw-Hill Prof.

— Clipper: dBASE Compiler. 1991. 24.95 (0-8306-6641-9) McGraw-Hill Prof.

— Clipper Programmers Guide, Five & One Quarter. 1991. 24.95 (0-8306-6079-8) McGraw-Hill Prof.

— Clipper Programmers Guide, Three & One Half. 1991. 24.95 (0-8306-6080-1) McGraw-Hill Prof.

— Clipper Programming. (Illus.). 320p. 1990. 32.95 (0-8306-8542-1, 3542); pap. 22.95 (0-8306-3542-4) McGraw-Hill Prof.

Beam, George & Simpson, Dick. Political Action: The Key to Understanding Politics. LC 84-5976. xiii, 253p. 1984. 24.95 (0-8040-0834-5); pap. 12.95 (0-8040-0835-3) Ohio U Pr.

Beam, Gordon, jt. ed. see Cohan, Tony.

Beam, Henry. Finance & Accounting for General Managers. 3rd ed. 154p. (C). 1998. per. 30.95 (0-7872-2051-5, 41205101) Kendall-Hunt.

Beam, Henry H. Finance & Accounting. 128p. (C). 1995. pap. text 19.95 (0-7872-1700-X) Kendall-Hunt.

Beam, Jack. Go Blue: A Great Lakes Novel. LC 99-32921. 280p. 1999. pap. 13.95 (1-883953-29-4, Face to Face) Midwest Trad.

Beam, Jeffery. The Fountain: Poems. LC 91-62197. 72p. 1992. 8.50 (0-933598-32-7) NC Wesleyan Pr.

— The Fountain: Poems. limited ed. LC 91-62197. 72p. 1992. 17.00 (0-933598-33-5) NC Wesleyan Pr.

— The Golden Legend. (Illus.). 48p. (Orig.). 1980. pap. 5.00 (0-912449-03-9) Floating Island.

— Midwinter Fires. 20p. (Orig.). 1990. pap. 8.00 (0-9622572-3-0) French Broad.

— Midwinter Fires. limited ed. 20p. (Orig.). 1990. 25.00 (0-9622572-4-9); 50.00 (0-9622572-5-7) French Broad.

— Visions of Dame Kind. (Illus.). 84p. 1995. 20.00 (0-912330-78-3); pap. 12.50 (0-912330-80-5) Jargon Soc.

Beam, Joan. Emily Louise. LC 93-79445. 192p. (Orig.). 1994. pap. 9.95 (0-9633919-8-4) Hells Canyon.

Beam, Joan & Branstad, Barbara. The Native American in Long Fiction: An Annotated Bibliography. LC 95-5636. (Native American Bibliography Ser.: No. 18). 384p. 1996. 56.00 (0-8108-3016-7) Scarecrow.

Beam, Joe. Becoming One: Emotionally, Spiritually, Sexually. LC 99-47709. 350p. 1999. 16.99 (1-58229-078-4) Howard Pub LA.

— Becoming One Workbook: Exercises in Intimacy. LC 99-47710. 150p. 1999. pap. 12.99 (1-58229-079-2) Howard Pub LA.

— Forgiven Forever: The Full Force of God's Tender Mercy. LC 98-13486. 256p. 1998. 16.99 (1-878990-66-7) Howard Pub LA.

— Seeing the Unseen: A Handbook for Spiritual Warfare. LC 95-173927. 344p. 1994. pap. 11.99 (1-878990-27-6) Howard Pub LA.

*Beam, Joe. Seeing the Unseen: Preparing Yourself for Spiritual Warfare. rev. ed. (Illus.). 342p. 2000. 16.99 (1-58229-139-X) Howard Pub LA.

Beam, Joe, jt. auth. see Stinnett, Nick.

Beam, Joseph, ed. In the Life: A Black Gay Anthology. (Illus.). 255p. 1986. pap. 8.95 (0-932870-73-2) Alyson Pubns.

Beam, Judy K. Ruffles & Flourishes: A Guide to Customs & Courtesies of the Military. (Illus.). 107p. 1999. reprint ed. text 20.00 (0-7881-6095-8) DIANE Pub.

Beam, Kathryn L. & Gagos, Traianos, eds. The Evolution of the English Bible: From Papyri to King James. LC 97-4518. (Illus.). (C). 1997. audio compact disk 59.95 (0-472-00249-X, 00249) U of Mich Pr.

*Beam, Lura. A Maine Hamlet. (Illus.). 256p. 2000. pap. 14.95 (0-88448-221-9) Tilbury Hse.

Beam, Lura, jt. auth. see Dickinson, Robert L.

Beam, Patricia. Collected Women. limited ed. 1985. 19.50 (0-935239-02-2) Seajay Society.

Beam, Philip C. Winslow Homer Watercolors. LC 83-70339. (Illus.). 1983. pap. 9.50 (0-916606-05-8) Bowdoin Coll.

Beam, Robert D., jt. auth. see Kuhn, Alfred.

*Beam, Thomas J. Consumers Digest Automotive Advisor: The Car Owner's A-to-Z Reference to Automotive Maintenance & Repair. (Illus.). 288p. 2000. pap. 19.95 (0-86730-807-9) Lebhar Friedman.

Beam, Thomas R., ed. Antibiotics, Hosts & Host Defences in Nosocomial Infections. 35.00 (0-915340-07-0) PJD Pubns.

Beam, Thomas R., Jr., ed. Recent Advances in Diagnosis & Treatment of Infections: Special Issue of Journal of Medicine. 1983. 35.00 (0-915340-12-7) PJD Pubns.

Beaman. System Dynamics & Control. (C). 1930. text. write for info. (0-06-040562-7) Addison-Wesley.

Beaman, Ardern H. M. Stambuloff. LC 70-135791. (Eastern Europe Collection). 1971. reprint ed. 23.95 (0-405-02733-8) Ayer.

— M. Stambuloff: With Six Portraits. LC 72-5471. (Select Bibliographies Reprint Ser.). 1977. reprint ed. 20.95 (0-8369-6896-4) Ayer.

Beaman, D. R., jt. ed. see Siegel, Benjamin M.

Beaman, David, ed. Multimedia Computing & Museums Vol. 1: ICHIM '95 Conference Proceedings. LC 96-113982. (Illus.). 388p. 1995. pap. 20.00 (1-885626-11-8) Archives & Mus.

Beaman, Dick. God's Justice, Administered in Love. LC 95-61392. 80p. 1995. per. 5.95 (1-57258-050-X) Teach Servs.

Beaman, Edmund A. Swedenborg & the New Age. LC 77-134422. (Communal Societies in America Ser.). reprint ed. 37.50 (0-404-08458-3) AMS Pr.

*Beaman, Jim. Interviewing for Radio. LC 00-25457. 2000. write for info. (0-415-22910-3) Routledge.

Beaman, John, ed. Messerschmitt BF 109 in Action, Pt. 2. (Aircraft in Action Ser.). (Illus.). 50p. 1993. pap. 9.95 (0-89747-138-5, 1057) Squad Sig Pubns.

Beaman, John H. Revision of Hieracium (Asteraceae) in Mexico & Central America. Anderson, Christiane, ed. (Systematic Botany Monographs: Vol. 29). (Illus.). 77p. 1990. pap. 9.00 (0-912861-29-0) Am Soc Plant.

*Beaman, John H. & Beaman, Reed S. Plants of Mt. Kinabalu, Vol. 3. (Illus.). 243p. 1998. 60.00 (983-812-026-X, Pub. by Royal Botnic Grdns) Balogh.

Beaman, Joseph J. Solid Freeform Fabrication: A New Direction in Manufacturing. LC 96-47010. 344p. (C). 1996. text 151.50 (0-7923-9834-3) Kluwer Academic.

Beaman, Joyce P. All for the Love of Cassie. 3rd ed. LC 73-86471. (Illus.). 102p. (gr. 4-12). 1973. 13.95 (0-87716-046-5) J Beaman.

— Bloom Where You Are Planted. 4th ed. LC 75-34645. 160p. (gr. 6-12). 1975. reprint ed. 13.95 (0-87716-060-0) J Beaman.

Beaman, Joyce Proctor. Teaching - Pure & Simple: One Way of Looking at Teaching. 2nd ed. LC 97-78037. 206p. (YA). (gr. 9-12). 1998. reprint ed. 13.95 (0-9658138-0-0) J Beaman.

Beaman, K. R., et al, eds. Proceedings of the First International Symposium on Turtles & Tortoises: Conservation & Captive Husbandry. 171p. 1991. pap. 25.00 (1-887945-00-8) CTTC.

*Beaman, Lori G. Shared Beliefs, Different Lives: Women's Identities in Evangelical Context. LC 99-50431. 1999. pap. 21.99 (0-8272-3444-9) Chalice Pr.

Beaman, Mark, jt. auth. see Madge, Steven.

Beaman, Middleton G. Index Analysis of the Federal Statutes: General & Permanent Law, 2 vols. LC 87-81280. vi, 2519p. 1987. reprint ed. 190.00 (0-89941-670-5, 201790) W S Hein.

— Index Analysis of the Federal Statutes: General & Permanent Law, Bk. 2. LC 87-81280. vi, 2519p. 1987. reprint ed. lib. bdg. 190.00 (0-89941-568-7, 201790) W S Hein.

Beaman, Peggy. No-Note Miracle Music: Mathematical Music. (Illus.). 100p. 1993. pap. 24.95 (1-929604-02-5) Beamans No-Note.

— No-Note Miracle Music Bk. 1: Gospel. unabridged ed. (Illus.). 31p. 1987. pap. 10.00 (1-929604-00-9) Beamans No-Note.

— No-Note Miracle Music Bk. 1: Traditional. (Illus.). 29p. 1987. pap. 10.00 (1-929604-01-7) Beamans No-Note.

Beaman, Reed S., jt. auth. see Beaman, John H.

Beaman, Ronda. Student Development & College Teaching. LC 96-138832. 140p. (Orig.). (C). 1995. pap. text 18.95 (0-943025-67-2) Cummngs & Hath.

Beame, Edmond M., ed. see Ariosto, Ludovico.

Beame, Paul W. & Buss, Samuel R., eds. Proof Complexity & Feasible Arithmetics: Dimacs Workshop, April 21-24, 1996. LC 97-29122. (DIMACS: Series in Discrete Mathematics & Theoretical Computer Science: Vol. 39). 320p. 1997. text 59.00 (0-8218-0577-0) Am Math.

Beame, Rona. Backyard Explorer Kit. LC 88-51582. (Illus.). 28p. (J). (gr. k-5). 1989. pap. 11.95 (0-89480-343-3, 1343) Workman Pub.

Beame-Rudman, Anne, et al. Given the Crime. LC 97-24075. 320p. 1998. 22.00 (0-671-00151-5) PB.

Beament, J. W., et al, eds. Advances in Insect Physiology, Vols. 2-13. Incl. Vol. 9. 1972. 77.00 (0-12-024209-5); write for info. (0-318-50192-9) Acad Pr.

Beament, James. The Violin Explained: Components, Mechanism, & Sound. LC 96-35558. (Illus.). 256p. 1997. text 65.00 (0-19-816623-0) OUP.

Beamer, Glenn. Creative Politics: Taxes & Public Goods in a Federal System. (Illus.). 190p. (C). pap. text 18.95 (0-472-08730-4, 08730) U of Mich Pr.

Beamer, Glenn. Creative Politics: Taxes & Public Goods in a Federal System. LC 98-58121. 190p. 1999. text 39.50 (0-472-11020-9, 11020) U of Mich Pr.

Beamer, Keola. Keola Beamer Teaches Hawaiian Slack Key Guitar: Fingerstyle Beauty & Elegance, Level 3. 1999. pap. text 19.95 (0-7935-9949-0) H Leonard.

Beamer, Keola, jt. auth. see Nelson, Mark.

Beamer, Linda, jt. auth. see Varner, Ira.

Beamer, Nona. Na Mele Hula: A Collection of Hawaiian Hula Chants. LC 87-751437. (Illus.). 96p. (C). 1987. pap. 21.95 incl. audio (0-939154-58-7, Pub. by Inst Polynesian) UH Pr.

— Na Mele Hula: A Collection of Hawaiian Hula Chants, Vol. 2. (Illus.). 96p. 2000. pap. 21.95 incl. audio (0-939154-57-9) Inst Polynesian.

Beamer, Shirley. A Face in the Window. 260p. 1997. pap. 11.95 (1-57502-714-3, PO1787) Morris Pubng.

Beamer, Winona D. Talking Story with Nona Beamer: Stories of a Hawaiian Family. LC 83-70357. (Illus.). 80p. (J). (gr. 2-6). 1984. 9.95 (0-935848-20-7) Bess Pr.

Beamer, Yvonne, jt. auth. see Hirschfelder, Arlene.

Beames. Wildlife Trust's Nature Photographer's Handbook. (Illus.). 160p. 1998. pap. 19.95 (0-7153-0791-6, Pub. by D & C Pub) Sterling.

Beames, Ian. The Wildlife Trusts Nature Photographer's Handbook. (Illus.). 160p. 1996. 27.95 (0-7153-9826-1, Pub. by D & C Pub) Sterling.

Beames, John. Memoirs of a Bengal Civilian: Lively Narrative of a Victorian District Officer. (Eland Travel Classics Ser.). 250p. (Orig.). 1991. pap. 14.95 (0-907871-75-5) Hippocrene Bks.

*Beames, John. Translation of Glanville. 362p. 1999. reprint ed. 125.00 (1-56169-531-9) Gaunt.

Beames, John, tr. see De Glanville, Ranulph.

Beames, Margaret. Juno Loves Barney. LC 93-20030. (Voyages Ser.). (Illus.). (J). 1994. pap. write for info. (0-383-03698-4) SRA McGraw.

— The Lunch That Mom Made. LC 92-21454. (Voyages Ser.). (Illus.). (J). 1993. 4.25 (0-383-03639-9) SRA McGraw.

Beamev, Erin. All Fired Up! Sparking the Flames of Leadership. (Illus.). xii, 104p. (Orig.). 1997. pap. 12.95 (0-9660220-0-9) WICT.

Beamis, John F., Jr. & Mathur, Praveen N., eds. Interventional Pulmonology. LC 98-15847. (Illus.). 528p. 1999. text 145.00 (0-07-005207-7) McGraw-Hill HPD.

Beamis, Paul W., jt. auth. see Baetz, Mark C.

Beamish. International Management. 4th ed. LC 99-31818. 656p. 1999. 84.38 (0-07-229072-2) McGraw.

Beamish, Caroline, tr. from FRE. Greece from the Air. LC 97-73769. (Illus.). 160p. 1997. 45.00 (0-8109-4125-2, Pub. by Abrams) Time Warner.

An Asterisk (*) at the beginning of an entry indicates that the title is appearing for the first time.

Beamish, Caroline, tr. see Jenger, Jean.

Beamish, Caroline, tr. see Jestaz, Bertrand.

Beamish, Caroline, tr. see Melot, Michel.

Beamish, Caroline, tr. see Piponnier, Fran C. & Mane, Perrine.

Beamish, David, jt. ed. see Shell, Donald.

Beamish, Ed. Windshear. 1995. 21.95 (*0-533-11392-X*) Vantage.

Beamish, F. E. Analytical Chemistry of Noble Metals. LC 65-17949. 1966. 271.00 (*0-08-011290-0*, Pub. by Pergamon Repr) Franklin.

Beamish, F. W., jt. ed. see Selley, L. J.

***Beamish, Paul W.** Asia-Pacific Cases in Strategic Management. LC 99-56029. 2000. write for info. (*0-07-239545-1*) McGrw-H Hghr Educ.

Beamish, Paul W. Multinational Joint Ventures in Developing Countries. 160p. 1988. lib. bdg. 52.50 (*0-318-35457-8*, Pub. by C Helm) Routldge.

Beamish, Paul W. & Casson, Mark, eds. Strategic Alliances. LC 98-21066. (Globalization of the World Economy Ser.: Vol. 2). 584p. 1998. 200.00 (*1-85898-694-X*) E Elgar.

Beamish, Paul W. & Killing, J. Peter. Cooperative Strategies Vol. 1: North American Perspectives. LC 96-50092. 1997. 51.00 (*0-7879-0812-6*) Lxngtn Bks.

Beamish, Paul W., et al. International Management: Text & Cases. 3rd ed. 576p. (C). 1996. text 66.50 (*0-256-19349-5*, Irwn McGrw-H) McGrw-H Hghr Educ.

— Japanese Multinationals in the Global Economy. LC 97-33199. (New Horizons in International Business Ser.). 352p. 1997. 90.00 (*1-85898-720-2*) E Elgar.

Beamish, R. E., et al, eds. Pathogenesis of Stress-Induced Heart Disease. (Developments in Cardiovascular Medicine Ser.). 1985. text 146.50 (*0-89838-710-8*) Kluwer Academic.

— Pathophysiology of Heart Disease. (Developments in Cardiovascular Medicine Ser.). 1987. text 161.50 (*0-89838-864-3*) Kluwer Academic.

— Stress & Heart Disease. (Developments in Cardiovascular Medicine Ser.). 1985. text 146.50 (*0-89838-709-4*) Kluwer Academic.

Beamish, Richard J. Getting the Word Out in the Fight to Save the Earth. LC 94-13724. (Illus.). 200p. 1995. text 49.95 (*0-8018-4894-6*); pap. text 24.95 (*0-8018-4895-4*) Johns Hopkins.

Beamish, Richard J., ed. Climate Change & Northern Fish Populations, Vol. 121. (Canadian Special Publication of Fisheries & Aquatic Sciences Ser.). 768p. (Orig.). (C). 1995. pap. 87.50 (*0-660-15780-2*, Pub. by NRC Res Pr) Accents Pubns.

Beamish, Richard J., ed. see Randorf, Gary.

Beamish, Rob. Marx, Method, & the Division of Labor. 208p. 1992. text 24.95 (*0-252-01878-8*) U of Ill Pr.

Beamish, Tony. The Arts of Malaya. LC 77-87022. (Illus.). reprint ed. 34.50 (*0-404-16794-2*) AMS Pr.

Beamon, Bob. Man Who Could Fly: The Bob Beamon Story. LC 99-226244. 175p. 1999. 18.95 (*1-885478-89-5*, Pub. by Genesis Press) BookWorld.

Beamon, Glenda W. Sparking the Thinking of Students, Ages 10-14: Strategies for Teachers. LC 97-4796. 168p. 1997. 51.95 (*0-8039-6582-6*, 80667); pap. 22.95 (*0-8039-6583-4*, 80668) Corwin Pr.

***Beamon-Isabell, Brenda.** Monday's Child. LC 00-190395. 2000. 25.00 (*0-7388-1629-9*); pap. 18.00 (*0-7388-1630-2*) Xlibris Corp.

Beamont, Roland P. Testing Early Jets: Compressibility & the Supersonic Era. (Illus.). 160p. (C). 1991. text 46.00 (*1-56098-109-1*) Smithsonian.

Beams, et al. Advanced Accounting. 7th ed. LC 98-32388. 899p. 1999. 100.00 (*0-13-597873-4*) P-H.

Beams, G. C., jt. auth. see Ellis, A. R.

Beams, John. Outlines of Indian Philology, ISSP Vol. 1, No. 2. 50p. 1974. reprint ed. 10.00 (*0-88065-053-2*) Scholarly Pubns.

Beams, Nick. The Significance & Implications of Globalization: A Marxist Assessment. (SEP Lecture Ser.). 61p. 1998. pap. 5.00 (*1-875639-26-8*) Mehring Bks.

Bean. Comparative Industry Relations. 2nd ed. 1994. pap. write for info. (*1-86152-495-1*, Pub. by ITBP) Thomson Learn.

Bean. Probability: The Science of Uncertainty. (Mathematics Ser.). 2002. pap. 65.00 (*0-534-36603-1*) Brooks-Cole.

Bean, jt. auth. see Ramage.

Bean, Adelaide, ed. see Bonosky, Phillip.

Bean, Alan. Apollo: An Eyewitness Account by Astronaut/Explorer Artist/Moonwalker Alan Bean. LC 98-19512. 176p. 1999. 45.00 (*0-86713-050-4*, 85128, Pub. by Greenwich Wrkshop) Workman Pub.

Bean, Anita. Complete Guide to Sports Nutrition. 2nd ed. pap. 15.95 (*0-7136-4388-9*, Pub. by A & C Blk) Midpt Trade.

***Bean, Anita.** The Complete Guide to Sports Nutrition. 3rd ed. 256p. 2000. pap. 14.95 (*0-7136-5389-2*, Pub. by A & C Blk) Midpt Trade.

Bean, Anita. The Complete Guide to Strength Training. (Illus.). 224p. 1997. pap. write for info. (*0-7136-4389-7*, Pub. by A & C Blk) Midpt Trade.

— Food for Fitness, 1 vol. 1998. pap. 17.95 (*0-7136-4794-9*) Adlard Coles Nautical.

— Sports Nutrition for Women. Wellington, Peggy, ed. pap. write for info. (*0-7136-4066-9*, 93384, Pub. by A & C Blk) Midpt Trade.

Bean, Annemarie. A Sourcebook on African-American Performance: Plays, People, Movements. LC 98-35340. (Worlds of Performance Ser.). 1999. write for info. (*0-415-18234-4*); pap. 24.99 (*0-415-18235-2*) Routledge.

Bean, Annemarie, et al, eds. Inside the Minstrel Mask: Readings in Nineteenth-Century Blackface Minstrelsy. LC 96-16572. (Illus.). 324p. 1996. pap. 22.95 (*0-8195-6300-5*, Wesleyan Univ Pr) U Pr of New Eng.

Bean, Barbara & Bennett, Shari. The Me Nobody Knows: A Guide for Teen Survivors. LC 97-26365. 1997. pap. 12.95 (*0-7879-3960-9*) Jossey-Bass.

Bean, Barton A., ed. Vascular Technology Review. 3rd ed. LC 88-34404. 1989. pap. text 55.00 (*0-941022-15-3*) Davies Pubng.

— Vascular Technology Review. 4th ed. 2000. pap. text 55.00 (*0-941022-19-6*) Davies Pubng.

Bean, Barton A., et al, eds. Vascular Physics Review. (Illus.). 180p. 1995. pap. text 55.00 (*0-941022-36-6*) Davies Pubng.

Bean, Barton A. & Oss, Kathleen A. Echocardiography Review. LC 89-18089. 1989. pap. 55.00 (*0-941022-16-1*) Davies Pubng.

Bean-Bayog, Margaret, ed. Children of Alcoholics. LC 87-23813. (Advances in Alcohol & Substance Abuse Ser.: Vol. 6, No. 4). 128p. 1987. text 39.95 (*0-86656-685-6*) Haworth Pr.

Bean, C., et al, eds. The Politics of Retribution: The 1996 Federal Election. LC 97-183720. (Illus.). 288p. 1997. pap. 24.95 (*1-86448-386-5*, Pub. by Allen & Unwin Pty) Paul & Co Pubs.

Bean, C. N. Altar Boys. 1999. mass mkt. 6.99 (*0-451-40660-5*, Onyx) NAL.

— Dust to Dust. 1998. mass mkt. 6.99 (*0-451-40804-7*, Onyx) NAL.

Bean, Charles, et al. Social Europe: One Policy for All? 8th ed. (Monitoring European Integration Ser.: No. 8). 120p. 1998. pap. 14.95 (*1-898128-33-2*, Pub. by Ctr Econ Policy Res) Brookings.

Bean, Charles R., jt. ed. see Dreze, Jacques H.

Bean, Constance A. Women Murdered by the Men They Loved. LC 91-23994. 196p. 1992. pap. 14.95 (*1-56023-003-7*, Harrington Park); lib. bdg. 39.95 (*1-56024-106-3*) Haworth Pr.

Bean, Cydne, jt. auth. see Bender, Deborah E.

Bean, David. Injunctions. 5th ed. 1991. pap. text. write for info. (*0-85121-695-1*) Addison-Wesley.

Bean, David, ed. Law Reform for All. 247p. 1996. pap. 34.00 (*1-85431-472-6*, Pub. by Blackstone Pr) Gaunt.

Bean, David, tr. see Buttiker, Urs.

Bean, Dawn, jt. auth. see Davis, Charlotte.

Bean, Deborah. Learn ACT! 3.0 for the Advanced User. LC 98-31103. 1998. pap. text 36.95 (*1-55622-588-1*) Wordware Pub.

***Bean, Deborah.** Learn Peach Tree Accounting: Configuration, Indtallation & Use. (Illus.). 2000. pap. text 29.95 (*1-55622-710-8*) Wordware Pub.

Bean, Deborah & Berkowitz, Neal. Learn ACT 3.0 for Windows 95. LC 97-10867. (Popular Applications Ser.). (Illus.). 250p. (Orig.). (C). 1997. pap. 19.95 (*1-55622-518-0*) Wordware Pub.

Bean, Deborah, jt. auth. see Berkowitz, Neal.

Bean, Delores. A Preacher Called David. 120p. 1998. pap. 11.95 (*1-880047-50-0*) Creative Des.

Bean, Donne L., jt. auth. see Kopp, Claire B.

Bean, Douglas E. And the Twain Shall Meet. LC 98-91089. 160p. 1999. pap. 12.95 (*0-533-13047-6*) Vantage.

— The Girl with Magic in Her Voice. 150p. 1996. pap. 10.95 (*0-9653609-0-3*) D E Bean.

Bean, E. William. New Treasures: A Perspective of New Testament Teachings Through Hebraic Eyes. rev. ed. 208p. (Orig.). 1999. pap. 13.95 (*0-9623950-2-1*) Cornerstn Pub.

Bean, Eli B., compiled by. History of Brownfield, Including Organization of the Town, Town Officers, Schools, Meeting Houses, Churches, Ministers. (Illus.). 165p. 1997. reprint ed. pap. 21.00 (*0-8328-5817-X*) Higginson Bk Co.

***Bean, Eric.** The ABC's of Parade. (Illus.). 32p. (YA). (ps up). 2000. pap. 10.00 (*1-56167-509-1*) Am Literary Pr.

Bean, Erik. Writing for Publication: The Online Magazine Article Writing Workshop Guide & Video Transcript. 82p. 1999. pap. 19.95 (*0-9665165-2-4*) Deadline MI.

— A Writing for Publication Guide. x, 90p. 1999. 39.95 (*0-9665165-3-2*) Deadline MI.

Bean, Eva M. East Bethel Road. 2nd ed. 750p. 1986. 50.00 (*0-9614153-0-4*) Bethel Hist Soc.

Bean, Frank D., et al, eds. At the Crossroads: Mexico & U. S. Immigration Policy. LC 96-50203. 322p. (Orig.). 1997. pap. 25.95 (*0-8476-8392-3*); text 66.00 (*0-8476-8391-5*) Rowman.

***Bean, Frank D. & Bell-Rose, Stephanie, eds.** Immigration & Opportunity: Race, Ethnicity & Employment in the United States. LC 99-37689. 412p. 1999. 39.95 (*0-87154-123-8*) Russell Sage.

Bean, Frank D. & Swicegood, Gray. Mexican American Fertility Patterns. (Mexican American Monographs: No. 10). 192p. 1985. text 20.00 (*0-292-75087-0*) U of Tex Pr.

Bean, Frank D. & Tienda, Marta. The Hispanic Population of the United States. LC 87-42621. (Population of the United States in the 1980s: A Census Monograph Ser.). 480p. 1988. 49.95 (*0-87154-104-1*) Russell Sage.

— The Hispanic Population of the United States. (Population of the United States in the 1980s: A Census Monograph Ser.). (Illus.). 480p. (C). 1990. pap. 18.95 (*0-87154-105-X*) Russell Sage.

Bean, Frank D., jt. ed. see Hamermesh, Daniel S.

Bean, Fred. Black Gold. LC 97-19361. 384p. 1997. text 23.95 (*0-312-86062-5*) St Martin.

— Black Gold. 1998. mass mkt. 5.99 (*0-8125-4597-4*, Pub. by Tor Bks) St Martin.

***Bean, Fred.** Ghost Riders. 2000. mass mkt. 5.99 (*0-451-20124-8*, Sig) NAL.

Bean, Fred. Lorena. 1998. mass mkt. 5.99 (*0-8125-4596-6*, Pub. by Forge NYC) St Martin.

Bean, Frederic. Blood Trail. 224p. 1993. mass mkt. 3.50 (*0-8217-4369-4*, Zebra Kensgtn) Kensgtn Pub Corp.

— Cry of the Wolf. 1992. mass mkt. 3.50 (*0-8217-3667-1*, Zebra Kensgtn) Kensgtn Pub Corp.

— Guns on the Cimarron. 224p. 1995. mass mkt. 3.99 (*0-8217-4843-2*, Zebra Kensgtn) Kensgtn Pub Corp.

— Hangman's Legacy. large type ed. 237p. 1992. reprint ed. lib. bdg. 15.95 (*1-56054-568-2*) Thorndike Pr.

***Bean, Frederic.** The Hangman's Tree. 288p. 2000. mass mkt. 5.99 (*0-553-58020-5*) Bantam.

Bean, Frederic. Hard Luck. large type ed. LC 93-30999. 250p. 1994. lib. bdg. 18.95 (*1-56054-718-9*) Thorndike Pr.

— Hell's Half Acre. 256p. (Orig.). 1996. mass mkt. 5.99 (*0-425-15584-6*) Berkley Pub.

— Lone Wolf. 256p. 1997. mass mkt. 4.99 (*0-7860-0359-6*, Pinncle Kensgtn) Kensgtn Pub Corp.

— Murder at the Spirit Cave. 336p. 1999. mass mkt. 5.99 (*0-553-58017-5*, Crimeline) Bantam.

— Pancho & Black Jack. 1995. mass mkt. 5.50 (*0-671-88691-6*) PB.

— Red River. (Rivers West Ser.). 272p. 1997. mass mkt. 5.50 (*0-553-56800-0*) Bantam.

— Santa Fe Showdown. 256p. 1993. mass mkt. 3.50 (*0-8217-4065-2*, Zebra Kensgtn) Kensgtn Pub Corp.

— Tom Spoon. large type ed. LC 90-46132. 236p. 1990. reprint ed. lib. bdg. 15.95 (*1-56054-075-3*) Thorndike Pr.

Bean, Frederic, jt. auth. see Jameson, W. C.

Bean, George. Yankee Auctioneer. (American Autobiography Ser.). 247p. 1995. reprint ed. lib. bdg. 79.00 (*0-7812-8452-X*) Rprt Serv.

Bean, George E. Lycian Turkey. (Illus.). 256p. 1990. pap. 24.95 (*0-7195-4764-4*, Pub. by John Murray) Trafalgar.

— Lycian Turkey: An Archaeological Guide. LC 78-326329. 197 p. 1978. write for info. (*0-510-03205-2*) Tolley UK.

Bean, Gerard M. Fiduciary Obligations & Joint Ventures: The Collaborative Fiduciary Relationship. 360p. 1995. text 95.00 (*0-19-825928-X*) OUP.

Bean, Greg. Internet Server Construction Kit for Windows3. LC 95-17368. 432p. 1995. pap. 39.95 incl. cd-rom (*0-471-12696-9*) Wiley.

— Internet Servers: A Step-by-Step Guide on How to Build Them. 155p. 1994. pap. 24.95 (*0-9642041-1-8*) CyberGrp.

Bean, Gregory. Grave Victory. LC 98-2825. 336p. 1998. text 23.95 (*0-312-18590-1*) St Martin.

— No Comfort in Victory: A Sheriff Harry Starbranch Mystery. 1996. mass mkt. 5.99 (*0-312-95877-3*) St Martin.

Bean, H. S. Fluid Meters, Their Theory & Application. 6th ed. 273p. 1970. 20.00 (*0-317-33526-X*, G00079) ASME.

Bean, Heike & Blanchard, Sarah. Carriage Driving: A Logical Approach Through Dressage Training. (Illus.). 256p. 1992. 30.00 (*0-87605-898-5*) Howell Bks.

Bean, Irean. Laguna Beach: Local Color. (Illus.). 76p. 1998. pap. 24.95 (*0-9660793-1-0*) Max Co.

Bean, J. C., et al, eds. Silicon Molecular Beam Epitaxy Vol. 220: Materials Research Society Symposium Proceedings. 649p. 1991. text 70.00 (*1-55899-114-X*) Materials Res.

— Strained Layer Epitaxy - Materials, Processing, & Device Applications. (Symposium Proceedings Ser.: Vol. 379). 521p. 1995. text 76.00 (*1-55899-282-0*) Materials Res.

Bean, J. P. The Sheffield Gang Wars. 135p. (C). 1992. pap. text 55.00 (*0-9507645-0-7*, Pub. by D&D Pubns) St Mut.

Bean, J. Ronald & O'Connor, Seamus. Alcohol a Problem? An Awareness Workbook. (Illus.). 48p. (Orig.). 1996. pap., wbk. ed. 9.95 (*0-9654052-2-2*) OConnor & Bean.

Bean, Jacob & Griswold, William M. Eighteenth Century Italian Drawings in The Metropolitan Museum of Art. (Illus.). 280p. 1990. 25.00 (*0-87099-585-5*, 0-8109-3250-4); pap. 20.00 (*0-87099-586-3*) Metro Mus Art.

Bean, Jacob & Turcic, Lawrence. Fifteenth Through Eighteenth Century French Drawings in the Metropolitan Museum of Art. (Illus.). 328p. 1987. pap. 19.95 (*0-317-56152-9*) Abrams.

Bean, James. Neurosurgery in Transition: The Sociol Economic Transformation of Neurological Surgery. 85.00 (*0-683-18345-1*) Lppncott W & W.

Bean, James H., ed. see Lynch, Don & Thompson, David.

***Bean, Jane.** Curing IBS Naturally with Chinese Medicine. 149p. 2000. pap. 12.95 (*1-891845-11-X*, Pub. by Blue Poppy Pr) IPG Chicago.

***Bean, John.** Communicating Successfully with Everyone: Bosses, Brothers & Sisters, Children, Co-Workers... And Yourself. Bean, Maureen, ed. LC 99-96485. 46p. 2000. pap. 14.95 (*0-9675764-0-7*) J Bean Pubg.

Bean, John C. Engaging Ideas: The Professor's Guide to Integrating Writing, Critical Thinking, & Active Learning in the Classroom. (Higher & Adult Education Ser.). 288p. (Orig.). 1996. pap. text 32.95 (*0-7879-0203-9*) Jossey-Bass.

Bean, John C., jt. auth. see Ramage, John D.

Bean, John C., ed. see International Symposium on Silicon Molecular Beam.

Bean, John C., jt. ed. see Kasper, Erich.

Bean, Jonathan J. Beyond the Broker State: Federal Policies Toward Small Business, 1936-1961. LC 96-10868. (Business, Society & the State Ser.). 336p. (C). 1996. 49.95 (*0-8078-2296-5*) U of NC Pr.

Bean, Joseph. Horsemen: Leathersex Short Fiction. LC 97-15478. 189p. 1997. pap. 14.95 (*0-943595-69-X*) Leyland Pubns.

Bean, Joseph, ed. see Baldwin, Guy.

Bean, Joseph, ed. see Nan, Mistress.

Bean, Joseph, ed. see Rinella, Jack.

Bean, Joseph W. Leathersex: A Guide for the Curious Outsider & the Serious Player. LC 94-71570. 236p. 1994. pap. 14.95 (*1-881943-05-4*) Daedalus Pub.

— Leathersex Q & A: Questions about Leathersex & the Leather Lifestyles Answered. LC 96-85421. 230p. (Orig.). 1996. pap. 16.95 (*1-881943-01-1*) Daedalus Pub.

Bean, Kenneth E., ed. see International Symposium on Very Large Scale Integr.

Bean, Kenneth L. Construction of Educational & Personnel Tests. LC 74-100141. 231p. 1970. reprint ed. lib. bdg. 59.50 (*0-8371-3247-9*, BEET, Greenwood Pr) Greenwood.

Bean, L. John & Lawton, Harry W. The Cahuilla Indians of Southern California. 1965. pap. 2.00 (*0-939046-08-3*) Malki Mus Pr.

Bean, L. L. Hunting Fishing & Camping. LC 93-9694. 104p. 1993. 19.95 (*1-55709-206-0*) Applewood.

Bean, Laurie. Your Opportunities As a Massage Therapist. (Illus.). 8p. 1994. pap. 2.50 (*1-884241-11-5*, OS115) Energeia Pub.

— Your Opportunities As a Secretary (Executive & Legal) (Illus.). 8p. 1994. pap. 2.50 (*1-884241-18-2*, OS122) Energeia Pub.

— Your Opportunities in Food Service. (Illus.). 8p. (Orig.). 1995. pap. 2.50 (*1-884241-06-9*, OS110) Energeia Pub.

— Your Opportunities in Legal Support. (Illus.). 8p. 1994. pap. 2.50 (*1-884241-09-3*, OS113) Energeia Pub.

— Your Opportunities in Real Estate. (Illus.). 8p. 1994. pap. 2.50 (*1-884241-14-X*, OS118) Energeia Pub.

— Your Opportunities in Recreation, Travel & Tourism. (Illus.). 8p. 1994. pap. 2.50 (*1-884241-15-8*, OS119) Energeia Pub.

— Your Opportunities in the Printing Industry. (Illus.). 8p. 1994. pap. 2.50 (*1-884241-13-1*, OS117) Energeia Pub.

Bean, Laurie, jt. auth. see Charette, Rick.

Bean, Louis H. How to Predict Elections. LC 78-141278. (Illus.). 196p. 1972. reprint ed. lib. bdg. 38.50 (*0-8371-5872-9*, BEPE, Greenwood Pr) Greenwood.

Bean, Louis H., compiled by. The Graphic Method of Curvilinear Correlation: Articles by Louis H. Bean, John D. Black, Mordecai Ezekiel, Richard E. Foote & Wilfred Malenbaum. LC 66-21654. 135p. 1969. 35.00 (*0-678-00282-7*) Kelley.

Bean, Lowell J. Mukat's People: The Cahuilla Indians of Southern California. LC 78-145782. (Illus.). 300p. 1972. pap. 15.95 (*0-520-02627-6*, Pub. by U CA Pr) Cal Prin Full Svc.

Bean, Lowell J., ed. The Ohlone Past & Present: Native Americans of the San Francisco Bay Region. (Anthropological Papers: No. 42). (Illus.). 408p. (C). 1994. 29.95 (*0-87919-130-9*) Ballena Pr.

— Seasons of the Kachina: Proceedings of the California State University Hayward Conferences on the Western Pueblos, 1987-1988. LC 89-6953. (Anthropological Papers: No. 34). (Illus.). 173p. 1989. pap. 21.95 (*0-87919-114-7*) Ballena Pr.

Bean, Lowell J. & Saubel, Katherine S. Temalpakh: Cahuilla Indian Knowledge & Usage of Plants. LC 72-85815. 1972. pap. 16.00 (*0-939046-24-5*) Malki Mus Pr.

Bean, Lowell J. & Vane, Sylvia B., eds. California Indian Shamanism. LC 92-6167. (Anthropological Papers: No. 39). (Illus.). 274p. 1992. text 34.00 (*0-87919-125-2*); pap. text 28.50 (*0-87919-124-4*) Ballena Pr.

— Ethnology of Alta California Indians Vol. II: Postcontact. LC 91-45781. (Spanish Borderlands Sourcebooks Ser.: Vol. 4). 1000p. 1992. text 50.00 (*0-8240-7119-0*) Garland.

— Ethnology of the Alta California Indians Vol. I: Precontact. LC 91-45781. (Spanish Borderlands Sourcebooks Ser.: Vol. 3). 928p. 1992. text 50.00 (*0-8240-0792-1*) Garland.

— The Ohlone Past & Present: Native Americans of the San Francisco Bay Region. (Anthropological Papers: No. 42). (Illus.). 376p. (C). 1994. pap. 23.95 (*0-87919-129-5*) Ballena Pr.

Bean, Lowell J., et al. The Cahuilla & the Santa Rosa Mountain Region: Places & Their Native American Association. 69p. (C). 1981. reprint ed. pap. text 8.13 (*1-55567-397-X*) Coyote Press.

— The Cahuilla Landscape: The Santa Rosa & San Jacinto Mountains. Vane, Sylvia B., ed. LC 91-8148. (Anthropological Papers: No. 37). (Illus.). 116p. 1991. text 27.00 (*0-87919-121-X*); pap. text 20.00 (*0-87919-120-1*) Ballena Pr.

Bean, Lowell J., jt. auth. see Vane, Sylvia B.

Bean, Lowell J., ed. see Knack, Martha C.

Bean, Lowell J., ed. see Sherer, Lorraine M.

Bean, M. Handsome Is As Handsome Does. LC 96-90871. (Illus.). 52p. (Orig.). (J). (gr. k-3). 1997. pap. 6.95 (*0-533-12191-4*) Vantage.

Bean, Malcolm. Political Culture in Modern Britain. 1987. text 57.50 (*0-231-06678-3*) Col U Pr.

Bean, Manya C. Too Shy to Surrender. 54p. (Orig.). 1993. pap. 8.95 (*0-9639821-0-9*) Osage.

Bean, Marian C. The Development of Word Order Patterns in Old English. LC 82-22722. (Illus.). 150p. (C). 1983. text 42.00 (*0-389-20356-4*, 07216) B&N Imports.

Bean, Maureen, ed. see Bean, John.

Bean, Michael J. The Evolution of National Wildlife Law. 1983. pap. text 15.95 (*0-03-063502-0*) Holt R&W.

Bean, Michael J. & Rowland, Melanie J. The Evolution of National Wildlife Law. 3rd ed. LC 97-8860. 568p. 1997. 79.50 (*0-275-95988-0*, Praeger Pubs); pap. 32.50 (*0-275-95989-9*, Praeger Pubs) Greenwood.

Bean, Michael J., et al. Reconciling Conflicts under the Endangered Species Act: The Habitat Conservation Planning Experience. LC 91-21750. 127p. reprint ed. pap. 39.40 (*0-608-09123-5*, 206975500006) Bks Demand.

Bean, Mimi & Perry, C. Michael, contrib. by. Cinderabbit! A Puppet Musical. 22p. (Orig.). (J). (gr. 1-7). 1986. pap. 3.50 (*1-57514-244-9*, 0015) Encore Perform Pub.

Bean, Orson. Too Much Is Not Enough. 192p. 1988. 14.95 (*0-8184-0465-5*) Carol Pub Group.

B

An Asterisk (*) at the beginning of an entry indicates that the title is appearing for the first time.

— Twenty-Five Ways to Cook a Mouse: Whisker-Licking Recipes for Your Gourmet Cat. LC 93-24145. (Illus.). 1993. 9.95 (*1-55972-199-5*, Birch Ln Pr) Carol Pub Group.

Bean, Philip. Compulsory Admissions to Mental Hospitals. LC 79-41786. 290p. reprint ed. pap. 89.90 (*0-608-18828-X*, 203048300069) Bks Demand.

Bean, Philip, ed. Adoption: Essays in Social Policy, Law, & Sociology. 336p. 1984. 47.50 (*0-422-78410-9*, NO. 9152, Pub. by Tavistock) Routldge.

— Mental Illness: Changes & Trends. LC 82-8603. 498p. reprint ed. pap. 154.40 (*0-608-15626-4*, 203175500076) Bks Demand.

Bean, Phillip, et al, eds. In Defense of Welfare. 250p. (C). 1985. pap. text 17.95 (*0-422-79090-7*, 9634, Pub. by Tavistock) Routldge.

Bean, Phillip W., et al. Precalculus. LC 92-27803. 672p. 1993. text 68.95 (*0-534-93160-X*) PWS Pubs.

Bean, R. International Labour Statistics. 320p. 1989. 125.00 (*0-415-02179-0*) Routledge.

Bean, R. J., ed. see Topology Seminar (1965: University of Wisconsin) S.

Bean, R. Mark. Cooperative Security in Northeast Asia: A China-Japan-South Korea Coalition Approach. 199p. (Orig.). (C). 1994. pap. text 40.00 (*0-7881-1077-2*) DIANE Pub.

Bean, R. S. It's Impossible to Learn Elevator Repair from Your Mother: A Guide to Finding a Job You Can Fit into Your Busy Time Schedule. (Illus.). 128p. 1992. pap. 9.95 (*0-8065-1327-6*, Citadel Pr) Carol Pub Group.

— People Watcher's Field Guide: People Watching at Its Funniest. Carle, Cliff, ed. 1992. pap. 5.95 (*0-918259-41-X*) CCC Pubns.

Bean, Reynold. Cooperation, Social Responsibility & Other Skills: Using the Four Conditions of Self-Esteem in Elementary & Middle Schools. LC 92-488. 1992. 21.95 (*1-56071-069-1*) ETR Assocs.

— Individuality, Self-Expression & Other Keys to Creativity: Using the Four Conditions of Self-Esteem in Elementary & Middle Schools. LC 92-20521. 1992. 21.95 (*1-56071-071-3*) ETR Assocs.

— Positive Risks, Challenges & Other Paths to Success: Busing the Four Conditions of Self-Esteem in Elementary & Middle Schools. LC 92-19096. 1992. 21.95 (*1-56071-070-5*) ETR Assocs.

***Bean, Richard.** Toast. 1999. pap. 10.95 (*1-84002-104-7*, Pub. by Theatre Comm) Consort Bk Sales.

Bean, Richard & Crane, Karen. The O. J. Syndrome: Confessions of an Abuser. (Illus.). 120p. 1995. pap. 11.95 (*0-933025-39-4*) Blue Bird Pub.

Bean, Richard N. The British Trans-Atlantic Slave Trade, Sixteen Fifty to Seventeen Seventy-Five. LC 75-2575. (Dissertations in American Economic History Ser.). (Illus.). 1978. 28.95 (*0-405-07256-2*) Ayer.

Bean, Rita M. & Wilson, Robert M. Effecting Change in School Reading Program: The Resource Role. LC 81-8231. 76p. reprint ed. pap. 30.00 (*0-8357-2632-0*, 204012000014) Bks Demand.

***Bean, Roger & Radford, Russell.** Powerful Products: Strategic Management of Successful New Product Development. LC 00-24828. 300p. 2000. 39.95 (*0-8144-0566-5*) AMACOM.

Bean, Ron. Comparative Industrial Relations: An Introduction to Cross-National Perspectives. 2nd ed. LC 93-29290. 256p. (C). 1994. pap. 26.95 (*0-415-07087-2*, B4066) Thomson Learn.

— Comparative Industrial Relations: An Introduction to Cross-National Perspectives. 2nd ed. LC 93-29290. 256p. (C). (gr. 13). 1994. pap. 60.95 (*0-415-07086-4*, B4062) Thomson Learn.

***Bean Sprouts Editors, ed.** Favorite Bible Stories. (Illus.). 2000. 14.99 (*0-7847-1212-3*) Standard Pub.

Bean, Susan L. Lava Beds National Monument. 48p. 1991. pap. 8.95 (*0-9631392-0-7*) Lava Beds NHA.

Bean, Susan S. Symbolic & Pragmatic Semantics: A Kannada System of Address. LC 77-18198. (Illus.). 1978. lib. bdg. 17.00 (*0-226-03989-7*) U Ch Pr.

— Symbolic & Pragmatic Semantics: A Kannada System of Address. LC 77-18198. 179p. Date not set. reprint ed. pap. 55.50 (*0-608-20999-6*, 205452700003) Bks Demand.

***Bean, Susan S.** Timeless Visions: Contemporary Art of India. (Illus.). 95p. 1999. pap. 25.00 (*0-88389-113-1*) Peabody Essex Mus.

***Bean, Susan S. & Sharf, Frederic A.** Korean Collection of the Peabody Essex Museum. (Peabody Essex Museum Collection: Vol. 133). (Illus.). 94p. 1999. pap. 25.00 (*0-88389-111-5*) Peabody Essex Mus.

Bean, Susan S., jt. auth. see Myers, Diana K.

Bean, Susan S., jt. ed. see Myers, Diana K.

Bean, Suzanne M., jt. auth. see Karnes, Frances A.

Bean, Suzanne M., jt. ed. see Karnes, Frances A.

Bean, Theodore W., ed. History of Montgomery County, Pennsylvania. (Illus.). 1295p. 1992. reprint ed. lib. bdg. 126.50 (*0-8328-1411-3*) Higginson Bk Co.

Bean, Tom, photos by. The Smithsonian Guides to Natural America: The Northern Plains - Minnesota, North Dakota, South Dakota. (Illus.). 1996. pap. 19.95 (*0-679-76477-1*) Random.

Bean, Vaughan. The ABCs of Meditation & More, (A Guide for Children) (Illus.). 96p. (Orig.). (J). (gr. 2-5). 1994. pap. 11.95 (*0-9631740-1-0*) Holographic Bks.

— The Dream Diary: Whose Dream Is This Anyway? (Illus.). 144p. (Orig.). pap. 16.95 (*0-9631740-0-2*) Holographic Bks.

***Bean, W. G.** Stonewall's Man: Sandie Pendleton. LC 99-89759. (Illus.). 272p. 2000. pap. 16.95 (*0-8078-4875-1*) U of NC Pr.

Bean, Walton. Boss Ruef's San Francisco: The Story of the Union Labor Party, Big Business, & the Graft Prosecution. 1952. pap. 15.95 (*0-520-00094-3*, Pub. by U CA Pr) Cal Prin Full Svc.

Bean, Walton, jt. auth. see Rawls, James J.

Bean, Wendy & Bouffler, Christine. Spell by Writing. LC 90-27028. 92p. (Orig.). (C). 1991. pap. text 17.00 (*0-435-08577-8*, 08577) Heinemann.

Bean, Wendy & Bouffler, Chrystine. Read, Write, Spell. LC 97-28849. 96p. 1997. pap. text 17.00 (*1-57110-075-X*) Stenhse Pubs.

Bean, Wiley E. The Morning of the Fourth Day. 2nd rev. ed. LC 94-94263. 363p. 1992. 18.00 (*0-9637650-0-0*) W E Bean.

Bean, William B. Walter Reed: A Biography. LC 81-16123. 208p. reprint ed. pap. 64.50 (*0-608-18484-5*, 203300500082) Bks Demand.

Bean, William C. Strategic Planning That Makes Things Happen. 300p. 1993. pap. 24.95 (*0-87425-212-1*) HRD Press.

Beanblossom, Gloria. The Tamarisk Tree. LC 99-70091. 352p. 1999. pap. 18.95 (*1-57197-170-X*) Pentland Pr.

Beanblossom, Ronald E., jt. ed. see Cady, Duane L.

Beanblossom, Ronald E., ed. see Reid, Thomas.

Beanblossom, Walter S. Harrison County, Indiana Marriage Affidavits & Certificates, 1809-1865. 243p. 1977. pap. 23.00 (*1-889221-19-8*) Ancestral Trails.

— Harrison County, Indiana School Enumeration, 1846 & 1847. 150p. 1977. pap. 16.00 (*1-889221-21-X*) Ancestral Trails.

Beane, Allan L. The Bully Free Classroom: Over 100 Tips & Strategies for Teachers K-8. LC 98-47202. 176p. (J). 1999. pap., teacher ed. 19.95 (*1-57542-054-6*) Free Spirit Pub.

Beane, Connie J., jt. ed. see Tribble, Edward J.

***Beane, Donald.** The United States & Gatt: A Relational Study. LC 99-41542. (International Business & Economics Ser.). 332p. 2000. 75.00 (*0-08-042759-6*, Pergamon Pr) Elsevier.

Beane, Donald, et al. The Singapore & Malaysia Electronics Industry. LC 97-146. (Electronics Industry Research Ser.). 128p. 1997. lib. bdg. 39.95 (*0-8493-3171-4*) CRC Pr.

Beane, Douglas C. As Bees in Honey Drown. 1998. pap. 5.25 (*0-8222-1651-5*) Dramatists Play.

Beane, Douglas Carter. The Country Club. Date not set. pap. 5.95 (*0-8222-1742-2*) Dramatists Play.

Beane, James A. Affect in the Curriculum: Toward Democracy, Dignity, & Diversity. 232p. (C). 1990. pap. text 17.95 (*0-8077-2999-X*) Tchrs Coll.

— Curriculum Integration: Designing the Core of Democratic Education. LC 97-26139. 1997. 35.00 (*0-8077-3684-8*); pap. 16.95 (*0-8077-3683-X*) Tchrs Coll.

— A Middle School Curriculum: From Rhetoric to Reality. 132p. (C). pap. text 18.00 (*1-56090-073-3*) Natl Middle Schl.

Beane, James A., ed. Toward a Coherent Curriculum. 184p. 1995. pap. 23.95 (*0-87120-311-1*) ASCD.

Beane, James A. & Lipka, Richard P. Self-Concept, Self-Esteem & the Curriculum. 272p. (C). 1986. pap. text 19.95 (*0-8077-2839-X*) Tchrs Coll.

— When the Kids Come First: Enhancing Self-Esteem. 86p. 1987. 5.00 (*1-56090-036-9*) Natl Middle Schl.

***Beane, James A. & Lipka, Richard P.** When the Kids Come First: Enhancing Self Esteem. LC 99-88512. 116p. 2000. pap. 18.95 (*1-891928-07-4*) Educ Intl Pr.

Beane, James A., jt. ed. see Apple, Michael W.

Beane, Leona, jt. auth. see Lakin, Leonard.

Beane, Marjorie N. From Framework to Freedom: A History of the Sister Formation Conference. 172p. (C). 1993. lib. bdg. 39.50 (*0-8191-9125-6*) U Pr of Amer.

Beane, Mildred B. Fine Arts: Performing Arts. 88p. 1989. pap. 10.95 (*0-8106-0303-9*) NEA.

Beane, Wendell C. The Truth Within You: Faith, Gnostic Visions, & Christ Consciousness. 1998. pap. 12.95 (*0-87604-412-7*) ARE Pr.

***Beaney, Gerry.** The Lost in the Sauce Cookbook. LC 99-91516. 285p. 1999. ring bd. 28.00 (*0-9677246-0-0*) Shorewood Cntrl.

Beaney, J., jt. auth. see Sgaravatti, E.

Beaney, Michael. The Frege Reader. LC 96-47027. (Readers Ser.). 320p. (C). 1997. text 68.95 (*0-631-19444-4*); pap. text 29.95 (*0-631-19445-2*) Blackwell Pubs.

Beaney, William M. The Right to Counsel in American Courts, Vol. 19--19. LC 72-5275. (University of Michigan Publications History & Political Science Ser.: Vol. 19). 268p. 1972. reprint ed. lib. bdg. 69.50 (*0-8371-5725-0*, BERC, Greenwood Pr) Greenwood.

***Beanland, Ame & Miles, Emily L.** It's A Chick Thing: Celebrating the Wild side of Women's Friendships. (Illus.). 215p. 2000. pap. 15.95 (*1-57324-196-2*) Conari Press.

Beans, Bruce E. Eagle's Plume: The Struggle to Preserve the Life & Haunts of America's Bald Eagle. LC 97-15433. (Illus.). 326p. 1997. pap. 17.95 (*0-8032-6142-X*) U of Nebr Pr.

Beans, Florence A. Canaan Tomorrow. LC 95-92671. 274p. 1995. pap. 10.00 (*0-9648833-0-9*) F A Beans.

Beans, Richard, et al. Process Improvement: A Guide for Teams. 225p. 1993. pap. 44.95 (*0-944533-06-X*) Coopers Total Qlty.

Bear. Stories from the Old Testament, Vol 1. (J). 1998. 16.00 (*0-671-88661-4*) S&S Bks Yung.

***Bear, Brown, pseud.** Loyalty, Betrayal, & Other Contact Sports: (Bravo) LC 99-91753. xxii, 317p. 2000. pap. write for info. (*0-9673933-2-9*) Erzse.

Bear, C. D. Digby: The Biggest Dog in the World. LC 74-9678. (Illus.). (YA). (gr. 5 up). 1940. lib. bdg. 12.89 (*0-200-00145-0*) HarpC Child Bks.

***Bear, Donald R.** Words Their Way: Word Study for Phonics, Vocabulary & Spelling Instruction. 2nd ed. 415p. 1999. pap. 28.00 (*0-13-021339-X*) P-H.

Bear, Donald R., jt. ed. see Templeton, Shane.

Bear, Dorothy & Stebbins, Beth. A Tour of Mendocino: Thirty-Two Historic Buildings along the Streets of Mendocino. 4th rev. ed. (Illus.). 32p. 1991. reprint ed. pap. 6.00 (*0-939431-06-8*) Bored Feet Pubns.

Bear, Dorothy, ed. see Jackson, W. Francis.

Bear, Edward. The Dark Night of Recovery: A Journey to Freedom. 164p. (Orig.). 1995. pap. 9.95 (*0-9644357-0-5*) M & J Pub.

— The Dark Night of Recovery: Conversations from the Bottom of the Bottle. LC 98-43235. 175p. (Orig.). 1999. pap. 9.95 (*1-55874-653-6*) Health Comm.

***Bear, Edward.** The Seven Deadly Needs. LC 99-54527. 150p. 2000. pap. 9.95 (*1-55874-776-1*) Health Comm.

Bear, Euan & Dimock, Peter T. Adults Molested As Children: A Survivor's Guide for Women & Men. (Safer Society Ser.). 67p. 1988. pap. 12.95 (*1-884444-03-2*) Safer Soc.

Bear, Euan, ed. see Allen, Craig M.

Bear, Euan, ed. see Blanchard, Geral T.

Bear, Euan, ed. see Carich, Mark S. & Adkerson, Donya L.

Bear, Euan, ed. see Cumming, Georgia & Buell, Maureen.

Bear, Euan, ed. see Cunningham, Carolyn & MacFarlane, Kee.

Bear, Euan, ed. see Donaldson, Stephen.

Bear, Euan, ed. see Freeman-Longo, Robert, et al.

Bear, Euan, ed. see Gray, A. & Wallace, R.

Bear, Euan, ed. see Haaven, J., et al.

Bear, Euan, ed. see Hocking, Phoenix J.

Bear, Euan, ed. see Johnson, S. A.

Bear, Euan, ed. see Kahn, Timothy J.

Bear, Euan, ed. see Knopp, Fay H.

Bear, Euan, ed. see Knopp, Fay H. & Benson, Anna.

Bear, Euan, ed. see Landry, Dorothy B.

Bear, Euan, ed. see Lewis, Alvin D.

Bear, Euan, ed. see Loiselle, Mindy B. & Wright, Leslie B.

Bear, Euan, ed. see Mathews, Ruth, et al.

Bear, Euan, ed. see Miletski, Hani.

Bear, Euan, ed. see Pithers, William, et al.

Bear, Euan, ed. see Rosencrans, Bobbie.

Bear, Euan, ed. see Roys, Deloris T. & Roys, Pat.

Bear, Euan, ed. see Steen, Charlene.

Bear, Euan, ed. see Tallmadge, Alice & Forster, Galyn.

Bear, Euan, ed. see Timms, Robert & Connors, Patrick.

Bear, Euan, ed. see Wasserman, Burt.

Bear, Euan, ed. see Wiehe, Vernon.

Bear, Firman E., et al. Earth: The Stuff of Life. 2nd rev. ed. LC 86-40043. (Illus.). 336p. 1990. pap. 17.95 (*0-8061-2244-7*) U of Okla Pr.

Bear, Fred. The Archer's Bible. rev. ed. LC 79-7585. (Outdoor Bible Ser.). (Illus.). 176p. 1980. pap. 8.95 (*0-385-15155-1*) Doubleday.

Bear, Fred. Fred Bear's Field Notes: The Adventures of Fred Bear. 288p. 1976. pap. 12.95 (*0-9619480-0-0*) F Bear.

Bear, Fred. Fred Bear's Filed Notes: The Adventures of Fred Bear. 288p. 1987. 10.95 (*0-318-23898-5*) F Bear.

Bear, George, et al, eds. Children's Needs II: Development, Problems & Alternatives. 3rd expanded ed. LC 97-3781. 930p. 1997. pap. text 80.00 (*0-932955-96-7*) Natl Assn Schl Psych.

Bear, George G. & Callahan, Carolyn M. On the Nose: Fostering Creativity, Problem Solving & Social Reasoning. (Orig.). 1984. pap. 14.95 (*0-936386-23-1*) Creative Learning.

Bear, George G., jt. ed. see Minke, Kathleen M.

Bear, Greg. Anvil of Stars. 480p. 1993. reprint ed. mass mkt. 6.99 (*0-446-36403-7*, Pub. by Warner Bks) Little.

— Bear's Fantasies: Six Stories in Old Paradigms. LC 95-200723. 160 p. 1992. write for info. (*1-880448-19-X*) Wildside.

— Blood Music. 256p. 1996. pap. 13.95 (*0-441-00348-6*) Ace Bks.

***Bear, Greg.** Corona. (Star Trek: No. 15). 192p. 2000. mass mkt. 3.99 (*0-7434-0372-X*) PB.

Bear, Greg. Corona. (Star Trek Ser.: No. 15). 1991. reprint ed. per. 5.50 (*0-671-74353-8*) PB.

— Darwin's Radio. LC 99-21833. 496p. 1999. 24.00 (*0-345-42333-X*, Del Rey) Ballantine Pub Grp.

***Bear, Greg.** Darwin's Radio. 2000. mass mkt. 6.99 (*0-345-43524-9*) Ballantine Pub Grp.

Bear, Greg. Dinosaur Summer. 1999. mass mkt. 6.99 (*0-446-60666-9*, Pub. by Warner Bks) Little.

— Eon. 512p. 1995. 5.99 (*0-8125-2047-5*, Pub. by Tor Bks) St Martin.

— Eternity. 1989. mass mkt. 5.99 (*0-445-20547-4*, Pub. by Warner Bks) Little.

— Eternity. 384p. 1994. reprint ed. mass mkt. 6.99 (*0-446-60188-8*, Pub. by Warner Bks) Little.

— The Forge of God. 448p. 1995. 5.99 (*0-8125-2433-0*, Pub. by Tor Bks) St Martin.

— Foundation & Chaos. LC 97-47274. (Foundation Trilogy Ser.: Vol. 2). 352p. 1998. 24.00 (*0-06-105242-6*, HarperPrism) HarpC.

— Foundation & Chaos Vol. 2: The Second Foundation Trilogy. (Second Foundation Trilogy Ser.: Vol. 2). 416p. 2000. mass mkt. 6.99 (*0-06-105640-5*, HarperPrism) HarpC.

— Heads. 160p. 1992. mass mkt. 3.99 (*0-8125-1996-5*, Pub. by Tor Bks) St Martin.

— Legacy, Vol. 1. 1996. mass mkt. 6.99 (*0-8125-2481-0*, Pub. by Tor Bks) St Martin.

— Moving Mars. 512p. 1994. mass mkt. 5.99 (*0-8125-2480-2*, Pub. by Tor Bks) St Martin.

— Queen of Angels. 482p. 1991. reprint ed. mass mkt. 6.99 (*0-446-36130-5*, Pub. by Warner Bks) Little.

***Bear, Greg.** Rogue Planet. (Star Wars Ser.). 400p. 2000. 26.00 (*0-345-43538-9*, Del Rey) Ballantine Pub Grp.

Bear, Greg. Slant. 1997. 23.95 (*0-614-27875-9*) Tor Bks.

— Slant. 505p. 1998. mass mkt. 6.99 (*0-8125-2482-9*, Pub. by Tor Bks) St Martin.

— Songs of Earth & Power. 560p. 1994. 24.95 (*0-312-85669-5*) Tor Bks.

— Songs of Earth & Power. 1996. mass mkt. 6.99 (*0-8125-3603-7*, Pub. by Tor Bks) St Martin.

— The Wind from a Burning Woman. LC 82-16395. (Illus.). 270p. 1983. 15.95 (*0-87054-094-7*) Arkham.

— The Wind from a Burning Woman. 1990. mass mkt. 4.95 (*0-445-20846-5*, Aspect) Warner Bks.

Bear, Greg, ed. New Legends. 384p. 1995. 22.95 (*0-312-85930-9*, Pub. by Tor Bks) St Martin.

— New Legends. 384p. 1996. pap. 13.95 (*0-312-86201-6*) Tor Bks.

Bear, Greg & Sennon, Olmy A. Legacy. 1996. pap. 6.99 (*0-614-98100-X*) Tor Bks.

Bear, Greg & Zahn, Timothy. Hardfought - Cascade Point. (Double Ser.: No. 2). 192p. 1988. pap. 2.95 (*0-8125-5971-1*, Pub. by Tor Bks) St Martin.

Bear, H. S. Differential Equations: A Concise Course. LC 99-13371. 224p. 1999. pap. text 8.95 (*0-486-40678-4*) Dover.

— Introduction to Mathematical Analysis. LC 97-8024. (Illus.). 400p. 1997. text 59.95 (*0-12-083940-7*) Acad Pr.

***Bear, H. S.** Understanding Calculus: A User's Guide. LC 00-33522. (Series on Understanding Science & Technology). (Illus.). 2001. write for info. (*0-7803-6018-4*) IEEE Standards.

Bear, Herbert S., ed. A Primer of Lebesgue Integration. LC 94-42043. (Illus.). 163p. 1995. text 21.00 (*0-12-083970-9*) Acad Pr.

Bear, Jacob. Dynamics of Fluids in Porous Media. (Illus.). 784p. 1988. reprint ed. pap. text 19.95 (*0-486-65675-6*) Dover.

— Hydraulics of Ground Water. (Water Resources & Environmental Engineering Ser.). (Illus.). 544p. (C). 1979. 116.25 (*0-07-004170-9*) McGraw.

— Modelling Groundwater Flow. (Theory & Applications of Transport in Porous Media Ser.). 1987. pap. text 59.00 (*1-55608-015-8*) Kluwer Academic.

***Bear, Jacob.** Seawater Intrusion in Coastal Aquifers. LC 98-53221. (Theory & Applications of Transport in Porous Media Ser.). 1999. write for info. (*0-7923-5573-3*) Kluwer Academic.

Bear, Jacob, et al, eds. Flow & Contaminant Transport in Fractured Rock. (Illus.). 560p. 1993. text 82.00 (*0-12-083980-6*) Acad Pr.

Bear, Jacob & Buchlin, J. M., eds. Modelling & Applications of Transport Phenomena in Porous Media. 396p. (C). 1991. text 215.00 (*0-7923-1443-3*) Kluwer Academic.

Bear, Jacob & Corapcioglu, M. Yavuz, eds. Advances in Transport Phenomena in Porous Media. (C). 1987. text 440.00 (*90-247-3533-5*) Kluwer Academic.

— Transport Processes in Porous Media. 840p. (C). 1991. text 369.50 (*0-7923-1363-1*) Kluwer Academic.

Bear, James A., ed. Jefferson at Monticello: Memoirs of a Monticello Slave. LC 67-17629. (Illus.). 144p. 1967. reprint ed. pap. text 9.50 (*0-8139-0022-0*) U Pr of Va.

Bear, James A., Jr. & Stanton, Lucia C., eds. Jefferson's Memorandum Books: Accounts, with Legal Records & Miscellany, 1767-1826, 2 vols. (Illus.). 656p. 1997. text 200.00 (*0-691-04719-7*, Pub. by Princeton U Pr) Cal Prin Full Svc.

Bear, James A., Jr., jt. auth. see Nichols, Frederick D.

Bear, James A., Jr., jt. ed. see Betts, Edwin M.

Bear, James A., jt. ed. see Mayo, Bernard.

***Bear, Jaya.** Amazon Magic: The Life Story of Ayahuasquero & Shaman Don Agustin Rivas Vasquez. (Illus.). 240p. 2000. pap. 15.95 (*0-9674255-0-6*) Colibri NM.

Bear, Joan A. Young, see Van Ahnan, Katherine & Young Bear, Joan A.

Bear, Joan A. Young, see Von Ahnen, Katherine & Young Bear, Joan A.

Bear, John. Best MBAs by Distance Learning. 1999. pap. text 17.95 (*1-893285-00-6*) DegreeNet.

— Best Technical Degrees by Distance Learning. 1999. pap. text 21.95 (*1-893285-01-4*) DegreeNet.

***Bear, John.** College Degrees by Mail & Internet 2001. 216p. 2000. pap. 14.95 (*1-58008-217-3*) Ten Speed Pr.

— College Degrees by Mail & Modem 2000. LC 98-664041. 216p. 2000. pap. text 12.95 (*1-58008-109-6*) Ten Speed Pr.

— Finding Money for College 2000-2001. 168p. 2001. pap. 8.95 (*1-58008-117-7*) Ten Speed Pr.

Bear, John. The Frog & the Princess, & the Prince & the Mole, & the Frog & the Mole, & the Prince & the Princess . . . LC 94-2802. (Illus.). 48p. (J). (gr. 1 up). 1994. 14.95 (*1-883672-07-4*) Tricycle Pr.

— Send This Jerk the Bedbug Letter: How Companies, Politicians, & the Mass Media Deal with Complaints & how to be a more effective complainer. LC 96-1526. 322p. (Orig.). 1996. pap. 12.95 (*0-89815-811-7*) Ten Speed Pr.

***Bear, John & Bear, Mariah.** Bears' Guide to Earning Degrees by Distance Learning: 25th Anniversary Edition. 14th rev. ed. 416p. 2000. pap. 29.95 (*1-58008-202-5*) Ten Speed Pr.

— Bears' Guide to the Best Computer Degrees by Distance Learning. 2001. pap. 17.95 (*1-58008-221-1*) Ten Speed Pr.

— Bears' Guide to the Best MBAs by Distance Learning. LC 00-29951. 2000. pap. 17.95 (*1-58008-220-3*) Ten Speed Pr.

Bear, John & Bear, Mariah. Complaint Letters for Busy People: When You're Unhappy with a Product, Company or Service, Here's How to Get the Satisfaction You Deserve. LC 99-21217. 240p. 1999. pap. 16.99 (*1-56414-403-8*) Career Pr Inc.

An Asterisk (*) at the beginning of an entry indicates that the title is appearing for the first time.

— Finding Money for College, 1998-1999. rev. ed. LC 98-121367. 168p. (C). 1997. text 8.95 (*0-89815-933-4*) Ten Speed Pr.

Bear, John, jt. auth. see Bear, Marina.

Bear, John, jt. auth. see Fox, Margaret S.

Bear, Larry A., jt. auth. see Maldonado-Bear, Rita.

Bear-Lehman, Jane, jt. ed. see Cromwell, Florence S.

Bear, Leroy Little, see Little Bear, Leroy.

Bear, Lily A. Beyond the Trail. (Illus.). 318p. 1993. 10.65 (*0-7399-0162-1*, 2341) Rod & Staff.

— Safe in His Care. (Illus.). 334p. (YA). (gr. 7-10). 1984. pap. 9.50 (*0-7399-0111-7*, 2373.) Rod & Staff.

— Smuggler's Quest. 1999. pap. 4.25 (*0-87813-587-1*) Christian Light.

— The Valley Between. (Illus.). 176p. 1996. 7.90 (*0-7399-0163-X*, 2241) Rod & Staff.

Bear, Luther S. Mia Indiana Knabeco. Harmon, William R., tr. from ENG. (ESP., Illus.). 88p. 1995. pap. 6.95 (*1-882251-09-1*) Eldonejo Bero.

Bear, Magadalene, jt. auth. see Jenkins, Gerald.

Bear, Magdalen. Days, Months & Years. (J). 1996. pap. 6.95 (*0-906212-71-5*, Pub. by Tarquin Pubns) Parkwest Pubns.

Bear, Magdalen, jt. auth. see Jenkins, Gerald.

Bear, Magdalene, jt. auth. see Jenkins, Gerald.

Bear, Mariah, jt. auth. see Bear, John.

Bear, Marina & Bear, John. How to Repair Food. rev. ed. LC 98-6444. 144p. 1998. pap. 8.95 (*0-89815-555-X*) Ten Speed Pr.

Bear, Marina C., jt. auth. see Everitt, Luba G.

Bear, Mark, et al. Neuroscience: Exploring the Brain. 2nd ed. 768p. 52.00 (*0-683-30596-4*) Lppncott W & W.

Bear, Mark F., et al. Neuroscience: Exploring the Brain. LC 95-13837. (Illus.). 680p. 1996. 49.00 (*0-683-00488-3*) Lppncott W & W.

Bear, Ray A. Young, see Young Bear, Ray A.

Bear, Richard. Desire for the Land. (Illus.). 58p. (Orig.). 1995. pap. write for info. (*0-9645574-0-1*) Stony Run Pr.

Bear Run Publishing Staff. Stories from the Old Testament, No. 5. (J). 1996. 16.00 (*0-671-88665-7*) S&S Childrens.

Bear, Sun, et al. Sun Bear the Path of Power: Sun Bear, Wabun & Barry Weinstock. (Illus.). 272p. (Orig.). 1987. pap. 9.95 (*0-13-653403-1*) S&S Trade.

Bear, Terry L. Meditation for Spiritual Growth. 56p. 1999. pap. 10.00 (*0-9655514-9-0*) Inspiring Word.

Bear, W. Forrest. Electric Motors, Principles, Controls, Service & Maintenance. rev. ed. Hoerner, Harry J. & Hoerner, Thomas A., eds. (Illus.). 208p. 1990. teacher ed. 3.35 (*0-913163-16-3*, 283); text 18.15 (*0-913163-24-4*, 183) Hobar Pubns.

Bear, W. Forrest & Hoerner, Thomas A. Rafter Layout with the Framing Square. rev. ed. (Illus.). 48p. 1982. pap. text 5.70 (*0-913163-02-3*, 166) Hobar Pubns.

— Torque & Torque Wrenches. (Illus.). 24p. 1971. pap. text 5.20 (*0-913163-05-8*, 171) Hobar Pubns.

Bear, W. Forrest & Hoerner, Thomas A., intros. Planning, Organizing & Teaching Agricultural Mechanics. rev. ed. (Illus.). 224p. 1986. pap. text 24.15 (*0-913163-18-X*, 178) Hobar Pubns.

— Sawhorse Layout with the Framing Square. rev. ed. (Illus.). 8p. 1971. pap. text 2.20 (*0-913163-01-5*, 165) Hobar Pubns.

Bear, W. Forrest, jt. auth. see Hoerner, Harry J.

Bear, W. Forrest, jt. auth. see Hoerner, Thomas A.

Bear, W. Forrest, jt. intro. see Hoerner, Thomas A.

Bear, Walter S. A Genealogy of the Bear Family & Biographical Record of the Descendants of Jacob Bear, 1747-1906. (Illus.). 216p. 1988. reprint ed. pap. 32.00 (*0-8328-0215-8*); reprint ed. lib. bdg. 40.00 (*0-8328-0214-X*) Higginson Bk Co.

Bearanger, Marie & Ethan, Eric. Colors of the Sea, 5 bks. Incl. Coral Reef Builders. LC 96-47568. (Illus.). 24p. (J). (gr. 1 up). 1997. lib. bdg. 18.60 (*0-8368-1737-0*); Coral Reef Feeders. LC 96-37056. (Illus.). 24p. (J). (gr. 1 up). 1997. lib. bdg. 18.60 (*0-8368-1738-9*); Coral Reef Hunters. LC 96-37057. (Illus.). 24p. (J). (gr. 1 up). 1997. lib. bdg. 18.60 (*0-8368-1739-7*); Coral Reef Partners. LC 96-47565. (Illus.). 24p. (J). (gr. 1 up). 1997. lib. bdg. 18.60 (*0-8368-1740-0*); Coral Reef Survival. LC 96-47569. (Illus.). 24p. (J). (gr. 1 up). 1997. lib. bdg. 18.60 (*0-8368-1736-2*); (Illus.). Set lib. bdg. 93.00 (*0-8368-1735-4*) Gareth Stevens Inc.

Bearbeitet, Thomas Von, see Deutsches Literaturarchiv Marbach Am Neckar, ed.

Bearce, George D. British Attitudes Towards India 1748-1858. LC 81-20244. 315p. 1982. reprint ed. lib. bdg. 69.50 (*0-313-23367-5*, BEBA, Greenwood Pr) Greenwood.

Bearce, Neil R. Minerals of Arizona: A Field Guide for Collectors. LC 98-44239. (Illus.). 224p. 1999. pap. 19.00 (*0-945005-33-4*) Geoscience Pr.

Beard. Vascular Surgery. (Illus.). 380p. (C). 1998. text 90.00 (*0-7020-2145-8*, W B Saunders Co) Harcrt Hlth Sci Grp.

Beard, Adelia, jt. auth. see Beard, Lina.

***Beard, Adrian.** Language of Politics. LC 99-23246. (Intertext Ser.). 2000. pap. write for info. (*0-415-20178-0*) Routledge.

Beard, Adrian. The Language of Sport. LC 97-15837. (Intertext Ser.). 128p. (C). 1998. pap. 14.99 (*0-415-16911-9*) Routledge.

Beard, Alan J., ed. see Delphos, William A.

Beard, Augustus F. Crusade of Brotherhood, a History of the American Missionary Association. LC 76-161728. reprint ed. 51.50 (*0-404-00004-5*) AMS Pr.

Beard, Barrett T. Wonderful Flying Machines: A History of U. S. Coast Guard Helicopters. LC 96-25922. (Illus.). 280p. 1996. 34.95 (*1-55750-086-X*) Naval Inst Pr.

Beard, Barrett T., ed. see Beard, Elihu B.

Beard, Belle B. Juvenile Probation: An Analysis of the Case Records of Five Hundred Children Studies at the Judge Baker Guidance Clinic & Placed on Probation in the Juvenile Court of Boston. LC 69-16224. (Criminology, Law Enforcement, & Social Problems Ser.: No. 95). 1969. reprint ed. 22.00 (*0-87585-095-2*) Patterson Smith.

Beard, Belle B., et al, eds. Centenarians: The New Generation. 20. LC 90-40899. (Contributions to the Study of Aging Ser.: No. 20). 304p. 1990. 65.00 (*0-313-27479-7*, WID, Greenwood Pr) Greenwood.

Beard, Bennie. Man's Made Hell. 104p. 1999. pap. 11.00 (*0-8059-4700-0*) Dorrance.

Beard, Bernice. Alaska at Your Own Pace: Traveling by RV Caravan. LC 98-92444. (Illus.). 272p. 1998. pap. 16.95 (*0-9653063-8-0*, Pub. by Arbor Hse) Seven Hills Bk.

— At Your Own Pace: Traveling Your Way in Your Motorhome. LC 96-95017. (Illus.). 1997. pap. 16.95 (*0-9653063-9-9*, Pub. by Arbor Hse) Seven Hills Bk.

— Colorado at Your Own Pace: Traveling by Motorhome with Friends. LC 98-94838. (Illus.). 1999. pap. 16.95 (*0-9653063-7-2*, Pub. by Arbor Hse) Seven Hills Bk.

Beard, Bodie J. & Zucker, Cher R. Forms for Office Building Management & Operations Manual Guidelines. LC 85-60205. (Illus.). 224p. 1986. ring bd. 79.95 (*0-912104-82-1*, NO. 953) Inst Real Estate.

Beard, Butch, et al. Butch Beard's Basic Basketball: The Complete Player. 2nd rev. ed. (Illus.). 144p. 1995. pap. 16.95 (*0-935576-48-7*) Kesend Pub Ltd.

Beard, Charles Austin. American City Government: A Survey of Newer Tendencies. LC 70-112522. (Rise of Urban America Ser.). (Illus.). 1974. reprint ed. 29.95 (*0-405-02435-5*) Ayer.

— Devil Theory of War: An Inquiry into the Nature of History & the Possibility of Keeping Out of War. LC 68-54771. (Illus.). 124p. 1969. reprint ed. lib. bdg. 35.00 (*0-8371-0300-2*, BEDT, Greenwood Pr) Greenwood.

— Economic Basis of Politics. 3rd rev. ed. LC 70-37513. (Essay Index Reprint Ser.). 1977. reprint ed. 20.95 (*0-8369-2535-1*) Ayer.

— An Economic Interpretation of the Constitution of the United States. LC 86-7675. 330p. 1986. pap. 15.95 (*0-02-902480-3*) Free Pr.

***Beard, Charles Austin.** An Economic Interpretation of the Constitution of the United States. LC 00-36834. 2000. write for info. (*1-58477-111-9*) Lawbk Exchange.

Beard, Charles Austin. An Economic Interpretation of the Constitution of the United States. LC 98-11613. 330p. 1998. pap. 24.95 (*0-7658-0457-3*) Transaction Pubs.

Beard, Charles Austin. The Industrial Revolution. 1973. 59.95 (*0-8490-0406-3*) Gordon Pr.

Beard, Charles Austin. Industrial Revolution. LC 69-13813. 105p. 1969. reprint ed. lib. bdg. 57.50 (*0-8371-2168-X*, BEIR, Greenwood Pr) Greenwood.

— Martin Luther & the Reformation in Germany until the Close of the Diet of Worms. LC 83-45638. reprint ed. 49.50 (*0-404-19822-8*) AMS Pr.

— The Nature of the Social Sciences: In Relation to Objectives of Instruction. LC 73-14148. (Perspectives in Social Inquiry Ser.). 256p. 1974. reprint ed. 18.95 (*0-405-05494-7*) Ayer.

***Beard, Charles Austin.** The Office of Justice of the Peace in England: In Its Origin & Development. LC 00-36237. 2000. write for info. (*1-58477-102-X*) Lawbk Exchange.

Beard, Charles Austin. Office of Justice of the Peace in England in Its Origin & Development. LC 74-18913. (Columbia University. Studies in the Social Sciences: No. 52). reprint ed. 31.50 (*0-404-51052-3*) AMS Pr.

— The Reformation of the Sixteenth Century in Its Relation to Modern Thought & Knowledge. LC 80-12915. 450p. 1980. reprint ed. lib. bdg. 45.50 (*0-313-22410-2*, BERF, Greenwood Pr) Greenwood.

— The Reformation of the 16th Century in Its Relations to Modern Thought & Knowledge. LC 77-27168. (Hibbert Lectures: 1883). reprint ed. 59.50 (*0-404-60404-8*) AMS Pr.

— The Rise of American Civilization. (History - United States Ser.). 824p. 1993. reprint ed. lib. bdg. 119.00 (*0-7812-4848-5*) Rprt Serv.

— The Supreme Court & the Constitution, 1912. LC 98-50368. vii, 127p. 1999. reprint ed. 45.00 (*1-886363-78-1*) Lawbk Exchange.

Beard, Charles Austin, ed. America Faces the Future. LC 73-90608. (Essay Index Reprint Ser.). 1977. 26.95 (*0-8369-1244-6*) Ayer.

— Century of Progress. LC 79-128205. (Essay Index Reprint Ser.). 1977. 30.95 (*0-8369-1903-3*) Ayer.

— Whither Mankind? LC 78-109708. 408p. 1973. reprint ed. lib. bdg. 75.00 (*0-8371-4199-0*, BEWM, Greenwood Pr) Greenwood.

— Whither Mankind? A Panorama of Modern Civilization. LC 72-128206. (Essay Index Reprint Ser.). 1977. reprint ed. 26.95 (*0-8369-2344-8*) Ayer.

Beard, Charles Austin & Smith, George H. The Future Comes: A Study of the New Deal. LC 73-143307. 178p. 1972. reprint ed. lib. bdg. 38.50 (*0-8371-5808-7*, BEFC, Greenwood Pr) Greenwood.

Beard, Charles Austin, tr. see Renan, Ernest.

Beard, Charles E., et al. Solutions to Your Public Relations Challenges: Great Ideas Selected from Entries in the 1991 John Cotton Dana Library Public Relations Award Contest by Members of the Library Administration & Management Association's Public Relations Section, John Cotton Dana Award Committee. LC 91-16674. vi, 26 p. 1991. 9.95 (*0-8389-7528-3*) ALA.

Beard, Charles R. Lucks & Talismans: A Chapter of Popular Superstition. LC 72-80494. 278p. 1972. reprint ed. 24.95 (*0-405-08246-0*, Pub. by Blom Pubns) Ayer.

Beard, Christine H. & Yntema, Sharon. New Vegetarian Baby. LC 99-47876. (Orig.). 1999. pap. 15.95 (*0-935526-63-3*) McBooks Pr.

Beard, Cindy W. His Messages. LC 98-60608. 144p. 1998. pap. 12.99 (*1-57921-117-8*, Pub. by WinePress Pub) BookWorld.

Beard, Cynthia A., et al. Pediatric Pocket Guide. unabridged ed. 22p. (Orig.). 1996. pap. 20.00 (*0-935890-07-6*, P31) Emerg Nurses IL.

***Beard, D. C.** Shelters, Shacks & Shanties. 1999. pap. text 9.95 (*1-893626-30-X*) Breakout Prods Inc.

Beard, D. C. Shelters, Shacks, & Shanties. LC 92-80292. 243p. 1992. reprint ed. pap. 10.95 (*0-936070-13-7*) Shelter Pubns.

Beard, Dan, ed. see Brown, Bellmore H.

Beard, Daniel C. The American Boy's Handy Book: What to Do & How to Do It. LC 82-3155. (Illus.). 448p. (J). (gr. 4 up). 1983. reprint ed. pap. 12.95 (*0-87923-449-0*) Godine.

— Moonblight & Six Feet of Romance. LC 74-22767. (Labor Movement in Fiction & Non-Fiction Ser.). (Illus.). 1976. reprint ed. 41.50 (*0-404-58405-5*) AMS Pr.

Beard, Darleen B. The Flim-Flam Man. LC 97-15606. (Illus.). 96p. (J). (gr. 2-6). 1998. 15.00 (*0-374-32346-1*) FS&G.

— The Pumpkin Man from Piney Creek. LC 94-34696. (Illus.). 32p. (J). (gr. k-3). 1995. 15.00 (*0-689-80215-X*) S&S Bks Yung.

— Twister. LC 95-13862. (Illus.). 32p. (J). (ps-3). 1999. 16.00 (*0-374-37977-7*) FS&G.

Beard, Elihu B. A Diary for 1849 Elihu Burritt Beard A Year in the Life of a College Student on the American Frontier. Beard, Barrett T., ed. LC 99-70474. 142p. 1999. pap. 11.95 (*0-7392-0178-6*, PO3144) Morris Pubng.

Beard, F., ed. see Hobbs, Bobbi.

***Beard, Frances J.** It's a Great Life: Stories & Sayings of Wisdom, Friendship & Love. (Illus.). 40p. 1999. pap. 5.00 (*0-9658370-3-3*) FJ Co.

Beard, Frances J. Kith & Kin: A Mystery Novel. LC 98-73285. 220p. 1998. pap. 13.95 (*0-9658370-2-5*) FJ Co.

— Nothing to Lose. LC 97-90378. 224p. 1997. pap. 13.95 (*0-9658370-1-7*) FJ Co.

Beard, Frank. Bible Symbols or the Bible in Pictures. (J). 1985. pap. 7.99 (*0-88019-170-8*) Schmul Pub Co.

Beard, Franklin. Gold Fields to Grazing Fields. 300p. 1989. text 37.50 (*0-945037-01-5*) Southern Mines Pr.

— The Way We Were Fifty Years Ago: East of Modesto to Empire & Beyond. 300p. 1985. text 37.50 (*0-945037-02-3*) Southern Mines Pr.

Beard, G. M., ed. Historical Records Survey: Check List of Washington Imprints, 1853-1876. 1942. 25.00 (*0-527-01930-5*) Periodicals Srv.

Beard, Geoffrey W. Craftsmen & Interior Decoration in England 1660 - 1820. LC 81-2648. (Illus.). 320p. 1981. 125.00 (*0-8419-0703-X*) Holmes & Meier.

— Upholsterers & Their Work in England, 1530-1840. LC 96-39874. (Bard Studies in the Decorative Arts). (Illus.). 360p. 1997. 80.00 (*0-300-07135-3*) Yale U Pr.

— The Work of Grinling Gibbons. LC 89-20460. (Illus.). 160p. 1999. 47.95 (*0-226-03992-7*) U Ch Pr.

Beard, George M. American Nervousness, Its Causes & Consequences: A Supplement to Nervous Exhaustion. LC 72-180552. (Medicine & Society in America Ser.). 382p. 1972. reprint ed. 24.95 (*0-405-03932-8*) Ayer.

— Sexual Neurasthenia, Its Hygiene, Causes, Symptoms & Treatment with a Chapter on Diet for the Nervous. 5th ed. Rockwell, A. D., ed. LC 76-180553. (Medicine & Society in America Ser.). 312p. 1972. reprint ed. 20.95 (*0-405-03933-6*) Ayer.

— Stimulants & Narcotics: Medically, Philosophically, & Morally Considered. Grob, Gerald N., ed. LC 80-1213. (Addiction in America Ser.). 1981. reprint ed. lib. bdg. 18.95 (*0-405-13569-6*) Ayer.

Beard, Gerald J. Me, Myself & I: Overcoming Inner Struggles. Beard, Tracie L., ed. 71p. 1998. pap. 9.99 (*1-57502-999-5*, PO2722) Morris Pubng.

***Beard, Gordon.** Basic Baltimorese III: An Illustrated Guide for Getting Around in Balamer, Murlip. 3rd ed. (Illus.). 32p. 1999. pap. 3.95 (*0-9603436-2-8*) Beard Armond and Gordon.

Beard, Henry. Golf Your Way. 1993. 15.00 (*0-385-46998-5*) Doubleday.

— Latin for All Occasions. (Illus.). 128p. 1990. 12.95 (*0-394-58660-3*) Villard Books.

— Latin for Even More Occasions (Lingua Latina Multo Pluribus Occasionibus) 96p. 1991. 13.00 (*0-679-40674-3*) Villard Books.

— Mulligan's Laws. (Illus.). 128p. 1998. pap. 9.95 (*0-385-49277-4*) Doubleday.

— The Official Exceptions to the Rules of Golf. 1992. 15.00 (*0-679-40886-X*) Villard Books.

— The Official Politically Correct Dictionary & Handbook. 1993. pap. 10.00 (*0-679-74944-6*) Villard Books.

— Poetry for Cats: The Definitive Anthology of Distinguished Feline Verse. (Illus.). 96p. 1994. 12.95 (*0-679-43582-4*) Villard Books.

— Zen for Cats. LC 97-19732. 1997. 10.95 (*0-375-50034-0*) Villard Books.

Beard, Henry, ed. Poetry for Cats: The Definitive Anthology of Distinguished Feline Verse. LC 94-15358. (Illus.). 1994. write for info. (*0-679-43502-6*) Villard Books.

Beard, Henry & Boswell, J. What's Worrying Gus? Date not set. pap. 12.00 (*0-679-77012-7*) McKay.

Beard, Henry & Boswell, John. Bill Gates' Personal Super-Secret, Private Laptop. LC 98-34241. (Illus.). 96p. 1998. pap. 13.95 (*0-684-85464-3*) Simon & Schuster.

— French for Cats: All the French Your Cat Will Ever Need. (Illus.). 96p. 1991. 10.00 (*0-679-40676-X*) Villard Books.

— The Official Exceptions to the Rules of Golf. LC 97-6647. 160p. 1997. pap. 15.95 (*0-679-74123-2*) Villard Books.

***Beard, Henry & McKie, Roy.** Com-Put-Ing (kum/pyoot/ing) A Dictionary for Web Surfers, Number-Crunchers, Desktop Publishers, & Space-Alien Zappers. LC 99-44187. (Illus.). 96p. 1999. pap. 7.95 (*0-7611-1774-1*) Workman Pub.

Beard, Henry & McKie, Roy. Cooking. LC 84-40678. (Illus.). 112p. (Orig.). 1985. pap. 6.95 (*0-89480-843-5*, 843) Workman Pub.

— Fishing. LC 82-40498. (Illus.). 96p. 1983. pap. 6.95 (*0-89480-355-7*, 355) Workman Pub.

— Gardening. LC 81-43783. (Illus.). 96p. 1982. pap. 6.95 (*0-89480-200-3*, 478) Workman Pub.

— Golfing. LC 86-40546. (Illus.). 96p. (Orig.). 1987. pap. 6.95 (*0-89480-322-0*, 1322) Workman Pub.

— Sailing. LC 80-54621. (Illus.). 96p. 1981. pap. 6.95 (*0-89480-144-9*, 448) Workman Pub.

— Ship's Log. (Illus.). 96p. 1983. pap. 7.95 (*0-89480-574-6*, 574) Workman Pub.

— Skiing. LC 89-40369. (Illus.). 96p. (Orig.). 1989. pap. 5.95 (*0-89480-650-5*, 1650) Workman Pub.

***Beard, Henry, et al.** The Mink Was Already Dead. LC 00-20108. 96p. 2000. pap. 7.95 (*0-7611-1636-2*) Workman Pub.

Beard, Henry, jt. auth. see Nielsen, Leslie.

Beard, J. Turfgrass: Science & Culture. (Illus.). 672p. 1972. 115.00 (*0-13-933002-X*) P-H.

Beard, J. S. Studies in Western Australian History Sheet 3: Great Victoria Desert. pap. 14.95 (*0-85564-085-5*, Pub. by Univ of West Aust Pr) Intl Spec Bk.

— Studies in Western Australian History Sheet 4: Nullarbor. pap. 14.95 (*0-85564-089-8*, Pub. by Univ of West Aust Pr) Intl Spec Bk.

— Vegetation Surveys of Western Australia Sheet 1: Kimberley. pap. 14.95 (*0-85564-091-X*, Pub. by Univ of West Aust Pr) Intl Spec Bk.

— Vegetation Surveys of Western Australia Sheet 5: Pilbara. pap. 14.95 (*0-85564-092-8*, Pub. by Univ of West Aust Pr) Intl Spec Bk.

— Vegetation Surveys of Western Australia Sheet 6: Murchison. (Vegetation Surveys of W. Australia Ser.). (Illus.). 1977. pap. 14.95 (*0-85564-093-6*, Pub. by Univ of West Aust Pr) Intl Spec Bk.

— Vegetation Surveys of Western Australia Sheet 7: Swan Memoir. (Illus.). 1977. pap. 22.50 (*0-85564-094-4*, Pub. by Univ of West Aust Pr) Intl Spec Bk.

Beard, J. S. & Webb, M. J. Studies in Western Australian History Sheet 2: Great Sandy Desert. pap. 14.95 (*0-85564-045-6*, Pub. by Univ of West Aust Pr) Intl Spec Bk.

***Beard, James.** Beard on Birds. 2000. 18.95 (*0-7624-0687-9*) Running Pr.

Beard, James. Beard on Bread. 1995. pap. 15.00 (*0-679-75504-7*) Knopf.

***Beard, James.** Beard on Food. (Illus.). 2000. 18.95 (*0-7624-0688-7*) Running Pr.

Beard, James. Calcium & Other Minerals Counter. 1996. mass mkt. write for info. (*0-614-25228-8*) Penguin Putnam.

— The Complete Book of Outdoor Cookery. 320p. 1997. pap. text 13.95 (*1-56924-752-8*) Marlowe & Co.

— Food Additives. 1997. mass mkt. write for info. (*0-614-25229-6*) Penguin Putnam.

— Food for Thought: The Armchair James Beard. Ferrone, John, ed. LC 98-29728. (Illus.). 360p. 1999. 24.95 (*1-55821-737-1*) Lyons Pr.

— Hors D'oeuvre & Canapes. 173p. 1999. 14.95 (*0-7624-0664-X*) Running Pr.

— The James Beard Cookbook. 3rd ed. Ferrone, John, ed. 470p. 1996. pap. 14.95 (*1-56924-809-5*) Marlowe & Co.

Beard, James. James Beard's American Cookery. 1996. 16.98 (*0-88365-958-1*) Galahad Bks.

Beard, James. James Beard's Menus for Entertaining. Ferrone, John, ed. (Illus.). 432p. 1996. pap. 14.95 (*1-56924-765-X*) Marlowe & Co.

— James Beard's New Fish Cookery. 512p. 1996. 12.98 (*0-88365-943-3*) Galahad Bks.

— James Beard's New Fish Cookery. 512p. 1994. pap. 18.00 (*0-316-08500-6*) Little.

— James Beard's Poultry. Ferrone, John, ed. LC 97-60237. (Illus.). 64p. (Orig.). 1997. pap. 7.95 (*0-614-30195-5*) Thames Hudson.

— James Beard's Salads. Ferrone, John, ed. LC 97-60241. (Illus.). 64p. (Orig.). 1997. pap. 7.95 (*0-500-27969-1*, Pub. by Thames Hudson) Norton.

— James Beard's Shellfish. Ferrone, John, ed. LC 97-60238. (Illus.). 64p. (Orig.). 1997. pap. 7.95 (*0-500-27967-5*, Pub. by Thames Hudson) Norton.

— James Beard's Simple Foods. 1994. pap. 12.00 (*0-02-030466-8*) Macmillan.

— James Beard's Soups. Ferrone, John, ed. LC 97-60239. (Illus.). 64p. (Orig.). 1997. pap. 7.95 (*0-500-27968-3*, Pub. by Thames Hudson) Norton.

— Love & Kisses & a Halo of Truffles: Letters to Helen Evans Brown. Ferrone, John, ed. (Illus.). 448p. 1995. pap. 13.45 (*1-55970-318-0*, Pub. by Arcade Pub Inc) Time Warner.

— Love & Kisses & a Halo of Truffles: Letters to Helen Evans Brown. Ferrone, John, ed. LC 94-9548. (Illus.). 416p. 1994. 25.45 (*1-55970-264-8*, Pub. by Arcade Pub Inc) Time Warner.

— Theory & Practice of Good Cooking. 430p. 1999. 22.95 (*0-7624-0613-5*) Running Pr.

Beard, James, intro. Portland Woman's Exchange Cookbook, 1913. LC 73-89993. (Illus.). 380p. 1987. spiral bd. 9.95 (*0-87595-045-0*) Oregon Hist.

Beard, James A. Barbecue with Beard. 240p. 1987. mass mkt. 9.95 (*0-446-38546-8*, Pub. by Warner Bks) Little.

— Beard on Birds. 1989. pap. 10.95 (*0-446-39032-1*) Warner Bks.

— James Beard's American Cookery. (Illus.). 877p. 1980. pap. 23.95 (*0-316-08566-9*) Little.

B

— James Beard's New Fish Cookery. rev. ed. 512p. 1989. mass mkt. 12.95 (*0-446-38647-2*, Pub. by Warner Bks) Little.

Beard, James B. Turf Management for Golf Courses. 2nd ed. LC 97-47205. (Illus.). 1000p. 2000. 95.00 (*1-57504-092-1*) Sleepng Bear.

— Turf Management of Golf Courses. 660p. 1982. 59.95 (*0-317-56418-8*) US Golf Assn.

Beard, James B., jt. auth. see Tani, Toshikazu.

Beard, James F. Cooper, Lafayette & the French National Budget. 1985. reprint ed. pap. 4.50 (*0-912296-74-7*) Am Antiquarian.

Beard, James F., ed. see Cooper, James Fenimore.

Beard, James F., ed. & intro. see Cooper, James Fenimore.

Beard, Jeff, jt. auth. see Lloyd, Chris.

Beard, Jeffrey L. & Duncan, Daniel W. Design Build: The Project Delivery System for Design & Construction. 420p. 1998. 59.95 (*0-07-006311-7*) McGraw-Hill Prof.

***Beard, Jo Ann.** The Boys of My Youth. 1998. mass mkt. 13.00 (*0-316-19134-5*, Back Bay) Little.

Beard, Jo Ann. The Boys of My Youth. 224p. 1999. pap. 13.00 (*0-316-08525-1*) Little.

Beard, Joan. Korea at Cost. (At Cost Travel Guide Ser.). (Illus.). 256p. 1996. pap. 14.95 (*1-86315-088-9*) Pelican.

— South Pacific at Cost. 2nd ed. (At Cost Travel Guide Ser.). (Illus.). 256p. 1996. pap. 16.95 (*1-86315-103-6*) Pelican.

Beard, JoAnn. The Boys of My Youth, Vol. 1. LC 97-29710. Vol. 1. 224p. (gr. 8). 1998. 22.95 (*0-316-08554-5*) Little.

Beard, Jocelyn, ed. The Best Men's Monologues of 1997. (Annual Best Monologues Ser.). 160p. 1998. pap. 11.95 (*1-57525-137-X*) Smith & Kraus.

— The Best Men's Stage Monologues of 1998. 128p. 1999. pap. 11.95 (*1-57525-185-X*) Smith & Kraus.

— The Best Stage Scenes of 1997. (Scene Anthologies Ser.). 256p. 1998. pap. 14.95 (*1-57525-139-6*) Smith & Kraus.

— The Best Women's Monologues of 1997. (Annual Best Monologues Ser.). 144p. 1998. pap. 11.95 (*1-57525-138-8*) Smith & Kraus.

— The Best Women's Stage Monologues of 1998. 128p. 1999. pap. 11.95 (*1-57525-184-1*) Smith & Kraus.

***Beard, Jocelyn, ed.** The Ultimate Scene Study Series Vol. 2: 102 Short Scenes for Two Actors. LC 99-89197. 480p. 1999. pap. 19.95 (*1-57525-153-1*) Smith & Kraus.

Beard, Jocelyn A., ed. The Best Men's Stage Monologue of 1996. (Annual Best Monologues Ser.). 136p. 1997. pap. 11.95 (*1-57525-075-6*) Smith & Kraus.

— The Best Men's Stage Monologues of 1990. LC 90-91798. (Monologue Audition Ser.). 74p. (Orig.). 1991. pap. 8.95 (*0-9622722-2-1*) Smith & Kraus.

— The Best Men's Stage Monologues of 1991. (Monologue Audition Ser.). 96p. 1992. pap. 8.95 (*1-880399-02-4*) Smith & Kraus.

— The Best Men's Stage Monologues of 1992. (Monologue Audition Ser.). 82p. 1993. pap. 8.95 (*1-880399-11-3*) Smith & Kraus.

— Best Men's Stage Monologues of 1993. (Monologue Audition Ser.). 100p. 1993. pap. 8.95 (*1-880399-43-1*) Smith & Kraus.

— The Best Men's Stage Monologues of 1994. (Monologue Audition Ser.). 100p. 1995. pap. 8.95 (*1-880399-64-4*) Smith & Kraus.

— The Best Men's Stage Monologues of 1995. (Annual Best Monologues Ser.). 96p. 1996. pap. 8.95 (*1-880399-70-9*) Smith & Kraus.

— The Best Stage Scenes of 1995. (Scene Anthologies Ser.). 256p. 1996. pap. 11.95 (*1-57525-015-2*) Smith & Kraus.

— The Best Stage Scenes of 1994. (Scene Anthologies Ser.). 256p. 1995. pap. 11.95 (*1-880399-66-0*) Smith & Kraus.

— The Best Stage Scenes of 1996. (Scene Anthologies Ser.). 256p. (Orig.). 1997. pap. 14.95 (*1-57525-077-2*) Smith & Kraus.

— The Best Stage Scenes of 1993. (Scene Anthologies Ser.). 256p. 1994. pap. 11.95 (*1-880399-44-X*) Smith & Kraus.

— The Best Stage Scenes of 1992. (Scene Anthologies Ser.). 202p. 1993. pap. 11.95 (*1-880399-18-0*) Smith & Kraus.

— The Best Women's Monologue of 1996. (Annual Best Monologues Ser.). 128p. 1997. pap. 11.95 (*1-57525-076-4*) Smith & Kraus.

— The Best Women's Stage Monologues of 1990. LC 90-91799. (Monologue Audition Ser.). 86p. (Orig.). 1991. pap. 8.95 (*0-9622722-1-3*) Smith & Kraus.

— The Best Women's Stage Monologues of 1991. (Monologue Audition Ser.). 98p. (Orig.). 1992. pap. 8.95 (*1-880399-01-6*) Smith & Kraus.

— The Best Women's Stage Monologues of 1992. (Monologue Audition Ser.). 88p. 1993. pap. 8.95 (*1-880399-10-5*) Smith & Kraus.

— The Best Women's Stage Monologues of 1993. (Monologue Audition Ser.). 104p. 1993. pap. 8.95 (*1-880399-42-3*) Smith & Kraus.

— The Best Women's Stage Monologues of 1994. (Monologue Audition Ser.). 104p. 1994. pap. 8.95 (*1-880399-65-2*) Smith & Kraus.

— The Best Women's Stage Monologues of 1995. (Annual Best Monologues Ser.). 96p. 1996. pap. 8.95 (*1-880399-62-8*) Smith & Kraus.

— Monologues from Classic Plays, 468 B. C. - 1960 A. D. LC 92-36194. (Monologue Audition Ser.). 236p. 1992. pap. 11.95 (*1-880399-09-1*) Smith & Kraus.

— 100 Great Monologues from the Neo-Classical Theatre. LC 94-33114. (Monologue Audition Ser.). 172p. 1994. pap. 9.95 (*1-880399-60-1*) Smith & Kraus.

— 100 Great Monologues from the 19th Century Romantic & Realistic Theatres. LC 94-33110. (Monologue Audition Ser.). 186p. 1994. pap. 9.95 (*1-880399-61-X*) Smith & Kraus.

— 100 Great Monologues from the Renaissance Theatre. LC 94-19393. (Monologue Audition Ser.). 186p. 1994. pap. 9.95 (*1-880399-59-8*) Smith & Kraus.

— 100 Men's Stage Monologues from the 1980s. (Monologue Audition Ser.). 170p. 1991. pap. 11.95 (*0-9622722-4-8*) Smith & Kraus.

— 100 Women's Stage Monologues from the 1980s. (Monologue Audition Ser.). 196p. 1991. pap. 11.95 (*0-9622722-9-9*) Smith & Kraus.

— Scenes from Classic Plays 468 B. C. to 1970 A. D. (Scene Study Ser.). 320p. 1993. pap. 11.95 (*1-880399-36-9*) Smith & Kraus.

— The Ultimate Audition Book: 222 Monologues, 2 Minutes & Under. LC 97-10471. (Audition Bks.). 256p. (Orig.). 1997. pap. 19.95 (*1-57525-066-7*) Smith & Kraus.

Beard, Jocelyn A. & Graham, Kristin, eds. The Best Stage Scenes for Men from the 1980's. (Scene Anthologies Ser.). 214p. 1991. pap. 8.95 (*0-9622722-8-0*) Smith & Kraus.

— The Best Stage Scenes for Women from the 1980's. (Scene Anthologies Ser.). 220p. 1991. pap. 8.95 (*0-9622722-7-2*) Smith & Kraus.

Beard, John, jt. auth. see Ferris, C. S.

Beard, John R. Life of Toussaint L'Ouverture, the Negro Patriot of Haiti. LC 75-109316. (Illus.). 335p. 1970. reprint ed. lib. bdg. 35.00 (*0-8371-3572-9*, BTL&) Greenwood.

Beard, John S. Plant Life of Western Australia. (Illus.). 319p. 1990. 37.50 (*0-86417-279-6*, Pub. by Kangaroo Pr) Seven Hills Bk.

— Proteas of Tropical Africa. (Illus.). 112p. 1993. 65.00 (*0-86417-449-7*, Pub. by Kangaroo Pr) Seven Hills Bk.

Beard, Jon W., ed. Impression Management & Information Technology. LC 95-14605. 224p. 1996. 57.95 (*0-89930-848-1*, Quorum Bks) Greenwood.

Beard, Jonathan P., et al. The Diagnosis & Treatment of Mental Illness: An Introduction. LC 88-5507. (Illus.). 216p. 1989. 34.95 (*0-8143-1920-3*); pap. 18.95 (*0-8143-1921-1*) Wayne St U Pr.

Beard, Jonathon & Gaines, Peter, eds. Vascular & Endovascular Surgery. (Companion Guide to Specialist Surgical Practice Ser.: Vol. 6). (Illus.). 380p. 1997. text 84.00 (*0-7020-2144-X*, Pub. by W B Saunders) Saunders.

Beard, Julie. A Dance in Heather. 384p. 1996. mass mkt. 5.99 (*0-515-11873-7*, Jove) Berkley Pub.

— Dance in Heather. 1998. mass mkt. 5.99 (*0-425-16424-1*) Berkley Pub.

— Falcon & the Sword. 352p. 1997. mass mkt. 5.99 (*0-515-12065-0*, Jove) Berkley Pub.

— Lady & the Wolf. 1998. mass mkt. 5.99 (*0-425-16425-X*) Berkley Pub.

— The Maiden's Heart. 352p. 1999. mass mkt. 6.50 (*0-515-12515-6*, Jove) Berkley Pub.

***Beard, Julie.** My Fair Lord. 352p. 2000. mass mkt. 6.99 (*0-425-17481-6*) Berkley Pub.

Beard, Julie. Romance of the Rose. 1998. mass mkt. 5.99 (*0-425-16342-3*) Berkley Pub.

Beard, Leo R. & Maxwell, W. H., eds. Water Resources Management in Industrial Areas. (Water Resources Ser.: Vol. 1). 463p. 1982. 75.00 (*0-907567-30-4*, Tycooly Pub); pap. 55.00 (*0-907567-31-2*, Tycooly Pub) Weidner & Sons.

Beard, Lina & Beard, Adelia. The American Girl's Handy Book: How to Amuse Yourself & Others. LC 86-46262. (Illus.). 480p. (J). 1987. pap. 12.95 (*0-87923-666-3*) Godine.

Beard, Madeleine. Acres & Heirlooms: The Survival of Britain's Historic. 256p. 1989. 25.00 (*0-415-03264-4*, A2094) Routledge.

— Faith & Fortune. 240p. 1998. pap. 21.00 (*0-85244-392-7*, 2492, Pub. by Gracewing) Morehouse Pub.

Beard, Margaret L. & Comstock, Roger W., eds. All Are Chosen: Stories of Lay Ministry & Leadership. LC 98-14659. 216p. 1998. pap. 15.00 (*1-55896-360-X*, Skinner Hse Bks) Unitarian Univ.

Beard, Margaret T., ed. Theory Construction & Testing. LC 95-60045. 328p. (C). 1996. pap. 45.95 (*0-923950-12-5*) Tucker IL.

***Beard, Mary.** The Invention of Jane Harrison. LC 99-86699. 2000. text write for info. (*0-674-00212-1*) HUP.

Beard, Mary & North, John, eds. Pagan Priests: Religion & Power in the Ancient World. LC 89-42954. 240p. 1989. text 47.50 (*0-8014-2401-1*) Cornell U Pr.

Beard, Mary, et al. Literacy in the Roman World. (JRA Supplementary Ser.: No. 3). (ENG & FRE., Illus.). 198p. 1991. 39.75 (*1-887829-03-2*) Jour Roman Arch.

— Religions of Rome Vol. 1: A History. LC 97-21302. (Illus.). 478p. (C). 1998. text 69.95 (*0-521-30401-6*); pap. text 24.95 (*0-521-31682-0*) Cambridge U Pr.

— Religions of Rome Vol. 2: A Sourcebook. 430p. 1998. text 69.95 (*0-521-45015-2*); pap. text 24.95 (*0-521-45646-0*) Cambridge U Pr.

Beard, Mary R. The American Labor Movement. LC 71-89717. (American Labor Ser., No. 1). 206p. 1971. reprint ed. 16.95 (*0-405-02103-8*) Ayer.

— On Understanding Women. LC 68-54773. (Illus.). 541p. 1969. reprint ed. lib. bdg. 59.75 (*0-8371-0302-9*, BEUW, Greenwood Pr) Greenwood.

— Woman As Force in History: A Study in Traditions & Realities. 365p. 1987. reprint ed. pap. 12.95 (*0-89255-113-5*) Persea Bks.

— Woman's Work in Municipalities. LC 72-2588. (American Women Ser.). 1978. reprint ed. 23.95 (*0-405-04446-1*) Ayer.

Beard, Mary R., ed. America Through Women's Eyes. LC 68-54772. 558p. 1969. lib. bdg. 65.00 (*0-8371-0301-0*, BEAT, Greenwood Pr) Greenwood.

— America Through Women's Eyes. (BCL1 - U. S. History Ser.). 558p. 1991. reprint ed. lib. bdg. 109.00 (*0-7812-6000-0*) Rprt Serv.

Beard, Michael, tr. see Hawi, Khalil.

Beard, Michael E. & Iske, S. D., eds. Lead in Paint, Soil, & Dust: Health Risks, Exposure Studies, Control Measures, Measurement Methods, & Quality Assurance. LC 95-17787. 1995. write for info. (*0-8031-1884-8*, STP1226) ASTM.

***Beard, Michael E. & Rook, Harry L., eds.** Advancements in Environmental Measurement Methods for Asbestos. LC 99-55148. (Illus.). 425p. 2000. text 95.00 (*0-8031-2616-6*, STP1342) ASTM.

Beard, Miriam, tr. see De Francesco, Grete.

Beard, Nick. Frontiers: Computing the Future. 300p. 1997. pap. 25.00 (*3-540-76138-1*) Spr-Verlag.

Beard, Oliver T. Bristling with Thorns: Facsimile of 1884 ed. LC 68-20006. (Americans in Fiction Ser.). (Illus.). 424p. reprint ed. pap. text 5.95 (*0-89197-687-6*); reprint ed. lib. bdg. 27.50 (*0-8398-0158-0*) Irvington.

Beard, Patricia. Good Daughters: Loving Our Mothers As They Age. LC 98-30861. 304p. 1999. 23.00 (*0-446-52359-3*, Pub. by Warner Bks) Little.

— Good Daughters: Loving Our Mothers As They Age. 289p. 1999. mass mkt. 13.99 (*0-446-67551-2*, Pub. by Warner Bks) Little.

***Beard, Patricia.** Growing up Republican: Christie Whitman - The Politics of Character. (Illus.). 262p. 1999. reprint ed. text 25.00 (*0-7881-6683-2*) DIANE Pub.

Beard, Patricia. Growing up Republican: Conversations with Christine Todd Whitman. 1996. 25.00 (*0-614-95702-8*) HarpC.

Beard, Paul, jt. auth. see Blanchard, David.

Beard, Pauline W. A Riddling Thing: A Study of Time in Five Twentieth-Century Novels. LC 94-12985. 1996. pap. 49.95 (*1-883255-70-8*) Intl Scholars.

Beard, Pauline Winsome. A Riddling Thing: A Study of Time in Five Twentieth-Century Novels. LC 94-12985. 174p. 1996. 69.95 (*1-883255-71-6*) Intl Scholars.

Beard, Peter. The Last Word from Paradise. write for info. (*0-679-40846-0*) Knopf.

— Resist & Masking Techniques. (Illus.). 128p. 1996. text write for info. (*90-5703-071-3*, Harwood Acad Pubs) Gordon & Breach.

Beard, Peter. Resist & Masking Techniques. (Illus.). 128p. 1997. pap. 22.50 (*0-8122-1611-3*) U of Pa Pr.

Beard, Peter. Zara's Tales. write for info. (*0-679-42659-0*) Knopf.

Beard, Peter, ed. Longing for Darkness: Kamante's Tales from Out of Africa. (Illus.). 264p. 1991. reprint ed. 25.00 (*0-87701-724-7*); reprint ed. pap. 24.95 (*0-87701-680-1*) Chronicle Bks.

***Beard, Peter H.** The End of the Game: The Last Word from Paradise. (Illus.). 288p. 2000. pap. 29.95 (*0-8118-2881-6*) Chronicle Bks.

Beard, Peter H. The End of the Game: The Last Word from Paradise. (Illus.). 288p. 1996. reprint ed. pap. 24.95 (*0-87701-516-3*) Chronicle Bks.

— Longing for Darkness: Kamante's Tales from Out of Africa. (Illus.). 264p. (ps up). 1998. pap. 24.95 (*0-8118-2105-6*) Chronicle Bks.

Beard, Philip L. & Kerens, E. Paul. How to Negotiate Capitation for Laboratory Services. 80p. 1996. pap. 79.00 (*0-915274-89-2*, 202686) Am Assn Clinical Chem.

Beard, R. W. & Sharp, Frank, eds. Early Pregnancy Loss. 465p. 1988. 101.00 (*0-387-19530-0*) Spr-Verlag.

Beard, Ray O., jt. auth. see Hoffman, Lee.

Beard, Richard. Basics of GMAW-GTAW Welding, Gas Metal Arc Welding, Gas Tungsten Arc Welding. Harrington, Lois G., ed. 20p. 1992. teacher ed. 3.00 (*0-89606-297-X*, 920TK); student ed. 5.00 (*0-89606-286-4*, 920) Am Assn Voc Materials.

— Damascus. LC 98-74755. 320p. 1999. 22.95 (*1-55970-460-8*, Pub. by Arcade Pub Inc) Time Warner.

— X20: A Novel of (Not) Smoking. LC 97-28214. 320p. 1997. 22.95 (*1-55970-399-7*, Pub. by Arcade Pub Inc) Time Warner.

— X20: A Novel of (Not) Smoking. 320p. 1999. pap. 12.00 (*0-380-73194-0*, Avon Bks) Morrow Avon.

Beard, Richard, et al, eds. Reproductive Health Care for Women & Babies: Policy & Ethics. (Illus.). 488p. 1995. text 85.00 (*0-19-262530-6*) OUP.

Beard, Richard W. & Nathanielsz, Peter W., eds. Fetal Physiology & Medicine: The Basis of Perinatology. 2nd rev. ed. LC 83-21028. (Reproductive Medicine Ser.: No. 6). 839p. 1984. reprint ed. pap. 200.00 (*0-608-01311-0*, 206205500001) Bks Demand.

Beard, Rick, ed. On Being Homeless: Historical Perspectives. (Illus.). 176p. (C). 1989. pap. 19.00 (*0-8135-1508-4*); text 35.00 (*0-8135-1507-6*) Rutgers U Pr.

Beard, Rick & Berlowitz, Leslie C., eds. Greenwich Village: Culture & Counterculture. LC 92-30445. (Illus.). 500p. (C). 1993. 32.95 (*0-8135-1946-2*) Rutgers U Pr.

Beard, Rick, ed. see Rothman, David, et al.

Beard, Robert. Lexeme-Morpheme Base Morphology: A General Theory of Inflection & Word Formation. LC 94-30216. (SUNY Series in Linguistics). 433p. (C). 1995. text 89.50 (*0-7914-2471-5*); pap. text 29.95 (*0-7914-2472-3*) State U NY Pr.

Beard, Robert & Szymanek, Bogdan, eds. Bibliography of Morphology, 1960-1985. LC 87-34172. (Library & Information Sources in Linguistics: Vol. 18). xiv, 193p. 1988. 38.00 (*90-272-3742-5*) J Benjamins Pubng Co.

Beard, Roger, jt. ed. see Oakhill, Jane.

Beard, Ross E. Carbine. 2nd ed. Phillips, Jim, ed. (Illus.). 320p. 1998. 29.95 (*0-932572-26-X*) Phillips Pubns.

Beard, Sam. Restoring Hope in America: The Social Security Solution. 220p. 1995. pap. 19.95 (*1-55815-489-2*) ICS Pr.

Beard, Shawn & Di Lima, Sara N. Emergency Department Manual Clinical & Administrative Forms, Checklists & Guidelines. LC 99-14034. 1999. 159.00 (*0-8342-1114-9*) Aspen Pub.

Beard, Shawn, ed. see Health & Administration Development Group (Aspen Publishers) Staff.

Beard, Sherrill L., ed. see Kelley, Richard D.

Beard, Steve. Logic Bomb: Transmissions from the Edge of Style Culture. LC 98-86427. (Illus.). 224p. 1999. pap. 16.00 (*1-85242-596-2*, Pub. by Serpents Tail) Consort Bk Sales.

— Mind Body in Action: MBA - Multi-Dimensional Health & Fitness. (Illus.). 165p. (Orig.). 1995. pap. 15.95 (*0-9642982-9-5*) NuLife Pubg.

***Beard, T. Randolph & Lozada, Gabriel A.** Economics, Entropy & the Environment: The Extraordinary Economics of Nicholas Georgescu-Roegen. LC 99-39679. 168p. 2000. 70.00 (*1-84064-122-3*) E Elgar.

Beard, Thomas R., ed. The Louisiana Economy. LC 69-17622. (Louisiana State University Studies: No. 15). 240p. 1969. pap. 74.40 (*0-7837-8462-7*, 204926700010) Bks Demand.

Beard, Timothy F., jt. auth. see Buck, J. Orton, Jr.

Beard, Tracie L., ed. see Beard, Gerald J.

Beard, Tyler. Art of the Boot. LC 99-26514. (Illus.). 144p. 1999. 39.95 (*0-87905-919-2*) Gibbs Smith Pub.

— The Cowboy Boot Book. LC 92-1968. (Illus.). 144p. 1992. pap. 19.95 (*0-87905-471-9*) Gibbs Smith Pub.

Beard, William A., 3rd. Blue Springs: A History of the Desperate Battles at Blue Springs for the Control of East Tennessee During the American Civil War. LC 98-164127. (Illus.). 100p. 1997. pap. write for info. (*0-9660640-1-1*) Strawberry Plains.

— History of the 79th New York Cameron Highlanders 1859-1876, with a Treatise on the Uniform & Equipment. (Illus.). 55p. 1996. pap. 12.00 (*0-9660640-0-3*) Strawberry Plains.

Beard, Yolande S. The Wappo: A Report. 1979. pap. 8.50 (*0-939046-26-1*) Malki Mus Pr.

Beardall, C. Douglas & Beardall, Jewel N. All about Angels: The Truth about Angels, Vol. 2. (Illus.). 155p. (Orig.). 1993. pap. 8.95 (*1-882371-27-5*) LDS Bk Pubns.

— All about Angels: The Truth about God's Angels, Vol. 1. (Illus.). 125p. (Orig.). 1993. pap. 8.95 (*1-882371-26-7*) LDS Bk Pubns.

— The Miracle of Love: General Authorities Counsel on Life & Love. 126p. (Orig.). 1993. pap. 8.95 (*1-882371-01-1*) LDS Bk Pubns.

— The Missionary Kit: Hints, Tips & Smart Advice for Missionaries. 208p. 1992. pap. 9.95 (*1-882371-00-3*) LDS Bk Pubns.

Beardall, Douglas. About the Three Nephites. 12th large type ed. Beardall, Jewel, ed. (Illus.). 254p. 1992. reprint ed. pap. 9.95 (*1-882371-25-9*) LDS Bk Pubns.

Beardall, Douglas C. Embarrassed by the Light: Unauthorized Biography of Betty Eadie & Her Book "Embraced by the Light" (Illus.). 188p. 1995. pap. 9.95 (*0-614-03637-2*) LDS Bk Pubns.

— Embarrassed by the Light: Unauthorized Biography of Betty Edie & Embraced by the Light. (Illus.). 190p. (Orig.). 1995. pap. 8.95 (*1-882371-50-X*) LDS Bk Pubns.

— A Missionary Handbook: Hints, Tips, & Smart Advice for Missionaries. Beardall, Jewel N., ed. & pref. by. 238p. (Orig.). 1995. pap. 11.95 (*1-882371-05-4*) LDS Bk Pubns.

Beardall, Douglas C. & Beardall, Jewel N. Passage to Light: Dealing with Death & Dying. 248p. 1979. pap. 12.95 (*1-882371-02-X*) LDS Bk Pubns.

Beardall, Douglas C., jt. auth. see Beardall, Jewel N.

Beardall, Douglas C., ed. & illus. see Beardall, Jewel N.

Beardall, Jewel, ed. The Miracle of Love: General Authorities Counsel on Love & Life. (Personal Enrichment Ser.). 108p. (Orig.). 1991. write for info. (*0-929985-57-5*) Jackman Pubng.

— Passage to Light. (Personal Enrichment Ser.). 139p. (Orig.). 1991. pap. write for info. (*0-929985-58-3*) Jackman Pubng.

Beardall, Jewel, ed. see Beardall, Douglas.

Beardall, Jewel N. The Greatest Little Christmas Book: Joyful Read-Aloud Christmas Stories. Beardall, Douglas C., ed. & illus. by. 128p. (Orig.). 1995. pap. 8.95 (*1-882371-30-5*) LDS Bk Pubns.

Beardall, Jewel N. & Beardall, Douglas C. Christmas Potpourri: Joyful Read-Aloud Short Stories. (Illus.). 130p. (Orig.). 1995. pap. 8.95 (*1-882371-29-1*) LDS Bk Pubns.

Beardall, Jewel N., jt. auth. see Beardall, C. Douglas.

Beardall, Jewel N., jt. auth. see Beardall, Douglas C.

Beardall, Jewel N., ed. & pref. see Beardall, Douglas C.

Beardeley, R. K. Temporal & Areal Relationships in Central California Archaeology, Pt. 2. fac. ed. (Reports of the University of California Archaeological Survey: No. 25). 79p. 1954. reprint ed. pap. 9.06 (*1-55567-345-7*) Coyote Press.

Bearden. Marketing. 3rd ed. 2000. 36.94 (*0-07-232297-7*) McGraw.

Bearden, ed. see Walker, Wilson L.

Bearden, Brian, ed. Fantasy Football 101: How to Build & Manage a Winning Team to the League Championship. (Orig.). 1993. pap. 19.95 (*0-9638525-0-7*) Bearden.

Bearden, Brian & Thomas, David. Fantasy Football Training Camp's the Playbook: A Draft Day Guide & Workbook. 50p. 1995. pap. text 19.95 (*0-9638525-2-3*) Bearden.

Bearden, Brian, et al. The Fantasy Football Training Camp Playbook. 75p. (Orig.). 1994. pap. text 19.95 (*0-9638525-1-5*) Bearden.

Bearden, Brian, jt. auth. see Chandler, Jim.

Bearden, Candace N. & Bearden, Michael D. Marus the Longneck & the Journey to Stone Mountain. (Marus the Longneck Ser.). (Illus.). 25p. (J). (ps-6). 1998. pap. 8.95 (*0-9667619-2-8*) Dino Tales.

An Asterisk (*) at the beginning of an entry indicates that the title is appearing for the first time.

— Marus the Longneck & the Rescue at Moss Hill. (Marus the Longneck Ser.). (Illus.). 25p. (J). (ps-6). 1998. pap. 8.95 (*0-9667619-1-X*) Dino Tales.

Bearden, Candace N., jt. auth. see Bearden, Michael D.

Bearden Et Al. Marketing-hardback. 2nd ed. 1997. 83.44 (*0-256-26907-6*) McGraw.

***Bearden, H. Joe & Fuquay, John W.** Applied Animal Reproduction. 5th ed. LC 99-25858. (Illus.). 400p. 1999. 94.00 (*0-13-081976-X*) P-H.

Bearden, Janet, jt. auth. see Bearden, Tim.

Bearden, Jean L. A History of Hoodsport: Gateway to the Olympics: Ida's Story. 4th rev. ed. (Illus.). 1994. pap. 20.00 (*0-9622337-5-7*) Perry Pub WA.

Bearden, Jim & Butler, Linda. Shadd: The Life & Times of Mary Shadd Cary. (Illus.). 256p. 1995. text 19.95 (*0-919600-76-X*, Pub. by NC Ltd) U of Toronto Pr.

Bearden, Lynn, ed. see Walker, Wilson L.

Bearden, Michael D. & Bearden, Candace N. Marus the Longneck Saves the Day. (Marus the Longneck Ser.). (Illus.). 25p. (J). (ps-6). 1998. pap. 8.95 (*0-9667619-0-1*) Dino Tales.

Bearden, Michael D., jt. auth. see Bearden, Candace N.

Bearden, Milton. The Black Tulip. LC 97-37224. 336p. 1998. 24.95 (*0-679-44791-1*) Random.

Bearden, Romare & Henderson, Harry. History of African-American Artists: From 1792 to the Present. 1993. 70.00 (*0-394-57016-2*) Pantheon.

Bearden, T. E. AIDS Biological Warfare. (Illus.). 484p. 1988. pap. 19.50 (*0-914119-04-4*) Tesla Bk Co.

— Cancer & the Unresolved Health Issues in the Biological Effect: EM Fields & Radiation. 56p. 1993. 9.50 (*0-914119-28-1*) Tesla Bk Co.

— Fer-de-Lance: A Briefing on Soviet Scalar Electromagnetic Weapons. LC 86-50553. (Illus.). 225p. (Orig.). 1986. pap. text 27.50 (*0-914119-03-6*) Tesla Bk Co.

— The Final Secret of Free Energy. 26p. 1993. 8.75 (*0-914119-29-X*) Tesla Bk Co.

— Gravitobiology: A New Biophysics. (Illus.). 178p. (Orig.). 1991. pap. 24.50 (*0-914119-07-9*) Tesla Bk Co.

— Solutions to Tesla's Secrets & the Soviet Tesla Weapons with Reference Articles for Solutions to Tesla's Secrets, 2 pts., Set. LC 81-85737. (Illus.). 188p. (Orig.). 1982. pap. 14.00 (*0-9603536-3-1*) Tesla Bk Co.

Bearden, Tim & Bearden, Janet. Youth on Mission Vol. 4: Transformed. (Illus.). 128p. (gr. 7). 1998. pap. text 15.95 (*1-56309-236-0*, W986102) Womans Mission Union.

Bearden, William. Marketing: Principles & Perspectives. 2nd ed. (C). 1997. text 12.25 (*0-256-26953-X*) McGraw.

Bearden, William O., et al. Handbook of Marketing Scales: Multi-Item Measures for Marketing & Consumer Behavior Research. LC 92-45241. 1993. 56.00 (*0-8039-5155-8*) Sage.

— Marketing. 520p. (C). 1995. text, student ed. 26.25 (*0-256-16344-8*, Irwn McGrw-H) McGrw-H Hghr Educ.

— Marketing: Principles & Perspectives. LC 94-31421. (Marketing Ser.). 631p. (C). 1994. text 68.95 (*0-256-11319-X*, Irwn Prfssnl) McGraw-Hill Prof.

— Marketing & Marketing Game. (C). 1994. text 87.90 (*0-256-19380-0*, Irwn McGrw-H) McGrw-H Hghr Educ.

— Marketing Career Guide. 160p. (C). 1995. text 10.25 (*0-256-18369-4*, Irwn McGrw-H) McGrw-H Hghr Educ.

Bearden, William O., et al. Marketing Principles & Perspectives. 2nd ed. LC 97-24735. (Irwin-McGraw-Hill Series in Marketing). (C). 1997. text 52.50 (*0-256-21897-8*, Irwn Prfssnl) McGraw-Hill Prof.

Bearden, William O., ed. see Netemeyer, Richard G.

Beardmore, Nellie. Memories Linger On. LC 97-91026. 1998. pap. 8.95 (*0-533-12542-1*) Vantage.

Beardon, A. F. The Iteration of Rational Functions. (Graduate Texts in Mathematics Ser.). (Illus.). xvi, 280p. 1995. 48.95 (*0-387-97589-6*) Spr-Verlag.

Beardon, Alan F. Complex Analysis: The Argument Principle in Analysis & Topology. LC 78-8540. 253p. reprint ed. pap. 78.50 (*0-8357-3393-9*, 203965000013) Bks Demand.

— The Geometry of Discrete Groups. (Graduate Texts in Mathematics Ser.: Vol. 91). (Illus.). 337p. 1995. 54.95 (*0-387-90788-2*) Spr-Verlag.

— The Geometry of Discrete Groups. rev. ed. (Graduate Tests in Mathematics Ser.: 91). 337p. 1996. 49.50 (*3-540-90788-2*) Spr-Verlag.

— Limits. LC 97-20490. (Undergraduate Texts in Mathematics Ser.). 1997. 34.95 (*0-387-98274-4*) Spr-Verlag.

Beardon, Colin, ed. Artificial Intelligence Terminology: A Reference Guide. 1989. text 19.95 (*0-470-21601-8*) P-H.

Beardon, Colin & Whitehouse, Diane. Computers & Society. 160p. (Orig.). 1994. pap. text 29.95 (*1-871516-41-2*, Pub. by Intellect) Cromland.

Beards, Andrew. Objectivity & Historical Understanding. (Series in Philosophy). 184p. 1997. 64.95 (*1-85972-521-X*, Pub. by Avebry) Ashgate Pub Co.

Beards, C. F. Vibration Analysis & Control System Dynamics. 2nd ed. LC 92-18183. (Ellis Horwood Series in Mechanical Engineering). 1992. 35.95 (*0-13-953332-X*, Pub. by Tavistock-E Horwood) Routldge.

Beards, Chris F. Analysis & Damping of Structural Vibration. (Illus.). 300p. 1996. pap. 90.00 (*0-470-23586-1*, Wiley-Interscience) Wiley.

— Engineering Vibration Analysis with Application to Control Systems. 426p. 1995. pap. text 65.95 (*0-470-23559-4*) Halsted Pr.

— Structural Vibration Analysis: Modelling, Analysis & Damping of Vibrating Structures. LC 82-25482. 153p. 1983. text 59.95 (*0-470-27422-0*) P-H.

— Vibrations & Control Systems. 1988. text 72.95 (*0-470-21165-2*) P-H.

Beards, Virginia, ed. see Ross, Martin.

Beardsell, Peter. A Theatre for Cannibals: Rodolfo Usigli & the Mexican State. LC 90-56174. 248p. 1992. 39.50 (*0-8386-3436-2*) Fairleigh Dickinson.

Beardsell, Peter, ed. & intro. see Cortazar, Julio.

***Beardsell, Peter R.** Europe & Latin America: Returning the Gaze. LC 99-55155. 2000. write for info. (*0-7190-5630-6*, Pub. by Manchester Univ Pr); pap. write for info. (*0-7190-5631-4*, Pub. by Manchester Univ Pr) St Martin.

Beardslee. Vision from the Hill. 1984. pap. 10.00 (*0-8028-0035-1*) Eerdmans.

***Beardslee, Clark S.** Memories Are Forever. 2000. write for info. (*1-58235-487-1*) Watermrk Pr.

Beardslee, Clark S. Second Thoughts. 1997. pap. write for info. (*1-57553-523-8*) Watermrk Pr.

Beardslee, Ed, jt. auth. see Seymour, Dale.

Beardslee, William A. First Corinthians: A Commentary for Today. LC 94-27009. 184p. (Orig.). 1994. pap. 14.99 (*0-8272-1018-3*) Chalice Pr.

Beardslee, William R. Breaking the Silence: Healing for Families with Depression: Healing for Families with Depression. 2000. write for info. (*0-316-08549-9*) Little.

Beardsley, A., jt. auth. see Orcutt, Samuel.

Beardsley, Aubrey. Aubrey Beardsley Bookplates. Theodore, Menten, ed. 1976. pap. 3.50 (*0-486-23350-2*) Dover.

— Best Works of Aubrey Beardsley. 44th ed. 144p. 1990. pap. 8.95 (*0-486-26273-1*) Dover.

— Illustrations for La Morte d'Arthur. (Illus.). 171p. 1972. pap. 8.95 (*0-486-22348-5*) Dover.

Beardsley, Aubrey & Glassco, John. The Story of Venus & Tannhauser. (Illus.). 148p. 1996. pap. 10.95 (*1-56201-089-1*) FoxRock.

Beardsley, Aubrey & Pope, Alexander. The Rape of the Lock. 1968. pap. 6.95 (*0-486-21963-1*) Dover.

Beardsley, Aubrey & Wilde, Oscar. Salome: A Tragedy in One Act. Douglas, Alfred, tr. (Illus.). 67p. 1967. pap. 6.95 (*0-486-21830-9*) Dover.

Beardsley, Aubrey, jt. auth. see Calloway, Stephen.

Beardsley, Audrey, jt. auth. see Wilde, Oscar.

Beardsley, Charles. Hollywood's Master Showman: The Legendary Sid Grauman. LC 80-69966. (Illus.). 192p. 1983. 25.00 (*0-8453-4703-9*, Cornwall Bks) Assoc Univ Prs.

Beardsley, D. B. History of Hancock County, Ohio. 472p. 1993. reprint ed. lib. bdg. 49.50 (*0-8328-2786-X*) Higginson Bk Co.

— History of Hancock County, Ohio. 472p. 1993. reprint ed. lib. bdg. 49.00 (*0-8328-2960-9*) Higginson Bk Co.

Beardsley, David, ed. First Do No Harm: A Practical Guide to Medication Safety & JCAHO Compliance. LC 99-212067. (Illus.). 150p. 1998. pap. text 87.00 (*1-57839-035-4*) Opus Communs.

Beardsley, David, ed. see Fritz, Albert L., et al.

Beardsley, David, ed. see Smith, Dean F.

Beardsley, Doug. Going Down Into History. 1976. pap. text 3.50 (*0-88982-002-3*, Pub. by Oolichan Bks) Genl Dist Srvs.

— Wrestling with Angels: New & Selected Poems, 1960-1995. Harris, Michael, ed. (Signal Editions Ser.). 176p. (Orig.). 1995. pap. 12.95 (*1-55065-063-7*, Pub. by Vehicule Pr) Genl Dist Srvs.

***Beardsley, Doug & Purdy, Al.** No One Else Is Lawrence: A Dozen of D. H. Lawrence's Best Poems with Introduction & Commentary. LC 99-216188. 80p. 1998. pap. 14.95 (*1-55017-194-1*) Harbour Pub Co.

Beardsley, Doug, jt. ed. see Purdy, Al.

Beardsley, E. Edwards. Life & Times of William Samuel Johnson. LC 72-4207. (Select Bibliographies Reprint Ser.). 1977. reprint ed. 20.95 (*0-8369-6872-7*) Ayer.

Beardsley, Edward H. Harry L. Russell & Agricultural Science in Wisconsin. LC 77-84950. 269p. reprint ed. pap. 83.40 (*0-608-13876-2*, 202372800033) Bks Demand.

— A History of Neglect: Health Care for Blacks & Mill Workers in the Twentieth-Century South. LC 86-24949. (Illus.). 400p. 1987. reprint ed. pap. 124.00 (*0-608-07987-1*, 206795200012) Bks Demand.

Beardsley, Elaine K. Working in Commercials: A Complete Sourcebook for Adult & Child Actors. (Illus.). 194p. 1993. pap. 27.95 (*0-240-80160-1*, Focal) Buttrwrth-Heinemann.

Beardsley, Fred G., III. Journey into Awareness: A Parent's Perspective on Children's Mental Health in Today's Society. (Illus.). viii, 203p. 1998. pap. 12.50 (*0-9664485-0-2*) Bridgtte Rose.

Beardsley, Gill. Exploring Play in the Primary Classroom. (Primary Curriculum Ser.). 1998. 25.95 (*1-85346-463-5*) Taylor & Francis.

Beardsley, Grace M. The Negro in Greek & Roman Civilization. 1979. 22.95 (*0-405-10581-9*) Ayer.

Beardsley, I. H. Genealogical History of the Beardsley - Beardslee Family in America, 1635-1902. (Illus.). 452p. 1993. reprint ed. pap. 69.50 (*0-8328-1683-3*); reprint ed. lib. bdg. 79.50 (*0-8328-1682-5*) Higginson Bk Co.

Beardsley, Jack. Elements of Subscription Fulfillment. 3rd rev. ed. (Illus.). 175p. 1999. 115.00 (*0-9669021-0-6*) Bardsey Pubg.

Beardsley, Joe. Mother Lode: Montana Poems & Narratives. LC 96-90781. (Illus.). ix, 104p. 1997. pap. 9.95 (*0-9654056-0-5*) Tobacco Root.

Beardsley, John. Art in Public Places. Harney, Andy L., ed. LC 81-85019. (Illus.). 149p. (Orig.). 1981. pap. 12.00 (*0-941182-05-3*) Partners Livable.

— Earthworks & Beyond: Contemporary Art in the Landscape. expanded ed. LC 83-21424. (Illus.). 176p. 1984. pap. 29.95 (*0-89659-963-9*) Abbeville Pr.

— Earthworks & Beyond: Contemporary Art in the Landscape. 3rd expanded ed. LC 96-46936. (Illus.). 224p. 1998. pap. 35.00 (*0-7892-0296-4*) Abbeville Pr.

— Elyn Zimmerman. (Illus.). 56p. (Orig.). 1991. pap. text 25.00 (*1-879293-02-1*) Contemp Art Mus.

— Gardens of Revelation: Environments by Visionary Artists. LC 94-23573. (Illus.). 224p. 1995. 60.00 (*1-55859-360-8*) Abbeville Pr.

— A Landscape for Modern Sculpture: Storm King Art Center. rev. ed. (Illus.). 112p. 1996. 39.95 (*0-7892-0246-8*) Abbeville Pr.

— Pablo Picasso. (Illus.). 92p. (J). 1991. 19.95 (*0-8109-3713-1*, Pub. by Abrams) Time Warner.

Beardsley, John, ed. Art & Landscape in Charleston & the Low Country: Spoletto Festival U. S. A. 1997. (Illus.). 168p. 1998. 45.00 (*1-888931-17-5*) Spacemkr Pr.

— John Ruppert: Natural Forces/Urban Context. (Illus.). 12p. 1996. pap. 6.00 (*0-938903-20-9*) Cty of Chicago.

Beardsley, John, et al. Functional Follies: 20 Architectural Objects of Delight. Brairton, Betsey, ed. LC 99-612742. (Illus.). 52p. 1999. pap. 15.00 (*1-893974-00-6*) Savannah Coll.

Beardsley, Levi. Otsego County Reminiscences: Personal & Other Incidents; Early Settlement of Otsego County Etc. (Illus.). 575p. 1997. reprint ed. lib. bdg. 59.50 (*0-8328-6197-9*) Higginson Bk Co.

Beardsley, Monroe C. Aesthetics: Problems in the Philosophy of Criticism. 2nd ed. LC 80-28899. (Illus.). 688p. (C). 1981. reprint ed. 49.95 (*0-915145-09-X*); reprint ed. pap. text 28.95 (*0-915145-08-1*) Hackett Pub.

— Aesthetics from Classical Greece to the Present: A Short History. LC 75-20138. (Studies in the Humanities). 416p. 1975. reprint ed. pap. text 19.95 (*0-8173-6623-7*) U of Ala Pr.

— Literature & Aesthetics. LC 68-57656. 1968. pap. 2.50 (*0-672-60903-7*, Bobbs) Macmillan.

— Modes of Argument. LC 67-18663. 1967. pap. 2.95 (*0-672-60893-6*, Bobbs) Macmillan.

— The Possibility of Criticism. LC 78-103416. (Criticism Monograph Ser.: No. 2). 124p. reprint ed. pap. 38.50 (*0-7837-3811-0*, 204363100010) Bks Demand.

Beardsley, Monroe C., ed. The European Philosophers from Descartes to Nietzsche. LC 92-50210. 912p. 1992. 22.00 (*0-679-60024-8*) Modern Lib NY.

Beardsley, Roger. The Hornby Companion. (Hornby Companion Ser.: Vol. 8). 628p. 1992. 85.00 (*0-904568-95-4*) Pincushion Pr.

Beardsley, Theodore S., Jr. Hispano-Classical Translations Printed Between 1482 & 1699. (Illus.). 176p. 1970. 15.00 (*0-87535-113-1*) Hispanic Soc.

Beardsley, Thomas R. Willimantic Industry & Community: The Rise & Decline of a Connecticut Textile City (Illus.). 264p. (Orig.). 1993. pap. 15.95 (*0-963452-4-0-1*) Windham Textile.

Beardsley, Thomas R., jt. ed. see Shuldiner, David P.

Beardsmore, Hugo B. Bilingualism: Basic Principles. 2nd ed. 205p. 1986. 49.00 (*0-905028-69-4*, MM1, Pub. by Multilingual Matters); pap. 19.00 (*0-905028-63-5*, Pub. by Multilingual Matters) Taylor & Francis.

Beardsmore, Hugo B., ed. European Models of Bilingual Education. LC 92-38546. (Multilingual Matters Ser.: No. 92). 184p. 1993. 79.00 (*1-85359-183-1*, Pub. by Multilingual Matters); pap. 29.95 (*1-85359-182-3*, Pub. by Multilingual Matters) Taylor & Francis.

Beardsmore, Hugo B., jt. ed. see Witte, Els.

Beardsmore, Valerie & Cox, Adele. Opinion Writing & Drafting in Tort. 347p. 1996. pap. 22.00 (*1-8594*-032-4*, Pub. by Cavendish Pubng) Gaunt.

Beardstown Ladies' Investment Club. Beardstown Ladies' Guide to Smart Spending: How to Save for a Rainy Day Without Sacrificing Your Lifestyle. large type ed. LC 97-7604. 1997. 27.95 (*0-7838-8124-X*) Mac Lib Ref.

— The Beardstown Ladies' Guide to Smart Spending for Big Savings: How to Save for a Rainy Day Without Sacrificing Your Lifestyle. LC 96-35857. (Illus.). 304p. (J). 1997. 19.45 (*0-7868-6265-3*, Pub. by Hyperion) Time Warner.

***Beardstown Ladies' Investment Club.** The Beardstown Ladies' Guide to Smart Spending for Big Savings: How to Save for a Rainy Day Without Sacrificing Your Lifestyle. (Illus.). 304p. (J). 1998. pap. 12.45 (*0-7868-8268-9*, Pub. by Hyperion) Time Warner.

Beardstown Ladies' Investment Club. Stitch-in-Time Guide to Growing Your Nest Egg. large type ed. pap. 23.95 (*1-56895-353-4*) Wheeler Pub.

Beardstown Ladies' Investment Club & Dellabough, Robin. The Beardstown Ladies' Pocketbook Guide to Picking Stocks. LC 97-46967. (Illus.). 288p. (J). 1998. mass mkt. 6.50 (*0-7868-8935-7*, Pub. by Hyperion) Time Warner.

— The Beardstown Ladies' Stitch-in-Time Guide to Growing Your Nest Egg: Step-by-Step Planning for a Comfortable Financial Future. (Illus.). 272p. (J). 1996. 19.45 (*0-7868-6192-4*, Pub. by Hyperion) Time Warner.

Beardstown Ladies' Investment Club & Whitaker, Leslie. The Beardstown Ladies' Common-Sense Investment Guide: How We Beat the Stock Market & How You Can Too. large type ed. LC 95-11350. 233p. 1996. pap. 21.95 (*0-7838-1407-0*, G K Hall Lrg Type) Mac Lib Ref.

Beardsworth, Alan & Keil, Teresa. Sociology on the Menu: An Invitation to the Study of Food & Society. LC 96-18305. 288p. (C). 1997. 80.00 (*0-415-11424-1*); pap. 24.99 (*0-415-11425-X*) Routledge.

Beardsworth, Gary. Recipes from the Moon. (Illus.). 124p. 1995. pap. 14.95 (*0-89815-681-5*) Ten Speed Pr.

Beardsworth, Richard. Derrida & the Political. LC 95-26620. (Thinking the Political Ser.). 192p. (C). 1996. pap. 22.99 (*0-415-10967-1*) Routledge.

Beardsworth, Richard, tr. see Stiegler, Bernard.

Beardwell, Ian & Holden, Len. Human Resources Management: A Contemporary Perspective. 2nd ed. (Illus.). 797p. 1997. pap. 67.50 (*0-273-62230-7*, Pub. by Pitman Pub) Trans-Atl Phila.

Beardwell, Ian J., ed. Contemporary Industrial Relations: A Critical Analysis. (Illus.). 254p. 1996. text 72.00 (*0-19-877387-0*); pap. text 32.00 (*0-19-877388-9*) OUP.

Beardwood, A. Records of the Trial of Walter Langeton. (Camden Fourth Ser.: No. 6). 27.00 (*0-901050-02-4*) David Brown.

Beardwood, Roger, jt. auth. see Tiller, Alan.

Beardwood, Roger, jt. auth. see Tillier, Alan.

Beardy, Flora & Coutts, Robert, eds. Voices from Hudson Bay: Cree Stories from York Factory. LC 98-121955. (Rupert's Land Record Society Ser.). (Illus.). 200p. 1996. 60.00 (*0-7735-1440-6*, Pub. by McG-Queens Univ Pr); pap. 22.95 (*0-7735-1441-4*, Pub. by McG-Queens Univ Pr) CUP Services.

Beare. Western Kentucky University. 1998. 81.45 (*0-323-00536-5*) Mosby Inc.

Beare, A. S., ed. Basic & Applied Influenza Research & Progress Towards Epidemiological Control. 288p. 1982. 119.95 (*0-8493-6250-4*, QR201) CRC Pr.

Beare, B. Ireland: Myths & Legends. 1996. 7.98 (*0-7858-0538-9*) Bk Sales Inc.

— Scotland: Myths & Legends. 1996. 7.98 (*0-7858-0537-0*) Bk Sales Inc.

Beare, Beryl. Discovering King Arthur. 1999. pap. text 16.95 (*0-572-02367-7*) Trans-Atl Phila.

— Dreams & Destinies: Your Dreams Explained. 96p. 1995. 19.95 (*1-57215-125-0*) World Pubns.

Beare, D. Effective Information Systems. 1996. pap. 140.00 (*1-85953-036-2*, Pub. by Tech Comm) St Mut.

Beare, David. Effective Information Systems. (Financial Times Management Briefings Ser.). 1997. pap. 94.50 (*0-273-63211-6*, Pub. by F T P-H) Trans-Atl Phila.

Beare, Geraldine, compiled by. Index to the Strand Magazine, 1891-1950. LC 82-11769. 859p. 1982. lib. bdg. 105.00 (*0-313-23122-2*, BIM/, Greenwood Pr) Greenwood.

***Beare, Hedley.** The Future's Schools: Coming, Ready or Not. LC 00-36780. (Student Outcomes & the Reform of Education Ser.). 2000. write for info. (*0-415-23869-2*) Routledge.

Beare, Hedley & Boyd, William L., eds. Restructuring Schools: An International Perspective on the Movement to Transform the Control & Performance of Schools. LC 92-39836. 1993. 95.00 (*0-7507-0121-8*, Falmer Pr); pap. 34.95 (*0-7507-0122-6*, Falmer Pr) Taylor & Francis.

Beare, Hedley & Slaughter, Richard. Education for the Twenty-First Century. (Educational Management Ser.). (Illus.). 192p. (C). 1994. pap. 22.99 (*0-415-11523-X*, B4070) Routledge.

Beare, Hedley, et al. Creating an Excellent School. (Educational Management Ser.). 224p. (C). 1988. lib. bdg. 45.00 (*0-415-00584-1*) Routledge.

— Creating an Excellent School. (Educational Management Ser.). 304p. (C). 1990. pap. 22.99 (*0-415-04717-X*) Routledge.

Beare, Jerry W. Ending Teenage Terrorism: A Parent Survival Guide. Finney, Rachael, ed. LC 98-92295. (Illus.). 147p. 1998. pap. 9.95 (*0-9668101-4-7*) J Beare.

Beare, John I. Greek Theories of Elementary Cognition: From Alcmaeon to Aristotle (1906 Edition) 366p. 1996. reprint ed. 64.00 (*1-85506-175-9*) Bks Intl VA.

Beare, Patricia G. Davis's NCLEX-RN Review. 3rd rev. ed. 816p. 2000. pap. text 34.95 (*0-8036-0577-3*) Davis Co.

— Principles & Practice of Adult Health Nursing. 2nd ed. 2328p. (C). (gr. 13). 1993. text, teacher ed. 38.00 (*0-8151-0423-5*, 24199) Mosby Inc.

Beare, Patricia G., et al, eds. Davis's NCLEX-PN Review Book. 2nd ed. LC 98-27802. (Illus.). 512p. 1998. pap. 31.95 (*0-8036-0403-3*) Davis Co.

— Davis's NCLEX-RN Review. 2nd ed. LC 95-41179. (Illus.). 705p. 1995. pap. text 33.95 incl. disk (*0-8036-0063-1*) Davis Co.

Beare, Patricia G. & Myers. Principles & Practice of Adult Health Nursing: With Study Guide. 3rd ed. (Illus.). 2048p. (C). (gr. 13). 1997. text, student ed. 74.00 (*0-8151-1032-4*, 29577) Mosby Inc.

***Beare, Patricia G. & Myers, Judith L.** Adult Health Nursing: Includes Testbank. 3rd ed. 1998. teacher ed. write for info. (*0-8151-1008-1*) Mosby Inc.

— Adult Health Nursing: Nursing Drug Guide Package. 3rd ed. (Illus.). 1920p. 1998. write for info. (*0-323-00497-0*) Mosby Inc.

Beare, Patricia G. & Myers, Judith L. Principles & Practice of Adult Health Nursing. 50p. 1990. 75.00 (*0-8016-0389-7*) Mosby Inc.

— Principles & Practice of Adult Health Nursing: Learning Guide. 3rd ed. 168p. (C). (gr. 13). 1997. pap. text 14.95 (*0-8151-1012-X*, 29579) Mosby Inc.

Beare, Patricia G. & Myers, Judith L., eds. Principles & Practice of Adult Health Nursing. 3rd ed. LC 97-35022. (Illus.). 1920p. (C). (gr. 13). 1997. text 67.00 (*0-8151-1006-5*, 29567) Mosby Inc.

Beare, Patricia G. & Thompson, Patricia E. Davis's Computerized Review for NCLEX-RN, 2 vols. 1998. 27.95 (*0-8036-0223-5*) Davis Co.

— Davis's Q & A for the NCLEX-RN. LC 97-29247. (Illus.). 648p. (C). 1998. pap. text 31.95 (*0-8036-0282-0*) Davis Co.

Beare, Patricia G., jt. auth. see Stanley, Mickey.

Beare, Paul. Functional Analysis Assessment: A Practical Manual. (Illus.). 116p. 1998. pap. 14.95 (*1-886979-12-X*) Practicl Pr.

Beare-Rogers, Joyce, ed. Methods for Nutritional Assessment of Fats. 264p. 1985. 40.00 (*0-935315-11-X*) Am Oil Chemists.

Beares, Paul R. Consumer Lending. (Illus.). 1978. teacher ed. 85.00 (*0-89982-001-8*) Am Bankers.

— Consumer Lending. 2nd ed. Lian, Tanja, ed. (Illus.). 360p. (C). 1992. pap. text 36.00 (*0-89982-334-3*) Am Bankers.

— Consumer Lending. 3rd ed. (Illus.). 1997. 60.00 (*0-89982-000-X*) Am Bankers.

Bearg, David W. Indoor Air Quality & HVAC Systems. 240p. 1993. boxed set 94.95 (*0-87371-574-8*, L574) Lewis Pubs.

B

***Bearg, Edson A.** Nebraska Cornhuskers: Tales, Traditions & Triumphs. LC 99-208694. 119p. 1999. write for info. (*1-892902-00-1*) Ramz Pubg.

Beargdyke, Nancy, jt. auth. see Wurmser, David.

***Bearinger, David, ed.** The Bill of Rights, The Courts, & The Law. 3rd ed. LC 98-61851. 1999. pap. text. write for info. (*0-9668919-1-0*) Virginia Fndt.

Bearison, David J. They Never Want to Tell You: Children Talk about Cancer. LC 90-49945. 192p. 1991. text 22.00 (*0-674-88370-5*, BEATHE) HUP.

Bearison, David J. & Mulhern, Raymond K., eds. Pediatric Psychooncology: Psychological Perspectives on Children with Cancer. (Illus.). 272p. 1994. text 60.00 (*0-19-507931-0*) OUP.

Bearison, David J. & Zimiles, Herbert, eds. Thought & Emotion: Developmental Perspectives. (Jean Piaget Society Ser.). 256p. (C). 1985. text 49.95 (*0-89859-530-4*) L Erlbaum Assocs.

Bearley, Joan M. All about Himalayan Cats. (Illus.). 160p. 1989. 17.95 (*0-86622-080-1*, PS-736) TFH Pubns.

Bearley, William L., jt. auth. see Jones, John E.

Bearman, David. Electronic Evidence: Strategies for Managing Records in Contemporary Organizations. (Archives & Museum Informatics Technical Reports). 1994. pap. text 30.00 (*1-885626-08-8*) Archives & Mus.

Bearman, David, ed. Hands on Hypermedia & Interactivity in Museums Vol. 2: ICHIM '95 Conference Proceedings. LC 96-113981. 293p. 1995. pap. 20.00 (*1-885626-12-6*) Archives & Mus.

Bearman, David & Trant, Jennifer, eds. Cultural Heritage Informatics, 1999. 1999. pap. text 50.00 (*1-885626-18-5*) Archives & Mus.

— Museum Interactive Multimedia, 1997. LC 98-160290. (Illus.). 234p. 1997. pap. 30.00 (*1-885626-14-2*) Archives & Mus.

— Museums & the Web, 1997: Selected Papers. LC 97-216909. 380p. 1997. pap. 30.00 (*1-885626-13-4*) Archives & Mus.

— Museums & the Web 99: Selected Papers from an International Conference. 1999. pap. text 50.00 incl. cd-rom (*1-885626-17-7*) Archives & Mus.

***Bearman, David & Traut, Jennifer, eds.** Museum & the Web, 2000: Selected Papers from an International Conference. (Illus.). 250p. 2000. pap. 50.00 incl. cd-rom (*1-885626-20-7*) Archives & Mus.

Bearman, Jane. David. LC 65-21753. (Illus.). (J). (gr. 3 up). 1975. 3.95 (*0-8246-0085-1*) Jonathan David.

— The Eight Nights: A Chanukah Counting Book. LC 78-60781. (Illus.). (J). (gr. k-3). 1979. pap. 6.00 (*0-8074-0237-0*, 102562) UAHC.

***Bearman, Jane.** Eight Nights: A Chanukah Counting Book. (Illus.). (J). 1999. pap. 6.00 (*0-8074-0025-4*) UAHC.

Bearman, Jane. Jonathan. LC 65-21754. (Illus.). (J). (gr. 3 up). 1975. 3.95 (*0-8246-0089-4*) Jonathan David.

Bearman, P. J., compiled by. Encyclopaedia of Islam: Index of Subjects to Volumes I - IX (Index des Matieres des Tomes I - IX) (ENG & FRE.). vi, 298p. 1998. pap. 94.25 (*90-04-11080-1*) Brill Academic Pubs.

— The Encyclopaedia of Islam: Index of Subjects to Volumes I-VII & the the Supplement, Fascicule 1-6. 220p. 1994. pap. text, per. 87.50 (*90-04-10073-3*) Brill Academic Pubs.

— Encyclopaedia of Islam: Index of Subjects to Volumes I-VIII & to the Supplements, Fasc. I-6/Index des Matieres des Tomes I-VIII et du Supplement, Livr. I-6. 300p. 1996. pap. 88.50 (*90-04-10594-8*) Brill Academic Pubs.

Bearman, P. J., ed. The Encyclopaedia of Islam: Index of Technical Terms to Volumes I-VII & to the Supplements. LC 95-44134. iv, 308p. 1995. pap. 118.50 (*90-04-09778-3*) Brill Academic Pubs.

***Bearman, P. J., et al, eds.** The Encyclopaedia of Islam. (Glossary & Index of Terms Ser.: Vols. I-IX). 400p. 1999. 97.50 (*90-04-11635-4*) Brill Academic Pubs.

— Encyclopaedia of Islam. 1000p. 2000. 609.00 (*90-04-11211-1*) Brill Academic Pubs.

Bearman, P. W., ed. Flow Induced Vibration: Proceedings 6th International Conference on Flow-Induced Vibration, London, UK, 10-12 April 1995. (Illus.). 688p. 1995. text 175.00 (*90-5410-547-X*, Pub. by A A Balkema) Ashgate Pub Co.

Bearman, Peter S. Relations into Rhetorics: Local Elite Social Structure in Norfolk England, 1540-1640. LC 92-35962. (Arnold & Caroline Rose Monograph Series of the American Sociological Association). 220p. (C). 1993. text 40.00 (*0-8135-1968-3*) Rutgers U Pr.

***Bearman, Peter S. & Bruckner, Hannah.** Power in Numbers: Peer Effects on Adolescent Girls Sexual Debut & Pregnancy. 65p. 1999. pap. 15.00 (*1-58671-011-7*) Natl Cpgn Teen Preg.

***Bearman, Peter S., et al.** Peer Potential: Making the Most of How Teens Influence Each Other. 115p. 1999. pap. 15.00 (*1-58671-010-9*) Natl Cpgn Teen Preg.

Bearman, Robert. Shakespeare in the Stratford Records. (Illus.). 96p. 1994. pap. 12.95 (*0-7509-0632-4*, Pub. by Sutton Pub Ltd) Intl Pubs Mktg.

Bearman, Robert, ed. The History of an English Borough: Stratford-upon-Avon 1196-1996. LC DA690.S92H57 1997. (Illus.). 240p. 1997. pap. 26.95 (*0-7509-1535-8*, Pub. by Sutton Pub Ltd) Intl Pubs Mktg.

Bearn, Alexander G. Archibald Garrod & the Individuality of Man. LC 92-27504. (Illus.). 248p. 1993. text 55.00 (*0-19-262145-9*, Clarendon Pr) OUP.

Bearn, Alexander G., et al, eds. Genetics of Neurological Disorders, Vol. 6. LC 85-508. (Progress in Medical Genetics: Vol. VI). 320p. 1985. 75.00 (*0-275-91331-7*, C13311, Praeger Pubs) Greenwood.

***Bearn, Alexander G. & American Philosophical Society Staff.** Useful Knowledge: The American Philosophical Society Millennium Program. LC 99-39406. (Memoirs of the American Philosophical Society Ser.: Vol. 234). 307p. 1999. 30.00 (*0-87169-234-1*) Am Philos.

Bearn, Alexander G., jt. ed. see Lasagna, Louis.

Bearn, Alexander G., jt. ed. see Steinberg, Arthur G.

Bearn, Gordon C. Waking to Wonder: Wittgenstein's Existential Investigations. LC 96-28483. (SUNY Series in Philosophy). 256p. (C). 1997. text 65.50 (*0-7914-3029-4*); pap. text 24.95 (*0-7914-3030-8*) State U NY Pr.

Bearne, Eve. Greater Expectations: Children Reading Writing. (Cassell Education Ser.). (Illus.). 160p. 1995. 100.00 (*0-304-33168-6*); pap. 33.95 (*0-304-33170-8*) Continuum.

— Making Progress in English. LC 97-32907. 376p. (C). 1998. pap. 39.99 (*0-415-15996-2*) Routledge.

— Use of Language Across the Secondary Curriculum. LC 98-21484. 288p. (C). 1998. pap. 25.99 (*0-415-16516-4*) Routledge.

Bearne, Eve, ed. Use of Language. LC 97-44627. 256p. (C). 1998. pap. 25.99 (*0-415-15851-6*) Routledge.

Bearne, Eve & Farrow, Cath. Writing Policy in Action: The Middle Years. (English, Language & Education Ser.). 160p. 1991. pap. 33.95 (*0-335-09444-9*) OpUniv Pr.

***Bearne, Eve & Watson, Victor.** Where Texts & Children Meet. LC 99-36160. 240p. 2000. pap. write for info. (*0-415-20663-4*) Routledge.

***Bearnson, Lisa.** Baby Memories: The Big Idea Book. (Illus.). 164p. 2000. 14.95 (*1-929180-30-6*, Creating Keepsakes) Porchswing Pub.

— Disney Memories: The Big Idea Book. 164p. 2000. 14.95 (*1-929180-05-5*, Creating Keepsakes) Porchswing Pub.

— Joy of Scrapbooking. LC 98-66930. 1998. 24.95 (*0-8487-1829-1*) Oxmoor Hse.

— Mom's Little Book of Displaying Children's Art. (Mom's Little Book Ser.). (Illus.). 96p. 2000. 16.95 (*1-929180-16-0*, Creating Keepsakes) Porchswing Pub.

Bearnson, Lisa & Humphreys, Gayle. Creating Keepsakes Joy of Scrapbooking: Creating Keepsakes. LC 98-66930. (Illus.). 160p. 1998. pap. 19.95 (*0-8487-1840-2*) Oxmoor Hse.

— Joy of Scrapbooking: Complete Guide to Preserving Your Treasured Memories. (Illus.). 128p. 1998. pap. 19.95 (*0-8069-9901-2*) Oxmoor Hse.

***Bearnson, Lisa & McGowan, Siobhan.** Mom's Little Book of Photo Tips. LC 99-39153. (Mom's Little Book of... Tips Ser.). (Illus.). 96p. 1999. 16.95 (*1-929180-12-8*, Creating Keepsakes) Porchswing Pub.

Bearor, Bob. The Battle on Snowshoes. (Illus.). xxiv, 95p. (Orig.). 1997. pap. 15.00 (*0-7884-0619-1*, B106) Heritage Bk.

***Bearor, Bob.** French & Indian War Battlesites: A Controversy. 141p. 2000. pap. 17.16 (*0-7884-1475-5*, 1475) Heritage Bk.

Bearor, Karen A. Irene Rice Pereira: Her Paintings & Philosophy. LC 92-46895. (American Studies). (Illus.). 336p. (C). 1993. 34.95 (*0-292-73858-7*) U of Tex Pr.

— Irene Rice Pereira's Early Work: Embarking on an Eastward Journey. 1994. write for info. (*0-318-72551-7*) Lowe Art Mus.

Bearpark, Keith. Protocols for Application Communication. LC 94-21734. 1994. write for info. (*0-07-709074-8*) McGraw.

Bearse, Alvah W. Physic Point: Memories of Hyannis (1914-1929) (Illus.). 100p. 1976. pap. 14.95 (*0-85699-203-8*) Chatham Pr.

Bearse, Austin. Reminiscences of Fugitive Slave Law Days in Boston. LC 74-82170. (Anti-Slavery Crusade in America Ser.). 1976. reprint ed. 18.95 (*0-405-00609-8*) Ayer.

Bearse, Peter J. The Evaluation of Business Incubation Projects. 98p. 1993. pap. 50.00 (*1-887183-19-1*) NBIA.

Bearsley, Richard K. Temporal & Areal Relationships in Central California Archaeology, Pt. 1. fac. ed. (Reports of the University of California Archaeological Survey: No. 24). (Illus.). 91p. 1954. reprint ed. pap. 10.31 (*1-55567-344-9*) Coyote Press.

Bearson, Jerome A. Chemical Creativity: Ideas From the Work of Woodward, Huckel, Meerwein & Others. LC 99-206238. 198p. 1999. pap. 62.95 (*3-527-29754-5*) Wiley.

Bearss, Ed. First Manassas Battlefield Map Study. (Virginia Civil War Battles & Leaders Ser.). (Illus.). 108p. 1991. 27.95 (*1-56190-015-X*) H E Howard.

— River of Lost Opportunities: The Civil War on the James River 1861-1862. (Virginia Civil War Battles & Leaders Ser.). (Illus.). 202p. 1995. 19.95 (*1-56190-078-8*) H E Howard.

Bearss, Ed & Calkins, Chris. The Battle of Five Forks. (Virginia Civil War Battles & Leaders Ser.). (Illus.). 131p. 1985. 19.95 (*0-930919-20-3*) H E Howard.

Bearss, Edwin C. The Battle of Cowpens: A Documented Narrative & Troop Movement Maps. (Illus.). 64p. 1996. reprint ed. pap. 6.95 (*1-57072-045-2*) Overmountain Pr.

— Hardluck Ironclad: The Sinking & Salvage of the Cairo. rev. ed. LC 79-25985. xiv, 258p. 1980. pap. 17.95 (*0-8071-0684-4*) La State U Pr.

— Vicksburg Campaign, 3 vols., Set. (Illus.). 2219p. 1991. 125.00 (*0-89029-308-2*) Morningside Bkshop.

— Vicksburg Campaign: Grant Strikes the Fatal Blow, Vol. II. (Illus.). 689p. 1991. 42.50 (*0-89029-313-9*) Morningside Bkshop.

— Vicksburg Campaign: Unvexed to the Sea, Vol. III. (Illus.). 761p. 1991. 42.50 (*0-89029-516-6*) Morningside Bkshop.

— Vicksburg Campaign: Vicksburg is the Key, Vol. I. (Illus.). 769p. 1991. 42.50 (*0-89029-312-0*) Morningside Bkshop.

Bearss, Edwin C. & Gibson, A. M. Fort Smith: Little Gibraltar on the Arkansas. LC 68-31377. (Illus.). 1988. reprint ed. pap. 13.95 (*0-8061-1232-8*) U of Okla Pr.

Bearss, Edwin C., jt. auth. see Wertz, Jay.

Bearup, George F., jt. auth. see Lowe, Richard C.

Bearup, Jeffrey T. Grip Check for Tennis: A Reference Guide to Grips. 28p. 1994. pap. 10.95 (*0-9640781-0-4*) Grip Check.

Beary, Evalena. Sugar Loaf Springs: Heber's Elegant Watering Place. (Illus.). 120p. 1985. write for info. (*0-318-59487-0*) River Road Pr.

Beary, Kevin. Florentine Locutions: A Study of Blasphemous & Obscene Expressions in Florentine Italian. 2nd ed. 96p. (Orig.). 1992. pap. 8.00 (*1-881355-00-4*) Intemprte Stage.

— In Medias Res: Including The Moment Before & Women's Williams. 104p. (Orig.). 1991. pap. 5.00 (*1-881355-02-0*) Intemprte Stage.

— The Savaged States of America. 323p. 1999. pap. 10.00 (*1-881355-04-7*, In Qua Urbe) Intemprte Stage.

— Sealed Containers. 28p. 1991. pap. 4.00 (*1-881355-03-9*) Intemprte Stage.

***Beary, Michael J.** Black Bishop: Edward T. Demby & the Struggle for Racial Equality in the Episcopal Church. LC 00-9541. (Studies in Anglican History). 2001. write for info. (*0-252-02618-7*) U Ch Pr.

Beary, Shaun. London's Good Coffee Shops. (Illus.). 76p. (Orig.). 1997. pap. 5.95 (*0-9528322-0-8*, Pub. by Portfolio) Seven Hills Bk.

Beas, Ricardo, tr. see Lozoff, Bo.

Beasant, John. Stalin's Silver. LC 99-21627. 224p. 1999. text 24.95 (*0-312-20590-2*) St Martin.

Beasant, Pam. Space. LC 92-53103. (One-Thousand Facts about...Ser.). (Illus.). 48p. (J). (gr. 4-7). 1992. pap. 8.95 (*1-85697-811-7*, Kingfisher) LKC.

Beasant, Pam & Findly, Ian. Electronics. (Introductions Ser.). (Illus.). 48p. (J). (gr. 6-12). 1985. pap. 7.95 (*0-86020-809-5*, Usborne) EDC.

Beasant, Pam & Smith, Alastair. How to Draw Maps & Charts. (How to Draw Ser.). (Illus.). 32p. (J). (gr. 4-7). 1993. pap. 4.95 (*0-7460-1002-8*, Usborne) EDC.

— How to Draw Maps & Charts. (How to Draw Ser.). (Illus.). 32p. (J). (gr. 4 up). 1993. lib. bdg. 12.95 (*0-88110-650-X*, Usborne) EDC.

Beasch, Anthony, tr. see John, Nicholas, ed.

Beaser, Richard. Outsmarting Diabetes: A Breakthrough Approach for Reducing the Effects of Insulin-Dependent Diabetes. 256p. 1994. pap. 14.95 (*0-471-34694-2*) Wiley.

Beaser, Richard S. Outsmarting Diabetes: A Breakthrough Approach for Reducing the Effects of Insulin-Dependent Diabetes. LC 94-11324. 256p. 1994. pap. 14.95 (*1-56561-051-2*) Wiley.

Beaser, Richard S. & Hill, Joan V. Manual Joslin para la Diabetes: The Joslin Guide to Diabetes. 352p. 1996. per. 15.00 (*0-684-82387-X*, Libros) S&S Trade Pap.

Beaser, Richard S., et al. The Joslin Guide to Diabetes: A Program for Managing Your Treatment. LC 95-12169. 352p. 1995. pap. 15.00 (*0-684-80208-2*) S&S Trade Pap.

Beaslai, P. S. Michael Collins & the Making of a New Ireland, 2 vols. 1985. reprint ed. 130.00 (*0-527-41198-1*) Periodicals Srv.

Beasley. Sexual Economyths. LC 94-9072. 1994. text 59.95 (*0-312-12234-9*) St Martin.

— Understanding EKGs: A Practical Approach. LC 99-14784. 192p. 1999. pap. text 37.00 (*0-8359-8571-7*) Global Press.

Beasley, jt. auth. see Henry.

Beasley, jt. auth. see Stack.

Beasley, A. W. Fellowship of Three. (Illus.). 84p. 1993. 29.95 (*0-86417-542-6*, Pub. by Kangaroo Pr) Seven Hills Bk.

Beasley, Amy, jt. auth. see Beasley, Bob.

Beasley, Angela. Minutes from the Great Women's Coffee Club. 1997. pap. text 6.95 (*1-887655-33-6*) Walnut Gr Pr.

Beasley, Barry. The Rivers of South Carolina. LC 99-35443. (Illus.). 128p. 1999. 39.95 (*1-56579-348-X*) Westcliffe Pubs.

Beasley, Bob. The Wisdom of Proverbs. 630p. Date not set. pap. 17.99 (*1-885358-53-9*, LP46831, Lgacy Pr) Rainbow CA.

Beasley, Bob & Beasley, Amy. Wisdom for Women: A Daily Devotional Based on Proverbs 31. 208p. pap. 9.99 (*1-885358-31-8*, LP46403) Rainbow CA.

Beasley, Bob & Getz, Gene. Proverbs for Promise Keeping. (Illus.). 192p. 1996. pap. 12.99 (*1-885358-21-0*, DB46401) Rainbow CA.

***Beasley, Brenda M. & West, Michael C.** Understanding 12 Lead EKG's: A Practical Approach. 288p. 2001. pap. text 38.67 (*0-13-027281-7*, Prentice Hall) P-H.

***Beasley, Bruce.** Signs & Abominations. LC 00-9415. (Wesleyan Poetry Ser.). 2000. write for info. (*0-8195-6456-7*, Wesleyan Univ Pr) U Pr of New Eng.

Beasley, Bruce. Summer Mystagogia. 96p. 1996. pap. 14.95 (*0-87081-438-9*) Univ Pr Colo.

***Beasley, Cecil W.** Atonement. 688p. 1998. pap. 31.00 (*0-8059-4350-1*) Dorrance.

Beasley, Chris. Sexual Economyths: Conceiving a Feminist Economics, Vol. 1. LC 94-9072. 1994. pap. 19.95 (*0-312-12235-7*) St Martin.

Beasley, Conger, Jr. The Blood of Dead Poets. Memmott, David, ed. LC 96-212363. (Wordcraft Speculative Writers Ser.). (Illus.). 96p. (Orig.). 1995. pap. 9.95 (*1-877655-15-5*) Wordcraft Oregon.

— Canyon De Chelly: The Timeless Fold. (Illus.). 128p. 1988. per. 8.95 (*0-9604462-4-9*) Sweetlight.

— Colorado Close-Up. LC 96-47460. (Illus.). 96p. (Orig.). 1997. pap. 11.95 (*1-55591-325-3*) Fulcrum Pub.

— Eyes Open in the Dark. LC 96-22241. 120p. (Orig.). 1996. pap. 14.45 (*1-886157-05-7*) BkMk.

— My Manhattan. 96p. (Orig.). 1986. pap. 3.95 (*0-9617499-0-3*) Woods Colt Pr.

— Stravinsky's Dream: A Story. 10p. (Orig.). 1994. pap. 3.00 (*1-884235-06-9*) Helicon Nine Eds.

— Sundancers & River Demons: Essays on Landscape & Ritual. LC 89-5168. 241p. (Orig.). 1990. pap. 18.00 (*1-55728-130-0*) U of Ark Pr.

— We Are a People in This World: The Lakota Sioux & the Massacre at Wounded Knee. LC 94-48101. 240p. 1995. pap. 16.00 (*1-55728-386-9*); text 20.00 (*1-55728-387-7*) U of Ark Pr.

Beasley, Conger, Jr., et al, texts. The Sierra Club Guide to the National Parks of the Rocky Mountains & the Great Plains: The Rocky Mountains & the Great Plains. rev. ed. LC 95-11447. (Sierra Club Guides to the National Parks Ser.). (Illus.). 280p. 1995. pap. 24.95 (*0-679-76496-8*) Stewart Tabori & Chang.

Beasley, Darryl A. Everything about Home Loans: A Financial Guide to Buying, Selling, Building, or Refinancing a Home. (Illus.). 333p. (Orig.). 1994. pap. 19.95 (*0-9636189-8-9*) Chase Pub LA.

***Beasley, David.** Aspects of Love: Helen, Caravetti, Adam. 168p. 2000. pap. 9.95 (*0-915317-11-7*, Pub. by Davus Pub) U of Toronto Pr.

Beasley, David. Chocolate for the Poor: A Story of Rape in 1805. LC 96-151015. 280p. 1996. pap. 11.95 (*0-915317-04-4*, Pub. by Davus Pub) U of Toronto Pr.

— Douglas MacAgy & the Foundations of Modern Art Curatorship. LC 98-154442. (Illus.). 168p. 1998. pap. 19.95 (*0-915317-09-5*, Pub. by Davus Pub) U of Toronto Pr.

— The Grand Conspiracy: A New York Library Mystery. LC 97-180268. 176p. 1997. pap. 10.95 (*0-915317-06-0*, Pub. by Davus Pub) U of Toronto Pr.

— Hamilton Romance: A Hamilton-Toronto Nexus. 224p. 1996. pap. 14.95 (*0-915317-05-2*, Pub. by Davus Pub) U of Toronto Pr.

— The Jenny: A New York Library Detective Novel. LC 95-146479. 110p. 1994. pap. 7.95 (*0-915317-03-6*, Pub. by Davus Pub) U of Toronto Pr.

— Pagan Summer. LC 96-900672. 256p. 1998. pap. 10.95 (*0-915317-07-9*, Pub. by Davus Pub) U of Toronto Pr.

— The Suppression of the Automobile: Skullduggery at the Crossroads, 81. LC 87-31788. (Contributions in Economics & Economic History Ser.: No. 81). 192p. 1988. 52.95 (*0-313-26144-X*, BSY/, Greenwood Pr) Greenwood.

— That Other God. 340p. 1993. pap. 18.95 (*0-915317-02-8*, Pub. by Davus Pub) U of Toronto Pr.

— Through Paphlagonia with a Donkey: An Adventure in the Turkish Isfendyars. (Illus.). 246p. 1983. pap. 9.95 (*0-915317-00-1*, Pub. by Davus Pub) U of Toronto Pr.

— Understanding Modern Art: The Boundless Spirit of Clay Edgar Spohn. LC 99-159703. (Illus.). 160p. 1999. pap. 34.95 (*0-915317-10-9*, Pub. by Davus Pub) U of Toronto Pr.

— Who Really Invented the Automobile? Skulduggery at the Crossroads. 2nd rev. ed. LC HD9710.A2B42 1966. (Illus.). 192p. 1997. pap. 13.95 (*0-915317-08-7*, Pub. by Davus Pub) U of Toronto Pr.

Beasley, Delilah L. Negro Trail Blazers of California. LC 73-88400. 317p. 1969. reprint ed. lib. bdg. 35.00 (*0-8371-1768-2*, BEN&) Greenwood.

Beasley, Donald E., et al, eds. National Heat Transfer Conference: Fundamental Experimental Techniques in Heat Transfer, Thermal Hydraulics of Advanced Nuclear Reactors, Heat & Mass Transfer in Supercritical Liquid Proceedings, National Heat Transfer Conference (32nd, 1997, Baltimore, Maryland. LC 97-74086. (HTD Ser.: Vol. 350). 255p. 1997. pap. 100.00 (*0-7918-1817-9*) ASME.

Beasley, Donald E., jt. auth. see Figliola, Richard J.

Beasley, Donald E., jt. auth. see Figliola, Richard S.

Beasley, Donna. Family Pride. 1997. pap. 12.95 (*0-614-25360-8*, Macmillan Ref) Mac Lib Ref.

Beasley, Ellen. The Alleys & Back Buildings of Galveston. LC 95-13938. (Illus.). 200p. 1996. 39.95 (*0-89263-328-X*) Tex A&M Univ Pr.

***Beasley, Ellen.** The Corner Store: An American Tradition, Galveston Style. (Illus.). 48p. 1999. pap. 16.95 (*0-9619752-9-6*) Natl Bldg Mus.

Beasley, Ellen & Fox, Stephen. Galveston Architecture Guidebook. LC 96-9889. (Illus.). 400p. (C). 1996. pap. 17.95 (*0-89263-346-8*) Tex A&M Univ Pr.

Beasley, Faith E. Revising Memory: Women's Fiction & Memoirs in Seventeenth-Century France. LC 90-31075. 296p. (C). 1991. text 45.00 (*0-8135-1585-8*) Rutgers U Pr.

Beasley, Faith E. & Jensen, Katharine A., eds. Approaches to Teaching Lafayette's Princess of Cleves. LC 98-35540. (Approaches to Teaching World Literature Ser.: No. 61). xi, 211 p. 1998. pap. 18.00 (*0-87352-746-1*, AP61P); lib. bdg. 37.50 (*0-87352-745-3*, AP61C) Modern Lang.

Beasley, Heather, jt. compiled by see Hammer, Patricia C.

***Beasley, Henry R.** The Eleanor Roosevelt Encyclopedia. Beasley, Maurine H. & Shulman, Holly C., eds. LC 00-23530. 2000. lib. bdg. write for info. (*0-313-30181-6*) Greenwood.

Beasley, Ina. Before the Wind Changed: People, Places & Education in the Sudan. Starkey, Janet, ed. (Oriental & African Archives, Ser.: No. 1). (Illus.). 524p. 1992. text 65.00 (*0-19-726110-8*) OUP.

Beasley, J. Michal, tr. see David, Thomas.

Beasley, J. W. & Grogan, E. W. Guide to Basic Electrocardiography. LC 90-7327. (Illus.). 180p. (C). 1990. spiral bd. 47.00 (*0-306-43296-X*, Kluwer Plenum) Kluwer Academic.

***Beasley, James M.** Witham: Inner & Outer Worlds, Paintings by Vernon Witham. (Illus.). 16p. 1999. 3.00 (*0-934306-21-4*) Springfield.

***Beasley, James M., intro.** Wayne Thiebaud: Works on Paper from the Family Collections. 32p. 1998. 15.00 (*0-934306-20-6*) Springfield.

Beasley, James R. Introduction to the Bible. LC 90-48377. 1991. pap. 24.95 (*0-687-19493-8*) Abingdon.

Beasley, Jerry. In Search of the Ultimate Martial Art: The Jeet Kune Do Experience. (Illus.). 208p. 1989. pap. 25.00 (*0-87364-516-2*) Paladin Pr.
— The Way of No Way. (Illus.). 160p. 1992. pap. 19.95 (*0-87364-668-1*) Paladin Pr.
Beasley, Jerry, ed. The Development of American Karate: History & Skills. LC 83-62681. (Illus.). 96p. 1983. pap. 9.95 (*0-943736-02-1*) Ormsby.
Beasley, Jerry, jt. auth. see Lewis, Joe.
Beasley, Jerry C. Tobias Smollett: Novelist. LC 97-37492. 1998. 45.00 (*0-8203-1971-6*) U of Ga Pr.
Beasley, Jerry C., jt. ed. see Hogan, Robert T.
Beasley, Jerry C., ed. see Hoywood, Eliza.
Beasley, Jerry C., ed. see Smollett, Tobias George.
Beasley, John E. Advances in Linear & Integer Programming. LC 97-158875. (Oxford Lectures Series in Mathematics & Its Applications: No. 4). (Illus.). 302p. 1996. text 75.00 (*0-19-853856-1*) OUP.
Beasley, Joseph D. & Knightly, Susan. Food for Recovery: The Next Step. LC 93-25244. 1994. 14.00 (*0-517-58694-0*, Crown) Crown Pub Group.
***Beasley, Mark S.** Auditing Cases. (Illus.). 250p. 1999. pap. text 30.00 (*0-13-080001-5*) P-H.
— Auditing Cases. (C). 2000. text. write for info. (*0-13-086688-1*) P-H.
Beasley, Mary. Mission on the Margins. 110p. 1998. pap. 13.95 (*0-7188-2966-2*, Lutterworth-Parkwest) Parkwest Pubns.
***Beasley, Mary Carlisle.** A Sister Is... 128p. 2000. pap. 4.95 (*1-58334-061-0*, Pub. by Walnut Gr Pr) Midpt Trade.
***Beasley, Mary Carlisle & Freeman, Criswell.** Girlfriends Forever. 128p. 2000. pap. 4.95 (*1-58334-064-5*, Pub. by Walnut Gr Pr) Midpt Trade.
— A Grandmother's Love Lasts a Lifetime. 128p. 2000. pap. 4.95 (*1-58334-059-9*, Pub. by Walnut Gr Pr) Midpt Trade.
— Mothers Change the World... One Child at a Time. 128p. 2000. pap. 4.95 (*1-58334-058-0*, Pub. by Walnut Gr Pr) Midpt Trade.
— Women Say the Wisest Things. 128p. 2000. pap. 4.95 (*1-58334-076-9*, Pub. by Walnut Gr Pr) Midpt Trade.
Beasley, Maureen. Five Centuries of Artists in Sutton: A Biographical Dictionary of Artists Associated with Sutton, London. (C). 1985. 90.00 (*0-907335-19-5*, Pub. by Sutton Libs & Arts) St Mut.
Beasley, Maurine H. Eleanor Roosevelt & the Media: A Public Quest for Self-Fulfillment. LC 86-19281. (Illus.). 258p. 1987. text 27.50 (*0-252-01376-X*) U of Ill Pr.
— The First Women Washington Correspondents, Vol. M4. 1976. 5.00 (*1-888028-02-5*) GWU Ctr WAS.
***Beasley, Maurine H. & Gibbons, Sheila J.** Taking Their Place: A Documentary History of Women in Journalism. 2nd ed. 384p. 2002. pap. 27.50 (*1-891136-07-0*) Strata Pub Co.
Beasley, Maurine H. & Theus, Kathryn T. The New Majority: A Look at What the Preponderance of Women in Journalism Education Means to the Schools & to the Professions. LC 88-2456. 186p. (Orig.). (C). 1988. pap. text 21.00 (*0-8191-6915-3*) U Pr of Amer.
Beasley, Maurine H., ed. see Beasley, Henry R.
Beasley, Maurine H., ed. see Hickok, Lorena.
Beasley, Michael. Reliability for Engineers, an Introduction. (Illus.). 270p. (C). 1991. pap. text 35.00 (*0-333-54238-X*, Pub. by Macmillan Ed) Scholium Intl.
Beasley-Murray, George. Word Biblical Commentary on John, Vol. 36. rev. ed. 592p. 1999. 29.99 (*0-7852-0940-9*) Nelson.
Beasley-Murray, George R. Gospel of Life: Theology in the Fourth Gospel. LC 91-34426. 132p. 1991. pap. 9.95 (*0-943575-76-1*) Hendrickson MA.
— Jesus & the Last Days: The Interpretation of the Olivet Discourse. LC 92-46769. 520p. 1993. 29.95 (*0-943575-37-0*) Hendrickson MA.
— John. (Biblical Commentary Ser.: Vol. 36). 29.99 (*0-8499-0235-5*) Word Pub.
— Preaching the Gospel from the Gospels. rev. ed. 282p. 1996. pap. 16.95 (*1-56563-166-8*) Hendrickson MA.
Beasley-Murray, Paul. Power for God's Sake: Power & Abuse in the Local Church. xiv, 194p. 1998. reprint ed. pap. 14.99 (*0-85364-899-9*, Pub. by Paternoster Pub) OM Literature.
Beasley, Norman. The Cross & the Crown. 1973. pap. 9.95 (*0-933062-12-5*) R H Sommer.
Beasley, Norman, jt. auth. see Smith, R.
Beasley, Norman, jt. auth. see Smith, Rixey.
Beasley, R. P., et al. Erosion & Sediment Pollution Control. 2nd ed. LC 83-12983. (Illus.). 366p. (C). 1972. text 49.95 (*0-8138-1530-4*) Iowa St U Pr.
Beasley, Reyna, jt. auth. see Roetzheim, William H,.
Beasley, Richard. Role of Beta Agonist Therapy in Asthma Mortality. 288p. 1993. lib. bdg. 199.00 (*0-8493-6761-1*, QR201) CRC Pr.
Beasley, Robert C. The Commandments of Christ: A Topical Study of Christian Discipleship. LC 98-50068. 176p. 1999. pap. 8.99 (*0-87552-171-1*) P & R Pubng.
Beasley, Ruth, jt. auth. see Reinisch, June M.
Beasley, Sonia. The Spirulina Cookbook: Recipes for Rejuvenating the Body. LC 81-40027. (Illus.). 184p. (Orig.). 1981. pap. 12.95 (*0-916438-39-2*) Dr Hills Technol.
Beasley, Spencer W., et al. Essential Pediatric Surgery. (Arnold Publication). (Illus.). 200p. 1996. text 89.50 (*0-340-56017-7*) OUP.
Beasley, Thomas T. Homebased Business - Your Guide to Success: How to Develop & Run Any Homebased Business. abr. ed. xv, 79p. pap. 9.95 (*0-9658763-0-6*) Cedar Ridge.
***Beasley-Topliffe, Keith.** Upper Room Spiritual Classics Series II. 1998. pap. text 24.00 (*0-8358-0853-X*) Upper Room Bks.
Beasley, Val R., ed. Trichothecene Mycotoxicosis: Pathophysiologic Effects, 2 Vols., Vol. I. 208p. 1989. 109.00 (*0-8493-5088-3*, RA1242, CRC Reprint) Franklin.
— Trichothecene Mycotoxicosis: Pathophysiologic Effects, 2 Vols., Vol. II. 224p. 1989. 121.00 (*0-8493-5089-1*, RA1242, CRC Reprint) Franklin.
Beasley, W. Conger, Jr. Over DeSoto's Bones. 2nd ed. Burmaster, Orvis C., ed. LC 78-74299. (Ahsahta Press Modern & Contemporary Poets of the West Ser.). 72p. 1979. pap. 6.95 (*0-916272-11-7*) Ahsahta Pr.
Beasley, W. G. The Japanese Experience: A Short History of Japan. LC 99-202382. 325p. 1999. 27.50 (*0-520-22050-1*, Pub. by U CA Pr) Cal Prin Full Svc.
***Beasley, W. G.** Japanese Experience: A Short History of Japan. (History of Civilization Ser.). 317p. 2000. pap. text 15.95 (*0-520-22560-0*, Pub. by U CA Pr) Cal Prin Full Svc.
Beasley, W. G. The Rise of Modern Japan. 306p. 1998. pap. text 15.00 (*0-7881-5583-0*) DIANE Pub.
***Beasley, W. G.** The Rise of Modern Japan: Political Economic & Social Change 1850. 2000. pap. 18.95 (*0-312-23373-6*) St Martin.
***Beasley, Walter.** The Bottom Line: On Tombstones, That Is. (Illus.). 128p. 1999. pap. 15.95 (*0-913383-67-8*) McClanahan Pub.
Beasley, Wendy. Beginner's Guide to Competitive Obedience. 1999. 12.95 (*1-85279-114-4*) TFH Pubns.
— Beginner's Guide to Working & Trials. 1999. 12.95 (*1-85279-113-6*) TFH Pubns.
Beasley, William G. Great Britain & the Opening of Japan, 1834-1858. LC 95-219761. (Japan Library). 248p. (Orig.). (C). 1996. pap. text 21.00 (*1-873410-43-3*, Pub. by Curzon Pr Ltd) UH Pr.
— Japan Encounters the Barbarian: Japanese Travellers in America & Europe, 1860 - 1873. LC 95-7979. 252p. 1995. 32.50 (*0-300-06324-5*) Yale U Pr.
Beasley, William G. Japanese Imperialism, 1894-1945. (Illus.). 294p. 1991. reprint ed. pap. text 28.00 (*0-19-822168-1*, 9233) OUP.
Beasley, William G. The Meiji Restoration. LC 72-78868. xiv, 514p. 1972. 65.00 (*0-8047-0815-0*) Stanford U Pr.
— The Rise of Modern Japan: Political, Economic & Social Change since 1850. 2nd ed. 336p. 1995. pap. 18.95 (*0-312-12751-0*) St Martin.
Beasom, Sam L. & Roberson, Sheila F., eds. Game Harvest Management. LC 84-72724. (Illus.). 300p. 1985. 20.00 (*0-912229-08-X*); pap. 15.00 (*0-912229-09-8*) CK Wildlife Res.
Beason. Now I Get. 2nd ed. 1999. pap. text 24.95 (*0-312-20135-4*) St Martin.
— Now I Get It. 1997. pap. text 5.00 (*0-312-15287-6*) St Martin.
— Now I Get It. 5th ed. 1996. pap. text 31.45 incl. audio compact disk (*0-312-15743-6*) St Martin.
Beason, Doug, jt. auth. see Anderson, Kevin.
Beason, Doug, jt. auth. see Anderson, Kevin J.
Beasor, Tom, jt. auth. see Steele, Paul T.
Beasse, Pierre. The New & Rational Treatise of Dowsing According to the Methods of Physical Radiesthesia. 214p. 1996. reprint ed. spiral bd. 18.50 (*0-7873-0083-7*) Hlth Research.
Beat, Nik, et al. Mad Angels & Amphetamines: An Anthology. LC 96-136690. 96p. pap. 12.95 (*1-895837-14-6*) Insomniac.
Beate, Bernardo, tr. see Tilling, Robert I., ed.
Beater, Jack. Pirates & Buried Treasure on Florida Islands. rev. ed. LC 65-1579. (Illus.). 118p. 1959. pap. 4.95 (*0-8200-1019-7*) Great Outdoors.
Beath, John & Katsoulacos, Yannis. The Economic Theory of Product Differentiation. (Illus.). 214p. (C). 1991. pap. text 19.95 (*0-521-33552-3*) Cambridge U Pr.
— The Economic Theory of Product Differentiation. (Illus.). 214p. (C). 1991. text 59.95 (*0-521-33526-4*) Cambridge U Pr.
Beath, Mary & Lopez, Barry. Land. (Illus.). (Orig.). 1989. pap. 12.95 (*0-685-26564-1*) P P Rindge.
Beath, Warren N. Bloodletter, Vol. 1. 1996. mass mkt. 4.99 (*0-8125-3393-3*) Tor Bks.
— The Death of James Dean. LC 86-45520. (Illus.). 224p. 1988. pap. 11.95 (*0-8021-3143-3*, Grove) Grove-Atltic.
— Shock Lines. 384p. 1993. mass mkt. 4.50 (*0-8217-4036-9*, Zebra Kensgtn) Kensgtn Pub Corp.
— Who Killed James Dean? (Orig.). 1995. 4.99 (*0-8125-3873-0*) Tor Bks.
Beatie, Russel H. Saddles. LC 79-6708. (Illus.). 408p. 1981. 69.95 (*0-8061-1584-X*) U of Okla Pr.
Beatina, Mary. Narayan: A Study in Transcendence. LC 93-4941. (Studies of World Literature in English: Vol. 3). XII, 154p. (C). 1994. text 41.95 (*0-8204-2137-5*) P Lang Pubng.
***Beating, Stephen.** Cut Throat: High Stakes & Killer Moves on the Electronic Frontier. LC 99-34764. (Illus.). 336p. 1999. pap. 18.00 (*1-55566-248-X*) Johnson Bks.
Beatles. The Beatles: Illustrated Lyrics. Aldridge, Alan, ed. LC 98-43707. (Illus.). 272p. 1999. 19.98 (*1-57912-058-X*) Blck Dog & Leventhal.
— The Beatles: 1962-1966. 120p. 1994. otabind 24.95 (*0-7935-3456-9*) H Leonard.
— The Complete Beatles Lyrics. 224p. 1992. per. 17.95 (*0-7935-1537-8*, 00308137) H Leonard.
Beatley, Janice C., jt. auth. see ERDA Technical Information Center Staff.
Beatley, Ralph, jt. auth. see Birkhoff, George D.
Beatley, Timothy. A Bibliography of Growth Management Sources. LC 85-31369. (CPL Bibliographies Ser.: No. 166). 1985. 10.00 (*0-86602-166-3*, Sage Prdcls Pr) Sage.
— Ethical Dilemmas in Hazard Mitigation. 57p. 1999. reprint ed. pap. text 20.00 (*0-7881-8033-9*) DIANE Pub.
— Ethical Land Use: Principles of Policy & Planning. LC 93-40870. 352p. (C). 1994. text 55.00 (*0-8018-4698-6*); pap. text 18.95 (*0-8018-4699-4*) Johns Hopkins.
— Habitat Conservation Planning: Endangered Species & Urban Growth. LC 93-22810. (Illus.). 272p. (Orig.). 1994. pap. 17.95 (*0-292-70806-8*) U of Tex Pr.
Beatley, Timothy & Brower, David. An Introduction to Coastal Zone Management. LC 94-13333. 272p. 1994. text 55.00 (*1-55963-280-1*); pap. text 32.50 (*1-55963-281-X*) Island Pr.
Beatley, Timothy & Manning, Kristy. The Ecology of Place: Planning for Environment, Economy & Community. LC 97-15863. 225p. 1997. pap. text. write for info. (*1-55963-478-2*) Island Pr.
Beatley, Timothy, jt. auth. see Berke, Philip R.
Beatley, Timothy, jt. auth. see Godschalk, David.
Beato, Felice, jt. auth. see Harris, David.
***Beato, Virgilio I., et al.** 40 Anos de Revolucion Cubana: El Legado de Castro. LC 99-62944. (Coleccion Cuba y Sus Jueces). (SPA.). 467p. 1999. 29.95 (*0-89729-901-9*) Ediciones.
Beato, Virgilio I., jt. auth. see Ros, Enrique.
Beaton, Alan. Left Side, Right Side. LC 85-52037. 370p. 1986. 47.50 (*0-300-03549-7*) Yale U Pr.
Beaton, Albert E. Mathematics Achievement in The Middle School Years: Third International Mathematics & Science Study. 248p. 1997. per. 21.00 (*0-16-063627-2*) USGPO.
— Science Achievement in the Middle School Years: Third International Mathematics & Science Study. 240p. 1997. per. 22.00 (*0-16-063628-0*) USGPO.
Beaton, Albert E., et al. Mathematics Achievement in the Middle School Years: IEA's 3rd International Mathematics. LC 96-71251. (Illus.). 244p. (Orig.). 1996. pap. 30.00 (*1-889938-02-5*) Intl Study Ctr.
— Science Achievement in the Middle School Years: IEA's Third International Mathematics & Science Study. LC 96-71250. (Illus.). 240p. (Orig.). 1996. pap. 30.00 (*1-889838-03-9*) Intl Study Ctr.
Beaton, Albert E., jt. ed. see Juster, Francis T.
Beaton, Betsy. Boy with Green Hair: Manuscript Edition. 1961. pap. 13.00 (*0-8222-0144-5*) Dramatists Play.
Beaton, C. F. & Hewitt, Geoffrey F., eds. Physical Property Data for the Design Engineer. 500p. 1988. 94.95 (*0-89116-739-0*) Hemisp Pub.
Beaton, Cecil. Cecil Beaton: Photographs 1920-1970. LC 95-69585. (Illus.). 320p. 1995. 85.00 (*1-55670-423-X*) Stewart Tabori & Chang.
— Indian Diary & Album. (Illus.). 96p. 1991. text 24.95 (*0-19-212299-1*) OUP.
Beaton, Charles R. & Maser, Chris. Reuniting Ecology & Economy. LC 99-199866. (Sustainable Community Development Ser.). 108p. 1999. 34.95 (*1-57444-189-2*) St Lucie Pr.
Beaton, Charles R., jt. auth. see Maser, Chris.
***Beaton, Claire.** One Moose, Twenty Mice. (Illus.). 32p. (J). (ps-k). 2000. pap. 6.99 (*1-84148-129-7*) Barefoot Bks NY.
Beaton, Clare. Animals/English-French. (Bilingual First Bks.). (ENG & FRE., Illus.). 24p. (J). (ps up). 1997. pap. text 3.95 (*0-7641-0037-8*) Barron.
— Animals/English-Spanish. LC 96-85829. (Bilingual First Bks.). (ENG & SPA., Illus.). 24p. (J). (ps up). 1997. pap. 3.95 (*0-7641-0038-6*) Barron.
***Beaton, Clare.** Are We There Yet? (Illus.). 24p. (J). (gr. k-4). 2000. pap. 5.95 (*1-874735-77-8*, Pub. by B Small Publishing) BHB Intl.
Beaton, Clare. Beads, Badges, & Bangles. LC 95-60777. (Fun to Do Ser.). (Illus.). 32p. (J). (gr. 2 up). 1995. lib. bdg. 15.95 (*1-887238-00-X*) Fitzgerald.
***Beaton, Clare.** The Box Book: Original Projects for All Ages. (Illus.). 103p. 1999. reprint ed. text 23.00 (*0-7881-6779-0*) DIANE Pub.
Beaton, Clare. Clothes/English-French. (Bilingual First Bks.). (FRE & ENG., Illus.). 24p. (J). (ps up). 1997. pap. 3.95 (*0-7641-0039-4*) Barron.
— Clothes/English-Spanish. LC 96-85824. (Bilingual First Bks.). (SPA & ENG., Illus.). 24p. (J). (ps up). 1997. pap. text 3.95 (*0-7641-0040-8*) Barron.
— Clown Activity Box: Book, Squirty Rose, Red Nose, & Face Paints. (Illus.). (J). (ps up). 1997. pap. 11.95 (*1-85479-207-5*) Trans-Atl Phila.
— The Clown Activity Box: Color Book, Red Nose, Squirting Flower & Face Paints. (Illus.). (J). (ps up). 1997. 11.95 (*1-85479-211-3*) Trans-Atl Phila.
— Colors/English-French. LC 96-85794. (Bilingual First Bks.). (FRE & ENG., Illus.). 24p. (J). (ps up). 1997. pap. 3.95 (*0-7641-0032-7*) Barron.
— Colors/English-Spanish. LC 96-85814. (Bilingual First Bks.). (SPA & ENG., Illus.). 24p. (J). (ps up). 1997. pap. 3.95 (*0-7641-0033-5*) Barron.
— The Easter Activity Book. (Illus.). 24p. (J). (gr. k-5). 1996. pap. 4.95 (*0-8120-9460-3*) Barron.
— Family: English/Spanish. LC 96-85809. (Bilingual First Bks.). (ENG & SPA., Illus.). 24p. (J). (ps up). 1997. pap. text 3.95 (*0-7641-0042-4*) Barron.
— Family/English-French. LC 96-85789. (Bilingual First Bks.). (FRE & ENG., Illus.). 24p. (J). (ps up). 1997. pap. 3.95 (*0-7641-0041-6*) Barron.
— Halloween Activity Book. (Illus.). 24p. (J). (ps-5). 1996. pap. 4.95 (*0-8120-9467-0*) Barron.
— Masks. LC 95-60779. (Fun to Do Ser.). (Illus.). 32p. (J). (gr. 2 up). 1995. lib. bdg. 15.95 (*1-887238-02-6*) Fitzgerald.
***Beaton, Clare.** Mother Goose Remembers. (Illus.). 64p. (J). (ps-2). 2000. 16.99 (*1-84148-073-8*) Barefoot Bks NY.
Beaton, Clare. Numbers/English-French. LC 96-85799. (Bilingual First Bks.). (FRE & ENG., Illus.). 24p. (J). (ps up). 1997. pap. 3.95 (*0-7641-0034-3*) Barron.
— Numbers/English-Spanish. LC 96-85834. (Bilingual First Bks.). (SPA & ENG., Illus.). 24p. (J). (ps up). 1997. pap. 3.95 (*0-7641-0035-1*) Barron.
***Beaton, Clare.** One Moose, Twenty Mice. (Illus.). 32p. (J). (ps). 2000. reprint ed. bds. 6.99 (*1-84148-285-4*) Barefoot Bks NY.
Beaton, Clare. Opposites - English-French. (Bilingual First Bks.). (FRE & ENG., Illus.). 24p. 1997. pap. text 3.95 (*0-7641-0030-0*) Barron.
— Opposites - English-Spanish. LC 96-85819. (Bilingual First Bks.). (SPA & ENG., Illus.). 24p. 1997. pap. text 3.95 (*0-7641-0031-9*) Barron.
***Beaton, Clare.** Zoe & Her Zebra. (Illus.). 32p. (J). (ps). 2000. reprint ed. bds. 6.99 (*1-84148-393-1*) Barefoot Bks NY.
Beaton, Clare. Animals Vol. 1: Los Animales. large type ed. (English-Spanish Bilingual First Bks.). (ENG & SPA.). 24p. (J). (ps up). 1998. lib. bdg. 14.45 (*1-56674-247-1*) Forest Hse.
***Beaton, Clare.** A Book of Cat Postcards. 12p. (J). (gr. k-4). 2000. pap. 3.95 (*1-874735-69-7*, Pub. by B Small Publishing) BHB Intl.
— A Book of Teddy Postcards. 4p. (J). (gr. k-4). 2000. pap. 3.95 (*1-874735-49-2*, Pub. by B Small Publishing) BHB Intl.
Beaton, Clare. Clothes (La Ropa), Vol. 2. large type ed. (English-Spanish Bilingual First Bks.). (ENG & SPA.). 24p. (J). (ps up). 1998. lib. bdg. 14.45 (*1-56674-248-X*) Forest Hse.
— Colors (Los Colores), Vol. 3. large type ed. (English-Spanish Bilingual First Bks.). (ENG & SPA.). 24p. (J). (ps up). 1998. lib. bdg. 14.45 (*1-56674-249-8*) Forest Hse.
— English-Spanish Bilingual First Books, 6 vols., Set. (J). (ps up). 1998. lib. bdg. 86.70 (*1-56674-944-1*) Forest Hse.
— Family (La Familia), Vol. 4. large type ed. (English-Spanish Bilingual First Bks.). (ENG & SPA.). 24p. (J). (ps up). 1998. lib. bdg. 14.45 (*1-56674-250-1*) Forest Hse.
— Numbers (Los Numeros), Vol. 5. large type ed. (English-Spanish Bilingual First Bks.). (ENG & SPA.). 24p. (J). (ps up). 1998. lib. bdg. 14.45 (*1-56674-251-X*) Forest Hse.
— One Moose, Twenty Mice. 32p. (J). (ps-k). 1999. 14.95 (*1-902283-37-6*) Barefoot Bks NY.
— Opposites (Los Contrarios), Vol. 6. large type ed. (English-Spanish Bilingual First Bks.). (ENG & SPA.). 24p. (J). (ps up). 1998. lib. bdg. 14.45 (*1-56674-252-8*) Forest Hse.
— Zoe & Her Zebra. 32p. (J). (ps-1). 1999. 14.95 (*1-902283-75-9*) Barefoot Bks NY.
Beaton, Clare. Let's Pretend. large type ed. (Craft & Project Books for Children). 48p. (J). (ps-4). 1998. lib. bdg. 17.95 (*1-56674-243-9*) Forest Hse.
Beaton, Clare, jt. auth. see Bruzzone, Catherine.
Beaton, Elizabeth. Ross & Cromarty: An Illustrated Architectural Guide. (Illus.). 112p. (C). 1992. pap. 35.00 (*1-873190-04-2*, Pub. by Rutland Pr) St Mut.
— Scotland's Traditional Houses: From Cottage to Tower-House. (Discovering Historic Scotland Ser.). (Illus.). 104p. 1997. pap. 22.00 (*0-11-495785-1*, Pub. by Statnry Office) Balogh.
***Beaton, Giff.** Birding Georgia. LC 99-86293. (Guide Ser.). (Illus.). 320p. 2000. pap. 22.95 (*1-56044-784-2*) Falcon Pub Inc.
Beaton, Harold & Johnston, Steve. Foundations of International Marketing. 320p. 1998. pap. 17.99 (*1-86152-164-2*) Thomson Learn.
Beaton, Jane, et al. Family Celebrations: Advent & Christmas. 64p. (J). 1984. pap. 2.95 (*0-8146-1389-6*) Liturgical Pr.
Beaton, Janet. After Frost, the Spring. large type ed. (Linford Romance Library). 1991. pap. 16.99 (*0-7089-7097-4*) Ulverscroft.
— Flower o' the Broom. large type ed. (Linford Romance Library). 1991. pap. 16.99 (*0-7089-7042-7*) Ulverscroft.
— Love Charade. large type ed. (Linford Romance Library). 1991. pap. 16.99 (*0-7089-7053-2*) Ulverscroft.
— Orchids for Love. large type ed. (Linford Romance Library). 1991. pap. 16.99 (*0-7089-7110-5*) Ulverscroft.
Beaton, Janet I., jt. ed. see Degner, Lesley F.
Beaton, K. B. A Practical Dictionary of German Usage. (GER.). 938p. 1997. text 153.00 (*0-19-824002-3*, Clarendon Pr) OUP.
Beaton, Leonard & Maddox, John. The Spread of Nuclear Weapons, No. 5--5. LC 76-16061. (Studies in International Security: No. 5). 216p. 1976. reprint ed. lib. bdg. 35.00 (*0-8371-8949-7*, BENW, Greenwood Pr) Greenwood.
Beaton, M. C., pseud. Agatha Raisin & the Fairies of Fryfam. mass mkt. write for info. (*0-312-97626-7*) St Martin.
— Agatha Raisin & the Fairies of Fryfam. 208p. 2000. 19.95 (*0-312-20496-5*, Minotaur) St Martin.
Beaton, M. C., pseud. Agatha Raisin & the Murderous Marriage. LC 96-19000. 208p. 1996. text 20.95 (*0-312-14538-1*) St Martin.
— Agatha Raisin & the Murderous Marriage. (An Agatha Raisin Mystery Ser.). 224p. 1997. mass mkt. 5.99 (*0-312-96186-3*) St Martin.
— Agatha Raisin & the Murderous Marriage. large type ed. LC 97-9696. (Large Print Book Ser.). 1997. pap. 21.95 (*1-56895-443-3*) Wheeler Pub.
— Agatha Raisin & the Potted Gardener. 1996. mass mkt. 5.50 (*0-8041-1359-9*) Ivy Books.
— Agatha Raisin & the Quiche of Death. 1993. mass mkt. 4.50 (*0-8041-1163-4*) Ivy Books.
— Agatha Raisin & the Quiche of Death. large type ed. LC 98-34460. 261p. 1998. 30.00 (*0-7838-0346-X*) Thorndike Pr.

B

B

***Beaton, M. C., pseud.** Agatha Raisin & the Terrible Tourist. LC 97-16903. (An Agatha Raisin Mystery Ser.). 198p. 1998. mass mkt. 5.99 (*0-312-96566-4*) St Martin.

— Agatha Raisin & the Terrible Tourist. LC 98-23999. 1998. 22.95 (*1-56895-574-X*) Wheeler Pub.

Beaton, M. C., pseud. Agatha Raisin & the Vicious Vet. 1994. mass mkt. 5.50 (*0-8041-1162-6*) Ivy Books.

— Agatha Raisin & the Vicious Vet. large type ed. LC 98-33784. 1998. 22.95 (*0-7838-0368-0*, G K Hall Lrg Type) Mac Lib Ref.

— Agatha Raisin & the Walkers of Dembley. (Agatha Raisin Ser.). 1996. mass mkt. 5.50 (*0-8041-1358-0*) Ivy Books.

— Agatha Raisin & the Wellspring of Death. LC 98-14177. (Agatha Raisin Mysteries). 272p. 1998. text 21.95 (*0-312-18523-5*) St Martin.

***Beaton, M. C., pseud.** Agatha Raisin & the Wellspring of Death. LC 98-14177. (Dead Letter Mysteries Ser.). 201p. 1999. mass mkt. 5.99 (*0-312-96695-4*) St Martin.

— Agatha Raisin & the Wellspring of Death. large type ed. LC 99-22152. (Large Print Book Ser.). 1999. write for info. (*1-56895-730-0*) Wheeler Pub.

Beaton, M. C., pseud. Agatha Raisin & the Witch of Wyckhadden. LC 99-15884. 208p. 1999. text 21.95 (*0-312-20494-9*) St Martin.

***Beaton, M. C., pseud.** Agatha Raisin & the Witch of Wyckhadden. 224p. 2000. mass mkt. 5.99 (*0-312-97369-1*) St Martin.

— Agatha Raisin & the Witch of Wyckhadden. LC 99-88720. (Mystery Ser.). 2000. 28.95 (*0-7862-2418-5*) Thorndike Pr.

Beaton, M. C., pseud. Agatha Raisin & the Wizard of Evesham. LC 98-50566. 208p. 1999. text 20.95 (*0-312-19822-1*) St Martin.

— Agatha Raisin & the Wizard of Evesham. 256p. 1999. mass mkt. 5.99 (*0-312-97062-5*, Minotaur) St Martin.

***Beaton, M. C., pseud.** Agatha Raisin & the Wizard of Evesham. large type ed. LC 00-26170. (Illus.). 284p. (J). 2000. 28.95 (*0-7862-2417-7*) Thorndike Pr.

— Death of a Cad. 1988. mass mkt. 4.99 (*0-8041-0225-2*) Ivy Books.

Beaton, M. C., pseud. Death of a Cad. large type ed. 265p. 1995. pap. 17.95 (*0-7838-1457-7*, G K Hall Lrg Type) Mac Lib Ref.

— Death of a Charming Man. 224p. 1994. 18.45 (*0-89296-529-0*, Pub. by Mysterious Pr) Little.

— Death of a Charming Man. 176p. 1995. mass mkt. 6.50 (*0-446-40338-5*, Pub. by Warner Bks) Little.

— Death of a Dentist. 1998. mass mkt. write for info. (*0-446-40494-2*, Mysterious Paperbk) Warner Bks.

— Death of a Dentist. 256p. 1998. mass mkt. 6.50 (*0-446-60601-4*, Pub. by Warner Bks) Little.

***Beaton, M. C., pseud.** Death of a Dustman. 224p. 2001. 22.95 (*0-89296-631-9*) Mysterious Pr.

— Death of a Dustman. 2001. mass mkt. write for info. (*0-446-60931-5*) Warner Bks.

Beaton, M. C., pseud. Death of a Glutton. 1995. mass mkt. 5.50 (*0-8041-1212-6*) Ivy Books.

— Death of a Gossip. 192p. 1999. mass mkt. 6.50 (*0-446-60713-4*, Pub. by Warner Bks) Little.

— Death of a Gossip. 160p. 1988. reprint ed. mass mkt. 4.99 (*0-8041-0226-0*) Ivy Books.

Beaton, M. C., pseud. Death of a Hussy. 1991. mass mkt. 5.50 (*0-8041-0768-8*) Ivy Books.

— Death of a Hussy. 2000. pap. 6.95 (*0-553-40967-0*, Pub. by Transworld Publishers Ltd) Trafalgar.

— Death of a Hussy. large type ed. LC 99-15670. 1999. 20.95 (*0-7838-8664-0*, G K Hall & Co) Mac Lib Ref.

Beaton, M. C., pseud. Death of a Macho Man. 240p. 1997. mass mkt. 5.99 (*0-446-40340-7*, Pub. by Warner Bks) Little.

— Death of a Nag. 224p. 1995. 18.45 (*0-89296-530-4*, Pub. by Mysterious Pr) Little.

— Death of a Nag. 1996. pap. 5.99 (*0-614-98075-5*) Mysterious Pr.

— Death of a Nag. 192p. 1996. mass mkt. 5.99 (*0-446-40339-3*, Pub. by Warner Bks) Little.

— Death of a Perfect Wife. 1990. mass mkt. 4.99 (*0-8041-0593-6*) Ivy Books.

— Death of a Prankster. (Hamish Macbeth Ser.). 1993. mass mkt. 5.99 (*0-8041-1102-2*) Ivy Books.

— Death of a Scriptwriter. (Hamish Macbeth Mystery Ser.). 198p. 1999. mass mkt. 6.50 (*0-446-60698-7*, Pub. by Warner Bks) Little.

— Death of a Snob. (Hamish Macbeth Ser.). 1992. mass mkt. 5.99 (*0-8041-0912-5*) Ivy Books.

***Beaton, M. C., pseud.** Death of a Snob. LC 99-42644. 2000. 30.00 (*0-7838-8755-8*, G K Hall Lrg Type) Mac Lib Ref.

Beaton, M. C., pseud. Death of a Travelling Man. 1996. mass mkt. 4.99 (*0-8041-1211-8*) Ivy Books.

— Death of an Addict: A Hamish Macbeth Mystery. LC 98-37555. (Hamish Macbeth Mystery Ser.). 215p. 1999. 22.00 (*0-89296-675-0*, Pub. by Mysterious Pr) Little.

— Death of an Outsider. 160p. 1990. mass mkt. 4.99 (*0-8041-0487-5*) Ivy Books.

***Beaton, M. C., pseud.** A Highland Christmas. LC 99-14588. (Illus.). 144p. 1999. 16.95 (*0-89296-699-8*, Pub. by Mysterious Pr) Little.

— A Highland Christmas. 2000. mass mkt. write for info. (*0-446-60919-6*) Warner Bks.

***Beaton, Paul.** Past, Present & Future. LC 99-65655. 200p. 1999. pap. 5.99 (*1-893181-29-4*, Simon & Northrop) Le Gesse Stevens.

Beaton, Rod. Fantasy Baseball Journal '97. 300p. (Orig.). 1997. pap. write for info. (*0-9636895-6-8*) Fantasy Spts.

Beaton, Roderick. George Seferis. (Studies in Modern Greek). xii, 130p. 1991. text 25.00 (*0-89241-527-4*) Caratzas.

— An Introduction to Modern Greek Literature. (Illus.). 440p. (C). 1994. text 65.00 (*0-19-815859-9*) OUP.

— An Introduction to Modern Greek Literature. 2nd ed. (Illus.). 438p. 1999. reprint ed. pap. text 29.95 (*0-19-815974-9*) OUP.

— The Medieval Greek Romance. 2nd rev. ed. LC 95-23528. 328p. (C). 1996. 85.00 (*0-415-12032-2*); pap. 27.99 (*0-415-12033-0*) Routledge.

Beaton, Roderick, ed. The Greek Novel A.D. 1 to 1985. 272p. 1988. lib. bdg. 57.50 (*0-7099-5093-4*, Pub. by C Helm) Routldge.

Beaton, Roderick & Ricks, David. Digenes Akrites: New Approaches to Byzantine Heroic Poetry. (Center for Hellenic Studies: Vol. 2). 208p. 1993. 76.95 (*0-86078-395-2*, Pub. by Variorum) Ashgate Pub Co.

Beaton, Roderick & Roueche, Charlotte, eds. The Making of Byzantine History: Studies Dedicated to Donald M. Nicol on His Seventieth Birthday. (Center for Hellenic Studies). 232p. 1993. 77.95 (*0-86078-385-5*, Pub. by Variorum) Ashgate Pub Co.

Beaton, Sarah R. & Voge, Susan A. Measurements for Long-Term Care. LC 97-33870. 1998. pap. 47.95 (*0-8039-5388-7*) Sage.

Beaton, W. Patrick, ed. Municipal Expenditures, Revenues, & Services: Economic Models & Their Use by Planners. LC 82-17786. 266p. 1983. pap. 1.00 (*0-88285-087-3*) Ctr Urban Pol Res.

Beaton, W. Patrick, jt. auth. see Sternlieb, George S.

Beaton, Welford. Know Your Movies. 1976. lib. bdg. 59.95 (*0-8490-2119-7*) Gordon Pr.

Beatrice, Jonelle A. Learning to Study Through Critical Thinking. LC 94-15557. 304p. (C). 1994. text 15.10 (*0-256-15449-X*, Irwn Prfssnl) McGraw-Hill Prof.

— Learning to Study Through Critical Thinking. 1995. teacher ed. 17.70 (*0-256-15450-3*, Irwn McGrw-H) McGrw-H Hghr Educ.

***Beatrice, Luca.** Salvo. 2000. pap. 25.00 (*88-8158-242-2*) Charta.

***Beatrice, William D.** Blue Lady. 2000. pap. 18.00 (*0-7388-2228-0*) Xlibris Corp.

Beatriz, Maria D. Latina Lite Cooking: 200 Delicious Lowfat Recipes from All over the Americas. LC 97-27741. 432p. (Orig.). 1998. mass mkt. 9.99 (*0-446-67297-1*, Pub. by Warner Bks) Little.

Beats, P. Supervisory Studies. 498p. (C). 1989. 140.00 (*0-7855-5686-9*, Pub. by Inst Pur & Supply) St Mut.

Beatson, J. Anson's Law of Contract. 27th ed. 800p. 1998. pap. text (*0-19-825262-5*) OUP.

Beatson, J., ed. Anson's Law of Contract. 27th ed. 800p. 1998. text 95.00 (*0-19-825261-7*) OUP.

Beatson, Jack. The Use & Abuse of Unjust Enrichment: Essays on the Law of Restitution. 292p. 1991. text 72.00 (*0-19-825425-3*, 3858) OUP.

Beatson, Jack, ed. Constitutional Reform in the United Kingdom - Principles & Practice: The University of Cambridge Centre for Public Law. 144p. 1998. pap. 30.00 (*1-901362-84-1*) Hart Pub.

Beatson, Jack & Friedmann, Daniel, eds. Good Faith & Fault in Contract Law. (Illus.). 578p. 1997. reprint ed. pap. text 38.00 (*0-19-826578-6*) OUP.

Beatson, Jack & Matthews, Martin H. Administrative Law: Cases & Materials. 2nd ed. (Illus.). 928p. 1989. 105.00 (*0-19-876206-2*) OUP.

Beatson, Jack & Tridimas, Takis, eds. New Directions in European Public Law. LC 98-196495. 300p. 1998. pap. 60.00 (*1-901362-24-8*, Pub. by Hart Pub) Northwestern U Pr.

Beatson, Robert. Naval & Military Memoirs of Great Britain, from 1727-1783, 6 vols., Set. LC 72-8675. (American Revolutionary Ser.). reprint ed. lib. bdg. 398.00 (*0-8398-0189-0*) Irvington.

— Naval & Military Memoirs of Great Britain, from 1727-1783, 6 vols., Vol. 1. LC 72-8675. (American Revolutionary Ser.). 543p. reprint ed. lib. bdg. 78.00 (*0-8290-1693-7*) Irvington.

— Naval & Military Memoirs of Great Britain, from 1727-1783, 6 vols., Vol. 2. LC 72-8675. (American Revolutionary Ser.). 464p. reprint ed. lib. bdg. 78.00 (*0-8290-1694-5*) Irvington.

— Naval & Military Memoirs of Great Britain, from 1727-1783, 6 vols., Vol. 3. LC 72-8675. (American Revolutionary Ser.). 615p. reprint ed. lib. bdg. 78.00 (*0-8290-1695-3*) Irvington.

— Naval & Military Memoirs of Great Britain, from 1727-1783, 6 vols., Vol. 4. LC 72-8675. (American Revolutionary Ser.). 594p. reprint ed. lib. bdg. 78.00 (*0-8290-1696-1*) Irvington.

— Naval & Military Memoirs of Great Britain, from 1727-1783, 6 vols., Vol. 5. LC 72-8675. (American Revolutionary Ser.). 131p. reprint ed. lib. bdg. 44.00 (*0-8290-1697-X*) Irvington.

— Naval & Military Memoirs of Great Britain, from 1727-1783, 6 vols., Vol. 6. LC 72-8675. (American Revolutionary Ser.). 516p. reprint ed. lib. bdg. 73.00 (*0-8290-1698-8*) Irvington.

Beatte, Brian & Defur, Brett. A River Valley Companion: A Nature Guide. (Show Me Missouri Ser.). (Illus.). 256p. (Orig.). 1997. pap. 14.95 (*0-9646625-1-5*, MG3490) Pebble Pub.

***Beattie.** Gratitude. MJF Books Staff, ed. 96p. 1999. 4.98 (*1-56731-367-1*, MJF Bks) Fine Comms.

Beattie. Healing the Home. 1992. 18.45 (*0-13-384967-8*) P-H.

— Health & Wellbeing. 1997. pap. 17.95 (*0-333-58717-0*) St Martin.

— Parent's Meditation Book. 1992. per. 7.95 (*0-13-650565-1*) P-H.

***Beattie-, Betsy.** Obligation & Opportunity: Single Maritime Women in Boston, 1870-1930. 192p. 2000. 60.00 (*0-7735-2018-X*, Pub. by McG-Queens Univ Pr) CUP Services.

Beattie, Alan, jt. auth. see Meredith, Philip.

Beattie, Allison, et al, eds. Sustainable Health Care Financing in Southern Africa: Papers from an EDI Health Policy Seminar Held in Johannesburg, South Africa, June 1996. LC 97-44593. (EDI Learning Resources Ser.). 192p. 1998. pap. 22.00 (*0-8213-4145-6*, 14145) World Bank.

Beattie, Andrew & Pepper, Timothy. Syria. (Rough Guide Ser.). (Illus.). 368p. 1998. pap. text 18.95 (*1-85828-331-0*, Pub. by Rough Guides) Penguin Putnam.

Beattie, Andrew J. The Evolutionary Ecology of Ant-Plant Mutualisms. (Cambridge Studies in Ecology). (Illus.). 192p. 1985. text 49.95 (*0-521-25281-4*) Cambridge U Pr.

Beattie, Ann. Another You. 1995. 24.00 (*0-614-15480-4*) Knopf.

— Another You. 336p. 1996. pap. 12.00 (*0-679-73464-3*) Vin Bks.

— The Burning House. 272p. 1995. pap. 12.00 (*0-679-76500-X*) Random.

— Chilly Scenes of Winter. LC 90-50186. (Vintage Contemporaries Ser.). 288p. 1991. pap. 13.00 (*0-679-73234-9*) Vin Bks.

— Falling in Place. LC 90-55707. 342p. 1991. pap. 14.00 (*0-679-73192-X*) Random.

— Falling in Place. 320p. 1987. mass mkt. 4.95 (*0-446-31454-4*, Pub. by Warner Bks) Little.

— Love Always: A Novel. LC 85-40866. (Vintage Contemporaries Ser.). 256p. 1986. pap. 12.00 (*0-394-74418-7*) Vin Bks.

— My Life, Starring Dara Falcon. 320p. 1998. pap. 13.00 (*0-679-78132-3*) Vin Bks.

— Park City: New & Selected Stories. 496p. 1999. pap. 14.00 (*0-679-78133-1*) Vin Bks.

— Picturing Will. LC 90-50167. (Vintage Contemporaries Ser.). 240p. 1991. pap. 12.00 (*0-679-73194-6*) Vin Bks.

— Secrets & Surprises. 1991. pap. 13.00 (*0-679-73193-8*) McKay.

— Secrets & Surprises. 320p. 1985. mass mkt. 3.95 (*0-446-31381-5*, Pub. by Warner Bks) Little.

— What Was Mine. 1992. pap. 12.00 (*0-679-73903-3*) Vin Bks.

— Where You'll Find Me. (Reading Group Guides Ser.). 1996. pap. write for info. (*0-684-00203-5*, Touchstone) S&S Trade Pap.

Beattie, Ann, ed. Ploughshares Fall, 1995: Living Rooms. 254p. (Orig.). 1995. pap. 8.95 (*0-933277-14-8*) Ploughshares.

Beattie, Arthur H., ed. & tr. see Pascal, Blaise.

Beattie, B. B., et al, eds. Temperate Fruit. (Postharvest Diseases of Horticultural Produce Ser.: Vol. 1). (Illus.). 84p. 1990. pap. 35.00 (*0-643-05051-5*, Pub. by CSIRO) Accents Pubns.

Beattie, Bruce R. & Taylor, C. Robert. The Economics of Production. LC 92-40378. 276p. (C). 1993. reprint ed. lib. bdg. 59.95 (*0-89464-534-X*) Krieger.

Beattie, C. P., jt. auth. see Dubey, J. P.

Beattie, Caroline, tr. see Bourdieu, Pierre & Darbel, Alain.

Beattie, Catherine. Healthy Breaks in Britain & Ireland: Health Farms, Spas, Hotels & Centres. rev. ed. (Illus.). 254p. 1995. pap. 17.95 (*0-9518511-1-X*, Pub. by JARR UK) Seven Hills Bk.

Beattie, D. R. & McIvor, J. S. The Targums of Ruth & Chronicles. (Aramaic Bible Ser.: Vol. 19). 270p. (Orig.). 1993. 79.95 (*0-8146-5455-X*, M Glazier) Liturgical Pr.

Beattie, D. R. G. & McNamara, M. J., eds. The Aramaic Bible: Targums in Their Historical Context. (JSOT Supplement Ser.: No. 166). 470p. 1994. 90.00 (*1-85075-454-3*, Pub. by Sheffield Acad) CUP Services.

Beattie, Don, jt. ed. see Lynch, Mary G.

Beattie, Donald, et al, eds. A Distant War Comes Home: Maine in the Civil War Era. LC 96-3332. (Illus.). 288p. (Orig.). 1996. pap. 14.95 (*0-89272-393-9*) Down East.

Beattie, Donald A., ed. History & Overview of Solar Heat Technologies. LC 96-34297. (Solar Heat Technologies Ser.: Vol. 1). (Illus.). 250p. (C). 1997. 39.50 (*0-262-02415-2*) MIT Pr.

Beattie, Donna K. Assessment in Art Education. (Art Education in Practice Ser.). 144p. 1997. pap. 15.55 (*0-87192-363-7*) Davis Mass.

Beattie, Edward. Diary of a Kriegie. (American Autobiography Ser.). 312p. 1995. reprint ed. lib. bdg. 89.00 (*0-7812-8453-8*) Rprt Serv.

Beattie, Edward J., et al. Thoracic Surgical Oncology. (Illus.). 405p. 1992. text 149.00 (*0-443-08589-7*) Church.

Beattie, Edward J., jt. auth. see Bloom, Norman.

Beattie, Edward J., jt. auth. see Harvey, James C.

***Beattie, G.** Head to Head. 1998. pap. text 22.95 (*0-575-06358-0*, Pub. by V Gollancz) Trafalgar.

Beattie, Genovieva, tr. see Grandjean, Samuel.

Beattie, Genovieva Sfatcu. Adam Si Eva... Pentru Mari Si Mici. (RUM., Illus.). 48p. (J). (gr. 4-7). 1991. write for info. (*1-893179-04-4*) Eastern Europe Aid.

— Adam Si Eva... Pentru Mari Si Mici. rev. ed. (RUM., Illus.). 64p. (J). (gr. 4-7). 1997. write for info. (*1-893179-11-7*) Eastern Europe Aid.

Beattie, Genovieva Sfatcu. Domnul Isus a Spus... La Toti Copiii. (RUM., Illus.). 116p. (J). (gr. 3-6). 1993. pap. text. write for info. (*1-893179-07-9*) Eastern Europe Aid.

— Dumnezeu a Creat Lumea... Pentru Toti Copiii. (RUM., Illus.). 60p. (J). (ps-3). 1990. write for info. (*1-893179-01-X*) Eastern Europe Aid.

— Dumnezeu a Creat Lumea... Pentru Toti Copiii. 2nd rev. ed. (RUM., Illus.). 60p. (J). (ps-3). 1992. write for info. (*1-893179-05-2*) Eastern Europe Aid.

— Festivalul Pastelui... Pentru Toti Copiii. (RUM., Illus.). 48p. (J). (gr. 3-6). 1990. write for info. (*1-893179-00-1*) Eastern Europe Aid.

— Festivalul Pastelui... Pentru Toti Copiii. rev. ed. (RUM., Illus.). 52p. (J). (gr. 3-6). 1991. write for info. (*1-893179-03-6*) Eastern Europe Aid.

— Sarbatori Fericite!... La Toti Copiii. (RUM., Illus.). 70p. (J). (gr. 1-4). 1990. write for info. (*1-893179-02-8*) Eastern Europe Aid.

— Sarbatori Fericite!... La Toti Copiii. 2nd rev. ed. (RUM., Illus.). 76p. (J). (gr. 1-4). 1994. text. write for info. (*1-893179-08-7*) Eastern Europe Aid.

Beattie, Genovieva Sfatcu, ed. see Marcu, Nichifor.

Beattie, Genovieva Sfatcu, tr. see Follette, John W.

***Beattie, Geoffrey.** The Corner Boys. 220p. 1999. 29.95 (*0-575-06432-3*, Pub. by Indigo) Trafalgar.

Beattie, Geoffrey. Hard Lines: Voices from Deep Within a Recession. LC 98-29834. (Illus.). 256p. 1998. text 69.95 (*0-7190-5362-5*, Pub. by Manchester Univ Pr) St Martin.

— Hard Lines: Voices from Deep Within a Recession. (Illus.). 256p. 1998. pap. 19.95 (*1-901341-08-9*, Pub. by Mandolin) St Martin.

Beattie, Geoffrey, jt. auth. see Ellis, Andrew W.

Beattie, Gregory & Johnson, Stephanie. Penguin 25 New Fiction. LC 98-199941. 249p. 1998. write for info. (*0-14-027502-9*) Viking Penguin.

Beattie, Gregory & Ransom, Richard. Use Value Assessment: Its Causes, Its Characteristics, Its Effects. LC KF6761.3.F2B. (Land Policy Roundtable Case Studies: No. 302). 47p. reprint ed. pap. 30.00 (*0-7837-2157-9*, 204245900004) Bks Demand.

Beattie, Honlee, ed. see Baggett, Bart A.

Beattie, Irene R., jt. auth. see Arum, Richard.

Beattie, J. M. Crime & the Courts in England, 1660-1800. LC 84-42875. (Illus.). 688p. 1986. reprint ed. pap. 200.00 (*0-608-07811-5*, 205987800010) Bks Demand.

Beattie, James. Elements of Moral Science. LC 75-45348. 1168p. 1976. reprint ed. lib. bdg. 100.00 (*0-8201-1167-8*) Schol Facsimiles.

— An Essay on the Nature & Immutability of Truth, in Opposition to Sophistry & Skepticism. LC 78-67645. (Scottish Enlightenment Ser.). reprint ed. 57.50 (*0-404-17122-2*) AMS Pr.

— The Minstrel: The Progress of Genius. LC 78-67646. (Scottish Enlightenment Ser.). reprint ed. 44.00 (*0-404-17176-1*) AMS Pr.

— The Philosophical & Critical Works, 4 vols., Set. Fabian, Bernhard, ed. (Anglistica & Americana Ser.: No. 104). 1975. 720.00 (*3-487-05160-5*) G Olms Pubs.

— The Philosophical & Critical Works: Elements of Moral Science, Edinburgh, 1790-1793, Vol. III & IV. (GER.). xxii, 1126p. 1974. reprint ed. write for info. (*3-487-05163-X*) G Olms Pubs.

— The Philosophical & Critical Works Vol. 1: On the Nature & Immutability of Truth. (Anglistica & Americana Ser.: No. 104a). 1975. reprint ed. 225.00 (*3-487-05161-3*) G Olms Pubs.

— The Philosophical & Critical Works Vol. 2: Dissertations Moral & Critical. Fabian, Bernhard, ed. (Anglistica & Americana Ser.: No. 104b). xvi, 677p. 1974. reprint ed. 200.00 (*3-487-05162-1*) G Olms Pubs.

— The Philosophical & Critical Works Vol. 4: Elements of Moral Science. Fabian, Bernhard, ed. (Anglistica & Americana Ser.: No. 4). xxii, 1126p. 1974. reprint ed. 160.00 (*3-487-05164-8*) G Olms Pubs.

— Poetical Works. LC 72-25. (Select Bibliographies Reprint Ser.). 1977. reprint ed. 19.95 (*0-8369-9953-3*) Ayer.

— Poetical Works of Beattie, Blair, & Falconer. Gilfillian, George, ed. LC 73-144580. reprint ed. 34.50 (*0-404-08552-0*) AMS Pr.

— Scoticisms, Arranged in Alphabetical Order, Designed to Correct Improprieties of Speech & Writing. LC 78-67647. (Scottish Enlightenment Ser.). reprint ed. 37.50 (*0-404-17177-X*) AMS Pr.

— Theory of Language, Pts. 1 & 2. LC 78-147953. reprint ed. 61.50 (*0-404-08201-7*) AMS Pr.

Beattie, James H. Traditional Lifeways to the Southern Maori. LC 94-159301. 640p. 1994. pap. 59.95 (*0-908569-79-3*, Pub. by Univ Otago Pr) Intl Spec Bk.

Beattie, John. The Breath of Angels: A True Story of Life & Death at Sea. LC 97-33. (Illus.). 270p. 1997. pap. 14.95 (*1-57409-028-3*) Sheridan.

— Bunyoro: An African Kingdom. LC 60-7331. 86p. (Orig.). (C). 1960. pap. text 23.50 (*0-03-004785-4*) Harcourt Coll Pubs.

— Drama in the Air: Extraordinary True Stories of Daring & Courage. (Illus.). 223p. 1992. pap. 10.95 (*0-86051-664-4*, Robson-Parkwest) Parkwest Pubns.

Beattie, John M. The English Court in the Reign of George I. LC 67-10776. 318p. reprint ed. pap. 90.70 (*0-608-12275-0*, 2024422) Bks Demand.

Beattie, Kate, et al, eds. Interactive Multimedia in University Education: Designing for Change in Teaching & Learning: Proceedings: IFIP TC3-WG3.2 Working Conference on the Design, Implementation, & Evaluation of Interactive Multimedia in University Settings (1994) LC 94-44970. (Computer Science Technology Ser.: No. A-59). 324p. 1994. pap. 123.50 (*0-444-82077-9*) Elsevier.

Beattie, Kathleen, jt. auth. see Gilstrap, Robert L.

Beattie, Keith. The Scar That Binds: American Culture & the Vietnam War. pap. text 20.00 (*0-8147-9869-1*) NYU Pr.

Beattie, Keith. The Scar That Binds: American Culture & the Vietnam War. 240p. 1998. text 40.00 (*0-8147-1326-2*) NYU Pr.

***Beattie, Kirk J.** Egypt During the Sadat Years. LC 00-40465. (Illus.). 2000. write for info. (*0-312-23639-5*) St Martin.

— Egyptian Politics During Sadat's Presidency. text. write for info. (*0-312-23246-2*) St Martin.

Beattie, Kurt, jt. auth. see Falls, Gregory A.

An Asterisk (*) at the beginning of an entry indicates that the title is appearing for the first time.

Beattie, L. Elisabeth. Conversations with Kentucky Writers II. LC 99-23215. (Kentucky Remembered Ser.). 320p. 1999. 29.95 (*0-8131-2124-8*) U Pr of Ky.

Beattie, L. Elisabeth, ed. Savory Memories. LC 97-32708. (Illus.). 184p. 1998. 19.95 (*0-8131-2046-2*) U Pr of Ky.

***Beattie, L. Elisabeth & Shaughnessey, Mary Angela.** Sisters in Pain: Battered Women Fight Back. LC HV6626.22.K4B43 2000. (Illus.). 240p. 2000. 29.95 (*0-8131-2151-5*) U Pr of Ky.

Beattie, Laura C. Discover African Wildlife: Activity Book. (Discover Ser.). (Illus.). 24p. (Orig.). (J). (gr. 3-8). 1994. pap., student ed. 2.95 (*0-911239-38-3*) Carnegie Mus.

— Discover Life Through the Ages. (Carnegie Museum Discover Ser.). (Illus.). 28p. (Orig.). (J). (gr. 3-8). 1995. pap. 3.95 (*1-57098-030-6*) Roberts Rinehart.

Beattie, Laura C. & Creative Company Staff. Discover Rocks & Minerals: Activity Book. (Discover Ser.). (Illus.). 24p. (Orig.). (J). (gr. 2-7). 1991. pap., student ed. 3.95 (*0-911239-36-7*) Carnegie Mus.

Beattie, Linda C. Becoming Me: An Autobiography for the Reader to Complete. (Illus.). 136p. 1998. pap. 19.95 (*0-9619634-3-3*) Kopacetic Ink.

— Making the Most of Your Llama: An Owner's Manual. 2nd rev. ed. Doll, Kathyrn, ed. LC 98-67195. (Illus.). 89p. (Orig.). 1998. pap. text 17.95 (*0-9619634-1-7*) Kopacetic Ink.

Beattie, M. The Language of Letting Go. (Meditations Ser.). 10.00 incl. audio (*0-89486-681-8*, 5608G) Hazelden.

Beattie, M. Language of Letting Go. LC 97-75444. 400p. 1998. reprint ed. 7.98 (*1-56731-238-1*, MJF Bks) Fine Comms.

***Beattie, Mary.** The Art of Learning to Teach: Preservice Teacher Narratives. LC 99-89710. 192p. 2000. pap. 24.00 (*0-13-791757-0*) P-H.

Beattie, Mary, jt. auth. see Eisner, Elliot W.

***Beattie, Mary E.** Obligation & Opportunity: Single, Maritime Women in Boston, 1870-1930. 192p. 2000. pap. 22.95 (*0-7735-2019-8*, Pub. by McG-Queens Univ Pr) CUP Services.

Beattie, May. Carpets of Central Persia. (Illus.). 104p. 1988. pap. 18.95 (*0-905035-17-8*) Interlink Pub.

Beattie, Melody. Beyond Codependency. (Discovery Ser.). 1989. 10.00 incl. audio (*0-89486-632-X*, 5609G) Hazelden.

— Beyond Codependency: And Getting Better All the Time. 252p. 1996. pap. 12.95 (*0-89486-583-8*, 5064A) Hazelden.

— Codependent No More: How to Stop Controlling Others & Start Caring for Yourself. LC 86-82660. 208p. pap. 12.95 (*0-89486-402-5*, 5014A) Hazelden.

— Codependent No More: How to Stop Controlling Others & Start Caring for Yourself. large type ed. LC 89-34356. 308p. 1989. pap. 16.95 (*0-8027-2631-3*) Walker & Co.

— Codependent No More & Beyond Codependency. (Illus.). 512p. 1997. reprint ed. 8.98 (*1-56731-218-7*, MJF Bks) Fine Comms.

— Codependents Guide to the Twelve Steps. 224p. 1992. per. 11.00 (*0-671-76227-3*) S&S Trade Pap.

— Codependents' Guide to the Twelve Steps. 1990. audio 9.95 (*0-671-72606-4*, Sound Ideas) S&S Audio.

— De Lenguaje Del Adios.Tr. of Language of Letting Go. (SPA.). 1998. pap. 15.00 (*968-39-1014-9*, Pub. by Edit Patria) Hazelden.

***Beattie, Melody.** Finding Your Way Home: A Soul Survival Kit, Set. abr. ed. 1998. audio 18.00 (*0-694-51933-2*) HarperAudio.

Beattie, Melody. Finding Your Way Home: A Soul Survivor Kit. LC 98-21059. 288p. (Orig.). 1998. pap. 13.00 (*0-06-251118-1*) HarpC.

Beattie, Melody. Journey to the Heart: Beattie,&Melody. abr. ed. 1996. audio 12.00 (*0-694-51679-1*) HarperAudio.

Beattie, Melody. Journey to the Heart: Daily Meditations on the Path to Freeing Your Soul. LC 95-42012. 384p. 1996. pap. 14.00 (*0-06-251121-1*, Pub. by Harper SF) HarpC.

— The Language of Letting Go: Daily Meditations for Codependents. 390p. pap. 14.95 (*0-89486-637-0*, 5076A) Hazelden.

— The Lessons of Love: Rediscovering Our Passion for Life When It All Seems Too Hard to Take. LC 94-14158. 240p. 1995. pap. 12.00 (*0-06-251078-9*, Pub. by Harper SF) HarpC.

— The Lessons of Love: Rediscovering Our Passion for Life When It All Seems Too Hard to Take. large type ed. 224p. 1995. pap. 12.95 (*0-8027-2685-2*) Walker & Co.

— Lighting the Path. abr. ed. audio 12.00 (*0-671-73952-2*, Audioworks) S&S Trade.

***Beattie, Melody.** More Language of Letting Go: 366 New Meditations by Melody Beattie. 400p. 2000. 15.00 (*1-56838-558-7*) Hazelden.

— Playing It by Heart: Taking Care of Yourself No Matter What. LC 99-58620. 250p. 1999. pap. text 15.00 (*1-56838-338-X*) Hazelden.

Beattie, Melody. Una Razon para Vivir.Tr. of Reason to Live. (SPA.). 173p. 1991. pap. 5.99 (*1-56063-210-0*, 498500) Editorial Unilit.

— Stop Being Mean to Yourself. LC 96-39644. 1997. 20.00 (*0-06-251119-X*, Pub. by Harper SF) HarpC.

— Stop Being Mean to Yourself: A Story about Finding the True Meaning of Self-Love. LC 98-37947. 229p. 1998. pap. 14.00 (*1-56838-286-3*) Hazelden.

Beattie, Melody. Stop Being Mean to Yourself: Beattie,&Melody. unabridged ed. 1997. audio 18.00 (*0-694-51854-9*, CPN 2663) HarperAudio.

Beattie, Melody. Ya No Seas Codependiente.Tr. of Codependent No More. (SPA.). 312p. pap. 15.00 (*968-39-0473-4*) Hazelden.

Beattie, Melody, et al. Talk, Trust & Feel: Keeping Codependency Out of Your Life. (Hazelden Recovery Bks.). 1991. mass mkt. 5.99 (*0-345-37455-X*) Ballantine Pub Grp.

Beattie, Melody L. Stop Being Mean to Yourself: A Story about Finding the True Meaning of Self-Love. 229p. 1998. text 20.00 (*0-7881-5825-2*) DIANE Pub.

Beattie, Michele, jt. auth. see Luc, Laura A.

Beattie, Mollie, et al. Working with Your Woodland: A Landowner's Guide. rev. ed. LC 92-56900. (Illus.). 302p. (C). 1993. pap. 22.00 (*0-87451-622-6*) U Pr of New Eng.

Beattie, Owen. Buried in Ice. (Time Quest Bks.). (J). 1992. 12.15 (*0-606-05773-0*, Pub. by Turtleback) Demco.

***Beattie, Owen.** Frozen in Time: The Fate of the Franklin Expedition. Geiger, John, ed. 216p. 2000. pap. 14.95 (*1-55054-616-3*) DGL.

Beattie, Owen, jt. auth. see Geiger, John.

Beattie, Patricia. Quester: The Journey of the Brave. LC 99-15430. (Illus.). 1999. text 24.95 (*1-86204-550-X*, Pub. by Element MA) Penguin Putnam.

***Beattie, Robert W.** Personalizing Your PC. 72p. 2000. pap. 6.95 (*0-7894-6854-9*) DK Pub Inc.

Beattie, Ronald H., jt. auth. see Morse, Wayne L.

Beattie, Sarah. 30-Minute Vegetarian Mexican Cookbook. 2nd ed. LC 97-51581. 160p. 1998. reprint ed. text 21.95 (*0-88001-598-5*) HarpC.

— 30-Minute Vegetarian Thai Cookbook. LC 97-51606. 160p. 1999. text 21.95 (*0-88001-599-3*) HarpC.

***Beattie, Sarah.** 30-Minute Vegetarian Turkish Cookbook. LC 98-36133. 1999. 21.95 (*0-88001-645-0*) HarpC.

***Beattie, Scott.** Legal & Justice Studies Workbook. 151p. 1999. pap. 25.00 (*1-86287-319-4*, Pub. by Federation Pr) Gaunt.

Beattie, Stephanie & Hall, Sue G. Parkwood. (Illus.). 68p. 1999. pap. 7.50 (*1-55046-300-4*, Pub. by Boston Mills) Genl Dist Srvs.

Beattie, Stephen, tr. see Grandjean, Samuel.

Beattie, Susan. The New Sculpture. LC 83-42876. (Studies in British Art). (Illus.). 240p. 1985. reprint ed. pap. 30.00 (*0-300-03359-1*, Y-517) Yale U Pr.

Beattie, Thomas F. Color Atlas of Pediatric Emergencies. (Illus.). 160p. (C). (gr. 13). 1997. text 64.95 (*0-8151-0550-9*, 21952) Mosby Inc.

***Beattie, Tina.** The Last Supper According to Martha & Mary. 2001. pap. 14.95 (*0-8245-1859-4*) Crossroad NY.

Beattie, Tina. Rediscovering Mary: Insights from the Gospels. 128p. (Orig.). 1994. pap. 20.00 (*0-86012-247-6*, Pub. by Srch Pr) St Mut.

Beattie, Vivien A., et al. Banks & Bad Debts: Accounting for Loan Losses in International Banking. 214p. 1995. 195.00 (*0-471-95317-2*) Wiley.

Beattie, William. Life & Letters of Thomas Campbell, 3 vols. LC 70-161729. reprint ed. 225.00 (*0-404-07630-0*) AMS Pr.

— The Scottish Tradition in Printed Books. 50p. 1986. 20.00 (*0-85411-004-6*, Pub. by Saltire Soc) St Mut.

Beattie, Donald. Tales of the Frisken Forest: The Adventures of Rusty Dusty Ripple the Rainbow Fish, Bk. I. (Illus.). 48p. 1990. 11.95 (*0-929212-01-0*) Donnie Corp.

Beattie, Melody. Denial. 28p. (Orig.). 1986. pap. 2.50 (*0-89486-343-6*, 5260B) Hazelden.

Beatty. Beaty Bus Law Nw Cent Pk. (C). 1997. 102.00 (*0-201-34439-4*) Addison-Wesley.

Beatty. Business Law New Century. 1997. teacher ed. 24.00 (*0-201-31673-0*) Addison-Wesley.

Beatty. Elect Image Bank-Prin Beh Neur. 1995. 19.74 (*0-697-31231-3*, WCB McGr Hill) McGrw-H Hghr Educ.

— Princ. Behavior: Pronunciation Guide. 1995. 2.25 (*0-697-29199-5*, WCB McGr Hill) McGrw-H Hghr Educ.

— Principles Behavioral Neurosciences. 3rd ed. 2000. pap. text, student ed. 14.30 (*0-697-36165-9*) McGraw.

— Principles of Behavior Neuroscience: Student Study Art Notebook. 1995. 15.74 (*0-697-29192-8*, WCB McGr Hill) McGrw-H Hghr Educ.

— Principles of Behavioral Neuroscience. 1995. 78.75 (*0-697-22876-2*, WCB McGr Hill) McGrw-H Hghr Educ.

Beatty & Samuelson. Business Law for a New Century. (Business Law Ser.). 1998. pap. 75.50 (*0-324-00342-0*) Sth-Wstrn College.

— Business Law for a New Century. (SWC-Business Law Ser.). 1998. pap., student ed. 18.00 (*0-324-00346-3*) Thomson Learn.

***Beatty & Samuelson.** Business Law for a New Century. 2nd ed. LC 99-86716. 2000. pap. 109.95 (*0-324-00350-1*) Sth-Wstrn College.

— Business Law for a New Century: Alternate Edition. 2001. pap. 40.00 (*0-324-01658-1*) Thomson Learn.

— Business Law for a New Century: Essentials Edition. 2001. pap. 65.00 (*0-324-01656-5*) Thomson Learn.

— Web Tutor on Webct to Accompany a Business Law for a New Century. 2nd ed. 2000. pap. 19.00 (*0-324-06592-2*) Sth-Wstrn College.

***Beatty, Al & Beatty, Gretchen, eds.** Federatino of Fly Fishers Fly Pattern Encyclopedia: Over 1600 of the Best Fly Patterns. (Illus.). 227p. 2000. pap. 39.95 (*1-57188-208-1*) F Amato Pubns.

— Federation of Fly Fishers Fly Pattern Encyclopedia: Over 1600 of the Best Fly Patterns. (Illus.). 227p. 2000. spiral bd. 49.95 (*1-57188-209-X*) F Amato Pubns.

Beatty, Alexandra, ed. see National Research Council Staff.

Beatty, Alexandra S. NAEP 1994 United States History Report Card: Findings from the National Assessment of Educational Progress. 136p. 1996. pap. 11.00 (*0-16-048645-9*) USGPO.

Beatty, Alice & Sargent, Mary. Basic Rug Hooking. rev. ed. LC 89-21684. (Illus.). 160p. 1990. pap. 18.95 (*0-8117-2306-2*) Stackpole.

Beatty, Andrew. Varieties of Javanese Religion: An Anthropological Account. LC 98-38613. (Studies in Social & Cultural Anthropology: No. III). (Illus.). 288p. (C). 1999. text 64.95 (*0-521-62444-4*); pap. text 23.95 (*0-521-62473-8*) Cambridge U Pr.

Beatty, Arthur. William Wordsworth, His Doctrine & Art in Their Historical Relations. 2nd ed. LC 75-28992. reprint ed. 41.50 (*0-404-14003-3*) AMS Pr.

Beatty, Barbara. Preschool Education in America: The Culture of Young Children from the Colonial Era to the Present. 270p. 1997. pap. 18.00 (*0-300-07273-2*) Yale U Pr.

Beatty, Bernard & Newey, Vincent, eds. Byron & the Limits of Fiction. LC 88-10438. 224p. (C). 1988. 59.00 (*0-389-20799-3*, N8357) B&N Imports.

Beatty, Bernard, jt. ed. see Gleckner, Robert F.

Beatty, Bess. Alamance: The Holt Family & Industrialization in a North Carolina County, 1837-1900. LC 99-23181. (Illus.). 248p. 1999. text 45.00 (*0-8071-2373-0*); pap. text 19.95 (*0-8071-2449-4*) La State U Pr.

— A Revolution Gone Backward: The Black Response to National Politics, 1876-1896, 105. LC 86-25747. (Contributions in Afro-American & African Studies: No. 105). 257p. 1987. 55.00 (*0-313-25533-4*, BRV/, Greenwood Pr) Greenwood.

Beatty, Betty R. Just for the Love of Flying. (Illus.). 2.5p. 1997. pap. 16.95 (*1-891118-00-5*, Wind Canyon Bks) Wind Canyon.

Beatty, Bev, jt. auth. see Beatty, Bill.

Beatty, Bill. Seven Steps Toward God. LC 85-82315. 112p. (Orig.). 1986. pap. 4.50 (*0-937779-01-6*) Greenlawn Pr.

Beatty, Bill & Beatty, Bev. Bill & Bev Beatty's Wild Plant Cookbook. LC 87-7802. (Illus.). 174p. 1987. pap. 9.95 (*0-87961-159-6*) Naturegraph.

Beatty, Bruce L. Lemon Belly Up: An Introduction to Economics. 4th ed. 272p. (C). 1995. per. 37.95 (*0-7872-1785-9*, 41178501) Kendall-Hunt.

Beatty, Charles C. Double Honour Due to the Laborious Gospel Minister. (Works of Charles Clinton Beatty). 1989. reprint ed. lib. bdg. 79.00 (*0-7812-1910-8*) Rprt Serv.

— Journal of a Two Months Tour among the Frontier Inhabitants of Pennsylvania. (Works of Charles Clinton Beatty). 1989. reprint ed. lib. bdg. 79.00 (*0-685-44798-7*) Rprt Serv.

— Journal of a Two-Months Tour, with a View to Promoting Religion. LC 72-108459. 1768. 25.00 (*0-403-00456-X*) Scholarly.

Beatty, Chris & Ledges, John. The Ecopress Complete Guide to Native Conifers of the Pacific Northwest. (Illus.). 6p. 1999. pap. 4.95 (*0-9639705-9-3*) Ecopress.

Beatty, Christine. Misery Loves Company. (Illus.). 80p. 1993. pap. 6.95 (*0-9637406-0-1*) Glamazon Pr.

Beatty, Christopher. The Susquehanna River Guide. LC 95-61569. (Illus.). 96p. (Orig.). 1995. pap. 9.95 (*0-9639705-7-7*) Ecopress.

— The Susquehanna River Guide: Fishing, Boating, Hiking & More from the Chesapeake to Northern Pennsylvania. 2nd rev. ed. LC 98-29619. (Illus.). 120p. 1998. pap. 12.95 (*0-9639705-6-9*) Ecopress.

Beatty, Dana, jt. auth. see Beatty, Denise.

Beatty, David. He That Wins Souls Is Wise. 1982. pap. 0.75 (*0-88144-005-1*, CPS-005) Christian Pub.

Beatty, David F., et al. Redevelopment in California. 2nd ed. 464p. (Orig.). 1995. pap. 42.00 (*0-923956-33-6*) Solano Pr.

Beatty, David M. Constitutional Law in Theory & Practice. 204p. 1995. text 50.00 (*0-8020-0701-5*); pap. text 19.95 (*0-8020-7650-5*) U of Toronto Pr.

— Putting the Charter to Work: Designing a Constitutional Labour Code. 264p. 1987. 65.00 (*0-7735-0600-4*, Pub. by McG-Queens Univ Pr); pap. 24.95 (*0-7735-0601-2*, Pub. by McG-Queens Univ Pr) CUP Services.

Beatty, David M., ed. Human Rights & Judicial Review: A Comparative Perspective. LC 94-21317. (International Studies in Human Rights: Vol. 34). 372p. 1994. lib. bdg. 142.50 (*0-7923-2968-6*) Kluwer Academic.

Beatty, Denise & Beatty, Dana. Weddings in Style: A Northern California Guide to Extraordinary Wedding & Party Sites. (Illus.). 300p. (Orig.). 1990. pap. 19.95 (*0-9625196-3-4*) D & D Beatty.

Beatty, Frederika. William Wordsworth of Rydal Mount. LC 74-161730. (Illus.). reprint ed. 32.50 (*0-404-07927-X*) AMS Pr.

Beatty, Grace J. ACT! 2.0 for Windows: The Visual Learning Guide. 304p. 1995. pap. 19.95 (*1-55958-739-3*) Prima Pub.

Beatty, Grace J. Excel X for Windows 95: The Visual Learning Guide, Vol. 1. 1995. pap. text 19.95 (*1-55958-736-9*) Prima Pub.

Beatty, Grace J. Excel 5 for the Mac: The Visual Learning Guide. 1995. pap. 19.95 (*1-55958-460-2*) Prima Pub.

Beatty, Grace J. Microsoft Works for Windows 95: Visual Learning Guide. 1996. pap. 19.95 (*0-7615-0385-4*) Prima Pub.

— PowerPoint: The Visual Learning Guide. LC 94-65674. (Illus.). 272p. 1994. pap. 19.95 (*1-55958-550-1*) Prima Pub.

— Procomm Plus for Windows: The Visual Learning Guide. 1995. pap. 19.95 (*1-55958-740-7*) Prima Pub.

— Wincomm Pro: The Visual Learning Guide. 1995. pap. text 19.95 (*0-7615-0090-1*) Prima Pub.

— Windows 95 Fast & Easy. 1995. pap. text 19.95 (*1-55958-738-5*) Prima Pub.

— WinFax Pro 7 for Windows: The Visual Learning Guide. 1996. pap. 19.95 (*0-7615-0380-3*) Prima Pub.

— WordPerfect 6.1 for Windows: Windows Fast & Easy 1995. pap. text 19.95 (*0-7615-0091-X*) Prima Pub.

Beatty, Grace J. & Gardner, David C. Excel for Windows: The Visual Learning Guide. (Illus.). 272p. (Orig.). 1992. pap. 19.95 (*1-55958-211-1*) Prima Pub.

Beatty, Grace J. & Gardner, David C. Excel 5 for Windows: The Visual Learning Guide. LC 93-86727. (Illus.). 272p. (Orig.). 1994. pap. 19.95 (*1-55958-392-4*) Prima Pub.

Beatty, Grace J. & Gardner, David C. Quicken 3 for Windows: The Visual Learning Guide. LC 93-10262. 1993. pap. 19.95 (*1-55958-342-8*) Prima Pub.

— Word for Windows Two: The Visual Learning Guide. LC 92-23807. (Illus.). 272p. (Orig.). 1992. pap. 19.95 (*1-55958-240-5*) Prima Pub.

Beatty, Grace J., et al. Discover Netscape Communicator. LC 97-72192. 416p. 1997. pap. 19.99 (*0-7645-3068-2*) IDG Bks.

Beatty, Grace J., jt. auth. see Gardner, David C.

Beatty, Grace J., jt. auth. see Joely, Grace.

Beatty, Gregg C. Developing a Hospital Emergency Preparedness Program. rev. ed. (Management & Compliance Ser.: Vol. 2). (Illus.). 110p. 1990. reprint ed. ring bd. 110.00 (*0-87258-451-8*, 055201) Am Hospital.

Beatty, Gregg C., jt. auth. see Wahle, Thomas.

Beatty, Gretchen, jt. ed. see Beatty, Al.

Beatty, Helen I. Wrap Me in My Dreams, Only Today, Country School. (Illus.). 180p. 1991. pap. 12.00 (*0-685-52572-4*) Fords Landing Pr.

Beatty, Homer G. & Homewood, A. E. Anatomical Adjustive Technic. rev. ed. 331p. (C). reprint ed. text 25.00 (*0-317-11382-8*) Parker Chiro.

Beatty, J. Changing Step. Date not set. pap. 6.99 (*1-871676-68-1*, Pub. by Christian Focus) Spring Arbor Dist.

Beatty, J. Kelly, et al, eds. The New Solar System. (Illus.). 432p. 1998. pap. 39.95 (*0-521-64587-5*) Cambridge U Pr.

— The New Solar System. (Illus.). 432p. 1999. text 59.95 (*0-521-64183-7*) Cambridge U Pr.

Beatty, J. Kelly & Chaikin, Andrew, eds. The New Solar System. 3rd ed. LC 89-38040. (Illus.). 336p. 1990. 24.95 (*0-933346-55-7*) Sky Pub.

Beatty, Jack. A Crime Against Civilization. 1998. write for info. (*0-201-62688-8*) Addison-Wesley.

— The Rascal King: The Life & Times of James Michael Curley. (Illus.). 592p. 1993. pap. 15.00 (*0-201-62617-9*) Addison-Wesley.

— The Rascal King: The Life & Times of James Michael Curley, 1874-1958. (Illus.). 608p. 1992. 25.00 (*0-201-17599-1*) Addison-Wesley.

***Beatty, Jack.** The Rascal King: The Life & Times of James Michael Curley, 1874-1958. 592p. 2000. pap. text 18.00 (*0-306-81002-6*, Pub. by Da Capo) HarpC.

Beatty, Jack. The World According to Peter Drucker. LC 97-36988. 204p. 1998. 24.50 (*0-684-83801-X*) Free Pr.

— The World According to Peter Drucker. LC 98-12378. 208p. 1998. reprint ed. pap. 13.00 (*0-7679-0302-1*) Broadway BDD.

Beatty, Jack, ed. Colossus: The Saga of the American Corporation. 432p. 30.00 (*0-7679-0352-8*) Broadway BDD.

Beatty, Jackson. Principles of Behavioral Neuroscience. LC 93-74861. 576p. (C). 1994. text 55.50 (*0-697-12741-9*) Brown & Benchmark.

— Principles of Behavioral Neuroscience. LC 93-74861. 224p. (C). 1995. text, student ed. 23.12 (*0-697-12743-5*) Brown & Benchmark.

Beatty, Jan. Mad River. LC 95-31468. (Poetry Ser.). 63p. 1996. pap. 10.95 (*0-8229-5570-9*) U of Pittsburgh Pr.

— Mad River. LC 95-31468. (Poetry Ser.). 63p. (C). 1996. text 24.95 (*0-8229-3897-9*) U of Pittsburgh Pr.

Beatty, Jan, ed. see Johnson, Ronald L.

Beatty, Jane N., jt. auth. see Harber, Jean R.

Beatty, Jerome. Arctic Rovings: or The Adventures of a New Bedford Boy on Sea & Land by Daniel Weston Hall. LC 91-40359. (Illus.). xiv, 144p. (J). (gr. 7-10). 1992. reprint ed. lib. bdg. 19.50 (*0-208-02324-0*, Linnet Bks) Shoe String.

— Matthew Looney & the Space Pirates. LC 84-40767. (Young Scott Bks.). (Illus.). (J). 1972. 9.95 (*0-201-09282-4*) HarpC Child Bks.

Beatty, John. The Citizen-Soldier: The Memoirs of a Civil War Volunteer. LC 97-43450. xvii, 376p. 1998. pap. 16.00 (*0-8032-6141-1*, Bison Books) U of Nebr Pr.

Beatty, John D. Vital Records of Biddeford, Maine Prior to 1856. LC 97-80802. (Maine Genealogical Society Special Publication Ser.: No. 28). 608p. 1998. 65.00 (*0-89725-338-8*, 1728) Picton Pr.

Beatty, John L. & Johnson, Oliver A. Heritage of Western Civilization, 2 vols., Vol. II. 6th ed. (Illus.). 400p. (C). 1987. pap. text write for info. (*0-318-61092-2*) P-H.

Beatty, John L. & Johnson, Oliver A., eds. Heritage of Western Civilization, 2 vols. 8th ed. LC 94-22933. Vol. 2. (Illus.). 448p. 1994. pap. text 41.00 (*0-13-104878-3*) P-H.

— The Heritage of Western Civilization. 8th ed. LC 94-22933. Vol. 1. (Illus.). 480p. 1994. pap. text 38.80 (*0-13-104860-0*) P-H.

Beatty, Kelly J., et al, eds. The New Solar System. 4th rev. ed. LC 98-34472. (Illus.). 422p. (C). 1997. pap. 39.95 (*0-933346-86-7*, 46867) Sky Pub.

Beatty, Kenneth J. Human Leopards: Account of the Trials of Human Leopards Before the Special Commisson Court. LC 74-15011. (Illus.). reprint ed. 39.50 (*0-404-12006-7*) AMS Pr.

Beatty-Kingston, W., tr. see Busch, Moritz.

Beatty, LaMond F. Filmstrips. Duane, James E., ed. LC 80-21338. (Instructional Media Library: Vol. 4). (Illus.). 104p. 1981. 27.95 (*0-87778-164-8*) Educ Tech Pubns.

— Instructional Materials Centers. Duane, James E., ed. LC 80-21451. (Instructional Media Library: Vol. 5). (Illus.). 104p. 1981. 27.95 (*0-87778-165-6*) Educ Tech Pubns.

— Motion Pictures. Duane, James E., ed. LC 80-21340. (Instructional Media Library: Vol. 8). (Illus.). 112p. 1981. 27.95 (*0-87778-168-0*) Educ Tech Pubns.

B

— Still Pictures. Duane, James E., ed. LC 80-21448. (Instructional Media Library: Vol. 14). (Illus.). 112p. 1981. 27.95 (*0-87778-174-5*) Educ Tech Pubns.

Beatty, Lynda, et al, eds. 1997 Directory of Mass Merchandisers. 1996. pap. 220.00 (*0-911790-36-5*) Trade Dimensns.

— 1997 Marketing Guidebook: The Book of Supermarket Distribution Facts. rev. ed. (Illus.). 949p. 1996. 325.00 (*0-911790-31-4*, Progress Grocer) Trade Dimensns.

Beatty, M. F. Principles of Engineering Mechanics Vol. 1: Kinematics: The Geometry of Motion. (Mathematical Concepts & Methods in Science & Engineering Ser.: Vol. 32). (Illus.). 414p. (C). 1986. 110.00 (*0-306-42131-3*, Plenum Trade) Perseus Pubng.

Beatty, M. T., et al, eds. Planning the Uses & Management of Land. (Agronomy Monograph Ser.: No. 21). (Illus.). 1028p. 1979. 30.00 (*0-89118-058-3*) Am Soc Agron.

Beatty, Marvin T., jt. ed. see Petersen, Gary W.

Beatty, Maura. Bootstrap Words: Pull Yourself Up! 112p. 1996. pap. text, per. 9.95 (*0-7872-1982-7*) Kendall-Hunt.

— Pizza & the Art of Life Management. 236p. 1996. pap. text 14.95 (*0-7872-2142-2*) Kendall-Hunt.

Beatty, Michael, et al. Studebaker: Less Than They Promised. LC 84-81548. (Illus.). 94p. (Orig.). 1984. 24.95 (*0-89708-150-1*); pap. 9.95 (*0-89708-129-3*) And Bks.

B

Beatty, Monica D. Blueberry Eyes. (Illus.). 32p. (J). (gr. k-6). 1996. pap. 8.95 (*0-929173-24-4*) Health Press.

— Fire Night. LC 99-37828. (Illus.). 32p. (J). (gr. 3-7). 1998. pap. 8.95 (*0-929173-31-7*) Health Press.

Beatty, Noelle, ed. see Pizzo, P., et al.

Beatty, Noelle B. Literary Byways of Boston & Cambridge. LC 90-26071. (Literary Cities Ser.). (Illus.). 80p. (Orig.). 1991. pap. 8.95 (*0-913515-60-4*, Starrhill Press) Black Belt Communs.

Beatty, Noelle Blackmer. Suriname: Major World Nations. LC 97-17786. (Major World Nations Ser.). (Illus.). 144p. (YA). (gr. 5 up). 1999. lib. bdg. 19.95 (*0-7910-4748-2*) Chelsea Hse.

Beatty, Patricia. Be Ever Hopeful Hannalee. 216p. (J). (gr. 5-9). 1990. pap. 3.95 (*0-8167-2259-5*) Troll Communs.

— Bonanza Girl. 1993. 10.05 (*0-606-05164-3*, Pub. by Turtleback) Demco.

— Charley Skedaddle. (J). 1997. pap. text 7.95 (*1-55734-565-1*) Tchr Create Mat.

— Charley Skedaddle. 186p. (J). (gr. 4-7). 1989. pap. 4.95 (*0-8167-1317-0*) Troll Communs.

Beatty, Patricia. Charley Skedaddle. (J). 1987. 10.05 (*0-606-04029-3*, Pub. by Turtleback) Demco.

Beatty, Patricia. The Coach That Never Came. LC 85-15213. 176p. (J). (gr. 7 up). 1985. 15.00 (*0-688-05477-3*, Wm Morrow) Morrow Avon.

— Eight Mules from Monterey. (J). 1993. 10.05 (*0-606-05251-8*, Pub. by Turtleback) Demco.

Beatty, Patricia. Jayhawker. LC 91-17890. 214p. (YA). (gr. 5 up). 1995. mass mkt. 5.95 (*0-688-14422-5*, Wm Morrow) Morrow Avon.

Beatty, Patricia. Jayhawker. 1995. 10.05 (*0-606-07734-0*, Pub. by Turtleback) Demco.

— Lupita Manana. LC 81-505. 192p. (J). (gr. 7 up). 1992. pap. 4.95 (*0-688-11497-0*, Wm Morrow) Morrow Avon.

***Beatty, Patricia.** Lupita Manana. LC 81-505. (SPA.). 192p. (J). 2000. mass mkt. 4.95 (*0-380-73247-5*) Morrow Avon.

Beatty, Patricia. Lupita Manana. (J). 1992. 10.05 (*0-606-01376-8*, Pub. by Turtleback) Demco.

Beatty, Patricia. Nickel-Plated Beauty. 1993. 10.05 (*0-606-05508-8*, Pub. by Turtleback) Demco.

Beatty, Patricia. O the Red Rose Tree. 1994. 10.05 (*0-606-06629-2*, Pub. by Turtleback) Demco.

— The Queen's Own Grove. (Illus.). 224p. (J). (gr. 4-6). 1999. pap. 8.95 (*0-9671154-5-0*) Imagine That CA.

Beatty, Patricia. Sarah & Me & the Lady from the Sea. 1994. 11.05 (*0-606-06712-4*, Pub. by Turtleback) Demco.

Beatty, Patricia. Sarah & Me & the Lady from the Sea. Cohn, Amy, ed. LC 89-33624. 224p. (YA). (gr. 5 up). 1994. reprint ed. mass mkt. 5.95 (*0-688-13626-5*, Wm Morrow) Morrow Avon.

— Turn Homeward, Hannalee. LC 84-8960. 208p. (J). (gr. 4-7). 1984. 16.00 (*0-688-03871-9*, Wm Morrow) Morrow Avon.

— Turn Homeward, Hannalee. 208p. 1999. mass mkt. 5.95 (*0-688-16676-8*, Wm Morrow) Morrow Avon.

— Turn Homeward, Hannalee. 193p. (J). (gr. 5-9). 1990. pap. 3.95 (*0-8167-2260-9*) Troll Communs.

— Turn Homeward, Hannalee. 1990. 9.05 (*0-606-12604-X*, Pub. by Turtleback) Demco.

Beatty, Patricia. Wait for Me, Watch for Me, Eula Bee. 1990. 9.05 (*0-606-04842-1*, Pub. by Turtleback) Demco.

Beatty, Patricia. Wait for Me, Watch for Me, Eula Bee. LC 78-12782. 224p. (J). (gr. 5 up). 1990. reprint ed. mass mkt. 4.95 (*0-688-10077-5*, Wm Morrow) Morrow Avon.

— Who Comes with Cannons? LC 92-6317. 192p. (YA). (gr. 5 up). 1992. 15.95 (*0-688-11028-2*, Wm Morrow) Morrow Avon.

Beatty, Paul. Big Bank Take Little Bank. LC 90-62908. (New Cafe Poets Ser.). 74p. (Orig.). 1990. pap. 9.95 (*0-9627842-7-3*) Nuyorican Poets.

***Beatty, Paul.** Tuff: A Novel. 2000. pap. write for info. (*0-375-70124-9*) Knopf.

— Tuff: A Novel. LC 99-40358. 272p. 2000. 23.00 (*0-375-40122-9*) Knopf.

Beatty, Paul. The White Boy Shuffle. 1997. pap. 10.00 (*0-8050-5351-4*) H Holt & Co.

Beatty, Paulette T. & Wolfe, Mary A. Connecting with Older Adults: Educational Responses & Approaches. LC 95-3088. (Professional Practices Ser.). (Illus.). 150p. (C). 1995. 19.00 (*0-89464-752-0*) Krieger.

***Beatty, Richard.** Copper. LC 99-54235. (Elements Ser.). (Illus.). (J). 2001. lib. bdg. 22.79 (*0-7614-0945-9*, Benchmark NY) Marshall Cavendish.

— Phosphorus. LC 99-88821. (Elements Ser.). 2001. lib. bdg. 22.79 (*0-7614-0946-7*) Marshall Cavendish.

— Sulfur. LC 99-86992. 2000. lib. bdg. 22.79 (*0-7614-0948-3*, Benchmark NY) Marshall Cavendish.

Beatty, Richard H. The Five-Minute Interview. 2nd ed. LC 97-22837. 206p. 1997. pap. 14.95 (*0-471-19295-3*) Wiley.

— The Interview Kit. LC 95-34905. 224p. 1995. pap. 12.95 (*0-471-12404-4*) Wiley.

***Beatty, Richard H.** The Interview Kit. 2nd ed. LC 99-52512. 256p. 2000. pap. 12.95 (*0-471-37948-4*) Wiley.

Beatty, Richard H. Interviewing & Selecting High Performers: Every Manager's Guide to Effective Interviewing Techniques. 213p. 1994. 79.95 (*0-471-59360-5*); pap. 17.95 (*0-471-59359-1*) Wiley.

— The New Complete Job Search. LC 91-41389. 320p. 1992. pap. 12.95 (*0-471-53494-3*) Wiley.

— 175 High-Impact Cover Letters. 2nd ed. LC 95-52821. 240p. 1996. pap. 10.95 (*0-471-12385-4*) Wiley.

— 175 High-Impact Resumes. 2nd ed. LC 98-24356. 288p. 1998. pap. 10.95 (*0-471-31476-5*) Wiley.

— The Perfect Cover Letter. 2nd ed. LC 96-20721. 192p. 1996. pap. 12.95 (*0-471-12400-1*) Wiley.

***Beatty, Richard H.** The Resume Kit. 4th ed. LC 99-55242. 368p. 2000. pap. 12.95 (*0-471-37949-2*) Wiley.

Beatty, Richard H. & Burkholder, Nicholas C. The Executive Career Guide for MBAs: Insider Advice on Getting to the Top from Today's Business Leaders. LC 95-17417. 238p. 1995. 17.95 (*0-471-55709-9*) Wiley.

Beatty, Richard W., jt. auth. see Schneier, Craig E.

Beatty, Richmond C., et al, eds. Vanderbilt Studies in the Humanities, Vol. 1. LC 52-1180. 283p. reprint ed. pap. 87.80 (*0-8357-3265-7*, 203948600001) Bks Demand.

Beatty, Robert. Journey of the Tern. LC 94-94102. (Illus.). 208p. (Orig.). 1994. pap. 7.95 (*0-9639705-8-5*) Ecopress.

— Sapo. LC 96-83915. 285p. 1996. 18.95 (*0-9639705-4-2*) Ecopress.

Beatty, Ronald L., et al, eds. Microwave Processing of Materials III. (Symposium Proceedings Ser.: Vol. 269). 623p. 1992. text 30.00 (*1-55899-164-6*) Materials Res.

Beatty, Susan & Woodfin Middleton, Karen. An Introduction to Home Education: How to Start Your Private Home School (In California) 7th rev. ed. Date not set. ring bd. 26.47 (*0-9660937-4-7*) CHEP.

Beatty, Susan, ed. see McLaughlin, Dan J.

***Beatty, Theresa M.** Food & Recipes of Africa. LC 98-11215. (Kids in the Kitchen Ser.). 24p. (J). (gr. k-4). 1999. 19.33 (*0-8239-5220-7*, PowerKids) Rosen Group.

Beatty, Theresa M. Food & Recipes of China. LC 98-11214. (Kids in the Kitchen Ser.). 24p. (J). (gr. k-4). 1999. 19.33 (*0-8239-5222-3*, PowerKids) Rosen Group.

— Food & Recipes of Greece. LC 98-11741. (Kids in the Kitchen Ser.). 24p. (J). (gr. k-4). 1999. 13.50 (*0-8239-5223-1*, PowerKids) Rosen Group.

— Food & Recipes of Mexico. LC 98-11776. (Kids in the Kitchen Ser.). 24p. (J). (gr. k-4). 1999. 13.50 (*0-8239-5224-X*, PowerKids) Rosen Group.

— Food & Recipes of the Caribbean. LC 98-11212. (Kids in the Kitchen Ser.). 24p. (J). (gr. k-4). 1999. 19.33 (*0-8239-5221-5*, PowerKids) Rosen Group.

***Beatty, Theresa M., contrib. by.** Food & Recipes of Japan. LC 98-11213. (Kids in the Kitchen Ser.). (Illus.). 24p. (J). 1999. 19.33 (*0-8239-5319-X*) Rosen Group.

Beatty, Willard W., ed. see Clark, Ann N.

Beatty, Willard W., ed. see Underhill, Ruth M.

Beaty, Barry J. & Marquardt, William C., eds. The Biology of Disease Vectors. (Illus.). 728p. 1996. lib. bdg. 85.00 (*0-87081-411-7*) Univ Pr Colo.

Beaty, Dave. Moths & Butterflies. LC 92-29741. (Nature Books Ser.). (Illus.). 32p. (J). (gr. 2-6). 1994. lib. bdg. 22.79 (*1-56766-001-0*) Childs World.

— Primates. (Nature Books Ser.). (Illus.). 32p. (J). (gr. 2-6). 1992. lib. bdg. 22.79 (*0-89565-851-8*) Childs World.

— Waterfowl. LC 92-32319. (Nature Books Ser.). (Illus.). 32p. (J). (gr. 2-6). 1994. lib. bdg. 22.79 (*1-56766-006-1*) Childs World.

***Beaty, David.** The Ghosts of the Eighth Attack. large type ed. 400p. 1999. 31.99 (*0-7089-4105-2*, Linford) Ulverscroft.

Beaty, David. He That Wins Souls is Wise: Minibook. 32p. 1989. pap. 1.00 (*0-89274-572-X*, HH-572) Harrison Hse.

Beaty, David T., jt. auth. see Harari, Oren.

Beaty, F. E. Sourcebook of HVAC Specifications. 608p. 1986. text 64.50 (*0-07-004192-X*) McGraw.

Beaty, Frank E., jt. auth. see Belk, William E.

Beaty, Frederick L. Byron the Satirist. LC 85-2943. 236p. 1985. 30.00 (*0-87580-109-9*) N Ill U Pr.

— The Ironic World of Evelyn Waugh: A Study of Eight Novels. LC 92-1305. 250p. 1992. pap. 16.00 (*0-87580-562-0*) N Ill U Pr.

— Light from Heaven: Love in British Romantic Literature. LC 70-157649. 288p. 1971. 28.00 (*0-87580-028-9*) N Ill U Pr.

Beaty, H. Wayne. Electric Power Distribution Systems: A Nontechnical Guide. LC 98-18533. 1998. 64.95 (*0-87814-731-4*) PennWell Bks.

— Electrical Engineering Materials Reference Guide. 320p. 1990. 49.00 (*0-07-004196-2*) McGraw.

Beaty, H. Wayne & Kirtley, James L., Jr. Electric Motor Handbook. (Illus.). 800p. 1998. 69.95 (*0-07-035971-7*) McGraw-Hill Prof.

Beaty, H. Wayne, jt. auth. see Fink, Donald G.

Beaty, J. Converting Conflict in Preschool. LC 94-75160. (C). 1994. pap. text 46.00 (*0-15-501223-1*, Pub. by Harcourt Coll Pubs) Harcourt.

Beaty, James H. & Price, Charles T., eds. A Selected Bibliography of Pediatric Orthopaedics. 4th ed. 400p. 1996. pap. 30.00 (*0-89203-158-1*) Amer Acad Ortho Surg.

Beaty, James H., jt. auth. see Canale, S. Terry.

Beaty, Janice J. Building Bridges with Multicultural Picture Books: For Children 3-5. LC 96-6854. 279p. 1996. pap. 41.00 (*0-13-400102-8*, Merrill Pub Co) Macmillan.

Beaty, Janice J. Observing Development of the Young Child. 4th ed. LC 97-2909. 402p. (C). 1997. pap. text 38.00 (*0-13-801986-X*) P-H.

— Preschool: Appropriate Practices. 2nd ed. (C). 1995. pap. text 42.00 (*0-15-502633-X*, Pub. by Harcourt Coll Pubs) Harcourt.

— Prosocial Guidance for the Preschool Child. LC 98-6519. (C). 1998. pap. text 32.00 (*0-13-633512-8*, Scribners Ref) Mac Lib Ref.

— Skills for Preschool Teachers. 6th ed. LC 98-51545. (Illus.). 352p. (C). 1999. pap. 33.00 (*0-13-096268-6*) P-H.

Beaty, Janice J. & Tucker, Hugh. The Computer As a Paintbrush: Creative Uses for the Personal Computer in the Preschool Classroom. 200p. (C). 1990. pap. text 30.80 (*0-675-20523-9*, Merrill Coll) P-H.

Beaty, Janice J., jt. auth. see Cunningham, Lawrence J.

Beaty, Jerome. Middlemarch from Notebook to Novel: A Study of George Eliot's Creative Method, 47. LC 81-6588. 134p. 1981. reprint ed. lib. bdg. 45.00 (*0-313-22412-9*, BEMF, Greenwood Pr) Greenwood.

— Misreading Jane Eyre: A Postformalist Paradigm. LC 96-2288. (Theory & Interpretation of Narrative Ser.). 259p. 1996. text 37.50 (*0-8142-0692-1*) Ohio St U Pr.

Beaty, Jerome. The Norton Introduction to Short Novels. 3rd ed. (C). 1999. pap., teacher ed. write for info. (*0-393-96832-4*) Norton.

***Beaty, Jerome.** The Norton Introduction to Short Novels. 3rd ed. LC 98-41702. (C). 1999. pap. 33.00 (*0-393-96831-6*) Norton.

Beaty, Jerome, ed. The Norton Introduction to Fiction. 6th ed. LC 95-4814. (C). 1995. pap. 41.75 (*0-393-96821-9*) Norton.

***Beaty, Jerome, et al, eds.** The Norton Introduction to Literature. 7th ed. LC 97-24449. 2200p. (C). 1998. text 53.00 (*0-393-97202-X*) Norton.

Beaty, Jerome & Hunter, J. Paul, eds. New Worlds of Literature: Writings from America's Many Cultures. LC 93-9921. (C). 1994. pap. text. write for info. (*0-393-96355-1*) Norton.

Beaty, Jerome & Hunter, J. Paul, eds. New Worlds of Literature: Writings from America's Many Cultures. 2nd ed. LC 93-9921. (C). 1994. pap. text 44.50 (*0-393-96354-3*) Norton.

***Beaty, Jerome, et al.** The Norton Introduction to Literature. 7th ed. LC 97-24451. (C). 1998. pap. text 32.50 (*0-393-97222-4*) Norton.

Beaty, John. Image of Life: The Degradation of American Standards & Its Worldwide Significance. 1991. lib. bdg. 79.95 (*0-8490-5056-1*) Gordon Pr.

— Iron Curtain over America. 1979. lib. bdg. 250.00 (*0-8490-2950-3*) Gordon Pr.

— Iron Curtain over America. 268p. 1951. reprint ed. pap. 9.00 (*0-913022-30-6*) CPA Bk Pub.

Beaty, John. The Iron Curtain over America. unabridged ed. 267p. 1951. reprint ed. pap. write for info. (*0-945001-14-2*) GSG & Assocs.

Beaty, Liz, jt. auth. see McGill, Ian.

Beaty, M., tr. see Calvin, John.

Beaty, Michael, ed. Christian Theism & the Problems of Philosophy. LC 90-70860. (Library of Religious Philosophy: Vol. 5). 380p. (C). 1990. pap. text 19.50 (*0-268-00781-0*) U of Notre Dame Pr.

Beaty, Monica D. My Sister Rose Has Diabetes. LC 97-35095. (Illus.). 32p. (J). (gr. 3-7). 1997. pap. 8.95 (*0-929173-27-9*) Health Press.

Beaty, Sandy & Wilkerson, J. L. Champion of Arbor Day: J. Sterling Morton. Parkison, Jami, ed. LC 98-71418. (Great Heartlanders Ser.). (Illus.). 130p. (YA). (gr. 4-12). 1999. pap. 8.95 (*0-9664470-1-8*) Acrn Bks.

Beaty, Seddon K. Butterflies Abound! 1993. pap. 24.95 (*0-201-81521-4*) Addison-Wesley.

— Dinosaurs Forever! 1992. pap. text 24.95 (*0-201-81523-0*) Addison-Wesley.

— Frogs & Toads. 200p. 1995. pap. text, student ed. 24.95 (*0-201-49501-5*) Addison-Wesley.

Beaty, Seddon K. & Fountas, Irene. Frogs & Toads: A Whole Language Resource Guide for K-4. Fowkes, Lois & Schottman, Elly, eds. (Theme Studies). (Illus.). 264p. (Orig.). 1995. pap., teacher ed. 24.95 (*0-201-49499-X*) Supplementary Div.

***Beaty, Wayne.** Handbook of Electric Power Calulations with CD-ROM. 3rd ed. (Illus.). 600p. 2000. 125.00 incl. cd-rom (*0-07-136298-3*) McGraw.

Beau, Bryan F. Le, see Le Beau, Bryan F.

Beau, Bryan F. Le, see Greenspoon, Leonard J. & Le Beau, Bryan F., eds.

Beau Chesne, John De, see De Beau Chesne, John.

Beau, Rosemary G., tr. see David, Serge.

Beaubaire, Nancy, ed. Native Perennials: North American Beauties. (21st-Century Gardening Ser.). (Illus.). 112p. (Orig.). 1996. pap. 9.95 (*0-945352-92-1*) Bklyn Botanic.

Beaubeau, Anne, tr. see Keckeis, M. B.

***Beaubien, Richard F. & Lamparski, Beata J.** What Every City Should Know about Intelligent Transportation Systems. (Illus.). 15p. 2000. pap. 5.00 (*0-935403-49-3*, IR-102) Inst Trans Eng.

Beaubien, Anne K., ed. Fee-Based Services - Issues & Answers: Second Conference on Fee-Based Research in College & University Libraries. LC 87-34900. 88p. 1987. pap. 15.00 (*0-9619861-0-7*) MI Info Transfer.

Beaubien, Michael P. & Wyeth, John S., Jr., eds. Views on the News: The Media & Public Opinion. LC 93-43679. (Illus.). 288p. (C). 1995. text 45.00 (*0-8147-3510-X*) NYU Pr.

Beauboeuf-Lafontant, Tamara & Augustine, D. Smith, eds. Facing Racism in Education. 2nd rev. ed. (Reprint Ser.: Vol. 28). 207p. 1996. pap. 25.95 (*0-916690-30-X*) Harvard Educ Rev.

***Beaubouef, R. T., et al, contrib. by.** Deep Water Sanstones: Brushy Canyon Formation, West Texas: Field Guide for AAPG Hedberg Field Research Conference - April 15-20, 1999. (Continuing Education Course Notes Ser.: Vol. 40). (Illus.). 50p. 1999. spiral bd. 59.00 (*0-89181-189-3*) AAPG.

Beaucamp, B. Boites en Porcelaines des Manufactures Europeennes au XVIII Siecle. (FRE.). 604p. 1991. 350.00 (*0-8288-7305-4*, 2859170499) Fr & Eur.

Beaucamp, Ernest & Hansen, Dorothea. Take Thirty Dictionary. (gr. 12). 1971. pap. 9.75 (*0-89420-099-2*, 219905) Natl Book.

— Take Thirty Shorthand: Student Syllabus, 2 vols., 1. (YA). (gr. 11-12). 1976. pap. text 9.95 (*0-89420-097-6*, 218999) Natl Book.

— Take Thirty Shorthand: Student Syllabus, 2 vols., 2. (YA). (gr. 11-12). 1976. 8.95 (*0-89420-098-4*, 219105); audio 192.75 (*0-89420-211-1*, 177700) Natl Book.

Beaucham, Tom L., ed. Intending Death: The Ethics of Assisted Suicide & Euthanasia. LC 95-4250. 234p. 1995. pap. text 34.20 (*0-13-199555-3*) P-H.

Beauchamp. Contemporary Issues in Bioethics. (Philosophy Ser.). 1978. pap. 18.50 (*0-8221-0200-5*) Wadsworth Pub.

— The Life & Times of Francis Marion & Her Friends. 1995. 25.00 (*0-02-508105-5*) Macmillan.

Beauchamp-Byrd, Mora. Transforming the Crown: African, Asian & Caribbean Artists in Britain, 1966-1996. Sirmans, M. Franklin, ed. (Illus.). 180p. 1997. pap. 39.95 (*0-9654082-0-5*) U Ch Pr.

Beauchamp, Cari. Without Lying Down: Frances Marion & the Powerful Women of Early Hollywood. 1997. 26.00 (*0-614-28027-3*, Scribner Pap Fic) S&S Trade Pap.

— Without Lying Down: Frances Marion & the Powerful Women of Early Hollywood. LC 97-641. (Illus.). 475p. 1997. 29.50 (*0-684-80213-9*, Lisa Drew) Scribner.

— Without Lying Down: Frances Marion & the Powerful Women of Early Hollywood. LC 97-44800. 475p. 1998. 17.95 (*0-520-21492-7*, Pub. by U CA Pr) Cal Prin Full Svc.

Beauchamp, Charlie. A Whale's Tale. 18p. (J). (gr. 1-4). 1995. pap. 4.95 (*0-9646498-4-5*) Pacific Tower.

Beauchamp, Dan E. Beyond Alcoholism: Alcohol & Public Health Policy. 240p. 1982. pap. 18.95 (*0-87722-286-X*) Temple U Pr.

— Health Care Reform & the Battle for the Body Politic. LC 95-33204. 173p. (C). 1996. 69.95 (*1-56639-413-9*); pap. 19.95 (*1-56639-414-7*) Temple U Pr.

— The Health of the Republic: Epidemics, Medicine, & Moralism As Challenges to Democracy. LC 87-35335. (Health, Society, & Policy Ser.). 312p. (C). 1988. 34.95 (*0-87722-558-3*) Temple U Pr.

— The Health of the Republic: Epidemics, Medicine, & Moralism As Challenges to Democracy. (Health, Society & Policy Ser.). 312p. 1990. pap. 22.95 (*0-87722-729-2*) Temple U Pr.

Beauchamp, Dan E. & Steinbock, Bonnie, eds. New Ethics for the Public's Health. LC 99-23617. (Illus.). 400p. 1999. text 67.50 (*0-19-512438-3*); pap. text 39.95 (*0-19-512439-1*) OUP.

Beauchamp, Darrell G., et al, eds. Imagery & Visual Literacy. (Illus.). 411p. (Orig.). (C). 1995. pap. text 25.00 (*0-614-04291-7*) Intl Visual.

— Visual Literacy in the Digital Age: Selected Readings from the 25th Annual Conference of the International Visual Literacy Association. (Illus.). 480p. (Orig.). (C). 1994. pap. text 25.00 (*0-945829-08-6*) Intl Visual.

Beauchamp, Darsi D., ed. see Perez, Jose A. & Mejias, Antonio I.

Beauchamp, Deanna, jt. auth. see Beauchamp, Gary.

Beauchamp, Edward, ed. see Nielsen, H. Dean & Cummings, William K.

Beauchamp, Edward, ed. see Rousmaniere, Kate, et al.

Beauchamp, Edward, ed. see Shimahara, Nobuo K.

Beauchamp, Edward R. An American Teacher in Early Meiji Japan. LC 75-45222. (Asian Studies at Hawaii: No. 17). (Illus.). 173p. reprint ed. pap. 53.70 (*0-8357-8529-7*, 203483100091) Bks Demand.

— Dimensions of Contemporary Japan: A Collection of Essays. 1998. 450.00 (*0-8153-2727-7*) Garland.

— Dissertations in the History of Education 1970-1980. LC 84-14125. 267p. 1984. 29.00 (*0-8108-1742-X*) Scarecrow.

— Preparing Teachers for Japan's Classrooms. LC 96-67186. (Fastback Ser.: No. 394). 44p. (Orig.). 1996. pap. 3.00 (*0-87367-594-0*) Phi Delta Kappa.

— Women & Women's Issues in Post World War II Japan. LC 98-45844. (Dimensions of Contemporary Japan Ser.: Vol. 4). (Illus.). 368p. 1998. reprint ed. 78.00 (*0-8153-2731-5*) Garland.

***Beauchamp, Edward R., ed.** Education & Schooling in Japan since 1945. LC 98-51524. (Dimensions of Contemporary Japan Ser.: Vol. 3). 328p. 1998. reprint ed. 75.00 (*0-8153-2730-7*) Garland.

Beauchamp, Edward R., ed. History of Contemporary Japan since World War II. LC 98-32323. (Dimensions of Contemporary Japan Ser.: Vol. 1). (Illus.). 376p. 1998. reprint ed. 80.00 (*0-8153-2728-5*) Garland.

— The Japanese Economy & Economic Issues since 1945. LC 98-51525. (Dimensions of Contemporary Japan Ser.: Vol. 5). (Illus.). 344p. 1998. reprint ed. 78.00 (*0-8153-2732-3*) Garland.

An Asterisk (*) at the beginning of an entry indicates that the title is appearing for the first time.

— Japanese Society since 1945. LC 98-45845. (Dimensions of Contemporary Japan Ser.: Vol. 2). (Illus.). 360p. 1998. reprint ed. 77.00 (*0-8153-2729-3*) Garland.

— Japan's Role in International Politics since World War II. LC 98-51523. (Dimensions of Contemporary Japan Ser.: Vol. 6). 376p. 1998. reprint ed. 75.00 (*0-8153-2733-1*) Garland.

— Windows on Japanese Education, 43. LC 90-45329. (Contributions to the Study of Education Ser.: No. 43). 344p. 1991. 65.00 (*0-313-26243-8*, BUE, Greenwood Pr) Greenwood.

Beauchamp, Edward R. & Vardaman, James M., Jr., eds. Japanese Education since 1945: A Documentary Study. LC 93-34744. 368p. (C). (gr. 13). 1994. text 90.95 (*0-87332-561-3*, East Gate Bk) M E Sharpe.

— Japanese Education since 1945: A Documentary Study. LC 93-34744. 368p. (C). (gr. 13). 1996. pap. text 42.95 (*1-56324-911-1*, East Gate Bk) M E Sharpe.

Beauchamp, Edward R., jt. ed. see Brunton, Richard H.

Beauchamp, Edward R., ed. see Glenn, Charles L. & De Jong, Ester J.

Beauchamp, Edward R., ed. see Graves, Karen.

Beauchamp, Edward R., ed. see Halasz, Gabor & Sadlak, Jan.

Beauchamp, Edward R., ed. see Lee, William.

Beauchamp, Edward R., ed. see Liu, Judith & Ross, Heidi A.

Beauchamp, Edward R., ed. see Long, Delbert & Long, Roberta.

Beauchamp, Edward R., jt. ed. see Mak, Grace C.

Beauchamp, Edward R., ed. see Paulston, Rolland.

Beauchamp, Edward R., ed. see Pollard, June, et al.

Beauchamp, Edward R., ed. see Postiglione, Gerard A. & Stites, Regie.

Beauchamp, Edward R., ed. see Ray, Douglas.

Beauchamp, Edward R., ed. see Sato, Nancy.

Beauchamp, Edward R., ed. see Scrase, Timothy.

Beauchamp, Edward R., ed. see Shafer, Susanne M.

Beauchamp, Edward R., ed. see Shimahara, Nobuo K. & Sakai, Akira.

Beauchamp, Edward R., jt. ed. see Sunal, Cynthia S.

Beauchamp, Edward R., ed. see Tjeldvoll, Arild.

Beauchamp, Edward R., ed. see Welch, Anthony R.

Beauchamp, G. A New Owner's Guide to Chow Chows. (Illus.). 160p. 1997. 12.95 (*0-7938-2780-9*, JG131) TFH Pubns.

Beauchamp, Gary & Beauchamp, Deanna. Religiously Mixed Marriage. 1981. pap. 7.15 (*0-89137-528-7*) Quality Pubns.

Beauchamp, Gerald & Cuny, Jean. Curtiss Hawk 75. (Illus.). 352p. (Orig.). 1997. pap. 49.95 (*0-934575-13-4*) Vip Pubs.

Beauchamp, Gorman. Jack London. Schlobin, Roger C., ed. LC 82-7345. (Starmont Reader's Guide Ser.: Vol. 15). 96p. 1984. pap. 17.00 (*0-916732-39-8*) Millefleurs.

Beauchamp, Henry K., jt. auth. see Dubois, J. A.

Beauchamp, K. G. Exhibiting Electricity. (History of Technology Ser.: No. 21). 337p. 1997. 85.00 (*0-85296-895-7*, HT021) INSPEC Inc.

Beauchamp, Kenneth G. Applications of Walsh & Related Functions. (Microelectronics & Signal Processing Ser.). 1984. text 138.00 (*0-12-084180-0*) Acad Pr.

Beauchamp, Kenneth G., ed. Information Technology & the Computer Network. (NATO ASI Series F: Computer & Systems Sciences, Special Programme AET: Vol. 6). x, 281p. 1984. 71.95 (*0-387-12883-2*) Spr-Verlag.

— Interlinking of Computer Networks. (NATO Advanced Study Institutes Ser.). 1979. text 135.00 (*90-277-0979-3*) Kluwer Academic.

Beauchamp, Kenneth G. & Poo, Gee S. Computer Communications. 3rd ed. (Illus.). 360p. 1995. mass mkt. 34.95 (*1-85032-168-X*) ITCP.

Beauchamp, Kenneth G. & Yuen, C. K. Digital Methods for Signal Analysis. (Illus.). 1979. text 65.00 (*0-04-621027-X*) Routledge.

Beauchamp, Kenneth G., ed. see NATO Advanced Study Institute Staff.

Beauchamp, Larry, jt. auth. see Parsons, Jim.

Beauchamp, Monte. Blab, Vol. 9. 1998. pap. text 18.95 (*1-56097-284-X*) Fantagraph Bks.

***Beauchamp, Monte.** Blab!, Vol. 10. 1999. pap. 19.95 (*1-56097-323-4*) Fantagraph Bks.

Beauchamp, Monte. The Life & Times of R. Crumb: Comments from Contemporaries. LC 98-18842. (Illus.). 192p. 1998. pap. 17.95 (*0-312-19571-0*) St Martin.

Beauchamp, Monte, ed. Blab!, No. 6. (Illus.). 128p. 1991. pap. 7.95 (*0-87816-131-7*) Kitchen Sink.

— Blab!, No. 7. (Illus.). 144p. 1992. pap. 8.95 (*0-87816-194-5*) Kitchen Sink.

Beauchamp, R. H. Twenty-Five Years at Brooklands Track with the "Railton Era" 108p. 1984. 39.00 (*0-7212-0619-0*, Pub. by Regency Pr GBR) St Mut.

Beauchamp, R. Mitchel. A Flora of San Diego County, California. 241p. 1986. 28.95 (*0-931950-01-5*); pap. 22.95 (*0-931950-00-7*) Sweetwater River Pr.

Beauchamp, R. Mitchel, ed. see Reid, C. & Dyer, R. Allen.

***Beauchamp, Richard.** American Eskimos. 1999. 12.95 (*0-7938-2781-7*) TFH Pubns.

Beauchamp, Richard. Doberman Pincsher: An Owner's Guide to a Happy Healthy Pet. LC 96-6040. (Illus.). 160p. 1996. 12.95 (*0-87605-481-5*) Howell Bks.

Beauchamp, Richard G. Australian Cattle Dog: Everything about Purchase, Care, Nutrition, Breeding, Behavior & Training. LC 96-29857. (Complete Pet Owner's Manual Ser.). 1997. pap. 6.95 (*0-8120-9854-4*) Barron.

— Bichon Frise: Everything about Purchase, Care, Nutrition, Breeding, Behavior, & Training. LC 95-39596. (Complete Pet Owner's Manual Ser.). 1996. pap. 6.95 (*0-8120-9465-4*) Barron.

***Beauchamp, Richard G.** Boxers for Dummies. (Illus.). 288p. 2000. pap. 15.99 (*0-7645-5285-6*) IDG Bks.

Beauchamp, Richard G. Owning, Raising & Training a Rottweiler. LC 99-62691. (Complete Idiot's Guides (Lifestyle) Ser.). (Illus.). 284p. 1999. pap. write for info. (*1-58245-041-2*) Macmillan Gen Ref.

***Beauchamp, Richard G.** Rottweilers for Dummies. (For Dummies (Lifestyles) Ser.). (Illus.). 334p. 2000. pap. 15.99 (*0-7645-5271-6*) IDG Bks.

Beauchamp, Richard G. The Truth about Bichons. unabridged ed. Allen, Michael, ed. & illus. by. 152p. 1998. 35.00 (*0-9623515-1-2*) Amer Cocker Mag.

***Beauchamp, Richard G.** Welsh Corgis: Pembroke & Cardigan. LC 98-31185. (Complete Pet Owner's Manual Ser.). (Illus.). 104p. 1999. pap. 6.95 (*0-7641-0557-4*) Barron.

Beauchamp, Rick, jt. contrib. by see Stamm, Miriam.

Beauchamp, Robert. Graymail. 290p. 1995. pap. 25.00 (*1-57087-062-4*) Prof Pr NC.

Beauchamp, Thomas L. Case Studies in Business, Society & Ethics. 4th ed. LC 97-25144. 281p. (C). 1997. pap. text, student ed. 31.80 (*0-13-398512-1*) P-H.

— Contemporary Issues in Bioethics. 5th ed. LC 98-48339. 1999. pap. 74.95 (*0-534-50476-0*) Brooks-Cole.

— Philosophical Ethics: An Introduction to Moral Philosophy. 2nd ed. 448p. (C). 1991. pap. 43.44 (*0-07-004256-X*) McGraw.

Beauchamp, Thomas L., et al, eds. Ethical Issues in Social Science Research. LC 81-12419. 448p. (C). 1982. pap. text 24.95 (*0-8018-2656-X*) Johns Hopkins.

Beauchamp, Thomas L. & Bowie, Norman E. Ethical Theory of Business. 5th ed. LC 96-8098. 661p. (C). 1996. pap. text 58.00 (*0-13-398520-2*) P-H.

Beauchamp, Thomas L. & Bowie, Norman E., eds. Ethical Theory & Business. 5th ed. LC 96-8098. 1997. write for info. (*0-01-339852-0*) P-H.

Beauchamp, Thomas L. & Childress, James F. Principles of Biomedical Ethics. 4th ed. LC 93-24390. 560p. (C). 1994. pap. text 29.95 (*0-19-508537-X*) OUP.

Beauchamp, Thomas L. & Pinkard, Terry P., eds. Ethics & Public Policy: Introduction to Ethics. 2nd ed. (Illus.). 416p. (C). 1982. pap. text 41.20 (*0-13-290957-X*) P-H.

Beauchamp, Thomas L. & Veatch, Robert M., eds. Ethical Issues in Death & Dying. 2nd ed. LC 95-9228. 458p. 1995. pap. text 47.00 (*0-13-282732-8*) P-H.

Beauchamp, Thomas L. & Walters, Leroy. Contemporary Issues in Bioethics. 4th ed. 752p. 1994. 49.25 (*0-534-22314-1*) Wadsworth Pub.

Beauchamp, Thomas L. & Walters, LeRoy, eds. Contemporary Issues in Bioethics. 2nd ed. 614p. (C). 1982. pap. write for info. (*0-534-01102-0*) Wadsworth Pub.

— Contemporary Issues in Bioethics. 3rd ed. 655p. (C). 1989. pap. 44.95 (*0-534-10182-8*) Wadsworth Pub.

Beauchamp, Thomas L., et al. Philosophy & the Human Condition. 2nd ed. 656p. (C). 1988. text 50.25 (*0-13-662537-1*) P-H.

Beauchamp, Thomas L., jt. auth. see Klaidman, Stephen.

Beauchamp, Thomas L., jt. ed. see Coughlin, Steven S.

Beauchamp, Thomas L., ed. see Hume, David.

***Beauchamp, Tom L.** Philosophical Ethics: An Introduction to Moral Philosophy. 3rd ed. LC 99-47187. 2001. write for info. (*0-07-229721-2*) McGrw-H Hghr Educ.

Beauchamp, Tom. L, ed. see Hume, David.

Beauchamp, William M. Aboriginal Chipped Stone Implements of New York. LC 76-43659. (New York State Museum Bulletin Ser.: Vol. 4, No. 16). reprint ed. 37.50 (*0-404-15495-6*) AMS Pr.

— Aboriginal Occupation of New York. LC 76-43660. (New York State Museum Bulletin Ser.: No. 32, Vol. 7). reprint ed. 45.00 (*0-404-15492-1*) AMS Pr.

— Aboriginal Occupation of New York. 190p. 1993. reprint ed. lib. bdg. 69.00 (*0-7812-5156-7*) Rprt Serv.

— Aboriginal Place Names of New York. 336p. 1993. reprint ed. lib. bdg. 89.00 (*0-7812-5155-9*) Rprt Serv.

— Aboriginal Use of Wood in New York. LC 76-43661. (New York State Museum Bulletin Ser.: No. 89). reprint ed. 49.50 (*0-404-15493-X*) AMS Pr.

— History of the New York Iroquois. 340p. 1993. reprint ed. lib. bdg. 89.00 (*0-7812-5154-0*) Rprt Serv.

— A History of the New York Iroquois, Now Commonly Called the Six Nations. LC 74-7925. (Illus.). reprint ed. 55.00 (*0-404-11811-9*) AMS Pr.

— Horn & Bone Implements of the New York Indians. LC 76-43662. (New York State Museum Bulletin Ser.: 50). reprint ed. 39.50 (*0-404-15494-8*) AMS Pr.

— Iroquois Folk Lore. LC 74-7926. reprint ed. 49.50 (*0-404-11812-7*) AMS Pr.

— The Iroquois Trail. LC 74-7927. reprint ed. 39.50 (*0-404-11813-5*) AMS Pr.

— Metallic Ornaments of the New York Indians. LC 74-7928. reprint ed. 31.50 (*0-404-11814-3*) AMS Pr.

— Moravian Journals Relating to Central New York. LC 72-8246. (Communal Societies in America Ser). reprint ed. 41.50 (*0-404-11000-2*) AMS Pr.

***Beauchamp, William M.** Moravian Journals Relating to Central New York, 1745-1766. 211p. 1999. reprint ed. pap. 22.50 (*0-7884-1311-2*, B112) Heritage Bk.

Beauchamp, William M. Perch Lake Mounds, with Notes on Other New York Mounds & Some Accounts of Indian Trails. LC 74-7929. reprint ed. 31.50 (*0-404-11815-1*) AMS Pr.

— Polished Stone Articles Used by the New York Aborigines Before & During European Occupation. LC 74-7930. reprint ed. 34.50 (*0-404-11816-X*) AMS Pr.

— Revolutionary Soldiers of Onondaga County, New York. 307p. 1993. reprint ed. lib. bdg. 35.00 (*0-8328-3511-0*) Higginson Bk Co.

— Wampum & Shell Articles Used by the New York Indians. LC 76-43663. (New York State Museum Bulletin Ser.: No. 41, Vol. 8). reprint ed. 49.50 (*0-404-15496-4*) AMS Pr.

Beauchamp, William M., ed. Iroquois Folk Lore, Gathered from the Six Nations of New York. 251p. 1997. reprint ed. lib. bdg. 34.00 (*0-8328-6083-2*) Higginson Bk Co.

***Beauchemin, Cyndi.** The Daycare Provider's Workbook: A Step by Step Guide to Assist Daycare Provider's in Setting... 1999. pap., wbk. ed. 24.95 (*0-9678010-1-X*) T C B Enterps.

Beauchemin, D. ICP-MS: Sample Introduction Methodology & Mixed Gas Plasmas. 1997. write for info. (*0-444-82029-9*) Elsevier.

Beauchemin, Katherine V., jt. auth. see Gallup, David A.

Beauchemin, Tim, ed. see Myers, Gene.

Beauchemin, Tim, ed. see Pierson, Frederick.

Beauchemin, Yves. The Alley Cat. 552p. 1996. pap. text 8.95 (*0-7710-3451-2*) McCland & Stewart.

— The Alley Cat. (C). 1989. 39.00 (*0-948353-18-X*, Pub. by Oldcastle Bks) St Mut.

— The Second Fiddle. Homel, David, tr. from FRE. LC 98-162035. 432p. 1999. 16.95 (*0-7737-3085-0*, Pub. by Stoddart Publ) Genl Dist Srvs.

Beauchesne, Alcide. Louis XVII, 2 vols. LC 78-161731. (Illus.). reprint ed. 164.50 (*0-404-07546-0*) AMS Pr.

Beauchet, Ludovic. Histoire du Droit Prive de la Republique Athenienne, 4 vols., Set. LC 75-13256. (History of Ideas in Ancient Greece Ser.). (FRE.). 1976. reprint ed. 169.95 (*0-405-07294-5*) Ayer.

— Histoire du Droit Prive de la Republique Athenienne, 4 vols., Vol. 1. LC 75-13256. (History of Ideas in Ancient Greece Ser.). (FRE.). 1976. reprint ed. 42.95 (*0-405-07295-3*) Ayer.

— Histoire du Droit Prive de la Republique Athenienne, 4 vols., Vol. 2. LC 75-13256. (History of Ideas in Ancient Greece Ser.). (FRE.). 1976. reprint ed. 42.95 (*0-405-07296-1*) Ayer.

— Histoire du Droit Prive de la Republique Athenienne, 4 vols., Vol. 3. LC 75-13256. (History of Ideas in Ancient Greece Ser.). (FRE.). 1976. reprint ed. 42.95 (*0-405-07297-X*) Ayer.

— Histoire du Droit Prive de la Republique Athenienne, 4 vols., Vol. 4. LC 75-13256. (History of Ideas in Ancient Greece Ser.). (FRE.). 1976. reprint ed. 42.95 (*0-405-07298-8*) Ayer.

Beauclair, Inez De, see De Beauclair, Inez.

Beauclair, Michelle M. Albert Camus, Marguerite Duras, & the Legacy of Mourning. LC 95-44272. (Francophone Cultures & Literatures Ser.: Vol. 21). 137p. (C). 1998. text 38.95 (*0-8204-3000-5*) P Lang Pubng.

Beauclerk, John. Hunters & Gatherers in Central Africa. (Oxfam Research Papers). 46p. (C). 1993. pap. 12.95 (*0-85598-191-1*, Pub. by Oxfam Pub) Stylus Pub VA.

Beauclerk, John, et al. Indigenous Peoples: A Fieldguide for Development. (Illus.). 128p. (C). 1988. pap. 12.95 (*0-85598-088-5*, Pub. by Oxfam Pub) Stylus Pub VA.

Beaucour, Fernand, et al. The Discovery of Egypt: Artists, Travellers & Scientists. Ballard, Bambi, tr. (Illus.). 272p. 1993. 50.00 (*2-08-013506-6*, Pub. by Flammarion) Abbeville Pr.

Beaucourt, C. Main-d'Oeuvre Potentielle et Emploi Regional en Union Sovietique. (Economies et Societes Series G: No. 24). 1966. pap. 34.00 (*0-8115-0715-7*) Periodicals Srv.

Beaucourt, Gaston L. Captivite et Derniers Moments de Louis-Seize, 2 vols. LC 71-161732. reprint ed. 35.00 (*0-404-07622-X*) AMS Pr.

Beaud, Michel. A History of Capitalism, 1500-1980. Dickman, Tom & Lefebvre, Anny, trs. from FRE. LC 83-42522. Orig. Title: Histoire du Capitalism. 288p. 1983. pap. 15.00 (*0-85345-627-5*, Pub. by Monthly Rev) NYU Pr.

— Socialism in the Crucible of History. Dickman, Tom, tr. from FRE. LC 92-15659. 232p. (C). 1993. text 55.00 (*0-391-03770-6*) Humanities.

Beaud, Michel & Dostaler, Gilles. Economic Thought since Keynes: A History & Dictionary of Major Economists. (Illus.). 512p. 1995. 165.00 (*1-85278-667-1*) E Elgar.

— Economic Thought since Keynes: A History & Dictionary of Major Economists. LC 97-12823. 512p. (C). 1997. pap. 32.99 (*0-415-16454-0*) Routledge.

Beaude, Pierre-Marie. The Book of Creation. Clements, Andrew, tr. LC 90-35418. (Illus.). 56p. (J). (gr. 5 up). 1991. pap. 16.95 (*0-88708-141-X*, Picture Book Studio) S&S Childrens.

Beaudet, Maurice & Erion, Tonya. Recipes from the Heart. (Illus.). 96p. 1988. 19.95 (*0-9617850-0-4*) Spot Press.

Beaudet, Pierre, ed. Under the Boardwalk in Quebec City. 199p. pap. 25.00 (*0-920717-52-7*) Guernica Editions.

Beaudet, Pierre, jt. ed. see Thede, Nancy.

***Beaudette, Charles G.** Excess Heat: Why Cold Fusion Research Prevailed. 360 p. 2000. pap. 26.95 (*0-9678548-1-4*) Oak Grove Pr.

— Excess Heat: Why Cold Fusion Research Prevailed. 360p. 2000. 36.95 (*0-9678548-0-6*, Pub. by Oak Grove Pr) Infinite Energy.

Beaudette, Therese. Adverse Reactions to Food. LC 91-31708. 1991. pap. 7.65 (*0-88091-093-3*, 0154) Am Dietetic Assn.

***Beaudin, Marc & Hellus, Al, eds.** Saginaw Songs: Poetry of Saginaw, Michigan. (Illus.). 36p. 1999. pap. text 5.00 (*1-56439-101-9*, Pub. by Ridgeway) Partners Pubs Grp.

Beaudine, Frank R. In Search of Success. LC 97-26579. 1997. pap. 9.99 (*0-8423-1721-X*) Tyndale Hse.

Beaudoin, Bernard, jt. ed. see Ginsburg, Robert N.

Beaudoin, David. The Hullabaloo Pt. I: A Little Bit of Heaven . . . A Whole Lot of Hell! unabridged ed. Beaudoin, Larissa, ed. & contrib. by by. LC 96-62037. (Illus.). 354p. 1998. pap., per. 37.75 (*0-9656341-6-7*) Tru-Bks.

Beaudoin, J.J., jt. auth. see Ramachandran, V.S.

Beaudoin, Larissa, ed. & contrib. by see Beaudoin, David.

Beaudoin, Luc J. Resetting the Margins: Russian Romantic Verse Tales & the Idealized Woman. LC 95-44269. (Berkeley Insights in Linguistics & Semiotics Ser.: Vol. 23). XII, 248p. (C). 1997. 47.95 (*0-8204-3048-X*) P Lang Pubng.

***Beaudoin, Marie-Jose, et al.** Bouillon de Poulet pour l'ame.Tr. of Chicken Soup for the Soul. (FRE.). 2000. boxed set 14.95 incl. audio (*2-89517-043-6*, Pub. by Coffragants) Penton Overseas.

— Bouillon de Poulet pour l'ame de la Femme.Tr. of Chicken Soup for the Woman's Soul. (FRE.). 1999. 14.95 incl. audio (*2-89517-038-X*, Pub. by Coffragants) Penton Overseas.

— Bouillon de Poulet pour l'ame des Ados.Tr. of Chicken Soup for the Teenage Soul. (FRE.). 1999. boxed set 14.95 incl. audio (*2-89517-039-8*, Pub. by Coffragants) Penton Overseas.

Beaudoin, Marie-Nathalie & Walden, Sue. Working with Groups to Enhance Relationships. LC 98-25401. 1998. pap. 24.95 (*1-57025-169-X*) Whole Person.

Beaudoin, Maurice, jt. auth. see Escaig, Roland.

Beaudoin, Michael, et al. Distance Education Symposium Papers: Selected Papers. (ACSDE Research Monograph Ser.: No. 4, Pt. 1). (C). 1991. pap. 20.00 (*1-877780-06-5*) ACSDE.

Beaudoin, Michael F., ed. Distance Education Symposium 3: Instruction. LC 98-146707. (ACSDE Research Monograph Ser.: No. 12). 119p. (Orig.). 1996. pap. text 30.00 (*1-877780-15-4*) ACSDE.

***Beaudoin, Tom.** Virtual Faith: The Irreverent Spiritual Quest of Generation X. 240p. 2000. pap. 16.00 (*0-7879-5527-2*) Jossey-Bass.

Beaudon, Tom. Virtual Faith: The Irreverent Spiritual Quest of Generation X. LC 97-33912. (Religion in Practice Ser.). 256p. 1998. mass mkt. 21.50 (*0-7879-3882-3*) Jossey-Bass.

Beaudot, William, jt. auth. see Herdegen, Lance.

Beaudot, William J. & Herdegen, Lance J., eds. An Irishman in the Iron Brigade: The Civil War Memoirs of James P. Sullivan, Sergeant, 6th Wisconsin Volunteers. LC 93-12574. (Irish in the Civil War Ser.: No. 3). (Illus.). xii, 189p. (C). 1993. 27.50 (*0-8232-1500-8*) Fordham.

Beaudouin, David, et al, eds. Gathering Voices: An Anthology of Baltimore Poets. 2nd ed. 160p. (Orig.). 1986. pap. 7.95 (*0-933837-72-0*) Dolphin-Moon.

Beaudouin-Lafon, M. Object-Oriented Languages: Basic Principles & Programming Techniques. 140p. 1994. mass mkt. 35.95 (*0-412-55800-9*, Chap & Hall NY) Chapman & Hall.

Beaudouin-Lafon, Michel. Computer Supported Co-operative Work. LC 98-42699. (Trends in Software Ser.). 274p. 1999. 115.00 (*0-471-96736-X*) Wiley.

Beaudoin-Ross, Jacqueline. Form & Fashion: Nineteenth-Century Montreal Dress. (Illus.). 96p. 1992. pap. 55.00 (*0-7735-0970-4*, Pub. by McG-Queens Univ Pr) CUP Services.

Beaudreau, Bernard C. Energy & Organization: Growth & Distribution Reexamined, 193. LC 97-37970. (Contributions in Economics & Economic History Ser.: Vol. 193). 208p. 1998. 65.00 (*0-313-30580-3*, Greenwood Pr) Greenwood.

— Energy & the Rise & Fall of Political Economy, 213. LC 99-25005. (Contributions in Economics & Economic History Ser.: No. 213). 240p. 1999. 65.00 (*0-313-31059-9*, GM1059, Greenwood Pr) Greenwood.

— Mass Production, the Stock Market Crash & the Great Depression: The Macroeconomics of Electrification, 175. LC 95-48363. (Contributions in Economics & Economic History: Vol. 175). 208p. 1996. 62.95 (*0-313-29920-X*, Greenwood Pr) Greenwood.

Beaudry, Ann & Schaeffer, Bob. Winning Local & State Elections: The Guide to Organizing, Financing, & Targeting Your Campaign. 208p. 1986. 35.00 (*0-02-902490-0*) Free Pr.

Beaudry, Catherine A. The Role of the Reader in Rousseau's "Confessions" LC 91-18783. (Age of Revolution & Romanticism: Interdisciplinary Studies: Vol. 2). 174p. (C). 1992. text 43.95 (*0-8204-1647-9*) P Lang Pubng.

***Beaudry-Corbett, Marilyn & Hardy, Ellen T., eds.** Early Scholars' Visits to Central America: Reports by Karl Sapper, Walter Lehmann & Franz Termer. Gutman, Theodore E., tr. from GER. LC 99-55214. (Occasional Papers: No. 18). (Illus.). 128p. 2000. pap. text 25.00 (*0-917956-95-8*) UCLA Arch.

Beaudry, Jo & Ketchum, Lynne. Carla Goes to Court. LC 82-2854. (Illus.). 32p. (J). (gr. 1-5). 1982. 16.95 (*0-89885-088-6*, Kluwer Acad Hman Sci); pap. 10.95 (*0-89885-354-0*, Kluwer Acad Hman Sci) Kluwer Academic.

Beaudry, Louis N. War Journal of Louis N. Beaudry, Fifth New York Cavalry: The Diary of a Union Chaplain, Commencing February 16, 1863. Beaudry, Richard E., ed. LC 96-24267. 260p. 1996. lib. bdg. 35.00 (*0-7864-0260-1*) McFarland & Co.

Beaudry, Mark H. Contemporary Lodging Security: Modern Hotel Security Management. LC 95-34236. 170p. 1996. 36.95 (*0-7506-9574-9*, BH Security) Buttrwrth-Heinemann.

Beaudry, Mary C. Domestic Pursuits: Historical Archaeology of American Households. 1994. write for info. (*0-8493-8884-8*) CRC Pr.

Beaudry, Mary C., ed. Art & Mystery of Historical Archaeology. 480p. 1992. lib. bdg. 95.00 (*0-8493-8854-6*, E159) CRC Pr.

— Documentary Archaeology in the New World. (New Directions in Archaeology Ser.). (Illus.). 224p. (C). 1993. pap. text 21.95 (*0-521-44999-5*) Cambridge U Pr.

B

Beaudry, Mary C., et al. Unearthing New England's Past: The Ceramic Evidence. LC 83-51504. 112p. (Orig.). (C). 1984. pap. 12.50 (*0-9621107-3-6*) Mus Our Natl Hertge.

Beaudry, Micheline. Battered Women. Huston, Lorne & Heap, Margaret, trs. from FRE. 118p. 1985. 41.99 (*0-920057-47-0*, Pub. by Black Rose); pap. 12.99 (*0-920057-46-2*, Pub. by Black Rose) Consort Bk Sales.

Beaudry, Michelle. How to Tell If You're Dead: Because You Just Never Know. (Illus.). 60p. (Orig.). 1996. pap. 6.00 (*0-9644347-1-7*) Laffbooks.

— Travellers Laffbook: 50 Reasons to Stay Home, Starting with Alabama. (Illus.). 128p. 1995. pap. 9.95 (*0-9644347-0-9*) Laffbooks.

Beaudry, Paul S. The Forgotten Regiment: History of the 151st New York Volunteer Infantry Regiment. LC 94-77362. 264p. (Orig.). 1995. pap. text 12.95 (*0-9642058-1-5*) InChem Pubng.

Beaudry, Richard E., ed. see Beaudry, Louis N.

Beaudry, Robert M. Only the Father Knows: An American Crisis. LC 94-77363. 232p. (Orig.). 1995. pap. 12.95 (*0-9642058-0-7*) InChem Pubng.

Beauer, Laurie. Vocabulary. LC 97-39921. (Language Workbooks Ser.). (Illus.). 104p. (C). 1998. pap. 14.99 (*0-415-16398-6*) Routledge.

Beaufait, Kathleen B., ed. see Luter, James G., Jr.

Beaufeaux, David F. Driving Self Defense. 1997. pap. 4.00 (*0-9658230-3-2*) Ready Serv.

— You & Your Credit: The Inside Story. 1996. pap. 4.00 (*0-9658230-1-6*) Ready Serv.

— You & Your Credit: The Inside Story. 2nd rev. ed. 14p. (YA). (gr. 7-12). 1997. write for info. (*0-9658230-0-8*) Ready Serv.

***Beauford, Fred.** The Rejected American: Reflections. unabridged ed. 219p. 1999. pap. 21.50 (*1-929188-00-5*) Morton Bks.

— The Womanizer. unabridged ed. 250p. (Orig.). 2000. pap. 21.99 (*1-929188-01-3*) Morton Bks.

***Beaufort, Anne.** Writing in the Real World: Making the Transition from School to Work. LC 99-43189. (Language & Literacy Ser.). 256p. 1999. text 59.00 (*0-8077-3901-4*); pap. text. write for info. (*0-8077-3900-6*) Tchrs Coll.

Beaufort, Francis. Karamania. 1988. reprint ed. lib. bdg. 75.00 (*0-685-21379-X*) Rprt Serv.

***Beaufort, Roxane.** Savage Bonds. 272p. 2000. pap. 9.95 (*1-901388-51-4*, Pub. by Chimera Pubns) Firebird Dist.

Beaufort, Simon. A Head for Poisoning. LC 99-21753. 384p. 1999. text 23.95 (*0-312-20549-X*) St Martin.

Beaufort, Simon De, see De Beaufort, Simon.

Beaufort Wijnholds, Onno De, see De Beaufort Wijnholds, Onno.

Beaufort, William M. DeBeaufort. Family of DeBeaufort in France, Holland, Germany & England. (Illus.). 163p. 1997. reprint ed. pap. 24.50 (*0-8328-8248-8*); reprint ed. lib. bdg. 34.50 (*0-8328-8247-X*) Higginson Bk Co.

Beauge, Luis A., et al, eds. Na/k-Atpase & Related Transport Atpases: The Surface Pumps on Which Every Living Creature Relies. LC 97-35157. (Annals of the New York Academy of Sciences Ser.: No. 834). 694p. 1997. 190.00 (*1-57331-060-3*) NY Acad Sci.

— Nalk-Atpase & Related Transport Atpases: The Surface Pumps on Which Every Living Creature Relies. LC 97-35157. (Annals of the New York Academy of Sciences Ser.: No. 834). 694p. 1997. pap. 190.00 (*1-57331-061-1*) NY Acad Sci.

Beaugrand. Manuel Pratique de Composition Francaise. 16.50 (*0-685-36705-3*, F140310); 7.95 (*0-8288-7608-8*, F140310) Fr & Eur.

Beaugrande, Robert de. Text Production: Forward a Science of Composition. Freedle, Roy O., ed. LC 83-25756. (Advances in Discourse Processes Ser.: Vol. 11). 416p. (C). 1984. pap. 42.50 (*0-89391-159-3*); text 78.50 (*0-89391-158-5*) Ablx Pub.

Beaugue, Jean de. L' Histoire de la Guerre d'Ecosse. Bain, Joseph, ed. LC 70-159993. (Maitland Club, Glasgow. Publications: No. 2). reprint ed. 17.50 (*0-404-52923-2*) AMS Pr.

Beaujard, P. Dictionary Malgache to French. (FRE.). 1998. 169.00 (*0-320-00278-0*) Fr & Eur.

Beaujeu-Garnier, Jacqueline. Geography of Population. 2nd ed. Beaver, Stanley H., tr. LC 77-30726. (Geographies for Advanced Study Ser.). (Illus.). 436p. reprint ed. pap. 135.20 (*0-8357-6127-4*, 203451100090) Bks Demand.

Beaujolais, Roxy. Home from the Inn Contented: A Cookbook of Simple, Popular Pub Food. (Illus.). 144p. 1997. pap. 22.95 (*1-85626-213-8*, Pub. by Cathie Kyle) Trafalgar.

***Beaujot, Rod.** Earning & Caring in Canadian Families. 250p. 1999. pap. 22.95 (*1-55111-166-7*) Broadview Pr.

Beaujot, Roderic P., et al. Family over the Life Course LC 96-140612. (Current Demographic Analysis Ser.). 173p. 1995. write for info. (*0-660-15565-6*) Stat Can Mktg.

Beaujouan, Guy. Par Raison de Nombres: L'Art du Calcul et les Savoirs Scientifiques Medievaux. (Collected Studies: No. CS 344). 336p. 1991. text 119.95 (*0-86078-281-6*, Pub. by Variorum) Ashgate Pub Co.

— Science Medievale d'Espagne et D'Alentour. (Collected Studies: No. CS374). 336p. 1992. 119.95 (*0-86078-304-9*, Pub. by Variorum) Ashgate Pub Co.

Beaujour, Elizabeth K. Alien Tongues: Bilingual Russian Writers of the "First" Emigration. LC 88-43287. (Studies of the Harriman Institute). 288p. 1989. text 39.95 (*0-8014-2251-5*) Cornell U Pr.

Beaujour, Michel. Poetics of the Literary Self-Portrait. (Studies in French Culture & Civilization). 419p. (C). 1992. pap. text 20.00 (*0-8147-1192-8*) NYU Pr.

Beaulac, Willard L. Franco: Silent Ally in World War II. LC 85-27896. (Illus.). 242p. 1986. 31.95 (*0-8093-1254-9*) S Ill U Pr.

Beaulieu, Andre & Morley, William F. La Province de Quebec. LC 72-151355. (Canadian Local Histories to 1950: A Bibliography Ser.: No. 2). 436p. reprint ed. pap. 135.20 (*0-8357-8199-2*, 203400500088) Bks Demand.

Beaulieu, Andre, jt. auth. see Johnson, Pierre M.

Beaulieu, Blandine. Maverick Column. 1996. 25.95 (*0-9660181-1-7*) Concept Arts.

— Maverick Column. large type ed. 545p. 1996. 24.95 (*0-9660181-0-9*) Concept Arts.

Beaulieu, Elizabeth Ann. Black Women Writers & the American Neo-Slave Narrative: Femininity Unfettered, 192. LC 98-33756. (Contributions in Afro-American & African Studies: Vol. 192). 200p. 1999. 49.95 (*0-313-30838-1*, Greenwood Pr) Greenwood.

Beaulieu, Gary. The Little Words That Grew: A Guide to Using Proverbs in the Therapeutic Process. LC 98-17909. 1998. pap. 18.00 (*1-882883-37-3*) Idyll Arbor.

Beaulieu, J. L., jt. auth. see Garreau, Bernard.

Beaulieu, Jane, et al. Trauma Pocket Guide. unabridged ed. 22p. 1997. pap. 20.00 (*0-935890-14-9*) Emerg Nurses IL.

Beaulieu, John. Music & Sound in the Healing Arts: An Energy Approach. Quasha, George, ed. LC 87-10076. 150p. (C). 1987. 19.95 (*0-88268-057-9*); pap. 12.95 (*0-88268-056-0*) Station Hill Pr.

Beaulieu, John E. & Granzin, Alex. Working Parents Can Raise Smart Kids: The "Time-Starved"Parent's Guide to Helping Your Child Succeed in School. LC 98-67442. (Illus.). 216 p. 1999. pap. 14.95 (*0-9666316-5-X*) Parkland Pr.

Beaulieu, Joyce E. & Berry, David E., eds. Rural Health Services: A Management Perspective. LC 94-20578. 350p. 1994. pap. 20.50 (*1-56793-018-2*, 0948) Health Admin Pr.

***Beaulieu, Linda.** Divine Providence: A Guide to the City's Best Restaurants. (Illus.). 48p. 2000. 18.95 (*1-58066-058-4*, Covered Brdge Pr) Douglas Charles Ltd.

Beaulieu, Michel, tr. see Robertson, Heather.

Beaulieu, Michele. Dictionnaire des Sculpteurs Francais du Moyen Age. (FRE.). 312p. 1992. 225.00 (*0-8288-9472-8*) Fr & Eur.

Beaulieu, Paul-Alain. Late Babylonian Texts in the Nies Babylonian Collection. Kasten, Ulla, ed. LC 94-5455. (Catalogue of the Babylonian Collection at Yale: Vol. 1). 103p. (C). 1994. 48.00 (*1-883053-04-8*) CDL Pr.

***Beaulieu, Paul-Alain.** Legal Administrative Texts from the Reign of Nabonidus. LC 99-88525. (Oriental Ser.: Vol. 19). (Illus.). 288p. 2000. 60.00 (*0-300-05770-9*) Yale U Pr.

Beaulieu, Robert J. Fashion Textiles. 3rd ed. LC 85-22008. 1985. wbk. ed., lab manual ed. 24.68 (*0-02-682830-8*) Macmillan.

Beaulieu, Thea K. The Color Love Journal: A Gift for Your Health & Happiness. (Illus.). 104p. (Orig.). 1992. pap. 9.95 (*0-9632758-0-1*) Polarity Wellness.

Beaulieu, Victor-Levy, jt. auth. see Atwood, Margaret.

Beaulou, John. The Polarity Therapy Workbook. 225p. 1994. write for info. (*0-9640604-0-X*) Bio Sonic Ent.

Beauman, Sally. Danger Zones. 1995. 23.00 (*0-614-96251-X*, Columbine) Fawcett.

— Danger Zones. 1997. mass mkt. 6.99 (*0-449-22561-5*, Crest) Fawcett.

— Danger Zones. large type ed. LC 96-19339. 1996. pap. 22.95 (*1-56895-343-7*) Wheeler Pub.

— Deception & Desire. 1998. mass mkt. 6.99 (*0-449-00248-9*, GM) Fawcett.

— Destiny. 848p. 1988. mass mkt. 7.50 (*0-553-27018-4*) Bantam.

— Lovers & Liars. 1995. mass mkt. 6.99 (*0-449-22368-X*, Crest) Fawcett.

— Lovers & Liars. 1997. pap. text 6.99 (*0-449-45793-1*) Fawcett.

— The Royal Shakespeare Company's Centenary Production of Henry V. 1976. 11.00 (*0-08-020874-6*, Pergamon Pr) Elsevier.

Beaumanoir, A. Continuous Spikes & Waves During Slow Sleep. 272p. 68.00 (*0-86196-488-8*, Pub. by J Libbey Med) Bks Intl VA.

— Falls in Epileptic & Non Epileptic Seizures During Childhood. 68.00 (*0-86196-540-X*, Pub. by J Libbey Med) Bks Intl VA.

Beaumarchais. Barber of Seville: Beaumarchais' Comedy in One-Act. (Illus.). 42p. 1968. pap. 3.25 (*0-88680-010-2*) I E Clark.

— Barber of Seville: Director's Script. (Illus.). 42p. 1968. pap. 10.00 (*0-88680-011-0*) I E Clark.

— Le Mariage de Figaro. (FRE.). (C). 1985. pap. 9.95 (*0-8442-1830-8*, VF1830-8) NTC Contemp Pub Co.

— Marriage of Figaro; Beaumarchais: One-Act Adaptation. (Illus.). 38p. 1968. pap. 3.25 (*0-88680-127-3*) I E Clark.

— Marriage of Figaro; Beaumarchais: One-Act Adaptation - Director's Script. (Illus.). 38p. 1968. pap. 10.00 (*0-88680-128-1*) I E Clark.

Beaumarchais, Jean P. Dictionnaire des Litteratures de la Langue Francaise. (FRE.). 665p. 1994. 700.00 (*0-7859-3952-0*) Fr & Eur.

— Dictionnaire des Litteratures de la Langue Francaise. 1995. 250.00 incl. audio compact disk (*0-7859-9547-1*) Fr & Eur.

Beaumarchais, Pierre De. The Barber of Seville & the Marriage of Figaro. Wood, John, tr. & intro. by. (Classics Ser.). 224p. 1964. pap. 9.95 (*0-14-044133-6*, Penguin Classics) Viking Penguin.

— Le Barbier de Seville Suivi de Jean Bete a la Foire. (FRE.). 1982. pap. 10.95 (*0-7859-1956-2*, 2070373770) Fr & Eur.

— Correspondance Vol. 2: 1773-1776. (FRE.). 282p. 1970. pap. 24.95 (*0-7859-6522-X*) Fr & Eur.

— Correspondance Vol. 3: 1777. (FRE.). 256p. 1972. pap. 24.95 (*0-7859-6523-8*) Fr & Eur.

— Correspondance Vol. 4: 1778. (FRE.). 334p. 1978. pap. 36.95 (*0-7859-6524-6*) Fr & Eur.

— The Figaro Plays: The Barber of Seville, The Marriage of Figaro, The Guilty Mother. Anderson, Graham, tr. 224p. 1994. pap. 15.95 (*0-948230-54-1*, Pub. by Absolute Classics) Theatre Comm.

— Lettres Inedites Publiees Par G. Chinard. (FRE.). 130p. 1929. pap. 39.95 (*0-7859-5345-0*) Fr & Eur.

— Le Mariage de Figaro. 192p. 1970. 5.95 (*0-686-54084-0*) Fr & Eur.

— Le Mariage de Figaro - La Mere Coupable. (FRE.). 1984. pap. 18.95 (*0-7859-1986-4*, 2070375277) Fr & Eur.

— Le Mariage de Figaro - Le Barbier de Seville. unabridged ed. (FRE.). pap. 5.95 (*2-87714-212-4*, Pub. by Bookking Intl) Distribks Inc.

— The Marriage of Figaro. 1991. pap. 6.95 (*0-88145-099-5*) Broadway Play.

— Oeuvres. deluxe ed. (FRE.). 1744p. 1988. 140.00 (*0-8288-3420-2*, F45970) Fr & Eur.

— Oeuvres. deluxe ed. (Pleiade Ser.). (FRE.). 1696p. 1988. 93.95 (*2-07-011137-7*) Schoenhof.

— Theatre Complet. 45.00 (*0-686-54088-3*) Fr & Eur.

Beaumarchais, Pierre De & Bonneville, Georges. Le Barbier de Seville. 64p. 1976. 5.95 (*0-686-54082-4*) Fr & Eur.

— Le Barbier de Seville. (FRE.). 64p. 1982. pap. 10.95 (*0-7859-3542-8*, F46074) Fr & Eur.

Beaumarchais, Pierre De & Pomeau, Rene. Theatre: Avec: Le Barbier de Seville, le Marriage de Figaro, la Mere Coupable. (FRE.). 320p. 1965. pap. 10.95 (*0-7859-0671-1*) Fr & Eur.

Beaumarchis, jt. ed. see Arnould.

Beaumariage, Robert, et al, eds. Object Oriented Simulation Conference. (Illus.). 148p. (Orig.). 1995. pap. 80.00 (*1-56555-043-9*, OOS-95) Soc Computer Sim.

Beaumariage, Robert & Roberts, eds. Conference on Object-Oriented Simulation, 1993. 190p. 1993. pap. 60.00 (*1-56555-022-6*, MC93-1) Soc Computer Sim.

Beaumariage, Terrence, jt. ed. see Ege, Raymond.

Beaumier, Pierre R. Napoleonic Era Daily Almanac: A Chronology of Important Events from 1769-1821. (Illus.). 455p. (Orig.). (C). 1993. pap. 25.00 (*1-883452-00-7*) Vive LEmpereur.

Beaumont, jt. ed. see Miller, Carey.

Beaumont, Phil B. Change in Industrial Relations: The Organization & Environment. LC 89-39096. 365p. reprint ed. pap. 113.20 (*0-608-20313-0*, 207156600002) Bks Demand.

Beaumont, A., et al, eds. Parallel Execution of Logic Programs: ICLP '91 Pre-Conference Workshop Paris, June 24, 1991 Proceedings. (Lecture Notes in Computer Science Ser.: Vol. 569). vii, 195p. 1991. 39.00 (*0-387-55038-0*) Spr-Verlag.

Beaumont, A. P. Intermediate Mathematical Statistics. 225p. (gr. 13). 1980. pap. text 36.95 (*0-412-15480-3*, 2890) Chapman & Hall.

Beaumont, Alison. Arthur Beaumont: Naval Artist, 1890-1978. (Illus.). 64p. 1989. pap. 20.00 (*0-685-25995-1*) Beaumont Pub.

Beaumont, Anne. Another Time, Another Love. large type ed. 257p. 1993. 27.99 (*0-7505-0569-9*, Pub. by Mgna Lrg Print) Ulverscroft.

— A Cinderella Affair. (Romance Ser.: No. 199). 1992. per. 2.89 (*0-373-03199-8*, 1-03199-6) Harlequin Bks.

— Images of Desire. large type ed. 1992. reprint ed. 18.95 (*0-263-13087-8*) Mac Lib Ref.

Beaumont, Anthony, tr. see Mahler-Werfel, Alma.

Beaumont, Antony. Busoni the Composer. LC 84-47699. (Illus.). 408p. 1985. 35.00 (*0-253-31270-1*) Ind U Pr.

— Ferruccio Busoni. 1987. text 81.00 (*0-231-06460-8*) Col U Pr.

***Beaumont, Antony.** Zemlinsky & His Art. LC 00-22272. 2000. 47.50 (*0-8014-3803-9*) Cornell U Pr.

Beaumont, Antony, ed. see Mahler-Werfel, Alma.

Beaumont, Barbara, tr. see Green, Julian.

Beaumont, Barbara, tr. see Lange, Monique.

Beaumont, Ben & Marcus, Hans. Chinese International Commercial Arbitration. LC 94-202308. 160p. 1994. 55.00 (*1-898029-04-0*, Pub. by Simmonds & Hill Pubng) Gaunt.

Beaumont, Ben & Yang, Philip. Chinese Maritime Law & Arbitration. LC 94-202301. 166p. 1994. 55.00 (*1-898029-03-2*, Pub. by Simmonds & Hill Pubng) Gaunt.

Beaumont, Ben, et al. Commentary on the Chinese Arbitration Act. 162p. 1995. pap. 55.00 (*1-898029-15-6*, Pub. by Simmonds & Hill Pubng) Gaunt.

Beaumont, Berry. Care of Drug Users in General Practice: A Harm-Minimization Approach. LC 97-20285. 1997. write for info. (*1-85775-236-8*, Radcliffe Med Pr) Scovill Paterson.

Beaumont, C. W. Vaslav Nijinsky. LC 74-1080. (Studies in Music: No. 42). (C). 1974. lib. bdg. 75.00 (*0-8383-1752-9*) M S G Haskell Hse.

***Beaumont, Charles.** A Touch of the Creature: Unpublished Stories. (Illus.). 175p. 1999. 40.00 (*1-892284-45-6*) Subtrrnean Pr.

Beaumont, Charles, ed. Hush, Child! Can't You Hear the Music? LC 81-10442. (Illus.). 128p. 1999. pap. 12.95 (*0-8203-2137-0*) U of Ga Pr.

Beaumont, Clive, jt. auth. see Carpentier, Tai.

Beaumont, Colleen, tr. see Newhauser, Johannes, ed.

Beaumont, Comyns. The Riddle of Prehistoric Britain. 208p. 1994. reprint ed. spiral bd. 24.50 (*0-7873-1205-3*) Hlth Research.

Beaumont, Cyril W. The Ballet Called Giselle. LC 72-77185. (Illus.). 141p. 1987. reprint ed. pap. 19.95 (*1-85273-004-8*) Princeton Bk Co.

— Bibliography of Dancing. LC 63-23181. 1978. reprint ed. 23.95 (*0-405-08247-9*, Pub. by Blom Pubns) Ayer.

— The History of Harlequin. LC 65-27909. (Illus.). 1972. reprint ed. 20.95 (*0-405-08248-7*, Pub. by Blom Pubns) Ayer.

— Michel Fokine & His Ballets. (Illus.). 170p. 1996. reprint ed. pap. 21.95 (*1-85273-050-1*) Princeton Bk Co.

Beaumont, Cyril W., ed. see Polunin, Vladimir.

Beaumont, De Leprince de, see De Leprince de Beaumont.

Beaumont, Diana & Beaumont, Michael. Forefathers: A History of the Working Class Beaumonts of West Riding, Yorkshire Decendants of Abraham Beaumont of Deershaw. LC 99-222893. (Illus.). 240p. 1999. pap. 23.00 (*0-7884-1072-5*, B100) Heritage Bk.

Beaumont, E. C. & Read, C. B., eds. Rio Chama Country. (Guidebook Ser.: No. 11). (Illus.). 129p. 1960. 15.00 (*1-58546-041-9*) NMex Geol Soc.

Beaumont, E. Larry. Faith in Motion. LC 97-61897. 384p. 1998. pap. 12.95 (*1-57921-069-4*) WinePress Pub.

Beaumont, Edward A., ed. Photogeology & Photogeomorphology. (Treatise of Petroleum Geology Reprint Ser.: No. 18). (Illus.). 555p. 1992. 15.00 (*0-89181-417-5*, 540); pap. 10.00 (*0-685-61029-2*, 539) AAPG.

— Structural Concepts & Techniques III: Detached Deformation. (Treatise of Petroleum Geology Reprint Ser.: No. 11). (Illus.). 651p. 1989. pap. 10.00 (*0-89181-410-8*, 737) AAPG.

— Structural Concepts & Techniques II: Basement-Involved Deformation. (Treatise of Petroleum Geology Reprint Ser.: No. 10). (Illus.). 479p. 1989. pap. 10.00 (*0-89181-409-4*, 735) AAPG.

Beaumont, Edward A. & Foster, Norman A. Geochemistry. LC 88-16671. (Treatise of Petroleum Geology Reprint Ser.: No. 8). 668p. 1988. pap. 200.00 (*0-608-05619-7*, 206607500006) Bks Demand.

— Reservoirs, Vol. 3. LC 87-19599. (Treatise of Petroleum Geology Reprint Ser.: No. 3, 4, & 5). 431p. 1987. pap. 133.70 (*0-608-05617-0*, 206607300003) Bks Demand.

Beaumont, Edward A. & Foster, Norman H. Reservoirs, Vol. 1. LC 87-19599. (Treatise of Petroleum Geology Reprint Ser.: No. 3, 4 & 5). 431p. 1987. pap. 133.70 (*0-608-05615-4*, 206607300001) Bks Demand.

— Reservoirs, Vol. 2. LC 87-19599. (Treatise of Petroleum Geology Reprint Ser.: No. 3, 4, & 5). 585p. 1987. pap. 181.40 (*0-608-05616-2*, 206607300002) Bks Demand.

Beaumont, Edward A. & Foster, Norman H., compiled by. Geophysics: Seismic Methods. LC 89-18158. (Treatise of Petroleum Geology Reprint Ser.: Vol. 12). (Illus.). 658p. reprint ed. pap. 200.00 (*0-608-20303-3*, 207155800001) Bks Demand.

— Geophysics Vol. 3: Geologic Interpretation of Seismic Data. LC 89-18158. (Treatise of Petroleum Geology Reprint Ser.: Vol. 14). (Illus.). 418p. reprint ed. pap. 129.60 (*0-608-20304-1*, 207155800003) Bks Demand.

Beaumont, Edward A. & Foster, Norman H., compiled by. Structural Traps Vol. 2: Traps Associated with Tectonic Faulting. LC 90-232052. (Treatise of Petroleum Geology Ser.). (Illus.). 279p. reprint ed. pap. 86.50 (*0-608-20302-5*, 207155700002) Bks Demand.

***Beaumont, Edward A. & Foster, Norman H., eds.** Exploring for Oil & Gas Traps. (Treatise of Petroleum Geology, Handbook of Petroleum Geology Ser.). (Illus.). 1150p. 1999. 59.00 (*0-89181-602-X*, 545) AAPG.

Beaumont, Edward A. & Foster, Norman H., eds. Structural Traps IV: Tectonic & Nontectonic Fold Traps, No. 4. (Treatise of Petroleum Geology Atlas of Oil & Gas Fields Ser.). (Illus.). 382p. 1990. 10.00 (*0-89181-584-8*, 020) AAPG.

— Structural Traps III: Tectonic Fold & Fault Traps, Vol. 3. (Treatise of Petroleum Geology Atlas of Oil & Gas Fields Ser.). (Illus.). 355p. 1990. 10.00 (*0-89181-583-X*, 019) AAPG.

Beaumont, Edward A., jt. auth. see Foster, Norman H.

Beaumont, Edward A., jt. compiled by see Foster, Norman H.

Beaumont, Edward A., jt. ed. see Foster, Norman H.

Beaumont, Francis. The Dramatic Works in the Beaumont & Fletcher Canon, Vol. 10. Turner, Robert K. et al, eds. 752p. (C). 1996. text 145.00 (*0-521-36189-3*) Cambridge U Pr.

— A King & No King: Beaumont & Fletcher. Turner, Robert K., Jr., ed. LC 63-14698. (Regents Renaissance Drama Ser.). 184p. reprint ed. pap. 57.10 (*0-608-12934-8*, 202469000038) Bks Demand.

— The Knight of the Burning Pestle. Hattaway, Michael, ed. (New Mermaid Ser.). (C). 1976. pap. text 9.75 (*0-393-90000-2*) Norton.

— The Knight of the Burning Pestle. Doebler, John, ed. LC 67-11462. (Regents Renaissance Drama Ser.). 169p. 1967. reprint ed. pap. 52.40 (*0-608-02736-7*, 206340100004) Bks Demand.

— Philaster - By Beaumont & Fletcher. Ashe, Dora J., ed. LC 75-127980. (Regents Renaissance Drama Ser.). 184p. reprint ed. pap. 57.10 (*0-8357-4103-6*, 203686900005) Bks Demand.

— The Works of Francis Beaumont & John Fletcher, 4 vols., Set. variorum ed. Bullen, Arthur H., ed. LC 75-41306. (BCL Ser. II). 1976. reprint ed. 210.00 (*0-404-14820-4*) AMS Pr.

Beaumont, Francis & Beaumont, John. Select Plays. reprint ed. 49.00 (*0-403-04257-7*) Somerset Pub.

Beaumont, Francis & Fletcher, John. The Knight of the Burning Pestle. LC 70-25848. (English Experience Ser.: No. 152). 76p. 1969. reprint ed. 20.00 (*90-221-0152-5*) Walter J Johnson.

— The Maides Tragedy. LC 70-38151. (English Experience Ser.: No. 431). 82p. 1972. reprint ed. 25.00 (*90-221-0431-1*) Walter J Johnson.

— The Maid's Tragedy. Craik, T. W., ed. (Revels Plays Ser.). 210p. 1990. pap. 17.95 (*0-7190-1636-3*, Pub. by Manchester Univ Pr) St Martin.

An Asterisk (*) at the beginning of an entry indicates that the title is appearing for the first time.

— Phylaster: or Love Lyes a Bleeding. LC 68-54617. (English Experience Ser.: No. 18). 66p. 1968. reprint ed. 20.00 (*90-221-0018-9*) Walter J Johnson.

— The Scornfyl Lady. LC 73-38152. (English Experience Ser.: No. 432). 70p. 1972. reprint ed. 15.00 (*90-221-0432-X*) Walter J Johnson.

— Songs & Lyrics from the Plays of Beaumont & Fletcher. Fellows, E. H., ed. LC 79-180038. 1972. reprint ed. 26.95 (*0-405-08249-5*, Pub. by Blom Pubns) Ayer.

— Wit Without Money: A Comedy. LC 73-25968. (English Experience Ser.: No. 264). 66p. 1970. reprint ed. 20.00 (*90-221-0264-5*) Walter J Johnson.

— Works, 10 vols. (BCL1-PR English Literature Ser.). 1992. reprint ed. lib. bdg. 900.00 (*0-7812-7235-1*) Rprt Serv.

— Works of Beaumont & Fletcher, 11 Vols, Set. LC 74-119953. (Select Bibliographies Reprint Ser.). 1977. 357.95 (*0-8369-5396-7*) Ayer.

Beaumont, Frank, ed. see Kaminski, Rosemary.

Beaumont, G. P. Elementary Mathematical Statistics. 1972. 11.50 (*0-07-084001-6*) McGraw.

Beaumont, Germaine. Le Chien Dans l'Arbre. (FRE.). 306p. 1978. pap. 10.95 (*0-7859-1869-8*, 2070370097) Fr & Eur.

Beaumont, Gustave A. De, see De Beaumont, Gustave A.

Beaumont, Heidi, ed. Notes Around Meadow Rise. 114p. (Orig.). 1996. pap. 15.95 (*0-943025-93-1*) Cummngs & Hath.

Beaumont, Hunter, jt. auth. see Hellinger, Bert.

Beaumont, I. Keyboarding Speed/Control Builders. 2nd ed. (TA - Typing/Keyboarding Ser.). 1984. mass mkt. 15.00 (*0-538-20080-4*) S-W Pub.

Beaumont, J., ed. Where to Now? Australia's Identity in the '90s. 216p. 1993. pap. 29.00 (*1-86287-124-8*, Pub. by Federation Pr) Gaunt.

Beaumont, J. Graham. Introduction to Neuropsychology. LC 83-24265. 314p. 1983. pap. text 25.00 (*0-89862-515-7*) Guilford Pubns.

— Textbook of Psychiatry. 530p. (C). (gr. 13). 1989. 54.95 (*0-86793-049-7*) Mosby Inc.

Beaumont, J. Graham, et al, eds. The Blackwell Dictionary of Neuropsychology. (Illus.). 816p. 1999. reprint ed. pap. 39.95 (*0-631-21435-6*) Blackwell Pubs.

Beaumont, Jeanette & Hole, W. Vere. Letters from Louisa: The Experiences of Louisa MacDonald. xiii, 202 p. 1996. pap. 24.95 (*1-86448-054-8*, Pub. by Allen & Unwin Pty) Paul & Co Pubs.

Beaumont, Jeanne M. Placebo Effects: Poems. 1997. 21.00 (*0-614-29433-9*) Norton.

— Placebo Effects: Poems. LC 97-3978. 96p. 1997. 21.00 (*0-393-04128-X*) Norton.

— Placebo Effects: Poems. 96p. 1999. pap. 11.00 (*0-393-31891-5*) Norton.

Beaumont, Joan, ed. Australia's War, 1939-45. LC 96-176215. (Illus.). 232p. 1997. pap. 19.95 (*1-86448-039-4*, Pub. by Allen & Unwin Pty) Paul & Co Pubs.

Beaumont, John. The Metamorphasis of Tobacco. LC 70-171734. (English Experience Ser.: No. 360). 44p. 1971. reprint ed. 25.00 (*90-221-0360-9*) Walter J Johnson.

Beaumont, John, et al. Managing the Environment. 283p. 1993. pap. text 44.95 (*0-7506-1574-5*) Buttrwrth-Heinemann.

Beaumont, John, jt. auth. see Beaumont, Francis.

Beaumont, John, jt. auth. see Carr, Christopher.

Beaumont, John, jt. auth. see Murphy, Peter.

Beaumont, John A., et al. Your Career in Marketing. 2nd ed. 1976. text 25.32 (*0-07-004245-4*) McGraw.

Beaumont, John E. Freemasonry at the Top. LC 96-147694. (Illus.). 140p. (Orig.). 1995. pap. 10.95 (*0-88053-089-8*) Macoy Pub.

Beaumont, John R. & Keys, Paul. Future Cities: Spatial Analysis of Energy Issues. LC 83-128760. (Geography & Public Policy Research Studies: No. 3). (Illus.). 216p. reprint ed. pap. 67.00 (*0-8357-6126-6*, 203421400089) Bks Demand.

Beaumont, John R. & Sutherland, Ewan. Information Resources Management: Management in Our Knowledge-Based Society & Economy. LC 93-110392. (BH Contemporary Business Ser.). (Illus.). 319p. 1992. reprint ed. pap. 98.90 (*0-608-07929-4*, 206790300012) Bks Demand.

Beaumont, John R., et al. Managing the Environment: Business Opportunity & Responsibility. LC 94-150146. (Illus.). 295p. reprint ed. pap. 91.50 (*0-608-07418-7*, 206764500009) Bks Demand.

Beaumont, Karen. Move over Rover. (J). 2005. write for info. (*0-15-201979-0*) Harcourt.

***Beaumont, Karen & Allen, Joy.** Being Friends. LC 00-35865. (Illus.). 2002. write for info. (*0-8037-2529-9*, Dial Yng Read) Peng Put Young Read.

Beaumont, Leland R. ISO 9001, the Standard Companion: The International Standard System for Assuring Product & Service Quality. 3rd ed. (Illus.). 44p. (Orig.). 1996. pap. 8.00 (*0-9636003-8-9*) ISO Easy.

— ISO 9001, the Standard Interpretation: The International Standard System for Assuring Product & Service Quality. 2nd ed. (Illus.). 128p. 1995. pap. 19.95 (*0-9636003-7-0*) ISO Easy.

Beaumont, Madeleine & Zibawi, Mahmoud. Eastern Christian Worlds. 272p. (Orig.). 1995. 89.95 (*0-8146-2375-1*, Liturg Pr Bks) Liturgical Pr.

Beaumont, Madeleine, tr. see Boismard, Marie-Emile, ed.

Beaumont, Madeleine, tr. see Deiss, Lucien.

Beaumont, Madeleine, tr. see Metzger, Marcel.

Beaumont, Madeleine M., tr. see Palazzo, Eric.

Beaumont-Maillet, Laure. Atget Paris. Britt, David, tr. from FRE. (Illus.). 788p. (Orig.). (C). 1993. pap. 55.00 (*3-927258-07-5*) Gingko Press.

Beaumont, Marc. Effective Mortgage Enforcement. 180p. 1998. pap. 66.00 (*1-85811-177-3*, Pub. by CLT Prof) Gaunt.

Beaumont, Marie. Le Bonheur Sans Entraves. (Amours d'Aujourd'Hui Ser.: No. 336). (FRE.). 1999. mass mkt. 5.50 (*0-373-38336-3*, 1-38336-3) Harlequin Bks.

— Combat Pour le Bonheur. (Amours d'Aujourd'Hui Ser.). (FRE.). 1997. pap. 4.99 (*0-373-38270-7*, 1-38270-4) Harlequin Bks.

— Halfway Home. (Superromance Ser.). 1993. per. 3.39 (*0-373-70538-7*, 1-70538-3) Harlequin Bks.

Beaumont, Marion S. Salary Systems in Public Higher Education: A Microeconomic Analysis. LC 85-5671. 240p. 1985. 49.95 (*0-275-90059-2*, C0059, Praeger Pubs) Greenwood.

Beaumont, Marion S. & Imperati, Kathryn B. Solar Access As a Property Right: Oregon & New Mexico. LC KF5698.7.B43. (Tax Policy Roundtable Property Tax Papers: No. TPR 14). 36p. reprint ed. pap. 30.00 (*0-7837-2158-7*, 204246000004) Bks Demand.

***Beaumont, Matt.** E: A Novel. 2000. pap. 13.00 (*0-452-28188-1*, Plume) Dutton Plume.

Beaumont, Michael, jt. auth. see Beaumont, Diana.

Beaumont, Mick, jt. auth. see Schwartz, Noa.

***Beaumont, Mike & O'Brien, Teresa.** Collaborative Research in Second Language Education. 160p. 2000. pap. 25.00 (*1-85856-171-X*, Trentham Bks) Stylus Pub VA.

Beaumont, Ned. Beat the Border: An Insider's Guide to How the U. S. Border Works & How to Beat It. (Illus.). 152p. 1995. pap. 18.00 (*0-87364-833-1*) Paladin Pr.

— Championship Streetfighting: Boxing As a Martial Art. LC 97-226705. (Illus.). 208p. 1997. pap. 20.00 (*0-87364-934-6*) Paladin Pr.

Beaumont, Nina. Across Time. (Historical Ser.). 1994. mass mkt. 3.99 (*0-373-28803-4*, 1-28803-4) Harlequin Bks.

— The Shadowed Heart. (Historical Ser.: Vol. 422). 1998. per. 4.99 (*0-373-29022-5*, 1-29022-0) Harlequin Bks.

— Surrender the Heart. 1997. per. 4.99 (*0-373-28962-6*, 1-28962-8) Harlequin Bks.

— Tapestry of Dreams. LC 96-319. (Historical Ser.). 299p. 1995. per. 4.50 (*0-373-28878-6*, 1-28878-6) Harlequin Bks.

— Tapestry of Fate. 1994. per. 3.99 (*0-373-28846-8*, 1-28846-3) Harlequin Bks.

— Twice upon Time. LC 96-7296. (Historical Ser.). 344p. 1996. per. 4.50 (*0-373-28903-0*, 1-28903-2) Harlequin Bks.

Beaumont, P. B. Government As Employer-Setting an Example. 79p. (C). 1981. 45.00 (*0-900628-20-0*) St Mut.

— Safety Legislation: The Trade Union Response. (C). 1988. text 30.00 (*0-7855-3170-X*, Pub. by Univ Nottingham) St Mut.

Beaumont, P. B., jt. auth. see Thomson, A. W.

Beaumont, Paul & McEleavy, Peter. The Hague Convention on International Child Abduction. LC 99-27432. 368p. 1999. text 110.00 (*0-19-826064-4*) OUP.

***Beaumont, Paul & Walker, Neil, eds.** Legal Framework of the Single European Currency. 224p. 1999. 54.00 (*1-84113-001-X*) Hart Pub.

***Beaumont, Paul R., ed.** Christian Perspectives on Human Rights & Legal Philosophy. viii, 147p. 1998. reprint ed. pap. 25.00 (*0-85364-901-4*, Pub. by Paternoster Pub) OM Literature.

— Christian Perspectives on Law & Relationism. 125p. 1999. pap. text 20.00 (*0-85364-994-4*, Pub. by Paternoster Pub) Eisenbrauns.

— Christian Perspectives on Law Reform. x, 154p. 1998. pap. text 20.00 (*0-85364-852-2*, Pub. by Paternoster Pub) Eisenbrauns.

Beaumont, Perry H. Fixed-Income Synthetic Assets: Packaging, Pricing & Trading Strategies for Financial Professionals. LC 92-10373. (Wiley Finance Editions Ser.). 320p. 1992. 55.00 (*0-471-55162-7*) Wiley.

Beaumont, Peter. Drylands: Environmental Management & Development. LC 93-3125. (Natural Environment: Problems & Management Ser.). (Illus.). 544p. (C). 1993. pap. 29.99 (*0-415-09663-4*, B2414) Routledge.

— Environmental Management & Development in Drylands. (Natural Environment: Problems & Management Ser.). 368p. 1989. 69.95 (*0-415-00457-8*) Routledge.

Beaumont, Peter & McLachlan, Keith, eds. Agricultural Development in the Middle East. fac. ed. LC 85-6414. 361p. pap. 112.00 (*0-7837-7372-2*, 204718200005) Bks Demand.

Beaumont, Peter W., et al. Delaware Composites Design Encyclopedia Vol. 4: Failure Analysis of Composite Materials. LC 89-51098. 1990. lib. bdg. 116.95 (*0-87762-702-9*) Technomic.

Beaumont, Philip. The Future of Employment Relations. 192p. 1995. 69.95 (*0-8039-7472-8*); pap. 26.95 (*0-8039-7473-6*) Sage.

— Human Resource Management: A Teaching Text. (Illus.). 256p. (C). 1993. text 59.95 (*0-8039-8814-1*); pap. text 22.95 (*0-8039-8815-X*) Sage.

Beaumont, R. P., jt. auth. see Adams, J. W.

Beaumont, Richard. Purdey's, the Guns & the Family. (Illus.). 248p. 1984. 32.50 (*0-940143-41-0*) Safari Pr.

Beaumont, Richard A., ed. People, Progress & Employee Relations: Proceedings. LC 76-54797. 178p. reprint ed. pap. 55.20 (*0-8357-9811-9*, 201148400078) Bks Demand.

Beaumont, Rod, ed. Ferguson's School to Work Guide: A Handbook of Information & Resources. LC 98-45081. (Illus.). 380p. (YA). (gr. 7-12). 1998. ring bd. 29.95 (*0-89434-269-X*) Ferguson.

***Beaumont, Roger.** The Nazis' March to Chaos: The Hitler Era Through the Lenses of Chaos-Complexity Theory. LC 99-32027. 224p. 2000. 59.95 (*0-275-96708-5*) Greenwood.

Beaumont, Roger A. Joint Military Operations: A Short History, 139. LC 92-36227. (Contributions in Military Studies Ser.: No. 139). 264p. 1993. 59.95 (*0-313-26744-8*, BJL, Greenwood Pr) Greenwood.

— Special Operations & Elite Units, 1939-1988: A Research Guide, 2. LC 88-25083. (Research Guides in Military Studies: No. 2). 258p. 1988. lib. bdg. 65.00 (*0-313-26001-X*, BUP/, Greenwood Pr) Greenwood.

— War, Chaos, & History. LC 94-19595. 232p. 1994. 59.95 (*0-275-94949-4*, Praeger Pubs) Greenwood.

Beaumont, Ross A. & Pierce, R. S. Torsion Free Groups of Rank Two. LC 52-42839. (American Mathematical Society Ser.: No. 38). 46p. reprint ed. pap. 30.00 (*0-608-09173-1*, 205267700002) Bks Demand.

Beaumont, Ross A. & Pierce, Richard S. Torsion-Free Groups of Rank Two. LC 52-42839. (Memoirs Ser.: No. 1/38). 41p. 1985. reprint ed. pap. 16.00 (*0-8218-1238-6*, MEMO/1/38) Am Math.

Beaumont, S. P. & Sotomayor-Torres, Cliva M., eds. Science & Engineering of One & Zero-Dimensional Semiconductors. (NATO ASI Ser.: Vol. 214). (Illus.). 350p. (C). 1990. text 132.00 (*0-306-43417-2*, Kluwer Plenum) Kluwer Academic.

Beaumont, Sally & Fay, Peter, trs. Observations Concerning the Planet Venus. LC 95-46763. 172p. 1995. 99.95 (*3-540-19980-2*) Spr-Verlag.

***Beaumont, Sebastian.** Cruelty of Silence. 2000. pap. text 15.95 (*1-873741-30-8*) Millivres Bks.

Beaumont, Sebastian. Heroes Are Hard to Find. (Orig.). 1993. pap. 14.95 (*1-873741-08-1*, Pub. by Millvres Bks) LPC InBook.

— On the Edge. 213p. (Orig.). 1992. pap. 13.95 (*1-873741-00-6*, Pub. by Millvres Bks) LPC InBook.

— Two: Learning to Drown - Addy, Laura & Old Jack Butler. 1994. pap. 13.95 (*1-873741-17-0*, Pub. by Millvres Bks) LPC InBook.

***Beaumont, Stephen.** Premium Beer Drinker's Guide: The World's Strongest, Boldest & Most Unusual Beers. (Illus.). 224p. 2000. pap. 24.95 (*1-55209-510-X*) Firefly Bks Ltd.

Beaumont, Stephen. Stephen Beaumont's Brewpub Cookbook: 100 Great Recipes from 30 Famous North American Brewpubs. LC 97-47323. (Illus.). 205p. 1998. pap. 18.95 (*0-937381-64-0*, Siris Bks) Brewers Pubns.

— A Taste for Beer. LC 95-11078. 256p. 1995. pap. 14.95 (*0-88266-907-9*, Garden Way Pub) Storey Bks.

***Beaumont, Stephen.** A Taste for Beer. 181p. 1999. reprint ed. pap. text 20.00 (*0-7881-6778-2*) DIANE Pub.

Beaumont, Ted, jt. auth. see Hoffman, Mark.

Beaumont, Tim. The End of the Yellowbrick Road: Ways & Means to the Sustainable Society. LC 98-175076. 160p. 1998. pap. 19.95 (*1-897766-36-X*, Pub. by Jon Carpenter) Paul & Co Pubs.

Beaumont, Timothy, ed. Modern Religious Verse. (Pocket Poet Ser.). 1966. pap. 3.95 (*0-8023-9039-0*) Dufour.

Beaumont, William. The Career of William Beaumont & the Reception of His Discovery: An Original Anthology. Cohen, I. Bernard, ed. LC 79-7949. (Three Centuries of Science in America Ser.). (Illus.). 1980. lib. bdg. 25.95 (*0-405-12530-5*) Ayer.

— William Beaumont's Formative Years. (American Autobiography Ser.). 87p. 1995. reprint ed. lib. bdg. 69.00 (*0-7812-8454-6*) Rprt Serv.

Beaumont, William & Osler, William. Experiments & Observations on the Gastric Juice & Physiology of Digestion: With a Biographical Essay, "William Beaumont: A Pioneer American Physiologist" unabridged ed. LC 96-23124. (Illus.). 320p. 1996. reprint ed. pap. text 10.95 (*0-486-69213-2*) Dover.

Beaumonte, Phyllis R. Roses & Thorns: Poetry & Prose. LC 93-74871. (Illus.). 67p. (Orig.). 1994. pap. text 8.95 (*0-9640059-0-5*) P R Beaumonte.

Beaune, Colette. The Birth of an Ideology: Myths & Symbols of Nation in Late-Medieval France. Cheyette, Fredric L., ed. Huston, Susan R., tr. from FRE. LC 90-24687. (Illus.). 424p. 1991. 60.00 (*0-520-05941-7*, Pub. by U CA Pr) Cal Prin Full Svc.

Beaunier, Andre & Besse, Jean M. Abbayes et Prieures de l'Ancienne France, 10 vols. lxviii, 2963p. reprint ed. write for info. (*0-318-71318-7*) Lubrecht & Cramer.

***Beaunoyer, Jean.** Celine The Real Story of Celine Dion. LC 99-38029. 1999. 22.50 (*1-55972-534-6*) Carol Pub Group.

Beauparlant, Marc. Buying Smart: How to Buy a Used Car. 1994. pap. 3.99 (*0-9641886-6-X*) Bee Pubng.

Beauplan, Sieur De, see Le Vasseur, Guillaume & De Beauplan, Sieur.

Beaupre, Gary S., jt. auth. see Carter, Dennis R.

Beaupre, Pierre-Paul, et al. Repertoire des Deces et Sepultures de Mont-Joli, Paroisses de--Notre Dame de Lourdes (1889-1992), Sainte-Bernadette-Soubirous (1957-1992), Suppl. 9. LC 95-22892. (FRE.). 189p. 1995. 26.00 (*2-9803120-9-6*) SGEQ.

Beauquier, C. Faune et Flore Populaires de Franche-Comte, 2 vols., 1 bk. LC 78-20142. (Collection de contes et de chansons populaires: Vols. 32-33). reprint ed. 43.00 (*0-404-60382-3*) AMS Pr.

Beauregard, David N. Virtue's Own Feature: Shakespeare & the Virtue Ethics Tradition. LC 95-5838. 264p. 1995. 41.50 (*0-87413-578-8*) U Delaware Pr.

Beauregard, Diane C. De, see De Beauregard, Diane C.

Beauregard, Diane Costa De, see Costa de Beauregard, Diane.

Beauregard, Erving E. Bingham of the Hills: Politician & Diplomat Extraordinary. (American University Studies: History: Ser. IX, Vol. 68). 327p. (C). 1989. text 54.50 (*0-8204-0918-9*) P Lang Pubng.

— History of Academic Freedom in Ohio: Case Studies in Higher Education, 1808-1976. (American University Studies: Language: Ser. XIV, Vol. 14). XII, 300p. (C). 1988. text 39.50 (*0-8204-0666-X*) P Lang Pubng.

***Beauregard, Erving E.** Notables of Harrison County, Ohio. LC 99-57089. (Studies in Local & Institutional History: Vol. 2). 452p. 2000. text 109.95 (*0-7734-7841-8*) E Mellen.

Beauregard, Erving E. Reverend John Walker: Renaissance Man. LC 89-39716. (American University Studies: History: Ser. IX, Vol. 87). X, 225p. (C). 1990. text 42.95 (*0-8204-1192-2*) P Lang Pubng.

Beauregard, Estelle. Correctional Administration Vocabulary. rev. expanded ed. (Terminology Bulletin Ser.: No. 224). (FRE.). 325p. (Orig.). 1994. pap. 29.95 (*0-660-59111-1*, Pub. by Canadian Govt Pub) Accents Pubns.

***Beauregard, Jack.** The Power of Balance: A New Process of Personal Transformation for the 21st Century. 232p. 2000. pap. 14.95 (*0-9662362-0-3*) Innervision Pr.

Beauregard, Michael, et al. Opening up the Statistical Toolbox: A Practical Guide to Statistical Quality Improvement. (Illus.). 400p. 1991. text 64.95 (*0-442-23439-2*) Chapman & Hall.

Beauregard, Monique. Emerger de la Nuit. 157p. 1993. 18.50 (*2-920083-68-6*) Edns Roseau.

— Integrer Sa Lumiere. 1997. 19.95 (*2-89466-009-X*) Edns Roseau.

Beauregard, Olivier Costa De, see Costa de Beauregard, Olivier.

Beauregard Parish Historical Society Staff. Beuregard, LA. (Illus.). 440p. 1986. reprint ed. text 60.00 (*0-88107-062-9*) Curtis Media.

Beauregard, Raymond A., jt. auth. see Fraleigh, John B.

Beauregard, Robert A. Atop the Urban Hierarchy. LC 88-18467. (Illus.). 324p. (C). 1989. 59.00 (*0-8476-7554-8*, R7554) Rowman.

Beauregard, Robert A., ed. Economic Restructuring & Political Response. (Urban Affairs Annual Review Ser.: Vol. 34). 320p. (C). 1989. text 62.00 (*0-8039-3184-0*) Sage.

— Economic Restructuring & Political Response, Pt. 34. (Urban Affairs Annual Review Ser.: Vol. 34). 320p. (C). 1989. pap. text 26.00 (*0-8039-3185-9*) Sage.

Beauregard, Robert A. & Indik, Bernard P. A Human Service Labor Market: Developmental Disabilities. LC 79-12391. 240p. 1979. pap. 21.95 (*0-88285-059-8*) Transaction Pubs.

— Labor Market Planning to Serve the Developmentally Disabled: A Literature Review & Bibliography. 1977. 8.00 (*0-686-19116-1*, 1258-1259, Sage Prdcls Pr) Sage.

Beaurline, L. A., ed. see Dryden, John.

Beaurline, L. A., ed. see Jonson, Ben.

Beaurline, L. A., ed. see Shakespeare, William.

Beaurline, Lester A. Jonson & Elizabethan Comedy: Essays in Dramatic Rhetoric. LC 77-75148. (Illus.). 365p. 1978. reprint ed. pap. 113.20 (*0-608-03166-6*, 206361900007) Bks Demand.

Beauroy, Jacques. Vin et Societe a Bergerac: Du Moyen Age aux Temps Modernes. (Stanford French & Italian Studies: No. 4). (FRE., Illus.). 294p. 1977. pap. 56.50 (*0-915838-32-X*) Anma Libri.

Beauroy, Jacques, jt. ed. see Hassall, William.

Beausay, Bill. Teenage Boys! Shaping the Man Inside; Surviving & Enjoying These Extraordinary Years. 256p. 1998. pap. 12.95 (*1-57856-042-X*) Waterbrook Pr.

Beausay, Kathryn, jt. auth. see Beausay, William.

Beausay, William. Boys: Shaping Ordinary Boys into Extraordinary Men. 224p. 1996. mass mkt. 6.50 (*0-7852-7262-3*) Nelson.

***Beausay, William.** Hijos! Haga de Ellos Grandes Hombres.Tr. of Boys! Shaping Ordinary Boys into Extraordinary Men. (SPA.). 256p. 1999. pap. text 9.50 (*0-311-46160-3*, Edit Mundo) Casa Bautista.

Beausay, William, II. The Leadership Genius of Jesus: Ancient Wisdom for Modern Business. LC 97-38372. 128p. 1998. 14.99 (*0-7852-7165-1*) Nelson.

— The People Skills of Jesus. LC 97-3897. 128p. 1997. 14.99 (*0-7852-7164-3*) Nelson.

Beausay, William & Beausay, Kathryn. Girls! Helping Your Little Girl Become an Extraordinary Woman. 240p. 1998. pap. 9.99 (*0-8007-5666-5*) Revell.

***Beausay, William & Beausay, Kathryn.** Hijas! Ayudeles A Ser Grandes Mujeres.Tr. of Girls! Help Them to Be Extraordinary Women. (SPA.). 224p. 1999. pap. text 8.50 (*0-311-46158-1*, Edit Mundo) Casa Bautista.

BeauSeigneur, James. Acts of God Bk. 3: Christ Clone Trilogy. LC 97-92165. 384p. (Orig.). 1998. pap. 12.95 (*0-9656948-7-9*) SelectiveHouse.

— Birth of an Age Bk. 2: Christ Clone Trilogy. LC 97-92166. 241p. 1997. pap. 12.95 (*0-9656948-6-0*) SelectiveHouse.

Beausobre, Isaac De, see De Beausobre, Isaac.

Beausobre, Julia De, see De Beausobre, Julia.

Beausoleil, Beau. Has That Carrying. 1985. 50.00 (*0-941220-10-9*) Jungle Garden.

— In Case - This Way Two Things Fell. 28p. (Orig.). 1982. pap. 5.50 (*0-937013-14-5*) Potes Poets.

— Witness. LC 76-39971. (Illus.). 60p. 1976. pap. 6.00 (*0-915572-23-0*) Panjandrum.

Beausoleil, Claude. Concrete City, Vol. 1. 110p. pap. 8.00 (*0-919349-23-4*) Guernica Editions.

Beausoleil, Laura. In the Absence of a Surface. (Illus.). 64p. (Orig.). 1985. pap. text 4.50 (*1-879594-10-2*) Androgyne Bks.

Beautiful House Editors, ed. Baths. LC 98-52686. 1999. 30.00 (*0-688-16750-0*, Hearst) Hearst Commns.

Beautiful House Editors, ed. see Maddex, Diane.

***Beautiful House Staff.** House Beautiful Fireplaces. LC 99-23317. 176p. 1999. 30.00 (*0-688-16950-3*, Wm Morrow) Morrow Avon.

Beauvais, Den, jt. auth. see Verheiden, Mark.

B

Beauvais, Fred & Trimble, Joseph E., eds. Sociocultural Perspectives on Volatile Solvent Use. LC 97-699. (Drugs & Society Monograph Ser.: Vol. 10, Nos. 1-2). 113p. (C). 1997. 39.95 (*1-56023-096-7*, Harrington Park) Haworth Pr.

***Beauvais-Godwin, Laura & Godwin, Raymond.** Complete Adoption Book. 2nd ed. 608p. 2000. pap. 16.95 (*1-58062-334-4*) Adams Media.

Beauveau, Borie. Farming & Folk Society: Threshing among the Pennsylvania Germans. Sharrow, Gregory, ed. LC 85-31818. (American Material Culture & Folklife Ser.). (Illus.). 155p. 1986. reprint ed. pap. 48.10 (*0-8357-1677-5*, 207052800097) Bks Demand.

Beauvert, Thierry. Opera Houses of the World. (Illus.). 210p. 1996. text 65.00 (*0-86565-977-X*) Vendome.

Beauville, Arnaud. Complex Algebraic Surfaces. LC 96-14064. (London Mathematical Society Student Texts Ser.: No. 34). 141p. (C). 1996. pap. text 24.95 (*0-521-49842-2*) Cambridge U Pr.

— Complex Algebraic Surfaces. 2nd ed. (London Mathematical Society Student Texts Ser.: No. 34). 141p. (C). 1996. text 64.95 (*0-521-49510-5*) Cambridge U Pr.

Beauvoir, Francine C. Raising Cooperative & Self-Confident Children: A Step-by-Step Handbook for Conscious Parenting. large type ed. Crapuchettes, Bruce, ed. (Illus.). 142p. 1997. pap. 20.00 (*0-9667298-0-3*) Pasadena Pr.

Beauvoir, Simone de. After the War. (Illus.). 276p. 1994. pap. 14.95 (*1-56924-982-2*) Marlowe & Co.

— All Men Are Mortal. Friedman, Leonard, tr. 1992. pap. 13.95 (*0-393-30845-6*) Norton.

— All Said & Done. (Illus.). 463p. 1994. pap. 16.95 (*1-56924-981-4*) Marlowe & Co.

— America Day by Day. LC 98-36823. 355p. 1999. 27.50 (*0-520-20979-6*, Pub. by U CA Pr) Cal Prin Full Svc.

***Beauvoir, Simone de.** America Day by Day. LC 98-36823. 408p. 2000. pap. 17.95 (*0-520-21067-0*) U CA Pr.

Beauvoir, Simone de. Belles Images. (Folio Ser.: No. 243). (FRE.). 1966. pap. 9.25 (*2-07-036243-4*) Schoenhof.

— Les Belles Images. (FRE.). 1972. pap. 10.95 (*0-8288-3621-3*, F85660) Fr & Eur.

— Les Bouches Inutiles. (FRE.). 1972. pap. 10.95 (*0-8288-9675-5*, 2070320359) Fr & Eur.

— Brigitte Bardot & the Lolita Syndrome. LC 78-169346. (Arno Press Cinema Program Ser.). (Illus.). 100p. 1980. reprint ed. 11.95 (*0-405-03912-3*) Ayer.

Beauvoir, Simone de. Ceremonie des Adieux. (Folio Ser.: No. 1805). (FRE.). pap. 13.95 (*2-07-037805-5*) Schoenhof.

— La Ceremonie des Adieux: Entretiens avec Sartre. (FRE.). 1987. pap. 16.95 (*0-8288-3623-X*) Fr & Eur.

Beauvoir, Simone de. The Coming of Age. O'Brian, Patrick, tr. 591p. 1996. pap. 14.00 (*0-393-31443-X*, Norton Paperbks) Norton.

— Deuxieme Sexe, 2 tomes, 17. (Folio Ser.: No. 37). (FRE.). 1949. pap. 14.95 (*2-07-032351-X*) Schoenhof.

— Deuxieme Sexe, 2 tomes, 38. (Folio Ser.: No. 37). (FRE.). 1949. pap. 15.95 (*2-07-032352-8*) Schoenhof.

— Le Deuxieme Sexe Vol. 1: Les Faits et les Mythes. (FRE.). 1986. pap. 16.95 (*0-8288-9676-3*, 207032351X) Fr & Eur.

— Le Deuxieme Sexe Vol. 2: L'Experience Vecue. (FRE.). 1986. pap. 18.95 (*0-8288-9677-1*, 2070323528) Fr & Eur.

— Djamila Boupacha. (FRE.). 292p. 1962. 49.95 (*0-8288-9678-X*, 207020524X) Fr & Eur.

— Ethics of Ambiguity. 168p. 1995. pap. 9.95 (*0-8065-0160-X*, 107, Citadel Pr) Carol Pub Group.

— Faut-Il Bruler Sade? (FRE.). 256p. 1972. pap. 10.95 (*0-8288-9679-8*, 2070352684) Fr & Eur.

Beauvoir, Simone de. Faut-Il Bruler Sade? (Idees Ser.). (FRE.). pap. 8.95 (*2-07-035268-4*) Schoenhof.

Beauvoir, Simone de. La Femme Rompue. (Folio Ser.: No. 960). (FRE.). pap. 8.95 (*2-07-036960-9*) Schoenhof.

— Femme Rompue: Monologue - L'Age de Discretion. (FRE.). 1978. pap. 10.95 (*0-8288-3622-1*) Fr & Eur.

— La Femme Rompue-Monologue-l'Age Du Discretion. (FRE.). 252p. 1978. pap. 11.95 (*0-7859-1855-8*, 2070369609) Fr & Eur.

— Force De L'age. (Folio Ser.: No. 1782). 1960. 15.95 (*2-07-037782-2*) Schoenhof.

— La Force De l'Age. (FRE.). 704p. 1986. pap. 16.95 (*0-7859-2052-8*, 2070377822) Fr & Eur.

— La Force De L'Age Vol. 1: La Force des Choses. (FRE.). 384p. 1977. pap. 10.95 (*0-8288-3624-8*) Fr & Eur.

— La Force De L'Age Vol. 2: La Force des Choses. (FRE.). 512p. 1978. pap. 12.95 (*0-8288-3650-7*) Fr & Eur.

— Force Des Choses, 1. (Folio Ser.: Nos. 764 & 765). (FRE.). 1963. 9.95 (*2-07-036764-9*) Schoenhof.

— Force Des Choses, 2. (Folio Ser.: Nos. 764 & 765). (FRE.). 1963. pap. 10.95 (*2-07-036765-7*) Schoenhof.

— La Force Des Choses, Tome I. (FRE.). 384p. 1977. pap. 11.95 (*0-7859-1820-5*, 2070367649) Fr & Eur.

— La Force Des Choses, Tome II. (FRE.). 512p. 1977. pap. 11.95 (*0-7859-1821-3*, 2070367657) Fr & Eur.

— Hard Times. (Illus.). 384p. 1994. pap. 16.95 (*1-56924-955-5*) Marlowe & Co.

— L' Invitee. (FRE.). 1977. pap. 13.95 (*0-8288-3651-5*, F85741); pap. 11.95 (*0-7859-1822-1*, 2070367681) Fr & Eur.

— Invitee: Roman. (Folio Ser.: No. 768). (FRE.). 1943. pap. 11.95 (*2-07-036768-1*) Schoenhof.

— Journal de Guerre. (Gallimard Ser.). (FRE.). pap. 32.95 (*2-07-071809-3*) Schoenhof.

— Journal de Guerre, Septembre, 1939-Janvier 1941. (FRE.). 374p. 1990. 45.00 (*0-8288-9680-1*, 2070718093) Fr & Eur.

— Letters to Sartre. Hoare, Quintin, ed. & tr. by. from FRE. 544p. (C). 1993. reprint ed. pap. 12.45 (*1-55970-212-5*, Pub. by Arcade Pub Inc) Time Warner.

— Lettres a Sartre, 1940 a 1963, Tomo 2. (Gallimard Ser.). (FRE.). 1990. pap. 35.95 (*2-07-071864-6*) Schoenhof.

— Lettres a Sartre, 1940-1963, Vol. 2. (FRE.). 448p. 1990. 49.95 (*0-8288-9674-7*, 2070718646) Fr & Eur.

— Lettres a Sartre, 1930 a 1939, Tome 1. (Gallimard Ser.). (FRE.). 1990. pap. 35.95 (*2-07-071829-8*) Schoenhof.

— Lettres a Sartre, 1930-1939, Vol. 1. (FRE.). 404p. 1990. 49.95 (*0-8288-9673-9*, 2070718298) Fr & Eur.

— Lettres au Castor et a Quelques Autres, 1926-1939, Vol. 1. (FRE.). 528p. 1983. 59.95 (*0-8288-9687-9*, 207026078X) Fr & Eur.

— Lettres au Castor et a Quelques Autres, 1940-1963, Vol. 2. (FRE.). 372p. 1983. 39.95 (*0-8288-9688-7*, 2070700399) Fr & Eur.

— Mandarins. 1999. pap. 16.00 (*0-393-31883-4*) Norton.

— Les Mandarins. LC 79-65852. 610p. 1979. reprint ed. pap. 9.95 (*0-89526-898-1*) Regnery Pub.

— Les Mandarins, 2 vols., Set. (Folio Ser.: Nos. 769 & 770). (FRE.). 1972. 10.95 (*0-685-57720-1*) Schoenhof.

— Les Mandarins, Vol. 1. (FRE.). 512p. 1978. pap. 10.95 (*0-8288-3652-3*, F85765) Fr & Eur.

— Les Mandarins, Vol. 1. (Folio Ser.: Nos. 769 & 770). (FRE.). 1972. pap. 11.95 (*2-07-036769-X*) Schoenhof.

— Les Mandarins, Vol. 2. (FRE.). 512p. 1978. pap. 10.95 (*0-8288-3653-1*, F85764) Fr & Eur.

— Les Mandarins, Vol. II. (Folio Ser.: Nos. 769 & 770). (FRE.). 1972. pap. write for info. (*2-07-036770-3*) Schoenhof.

— Memoires d'une Jeune Fille Rangee. (FRE.). 1972. pap. 13.95 (*0-8288-3658-2*, F85771) Fr & Eur.

— Memoires d'une Jeune Fille Rangee. (Folio Ser.: No. 786). (FRE.). 1972. pap. 11.95 (*2-07-036786-X*) Schoenhof.

— Memoirs of a Dutiful Daughter. Kirkup, James, tr. from FRE. 368p. 1974. reprint ed. pap. 13.00 (*0-06-090351-1*, CN351, Perennial) HarperTrade.

— Une Mort Tres Douce. (FRE.). 160p. 1972. pap. 10.95 (*0-8288-3654-X*) Fr & Eur.

— Une Mort Tres Douce. (Folio Ser.: No. 137). (FRE.). 160p. 1972. pap. 6.95 (*2-07-036137-3*) Schoenhof.

***Beauvoir, Simone de.** Must We Burn Sade? LC 99-40738. 375p. 2000. text 59.95 (*1-57392-726-0*, Humanity Bks) Prometheus Bks.

Beauvoir, Simone de. Pour une Morale de l'Ambiguite: Pyrrhus et Cineas. (FRE.). 384p. 1963. pap. 10.95 (*0-8288-9682-8*, 2070350215) Fr & Eur.

— Prime of Life. (Illus.). 479p. 1994. pap. 14.95 (*1-56924-956-3*) Marlowe & Co.

— Quand Prime le Spirituel. (FRE.). 250p. 1980. 29.95 (*0-8288-9681-X*, 2070286223) Fr & Eur.

— Le Sang Des Autres. (FRE.). 320p. 1973. pap. 11.95 (*0-7859-1740-3*, 2070363635) Fr & Eur.

— Le Sang Des Autres. (Folio Ser.: No. 363). (FRE.). 320p. 1973. pap. 9.95 (*2-07-036363-5*) Schoenhof.

— Le Sang des Autres. (FRE.). 1973. pap. 11.95 (*0-8288-3655-8*, M3058) Fr & Eur.

— The Second Sex. Pashley, H. N., ed. & tr. by. LC 92-54303. 1993. 20.00 (*0-679-42016-9*) Everymns Lib.

— The Second Sex. 1990. pap. 16.00 (*0-679-72451-6*) Vin Bks.

— She Came to Stay. 1999. reprint ed. pap. 14.00 (*0-393-31884-2*) Norton.

— Simone de Beauvoir Aujourd'hui, Six Entretiens. (FRE.). 128p. 1984. 24.95 (*0-8288-9683-6*, 271520180X) Fr & Eur.

— Simone de Beauvoir et le Cours du Monde. (FRE.). 170p. 1978. 95.00 (*0-8288-9684-4*, 225202058X) Fr & Eur.

— Tous les Hommes Sont Mortels. (FRE.). 544p. 1974. pap. 15.95 (*0-8288-3656-6*, F85820) Fr & Eur.

— Tous les Hommes Sont Mortels. (Folio Ser.: No. 533). (FRE.). 544p. (J). 1974. pap. 12.50 (*2-07-036533-6*) Schoenhof.

— Tout Compte Fait. (FRE.). 1978. pap. 16.95 (*0-8288-3657-4*) Fr & Eur.

— Tout Compte Fait. (Folio Ser.: No. 1022). (FRE.). 633p. 1978. pap. 13.95 (*2-07-037022-4*) Schoenhof.

— A Transatlantic Love Affair: Letters to Nelson Algren. Reeves, Ellen G., tr. LC 97-53085. (Illus.). 608p. 1998. 27.50 (*1-56584-422-X*, Pub. by New Press NY) Norton.

— A Transatlantic Love Affair: Letters to Nelson Algren. 560p. 1999. pap. text 18.95 (*1-56584-560-9*, Pub. by New Press NY) Norton.

— A Very Easy Death. O'Brian, Patrick, tr. 1985. pap. 11.00 (*0-394-72899-8*) Pantheon.

— La Vieillesse, 2 vols., 1. (Idees Ser.). (FRE.). pap. 10.95 (*2-07-035408-3*) Schoenhof.

— La Vieillesse, 2 vols., 2. (Idees Ser.). (FRE.). pap. 9.95 (*2-07-035409-1*) Schoenhof.

— La Vieillesse, 2 vols., Set. (Idees Ser.). (FRE.). 10.95 (*0-685-37193-X*) Schoenhof.

— La Viellesse, Vol. 1. (FRE.). 1979. pap. 13.95 (*0-8288-9685-2*, 2070354083) Fr & Eur.

— La Viellesse, Vol. 2. (FRE.). 1979. pap. 13.95 (*0-8288-9686-0*, 2070354091) Fr & Eur.

— The Woman Destroyed. O'Brian, Patrick, tr. LC 84-1846. 256p. 1987. pap. 14.00 (*0-394-71103-3*) Pantheon.

Beauvoir, Simone de, ed. see Sartre, Jean-Paul.

Beauvois. Schemas. (C). 1996. pap. text 32.50 (*0-15-501282-7*) Harcourt Coll Pubs.

— Schemas. (C). 1996. pap. text, teacher ed. 28.00 (*0-15-501702-0*) Harcourt Coll Pubs.

Beauvois, D. Le Noble, le Serf et le Revizor. 356p. 1985. write for info. (*2-903928-31-2*) Gordon & Breach.

— Le Noble, le Serf et le Revizor. 2nd ed. vi, 365p. 1991. pap. text 46.00 (*2-88124-075-5*) Gordon & Breach.

Beauvois, Jean-Leon, jt. auth. see Joule, R. V.

Beauvy, Francois. Dictionnaire Picard des Parlers et Traditions du Beauvaisis. (FRE.). 1990. write for info. (*0-7859-8110-1*, 2-85706-020-3) Fr & Eur.

Beaux Arts Societe Staff. Idaho a la Carte: A Gallery of Treasures, Traditions & Tastes from the Beaux Arts Societe. LC 95-61734. (Illus.). 240p. (C). 1995. 24.95 (*0-9648326-0-7*) Beaux Arts Soc.

Beauzamy, B. Introduction to Operator Theory & Invariant Subspaces. (Mathematical Library: Vol. 42). 358p. 1988. 138.00 (*0-444-70521-X*, North Holland) Elsevier.

***Beavan, Colin.** Fingerprints: The Origins & Pioneers of Scientific Crime Dectection. 2001. 22.95 (*0-7868-6607-1*, Pub. by Disney Pr) Time Warner.

— Fingerprints: The Origins & Pioneers of Scientific Crime Dectection. 2002. pap. 14.95 (*0-7868-8528-9*, Pub. by Disney Pr) Time Warner.

***Beaven, Derek.** Acts of Mutiny. LC 99-53129. 280p. 2000. text 24.00 (*0-312-24100-3*, Picador USA) St Martin.

Beaven, Donald W. A Color Atlas of the Nail in Clinical Diagnosis. 2nd ed. 256p. 1994. 39.95 (*0-7234-1991-4*) Mosby Inc.

Beaven, Donald W. & Brooks, E. A Color Atlas of the Nail in Clinical Diagnosis. 2nd ed. 1994. write for info. (*0-7234-2026-2*, Pub. by Martin Dunitz) Mosby Inc.

Beaven, G. L., et al. Optical Fibres, Vol. 5. (EPO Applied Technology Ser.). (Illus.). 650p. 1986. 280.00 (*0-08-030577-6*, Pub. by Pergamon Repr) Franklin.

Beaven, Guy W. Hello Suckers! Inside the Brutal World of Stock Market Scams & How to Prevent Falling Victim. LC 95-94971. 192p. (Orig.). 1995. pap. 19.95 (*0-9650508-0-7*) Gordon-Richardson.

Beaven, M. A. Histamine: Its Role in Physiological & Pathological Processes. (Monographs in Allergy: Vol. 13). (Illus.). 1978. pap. 33.25 (*3-8055-2887-6*) S Karger.

Beaven, Marilyn, ed. see National Gallery of Art Staff.

Beaven, P. M. Which Three Till Now. 231p. 1978. 75.00 (*0-906204-04-6*) St Mut.

Beaver. Cajun Men Cook: Recipes, Stories & Food Experiences from Louisiana Cajun Country. 1994. 16.95 (*0-9642486-0-3*) Beaver Club.

— Introduction to Probability & Statistics: Partial Solutions Manual. 7th ed. 125p. (C). 1987. pap. 11.00 (*0-87150-049-3*, 36G0154) PWS Pubs.

— Introduction to Probability & Statistics: Study Guide. 7th ed. 408p. (C). 1987. pap., student ed. 16.50 (*0-87150-050-7*, 36G0155) PWS Pubs.

Beaver, jt. auth. see Mendenhall.

Beaver, jt. auth. see Mendenhall, William.

Beaver, Benjamin, jt. auth. see Deans, David.

Beaver, Bonnie G., jt. auth. see Shively, Michael J.

Beaver, Bonnie V. Canine Behavior: A Guide for Veterinarians. Kersey, Ray, ed. LC 98-17176. (Illus.). 368p. (C). 1998. pap. 29.95 (*0-7216-5965-9*, W B Saunders Co) Harcrt Hlth Sci Grp.

— Comparative Anatomy of Domestic Animals: A Guide. LC 80-148036. 219p. reprint ed. pap. 67.90 (*0-608-17353-3*, 202982200065) Bks Demand.

— Feline Behavior: A Guide for Veterinarians. 2nd ed. (Illus.). 272p. 1992. pap. text 34.00 (*0-7216-3992-5*, W B Saunders Co) Harcrt Hlth Sci Grp.

— The Veterinarian's Encyclopedia of Animal Behavior. LC 94-27257. (Illus.). 320p. 1994. text 34.95 (*0-8138-2114-2*) Iowa St U Pr.

Beaver, Bruce. Bruce Beaver: New & Selected Poems 1960-1990. 1991. pap. 19.95 (*0-7022-2338-7*, Pub. by Univ Queensland Pr) Intl Spec Bk.

— Charmed Lives. LC 88-17306. (Poetry Ser.). 131p. (Orig.). 1989. pap. text 16.95 (*0-7022-2141-4*, Pub. by Univ Queensland Pr) Intl Spec Bk.

Beaver County Research Center Staff & Closson Press Staff. Beaver County, PA Cemeteries, Vol. 1. 85p. 1982. per. 11.00 (*0-933227-54-X*, 472) Closson Pr.

— Beaver County, PA Cemeteries, Vol. 2. 109p. 1986. pap. text 11.00 (*0-933227-53-1*, 473) Closson Pr.

— Beaver County, PA Cemeteries, Vol. 4. 58p. 1986. pap. text 11.00 (*0-933227-27-2*, 475) Closson Pr.

Beaver County Times Staff. Celebrate the Valley: Life in Beaver & Western Allegheny Counties, 2 vols. LC 99-187318. (Illus.). 120p. 1998. 24.95 (*0-9668109-0-2*) Beaver News.

Beaver, D. Lazy Learning: Making the Most of the Brains You Were Born With. 1994. pap. 12.95 (*1-85230-503-7*, Pub. by Element MA) Penguin Putnam.

Beaver, Daniel. More Than Just Sex: A Committed Couple's Guide to Keeping Relationships Lively, Intimate & Gratifying. LC 91-42286. 240p. (Orig.). 1992. pap. 12.95 (*0-944031-35-8*) Aslan Pub.

Beaver, Daniel C. Parish Communities & Religious Conflict in the Vale of Gloucester, 1590-1690, Vol. 129. LC 98-16295. (Harvard Historical Studies). 480p. 1998. 49.50 (*0-674-75845-5*) HUP.

Beaver, Daniel R., ed. Some Pathways in Twentieth-Century History: Essays in Honor of Reginald Charles McGrane. LC 69-11348. 316p. reprint ed. pap. 98.00 (*0-7837-3791-2*, 204361100010) Bks Demand.

Beaver, David. What Comes First in Dynamic Semantics: A Critical Review of Linguistic Theories of Presupposition & a Dynamic Alternative. (Studies in Logic, Language & Information). 250p. (C). 1998. 64.95 (*1-57586-121-6*); pap. 24.95 (*1-57586-120-8*) CSLI.

Beaver, Diana. NLP for Lazy Learning: Superlearning Strategies for Business & Personal Development. 208p. 1998. pap. 14.95 (*1-86204-412-0*, Pub. by Element MA) Penguin Putnam.

Beaver, Donald. Ecology Laboratory Bot/Zol 355L: A Course Manual. 272p. (C). 1998. spiral bd. 34.95 (*0-7872-5524-6*, 41552401) Kendall-Hunt.

Beaver, Donald D. The American Scientific Community, 1800 to 1860: A Statistical Historical Study. Zuckerman, Harriet & Merton, Robert K., eds. LC 79-8973. (Dissertations on Sociology Ser.). 1980. lib. bdg. 36.95 (*0-405-12950-5*) Ayer.

Beaver, Edmund. Travel Games. (J). (gr. 2 up). 1974. pap. 2.00 (*0-910208-01-8*) Beavers.

Beaver, Floyd. The Homeward Bounder & Other Sea Stories. LC 95-75695. 256p. 1996. pap. 17.95 (*0-9637586-3-2*) Glencannon Pr.

— White Hats: Stories of the U. S. Navy Before World War II. 256p. 1998. pap. 17.95 (*1-889901-11-3*) Glencannon Pr.

Beaver, Frank. Dictionary of Film Terms: The Aesthetic Companion to Film Analysis. rev. ed. (Twayne's Filmmakers Ser.). (Illus.). 324p. 1994. 33.00 (*0-8057-9333-X*, Twyne); pap. 20.00 (*0-8057-9334-8*, Twyne) Mac Lib Ref.

— Oliver Stone: Maverick Filmmaker. (Twayne's Filmmakers Ser.). (Illus.). 175p. 1994. 26.95 (*0-8057-9326-7*, Twyne) Mac Lib Ref.

Beaver, Frank E. Bosley Crowther: Social Critic of the Film, 1974. LC 73-21589. (Dissertations on Film Ser.: Vol. 8). 202p. 1977. 15.95 (*0-405-04870-X*) Ayer.

— Oliver Stone: Maverick Filmmaker. (Twayne's Filmmakers Ser.). (Illus.). 175p. 1994. pap. 20.00 (*0-8057-9332-1*, Twyne) Mac Lib Ref.

***Beaver, Frank E.** 100 Years of American Film. LC 99-48482. 1999. write for info. (*0-02-865380-7*) Macmillan Gen Ref.

Beaver, Harold. The Great American Masquerade. LC 85-13426. (Critical Studies). 238p. 1985. 50.00 (*0-389-20585-0*, N8143) B&N Imports.

— Huckleberry Finn: Unwin Critical Library. 192p. 1987. text 34.95 (*0-04-800077-9*) Routledge.

Beaver, Harold, ed. see Melville, Herman.

Beaver, Harold, ed. & compiled by see Poe, Edgar Allan.

Beaver, I. M. Bieber: History & Genealogy of the Bieber, Beaver, Biever, Beeber Family (Desc. of George Bieber of Germany & Penna.) (Illus.). 984p. 1996. reprint ed. pap. 129.50 (*0-8328-5599-5*); reprint ed. lib. bdg. 139.50 (*0-8328-5598-7*) Higginson Bk Co.

Beaver Island Historical Society Staff. Journal of Beaver Island History, Vol. I. (Illus.). 218p. (Orig.). 1987. reprint ed. 12.00 (*0-944216-01-3*) Beaver Island.

— Journal of Beaver Island History, Vol. II. 2nd ed. LC 81-642940. (Illus.). 183p. (Orig.). 1980. reprint ed. pap. 12.00 (*0-944216-02-1*) Beaver Island.

— Journal of Beaver Island History, Vol. III. Frank, Florence C., ed. LC 81-642940. (Illus.). 240p. (Orig.). 1988. pap. 12.00 (*0-944216-03-X*) Beaver Island.

Beaver, Jason. Late Night Netscape IFC. 574p. 1997. pap. text 49.99 (*1-56276-540-X*, Ziff-Davis Pr) Que.

Beaver, John F. Putting Microsoft Works to Work in Your Classroom. LC 97-146940. (Illus.). 496p. (Orig.). (C). 1997. pap. text 39.95 (*0-943025-95-8*) Cummngs & Hath.

Beaver, Margaret. He Mau Mikilima Hau No Ioane. Perreira, Hiapo K., tr. from ACE. (HAW., Illus.). 12p. (J). (gr. 1-2). 1996. pap. 6.95 incl. audio (*1-890270-28-8*) Aha Punana Leo.

***Beaver, Marian, et al.** Babies & Young Children: Boook 1: Early Years Development. 2nd ed. (Illus.). 404p. 1999. pap. 33.50 (*0-7487-3974-2*, Pub. by S Thornes Pubs) Trans-Atl Phila.

Beaver, Marian, et al. Babies & Young Children Bk. 1: Development 0-7. 296p. 1994. pap. 33.50 (*0-7487-1785-4*, Pub. by S Thornes Pubs) Trans-Atl Phila.

***Beaver, Marian, et al.** Babies & Young Children Bk. 2: Early Years Care & Education. 2nd ed. (Illus.). 488p. 1999. pap. 33.50 (*0-7487-3975-0*, Pub. by S Thornes Pubs) Trans-Atl Phila.

Beaver, Marian, et al. Babies & Young Children Bk. 2: Work & Care. 336p. 1995. pap. 33.50 (*0-7487-1787-0*, Pub. by S Thornes Pubs) Trans-Atl Phila.

Beaver, Marion L. & Miller, Don A. Clinical Social Work Practice with the Elderly: Primary, Secondary, & Tertiary Intervention. 2nd ed. 414p. (C). 1992. pap. 37.95 (*0-534-17130-3*) Brooks-Cole.

Beaver, Marion L., jt. auth. see Miller, Don A.

Beaver, Michael D. & Borsarello, J. F. Camouflage Uniforms of the Waffen-SS: A Photographic Reference. LC 95-68165. (Illus.). 296p. 1995. 59.95 (*0-88740-803-6*) Schiffer.

Beaver, Patricia D. Rural Community in the Appalachian South. rev. ed. 182p. (C). 1992. reprint ed. pap. text 11.95 (*0-88133-656-4*) Waveland Pr.

Beaver, Patricia D., jt. auth. see Hill, Carole E.

Beaver, Patrick. A History of Lighthouses. (Illus.). 182p. 1973. 7.95 (*0-8065-0368-8*, Citadel Pr) Carol Pub Group.

— A Taste of Tradition: The Story of a Family Business 1950-1996. (Illus.). 220p. 1997. 49.95 (*0-485-11510-7*, Pub. by Athlone Pr) Humanities.

***Beaver, R. Pierce.** All Loves Excelling: American Protestant Women in World Mission. 228p. 1998. pap. 23.00 (*1-57910-190-9*) Wipf & Stock.

Beaver, R. Pierce. American Protestant Women in World Mission. LC 80-14366. Orig. Title: All Loves Excelling. 237p. reprint ed. 73.50 (*0-8357-9122-X*, 201931700011) Bks Demand.

Beaver, R. Pierce, ed. American Missions in Bicentennial Perspective. LC 77-7569. 438p. 1977. pap. 11.95 (*0-87808-153-4*) William Carey Lib.

Beaver, Rachel. All About the St. Bernard. 3rd ed. 1999. 39.95 (*1-85279-078-4*) TFH Pubns.

Beaver, Rick. Educational Psychology Casework: A Practical Guide. LC 96-195370. 200p. 1996. pap. 26.95 (*1-85302-364-7*, Pub. by Jessica Kingsley) Taylor & Francis.

Beaver, Robert J. & Mendenhall, William. Programmed Study Guide for Introduction to Probability & Statistics. 4th ed. 1975. pap. 6.75 (*0-87872-095-2*) PWS Pubs.

Beaver, Robert J., jt. auth. see Mendenhall, William.

Beaver, Robert P. Christianity & African Education: The Papers of a Conference at the University of Chicago. LC 65-25184. 233p. reprint ed. pap. 72.30 (*0-608-10781-6*, 201294000083) Bks Demand.

An Asterisk (*) at the beginning of an entry indicates that the title is appearing for the first time.

Beaver, Stanley H., jt. auth. see Stamp, L. Dudley.

Beaver, Stanley H., jt. auth. see Stamp, Laurence D.

Beaver, Stanley H., tr. see Beaujeu-Garnier, Jacqueline.

Beaver, Teri. The Author's Profile: Assessing Writing in Context. LC 97-39401. (Illus.). 176p. 1998. pap. text 16.00 (*1-57110-059-8*) Stenhse Pubs.

Beaver, Wilfred N. Unexplored New Guinea. LC 75-32799. (Illus.). reprint ed. 74.50 (*0-404-14102-1*) AMS Pr.

Beaver, William. Nuclear Power Goes On-Line: A History of Shippingport, 105. LC 89-26065. (Contributions in Economics & Economic History Ser.: No. 105). 208p. 1990. 55.00 (*0-313-27244-1*, BVS/, Greenwood Pr) Greenwood.

— Practical Martial Arts for Special Forces. (Illus.). 112p. 1996. pap. 17.00 (*0-87364-866-8*) Paladin Pr.

— Wealth-Building Secrets As Practiced by the World's Richest People: What the Kuwaitis Can Teach You about Getting Rich - And Staying Rich. LC 98-157595. (Illus.). 128p. 1998. pap. 16.00 (*0-87364-976-1*) Paladin Pr.

Beaver, William, jt. auth. see Parker, George G.

Beaver, William H. Financial Reporting: An Accounting Revolution. (Contemporary Topics in Accounting Ser.). (Illus.). 240p. (C). 1981. text 20.95 (*0-685-03858-0*) P-H.

— Financial Reporting: An Accounting Revolution. 3rd ed. LC 97-25886. (Contemporary Topics in Accounting Ser.). (Illus.). 180p. 1997. pap. text 52.00 (*0-13-737149-7*) P-H.

Beaver, William H. & Landsman, Wayne R. Incremental Information Content of Statement Thirty-Three Disclosures. LC 83-82489. (Financial Accounting Standards Board Research Report Ser.). (Illus.). (Orig.). 1983. pap. 25.00 (*0-910065-19-5*) Finan Acct Found.

***Beaverhead, Pete, et al.** Mary Quequesah's Love Story: A Pend D'Oreille Indian Tale. LC 00-24101. 2000. pap. write for info. (*0-917298-71-3*) MT Hist Soc.

Beavers. Essential Math Custom. 2nd ed. (C). 1998. pap. text 48.00 (*0-201-43514-4*) Addison-Wesley.

— Essential Mathematics. 864p. (C). 1995. pap. text 38.00 (*0-06-406020-9*) Addson-Wesley Educ.

— Introduction to Management Accounting. 362p. (C). 1997. pap. text 36.40 (*0-536-59994-7*) Pearson Custom.

Beavers, Anthony F. Levinas Beyond the Horizons of Cartesianism: An Inquiry into the Metaphysics of Morals. LC 93-35785. (American University Studies: Vol. 150). 146p. (C). 1995. text 34.95 (*0-8204-2173-1*) P Lang Pubng.

Beavers, David P. The Jackal Awakens. 1995. pap. 11.95 (*1-873741-22-7*) LPC InBook.

— Jackal in the Dark. 1994. pap. 13.95 (*1-873741-16-2*, Pub. by Millvres Bks) LPC InBook.

— Thresholds. 1997. pap. text 12.95 (*1-873741-28-6*, Pub. by Millvres Bks) LPC InBook.

Beavers, Dorothy J. Autism: Nightmare Without End. Hammond, Debbie, ed. LC 79-27669. 1982. 24.95 (*0-87949-167-1*) Ashley Bks.

Beavers, Dustin. Nearly Normal, Vol. I. (Illus.). 1994. pap. 5.95 (*0-911505-09-1*) Lifecraft.

Beavers, Herman. Wrestling Angels into Song: The Fictions of Ernest J. Gaines & James Alan McPherson. (Penn Studies in Contemporary American Fiction). 304p. (C). 1995. text 36.50 (*0-8122-3150-3*) U of Pa Pr.

Beavers, Kenneth A. A Self-Esteem Guidebook: Learning to Embrace Your Imperfect Self. 339p. (Orig.). 1992. pap. 17.95 (*1-883660-23-8*) Galloway Pr.

— A Self-Esteem Guidebook: Learning to Embrace Your Imperfect Self. LC 91-90244. (Illus.). 346p. (Orig.). 1992. pap. 24.95 (*1-880025-16-7*) Psych-Care Pub.

— Self-Worth Without Self-Worship: The Bible-Based Approach to Self-Acceptance. LC 94-76801. 256p. (Orig.). 1995. pap. 9.95 (*1-883660-39-4*) Galloway Pr.

— Your Mental Mythology: 100 Lies That Shatter Self-Esteem. LC 93-81043. 304p. 1995. pap. 11.95 (*1-883660-32-7*) Galloway Pr.

Beavers, Marion C. The Wedding. LC 96-61785. 208p. (Orig.). 1997. pap. 10.99 (*1-883893-83-6*) WinePress Pub.

Beavers, Mary Kay. Essential Mathematics. 2nd ed. (C). 1995. pap., student ed. 10.00 (*0-06-501955-5*) Addson-Wesley Educ.

Beavers, Mary Kay. Essential Mathematics. 2nd ed. LC 94-12269. 830p. (C). 1997. pap. text 80.00 (*0-06-040602-X*) Addson-Wesley Educ.

Beavers, Mary Kay, ed. Essential Math Brief. (C). 1997. text 62.00 (*0-673-67619-6*) Addison-Wesley.

Beavers, Randell A. The Birds of Tikal: An Annotated Checklist for Tikal National Park & Peten, Guatemala. LC 92-2919. (W. L. Moody, Jr. Natural History Ser.: No. 12). (Illus.). 168p. 1992. 29.50 (*0-89096-525-0*); pap. 12.95 (*0-89096-518-8*) Tex A&M Univ Pr.

Beavers, W. Robert & Hampson, Robert B. Successful Families: Assessment & Intervention. (C). 1990. 27.95 (*0-393-70091-7*) Norton.

Beavers, William A., jt. auth. see Bates, Robert B.

***Beaverson, Aiden.** The Hidden Arrow of Maether. LC 00-26105. (Illus.). (J). 2000. pap. 14.95 (*0-385-32750-1*) Delacorte.

***Beaverstock, Jonathan.** The Global City. 288p. 2000. pap. 24.95 (*0-340-73116-8*); text 65.00 (*0-340-73115-X*, Pub. by E A) OUP.

Beavis. Insects & Other Invertebrates in Classical Antiquity. 286p. 1988. text 99.00 (*0-85989-284-0*, Pub. by Univ Exeter Pr) Northwestern U Pr.

Beavis, Bill & McCloskey, Richard G. Salty Dog Talk: The Nautical Origins of Everyday Expressions. 1994. pap. 6.95 (*0-924486-82-1*) Sheridan.

Beavis, Catherine, jt. auth. see Green, Bill.

***Beavis, John & Hunt, Alan, eds.** Communicating Archaeology. (Bournemouth University School of Conversation Sciences Occasional Paper Ser.: Vol. 8). 120p. 1999. pap. 19.95 (*1-900188-93-7*, Pub. by Oxbow Bks) David Brown.

Beavis, Mary Ann. Mark's Audience: The Literary & Social Setting of Mark 4.11-12. (JSNT Supplement Ser.: No. 33). 262p. 1989. 75.00 (*1-85075-215-X*, Pub. by Sheffield Acad) CUP Services.

Beavo, Joe & Houslay, Miles D., eds. Cyclic Nucleotide Phosphodiesterases: Structure, Regulation, & Drug Action. LC 90-11982. (Molecular Pharmacology Ser.). 358p. 1990. 295.00 (*0-471-92707-4*) Wiley.

Beavon, Chester. Only Virgins Need Apply. 1990. 16.95 (*0-9617572-2-1*) Times Journal Pub.

***Beazely, Jan.** The Strength of Mercy: Making a Difference in the World One Child at a Time. LC 98-53168. 160p. 1999. pap. 8.95 (*1-57856-194-9*) Waterbrook Pr.

Beazer, William F. The Commercial Future of Hong Kong. LC 76-24343. 176p. 1978. 55.00 (*0-275-90284-6*, C0284, Praeger Pubs) Greenwood.

Beazley, et al. Local Communities & Mega-Project Development. 59.95 (*1-85972-520-1*) Ashgate Pub Co.

Beazley, Angela. Next Steps in Cross Stitch. 1999. 16.95 (*1-85391-529-7*) Merehurst Ltd.

— Traditional Cottages in Cross Stitch. (Illus.). 1999. pap. 6.95 (*1-85391-721-4*) Tuttle Pubng.

Beazley, Bob. Kayaking Essentials. (Nuts-n-Bolts Guides Ser.). (Illus.). 32p. 1995. pap. 4.95 (*0-89732-169-3*) Menasha Ridge.

— Open-Cockpit Kayaks. (Nuts-N-Bolt Guides Ser.). (Illus.). 32p. (Orig.). 1996. pap. 4.95 (*0-89732-215-0*) Menasha Ridge.

Beazley, Charles R. A Note-Book of Medieval History, A.D. 323 - A. D. 1453. LC 70-160957. (Select Bibliographies Reprint Ser.). 1977. reprint ed. 20.95 (*0-8369-5824-1*) Ayer.

Beazley, Frank, jt. auth. see Norman, Jane.

Beazley, John D. Attic Black Figure Vase-Painters. LC 75-44909. 1978. reprint ed. lib. bdg. 60.00 (*0-87817-191-6*) Hacker.

— Attic Red-Figure Vase-Painters, 3 Vols., Set. 2036p. 1983. reprint ed. 125.00 (*0-87817-289-0*) Hacker.

— The Development of the Attic Black-Figure. rev. ed. Von Bothmer, Dietrich & Moore, Mary B., eds. (Sather Classical Lectures: No. 24). 248p. (C). 1986. 100.00 (*0-520-05593-4*, Pub. by U CA Pr) Cal Prin Full Svc.

— Greek Vases: Lectures by J. D. Beazley. Kurtz, Donna C., ed. (Illus.). 234p. (C). 1990. 89.00 (*0-19-813412-6*) OUP.

— Some Attic Vases in the Cyprus Museum. rev. ed. (Illus.). 46p. 1989. pap. 14.95 (*0-947816-27-5*, Pub. by Oxford Univ Comm Arch) David Brown.

— The Way Nature Works. (Illus.). 360p. 1992. 35.00 (*0-02-508110-1*) Macmillan.

Beazley, John D., tr. see Pfuhl, Ernst.

Beazley, John M., jt. ed. see Kurjak, Asim.

Beazley, Ken. Surface Coating: A Literature Review. 122p. 1996. pap. 95.00 (*0-902799-84-3*, Pub. by Pira Internatl) Bks Intl VA.

Beazley, Kenoo. Papermaking Fillers. 1998. 100.00 (*1-85802-034-4*, Pub. by Pira Pub) Bks Intl VA.

Beazley, Mitchell. American Express Dublin & Cork. 1993. pap. 13.00 (*0-13-092743-0*) P-H.

— The American Express Pocket Guide to Boston. 1992. pap. 13.00 (*0-671-84930-1*) S&S Trade.

— American Express Pocket Travel Guide to Moscow & St. Petersburg. 1994. pap. 13.00 (*0-671-84931-X*) S&S Trade.

Beazley, Mitchell, jt. auth. see Sala, Orietta.

Beazley, Mitchell, jt. auth. see Seddon, George.

Beazley, Mitchell, jt. auth. see Titchmarsh, Alan.

Beazley, William G. Cad/Cam, CAE: Purchase Specification Templates. Jenkins, Bruce L., ed. (Series in CAD-CAM, CAE). 230p. 1987. ring bd. 240.00 (*0-938484-22-2*) Daratech.

Beazley, William O. Amos, the Cowboy Mouse. large type ed. (Illus.). 48p. (Orig.). (J). (gr. k-5). 1996. pap. 8.95 (*1-884758-10-X*) W O Beazley.

— Apache, the Horse Who Needs a Friend. large type ed. (White Horse Ser.). (Illus.). 46p. (Orig.). (J). (gr. k-5). 1995. pap. 7.95 (*1-884758-09-6*) W O Beazley.

— Casper, the Horse Who Hates Bands. large type ed. (Illus.). 50p. (Orig.). (J). (gr. k-5). 1994. pap. 7.95 (*1-884758-08-8*) W O Beazley.

— Chuck, the Horse Who Cared. large type ed. (Illus.). 44p. (J). (gr. k-5). 1993. reprint ed. pap., spiral bd. 7.95 (*1-884758-03-7*) W O Beazley.

— Clovis: The Patient Horse. large type ed. (Illus.). 50p. (J). (gr. 3-9). 1997. pap., spiral bd. 8.95 (*1-884758-12-6*) W O Beazley.

— Cotton, the Nosey Horse. large type ed. (Illus.). 48p. (J). (gr. k-5). 1993. reprint ed. pap., spiral bd. 7.95 (*1-884758-01-0*) W O Beazley.

— Horses I Have Known. LC 84-63049. (Illus.). 263p. 1985. 12.95 (*0-910075-03-4*) Hardin-Simmons.

— Princess, the Lucky Horse. large type ed. (White Horse Ser.). (Illus.). 47p. (J). (gr. k-5). 1994. reprint ed. spiral bd. 7.95 (*1-884758-07-X*) W O Beazley.

— Ragweed, the Horse Who Lost Her Cool. large type ed. (Illus.). 45p. (J). (gr. k-5). 1993. reprint ed. pap., spiral bd. 7.95 (*1-884758-02-9*) W O Beazley.

— Smokey, the Horse Who Ate Too Much. large type ed. (Illus.). 36p. (Orig.). (J). (gr. k-5). 1993. pap., spiral bd. 7.95 (*1-884758-06-1*) W O Beazley.

— Swede, the Horse Who Didn't Forget. large type ed. (White Horse Ser.). (Illus.). 46p. (J). (gr. k-5). 1989. reprint ed. spiral bd. 7.95 (*1-884758-11-8*) W O Beazley.

— Trouble, the Horse Who Is Different. large type ed. (Illus.). 42p. (J). (gr. k-5). 1989. reprint ed. pap., spiral bd. 7.95 (*1-884758-04-5*) W O Beazley.

— White-Boy, the Proud Horse. large type ed. (Illus.). 44p. (J). (gr. k-5). 1993. reprint ed. pap., spiral bd. 7.95 (*1-884758-05-3*) W O Beazley.

***Bebarta, K. C.** Teak: Ecology, Silviculture, Management & Profitability. LC 99-936618. (Illus.). 1999. pap. 475.00 (*81-7089-262-7*, Pub. by Intl Bk Distr) St Mut.

— Teak: Ecology, Silviculture, Management & Profitability. 1998. pap. 90.00 (*0-7855-7662-2*) St Mut.

Bebb, Evelyn D. Nonconformity & Social & Economic Life, 1660-1800. LC 80-21180. 198p. 1980. reprint ed. lib. bdg. 35.00 (*0-87991-867-5*) Porcupine Pr.

Bebb, Lynn. Welsh Pottery. (Illus.). 40p. 1997. pap. 8.50 (*0-7478-0339-0*, Pub. by Shire Pubns) Parkwest Pubns.

Bebb, Phillip, jt. auth. see Sessions, Kyle.

Bebb, Phillip N. & Marshall, Sherrin D., eds. The Process of Change in Early Modern Europe: Essays in Honor of Miriam Usher Chrisman. LC 88-19497. (Illus.). 250p. 1988. lib. bdg. 36.95 (*0-8214-0900-X*) Ohio U Pr.

Bebb, Prudence. The Eleventh Emerald. large type ed. (General Ser.). 384p. 1993. 27.99 (*0-7089-2872-2*) Ulverscroft.

***Bebb, Prudence.** Georgian Popoleton (1714-1830) 1999. pap. 21.00 (*1-85072-156-4*, Pub. by W Sessions) St Mut.

— Life in Regency Harrogate. 1999. pap. 21.00 (*1-85072-174-2*, Pub. by W Sessions) St Mut.

— Life in Regency Scarborough, 1811-1820. 1999. pap. 21.00 (*1-85072-194-7*, Pub. by W Sessions) St Mut.

Bebb, Prudence. Life in Regency York, 1811-1820. 1999. pap. 21.00 (*1-85072-095-9*, Pub. by W Sessions) St Mut.

— The Nabob's Nephew. large type ed. (Linford Romance Library). 304p. 1993. pap. 16.99 (*0-7089-7462-7*, Linford) Ulverscroft.

— The Ridgeway Ruby. large type ed. 1995. 27.99 (*0-7089-3387-4*) Ulverscroft.

— Shopping in Regency York. LC 95-151279. 1999. pap. 21.00 (*1-85072-148-3*, Pub. by W Sessions) St Mut.

— The White Swan. large type ed. (Linford Romance Library). 1996. pap. 16.99 (*0-7089-7834-7*, Linford) Ulverscroft.

***Bebb, Richard.** Welsh Country Furniture, 301. (Illus.). 32p. 1999. pap. 5.25 (*0-7478-0236-X*, Pub. by Shire Pubns) Parkwest Pubns.

Bebb, Russ. The Big Orange: A Story of Tennessee Football. LC 73-86998. (College Sports Bks.). 1982. 12.95 (*0-87397-214-7*, Strode Pubs) Circle Bk Service.

Bebbington, Andrew & Bleddyn, Davies. Resources, Needs & Outcomes in Community-Based Care. 497p. 1990. text 91.95 (*1-85628-130-2*, Pub. by Avebry) Ashgate Pub Co.

Bebbington, Anthony & Thiele, Graham, eds. Non-Governmental Organisations & the State in Latin America: Rethinking Roles in Sustainable Agricultural Development. (Non-Governmental Organizations Ser.). (Illus.). 320p. (C). 1993. pap. 27.99 (*0-415-08846-1*, B0856) Routledge.

Bebbington, David W. Evangelicalism in Modern Britain: A History from the 1730's to the 1980's. 384p. (C). 1989. pap. 24.99 (*0-04-941019-9*) Routledge.

— William Ewart Gladstone: Faith & Politics in Victorian Britain. (Library of Religious Biography). 287p. (C). 1993. pap. 16.00 (*0-8028-0152-8*) Eerdmans.

Bebbington, Paul E., ed. Social Psychiatry: Theory, Methodology, & Practice. 420p. (C). 1991. 49.95 (*0-88738-403-X*) Transaction Pubs.

Bebbington, Warren, ed. Dictionary of Australian Music. LC 99-212780. (Illus.). 384p. 1999. 45.00 (*0-19-550839-4*) OUP.

— The Oxford Companion to Australian Music. (Illus.). 704p. 1998. text 75.00 (*0-19-553432-8*) OUP.

Bebchuk, Lucian A., ed. Corporate Law & Economic Analysis. (Illus.). 324p. (C). 1990. text 59.95 (*0-521-36054-4*) Cambridge U Pr.

Bebel, August. My Life, by August Bebel. LC 83-1556. 343p. (C). 1983. reprint ed. lib. bdg. 69.50 (*0-313-23927-4*, BEMY, Greenwood Pr) Greenwood.

— Woman in the Past, Present & Future. (C). 1988. text 21.50 (*0-7453-0353-6*) Westview.

— Woman in the Past, Present & Future. LC 72-9616. (International Library of Social Sciences: Vol. 1). reprint ed. 44.50 (*0-404-57409-2*) AMS Pr.

Bebel-Gisler, Dany. Leonora: The Buried Story of Guadeloupe. Leskes, Andrea, tr. from CRP. 284p. (C). 1994. text 50.00 (*0-8139-1515-5*) U Pr of Va.

— Leonora: The Buried Story of Guadeloupe. Leskes, Andrea, tr. from CRP. 320p. (C). 1995. pap. 18.50 (*0-8139-1518-X*) U Pr of Va.

Bebel, Heinrich. Facetien. Drei Bucher. xxix, 208p. 1967. reprint ed. 55.00 (*0-318-71255-5*) G Olms Pubs.

Beben, Mary & Meehan, Bridget M. Walking the Prophetic Journey: Eucharistic Liturgies for 21st Century Small Faith Communities. LC 98-60910. 90p. 1998. spiral bd. 12.00 (*0-9658137-8-9*) Woven Word.

Bebenroth, Charlotta M. Childhood of Famous Americans: Meriwether Lewis. (Illus.). 192p. (J). (gr. 3-7). 1997. per. 4.99 (*0-689-81740-1*) S&S Childrens.

— Meriwether Lewis: Boy Explorer. 1997. 10.09 (*0-606-13605-3*, Pub. by Turtleback) Demco.

Bebensee, Lyle. Indian Summer. LC 98-182189. 294p. 1997. write for info. (*0-919581-17-X*) Thrd Eye.

Beberdick, Frank. Chicago's Historic Pullman District. LC 98-87700. (Images of America Ser.). 1998. 18.99 (*0-7385-0029-1*) Arcadia Publng.

Beberdick, Frank H. The Beberdick Family Germany to America. LC 99-188512. 118p. 1999. write for info. (*0-9654355-5-5*) Fmly History.

Beberfall, Lester, tr. see Blasco-Ibanez, Vicente.

Bebermeyer, Gustav. Tubinger Dichterhumanisten. Bebel, Frischlin, Flayder. vii, 108p. 1967. reprint ed. 25.00 (*0-318-71256-3*) G Olms Pubs.

Bebermeyer, Gustav & Bebermeyer, Renate. Worterbuch zu Martin Luthers Deutschen Schriften Lieferung 3: Hartiglich - Heil. 206p. 1997. reprint ed. 90.00 (*3-487-09879-2*) G Olms Pubs.

Bebermeyer, Gustav, jt. auth. see Bebermeyer, Renate.

Bebermeyer, Renate & Bebermeyer, Gustav. Worterbuch zu Martin Luthers Deutschen Schriften Lieferung 2: Hals-Hartigkeit. (GER.). xiii, 200p. 1993. 85.00 (*3-487-09715-X*) G Olms Pubs.

Bebermeyer, Renate, jt. auth. see Bebermeyer, Gustav.

Bebessay, Araya, jt. auth. see Bloom, Robert.

Bebey, Francis. African Music: A People's Art. Bennett, Josephine, tr. from FRE. LC 74-9348. (Illus.). 192p. 1975. pap. 16.95 (*1-55652-128-6*, Lawrence Hill) Chicago Review.

Bebhardt, Richard C. & Gebhardt, Barbara G., eds. Academic Advancement in Composition Studies: Scholarship, Publication, Promotion, Tenure. LC 96-18456. 224p. 1996. 45.00 (*0-8058-2101-5*) L Erlbaum Assocs.

Bebie, Philip. The Warning. 96p. 1986. pap. 4.50 (*1-890137-30-8*) One Hund-One Fnd.

Bebin, J., jt. auth. see Bontoux, J.

Bebis, George S. The Mind of the Fathers. LC 93-50532. 147p. 1994. pap. 9.95 (*0-916586-73-1*, Pub. by Holy Cross Orthodox) BookWorld.

— The Mind of the Fathers: Essays in Patristic Studies. LC 93-50532. 1994. pap. 9.95 (*0-917651-73-1*) Holy Cross Orthodox.

Bebko, Anne R., et al. Language! Roots. (Language! Ser.). 716p. 1997. ring bd. 65.00 (*1-57035-136-8*, 99ROOT) Sopris.

Bebler, Anton A. The Scientific - Technological Challenge & East European Socialism. (CISA Working Papers: No. 65). 25p. (Orig.). 1989. pap. 15.00 (*0-86682-082-5*) Ctr Intl Relations.

Bebler, Anton A., ed. The Challenge of NATO Expansion. LC 98-45035. 256p. 1999. 65.00 (*0-275-96108-7*, Praeger Pubs) Greenwood.

— Civil-Military Relations in Post-Communist States: Central & Eastern Europe in Transition. LC 96-20686. 176p. 1997. 57.95 (*0-275-95350-5*, Praeger Pubs) Greenwood.

Bebler, Anton A. & Seroka, Jim, eds. Contemporary Political Systems: Classifications & Typologies. LC 89-39943. 384p. 1990. lib. bdg. 55.00 (*1-55587-147-X*) L Rienner.

Bebnek, H. D., et al, eds. Progress in Botany. Vol. 51. (Illus.). 455p. 1990. 257.95 (*0-387-51785-5*) Spr-Verlag.

Bebout, D. G., et al. Depositional & Diagenetic History of the Sligo & Hosston Formations (Lower Cretaceous) in South Texas. (Reports of Investigations: RI 109). (Illus.). 69p. 1981. pap. 4.00 (*0-686-36993-9*) Bur Econ Geology.

Bebout, Don G., et al, eds. Atlas of Major Central & Eastern Gulf Coast Gas Reservoirs. (Illus.). 88p. 1992. pap. 38.00 (*0-317-05180-6*, AT0005) Bur Econ Geology.

Bebout, Don G. & Loucks, R. G., eds. Cretaceous Carbonates of Texas & Mexico--Applications to Subsurface Exploration. (Reports of Investigations: RI. 89). 322p. 1977. reprint ed. pap. 11.00 (*0-686-36611-5*) Bur Econ Geology.

Bebout, Don G., et al. Frio Sandstone Reservoirs in the Deep Subsurface along the Texas Gulf Coast: Their Potential for the Production of Geopressured Geothermal Energy. (Reports of Investigations: RI 91). (Illus.). 92p. 1978. reprint ed. pap. 5.50 (*0-318-03230-9*) Bur Econ Geology.

— Geology of Carbonate Porosity: Sunday, April 1, 1979 in Conjunction with the AAPG-SEPM Convention April 1-4, 1979, Houston, TX. LC TN0870.5.A44. (AAPG Continuing Education Course Note Ser.: Vol. 11). (Illus.). 261p. reprint ed. pap. 81.00 (*0-608-08727-0*, 206936600004) Bks Demand.

— Wilcox Sandstone Reservoirs in the Deep Subsurface along the Texas Gulf Coast, Their Potential for Production of Geopressured Geothermal Energy. (Reports of Investigations: RI 117). (Illus.). 125p. 1982. pap. 5.00 (*0-318-03251-1*) Bur Econ Geology.

Bebout, Gray E., et al, eds. Subduction Top to Bottom. LC 96-35932. (Geophysical Monograph Ser.: Vol. 96). 1996. 60.00 (*0-87590-078-X*) Am Geophysical.

Bebr, Gerhard. Development of Judicial Control of the European Communities. 840p. 1981. lib. bdg. 345.00 (*90-247-2541-0*) Kluwer Academic.

***Bebris, Carrie A.** Pool of Radiance: The Ruins of Myth Drannor. (Forgotten Realms Ser.). 2000. mass mkt. 6.99 (*0-7869-1387-8*) Wizards Coast.

Bebuawu, Gazen & Luciani, Giacomo. Nation, State & Integration in the Arab World Vol. 2: The Rentier State. 256p. 1987. lib. bdg. 57.50 (*0-7099-4144-7*, Pub. by C Helm) Routldge.

Bec, Pierre. The Fundus Periphery. Blodi, Frederick C., tr. (Illus.). 484p. (C). (gr. 13). 1986. text 113.50 (*0-89352-211-2*) Mosby Inc.

Becam, Susan. Rhyme in Gace Brule's Lyric: Formal & Semantic Interplay. LC 96-48090. (Studies in the Humanities: Vol. 34). XII, 230p. (C). 1998. text 46.95 (*0-8204-3700-X*) P Lang Pubng.

Becan-McBride, Kathleen, et al. Phlebotomy. 1993. 65.00 (*0-89189-328-8*) Am Soc Clinical.

Beccaceci, Marcelo D. Natural Patagonia - Patagonia Natural: Argentina & Chile. LC 97-28419. (ENG & SPA., Illus.). 136p. 1998. pap. 24.95 (*0-9630180-3-5*) Pangaea Pub.

— Natural Patagonia - Patagonia Natural: Argentina & Chile. Hayskar, Bonnie J., ed. LC 97-28419. (ENG & SPA., Illus.). 136p. 1998. 32.95 (*0-9630180-4-3*) Pangaea Pub.

Beccari, O. Asiatic Palms: Lepidocaryeae, Pts. 1-2: The Species Daemonorops, 2 vols., Set. (C). 1988. 1140.00 (*0-7855-3236-6*, Pub. by Scholary) St Mut.

— Asiatic Palms Pt. I: Lepidocaryeae: The Species of

B

Calamus, 2 vols. (Annals of Royal Botanic Garden, Calcutta Ser.: Vol. XI Supp.). 160p. 1986. 500.00 (*1-55528-003-X*, Pub. by Today Tomorrow) Scholarly Pubns.

— Asiatic Palms Pts. I & II: Lepidocaryeary: The Species of Daemonorops, 2 vols. (Annals of Royal Botanic Garden, Calcutta Ser.: Vol. XII). 239p. 1985. 650.00 (*0-317-64510-2*, Pub. by Today Tomorrow) Scholarly Pubns.

— Asiatic Palms Pts. 2-3: Lepidocaryeae: The Species of General Ceratolobus to Eugelssona, 2 vols., Set. (C). 1988. 1400.00 (*0-7855-3235-8*, Pub. by Scientific) St Mut.

— Asiatic Palms Pts. II & III: Lepidocarea: The Species of Genera Ceratobus to Eugelssona, 2 vols. (Annals of Royal Botanic Garden, Calcutta Ser.: Vol. XII, Pt. 2). 231p. 1986. 825.00 (*1-55528-008-0*, Pub. by Today Tomorrow) Scholarly Pubns.

— Systematic Enumeration of the Species of Calmus & Daemonorops with Diagnoses of the New Ones. 230p. 1979. reprint ed. 40.00 (*0-7855-6641-4*, Pub. by Intl Bk Distr) St Mut.

Beccari, Odoardo. Wanderings in the Great Forests of Borneo. (Oxford in Asia Hardback Reprints Ser.). (Illus.). 456p. 1990. pap. 18.95 (*0-19-588923-1*) OUP.

Beccaria, Cesare. Of Crimes & Punishments. 200p. 1998. pap. text 11.95 (*1-56886-054-4*) Marsilio Pubs.

— On Crimes & Punishments. (International Pocket Library). 1992. pap. 5.95 (*0-8283-1800-X*) Branden Bks.

— On Crimes & Punishments. Young, David, ed. & tr. by. from ITA. LC 85-17578. (HPC Classics Ser.). 129p. (C). 1986. pap. 6.95 (*0-915145-97-9*); lib. bdg. 27.95 (*0-915144-99-9*) Hackett Pub.

— On Crimes & Punishments. Paolucci, Henry, tr. LC 61-18589. 128p. (C). 1963. pap. text 5.80 (*0-02-391360-6*, LLA107, Macmillan Coll) P-H.

— On Crimes & Punishments: Beccaria. 10th ed. Paolucci, Henry, tr. 99p. 1963. pap. 15.00 (*0-672-60302-0*, Bobbs) Macmillan.

— On Crimes & Punishments & Other Writings. Bellamy, Richard, ed. (Cambridge Texts in the History of Political Thought Ser.). (Illus.). 229p. (C). 1995. pap. text 19.95 (*0-521-47982-7*) Cambridge U Pr.

Becchetti, Claudio, jt. auth. see Ricotti, Lucio P.

Becchetti, Fred. Physics 128 & 241: Lab Manual. (C). 1993. 30.00 (*1-881592-12-X*) Hayden-McNeil.

— Physics 127 & 141: Lab Manual. (C). 1993. 30.00 (*1-881592-13-8*) Hayden-McNeil.

Becchetti, L., jt. ed. see Bagella, M.

Becchio, Bruno. Swiss Company Law. LC 96-3332. 1996. lib. bdg. 114.50 (*90-411-0967-6*) Kluwer Academic.

Becconsall, Jack, tr. see Berger, Stefan, et al.

Becconsall, Jack K., tr. see Friebolin, Horst.

Becerra. College Algebra From A Unified Perspective. (Mathematics Ser.). 1998. student ed. 16.00 (*0-534-34564-6*) Brooks-Cole.

Becerra, A. T., ed. see International Symposium on Peritoneal Dialysis Staff.

Becerra, Juan J. & Friedman, Eby G. Analog Design Issues in Digital VlSI Circuits & Systems. LC 97-17677. 1997. text 93.50 (*0-7923-9950-1*) Kluwer Academic.

Becerra, Linda & Sirisaengtaksin, Ongard. College Algebra from a Unified Laboratory Perspective. LC 97-23246. (Mathematics Ser.). 320p. 1997. mass mkt. 65.95 (*0-534-34403-8*) Wadsworth Pub.

Becerra, Linda, et al. College Algebra From Unif Pers:prelim Ed. (Math). 256p. (C). 1996. mass mkt. 18.25 (*0-534-34470-4*) Brooks-Cole.

Becerra, Linda, jt. auth. see Stewart, James.

Becerra, Ricardo, et al. La Reforma Electoral de 1996 (The Electoral Reform of 1996) (SPA.). 237p. 1997. pap. 7.99 (*968-16-5185-5*, Pub. by Fondo) Continental Bk.

Becerra, Rosina M. & Shaw, David. The Hispanic Elderly: A Research Reference Guide. 152p. (Orig.). 1984. pap. text 22.50 (*0-8191-3627-1*) U Pr of Amer.

Becerra, Rosina M., jt. auth. see De Anda, Diane.

Becerra, Rosina M., jt. auth. see Iglehart, Alfreda P.

Bech, C. & Reinertsen, R. E., eds. Physiology of Cold Adaptation in Birds. (NATO ASI Series A, Life Sciences: Vol. 173). (Illus.). 394p. 1989. 120.00 (*0-306-43237-4*, Plenum Trade) Perseus Pubng.

Bech, David, ed. 1997 Managed Home Care Sourcebook. LC 98-233104. (Illus.). 575p. 1997. pap. text 195.00 (*1-881393-97-6*) Faulkner & Gray.

Bech, Henning. When Men Meet: Homosexuality & Modernity. Mesquit, Teresa & Davies, Tim, trs. LC 96-46557. 1997. pap. 18.95 (*0-226-04022-4*); lib. bdg. 42.00 (*0-226-04021-6*) U Ch Pr.

Bech, Per. The Bech, Hamilton, & Zung Scales for Mood Disorders: Screening & Listening: A Twenty Years Update with References to DSM & ICD-10. LC 95-15491. 1995. write for info. (*0-387-59104-4*) Spr-Verlag.

— The Bech, Hamilton, & Zung Scales for Mood Disorders: Screening & Listening: A Twenty Years Update with References to DSM & ICD-10. LC 95-15491. (Illus.). 80p. 1995. 69.00 (*3-540-59104-4*) Spr-Verlag.

— The Bech, Hamilton & Zung Scales for Moods Disorders Screening & Listening. 2nd rev. ed. 1996. pap. 89.95 (*3-540-61245-9*) Spr-Verlag.

— Rating Scales for Psychopathology, Health Status, & Quality of Life: A Compendium on Documentation in Accordance with the DSM-III-R & WHO Systems. LC 92-49556. 1993. 159.00 (*0-387-55903-5*) Spr-Verlag.

Bechamp, A. The Blood & Its Third Anatomical Element. 1991. lib. bdg. 250.00 (*0-87700-927-9*) Revisionist Pr.

— The Blood & Its Third Anatomical Element. 1996. reprint ed. spiral bd. 28.50 (*0-7873-1163-4*) Hlth Research.

Bechamp, A., contrib. by. The Blood & Its Third Anatomical Element (1921) 255p. 1996. reprint ed. pap. 24.95 (*1-56459-712-1*) Kessinger Pub.

Bechard, Gorman. Good Neighbors. LC 98-6957. 304p. 1998. 24.00 (*0-7867-0512-4*) Carroll & Graf.

— Second Greatest Story Ever Told. 1991. 17.95 (*0-8065-1263-6*, Citadel Pr) Carol Pub Group.

Bechard, Margaret. If It Doesn't Kill You. LC 98-49553. 156p. (YA). (gr. 7-12). 1999. 15.99 (*0-670-88547-9*) Viking Penguin.

— My Mom Married the Principal. LC 97-22653. (J). 1998. 14.99 (*0-670-87394-2*) Viking Penguin.

— My Sister, My Science Report. (Illus.). 96p. (J). 1992. pap. 4.99 (*0-14-034408-X*, PuffinBks) Peng Put Young Read.

— Really No Big Deal. LC 93-31065. (Illus.). 160p. (J). (gr. 3-7). 1996. pap. 3.99 (*0-14-036912-0*, PuffinBks) Peng Put Young Read.

— Really No Big Deal. 1996. 9.09 (*0-606-09781-3*, Pub. by Turtleback) Demco.

— Star Hatchling. 1997. 9.60 (*0-606-13038-1*, Pub. by Turtleback) Demco.

Bechard, Margaret E. My Sister, My Science Report. (J). 1992. 9.09 (*0-606-01724-0*, Pub. by Turtleback) Demco.

Bechard, Matthew. International Online Markets 2000: Strategic Outlook & Forecast. 3rd rev. ed. Kopp, Linda et al, eds. 200p. 1999. 1995.00 (*0-88709-099-0*) Simba Info Inc.

— Publishing for Professional Markets: 99-2003 Review, Trends & Forcast. 3rd rev. ed. Martucci, Kathleen & Robell, Victor, eds. (Illus.). 282p. 1999. 1995.00 (*0-88709-155-5*) Simba Info Inc.

Bechard, Matthew, et al. Publishing for Professional Markets: 99-2000 Review, Trends & Forecast. Kopp, Linda, ed. 282p. 1999. 1995.00 (*0-88709-109-1*) Simba Info Inc.

Bechdel, Alison. Dykes to Watch Out For. LC 86-22760. (Illus.). 80p. (Orig.). 1986. pap. 9.95 (*0-932379-17-6*); lib. bdg. 18.95 (*0-932379-18-4*) Firebrand Bks.

— Dykes to Watch Out For: The Sequel. LC 92-4452. 136p. 1992. pap. 10.95 (*1-56341-008-7*); lib. bdg. 22.95 (*1-56341-009-5*) Firebrand Bks.

— Hot, Throbbing Dykes to Watch Out For: Cartoons. LC 97-15167. (Illus.). 144p. (C). 1997. pap. 10.95 (*1-56341-086-9*); lib. bdg. 22.95 (*1-56341-087-7*) Firebrand Bks.

— The Indelible Alison Bechdel: Confessions, Comix & Miscellaneous Dykes to Watch Out For. LC 98-9305. (Illus.). 224p. 1998. pap. 16.95 (*1-56341-096-6*); lib. bdg. 26.95 (*1-56341-097-4*) Firebrand Bks.

— More Dykes to Watch Out For. LC 88-6892. (Illus.). 112p. (Orig.). 1988. pap. 10.95 (*0-932379-45-1*); lib. bdg. 20.95 (*0-932379-46-X*) Firebrand Bks.

— New, Improved! Dykes to Watch Out For. LC 90-3184. (Illus.). 120p. 1990. pap. 10.95 (*0-932379-79-6*); lib. bdg. 22.95 (*0-932379-80-X*) Firebrand Bks.

***Bechdel, Alison.** Post-Dykes to Watch Out For. (Illus.). 144p. 2000. pap. 11.95 (*1-56341-122-9*, Pub. by Firebrand Bks); lib. bdg. 24.95 (*1-56341-123-7*, Pub. by Firebrand Bks) LPC InBook.

Bechdel, Alison. Spawn of Dykes to Watch Out For: Cartoons. LC 93-37734. (Illus.). 136p. 1993. pap. 10.95 (*1-56341-039-7*); lib. bdg. 22.95 (*1-56341-040-0*) Firebrand Bks.

— Split-Level Dykes to Watch Out For: Cartoons. (Illus.). 128p. 1998. pap. 10.95 (*1-56341-102-4*) Firebrand Bks.

— Split-Level Dykes to Watch Out For: Cartoons. LC 98-44382. (Illus.). 128p. 1998. 22.95 (*1-56341-103-2*) Firebrand Bks.

— Unnatural Dykes to Watch Out For: Cartoons. LC 95-36092. 144p. 1995. pap. 10.95 (*1-56341-067-2*); lib. bdg. 22.95 (*1-56341-068-0*) Firebrand Bks.

Bechdel, Les & Ray, Slim. River Rescue: A Manual for Whitewater Safety. 3rd rev. ed. LC 96-53448. (Illus.). 336p. 1997. pap. 16.95 (*1-878239-55-4*) AMC Books.

Bechdolt, Fred R., jt. auth. see Hopper, James M.

Bechdolt, Frederick R. Giants of the Old West. LC 73-80382. (Essay Index Reprint Ser.). 1977. 18.95 (*0-8369-1020-6*) Ayer.

— Tales of the Old-Timers. 1993. reprint ed. lib. bdg. 75.00 (*0-7812-5915-0*) Rprt Serv.

Bechdolt, Lucile. How Many Miles to Jesus. 1991. pap. 4.95 (*0-89137-460-4*) Quality Pubns.

— Let Me Tell You about Jesus. 1990. 4.35 (*0-89137-058-7*) Quality Pubns.

Becher & Yudenfreund. Emulsions, Latices & Dispersions. (Illus.). 344p. 1978. text 150.00 (*0-8247-6797-7*) Dekker.

Becher, Albert E. Groundwater Resources in & Near the Anthracite Basins of Schuylkill & Adjacent Counties, Pennsylvania. (Water Resource Reports: No. 64). (Illus.). 59p. (Orig.). 1991. pap. 12.00 (*0-8182-0121-5*) Commonweal PA.

***Becher, Anne.** American Environmental Leaders: A Biographical Dictionary. 2000. lib. bdg. 60.00 (*1-57607-162-6*) ABC-CLIO.

Becher, Anne. Biodiversity: A Reference Handbook. LC 97-42890. 275p. 1998. lib. bdg. 45.00 (*0-87436-923-1*) ABC-CLIO.

Becher, Bernd & Becher, Hilla. Bernd & Hilla Becher: Pennsylvania Coal Mine Tipples. (Illus.). 136p. 1991. 45.00 (*0-944521-23-1*) Dia Ctr Arts.

— Gas Tanks. LC 93-10026. (Illus.). 119p. 1993. 65.00 (*0-262-02361-X*) MIT Pr.

— Water Towers. (Illus.). 223p. 1988. 70.00 (*0-262-02277-X*) MIT Pr.

Becher, Bernd, jt. auth. see Becher, Hilla.

Becher, Erich. Der Begriff des Attributes Bei Spinoza. (Abhandlungen Zur Philosophie und Ihrer Geschichte Ser.: No. 19). (GER.). 61p. 1980. reprint ed. write for info. (*3-487-06777-3*) G Olms Pubs.

Becher, G., jt. auth. see Bjorseth, Alf.

Becher, Gerhard & Kuhlmann, Stefan, eds. Evaluation of Technology Policy Programmes in Germany. LC 94-23182. (Economics of Science, Technology & Innovation Ser.: Vol. 4). 372p. (C). 1994. lib. bdg. 136.00 (*0-7923-3115-X*) Kluwer Academic.

***Becher, H. & Burns, P.** Handbook of Contrast Echocardiography: LV Function & Myocardial Perfusion. (Illus.). 150p. 2000. 54.00 (*3-540-67083-1*) Spr-Verlag.

Becher, Herbert J. Woerterbuche der Rechtssprache & Wirtschaftssprache Vol. 1: Spanish-German. 3rd ed. (GER & SPA.). 1142p. 1988. 250.00 (*0-7859-6881-4*, 3406321852) Fr & Eur.

— Woerterbuche der Rechtssprache und Wirtschaftssprache, Vol. 2. 3rd ed. (GER & SPA.). 1019p. 1989. 250.00 (*0-8288-6432-2*, M7022) Fr & Eur.

Becher, Hilla & Becher, Bernd. Industrial Facades. (Illus.). 240p. 1995. 75.00 (*0-262-02388-1*) MIT Pr.

— Mineheads. LC 97-72280. (Illus.). 180p. 1997. 75.00 (*0-262-02430-6*) MIT Pr.

Becher, Hilla, jt. auth. see Becher, Bernd.

Becher, I. Recent Developments in the Synthesis & Chemistry of 2(1H)-Pyridinethiones & Related Compounds, Vol. 8, No. 3. Stidsen, C. E. & Senning, Alexander, eds. (Sulfur Reports: Vol. 8, Pt. 3). 48p. 1988. pap. text 77.00 (*3-7186-4835-0*) Gordon & Breach.

Becher, Ilse. Lateinisch-Griechisch Wortschatz in der Medizin. 3rd ed. (GER, GRE & LAT.). 255p. 1991. 59.95 (*0-7859-6874-1*, 3333006278) Fr & Eur.

— Latin to Greek Wortschatz In der Medizin. 4th ed. (GRE & LAT.). 255p. 1995. 69.95 (*0-320-00554-2*) Fr & Eur.

Becher, J. & Pedersen, Carl T., eds. Developments in the Organic Chemistry of Sulfur: Proceedings of the XIII International Symposium on the Organic Chemistry of Sulfur, August 7-12, 1988, Odense, Denmark. 394p. 1989. text 114.00 (*0-677-22140-1*) Gordon & Breach.

Becher, J. J. Chymischer Gluckshafen Oder Grobe Chymische Concordanz und Collection von Funffzenhenhundert Chymischen Processen. (GER.). 1997. write for info. (*3-487-05133-8*) G Olms Pubs.

Becher, James P. When You Marry. (Stepping Stones Ser.). 32p. (Orig.). 1992. pap. 1.95 (*0-8100-0458-5*, 12N2005) Northwest Pub.

Becher, Jan & Schaumburg, Kjeld, eds. Molecular Engineering for Advanced Materials. LC 94-48060. (NATO ASI Ser.: Series C, Mathematical & Physical Sciences: Vol. 456). 1995. text 217.50 (*0-7923-3347-0*) Kluwer Academic.

Becher, Jeanne, ed. Women, Religion & Sexuality: Studies on the Impact of Religious Teaching on Women. LC 91-10003. 278p. (Orig.). (C). 1991. pap. 17.00 (*1-56338-013-7*) TPI PA.

Becher, Max, jt. photos by see Robbins, Andrea.

Becher, Mordechai & Newman, Moshe. After the Return. LC 94-30794. 1994. 18.95 (*0-87306-688-X*) Feldheim.

Becher, Norman. The Complete Guide of Home Inspection. 2nd ed. 288p. 1993. pap. 19.95 (*0-07-004535-6*) McGraw.

Becher, P. F., et al, eds. Advances in Structural Ceramics. (MRS Symposium Proceedings Ser.: Vol. 78). 1987. text 17.50 (*0-931837-43-X*) Materials Res.

Becher, Paul. Dictionary of Colloid & Surface Science. (Illus.). 216p. 1989. text 125.00 (*0-8247-8326-3*) Dekker.

***Becher, Paul.** Emulsions: Theory & Practice. 3rd ed. LC 99-43770. 2000. write for info. (*0-8412-3496-5*) Am Chemical.

Becher, Paul. Encyclopedia of Emulsion Technology, Vol. 2. (Illus.). 536p. 1985. text 182.75 (*0-8247-1877-1*) Dekker.

— Encyclopedia of Emulsion Technology, Vol. 3. (Illus.). 452p. 1987. text 182.75 (*0-8247-1878-X*) Dekker.

— Encyclopedia of Emulsion Technology, Vol. 4. (Illus.). 376p. 1996. text 182.75 (*0-8247-9380-3*) Dekker.

Becher, Paul, tr. see Shinoda, Kozo.

Becher, Peter. Gauge Theories of Strong & Electroweak Interactions. Cottrell, Valerie H., tr. LC 83-6456. (Illus.). 318p. reprint ed. pap. 98.60 (*0-8357-4313-6*, 203711200007) Bks Demand.

Becher, Ronald. Massacre Along the Medicine Road: A Social History of the Indian War of 1864 in Nebraska Territory. LC 98-48924. 1999. pap. 22.95 (*0-87004-387-0*) Caxton.

— Massacre along the Medicine Road: A Social History of the Indian War of 1864 in Nebraska Territory. Cornell, Wayne, ed. LC 98-48924. 500p. 1999. 32.95 (*0-87004-389-7*, 038970) Caxton.

Becher, Siegfried. Erkenntnistheoretische Untersuchungen Zu Stuart Mills Theorie der Kausalitaet. (Abhandlungen Zur Philosophie und Ihrer Geschichte Ser.: Bd. 25). (GER.). 149p. 1980. reprint ed. write for info. (*3-487-06782-X*) G Olms Pubs.

Becher, Thomas. Boeing 757 & 767. (Illus.). 200p. 1999. 52.95 (*1-86126-197-7*) Motorbooks Intl.

Becher, Tony. Academic Tribes & Territories: Intellectual Enquiry & the Cultures of Disciplines. 192p. 1989. pap. 33.95 (*0-335-09220-9*) OpUniv Pr.

— Professional Practices: Commitment & Capability in a Changing Environment. 289p. 1999. 34.95 (*1-56000-414-2*) Transaction Pubs.

Becher, Tony, ed. Governments & Professional Education. LC 93-1136. 190p. 1994. 123.00 (*0-335-19135-5*) OpUniv Pr.

Becher, Tony, et al. Graduate Education in Britain. (Higher Education Policy Ser.: No. 17). 240p. 1993. 55.00 (*1-85302-531-3*) Taylor & Francis.

***Becher, William D.** An Ocean Between. xiv 672p. 2000. 27.95 (*0-9677283-4-7*) Barton.

Becher, Wolfgang. MS Works 2.0 Musterlosungen. (GER.). (C). 1990. text. write for info. (*0-201-55915-3*) Addison-Wesley.

Becherelle, Louis-Michel. La Conjugaison Dictionnaire de Douze Milles Verbes. rev. ed. (FRE.). 175p. 1990. 17.95 (*0-7859-7783-X*, 2218016605) Fr & Eur.

Becherer, Elsy, tr. see Rieker, Hans-Ulrich.

Becherer, Joseph A., et al. Pietro Perugino: Master of the Italian Renaissance. LC 97-33981. 1997. pap. write for info. (*0-942159-20-9*) Rizzoli Intl.

— Pietro Perugino: Master of the Italian Renaissance. LC 97-33981. 317p. 1997. 60.00 (*0-8478-2076-9*, Pub. by Rizzoli Intl) St Martin.

Becherer, Richard J. Science Plus Sentiment: Cesar Daly's Formula for Modern Architecture. LC 84-2453. (Studies in the Fine Arts - Architecture: No. 7). (Illus.). 451p. reprint ed. pap. 139.90 (*0-8357-1566-3*, 207049300097) Bks Demand.

Becherer, Richard J., ed. Laser Radar VII: Advanced Technology for Applications. 1992. 20.00 (*0-8194-0779-8*, 1633) SPIE.

Bechert, Frank. Keine Versohnung Mit Dem Nichts: Zur Rezeption Von Samuel Beckett in der DDR. (Illus.). 428p. 1997. 63.95 (*3-631-31980-0*) P Lang Pubng.

Bechert, Heinz, ed. When Did the Buddha Live? Controversy on the Dating of the Historical Buddha. LC 95-904176. (C). 1995. 98.50 (*81-7030-469-5*, Pub. by Sri Satguru Pubns) S Asia.

Bechert, Heinz & Gombrich, Richard F., eds. The World of Buddhism. LC 91-65147. (Illus.). 308p. 1991. reprint ed. pap. 29.95 (*0-500-27628-5*, Pub. by Thames Hudson) Norton.

Bechert, Johannes, et al, eds. Toward a Typology of European Languages. (Empirical Approaches to Language Typology Ser.: No. 8). x, 388p. (C). 1990. lib. bdg. 121.55 (*3-11-012108-5*) Mouton.

Beches, Annette, jt. ed. see Wang, Wilfried.

Bechet, Sidney. Treat It Gentle: An Autobiography. LC 74-23412. (Roots of Jazz Ser.). (Illus.). vi, 245p. 1978. reprint ed. pap. 12.95 (*0-306-80086-1*) Da Capo.

Bechett, Wendy M., tr. John of Ford: Sermons on the Song of Songs I. LC 77-3697. (Cistercian Fathers Ser.: No. 29). 1977. 14.95 (*0-87907-629-1*) Cistercian Pubns.

Bechham, Dow. Stars in the Dark: Coal Mines of Southwestern Oregon. (Illus.). 226p. (C). 1995. pap. text 15.95 (*0-930998-06-5*) Arago Bks.

Bechhoefer, Ina S., ed. Guide to Real Estate & Mortgage Banking Software. 9th ed. 1200p. Date not set. write for info. (*0-917935-19-5*) Real Est Sol.

Bechhofer, C. E. In Denikin's Russia & the Caucasus, 1919-1920. LC 76-115507. (Russia Observed Ser.). (Illus.). 1971. reprint ed. 34.95 (*0-405-03077-0*) Ayer.

Bechhofer, C. E., tr. Five Russian Plays with One from the Ukrainian. LC 77-89719. (One-Act Plays in Reprint Ser.). 1977. 25.00 (*0-8486-2016-X*) Roth Pub Inc.

***Bechhofer, Frank & Paterson, Lindsay.** Principles of Research Design in Social Sciences. LC 99-44348. 192p. (C). 2000. text. write for info. (*0-415-21442-4*) Routledge.

— Principles of Research Design in the Social Sciences. LC 99-44348. 2000. pap. 24.99 (*0-415-21443-2*) Routledge.

Bechhofer, Laurie, jt. ed. see Parrot, Andrea.

Bechhofer, Robert E. & Dunnett, Charles W. Percentage Points of Multivariate Student Distributions. LC 74-6283. (Selected Tables in Mathematical Statistics Ser.: Vol. 11). 371p. 1988. text 58.00 (*0-8218-1911-9*, TABLES/11C) Am Math.

Bechhofer, Robert E., et al. Design & Analysis of Experiments for Statistical Selection, Screening & Multiple Comparisons. LC 94-41843. (Probability & Mathematical Statistics Ser.). 344p. 1995. 89.95 (*0-471-57427-9*) Wiley.

***Bechko, Peggy A.** Cloud Dancer. LC 99-54986. 2000. 26.95 (*0-7862-2332-4*) Five Star.

Bechko, Peggy A. Dark Side of Love. large type ed. LC 97-49960. 1998. 22.95 (*0-7862-1314-0*) Thorndike Pr.

— The Eye of the Hawk: A Western Story. LC 97-38393. 213p. 1998. 18.95 (*0-7862-0991-7*) Thorndike Pr.

— The Eye of the Hawk: A Western Story. large type ed. LC 98-43049. 1999. pap. 18.95 (*0-7862-1030-3*) Thorndike Pr.

— Gunman's Justice. large type ed. LC 96-19290. (Sagebrush Large Print Westerns Ser.: Vol. 1). 176p. 1996. lib. bdg. 18.95 (*1-57490-012-9*) T T Beeler.

— The Tin-Pan Man. LC 96-43957. (Five Star Ser.). 246p. 1997. 17.95 (*0-7862-0736-1*) Five Star.

— The Tin-Pan Man. large type ed. 1999. 20.00 (*0-7862-0759-0*) Thorndike Pr.

***Bechko, Peggy A.** Tumbleweeds Frontier Stories. large type ed. 2000. 30.00 (*0-7862-1337-X*) Thorndike Pr.

Bechky, Allen. Adventuring in East Africa: The Sierra Club Travel Guide to the Great Safaris of Kenya, Tanzania, Rwanda, Eastern Zaire & Uganda. LC 89-10572. (Adventure Travel Guide Ser.). (Illus.). 464p. 1990. pap. 15.00 (*0-87156-747-4*, Pub. by Sierra) Random.

— Adventuring in Southern Africa. LC 97-8048. (Illus.). 416p. 1997. pap. 18.00 (*0-87156-593-5*, Pub. by Sierra) Random.

Bechle, Joyce M. Butterfly. 125p. (Orig.). (C). 1996. pap., per. 8.00 (*0-9654210-0-7*) J Bechle.

Bechler, Zav. Contemporary Newtonian Research. 247p. 1982. text 135.00 (*90-277-1303-0*, D Reidel) Kluwer Academic.

— Newton's Physics & the Conceptual Structure of the Scientific Revolution. 624p. (C). 1991. lib. bdg. 292.50 (*0-7923-1054-3*, Pub. by Kluwer Academic) Kluwer Academic.

Bechler, Zev. Aristotle's Theory of Actuality. LC 94-1045. (SUNY Series in Ancient Greek Philosophy). 270p. (C). 1995. text 69.50 (*0-7914-2239-9*); pap. text 23.95 (*0-7914-2240-2*) State U NY Pr.

Bechlin, Earl. Maine. (Adventure Guide Ser.). (Illus.). 360p. (Orig.). 1999. pap. 16.95 (*1-55650-860-3*) Hunter NJ.

An Asterisk (*) at the beginning of an entry indicates that the title is appearing for the first time.

Bechner, John F. True Wealth by the Book: How 100 Inspirational Americans Encountered Character, Moral & Spiri. 1999. pap. text. write for info. (*0-9655745-2-0*) By The Book Pub.

Bechoefer, Ina, ed. At the Forefront of Mortgage Banking Technology. 3rd ed. 150p. (Orig.). (C). 1997. pap. 60.00 (*1-57599-022-9*, PB6-110190-BK-P, Real Est Fin Pr) Mortgage Bankers.

***Becht, J. Terryl.** Bubba's Book. (Illus.). 125p. 1999. write for info. (*1-890933-00-7*) Ashton Prods.

Becht, Kenneth R. Just the Facts: A Case for Impeachment. 1997. pap. 15.95 (*1-881116-96-4*) Black Forest Pr.

— Just the Facts - A Case for Impeachment: Over 200 Documented Lies, Misrepresentations & Contradictory Statements by William Jefferson Clinton. Crain, Duran, ed. 319p. 1997. pap. 19.95 (*0-9662726-0-9*) Putting Am First.

Becht, Linda, ed. see Guyton, Bill.

Becht, R. Revision der Sektion Alopecuroideae DC. der Gattung Astragalus L. (Phanerogamarum Monographiae: No. 10). (Illus.). 1979. lib. bdg. 48.00 (*3-7682-1188-6*) Lubrecht & Cramer.

Bechtal, Stefan, et al. Sex: A Man's Guide. 656p. 1998. pap. 7.99 (*0-425-16580-9*) Berkley Pub.

Bechtel, jt. auth. see Nunley, William.

Bechtel, Bernard. Reptile & Amphibian Variants: Colors, Patterns, & Scales. LC 94-6665. (Illus.). 224p. 1995. 64.50 (*0-89464-862-4*) Krieger.

Bechtel, Carol B. Glimpses of Glory: Daily Reflections on the Bible. LC 97-41414. 128p. 1998. pap. 10.00 (*0-664-25743-7*) Westminster John Knox.

Bechtel, D. B., ed. New Frontiers in Food Microstructure. LC 83-70795. (Illus.). 392p. 1983. text 76.00 (*0-913250-32-5*) Am Assn Cereal Chem.

Bechtel, Dave A. Digital Electronics. 4th ed. 1995. pap. text, student ed. 32.80 (*0-13-399452-X*) P-H.

Bechtel, Delphine. Der Nister's Work, 1907-1929: A Study of a Yiddish Symbolist. Valentin, Jean-Marie, ed. (Contacts: Series Three, Etudes et Documents: Vol. 11). (Illus.). 306p. 1991. pap. 53.00 (*3-261-04239-7*) P Lang Pubng.

Bechtel, Faythelma. Creative Touch, No. 3. 1988. 4.40 (*0-87813-923-0*) Christian Light.

***Bechtel, Faythelma.** God's Marvelous Gifts. rev. ed. (Christian Day School Ser.). (J). (gr. 5). 2000. 14.95 (*0-87813-936-2*) Christian Light.

Bechtel, Friedrich. Die Griechischen Dialekte Bd. 1: Der Lesbische, Thessalische, Bootische, Arkadische und Kyprische Dialekt. (GER.). vi, 447p. 1963. 105.00 (*3-296-10611-1*) G Olms Pubs.

— Die Griechischen Dialekte Bd. 3: Der Ionische Dialekt. (GER.). ix, 353p. 1963. 80.00 (*3-296-10613-8*) G Olms Pubs.

— Die Historischen Personennamen Des Griechischen Bis Zur Kaiserzeit. xvi, 637p. 1982. reprint ed. 160.00 (*3-487-00497-6*) G Olms Pubs.

— Lexilogus Zu Homer. viii, 314p. 1964. reprint ed. 80.00 (*0-318-70873-6*) G Olms Pubs.

— Die Vocalcontraction Bei Homer. xi, 314p. 1976. reprint ed. 80.00 (*3-487-05837-5*) G Olms Pubs.

Bechtel, Gordon C. Multidimensional Preference Scaling. (Methods & Models in the Social Sciences Ser.: No. 6). 1976. pap. 32.35 (*90-279-7592-1*) Mouton.

Bechtel, Guy. Dictionnaire de la Betise et des Erreurs de Jugement. (FRE.). 820p. 1991. pap. 55.00 (*0-7859-7808-9*, 2221067479) Fr & Eur.

Bechtel, H. Kenneth. State Police in the United States: A Socio-Historical Analysis, 47. LC 94-30929. (Contributions in Criminology & Penology Ser.: Vol. 47). 192p. 1995. 59.95 (*0-313-26380-9*, Greenwood Pr) Greenwood.

Bechtel, Helen R. My Walk with Jesus: Miracles in the Snow. LC 98-61307. (Illus.). 64p. 1998. pap. 11.99 (*1-57921-151-8*, Pub. by WinePress Pub) BookWorld.

Bechtel, Helmut, et al. The Manual of Cultivated Orchard Species. 3rd ed. (Illus.). 500p. 1992. 85.00 (*0-262-02339-3*) MIT Pr.

Bechtel, John H., ed. Select Speeches for Declamation. LC 75-103083. (Granger Index Reprint Ser.). 1977. 19.95 (*0-8369-6098-X*) Ayer.

— Temperance Selections. LC 71-116393. (Granger Index Reprint Ser.). 1977. 17.95 (*0-8369-6134-X*) Ayer.

Bechtel, Judith & Franzblau, Bettie. Reading in the Science Classroom. 64p. 1980. pap. 8.95 (*0-8106-3201-2*) NEA.

***Bechtel, Louis.** Thailand Guide. 2nd ed. 528p. 1999. pap. 18.95 (*1-892975-16-5*) Open Rd Pub.

Bechtel, Peter J., ed. Muscle As Food. (Food Science & Technology Ser.). 1986. text 153.00 (*0-12-084190-8*) Acad Pr.

Bechtel, Robert B. Environment & Behavior Research: An Introduction. LC 96-25246. 722p. 1996. 40.00 (*0-8039-5795-5*) Sage.

Bechtel, Rose, tr. see Saltman, David.

Bechtel, Stefan & Stains, Laurence R. The Good Luck Book. LC 97-4102. (Illus.). 384p. 1997. pap. 7.95 (*0-7611-0541-7*, 10541) Workman Pub.

***Bechtel, Stefan & Stains, Laurence Roy.** What Women Want: What Every Man Needs to Know about Sex, Romance, Passion, & Pleasure. LC 99-59608. 480p. 2000. 31.95 (*1-57954-093-7*) Rodale Pr Inc.

Bechtel, Stefan, jt. auth. see Castle, Kit.

Bechtel, Stefan, jt. auth. see Prevention Magazine Editors.

Bechtel, Stephan. Sex: A Man's Guide. (Illus.). 512p. 1997. pap. 17.95 (*0-87596-458-3*) Rodale Pr Inc.

***Bechtel, William.** Companion to Cognitive Science. (Companions to Philosophy Ser.). 800p. 1999. pap. 34.95 (*0-631-21851-3*) Blackwell Pubs.

Bechtel, William. Philosophy of Mind: An Overview for Cognitive Science. (Tutorials in Cognitive Science Ser.). 176p. 1988. text 36.00 (*0-8058-0218-5*); pap. text 21.50 (*0-8058-0234-7*) L Erlbaum Assocs.

— Philosophy of Science: An Overview for Cognitive Science. (Tutorial Essays in Cognitive Science Ser.). 152p. 1988. 36.00 (*0-89859-695-5*); pap. text 19.95 (*0-8058-0221-5*) L Erlbaum Assocs.

Bechtel, William, ed. Integrating Scientific Disciplines. 360p. (C). 1986. lib. bdg. 173.50 (*90-247-3242-5*, Pub. by M Nijhoff) Kluwer Academic.

Bechtel, William & Abrahamsen, Adele, eds. Connectionism & the Mind: Parallel Processing, Dynamics, & Evolution. 2nd ed. 356p. 1998. 64.95 (*0-631-20712-0*); pap. 29.95 (*0-631-20713-9*) Blackwell Pubs.

Bechtel, William & Abrahamson, Adele. Connectionism & the Mind: An Introduction to Parallel Processing in Network. (Illus.). 1994. pap. 28.95 (*0-631-16577-0*) Blackwell Pubs.

***Bechtel, William & Graham, George, eds.** A Companion to Cognitive Science. LC 97-38757. (Companions to Philosophy Ser.). (Illus.). 800p. 1999. 99.95 (*1-55786-542-6*) Blackwell Pubs.

Bechtel, William & Richardson, Robert C. Discovering Complexity: Decomposition & Localization as Strategies in Scientific Research. (Illus.). 328p. 1992. text 49.50 (*0-691-08762-8*, Pub. by Princeton U Pr) Cal Prin Full Svc.

Bechtel, William, jt. auth. see Luckhardt, C. Grant.

Bechteler, W., ed. Transport of Suspended Solids in Open Channels: Proceedings of Euromech 192, Munich - Neubibiberg, 11-15 June 1985. 278p. (C). 1986. text 136.00 (*90-6191-644-5*, Pub. by A A Balkema) Ashgate Pub Co.

Bechtell, Michelle L. Untangling Organizational Gridlock: Strategies for Building a Customer Focus. 224p. 1993. 27.95 (*0-8144-0203-8*) AMACOM.

Bechterev, Vladimir M. General Principles of Human Reflexology: An Introduction to the Objective Study of Personality. LC 73-2961. (Classics in Psychology Ser.). 1976. reprint ed. 30.95 (*0-405-05134-4*) Ayer.

Bechtereva, N. P. Psychophysiology Today & Tomorrow. 1981. 126.00 (*0-08-025930-8*, Pub. by Pergamon Repr) Franklin.

Bechthold, W., et al. Direct Disposal of Spent Nuclear Fuel. (C). 1987. text 152.50 (*1-85333-079-5*) Kluwer Academic.

Bechtler, Cristina, ed. see Gehry, Frank O. & Forster, Kurt W.

Bechtloff, Carol A. Recipes from the Whitegate Inn: A Collection of Bed & Breakfast Recipes from the Kitchen of Carol Amato Bechtloff. LC 98-91021. 132p. 1999. pap. 14.95 (*0-9668803-0-7*) Whitegate Inn.

Bechtold, Brigitte. Economy & Society: A Long View of Economic Ideas. 325p. (C). 1996. pap. text 24.80 (*0-87563-653-5*) Stipes.

Bechtold, Gottfried. Monograph. (Illus.). 447p. 1997. 95.00 (*3-908162-58-0*) Dist Art Pubs.

Bechtold, Lisze. Buster, the Very Shy Dog. LC 97-12452. (Illus.). 48p. (J). (gr. 1-4). 1998. 15.00 (*0-395-85008-8*) HM.

***Bechtold, Lisze.** Edna's Tale. LC 00-36945. (Illus.). (J). 2001. write for info. (*0-618-09164-5*) HM.

Bechtold, Paul. Catholic Theology Union at Chicago: The Founding Years. LC 93-71237. (Illus.). 350p. 1993. pap. 10.95 (*0-9636659-0-1*) Cath Theol Union.

***Bechtold, Richard.** Essentials of Software Project Management. (Illus.). 409p. 1999. 59.00 (*1-56726-084-5*); pap. 59.00 (*1-56726-085-3*) Mgmt Concepts.

Bechtold, Richard L. Alternative Fuels Guidebook: Properties, Storage, Dispensing, & Vehicle Facility Modifications. LC 97-27727. 214p. 1997. 39.00 (*0-7680-0052-1*, R-180) Soc Auto Engineers.

Bechtolsheim, Lulu, tr. see Nachbin, Leopoldo.

Bechtolsheim, Stephen V. TEX in Practice, 4 vols., Set. Rogers, David F., ed. (Monographs in Visual Communication). (Illus.). 1872p. 1994. 225.95 (*0-387-97296-X*) Spr-Verlag.

— TEX in Practice, 4 vols., Vol. I: Basics. Rogers, David F., ed. (Monographs in Visual Communication). (Illus.). 384p. 1994. 65.95 (*0-387-97595-0*) Spr-Verlag.

— TEX in Practice, 4 vols., Vol. II: Paragraphs, Math & Fonts. Rogers, David F., ed. (Monographs in Visual Communication). (Illus.). 368p. 1994. 65.95 (*0-387-97596-9*) Spr-Verlag.

— TEX in Practice, 4 vols., Vol. III: Tokens, Macros. Rogers, David F., ed. (Monographs in Visual Communication). (Illus.). 544p. 1994. 65.95 (*0-387-97597-7*) Spr-Verlag.

Beck. Hyperbook Computer-Englisch. (ENG & GER.). 1993. 49.95 (*0-7859-7431-8*, 3423505338) Fr & Eur.

— In the Best of Health? The Status & Future of Health Care in the U. K. 376p. 1992. pap. 47.75 (*1-56593-039-8*, 0287) Thomson Learn.

— Managerial Commmunication: The Lifeline. (C). 1996. text. write for info. (*0-03-015368-9*) Harcourt Coll Pubs.

— NCA Review for the Clinical Laboratory Sciences. 3rd ed. LC 96-16315. 254p. 1996. pap. text 35.00 (*0-316-59942-5*, Little Brwn Med Div) Lppncott W & W.

— A Practical Approach to the Drumset. 48p. 1985. pap. 7.95 (*0-7935-2320-6*, 00123245) H Leonard.

— Reading Today & Tomorrow. (Reading Ser.). (J). 1989. pap., teacher ed. 78.75 (*0-15-718371-8*) Harcourt Schl Pubs.

— Reading Today & Tomorrow: End of Book Test. (Reading Ser.). (J). 1989. pap., teacher ed. 17.00 (*0-15-718335-1*); pap., teacher ed. 17.00 (*0-15-718345-9*); pap., teacher ed. 17.00 (*0-15-718355-6*); pap., teacher ed. 17.00 (*0-15-718365-3*); pap., teacher ed. 17.00 (*0-15-718375-0*); pap., teacher ed. 17.00 (*0-15-718385-8*) Harcourt Schl Pubs.

— Reading Today & Tomorrow: End of Unit Test. (Reading Ser.). (YA). (gr. 11). 1989. pap., teacher ed. 17.00 (*0-15-718109-X*) Harcourt Schl Pubs.

— Reading Today & Tomorrow: End of Unit Test A. (Reading Ser.). (J). 1989. pap., teacher ed. 17.00 (*0-15-718129-4*); pap., teacher ed. 17.00 (*0-15-718139-1*) Harcourt Schl Pubs.

— Reading Today & Tomorrow: End of Unit Test A. (Reading Ser.). (J). (gr. 5). 1989. pap., teacher ed. 17.00 (*0-15-718049-2*) Harcourt Schl Pubs.

— Reading Today & Tomorrow: End of Unit Test A. (Reading Ser.). (J). (gr. 7). 1989. pap., teacher ed. 17.00 (*0-15-718069-7*) Harcourt Schl Pubs.

— Reading Today & Tomorrow: End of Unit Test A. (Reading Ser.). (YA). (gr. 9). 1989. pap., teacher ed. 17.00 (*0-15-718089-1*) Harcourt Schl Pubs.

— Reading Today & Tomorrow: End of Unit Test A. (Reading Ser.). (YA). (gr. 12). 1989. pap., teacher ed. 17.00 (*0-15-718119-7*) Harcourt Schl Pubs.

— Reading Today & Tomorrow: End Unit Test A. (Reading Ser.). (J). (gr. 6). 1989. pap., teacher ed. 17.00 (*0-15-718059-X*) Harcourt Schl Pubs.

— Reading Today & Tomorrow: End Unit Test A. (Reading Ser.). (J). (gr. 8). 1989. pap., teacher ed. 17.00 (*0-15-718079-4*) Harcourt Schl Pubs.

— Reading Today & Tomorrow: End Unit Test B. (Reading Ser.). (J). 1989. pap., teacher ed. 17.00 (*0-15-718252-2*); pap., teacher ed. 17.00 (*0-15-718272-X*) Harcourt Schl Pubs.

— Reading Today & Tomorrow: Kingdoms. (Reading Ser.). (J). (gr. 4). 1989. pap., teacher ed. 45.00 (*0-15-718031-X*) Harcourt Schl Pubs.

— Reading Today & Tomorrow: Kingdoms, Level 15. (J). (gr. 4). 1989. pap., wbk. ed. 21.50 (*0-15-718037-9*) Harcourt Schl Pubs.

— Reading Today & Tomorrow Level 1: Sundrops. 1989th ed. (J). (gr. 1). 1989. pap., teacher ed. 61.75 (*0-15-718001-8*) Harcourt Schl Pubs.

— Reading Today & Tomorrow Levels 9-15: Placement Tests. (Reading Ser.). (J). 1989. pap., teacher ed. 13.50 (*0-15-718233-9*) Harcourt Schl Pubs.

— Reading Today & Tomorrow Skill Master Level 1: End of Book Test. (J). (gr. 1). 1989. pap., teacher ed. 17.00 (*0-15-718007-7*) Harcourt Schl Pubs.

— Skill Master for Reading Today & Tomorrow Level 3: End of Book Test. (Reading Ser.). (J). (gr. 3). 1989. pap., teacher ed. 17.00 (*0-15-718027-1*) Harcourt Schl Pubs.

— Skill Master for Reading Today & Tomorrow Level 6: End of Book Tests. (Reading Ser.). (J). (gr. 6). 1989. pap., teacher ed. 17.00 (*0-15-718057-3*) Harcourt Schl Pubs.

— Skill Master for Reading Today & Tomorrow Level 7: End of Book Test. (Reading Ser.). (J). (gr. 7). 1989 pap., teacher ed. 17.00 (*0-15-718067-0*) Harcourt Schl Pubs.

— Skill Master for Reading Today & Tomorrow Level 8: End of Book Test. (Reading Ser.). (J). (gr. 8). 1989 pap., teacher ed. 17.00 (*0-15-718077-8*) Harcourt Schl Pubs.

— Skill Master for Reading Today & Tomorrow Level 9: End of Book Test. (Reading Ser.). (YA). (gr. 9). 1989. pap., teacher ed. 17.00 (*0-15-718087-5*) Harcourt Schl Pubs.

— Skill Master for Reading Today & Tomorrow Level 11: End of Book Test. (Reading Ser.). (YA). 1989. pap., teacher ed. 17.00 (*0-15-718107-3*) Harcourt Schl Pubs.

— Skill Master for Reading Today & Tomorrow Level 12: End of Book Test. (Reading Ser.). (YA). (gr. 12). 1989. pap., teacher ed. 17.00 (*0-15-718117-0*) Harcourt Schl Pubs.

— Skill Master for Reading Today & Tomorrow Level 13: End of Book Test. (Reading Ser.). (J). 1989. pap., teacher ed. 17.00 (*0-15-718127-8*) Harcourt Schl Pubs.

— Skill Master for Reading Today & Tomorrow Level 14: End of Book Test. (Reading Ser.). (J). 1989. pap., teacher ed. 17.00 (*0-15-718137-5*) Harcourt Schl Pubs.

— Skill Master Reading Today & Tomorrow Level 2: End of Book Test. (Reading Ser.). (J). (gr. 2). 1989. pap., teacher ed. 17.00 (*0-15-718017-4*) Harcourt Schl Pubs.

— Skill Master Reading Today & Tomorrow Level 5: End of Book Test. (Reading Ser.). (J). (gr. 5). 1989. pap., teacher ed. 17.00 (*0-15-718047-6*) Harcourt Schl Pubs.

— Teacher Idea Book for Reading Today & Tomorrow Level 1. (Reading Ser.). 1989. pap., teacher ed. 39.75 (*0-15-718271-1*) Harcourt Schl Pubs.

— Teacher Idea Book for Reading Today & Tomorrow Level 7-8. (Reading Ser.). 1989. pap., teacher ed. 39.75 (*0-15-718301-7*) Harcourt Schl Pubs.

— Teacher Idea Book for Reading Today & Tomorrow Level 11. (Reading Ser.). 1989. pap., teacher ed. 39.75 (*0-15-718321-1*) Harcourt Schl Pubs.

— Teacher's Idea Book for Reading Today & Tomorrow. 1989. pap., teacher ed. 45.75 (*0-15-718391-2*) Harcourt Schl Pubs.

***Beck.** The Teddy Robber. 2000. pap. 8.95 (*0-552-52593-6*, Pub. by Transworld Publishers Ltd) Trafalgar.

— Theory & Practice Massage Workbook. 3rd ed. 184p. 1999. wbk. ed. 25.95 (*1-56253-405-X*) Thomson Learn.

Beck. The Theory & Practice of Therapeutic Massage. 3rd ed. LC 98-49279. (Massage Ser). 720p. 1999. text 53.95 (*1-56253-404-1*) Thomson Learn.

— Theory & Practice of Therapeutic Message. 3rd ed. LC 98-49279. (Massage Ser.). 720p. 1999. text 48.95 (*1-56253-536-6*) Thomson Learn.

— Theory & Practice Therapeutic Massage Curriculum Guide. (Cosmetology Ser.). 1982. 2.75 (*0-87350-372-4*, VNR) Wiley.

— Workbook for Reading Today & Tomorrow. (Reading Ser.). (YA). (gr. 12). 1989. pap., teacher ed. 21.50 (*0-15-718113-8*) Harcourt Schl Pubs.

Beck & Goplerud. Waters & Water Rights Vol. 3: 1998 Edition, 1990 Supplement. 1987. text. write for info. (*0-87473-397-9*, 60780-10, MICHIE) LEXIS Pub.

Beck & Well. Patient Care in Colorectal Surgery. 1991. 50.00 (*0-316-08653-3*, Little Brwn Med Div) Lppncott W & W.

Beck, et al. Laboratory Notes for Physics. 16th ed. 242p. (C). 1998. spiral bd. 31.95 (*0-7872-5357-X*, 41535701) Kendall-Hunt.

— Online Diaries: The Lollapalooza '95 Tour Journals. 128p. 1996. 6.00 (*1-887128-20-4*) Soft Skull Pr.

Beck, Gregor, jt. auth. see Dobson, Clive.

Beck, A. Gases & Vacua Pts. 1-3: Vacuum Tech Applied Continuously Pumped Systems. LC 63-214430. (Handbook of Vacuum Physics Ser.). 1964. 95.00 (*0-08-010425-8*, Pub. by Pergamon Repr) Franklin.

Beck, A., et al, eds. Probability in Banach Spaces V. (Lecture Notes in Mathematics Ser.: Vol. 1153). vi, 457p. 1985. 59.95 (*0-387-15704-2*) Spr-Verlag.

Beck, A. C. That Lawyer Girl: The Unauthorized Guide to Ally's World. LC 98-55396. (Illus.). 240p. 1999. pap. 14.95 (*1-58063-044-8*, Pub. by Renaissance) St Martin.

Beck, A. David. The Chicago American Indian Community, 1893-1988: Annotated Bibliography & Guide to Sources in Chicago. ii, 284p. 1988. pap. 19.95 (*0-944898-01-7*) Am Indian Pr.

Beck, A. E., et al, eds. Hydrogeological Regimes & Their Subsurface Thermal Effects, Vol. 47, IUGG 2. (Geophysical Monograph Ser.). 158p. 1989. 27.00 (*0-87590-451-3*) Am Geophysical.

Beck, A. H. Handbook of Vacuum Physics, Vol. 3, Pts. 1-3. 1965. pap. 91.00 (*0-08-011051-7*, Pub. by Pergamon Repr) Franklin.

Beck, A. J., et al, eds. Organic Substances in Soil & Water: Natural Constituents & Their Influences on Contaminant Behaviour. 200p. 1993. 126.00 (*0-85186-635-2*) CRC Pr.

Beck, Aaron. Cognitive Therapy of Depression. 1992. pap. 20.95 (*0-15-804591-2*, Gulliver Bks) Harcourt.

Beck, Aaron T. Cognitive Therapy & Emotional Disorders. LC 75-33518. 365p. (Orig.). 1976. 52.50 (*0-8236-1005-5*) Intl Univs Pr.

— Cognitive Therapy & the Emotional Disorders. 1979. pap. 15.95 (*0-452-00928-6*) NAL.

— Depression: Causes & Treatment. LC 67-23826. 374p. (C). 1972. reprint ed. pap. text 20.95 (*0-8122-1032-8*) U of Pa Pr.

— Love Is Never Enough: How Couples Can Overcome Misunderstandings, Resolve Conflicts, & Solve Relationship Problems Through Cognitive Therapy. LC 88-45010. 432p. 1989. reprint ed. pap. 14.00 (*0-06-091604-4*, Perennial) HarperTrade.

***Beck, Aaron T.** Prisoners Of Hate: The Cognitive Basis of Anger, Hostility, & Violence. LC 99-22651. (Illus.). 368p. 1999. 26.00 (*0-06-019377-8*) HarpC.

Beck, Aaron T., et al, eds. The Prediction of Suicide. LC 86-71588. 256p. 1987. reprint ed. pap. 19.95 (*0-914783-16-5*) Charles.

Beck, Aaron T. & Freeman, Arthur. Cognitive Therapy of Personality Disorders. LC 90-33575. 396p. 1990. lib. bdg. 44.00 (*0-89862-434-7*) Guilford Pubns.

Beck, Aaron T., et al. Anxiety Disorders & Phobias: A Cognitive Perspective. 372p. 1990. pap. 18.00 (*0-465-00385-0*, Pub. by Basic) HarpC.

— Cognitive Therapy of Depression. LC 79-19967. (Guilford Clinical Psychology & Psychotherapy Ser.). 425p. 1979. lib. bdg. 46.95 (*0-89862-000-7*) Guilford Pubns.

— Cognitive Therapy of Depression. LC 79-19967. (Clinical Psychology & Psychotherapy Ser.). 425p. 1987. pap. text 27.00 (*0-89862-919-5*) Guilford Pubns.

— Cognitive Therapy of Substance Abuse. LC 93-5208. 354p. 1993. lib. bdg. 42.00 (*0-89862-115-1*) Guilford Pubns.

Beck, Aaron T., jt. auth. see Alford, Brad A.

Beck, Adams, jt. auth. see Moresby, Lily.

***Beck, Adolf, et al.** Friedrich Gottlie Klopstock Werke Und Briefe. 464p. 1999. 216.00 (*3-11-016321-7*) De Gruyter.

Beck, Al. Beaucoup Haiku: And Divergent Verse. LC 98-67835. (Illus.). 180p. 1999. pap. 10.00 (*0-934852-66-9*) Lorien Hse.

— Gnomes & Poems. (Illus.). 75p. (Orig.). 1992. pap. 10.00 (*0-934852-59-6*) Lorien Hse.

***Beck, Al.** God Is in the Glove Compartment. (Illus.). 192p. 2000. pap. 10.00 (*0-934852-67-7*, AB-5) Lorien Hse.

Beck, Al. Sight Lines. (Illus.). 87p. (Orig.). 1996. pap. 6.00 (*0-934852-63-4*) Lorien Hse.

— Songs from the Rainbow Worm: Poems, Drawings, Ceremonial Masks & Photographs. (Illus.). 112p. (Orig.). 1997. pap. 9.50 (*0-934852-65-0*) Lorien Hse.

Beck, Alan & Katcher, Aaron. Between Pets & People: The Importance of Animal Companionship. rev. ed. LC 96-6044. (Illus.). 344p. (C). 1996. pap. 18.95 (*1-55753-077-7*) Purdue U Pr.

Beck, Alfred M. U. S. Army in World War II, Technical Services, the Corps of Engineers: The War Against Germany. LC 84-11376. (Center for Military History Publication German Report Series, DA Pam: No. 10-22). (Illus.). 626p. 1985. 40.00 (*0-16-001938-9*, S/N 008-029-00131-4) USGPO.

Beck, Alfred M., ed. see Nalty, Bernard C., et al.

***Beck, Alison & Binetti, Marianne.** Perennials for British Columbia. (Illus.). 352p. 2000. pap. 18.95 (*1-55105-258-X*) Lone Pine.

Beck, Alison, jt. auth. see Binetti, Marianne.

***Beck, Allen & Maruschak, Laura.** State & Federal Corrections Information Systems: An Inventory of Data Elements & an Assessment of Reporting Capabilities. (Illus.). 192p. (C). 1999. pap. text 35.00 (*0-7881-7587-4*) DIANE Pub.

B

An Asterisk (*) at the beginning of an entry indicates that the title is appearing for the first time.

Beck, Anatole, et al. Excursions into Mathematics. LC 68-57963. (Illus.). (C). 1969. text 49.95 (0-87901-004-5) Worth.

***Beck, Anatole, et al.** Excursions into Mathematics: The Millennium Edition. 2nd rev. ed. LC 99-58794. (Illus.). 500p. 2000. pap. 34.00 (1-56881-115-2) AK Peters.

Beck, Andre T. Prisoners Of Hate: The Cognitive Basis of Anger, Hostility, & Violence. 368p. 2000. pap. 14.00 (0-06-093200-7, Perennial) HarperTrade.

Beck, Andrea. Elliot Bakes a Cake. (Illus.). 32p. (J). (ps-2). 1999. 12.95 (1-55074-443-7, Pub. by Kids Can Pr) Genl Dist Srvs.

***Beck, Andrea.** Elliot Bakes a Cake. (Elliot Moose Story Ser.). (Illus.). 32p. (J). (ps-k). 2000. pap. 5.95 (1-55074-696-0, Pub. by Kids Can Press) Genl Dist Srvs.

Beck, Andrea. Elliot's Emergency. (Elliot Moose Story Ser.). (Illus.). 32p. (J). (ps-2). 1998. 12.95 (1-55074-441-0, Pub. by Kids Can Pr) Genl Dist Srvs.

— Elliot's Emergency. (Elliot Moose Story Ser.). (Illus.). 32p. (J). (ps-2). 1999. pap. 5.95 (1-55074-687-1, Pub. by Kids Can Pr) Genl Dist Srvs.

***Beck, Andrea.** Elliot's Shipwreck. (Elliot Moose Story Ser.). (Illus.). 32p. (J). (ps-2). 2000. pap. 5.95 (1-55074-698-7, Pub. by Kids Can Press) Genl Dist Srvs.

Beck, Andreas. Percutaneous Transluminal Angioscopy. LC 92-48747. 1993. write for info. (3-540-51066-4); 164.45 (0-387-51066-4) Spr-Verlag.

Beck, Ann. History of the British Medical Administration of East Africa, 1900-1950. LC 70-115472. (Commonwealth Fund Publications). 277p. 1970. 29.95 (0-674-40170-0) HUP.

— Medicine, Tradition, & Development in Kenya & Tanzania, 1920-1970. 114p. 1981. 12.00 (0-918456-44-4) African Studies Assn.

Beck, Anna R., jt. auth. see Beck, Howard.

***Beck, Araidne P. & Lewis, Carol M., eds.** The Process of Group Psychotherapy: Systems for Analyzing Change. 494p. 2000. 49.95 (1-55798-658-4, 4318930) Am Psychol.

Beck, Arlene. Painting Realistic Flowers in Acrylic. LC 97-17884. (Illus.). 128p. 1998. pap. 24.99 (0-89134-776-3, North Lght Bks) F & W Pubns Inc.

Beck, Art. Enlightenment: Shorthand for a Scurillious Life (the Re-Discovered Poems of Giacoma Casanova) 1977. pap. 3.00 (0-88031-035-9) Invisible-Red Hill.

— Rilke. LC 82-84119. 70p. (Orig.). 1983. pap. 3.95 (0-941692-06-X) Elysian Pr.

Beck, Art, tr. Luxorius: Simply to See. 64p. 1990. pap. 80.00 (0-918395-12-7) Poltroon Pr.

Beck, Astrid. The Leningrad Codex. fac. ed. Freedman, David N. & Sanders, James A., eds. 1072p. 1998. 255.00 (0-8028-3786-7) Eerdmans.

Beck, Astrid B., et al, eds. The Leningrad Codex: A Facsimile Edition. fac. ed. (Illus.). 1024p. 1997. 250.00 (90-04-10854-8) Brill Academic Pubs.

Beck, Astrid B., tr. see Barth, Markus & Blanke, Helmut.

Beck, Audrey J. The Collection of John A. & Audrey Jones Beck. 1998. write for info. (0-89090-088-4); pap. write for info. (0-89090-090-6) Mus Fine TX.

Beck, B., ed. Perspectives on a Regional Culture. 212p. 1979. 19.95 (0-318-36977-X) Asia Bk Corp.

Beck, B. D. Assessing Health Risks from Contaminated Soil. 1987. text 77.00 (2-88124-419-X) Gordon & Breach.

Beck, Barbara. The Bryn & Llangattock-nigh-Usk: A Short History, Reminiscences & Photographs. 187p. (C). 1989. 59.00 (0-905928-24-5, Pub. by D Brown & Sons Ltd) St Mut.

Beck, Barbara, jt. auth. see Beck, Thomas A.

Beck, Barry & Beck, Cathy. Fly-Fishing the Flats. LC 98-30317. 1999. 39.95 (0-8117-2764-5) Stackpole.

— Fly-Fishing the Flats. LC 98-30317. (Illus.). 160p. 1999. 39.95 (0-8117-0626-5) Stackpole.

***Beck, Barry & Beck, Cathy.** Pennsylvania Blue-Ribbon Fly Fishing Guide. (Illus.). 96p. 2000. pap. 24.95 (1-57188-158-1) F Amato Pubns.

Beck, Barry F., ed. Applied Karst Geology: The Proceedings of the Fourth Multidisciplinary Conference on Sinkholes & the Engineering & Environmental Impacts of Karst. (Illus.). 304p. (C). 1993. 126.00 (90-5410-305-1, Pub. by A A Balkema) Ashgate Pub Co.

— Engineering & Environmental Impacts of Sinkholes & Karst: Proceedings of the Third Multidisciplinary Conference, St. Petersburg-Beach, Florida, 2 - 4 October 1989. (Illus.). 392p. (C). 1989. text 155.00 (90-6191-987-8, Pub. by A A Balkema) Ashgate Pub Co.

— Karst Geohazards: Engineering & Environmental Problems in Karst Terrane: Proceedings of the 5th Multidisciplinary Conference on Sinkholes & the Engineering & Environmental Impacts of Karst, Gatlinburg, Tennessee, 2-5 April 1995. (Illus.). 304p. (C). 1995. text 123.00 (90-5410-535-6, Pub. by A A Balkema) Ashgate Pub Co.

Beck, Barry F., et al, eds. The Engineering Geology & Hydrogeology of Karst Terranes: Proceedings of the Sixth Multidisciplinary International Conference, Springfield, Missouri, 6-9 April 1997. (Illus.). 528p. (Orig.). (C). 1997. text 136.00 (90-5410-867-3, Pub. by A A Balkema) Ashgate Pub Co.

***Beck, Barry F., et al, eds.** Hydrogeology & Engineering Geology of Sinkholes & Karst 1999: Proceedings of the 7th Multidisciplinary Conference, Harrisburg-Hershey, PA, USA, 10-14 April. (Illus.). 16p. 1999. text 115.00 (90-5809-046-9, Pub. by A A Balkema) Ashgate Pub Co.

Beck, Beatrice M. Ethnobotany of the California Indians Vol. 1: A Bibliobraphy & Index. (Illus.). 160p. 1994. pap. write for info. (1-878762-50-8) Balogh.

Beck, Beatrix. Leon Morin, Pretre. (FRE.). 192p. 1972. pap. 10.95 (0-7859-1711-X, 2070362175) Fr & Eur.

— Une Mort Irreguliere. (FRE.). 1981. pap. 10.95 (0-685-66710-3, 2070372782) Fr & Eur.

Beck, Bill. Good Chemistry: The Story of P. C. Reilly & Reilly Industries. Hackett, Kim, ed. (Illus.). 224p. 1996. write for info. (0-9651415-0-0); pap. write for info. (0-9651415-1-9) Reilly Indust.

— Interconnections: The History of the Mid-Continent Area Power Pool. (Illus.). 200p. (Orig.). 1988. pap. write for info. (0-318-63154-7) MCAPP.

— Light Across the Prairies: An Illustrated History of Northwestern Public Service Company. (Illus.). 260p. (Orig.). (C). 1989. write for info. (0-318-65405-9) NW Pub Serv.

— The People Process: A Manufacturing Story. Westmoreland Larson Webster, Inc., Staff, ed. & illus. by. LC 95-75072. 133p. 1994. text. write for info. (0-9644463-0-8); pap. text 24.00 (0-9644463-1-6) Phillips Plastics.

— PP&L: 75 Years of Powering the Future: An Illustrated History of Pennsylvania Power & Light Co. 450p. 1995. text. write for info. (0-9645915-0-2); pap. text. write for info. (0-9645915-1-0) PA Power & Light.

Beck, Bill, jt. auth. see Ruskin, John.

Beck, Bodog. The Bible of Bee Venom Therapy. rev. ed. xii, 238p. 1997. pap. 29.95 (1-890708-00-3) Health Res Pr.

Beck, Bodog & Smedley, Doree. Honey & Your Health: A Nutritional, Medicinal & Historical Commentary. rev. ed. (Illus.). 246p. 1997. pap. 27.95 (1-890708-02-X) Health Res Pr.

Beck-Bornholdt, Hans-Peter. Current Topics in Clinical Radiobiology of Tumors. (Illus.). 160p. 1993. write for info. (3-540-56512-4) Spr-Verlag.

Beck-Bornholdt, Hans-Peter, ed. Current Topics in Clinical Radiobiology of Tumors. LC 93-22941. 1993. 125.00 (0-387-56512-4) Spr-Verlag.

Beck, Brandon. 3rd Winchester. (Virginia Civil War Battles & Leaders Ser.). (Illus.). 127p. 1997. 19.95 (1-56190-101-6) H E Howard.

Beck, Brandon H., ed. Third Alabama! The Civil War Memoir of Brigadier General Cullen Andrews Battle, CSA. LC 99-6491. 1999. 29.95 (0-8173-1001-0) U of Ala Pr.

Beck, Brandon H. & Grunder, Charles. The First Battle of Winchester. (Virginia Civil War Battles & Leaders Ser.). (Illus.). 111p. 1992. 19.95 (1-56190-038-9) H E Howard.

Beck, Brandon H., jt. auth. see Grunder, Charles S.

***Beck, Brenda E.** Folktales of India. (Illus.). 358p. 1999. pap. 15.00 (0-226-04083-6) U Ch Pr.

Beck, Brenda E., et al, eds. Folktales of India. LC 86-7112. (Folktales of the World Ser.). (Illus.). xxxii, 358p. (C). 1987. 29.95 (0-226-04080-1) U Ch Pr.

Beck, Bruce, jt. ed. see Young, Bruce.

Beck, Bryan. Clinical Trials: Decision Tools for Measuring & Improving Performance. (Illus.). 152p. 1996. 169.00 (1-57491-019-1) Interpharm.

***Beck-Burridge, Martin & Walton, Jeremy.** Britain's Winning Formula: Achieving World Leadership in Motorsports. LC 99-49414. 2000. text 75.00 (0-312-23064-8) St Martin.

Beck, C. Andrew. Turning Hobbies into Cash. LC 94-70101. (Illus.). 128p. (Orig.). 1994. pap. 8.95 (0-9640401-0-7) Four Crnrs Grp.

— Turning Hobbies into Cash. LC 91-77197. (Illus.). 144p. (Orig.). 1991. pap. 11.95 (0-9631520-0-9) Monterey Prods.

Beck, C. Malcolm & Garrett, Howard. Texas Bug Book: Understanding Insects. LC 98-3594. 192p. 1999. 40.00 (0-292-70868-8); pap. 24.95 (0-292-70869-6) U of Tex Pr.

Beck, C. Malcolm, jt. auth. see Garrett, J. Howard.

Beck, Camilla. Our Feet Are the Feet of Dogs. 1997. 12.00 (1-891051-08-3) Back Cover Pr.

Beck, Carl, ed. Law & Justice: Essays in Honor of Robert S. Rankin. LC 74-86476. 370p. reprint ed. pap. 114.70 (0-608-14660-9, 202336700032) Bks Demand.

Beck, Carl, et al. Political Science Thesaurus. LC 75-326011. 471p. reprint ed. pap. 146.10 (0-608-11111-2, 201779900008) Bks Demand.

Beck, Carl, jt. ed. see Mesa-Lago, Carmelo.

Beck, Carol, jt. auth. see Allison, Nan.

Beck, Carolyn, ed. see Christlieb, Don.

Beck, Carolyn S. Our Own Vine & Fig Tree: The Persistence of the Mother Bethel Family. LC 88-35114. (Immigrant Communities & Ethnic Minorities in the U. S. & Canada Ser.: No. 36). 1989. 57.50 (0-404-19446-X) AMS Pr.

Beck, Cathy. Cathy Beck's Fly Fishing Handbook. LC 95-44809. (Illus.). 184p. 1996. 24.95 (1-55821-340-6) Lyons Pr.

— Cathy Beck's Fly-Fishing Handbook. (Illus.). 184p. 1996. pap. 16.95 (1-55821-471-2) Lyons Pr.

Beck, Cathy, jt. auth. see Beck, Barry.

Beck, Charles B. The Origin & Early Evolution of Angiosperms. 1976. text 97.00 (0-231-03857-7) Col U Pr.

Beck, Charles B., ed. Origin & Evolution of Gymnosperms. (Illus.). 552p. 1988. text 91.00 (0-231-06358-X) Col U Pr.

Beck, Charles E. Managerial Communication: Bridging Theory & Practice. LC 98-8141. 500p. 1998. 70.00 (0-13-849886-5) P-H.

Beck, Charles L. Model for Leading Change: Making Acquisition Reform Work. 136p. 1997. per. 10.00 (0-16-061209-8) USGPO.

Beck, Charlotte. Dating in Exposed & Surface Contexts. LC 94-7113. 1994. pap. 19.95 (0-8263-1523-2) U of NM Pr.

***Beck, Charlotte, ed.** Models for the Millennium: Great Basin Anthropology Today. LC 99-45381. (Illus.). 314p. 1999. 65.00 (0-87480-593-7) U of Utah Pr.

Beck, Charlotte, tr. see Barnes, Peter.

***Beck, Charlotte H.** The Fugitive Legacy: A Critical History. (Southern Literary Studies). (Illus.). 312p. 2000. 49.95 (0-8071-2590-3) La State U Pr.

Beck, Charlotte J. Everyday Zen: Love & Work. Smith, Steve, ed. LC 88-45692. 224p. 1989. pap. 13.00 (0-06-060734-3) HarperTrade.

Beck, Charlotte J. & Smith, Steve. Nothing Special: Living Zen. LC 92-56131. 288p. 1994. reprint ed. pap. 13.00 (0-06-251117-3, Pub. by Harper SF) HarpC.

Beck, Chip, jt. auth. see Glad, Wayne.

Beck, Christa & Forsting, Christine. Istanbul. (Architecture Guides Ser.). (Illus.). 320p. 1998. pap. 5.95 (3-89508-638-X, 520206) Konemann.

Beck, Christian & Schlogl, Friedrich. Thermodynamics of Chaotic Systems: An Introduction. (Nonlinear Science Ser.: No. 4). (Illus.). 306p. (C). 1995. pap. text 30.95 (0-521-48451-0) Cambridge U Pr.

Beck, Christina S., et al. Partnership for Health: Building Relationships Between Women & Health Caregivers. LC 96-54801. (Communication Ser.). 232p. 1997. pap. 21.50 (0-8058-2445-6); text 45.00 (0-8058-2444-8) L Erlbaum Assocs.

Beck, Christine S. Spirit of Summit County, Colorado: A Photographic Celebration. LC 95-71871. (Illus.). 128p. 1996. 25.95 (0-9649005-0-5) PrismLght Pr.

***Beck-Clark, Denise.** Concurrent Sentences: A True Story of Murder, Love & Redemption. LC 99-70155. 340p. 1999. 24.95 (0-88282-188-1, No. 0882821881, Pub. by New Horizon NJ) Natl Bk Netwk.

Beck, Clark L. & Burks, Ardath W. Aspects of Meiji Modernization: The Japan Helpers & the Helped. 45p. 1983. pap. text 24.95 (0-87855-936-1) Transaction Pubs.

Beck, Curt & Shennan, Stephen. Amber in Prehistoric Britain. (Oxbow Monographs in Archaeology: No. 8). (Illus.). 231p. 1991. pap. 36.00 (0-946897-30-1, Pub. by Oxbow Bks) David Brown.

Beck, Curt W., ed. Archaeological Chemistry. LC 74-22372. (Advances in Chemistry Ser.: No. 138). 254p. 1974. 43.95 (0-8412-0211-7) Am Chemical.

— Archaeological Chemistry. LC 74-22372. (Advances in Chemistry Ser.: Vol. 138). 264p. 1974. reprint ed. pap. 81.90 (0-608-03903-9, 206435000008) Bks Demand.

Beck, D. & Materon, L. A. Nitrogen Fixation by Legumes in Mediterranean Agriculture. (Developments in Plants & Soil Sciences Ser.). (C). 1988. text 271.50 (90-247-3624-2) Kluwer Academic.

Beck, David. Flames of Wisdom: Patristic Counsels for Contemporary Life. 1994. pap. 8.95 (0-937032-96-4) Light&Life Pub Co MN.

— For They Shall See God: Purifying Our Hearts That We May See God. 131p. 1995. pap. 10.95 (1-880971-08-9) Light&Life Pub Co MN.

***Beck, David, ed.** O'Connor's Annotated CPRC Plus, 1999. annot. ed. (Texas Annotated Codes Plus Ser.). 1018p. 1999. pap. 34.95 (1-884554-31-8) J McClure Pubng.

Beck, David, ed. see Thurman, Beverly J.

Beck, David E., ed. Handbook of Colorectal Surgery. (Illus.). 485p. 1996. text 39.00 (1-57626-012-7) Quality Med Pub.

Beck, David E. & Wexner, Steven D., eds. Fundamentals of Anorectal Surgery. LC 92-2983. 509p. 1992. text 97.00 (0-07-105436-7, RD544) McGraw-Hill HPD.

Beck, David R. The Discipleship Paradigm: Readers & Anonymous Characters in the Fourth Gospel. LC 97-19022. viii, 174p. 1997. 69.50 (90-04-10700-2) Brill Academic Pubs.

Beck, Debra, ed. see Fisser, Herbert G.

Beck, Deva & Beck, James. The Pleasure Connection: How Endorphins Affect Our Health & Happiness. LC 87-60379. 235p. (Orig.). 1987. pap. 12.95 (0-9617972-0-7) Synthesis Pr.

Beck, Don & Cowan, Chris. Spiral Dynamics. (Illus.). 400p. (Orig.). 1996. 38.95 (1-55786-940-5) Blackwell Pubs.

Beck, Donald. Down to Earth Landlording: An Investor's Guide to Successful Property Management. 2nd rev. ed. (Illus.). 125p. 1993. pap. 25.00 (0-9633163-0-3) M-M Prodns.

***Beck, Donald.** The Second Coming: Finality. LC 99-91574. 1999. 25.00 (0-7388-0892-X); pap. 18.00 (0-7388-0893-8) Xlibris Corp.

Beck, Donald F. Basic Hospital Financial Management. 2nd ed. LC 80-19598. 347p. (C). 1989. 62.00 (0-8342-0017-1) Aspen Pub.

Beck, Donald R., jt. ed. see Nicolaides, Cleanthes A.

Beck, Dorothy F. Marriage & the Family under Challenge: An Outline of Issues, Trends, & Alternatives. 2nd ed. LC 76-26307. 107p. reprint ed. pap. 33.20 (0-608-18322-9, 203159600075) Bks Demand.

Beck, Dorothy F. & Jones, Mary A. Progress on Family Problems: A Nationwide Study of Clients' & Counselors' Views on Family Agency Services. LC 73-81256. 205p. reprint ed. pap. 63.60 (0-8357-2760-2, 203988400014) Bks Demand.

Beck, Dorothy G. No Peeping under the Curtain: Tips & Scripts for School Drama Productions. LC 93-40075. (Illus.). 330p. 1994. 39.50 (0-8108-2545-7) Scarecrow.

Beck, Dorothy S. Mrs. Beck's Cookie Cookbook. Demou, Doris B., ed. & pref. by. 138p. (YA). (gr. 6-12). 1988. 10.00 (0-9604794-2-2) Doris Demou.

Beck, Douglas L. Handbook of Intraoperative Monitoring. LC 94-12881. (Illus.). 254p. (Orig.). (C). 1994. pap. text 55.00 (1-56593-210-2, 0468) Thomson Learn.

Beck, E., jt. auth. see Resch, H.

Beck, E. M., jt. auth. see Tolnay, Stewart E.

Beck, Earl C. Lore of the Lumber Camps. enl. rev. ed. LC 49-7123. (University of Michigan Studies & Publications). (Illus.). 378p. reprint ed. pap. 117.20 (0-608-10836-7, 205107800074) Bks Demand.

— Songs of the Michigan Lumberjacks. LC M 1629.B34S6. (University of Michigan Studies & Publications). 316p. reprint ed. pap. 98.00 (0-608-13968-8, 205562000029) Bks Demand.

— They Knew Paul Bunyan. Dorson, Richard M., ed. LC 80-789. (Folklore of the World Ser.). 1981. reprint ed. lib. bdg. 29.95 (0-405-13328-6) Ayer.

Beck, Earl R. The Death of the Prussian Republican: A Study of Reich-Prussian Relations, 1932-1934. LC 59-9600. (Florida State University Studies: No. 31). 293p. reprint ed. pap. 90.90 (0-7837-5021-8, 204468900004) Bks Demand.

— European Home Fronts, 1939-1945. Eubank, Keith, ed. (European History Ser.). 175p. (C). 1993. pap. text 11.95 (0-88295-906-9) Harlan Davidson.

— Germany Rediscovers America. LC 68-54592. 347p. reprint ed. pap. 107.60 (0-7837-5075-7, 204477300004) Bks Demand.

— A Time of Triumph & of Sorrow: Spanish Politics During the Reign of Alfonso XII, 1874-1885. LC 78-23282. 320p. 1979. 31.95 (0-8093-0902-5) S Ill U Pr.

— Under the Bombs: The German Home Front, 1942-1945. (Illus.). 280p. 1999. reprint ed. pap. 18.00 (0-8131-0977-9) U Pr of Ky.

Beck, Ed. Billie: A Love That Couldn't Die. rev. ed. LC 89-62541. 260p. 1989. reprint ed. pap. 7.95 (0-917851-37-4) Bristol Hse.

Beck, Edward, et al. Evaluation, Repair, Modification & Design of Welded Steel Moment Frame Structures: Interm Guidelines. (Illus.). 227p. (C). 1997. reprint ed. pap. text 50.00 (0-7881-4252-6) DIANE Pub.

Beck, Eileen, ed. see Dibble, Peter C.

Beck, Elizabeth J., ed. see Beck, John R.

Beck, Eric R., et al. Tutorials in Differential Diagnosis. 3rd ed. (Illus.). 236p. (Orig.). 1992. pap. text 33.00 (0-443-04472-4) Church.

Beck, Ernest, jt. auth. see Bachin, Peter.

Beck, Evelyn T. Kafka & the Yiddish Theater: Its Impact on His Work. LC 75-143763. 270p. 1971. reprint ed. pap. 77.00 (0-7837-9776-1, 2060505) Bks Demand.

Beck, Evelyn T., jt. ed. see Sherman, Julia A.

Beck, F., et al, eds. The Catecholaminergic Innervation of the Rat Amygdala, Vol. 142. LC 97-45951. (Advances in Anatomy, Embryology, & Cell Biology Ser.). (Illus.). xii, 112p. 1998. pap. 99.00 (3-540-63903-9) Spr-Verlag.

Beck, F., ed. see Angelov, D. N., et al.

Beck, F., jt. ed. see Barsukov, V.

Beck, F., ed. see Funke, C. & Kuhn, H. J.

Beck, F., ed. see Kasper, Michael.

Beck, F., jt. ed. see Lierse, W.

Beck, F., ed. see Muller-Gerbl, Magdalena.

Beck, F., ed. see Reznikov, K. Y.

Beck, F., ed. see Schmidt, Walter.

Beck, F., ed. see Snipes, Robert L.

Beck, F., ed. see Spornitz, U. M.

Beck, F., ed. see Stichel-Gunkel, Christine C.

Beck, F., ed. see Usunoff, Kamen G., et al.

Beck, F., ed. see Van Domburg, P. H. & Ten Donkelaar, H. J.

Beck, F A., et al, eds. New Nuclear Physics with Advanced Techniques: Proceedings of the International Conference, Crete, Greece, 23-29 June 1991. 450p. 1992. text 124.00 (981-02-0861-8) World Scientific Pub.

Beck, F Barry & Wilson, William L., eds. Karst Hydrogeology: Engineering & Environmental Applications: Proceedings of the Second Multidisciplinary Conference on Sinkholes & the Environmental Impact of Karst, Orlando, FL, 9-11 February 1987. 475p. (C). 1987. text 155.00 (90-6191-692-5, Pub. by A A Balkema) Ashgate Pub Co.

Beck, F. H., jt. auth. see Roach, Donald B.

Beck, Francine. Mega Sex: Achieving Unlimited Sexual Potency Forever. LC 96-26763. 352p. 1997. pap. text 14.95 (0-935016-08-2, Dunhill Pub Co) Zinn Pub Grp.

— Unlimited Sex: Beck's Three-Step Method for Achieving Unlimited Male Potency Forever. 1996. pap. text 14.95 (0-935016-37-6) Arrowood Pr.

***Beck, Frank O.** Hobomania: Guide to Bugause SQ & Chicago's Bohemia of the Early 1900s. 160p. 2000. pap. 14.00 (0-88286-251-0) C H Kerr.

Beck, Frederick. Second Carrot from the End. (American Autobiography Ser.). 160p. 1995. reprint ed. lib. bdg. 69.00 (0-7812-8455-4) Rprt Serv.

Beck, Friedrich. Preparation Techniques for the Failure Analysis of Integrated Circuits. LC 97-11255. (Wiley Series in Quality & Reliability Engineering). 190p. 1998. 115.00 (0-471-97401-3) Wiley.

***Beck, G. A.** Love from the Spirit: A Compilation of Poetry. LC 99-96655. 2000. pap. 7.95 (0-533-13282-7) Vantage.

***Beck, Gad.** An Underground Life: Memoirs of a Gay Jew in Nazi Berlin. Orig. Title: Und Gad Ging Zu David. 2000. pap. 16.95 (0-299-16504-3) U of Wis Pr.

Beck, Gad & Heibert, Frank. An Underground Life: Memoirs of a Gay Jew in Nazi Berlin. Brown, Allison, tr. from GER. LC 99-6441. (Living Out Ser.). (Orig. Title: Und Gad Ging Zu David. (Illus.). 168p. 1999. text 24.95 (0-299-16500-0) U of Wis Pr.

Beck, George A., et al. Minnesota Administrative Procedure. 2nd ed. LC 98-61176. 450p. 1998. ring bd. 115.00 (0-9666567-0-9) Weekend Pubns.

Beck-Gernsheim, Elisabeth. The Social Implications of Bioengineering. Mazzarins, Laimdota, tr. LC 95-12912. 144p. (C). 1995. pap. 15.00 (0-391-03842-7); text 45.00 (0-391-03841-9) Humanities.

Beck-Gernsheim, Elisabeth, jt. auth. see Beck, Ulrich.

***Beck, Gregor G. & Littlejohn, Bruce, eds.** Voices for the Watershed: Environmental Issues in the Great Lakes - St. Lawrence Drainage Basin. (Illus.). 208p. 2000. 24.95 (0-7735-2003-1, Pub. by McG-Queens Univ Pr) CUP Services.

Beck, Gregory, ed. Primordial Immunity: Foundations for the Verterbrate Immune System. LC 94-4703. (Annals Ser.). 1994. pap. 100.00 (0-89766-840-5) NY Acad Sci.

Beck, Guy L. Sonic Theology: Hinduism & Sacred Sound. LC 92-42734. (Studies in Comparative Religion). 306p. (C). 1993. text 39.95 (0-87249-855-7) U of SC Pr.

An Asterisk (*) at the beginning of an entry indicates that the title is appearing for the first time.

Beck, H. & Gundtherodt, H. J., eds. Glassy Metals I. (Topics in Applied Physics Ser.: Vol. 46). (Illus.). 350p. 1981. 84.95 (*0-387-10440-2*) Spr-Verlag.

Beck, H. & Guntherodt, H. J., eds. Glassy Metals, Vol. 3. (Topics in Applied Physics Ser.: Vol. 72). (Illus.). 280p. 1994. 96.95 (*0-387-57440-9*) Spr-Verlag.

Beck, H., jt. ed. see Guntherodt, H. J.

Beck, H. G., et al, eds. Kyklos: Griechisches und Byzantinisches: Rudolf Keydell zum 90. Geburstag. (C). 1978. 115.40 (*3-11-007211-4*) De Gruyter.

***Beck, Haig.** Parliament House, Canberra: A Building for the Nation. (Illus.). 280p. 2000. 49.95 (*0-949284-33-5*, Pub. by Watermark) Antique Collect.

***Beck, Haig & Cooper, Jackie.** Denton, Corker, Marshall: Rule Playing & the Ratbag Element. LC 99-87032. (Illus.). 240p. 2000. 70.00 (*3-7643-6161-1*) Birkhauser.

Beck, Hallie. Roses in a Desert Garden. Harper, Judy, ed. (Illus.). 150p. 1996. 14.95 (*0-9625961-1-6*) PHG AZ.

Beck, Hamilton H. H. The Elusive "I" in the Novel: Hippel, Sterne, Diderot, Kant. (American University Studies: Germanic Languages & Literature: Ser. I, Vol. 46). X, 161p. (C). 1987. text 31.00 (*0-8204-0279-6*) P Lang Pubng.

Beck, Hanno, et al. Citizens' Guide to Environmental Tax Shifting: For a Cleaner Environment, Stronger Economy, Fairer Tax Code. Erskine, Lynn, ed. (Illus.). 59p. 1998. pap. 15.00 (*0-913890-81-2*) Friends of Earth.

Beck, Hans-Georg. Byzantinistik Heute. (C). 1977. 8.95 (*3-11-007220-3*) De Gruyter.

Beck, Hans T., ed. Useful Palms of the World: A Synoptic Bibliography. 752p. 1990. text 64.50 (*0-231-06676-7*) Col U Pr.

Beck, Harry. A Gun-Handy Stranger. large type ed. (Linford Western Large Print Ser.). 240p. 1996. pap. 16.99 (*0-7089-7816-9*, Linford) Ulverscroft.

Beck, Heinrich, et al, eds. Germanische Religionsgeschichte: Quellen und Quellenprobleme. (Ergaenzungsbaende zum Reallexicon der Germanischen Altertumskunde Ser.: Bd. 5). (GER.). viii, 751p. (C). 1992. lib. bdg. 275.40 (*3-11-012872-1*) De Gruyter.

— Kreativer Friede Durch Begegnung der Weltkulturen: Im Auftrag der Hanns-Seidel-Stiftung. (Schriften zur Triadik und Ontodynamik Ser.: Bd. 9). (GER.). 370p. 1995. 61.95 (*3-631-48934-X*) P Lang Pubng.

Beck, Henry C. Forgotten Towns of Southern New Jersey. 1984. pap. 14.95 (*0-8135-1016-3*) Rutgers U Pr.

— The Jersey Midlands. LC 83-15930. (Illus.). 462p. 1984. reprint ed. pap. 143.30 (*0-608-02734-0*, 206339900004) Bks Demand.

— More Forgotten Towns of Southern New Jersey. 1984. reprint ed. pap. 14.95 (*0-8135-0432-5*) Rutgers U Pr.

— The Roads of Home: Lanes & Legends of New Jersey. 301p. 1983. reprint ed. pap. 15.95 (*0-8135-1018-X*) Rutgers U Pr.

— Tales & Towns of Northern New Jersey. 357p. (Orig.). (C). 1983. reprint ed. pap. 14.95 (*0-8135-1019-8*) Rutgers U Pr.

Beck, Henry H. On the Texas Frontier. 2nd ed. LC 98-51155. (Illus.). 308p. 1999. reprint ed. 24.95 (*1-56474-303-9*) Fithian Pr.

Beck, Herman L. L' Image d'Idris Second, ses Descendants de Fas et la Politique Sharifienne des Sultans Marinides (656-869 - 1258-1465) LC 88-38592. (Asfar - Publications of the Research Institute for the History of Muslim-Christian Relations, Leiden University: Vol. 3). (FRE.). iv, 292p. 1989. 83.50 (*90-04-09054-1*) Brill Academic Pubs.

Beck, Hermann. The Origins of the Authoritarian Welfare State in Prussia: Conservatives, Bureaucracy & the Social Question, 1815-70. (Social History, Popular Culture, & Politics in Germany Ser.). 320p. 1995. text 54.50 (*0-472-10546-9*, 10546) U of Mich Pr.

— The Origins of the Authoritarian Welfare State in Prussia: Conservatives, Bureaucracy & the Social Question, 1815-70. 320p. (C). 1997. reprint ed. pap. text 24.95 (*0-472-08428-3*, 08428) U of Mich Pr.

Beck, Hope P. Sunday School Plays for Preschoolers. LC 96-52622. 55p. 1997. pap. 7.95 (*0-7880-1062-X*) CSS OH.

Beck, Horace. Classification & Nomenclature of Beads & Pendants. (Illus.). 80p. 1973. pap. 15.00 (*0-87387-083-2*) Shumway.

— Folklore & the Sea. 4th rev. ed. (American Maritime Library: Vol. 6). (Illus.). 545p. 1981. pap. 24.95 (*0-913372-36-6*) Mystic Seaport.

***Beck, Horace.** Folklore & the Sea, Vol. 1. 1999. 12.99 (*0-7858-1119-2*) Bk Sales Inc.

Beck, Howard. The William Wordsworth Way. LC 99-221591. (Illus.). 192p. 1998. 19.95 (*1-85158-978-3*, Pub. by Mainstream Pubng) Trafalgar.

Beck, Howard, ed. Whole Wheat Cookery Treasures from the Wheat Bin. LC 86-72596. 165p. 1986. reprint ed. spiral bd. 12.95 (*0-9617875-0-3*) Wheat Bin.

Beck, Howard & Beck, Anna R. Whole Wheat Cookery: Treasures from the Wheat Bin. 166p. 1993. pap., spiral bd. 12.95 (*1-882420-00-4*) Hearth KS.

Beck, Hubert F. Como Responder a... Las Sectas. (Serie Respuesta). (SPA.). 1990. pap. 2.95 (*0-570-09904-8*) Concordia.

Beck, Hubert F. The Cults: How to Respond. rev. ed. LC 95-10751. (How to Respond Ser.). Orig. Title: How to Respond to...the Cults. 64p. 1995. 3.99 (*0-570-04668-8*, 12-6001) Concordia.

Beck, Ian. The Diver's Reluctance to Ascend: Short Stories LC 89-173517. 100 p. 1986. write for info. (*0-207-15259-4*) Ang Robertson.

— Emily & the Golden Acorn. LC 91-4510. (J). (ps-3). 1992. pap. 14.00 (*0-671-75979-5*) S&S Bks Yung.

— Five Little Ducks. LC 92-27193. (Illus.). 32p. (J). (ps-2). 1995. 14.95 (*0-8050-2525-1*, Bks Young Read) H Holt & Co.

***Beck, Ian.** Home Before Dark. LC 00-29137. 2001. pap. write for info. (*0-439-17523-2*) Scholastic Inc.

— Lost in the Snow. LC 99-47802. 2000. pap. write for info. (*0-439-17521-6*) Scholastic Inc.

— Peter & the Wolf. (J). 2000. pap. 8.95 (*0-552-52755-6*, Pub. by Transworld Publishers Ltd) Trafalgar.

Beck, Ian. The Teddy Robber. 32p. 1993. 7.50 (*0-385-40369-0*) Doubleday.

Beck, Ian. Read Me a Fairy Tale: A Child's Book of Classic Fairy Tales. LC 92-41949. 128p. (J). (gr. k up). 1993. 16.95 (*0-590-49431-7*) Scholastic Inc.

Beck, Ian. Peter & the Wolf. LC 95-75918. 32p. (J). (gr. 4-6). 1995. 13.00 (*0-689-80336-2*) Atheneum Yung Read.

***Beck, Ingrid.** Building Preservation Knowledge in Brazil. (Illus.). 37p. 1999. pap. 15.00 (*1-887334-71-8*) Coun Lib & Info.

— The Lord Is My Shepherd: From Psalm 23. 1999. pap. 7.99 (*1-85608-400-0*) Hunt GBR.

Beck, Ingrid. Die Ringkomposition Bei Herodot und Ihre Bedeutung Fur die Beweistechnik. (GER.). iii, 136p. 1971. 30.00 (*0-318-70627-X*) G Olms Pubs.

Beck, Ingrid. The Lord Is My Shepherd: From Psalm 23. 32p. 1999. 10.00 (*0-664-22135-1*) Westminster John Knox.

Beck, Isabel L., et al. Questioning the Author: An Approach for Enhancing Student Engagement with Text. LC 96-52260. 130p. 1997. pap. 17.95 (*0-87207-242-8*, 242) Intl Reading.

Beck, Isabel L., jt. ed. see Leinhardt, Gaea.

Beck, J. Gayle, jt. auth. see Rosen, Raymond C.

Beck, J. Murray. Joseph Howe: Conservative Reformer, 1804-1848. 400p. 1984. pap. 24.95 (*0-7735-0445-1*, Pub. by McG-Queens Univ Pr) CUP Services.

— Joseph Howe: Conservative Reformer, 1804-1848, Vol. 1. 400p. 1982. 65.00 (*0-7735-0387-0*, Pub. by McG-Queens Univ Pr) CUP Services.

— Joseph Howe: The Briton Becomes Canadian, 1848-1873. 359p. 1983. 65.00 (*0-7735-0388-9*, Pub. by McG-Queens Univ Pr) CUP Services.

— Joseph Howe: The Briton Becomes Canadian, 1848-1873. 448p. 1984. pap. 24.95 (*0-7735-0447-8*, Pub. by McG-Queens Univ Pr) CUP Services.

Beck, J. S., et al, eds. Microporous & Macroporous Materials. (MRS Symposium Proceedings Ser.: Vol. 431). 551p. 1996. 73.00 (*1-55899-334-7*, 431) Materials Res.

Beck, J. Spencer. Hollywood Christmas. (Hollywood Ser.). (Illus.). 80p. 1994. 12.95 (*1-56566-069-2*) Thomasson-Grant.

— Hollywood Doctors. Suares, Jean-Claude, ed. (Hollywood Ser.). (Illus.). 80p. 1994. 12.95 (*1-56566-068-4*) Thomasson-Grant.

— Hollywood Drag. LC 95-128565. (Illus.). 80p. 1994. 12.95 (*1-56566-056-0*) Thomasson-Grant.

— Hollywood Heavies. LC 95-128569. (Illus.). 80p. 1994. 12.95 (*1-56566-057-9*) Thomasson-Grant.

— Hollywood Kids. Suares, Jean-Claude, ed. (Hollywood Ser.). (Illus.). 80p. 1994. 12.95 (*1-56566-067-6*) Thomasson-Grant.

— Hollywood Lovers. LC 95-128567. (Illus.). 80p. 1994. 12.95 (*1-56566-058-7*) Thomasson-Grant.

— Hollywood Trains. Suares, Jean-Claude, ed. (Hollywood Ser.). (Illus.). 80p. 1994. 12.95 (*1-56566-066-8*) Thomasson-Grant.

— Hollywood Weddings. LC 95-128566. (Illus.). 80p. 1994. 12.95 (*1-56566-059-5*) Thomasson-Grant.

— Uncommon Grace: Reminiscences & Photographs of Jacqueline Bouvier Kennedy Onassis. LC 94-32337. (Illus.). 128p. 1994. 24.95 (*1-56566-077-3*) Thomasson-Grant.

Beck, J. Swanson, jt. auth. see Brown, R. A.

Beck, J. Swanson, jt. ed. see Brown, R. A.

Beck, J. V., et al. Heat Conduction Using Green's Functions. (Series in Computational Methods & Physical Processes in Mechanics & Thermal Sciences). 550p. 1992. 87.95 (*1-56032-096-6*) Hemisp Pub.

Beck, J. V., ed. see American Society of Mechanical Engineers Staff.

Beck, J. V., jt. ed. see Bryan, W. J.

Beck, James. Italian Renaissance Painting. (Illus.). 500p. 1999. 29.95 (*3-8290-0486-9*, 520632) Konemann.

— Jacopo Della Quercia, 2 vols., Set. (Illus.). 616p. 1992. text 109.50 (*0-231-07200-7*) Col U Pr.

— Jacopo Della Querica, Vol. 1. 1992. text 52.50 (*0-231-07684-3*) Col U Pr.

— Jacopo Della Querica, Vol. 2. 1992. text 58.50 (*0-231-07686-X*) Col U Pr.

— Massacio the Documents with the Collaboration of Gino Corti. LC 78-67679. 1978. 28.00 (*0-686-92649-8*) J J Augustin.

— Raphael: The Stanza della Segnatura, Rome. LC 93-13059. (Great Fresco Cycles of the Renaissance Ser.). (Illus.). 96p. 1992. 25.00 (*0-8076-1314-2*) Braziller.

Beck, James & Daley, Michael. Art Restoration: The Culture, the Business, & the Scandal. (Illus.). 272p. 1996. pap. 14.95 (*0-393-31297-6*, Norton Paperbks) Norton.

Beck, James, et al. Patricia Nix. 192p. 1995. 100.00 (*0-9648340-0-6*) Dillon Gallery.

Beck, James, jt. auth. see Beck, Deva.

Beck, James, ed. see National Gallery of Art Staff.

Beck, James C. The Potentially Violent Patient & the Tarasoff Decision in Psychiatric Practice. LC 84-28241. 153p. reprint ed. pap. 47.50 (*0-8357-2806-4*, 203620200011) Bks Demand.

Beck, James C., ed. Confidentiality Versus the Duty to Protect: Foreseeable Harm in the Practice of Psychiatry. LC 90-13. (Issues in Psychiatry Ser.). 212p. 1990. text 16.95 (*0-88048-170-6*, 8170) Am Psychiatric.

Beck, James H. Raphael. LC 93-39102. (Illus.). 128p. 1994. 24.95 (*0-8109-3777-8*, Pub. by Abrams) Time Warner.

Beck, James H. & di Lodovico Buonarroti Simoni, Michelangelo. Three Worlds of Michelangelo. LC 98-21538. (Illus.). 256p. 1999. 25.95 (*0-393-04524-2*) Norton.

Beck, James M. May It Please the Court. McGuire, O. R., ed. LC 75-121447. (Essay Index Reprint Ser.). 1977. 30.95 (*0-8369-1694-8*) Ayer.

— May It Please the Court. McGuire, O. R., ed. xx, 51 p. 1996. reprint ed. 132.00 (*1-56169-203-4*) Gaunt.

— The Vanishing Rights of the States: A Discussion of the Right of the Senate to Nullify the Action of a Sovereign State in the Selection of Its Representatives in the Senate. LC 97-74796. 126p. 1997. reprint ed. 45.00 (*1-56169-336-7*) Gaunt.

Beck, James M., jt. ed. see Rosen, Mark J.

***Beck, James R.** Dorothy Carey: The Tragic & Untold Story of Mrs. William Carey. 253p. 2000. pap. 23.00 (*1-57910-341-3*) Wipf & Stock.

Beck, James R., contrib. by. Jesus & Personality Theory: Exploring the Five-Factor Model. LC 98-54077. 240p. 1999. pap. 15.99 (*0-8308-1925-8*, 1925) InterVarsity.

Beck, James R., jt. ed. see Kroeger, Catherine C.

Beck, Jan-Wilhelm, ed. see Maurus, Terentianus.

Beck, Janalee. How to Have Mult.orgasms. 224p. 1993. mass mkt. 5.99 (*0-380-76938-7*, Avon Bks) Morrow Avon.

Beck, Jane C. The General Store in Vermont: An Oral History. 44p. 1988. 7.50 (*0-934720-23-1*) VT Folklife Ctr.

— Memories Touched by Fancy: Bessie Drennan, Vermont Artist. (Illus.). 40p. (Orig.). 1990. pap. 8.95 (*0-916718-10-7*) VT Folklife Ctr.

Beck, Jane C., ed. Always in Season: Folk Art & Traditional Culture in Vermont. LC 82-70924. (Illus.). 144p. 1982. pap. 17.95 (*0-916718-09-3*) U Pr of New Eng.

— Always in Season: Folk Art & Traditional Culture in Vermont. LC 82-70924. (Illus.). 144p. 1982. pap. 14.95 (*0-685-05821-2*) VT Folklife Ctr.

Beck, Jane C. & Ives, Edward D., eds. Vermont Recollections: Sifting Memories Through the Interview Process. LC 96-229967. (Northeast Folklore Ser.: Vol. XXX). (Illus.). 191p. (Orig.). (C). 1995. pap. 15.00 (*0-943197-22-8*) ME Folklife Ctr.

Beck, Janet P. Too Good to Be True: The Story of Denise Redlick's Murder. LC 90-53558. 360p. 1990. 21.95 (*0-88282-066-4*) New Horizon NJ.

Beck, Jansen de, see De Beck, Jansen.

Beck, Jay V. General Microbiology. 3rd ed. 1997. pap., student ed., lab manual ed. 25.80 (*0-02-307762-X*, Macmillan Coll) P-H.

Beck, Jean & Beck, Louise, eds. Manuscrit du Roi, 2 vols. (Chansonniers des troubadours et des trouveres Ser.: Vol. 2). (Illus.). 1970. reprint ed. lib. bdg. 200.00 (*0-8450-0003-9*) Broude.

Beck, Jean, jt. auth. see Amanat, Ebrahim.

Beck, Jeff. Jeff Beck Anthology. (Illus.). 280p. 1991. pap. 24.95 (*0-8256-1262-4*, AM73024) Music Sales.

Beck, Jeffrey, jt. compiled by see Adams, Mignon.

Beck, Jerome & Rosenbaum, Marsha. Pursuit of Ecstasy: The MDMA Experience. LC 93-3371. (SUNY Series in New Social Studies on Alcohol & Drugs). 239p. (C). 1994. pap. text 19.95 (*0-7914-1818-9*) State U NY Pr.

Beck, Jerri & George, Anne Carroll, eds. A Baker's Dozen: Contemporary Women Poets of Alabama. (Orig.). 1988. pap. 10.00 (*0-945301-03-0*) Druid Pr.

Beck, Jerry. 50 Greatest Cartoons. 192p. 1998. write for info. (*1-57215-271-0*) World Pubns.

— I Tawt I Taw a Puddy Tat: Fifty Years of Sylvester & Tweety. (Illus.). 88p. 1995. pap. 19.95 (*0-8050-3598-7*) H Holt & Co.

— I Tawt I Taw a Puddy Tat: Tweety & Sylvester's Golden Jubilee. 88p. (J). 1995. 35.00 (*0-8050-1644-9*) H Holt & Co.

Beck, Jerry & Friedwald, Will. Looney Tunes & Merrie Melodies. (Illus.). 396p. 1995. pap. 15.95 (*0-8050-0894-2*, Owl) H Holt & Co.

Beck, Jerry, jt. auth. see Friedwald, Will.

Beck, Jill. Children on the Hill: A Critical Analysis. (Educational Performance Collection). 42p. (C). 1986. pap. text. write for info. (*0-932582-51-6*) Dance Notation.

— Falling Off the Back Porch: A Critical Analysis. (Educational Performance Collection). 53p. (C). 1986. pap. text. write for info. (*0-932582-47-8*) Dance Notation.

— Not for Love Alone: A Critical Analysis. (Educational Performance Collection). 30p. 1985. pap. write for info. (*0-932582-49-4*) Dance Notation.

— Scenes from the Music of Charles Ives: A Critical Analysis. (Educational Performance Collection). 59p. (C). 1985. pap. text. write for info. (*0-932582-43-5*) Dance Notation.

— What's Remembered: A Critical Analysis. (Educational Performance Collection). 52p. (C). 1986. pap. text. write for info. (*0-932582-45-1*) Dance Notation.

Beck, Jill, ed. A Revival of Nijinsky's Original l'Apres-Midi d'un Faune, Vol. 1, Part 3. 96p. 1991. pap. text 15.00 (*3-7186-5117-3*, Harwood Acad Pubs) Gordon & Breach.

Beck, Jill & Reiser, Joseph C. Moving Notation: A Handbook of Musical Rhythm & Elementary Labanotation for the Dancer. (Performing Arts Studies). 367p. 1998. pap. 42.00 incl. cd-rom (*90-5702-179-X*, Harwood Acad Pubs) Gordon & Breach.

***Beck, Jill & Reiser, Joseph C.** Moving Notation: A Handbook of Musical Rhythm & Elementary Labanotation for the Dancer. 367p. 1998. text 108.00 (*90-5702-178-1*, Harwood Acad Pubs) Gordon & Breach.

Beck, Joan. How to Raise a Brighter Child: The Case for Early Learning. 352p. 1991. per. 6.99 (*0-671-73999-9*) PB.

***Beck, Joan.** How to Raise Brighter Child: The Case for Early Learning. LC 99-26646. 352p. 1999. per. 14.00 (*0-671-03575-4*) PB.

Beck, Johann B. Die Melodien der Troubadours. LC 70-39420. reprint ed. 49.50 (*0-404-08347-1*) AMS Pr.

— La Musique des Troubadours. (Illus.). reprint ed. 34.50 (*0-404-56526-3*) AMS Pr.

***Beck, Johannes & Clanton, Robert.** Life & Music of Nick Cave. 1999. pap. 39.99 (*3-931126-27-7*, Pub. by Die Gestalten) Consort Bk Sales.

Beck, John. Morality & Citizenship. LC 98-221244. 1998. pap. 24.95 (*0-304-70187-4*) Continuum.

Beck, John, et al, eds. Toward a Sociology of Education. LC 77-80869. Orig. Title: World's Apart: Readings for a Sociology of Education. 570p. 1978. reprint ed. pap. text 24.95 (*0-87855-643-5*) Transaction Pubs.

Beck, John & Starr, Ronald. Complete Guide to Real Estate Foreclosure Super Bargains in California. rev. ed. Albert, Jonathan, ed. 355p. (Orig.). pap. 149.00 (*0-934521-04-2*); spiral bd. 79.00 (*0-934521-03-4*) Unlimited Golden Pr.

— Take This House, Please! The Complete Guide to Buying Real Estate Owned by Lenders, 2 vols., 1. Albert, Jonathan, ed. 535p. (Orig.). 1985. pap. 65.00 (*0-934521-00-X*) Unlimited Golden Pr.

— Take This House, Please! The Complete Guide to Buying Real Estate Owned by Lenders, 2 vols., 2. Albert, Jonathan, ed. 535p. (Orig.). 1985. pap. 65.00 (*0-934521-01-8*) Unlimited Golden Pr.

— Take This House, Please! The Complete Guide to Buying Real Estate Owned by Lenders, 2 vols., Set. Albert, Jonathan, ed. 535p. (Orig.). 1985. spiral bd. 95.00 (*0-934521-02-6*) Unlimited Golden Pr.

***Beck, John A.** Translators As Storytellers: A Study in Septuagint Translation Technique. LC 99-48695. (Studies in Biblical Literature: Vol. 25). 248p. (C). 2000. 50.95 (*0-8204-4850-8*) P Lang Pubng.

Beck, John A. & Ellis, John T. Guide to the ASI Real Estate License Examinations. 2nd ed. 400p. (C). 1998. pap. 27.20 (*0-13-365941-0*) P-H.

Beck, John C. & Beck, Martha N. The Change of a Lifetime: Employment Patterns among Japan's Managerial Elite. LC 93-41946. (Illus.). 334p. (C). 1994. text 40.00 (*0-8248-1503-3*); pap. text 15.75 (*0-8248-1529-7*) UH Pr.

***Beck, John D. & Yeager, Neil M.** The Leader's Window: Mastering the Four Styles of Leadership to Build High-Performing Teams. (Illus.). 242p. 1999. text 30.00 (*0-7881-5982-8*) DIANE Pub.

Beck, John D. W. & Yeager, Neil M. The Leader's Window: Mastering the Four Styles of Leadership to Build High-Perfoming Teams. 242p. 1994. 90.00 (*0-471-58525-4*); pap. 19.95 (*0-471-02554-2*) Wiley.

Beck, John E. & Cox, Charles, eds. Advances in Management Education. LC 80-40117. (Illus.). 370p. reprint ed. pap. 114.70 (*0-8357-5169-4*, 203304800083) Bks Demand.

Beck, John H., ed. Encyclopedia of Percussion. LC 93-48846. (Illus.). 448p. 1994. text 85.00 (*0-8240-4788-5*, H947) Garland.

— Encyclopedia of Percussion. (Illus.). 448p. 1997. pap. text 27.95 (*0-8153-2894-X*, H947) Garland.

Beck, John R. Managing Service for Success. Beck, Elizabeth J., ed. 128p. (Orig.). (C). 1987. pap. 25.00 (*0-9619359-0-1*) Intl Pest Mgmt.

Beck, Joseph R., jt. auth. see Trzyna, Thomas N.

Beck, Judith S. Cognitive Therapy: Basics & Beyond. LC 95-12521. 338p. 1995. lib. bdg. 38.00 (*0-89862-847-4*) Guilford Pubns.

Beck, June D., ed. The Quiet Land: The Diaries of Frank Debenham. 208p. 1998. pap. 135.00 (*1-85297-037-5*) St Mut.

Beck, K. K. Amateur Night. 288p. 1993. 18.95 (*0-89296-480-4*) Mysterious Pr.

— The Body in the Volvo. large type ed. LC 92-795. 260p. 1992. reprint ed. lib. bdg. 17.95 (*1-56054-379-5*) Thorndike Pr.

— Cold Smoked: A Jane Da Silva Mystery. 240p. 1996. mass mkt. 5.99 (*0-446-40351-2*, Pub. by Warner Bks) Little.

— Death in a Deck Chair. 1984. 12.95 (*0-8027-5601-8*) Walker & Co.

— Electric City. 224p. 1995. mass mkt. 5.50 (*0-446-40350-4*, Pub. by Warner Bks) Little.

— Electric City. large type ed. LC 94-3762. 434p. 1994. lib. bdg. 20.95 (*0-7862-0316-1*) Thorndike Pr.

— A Hopeless Case. 272p. 1993. mass mkt. 4.99 (*0-446-40144-7*, Pub. by Warner Bks) Little.

— Peril under the Palms. 208p. 1989. 18.95 (*0-8027-5715-4*) Walker & Co.

— The Revenge of Kali-Ra. LC 98-35772. 229p. 1999. 22.00 (*0-89296-670-X*, Pub. by Mysterious Pr) Little.

— Rule of Law. 1996. write for info. (*0-614-14425-6*) Warner Bks.

— Unwanted Attentions. 192p. 1988. 17.95 (*0-8027-5729-4*) Walker & Co.

— Unwanted Attentions. large type ed. LC 89-4340. 329p. 1989. reprint ed. lib. bdg. 17.95 (*0-89621-868-6*) Thorndike Pr.

— We Interrupt This Broadcast. LC 97-34456. 240p. 1997. 19.50 (*0-89296-642-4*, Pub. by Mysterious Pr) Little.

Beck-Kapphan, Cornelia. Geschlechtsspezifische Musikerziehung in Wandervogel und Jugendmusikbewegung. Nolte, Eckhard & Weyer, Reinhold, eds. (Beitrage zur Geschichte der Musikpadagogik Ser.: Bd. 7). (Illus.). 299p. 1998. pap. 51.95 (*3-631-32696-3*) P Lang Pubng.

Beck, Katie. The Moas. Thatch, Nancy R., ed. LC 99-18079. (Books for Students by Students). (Illus.). 29p. (J). (gr. 4-7). 1999. lib. bdg. 15.95 (*0-933849-73-7*) Landmark Edns.

***Beck, Ken.** Extreme Programming Explained: Embracing Change. LC 99-36995. 224p. 1999. pap. text 29.95 (*0-201-61641-6*) Addison-Wesley.

Beck, Ken. Terrific Tennessee. LC 96-71358. 128p. 1999. pap. 6.95 (*1-887654-23-2*) Premium Pr TN.

Beck, Ken & Beck, Terry. Amazing Arkansas. 2nd rev. ed. LC 97-69523. 128p. 1997. pap. 6.95 (*1-887654-21-6*) Premium Pr TN.

Beck, Ken & Clark, Jim. Aunt Bee's Mealtime in Mayberry. LC 98-55326. (Illus.). 224p. 1999. 19.95 (*1-55853-737-6*) Rutledge Hill Pr.

***Beck, Ken & Clark, Jim.** Mayberry Memories. (Illus.). 2000. 34.99 (*1-55853-830-5*) Rutledge Hill Pr.

Beck, Ken & Downs, David. Titanic Trivia. LC 98-66159. (Illus.). 128p. 1998. pap. 6.95 (*1-887654-42-9*) Premium Pr TN.

***Beck, Ken, et al.** Animal Magnetism: An Illustrated Guide to TV's Most Famous Pets. (Illus.). 196p. 2001. pap. 16.95 (*1-57500-178-0*, Pub. by TV Bks) HarpC.

Beck, Ken, et al. Cats Out of the Bag: 401 Purr-fectly Pleasing Tidbits for Cat Lovers. LC 96-69012. 128p. (Orig.). 1996. pap. 6.95 (*1-887654-16-X*) Premium Pr TN.

Beck, Ken, ed. see Early, Donna P. & Hand, Edie.

Beck, Ken, ed. see Hemphill, Bethni & McClain, Brenda.

***Beck, Kenneth.** The Andy Griffith Show Book: From Miracle Salve to Kerosene Cucumbers, the Complete Guide to One of Television's Best-Loved Shows. (Illus.). 240p. 2000. pap. 14.95 (*0-312-26287-6*) St Martin.

Beck, Kenneth & Beck, Terry. I'll Be Doggone: A Tail-Wagging Tribute to Man's Best Friend. LC 95-70714. 128p. 1996. pap. 6.95 (*1-887654-01-1*) Premium Pr TN.

Beck, Kenneth & Clark, Jim. Aunt Bee's Delightful Desserts. LC 96-13202. 276p. 1996. spiral bd. 14.95 (*1-55853-402-4*) Rutledge Hill Pr.

Beck, Kenneth, jt. auth. see Clark, Jim.

Beck, Kent. CRC: The Essence of Objects. (C). 1998. pap. text 28.00 (*0-13-311523-2*) P-H.

— Kent Beck's Guide to Better Smalltalk. LC 98-39476. (SIGS Reference Ser.: No. 14). 336p. (C). 1998. pap. 44.95 (*0-521-64437-2*) Cambridge U Pr.

— Smalltalk Best Practice Patterns. LC 96-2941. 240p. 1996. pap. 48.00 (*0-13-476904-X*) P-H.

***Beck, Kent & Fowler, Martin.** Steering & Planning with Extreme Programming. 256p. 2000. pap. text 29.95 (*0-201-71091-9*) Addison-Wesley.

Beck, Kristin, jt. auth. see Dockett, Lauren.

Beck, L. Fundamentals of Yiddish Usage: Text & Workbook of Basic Yiddish Language. (YID., Illus.). 141p. (Orig.). 1989. write for info. (*0-9622198-1-9*) CCTV.

— Fundamentals of Yiddish Usage: Text & Workbook of Basic Yiddish Language. (YID., Illus.). 135p. (Orig.). 1992. text 13.00 (*0-9622198-2-7*) CCTV.

Beck, L., et al, eds. Hormone-Related Malignant Tumors. (Recent Results in Cancer Research Ser.: Vol. 118). (Illus.). 296p. 1990. 137.00 (*0-387-51258-6*) Spr-Verlag.

Beck, L., jt. ed. see Grundmann, Ekkehard.

Beck, L. A. Regional Approaches to Mortuary Analysis: Alexander. LC 94-49728. (Interdisciplinary Contributions to Archaeology Ser.). (Illus.). 300p. (C). 1995. 49.50 (*0-306-44931-5*, Plenum Trade) Perseus Pubng.

Beck, L. Adams. The House of Fulfilment. 342p. 1997. pap. 27.00 (*0-89540-304-8*, SB-304) Sun Pub.

— Legend of the Buddha. (C). 1993. text 26.00 (*81-7305-022-8*, Pub. by Aryan Bks Intl) S Asia.

— The Openers of the Gate. 368p. 1986. reprint ed. pap. 11.95 (*0-87516-561-3*) DeVorss.

— The Way of Power: Studies in the Occult (1927) 290p. 1998. reprint ed. pap. 22.50 (*0-7661-0303-X*) Kessinger Pub.

Beck, L. W., ed. see International Kant Congress Staff.

Beck, L. W., ed. see Kant International Congress Staff.

Beck, Larry & Cable, Ted. Interpretation for the 21st Century: Fifteen Guiding Principles. LC 99-181163. 1997. pap. 24.95 (*1-57167-133-1*) Sagamore Pub.

Beck, Laura, jt. auth. see Wiles, Julian.

Beck, Laurie R., et al. A User's Guide to New York City Public Elementary & Intermediate Schools: Selected Statistics, 1992-1993. 106p. 1995. 17.50 (*0-88156-165-7*) Comm Serv Soc NY.

Beck, Lawrence H., jt. ed. see Cebul, Randall D.

Beck, Lee & Malks, Josh B. Auburn & Cord. LC 96-10496. (Illus.). 160p. 1996. 32.95 (*0-7603-0172-7*) MBI Pubg.

Beck, Leif C. The Physician's Office. LC 77-87555. (Illus.). 1977. 14.95 (*90-219-0346-6*) Excerpta Princeton.

Beck, Leland L. Lab Manual to Accompany Pascal - A Guided Tour: Turbo Pascal Version. 168p. (C). 1994. pap. text 12.95 (*1-884808-02-6*) Comp Educ Pr.

— Lab Manual to Accompany Pascal - A Guided Tour: UNIX Version. 168p. 1994. pap. text 12.95 (*1-884808-01-8*) Comp Educ Pr.

— System Software: An Introduction to Systems Programming. 496p. 1985. text. write for info. (*0-201-10950-6*) Addison-Wesley.

— System Software: An Introduction to Systems Programming. 3rd ed. LC 96-22968. 480p. (C). 1996. 63.00 (*0-201-42300-6*) Addison-Wesley.

***Beck, Leslie.** Leslie Beck's Coordinated Kitchen: Creative Projects You Can Make. (Illus.). 128p. 2000. pap. 27.95 (*1-56477-350-7*) Martingale & Co.

— Managing Menopause with Diet, Vitamins & Herbs: An Essential Guide for the Pre & Post-Menopausal Years. 288p. 2000. pap. 29.95 (*0-13-017966-3*) P-H.

— The Quilted Nursery: More Than 50 Coordinated Projects for Baby. LC 99-44335. (Illus.). 128p. 1999. pap. 29.95 (*1-56477-288-8*, B410) Martingale & Co.

Beck, Levitt. Fighter Pilot. (American Autobiography Ser.). 200p. 1995. reprint ed. lib. bdg. 69.00 (*0-7812-8456-2*) Rprt Serv.

Beck, Lewis C. A Gazetteer of the States of Illinois & Missouri. LC 75-84. (Mid-American Frontier Ser.). 1975. reprint ed. 37.95 (*0-405-06853-0*) Ayer.

Beck, Lewis W. The Actor & the Spectator: 1975 Edition. (Key Texts Ser.). 152p. 1998. pap. 15.00 (*1-85506-557-6*) Thoemmes Pr.

— A Commentary of Kant's "Critique of Practical Reason" LC 60-5464. (Midway Reprint Ser.). xiv, 306p. 1984. reprint ed. pap. text 22.00 (*0-226-04076-3*) U Ch Pr.

— A Commentary on Kant's Critique of Practical Reason. 306p. 1996. reprint ed. pap. text 15.95 (*0-226-04075-5*) U Ch Pr.

— Early German Philosophy: Kant & His Predecessors. 567p. 1996. pap. 29.95 (*1-85506-447-2*) Bks Intl VA.

***Beck, Lewis W.** Early German Philosophy: Kant & His Predecessors. LC 99-52248. 570p. 2000. pap. text 27.00 (*1-890318-17-5*) St Augustines Pr.

Beck, Lewis W. Early German Philosophy: Kant & His Predecessors. LC 79-75427. 570p. reprint ed. pap. 176.70 (*0-7837-1670-2*, 205720200024) Bks Demand.

— Essays on Kant & Hume. LC 77-19999. 231p. reprint ed. pap. 71.70 (*0-7837-2786-0*, 204317800006) Bks Demand.

— Kant Selections. (Great Philosophers Ser.). 496p. (C). 1988. pap. text 13.60 (*0-02-307821-9*, Macmillan Coll) P-H.

— Kant's Three Critiques, 5 vols., Set. 3144p. (C). (gr. 13 up). 1993. text, boxed set 785.00 (*0-415-10505-6*) Routledge.

— Perpetual Peace: Kant. 80p. (C). 1957. pap. text 6.00 (*0-02-307750-6*, Macmillan Coll) P-H.

— Six Secular Philosophers. (Key Texts). 126p. 1997. reprint ed. pap. 15.00 (*1-85506-518-5*) Thoemmes Pr.

— Studies in the Philosophy of Kant. LC 81-7247. (Essay & Monograph Series of the Liberal Arts Press). 242p. 1981. reprint ed. lib. bdg. 55.00 (*0-313-23183-4*, BESK, Greenwood Pr) Greenwood.

Beck, Lewis W., ed. Eighteenth Century Philosophy. LC 66-10364. (Orig.). 1966. pap. 15.95 (*0-02-902100-6*) Free Pr.

Beck, Lewis W., tr. Kant Foundations of the Metaphysics. 2nd ed. 128p. (C). 1989. pap. text 8.20 (*0-02-307825-1*, Macmillan Coll) P-H.

Beck, Lewis W., et al. Kant's Latin Writings in English Translation. LC 84-48030. (American University Studies: Philosophy: Ser. V, Vol. 9). (C). 1986. text 29.95 (*0-8204-0167-6*) P Lang Pubng.

— On History Kant. 192p. (C). 1963. pap. text 8.00 (*0-02-307860-X*, Macmillan Coll) P-H.

Beck, Lewis W., jt. auth. see Mahaffy, Carcus.

Beck, Lewis W., ed. see Vaihinger, Hans.

Beck, Lewis W., ed. see Ward, James.

Beck, Lewis W., tr. see Kant, Immanuel.

Beck, Lily A. Gallants. LC 76-128207. (Essay Index Reprint Ser.). 1977. 21.95 (*0-8369-1864-9*) Ayer.

— The Ladies' A Shining Constellation of Wit & Beauty. LC 71-156612. (Essay Index Reprint Ser.). 1977. reprint ed. 23.95 (*0-8369-2268-9*) Ayer.

Beck, Lois. Nomad: A Year in the Life of a Qashqa'i Tribesman in Iran. (Illus.). 482p. 1991. 65.00 (*0-520-07003-8*, Pub. by U CA Pr); pap. 22.50 (*0-520-07495-5*, Pub. by U CA Pr) Cal Prin Full Svc.

— The Qashqa'i of Iran. LC 85-23404. (Illus.). 422p. reprint ed. pap. 130.90 (*0-7837-2498-5*, 208029200004) Bks Demand.

Beck, Lois & Keddie, Nikki R., eds. Women in the Muslim World. LC 78-3633. 712p. 1980. pap. 18.95 (*0-674-95481-5*) HUP.

Beck, Louise, jt. ed. see Beck, Jean.

Beck, Lynn G. Reclaiming Educational Administration As a Caring Profession. (Critical Issues in Educational Leadership Ser.). 176p. (C). 1994. text 43.00 (*0-8077-3314-8*); pap. text 18.95 (*0-8077-3313-X*) Tchrs Coll.

Beck, Lynn G. & Murphy, Joseph. Ethics in Educational Leadership Programs: An Expanding Role. 136p. 1994. pap. 19.95 (*0-8039-6150-2*) Corwin Pr.

— Ethics in Educational Leadership Programs: An Expanding Role. LC 94-27450. 136p. 1994. 45.95 (*0-8039-6149-9*) Corwin Pr.

— The Four Imperatives of a Successful School. LC 96-1008. (1-Off Ser.). 160p. 1996. 51.95 (*0-8039-6279-7*) Corwin Pr.

— The Four Imperatives of a Successful School. LC 96-10089. 160p. 1996. pap. 22.95 (*0-8039-6280-0*) Corwin Pr.

— Understanding the Principalship: Metaphorical Themes, 1920s-1990s. 272p. (C). 1992. text 47.00 (*0-8077-3208-7*); pap. text 22.95 (*0-8077-3207-9*) Tchrs Coll.

Beck, Lynn G., jt. auth. see Murphy, Joseph.

Beck, M. B., ed. Systems Analysis in Water Quality Management: Proceedings of a Symposium Held in London, U. K., 30 June-2 July 1987. (Advances in Water Pollution Control Ser.: No. 3). (Illus.). 445p. 1987. 112.50 (*0-08-035585-4*, Pergamon Pr) Elsevier.

Beck, M. B., et al, eds. Watermatex 'Ninety-One: Proceedings of the Second International Conference on Systems Analysis in Water Quality Management, Held in Durham, New Hampshire, USA, 3-6 June 1991. (Water Science & Technology Ser.: No. 24). (Illus.). 366p. 1991. pap. 157.00 (*0-08-041161-4*, Pergamon Pr) Elsevier.

Beck, M. B. & Lessard, P., eds. Watermatex '97: Systems Analysis & Computing in Water Quality Management: Towards a New Agenda. 392p. 1997. pap. write for info. (*0-08-043373-1*) Elsevier.

Beck, M. B. & Schilling, W., eds. Uncertainty, Risk & Transient Pollution Events: Selected Proceedings of the IAWQ Interdisciplinary International Symposium on Uncertainty, Risk & Transient Pollution Events, Held in Exeter, UK, 26-28 July 1995. (Water Science & Technology 33 Ser.: 33). 236p. 1996. pap. text 130.00 (*0-08-042893-2*, Pergamon Pr) Elsevier.

Beck, M. S., et al, eds. Tomographic Techniques for Process Design & Operation. 504p. 1993. 172.00 (*1-85312-246-7*) Computational Mech MA.

Beck, M. S., et al, eds. Tomographic Techniques for Process Design & Operation. LC 93-70678. 504p. 1993. 172.00 (*1-56252-170-5*, 2467) Computational Mech MA.

Beck, M. S. & Plaskowski, A. Cross Correlation Flowmeters - Their Design & Application. (Illus.). 256p. 1987. 144.00 (*0-85274-532-X*) IOP Pub.

Beck, M. S., jt. ed. see Williams, R. A.

Beck, Malcolm. The Secret Life of Compost: A "How-to" & "Why" Guide to Composting-Lawn, Garden, Feedlot or Farm. LC 96-85733. (Illus.). 140p. (Orig.). 1997. pap. 19.00 (*0-911311-52-1*); text 25.00 (*0-911311-53-X*) Acres USA.

Beck-Managetta, G., et al, eds. Genetics of the Epilepsies. (Illus.). 230p. 1989. 118.00 (*0-387-18421-X*) Spr-Verlag.

Beck-Managetta, Gertrud, jt. auth. see Ried, Sibylle.

Beck, Maria-Luise, ed. Morphology & Its Interfaces in Second-Language Knowledge. LC 98-44714. (Language Acquisition & Language Disorders Ser.: Vol. 19). x, 387p. 1998. 75.00 (*1-55619-784-5*) J Benjamins Pubng Co.

Beck, Marianna. The Ecstatic Moment: The Best of Libido Magazine. LC 96-49404. 336p. 1997. pap. 12.95 (*0-385-31586-4*) Doubleday.

Beck, Mark F. Milady's Theory & Practice of Therapeutic Massage. 2nd ed. 693p. 1994. pap. 48.95 (*1-56253-120-4*) Thomson Learn.

— Milady's Theory & Practice of Therapeutic Massage: Curriculum Guide. 2nd ed. 3p. 1993. 2.75 (*1-56253-121-2*) Milady Pub.

— Milady's Theory & Practice of Therapeutic Massage: Workbook-Answer Key. 2nd ed. 161p. 1994. text, teacher ed. 20.00 (*1-56253-217-0*) Milady Pub.

— Theory/Practice Therapy Massage. 2nd ed. (MASSAGE). 161p. 1994. 20.75 (*1-56253-216-2*) Thomson Learn.

Beck, Martha. Expecting Adam: A True Story of Birth, Rebirth & Everyday Magic. LC 98-26142. 328p. 1999. 23.95 (*0-8129-2980-2*, Times Bks) Crown Pub Group.

***Beck, Martha.** Expecting Adam: A True Story of Birth, Rebirth, & Everyday Magic. 336p. 2000. pap. 13.95 (*0-425-17448-4*) Berkley Pub.

— Finding Your Own North Star. 2000. 24.00 (*0-8129-3217-X*) Random Hse Chldrns.

***Beck, Martha C.** Plato's Self-Corrective Development of the Concepts of Soul, Forms & Immortality in Three Arguments of the Phaedo. LC 99-27736. (Studies in the History of Philosophy: Vol. 52). 276p. 1999. text 89.95 (*0-7734-7950-3*) E Mellen.

Beck, Martha N. Breaking Point: Why Women Fall Apart & How They Can Recreate Their Lives. 1997. 24.00 (*0-614-28158-X*, Times Bks) Crown Pub Group.

Beck, Martha N., jt. auth. see Beck, John C.

Beck, Mary Ann, et al, eds. The Analysis of Hispanic Texts: Current Trends in Methodology. LC 76-5741. (First York College Colloquium). 1976. pap. 20.00 (*0-916950-00-X*) Biling Rev-Pr.

Beck, Mary E. Nutrition & Dietetics for Nurses. 7th ed. (Churchill Livingstone Nursing Text Ser.). (Illus.). 1984. pap. text 24.00 (*0-443-03121-5*) Church.

— Nutrition & Dietetics for Nurses. 8th ed. (Illus.). 221p. 1991. pap. text. write for info. (*0-443-03557-1*) Church.

Beck, Mary Giraudo. Ka gun da - George James Beck: Alaskan Pioneer Teacher, Missionary, Leader. LC 98-83194. (Illus.). 142p. 1999. pap. 14.95 (*0-9669478-1-9*, 3366) Rocky Pt Pubg.

Beck, Maysel. Leena's Ribbon. 106p. 1995. pap. 10.00 (*0-87012-529-X*) McClain.

An educating children's book about a young girl & her desire to race her horse, Ribbon, in a real horse race. Leena shows her dedication to her dream & to her best friend, Ribbon, as she endures her daily chores on the Coy Ranch & the responsibility of working with her trainer to make her horse a winner.
Publisher Paid Annotation.

Beck, Melissa, compiled by. The Typographic Bookplates of Ward Ritchie. limited ed. (Illus.). 108p. 1990. 45.00 (*0-931043-03-4*) K Karmiole.

Beck, Mervyn. Soccer Fit: Training & Health for Soccer Players. (Illus.). 96p. 1992. pap. 22.95 (*1-85223-472-5*, Pub. by Crolwood) Trafalgar.

Beck, Mervyn, et al. Soccer Training. (Illus.). 128p. 1996. pap. 22.95 (*1-85223-896-8*, Pub. by Crolwood) Trafalgar.

Beck, Michael, compiled by. Promises of the Proverbs. 256p. 1998. lthr. 4.97 (*1-57748-202-6*) Barbour Pub.

Beck, Michael, et al. Linux Kernel Internals. 2nd ed. LC 98-120732. (Illus.). 496p. 1997. pap. text 49.95 (*0-201-33143-8*) Peachpit Pr.

Beck, Michael J., et al. 365 Questions for Couples. LC 98-47859. 1999. pap. 6.95 (*1-58062-068-X*) Adams Media.

Beck, Mihaly T. Chemistry of Complex Equilbria. 1989. text 119.00 (*0-470-21499-6*) P-H.

Beck, Morris. Government Spending: Trends & Issues. LC 81-5007. 135p. 1981. 45.00 (*0-275-90582-9*, C0582, Praeger Pubs) Greenwood.

Beck, Morris, jt. auth. see Guttentag, Jack M.

Beck, Nathaniel & Katz, Jonathan. The Analysis of Time-Series Cross Sectional Data. (Illus.). (C). text. write for info. (*0-472-09700-8*); pap. text. write for info. (*0-472-06700-1*) U of Mich Pr.

Beck, Norman A. Anti-Roman Cryptograms in the New Testament: Symbolic Messages of Hope & Liberation. LC 95-1461. (Westminster College Library of Biblical Symbolism: Vol. 1). 191p. (Orig.). (C). 1997. pap. 29.95 (*0-8204-2771-3*) P Lang Pubng.

— Mature Christianity in the 21st Century: The Recognition & Repudiation of the Anti-Jewish Polemic of the New Testament. rev. ed. LC 93-46884. (Shared Ground among Jews & Christians Ser.: Vol. 5). 320p. 1994. 26.95 (*0-8245-1358-4*) Crossroad NY.

— Scripture Notes Ser. C: (Common Consensus Lectionary) 1985. 12.25 (*0-89536-755-6*, 5861) CSS OH.

— Scripture Notes Ser. B: (Common Consensus Lectionary), Pt. B. 1984. 12.25 (*0-89536-687-8*, 4863) CSS OH.

Beck, Nuala. Excelerate: Growing in the New Economy. (Illus.). 350p. 1998. text 28.00 (*0-7881-5816-3*) DIANE Pub.

***Beck, Nuala.** The Next Century: Why Canada Wins. LC 99-182175. 2000. pap. 18.00 (*0-00-638527-3*) HarpC.

Beck, Nuala. Shifting Gears: Thriving in the New Economy. 209p. 1998. pap. 18.00 (*0-00-638480-3*) Collins SF.

Beck, Otto W. Art Principles of Portrait Photography. LC 72-9181. (Literature of Photography Ser.). 1973. reprint ed. 23.95 (*0-405-04892-0*) Ayer.

Beck, P. G. & Forster, M. C. Six Rural Problem Areas: Relief-Resources-Rehabilitation. LC 71-165679. (Research Monographs: Vol. 1). 1971. reprint ed. lib. bdg. 22.50 (*0-306-70333-5*) Da Capo.

Beck, Pamela H. Discovering Cued Speech. 2nd rev. ed. (Illus.). 107p. 1988. teacher ed. 18.00 (*1-892917-00-9*, BECIA) N Coast Cued.

— Discovering Cued Speech Learner's Workbook. 6th rev. ed. (Illus.). 43p. 1996. student ed., wbk. ed. 8.00 (*1-892917-01-7*) N Coast Cued.

— Kids Discovering Cued Speech. 2nd rev. ed. (Illus.). 89p. 1990. teacher ed. 15.00 (*1-892917-02-5*) N Coast Cued.

Beck, Pamela H. & Walker, Beth. Discovering Cued Speech Children's Calendar. (Illus.). 18p. 1997. 6.00 (*1-892917-04-1*, BECIEC) N Coast Cued.

— Discovering Cued Speech Progress Calendar. (Illus.). 16p. 1997. 6.00 (*1-892917-03-3*) N Coast Cued.

Beck, Paul. Case Exercises in Clinical Reasoning. LC 81-10414. (Illus.). 334p. reprint ed. pap. 103.60 (*0-8357-7587-9*, 205690800096) Bks Demand.

— The Disobedient Children Punished: A Story of Two Children That Killed Each Other. (Illus.). 25p. 1933. reprint ed. pap. 25.00 (*0-87556-842-4*) Saifer.

Beck, Paul, et al. Eastern Europe for Beginners. (Illus.). 176p. 1997. pap. 11.00 (*0-86316-237-1*) Writers & Readers.

Beck, Paul A. Party Politics in America. 8th ed. LC 96-13789. 467p. (C). 1997. pap. 53.00 (*0-673-99578-X*) Addison-Wesley Educ.

Beck, Paul A., ed. Electronic Structure & Alloy Chemistry of the Transition Elements. LC 62-18701. 261p. reprint ed. pap. 81.00 (*0-608-09950-3*, 200067900038) Bks Demand.

Beck, Paul A., jt. ed. see Rowland, T. J.

***Beck, Paul N.** Soldier, Settler, Sioux: Fort Ridgely & the Minnesota River Valley, 1853-1867. (Prairie Plains Ser.: Vol. 8). (Illus.). 150p. 2000. pap. 12.95 (*0-931170-75-3*) Ctr Western Studies.

Beck, Peggy V. Oremos, Oremos: New Mexican Midwinter Masquerades. (Illus.). (Orig.). 1987. pap. text 5.95 (*0-9609818-2-9*) M Rogers Mus.

Beck, Peggy V. & Walters, Anna L. The Sacred: Ways of Knowledge, Sources of Life. (Illus.). 384p. 1977. pap. 24.95 (*0-912586-24-9*) Dine College Pr.

Beck, Peter. The Falkland Islands As an International Problem. 208p. (C). 1989. lib. bdg. 62.50 (*0-415-00909-X*) Routledge.

— The Falkland Islands As an International Problem. LC 88-32128. (Illus.). 223p. reprint ed. pap. 69.20 (*0-608-20314-9*, 207156700002) Bks Demand.

— Prospects & Strategies for Nuclear Power: Global Boon or Dangerous Diversion? 144p. (C). 1994. pap. 19.95 (*1-85383-217-0*) Brookings.

Beck, Peter, et al. British Documents on Foreign Affairs: Series J: The League of Nations, 10 vols. LC 91-43084. Date not set. lib. bdg. 1525.00 (*0-89093-614-5*) U Pubns Amer.

Beck, Peter J. Scoring for Britain: International Football & International Politics, 1900-1939. LC 98-47283. (Sport in the Global Society Ser.: No. 9). 2p. 1999. 59.50 (*0-7146-4899-X*, Pub. by F Cass Pubs); pap. 26.50 (*0-7146-4454-4*, Pub. by F Cass Pubs) Intl Spec Bk.

Beck, R., et al, eds. Galactic & Intergalactic Magnetic Fields. (C). 1990. lib. bdg. 184.00 (*0-7923-0704-6*) Kluwer Academic.

— Galactic & Intergalactic Magnetic Fields. (C). 1990. pap. text 86.00 (*0-7923-0705-4*) Kluwer Academic.

Beck, R. & Grave, R., eds. Interstellar Magnetic Field. (Illus.). 290p. 1987. 60.95 (*0-387-17751-5*) Spr-Verlag.

Beck, R., jt. auth. see Heywang-Kobrunner, S.

Beck, R. L. & Schrader, Daryl. America's Planetariums & Observatories: A Sampling. (Illus.). 230p. 1991. pap. 16.95 (*0-9630565-0-6*) Sunwest Space.

Beck, Rachael. Plainverse: For People Who Can't Stand Obscure Poetry. LC 91-58773. 120p. 1991. 17.95 (*1-878208-11-X*) Guild Pr IN.

An Asterisk (*) at the beginning of an entry indicates that the title is appearing for the first time.

Beck, Rainer, intro. Lichtner-Aix: Arbeiten der Letzten Jahre Mit Vollstandigem Oeuvre-Verzeichnis der Druckgraphik Von 1984 Bis 1987. (GER., Illus.). 144p. (C). 1988. 82.00 (*3-8170-2013-9*, Pub. by Knstvrlag Weingrtn) Intl Bk Import.

— Lichtner-Aix, Malerei und Graphik: Mit Vollstandigem Oeuvre-Verzeichnis der Druckgraphik Von 1967 Bis 1983. (GER., Illus.). 143p. (C). 1983. 82.00 (*3-921617-77-4*, Pub. by Knstvrlag Weingrtn) Intl Bk Import.

Beck, Rainer, et al. Solar Astronomy Handbook. LC 95-46338. 1995. 24.95 (*0-943396-47-6*) Willmann-Bell.

Beck, Ray. Project RIDE Program Manual: Secondary Version. 3rd ed. (Project RIDE Ser.). (Illus.). 128p. 1996. pap. text. write for info. (*1-57035-110-4*) Sopris.

Beck, Ray, et al. Basic Skill Builder Sheets: Basic Addition, Subtraction, Multiplication, Division. (Basic Skill Builders Ser.). 376p. 1995. ring bd. 39.00 (*1-57035-050-7*, 16MATH1) Sopris.

— Basic Skill Builder Sheets: Complex Addition & Subtraction. (Basic Skill Builders Ser.). 84p. (J). (gr. k-12). 1996. ring bd. 10.00 (*1-57035-089-2*, 16COMP) Sopris.

— Basic Skill Builder Sheets: Count Bys. (Basic Skill Builders Ser.). 90p. 1996. ring bd. 10.00 (*1-57035-108-2*, 16COUNT) Sopris.

— Basic Skill Builder Sheets: Decimals. (Basic Skill Builders Ser.). 64p. (YA). 1996. ring bd. 10.00 (*1-57035-093-0*, 16DEC) Sopris.

— Basic Skill Builder Sheets: Fractions. (Basic Skill Builders Ser.). 94p. (J). (gr. k-12). 1996. ring bd. 10.00 (*1-57035-091-4*, 16FRAC) Sopris.

— Basic Skill Builder Sheets: Handwriting. (Basic Skill Builders Ser.). 122p. (J). (gr. k-12). 1996. ring bd. 10.00 (*1-57035-092-2*, 16WRIT) Sopris.

— Basic Skill Builder Sheets: Language. (Basic Skill Builders Ser.). 512p. (J). (gr. k-12). 1995. ring bd. 39.00 (*1-57035-067-1*, 16LANG1) Sopris.

— Basic Skill Builder Sheets: Math Tool Skills. (Basic Skill Builders Ser.). 126p. (J). (gr. k-12). 1996. ring bd. 10.00 (*1-57035-090-6*, 16TOOL) Sopris.

— Basic Skill Builder Sheets: Metric Units. (Basic Skill Builders Ser.). 128p. (J). (gr. k-12). 1996. ring bd. 10.00 (*1-57035-094-9*, 16MET) Sopris.

— Basic Skill Builder Sheets: Reading Set. (Basic Skill Builders Ser.). 247p. 1997. ring bd. 39.00 (*1-57035-120-1*, 16-READ-1) Sopris.

— Basic Skill Builder Sheets: Roman Numerals. (Basic Skill Builders Ser.). 66p. 1996. ring bd. 10.00 (*1-57035-109-0*, 16RN) Sopris.

— Basic Skill Builder Sheets: Story Problems. (Basic Skill Builders Ser.). 110p. 1996. ring bd. 10.00 (*1-57035-111-2*, 16STORY) Sopris.

— Basic Skill Builder Sheets: Telling Time. (Basic Skill Builders Ser.). 82p. (J). (gr. k-12). 1996. ring bd. 10.00 (*1-57035-088-4*, 16TIME) Sopris.

— Basic Skill Builder Sheets: U. S. Maps. (Basic Skill Builders Ser.). 92p. (J). (gr. k-12). 1995. ring bd. 10.00 (*1-57035-073-6*, 16MAP) Sopris.

***Beck, Ray, et al.** Basic Skill Builders: Spelling Skill Builder Timings. (Basic Skill Builders Ser.). 80p. 1999. ring bd. 15.00 (*1-57035-202-X*, 16SPELL) Sopris.

Beck, Ray, et al. Basic Skill Builders Handbook. (Basic Skill Builders Ser.). 92p. 1995. pap. text 15.00 (*1-57035-048-5*, 16HAND) Sopris.

***Beck, Ray, et al.** Basic Skill Builders Sheets: Money. (Basic Skill Builders). 38p. 1999. ring bd. 10.00 (*1-57035-210-0*, 16 MONEY) Sopris.

Beck, Ray, jt. auth. see Witt, Joe.

***Beck, Raymond W.** A Chronology of Microbiology in Historical Context. 352p. 2000. pap. 43.95 (*1-55581-193-0*) ASM Pr.

Beck, Reinhart. Dictionary of Politics: Sachwoerterbuch der Politik. 2nd ed. (ENG & GER.). 1111p. 1986. 75.00 (*0-8288-2255-7*, M8026) Fr & Eur.

Beck, Renee & Metrick, Sydney B. The Art of Ritual. LC 89-33894. 192p. 1995. pap. 11.95 (*0-89087-582-0*) Celestial Arts.

Beck, Richard. The Achromatic Microscope. (History of Microscopy Ser.). 272p. 1987. reprint ed. 27.00 (*0-940095-06-8*) Sci Heritage Ltd.

— African-American History. 1994. pap., teacher ed. 10.00 (*0-88092-153-6*); pap., student ed. 15.00 (*0-88092-152-8*) Royal Fireworks.

— A Proud Tradition, a Bright Future: A Sesquicentennial History of St. Johnsbury Academy. LC 92-62022. (Illus.). 320p. 1992. 7.00 (*0-9634640-0-0*) St Johns Acad.

Beck, Richard, ed. Icelandic Poems & Stories. LC 68-57059. (Short Story Index Reprint Ser.). 1977. 23.95 (*0-8369-6001-7*) Ayer.

***Beck, Richard J.** Case Management: A Heuristic Approach. 216p. 2000. write for info. (*1-58692-023-5*) Copyright Mgmt.

Beck, Richard J. Famous Idahoans. (Illus.). 121p. (Orig.). 1989. pap. 6.95 (*0-9623034-0-2*) R J Beck.

Beck, Richard K. Pharmacology Field Reference Guide. LC 95-50500. (Illus.). 122p. (C). 1996. pap. 20.95 (*0-8036-0133-6*) Thomson Learn.

— Pharmacology for Prehospital Emergency Care. 2nd ed. Vance, James R., ed. LC 93-33629. 307p. (C). 1994. pap. 23.95 (*0-8036-0692-3*) Thomson Learn.

***Beck, Robert.** Naked Soul of Iceberg Slim. 256p. 1998. mass mkt. 6.99 (*0-87067-998-8*) Holloway.

Beck, Robert. Waters & Water Rights: 1994 Edition, Vol. 6. 1097p. 1994. text 100.00 (*1-55834-186-2*, 60756-11, MICHIE) LEXIS Pub.

Beck, Robert, jt. auth. see Slim, Iceberg.

Beck, Robert C. Motivation: Theories & Principles. 4th ed. LC 99-12289. 477p. (C). 1999. 73.00 (*0-13-011292-5*) P-H.

Beck, Robert E. Career Patterns: The Liberal Arts Major in Bell System Management. 13p. (Orig.). 1981. pap. text 2.00 (*0-911696-07-5*) Assn Am Coll.

Beck, Robert E., ed. 1998 Cumulative Supplement, Waters & Water Rights Vol. 1: 1991 Edition. 1998. write for info. (*0-327-00777-X*, 52691-16) LEXIS Pub.

— 1998 Cumulative Supplement, Waters & Water Rights Vol. 2: 1991 Edition. 1998. write for info. (*0-327-00778-8*, 526592-16) LEXIS Pub.

— 1998 Cumulative Supplement, Waters & Water Rights Vol. 3: 1991 Edition. 1998. write for info. (*0-327-00779-6*, 52693-16) LEXIS Pub.

— 1998 Cumulative Supplement, Waters & Water Rights Vol. 4: 1991 Edition. 1998. write for info. (*0-327-00780-X*, 52694-16) LEXIS Pub.

— 1998 Cumulative Supplement, Waters & Water Rights Vol. 6: 1991 Edition. 1998. write for info. (*0-327-00781-8*, 52696-16) LEXIS Pub.

— 1998 Cumulative Supplement, Waters & Water Rights Vol. 7: 1991 Edition. 1998. write for info. (*0-327-00782-6*, 52697-16) LEXIS Pub.

— Waters & Water Rights: 1991 Edition, 7 vols. 1991. 695.00 (*0-87473-753-2*, 60748-10, MICHIE) LEXIS Pub.

***Beck, Robert E., ed.** Waters & Water Rights: 1999 Tables. 600p. 1999. write for info. (*0-327-10006-0*, 6075711) LEXIS Pub.

Beck, Robert E., et al. Waters & Water Rights, 1991 Edition, 1998 Replacement, Vol. 5. LC 67-5399. 800p. 1998. 130.00 (*0-327-00604-8*, 6075511) LEXIS Pub.

— Cases & Materials on Mineral Law. (American Casebook Ser.). 765p. (C). 1994. 60.00 (*0-314-02916-8*) West Pub.

Beck, Robert E., jt. auth. see Kolman, Bernard.

Beck, Robert H. Change & Harmonization in European Education. LC 75-167299. 222p. reprint ed. pap. 68.90 (*0-608-14096-1*, 205584100039) Bks Demand.

Beck, Robert H., et al. The Changing Structure of Europe: Economic, Social, & Political Trends. LC 73-110659. 296p. reprint ed. pap. 91.80 (*0-608-14097-X*, 205584000039) Bks Demand.

Beck, Robert J. Oil Industry Outlook, 1997-2001. 13th ed. 290p. 1993. 175.00 (*0-685-71333-4*) PennWell Bks.

***Beck, Robert J.** WW Petro Industry Outlook. 16th ed. 324p. 1999. 195.00 (*0-87814-773-X*) PennWell Bks.

Beck, Robert J., et al, eds. Approaches to International Law: An Interdisciplinary Anthology. (Illus.). 328p. 1996. pap. text 27.95 (*0-19-508540-X*) OUP.

— International Rules: Approaches from International Law & International Relations. (Illus.). 328p. 1996. text 49.95 (*0-19-508539-6*) OUP.

***Beck, Robert J. & Ambrosio, Thomas.** International Law & the Rise of Nations. (Illus.). 304p. (C). 2000. pap. 34.95 (*1-889119-30-X*, Chatham House Pub) Seven Bridges.

Beck, Robert J., jt. auth. see Wood, Denis.

Beck, Robert M., et al. Business Formations & Terminations in Kentucky. xiii, 118p. 1993. pap. 40.00 (*1-58757-002-5*, BM013) Univ of KY.

Beck, Robert M., Jr., jt. auth. see D'Angelo, Laura A.

Beck, Robert R. Nonviolent Story: Narrative Conflict Resolution in the Gospel of Mark. LC 95-42415. 210p. (Orig.). 1996. pap. 16.00 (*1-57075-061-0*) Orbis Bks.

***Beck, Roger B.** The History of South Africa. LC 99-58880. (The Greenwood Histories of the Modern Nations Ser.). 280p. 2000. 35.00 (*0-313-30730-X*, GR0730, Greenwood Pr) Greenwood.

Beck, Roger B., tr. see Van der Merwe, Petrus J.

Beck, Roy. Prophets & Politics: A Handbook on the Washington Offices of the U. S. Churches. (Illus.). 193p. (Orig.). 1994. pap. 8.95 (*1-881780-08-2*) Social Contract.

— Re-Charting America's Future: Responses to Arguments Against Stabilizing U. S. Population & Limiting Immigration. (Illus.). 217p. (Orig.). 1994. pap. 9.95 (*1-881780-06-6*) Social Contract.

Beck, Roy A. Play Production Today! 4th ed. 336p. 1989. 26.60 (*0-8442-5085-6*) NTC Contemp Pub Co.

— Stagecraft. (Illus.). 96p. 1994. pap. 10.95 (*0-8442-5134-8*, 51348, Natl Textbk Co) NTC Contemp Pub Co.

Beck, Roy W. & Smith, Craig H. Neuroophthalmology. (Illus.). 256p. 1987. 64.95 (*0-316-08651-7*, Little Brwn Med Div) Lppncott W & W.

Beck, Rudolf H., ed. The Feedback Society. LC 99-180219. 1997. pap. write for info. (*0-9660429-0-5*) Rubivar.

Beck, S. Our Fathers Have Told Us. 224p. 1993. write for info. (*1-883704-01-4*) Cleaveland.

Beck, Sally. Banners on Favorite Bible Verses. LC 98-148332. 80p. 1998. pap. 9.99 (*0-570-04988-1*, 12-3337) Concordia.

Beck, Sam. Manny Almeida's Ringside Lounge: The Cape Verdeans' Struggle for Their Neighborhood. LC 92-72593. (Illus.). 118p. (Orig.). 1992. pap. text 12.50 (*0-943722-18-7*) Gavea-Brown.

***Beck, Sara Ramser, ed.** Library Training for Staff & Customers. LC 00-23133. 108p. 2000. 39.95 (*0-7890-0965-X*); pap. text 14.95 (*0-7890-0983-8*) Haworth Pr.

Beck, Sharon E., jt. auth. see Jones, Rebecca A.

Beck, Shirley, ed. see Association for Childhood Education International Staff.

Beck-Sickinger, jt. ed. see Jung, Gunther.

Beck, Simone & Simon, Patricia. Simca's Cuisine: One Hundred Classic French Recipes for Every Occasion. LC 98-19912. (Cook's Classic Library). (Illus.). 368p. 1998. reprint ed. pap. 16.95 (*1-55821-755-X*) Lyons Pr.

Beck, Stanley M. & Bernier, Ivan, eds. Canada & the New Constitution: The Unfinished Agenda, 2 Vols., Vol. 1. 399p. 1983. 16.95 (*0-920380-73-5*, Pub. by Inst Res Pub) Ashgate Pub Co.

Beck, Stephen V., jt. ed. see Kiple, Kenneth F.

***Beck, Steve.** Trout Fishing the John Muir Trail. 2000. pap. 19.95 (*1-57188-188-3*, MUIR) F Amato Pubns.

Beck, Steve. Yosemite Trout Fishing Guide. (Illus.). 158p. 1996. pap. text 14.95 (*1-57188-042-9*) F Amato Pubns.

Beck, Stevie, et al. Winning Ways on the Autoharp, 2 vols., Vol. 1. Blackley, Becky, ed. (Illus.). 52p. 1985. pap 8.95 (*0-912827-05-X*) I A D Pubns.

— Winning Ways on the Autoharp, 2 vols., Vol. 2. Blackley, Becky, ed. (Illus.). 52p. 1985. pap. 8.95 (*0-912827-06-8*) I A D Pubns.

Beck, Sue, pseud. How to Buy Your Home... & Do It Right. 252p. 1984. pap. 10.95 (*0-9614583-0-5*) Evans Pub.

Beck, Susan. Beading with the Sewing Machine & Serger. (Illus.). 128p. 1998. 14.95 (*0-8069-9484-3*, Sterling-SIR) Sterling.

— Great Clothing from Sweatshirts & T-Shirts. LC 98-183752. (Illus.). 128p. 1998. 27.95 (*0-8069-0792-4*) Sterling.

***Beck, Susan.** Great Clothing from Sweatshirts, T-Shirts & Denim. 128p. 1999. pap. text 14.95 (*0-8069-7803-1*) Sterling.

Beck, Susan. Language Acquisition & Development. (C). 2002. 35.00 (*0-13-523515-4*, Macmillan Coll) P-H.

— Quick Sewing Projects from Placemats: Sew-Fast Gift Ideas. (Illus.). 128p. 1997. pap. text 14.95 (*0-8069-9486-X*) Sterling.

Beck, Susan B. Conestoga Stories. 50p. (J). (gr. 1-6). 1995. pap. 6.50 (*0-87602-332-4*) Anchorage.

***Beck, Susan E.** God Loves Me Bible. (J). 1999. 7.97 (*0-310-95846-6*); 7.97 (*0-310-95847-4*) Zondervan.

Beck, Susan E. God Loves Me Bible. large type ed. (Illus.). 160p. (J). (ps). 1993. 7.99 (*0-310-91652-6*) Zondervan.

Beck, Susan E., see Beck, Sue, pseud.

Beck, Susan J., ed. Outline for Online Ready Reference Services: Occasional Paper, No. 3. (C). 1989. pap. text 12.00 (*0-8389-7317-5*) ALA.

Beck, Susan P. Quick Sewing Projects from Placemats: Sew-Fast Gift Ideas. LC 96-26162. (Illus.). 128p. 1996. 27.95 (*0-8069-9487-8*) Sterling.

Beck, Susan P. & Jennings, Pat. Elegant Beading for Sewing Machine & Serger. LC 96-22388. (Great Sewing Projects Ser.). (Illus.). 128p. 1996. 24.95 (*0-8069-9485-1*) Sterling.

***Beck, Terry.** High Performance Selling: Advice, Tactics & Tools: The Complete Guide to Sales Success. 224p. 2000. pap. 15.00 (*0-00-638628-8*) HarpC.

Beck, Terry, jt. auth. see Beck, Ken.

Beck, Terry, jt. auth. see Beck, Kenneth.

Beck, Theodore, tr. see Underhill, Evelyn.

Beck, Theodore R., et al, eds. Electrochemical Contributions to Environmental Protection. LC 72-89668. (Illus.). 180p. reprint ed. pap. 55.80 (*0-608-11430-8*, 205200100024) Bks Demand.

Beck, Theodoric R. Elements of Medical Jurisprudence, 1823, 2 vols. LC 96-35845. 931p. 1997. reprint ed. 125.00 (*1-886363-24-2*) Lawbk Exchange.

***Beck, Thomas A. & Beck, Barbara.** The Hatch Chile Cookbook: Authentic New Mexican Recipes. 6th rev. ed. (Illus.). 135p. 1999. pap. 15.95 (*0-9666056-0-8*) New Mexican Conn.

Beck, Thomas D. French Legislators, Eighteen Hundred to Eighteen Thirty Four: A Study in Quantitative History. LC 73-83059. 212p. reprint ed. pap. 65.80 (*0-608-15834-8*, 203142400074) Bks Demand.

Beck, Thomasina. Embroiderer's Flowers. (Illus.). 160p 1997. pap. 19.95 (*0-7153-0692-8*) Sterling.

— The Embroiderer's Garden. (Illus.). 192p. 1989. 29.95 (*0-7153-9117-8*, Pub. by D & C Pub) Sterling.

— Embroiderer's Garden. (Illus.). 192p. 1997. pap. 19.95 (*0-7153-0691-X*) Sterling.

— The Embroiderer's Story: Needlework from the Renaissance to the Present Day. (Illus.). 160p. 1996. 29.95 (*0-7153-0238-8*, Pub. by D & C Pub) Sterling.

***Beck, Thomasina.** The Embroiderer's Story: Needlework from the Renaissance to the Present Day. 160p. 1999. pap. text 21.95 (*0-7153-0962-5*) Strlng Pub CA.

Beck, Thomasina. Gardening with Silk & Gold. LC 98-127432. (Illus.). 160p. 1998. 29.95 (*0-7153-0487-9*, Pub. by D & C Pub) Sterling.

Beck, Tom. An American Vision: John G. Bullock & the Photo-Secession. 160p. 1989. 44.95 (*0-89381-405-9*) Aperture.

Beck, Tom, tr. see Komenda-Soentgerath, Olly.

Beck, Tony. The Experience of Poverty: Fighting for Respect & Resources in Village India. 221p. 1994. pap. 19.95 (*1-85339-218-9*, Pub. by Intermed Tech) Stylus Pub VA.

Beck, Trudy, jt. auth. see Green, Laurel.

***Beck, Ulrich.** The Brave New World of Work. Camiller Patrick, tr. from GER. LC 99-58486.Tr. of Schone neue Arbeitswelt. 200p. 2000. text 59.95 (*0-7456-2397-2*, Pub. by Polity Pr); pap. text 26.95 (*0-7456-2398-0*, Pub. by Polity Pr) Blackwell Pubs.

Beck, Ulrich. Ecological Enlightenment: Essays on the Politics of the Risk Society. Ritter, Mark A., tr. LC 93-1682. (Illus.). 152p. (C). 1995. pap. 15.00 (*0-391-03832-X*) Humanities.

— Ecological Politics in An Age of Risk. Weisz, Amos, tr. LC 95-15380. 209p. 1995. pap. 31.95 (*0-7456-1377-2*) Blackwell Pubs.

— The Reinvention of Politics: Rethinking Modernity in the Global Social Order. Ritter, Mark, tr. LC 96-45035.Tr. of Die Erfurdung des Politischen. (GER.). 200p. 1996. 58.95 (*0-7456-1366-7*); pap. 25.95 (*0-7456-1758-1*) Blackwell Pubs.

— What Is Globalization? Camiller, Patrick, tr. from GER. LC 99-27522. Orig. Title: Was Ist Globalisierung?. 208p. (C). 2000. text 59.95 (*0-7456-2125-2*, Pub. by Polity Pr); pap. text 26.95 (*0-7456-2126-0*, Pub. by Polity Pr) Blackwell Pubs.

— World Risk Society. LC 99-16938. 148p. (C). 1999. 59.95 (*0-7456-2220-8*, Pub. by Polity Pr) Blackwell Pubs.

— World Risk Society. LC 99-16938. 148p. (C). 1999. pap. text 24.95 (*0-7456-2221-6*, Pub. by Polity Pr) Blackwell Pubs.

Beck, Ulrich, tr. Democracy Without Enemies. LC 98-6186. 144p. 1998. 52.95 (*0-7456-1822-7*); pap. 23.95 (*0-7456-1823-5*) Blackwell Pubs.

Beck, Ulrich & Beck-Gernsheim, Elisabeth. The Normal Chaos of Love. Ritter, Mark & Wiebel, Jane, trs. from GER. 227p. 1995. text 66.95 (*0-7456-1071-4*); pap. text 26.95 (*0-7456-1382-9*) Blackwell Pubs.

Beck, Ulrich, et al. Reflexive Modernization: Politics, Tradition, & Aesthetics in the Modern Social Order. LC 94-67058. 230p. (C). 1995. pap. 14.95 (*0-8047-2472-5*) Stanford U Pr.

Beck, Ulrick. Risk Society: Towards a New Modernity. Ritter, Mark, tr. (Theory, Culture & Society Ser.: Vol. 17). (Illus.). 304p. 1992. 65.00 (*0-8039-8345-X*); pap. 24.95 (*0-8039-8346-8*) Sage.

Beck, V. Dictionary of Technical Information: Agriculture & Feeding, 2 vols. 891p. (C). 1980. 250.00 (*0-569-08636-1*, Pub. by Collets) St Mut.

— Dictionary of Technical Information: Agriculture & Feeding, 2 vols., Set. 891p. (C). 1980. 150.00 (*0-89771-914-X*, Pub. by Collets) St Mut.

Beck, Van, et al, eds. Reallexikon der Germanischen Altertumskunde Band 5: Chronos - Dona. (Lieferungswerke - Serials Ser.). (GER.). vi, 605p. 1984. 300.00 (*3-11-009635-8*) De Gruyter.

Beck, Victoria J., jt. auth. see Barilleaux, Rene P.

Beck, Virgil. Salmon Coast to Coast. LC 91-66690. (Complete Angler's Library). 250p. 1991. write for info. (*0-914697-43-9*) N Amer Outdoor Grp.

Beck, Vladimir. Dictionary of Food & Agriculture. (ENG, FRE, GER, HUN & RUS.). 278p. 1980. 75.00 (*0-8288-0033-2*, M15600) Fr & Eur.

— Mezogazdasac es Elelmezesugy: Agriculture & Food Dictionary. (ENG, FRE, GER, HUN & RUS.). 513p. 1980. 45.00 (*0-8288-0034-0*, M169) Fr & Eur.

Beck, Von, et al, eds. Antike und Abendland Band 44: Beitrage Zum Verstandnis der Griechen und Romer und Ihres Nachlebens. Jahrbuch, 1998. (GER.). vi, 190p. 1998. 157.35 (*3-11-015796-9*) De Gruyter.

— Reallexikon der Assyriologie und Vorderasiatischen Archaologie: Musik - Mythologie. (Lieferungswerke - Serials Ser.). (GER.). 109p. 1997. 75.00 (*3-11-014812-9*) De Gruyter.

— Fruhmittelalterliche Studien Band 31: Jahrbuch des Instituts fur Fruhmittelalterforschung der Universitat Munster, 1997. (GER.). 512p. 1997. 225.00 (*3-11-015871-X*) De Gruyter.

— Reallexikon der Assyriologie und Vorderasiatischen Archaologie Band 8, Lieferung 5/6: Moab - Musik. (Lieferungswerke - Serials Ser.). (GER.). 160p. 1995. 84.00 (*3-11-014811-0*) De Gruyter.

— Reallexikon der Assyriologie und Vorderasiatischen Archaologie Band 8, Liegerung 1/2: Meek - Miete. (Lieferungswerke - Serials Ser.). (GER.). 160p. 1993. 78.00 (*3-11-013503-5*) De Gruyter.

— Reallexikon der Assyriologie und Vorderasiatischen Archaologie Band 8, Liegerung 3/4: Miete - Moab. (Lieferungswerke - Serials Ser.). (GER.). 160p. 1994. 80.00 (*3-11-014264-3*) De Gruyter.

— Reallexikon der Germanischen Altertumskunde Band 3: Bilrost - Brunichilde, 3. (Lieferungswerke - Serials Ser.). (GER.). vi, 589p. 1978. 300.00 (*3-11-006512-6*) De Gruyter.

— Reallexikon der Germanischen Altertumskunde Band 4: Brunnen - Chronologie. (Lieferungswerke - Serials Ser.). (GER.). vi, 674p. 1981. 300.00 (*3-11-006513-4*) De Gruyter.

— Reallexikon der Germanischen Altertumskunde Band 6: Donar-Porr - Einbaum. (Lieferungswerke - Serials Ser.). (GER.). vi, 613p. 1986. 300.00 (*3-11-010468-7*) De Gruyter.

— Reallexikon der Germanischen Altertumskunde Band 7: Einfache Formen - Eugippius. (Lieferungswerke - Serials Ser.). (GER.). vi, 622p. 1989. 300.00 (*3-11-011445-3*) De Gruyter.

— Reallexikon der Germanischen Altertumskunde Band 8: Euhemerismus - Fichte. (Lieferungswerke - Serials Ser.). (GER.). vi, 613p. 1994. 300.00 (*3-11-013188-9*) De Gruyter.

— Reallexikon der Germanischen Altertumskunde Band 9: Fidel - Friedlosigkeit. (Lieferungswerke - Serials Ser.). (GER.). 621p. 1995. 300.00 (*3-11-014642-8*) De Gruyter.

— Reallexikon der Germanischen Altertumskunde Band 10, Lieferung 3/4: Furstengraber - Gamla Uppsala. (Lieferungswerke - Serials Ser.). (GER.). 1996. 86.00 (*3-11-015100-6*) De Gruyter.

— Reallexikon der Germanischen Altertumskunde Band 10, Lieferung 5/6: Gamleborg - Gelubde. (Lieferungswerke - Serials Ser.). (GER.). 200p. 1998. 94.00 (*3-11-015101-4*) De Gruyter.

Beck, Warren. Joyce's Dubliners: Substance, Vision & Art. LC 78-86477. 383p. reprint ed. pap. 118.80 (*0-608-14810-5*, 202618600048) Bks Demand.

Beck, Warren A. & Haase, Ynez D. Historical Atlas of California. LC 74-5952. (Illus.). 240p. 1975. pap. 19.95 (*0-8061-1212-3*) U of Okla Pr.

— Historical Atlas of New Mexico. LC 68-31366. (Illus.). 152p. 1969. reprint ed. pap. 19.95 (*0-8061-0817-7*) U of Okla Pr.

— Historical Atlas of the American West. LC 88-40540. (Illus.). 200p. 1992. pap. 19.95 (*0-8061-2456-3*) U of Okla Pr.

Beck, William, ed. Hemavid Version 3.0, CD-ROM. 1995. pap. 95.00 incl. disk (*0-262-52189-X*) MIT Pr.

Beck, William C. & Meyer, Ralph, eds. Health Care Environment: The User's Viewpoint. 272p. 1982. 154.00 (*0-8493-6150-8*, RA967, CRC Reprint) Franklin.

Beck, William J., tr. see Leschmelle, Pierre.

B

Beck, William J., tr. see Stephane, Roger.

Beck, William S., ed. Hematology. 5th ed. (Illus.). 664p. 1991. 60.00 (*0-262-02316-4*); pap. text 34.50 (*0-262-52157-1*) MIT Pr.

Beck, William W., Jr. Obstetrics & Gynecology. 3rd ed. LC 92-48888. (National Medical Series for Independent Study). (Illus.). 504p. 1993. pap. 27.00 (*0-683-06241-7*) Lppncott W & W.

Beck, William W. Obstetrics & Gynecology. 4th ed. LC 96-29165. (National Medical Series for Independent Study). 510p. 1996. write for info. (*0-683-18015-0*) Lppncott W & W.

Beck, Wolfgang, et al, eds. The Social Quality of Europe. LC 97-25286. (Studies in Social Policy: Vol. 1). 352p. 1997. 108.00 (*90-411-0456-9*) Kluwer Law Intl.

Beck, Wolfgang, ed. see Friedlaender, Saul, et al.

Becka, Anne Marie, ed. see Rutter, Bryce G. & Dainoff, Marvin J.

Becka, Brenda, ed. see Riccardo, Thomas.

Becka, Jan. Historical Dictionary of Myanmar. LC 93-48303. (Asian Historical Dictionaries Ser.: No. 15). (Illus.). 352p. 1995. 52.00 (*0-8108-2840-5*) Scarecrow.

Beckage, et al, eds. Parasites & Pathogens of Insects, 2 vols., Set. (Illus.). 740p. 1993. 188.00 (*0-12-084440-0*) Acad Pr.

Beckage, N. E., et al. Parasites & Pathogens of Insects Vol. 1: Parasites. (Illus.). 364p. 1993. text 100.00 (*0-12-084441-9*) Acad Pr.

— Parasites & Pathogens of Insects Vol. 2: Pathogens. (Illus.). 294p. 1993. text 100.00 (*0-12-084442-7*) Acad Pr.

Beckdett, Fiona. Wine by Style: A Practical Guide to Choosing Wine by Flavor, Weight & Color. (Illus.). 120p. 1998. pap. 24.95 (*1-84000-030-9*, Pub. by Mitchell Beazley) Antique Collect.

Becke, Archibald F. Napoleon & Waterloo: The Emperor's Campaign with the Armee Du Nord, 1815. LC 95-12756. (Napoleonic Library: Vol. 29). 352p. 1995. write for info. (*1-85367-206-8*, Pub. by Greenhill Bks) Stackpole.

— Napoleon & Waterloo: The Emperor's Campaign with the Armee Du Nord 1815, 2 vols, Set. LC 73-160958. (Select Bibliographies Reprint Ser.). 1977. reprint ed. 72.95 (*0-8369-5825-X*) Ayer.

Becke, Louis. By Reef & Palm. LC 75-116938. (Short Story Index Reprint Ser.). 1977. 19.95 (*0-8369-3440-7*) Ayer.

— Pacific Tales. LC 70-98561. (Short Story Index Reprint Ser.). 1977. 21.95 (*0-8369-3135-1*) Ayer.

— Pacific Tales. (Pacific Basin Ser.). 1998. pap. 31.00 (*0-7103-0254-1*, Pub. by Kegan Paul Intl) Col U Pr.

— Rodman the Boat-Steerer, & Other Stories. LC 70-125206. (Short Story Index Reprint Ser.). 1977. 21.95 (*0-8369-3573-X*) Ayer.

— South Sea Supercargo. Day, A. Grove, ed. 200p. reprint ed. pap. 57.00 (*0-8357-8530-0*, 2034832) Bks Demand.

— Under Tropic Skies. LC 73-113650. (Short Story Index Reprint Ser.). 1977. 19.95 (*0-8369-3379-6*) Ayer.

— Yorke the Adventurer, & Other Stories. LC 71-37535. (Short Story Index Reprint Ser.). 1977. reprint ed. 20.95 (*0-8369-4094-6*) Ayer.

Beckel, Lothar. Atlas of Global Change. LC 98-2955. (Illus.). 160p. 1998. 90.00 (*0-02-864956-7*, Schirmer Books) Mac Lib Ref.

Beckelman, Laurie. Anger. LC 93-40641. 48p. (J). 1994. pap. 5.95 (*0-382-24744-2*, Crstwood Hse); text 13.95 (*0-89686-841-9*, Crstwood Hse) Silver Burdett Pr.

Beckelman, Laurie. Anger. LC 93-40641. (Hotline Ser.). 1994. 11.15 (*0-606-10216-7*, Pub. by Turtleback) Demco.

Beckelman, Laurie. Body Blues. LC 93-31778. (Hot Line Ser.). 48p. (J). 1994. pap. 5.95 (*0-382-24743-4*, Crstwood Hse); lib. bdg. 5.95 (*0-89686-842-7*, Crstwood Hse) Silver Burdett Pr.

Beckelman, Laurie. Body Blues. LC 93-31778. (Hotline Ser.). 1994. 11.15 (*0-606-10217-5*, Pub. by Turtleback) Demco.

Beckelman, Laurie. Boredom. LC 94-37309. (Hot Line Ser.). (YA). (gr. 5 up). 1995. lib. bdg. 13.95 (*0-89686-844-3*) Silver Burdett Pr.

— Boredom. LC 94-37309. (Hot Line Ser.). (Illus.). 48p. (J). (gr. 6 up). 1995. pap. 5.95 (*0-382-24955-0*) Silver Burdett Pr.

— Censorship. LC 98-23174. (You Decide! Ser.). (J). 1999. lib. bdg. 13.95 (*0-382-39346-5*, Crstwood Hse) Silver Burdett Pr.

— Depression. (Hot Line Ser.). (Illus.). 48p. (YA). (gr. 6 up). 1995. pap. 5.95 (*0-382-24956-9*, Crstwood Hse) Silver Burdett Pr.

— Depression. LC 94-30976. (Hot Line Ser.). (YA). 1995. lib. bdg. 13.95 (*0-89686-845-1*) Silver Burdett Pr.

— Envy. LC 94-29744. (Hot Line Ser.). (Illus.). 48p. (J). (gr. 6 up). 1995. pap. 5.95 (*0-382-24957-7*, Crstwood Hse) Silver Burdett Pr.

— Gambling. LC 98-23172. (You Decide! Ser.). (J). 1999. lib. bdg. 13.95 (*0-382-39354-6*, Crstwood Hse) Silver Burdett Pr.

— Grief. LC 94-45692. (Hot Line Ser.). (J). 1995. lib. bdg. 13.95 (*0-89686-847-8*, Crstwood Hse) Silver Burdett Pr.

— Grief. LC 94-45692. (Hot Line Ser.). (Illus.). 48p. (YA). (gr. 6 up). 1995. pap. 5.95 (*0-382-24958-5*, Crstwood Hse) Silver Burdett Pr.

— Gun Control. LC 98-23188. (You Decide! Ser.). (J). 1999. lib. bdg. 13.95 (*0-382-39348-1*, Crstwood Hse) Silver Burdett Pr.

***Beckelman, Laurie.** Human Body. (On the Spot Ser.). (Illus.). 16p. (J). (gr. k-2). 2001. 7.99 (*1-57584-806-6*, Pub. by Rdrs Digest) S&S Trade.

Beckelman, Laurie. The Human Body. LC 98-53122. (Pathfinders Ser.). (Illus.). 64p. (YA). (gr. 3-8). 1999. 16.99 (*1-57584-289-0*, Pub. by Rdrs Digest) Random.

— Loneliness. LC 93-5625. (Hot Line Ser.). 48p. (J). 1994. pap. 5.95 (*0-382-24745-0*); text 13.95 (*0-89686-843-5*, Crstwood Hse) Silver Burdett Pr.

— Loneliness. LC 93-5625. (Hotline Ser.). 1994. 11.15 (*0-606-10218-3*, Pub. by Turtleback) Demco.

— Media Violence. LC 98-23178. (You Decide! Ser.). (J). 1999. lib. bdg. 13.95 (*0-382-39351-1*, Crstwood Hse) Silver Burdett Pr.

— Stress. 48p. 1994. pap. 5.95 (*0-382-24746-9*) Silver Burdett Pr.

— Stress. LC 94-2735. (J). 1994. text 13.95 (*0-89686-848-6*, Crstwood Hse) Silver Burdett Pr.

Beckelman, Laurie. Stress. LC 94-2735. (Hotline Ser.). 1994. 11.15 (*0-606-10219-1*, Pub. by Turtleback) Demco.

Beckemeyer, Curt A. Rural Road Condition Survey Guide. (Illus.). 79p. (Orig.). (C). 1996. pap. text 30.00 (*0-7881-3147-8*) DIANE Pub.

Becken, H. J., jt. ed. see Oosthuizen, Gerhardus C.

Becken, Hans-Jurgen, tr. see Hexham, Irving & Oosthuizen, G. C., eds.

Becken, Hans-Jurgen, tr. see Hexham, Irving & Oosthuizen, Gerhardus C., eds.

Beckenbach. Modern College Algebra & Trig. 2nd ed. (Math). 1972. 13.50 (*0-534-00110-6*) Brooks-Cole.

— Modern College Algebra & Trig. 3rd ed. (Math). 1977. 17.75 (*0-534-00468-7*) Brooks-Cole.

— S.g. College Algebra. 6th ed. (Math). 1985. student ed. 8.75 (*0-534-03654-6*) Brooks-Cole.

— Stdt Guide-college Algebra,4th. 4th ed. (Math). 1978. student ed. 6.75 (*0-534-00537-3*) Brooks-Cole.

— Stdt Sm College Algebra. 6th ed. (Math). 1985. student ed. 8.75 (*0-534-03655-4*) Brooks-Cole.

— Stdt Sol - College Algebra, 5th. 5th ed. (Math). 1982. student ed. 6.75 (*0-534-01166-7*) Brooks-Cole.

— Stdt Sol-mod Coll Alg Trig, 4th. 4th ed. (Math). 1981. student ed. 8.75 (*0-534-00952-2*) Brooks-Cole.

Beckenbach & Drooyan. College Algebra, 4th. 4th ed. (Math). 1978. 19.75 (*0-534-00536-5*) Brooks-Cole.

— Stdt Sm & S.g. College Algebra. 7th ed. (Math). 1988. student ed. 11.25 (*0-534-08557-1*) Brooks-Cole.

Beckenbach, Edwin F. College Algebra. 5th ed. (Math). 1982. student ed. 8.75 (*0-534-01119-5*) Brooks-Cole.

Beckenbach, Edwin F., ed. Applied Combinatorial Mathematics. LC 80-12457. 630p. 1981. reprint ed. lib. bdg. 58.00 (*0-89874-172-6*) Krieger.

— General Inequalities II. (International Series of Numerical Mathematics: No. 47). 505p. 1980. 87.50 (*0-8176-1056-1*) Birkhauser.

Beckenbach, Edwin F. & Bellman, R. An Introduction to Inequalities. LC 61-6228. (New Mathematical Library: No. 3). 133p. 1961. pap. text 8.00 (*0-88385-603-4*, NML-03) Math Assn.

Beckenbach, Edwin F. & Walter, Wolfgang. General Inequalities III. (International Series of Numerical Mathematics: Vol. 64). 592p. (C). 1983. text 80.65 (*3-7643-1539-3*) Birkhauser.

Beckenbach, Edwin F., et al. College Algebra. 6th ed. (Math). (C). 1984. mass mkt. 30.75 (*0-534-03653-8*) PWS Pubs.

Beckendorf, Charles. Charles Beckendorf--Texas. LC 86-71956. (Illus.). 160p. 1986. 75.00 (*0-939929-05-8*, GB/T-1) C Beckendorf Gallery.

***Beckensall, Stan.** British Prehistoric Rock Art. (History & Archaeology Ser.). (Illus.). 176p. 1999. 29.99 (*0-7524-1471-2*, Pub. by Tempus Pubng) Arcadia Publng.

Beckensall, Stan. Rock Carvings of Northern Britain. 1989. pap. 40.00 (*0-85263-760-8*, Pub. by Shire Pubns) St Mut.

Beckenstein. Cpsm Rdgs for Bus & the Polit. 1998. pap. text 29.00 (*0-07-230291-7*) McGraw.

Beckenstein, Edward, jt. auth. see Narici, Lawrencel.

***Becker.** Biocore Syllabus. 1998. pap. text 3.00 (*0-201-60673-9*) Addison-Wesley.

Becker. Course Syllabus Cell Biology. (C). 1997. text 3.20 (*0-201-30738-3*) Addison-Wesley.

— Drug Handbook for the Dental Patient. 1999. pap. text. write for info. (*0-7216-7323-6*, W B Saunders Co) Harcrt Hlth Sci Grp.

— Essentials of Surgery. (C). 2000. pap. text. write for info. (*0-7216-8186-7*, W B Saunders Co) Harcrt Hlth Sci Grp.

— Georges Simenon. rev. ed. LC 99-33697. 1999. 22.95 (*0-8057-4557-2*, Twyne) Mac Lib Ref.

— Gothic Forms of Feminine Fiction. (Illus.). 224p. 1999. text 79.95 (*0-7190-5330-7*) Manchester Univ Pr.

— Heart Smart. 1984. pap. 3.50 (*0-671-30924-2*) PB.

— High Resolution NMR. 3rd ed. 424p. (C). 1999. 79.95 (*0-12-084662-4*) Acad Pr.

— Managed Care Manual. LC 99-182082. 1998. pap. text 39.95 (*0-323-00077-0*) Mosby Inc.

— The New S Language. 1988. lib. bdg. 64.95 (*0-412-74150-4*) Chapman & Hall.

— Perpetual Estate Planning. 1993. 125.00 (*0-316-08663-0*, Aspen Law & Bus) Aspen Pub.

— Programming Web Advertising. (C). 1998. text. write for info. (*1-55860-522-3*) Morgan Kaufmann.

— Reformed Jesuits, Vol. 2. 1997. pap. text 11.95 (*0-89870-627-0*) Ignatius Pr.

— Soviet & Russian Press Coverage of the United States: Press, Politics & Identity in Transition. LC 98-47674. 272p. 1999. text 72.00 (*0-312-21907-5*) St Martin.

— Sunday School Tooter: Tonette, Soprano Recorder Flutophone & Song Flute. 1990. 6.95 (*0-685-32151-7*, H859) Hansen Ed Mus.

— Sweet & Low. 1988. pap. 7.95 (*0-671-64991-4*) PB.

***Becker.** World of the Cell & the Biology Place. 4th ed. 2000. pap. text 86.00 (*0-8053-4531-0*) Benjamin-Cummings.

Becker & Greenberg, R. A., eds. Educational Rehabilitation of the Handicapped in the German Democratic Republic & in the United States of America: An Overview. 303p. 1986. 45.00 (*0-317-66819-6*, Pergamon Pr) Elsevier.

Becker & Wheeler, William B. Discovering the American Past: A Look at the Evidence, 2 vols. 2nd ed. (C). 1990. pap. text 2.76 (*0-395-52708-2*) HM.

Becker, Philippe M., et al. Erbium-Doped Fiber Amplifiers: Fundamentals & Technology. LC 97-29070. (Optics & Photonics Ser.). (Illus.). 480p. (C). 1999. 95.00 (*0-12-084590-3*) Acad Pr.

Becker & Mayer, Ltd. Staff. Parlor Cards, Vol. 3. 1999. text 14.50 (*0-670-86518-4*) Viking Penguin.

— Parlor Cards, Vol. 4. 1999. text 14.95 (*0-670-86519-2*) Viking Penguin.

***Becker & Mayer Staff, prod.** First Impressions: A Keepsake Baby Book & Plaster Casting Kit with Other. (Illus.). 48p. 1999. 19.98 (*0-7651-0917-4*) Smithmark.

Becker, A., tr. see Keller, Conrad P.

Becker, A. A. Boundary Element Method in Engineering. 352p. 1992. 33.50 (*0-07-707415-7*) McGraw.

Becker, A. C. A. C. Becker's Speckled Trout: How, When & Where. LC 88-92412. (Illus.). 1988. pap. text. write for info. (*0-929980-00-X*) TX Fish & Game.

Becker, A. C., Jr. A. C. Becker's Speckled Trout Vol. 1: How, When & Where. Robertson, Barbara A., ed. (Illus.). 128p. (Orig.). 1988. pap. 11.95 (*0-685-44287-X*) TX Fish & Game.

Becker, A. L. Beyond Translation: Essays Towards a Modern Philosophy. LC 94-47089. 456p. 1995. text 54.50 (*0-472-10573-6*, 10573) U of Mich Pr.

Becker, A. L., ed. Writing on the Tongue. LC 88-63411. (Michigan Papers on South & Southeast Asia: No. 33). (Illus.). 321p. 1989. 31.95 (*0-89148-047-1*); pap. 17.95 (*0-89148-048-X*) Ctr S&SE Asian.

Becker, A. L. & Yengoyan, Aram, eds. Imagination of Reality: Essays in Southeast Asian Coherence Systems. LC 79-15675. (Language & Being Ser.). (Illus.). 352p. 1979. text 73.25 (*0-89391-021-X*) Ablx Pub.

Becker, Aaron M. Whose Death in the Tunnel? LC 99-12659. 350p. 1999. 25.00 (*1-885003-20-X*) R D Reed Pubs.

Becker, Abraham S. Economic Leverage on the Soviet Union in the 1980's. LC 84-11700. 1984. pap. text 7.50 (*0-8330-0577-4*, R-3127-USDP) Rand Corp.

— Soviet National Income, 1958 to 1964: National Accounts of the U. S. S. R. in the Seven Year Plan Period. LC 70-77483. 626p. reprint ed. pap. 194.10 (*0-608-17463-7*, 202994400066) Bks Demand.

Becker, Abraham S., et al. The Economics & Politics of the Middle East. LC 74-14466. (Middle East Economic & Political Problems & Prospects Ser.). 144p. reprint ed. pap. 44.70 (*0-608-16395-3*, 202627700049) Bks Demand.

Becker, Alexander. Transferbeziehungen Zwischen den Generationen: Unter Besonderer Berucksichtigung der Intragenerationalen Verteilungswirkungen. (GER., Illus.). 353p. 1996. 61.95 (*3-631-30151-0*) P Lang Pubng.

Becker, Alida. The Tolkien Scrapbook. LC 78-65276. 192 p. 1978. write for info. (*0-448-16455-8*, G & D) Peng Put Young Read.

Becker, Aliza. Contemporarys Citizenship Now. 1995. 22.53 (*0-8092-3271-5*) NTC Contemp Pub Co.

Becker, Aliza & Edwards, Laurie. Contemporary's Citizenship Now. (Illus.). 165p. 1997. pap. 23.95 incl. audio (*0-8442-0661-X*, 0661X) NTC Contemp Pub Co.

Becker, Aliza, et al. Citizenship Now: A Guide for Naturalization. 165p. 1995. pap. 10.60 (*0-8092-3270-7*); pap. 31.86 incl. audio (*0-8092-3269-3*) NTC Contemp Pub Co.

***Becker, Allienne R.** The Divine & Human Comedy of Andrew M. Greeley, 7. LC 00-25114. (Contributions to the Study of American Literature Ser.: Vol. 7). 240p. 2000. 59.00 (*0-313-31564-7*, GM1564, Greenwood Pr) Greenwood.

Becker, Allienne R. The Lost Worlds Romance: From Dawn till Dusk, 51. LC 92-1130. (Contributions to the Study of Science Fiction & Fantasy Ser.: No. 51). 184p. 1992. 55.00 (*0-313-26123-7*, BKR/, Greenwood Pr) Greenwood.

Becker, Allienne R., ed. Visions of the Fantastic: Selected Essays from the Fifteenth International Conference on the Fantastic in the Arts, 68. LC 95-39493. (Contributions to the Study of Science Fiction & Fantasy Ser.: Vol. 68). 232p. 1996. 59.95 (*0-313-29725-8*, Greenwood Pr) Greenwood.

Becker, Andrew S. The Shield of Achilles & the Poetics of Ekphrasis: Theory, Philology, & the Shield of Achilles. 200p. (C). 1995. pap. text 25.95 (*0-8476-7998-5*); lib. bdg. 56.00 (*0-8476-7997-7*) Rowman.

Becker, Angelika & Carroll, Mary, eds. The Acquisition of Spatial Relations in a Second Language: In Co-Operation with Jorge Giacobbe, Clive Perdue & Remi Porquier. LC 97-8791. (Studies in Bilingualism: Vol. 11). xix, 212p. 1997. lib. bdg. 45.00 (*1-55619-545-1*) J Benjamins Pubng Co.

Becker, Ann, ed. see Kirkpatrick, Stephen.

Becker, Ann W. Faith for the Journey: Youth Explore the Confession of Faith. LC 97-61154. 120p. (YA). (gr. 9-12). 1997. pap. 8.95 (*0-87303-313-2*) Faith & Life.

Becker, Anne. The Transmutation Notebooks: Poems in the Voices of Charles & Emma Darwin. Cavalieri, Grace & Comitz, Cindy, eds. 120p. (Orig.). 1995. pap. 10.00 (*0-938572-12-1*) Bunny Crocodile.

Becker, Anne E. Body, Self, & Society: The View from Fiji. (Illus.). 224p. 1995. pap. text 14.95 (*0-8122-1397-1*) U of Pa Pr.

— Body, Self, & Society: The View from Fiji. (Illus.). 224p. 1995. text 34.95 (*0-8122-3180-5*) U of Pa Pr.

Becker, Annette. War & Faith: The Religious Imagination in France, 1914-1930. McPhail, Helen, tr. from FRE. LC 98-219500. (Legacy of the Great War Ser.). xiii, 191p. 1998. 65.00 (*1-85973-173-2*, Pub. by Berg Pubs) NYU Pr.

Becker, Annette, et al, eds. DAM Architecture Annual, 1997. (Illus.). 200p. 1997. 45.00 (*3-7913-1849-7*, Pub. by Prestel) te Neues.

— 20th Century Architecture in Ireland. LC 97-3740. (Illus.). 192p. 1997. 65.00 (*3-7913-1719-9*, Pub. by Prestel) te Neues.

Becker, Annette, jt. ed. see Wang, Wilfried.

Becker, Anton E., jt. auth. see Anderson, Robert H.

Becker, Anton E., jt. auth. see Kurosawa, H.

Becker, Art. Transcendence. 16p. 1995. pap. 7.95 (*0-9646065-0-X*) A Becker Photo.

Becker, Arthur H. The Compassionate Visitor: Resources for Ministering to People Who Are Ill. LC 84-28370. 128p. (Orig.). 1985. pap. 11.99 (*0-8066-2094-3*, 10-1620, Augsburg) Augsburg Fortress.

Becker, Arthur P., ed. Land & Building Taxes: Their Effect on Economic Development. LC 70-84951. (Publications of the Committee on Taxation, Resources & Economic Development: Vol. 4). 324p. 1969. reprint ed. pap. 100.50 (*0-608-01931-3*, 206258600003) Bks Demand.

Becker, Audrey. Dying Dreams. Regan, Judith, ed. 360p. (Orig.). 1993. mass mkt. 5.99 (*0-671-73232-3*) PB.

Becker, B., ed. Free Stuff for Everyone. deluxe ed. (Illus.). 192p. 1999. pap. 7.95 (*1-893128-05-9*) Prime Pub.

— Prime's Work-at-Home Directory: Work at Home. rev. ed. (Illus.). 32p. 1999. pap. 3.95 (*1-893128-04-0*) Prime Pub.

Becker, B. F., jt. ed. see Gerlach, E.

Becker, Barbara, jt. auth. see Kelly, Eric D.

Becker, Barbara L., jt. auth. see Gilmore, Gary D.

Becker, Benjamin M., et al. Legal Checklists, 1965-1991, 2 vols. LC 82-4513. 1989. 240.00 (*0-685-09240-2*) West Group.

— Legal Checklists Specially Selected Forms, 1977-1990. LC 76-56745. 130.00 (*0-317-12018-2*) West Group.

Becker, Bernard H. Scientific London. 340p. 1968. reprint ed. 30.00 (*0-7146-2328-8*, Pub. by F Cass Pubs) Intl Spec Bk.

Becker, Betty G. & Fender, Dolores T. Vocational & Personal Adjustments in Practical Nursing. 7th ed. (Illus.). 194p. 1994. teacher ed. write for info. (*0-8151-4419-9*) Mosby Inc.

Becker, Betty G. & Fendler, Dolores T. Vocational & Personal Adjustments in Practical Nursing. 7th ed. LC 93-8185. (Illus.). 194p. (C). (gr. 13). 1993. pap. text 24.95 (*0-8016-6839-5*, 06839) Mosby Inc.

Becker, Bob. Grampa's Stories . . . for Little Kids. (Illus.). 46p. (J). 1998. pap. 8.95 (*1-885548-00-1*) Boot Prints.

— Twenty Demonstrations Guaranteed to Knock Your Socks Off, Vol. II. (Illus.). 104p. (Orig.). 1997. pap. text 14.95 (*1-877991-42-2*) Flinn Scientific.

— Ya, Ya! Those Were the Days! Nostalgic Tales of the Past. (Illus.). 197p. 1993. pap. 8.95 (*1-885548-01-X*) Boot Prints.

Becker, Bob, ed. Contemporary Percussion: Performers' Perspectives. (Contemporary Music Review Ser.). 70p. 1992. pap. text 15.00 (*3-7186-5286-2*, Harwood Acad Pubs) Gordon & Breach.

— Fishing Stories: Adventures on Lakes & Streams. 234p. 1994. pap. 8.95 (*1-885548-02-8*) Boot Prints.

Becker, Bonny. Ants Day Off. LC 99-22598. (J). (gr. k-3). 2002. pap. 16.00 (*0-689-82274-X*) S&S Childrens.

— The Christmas Crocodile. LC 96-53140. (Illus.). 40p. (J). (ps-2). 1998. per. 16.00 (*0-689-81503-4*) Aladdin.

— The Quiet Way Home. LC 95-6066. (Illus.). 88p. (J). (gr. k-2). 1995. 15.95 (*0-8050-3530-3*) H Holt & Co.

***Becker, Bonny.** Tickly Prickly. LC 98-70967. (Growing Tree Ser.). (Illus.). 24p. (YA). (ps-k). 1999. 9.95 (*0-694-01239-4*, HarpFestival) HarpC Child Bks.

Becker, Brandon Charles, et al. Securities Law & the Internet: Doing Business in a Rapidly Changing Marketplace. LC 98-178634. (Corporate Law & Practice Course Handbook Ser.). 920 p. 1998. 129.00 (*0-87224-444-X*) PLI.

Becker, Brenda L., jt. auth. see Moser, Marvin.

Becker, Brent. Changing Structure of the Electric Power Industry 1999: Mergers & Other Corporate Combinations. 115p. (C). pap. text 25.00 (*0-7567-0009-4*) DIANE Pub.

Becker, Bruce & Hanson, Handt. Victory Feast: A Worship Celebration of Word, Sacrament & Song. 10p. 1989. pap. 7.95 (*0-933173-19-9*) Chging Church Forum.

Becker, Bruce E. & Cole, Andrew J., eds. Comprehensive Aquatic Therapy. LC 97-12662. 184p. 1997. text 52.50 (*0-7506-9649-4*) Buttrwrth-Heinemann.

***Becker-Burridge, Kate.** News Releases: Working with the Media & Getting the Media to Work for You. Steis, Sally & Steis, Drew, eds. (Art Calendar Guide Ser.). (Illus.). 48p. 1999. pap. 9.95 (*0-945388-28-4*) Art Calendar.

Becker, C. Dale & Neitzel, Duane A., eds. Water Quality in North American River Systems. LC 92-4935. 328p. 1992. per. 44.95 (*0-935470-50-6*) Battelle.

Becker, Calvin. First & Second Timothy & Titus. (Teach Yourself the Bible Ser.). pap. 5.99 (*0-8024-2646-8*, 532) Moody.

Becker-Cantarino, Barbara, ed. Berlin in Focus: Cultural Transformations in Germany. LC 95-50531. 224p. 1996. 57.95 (*0-275-95507-9*, Praeger Pubs) Greenwood.

— Daniel Heinsius: Nederduytsche Poemata. (GER., Illus.). 288p. 1983. 36.00 (*3-261-03169-7*) P Lang Pubng.

Becker-Cantarino, Barbara, ed. see Handke, Peter.

Becker, Carl B. Breaking the Circle: Death & the Afterlife in Buddhism. LC 92-43710. 216p. (C). 1993. 16.95 (*0-8093-1845-8*); pap. 16.95 (*0-8093-1932-2*) S Ill U Pr.

— Paranormal Experience & Survival of Death. LC

An Asterisk (*) at the beginning of an entry indicates that the title is appearing for the first time.

92-37751. (SUNY Series in Western Esoteric Traditions). 257p. (C). 1993. pap. text 23.95 (*0-7914-1476-0*) State U NY Pr.

Becker, Carl B., ed. Asian & Jungian View of Ethics, 66. LC 98-20069. 160p. 1999. 49.95 (*0-313-30452-1*, Greenwood Pr) Greenwood.

Becker, Carl F. Poems for Seniors, No. 2. 100p. (Orig.). 1991. pap. 8.00 (*0-9633350-0-6*) C F Becker.

— Die Tonwerke des XVI. und XVII. Jahrhunderts. 1969. reprint ed. 70.00 (*0-318-71735-2*) G Olms Pubs.

Becker, Carl H. Beitraege zur Geschicte Agyptens unter Dem Islam, 2 vols. in 1. LC 77-10579. (Studies in Islamic History: No. 5). (GER.). 198p. 1977. reprint ed. lib. bdg. 37.50 (*0-87991-454-8*) Porcupine Pr.

— Islamstudien, 2 vols., Set. xxi, 1084p. 1967. reprint ed. 240.00 (*0-318-71488-4*) G Olms Pubs.

Becker, Carl L. Carl Lotus Becker. (BCL1 - U. S. History Ser.). 279p. 1991. reprint ed. lib. bdg. 79.00 (*0-7812-6095-7*) Rprt Serv.

— Declaration of Independence: A Study in the History of Political Ideas. 1958. pap. 10.00 (*0-394-70060-0*, V-60) Vin Bks.

— Detachment & the Writing of History: Essays & Letters of Carl L. Becker. Snyder, Phil L., ed. LC 70-152590. 240p. 1972. reprint ed. lib. bdg. 55.00 (*0-8371-6023-5*, BEWH, Greenwood Pr) Greenwood.

— The Eve of the Revolution: A Chronicle of the Breach with England. (BCL1 - U. S. History Ser.). 267p. 1991. reprint ed. lib. bdg. 79.00 (*0-7812-6110-4*) Rprt Serv.

— Freedom & Responsibility in the American Way of Life, V. 1. LC 80-11156. (University of Michigan, William W. Cook Foundation Lectures: Vol. 1). 122p. 1980. reprint ed. lib. bdg. 35.00 (*0-313-22361-0*, BEFA, Greenwood Pr) Greenwood.

— Heavenly City of the Eighteenth-Century Philosophers. (Storrs Lectures). (C). 1959. pap. 14.00 (*0-300-00017-0*, Y5) Yale U Pr.

— The History of Political Parties in the Province of New York, 1760-1776. LC 10-7312. (Bulletin of the University of Wisconsin History Ser.: No. 286). 323p. reprint ed. pap. 100.20 (*0-7837-2648-1*, 204300200006) Bks Demand.

— History of Political Parties in the Province of New York, 1760-76. 1993. reprint ed. lib. bdg. 89.00 (*0-7812-5166-4*) Rprt Serv.

— How New Will the Better World Be? A Discussion of Post-War Reconstruction. LC 72-134051. (Essay Index Reprint Ser.). 1977. reprint ed. 23.95 (*0-8369-2482-7*) Ayer.

— Progress & Power. LC 83-45701. reprint ed. 32.50 (*0-404-20023-0*) AMS Pr.

— Safeguarding Civil Liberty Today. 1949. 16.50 (*0-8446-1064-X*) Peter Smith.

— Social Responsibility & the Place of the Artist in Society. 22p. (C). 1990. pap. text 3.00 (*0-941702-28-6*) Lake View Pr.

— Zones of Contention: Essays on Art, Institutions, Gender, & Anxiety. LC 95-32373. (SUNY Series, Interruptions). (Illus.). 268p. (C). 1996. text 54.50 (*0-7914-2937-7*); pap. text 17.95 (*0-7914-2938-5*) State U NY Pr.

Becker, Carl L., ed. The Subversive Imagination: The Artist, Society, & Social Responsibility. LC 93-36230. (Illus.). 256p. (C). (gr. 13). 1994. pap. 18.99 (*0-415-90592-3*) Routledge.

***Becker, Carl L. & Kammen, Michael G.** The United States. 334p. 2000. pap. 24.95 (*0-7658-0637-1*) Transaction Pubs.

Becker, Carl L., et al. The Spirit of '76 & Other Essays. (Brookings Institution Reprint Ser.). reprint ed. lib. bdg. 30.00 (*0-697-00150-4*) Irvington.

— The Spirit of '76 & Other Essays. (BCL1 - U. S. History Ser.). 135p. 1991. reprint ed. lib. bdg. 69.00 (*0-7812-6102-3*) Rprt Serv.

Becker, Carl L., ed. see Acker, Kathy, et al.

Becker, Carl L., tr. see Uehiro, Eiji.

Becker, Carl M. Home & Away: The Rise & Fall of Professional Football on the Banks of the Ohio, 1919-1394. LC 98-23470. 448p. 1998. pap. 19.95 (*0-8214-1238-8*) Ohio U Pr.

— Home & Away: The Rise & Fall of Professional Football on the Banks of the Ohio, 1919-1934. LC 98-23470. 448p. 1998. text 36.95 (*0-8214-1237-X*) Ohio U Pr.

Becker, Carl M. & Thobaben, Robert G. Common Warfare: Parallel Memoirs by Two World War II GIs in the Pacific. LC 91-51003. (Illus.). 224p. 1992. lib. bdg. 28.95 (*0-89950-699-2*) McFarland & Co.

Becker, Carl M. & Thomas, Ritchie, eds. An American Pursuit Pilot in France: Roland W. Richardson's Diaries & Letters, 1917-1919. LC 91-14178. (Illus.). 198p. 1994. 24.95 (*0-942597-64-8*) White Mane Pub.

Becker, Carol A. Community Information Service: A Directory of Public Library Involvement. LC 74-620019. (Student Contribution Ser.: No. 5). 1974. pap. 5.00 (*0-911808-09-4*) U of Md Lib Serv.

***Becker, Carol E.** Becoming Colleagues: Women & Men Serving Together in Faith. LC 00-27383. 2000. 22.00 (*0-7879-4709-1*) Jossey-Bass.

Becker, Carol E. & Shawchuck, Norman. Leading Women: How Church Women Can Avoid Leadership Traps & Negotiate the Gender Maze. 176p. (Orig.). 1995. pap. 14.95 (*0-687-45964-8*) Abingdon.

Becker, Carol S. Living & Relating: An Introduction to Phenomenology. (Illus.). 224p. 1992. 48.00 (*0-8039-3902-7*); pap. 23.50 (*0-8039-3903-5*) Sage.

Becker, Catherine. Mana Karten: Verbinde Dich Mit der Kraft Uralter Hawaiianischer Weisheit. Lamontagne, Tara, tr.Tr. of Mana Cards. (GER., Illus.). 100p. 1998. pap. 30.50 (*0-9660142-1-9*) Radiance Netwk.

Becker, Catherine Kalama. Mana Cards: The Power of Hawaiian Wisdom. LC 97-76453. (Illus.). 44p. 1998. pap. 36.50 (*0-9660142-0-0*) Radiance Netwk.

Becker, Charles H. Plant Manager's Handbook. 304p. 1974. 42.00 (*0-685-03897-1*) P-H.

Becker, Charles M., et al. Beyond Urban Bias in Africa: Urbanization in an Era of Structural Adjustment. LC 93-32405. (Social History of Africa Ser.). 294p. (C). 1994. 60.00 (*0-435-08091-1*, 08091); pap. 27.50 (*0-435-08093-8*, 08093) Heinemann.

— Indian Urbanization & Economic Growth since 1960. LC 90-28392. (Studies in Development). 360p. 1991. text 65.00 (*0-8018-4179-8*) Johns Hopkins.

Becker, Charles M., jt. auth. see Mills, Edwin S.

Becker, Charlotte, jt. ed. see Becker, Lawrence C.

Becker, Charlotte B., jt. ed. see Becker, Lawrence C.

***Becker, Cheri.** Synergistic Food Production Management: The Comprehensive Workbook. LC 98-50351. 219p. 1998. pap. text, wbk. ed. 30.40 (*0-13-083389-4*) P-H.

Becker, Christine. Cockroaches, Stinkbugs, & Other Creepy Crawlers. (Draw Science Ser.). 1996. 13.15 (*0-606-09214-5*, Pub. by Turtleback) Demco.

— Color Anatomy! The Human Body from Head to Toe. LC 97-74875. (Illus.). 64p. (J). 1997. pap. 7.95 (*1-56565-738-1*, 07381W, Pub. by Lowell Hse Juvenile) NTC Contemp Pub Co.

— Draw Gross. LC 97-180021. (Illus.). 64p. (J). (gr. 3-7). Date not set. pap. 7.95 (*1-56565-588-5*, 05885W) NTC Contemp Pub Co.

Becker, Christine S., ed. Performance Evaluation: An Essential Management Tool. (Practical Management Ser.). 209p. 1988. pap. text 23.95 (*0-87326-051-1*) Intl City-Cnty Mgt.

Becker, Christoph. History of the Catholic Missions in Northeast India. 1980. 32.00 (*0-8364-0600-1*, Pub. by Mukhopadhyaya) S Asia.

— Sprachkonzeptionen der Deutschen Fruehaufklarung: Woerterbuch und Untersuchung. (Europaische Hochschulschriften Ser.: Reihe 1, Band 1659). (GER.). 422p. 1998. pap. 56.95 (*3-631-33020-0*) P Lang Pubng.

Becker, Christoph, et al. Tahiti. (Illus.). 181p. 1998. 45.00 (*3-7757-0744-1*, Pub. by Gerd Hatje) Dist Art Pubs.

Becker, Clarence F. Solar Radiation Availability on Surfaces in the U. S. as Affected by Season, Orientation, Latitude, Altitude, & Cloudiness. Bruchey, Stuart, ed. LC 78-22659. (Energy in the American Economy Ser.). (Illus.). 1979. lib. bdg. 17.95 (*0-405-11963-1*) Ayer.

Becker, Claudia, tr. see Lachner, Bert.

Becker, Colette. Dictionnaire d'Emile Zola: Dictionnaire des Rougon-Macquart. (FRE.). 720p. 1993. pap. 49.95 (*0-7859-7813-5*, 2221076125) Fr & Eur.

Becker, Colette, ed. see Zola, Emile.

Becker Cotto, Deborah. On the Write Track: Beginning Literacy for Secondary Students. (Illus.). 178p. (YA). (gr. 6-12). 1997. pap. text 16.95 (*1-882483-38-3*) Alta Bk Ctr.

Becker, D. H. & Gardner, L. B. Prevention in Clinical Practice. LC 88-12568. (Illus.). 468p. (C). 1988. text 85.00 (*0-306-42624-2*, Kluwer Plenum) Kluwer Academic.

Becker, Dana. Through the Looking Glass: Women & Borderline Personality Disorders. LC 97-8091. (New Directions in Theory & Psychology Ser.). 224p. 1997. text 69.00 (*0-8133-3309-1*, Pub. by Westview) HarpC.

— Through the Looking Glass: Women & Borderline Personality Disorders. LC 97-8091. (New Directions in Theory & Psychology Ser.). 224p. (C). 1997. pap. text 24.00 (*0-8133-3310-5*, Pub. by Westview) HarpC.

Becker, Daniel E. Pharmacology. (C). 1993. student ed. 20.39 (*1-56870-094-6*) RonJon Pub.

Becker, Daniel G., jt. auth. see Toriumi, Dean M.

Becker, David. General Chemistry. 3rd ed. (C). 1997. pap. text, student ed. 23.95 (*0-7167-3032-4*) W H Freeman.

— Watercolor Composition Made Easy. LC 98-56085. (Illus.). 128p. 1999. 27.99 (*0-89134-891-3*, 31379, North Lght Bks) F & W Pubns Inc.

Becker, David G. The New Bourgeoisie & the Limits of Dependency; Mining, Class, & Power in "Revolutionary" Peru. LC 82-61352. 457p. 1983. reprint ed. pap. 141.70 (*0-608-02576-3*, 206322100004) Bks Demand.

Becker, David G. & Sklar, Richard L., eds. Postimperialism & World Politics. LC 98-56626. (Illus.). 408p. 1999. 69.50 (*0-275-96613-5*, C6613, Praeger Pubs) Greenwood.

Becker, David P. Old Master Drawings at Bowdoin College. LC 84-72390. (Illus.). 260p. (Orig.). 1985. 30.00 (*0-916606-08-2*); pap. 14.95 (*0-685-73717-9*) Bowdoin Coll.

— Vinalhaven at Bowdoin: One Press, Multiple Impressions. (Illus.). 24p. (Orig.). 1992. pap. 10.00 (*0-916606-23-6*) Bowdoin Coll.

Becker, David P., jt. auth. see Cohn, Marjorie B.

Becker, Dennis & Becker, Paula B. Customer Service & the Telephone. LC 94-340. (Business Skills Express Ser.). 112p. 1994. text 10.95 (*0-7863-0224-0*, Irwn Prfssnl) McGraw-Hill Prof.

— Powerful Presentation Skills. LC 93-16149. (Business Skills Express Ser.). 96p. 1993. pap. 10.95 (*1-55623-870-3*, Irwn Prfssnl) McGraw-Hill Prof.

Becker, Dennis, jt. auth. see Becker, Paula B.

Becker, Dennis, ed. see Becker, Nancy, et al.

Becker, Dianne, ed. see Long, Caroline B.

Becker, Dianne G., ed. see Long, Caroline C.

Becker, Dirk K., jt. auth. see Hoffman, Randy.

Becker, Don, ed. see Becker, Greg.

Becker, Donald. Reverse Dictionary of Urdu. (URD.). 1980. 38.00 (*0-8364-0656-7*, Pub. by Manohar) S Asia.

Becker, Donald C. Security Administration: A Practical Systems Approach. (Illus.). 224p. (C). 1985. 40.95 (*0-398-05064-3*) C C Thomas.

Becker, Donald P., et al. Textbook of Head Injury. (Illus.). 576p. 1989. text 220.00 (*0-7216-1614-3*, W B Saunders Co) Harcrt Hlth Sci Grp.

Becker, Donna L., jt. auth. see Becker, Harold K.

Becker-Donner, Etta. Hinterland Liberia. LC 74-15030. reprint ed. 56.00 (*0-404-12037-7*) AMS Pr.

Becker, Dotti, jt. auth. see Becker, Jim.

Becker, E., ed. see Burgisser, Peter.

Becker, E., ed. see Jungnickel, D.

Becker, E., ed. see Saito, Mutsumi, et al.

Becker, E. B., jt. auth. see Oden, J. Tinsley.

Becker, E. Lovell, ed. Membrane Activation in Immunologically Relevant Cells. (Progress in Allergy Ser.: Vol. 42). (Illus.). xiv, 312p. 1988. 191.50 (*3-8055-4699-8*) S Karger.

Becker, E. Robert & Pereira, Carmo J., eds. Computer-Aided Design. (Chemical Industries Ser.: Vol. 51). (Illus.). 640p. 1993. text 235.00 (*0-8247-9003-0*) Dekker.

Becker, E. W. Microalgae: Biotechnology & Microbiology. (Studies in Biotechnology: No. 10). (Illus.). 301p. (C). 1994. text 74.95 (*0-521-35020-4*) Cambridge U Pr.

Becker, Edwin D. High Resolution NMR: Theory & Clinical Applications. 2nd ed. (Illus.). 354p. 1995. reprint ed. pap. text 42.00 (*0-12-084661-6*) Acad Pr.

***Becker, Egon.** Sustainability & Social Science. LC 99-24860. 1999. spiral bd. 69.95 (*1-85649-708-9*) Zed Books.

***Becker, Egon & Jahnige, Thomas P., eds.** Sustainability & the Social Sciences. LC 99-24860. 336p. 1999. pap. 29.95 (*1-85649-709-7*) Zed Books.

***Becker, Eike.** Verbundnetz Gas AG, Leipzig: Headquarters Building becker gewers kuhn & kuhn architects. 1999. 29.95 (*3-7913-2130-7*) Prestel.

***Becker, Elizabeth.** Untitled or Spot Diner. 2001. (*0-8129-3162-9*) Random.

Becker, Elizabeth. When the War Was Over: Cambodia & the Khmer Rouge Revolution. rev. ed. LC 98-37790. 624p. 1998. pap. text 17.00 (*1-891620-00-2*, Pub. by PublicAffairs NY) HarpC.

— When the War Was Over: Cambodia's Revolution & the Voices of Its People. (Illus.). 502p. 1986. 19.95 (*0-671-41787-8*) S&S Trade.

Becker, Elle. How to Live with a Spinal Cord Injury. LC 89-85624. (Illus.). 96p. (Orig.). 1989. pap. 6.95 (*0-915708-27-2*) Cheever Pub.

— Love - Where to Find It, How to Keep It. 106p. (Orig.). 1991. pap. 6.95 (*0-915708-32-9*) Cheever Pub.

Becker, Elle & Mauro, Robert. How to Live Longer with a Disability. Garee, Betty, ed. LC 94-70772. 300p. 1994. pap. 11.50 (*0-915708-38-8*) Cheever Pub.

Becker, Ellen. Gold Leaf Application & Antique Restoration. LC 98-86263. (Illus.). 96p. (Orig.). 1999. pap. 19.95 (*0-7643-0632-4*) Schiffer.

Becker, Eric V. De, see De Becker, Eric V.

Becker, Ernest. The Birth & Death of Meaning. 2nd ed. LC 62-15359. 228p. 1971. pap. 16.95 (*0-02-902190-1*) Free Pr.

— The Denial of Death. LC 73-1860. 1985. pap. 14.95 (*0-02-902380-7*) Free Pr.

— The Denial of Death. 320p. 1997. per. 12.00 (*0-684-83240-2*) Free Pr.

— The Denial of Death. 1998. 25.25 (*0-8446-6932-6*) Peter Smith.

— Escape from Evil. LC 75-12059. 1985. pap. 14.95 (*0-02-902450-1*) Free Pr.

Becker, Ethel A. Klondike 98: E. A. Hegg's Gold Rush Album. rev. ed. LC 67-27689. 1967. 14.95 (*0-8323-0000-4*) Binford Mort.

Becker, Eve. Sarah Michelle Geller, Scene 4. (Illus.). 32p. (J). (gr. 4-9). 1998. pap. 6.99 (*0-689-82406-8*) Aladdin.

Becker, Evvie, et al. High-Risk Sexual Behavior: Interventions with Vulnerable Populations. LC 98-28252. (Prevention in Practice Library). (Illus.) 180p. (C). 1998. pap. text 22.50 (*0-306-45858-6*, Kluwer Plenum) Kluwer Academic.

— High-Risk Sexual Behavior: Interventions with Vulnerable Populations. LC 98-28252. (Prevention in Practice Library). (Illus.). 180p. (C). 1998. 39.50 (*0-306-45857-8*, Plenum Trade) Perseus Pubng.

Becker, Evvie, jt. auth. see Rickel, Annette U.

Becker, F. Satellite Remote Sensing for Operational Hydrology, Vol. 4. (Remote Sensing Reviews Ser.). 472p. 1990. text 299.00 (*3-7186-5056-8*, Harwood Acad Pubs) Gordon & Breach.

Becker, F., ed. see Ismailov, T. K.

Becker, F., ed. see Kobayashi, T.

Becker, F., ed. see Matzler, C.

Becker, F., ed. see Tsuchiya, K.

Becker, Franklin & Steele, Fritz. Workplace by Design: Mapping the High-Performance Workscape. LC 94-32960. (Management Ser.). 246p. 1995. mass mkt. 27.00 (*0-7879-0047-8*) Jossey-Bass.

Becker, Frawley. 411 Joseph. 115p. (C). Date not set. pap. 5.60 (*0-87129-883-X*, F63) Dramatic Pub.

Becker, Frederick F., ed. Cancer: A Comprehensive Treatise. Incl. Biology of Tumors: Surfaces, Immunology & Comparative Pathology. 440p. 1975. 75.00 (*0-306-35204-4*, Kluwer Plenum); Chemotherapy. 566p. 1977. 75.00 (*0-306-35205-2*, Kluwer Plenum); Radiotherapy, Surgery & Immunotherapy. 544p. 1977. 75.00 (*0-306-35206-0*, Kluwer Plenum); Vol. 2. Etiology: Viral Carcinogenesis. 440p. 1975. 75.00 (*0-306-35202-8*, Kluwer Plenum); Vol. 3. Biology of Tumors: Cellular Biology & Growth. 474p. 1975. 75.00 (*0-306-35203-6*, Kluwer Plenum); (Illus.). write for info. (*0-318-55312-0*, Plenum Trade) Perseus Pubng.

— The Liver: Normal & Abnormal Functions, 2 pts., Pt. 1. LC 74-77112. (Biochemistry of Disease Ser.: No. 5). (Illus.). 590p. reprint ed. pap. 182.90 (*0-7837-0894-7*, 204120000001) Bks Demand.

— The Liver: Normal & Abnormal Functions, 2 pts., Pt. 2. LC 74-77112. (Biochemistry of Disease Ser.: No. 5). (Illus.). 465p. reprint ed. pap. 144.20 (*0-7837-0895-5*, 204120000002) Bks Demand.

Becker, Frederick F., et al, eds. Cancer Vol. 1: A Comprehensive Treatise, Etiology: Chemical & Physical Carcinogenesis. 2nd ed. LC 81-21050. 736p. 1982. 125.00 (*0-306-40701-9*, Plenum Trade) Perseus Pubng.

Becker, Friedrich. Friedrich Becker, Kinetic Jewelry. 1997. 108.00 (*3-925369-76-7*, Pub. by Arnoldsche Art Pubs) Antique Collect.

Becker, G. & Sabatier, Roland. Le Gratin des Champignons. (FRE., Illus.). 224p. 1986. lib. bdg. 55.00 (*2-7234-0624-5*) Lubrecht & Cramer.

Becker, G. & Slattery, Kathy. A System Administrator's Guide to Sun Workstations. (Sun Technical Reference Library). (Illus.). 296p. 1994. 53.95 (*0-387-97250-1*) Spr-Verlag.

Becker, G. & Theden, G., eds. Annual Report on Wood Protection, 1955.Tr. of Jahresberichte Ueber Holzschutz. viii, 170p. 1956. 36.95 (*0-387-02057-8*) Spr-Verlag.

— Annual Report on Wood Protection, 1959-1960.Tr. of Jahresberichte Ueber Holzschutz. v, 481p. 1969. 92.95 (*0-387-04576-7*) Spr-Verlag.

— Annual Report on Wood Protection, 1961-62. 1972. 79.95 (*0-387-05827-3*) Spr-Verlag.

Becker, G. F., jt. auth. see Emmons, S. F.

Becker, Gail. Anti-Oxidant Pocket Counter: A Guide to the Essential Nutrients That Help Fight Cancer. 1993. pap. 3.99 (*0-8129-2143-7*, Times Bks) Crown Pub Group.

Becker, Gail L. Supplement Savvy: A Shopper's Guide to Brand-Name Supplements. LC 97-212521. 480p. 1997. mass mkt. 6.50 (*0-440-22304-0*) Dell.

Becker, Gary. Accounting for Tastes. (Illus.). 256p. 1996. 35.00 (*0-674-54356-4*) HUP.

Becker, Gary & Becker, Guity N. The Economics of Life: From Baseball to Affirmative Action to Immigration, How Real-World Issues Affect Our Everyday Life. 352p. 1998. pap. 14.95 (*0-07-006709-0*, BusinessWeek Bks) McGraw.

Becker, Gary D., jt. auth. see Radford, Elaine R.

Becker, Gary J., jt. auth. see Perler, Bruce A.

Becker, Gary J., jt. ed. see Perler, Bruce A.

Becker, Gary Stanley. Accounting for Tastes. (Illus.). 288p. 1998. pap. text 17.95 (*0-674-54357-2*) HUP.

— The Economic Approach to Human Behavior. LC 75-43240. 320p. 1978. reprint ed. pap. text 17.00 (*0-226-04112-3*, P803) U Ch Pr.

— The Economic Way of Looking At Behavior: The Nobel Lecture. LC 96-20372. (Essays in Public Policy Ser.: No. 69). 31p. 1996. pap. 5.00 (*0-8179-5742-1*) Hoover Inst Pr.

— Economics of Discrimination. 2nd rev. ed. LC 73-157422. (Economic Research Studies). 178p. 1971. pap. text 11.95 (*0-226-04116-6*, P393) U Ch Pr.

— Human Capital: A Theoretical & Empirical Analysis, with Special Reference to Education. LC 93-24690. 412p. 1994. pap. text 18.00 (*0-226-04120-4*) U Ch Pr.

— Human Capital: A Theoretical & Empirical Analysis, with Special Reference to Education. LC 93-24690. 1994. lib. bdg. 50.00 (*0-226-04119-0*) U Ch Pr.

— Human Capital: A Theoretical & Empirical Analysis with Special Reference to Education. 2nd ed. xx, 268p. 1983. pap. text 15.95 (*0-226-04109-3*, Midway Reprint) U Ch Pr.

***Becker, Gary Stanley.** Social Economics: Market Behavior in a Social Environment. 224p. 2001. 29.95 (*0-674-00337-3*) HUP.

Becker, Gary Stanley. A Treatise on the Family. enl. ed. 424p. 1993. pap. 24.95 (*0-674-90699-3*) HUP.

— A Treatise on the Family. enl. ed. LC 90-4975. (Illus.). 432p. 1994. 55.50 (*0-674-90698-5*, BECTRR) HUP.

Becker, Gary Stanley & Becker, Guity N. The Economics of Life: From Baseball to Affirmative Action to Immigration, How Real-World Issues Affect Our Everyday Life. LC 96-24445. 352p. 1996. 25.00 (*0-07-005943-8*) McGraw.

Becker, Gary Stanley & Landes, William M., eds. Essays in the Economics of Crime & Punishment. LC 73-88507. (Human Behavior & Social Institutions Ser.: No. 3). 288p. reprint ed. pap. 89.30 (*0-608-10824-3*, 205170300005) Bks Demand.

— Essays in the Economics of Crime & Punishment. 287p. 1974. reprint ed. 72.00 (*0-87014-263-1*) Natl Bur Econ Res.

Becker, Gary Stanley, jt. auth. see Ghez, Gilbert R.

Becker, Gavin J., et al. Clinical Nephrology in Medical Practice. (Essentials Ser.). (Illus.). 400p. 1992. 100.00 (*0-632-03167-0*) Blackwell Sci.

Becker, Gay. Disrupted Lives: How People Create Meaning in a Chaotic World. LC 96-52482. 275p. 1997. 27.50 (*0-520-20913-3*, Pub. by U CA Pr) Cal Prin Full Svc.

***Becker, Gay.** The Elusive Embryo: How Women & Men Approach New Reproductive Technologies. 368p. 2000. 45.00 (*0-520-22430-2*); pap. 17.95 (*0-520-22431-0*) U CA Pr.

Becker, Gaylene. Growing Old in Silence. LC 79-63548. 160p. 1980. pap. 16.95 (*0-520-05058-4*, Pub. by U CA Pr) Cal Prin Full Svc.

— Healing the Infertile Family: Strengthening Your Relationship in the Search for Parenthood. LC 97-8565. 327p. 1997. pap. 15.95 (*0-520-21180-4*, Pub. by U CA Pr) Cal Prin Full Svc.

Becker, Geoffrey. Bluestown. 1997. pap. 11.95 (*0-312-15481-X*) St Martin.

— Dangerous Men. 161p. (C). 1995. 22.50 (*0-8229-3899-5*) U of Pittsburgh Pr.

Becker, George. The Mad Genius Controversy: A Study in the Sociology of Deviance. LC 78-875. (Sociological Observations Ser.: No. 5). 152p. reprint ed. pap. 47.20 (*0-608-09954-6*, 202186900026) Bks Demand.

B

Becker, George J. Ornamental Calligraphy. LC 93-2454. (Illus.). 64p. 1993. reprint ed. pap. text 5.95 (*0-486-27678-3*) Dover.

— Television & the Classroom Reading Program: If You Can't Beat 'Em Join 'Em. LC 73-89304. (Reading Aids Ser.). 32p. reprint ed. pap. 30.00 (*0-608-16692-8*, 202679200052) Bks Demand.

Becker, George J., ed. Documents of Modern Literary Realism. LC 63-7064. 621p. reprint ed. pap. 192.60 (*0-8357-8863-6*, 203338000085) Bks Demand.

Becker, George J., tr. see Sartre, Jean-Paul.

Becker, Gerhold K., ed. Ethics in Business & Society: Chinese & Western Perspectives. LC 96-3976. (Studies in Economic Ethics & Philosophy Ser.). (Illus.). 232p. 1996. text 79.00 (*3-540-60773-0*) Spr-Verlag.

Becker, Gerhold K. & Buchanan, James P., eds. Changing Nature's Course: The Ethical Challenge of Biotechnology. LC 97-143402. 208p. (Orig.). 1996. pap. 39.50 (*962-209-403-1*, Pub. by HK Univ Pr) Coronet Bks.

Becker, Greg. The Seagoing Hitchhiker's Handbook: Roaming the Earth on Other People's Yachts. Marin, Estela, ed. LC 95-126387. 224p. (Orig.). 1994. pap. 11.95 (*0-9639712-0-4*) High Adventure.

— So You Want to Buy a Diamond: A No-Nonsense Guide. Becker, Don & Hines, Bill, eds. (Illus.). (Orig.). 1994. pap. 3.95 (*0-9639712-1-2*) High Adventure.

B

Becker, Guity N., jt. auth. see Becker, Gary.

Becker, Guity N., jt. auth. see Becker, Gary Stanley.

Becker, Gustav. Catalogi Bibliothecarum Antiqui, 2 vols. in 1. iv, 350p. 1973. reprint ed. 168.00 (*3-487-04752-7*) G Olms Pubs.

Becker, H. & Kechris, A. S. The Descriptive Set Theory of Polish Group Actions. (London Mathematical Society Lecture Note Ser.: No. 232). 147p. (C). 1996. pap. text 37.95 (*0-521-57605-9*) Cambridge U Pr.

Becker, H. & Manz, A., eds. Microsystem Technology in Chemistry & Life Sciences. (Topics in Current Chemistry Ser.: Vol. 194). (Illus.). 262p. 1997. text 159.00 (*3-540-63424-X*) Spr-Verlag.

Becker, H., jt. ed. see Manz, A.

Becker, H. D., et al, eds. Surgery of the Stomach. (Illus.). 390p. 1988. 284.00 (*0-387-17116-9*) Spr-Verlag.

Becker, H. D. & Caspary, W. F. Postgastrectomy & Postvagatomy Syndromes. (Illus.). 500p. 1980. 108.00 (*0-387-09445-8*) Spr-Verlag.

Becker, H. Neil, et al. Care & Management of Miniature Pet Pigs: Guidelines for the Veterinary Practitioner. Reeves, David E., ed. (Illus.). 117p. (Orig.). Date not set. pap. 40.00 (*0-9603534-3-7*) Vet Practice.

***Becker, Hal.** At Your Service: Calamities, Catastrophes, & Other Curiosities of Customer Service. LC 98-16190. 288p. 1998. pap. 17.95 (*0-471-25542-4*) Wiley.

Becker, Hal. Can I Have 5 Minutes of Your Time? A No-Nonsense, Fun Approach to Sales. 160p. 1999. reprint ed. pap. 12.95 (*0-9619590-7-X*) OakHill Pr VA.

Becker, Hans J. Das Tomale Guigos I. (GER.). xxvi, 283p. 1975. 44.80 (*3-615-00156-7*, Pub. by Weidmann) Lubrecht & Cramer.

Becker, Harold K. & Becker, Donna L. Handbook of the World's Police. LC 85-26253. (Illus.). 350p. 1985. 34.50 (*0-8108-1863-9*) Scarecrow.

Becker, Heiko, jt. auth. see Diepenbrock, Wulf.

Becker, Helene. Teaching ESL K-12: Views from the Classroom. (Teachersource Ser.). 2001. 20.95 (*0-8384-7901-4*) Heinle & Heinle.

Becker, Helmut, jt. ed. see Thorelli, Hans B.

Becker, Henk. Social Impact Assessment Method & Experience in Europe, North America & the Developing World. LC 98-102226. 320p. 1997. 65.00 (*1-85728-346-5*, Pub. by UCL Pr Ltd); pap. 27.50 (*1-85728-347-3*, Pub. by UCL Pr Ltd) Taylor & Francis.

Becker, Henk A. & Porter, Alan L. Methods & Experiences in Impact Assessment. 1986. text 158.50 (*90-277-2264-1*) Kluwer Academic.

Becker, Herbert L. John Lennon - Between the Lines. 200p. 1997. pap. 29.99 (*1-890167-01-0*) MagicWeb.

— More Magic Secrets . . . All the Secrets of Magic Revealed. (Illus.). 1997. pap. 29.99 incl. cd-rom (*1-890167-26-6*) MagicWeb.

— More Magic Secrets . . . All the Secrets of Magic Revealed. rev. ed. (Illus.). 190p. (YA). 1997. pap. 19.99 (*1-890167-25-8*) MagicWeb.

***Becker, Herbert L.** 101 Greatest Magic Secrets: A Tell-All Guide to the Most Amazing Tricks & Illusions of All Time. 1999. pap. text 14.00 (*0-8065-2154-6*, Birch Ln Pr) Carol Pub Group.

Becker, Herbert L., ed. see Hobby Maker Incorporated Staff.

Becker, Hilton. What Are You Putting on Your Skin. 80p. 1997. pap. write for info. (*1-883928-24-9*) Longwood.

Becker Holstein, Barbara. The Enchanted Self: A Positive Therapy. LC 99-458455. 144p. 1997. 55.00 (*90-5702-502-7*, Harwood Acad Pubs); pap. text 18.00 (*90-5702-503-5*, Harwood Acad Pubs) Gordon & Breach.

Becker, Howard & Barnes, Harry E. Social Thought from Lore to Science, Vols. 2 & 3. 3rd ed. 1990. 37.00 (*0-8446-1620-6*) Peter Smith.

Becker, Howard P. Through Values to Social Interpretation: Essays on Social Contexts, Actions, Types & Prospects. LC 69-10068. 341p. 1968. reprint ed. lib. bdg. 35.00 (*0-8371-0014-3*, BESI, Greenwood Pr) Greenwood.

Becker, Howard S. Art Worlds. LC 81-2694. (Illus.). 408p. 1982. pap. 19.95 (*0-520-05218-8*, Pub. by U CA Pr) Cal Prin Full Svc.

— Becoming a Marihuana User. (Reprint Series in Sociology). (C). 1993. reprint ed. pap. text 1.00 (*0-8290-2619-3*, S-9) Irvington.

— Boys in White: Student Culture in Medical School. LC 91-16622. 456p. Date not set. reprint ed. pap. 141.40 (*0-608-21000-5*, 205452800003) Bks Demand.

Becker, Howard S. Exploring Society Photographically. 1981. pap. 11.95 (*0-226-04097-6*) U Ch Pr.

Becker, Howard S. Outsiders. 224p. 1997. 14.95 (*0-684-83635-1*) Free Pr.

— Outsiders: Studies in the Sociology of Deviance. LC 63-8413. 1966. pap. 14.95 (*0-02-902140-5*) Free Pr.

— Problems of Inference & Proof in Participant Observation. (Reprint Series in Social Sciences). (C). 1993. reprint ed. pap. text 1.00 (*0-8290-3493-5*, S-337) Irvington.

— The Professional Dance Musician & His Audience. (Reprint Series in Sociology). (C). 1993. reprint ed. pap. text 5.00 (*0-8290-2620-7*, S-10) Irvington.

— Role & Career Problems of the Chicago Public School Teacher. Zuckerman, Harriet & Merton, Robert K., eds. LC 79-8974. (Dissertations on Sociology Ser.). 1980. lib. bdg. 31.95 (*0-405-12951-3*) Ayer.

— Tricks of the Trade: How to Think about Your Research While You're Doing It. LC 97-19618. 264p. 1997. 35.00 (*0-226-04123-9*); pap. 14.00 (*0-226-04124-7*) U Ch Pr.

— Writing for Social Scientists: How to Start & Finish Your Thesis, Book, or Article. LC 85-16504. (Chicago Guides to Writing, Editing & Publishing Ser.). xii, 192p. 1986. pap. 10.00 (*0-226-04108-5*); lib. bdg. 20.00 (*0-226-04107-7*) U Ch Pr.

Becker, Howard S., ed. Campus Power Struggle. rev. ed. LC 72-91466. 191p. (C). 1970. reprint ed. pap. text 19.95 (*0-87855-556-0*) Transaction Pubs.

— Campus Power Struggle. 2nd rev. ed. LC 72-91466. 191p. (C). 1970. reprint ed. 32.95 (*0-87855-059-3*) Transaction Pubs.

— Culture & Civility in San Francisco. (Illus.). 164p. 1971. reprint ed. pap. text 19.95 (*0-87855-568-4*) Transaction Pubs.

— Exploring Society Photographically. (C). 1981. 11.95 (*0-941680-00-2*, 04097-6) M&L Block.

Becker, Howard S., et al, eds. Boys in White: Student Culture in Medical School. rev. ed. LC 76-26951. 456p. 1991. reprint ed. pap. text 24.95 (*0-87855-622-2*) Transaction Pubs.

Becker, Howard S. & McCall, Michal M., eds. Symbolic Interaction & Cultural Studies. LC 89-48060. 294p. 1990. pap. text 17.95 (*0-226-04118-2*) U Ch Pr.

— Symbolic Interaction & Cultural Studies. LC 89-48060. 296p. 1993. lib. bdg. 37.50 (*0-226-04117-4*) U Ch Pr.

Becker, Howard S. & Strauss, Anslem L. Careers, Personality, & Adult Socialization. (Reprint Series in Social Sciences). (C). 1993. reprint ed. pap. text 5.00 (*0-8290-2731-9*, S-11) Irvington.

Becker, Howard S., et al. Boys in White: Student Culture in Medical School. LC 61-16622. 470p. reprint ed. pap. 145.70 (*0-608-09383-1*, 205412800004) Bks Demand.

— Exploring Society Photographically. LC 81-83668. (Illus.). 96p. 1981. pap. 8.00 (*0-317-60926-2*) M&L Block.

— Making the Grade: The Academic Side of College Life. LC 94-41458. 1995. pap. 21.95 (*1-56000-807-5*) Transaction Pubs.

Becker, Howard S., jt. ed. see Ragin, Charles C.

Becker, Howard S., ed. & tr. see Candido, Antonio.

Becker, Hugh, jt. auth. see Glad, Ernest.

Becker, Hyam Y. The Temple of Hashem. LC 97-42614. 312p. 1998. text 10.95 (*965-229-156-0*) Gefen Bks.

Becker, I. Antiviral Drugs. Melnick, Joseph L., ed. (Monographs in Virology: Vol. 11). (Illus.). 1976. 65.25 (*3-8055-2248-7*) S Karger.

Becker, Irving, jt. auth. see Ellis, Albert.

Becker, J. D., et al, eds. Parallelism, Learning, Evolution: Workshop on Evolutionary Models & Strategies, Neubiberg, Germany, March 10-11, 1989 Workshop on Parallel Processing: Logic, Organization & Technology - WOPPLOT 89, Wildbad Kreuth, Germany, July 24-28, 1989 Proceedings. (Lecture Notes in Artificial Intelligence Ser.: Vol. 565). viii, 525p. 1991. 69.95 (*0-387-55027-5*) Spr-Verlag.

Becker, J. D. & Eisele, I., eds. WOPPLOT 86 Parallel Processing-Logic, Organization, & Technology. (Lecture Notes in Computer Science Ser.: Vol. 253). v, 226p. 1987. 33.00 (*0-387-18022-2*) Spr-Verlag.

Becker, J. J ., et al, eds. Magnetism & Magnetic Materials: Proceedings, 1975. LC 76-10931. (AIP Conference Proceedings Ser.: No. 29). 693p. 1976. 30.00 (*0-88318-128-2*) Am Inst Physics.

Becker, J. R. Corrosion & Scale Handbook. LC 98-39571. 1998. 74.95 (*0-87814-749-7*) PennWell Bks.

— Crude Oil Waxes, Emulsions, & Asphaltenes. LC 97-31816. 1997. 74.95 (*0-87814-737-3*) PennWell Bks.

Becker, Jack, jt. auth. see Wolschke-Bulmahn, Joachim.

Becker, Jack D. & Hassan, Nik R. International Directory of Information Systems - Technology Research Centers, 1993. 80p. (Orig.). 1992. pap. 15.00 (*0-9635569-0-8*) U NTX Col Busn.

Becker, James. Mentoring High-Risk Kids. LC 93-46107. 51p. 1994. pap. 6.50 (*1-56246-092-7*, 3209, Hazelden/Johnson Inst) Hazelden.

Becker, James F. Marxian Political Economy: An Outline. LC 76-9172. 336p. reprint ed. pap. 95.80 (*0-608-18409-8*, 2030580) Bks Demand.

Becker, Jan, et al. Enhance Chance. (Illus.). 58p. (Orig.). (J). (gr. k-9). 1995. pap. 8.50 (*0-918932-10-6*, A-1107) Activity Resources.

Becker, Jane & Franco, Barbara. Folkroots, New Roots: Folklore in American Life. LC 88-50979. (Illus.). 196p. 1989. pap. 17.95 (*0-9622107-2-2*) H Sanoff.

Becker, Jane & Franco, Barbara, eds. Folk Roots, New Roots: Folklore in American Life. (Illus.). xvii, 196p. 1988. pap. 17.95 (*0-9621107-2-8*) Mus Our Natl Hertge.

Becker, Jane R., jt. ed. see Weisberg, Gabriel P.

Becker, Jane S. Selling Tradition: Appalachia & the Construction of an American Folk, 1930-1940. LC 97-40858. (Illus.). 360p. 1998. pap. 18.95 (*0-8078-4715-1*); lib. bdg. 55.00 (*0-8078-2408-9*) U of NC Pr.

Becker, Jaqueline H. Staying Alive & Other Poems. 56p. 1994. pap. 9.95 (*0-9644685-0-6*) ICA Becker Ent.

Becker, Jared. Eugenio Montale (TWAS 778 Italy) (Twayne's World Authors Series, Italy: No. 778). 224p. (C). 1986. 32.00 (*0-8057-6633-2*) Macmillan.

Becker, Jared M. Nationalsim & Culture Vol. 11: Gabriele D'Annunzio & Italy after the Risorgimento. LC 93-16377. (Studies in Italian Culture: Vol. 11). 226p. (C). 1995. text 46.95 (*0-8204-2085-9*) P Lang Pubng.

***Becker, Jasper.** The Chinese. 2001. 26.00 (*0-684-84412-5*) Free Pr.

Becker, Jasper. Hungry Ghosts. LC 97-44007. (Illus.). 352p. 1998. 14.95 (*0-8050-5668-8*, Owl) H Holt & Co.

— Hungry Ghosts: Mao's Secret Famine. LC 96-32803. (Illus.). 352p. 1997. 24.50 (*0-684-83457-X*) Free Pr.

— The Lost Country: Mongolia Revealed. (Illus.). 325p. 1992. lib. bdg. 35.00 (*0-340-55665-X*, Pub. by Hodder & Stought Ltd) Lubrecht & Cramer.

Becker, Jasper B. Truth or Consequences: New Vision for Health & Healing. (Illus.). 176p. 1998. pap. 16.00 (*0-9664194-0-5*) J Becker.

Becker, Jay, et al. Practice Book for the RCT in U. S. History & Government. 157p. 1990. student ed. 8.95 (*0-910307-23-7*) Comp Pr.

Becker, Jean, jt. auth. see Hinds, Joan.

Becker, Jean-Jacques. The Great War & the French People. 344p. 1986. pap. 19.50 (*0-907582-53-2*, Pub. by Berg Pubs) NYU Pr.

Becker, Jeffrey M., et al. Biotechnology: A Laboratory Course. 2nd ed. (Illus.). 261p. 1996. spiral bd. 33.95 (*0-12-084562-8*) Acad Pr.

Becker, Jerry P. & Shimada, Shigeru, eds. The Open-Ended Approach: A New Proposal for Teaching Mathematics. LC 97-12708. (Illus.). 175p. 1997. pap. 23.95 (*0-87353-430-1*) NCTM.

Becker, Jill B., et al, eds. Behavioral Endocrinology. (Illus.). 688p. 1992. pap. text 42.00 (*0-262-52171-7*, Bradford Bks) MIT Pr.

Becker, Jillian. The Soviet Connection: State Sponsorship of Terrorism. (C). 1990. 40.00 (*0-907967-60-4*, Pub. by Inst Euro Def & Strat) St Mut.

— The Soviet Connection: State Sponsorship of Terrorism. (C). 1981. pap. 29.00 (*0-907967-69-8*) St Mut.

Becker, Jim. The Glove Compartment Car Care Book: Everything You Need to Keep Your Car Running Smoothly & Cheaply! 72p. 1994. pap. 3.49 (*0-393-30991-6*) Norton.

— Where Does All the Money Go? 1992. pap. 69.80 (*0-393-30900-2*) Norton.

— You Can Name 100 Trucks! (Illus.). 14p. (J). (ps-k). 1994. bds. 8.95 (*0-590-46402-0*, Cartwheel) Scholastic Inc.

Becker, Jim & Becker, Dotti. An Everlasting Garden. 2nd rev. ed. Ligon, Linda C., ed. (Illus.). 96p. 1994. pap. 12.95 (*0-934026-92-0*) Interweave.

Becker, Jim & Brawner, Faye. Scented Geraniums: Knowing, Growing, & Enjoying More Than 100 Varieties. (Illus.). 96p. 1996. pap. 14.95 (*1-883010-18-7*) Interweave.

Becker, Jim & Mayer, Andy. Build Your Own Radio. LC 91-52875. (Discovery Kit Ser.). (Illus.). 64p. (Orig.). (J). (gr. 4-7). 1992. student ed. 19.95 (*1-56138-071-7*) Running Pr.

— Mouse House. LC 95-183060. (Illus.). 44p. (Orig.). 1995. pap. 9.95 (*0-14-024441-7*, Penguin Bks) Viking Penguin.

— Where Does All the Money Go? Taking Control of Your Personal Expenses. 1992. pap. 3.49 (*0-393-30899-5*) Norton.

Becker, Jim, et al. Golf Dirty Tricks: Fifty Ways to Lie, Cheat & Steal Your Way to Victory. LC 93-41142. (Illus.). 112p. 1994. 8.95 (*0-8362-4224-6*) Andrews & McMeel.

— Good Dog, Millie: A Day in the Life of America's Most Influential Canine. LC 92-9152. 1992. 107.40 (*0-02-508202-7*) Macmillan.

— You Can Be a Doctor in Thirty Minutes. LC 84-3638. 12p. (Orig.). 1984. mass mkt. 6.95 (*0-446-38101-2*, Pub. by Warner Bks) Little.

Becker, Jim, jt. auth. see Mayer, Andy.

Becker, Joachim. Messianic Expectation in the Old Testament. 1996. 35.95 (*0-567-09302-6*) Bks Intl VA.

— Messianic Expectation in the Old Testament. Green, David E., tr. LC 79-8891. 96p. reprint ed. pap. 30.00 (*0-608-17175-1*, 202787500056) Bks Demand.

Becker, Joachim, ed. see Schmid, Wolfgang P.

Becker, Jocelyn. How to Program Bongo. 326p. 1997. pap. text 39.99 incl. cd-rom (*1-56276-534-5*, Ziff-Davis Pr) Que.

— San Francisco Bay Tripper: Twenty Exciting Day Trips in the San Francisco Bay Area. (Illus.). 208p. (Orig.). 1994. pap. 10.00 (*0-9637073-0-2*) Brighter Bks.

Becker, John. Seven Little Rabbits. LC 72-86974. (Illus.). 32p. (J). (ps-k). 1991. pap. 4.99 (*0-590-44849-8*, Blue Ribbon Bks) Scholastic Inc.

— Seven Little Rabbits. 2nd ed. Cooney, Barbara, tr. (Illus.). 32p. (J). (ps-3). 1994. reprint ed. 5.95 (*0-8027-8311-2*) Walker & Co.

Becker, John Leonard. Seven Little Rabbits. (Blue Ribbon Bks.). (J). 1973. 10.19 (*0-606-01183-8*, Pub. by Turtleback) Demco.

Becker, John W. If Silence Should Speak. 182p. (Orig.). 1994. pap. 8.50 (*0-9641319-0-0*) Legation Pr.

***Becker, Jonathan J.** Great Dads. LC 00-28868. 256p. 2000. pap. 10.95 (*1-58062-277-1*) Adams Media.

Becker, Jonathan J. Neogene Avian Localities of North America. LC 87-42557. 200p. (Orig.). (C). 1987. pap. text 19.95 (*0-87474-225-0*) Smithsonian.

Becker, Joni, et al. Themestorming. (Illus.). 308p. (Orig.). 1994. pap. text 24.95 (*0-87659-170-5*) Gryphon Hse.

Becker, Jorg, et al, eds. Communication & Domination: Essays in Honor of Herbert I. Schiller. (Communication & Information Science Ser.). 288p. 1986. text 73.25 (*0-89391-380-4*) Ablx Pub.

Becker, Josef & Knipping, Franz, eds. Power in Europe? Great Britain, France, Italy & Germany in a Postwar World, 1945-1950, Contributions to an International Colloquim at Augsburg, April 1984. viii, 583p. 1986. lib. bdg. 169.25 (*3-11-010608-6*) De Gruyter.

Becker, Joseph & Hayes, Robert M. Information Storage & Retrieval: Tools, Elements, Theories. LC 63-12279. (Information Sciences Ser.). 460p. reprint ed. pap. 142.60 (*0-608-11145-7*, 201953300013) Bks Demand.

Becker, Joseph & Kleinman, Arthur, eds. Psychosocial Aspects of Depression. 272p. (C). 1990. text 89.95 (*0-8058-0079-4*) L Erlbaum Assocs.

Becker, Joseph E. De, see De Becker, Joseph E.

Becker, Joseph F., et al. Novel Laser Sources & Applications: Proceedings of a Workshop Held November 12-13, 1993, San Jose, California, USA. LC 94-29108. 1994. 30.00 (*0-8194-1512-X*, PM16) SPIE.

Becker, Joseph M. Experience Rating in Unemployment Insurance: An Experiment in Competitive Socialism. LC 72-4026. 422p. reprint ed. pap. 130.90 (*0-608-13619-0*, 202076300018) Bks Demand.

— In Aid of the Unemployed. LC 78-17906. (Illus.). 317p. 1978. reprint ed. lib. bdg. 69.50 (*0-313-20534-5*, BEIA, Greenwood Pr) Greenwood.

Becker, Joyce R. Nature's Patterns: Inspirations & Techniques for Quilt Makers. LC 95-38016. (Illus.). 176p. 1996. pap. 24.95 (*0-8442-2648-3*, Quilt Dgst Pr) NTC Contemp Pub Co.

Becker, Judith. Gamelan Stories: Tantrism, Islam, & Aesthetics in Central Java. LC 98-127916. (Illus.). iv, 222p. (Orig.). 1993. pap. 24.95 (*1-881044-06-8*) ASU Prog SE Asian.

Becker, Judith, ed. Karawitan: Source Readings in Javanese Gamelan & Vocal Music, Vol. 1-3. (Illus.). (C). pap. text 105.00 (*0-472-53005-4*) Ctr S&SE Asian.

Becker, Judith & Feinstein, Alan H., eds. Karawitan: Source Readings in Javanese Gamelan & Vocal Music. LC 82-72445. (Michigan Papers on South & Southeast Asia: No. 31). 503p. (C). 1988. 41.95 (*0-89148-041-2*) Ctr S&SE Asian.

— Karawitan: Source Readings in Javanese Gamelan & Vocal Music, Vol. 1. LC 82-72445. (Michigan Papers on South & Southeast Asia: No. 23). xviii, 526p. 1984. 41.95 (*0-89148-027-7*) Ctr S&SE Asian.

— Karawitan: Source Readings in Javanese Gamelan & Vocal Music, Vol. 2. LC 82-72445. (Michigan Papers on South & Southeast Asia: No. 30). 401p. (C). 1987. 41.95 (*0-89148-034-X*) Ctr S&SE Asian.

Becker, Judith, et al. Fine-Tuning: An NCCB Report on Noncommercial Radio. 1980. pap. 5.00 (*0-9603466-4-3*) T R A C.

Becker, Judith, jt. auth. see Becker, Ross.

Becker, Judith O. Traditional Music in Modern Java: Gamelan in Changing Society. LC 80-19180. (Illus.). 271p. reprint ed. pap. 77.30 (*0-608-18188-9*, 2032916) Bks Demand.

Becker, Judy. The Missing Message of Revelation: Natural Catastrophes Ordained by God. (Illus.). 374p. (Orig.). 1986. pap. 9.95 (*0-9617493-0-X*) Judy Becker.

Becker, Juergen. Annaeherungen: Zur Urchristlichen Theologiegeschichte und zum Umgang mit Ihren Quellen. Bd. 76. (GER.). 508p. (C). 1994. lib. bdg. 136.95 (*3-11-014551-0*) De Gruyter.

— Jesus von Nazaret. (GER.). xi, 460p. (C). 1995. pap. text 29.95 (*3-11-014882-X*); lib. bdg. 56.95 (*3-11-014881-1*) De Gruyter.

Becker, Jules. The Course of Exclusion, 1882-1924: San Francisco Newspaper Coverage of the Chinese & Japanese in the United States. LC 91-25795. 344p. 1991. lib. bdg. 99.95 (*0-7734-9874-5*) E Mellen.

***Becker, Juliette.** A Carefree Wedding: Postcards from Your Mind's Eye - Creative Stress Management. unabridged ed. 1999. 19.95 incl. audio (*1-928667-02-3*); 19.95 incl. audio compact disk (*1-928667-00-7*) Postcards MindsEye.

Becker, Jurek. Bronstein's Children. Vennewitz, Leila, tr. 1988. pap. 19.95 (*0-15-114350-1*) Harcourt.

— Bronstein's Children. LC 98-51315. 1999. pap. 15.00 (*0-226-04127-1*) U Ch Pr.

— Jacob the Liar. Vennewitz, Leila, tr. from GER. LC 95-18096. (Illus.). 256p. 1996. 21.45 (*1-55970-315-6*, Pub. by Arcade Pub Inc) Time Warner.

***Becker, Jurek.** Jakob the Liar. 1999. pap. 11.95 (*0-452-28170-9*, Plume) Dutton Plume.

Becker, Jurgen. Jesus of Nazareth. Crouch, James E., tr. LC 97-48488. 386p. 1998. 49.95 (*3-11-015773-X*); pap. 24.95 (*3-11-015772-1*) De Gruyter.

— Paul: Apostle to the Gentiles. Dean, O. C., Jr., tr. LC 92-28776. 448p. 1993. pap. 34.95 (*0-664-25707-0*) Westminster John Knox.

Becker, Jurgen & Rehbinder, Manfred, eds. European Coproduction in Film & Television. 164p. 1989. pap. 26.50 (*3-7890-1874-0*, Pub. by Nomos Verlags) Intl Bk Import.

Becker, K. H. & Dorfler, M. Dynamical Systems & Fractals: Computer Graphics Experiments with Pascal. Stewart, Ian, tr. (Illus.). 416p. (C). 1989. pap. text 27.95 (*0-521-36910-X*) Cambridge U Pr.

— Dynamical Systems & Fractals: Computer Graphics Experiments with Pascal. Stewart, Ian, tr. (Illus.). 416p. (C). 1989. text 85.00 (*0-521-36025-0*) Cambridge U Pr.

Becker, K. H., jt. ed. see Niki, Hiromi.

An Asterisk (*) at the beginning of an entry indicates that the title is appearing for the first time.

Becker, Karin E. Dorothea Lange & the Documentary Tradition. fac. ed. LC 79-20841. 295p. 1980. reprint ed. pap. 91.50 (*0-7837-7813-9*, 204756900007) Bks Demand.

***Becker, Katja.** Trimenonkoliken Als Elterliche Klage in Der Padiatrischen Praxis: Merkmale Von Mutter Und Kind. (Illus.). 222p. 1999. 37.95 (*3-631-34499-6*) P Lang Pubng.

***Becker, Kenneth D., tr. from GRE.** The Gospel & Epistles of John the Apostle. LC 99-68896. 96p. 1999. pap. 9.95 (*1-57736-173-3*) Providence Hse.

Becker, Kenneth L. & Bilezikian, John P., eds. Principles & Practice of Endocrinology & Metabolism. 2nd ed. LC 94-42416. 2,208p. 1995. text 194.00 (*0-397-51404-2*) Lppncott W & W.

Becker, Kenneth L., et al. Principles & Practice of Endocrinology & Metabolism. 3rd ed. 2208p. text 199.00 (*0-7817-1750-7*) Lppncott W & W.

***Becker, Kip, ed.** Culture & International Business. LC 99-57752. 172p. 1999. 49.95 (*0-7890-0969-2*, Intl Busn Pr) Haworth Pr.

— Culture & International Business. LC 99-57752. 172p. 2000. pap. text 24.95 (*0-7890-0987-0*, Intl Busn Pr) Haworth Pr.

Becker, Kip, jt. auth. see Beliroglu, Haluk.

Becker, Kurt H. Novel Aspect of Electron-Molecule Collisions. 1998. 78.00 (*981-02-3469-4*) World Scientific Pub.

Becker, Kurt H., et al. Phenomena in Ionized Gases: XXII ICPIG. (AIP Press Conference Proceedings Ser.: No. 363). (Illus.). 400p. 1996. 130.00 (*1-56396-550-X*, CP 363, AIP Pr) Spr-Verlag.

Becker, L. B. & Schoenbach, K., eds. Audience Responses to Media Diversification: Coping with Plenty. (Communication Ser.). 400p. 1989. 89.95 (*0-8058-0229-0*) L Erlbaum Assocs.

***Becker, Laney K.** Dear Stranger, Dearest Friend. 304p. 2000. 24.00 (*0-380-97853-9*, Wm Morrow) Morrow Avon.

Becker, Laura, ed. see Schwartz, Jeffrey I.

***Becker, Lawrence C.** A New Stoicism. 272p. 1999. pap. 16.95 (*0-691-00964-3*, Pub. by Princeton U Pr) Cal Prin Full Svc.

Becker, Lawrence C. Property Rights: Philosophic Foundations. 148p. 1980. pap. 14.95 (*0-7100-0606-3*, Routledge Thoemms) Routledge.

— Reciprocity. 448p. 1986. 35.00 (*0-7102-0828-6*, 08286, Routledge Thoemms) Routledge.

— Reciprocity. LC 85-19431. x, 448p. 1990. pap. text 22.50 (*0-226-04106-9*) U Ch Pr.

— Virtue. (Focus Ser.). (C). 1996. text 34.95 (*0-8133-8160-6*); pap. text 11.95 (*0-8133-8161-4*) Westview.

Becker, Lawrence C. & Becker, Charlotte, eds. Encyclopedia of Ethics, 2 vols. LC 91-4978. 1462p. 1992. text 175.00 (*0-8153-0403-X*, H925) Garland.

Becker, Lawrence C. & Becker, Charlotte B., eds. A History of Western Ethics. LC 92-10219. 224p. 1992. text 15.00 (*0-8153-0726-8*, H01540); pap. text 22.95 (*0-8153-0728-4*) Garland.

Becker, Leah B. Becker. Biographical History of the Becker Family & Their Early Settlement in America. (Illus.). 136p. 1997. reprint ed. pap. 21.00 (*0-8328-7459-0*); reprint ed. lib. bdg. 31.00 (*0-8328-7458-2*) Higginson Bk Co.

Becker, Lee, ed. see Abrahamson, David.

Becker, Lee, ed. see Drucker, Susan J. & Cathcart, Robert S.

Becker, Lee, ed. see Greenberg, Bradley S., et al.

Becker, Lee, ed. see Smith, Joel.

Becker, Lee B., et al. Training & Hiring of Journalists. Voigt, Melvin J., ed. LC 86-17419. (Communication & Information Science Ser.). 192p. 1987. text 73.25 (*0-89391-337-5*) Ablx Pub.

Becker, Leslee. The Sincere Cafe: Stories by Leslee Becker. LC 96-31638. (First Ser.). 184p. (Orig.). 1996. pap. 14.00 (*0-922811-28-8*) Mid-List.

Becker, Leslie. The Organized Actor: A Ready-to-Use Workbook for the Serious Actor. 3rd ed. 100p. 1994. spiral bd., wbk. ed. 16.95 (*0-9667365-0-8*) Pizazz Prods.

— The Organized Actor: The Workbook & Planner for the Serious Actor. 3rd ed. 139p. 1998. pap. text, wbk. ed. 17.95 (*0-9667365-1-6*) Pizazz Prods.

Becker, Lois & Stratton, Mark. ABC & T for Teddy. Becker, Mary et al, eds. (Teddy Ruxpin Tell Me Again Ser.). (Illus.). 24p. (J). 1995. pap. 11.95 incl. audio (*0-934323-82-8*) Alchemy Comms.

— All Around Town. Becker, Mary et al, eds. (Teddy Ruxpin Tell Me Again Ser.). (Illus.). 24p. (J). 1995. pap. 11.99 incl. audio (*0-934323-81-X*) Alchemy Comms.

Becker, Luc De. Immobilised Living Cell Systems: Modelling & Experimental Methods. Willaert, Ronnie G. & Baron, Gino V., eds. LC 95-34969. 386p. 1996. 175.00 (*0-471-95734-8*) Wiley.

Becker, Lucille F. Louis Aragon. LC 70-110702. (Twayne's World Authors Ser.). 1971. lib. bdg. 20.95 (*0-8057-2056-1*) Irvington.

— Pierre Boulle. LC 95-37767. (Twayne's World Authors Ser.: Vol. 859). 1996. 32.00 (*0-8057-8272-9*, Twyne) Mac Lib Ref.

— Twentieth-Century French Women Novelists. (World Authors Ser.). 256p. 1989. 26.95 (*0-8057-8251-6*, TWAS 813) Macmillan.

Becker, Lucille Frackman, see Frackman Becker, Lucille.

***Becker, Luverne R.** The Journey Begins. 132p. 2000. pap. 15.00 (*0-9676176-0-X*) L R Becker.

Becker, Lyle M. King of the Gumballs: An Entrepreneur's Spiritual Journey Building a Business While Raising Eight Kids & Surviving the Feminist Movement & a 50-Year Marriage. LC 97-94643. 1997. pap. 11.95 (*0-9661143-0-2*) Caliana Pub.

***Becker, Lyle M.** Listen to Your Body: And Add 10-15 Happy Healthy Years to Your Life. Marriott, Nancy, ed. LC 99-98131. 126p. 2000. pap. 9.95 (*0-9661143-1-0*) Caliana Pub.

Becker, M. & Haberfellner, Liebetrau G. Electronic Data Processing in Practice: A Handbook for Users. 1989. text 49.95 (*0-470-21402-3*) P-H.

Becker, M., et al. Transputers, '94: Advanced Research & Industrial Applications: Proceedings of the International Conference Actes de la Conference International, Seriens, France, Sept. 21-23, 1994. LC 94-77519. (Transputer & Occam Engineering Ser.: Vol. 40). 316p. (YA). (gr. 12). 1994. 99.00 (*90-5199-179-7*) IOS Press.

Becker, M., jt. auth. see Lewins, J.

Becker, M. E., et al. LCD Optical Performance: Measuring & Modelling LCDs. (World Scientific Series on Information Display). 250p. 1997. text 48.00 (*981-02-2296-3*) World Scientific Pub.

Becker, M. J., et al. The German-American Forty-Eighters, 1848-1998. LC 98-144782. (Illus.). 126p. (C). 1998. pap. 16.00 (*1-880788-10-1*) MKGAC & IGHS.

Becker, Marc. Mariategui & Latin American Marxist Theory. LC 93-3211. (Monographs in International Studies, Latin America Ser.: No. 20). 239p. (C). 1993. pap. text 20.00 (*0-89680-177-2*) Ohio U Pr.

***Becker, Margaret.** Growing up Together: Sisters & Brothers We'll Always Be. gif. ed. (Illus.). 64p. 2000. 15.99 (*0-7369-0224-4*) Harvest Hse.

Becker, Margaret. Rhino Modeling & Visualization. LC 99-64947. 512p. 1999. 45.00 (*0-7357-0925-4*) New Riders Pub.

— With New Eyes. LC 98-4078. 180p. 1998. 12.99 (*1-56507-847-0*) Harvest Hse.

Becker, Marilyn R. Last Touch: Preparing for a Parent's Death. LC 92-81726. 160p. (Orig.). 1993. pap. 11.95 (*1-879237-34-2*) New Harbinger.

Becker, Marion R., jt. auth. see Rombauer, Irma.

Becker, Marjorie. Setting the Virgin on Fire: Lazaro Cardenas, Michoacan Peasants & the Mexican Revolution. LC 94-40327. (Twentieth-Century Japan Ser.). (Illus.). 194p. 1996. pap. 18.95 (*0-520-08419-5*, Pub. by U CA Pr) Cal Prin Full Svc.

Becker, Mark, jt. ed. see Sobel, Michael.

Becker, Marsha J. The Odd-Lot Couple. 10p. 1992. write for info. (*1-881124-10-X*) Ctr Creat Endeavors.

Becker, Marshall J. & Betancourt, Philip P. Richard Berry Seager: Pioneer Archaeologist & Proper Gentleman. LC 97-4625. (Illus.). xvi, 255p. 1997. 20.00 (*0-924171-47-2*) U Museum Pubns.

***Becker, Marshall J., et al.** Excavations in Residential Areas of Tikal. LC 99-6966. (Tikal Reports Ser.). 1999. write for info. (*0-924171-71-5*) U Museum Pubns.

Becker, Martin. Becoming Your Dog's Best Friend. (Illus.). 64p. 1994. 8.95 (*0-7938-0087-0*, TS220) TFH Pubns.

— Heat Transfer: A Modern Approach. LC 86-18661. (Illus.). 440p. (C). 1986. 78.00 (*0-306-42316-2*, Plenum Trade) Perseus Pubng.

Becker, Martin, et al, eds. Solar Thermal Energy Utilization: German Studies on Technology & Applications, Vol. 6: Final Reports 1990. 350p. 1993. 89.95 (*0-387-54836-X*) Spr-Verlag.

— Solar Thermal Energy Utilization V: Final Reports, 1989. (German Studies on Technology & Applications). 520p. 1991. pap. 77.00 (*0-387-53269-2*) Spr-Verlag.

Becker, Martin & Bohmer, M., eds. GAST: The Gas-Cooled Solar Tower Technology Program. 350p. 1989. 118.95 (*0-387-50121-5*) Spr-Verlag.

Becker, Martin & Funken, K. H., eds. Solar Thermal Energy Utilization IV: Final Reports, 1988. (German Studies on Technology & Applications). 460p. 1991. pap. 64.00 (*0-387-53268-4*) Spr-Verlag.

Becker, Martin, et al. Larousse des Arbres, des Arbustes et des Arbrisseaux de l'Europe Occidentale. (FRE.). 336p. 1982. 75.00 (*0-8288-1242-X*, F12280) Fr & Eur.

Becker, Martin, jt. ed. see Carasso, M.

Becker, Martin, ed. see Funken, K. H. & Schneider, G. E.

Becker, Martin, jt. ed. see Lewins, Jeffery D.

Becker, Martin J. A History of Catholic Life in the Diocese of Albany, 1609-1864. LC 77-359170. (Monographs: No. 31). (Illus.). 1975. 15.00 (*0-930060-11-3*) US Cath Hist.

Becker, Marvin, ed. see LeBlanc, Joseph.

Becker, Marvin, ed. see Watts, James.

Becker, Marvin B. Civility & Society in Western Europe, 1300-1600. LC 87-46252. 238p. 1988. reprint ed. pap. 73.80 (*0-608-01047-2*, 205935500001) Bks Demand.

— The Emergence of Civil Society in the Eighteenth Century: A Privileged Moment in the History of England, Scotland, & France. LC 93-46327. 196p. (C). 1994. 27.50 (*0-253-31129-2*) Ind U Pr.

Becker, Mary & American Bar Association Staff. Don't Just Hear It Through the Grapevine: Studying Gender Questions at Your Law School. LC 98-135307. 96 p. 1998. write for info. (*1-57073-534-4*) Amer Bar Assn.

Becker, Mary, et al. Animals I'd Like to Be. (Teddy Ruxpin Tell Me Again Ser.). (Illus.). 24p. (J). 1995. pap. 11.95 incl. audio (*0-934323-80-1*) Alchemy Comms.

— Let's Play Today. (Teddy Ruxpin Tell Me Again Ser.). (Illus.). 24p. (J). 1995. pap. 11.95 incl. audio (*0-934323-83-6*) Alchemy Comms.

— Welcome to the Hospital. (Illus.). 28p. (J). 1994. pap. write for info. incl. audio (*0-934323-79-8*) Alchemy Comms.

Becker, Mary, jt. auth. see Schmidt, Richard O.

Becker, Mary, ed. see Baron, Phil.

Becker, Mary, ed. see Becker, Lois & Stratton, Mark.

Becker, Mary, ed. see Forsse, Ken & Hughes, Margaret A.

Becker, Mary, ed. see Hughes, Margaret A.

Becker, Mary, ed. see Ryan, Will.

Becker, Mary, tr. see Petren, Birgitta & Putini, Elisabetta.

Becker, Mary E., et al. Cases & Materials on Feminist Jurisprudence: Taking Women Seriously. 926p. (C). 1993. 60.00 (*0-314-02807-2*) West Pub.

Becker, Maurice. Biology Flipper. (Illus.). 49p. (YA). (gr. 7 up). 1988. reprint ed. 6.95 (*1-878383-05-1*) C Lee Pubns.

Becker, May, ed. Golden Tales of Canada. LC 75-37536. (Short Story Index Reprint Ser.). (Illus.). 1977. reprint ed. 20.95 (*0-8369-4095-4*) Ayer.

Becker, Melissa. My Family Helps. Gross, Karen, ed. (Illus.). 24p. (J). (ps-1). 1993. pap. text 4.95 (*1-56309-080-5*, N938102, New Hope) Womans Mission Union.

Becker, Meryl. Samantha: A Soap Opera & Vocabulary Book for Adult Students of English As a Second Language. LC 92-63209. 334p. 1993. pap., teacher ed. 9.95 (*0-472-08190-X*, 08190); pap. text 15.95 (*0-472-08178-0*, 08178) U of Mich Pr.

Becker, Meryl R. Samantha: The Sequel. (Illus.). 272p. (C). pap., teacher ed. 9.95 (*0-472-08664-2*, 08664); pap. text 18.95 (*0-472-08595-6*, 08595) U of Mich Pr.

***Becker, Michael A. & Fenske, Wolfgang.** Das Ende Der Tage Und Die Gegenwart des Heils: Begegnungen Mit Dem Neuen Testament Und Seiner Umwelt. Festschrift Fur Prof. Heinz-Wolfgang Kuhn (65) (Arbeiten zur Geschichte des Antiken Judentums und des Urchristentums Ser.). (Illus.). 306p. 1999. 100.00 (*90-04-11135-2*) Brill Academic Pubs.

Becker, Michael A., jt. auth. see Jaccard, James.

Becker, Mike. Die Clipper - Befehsreferenz Clipper 87 Bis 5.01 and Tools. (GER.). (C). 1992. text. write for info. (*0-201-57865-4*) Addison-Wesley.

— Netzwerkprogrammierung Mit Clipper. (GER.). (C). 1990. text. write for info. (*0-201-55913-7*) Addison-Wesley.

— Novell Netware Story, Vol. 1. (C). 1992. text. write for info. (*0-201-55974-9*) Addison-Wesley.

— Novell Netware Story Vol. 2: Novell Netware 286. (C). 1992. text. write for info. (*0-201-55995-1*) Addison-Wesley.

— Novell Netware Story Vol. 4: Novell Netware C Compiler. (C). 1992. text. write for info. (*0-201-55997-8*) Addison-Wesley.

— Novell Netware Story Vol. 5: Novell Netware Datenbankprodukte. (GER.). (C). 1993. text. write for info. (*0-201-55998-6*) Addison-Wesley.

Becker, Monica & Geiser, Ken. Evaluating Progress: A Report on the Findings of the Massachusetts Toxics Use Reduction Program Evaluation. (Illus.). 95p. (C). 1998. pap. text 25.00 (*0-7881-7461-4*) DIANE Pub.

Becker, Monique, et al, eds. Transputers, 1992: Advanced Research & Industrial Applications, Proceedings of the International Conference, 20-22 May 1992, Bensancon, France. LC 91-59039. (Transputer & Occam Engineering Ser.: Vol. 26). 381p. (YA). (gr. 12). 1992. 105.00 (*90-5199-081-2*, Pub. by IOS Pr) IOS Press

Becker, N . G. Analysis of Infectious Disease Data. (Monographs on Statistics & Applied Probability). 240p. (gr. 13). 1989. boxed set 62.95 (*0-412-30990-4*, A2302, Chap & Hall CRC) CRC Pr.

Becker, Nancy. Bagel Book & Slicer: Recipes for Bagel Lovers. (Illus.). 144p. 1996. pap. 9.95 (*0-8362-2140-0*) Andrews & McMeel.

Becker, Nancy, et al. Family Night at Home: A Manual for Growing Families. Martens, Phyllis & Becker, Dennis, eds. LC 81-67635. (Illus.). 100p. 1981. reprint ed. pap. 3.95 (*0-9606436-0-5*) Kindred Prods.

Becker, Nettie & Becker, Paul. A Comprehensive Guide for Caregivers in Day-Care Settings: Training Child Care Workers & Parents to Reduce the At-Risk Factor in Infants & Young Children. LC 98-48433. 226p. 1999. 52.95 (*0-398-06930-1*); pap. text 35.95 (*0-398-06931-X*) C C Thomas.

Becker, Norman. The Complete Book of Home Inspection. 2nd ed. (Illus.). 192p. (Orig.). 1992. 19.95 (*0-8306-3786-9*, 4100); pap. 12.95 (*0-8306-3785-0*, 4100) McGraw-Hill Prof.

Becker, P. W., ed. see CISM (International Center for Mechanical Sciences.

Becker, Palmer. Called to Care: A Training Manual for Small Group Leaders. LC 93-12086. 144p. (Orig.). 1993. pap. 6.99 (*0-8361-3622-5*) Herald Pr.

— Called to Equip: A Training & Resource Manual for Pastors. LC 93-12085. 120p. (Orig.). 1993. pap. 6.99 (*0-8361-3623-3*) Herald Pr.

Becker, Paul, jt. auth. see Becker, Nettie.

Becker, Paula B. & Becker, Dennis. Business Speaking. LC 92-27382. 200p. (C). 1992. text 14.80 (*0-256-12630-5*, Irwn McGrw-H) McGrw-H Hghr Educ.

Becker, Paula B., jt. auth. see Becker, Dennis.

Becker, Penny E. & Eiesland, Nancy L., eds. Contemporary American Religion: An Ethnographic Reader. LC 97-33744. 272p. 1997. 65.00 (*0-7619-9195-6*); pap. 24.95 (*0-7619-9196-4*) AltaMira Pr.

Becker, Peter & Clark, William, eds. Little Tools of Knowledge. (Social History, Popular Culture & Politics in Germany Ser.). (Illus.). 424p. (C). text 52.50 (*0-472-11108-6*, 11108) U of Mich Pr.

Becker, Peter, jt. auth. see Dorn, Charlotte.

Becker, Peter B. Chromatin Protocols. LC 99-10955. (Methods in Molecular Biology Ser.: Vol. 119). (Illus.). 544p. 1999. 89.50 (*0-89603-665-0*) Humana.

Becker, Peter M., et al. Children in Worship: Lessons from Research. 1999. pap. write for info. (*1-893989-01-*) Pillars Pr.

Becker, Petrus. Germania Sacra: Historisch-Statistische Beschreibung der Kirche des Alten Reiches, Vol. 34. Max-Plank-Institut fuer Geschichte Staff, ed. (GER., Illus.). xvi, 930p. (C). 1996. lib. bdg. 333.35 (*3-11-015023-9*) De Gruyter.

Becker, Pierre. Phosphates & Phosphoric Acid: Raw Materials, Technology, & Economics of the Wet Process. 2nd expanded rev. ed. (Fertilizer Science & Technology Ser.: No. 6). (Illus.). 760p. 1988. text 255.00 (*0-8247-7976-2*) Dekker.

Becker, R., et al, eds. Psychopathological & Neurological Dysfunctions Following Open-Heart Surgery, Milwaukee 1980: Proceedings. (Illus.). 384p. 1983. 103.00 (*0-387-11621-4*) Spr-Verlag.

Becker, R. & Burmeister, E., eds. Growth Theory, 3 vols., Set. (International Library of Critical Writings in Economics: Vol. 10). 1296p. 1990. text 520.00 (*1-85278-189-0*) E Elgar.

Becker, R. C. & Alpert, J. S., eds. Cardiovascular Disease in Women. (Journal: Cardiology: Vol. 77, Suppl. 2). (Illus.). iv, 140p. 1990. pap. 43.50 (*3-8055-5222-X*) S Karger.

— Cardiovascular Disease in Women: Journal: Cardiology, 1995. (Journal: Cardiology: Vol. 86, No. 4, 1995). (Illus.). 98p. 1995. pap. 22.75 (*3-8055-6197-0*) S Karger.

Becker, R. D. Movements High Plains: Poetry by R. D. Becker. (Illus.). 122p. 1998. pap. 20.00 (*1-57502-737-2*, PO2052) Morris Pubng.

Becker R., Margot. Ann M. Martin: The Story of the Author of the Baby-Sitters Club. 160p. (J). (gr. 4-6). 1993. pap. 3.99 (*0-590-45877-9*) Scholastic Inc.

Becker, R. P. & Johari, Om. Scanning Electron Microscopy, 1980, Pt. II. LC 72-626068. (Illus.). xiv, 658p. 1980. 52.00 (*0-931288-12-6*) Scanning Microscopy.

Becker, R. P., ed. see Carter, H. W., et al.

Becker, R. P., jt. ed. see Johari, Om.

Becker, Ralph. Lent, Good Friday & Easter. pap. 0.99 (*0-87377-011-0*) GAM Pubns.

Becker, Ralph E. Miracle on the Potomac: The Kennedy Center from the Beginning. (Illus.). 240p. 1989. 24.95 (*0-910155-15-1*) Bartleby Pr.

Becker-Reems, Elizabeth D. Self-Managed Work Teams in Health Care Organizations. LC 94-1253. 245p. 1994. pap. 49.00 (*1-55648-122-5*, 169109) AHPI.

Becker-Reems, Elizabeth D. & Garrett, Daniel G. Testing the Limits of Teams: How to Implement Self-Management in Health Care. LC 97-53189. 1998. 50.00 (*1-55648-215-9*) AHPI.

Becker, Reinhard P., ed. see Erasmus, Desiderius, et al.

Becker, Reinhold, ed. see Lungwitz, Hans.

Becker, Richard. Electromagnetic Fields & Interactions. (Illus.). 864p. (C). 1982. reprint ed. pap. 17.95 (*0-486-64290-9*) Dover.

Becker, Richard, ed. see Benn, Gottfried.

Becker, Richard A., et al. The New S Language: A Programming Environment for Data Analysis & Graphics. 702p. (C). (gr. 13). 1988. per. 69.95 (*0-534-09193-8*, Chap & Hall CRC) CRC Pr.

— The New S Language: A Programming Environment for Data Analysis & Graphics. (Wadsworth & Brooks-Cole Statistics-Probability Ser.). 702p. (C). 1988. mass mkt. 44.50 (*0-534-09192-X*) Chapman & Hall.

***Becker, Richard C.** Chest Pain. LC 99-87184. 136p. 2000. pap. 25.00 (*0-7506-7141-6*) Buttrwrth-Heinemann.

Becker, Richard C. Fibrinolytic & Antithrombotic Therapy: Theory, Practice & Management. (Illus.). 656p. 2000. pap. text 49.95 (*0-19-512331-X*) OUP.

Becker, Richard C., ed. The Modern Era of Coronary Thrombolysis, 160. LC 94-30680. (Developments in Cardiovascular Medicine Ser.). 320p. (C). 1994. text 180.00 (*0-7923-3063-3*) Kluwer Academic.

— Textbook of Coronary Thrombosis & Thrombolysis. LC 97-16368. (Developments in Cardiovascular Medicine Ser.). 704p. 1998. 398.00 (*0-7923-9923-4*) Kluwer Academic.

Becker, Richard S. Journey into Destiny. (Illus.). 47p. (C). 1989. pap. write for info. (*0-318-65863-1*) R S Becker.

— Reflections of the Heart. (Illus.). 53p. (C). 1989. pap. write for info. (*0-318-65862-3*) R S Becker.

Becker-Ritterspach, Raimund. Water Conduits in the Kathmandu Valley, Set. LC 96-900896. (Illus.). 119p. (C). 1995. 147.50 (*81-215-0690-5*, Pub. by M Manoharial) Coronet Bks.

Becker-Ritterspach, Raimund O. Water Conducts in the Kathmandu Valley, 2 vols. 1994. pap. 384.00 (*0-7855-7505-7*, Pub. by Ratna Pustak Bhandar) St Mut.

***Becker, Robert.** The Anatomy of Depression: An Autobiography by Robert Becker. 114p. 1999. pap. write for info. (*0-7392-0357-6*, PO3549) Morris Pubng.

Becker, Robert. Nancy Lancaster: Her Life, Her World, Her Art. LC 95-34170. (Illus.). 416p. 1996. 50.00 (*0-394-56791-9*) Knopf.

— The Socialization of Jamie McFee: A Novel. 138p. 1998. pap. 10.00 (*0-7392-0023-2*, PO2781) Morris Pubng.

Becker, Robert A. Revolution, Reform & the Politics of American Taxation, 1763-1783. LC 79-19729. 335p. 1980. reprint ed. pap. 103.90 (*0-608-00862-1*, 206165300010) Bks Demand.

Becker, Robert A. & Borck, Jim S., eds. The Eighteenth Century: A Current Bibliography. (New Ser.: No. 12). (Illus.). 600p. 84.60 (*0-404-62217-8*) AMS Pr.

Becker, Robert A. & Boyd, John H., III. Capital Theory, Equilibrium Analysis & Recursive Utility. LC 96-41656. (Illus.). 400p. 1997. text 75.95 (*1-55786-413-6*) Blackwell Pubs.

Becker, Robert A., jt. ed. see Jensen, Merrill.

Becker, Robert E. & Giacobini, Ezio, eds. Alzheimer Disease: From Molecular Biology to Therapy. LC 96-30911. (Advances in Alzheimers Disease Therapy Ser.). 620p. 1996. 89.50 (*0-8176-3879-2*) Birkhauser.

— Alzheimer's Disease: Current Research in Early Diagnosis. 300p. 1990. 85.00 (*0-8448-1659-0*, Crane Russak) Taylor & Francis.

— Cholinergic Basis for Alzheimer Therapy. (Advances in Alzheimers Disease Therapy Ser.). (Illus.). x, 480p. 1991. 87.50 (*0-8176-3566-1*) Birkhauser.

B

Becker, Robert E., ed. see Giacobini, Ezio.

Becker, Robert E., jt. ed. see Giacobini, Ezio.

Becker, Robert H., ed. Thomas Christy's Road Across the Plains. limited ed. 1969. 50.00 (*0-912094-13-3*) Old West.

Becker, Robert H., ed. see Wagner, Henry R.

Becker, Robert O. Cross Currents: The Perils of Electropollution, the Promise of Electromedicine. LC 89-5067. (Illus.). 352p. 1990. pap. 14.95 (*0-87477-609-0*, Tarcher Putnam) Putnam Pub Group.

***Becker, Robert O. & Selden, Gary.** The Body Electric: Electromagnetism & the Foundation of Life. Guarnaschelli, Maria D., ed. LC 86-25168. (Illus.). 368p. 1998. pap. 13.00 (*0-688-06971-1*, Quil) HarperTrade.

Becker, Robert P. & Johari, Om. Cell Surface Labeling. (Illus.). 100p. 1979. pap. text 10.00 (*0-931288-07-X*) Scanning Microscopy.

Becker, Robert P., jt. ed. see Johari, Om.

Becker, Robin. All-American Girl. (Poetry Ser.). Orig. Title: Cross Dressing for the Girls. 69p. 1996. pap. 10.95 (*0-8229-5580-6*); text 24.95 (*0-8229-3917-7*) U of Pittsburgh Pr.

— Backtalk. LC 81-72094. 74p. (C). 1982. pap. 9.95 (*0-914086-36-7*) Alice James Bks.

— Giacometti's Dog. LC 89-39342. (Poetry Ser.). 72p. 1990. pap. 10.95 (*0-8229-5428-1*); text 19.95 (*0-8229-3636-4*) U of Pittsburgh Pr.

***Becker, Robin.** The Horse Fair. 96p. 2000. pap. 12.95 (*0-8229-5720-5*) U of Pittsburgh Pr.

Becker, Robin, et al. Personal Effects. LC 75-46406. 88p. 1976. pap. 3.95 (*0-914086-15-4*) Alice James Bks.

Becker, Roger J., jt. auth. see Buettner, Donald R.

***Becker, Rolf.** Umweltschutz im Jahresabschlua: Rechtliche und Okonomische Analyse: Auswirkungen des Handels- und Steuerrechts de Lege Lata und de Lege Ferenda auf die Entscheidung Zur Durchfuhrung von Umweltschutzmaanahmen. (Europaische Hochschulschriften Ser.: Bd. 2540). Xiv, 256p. 1999. 45.95 (*3-631-35724-9*) P Lang Pubng.

***Becker, Ronald F.** Criminal Investigation. LC 99-51397. 436p. 1999. 68.00 (*0-8342-1711-2*) Panel Pubs.

Becker, Ronald F. Scientific Evidence & Expert Testimony Handbook: A Guide for Lawyers, Criminal Investigators & Forensic Specialists. LC 96-53287. 246p. 1997. pap. text 42.95 (*0-398-06762-7*) C C Thomas.

— The Underwater Crime Scene: Underwater Crime Investigative Techniques. LC 94-48036. (Illus.). 148p. (C). 1995. text 44.95 (*0-398-05979-9*); pap. text 31.95 (*0-398-05980-2*) C C Thomas.

Becker, Ross. The Good Dog! Dog Product Buyers Guide. 2nd rev. ed. (Illus.). 168p. 1998. pap. 17.95 (*0-937776-03-3*, Good Dog Bks) Good Commun Inc.

Becker, Ross & Becker, Judith. Scotties at the FDR Memorial: Fala, Franklin D. Roosevelt & Scotties. (Illus.). 32p. 1998. pap. 4.95 (*0-937776-04-1*, Good Dog Bks) Good Commun Inc.

Becker, Ross, jt. auth. see Weitzman, Nan.

Becker, Samuel L., ed. Discovering Mass Communication. 4th ed. (C). 1998. text. write for info. (*0-321-01548-7*) Addson-Wesley Educ.

Becker, Samuel L. & Roberts, Churchill L. Discovering Mass Communication. 3rd ed. 450p. (C). 1997. pap. 68.00 (*0-673-46119-X*) Addson-Wesley Educ.

Becker, Sandi, jt. auth. see Kaplan, Carol.

Becker, Saul. Responding to Poverty: The Politics of Cash & Care. LC 96-50040. (Longman Social Policy in Britain Ser.). 1997. write for info. (*0-582-24322-X*, Pub. by Addison-Wesley) Longman.

Becker, Scott. Health Care Law: A Practical Guide. 1985. ring bd. 220.00 (*0-8205-1398-9*) Bender.

— Revolutions Per Minute: The Triumph of Electronic Music & DJ Culture. 1999. pap. text 15.00 (*1-888277-16-5*) Incommcdo San Diego.

Becker, Scott, ed. We Rock, So You Don't Have To: The Option Reader. 256p. 1998. pap. text 15.00 (*1-888277-07-6*) Incommcdo San Diego.

Becker, Scott & Cassidy, Michael A., eds. Health Care Law Monthly. text 275.00 (*0-8205-2068-3*) Bender.

Becker, Selwyn W., jt. auth. see Daft, Richard L.

Becker, Seymour. Nobility & Privilege in Late Imperial Russia. 273p. 1988. pap. 16.00 (*0-87580-539-6*) N Ill U Pr.

— Russia's Protectorates in Central Asia: Bukhara & Khiva, 1865-1924. LC 67-30825. (Russian Research Center Studies: No. 54). (Illus.). 434p. 1968. reprint ed. pap. 134.60 (*0-7837-4446-3*, 205797600012) Bks Demand.

Becker, Shirley. Buddy's Shadow. large type ed. (Turtle Bks.). (Illus.). 32p. (J). (ps-2). 1991. pap. 7.95 (*0-944727-08-5*) Jason & Nordic Pubs.

— Buddy's Shadow. large type ed. (Turtle Bks.). (Illus.). 32p. (J). (ps-2). 1992. reprint ed. lib. bdg. 13.95 (*0-944727-19-0*) Jason & Nordic Pubs.

Becker, Shirley A. & Whittaker, James A., eds. Cleanroom Software Engineering Practices. LC 96-27545. (Series in Software Engineering Management). 208p. 1997. pap. text 39.95 (*1-878289-34-9*) Idea Group Pub.

Becker, Sidney. Law Enforcement Inc. 191p. 1973. 25.00 (*0-685-42287-9*) Okpaku Communications.

Becker, Sidney G., jt. auth. see Skidell, Myrna B.

Becker, Siegbert W. Foolishness of God. 276p. 1982. 11.99 (*0-8100-0155-1*, 15N0383) Northwest Pub.

— The Holy Ghost & His Work. 48p. (Orig.). 1984. pap. 5.00 (*0-8100-0191-8*, 22N0773) Northwest Pub.

— Revelation Distant Triumph Song. 1985. 27.99 (*0-8100-0190-X*, 15N0410) Northwest Pub.

— Wizards That Peep. Kujath, Mentor, ed. 1978. pap. 8.99 (*0-8100-0054-7*, 15N0366) Northwest Pub.

— The Word Goes On. LC 92-61630. 1992. 27.99 (*0-8100-0440-2*, 15N0550) Northwest Pub.

Becker, Stefan P. Erkenntnis und Gebet: Die Pneumatologische Grundstruktur von Karl Barths Dogmatischer Arbeit. (Basler und Berner Studien zur Historischen und Systematischen Theologie: Bd. 65). (GER.). 291p. 1995. 47.95 (*3-906753-45-X*, Pub. by P Lang) P Lang Pubng.

Becker, Stephen, tr. see Malraux, Andre.

Becker, Stephen, tr. see Schwarz-Bart, Andre.

Becker, Stephen, tr. see Wiesel, Elie.

Becker, Susan C. Living with a Deaf Dog. (Illus.). viii, 84p. 1997. pap. 15.95 (*0-9660058-0-5*) S C Becker.

Becker, Susan D. Origins of the Equal Rights Amendment: American Feminism Between the Wars, 23. LC 80-23633. (Contributions in Women's Studies: No. 23). 300p. 1981. 55.00 (*0-313-22818-3*, BOE/, Greenwood Pr) Greenwood.

Becker, Susan D., jt. auth. see Wheeler, William B.

Becker, Susanne. Gothic Forms of Feminine Fiction. (Illus.). 224p. 1999. 24.95 (*0-7190-5331-5*, Pub. by Manchester Univ Pr) St Martin.

***Becker, Susanne.** Lyrik Chinesischer Dichterinnen: Von Den Anfangen (11. JH. V. CHR.) Bis Zum 10. JH. N. CHR. (Frankfurter China-Studien. BD. 5 Ser.). 307p. 1999. 52.95 (*3-631-34861-4*) P Lang Pubng.

Becker, Suzy. The All Better Book. LC 92-50282. (Illus.). 96p. 1992. pap. 5.95 (*1-56305-314-4*, 3314) Workman Pub.

— All I Need to Know I Learned from My Cat. LC 90-50365. (Illus.). 96p. 1991. pap. 5.95 (*0-89480-824-9*, 1824) Workman Pub.

Becker, Suzy. Bud & Scooter. 48p. pap. 3.95 (*0-06-444286-1*) HarpC.

— Bud & Scooter. (Illus.). 48p. (J). (gr. k-3). 14.89 (*0-06-028971-6*); 14.95 (*0-06-028970-8*) HarpC Child Bks.

Becker, Suzy. My Dog's the World's Best Dog. LC 95-34378. (Illus.). 96p. 1995. pap. 6.95 (*0-7611-0105-5*, 10105) Workman Pub.

Becker, Svea & Winn, Laurie. Modern Jazz New York. Cook, Ray, ed. (Illus.). 56p. (Orig.). (C). 1982. pap. text 15.00 (*0-9602002-4-X*) Ray Cook.

Becker, Sylvia. How to Make Ceramic Character Dolls: And Their Accessories. (Illus.). 80p. (Orig.). 1993. pap. 18.95 (*0-85532-721-9*, 721-9, Pub. by Srch Pr) A Schwartz & Co.

***Becker, Ted Daryl & Slaton, Christa D.** The Future of Teledemocracy: Visions & Theories * Action Experiments * Global Practices. LC 99-55169. 248p. 2000. 65.00 (*0-275-96632-1*, Praeger Pubs); pap. 24.95 (*0-275-97090-6*, Praeger Trade) Greenwood.

Becker, Theodore & Dodson, Anthony. Live This Book: Abbie Hoffman's Philosophy for a Free & Green America. LC 90-63430. 120p. (Orig.). 1991. pap. 8.95 (*0-9622683-9-9*) Noble Pr.

Becker, Theodore L. Comparative Judicial Politics: The Political Functionings of Courts. LC 87-10878. 424p. 1987. reprint ed. pap. text 32.00 (*0-8191-6343-0*) U Pr of Amer.

Becker, Theodore L., ed. An Introduction to Quantum Politics. LC 90-49219. 248p. 1991. 57.95 (*0-275-93310-5*, C3310, Praeger Pubs) Greenwood.

— Political Trials. LC 78-126303. (C). 1971. pap. write for info. (*0-672-60744-1*, Bobbs) Macmillan.

Becker, Theodore L. & Couto, Richard A., eds. Teaching Democracy by Being Democratic. LC 96-20930. (Transformational Politics & Political Science Ser.). 200p. 1996. 65.00 (*0-275-95552-4*, Praeger Pubs); pap. 20.95 (*0-275-95553-2*, Praeger Pubs) Greenwood.

Becker, Thomas. Die Hegemonie der Moderne: Zur Neubestimmung Politischer Romantik im Naturrecht Kants & Hegels. (Studien & Materialien zur Geschichte der Philosophie: Vol. 40). (GER.). viii, 213p. 1996. write for info. (*3-487-10134-3*) G Olms Pubs.

— Werke Bd. 1: Der Begriff der Religion Im System der Philosophie. (GER.). 216p. 1996. reprint ed. write for info. (*3-487-06400-6*) G Olms Pubs.

Becker, Thomas & Weispfenning, Volker. Grobner Bases: A Computational Approach to Commutative Algebra. LC 92-37955. (Graduate Texts in Mathematics Ser.). 592p. 1993. 59.95 (*0-387-97971-9*) Spr-Verlag.

Becker, Thomas M., et al, eds. Racial & Ethnic Patterns of Mortality in New Mexico. LC 92-29585. (Illus.). 253p. 1993. reprint ed. pap. 78.50 (*0-608-07865-4*, 205404800011) Bks Demand.

Becker, Truman. The Revolution. 169p. (Orig.). 1987. pap. 12.50 (*971-10-0322-8*, Pub. by New Day Pub) Cellar.

Becker, U. & Shirley, D. A. Vuv & Soft X-Ray Photoionization. (Physics of Atoms & Molecules Ser.). (Illus.). 651p. (C). 1996. text 179.00 (*0-306-45038-0*, Kluwer Plenum) Kluwer Academic.

Becker, Udo. Diccionario Riodeuro: Fisica del Espacio: Astro-Physics. (SPA.). 264p. 1978. pap. 14.95 (*0-8288-5152-2*, S50163) Fr & Eur.

— Dictionary of Commercial Law: English, German & French. (ENG, FRE & GER.). 1000p. 1980. 150.00 (*0-7859-7459-8*, 285608012X) Fr & Eur.

— Dictionary of Commerical Law. 2nd ed. (ENG, FRE & GER.). 1000p. 1980. 159.50 (*2-85608-012-X*) IBD Ltd.

— Herder-Lexikon Umwelt. (GER.). 216p. 1976. 35.00 (*0-8288-5707-5*, M7460) Fr & Eur.

— Herder-Lexikon Weltaumphysik. (GER.). 240p. 1975. pap. 35.00 (*0-8288-5903-5*, M7461) Fr & Eur.

— Lexicon of Astrology: Lexikon der Astrologie. (GER.). 320p. 1986. 45.00 (*0-8288-1190-3*, M15271) Fr & Eur.

— Lexikon der Symbole. (GER.). 352p. 1992. 150.00 (*0-7859-8376-7*, 3451224836) Fr & Eur.

Becker, Udo, ed. The Continuum Encyclopedia of Symbols. Garmer, Lance W., tr. from GER. LC 77-6948. (Illus.). 500p. 1994. 39.50 (*0-8264-0644-0*) Continuum.

***Becker, Udo, ed.** Continuum Encyclopedia of Symbols. (Illus.). 368p. 2000. pap. text 24.95 (*0-8264-1221-1*) Continuum.

Becker, Ulrich. Das Uberleben Multinationaler Unternehmungen: Generierung & Transfer von Wissen im Internationalen Wettbewerb. (GER., Illus.). xliv, 373p. 1996. 63.95 (*3-631-49633-8*) P Lang Pubng.

Becker, Uwe. Richterzeit & Konigtum: Redaktionsgeschichtliche Studien Zum Richterbuch. (Beiheft zur Zeitschrift fuer die Alttestamentliche Wissenschaft Ser.: Band 192). ix, 326p. (C). 1990. lib. bdg. 90.80 (*3-11-012440-8*) De Gruyter.

Becker, Uwe, ed. Studies of Vacuum Ultraviolet & X-Ray Processes, 3 vols., Set, Vols. 1-3. 1993. write for info. (*0-404-69950-2*) AMS Pr.

Becker, Uwe & Heinzmann, Ulrich, eds. Proceedings of the International Workshop on Photoionization 1992, Berlin, Germany, August 24-28, 1992. LC 93-4230. (Studies of Vacuum Ultraviolet & X-Ray Processes: No. 1). 204p. 1993. 75.00 (*0-404-69951-0*) AMS Pr.

Becker, Verne, jt. auth. see Johnson, Dave.

Becker, Verne, jt. auth. see Liefeld, Olive F.

Becker, Verne, jt. auth. see Stribling, Thomas B.

Becker, Vitor O. Oxytenidae. Heppner, J. B., ed. (Lepidopterorum Catalogus Ser.: Vol. 19: Fasc. 115). (Illus.). 10p. 2000. pap. text 4.50 (*0-945417-69-1*) Sci Pubs.

Becker, Vivian. Antique & 20th Century Jewellery. 2nd ed. (Illus.). 319p. 1989. 69.50 (*0-7198-0171-0*, Pub. by NAG Press) Antique Collect.

Becker, Vivienne. Art Nouveau Jewelry. LC 98-60309. (Illus.). 240p. 1998. pap. 29.95 (*0-500-28078-9*, Pub. by Thames Hudson) Norton.

— Fabulous Costume Jewelry: History of Fantasy & Fashion in Jewels. LC 93-84625. (Illus.). 232p. 1993. 39.95 (*0-88740-531-2*) Schiffer.

Becker, W., et al, eds. Current Oculomotor Research: Physiological & Psychological Aspects. LC 98-31568. (Illus.). 492p. (C). 1999. text 135.00 (*0-306-46049-1*, Kluwer Plenum) Kluwer Academic.

Becker, W., ed. see International Astronomical Union Staff.

Becker, W. E., ed. Production & Use of Microalgae. (Ergebnisse der Limnologie Ser.: Heft 20). (GER., Illus.). vi, 198p. 1985. pap. 57.00 (*3-510-47018-4*, Pub. by E Schweizerbartsche) Balogh.

Becker, W. Victoria. Legal Issues Affecting Interstate Disposal. Glass, Karen, ed. (Hazardous Waste Management in the States Ser.). 48p. (Orig.). 1989. pap. text 15.00 (*1-55877-045-3*) Natl Governor.

— Siting Hazardous Waste Facilities: Guiding Principles. Feinstein, Gerry, ed. 40p. (Orig.). 1993. pap. text 15.00 (*1-55877-209-X*) Natl Governor.

***Becker, Walt.** Link. LC 98-24615. 432p. 2000. mass mkt. 6.99 (*0-380-73161-4*, Avon Bks) Morrow Avon.

— Link. (Illus.). (J). 2000. 12.34 (*0-606-17976-3*) Turtleback.

Becker, Walt. Link: A Novel. LC 98-24615. (Illus.). 384p. 1998. 25.00 (*0-688-15822-6*, Wm Morrow) Morrow Avon.

Becker, Walter, et al. Ear, Nose, & Throat Diseases: A Pocket Reference. 2nd ed. 1994. 29.90 (*0-86577-536-2*) Thieme Med Pubs.

Becker, Walter Alvin. Full Speed Ahead! An Autobiography. LC 91-76388. 227 p. (Orig.). 1997. pap. 14.95 (*0-931399-04-1*) Academic Enter.

— Manual de Genetica Cuantitativa. rev. ed. Deaton, Oliver & Vera, Rafael, trs. from ENG. LC 86-71091.Tr. of Manual of Quantitative Genetics. (SPA.). 176p. (C). 1986. pap. 19.95 (*0-931399-01-7*) Academic Enter.

— Manual of Quantitative Genetics. 5th ed. LC 91-71883. 192p. (C). 1992. pap. text 29.95 (*0-931399-11-4*) Academic Enter.

Becker, Walter E., ed. Reaction Injection Molding (RIM) (Illus.). 336p. 1979. 66.00 (*0-938648-31-4*) T-C Pr CA.

Becker, Warren, jt. auth. see Gleason, Harold.

Becker, Wayne M. World of the Cell. 2nd ed. (C). 1991. pap. text, student ed. 28.50 (*0-8053-0871-7*) Addison-Wesley.

Becker, Werner, et al, eds. Universities in Germany. (ENG & GER., Illus.). 304p. 1997. 55.00 (*3-7913-1496-3*, Pub. by Prestel) te Neues.

Becker, Wesley C. Parents Are Teachers: A Child Management Program. LC 72-75091. (Illus.). 200p. (Orig.). 1971. pap. text 12.95 (*0-87822-019-4*, 0194) Res Press.

Becker, William C. & O'Melia, Charles R. Optimizing Ozonation for Turbidity & Organics (TOC) Removal by Coagulation & Filtration. (Illus.). 236p. 1996. pap. 195.00 (*0-89867-878-1*, 90703) Am Water Wks Assn.

Becker, William E. Statistics for Business & Economics Using Microsoft Excel 97. LC 97-93693. (Illus.). xvi, 571p. (C). 1997. pap. text 32.00 (*0-9658576-0-3*) S R B Publishing.

— Student Solutions Manual with Practice Tests to Accompany Statistics for Business & Economics Using Microsoft Excel 97. (Illus.). (C). 1997. pap. text 10.00 (*0-9658576-1-1*) S R B Publishing.

Becker, William E., ed. The Economics of American Higher Education. 368p. (C). 1992. lib. bdg. 175.00 (*0-7923-9164-0*) Kluwer Academic.

— Higher Education & Economic Growth. 192p. (C). 1992. lib. bdg. 139.50 (*0-7923-9235-3*) Kluwer Academic.

Becker, William E. & Baumol, William J., eds. Assessing Educational Practices: The Contribution of Economics. (Illus.). 285p. (C). 1995. 39.50 (*0-262-02398-9*) MIT Pr.

Becker, William E. & Harnett, Donald L. Business & Economics Statistics with Computer Applications. LC 85-9025. (C). 1987. text 39.16 (*0-201-10956-5*) Addison-Wesley.

***Becker, William E. & Watts, Michael, eds.** Teaching Economics to Undergraduates: Alternatives to Chalk & Talk. LC 98-48149. 296p. 1999. 90.00 (*1-85898-972-8*) E Elgar.

— Teaching Economics to Undergraduates: Alternatives to Chalk & Talk. LC 98-48149. 296p. 2000. pap. 30.00 (*1-84064-270-X*) E Elgar.

Becker, William H. The Dynamics of Business-Government Relations: Industry, & Exports, 1893 to 1921. LC 81-10318. (Chicago Original Paperback Ser.). 256p. 1982. pap. text 24.00 (*0-226-04121-2*) U Ch Pr.

Becker, William H., jt. ed. see Seely, Bruce E.

Becker-Wortham, Roxanne, jt. auth. see Wortham, Robert.

Becker, Y. The Agent of Trachoma: Recent Studies of the Biology, Biochemistry & Immunology of a Prokaryotic Obligate Parasite of Eukaryocytes. (Monographs in Virology: Vol. 7). (Illus.). 99p. 1974. 55.75 (*3-8055-1657-6*) S Karger.

Becker, Yechiel. Antiviral Drugs & Interferon: The Molecular Basis of Their Activity. (Developments in Molecular Virology Ser.). 464p. 1984. text 159.00 (*0-89838-643-8*) Kluwer Academic.

— Molecular Virology. 1983. text 102.00 (*90-247-2742-1*) Kluwer Academic.

Becker, Yechiel, ed. Herpesvirus DNA. 1981. text 206.50 (*90-247-2512-7*) Kluwer Academic.

— Molecular Evolution of Viruses - Past & Present. 302p. (C). 1996. text 181.50 (*0-7923-9739-8*) Kluwer Academic.

— Recombinant DNA Research & Viruses. (Developments in Molecular Virology Ser.). 1984. text 161.00 (*0-89838-683-7*) Kluwer Academic.

— Replication of Viral & Cellular Genomes. (Developments in Molecular Virology Ser.). 1983. text 163.50 (*0-89838-589-X*) Kluwer Academic.

— Skin Langerhans (Dendritic) Cells in Virus Infections & AIDS. (Developments in Medical Virology Ser.). (C). 1990. text 208.00 (*0-7923-1015-2*) Kluwer Academic.

— Viral Messenger RNA. (Developments in Molecular Virology Ser.). 1985. text 167.00 (*0-89838-706-X*) Kluwer Academic.

— Virus Infections & Diabetes Mellitus. (Developments in Medical Virology Ser.). (C). 1987. text 159.00 (*0-89838-970-4*) Kluwer Academic.

Becker, Yechiel, et al, eds. Molecular Aspects of Human Cytomegalovirus Diseases. LC 92-49467. (Frontiers of Virology Ser.: Vol. 2). 1993. write for info. (*3-540-55948-5*); 149.95 (*0-387-55948-5*) Spr-Verlag.

Becker, Yechiel & Darai, G., eds. Diagnosis of Human Viruses by Polymerase Chain Reaction Technology. LC 92-49412. (Frontiers of Virology Ser.: Vol. 1). (Illus.). 340p. 1992. 154.00 (*0-387-55461-0*) Spr-Verlag.

— Pathogenicity of Human Herpesviruses Due to Specific Pathogenicity Genes. LC 93-38678. 1994. 174.95 (*0-387-57127-2*) Spr-Verlag.

Becker, Yechiel, jt. ed. see Darai, Gholamreza.

Becker, Yechiel, jt. ed. see Wittman, G.

Beckerdite, Luke, ed. American Furniture 1997. (Illus.). 421p. 1997. pap. 55.00 (*0-87451-851-2*) U Pr of New Eng.

— American Furniture 1994. (Illus.). 276p. 1994. pap. 55.00 (*0-87451-681-1*) U Pr of New Eng.

— American Furniture 1996. (Illus.). 356p. 1996. pap. 55.00 (*0-87451-793-1*) U Pr of New Eng.

— American Furniture, 1998. (Illus.). 309p. 1998. pap. 55.00 (*0-87451-892-X*) U Pr of New Eng.

***Beckerdite, Luke, ed.** American Furniture, 1999. (Illus.). 335p. 2000. pap. 55.00 (*1-58465-014-1*) U Pr of New Eng.

Beckerdite, Luke & Hosley, William H., eds. American Furniture 1995. (Illus.). 312p. 1995. pap. 55.00 (*0-87451-727-3*) U Pr of New Eng.

Beckerer, Frank S. Beckson Memory-Mate Commerical Log MM205. 112p. 1984. 23.95 (*1-928769-02-0*) Beckson Marine.

— Beckson Memory-Mate Cruise Log MM203. 94p. 1972. 23.95 (*1-928769-01-2*) Beckson Marine.

Beckerer, Frank S. Beckson Memory-Mate Cruise Log MM403. 80p. 1965. ring bd. 19.95 (*1-928769-08-X*) Beckson Marine.

Beckerer, Frank S. Beckson Memory-Mate Cruise Log MM303. 108p. 1965. 28.95 (*1-928769-04-7*) Beckson Marine.

Beckerer, Frank S. Beckson Memory-Mate Fish-Tales Log MM504. 48p. 1977. ring bd. 10.95 (*1-928769-11-X*) Beckson Marine.

— Beckson Memory-Mate GPS Register MM506. 60p. 1996. ring bd. 10.95 (*1-928769-12-8*) Beckson Marine.

— Beckson Memory-Mate GPS/Loran Log MM406. 72p. 1993. ring bd. 19.95 (*1-928769-09-8*) Beckson Marine.

Beckerer, Frank S. Beckson Memory-Mate GPS/Loran Log MM206. 110p. 1993. 23.95 (*1-928769-03-9*) Beckson Marine.

Beckerer, Frank S. Beckson Memory-Mate Guest Log MM402. 70p. 1965. ring bd. 19.95 (*1-928769-07-1*) Beckson Marine.

Beckerer, Frank S. Beckson Memory-Mate Guest Log MM202. 94p. 1974. 23.95 (*1-928769-00-4*) Beckson Marine.

Beckerer, Frank S. Beckson Memory-Mate Radio Log MM401. 70p. 1965. ring bd. 19.95 (*1-928769-06-3*) Beckson Marine.

— Beckson Memory-Mate Small Boat Log MM503. 48p. 1969. ring bd. 10.95 (*1-928769-10-1*) Beckson Marine.

Beckerer, Frank S. Beckson Memory-Mate 303 Refill MM304. 60p. 1965. 10.95 (*1-928769-05-5*) Beckson Marine.

Beckerhoff, Tom. Treupflichten bei der Stimmrechtsausubung & Eigenhaftung des Stimmrechtsvertreters. (GER.). 240p. 1996. 44.95 (*3-631-30915-5*) P Lang Pubng.

Beckerlegge, Elizabeth. Criminal Litigation Manual. 162p. 1997. pap. 30.00 (*1-85811-120-X*, Pub. by CLT Prof) Gaunt.

***Beckerlegge, Gwilym.** The Ramakrishna Mission: The Making of a Modern Hindu Movement. (Illus.). 240p. 2000. text 24.95 (*0-19-565133-2*) OUP.

Beckerlegge, Gwilym. The World Religions Reader. LC 97-25948. (Illus.). 512p. (C). 1998. 80.00 (*0-415-17487-2*); pap. 24.99 (*0-415-17488-0*) Routledge.

Beckerlegge, Oliver A., jt. ed. see Kimbrough, S. T., Jr.

Beckerley, James G., ed. see AEC Technical Information Center Staff.

Beckerling, Louis. Singapore: Financing Asia's Growth. (Euromoney Country Guide Ser.). 166p. 1996. 170.00 (*1-85564-474-6*, Pub. by Euromoney) Am Educ Systs.

Beckerman. Viewer's Guide 1 FAUSA, Vol. 1. 1990. pap. text 20.00 (*0-02-332771-5*, Macmillan Coll) P-H.

— Viewer's Guide 2 FAUSA, Vol. 2. 1990. pap. text 20.00 (*0-02-332772-3*, Macmillan Coll) P-H.

Beckerman, Anita & Tappen, Ruth M. It Takes More Than Love: A Practical Guide to Taking Care of an Aging Adult. LC 99-28049. 1999. 19.50 (*1-878812-50-5*) Hlth Prof Pr.

Beckerman, Bernard, ed. see Binnie, Eric.

Beckerman, Bernard, ed. see DeHart, Steven.

Beckerman, Bernard, ed. see Herzel, Roger W.

Beckerman, Bernard, ed. see Jensen, Ejner J.

Beckerman, Bernard, ed. see Ryan, Betsy A.

Beckerman, Bernard, ed. see Staples, Shirley.

Beckerman, Edwin. Politics & the American Public Library: Creating Political Support for Library Goals. LC 95-50135. 224p. 1996. 37.50 (*0-8108-3115-5*) Scarecrow.

Beckerman, Edwin, ed. A History of New Jersey Libraries, 1750-1996. LC 96-45323. 336p. 1997. 58.00 (*0-8108-3272-0*) Scarecrow.

Beckerman, Edwin, jt. auth. see Gertzog, Alice.

Beckerman, Howard S. Animation, the Whole Story. 31.95 (*0-8488-0867-3*) Amereon Ltd.

— Heartworks: Inspirations for English as Second Language. 260p. (C). 1989. pap. text 30.40 (*0-13-385220-2*) P-H.

***Beckerman, Howard S.** Rush Hour French. (FRE.). 120p. 2000. pap. 21.95 incl. audio compact disk (*2-8315-7714-4*, Pub. by Berlitz); pap. 19.95 incl. audio (*2-8315-7107-3*) Berlitz.

— Rush Hour Spanish. (SPA.). 120p. 2000. pap. 21.95 incl. audio compact disk (*2-8315-7717-9*, Pub. by Berlitz); pap. 19.95 incl. audio (*2-8315-7108-1*) Berlitz.

Beckerman, Ilene. Love, Loss, & What I Wore. LC 95-20460. (Illus.). 164p. 1995. 14.95 (*1-56512-111-2*, 72111) Algonquin Bks.

***Beckerman, Ilene.** Mother of the Bride: The Dream, the Reality, the Search for a Perfect Dress. 2000. 17.95 (*1-56512-288-7*) Algonquin Bks.

— Mother of the Bride: The Dream, the Reality, the Search for a Perfect Dress. LC 99-88845. (Illus.). 192p. 2000. 17.95 (*1-56512-259-3*, 72259) Algonquin Bks.

Beckerman, Ilene. What We Do for Love. LC 97-16640. 144p. 1997. 14.95 (*1-56512-180-5*) Algonquin Bks.

Beckerman, Martin. Adaptive Cooperative Systems. LC 96-44719. (Adaptive & Learning Systems for Signal Processing, Communications & Control Ser.). 427p. 1997. 76.95 (*0-471-01287-4*) Wiley.

***Beckerman, Marty.** Death to All Cheerleaders: One Adolescent Journalist's Cheerful Diatribe Against Teenage Plasticity. LC 00-132434. 184p. 2000. 12.95 (*0-9700629-0-7*) Infected Pr.

Beckerman, Michael. The Dvorak New World Symphony. (Critical Editions Ser.). (C). Date not set. pap. text. write for info. (*0-393-96678-X*, Norton Paperbks) Norton.

— Janacek As Theorist. (Studies in Czech Music: No. 3). 200p. 1994. lib. bdg. 54.00 (*0-945193-03-3*) Pendragon NY.

Beckerman, Michael, ed. Dvorak & His World. LC 93-4037. (Illus.). 325p. 1993. text 60.00 (*0-691-03386-2*, Pub. by Princeton U Pr); pap. text 22.95 (*0-691-00097-2*, Pub. by Princeton U Pr) Cal Prin Full Svc.

Beckerman, Michael & Bauer, Glen, eds. Janacek & Czech Music: Proceedings of the International Conference. (Studies in Czech Music: No. 1). 300p. 1995. lib. bdg. 54.00 (*0-945193-36-X*) Pendragon NY.

Beckerman, Michael B. New Worlds of Dvorak. (Illus.). 200p. 1999. 27.95 (*0-393-04706-7*) Norton.

Beckerman, Richard, ed. see Eklund, Ken & Baylon, David.

Beckerman, Robert C., et al. Respiratory Control Disorders in Infants & Children. (Illus.). 448p. 1992. 72.00 (*0-683-00498-0*) Lppncott W & W.

Beckerman-Rodau, Andrew. Business Associations: Cases & Materials on Agency, Partnership, & the Legal Problems of Business Enterprise. 630p. (C). 1995. ring bd. 71.00 (*1-879581-25-6*) Lupus Pubns.

***Beckerman-Rodau, Andrew.** Business Organizations: Cases & Materials on Partnerships, Limited Liability Companies & Corporations. 754p. (C). 1998. ring bd. 73.00 (*1-879581-52-3*) Lupus Pubns.

Beckerman, Wilfred. Growth, the Environment & the Distribution of Incomes: Essays by a Sceptical Optimist. LC 95-30416. (Economists of the Twentieth Century Ser.). (Illus.). 528p. 1995. 120.00 (*1-85898-262-6*) E Elgar.

— The Labour Government's Economic Record 1964-1970. LC 72-184050. 343p. 1972. write for info. (*0-7156-0608-5*) G Duckworth.

— The Labour Government's Economic Record 1964-1970. LC 76-351014. (Paperduck Ser.). 343p. 1975. write for info. (*0-7156-0890-8*) G Duckworth.

— Through Green-Colored Glasses: Environmentalism Reconsidered. LC 96-30858. 230p. 1996. 21.95 (*1-882577-35-3*); pap. text 11.95 (*1-882577-36-1*) Cato Inst.

Beckerman, Wilfred, ed. Wage Rigidity & Umemployment. LC 86-45446. 231p. reprint ed. pap. 71.70 (*0-7837-2192-7*, 204253000004) Bks Demand.

***Beckermann, Ansgar.** Analytische Einfuhrung in Die Philosophie des Geistes. 480p. 1999. 43.00 (*3-11-015776-4*) De Gruyter.

Beckermann, Ansgar. Einfuhrung in die Logik. 314p. 1997. 21.00 (*3-11-014774-2*) De Gruyter.

Beckermann, Ansgar, et al, eds. Emergence or Reduction? Essays on the Prospects of Nonreductive Physicalism. (Foundations of Communication & Cognition Ser.). vii, 315p. (C). 1992. lib. bdg. 116.95 (*3-11-012880-2*, 51-92) De Gruyter.

Beckermann, Christoph, et al, eds. Micro - Macro Scale Phenomena in Solidification. (HTD Series, Vol. 218: AMD: Vol. 139). 160p. 1992. 45.00 (*0-7918-1060-7*, G00704) ASME.

— Transport Phenomena in Solidification: Proceedings: International Mechanical Engineering Congress & Exposition (1994: Chicago, IL) LC 94-78966. (HTD - AMD Ser.: Vol. 284, Vol. 182). 279p. 1995. pap. 90.00 (*0-7918-1392-4*, G00887) ASME Pr.

Beckermann, Christoph, ed. see International Conference on Modeling of Casting & & Engineering Foundation (U.S.) Staff.

Beckers, C., et al, eds. Positron Emission Tomography in Clinical Research: Tracer Modelling & Radioreceptors. (C). 1989. text 171.00 (*0-7923-0254-0*) Kluwer Academic.

Beckers, Marion & Moorgat, Elisabeth. Atelier Lotte Jacobi: Berlin, New York. (Illus.). 223p. 1998. 60.00 (*3-87584-636-2*) Nicolaische Verlagsbuchhandlung.

Beckers, Mirion & Moortgat, Elisabeth. Atelier Lotte Jacobi: Berlin-New York. 224p. 1997. 60.00 (*3-87584-646-X*) Dist Art Pubs.

Beckert, Charles. Happy Children, Happy Families. 1996. pap. 6.95 (*1-55503-775-5*, 01111809) Covenant Comms.

Becket. Le Corbusier's Poeme de l'angl. text. write for info. (*0-471-48947-6*) Wiley.

Becket, Andrew. Concordance to Shakespeare. LC 77-134319. reprint ed. lib. bdg. 74.50 (*0-404-00698-1*) AMS Pr.

Becket, Fiona. D. H. Lawrence: The Thinker As Poet. LC 97-5826. 224p. 1997. text 55.00 (*0-312-17503-5*) St Martin.

Becket, Jan & Singer, Joseph, photos by. Pana O'ahu: Sacred Stones, Sacred Land. LC 98-31995. (Illus.). 232p. 1999. text 42.00 (*0-8248-1828-8*, Latitude Twenty) UH Pr.

***Becket, Thomas.** The Correspondence of Thomas Becket, Archbishop of Canterbury. Duggan, Anne, ed. 780p. 2000. text 140.00 (*0-19-822265-3*) OUP.

Becket, Wendy & Pattison, George. Pains of Glass: The Story of the Passion from King's College Chapel, Cambridge. (Illus.). 48p. 1996. 12.95 (*0-563-37170-6*, BBC-Parkwest) Parkwest Pubns.

***Beckett.** The Eastern Dada Orbit Vol. 4: Russia, Georgia, The Ukraine, Central Europe, Japan. 1998. 95.00 (*0-8161-0588-X*, G K Hall Lrg Type) Mac Lib Ref.

Beckett & Alexandrou. Introduction to Eurocode 2: Design of Concrete Structures. LC 98-211102. (Illus.). 248p. 1997. mass mkt. 54.95 (*0-419-20140-8*, E & FN Spon) Routledge.

Beckett, et al. Science Probe 9. (UK - Science Ser.). 1995. text 62.95 (*0-17-604716-6*) S-W Pub.

Beckett, A. H. & Stenlake, J. B. Practical Pharmaceutical Chemistry, Vol. 1, Part I. 4th rev. ed. LC 87-14470. 382p. (C). 1988. text 55.00 (*0-485-11322-8*, Pub. by Athlone Pr) Humanities.

— Practical Pharmaceutical Chemistry, Vol. 2, Part II. 4th rev. ed. LC 87-14470. 560p. (C). 1988. text 75.00 (*0-485-11323-6*, Pub. by Athlone Pr) Humanities.

Beckett, Alison. Miller's Collecting Teddy Bears & Dolls: The Facts at Your Fingertips. (Illus.). 176p. 1996. 19.95 (*1-85732-893-0*, Pub. by Reed Illust Books) Antique Collect.

***Beckett, Beth.** Lipstick, Sweat & Sweatrag. 1998. pap. 24.95 (*1-875998-37-3*, Pub. by Central Queensland) Accents Pubns.

Beckett, Bob & Sytsema, Rebecca Wagner. Commitment to Conquer: Redeeming Your City by Strategic Intercession. LC 97-1373. 176p. (Orig.). 1997. pap. 9.99 (*0-8007-9252-1*) Chosen Bks.

Beckett, Bonnie A. The Reception of Pablo Neruda's Works in the German Democratic Republic. (Germanic Studies in America: Vol. 42). 258p. 1981. 43.00 (*3-261-04896-4*) P Lang Pubng.

Beckett, Brian. Introduction to Cryptolology & PC Security. LC 97-6936. 1997. write for info. (*0-07-709235-X*) McGraw.

— Weapons of Tomorrow. 160p. 1983. 17.95 (*0-306-41383-3*, Plenum Trade) Perseus Pubng.

Beckett, Cheryl. Growing up Inside Out. Barton, B. J., ed. (Illus.). 167p. (Orig.). 1994. pap. 13.95 (*0-9642255-0-6*) Higher States.

Beckett, Cynthia, et al. Working with Governors in Schools: Developing a Professional Partnership. 176p. 1991. pap. 34.95 (*0-335-09427-9*) OpUniv Pr.

Beckett, Denis. Madibaland. LC 98-137586. 211p. 1998. write for info. (*0-14-027456-1*, Penguin Bks) Viking Penguin.

Beckett, Derrick. The Ultimate Load Design of Continuous Concrete Beams. LC 67-31269. 126p. reprint ed. pap. 39.10 (*0-608-30944-3*, 202070700018) Bks Demand.

Beckett, Edmond. Clocks & Watches: 1874-1990. 6th ed. (Illus.). 322p. 1991. pap. 25.00 (*0-87556-182-9*) Saifer.

Beckett, Edmund. Clocks & Watches. 322p. 25.00 (*0-87556-952-8*) Saifer.

Beckett, Elspeth. Wild Flowers of Majorca, Minorca & Ibiza: With Keys to the Flora of the Balearic Islands. (Illus.). 231p. (C). 1988. text 82.00 (*90-6191-634-8*, Pub. by A A Balkema) Ashgate Pub Co.

Beckett, Fiona. Wine Uncorked: A Practical Introduction to Tasting & Enjoying Wine. (Illus.). 144p. 1999. 24.95 (*1-57223-201-3*, 2013) Willow Creek Pr.

***Beckett, Francis.** Enemy Within: The Rise & Fall of the British Communist Party. 253p. 1999. pap. 19.95 (*0-85036-477-9*, Pub. by MRLN) Paul & Co Pubs.

— Rebel Who Lost His Cause: The Tragedy of John Beckett MP. 2000. 35.00 (*1-902809-04-1*, London House) Allison & Busby.

Beckett, Frederick E. College Composition: The Course Where a Student Doesn't Learn to Write. LC 74-78204. 176p. (C). 1974. 16.00 (*0-9600740-1-5*) Calcon Pr.

Beckett, Gilbert A. The Comic History of Rome. LC 96-17098. (Illus.). xii, 308p. 1996. reprint ed. pap. 19.00 (*0-86516-333-2*) Bolchazy-Carducci.

***Beckett, Gilbert Abbott & Cruikshank, George.** The Comic Blackstone. LC 00-36242. 2000. write for info. (*1-58477-104-6*) Lawbk Exchange.

Beckett, Harry. Alberta. LC 97-12435. (Journey Across Canada Ser.). 24p. (J). (gr. 2-5). 1997. lib. bdg. 18.60 (*1-55916-205-8*) Rourke Bk Co.

— British Columbia. LC 97-13887. (Journey Across Canada Ser.). 24p. (J). (gr. 2-5). 1997. lib. bdg. 18.60 (*1-55916-206-6*) Rourke Bk Co.

***Beckett, Harry.** Lake Erie. LC 99-14508. 32p. (J). (gr. 3-5). 1999. lib. bdg. 17.45 (*0-86593-527-0*) Rourke Corp.

— Lake Ontario. LC 99-13175. 32p. 1999. lib. bdg. write for info. (*0-86593-526-2*) Rourke Corp.

— Lake Superior. LC 98-47525. (Great Lakes of North America Ser.). 32p. (J). (gr. 3-5). 1999. lib. bdg. 17.45 (*0-86593-528-9*) Rourke Corp.

Beckett, Harry. Manitoba. LC 97-7672. (Journey Across Canada Ser.). 24p. (J). (gr. 3-5). 1997. lib. bdg. 18.60 (*1-55916-203-1*) Rourke Bk Co.

— New Brunswick. LC 97-932. (Journey Across Canada Ser.). 24p. (J). (gr. 3-5). 1997. lib. bdg. 18.60 (*1-55916-202-3*) Rourke Bk Co.

— Newfoundland. LC 97-2211. (Journey Across Canada Ser.). 24p. (J). (gr. 3-5). 1997. lib. bdg. 18.60 (*1-55916-197-3*) Rourke Bk Co.

— The Northwest Territories. LC 97-22219. (Journey Across Canada Ser.). 24p. (J). (gr. 3-5). 1997. lib. bdg. 18.60 (*1-55916-207-4*) Rourke Bk Co.

— Nova Scotia. LC 97-6136. (Journey Across Canada Ser.). 24p. (J). (gr. 3-5). 1997. lib. bdg. 18.60 (*1-55916-199-X*) Rourke Bk Co.

— Ontario. LC 97-2214. (Journey Across Canada Ser.). 24p. (J). (gr. 3-5). 1997. lib. bdg. 18.60 (*1-55916-198-1*) Rourke Bk Co.

— Prince Edward Island. LC 97-1421. (Journey Across Canada Ser.). 24p. (J). (gr. 3-5). 1997. lib. bdg. 18.60 (*1-55916-200-7*) Rourke Bk Co.

— Quebec. LC 97-1422. (Journey Across Canada Ser.). 24p. (J). (gr. 3-5). 1997. lib. bdg. 18.60 (*1-55916-201-5*) Rourke Bk Co.

— Saskatchewan. LC 97-12866. (Journey Across Canada Ser.). 24p. (J). (gr. 3-5). 1997. lib. bdg. 18.60 (*1-55916-204-X*) Rourke Bk Co.

— Waterways to the Great Lakes. LC 99-23310. (Great Lakes of North America Ser.). 32p. (J). (gr. 3-5). 1999. 17.45 (*0-86593-529-7*) Rourke Corp.

— Yukon. LC 97-20690. (Journey Across Canada Ser.). 24p. (J). (gr. 3-5). 1997. lib. bdg. 18.60 (*1-55916-208-2*) Rourke Bk Co.

***Beckett, Harry, contrib. by.** Lake Huron. LC 99-13024. (Great Lakes of North America Ser.). 32p. 1999. lib bdg. write for info. (*0-86593-525-4*) Rourke Corp.

— Lake Michigan. LC 99-13023. (Great Lakes of North America Ser.). 32p. 1999. lib. bdg. write for info. (*0-86593-524-6*) Rourke Corp.

Beckett, Hazael W. Growing up in Dallas. (Illus.). 1985. 37.50 (*0-911796-07-X*) Beacham.

***Beckett-Hoffmann, Bonnie.** Aviation Safety: FAA's Use of Emergency Orders to Revoke or Suspend Operating Certificates. 55p. (C). 2000. reprint ed. pap. text. write for info. (*0-7881-8853-4*) DIANE Pub.

***Beckett, I. F.** Encyclopedia of Guerrilla Warfare. LC 98-55119. xxiii, 303p. 1999. write for info. (*1-57607-189-8*) ABC-CLIO.

Beckett, I. F. W. Victoria's Wars. (Hidden in Camera Ser.: Vol. 2). (Illus.). 88p. 1999. pap. text 12.50 (*0-7478-0388-9*, Pub. by Shire Pubns) Parkwest Pubns.

***Beckett, Ian.** The Great War. 352p. 1999. write for info. (*0-582-32249-9*); pap. write for info. (*0-582-32248-0*) Addison-Wesley.

Beckett, Ian F. Buckinghamshire. (Country Guide Ser.: No. 13). (Illus.). 104p. pap. 12.50 (*0-7478-0270-X*, Pub. by Shire Pubns) Parkwest Pubns.

— War Correspondents American Civil War. (War Correspondents Ser.). (Illus.). 256p. 1993. 31.95 (*0-7509-0044-X*, Pub. by Sutton Pub Ltd) Intl Pubs Mktg.

Beckett, Ian F., jt. ed. see Chandler, David.

Beckett, Ian F., ed. see Laband, John P.

***Beckett, Ian F. W.** Discovering British Regimental Traditions. 136p. 1999. pap. 25.00 (*0-7478-0410-9*, Pub. by Shire Pubns) St Mut.

Beckett, Ian F. W. Encyclopedia of Guerrilla Warfare. LC 98-55119. 303p. 1999. lib. bdg. 75.00 (*0-87436-929-0*) ABC-CLIO.

Beckett, Ian F. W. Johnnie Gough, VC: A Biography of Brig-Gen Sir John Gough, VC, KCB, CMG. 247p. 1997. (*1-871085-01-2*) Donovan Pub.

Beckett, J. Steven. Baseball Card Alphabetical Checklist, No. 6. (Sport Americana Ser.). 1994. pap. 15.95 (*0-937424-73-0*) Edgewater.

Beckett, J. V. A Centenary History of Nottingham. LC 96-9834. (Illus.). 400p. 1997. text 89.95 (*0-7190-4001-9*) Manchester Univ Pr.

— Coal & Tobacco: The Lowthers & the Economic Development of West Cumberland, 1660-1760. LC 80-40785. 295p. reprint ed. pap. 84.10 (*0-608-15693-0*, 2031620) Bks Demand.

Beckett, J. V. & Brand, Ken. Nottingham: An Illustrated History. LC 96-46265. (Illus.). 1997. write for info. (*0-7190-4002-7*, Pub. by Manchester Univ Pr) St Martin.

Beckett, James. Andre Agassi. (Great Sport Heroes Ser.). 1997. 15.00 (*0-676-60104-9*) Random.

— Baseball Cards 2000. 19th ed. 1999. pap. 7.99 (*0-676-60156-1*) Hse Collectbls.

— Basketball Card Price Guide No. 6, No. 6. 1997. pap. 19.95 (*0-676-60083-2*) Random.

— Basketball Cards. 1997. pap. 14.95 (*0-676-60124-3*) Hse Collectbls.

— Beckett Almanac of Baseball No. 2, Vol. 2. 1997. pap. 34.95 (*0-676-60135-9*) Hse Collectbls.

— Beckett Almanac of Baseball Cards. unabridged ed. 1996. pap. 29.95 (*0-676-60059-X*) Random.

— Beckett Baseball Card Alphabet. 1997. pap. 19.95 (*0-676-60125-1*) Hse Collectbls.

— Beckett Football Card Alphabetical Checklist No. 1, Vol. 1. 1997. pap. 14.95 (*0-676-60123-5*) Hse Collectbls.

***Beckett, James.** Beckett Football Card Price Guide, 16. 1999. pap. text 19.95 (*1-887432-76-0*) Beckett Pubns.

Beckett, James. Beckett Football Card Price Guide, No. 13. 13th ed. 1996. pap. 19.95 (*0-676-60060-3*) Random.

— Beckett Football Card Price Guide No. 14, Vol. 14. (J). 1997. pap. 19.95 (*0-676-60121-9*, Pub. by Random Bks Yng Read) Random.

— Beckett Hockey Card Price Guide No. 7. 1997. pap. 24.95 (*0-676-60119-7*) Hse Collectbls.

— Beckett Racing Card Price Guide No. 1, No. 1. 1996. pap. 14.95 (*0-676-60058-1*) Random.

— Beckett Racing Price Guide & Alphabetical Checklist No. 2, Vol. 2. 2nd ed. 1997. pap. 14.95 (*0-676-60120-0*) Random.

***Beckett, James.** Official Price Guide to Baseball Cards: 2001 Edition. 20th ed. (Illus.). 910p. 2000. pap. 6.99 (*0-676-60191-X*) Hse Collectbls.

— The Official Price Guide to Basketball Cards. 9th ed. 464p. 1999. pap. write for info. (*0-676-60182-0*) Hse Collectbls.

— The Official Price Guide to Football Cards. 19th ed. (Illus.). 672p. 1999. pap. 6.99 (*0-676-60183-9*) Hse Collectbls.

Beckett, James. Tiger Woods. (Beckett Great Sports Heroes Ser.). 1997. pap. text 24.95 (*1-887432-36-1*) Beckett Pubns.

Beckett, James, ed. Joe Montana. 1995. pap. 15.00 (*0-614-15516-9*, Harvest Bks) Harcourt.

— Mickey Mantle. 1995. pap. 15.00 (*0-614-15517-7*, Harvest Bks) Harcourt.

— Shaquille O'Neal. 1995. pap. 15.00 (*0-614-15518-5*, Harvest Bks) Harcourt.

Beckett, John D. Loving Monday: Succeeding in Business Without Selling Your Soul. LC 98-17886. 177p. 1998. 15.99 (*0-8308-1926-6*, 1926) InterVarsity.

***Beckett, Justin F. & Sudarkasa, Michael E. M.** Investing in Africa: An Insiders Guide to the Ultimate Emerging Market. 224p. 2000. 49.95 (*0-471-37951-4*) Wiley.

***Beckett, Katherine.** Making Crime Pay: Law & Order in Contemporary American Politics. (Studies in Crime & Public Policy). (Illus.). 168p. 1999. pap. 14.95 (*0-19-513626-8*) OUP.

Beckett, Kathleen. Fashion. (Careers Without College Ser.). 1992. 13.15 (*0-606-05186-4*, Pub. by Turtleback) Demco.

— Virtue's Prize, Vol. 1. (Zebra Regency Romance Ser.). 1999. mass mkt. 4.99 (*0-8217-6358-X*, Zebra Kensgtn) Kensgtn Pub Corp.

Beckett, Kenneth A. Gardening Basics: How to Design, Plant & Maintain Your Garden. LC 99-20247. (Illus.). 276p. 1999. 29.95 (*0-8069-2453-5*) Sterling.

— The Step-by-Step Guide to Growing Under Glass. LC 80-5911. (Step-by-Step Encyclopedia of Gardening). 1982. pap. 8.95 (*0-671-42256-1*) S&S Trade.

Beckett, Leslie & Sabine, B. E. Revenue Investigations & Appeals Manuals. 2nd ed. pap. 84.00 (*0-406-50152-1*, U.K., MICHIE) LEXIS Pub.

***Beckett, Lucy.** Time Before You Die: A Novel of the Reformation. 1999. pap. 14.95 (*0-89870-743-9*) Ignatius Pr.

Beckett, Margaret, jt. auth. see Meacher, Michael.

Beckett, Mary. A Belfast Woman. 112p. 1996. pap. 10.95 (*0-905169-85-9*, Pub. by Poolbeg Pr) Dufour.

Beckett, Melvin L. Deep Breathing to Fitness. (Illus.). 17p. 1981. pap. 2.95 (*0-686-32543-5*) MLB Pub.

Beckett, Oliver. J. F. Herring & Sons. 200p. 1990. 110.00 (*0-85131-335-3*, Pub. by J A Allen) St Mut.

Beckett, Paul & Alli, Warisu O. Democracy & the Elite in Nigeria: Perspectives from Survey Research. LC 98-39687. 1998. write for info. (*0-942615-37-9*) U Wis African Stud.

Beckett, Paul A. & Young, Crawford, eds. Dilemmas of Democracy in Nigeria. LC 97-17411. (Rochester Studies in African History & the Diaspora: Vol. 2). 448p. 1997. 65.00 (*1-878822-98-5*) Univ Rochester Pr.

Beckett, Peter G. Adolescents out of Step: Their Treatment in a Psychiatric Hospital. LC 65-13538. (Lafayette Clinic Monographs in Psychiatry: No. 2). 191p. reprint ed. pap. 59.30 (*0-8357-5115-5*, 202765300055) Bks Demand.

Beckett, Peter G., et al. A Teaching Program in Psychiatry, Vol. 2. LC 67-64750. 278p. pap. 86.20 (*0-608-16061-X*, 203319100084) Bks Demand.

Beckett Publications. Hot Cars: A Collector's Ultimate Source for Hot Wheels, Matchbox & Johnny Lightning. LC 99-227416. 1999. pap. text 24.95 (*1-887432-69-8*) Beckett Pubns.

Beckett Publications Editors. Autographs: A Reference & Price Guide for Sports & Celebrity Autographs. 1999. pap. text 24.95 (*1-887432-68-X*) Beckett Pubns.
— Baseball Card Alphabetical Checklist. 1998. pap. 14.95 (*1-887432-44-2*); pap. 19.95 (*1-887432-45-0*) Beckett Pubns.
— Basketball Card Alphabetical Checklist, Vol. 1. 1998. pap. text 14.95 (*1-887432-31-0*) Beckett Pubns.
— Basketball Card Price Guide. 1998. pap. 19.95 (*1-887432-43-4*) Beckett Pubns.
— Basketball Card Price Guide, Vol. 6. 1998. pap. text 19.95 (*1-887432-27-2*) Beckett Pubns.
— Beanies & Plush Toys: Everything You Need to Know about Collecting Beanies & Other Plush Toys. LC 98-235160. 1998. pap. 24.95 (*1-887432-58-2*) Beckett Pubns.
— Beckett Almanac of Baseball Cards & Collectibles. (Almanac of Baseball Ser.). 1998. pap. 34.95 (*1-887432-39-6*) Beckett Pubns.
***Beckett Publications Editors.** Beckett Almanac of Baseball Cards & Collectibles, 4. 1999. pap. text 34.95 (*1-887432-54-X*) Beckett Pubns.
Beckett Publications Editors. Beckett Baseball Card Price Guide. 1998. pap. text 19.95 (*1-887432-37-X*) Beckett Pubns.
— Beckett Baseball Card Price Guide #21. 1999. pap. text 19.95 (*1-887432-70-1*) Beckett Pubns.
— Beckett Racing Collectibles Price Guide & Alphabetical Checklist #04: The World's Most Trusted. 1999. pap. text 14.95 (*1-887432-71-X*) Beckett Pubns.
— Beckett Racing Price Guide & Alphabetical Checklist. 1998. pap. text 14.95 (*1-887432-38-8*) Beckett Pubns.
— Christmas Collectibles: Everything You Need to Know about Christmas Collectibles. LC 99-188073. 1998. pap. 24.95 (*1-887432-57-4*) Beckett Pubns.
***Beckett Publications Editors.** Collectible Christmas Tree Pins: A Comprehensive Price Guide for Vintage & Contemporary Holida. 1999. pap. text 24.95 (*1-887432-83-3*) Beckett Pubns.
Beckett Publications Editors. Collectibles from a Galaxy Far, Far Away: A Movie Fan's Extreme Guide. LC 99-227418. (Illus.). 256p. 1999. pap. 24.95 (*1-887432-73-6*) Beckett Pubns.
— Dale Earnhardt: The Intimidator. LC 98-235192. 1998. 19.95 (*1-887432-59-0*) Beckett Pubns.
***Beckett Publications Editors.** Dan Marino: The Making of A Legend. 1999. 19.95 (*1-887432-78-7*) Beckett Pubns.
Beckett Publications Editors. Fathers & Sons (Hill) Stories of How Sports Builds Lifetime Bonds. 128p. 1999. 19.95 (*1-887432-66-3*) Beckett Pubns.
— Fathers & Sons (McGwire) Stories of How Sport Builds Lifelong Bonds. (Illus.). 128p. 1999. 19.95 (*1-887432-75-2*) Beckett Pubns.
— Football Card Alphabetical Checklist. 1998. pap. 14.95 (*1-887432-41-8*) Beckett Pubns.
— Football Card Price Guide. 1998. pap. 19.95 (*1-887432-40-X*) Beckett Pubns.
— Football Card Price Guide, Vol. 14. 1998. pap. text 19.95 (*1-887432-29-9*) Beckett Pubns.
***Beckett Publications Editors.** Good Sports: Athletes Your Kids Can Look Up to. 1999. 19.95 (*1-887432-62-0*) Beckett Pubns.
Beckett Publications Editors. Hockey Card Price Guide & Alphabetical Checklist. 1998. pap. 24.95 (*1-887432-42-6*) Beckett Pubns.
— Hockey Card Price Guide & Alphabetical Checklist, Vol. 17. 1998. pap. text 24.95 (*1-887432-30-2*) Beckett Pubns.
— Joe DiMaggio: The Yankee Clipper. LC 98-235193. (Illus.). 1998. 19.95 (*1-887432-60-4*) Beckett Pubns.
— John Elway. LC 99-197338. 126p. 1999. write for info. (*1-887432-74-4*) Beckett Pubns.
— Ken Griffry, Jr. LC 99-218306. 1999. 19.95 (*1-887432-64-7*) Beckett Pubns.
***Beckett Publications Editors.** Mark McGwire: On the Record, 1. LC 98-232598. 1998. 19.95 (*1-887432-63-9*) Beckett Pubns.
Beckett Publications Editors. Memories of Mike. LC 99-227075. 1999. 19.95 (*1-887432-67-1*) Beckett Pubns.
— Michael Jordan: An Illustrated Tribute to the World's Greatest Athlete. 1998. pap. 24.95 (*1-887432-61-2*) Beckett Pubns.
— Michael Jordan Memorabilia: Everything You Need to Know about Collecting. LC 99-189068. 1998. pap. 24.95 (*1-887432-55-8*) Beckett Pubns.
— New York Yankees Collectibles: An Exhaustive Guide to Memorabilia for America's Favorite Team. LC 99-236284. 1999. pap. text 24.95 (*1-887432-65-5*) Beckett Pubns.
— No Fear. LC 99-192215. 1998. pap. 24.95 (*1-887432-53-1*) Beckett Pubns.
— Sports Art of Bart Forbes. LC 99-190383. 1998. 39.95 (*1-887432-51-5*) Beckett Pubns.
— Star Wars Collectibles: Everything You Need to Know about Star Wars Collectibles. LC 99-188148. 1998. pap. 24.95 (*1-887432-56-6*) Beckett Pubns.
— Super Sunday: The Inside Slant on the Ultimate Game. LC 99-184114. 1998. pap. 39.95 (*1-887432-52-3*) Beckett Pubns.
***Beckett Publications Editors.** 300 Great Baseball Cards of the 20th Century: A Historical Tribute by The Hobby's Most Relied Up. 1999. 19.95 (*1-887432-80-9*) Beckett Pubns.
Beckett Publications Editors. 12 Rounds with Oscar de la Hoya. LC 99-187017. 1998. pap. 24.95 (*1-887432-50-7*) Beckett Pubns.
***Beckett Publications Staff.** Beckett Football Card Alphabetical Checklist. LC 97-222463. 1998. pap. write for info. (*1-887432-32-9*) Beckett Pubns.
***Beckett Publications Staff, ed.** Beckett Pokemon Collector Price Guide. (Illus.). 2000. pap. 9.95 (*1-887432-96-5*) Beckett Pubns.
— Beckett Racing Collectibles & Die-Cast Price Guide. (Illus.). 2000. pap. 14.95 (*1-887432-91-4*) Beckett Pubns.
— Coca-Cola Collectible Bean Bags & Plush. (Collector's Guide to Coca Cola Items Ser.). (Illus.). 2000. pap. 24.95 (*1-887432-97-3*) Beckett Pubns.
— Coca-Cola Collectible Cars & Trucks. (Collector's Guide to Coca Cola Items Ser.). (Illus.). 2000. pap. 24.95 (*1-887432-99-X*) Beckett Pubns.
— Coca-Cola Collectible Polar Bears. (Collector's Guide to Coca Cola Items Ser.). (Illus.). 2000. pap. 24.95 (*1-887432-92-2*) Beckett Pubns.
— Coca-Cola Collectible Santas. (Collector's Guide to Coca Cola Items Ser.). (Illus.). 2000. pap. 24.95 (*1-887432-93-0*) Beckett Pubns.
***Beckett Publishing Staff, PUBLISHING.** Beckett Baseball Card Alphabetical Checklist. 1999. pap. text 19.95 (*1-887432-77-9*) Beckett Pubns.
— Beckett Football Card Alphabetical Checklist No. 1, 3. 1999. pap. text 14.95 (*1-887432-79-5*) Beckett Pubns.
— Beckett Hockey Card Price Guide & Alphabetical Checklist, 9. 1999. pap. text 24.95 (*1-887432-84-1*) Beckett Pubns.
Beckett, R. Surface & Colloid Chemistry in Natural Waters & Water Treatment. LC 90-21580. (Illus.). 166p. (C). 1990. 75.00 (*0-306-43802-X*, Plenum Trade) Perseus Pubng.
***Beckett, S. T.** Industrial Chocolate Manufacture & Use. 3rd ed. LC 99-36702. 1999. write for info. (*0-632-05433-6*) Blackwell Sci.
Beckett, Samuel. All Strange Away. 1991. pap. 6.95 (*0-7145-3858-2*) Riverrun NY.
— As the Story Was Told. 96p. 1990. 20.95 (*0-7145-4113-3*) Riverrun NY.
— En Attendant Godot. Bree, Germaine & Schoenfeld, Eric, eds. (C). 1963. pap. text 30.75 (*0-13-276957-3*) P-H.
— Cascando & Other Short Dramatic Pieces. LC 68-22023. 96p. 1969. pap. write for info. (*0-8021-5099-3*, Grove) Grove-Atltic.
— Collected Poems in English & French. LC 77-77855. (ENG & FRE.). 144p. 1977. pap. 11.00 (*0-8021-3096-8*, Grove) Grove-Atltic.
— Collected Poems, 1930-1989. 350p. 29.95 (*0-7145-4186-9*) Riverrun NY.
— The Collected Shorter Plays of Samuel Beckett. LC 83-49371. 320p. (Orig.). 1984. pap. 15.95 (*0-8021-5055-1*, Grove) Grove-Atltic.
— Collected Shorter Prose, 1945-1988. 320p. pap. 19.95 (*0-7145-4211-3*) Riverrun NY.
— Comedies et Actes Divers. Incl. Actes sans Paroles II. 1966. Cascando. 1966. Comedie. 1966. Dis Joe. 1966. Film. 1966. Paroles et Musique. 1966. Souffle. 1966. Va-Et-Vient. 1966. 1966. Set pap. 16.95 (*0-7859-0925-7*, F85940) Fr & Eur.
— Comedies et Actes Divers: Comedie; Va-et-Vient; Cascando; Parole et Musique; Dis. (FRE.). 104p. 1972. pap. 16.95 (*0-7859-1193-6*, F85940) Fr & Eur.
— Comment C'est. (FRE.). 180p. 1961. pap. 19.95 (*0-7859-0593-6*, F86010) Fr & Eur.
— The Complete Short Prose of Samuel Beckett, 1929-1989. Gontarski, S. E., ed. & intro. by. LC 95-13074. 294p. 1996. 23.00 (*0-8021-1577-2*, Grove) Grove-Atltic.
— The Complete Short Prose of Samuel Beckett, 1929-1989. Gontarski, S. E., ed. & intro. by. LC 95-13074. 336p. 1997. reprint ed. pap. 14.00 (*0-8021-3490-4*, Grove) Grove-Atltic.
— Le Depeupleur. (FRE.). 58p. 1970. pap. 12.95 (*0-7859-0631-2*, F86020) Fr & Eur.
— Derniere Bande. (FRE.). 76p. 1960. pap. 9.95 (*0-7859-0594-4*, F85950) Fr & Eur.
— Disjecta. 1995. 14.95 (*0-7145-3974-0*) Riverrun NY.
— Disjecta: Miscellaneous Writings & a Dramatic Fragment. Cohn, Ruby, ed. LC 83-48308. 176p. 1984. pap. 12.00 (*0-8021-5129-9*, Grove) Grove-Atltic.
— Dramaticules. 80p. (Orig.). pap. 7.95 (*0-7145-4214-8*) Riverrun NY.
— Dream of Fair to Middling Women. LC R6003.E282D74 1992 9. Date not set. write for info. (*0-7145-4212-1*, Pub. by Calder Pubns Ltd) Riverrun NY.
— Dream of Fair to Middling Women. 252p. 1996. pap. 15.95 (*0-7145-4213-X*) Riverrun NY.
— Eleutheria. Brodsky, Michael, tr. 200p. 1995. pap. 12.95 (*1-56201-110-3*) FoxRock.
— En Attendant Godot. (FRE.). 164p. 1952. pap. 19.95 (*0-7859-0596-0*, FC1883) Fr & Eur.
— En Attendant Godot. (FRE.). (C). 1952. pap. 13.95 (*0-8442-1997-5*, VF1997-5) NTC Contemp Pub Co.
— Endgame. 264p. 1993. 21.45 (*1-55970-217-6*, Pub. by Arcade Pub Inc) Time Warner.
— Endgame: Production Notebook. rev. ed. LC 92-44042. (Theatrical Notebooks of Samuel Beckett Ser.: Vol. 2).Tr. of Fin de Partie. (ENG & FRE.). 256p. 1993. 75.00 (*0-8021-1089-4*, Grove) Grove-Atltic.
— Endgame & Act Without Words. LC 81-47545. 96p. 1983. pap. 10.00 (*0-8021-5024-1*, Grove) Grove-Atltic.
— Ends & Odds. LC 76-14510. 128p. 1976. pap. 8.95 (*0-8021-5046-2*, Grove) Grove-Atltic.
— Fin de Partie. (FRE.). 128p. 1957. pap. 11.95 (*0-7859-0597-9*, F85979) Fr & Eur.
— First Love & Other Shorts. LC 73-15463. 96p. 1974. pap. 11.00 (*0-8021-5131-0*, Grove) Grove-Atltic.
— Happy Days. LC 61-16911. 64p. 1987. pap. 8.95 (*0-8021-3076-3*, Grove) Grove-Atltic.
— How It Is. LC 63-16998. 160p. 1965. pap. 12.00 (*0-8021-5066-7*, Grove) Grove-Atltic.
— I Can't Go on, I'll Go On: A Samuel Beckett Reader. LC 91-21178. 672p. 1992. pap. 15.95 (*0-8021-3287-1*, Grove) Grove-Atltic.
— Innomable. (FRE.). 210p. 1953. pap. 27.95 (*0-7859-0600-2*, F86030) Fr & Eur.
— Krapp's Last Tape & Other Dramatic Pieces: Krapp's Last Tape; All That Fall; Act Without Words I; Act Without Words II. LC 60-8388. 144p. 1957. reprint ed. pap. 10.00 (*0-8021-5134-5*, Grove) Grove-Atltic.
— The Lost Ones. LC 72-84341. Orig. Title: Le Depeupleur. 63p. 1988. reprint ed. pap. 9.95 (*0-8021-3092-5*, Grove) Grove-Atltic.
— Malone Meurt. (FRE.). 208p. 1947. write for info. (*0-318-72557-6*) Fr & Eur.
— Malone Meurt. (FRE.). 224p. 1951. pap. 28.95 (*0-7859-0922-2*, F86041) Fr & Eur.
— Mercier & Camier. 24.95 (*0-685-37198-0*, F86050) Fr & Eur.
— Mercier & Camier. LC 74-21639. 128p. 1991. pap. 11.00 (*0-8021-3235-9*, Grove) Grove-Atltic.
— Molloy. 15.95 (*0-685-37199-9*, F86060) Fr & Eur.
— Molloy. Bowles, Patrick, tr. from FRE. LC 55-5113. 256p. 1978. pap. 12.95 (*0-8021-5136-1*, Grove) Grove-Atltic.
— Molloy, Malone Dies, The Unnamable: A Triology. LC 98-119494. 1997. 20.00 (*0-375-40070-2*) Everymns Lib.
— More Pricks Than Kicks. LC 72-119923. 191p. 1972. pap. 11.00 (*0-8021-5137-X*, Grove) Grove-Atltic.
— More Pricks Than Kicks. 1995. pap. 11.95 (*0-7145-0705-9*) Riverrun NY.
— More Pricks Than Kicks. large type ed. 254p. 1990. 22.95 (*1-85290-015-6*, Pub. by ISIS Lrg Prnt) Transaction Pubs.
— Murphy. 208p. 1947. pap. write for info. (*0-7859-4710-8*) Fr & Eur.
— Murphy. LC 57-6939. 288p. 1969. pap. 12.00 (*0-8021-5037-3*, Grove) Grove-Atltic.
— Nohow On. 128p. 1993. pap. 12.95 (*0-7145-4112-5*) Riverrun NY.
— Nohow On: Company, Ill Seen, Ill Said, Worstward Ho. LC 95-43710. 144p. 1995. pap. 11.00 (*0-8021-3426-2*, Grove) Grove-Atltic.
— Nouvelles et Textes pour Rien. (FRE.). 208p. 1955. pap. 28.95 (*0-7859-0605-3*, F86090) Fr & Eur.
— Oh les Beaux Jours. 2nd ed. (FRE.). 92p. 1975. pap. 12.95 (*0-7859-0607-X*, F85980) Fr & Eur.
— Ohio Impromptu: Three Plays, Ohio Impromptu; Catastrophe; What Where. LC 83-49372. 64p. (Orig.). 1984. pap. 6.95 (*0-8021-5116-7*, Grove) Grove-Atltic.
— Paroles et Musique. (Coll. Bilingue). (ENG & FRE.). pap. 4.50 (*0-685-37196-4*, F85990) Fr & Eur.
— Pour Finir Encore. (FRE.). 56p. 1976. pap. 10.95 (*0-7859-0659-2*, M3063) Fr & Eur.
— Premier Amour. pap. 8.95 (*0-685-37200-6*, F86100) Fr & Eur.
— Le Premier Amour. (FRE.). 298p. 1970. 14.95 (*0-7859-4776-0*) Fr & Eur.
— Rockaby & Other Short Pieces. LC 80-8916. 80p. 1981. pap. 10.00 (*0-8021-5138-8*, Grove) Grove-Atltic.
— Samuel Beckett's Company - Compagnie & a Piece of Monologue - Solo: A Bilingual Variorum Edition. Krance, Charles, ed. LC 91-37752. (Illus.). 232p. 1993. text 15.00 (*0-8240-9610-X*, H1400) Garland.
— Shorter Plays Vol. 4: The Theatrical Notebooks of Samuel Beckett. deluxe ed. Gontarski, S. E., ed. LC 99-42689. 1999. 125.00 (*0-8021-1654-X*) Grove-Atltic.
— Stirrings Still. 46p. 1991. pap. 5.95 (*1-56201-015-8*) FoxRock.
— Stories & Texts for Nothing. Seaver, Richard, tr. from FRE. LC 67-20341. 160p. 1988. pap. 11.00 (*0-8021-5062-4*, Grove) Grove-Atltic.
— Tetes Mortes. pap. 8.95 (*0-685-37201-4*, F86110) Fr & Eur.
— Theatre One. Incl. Acte sans paroles I et II. En Attendant Godot. Fin de Partie. 29.95 (*0-685-37195-6*) Fr & Eur.
— Three Novels: Molloy; Malone Dies; The Unnamable. LC 59-13886. 416p. 1955. reprint ed. pap. 14.00 (*0-8021-5091-8*, Grove) Grove-Atltic.
— Tous Ceux Qui Tombent.Tr. of All That Fall. (FRE.). 80p. 1957. pap. 10.95 (*0-7859-0611-8*, F86000) Fr & Eur.
— Waiting for Godot. LC 54-6803. 128p. 1987. pap. 10.00 (*0-8021-3034-8*, Grove) Grove-Atltic.
— Watt. 29.95 (*0-685-37202-2*, F86120) Fr & Eur.
— Watt. LC 58-9097. 256p. 1970. pap. 12.95 (*0-8021-5140-X*, Grove) Grove-Atltic.
— Watt. 1994. pap. 14.95 (*0-7145-0610-9*) Riverrun NY.
Beckett, Samuel, tr. from SPA. Anthology of Mexican Poetry. (ENG & SPA.). 213p. (Orig.). pap. 13.95 (*0-7145-0086-0*) Riverrun NY.
Beckett, Samuel, et al. An Examination of James Joyce. LC 74-1307. (Studies in Joyce: No. 96). 1974. lib. bdg. 75.00 (*0-8383-2025-2*) M S G Haskell Hse.
— No Author Better Served: The Correspondence of Samuel Beckett & Alan Schneider. LC 98-5207. 512p. 1998. 35.00 (*0-674-62522-6*) HUP.
Beckett, Samuel, jt. auth. see Monarch Notes Staff.
Beckett, Samuel, tr. see Bosquet, Alain.
Beckett, Samuel, tr. see Paz, Octavio, ed.
Beckett, Sandra L. Les Reflets, les Echos & les Ombres Chez Henri Bosco: Une Etude Du Double Obscur. LC 93-15152. (FRE.). 296p. 1993. 89.95 (*0-7734-2898-4*) E Mellen.
Beckett, Sandra L., ed. Reflections of Change: Children's Literature since 1945. 74. LC 96-22004. (Contributions to the Study of World Literature Ser.: 74). 216p. 1997. 55.00 (*0-313-30145-X*, Greenwood Pr) Greenwood.
***Beckett, Sandra L., ed.** Transcending Boundaries: Writing for a Dual Audience of Children & Adults. LC 99-39096. (Children's Literature & Culture Ser.: No. 13). 304p. 1999. 55.00 (*0-8153-3359-5*, H2152, Pub. by Garland) Taylor & Francis.
***Beckett Sci Fi Collector Staff.** Sci-fi Collectiblest: A Comprehensive Price Guide & Checklist. 1999. pap. text 24.95 (*1-887432-82-5*) Beckett Pubns.
Beckett, Sheilah. Beauty & the Beast: Full-Color Sturdy Book. LC 95-14521. (Little Activity Bks.). (Illus.). 16p. (Orig.). (J). 1996. pap. text 1.00 (*0-486-28824-2*) Dover.
— Little Red Riding Hood: Full-Color Sturdy Book. LC 95-53008. (Illus.). 16p. (J). 1996. pap. 1.00 (*0-486-29168-5*) Dover.
— Pegatinas de Blancanieves. 1995. pap. text 1.00 (*0-486-28839-0*) Dover.
— Snow White: Full-Color Picture Book. LC 94-48705. (Little Activity Bks.).Tr. of Schneewittchen. (ENG & GER., Illus.). 16p. (Orig.). (J). 1995. pap. text 1.00 (*0-486-28516-2*) Dover.
— Stickers - Make Your Own Sleeping Beauty. (Illus.). (J). (ps-3). 1996. pap. 1.00 (*0-486-29392-0*, 256194Q) Dover.
Beckett, Sheilah, retold by. The Little Mermaid: Full-Color Sturdy Book. LC 95-18749. (Little Activity Bks.). (Illus.). 16p. (Orig.). (J). 1995. pap. text 1.00 (*0-486-28825-0*) Dover.
Beckett, Sheilah & Perrault, Charles. Sleeping Beauty. LC 97-19552. (Illus.). 12p. (J). 1997. pap. 1.00 (*0-486-29915-5*) Dover.
Beckett, Simon. Fine Lines: A Novel. LC 94-13613. 304p. 1994. 22.00 (*0-671-89206-1*) S&S Trade.
Beckett, Thomas. The Accountant's Assistant. Brief, Richard P., ed. LC 80-1471. (Dimensions of Accounting Theory & Practice Ser.). 1980. reprint ed. lib. bdg. 18.95 (*0-405-13501-7*) Ayer.
Beckett, Tom. Separations. (Chapbook Ser.). 24p. 1988. pap. 5.00 (*0-945112-06-8*) Generator Pr.
***Beckett, Tom, et al, eds.** A Wild Salience: The Writing of Rae Armantrout. 180p. 2000. pap. 15.00 (*1-58711-025-3*) Burning Pr.
Beckett, W. H. Akokoaso, a Survey of a Gold Coast Village. LC 76-44689. reprint ed. 32.50 (*0-404-15905-2*) AMS Pr.
Beckett, Wendy. Beckmann & the Self. LC 97-3597. 1997. write for info. (*3-7913-1793-8*, Pub. by Prestel) te Neues.
— A Child's Book of Prayer in Art. LC 94-40362. (Illus.). 32p. (J). (ps-4). 1995. 14.95 (*1-56458-875-0*) DK Pub Inc.
***Beckett, Wendy.** In the Midst of Chaos, Peace. 1999. 19.95 (*0-89870-764-1*) Ignatius Pr.
— Love: Meditations on Love. 48p. 2000. 9.95 (*0-7894-5338-X*, D K Ink) DK Pub Inc.
Beckett, Wendy. Meditations on Joy. LC 95-11886. (Sr. Wendy's Meditations Ser.). (Illus.). 48p. 1995. 8.95 (*0-7894-0179-7*, 6-70486) DK Pub Inc.
— Meditations on Love. LC 95-11885. (Sr. Wendy's Meditations Ser.). (Illus.). 48p. 1995. 8.95 (*0-7894-0178-9*, 6-70485) DK Pub Inc.
— Meditations on Peace. LC 95-11884. (Sr. Wendy's Meditations Ser.). (Illus.). 48p. 1995. 8.95 (*0-7894-0177-0*, 6-70484) DK Pub Inc.
— Meditations on Silence. LC 95-11883. (Sr. Wendy's Meditations Ser.). (Illus.). 48p. 1995. 8.95 (*0-7894-0180-0*, 6-70487) DK Pub Inc.
— My Favorite Things: 75 Works of Art from Around the World. LC 98-53881. (Illus.). 160p. 1999. 29.95 (*0-8109-4387-5*, Pub. by Abrams) Time Warner.
— The Mystical Now: Art & the Sacred. LC 92-24967. 1993. 25.95 (*0-87663-647-4*, Pub. by Universe) St Martin.
***Beckett, Wendy.** Sister Wendy's American Collection. 288p. 2000. 40.00 (*0-06-019556-8*) HarpC.
— Sister Wendy's Book of Muses. LC 98-44325. 48p. (Orig.). 2000. 14.95 (*0-8109-4388-3*, Pub. by Abrams) Time Warner.
Beckett, Wendy. Sister Wendy's Book of Saints. LC 97-33492. 96p. 1998. 19.95 (*0-7894-2398-7*) DK Pub Inc.
— Sister Wendy's Book of Saints. (Illus.). 96p. 1998. 19.95 (*0-8294-1270-0*) Loyola Pr.
— Sister Wendy's Grand Tour: Discovering Europe's Great Art. LC 96-69110. (Illus.). 166p. 1996. 24.95 (*1-55670-509-3*) Stewart Tabori & Chang.
— Sister Wendy's Meditations. LC 94-6322. 160p. 1998. 19.95 (*0-7894-3746-5*) DK Pub Inc.
— Sister Wendy's Nativity. LC 99-167653. (Illus.). 96p. 1998. 24.95 (*0-06-019336-0*) HarpC.
***Beckett, Wendy.** Sister Wendy's Nativity. (Illus.). 1998. 19.95 (*0-8294-1367-7*) Loyola Pr.
Beckett, Wendy. Sister Wendy's Odyssey: A Journey of Artistic Discovery. 96p. 1998. 24.95 (*1-55670-857-2*) Stewart Tabori & Chang.
— Sister Wendy's 1000 Masterpieces. LC 99-20355. 512p. 1999. 40.00 (*0-7894-4603-0*) DK Pub Inc.
— Sister Wendy's Story of Painting. LC 94-6322. (Illus.). 400p. 1997. 39.95 (*1-56458-615-4*) DK Pub Inc.
***Beckett, Wendy.** Story of Painting. (Illus.). 736p. 2000. 40.00 (*0-7894-6805-0*) DK Pub Inc.
Beckett, Wendy, jt. auth. see Moyers, Bill.
Beckett, Wendy M., tr. see John Abbot of Ford.
Beckett, William. Metamorphosis: A Programmer Looks at the Software Crisis. 362p. 1997. pap. text 15.00 (*0-9660333-9-6*) Numerical Analog.
Beckey, Fred. Cascade Alpine Guide: Columbia River to Stevens Pass. 2nd ed. LC 86-23899. (Climbing & High Routes Ser.: Vol. 1). (Illus.). 350p. 1987. vinyl bd. 29.95 (*0-89886-127-6*) Mountaineers.
— Cascade Alpine Guide: Rainy Pass to Fraser River. 2nd ed. (Climbing & High Routes Ser.: Vol. 3). (Illus.). 350p. 1995. vinyl bd. 29.95 (*0-89886-423-2*) Mountaineers.
— Cascade Alpine Guide: Stevens Pass to Rainy Pass. 2nd ed. LC 86-23899. (Climbing & High Routes Ser.: Vol. 2). (Illus.). 350p. 1989. vinyl bd. 29.95 (*0-89886-152-7*) Mountaineers.
— Challenge of the North Cascades. (Illus.). 292p. 1996. pap. text 14.95 (*0-89886-479-8*) Mountaineers.

An Asterisk (*) at the beginning of an entry indicates that the title is appearing for the first time.

*Beckey, Fred. Columbia River to Stevens Pass. 3rd ed. (Cascade Alpine Guide Ser. : Vol. 1). (Illus.). 384p. 2000. pap. 34.95 (0-89886-577-8) Mountaineers.
Beckey, Fred. Mount McKinley: Icy Crown of North America. (Illus.). 320p. 1993. 29.95 (0-89886-362-7) Mountaineers.
— Mount McKinley: Icy Crown of North America. 320p. 1999. pap. 19.95 (0-89886-646-4) Mountaineers.
— Mountains of North America. LC 82-3315. (Illus.). 288p. 1982. 35.00 (0-87156-320-7, Pub. by Sierra) Random.
— A Range of Glaciers: The Exploration & Survey of the Northern Cascade Range. LC 98-34488. (Illus.). 750p. 2000. 60.00 (0-87595-243-7) Oregon Hist.
Beckey, H. D. Field Ionization & Field Desorption Mass Spectroscopy. 1978. 157.00 (0-08-020612-3, Pub. by Pergamon Repr) Franklin.
Beckfield, Denise F. Master Your Panic . . . & Take Back Your Life! Twelve Treatment Sessions to Overcome High Anxiety. 2nd ed. LC 97-51465. 304p. 1998. pap. 15.95 (1-886230-08-0) Impact Pubs CA.
Beckford, James A. Religion & Advanced Industrial Society. 160p. 1989. text 34.95 (0-04-301228-0); pap. text 16.95 (0-04-301229-9) Routledge.
Beckford, James A., ed. New Religious Movements & Rapid Social Change. 272p. (C). 1987. text 47.50 (0-8039-8003-5); pap. text 19.95 (0-8039-8591-6) Sage.
Beckford, James A. & Gilliat, Sophie. Religion in Prison: Equal Rites in a Multi-Faith Society. LC 97-38738. 250p. (C). 1998. 54.95 (0-521-62246-8) Cambridge U Pr.
Beckford, James A. & Luckmann, Thomas, eds. The Changing Face of Religion. (International Sociology Ser.: Vol. 37). 192p. (C). 1989. 39.95 (0-8039-8211-9); pap. text 18.95 (0-8039-8592-4) Sage.
Beckford, John. Quality: A Critical Introduction. LC 97-51904. 352p. (C). 1998. 100.00 (0-415-18163-1); pap. 34.99 (0-415-18164-X) Routledge.
Beckford, Joseph G. Bank Compliance Law, 2 vols., Set. 1400p. 1995. 245.00 (0-7913-2535-0) Warren Gorham & Lamont.
— Bank Compliance Law, Vol. 1. 1995. write for info. (0-7913-2533-4) Warren Gorham & Lamont.
— Bank Compliance Law, Vol. 2. 1995. write for info. (0-7913-2534-2) Warren Gorham & Lamont.
— Bank Holding Company Compliance Manual. 1986. ring bd. 285.00 (0-8205-1507-8) Bender.
*Beckford, Peter. Thoughts on Hunting. LC 99-58353. (Illus.). 300p. 2000. lthr. 150.00 (1-56416-172-2) Derrydale Pr.
— Thoughts on Hunting. LC 99-58353. (Illus.). 300p. 2000. 35.00 (1-56833-151-7) Derrydale Pr.
Beckford, Ruth. Katherine Dunham, a Biography. LC 79-4577. (Dance Program Ser.: No. 14). (Illus.). 183p. reprint ed. pap. 56.80 (0-7837-0820-3, 204113400019) Bks Demand.
*Beckford, Ruth. Still Groovin' Affirmations for Women in the Second Half of Life. LC 99-34099. 160p. 1999. 19.95 (0-8298-1337-3) Pilgrim OH.
— Still Groovin' Affirmations for Women in the Second Half of Life. 176p. 2000. pap. 12.95 (1-57071-529-7) Sourcebks.
Beckford, William. Biographical Memoirs of Extraordinary Painters. Gemmett, Robert J., ed. LC 69-19434. (Illus.). 112p. 1975. 24.50 (0-8386-7367-8) Fairleigh Dickinson.
— Biographical Memoirs of Extraordinary Painters (1780) Ward, Philip, ed. (Language & Literature Ser.: Vol. 6). 1977. pap. 25.00 (0-900891-13-0) Oleander Pr.
— The Episodes of Vathek. (Dedalus European Classics Ser.). 208p. 1995. pap. 16.95 (0-7818-0413-2) Hippocrene Bks.
— The Episodes of Vathek. 2nd ed. Jack, Malcolm R., ed. Marzials, Frank, tr. from FRE. (European Classics). 207p. 1999. reprint ed. pap. 11.99 (1-873982-61-5, Pub. by Dedalus) Hippocrene Bks.
— Modern Novel Writing: Azemia, 4 vols. LC 74-81366. 264p. 1970. reprint ed. 50.00 (0-8201-1063-9) Schol Facsimiles.
— The Travel-Diaries of William Beckford of Fonthill, 2 vols. (BCL1-PR English Literature Ser.). 1992. reprint ed. lib. bdg. 150.00 (0-7812-7435-4) Rprt Serv.
— Vathek. Lonsdale, Richard, ed. & intro. by. LC 99-208231. (Oxford World's Classics Ser.). 224p. 1999. pap. 9.95 (0-19-283656-0) OUP.
*Beckford, William. Vathek. Reed, Jeremy, ed. (Classics). 160p. 2000. reprint ed. pap. 12.95 (1-84068-018-0, Pub. by Creation Books) Subterranean Co.
Beckford, William. Vathek: The English Translation by Samuel Henley (1786) & the French Editions of Lausanne & Paris -1787., 3 vols. in 1. LC 72-4324. (FRE.). 768p. 1972. reprint ed. 90.00 (0-8201-1102-3) Schol Facsimiles.
Beckford, William & Jack, Malcolm. Vathek & Other Stories: A William Beckford Reader. LC 94-109361. 314 p. 1993. 59.95 (1-85196-049-X, Pub. by Pickering & Chatto) Ashgate Pub Co.
Beckh, ed. Geoponica. (GRE.). 1994. reprint ed. 125.00 (3-519-01387-8, T1387, Pub. by B G Teubner) U of Mich Pr.
Beckham, Allidees N. In Praise of the Bridge that Brought Us Over: Favorite Sermons of the Rev. Allidees Nicholson Beckham. 120p. Date not set. pap. write for info. (0-9652186-0-0) Saint Marks Church.
Beckham, Barry. The Black Student's Guide to Colleges: Profiles of 182 Colleges, Black & White. 3rd ed. 496p. 1995. pap. 16.95 (0-931761-07-7) Beckham Pubns.
— College Selection Workbook: Self-Paced Exercises to Help You Choose the Right College. 64p. 1995. pap. 6.95 (0-931761-10-7) Beckham Pubns.
— Double Dunk: The Inspiring Story of a Harlem Basketball Legend. 192p. 1995. pap. 9.95 (0-931761-22-0) Beckham Pubns.
— Runner Mack. LC 83-6140. (Howard University Press Library of Contemporary Literature). 213p. 1984. pap. 14.95 (0-88258-116-3) Howard U Pr.
Beckham, Barry, ed. The Black Student's Guide to Colleges. 4th ed. 480p. 1996. pap. 19.95 (1-56833-080-4) Madison Bks UPA.
— The Black Student's Guide to Scholarships. 5th ed. 216p. 1998. pap. 17.95 (1-56833-117-7, Pub. by Madison Bks UPA) Natl Bk Netwk.
— The Black Student's Guide to Scholarships: 500+ Private Money Sources for Black & Minority Students. rev. ed. 224p. 1996. pap. 14.95 (1-56833-079-0) Madison Bks UPA.
Beckham, Beverly. A Gift of Time. Kromer, Ed, ed. (Illus.). 244p. 1991. pap. 12.95 (1-879688-00-X) Host Comns Inc.
Beckham, Carole. Cycles of Opportunity. LC 97-32068. (Illus.). 368p. 1998. pap. 19.95 (0-9635766-3-1) Source.
Beckham, Claire, ed. see Nisbet, James D.
Beckham, Diane B. Federal Rules, Annotated. 1995th ed. LC 99-211520. 404p. 1995. write for info. (1-57625-014-8) Amer Law Media.
Beckham, Dow. Swift Flows the River: Log Driving in Oregon. (Illus.). 207p. (Orig.). (C). 1992. pap. text 15.95 (0-930998-04-9) Arago Bks.
Beckham, E. Edward & Leber, William R., eds. Handbook of Depression. 2nd ed. LC 94-49600. 628p. 1995. lib. bdg. 65.00 (0-89862-841-5) Guilford Pubns.
Beckham, Edward E. & Leber, William R., eds. Handbook of Depression. 2nd ed. LC 94-49600. 628p. 1997. pap. 37.00 (1-57230-224-0, 0224) Guilford Pubns.
Beckham, James M. Genealogy of the Beckham Family in Virginia. (Illus.). 98p. 1991. reprint ed. pap. 20.00 (0-8328-0221-2); reprint ed. lib. bdg. 28.00 (0-8328-0220-4) Higginson Bk Co.
Beckham, Joseph. Faculty Staff Nonrenewal & Dismissal for Cause in Institutions of Higher Education. LC 98-7646. (The Higher Education Administration Ser.). 1998. 18.95 (0-912557-21-4) Coll Admin Pubns.
Beckham, Joseph C. Faculty-Staff Dismissal for Cause in Institutions of Higher Education. Hardin, Julia P., ed. LC 86-18767. (Higher Education Administration Ser.). 68p. 1994. pap. 18.95 (0-912557-06-0) Coll Admin Pubns.
— Meeting Legal Challenges. LC 96-60048. (School Leader's Library). 203p. 1996. pap. 39.95 (1-56676-407-6) Scarecrow.
Beckham, Laura. A Bad Seed. LC 98-89499. 375p. 1998. text 25.00 (0-7388-0239-5); pap. text 15.00 (0-7388-0240-9) Xlibris Corp.
Beckham, Sheila & O'Conner, Helen K. Waianae Diet CookBook. 89p. 1993. pap. text 7.25 (0-9646023-1-8) Waianae Coast CHC.
Beckham, Stephen D. The Land of the Umpqua: A History of Douglas County, Oregon. (Illus.). 288p. (Orig.). 1986. pap. 15.00 (0-9616574-1-3); text 25.00 (0-9616574-0-5) Douglas Cty Planning.
— Lewis & Clark College. LC 91-71222. (Illus.). 160p. 1991. 29.95 (0-9630866-1-8) L&C Coll.
— Requiem for a People: The Rogue Indians & the Frontiersmen. LC 96-22808. (Northwest Reprints Ser.). (Illus.). 232p. 1996. reprint ed. pap. 15.95 (0-87071-521-6) Oreg St U Pr.
— The Simpsons of Shore Acres. (Illus.). 54p. 1992. pap. text 6.95 (0-685-53206-2) Arago Bks.
— The Simpsons of Shore Acres. 2nd ed. (Illus.). 64p. reprint ed. pap. 6.95 (0-930998-05-7) Arago Bks.
Beckham, Stephen D., ed. Many Faces: An Anthology of Oregon Autobiography. (Oregon Literature Ser.: Vol. 2). (Illus.). 352p. (Orig.). 1993. pap. 21.95 (0-87071-372-8); text 35.95 (0-87071-371-X) Oreg St U Pr.
Beckham, William A. The Second Reformation: Reshaping the Church for the 21st Century. (Illus.). 253p. (Orig.). 1995. pap. 12.95 (1-880828-90-1) Touch Pubns.
Beckhand, Richard & Harris, Reubin T. Organizational Transitions: Managing Complex Change. 2nd ed. (Organization Development Ser.). (Illus.). 117p. (C). 1987. pap. text 40.00 (0-201-10887-9) Addison-Wesley.
Beckhard, Richard. Agent of Change: My Life, My Practice. LC 97-21159. 304p. 1997. 32.95 (0-7879-1012-0) Jossey-Bass.
Beckhard, Richard. Participant Workbook. 1985. pap. text 14.95 (0-201-10722-8) Addison-Wesley.
Beckhard, Richard & Pritchard, Wendy. Changing the Essence: The Art of Creating & Leading Fundamental Change in Organizations. LC 91-37204. (Management Ser.). 125p. 1992. mass mkt. 25.00 (1-55542-412-0) Jossey-Bass.
Beckhart, Benjamin H., ed. New York Money Market, 4 vols. LC 79-155152. reprint ed. 210.00 (0-404-04550-2) AMS Pr.
Beckhaus, Neil, tr. see Hemmer, H.
Beckheuer, Burkhard. Paulus und Jerusalem: Kollekte und Mission im Theologischen Denken des Heidenapostels. (Europaische Hochschulschriften Ser.: Reihe 23, Bd. 611). (GER.). 287p. 1997. 54.95 (3-631-32093-0) P Lang Pubng.
*Beckhorn, Susan. In the Morning of the World: Six Woodland Why Stories. (Illus.). 48p. (J). 2000. 15.95 (0-89272-503-6) Down East.
Becking, Bob. The Fall of Samaria: A Historical & Archeological Study. LC 92-15670. (Studies in the History of the Ancient Near East: Vol. 2). xvi, 153p. 1992. 65.50 (90-04-09633-7) Brill Academic Pubs.
Becking, Bob & Dijkstra, Meindert, eds. On Reading Prophetic Texts: Gender-Specific & Related Studies in Memory of Fokkelien van Dijk-Hemmes. LC 95-46889. (Biblical Interpretation Ser.: Vol. 18). 1996. 98.00 (90-04-10274-4) Brill Academic Pubs.
Becking, Bob & Korpel, Marjo C. A. The Crisis of Israelite Religion: Transformation of Religious Tradition in Exilic & Post-Exilic Times. LC 99-22793. (Oudtestamentische Studien). 1999. write for info. (90-04-11496-3) Brill Academic Pubs.
Becking, L. G. Baas, see Veendorp, H. & Baas Becking, L. G.
Beckingham, Ann C. Promoting Healthy Aging: A Nursing & Community Perspective. 496p. (C). (gr. 13). 1993. pap. text 30.00 (0-8016-0916-X, 00916) Mosby Inc.
Beckingham, Charles F., jt. ed. see Hamilton, Bernard.
Beckingham, Charles F., ed. see John, Prester.
*Beckingham, Dolores. Heavenly Poetry. 1999. pap. write for info. (1-58235-392-1) Watermrk Pr.
Beckington, Thomas. Memorials of the Reign of King Henry VI: Official Correspondence of Thomas Bekynton, Secretary to Henry VI & Bishop of Bath & Wells, 2 vols. Williams, George, ed. (Rolls Ser.: No. 56). 1974. reprint ed. 140.00 (0-8115-1118-9) Periodicals Srv.
Beckinsale, Monica & Beckinsale, Robert P. Southern Europe: A Systematic Geographical Study. LC 74-14940. (Illus.). 352p. 1975. 55.00 (0-8419-0178-3) Holmes & Meier.
Beckinsale, Robert P., jt. auth. see Beckinsale, Monica.
Becklake, John, ed. History of Rocketry & Astronautics. (AAS History Ser.: Vol. 17). (Illus.). 480p. 1995. 60.00 (0-87703-395-1, Am Astronaut Soc); pap. 40.00 (0-87703-396-X, Am Astronaut Soc) Univelt Inc.
Becklake, Sue. Space. World Book Staff, ed. LC 97-12158. (Picture Reference Ser.). (Illus.). 48p. (J). (gr. 2-6). 1997. write for info. (0-7166-9900-1) World Bk.
— Space: The Official Planetarium Book. 128p. 1994. pap. 14.95 (1-55958-583-8) Prima Pub.
— Traveling in Space. LC 90-11017. (Exploring the Universe Ser.). (Illus.). 32p. (J). (gr. 4-6). 1991. lib. bdg. 18.60 (0-8167-2136-X) Troll Communs.
— Traveling in Space. LC 90-11017. (Exploring the Universe Ser.). 32p. (J). (gr. 4-6). 1996. pap. 4.95 (0-8167-2137-8) Troll Communs.
— The Visual Dictionary of the Universe. LC 93-22419. (Eyewitness Visual Dictionaries Ser.). (Illus.). (J). (gr. 4 up). 1993. 18.95 (1-56458-336-8) DK Pub Inc.
Becklake, Sue, et al. All about Space. LC 97-29790. (Scholastic First Encyclopedia Ser.). (Illus.). 80p. (J). (gr. k-3). 1998. 14.95 (0-590-10471-3) Scholastic Inc.
*Beckland, Jack. Summers with the Bears: Six Seasons in the North Woods. (Illus.). 192p. 2000. pap. 11.95 (0-7868-8537-8, Pub. by Disney Pr) Time Warner.
*Becklane, Susan. Space. (Picture Reference Ser.). (Illus.). (J). (gr. 2-6). 2000. pap. 13.95 (1-58728-654-8) Two Can Pub.
Beckler, Steve. Dirty Hands: The Problem of Political Morality. (Avebury Series in Philosophy). 163p. 1993. 71.95 (1-85628-489-1, Pub. by Avebury) Ashgate Pub Co.
Beckles. Basic Economics. (C). 1995. pap. text 18.36 (0-395-76170-0) HM.
Beckles, Frances N. Green Book Scholarship Directory: Premier National Edition 1997/1998. 40p. 1996. 21.95 (0-9654830-0-2) Coll Cost Cnslting.
Beckles, Hilary. The Development of West Indies Cricket. LC 98-45481. 208p. 1999. 59.95 (0-7453-1477-5, Pub. by Pluto GBR) Stylus Pub VA.
*Beckles, Hilary. The Development of West Indies Cricket. 208p. 1999. pap. 24.95 (0-7453-1472-4, Pub. by Pluto GBR) Stylus Pub VA.
Beckles, Hilary. The Development of West Indies Cricket. LC 98-45481. (Illus.). 256p. 1999. 59.95 (0-7453-1467-8, Pub. by Pluto GBR) Stylus Pub VA.
*Beckles, Hilary. The Development of West Indies Cricket. (Illus.). 256p. 1999. pap. 24.95 (0-7453-1462-7, Pub. by Pluto GBR) Stylus Pub VA.
Beckles, Hilary & Sheperd, Verene, eds. Caribbean Slavery in the Atlantic World. rev. ed. LC 99-48681. Orig. Title: Caribbean Slave Society & Economy. (Illus.). 1200p. (C). 2000. pap. text 34.95 (1-55876-185-3) Wiener Pubs Inc.
Beckles, Hilary M. Caribbean Slave Society & Economy. 496p. 1993. 40.00 (1-56584-085-2, Pub. by New Press NY) Norton.
— Centering Woman: Gender Relations in Caribbean Slave Society. LC 98-43652. 226p. (C). 1999. text 39.95 (1-55876-204-3); pap. text 16.95 (1-55876-205-1) Wiener Pubs Inc.
— A History of Barbados: From Amerindian Society to Nation State. (Illus.). 240p. (C). 1990. pap. text 22.95 (0-521-35879-5) Cambridge U Pr.
— Natural Rebels: A Social History of Enslaved Women in Barbados. LC 89-10767. 224p. (Orig.). (C). 1990. text 40.00 (0-8135-1510-6); pap. text 16.00 (0-8135-1511-4) Rutgers U Pr.
Beckles, Hilary M. & Shepherd, Verene, eds. Caribbean Freedom: Economy & Society from Emancipation to the Present. LC 95-52867. 596p. (C). 1998. pap. text 26.95 (1-55876-128-4) Wiener Pubs Inc.
— Caribbean Slave Society & Economy: A Student Reader. LC 93-6739. 496p. 1993. pap., student ed. 20.00 (1-56584-086-0, Pub. by New Press NY) Norton.
Beckles, Hilary M. & Stoddart, Brian, eds. Liberation Cricket: West Indies Cricket Culture. LC 94-11595. (Sport, Society, & Politics Ser.). 1995. text 29.95 (0-7190-4315-8, Pub. by Manchester Univ Pr) St Martin.
Beckles, Reuben. A Collection of Twelve Short Stories. LC 99-201284. 192p. 1998. pap. text 12.95 (0-9657004-3-7) Aquarian Pub Co.
— A Delcaration of Independence! A Statement of Truth! Black Power! 426p. (Orig.). 1996. pap. text 19.95 (0-9657004-0-2) Aquarian Pub Co.
Beckley, Bill & Shapiro, David, eds. Uncontrollable Beauty: Toward a New Aesthetics. LC 98-70100. 448p. 1998. 24.95 (1-880559-90-0) Allworth Pr.
Beckley, Catherine, jt. ed. see Donegan, Thomas.
Beckley, Harlan R., ed. The Annual of the Society of Christian Ethics, 1996. 300p. (Orig.). 1993. pap. 18.00 (0-685-66864-9) Georgetown U Pr.
Beckley, Harlan R. & Swezey, Charles M., eds. James M. Gustafson's Theocentric Ethics: Interpretations & Assessments. LC 88-21836. 304p. (C). 1988. text 34.95 (0-86554-307-0, MUP/H253) Mercer Univ Pr.
Beckley, Harlan R., ed. & intro. see Ryan, John A.
Beckley, Jeff, et al. Eudora Light: Version 3 for Windows User Manual. (Illus.). 133p. 1998. reprint ed. pap. 9.95 (1-888725-20-6) Sci & Human Pr.
Beckley, John James. Justifying Jefferson: The Political Writings of John James Beckley. 281p. 1996. pap. 22.00 (0-16-048431-6, Library of Cong) USGPO.
Beckley, John L. The Power of Little Words: Some Ideas to Improve Your Writing. (Illus.). 128p. 1984. 14.95 (0-910187-02-9) Economics Pr.
— Some Curious Facts about How We Make Our Living: Why Didn't Somebody Tell Us. Flint, Helen, ed. LC 82-12987. (Illus.). 136p. (Orig.). 1986. 14.95 (0-910187-00-2) Economics Pr.
— Working with People. 158p. 1985. 14.95 (0-910187-03-7) Economics Pr.
Beckley, John L., ed. see Rowland, Daniel.
Beckley, Judi & West, Randy. Rose-a-Down Dilly. (Illus.). 32p. (Orig.). 1981. pap. 4.95 (0-942478-01-0) Photopia Pr.
Beckley, Pedr. Revelando el Futuro (Unlocking the Future) Lo Que-Horoscopo (What-Horoscope) (SPA.). 1.50 (0-685-74981-9, 490256) Editorial Unilit.
Beckley, Rene. Ancient Walls of East Anglia. 144p. (C). 1988. 50.00 (0-900963-93-X, Pub. by T Dalton) St Mut.
Beckley, Robert M. & Myers, Sherrill M. Theater Facility Impact Study: Theater Facilities: Guidelines & Strategies, Vol. 1. (Publications in Architecture & Urban Planning: No. R81-9). (Illus.). vi, 139p. 1981. per. 15.00 (0-938744-21-6) U of Wis Ctr Arch-Urban.
Beckley, Ross A., jt. auth. see Fisher, Barbara C.
Beckley, Timothy G. Book of Space Contacts. (Illus.). 72p. 1981. pap. 9.95 (0-938294-05-9) Inner Light.
— MIB, Aliens among Us. 30p. 1996. reprint ed. spiral bd. 9.50 (0-7873-0085-3) Hlth Research.
— Psychic & UFO Revelations in Last Days. 2nd ed. (Illus.). 189p. 1989. pap. 15.00 (0-938294-01-6) Inner Light.
— Revelation - The Divine Fire. 1988. pap. 12.95 (0-938294-60-1) Inner Light.
— The Shaver Mystery & the Inner Earth. 95p. 1985. reprint ed. spiral bd. 14.00 (0-7873-0084-5) Hlth Research.
— Strange Encounters: Bizarre & Eerie Contact with UFO Occupants. 96p. 1992. 15.00 (0-938294-21-0) Inner Light.
— Subterranean Worlds Inside Earth. 1992. 15.00 (0-938294-22-9) Inner Light.
— The UFO Silencers: Mystery of the Men in Black. (Illus.). 160p. 1992. 21.95 (0-938294-87-3) Inner Light.
— UFOs among the Stars: Close-Encounters of the Famous. (Illus.). 112p. 1992. 15.00 (0-938294-45-8) Inner Light.
— The Visitation: Modern Miracles & Signs. 14p. 1981. spiral bd. 7.00 (0-7873-1207-X) Hlth Research.
Beckley, Timothy G., ed. Messages from the People of the Planet Clarion: The True Experiences of Truman Bethurum. 150p. 1997. 14.95 (0-938294-55-5) Inner Light.
Beckley, Timothy G. & Crockett, Arthur. Prophecies of the Presidents: The Spiritual Destiny of America Revealed! 1992. 15.00 (0-938294-39-3) Inner Light.
Beckley, Timothy G. & Tessman, Diane. Your Passport to Heaven. 150p. 14.95 (0-938294-88-1) Inner Light.
Beckley, Timothy G., jt. auth. see Crockett, Arthur.
Beckley West, Judi. The Brothers: A Protohistory. 2nd abr. rev. ed. West, Randall, ed. 85p. (Orig.). 1981. pap. 17.95 (0-942478-00-2) Photopia Pr.
Beckley, William. Creating a Classroom Portfolio System. 134p. 1997. pap. text, spiral bd. 19.95 (0-7872-3483-4) Kendall-Hunt.
*Becklin, Karonne & Stunnarborg, Edith. Medical Office Procedures. 1999. teacher ed. 14.00 (0-02-804746-X) Glencoe.
— Medical Office Procedures. 4th ed. 1999. wbk. ed. 35.00 incl. disk (0-02-804881-4) Glencoe.
Becklin, Karonne & Sunnarborg, Edith. Medical Office Procedures: With Computer Simulation. 4th ed. 128p. teacher ed. 14.04 (0-02-802533-4) Glencoe.
— Medical Office Transcription: An Introduction to Medical Transcription. 128p. 1998. text, wbk. ed. 27.50 incl. disk (0-02-802240-8) Glencoe.
*Becklin, Karonne & Sunnarborg, Edith M. Medical Office Transcription: An Introduction to Medical Transcription. 1998. teacher ed. 9.60 incl. disk (0-02-802242-4) Glencoe.
Becklin, Karonne J. Medical Office Procedures. 3rd ed. 1994. pap. 34.50 (0-02-800120-6) Glencoe.
Becklin, Karonne J. & Sunnarborg, Edith M. Medical Office Procedures. 4th ed. 1995. pap. 42.95 (0-02-802531-8) Glencoe.
Beckloff, Mark, jt. auth. see Dye, Dan.
Becklund, Jack. Summers with the Bears: Six Seasons in the North Woods. LC 98-10908. 192p. (J). 1999. 21.00 (0-7868-6393-5, Pub. by Hyperion) Time Warner.
Becklund, Laurie, jt. auth. see Strasser, J. B.
Becklund, Patti. In His Hand. 168p. 1999. 14.99 (1-56322-068-7) Hensley Pub.
Beckman. Le Marketing. 4th ed. (C). 1990. pap. write for info. (0-03-998099-5) Harcourt Coll Pubs.
*Beckman. Nuclear Predicament. 3rd ed. LC 99-47280. 340p. 1999. pap. text 33.60 (0-13-680638-4) P-H.
Beckman, A. L., ed. The Neural Basis of Behavior. (Illus.). 350p. 1982. text 53.95 (0-88331-162-3) R B Luce.
Beckman, Barbara, jt. auth. see Butler, Narda.

B

Beckman, Betsey, et al. A Retreat with Our Lady, Dominic & Ignatius: Praying with Our Bodies. Hutchinson, Gloria, ed. LC 98-101318. 192p. (Orig.). 1997. pap. 9.95 (0-86716-256-2, B2562) St Anthony Mess Pr.

Beckman, Bjorn. Organising the Farmers: Cocoa Politics & National Development in Ghana. 299p. 1976. write for info. (91-7106-101-0, Pub. by Nordic Africa) Transaction Pubs.

Beckman, Bjorn, jt. auth. see Andrae, Gunilla.

Beckman, C. H. The Nature of Wilt Diseases of Plants. LC 87-70385. (Illus.). 182p. 1987. 38.00 (0-89054-074-8) Am Phytopathol Soc.

Beckman, C. H., jt. ed. see Tjamos, E. C.

Beckman, Carol, et al. Channels to Children: Early Childhood Activity Guide for Holidays & Seasons. (Illus.). (C). 1982. pap., spiral bd. 24.95 (0-9616396-0-1) Channels Children.

Beckman, David. Under Pegasus: A Novel. LC 96-52223. 200p. 1997. 19.95 (0-9651244-1-X, Gldengrove Bks) Derrynane Pr.

Beckman, Ericka & Snyder, David. The Beanstalk & Jack. (Artists' Bks.). (Illus.). 32p. 1988. 5.00 (0-936739-12-6) Hallwalls Inc.

Beckman, Erik. The Criminal Justice Dictionary. 2nd rev. ed. LC 78-72049. 1983. pap. 25.00 (0-87650-152-8) Pierian.

Beckman, Frank S. Mathematical Foundations of Programming. LC 79-1453. 1980. text. write for info. (0-201-14462-X) Addison-Wesley.

Beckman, G. M., jt. ed. see Hoffner, H. A., Jr.

***Beckman, Gary.** Catalogue of the Babylonian Collections at Yale. Kasten, Ulla, ed. LC 99-44915. (Old Babylonian Archival Texts in the Yale Babylonian Collection: Vol. 4). 280p. 2000. 48.00 (1-883053-54-4) CDL Pr.

Beckman, Gary M. Hittite Fragments in American Collection. (Texts from the Babylonian Collection: Vol. 2). 60p. 1986. pap. write for info. (0-9667495-1-0) Yale Babylonian.

Beckman, Gary M. Old Babylonian Archival Texts in the Nies Babylonian Collection. Kasten, Ulla, ed. (Catalogue of the Babylonian Collection at Yale: No. 2). viii, 173p. (C). 1995. 48.00 (1-883053-11-0) CDL Pr.

Beckman, Howard. An Introduction to Vedic Astrology... Spiritual Science of the Ancients. 2nd ed. (Illus.). 1995. pap. write for info. (0-9525172-0-5) Balaji Pub.

— Mantras, Yantras, & Fabulous Gems... Healing Secrets of the Ancient Vedas. deluxe ed. (Illus.). 1995. write for info. (0-9525172-5-6) Balaji Pub.

Beckman, J. E., ed. The Nearest Active Galaxies. 236p. (C). 1993. text 138.50 (0-7923-2528-1) Kluwer Academic.

***Beckman, J. E. & Mahoney, T. J., eds.** The Evolution of Galaxies on Cosmological Timescales. LC 99-67762. (Conference Series Proceedings: Vol. 187). 359p. 1999. text 52.00 (1-58381-013-7) Astron Soc Pacific.

Beckman, Jan P., ed. Fragen & Probleme Einer Medizinischen Ethik. (Philosophie & Wissenschaft - Transdiziplinaere Studien: Vol. 10). (GER.). vii, 415p. 1995. pap. text 44.65 (3-11-014782-3) De Gruyter.

Beckman, Jean, ed. see Lindstrom, Marilyn.

Beckman, Jean E. Why? There Is More to You Than Meets the Eye. (Illus.). 50p. (Orig.). (J). (gr. 9-12). 1981. pap. 4.25 (0-941992-00-4) Los Arboles Pub.

***Beckman, Jeffrey W.** Little League Lessons for Parents & Coaches. LC 99-93306. (Little League Tips Ser.: No. 1). 50p. 1999. pap. 7.50 (0-9672268-0-5) Christ Dev Res.

***Beckman, Jeffrey W., contrib. by.** Career Success Begins with Jesus: The One-Hour Guide. LC 99-93305. 56p. 1999. pap. 7.50 (0-9672268-1-3, 11) Christ Dev Res.

***Beckman, Jill N.** Positional Faithfulness: An Optimality Theoretic Treatment of Phonological Asymmetries. LC 99-27980. 250p. 1999. 69.00 (0-8153-3348-X) Garland.

Beckman, John E. & Crivellari, Lucio, eds. Progress in Stellar Spectral Line Formation Theory. 1985. text 203.00 (90-277-2007-X) Kluwer Academic.

Beckman, Joshua. Things Are Happening. LC 98-71446. 80p. 1998. write for info. (0-9663395-0-9); pap. 14.00 (0-9663395-1-7) Amer Poet.

Beckman, Joshua, jt. auth. see Salamun, Tomaz.

Beckman, Julie. Kids on the Internet: Elementary Social Studies Projects. 48p. (J). (gr. 1-4). 1999. teacher ed., spiral bd. 12.95 (1-58108-039-5) Pencil Point.

Beckman, L., ed. see International Symposium on Inborn Errors of Metabo.

Beckman, Linda, jt. ed. see Eiduson, Bernice T.

***Beckman, Linda Hunt.** Amy Levy: Her Life & Letters. 384p. 2000. pap. 24.95 (0-8214-1330-9, Ohio U Ctr Intl) Ohio U Pr.

— Amy Levy: Her Life & Letters. LC 99-86688. (Illus.). 384p. 2000. text 49.95 (0-8214-1329-5, Ohio U Ctr Intl) Ohio U Pr.

Beckman, Linda J. & Harvey, S. Marie, eds. The New Civil War: The Psychology, Culture & Politics of Abortion. LC 98-3553. (Psychology of Women Book Ser.: Div. 35). (Illus.). 432p. 1998. text 49.95 (1-55798-517-0) Am Psychol.

Beckman, Linda J., jt. ed. see Wilsnack, Sharon C.

Beckman, M. J. Lectures on Location Theory. LC 99-25888. (Illus.). xiv, 195p. 1999. 69.95 (3-540-65736-3) Spr-Verlag.

Beckman, Martha J. Meditations to Make You Smile. LC 94-30674. (Illus.). 128p. 1995. pap. 8.00 (0-687-00781-X) Dimen for Liv.

— More Meditations to Make You Smile. 112p. 1997. pap. 8.00 (0-687-00952-9) Dimen for Liv.

Beckman, Mary E., jt. auth. see Pierrehumbert, Janet.

Beckman, Mary E., jt. ed. see Kingston, John A.

Beckman, Max. Max Beckmann. Selz, Peter H. et al, eds. 1981. 24.95 (0-405-12888-6) Ayer.

Beckman, Morris. Atlantic Roulette: A Merchantman at War, June 1940, Running the Gauntlet of U-Boat Alley, E-Boat Alley & the Luftwaffe. 144p. 1997. (1-871085-32-2) Donovan Pub.

Beckman, Morris. The Hackney Crucible. LC 95-17505. (Illus.). 200p. (C). 1996. pap. 19.50 (0-85303-286-6, Pub. by M Vallentine & Co) Intl Spec Bk.

Beckman, Morris. The Jewish Brigade: An Army with Two Masters, 1944-1945. (Illus.). 240p. 1999. 24.95 (1-885119-56-9) Sarpedon.

Beckman, Morris. The Jewish Brigade: An Army with Two Masters, 1944-1945. 176p. 1997. 80.00 (1-86227-032-5, Pub. by Spellmnt Pubs) St Mut.

Beckman, N. Norwegian-Swedish Dictionary: Norsk-Svensk Ordbok. rev. ed. (NOR & SWE.). 210p. 1985. 49.95 (0-8288-1035-4, M3320) Fr & Eur.

Beckman, Norman, ed. New Directions in Public Administration: The Federal View. 209p. 1975. pap. text 24.95 (0-87855-650-8) Transaction Pubs.

Beckman, Olof. Angstrom: Father & Son. LC 97-214391. (Acta Universitatis Upsaliensis: No. 60). (Illus.). 44p. 1997. pap. 36.50 (91-554-3960-8, Pub. by Almqvist Wiksell) Coronet Bks.

Beckman, P. & Spizzichino, A. The Scattering of Electromagnetic Waves from Rough Surfaces. LC 63-10108. (International Series of Monographs on Electronics & Instrumentation: Vol. 4). 1963. 224.00 (0-08-010007-4, Pub. by Pergamon Repr) Franklin.

Beckman, Pat R. From the Ashes. LC 95-69275. (Council for Indian Education Ser.). (Illus.). 160p. (J). (gr. 3-7). 1995. pap. 9.95 (1-57098-011-X) Roberts Rinehart.

Beckman, Paul. Come! Meet My Family. 140p. 1995. pap. 12.00 (0-9645520-0-0) Weighted Anchor.

Beckman, Paula, ed. Strategies for Working with Families of Young Children with Disabilities. 304p. (Orig.). 1996. pap. text 33.00 (1-55766-257-6, 2576) P H Brookes.

Beckman, Paula & Boyes, Gayle B. Deciphering the System: A Guide for Families of Young Children with Disabilities. 208p. 1993. pap. text 14.95 (0-914797-87-5) Brookline Bks.

Beckman, Peter R. & D'Amico, Francine, eds. Women, Gender & World Politics: Perspectives, Policies & Prospects. LC 94-15857. 264p. 1994. 69.50 (0-89789-305-0, Bergin & Garvey); pap. 20.95 (0-89789-306-9, Bergin & Garvey) Greenwood.

Beckman, Peter R., jt. ed. see D'Amico, Francine.

Beckman, Pierina E. El Valor Literario del Lazaro de 1555: Genero, Evolucion, y Metamorfosis. LC 90-35787. (American University Studies: Romance Languages & Literature: Ser. II, Vol. 153). XIII, 174p. (C). 1991. text 33.95 (0-8204-1378-X) P Lang Pubng.

Beckman, Ray. Paper Coins. LC 84-71865. (Illus.). 250p. (Orig.). 1985. pap. 9.95 (0-9611240-3-2) Basement Pr.

Beckman, Richard J. A Beginner's Guide to Prayer. LC 94-1577. 1994. pap. 10.99 (0-8066-2674-7, 9-2674, Augsburg) Augsburg Fortress.

Beckman, Robert C. Elliot Wave Explained: A Real-World Guide to Predicting & Profiting from Market Turns. 2nd ed. 1995. per. 29.95 (1-55738-887-3, Irwn Prfssnl) McGraw-Hill Prof.

Beckman, Sharon T. Caring Together: Creating & Guiding a Safe, Christian Support Group. Ellison, Pat T. & Stack-Nelson, Judy, eds. (People Together Ser.). (Illus.). 60p. 1998. pap. text, wbk. ed. 12.95 (1-890676-15-2) Beavers Pond.

Beckman, Stephan D., jt. ed. see Munnick, Harriet D.

Beckman, Steven D., tr. see De La Bathie, H. Perrier.

Beckman, Theodore N. & Nolen, Herman C. The Chain Store Problem: A Critical Analysis. LC 75-39231. (Illus.). 1976. reprint ed. 29.95 (0-405-08008-5) Ayer.

Beckman, William A., jt. auth. see Duffie, John A.

Beckmann. Plant Genomes. 1992. pap. text. write for info. (0-7923-1631-2) Kluwer Academic.

Beckmann, Aike, jt. auth. see Haidvogel, Dale B.

Beckmann, Annie, ed. see Bell, Mary.

Beckmann, Beverly Ann. Activities & Patterns for the Early Childhood Classroom. LC 99-186973. (Illus.). 304p. (J). 1997. pap., teacher ed. 24.95 (1-57690-470-9, TCM2470) Tchr Create Mat.

Beckmann, Charles R., et al. Obstetrics & Gynecology. 2nd ed. LC 94-40390. (Illus.). 560p. 1995. (0-683-00503-0) Lppncott W & W.

— Obstetrics & Gynecology. 3rd ed. LC 97-49309. 1998. 37.00 (0-683-30391-0) Lppncott W & W.

— Obstetrics & Gynecology for Medical Students. (Illus.). 496p. 1992. pap. 33.00 (0-683-00500-6) Lppncott W & W.

Beckmann, David & Simon, Arthur. Grace at the Table: Ending Hunger in God's World. 204p. 1999. pap. 10.99 (0-8308-2217-8, 2217) InterVarsity.

— Grace at the Table: Ending Hunger in God's World. LC 99-13994. 224p. 1999. pap. 10.95 (0-8091-3866-2) Paulist Pr.

Beckmann, David, et al. Friday Morning Reflections at the World Bank: Essays on Values & Development. 96p. (Orig.). 1991. pap. 10.95 (0-932020-78-X) Seven Locks Pr.

Beckmann, Dorothee. Hippokratisches Ethos und Arztliche Verantwortung: Zur Genese Eines Anthropologischen Selbstverstandnisses Griechischer Heilkunst Im Spannungsfeld Zwischen Arztlichem Konnen und Moralischer Wahrnehmung. (Forum Interdisziplinare Ethik Ser.: Bd. 10). (GER., Illus.). 549p. 1995. 79.95 (3-631-48400-3) P Lang Pubng.

Beckmann, Dorothee, jt. auth. see Hunold, Gerfried W.

Beckmann, Frank. Untersuchungen zur Grammatik von Adjunkten im Deutschen. (GER.). 298p. (C). 1997. lib. bdg. 146.70 (3-11-014594-4) De Gruyter.

Beckmann, Frank & Heyer, Gerhard, eds. Theorie und Praxis des Lexikons. (Grundlagen der Kommunikation & Kognition (Foundations of Communication & Cognition) Ser.). (GER.). viii, 348p. (C). 1993. lib. bdg. 152.35 (3-11-013502-7) De Gruyter.

Beckmann, Friedrich & Schmidt, Eckart W. N-Gons. Garner, Cyril W., tr. LC 70-185699. (Mathematical Expositions Ser.: No. 18). 207p. reprint ed. pap. 64.20 (0-608-30880-3, 201944800011) Bks Demand.

Beckmann, G. & Gilli, P. V. Thermal Energy Storage. (Topics in Energy Ser.). (Illus.). 240p. 1984. 69.95 (0-387-81764-6) Spr-Verlag.

Beckmann, George M. The Making of the Meiji Constitution: The Oligarchs & the Constitutional Development of Japan, 1868-1891. LC 72-7963. 158p. 1975. reprint ed. lib. bdg. 38.50 (0-8371-6553-9, BEMC, Greenwood Pr) Greenwood.

Beckmann, H. & Lanczik, M., eds. Leonhard Classification of Endogenous Psychoses: Cycloid Psychoses, Differentiated Nosology, Differentiated Therapy & Historical Aspects - Journal: Psychopathology, 1990, Vol. 23, Nos. 4-6. (Illus.). 164p. 1991. pap. 106.25 (3-8055-5373-0) S Karger.

Beckmann, H. & Riederer, P., eds. Monoamine Oxidase & Its Selective Inhibitors. (Modern Problems of Pharmacopsychiatry Ser.: Vol. 19). (Illus.). x, 354p. 1983. 172.25 (3-8055-3595-3) S Karger.

Beckmann, H., jt. auth. see Franzek, Ernest.

Beckmann, H., ed. see Leonhard, K.

Beckmann, J. Nursing Malpractice: Implications for Clinical Practice & Nursing Education. LC 94-10802. 298p. 1994. pap. 22.50 (0-295-97373-0) U of Wash Pr.

Beckmann, J., jt. ed. see Kuhl, Julius.

Beckmann, Jacques S. & Osborn, Thomas C., eds. Plant Genomes Methods for Genetic & Physical Mapping. (C). 1992. text 189.00 (0-7923-1630-4) Kluwer Academic.

Beckmann, Janet P. Nursing Negligence: Analyzing Malpractice in the Hospital Setting. LC 95-41787. (Illus.). 400p. 1996. 55.00 (0-7619-0225-2); pap. 25.95 (0-7619-0226-0) Sage.

Beckmann, Johann. Physikalisch-Okonomische Bibliothek, 23 vols. write for info. (0-318-71736-0) G Olms Pubs.

Beckmann, John, ed. The Virtual Dimension: Architecture, Representation, & Crash Culture. LC 97-24469. (Illus.). 350p. (Orig.). 1998. pap. 24.95 (1-56898-120-1) Princeton Arch.

***Beckmann, Jon.** After-Dinner Drinks: Choosing, Serving & Enjoying. LC 98-51736. (Illus.). 120p. 1999. 18.95 (0-8118-2094-7) Chronicle Bks.

Beckmann, Jurgen, jt. ed. see Kuhl, Julius.

Beckmann, Leo. Lasers in Materials Processing. LC 98-125173. 98p. 1997. pap. 132.00 (0-8194-2517-6) SPIE.

Beckmann, Martin J. Tinbergen Lectures on Organization Theory. 2nd rev. ed. (Texts & Monographs in Economics & Mathematical Systems). 280p. 1988. 49.95 (0-387-18515-1) Spr-Verlag.

Beckmann, Martin J., et al, eds. Bootstrapping & Related Techniques: Proceedings of an International Conference Held in Trier, FRG, June 4-8, 1990. (Lecture Notes in Economics & Mathematical Systems Ser.: Vol. 376). (Illus.). viii, 247p. 1992. pap. 50.00 (0-387-55003-8) Spr-Verlag.

— Knowledge & Networks in a Dynamic Economy: Festschrift in Honor of Ake E. Andersson. LC 98-20863. (Illus.). x, 421p. 1998. 55.00 (3-540-64245-5) Spr-Verlag.

— Simulation & Optimization: Proceedings of the International Workshop on Computationally Intensive Methods in Simulation & Optimization Held at the International Institute for Applied Systems Analysis (IIASA) Laxenburg, Austria, August 23-25, 1990. (Lecture Notes in Economics & Mathematical Systems Ser.: Vol. 374). (Illus.). x, 162p. 1992. 45.95 (0-387-54980-3) Spr-Verlag.

— Stochastic Processes & Their Applications: Proceedings of the Symposium Held in Honour of Professor S. K. Srinivasan at the Indian Institute of Technology Bombay, India, December 27-30, 1990. (Lecture Notes in Economics & Mathematical Systems Ser.: Vol. 370). (Illus.). xi, 292p. 1991. 65.00 (0-387-54635-9) Spr-Verlag.

Beckmann, Martin J. & Puu, Tonu. Spatial Structures. (Advances in Spatial & Network Economics Ser.). (Illus.). 144p. 1990. 55.95 (0-387-51957-2) Spr-Verlag.

Beckmann, Martin J., jt. auth. see Bartmann, Dieter.

Beckmann, Martin J., ed. see Chen, S. J. & Hwang, C. L.

Beckmann, Martin J., ed. see Esteban, J.

Beckmann, Martin J., ed. see Gardeazabal, J. & Regulez, M.

Beckmann, Martin J., ed. see Heuer, Gerald A. & Leopold-Wildburger, U.

Beckmann, Martin J., ed. see Horvath, B.

Beckmann, Martin J., ed. see Koblo, R. B.

Beckmann, Martin J., ed. see Pfann, G.

Beckmann, Martin J., ed. see Puppe, C.

Beckmann, Martin J., jt. ed. see Sato, R.

Beckmann, Martin J., ed. see Schmutzler, A.

Beckmann, Martin J., ed. see Stalder, P.

Beckmann, Martin J., ed. see Stormer, H.

Beckmann, Martin J., ed. see Uhlich, G. R.

Beckmann, Martin J., ed. see Villar, Antonio.

Beckmann, Martin J., ed. see Zornig, P.

***Beckmann, Max.** Max Beckmann: Zeichnungen. (Ill.). 256p. 2000. 60.00 (3-87909-613-9, Pub. by Wienand) Nazraeli Press.

Beckmann, Max. On My Painting. 2nd ed. Scrivani, George, tr. from GER. 125p. (Orig.). 1994. reprint ed. pap. 5.95 (0-937815-19-5) Hanuman Bks.

— Self-Portrait in Words: Collected Writings & Statements, 1903-1950. Buenger, Barbara C., ed. Heller, Reinhold & Britt, David, trs. (Illus.). 496p. (C). 1997. 34.95 (0-226-04135-2) U Ch Pr.

Beckmann, Max & Buenger, Barbara C. Self-Portrait in Words: Collected Writings & Statements, 1903-1950. LC 96-23422. 1999. pap. text 20.00 (0-226-04136-0) U Ch Pr.

Beckmann, Nicolau, ed. Carbon-13 NMR Spectroscopy in Biological Systems. (Illus.). 334p. 1995. text 74.00 (0-12-084370-6) Acad Pr.

Beckmann, Petr. Einstein Plus Two. LC 85-82516. (Illus.). 1987. text 40.00 (0-911762-39-6) Golem.

— Elementary Queuing Theory & Telephone Traffic. rev. ed. LC 76-57827. (Traffic Ser.). (Illus.). 48p. (C). 1981. spiral bd. 19.95 (1-56016-066-7) ABC TeleTraining.

— The Health Hazards of NOT Going Nuclear. LC 76-12720. (Illus.). 188p. 1976. pap. 15.00 (0-911762-17-5) Golem.

— A History of Pi. 19th ed. 1976. pap. 11.95 (0-312-38185-9) St Martin.

— Musical Musings. LC 89-84833. (Illus.). 197p. (Orig.). 1989. pap. 15.00 (0-911762-40-X) Golem.

— Orthogonal Polynomials for Engineers & Physicists. LC 72-87318. 1973. 35.00 (0-911762-14-0) Golem.

Beckmann, Petr & Spizzichino, Andre. The Scattering of Electromagnetic Waves from Rough Surfaces. LC 87-70042. (Artech House Radar Library). (Illus.). 511p. reprint ed. pap. 158.50 (0-8357-4231-8, 203701800002) Bks Demand.

Beckmann, Petr, tr. see Shevchenko, Viktor V.

Beckmann, Petr, tr. see Shifrin, A. S.

Beckmann, Petr, tr. see Zakharyev, L. N., et al.

***Beckmann, Roberta.** Children Who Grieve: A Manual for Conducting Support Groups. rev. ed. 1999. pap. 21.95 (1-55691-157-2) Learning Pubns.

— It's Okay to Feel. rev. ed. 1999. pap. 11.50 (1-55691-171-8) Learning Pubns.

***Beckmann, S. & Haug, G., eds.** Stressechocardiography Interactive: Strategies for Interpretation. 160p. 1999. 109.00 incl. cd-rom (3-7985-1150-0, Pub. by D Steinkopff) Spr-Verlag.

Beckmen, Richard J. Prayer: Beginning Conversations with God. LC 94-42239. (Face to Face with God Ser.). 80p. 1995. pap. text 8.99 (0-8066-2768-9, 10-27689) Augsburg Fortress.

— Praying for Wholeness & Healing. LC 95-4053. (Face to Face with God Ser.). 80p. 1995. pap. 8.99 (0-8066-2770-0, 10-27700) Augsburg Fortress.

Becknell, John. Medic Life: Creating Success in EMS. LC 95-872. 1995. pap. text 9.95 (0-8151-3046-5) Jems Comm.

Becknell, John M. The Mastiff: An Owner's Guide to a Healthy Pet. (Owner's Guide to a Happy, Healthy Pet Ser.). 128p. 1998. 12.95 (0-87605-609-5) Howell Bks.

Becknell, Thomas & Ashcroft, Mary E., eds. The Beginning of Wisdom: Prayers for Growth & Understanding. 160p. 1995. 14.99 (0-345-39651-0, Moorings) Ballantine Pub Grp.

Beckner, Chrisanne. 100 African-Americans Who Shaped American History. 1995. pap. text 7.95 (0-912517-18-2) Bluewood Bks.

— 100 Great Cities of World History. (One Hundred Ser.). (Illus.). 112p. 1995. pap. 7.95 (0-912517-14-X) Bluewood Bks.

Beckner, Everet. Techniseasonal Commodity Trading. 1984. 65.00 (0-930233-22-0) Windsor.

Beckner, Steven K. Back from the Brink: The Greenspan Years. LC 96-36171. 464p. 1996. 29.95 (0-471-16127-6) Wiley.

***Beckner, Steven K.** Back from the Brink: The Greenspan Years. 452p. 1999. pap. 16.95 (0-471-32574-0) Wiley.

Beckoff, Marc & Byers, John A., eds. Animal Play: Evolutionary, Comparative & Ecological Perspectives. LC 97-22056. (Illus.). 209p. (C). 1998. text 80.00 (0-521-58383-7); pap. text 32.95 (0-521-58656-9) Cambridge U Pr.

Beckoff, Samuel. Monarch Notes on Updike's Rabbit Run & Rabbit Redux. 1974. 4.25 (0-671-00947-8, Arco) Macmillan Gen Ref.

— The Volcano Disaster. (J). 1998. per. 3.99 (0-671-00968-0, Minstrel Bks) PB.

Beckom, Jesse, Jr. Gangs, Drugs & Violence Chicago Style. Baker, Derrick K., ed. (Illus.). 73p. 1995. teacher ed. 19.95 (0-9645051-0-X) GDVPC.

Beckom, Jesse & Beckom, Venus. Heart to Heart. 20p. 1995. pap. 15.00 (0-9645051-4-2) GDVPC.

Beckom, Rosalie. Eating Desirable Foods While Toning Your Body: Health & Weight Maintenance Guide. rev. ed. Baker, Derrick K., ed. (Illus.). 135p. pap. 29.99 (0-9645051-5-0) GDVPC.

Beckom, Venus, jt. auth. see Beckom, Jesse.

Beckon, Madge. At His Feet: Lessons Learned from the Master. 198p. (Orig.). 1994. pap. 8.95 (1-882701-06-2) Uplook Min.

— In His Hands: A Memorial to God's Faithfulness. Nicholson, J. B., Jr., ed. (Orig.). 1997. pap. 9.95 (1-882701-27-5) Uplook Min.

***Beckon, Madge.** On His Heart: Our High Priest's Loving Care. 167p. 1999. pap. 8.99 (1-882701-59-3, Gospel Folio Pr) Uplook Min.

Beckos, Barbara. Traditions in American Basketry. (Illus.). 11p. 1977. 10.00 (0-685-70735-0) Gal Assn NY.

Becks, K-H. & Perret-Gallix, D. New Computing Techniques in Physics Research III: Proceedings of the 3rd International Workshop on Software Engineering. 684p. 1994. text 150.00 (981-02-1699-8) World Scientific Pub.

Becks-Malorny, Ulrike. Cezanne. (Illus.). 96p. 1995. pap. 9.99 (3-8228-8906-7) Taschen Amer.

Becks-Malorny, Ulrike. Cezanne. (SPA.). 1996. pap. 9.99 (*3-8228-8830-3*) Taschen Amer.

***Becks-Malorny, Ulrike.** Ensor. 1999. pap. text 9.99 (*3-8228-7026-9*) Benedikt Taschen.

Becks-Malorny, Ulrike. Kandinsiky. (SPA.). 1996. pap. 19.99 (*3-8228-9557-1*) Taschen Amer.

— Kandinsky. 1995. pap. 19.99 (*3-8228-9045-6*) Taschen Amer.

***Becks-Malorny, Ulrike.** Kandinsky. 1999. 19.99 (*3-8228-7013-7*) Taschen Amer.

Becks-Malorny, Ulrike. Kandinsky, Wassily. (Big Art Ser.). (Illus.). 200p. 1999. 19.99 (*3-8228-7079-X*) Taschen Amer.

Becks-Malovny, Ulrike. Cezanne, 11 vols. (Thunder Bay Artists Ser.). (Illus.). 96p. 1997. pap. text 4.99 (*1-57145-095-5*, Thunder Bay) Advantage Pubs.

Beckson, Karl. Arthur Symons: A Life. (Illus.). 412p. 1987. text 90.00 (*0-19-812882-7*) OUP.

Beckson, Karl, ed. Oscar Wilde. (Critical Heritage Ser.). 448p. (C). 1997. 140.00 (*0-415-15952-0*) Routledge.

Beckson, Karl, ed. Aesthetes & Decadents of the 1890s: An Anthology of British Poetry & Prose. (Illus.). 382p. 1993. reprint ed. pap. 14.00 (*0-89733-044-7*) Academy Chi Pubs.

Beckson, Karl & Ganz, Arthur. Literary Terms: A Dictionary. 3rd rev. ed. LC 88-34368. 308p. 1989. pap. 11.00 (*0-374-52177-8*) FS&G.

Beckson, Karl & Munro, John M., eds. Arthur Symons: Selected Letters, 1880-1935. LC 87-51647. (Illus.). 321p. 1989. text 44.95 (*0-87745-213-X*) U of Iowa Pr.

Beckson, Karl, et al. Arthur Symons: A Bibliography. LC 89-84406. (British Authors, 1880-1920 Ser.: No. 5). 330p. (C). 1990. lib. bdg. 30.00 (*0-944318-04-5*) ELT Pr.

Beckson, Karl, jt. ed. see Lago, Mary M.

Beckson, Karl, ed. see Wilde, Oscar.

Beckson, Karl E. The Oscar Wilde Encyclopedia. LC 97-36303. (Studies in the Nineteenth Century). 456p. 1998. 125.00 (*0-404-61498-1*) AMS Pr.

Beckstead, Gayle & Kozub, Mary L. Searching in Illinois: A Reference Guide to Public & Private Records. LC 84-80217. (ISC State Search Bks.: No. 3). 210p. (Orig.). 1984. pap. text 12.95 (*0-942916-05-0*) ISC Pubns.

Beckstead, Lee A. Beckstead. Descendants of John Beckstead, b. about 1738, Saxony, Germany, d. 1808, Schoharie County, N. Y. (Illus.). 901p. 1997. reprint ed. pap. 129.00 (*0-8328-7461-2*); reprint ed. lib. bdg. 139.00 (*0-8328-7460-4*) Higginson Bk Co.

Beckstead, Robert M. A Survey of Medical Neuroscience. 437p. 1996. pap. 34.95 (*0-387-94488-5*) Spr-Verlag.

Beckstrom, John H. Darwinism Applied: The Evolutionary Path to Social Goals. LC 93-2863. (Human Evolution, Behavior & Intelligence Ser.). 184p. 1993. 49.95 (*0-275-94568-5*, C4568, Praeger Pubs) Greenwood.

— Evolutionary Jurisprudence: Prospects & Limitations on the Use of Modern Darwinism Throughout the Legal Process. 152p. 1989. text 24.95 (*0-252-01621-1*) U of Ill Pr.

— Sociobiology & the Law: The Biology of Altruism in the Courtroom of the Future. LC 84-16415. 160p. 1985. text 24.95 (*0-252-01171-6*) U of Ill Pr.

Beckstrom, Kurt & Taylor, Buck. Fishing with Marine Electronics. LC 92-81043. (Complete Angler's Library). 233p. 1992. write for info. (*0-914697-47-1*) N Amer Outdoor Grp.

Beckstrom, Robert J. Decks & Patios for Dummies. National Gardening Association Editors, ed. LC 98-84304. (For Dummies Ser.). (Illus.). 384p. 1998. pap. 16.99 (*0-7645-5075-6*) IDG Bks.

— Ortho's Home Improvement Encyclopedia. Shakery, Karin, ed. LC 85-70877. (Illus.). 512p. 1985. 24.95 (*0-89721-066-2*, Ortho Bks) Meredith Bks.

Beckstrom, Robert J. & Ortho Books-How to Staff. Ortho's Home Improvement Encyclopedia. rev. ed. Ahlstrand, Alan, ed. LC 94-65698. (Illus.). 512p. 1994. 29.95 (*0-89721-270-3*, UPC 05620A) Meredith Bks.

Beckstrom, Robert J., ed. see Birchard, John.

Beckstrom, Robert J., ed. see Ross, Sharon M.

Beckstrom-Sternberg, Steve M., jt. auth. see Duke, James A.

Becksvoort, Christian. The Shaker Legacy: Perspectives on an Enduring Furniture Style. LC 98-6987. (Illus.). 240p. 1998. 40.00 (*1-56158-218-2*, 070349) Taunton.

***Becksvoort, Christian.** The Shaker Legacy: Perspectives on an Enduring Furniture Style. (Illus.). 2000. reprint ed. pap. 24.95 (*1-56158-357-X*) Taunton.

Beckton, Clare. The Courts & the Charters. (Collected Research Studies of the Royal Commission on the Economic Union & Development Prospects for Canada: Vol. 58). 1985. pap. text 21.95 (*0-8020-7305-0*) U of Toronto Pr.

Beckum, William Forrest, Jr. & Langley, Albert M., Jr. Central of Georgia Railway Album. LC 86-50539. (Illus.). 144p. (Orig.). 1986. pap. 19.95 (*0-9615257-1-1*) Union Sta.

— Georgia Railroad Album. LC 85-51239. (Illus.). 72p. (Orig.). 1985. pap. 10.95 (*0-9615257-0-3*) Union Sta.

Beckvermit, John J., 3rd. African Art Playing Card Deck. 1995. pap. 7.00 (*0-88079-701-0*, BLA55) US Games Syst.

Beckwell, Robert E. Hi...Goodbye, Detroit! (Illus.). 400p. (Orig.). 1993. pap. 12.95 (*0-9634988-0-0*) R E Beckwell.

Beckwith. Do the Right Thing. (Philosophy Ser.). (C). 1996. 50.95 (*0-534-54244-1*) Wadsworth Pub.

***Beckwith.** Do the Right Thing. 2nd ed. 2001. pap. 38.00 (*0-534-54335-9*) Thomson Learn.

Beckwith, Agnes. Zar Meets Rahbue: From the Land of Senga. (Illus.). 16p. (J). (gr. 3-6). 1998. pap. 6.00 (*0-8059-4263-7*) Dorrance.

Beckwith, Alice. Victorian Bibliomania: The Illuminated Book in 19th-Century Britain. Phillips, Janet, ed. LC 86-62734. (Illus.). 83p. (Orig.). 1987. pap. 18.00 (*0-911517-45-6*) Mus of Art RI.

Beckwith, Bill E. Neuropeptides in Development & Aging. LC 97-5944. (Annals of the New York Academy of Sciences Ser.). 1997. pap. 120.00 (*1-57331-067-0*) NY Acad Sci.

Beckwith, Bill E., et al, eds. Neuropeptides Development & Aging. Vol. 814. LC 97-5944. 1997. 120.00 (*1-57331-066-2*) NY Acad Sci.

Beckwith, Bob & Craig, Drew. Hypotheses: Superatomb, Neutrinos & Extraterrestrials. (Illus.). 154p. (Orig.). 1998. pap. 20.00 (*0-9657178-0-1*) R W Beckwith.

Beckwith, Burnham Putnam. Beyond Tomorrow, a Rational Utopia. 188p. (C). 1986. reprint ed. 9.00 (*0-9603262-5-1*) Beckwith.

Beckwith, Carol. Maasai. (Illus.). 276p. 1990. pap. 34.98 (*0-8109-8099-1*, Pub. by Abrams) Time Warner.

Beckwith, Carol, photos by. Nomads of Niger. LC 93-14899. (Illus.). 224p. 1993. pap. 29.98 (*0-8109-8125-4*, Pub. by Abrams) Time Warner.

***Beckwith, Carol & Fisher, Angela.** Passages: Photographs in Africa. LC 00-31317. (Illus.). 112p. 2000. pap. 24.95 (*0-8109-2948-1*, Pub. by Abrams) Time Warner.

Beckwith, Carol & Fisher, Angela, photos by. African Ark: People & Ancient Cultures of Ethiopia & the Horn of Africa. (Illus.). 320p. 1990. 65.00 (*0-8109-1902-8*, Pub. by Abrams) Time Warner.

***Beckwith, Carol, et al.** African Ceremonies. 2 vols. LC 99-24434. (Illus.). 744p. 2000. boxed set 150.00 (*0-8109-4205-4*, Pub. by Abrams) Time Warner.

Beckwith, Carol, jt. auth. see Van Offelen, Marion.

Beckwith, Carrie, et al. Editor in Chief A2: Grammar Disasters & Punctuation Faux Pas. (Illus.). 72p. (J). (gr. 4-6). 1999. pap. 14.95 (*0-89455-719-X*, MP9704) Crit Think Bks.

— Editor in Chief B2: Grammar Disasters & Punctuation Faux Pas. (Illus.). 93p. (YA). (gr. 6-8). 1999. pap. 15.95 (*0-89455-720-3*, MP9705) Crit Think Bks.

***Beckwith, Carrie, et al.** Editor in Chief C2: Grammar Disasters & Punctuation Faux Pas. (Illus.). (gr. 8 up). 1999. pap. 16.95 (*0-89455-721-1*, MP9706) Crit Think Bks.

***Beckwith, Charlie A.** Delta Force: The Army's Elite Counterterrorist Unit. 384p. 2000. mass mkt. 6.99 (*0-380-80939-7*, Avon Bks) Morrow Avon.

***Beckwith, Christian, ed.** The American Alpine Journal, 1999. (American Alpine Journal: Vol. 41, No. 73). (Illus.). 500p. 1999. pap. 30.00 (*0-930410-84-X*) Amer Alpine Club.

Beckwith, Christian, ed. The American Alpine Journal, 1997. (Illus.). 444p. 1997. pap. 30.00 (*0-930410-65-3*) Amer Alpine Club.

— The American Alpine Journal, 1996. (Illus.). 428p. 1996. pap. 30.00 (*0-930410-64-5*) Amer Alpine Club.

— American Alpine Journal, 1998, Vol. 40, No. 72. (Illus.). 450p. 1998. pap. 30.00 (*0-930410-78-5*) Amer Alpine Club.

***Beckwith, Christian, ed.** The American Alpine Journal, 2000, Vol. 42, No. 74. (Illus.). 500p. 2000. pap. 30.00 (*0-930410-87-4*, Pub. by Amer Alpine Club) Mountaineers.

Beckwith, F. W. Beckwith: Additional Beckwith Notes, Including Avery, Ely, Gilbert, Holmes, Lee, Smith, Southerland, Wightman & Williams Families. 49p. 1993. reprint ed. pap. 10.00 (*0-8328-3763-6*); reprint ed. lib. bdg. 20.00 (*0-8328-3762-8*) Higginson Bk Co.

Beckwith, Francis J. Bahai. LC 85-20161. 64p. 1985. pap. 4.99 (*0-87123-848-9*) Bethany Hse.

— David Hume's Argument Against Miracles: A Critical Analysis. LC 89-33135. 160p. (C). 1989. lib. bdg. 34.00 (*0-8191-7487-4*) U Pr of Amer.

— Politically Correct Death: Answering the Arguments for Abortion Rights. LC 92-31659. 256p. 1993. pap. 19.99 (*0-8010-1050-0*) Baker Bks.

— Public Education, the First Amendment, & the Influence of New Religious Movements: A Policy Analysis. 22p. 1993. 10.00 (*1-886306-07-9*) Nevada Policy.

Beckwith, Francis J. & Jones, Todd E., eds. Affirmative Action: Social Justice or Reverse Discrimination? LC 97-25098. (Contemporary Issues Ser.). 250p. 1997. pap. text 16.95 (*1-57392-157-2*) Prometheus Bks.

Beckwith, Francis J. & Koukl, Gregory. Relativism: Feet Firmly Planted in Mid-Air. LC 98-17425. 192p. 1998. pap. 14.99 (*0-8010-5806-6*) Baker Bks.

Beckwith, Francis J. & Parrish, Stephen E. The Mormon Concept of God: A Philosophical Analysis. LC 91-15131. (Studies in American Religion: Vol. 55). 156p. 1991. lib. bdg. 69.95 (*0-7734-9787-0*) E Mellen.

— See the Gods Fall: Four Rivals to Christianity. LC 97-35176. 1997. 21.99 (*0-89900-794-5*) College Pr Pub.

Beckwith, Francis J., jt. auth. see Pojman, Louis P.

Beckwith, Francis J., jt. ed. see Bauman, Michael.

Beckwith, George C. The Peace Manual or War & Its Remedies. LC 73-137529. (Peace Movement in America Ser.). 252p. 1972. reprint ed. lib. bdg. 31.95 (*0-89198-056-3*) Ozer.

Beckwith, George C., ed. The Book of Peace: A Collection of Essays on War & Peace. LC 70-137528. (Peace Movement in America Ser.). iv, 500p. 1972. reprint ed. lib. bdg. 59.95 (*0-89198-055-5*) Ozer.

Beckwith, H. W. History of Fountain County, Indiana. (Illus.). 982p. 1993. reprint ed. lib. bdg. 97.50 (*0-8328-2922-6*) Higginson Bk Co.

— History of Montgomery County: Together with Historic Notes on the Wabash Valley, Gleaned from Early Authors, Old Maps & Manuscripts...& Other Authentic...Sources. (Illus.). 607p. 1997. reprint ed. lib. bdg. 63.50 (*0-8328-6660-1*) Higginson Bk Co.

— History of Vermilion County, Illinois. (Illus.). 1041p. 1993. reprint ed. lib. bdg. 99.00 (*0-8328-3516-1*) Higginson Bk Co.

***Beckwith, Harry.** The Invisible Touch: The Four Keys to Modern Marketing. LC 99-48663. 256p. 2000. 21.95 (*0-446-52417-4*, Pub. by Warner Bks) Little.

Beckwith, Harry. Selling the Invisible: A Field Guide to Modern Marketing. LC 96-16774. 252p. 1997. 19.95 (*0-446-52094-2*, Pub. by Warner Bks) Little.

— Selling the Invisible: A Field Guide to Modern Marketing. 272p. 1999. pap. 12.00 (*0-446-67231-9*) Warner Bks.

Beckwith, Hiram W. The Illinois & Indiana Indians. LC 75-86. (Mid-American Frontier Ser.). 1980. reprint ed. 16.95 (*0-405-06854-9*) Ayer.

Beckwith, Ivy. Quick Relief for Children's Ministry Leaders. Wolf, Beth, ed. LC 98-12668. (Illus.). 80p. 1998. pap. 9.99 (*0-7644-2072-0*) Group Pub.

Beckwith, Ivy, ed. Children's Church Specials. LC 98-15018. (Illus.). 128p. (J). 1998. per. 16.99 (*0-7644-2063-1*, Vital Ministry) Group Pub.

Beckwith, Jack, jt. auth. see Cecil, Larry.

Beckwith, Jay. How to Design & Build Children's Play Equipment. LC 86-71055. (Illus.). 96p. 1986. pap. 9.95 (*0-89721-075-1*, Ortho Bks) Meredith Bks.

Beckwith, John. Early Christian & Byzantine Art. 2nd ed. (Pelican History of Art Ser.). (Illus.). 405p. (C). 1979. reprint ed. 55.00 (*0-300-05295-2*) Yale U Pr.

— Early Christian & Byzantine Art. 2nd ed. (Pelican History of Art Ser.). (Illus.). 405p. (C). 1986. reprint ed. pap. 27.50 (*0-300-05296-0*) Yale U Pr.

— Early Medieval Art. LC 84-51844. (World of Art Ser.) (Illus.). 270p. 1985. pap. 14.95 (*0-500-20019-X*, Pub. by Thames Hudson) Norton.

Beckwith, John, ed. see International Conference of Composers (1960: Strat.

Beckwith, John A. Gem Minerals of Idaho. enl. ed. LC 70-150817. (Illus.). (Orig.). 1972. pap. 9.95 (*0-87004-228-9*) Caxton.

Beckwith, John A. & Coope, Geoffrey G., eds. Contemporary American Biography. LC 77-142607. (Essay Index Reprint Ser.). 1977. reprint ed. 24.95 (*0-8369-2483-5*) Ayer.

Beckwith, Jon, et al, eds. Gene Function in Prokaryotes. LC 83-15229. (Monographs: Vol. 15). 328p. 1984. reprint ed. pap. 35.00 (*0-87969-176-X*) Cold Spring Harbor.

Beckwith, Jonathan & Silhavy, Thomas J. The Power of Bacterial Genetics: A Literature-Based Course. LC 92-11643. (Illus.). 842p. Date not set. reprint ed. pap. 200.00 (*0-608-20710-1*, 207180800002) Bks Demand.

Beckwith, Karen. American Women & Political Participation: The Impacts of Work, Generation & Feminism, 68. LC 85-27284. (Contributions in Women's Studies: No. 68). 199p. 1986. 52.95 (*0-313-24507-X*, BAW/, Greenwood Pr) Greenwood.

Beckwith, Kathy. Don't Shoot! We May Both Be on the Same Side: A Curriculum Guide for Working Together & Resolving Conflicts. LC 98-72135. (Illus.). 254p. 1998. pap. text 39.95 (*0-932796-86-9*) Ed Media Corp.

Beckwith, L. D. Onward & Upward Ourselves. 181p. 1986. 12.95 (*0-317-68201-6*) L D Beckwith.

Beckwith, Lillian. Beautiful Just! large type ed. 1989. 12.00 (*0-7089-0348-7*) Ulverscroft.

— The Small Party. large type ed. 1991. 27.99 (*0-7089-2274-0*) Ulverscroft.

Beckwith, Martha W. Black Roadways: A Study of Jamaican Folk Life. LC 69-16597. (Illus.). 243p. 1971. reprint ed. lib. bdg. 59.50 (*0-8371-1144-7*, BEB&) Greenwood.

— Hawaiian Mythology. LC 70-97998. 606p. 1982. pap. 16.95 (*0-8248-0514-3*) UH Pr.

— Jamaica Anansi Stories. LC 26-10368. (American Folklore Society Memoirs Ser.: Vol. 17). 1969. reprint ed. 30.00 (*0-527-01069-3*) Periodicals Srv.

— Jamaica Folk-Lore. LC 30-18643. (American Folklore Society Memoirs Ser.). 1969. reprint ed. 35.00 (*0-527-01073-1*) Periodicals Srv.

— Jamaica Proverbs. LC 70-100278. 137p. 1970. reprint ed. lib. bdg. 49.50 (*0-8371-2938-9*, BEJ&) Greenwood.

— Myths & Hunting Stories of the Mandan & Hidatsa Sioux. LC 76-43665. (Vassar College Folklore Foundation: Publication No. 10). 1977. reprint ed. 39.50 (*0-404-15498-0*) AMS Pr.

Beckwith, Martha W., ed. The Kumulipo: A Hawaiian Creation Chant. LC 79-188978. 276p. 1981. reprint ed. pap. 12.95 (*0-8248-0771-5*) UH Pr.

Beckwith, Martha W., et al. Pushkin. LC 75-168509. (Black Heritage Library Collection). 1977. reprint ed. 27.95 (*0-8369-8862-0*) Ayer.

Beckwith, Mary Ann. Creative Watercolor: A Step-by-Step Guide & Showcase. (Illus.). 144p. 1996. 29.99 (*1-56496-172-9*, Quarry Bks) Rockport Pubs.

Beckwith, Nina. Opera's Great Voices. LC 97-14048. (Life, Times, & Music Ser.). 1997. pap. write for info. (*1-56799-502-0*, Friedman-Fairfax) M Friedman Pub Grp Inc.

Beckwith, Osmond. Vernon: An Anecdotal Novel. LC 81-65121. (Illus.). 204p. 1981. 10.00 (*0-917020-02-2*) Breaking Point.

Beckwith, P. Creoles of St. Louis. 174p. 1993. reprint ed. pap. 26.00 (*0-8328-1345-1*); reprint ed. lib. bdg. 36.00 (*0-8328-1344-3*) Higginson Bk Co.

Beckwith, Paul. The Beckwiths. 384p. 1988. reprint ed. pap. 59.50 (*0-8328-0223-9*); reprint ed. lib. bdg. 69.50 (*0-8328-0222-0*) Higginson Bk Co.

Beckwith, Paul, et al, eds. Hymns II. LC 76-47503. 1976. 16.99 (*0-87784-898-X*, 898); pap. 11.99 (*0-87784-783-5*, 783); spiral bd. 18.99 (*0-87784-750-9*, 750) InterVarsity.

Beckwith, Roger T. Calendar & Chronology, Jewish & Christian: Biblical, Intertestamental & Patristic Studies. LC 96-33630. (Arbeiten Zur Geschichte des Antiken Judentums & des Urchristentums Ser.: No. 33). 320p. 1996. 114.00 (*90-04-10586-7*) Brill Academic Pubs.

— The Old Testament Canon of the New Testament Church & Its Background in Early Judaism. fac. ed. LC 85-6850. 572p. 1986. reprint ed. pap. 177.40 (*0-7837-7944-5*, 204770000008) Bks Demand.

Beckwith, Roger T. & Scott, Wilfrid. This Is the Day: The Biblical Doctrine of the Christian Sunday in it's Jewish & Early Church Setting. 392p. 1978. 12.00 (*0-551-05568-5*) Attic Pr.

Beckwith, S., ed. see Ray, Thomas P.

Beckwith, S. V. Disks & Outflows Around Young Stars: Proceedings of a Conference Held at Heidelberg, Germany, 6-9 September 1994. LC 96-26661. (Lecture Notes in Physics Ser.: Vol. 465). 361p. 1996. 84.95 incl. cd-rom (*3-540-61389-7*) Spr-Verlag.

Beckwith, S. V., et al, eds. Disk & Outflows Around Young Stars: Proceedings of a Conference Held at Heidelberg, Germany 6-9 September 1994. 400p. 1996. 49.50 incl. cd-rom (*3-540-14583-4*) Spr-Verlag.

Beckwith, Sarah. Christ's Body. 216p. (C). 1996. pap. 25.99 (*0-415-14426-4*) Routledge.

Beckwith, Sarah, et al, eds. Catholicism & Catholicity: Eucharistic Communities in Historical & Contemporary Perspectives. 1999. pap. 24.95 (*0-631-21501-8*) Blackwell Pubs.

***Beckwith, Stacy N.** Charting Memory: Recalling Medieval Spain. LC 99-48637. (Hispanic Issues Ser.). 1999. write for info. (*0-8153-3325-0*) Garland.

Beckwith, Thomas. Mechanical Measurements. 6th ed. 1999. text. write for info. (*0-201-84765-5*) Addison-Wesley.

Beckwith, Thomas G. & Marangoni, Roy D. Mechanical Measurements. 4th ed. (Illus.). (C). 1990. text 65.75 (*0-201-17866-4*) Addison-Wesley.

Beckwith, Thomas G., et al. Mechanical Measurements. 3rd ed. 1982. text 39.96 (*0-201-00036-9*) Addison-Wesley.

— Mechanical Measurements. 5th ed. LC 92-23515. (Illus.). 895p. (C). 1993. 100.00 (*0-201-56947-7*) Addison-Wesley.

— Mechanical Measurements: Solutions Manual. 3rd ed. 1982. pap. text, teacher ed. 1.25 (*0-201-00037-7*) Addison-Wesley.

Beckwith, Thomas G., et al. Mechanical Measurements: Solutions Manual. 5th ed. 1994. pap. text 23.33 (*0-201-90913-8*) Addison-Wesley.

Beckwourth, James P. The Life & Adventures of James P. Beckwourth. LC 73-88092. 663p. reprint ed. pap. 200.00 (*0-608-08690-8*, 206921300003) Bks Demand.

— The Life & Adventures of James P. Beckwourth. (American Biography Ser.). 547p. 1991. reprint ed. lib. bdg. 99.00 (*0-7812-8015-X*) Rprt Serv.

Beckylane. Where the Rivers Join: A Personal Account of Healing from Ritual Abuse. 264p. 1995. pap. 14.95 (*0-88974-043-7*, Pub. by Press Gang Pubs) LPC InBook.

Beclard, Leon. Sebastien Mercier. x, 810p. 1982. reprint ed. 130.00 (*3-487-07262-9*) G Olms Pubs.

Becnel. Crips & Bloods. 1994. 25.00 (*0-02-508240-X*) Macmillan.

Becnel, Barbara C. The Co-Dependent Parent: Free Yourself by Freeing Your Child. LC 90-84718. 272p. 1991. pap. 14.00 (*0-06-250126-7*, Pub. by Harper SF) HarpC.

Becnel, Barbara C., jt. auth. see Williams, Stanley T.

Becnel, Irwin J., Jr. & Nicholson, Kenneth E. The Impact of Digital Technology on Image Suppliers in the Printing & Publishing Industry: A Study of Futures & Strategies. Cripe, Helen, ed. LC 94-69082. (Illus.). 118p. (Orig.). (C). 1994. pap. text 65.00 (*0-9643916-2-7*) Integ Tech Res.

Becnel, Kenneth J. Simon Said ... 233p. 1997. pap. 10.95 (*0-9655108-0-8*) K J Becnel.

— Simon Said... (Too) What God Wants You to Know. LC 98-93127. 357p. 1998. pap. 17.50 (*0-9655108-1-6*) K J Becnel.

Becnel, Rexanne. The Bride of Rosecliffe. 378p. 1998. mass mkt. 6.50 (*0-312-96649-0*) St Martin.

— Heart of the Storm, Vol. 1. 368p. 1995. mass mkt. 5.99 (*0-312-95608-8*) St Martin.

— Knight of Rosecliffe. 336p. 1999. mass mkt. 6.50 (*0-312-96905-8*) St Martin.

— The Maiden Bride, Vol. 1. 4th ed. 336p. 1996. mass mkt. 5.99 (*0-312-95978-8*) St Martin.

***Becnel, Rexanne.** The Matchmaker. 2001. pap. write for info. (*0-312-97699-2*, St Martins Paperbacks) St Martin.

— The Mistress of Rosecliffe. 304p. 2000. mass mkt. 6.50 (*0-312-97402-7*, St Martins Paperbacks) St Martin.

Becnel, Rexanne. The Rose of Blacksword. 448p. 1992. mass mkt. 5.99 (*0-440-20910-2*) Dell.

Becnel, Rexanne, et al. A Dance with Devil, Vol. 1. 1997. mass mkt. 5.99 (*0-312-96318-1*) St Martin.

Becnel, Thomas A. Senator Allen Ellender of Louisiana: A Biography. LC 95-35101. (Southern Biography Ser.). (Illus.). 344p. (C). 1995. text 40.00 (*0-8071-1978-4*) La State U Pr.

Becnel, Thomas A. & Conrad, Glen R., eds. Agriculture & Economic Development in Louisiana. LC 96-84494. (Louisiana Purchase Bicentennial Series in Louisiana History: Vol. XVI). (Illus.). 699p. 1998. 40.00 (*1-887366-15-6*) Univ LA Lafayette.

Becom, Jeffrey. Mediterranean Color. (Illus.). 192p. 1990. 45.00 (*0-89659-925-6*) Abbeville Pr.

Becom, Jeffrey & Aberg, Sally J. Maya Color: The Painted Villages of Mesoamerica. LC 97-8347. (Illus.). 180p. 1997. 50.00 (*0-7892-0215-8*) Abbeville Pr.

Becon-McBride, Kathleen & Garza, Diane. Phlebotomy Blood Collection: A & L Quick Review. 4th rev. ed. LC 97-30652. 168p. (C). 1997. 29.95 (*0-8385-0334-9*, A-0334-1) Appleton & Lange.

Becon, Thomas. The Demaundes of Holy Scripture, with Answers to the Same. LC 79-84087. (English Experience Ser.: No. 907). 116p. 1979. reprint ed. lib. bdg. 15.00 (*90-221-0907-0*) Walter J Johnson.

— The Physyke of the Soule. LC 74-28831. (English Experience Ser.: No. 713). 1975. reprint ed. 20.00 (90-221-0713-2) Walter J Johnson.

— The Principles of Christian Religion. LC 76-57355. (English Experience Ser.: No. 774). 1977. reprint ed. lib. bdg. 25.00 (90-221-0774-4) Walter J Johnson.

Becque, Hari. La Parisienne. (Livret Ser.). pap. 6.95 (0-685-34881-4) Fr & Eur.

Becquer, Gustavo A. Legends & Letters. Fedorchek, Robert M., tr. from SPA. LC 95-10321. (Illus.). 1996. 38.50 (0-8387-5307-8) Bucknell U Pr.

***Becquer, Gustavo A.** Rimas. (SPA.). 1999. pap. text 13.00 (84-481-0620-2, McGrw-H College) McGrw-H Hghr Educ.

Becquer, Gustavo A. Rimas. unabridged ed. (SPA.). pap. 7.95 (84-410-0001-8, Pub. by Bookking Intl) Distribks Inc.

Becquer, Gustavo A. Rimas, Narraciones y Leyendas. (SPA.). 1997. pap. 8.98 (968-15-0103-9) Ed Mex.

Becquer, Gustavo A. Rimas y Declaraciones Poeticas. (SPA.). 279p. 1989. 11.95 (0-8288-7077-2) Fr & Eur.

— Rimas y Leyendas. (SPA.). 9.95 (0-8288-2553-X) Fr & Eur.

— Rimas y Leyendas. (Clasicos Ser.). (SPA.). 136p. 1996. pap. write for info. (0-929441-85-0) Pubns Puertorriquenas.

— Rimas y Leyendas. (Clasicos Esenciales Ser.). (SPA.). (C). 1998. pap. 9.95 (84-294-4626-5) Santillana.

— Romantic Legends of Spain. Bates, Cornelia F. & Bates, Katharine L., trs. LC 78-169539. (Short Story Index Reprint Ser.). 1977. reprint ed. 22.95 (0-8369-4000-8) Ayer.

Becquer, Gustavo A., jt. auth. see Armanet, J.

Becquer, Gustavo Adolfo, see Adolfo Becquer, Gustavo, adapted by.

Becquet, Jean. Vie Canoniale en France aux Xe-XIIe Siecles. (Collected Studies: No. CS220). (FRE.). 292p. (C). 1985. reprint ed. lib. bdg. 113.95 (0-86078-168-2, Pub. by Variorum) Ashgate Pub Co.

Becquet, Marc C., ed. Teleoperation: Numerical Simulation & Experimental Validation. (C). 1992. text 152.50 (0-7923-1584-7) Kluwer Academic.

Becraft, Melvin E. Picasso's Guernica: Images Within Images. 2nd rev. ed. LC 85-73564. (Illus.). 146p. 1987. 23.95 (0-9615981-0-7) M E Becraft.

Becroft, Andrew. Dixon's Road Traffic Law, 2 vols., Set. ring bd. write for info. (0-409-79048-6, NZ, MICHIE) LEXIS Pub.

Becton, F. Julian & Morschauser, Joseph, III. The Ship That Would Not Die: The USS Laffey. LC 80-16263. (Illus.). 316p. 1987. pap. 9.95 (0-933126-87-5) Pictorial Hist.

Becton, Randy. The Beauty of God's Whisper. 1979. pap. 6.35 (0-89137-310-1) Quality Pubns.

— Everyday Comfort: Readings for the First Month of Grief. LC 93-3971. 112p. (gr. 10). 1993. pap. 7.99 (0-8010-1066-7) Baker Bks.

— Everyday Evangelism: Making a Difference for Christ Where You Live. LC 96-41598. 128p. (gr. 11). 1997. pap. 7.99 (0-8010-5740-X) Baker Bks.

— Everyday Strength: A Cancer Patient's Guide to Spiritual Survival. 160p. (Orig.). (gr. 10). 1989. pap. 8.99 (0-8010-0975-8) Baker Bks.

Becvar, Dorothy & Becvar, Ray. Hot Chocolate for a Cold Winter Night: Exercises for Relationship Enhancement. 1994. pap. 14.95 (0-89108-233-6, 9401) Love Pub Co.

Becvar, Dorothy S. Soul Healing: A Spiritual Orientation in Counseling & Therapy. LC 96-45051. 256p. 1997. 35.00 (0-465-09552-6, Pub. by Basic) HarpC.

Becvar, Dorothy S., ed. The Family, Spirituality, & Social Work. LC 97-47663. 121p. 1998. 29.95 (0-7890-0503-4) Haworth Pr.

Becvar, Dorothy S. & Becvar, Raphael J. Systems Theory & Family Therapy: A Primer. 2nd ed. LC 98-46481. 144p. 1998. pap. 16.50 (0-7618-1295-4) U Pr of Amer.

Becvar, Dorothy S., jt. auth. see Becvar, Raphael J.

***Becvar, Dorothy Stroh & Becvar, Raphael J.** Family Therapy: A Systematic Integration. 4th ed. LC 98-31604. 416p. (C). 1999. 60.00 (0-205-28531-7, Macmillan Coll) P-H.

Becvar, Raphael J. & Becvar, Dorothy S. Systems Theory & Family Therapy: A Primer. LC 81-43721. 104p. (Orig.). (C). 1982. pap. text 14.75 (0-8191-2444-3); lib. bdg. 49.00 (0-8191-2443-5) U Pr of Amer.

Becvar, Raphael J., et al. Group Work: Cybernetic, Constructivist, & Social Constructionist Perspectives. 168p. (C). 1997. pap. text 29.95 (0-89108-252-2, 9703) Love Pub Co.

Becvar, Raphael J., jt. auth. see Becvar, Dorothy S.

Becvar, Raphael J., jt. auth. see Becvar, Dorothy Stroh.

Becvar, Ray, jt. auth. see Becvar, Dorothy.

***Bed & Breakfast Association of Alaska, Anchorage Chapter Staff, compiled by.** Bed & Breakfast Directory, Anchorage, AK. 4th ed. (ENG.). 40p. 1998. spiral bd. 5.00 (1-57833-036-X) Todd Commns.

Bed & Breakfast Innkeepers of South Dakota Staff. South Dakota Sunrise: A Collection of Breakfast Recipes. LC 97-62263. (Illus.). 96p. 1997. pap. 10.95 (1-883651-08-5) Winters IN.

BED Publishing Staff, ed. see Gates, Donna.

Beda. The History of the Church of England. (English Experience Ser.: No. 234). 382p. 1970. reprint ed. 55.00 (90-221-0234-3) Walter J Johnson.

Beda Venerabilis Staff. Bedae Opera De Temporibus. Jones, C. W., ed. (Medieval Academy Bks.: No. 41). 1966. reprint ed. 25.00 (0-910956-17-0) Medieval Acad.

Bedani, Gino. Politics & Ideology in the Italian Workers' Movement: Union Development & the Changing Role of the Catholic & Communist Subcultures in Postwar Italy. LC 95-145333. (Illus.). 365p. 1995. 53.00 (0-85496-827-X) Berg Pubs.

— Vico Revisited: Orthodoxy, Naturalism & Science in the Scienza Nuova. LC 88-11117. 308p. 1989. 19.50 (0-85496-266-2) Berg Pubs.

***Bedani, Gino & Haddock, Bruce, eds.** The Politics of Italian National Identity. 224p. 2000. 75.00 (0-7083-1622-0, Pub. by U Wales Pr) Paul & Co Pubs.

***Bedaque, Paulo F.** Nuclear Physics with Effective Field Theory II: University of Washington, Seattle, U. S. A. 25-26 Feb. 1999. 75.00 (981-02-4181-X) World Scientific Pub.

Bedard. Clay Ladies. 1999. 16.00 (0-689-81184-5) S&S Childrens.

Bedard, Bob. Companion's of the Cross. LC 94-66590. 195p. 1994. pap. 8.00 (1-882972-36-8, 3241) Queenship Pub.

— Evangelization: A Challenge for the Catholic Church. 32p. 1995. pap. 1.95 (1-882972-41-4, 3242) Queenship Pub.

Bedard, Brian. Hour of the Beast & Other Stories. LC 84-12642. 110p. (Orig.). 1984. pap. 10.00 (0-933428-04-9) Chariton Review.

Bedard, David J. Blue Confessions. (Illus.). 1993. 24.95 (0-07-004789-8) McGraw.

— Blue Confessions: Favorite Stories From Private Pilot. (Illus.). 240p. 1992. 24.95 (0-8306-4097-5, 4214); pap. 14.95 (0-8306-4098-3, 4214) McGraw-Hill Prof.

Bedard, George. Mirabelle House. Inbody, Mary & Knox, Dahk, eds. (Illus.). 116p. 1996. pap. 11.95 (1-881116-83-2) Black Forest Pr.

Bedard, Hank. Lucky Thirteen. 1980. pap. 1.75 (0-686-38385-0) Eldridge Pub.

Bedard, Jim. Lotus in the Fire: The Healing Power of Zen. LC 98-31120. 160p. 1999. pap. 14.00 (1-57062-430-5, Pub. by Shambhala Pubns) Random.

Bedard, John M. Border Guards. LC 96-83030. 250p. (Orig.). 1996. pap. 14.95 (0-9650269-0-6, 51495) Alouette Pub.

Bedard, Marcia E. Breaking with Tradition: Diversity, Conflict & Change in Contemporary American Families. LC 91-75940. 228p. 1992. pap. text 22.95 (0-930390-14-8); lib. bdg. 38.95 (0-930390-15-6) Gen Hall.

Bedard, Michael. The Clay Ladies. LC 98-61336. (Illus.). 40p. (J). (gr. 3-6). 1999. 16.95 (0-88776-385-5) Tundra Bks.

— A Darker Magic. 192p. (J). 1989. pap. 2.95 (0-380-70611-3, Avon Bks) Morrow Avon.

— The Divide. LC 96-14726. (Illus.). 32p. (J). (gr. k-3). 1997. 16.95 (0-385-32124-4, DD Bks Yng Read) BDD Bks Young Read.

— Emily. LC 91-41806. (Illus.). 40p. (J). (gr. k-3). 1992. 16.95 (0-385-30697-0) Doubleday.

— Glasstown. LC 96-41675. (Illus.). 40p. (J). (gr. 1-4). 1997. 16.00 (0-689-81185-3) S&S Childrens.

— Painted Devil. LC 92-35637. 224p. (J). (gr. 5-9). 1994. 15.95 (0-689-31827-8) Atheneum Yung Read.

— Redwork. 224p. (YA). 1992. pap. 3.50 (0-380-71612-7, Avon Bks) Morrow Avon.

— Sitting Ducks. LC 97-50355. 40p. (J). 1998. 15.99 (0-399-22847-0) Putnam Pub Group.

— The Tinder Box. (Illus.). 32p. (J). (gr. k-3). 1995. 12.95 (0-19-540767-9) Stoddart Publ.

Bedard, Patrick. Expert Driving. LC 87-51170. (Illus.). 96p. (Orig.). 1987. pap. 9.95 (0-9619417-0-7) Valentine Res.

Bedard, Pauline. Baby's First Bible Songs. LC 97-216135. (Illus.). 1997. write for info. (0-7853-2318-X) Pubns Intl Ltd.

— Baby's First Silly Songs. LC 97-216205. (Illus.). 1997. write for info. (0-7853-2320-1) Pubns Intl Ltd.

Bedard, Richard. In the Shadow of the Tornado: Stories & Adventures from the Heart of Storm Country. LC 95-81642. (Illus.). 170p. (Orig.). 1996. pap. 11.95 (0-9649527-1-8) Gilco Pubng.

Bedard, Roger L. Dramatic Literature for Children: A Century in Review. 1983. pap. text 40.00 (0-87602-020-1) Anchorage.

Bedard, Roger L. & Tolch, C. John, eds. Spotlight on the Child: Studies in the History of American Children's Theatre, 28. LC 88-21336. (Contributions in Drama & Theatre Studies: No. 28). 207p. 1989. 52.95 (0-313-25793-0, BDT/, Greenwood Pr) Greenwood.

Bedard, Vicki W., jt. auth. see Rabior, William.

Bedarida, Francois. A Social History of England, 1851-1990. LC 90-44716. (Illus.). 384p. (C). 1991. pap. 27.99 (0-415-01614-2, A1963) Routledge.

— The Social Responsibility of the Historian. 120p. (C). 1995. pap. 12.95 (1-57181-896-0) Berghahn Bks.

Bedate, Pilar Gomez, see Gomez Bedate, Pilar.

***Bedau.** Punishment. 2000. 65.00 (0-8133-6604-6, Pub. by Westview); pap. 19.00 (0-8133-6605-4, Pub. by Westview) HarpC.

Bedau, Hugo A. Death Is Different: Studies in the Morality, Law, & Politics of Capital Punishment. 360p. 1987. text 45.00 (1-55553-008-7) NE U Pr.

— The Death Penalty in America: Current Controversies. LC 96-7028. (Illus.). 544p. 1997. 40.00 (0-19-510438-2) OUP.

— Making Mortal Choices: Three Exercises in Moral Casuistry. 136p. 1997. pap. 15.95 (0-19-510878-7); text 39.95 (0-19-510877-9) OUP.

— Writing Philosophy Papers. 163p. 1996. pap. text 19.95 (0-312-10082-5) St Martin.

Bedau, Hugo A., ed. Civil Disobedience in Focus. (Philosophers in Focus Ser.). 256p. (C). (gr. 13). 1991. pap. 25.99 (0-415-05055-3, A5482); text 89.95 (0-415-05054-5, A5478) Routledge.

— The Death Penalty in America: Current Controversies. (Illus.). 544p. 1998. reprint ed. pap. 18.95 (0-19-512286-0) OUP.

***Bedau, Mark A., et al, eds.** Artificial Life Vol. VII: Proceedings of the Seventh International Conference on Artificial Life. (Complex Adaptive Systems Ser.). 500p. 2000. 75.00 (0-262-52290-X, Bradford Bks) MIT Pr.

Bedaux, J. J., jt. auth. see Kooijman, S. A.

Bedborough, Sheena, jt. auth. see McLullich, Helen.

Bedbrook, Gerald S. Keyboard Music from the Middle Ages to the Beginnings of the Baroque. 2nd ed. LC 69-15605. (Music Ser.). (Illus.). 1973. reprint ed. 29.50 (0-306-71056-0) Da Capo.

— Keyboard Music from the Middle Ages to the Beginnings of the Baroque: Music Book Index. 170p. 1993. reprint ed. lib. bdg. 69.00 (0-7812-9640-4) Rprt Serv.

Bedbury, Scott & Fenichell, Stephen. A New Brand World: Ten Principles for Achieving Brand Leadership in the Twenty-First Century... 320p. 2000. write for info. (0-316-08463-8) Little.

***Beddard, Phil.** Nocturnal: Global Highflyers. 2000. pap. 27.50 (1-86154-169-4) Abrams.

Beddard, Ralph. Human Rights & Europe. 300p. (C). 1993. 150.00 (1-85701-014-0, Pub. by Grotius Pubns Ltd) St Mut.

Bedding, Robin, et al. Nematodes & the Biological Control of Insect Pests. 178p. 1995. 60.00 (0-643-05479-0, Pub. by CSIRO) Accents Pubns.

Beddoe, A. F. Biologic Ionization Applied to Farming & Soil Management: Principles & Techniques. 210p. 1992. pap. text 100.00 (1-881201-06-6); spiral bd. 100.00 (1-881201-00-7) S & J Unltd.

— Biologic Ionization As Applied to Human Nutrition: Principles & Technique. 310p. 1992. pap. text 100.00 (1-881201-05-8); spiral bd. 100.00 (1-881201-01-5) S & J Unltd.

— Nourishment Home Grown: How to Grow Real Nutritious Foods in Your Back Yard. 300p. 1992. 25.00 (1-881201-04-X); pap. 20.00 (1-881201-02-3) S & J Unltd.

Beddoe, A. F., jt. auth. see Brobst, Lee.

Beddoe, Deirdre. Back to Home & Duty: Women Between the Wars, 1918-1939. (Illus.). 178p. 1989. pap. text 13.00 (0-04-440515-4) NYU Pr.

Beddoe, John. The Anthropological History of Europe. 190p. (C). 1996. pap. 18.00 (1-878465-16-3) Scott-Townsend Pubs.

— The Races of Britain. 300p. 1983. reprint ed. 36.00 (0-941694-13-5) Cliveden Pr.

Beddoes, Jonathan & Parr, J. Gordon. Introduction to Stainless Steels. 3rd ed. LC 99-231555. (Illus.). 315p. 1999. 128.00 (0-87170-673-3, 06685G CU) ASM.

Beddoes, Thomas L. The Brides' Tragedy, 1822. LC 93-17412. (Revolution & Romanticism Ser.). 150p. 1993. reprint ed. 48.00 (1-85477-130-2) Continuum.

— The Letters of Thomas Lovell Beddoes. Gosse, Edmund W., ed. LC 70-173168. 270p. 1972. reprint ed. 24.95 (0-405-08250-9, Pub. by Blom Pubns) Ayer.

— The Letters of Thomas Lovell Beddoes. (Anglistica & Americana Ser.: No. 142). viii, 270p. 1973. reprint ed. 50.00 (3-487-04828-0) G Olms Pubs.

— The Works of Thomas Lovell Beddoes. Donner, H. W., ed. LC 75-41023. (BCL Ser. II). 1976. reprint ed. 72.50 (0-404-14507-8) AMS Pr.

Beddome, R. H. The Ferns of British India, 2 vols., Set. (C). 1988. 115.00 (0-7855-3263-3, Pub. by Scientific) St Mut.

— Ferns of Southern India. (C). 1988. 130.00 (0-7855-3262-5, Pub. by Scientific) St Mut.

— Ferns of Southern India. 1969. reprint ed. 60.00 (0-934454-31-0) Lubrecht & Cramer.

— Flora Sylvatica for Southern India, Set, Vols. 1 & 2. 800p. (C). 1978. text 2500.00 (0-89771-547-0, Pub. by Intl Bk Distr) St Mut.

— Flora Sylvatica for Southern India, Vols. 1-3. (C). 1988. 800.00 (0-7855-3234-X, Pub. by Scientific) St Mut.

— Handbook to the Ferns of British India Ceylon & Malay Peninsula. 1969. reprint ed. 45.00 (0-934454-47-7) Lubrecht & Cramer.

— Handbook to the Ferns of British India, Ceylon & Malaya Peninsula. 502p. 1977. suppl. ed. 20.00 (0-88065-054-0) Scholarly Pubns.

— Icones Plantrum Indiae Orientalis. (Illus.). 70p. 1972. reprint ed. 40.00 (0-88065-055-9) Scholarly Pubns.

— Supplement to the Ferns of Southern India & British India. 1997. pap. 100.00 (81-7089-238-4, Pub. by Intl Bk Distr) St Mut.

Beddome, R. H., ed. Handbook of the Fern of British India, Ceylon & the Malay Peninsula A. K. with Supplement. (C). 1988. 40.00 (0-7855-3264-1, Pub. by Scientific) St Mut.

Beddow, ed. Fine Particle Science & Technology Series. 1991. 628.80 (0-8493-5780-2) CRC Pr.

Beddow, J.K. Image Analysis Sourcebook. LC 97-222761. 1997. bds. 110.00 (0-9617531-7-X) Am Univ Sci & Tech.

Beddow, John K. Particle Characterization in Technology. Incl. Vol. I. Applications & Microanalysis. 264p. 1984. 147.00 (0-8493-5784-5, TA418, CRC Reprint); Vol. II. Morphological Analysis. 288p. 1984. 157.00 (0-8493-5785-3, TA418, CRC Reprint); 1984. 170.00 (0-318-60684-4) CRC Pr.

Beddow, John K., ed. see Luerkens, David W.

Beddow, Margery. Bob Fosse's Broadway. LC 96-10858. 116p. 1996. pap. 15.95 (0-435-07002-9) Heinemann.

Beddow, Michael. Mann: Doctor Faustus. LC 93-49364. (Landmarks of World Literature Ser.). 132p. (C). 1994. text 34.95 (0-521-37575-4); pap. text 12.95 (0-521-37592-4) Cambridge U Pr.

Beddow, Nicholas, ed. The Book of Escomb: Prayers in the Escomb Tradition. 48p. 1997. pap. text 9.99 (1-900507-29-3, Pub. by Solway) Eisenbrauns.

Beddows. Speak up for Yourself. 1989. pap. text. write for info. (0-273-03025-6) Addison-Wesley.

Bede. Bede's Ecclesiastical History of the English People. 2nd rev. ed. Mynors, Roger A. & Colgrave, Bertram, eds. & trs. by. 694p. 1993. text 110.00 (0-19-822173-8) OUP.

— Bede's Historia Ecclesiastica. Garforth, F. W., ed. (LAT., Illus.). 158p. (C). 1988. reprint ed. pap. 13.00 (0-86516-218-2) Bolchazy-Carducci.

— Commentary on the Acts of the Apostles by the Venerable Bede. Martin, Lawrence T., tr. from LAT. & intro. by. (Cistercian Studies: No. 117). 212p. 1989. 29.95 (0-87907-617-8); pap. 14.95 (0-87907-917-7) Cistercian Pubns.

— Ecclesiastical History of the English People: The Greater Chronicle; Bede's Letter to Egbert. (Illus.). 484p. 1999. pap. 10.95 (0-19-283866-0) OUP.

Bede, Adam. Adam Beade. (Classics Library). 1998. pap. 3.95 (1-85326-192-0, 1920WW, Pub. by Wrdsworth Edits) NTC Contemp Pub Co.

Bede, Barry, jt. auth. see Piekalkiewicz, Jaroslaw.

Bede, Brandt A. Tales of a Country Doctor: One Hundred Years of Health Care in Lewis County. LC 92-85175. 124p. (C). 1993. pap. 13.50 (1-880222-12-4) Red Apple Pub.

Bede, Elbert. Fabulous Opal Whiteley. (Illus.). 190p. 1978. pap. 9.95 (0-8323-0360-7) Binford Mort.

— Five-Fifteen Minute Talks. x, 126p. 1994. reprint ed. pap. 7.25 (0-88053-042-1, M 091) Macoy Pub.

— The Landmarks of Freemasonry. 56p. 1980. reprint ed. pap. text 3.95 (0-88053-020-0, M 069) Macoy Pub.

— Three-Five-Seven Minute Talks on Freemasonry. 9th ed. xii, 116p. 1993. reprint ed. pap. 7.25 (0-88053-048-0, M-306) Macoy Pub.

Bede, Jean-Albert & Edgerton, William, eds. Columbia Dictionary of Modern European Literature. 2nd ed. LC 80-17082. 800p. 1980. text 226.00 (0-231-03717-1) Col U Pr.

Bede the Venerable. Ecclesiastical History of England. Giles, John A., ed. LC 78-136367. (Bohn's Antiquarian Library). (Illus.). reprint ed. 72.50 (0-404-50001-3) AMS Pr.

Bedeaux, Ed. Lannigan. large type ed. (Linford Western Library). 256p. 1993. pap. 16.99 (0-7089-7305-1) Ulverscroft.

Bedee, Henk. International Guide to Social Security. 1995. lib. bdg. 157.00 (90-6544-874-8) Kluwer Academic.

Bedeian, Arthur. Management Lauretes: A Collection of Autobiographical Essays, Vol. 5. 1998. 86.25 (0-7623-0178-3) Jai Pr.

Bedeian, Arthur G., ed. Management Laureates: A Collection of Autobiographical Essays, Vol. 2. 439p. 1993. 86.25 (1-55938-470-0) Jai Pr.

Bedeian, ARthur G., ed. Management Laureates: A Collection of Autobiographical Essays, Vol. 3. 414p. 1993. 86.25 (1-55938-471-9) Jai Pr.

— Management Laureates: A Collection of Autobiographical Essays, Vol. 4. 1996. 86.25 (1-55938-730-0) Jai Pr.

Bedeian, Arthur G. & Zammuto, Raymond F. Organizations: Theory & Design. (Illus.). 624p. (C). 1991. text 56.00 (0-03-012583-9) Dryden Pr.

Bedeian, Arthur G., ed. see Ansoff, H. Igor.

Bedel, Jean. Dictionnaire Illustre des Antiquites et de la Brocante. (FRE.). 1988. write for info. (0-7859-7668-X, 2035091063) Fr & Eur.

Bedeladze, T., ed. English-Uzbek-Russian Commercial Dictionary. 344p. (C). 1995. 32.95 (0-8285-5542-7) Firebird NY.

Bedell, Clyde B. The Basic Total Selling & Advertising Service - Floorcoverings. 2nd ed. LC 75-27670. 366p. 1984. spiral bd. 295.00 (0-916014-00-2) BASIC Bedell.

— Concordex of the URANTIA Book. 3rd rev. ed. LC 85-18502. 512p. 1987. 17.95 (0-916014-75-4) BASIC Bedell.

— How to Convert White Space Into Advertising That Sells - a Basic Short Course in Advertising Creation. 256p. 1964. 99.95 (0-916014-02-9) BASIC Bedell.

Bedell, Clyde B. & Alexander, J. A. 131 Stress Reducin' Recession Bustin' Profit Proven Furniture Ads. LC 82-71190. 288p. 1982. 129.00 (0-916014-01-0) BASIC Bedell.

Bedell, Cornelia F., compiled by. Now & Then & Long Ago in Rockland County, New York. 2nd ed. LC 92-36972. (Illus.). 399p. 1992. reprint ed. 25.00 (0-911183-45-0) Rockland County Hist.

***Bedell, Gene.** Three Steps to Yes: The Gentle Art of Getting Your Way. 192p. 2000. 23.00 (0-609-60698-0) Crown Pub Group.

Bedell, George C., et al. Religion in America. 2nd ed. LC 81-8239. 560p. (C). 1982. text 45.80 (0-02-307810-3, Macmillan Coll) P-H.

Bedell, Jack. At the Bonehouse. LC 97-44278. (Southern & Southwestern Writers Breakthrough Ser.). 64p. 1998. pap. 11.00 (1-881515-16-8) TX Review Pr.

Bedell, Jane. Mischief & Eve: A Halloween Beginning. (Illus.). 22p. (J). (gr. 2-4). 1998. pap. 3.99 (0-9665837-0-1) J M Bedell.

Bedell, Jeffrey E. Overcome Your Foreign Accent & Speak English with Confidence. 1987. pap. 7.00 (0-916014-51-7) Am Spch Imprvmnt.

— Overcome Your Foreign Accent & Speak English with Confidence. rev. ed. 32p. 1987. 129.95 incl. audio (0-916014-50-9) Am Spch Imprvmnt.

Bedell, Jeffrey R. & Lennox, Shelley S. Handbook for Communication & Problem Solving: Skills Training: A Cognitive-Behavioral Approach. LC 96-24667. (Publication Series of the Einstein-Monte). 288p. 1996. 69.50 (0-471-08250-3) Wiley.

Bedell, K. S. Cellular/Wireless Managment. LC 98-53242. 1999. 49.95 (0-07-134645-7) McGraw.

Bedell, Kenneth. Yearbook of American & Canadian Churches, 1994. 1994. pap. 29.95 (0-687-46650-4) Abingdon.

B

An Asterisk (*) at the beginning of an entry indicates that the title is appearing for the first time.

Bedell, Kenneth B. Yearbook of American & Canadian Churches, 1995. (Orig.). 1995. pap. 29.95 (*0-687-00826-3*) Abingdon.
— Yearbook of American & Canadian Churches, 1996. 312p. 1996. pap. 29.95 (*0-687-05589-X*) Abingdon.
Bedell, Kevin S., ed. Strongly Correlated Electronic Materials: The Los Alamos Symposium, 1993. LC 94-28602. (C). 1994. 54.00 (*0-201-40930-5*) Addison-Wesley.
Bedell, L. Frank. Crew Genealogy, 1397-1966. (Illus.). 59p. 1995. reprint ed. pap. 17.00 (*0-8328-4906-5*); reprint ed. lib. bdg. 27.00 (*0-8328-4905-7*) Higginson Bk Co.
— Ellyson: Dr. Robert & Elizabeth Ellyson, Their Ancestors & Descendants. (Illus.). 283p. 1995. reprint ed. pap. 37.00 (*0-8328-4910-3*); reprint ed. lib. bdg. 47.00 (*0-8328-4909-X*) Higginson Bk Co.
Bedell, Mella W., jt. auth. see Bangerter, Alisa D.
Bedenbaugh, Angela O., et al. Determining the Proportionality Constant, R, in the Ideal Gas Equation. Neidig, H. Anthony, ed. (Modular Laboratory Program in Chemistry Ser.). 12p. (C). 1990. pap. text 1.50 (*0-87540-379-4*, PROP 379-4) Chem Educ Res.
— Determining the Mass Percent Composition of an Aqueus Hydrogen Peroxide Solution. Neidig, H. Anthony, ed. (Modular Laboratory Program in Chemistry Ser.). 12p. (C). 1990. pap. text 1.50 (*0-87540-378-6*, ANAL 378-6) Chem Educ Res.
— Determining the Molar Volume of Oxygen. Neidig, H. Anthony, ed. (Modular Laboratory Program in Chemistry Ser.). 12p. (C). 1990. pap. text 1.50 (*0-87540-377-8*, PROP 377-8) Chem Educ Res.
***Bedenick, B. & Besant, C. B.** Analysis of Engineering Structures. 2000. 45.00 (*1-898563-55-1*, Pub. by Horwood Pub) Paul & Co Pubs.
Beder, Harold W. & Darkenwald, Gordon G. Development, Demonstration, & Dissemination: Case Studies of Selected Special Projects in Adult Basic Education. LC 74-23656. (Occasional Papers: No. 42). 59p. 1974. pap. 2.75 (*0-87060-067-2*, OCP 42) Syracuse U Cont Ed.
Beder, Harold W. & Smith, Franceska. Developing an Adult Education Program Through Community Linkages. 1977. 7.00 (*0-88379-009-2*) A A A C E.
Beder, Sharon. Global Spin: The Corporate Assault on Environmentalism. LC 97-47111. (Illus.), 288p. 1998. pap. 19.95 (*1-890132-12-8*) Chelsea Green Pub.
— The New Engineer: Management & Professional Responsibility in a Changing World. LC 98-185063. 350p. 1998. 84.95 (*0-7329-4675-1*, Pub. by Macmill Educ); pap. 42.95 (*0-7329-4676-X*, Pub. by Macmill Educ) Paul & Co Pubs.
***Beder, Sharon.** Noses to the Grindstone: Shaping Industrial Servitude. LC 00-43285. 2000. boxed set. write for info. (*1-85649-885-9*, Pub. by Zed Books) St Martin.
Bederman, Gail. Manliness & Civilization: A Cultural History of Gender & Race in the United States, 1880-1917. xiv, 308p. 1996. pap. text 19.00 (*0-226-04139-5*) U Ch Pr.
— Manliness & Civilization: A Cultural History of Gender & Race in the United States, 1880-1917. LC 94-26936. (Women in Culture & Society Ser.). 322p. 1998. 27.50 (*0-226-04138-7*) U Ch Pr.
Bederman, Sanford H. Africa, a Bibliography of Geography & Related Disciplines: A Selected Listing of Recent Literature Published in the English Language. 3rd fac. ed. LC 74-22175. 342p. 1994. pap. 106.10 (*0-7837-7677-2*, 204743000007) Bks Demand.
Bederson, Benjamin, ed. More Things in Heaven & Earth: A Celebration of Physics at the Millennium. LC 98-53116. (Illus.). 600p. 1999. 75.00 (*0-387-98662-6*) Spr-Verlag.
Bederson, Benjamin, et al, eds. Advances in Atomic, Molecular, & Optical Physics, Vol. 37. (Illus.). 388p. (C). 1996. text 125.00 (*0-12-003837-4*) Acad Pr.
Bederson, Benjamin & Dalgarno, Alexander, eds. Advances in Atomic, Molecular, & Optical Physics, Vol. 32. (Illus.), 464p. (C). 1993. text 155.00 (*0-12-003832-3*) Acad Pr.
Bederson, Benjamin & Walther, Herbert, eds. Advances in Atomic, Molecular, & Optical Physics, Vol. 34. (Illus.). 497p. (C). 1995. text 137.00 (*0-12-003834-X*) Acad Pr.
— Advances in Atomic, Molecular, & Optical Physics, Vol. 35. (Illus.). 408p. (C). 1995. text 137.00 (*0-12-003835-8*) Acad Pr.
— Advances in Atomic, Molecular, & Optical Physics, Vol. 36. (Illus.). 295p. (C). 1996. text 125.00 (*0-12-003836-6*) Acad Pr.
— Advances in Atomic, Molecular Optical Physics, Vol. 38. (Illus.). 256p. (C). 1997. text 125.00 (*0-12-003838-2*) Morgan Kaufmann.
— Advances in Atomic, Molecular, & Optical Physics, Vol. 40. 321p. 1998. boxed set 140.00 (*0-12-003840-4*) Acad Pr.
— Advances in Atomic, Molecular, & Optical Physics, Vol. 41. (Illus.). 320p. 1998. boxed set 140.00 (*0-12-003841-2*) Acad Pr.
— Advances in Atomic, Molecular & Optical Physics Vol. 39: Subject & Author Cumulative Index. (Illus.). 480p. (C). 1998. text 140.00 (*0-12-003839-0*) Acad Pr.
***Bederson, Benjamin & Walther, Herbert, eds.** Advances in Atomic, Molecular & Optical Physics Vol. 42. 440p. 1999. 145.00 (*0-12-003842-0*) Acad Pr.
Bederson, Joshua B. & Tuhrim, Stanley, eds. Treatment of Carotid Disease: A Practitioner's Manual. 255p. 40.00 (*1-879284-55-3*) Am Assn Neuro.
Bedeski, Robert E. The Transformation of South Korea: Reform & Reconstitution in the Sixth Republic under Roe Tae Woo, 1987-1992. LC 93-30537. 208p. (C). 1994. pap. 27.99 (*0-415-10604-4*) Routledge.
Bedessem, Anne & McIver, Peter B. The Stations of the Cross: Arranged for Readers Theatre. (Orig.). 1994. pap. text 5.95 (*1-56929-023-7*, Pastoral Press) OR Catholic.
Bedessem, Edward N. Central Europe: The United States Army Campaigns of World War 2. 35p. 1996. pap. 2.00 (*0-16-048136-8*) USGPO.
***Bedford.** Bedford World History Atlas. 2002. pap. write for info. (*0-312-17186-2*) St Martin.
Bedford. Legal Keys: Keyboard Drills. (C). 1991. pap. text. write for info. (*0-7730-5032-9*) Addison-Wes.
Bedford. What Do You Do with a Political Science Major? pap. text. write for info. (*0-312-24871-7*) St Martin.
Bedford, A. & Drumheller, D. S. Introduction to Elastic Wave Propagation. 312p. 1996. pap. 90.00 (*0-471-96700-9*) Wiley.
Bedford, A. & Fowler, Wallace. Engineering Mechanics. Incl. Statics. 624p. 1995. (*0-201-49866-9*); 1200p. 1996. 1.07 (*0-201-49868-5*) Addison-Wesley.
Bedford, A. Marc. Dynamics: Windows Version. 1995. pap. text. write for info. (*0-201-84551-2*) Addison-Wesley.
— Dynamics Engineering Mechanics: SI Version. LC 97-207509. (C). 1996. pap. text 69.95 (*0-201-40341-2*) Addison-Wesley.
— Engineering Mechanics: Dynamics & Working Model Windows Bundle. (C). 1995. 109.95 (*0-201-85951-3*) Addison-Wesley.
— Engineering Mechanics: Statics & Student Edition of Working Model Windows Bundle. (C). 1995. 109.95 (*0-201-85954-8*) Addison-Wesley.
— Statics: Windows Version. (C). 1995. pap. text. write for info. (*0-201-84558-X*) Addison-Wesley.
— Statics Engineering Mechanics: SI Version. LC 97-18607. (C). 1996. pap. text 69.95 (*0-201-40340-4*) Addison-Wesley.
Bedford, Anthony. Engineering Mechanics: Dynamics. 2nd ed. LC 98-34437. 600p. (C). 1998. 96.00 (*0-201-18071-5*, Prentice Hall) P-H.
— Engineering Mechanics: Statics. 2nd ed. LC 98-18289. (Engineering Ser.). 650p. (C). 1998. 96.00 (*0-201-18070-7*, Prentice Hall) P-H.
***Bedford, Anthony & Fowler, Wallace.** Statics & Dynamics. 2nd ed. 1250p. (C). 1998. 125.20 (*0-201-44497-6*) Peachpit Pr.
***Bedford, Anthony M. & Liechti, Kenneth M.** Mechanics of Materials. 855p. 2000. pap. 101.33 (*0-201-89552-8*) P-H.
Bedford, Arthur. The Great Abuse of Music in Two Parts. fac. ed. (Monuments of Music & Music Literature in Facsimile Ser., Series II: Vol. 12). 1965. lib. bdg. 40.00 (*0-8450-2212-1*) Broude.
— Serious Reflections on the Scandalous Abuse & Effects of the Stage. (English Stage Ser.: Vol. 41). 1974. lib. bdg. 61.00 (*0-8240-0624-0*) Garland.
Bedford, B., jt. ed. see Ives, C.
Bedford, Barbara L., jt. auth. see Geisler, Charles C.
Bedford, Bruce, jt. auth. see Maredia, Karen.
Bedford, C. Harold. The Seeker: D. S. Merezhkovskiy. LC 74-28496. x, 222p. 1975. 27.50 (*0-7006-0131-7*) U Pr of KS.
Bedford, Debbi. After the Promise. (Superromance Ser.). 1993. mass mkt. 3.39 (*0-373-70546-8*, 1-70546-6) Harlequin Bks.
— Blessing. (Historical Ser.). 1993. mass mkt. 3.99 (*0-373-28787-9*, 1-28787-9) Harlequin Bks.
Bedford, Denise. Selecting & Designing an Integrated Library System. 2000. 39.50 (*1-57387-064-1*) Info Today Inc.
Bedford, Denton R. Tsali. LC 72-91136. (Illus.). 256p. 1972. pap. 15.00 (*0-913436-24-0*) Indian Hist Pr.
Bedford, Faith A. Benson, Frank W. American Impressionist. LC 94-4638. 240p. 1994. 50.00 (*0-8478-1609-5*, Pub. by Rizzoli Intl) St Martin.
Bedford, Faith A., et al. Frank W. Benson: His Sporting Art. (Illus.). 112p. (Orig.). 1996. pap. 35.00 (*0-9654609-0-8*) G E Nelson.
***Bedford, Faith Andrews.** The Sporting Art of Frank Weston Benson. (Illus.). 272p. 2000. 70.00 (*1-56792-112-6*) Godine.
Bedford, Frances. Harpsichord & Clavichord Music of the Twentieth Century. LC 93-27827. (Reference Books in Music: No. 22). (Illus.). liv, 609p. 1993. 69.50 (*0-914913-19-0*, Fallen Lef Pr) Scarecrow.
Bedford, Henry F. Seabrook Station: Citizen Politics & Nuclear Power. LC 89-77123. (Illus.). 248p. (C). 1990. 30.00 (*0-87023-711-X*) U of Mass Pr.
— Seabrook Station: Citizen Politics & Nuclear Power. LC 89-77123. (Illus.). 248p. (C). 1992. reprint ed. pap. 17.95 (*0-87023-785-3*) U of Mass Pr.
— Socialism & the Workers in Massachusetts, 1886-1912. LC 66-15794. (Illus.). 234p. 1966. 30.00 (*0-87023-019-7*) U of Mass Pr.
Bedford, Henry F., ed. Their Lives & Numbers: The Condition of Working People in Massachusetts, 1870-1900. LC 94-23402. (Documents in American Social History Ser.). (Illus.). 264p. 1995. pap. text 17.95 (*0-8014-8255-5*) Cornell U Pr.
Bedford, Henry F. & Colt, Thomas C. Main Problems in American History Vol. 1: Reconstruction: The Nation's Unfinished Business Black Life after Reconstruction, 1877-1910. abr. ed. (PaperBook Series in History). (Illus.). 128p. (C). 1996. pap. text 2.25 (*1-877891-32-0*) Paperbook Fr Inc.
Bedford, Jim. Flyfisher's Guide to Michigan. LC 99-88741. 2000. pap. 26.95 (*1-885106-76-9*) Wild Adven Pr.
— Steelhead Savvy. LC 95-165860. (Illus.). 88p. 1995. pap. 12.95 (*1-878175-94-7*) F Amato Pubns.
Bedford, Jimmy, ed. see Brown, Emily I.
Bedford, John. Moment in Time. large type ed. (Dales Mystery Ser.). 292p. 1992. pap. 18.99 (*1-85389-318-8*, Dales) Ulverscroft.
Bedford, John R. Graphic Engineering Geometry. LC 78-67438. (Illus.). 159p. (Orig.). reprint ed. pap. 49.30 (*0-608-17456-4*, 202992400066) Bks Demand.
Bedford, Kristina. Coriolanus at the National: The Interpretation of the Time. LC 90-55697. (Illus.). 352p. 1992. 55.00 (*0-945636-18-0*) Susquehanna U Pr.
***Bedford, M. & Partridge, G., eds.** Enzymes in Farm Animal Nutrition. (CABI Publishing Ser.). (Illus.). 256p. 2000. text. write for info. (*0-85199-393-1*) OUP.
Bedford, Marc A. Engineering Mechanics: Statistics & Student Edition of Working Model Macintosh. (C). 1996. 117.33 (*0-201-85948-3*) Addison-Wesley.
— Statics & Dynamics. 1995. 99.25 (*0-201-85949-1*) Addison-Wesley.
— Statistics & Dynamics & Student Edition of Working Model Bundle. (C). 1995. 123.95 (*0-201-85953-X*) Addison-Wesley.
Bedford, Martyn. Acts of Revision. 256p. 1998. mass mkt. 19.95 (*0-552-99674-2*) Bantam.
Bedford, Martyn. The Houdini Girl. LC 98-35826. 320p. 1999. 24.00 (*0-375-40527-5*) Pantheon.
***Bedford, Martyn.** The Houdini Girl. (Crime - Black Lizard Ser.). 320p. 2000. pap. 13.00 (*0-375-70476-0*) Vin Bks.
Bedford, Michael & Dettman, B. The Horror Factory: Universal Pictures & the Horror Film, 1925-1950. 1975. lib. bdg. 250.00 (*0-87968-443-7*) Gordon Pr.
Bedford, Nancy A., tr. see Price, Max B.
Bedford, Nancy K., jt. auth. see Brown, Jerilyn B.
Bedford, Norton M. The Future of Accounting in a Changing Society. (Arther Andersen Lecture Ser.). 101p. 1970. pap. text 5.00 (*0-87563-214-9*) Stipes.
— Introduction to Modern Accounting. LC 68-12885. 756p. reprint ed. pap. 200.00 (*0-608-10969-X*, 201239200081) Bks Demand.
Bedford, P. G. An Atlas of Canine Surgical Techniques. (Illus.). 194p. 1996. pap. write for info. (*0-632-01814-3*) Blackwell Sci.
***Bedford, Peter R.** Temple Restoration in Early Achaemenid Judah. (Supplements to the Journal for the Study of Judaism Ser.). 208p. 2000. text 65.00 (*90-04-11509-9*) Brill Academic Pubs.
Bedford-Pierce, Sophia. African Proverbs. 1962. 7.99 (*0-88088-025-2*) Peter Pauper.
— A Friend Is a Special Treasure. LC 97-198538. (Keepsakes Ser.). (Illus.). 56p. 1997. 7.99 (*0-88088-891-1*) Peter Pauper.
— The Key to Happiness. (Charming Petites Ser.). (Illus.). 80p. 1997. 4.95 (*0-88088-822-9*) Peter Pauper.
— The Key to Life. (Charming Petites Ser.). (Illus.). 80p. 1995. 4.95 (*0-88088-790-7*) Peter Pauper.
Bedford-Pierce, Sophie, jt. auth. see Conny, Beth Mende.
Bedford, R. D. Dialogues with Convention: Essays in Renaissance Poetry. LC 89-20269. 204p. 1990. text 42.50 (*0-472-10171-4*, 10171) U of Mich Pr.
Bedford, Richard C. English Experienced: Teaching Foreign Students by Staging Communication. LC 70-156068. (Savoyard Book Ser.). 228p. reprint ed. pap. 70.70 (*0-7837-3586-3*, 204344600009) Bks Demand.
Bedford, Simi. Yoruba Girl Dancing. 192p. 1994. pap. 10.95 (*0-14-023293-1*, Penguin Bks) Viking Penguin.
Bedford Staff. Bedford History. 2000. pap. text 61.50 (*0-312-13676-5*) St Martin.
Bedford, Steven. The Long Island Country House, 1870-1930. LC 87-63536. (Illus.). 100p. (C). 1988. pap. 15.00 (*0-943526-17-5*) Parrish Art.
Bedford, Steven M. John Russell Pope: Architect of Empire. LC 97-49820. (Illus.). 240p. 1998. 60.00 (*0-8478-2086-6*, Pub. by Rizzoli Intl) St Martin.
Bedford, Stewart. Instant Replay. (Illus.). 1974. pap. 1.95 (*0-917476-00-X*) A Ellis Institute.
***Bedford, Sybille.** Legacy. LC 75-34600. (Neglected Books of the 20th Century Ser.). 380p. 1999. reprint ed. pap. 8.50 (*0-912946-26-1*, Ecco Press) HarperTrade.
Bedford, Victoria H., jt. ed. see Blieszner, Rosemary H.
Bedford, W. K. Riland: Three Hundred Years of a Family Living, Being a History of the Rilands of Sutton Coldfield, England. 175p. 1993. reprint ed. pap. 28.00 (*0-8328-3739-3*); reprint ed. lib. bdg. 38.00 (*0-8328-3738-5*) Higginson Bk Co.
Bedford, William K. The Order or the Hospital of St. John of Jerusalem. LC 76-29831. reprint ed. 44.50 (*0-404-15412-3*) AMS Pr.
Bedgood, Lorenza. Powerful Inspirational Thoughts: Reach for the Stars. 2nd ed. LC 91-72524. (Illus.). 96p. 1991. pap. 7.95 (*1-879926-05-9*) D M K D Pubns.
***Bedi, Ashok.** Path to the Soul: The Union of Eastern & Western Wisdom to Heal Your Body, Mind & Soul. LC 00-26122. (Illus.). 272p. 2000. pap. 16.95 (*1-57863-187-4*) Weiser.
Bedi, Hari. Understanding the Asian Manager. 192p. (Orig.). pap. 19.95 (*1-86373-029-X*, Pub. by Allen & Unwin Pty) Paul & Co Pubs.
Bedi, Joyce, jt. auth. see Collins, Douglas.
***Bedi, Kiran.** It's Always Possible: Transforming One of the Largest Prisons in the World. (Illus.). 400p. 1999. pap. 24.95 (*0-9585805-3-7*, Pub. by Indra Pubng) Intl Spec Bk.
Bedi, Kiran. It's Always Possible: Transforming One of the Largest Prisons in the World. LC 98-909055. xvi, 400p. 1998. write for info. (*81-207-2049-0*) Sterling Pubs.
Bedi, Rajesh. India's Wild Wonders. 1993. 59.95 (*81-7107-029-9*) Mandala Pub Grp.
— Sadhus: The Holy Men of India. 1993. 44.95 (*81-7107-021-3*) Mandala Pub Grp.
***Bedi, S., ed.** Gods & Goddesses of India. 1998. pap. 100.00 (*81-86982-04-3*, Pub. by Business Pubns) St Mut.
Bedi, Satya D. Extradition in International Law & Practice. LC 67-93868. 1968. lib. bdg. 45.00 (*0-89941-367-5*, 500240) W S Hein.
Bedi, Sohinder S. Folklore of the Punjab. 160p. 1980. 6.95 (*0-318-36322-4*) Asia Bk Corp.
Bedi, Susham. The Fire Sacrifice. (Asian Writers Ser.). 182p. 1994. pap. 9.95 (*0-435-95087-8*, 95087) Heinemann.
Bediako, Abraham. Conforming into His Image. 79p. 1989. pap. 3.95 (*0-88144-133-3*) Christian Pub.
Bediako, Gillian M. Primal Religion & the Bible: William Robertson Smith & His Heritage. LC 97-205426. (JSOT Supplement Ser.: No. 246). 402p. 1997. 90.75 (*1-85075-672-4*, Pub. by Sheffield Acad) CUP Services.
Bediako, Kwame. Christianity in Africa: The Renewal of Non-Western Religion. LC 95-24225. 276p. 1996. pap. 25.00 (*1-57075-048-3*) Orbis Bks.
Bedicheck, Jane G., compiled by. The Roy Bedicheck Family Letters. LC 97-29539. (Illus.). 464p. 1998. 29.95 (*1-57441-032-6*) UNTX Pr.
Bedichek, Roy. Adventures with a Texas Naturalist. (Illus.). 360p. (C). 1994. pap. 14.95 (*0-292-70311-2*) U of Tex Pr.
— Adventures with a Texas Naturalist. (American Autobiography Ser.). 330p. 1995. reprint ed. lib. bdg. 89.00 (*0-7812-8457-0*) Rprt Serv.
Bedichek, Wendell M., jt. auth. see Tannahill, Neal R.
Bedient, Cal. Candy Necklace. LC 96-20013. (Wesleyan Poetry Ser.). 99p. 1997. pap. 12.95 (*0-8195-1221-4*, Wesleyan Univ Pr); text 25.00 (*0-8195-2234-1*, Wesleyan Univ Pr) U Pr of New Eng.
Bedient, Calvin. He Do the Police in Different Voices: The Waste Land & Its Protagonist. LC 86-11302. (A Chicago Original Paperback Ser.). 236p. Date not set. reprint ed. pap. 73.20 (*0-608-21001-3*, 205452900003) Bks Demand.
— He Do the Police in Different Voices: The Wasteland & Its Protagonist. LC 86-11302. 240p. (C). 1987. pap. text 13.95 (*0-226-04141-7*) U Ch Pr.
— In the Heart's Last Kingdom. 264p. 1986. pap. 15.50 (*0-674-44547-3*) HUP.
— In the Heart's Last Kingdom: Robert Penn Warren's Major Poetry. 264p. 1984. 32.00 (*0-674-44546-5*) HUP.
Bedient, John. Marketing Decision Making Using Lotus 1-2-3. 176p. (C). 1989. pap. text. write for info. incl. 5.25 hd (*0-538-80358-4*, SS80A81); pap. text. write for info. incl. 3.5 hd (*0-538-80480-7*, SS80A8H88) S-W Pub.
Bedient, Philip B. Ground Water Contamination: Transport & Remediation. 560p. 1994. text 89.00 (*0-13-362592-3*) P-H.
***Bedient, Philip B.** Ground Water Contamination: Transport & Remediation. 2nd ed. LC 99-38305. (Illus.). 604p. 1999. 93.00 (*0-13-013840-1*) P-H.
Bedient, Philip B., et al. Hydrology & Floodplain Analysis. LC 87-14308. (Illus.). 650p. (C). 1988. student ed. write for info. (*0-201-14589-8*) Addison-Wesley.
— Hydrology & Floodplain Analysis. 2nd ed. (Illus.). 712p. (C). 1992. 105.00 (*0-201-51711-6*) Addison-Wesley.
Bedient, Shirle. How to Paint Flowers in Watercolor. (How to Draw & Paint Ser.). (Illus.). 32p. pap. 6.95 (*1-56010-078-8*, HT 237) W Foster Pub.
Bedier, Joseph. Les Legendes Epiques: Recherches sur la formation des chansons de geste, 4 vols., Set. LC 78-63487. reprint ed. 159.00 (*0-404-17130-3*) AMS Pr.
— The Romance of Tristan & Iseult. 1965. pap. 5.56 (*0-394-70271-9*) Vin Bks.
— The Romance of Tristan & Iseult. 208p. 1994. pap. 10.00 (*0-679-75016-9*) Vin Bks.
***Bedier, Joseph, et al.** Une Amitie de Jeunesse. (Illus.). x, 322p. 1999. 49.95 (*3-906763-48-X*, Pub. by P Lang) P Lang Pubng.
Bedik, Shelly. Our President: Bill Clinton. 32p. (J). (gr. k-3). 1993. pap. 2.50 (*0-590-47126-0*) Scholastic Inc.
— Thomas Edison: Great American Inventor. 32p. (J). (ps-3). 1995. pap. 2.50 (*0-590-48357-9*) Scholastic Inc.
***Bedillion, A. Mark.** Psychiatric Survivor: From Misdiagnosed Mental Patient to Hospital Director. Breggin, Peter, ed. LC 99-70433. 206p. 1999. pap. 14.95 (*1-880451-41-7*) Rainbows End.
Bedinger. Teen Counseling. 272p. (C). 1992. per. 28.95 (*0-8403-8193-X*) Kendall-Hunt.
Bedinger, M. S., et al, eds. Site Characterization & Design of On-Site Septic Systems Vol. 132: STP 1324. LC 97-40555. 325p. 1997. 74.00 (*0-8031-2420-1*, STP1324) ASTM.
Bedingfeld, T., tr. see Machiavelli, Niccolo.
Bedingfield, T., ed. see Cardano, Girolamo.
Bedington, Glynn. Who Do You Want to Be? The Art of Presenting Yourself with Ease. 168p. (Orig.). 1995. pap. 10.95 (*0-9624945-9-3*) Silvercat Pubns.
Bedini, Annabel, tr. see Sordi, Marta.
Bedini, Silvio A. The Life of Benjamin Banneker: The First African American Man of Science. LC 98-22848. Date not set. pap. write for info. (*0-938420-63-1*) MD Hist.
— The Life of Benjamin Banneker: The First African-American Man of Science. 2nd rev. expanded ed. LC 98-22848. (Illus.). 448p. 1998. 35.00 (*0-938420-59-3*) MD Hist.
— The Mace & the Gavel. LC 97-30718. (Transactions Ser.: Vol. 87, Pt. 4). (Illus.). 84p. 1997. pap. 15.00 (*0-87169-874-9*, T874-bes) Am Philos.
— Patrons, Artisans & Instruments of Science, 1600-1750. LC 98-53851. (Variorum Collected Studies Ser.). (Illus.). 12p. 1999. text 120.95 (*0-86078-781-8*) Ashgate Pub Co.
Bedini, Silvio A. The Pope's Elephant. LC 98-121003. (Illus.). 320p. 1998. 55.00 (*1-85754-277-0*, Pub. by Carcanet Pr) Paul & Co Pubs.
— The Pope's Elephant. LC 98-36227. (Illus.). 312p. 1998. 29.95 (*1-879941-41-4*, Pub. by J S Sanders) Natl Bk Netwk.
***Bedini, Silvio A.** The Pope's Elephant. (Illus.). 320p. 2000. pap. 14.95 (*0-14-028862-7*, Penguin Bks) Viking Penguin.

B

An Asterisk (*) at the beginning of an entry indicates that the title is appearing for the first time.

B

Bedini, Silvio A., ed. Christopher Columbus & the Age of Exploration: An Encyclopedia. LC 98-19964. Orig. Title: The Christopher Columbus Encyclopedia. (Illus.). 824p. 1998. reprint ed. pap. 39.50 (0-306-80871-4) Da Capo.

Bedjan, Paul, ed. Acta Martyrum et Sanctorum Syriace, 7 vols. (GER.). lxxvii, 5008p. 1968. reprint ed. 1050.00 (0-318-70601-6) G Olms Pubs.

Bedjaoui, Mohammed. The New World Order & the Security Council: Testing the Legality of Its Acts. LC 93-41072. 1993. write for info. (0-7923-2562-1) Kluwer Academic.

— Towards a New International Economic Order. LC 79-22943. Orig. Title: Pour un Nouvel Ordre Economique International. 287p. 1979. pap. 29.95 (0-8419-0588-6) Holmes & Meier.

Bedke, John, jt. auth. see Sandage, Allan.

Bedley, Gene. ABCDs of Discipline. LC 79-90307. 128p. 1979. pap. 10.95 (1-888353-00-7) People-Wise.

— Climate Creators Dynamic Principles for Promoting Self Esteem. LC 82-90185. 126p. 1982. pap. 10.95 (1-888353-02-3) People-Wise.

— Game Time: Mental Messages for Teams & Life. LC 94-93856. 95p. 1994. pap. 24.00 (1-888353-16-3) People-Wise.

— How Do You Recognize a Good School When You Walk into One? LC 80-83308. 134p. 1980. pap. 19.95 (1-888353-01-5) People-Wise.

— Self Manager Program, 11 booklets, Set. 1985. pap. 40.00 (1-888353-06-6) People-Wise.

— Value Driven Discipline. 150p. 1996. pap. text 24.95 (1-888353-18-X) People-Wise.

— Values in Action, Set. LC 93-92737. 411p. 1994. teacher ed. 169.00 (1-888353-14-7) People-Wise.

Bedley, Gene & Greene, Gary. Success Is a Fly in the Eye of a Frog. LC 94-68954. 56p. (J). 1995. 20.00 (1-888353-17-1) People-Wise.

Bedley, Gene A. The Big "R" Responsibility, Who Left the Milk Out? LC 84-62568. (Illus.). 139p. (Orig.). 1985. pap. 10.95 (1-888353-03-1) People-Wise.

Bedley, Janet Q. Promises Broken, Promises Kept. LC 91-6306. 224p. (J). 1991. pap. 6.99 (1-55513-609-5, 36095, LifeJourney) Chariot Victor.

***Bedley, Tim.** Mr. Tim's Tips for New Teachers. (Illus.). 32p. 1999. spiral bd. 12.95 (0-9667145-1-2) Inspiring Teachers Pubg.

Bedmer, et al. North American Indian Portfolios. (Tiny Folios Ser.). (Illus.). 272p. 1996. pap. 11.95 (1-55859-601-1) Abbeville Pr.

***Bednair, Miloslav.** Human Dignity: Values & Justice. LC 99-50277. (Cultural Heritage & Contemporary Change Ser.). 1999. pap. write for info. (1-56518-140-9) Coun Res Values.

Bednar, Agnes, ed. see Bednar, Nancy & Walter, Kelly.

Bednar, Chuck. College Football. 150p. 1999. pap. 9.99 (1-58365-017-2) BT Pub.

Bednar, Gerald J. Faith As Imagination: The Contribution of William F. Lynch, S. J. 224p. (Orig.). 1996. pap. 16.95 (1-55612-907-6, LL1907) Sheed & Ward WI.

Bednar, Henry H. Pressure Vessel Design Handbook. 2nd ed. LC 90-5043. 446p. (C). 1990. 62.50 (0-89464-503-X) Krieger.

Bednar, J. B., ed. Geophysical Inversion. LC 91-39015. (Proceedings in Applied Mathematics Ser.: No. 52). x, 453p. 1992. pap. text 96.50 (0-89871-273-4) Soc Indus-Appl Math.

Bednar, J. B., et al, eds. Conference on Inverse Scattering: Theory & Application. LC 85-51381. (Proceedings in Applied Mathematics Ser.: No. 11). x, 290p. 1984. 36.00 (0-89871-190-8) Soc Indus-Appl Math.

Bednar, Jaroslav. Theoretical Foundations of Radiation Chemistry. 282p. 1990. text 195.50 (90-277-2668-X) Kluwer Academic.

Bednar, Kamil. Our Garden Our Friend. Velinsky-Ondrujova, Ludmila, tr. from CZE. (Illus.). 180p. 1994. pap. 9.95 (0-685-71273-7) Kabel Pubs.

— Our Garden Our Friend. (Illus.). 182p. 1994. text 29.50 (0-930329-65-1) Kabel Pubs.

Bednar, Mike. Anthracite Rebirth: Story of the Reading & Northern Railroad. LC 98-22453. 1998. 55.00 (0-9620844-9-2) Garrigues Hse.

— Lehigh Valley Railroad, the New York Division: An Illustrated Operational History Covering the Last Twenty Years of the Railroad & the People Who Were There. LC 93-38099. xiv, 138p. 1993. 52.50 (0-9620844-5-X) Garrigues Hse.

Bednar, Milosav, jt. ed. see Vejrazka, Michael.

Bednar, Nancy. Silk Ribbon Machine Embroidery. LC 96-52099. (Great Sewing Projects Ser.). (Illus.). 144p. 1997. 27.95 (0-8069-9493-2) Sterling.

— Silk Ribbon Machine Embroidery. (Illus.). 144p. 1998. 14.95 (0-8069-9492-4, Sterling-SIR) Sterling.

Bednar, Nancy & Walter, Kelly. Gold Rush: Thematic Unit. Bednar, Agnes, ed. (Thematic Units Ser.). (J). (gr. 3-5). 1994. 9.95 (1-55734-241-5) Tchr Create Mat.

Bednar, Richard L. & Peterson, Scott R. Doing the Right Things for the Right Reasons. LC 95-12512. v, 138p. 1995. 13.95 (0-87579-870-5) Deseret Bk.

— Self-Esteem: Paradoxes & Innovations in Clinical Theory & Practice. 2nd ed. 433p. 1995. text 34.95 (1-55798-305-4); pap. text 24.95 (1-55798-290-2) Am Psychol.

— Spirituality & Self-Esteem. LC 90-40728. ix, 157p. 1994. pap. 7.95 (0-87579-840-3) Deseret Bk.

Bednar, Richard L., et al. Psychotherapy with High-Risk Clients: Legal & Professional Standards. 226p. (C). 1991. text 45.95 (0-534-15408-5) Brooks-Cole.

Bednar, Zdenek F. Where Is My Home? A Theology of Hope As the Outcome of Despair; A Survivor of Nazism, Communism & Exile Remembers the Forces That Shaped His Faith. Hadidian, Dikran Y., ed. (Princeton Theological Monograph Ser.: Vol. 45). (Illus.). xii, 340p. 1998. pap. 35.00 (1-55635-036-8) Pickwick.

Bednarczyk, Angela & Weinstock, Janet. Happy Birthday: A Beginner's Book of Signs. LC 96-67577. (Illus.). 16p. (J). (ps). 1997. bds. 4.95 (1-887734-05-8) Star Brght Bks.

— Opposites: A Beginner's Book of Signs. LC 96-67576. (Illus.). 16p. (J). (ps). 1997. bds. 4.95 (1-887734-06-6) Star Brght Bks.

Bednarek, A. R., ed. see Ulam, Stanislaw M.

Bednarek, Janet R., ed. The Enlisted Experience: A Conversation with the Chief Master Sergeants of the Air Force. (Special Studies). (Illus.). 166p. 1995. pap. 9.00 (0-16-048692-0) AFH & MP.

— The Enlisted Experience: A Conversation with the Chief Master Sergeants of the Air Force. (Illus.). 166p. 1998. pap. text 30.00 (0-7881-2824-8) DIANE Pub.

Bednarik, Joseph, ed. The Sumac Reader. LC 96-18730. 1997. 17.95 (0-87013-462-0) Mich St U Pr.

Bednarik, Karl. The Male in Crisis. Sebba, Helen, tr. from GER. LC 81-7122. 194p. 1981. reprint ed. lib. bdg. 45.50 (0-313-22713-6, BEMS, Greenwood Pr) Greenwood.

Bednarowski, Mary F. New Religions & the Theological Imagination in America. LC 88-46038. (Religion in North America Ser.). 192p. 1989. text 25.00 (0-253-31137-3) Ind U Pr.

— New Religions & the Theological Imagination in America. LC 88-46038. (Religion in North America Ser.). 192p. 1995. pap. 12.95 (0-253-20952-8) Ind U Pr.

***Bednarowski, Mary Farrell.** The Religious Imagination of American Women. LC 99-23096. (Religion in North America Ser.). 256p. 1999. 35.00 (0-253-33594-9) Ind U Pr.

Bednarowski, Mary Farrell. The Religious Imagination of American Women. LC 99-23096. (Religion in North America Ser.). 1999. pap. 15.95 (0-253-21338-X) Ind U Pr.

Bednarski, Betty, tr. see Ferron, Jacques.

Bednarski, Mark D. & Simon, Ethan S., eds. Enzymes in Carbohydrate Synthesis. LC 91-18662. (ACS Symposium Ser.: No. 466). (Illus.). 131p. 1991. text 42.00 (0-8412-2097-2, Pub. by Am Chemical) OUP.

Bednarz, John, Jr., tr. see Bergmann, Jorg R.

Bednarz, John, Jr., tr. see Luhmann, Niklas.

Bednarz, Nadine, ed. Approaches to Algebra: Perspectives for Research & Teaching. (Mathematics Education Library: Vol. 18). 364p. (C). 1996. pap. text 73.50 (0-7923-4168-6) Kluwer Academic.

Bednarz, Nadine, et al. Approaches to Algebra: Perspectives for Research & Teaching. LC 96-26715. (Mathematics Education Library). 364p. 1996. lib. bdg. 145.00 (0-7923-4145-7) Kluwer Academic.

Bednarz, Robert S. The Effect of Air Pollution on Property Value in Chicago. LC 75-23057. (University of Chicago, Department of Geography, Research Paper Ser.: No. 166). 122p. 1975. reprint ed. pap. 37.90 (0-608-02247-0, 206288800004) Bks Demand.

Bednarz, Sarah W., et al. Geography for Life: National Geography Standards, 1994. LC 96-195508. (Illus.). 272p. 1994. pap. 7.00 (0-7922-2775-1) NCFGE.

Bednenko, V. S., jt. auth. see Atkov, Oleg.

Bednersh, Wayne. Collectible Souvenir Spoons: Identification & Values. 1998. pap. text 19.95 (1-57432-063-7) Collector Bks.

***Bednersh, Wayne.** Collectible Souvenir Spoons: Identification & Values. 2nd ed. (Illus.). 192p. 2000. pap. 29.95 (1-57432-189-7) Collector Bks.

Bedney, Steve, ed. see Hertzberg, Mark.

Bednorz, Achim, jt. auth. see Barrucand, Marianne.

Bednorz, J. G., et al, eds. Earlier & Recent Aspects of Superconductivity: Lectures from the International School, Erice, Trapani, Sicily, July 4-16, 1989. (Solid-State Sciences Ser.: Vol. 90). ix, 529p. 1990. 43.95 (0-387-52156-9) Spr-Verlag.

Bednorz, J. G. & Muller, K. A., eds. Earlier & Recent Aspects of Superconductivity: Lectures from the International School Erice, Trapani, Sicily, July 4-16, 1989. 2nd ed. (Solid-State Sciences Ser.: Vol. 90). (Illus.). 529p. 1991. reprint ed. 39.95 (0-387-53498-9) Spr-Verlag.

Bednowitz, Allan L. & Segmuller, Armin P., eds. World Dictionary of Crystallographers. 7th ed. 1986. pap. text 17.50 (90-277-2094-0) Kluwer Academic.

Bedny, Gregory & Meister, David. Current Theory of Activity: Application to Design & Learning. LC 97-12608. (Applied Psychology Ser.). 350p. 1996. 99.95 (0-8058-1771-9) L Erlbaum Assocs.

Bedogni, G. Operative Endoscopy of the Digestive Tract. (Illus.). 274p. 1984. text 106.00 (88-299-0140-7, Pub. by Piccin Nuova) Gordon & Breach.

Bedogni, G., et al. Operative Endoscopy of the Digestive Tract. 274p. 1984. text 96.00 (1-57235-014-8, Pub. by Piccin Nuova) Gordon & Breach.

Bedolla, Miguel. Essential Spanish for Healthcare. LC 97-226345. 1997. pap. 18.00 (0-609-80138-4) Liv Lang.

— Spanish for Health Care Pro. 1997. pap. 35.00 incl. audio (0-609-60089-3) Liv Lang.

Bedor, Deborah, jt. auth. see Bamberger, David.

Bedord, Russ. New Beginnings: Healing Through Communication. LC 94-93982. 272p. (Orig.). 1995. pap. 24.95 (0-9644918-6-9) Regenics Pr.

Bedore, Bernie. Mythical Mufferaw. (Illus.). 96p. (J). Date not set. pap. 10.95 (1-55082-087-7, Pub. by Quarry Pr) LPC InBook.

Bedore, James, jt. auth. see Turner, Louis.

Bedos-Rezak, Brigitte. Form & Order in Medieval France: Studies in Social & Quantitative Sigillography. (Collected Studies: No. CS 424). 328p. 1993. 124.95 (0-86078-355-3, Pub. by Variorum) Ashgate Pub Co.

Bedoucha, G., ed. L' Eau, L'Amie du Puissanterries: Une Communaute Oasienne du Sud-Tunisien. (FRE.). xvi, 428p. 1987. pap. text 71.00 (2-88124-187-5) Gordon & Breach.

Bedouelle, Guy. Controversies. 392p. 1997. text 100.00 (0-8020-4310-0) U of Toronto Pr.

— Dictionnaire d'Histoire de l'Eglise. (FRE.). 333p. 1994. 79.95 (0-7859-8095-4, 2854432517) Fr & Eur.

— In the Image of Saint Dominic: Nine Portraits of Domican Life. LC 93-78534. 161p. pap. 9.95 (0-89870-467-7) Ignatius Pr.

Bedoukian, Kerop. Some of Us Survived: The Story of an Armenian Boy. LC 79-10601. 186p. (J). (gr. 6 up). 1979. 13.95 (0-374-37132-6) FS&G.

Bedoukian, P. Z. Coinage of the Artaxiads of Armenia. (Illus.). 1978. lib. bdg. 45.00 (1-886720-03-7) S J Durst.

Bedoukian, Paul Z. Armenian Coin Hoards. 64p. (Orig.). 1987. 8.00 (0-9606842-4-7) ANS.

— Coinage of the Armenian Kingdoms of Sophene & Commagene. (ARM & ENG., Illus.). 39p. 1985. 6.00 (0-9606842-3-9) ANS.

— A Hoard of Copper Coins of Tigranes the Great & a Hoard of Artaxiad Coins. (Special Publication Ser.: No. 7). (ARM & ENG., Illus.). 32p. 1991. 5.50 (0-9606842-7-1) ANS.

— Perfumery & Flavoring Materials: Annual Review Articles, 1945-1982. LC TP0983.. 443p. reprint ed. pap. 137.40 (0-7837-2433-0, 20425810005) Bks Demand.

— Selected Numismatic Studies. (ARM & ENG.). 570p. 1981. boxed set 35.00 (0-9606842-0-4) ANS.

Bedoun, Nawja. A Taste from the Mediterranean. 106p. (Orig.). 1997. pap. 12.95 (0-910119-54-6) SOCO Pubns.

Bedoya, Roberto, ed. Organizing Artists: A Document & Directory of the National Association of Artists' Organizations, 1998. LC 98-66539. (Illus.). 163p. 1998. pap. 25.00 (0-927851-05-9) NAAO.

Bedoya, Roberto, et al. Inheritance. (Illus.). 48p. (Orig.). (C). 1992. pap. 5.00 (0-937335-11-8) LA Contemp Exhib.

Bedoyere, Charlotte De La, see De la Bedoyere, Charlotte, tr.

Bedoyere, Guy de la, see de la Bedoyere, Guy.

Bedoyere, Michael De La, see De La Bedoyere, Michael.

Bedoyere, Quentin De La, see De la Bedoyere, Quentin.

Bedrani, S. & Chole, Esbetu. Social Development in Africa: Strategies, Policies & Programs since the Lagos Plan. (African Social Challenges Ser.: No. 4). 224p. 1991. lib. bdg. 65.00 (0-905450-28-0, Pub. by H Zell Pubs) Seven Hills Bk.

Bedrick, Claudia Z., tr. see Larroche, Caroline.

Bedrick, Claudia Z., tr. see Sellier, Marie.

Bedrikovetsky, Pavel. Mathematical Theory of Oil & Gas Recovery: With Applications to Ex-U. S. S. R. Oil & Gas Fields. LC 93-14525. (Petroleum Engineering Studies & Development Ser.). 600p. (C). 1993. text 313.00 (0-7923-2381-5) Kluwer Academic.

Bedrin, George & Tamoush, Philip, eds. A New Era Begins: Proceedings of the Conference of Orthodox Bishops, Ligonier, Pennsylvania, 1994. 189p. 1996. per. 7.95 (1-879038-27-7) Oakwood Pubns.

Bedrosian, Carol A. Home Health Nursing: Nursing Diagnosis & Care Plans. 622p. (C). 1988. pap. text 39.95 (0-8385-3842-8, A3842-0) Appleton & Lange.

Bedrosian, Dave. 2 Bass Hits: Learn the Fundamentals of Playing Two Bass Drums. (Illus.). 36p. 1999. pap. 19.95 incl. cd-rom (1-57424-049-8) Centerstream Pub.

Bedrosian, Edward. Mutual Interference in Fast-Frequency-Hopped, Multiple Frequency-Shift-Keyed, Spread-Spectrum Communication Satellite Systems. LC 96-19534. (Illus.). 83p. (Orig.). 1996. pap. 15.00 (0-8330-2393-4, MR-672-AF/A) Rand Corp.

Bedrosian, Edward & Huth, Gaylord. Concept-Level Analytical Procedures for Loading Nonprocessing Communication Satellites with Direct-Sequence, Spread-Spectrum Signals. LC 95-26272. 42p. (Orig.). 1996. pap. text 15.00 (0-8330-2340-3, MR-640-AF/A) Rand Corp.

— Concept-Level Analytical Procedures for Loading Nonprocessing Communication Satellites with Nonantijam Signals. LC 95-47565. 94p. (Orig.). 1996. pap. text 15.00 (0-8330-2339-X, MR-639-AF/A) Rand Corp.

Bedrosian, Maggie M. Life Is More Than Your To-Do List: Blending Business Success with Personal Satisfaction. (Illus.). 192p. (Orig.). 1995. pap. 12.95 (1-884798-26-8) B C I Press.

— Speak Like a Pro. LC 93-74966. 1994. 25.00 (1-884798-25-X) B C I Press.

Bedrosian, Margaret. The Magical Pine Ring: Culture & the Imagination in Armenian-American Literature. LC 91-17264. 256p. 1991. 34.95 (0-8143-2339-1) Wayne St U Pr.

Bedrosian, Margaret M. Delights, Dilemmas & Decisions: The Gift of Living Lightly. (Illus.). 234p. 1992. 18.95 (1-879198-05-3) Knwldg Ideas & Trnds.

Bedrosian, Richard C. & Bozicas, George D. Treating Family of Origin Problems: A Cognitive Approach. LC 93-33386. 384p. 1994. lib. bdg. 40.00 (0-89862-178-X) Guilford Pubns.

Bedrosian, Robert. Armenia in Ancient & Medieval Times. 96p. 1985. pap. 9.95 (0-685-37410-6) Armenian Natl Educ.

Bedrosian, Robert Der, see Der Bedrosian, Zabel & Der Bedrosian, Robert, eds.

Bedrosian, S. D. & Porter, W. A., eds. Recent Trends in Systems Theory. 1976. pap. 40.00 (0-08-020590-9, Pergamon Pr) Elsevier.

Bedrosian, Zabel Der, see Der Bedrosian, Zabel, ed.

Bedrossian, Analia, jt. auth. see De Bedrossian, Nydia.

Bedrossian, Carlos. Malignant Effusions: A Multimodal Approach to Cytologic Diagnosis. LC 91-7105. (Illus.). 288p. 1994. 145.00 (0-89640-196-0) Igaku-Shoin.

Bedrossian, Matthias. New Armenian-English Dictionary. (ARM & ENG.). 816p. 49.95 (0-86685-122-4, LDL1224, Pub. by Librairie du Liban) Intl Bk Ctr.

Bedsole, Betty. Stepping Stones: Early Elementary Level, Year 1. Hawn, C. Michael, ed. (Stepping Stones Ser.). 64p. 1995. reprint ed. pap. text 22.95 (1-929187-05-X, CGBK56) Choristers.

Bedsworth, Joyce, jt. auth. see Bedsworth, Philip.

Bedsworth, Philip & Bedsworth, Joyce. Fight the Good Fight. LC 91-20148. 128p. (Orig.). 1991. pap. 7.99 (0-8361-3568-7) Herald Pr.

***BeDuhn, Jason.** The Manichaean Body: In Discipline & Ritual. LC 99-45879. 2000. 42.50 (0-8018-6270-1) Johns Hopkins.

BeDuhn, Jason & Mirecki, Paul A. Emerging from Darkness: Studies in the Recovery of Manichaean Sources. x, 310p. 1997. 123.00 (90-04-10760-6) Brill Academic Pubs.

Bedula, Jane, ed. see Chambers, Kareen S.

Bedurftig, Friedmann, jt. ed. see Zentner, Christian.

***Bedward, Diana.** Quantitative Methods: A Business Perspective. 281p. 1999. pap. text 39.95 (0-7506-4093-6) Buttrwrth-Heinemann.

Bedward, Diana, et al. First Line Management: A Practical Approach. LC 97-212620. 320p. 1997. pap. text 34.95 (0-7506-2799-9, HF5001) Buttrwrth-Heinemann.

Bedward, Marvin V. & Anderson, Mark V. Growing Your Business Internationally: How to Form Profitable Overseas Partnerships, Alliances & Joint Ventures. 200p. 1992. per. 24.95 (1-55738-464-9, Irwn Prfssnl) McGraw-Hill Prof.

Bedwell, C. E. A Catalogue of the Printed Books in the Library of the Honourable Society of the Middle Temple, 4 vols. 1961. reprint ed. lib. bdg. 150.00 (0-89941-352-8, 500070) W S Hein.

Bedwell, C. H., tr. see Aust, W.

Bedwell, Carol, tr. see Meckel, Christoph.

***Bedwell, Don.** Silverbird: The American Airlines Story. Wegg, John, ed. (Illus.). 300p. 2000. 69.95 (0-9653993-6-2, A-20) Airways Intnl.

Bedwell, Randall. Christmas in the South: Stories & Tales of Yuletides Past. Booker, Trent & Boker, Carol, eds. (Illus.). 76p. 1998. pap. 9.95 (1-889709-04-2) Spiridon Pr.

— General Lee & Santa Claus: An Adaptation. LC 97-60758. (Illus.). 40p. (J). (gr. 2-5). 1997. pap. 9.95 (1-889709-01-8) Spiridon Pr.

— General Lee's Christmas. Booker, Trent, ed. (Illus.). 40p. 1998. pap. 9.95 (1-889709-11-5) HEAL Found.

— May I Quote You, General Grant? (May I Quote You Ser.). (Illus.). 96p. 1998. pap. 7.95 (1-888952-95-4) Cumberland Hse.

***Bedwell, Randall.** Millennium Madness Vol. 1: The Future Is Now. Fones, Mardy, ed. LC 99-70380. 128p. 1999. pap. 6.95 (1-887654-74-7) Premium Pr TN.

Bedwell, Randall. Vintage Virginia. Baker, Carol, ed. LC 98-66163. 128p. 1998. pap. 6.95 (1-887654-38-0) Premium Pr TN.

***Bedwell, Randall, ed.** Brink of Destruction: A Quotable History of the Civil War. LC 99-18835. 240p. 1999. pap. 10.95 (1-58182-005-4) Cumberland Hse.

Bedwell, Randall, ed. May I Quote You, General Chamberlain? (May I Quote You Ser.). (Illus.). 96p. 1998. pap. 7.95 (1-888952-96-2) Cumberland Hse.

— May I Quote You, General Forrest? LC 96-51932. (May I Quote You Ser.). (Illus.). 96p. (Orig.). 1997. pap. 7.95 (1-888952-35-0) Cumberland Hse.

— May I Quote You, General Lee? LC 96-51927. (May I Quote You Ser.). (Illus.). 96p. 1997. pap. 7.95 (1-888952-34-2) Cumberland Hse.

— May I Quote You, General Lee?, Vol. 2. (May I Quote You Ser.). (Illus.). 96p. 1998. pap. 7.95 (1-888952-94-6) Cumberland Hse.

— May I Quote You, General Longstreet? LC 96-51928. (May I Quote You Ser.). (Illus.). 96p. (Orig.). 1997. pap. 7.95 (1-888952-37-7) Cumberland Hse.

— May I Quote You, Stonewall Jackson? LC 96-52697. (May I Quote You Ser.). (Illus.). 96p. (Orig.). 1997. pap. 7.95 (1-888952-36-9) Cumberland Hse.

— Unbroken Circle: A Quotable History of the Grand Ole Opry. LC 99-41844. (Illus.). 212p. 1999. pap. 12.95 (1-58182-014-3) Cumberland Hse.

Bedwell, Randall, ed. see Jones, Palmer T.

Bedwell, Randall, ed. see Robilio, Victor.

Bedwell, Randall, ed. see Williams, Edward F., 3rd.

Bedwell, William. Mesolabium Architectonicum That Is a Most Rare Instrument of Measuring. LC 72-172. (English Experience Ser.: No. 224). 24p. 1970. reprint ed. 25.00 (90-221-0224-6) Walter J Johnson.

Bedwell, William, tr. see Salignacus, Bernard.

Bedworth, Albert E., jt. auth. see Bedworth, David A.

Bedworth, David A. & Bedworth, Albert E. The Profession & Practice of Health Education. 496p. (Orig.). (C). 1991. text. write for info. (0-697-12160-7) Brown & Benchmark.

Bedworth, David D. & Bailey, James E. Integrated Production Control Systems: Management, Analysis, Design. 2nd ed. LC 86-23379. 496p. 1987. text 99.95 (0-471-82179-9) Wiley.

Bedworth, David D., et al. Computer Integrated Design & Manufacturing. 672p. (C). 1991. 93.75 (0-07-004204-7) McGraw.

***Bee.** Constructive Feedback. 96p. 2000. pap. 17.95 (0-8464-5015-1) Beekman Pubs.

Bee. Developing Child Study Guide. 9th ed. 1999. pap. text 15.00 (0-321-04710-9) Addson-Wesley Educ.

An Asterisk (*) at the beginning of an entry indicates that the title is appearing for the first time.

— Developing Child Telecourse: Text & Study Guide. 6th ed. (C). 1997. pap., student ed. 91.00 (*0-06-501334-4*) Addson-Wesley Educ.

*Bee. Supplement The Developing Child. 9th ed. 2000. 76.00 incl. cd-rom (*0-205-32458-4*) Allyn.

***Bee & Bee.** Customer Care. 96p. 2000. pap. 17.95 (*0-8464-5025-9*) Beekman Pubs.

— Facilitation Skills. 190p. 2000. pap. 44.95 (*0-8464-5056-9*) Beekman Pubs.

— Managing Information & Statistics. 336p. 2000. pap. 44.95 (*0-8464-5113-1*) Beekman Pubs.

— Project Management: The People Challenge. 168p. 2000. pap. 56.95 (*0-8464-5135-2*) Beekman Pubs.

— Training Needs Analysis & Evaluation. 320p. 2000. pap. 50.95 (*0-8464-5152-2*) Beekman Pubs.

Bee, jt. auth. see Bee.

Bee, Abby. Nauseous in Paradise. (Illus.). 40p. (Orig.). 1986. pap. 6.95 (*0-939821-13-3*) HerBooks.

Bee, Becky. The Cob Builders Handbook: You Can Hand-Sculpt Your Own Home. 3rd ed. McMillan, Alex & Spiralstone, Mitch, eds. LC 97-90728. (Illus.). 173p. 1998. reprint ed. pap. 23.95 (*0-9659082-0-8*, Pub. by Groundworks) Chelsea Green Pub.

Bee-Books Staff. Euro-Woerterbook: German-English-French-Italian-Portuguese-Spanish CD-ROM Version. (ENG, FRE, GER, ITA & POR.). 1994. 49.95 (*0-7859-7432-6*, 3570080145) Fr & Eur.

Bee, Cindy. A Big House, a Little Girl & a Few Things That Made Them Laugh. (Illus.). 20p. (Orig.). (J). (ps-5). 1990. pap. 2.75 (*0-9616308-1-7*) Hearthstn Inn.

***Bee, Clair.** Backboard Fever. LC 99-38412. (Chip Hillon Sports Ser.: No. 10). 208p. (YA). 1999. reprint ed. pap. 5.99 (*0-8054-1992-6*) Broadman.

Bee, Clair. Championship Ball. rev. ed. Farley, Cynthia B. & Farley, Randall, eds. LC 98-28095. (Chip Hilton Ser.: Vol. 2). (J). 1998. pap. 5.99 (*0-8054-1815-6*) Broadman.

— Clutch Hitter. 17.95 (*0-8488-1246-8*) Amereon Ltd.

— Clutch Hitter. rev. ed. Farley, Cynthia B. & Farley, Randall K., eds. LC 98-28093. (Chip Hilton Ser.: Vol. 4). (J). 1998. pap. 5.99 (*0-8054-1817-2*) Broadman.

— Dugout Jinx. 17.95 (*0-8488-1247-6*) Amereon Ltd.

— Dugout Jinx. LC 98-43531. (Chip Hilton Sports Ser.: Vol. 8). 208p. (YA). 1999. reprint ed. pap. 5.99 (*0-8054-1990-X*) Broadman.

***Bee, Clair.** Fence Busters, 24 vols., Vol. 11. LC 99-26656. (Chip Hilton Sports Ser.). 208p. (YA). 1999. reprint ed. pap. 5.99 (*0-8054-1993-4*) Broadman.

— Fourth down Shutdown. rev. ed. LC 99-47979. (Chip Hilton Sports Ser.: No. 13). 208p. 2000. pap. 5.99 (*0-8054-2092-4*) Broadman.

Bee, Clair. Freshman Quarterback, Vol. 9. LC 99-32367. (Chip Hilton Sports Ser.). 208p. (J). 1999. reprint ed. pap. 5.99 (*0-8054-1991-8*) Broadman.

***Bee, Clair.** Hardcourt Upset. rev. ed. (Chip Hilton Sports Ser.: No. 15). 208p. (YA). 2000. pap. 5.99 (*0-8054-2094-0*) Broadman.

Bee, Clair. Hoop Crazy! LC 98-43540. (Chip Hilton Sports Ser.: Vol. 6). 208p. (YA). 1999. reprint ed. pap. 5.99 (*0-8054-1988-8*) Broadman.

— A Pass & a Prayer. LC 98-50759. (Chip Hilton Sports Ser.: Vol. 5). 208p. (YA). 1999. reprint ed. pap. 5.99 (*0-8054-1987-X*) Broadman.

***Bee, Clair.** Pay-Off Pitch. rev. ed. (Chip Hilton Sports Ser.: No. 16). 208p. 2000. pap. 5.99 (*0-8054-2095-9*) Broadman.

Bee, Clair. Pitchers Duel. LC 98-50758. (Chip Hilton Sports Ser.: Vol. 7). 208p. (YA). 1999. reprint ed. pap. 5.99 (*0-8054-1989-6*) Broadman.

— Strike Three! 17.95 (*0-8488-1248-4*) Amereon Ltd.

— Strike Three. rev. ed. Farley, Cynthia B. & Farley, Randall K., eds. LC 98-28094. (Chip Hilton Ser.: Vol. 3). (J). 1998. pap. 5.99 (*0-8054-1816-4*) Broadman.

***Bee, Clair.** Ten Seconds to Play!, 24 vols., Vol. 12. LC 99-39092. (Chip Hilton Sports Ser.). 208p. (YA). 1999. reprint ed. pap. text 5.99 (*0-8054-1994-2*) Broadman.

Bee, Clair. Touchdown Pass. 1993. reprint ed. lib. bdg. 25.95 (*1-56849-182-4*) Buccaneer Bks.

— Touchdown Pass. rev. ed. Farley, Cynthia B. & Farley, Randall, eds. LC 98-28092. (Chip Hilton Ser.: Vol. 1). (J). 1998. pap. 5.99 (*0-8054-1686-2*) Broadman.

***Bee, Clair.** Tournament Crises. Farley, Cynthia Bee & Farley, Randall, eds. LC 99-51788. (Chip Hilton Sports Ser.: Vol. 14). 208p. (YA). 2000. reprint ed. pap. 5.99 (*0-8054-2093-2*) Broadman.

Bee, Frances & Bee, Roland. Training Needs Analysis & Evaluation. 200p. 1993. pap. 125.00 (*0-85292-547-6*, Pub. by IPM Hse) St Mut.

Bee, Frances, jt. auth. see Bee, Roland.

Bee Gees. Bee Gees Anthology: Tales from the Brothers Gibb - a History in Song 1967-1990. (Piano-Vocal-Guitar Ser.). 192p. (Orig.). 1991. otabind 17.95 (*0-7935-0413-9*, 00490567) H Leonard.

Bee, Helen L. Developing Child. 6th ed. (C). 1993. pap., student ed. 26.00 (*0-06-500516-3*) Addson-Wesley Educ.

***Bee, Helen L.** The Developing Child. 9th ed. LC 98-31711. 575p. (C). 1999. text 79.00 (*0-321-04709-5*) Allyn.

Bee, Helen L. The Growing Child. LC 94-37748. (C). 1996. pap. text, student ed. 23.44 (*0-673-99361-2*) Addson-Wesley Educ.

— Growing Child: Applied Approach. 2nd ed. (C). 1999. pap. text, student ed. 18.75 (*0-321-03478-3*) Addson-Wesley Educ.

— The Journey of Adulthood. 4th ed. LC 99-24184. 492p. 1999. 70.67 (*0-13-010953-3*) P-H.

— Lifespan Development. LC 93-20091. (C). 1997. pap., student ed. 28.00 (*0-06-500983-5*) Addson-Wesley Educ.

— Lifespan Development. 2nd ed. (C). 1998. pap. text, student ed. 22.50 (*0-321-00445-0*) Addson-Wesley Educ.

Bee, Helen L., ed. The Growing Child: An Applied Approach. 2nd ed. LC 97-45180. 636p. (C). 1998. text 81.00 (*0-321-01346-8*) Allyn.

Bee, Helen L., ed. Lifespan Development. 2nd ed. LC 97-5362. 640p. (C). 1997. text 82.00 (*0-321-01121-X*) Allyn.

Bee, James W., et al. Mammals in Kansas. (Public Education Ser.: No. 7). (Illus.). x, 302p. 1981. pap. 12.95 (*0-89338-014-8*) U KS Nat Hist Mus.

— Mammals in Kansas. Collins, Joseph T., ed. (Public Education Ser.: No. 7). (Illus.). x, 302p. 1981. 17.95 (*0-89338-015-6*) U KS Nat Hist Mus.

Bee, Jaymz. Cocktail Parties for Dummies. LC 97-80183. (For Dummies Ser.). 272p. 1997. pap. 14.99 (*0-7645-5026-8*) IDG Bks.

Bee, Lucy H. Daughter of Spies. 453p. 1999. pap. 12.95 (*0-7392-0163-8*, PO3117) Morris Pubng.

Bee, Marc J. Quasielastic Neutron Scattering: Principles & Applications in Solid State Chemistry, Biology & Materials Science. (Illus.). 452p. 1988. 229.00 (*0-85274-371-8*) IOP Pub.

Bee, Noah. The Impossible Takes Longer. (History of Israel in Cartoons Ser.: Vol. II). (Illus.). 207p. 1983. 11.95 (*0-8197-0491-1*) Bloch.

— In Spite of Everything: History of the State of Israel. LC 73-77304. (Illus.). 200p. 1973. 11.95 (*0-8197-0297-8*) Bloch.

— Years of Triumphs, Trials & Errors. 208p. 1988. 13.95 (*0-8197-0555-1*) Bloch.

Bee, Ooi J. Tropical Deforestation: The Tyranny of Time. (Orig.). 1993. 55.00 (*9971-69-184-1*, Pub. by Sngapore Univ Pr) Coronet Bks.

— Tropical Deforestation: The Tyranny of Time. 190p. (Orig.). 1994. pap. 38.50 (*9971-69-183-3*, Pub. by Sngapore Univ Pr) Coronet Bks.

***Bee, Peta.** The Body Bible. (Illus.). 192p. 2000. pap. 22.50 (*1-899807-05-5*, Pub. by SportsBooks Ltd) Trans-Atl Phila.

***Bee, Peta.** Living with Asthma. (Living with... Ser.). 32p. 1999. lib. bdg. 22.83 (*0-8172-5576-1*) Raintree Steck-V.

Bee, Peta. Living with Asthma. LC 98-18852. 32 p. (J). 2000. write for info. (*0-8172-5568-0*) Raintree Steck-V.

***Bee, Queen.** Little Bitz. 64p. 2000. pap. 10.00 (*0-9679509-0-2*) Aura Pubng MA.

Bee, R. D., et al. Food Colloids, No. 75. Mingins, J., ed. 1989. 154.00 (*0-85186-826-6*) CRC Pr.

Bee, Robert L. Crosscurrents along the Colorado: The Impact of Government Policy on the Quechan Indians. LC 81-7446. 204p. reprint ed. pap. 63.30 (*0-7837-1903-5*, 204210700001) Bks Demand.

— Patterns & Processes: An Introduction to Anthropological Strategies for the Study of Sociocultural Change. LC 73-10791. (C). 1974. pap. 17.95 (*0-02-902090-5*) Free Pr.

Bee, Robert L., ed. The Boys from Rockville: Civil War Narratives of Sgt. Benjamin Hirst, Company D, 14th Connecticut Volunteers. LC 97-33769. (Voices of the Civil War Ser.). (Illus.). 256p. 1998. 35.00 (*1-57233-005-8*) U of Tenn Pr.

Bee, Robert L., jt. ed. see Castile, George P.

Bee, Roger & Browne, Gary F. The Chicago Great Western in Minnesota. (Illus.). 115p. 1984. write for info. (*0-930431-00-6*) Blue River Pubns.

Bee, Roland & Bee, Frances. Constructive Feedback. 1996. pap. 25.00 (*0-85292-629-4*, Pub. by IPM Hse) St Mut.

— Management Information Systems & Statistics. 250p. (C). 1990. 75.00 (*0-85292-435-6*, Pub. by IPM Hse) St Mut.

Bee, Roland, jt. auth. see Bee, Frances.

Bee, Ronald J. Nuclear Proliferation: The Post-Cold-War Challenge. Hoepli-Phalon, Nancy L., ed. LC 94-61086. (Headline Ser.: No. 303). (Illus.). 72p. (Orig.). 1995. pap. 5.95 (*0-87124-160-9*, HS 303) Foreign Policy.

Bee, Ronald J., jt. auth. see Feldbaum, Carl B.

***Bee, Susan.** M/E/A/N/I/N/G: An Anthology of Artists' Writings, Theory & Criticism. 2000. 64.95 (*0-8223-2534-9*) Duke.

***Bee, Susan & Schor, Mira, eds.** M/E/A/N/I/N/G: An Anthology of Artists' Writing, Theory & Criticism. 2000. pap. 21.95 (*0-8223-2566-7*) Duke.

Bee, Tan O., jt. auth. see Pheng, Low S.

Beeaff, Dianne E. A Grand Madness: Ten Years on the Road with U2. LC 99-71601. (Illus.). 345p. 2000. pap. 16.95 (*0-9656188-1-1*) Hawkmoon Pubns.

— Homecoming. LC 96-79342. (Illus.). 65p. (Orig.). (C). 1997. pap. 12.95 (*0-9656188-0-3*) Hawkmoon Pubns.

***Beebe.** Communication: Principles For A Lifetime. 2000. pap. 20.67 (*0-205-32778-8*) S&S Trade.

Beebe. Interpersonal Communication: Relating to Others. 2nd ed. LC 98-25281. 432p. 1998. pap. text 50.00 (*0-205-28757-3*) Allyn.

***Beebe.** Interpersonal Communication: Relating to Others. 2nd ed. 1999. cd-rom 48.00 (*0-205-31984-X*) Allyn.

Beebe. Public Speaking. 3rd ed. 1997. text 53.27 (*0-205-28003-X*, Longwood Div) Allyn.

***Beebe.** Public Speaking: An Audience-Centered Approach. 4th ed. LC 99-14266. 454p. 1999. pap. text 50.00 (*0-205-29559-2*) Allyn.

***Beebe & Funk.** Emergency Medical Care: Basic Sc. (C). 2001. pap., wbk. ed. 19.50 (*0-7668-1493-9*) Thomson Learn.

Beebe, Gayle D. The Interpretive Role of the Religious Community in Friedrich Schleiermacher & Josiah Royce: Heavenly Bonds. LC 98-43822. 208p. 1999. text 89.95 (*0-7734-1977-2*) E Mellen.

Beebe, B. W., et al, eds. Natural Gases of North America: A Symposium, Vol. 1. LC 68-15769. (American Association of Petroleum Geologists. Memoir Ser.: No. 9). 1236p. reprint ed. pap. 200.00 (*0-608-11197-X*, 205002500057) Bks Demand.

— Natural Gases of North America: A Symposium, Vol. 2. LC 68-15769. (American Association of Petroleum Geologists. Memoir Ser.: No. 9). 1253p. reprint ed. pap. 200.00 (*0-608-11198-8*, 205002500058) Bks Demand.

Beebe, C., jt. auth. see Fisher, J. B.

Beebe, Catherine. St. Dominic & the Rosary. LC 95-79886. 216p. (J). (gr. 4-8). 1996. reprint ed. pap. 9.95 (*0-89870-518-5*) Ignatius Pr.

— Saint John Bosco. 2nd ed. LC 92-71930. (Vision Bks.). 157p. (J). (gr. 4-9). 1992. pap. 9.95 (*0-89870-416-2*) Ignatius Pr.

***Beebe, Channing.** Cannibals & Big Game. (Illus.). 250p. 2001. Price not set. (*1-57157-202-3*) Safari Pr.

— Cannibals & Big Game. limited ed. (Illus.). 250p. 2001. 70.00 (*1-57157-126-4*) Safari Pr.

Beebe, Clarence. A Monograph of the Descent of the Family of Beebe. (Illus.). 127p. 1988. reprint ed. pap. 25.00 (*0-8328-0225-5*); reprint ed. lib. bdg. 33.00 (*0-8328-0224-7*) Higginson Bk Co.

Beebe, Ellen S., tr. see Meier, Bernhard.

Beebe, Frank. A Falconry Manual. (Illus.). 200p. 1984. pap. 17.95 (*0-88839-978-2*) Hancock House.

Beebe, Frank L. The Compleat Falconer. (Illus.). 300p. 1982. 70.00 (*0-88839-253-2*) Hancock House.

Beebe, Frank L. & Webster, Harold M., eds. North American Falconry & Hunting Hawks. 5th ed. (Illus.). 490p. 1995. 40.00 (*0-685-66290-X*); 55.00 (*0-912510-01-3*) North Am Fal Hunt.

Beebe, Gilbert W. Contraception & Fertility in the Southern Appalachians. LC 79-169373. (Family in America Ser.). (Illus.). 396p. 1972. reprint ed. 20.95 (*0-405-03849-6*) Ayer.

Beebe, Glenn. Toxic Carpet, No. III. 368p. 1991. pap. 12.95 (*0-9637095-0-X*) AOPR.

Beebe, Hank. The Other Person's Shoes: One Act Musical. (Illus.). 20p. (YA). (gr. 6-12). 1992. pap. 3.25 (*0-88680-366-7*) I E Clark.

Beebe, John. Integrity in Depth. Rosen, David H., ed. & frwd. by. LC 94-44336. (Psychology Ser.). 192p. 1995. pap. 12.95 (*0-88064-213-0*) Fromm Intl Pub.

— Integrity in Depth. LC 91-27214. (Carolyn & Ernest Fay Series in Analytical Psychology: No. 2). 192p. 1992. 19.50 (*0-89096-493-9*) Tex A&M Univ Pr.

Beebe, Joyce. Reflections of Joy: Acrylic Painting Techniques. (Designer Ser.). (Illus.). 32p. (Orig.). 1986. pap. 8.95 (*0-917121-13-9*, 50-100) M F Weber Co.

***Beebe, Kenneth R., et al.** Chemometrics: A Practical Guide. LC 97-17970. (Series on Laboratory Automation). 348p. 1998. 74.95 (*0-471-12451-6*, Wiley-Interscience) Wiley.

Beebe, L. Super Fun Math. 48p. 1998. pap. 12.95 (*0-590-25541-X*, 893239Q) Scholastic Inc.

Beebe, Lewis. Journal of Dr. Lewis Beebe, a Physician on the Expedition Against Quebec, 1776. Kirkland, Frederic R., ed. LC 77-140854. (Eyewitness Accounts of the American Revolution Ser.). (Illus.). 1971. reprint ed. 14.95 (*0-405-01201-2*) Ayer.

Beebe, Linda, ed. Professional Writing for the Human Services. LC 92-39534. 325p. (C). 1993. 31.95 (*0-87101-199-9*) Natl Assn Soc Wkrs.

Beebe, Lucius & Clegg, Charles. Virginia & Truckee: A Story of Virginia City & Comstock Times. 7th ed. (Illus.). 72p. 1991. reprint ed. pap. 5.95 (*1-879897-00-8*) NV St Rail Mus.

Beebe, Marjorie H. Art at Pomona, Eighteen Eighty-Seven to Nineteen Eighty-Seven: A Centennial Celebration. 88p. 1988. 5.00 (*0-915478-57-9*) Montgomery Gallery.

— Early Twentieth Century German Prints from the Pomona College Collection. (Illus.). 30p. 1983. 4.00 (*0-915478-49-8*) Montgomery Gallery.

— Printmaking in France, 1850-1900. 1982. 3.00 (*0-915478-48-X*) Montgomery Gallery.

Beebe, Morton, photos by. Cascadia: A Tale of Two Cities, Seattle & Vancouver, B. C. LC 96-11525. (Illus.). 208p. 1996. 49.50 (*0-8109-4048-5*) Abrams.

Beebe, Philip J. The Codependent Counselor: Guidelines for Self-Assessment & Change. 178p. 1990. pap. 13.00 (*0-8309-0560-X*) Herald Pub Hse.

Beebe, Ralph, jt. auth. see Lamoreau, John.

Beebe, Ralph, jt. auth. see Rantisi, Audeh.

Beebe, Ralph A., jt. auth. see Langford, Cooper H.

Beebe, Ralph K. A Garden of the Lord: A History of Oregon Yearly Meeting of Friends Church. LC 68-56609. (Illus.). 288p. 1968. 8.95 (*0-913342-13-0*) Barclay Pr.

— A Heritage to Honor, a Future to Fulfill: A History of George Fox College, 1891-1991. 152p. 1991. 24.95 (*0-913342-71-8*) Barclay Pr.

Beebe, Reta. Jupiter: The Giant Planet. 2nd rev. ed. LC 96-38604. (Smithsonian Library of the Solar System). (Illus.). 250p. 1996. 29.95 (*1-56098-731-6*); pap. 17.95 (*1-56098-685-9*) Smithsonian.

Beebe, Robert P. Voyaging under Power. 22.95 (*0-8488-0913-0*) Amereon Ltd.

Beebe, Rose M., ed. & tr. see Osio, Antonio M.

Beebe, Steven A. Skill Builders & Problem Solvers. 2nd ed. 1998. pap. text 15.00 (*0-205-28937-1*) Allyn.

***Beebe, Steven A. & Beebe, Susan J.** Communication: Principles for a Lifetime. 496p. 2000. pap. 48.00 (*0-205-32287-5*) Allyn.

***Beebe, Steven A. & Masterson, John T.** Communicating in Small Groups: Principles & Practices. 6th ed. LC 99-26288. 389p. (C). 1999. pap. text 52.00 (*0-321-03648-4*) Addison-Wesley.

Beebe, Steven A. & Masterson, John T. Family Talk. LC 94-48522. 320p. (C). 1985. pap. text 38.25 (*0-07-554896-8*) McGraw.

Beebe, Susan J., jt. auth. see Beebe, Steven A.

Beebe, Thomas O., et al, intros. Zum 40. Jahrestag der Beendigung des Krieges in Europa und der Natianlsozialistischen Gewaltherrschaft: Speech by Richard von Weizsacker. (GER.). 30p. 1987. pap. 15.00 (*0-942017-29-3*, 04-6450S) Amer Assn Teach German.

Beebe, Von N. & Mackey, William F. Bilingual Schooling & the Miami Experience. (Illus.). 223p. (C). 1990. pap. text 21.95 (*0-935501-20-7*, CP332) Transaction Pubs.

Beebe, William. Edge of the Jungle. 22.95 (*0-88411-839-8*) Amereon Ltd.

— Galapagos: World's End. (Illus.). 520p. 1988. reprint ed. pap. 13.95 (*0-486-25642-1*) Dover.

— Jungle Peace. 313p. Date not set. 24.95 (*0-8488-2209-9*) Amereon Ltd.

— Monograph of the Pheasants, Vol. 1. 1990. 50.00 (*0-486-26579-X*) Dover.

— Monograph of the Pheasants, Vol. 2. 1990. 50.00 (*0-486-26580-3*) Dover.

— Nonsuch: Land of Water. 277p. Date not set. 23.95 (*0-8488-2208-0*) Amereon Ltd.

— Pheasant Jungles. (Illus.). 248p. 1995. reprint ed. 29.95 (*0-88839-373-3*) Hancock House.

Beebe, William S. Cosmic Theory of Primes. (LC History-America-E). 99p. 1999. reprint ed. lib. bdg. 99.00 (*0-7812-4307-6*) Rprt Serv.

Beebee, T. & Burke, J. E. Gene Structure & Transcription: In Focus. 2nd ed. (In Focus Ser.). (Illus.). 104p. 1992. pap. text 16.95 (*0-19-963317-7*) OUP.

Beebee, Thomas O. Clarissa on the Continent: Translation & Seduction. LC 89-23223. 248p. 1990. lib. bdg. 35.00 (*0-271-00693-5*) Pa St U Pr.

— Epistolary Fiction in Europe, 1500-1850. LC 98-35812. (Literature, Culture, Theory Ser.). (Illus.). 270p. (C). 1999. text 64.95 (*0-521-62275-1*) Cambridge U Pr.

— The Ideology of Genre: A Comparative Study of Generic Instability. LC 93-8462. 1994. 50.00 (*0-271-01022-3*); pap. 19.95 (*0-271-01023-1*) Pa St U Pr.

Beebee, Thomas O., tr. see Bai, Hua.

Beebee, Trevor J. Frogs & Toads. (Illus.). 120p. text 19.95 (*0-905483-38-3*, Pub. by Whittet Bks) Diamond Farm Bk.

— The Natterjack Toad. (Illus.). 1983. 24.95 (*0-19-217709-5*) OUP.

— Pond Life. (Illus.). 128p. text 19.95 (*0-905483-99-5*, Pub. by Whittet Bks) Diamond Farm Bk.

Beebee, Yale, ed. see Merriam, Daniel B.

Beeber, Peggy K. You Don't Need a Ph. D. to Understand Me: (You Just Need to Have Known My Mother) unabridged ed. 79p. 1998. pap. 10.95 (*1-892896-64-8*) Buy Books.

Beeber, Stuart, ed. see Samberg, Sandra.

Beebout, Harold, jt. auth. see Ohls, James C.

Beeby, A. W. & Narayanan, R. S. Designer's Handbook to Eurocode 2 Pt. 1.1: Design of Concrete Structures. LC 95-183349. 250p. 1994. 11.00 (*0-7277-1668-9*) Am Soc Civil Eng.

Beeby, A. W., jt. auth. see Narayanan, R. S.

***Beeby, Betty.** Breath Escaping Envelopes: Letters & Photographs from the Grand Traverse Bay Region, 1875-1905. (Illus.). 256p. 2000. 40.00 (*0-9674525-0-3*); pap. 25.00 (*0-9674525-1-1*) Pearl MI.

Beeby, Clarence E. Quality of Education in Developing Countries. LC 66-14438. 149p. 1966. 22.00 (*0-674-74050-5*) HUP.

Beeby, Dean. Cargo of Lies: The True Story of a Nazi Double-Agent in Canada. (Illus.). 256p. 1996. text 29.95 (*0-8020-0731-7*) U of Toronto Pr.

— In a Crystal Land: Canadian Explorers in Antarctica. (Illus.). 262p. (C). 1994. text 29.95 (*0-8020-0362-1*) U of Toronto Pr.

***Beeby, H. D.** Canon & Mission. (Christian Mission & Modern Culture Ser.). 128p. (Orig.). 1998. pap. 11.00 (*1-56338-258-X*) TPI PA.

Beeby, J. L., et al, eds. Condensed Systems of Low Dimensionality. (NATO ASI Series B, Physics: Vol. 253). (Illus.). 844p. (C). 1991. 210.00 (*0-306-43887-9*, Plenum Trade) Perseus Pubng.

Beeby, John. Future Fertility: Transforming Human Waste into Human Wealth. (Illus.). 164p. 1995. pap. 18.50 (*0-614-11406-3*) Ecology Action.

***Beeby, John.** Future Fertility: Transforming Human Waste into Human Wealth. 164p. 1998. 18.50 (*0-9600772-3-5*) Ecology Action.

— Test Your Soil with Plants. 91p. 1997. 12.50 (*0-9600772-2-7*) Ecology Action.

Beeby, Mary Kay, ed. see Shandler, Donald.

***Beeby, Max & Beeby, Rosie.** Cafe Max & Rosie: Vegetarian Cooking with Health & Spirit. (Illus.). 192p. 2000. pap. 19.95 (*1-58008-237-8*) Ten Speed Pr.

Beeby, Rosie, jt. auth. see Beeby, Max.

Beeby, Suzi. Important Things. (Illus.). 87p. (Orig.). 1996. pap. 9.95 (*0-9653502-0-7*) MTW.

Beeby, W. & Collier, P. New Directions Through CAD-CAM. 230p. 1986. 37.00 (*0-87263-217-2*) SME.

Beech. Waterbirth Unplugged: International Perspectives on Waterbirth. 160p. 1997. pap. text 31.50 (*1-898507-53-8*) Buttrwrth-Heinemann.

Beech, D., ed. Concepts in User Interfaces. (Lecture Notes in Computer Science Ser.: Vol. 234). x, 116p. 1986. 26.00 (*0-387-16791-9*) Spr-Verlag.

Beech, Elizabeth. Fast Food Figures. 126p. 1998. pap. 19.95 (*0-7643-0576-X*) Schiffer.

Beech, G., ed. Computer Assisted Learning in Science Education. LC 78-40566. 1979. pap. 55.00 (*0-08-023010-5*, Pergamon Pr) Elsevier.

Beech, George T. A Rural Society in Medieval France: The Gatine of Poitou in the Eleventh & Twelfth Centuries. LC 78-64241. (Johns Hopkins University. Studies in the Social Sciences. Thirtieth Ser. 1912: 1). reprint ed. 32.50 (*0-404-61346-2*) AMS Pr.

Beech, Graham. FORTRAN Four in Chemistry: An Introduction to Computer-Assisted Methods. LC 75-2488. 313p. reprint ed. pap. 97.10 (*0-608-17673-7*, 203039000069) Bks Demand.

Beech, H. R. & Vaughan, M. Behavioral Treatment of Obsessional States. LC 78-4552. 197p. reprint ed. pap. 61.10 (*0-8357-4317-9*, 203711600007) Bks Demand.

B

Beech, J. C. & Wolf. Durability of Building Sealants: Proceedings of the International Rilem Symposium. (Rilem Proceedings Ser.). (Illus.). 160p. (C). 1995. 100.00 (*0-419-21070-9*, E & FN Spon) Routledge.

Beech, Jill, ed. Equine Respiratory Disorders. LC 90-5885. (Illus.). 458p. 1991. 89.50 (*0-8121-1325-X*) Lppncott W & W.

Beech, John. Learning to Read: A Cognitive Approach to Reading & Poor Reading. 160p. 1985. 22.50 (*1-56593-518-7*, 0008) Singular Publishing.

Beech, John R. & Harding, Leonora, eds. Assessment in Neuropsychology. LC 95-15757. (Assessment Library). 216p. (C). 1996. pap. 25.99 (*0-415-12953-2*) Routledge.

— Assessment in Neuropsychology. LC 95-15757. (Assessment Library). 216p. (C). (gr. 13). 1996. 75.00 (*0-415-09390-2*) Routledge.

Beech, John R. & Singleton, Chris. The Psychological Assessment of Reading. LC 97-3684. (Routledge Assessment Library). (Illus.). 368p. (C). 1997. 85.00 (*0-415-12858-7*); pap. 29.99 (*0-415-12859-5*) Routledge.

Beech, John R., jt. ed. see Colley, Ann M.

Beech, Len & Day, Martin. Another Girl, Another Planet. 1998. pap. 6.95 (*0-426-20528-6*, Pub. by Virgin Bks) London Brdge.

Beech, Linda. El Autobus Magico Dentro De Un Pastel: Un Libro Sobre Cocina. (J). 1995. 7.70 (*0-606-07468-6*, Pub. by Turtleback) Demco.

— El Autobus Magico En El Museo Encantado: Un Libro Sobre Los Sonidos. (J). 1995. 7.70 (*0-606-07470-8*, Pub. by Turtleback) Demco.

— Fun Phonics Cut & Paste. 1999. pap. text 7.95 (*0-439-04762-5*) Scholastic Inc.

***Beech, Linda.** The Magic School Bus Gets Ants in Its Pants: A Book about Ants. (Magic School Bus Ser.). (Illus.). (J). (ps-3). 1999. pap. 9.95 (*0-7857-7531-5*) Econo-Clad Bks.

Beech, Linda. The Magic School Bus Gets Ants in Its Pants: A Book about Ants. Duchesne, Lucie, tr. (Magic School Bus Ser.). (FRE., Illus.). (J). (gr. k-2). 1996. pap. 5.99 (*0-590-16037-0*) Scholastic Inc.

— The Magic School Bus Gets Ants in Its Pants: A Book about Ants. (Magic School Bus Ser.). (Illus.). (J). (ps-3). 1996. pap. 2.99 (*0-590-40024-X*) Scholastic Inc.

— The Magic School Bus Gets Ants in Its Pants: A Book about Ants. (Magic School Bus Ser.). (Illus.). (J). (gr. k-2). 1996. 8.19 (*0-606-09586-1*, Pub. by Turtleback) Demco.

***Beech, Linda.** The Magic School Bus Gets Baked in a Cake: A Book about Kitchen Chemistry. (Magic School Bus Ser.). (Illus.). (J). (ps-3). 1999. pap. 10.55 (*0-7857-5622-1*) Econo-Clad Bks.

Beech, Linda. The Magic School Bus Gets Baked in a Cake: A Book about Kitchen Chemistry. Duchesne, Lucie, tr. from ENG. (Magic School Bus Ser.). (FRE., Illus.). 32p. (J). (gr. k-2). pap. 5.99 (*0-590-24660-7*) Scholastic Inc.

— The Magic School Bus Gets Baked in a Cake: A Book about Kitchen Chemistry. LC 94-38834. (Magic School Bus Ser.). (Illus.). 32p. (J). (ps-3). 1995. pap. 2.99 (*0-590-22295-3*) Scholastic Inc.

— The Magic School Bus Gets Baked in a Cake: A Book about Kitchen Chemistry. (Magic School Bus Ser.). (Illus.). (J). (gr. k-2). 1995. 8.19 (*0-606-07820-7*, Pub. by Turtleback) Demco.

***Beech, Linda.** The Magic School Bus in the Haunted Museum: A Book about Sound. (Magic School Bus Ser.). (Illus.). (J). (ps-3). 1999. pap. 10.55 (*0-7857-5623-X*) Econo-Clad Bks.

Beech, Linda. The Magic School Bus in the Haunted Museum: A Book about Sound. Duchesne, Lucie, tr. (Magic School Bus Ser.). (FRE., Illus.). 32p. (J). (gr. k-2). pap. 5.99 (*0-590-24657-7*) Scholastic Inc.

— The Magic School Bus in the Haunted Museum: A Book about Sound. LC 94-25970. (Magic School Bus Ser.). (Illus.). 32p. (J). (gr. k-2). 1995. pap. 2.50 (*0-590-48412-5*) Scholastic Inc.

— The Magic School Bus in the Haunted Museum: A Book about Sound. (Magic School Bus Ser.). (Illus.). (J). (gr. k-2). 1995. 7.70 (*0-606-07822-3*, Pub. by Turtleback) Demco.

***Beech, Linda.** The Magic School Bus Meets the Rot Squad: A Book about Decomposition. (Magic School Bus Ser.). (Illus.). (J). (ps-3). 1999. pap. text 10.55 (*0-7857-7509-9*) Econo-Clad Bks.

Beech, Linda. The Magic School Bus Meets the Rot Squad: A Book about Decomposition. LC 94-44652. (Magic School Bus Ser.). (Illus.). 32p. (J). (ps-3). 1995. pap. 2.50 (*0-590-40023-1*) Scholastic Inc.

— The Magic School Bus Meets the Rot Squad: A Book about Decomposition. Duchesne, Lucie, tr. (Magic School Bus Ser.). (FRE., Illus.). 32p. (J). (gr. k-2). 1996. pap. 5.99 (*0-590-16036-2*) Scholastic Inc.

— The Magic School Bus Meets the Rot Squad: A Book about Decompostion. (Magic School Bus Ser.). (Illus.). (J). (gr. k-2). 1995. 8.19 (*0-606-07825-8*, Pub. by Turtleback) Demco.

Beech, Linda, jt. auth. see Cole, Joanna.

Beech, Linda W., et al. America & the Americas. Evento, Susan, ed. (Literature Based Reading Activities/ Conversion Ser.). 64p. 1995. pap. 9.95 (*1-56784-516-9*) Newbridge Educ.

— Family Times. Evento, Susan, ed. (Literature Based Reading Activities/Conversion Ser.). 64p. 1995. pap. 9.95 (*1-56784-515-0*) Newbridge Educ.

— Long Ago. Evento, Susan, ed. (Literature Based Reading Activities/Conversion Ser.). 64p. 1995. pap. 9.95 (*1-56784-517-7*) Newbridge Educ.

Beech, Linda Ward. El Autobus Magico Conoce Al Escuadron De La Desintegracion: Un Libro Sobre La Descomposicion. (J). 1995. 8.19 (*0-606-07467-8*, Pub. by Turtleback) Demco.

***Beech, Linda Ward.** Fun Phonics Puzzles & Games. 48p. 1999. pap. 7.95 (*0-439-04760-9*) Scholastic Inc.

— Great Grammar Skill Builders: Grades 4-5. (Ready-to-Go Reproducibles Ser.). (Illus.). 48p. (J). 2000. pap. 8.95 (*0-439-10543-9*) Scholastic Inc.

— Great Grammar Skill Builders: Grades 6-8. (Ready-to-Go Reproducibles Ser.). (Illus.). 48p. (YA). (gr. 6-8). 2000. pap. 8.95 (*0-439-10544-7*) Scholastic Inc.

— Great Grammar Skills Builders, Vol. 1. (Illus.). 48p. 1999. pap. 8.95 (*0-439-10542-0*) Scholastic Inc.

— Instant File Folder Games for Math. (Illus.). 64p. (J). 2000. pap. 10.95 (*0-439-13730-6*) Scholastic Inc.

Beech, Linda Ward. Ready to Go. (Illus.). 48p. 1999. pap. text 7.95 (*0-439-04761-7*) Scholastic Inc.

***Beech, M.** The A to Z Names in Rock. 250p. 1999. pap. text 17.95 (*1-86105-059-3*) Robson.

Beech, Nic, jt. auth. see McKenna, Eugene.

Beech, Tamara, jt. auth. see Smith, Nancy C.

***Beech, Wendy.** The Black Enterprise Guide to Starting Your Own Business. LC HD62.5.B43 1999. (Black Enterprise Ser.). 480p. 1999. pap. 19.95 (*0-471-32454-X*) Wiley.

Beecham, B. Julian, jt. auth. see Hall, Peter J.

Beecham, Caroline. Rainbow. (J). (gr. 2 up). 1996. pap. 3.99 (*0-614-15723-4*) Random.

Beecham, Jennifer, jt. auth. see Netten, Ann.

Beecham, John J. & Rohlman, Jeff. A Shadow in the Forest: Idaho's Black Bear. LC 94-1537. (Northwest Naturalist Bks.). 273p. 1994. pap. 18.95 (*0-89301-172-X*) U of Idaho Pr.

Beecham, Lenore. Song of the Soul: In Celebration of Korea. LC 83-16526. (Illus.). 44p. 1984. reprint ed. pap. 30.00 (*0-608-00234-8*, 206073600006) Bks Demand.

Beecham, R. K. & Stevens, Michael E. As If It Were Glory: Robert Beecham's Civil War from the Iron Brigade to the Black Regiments. LC 97-26826. xx, 236p. 1998. 28.95 (*0-945612-55-9*) Madison Hse.

Beecham, Sir Thomas, Society Staff. Sir Thomas Beecham Discography. LC 78-2261. 77p. 1978. reprint ed. lib. bdg. 55.00 (*0-313-20367-9*, STBD, Greenwood Pr) Greenwood.

Beecham, Thomas. A Mingled Chime: An Autobiography. LC 76-40182. (Music Ser.). 1976. reprint ed. 39.50 (*0-306-70791-8*) Da Capo.

— A Mingled Chime: An Autobiography. LC 76-40238. 330p. 1977. reprint ed. lib. bdg. 35.00 (*0-8371-9274-9*, BEMCH, Greenwood Pr) Greenwood.

— A Mingled Chime, an Autobiography. (Music Book Index Ser.). 330p. 1992. reprint ed. lib. bdg. 89.00 (*0-7812-9462-2*) Rprt Serv.

***Beechen, Adam.** Wild Thornberrys Survival Guide, Vol. 2. 48p. (J). (gr. 4-6). 2000. pap. 2.99 (*0-689-83277-X*, Simon Spot) Litle Simon.

Beechen, Paul D., jt. auth. see Starr, V. Hale.

Beecher, jt. auth. see Bittinger.

Beecher, jt. auth. see Bittinger, Marvin L.

Beecher, Anne, jt. auth. see Blake, Beatrice.

Beecher, Catharine E. Essay on Slavery & Abolitionism. LC 74-133147. (Black Heritage Library Collection). 1977. 20.95 (*0-8369-8703-9*) Ayer.

— Letters to the People on Health & Happiness. LC 70-180554. (Medicine & Society in America Ser.). (Illus.). 228p. 1972. reprint ed. 18.95 (*0-405-03934-4*) Ayer.

Beecher, Catharine E. & Stowe, Harriet Beecher. American Woman's Home: Or, Principles of Domestic Science. LC 77-165703. (American Education Ser.: No. 2). 1977. reprint ed. 27.95 (*0-405-03692-2*) Ayer.

Beecher, Catherine E. Letters to the People on Health & Happiness. (Works of Catherine E. Beecher). vi, 222p. reprint ed. lib. bdg. 49.00 (*0-932051-03-0*) Rprt Serv.

Beecher, Catherine E. & Stowe, Harriet Beecher. American Woman's Home. LC 75-22526. (Illus.). 557p. (C). 1996. pap. 17.95 (*0-917482-04-2*) Rutgers U Pr.

Beecher, Charles. Harriet Beecher Stowe in Europe: The Journal of Charles Beecher. Van Why, Joseph S. & French, Earl, eds. (Illus.). 382p. 1986. 15.00 (*0-917482-20-4*) Stowe-Day.

Beecher, Charles E. Studies in Evolution. Gould, Stephen Jay, ed. LC 79-8324. (History of Paleontology Ser.). (Illus.). 1980. reprint ed. lib. bdg. 61.95 (*0-405-12704-9*) Ayer.

Beecher, Donald, ed. Barnabe Riche: His Farewell to Military Profession. (Medieval & Renaissance Texts & Studies: Vol. 91). 336p. 1992. 28.00 (*0-86698-105-5*, MR91) MRTS.

Beecher, Donald & Ciavolella, Massimo, eds. Comparative Critical Approaches to Renaissance Comedy. (Carleton Renaissance Plays Ser.: No. 9). 165p. 1986. pap. 10.00 (*0-919473-55-5*, Pub. by Dovehouse) Sterling.

Beecher, Donald, ed. & tr. see Bernini, Gian Lorenzo.

Beecher, Donald A., ed. Barnabe Riche: His Farewell to the Military Profession. (Medieval & Renaissance Texts & Studies: Vol. 91). 335p. 1992. pap. 14.95 (*0-86698-104-7*, P9) Pegasus Pr.

Beecher, Donald A., ed. see Ferrand, Jacques.

Beecher, Donald A., ed. see Lodge, Thomas.

Beecher, Donald A., ed. & tr. see Ferrand, Jacques.

Beecher, Donald A., jt. tr. see Ciavolella, Massimo.

Beecher, Edward. Narrative of Riots at Alton. LC 70-115858. (Studies in Black History & Culture: No. 54). 1970. reprint ed. lib. bdg. 75.00 (*0-8383-1072-9*) M S G Haskell Hse.

— Narrative of the Riots at Alton: In Connection with the Death of Rev. Elijah P. Lovejoy. LC 77-89425. (Black Heritage Library Collection). 1977. 17.95 (*0-8369-8509-5*) Ayer.

— The Papal Conspiracy Exposed & Protestantism Defended. LC 76-46066. (Anti-Movements in America Ser.). (Illus.). 1977. reprint ed. lib. bdg. 35.95 (*0-405-09940-1*) Ayer.

Beecher, Gary R., ed. Human Nutrition Research. LC 79-91006. (Beltsville Symposia in Agricultural Research Ser.: No. 4). (Illus.). 318p. 1981. text 53.50 (*0-916672-48-4*) Rowman.

— Research Instrumentation for the 21st Century. (Beltsville Symposia in Agricultural Research Ser.). (C). 1988. text 255.50 (*90-247-3595-5*) Kluwer Academic.

Beecher, George. Learning & Self-Governing: Questions on the Future of Democracy in America. LC 94-31043. 192p. 1994. 20.00 (*0-912362-12-X*) Adamant Pr.

— My World Is Burning & Other Poems. 1998. pap. write for info. (*1-57553-985-3*) Watermrk Pr.

— The Sandspur. 1997. pap. 56.95 (*1-57553-622-6*) Watermrk Pr.

***Beecher, George.** A Wonder World. 1999. pap. write for info. (*1-58235-305-0*) Watermrk Pr.

Beecher, H. H. Record of the 114th Regiment of New York: State Volunteers of the Civil War. 592p. 1996. reprint ed. 82.00 (*1-887530-05-3*) RSG Pub.

Beecher, Harris H. Record of the 114th Regiment, N. Y. S. V. Where It Went, What It Saw, & What It Did. 592p. 1996. reprint ed. pap. 34.00 (*1-887530-08-8*) RSG Pub.

Beecher, Henry E., jt. auth. see Wawrukiewicz, Anthony S.

Beecher, Henry K. & Altschule, Mark D. Medicine at Harvard: The First Three Hundred Years. LC 75-40869. 603p. reprint ed. pap. 187.00 (*0-608-14819-9*, 202563300045) Bks Demand.

Beecher, Henry W. American Rebellion. LC 70-168510. (Black Heritage Library Collection). 1977. reprint ed. 22.95 (*0-8369-8863-9*) Ayer.

— Evolution & Religion. (Works of Henry Ward Beecher). 1989. reprint ed. lib. bdg. 79.00 (*0-7812-1925-6*) Rprt Serv.

— Freedom & War. LC 70-157361. (Black Heritage Library Collection). 1977. 32.95 (*0-8369-8799-3*) Ayer.

— Lectures & Orations. Hillis, Newell D., ed. LC 72-126662. (BCL Ser. II). 1970. reprint ed. 47.50 (*0-404-00699-X*) AMS Pr.

— Lectures & Orations. (BCL1-PS American Literature Ser.). 330p. 1992. reprint ed. lib. bdg. 79.00 (*0-7812-6674-2*) Rprt Serv.

— Life of Jesus the Christ. (Works of Henry Ward Beecher). 1989. reprint ed. lib. bdg. 79.00 (*0-7812-0919-6*) Rprt Serv.

— New Star Papers. (Works of Henry Ward Beecher). 1989. reprint ed. lib. bdg. 79.00 (*0-685-44799-5*) Rprt Serv.

— Patriotic Addresses In. (Works of Henry Ward Beecher). 857p. 1985. reprint ed. lib. bdg. 99.00 (*0-932051-04-9*) Rprt Serv.

— Plain & Pleasant Talks about Fruits, Flowers & Farming. (Works of Henry Ward Beecher). 1989. reprint ed. lib. bdg. 79.00 (*0-685-44727-8*) Rprt Serv.

— Seven Lectures to Young Men. (Works of Henry Ward Beecher). 1989. reprint ed. lib. bdg. 79.00 (*0-7812-1918-3*) Rprt Serv.

— Star Papers: Experience of Art & Nature. (Works of Henry Ward Beecher). vi, 359p. reprint ed. lib. bdg. 49.00 (*0-932051-01-4*) Rprt Serv.

— Star Papers: Or, Experiences of Art & Nature. LC 75-39679. (Essay Index Reprint Ser.). 1977. reprint ed. 26.95 (*0-8369-2745-1*) Ayer.

— The Works of Henry Ward Beecher, 1813-1887, Set. 1987. reprint ed. 800.00 (*0-685-18614-8*) Rprt Serv.

— Yale Lectures on Preaching. (Works of Henry Ward Beecher). vii, 359p. reprint ed. lib. bdg. 59.00 (*0-7812-0911-0*) Rprt Serv.

— Yale Lectures on Preaching. 1976. reprint ed. 49.00 (*0-403-06546-1*, Regency) Scholarly.

Beecher, Henry W. & Wanrukiewicz, Anthony S. U. S. Domestic Postal Rates, 1872-1999. 2nd rev. ed. (Illus.). xiv, 338p. 1999. 50.00 (*0-9672782-2-8*); pap. 40.00 (*0-9672782-3-6*) CAMA.

Beecher, Henry W., jt. auth. see Wawrukiewicz, Anthony S.

***Beecher, Henry Ward.** Norwood: or Village in New England. 252p. 2000. pap. 9.95 (*0-594-03590-2*) Eightn Hundrd.

Beecher, Jo. Texas Beau. LC 98-163466. (Illus.). 32p. (J). (gr. 3-5). 1999. 14.95 (*1-57168-204-X*, Eakin Pr) Sunbelt Media.

Beecher, John. Report to the Stockholders & Other Poems. 3rd ed. LC 62-6046. (Illus.). 1971. reprint ed. 5.00 (*0-911234-02-0*) Red Mtn.

— To Live & Die in Dixie, & Other Poems. LC 66-28695. (Illus.). 1966. 5.00 (*0-911234-00-4*) Red Mtn.

***Beecher, Jonathan.** Victor Considerant & the Rise & Fall of French Romantic Socialism. LC 00-28717. (Illus.). 604p. 2001. 65.00 (*0-520-22297-0*) U CA Pr.

Beecher, Jonathon F. & Bienvenu, Richard, eds. The Utopian Vision of Charles Fourier: Selected Texts on Work, Love & Passionate Attraction. LC 83-5897. 448p. 1982. text 42.00 (*0-8262-0426-0*) U of Mo Pr.

Beecher, Judith A., jt. auth. see Bittinger, Marvin L.

Beecher, Lyman. Autobiography, 2 vols., Set. (American Biography Ser.). 1991. reprint ed. lib. bdg. 180.00 (*0-7812-8016-8*) Rprt Serv.

— Lyman Beecher & the Reform of Society: Four Sermons, 1804-1828. LC 71-38437. (Religion in America, Ser. 2). 214p. 1977. reprint ed. 21.95 (*0-405-04058-X*) Ayer.

— A Plea for the West. Grob, Gerald N., ed. LC 76-46067. 1977. lib. bdg. 19.95 (*0-405-09941-X*) Ayer.

— A Plea for the West. (Works of Lyman Beecher). 190p. 1985. reprint ed. lib. bdg. 49.00 (*0-932051-00-6*) Rprt Serv.

Beecher, Margaret. Developing the Gifts & Talents of All Students in the Regular Classroom: An Innovative Curriculum Design Based on the Enrichment Trial Model. Briatico, Debra, ed. 292p. 1995. pap. text 42.95 (*0-936386-68-1*, 730) Creative Learning.

Beecher, Marguerite, jt. auth. see Beecher, Willard.

Beecher, Mark H. The Tool That Built Niagara. (Illus.). 62p. (Orig.). 1976. pap. 4.00 (*0-685-29129-4*) Niagara Cnty Hist Soc.

Beecher, Maureen U. & Anderson, Lavina F., eds. Sisters in Spirit: Mormon Women in Historical & Cultural Perspective. LC 86-30757. 304p. (C). 1992. pap. text 15.95 (*0-252-06296-5*) U of Ill Pr.

Beecher, Maureen U., jt. ed. see Bitton, Davis.

Beecher, Michael D., jt. ed. see Bolles, Robert C.

Beecher, Pamela. Douglas Arthur Teed: An American Romantic, 1860-1929. (Illus.). 54p. (Orig.). 1982. pap. 5.00 (*1-877885-02-9*) Arnot Art.

Beecher, Sean. Day by Day: A Miscellany of Cork History. 370p. 1992. pap. 16.95 (*0-9516036-7-1*) Dufour.

Beecher, Wendy, compiled by. Directory of Community Social Work Initiatives: Scotland. (C). 1987. 45.00 (*0-7855-3745-7*, Pub. by Natl Inst Soc Work) St Mut.

Beecher, Willard & Beecher, Marguerite. Beyond Success & Failure: Ways to Emotional Maturity. rev. ed. LC 66-24877. 230p. 1986. reprint ed. pap. 11.95 (*0-87516-569-9*) Beecher Found.

— Parents on the Run. LC 73-83773. 238p. 1983. reprint ed. pap. 6.95 (*0-87516-522-2*) DeVorss.

— The Sin of Obedience: "Parents on The Run" 88p. (Orig.). 1982. pap. 7.75 (*0-942350-00-6*) Beecher Found.

Beechert, Alice, ed. see Reinecke, John E.

Beechert, Alice M., ed. see Reinecke, John E.

Beechert, Edward D. Aupuni I La'au: A History of Hawai'i's Carpenters Union Local 745. pap. 7.95 (*0-681-02743-6*) Booklines Hawaii.

— Working in Hawaii: A Labor History. LC 85-8640. 414p. 1985. 24.95 (*0-8248-0890-8*) UH Pr.

Beechert, Edward D., ed. see Reinecke, John E.

Beechey. Murdering Ministers. LC 99-36337. 1999. text 24.95 (*0-312-20902-9*) St Martin.

Beechey, Alan. An Embarrassment of Corpses. LC 97-17819. 265p. 1997. 22.95 (*0-312-16936-1*, Thomas Dunne) St Martin.

Beechey, Gwilym, ed. see Bennett, John, et al.

Beechey, Gwilym, ed. see Corrette, Michel.

Beechey, Gwilym, ed. see Greene, Maurice.

Beechey, Gwilym, ed. see Linley, Thomas, Jr.

Beechey, James, ed. see Bradshaw, Tony.

Beechey, K. A. Daily Meditations. 1994. 8.95 (*0-8356-7574-2*) Theos Pub Hse.

Beechey, Katherine, ed. Daily Meditations: Extracts from Letters to the Masters of the Wisdom. 166p. 1990. 8.95 (*81-7059-144-9*) Theos Pub Hse.

Beechhoefer, Ina S., ed. Guide to Real Estate & Mortgage Banking Software. 8th ed. LC 95-61422. 640p. 1995. pap., per. 89.95 (*0-917935-18-7*) Real Est Sol.

— Guide to Real Estate & Mortgage Banking Software. 9th ed. 1997. per. 89.95 (*0-614-30273-0*) Real Est Sol.

Beechick, Ruth. Adam & His Kin: The Lost History of Their Lives & Times. (Illus.). 176p. 1990. pap. 9.00 (*0-940319-07-1*) Mott Media.

— The Cabin & the Ice Palace. LC 95-83675. 148p. (YA). (gr. 5 up). 1996. pap. 9.00 (*0-940319-10-1*) Mott Media.

— Dr. Beechick's Homeschool Answer Book. Strayer, Debbie, ed. LC 98-71003. 224p. 1998. pap. 12.00 (*0-940319-12-8*) Mott Media.

— An Easy Start in Arithmetic: Grades K-3. (Three R's Ser.). 32p. (gr. k-3). 1986. pap. 4.00 (*0-940319-01-2*) Mott Media.

— Genesis: Finding Our Roots. LC 97-70526. 112p. 1997. text 17.50 (*0-940319-11-X*) Mott Media.

Beechick, Ruth. A Home Start in Reading: Grades K-3. (Three R's Ser.). 32p. (Orig.). 1985. pap. 4.00 (*0-940319-00-4*) Mott Media.

Beechick, Ruth. The Language Wars: And Other Writings for Homeschoolers. LC 95-78025. 252p. 1995. pap. 12.00 (*0-940319-09-8*) Mott Media.

— A Strong Start in Language: Grades K-3. (Three R's Ser.). 32p. (Orig.). 1986. pap. 4.00 (*0-940319-02-0*) Mott Media.

— The Three R's: Grades K-3, 3 vols. & poster. 96p. 1986. pap. 12.00 (*0-940319-06-3*) Mott Media.

— You Can Teach Your Child Successfully: Grades 4-8. 2nd ed. LC 88-20014. (Illus.). 388p. 1992. 19.00 (*0-940319-05-5*); pap. 14.00 (*0-940319-04-7*) Mott Media.

Beechick, Ruth & Nelson, Jeannie. Language & Thinking for Young Children. (J). 1987. pap. 7.99 (*0-88062-152-4*) Mott Media.

Beeching. Case Histories in Infectious Diseases. 1993. 35.00 (*0-7234-1799-7*) Mosby Inc.

— Illustrated Case Histories in Infectious Disease. 1993. 24.95 (*0-685-65362-5*) Mosby Inc.

Beeching, Cyril L. A Dictionary of Dates. LC 92-40815. (C). 1993. 15.95 (*0-19-211693-2*) OUP.

— A Dictionary of Dates: New Edition. 2nd ed. (Oxford Paperback Reference Ser.). 350p. 1997. pap. 11.95 (*0-19-280056-6*) OUP.

— A Dictionary of Eponyms. 3rd ed. LC 89-38629. 228p. Date not set. reprint ed. pap. 70.70 (*0-608-20723-3*, 207182100002) Bks Demand.

Beeching, Henry C. William Shakespeare, Player, Playmaker & Poet. LC 77-168571. (Illus.). reprint ed. 29.50 (*0-404-00724-4*) AMS Pr.

Beeching, Jack. The Invention of Love. 71p. (Orig.). 1997. pap. 10.00 (*1-882191-03-X*) Spirit Horse Pr.

— A Memoir of Thomas McGrath. 30p. (Orig.). 1993. pap. 4.00 (*1-882191-02-1*) Spirit Horse Pr.

Beeching, Jack, ed. & abr. see Hakluyt, Richard.

Beeching, Kate. Basic French. 1988. pap. text 19.44 (*0-582-22481-0*, 78060); audio 23.00 (*0-582-22482-9*, 78059) Longman.

Beeching, Kate & Le Guilloux, Isabelle. La Passerelle: French Grammar in Use. (Illus.). 232p. (C). 1993. pap. 31.95 (*0-521-36857-X*); audio 31.95 (*0-521-36471-X*) Cambridge U Pr.

An Asterisk (*) at the beginning of an entry indicates that the title is appearing for the first time.

Beeching, Nick J. & Nye, Fred J. Diagnostic Picture Tests in Clinical Infectious Disease. 124p. 1996. pap. 18.00 (*0-7234-2451-9*, 70082) Mosby Inc.

Beeching, Paul Q. Awkward Reverence: Reading the New Testament Today. LC 96-45038. 260p. 1997. 24.95 (*0-8264-1000-6*) Continuum.

***Beeching, Steve.** Servicing Video Equipment & Camcorders. 320p. 2001. pap. 59.95 (*0-7506-5039-7*, Newnes) Buttrwrth-Heinemann.

Beeching, Steve. Servicing Videocassette Recorders. 4th ed. (Illus.). 250p. 1993. text 59.95 (*0-7506-0935-4*) Buttrwrth-Heinemann.

— Videocassette Recorders: A Servicing Guide. 1988. 44.00 (*0-434-90123-7*) CRC Pr.

Beechler, Schon & Stucker, Kristin. Japanese Business, 4 vols. LC 96-51809. (Illus.). 1840p. (C). 1998. 700.00 (*0-415-15801-X*) Routledge.

Beechler, Schon L. & Bird, Allan, eds. Japanese Multinationals Abroad: Individual & Organizational Learning. LC 98-20135. (Japan Business & Economics Ser.). (Illus.). 288p. 1999. text 49.95 (*0-19-511925-8*) OUP.

Beechman, Dolly, jt. auth. see Sternberg, Pat.

Beechy. Canadian Advanced Financial Accounting. (FRE.). (C). 1990. pap. write for info. (*0-03-998106-1*) Harcourt Coll Pubs.

Beeck, Bart Op De, see Callewaert, Winand M.

Beeck, Bart Op De, see Callewaert, Winand M. & Op De Beeck, Bart.

Beeck, Bart Op De, see Callewaert, Winand M.

Beeck, Bart Op De, see Callewaert, Winand M. & Op De Beeck, Bart.

Beeck, Bart Op De, see Callewaert, Winand M.

Beeck, Bart Op De, see Callewaert, Winand M. & Op De Beeck, Bart.

Beeck, Bart Op De, see Callewaert, Winand M.

Beeck, Johannes, et al. Telefon. (GER., Illus.). 50p. (YA). (gr. 7 up). 1990. 25.00 incl. audio (*0-939990-70-9*) Intl Linguistics.

Beecroft, Vanessa, et al, contrib. by. ID: An International Survey on the Notion of Identity in Contemporary Art. (Illus.). 127p. 1999. pap. 30.00 (*90-70149-59-1*, 910552, Pub. by NAi Uitgevers) Dist Art Pubs.

— Parkett, No. 56. 250p. 1999. pap. 32.00 (*3-907582-06-3*, Pub. by Parkett Verlag AG) Dist Art Pubs.

Beecroft, K. A. & Palmer, R. E., eds. Library Association Yearbook, 1998-99. 518p. 1998. pap. 80.00 (*1-85604-285-5*, LAP42855, Pub. by Library Association) Bernan Associates.

***Beecroft, K. A. & Palmer, R. E., eds.** Library Association Yearbook, 2000-2001. 432p. 2000. pap. 80.00 (*1-85604-368-1*, LAP3681, Pub. by Library Association) Bernan Associates.

***Beecroft, Simon.** The New Book of El Nino. LC 98-55560. 1999. pap. 9.95 (*0-7613-0797-4*) Millbrook Pr.

Beecroft, Simon. The New Book of El Nino. LC 98-55560. (Illus.). 31p. (J). (gr. 4-6). 1999. lib. bdg. 24.90 (*0-7613-0920-9*) Millbrook Pr.

— Superhumans: A Beginner's Guide to Bionics. LC 97-41602. (Future Files Ser.). (Illus.). 32p. (J). (gr. 4-6). 1998. pap. 8.95 (*0-7613-0636-6*, Copper Beech Bks); lib. bdg. 22.40 (*0-7613-0621-8*, Copper Beech Bks) Millbrook Pr.

Beecroft, Vanessa. Vanessa Beecroft: Performaces. 152p. 1999. 39.95 (*3-89322-964-7*) Dist Art Pubs.

Beed, Terence W. & Stimson, Robert J., eds. Survey Interviewing: Theory & Techniques. 224p. (C). 1985. text 34.95 (*0-86861-436-X*) Routledge.

Beede, Benjamin R., compiled by. Military & Strategic Policy: An Annotated Bibliography, 2. LC 89-25616. (Bibliographies & Indexes in Military Studies: No. 2). 355p. 1990. lib. bdg. 89.50 (*0-313-26000-1*, BMZ/, Greenwood Pr) Greenwood.

Beede, Benjamin R., ed. The War of 1898 & U. S. Interventions, 1898-1934: An Encyclopedia. LC 93-49579. (Military History of the U. S. Ser.: Vol. 2). 784p. 1994. text 100.00 (*0-8240-5624-8*, H933) Garland.

Beede, Benjamin R. & Brugh, Anne. Politics & Government of N.J., 1900-1980: An Annotated Bibliography, Vol. XXIII. 420p. 1989. 40.00 (*0-911020-22-5*) NJ Hist Soc.

Beede, Bob. Raising Healty Horses. (Illus.). Date not set. pap. write for info. (*1-886532-09-5*) Christian Vet.

***Beede, Martha & Burnett, Darlene, eds.** Planning for Student Services: Best Practices for the 21st Century. (Illus.). 160p. 1999. pap. 45.00 (*0-9601608-9-2*) Soc Coll & Univ Planning.

Beedell, Ann. The Decline of the English Musician, 1788-1888: A Family of English Musicians in Ireland, England, Mauritius, & Australia. LC 92-10038. (Illus.). 352p. 1992. 85.00 (*0-19-816294-4*, Clarendon Pr) OUP.

Beeding, Francis. The Nine Waxed Faces. 1994. lib. bdg. 21.95 (*1-56849-472-6*) Buccaneer Bks.

Beedle, Joyce. The Carebook: A Workbook for Caregiver Peace of Mind. Dunn, Louise, ed. 51p. 1991. ring bd., wbk. ed. 24.50 (*0-9630730-5-2*) Lady Bug.

— The Carebook: A Workbook for Caregiver Peace of Mind. rev. ed. 51p. 1993. reprint ed. student ed., ring bd. 24.50 (*0-9630730-8-7*) Lady Bug.

Beedle, Lynn S. Stability of Metal Structures: A World View. 2nd ed. 940p. 1991. 75.00 (*1-879749-50-5*) Structural Stability.

Beedle, Lynn S. & Rice, Dolores B., eds. Collected Papers of Habitat & the High-Rise: Tradition & Innovation. (Illus.). 557p. 1996. text 45.00 (*0-939493-14-4*) Coun Tall Bldg.

— Habitat & the High Rise: Tradition & Innovation. 191p. (C). 1995. text 60.00 (*0-939493-09-8*) Coun Tall Bldg.

Beedle, Michael A. Enterprise Architectural Patterns: Building Blocks of the Agile Company. (Managing Object Technology Ser.: No. 19). 300p. (C). 1998. pap. 39.95 (*0-521-64546-8*) Cambridge U Pr.

Beedy, Jeffrey P. Sports PLVS. LC 97-76605. (Illus.). 200p. (Orig.). 1997. pap. 16.00 (*0-934387-13-3*) Project Advent.

Beeferman, Larry W. Images of the Citizen & the State: Resolving the Paradox of Public & Private Power in Constitutional Law. 502p. (C). 1996. lib. bdg. 69.50 (*0-7618-0231-2*) U Pr of Amer.

Beeferman, Larry W. Images of the Citizen & the State: Resolving the Paradox of Public & Private Power in Constitutional Law. 502p. (C). 1996. pap. text 44.50 (*0-7618-0232-0*) U Pr of Amer.

Beeftink, Wim G., ed. Vegetation Dynamics. 135p. 1980. pap. text 99.50 (*90-6193-606-3*) Kluwer Academic.

Beegel, Susan F., ed. Hemingway's Neglected Short Fiction: New Perspectives. LC 91-34441. 392p. 1991. reprint ed. pap. text 22.95 (*0-8173-0586-6*) U of Ala Pr.

Beegel, Susan F., et al, eds. Steinbeck & the Environment: Interdisciplinary Approaches. LC 96-36276. 384p. 1997. text 34.95 (*0-8173-0846-6*) U of Ala Pr.

Beeger, Dieter & Quellmalz, Werner. Dresden und Umgebung. (Sammlung Geologischer Fuehrer Ser.: Band 87). (GER., Illus.). viii, 205p. 1994. spiral bd. 29.00 (*3-443-15062-4*, Pub. by Gebruder Borntraeger) Balogh.

Beeghley. Angles of Vision. 1998. pap. text. write for info. (*0-8133-3526-4*) Westview.

— Social Problems. (C). 1995. text 36.75 (*0-15-501579-6*) Harcourt Coll Pubs.

***Beeghley.** Social Stratification in the United States. 3rd ed. LC 99-26838. 306p. (C). 1999. 70.00 (*0-205-27835-3*, Macmillan Coll) P-H.

Beeghley, Leonard. Angles of Vision: How to Understand Social Problems. LC 98-13958. 258p. 1998. text 79.00 (*0-8133-2948-5*, Pub. by Westview); pap. 29.00 (*0-8133-2949-3*, Pub. by Westview) HarpC.

— The Structure of Social Stratification in the United States. 2nd ed. LC 95-15287. 1995. text 66.00 (*0-205-16805-1*) Allyn.

— What Does Your Wife Do? Gender & the Transformation of Family Life. (New Perspectives in Sociology Ser.). (C). 1996. pap. 69.00 (*0-8133-2634-6*, Pub. by Westview) HarpC.

Beeghly, Marjorie, jt. ed. see Cicchetti, Dante.

Beegle, Dewey M. God's Word into English. LC 79-84556. 1965. pap. 8.95 (*0-933462-02-6*) Pryor Pettengill.

— Moses, the Servant of Yahweh. LC 79-84558. 368p. 1972. reprint ed. pap. text 8.95 (*0-933462-03-4*) Pryor Pettengill.

— Prophecy & Prediction. 274p. 1978. write for info. (*0-933462-00-X*); pap. text 8.95 (*0-933462-01-8*) Pryor Pettengill.

— Scripture, Tradition & Infallibility. LC 79-84557. Orig. Title: The Inspiration of Scripture. 332p. 1980. reprint ed. pap. text 8.95 (*0-933462-04-2*) Pryor Pettengill.

Beegle, Kathleen. The Quality & Availability of Family Planning Services & Contraceptive Use in Tanzania. LC 95-13435. (LSMS Working Papers: No. 114). 66p. 1995. pap. 22.00 (*0-8213-3198-1*, 13198) World Bank.

Beegle, Margaret, jt. auth. see Korth, Philip A.

Beegle, Shirley. Bible Women Crossword Puzzles. Fittro, Pat, ed. 48p. (Orig.). (J). (gr. 5). 1996. pap. 3.99 (*0-7847-0456-2*, 02696) Standard Pub.

— Favorite Bible Verses Find-a-Word. Fittro, Pat, ed. 48p. (Orig.). (J). (gr. 7). 1996. pap. 1.49 (*0-7847-0498-8*, 02598) Standard Pub.

Beegle, Shirley, ed. see Anderson, Debby.

Beegle, Shirley, ed. see Bennett, Marian.

Beegle, Shirley, ed. see Brooks, Sandra.

Beegle, Shirley, ed. see Cachiaras, Dot.

Beegle, Shirley, ed. see Eberle, Sarah.

Beegle, Shirley, ed. see Gambill, Henrietta D.

Beegle, Shirley, ed. see Hayes, Wanda.

Beegle, Shirley, ed. see Horlacher, Bill & Horlacher, Kathy.

Beegle, Shirley, ed. see Mahany, Patricia S.

Beegle, Shirley, ed. see Matranga, Frances C.

Beegle, Shirley, ed. see Meyer, Kathleen A.

Beegle, Shirley, ed. see Mueller, Virginia.

Beegle, Shirley, ed. see Odor, Ruth S.

Beegle, Shirley, ed. see Stewart, Kristine K.

Beegle, Shirley, ed. see Watson, E. Elaine.

Beeharry, Girindre K., jt. auth. see Brodie, Joseph W.

Beehler, Bruce, et al. Birds of New Guinea. LC 85-42673. (Illus.). 370p. 1985. pap. 49.50 (*0-691-02394-8*, Pub. by Princeton U Pr) Cal Prin Full Svc.

Beehler, Bruce M. A Naturalist in New Guinea. (Corrie Herring Hooks Ser.: No. 17). (Illus.). 251p. 1991. 29.95 (*0-292-75541-4*) U of Tex Pr.

Beehler, Bruce M., jt. auth. see Frith, Clifford B.

Beehler, Roger & Drengson, Alan R., eds. The Philosophy of Society. 1978. pap. 15.95 (*0-416-83490-6*, NO. 2083) Routledge.

Beehr, Terry A. Basic Organizational Psychology. LC 95-17938. 256p. 1995. pap. text 35.00 (*0-205-14811-5*) Allyn.

Beehr, Terry A. Psychological Stress in the Workplace. LC 94-9357. (Illus.). 288p. (C). (gr. 13). 1995. 75.00 (*0-415-09426-7*, A8201) Routledge.

***Beek, B., ed.** Bioaccumulation: New Aspects & Developments. (Handbook of Environmental Chemistry Ser.: Vol. 2, Pt. J). xiv, 284p. 2000. 143.00 (*3-540-62575-5*) Spr-Verlag.

Beek, Frits Van, see Van Beek, Frits.

Beek, Gus W. Van, see Van Beek, Gus W.

Beek, Jan M. V. D. Dutch Business Law. Schuit, Steven R. et al, eds. 1984. ring bd. 284.00 (*90-6544-974-4*) Kluwer Law Intl.

Beek, Johannes H. Van, see Dahan, Albert & Van Beek, Johannes H.

Beek, M. A., et al, eds. Symbolae Biblicae et Mesopotamicae: Francisco Mario Theodoro De Liagre Bohl Dedicatae. (Illus.). viii, 416p. 1973. pap. text 175.00 (*0-614-03987-8*, Pub. by Netherlands Inst) Eisenbrauns.

Beek, Stephen D. Van, see Van Beek, Stephen D.

Beek, T. A. Van, see Van Beek, T. A., ed.

Beek, To De Haan-van, see De Haan-van Beek, To.

Beek, Tom Van, see Van Beek, Tom.

***Beek, W. J.** Transport Phenomena. 2nd ed. LC 99-13161. 342p. 1999. 185.00 (*0-471-99977-6*) Wiley.

***Beek, W. J., et al.** Transport Phenomena. 2nd ed. LC 99-13161. 342p. 1999. pap. 59.95 (*0-471-99990-3*) Wiley.

Beek, Walter E. Van, see Blakely, Thomas D.

***Beeke, Jemma.** The Brand New Creature. (Illus.). 32p. (J). (ps-2). 1999. pap. text 6.95 (*1-86233-037-9*) Levinson Bks.

— The Rickety Barn Show. LC 00-24835. (Illus.). (J). 2001. 14.95 (*0-385-32795-1*, DD Bks Yng Read) BDD Bks Young Read.

Beeke, Jemma & Beeke, Tiphanie. The Brand New Creature. LC 99-162377. (Illus.). 32p. (J). 1998. 14.95 (*1-899607-66-8*) Sterling.

***Beeke, Joel.** The Quest for Full Assurance: Legacy of Calvin & His Successors. 395p. 1999. pap. 14.99 (*0-85151-745-5*) Banner of Truth.

Beeke, Joel R. Backsliding: Disease & Cure. 92p. 1982. pap. 2.00 (*1-892777-09-6*) Reform Heritage Bks.

— Holiness: God's Call to Sanctification. 25p. 1994. pap. 2.00 (*0-85151-671-8*) Banner of Truth.

— Jehovah Shepherding His Sheep: Sermons on the Twenty-Third Psalm. 2nd ed. 379p. 1997. 9.00 (*1-892777-06-1*) Reform Heritage Bks.

— Justification by Faith: Selected Bibliography. 43p. 1995. pap. 5.00 (*1-892777-12-6*) Reform Heritage Bks.

— Truth That Frees. (YA). (gr. 5-12). 1998. 19.00 (*1-892777-13-4*) Reform Heritage Bks.

Beeke, Joel R., intro. 1998-1999 Yearbook: Church & School Directory of Heritage Netherlands Reformed Congregations. 91p. 1998. pap. 4.00 (*1-892777-03-7*) Reform Heritage Bks.

Beeke, Joel R. & Ferguson, Sinclair B., eds. Reformed Confessions Harmonized. LC 98-50178. 271p. (gr. 13). 1999. pap. 19.99 (*0-8010-5222-X*) Baker Bks.

Beeke, Joel R. & Greendyk, James D. Knowing & Living the Christian Life: Weekly Devotions. 295p. 1997. 15.00 (*1-892777-04-5*) Reform Heritage Bks.

Beeke, Joel R., et al. Sola Scriptura: The Protestant Position on the Bible. Kistler, Don, ed. LC 97-105530. 280p. (Orig.). 1996. pap. 14.95 (*1-57358-028-7*) Soli Deo Gloria.

Beeke, Joel R., jt. auth. see Vander Zwaag, Foppe.

Beeke, Joel R., ed. see Halyburton, Thomas.

Beeke, Joel R., ed. see Watson, Thomas.

Beeke, Joel R., tr. see Dathenus, Petrus.

Beeke, Joel R., tr. see Hellenbroek, Abraham.

Beeke, Joel R., tr. see VanderKemp, Johannes.

Beeke, Tiphanie, jt. auth. see Beeke, Jemma.

Beeker, John. Implementing Tailpipe Tests: What Factors Influence States to Respond to National Environmental Policy Goals? LC 90-45125. (Environment: Problems & Solutions Ser.: Vol. 4). 240p. 1990. text 20.00 (*0-8240-0420-5*) Garland.

***Beeker, Simon.** The Handbook of Chinese Hematology. Orig. Title: The Treatment of Blood Diseases with Chinese Medicine. 240p. 2000. pap. text 39.95 (*1-891845-16-0*) Blue Poppy Pr.

Beekes, R. S. Development of the Proto-Indo-European Laryngeals in Greek. (Janua Linguarum, Ser. Practica: No. 42). 1969. pap. text 89.25 (*90-279-0693-9*) Mouton.

Beekes, Robert S. P. Comparative Indo-European Linguistics: An Introduction. LC 95-16596. xxii, 376p. 1995. pap. 29.95 (*1-55619-505-2*); lib. bdg. 95.00 (*1-55619-504-4*) J Benjamins Pubng Co.

Beekman. Comput Current Dos5 DBAs. (C). 1996. text 76.66 (*0-8053-5133-7*) Benjamin-Cummings.

— COMPUT CURRENT DOS6 WRK3. (C). 1997. text 86.00 (*0-8053-5145-0*) Benjamin-Cummings.

— Computer Currents. (C). 1996. text 81.00 (*0-8053-5140-X*) Benjamin-Cummings.

— Computer Currents Win R5. (C). 1996. text 68.00 (*0-8053-5265-1*) Benjamin-Cummings.

— Qbasic. (C). 1996. text 76.00 (*0-8053-5149-3*) Benjamin-Cummings.

***Beekman.** Techsuite: Computer Confluence: Exploring Tomorrow's Technology. 3rd ed. 1998. 84.00 (*0-201-47425-5*) Addison-Wesley.

Beekman, Allan. Crisis: The Japanese Attack on Pearl Harbor & Southeast Asia. (Illus.). 456p. 1992. 25.95 (*0-9609132-3-8*) Heritage Pac.

— The Niihau Incident. LC 82-83137. (Illus.). 128p. 1982. pap. 6.95 (*0-9609132-0-3*) Heritage Pac.

Beekman, Amy. Partnering for Growth: Entrepreneurial Strategies for Value-Chain Management. rev. ed. LC 99-33043. (Studies in Entrepreneurship). (Illus.). 132p. 1999. 43.00 (*0-8153-3402-8*) Garland.

Beekman, Daniel. Forest, Village, Town, City. LC 79-7819. (Illus.). 32p. (J). (gr. 3-6). 1982. lib. bdg. 11.89 (*0-690-04085-7*) HarpC Child Bks.

Beekman, E. M. Troubled Pleasures: Dutch Colonial Literature from the East Indies, 1600-1950. LC 95-17849. 672p. (C). 1996. text 135.00 (*0-19-815853-1*, Clarendon Pr) OUP.

Beekman, E. M., ed. Patriotism, Inc & Other Tales by Paul van Ostaijen. LC 79-150314. 192p. 1971. 27.50 (*0-87023-084-0*); pap. 13.95 (*0-87023-097-2*) U of Mass Pr.

Beekman, E. M., ed. Fugitive Dreams: An Anthology of Dutch Colonial Literature. LC 87-19031. (Library of the Indies). 344p. (C). 1988. lib. bdg. 40.00 (*0-87023-575-3*) U of Mass Pr.

— The Oyster & the Eagle: Selected Aphorisms & Parables of Multatuli. LC 73-93171. 124p. 1974. lib. bdg. 20.00 (*0-87023-123-5*) U of Mass Pr.

Beekman, E. M., jt. auth. see Rumpf, Georg E.

Beekman, E. M., ed. see Alberts, A.

Beekman, E. M., ed. see Daum, P. A.

Beekman, E. M., ed. see Du Perron, E.

Beekman, E. M., ed. see Nieuwenhuys, Rob.

Beekman, E. M., ed. see Nijs, E. Breton de.

Beekman, E. M., ed. see Van Schendel, Arthur.

Beekman, E. M., tr. see Rumphius.

Beekman, George. Beekman Book Including Word 6.0 for Windows, Access 2.0 for Windows & Excel 5.0 for Windows Modules. 1995. pap. text 84.33 (*0-8053-2658-8*) Benjamin-Cummings.

— Beekman Computer Currents: DOS 6.0-Windows 3.1, MS Works for Windows. (C). 1995. pap. text 76.66 (*0-8053-2682-0*) Addison-Wesley.

— Beekman Computer Currents: Lotus 1-2-3 Release 2.3/2.4, Wordperfect 6.0 for Winbase 3 Plus, Structured Basic. 1995. pap. text 76.66 (*0-8053-3425-4*) Addison-Wesley.

— Beekman D6 Lo Wo for Bundle or Canada. 1994. pap. text. write for info. (*0-8053-8853-2*) Addison-Wesley.

— Compt Confl: Expr Tomorr. (C). 1997. pap. text 42.00 (*0-201-33912-9*) Addison-Wesley.

— Computer Confluence. 2nd ed. (C). 1997. text 74.06 (*0-201-76566-7*) Addison-Wesley.

— Computer Confluence. 3rd ed. LC 98-34363. 480p. (C). 1998. pap. text 58.00 (*0-201-35213-3*) Addison-Wesley.

— Computer Confluence: Exploring Tomorrow's Technology. 2nd ed. LC 96-38494. 1996. pap. text 105.00 incl. cd-rom (*0-8053-2289-2*) Benjamin-Cummings.

— Computer Confluence: Exploring Tomorrow's Technology. 3rd ed. 480p. (C). 1998. pap. text 56.00 incl. audio compact disk (*0-201-43855-0*, Prentice Hall) P-H.

***Beekman, George.** Computer Confluence: Exploring Tomorrow's Technology. 4th ed. 572p. 2000. pap. 60.00 (*0-13-088237-2*) P-H.

Beekman, George. Computer Confluence: Exploring Tomorrow's Technology, Concise Edition. LC 98-48650. 320p. (C). 1998. pap. text 43.00 incl. audio compact disk (*0-201-33945-5*, Prentice Hall) P-H.

— Computer Confluence: Exploring Tomorrow's Technology Instructor's Manual. 3rd ed. 448p. 1998. 22.00 (*0-201-42876-8*) Addison-Wesley.

— Computer Confluence Business Edition. 2nd ed. (C). 1997. pap. text. write for info. (*0-8053-0434-7*) Longman.

— Computer Confluence Business Edition 2. 2nd ed. LC 99-11958. 592p. (C). 1999. pap. text 57.00 (*0-201-42881-4*) Addison-Wesley.

— Computer Confluence 3. 3rd annot. ed. LC 98-34363. 480p. (C). 1998. pap. text, teacher ed. 55.00 (*0-201-42880-6*) Addison-Wesley.

— Computer Currents. (C). 1996. text 53.00 (*0-8053-5129-9*) Benjamin-Cummings.

— Computer Currents: Navigating Tomorrow a Technology. 432p. 1994. pap. text, teacher ed. 40.00 (*0-8053-2454-2*) Benjamin-Cummings.

— Computer Influence: Book Only. 2nd ed. (C). 1997. pap. text 55.00 (*0-8053-0427-4*) Benjamin-Cummings.

— Condensed Pascal: Oh! Macintosh Pascal! (C). 1990. pap. text 55.00 (*0-393-96120-6*) Norton.

— DOS6.0WIN3.1 REL2.3 CUST. 1995. pap. text 44.66 (*0-8053-2599-9*) Addison-Wesley.

— Hypercard 2.2 in a Hurry. 384p. 1994. pap. text 22.95 (*0-201-40887-2*) Addison-Wesley.

— HyperCard 2.2 in a Hurry: The Fast Track to Multimedia. 2nd ed. 353p. (C). 1994. mass mkt. 43.95 (*0-534-25116-1*) Wadsworth Pub.

— HyperCard 2.3 in a Hurry: The Fast Track to Multimedia. 1995. mass mkt. 43.95 (*0-534-51300-X*) Wadsworth Pub.

— INCLD DOS 6.0&WIN3.1 CB. 1995. pap. text 91.33 (*0-8053-2641-3*) Benjamin-Cummings.

— INCLD DOS6.0&WIN3.1 CB. 1995. pap. text 76.66 (*0-8053-2652-9*) Benjamin-Cummings.

— INCLDG QUATTRO PRO1.0 CB. 1995. pap. text 44.66 (*0-8053-2606-5*) Benjamin-Cummings.

— INCLDNG DOS6.0&WIN3.1 CB. 1995. pap. text 44.66 (*0-8053-2610-3*) Benjamin-Cummings.

— Internet. 2nd ed. 54p. (C). 1996. pap. text. write for info. (*0-8053-2111-X*) Addison-Wesley.

— Printed Testbank Computer. 432p. 1994. pap. text 11.50 (*0-8053-2457-7*) Benjamin-Cummings.

— Select Computer Currents. 1995. pap. text 70.00 (*0-8053-3354-1*) Addison-Wesley.

— Trans Computr Currents. 432p. 1994. pap. text 89.00 (*0-8053-2449-6*) Benjamin-Cummings.

***Beekman, George & Rathswohl, Eugene.** Computer Confluence Business with Cd & Web Guide. 2nd ed. 592p. 1999. pap. text 60.00 (*0-201-43857-7*) Addison-Wesley.

Beekman, George C. Early Dutch Settlers of Monmouth County. (Illus.). 162p. 1997. reprint ed. pap. 21.00 (*0-8328-6059-X*) Higginson Bk Co.

— Early Dutch Settlers of Monmouth County. 2nd ed. 1974. 12.00 (*0-686-11781-6*) Neptune His Soc.

Beekman, J. F., tr. see Broekman, Jan M.

Beekman, John & Callow, John. Translating the Word of God: With Scripture & Topical Indexes. LC 83-51850. 412p. 1974. pap. 29.00 (*1-55671-098-4*) S I L Intl.

Beekman, John A., jt. auth. see Andrews, George H.

Beekman-Love, Gilian & Neiger, L. Materials Management. (Applied Business Logistics Ser.: Vol. 1). 1978. pap. text 78.50 (*90-207-0748-5*) Kluwer Academic.

Beekman, Susan & Holmes, Jeanne. Battles, Hassles, Tantrums & Tears. LC 92-37608. 1993. pap. 13.00 (*0-688-11937-9*, Hearst) Hearst Commns.

Beekman, W. Boerhave. Elsevier's Wood Dictionary Vol. 1: Commercial & Botanical Nomenclature of World Timbers, Sources of Supply. (DUT, ENG, FRE, GER & ITA.). 480p. 1964. 295.00 (*0-8288-9199-0*) Fr & Eur.

— Elsevier's Wood Dictionary Vol. 2: Production, Transport, Trade. (DUT, ENG, FRE, GER & ITA.). 642p. 1966. 295.00 (*0-8288-9200-8*) Fr & Eur.

— Elsevier's Wood Dictionary Vol. 3: Research, Manufacture, Utilization. (DUT, ENG, FRE, GER & ITA.). 460p. 1968. 295.00 (*0-8288-9201-6*) Fr & Eur.

Beeksma, Deborah, ed. see Knowles, Claire.

Beeksma, Deborah L., ed. The Fool's Journey. (Illus.). 94p. (Orig.). 1995. pap. text 9.99 (*0-9648972-0-2*, Quiddity) OnQ.

Beekun, Rafik I. Islamic Business Ethics. LC 96-16857. (Human Development Ser.). 1996. write for info. (*1-56564-242-2*) IIIT VA.

***Beekun, Rafik I. & Badawi, Jamal A.** Leadership, an Islamic Perspective. LC 99-42025. 1999. write for info. (*0-915957-94-9*) amana pubns.

Beel, C. Gordon, et al. High-Tech Ventures: The Guide for Entrepreneurial Success. 387p. 1991. 35.00 (*0-201-56321-5*) Addison-Wesley.

Beel, Cecil H., Jr., jt. auth. see Spady, Richard J.

Beel, Marianne, ed. A Sandhill Century, Eighteen Eighty-Three to Nineteen Eighty-Three, 2 vols. set, Bk. I. LC 85-70605. (Illus.). 400p. 1986. write for info. (*0-9614508-0-0*) Cherry County Cent.

— A Sandhill Century, Eighteen Eighty-Three to Nineteen Eighty-Three, 2 vols. set, Bk. II. LC 85-70605. (Illus.). 562p. 1986. write for info. (*0-9614508-1-9*) Cherry County Cent.

— A Sandhill Century, Eighteen Eighty-Three to Nineteen Eighty-Three, 2 vols. set, Set. LC 85-70605. (Illus.). 1986. 61.00 (*0-9614508-2-7*) Cherry County Cent.

Beelen, D. W., jt. auth. see Schaefer, U. W.

Beeler, Barbara J. According to the Word of God: Personal Prayers & Confessions. (Illus.). 100p. (Orig.). 1994. pap. text 10.00 (*0-9643586-0-3*) REED IT.

— Spiritual Warfare Manual. (Illus.). 38p. 1994. student ed. 10.00 (*0-9643586-1-1*) REED IT.

Beeler, Cecil F. Boys in the Well. (Northern Lights Young Novels Ser.). 128p. (Orig.). (J). (gr. 3-9). 1996. pap. 7.95 (*0-88995-136-5*, Pub. by Red Deer) Genl Dist Srvs.

— No Room in the Well. (Northern Lights Young Novels Ser.). 176p. (J). (gr. 4-9). 1993. pap. 7.95 (*0-88995-099-7*, Pub. by Red Deer) Genl Dist Srvs.

Beeler, Cecil Freeman. The Girl in the Well. (Northern Lights Young Novels Ser.). 128p. (J). (gr. 4-9). 1991. pap. 7.95 (*0-88995-075-X*, Pub. by Red Deer) Genl Dist Srvs.

Beeler, Charlene. American Nostalgia. (Simulation Ser.). 62p. 1991. pap. 14.95 (*1-882664-01-9*) Prufrock Pr.

— Earth Friendly. (Simulation Ser.). 44p. 1994. pap. 14.95 (*1-882664-10-8*) Prufrock Pr.

— Endangered Species. (Simulation Ser.). 44p. 1994. pap. 14.95 (*1-882664-11-6*) Prufrock Pr.

— Introduction Pack. (Simulation Ser.). 44p. 1991. pap. 14.95 (*1-882664-04-3*) Prufrock Pr.

— Medieval Destinations. (Simulation Ser.). 44p. 1991. pap. 14.95 (*1-882664-02-7*) Prufrock Pr.

— Western Explorations. (Simulation Ser.). 51p. 1991. pap. 19.95 (*1-882664-03-5*) Prufrock Pr.

Beeler, Duane. Arbitration for the Local Union. 105p. (Orig.). 1977. pap. 3.95 (*0-317-12246-0*) Union Rep.

— Book of Roots: A Full Study of Our Families of Words. 256p. (Orig.). (C). 1988. pap. 10.00 (*0-918515-00-9*) Union Rep.

— Discipline & Discharge. 225p. (Orig.). 1978. pap. 5.95 (*0-317-12244-4*) Union Rep.

— Labor Law for the Union Officer. rev. ed. 103p. 1979. reprint ed. pap. 3.95 (*0-317-12248-7*) Union Rep.

— Negotiating the Contract. 139p. (Orig.). 1981. pap. 4.95 (*0-317-12243-6*) Union Rep.

— Speak up to Move Up: Public Speaking for the Union Representative. 101p. (Orig.). 1979. pap. 3.95 (*0-317-12254-1*) Union Rep.

— Union Professional: The Staff Rep in Action. 109p. 1977. pap. 3.95 (*0-317-12247-9*) Union Rep.

Beeler, Duane & Krushenbaum, Harry. How to Be a More Effective Union Representative. 125p. (Orig.). 1965. pap. 3.95 (*0-317-12245-2*) Union Rep.

— Roles of the Labor Leader. 131p. (Orig.). 1969. pap. 3.95 (*0-317-12249-5*) Union Rep.

Beeler, Duane, et al. Why Workers Behave the Way They Do. 240p. (Orig.). 1983. pap. 7.95 (*0-317-12241-X*) Union Rep.

Beeler, John. Warfare in Feudal Europe, 730-1200. LC 74-148018. (Illus.). 288p. 1973. pap. text 15.95 (*0-8014-9120-7*) Cornell U Pr.

Beeler, John, ed. see Schurman, Donald Mackenzie.

Beeler, John F. British Naval Policy in the Gladstone-Disraeli Era, 1866-1880. LC 97-33038. 1998. write for info. (*0-8047-2981-6*) Stanford U Pr.

Beeler, John F., jt. auth. see Schurman, D. M.

Beeler, John H., ed. see Oman, Charles W.

Beeler, Myrton F., jt. auth. see Freeman, James A.

Beeler-Port, Josef. Verklarung des Auges: Konstruktionsanalyse der Ersten Wissenschaftslehre J. G. Fichtes von 1804. (Europaische Hochschulschriften Ser.: Reihe 20, Bd. 458). (GER.). 333p. 1997. 49.95 (*3-906753-63-8*, Pub. by P Lang) P Lang Pubng.

Beeler, Ronald & Noll, Rhona S. Beginning Algebra. 176p. (C). 1993. text, student ed. 18.75 (*0-697-17227-9*, WCB McGr Hill) McGrw-H Hghr Educ.

— Intermediate Algebra. 224p. (C). 1993. text, student ed. 18.13 (*0-697-17228-7*, WCB McGr Hill) McGrw-H Hghr Educ.

Beeler, Selby B. Throw Your Tooth on the Roof: Tooth Traditions from Around the World. LC 97-46042. (Illus.). 32p. (J). (gr. 1-4). 1998. 16.00 (*0-395-89108-6*) HM.

Beeler, Stanley W. The Invisible College: A Study of the Three Original Rosicrucian Texts. LC 91-12215. (Studies in German Literature & Culture: No. 4). 1991. 37.50 (*0-404-64054-0*) AMS Pr.

Beeley, Arthur L. An Experimental Study in Left-Handedness, with Practical Suggestions for Schoolroom Tests. LC 78-72787. (Brainedness, Handedness, & Mental Abilities Ser.). reprint ed. 39.50 (*0-404-60852-3*) AMS Pr.

Beeley, Brian W., jt. auth. see Boswell, David M.

Beeley, Linda. Safer Prescribing: A Guide to Some Problems in the Use of Drugs. 5th ed. 128p. 1991. pap. 16.95 (*0-632-03292-8*) Blackwell Sci.

Beeley, Linda, jt. auth. see Wade, O. L.

Beeley, P. R. & Smart, R. F., eds. Investment Casting. 486p. 1995. 160.00 (*0-901716-66-9*, Pub. by Inst Materials) Ashgate Pub Co.

***Beeley, Peter R.** Foundry Technology. 2nd ed. 2000. 99.95 (*0-7506-4567-9*) Buttrwrth-Heinemann.

Beeley, Ray. The Roaring of the Lion. 117p. 1997. reprint ed. pap. 7.99 (*0-85151-715-3*) Banner of Truth.

Beell, Thomas & Washington Post Writers Staff. Messages 4: The Washington Post Media Companion. 4th ed. 333p. 1996. pap. text 23.00 (*0-205-26559-6*) Allyn.

Beels, Richard, et al. GroupWise 5.2 Administrator's Guide. LC 97-65904. 864p. 1997. pap. text 44.99 incl. cd-rom (*0-7821-1993-X*) Sybex.

Beem, Christopher. Pluralism & Consensus: Conceptions of the Good in the American Polity. LC 97-68132. (Studies in Religion, Society & Personality). ix, 153p. 1998. text 29.95 (*0-913348-29-5*) Ctr Sci Study.

— Weaving The Moral Fabric: Reclaiming American Public Life. LC 98-49098. (Morality & Society Ser.). 256p. 1999. 28.00 (*0-226-04144-1*) U Ch Pr.

Beem, David. Beem. Daniel Beem & His Descendants, Embracing Some Facts Relating to the Early History of Spencer & Owen Counties, Ind., & Personal Recollections by the Author. (Illus.). 102p. 1997. reprint ed. pap. 17.00 (*0-8328-7465-5*); reprint ed. lib. bdg. 27.00 (*0-8328-7464-7*) Higginson Bk Co.

***Beem, Edgar Allen.** Maine: The Spirit of America. LC 99-55231. (Illus.). 96p. 2000. 12.95 (*0-8109-5570-9*, Pub. by Abrams) Time Warner.

Beem, J. K. & Woo, P. Y. Doubly Timelike Surfaces. LC 52-42839. (Memoirs Ser.: No. 1/92). 115p. 1969. pap. 16.00 (*0-8218-1292-0*, MEMO/1/92) Am Math.

Beem, John & Duggal, Krishan L., eds. Differential Geometry & Mathematical Physics. LC 94-20799. (Contemporary Mathematics Ser.: Vol. 170). 224p. 1994. pap. 41.00 (*0-8218-5172-1*, CONM/170) Am Math.

Beem, John K. & Woo, Peter Y. Doubly Timelike Surfaces. LC QA0003.A57. (American Mathematical Society Ser.: No. 92). 118p. 1969. reprint ed. pap. 36.60 (*0-608-00213-5*, 206099600006) Bks Demand.

Beem, John K., et al. Global Lorentzian Geometry. 2nd ed. LC 96-957. (Monographs & Textbooks in Pure & Applied Mathematics: Vol. 202). (Illus.). 656p. 1996. text 189.00 (*0-8247-9324-2*) Dekker.

Beem, Nelson. Beem. History of the Michael Beem Family. (Illus.). 96p. 1997. reprint ed. pap. 18.00 (*0-8328-7467-1*); reprint ed. lib. bdg. 28.00 (*0-8328-7466-3*) Higginson Bk Co.

— Facts & Fiction about Loudonville & the Area. (Illus.). 1991. pap. 4.50 (*1-879377-04-7*) Truax Print.

Beeman, D., jt. auth. see Bower, J.

Beeman, Judith, jt. auth. see Beeman, Martin.

Beeman, Mark & Chiarello, Christine. Right Hemisphere Language Comprehension: Perspectives from Cognitive Neuroscience. LC 96-46733. 360p. 1997. text. write for info. (*0-8058-1925-8*) L Erlbaum Assocs.

— Right Hemisphere Language Comprehension: Perspectives from Cognitive Neuroscience. LC 96-46733. 360p. 1997. pap. 39.95 (*0-8058-1926-6*) L Erlbaum Assocs.

Beeman, Marsha L. Where Am I? Clue-by-Clue Descriptive Sketches of American Historical Places. LC 96-42227. 319p. (Orig.). 1996. pap. 32.50 (*0-7864-0243-1*) McFarland & Co.

— Who Am I? Clue-by-Clue Biographical Sketches of American Historical Figures. LC 92-56629. (Illus.). 212p. 1993. pap. 27.50 (*0-89950-899-5*) McFarland & Co.

Beeman, Marsha Lynn. Joan Fontaine: A Bio-Bibliography, 50. LC 93-45311. (Bio-Bibliographies in the Performing Arts Ser.: No. 50). 360p. 1994. lib. bdg. 69.50 (*0-313-28409-1*, Greenwood Pr) Greenwood.

Beeman, Martin & Beeman, Judith. Joys of Hawaiian Cooking. (Illus.). 1981. pap. 10.95 (*0-912180-41-2*) Petroglyph.

Beeman, Richard, et al, eds. Beyond Confederation: Origins of the Constitution & American National Identity. LC 86-16150. (Institute of Early American History & Culture Ser.). x, 366p. (C). 1987. 45.00 (*0-8078-1719-8*); pap. 18.95 (*0-8078-4172-2*) U of NC Pr.

Beeman, William & Frank, Isaiah. New Dynamics in the Global Economy. 43p. 1988. pap. 9.50 (*0-87186-248-4*) Comm Econ Dev.

Beeman, William O. Language, Status, & Power in Iran. LC 84-48490. (Advances in Semiotics Ser.). (Illus.). 276p. (C). 1986. 15.95 (*0-253-33139-0*) Ind U Pr.

Beeman, William O., jt. auth. see Helfgot, Daniel.

Beemer, jt. auth. see Peters, Chester.

Beemer, A. M., ed. see Annual Oholo Biological Conference Staff.

Beemer, C. Britt & Shook, Robert L. Predatory Marketing. LC 97-43240. 304p. 1998. pap. 14.00 (*0-7679-0189-4*) Broadway BDD.

Beemer, Rod & Peterson. Ford Tractor Implements. LC 98-23726. (Tractor Color History Ser.). (Illus.). 128p. 1998. pap. 21.95 (*0-7603-0428-9*) Motorbooks Intl.

Beemer, Rod, jt. auth. see Peterson, Chester, Jr.

Beemer, Rod, jt. auth. see Peterson, Chester.

Beemyn, Brett. Creating a Place for Ourselves: Lesbian, Gay & Bisexual Community Histories. LC 96-46104. 320p. 1997. pap. 16.99 (*0-415-91390-X*) Routledge.

— Creating a Place for Ourselves: Lesbian, Gay & Bisexual Community Histories. LC 96-46104. 320p. (C). 1997. 70.00 (*0-415-91389-6*) Routledge.

Beemyn, Brett & Eliason, Mickey, eds. Queer Studies: A Lesbian, Gay, Bisexual, & Transgender Anthology. LC 96-25709. (Illus.). 318p. (C). 1996. text 60.00 (*0-8147-1257-6*); pap. text 25.00 (*0-8147-1258-4*) NYU Pr.

Been, jt. ed. see Jefferies.

Been, Diana B. The Jamaican Herbalist: Use of Herbs in Jamaica. 200p. (Orig.). Date not set. pap. text 15.00 (*0-9649550-2-4*) Been Bks.

Been, Margaret L. Wilderness & Gardens: An American Lady's Prospect. Westburg, John E., ed. (Illus.). 1974. pap. 6.00 (*0-87423-011-X*) Westburg.

Been, Marta. Say It Right, Write It Right: The Secretary's Guide to Solving Business Communications Problems. 384p. (C). 1994. text 29.95 (*0-13-791492-X*) P-H.

Beena, C. Personality Typologies: A Comparison of Western & Ancient Indian Approaches. 1990. 59.00 (*81-7169-092-0*, Commonwealth) S Asia.

Beenackers, A. A. & Van Swaay, W., eds. Advanced Gasification: Methanol Production from Wood-Results of the EEC Pilot Programme. 1986. text 129.50 (*90-277-2212-9*) Kluwer Academic.

Beene. College English. (C). 1992. pap. text, wbk. ed. 21.56 (*0-395-64584-0*) HM.

— College English. (C). 1992. pap., suppl. ed. 2.76 (*0-395-64585-9*) HM.

— Options. (C). 1992. pap., wbk. ed. 21.56 (*0-395-59963-6*) HM.

Beene, Charles. Police Crowd Control: Risk-Reduction Strategies for Law Enforcement. (Illus.). 128p. 1992. pap. 16.00 (*0-87364-674-6*) Paladin Pr.

Beene, Lynn. A Guide to British Prose Explication: Nineteenth & Twentieth Century. LC 96-27135. 1996. 55.00 (*0-8161-1987-2*, G K Hall & Co) Mac Lib Ref.

— The Riverside Handbook. (C). 1992. text, teacher ed. 32.76 (*0-395-59961-X*) HM.

Beene, Lynn & Kopple, William V. The Riverside Handbook. (C). 1992. pap. text, teacher ed. 3.96 (*0-395-59962-8*) HM.

Beene, Lynn & Vande Kopple, William J. The Riverside Handbook. (C). 1991. text 31.56 (*0-395-52372-9*) HM.

Beene, Lynn D. & White, Peter. Solving Problems in Technical Writing. (Illus.). 256p. (C). 1988. pap. text 23.95 (*0-19-505331-1*) OUP.

Beene, LynnDianne. John Le Carre. LC 92-18671. (Twayne's English Authors Ser.). 170p. 1992. 32.00 (*0-8057-7013-5*) Macmillan.

Beene, Wayne, ed. A Dictionary of Iraqi-Arabic: Arabic-English. (ARA & ENG.). 523p. (C). 1991. reprint ed. pap. text 24.95 (*0-87840-281-0*) Georgetown U Pr.

Beenet, S. S. An Introduction to Plant Nomenclature. (C). 1979. text 60.00 (*0-89771-549-7*, Pub. by Intl Bk Distr) St Mut.

***Beenhakker, Henri L.** The Global Economy & International Financing. LC 00-37265. 2000. write for info. (*1-56720-401-5*) Greenwood.

Beenhakker, Henri L. Handbook for the Analysis of Capital Investments. LC 76-5324. (Illus.). 452p. (Orig.). 1976. 55.00 (*0-8371-8901-2*, BCI/, Greenwood Pr) Greenwood.

— Investment Decision Making in the Private & Public Sectors. LC 96-913. 264p. 1996. 72.95 (*1-56720-028-1*, Quorum Bks) Greenwood.

— Risk Management in Project Finance & Implementation. LC 97-8856. 296p. 1997. 69.50 (*1-56720-106-7*, Quorum Bks) Greenwood.

Beenham, Rosemary & Harrison, Colin. The Basics of Librarianship. 3rd ed. LC 90-45271. 245p. reprint ed. pap. 76.00 (*0-608-09587-7*, 205438900006) Bks Demand.

Beenker, Eric. Jan van der Vaart. 1993. 45.00 (*90-6918-082-0*, Pub. by Boymans Mus) U of Wash Pr.

Beenker, F. P., et al. Testability Concepts for Digital ICs: The Macro Test Approach. (Frontiers in Electronic Testing Ser.). 224p. (C). 1995. text 118.50 (*0-7923-9658-8*) Kluwer Academic.

Beenler, Bruce M., jt. auth. see Ripley, Sidney.

Beenstock, Michael. Work, Welfare & Taxation: A Study of Labour Supply Incentives in the U. K. 220p. (C). 1987. text 55.00 (*0-04-331104-0*); pap. text 18.95 (*0-04-331105-9*) Routledge.

— The World Economy in Transition. 2nd ed. 250p. 1984. pap. text 19.95 (*0-04-339035-8*) Routledge.

Beenstock, Michael, ed. Modelling the Labour Market. 250p. (gr. 13). 1988. text 110.00 (*0-412-28830-3*) Chapman & Hall.

***Beentje, Henk.** Flora of Tropical East Africa: Surianaceae. 8p. 1998. 3.00 (*90-6191-381-0*, Pub. by A A Balkema) Ashgate Pub Co.

Beentje, Henk. Kenya Trees, Shrubs & Lianas. LC 94-983457. (Illus.). ix, 722p. 1994. 60.00 (*9966-9861-0-3*, Pub. by Royal Botnic Grdns) Balogh.

Beentje, Henk, jt. auth. see Coe, Malcolm.

Beentje, Henk, jt. auth. see Dransfield, John.

Beentjes, Pancratius C. Book of Ben Sira in Hebrew: A Text Edition of All Extant Hebrew Manuscripts & A Synopsis Of All Parallel Hebrew Ben Sira Texts. Vol. 68. (Illus.). Viii, 182p. 1997. text 89.00 (*90-04-10767-3*) Brill Academic Pubs.

Beentjes, Pancratius C., ed. The Book of Ben Sira in Modern Research: Proceedings of the First International Ben Sira Conference (28 - 31 July 1996) LC 97-34015. 234p. 1997. text 101.35 (*3-11-015673-3*) De Gruyter.

Beer. In These Hills, Vol. 1. 1999. text 22.50 (*0-8050-3726-8*) St Martin.

— Mechanical Engineering: Dynamics. 4th ed. 1987. student ed. 42.81 (*0-07-004583-6*) McGraw.

— Mechanical Engineering/Statics. 4th ed. 1987. 27.50 (*0-07-004581-X*) McGraw.

— Mechanics Materials. 2nd ed. 1992. teacher ed. 12.95 (*0-07-004341-8*) McGraw.

Beer. Prealgebra: Student's Solution Manual. 272p. (C). 1997. student ed. 21.00 (*0-321-01274-7*) Addison-Wesley.

— Programming the Boundary Elements. 1969. text. write for info. (*0-471-85722-X*) Wiley.

Beer. Sir Walter Raleigh & His Readers in the Seventeenth Century: Speaking to the People. LC 97-3277. 210p. 1997. text 55.00 (*0-312-17610-4*) St Martin.

— Stafford Beer Classics Library, 6 vols., Set. 2350p. 1994. text 233.00 (*0-471-95154-4*) Wiley.

— Vector Mechanical Engineering: Dynamics of Over-Head. 5th ed. 1988. 57.50 (*0-07-004587-9*) McGraw.

— Vector Mechanics Engineering. 7th ed. 2002. 91.25 (*0-07-230491-X*); 71.00 (*0-07-230492-8*) McGraw.

— Vector Mechanics Engineering: Statics. 7th ed. 2002. 73.50 (*0-07-230493-6*) McGraw.

***Beer & Peake.** Prealgebra Algebra. 540p. 1999. pap. text 72.00 (*0-201-59768-3*) Addison-Wesley.

Beer, A. Vistas in Astronomy, Vol. 17. 1975. 115.00 (*0-08-017878-2*, Pergamon Pr) Elsevier.

Beer, A. E., jt. ed. see Toder, V.

Beer, Albert, et al, eds. Semiconductors & Semimetals Vol. 45: Effect of Disorder & Defects in Ion-Implanted Semiconductors: Electrical & Physicochemical Characterization. (Illus.). 300p. 1997. text 130.00 (*0-12-752145-3*) Morgan Kaufmann.

Beer, Albert C. Vistas in Astronomy, 22 vols., Vol. 4. 1979. pap. 39.00 (*0-08-023071-7*, Pergamon Pr) Elsevier.

Beer, Albert C., et al, eds. Semiconductors & Semimetals: Spectroscopy of Semiconductors, Vol. 36. (Illus.). 435p. 1992. text 123.00 (*0-12-752136-4*) Acad Pr.

Beer, Albert C., jt. auth. see Beer, P.

Beer, Ann, jt. ed. see Gillett, Margaret.

Beer, Anne R. Environmental Planning for Site Development. (Illus.). 336p. (Orig.). (C). 1990. pap. 45.00 (*0-419-15300-4*, E & FN Spon) Routledge.

***Beer, Anne R. & Higgins, Catherine.** Environmental Planning for Site Development 2nd ed. LC 99-16704. 2000. 41.99 (*0-419-24460-3*, E & FN Spon) Routledge.

Beer, Arthur & Beer, Peter, eds. Vistas in Astronomy. Incl. Vol. 8. Aspects of Stellar Evolution. LC 50-111295. 1966. 140.00 (*0-08-011649-3*); Vol. 9. New Aspects in the History & Philosophy of Astronomy. LC 50-111295. 1968. 140.00 (*0-08-012089-X*); Vol. 12. Henry Norris Russell Memorial Volume. LC 50-111295. 1970. 155.00 (*0-08-006765-4*); Vol. 17. Copernicus: Yesterday & Today. LC 50-111295. 1975. 290.00 (*0-08-017879-0*); Vol. 18. Kepler: Four Hundred Years. LC 50-111295. 1975. 185.00 Vol. 19, Pt. 2. New Aspects in the History & Philosophy of Astronomy. LC 50-111295. 1975. pap. 29.00 (*0-08-018945-8*); Vol. 19, Pt. 4. From Newton to Black Holes. LC 50-111295. 1976. pap. 24.00 (*0-08-020257-8*); Vol. 1. LC 50-111295. 1962. 140.00 (*0-08-009565-8*); Vol. 5. LC 50-111295. 1962. 155.00 (*0-08-009630-1*); Vol. 6. LC 50-111295. 1965. 155.00 (*0-08-010999-3*); Vol. 7. LC 50-111295. 1966. 140.00 (*0-08-011648-5*); Vol. 10. LC 50-111295. 1968. 155.00 (*0-08-012363-5*); Vol. 11. LC 50-111295. 1969. 155.00 (*0-08-012660-X*); Vol. 13. LC 50-111295. 1972. 155.00 (*0-08-015618-5*); Vol. 14. LC 50-111295. 1972. 140.00 (*0-08-015870-6*); Vol. 15. LC 50-111295. 1974. 140.00 (*0-08-017118-4*); 16. LC 50-111295. 1974. 155.00 (*0-08-017141-9*); Set. The Kepler & Copernicus Memorial Volume. LC 50-111295. 1334p. 1975. 395.00 (*0-08-018139-2*); Vol. 19, Pt. 1. LC 50-111295. 1975. pap. 35.00 (*0-08-018944-X*); Vol. 19, Pt. 3. LC 50-111295. 1976. pap. 32.00 (*0-08-020255-1*); LC 50-111295. write for info. (*0-318-55237-X*) Elsevier.

Beer, Barrett L. Northumberland: The Political Career of John Dudley, Earl of Warwick & Duke of Northumberland. LC 73-77386. 247p. reprint ed. pap. 76.60 (*0-7837-1340-1*, 204148800020) Bks Demand.

— Rebellion & Riot: Popular Disorder in England During the Reign of Edward VI. LC 81-19341. 270p. reprint ed. pap. 83.70 (*0-7837-0574-3*, 204091800019) Bks Demand.

— Tudor England Observed: The World of John Stow. LC 99-193394. (Illus.). 224p. 1998. 39.95 (*0-7509-1943-4*, Pub. by Sutton Pub Ltd) Intl Pubs Mktg.

Beer, Barrett L., ed. The Life & Raigne of King Edward the Sixth by John Hayward. LC 92-26984. (Illus.). 208p. 1993. lib. bdg. 35.00 (*0-87338-475-X*) Kent St U Pr.

Beer, Bill. Speak French in Fifteen Minutes. 108p. (Orig.). 1993. pap. 3.50 (*0-9634055-1-9*) Fifteen Minute Pr.

— Speak Spanish in Fifteen Minutes. 104p. (Orig.). 1992. pap. 3.50 (*0-9634055-0-0*) Fifteen Minute Pr.

— We Swam the Grand Canyon: The True Story of a Cheap Vacation That Got a Little Out of Hand. 171p. 1995. pap. 12.00 (*0-9634055-9-4*) Fifteen Minute Pr.

Beer, Carel De, see Jackson, Melvin H.

Beer, Carel De, see Jackson, Melvin H. & De Beer, Carel.

Beer, Cecilia. Temple-Boys Pt. 1: A Study of Cypriote Votive Sculpture, Catalogue. (Studies in Mediterranean Archaeology: Vol. CXIII). (Illus.). 305p. 1994. 99.95 (*91-7081-013-3*, Pub. by P Astroms) Coronet Bks.

B

An Asterisk (*) at the beginning of an entry indicates that the title is appearing for the first time.

Beer, Colin, jt. auth. see Immelmann, Klaus.

Beer, David & McMurrey, David. A Guide to Writing As an Engineer. LC 96-13162. 272p. 1996. pap. 37.95 (*0-471-11715-3*) Wiley.

Beer, David F., ed. Writing & Speaking in the Technology Professions: A Practical Guide. LC 91-21418. (Illus.). 278p. (C). 1991. pap. text 34.95 (*0-87942-284-X*, PP0278-2) Inst Electrical.

***Beer, Edith Hahn.** The Nazi Officer's Wife: How One Jewish Woman Survived The Holocaust. 320p. 2000. pap. 14.00 (*0-688-17776-X*, Perennial) HarperTrade.

Beer, Edith Hahn & Dworkin, Susan. The Nazi Officer's Wife: How One Jewish Woman Survived the Holocaust. LC 99-43362. 320p. 1999. 26.00 (*0-688-16689-X*, Wm Morrow) Morrow Avon.

Beer, Ferdinand P. & Johnston, E. Russell. Mechanics of Materials. 2nd ed. 1995. 88.44 incl. disk (*0-07-911388-5*, WCB McGr Hill) McGraw-H Hghr Educ.

— Vector Mechanics for Engineers: Statics & Dynamics. 6th ed. LC 96-42906. 1280p. 1997. 114.14 incl. disk (*0-07-847129-X*, TA350) McGraw.

Beer, Ferdinand Pierre. Vector Mechanics for Engineers: Statics. 6th ed. 599p. 1996. pap. text 79.75 (*0-07-114057-3*, TA351) McGraw.

Beer, Ferdinand Pierre & Johnston, E. Russel. Vector Mechanics for Engineers: Statics. 6th ed. (C). 1995. text 72.00 incl. disk (*0-07-912966-8*) McGraw.

Beer, Ferdinand Pierre & Johnston, E. Russell, Jr. Mechanics for Engineers: Combined, Vol. 99. 4th ed. 944p. (C). 1987. text 90.25 (*0-07-004584-4*) McGraw.

Beer, Ferdinand Pierre & Johnston, E. Russell. Mechanics for Engineers: Dynamics, Vol. 2. 4th ed. (C). 1987. text 71.00 (*0-07-004582-8*) McGraw.

Beer, Ferdinand Pierre & Johnston, E. Russell, Jr. Mechanics for Engineers: Statics. 4th ed. 496p. (C). 1986. text 72.50 (*0-07-004580-1*) McGraw.

Beer, Ferdinand Pierre & Johnston, E. Russell. Vector Mechanics for Engineers: Dynamics. 5th ed. (C). 1992. pap. text, suppl. ed. 47.00 (*0-07-911461-X*) McGraw.

— Vector Mechanics for Engineers: Statics. 5th ed. (C). 1992. pap. text, suppl. ed. 51.00 (*0-07-911462-8*) McGraw.

— Vector Mechanics for Engineers: 800 Solved Problems in Vector Mechanics for Engineers Statistics. 5th ed. (C). 1990. text 79.74 (*0-07-909914-9*) McGraw.

Beer, Ferdinand Pierre & Russell, Johnston E. Vector Mechanics for Engineers: Combined. 5th ed. 1088p. (C). 1988. text 94.00 (*0-07-079923-7*) McGraw.

— Vector Mechanics for Engineers: Dynamics. 5th ed. 592p. (C). 1992. text 14.50 (*0-07-005009-0*) McGraw.

— Vector Mechanics for Engineers: Statics. 5th ed. 496p. 1992. 44.95 (*0-07-004507-0*) McGraw.

— Vector Mechanics for Engineers: Statics. 5th ed. 496p. (C). 1992. pap. text 14.50 (*0-07-005011-2*) McGraw.

Beer, Ferdinand Pierre, et al. Vector Mechanics for Engineers: Dynamics. 6th ed. LC 96-42905. 1997. write for info. (*0-07-005366-9*) McGraw.

— Vector Mechanics for Engineers: Dynamics. 6th ed. LC 96-42905. 626p. 1997. 90.63 (*0-07-913034-8*); 90.63 (*0-07-912637-5*) McGraw.

— Vector Mechanics for Engineers: Statics. 6th ed. LC 95-39089. 1995. write for info. (*0-07-005367-7*) McGraw.

— Vector Mechanics for Engineers: Statics & Dynamics. 6th ed. LC 96-42906. 1997. write for info. (*0-07-005365-0*) McGraw.

— Vector Mechanics for Engineers: Statics & Dynamics. 6th ed. LC 96-42906. 1997. 94.00 (*0-07-847126-5*) McGraw.

Beer, Frances, tr. Julian of Norwich: Revelations of Divine Love & the Motherhood of God. LC 97-40649. (Library of Medieval Women). 102p. 1999. pap. 17.95 (*0-85991-453-4*) Boydell & Brewer.

Beer, Frances, ed. see Austen, Jane & Bronte, Charlotte.

Beer, Francis A. & Hariman, Robert, eds. Post-Realism: The Rhetorical Turn in International Relations. 280p. (Orig.). 1996. 35.95 (*0-87013-422-1*); pap. 24.95 (*0-87013-461-2*, 0-87013-422-1) Mich St U Pr.

Beer, Francis De, see De Beer, Francis.

Beer, G., et al, eds. Computer Methods & Advances in Geomechanics: Proceedings of the Seventh International Conference, Cairns, 6-10 May 1991, 3 vols. 2000p. (C). 1991. text 388.00 (*90-6191-189-3*, Pub. by A A Balkema) Ashgate Pub Co.

Beer, George A. The Coming of the Italian-Ethiopian War. LC 67-14336. 420p. reprint ed. pap. 130.20 (*0-608-11804-4*, 201725800006) Bks Demand.

Beer, George L. British Colonial Policy. 327p. 1993. reprint ed. lib. bdg. 89.00 (*0-7812-5167-2*) Rprt Serv.

— British Colonial Policy, 1754-1765. 1990. 16.50 (*0-8446-1065-8*) Peter Smith.

Beer, Gerald. Topologies on Closed & Closed Convex Sets. LC 93-31538. (Mathematics & Its Applications Ser.: Vol. 268). 352p. 1993. text 214.50 (*0-7923-2531-1*) Kluwer Academic.

***Beer, Gillian.** Alice in Space. 1999. lib. bdg. 25.00 (*0-226-04150-6*) U Ch Pr.

Beer, Gillian. Arguing with the Past: Essays in Narrative from Woolf to Sidney. 208p. 1989. 39.50 (*0-415-02607-5*, A3480); pap. 14.95 (*0-415-02608-3*, A3484) Routledge.

— Darwin's Plots: Evolutionary Narrative in Darwin, George Eliot, & Nineteenth-Century Fiction. 384p. 1985. pap. 10.95 (*0-7448-0021-8*, Routledge Thoemms) Routledge.

***Beer, Gillian.** Darwin's Plots: Evolutionary Narrative in Darwin, George Eliot & Nineteenth-Century Fiction. 2nd ed. LC PR878.E95B43 2000. 312p. 2000. 54.95 (*0-521-78008-X*); pap. 19.95 (*0-521-78392-5*) Cambridge U Pr.

Beer, Gillian. Meredith: A Change of Masks. LC 70-546357. (A Study of the Novels). 1970. 23.25 (*0-485-11122-5*) Athlone Pr.

— Open Fields: Science in Cultural Encounter. (Illus.). 350p. (C). 1996. text 45.00 (*0-19-818369-0*) OUP.

— Open Fields: Science in Cultural Encounter. (Illus.). 350p. 1999. pap. text 27.50 (*0-19-818635-5*) OUP.

— Virginia Woolf: The Common Ground. LC 96-40084. 192p. (Orig.). 1997. pap. text 18.95 (*0-472-08463-1*, 08463) U of Mich Pr.

Beer, Gillian, ed. see Woolf, Virginia.

Beer, Gillian, ed. & intro. see Austen, Jane.

Beer, Gillian, ed. & intro. see Darwin, Charles.

Beer, Gretel. Austria. (Exploring Rural Europe Ser.). (Illus.). 168p. 1993. pap. 12.95 (*0-8442-9463-2*, 94632, Natl Textbk Co) NTC Contemp Pub Co.

***Beer, Gretel.** Austrian Cooking. (Cookery Classics). 256p. 1999. 19.95 (*0-233-99471-8*, Pub. by Andre Deutsch) Trafalgar.

Beer, Gretel. Austrian Cooking & Baking. 224p. 1975. reprint ed. pap. 5.95 (*0-486-23220-4*) Dover.

Beer-Hofmann, Richard. Jacob's Dream. Wynn, Ida B., tr. from GER. Orig. Title: Jaakobs Traum. 1946. 17.50 (*0-917324-06-4*) German Bk Ctr.

Beer, J. Concepts, Design & Performance Analysis of a Parallel Prolog Machine. (Lecture Notes in Computer Science Ser.: Vol. 404). vi, 128p. 1989. 27.00 (*0-387-52053-8*, 3833) Spr-Verlag.

Beer, Jeanette, tr. see De Fournival, Richard.

Beer, Jeanette M. Translation Theory & Practice in the Middle Ages. LC 97-12898. (Studies in Medieval Culture). 1997. 40.00 (*1-879288-81-8*); pap. 20.00 (*1-879288-82-6*) Medieval Inst.

Beer, Jeanette M., ed. Early Prose in France: Contexts of Bilingualism & Authority. 1992. boxed set 25.00 (*1-879288-12-5*) Medieval Inst.

— Medieval Translators & Their Craft. (Studies in Medieval Culture: No. 25). 1988. boxed set 37.95 (*0-918720-95-8*) Medieval Inst.

— Medieval Translators & Their Craft. (Studies in Medieval Culture: No. 25). 1988. pap. 17.95 (*0-918720-96-6*) Medieval Inst.

Beer, Jeanette M. & Lloyd-Jones, Kenneth, eds. Translation & the Transmission of the Culture 1300-1600. LC 95-30225. (Studies in Medieval Culture: Vol. 35). 1995. pap. 18.00 (*1-879288-56-7*); boxed set 38.00 (*1-879288-55-9*) Medieval Inst.

Beer, Jennifer E. Mediator's Handbook (Neighborhoods) 4th rev. ed. Adams, Sandi et al, eds. (Illus.). 80p. 1995. reprint ed. pap. 12.00 (*0-941308-12-X*) Frnds Conflict Res Prog.

Beer, Jennifer E. & Stief, Eileen. The Mediator's Handbook. 3rd rev. ed. (Illus.). 176p. 1997. pap. 19.95 (*0-86571-359-6*) New Soc Pubs.

***Beer, Jeroen de.** Potential for Industrial Energy-Efficiency Improvement in the Long Term. LC 00-35746. (Eco-Efficiency in Industry & Science Ser.). 2000. write for info. (*0-7923-6282-9*) Kluwer Academic.

Beer, Johann. German Winter Nights. Russell, John, tr. LC 98-39707. (Studies in German Literature, Linguistics, & Culture). 270p. 1999. 50.00 (*1-57113-195-7*) Camden Hse.

— Samtliche Werke. Bratenwender, Kehrer et al, eds. (Mittlere Deutsche Literatur in Neu- und Nachdrucken Ser.: Bd. 6). 226p. 1997. 89.95 (*3-906755-98-3*, Pub. by P Lang) P Lang Pubng.

— Samtliche Werke, Bd. 6, Sonderausgabe. Bratenwender, Kehrer et al, eds. (Mittlere Deutsche Literatur in Neu- und Nachdrucken Ser.: Bd. 6). 226p. 1997. 89.95 (*3-906755-99-1*, Pub. by P Lang) P Lang Pubng.

Beer, John. Providence & Love: Studies in Wordsworth, Channing, Myers, George Eliot & Ruskin. LC 98-29841. (Illus.). 356p. 1999. text 80.00 (*0-19-818436-0*) OUP.

Beer, John, ed. Samuel Taylor Coleridge. (Everyman's Poetry Ser.). 116p. 1997. pap. 1.95 (*0-460-87826-3*, Everyman's Classic Lib) Tuttle Pubng.

Beer, John B. Against Finality: Inaugural Lecture, Delivered 4th February 1993. 48p. (C). 1994. pap. text 9.95 (*0-521-45954-0*) Cambridge U Pr.

— Blake's Visionary Universe. LC 72-455136. 394p. 1969. write for info. (*0-389-01093-6*) B&N Imports.

— Coleridge the Visionary. LC 78-2445. 367p. 1978. reprint ed. lib. bdg. 35.00 (*0-313-20360-1*, BECO, Greenwood Pr) Greenwood.

— The Emergence of the German Dye Industry. Cohen, I. Bernard, ed. LC 80-2115. (Development of Science Ser.). (Illus.). 1981. lib. bdg. 18.95 (*0-405-13835-0*) Ayer.

— Romantic Influences: Contemporary, Victorian, Modern. LC 93-29451. 256p. 1993. text 49.95 (*0-312-10639-4*) St Martin.

— Wordsworth & the Human Heart. LC 79-305199. 277 p. 1978. write for info. (*0-333-24104-5*) Macmillan.

Beer, John B., ed. The Collected Works of Samuel Taylor Coleridge: Aids of Reflection. (Bollingen Ser.: Vol. LXXV, No. 9). (Illus.). 950p. 1993. text 135.00 (*0-691-09876-X*, Pub. by Princeton U Pr) Cal Prin Full Svc.

— A Passage to India: Essays in Interpretation. LC 85-22947. 176p. 1985. 56.00 (*0-389-20601-6*, N8159) B&N Imports.

— Questioning Romanticism. LC 94-49331. 328p. 1995. text 48.50 (*0-8018-5052-5*); pap. text 18.95 (*0-8018-5053-3*) Johns Hopkins.

Beer, John B., ed. see Coleridge, Samuel Taylor.

Beer, John De, see Killen, Patricia O. & De Beer, John.

***Beer, Joop D. & Wissen, Leo V., eds.** Europe: One Continent, Different Worlds Population Scenarios for the 21st Century. LC 99-34299. (European Studies of Population). 208p. 1999. 100.00 (*0-7923-5840-6*) Kluwer Academic.

Beer, Joop de, see de Beer, Joop.

Beer, Lawre. Constitutional System - Asia. LC 91-5165. (Asian Law Ser.: No. 12). 752p. 1992. 75.00 (*0-295-97174-6*) U of Wash Pr.

Beer, Lawrence W. & Itoh, Hiroshi. The Constitutional Case Law of Japan, 1970 Through 1990. LC 96-10968. (Asian Law Ser.: Vol. 13). 704p. 1996. text 65.00 (*0-295-97549-0*) U of Wash Pr.

Beer, Lawrence W., jt. auth. see Itoh, Hiroshi.

Beer, Lisl, ed. Punch & Judy. (Silver Series of Puppet Plays). 1997. pap. 3.95 (*0-8283-1244-3*) Branden Bks.

— Second Shepherd's Play. (Silver Mosque Ser.). 1997. pap. 3.95 (*0-8283-1246-X*) Branden Bks.

Beer, Max. A History of British Socialism. 300p. 1984. 40.00 (*0-7855-2945-4*) St Mut.

— A History of British Socialism, 2 vols. Mayer, J. P., ed. LC 78-67332. (European Political Thought Ser.). 1979. reprint ed. lib. bdg. 61.95 (*0-405-11578-0*) Ayer.

Beer, Michael. Critical Path: Mobilizing Human Resources for Corporate Renewal. 300p. 1991. 29.95 (*0-07-103294-0*) McGraw.

***Beer, Michael & Nohria, Nitin.** Breaking the Code of Change. LC 00-25425. 2000. write for info. (*1-57851-331-6*) Harvard Busn.

Beer, michael & Spector, Bert A. Readings in Human Resource Management. LC 84-25977. 752p. 1985. pap. 24.95 (*0-02-902370-X*) Free Pr.

Beer, Michael, et al. The Critical Path to Corporate Renewal. 304p. 1990. 27.95 (*0-87584-239-9*) Harvard Busn.

***Beer, Nick.** Audio Hi-Fi Troubleshooting & Repair. 256p. 2000. pap. 39.95 (*0-7506-7242-0*) Buttrwrth-Heinemann.

— Newnes Guide to Audio & Hi-Fi: A Conprehensive Introduction to Audio & Hi-Fi Systems. 384p. 1999. pap. text 28.95 (*0-7506-4418-4*, Newnes) Buttrwrth-Heinemann.

Beer, Nick. Servicing Audio & Hi-Fi Equipment. 2nd rev. ed. LC 94-22230. (Illus.). 304p. 1995. text 56.95 (*0-7506-2117-6*) Buttrwrth-Heinemann.

— Servicing Satellite TV Equipment. LC 98-179275. 176p. 1998. text 56.95 (*0-7506-3425-1*, Newnes) Buttrwrth-Heinemann.

Beer, P., ed. Vistas in Astronomy, Vol. 26. (Illus.). 426p. 1985. 180.00 (*0-08-032314-6*, Pergamon Pr) Elsevier.

Beer, P., et al, eds. Longitude Zero, 1884 to 1984: Proceedings of an International Symposium held at the National Maritime Museum, Greenwich, London, 9-13 July 1984 to Mark the Centenary of the Adoption of the Greenwich Meridian. (Illus.). 408p. 1985. pap. 89.00 (*0-08-032726-5*, Pub. by PPL) Elsevier.

— Vistas in Astronomy, Vol. 27. (Illus.). 486p. 1986. write for info. (*0-685-01782-6*) Elsevier.

— Vistas in Astronomy, Vol. 27. (Illus.). 486p. 1986. 162.00 (*0-08-033235-8*, C150, Pub. by PPL) Elsevier.

— Vistas in Astronomy, Vol. 28. (Illus.). 650p. 1986. 162.00 (*0-08-034129-2*, Pub. by PPL) Elsevier.

Beer, P. & Beer, Albert C. Vistas in Astronomy, Vol. 23. 1980. 140.00 (*0-08-026046-2*, Pergamon Pr) Elsevier.

Beer, P. & Pounds, K., eds. Vistas in Astronomy, Vol. 25. (Illus.). 436p. 1984. 160.00 (*0-08-031042-7*, Pergamon Pr) Elsevier.

Beer, Patricia. Autumn. LC 98-117235. 56p. 1998. pap. 12.95 (*1-85754-331-9*, Pub. by Carcanet Pr) Paul & Co Pubs.

— Just Like the Resurrection: Poems. LC 67-11109. 1967. 15.95 (*0-8023-1131-8*) Dufour.

Beer, Peter, jt. ed. see Beer, Arthur.

Beer, Peter H. De, see Leonard, Robert J.

Beer, Peter H. De, see Leonard, Robert J. & De Beer, Peter H.

Beer, Peter H. De, see Leonard, Robert J.

Beer, Pieter De, see Braster, Patrick & De Beer, Pieter.

Beer-Poitevin, F. Diccionario Medico.Tr. of Medical Dictionary. (SPA.). 352p. 1979. 95.00 (*0-8288-4776-2*, S3751) Fr & Eur.

Beer-Poitevin, Frank. Enciclopedia Medica para la Familia Moderna, Vol. 1. (SPA.). 368p. 1985. pap. 125.00 (*0-7859-5030-3*) Fr & Eur.

— Enciclopedia Medica para la Familia Moderna, Vol. 2. (SPA.). 368p. 1985. pap. 125.00 (*0-7859-6397-9*, 8486452023) Fr & Eur.

— Enciclopedia Medica para la Familia Moderna, Vol. 3. (SPA.). 368p. 1985. pap. 125.00 (*0-7859-6398-7*, 8486452031) Fr & Eur.

***Beer, R., et al.** Endodontology: Color Atlas of Dental Medicine. LC 99-28377. (Illus.). 1999. write for info. (*0-86577-856-6*) Thieme Med Pubs.

Beer, Randall D. Intelligence As Adaptive Behavior: An Experiment in Computational Neuroethology. (Perspectives in Artificial Intelligence Ser.: Vol. 6). 213p. 1990. text 47.00 (*0-12-084730-2*) Acad Pr.

Beer, Randall D., et al, eds. Biological Neural Networks in Invertebrate Neuroethology & Robotics. (Neural Networks: Foundations to Applications Ser.). (Illus.). 417p. 1992. text 77.00 (*0-12-084728-0*) Acad Pr.

Beer, Reinhard. Remote Sensing by Fourier Transform Spectrometry. LC 91-33607. (Chemical Analysis: A Series of Monographs on Analytical Chemistry & Its Applications). 156p. 1992. 105.00 (*0-471-55346-8*) Wiley.

Beer, Richard L. & Field, Judith J. Michigan Legal Literature: An Annotated Guide. 2nd ed. LC 90-5205. 200p. 1991. pap. 27.50 (*1-57588-330-9*); lib. bdg. 37.50 (*0-89941-740-X*, 306390) W S Hein.

Beer, Robert. The Encyclopedia of Tibetan Symbols & Motifs. LC 98-19865. (Illus.). 400p. 1999. 60.00 (*1-57062-416-X*, Pub. by Shambhala Pubns) Random.

Beer, Samuel Hutchison. Britain Against Itself: The Political Contradictions of Collectivism. 256p. (C). 1982. pap. text 12.50 (*0-393-95288-6*) Norton.

— The National Idea & American Federalism. LC 92-12077. 1993. write for info. (*0-674-60212-9*) HUP.

— To Make a Nation: The Rediscovery of American Federalism. 496p. 1994. pap. text 18.95 (*0-674-89318-2*, BEEMAX) Belknap Pr.

— To Make a Nation: The Rediscovery of American Federalism. 496p. (C). 1993. text 29.95 (*0-674-89317-4*) HUP.

— Treasury Control: The Co-Ordination of Financial & Economic Policy in Great Britain. LC 82-11843. 138 p. 1982. write for info. (*0-313-23626-7*) Greenwood.

Beer, Samuel Hutchison, ed. see Marx, Karl & Engels, Friedrich.

Beer, Shane R. De, see De Beer, Shane R.

Beer, Stafford. Beyond Dispute: The Invention of Team Syntegrity. LC 94-2439. (Managerial Cybernetics of Organization Ser.). 380p. 1994. 115.95 (*0-471-94451-3*) Wiley.

— Brain of the Firm. LC 80-49979. (Stafford Beer Classic Library). 432p. 1995. pap. 89.95 (*0-471-94839-X*) Wiley.

— Decision & Control: The Meaning of Operational Research & Management Cybernetics. (Stafford Beer Classic Library). 568p. 1995. pap. 89.95 (*0-471-94838-1*) Wiley.

— Designing Freedom. LC 95-127450. (Stafford Beer Classic Library). 108p. 1995. pap. 89.95 (*0-471-95165-X*) Wiley.

— Diagnosing the System for Organizations. LC 66-25668. (Stafford Beer Classic Library). 178p. 1995. pap. 89.95 (*0-471-95136-6*) Wiley.

— The Heart of Enterprise. (Stafford Beer Classic Library). 596p. 1995. pap. 89.95 (*0-471-94837-3*) Wiley.

— The Heart of Enterprise. LC 79-40532. (Managerial Cybernetics of Organization Ser.: No. 2). (Illus.). 596p. reprint ed. pap. 184.80 (*0-608-18837-9*, 203048700069) Bks Demand.

— Platform for Change. LC 73-10741. (Stafford Beer Classic Library). 468p. 1995. pap. 89.95 (*0-471-94840-3*) Wiley.

Beer, Sylvan Z., ed. Liquid Metals: Chemistry & Physics. LC 78-157836. (Monographs & Textbooks in Material Science: No. 4). (Illus.). 743p. reprint ed. pap. 200.00 (*0-7837-0830-0*, 204114400019) Bks Demand.

Beer, T. Environmental Oceanography: An Introduction to the Behaviour of Coastal Waters. LC 82-18099. (PIL Ser.). (Illus.). 109p. 1983. text 126.00 (*0-08-026291-0*, Pub. by Pergamon Repr) Franklin.

Beer, T. Hydrological Tables. 1991. 222.00 (*1-85312-304-8*) Computational Mech MA.

— Meteorological Tables. 1990. 222.00 (*1-85312-305-6*) Computational Mech MA.

— Oceanographic Tables. 1989. 222.00 (*1-85312-306-4*) Computational Mech MA.

Beer, Thomas. Hanna. (History - United States Ser.). 325p. 1992. reprint ed. lib. bdg. 89.00 (*0-7812-6196-1*) Rprt Serv.

— The Mauve Decade. LC 97-17485. 272p. 1997. pap. 11.95 (*0-7867-0501-9*) Carroll & Graf.

— Stephen Crane: A Study in American Letters. (BCL1-PS American Literature Ser.). 248p. 1992. reprint ed. lib. bdg. 79.00 (*0-7812-6696-3*) Rprt Serv.

Beer, Tom. Applied Environmentrics Oceanographic Tables, 1989. 1991. 215.00 (*0-9590809-2-9*) CRC Pr.

— Applied Environmetrics Hydrological Tables. 1992. lib. bdg. 137.00 (*0-9590809-3-7*) CRC Pr.

— Applied Environmetrics Meteorological Tables, 1990. 1991. 215.00 (*0-9590809-1-0*) CRC Pr.

— Environmental Oceanography. 2nd ed. LC 96-18708. (Marine Science Ser.). 400p. 1996. boxed set 104.95 (*0-8493-8425-7*) CRC Pr.

Beer, Ulrich, et al. Delivering the Future Organization, Key Levers for Success: Corporate Sponsor Forum Proceedings, 1991. 192p. 1992. pap. 29.95 (*1-881115-00-3*) Human Res Plan.

***Beer, Valorie.** Web Learning Fieldbook: Using the World Wide Web to Build Workplace Learning Environments. LC 99-50487. 256p. 2000. pap. 39.95 (*0-7879-5023-8*, Pfffr & Co) Jossey-Bass.

Beer, Valorie, jt. auth. see Carr, Clay.

Beer, Walter. Methodische und Standortoekologische Untersuchungen Zum Naehrstoffumsatz Im Gruenland. (Dissertationes Botanicae Ser.: Band 242). (Illus.). vi, 216p. 1995. pap. 56.00 (*3-443-64154-7*, Pub. by Gebruder Borntraeger) Balogh.

Beer, William, tr. see Crozier, Michel.

Beer, William R. American Stepfamilies. 226p. (C). 1991. text 44.95 (*0-88738-436-6*) Transaction Pubs.

— Househusbands: Men & Housework in American Families. LC 82-12079. 153p. 1982. 52.95 (*0-275-91707-X*, C1707, Praeger Pubs) Greenwood.

Beer, William R., ed. Relative Strangers: Studies of Stepfamily Processes. LC 88-6697. 192p. (C). 1989. 52.00 (*0-8476-7570-X*) Rowman.

— Strangers in the House: The World of Stepsiblings & Half-Siblings. 276p. 1989. 34.95 (*0-88738-262-2*) Transaction Pubs.

Beerbohm, Max. Letters to Reggie Turner. Hart-Davis, Rupert, ed. LC 79-8052. reprint ed. 39.50 (*0-404-18362-X*) AMS Pr.

— Lytton Strachey. LC 74-7186. (English Literature Ser.: No. 33). 1974. lib. bdg. 75.00 (*0-8383-1936-X*) M S G Haskell Hse.

— Mainly on the Air. LC 72-287. (Essay Index Reprint Ser.). 1977. reprint ed. 19.95 (*0-8369-2785-0*) Ayer.

— Max Beerbohm: Collected Verse. Riewald, J. G., ed. & notes by. LC 93-36129. (Illus.). xxx, 222p. (C). 1994. lib. bdg. 42.50 (*0-208-02390-9*, Archon Bks) Shoe String.

— More. LC 67-28730. (Essay Index Reprint Ser.). 1977. 19.95 (*0-8369-0181-9*) Ayer.

— Observations. LC 71-163891. (English Literature Ser.: No. 33). 1971. reprint ed. lib. bdg. 75.00 (*0-8383-1249-7*) M S G Haskell Hse.

B

An Asterisk (*) at the beginning of an entry indicates that the title is appearing for the first time.

***Beerbohm, Max.** Seven Men. (Classics Ser.). 200p. 2000. pap. 12.95 (0-940322-54-4, Pub. by NY Rev Bks) Midpt Trade.
— Seven Men. (Twelve-Point Ser.). 130p. 2000. reprint ed. lib. bdg. 22.00 (1-58287-125-6) North Bks.
Beerbohm, Max. Works & More. LC 12-30603. 49.00 (0-403-00144-7) Scholarly.
— Works & More. 1988. reprint ed. lib. bdg. 79.00 (0-7812-0152-7) Rprt Serv.
— The Works of Max Beerbohm. 192p. 1985. reprint ed. lib. bdg. 39.00 (0-932051-90-1) Rprt Serv.
— Zuleika Dobson. 22.95 (0-8488-0914-9) Amereon Ltd.
— Zuleika Dobson. LC 98-19544. 1998. pap. 10.95 (0-375-75248-X) Random.
Beerbohm, Max, compiled by. Herbert Beerbohm Tree: Some Memories of Him & of Art. LC 75-91895. (Illus.). 1972. reprint ed. 24.95 (0-405-08251-7, Pub. by Blom Pubns) Ayer.
Beere, Carole A. Gender Roles: A Handbook of Tests & Measures. LC 89-17033. 592p. 1990. lib. bdg. 99.50 (0-313-26278-0, BHK/, Greenwood Pr) Greenwood.
— Sex & Gender Issues: A Handbook of Tests & Measures. LC 90-32466. 448p. 1990. lib. bdg. 105.00 (0-313-27462-2, BGC, Greenwood Pr) Greenwood.
— Women & Women's Issues: A Handbook of Tests & Measures. LC 79-88106. (Jossey-Bass Social & Behavioral Science Ser.). 568p. reprint ed. pap. 176.10 (0-8357-4815-4, 203775200009) Bks Demand.
***Beere, Joel R.** Gisbertus Voetius: Toward a Reformed Marriage of Knowledge & Piety. 36p. (Orig.). 1999. pap. 2.50 (1-892777-18-5) Reform Heritage Bks.
— Puritan Evangelism/A Biblical Approach. 52p. (Orig.). 1999. pap. 2.50 (1-892777-16-9) Reform Heritage Bks.
— A Reader's Guide to Reformed Literature: An Annotated Bibliography of Reformed Theology. 98p. 1998. pap. 4.50 (1-892777-15-0) Reform Heritage Bks.
***Beere, Joel R., ed.** Doctrinal Standards, Liturgy, & Church Order. 189p. (Orig.). 1999. pap. 3.50 (1-892777-17-7) Reform Heritage Bks.
***Beere, Ken.** The Bluffer's Guide to the Flight Deck: Bluff Your Way in the Flight Deck. (Bluffer's Guides Ser.). 64p. 1999. pap. 5.95 (1-902825-50-0) Oval Bks.
Beere, Peter. Kiss of Death. 176p. (YA). (gr. 7-9). 1995. pap. 3.50 (0-590-20372-X) Scholastic Inc.
— Kiss of Death. (Point Crime Ser.). 1994. 8.60 (0-606-07764-2, Pub. by Turtleback) Demco.
— School for Terror: Going to School Can Be Murder. 160p. (YA). (gr. 7-9). 1994. pap. 3.50 (0-590-48319-6) Scholastic Inc.
Beerel, Annabel. Lead Through Strategic Planning. LC 99-208034. (ITBP PROFESSIONAL). 320p. 1998. pap. 19.99 (1-86152-208-8) Thomson Learn.
Beerel, Annabel C. Expert Systems: Strategic Implications & Applications. 1987. text 43.95 (0-470-20974-7) P-H.
Beerel, Annabel C., jt. auth. see Barrett, Michael L.
***Beerens, Dan.** Evaluating Teachers for Professional Growth: Creating a Culture of Motivation & Learning. LC 99-6723. (One-Off Ser.). 184p. 1999. pap. 29.95 (0-7619-7567-5); lib. bdg. 69.95 (0-7619-7566-7) Corwin Pr.
Beeri, C., et al, eds. Third International Conference on Data & Knowledge Bases. 400p. 1988. pap. text 30.95 (0-934613-95-8) Morgan Kaufmann.
Beeri, C. Onal, ed. see Conference on Database Theory Staff, et al.
Beeri, Catriel, et al, eds. Database Programming Languages, DBPL-4: Proceedings of the Fourth International Workshop on Database Programming Languages, Manhattan, New York City, 30 August-1 September 1993. LC 93-45322. (Workshops in Computing Ser.). viii, 436p. 1994. 93.95 (0-387-19853-9) Spr-Verlag.
Beerman, Bob D. A View from the Stands - A Season with Bob the Beerman. LC 94-65390. 139p. 1994. pap. 9.95 (0-9640341-0-7) Successful Concepts.
Beerman, David R. 102 Questions Children Ask about the Bible. LC 93-41888. 208p. 1994. pap. 9.99 (0-8423-4570-1) Tyndale Hse.
Beerman, Dorothee, et al, eds. Rightward Movement. LC 97-38870. (Linguistik Aktuell/Linguistics Today Ser.: Vol. 17). vi, 410p. 1997. lib. bdg. 83.00 (1-55619-901-5) J Benjamins Pubng Co.
Beerman, Merlin. Steps to Christ Bible Study Guide. Nelson, Velda, ed. (Illus.). 96p. 1998. pap., student ed. 2.99 (0-9668482-0-9) Revelation Hymn.
Beermann, D. Quinolone Antibacterials. Kuhlmann, J. et al, eds. LC 97-455. (Handbook of Experimental Pharmacology Ser.: No. 127). (Illus.). 480p. 1997. 359.00 (3-540-62512-7) Spr-Verlag.
***Beermann, Jack M.** Administrative Law. (Aspen RoadMap Law Course Outline Ser.). 375p. 2000. pap. text 21.95 (0-7355-1246-9) Panel Pubs.
Beers. Writing Instructions in Elementary & Middle School. (C). 1993. 30.00 (0-205-14184-6, Macmillan Coll) P-H.
Beers, et al. The History of Brown County, Ohio: Biographical Sketches. 328p. 1996. pap. 27.00 (0-7884-0427-X, B123) Heritage Bk.
Beers, Alma, jt. auth. see Coker, William C.
Beers, Alma H., jt. auth. see Coker, William C.
Beers, B. J. FRANK - The Design of a New Landsurveying System Using Panoramic Images. (Illus.). xx, 137p. (Orig.). 1995. pap. 67.50 (90-407-1166-6, Pub. by Delft U Pr) Coronet Bks.
***Beers, Bob.** The Complete Color Guide to Aurora H. O. Slot Cars. (Illus.). 200p. 2000. pap. write for info. (0-9700213-0-5) A J Loring.
Beers, Bonnie & Gellerman, Denny. Come & Git It. LC 89-161287. (Illus.). 341p. (Orig.). reprint ed. pap. 13.95 (0-685-29806-X) B-D Pubns.
***Beers, Bonnie & Saunders-Smith, Gail.** Earth's Land & Water. LC 00-36503. (Illus.). (J). 2001. write for info. (0-7368-0737-3) Capstone Pr.
Beers, Burt, et al. Inside Secrets to Finding a Teaching Job. LC 97-8988. (Illus.). 200p. (Orig.). 1997. pap. 12.95 (1-57112-079-3, PO793) Park Ave.
Beers, Burton, jt. auth. see Clyde, Paul.
Beers, Burton F. Living in Africa, Southern Asia & the Pacific Realm. (J). (gr. k-12). 1997. text. write for info. (1-885647-28-X) NCSU Hum Ext.
— Living in North Carolina (Living in Our World) (J). (gr. k-12). 1997. text. write for info. (1-885647-27-1) NCSU Hum Ext.
— Vain Endeavor: Robert Lansing's Attempts to End the American-Japanese Rivalry. LC 61-16907. 219p. reprint ed. 67.90 (0-8357-9119-X, 201788400010) Bks Demand.
Beers, Clifford W. A Mind That Found Itself. 5th ed. LC 80-5256. (Contemporary Community Health Ser.). 228p. (C). 1981. reprint ed. pap. 15.95 (0-8229-5324-2) U of Pittsburgh Pr.
— A Mind That Found Itself: An Autobiography. (American Biography Ser.). 205p. 1991. reprint ed. lib. bdg. 69.00 (0-7812-8017-6) Rprt Serv.
Beers, D. G. Atlas of Northampton County, Pennsylvania. 56p. 1990. reprint ed. pap. 19.00 (1-877701-16-5) NCH&GS.
Beers, David. Blue Sky Dream. LC 97-25493. 1997. pap. 13.00 (0-15-600531-X) Harcourt.
Beers, Donald O. Generic & Innovator Drugs: A Guide to FDA Approval Requirements. 3rd ed. 1280p. 1992. ring bd. 136.00 (0-13-225111-6) Aspen Law.
— Generic & Innovator Drugs: A Guide to FDA Approval Requirements. 4th ed. LC 95-13937. 1995. ring bd. write for info. (0-614-05430-3) Aspen Law.
— Generic & Innovator Drugs: A Guide to FDA Approval Requirements. 4th ed. 1280p. 1995. 196.00 (1-56706-157-5) Panel Pubs.
— Generic & Innovator Drugs: A Guide to FDA Approval Requirements. 5th ed. LC 98-37519. 1998. boxed set 210.00 (0-7355-0281-1) Panel Pubs.
Beers, Fred G. The First Generation: A Half Century of Pioneering in Perry, Oklahoma. LC 91-61776. (Oklahoma Legacies Ser.). (Illus.). 384p. 1991. 19.95 (0-913507-22-9) New Forums.
Beers, G. Kylene, jt. ed. see Samuels, Barbara G.
Beers, Gilbert. It's Mine! The Muffin Family Learns about Sharing. (Illus.). 32p. (J). 1995. pap. 2.99 (1-56476-315-3, 6-3315, Victor Bks) Chariot Victor.
Beers, Gilbert V. The Busy Bee. LC 94-239639. (Muffin Family Ser.). (Illus.). 32p. (Orig.). (J). 1994. pap. 3.50 (1-56476-313-7, 6-3313, Victor Bks) Chariot Victor.
— It's Not Fair. LC 94-239563. (Muffin Family Ser.). (Illus.). 32p. (Orig.). (J). 1994. pap. 3.50 (1-56476-312-9, 6-3312, Victor Bks) Chariot Victor.
— The Lost Car. LC 94-239890. (Muffin Family Ser.). (Illus.). 32p. (Orig.). (J). 1994. pap. 3.50 (1-56476-314-5, 6-3314, Victor Bks) Chariot Victor.
— Precious Moments Through-the-Day Stories. LC 90-1265. (Precious Moments for Children Ser.). (Illus.). 256p. (J). (gr. k-7). 1991. pap. 12.99 (0-8010-4099-X) Baker Bks.
— Who Spilled That Stuff? The Muffin Family Learns about Forgiving. (J). 1995. pap. 2.99 (1-56476-316-1, 6-3316, Victor Bks) Chariot Victor.
Beers, Henry A. Connecticut Wits, & Other Essays. LC 70-153303. reprint ed. 24.50 (0-404-04643-6) AMS Pr.
— The Connecticut Wits & Other Essays. (BCL1-PR English Literature Ser.). 262p. 1992. reprint ed. lib. bdg. 79.00 (0-7812-7006-5) Rprt Serv.
— Four Americans. LC 68-54324. (Essay Index Reprint Ser.). 1977. 16.95 (0-8369-0182-7) Ayer.
— History of English Romanticism in the Eighteenth Century. LC 66-29374. 464p. 1966. reprint ed. 75.00 (0-87752-006-2) Gordian.
— Milton's Tercentenary. LC 73-39421. reprint ed. 19.50 (0-404-00725-2) AMS Pr.
— Nathaniel Parker Willis. LC 70-89458. (BCL Ser. I). reprint ed. 24.50 (0-404-00726-0) AMS Pr.
— Nathaniel Parker Willis. (BCL1-PS American Literature Ser.). 365p. 1992. reprint ed. lib. bdg. 89.00 (0-7812-6906-7) Rprt Serv.
— Points at Issue, & Some Other Points. LC 67-22055. (Essay Index Reprint Ser.). 1977. 19.95 (0-8369-0183-5) Ayer.
Beers, Henry A., ed. see Willis, Nathaniel P.
Beers, Henry P. The Confederacy: Guide to the Archives of the Government of the Confederate States of America. LC 86-8362. 536p. 1986. reprint ed. text 25.00 (0-911333-18-5, 100010) National Archives & Recs.
— The French & British in the Old Northwest: A Bibliographical Guide to Archive & Manuscript Sources. LC 64-13305. 308p. reprint ed. pap. 95.50 (0-608-16595-6, 202767400055) Bks Demand.
— French & Spanish Records of Louisiana: A Bibliographical Guide to Archive & Manuscript Sources. LC 88-13619. 368p. 1989. text 50.00 (0-8071-1444-8) La State U Pr.
— Spanish & Mexican Records of the American Southwest: A Bibliographical Guide to Archive & Manuscript Sources. fac. ed. LC 79-4313. 507p. reprint ed. pap. 157.20 (0-7837-6956-3, 204690600003) Bks Demand.
— The Western Military Frontier, 1815-1846. LC 75-25798. (Perspectives in American History Ser.: No. 35). (Illus.). vi, 227p. 1975. reprint ed. lib. bdg. 35.00 (0-87991-359-2) Porcupine Pr.
Beers, Henry P., jt. auth. see Munden, Kenneth W.
Beers, Howard W. Indonesia: Resources & Their Technological Development. LC 78-111503. 288p. reprint ed. 89.30 (0-8357-9786-4, 201351500086) Bks Demand.
Beers, James, jt. auth. see Ward-Beech, Linda.
Beers, Joan, ed. Campus Vacations Directory. 4th rev. ed. 45p. 1989. pap. 10.75 (0-317-93127-X) Campus Vacations.
Beers, Kylene & Samuels, Barbara G., eds. Into Focus: Understanding & Creating Middle School Readers. LC 98-106187. (Illus.). 502p. (YA). (gr. 5-9). 1998. pap. text 49.95 (0-926842-64-1) CG Pubs Inc.
Beers, Larry. The Right Angle Countertop. 13p. (YA). (gr. 10 up). 1987. pap., wbk. ed. 7.00 (0-8064-1409-X, W30) Bergwall.
Beers, Leland. Towpath Topsy: The Story of the Ohio Canal at Dresden. Jones, Proctor, ed. & intro. by. LC 94-78060. 260p. (Orig.). (YA). 1994. pap. 9.95 (1-885446-00-4) Proctor Jones.
Beers, P. & Murdin, P., eds. The Observatories of the Canaries: On the Occasion of Their Inauguration, June 28-29, 1985. (Illus.). 168p. 1985. pap. 44.00 (0-08-033676-0, C150, Pub. by PPL) Elsevier.
Beers, Paul B. Pennsylvania Politics Today & Yesterday: The Tolerable Accommodation. LC 79-65826. (Keystone Bks.). (Illus.). 416p. (C). 1980. 45.00 (0-271-00238-7) Pa St U Pr.
***Beers, Paul B., et al.** Supramolecular Chemistry. LC 99-10286. 74. (Illus.). 96p. 1999. pap. text 12.95 (0-19-850447-0) OUP.
Beers, Portia. Encyclopedie de la Femme, 4: Comment Plaire aux Hommes. (ENG & FRE.). 144p. 1974. 29.95 (0-8288-6038-6, M6026) Fr & Eur.
Beers, Red. How to Catch! Sand Bass, Stripers & Hybrids on Lake Lewisville. 130p. 1993. pap. 12.95 (0-9636622-5-2) Catch All Pub.
Beers, Roland F., Jr., et al, eds. Molecular & Cellular Repair Processes Johns Hopkins Medical Journal Supplement, No. 1. LC 78-184199. (Miles International Symposia on Molecular Biology Ser.). 287p. (C). reprint ed. 89.00 (0-8357-9278-1, 201568500095) Bks Demand.
Beers, Roland F. & Basset, Edward, eds. The Role of Immunological Factors in Infectious, Allergic, & Autoimmune Processes. LC 75-25109. (Miles International Symposium Ser.: No. 8). (Illus.). 556p. 1976. reprint ed. pap. 172.40 (0-608-00630-0, 206121800007) Bks Demand.
Beers, Roland F., Jr. & Bassett, Edward G., eds. Cell Fusion: Gene Transfer & Transformation. LC 83-20194. (Miles International Symposium Ser.: No. 14). (Illus.). 437p. 1984. reprint ed. pap. 135.50 (0-608-00584-3, 206117100007) Bks Demand.
— Mechanisms of Pain & Analgesic Compounds. fac. ed. LC 78-52524. (Miles International Symposium Ser.: No. 11). (Illus.). 510p. pap. 158.10 (0-7837-7500-8, 204700600005) Bks Demand.
— Polypeptide Hormones. LC 79-66512. (Miles International Symposium Ser.: No. 12). (Illus.). 544p. 1980. reprint ed. pap. 168.70 (0-608-00591-6, 206117800007) Bks Demand.
— Recombinant Molecules: Impact on Science & Society. fac. ed. LC 76-5675. (Miles International Symposium Ser.: No. 10). (Illus.). 554p. pap. 171.80 (0-7837-7512-1, 204699300005) Bks Demand.
Beers, Ronald A., jt. auth. see Beers, V. Gilbert.
Beers, Sue R., jt. ed. see Goldstein, Gerald.
Beers, Susan E., ed. see Salem Press Editors.
Beers, Susan-Jane. Jamu: The Ancient Art of Herbal Healing. 1999. pap. text 19.95 (962-593-503-7) Periplus.
Beers, Terry. A Thousand Graceful Subtleties: Rhetoric in the Poetry of Robinson Jeffers. LC 94-21930. Vol. 3. XIII, 113p. (C). 1995. text 38.95 (0-8204-2592-3) P Lang Pubng.
***Beers, Terry, ed.** Unfolding Beauty: Celebrating California's Landscapes. (California Legacy Ser.). 452p. 2000. pap. 17.95 (1-890771-34-1) Heyday Bks.
Beers, Todd, ed. Waiting Room: Writing by Children & Adult Patients in a Hospital Setting. (Illus.). 64p. (Orig.). 1991. pap. 5.95 (0-9618487-2-3) Writers & Bks.
Beers, V. Gilbert. ABC: Learn about Letters from 5 Bible Stories. (J). 1995. 9.99 incl. VHS (89-00-88140-X, Victor Bks) Chariot Victor.
Beers, V Gilbert. Baby Jesus. 1999. bds. 3.99 (0-7814-3335-5) Chariot Victor.
Beers, V. Gilbert. A Birthday Gift for Mommi. LC 94-239548. (Muffin Family Ser.). (Illus.). 32p. (Orig.). (J). 1994. pap. 3.50 (1-56476-311-0, 6-3311, Victor Bks) Chariot Victor.
Beers, V Gilbert. David Fights a Giant. 1999. 3.99 (0-7814-3336-3) Chariot Victor.
Beers, V. Gilbert. The Early Reader's Big Book of Bible Learning. LC 96-109269. (Illus.). 528p. (J). 1995. 12.99 (0-88070-774-7, Gold n Honey) Zondervan.
— Finding Purpose from Your Pain. LC 97-44748. 160p. 1998. mass mkt. 5.99 (0-8007-8649-1, Spire) Revell.
— God's Little Devotional for Kids. (God's Little Devotional Bks.). 160p. (J). (gr. 1-6). 1997. 12.99 (1-56292-362-5) Honor Bks OK.
— Jesus & Me: Five-Minute Virtues to Grow On. LC 97-42560. (Illus.). 64p. (J). (gr. 1-5). 1998. 10.99 (1-56507-926-4) Harvest Hse.
— My Picture Reading Bible to See & Share. (Illus.). 384p. (J). 1994. 15.99 (1-56476-297-1, 6-3297, Victor Bks) Chariot Victor.
— Noah Builds a Big Boat. 1999. 3.99 (0-7814-3334-7) Chariot Victor.
— 1-2-3: Learn about Counting with Noah & Other Friends. (J). 1995. VHS 9.99 (89-00-88056-X, Victor Bks) Chariot Victor.
***Beers, V. Gilbert.** Pequeno Libro Devocional de Dios Para Ninos. (SPA.). (J). (gr. 4-7). 2000. 10.99 (0-7899-0718-6) Spanish Hse Distributors.
Beers, V. Gilbert. Precious Moments Storybook Collection: Stories That Celebrate Everyday Joys. (Illus.). 416p. (J). 1997. 19.99 (0-88486-182-1, Inspirational Pr) Arrowood Pr.
— Preschooler's Bible Paint with Water. (Preschoolers Bible Ser.). (J). 1995. pap. 2.99 (1-56476-531-8, 6-3531, Victor Bks) Chariot Victor.
— Preschooler's Bible Sticker Book. (Preschoolers Bible Ser.). (J). 1995. pap. 2.99 (1-56476-530-X, 6-3530, Victor Bks) Chariot Victor.
— Preschooler's Family Story. (Preschoolers Bible Ser.). 256p. (J). 1995. 16.99 (1-56476-492-3, 6-3492, Victor Bks) Chariot Victor.
— Step by Step Bible Story: God's Word in One Sweeping Narrative for Children. LC 99-35209. 1999. write for info. (0-7814-3307-X) Chariot Victor.
— Teaching Toddlers the Bible. LC 93-19696. (Toddlers Ser.). (Illus.). 120p. 1993. pap. 5.99 (1-56476-155-X, 6-3155, Victor Bks) Chariot Victor.
— Toddler SingAlong Time. (J). 1995. 14.99 (89-00-88168-X, 3-1230, Victor Bks) Chariot Victor.
— The Toddlers Bedtime Storybook. (Toddlers Ser.). (Illus.). 352p. (J). (ps). 1993. 15.99 (1-56476-181-9, 6-3181, Victor Bks) Chariot Victor.
— Toddler's Bible Coloring Book: New Testament. (Toddlers Ser.). (Illus.). 48p. (Orig.). (J). 1994. pap. 2.50 (1-56476-302-1, 6-3302, Victor Bks) Chariot Victor.
— Toddler's Bible Coloring Book: Old Testament. (Toddlers Ser.). (Illus.). 48p. (Orig.). (J). 1994. pap. 2.50 (1-56476-301-3, 6-3301, Victor Bks) Chariot Victor.
— Toddlers Bible Easter Book. 32p. (J). 1995. 5.99 (1-56476-526-1, 6-3526, Victor Bks) Chariot Victor.
— Toddler's Bible Paint with Water. (Illus.). (J). 1995. pap. 4.99 (1-56476-529-6, 6-3529, Victor Bks) Chariot Victor.
— Toddlers Bible Sticker Book. (Illus.). (J). (ps). 1995. pap. 4.99 (1-56476-528-8, 6-3528, Victor Bks) Chariot Victor.
— Toddlers Book of Prayers. 96p. (J). 1996. 7.99 (1-56476-557-1, 6-3557, Victor Bks) Chariot Victor.
— Toddlers Christmas Book. (Toddlers Ser.). (Illus.). 32p. (J). (ps). 1995. 5.99 (1-56476-527-X, 6-3527, Victor Bks) Chariot Victor.
— Toddlers Devotions. 1998. 16.99 (0-7814-3063-1) Chariot Victor.
— The Toddler's First Songbook. (Toddlers Bible Video Ser.). 168p. (J). 1994. 16.99 incl. audio (1-56476-300-5, 6-3300, Victor Bks) Chariot Victor.
— Toddler's Home Learning Kit. (Toddlers Bible Video Ser.). 1995. 79.99 Chariot Victor.
— Toddlers Tiny Bible. 96p. (J). 1996. 7.99 (1-56476-556-3, 6-3556, Victor Bks) Chariot Victor.
— Toddy Bear's Good Food Book. LC 95-142723. (Toddy Bear Bks.). (Illus.). 24p. (J). 1994. 5.99 (1-56476-165-7, 6-3165, Victor Bks) Chariot Victor.
— Toddy Bear's Good Morning Book. (Toddy Bear Bks.). (Illus.). 24p. (J). 1994. 5.99 (1-56476-166-5, 6-3166, Victor Bks) Chariot Victor.
— Toddy Bear's One-Two-Three Counting Book. (Toddy Bear Bks.). (Illus.). 24p. (J). 1994. 5.99 (1-56476-167-3, 6-3167, Victor Bks) Chariot Victor.
— Toddy Bear's Tall & Short Book. (Toddy Bear Bks.). (Illus.). 24p. (J). 1994. 5.99 (1-56476-168-1, 6-3168, Victor Bks) Chariot Victor.
— The Victor Journey Through the Bible. LC 95-48853. 416p. 1996. 34.99 (1-56476-480-X, 63480, Victor Bks) Chariot Victor.
Beers, V. Gilbert, retold by. The PreSchooler's Bible. LC 94-211236. (Illus.). 432p. (J). (ps-k). 1994. 17.99 (1-56476-317-X, 6-3317, Victor Bks) Chariot Victor.
Beers, V. Gilbert & Beers, Ronald A. Big Book of All-Time Favorite Bible Stories: 150 Great Stories for Little People. (Illus.). 324p. (J). 1997. 9.99 (0-88486-183-X, Inspirational Pr) Arrowood Pr.
— Choosing God's Way to See & Share. (J). 1983. 14.99 (0-88207-819-4, Victor Bks) Chariot Victor.
— Little People in Tough Spots: Bible Answers for Young Children. (Illus.). 154p. (J). (ps-3). 1992. 7.99 (0-8407-9157-7) Nelson.
Beers, W. H., & Co. Staff. The History of Brown County, Ohio. (Illus.). 534p. 1995. reprint ed. pap. 33.50 (0-7884-0271-4) Heritage Bk.
— The History of Union County, Ohio. LC 96-222802. (Illus.). 1417p. 1996. reprint ed. pap. 107.50 (0-7884-0534-9, B121) Heritage Bk.
— The History of Warren County, Ohio. abr. ed. (Illus.). 940p. 1994. reprint ed. pap. 52.00 (1-55613-978-0) Heritage Bk.
Beers, William. Women & Sacrifice: Male Narcissism & the Psychology of Religion. LC 92-13007. 214p. (C). 1992. 28.95 (0-8143-2377-4) Wayne St U Pr.
Beersmans, F. Langenscheidts Euroworterbucher: Niederlandisch. 1997. pap. write for info. (3-468-12230-6) Langenscheidt.
Beersmans, F. Universal Dutch/German/Dutch Pocket Edition. 4th ed. (GER & DUT.). 432p. 1995. 29.95 (0-320-01024-4) Fr & Eur.
Beerworth, Ellen E. Contemporary Issues in Product Liability Law. 122p. 1991. pap. 37.50 (1-86287-048-9, Pub. by Federation Pr) Gaunt.
— Product Liability. 220p. 1989. pap. 48.00 (1-86287-011-X, Pub. by Federation Pr) Gaunt.
Beery, Gladys B. Sinners & Saints: Tales of Old Laramie City. LC 93-38315. 280p. (Orig.). 1993. pap. 12.95 (0-931271-23-1) Hi Plains Pr.
Beery, Mike. Readings on Modern American Social Issues. 128p. (C). 1996. pap. text, per. 23.95 (0-7872-2696-3, 41269601) Kendall-Hunt.
Beery, T. Prentice Hall Handbook for Writers Basic Workbook. 12th ed. 1994. pap. text, wbk. ed. 26.60 (0-13-149154-7) P-H.
Bees, N. A. Chronicon Monembasiae. 50p. 1979. 12.50 (0-89005-279-4) Ares.
— Corpus der Griechisch Christlichen Inschriften von Hellas. 1978. 30.00 (0-89005-238-7) Ares.
Bees, William J., ed. Design Analysis, Robust Methods, & Stress Classification. (PVP Ser.: Vol. 265). 344p. 1993. 70.00 (0-7918-0992-7, H00824) ASME.

Bees, William J., et al, eds. Approximate Methods in the Design & Analysis of Pressure Vessels & Piping Components, 1997: Proceedings ASME Pressure Vessels & Piping Conference (1997, Orlando, FL) LC 97-72851. 267p. 1997. pap. 112.00 (0-7918-1563-3) ASME.
— Developments in a Progressing Technology: Proceedings, 1994. LC 94-71578. (PVP Ser.: Vol. 279). 189p. 1995. pap. 50.00 (0-7918-1352-5) ASME Pr.
Bees, William J., ed. see Newaz, Golam M.
Beesch, Ruth K. Florida Visionaries, 1870-1930. (Illus.). 68p. 1989. pap. 13.95 (0-8130-0929-4) U Press Fla.
Beesch, Ruth K. & Murray, Mary E. Height x Length x Width: Contemporary Sculpture from the Weatherspoon Collection. (Illus.). 32p. 1991. pap. text 10.00 (0-9627541-1-0) UNC Greensboro.
Beesch, Ruth K., et al. Changing Perceptions: The Evolution of Twentieth Century American Art. (Illus.). 112p. (C). 1990. per. 15.00 (0-9627541-0-2) UNC Greensboro.
Beesch, Ruth K., ed. see Henry, Gerrit.
Beesch, Ruth K., ed. see Richardson, Trevor.
Beese, Gerhard, jt. auth. see Lotschert, Wilhelm.
Beese, Gerhard, jt. auth. see Lotschert, William.
Beese, T. J. & Hamilton, Todd C. The Guardsman. 1988. pap. 2.95 (0-517-00665-0) Random Hse Value.
Beesing, Maria, et al. The Enneagram: A Journey of Self Discovery. 1984. pap. 14.95 (0-87193-214-8) Dimension Bks.
Beesley. Chiral Chromotography. LC 98-50612. 506p. 1999. 210.00 (0-471-97427-7) Wiley.
***Beesley, Amanda.** Something New: Reflections on the Beginnings of a Marriage. LC 99-40425. 192p. 2000. 21.95 (0-385-49905-1) Doubleday.
Beesley, Amanda, jt. auth. see Bayone, Jeff.
Beesley, John. Verse on Understanding. 68p. 1987. boxed set 25.00 (0-7223-2078-7, Pub. by A H S Ltd) St Mut.
***Beesley, Julian E.** Immunocytochemistry & In-Situ Hybridization in the Biomedical Sciences. (Illus.). 264p. 1999. 69.95 (0-8176-4065-7, Pub. by Birkhauser) Spr-Verlag.
Beesley, Julian E., ed. Immunocytochemistry: A Practical Approach. LC 92-48716. (Practical Approach Ser.). (Illus.). 266p. (C). 1993. pap. text 45.00 (0-19-963269-3); spiral bd. 75.00 (0-19-963270-7) OUP.
Beesley, Lawrence. Loss of the S. S. Titanic. Date not set. 24.95 (0-8488-2190-4) Amereon Ltd.
***Beesley, Lawrence.** The Loss of the S. S. Titanic: Its Story & Its Lessons. LC 99-462121. (Illus.). 224p. 2000. pap. 13.00 (0-618-05531-2) HM.
Beesley, M. E. Privatization Regulation & Deregulation. 2nd ed. 480p. (C). 1997. pap. 29.99 (0-415-16453-2) Routledge.
Beesley, M. E., ed. Regulating Utilities: Broadening the Debate. (IEA Reading Ser.: No. 46). 312p. 1997. pap. 47.50 (0-255-36406-7, Pub. by Inst Economic Affairs) Coronet Bks.
Beesley, M. E., et al, eds. Regulating Utilities: The Way Forward. (IEA Readings Ser.: No. 41). 160p. 1994. pap. 41.50 (0-255-36337-0, Pub. by Inst Economic Affairs) Coronet Bks.
Beesley, M. E., et al. Britain in the Common Market: A New Business Opportunity. LC 73-86106. xii, 298 p. 1974. 14.00 (0-582-44308-3) Longman.
Beesley, M. E., et al. Markets & the Media: Competition, Regulation & the Interests of Consumers. (IEA Readings Ser.: No. 43). 146p. 1996. pap. 37.50 (0-255-36378-8, Pub. by Inst Economic Affairs) Coronet Bks.
Beesley, Michael. Privatization Regulation & Deregulation. 2nd ed. 480p. (C). 1997. 100.00 (0-415-16452-4) Routledge.
Beesley, Ronald P. The Creative Ethers. 1978. reprint ed. pap. 4.95 (0-87516-268-1) DeVorss.
— Yoga of the Inward Path. 1978. reprint ed. pap. 5.95 (0-87516-269-X) DeVorss.
Beesley, Stanley W. Vietnam: The Heartland Remembers. 208p. 1987. 21.95 (0-8061-2062-2) U of Okla Pr.
Beesley, Ted. Guild Guitars: Guitar History, Vol. 5. (Illus.). 180p. 1997. pap. 19.95 (0-933224-78-8, T305) Bold Strummer Ltd.
Beesley, Terrece. Fabric Mosaics. LC 98-49857. 1999. pap. text 21.95 (1-56477-267-5, Fiber Studio Pr) Martingale & Co.
Beesley, Terrece & Boerens, Trice. Applique for Baby: 20 Charming Projects for the Nursery. LC 99-35377. (Illus.). 128p. 1999. pap. 26.95 (1-56477-283-7) Martingale & Co.
— Garden Applique. LC 99-22867. (Illus.). 128p. 1999. pap. 26.95 (1-56477-292-6, B404) Martingale & Co.
***Beesley, Terrece & Boerens, Trice.** Your Family Heritage: Projects in Applique. (Illus.). 96p. 2000. pap. 24.99 (1-56477-308-6, B446, Pub. by Martingale & Co) F & W Pubns Inc.
Beesley, Terrece, jt. auth. see Boerens, Trice.
Beesly, Edward S. Queen Elizabeth. LC 74-39408. (Select Bibliographies Reprint Ser.). 1977. reprint ed. 18.95 (0-8369-9901-0) Ayer.
***Beesly, Patrick.** Very Special Intelligence: The Story of the Admiralty's Operational Centre, 1939-1945. 2000. 34.95 (1-85367-398-6) Greenhill Bks.
Beeson, jt. auth. see Plante.
Beeson, Bob. Ten Little Circus Mice. (Illus.). 32p. (J). (ps-1). 1993. 11.95 (0-8249-8616-4, Ideals Child) Hambleton-Hill.
— What Time Is It, Mr. Wolf? (Illus.). 32p. (J). (ps-1). 1994. 12.95 (0-8249-8649-0, Ideals Child) Hambleton-Hill.
Beeson, Bob, jt. auth. see Dalton, Sheila.
Beeson, Charles H. A Primer of Medieval Latin: An Anthology of Prose & Poetry. LC 86-8301. 390p. (C). 1986. reprint ed. pap. 14.95 (0-8132-0635-9) Cath U Pr.
Beeson, Colin R. The Glider Pilot War at Home & Overseas. 263p. (Orig.). 1978. pap. 40.00 (0-89126-063-3) MA-AH Pub.
Beeson, D. R. In the Spirit of Adventure: A Hike in the Great Smoky Mountains. Maynard, Charles W. et al, eds. 110p. 1994. text 12.95 (0-9630682-8-8); pap. text 7.95 (0-9630682-7-X) Panther TN.
— In the Spirit of Adventure: A Mount Mitchell Hiking Journal. Maynard, Charles W. et al, eds. 112p. 1995. text 12.95 (1-887205-01-2); pap. text 7.95 (1-887205-00-4) Panther TN.
— In the Spirit of Adventure: A 1913 Roan & Grandfather Mountain Hiking Journal. Maynard, Charles et al, eds. 112p. Date not set. 12.95 (1-887205-03-9); pap. 7.95 (1-887205-02-0) Panther TN.
— In the Spirit of Adventure: A 1914 Table Rock Mountain Hiking Journal. Maynard, Charles et al, eds. 112p. Date not set. pap. 7.95 (1-887205-04-7); text 12.95 (1-887205-05-5) Panther TN.
***Beeson, Dan L.** Assembling & Repairing Personal Computers. 2nd ed. LC 98-50976. (Illus.). 458p. 1999. pap. text 87.00 incl. disk (0-13-081949-2) P-H.
Beeson, David, ed. see Philippot, Patrick.
***Beeson, Diane & Stempel, Carl.** Sex, Gender & Intimacy: Selected Readings. 402p. (C). 1999. pap. text 41.95 (0-7872-5889-X, 41588901) Kendall-Hunt.
***Beeson, Harold Deck, et al, eds.** Safe Use of Oxygen & Oxygen Systems: Guidelines of Oxygen System Design, Materials Selection, Operations, Storage & Transportation. LC 99-54559. (Manual Ser.). (Illus.). 106p. 1999. pap. 54.00 (0-8031-2083-4, MNL36) ASTM.
Beeson, Jasper L. Beeson Genealogy. 144p. 1994. reprint ed. pap. 25.00 (0-8328-4196-X); reprint ed. lib. bdg. 35.00 (0-8328-4195-1) Higginson Bk Co.
Beeson, John. John Beeson's Plea for the Indians, His Lone Cry in the Wilderness for Indian Rights: Oregon's First Civil Rights Advocate. LC 94-8879. (Illus.). 176p. 1994. pap. 12.95 (0-936738-80-4) Webb Research.
***Beeson, John.** A Plea for the Indians. (Illus.). 149p. 1998. pap. 11.95 (0-87770-676-X) Ye Galleon.
Beeson, Kenneth C. & Matrone, Gennard. The Soil Factor in Nutrition: Animal & Human. LC 76-18421. (Nutrition & Clinical Nutrition Ser.: No. 2). 168p. reprint ed. pap. 52.10 (0-7837-0702-9, 204103400019) Bks Demand.
Beeson, M. Foundations of Constructive Mathematics. (Ergebnisse der Mathematik Ser.: Vol. 6). 480p. 1985. 179.95 (0-387-12173-0) Spr-Verlag.
Beeson, Margaret, et al. Hispanic Writers in French Journals: An Annotated Bibliography. LC 77-93922. (SSSAS Bibliographies Ser.: No. 102). 155p. 1978. pap. 25.00 (0-89295-002-1) Society Sp & Sp-Am.
Beeson, Margaret E., tr. see Hernandez, Ramon.
Beeson, Richard D. & Crutcher, Ernest R. Hardware Cleaning & Sampling for Cleanliness Verification & Contamination Control Microscopy. LC 61-38584. 34p. 1983. pap. text 60.00 (0-915414-72-4) IEST.
Beeson, Steve, jt. auth. see Wyckoff, Susan.
***Beeson, Trevor.** Rebels & Reformers. 1998. pap. 23.00 (0-334-02792-6) TPI PA.
Beeson, W. & Tobin, H., eds. Developing a Practice in Ambulatory Surgery. (American Academy of Facial Plastic & Reconstructive Surgery Monograph). (Illus.). 320p. 1993. pap. text 92.00 (0-86577-412-9) Thieme Med Pubs.
Beestman, G. B. & Vander Hooven, D. I., eds. Pesticide Formulations & Application Systems, Vol. 7. LC 87-14461. (Special Technical Publication Ser.: No. 968). (Illus.). 275p. 1987. text 39.00 (0-8031-0970-9, STP968) ASTM.
Beeston, ed. see al-Jahiz.
Beeston, Alfred F. Arabic Historical Phraseology: Supplement to Written Arabic: an Approach to the Basic Structures. LC 68-18342. 150p. reprint ed. pap. 42.80 (0-8357-5705-6, 2022439) Bks Demand.
— Dictionnaire Sabeen, Vol. 3.Tr. of Anglais-Francais-Arabe. (ARA, ENG & FRE.). 173p. 1985. pap. 125.00 (0-8288-1448-1, F1940) Fr & Eur.
— Sabaic Dictionary: English-French-Arabic Dictionary. (ARA, ENG & FRE.). 183p. 1982. 22.00 (0-86685-359-6, LDL3596, Pub. by Librairie du Liban) Intl Bk Ctr.
— Written Arabic: An Approach to the Basic Structures. 124p. (Orig.). (C). 1968. pap. text 23.95 (0-521-09559-X) Cambridge U Pr.
Beeston, Alfred F., et al, eds. Arabic Literature to the End of the Umayyad Period. LC 82-23528. (Cambridge History of Arabic Literature Ser.). (Illus.). 576p. 1984. text 125.00 (0-521-24015-8) Cambridge U Pr.
Beeston, Blanche. The Way of the Levites. 186p. 1989. pap. text 7.95 (0-9616488-6-4) Alef Bet Comns.
***Beeston, John.** The Wine Regions of Australia. (Illus.). 544p. 2000. 50.00 (1-86448-641-4, Pub. by Allen & Unwin Pty) IPG Chicago.
Beeston, Richard. Looking for Trouble: The Life & Times of a Foreign Correspondent. LC 97-12843. (Illus.). 178p. 1997. 42.50 (1-85753-251-1, Pub. by Brasseys) Brasseys.
Beet, J. Agar. Ephesians, Philippians, Colossians & Philemon. pap. 12.99 (0-88019-058-2) Schmul Pub Co.
— First Corinthians. 1988. pap. 13.99 (0-88019-240-2) Schmul Pub Co.
— Galatians. 1981. pap. 11.99 (0-88019-030-2) Schmul Pub Co.
— Holiness As Understood by the Writers of the Bible. pap. 3.99 (0-88019-174-0) Schmul Pub Co.
— Second Corinthians. 1989. pap. 13.99 (0-88019-242-9) Schmul Pub Co.
Beet, S. W., jt. auth. see Cooke, M.
***Beeteson, J. S.** Visualising Magnetic Fields. 120p. 1999. boxed set 80.00 incl. disk (1-898326-70-3, Pub. by CISP) Balogh.
Beeth, Howard & Wintz, Cary D., eds. Black Dixie: Afro-Texan History & Culture in Houston. LC 91-39257. (Centennial Series of the Association of Former Students: No. 41). 312p. 1992. 49.95 (0-89096-494-7) Tex A&M Univ Pr.
Beetham, David. Bureaucracy. Parkin, Frank, ed. (Concepts in the Social Sciences Ser.). 132p. 1996. 9.00 (0-335-19655-1) OpUniv Pr.
— Bureaucracy. Parkin, Frank, ed. (Concepts in the Social Sciences Ser.). (Illus.). 132p. 1996. pap. 2.00 (0-335-19654-3) OpUniv Pr.
— Bureaucracy. 2nd rev. ed. (Concepts in Social Thought Ser.). 120p. 1996. pap. 14.95 (0-8166-2939-0); text 37.95 (0-8166-2938-2) U of Minn Pr.
— Democracy & Human Rights. LC 98-52192. 250p. (C). 1999. text 62.95 (0-7456-1108-7, Pub. by Polity Pr); pap. text 29.95 (0-7456-2315-8, Pub. by Polity Pr) Blackwell Pubs.
Beetham, David, ed. Defining & Measuring Democracy. (Sage Modern Politics Ser.: Vol. 36). 224p. 1995. 69.95 (0-8039-7788-3); pap. 29.95 (0-8039-7789-1) Sage.
Beetham, David & Boyle, Kevin. Introducing Democracy: Eighty Questions & Answers. (Illus.). 150p. (C). 1995. text 39.95 (0-7456-1519-8, Pub. by Polity Pr); pap. text 17.95 (0-7456-1520-1, Pub. by Polity Pr) Blackwell Pubs.
Beetham, Donald W., jt. ed. see Walker, Sandra C.
Beetham, Frank J. Beginning Greek with Homer. (Bristol Classic Press Ser.). 256p. 1996. pap. text 29.95 (1-85399-480-4, Pub. by Brist Class Pr) Focus Pub-R Pullins.
Beetham, John. Creating a Competitive Company: A Manual for Energy Utilities. LC 98-46195. (Illus.). 256p. 1998. pap. 79.00 (0-910325-72-3) Public Util.
Beetham, Margaret. A Magazine of Her Own? Domesticity & Desire in the Woman's Magazine, 1800-1914. (Illus.). 256p. (C). 1996. pap. 29.99 (0-415-14112-5) Routledge.
Beetham, P. & Mason, A. Production of Pathogen Tested Sweet Potato. 1992. pap. 69.00 (1-86320-063-0, Pub. by ACIAR) St Mut.
Beethoven, Jane & Moore, Carman. Rock-It: An Exciting Trip Through the History of American Popular Music. 32p. 1980. pap., wbk. ed. 3.50 (0-88284-474-1, 1951); pap. text 4.50 (0-88284-473-3, 1950) Alfred Pub.
Beethoven, Ludwig van. Adagio Cantabile (Sonata in C Minor Op13) 12p. 1997. per. 4.95 (0-7935-8320-9) H Leonard.
— Bagatelles, Rondos & Other Shorter Works for Piano. 128p. pap. 8.95 (0-486-25392-9) Dover.
— Beethoven. 64p. 1996. pap. 9.95 (0-7935-6736-X) H Leonard.
— Beethoven: Letters, Journals & Conversations. Hamburger, Michael, ed. LC 77-13799. 282p. 1978. reprint ed. lib. bdg. 47.50 (0-8371-9899-2, BELJ, Greenwood Pr) Greenwood.
***Beethoven, Ludwig van.** Beethoven: Piano Pieces. (Cloth Bound Pocket Ser.). 1999. 7.95 (963-9155-57-8) Konemann.
— Beethoven: Piano Solo - Complete Edition, 7 Vols. (Urtext Editions for Piano). 1999. boxed set 79.95 (963-9059-95-1) Konemann.
— Beethoven: Piano Solo - Sonatas, 3 Vols. (Urtext Editions for Piano). 688p. boxed set 49.95 (963-9059-00-5) Konemann.
Beethoven, Ludwig van. Beethoven: Symphony No. Five in C Minor. Forbes, Elliot, ed. LC 73-98890. (Critical Scores Ser.). (C). 1971. pap. text 16.75 (0-393-09893-1) Norton.
***Beethoven, Ludwig van.** Beethoven: Variations. (Cloth Bound Pocket Ser.). 1999. 7.95 (963-9155-56-X) Konemann.
— Beethoven: 32 Piano Sonatas, 2 vols. (Cloth Bound Pocket Ser.). 1999. boxed set 14.95 (963-9155-53-5) Konemann.
Beethoven, Ludwig van. Beethoven's Letters. Eaglefield-Hull, A., ed. Shedlock, J. S., tr. from GER. LC 73-159687. 410p. 1972. reprint ed. pap. 9.95 (0-486-22769-3) Dover.
— Beethoven's Letters: A Critical Edition with Explanatory Notes, 2 Vols, Set. Kalischer, Alf C., ed. LC 74-102225. (Select Bibliographies Reprint Ser.). 1977. 56.95 (0-8369-5110-7) Ayer.
— Beethoven's Letters, Seventeen Ninety to Eighteen Twenty-Six, from the Collection of Dr. Ludwig Nohl, Also His Letters to the Archduke Rudolph, Cardinal-Archbishop of Olmutz, K. W. from the Collection of Dr. Ludwig Ritter Von Kochel, 2 Vols. LC 77-114868. (Select Bibliographies Reprint Ser.). 1977. 35.95 (0-8369-5273-1) Ayer.
***Beethoven, Ludwig van.** The Complete Music for Wind Ensembles. 1999. pap. text 15.95 (0-486-40860-4) Dover.
Beethoven, Ludwig van. Complete Piano Concertos in Full Score. (Music Ser.). 384p. 1983. reprint ed. pap. 15.95 (0-486-24563-2) Dover.
— Complete Piano Sonatas, 2 vols., 1. Schenker, Heinrich, ed. LC 74-83473. 1975. reprint ed. pap. 12.95 (0-486-23134-8) Dover.
— Complete Piano Sonatas, 2 vols., 2. Schenker, Heinrich, ed. LC 74-83473. 1975. reprint ed. pap. 12.95 (0-486-23135-6) Dover.
— Complete Sonatas & Variations for Cello & Piano. 176p. 1990. pap. 10.95 (0-486-26441-6) Dover.
— Complete String Quartets. LC 75-104809. 434p. 1970. reprint ed. pap. 16.95 (0-486-22361-2) Dover.
— Complete String Quartets Transcribed for Four-Hand Piano, 2 series. unabridged ed. 256p. 1980. pap. 14.95 (0-486-23975-6) Dover.
— Complete Variations for Solo Piano. 240p. pap. 12.95 (0-486-25188-8) Dover.
— Complete Violin Sonatas. 256p. 1990. pap. 13.95 (0-486-26277-4) Dover.
Beethoven, Ludwig van. Concerto in C Major, Op. 56 (Triple Concerto) & Fantasia in C Minor, Op. 80 (Choral Fantasy) in Full Score. 176p. Date not set. 13.95 (0-486-40148-0) Dover.
Beethoven, Ludwig van. Concerto in D Major Opus 61: Violin & Piano. 40p. 1987. pap. 13.95 (0-7935-4870-5) H Leonard.
— Concerto No. 4 in G Major Opus 58 2 Pianos 4 Hands. 80p. 1986. pap. 7.95 (0-7935-5192-7) H Leonard.
— Fidelio. 1998. pap. 7.95 (963-8303-07-7) Konemann.
— Fidelio. John, Nicholas, ed. Hammond, Tom, tr. from GER. (English National Opera Guide Series: Bilingual Libretto, Articles: No. 4). (Illus.). 1981. pap. 9.95 (0-7145-3823-X) Riverrun NY.
— Fidelio in Full Score. 272p. 1984. pap. 14.95 (0-486-24740-6) Dover.
Beethoven, Ludwig van. Fidelio Vocal Score. (ENG & GER.). 1986. pap. 24.95 (0-7935-2011-8, 50337350) H Leonard.
Beethoven, Ludwig van. Five Great Piano Sonatas. 1999. pap. text 9.95 (0-486-40848-5) Dover.
***Beethoven, Ludwig van.** Five Piano Trios: Opp. 11, 44, 121a & WoO 38 & 39. 2000. pap. 10.95 (0-486-41168-0) Dover.
— Fur Elise Albumblatt: For the Piano. 8p. 1986. pap. 3.95 (0-7935-5287-7, 50280640) H Leonard.
— Hallelujah from Mount of Olives. 16p. 1986. pap. 1.25 (0-7935-5473-X, 50293600) H Leonard.
Beethoven, Ludwig van. Late String Quartets & the Grosse Fugue, Opp. 127, 130-133, 135. (Miniature Scores Ser.). 1998. pap. 4.95 (0-486-40111-1) Dover.
— Mass in C & Christ on the Mount of Olives in Full Score. 272p. pap. 16.95 (0-486-29346-7) Dover.
— Missa Solemnis in Full Score. 272p. pap. 15.95 (0-486-26894-2) Dover.
— My First Book of Classics: Beethoven. (Easy Classics Ser.). 1990. 6.95 (0-685-32054-5, H702) Hansen Ed Mus.
— New Beethoven Letters. MacArdle, Donald W., tr. LC 57-7331. 628p. reprint ed. pap. 194.70 (0-608-11008-6, 201009700068) Bks Demand.
— Notturno for Viola & Piano Centennial Edition. 1992. pap. 7.95 (0-7935-2022-3) H Leonard.
***Beethoven, Ludwig van.** Piano Concerto No. 5 in E-Flat Major, Op. 73. unabridged ed. 96p. 1999. pap. 3.95 (0-486-40636-9) Dover.
Beethoven, Ludwig van. Piano Concertos Nos. 4 & 5 ("Emperor") With Orchestral Reduction for Second Piano. 160p. pap. 10.95 (0-486-28442-5) Dover.
— Piano Variations Bk. 1: Piano. 152p. 1986. per. 13.95 (0-7935-3580-8) H Leonard.
***Beethoven, Ludwig van.** The Ruins of Athens & Other Overtures in Full Score. 208p. 1999. pap. text 15.95 (0-486-40628-8) Dover.
Beethoven, Ludwig van. Six Great Piano Trios in Full Score. 224p. pap. 11.95 (0-486-25398-8) Dover.
Beethoven, Ludwig van. Sonata in C Minor, Opus 13, Piano Solo Sonata Pathetique. 24p. 1986. pap. 3.95 (0-7935-5296-6, 50266370) H Leonard.
— Sonata I. (Music Scores Ser.). 1998. pap. text 7.98 (963-8303-20-4) Kone Music.
— Sonata III. (Music Scores Ser.). 1998. pap. 7.98 (963-8303-22-0) Kone Music.
Beethoven, Ludwig van. Sonatas for Violin & Piano, No. 5 ("Spring"), No. 8 & No. 9 ("Kreutzer") With Separate Violin Part, Vols. 5, 8 & 9. pap. 9.95 (0-486-29142-1) Dover.
— Sonatina Album for Piano: Centennial Edition. 64p. 1992. pap. 7.95 (0-7935-2023-1) H Leonard.
— Songs for Solo Voice & Piano. 192p. 1986. pap. 10.95 (0-486-25125-X) Dover.
Beethoven, Ludwig van. String Quartets Opus 18, Nos. 1-6. 1986. pap. text 40.00 (0-7935-3888-2, 50261890) H Leonard.
— Symphonies: Piano, Bk. 1. 152p. 1986. per. 15.95 (0-7935-1538-6, 50260120) H Leonard.
— Symphonies: Piano, Bk. 2. 164p. 1986. per. 15.95 (0-7935-4084-4, 50260130) H Leonard.
Beethoven, Ludwig van. Symphonies Nos. 8 & 9 in Full Score. 256p. pap. 11.95 (0-486-26035-6) Dover.
— Symphonies Nos. 5, 6 & 7 in Full Score. 272p. 1989. pap. 11.95 (0-486-26034-8) Dover.
— Symphonies Nos. 1, 2, 3, & 4 in Full Score. 272p. pap. 11.95 (0-486-26033-X) Dover.
Beethoven, Ludwig van. Symphony No. 6 in F Major, Op. 68 ("Pastorale") 96p. Date not set. 2.95 (0-486-40123-5) Dover.
— Symphony No. 8 in F Major, OP 93. (Miniature Scores Ser.). 2000. pap. 3.95 (0-486-41169-9) Dover.
— Symphony No. 7 in A Major, Op. 92. (Miniature Scores Ser.). 1998. pap. 2.95 (0-486-40418-8) Dover.
Beethoven, Ludwig van. Symphony Number 3 in E Flat Major. 1998. 2.95 (0-486-29796-9, 741718Q) Dover.
— Symphony Number 5 in C Minor OP 67. 1998. 2.95 (0-486-29850-7, 741722Q) Dover.
— Symphony Number 9 in D Minor OP 12. 1998. 4.95 (0-486-29924-4, 741724Q) Dover.
— The Symphony of Life: Letters by Ludwig van Beethoven. Steindorff, Ulrich L., tr. LC 74-24037. reprint ed. 17.50 (0-404-12860-2) AMS Pr.
— Thirty-Two Sonatas for the Pianoforte, 2 Vols. Schnabel, Arthur, ed. 1935. pap. 15.00 (0-686-66528-7, Fireside) S&S Trade Pap.
— Thirty-Two Sonatas for the Pianoforte, 2 Vols, 1. Schnabel, Arthur, ed. 1935. pap. 7.50 (0-685-73425-0, 07100, Fireside) S&S Trade Pap.
— Thirty-Two Sonatas for the Pianoforte, 2 Vols, 2. Schnabel, Arthur, ed. 1935. pap. 7.50 (0-685-73426-9, 07110, Fireside) S&S Trade Pap.

B

An Asterisk (*) at the beginning of an entry indicates that the title is appearing for the first time.

Beethoven, Ludwig van, et al. Great Romantic Violin Concertos in Full Score. 224p. pap. 12.95 (0-486-24989-1) Dover.

Beetle, Alan A. Distribution of Native Grasses in California. (Illus.). 52p. 1987. reprint ed. pap. 5.00 (0-933421-11-7) Redwood Seed.

Beetle, Alan A., et al. Grasses of Wyoming. 3rd ed. (Illus.). 440p. 1988. 22.00 (0-941570-07-X) U of Wyoming.

Beetle, David H. Up Old Forge Way. limited ed. (Illus.). 432p. 1984. 12.95 (0-932052-14-2) North Country.

***Beetles, Chris.** Mabel Lucie Attwell. (Illus.). 110p. 1999. pap. 19.50 (1-871136-56-3, Pub. by Beetles Ltd) Antique Collect.

Beetley, Phil. Web Server Technologies, Professional Reference. 1997. pap. text 50.00 (1-56205-772-3) New Riders Pub.

Beeton, Douglas R. & Dorner, Helene T. A Dictionary of English Usage in Southern Africa. 1976. 19.95 (0-19-570069-4) OUP.

Beeton, Isabella. Beeton's Book of Needlework. 1991. pap. 4.95 (0-671-08154-3) S&S Trade.

***Beeton, Isabella.** Mrs. Beeton's Book of Household Management. Humble, Nicola, ed. LC 99-54236. (Oxford World's Classic Ser.). (Illus.). 672p. 2000. pap. 13.95 (0-19-283345-6) OUP.

Beeton, Mayson M., ed. see Defoe, Daniel.

***Beeton, Sue.** Ecotourism: A Practical Guide for Rural Communities. 220p. 1998. pap. 29.95 (0-643-06359-5, Pub. by CSIRO) Accents Pubns.

Beets, G. C., et al, eds. Population & Family in the Low Countries, 1992: Family & Labour. (NIDI-CBGS Publications: Vol. 26). viii, 272p. 1993. pap. 52.00 (90-265-1342-9) Swets.

Beets, Willem C. Environmentally Sound Agriculture - A Global Perspective. (Illus.). 450p. 1998. 60.00 (981-00-7989-3, Pub. by AgBe Pub) Balogh.

Beetz. Software Engineering. (C). 1990. text. write for info. (0-201-55905-6) Addison-Wesley.

Beetz, Carl P. & Satterthwaite, Linton, Jr. The Monuments & Inscriptions of Caracol, Belize. (University Museum Monographs: No. 45). (Illus.). xiv, 188p. 1981. text 40.00 (0-934718-41-5) U Museum Pubns.

Beetz, Kirk H. Algernon Charles Swinburne: A Bibliography of Secondary Works, 1861-1980. LC 82-3359. (Author Bibliographies Ser.: No. 61). 238p. 1982. 26.50 (0-8108-1541-9) Scarecrow.

***Beetz, M., ed.** Concurrent Reactive Plans: Anticipating & Forestalling Execution Failures. (Lecture Notes in Artificial Intelligence: Vol. 1772). xvi, 213p. 2000. pap. 45.00 (3-540-67241-9) Spr-Verlag.

Beevar, Dorothy S. & Beevar, Raphael J. Pragmatics of Human Relationships. (C). 1998. pap. text 29.95 (1-884228-26-7) Geist & Russell.

Beevar, Raphael J., jt. auth. see Beevar, Dorothy S.

Beever, Jessica, et al. Mosses of New Zealand. 1996. 79.95 (0-908569-52-1, Pub. by Univ Otago Pr) Intl Spec Bk.

Beevers, D. G. & MacGregor, G. A. Hypertension in Practice. 3rd ed. 286p. 1999. 89.95 (1-85317-591-9) Martin Dunitz.

Beevers, Geoffrey & Eliot, George. George Eliot's Adam Bede. LC 92-195139. 70 p. 1990. write for info. (0-573-11049-2) French.

Beevers, John. Autobiography of Saint Therese of Lisieux: The Story of a Soul. 160p. 1987. pap. 9.95 (0-385-02903-9, D56, Image Bks) Doubleday.

— St. Joan of Arc. 1995. reprint ed. pap. 9.00 (0-89555-043-1) TAN Bks Pubs.

— St. Therese, the Little Flower: The Making of a Saint. LC 73-80147. (Orig.). 1994. pap. 6.00 (0-89555-035-0) TAN Bks Pubs.

Beevers, L. Nitrogen Metabolism in Plants. 333p. (C). 1979. text 120.00 (0-89771-548-9, Pub. by Intl Bk Distr) St Mut.

— Nitrogen Metabolism in Plants. 333p. 1979. reprint ed. 100.00 (0-7855-6640-6, Pub. by Intl Bk Distr) St Mut.

Beevis, D., et al. Applications of Human Performance Models to Systems Design. (Defense Research Ser.: Vol. 2). (Illus.). 568p. 1989. 125.00 (0-306-43242-0, Plenum Trade) Perseus Pubng.

Beevor, Antony. Stalingrad. LC 98-19346. (Illus.). 494p. 1998. 35.00 (0-670-87095-1) Viking Penguin.

— Stalingrad: The Fateful Siege, 1942-1943. (Illus.). 624p. 1999. pap. 16.95 (0-14-028458-3) Viking Penguin.

***Beevor, Kinta.** A Tuscan Childhood. 271p. 2000. pap. 13.00 (0-375-70426-4) Vin Bks.

Beezer, Anne, jt. ed. see Barker, Martin.

Beezer, Bruce. North Carolina Teachers' Professional Competencies Handbook. LC 91-76030. 176p. (C). 1992. pap. 14.00 (0-89089-443-4) Carolina Acad Pr.

Beezley, William H. Insurgent Governor: Abraham Gonzalez & the Mexican Revolution in Chihuahua. LC 72-86257. (Illus.). 219p. reprint ed. pap. 67.90 (0-7837-6875-3, 204670500003) Bks Demand.

— Judas at the Jockey Club & Other Episodes of Porfirian Mexico. LC 86-11320. x, 187p. 1987. pap. text 11.00 (0-8032-6102-0, Bison Books) U of Nebr Pr.

***Beezley, William H.** Viva Mexico! Viva Independencia! Celebrations of September 16. (Illus.). 2000. 60.00 (0-8420-2914-1) Scholarly Res Inc.

Beezley, William H., et al, eds. Rituals of Rule, Rituals of Resistance: Public Celebrations & Popular Culture in Mexico. LC 94-884. (Latin American Silhouettes Ser.). (Illus.). 404p. 1994. 55.00 (0-8420-2416-6); pap. 19.95 (0-8420-2417-4) Scholarly Res Inc.

***Beezley, William H. & Curcio-Nagy, Linda.** Latin American Popular Culture: An Introduction. 286p. 2000. 55.00 (0-8420-2710-6); 21.95 (0-8420-2711-4) Scholarly Res Inc.

Beezley, William H. & Ewell, Judith, eds. The Human Tradition in Latin America: The Twentieth Century. LC 87-12906. (Latin American Silhouettes Ser.). 311p. (C). 1987. 45.00 (0-8420-2283-X); pap. 17.95 (0-8420-2284-8) Scholarly Res Inc.

— The Human Tradition in Modern Latin America. LC 97-20943. (Latin American Silhouettes Ser.). 312p. (C). 1997. 50.00 (0-8420-2612-6, SR Bks); pap. 18.95 (0-8420-2613-4, SR Bks) Scholarly Res Inc.

***Beezley, William H. & Lorey, David E., eds.** Viva Mexico! Viva Independencia! Celebrations of September 16. (Illus.). 2000. pap. 21.95 (0-8420-2915-X, SR Bks) Scholarly Res Inc.

Beezley, William H. & MacLachlan, Colin M. Latin America: The Peoples & Their History. LC 98-88398. 336p. (C). 1999. pap. text 41.50 (0-15-501563-X) Acad Pr.

Beezley, William H., jt. auth. see MacLachlan, Colin M.

Beezley, William H., jt. ed. see Ewell, Judith.

Beezley, William H., ed. see Gilderhus, Mark T.

Beezley, William H., jt. ed. see Meyer, Michael C.

Beezley, William H., ed. see Nibb, Stephen R.

Beezley, William H., jt. ed. see Raat, W. Dirk.

Beffart, Mark. Paris for Free (or Extremely Cheap) Hundreds of Free & Inexpensive Things to Do in Paris. 2nd rev. ed. LC 96-49219. (Illus.). 192p. 1997. pap. 10.95 (0-914457-87-X) Mustang Pub.

Befu, Harumi, ed. Cultural Nationalism in East Asia. (Research Papers & Policy: No. 39). 208p. 1993. pap. 17.00 (1-55729-039-3) IEAS.

Befus, A. Dean, et al, eds. Mast Cell Differentiation & Heterogeneity. LC 86-6589. 448p. 1986. reprint ed. pap. 138.90 (0-608-03385-5, 206408200008) Bks Demand.

Beg, Anwer, ed. see Azami, Mustafa.

Beg, Mirza Masum. Christ Is Come: Prophecies about the Advent of the Promised Messiah. 4th ed. 1996. pap. 3.95 (0-913321-63-X) Ahmadiyya Anjuman.

Begail, Vivian. Head Injury in Children & Adolescents: A Resource & Review for School & Allied Professionals. 2nd ed. 280p. 1996. 80.50 (0-471-16194-2) Wiley.

— Head Injury in Children & Adolescents: A Resource for School & Allied Professionals. 2nd ed. LC 92-52847. (Illus.). 248p. 1992. pap. 29.95 (0-88422-098-2) Clinical Psych.

***Begala, Kathye.** Kathye's Inspirations. (Illus.). 34p. 1999. 10.95 (1-57377-071-X, 19884-2288) Easl Pubns.

— Kathye's Inspirations, Vol. 2. (Illus.). 36p. 10.95 (1-57377-103-1, 0-19884-02544-9) Easl Pubns.

Begam, Richard. Samuel Beckett & the End of Modernity. LC 96-27406. 1996. write for info. (0-8047-2731-7) Stanford U Pr.

Begamudre, Ven. Laterna Magika. LC 98-119639. 208p. 1997. pap. 16.95 (0-88982-166-6, Pub. by Oolichan Bks) Genl Dist Srvs.

Begamudre, Ven. Van de Graaff Days. 272p. 1993. pap. text 14.95 (0-88982-126-7, Pub. by Oolichan Bks) Genl Dist Srvs.

Begamudre, Ven & Krause, Judith, eds. Out of Place: Stories & Poems. 216p. 1990. pap. 12.95 (1-55050-019-8, Pub. by Coteau) Genl Dist Srvs.

Begaud, B., ed. Methodological Approaches in Pharmacoepidemiology: Application to Spontaneous Reporting. 180p. 1993. 149.50 (0-444-81577-5) Elsevier.

Begawan, Bandar S. & Darussalam, Brunei. The Integrated Management Plan for the Coastal Zone of Brunei Darussalam. (ICLARM Technical Reports: No. 29). 122p. 1992. per. write for info. (971-8709-15-0, Pub. by ICLARM) Intl Spec Bk.

Begay, Shonto. Navajo: Visions & Voices Across the Mesa. LC 93-31610. (Illus.). 48p. (J). (ps-3). 1995. 15.95 (0-590-46153-2) Scholastic Inc.

Begay, Shonto. The Mud Pony: A Traditional Skidi Pawnee Tale. LC 87-23451. 32p. (J). (gr. k-4). 1988. 15.95 (0-590-41525-5) Scholastic Inc.

Begay, Shonto W., ed. see White Deer of Autumn Staff.

Begaye, Lisa Shook. Building a Bridge. (Illus.). 32p. (J). (gr. k-3). 1998. pap. 7.95 (0-87358-727-8, Rising Moon Bks) Northland AZ.

Begbie, William H. & Joseph, Abraham. A Vocabulary, English, Burmese, Hindustani & Tamil In English Characters, With the Burmese Also in the Native Letters, to Which Are Added a Few Sentences Likely to Be Useful in Daily Life. LC 98-902745. (INC & TAM.). xii, 153p. 1996. write for info. (81-206-1249-3) Asian Educ Servs.

Begbie, Harold. Mirrors of Downing Street. LC 79-121448. (Essay Index Reprint Ser.). 1977. 20.95 (0-8369-1695-6) Ayer.

— Souls in Action: The Crucible of the New Life. LC 95-75902. 308p. 1995. 14.95 (1-886787-00-X) Messengers Hope.

— Twice-Born Men: A Clinic in Regeneration. LC 94-79790. 280p. 1995. 14.95 (0-9605642-9-2) Messengers Hope.

— Windows of Westminster. LC 77-104993. (Essay Index Reprint Ser.). 1977. 21.95 (0-8369-1447-3) Ayer.

***Begbie, Jeremy S.** Theology, Music & Time. (Cambridge Studies in Christian Doctrine). (Illus.). 288p. 2000. write for info. (0-521-44464-0); pap. write for info. (0-521-78568-5) Cambridge U Pr.

Begbie, Jeremy S. Voicing Creation's Praise: Towards a Theology of the Arts. 286p. 1991. pap. 31.95 (0-567-29188-X, Pub. by T & T Clark) Bks Intl VA.

***Begbie, Jeremy S., ed.** Beholding the Glory: Incarnation Through the Arts. 188p. (C). 2000. pap. 13.99 (0-8010-2244-4) Baker Bks.

Begehr. Partial Differential Equations. 232p. (C). 1992. ring bd. 60.95 (0-582-09640-5) CRC Pr.

Begehr, H. & Gilbert, Robert. Transformation, Transmutations & Kernel Functions, Vol. 58. 416p. 1992. ring bd. 168.95 (0-582-02695-4, LM2695, Chap & Hall CRC) CRC Pr.

Begehr, Heinrich, tr. see Bliev, N.

Begehr, Heinrich G. Mathematics in Berlin. LC 98-21860. 1998. 32.00 (0-8176-5943-9) Birkhauser.

Begehr, Heinrich G., et al, eds. Mathematics in Berlin. LC 98-21860. (Illus.). 200p. 1998. pap. 22.00 (3-7643-5943-9) Spr-Verlag.

***Begehr, Heinrich G., et al.** Complex Methods for Partial Differential Equations. LC 99-46860. (International Society for Analysis, Applications & Computation Ser.). 1999. pap. write for info. (0-7923-6000-1) Kluwer Academic.

Begehr, Heinrich G. W. Complex Analytic Methods for Partial Differential Equations: An Introductory Text. LC 94-34414. 250p. 1994. text 44.00 (981-02-1550-9) World Scientific Pub.

Begehr, Heinrich G. W., et al. Partial Differential & Integral Equations. LC 98-47337. (International Society for Analysis, Applications & Computation Ser.). 1998. write for info. (0-7923-5482-6) Kluwer Academic.

Begehr, Heinrich G. W., jt. auth. see Wen, Guo C.

Begehr, Henrich G. & Dzhuraev, Abduhamid. Introduction to Several Complex Variables & Partial Differential Equations. 1996. 130.00 (0-582-25500-7, Pub. by Addison-Wesley) Longman.

***Begel, Daniel.** Sports Psychology. LC 99-35444. 276p. 2000. text 40.00 (0-393-70295-2) Norton.

***Begelman, Mitchell.** Turn Right at Orion: Travels Through the Cosmos. 256p. 2000. text 25.00 (0-7382-0207-X, Pub. by Perseus Pubng) HarpC.

Begelman, Mitchell & Rees, Martin. Gravity's Fatal Attraction: Black Holes in the Universe. (Illus.). 246p. 1998. pap. text 19.95 (0-7167-6029-0) W H Freeman.

Begemann, H. & Rastetter, J. W. Atlas of Clinical Hematology. (Illus.). 325p. 1989. 365.00 (0-387-50851-1) Spr-Verlag.

— Atlas of Clinical Hematology. 3rd ed. Heilmeyer, Ludwig M., ed. Hirsch, H. J., tr. from GER. LC 72-86892. (Illus.). xv, 324p. 1979. 217.00 (0-387-09404-0) Spr-Verlag.

Begendahl, Timothy J., et al. Rating Maintenance Phase Version 2: Program Document. 55p. (Orig.). (C). 1995. pap. text 30.00 (0-7881-1905-2) DIANE Pub.

Beger, H. G., et al, eds. Cancer Therapy. 305p. 1988. 103.00 (0-387-19293-X) Spr-Verlag.

— Chronic Pancreatitis: Research & Clinical Management. (Illus.). xvi, 574p. 1990. 139.00 (0-387-52034-1) Spr-Verlag.

— The Role of Enzyme Treatment in Pancreatic Disease. (Journal: Digestion: Vol. 54, Suppl. 2, 1993). (Illus.). vi, 54p. 1993. pap. 26.25 (3-8055-5861-9) S Karger.

Beger, H. G. & Buechler, M. W., eds. European Pancreatic Club EPC, Abstracts 24th Meeting, Ulm, October 1992: Journal: Digestion, Vol. 52, No. 2, 1992. 76p. 1992. pap. 36.75 (3-8055-5693-4) S Karger.

***Beger, H. G., et al.** The Pancreas, Vol. 2. LC 97-7000. Vol. 2. (Illus.). 1664p. 1998. 499.95 (0-86542-420-9) Blackwell Sci.

Begerud, Marly & Busche, Don. Microsoft Windows 95. (Quicktorial Ser.). 1996. mass mkt. 21.95 (0-538-66409-6) S-W Pub.

Begg, Alexander. Red River Journal & Other Papers Relative to the Red River Resistance of 1869-1870, Vol. 34. Morton, W. L., ed. LC 69-14506. 636p. 1969. reprint ed. lib. bdg. 85.00 (0-8371-5074-4, BERR, Greenwood Pr) Greenwood.

***Begg, Alistair.** The Hand of God. 1999. 6.99 (0-8024-1703-5) Moody.

— Lasting Love. 1997. 14.99 incl. audio (0-8024-3402-9) Moody.

Begg, Alistair. Lasting Love: How to Avoid Marital Failure. LC 97-207335. 264p. 1997. 14.99 (0-8024-3401-0) Moody.

— Made for His Pleasure: Experiencing Our Father's Pleasure As We Glorify Him. LC 96-200721. 12.99 (0-8024-7138-2, 212) Moody.

— Nehemiah. 1999. pap. 16.99 (0-8024-1719-1) Moody.

***Begg, Alistair.** Preaching for God's Glory. LC 99-36911. (Today's Issues Ser.). 48p. 1999. pap. 4.99 (1-58134-123-7) Crossway Bks.

— Putting God First. 2000. 19.99 (0-8024-1716-7) Moody.

Begg, Alistair. What Angels Wish They Knew: The Basics of True Christianity. 1998. 16.99 (0-8024-1718-3); mass mkt. 5.99 (0-8024-1708-6) Moody.

***Begg, Alistair.** What Angels Wish They Knew: The Basics of True Christianity. 1998. pap. 19.99 (0-8024-1709-4) Moody.

***Begg, C. T.** Josephus' Story of the Later Monarchy: AJ 9,1-10,185. x, 650p. 2000. 86.00 (90-429-0785-1, Pub. by Peeters Pub) Bks Intl VA.

Begg, David. Impact of Eastern Europe. 1994. pap. 14.95 (1-898128-04-9, Pub. by Ctr Econ Policy Res) Brookings.

— Independent & Accountable: A New Mandate for the Bank of England? 96p. (C). 1994. pap. 9.95 (1-898128-02-2) Brookings.

— Making of Monetary Union. 1994. pap. text, student ed. 14.95 (1-898128-05-7, Pub. by Ctr Econ Policy Res) Brookings.

Begg, David, et al, eds. Economic Policy, No. 27. 240p. 1998. pap. 39.95 (0-631-21177-2) Blackwell Pubs.

***Begg, David, et al, eds.** Economic Policy: A European Forum, No. 29. 240p. 1999. pap. text 39.95 (0-631-21809-2) Blackwell Pubs.

Begg, David, et al, eds. Economic Policy: A European Forum, Vol. 28. (ECOP Ser.). 240p. 1999. pap. 39.95 (0-631-21497-6) Blackwell Pubs.

— Emu: Prospects & Challenges for the Euro. (Illus.). 360p. 1998. 68.95 (0-631-20997-2) Blackwell Pubs.

***Begg, David, et al.** Economic Policy No. 30. (Economic Policy Ser.). 240p. 2000. pap. 39.95 (0-631-22159-X) Blackwell Pubs.

Begg, David, et al. EMU: Getting the End-Game Right. (Monitoring European Integration Ser.: Vol. 7). 75p. 1997. pap. 14.95 (1-898128-26-X, Pub. by Ctr Econ Policy Res) Brookings.

— Making Sense of Subsidiarity: How Much Centralization for Europe? 192p. (C). 1994. pap. 14.95 (1-898128-03-0) Brookings.

— Monitoring the European Central Bank, Report No. 1. 120p. 1998. pap. 14.95 (1-898128-39-1, Pub. by Ctr Econ Policy Res) Brookings.

Begg, David K. The Rational Expectations Revolution in Macroeconomics: Theories & Evidence. LC 82-47785. (Illus.). 303p. reprint ed. pap. 94.00 (0-608-06039-9, 206637100008) Bks Demand.

Begg, Deborah, jt. auth. see Atkinson, Phillip S.

Begg, Deike. Rebirthing - Freedom from Your Past: A Revolutionary Way to Change Your Life in 20 Hours. 1999. pap. 16.00 (0-7225-3704-2) Thorsons PA.

Begg, Desmond. A Traveller's Wine Guide to Spain. LC 96-45976. (Traveller's Wine Guides Ser.). (Illus.). 144p. 1998. pap. write for info. (1-56656-224-4) Interlink Pub.

— The Vodka Companion: A Connoisseur's Guide. (Illus.). 192p. 1998. 19.95 (0-7624-0252-0) Running Pr.

Begg, Ean. Cult of the Black Virgin. LC 97-190570. 1997. pap. 12.95 (0-14-019510-6) Viking Penguin.

— Myth & Today's Consciousness. 1991. pap. 10.95 (0-904575-30-6) Sigo Pr.

Begg, Ean & Rich, Deike. On the Trail of Merlin: A Guidebook to the Western Mystery Tradition. 1991. 30.00 (0-85030-939-5, Pub. by Aqrn Pr) Harper SF.

***Begg, Iain.** EU Investment Grants Review. LC 99-28066. (Technical Papers). 48p. 1999. pap. 22.00 (0-8213-4499-4) World Bank.

Begg, Iain & Grimwade, Nigel. Paying for Europe. (Contemporary European Studies: Vol. 2). 208p. 1998. pap. 15.00 (1-85075-858-1, Pub. by Sheffield Acad) CUP Services.

Begg, Iain & Henry, S. G., eds. Applied Economics & Public Policy. LC 97-44533. (Department of Applied Economics Occassional Papers: No. 63). 318p. (C). 1998. text 64.95 (0-521-62414-2) Cambridge U Pr.

Begg, James D. Abdominal X-Rays Made Easy. LC 99-27853. 1999. pap. write for info. (0-443-06205-6, W B Saunders Co) Harcrt Hlth Sci Grp.

Begg, Patrick. Late Cypriot Terracotta Figurines: A Study in Context. (Studies in Mediterranean Archaeology & Literature: No. 101). (Illus.). 108p. (Orig.). 1991. pap. 29.50 (91-7081-036-2, Pub. by P Astroms) Coronet Bks.

Begg, Paul. City Walks of London. (Illus.). 181p. 1992. pap. 8.95 (0-86051-647-4, Robson-Parkwest) Parkwest Pubns.

— Jack the Ripper: The Uncensored Facts. (Illus.). 256p. 1992. pap. 12.95 (0-86051-583-4, Robson-Parkwest) Parkwest Pubns.

Begg, Paul, et al. The Jack the Ripper A to Z. 3rd ed. (Illus.). 560p. 1994. pap. 15.95 (0-7472-5522-9, Pub. by Headline Bk Pub) Trafalgar.

Begg, Peter F. Corporate Acquisitions & Mergers: 1988 Basic Work & 1989 Supplement Service. (C). 1988. suppl. ed. 150.50 (1-85333-264-X, Pub. by Graham & Trotman); ring bd. 99.00 (1-85333-012-4, Pub. by Graham & Trotman) Kluwer Academic.

— Corporate Acquisitions & Mergers: 1989 Basic Work & Supplement Service. (C). 1989. ring bd. 167.00 (1-85333-265-8, Pub. by Graham & Trotman) Kluwer Academic.

— Corporate Acquisitions & Mergers: 1991 Basic Work & Supplement Service, 2 vols., Set. 850p. 1991. lib. bdg. 199.00 (1-85333-485-5, Pub. by Graham & Trotman) Kluwer Academic.

— Corporate Acquisitions & Mergers Vols. 1-2: U. K. & Continental Europe, 2 vols., Set. 1000p. (C). 1995. ring bd. 405.00 (1-85333-832-X, Pub. by Graham & Trotman) Kluwer Academic.

— Corporate Acquisitions & Mergers Vols. 1 & 2: 1992 Basic Work & Supplement Service. 850p. 1992. suppl. ed. 159.00 (1-85333-649-1, Pub. by Graham & Trotman) Kluwer Academic.

Begg, Peter F., ed. Corporate Acquisitions & Mergers. (C). 1990. ring bd. 190.00 (1-85333-307-7, Pub. by Graham & Trotman) Kluwer Academic.

— Corporate Acquisitions & Mergers: A Practical Guide to the Legal, Financial & Administrative Implications. 3rd ed. 672p. (C). 1991. lib. bdg. 177.00 (1-85333-625-4, Pub. by Graham & Trotman) Kluwer Academic.

Begg, R. W., ed. see Canadian Cancer Conference Staff.

Begg, Tom. The Excellent Women. 240p. (C). 1996. pap. 45.00 (0-85976-404-4, Pub. by J Donald) St Mut.

— Housing Policy in Scotland. 240p. 1996. pap. 48.00 (0-85976-433-8, Pub. by J Donald) St Mut.

Begg, Virginia Lopez. Seasons of My Garden: A Two-Year Recordkeeper. (Illus.). 128p. 1996. spiral bd. 16.00 (1-56799-692-2, Friedman-Fairfax) M Friedman Pub Grp Inc.

Begg, Vivienne. Developing Expert CAD Systems. (High Technology Modular Ser.). 128p. 1984. 19.95 (0-89059-042-7, 0155) Productivity Inc.

Beggiani, Seely J. Early Syriac Theology: With Special Reference to the Maronite Tradition. LC 83-3658. 172p. (Orig.). (C). 1983. pap. text 19.50 (0-8191-3153-9) U Pr of Amer.

Beggs, Alan, et al. Mental & Physical Fitness for Sailing. 96p. (C). 1993. text 18.95 (0-906754-94-1, Pub. by Fernhurst Bks) St Mut.

Beggs, Beth. Just Passing Through. LC 94-14512. 160p. 1994. pap. 10.95 (1-55622-376-5, Seaside Pr) Wordware Pub.

Beggs, David W. America's Schools & Churches. LC 65-12279. 253p. reprint ed. pap. 78.50 (0-8357-5409-X, 205519000011) Bks Demand.

Beggs, David W., 3rd, ed. Team Teaching: Bold New Venture. LC 64-17456. (Bold New Venture Ser). (Illus.). 192p. reprint ed. 59.60 (*0-8357-9245-5*, 201581000097) Bks Demand.

Beggs, Edward L. Huckleberry's for Runaways: Parents & Teenagers Working with Conflict. rev. ed. LC 96-92580. (Illus.). 320p. (YA). 1997. pap. 9.95 (*1-889607-02-9*) Self-Reliance Pr.

— Skateland: California Portraits. LC 96-92583. (Illus.). 250p. (Orig.). (YA). 1997. pap. 14.95 (*1-889607-01-0*) Self-Reliance Pr.

Beggs, H. Dale. Production Optimization Using Nodal Analysis. 411p. 1991. 64.00 (*0-930972-14-7*, P7479) Oil & Gas.

Beggs, James S. Naming of Parts: An Analytical Study of Henry Reed. 190p. 1998. pap. 19.95 (*0-85958-671-5*, Pub. by Univ of Hull Pr) Paul & Co Pubs.

Beggs, Jim. The Little Book of Inspiration. LC 93-36646. (Illus.). 64p. (Orig.). 1994. 6.95 (*0-87573-028-0*) Jain Pub Co.

***Beggs, John.** The Police & Criminal Evidence Act 1984 Explained. 2000. 50.00 (*0-11-702396-5*, Pub. by Statnry Office) Balogh.

Beggs, Joseph S. Kinematics. LC 82-15835. (Illus.). 223p. 1983. text 65.00 (*0-89116-355-7*) Hemisp Pub.

Beggs, Josh & Thede, Dylan. Designing Web Audio. Koman, Richard, ed. (Illus.). 250p. 1999. pap. 29.95 (*1-56592-353-7*) OReilly & Assocs.

Beggs, Marck L. Godworm: Poems. LC 95-41335. 64p. 1995. pap. 14.95 (*0-7734-0023-0*, Mellen Poetry Pr) E Mellen.

Beggs, Marjorie. Breaking the Cycle of Failure: Family Enrichment Network. 28p. (Orig.). 1989. pap. 5.00 (*0-936434-60-0*, Pub. by Zellerbach Fam Fund) Intl Spec Bk.

— Dual Diagnosis: Challenges of Serving Mentally Ill Substance Abusers. 48p. 1998. pap. 8.95 (*0-936434-99-6*, Study Ctr Pr) SF Study Ctr.

— Family Preservation Programs: State's Successful New Strategy to Keep Children at Home. 28p. 1993. pap. 5.00 (*0-936434-63-5*, Pub. by Zellerbach Fam Fund) Intl Spec Bk.

— Foster Families As Partners in Therapy. 52p. 1987. pap. 5.00 (*0-936434-23-6*, Pub. by Zellerbach Fam Fund) Intl Spec Bk.

— Foster Kids Survival Groups: Lessons from a Mental Health-Social Services Collaborative. 28p. (Orig.). 1994. pap. 5.00 (*0-936434-76-7*, Pub. by Zellerbach Fam Fund) Intl Spec Bk.

— The Future of Families: Challenges & Obstacles. 40p. (Orig.). 1992. pap. 5.00 (*0-936434-68-6*, Pub. by Zellerbach Fam Fund) Intl Spec Bk.

— In a Day's Work: Four Child Welfare Workers in California. unabridged ed. LC 96-92019. (Illus.). 84p. (Orig.). 1996. pap. 14.95 (*0-936434-96-1*, DW, Study Ctr Pr) SF Study Ctr.

— No Strings Attached Grant Program. 36p. (Orig.). 1995. pap. 5.00 (*0-936434-86-4*, Pub. by Zellerbach Fam Fund) Intl Spec Bk.

— OK in My Backyard: Issues & Rights in Housing for the Mentally Ill. 34p. 1993. pap. 5.00 (*0-936434-64-3*, Pub. by Zellerbach Fam Fund) Intl Spec Bk.

— Preserving the Cultural Legacy: Black Adoption Placement & Research Center. 28p. (Orig.). 1992. pap. 5.00 (*0-936434-62-7*, Pub. by Zellerbach Fam Fund) Intl Spec Bk.

— A Tree with 3 Branches: California Partnership for Children. 54p. 1998. pap. 5.00 (*1-888956-02-X*) SF Study Ctr.

Beggs, Marjorie, ed. North Richmond: A Community in Transition. 35p. (Orig.). 1995. pap. 5.00 (*0-936434-82-1*, Pub. by Zellerbach Fam Fund) Intl Spec Bk.

Beggs, Marjorie & Walker, Ellen B. Clients Serving Clients: Mental Health Client Self-Help Projects in Northern California. 28p. (Orig.). 1989. pap. 5.00 (*0-936434-61-9*, Pub. by Zellerbach Fam Fund) Intl Spec Bk.

Beggs, Marjorie, jt. auth. see Link, Geoffrey.

Beggs, Marjorie, jt. ed. see Link, Terry.

Beggs, Marjorie, ed. see Manian, Padma.

Beggs, Marjorie, ed. see Romines, Ken.

Beggs, Mary J. Choosing to Cope. LC 87-82988. 128p. 1988. pap. 2.95 (*0-88243-510-8*, 02-0510) Gospel Pub.

Beggs, Pauline. Birds of Prey. (Eye to Eye Ser.). (Illus.). 32p. (J). (gr. 1-5). 1998. pap. 11.99 (*1-58184-002-0*, Pub. by S1omerville Hse) Penguin Putnam.

***Beggs, Pauline.** Birds of Prey. (Eye to Eye Bks.). (Illus.). 32p. (J). (gr. 1-7). 1998. pap. 11.99 (*1-894042-02-6*) Somerville Hse.

Beggs, Sara. No Nonsense Guide to Teaching Art. (Illus.). 1991. pap. text 11.95 (*0-513-02051-9*) Denison.

Beghi, Giogio. Energy Storage & Transportation: Prospects for New Technologies. 1981. text 106.00 (*90-277-1166-6*) Kluwer Academic.

— Performance of Solar Energy Converters: Thermal Collectors & Photovoltaic Cells. 1983. text 226.00 (*90-277-1545-9*) Kluwer Academic.

— Synthetic Fuels. 1985. text 208.00 (*90-277-2016-9*) Kluwer Academic.

Beghi, Giogio, ed. Thermal Energy Storage. 1982. text 199.50 (*90-277-1428-2*) Kluwer Academic.

Beghin, I., et al. A Guide to Nutritional Assessment. (Nonserial Publication). 80p. 1988. pap. text 17.00 (*92-4-154221-7*, 1150286) World Health.

Beghtol, Clare. The Classification of Fiction: The Development of a System Based on Theoretical Principles. LC 93-45409. 1993. 41.50 (*0-8108-2828-6*) Scarecrow.

Begich, Nick. Angels Don't Play This Haarp: Advances in Tesla Technology. 215p. 1997. pap. 14.95 (*0-9648812-0-9*) Earthpulse Pr.

— Earthpulse Flashpoints. (Earthpulse Flashpoints: 5). 64p. (Orig.). 1998. pap. 4.95 (*1-890693-14-6*) Earthpulse Pr.

— Earthpulse Flashpoints, 2. (Earthpulse Flashpoints Ser.: II). 64p. (Orig.). 1999. pap. 4.95 (*1-890693-17-0*) Earthpulse Pr.

— Earthpulse Flashpoints, 6. (Earhpulse Flashpoints: 6). 64p. (Orig.). 1998. pap. 4.95 (*1-890693-15-4*) Earthpulse Pr.

— Earthpulse Flashpoints: Series 2, No. 1, Vols. 1-6. (Illus.). 1998. pap. 4.95 (*1-890693-16-2*) Earthpulse Pr.

Begich, Nick. Towards a New Alchemy Vol. 1: The Millennium Science. Begich, Thomas, ed. (Illus.). 180p. (Orig.). 1996. pap. 14.95 (*0-9648812-2-5*) Earthpulse Pr.

Begich, Nick, ed. Earthpulse Flashpoints: Series 1, No. 4. (Illus.). 64p. 1998. 4.95 (*0-9648812-8-4*) Earthpulse Pr.

***Begich, Nick & Roderick, James.** Earth Rising - The Revolution: Toward a Thousand Years of Peace. 304p. 2000. pap. 17.95 (*1-890693-43-X*) Earthpulse Pr.

Begich, Nick, et al. Earthpulse Flashpoints: New Text, No. 1. 68p. 1996. pap. 4.95 (*0-9648812-1-7*) Earthpulse Pr.

— Earthpulse Flashpoints: New Text, No. 2. 64p. 1996. pap. 4.95 (*0-9648812-3-3*) Earthpulse Pr.

Begich, Thomas, et al. Earthpulse Flashpoints: New Text, No. 3. 52p. 1996. pap. 4.95 (*0-9648812-4-1*) Earthpulse Pr.

Begich, Thomas, ed. see Begich, Nick.

Begiebing, Robert J. Acts of Regeneration: Allegory & Archetype in the Works of Norman Mailer. LC 80-50416. 223p. reprint ed. pap. 69.20 (*0-7837-2361-X*, AU0042600006) Bks Demand.

— The Adventures of Allegra Fullerton: Or a Memoir of Startling & Amusing Episodes from Itinerant Life- A Novel. LC 99-34280. (Hardscrabble Bks.). (Illus.). 326p. 1999. 24.95 (*0-87451-947-0*) U Pr of New Eng.

— The Strange Death of Mistress Coffin. LC 90-19528. 240p. 1996. pap. 9.95 (*1-56512-145-7*, 72145) Algonquin Bks.

— Toward a New Synthesis: John Fowles, John Gardner, Norman Mailer. LC 88-34076. 162p. 1989. reprint ed. pap. 50.30 (*0-608-02655-7*, AU0047900006) Bks Demand.

Begiebing, Robert J. & Grumbling, Owen. The Literature of Nature: The British & American Traditions. (Illus.). 730p. 1990. 49.00 (*0-937548-16-2*) Plexus Pub.

Begiebing, Robert J. & Grumbling, Owen, eds. The Literature of Nature: The British & American Traditions. (Illus.). 730p. 1990. pap. 37.50 (*0-937548-17-0*) Plexus Pub.

Begin, Carmelle & Nebel, Constance. Opus: The Making of Musical Instruments in Canada. (Illus.). 148p. 1992. 29.95 (*0-660-14006-3*, Pub. by CN Mus Civilization) U of Wash Pr.

Begin, James P. Dynamic Human Resource Systems: Cross-National Comparisons. LC 97-19625. (Studies in Organization: Vol. 79). xx, 377p. (C). 1997. text 84.95 (*3-11-015514-1*); pap. text 24.95 (*3-11-015515-X*) De Gruyter.

Begin, R. O., jt. ed. see Mossman, B. T.

Begin, Raymond F. Fundamentals of Insurance. 1977. write for info. (*0-672-61413-8*, Bobbs) Macmillan.

Begin, S., et al. Traditional Ties: Cultural Awareness & Listening Skills. 112p. 1992. audio 46.50 (*0-8013-0817-8*, 79184) Longman.

Begin, Ze'ev B. A Zionist Stand. 1993. pap. 17.50 (*0-7146-4089-1*, Pub. by F Cass Pubs) Intl Spec Bk.

Beginners Bible Staff. Beginner's Bible, Lift & Peek into Noah's Ark. LC 95-78417. (Illus.). (J). 1996. 10.99 (*0-679-87530-1*) McKay.

Beglar, David, et al. Cassette Contemporary Topics. LC 92-39791. (Longman Listening Ser.). 1993. audio 66.00 (*0-8013-0929-8*) Longman.

— Contemporary Topics. LC 92-39791. (Longman Listening Ser.). 144p. 1993. pap. text 24.97 (*0-8013-0928-X*) Longman.

Begleiter, Henri & Kissin, Benjamin, eds. The Biology of Alcoholism Vol. 7: Pathogenesis of Alcoholism: Biological Factors. LC 82-22284. 666p. 1983. 120.00 (*0-306-41053-2*, Plenum Trade) Perseus Pubng.

— The Biology of Alcoholism Vol. 7: Pathogenesis of Alcoholism: Biological Factors, Vols. 6 & 7. LC 82-22284. 666p. 1983. 175.00 (*0-685-06438-7*, Plenum Trade) Perseus Pubng.

— The Genetics of Alcoholism. LC 93-35497. (Alcohol & Alcoholism Ser.: No. 1). (Illus.). 416p. 1995. text 79.50 (*0-19-508877-8*) OUP.

— The Pharmacology of Alcohol & Alcohol Dependence. (Alcohol & Alcoholism Ser.: No. 2). (Illus.). 536p. (C). 1996. text 99.50 (*0-19-510094-8*) OUP.

Begleiter, Henri, jt. ed. see Cloninger, C. Robert.

Begleiter, Henri, jt. ed. see Kissin, Benjamin.

***Begleiter, Marcie.** From Word to Image: Storyboarding & the Filmmaking Process. LC 00-33441. (Illus.). 2000. write for info. (*0-941188-28-0*) M Wiese.

Begleiter, Steven. Fathers & Sons. (Illus.). 180p. 1989. 9.98 (*0-89659-968-X*) Abbeville Pr.

Begley, Adam. Literary Agents: A Writer's Guide. 96p. 1993. pap. 12.95 (*0-14-017215-7*, Penguin Bks) Viking Penguin.

Begley, Adam, ed. Literary Agents: A Writer's Guide. LC 83-617350. 192p. 1993. pap. 10.00 (*0-913734-17-9*) Poets & Writers.

Begley, Adam, ed. see Garner, Dwight L.

Begley, Alice C. & Johnson, Mary Ellen. Guilderland. (Images of America Ser.). 1997. pap. 18.99 (*0-7385-0112-3*) Arcadia Publng.

Begley, Charles E., jt. ed. see Agich, George J.

Begley, David L. Selected Papers on Free-Space Laser Communications II. LC 94-11393. (Milestone Ser.: Vol. MS 100). 1994. pap. 45.00 (*0-8194-1636-3*) SPIE.

— Selected Papers on Free-Space Laser Communications II. LC 94-11393. (Milestone Ser.: Vol. MS 100/HC). 1994. 55.00 (*0-8194-1637-1*) SPIE.

Begley, David L., ed. Free-Space Laser Communications: Selected Papers. (Milestone Ser.: Vol. MS30). 608p. 1991. 45.00 (*0-8194-0626-0*); pap. 35.00 (*0-8194-0627-9*) SPIE.

Begley, Donal F. The Ancestor Trail in Ireland. (Illus.). 32p. (Orig.). 1982. pap. 5.95 (*0-9502455-8-5*, Pub. by Heraldic Art) Irish Bks Media.

Begley, Edwin P., jt. ed. see Sturrock, Charles P.

Begley, Jackson A. Allen. History & Genealogical Record of the Allens-Begleys-Mays of Kentucky: Descendants of John Allen from 175- to the Present Time (1953) rev. ed. (Illus.). 147p. 1998. reprint ed. pap. 21.00 (*0-8328-7241-5*); reprint ed. lib. bdg. 31.00 (*0-8328-7240-7*) Higginson Bk Co.

Begley, Janet, ed. see Rattenbury, Richard C.

***Begley, John J.** Christian Initiation: A Handbook of Sources. LC 00-34361. 2000. pap. write for info. (*0-940866-90-0*) U Scranton Pr.

Begley, Loren, Jr., jt. auth. see Funk, Paul E.

Begley, Lorraine, ed. Crossing That Bridge: A Critical Look at the PEI Fixed Link. 192p. 1993. pap. 10.95 (*0-921556-39-X*, Pub. by Gynergy-Ragweed) U of Toronto Pr.

Begley, Louis. About Schmidt. 288p. 1997. pap. 12.00 (*0-449-91116-0*, Columbine) Fawcett.

— As Max Saw It. 160p. 1995. pap. 10.00 (*0-449-90947-6*) Fawcett.

— As Max Saw It. 1994. 21.00 (*0-679-43307-4*) Random.

— The Man Who Was Late. 256p. 1994. pap. 10.00 (*0-449-90911-5*, Columbine) Fawcett.

— Mistler's Exit. 1999. pap. 12.00 (*0-449-00422-8*) Ballantine Pub Grp.

— Mistler's Exit. LC 98-14566. 224p. 1998. 22.00 (*0-375-40262-4*) Random.

***Begley, Louis.** Schmidt Delivered. 272p. 2000. 25.00 (*0-375-41088-0*) Knopf.

Begley, Louis. Wartime Lies. 1997. pap. 12.00 (*0-449-00117-2*) Fawcett.

— Wartime Lies. 192p. 1992. mass mkt. 5.99 (*0-8041-0990-7*) Ivy Books.

Begley, Louis & Bradley, David. Obsession. (Illus.). 1994. boxed set 100.00 (*1-883060-02-X*) Quill & Brush Pr.

Begley, Louis, et al. Obsession. (Illus.). 116p. 1994. pap. 15.00 (*1-883060-03-6*) Quill & Brush Pr.

Begley, Melinda, ed. see Clifton, Lisa.

Begley, Melinda J., ed. see Zerbst, Elizabeth Lipiec.

Begley, Paul & Leonard, Pauline, eds. The Values of Educational Administration: A Book of Readings. LC 99-491960. 256p. 1999. 79.95 (*0-7507-0937-5*, Falmer Pr); pap. 30.95 (*0-7507-0936-7*, Falmer Pr) Taylor & Francis.

Begley, Paul R., et al. African American Genealogical Research. rev. ed. Andrews, Judith M., ed. (Illus.). 28p. 1997. pap. 5.00 (*1-880067-40-4*) SC Dept of Arch & Hist.

Begley, Paul T., ed. Values & Educational Leadership. LC 99-26254. (SUNY Series, Educational Leadership). (Illus.). 384p. (C). 1999. text 59.50 (*0-7914-4291-8*); pap. text 19.95 (*0-7914-4292-6*) State U NY Pr.

Begley, Philip A. & Jacobs, Mark B. Catching Fire: A Process for Building Leadership & Organizational Character. (Illus.). 261p. 1996. ring bd., wbk. ed. 225.00 (*1-890071-00-5*) Perform IN.

Begley, Phillip A. & Jacobs, Mark B. Catching Fire: Reality Leadership. LC 98-137378. (Reality Leadership Ser.). (Illus.). 200p. (Orig.). 1997. pap. 19.95 (*1-890071-02-1*) Perform IN.

Begley, T., jt. auth. see Broumas, Olga.

Begley, T., tr. see Elytis, Odysseus.

***Begley, Thomas D. & Jeffreys, Jo-Anne.** Representing the Elderly Client: Law & Practice LC 99-35522. 1999. ring bd. 145.00 (*0-7355-0367-2*) Panel Pubs.

Begley, Vimala & De Puma, Richard D., eds. Rome & India: The Ancient Sea Trade. LC 91-6579. (Wisconsin Studies in Classics). (Illus.). 248p. reprint ed. pap. 76.90 (*0-608-09844-2*, 206923200003) Bks Demand.

Begley, Vincent J. The Adventures of Tom Tinker. (J). (ps-3). 1993. pap. 14.95 (*0-933905-21-1*) Claycomb Pr.

— Missing Links. 224p. 1988. 15.95 (*0-933905-17-3*); pap. 9.95 (*0-933905-06-8*) Claycomb Pr.

Begley, W. E. Monumental Islamic Calligraphy from India. LC 84-29717. (Illus.). 144p. 1985. 17.95 (*0-932815-00-6*); pap. 10.95 (*0-932815-01-4*) Islamic Found.

Begley, Walter. Biblia Anagramatica. 212p. 1992. reprint ed. pap. 15.95 (*1-56459-016-X*) Kessinger Pub.

Begley, Walter, ed. Biblia Cabalistica. 158p. 1992. reprint ed. pap. 15.95 (*1-56459-017-8*) Kessinger Pub.

Begley, Wayne Edison. Taj Mahal: Illumined Tomb. (Illus.). 392p. 1990. 45.00 (*0-295-96944-X*) U of Wash Pr.

Beglinger, C., ed. European Pancreatic Club EPC, Twenty-Second Meeting, Basel, October 1990: Abstracts. (Journal: Digestion: Vol. 46, No 3, 1990). 72p. 1990. pap. 38.50 (*3-8055-5315-3*) S Karger.

Beglinger, C. & Buchler, M. W., eds. Role of Somatostatin-Analogues in Gastrointestinal Diseases. (Digestion Ser.: Vol. 60, Suppl. 2 (1999)). (Illus.). iv, 58p. 1999. pap. 25.25 (*3-8055-6878-9*) S Karger.

Beglinger, C. & Marbet, U., eds. Controversies about Inflammatory Diseases of the Pancreas. (Journal: Digestive Diseases: Vol. 10, No. 6, 1992). (Illus.). iv, 56p. 1992. pap. 36.75 (*3-8055-5719-1*) S Karger.

Beglinger, C., jt. ed. see Adler, G.

Begly, Carolyn. RGP Lens Fitting. (Contact Lens Update Ser.). 120p. 1999. 45.00 (*0-7506-9677-X*) Buttrwrth-Heinemann.

Begmen, Ronald & Strom, Mark. California Employee Survival Handbook. 3rd ed. (Illus.). 1998. pap. 17.95 (*0-9639232-2-6*) Pro Per Pubns.

Begnal, Kate. Iris Murdoch: A Reference Guide. (Reference Guides to Literature Ser.). 192p. 1987. 45.00 (*0-8161-8646-4*, Hall Reference) Macmillan.

Begnal, Michael H. Dreamscheme: Narrative & Voice in "Finnegans Wake" 127p. 1988. 34.95 (*0-8156-2426-3*) Syracuse U Pr.

— Joseph Sheridan Lefanu. LC 71-126032. (Irish Writers Ser.). 87p. 1975. pap. 1.95 (*0-8387-7735-X*) Bucknell U Pr.

Begnal, Michael H., ed. On Miracle Ground: Essays on the Fiction of Lawrence Durrell. LC 89-43051. 216p. 1990. 38.50 (*0-8387-5158-X*) Bucknell U Pr.

Begnal, Michael H. & Eckley, Grace. Narrator & Character in "Finnegans Wake" LC 73-4957. 241p. 1975. 34.50 (*0-8387-1337-8*) Bucknell U Pr.

Begnal, Thomas. The Woodworking Handbook. LC 97-11378. (Illus.). 224p. 1997. 21.99 (*1-55870-463-9*, Betrwy Bks) F & W Pubns Inc.

Begnal, Tom. The Woodworker's Guide to Shop Math. LC 98-18133. (Illus.). 208p. 1998. pap. 22.99 (*1-55870-485-X*, Popular Woodwking Bks) F & W Pubns Inc.

Bego, Mark. Alan Jackson: Gone Country. LC 96-18215. (Illus.). 200p. (Orig.). 1996. pap. 19.95 (*0-87833-919-1*) Taylor Pub.

***Bego, Mark.** Aretha Franklin. 2000. mass mkt. 18.00 (*0-306-80935-4*, Pub. by Da Capo) HarpC.

Bego, Mark. Bonnie Raitt: Just in the Nick of Time. (Illus.). 368p. 1995. 22.50 (*1-55972-315-7*, Birch Ln Pr) Carol Pub Group.

— Bonnie Raitt: Just in the Nick of Time. LC 97-5010. (Illus.). 272p. 1997. mass mkt. 6.99 (*0-8065-8011-9*, Citadel Stars) Carol Pub Group.

Bego, Mark. Bonnie Raitt: Just in the Nick of Time. abr. ed. 1996. 16.95 incl. audio (*1-882071-65-4*) B&B Audio.

Bego, Mark. George Strait: The Story of Country Music's Living Legend. LC 96-78891. (Illus.). 304p. 1997. 22.95 (*1-57566-116-0*) Kensgtn Pub Corp.

— George Strait: The Story of Country's Living Legend. 208p. 1998. pap. 12.00 (*1-57566-349-X*) Kensgtn Pub Corp.

— George Strait The Story of Country's Living Legend. 1999. mass mkt. 5.99 (*0-7860-0671-4*) Kensgtn Pub Corp.

— LeAnn Rimes. LC 98-23936. (Illus.). 80p. 1998. pap. 9.99 (*0-312-19378-5*) St Martin.

— Leonardo DiCaprio: Romantic Hero. 96p. 1998. pap. 10.95 (*0-8362-6972-1*) Andrews & McMeel.

***Bego, Mark.** Madonna: Blonde Ambition. expanded ed. (Illus.). 2000. pap. 18.95 (*0-8154-1051-4*) Cooper Sq.

Bego, Mark. The Rock & Roll Almanac. 288p. 1996. 12.95 (*0-02-860432-6*) Macmillan Info.

— The Rock & Roll Almanac: The Songs, the Stars, the Scandals, the Stories. (Illus.). 308p. 1999. reprint ed. pap. text 13.00 (*0-7881-6482-1*) DIANE Pub.

***Bego, Mark.** Story of Jewel. 1998. pap. text 14.95 (*0-8256-1685-9*) Music Sales.

— Vince Gill: An Unauthorized Biography of the Country Music Superstar. (Illus.). 256p. 2000. 22.95 (*1-58063-097-9*) Renaissance.

Bego, Mark, jt. auth. see Reeves, Martha.

Bego, Mark, jt. auth. see Stanley, David.

Begolly, Michael J. Leading the Assembly in Prayer: A Practical Guide for Lay & Ordained Presiders. LC 97-5326. 160p. (Orig.). 1997. pap. text 17.95 (*0-89390-398-1*) Resource Pubns.

Begon, M. Advances in Ecological Research, 28. 240p. 1999. 99.95 (*0-12-013928-6*) Acad Pr.

Begon, Michael. Ecology: Individuals, Populations, & Communities. 3rd ed. 1996. pap. text 54.95 (*0-632-03801-2*) Blackwell Sci.

Begon, Michael & Fitter, Alastair H., eds. Advances in Ecological Research, Vol. 23. (Illus.). 355p. 1992. text 104.00 (*0-12-013923-5*) Acad Pr.

— Advances in Ecological Research, Vol. 24. (Illus.). 410p. 1993. text 104.00 (*0-12-013924-3*) Acad Pr.

— Advances in Ecological Research, Vol. 25. (Illus.). 320p. 1994. text 104.00 (*0-12-013925-1*) Acad Pr.

— Advances in Ecological Research, Vol. 26. (Illus.). 408p. 1995. text 84.00 (*0-12-013926-X*) Acad Pr.

Begon, Michael, et al. Ecology. 3rd ed. (Illus.). 1996. pap. 69.95 (*0-632-04393-8*) Blackwell Sci.

Begona, Mauricio De, see De Begona, Mauricio.

Begos, Jane. A Women's Diaries Miscellany. 302p. 1989. 30.00 (*0-913660-23-X*); pap. 22.00 (*0-913660-24-8*) Magic Cir Pr CT.

Begoun, Paula. The Beauty Bible: From Acne to Wrinkles & Everything in Between. (Illus.). 388p. (Orig.). 1997. pap. 16.95 (*1-877988-22-7*) Beginning Pr.

***Begoun, Paula.** Don't Go to the Cosmetics Counter Without Me. 5th ed. 1000p. 2000. pap. 24.95 (*1-877988-28-6*) Beginning Pr.

Begoun, Paula. Don't Go to the Cosmetics Counter Without Me: An Eye-Opening Guide to Brand-Name Cosmetics. 4th ed. Asmus, Sigrid, ed. 754p. 1998. pap. 19.95 (*1-877988-23-5*) Beginning Pr.

Begoun, Paula & Bell, Stephanie. There Must Be Something for the Groom to Do: How to Plan Your Wedding Together. 176p. 1996. pap. 12.95 (*1-877988-16-2*) Beginning Pr.

Begoun, Paula & Iulsaas, Kris. Don't Go Shopping for Hair Care Products Without Me. 2nd rev. ed. Asmus, Sigrid, ed. (Illus.). 656p. 1999. pap. 19.95 (*1-877988-26-X*) Beginning Pr.

Begovic, B. The Economic Approach to Optimal City Size. (Progress in Planning Ser.: No. 36). 68p. 1991. pap. 56.50 (*0-08-041838-4*, Pergamon Pr) Elsevier.

B

An Asterisk (*) at the beginning of an entry indicates that the title is appearing for the first time.

Begovic, Tomislav. Gott - Der Weg des Menschen Zu Sich Selbst: Zur Theologischen Anthropologie in der Mystischen Lehre des Heiligen Johannes vom Kreuz. (Europaische Hochschulschriften Ser.: Reihe 23, Bd. 379). (GER.). IV, 256p. 1989. 51.80 (*3-631-40396-8*) P Lang Pubng.

Begrich, Joachim, jt. auth. see Gunkel, Hermann.

Begrmann. Woerterbuch Althochdeutschen. (GER.). 800p. 1990. 395.00 (*0-7859-7437-7*, 3484106638) Fr & Eur.

Beguad, Lenore. Ana Banana y Yo. 1995. pap. text 6.95 (*84-372-4017-4*) Santillana.

Begue, Claude M., ed. see Duras, Marguerite.

Begue, Yvette, ed. Judicial Discipline & Disability Digest: 1981-1986 Supplement. LC 81-65601. 1988. 190.00 (*0-938870-40-8*) Am Judicature.

Beguelin, Marie-Josee, jt. text see Moeschler, Jacques.

Beguerie, Philippe & Duchesneau, Claude. How to Understand the Sacraments. (Adult Christian Formation Program Ser.). (Illus.). 192p. (Orig.). 1990. pap. 16.95 (*0-8245-1026-7*) Crossroad NY.

Beguin, ed. see Nerval, Gerard De.

Beguin, A., et al. Sources of Thermodynamic Data on Mesogens: A Special Issue of the Journal of Molecular Crystals & Liquid Crystals. 340p. 1984. pap. text 348.00 (*0-677-16575-7*) Gordon & Breach.

Beguin, Andre. Dictionnaire Technique de la Peinture, 6 vols. (FRE.). 202p. 1981. pap. 395.00 (*0-7859-8217-5*, 2903319146) Fr & Eur.

— Dictionnaire Technique de la Peinture Vol. 1: A-B. (FRE.). 230p. 1978. pap. 59.95 (*0-7859-8215-9*, 2903319073) Fr & Eur.

— Dictionnaire Technique de la Peinture Vol. 2: C-E. (FRE.). 202p. 1979. pap. 59.95 (*0-7859-8665-0*, 290331909x) Fr & Eur.

— Dictionnaire Technique de la Peinture Vol. 3: F-H. (FRE.). 204p. 1980. pap. 59.95 (*0-7859-8216-7*, 2903319111) Fr & Eur.

— Dictionnaire Technique de la Peinture Vol. 5: N-P. (FRE.). 230p. 1982. pap. 59.95 (*0-7859-8218-3*, 2903319162) Fr & Eur.

— Dictionnaire Technique de la Peinture Vol. 6: Q-Z. (FRE.). 270p. 1984. pap. 59.95 (*0-7859-8219-1*, 2903319189) Fr & Eur.

— Dictionnaire Technique et Critique du Dessin. (FRE.). 1978. 150.00 (*0-8288-5202-2*, M6027) Fr & Eur.

Beguin, Antoinette, intro. Profiles of Rural Poverty. (Illus.). v, 50p. (Orig.). 1979. pap. 6.75 (*92-2-102142-4*) Intl Labour Office.

Beguin, Gilles & Morel, Dominique. The Forbidden City: Center of Imperial China. LC 97-7637. (Discoveries Ser.). (Illus.). 143p. 1997. pap. 12.95 (*0-8109-2822-1*, Pub. by Abrams) Time Warner.

Beguin, Louis-Paul. General Lexicon of Insurance: French - English, English - French. (ENG & FRE.). 267p. 1990. pap. 59.95 (*0-8288-9389-6*) Fr & Eur.

— Technical Vocabulary of Life Insurance, English-French Vocabulary. (ENG & FRE.). 135p. 1990. pap. 29.95 (*0-8288-4844-0*, M9245) Fr & Eur.

Beguin, Louis-Paul, et al. Technical Vocabulary of Life Insurance: Vocabulaire Technique des Assurances sur la Vie, Vol. 1, French-English. (ENG & FRE.). 309p. 1990. pap. 14.95 (*0-8288-4843-2*, M9244) Fr & Eur.

Beguin, Rebecca. Hers Was the Sky. LC 92-47053. 200p. (Orig.). 1993. pap. 8.95 (*0-934678-47-2*) New Victoria Pubs.

— In Unlikely Places: Searching for Miss Poole. LC 90-5940. 200p. (Orig.). 1990. pap. 8.95 (*0-934678-25-1*) New Victoria Pubs.

— Runway at Eland Springs. LC 87-60528. 240p. (Orig.). 1987. pap. 7.95 (*0-934678-10-3*) New Victoria Pubs.

— Torrid Zone. LC 96-45121. 200p. (Orig.). 1997. pap. 10.95 (*0-934678-81-2*) New Victoria Pubs.

Beguinot, Brigitte. The Mouse Party: An Open-the-Door Book. LC 91-77598. (Illus.). 12p. (J). (ps-3). 1992. bds. 10.95 (*1-878093-50-9*) Boyds Mills Pr.

Beguiristain, Rosa D. & Dihigo, Mario E. Cosas de Muchachos: Anecdotas Infantiles. (Coleccion Caniqui Ser.). (SPA., Illus.). 149p. 1998. pap. 12.00 (*0-89729-865-9*) Ediciones.

Begum, Anwara. Inter-Republican Co-Operation of the Russian Republic. LC 97-470. (Illus.). 168p. 1997. text 72.95 (*1-85521-940-9*, Pub. by Ashgate Pub) Ashgate Pub Co.

Begum, Khurshida. Tension over the Farakka Barrage: A Techno-Political Tangle in South Asia. 1988. 34.00 (*0-8364-2271-6*, Pub. by KP Bagchi) S Asia.

***Begun, Abbey M., ed.** Prisons & Jails: A Deterrent to Crime. rev. ed. (Information Plus Reference Ser.). (Illus.). 184p. 1999. pap. text 26.95 (*1-57302-102-4*) Info Plus TX.

— Transportation: America's Lifeline. rev. ed. (Information Plus Reference Ser.). (Illus.). 144p. 1999. pap. text 25.95 (*1-57302-103-2*) Info Plus TX.

Begun, Abbey M., et al, eds. AIDS. 5th rev. ed. (Information Plus Reference Ser.). (Illus.). 120p. (YA). 1998. pap. text 25.95 (*1-57302-072-9*) Info Plus TX.

***Begun, Abbey M., et al, eds.** Growing up in America. 7th rev. ed. (Reference Ser.). (Illus.). 176p. (YA). (gr. 9-12). 1999. pap. text 26.95 (*1-57302-087-7*) Info Plus TX.

— Health: A Concern for Every American. 10th rev. ed. (Reference Ser.). (Illus.). 192p. 1999. pap. text 26.95 (*1-57302-086-9*) Info Plus TX.

Begun, Abbey M., et al, eds. Minorities: A Changing Role in American Society. 10th rev. ed. (Information Plus Reference Ser.). (Illus.). 180p. 1998. pap. text 26.95 (*1-57302-077-X*) Info Plus TX.

— Women's Changing Role. 10th rev. ed. (Information Plus Reference Ser.). (Illus.). 184p. 1998. pap. text 26.95 (*1-57302-067-2*) Info Plus TX.

Begun, Abbey M., ed. see Information Plus Staff.

Begun, Abbey M., ed. see Sutton, Diane Le Clair.

Begun, David R., et al, eds. Function, Phylogeny, & Fossils: Miocene Hominoid Evolution & Adaptations. LC 96-40485. (Advances in Primatology Ser.). 436p. (C). 1997. 120.00 (*0-306-45457-2*, Kluwer Plenum) Kluwer Academic.

Begun, Ruth, et al, eds. Ready-to-Use Violence Prevention Skills Lessons & Activities: Activities for Elementary Students. LC 99-30609. (Illus.). 256p. 1998. spiral bd. 27.95 (*0-87628-136-6*) Ctr Appl Res.

Begun, Ruth W., ed. Ready-to-Use Social Skills Lessons & Activities for Grades PreK-K. LC 95-5194. 280p. 1995. pap. text, student ed. 27.95 (*0-87628-863-8*) Ctr Appl Res.

— Ready-to-Use Social Skills Lessons & Activities for Grades PreK-K. (Illus.). 240p. 1998. pap. 27.50 (*0-87628-472-1*) Ctr Appl Res.

— Ready-to-Use Social Skills Lessons & Activities for Grades 1-3. LC 95-24335. 280p. 1995. pap. text, student ed. 27.95 (*0-87628-864-6*) Ctr Appl Res.

— Ready-to-Use Social Skills Lessons & Activities for Grades 1-3. (Illus.). 240p. (gr. 1). 1998. pap. 27.50 (*0-87628-473-X*) Ctr Appl Res.

— Ready-to-Use Social Skills Lessons & Activities for Grades 4-6. 280p. 1996. pap. text 27.95 (*0-87628-865-4*) Ctr Appl Res.

— Ready-to-Use Social Skills Lessons & Activities for Grades 4-6. (Illus.). 240p. 1998. pap. 27.50 (*0-87628-474-8*) Ctr Appl Res.

— Ready-to-Use Social Skills Lessons & Activities for Grades 7-12. 280p. 1995. pap. text 27.95 (*0-87628-866-2*) Ctr Appl Res.

— Ready-to-Use Social Skills Lessons & Activities for Grades 7-12. (Illus.). 240p. 1998. pap. 27.50 (*0-87628-475-6*) Ctr Appl Res.

Begun, Ruth W., et al. Ready-to-Use Violence Prevention Skills Lessons & Activities for Secondary Students. LC 97-47478. (Illus.). 256p. 1998. spiral bd. 27.95 (*0-87628-917-0*) Ctr Appl Res.

Beh-Eger, Dorita, jt. auth. see Marx, Trish.

Beh, Lois C. Chicago, the Coloring Book. 16p. (J). (gr. 3). 1990. pap. 3.95 (*0-9641328-0-X*) Passport Coloring.

Beh, Su-Ping. Vom Ursprung Politischer Kontrolle in Ihren Zeitlosen Dimensionen Geistigen Verfassungslebens. XXVI, 234p. 1998. 48.95 (*3-631-33243-2*) P Lang Pubng.

Beha ed-Din. The Life of Saladin. 1972. lib. bdg. 250.00 (*0-87968-480-1*) Krishna Pr.

Beha, Phillipe, jt. auth. see Luppens, Michel.

Behagg, Clive. Politics & Production in the Early Nineteenth Century. LC 89-34005. 283p. reprint ed. pap. 87.80 (*0-608-20315-7*, 207156800002) Bks Demand.

Behague, Gerard. Heitor Villa-Lobos: The Search for Brazil's Musical Soul. LC 94-21638. (ILAS Special Publication Ser.). (Illus.). 220p. (Orig.). (C). 1994. pap. text 14.95 (*0-292-70823-8*, Pub. by Inst Latin Am) U of Tex Pr.

Behague, Gerard, ed. Performance Practice: Ethnomusicological Perspectives, 12. LC 83-10842. (Contributions in Intercultural & Comparative Studies: No. 12). (Illus.). 262p. 1984. 62.95 (*0-313-24160-0*, BPE/, Greenwood Pr) Greenwood.

Behague, Gerard H., ed. Music & Black Ethnicity: The Caribbean & South America. LC 94-503. 352p. (C). 1998. pap. 25.95 (*1-56000-708-7*, Pub. by U Miami N-S Ctr) L Rienner.

Behaim, Albert Von, see Von Behaim, Albert.

Behal & Melilli, Albert S., eds. Stainless Steel Castings - STP 756. 454p. 1982. 45.00 (*0-8031-0740-4*, STP756) ASTM.

Behal-Thomsen, et al. Typisch Deutsch. 144p. 1993. 24.50 (*3-468-49446-7*) Langenscheidt.

Behan, Beatrice. The Dubbalin Man - Brendan Behan: A New Selection from Brendan Behan's Irish Press Column. LC 98-120432. (Illus.). 134p. 1998. pap. 15.95 (*1-899047-15-8*, Pub. by A A Farmar) Irish Bks Media.

Behan, Beverly. Jumping Ship: How to Navigate Your Way to a More Satisfying Job or Career. LC 98-933093. 158p. 1999. pap. 15.95 (*0-7737-6051-2*) Genl Dist Srvs.

— Jumping Ship: Strategies for Career Changes & Job Hunters. 1999. 19.95 (*0-7737-3159-8*) Genl Dist Srvs.

Behan, Brendan. After the Wake. Fallon, Peter, ed. LC 82-159911. (Classic Irish Fiction Ser.). 156p. 1983. 15.95 (*0-905140-97-4*) Devin.

***Behan, Brendan.** Borstal Boy. 386p. 1999. pap. 14.95 (*1-56792-105-1*, Non Pareil Bk) Godine.

Behan, Brendan. The Complete Plays. Incl. Hostage. 1978. Quare Fellow. 1978. Richard's Cork Leg. 1978. Three One Act Plays for Radio. 1978. 1978. Set pap. 8.95 (*0-394-17052-0*, B411) Grove-Atltic.

— The Complete Plays of Behan: The Hostage, The Quare Fellow, Richard's Cork Leg. LC 78-53931. 352p. (Orig.). 1988. pap. 14.00 (*0-8021-3070-4*, Grove) Grove-Atltic.

— An Giall: The Hostage. Wall, Richard, ed. & tr. by. LC 87-20864. (Irish Dramatic Texts Ser.). 182p. 1987. reprint ed. pap. 56.50 (*0-7837-9185-2*, 204988500003) Bks Demand.

— The King of Ireland's Son. LC 96-28377. (Illus.). 40p. (J). (gr. 1 up). 1997. 16.95 (*0-531-09549-5*) Orchard Bks Watts.

— The Letters of Brendan Behan. Mikhail, E. H., ed. (Illus.). 272p. 1991. 60.00 (*0-7735-0888-0*, Pub. by McG-Queens Univ Pr) CUP Services.

— Poems & a Play in Irish. 76p. 1989. pap. 12.95 (*0-904011-15-1*) Dufour.

— The Scarperer. reprint ed. lib. bdg. 18.95 (*0-89190-573-1*, Rivercity Pr) Amereon Ltd.

Behan, Brian. Mother of All the Behans: The Autobiography of Kathleen Behan. 138p. 1995. pap. 12.95 (*1-85371-337-6*, Pub. by Poolbeg Pr) Dufour.

Behan, Brian & Dillon-Malone, A. The Brothers Behan. LC 98-230776. 237 p. 1998. write for info. (*1-901658-16-3*) Ashfield Pr.

Behan, Dominic. Ireland Sings. (Illus.). 156p. 1973. pap. 12.95 (*0-8256-9341-1*, AM26725) Music Sales.

Behan, Eileen. Cooking Well for the Unwell: More Than One Hundred Nutritious Recipes. 384p. 1997. reprint ed. pap. 15.00 (*0-688-15558-8*, Quil) HarperTrade.

— Eat Well, Lose Weight While Breastfeeding: The Complete Nutrition Book for Nursing Mothers. LC 92-632. 235p. 1992. pap. 11.95 (*0-679-73355-8*) Villard Books.

— Meals That Heal: For Babies & Toddlers. 1999. pap. write for info. (*0-671-52985-4*) S&S Trade.

— Meals That Heal for Babies & Toddlers. 304p. 1996. pap. 12.00 (*0-671-52986-2*) S&S Trade.

— The Pregnancy Diet. 336p. 1998. pap. 14.00 (*0-671-74794-0*, PB Trade Paper) PB.

— The Pregnancy Diet: A Healthy Weight Control Program for Pregnant Women. LC 98-53461. 288p. 1999. pap. 12.00 (*0-671-00393-3*) S&S Trade.

Behan, Peter, et al, eds. Postviral Fatigue Syndrome. (British Medical Bulletin Ser.: Vol. 47, No. 4). (Illus.). 264p. 1992. text. write for info. (*0-443-04490-2*) Church.

Behan, Tom. The Camorra. LC 95-22481. 240p. (C). 1996. 70.00 (*0-415-09987-0*) Routledge.

***Behan, Tom.** Dario Fo: Revolutionary Theatre. LC 99-42772. 160p. 2000. 59.95 (*0-7453-1362-0*, Pub. by Pluto GBR); pap. 17.95 (*0-7453-1357-4*, Pub. by Pluto GBR) Stylus Pub VA.

Behan, Tom. The Long Awaited Moment: The Working Class & the Italian Communist Party in Milan, 1943-1948. LC 95-21799. (American University Studies: Vol. 174). (Illus.). XII, 310p. (C). 1997. 49.95 (*0-8204-2674-1*) P Lang Pubng.

Behana. Child Abuse: Detection, Intervention & Prevention. (C). 1996. pap. text, teacher ed. 40.00 (*0-15-503958-X*) Harcourt Coll Pubs.

Behar. Crisis & the Arts, the History of Dada Vol. 6: Paris. 2000. 85.00 (*0-8161-7374-5*, G K Hall & Co) Mac Lib Ref.

***Behar, Alberto.** Noise Handbook. LC 99-40683. 131p. 1999. pap. 43.95 (*1-56593-992-1*) Singular Publishing.

Behar-Horenstein, ed. Curriculum Issues & the Postsecondary Preparation of Educators: A Special Issue of the Peabody Journal of Education, Vol. 70, No. 3, 1996. 1996. reprint ed. pap. 20.00 (*0-8058-9893-X*) L Erlbaum Assocs.

Behar-Horenstein, Linda S., jt. auth. see Glanz, Jeffrey.

Behar-Horenstein, Linda S., jt. auth. see Ornstein, Allan C.

***Behar, J.** Cooperation & Competition in a Common Market: Studies on the Formation of MERCOSUR. Muller, W. A. & Bihn, M., eds. (Contributions to Economics Ser.). viii, 152p. 2000. pap. text (*3-7908-1280-3*) Spr-Verlag.

Behar, Jaime. Trade & Employment in Mexico. (Swedish Institute for Social Research Ser.: No. 7). (Illus.). 296p. 1989. pap. 48.50 (*91-7604-029-1*) Coronet Bks.

Behar, Jaime & Malaki, Akhil, eds. Regional Integration & Economic Reform in Central America. LC 96-209679. (Institute of Latin American Studies). (Illus.). 198p. 1996. pap. 69.50 (*91-85894-47-8*, Pub. by Almqvist Wiksell) Coronet Bks.

Behar, Joseph E. Mapping Cyberspace: Social Research on the Electronic Frontier. (Dowling Studies in the Humanities & the Social Sciences). 256p. 1997. pap. 17.00 (*1-883058-43-0*, Dowling College) Global Pubns.

Behar, Joseph E., jt. auth. see Cuzan, Alfred G.

***Behar, Joy.** Joy Shtick: Or What Is the Existential Vaccuum & Does It Come with Attach. 208p. 2000. pap. 12.95 (*0-7868-8545-9*, Pub. by Disney Pr) Time Warner.

Behar, Joy. Joy Shtick: Or What Is the Existential Vacuum & Does It Come with Attachments? LC 98-42761. (Illus.). 191p. 1999. 19.95 (*0-7868-6423-0*, Pub. by Hyperion) Time Warner.

Behar, June, ed. see Nasmyth, Virginia & Nasmyth, Spike.

Behar, Larry J. Comment Immigrer aux U. S. A. Les Affaires en Amerique. 296p. 1993. pap. text 19.95 (*0-9637164-1-7*) L J Behar.

— How to Immigrate to the U. S. A. Doing Business in America. 296p. 1993. pap. text 19.95 (*0-9637164-0-9*) L J Behar.

Behar, Linda S. The Knowledge Base of Curriculum: An Empirical Analysis. 188p. (Orig.). (C). 1993. pap. text 27.50 (*0-8191-9267-8*); lib. bdg. 49.50 (*0-8191-9266-X*) U Pr of Amer.

Behar, Ruth. The Presence of the Past in a Spanish Village. (Illus.). 426p. 1991. pap. text 21.95 (*0-691-02866-4*, Pub. by Princeton U Pr) Cal Prin Full Svc.

— Translated Woman: Crossing the Border with Esperanza's Story. LC 92-5588. 400p. 1994. pap. 16.00 (*0-8070-7053-X*) Beacon Pr.

— The Vulnerable Observer: Anthropology That Breaks Your Heart. LC 96-11409. 208p. 1997. reprint ed. pap. 15.00 (*0-8070-4631-0*) Beacon Pr.

Behar, Ruth, ed. Bridges to Cuba/Puentes a Cuba. LC 95-34522. 448p. (Orig.). 1995. text 49.50 (*0-472-09611-7*, 09611) U of Mich Pr.

— Bridges to Cuba/Puentes a Cuba. LC 95-34522. (Illus.). 448p. (Orig.). 1995. pap. 18.95 (*0-472-06611-0*, 06611) U of Mich Pr.

Behar, Ruth & Gordon, Deborah A., eds. Women Writing Culture. (Illus.). 470p. 1995. pap. 19.95 (*0-520-20208-2*, Pub. by U CA Pr) Cal Prin Full Svc.

Behar, Stella. Georges Perec: Ecire pour Ne Pas Dire. LC 94-9795. (Currents in Comparative Romance Languages & Literatures Ser.: Vol. 28). (FRE.). 246p. (C). 1995. text 53.95 (*0-8204-2467-6*) P Lang Pubng.

***Behar, Susie.** Grasslands. LC 99-45543. (Closer Look at... Ser.). (Illus.). 32p. (J). (gr. 4-6). 2000. lib. bdg. 21.90 (*0-7613-1153-X*, Copper Beech Bks) Millbrook Pr.

Behar, Unda S., jt. ed. see Ornstein, Allan C.

Behar-Velay, Lydia. Dictionnaire de Poche: Espagnol-Francais - Francais-Espagnol. (FRE & SPA.). 660p. 1994. pap. 19.95 (*0-7859-7860-7*, 2253064483) Fr & Eur.

Behara, Minaketan, et al, eds. Symposia Gaussina Conference A: Mathematics & Theoretical Physics: Proceedings of the 2nd Gauss Symposium, Munich, Germany, August 2-7, 1993. LC 95-14935. (Symposia Gaussiana Ser.). xx, 745p. (C). 1995. lib. bdg. 198.95 (*3-11-014476-X*) De Gruyter.

Behari, Bankey, tr. see Attar, Farid Al-Din.

Behari, Bepin. Fundamentals of Vedic Astrology: Vedic Astrologer's Handbook, Vol. 1. 280p. 1993. pap. 14.95 (*1-878423-09-6*) Morson Pub.

— Mismanagement of Indian Economy. (C). 1991. 23.50 (*81-7018-659-5*, Pub. by BR Pub) S Asia.

— Myths & Symbols of Vedic Astrology. 280p. (Orig.). (C). 1990. pap. 14.95 (*1-878423-06-1*) Morson Pub.

— Planets in the Signs & Houses, Vol. 2. 256p. 1990. pap. 14.95 (*1-878423-10-X*) Morson Pub.

— Rural Poverty & Unemployment. 304p. 1990. text 50.00 (*0-7069-4954-4*, Pub. by Vikas) S Asia.

Behari, Bepin & Behari, Madhuri. Introduction to Esoteric Astrology. 1998. pap. 14.50 (*0-8364-5539-8*) S Asia.

Behari, Madhuri, jt. auth. see Behari, Bepin.

Behavioral Research Conference Staff. Strategic Decisions from Behavioral Research: 1st Annual Behavioral Research Conference, January 24-26, 1990, Axioms under Review: Challenging the Conventional Wisdom of Marketing & Attitude Research. LC 90-1051. (Illus.). 238p. 1990. reprint ed. pap. 73.80 (*0-7837-9764-8*, 206049200005) Bks Demand.

Behbahani, Simin. A Cup of Sin: Selected Poems. Milani, Farzaneh & Safa, Kaveh, trs. from PER. LC 98-53791. (Middle East Literature in Translation Ser.). 182p. 1998. 24.95 (*0-8156-0554-4*) Syracuse U Pr.

Behbehani, Abbas M. The Smallpox Story: In Words & Pictures. LC 88-20846. (Illus.). (Orig.). (C). 1988. pap. text 15.95 (*0-685-24022-3*) Univ KS Med Ctr.

Behbehani, Hashim S. China's Foreign Policy in the Arab World 1955-75: Three Case Studies. (Illus.). 425p. 1981. pap. text 29.95 (*0-7103-0125-1*) Routledge.

Behbehani, Hashim S., ed. China & the People's Democratic Republic of Yemen: A Report. 425p. 1985. 45.00 (*0-7103-0097-2*) Routledge.

Behbehani, Soraya S. The Messenger Within: Discovering Love & Wholeness Through Meditation. 230p. 1996. pap. 16.90 (*0-614-21311-8*, 1369) Kazi Pubns.

***Behbehani, Soraya Susan.** The Messenger Within: Discovering Love & Wholeness Through Meditation. 3rd ed. 250p. 1999. pap. 16.95 (*0-910735-68-9*, Pub. by MTO Printing & Pubn Ctr) ACCESS Pubs Network.

Behbudi, Muhammad B. & Turner, Colin. The Quran: A New Interpretation: In English with Arabic Text. (ARA & ENG.). 688p. 1998. 85.00 (*0-7007-0407-8*, Pub. by Curzon Pr Ltd) Paul & Co Pubs.

Behdad, Ali. Belated Travelers: Orientalism in the Age of Colonial Dissolution. LC 93-44399. (Post-Contemporary Interventions Ser.). (Illus.). 208p. 1994. text 49.95 (*0-8223-1454-1*); pap. text 16.95 (*0-8223-1471-1*) Duke.

Behdad, Sohrab & Nomani, Farhad, eds. Islam & Public Policy. (International Review of Comparative Public Policy Ser.: Vol. 9). 1997. 78.50 (*0-7623-0268-2*) Jai Pr.

Behdad, Sohrab, jt. ed. see Rahnema, Saeed.

Behe, George. Titanic: Safety, Speed & Sacrifice. Harris, Marion, ed. LC 97-6521. (Illus.). 88p. 1997. pap. 12.50 (*0-933449-31-3*) Transport Trails.

Behe, George, jt. auth. see Goss, Michael.

Behe, Michael J. Darwins Black Box. 1996. 25.00 (*0-02-874101-3*) Free Pr.

— Darwin's Black Box: The Biochemical Challenge to Evolution. (Illus.). 320p. 1996. 24.50 (*0-684-82754-9*) Free Pr.

— Darwin's Black Box: The Biochemical Challenge to Evolution. LC 96-695. (Illus.). 307p. 1998. pap. 13.00 (*0-684-83493-6*, Touchstone) S&S Trade Pap.

Behee, John R. Fielding Yost's Legacy. LC 77-173360. (Illus.). 210p. 1971. 9.95 (*0-914464-00-0*) J & J Bks.

— Hail to the Victors. LC 74-75995. (Illus.). 140p. 1974. pap. 9.95 (*0-914464-01-9*) J & J Bks.

Behee, John R. & Saylor, Tom. Wave the Flag for Hudson High. LC 77-89960. (Illus.). 1977. pap. 9.95 (*0-914464-02-7*) J & J Bks.

***Beheler.** Networking Using Novell Netware 5.0. 304p. 2001. pap. text 45.00 (*0-13-270588-5*) P-H.

***Beheler, Ann.** Data Communications & Networking Fundamentals Using Novell NetWare (4.11) LC 98-28513. 500p. 1998. pap. 77.00 (*0-13-592007-8*) P-H.

— Networking Fundamentals Using Novell NetWare (4.11) LC 98-29725. 252p. 1998. pap. 61.00 (*0-13-409806-4*) P-H.

Beheler, Ann. Using Novell Network 4.11: Introduction to Data Communications Using Netware. LC 98-9673. 272p. 1998. pap. 63.00 (*0-13-270570-2*) P-H.

Beheler, Laura. The Dragon Thread. LC 80-84202. 164p. 1981. 9.95 (*0-937884-00-6*) Hystry Mystry.

— The Snow Moon. 1986. 20.00 (*0-946270-30-9*, Pub. by Pentland Pr) St Mut.

Behem, Jacob. Three Principles of the Divine Essence. 1978. reprint ed. 18.00 (*0-911662-65-0*) Yoga.

Beher, W. T. Chemistry & Physiology of Bile Acids & Their Influence on Atherosclerosis. (Monographs on Atherosclerosis: Vol. 6). (Illus.). 1976. 85.25 (*3-8055-2242-8*) S Karger.

Behera, Deepak K., jt. ed. see Pfeffer, Georg.

An Asterisk (*) at the beginning of an entry indicates that the title is appearing for the first time.

Behera, G. A., ed. Electronic Correlation & Disorder Effects in Metals. 400p. (C). 1991. text 100.00 (*9971-5-0887-7*) World Scientific Pub.

Behera, K. S. Konark - The Heritage of Mankind Vol. 1: Religion, History & Architecture. (Illus.). xxix, 171p. 1996. 89.00 (*81-7305-074-0*, Pub. by Aryan Bks Intl) Nataraj Bks.

— Konark - The Heritage of Mankind Vol. 2: Art & Culture. LC 96-900172. (Illus.). xi, 190p. 1996. 89.00 (*81-7305-075-9*, Pub. by Aryan Bks Intl) Nataraj Bks.

***Behera, K. S. & Donaldson, Thomas.** Sculpture Masterpieces from Orissa: Style & Iconography. LC 98-907370. 1998. 130.00 (*81-7305-131-3*, Pub. by Aryan Bks Intl) S Asia.

Behera, K. S., jt. auth. see Saha, S. P.

***Behera, M. C.** Pilgrim Centre Parshuram Kund: Articulation of Indian Society, Culture & Economic Dimension. LC 98-908717. 1998. 24.00 (*81-7169-503-5*, Pub. by Commonwealth) S Asia.

Behera, S. N., jt. auth. see Rao, B. K.

Behera, S. N., jt. ed. see Jena, P.

Behery, Hassan M. Short Fibre Content & Uniformity Index in Cotton. 48p. 1993. pap. 45.00 (*0-85198-781-8*) OUP.

Beheshti, Ayatullah. Ownership in Islam. Afghari, Ali R., tr. 80p. (Orig.). 1989. pap. text 5.60 (*1-871031-28-1*) Abjad Bk.

Behforooz, Ali & Hudson. Instructor's Guide & Transparency Masters to Accompany Software Engineering Fundamentals. (Illus.). 262p. 1996. text, teacher ed. write for info. (*0-19-511153-2*) OUP.

Behforooz, Ali & Hudson, Frederick J. Software Engineering Fundamentals. (Illus.). 688p. (C). 1996. text 79.95 (*0-19-510539-7*) OUP.

Behiels, Michael D. Prelude to Quebec's Quiet Revolution: Liberalism vs. Neo-Nationalism, 1945-60. 400p. 1985. 60.00 (*0-7735-0423-0*, Pub. by McG-Queens Univ Pr); pap. 22.95 (*0-7735-0424-9*, Pub. by McG-Queens Univ Pr) CUP Services.

***Behiels, Michael D. & Martel, Marcel, eds.** A Rare Bird on Earth: Essays in Honour of Ramsay Cook. (Illus.). 320p. 2000. pap. 19.95 (*0-19-541463-2*) OUP.

Behiels, Michael D. & Mathew, K. S. Canada, Its Regions & People. LC 98-901309. 1998. 42.50 (*81-215-0803-7*, Pub. by M Manoharial) Coronet Bks.

Behing, Paul L. Taxation of 401(K) & Other Salary Reduction Plans. 800p. 1994. 145.00 (*0-7913-1979-2*) Warren Gorham & Lamont.

Behkalam, Akbar. Akbar Behkalam: Movement & Change, Paintings & Sketches. (Illus.). 117p. (Orig.). 1989. pap. 25.00 (*0-939214-37-7*) Mazda Pubs.

***Behl, Aditya & Weightman, Simon, eds.** Madhumalati: An Indian Sufi Romance. (Oxford World's Classics Ser.). 240p. 2001. 10.95 (*0-19-284037-1*) OUP.

Behl, Benoy K. & Nigam, Sangitika. The Ajanta Caves: Artistic Wonder of Ancient Buddist India. LC 97-32237. (Illus.). 256p. 1998. 65.00 (*0-8109-1983-4*, Pub. by Abrams) Time Warner.

Behl, Y. S. & Tangri, O. P., eds. Integrated Urban Pest Management. 195p. (C). 1986. 250.00 (*0-7855-6736-4*, Pub. by Himalayan Bks) St Mut.

Behle, Klaus. Ein Generatororientiertes Makrookonometrisches Modell fur die BRD zur Simulation der Gesamtwirtschaftlichen Entwicklung bis zum Jahre 2005. (GER., Illus.). XXIII, 830p. 1996. 127.95 (*3-631-30839-6*) P Lang Pubng.

Behle, William H. Utah Birds: Geographic Distribution & Systematics. pap. 12.95 (*0-940378-06-X*) Utah Mus Natural Hist.

— Utah Birds: Historical Perspective & Bibliography. 25.00 (*0-940378-11-6*) Utah Mus Natural Hist.

Behlen, Charles. Perdition's Keepsake. Oliphant, Dave, ed. (Illus.). 1978. pap. 5.00 (*0-933384-00-9*) Prickly Pear.

Behler, Constantin. Nostalgic Teleology: Friedrich Schiller & the Schemata of Aesthetic Humanism. LC 95-36517. (Stanford German Studies: Vol. 26). 259p. 1995. 46.95 (*3-906755-22-3*) P Lang Pubng.

Behler, Deborah, jt. auth. see Behler, John.

Behler, Ernst. Confrontations: Derrida - Heidegger - Nietzsche. Taubeneck, Steven, tr. from GER. 200p. (C). 1991. 39.50 (*0-8047-1945-4*); pap. 13.95 (*0-8047-1968-3*) Stanford U Pr.

— German Romantic Literary Theory. LC 92-22039. (Cambridge Studies in German). (Illus.). 368p. (C). 1993. text 74.95 (*0-521-32585-4*) Cambridge U Pr.

— Irony & the Discourse of Modernity. LC 90-11960. 160p. (C). 1990. 20.00 (*0-295-96998-9*) U of Wash Pr.

Behler, Ernst, ed. see Hegel, Georg Wilhelm Friedrich.

Behler, Ernst, ed. see Nietzsche, Friedrich Wilhelm.

Behler, Ernst, ed. see Rey, William H.

Behler, Ernst, tr. see Schlegel, Friedrich von.

Behler, John, contrib. by. Familiar Reptiles & Amphibians of North America. (Illus.). 192p. 1988. pap. 9.00 (*0-394-75793-9*) Knopf.

Behler, John & Behler, Deborah. Alligators & Crocodiles. LC 97-28583. (WorldLife Library). 72p. (Orig.). (YA). (gr. 5 up). 1998. pap. 16.95 (*0-89658-370-8*) Voyageur Pr.

Behler, John L. National Audubon Society First Field Guide. LC 98-8332. (Illus.). 160p. (J). (gr. 3-7). 1999. 17.95 (*0-590-05467-8*); pap. 11.95 (*0-590-05487-2*) Scholastic Inc.

Behlim, S. A. Quran Made Easy (Yassar nal Quran) 1987. pap. 7.50 (*0-933511-01-9*) Kazi Pubns.

Behling, Bill & Hunt, Michael. Pepsi-Cola Collectibles, Vol. III. 2nd rev. ed. (Illus.). 156p. 1994. pap. 17.95 (*0-89538-021-8*) L-W Inc.

Behling, Brett & Harville, Bruce. Mastering Fee Management: All Factors Accounted For. 86p. (Orig.). 1993. pap. 89.00 (*1-889394-28-9*) Credit Union Execs.

Behling, Hermann. Untersuchungen Zur Spaetpleistozaenen und Holozaenen Vegetations- und Klimageschichte. (Dissertationes Botanicae Ser.: Band 206). (Illus.). ii, 149p. 1993. pap. 65.00 (*3-443-64118-0*, Pub. by Gebruder Borntraeger) Balogh.

Behling, John H. Guidelines for Preparing the Research Proposal. rev. ed. LC 83-23362. 88p. 1884. pap. text 14.50 (*0-8191-3734-0*) U Pr of Amer.

***Behling, Orlando & Law, Kenneth S.** Translating Questionnaires & Other Research Instruments: Problems & Solutions 1. LC 00-8368. (Quantitative Application in the Social Sciences Ser.). 2000. write for info. (*0-7619-1824-8*) Sage.

Behling, Richard. Exercises in Sentential Logic. 3rd ed. 208p. (C). 1997. per. 32.95 (*0-7872-4511-9*) Kendall-Hunt.

Behling, Richard, jt. auth. see Clarke, D. S.

Behling, Richard W. Exercises in Sentential Logic. 3rd ed. 224p. (C). 1994. per. 25.95 (*0-8403-9506-X*) Kendall-Hunt.

Behling, Robert E. Geology in West Virginia: A Study Guide for Physical Geology at West Virginia University. 112p. 1995. spiral bd. 17.95 (*0-8403-7939-0*) Kendall-Hunt.

***Behling, Sophia.** Glass: Structure & Technology in Architecture. (Illus.). 152p. 2000. 59.95 (*3-7913-2155-2*) Prestel Pub NY.

— Solar Power: The Evolution of Sustainable Architecture. (Illus.). 240p. 2000. pap. 29.95 (*3-7913-2411-X*) Prestel.

Behling, Sophia & Behling, Stefan. Sol Power: The Evolution of Solar Architecture. (Illus.). 240p. 1996. 65.00 (*3-7913-1670-2*, Pub. by Prestel) te Neues.

Behling, Stefan, jt. auth. see Behling, Sophia.

Behling, Thomas A. Introducing Life into Physics. Nolan-Rosager, Sharon, ed. (Illus.). 147p. (C). 1990. text 25.00 (*0-9626256-0-4*) T A Behling.

Behlke, J., et al, eds. Analytical Ultracentrifugation. (Progress in Colloid & Polymer Science Ser.: Vol. 99). 212p. 1996. 99.00 (*3-7985-1038-5*) Spr-Verlag.

Behlmer, George K. Friends of the Family: The English Home & Its Guardians, 1850-1940. LC 98-11235. 472p. 1998. 55.00 (*0-8047-3313-9*) Stanford U Pr.

***Behlmer, George K. & Leventhal, F. M.** Singular Continuities: Tradition, Nostalgia & Identity in Modern British Culture. LC 00-39487. (Illus.). 2000. write for info. (*0-8047-3489-5*) Stanford U Pr.

Behlmer, Rudy. Behind the Scenes. LC 89-84945. (Illus.). 340p. 1989. pap. 14.95 (*0-573-60600-5*) S French Trade.

— W. S. Van Dyke's Journal: White Shadows in the South Seas, 1927-28, & Other Van Dyke on Van Dyke, Vol. 47. LC 95-34206. (Filmmakers Ser.: No. 47). 160p. 1996. 34.50 (*0-8108-3028-0*) Scarecrow.

Behlmer, Rudy, ed. Memo from Darryl F. Zanuck: The Golden Years at 20th Century-Fox. LC 92-32865. (Illus.). 288p. 1995. pap. 14.00 (*0-8021-3332-0*, Grove) Grove-Atltic.

— The Sea Hawk. LC 81-70418. (Wisconsin-Warner Bros. Screenplay Ser.). (Illus.). 244p. 1982. pap. 9.95 (*0-299-09014-0*) U of Wis Pr.

Behlmer, Rudy, selected by. Memo from David O. Selznick. LC 89-36530. (Illus.). 518p. 1989. pap. 18.95 (*0-573-60601-3*) S French Trade.

Behlmer, Rudy, ed. see Selznick, David O.

Behlmer, Stacey Endress, jt. auth. see Cushman, Robert.

Behlolavek, John M. & Wynne, Lewis N., eds. Divided We Fall: Essays on Confederate Nation-Building. LC 91-60159. (Illus.). 264p. 1991. pap. 15.95 (*0-945759-03-7*) St Leo Col Pr.

Behm, Barbara J. Animal Opposites. Incl. Daytime & Nighttime Animals. Camm, Martin. LC 99-32254. 24p. (J). (ps up). 1999. lib. bdg. 18.60 (*0-8368-2459-8*); Prickly & Soft Animals. Twinney, Dick. LC 99-33300. 24p. (J). (ps up). 1999. lib. bdg. 18.60 (*0-8368-2460-1*); Quick & Slow Animals. Camm, Martin. LC 99-31623. 24p. (J). (ps up). 1999. lib. bdg. 18.60 (*0-8368-2461-X*); Sleepy & Busy Animals. LC 99-33354. (Illus.). 24p. (J). (ps up). 1999. lib. bdg. 18.60 (*0-8368-2462-8*); (Illus.). 24p. (J). (ps up). Set lib. bdg. 74.40 (*0-8368-2458-X*) Gareth Stevens Inc.

— Tears of Joy. unabridged ed. LC 98-91062. (Illus.). 32p. (J). (gr. 1 up). 1999. lib. bdg. 19.95 (*0-9669647-0-5*) WayWord.

Behm, Barbara J., jt. auth. see Balouet, Jean-Christopher.

Behm, Carl, III, jt. auth. see Hahn, H. George.

Behm, Carol, jt. auth. see Bryant, C.

Behm, Douglas R. An Advent Covenant Wreath. 16p. 1981. pap. text 3.95 (*0-89536-482-4*, 0102) CSS OH.

***Behm, Kim, contrib. by.** 16,000 Suspects. unabridged ed. (Ragbrai Mystery Ser.). 190p. 1999. pap. 10.95 (*0-9662041-2-3*) KUNI.

***Behm, Marc.** Eye of the Beholder. 1999. mass mkt. 6.99 (*0-345-42799-8*, Ballantine) Ballantine Pub Grp.

Behm, Marc. Mortelle Randonnee. (FRE.). 247p. 1987. pap. 10.95 (*0-7859-2070-6*, 2070378594) Fr & Eur.

Behm, Mary & Behm, Richard. One Hundred One Ideas to Help Your Child Learn to Read & Write. Shermis, Michael, ed. LC 89-49266. (Illus.). 39p. 1989. pap. 6.50 (*0-927516-13-6*) ERIC-REC.

— 101 Ways to Help Your Child Learn to Read & Write. LC 95-18220. (Illus.). 58p. (Orig.). 1995. pap. 5.99 (*1-883790-16-6*, EDINFO Pr) Grayson Bernard Pubs.

Behm, Mary, jt. auth. see Behm, Richard.

Behm, R. J., et al, eds. Scanning Tunneling Microscopy & Related Methods. (C). 1990. text 264.50 (*0-7923-0861-1*) Kluwer Academic.

Behm, Richard & Behm, Mary. Leamos! (Let's Read!) Prepare a Sus Hijos a Leer y Escribir (One Hundred One Ideas to Help Your Child Learn to Read & Write) Lewis, Warren W., ed. Hoffman, Joan & Lizarraga, Angelica, trs. LC 93-781. (ENG & SPA., Illus.). 128p. (Orig.). 1993. pap. 8.95 (*0-927516-36-5*) ERIC-REC.

— Leamos! (Let's Read) 101 Ideas Para Ayundar a Sus Hijos a Que Apprendan a Leer y a Escribir - 101 Ideas to Help Your Child Learn to Read & Write. Lewis, Warren W., ed. Hoffman, Joan et al, trs. LC 94-21536. (ENG & SPA.). 48p. 1995. pap. 8.95 (*0-927516-60-8*, AG45) ERIC-REC.

Behm, Richard, jt. auth. see Behm, Mary.

Behm, Ronald, jt. auth. see Salley, Columbus.

Behm, Tom. How Things Happen in Three: A Participation Musical(Playscript) (J). (gr. k-3). 1993. pap. 6.00 (*0-87602-317-0*) Anchorage.

Behm, Tom, adapted by. Tarheel Tales. 35p. (J). 1991. pap. 6.00 (*0-87602-292-1*) Anchorage.

Behman, Jacob & Rainy, Charlotte A., trs. Thoughts on the Spiritual Life. 87p. 1996. reprint ed. spiral bd. 8.00 (*0-7873-0086-1*) Hlth Research.

Behmen, Jacob. The Epistles of Jacob Behmen: The Life of Christ. 216p. (Orig.). 1992. reprint ed. pap. 17.95 (*1-56459-031-3*) Kessinger Pub.

Behn, Aphra. The Complete Works of Aphra Behn Vol. I: Poems. Todd, Janet, ed. LC 92-17972. 481p. 1992. text 75.00 (*0-8142-0578-X*) Ohio St U Pr.

— The Complete Works of Aphra Behn Vol. II: Love-Letters Between & Nobleman & His Sister. Todd, Janet, ed. LC 92-17972. 473p. 1993. text 75.00 (*0-8142-0610-7*) Ohio St U Pr.

— The Complete Works of Aphra Behn Vol. III: "The Fair Jilt" & Other Short Stories. Todd, Janet, ed. LC 92-17972. 468p. 1995. text 75.00 (*0-8142-0616-6*) Ohio St U Pr.

— The Complete Works of Aphra Behn Vol. IV: "Seneca Unmasqued" & Other Prose Translations. Todd, Janet, ed. LC 92-17972. 434p. 1994. text 75.00 (*0-8142-0627-1*) Ohio St U Pr.

— The Complete Works of Aphra Behn Vol. V: The Plays, 1671-1677. Todd, Janet, ed. LC 92-17972. 583p. (C). 1996. text 75.00 (*0-8142-0677-8*) Ohio St U Pr.

— The Complete Works of Aphra Behn Vol. VI: The Plays, 1677-1682. Todd, Janet, ed. LC 92-17972. 486p. (C). 1996. text 75.00 (*0-8142-0678-6*) Ohio St U Pr.

— The Complete Works of Aphra Behn Vol. VII: The Plays, 1682-1696. Todd, Janet, ed. LC 92-17972. 474p. (C). 1996. text 75.00 (*0-8142-0679-4*) Ohio St U Pr.

— The Novels of Mrs. Aphra Behn. LC 72-98183. 380p. 1970. reprint ed. lib. bdg. 65.00 (*0-8371-2824-2*, BENB, Greenwood Pr) Greenwood.

— The Novels of Mrs. Aphra Behn. (BCL1-PR English Literature Ser.). 380p. 1992. reprint ed. lib. bdg. 89.00 (*0-7812-7320-X*) Rprt Serv.

***Behn, Aphra.** Oroonoko. 368p. 1999. text 39.95 (*0-312-21065-5*) St Martin.

Behn, Aphra. Oroonoko & Other Prose Narratives. LC 67-25151. 1993. 14.95 (*0-88143-154-0*) Ayer.

— Oroonoko & Other Prose Narratives. LC 67-25151. 1972. 40.95 (*0-405-08252-5*, Pub. by Blom Pubns) Ayer.

— Oroonoko, & Other Writings. Salzman, Paul, ed. & intro. by. LC 99-186652. (Oxford World's Classics Ser.). 320p. 1998. pap. 8.95 (*0-19-283460-6*) OUP.

— Oroonoko: or The Royal Slave. 96p. 1997. pap. 8.95 (*0-393-31205-4*) Norton.

— Oroonoko, the Rover & Other Works. Todd, Janet, ed. & intro. by. 384p. 1999. pap. text 6.00 (*0-14-043338-4*) Addson-Wesley Educ.

— The Rover. 69p. (C). 1995. pap. write for info. (*0-413-66880-0*, A0680, Methuen Drama) Methn.

***Behn, Aphra.** The Rover. 102p. 1999. pap. text 7.95 (*1-85459-178-9*, Pub. by Theatre Comm) Consort Bk Sales.

Behn, Aphra. The Rover. Link, Frederick M., ed. LC 66-20828. (Regents Restoration Drama Ser.). xvi, 144p. (C). 1967. pap. text 9.95 (*0-8032-5350-8*) U of Nebr Pr.

— The Rover. 2nd ed. Russell, Anne, ed. (Literary Texts Ser.). 200p. 1999. pap. 8.95 (*1-55111-214-0*) Broadview Pr.

— The Rover & Other Plays: The Rover; The Feigned Courtesans; The Lucky Chance; The Emperor of the Moon. Spencer, Jane, ed. & intro. by. (Oxford World's Classics Ser.). 430p. 1998. pap. 8.95 (*0-19-283451-7*) OUP.

— The Works of Aphra Behn, 6 vols., 1. Summers, Montague, ed. LC 67-22243. 1972. reprint ed. 30.95 (*0-405-08254-1*, Pub. by Blom Pubns) Ayer.

— The Works of Aphra Behn, 6 vols., 2. Summers, Montague, ed. LC 67-22243. 1972. reprint ed. 30.95 (*0-405-08255-X*, Pub. by Blom Pubns) Ayer.

— The Works of Aphra Behn, 6 vols., 3. Summers, Montague, ed. LC 67-22243. 1972. reprint ed. 30.95 (*0-405-08256-8*, Pub. by Blom Pubns) Ayer.

— The Works of Aphra Behn, 6 vols., 4. Summers, Montague, ed. LC 67-22243. 1972. reprint ed. 30.95 (*0-405-08257-6*, Pub. by Blom Pubns) Ayer.

— The Works of Aphra Behn, 6 vols., 5. Summers, Montague, ed. LC 67-22243. 1972. reprint ed. 30.95 (*0-405-08258-4*, Pub. by Blom Pubns) Ayer.

— The Works of Aphra Behn, 6 vols., 6. Summers, Montague, ed. LC 67-22243. 1972. reprint ed. 30.95 (*0-405-08259-2*, Pub. by Blom Pubns) Ayer.

— Works of Aphra Behn, 6 vols., Set. Summers, Montague, ed. LC 67-22243. 1972. reprint ed. 179.95 (*0-405-08253-3*, Pub. by Blom Pubns) Ayer.

— The Works of Aphra Behn, 6 vols., Set. (BCL1-PR English Literature Ser.). 1992. reprint ed. lib. bdg. 450.00 (*0-7812-7319-6*) Rprt Serv.

Behn, Darnell. The Future Commandments. 24p. 1998. pap. 6.00 (*0-8059-4143-6*) Dorrance.

Behn, Harry. Trees. (Illus.). (J). (gr. 3). 1995. pap. 5.95 (*0-8050-3550-8*, Bks Young Read) H Holt & Co.

— Trees. LC 91-25179. (Illus.). 89p. (J). (ps-2). 1995. 14.95 (*0-8050-1926-X*, B Martin BYR) H Holt & Co.

Behn, Harry, ed. see Giddings, Ruth W.

Behn, Noel. Lindbergh: The Crime. 512p. 1995. mass mkt. 5.99 (*0-451-40589-7*, Onyx) NAL.

Behn, Robert D. Leadership Counts: Lessons for Public Managers from the Massachusetts Welfare, Training, & Employment Program. (Illus.). 264p. 1994. pap. text 21.00 (*0-674-51853-5*, BEHLEX) HUP.

— Leadership Counts: Lessons for Public Managers from the Massachusetts Welfare, Training & Employment Program. 272p. (C). 1992. 32.00 (*0-674-51852-7*) HUP.

***Behn, Robert D.** Rethinking Democratic Accountability. 192p. 2000. 41.95 (*0-8157-0862-9*); pap. 16.95 (*0-8157-0861-0*) Brookings.

Behn, Robert D., ed. Governors on Governing. LC 90-43216. 192p. (Orig.). (C). 1991. text 43.50 (*0-8191-7890-X*); pap. text 22.50 (*0-8191-7891-8*) Natl Governor.

Behn, Robert D., jt. ed. see Altshuler, Alan A.

Behn, Robin. Paper Bird. LC 87-51682. 88p. 1988. 15.95 (*0-89672-164-7*); pap. 9.95 (*0-89672-163-9*) Tex Tech Univ Pr.

Behn, Robin & Twichell, Chase, eds. The Practice of Poetry: Writing Exercises from Poets Who Teach. LC 92-52535. 320p. 1992. pap. 15.00 (*0-06-273024-X*, Harper Ref) HarpC.

Behnam, A. M. To Your Health. 75p. 1993. pap. 3.95 (*0-88172-181-6*) Believers Bkshelf.

Behnam, M. Reza. Cultural Foundations of Iranian Politics. LC 86-15871. 198p. reprint ed. pap. 61.40 (*0-8357-6843-0*, 203553800095) Bks Demand.

***Behnam, Mariam.** Heirloom: Evening Tales of the East. (Illus.). 354p. 2000. pap. text 12.95 (*0-19-579329-3*) OUP.

Behncke, F. H. Pioneer Teachers. 114p. 1996. reprint ed. spiral bd. 11.00 (*0-7873-0087-X*) Hlth Research.

— Pioneer Teachers (1920) 114p. 1996. reprint ed. pap. 9.95 (*1-56459-887-X*) Kessinger Pub.

Behne, Adolf. The Modern Functional Building. Robinson, Michael, tr. from GER. LC 96-1970. (Texts & Documents Ser.). (Illus.). 280p. 1996. 40.00 (*0-89236-363-0*, Pub. by J P Getty Trust); pap. 24.95 (*0-89236-364-9*, Pub. by J P Getty Trust) OUP.

Behne, Frank. Heinrich Siber und das Romische Staatsrecht von Theodor Mommsen: Ein Beitrag zur Rezeptionsgeschichte Mommsens im 20. (Beitrage zur Altertumswissenschaft Ser.: Bd. 12). (GER.). viii, 278p. 1999. 60.00 (*3-487-10910-7*, Pub. by G Olms Verlag) Lubrecht & Cramer.

Behnert, Gabriele J. Anatomie Eines Genres. (Studien Zur Filmgeschichte Ser.: Vol. 6). (GER.). x, 142p. 1992. write for info. (*3-487-09485-1*) G Olms Pubs.

Behney, J.Bruce & Eller. The History of the Evangelical United Brethren Church. Krueger, Kenneth W., ed. LC 79-14738. (Illus.). 1979. 19.95 (*0-687-17206-3*) Abingdon.

Behning, Arvid. Das Leben der Wolga: Zugleich eine Einfuhrung in die Flussbiologie. (Binnengewaesser Ser.: Band V). (GER., Illus.). vi, 162p. 1928. 25.00 (*3-510-40705-9*, Pub. by E Schweizerbartsche) Balogh.

Behnisch, Georg C. On Colour. 100p. 1994. pap. 35.00 (*3-7757-0474-4*, Pub. by Gerd Hatje) Dist Art Pubs.

Behnisch, Gunther. Tour Through the Exhibition. 1994. pap. 35.00 (*3-7757-0480-9*, Pub. by Gerd Hatje) Dist Art Pubs.

Behnke, jt. auth. see Moore.

Behnke, Donna A. Religious Issues in Nineteenth Century Feminism. LC 80-52544. viii, 299p. (C). 1982. 22.50 (*0-87875-203-X*) Whitston Pub.

Behnke, H., et al, eds. Fundamentals of Mathematics, 3 vols. 1984. reprint ed. pap. 40.00 (*0-685-07932-5*); reprint ed. pap. 16.50 (*0-685-57870-4*) MIT Pr.

— Fundamentals of Mathematics, 3 vols., Set. 1984. reprint ed. 75.00 (*0-685-07931-7*) MIT Pr.

— Progress in Botany: Structural Botany, Physiology, Genetics, Taxonomy, Geobotany, 57, Vol. 57. 424p. 1996. 230.00 (*3-540-59460-4*) Spr-Verlag.

Behnke, H. & Courant, Richard, eds. Contributions to Functional Analysis. (ENG, FRE & GER.). 1976. 74.00 (*0-387-07768-5*) Spr-Verlag.

Behnke, H. D., et al, eds. Progress in Botany: Structural Botany, Physiology, Genetics, Taxonomy, Geobotany Fortschritte der Botanik, Vol. 52. (Illus.). xv, 420p. 1991. 238.95 (*0-387-53471-7*) Spr-Verlag.

— Progress in Botany: Structural Botany, Physiology, Genetics, Taxonomy, Geobotany Fortschritte der Botanik, Vol. 53. (Illus.). 450p. 1992. 272.95 (*0-387-54734-7*) Spr-Verlag.

— Progress in Botany: Structural Botany, Physiology, Genetics, Taxonomy, Geobotany Fortschritte der Botanik, Vol. 55. (Illus.). 470p. 1994. 238.95 (*0-387-57321-6*) Spr-Verlag.

— Structural Botany, Physiology, Genetics, Taxonomy, Geobotany. (Progress in Botany Ser.: Vol. 54). (Illus.). 576p. 1993. 262.95 (*0-387-56358-X*) Spr-Verlag.

— Structural Botany, Physiology, Genetics, Taxonomy, Geobotany. (Progress in Botany Ser.: Vol. 58). (Illus.). 616p. 1996. 269.00 (*3-540-61329-3*) Spr-Verlag.

Behnke, H. D. & Esser, Karl, eds. Structural Botany, Physiology, Genetics, Taxomony & Geobotany. (Progress in Botany Ser.: Vol. 56). 400p. 1995. 235.95 (*3-540-58407-2*) Spr-Verlag.

Behnke, H. D. & Mabry, Tom J., eds. Caryophyllales: Evolution & Systematics. LC 93-21309. xiv, 334 p. 1994. 219.95 (*0-387-56695-3*) Spr-Verlag.

Behnke, H. D. & Sjolund, R. D., eds. Sieve Elements. (Illus.). 240p. 1990. 163.95 (*0-387-50783-3*) Spr-Verlag.

Behnke, H. D., et al. Structural Botany, Physiology, Genetics, Taxonomy, Geobotany. (Progress in Botany Ser.: Vol. 59). (Illus.). 708p. 1998. 275.00 (*3-540-63214-X*) Spr-Verlag.

Behnke, J. M., ed. Parasites: Immunity & Pathology: The Consequences of Parasitic Infections in Mammals. 250p. 1990. 143.00 (*0-85066-499-3*) Taylor & Francis.

B

An Asterisk (*) at the beginning of an entry indicates that the title is appearing for the first time.

Behnke, J. M., jt. ed. see Barnard, C. J.

***Behnke, John.** 90 Days, One Day at a Time: A New Beginning for People in Recovery. LC 99-29235. 160p. 1999. pap. 7.95 (*0-8091-3881-6*) Paulist Pr.

Behnke, Leo, ed. see Buffum, Richard.

Behnke, Marian. Notes from Baby Angel Grace. 2nd ed. (Illus.). 64p. (Orig.). 1995. spiral bd. 10.00 (*0-9646614-0-3*) Azure Pub.

***Behnke, Patricia C.** A Victorian Justice. (New Voices in American Fiction Ser.). 200p. 2000. pap. 14.95 (*1-883938-82-1*) Dry Bones Pr.

Behnke, R. J. Native Trout of Western North America. LC 92-72941. (AFS Monograph Ser.: No. 6). 275p. 1992. pap. 40.00 (*0-913235-78-4*, 520.06P) Am Fisheries Soc.

***Behnke, Robert S.** Kinetic Anatomy. (Illus.). 236p. 2000. pap. write for info. (*0-7360-0016-X*) Human Kinetics.

Behnke, Robert W. German "Smart-Bus" Systems: Potential for Application in Portland, Oregon: Volume 1, Technical Report. (Illus.). 100p. (Orig.). (C). 1995. pap. text 40.00 (*0-7881-2025-5*) DIANE Pub.

Behnke, Roy H., Jr. The Herders of Cyrenaica: Ecology, Economy, & Kinship Among the Bedouin of Eastern Libya. LC 79-10605. (Illinois Studies in Anthropology: No. 12). (Illus.). 207p. 1980. pap. text 14.50 (*0-252-00729-8*) U of Ill Pr.

Behnke, S. The Essentials of Florida Mental Health Law. (Professional Bks.). 240p. 1999. 35.00 (*0-393-70309-6*) Norton.

— The Essentials of New York Mental Health Law. (Professional Bks.). 240p. 1999. 35.00 (*0-393-70308-8*) Norton.

Behnke, Stephen. The Essentials of Massachusetts Mental Health Law: Mass. LC 97-32855. 224p. 1998. 35.00 (*0-393-70249-9*) Norton.

Behnke, Stephen H. The Essentials of California Mental Health Law. LC 98-26013. 224p. 1998. 35.00 (*0-393-70250-2*) Norton.

Behnke, Stephen H., jt. auth. see Saks, Elyn R.

Behnken, H., jt. auth. see Hauk, V.

***Behnken, Kenneth W.** Planting Missions Across Cultures. 220p. 2000. teacher ed., ring bd. 39.95 (*0-570-05251-3*, 12-4061) Concordia.

Behnken, Patricia A. Bayless. Heavenly Dreams. (Illus.). 192p. 1998. pap. 10.95 (*0-9637811-2-X*) Morning Joy.

— Pathways of My Journey. LC 93-90621. (Illus.). 152p. (Orig.). 1993. pap. 9.95 (*0-9637811-0-3*) Morning Joy.

***Behoff, Marc, ed.** The Smile of a Dolphin: Remarkable Accounts of Animal Emotions. (Illus.). 224p. 2000. 35.00 (*1-56331-925-X*) Discovery.

***Behor, G.** Ancient Greece: Monuments Past & Present. (Illus.). 72p. 2000. pap. 24.95 (*88-8162-067-7*, Pub. by Vision Srl) J P Getty Trust.

Behoriam, Ellen. Adobe Illustrator 7.0: An Introduction to Digital Illustration. LC 98-10913. (Against the Clock Ser.). 328p. (C). 1998. pap. text 33.33 (*0-13-080166-6*) P-H.

***Behoriam, Ellenn.** Adobe Illustrator 8: Advanced Digital Illustration. LC 99-24453. 440p. (C). 1999. spiral bd. 33.33 (*0-13-084000-9*) P-H.

— Adobe Pagemaker 6.5: Advanced Electronic Mechanicals & Student Cd Package. 360p. (C). 1998. pap. text 33.33 (*0-13-096160-4*) P-H.

— Adobe Pagemaker 6.5: An Introduction to Electronic Mechanicals & Student Cd Package. 312p. (C). 1998. pap. text 33.33 (*0-13-096169-8*) P-H.

— Adobe Photoshop 4: Advanced Digital Images & Student Cd Package. 368p. (C). 1999. pap. text 33.33 (*0-13-083902-7*) P-H.

— Freehand 8: Advanced Digital Illustration & Student Cd Package. 304p. (C). 1998. pap. text 33.33 (*0-13-096172-8*) P-H.

— Presswise: Digital Imposition & Student CD Package. 304p. (C). 1999. pap. text 33.33 (*0-13-020815-9*) P-H.

Behr, jt. auth. see Bowen, B. A.

Behr, A. Architektur in Der DDR. 212p. 1980. 81.00 (*0-7855-1491-0*) St Mut.

Behr, A. L., et al. An Educational Psychology for Schools in Africa. 156p. (C). 1987. pap. 24.95 (*0-409-10255-5*) Buttrwrth-Heinemann.

Behr, Arno. Carbon Dioxide Activation by Metal Complexes. LC 88-14873. 161p. 1988. 125.00 (*3-527-26903-7*, Wiley-VCH) Wiley.

Behr, Ashley F. Camp ICMI. (21st Century Kids Ser.). (Illus.). 32p. (J). (ps-3). 1998. per. 5.95 (*0-9660533-0-3*) D J Behr.

— Nailah's Surprise. O'Neill, Terry, ed. (Illus.). 32p. (J). (ps-3). 1998. pap., per. 5.95 (*0-9660533-1-1*) D J Behr.

Behr, C. A., tr. see Aristides.

Behr, Charles & Aristides, P. Aelius. The Complete Works: With an Appendix Containing the Fragments & Inscriptions, Vol. 1. viii, 538p. 1986. 164.00 (*90-04-07844-4*) Brill Academic Pubs.

Behr, Charles Allison, tr. see Aristides, P. Aelius.

Behr, E., tr. see Kostrikin, Alexei I. & Shafarevich, I. R., eds.

Behr, E. Thomas. Tao of Sales: The Easy Way to Sell in Tough Times. LC 96-35236. 176p. 1997. pap. 21.95 (*1-86204-058-3*, Pub. by Element MA) Penguin Putnam.

Behr, Edward. The Algerian Problem. LC 75-43947. (Illus.). 256p. 1976. reprint ed. lib. bdg. 35.00 (*0-8371-8722-2*, BEAPR, Greenwood Pr) Greenwood.

— Indonesia: A Voyage Through the Archipelago by 45 of the Worldm S Leading Photographers, August the 26th to September the 4th 1989, in Commemoration of the 45th Anniversary of the Proclamation of Independence LC 94-185155. 1990. write for info. (*2-87868-003-0*) Ed Pacifique.

— Les Miserables. 1996. pap. 21.45 (*1-55970-370-9*, Pub. by Arcade Pub Inc) Time Warner.

Behr, Edward. Prohibition: Thirteen Years That Changed America. LC 96-24063. 256p. 1996. 24.45 (*1-55970-356-3*, Pub. by Arcade Pub Inc) Time Warner.

Behr, Edward. Prohibition: Thirteen Years That Changed America. LC 96-24063. (Illus.). 272p. 1997. pap. 13.45 (*1-55970-394-6*, Pub. by Arcade Pub Inc) Time Warner.

Behr, Edward, text. Indonesia: A Voyage Through the Archipelago. (Illus.). 288p. 39.95 (*962-593-225-9*) Tuttle Pubng.

Behr, Gustavus E., Jr., jt. auth. see Richards, Theodore W.

Behr, H. J., et al, eds. Observation of the Continental Crust Through Drilling II. (Exploration of the Deep Continental Crust Ser.). (Illus.). 230p. 1987. 60.00 (*0-387-17348-X*) Spr-Verlag.

Behr, H. J. & Raleigh, C. B., eds. Crustal Structure of the Bohemian Massif & the West Carpathians. LC 95-127051. 372p. 1995. 157.95 (*0-387-57986-9*) Spr-Verlag.

Behr, Ira S. Star Trek Deep Space Nine: Deep Space Nine Legends of the Ferengi. (U Ser.). 1997. per. 12.00 (*0-671-00728-9*) PB.

Behr, Ira S. & Wolfe, Robert H. Star Trek: Deep Space Nine: Legends of the Ferengi. abr. ed. 1997. audio 12.00 (*0-671-57901-0*) S&S Audio.

Behr, Ira S., jt. auth. see Quark.

Behr, Jean-Paul, ed. The Lock-and-Key Principle: The State of the Art--100 Years On, Vol. 1, The State of the Art--100 Years On. 336p. 1995. 260.00 (*0-471-93902-1*) Wiley.

Behr, Joan H., ed. Accounting Issues & Credit Evaluation. (Special Collection from the Journal of Commercial Bank Lending). 128p. (Orig.). 1992. pap. 45.00 (*0-936742-88-7*, 36047) Robt Morris Assocs.

— Banking Services for the Affluent: A Special Collection from the Journal of Commercial Lending. LC 92-32158. 132p. (Orig.). 1992. pap. 45.00 (*0-936742-90-9*, 36048) Robt Morris Assocs.

— Cash Flow: A Special Collection from the Journal of Commercial Bank Lending. 108p. 1989. pap. text 45.00 (*0-936742-62-3*, 36038) Robt Morris Assocs.

— Community Bank Lending: A Special Collection from the Journal of Commercial Bank Lending. LC 89-29965. 104p. (Orig.). 1989. pap. text 45.00 (*0-936742-69-0*, 36040) Robt Morris Assocs.

— Credit Analysis Vol. 2: A Special Collection from the Journal of Commercial Bank Lending. 88p. (Orig.). 1990. pap. 45.00 (*0-936742-79-8*, 36043) Robt Morris Assocs.

— Environmental Risk: A Special Collection from the Journal of Commercial Bank Lending. LC 91-21019. (Special Collection from the Journal of Commercial Bank Lending). 132p. (Orig.). 1991. pap. 45.00 (*0-936742-82-8*, 36045) Robt Morris Assocs.

— Financial Statement Analysis - A Special Collection from the Journal of Commercial Bank Lending. LC 91-40900. 132p. (Orig.). 1991. pap. 45.00 (*0-936742-86-0*, 36046) Robt Morris Assocs.

— Lending to Different Industries, Vol. 3. LC 90-5900. 232p. 1992. pap. 85.00 (*0-936742-91-7*, 36058) Robt Morris Assocs.

— Loan Portfolio Management. LC 88-29760. (Special Collection from the Journal of Commercial Bank Lending). 108p. (Orig.). 1988. pap. 45.00 (*0-936742-58-5*, 36037) Robt Morris Assocs.

— Loan Pricing: A Special Collection from the Journal of Commercial Bank Lending. LC 89-12259. (Illus.). 100p. 1989. pap. 45.00 (*0-936742-66-6*, 36039) Robt Morris Assocs.

— Loan Training: A Special Collection from the Journal of Commercial Bank Lending. LC 90-32862. (Illus.). 104p. 1990. pap. 45.00 (*0-936742-73-9*, 36041) Robt Morris Assocs.

— Preparing a Commercial Credit Information Policy. 2nd ed. LC 89-13522. 156p. 1989. 64.00 (*0-936742-70-4*, 32091) Robt Morris Assocs.

— Real Estate & Construction Lending: A Special Collection from the Journal of Commercial Bank Lending, Vol. 2. LC 86-8567. (Illus.). 128p. 1990. pap. text 45.00 (*0-936742-76-3*, 36042) Robt Morris Assocs.

Behr, Joan H. & Burke, Sarah A., eds. Lending to Different Industries, Vol. 2. 2nd ed. (Illus.). 396p. 1990. pap. 85.00 (*0-936742-77-1*, 36030) Robt Morris Assocs.

Behr, Joan H., ed. see Bond, Elizabeth.

Behr, Joan H., ed. see Clarke, Richard.

Behr, Joan H., ed. see Darling, George K. & Chaston, James F., Jr.

Behr, Joan H., ed. see Davis, John A., Jr.

Behr, Joan H., ed. see Dickerson, Charles S.

Behr, Joan H., ed. see Harlan, James C.

Behr, Joan H., ed. see McGinty, Kevin J.

Behr, Joan H., ed. see Morsman, Edgar M., Jr.

Behr, Joan H., jt. ed. see Smith, Daphne.

Behr, Joan H., ed. see Stampleman, Arthur H.

Behr, Joan H., ed. see Strischek, Dev.

Behr, Joan H., jt. ed. see Welsh, Nancy.

Behr, Johann Von, see Von Behr, Johann.

***Behr, John.** Asceticism & Anthropology in Irenaeus & Clement. LC 99-56664. (Oxford Early Christian Studies). 250p. 2000. text. write for info. (*0-19-827000-3*) OUP.

Behr, John, tr. see Irenaeus.

Behr, Mark. The Smell of Apples. LC 95-21658. 200p. 1997. pap. 12.00 (*0-312-15209-4*, Picador USA) St Martin.

— The Smell of Apples: A Novel. LC 95-21658.Tr. of Reuk van Appels. 224p. 1995. 21.95 (*0-312-13604-8*) St Martin.

Behr, Merlyn & Hiebert, J., eds. Number Concepts & Operations in the Middle Grades: The Research Agenda for Mathematics Education, Vol. 2. 280p. 1988. text 59.95 (*0-8058-0353-X*) L Erlbaum Assocs.

Behr, Mitchell. The Beautiful Bride Book. LC 97-24291. (Illus.). 192p. 1998. pap. 12.00 (*0-399-52373-1*, Perigee Bks) Berkley Pub.

***Behr, Richard.** Under the Headset: Surviving Dispatcher Stress. 118p. 2000. pap. 29.95 (*0-9661970-4-6*) Staggs Pub.

***Behr, Shulamith.** Expressionism. (Movements in Modern Art Ser.). (Illus.). 100p. 2000. text 39.95 (*0-521-78299-6*) Cambridge U Pr.

— Expressionism. (Movements in Modern Art Ser.). (Illus.). 100p. (C). 2000. pap. text 15.95 (*0-521-78847-1*) Cambridge U Pr.

Behr, Shulamith, et al. Expressionism Reassessed. LC 93-2709. 1994. text 29.95 (*0-7190-3844-8*, Pub. by Manchester Univ Pr) St Martin.

Behr-Sigel, Elisabeth. The Ministry of Women in the Church. LC 89-63746. 235p. 1990. per. 8.95 (*0-9618545-6-1*) Oakwood Pubns.

— The Place of the Heart: An Introduction to Orthodox Spirituality. Bigham, Stephen, tr. from FRE. 192p. (Orig.). 1992. per. 8.95 (*1-879038-04-8*) Oakwood Pubns.

Behr, Steve. Mountain Biking. LC 98-3983. (Extreme Sports Ser.). (Illus.). 32p. (J). (gr. 5-9). 1998. pap. 6.95 (*0-7641-0796-8*) Barron.

Behrangi, Samad. The Little Black Fish: Mahi Siah Kuchulu. Amuzegar, Hooshang, tr. LC 96-36970. (Classics of Persian Literature Ser.: Vol. 2). (Illus.). 64p. (Orig.). (J). 1997. pap. 8.50 (*0-936347-78-3*) IBEX.

— The Tale of the Little Black Fish: Mahi Siah Kuchulu. Amuzegar, Hooshang, tr. LC 91-73480. (ENG & PER., Illus.). 72p. (Orig.). (J). 1992. pap. 8.50 (*0-936347-20-1*) IBEX.

Behranqi, Samad. The Little Black Fish & Other Modern Persian Stories. 2nd ed. Hegland, Mary & Hooglund, Eric, trs. from PER. LC 87-26680. 106p. 1987. reprint ed. pap. 10.00 (*0-89410-621-X*, Three Contnts) L Rienner.

Behravesh, Mohamad M., et al, eds. NDE Performance Demonstration, Planning & Research: Proceedings ASME Pressure Vessels & Piping Conference (1997, Orlando, FL) LC 97-73339. (PVP Ser.: Vol. 352, NDE-Vol. 16). 71p. 1997. pap. 84.00 (*0-7918-1569-2*) ASME.

Behravesh, Mohamad M., jt. auth. see Mansfield.

Behravesh, Nariman, jt. auth. see Mansfield, Edwin.

Behre, H. M., jt. auth. see Nieschlag, E.

Behre, H. M., ed. see Brinkworth, M.

Behre, H. M., jt. ed. see Nieschlag, E.

Behre, K. E., ed. Anthropogenic Indicators in Pollen Diagrams. 245p. (C). 1986. 123.00 (*90-6191-673-9*, Pub. by A A Balkema) Ashgate Pub Co.

Behren, Ronald Von, see Von Behren, Ronald.

Behrend. German Unification: The Destruction of an Economy. Date not set. 54.95 (*0-7453-1004-4*, Pub. by Pluto GBR); pap. 19.95 (*0-7453-1003-6*, Pub. by Pluto GBR) Stylus Pub VA.

Behrend, Arthur. As from Kemmel Hill: An Adjutant in France & Flanders, 1917 & 1918. LC 75-3861. (Illus.). 176p. 1975. reprint ed. lib. bdg. 39.75 (*0-8371-8087-2*, BEKH, Greenwood Pr) Greenwood.

Behrend, Genevieve. Your Invisible Power. 92p. 1996. reprint ed. spiral bd. 10.50 (*0-7873-0088-8*) Hlth Research.

— Your Invisible Power: The Mental Science of Thomas Troward. 95p. 1951. pap. 7.95 (*0-87516-004-2*) DeVorss.

— Your Invisible Power: Working Principles & Concrete Examples in Applied Mental Science (1927) 92p. 1996. reprint ed. pap. 9.95 (*1-56459-889-6*) Kessinger Pub.

***Behrend, Heike.** Alice Lakwena & the Spirits: War in Northern Uganda, 1985-96. LC 99-88653. (Eastern African Studies). 224p. 2000. text 42.95 (*0-8214-1310-4*, Ohio U Ctr Intl) Ohio U Pr.

— Alice Lakwena & the Spirits: War in Northern Uganda, 1985-96. LC 99-88653. (Eastern African Studies). 224p. 2000. pap. text 19.95 (*0-8214-1311-2*, Ohio U Ctr Intl) Ohio U Pr.

***Behrend, Heike & Luig, Ute, eds.** Spirit Possession, Modernity & Power in Africa. LC 99-31300. (Illus.). 192p. 2000. text 49.95 (*0-299-16630-9*); pap. text 22.95 (*0-299-16634-1*) U of Wis Pr.

Behrend, Jackie. The Hauntings of Williamsburg, Yorktown, & Jamestown. LC 98-2973. (Illus.). 1998. pap. 9.95 (*0-89587-210-2*) Blair.

Behrend, Jodi, jt. auth. see Adelman, Todd.

***Behrend, Katrin.** Cats: Everything about Purchase, Care, Nutrition, Grooming & Behavior. LC 99-12278. (Barron's Pet Owner's Manuals Ser.). 104p. 1999. 6.95 (*0-7641-0933-2*) Barron.

— Cats: How to Take Care of Them & Understand Them. 1990. 12.15 (*0-606-05059-0*, Pub. by Turtleback) Demco.

Behrend, Katrin. Guinea Pigs. Niewisch, Helgard, tr. LC 98-18038. (Barron's Complete Pet Owner's Manuals). (Illus.). 64p. 1998. pap. 6.95 (*0-7641-0670-8*) Barron.

Behrend, Katrin. Guinea Pigs: Proper Care & Understanding: Expert Advice for Appropriate Maintenance. (J). 1991. 12.15 (*0-606-03154-5*, Pub. by Turtleback) Demco.

Behrend, Katrin. Indoor Cats. LC 99-19207. (Complete Pet Owner's Manual Ser.). 104p. 1999. 6.95 (*0-7641-0935-9*) Barron.

Behrend, Katrin & Wegler, Monika A. The Complete Book of Cat Care. 144p. 1991. pap. 12.95 (*0-8120-4613-7*) Barron.

Behrend, Louise. A Suzuki Approach. 72p. 1998. pap. text 8.95 (*0-87487-768-7*) Summy-Birchard.

Behrend, Ute. Girls: Photographs 1994-1995. LC 97-115203. (Illus.). 144p. 1996. 40.00 (*3-931141-19-5*, Pub. by Scalo Pubs) Dist Art Pubs.

Behrend, William. Ludwig Van Beethoven's Pianoforte Sonatas. Lund, Ingeborg, tr. LC 74-24038. (Illus.). reprint ed. 54.50 (*0-404-12861-0*) AMS Pr.

Behrends, Rainer, et al. Biblia Pauperum: Apocalypsis. LC 77-88869. (Illus.). 1978. boxed set 750.00 (*0-87817-239-4*) Hacker.

Behrends, Steve, et al, eds. Strange Shadows: The Uncollected Fiction & Essays of Clark Ashton Smith, 36. LC 88-24632. (Contributions to the Study of Science Fiction & Fantasy Ser.: No. 36). 295p. 1989. 59.95 (*0-313-26611-5*, BEQ) Greenwood.

Behrends, Steve, ed. see Smith, Clark A.

Behrendt, Axel & Behrendt, Bibiana. Cognac: The Guide for Cognac Lovers & Connoisseurs. Stockman, Russell, tr. from GER. LC 96-37075. (Illus.). 232p. 1997. bds. 25.00 (*0-7892-0223-9*) Abbeville Pr.

— Grappa: A Guide to the Best. (Illus.). 276p. (J). 2000. 25.00 (*0-7892-0339-1*, Abbeville Kids) Abbeville Pr.

Behrendt, Bibiana, jt. auth. see Behrendt, Axel.

Behrendt, Bill C. Conquering PCJr Kinks. 1985. 14.95 (*0-13-167891-4*) P-H.

Behrendt, Bill L. Music & Sound for the Macintosh. write for info. (*0-318-58192-2*) P-H.

— Pocket Magic: Graphic Games for the Pocket Computer. LC 82-80271. (Illus.). 96p. (Orig.). (YA). 1982. 17.95 (*0-685-05521-3*); pap. 9.95 (*0-942412-01-X*); audio 8.95 (*0-686-87025-5*) Micro Text Pubns.

— Thirty Games for the Timex-Sinclair Computer. 1983. write for info. (*0-318-57970-7*) P-H.

Behrendt, Donna J. & Cleveland Clinic Foundation Staff. Clinical Guidelines for Managed Home Care. LC 96-44666. 1996. 169.00 (*0-8342-0815-6*) Aspen Pub.

Behrendt, Fred. Children of the Deep: 1930's Adventures in Innsmouth for Call of Cthulhu. 1998. pap. text 12.95 (*1-56882-139-5*) Chaosium.

Behrendt, Fred, et al. Perils of the Young Kingdoms. Brooks, Les, ed. (Stormbringer Roleplaying Game System Ser.). (Illus.). 128p. (Orig.). (YA). (gr. 7 up). 1991. pap. 18.95 (*0-933635-82-6*, 2113) Chaosium.

Behrendt, H. M. Horsethief Ranch: An Oral History. (Illus.). 130p. (Orig.). 1985. pap. 7.95 (*0-9613777-0-4*) Horsethief Pubns.

Behrendt, John C. Innocents on the Ice: A Memoir of Antarctic Exploration, 1957. LC 98-26379. (Illus.). 408p. 1998. 29.95 (*0-87081-493-1*) Univ Pr Colo.

— Innocents on the Ice: A Memoir of Antarctic Exploration, 1957. 456p. 1999. pap. text 19.95 (*0-87081-551-2*) Univ Pr Colo.

Behrendt, Larissa. Aboriginal Dispute Resolution: A Step Towards Self-Determination & Community Autonomy. LC 95-222230. 115p. 1995. pap. 21.00 (*1-86287-178-7*, Pub. by Federation Pr) Gaunt.

Behrendt, Leo. Ethical Teaching of Hugo of Trimberg. LC 77-140042. (Catholic University of America. Studies in Romance Languages & Literatures: No. 1). reprint ed. 37.50 (*0-404-50221-0*) AMS Pr.

***Behrendt, Manfred.** Von Teotihuacan Bis Tiwanaku: Altamerikanische Motive in der Spanisch-Amerikanischen Lyrik des 20. Jahrhunderts. (Europaische Hochschulschriften Ibero-Romanische Sprachen und Literaturen Ser.). 386p. 1999. 52.95 (*3-631-35237-9*) P Lang Pubng.

Behrendt, Roland, tr. see Arnold, Klaves, ed.

Behrendt, S., et al, eds. Life Cycle Design: A Manual for Small & Medium Sized Companies. LC 97-30264. (Illus.). 204p. 1997. 99.95 incl. cd-rom (*3-540-62793-6*) Spr-Verlag.

Behrendt, Stephen C. Instruments of the Bones. LC 91-35762. (First Poetry Ser.). 104p. 1992. pap. 9.95 (*0-922811-14-8*) Mid-List.

— The Moment of Explosion: Blake & the Illustration of Milton. LC 82-13561. (Illus.). xvi, 235p. 1983. text 60.00 (*0-8032-1169-4*) U of Nebr Pr.

— Reading William Blake. 1992. text 49.95 (*0-312-06835-2*) St Martin.

— Romanticism, Radicalism & the Press. LC 96-51736. (Illus.). 240p. 1997. pap. text 23.95 (*0-8143-2568-8*) Wayne State Univ Ctr for.

— Royal Mourning & Regency Culture: Elegies & Memorials of Princess Charlotte. LC 97-22795. 270p. 1997. text 65.00 (*0-312-21049-3*) St Martin.

— Shelley & His Audiences. LC 88-31621. 309p. 1989. reprint ed. pap. 95.80 (*0-608-02689-1*, 206334200004) Bks Demand.

— A Step in the Dark. LC 96-25034. (Orig.). 1996. pap. 11.00 (*0-922811-27-X*) Mid-List.

Behrendt, Stephen C., ed. Approaches to Teaching Shelley's Frankenstein. LC 90-43124. (Approaches to Teaching World Literature Ser.: No. 33). x, 190p. 1990. pap. text 18.00 (*0-87352-540-X*, AP33P); lib. bdg. 37.50 (*0-87352-539-6*, AP33C) Modern Lang.

— History & Myth: Essays on English Romantic Literature. LC 89-16728. 252p. reprint ed. pap. 78.20 (*0-608-10561-9*, 207118100009) Bks Demand.

Behrendt, Stephen C. & Linkin, Harriet K., eds. Approaches to Teaching British Women Poets of the Romantic Period. LC 97-34319. (Approaches to Teaching World Literature Ser.: No. 60). xiii, 207p. 1997. pap. 18.00 (*0-87352-744-5*, AP60P); lib. bdg. 37.50 (*0-87352-743-7*, AP60C) Modern Lang.

Behrendt, Stephen C., jt. ed. see Linkin, Harriet K.

Behrendt, W., et al, eds. Organversagen in der Intensivmedizin. (Beitraege zur Intensiv und Notfallmedizin Ser.: Vol. 1). (Illus.). xii, 182p. 1983. pap. 55.00 (*3-8055-3794-8*) S Karger.

Behrendt, W., et al. Intensivmedizin und Organversagen. (Beitraege zur Intensiv und Notfallmedizin Ser.: Vol. 3). (Illus.). viii, 188p. 1985. 58.50 (*3-8055-4016-7*) S Karger.

An Asterisk (*) at the beginning of an entry indicates that the title is appearing for the first time.

— Landscape over Zero. Hinton, David, tr. from ENG. LC 96-20854. (CHI.). 112p. 1996. pap. 9.95 (*0-8112-1334-X*, NDP830, Pub. by New Directions) Norton.

— Old Snow. McDougall, Bonnie S., tr. from CHI. LC 91-16507. 96p. 1991. 16.95 (*0-8112-1182-7*, Pub. by New Directions); pap. 8.95 (*0-8112-1183-5*, NDP727, Pub. by New Directions) Norton.

— Waves. McDougall, Bonnie S. & Cooke, Susette T., trs. from CHI. LC 89-13346. Vol. 693. 224p. 1990. 22.95 (*0-8112-1133-9*, Pub. by New Directions); pap. 10.95 (*0-8112-1134-7*, NDP693, Pub. by New Directions) Norton.

Beibel, David B., jt. auth. see Zylstra, Mignon M.

***Beiber, Janet.** In Name Only. 2000. mass mkt. 6.50 (*0-449-00285-3*) Fawcett.

Beich, Carol. That Crazy Vacuum. LC 96-96441. (Illus.). 25p. (Orig.). (J). (gr. k-4). 1996. pap. 4.95 (*0-9631098-1-2*) Beich Pubng.

Beich, Everett. Reaching for the Gold. 125p. 1992. pap. 9.95 (*0-9631098-0-4*) Beich Pubng.

Beicher, H. A. All about Klondike. 40p. 1995. pap. 5.95 (*1-881147-15-0*) Lowell Print.

Beicher, Robert J., jt. auth. see Serway, Raymond A.

Beichman, Arnold. Anti-American Myths: Their Causes & Consequences. 358p. (C). 1992. pap. 24.95 (*1-56000-590-4*) Transaction Pubs.

— Herman Wouk: The Novelist As Social Historian. 114p. 1984. 34.95 (*0-87855-498-X*) Transaction Pubs.

— The Long Pretense: Soviet Treaty Diplomacy from Lenin to Gorbachev. 296p. (C). 1990. 39.95 (*0-88738-360-2*) Transaction Pubs.

***Beichman, Arnold, ed.** CNN's Cold War Documentary: Issues & Controversy. LC 99-37156. (Publication Ser: Vol. 466). 173p. 2000. pap. 17.95 (*0-8179-9742-3*) Hoover Inst Pr.

Beichman, Janine. The End of Summer. 152p. 1993. pap. 8.00 (*4-7700-1746-4*) Kodansha.

Beichman, Janine, tr. from JPN. A Poet's Anthology: The Range of Japanese Poetry. (Reflections Ser.: No. 3). (ENG.). 224p. (C). 1994. pap. text 19.95 (*0-942668-38-3*) Katydid Bks.

Beichman, Janine, tr. see Fitzsimmons, Thomas, ed.

Beichman, Janine, tr. see Makoto, Ooka.

Beichman, Janine, tr. see Ooka, Makoto.

Beichman, Janine, tr. see Setouchi, Harumi.

Beichner, Robert J., jt. auth. see Schwartz, James E.

Beicken, Peter, jt. auth. see Kolker, Robert P.

Beidar, K. I., et al, eds. Rings with Generalized Polynomial Identities. (Pure & Applied Mathematics Ser.: Vol. 196). (Illus.). 544p. 1995. text 199.00 (*0-8247-9325-0*) Dekker.

Beidel, Deborah C. & Turner, Samuel M. Shy Children, Phobic Adults: Nature & Treatment of Social Phobia. LC 97-33477. 324p. 1997. 39.95 (*1-55798-461-1*) Am Psychol.

Beidelman, T. O. The Cool Knife: Imagery of Gender, Sexuality, & Moral Education in Kaguru Initiation Ritual. LC 96-43928. (Series in Ethnographic Inquiry). (Illus.). 336p. 1997. pap. text 18.95 (*1-56098-714-6*) Smithsonian.

Beidelman, Thomas O. Colonial Evangelism: A Socio-Historical Study of an East African Mission at the Grassroots. LC 81-47771. (Illus.). 296p. 1982. 35.00 (*0-253-31386-4*) Ind U Pr.

— Colonial Evangelism: A Socio-Historical Study of an East African Mission at the Grassroots. LC 81-47771. 293p. reprint ed. pap. 90.90 (*0-608-09269-X*, 205407100002) Bks Demand.

— A Comparative Analysis of the Jajmani System. 15.00 (*0-685-71736-4*) J J Augustin.

— The Cool Knife: Imagery of Gender, Sexuality, & Moral Education in Kaguru Initiation Ritual. LC 96-43928. (Series in Ethnographic Inquiry). (Illus.). 336p. 1997. text 35.00 (*1-56098-713-8*) Smithsonian.

— The Kaguru: A Matrilineal People of East Africa. (Illus.). 134p. (C). 1983. reprint ed. pap. text 10.50 (*0-88133-060-4*) Waveland Pr.

— The Matrilineal Peoples of Eastern Tanzania (Zaramo, Luguru, Kaguru, Ngulu, Etc.) LC 67-112486. (Ethnographic Survey of Africa - East Central Africa Ser.: Pt. 16). (Illus.). 96p. reprint ed. pap. 30.00 (*0-8357-3212-6*, 205708300010) Bks Demand.

— Moral Imagination in Kaguru Modes of Thought. 240p. (C). 1993. pap. text 16.95 (*1-56098-236-5*) Smithsonian.

— W. Robertson Smith & the Sociological Study of Religion. LC 74-7568. 106p. reprint ed. pap. 32.90 (*0-608-18218-4*, 205662500078) Bks Demand.

Beidelman, Thomas O., jt. auth. see Middleton, John.

Beideman, Ronald P. In the Making of a Profession: The National College of Chiropractic 1906-1981. Lawrence, Dana J., ed. (Illus.). (C). 1995. text 49.95 (*0-9615849-2-0*) Natl Coll Chiro.

Beider, Alexander. A Dictionary of Jewish Surnames from the Kingdom of Poland. LC 96-14963. (Illus.). 608p. 1996. 69.50 (*0-9626373-9-4*) Avotaynu.

— A Dictionary of Jewish Surnames from the Russian Empire. LC 92-46252. (Illus.). 784p. 1993. 75.00 (*0-9626373-3-5*) Avotaynu.

— Jewish Surnames in Prague (15th-18th Centuries) LC 94-31620. viii, 40p. 1995. pap. 11.00 (*0-9626373-5-1*) Avotaynu.

Beiderman, Charles & Johnston, William. The Beginner's Handbook of Woodcarving: With Projects Patterns for Line Carving, Relief Carving, Carving in the Round, & Bird Carving. (Illus.). 192p. 1988. reprint ed. pap. 7.95 (*0-486-25687-1*) Dover.

Beiderwell. Thinking Through Literature & Film. (C). 1996. pap. text. write for info. (*0-15-501770-5*) Harcourt Coll Pubs.

Beiderwieden, George. Heaven. 32p. 1966. pap. 1.99 (*0-570-03680-1*, 74-1008) Concordia.

— Heaven. large type ed. spiral bd. write for info. (*0-318-66318-X*, 8015) LBW.

Beidleman, Carl R. Interest Swaps. 544p. 1990. text 80.00 (*1-55623-207-1*, Irwn Prfssnl) McGraw-Hill Prof.

— Valuation of Used Capital Assets, Vol. 7. (Studies in Accounting Research). 84p. 1973. 12.00 (*0-86539-019-3*) Am Accounting.

Beidleman, Carl R., ed. Cross Currency Swaps. 750p. 1991. text 80.00 (*1-55623-316-7*, Irwn Prfssnl) McGraw-Hill Prof.

Beidleman, Linda H., jt. auth. see Kozloff, Eugene N.

***Beidleman, Richard G.** Plants of Rocky Mountain National Park. (Illus.). 2000. pap. 29.95 (*1-56044-910-1*) Falcon Pub Inc.

***Beidleman, Richard G., et al.** Colorado Vertebrate Zoology: A Comprehensive Annotated Bibliography. 500p. 2000. 125.00 (*0-87081-557-1*, Pub. by Univ Pr Colo) U of Okla Pr.

Beidler, J. Data Structures & Algorithms: An Object-Oriented Approach Using Ada 95. LC 96-23982. (Undergraduate Texts in Computer Science Ser.). 364p. 1996. 49.95 (*0-387-94834-1*) Spr-Verlag.

Beidler, Michelle. Rosita y Mateo Coloring Book. (SPA & ENG.). 40p. (J). (ps-4). 1988. pap. 1.90 (*0-7399-0181-8*, 29.35.1) Rod & Staff.

Beidler, Peter G. Fig Tree John: An Indian in Fact & Fiction. LC 76-26345. 176p. 1977. reprint ed. pap. 54.60 (*0-608-02347-7*, 206298800004) Bks Demand.

— Ghosts, Demons & Henry James: The Turn of the Screw at the Turn of the Century. LC 88-39776. 272p. 1989. text 32.50 (*0-8262-0684-0*) U of Mo Pr.

— Writing Matters. (Illus.). 160p. (Orig.). (C). 1991. pap. text 31.00 (*0-02-307865-0*, Macmillan Coll) P-H.

Beidler, Peter G., ed. Distinguished Teachers on Effective Teaching. LC 85-81906. (New Directions for Teaching & Learning Ser.: No. TL 28). (Orig.). 1986. pap. 22.00 (*1-55542-995-5*) Jossey-Bass.

Beidler, Peter G. & Barton, Gaynor. A Reader's Guide to the Novels of Louise Erdrich. LC 99-12592. 280p. 1999. 34.95 (*0-8262-1212-3*) U of Mo Pr.

***Beidler, Peter G. & Barton, Gaynor.** A Reader's Guide to the Novels of Louise Erdrich. 280p. 1999. pap. 19.95 (*0-8262-1239-5*) U of Mo Pr.

Beidler, Peter G. & Biebel, Elizabeth M., eds. Chaucer's Wife of Bath's Prologue & Tale: An Annotated Bibliography, 1900-1995. LC 98-230240. (Chaucer Bibliographies Ser.). 426p. 1999. text 85.00 (*0-8020-4366-6*) U of Toronto Pr.

Beidler, Peter G., ed. see Chaucer, Geoffrey.

Beidler, Peter G., ed. see James, Henry.

Beidler, Philip D. American Literature & the Experience of Vietnam. LC 81-19845. 240p. 1982. 35.00 (*0-8203-0612-6*) U of Ga Pr.

— The Art of Fiction in the Heart of Dixie: An Anthology of Alabama Writers. LC 86-6919. 352p. (C). 1986. pap. 22.95 (*0-8173-0314-6*) U of Ala Pr.

— First Books: The Printed Word & Cultural Formation in Early Alabama. LC 99-6084. 216p. 1999. 34.95 (*0-8173-0985-3*) U of Ala Pr.

— The Good War's Greatest Hits: World War II & American Remembering. x, 220p. 1998. 29.95 (*0-8203-2001-3*) U of Ga Pr.

Beidler, Philip D., ed. Many Voices, Many Rooms: A New Anthology of Alabama Writers. LC 97-13084. 384p. 1997. pap. 22.95 (*0-8173-0904-7*); text 39.95 (*0-8173-0867-9*) U of Ala Pr.

Beier, Ann E., jt. auth. see McElfish, James M., Jr.

Beier, Ernst G. & Valens, Evans G. People-Reading: How We Control Others, How They Control Us. LC 84-43053. 228p. 1980. pap. 12.95 (*0-8128-6263-5*, Scrbrough Hse) Madison Bks UPA.

Beier, Ernst G. & Young, David M. The Silent Language of Psychotherapy: Social Reinforcement of Unconscious Processing. 3rd rev. ed. LC 97-48669. 323p. 1998. pap. text 25.95 (*0-202-30610-0*); lib. bdg. 49.95 (*0-202-30609-7*) Aldine de Gruyter.

Beier, Freidrich-Karl, ed. see Bochnovic, John.

***Beier, Friedrich-Karl, et al, eds.** German Industrial Property, Copyright & Antitrust Laws. 3rd ed. 2000. 65.00 (*3-527-28762-0*) Wiley.

— German Industrial Property, Copyright & Antitrust Laws. 3rd enl. rev. ed. LC 97-148801. (Illus.). 455p. 1996. 159.00 (*3-527-28730-2*, Wiley-VCH) Wiley.

Beier, Friedrich-Karl & Schricker, G., eds. From GATT to TRIPS. LC 97-190540. 504p. 1996. pap. 175.00 (*3-527-28782-5*, Wiley-VCH) Wiley.

Beier, H. M. & Karlson, P., eds. Proteins & Steroids in Early Pregnancy. (Illus.). 346p. 1982. 65.95 (*0-387-10457-7*) Spr-Verlag.

Beier, H. M., et al. The Endometrium as a Target for Contraception. LC 96-29098. (Ernst Schering Research Foundation Workshop Ser.). 1996. write for info. (*0-387-61257-2*); 79.50 (*3-540-61257-2*) Spr-Verlag.

Beier, H. M., jt. ed. see Herrier, A.

Beier, H. M., tr. & intro. see Kuhnel, Wolfgang.

Beier, Lucinda M. A Matter of Life & Death: Health, Illness & Medicine in McLean County. (Illus.). 312p. (Orig.). 1996. 40.00 (*0-943788-09-9*); pap. 15.00 (*0-943788-08-0*) McLean County.

— Sufferers & Healers: The Experience of Illness in Seventeenth-Century England. (Social & Economic History Ser.). (Illus.). 288p. 1988. text 69.95 (*0-7102-1053-1*, Routledge Thoemms) Routledge.

Beier, Richard A., jt. auth. see Hardy, H. H.

Beier, Ross C. & Stanker, Larry H., eds. Immunoassays for Residue Analysis: Food Safety. LC 95-50870. (ACS Symposium Ser.: No. 621). (Illus.). 544p. 1996. text 135.00 (*0-8412-3379-9*, Pub. by Am Chemical) OUP.

Beier, Rudolf. Sprache - System und Funktion: Festschrift Fur Gunter Weise. Augst, Gerhard, ed. (Theorie und Vermittlung der Sprache Ser.: Bd. 25). (GER., Illus.). x, 262p. 1996. 51.95 (*3-631-49815-2*) P Lang Pubng.

Beier, T. Vlli, jt. auth. see Ijimere, Obotunde.

Beier, Ulli. Art in Nigeria, 1960. LC 61-16002. 67p. reprint ed. pap. 25.00 (*0-8357-5760-9*, 2051428) Bks Demand.

— Introduction to African Literature: An Anthology of Critical Writing from Black Orpheus. LC 66-30612. 282p. reprint ed. pap. 87.50 (*0-608-10961-4*, 200693500060) Bks Demand.

Beier, Ulli. The Origin of Life & Death: African Creation Myths. (African Writers Ser.). 65p. (C). 1966. pap. 7.95 (*0-435-90023-4*, 90023) Heinemann.

Beier, Ulli. Yoruba Poetry: An Anthology of Traditional Poems. LC 77-92244. 126p. reprint ed. pap. 36.00 (*0-608-12270-X*, 2024420) Bks Demand.

Beier, Ulli, ed. Words of Paradise: Poetry of Papua New Guinea. Laycock, Don & Natachee, Allan, trs. LC 72-77912. (Illus.). 112p. 1973. 15.00 (*0-87775-031-9*); pap. 7.50 (*0-87775-081-5*) Unicorn Pr.

Beier, Ulli, jt. auth. see Gbadanosi, Bakare.

Beierel, Marlene & Sylvan, Anne. What Comes in Threes?, Vol. 3758. (Emergent Reader Big Bks.). (Illus.). 8p. (J). (gr. k-2). 1996. pap. 8.98 (*1-57471-096-6*) Creat Teach Pr.

Beierle, Christoph & Plumer, Lutz, eds. Logic Programming: Formal Methods & Practical Applications. LC 94-40114. (Studies in Computer Science & Artificial Intelligence). 418p. 1994. 158.50 (*0-444-82092-2*) Elsevier.

Beierle, Herbert L. The Art & Science of Wholeness. 1975. 20.00 (*0-940480-00-X*) UNIPress.

— L' Arte e la Scienza della Totalita. 1986. pap. 20.00 (*0-940480-32-8*) UNIPress.

— Autobiography of God. 2nd rev. ed. 1996. pap. 12.95 (*0-940480-38-7*) UNIPress.

— Un Dono del Se Fatto al Se. 1984. pap. 9.95 (*0-940480-31-X*) UNIPress.

— A Gift from Self to Self. 1981. pap. 9.95 (*0-940480-12-3*) UNIPress.

— How to Give a Healing Treatment. rev. ed. 1995. pap. 2.00 (*0-940480-34-4*) UNIPress.

— I Am Number One. LC 90-70207. 1992. pap. 12.95 (*0-940480-21-2*) UNIPress.

— Illumination: Handbook of Ascended Masters. 1978. 20.00 (*0-940480-02-6*) UNIPress.

— The Inexhaustible Laughter of Heaven: Bliss. (Illus.). 1997. pap. 2.00 (*0-940480-39-5*) UNIPress.

— Kunst und Wissenschaft der Goettlichen Ganzheit. 1981. pap. 20.00 (*0-940480-13-1*) UNIPress.

— The Law of Cause & Effect. 1991. pap. 2.00 (*0-940480-23-9*) UNIPress.

— Practice Reality. 1982. pap. 2.00 (*0-940480-27-1*) UNIPress.

— Practice Reality. rev. ed. 1995. pap. 2.00 (*0-940480-35-2*) UNIPress.

— Quiet, Healing Zone! (C). 1980. pap. 14.95 (*0-940480-10-7*) UNIPress.

— The Relative. 1990. pap. 20.00 (*0-940480-22-0*) UNIPress.

— School for Masters. 1979. pap. 2.00 (*0-940480-11-5*) UNIPress.

— Song of the Spirit. 1978. 20.00 (*0-940480-01-8*) UNIPress.

— The Three Hour Meditation. 1995. pap. 2.00 (*0-940480-29-8*) UNIPress.

— Warum Ich Sagen Kann Ich Bin Gott. 1995. pap. 2.00 (*0-940480-15-8*) UNIPress.

— Why I Can Say I Am God. rev. ed. 1995. pap. 2.00 (*0-940480-33-6*) UNIPress.

Beierle, Herbert L., ed. The Minister's Manual. 6th ed. 283p. (C). 1997. pap. 14.95 (*0-940480-03-4*) UNIPress.

Beierle, Herbert L., et al, eds. Practitioners Manual. LC 96-137657. 1995. pap. 12.95 (*0-940480-26-3*) UNIPress.

Beierle, Marlene & Sylvan, Anne. Que Viene en Grupos de Tres?, Vol. 4081. Hood, Christine, ed. Rancho Park Publishing Staff, tr. (Math Spanish Learn to Read Ser.).Tr. of What Comes in Threes. (SPA., Illus.). 8p. (J). (ps-2). 1996. pap. 1.75 (*1-57471-155-5*, 4081) Creat Teach Pr.

— What Comes in Threes?, Vol. 3701. (Emergent Reader Bk.). 8p. (J). (gr. k-2). 1995. pap. 1.75 (*0-916119-85-8*) Creat Teach Pr.

Beierle, Thomas C., jt. auth. see Probst, Katherine N.

Beierlein, James G., et al. Principles of Agribusiness Management. 2nd rev. ed. (Illus.). 328p. (C). 1995. text 36.95 (*0-88133-844-3*) Waveland Pr.

Beiersdorf, H., jt. auth. see Von Stackelberg, U.

Beiersdorf, Horst. Bridgebuilding Equipment of the Wehrmacht, 1939-1945. LC 98-182564. 48p. 1998. pap. 9.95 (*0-7643-0571-9*) Schiffer.

— German Military Trailers & Towed Equipment in World War II, 1935-1945. Force, Edward, tr. from GER. (Illus.). 48p. (Orig.). 1995. pap. 9.95 (*0-88740-757-9*) Schiffer.

Beifuss, John. Armadillo Ray. LC 94-44527. (Illus.). 32p. (J). (gr. k-4). 1995. 13.95 (*0-8118-0334-1*) Chronicle Bks.

— Armadillo Ray. (SPA., Illus.). (J). (gr. k-4). 1998. 15.95 (*0-8118-2277-X*); pap. 6.95 (*0-8118-2211-7*) Chronicle Bks.

— Armadillo Ray. (Illus.). (J). (gr. k-4). 1998. pap. 6.95 (*0-8118-2135-8*) Chronicle Bks.

Beifuss, Will. Psychedelic Source Book. (Illus.). 72p. (Orig.). 1996. pap., per. 12.95 (*0-9647946-2-4*) Flowers Pubng.

Beig, Maria. Lost Weddings: A Novel. Blickle, Peter & Gordon, Jaimy, trs. from GER. 140p. 1990. 17.95 (*0-89255-145-3*) Persea Bks.

Beigbeder Atienza, F. Polytechnic Dictionary of Spanish & English Languages - English-Spanish. 2nd ed. (ENG & SPA.). 1543p. 1997. 180.00 (*84-7978-299-4*, Pub. by Ediciones Diaz) IBD Ltd.

Beigbeder-Atienza, F. Technical Directory Spanish-English - English-Spanish. (ENG & SPA.). 1253p. 1996. 70.00 (*84-7978-221-8*, Pub. by Ediciones Diaz) IBD Ltd.

Beigbeder, F. Dictionary of Technical Terms: Spanish-English/English-Spanish. (ENG & SPA.). 1300p. 1996. 195.00 (*0-7859-9258-8*) Fr & Eur.

Beigbeder, Frederick. Barbie. 1998. 18.95 (*0-7893-0247-0*, Pub. by Universe) St Martin.

Beigbeder, Olivier. Dictionnaire des Sciences Occultes de l'Esoterisme et des Arts Divinitoires. (FRE.). 436p. 1989. 95.00 (*0-7859-4806-6*) Fr & Eur.

Beigbeder, Yves. International Monitoring of Plebiscites, Referenda & National Elections: Self-Determination & Transition to Democracy. LC 93-39167. (International Studies on Human Rights). 340p. (C). 1994. lib. bdg. 149.00 (*0-7923-2563-X*) Kluwer Academic.

— The Role & Status of International Humanitarian Volunteers & Organizations: The Right & Duty to Humanitarian Assistance. 432p. (C). 1991. lib. bdg. 169.00 (*0-7923-1190-6*) Kluwer Academic.

— Threats to the International Civil Service: Past Pressures & New Trends. 220p. 1988. text 54.00 (*0-86187-953-8*) St Martin.

Beigbeder, Yves, et al. The World Health Organization. LC 98-43179. (International Organization & the Evolution of World Society Ser.). 1998. 84.00 (*90-411-1096-8*) Kluwer Academic.

Beigbock, W., ed. see Busch, Paul, et al.

Beigel, jt. auth. see Floyd.

Beigel, Allan, et al. World Congress of Psychiatry. LC 95-166269. 1548p. 1994. text 202.00 (*981-02-1500-2*) World Scientific Pub.

Beigel, Allan, jt. auth. see Russell, Harold E.

Beigel, Gerard. Faith & Social Justice in the Teaching of Pope John Paul II. LC 95-53179. (American University Studies: Vol. 191). 176p. (C). 1997. 38.95 (*0-8204-3090-0*) P Lang Pubng.

***Beigel, Harvey M.** USS Los Angeles: Cold War Sentinel. (Illus.). 64p. 2000. pap. 9.95 (*1-57510-067-3*, 129962AE, Pub. by Pictorial Hist) Motorbooks Intl.

Beigel, Herbert. The Closed Fraternity of Police & the Development of the Corrupt Attitude. (Criminal Justice Center Monographs). 1978. pap. text 3.25 (*0-318-37485-4*) John Jay Pr.

Beigel, Joan K. & Earle, Ralph H. Successful Private Practice in the 1990s: A New Guide for the Mental Health Professional. LC 90-2053. 224p. 1990. pap. text 25.95 (*0-87630-586-9*, 5869) Brunner-Mazel.

Beigel, R. Lighting Your Home. 1994. pap. 9.95 (*1-870948-94-7*) St Mut.

Beigel, Renate, jt. auth. see Lyons, Stanely.

Beigel, Richard, jt. auth. see Floyd, Robert W.

Beiger, jt. auth. see Crandell.

Beighley, Colette, jt. see Beighley, David.

Beighley, David & Beighley, Colette. Dancing with Yesterday's Shadows Series, 6 progs. on 3 cass.; set. pap., student ed., wbk. ed. 69.95 incl. VHS (*1-55568-177-8*) Gospel Communs.

Beighley, David G. Dancing with Yesterday's Shadows. 166p. 1997. 19.95 (*1-55568-201-4*); pap., student ed. 4.95 (*1-55568-203-0*) Gospel Communs.

Beighley, Jay C. Workplace Violence Prevention. 158p. 1998. ring bd. 49.95 (*1-879876-08-6*, 30301) Mgmt Advantage.

Beighton, G. J., jt. auth. see Beighton, Peter H.

Beighton, Greta, jt. auth. see Beighton, Peter.

Beighton, Greta, jt. auth. see Beighton, Peter H.

Beighton, Peter & Beighton, Greta. The Man Behind the Syndrome. 240p. 1986. 54.95 (*3-540-16218-6*) Spr-Verlag.

Beighton, Peter, et al. Hypermobility of Joints. 3rd ed. LC 99-10453. 200p. 1999. 149.00 (*1-85233-142-9*, Pub. by Spr-Verlag) Spr-Verlag.

Beighton, Peter H. & Beighton, G. J. The Man Behind the Syndrome. (Illus.). 250p. 1991. reprint ed. 60.95 (*0-387-16218-6*) Spr-Verlag.

Beighton, Peter H. & Beighton, Greta. The Person Behind the Syndrome. LC 96-17384. (Illus.). 248p. 1996. 59.00 (*3-540-76044-X*) Spr-Verlag.

Beighton, Peter H., et al. Hypermobility of Joints. (Illus.). 105p. 1983. 75.00 (*0-387-12113-7*) Spr-Verlag.

Beighton, Peter H., jt. auth. see Kozlowski, Kazimierz.

Beigie, Carl E. Inflation Is a Social Malady. LC 78-70536. (British-North American Committee Ser.). 92p. 1979. 4.00 (*0-902594-34-6*) Natl Planning.

Beigie, Carl E. & Hero, Alfred O., Jr., eds. Natural Resources in U. S.-Canadian Relations: Patterns & Trends in Resource Supplies & Policies, Vol. 2. 1980. pap. text 14.50 (*0-89158-878-7*) Westview.

— Natural Resources in U. S.-Canadian Relations: Patterns & Trends in Resource Supplies & Policies, Vol. 2. 1980. text 43.00 (*0-89158-555-9*) Westview.

— Natural Resources in U. S.-Canadian Relations: The Evolution of Policies & Issues, Vol. 1. (Illus.). 362p. 1980. text 42.00 (*0-89158-554-0*) Westview.

Beigie, Carl E., jt. auth. see Maxwell, Judith B.

Beigl, William. Adventures in Hypnosis. limited ed. Strnad, Wayne, ed. & illus. by. LC 89-92466. (Adventure in Hypnosis Reprint Ser.: Vol. I). 200p. (Orig.). 1990. pap. text 500.00 (*0-9624961-0-3*) Rainbow News.

— Adventures in Hypnosis. 2nd ed. Strong, Wayne, ed. LC 91-7651. (Adventure in Hypnosis Reprint Ser.: Vol. 2). (Illus.). 200p. (Orig.). 1991. pap. text 19.95 (*0-9624961-1-1*) Rainbow News.

An Asterisk (*) at the beginning of an entry indicates that the title is appearing for the first time.

Beiglbock, W., et al, eds. Quantum Relativity: A Synthesis of the Ideas of Einstein & Heisenberg. (Texts & Monographs in Physics). (Illus.). 600p. 1996. 89.00 (*3-540-57084-5*) Spr-Verlag.
— White Dwarfs: Proceedings of the 9th European Workshop on White Dwarfs Held at Kiel, Germany, 29 August-1 September 1994. (Lecture Notes in Physics Ser.: Vol. 443). xii, 346p. 1995. 92.95 (*3-540-59157-5*) Spr-Verlag.
Beiglbock, W., ed. see Akulin, V. M. & Karlov, N. V.
Beiglbock, W., ed. see Alkofer, Reinhard & Reinhardt, Hugo.
Beiglbock, W., ed. see Balian, R. M.
Beiglbock, W., ed. see Bendjaballah, Cherif.
Beiglbock, W., ed. see Blanchard, P. & Bruning, E.
Beiglbock, W., ed. see Childress, Stephen & Gilbert, A. D.
Beiglbock, W., ed. see Derdzinski, A.
Beiglbock, W., ed. see Dunne, Gerald.
Beiglbock, W., ed. see Elizalde, Emilio.
Beiglbock, W., ed. see Fernandez, R., et al.
Beiglbock, W., ed. see Galindo, A.
Beiglbock, W., ed. see Greer, Allan J. & Kossler, William J.
Beiglbock, W., ed. see Haag, Rudolf.
Beiglbock, W., ed. see Hora, Heinrich.
Beiglbock, W., ed. see International Winter School on Theoretical Physics Staff & Kowalski-Glikman, Jerzy.
Beiglbock, W., ed. see Kuo, T. T. & Osnes, E.
Beiglbock, W., ed. see Mittelstaedt, P., et al.
Beiglbock, W., ed. see Morandi, G.
Beiglbock, W., ed. see Namiki, Mikio, et al.
Beiglbock, W., ed. see Scadron, Michael D.
Beiglbock, W., ed. see Scharf, Gunter.
Beiglbock, W., ed. see Sibgatullin, N. R.
Beiglbock, W., ed. see Spohn, H.
Beiglbock, W., ed. see Ting, L. & Klein, R.
Beiglbock, W., ed. see Woodhouse, N. M.
Beiglbock, W., ed. see Yaghjian, Arthur D.
Beiglbock, W., ed. see Zak, Michail, et al.
Beiglbock, W., ed. see Zeytounian, R. K.
Beiglbock, W., ed. see Zubov, Leonid M.
Beiglbsck, W., ed. see Ambjorn, Jan, et al.
Beiglbsck, W., ed. see Elbaz, E.
Beiglbsck, W., ed. see Landi, Giovanni.
Beigum Kaplan, Barbara. Land & Heritage in the Virginia Tidewaters: A History of King & Queen County. (Illus.). viii, 279p. 1993. 25.00 (*0-9664788-1-9*) King & Queen.
Beije, P. R., et al. A Competitive Future for Europe? Towards a New European Industrial Policy. 304p. 1987. lib. bdg. 69.95 (*0-7099-5032-2*, Pub. by C Helm) Routldge.
Beije, Paul. Technological Change in the Modern Economy: Basic Topics & New Developments. LC 98-3824. 304p. 1999. 95.00 (*1-85898-331-2*) E Elgar.
***Beije, Paul.** Technological Change in the Modern Economy: Basic Topics & New Developments. LC 98-38242. 304p. 2000. pap. 30.00 (*1-84064-462-1*) E Elgar.
Beijer, Agne. Court Theatres of Drottningholm & Gripsholm. LC 77-180032. (Illus.). 1972. reprint ed. 38.95 (*0-405-08260-6*) Ayer.
Beijeren, H. Van, see Van Beijeren, H., ed.
Beijing Institute Staff. Chinese-English Dictionary of Architecture & Construction. (CHI & ENG.). 1027p. 1992. 35.00 (*0-7859-8831-9*) Fr & Eur.
***Beijing International Conference on Group Theory Staff, et al.** Group Theory: Proceedings of the 1996 Beijing International Conference on... LC 98-10805. xii, 143 p. 1998. write for info. (*981-3083-85-9*, Pub. by Spr-Verlag) Spr-Verlag.
Beijing Language Institute Staff. Chinese for Today, Vol. 1. 2nd ed. 428p. 1997. 38.95 (*962-07-4290-7*, Pub. by Commercial Pr) Cheng & Tsui.
— Chinese for Today, Vol. 2. 2nd ed. 428p. 1997. 38.95 (*962-07-4294-X*, Pub. by Commercial Pr) Cheng & Tsui.
— New Chinese Three Hundred. 1990. audio 40.00 (*0-88727-121-9*) Cheng & Tsui.
— The Pinyin Chinese-English Dictionary. Wu Jingrong, ed. (CHI & ENG.). 976p. 1982. pap. 59.95 (*0-471-86796-9*) Wiley.
— Practical Chinese Reader, Elementary Course Bk. 1: Traditional Character Edition. (C & T Asian Language Ser.). 394p. (C). 1990. pap. text 18.95 (*0-88727-229-0*) Cheng & Tsui.
Beijing Language Institute Staff, ed. Chinese Character Exercise Book for Practical Chinese Reader. (Practical Chinese Reader Ser.: No. 1). 208p. (Orig.). (C). 1982. pap. 4.95 (*0-8351-1146-6*) China Bks.
— Chinese Character Exercise Book for Practical Chinese Reader. (Practical Chinese Reader Ser.: No. 2). 108p. (Orig.). (C). 1982. pap. 4.95 (*0-8351-1147-4*) China Bks.
Beijing Language Institute Staff, jt. auth. see Bejing Language Institute Staff.
Beijing Military Science Staff. Dictionary of the Military. (ARA, CHI, ENG, FRE & GER.). 1030p. 1989. 75.00 (*0-8288-9445-0*) Fr & Eur.
Beijing Normal University Staff, jt. compiled by see People's Insurance Company of China Staff.
Beijing University Department of Foreign Languages, ed. A Chinese-English Dictionary. 1444p. 1995. 128.00 (*7-5600-0739-2*, Pub. by Foreign Lang Pr) Cheng & Tsui.
Beik, Mildred A. The Miners of Windber: The Struggles of New Immigrants for Unionization, 1890s-1930s. LC 95-47701. 1996. 65.00 (*0-271-01566-7*); pap. 22.95 (*0-271-01567-5*) Pa St U Pr.
Beik, Paul, ed. Flora Tristan, Utopian Feminist: Her Travel Diaries & Personal Crusade. LC 92-15235. 224p. (C). 1993. 32.00 (*0-253-31163-2*); pap. 17.95 (*0-253-20766-5*, MB 766) Ind U Pr.
Beik, Paul H. Judgment of the Old Regime. LC 44-2365. (Columbia University. Studies in the Social Sciences: No. 509). reprint ed. 24.50 (*0-404-51509-6*) AMS Pr.
Beik, William. Absolutism & Society in Seventeenth-Century France: State Power & Provincial Aristocracy in Languedoc. LC 84-9561. (Cambridge Studies in Early Modern History). (Illus.). 398p. 1989. pap. text 22.95 (*0-521-36782-4*) Cambridge U Pr.
***Beik, William.** Louis the Fourteenth & Absolutism. 2000. pap. 15.95 (*0-312-13309-X*) St Martin.
— Louis XIV & Absolutism: A Brief Study with Documents. 2000. text 39.95 (*0-312-22743-4*) St Martin.
Beik, William. Urban Protest in Seventeenth-Century France: The Culture of Retribution. LC 96-2951. (Illus.). 296p. (C). 1997. pap. text 19.95 (*0-521-57585-0*) Cambridge U Pr.
— Urban Protest in Seventeenth-Century France: The Culture of Retribution. LC 96-2951. (Illus.). 296p. (C). 1997. text 59.95 (*0-521-57308-4*) Cambridge U Pr.
Beil, Daric, ed. Twelve Tattoos. LC 93-37371. (Illus.). 176p. 1998. 16.95 (*0-913720-89-5*) Beil.
Beil, Drake. Managing for the '90s: The Book of Solutions. Magisa, Lenore, ed. (Illus.). 212p. 1992. pap. 7.95 (*0-89610-266-1*) Island Heritage.
Beil, Karen M. A Cake All for Me. LC 97-41951. (Illus.). (J). (ps-3). 1998. lib. bdg. 16.95 (*0-8234-1368-3*) Holiday.
— Grandma According to Me. (Illus.). 32p. (J). 1994. pap. 4.99 (*0-440-40995-0*) Dell.
Beil, Karen Magnuson. Fire in Their Eyes: Wildfires & the People Who Fight Them. LC 98-6378. (Illus.). 64p. (J). 1999. 18.00 (*0-15-201043-2*); pap. 10.00 (*0-15-201042-4*) Harcourt.
Beil, Karen Magnuson. Grandma According to Me. 1994. 10.19 (*0-606-06992-5*, Pub. by Turtleback) Demco.
Beilan, Michael H. Your Offshore Doctor: A Manual of Medical Self-Sufficiency at Sea. 2nd ed. (Illus.). 184p. 1996. pap. 17.50 (*1-57409-013-5*) Sheridan.
Beilby, Alvin L., ed. Modern Classics in Analytical Chemistry, Vol. 1. LC 75-125864. (ACS Reprint Collection). 1970. pap. 8.95 (*0-8412-0315-6*) Am Chemical.
— Modern Classics in Analytical Chemistry, Vol. 2. LC 75-125864. (ACS Reprint Collection). 1976. pap. 10.95 (*0-8412-0332-6*) Am Chemical.
— Modern Classics in Analytical Chemistry: A Collection of Articles from Analytical Chemistry Selected for Their Value As Supplementary Reading about Modern Chemical Instrumentation & Analytical Methods, Vol. 2. LC 75-125864. (ACS Reprint Collection). (Illus.). 314p. 1976. reprint ed. pap. 97.40 (*0-608-04351-6*, 206513200002) Bks Demand.
Beilby, M. H., et al. Scientific Programmer's Toolkit: Turbo Pascal Edition. (Illus.). 438p. 1990. 198.00 incl. disk (*0-7503-0038-8*) IOP Pub.
— Scientific Programmer's Toolkit: Turbo Pascal Edition. (Illus.). 438p. 1991. 198.00 incl. disk (*0-7503-0127-9*) IOP Pub.
Beilenson, Edna. Golden Treasury of Psalms & Prayer. large type ed. 1986. 5.95 (*0-8027-2555-4*) Walker & Co.
Beilenson, Esther, compiled by. Congratulations on Your Graduation! (Pocket Gift Editions Ser.). (Illus.). 64p. 1999. 4.95 (*0-88088-099-6*) Peter Pauper.
***Beilenson, Esther L.** Beacon of Light. (Pocket Gold Ser.). (Illus.). 64p. 2000. 4.95 (*0-88088-116-X*) Peter Pauper.
— Love Is a Beautiful Thing. (Pocket Gold Ser.). (Illus.). 64p. 1999. 5.95 (*0-88088-110-0*) Peter Pauper.
Beilenson, Evelyn. First Aid for a Mother's Soul. (Charming Petites Ser.). (Illus.). 80p. 1998. 4.95 (*0-88088-383-9*) Peter Pauper.
Beilenson, Evelyn, compiled by. Con Amor. (Petites Ser.).Tr. of With Love. (SPA., Illus.). 80p. 1998. 4.95 (*0-88088-237-9*) Peter Pauper.
***Beilenson, Evelyn, ed.** First Aid for the Jewish Soul. (Charming Petites Ser.). (Illus.). 80p. 2000. 4.95 (*0-88088-332-4*) Peter Pauper.
Beilenson, Evelyn L. Dreams Can Come True. LC 99-203075. (Charming Petites Ser.). (Illus.). 80p. 1998. 4.95 (*0-88088-839-3*) Peter Pauper.
***Beilenson, Evelyn L.** My Bridal Shower Record Keeper & Photo Album. (Illus.). 48p. 2000. 11.99 (*0-88088-648-X*) Peter Pauper.
— True Friends. (Charming Petites Ser.). (Illus.). 80p. 1996. 4.95 (*0-88088-797-4*) Peter Pauper.
***Beilenson, Evelyn L.** True Friends. (Matchbook Mailers Ser.). (Illus.). 80p. 2000. 4.95 (*0-88088-526-2*) Peter Pauper.
Beilenson, Evelyn L., ed. With Love. (Charming Petites Ser.). (Illus.). 80p. 1991. 4.95 (*0-88088-735-4*) Peter Pauper.
— Women. (Charming Petites Ser.). (Illus.). 80p. 1991. 4.95 (*0-88088-748-6*) Peter Pauper.
Beilenson, Evelyn L. & Kaufman, Lois L. Amor Verdadero. (Petites Ser.).Tr. of True Love. (SPA., Illus.). 80p. 1998. text 4.95 (*0-88088-232-8*) Peter Pauper.
— True Love. (Charming Petites Ser.). (Illus.). 80p. 1995. 4.95 (*0-88088-771-0*) Peter Pauper.
Beilenson, John P. The Book of Tea. LC 96-168700. (Die-Cuts Ser.). (Illus.). 80p. 1995. pap. 5.99 (*0-88088-928-4*) Peter Pauper.
— Prayers for Inner Strength. large type ed. (Large Print Inspirational Ser.). 1987. pap. 5.95 (*0-8027-2582-1*) Walker & Co.
— Time-Honored Friends: The Best Is Yet to Come. (Keepsakes with Ribbons Ser.). (Illus.). 56p. 1995. 7.99 (*0-88088-888-1*) Peter Pauper.
Beilenson, John P., ed. Voices of Struggle, Voices of Pride: Quotes by Great African-Americans. (Illus.). 64p. 1992. 7.99 (*0-88088-563-7*) Peter Pauper.
***Beilenson, Laurence L., ed.** Happy Birthday. (Matchbook Mailers Ser.). (Illus.). 80p. 2000. 4.95 (*0-88088-550-0*) Peter Pauper.
Beilenson, Nick. The First 100 Years Are the Hardest. LC 98-141010. (Charming Petites Ser.). (Illus.). 80p. 1997. 4.95 (*0-88088-823-7*) Peter Pauper.
— Get Well Soon. (Charming Petites Ser.). (Illus.). 80p. 1997. 4.95 (*0-88088-825-3*) Peter Pauper.
***Beilenson, Nick.** A Moment in Time: My Life at the Dawn of the New Millennium. (Guided Journals). (Illus.). 128p. 1999. 11.99 (*0-88088-222-0*) Peter Pauper.
Beilenson, Nick. Thomas Jefferson, His Words & Vision. LC 98-219847. (Pocket Gift Editions Ser.). 1998. 4.95 (*0-88088-082-1*) Peter Pauper.
Beilenson, Nick, compiled by. Para Mi Amigo. (Petites Ser.).Tr. of For My Friend. (SPA., Illus.). 80p. 1998. text 4.95 (*0-88088-231-X*) Peter Pauper.
Beilenson, Nick, ed. For My Friend. (Petites Ser.). (Illus.). 80p. 1991. 4.95 (*0-88088-730-3*) Peter Pauper.
***Beilenson, Peter, tr.** The Four Seasons Guided Journal. (Guided Journals). (Illus.). 128p. 2000. 11.99 (*0-88088-224-7*) Peter Pauper.
Beilenson, Suzanne. Cat's Meow. (Charming Petites Ser.). (Illus.). 80p. 1993. 4.95 (*0-88088-762-1*) Peter Pauper.
— Crazy about Cats. LC 99-170281. (Pocket Gift Editions Ser.). 1998. 4.95 (*0-88088-076-7*) Peter Pauper.
— Happy Anniversary. (Charming Petites Ser.). (Illus.). 80p. 1995. 4.95 (*0-88088-774-5*) Peter Pauper.
— Mothers & Daughters: That Special Bond. LC 98-232376. (Pocket Gift Editions Ser.). 1998. 4.95 (*0-88088-072-4*) Peter Pauper.
Beilenson, Suzanne & Wolk, Daniel S. The Eight Nights of Hanukah. (Charming Petites Ser.). (Illus.). 80p. 1993. 5.95 (*0-88088-781-8*) Peter Pauper.
Beiler, Albert H. Recreations in the Theory of Numbers. (Orig.). 1964. pap. 9.95 (*0-486-21096-0*) Dover.
***Beiler, Allen R.** Family History & Genealogy of Pioneer Jacob Beiler (1698-1771) Beiler - Boiler - Byler. (Illus.). 596p. 1998. 39.95 (*1-930353-01-4*) Masthof Pr.
Beiler, Edna. Mattie Mae. LC 67-24800. (Illus.). 128p. (J). (gr. 3-7). 1967. pap. 5.99 (*0-8361-1789-1*) Herald Pr.
***Beiler, Edna.** Mattie Mae. 2nd ed. LC 99-58469. (Illus.). (J). 2000. 6.99 (*0-8361-9143-9*) Herald Pr.
— Mattie Mae. 2nd ed. (Illus.). 112p. (J). (ps-4). 2000. pap. 6.99 (*0-8361-9141-2*) Herald Pr.
Beilhart, Jacob. Love Letters from Spirit to You. 2nd ed. 112p. 1986. reprint ed. pap. 4.95 (*0-918588-07-3*, 505-100) Barksdale Foun.
— Spirit Fruit & Voice. 2nd ed. (Illus.). 176p. 1986. reprint ed. pap. 6.95 (*0-918588-08-1*, 507-100) Barksdale Foun.
Beilharz, Peter. Imagining the Antipodes: Culture, Theory & the Visual in the Work of Bernard Smith. LC 96-52054. 232p. (C). 1997. text 49.95 (*0-521-58355-1*) Cambridge U Pr.
— Postmodern Socialism: Romanticism, City & State. (Interpretations Ser.). 160p. 1994. pap. 19.95 (*0-522-84535-5*, Pub. by Melbourne Univ Pr) Paul & Co Pubs.
— Transforming Labor: Labour Tradition & the Labor Decade in Australia. LC 93-37970. 244p. (C). 1993. pap. write for info. (*0-521-43821-7*) Cambridge U Pr.
— Transforming Labor: Labour Tradition & the Labor Decade in Australia. LC 93-37970. 261p. (C). 1994. text 64.95 (*0-521-43237-5*) Cambridge U Pr.
— Trotsky, Trotskyism & the Transition to Socialism. 208p. 1987. 53.00 (*0-389-20698-9*, N 8256) B&N Imports.
***Beilharz, Peter, ed.** The Bauman Reader. 2000. 64.95 (*0-631-21491-7*); pap. 27.95 (*0-631-21492-5*) Blackwell Pubs.
Beilharz, Peter, ed. Social Theory: A Guide to Central Thinkers. 256p. (Orig.). pap. 22.95 (*1-86373-163-6*, Pub. by Allen & Unwin Pty) Paul & Co Pubs.
***Beilharz, Peter & Nyland, Chris, eds.** The Webbs, Fabianism & Feminism: Fabianism & the Political Economy of Everyday Life. LC 98-71957. (Avebury Series in Philosophy). 176p. 1998. text 55.95 (*1-84014-307-X*, Pub. by Ashgate Pub) Ashgate Pub Co.
Beilharz, Peter, et al. Arguing about the Welfare State: The Australian Experience. 176p. (C). 1992. pap. text 19.95 (*1-86373-096-6*, Pub. by Allen & Unwin Pty) Paul & Co Pubs.
Beilharz, Peter, ed. see Rundell, John.
Beilin, Elaine V. Early Modern Englishwoman Part. 2, Vol. 12. LC 99-55939. 1905. 47.95 (*1-84014-225-1*) Ashgate Pub Co.
Beilin, Elaine V., ed. see Askew, Anne.
Beilin, Harry & Pufall, Peter, eds. Piaget's Theory: Prospects & Possibilities. (Jean Piaget Symposia Ser.). 360p. 1992. text 79.95 (*0-8058-1050-1*) L Erlbaum Assocs.
***Beilin, Yossi.** His Brother's Keeper: Israel & Diaspora Jewry in the Twenty-First Century. LC 99-89429. 288p. 2000. 24.00 (*0-8052-4175-2*) Schocken.
— Touching Peace. 1999. 50.00 (*0-297-64316-9*, Pub. by Weidenfeld & Nicolson) Trafalgar.
Beilis, Mendel. Scapegoat on Trial. (C). 1993. 19.95 (*1-56062-166-4*); pap. 14.95 (*1-56062-167-2*) CIS Comm.
Beilke, Ines. Career Motivation & Self-concept: Get Your Life on Track. 4th ed. 304p. (C). per. write for info. (*0-7872-6392-3*) Kendall-Hunt.
Beilke, Marlan. Family, Friends & Poetry. 12p. 1980. pap. 5.00 (*0-918466-09-1*) Quintessence.
Beilke, Marlan, ed. see Harte, F. Bret.
Beilke, S. & Elshout, A. J., eds. Acid Deposition. 1983. text 106.00 (*90-277-1588-2*) Kluwer Academic.
Beillo, Lisa, ed. see Weiss, Robert C.
Beilner, Heinz, et al, eds. Quantitative Evaluation of Computing & Communication Systems: 8th International Conference on Modeling Techniques & Tools for Computer Performance Evaluation, Heidelberg, Germany, September 20-22, 1995, Proceedings, Vol. X. (Lecture Notes in Computer Science Ser.: Vol. 977). 415p. 1995. 68.00 (*3-540-60300-X*) Spr-Verlag.
Beilstein. Beilstein Handbook. 5th ed. 1992. suppl. ed. 1945.00 (*0-387-55630-3*) Spr-Verlag.
Beilstein, Christian W., ed. see Fukui, Shizuo.
Beilstein Institut fur Literatur der Organischen Chemie. Acyclische Kohlenwasserstoffe, Hydroxy-Verbindungen und Oxo-Verbindungen. (Beilsteins Handbuch der Organischen Chemie Ser., 4th Ed., 4th Suppl.: Vol. 1, Pt. 6). 569p. 1975. 695.00 (*0-387-07221-7*) Spr-Verlag.
— Acyclische Verbindungen. Boit, H. G., ed. LC 72-95756. (Beilsteins Handbuch der Organischen Chemie Ser., 4th Ed., 4th Suppl.: Vol. 2, Pt. 1). 692p. 1975. 795.00 (*0-387-07311-6*) Spr-Verlag.
— Beilstein Handbook of Organic Chemistry: Heterocyclic Compounds. Luckenbach, R., ed. (Fifth Supplementary Ser.: Vol. 25, Pt. 18). 820p. 1993. 2060.00 (*0-387-56117-X*) Spr-Verlag.
— Beilstein Handbook of Organic Chemistry: Heterocyclic Compounds. Luckenbach, R., ed. (Fifth Supplementary Ser.: Vol. 25, Pt. 17). (Illus.). 74p. 1993. 2270.00 (*0-387-56116-1*) Spr-Verlag.
— Beilstein-Leitfaden: Eine Anleitung Zur Benutzung Von Beilsteins Handbuch der Organischen Chemie. 56p. 1975. 525.00 (*0-387-07431-7*) Spr-Verlag.
— Heterocyclische Verbindungen. Boit, H. G., ed. (Beilsteins Handbuch der Organischen Chemie Ser., 4th Ed., 4th Suppl.: Vol. 17, Pt. 6). 868p. 1975. 1165.00 (*0-387-07359-0*) Spr-Verlag.
— Heterocyclische Verbindungen, Pt. 3. (Beilsteins Handbuch der Organischen Chemie Ser., 4th Ed., 4th Suppl.: Vol. 17, Pts. 3-5). 1975. 1210.00 (*0-387-07084-2*) Spr-Verlag.
— Heterocyclische Verbindungen, Pt. 4. (Beilsteins Handbuch der Organischen Chemie Ser., 4th Ed., 4th Suppl.: Vol. 17, Pts. 3-5). 1975. 1675.00 (*0-387-07220-9*) Spr-Verlag.
— Heterocyclische Verbindungen, Pt. 5. (Beilsteins Handbuch der Organischen Chemie Ser., 4th Ed., 4th Suppl.: Vol. 17, Pts. 3-5). 1975. 1055.00 (*0-387-07310-8*) Spr-Verlag.
Beilstein Institut fur Literatur der Organischen Chemie, compiled by. Beilstein: Centennial Index - Generalregister: General Formula Index - General-Formelregister, Vol. 29, Pt. 4. 4th ed. (Handbook of Organic Chemistry Ser.). 1280p. 1992. 775.00 (*0-387-55572-2*) Spr-Verlag.
— Beilstein: Centennial Index - Generalregister: General Formula Index - General-Formelregister, Vol. 29, Pt. 5. 4th ed. (Handbook of Organic Chemistry Ser.). 1280p. 1992. 775.00 (*0-387-55573-0*) Spr-Verlag.
— Beilstein Handbook of Organic Chemistry: Centennial Index - Generalregister, 3 pts., Vol. 28, Pt. 8: P - Propanol. 4th ed. iv, 1401p. 1991. 775.00 (*0-387-54088-1*) Spr-Verlag.
— Beilstein Handbook of Organic Chemistry: Centennial Index - Generalregister, 3 pts., Vol. 28, Pt. 9: Propanon. 4th ed. 1600p. 1991. 775.00 (*0-387-54089-X*) Spr-Verlag.
— Beilstein Handbook of Organic Chemistry: Centennial Index - Generalregister, 3 pts., Vol. 28, Pt. 10: S-Z. 4th ed. 1600p. 1991. 775.00 (*0-387-54090-3*) Spr-Verlag.
— Beilstein Handbook of Organic Chemistry: Heterocyclic Compounds, Pt. 15. 4th ed. (Supplementary Series 5: Vol. 25). xxii, 807p. 1993. 2490.00 (*0-387-56114-5*) Spr-Verlag.
— Centennial Index - General Register Vol. 29. Pt. 10: C19 - C20 H24. 1280p. 1992. 775.00 (*0-387-55682-6*) Spr-Verlag.
— Centennial Index - General Register Vol. 29, Pt. 11: C20 H26 - C22 H28. 1280p. 1992. 775.00 (*0-387-55683-4*) Spr-Verlag.
— Centennial Index - General Register Vol. 29. Pt. 12: C22 H29 - C25. 1280p. 1992. 775.00 (*0-387-55684-2*) Spr-Verlag.
— Centennial Index - General Register Vol. 29, Pt. 13: C26 - C372. 1280p. 1992. 775.00 (*0-387-55685-0*) Spr-Verlag.
Beilstein Institut fur Literatur der Organischen Chemie, ed. Heterocyclic Compounds. 4th ed. (Beilstein Handbook of Organic Chemistry Ser.: 5th Suppl.: Vol. 22, Pt. 14). 770p. 1991. 3090.00 (*0-387-53403-2*) Spr-Verlag.
— Molkick: Version 2.0. 200p. 1992. student ed. 895.95 incl. disk (*0-387-14107-3*) Spr-Verlag.
Beilstein Institut fur Literatur der Organischen Chemie & Luckenbach, R., eds. Beilstein: Centennial Index - Generalregister. 4th ed. (Handbook of Organic Chemistry Ser.: Vol. 28, Pt. 2). iv, 1419p. 1991. 775.00 (*0-387-54048-2*) Spr-Verlag.
— Heterocyclic Compounds. 4th ed. (Beilstein Handbook of Organic Chemistry Ser.: 5th Suppl.: Vol. 23, Pt. 6). 720p. 1991. 1870.00 (*0-387-53892-5*) Spr-Verlag.
Beilstein Institut fur Literatur der Organischen Chemie, jt. ed. see Luckenbach, R.
Beim, George & Stevens, Julia R. Babe Ruth: A Family Portrait. LC 98-9548. 1998. 29.95 (*0-87833-995-7*) Taylor Pub.
Beim, Howard J., et al. Rapid Guide to Hazardous Air Pollutants. 582p. 1997. pap. 43.95 (*0-471-29234-6*, VNR) Wiley.
Beim, Howard J., jt. auth. see Theodore, Louis.
Beim, Norman. Hymie & the Angel. LC 98-14194. 198p. 1999. pap. 12.95 (*0-931231-09-4*) Newconcept Pr.
— My Family, the Jewish Immigrants: The Jewish Immigrants. LC 97-19410. (Illus.). 400p. 1997. pap. 18.95 (*0-931231-08-6*) Newconcept Pr.
— Plays at Home & Abroad. LC 96-21006. 524p. 1996. pap. 19.95 (*0-931231-07-8*) Newconcept Pr.
— Six Award Winning Plays. 251p. 1995. pap. 17.95 (*0-931231-06-X*) Newconcept Pr.

B

Beim, Richard N. Personal Relationships. 1992. mass mkt. 4.99 (*0-8125-1884-5*, Pub. by Tor Bks) St Martin.

Beima, Janice, jt. auth. see Stone, Carolyn.

Beimborn, Edward, et al. Strategies for Private Sector Participation in the Provision of Transportation Facilities. (Publications in Architecture & Urban Planning: No. R85-4). v, 18p. 1985. 5.00 (*0-938744-40-2*) U of Wis Ctr Arch-Urban.

Beimer, Dorothy S. Hovels, Haciendas & House Calls: The Life of Carl H. Gellenthien, M.D. LC 85-14881. (Illus.). 320p. (Orig.). 1986. pap. 16.95 (*0-86534-074-9*) Sunstone Pr.

Beimler, Rosalind R. The Days of the Dead (Los Dias de Muertos) Mexico's Festival of Communion with the Departed (Un Festival de Comunion con los Muertos en Mexico) LC 97-50140. (ENG & SPA., Illus.). 112p. 1998. reprint ed. pap. 25.00 (*0-7649-0619-4*, A924) Pomegranate Calif.

Beimling, Barbara. Botticelli. (SPA.). 1996. pap. 9.99 (*3-8228-9541-5*) Taschen Amer.

Bein, Alex. Hier Kannst Du Nicht Jeden Gruben. (Haskala - Wissenschaftliche Abhandlungen Ser.: Vol. 14). (GER.). 328p. 1995. write for info. (*3-487-10046-0*) G Olms Pubs.

— The Jewish Question: Biography of a World Problem. Zohn, Harry, tr. from GER. LC 87-46422. 784p. 1990. 60.00 (*0-8386-3252-1*) Fairleigh Dickinson.

B

Bein, G. German-English Dictionary of International Transport. (ENG & GER.). 232p. 1980. 45.00 (*0-569-05117-7*) St Mut.

Bein, Sarah. Instead of Indonesia. 64p. pap. 9.95 (*1-888996-10-2*, Red Hen Press) Valentine CA.

Bein, Thomas, ed. Supramolecular Architecture: Synthetic Control in Thin Films & Solids. LC 92-14921. (ACS Symposium Ser.: Vol. 499). (Illus.). 441p. 1992. text 110.00 (*0-8412-2460-9*, Pub. by Am Chemical) OUP.

Beinart, Haim. Moreshet Sephard: The Sephardi Legacy, Vol. 1. 492p. 1992. 45.00 (*965-223-793-0*) Gefen Bks.

— Moreshet Sephard: The Sephardi Legacy, Vol. 2. 478p. 1992. 45.00 (*965-223-822-8*) Gefen Bks.

Beinart, Haim, ed. Jews in Italy: Studies Dedicated to the Memory of Umberto Cassuto on the 100th Anniversary of His Birth. 390p. 1988. text 20.00 (*965-223-623-3*, Pub. by Magnes Pr) Eisenbrauns.

***Beinart, Haim & Green, Jeffrey M.** The Expulsion of the Jews from Spain. (Illus.). 656p. 2000. (*1-874774-41-2*) Intl Spec Bk.

Beinart, Jenifer. A History of the Nuffield Department of Anaesthetics, Oxford, 1937-1987. (Illus.). 228p. 1987. 49.95 (*0-19-261648-X*) OUP.

Beinart, William. Twentieth-Century South Africa. LC 93-50619. 310p. 1994. pap. text 17.95 (*0-19-289239-8*) OUP.

Beinart, William & Coates, Peter. Environment & History: The Taming of Nature in the U. S. A. & South Africa. LC 94-49712. (Historical Connections Ser.). 136p. (C). 1995. pap. 16.99 (*0-415-11468-3*) Routledge.

Beinart, William & Dubow, Saul. Segregation & Apartheid in Twentieth Century South Africa. LC 94-36134. (Rewriting Histories Ser.). 256p. (C). (gr. 13). 1995. 70.00 (*0-415-10356-8*, B4358) Routledge.

Beinart, William & Dubow, Saul, eds. Segregation & Apartheid in Twentieth Century South Africa. (Rewriting Histories Ser.). 256p. (C). 1998. pap. 22.99 (*0-415-10357-6*, B4362) Routledge.

Beinat, Euro & Nijkamp, Peter. Multicriteria Analysis for Land-Use Management. LC 98-35417. (Environment & Management Ser.). vii, 372 p. 1998. 159.00 (*0-7923-5198-3*) Kluwer Academic.

Beinecke, Mary A. Basic Needlery Stitches on Mesh Fabrics. LC 73-77444. (Illus.). 64p. (Orig.). 1973. pap. 4.50 (*0-486-21713-2*) Dover.

Beinecke Rare Book-Manuscript Library Staff. The Beinecke Rare Book & Manuscript Library: A Guide to Its Collections. rev. ed. Sammons, Christa, ed. LC 94-14511. (Illus.). 1994. pap. write for info. (*0-8457-3127-0*) Yale U Lib.

Beinecke Rare Book-Manuscript Library Staff, jt. auth. see Marciari, John.

***Beinecke, William S. & Kabaservice, Geoffrey M.** Through Mem'ry's Haze: A Personal Memoir. LC 99-462317. 2000. write for info. (*0-9676987-0-7*) Prospect Hill.

Beineke, John A. And There Were Giants in the Land: The Life of William Heard Kilpatrick. LC 97-8539. (History of Schools & Schooling: Vol. 5). XX, 500p. 1998. pap. 32.95 (*0-8204-3773-5*) P Lang Pubng.

Beineke, Lowell W. & Wallace, Robin J., eds. Graph Connections: Relationships Between Graph Theory & Other Areas of Mathematics. LC 97-164766. (Oxford Lecture Series in Mathematics & Its Applications: No. 5). (Illus.). 304p. 1997. text 65.00 (*0-19-851497-2*) OUP.

Beiner, G. Shakespeare's Agonistic Comedy: Poetics, Analysis, Criticism. LC 91-58238. 1993. 44.50 (*0-8386-3467-2*) Fairleigh Dickinson.

Beiner, Ronald. Philosophy in a Time of Lost Spirit: Essays on Contemporary Theory. LC 97-228621. 192p. 1997. pap. text 24.95 (*0-8020-8067-7*) U of Toronto Pr.

— Philosophy in a Time of Lost Spirit: Essays on Contemporary Theory. LC 97-228621. 192p. 1997. text 50.00 (*0-8020-4210-4*) U of Toronto Pr.

— Political Judgment. LC 83-50829. 215p. Date not set. reprint ed. pap. 66.70 (*0-608-21002-1*, 205453000003) Bks Demand.

— Theorizing Nationalism. LC 98-6505. (SUNY Series in Political Theory). 288p. (C). 1998. pap. text 21.95 (*0-7914-4066-4*) State U NY Pr.

— Theorizing Nationalism. LC 98-6505. (SUNY Series in Political Theory). 288p. (C). 1999. text 65.50 (*0-7914-4065-6*) State U NY Pr.

Beiner, Ronald S. Kant & Political Philosophy: The Contemporary Legacy. 1996. pap. 19.00 (*0-300-06641-4*) Yale U Pr.

— Political Judgement. LC 83-50829. (C). 1984. pap. text 9.50 (*0-226-04165-4*) U Ch Pr.

— Political Judgment. LC 83-50829. (C). 1984. lib. bdg. 20.00 (*0-226-04164-6*) U Ch Pr.

— What's the Matter with Liberalism? 208p. (C). 1992. 45.00 (*0-520-07793-8*, Pub. by U CA Pr) Cal Prin Full Svc.

— What's the Matter with Liberalism? LC 91-29453. 205p. 1995. pap. 16.95 (*0-520-20335-6*, Pub. by U CA Pr) Cal Prin Full Svc.

Beiner, Ronald S., ed. Theorizing Citizenship. LC 94-10401. (SUNY Series in Political Theory: Contemporary Issues). 335p. (C). 1994. pap. text 21.95 (*0-7914-2336-0*) State U NY Pr.

Beiner, Ronald S. & Booth, William J., eds. Kant & Political Philosophy: The Contemporary Legacy. LC 93-2945. 416p. 1993. 47.00 (*0-300-05687-7*) Yale U Pr.

Beiner, Ronald S., ed. see Arendt, Hannah.

Beiner, Stan J. Bible Scenes: Joshua to Solomon. LC 88-70868. 235p. 1988. pap. text 11.95 (*0-86705-022-5*) A R E Pub.

— Class Acts: Plays & Skits for Jewish Settings. LC 92-71967. 300p. 1992. pap. text 11.95 (*0-86705-028-4*) A R E Pub.

— Sedra Scenes: Skits for Every Torah Portion. LC 82-71282. 225p. (J). (gr. 6-12). 1982. pap. text 11.95 (*0-86705-007-1*) A R E Pub.

Beinert, Dieter. Corporate Acquisitions & Mergers in Germany. 2nd ed. LC 97-224629. 1997. text 90.00 (*90-411-0677-4*) Kluwer Law Intl.

Beinert, Richard, jt. ed. see Hancock, Maxine.

Beinert, Wolfgang, ed. see Fritsch, Matthias J.

Beinfeld, Solon, ed. see Ford, M.

Beinfield, Harriet & Korngold, Efrem. Between Heaven & Earth: A Guide to Chinese Medicine. 448p. 1992. pap. 14.00 (*0-345-37974-8*) Ballantine Pub Grp.

Beinhardt, Roger & Jacobus, Charles J. WG&L Texas Real Estate Law Deskbook. 816p. 99.50 (*0-7913-2005-7*) Warren Gorham & Lamont.

Beinhart, Larry. American Hero. 1994. mass mkt. 6.99 (*0-345-91246-2*) Ballantine Pub Grp.

— American Hero. 1994. reprint ed. mass mkt. 6.99 (*0-345-36663-8*) Ballantine Pub Grp.

— How to Write a Mystery. LC 96-3516. 240p. (Orig.). 1996. pap. 11.00 (*0-345-39758-4*) Ballantine Pub Grp.

— No One Rides for Free. 240p. 1987. pap. 3.95 (*0-380-70283-5*, Avon Bks) Morrow Avon.

Beinhorn, George, ed. Food for Fitness. LC 74-16792. (Illus.). 144p. 1975. pap. 3.95 (*0-89037-084-2*) Anderson World.

Beinhorn, George, tr. see Steffny, Manfred.

Beinhorn, George, tr. see Van Aaken, Ernst.

Beinin, Joel. The Dispersion of Egyptian Jewry. LC 97-28043. (Contraversions Ser.). 318p. 1998. 45.00 (*0-520-21175-8*, Pub. by U CA Pr) Cal Prin Full Svc.

— Was the Red Flag Flying There? Marxist Politics & the Arab-Israeli Conflict in Egypt & Israel, 1948-1965. LC 89-49036. 328p. 1990. 55.00 (*0-520-07035-6*, Pub. by U CA Pr); pap. 17.95 (*0-520-07036-4*, Pub. by U CA Pr) Cal Prin Full Svc.

***Beinin, Joel & Lockman, Zachary.** Workers on the Nile: Nationalism, Communism, Islam, & the Egyptian Working Class, 1882-1954. 488p. 1998. 29.50 (*977-424-482-6*, Pub. by Am Univ Cairo Pr) Col U Pr.

Beinin, Joel & Stork, Joe, eds. Political Islam: Essay from Middle East Report. LC 95-39810. 383p. (C). 1996. 55.00 (*0-520-20447-6*, Pub. by U CA Pr) Cal Prin Full Svc.

— Political Islam: Essay from Middle East Report. LC 95-39810. (Illus.). 383p. 1996. pap. 22.50 (*0-520-20448-4*, Pub. by U CA Pr) Cal Prin Full Svc.

Beinin, Joel, jt. ed. see Lockman, Zachary.

Beinin, L. Medical Consequences of Natural Disasters. (Illus.). 195p. 1985. pap. 78.00 (*0-387-15506-6*) Spr-Verlag.

Beining, Guy. M-Factor. 36p. (Orig.). 1993. pap. 5.00 (*0-926935-82-8*) Runaway Spoon.

— Piecemeal, Pt. 1. (Illus.). 42p. (Orig.). 1988. pap. 3.00 (*0-926935-25-9*) Runaway Spoon.

— Piecemeal, Pt. 2. (Illus.). 44p. (Orig.). 1988. pap. 3.00 (*0-926935-26-7*) Runaway Spoon.

— Piecemeal, Pt. 3. (Illus.). 36p. (Orig.). 1989. pap. 3.00 (*0-926935-27-5*) Runaway Spoon.

— Piecemeal, Pt. 4. (Illus.). 36p. (Orig.). 1989. pap. 3.00 (*0-926935-28-3*) Runaway Spoon.

— Piecemeal, Pt. 5. (Illus.). 36p. (Orig.). 1989. pap. 3.00 (*0-926935-29-1*) Runaway Spoon.

— Piecemeal, Pt. 6. (Illus.). 36p. (Orig.). 1989. pap. 3.00 (*0-926935-30-5*) Runaway Spoon.

— Piecemeal, Pt. 7. (Illus.). 36p. (Orig.). 1989. pap. 3.00 (*0-926935-31-3*) Runaway Spoon.

— Piecemeal, Pt. 8. (Illus.). 42p. (Orig.). 1989. pap. 3.00 (*0-926935-32-1*) Runaway Spoon.

— Piecemeal, Pts. 1-8. (Illus.). 308p. (Orig.). 1989. pap. 20.00 (*0-926935-33-X*) Runaway Spoon.

Beining, Guy & Ryder, Laura. Beining & Ryder: London Born. limited ed. (Illus.). 1994. pap. 10.00 (*1-884185-04-5*) O Zone.

Beining, Guy R. Axiom of a Torn Pulley. limited ed. 60p. 1995. 18.00 (*0-937013-61-7*) Potes Poets.

— 100 Haiku Selected from a Decade (1982-1991) limited ed. (Codex Edition Ser.). (Illus.). 30p. 1993. 6.50 (*1-884185-00-2*) O Zone.

— Stoma: Selected Poems 1985-1989. LC 90-579. (Illus.). 64p. (Orig.). 1990. pap. 10.50 (*0-941749-14-2*) Black Tie Pr.

— Unwrapping Spheres of Clouds & Skulls. deluxe limited ed. (Illus.). 1994. spiral bd. 22.00 (*1-884185-07-X*) O Zone.

— Vanishing Whores & the Insomniac. (Illus.). 40p. (Orig.). 1991. pap. 3.00 (*0-926935-57-7*) Runaway Spoon.

Beinke, Janiece M. Miss Garbo: An Unusual Dog. (Illus.). 20p. (J). (gr. 1-4). 1998. pap. 8.95 (*1-880726-14-9*) Turnage Pub.

Beinlich, Horst. Corpus der Hieroglyphischen Inschriften aus dem Grab des Tutanchamun: Tutankhamuns Tomb. 298p. 1989. 110.00 (*0-900416-53-X*, Pub. by Aris & Phillips) David Brown.

Beinssen-Hesse, Silke & Rigby, Catherine. Out of the Shadows: Contemporary German Feminism. LC 97-187653. (Interpretations Ser.). 160p. 1996. pap. 14.95 (*0-522-84592-4*, Pub. by Melbourne Univ Pr) Paul & Co Pubs.

Beintema, David, jt. auth. see Prechtl, Heinz F.

Beintema, Rita. Salutation to the Sun: A Daily Exercise for a Vital Life. Penton, Jill, tr. (Illus.). 80p. 1997. pap. 7.95 (*0-85207-304-6*, Pub. by C W Daniel) Natl Bk Netwk.

Beintema, William J., ed. Clergy Malpractice: An Annotated Bibliography. LC 90-80945. 82p. 1990. lib. bdg. 28.50 (*0-89941-738-8*, 306420) W S Hein.

Beinum, Ingrid Ljungberg van, see van Beinum, Ingrid Ljungberg.

Beirendonck, Walter Van, see Van Beirendonck, Walter.

Beiriger, Eugene. Churchill, Munitions & Mechanical Warfare: The Politics of Supply & Strategy. LC 97-13088. (American University Studies IX: Vol. 183). XIV, 188p. (C). 1998. text 39.95 (*0-8204-3314-4*) P Lang Pubng.

Beirlant, Jan, et al. Practical Analysis of Extreme Values. (Illus.). 170p. (Orig.). 1996. pap. 52.50 (*90-6186-768-1*, Pub. by Leuven Univ) Coronet Bks.

Beirne. Criminology. 2nd ed. (C). 1995. pap. text, teacher ed. 33.75 (*0-15-501930-9*) Harcourt Coll Pubs.

***Beirne.** Criminology. 3rd ed. LC 99-41263. 1999. 65.00 (*0-8133-6655-0*) Westview.

Beirne, Barbara. Children of the Ecuadorian Highlands. (J). 1996. lib. bdg. 21.72 (*1-57505-000-5*) Lerner Pub.

Beirne, Charles J. The Problem of Americanization in the Catholic Schools of Puerto Rico. 144p. (Orig.). 1974. pap. 4.00 (*0-8477-2725-4*) U of PR Pr.

— El Problema de la "Americanizacion" en las Escuelas Catolicas de Puerto Rico. Estades De Camara, Maria E., tr. LC 76-10347. (SPA.). 154p. 1974. pap. 4.00 (*0-8477-2726-2*) U of PR Pr.

Beirne, Elizabeth. The Greater New York Centennial. (Illus.). 120p. 1999. pap. 24.00 (*0-9652331-3-8*) Hist NYCP.

— The Hudson River: Inspiration & Challenge. LC 97-213715. (Illus.). 136p. 1997. pap. 26.00 (*0-9652331-1-1*) Hist NYCP.

— The Logic of Disclosures. 144p. (Orig.). (C). 1996. pap. write for info. (*1-57502-250-8*) Morris Pubng.

— Sports & Athletics in New York. (Illus.). 120p. 1998. pap. 24.00 (*0-9652331-2-X*) Hist NYCP.

Beirne, Elizabeth, ed. New York City at the Turn of Century. (Illus.). 160p. (Orig.). 1996. pap. write for info. (*0-9652331-0-3*) Hist NYCP.

Beirne, Elizabeth, ed. see Poe, Edgar Allan.

Beirne, Francis F. The Amiable Baltimoreans. LC 84-47953. (Maryland Paperback Bookshelf Ser.). 400p. 1951. reprint ed. pap. 124.00 (*0-608-07328-8*, 206755600009) Bks Demand.

— The War of 1812. (History - United States Ser.). 410p. 1993. reprint ed. lib. bdg. 99.00 (*0-7812-4825-6*) Rprt Serv.

Beirne, Gerard. Digging My Own Grave. LC 97-143523. 80p. 1997. 24.95 (*1-873790-43-0*); pap. 12.95 (*1-873790-46-5*) Dufour.

Beirne, Martin & Ramsay, Harvie, eds. Information Technology & Workplace Democracy. LC 92-1005. 288p. (C). 1992. pap. 77.95 (*0-415-00417-9*, A7639) Thomson Learn.

Beirne, Piers. Inventing Criminology: Essays on the Rise of "Homo Criminalis" LC 91-46327. (SUNY Series in Deviance & Social Control). 274p. 1993. pap. text 21.95 (*0-7914-1276-8*) State U NY Pr.

— Inventing Criminology: Essays on the Rise of "Homo Criminalis" LC 91-46327. (SUNY Series in Deviance & Social Control). 274p. 1993. text 64.50 (*0-7914-1275-X*) State U NY Pr.

Beirne, Piers, ed. The Origins & Growth of Criminology: Essays on Intellectual History, 1760-1945. (International Library of Criminology & Criminal Justice). 416p. 1994. 159.95 (*1-85521-418-0*, Pub. by Dartmth Pub) Ashgate Pub Co.

— Revolution in Law: Contributions to the Development of Soviet Legal Theory, 1917-1938. LC 89-29816. 216p. (gr. 13). 1990. text 106.95 (*0-87332-560-5*) M E Sharpe.

Beirne, Piers & Messerschmidt, James. Criminology. 2nd ed. LC 94-77147. (Illus.). 680p. (C). 1994. text 78.00 (*0-15-501926-0*, Pub. by Harcourt Coll Pubs) Harcourt.

Beirne, Piers & Nelken, David, eds. Issues in Comparative Criminology. LC 97-6073. (International Library of Criminology, Criminal Justice, & Penology). 528p. 1997. text 179.95 (*1-85521-601-9*, Pub. by Ashgate Pub) Ashgate Pub Co.

Beirne, S. J., et al. Jesuit Education & Social Change in El Salvador. LC 96-4173. (Studies in Higher Education: Vol. 05). 280p. 1996. text 55.00 (*0-8153-2121-X*, SS1055) Garland.

Beirness, Douglas, et al. DWI Repeat Offenders: A Review & Synthesis of the Literature (In Canada) (Illus.). 156p. (C). 1998. pap. text 30.00 (*0-7881-7448-7*) DIANE Pub.

Beiruti, Sonia. Al Chami. Kaliffe, Ramzi, ed. (Silsilat Atbak Min Alaalam (Meals of the World) Ser.: No. 11).Tr. of Damascus Cuisine. (ARA., Illus.). 40p. 1991. pap. 9.50 (*1-58311-022-4*) Eastern Corp.

— Al Chorba. Kaliffe, Ramzi, ed. (Silsilat Daliluki Sayidati (Woman's Guide) Ser.: No. 2).Tr. of Soups. (ARA., Illus.). 40p. 1990. pap. 8.50 (*1-58311-025-9*) Eastern Corp.

— Al Faransi. Kaliffe, Ramzi, ed. (Silsilat Atbak Min Alaalam (Meals of the World) Ser.: No. 3).Tr. of French Cuisine. (ARA., Illus.). 40p. 1991. pap. 9.50 (*1-58311-014-3*) Eastern Corp.

— Al Hindi. Kaliffe, Ramzi, ed. (Silsilat Atbak Min Alaalam (Meals of the World) Ser.: No. 2).Tr. of Indian Cuisine. (ARA., Illus.). 40p. 1991. pap. 9.50 (*1-58311-013-5*) Eastern Corp.

— Al Itali. Kaliffe, Ramzi, ed. (Silsilat Atbak Min Alaalam (Meals of the World) Ser.: No. 12).Tr. of Italian Cuisine. (ARA., Illus.). 40p. 1991. pap. 9.50 (*1-58311-023-2*) Eastern Corp.

— Al Kabab. Kaliffe, Ramzi, ed. (Silsilat Daliluki Sayidati (Woman's Guide) Ser.: No. 10).Tr. of Kabab. (ARA., Illus.). 40p. 1990. pap. 8.50 (*1-58311-033-X*) Eastern Corp.

— Al Khaligi. Kaliffe, Ramzi, ed. (Silsilat Atbak Min Alaalam (Meals of the World) Ser.: No. 10).Tr. of Gulf Cuisine. (ARA., Illus.). 40p. 1991. pap. 9.50 (*1-58311-021-6*) Eastern Corp.

— Al Lobnani. Kaliffe, Ramzi, ed. (Silsilat Atbak Min Alaalam Ser.: No. 6).Tr. of Lebanese Cuisine. (ARA., Illus.). 40p. 1991. pap. 9.50 (*1-58311-017-8*) Eastern Corp.

— Al Maghribi. Kaliffe, Ramzi, ed. (Silsilat Atbak Min Alaalam (Meals of the World) Ser.: No. 7).Tr. of Moroccan Cuisine. (ARA., Illus.). 40p. 1991. pap. 9.50 (*1-58311-018-6*) Eastern Corp.

— Al Masri. Kaliffe, Ramzi, ed. (Silsilat Atbak Min Alaalam (Meals of the World) Ser.: No. 9).Tr. of Egyptian Cuisine. (ARA., Illus.). 40p. 1991. pap. 9.50 (*1-58311-020-8*) Eastern Corp.

— Al Mexiqui. Kaliffe, Ramzi, ed. (Silsilat Atbak Min Alaalam (Meals of the World) Ser.: No. 8).Tr. of Mexican Cuisine. (ARA., Illus.). 40p. 1991. pap. 9.50 (*1-58311-019-4*) Eastern Corp.

— Al Salata. Kaliffe, Ramzi, ed. (Silsilat Daliluki Sayidati (Woman's Guide) Ser.: No. 18).Tr. of Salads. (ARA., Illus.). 40p. 1990. pap. 8.50 (*1-58311-041-0*) Eastern Corp.

— Al Sini. Kaliffe, Ramzi, ed. (Silsilat Atbak Min Alaalam (Meals of the World) Ser.: No. 5).Tr. of Chinese Cuisine. (ARA., Illus.). 40p. 1991. pap. 9.50 (*1-58311-016-X*) Eastern Corp.

— Al Tabak Al Zaiti. Kaliffe, Ramzi, ed. (Silsilat Daliluki Sayidati (Woman's Guide) Ser.: No. 3).Tr. of Vegetarian. (ARA., Illus.). 40p. 1990. pap. 8.50 (*1-58311-026-7*) Eastern Corp.

— Al Tabak Alitaly. Kaliffe, Ramzi, ed. (Silsilat Daliluki Sayidati (Woman's Guide) Ser.: No. 4).Tr. of Italian Dishes. (ARA., Illus.). 40p. 1990. pap. 8.50 (*1-58311-027-5*) Eastern Corp.

— Al Turkey. Kaliffe, Ramzi, ed. (Silsilat Atbak Min Alaalam (Meals of the World) Ser.: No. 1).Tr. of Turkish Cuisine. (ARA., Illus.). 40p. 1991. pap. 9.50 (*1-58311-012-7*) Eastern Corp.

— Al Younani. Kaliffe, Ramzi, ed. (Silsilat Atbak Min Alaalam (Meals of the World) Ser.: No. 4).Tr. of Greek Cuisine. (ARA., Illus.). 40p. 1991. pap. 9.50 (*1-58311-015-1*) Eastern Corp.

— Alamrad Alnisaiya. Kaliffe, Ramzi, ed. (Silsilat Daliluki Sayidati (Woman's Guide) Ser.: No. 9).Tr. of Female Diseases. (ARA., Illus.). 40p. 1990. pap. 8.50 (*1-58311-032-1*) Eastern Corp.

— Aldajaj Alchahi. Kaliffe, Ramzi, ed. (Silsilat Daliluki Sayidati (Woman's Guide) Ser.: No. 20).Tr. of Chicken. (ARA., Illus.). 40p. 1990. pap. 8.50 (*1-58311-043-7*) Eastern Corp.

— Alhalawyat Alarabia. Kaliffe, Ramzi, ed. (Silsilat Daliluki Sayidati (Woman's Guide) Ser.: No. 15).Tr. of Arab Sweets. (ARA., Illus.). 40p. 1990. pap. 8.50 (*1-58311-038-0*) Eastern Corp.

— Almouajanat Al Mihchiya. Kaliffe, Ramzi, ed. (Silsilat Daliluki Sayidati (Woman's Guide) Ser.: No. 22).Tr. of Baked Pasta. (ARA., Illus.). 40p. 1990. pap. 8.50 (*1-58311-045-3*) Eastern Corp.

— Almouajanat Alitaliya. Kaliffe, Ramzi, ed. (Silsilat Daliluki Sayidati (Woman's Guide) Ser.: No. 21).Tr. of Italian Pasta. (ARA., Illus.). 40p. 1990. pap. 8.50 (*1-58311-044-5*) Eastern Corp.

— Almourabbayat. Kaliffe, Ramzi, ed. (Silsilat Daliluki Sayidati (Woman's Guide) Ser.: No. 14).Tr. of Jams. (ARA., Illus.). 40p. 1990. pap. 8.50 (*1-58311-037-2*) Eastern Corp.

— Alrashaka. Kaliffe, Ramzi, ed. (Silsilat Daliluki Sayidati (Woman's Guide) Ser.: No. 7).Tr. of Agility. (ARA., Illus.). 40p. 1990. pap. 8.50 (*1-58311-030-5*) Eastern Corp.

— Alsamak. Kaliffe, Ramzi, ed. (Silsilat Daliluki Sayidati (Woman's Guide) Ser.: No. 16).Tr. of Fish. (ARA., Illus.). 40p. 1990. pap. 8.50 (*1-58311-039-9*) Eastern Corp.

— Atbak Alforn. Kaliffe, Ramzi, ed. (Silsilat Daliluki Sayidati (Woman's Guide) Ser.: No. 1).Tr. of Oven Dishes. (ARA., Illus.). 40p. 1990. pap. 8.50 (*1-58311-024-0*) Eastern Corp.

— Charaeh Allahem. Kaliffe, Ramzi, ed. (Silsilat Daliluki Sayidati (Woman's Guide) Ser.: No. 11).Tr. of Meats. (ARA., Illus.). 40p. 1990. pap. 8.50 (*1-58311-034-8*) Eastern Corp.

— Chrab Aldiyafa. Kaliffe, Ramzi, ed. (Silsilat Daliluki Sayidati (Woman's Guide) Ser.: No. 12).Tr. of Drinks. (ARA., Illus.). 40p. 1990. pap. 8.50 (*1-58311-035-6*) Eastern Corp.

— Daliluki Sayidati. Kaliffe, Ramzi, ed.Tr. of Woman's Guide. (ARA., Illus.). 1900p. 1989. 439.00 (*1-58311-004-6*) Eastern Corp.

An Asterisk (*) at the beginning of an entry indicates that the title is appearing for the first time.

— Giza Altifl. Kaliffe, Ramzi, ed. (Silsilat Daliluki Sayidati (Woman's Guide) Ser.: No. 13).Tr. of Child Nutrition. (ARA., Illus.). 40p. 1990. pap. 8.50 (*1-58311-036-4*) Eastern Corp.

— Jamal Al Chaar. Kaliffe, Ramzi, ed. (Silsilat Daliluki Sayidati (Woman's Guide) Ser.: No. 19).Tr. of Hair Beauty. (ARA., Illus.). 40p. 1990. pap. 8.50 (*1-58311-042-9*) Eastern Corp.

— Mahrajan Alijja. Kaliffe, Ramzi, ed. (Silsilat Daliluki Sayidati (Woman's Guide) Ser.: No. 6).Tr. of Omelets. (ARA., Illus.). 40p. 1990. pap. 8.50 (*1-58311-029-1*) Eastern Corp.

— Ma'Koulat Bahriya. Kaliffe, Ramzi, ed. (Silsilat Daliluki Sayidati (Woman's Guide) Ser.: No. 17).Tr. of Seafood Appetizers. (ARA., Illus.). 40p. 1990. pap. 8.50 (*1-58311-040-2*) Eastern Corp.

— Matbakh Sayidata. Kaliffe, Ramzi, ed.Tr. of Lady's Kitchen. (ARA., Illus.). 318p. 1990. 62.99 (*1-58311-009-7*) Eastern Corp.

— Mawaed Al Aalam. Kaliffe, Ramzi, ed.Tr. of Meals of the World. (ARA., Illus.). 463p. 1991. 73.50 (*1-58311-010-0*) Eastern Corp.

— Mawsouat Al Tabekh. Kaliffe, Ramzi, ed.Tr. of Cooking Encyclopedia. (ARA., Illus.). 2880p. 1990. 699.00 (*1-58311-001-1*) Eastern Corp.

— Moukabilat Arabia. Kaliffe, Ramzi, ed. (Silsilat Daliluki Sayidati (Woman's Guide) Ser.: No. 5).Tr. of Arab Appetizer. (ARA., Illus.). 40p. 1990. pap. 8.50 (*1-58311-028-3*) Eastern Corp.

— Sohat Altifl. Kaliffe, Ramzi, ed. (Silsilat Daliluki Sayidati (Woman's Guide) Ser.: No. 8).Tr. of Child Health. (ARA., Illus.). 40p. 1990. pap. 8.50 (*1-58311-031-3*) Eastern Corp.

***Beisbart, Ortwin & Mieth, Annemarie.** Deutschlehrer-Bildung im Wandel: Konzepte und Strukturen Von der Mitte des 19. Jahrhunderts Bis Zur Gegenwart. (Beitrage zur Geschichte des Deutschunterrichts. Bd. 41 Ser.). 227p. 1999. 38.95 (*3-631-34678-6*) P Lang Pubng.

Beisbier, Beverly. Sounds Great. (College ESL Ser.: Bk. 1). (J). 1994. pap., teacher ed. 7.95 (*0-8384-4272-2*) Heinle & Heinle.

— Sounds Great. (College ESL Ser.: Bk. 2). (J). 1994. mass mkt., teacher ed. 7.95 (*0-8384-4275-7*) Heinle & Heinle.

— Sounds Great. (College ESL Ser.: Bk. 2). (J). 1994. suppl. ed. 90.00 incl. audio (*0-8384-4274-9*) Heinle & Heinle.

— Sounds Great, Bk. 1. LC 93-41029. 203p. (J). 1994. mass mkt. 15.00 (*0-8384-3964-0*) Heinle & Heinle.

— Sounds Great, Bk. 2. (College ESL Ser.). 192p. (C). 1994. mass mkt. 15.00 (*0-8384-4273-0*) Heinle & Heinle.

Beischer, Norman A. Obstetrics & Newborn: Illustrated Text. 3rd ed. (Illus.). 1997. pap. text 55.00 (*0-7020-2123-7*) Bailliere Tindall.

Beischer, Norman A., et al. Care of the Pregnant Woman & Her Baby. 2nd ed. (Illus.). 424p. 1990. text 45.95 (*0-7295-0297-X*) Bailliere Tindall.

Beise, E. J., jt. ed. see McKeown, R. D.

Beisel, Christopher. Window on the West: The Collectors' El Palacio. 200p. (Orig.). 1989. pap. 19.95 (*0-9623304-0-X*) MNMF.

Beisel, John L. Contemporary Retailing. 2nd ed. (Illus.). 720p. (C). 1993. teacher ed. write for info. (*0-318-69281-3*) Macmillan.

Beisel, Nicola. Inperiled Innocents: Anthony Comstock & Family Reproduction in Victorian America. (Princeton Studies in American Politics). 288 pages 2 linp. 1997. pap. text 15.95 (*0-691-02778-1*, Pub. by Princeton U Pr) Cal Prin Full Svc.

Beisel, Nicola K. Imperiled Innocents: Anthony Comstock & Family Reproduction in Victorian America. LC 96-3013. (Princeton Studies in American Politics). 296p. 1997. text 35.00 (*0-691-02779-X*, Pub. by Princeton U Pr) Cal Prin Full Svc.

Beisel, William R., jt. ed. see Kjohhede, Chris.

Beisembiev, Timur. The Life of Alimqul: A Native Chronicle of Nineteenth Century Central Asia. (Illus.). 388p. 1998. 95.00 (*0-7007-1114-7*, Pub. by Curzon Pr Ltd) Paul & Co Pubs.

Beisenherz, Paul C. & Dantonio, Marylou. Using the Learning Cycle to Teach Physical Science: A Hands on Approach for the Middle Grades. LC 95-24856. 256p. 1996. pap. text 26.50 (*0-435-08376-7*, 08376) Heinemann.

Beiser. Concepts of Modern Physics. 5th ed. 1994. teacher ed. 20.00 (*0-07-004815-0*) McGraw.

— Concepts of Modern Physics. 5th ed. 1994. student ed. 24.06 (*0-07-005181-X*) McGraw.

Beiser, Arthur. Basic Concepts of Physics. 2nd ed. LC 70-168762. (C). 1972. text 45.25 (*0-201-00491-7*) Addison-Wesley.

— Concepts of Modern Physics. 4th ed. (C). 1987. text 80.25 (*0-07-004473-2*) McGraw.

— Concepts of Modern Physics. 5th ed. LC 94-17477. 544p. (C). 1994. 88.44 (*0-07-004814-2*) McGraw.

— Manual to Physics. 5th ed. (C). 1991. pap. text, student ed. 28.00 (*0-201-16868-5*) Addison-Wesley.

— Modern Technical Physics. 6th ed. (Illus.). 860p. (C). 1991. 80.00 (*0-201-57899-9*) Addison-Wesley.

— Physics Study Guide. 5th ed. 368p. (C). 1991. pap. text 28.00 (*0-201-50320-4*) Addison-Wesley.

— Schaum's Outline of Physical Science. 2nd ed. 368p. (C). 1988. pap. 14.95 (*0-07-004419-8*) McGraw.

— Schaum's Outline of Theory & Problems of Applied Physics. 3rd ed. LC 94-24928. (Schaum's Outline Ser.). 465p. (C). 1995. pap. 14.95 (*0-07-005201-8*) McGraw.

— Schaum's Outline of Theory & Problems of Basic Mathematics for Electricity & Electronics. 2nd ed. LC 92-30096. 224p. (C). 1993. pap. 14.95 (*0-07-004439-2*) McGraw.

Beiser, Arthur & Krauskopf, Konrad B. Introduction to Earth Science. (Illus.). 320p. (C). 1975. text. write for info. (*0-07-004368-X*) McGraw.

Beiser, Arthur, jt. auth. see Krauskopf, Konrad B.

Beiser, Arthur, jt. auth. see Krauskopf, Konrad Bates.

Beiser, Frederick C. Enlightenment, Revolution, & Romanticism: The Genesis of Modern German Political Thought, 1790-1800. 448p. 1992. 55.00 (*0-674-25727-8*) HUP.

— The Fate of Reason: German Philosophy from Kant to Fichte. LC 86-14303. 409p. 1987. 46.95 (*0-674-29502-1*) HUP.

— The Fate of Reason: German Philosophy from Kant to Fichte. 416p. 1993. pap. 23.95 (*0-674-29503-X*) HUP.

— The Sovereignty of Reason: The Defense of Rationality in the Early English Enlightenment. LC 96-14461. 328p. 1997. text 39.50 (*0-691-03395-1*, Pub. by Princeton U Pr) Cal Prin Full Svc.

Beiser, Frederick C., ed. The Cambridge Companion to Hegel. LC 92-15572. (Cambridge Companions to Philosophy Ser.). 528p. (C). 1993. text 69.95 (*0-521-38274-2*); pap. text 23.95 (*0-521-38711-6*) Cambridge U Pr.

— The Early Political Writings of the German Romantics. (Cambridge Texts in the History of Political Thought Ser.). 248p. (C). 1996. text 59.95 (*0-521-44501-9*); pap. text 20.95 (*0-521-44951-0*) Cambridge U Pr.

Beiser, Helen R. Travel Is in My Genes. LC 97-91430. 1998. pap. 11.95 (*0-533-12677-0*) Vantage.

Beiser, Leo. Laser Scanning Notebook. 24p. 1992. 18.00 (*0-8194-1157-4*) SPIE.

Beiser, Leo, ed. Selected Papers on Laser Scanning & Recording. 504p. 1985. 35.00 (*0-89252-413-8*, 378) SPIE.

***Beiser, Leo, et al, eds.** Optical Scanning. 280p. 1999. pap. text 72.00 (*0-8194-3273-3*) SPIE.

Beiser, Leo & Sagan, Stephen F., eds. Optical Scanning Systems: Design & Applications. LC 98-125246. 35p. 1997. pap. 69.00 (*0-8194-2553-2*) SPIE.

Beiser, Morley. Strangers at the Gate: The 'Boat People's' First Ten Years in Canada. (Illus.). 224p. 1999. pap. 17.95 (*0-8020-8117-7*); lib. bdg. 50.00 (*0-8020-4282-1*) U of Toronto Pr.

Beisgen, Beverly A. Life Enhancing Activities for Mentally Impaired Adults. 336p. 1989. pap. 39.95 (*0-8261-6790-X*) Springer Pub.

Beishir, Lois. Microbiology: Lab Manual & Instructor Manual. 6th ed. 544p. 1997. text, teacher ed. 18.00 (*0-673-55987-4*) Addson-Wesley Educ.

— Microbiology in Practice: A Self-Instructional Laboratory Course. 6th ed. 522p. (C). 1996. pap. text 52.00 (*0-673-99559-3*) Addson-Wesley Educ.

Beishuizen, J. J., et al. The Use of the Microcomputer in Teaching & Learning. xiv, 258p. 1988. 42.50 (*90-265-0894-8*) Swets.

***Beisley-Guiotto, David.** Sawtooth Country. 2000. pap. 15.00 (*0-931659-64-7*) Limberlost Pr.

— Sawtooth Country. aut. limited ed. 2000. 55.00 (*0-931659-65-5*) Limberlost Pr.

Beisly, Sidney. Shakspere's Garden. LC 79-113551. reprint ed. 39.50 (*0-404-00727-9*) AMS Pr.

Beisman, Mark. Guide to Rotational Atherectomy. (Illus.). 317p. (C). Date not set. pap. text 59.95 (*1-890114-02-2*) Physicians Pr.

Beisner, E. Calvin. Answers for Atheists, Agnostics, & Other Thoughtful Skeptics: A Dialogue about Christian Faith & Life. rev. ed. LC 92-41614. 1993. pap. 12.99 (*0-89107-700-6*) Crossway Bks.

— Answers for Atheists, Agnostics, & Other Thoughtful Skeptics: Dialogs about Christian Faith & Life. large type ed. LC 94-11888. 225p. 1994. lib. bdg. 20.95 (*0-8161-5993-9*, G K Hall Lrg Type) Mac Lib Ref.

— Jesus Only Churches. LC 96-21589. (Zondervan Guide to Cults & Religious Movements Ser.). 96p. 1998. pap. 5.99 (*0-310-48871-0*) Zondervan.

— Psalms of Promise: Celebrating the Majesty & Faithfulness of God. 2nd ed. 304p. 1994. reprint ed. pap. 9.99 (*0-87552-107-X*) P & R Pubng.

Beisner, Monika. Monika Beisner's Book of Riddles. LC 83-81529. (Sunburst Ser.). (Illus.). 32p. (gr. 2 up). 1987. pap. 3.95 (*0-374-45317-9*, Sunburst Bks) FS&G.

Beisner, Robert L. From the Old Diplomacy to the New, 1865-1900. 2nd ed. Eisenstadt, A. S. & Franklin, John H., eds. LC 85-17649. (American History Ser.). 208p. (C). 1986. pap. text 11.95 (*0-88295-833-X*) Harlan Davidson.

***Beisner, Robert L.** Shafr Guide to American Foreign Relations Since 1700. 2nd ed. 2001. lib. bdg. 175.00 (*1-57607-080-8*) ABC-CLIO.

Beisner, Robert L. Twelve Against the Empire: The Anti-Imperialists, 1898-1900. 336p. 1992. reprint ed. pap. 15.95 (*1-879176-10-6*) Imprint Pubns.

— Twelve Against the Empire: The Anti-Imperialists, 1898-1900. LC 84-24116. 310p. (C). 1985. reprint ed. pap. text 9.95 (*0-226-04171-9*) U Ch Pr.

Beisner, Robert L., jt. ed. see Challinor, Joan R.

Beiss, Fern. The Sex Diet: Eating for Impotence & Female Sexual Disorder. 288p. 2000. pap. 24.95 (*1-893290-40-9*) Peanut Butt & Jelly.

Beisse. Guide to Computer User Support. (Miscellaneous/Catalogs Ser.). (C). 1998. mass mkt. 39.95 (*0-7600-7001-6*) Course Tech.

***Beisse.** A Guide to Computer User Support. 2nd ed. (C). 2000. pap. 30.00 (*0-619-03363-0*) Course Tech.

Beissel, Henry. Cantos North. 63p. 1982. 6.95 (*0-920806-41-4*, Pub. by Penumbra Pr) U of Toronto Pr.

Beissel, James D., Sr. Powwow Power. Rogers, Joseph M., ed. LC 97-94645. 1998. 33.95 (*0-9623159-3-1*) Crystal Educn.

— The Wedge: History & Genealogy. Stoltzfus, Janice M., ed. LC 90-80964. (Illus.). 462p. 1991. text 60.00 (*0-9623159-0-7*) Crystal Educn.

Beisser, Arnold R. Flying Without Wings: Personal Reflections on Being Disabled. large type ed. LC 91-34133. (General Ser.). 216p. 1992. pap. 15.95 (*0-8161-5337-X*, G K Hall Lrg Type) Mac Lib Ref.

***Beisser, Deanna.** Is It Time to Make a Change? LC 99-16856. 64p. 2000. 16.95 (*0-88396-528-3*) Blue Mtn Art.

Beisser, Deanna. Is It Time to Make a Change? Positive Thoughts for When Life Presents You with a New Direction. LC 97-9946. 48p. 1997. pap. 8.95 (*0-88396-451-1*) Blue Mtn Art.

Beissinger, Margaret H., et al. Epic Traditions in the Contemporary World: The Poetics of Community. LC 98-49047. (Joan Palevsky Classic Literature Books). 333p. 1999. 48.00 (*0-520-21037-9*, Pub. by U CA Pr) Cal Prin Full Svc.

***Beissinger, Margaret H., et al.** Epic Traditions in the Contemporary World: The Poetics of Community. LC 98-49047. 333p. 1999. pap. 17.95 (*0-520-21038-7*, Pub. by U CA Pr) Cal Prin Full Svc.

Beissinger, Mark R. Scientific Management, Socialist Discipline, & Soviet Power. LC 87-30887. (Russian Research Center Studies: No. 84). 376p. 1988. 46.50 (*0-674-79490-7*) HUP.

Beissinger, Steven R. & Snyder, Noel F., eds. New World Parrots in Crisis: Solutions from Conservation Biology. LC 91-52867. (Illus.). 256p. (C). 1991. pap. text 17.95 (*1-56098-136-9*) Smithsonian.

***Beistegui, Miguel de & Sparks, Simon, eds.** Philosophy & Tragedy. (Warwick Studies in European Philosophy Ser.). 256p. (C). 2000. text 85.00 (*0-415-19141-6*) Routledge.

Beistegui, Miguel de, see Sparks, Simon & De Beistegui, Miguel.

Beistegui, Miguel de, see De Beistegui, Miguel.

Beiswinger, George L. Growing Older: If I Can't Complain Now, When? LC 97-92616. (Illus.). 128p. 1998. pap. 6.95 (*0-9661123-0-X*) Mirage Pubns.

— One to One: The Story of the Big Brothers-Big Sisters Movement in America. LC 84-20399. (Illus.). 290p. 1985. 15.95 (*0-9613820-0-7*) Big Brothers-Big Sisters.

Beit-Arie, Malachi. Catalogue of the Hebrew Manuscripts in the Bodleian Library & in the College Libraries of Oxford: Supplement of Addenda & Corrigenda to Volume I. May, R. A., ed. (Illus.). 330p. (C). 1995. text 98.00 (*0-19-817386-5*) OUP.

— The Makings of the Medieval Hebrew Book. (Studies in Palaeography & Codicology). (Illus.). 284p. 1993. 40.00 (*965-223-804-X*, Pub. by Magnes Pr) Gefen Bks.

***Beit-Arieh, Itzhaq, ed.** Tel 'Ira: A Stronghold in the Biblical Negev. (Monograph Series of the Sonia & Marco Nadler Institute of Archaeology: Vol. 15). (Illus.). xxii, 521p. 1999. text 60.00 (*965-440-008-1*, Pub. by Friends Archeol Inst) Eisenbrauns.

Beit-Arieh, Itzhaq, ed. Horvat Qitmit: An Edodmite Shrine in the Biblical Negev. (Monograph Series of the Sonia & Marco Nadler Institute of Archaeology: Vol. 11). xvi, 319p. 1995. text 60.00 (*965-440-004-9*, Pub. by Friends Archeol Inst) Eisenbrauns.

Beit-Hallahmi, Benjamin. Despair & Deliverance: Private Salvation in Contemporary Israel. LC 91-16392. (SUNY Series in Israeli Studies). 221p. (C). 1992. pap. text 21.95 (*0-7914-1000-5*) State U NY Pr.

— The Illustrated Encyclopedia of Active New Religions, Sects & Cults. rev. ed. Rosen, Roger, ed. (Illus.). 350p. 1998. lib. bdg. 59.95 (*0-8239-2586-2*) Rosen Group.

— Original Sins: Reflections on the History of Zionism & Israel. LC 93-13551. 240p. 1993. 29.95 (*1-56656-130-2*, Olive Branch Pr); pap. 14.95 (*1-56656-131-0*, Olive Branch Pr) Interlink Pub.

— Prolegomena to the Psychological Study of Religion. LC 88-48020. 128p. 1989. 28.50 (*0-8387-5159-8*) Bucknell U Pr.

Beit-Hallahmi, Benjamin & Argyle, Michael. Psychology of Religious Behaviour, Belief, & Experience. LC 97-205504. 336p. (C). 1997. 80.00 (*0-415-12330-5*); pap. 24.99 (*0-415-12331-3*) Routledge.

Beit-Hallahmi, Benjamin, jt. ed. see Sobel, Zvi.

Beitchman, Joseph H., et al, eds. Language, Learning, & Behavior Disorders: Developmental, Biological, & Clinical Perspectives. (Illus.). 582p. (C). 1996. text 129.95 (*0-521-47229-6*) Cambridge U Pr.

Beitchman, Philip. Alchemy of the Word: Cabala of the Renaissance. LC 97-37506. (SUNY Series in Western Esoteric Traditions). 364p. (C). 1998. text 65.50 (*0-7914-3737-X*); pap. text 21.95 (*0-7914-3738-8*) State U NY Pr.

— I Am a Process with No Subject. LC 88-1344. (University of Florida Humanities Monographs: No. 61). 320p. 1988. 49.95 (*0-8130-0888-3*) U Press Fla.

Beitchman, Philip, tr. see Baudrillard, Jean.

Beitchman, Philip, tr. see Virilio, Paul.

Beite, A. M. Basic Swedish Grammar. 3rd ed. (ENG & SWE.). 1989. 85.00 (*0-7859-7460-1*, 9121015511) Fr & Eur.

Beitel, J. M., jt. auth. see Mickel, J. T.

Beith, Alan. The Case for the Liberal Party & the Alliance. LC 82-17168. 182p. reprint ed. pap. 56.50 (*0-608-30930-3*, 202252200027) Bks Demand.

Beith, G. A. Edward Carpenter. LC 72-3568. (English Literature Ser.: No. 33). 1972. reprint ed. lib. bdg. 75.00 (*0-8383-1558-5*) M S G Haskell Hse.

Beith, Mary. Healing Threads: Traditional Medicines of the Highlands & Islands. 232p. (Orig.). 1995. pap. 19.95 (*0-7486-6199-9*, Pub. by Polygon) Subterranean Co.

Beitl, Richard. Dictionary of German Folklore: Woerterbuch der Deutschen Volkskunde. 3rd ed. (GER.). 1005p. 1981. 59.95 (*0-8288-1186-5*, M7112) Fr & Eur.

Beitler, Stephen, jt. auth. see Atalla, Bill M.

Beitman, Bernard D. The Psychotherapist's Guide to Cost Containment: How to Survive & Thrive in an Age of Managed Care. LC 97-33921. 1998. write for info. (*0-8039-7381-0*) Sage.

— The Structure of Individual Psychotherapy. LC 86-3160. 330p. 1990. reprint ed. pap. text 23.00 (*0-89862-461-4*) Guilford Pubns.

Beitman, Bernard D. & Klerman, Gerald L., eds. Combining Psychotherapy & Drug Therapy in Clinical Practice. LC 84-14144. 288p. 1984. text 39.95 (*0-88331-120-8*) R B Luce.

— Integrating Pharmacotherapy & Psychotherapy. LC 90-14510. 458p. 1991. text 58.00 (*0-88048-350-4*, 8350) Am Psychiatric.

***Beitman, Bernard D. & Yue, Dongmei.** Learning Psychotherapy: A Time-Efficient, Research-Based, & Outcome-Measured Training Program. LC 98-50157. (Illus.). 350p. 1999. pap. 40.00 (*0-393-70296-0*) Norton.

Beitman, Bernard D. & Yue, Dongmei. Learning Psychotherapy: A Time-Efficient, Research-Based, & Outcome-Measured Training Program. 88p. 1999. pap. 30.00 (*0-393-70305-3*) Norton.

Beitman, Hartford. Financial Services Marketing: Proven Techniques for Advertising, Direct Mail, & Telemarketing. 1990. 29.95 (*0-8306-8062-4*) McGraw-Hill Prof.

Beitman, Ronald S. Practitioner's Guide to Liquor Liability Litigation: 1991 Supplement. LC 87-71248. 89p. 1991. pap. 15.00 (*0-8318-0668-0*, B668) Am Law Inst.

***Beitman, Ronald S., et al.** Liquor Liability: A Primer for Winning Your Case. LC 99-61271. 344p. 1999. 125.00 (*0-8318-0792-X*, B792) Am Law Inst.

Beitman, Ronald S., ed. see Institutional Staff.

Beitner, Rivka. Regulation of Carbohydrate Metabolism, 2 vols., Vol. 1. LC 84-12060. 176p. 1985. 105.00 (*0-8493-5262-2*, QP701, CRC Reprint) Franklin.

Beitner, Rivka, ed. Regulation of Carbohydrate Metabolism, 2 vols., Vol. 2. LC 84-12060. 224p. 1985. 132.00 (*0-8493-5263-0*, QP701, CRC Reprint) Franklin.

***Beito, David T.** From Mutual Aid to the Welfare State: Fraternal Societies & Social Services, 1890-1967. LC 99-41895. 424p. 2000. pap. 24.95 (*0-8078-4841-7*) U of NC Pr.

— From Mutual Aid to the Welfare State: Fraternal Societies & Social Services, 1890-1967. LC 99-41895. (Illus.). 424p. 2000. lib. bdg. 55.00 (*0-8078-2531-X*) U of NC Pr.

Beito, David T. Taxpayers in Revolt: Tax Resistance During the Great Depression. LC 88-26032. 232p. 1989. reprint ed. pap. 72.00 (*0-7837-9016-3*, 204976800003) Bks Demand.

Beito, Gretchen U. Coya Come Home: A Congresswoman's Journey. (Illus.). 336p. 1990. 19.95 (*0-938817-02-7*) Pomegranate Pr.

Beitone, Alane. Economic & Historical Analysis of Contemporary Societies. 1998. pap. 17.95 (*0-9646073-6-0*) Algora Pubng.

Beittel, Joan N., jt. auth. see Beittel, Kenneth R.

Beittel, Kenneth R. Zen & the Art of Pottery. 2nd ed. (Illus.). 148p. 1989. 14.95 (*0-8348-0221-X*) Weatherhill.

Beittel, Kenneth R. & Beittel, Joan N. A Celebration of Art & Consciousness. 304p. (Orig.). 1991. pap. 14.95 (*0-9628511-1-6*) HVHA.

— Ralph & Deno in Vermont. LC 90-86028. (Illus.). 32p. (Orig.). (J). (gr. 5 up). 1990. pap. 6.00 (*0-9628511-0-8*) HVHA.

Beitter, Ursula, ed. Schreiben im Heutigen Deutschland: Die Literarische Szene nach der Wende. (Loyola College in Maryland Berlin Seminar). (GER.). XXVIII, 196p. (C). 1998. text 46.95 (*0-8204-3319-5*) P Lang Pubng.

Beitter, Ursula E., ed. The New Europe at the Crossroads. XXV, 305p. (C). 1999. text 57.95 (*0-8204-3923-1*) P Lang Pubng.

— Schreiben im heutigen Deutschland: Fragen an die Vergangenheit. LC 98-20813. (Loyola College in Maryland Berlin Seminar: Vol. 2). XXII, 251p. 1998. 49.95 (*0-8204-3831-6*) P Lang Pubng.

Beitz, Alvin J. & Anderson, John H. Neurochemistry of the Vestibular System. LC 99-38971. 432p. 1999. boxed set 129.95 (*0-8493-7679-3*) CRC Pr.

Beitz, Charles, jt. ed. see Kuperberg, Mark.

Beitz, Charles R. Political Theory & International Relations. LC 79-83976. 212p. 1979. pap. text 14.95 (*0-691-02192-9*, Pub. by Princeton U Pr) Cal Prin Full Svc.

— Political Theory & International Relations, Revised Edition. LC 99-12992. 1999. pap. text 14.95 (*0-691-00915-5*, Pub. by Princeton U Pr) Cal Prin Full Svc.

Beitz, Charles R., et al, eds. International Ethics: A Philosophy & Public Affairs Reader. LC 84-42938. 352p. 1985. pap. text 17.95 (*0-691-02234-8*, Pub. by Princeton U Pr) Cal Prin Full Svc.

Beitz, Ursula, jt. auth. see LeRoy, Gaylord C.

Beitz, Wolfgang. Engineering Design. Wallace, K., ed. (Illus.). 460p. 1984. 78.40 (*0-387-13601-0*) Spr-Verlag.

— Engineering Design. (Illus.). 420p. 1993. pap. 39.00 (*0-387-50442-7*) Spr-Verlag.

Beitz, Wolfgang, jt. auth. see Pahl, Gerald.

Beitz, Wolfgang, ed. see Dubbel, Heinrich.

Beitzel, Barry. The Moody Atlas of Bible Lands. 42.99 (*0-8024-0438-3*, 218) Moody.

Beitzel, Barry J. & Young, Gordon D., eds. Amarna in Retrospect: A Centennial Celebration. 700p. Date not set. text 54.50 (*1-57506-010-8*) Eisenbrauns.

Beitzel, Richard. Infrared Portrait Photography. 128p. 2000. pap. 29.95 (*1-58428-012-3*, Pub. by Amherst Media) IPG Chicago.

Beitzel, Wallace D., jt. auth. see Harter, James H.

B

Beitzell, Robert, ed. Tehran - Yalta - Potsdam: The Soviet Protocols. (Russian Ser.: Vol. 17). 35.00 (*0-87569-013-0*) Academic Intl.

Beitzinger, A. J. A History of American Political Thought. 640p. 1986. reprint ed. pap. 38.95 (*0-935005-94-3*); reprint ed. lib. bdg. 57.95 (*0-935005-31-5*) Lincoln-Rembrandt.

Beitzinger, Alfons J. Edward G. Ryan: Lion of the Law. LC 59-63607. (Illus.). 224p. 1960. pap. 12.95 (*0-87020-002-X*) State Hist Soc Wis.

Beixedon, S. Yvette De, see De Beixedon, S. Yvette.

Beizer, Arnold L. If You Don't Ask You Will Never Know! (Illus.). 528p. 1991. pap. write for info. (*0-9629291-0-7*) Sword Messianic.

Beizer, Boris. The Black Box Testing: Techniques for Functional Testing of Software. LC 94-44711. 320p. 1995. pap. 44.99 (*0-471-12094-4*) Wiley.

— Software Testing Techniques. 2nd ed. 576p. 1990. text 55.95 (*1-85032-880-3*) ITCP.

Beizer, Janet. Ventriloquized Bodies: Narratives of Hysteria in Nineteenth-Century France. (Illus.). 312p. 1994. text 49.95 (*0-8014-2914-5*); pap. text 18.95 (*0-8014-8142-2*) Cornell U Pr.

Beizer, Mikhail. Jews of St. Petersburg: Excursions Through a Noble Past. 360p. 1989. 29.95 (*0-8276-0321-5*) JPS Phila.

— Jews of St. Petersburg: Excursions Through a Noble Past. Gilbert, Martin, ed. Sherbourne, Michael, tr. from RUS. (Illus.). 328p. 1999. reprint ed. text 25.00 (*0-7881-6115-6*) DIANE Pub.

Beja, Morris. James Joyce: A Literary Life. LC 92-20068. (Illus.). 150p. 1992. pap. text 16.95 (*0-8142-0599-2*) Ohio St U Pr.

— Joyce, the Artist Manque & Indeterminacy. 34p. 1990. pap. 8.95 (*0-86140-320-7*, Pub. by Smyth) Dufour.

— Perspective on Orson Welles. 1995. 55.00 (*0-8161-7344-3*, G K Hall & Co) Mac Lib Ref.

Beja, Morris, ed. Critical Essays on Virginia Woolf. (Critical Essays on British Literature Ser.). 264p. 1985. 48.00 (*0-8161-8753-3*, G K Hall & Co) Mac Lib Ref.

Beja, Morris, et al, eds. James Joyce: The Centennial Symposium. LC 85-24591. (Illus.). 256p. 1986. text 27.50 (*0-252-01291-7*) U of Ill Pr.

— Samuel Beckett: Humanistic Perspectives. LC 82-12468. (Illus.). 234p. 1983. reprint ed. pap. 72.60 (*0-608-04444-X*, 206497600012) Bks Demand.

Beja, Morris & Norris, David, eds. Joyce in the Hibernian Metropolis: Essays. LC 95-50446. 312p. 1996. text 62.50 (*0-8142-0685-9*) Ohio St U Pr.

Bejan. Solutions Manual for Convection Heat Transfer. 2nd ed. 1995. pap. text. write for info. (*0-471-12922-4*) Wiley.

— Thermal Design & Optimization: Solutions Manual. 1996. pap. text. write for info. (*0-471-16010-5*) Wiley.

— Thermodynamics. 2nd ed. 1997. pap. text, student ed. write for info. (*0-471-19761-0*) Wiley.

Bejan, Adrian. Advanced Engineering Thermodynamics. 2nd ed. LC 97-5543. 896p. 1997. 99.00 (*0-471-14880-6*) Wiley.

— Convection Heat Transfer. 2nd ed. 656p. 1994. 110.00 (*0-471-57972-6*) Wiley.

— Entropy Generation Minimization. 47p. 1995. lib. bdg., lab manual ed. 0.50 (*0-8493-9655-7*) CRC Pr.

— Entropy Generation Minimization: The Method of Thermodynamic Optimization of Finite-Size Systems & Finite-Time Processes. Kulacki, Frank A., ed. LC 95-11954. (Mechanical Engineering Ser.). 400p. 1995. boxed set 104.95 (*0-8493-9651-4*, 9651) CRC Pr.

— Heat Transfer with Software IBM 3.5 & IBM 5.25 Set. 675p. 1993. text 108.50 incl. 5.25 ld (*0-471-59503-9*) Wiley.

***Bejan, Adrian.** Shape & Structure, from Engineering to Nature. (Illus.). 384p. 2000. write for info. (*0-521-79049-2*); pap. write for info. (*0-521-79388-2*) Cambridge U Pr.

Bejan, Adrian & Jones, J. S. Modern Heat Transfer. LC 92-25535. 704p. (C). 1993. text 105.95 (*0-471-50290-1*) Wiley.

Bejan, Adrian & Mamut, Eden. Theromodynamic Optimization of Complex Energy Systems LC 99-22954. (NATO ASI Ser.). 1999. write for info. (*0-7923-5725-6*). Kluwer Academic.

Bejan, Adrian, et al. Energy & the Environment. LC 99-10164. (Environmental Science & Technology Library). 1999. write for info. (*0-7923-5596-2*) Kluwer Academic.

— Thermal Design & Optimization. LC 95-12071. 560p. 1995. 99.00 (*0-471-58467-3*) Wiley.

Bejan, Adrian, jt. auth. see Nield, D. A.

Bejan, Adrian, jt. auth. see Nield, Donald A.

Bejancu, Aurel. Geometry of CR-Submanifolds. (Mathematics & Its Applications East European Ser.). 1986. text 132.50 (*90-277-2194-7*) Kluwer Academic.

Bejancu, Aurel, jt. auth. see Duggal, Krishan L.

Bejar, Eduardo, jt. auth. see Barreda, Pedro.

Bejar, I. I., et al. Cognitive & Psychometric Analysis of Analogical Problem Solving. (Recent Research in Psychology Ser.). (Illus.). 224p. 1990. 63.95 (*0-387-97321-4*) Spr-Verlag.

Bejar, Isaac I. Achievement Testing. LC 83-50514. (Quantitative Applications in the Social Sciences Ser.: Vol. 36). 88p. 1983. pap. text 10.95 (*0-8039-2047-4*) Sage.

Bejar-Rivera, Hector. Peru, 1965: Notes on a Guerrilla Experience. Rose, William, tr. LC 75-105309. 142p. 1970. reprint ed. pap. 44.10 (*0-608-08300-3*, 205617400054) Bks Demand.

***Bejarano, Luis Guillermo.** Versatilidad y Unidad Estetica en Guillermo Valencia a la luz del Simbolismo Frances. (Currents in Comparative Romance Languages & Literatures Ser.: Vol. 85). (SPA.). 232p. (C). 1999. text 49.95 (*0-8204-4440-5*) P Lang Pubng.

Bejczy, A., jt. ed. see Fijany, A.

Bejel, Emilio. Escribir en Cuba. (SPA.). 402p. 1991. pap. 12.95 (*0-8477-3661-X*) U of PR Pr.

Bejel, Emilio & Fernandez, Ramiro. La Subversion de la Semiotica Analisis Estructural de Textos Hispanicos. LC 88-72319. 270p. 1988. 20.00 (*0-935318-15-1*) Edins Hispamerica.

Bejel, Emilio & Panico, Marie J. Huellas-Footprints. LC 82-71933. (ENG & SPA.). 122p. 1982. pap. 6.50 (*0-935318-07-0*) Edins Hispamerica.

Bejel, Emilio F. Jose Lezama Lima, Poet of the Image. (Illus.). 192p. 1990. 49.95 (*0-8130-0980-4*) U Press Fla.

Bejenar, G. Dictionary of Medicine: Russian - French. (FRE & RUS.). lib. bdg. 75.00 (*0-8288-2615-3*, F12776) Fr & Eur.

Bejger, Aleksander. Mission und Kirche in Sambia (1875-1994) (Europaische Hochschulschriften Ser.: Reihe 23, Bd. 584). (GER., Illus.). 818p. 1996. 114.95 (*3-631-30154-5*) P Lang Pubng.

Bejing Language Institute Staff & Beijing Language Institute Staff. New Chinese Three Hundred: A Beginning Language Course, Set. unabridged ed. (C & T Asian Language Ser.). 355p. 1994. boxed set 49.95 incl. audio (*0-88727-002-6*) Cheng & Tsui.

***Bejjani, Ghassan K. & Wright, Donald.** Surgical Anatomy for Neurosurgeons: Anatomy Review & Dissection Manual. (Illus.). 448p. 2001. 149.00 (*0-86577-879-5*) Thieme Med Pubs.

***Bejoint, Henri.** Modern Lexicography. 288p. 2000. pap. 24.95 (*0-19-829951-6*) OUP.

Bejoint, Henri. Tradition & Innovation in Modern English Dictionaries. (Studies in Lexicography & Lexicology). 288p. 1994. text 55.00 (*0-19-823919-X*) OUP.

Bejoint, Henri, jt. ed. see Wakely, Richard.

***Bek, Alii M.** Children of the Anarii. (Illus.). 2000. pap. 12.95 (*0-9651543-1-9*) Full Cir Pr.

— Children of the Anarii III. (Illus.). 2000. pap. 12.95 (*0-9651543-3-5*) Full Cir Pr.

Bek, Lilla & Pullar, Philippa. Healing with Chakra Energy: Restoring the Natural Harmony of the Body. LC 94-12262. 160p. 1995. pap. 10.95 (*0-89281-513-2*, Destiny Bks) Inner Tradit.

— The Seven Levels of Healing. 160p. 1987. pap. 17.95 (*0-7126-9473-0*, Pub. by CEN3) Trafalgar.

Bek, Lilla, jt. auth. see Wilson, Annie.

Bek, Lise. Towards Paradise on Earth: Modern Space Conception in Architecture--A Creation of Renaissance Humanism. (Analecta Romana Ser.: Suppl. IX). (Illus.). 274p. (Orig.). 1980. pap. 49.50 (*87-7492-310-2*, Pub. by Odense Universitets Forlag) Coronet Bks.

Bek, William G., tr. see Tolzmann, Don Heinrich, ed.

Bekaert, Jacques. Vietnam: A Portrait. (Illus.). 200p. 1996. 45.00 (*962-7787-02-7*, Pub. by O&A Edits) Weatherhill.

Bekaert, Rosemary K. Word Processing Simplified for Superscript: TRS 80 Models III IV & IVP. (Illus.). 208p. (Orig.). 1985. pap. 25.00 (*0-9615582-0-2*) Kelly Ent.

***Bekakos, M. P. & Sambandham, M.** Computational Methods & Neural Networks: Parallel, Systolic & Neurocomputing. LC 99-47140. 1999. write for info. (*0-9640398-6-9*) Dynamic Pubs.

Bekalo, Isaac. Participatory Approach to Rural AIDS Education: A Workshop Manual. limited ed. 94p. 1992. 4.00 (*0-942717-40-6*) Intl Inst Rural.

Beke, B. The Process of Fine Grinding. 1981. text 99.50 (*90-247-2462-7*) Kluwer Academic.

Beke, D. L. & Gas, P., eds. Diffusion in Semiconductors & Non-Metallic Solids, Subvolume A. (Numerical Data & Functional Relationships in Science & Technology Ser.). xiii, 480p. 1998. 2646.00 incl. cd-rom (*3-540-60964-4*) Spr-Verlag.

Beke, D. L. & Szabo, I. A, eds. Diffusion & Stresses. (Defect & Diffusion Forum: 129-130). (Illus.). 356p. 1996. 192.00 (*3-908450-16-0*, Pub. by Scitec Pubns) Enfield Pubs NH.

Beke, D. L., jt. ed. see Kedves, F. J.

Beke, D. L., jt. ed. see Martienssen, W.

Beke, Laszlo, et al. Nightmare Works: Tibor Hajas. (Illus.). 82p. (Orig.). 1990. 10.00 (*0-935519-11-4*) Anderson Gal.

Bekefi, George. Electromagnetic Vibrations, Waves, & Radiation. Barrett, Alan H., ed. LC 77-10421. 1977. pap. text 42.00 (*0-262-52047-8*) MIT Pr.

Bekele, Gaitachew. The Emperor's Clothes: A Personal Viewpoint on Politics & Administration in the Imperial Ethiopian Government, 1941-1974. LC 93-19273. (African Studies: No. 3). (Illus.). 125p. (C). 1993. text 24.95 (*0-87013-325-X*) Mich St U Pr.

***Bekemans, Leonce & Mira, Eduard, eds.** Civitas Europa: Cities, Urban Systems, & Cultural Regions Between Diversity & Convergence. LC 99-53172. 292p. 2000. pap. 35.95 (*0-8204-4651-3*) P Lang Pubng.

Bekemeier, H., ed. see Hirschelmann, R.

***Beken of Cowes Ltd.** The Golden Age of Sailing: The Classic Yacht Photographs by Beken of Cowes. (Illus.). 2000. 25.00 (*0-8129-3283-8*, Times Bks) Crown Pub Group.

Beken of Cowes Ltd. Hundred Years of Sail. (Illus.). 220p. 1993. 65.00 (*1-86046-253-7*, Pub. by Harvill Press) HarpC.

Beker, Avi. Disarmament Without Order: The Politics of Disarmament at the United Nations, 118. LC 84-6722. (Contributions in Political Science Ser.: No.118). (Illus.). 212p. 1985. 57.95 (*0-313-24362-X*, BDW/, Greenwood Pr) Greenwood.

— Jewish Communities of the World. LC 97-19189. (Illus.). 256p. 1997. lib. bdg. 26.95 (*0-8225-1934-8*, Lerner Publctns) Lerner Pub.

— Jewish Communities of the World. (Illus.). 256p. (J). 1998. pap. text 19.95 (*0-8225-9822-1*) Lerner Pub.

***Beker, Avi.** The Plunder of Jewish Property During the Holocaust. LC 00-55041. 2000. write for info. (*0-8147-9867-5*) NYU Pr.

Beker, Avi, jt. ed. see Ro'i, Yaacov.

Beker, Henry J. & Piper, F. C. Secure Speech Communications: A Monograph. (Microelectronics & Signal Processing Ser.). 1985. text 125.00 (*0-12-084780-9*) Acad Pr.

Beker, J. Christiaan. The New Testament: A Thematic Introduction. LC 93-32244. 152p. 1994. pap. 15.00 (*0-8006-2775-X*, 1-2775) Augsburg Fortress.

— Paul the Apostle: The Triumph of God in Life & Thought. LC 79-8904. 480p. 1980. pap. 25.00 (*0-8006-1811-4*, 1-1811) Augsburg Fortress.

— The Triumph of God: The Essence of Paul's Thought. Stuckenbruck, Loren T., tr. from GER. LC 90-35463. 168p. 1990. pap. 15.00 (*0-8006-2438-6*, 1-2438) Augsburg Fortress.

Beker, Jerome & Eisikovits, Zvi C., eds. Knowledge Utilization in Residential Child & Youth Care Practice. 1991. pap. 14.50 (*0-87868-427-1*) Child Welfare.

Beker, Jerome & Lewis, William L. Helping the Youthful Offender: Individual & Group Therapies That Work. LC 89-33070. (Child & Youth Services Ser.: Vol. 11, No. 2). (Illus.). 153p. 1989. text 49.95 (*0-86656-900-6*) Haworth Pr.

Beker, Jerome & Magnuson, Douglas, eds. Residential Education As an Option for At-Risk Youth. LC 96-12415. 133p. 1996. text 39.95 (*1-56024-818-1*) Haworth Pr.

Beker, Jerome, jt. auth. see Willie, Charles V.

Beker, Jerome, ed. see Eisikovits, Zvi C.

Beker, Jerry, et al. What Do I Do Now? Challenges & Choices for Camp Counselors & Other Youth Workers. rev. ed. 160p. (C). 1996. pap. 15.95 (*0-87603-151-3*) Am Camping.

Bekerian, Debra A., jt. ed. see Jackson, Janet L.

Bekerie, Ayele. Ethiopic, an African Writing System: Its History & Principles. LC 96-10408. 180p. 1996. 59.95 (*1-56902-020-5*); pap. 18.95 (*1-56902-021-3*) Red Sea Pr.

Bekerman, Gerard. Basic Vocabulary of Marxism: Vocabulario Basico del Marxismo. (SPA.). 278p. 1983. pap. 19.95 (*0-8288-2265-4*, S40317) Fr & Eur.

— Vocabulary of Marxism: Vocabulaire du Marxisme. (FRE & GER.). 360p. 1981. 65.00 (*0-8288-2254-9*, F70762) Fr & Eur.

Bekes, Ferec & Lasztity, Radomir, eds. Gluten Proteins: Proceedings of the 3rd International Workshop on Gluton Proteins. 636p. (C). 1988. text 141.00 (*9971-5-0493-6*) World Scientific Pub.

Bekes, Ferenc & MacRitchie, Finlay. Protein-Lipid Association in Wheat. 1991. 129.95 (*0-8493-5179-0*, CRC Reprint) Franklin.

Bekessy, Emery & Lagerkvist, Par. Barabbas. reprint ed. lib. bdg. 21.95 (*0-89190-574-X*, Rivercity Pr) Amereon Ltd.

Beketov, V. G., jt. auth. see Rabinovich, V. A.

Bekey, George A. Autonomous Agents. LC 98-5209. 1998. 110.00 (*0-7923-8137-8*) Kluwer Academic.

Bekey, George A. & Goldberg, Kenneth Y., eds. Neural Networks in Robotics. LC 92-27162. (C). 1992. text 210.50 (*0-7923-9268-X*) Kluwer Academic.

Bekey, George A. & Schwartz, Morton D., eds. Hospital Information Systems. LC 70-190097. (Biomedical Engineering Ser.: Vol. 1). 416p. reprint ed. pap. 129.00 (*0-608-16573-5*, 202780800054) Bks Demand.

Bekey, George A. & Ura, Tamaki. Underwater Robots. Yuh, Junku, ed. LC 96-23420. 256p. (C). 1996. text 157.50 (*0-7923-9754-1*) Kluwer Academic.

Bekey, Ivan, ed. Permanent Presence - Making It Work, 22nd Goddard Memorial Symposium, Mar. 15-16, 1984, Greenbelt, MD. (Science & Technology Ser.: Vol. 60). (Illus.). 190p. 1985. 40.00 (*0-87703-207-6*, Am Astronaut Soc); pap. 30.00 (*0-87703-208-4*, Am Astronaut Soc) Univelt Inc.

Bekey, Ivan & Herman, Daniel, eds. Space Stations & Space Platforms: Concepts, Design, Infrastructure, & Uses. LC 85-19972. (PAAS Ser.: Vol. 99). 392p. 1986. 69.95 (*0-930403-01-0*, V-99) AIAA.

Bekh, Olena & Dingley, James. Teach Yourself Ukrainian: A Complete Course for Beginners. (ENG & UKR.). 320p. 1998. pap. 29.95 incl. audio (*0-8442-3852-X*, Teach Yrslf) NTC Contemp Pub Co.

Bekh, Olena & Dingley, Jim. Ukrainian Phrasebook: Language Survival Kit. (Illus.). 176p. 1996. pap. 5.95 (*0-86442-339-X*) Lonely Planet.

Bekh, Olena, jt. auth. see Dingley, Jame.

Bekhor, Isaac, ed. Progress in Non-Histone Protein Research, Vol. I. 224p. 1985. 130.00 (*0-8493-5528-1*, QP552, CRC Reprint) Franklin.

— Progress in Non-Histone Protein Research, Vol. II. 240p. 1985. 137.00 (*0-8493-5529-X*, CRC Reprint) Franklin.

— Progress in Non-Histone Protein Research, Vol. III. 224p. 1989. 121.00 (*0-8493-5530-3*, QP552, CRC Reprint) Franklin.

***Bekhterev, V. M.** Collective Reflexology: The Complete Edition. Strickland, Lloyd H., ed. Lockwood, Eugenia & Lockwood, Alisa, trs. 452p. 2000. 54.95 (*0-7658-0009-8*) Transaction Pubs.

Bekhterev, V. M. Suggestion: Its Role in Social Life. Strickland, Lloyd H., ed. Dobreva-Martinova, Tzvetanka, tr. from RUS. LC 97-51701. 187p. 1997. text 39.95 (*1-56000-340-5*) Transaction Pubs.

Bekhtereva, Natal'ia P. Biopotentials of Cerebral Hemispheres in Brain Tumors. Haigh, Basil & Bailey, Percival, trs. LC 61-17724. (International Behavioral Sciences Ser.). 191p. reprint ed. pap. 59.30 (*0-8357-7254-3*, 202064400018) Bks Demand.

Bekier, Matthias. Marketing of Hedge Funds: A Key Strategic Variable in Defining Possible Roles of an Emerging Investment Force. 2nd ed. (European University Studies: Vol. 1902). 557p. (C). 1997. pap. text 63.95 (*3-906759-43-1*) P Lang Pubng.

Bekiroglu. Simulation in Inventory & Production Control. 64p. 1983. pap. 20.00 (*0-685-67787-7*, MC83-1) Soc Computer Sim.

***Bekka, B. & Mayer, M.** Ergodic Theory & Topological Dynamics of Group Actions on Homogeneous Spaces. (London Mathematical Society Lecture Note Ser.: No. 269). (Illus.). 224p. (C). 2000. pap. 39.95 (*0-521-66030-0*) Cambridge U Pr.

Bekkali, M. Topics in Set Theory: Lebesgue Measurability, Large Cardinals, Forcing Axioms, Rho-Functions. (Lecture Notes in Mathematics Ser.: Vol. 1476). vii, 120p. 1991. pap. 24.00 (*0-387-54121-7*) Spr-Verlag.

***Bekkar, Bruce & Wahn, Udo.** Your Guy's Guide to Gynecology: A Resource for Men & Women. (Illus.). 325p. 2000. 24.95 (*0-9655067-4-6*, Pub. by N Star Pubns) Midpt Trade.

Bekkari, Muhammad, tr. see Badawi, Jamal A.

Bekke, Hans A., et al, eds. Civil Service Systems in Comparative Perspective. LC 95-22444. (Public Affairs Ser.). 1995. pap. 19.95 (*0-253-21032-1*) Ind U Pr.

Bekken, Bonnie B. Opportunities in Performing Arts Careers. (Opportunities In . . . Ser.). (Illus.). 160p. pap. 11.95 (*0-8442-8567-6*, 85676, VGM Career) NTC Contemp Pub Co.

— Opportunities in Performing Arts Careers. (Illus.). 160p. 1992. 14.95 (*0-8442-8566-8*, VGM Career) NTC Contemp Pub Co.

***Bekken, Bonnie Bjorguine.** Opportunites in Performing Arts. rev. ed. LC 00-39269. (Opportunities Ser.). (Illus.). 2000. pap. 11.95 (*0-658-00471-9*) NTC Contemp Pub Co.

— Performing Arts Careers. rev. ed. (Opportunities in . . . Ser.). 2000. 14.95 (*0-658-00470-0*, VGM Career) NTC Contemp Pub Co.

Bekken, Dean, jt. auth. see Cooper, Irving S.

Bekker, Cajus. Hitler's Naval War. (YA). (gr. 7 up). 1981. mass mkt. 2.75 (*0-89083-759-7*, Zebra Kensgtn) Kensgtn Pub Corp.

— The Luftwaffe War Diaries: The German Air Force in World War II. Ziegler, Frank H., tr. from GER. LC 94-11183.Tr. of Angriffsh Ohe 4000. (Illus.). 447p. 1994. reprint ed. pap. 17.50 (*0-306-80604-5*) Da Capo.

Bekker, Frans & Staude, Gavin. Starting & Managing a Small Business. 553p. (C). 1994. reprint ed. pap. text 41.50 (*0-7021-2128-2*, Pub. by Juta & Co) Intl Spec Bk.

Bekker, Hugo. Gottfried's "Tristan" Journey Through the Realm of Eros. LC 86-72130. (GERM Ser.: Vol. 29). (Illus.). 310p. 1987. 45.00 (*0-938100-49-1*) Camden Hse.

Bekker, Immanuel, ed. see Sophista, Apollonius.

Bekker, J. C. Butterworth Selection of Statutes: Constitutional Law. 158p. 1990. pap. 35.00 (*0-409-01219-X*, SA, MICHIE) LEXIS Pub.

— Family Law: An Introduction. 146p. 1990. pap. write for info. (*0-7021-2388-9*, Pub. by Juta & Co) Gaunt.

— Seymour's Customary Law in Southern Africa. 5th ed. 520p. 1989. pap. 50.00 (*0-7021-2219-X*, Pub. by Juta & Co) Gaunt.

Bekker, J. C. & Carpenter, G. Butterworths Selection of Statutes: Constitutional Law. 2nd ed. 158p. 1994. pap. write for info. (*0-409-01220-3*, MICHIE) LEXIS Pub.

Bekker-Nielsen, Hans. Old Norse - Icelandic Studies: A Select Bibliography. LC Z 2556.. 95p. reprint ed. pap. 30.00 (*0-608-11160-0*, 201915700011) Bks Demand.

Bekker-Nielsen, Hans, jt. ed. see Nyberg, Tore.

Bekker, Paul. Beethoven. Bozman, M. M., tr. LC 75-175938. (BCL Ser. I). (Illus.). 1972. reprint ed. 42.50 (*0-404-00728-7*) AMS Pr.

— Beethoven. 391p. 1990. reprint ed. lib. bdg. 79.00 (*0-7812-9042-2*) Rprt Serv.

— The Changing Opera. Mendel, Arthur, tr. LC 80-2256. reprint ed. 42.50 (*0-404-18803-6*) AMS Pr.

— Richard Wagner: His Life in His Work. Bozman, M. M., tr. LC 70-107792. (Select Bibliographies Reprint Ser.). 1977. 35.95 (*0-8369-5176-X*) Ayer.

— Richard Wagner: His Life in His Work. Bozman, M. M., tr. LC 74-106713. 522p. 1971. reprint ed. lib. bdg. 35.00 (*0-8371-3443-9*, BERW, Greenwood Pr) Greenwood.

— Richard Wagner - His Life in His Work: Music Book Index. 522p. 1993. reprint ed. lib. bdg. 99.00 (*0-7812-9707-9*) Rprt Serv.

— Story of Music: An Historical Sketch of the Changes in Musical Form. LC 74-124592. (BCL Ser. I). (Illus.). 1970. reprint ed. 34.50 (*0-404-00729-5*) AMS Pr.

— The Story of Music: An Historical Sketch of the Changes in Musical Form. 277p. 1990. reprint ed. lib. bdg. 69.00 (*0-7812-9020-1*) Rprt Serv.

— The Story of the Orchestra. (Music Book Index Ser.). 320p. 1992. reprint ed. lib. bdg. 89.00 (*0-7812-9469-X*) Rprt Serv.

Bekker, Peter. Country. (Illus.). 64p. 1997. 13.50 incl. audio compact disk (*1-56799-542-X*, Friedman-Fairfax) M Friedman Pub Grp Inc.

Bekker, Peter H. The Legal Position of Intergovernmental Organizations. (Legal Aspects of International Organizations Ser.). 284p. 1994. lib. bdg. 86.00 (*0-7923-2904-X*, Pub. by M Nijhoff) Kluwer Academic.

Bekker, Peter H. & International Court of Justice Staff. Commentaries on World Court Decisions (1987-1996) LC 97-42564. 324p. 1998. 99.50 (*90-411-0558-1*) Kluwer Law Intl.

Bekker, Peter O. Roots of Country: The Story of Country Music. LC 96-29063. 1996. write for info. (*1-56799-376-1*, Friedman-Fairfax) M Friedman Pub Grp Inc.

— The Story of the Blues. LC 96-38465. (The Life, Times &

An Asterisk (*) at the beginning of an entry indicates that the title is appearing for the first time.

Music Ser.). 1997. 13.50 (*1-56799-357-5*, Friedman-Fairfax); pap. write for info. (*1-56799-081-9*, Friedman-Fairfax) M Friedman Pub Grp Inc.

Bekker, W. G. Historical & Critical Review of Samuel Butlers' Literary Works. LC 67-8773. (Studies in Fiction: No. 34). 1969. reprint ed. lib. bdg. 75.00 (*0-8383-0509-1*) M S G Haskell Hse.

Bekker, Willem G. An Historical & Critical Review of Samuel Butler's Literary Works. (BCL1-PR English Literature Ser.). 258p. 1992. reprint ed. lib. bdg. 79.00 (*0-7812-7470-2*) Rprt Serv.

Bekker, Z. S. Growth Patterns - Dynamic Branches: A Contribution to the Description of the Socialist Growth Pattern. 245p. 1988. 90.00 (*0-7855-2767-2*, Pub. by Akade Kiado) St Mut.

Bekkers, Gasten, jt. auth. see Thijssepark, Jac P.

Bekkers, Rudi. Mobile Telecommunications: Standards, Regulations & Applications - Wireless Communications Engineering. LC 98-41588. 1998. 99.00 (*0-89006-806-2*) Artech Hse.

Bekkers, Victor & Koops, Bert-Jaap, eds. Emerging Electronic Highways: New Challenges for Politics & Law. LC 95-26542. 187p. 1995. 87.50 (*90-411-0183-7*) Kluwer Law Intl.

Bekkers, Y. & Cohen, J., eds. Memory Management: International Workshop IWMM '92, St. Malo, France, September 17-19, 1992 - Proceedings. LC 92-30705. (Lecture Notes in Computer Science Ser.: Vol. 637). xi, 525p. 1992. 76.95 (*0-387-55940-X*) Spr-Verlag.

Bekkum, H. Van, see Van Bekkum, H.

Bekkum, Wout J. Van, see Van Bekkum, Wout J., comment.

Beklemishev, Lev D., et al. Provability, Complexity, Grammars. LC 99-20177. (Translations Ser.). 12p. 1999. write for info. (*0-8218-1078-2*) Am Math.

Beklemishev, V. N. Principles of Comparative Anatomy of Invertebrates, 2 vols. Kabata, Z., ed. McLennan, J. M., tr. LC 70-97749. 1970. lib. bdg. 72.00 (*0-226-04175-1*) U Ch Pr.

Beknasarov, A. A., tr. see Gorbatkina, J. A.

Beknazarov, A., tr. see Abrikosov, A. A.

Beknazarov, A., tr. see Volkenstein, Michael V., ed.

***Bekoff, Marc.** Strolling with Our Kin: Speaking for & Respecting Voiceless Animals. 2000. pap. 9.95 (*1-881699-02-1*, Pub. by Am Anti-Viv Soc) Lantern Books.

Bekoff, Marc & Jamieson, Dale, eds. Readings in Animal Cognition. LC 95-386. (Illus.). 496p. 1995. pap. text 32.50 (*0-262-52208-X*, Bradford Bks) MIT Pr.

Bekoff, Marc, jt. auth. see Allen, Colin.

Bekoff, Marc, jt. auth. see Carrier, Jim.

***Bekoff, Marc A.** Encyclopedia of Animal Rights & Animal Welfare. (Illus.). 480p. 1999. lib. bdg. 75.00 (*1-57958-082-3*) Fitzroy Dearborn.

Bekoff, Marc A. & Meaney, Carron, eds. Encyclopedia of Animal Rights & Animal Welfare. LC 97-35098. 472p. 1998. 59.95 (*0-313-29977-3*, Greenwood Pr) Greenwood.

Bekon of Cowes. A Hundred Years of Sail. (Illus.). 200p. 1993. 70.00 (*0-00-216811-1*) T Reed Pubns.

Beksinski, Zdzislaw. The Fantastic Art of Beksinski. 80p. 1998. 24.95 (*1-883398-38-X*) Morpheus Intl.

Bel, Ami. Ben Ami: Intimate Friends. 1996. pap. text 39.95 (*3-86187-065-7*) Bookazine Co Inc.

— Euros Edition: Photos of Johan. 8th ed. (Illus.). 1997. 16.95 (*3-86187-090-8*, Pub. by B Gmunder) Bookazine Co Inc.

***Bel Ami Books Staff.** Frisky Summer. 2000. pap. 15.95 (*1-902644-26-3*) Prowler Pr.

— Luka's Story. 2000. pap. 15.95 (*1-902644-25-5*) Prowler Pr.

Bel-Ami, Jean. La Chanson de Bel-Ami: Bel Ami's Song. (FRE.). 275p. pap. 17.50 (*0-9646926-4-3*) Montreux Media.

Bel, Art J. van, see Van Bel, Art J., ed.

Bel Geddes, Joan. Childhood & Children: A Compendium of Customs, Superstitions, Theories, Profiles & Facts. LC 96-48258. (Illus.). 680p. 1997. boxed set 69.95 (*0-89774-880-8*) Oryx Pr.

***Bel Geddes, Joan.** Children Praying: Why & How to Pray with your Children. LC 99-61899. 124p. 1999. pap. 11.95 (*1-893732-04-5*) SORIN BKS.

Bel Geddes, Norman. Horizons. LC 72-92. (Select Bibliographies Reprint Ser.). 1977. reprint ed. 41.95 (*0-8369-9954-1*) Ayer.

Bel-Ka, Abdul. Letters from Saudi Arabia. (Illus.). 120p. (Orig.). 1987. pap. 29.50 (*0-930329-17-1*) Kabel Pubs.

***Bel, M. Antonia.** La Historia de las Mujeres Desde los Textos. (SPA.). 224p. 2000. pap. 12.95 (*84-344-2858-X*) Planeta Edit.

Bela-Elek, P. S., jt. auth. see Csikos-Nagy, B.

Bela, Szende, jt. ed. see Hoskins, John A.

Belady, L. A., jt. auth. see Lehman, M. M.

Belady, L. A., jt. ed. see Maekawa, M.

***Belafi-Bakbo, Katalin, et al.** Integration of Membrane Processes into Bioconversions. LC 00-42338. 2000. write for info. (*0-306-46437-3*) Plenum.

Belafonte, Harry, et al. Island in the Sun. Fogelman, Phyllis, ed. LC 98-36175. (Illus.). 32p. (J). (ps-3). 1999. 15.99 (*0-8037-2387-3*, Dial Yng Read) Peng Put Young Read.

***Belag, Andrea.** Andrea Belag, New York-koln. 1999. 39.95 (*3-931135-36-5*) Hard Pressed Bks.

Belai, Margrita A., et al. Song of Nightingale: An Anthology of Modern Soviet Short Stories. Bhatnagar, Y. C., tr. 214p. (C). 1987. 17.50 (*81-202-0189-2*, Pub. by Ajanta) S Asia.

Belaich, J. P., et al. Microbiology & Biochemistry of Strict Anaerobes Involved in Interspecies Hydrogen Transfer. LC 90-7023. (FEMS Symposium Ser.: No. 54). (Illus.). 556p. (C). 1990. text 155.00 (*0-306-43517-9*, Kluwer Plenum) Kluwer Academic.

Belaief, Gail. Spinoza's Philosophy of Law. LC 78-118275. (Studies in Philosophy: No. 24). (Illus.). 151p. (Orig.). 1971. pap. text 33.85 (*90-279-1851-1*) Mouton.

Belair, Fernando, ed. see Sutton, Gart.

Belair, Jacques & Dubuc, Serge, eds. Fractal Geometry & Analysis. 488p. (C). 1991. text 259.00 (*0-7923-1399-2*) Kluwer Academic.

Belair, Richard L. The Fathers. 250p. (Orig.). 1991. pap. 9.95 (*0-8283-1936-7*) Branden Bks.

Belaire, David. A Guide to the Big Band Era: A Comprehensive Review of All the Recorded Hits & all the Hitmakers. LC 96-90496. 269p. (Orig.). 1996. pap. 16.95 (*0-9653681-0-6*) Winged Note.

Belamri, Rabah. Shattered Vision. Harter, Hugh A., tr. from FRE. (French Expressions Ser.). 180p. 1994. 19.95 (*0-8419-1258-0*) Holmes & Meier.

Beland, Bernard. Electricity As a Cause of Fires. 1984. 5.35 (*0-318-03822-6*, TR84-5) Society Fire Protect.

***Beland, Claire Doyle.** Luck Doesn't Happen by Chance. 1999. pap. 12.95 (*1-886940-05-3*) Ozark Mountn.

Beland, F. A., jt. ed. see Poirier, Miriam C.

Beland, Pierre. Beluga: A Farewell to Whales. (Illus.). 240p. 1996. 25.00 (*1-55821-398-8*, 13988) Lyons Pr.

Beland, Sylvie. High Performance Thermoplastic Resins & Their Composites. LC 90-27388. (Illus.). 177p. 1991. 89.00 (*0-8155-1278-3*) Noyes.

***Belandres, Praxedes V.** Textbook of Military Medicine, Surgical Combat Casualty Care Pt. 4: Rehabilitation of Injured Combatant, Vol. 2. 556p. 2000. boxed set 51.00 (*0-16-059129-5*) USGPO.

Belanger. Raising Milk Goats the Modern Way. 1983. pap. 6.95 (*0-88266-062-4*) Storey Bks.

Belanger, Alain Yvan. Pocket Guide to Physical Agents. 352p. spiral bd. write for info. (*0-7817-2108-3*) Lppncott W & W.

Belanger, Andre J. The Ethics of Catholicism & the Consecration of the Intellectual. 248p. 1997. 55.00 (*0-7735-1517-8*, Pub. by McG-Queens Univ Pr) CUP Services.

— Framework for a Political Sociology. 256p. 1985. pap. 18.95 (*0-8020-6571-6*); text 32.50 (*0-8020-5666-0*) U of Toronto Pr.

Belanger, Ann C. Vascular Anatomy & Physiology: An Introductory Text. LC 90-925. 200p. 1990. pap. 39.95 (*0-941022-11-0*) Davies Pubng.

— Vascular Anatomy & Physiology: An Introductory Text. 2nd ed. Date not set. pap. 39.95 (*0-941022-40-4*) Davies Pubng.

***Belanger, B.** Lost Source Exercise, 1997: Exercise of Radiological Response Through Cooperation & Coordination of Local, State & Federal Agency Resources under the National Contingency Plan. 48p. 1998. pap. 4.25 (*0-16-062758-3*) USGPO.

Belanger, Charles A. The Chinese Herb Selection Guide: A Traditional & Modern Clinical Repertory with a Summary Materia Medica for the Health Care Practitioner. LC 97-91745. xxiv, 892p. (Orig.). 1997. pap. 59.95 (*0-9657310-3-0*) Phytotech Database.

Belanger, Claude, jt. auth. see Trudel, Pierre.

Belanger, Dian O. Enabling American Innovation: Engineering & the National Science Foundation. LC 97-28311. (Purdue University Press History of Technology Ser.). 1997. 39.95 (*1-55753-111-0*) Purdue U Pr.

— Managing American Wildlife: A History of the International Association of Fish & Wildlife Agencies. LC 87-30065. 264p. 1988. pap. 18.95 (*0-87023-609-1*) U of Mass Pr.

***Belanger, France & Jordan, Dianne.** Evaluation & Implementation of Distance Learning: Technologies, Tools & Techniques. LC 99-47580. (Illus.). 250p. (C). 2000. pap. 69.95 (*1-878289-63-2*) Idea Group Pub.

Belanger, Francine & Duplain, Jacques. English - French Vocabulary of Office Computers, Electronics & Telecommunications. (ENG & FRE.). 89p. 1992. pap. 29.95 (*0-8288-9410-8*) Fr & Eur.

Belanger, Francine, jt. auth. see Mercier, Jean.

***Belanger Grafton, Carol.** Old-Fashioned Fruit & Vegetable Stickers: 62 Full-Color Pressure-Sensitive Stickers. (Illus.). (J). 1998. pap. 4.95 (*0-486-40388-2*) Dover.

— Old-Fashioned Wild Animals Stickers: 84 Full-Color Pressure-Sensitive Designs. (Illus.). (J). 1998. pap. 4.95 (*0-486-40389-0*) Dover.

— Santa Claus Stickers. (Illus.). (J). 1999. pap. 4.95 (*0-486-40595-8*) Dover.

Belanger Grafton, Carol, ed. 504 Decorative Vignettes in Full Color. (Illus.). 48p. 1999. pap. text 9.95 (*0-486-40467-6*) Dover.

— Medieval Woodcut Illustrations: City Views & Decorations from the Nuremberg Chronicle. LC 99-26476. (Illus.). 96p. 1999. pap. 8.95 (*0-486-40458-7*) Dover.

Belanger, J. L., tr. see Morin, Edgar.

Belanger, J. M. & Pare, J. R., eds. Instrumental Methods in Food Analysis. 1996. write for info. (*0-614-17928-9*) Elsevier.

Belanger, J. M., jt. auth. see Pare, J. R.

***Belanger, Jacque.** Being Local Worldwide: Abb & The Challenge of Global Management. LC 99-33981. 1999. 39.95 (*0-8014-3650-8*) Cornell U Pr.

Belanger, Jacque, et al, eds. Workplace Industrial Relations & the Global Challenge. LC 94-1668. (Cornell International Industrial & Labor Relations Reports: No. 25). 352p. 1994. text 59.95 (*0-87546-327-4*, ILR Press); pap. text 29.95 (*0-87546-328-2*, ILR Press) Cornell U Pr.

Belanger, Jean-Pierre, tr. A Great Lakes Fur Trade Coloring Book.Tr. of Les/Fourrures et les Grands lacs cahier a colorier. (ENG & FRE., Illus.). 32p. 1981. pap. 3.50 (*0-87351-154-9*) Minn Hist.

Belanger, Jerry. Raising Milk Goats the Modern Way. rev. ed. LC 89-45737. (Illus.). 208p. 1990. pap. 12.95 (*0-88266-576-6*) Storey Bks.

***Belanger, Jerry.** Storey's Guide to Raising Dairy Goats: Breeds, Care, Dairying. 288p. 2000. pap. 18.95 (*1-58017-259-8*) Storey Bks.

***Belanger, Joe.** Catalina Island: All You Need to Know. LC 00-190798. (Illus.). 224p. 2000. pap. 18.95 (*0-9700086-0-0*) Roundtable.

Belanger, Joseph L. China Prism: Yellow - Red - Green. LC 99-68263. 96p. 1999. pap. 10.00 (*1-57197-162-9*) Pentland Pr.

Belanger, Louis, jt. auth. see Mace, Gordon.

Belanger, Pamela J. Inventing Acadia: Artists & Tourists at Mount Desert. Hall, Dawn, ed. LC 99-7192. (Illus.). 170p. 1999. pap. 39.95 (*0-918749-09-3*, Pub. by W A Farnsworth) U Pr of New Eng.

— Maine in America: American Art at the Farnsworth Art Museum. (Illus.). 256p. 1999. 55.00 (*0-918749-08-5*) U Pr of New Eng.

Belanger, Paul, et al, eds. Literacy & Basic Education on the Eve of the 21st Century: Report of the 6th European Conference of Directors of Educational Research Institutions, Bled (Yugoslavia), 9-12 October 1991. LC 92-27540. 258p. 1992. 76.00 (*90-265-1264-3*) Swets.

Belanger, Paul & Gelpi, Ettore, eds. Lifelong Education. LC 95-9153. 220p. (C). 1995. pap. text 26.50 (*0-7923-3510-4*) Kluwer Academic.

Belanger, Paul & Tuijnman, Albert. New Patterns of Adult Learning: A 6-Country Comparative Study. LC 97-30104. 200p. 1997. 78.75 (*0-08-043069-4*, Pergamon Pr) Elsevier.

Belanger, Paul & Tuijnman, Sofia. The Emergence of Learning Societies: Who Participates in Adult Learning. LC 97-17791. 200p. 1997. 73.50 (*0-08-043068-6*, Pergamon Pr) Elsevier.

Belanger, Pierre. Modern Control Engineering: International Edition. 494p. (C). 1995. pap. text 27.95 (*0-03-015247-X*) OUP.

Belanger, Pierre-Andre. Optical Fiber Theory: A Supplement to Applied Electromagnetics. 244p. 1993. text 52.00 (*981-02-1491-X*) World Scientific Pub.

Belanger, Pierre R. Control Engineering: A Modern Approach. LC 94-67281. (Illus.). 494p. (C). 1994. text 76.95 (*0-03-013489-7*) OUP.

Belanger, Pierre R., et al. Introduction to Circuits with Electronics: An Integrated Approach. LC 85-760. (Illus.). 720p. (C). 1995. text 86.95 (*0-03-064008-3*) OUP.

— Introduction to Circuits with Electronics: An Integrated Approach. LC 85-760. 702p. (C). 1985. teacher ed. write for info. (*0-03-064009-1*) SCP.

***Belanger, Ronnie.** The Wedding Book - Making Memories. (Illus.). 2000. 19.99 (*0-88270-802-3*) Bridge-Logos.

Belanger, Ronnie & Mast, Brian, eds. Profiles of Success: The Best of Christian Businessmen's Magazine, Vol. 1. LC 99-64057. (Illus.). 170p. 1999. pap. 15.99 (*0-88270-775-2*, Pub. by Bridge-Logos) Spring Arbor Dist.

Belanger, Sandra E., compiled by. Better Said & Clearly Written: An Annotated Guide to Business Communication Sources, Skills & Samples, 3. LC 89-17227. (Bibliographies & Indexes in Mass Media & Communications Ser.: No. 3). 210p. 1989. lib. bdg. 49.95 (*0-313-26641-7*, BBF/) Greenwood.

Belanger, Terry. Lunacy & the Arrangement of Books. ii, 28p. 1985. pap. 10.00 (*0-938768-08-5*) Oak Knoll.

Belanger, Terry, jt. ed. see Young, Heartsill.

Belanger, Thomas C. The Complete Planning Guide for Microsoft Project for Windows 95 & Windows 3.1. (Illus.). 288p. 1996. pap. text 34.95 (*0-7506-9777-6*, Digital DEC) Buttrwrth-Heinemann.

— How to Plan Any Project: A Guide for Teams & Individuals. 2nd ed. (Illus.). 224p. 1995. pap., wbk. ed. 29.95 (*0-9631465-1-3*) Sterling Planning Grp.

Belanina, V. Pavlovsk: A Guide. (Illus.). 88p. (C). 1987. 30.00 (*0-7855-5190-5*, Pub. by Collets) St Mut.

Belanoff, Pat, et al, eds. Nothing Begins with N: New Investigations of Freewriting. LC 89-26290. 304p. (C). 1991. 36.95 (*0-8093-1657-9*); pap. 21.95 (*0-8093-1658-7*) S Ill U Pr.

Belanoff, Patricia & Dickson, Marcia. Portfolios: Process & Product. LC 91-3804. 315p. (C). 1991. pap. text 25.00 (*0-86709-275-0*, 0275, Pub. by Boynton Cook Pubs) Heinemann.

Belanoff, Patricia, et al. The Right Handbook: Grammar & Usage in Context. 2nd rev. ed. LC 92-28851. 294p. 1992. pap. text 21.00 (*0-86709-316-1*, 0316, Pub. by Boynton Cook Pubs) Heinemann.

Belanoff, Patricia, jt. auth. see Elbow, Peter.

Belar, Cynthia D. & Deardorff, William W. Clinical Health Psychology in Medical Settings: A Practitioner's Handbook. 2nd rev. ed. LC 94-49604. 296p. 1995. text 29.95 (*1-55798-277-5*); pap. text 24.95 (*1-55798-287-2*) Am Psychol.

Belardinelli, Luiz, jt. auth. see Pelleg, Amir.

Belardinelli, Luiz, ed. see International Symposium on Adrenosine & Adenine Staff.

Belardo, Sal & Weinroth, Jay, eds. Proceedings of a Conference on Simulation in Business & Management, 1990. (Simulation Ser.: Vol. 21, No. 4). 160p. 1990. 48.00 (*0-911801-63-4*, SS21-4) Soc Computer Sim.

***Belasco.** Brothers of New Essex: Afro-Erotic Adventures. (Illus.). 200p. 2000. pap. 24.95 (*1-57344-111-2*, Pub. by Cleis Pr) Publishers Group.

Belasco, Amy. Paying for Military Readiness & Upkeep: Trends in Operation & Maintenance Spending. (Illus.). 75p. (C). 1998. pap. text 20.00 (*0-7881-7381-2*) DIANE Pub.

Belasco, Amy & Musell, R. Mark. Reducing the Size of the Federal Civilian Work Force. (Illus.). 72p. (Orig.). (C). 1994. pap. text 30.00 (*0-7881-0702-X*) DIANE Pub.

Belasco, Bernard. The Entrepreneur As Culture Hero: Pre-Adaptations for Nigerian Economic Development. LC 79-10475. (Illus.). 239p. 1980. 59.95 (*0-275-90451-2*, C0451, Praeger Pubs) Greenwood.

Belasco, David. The Girl of the Golden West. Meserve, Walter J., ed. & intro. by. (On Stage, America! Ser.). 73p. 1996. spiral bd. 4.95 (*0-937657-34-4*) Feedbk Theabks & Prospero.

***Belasco, David.** The Heart of Maryland. (Americana Series). 71p. 2000. reprint ed. pap. 4.95 (*0-937657-60-3*) Feedbk Theabks & Prospero.

Belasco, David. The Theatre Through Its Stage Door. Defoe, Louis V., ed. LC 69-56534. (Illus.). 1972. reprint ed. 24.95 (*0-405-08261-4*, Pub. by Blom Pubns) Ayer.

Belasco, James A. Teaching the Elephant to Dance: The Manager's Guide to Empowering Change. 288p. (C). 1991. reprint ed. pap. 13.95 (*0-452-26629-7*) Dutton Plume.

***Belasco, James A.** The Ten Commandments: Ancient Wisdom for Future Success. LC 00-29200. 2000. write for info. (*1-893224-16-3*, New Millenn Pr) New Millenn Enter.

Belasco, James A. & Stayer, Ralph C. Flight of the Buffalo: Soaring to Excellence, Learning to Let Employees Lead. 370p. 1999. reprint ed. 32.95 (*0-7351-0057-8*) Replica Bks.

— Flight of the Buffalo: Soaring to Excellence, Learning to Let Employees Lead. 368p. 1994. reprint ed. mass mkt. 14.99 (*0-446-67008-1*, Pub. by Warner Bks) Little.

***Belasco, James A. & Stead, Jerre.** Seize Tomorrow, Start Today: Renew Your Vision, Revitalize Your Organization, & Stay Ahead of the Future. 496p. 2000. mass mkt. 14.95 (*0-446-67604-7*) Warner Bks.

Belasco, James A. & Stead, Jerre. Soaring with the Phoenix: Renewing the Vision, Reviving the Spirit & Re-Creating the Success of Your Company. LC 98-34785. 320p. 1999. 25.00 (*0-446-52400-X*, Pub. by Warner Bks) Little.

Belasco, Joel & Brawerman, George, eds. Control of Messenger RHA Stability. (Illus.). 517p. 1993. text 94.00 (*0-12-084782-5*) Acad Pr.

Belasco, Kent S. Analyzing Bank Staffing Levels: A Model for Establishing & Maintaining Optimal Employee Productivity. 300p. 1991. text 65.00 (*1-55738-306-5*, Irwn Prfssnl) McGraw-Hill Prof.

— Bank Productivity: Improvement Techniques. 1991. text 45.00 (*1-55520-168-7*, Irwn Prfssnl) McGraw-Hill Prof.

— Bank Systems Management: The Project Management Guide to Planning & Implementing System Installations, Conversions & Mergers. (Illus.). 314p. 1998. reprint ed. lib. bdg. 62.50 (*0-7351-0032-2*) Replica Bks.

— Bank Systems Management: The Project Management Guide to Planning & Implementing Systems. LC 94-146253. 1993. text 62.50 (*1-55738-380-4*, Irwn Prfssnl) McGraw-Hill Prof.

— Earnings Enhancement. 1990. write for info. (*1-55520-199-7*, Irwn Prfssnl) McGraw-Hill Prof.

— Financial Institution Staffing: Analyzing & Modeling Staff Levels in a Competitive & Consolidating Industry. LC 97-9645. 375p. 1997. 60.00 (*0-7863-1106-1*, Irwn Prfssnl) McGraw-Hill Prof.

— Managing Bank Conversions. LC 96-3563. 1996. text 60.00 (*0-7863-0735-8*, Irwn Prfssnl) McGraw-Hill Prof.

Belasco, Leonard, ed. Northwords. LC 80-85225. 66p. (Orig.). 1981. pap. 12.95 (*0-915032-23-6*) Natl Poet Foun.

Belasco, Susan, jt. auth. see Ammons, Elizabeth.

Belasco, Warren J. Americans on the Road: From Autocamp to Motel, 1910-1945. LC 97-13502. (Illus.). 224p. 1997. reprint ed. pap. 15.95 (*0-8018-5734-1*) Johns Hopkins.

— Appetite for Change: How the Counterculture Took on the Food Industry & What Happened When It Did, 1966-1988. LC 93-18124. 328p. 1993. pap. text 17.95 (*0-8014-8128-7*) Cornell U Pr.

Belasen, Alan T. Leading the Learning Organization: Communication & Competencies for Managing Change. LC 99-11338. (SUNY Series, Human Communication Processes). (Illus.). 480p. (C). 1999. text 71.50 (*0-7914-4367-1*); pap. text 23.95 (*0-7914-4368-X*) State U NY Pr.

Belash, Constance A. Braiding & Knotting: Techniques & Projects. LC 74-75266. (Illus.). 126p. 1974. reprint ed. pap. 5.95 (*0-486-23059-7*) Dover.

Belasic, David & Schmidt, Paul. The Penguin Principles. LC 85-15524. 1986. 7.95 (*0-89536-799-8*, 6817) CSS OH.

Belasich, Deborah K. Enterprise Zones: Policy Perspectives of Economic Development. LC 92-34841. (Studies in Entrepreneurship). 152p. 1993. text 15.00 (*0-8153-0994-5*) Garland.

Belasik, Paul. Exploring Dressage Technique. 1993. pap. 30.00 (*0-85131-606-9*, Pub. by J A Allen) Trafalgar.

— Riding Towards the Light: An Apprenticeship in the Art of Dressage Riding. 152p. 1990. 40.00 (*0-85131-509-7*, Pub. by J A Allen) Trafalgar.

***Belasik, Paul.** Songs of the Horses. 2000. pap. 17.95 (*0-85131-758-8*, Pub. by J A Allen) Trafalgar.

Belavadi, S. H. Theories & Practice of Parliamentary Procedure in India. (C). 1989. 135.00 (*0-7855-3716-3*) St Mut.

— Theory & Practice of Parliamentary Procedure in India. (C). 1988. 135.00 (*0-7855-4739-8*) St Mut.

Belaval, Domitila, jt. ed. see Nash, Rose.

Belaval, Yvon. Histoire de la Philosophie: De la Renaissance a la Revolution, Vol. 2. (Historique Ser.). 1168p. 75.00 (*0-686-56455-3*) Fr & Eur.

— Histoire de la Philosophie: Du XIX Siecle a nos Jours, Vol. 3. (Historique Ser.). 1408p. 52.50 (*0-686-56456-1*) Fr & Eur.

— Histoire de la Philosophie, Vol. 2: De la Renaissance a la Revolution Kantienne. (FRE.). 1168p. 1973. 115.00 (*0-7859-5216-0*, 2070107604) Fr & Eur.

B

— Histoire de la Philosophie, Vol. 3: Du XIX Siecle a Nos Jours. (FRE.). 1408p. 1974. 130.00 (*0-7859-5217-9*, 2070108252) Fr & Eur.

— Philosophers & Their Language. Guterman, Norbert, tr. LC 66-18481. 157p. reprint ed. pap. 48.70 (*0-608-10097-8*, 200523000052) Bks Demand.

Belavich-Ivac, Lois, jt. auth. see Bartram, Greg.

Belavin, A. A. & Drinfield, V. G. Triangle Equations & Simple Lie Algebras. 100p. 1998. text 19.00 (*90-5702-269-9*, ECU25) Gordon & Breach.

Belavkin, V. P., et al. Quantum Communications & Measurement: Proceedings of an International Workshop Held in Nottingham, England, July 11-16, 1994. LC 95-32969. (Illus.). 544p. (C). 1995. text 162.00 (*0-306-45128-X*, Kluwer Plenum) Kluwer Academic.

Belbase, Narayan. The Implementation of International Environmental Law in Nepal. 1997. pap. 25.00 (*0-7855-7420-4*, Pub. by Ratna Pustak Bhandar) St Mut.

Belben, Rosalind. Dreaming of the Dead People. (Masks Ser.). 160p. (Orig.). 1991. reprint ed. pap. text 10.95 (*1-85242-150-9*) Serpents Tail.

— Is Beauty Good? (Masks Ser.). 128p. (Orig.). 1991. pap. text 10.95 (*1-85242-153-3*) Serpents Tail.

Belbin, David. Avenging Angel. 224p. (YA). (gr. 7-9). 1994. pap. 3.50 (*0-590-48890-2*) Scholastic Inc.

— Deadly Secrets. 176p. (YA). (gr. 7-9). 1994. pap. 3.50 (*0-590-48318-8*) Scholastic Inc.

— Final Cut. 224p. (YA). (gr. 7 up). 1994. pap. 3.50 (*0-590-48972-0*) Scholastic Inc.

— Final Cut. (Point Crime Ser.). 1994. 8.60 (*0-606-07511-9*, Pub. by Turtleback) Demco.

Belbin, Meredith. Changing the Way We Work. LC 97-144717. 160p. 1997. text 57.95 (*0-7506-2874-X*) Buttrwrth-Heinemann.

— The Coming Shape of the Organization. (Illus.). 144p. 1996. text 56.95 (*0-7506-2356-X*) Buttrwrth-Heinemann.

Belbin, Meredith. How to Build a Successful Team... the Belbin Way. 1996. cd-rom 125.00 (*0-7506-2777-8*) Buttrwrth-Heinemann.

Belbin, R. M. The Job Promoters: A Journey to a New Profession. LC 91-100771. 204p. 1990. reprint ed. pap. 63.30 (*0-608-07426-8*, 206765300009) Bks Demand.

***Belbin, R. Meredith.** Beyond the Team. (Illus.). 160p. 2000. 32.95 (*0-7506-4641-1*) Buttrwrth-Heinemann.

Belbin, R. Meredith. Changing the Way We Work. 115p. 1999. pap. text 32.95 (*0-7506-4288-2*) Buttrwrth-Heinemann.

— Coming Shape of Organization. LC 98-208253. 148p. 1998. pap. text 34.95 (*0-7506-3950-4*) Buttrwrth-Heinemann.

Belcaro. Handbook of Venous Diseases. 1995. pap. text 39.00 (*0-7020-2016-8*, W B Saunders Co) Harcrt Hlth Sci Grp.

Belcaro, G. & Nicolaides, A. Venous Clinic. 100p. 1997. pap. text 16.00 (*1-86094-051-X*) World Scientific Pub.

Belcastro, Patricia. Evaluating Library Staff: A Performance Appraisal System. LC 97-32669. 253p. 1998. 35.00 (*0-8389-0731-8*) ALA.

Belcastro, Philip A. The Birth Control Book. 144p. (C). 1986. pap. 32.50 (*0-86720-068-5*) Jones & Bartlett.

Belch. Introduction to Advertising Promotion. 5th ed. 2001. 66.00 (*0-07-231445-1*) McGraw.

— Introduction to Advertising Promotion Myth Makers. 3rd ed. 1996. 67.50 (*0-256-26091-5*) McGraw.

Belch, et al. Color Atlas of Pericardial Vascular Diseases. 2nd ed. 1996. text 76.95 (*0-7234-2074-2*, Pub. by Martin Dunitz) Mosby Inc.

Belch, George & Belch, Michael A. CPS - Introduction to Advertising & Promotion: Course Syllabus For Market 607. 3rd ed. (C). 1995. 0.50 (*0-256-20022-X*, Irwn McGrw-H) McGrw-H Hghr Educ.

Belch, George E. & Belch, Michael A. Advertising & Promotion: An Integrated Marketing Communications Perspective. 4th ed. LC 97-28715. (Irwin-McGraw-Hill Series in Marketing). 1997. 76.25 (*0-256-21899-4*, Irwn Prfssnl) McGraw-Hill Prof.

— Introduction to Advertising & Promotion: An Integrated Marketing Communications Perspective. 2nd ed. LC 92-22766. (Illus.). 864p. (C). 1992. text, student ed. 31.50 (*0-256-10825-0*, Irwn McGrw-H) McGrw-H Hghr Educ.

— Introduction to Advertising & Promotion: An Integrated Marketing Communications Perspective. 3rd ed. LC 94-22646. 762p. (C). 1994. text 69.95 (*0-256-13696-3*, Irwn McGrw-H) McGrw-H Hghr Educ.

***Belch, Jerry.** Simulating the Medical Office Software for Windows 95, 7 Modules, Set. Harris, Valerie et al, eds. (Illus.). 600p. 1999. teacher ed., ring bd. 249.95 incl. disk (*0-89262-528-7*); student ed., spiral bd. 49.95 incl. cd-rom (*0-89262-529-5*) Career Pub.

— Simulating the Medical Office Software for Windows 95: Appointments Instructor's Guide. Harris, Valerie et al, eds. (Illus.). 42p. 1999. teacher ed., spiral bd. 49.95 incl. disk (*0-89262-540-6*) Career Pub.

— Simulating the Medical Office, Software for Windows 95: Appointments Module. Harris, Valerie et al, eds. (Illus.). 58p. 1999. spiral bd. 7.95 (*0-89262-533-3*) Career Pub.

— Simulating the Medical Office Software for Windows 95: Business Checking Instructor's Guide. Harris, Valerie et al, eds. (Illus.). 44p. 1999. teacher ed., spiral bd. 49.95 incl. disk (*0-89262-541-4*) Career Pub.

— Simulating the Medical Office, Software for Windows 95: Business Checking Module. Harris, Valerie et al, eds. (Illus.). 82p. 1999. spiral bd. 7.95 (*0-89262-534-1*) Career Pub.

— Simulating the Medical Office Software for Windows 95: Correspondence Instructor's Guide. Harris, Valerie et al, eds. (Illus.). 50p. 1999. teacher ed., spiral bd. 49.95 incl. disk (*0-89262-539-2*) Career Pub.

— Simulating the Medical Office, Software for Windows 95: Correspondence Module. Harris, Valerie et al, eds. (Illus.). 94p. 1999. spiral bd. 7.95 (*0-89262-532-5*) Career Pub.

— Simulating the Medical Office Software for Windows 95: Insurance Claims Instructor's Guide. Harris, Valerie et al, eds. (Illus.). 36p. 1999. teacher ed., spiral bd. 49.95 incl. disk (*0-89262-544-9*) Career Pub.

— Simulating the Medical Office, Software for Windows 95: Insurance Claims Module. Harris, Valerie et al, eds. (Illus.). 58p. 1999. spiral bd., wbk. ed. 7.95 (*0-89262-537-6*) Career Pub.

— Simulating the Medical Office Software for Windows 95: Patient Billing Instructor's Guide. Harris, Valerie et al, eds. (Illus.). 80p. 1999. teacher ed., spiral bd. 49.95 incl. disk (*0-89262-543-0*) Career Pub.

— Simulating the Medical Office, Software for Windows 95: Patient Billing Module. Harris, Valerie et al, eds. (Illus.). 96p. 1999. spiral bd. 9.95 (*0-89262-536-8*) Career Pub.

— Simulating the Medical Office Software for Windows 95: Purchase Orders Instructor's Guide. Harris, Valerie et al, eds. (Illus.). 32p. 1999. teacher ed., spiral bd. 49.95 incl. disk (*0-89262-542-2*) Career Pub.

— Simulating the Medical Office, Software for Windows 95: Purchase Orders Module. Harris, Valerie et al, eds. (Illus.). 66p. 1999. spiral bd., wbk. ed. 7.45 (*0-89262-535-X*) Career Pub.

— Simulating the Medical Office Software for Windows 95: Record Management Instructor's Guide. Harris, Valerie et al, eds. (Illus.). 52p. 1999. teacher ed., spiral bd. 49.95 incl. disk (*0-89262-538-4*) Career Pub.

— Simulating the Medical Office Software, for Windows 95: Record Management Module. Harris, Valerie et al, eds. (Illus.). 76p. 1998. spiral bd. 7.95 (*0-89262-531-7*) Career Pub.

Belch, Jill J. F. & Zurier, Robert B., eds. Connective Tissue Diseases. (Illus.). 408p. 1995. text 99.00 (*0-412-48620-2*, Pub. by E A) OUP.

Belch, Michael A., jt. auth. see Belch, George.

Belch, Michael A., jt. auth. see Belch, George E.

Belchem, John. Dictionary of Nineteenth Century History. 768p. 1997. pap. 16.95 (*0-14-051269-1*) Viking Penguin.

— Orator Hunt: Henry Hunt & English Working-Class Radicalism. 320p. 1985. 59.00 (*0-19-822759-0*) OUP.

— Popular Radicalism in Nineteenth-Century Britain. (Social History in Perspective Ser.). 160p. 1996. pap. 19.95 (*0-312-15806-8*); text 49.95 (*0-312-15799-1*) St Martin.

Belchem, John & Kirk, Neville, eds. Languages of Labour. LC 97-18807. 232p. 1997. text 74.95 (*1-85928-428-0*, Pub. by Scolar Pr) Ashgate Pub Co.

Belchem, John & Price, Richard, eds. A Dictionary of Nineteenth-Century World History. (Illus.). 840p. 1994. 72.95 (*0-631-18352-3*) Blackwell Pubs.

Belchen, Richard P. Ministry Helps in Acts. 72p. (C). reprint ed. pap. 6.95 (*0-925703-62-1*) Crown MA.

— Ministry Helps in John. 60p. pap. 6.95 (*0-925703-18-4*) Crown MA.

— Teaching Helps in Hebrews. 56p. pap. 6.95 (*0-925703-16-8*) Crown MA.

— Teaching Helps in James. 64p. pap. 6.95 (*0-925703-17-6*) Crown MA.

— Teaching Helps in Malachi. 38p. pap. 6.95 (*0-925703-63-X*) Crown MA.

— Teaching Helps in II Corinthians. 38p. pap. 6.95 (*0-925703-15-X*) Crown MA.

Belchen, Richard P. & Mattia, Anthony. Seventeenth Century Baptist Confessions of Faith. 56p. pap. 5.95 (*0-925703-23-0*) Crown MA.

Belcher. City Parochial Foundation. 378p. 1991. 78.95 (*0-85967-879-2*) Ashgate Pub Co.

Belcher. The Mutineers of the Bounty & Their Descendants in Pitcairn. 1972. 250.00 (*0-87968-342-2*) Gordon Pr.

Belcher, Alice, et al, eds. R&D Decisions: Strategy, Policy, & Disclosure. LC 95-50137. (Research in Organizational Behaviour & Strategy Ser.). 304p. (C). 1996. 90.00 (*0-415-13777-2*) Routledge.

Belcher, Anne E. Hematolymphatic & Neoplastic Disorders. (Illus.). 288p. (C). (gr. 13). 1992. text 36.00 (*0-8016-1809-6*, 01809) Mosby Inc.

Belcher, Betty. Creative Flower Arranging: Floral Design for Home & Flower Show. (Illus.). 168p. 1993. pap. 29.95 (*0-88192-247-1*) Timber.

Belcher, C. Francis. Logging Railroads of the White Mountains. rev. ed. (Illus.). 256p. 1980. pap. 14.95 (*0-910146-32-2*) AMC Books.

Belcher, Diana. The Mutineers of the Bounty & Their Descendants in Pitcairn & Norfolk Islands. LC 75-3439. reprint ed. 49.50 (*0-404-14443-8*) AMS Pr.

Belcher, Diane & Braine, George. Academic Writing in a Second Language: Essays on Research & Pedagogy. LC 94-13814. 336p. 1995. pap. 39.50 (*1-56750-116-8*); text 73.25 (*1-56750-115-X*) Ablx Pub.

Belcher, Diane D. & Hirvela, Alan R., eds. Linking Literacies: Perspectives on L2 Reading - Writing Connections. (Illus.), 300p. (C). text 44.50 (*0-472-09753-9*); pap. text 29.95 (*0-472-06753-2*) U of Mich Pr.

Belcher, Edward & Simpkinson, F. G. H. M. S. Sulphur on the Northwest & California Coasts, 1837 & 1839. Pierce, Richard A., ed. (Alaska History Ser.: No. 12). (Illus.). 1979. 18.00 (*0-919642-65-9*) Limestone Pr.

Belcher, George F., jt. auth. see Aumonier, Stacy.

Belcher, H. W. & D'Itri, Frank M. Subirrigation & Controlled Drainage. LC 94-30888. 496p. 1994. lib. bdg. 85.00 (*1-56670-139-2*, L1139) Lewis Pubs.

Belcher, J. A., ed. Sign Language Dot-to-Dot. 32p. (J). (ps-3). 1979. 6.95 (*0-917002-40-7*) Joyce Media.

Belcher, James. The Diamond Ring River Valley: The Story of Sara Gail & Her Battle Against the Forces of Solitude. 90p. 1988. pap. 10.00 (*0-944754-13-9*) Pudding Hse Pubns.

***Belcher, James.** Feelings. 1999. pap. write for info. (*1-58235-258-5*) Watermrk Pr.

Belcher, James O., jt. auth. see Norton, Robert E.

Belcher, James O., tr. see Li Cunbao.

Belcher, Jane C. & Jacobsen, Julia M. From Idea to Funded Project: Grant Proposals That Work. 4th ed. LC 91-41706. (Illus.). 144p. 1992. pap. 26.50 (*0-89774-710-0*) Oryx Pr.

Belcher, Jennifer D. Managing Costs for Profitability. (Orig.). 1996. pap. 9.95 (*0-942477-00-6*) Emprise Intl.

Belcher, John G. Gain Sharing. LC 91-15351. (Illus.). 214p. 1991. pap. 66.40 (*0-608-05076-8*, 206563100005) Bks Demand.

Belcher, John G., Jr. How to Design & Implement a Results-Oriented Variable Pay System. 256p. 1996. 55.00 (*0-8144-0296-8*) AMACOM.

— Productivity Plus. LC 87-9222. 240p. 1987. 26.95 (*0-87201-451-7*, 1451) Gulf Pub.

Belcher, Jon B. Short Wings Forever. (Illus.). 224p. 1998. pap. 24.95 (*1-893904-00-8*) BCo.

Belcher, Jwaundace, jt. auth. see Bell, Marchella.

Belcher, Lou & Fischl, Donna. Footsteps: Unforgettable Walks in Southeastern Virginia. LC 97-90117. (Illus.). 250p. 1997. pap. 12.95 (*0-9657022-0-0*, 0001) Footsteps Inc.

Belcher, M. A. W. N. Pugin: An Annotated Bibliography. 560p. 1987. text 199.90 (*0-7201-1774-7*) Continuum.

Belcher, Martha & Gennino, Angela, eds. Southeast Asia Rainforests: A Resource Guide & Directory. (Illus.). 100p. (Orig.). 1993. pap. 8.50 (*0-9628033-2-4*) Rainforest Act.

Belcher, Max. A Land & Life Remembered: Americo-Liberian Folk Architecture. LC 88-20531. (Illus.). 224p. 1988. pap. 19.95 (*0-8203-1086-7*) U of Ga Pr.

— A Land & Life Remembered: Americo-Liberian Folk Architecture. LC 88-20531. (Illus.). 224p. 1988. 35.00 (*0-8203-1085-9*) U of Ga Pr.

Belcher, Michael. Exhibitions in Museums. (Illus.). 248p. (C). 1993. reprint ed. pap. text 17.95 (*1-56098-324-8*) Smithsonian.

Belcher, R., jt. auth. see Breene, R.

Belcher, R., jt. auth. see Critchfield, F.

Belcher, R., jt. auth. see Gorsuch, T.

Belcher, R., jt. auth. see Nielsen, A.

Belcher, Richard P. Arthur W. Pink - Born to Write. 165p. 1993. reprint ed. pap. 7.95 (*1-883265-01-0*) Richbarry Pr.

— Diagramming the Greek New Testament. 62p. 1993. reprint ed. pap. 10.00 (*1-883265-06-1*) Richbarry Pr.

— A Journey in Authority, Vol. 3. 183p. 1996. pap. 8.95 (*1-883265-11-8*) Richbarry Pr.

***Belcher, Richard P.** A Journey in Eschatology. 240p. 2000. write for info. (*1-883265-21-5*) Richbarry Pr.

Belcher, Richard P. A Journey in Grace. 4th ed. (Journey Bks.: Vol. 5). 154p. 1990. reprint ed. 8.95 (*0-925703-11-7*) Richbarry Pr.

— A Journey in Inspiration, Series 5. (Journey Bks.: Vol. 5). 170p. 1998. pap. 8.95 (*1-883265-14-2*) Richbarry Pr.

— A Journey in Providence. 204p. 1999. pap. 10.95 (*1-883265-19-3*) Richbarry Pr.

— A Journey in Purity: A Theological Novel. (Journey Bks.: Vol. 2). 213p. 1996. pap. 10.95 (*0-925703-39-7*) Richbarry Pr.

— A Journey in the Spirit, Vol. 4. 220p. 1997. pap. 10.95 (*1-883265-12-6*) Richbarry Pr.

— A Layman's Guide to the Lordship Controversy. 123p. 1990. pap. 7.95 (*0-925703-13-3*) Richbarry Pr.

— A Layman's Guide to the Sabbath Question. 161p. 1991. pap. 7.95 (*0-925703-43-5*) Richbarry Pr.

— Ministry Helps in Amos. 48p. 1995. pap. 6.95 (*1-883265-16-9*) Richbarry Pr.

— Ministry Helps in Ephesians. 44p. 1996. pap. 6.95 (*1-883265-18-5*) Richbarry Pr.

— Ministry Helps in Galatians. 50p. 1996. pap. 6.95 (*1-883265-17-7*) Richbarry Pr.

— Ministry Helps in Hosea. 60p. (Orig.). 1993. pap. 6.95 (*1-883265-08-8*) Richbarry Pr.

— Ministry Helps in Isaiah. 132p. 1994. pap. 6.95 (*1-883265-15-0*) Richbarry Pr.

***Belcher, Richard P.** Ministry Helps in Thessalonians. 70p. 2000. pap. write for info. (*1-883265-20-7*) Richbarry Pr.

Belcher, Richard P. A Practical Approach to the Greek New Testament. 58p. 1993. reprint ed. pap. 10.00 (*1-883265-03-7*) Richbarry Pr.

— Preaching the Gospel: A Theological Perspective & a Personal Method. 120p. (C). 1995. pap. 7.95 (*1-883265-10-X*) Richbarry Pr.

— Teaching Helps in First Corinthians. (Ministry Helps Ser.). 58p. 1993. reprint ed. pap. 6.95 (*1-883265-04-5*) Richbarry Pr.

— Teaching Helps in First Peter. (Minstry Helps Ser.). 76p. 1993. reprint ed. pap. 6.95 (*1-883265-05-3*) Richbarry Pr.

— Teaching Helps in Psalms. (Ministry Helps Ser.). 53p. 1993. reprint ed. pap. 6.95 (*1-883265-02-9*) Richbarry Pr.

Belcher, Richard P., ed. Arthur W. Pink - Letters from Spartanburg, 1917-1920. 287p. 1993. 10.95 (*1-883265-00-2*) Richbarry Pr.

— Arthur W. Pink - Letters of an Itinerant Preacher 1920-21. 1994. pap. 5.95 (*1-883265-09-6*) Richbarry Pr.

Belcher, Roger, jt. auth. see Varrall, Geoff.

Belcher, S. E., jt. ed. see Perkins, R. J.

Belcher, Sandy, ed. see Sentell, Gerald D.

Belcher, Stephen. Epic Traditions of Africa. LC 98-55990. 288p. 1999. pap. 19.95 (*0-253-21281-2*); text 39.95 (*0-253-33501-9*) Ind U Pr.

Belcher, Supply. The Harmony of Maine. Hitchcock, H. Wiley, ed. LC 77-169607. (Earlier American Music Ser.: No. 6). 104p. 1972. reprint ed. lib. bdg. 25.00 (*0-306-77306-6*) Da Capo.

Belcher, Wyatt W. Economic Rivalry Between St. Louis & Chicago, 1850-1880. LC 68-58548. (Columbia University. Studies in the Social Sciences: No. 529). reprint ed. 24.50 (*0-404-51529-0*) AMS Pr.

Belchetz, Ruth. On the Tightrope. 32p. (Orig.). 1993. pap. 7.50 (*0-9636459-0-0*) Harpswell Rd.

Belchez, Chito & Moguet, Pamela J. Bikol Newspaper Reader. LC 91-70529. (Philippine Language Ser.). xxv, 143p. 1992. 48.00 (*0-931745-76-4*) Dunwoody Pr.

Belchior, Maria D. & Martinez-Lopez, Enrique, eds. Camoniana Californiana: Commemorating the Quadricentennial of the Death of Luis Vaz de Camoes. LC 85-82255. (ENG & POR.). 266p. (Orig.). 1985. pap. 20.00 (*0-942208-21-8*) Bandanna Bks.

Belcove-Shalin, Janet S., ed. New World Hasidim: Ethnographic Studies of Hasidic Jews in America. LC 94-300. (SUNY Series in Anthropology & Judaic Studies). 285p. (C). 1995. text 57.50 (*0-7914-2245-3*); pap. text 18.95 (*0-7914-2246-1*) State U NY Pr.

Beld, A. Van den, see Van den Beld, A.

Beld, Gordon. A Gentle Breeze from Gossamer Wings: A Fictionap Depiction of Refugees from the Pol Pot Era. LC 98-50636. (Judeo-Christian Ethics Ser.). 320p. 1999. pap. 18.00 (*1-885288-07-7*, Pub. by PREP Pubng) BookWorld.

Beld, Scott G. Two Terminal Archaic/Early Woodland Sites in Central Michigan. (Technical Reports Ser.: No. 22). xii, 140p. (Orig.). (C). 1992. pap. 12.00 (*0-915703-27-0*) U Mich Mus Anthro.

Beld, Scott G., et al. The Tablets of Ebla: Concordance & Bibliography. LC 84-5939. x, 70p. (Orig.). (C). 1984. pap. text 10.00 (*0-931464-21-8*) Eisenbrauns.

Belda, Manuel, et al, eds. Holiness & the World: Studies in the Teachings of Blessed Josemaria Escriva.Tr. of Santita e Mondo. 296p. 1998. pap. 12.95 (*1-890177-04-0*) Midwest Theol.

Beldecos, Nick, ed. see Poliquin, Charles.

Beldegreen, Alecia. The Bed. (Illus.). 256p. 1995. pap. 27.50 (*1-55670-394-5*) Stewart Tabori & Chang.

Belden. Snake Blossoms. 64p. (Orig.). 1976. pap. 9.95 (*0-917658-06-X*) BPW & P.

Belden, Elionne L. Claiming Chinese Identity. LC 97-31033. (Asian Americans Ser.). 192p. 1997. text 51.00 (*0-8153-2991-1*) Garland.

Belden, Gael. Roam: Ojai's Little Hip Hiking Book. (Illus.). 30p. 1999. pap. 10.00 (*0-9670232-0-3*) Bigger Love.

Belden, Jack. China Shakes the World. LC 77-105312. 544p. reprint ed. pap. 168.70 (*0-8357-6054-5*, 203435800089) Bks Demand.

— Retreat with Stillwell. (China in the 20th Century Ser.). (Illus.). 368p. 1975. reprint ed. lib. bdg. 32.50 (*0-306-70734-9*) Da Capo.

— Still Time to Die. (China in the 20th Century Ser.). xi, 322p. 1975. reprint ed. lib. bdg. 32.50 (*0-306-70735-7*) Da Capo.

Belden, Jessie P. Concerning Some of the Ancestors & Descendants of Royal Denison Belden & Olive Cadwell Belden. (Illus.). 248p. 1988. reprint ed. pap. 37.00 (*0-8328-0229-8*); reprint ed. lib. bdg. 47.00 (*0-8328-0228-X*) Higginson Bk Co.

Belden, Joseph & Wiener, Robert. Housing in Rural America: Building Affordable & Inclusive Communities. LC 98-40091. 218p. 1998. write for info. (*0-7619-1380-7*); pap. write for info. (*0-7619-1381-5*) Sage.

Belden, Joseph N., et al. Dirt Rich, Dirt Poor: America's Food & Farm Crisis. LC 85-8274. (Alternative Policies for America Ser.). 185p. 1986. pap. 14.95 (*0-7102-0666-6*, Routledge Thoemms) Routledge.

Belden, Kenneth. Husband & Wife Are One - But Which One? Belden, Stella, ed. 1982. 1.00 (*0-901269-71-9*) Grosvenor USA.

— Meeting Moral Re-Armament. 1979. 2.00 (*0-901269-46-8*) Grosvenor USA.

— Reflections on Moral Re-Armament. 1983. 4.25 (*0-901269-77-8*) Grosvenor USA.

Belden, Kenneth, ed. The Revolutionary Path. 1975. 2.25 (*0-901269-14-X*) Grosvenor USA.

Belden, Kim. Computer Solutions: An Accounting Practice Case. 176p. (C). 1996. pap. text 19.95 (*0-9650364-0-5*) Busn Educ Pub.

Belden, Kim, jt. auth. see Noble, Kathleen N.

Belden, L. Burr. Goodbye, Death Valley. (Illus.). 64p. 1956. 5.95 (*0-936932-01-5*) Death Valley Fortyniners.

— Mines of Death Valley. 1996. pap. 4.50 (*0-87505-410-2*) Borden.

Belden, L. Burr, et al. Death Valley to Yosemite: Frontier Mining Camps & Ghost Towns: The Men, the Women, Their Mines & Stories LC 98-37278. 192p. 1998. write for info. (*0-9647530-8-1*) Spotted Dog CA.

Belden, Louise C. Marks of American Silversmiths in the Ineson-Bissell Collection. LC 78-31816. 518p. reprint ed. pap. 160.60 (*0-7837-1766-0*, 204190900001) Bks Demand.

Belden, Stella, ed. see Belden, Kenneth.

Belden, Thomas G., jt. auth. see Cavitch, Zolman.

Belden, Wilanne S. Frankie! LC 86-33507. (Illus.). 163p. (J). (gr. 3-7). 1987. 14.95 (*0-15-229380-9*) Harcourt.

— Mind-Find. LC 87-11979. 191p. (YA). (gr. 7 up). 1988. 14.95 (*0-15-254270-1*) Harcourt.

— Mind-Hold. LC 86-19370. 256p. 1987. 14.95 (*0-15-254280-9*) Harcourt.

Belderbos, Rene A. Japanese Electronics Multinationals & Strategic Trade Policies. LC 96-50048. (Illus.). 418p. 1998. text 55.00 (*0-19-823332-9*) OUP.

***Belderok, B., et al.** Bread-Making Quality of Wheat: A Century of Breeding in Europe. LC 00-33080. 2000. write for info. (*0-7923-6383-3*) Kluwer Academic.

Beldi, Lino G. The Fisher of Children. LC 90-72074. 80p. (Orig.). 1991. pap. 10.00 (*0-910147-95-7*) World Poetry Pr.

Belding, Carol A. Life Prints. 10p. 1996. pap. 1.98 (*1-888923-01-6*) Poetic License.

Belding, David & Mitchell, Kevin. Foundations of Analysis. 448p. (C). 1991. text 47.20 (*0-13-326679-6*, 540103) P-H.

Belding, Patricia W. Through Hell & High Water in Barre, Vermont: 25 Eyewitness Accounts of the Flood of '27. LC 98-92174. (Illus.). 130p. 1998. pap. 12.95 (*0-9650699-1-5*) Potash Brook.

— Where the Books Are: History & Architecture of Vermont's Public Libraries with Photos & Anecdotes. LC 95-92807. (Illus.). 184p. 1996. pap. 22.50 (*0-9650699-0-7*) Potash Brook.

***Belding, Shaun.** Dealing with the Customer from Hell: A Survival Guide. 192p. 2000. pap. 13.95 (*0-7737-6103-9*) Stoddart Publ.

Belding, W. G., ed. ASM Handbook of Engineering Mathematics. 697p. 1983. 142.00 (*0-87170-157-X*, 6113) ASM.

Belding, William G. & Widness, Roger W. America's Productivity Slump: Are We Working Hard Enough? (Illus.). 216p. (Orig.). 1989. pap. 11.95 (*0-685-29366-1*) PTV Pubns.

Beldiushkin, V. Adverbial Relations in Russian & Their English Equivalents. 240p. (C). 1988. 50.00 (*0-7855-4229-9*, Pub. by Collets) St Mut.

Beldock, John. Little Book of Love. 1994. pap. 5.95 (*1-85230-471-5*, Pub. by Element MA) Penguin Putnam.

Belefant, Arthur. Facilities Engineering Design. 100p. (C). 1994. pap. text 20.00 (*0-9629555-9-0*, Iban Bks) Benjamin Ross & Lane.

— Frankenstein, the Man & the Monster. 125p. (Orig.). (C). 1996. pap. text 19.95 (*0-9629555-8-2*, Iban Bks) Benjamin Ross & Lane.

Belegundu, Ashok D. & Mistree, Farrokh, eds. Optimization in Industry, 1997: Proceedings. LC 98-760034. 283p. 1998. pap. 90.00 (*0-7918-1248-0*) ASME Pr.

Belegundu, Ashok D., jt. auth. see Chandrupatla, Tirupathi R.

Belekhova. Fotex Manual on Business Accounting: Russian-English with English Russian Dictionary for Stock Purchase Agreements. (ENG & RUS.). 576p. 1992. pap. 39.95 (*0-7859-1080-8*, 5900134016) Fr & Eur.

Belen, M., et al. The Archaeology of Early Roman Baetica. Keay, Simon, ed. (Journal of Roman Archaeology Supplementary Ser.: No. 29). (Illus.). 246p. 1998. 79.50 (*1-887829-29-6*) Jour Roman Arch.

Belenger, Claire, jt. ed. see Ghorayshi, Parvin.

Belenkii, B. G., et al, eds. Capillary Liquid Chromatography. (Macromolecular Compounds Ser.). (Illus.). 262p. (C). 1987. text 114.00 (*0-306-10994-8*, Kluwer Plenum) Kluwer Academic.

Belenko, Steven R. Crack & the Evolution of Anti-Drug Policy, 42. LC 93-9312. (Contributions in Criminology & Penology Ser.: No. 42). 216p. 1993. 59.95 (*0-313-28030-4*, BKE, Greenwood Pr) Greenwood.

— Drugs & Drug Policy In America: A Documentary History. LC 99-32530. 416p. 2000. 49.95 (*0-313-29902-1*) Greenwood.

Belenky, Alexander S. Operations Research in Transportation Systems: Ideas & Schemes of Optimization Methods for Strategic Planning & Operations Management. LC 98-26529. (Applied Optimization Ser.). 1998. 195.00 (*0-7923-5157-6*) Kluwer Academic.

Belenky, Gregory, ed. Contemporary Studies in Combat Psychiatry, 62. LC 86-33660. (Contributions in Military Studies Ser.: No. 62). 291p. 1987. 62.95 (*0-313-25513-X*, BYT/, Greenwood Pr) Greenwood.

Belenky, Mary F., ed. WOMENS WAYS OF KNOWING 10TH ANIV. 10th anniversary ed. LC 97-145594. 272p. 1996. pap. 17.50 (*0-465-09099-0*) HarpC.

Belenky, Mary F., et al. A Tradition That Has No Name: Women's Ways of Leading. 384p. 1999. pap. 20.00 (*0-465-08681-0*, Pub. by Basic) HarpC.

***Belentschikow, Renate.** Neue Wege der Slavistischen Wortbildungsforschung: Tagung der Internationalen Kommission fur Slavische Wortbildung, Magdeburg, 9-11, 10, 97. (GER., Illus.). 358p. 1999. 57.00 (*3-631-34528-3*) P Lang Pubng.

Belentschikow, Renate & Ibler, Reinhard, eds. Forschungen Zur Linguistik und Poetik: Zum Andenken an Grigorij O. Vinokur (1896-1947) (Vergleichende Studien Zu den Slavischen Sprachen und Literaturen: Vol. 1). (Illus.). 264p. 1997. pap. 48.95 (*3-631-32277-1*) P Lang Pubng.

Belentschikow, Renate, ed. see Belentschikow, Valentin.

Belentschikow, Valentin. Die Russische Expressionistische Lyrik, 1919-1922. (GER., Illus.). 407p. 1996. 63.95 (*3-631-30160-X*) P Lang Pubng.

— Zur Poetik Boris Pasternaks: Der Berliner Gedichtzyklus, 1922-1923. Belentschikow, Renate & Ibler, Reinhard, eds. (Vergleichende Studien zu den Slavischen Sprachen und Literaturen: Vol. 2). 157p. 1997. pap. 31.95 (*3-631-32274-7*) P Lang Pubng.

Beletic, James W. & D'Amico, Paolo, eds. Optical Detectors for Astronomy: October 8-10, 1996, Garching, Germany. LC 97-49807. (Astrophysics & Space Science Library). 228p. 1998. 72.00 (*0-7923-4925-3*) Kluwer Academic.

Beletich, A. S. & Hall, D. P. Design Handbook for Reinforced Concrete Elements. 512p. 1998. reprint ed. 49.95 (*0-908237-76-6*, Pub. by New South Wales Univ Pr) Intl Spec Bk.

Beletsky, Les. Belize & Northern Guatemala: The Ecotravellers' Wildlife Guide. LC 99-178258. (AP Natural World Ser.). (Illus.). 400p. (C). 1998. pap. 27.95 (*0-12-084811-2*) Acad Pr.

— Costa Rica: The Ecotravellers' Wildlife Guide. LC 97-45871. (Illus.). xii, 426p. 1998. pap. 27.95 (*0-12-084810-4*) Acad Pr.

— Tropical Mexico: The Ecotravellers' Wildlife Guide. (Ecotravellers' Wildlife Guides Ser.). (Illus.). 512p. (C). 1999. 27.95 (*0-12-084812-0*) Acad Pr.

Beletsky, Les D. Ecuador-The Galapagos Islands. (Ecotravellers' Wildlife Guides Ser.). 350p. 1999. 27.95 (*0-12-084814-7*) Acad Pr.

— Hawaii. (Ecotravellers' Wildlife Guides Ser.). 350p. 1999. pap. 27.95 (*0-12-084813-9*) Acad Pr.

— The Red-Winged Blackbird: The Biology of a Strongly Polygynous Songbird. (Illus.). 352p. 1996. text 64.95 (*0-12-084745-0*) Acad Pr.

Beletsky, Les D. & Orians, Gordon H. Red-Winged Blackbirds: Decision-Making & Reproductive Success. LC 96-18894. (Illus.). 288p. 1996. pap. text 21.95 (*0-226-04187-5*); lib. bdg. 65.00 (*0-226-04186-7*) U Ch Pr.

Beletsky, Vladimir V. & Levin, Evgenii M. Dynamics of Space Tether Systems (English Language Edition) LC 57-43761. (Advances in the Astronautical Sciences Ser.: Vol. 83). (Illus.). 508p. 1993. 120.00 (*0-87703-370-6*, Am Astronaut Soc); pap. 90.00 (*0-87703-371-4*, Am Astronaut Soc) Univelt Inc.

Belev, George C. Minimizing Risk. 156p. (Orig.). 1995. pap. 37.45 (*0-940343-68-1*, MRIS) Natl Contract Mgmt.

Belev, Georgi, jt. ed. see Sapinkopf, Lisa.

Belevan, Harry. The Heirs of Ariadne. LC 97-15106. (Cultural Ser.). 1997. write for info. (*0-8270-3642-6*) OAS.

Belew, Elizabeth. The Little Book of Happies. 128p. (Orig.). 1996. pap. 5.95 (*1-889116-03-3*) Penbrooke Pub.

Belew, Elizabeth, ed. The Enchantment of Gardening. 128p. 1998. pap. 5.95 (*1-889116-11-4*) Penbrooke Pub.

— Everlasting Friendship: An Inspired Collection of Writings. LC 97-107130. 96p. (Orig.). 1996. boxed set 12.95 (*1-889116-04-1*) Penbrooke Pub.

— Letters to Mother: Expressions of Love from Famous People. LC 96-203667. (Illus.). 96p. 1996. boxed set 15.95 (*1-889116-00-9*) Penbrooke Pub.

— Love Letters to Remember: A Collection of Romance & Passion. LC 96-204759. (Illus.). 96p. 1996. boxed set 15.95 (*1-889116-02-5*) Penbrooke Pub.

— Sister of Mine: A Heartwarming Collection of Letters, Writings & Poetry. (Illus.). 96p. 1996. boxed set 13.95 (*1-889116-08-4*) Penbrooke Pub.

— A Tribute to Dad. 128p. 1997. pap. 5.95 (*1-889116-13-0*) Penbrooke Pub.

— A Tribute to Mom. 128p. 1997. pap. 5.95 (*1-889116-12-2*) Penbrooke Pub.

Belew, Julia E. The Everyday Low Fat Cooking Book. 64p. 1992. pap. text 3.95 (*0-9642867-0-X*) HomeBound Pr.

Belew, Linda, ed. see Smith, Patricia.

Belew, M. Wendell & Wahl, Dick. Ken Prickett: Man of Joy. (Meet the Missionary Ser.). 57p. (J). (gr. 4-6). 1996. pap. text 5.99 (*1-56309-148-8*, W947123) Womans Mission Union.

Belew, Richard. Adapting Individuals in Evolving Populations: Models & Algorithms. (C). 1996. pap. 42.00 (*0-201-48369-6*) Addison-Wesley.

***Belew, Richard K.** Finding Out About: Search Engine Technology from a Cognitive Perspective. LC 99-87329. (Illus.). 325p. (C). 2000. write for info. (*0-521-63028-2*) Cambridge U Pr.

Belew, Richard K., ed. Genetic Algorithms: Proceedings of the 4th International Conferences. 576p. (C). 1991. pap. text 49.95 (*1-55860-208-9*) Morgan Kaufmann.

Belew, Richard K. & Vose, Michael D., eds. Foundations of Genetic Algorithms. rev. ed. 475p. 1998. text 74.95 (*1-55860-460-X*, FOGA 4) Morgan Kaufmann.

Beley, Jim, ed. Basic Masonry Techniques. LC 85-60003. (Illus.). 1985. 9.95 (*0-89721-045-X*, Ortho Bks) Meredith Bks.

Beley, Jim, ed. see Galle, Fred C., et al.

Beley, Jim, ed. see Williams, T. Jeff.

Beleznay, F., jt. ed. see Ferenczi, G.

Belf, Teri-E & Ward, Charlotte. Simply Live It Up: Brief Solutions. 2nd rev. ed. LC 96-72247. (Illus.). 224p. 1997. mass mkt. 16.95 (*0-9646842-1-7*) Purposeful Pr.

***Belfer, Lauren.** City of Light. 518p. 1999. pap. 24.95 (*0-385-22401-X*) Delacorte.

— City of Light. LC 98-52917. 518p. 1999. 24.95 (*0-385-33401-X*, Dial Pr) Dell.

— City of Light. 39p. 2000. mass mkt. 6.99 (*0-440-23512-X*) Dell.

Belfer, Lauren. City of Light. large type ed. LC 99-25617. (Basic Ser.). 1999. pap. 28.95 (*0-7862-1991-2*) Mac Lib Ref.

Belfer, Nancy. Batik & Tie Dye Techniques. rev. ed. Orig. Title: Designing in Batik & Tie Dye. (Illus.). 160p. 1992. reprint ed. pap. 8.95 (*0-486-27131-5*) Dover.

Belfi, V. A., jt. auth. see Doran, R. S.

Belfield, ed. see Everest Staff.

Belfield, E. M., jt. auth. see Parham, H. J.

Belfield, Eversley. The Boer War. (Concise Campaigns Ser.). (Illus.). 181p. 1993. reprint ed. 34.50 (*0-85052-369-9*, Pub. by Leo Cooper) Trans-Atl Phila.

Belfield, Wendell O. & Zucker, Martin. How to Have a Healthier Dog: The Benefits of Vitamins & Minerals for Your Dog's Life Cycles. rev. ed. pap. 11.95 (*0-9629947-1-5*) Orthomolecular.

— The Very Healthy Cat Book. 247p. 1983. write for info. (*0-9629947-0-7*) Orthomolecular.

Belfiglio, Ellie K. The Rain Stops in Texas: One Woman's Struggle from Oppression to Freedom. LC 97-14519. (Illus.). 200p. 1997. pap. 16.95 (*1-57168-191-4*, Eakin Pr) Sunbelt Media.

Belfiglio, Jeff. Washington Environmental Regulations & Liability. 450p. 1994. ring bd. 90.00 (*1-56257-193-1*, MICHIE) LEXIS Pub.

Belfiglio, Jeff, et al. Hazardous Waste Disposal Sites: A Handbook for Public Input & Review. LC 82-121857. x, 200p. 1982. 12.00 (*0-685-06772-6*) Stanford Enviro.

Belfiglio, Val. Pride of the Southwest: Outstanding Athletes of the Southwest Conference. (Illus.). 144p. (J). (gr. 6-7). 1992. 14.95 (*0-89015-822-3*) Sunbelt Media.

Belfiglio, Valentine J. Honor, Pride, Duty: History of the Texas State Guard. LC 95-5808. 1995. 18.95 (*1-57168-030-6*) Sunbelt Media.

— The Italian Experience in Texas: A Closer Look. (Illus.). 192p. 1997. 19.95 (*0-89015-969-6*, Eakin Pr) Sunbelt Media.

Belfiore, Elizabeth. Tragic Pleasures: Aristotle on Plot & Emotion. 408p. 1992. text 57.50 (*0-691-06899-2*, Pub. by Princeton U Pr) Cal Prin Full Svc.

Belfiore, F. Current Diabetology. (Frontiers in Diabetes Ser.: Vol. 6). viii, 284p. 1985. 154.00 (*3-8055-4029-9*) S Karger.

— Enzyme Regulation & Metabolic Diseases. (Illus.). xxiv, 880p. 1981. 216.75 (*3-8055-0005-X*) S Karger.

— New Events & Facts in Diabetes. (Frontiers in Diabetes Ser.: Vol. 2). (Illus.). x, 190p. 1982. 99.25 (*3-8055-3541-4*) S Karger.

— Reviewed Contents of Major Diabetes Congresses. (Frontiers in Diabetes Ser.: Vol. 1). xii, 162p. 1981. 77.50 (*3-8055-3414-0*) S Karger.

Belfiore, F., et al, eds. Current Topics in Diabetes Research. (Frontiers in Diabetes Ser.: Vol. 12). (Illus.). x, 236p. 1993. 259.25 (*3-8055-5779-5*) S Karger.

— Diabetes Mellitus: Etiopathogenesis & Metabolic Aspects. (Frontiers in Diabetes Ser.: Vol. 4). (Illus.). x, 282p. 1984. 184.50 (*3-8055-3771-9*) S Karger.

— Endothelial Cell Function in Diabetic Microangiopathy: Problems in Methodology & Clinical Aspects. (Frontiers in Diabetes Ser.: Vol. 9). (Illus.). 212p. 1990. pap. 168.75 (*3-8055-5052-9*) S Karger.

— Obesity: Basic Concepts & Clinical Aspects. (Frontiers in Diabetes Ser.: Vol. 11). (Illus.). viii, 220p. 1991. 214.00 (*3-8055-5405-2*) S Karger.

— Vascular & Neurologic Complications of Diabetes Mellitus. (Frontiers in Diabetes Ser.: Vol. 8). (Illus.). xii, 256p. 1987. 172.25 (*3-8055-4452-9*) S Karger.

Belfiore, F. & Gregorio, S., eds. Tissue-Specific Metabolic Alterations in Diabetes. (Frontiers in Diabetes Ser.: Vol. 10). viii, 192p. 1990. 168.00 (*3-8055-5171-1*) S Karger.

Belfiore, F. & Iannello, Silvia. Advances in World Diabetes Research. (Frontiers in Diabetes Ser.: Vol. 5). x, 258p. 1984. 143.50 (*3-8055-3810-3*) S Karger.

***Belfiore, F. & Mogensen, C. E., eds.** New Concepts in Diabetes & Its Treatment. (Illus.). 2000. 172.25 (*3-8055-6907-6*) S Karger.

Belfiore, F. & Rabuazzo, Agata M. Latest Achievements of Diabetes Research. (Frontiers in Diabetes Ser.: Vol. 7). x, 298p. 1986. 276.25 (*3-8055-4261-5*) S Karger.

Belfiore, Francesco, et al, eds. Molecular & Cell Biology of Type 2 Diabetes & Its Complications: 5th International Diabetes Conference, Turin, April 10 - 12, 1997. LC 98-10210. (Frontiers in Diabetes Ser.: Vol. 14). (Illus.). x, 260p. 1998. 97.50 (*3-8055-6644-1*) S Karger.

Belfiore, Phillip J. Recognizing Community Choices by Individuals with Profound Disabilities: An Assessment. LC 93-48120. (Innovations Ser.: No. 1). 1994. 21.95 (*0-940898-33-0*) Am Assn Mental.

Belfon, Vastiana. The Amistad International Dictionary of Black Quotations. 480p. 1994. 34.95 (*1-56743-066-X*, Amistad) HarperTrade.

***Belford, Barbara.** Oscar Wilde: A Certain Genius. (Illus.). 416p. 2000. 29.95 (*0-679-45734-8*) Random.

Belford, Fontaine M. Uses of the Heart. Campbell, Judith & Ochs, Carol, eds. (Illus.). 168p. 1998. pap. write for info. (*1-891180-52-5*) Campbell & Lockwood.

Belford, James N. & Dunlop, Jack. The Mauser Self-Loading Pistol. (Illus.). 208p. 1969. 29.95 (*0-87505-108-1*) Pioneer Pr.

Belford, Kathi. The Purple Turtles Mystery: The Legend of Lost Boy. LC 97-169128. (Illus.). 90p. (J). (ps-5). 1996. 14.95 (*0-9646803-2-7*) Plant Speak Prods.

— The Traveling Basket: or Mrs. Carey's Christmas Call. LC 95-68984. (Illus.). 160p. 1995. 19.95 (*0-9646803-6-X*) Plant Speak Prods.

Belford, Ros & Palmer, Rodney. Rome. LC 92-53473. (Eyewitness Travel Guides Ser.). (Illus.). 432p. 1993. pap. 24.95 (*1-56458-186-1*) DK Pub Inc.

Belford, Ross, et al. Italy. (New Rough Guides Ser.). 1996. pap. 19.95 (*0-614-97917-X*, Penguin Bks) Viking Penguin.

Belford Ulanov, Ann. Religion & the Spiritual in Carl Jung: Essays on Jung & Religion. LC 99-41154. 288p. 2000. pap. 24.95 (*0-8091-3907-3*) Paulist Pr.

Belford, William. Parish Liturgy Basics. (Orig.). 1992. pap. text 9.95 (*0-912405-96-1*, Pastoral Press) OR Catholic.

Belford, William J. Special Ministers of the Eucharist. 64p. 1992. pap. 2.95 (*0-8146-6039-8*, Pueblo Bks) Liturgical Pr.

Belfort, Anne Marie, jt. auth. see Camard, Jean Pierre.

Belforte, David A., jt. ed. see Levitt, M.

Belfour, A. O., ed. Twelfth-Century Homilies in Ms. Bodley 343 Pt. I: Text. (EETS, OS Ser.: Vol. 137). 1974. reprint ed. pap. 36.00 (*0-8115-3369-7*) Periodicals Srv.

Belfour, Charles, jt. auth. see Haywood, Mary Ellen.

Belfrage, Bertil. George Berkeley's Manuscript: 1987 Edition. 159p. 1996. reprint ed. 58.00 (*1-85506-364-6*) Bks Intl VA.

Belfrage, Cedric, tr. see Galeano, Eduardo.

Belfrage, Cedric, tr. see Quintero Rivera, Angel.

Belfrage, Cedric, tr. see Selser, Gregorio.

Belfrage, Cedric, tr. see Silen, Juan A.

Belfrage, Nicolas. Barolo to Valpolicella: The Wines of Northern Italy. 368p. 1999. 35.00 (*0-571-17851-0*) Faber & Faber.

— Barolo to Valpolicella: The Wines of Northern Italy. (Illus.). 272p. 1999. pap. 18.00 (*0-571-17852-9*) Faber & Faber.

Belfrage, Sally. Freedom Summer. (Carter G. Woodson Institute Series in Black Studies). 246p. 1990. reprint ed. pap. 14.50 (*0-8139-1299-7*) U Pr of Va.

Belgacem, Fethi. Elliptic Boundary Value Problems with Indefinite Weights: Variational Formulations of the Principal Eigenvalue & Applications. 1997. lib. bdg. 59.95 (*0-582-31597-2*, Pub. by Addison-Wesley) Longman.

Belgardt, Raimund. Romantische Poesie. 1970. text 61.55 (*90-279-1248-3*) Mouton.

Belge, Robert. Arithmetic Made Simple. rev. ed. LC 87-24716. 176p. 1988. pap. 12.95 (*0-385-23938-6*) Doubleday.

Belgion, Montgomery. Human Parrot, & Other Essays. LC 67-22056. (Essay Index Reprint Ser.). 1977. 19.95 (*0-8369-0184-3*) Ayer.

Belgion, Montgomery, tr. see De Rougemont, Denis.

Belgrad, Daniel. Culture of Spontaneity. LC 97-29793. (Illus.). 343p. 1998. 29.00 (*0-226-04188-3*) U Ch Pr.

— Culture of Spontaneity: Improvisation & the Arts in Postwar America. 1999. pap. text 17.00 (*0-226-04190-5*) U Ch Pr.

Belgrad, Eric A. & Nachmias, Nitza, eds. The Politics of International Humanitarian Aid Operations. LC 96-44677. 240p. 1997. 62.95 (*0-275-95273-8*, Praeger Pubs) Greenwood.

Belgrano Action Group Staff, ed. The Unnecessary War: Proceedings of the Belgrano Enquiry, November 1986. 184p. 1988. 42.50 (*0-85124-455-6*, Pub. by Spkesman) Coronet Bks.

Belgrano, Giovanni. Let's Make a Movie. LC 72-90235. (Illus.). 48p. (J). (gr. 4-9). 1973. 12.95 (*0-87592-028-4*) Scroll Pr.

Belgrave, Anne. How to Make Felt: Create Hats, Bags, Rugs, Masks & Much More. 1996. pap. 17.95 (*0-85532-795-2*, Pub. by Srch Pr) A Schwartz & Co.

Belgrave, Charles. Personal Column. (Illus.). 248p. 1996. 45.00 (*0-86685-004-X*) Intl Bk Ctr.

Belgrave, Faye Z. Psychosocial Aspects of Chronic Illness & Disability among African Americans. LC 98-9635. 176p. 1998. 59.95 (*0-86569-242-4*, Auburn Hse) Greenwood.

***Belgrave, Laura.** In the Spirit of Murder. (Claudia Hershey Mysteries Ser.). 204p. 2000. 24.50 (*1-57072-108-4*); pap. 15.00 (*1-57072-124-6*, Silver Dagger) Overmountain Pr.

Belgrave, Robert & Cornell, Margaret. Energy Self-Sufficiency for the U. K. 200p. 1985. text 77.95 (*0-566-00992-7*, Pub. by Dartmth Pub) Ashgate Pub Co.

***Belgum, David.** A Clearer Vision: Lenten Mid-Week Sermons. 2000. pap. 6.95 (*0-7880-1537-0*) CSS OH.

Belgum, David. Cultural Diversity: Fabrics of Society. 1997. pap. 9.95 (*0-9657862-0-X*) Rose Sharon Pub.

***Belgum, David.** Excuse Me: I'm Just Passing By. 236p. 2000. pap. 9.95 (*0-7880-1617-2*, Fairway Pr) CSS OH.

Belgum, Erik. Artificial Intelligence: Opposing Viewpoints. LC 90-3519. (Great Mysteries Ser.). (Illus.). 96p. (J). (gr. 5-8). 1990. lib. bdg. 22.45 (*0-89908-085-5*) Greenhaven.

— Star Fiction. 1996. write for info. (*1-886214-01-8*) Detour Pr.

Belgum, Kirsten. Interior Meaning: Design of the Bourgeois Home in the Realist Novel. LC 91-713. (German Life & Civilization Ser.: Vol. 9). 237p. (C). 1992. text 46.95 (*0-8204-1627-4*) P Lang Pubng.

Belgum, Kirsten, contrib. by. Popularizing the Nation: Audience, Representation, & the Production of Identity in "Die Gartenlaube," 1853-1900. LC 97-29654. (Modern German Culture & Literature Ser.). (Illus.). xxxi, 237p. 1998. text 50.00 (*0-8032-1283-6*) U of Nebr Pr.

Belhassen, Eric, ed. Drought Tolerance in Higher Plants: Genetical, Physiological & Molecular Biological Analysis. LC 96-9021. 152p. (C). 1996. text 110.50 (*0-7923-4123-6*) Kluwer Academic.

Belhayes, Iris. Spirit Guides: We Are Not Alone. 200p. (Orig.). 1984. pap. 12.95 (*0-917086-80-5*) ACS Pubns.

Belhoste, B. Augustin-Louie Cauchy: A Biography. Toomer, G. J., ed. (Studies in the History of Mathematics & Physical Sciences: Vol. 16). (Illus.). 392p. 1991. 95.95 (*0-387-97220-X*) Spr-Verlag.

Beliaev, Ilia. Tausha: The Life & Teachings of a Russian Mystic. LC 99-87510. (Illus.). 176p. 2000. pap. text 14.95 (*1-58177-024-3*, Pub. by Barrytown Ltd) Consort Bk Sales.

Beliard, O. The Marquis de Sade. (FRE.). 317p. 1958. pap. 25.00 (*0-87556-953-6*) Saifer.

Beliavance-Johnson, Marsha. John Fitzgerald Kennedy in Massachusetts: A Guide. (Famous Footsteps Ser.). (Illus.). 48p. 1996. pap. 4.95 (*0-929709-11-X*) Computer Lab.

***Beliavsky, Alexander.** Two Knight's Defence: Tournament. (Chess Bks.). (Illus.). 176p. 1999. pap. text 16.95 (*0-7134-8441-1*) B T B.

Beliavsky, Alexander. Winning Endgame Technique. 1995. pap. 21.00 (*0-8050-3905-8*, Pub. by Batsford Chess) H Holt & Co.

Belic, Cintr J. Slovnik Spisovneho Jazyka Ceskeho, 8 vols. 1989. 196.00 (*0-614-25058-7*) Szwede Slavic.

Belic, D., jt. ed. see Puric, J.

Belich, James. I Shall Not Die: Titokowaru's War, New Zeland 1868-9. LC 89-208945. 1996. pap. 24.95 (*0-04-614022-0*) Routledge.

— Making Peoples: A History of the New Zealanders: From Polynesian Settlement to the End of the Nineteenth Century. 484p. 1996. text 34.00 (0-8248-1890-3) UH Pr.
— The Victorian Interpretation of Racial Conflict: The Maori, the British, & the New Zealand Wars. (McGill-Queen's Studies in Ethnic History). 400p. (C). 1989. pap. text 24.95 (0-7735-0739-6, Pub. by McG-Queens Univ Pr) CUP Services.
— The Victorian Interpretation of Racial Conflict: The Maori, the British & the New Zealand Wars. (McGill-Queen's Studies in Ethnic History). 400p. (C). 1989. text 60.00 (0-7735-0750-7, Pub. by McG-Queens Univ Pr) CUP Services.
Belichko, Iu. V. & Pidgora, V. O. Through the Centuries. 336p. 1982. 155.00 (0-7855-1677-8) St Mut.
Beliele, Kelvin. If the Shoe Fits. (Orig.). 1994. mass mkt. 4.95 (1-56333-223-X, Badboy) Masquerade.
Belier, Wouter W. Decayed Gods: Origin & Development of Georges Dumezil's 'Ideologie Tripartie' LC 91-18815. (Religions in the Graeco-Roman World Ser.: No. 7). (Illus.). xv, 254p. 1991. 89.50 (90-04-09487-3) Brill Academic Pubs.
Belieu, Erin. Infanta. LC 95-14192. (National Poetry Ser.). 150p. (Orig.). 1995. pap. 12.00 (1-55659-101-2) Copper Canyon.
***Belieu, Erin.** One Above & One Below: New Poems. 85p. 2000. pap. 14.00 (1-55659-144-6) Copper Canyon.
Belikoff, Kathleen. Opportunities in Eye Care Careers. LC 97-39478. (Opportunities in...Ser.). (Illus.). 160p. 1998. 14.95 (0-8442-2302-6, 23026, VGM Career); pap. 11.95 (0-8442-2303-4, 23034, VGM Career) NTC Contemp Pub Co.
Belikove, Ruth K. The Rugs of Teec Nos Pos: Jewels of the Navajo Loom. LC 94-7094. (Illus.). 48p. (Orig.). (C). 1994. pap. 22.50 (0-9633710-1-0) Adobe Gallery.
Belile, Elisabeth A. Polishing the Bayonet. LC 97-130533. 150p. (Orig.). 1994. pap. 12.00 (1-884615-05-8) Incommcdo San Diego.
***Beliles, David B.** Theoretically-Informed Criticism of Donne's Love Poetry: Towards a Pluralist Hermeneutics of Faith. LC 98-30523. (Studies in Literary Criticism & Theory: Vol. 12). 147p. (C). 1999. text 43.00 (0-8204-4277-1) P Lang Pubng.
Beliles, Mark, jt. auth. see McDowell, Stephen.
Beliles, Mark A., ed. Thomas Jefferson's Abridgement of the Words of Jesus of Nazareth. 80p. 1993. pap. 5.95 (1-887456-04-X) Providence Found.
Beliles, Mark A. & McDowell, Stephen K. America's Providential History. 300p. 1989. pap. 15.95 (1-887456-00-7) Providence Found.
Beliles, Mark A., jt. auth. see McDowell, Stephen K.
Belin, David W. Leaving Money Wisely: A Guide for Middle- & Upper-Income Americans for the 1990s. 320p. 1991. 21.00 (0-684-19227-6, Scribners Ref) Mac Lib Ref.
— Leaving Money Wisely: Creative Estate Planning for Middle- & Upper- Income Americans for the 1990s. 320p. 1993. reprint ed. pap. 12.00 (0-02-008092-1) Macmillan.
Belin, Esther C. From the Belly of My Beauty. LC 99-6335. 104p. 1999. pap. 14.95 (0-8165-1954-4) U of Ariz Pr.
***Belin-Ferre, Esther, et al, eds.** Quasicrystals. 600p. 2000. 118.00 (981-02-4281-6) World Scientific Pub.
Belin, J. C. & Ball, Braden L. The Edward Ball We Knew: An Untold Story of the Man Who Really Discovered Florida. LC 98-60891. (Illus.). 288p. 1998. 24.95 (0-9659142-1-6) U of West Fla.
Belin, Jean-Paul. Le Mouvement Philosophique de 1748 a 1789. 381p. 1973. reprint ed. 80.00 (3-487-04822-1) G Olms Pubs.
Belin, Mel. Flesh That Was Chrysalis. LC 98-60612. (Capital Collection). 72p. 1999. pap. 10.00 (0-915380-40-4) Word Works.
Belin, Susan S., ed. & intro. see Peck, Rasamond.
Belina, T. Flight to Fear. pap. 16.25 (0-8224-5252-9) Fearon Teacher Aids.
Belinda, Coote. NAFTA: Poverty & Free Trade in Mexico:, Oxfam Insight. (Oxfam Insight Ser.). 64p. (C). 1995. pap. 7.50 (0-85598-302-7, Pub. by Oxfam Pub) Stylus Pub VA.
Belindo, John. An Historical Chronology of the Kiowa Tribe. (Treaty Manuscripts Ser.: No. 22). 12p. 5.50 (0-317-57454-X) Inst Dev Indian Law.
Belinfante, F. J. Measurements of Time Reversal in Objective Quantum Theory. 1975. 62.00 (0-08-018152-X, Pub. by Pergamon Repr) Franklin.
— Survey of Hidden Variables Theories. 376p. (C). 1973. text 166.00 (0-08-017032-3, Pub. by Pergamon Repr) Franklin.
Belinfante, J. G. & Kolman, Bernard. A Survey of Lie Groups & Lie Algebras with Applications & Computational Methods. LC 89-19699. (Classics in Applied Mathematics Ser.: No. 02). xi, 164p. 1989. pap. 35.50 (0-89871-243-2, CL02) Soc Indus-Appl Math.
***Beling, Stephanie.** Power Foods: Good Food, Good Health with Phytochemicals, Nature's Own Energy Boosters. 372p. 2000. text 25.00 (0-7881-9021-0) DIANE Pub.
Beling, Stephanie. PowerFoods: Good Food, Good Health with Phytochemicals, Nature's Own Energy Boosters. 384p. 1998. pap. 15.00 (0-06-092954-5, Perennial) HarperTrade.
Beling, Willard A., ed. Middle East Peace Plans. (WVSS on the Middle East Ser.). (C). 1996. pap. text 22.50 (0-8133-7125-2) Westview.
Beling, Willard A., ed. The Middle East: Quest for an American Policy. LC 73-4281. (Illus.). 347p. (C). 1976. text 24.50 (0-87395-228-6) State U NY Pr.
Belinorlec, jt. auth. see Pendleton-Lee, Shaun.
Belinski, Steve E., et al, eds. Vacuum Mechatronics, First International Workshop. LC 89-45905. (AIP Conference Proceedings Ser.: No. 192). 192p. 1990. lib. bdg. 70.00 (0-88318-394-3) Am Inst Physics.
Belinski, Steve E., et al. Vacuum Mechatronics. (Materials Library). 388p. 1990. text 20.00 (0-89006-456-3) Artech Hse.
Belinson, Jerome L., jt. ed. see Markman, Maurie.
Beliroglu, Haluk & Becker, Kip. Publishing Guide for Engineering Sciences. (Topics in Operations Research Ser.). xxv, 506p. 1986. pap. 10.00 (1-877640-13-1) INFORMS.
Belis, Cynthia. Learning Works 4 for Windows 95. 1996. 27.00 (1-56243-298-2, Z-8) DDC Pub.
Belis, Cynthia, jt. auth. see Dembo, Shirley.
Belisle, Augustin. Into the Heart of God: Spiritual Reflections. LC 88-24016. 79p. (Orig.). 1989. pap. 8.95 (0-932506-58-5) St Bedes Pubns.
— The Wheel of Becoming: Personal Growth Through the Liturgical Year. LC 87-26493. 87p. (Orig.). 1987. pap. 9.95 (0-932506-57-7) St Bedes Pubns.
Belisle, Lisette. Just Jessie. 1997. per. 3.99 (0-373-24134-8, 1-24134-8) Silhouette.
Belisle, Louis-Alexandre. North American Dictionary of the French Language. (FRE.). 1979. 125.00 (0-8288-7286-4, M8528) Fr & Eur.
Belisle, Lyn. Coloring the Folk Art of Mexico. (Illus.). 40p. (J). (gr. k-4). 1987. pap. 5.95 (0-931722-62-4) Corona Pub.
Belisle, Peter-Damian, tr. see Vigilucci, Lino.
Belita, Christopher, ed. see Ludlum, James S.
Belitskii, G. R. & Lyubich, Y. I. Matrix Norms & Their Applications. (Operator Theory Ser.: No. 36). 216p. 1988. 156.00 (0-8176-2220-9) Birkhauser.
Belitskus, David. Fiber & Whisker Reinforced Ceramics for Structural Applications. (Materials Engineering Ser.: Vol. 4). (Illus.). 360p. 1993. text 175.00 (0-8247-9111-8) Dekker.
Belitsos, Byron, jt. auth. see Harris, Fred.
Belitt, Ben. The Enemy Joy: New & Selected Poems. LC 64-15805. 1965. pap. 1.95 (0-226-04192-1, PP2) U Ch Pr.
— The Forged Feature: Towards a Poetics of Uncertainty, New & Selected Essays. xii, 279p. 1994. 30.00 (0-8232-1603-9); pap. 17.95 (0-8232-1604-7) Fordham.
— Literature & Belief: Three Spiritual Exercises. (Chapbooks in Literature Ser.). (Illus.). 29p. (Orig.). 1985. pap. text 5.00 (1-878603-02-7) Bennington Coll.
— Possessions: New & Selected Poems 1938-1985. LC 85-45969. 160p. 1986. 20.00 (0-87923-626-4) Godine.
— Possessions: New & Selected Poems 1938-1985. LC 85-45969. 160p. 1986. pap. 12.95 (0-87923-633-7) Godine.
— This Scribe My Hand: Complete Poems. LC 98-42512. 226p. 1998. pap. 19.95 (0-8071-2324-2); text 26.95 (0-8071-2323-4) La State U Pr.
Belitt, Ben, ed. & tr. see Neruda, Pablo.
Belitt, Ben, tr. see Rimbaud, Jean N.
Belitz, Charlene & Lundstrom, Meg. The Power of Flow: Practical Ways to Transform Your Life with Meaningful Coincidence. LC 98-25300. 304p. 1998. pap. 12.00 (0-609-80197-X) Crown Pub Group.
— The Power of Flow: Practical Ways to Transform Your Life with Meaningful Coincidence. LC 97-183204. 276p. 1997. 22.00 (0-517-70558-3) Random.
Belitz, H. D. & Grosch, W. Food Chemistry. (Illus.). xxxviii, 769p. 1987. 139.95 (0-387-15043-9) Spr-Verlag.
— Food Chemistry. (Illus.). xxxvii, 774p. 1992. 47.95 (0-387-97373-7) Spr-Verlag.
— Food Chemistry. 2nd ed. Burghagen, M. M., tr. from GER. LC 99-10777. (Illus.). 800p. 1999. 139.00 (3-540-64704-X); pap. 59.95 (3-540-64692-2) Spr-Verlag.
***Beliveau, Beverly Hicks.** Grace. LC 00-90445. 2000. 8.95 (0-533-13512-5) Vantage.
***Beliveau, Caroline.** San Diego. (Illus.). 2001. pap. 12.95 (2-89464-389-6) Ulysses Travel.
Beliveau, Jean. Jean Beliveau: My Life In Hockey. (Illus.). 336p. 1995. text 21.95 (0-7710-1107-5) McCland & Stewart.
Beliveau, Jean, et al. Jean Beliveau: My Life in Hockey. (Illus.). 336p. 1996. pap. 19.99 (0-7710-1108-3) McCland & Stewart.
Beljame, Alexandre. Men of Letters & the English Public in the 18th Century, 1660-1744. 1988. reprint ed. lib. bdg. 69.00 (0-7812-0367-8) Rprt Serv.
— Men of Letters & the English Public in the 18th Century, 1660-1744: Dryden, Addison, Pope. Dobree, Bonamy, ed. Lormier, E. O., tr. LC 71-159815. 1971. reprint ed. 89.00 (0-403-03645-3) Scholarly.
Beljanski, M. The Regulation of DNA Replication & Transcription. (Experimental Biology & Medicine Ser.: Vol. 8). (Illus.). x, 190p. 1983. pap. 108.00 (3-8055-3631-3) S Karger.
Belk, Bradford, jt. auth. see Gangelhoff, Jeanne M.
Belk, C. Seejoy. Myart. 1998. pap. text 11.95 (0-9620258-8-7, 26A) Babe Pub.
Belk, Clothilde. Conscious Directional Recipes for the 90s. (Illus.). 50p. (Orig.). (YA). 1990. pap. text 8.95 (0-9620258-3-6) Babe Pub.
— Polish & Publish. Nee, Kathie, ed. (Illus.). 70p. (Orig.). 1995. pap. text 6.95 (0-9620258-7-9) Babe Pub.
— Write, Wright, Right. Nee, Kathie, ed. LC 95-94494. (Illus.). 70p. (Orig.). pap. text 6.95 (0-9620258-6-0) Babe Pub.
— You Are a Star. (Illus.). (Orig.). (C). 1991. pap. 6.95 (0-9620258-0-1) Babe Pub.
Belk, D., et al, eds. Studies on Large Branchiopod Biology & Aquaculture. (Developments in Hydrobiology Ser.). 320p. 1991. text 267.50 (0-7923-1169-8) Kluwer Academic.
— Studies on Large Branchiopod Biology & Aquaculture II. LC 94-43529. (Developments in Hydrobiology Ser.: Vol. 103). 1995. text 257.50 (0-7923-3292-X) Kluwer Academic.
Belk, Denton, jt. auth. see Eriksen, Clyde.
***Belk, G. W.** Floreen: The Story of Mitchell. 19p. 1999. pap. 4.95 (1-57072-095-9, Silver Dagger) Overmountain Pr.
Belk, Gordon G., ed. see Schmid-Belk, Donna D.
Belk, Jon & Jainchill, Michael C. Supplement to Connecticut Law of Uninsured & Underinsured Motorist Coverage 1994. 84p. 1994. pap. 50.00 (1-878698-27-3) Atlantic Law.
Belk, Russel, ed. Highways & Byways: Proceedings of the 1991 Conference. 238p. 1991. 19.00 (0-915552-29-9) Assn Consumer Res.
Belk, Russell, jt. ed. see Groves, Ron.
Belk, Russell W. Collecting in a Consumer Society. LC 94-39979. 224p. (C). (gr. 13). 1995. 75.00 (0-415-10534-X, C0484) Routledge.
Belk, Russell W., et al, eds. AMA Winter Educators' Conference, 1987: Marketing Theory. LC 87-944. (Illus.). 419p. 1987. reprint ed. pap. 129.90 (0-7837-9762-1, 206049000005) Bks Demand.
Belk, Russell W., et al, eds. Consumption & Marketing: Macro Dimensions. LC 95-13608. 1995. pap. 50.95 (0-538-85050-7) S-W Pub.
Belk, Russell W., jt. auth. see Gardner, David M.
Belk, Russell W., ed. see American Marketing Association Staff.
Belk, Sarah. Around the Southern Table: Innovative Recipes Celebrating 300 Years of Eating & Drinking. 528p. 1997. 12.99 (0-88365-972-7) Galahad Bks.
Belk, Tom. Wellhead Protection: A Guide for Small Communities. (Illus.). 144p. (Orig.). (C). 1994. pap. text 40.00 (0-7881-1470-0) DIANE Pub.
Belk, William E. & Beaty, Frank E. Art at Auction in America 1995-96. 525p. 1996. pap. 49.95 (0-9651184-0-1) Frontier Pubng.
— Art at Auction in America 1997. 350p. 1997. pap. 39.95 (0-9651184-1-X) Frontier Pubng.
Belka, David E. Teaching Children Games. (Becoming a Master Teacher Ser.). 144p. 1994. pap. text 31.95 incl. VHS (0-87322-701-8, AMTP0306) Human Kinetics.
— Teaching Children Games: Becoming a Master Teacher. LC 93-30702. (Illus.). 144p. 1994. pap. text 16.00 (0-87322-481-7, BBEL0481) Human Kinetics.
Belkacem, Charles, jt. auth. see Sedira, Ben.
***Belkadi, Jean Marc.** Advanced Scale Concepts & Licks for Guitar: Private Lessons. 48p. 1999. pap. 12.95 incl. audio compact disk (0-7935-9288-7) H Leonard.
Belkaoui. Accounting Theory. 3rd ed. 1998. pap. 32.95 (1-86152-420-X) Thomson Learn.
— International & Multinational Accounting. 1998. pap. 32.95 (1-86152-421-8) Thomson Learn.
Belkaoui, A. K. Conjugal Blues. 190p. (Orig.). 1998. mass mkt. 11.95 (1-57532-114-9) Press-Tige Pub.
— So You Want to Be Sophisticated. O'Donnell, Kelly, ed. (Illus.). 126p. 1997. mass mkt. 8.95 (1-57532-075-4) Press-Tige Pub.
Belkaoui, Ahmed R. Accounting Theory. 3rd ed. 106p. (C). 1993. student ed. 4.75 (0-03-097205-1) Dryden Pr.
— Baraka. 185p. (Orig.). 1997. pap. 11.95 (1-57532-084-3) Press-Tige Pub.
— Behavioral Accounting: The Research & Practical Issues. LC 88-32147. 190p. 1989. 59.95 (0-89930-341-2, BBV, Quorum Bks) Greenwood.
— The Coming Crisis in Accounting. LC 88-35741. 196p. 1989. 59.95 (0-89930-379-X, BKG/, Quorum Bks) Greenwood.
— Conceptual Foundations of Management Accounting. LC 80-16086. (A-W Paperback Series in Accounting). 125p. 1980. pap. write for info. (0-201-00097-0) Addison-Wesley.
— Handbook of Management Control Systems. LC 86-3262. (Illus.). 369p. 1986. 85.00 (0-89930-178-9, BHC/, Quorum Bks) Greenwood.
— Human Information Processing in Accounting. LC 88-32148. 310p. 1989. 72.95 (0-89930-378-1, BHN, Quorum Bks) Greenwood.
— Industrial Bonds & the Rating Process. LC 83-4600. (Illus.). 198p. 1983. 57.95 (0-89930-046-4, BEB/, Quorum Bks) Greenwood.
— Inquiry & Accounting: Alternate Methods & Research Perspectives. LC 87-2496. 451p. 1987. 85.00 (0-89930-222-X, BUI/, Quorum Bks) Greenwood.
— International Accounting: Issues & Solutions. LC 84-11514. (Illus.). 364p. 1985. 75.00 (0-89930-089-8, BLN/, Quorum Bks) Greenwood.
— Judgment in International Accounting: A Theory of Cognition, Cultures, Language, & Contracts. LC 89-10789. 140p. 1990. 49.95 (0-89930-471-0, BIH/, Greenwood Pr) Greenwood.
— The Learning Curve: A Management Accounting Tool. LC 85-9438. (Illus.). 258p. 1986. 72.95 (0-89930-132-0, BLV/, Quorum Bks) Greenwood.
— Multinational Financial Accounting. LC 91-8400. 240p. 1991. 72.95 (0-89930-614-4, BKM, Quorum Bks) Greenwood.
— Multinational Management Accounting. LC 90-8896. 304p. 1991. 77.50 (0-89930-529-6, BMJ/, Quorum Bks) Greenwood.
— The New Environment in International Accounting: Issues & Practices. LC 87-7252. 232p. 1988. 75.00 (0-89930-267-X, BDV/, Quorum Bks) Greenwood.
— Public Policy & the Practice & the Problems of Accounting. LC 85-3568. (Illus.). 204p. 1985. 62.95 (0-89930-105-3, BIF/, Quorum Bks) Greenwood.
— Quantitative Models in Accounting: A Procedural Guide for Professionals. LC 86-16993. 373p. 1987. 85.00 (0-89930-186-X, BQU/, Quorum Bks) Greenwood.
— Socio-Economic Accounting. LC 83-17682. (Illus.). 324p. 1984. 75.00 (0-89930-065-0, BSE, Quorum Bks) Greenwood.
— Value Added Reporting: Lessons for the U. S. LC 91-14827. 192p. 1992. 55.00 (0-89930-651-9, BVE, Quorum Bks) Greenwood.
Belkaoui, Ahmed R., jt. auth. see Belkaoui, Janice M.
Belkaoui, Ahmed R., jt. auth. see Pavlik, Ellen L.
Belkaoui, Janice M. & Belkaoui, Ahmed R. Accounting in the Dual Economy. LC 91-17. 176p. 1991. 59.95 (0-89930-615-2, BKB/, Quorum Bks) Greenwood.
Belke, Robert E. Arts & Crafts Woodworking Projects: 11 New Designs in the Stickley Tradition. LC 97-51530. (Illus.). 112p. 1998. 19.95 (0-8117-2662-2) Stackpole.
***Belke, Robert E.** Classic Country Furniture. (Illus.). 128p. 2000. pap. 19.99 (1-55870-544-9, Popular Woodwking Bks) F & W Pubns Inc.
***Belke, Thomas J.** Juche: A Christian Study of North Korea's State Religion. LC 99-30315. (Illus.). 416p. 1999. pap. 15.00 (0-88264-329-0) Living Sacrifice Bks.
Belker, Heiner, ed. see Kropotkin, Peter.
Belker, Loren. Seems Like Old Times: The Big Bands of the Midwest. (Illus.). 131p. (Orig.). 1992. pap. 16.95 (0-934904-30-8) J & L Lee.
Belker, Loren B. The First-Time Manager. 3rd ed. LC 92-33135. 208p. 1993. pap. 16.95 (0-8144-7802-6) AMACOM.
— The First-Time Manager. 4th ed. LC 96-39055. 224p. 1997. pap. 17.95 (0-8144-7940-5) AMACOM.
— The First-Time Manager: A Practical Guide to the Management of People. LC 85-48217. 204p. reprint ed. pap. 63.30 (0-7837-6470-7, 204647400001) Bks Demand.
— Organizing for Political Victory. LC 82-7855. 208p. (C). 1982. text 30.95 (0-88229-727-9) Burnham Inc.
— The Successful Secretary: You, Your Boss, & the Job. LC 81-66239. 224p. reprint ed. pap. 69.50 (0-608-12853-8, 202359000033) Bks Demand.
***Belkic, D. S.** Principles of Quantum Scattering Theory. 1999. 145.00 (0-7503-0496-0) IOP Pub.
Belkin, Aaron, jt. ed. see Tetlock, Philip E.
Belkin, David, jt. ed. see Roosevelt, Frank.
Belkin, Gary S. Introduction to Counseling. 3rd ed. 648p. (C). 1988. text. write for info. (0-697-06693-2) Brown & Benchmark.
Belkin, Gary S., jt. auth. see Faw, Terry.
Belkin, Gary S., jt. auth. see Wittig, Arno F.
Belkin, Gary S., jt. ed. see Morone, James A.
Belkin, Janet, et al. TOEIC - Test of English for International Communication. 768p. 1997. pap. 18.95 (0-87891-140-5); pap. 39.95 incl. audio (0-87891-796-9) Res & Educ.
Belkin, Kristin L. Rubens. LC 98-229704. (Illus.). 352p. 1998. pap. 19.95 (0-7148-3412-2, Pub. by Phaidon Press) Phaidon Pr.
Belkin, Lisa. First, Do No Harm. 1994. mass mkt. 5.99 (0-449-22290-X, Crest) Fawcett.
— Show Me a Hero: A Tale of Murder, Suicide, Race, & Redemption. LC 98-14281. 352p. (YA). (gr. 8). 1999. 25.00 (0-316-08805-6) Little.
***Belkin, Lisa.** Show Me a Hero: The Story of an Urban Tragedy - & of the Housing Revolution that is Changing America's Neighborhoods. 352p. 2000. pap. 14.95 (0-316-08864-1) Little.
Belkin, Michael, jt. ed. see Stuck, Bruce E.
Belkin, R. S. Concise Encyclopedia of Criminalistics. (Illus.). 111p. 1996. 74.95 (5-85270-088-6) Austin & Winfield.
Belkin, Samuel. The Midrash of Philo Vol. 1: The Oldest Recorded Midrash, Genesis II-XVII. Hurvitz, Elazar, ed. (HEB.). 1989. 49.50 (0-88125-149-6) Ktav.
Belkind, Allen. Dos Passos: The Critics & the Writer's Intention. LC 70-156782. (Crosscurrents-Modern Critiques Ser.). 352p. reprint ed. pap. 109.20 (0-608-15481-4, AU0034400062) Bks Demand.
Belkind, Allen J. Jean-Paul Sartre, Sartre Existentialism in English: A Bibliographical Guide. LC 76-95708. (Serif Ser.: No. 10). 254p. reprint ed. 78.80 (0-8357-9367-2, 201610700098) Bks Demand.
Belkindas, Misha V. Regional Economic Modeling in the Soviet Union. Johnson, Anne H., ed. (Illus.). ix, 102p. (Orig.). 1989. pap. text 75.00 (1-55831-089-4) Delphic Associates.
— Soviet Regional Economic Autonomy Baltics vs. Moscow. Possehl, Suzanne R., ed. Sargent, Peter, tr. from RUS. (Illus.). x, 103p. (Orig.). 1989. pap. 75.00 (1-55831-109-2) Delphic Associates.
Belkindas, Misha V. & Ivanova, Olga V., eds. Foreign Trade Statistics in the USSR & Successor States: Statistika Vneshnei Torgovli v SSSR i Godsudarstvakh-Preemnikakh. LC 95-13209. (Studies of Economies in Transformation: No. 18). 248p. 1996. pap. 22.00 (0-8213-3226-0, 13226) World Bank.
Belknap. The Invisible Woman: Gender, Crime & Justice. 2nd ed. (Criminal Justice Ser.). 2000. pap. 25.00 (0-534-54209-3) Wadsworth Pub.
Belknap, Bryan. Freestylin' Bustin' Out from Law to Life - A Creative Study of the Book of Galatians. Reeves, Dale, ed. (Empowered Youth Products Ser.). (Illus.). 64p. 1999. 8.99 (0-7847-0903-3, 23313) Standard Pub.
***Belknap, Bryan.** Stormchaser: The Peril of Life Without God. Reeves, Dale & Durden, Leslie, eds. 64p. 2000. pap. text 8.99 (0-7847-1151-8) Standard Pub.
Belknap, Buzz & Evans, Laura. Grand Canyon River Guide. rev. ed. (Illus.). 1995. 18.95 (0-916370-10-0) Westwater.
Belknap, Buzz, jt. auth. see Evans, Laura.
Belknap, Donald J. What & Where Is Religious Truth Today? Earth's Only Way Out! (Illus.). 512p. 1991. 18.95 (0-9628767-0-4) SERFI.
Belknap, George N. And Still More Addenda to Belknap's Oregon Imprints, 1845-1870. 35p. 1986. pap. 5.95 (0-912296-86-0) Am Antiquarian.
— Early Oregon Imprints in the Oregon State Archives. 17p. 1981. pap. 6.50 (0-912296-52-6) Am Antiquarian.

An Asterisk (*) at the beginning of an entry indicates that the title is appearing for the first time.

Belknap, Henry W. Forrester: Simon Forrester of Salem & His Descendants. (Illus.). 48p. 1997. reprint ed. pap. 10.00 (*0-8328-8616-5*); reprint ed. lib. bdg. 20.00 (*0-8328-8615-7*) Higginson Bk Co.

Belknap, Ivan. Human Problems of a State Mental Hospital. Grob, Gerald N., ed. LC 78-22548. (Historical Issues in Mental Health Ser.). (Illus.). 1980. reprint ed. lib. bdg. 23.95 (*0-405-11902-X*) Ayer.

Belknap, Jeremy. The Foresters: An American Tale. LC 78-104413. reprint ed. lib. bdg. 19.00 (*0-8398-0159-9*) Irvington.

— The Foresters: An American Tale. 216p. 1985. reprint ed. lib. bdg. 79.00 (*0-7812-0519-0*) Rprt Serv.

— Foresters: An American Tale. reprint ed. pap. text 6.95 (*0-8290-2113-2*) Irvington.

— Foresters, an American Tale, 1792. LC 71-100127. 230p. 1969. reprint ed. 50.00 (*0-8201-1071-X*) Schol Facsimiles.

— History of New Hampshire, 3 vols. LC 73-141081. (Research Library of Colonial Americana). (Illus.). 1972. reprint ed. 132.95 (*0-405-03272-2*) Ayer.

— History of New Hampshire, 3 vols., Vol. 1. LC 73-141081. (Research Library of Colonial Americana). (Illus.). 1972. reprint ed. 44.95 (*0-405-03273-0*) Ayer.

— History of New Hampshire, 3 vols., Vol. 2. LC 73-141081. (Research Library of Colonial Americana). (Illus.). 1972. reprint ed. 44.95 (*0-405-03274-9*) Ayer.

— History of New Hampshire, 3 vols., Vol. 3. LC 73-141081. (Research Library of Colonial Americana). (Illus.). 1972. reprint ed. 44.95 (*0-405-03275-7*) Ayer.

Belknap, Joanne. The Invisible Woman: Gender, Crime & Justice. LC 95-8840. 1995. 33.95 (*0-534-15870-6*) Wadsworth Pub.

Belknap, Jodi P. Majesty: The Exceptional Trees of Hawaii. Cazimero, Momi, ed. LC 82-60598. (Illus.). 72p. 1982. 12.95 (*0-686-38728-7*) Outdoor Circle.

Belknap, Joel R. The Story of Free Enterprise. 1963. 9.95 (*0-8159-6825-6*) Devin.

Belknap, Leora E. Farnum: Know Thyself: A Genealogy. (Illus.). 105p. 1997. reprint ed. pap. 16.50 (*0-8328-8534-7*); reprint ed. lib. bdg. 26.50 (*0-8328-8533-9*) Higginson Bk Co.

Belknap, Maria. The Equine Dictionary. 450p. 1997. pap. (*0-85131-696-4*) J A Allen.

— Horseman's Spanish/English Dictionary. 1996. pap. text 19.95 (*0-914327-68-2*) Breakthrgh NY.

— HorseWords: The Equine Dictionary: The Ultimate Reference Book for the Horse Owner. 472p. 1998. 22.95 (*1-57076-101-9*) Trafalgar.

Belknap, Martha. Mind-Body Magic: Creative Activities for Any Audience. LC 96-35696. 160p. (Orig.). 1997. pap. 21.95 (*1-57025-126-6*) Whole Person.

— Taming More Dragons: Another Collection of Creative Relaxation Activities for Home & School. (Illus.). 48p. 1994. pap. 9.00 (*0-9643459-1-9*) M Belknap.

— Taming Your Dragons: A Collection of Creative Relaxation Activities for Home & School. (Illus.). 44p. 1994. pap. 9.00 (*0-9643459-0-0*) M Belknap.

Belknap, Michal R. Cold War Political Justice: The Smith Act, the Communist Party, & American Civil Liberties, 66. LC 77-4566. (Contributions in American History Ser.: No. 66). 322p. 1977. 47.95 (*0-8371-9692-2*, BCW/, Greenwood Pr) Greenwood.

— Federal Law & Southern Order: Racial Violence & Constitutional Conflict in the Post-Brown South. LC 86-19237. 416p. 1995. pap. 20.00 (*0-8203-1735-7*) U of Ga Pr.

— To Improve the Administration of Justice: A History of the American Judicature Society. LC 92-72983. 320p. (C). 1992. 14.95 (*0-938870-57-2*) Am Judicature.

***Belknap, Michal R.** The Vinson Court: Justices, Rulings, & Legacy. 2002. lib. bdg. 55.00 (*1-57607-201-0*) ABC-CLIO.

Belknap, Michal R., ed. Administrative History of the Civil Rights Division of the Department of Justice During the Johnson Administration, 2 vols., Set. LC 91-3627. (Civil Rights, White House & Justice Dept. Ser.: Vol. 17). 1152p. 1992. text 100.00 (*0-8240-3385-X*) Garland.

— American Political Trials. exp. rev. ed. LC 93-30888. (Contributions in American History Ser.: No. 152). 352p. 1994. pap. 26.95 (*0-275-94437-9*, Greenwood Pr) Greenwood.

— American Political Trials, 152. exp. rev. ed. LC 93-30888. (Contributions in American History Ser.: No. 152). 352p. 1994. 75.00 (*0-313-28687-6*, Greenwood Pr) Greenwood.

— Attitudes, Goals & Priorities. LC 91-3629. (Civil Rights, White House & Justice Dept. Ser.: Vol. 1). 488p. 1991. text 45.00 (*0-8240-3366-3*) Garland.

— Combatting Housing Discrimination. LC 91-3622. (Civil Rights, White House & Justice Dept. Ser.: Vol. 6). 208p. 1991. text 23.00 (*0-8240-3374-4*) Garland.

— Desegregation of Public Education. LC 91-3621. (Civil Rights, White House & Justice Dept. Ser.: Vol. 7). 584p. 1991. text 52.00 (*0-8240-3375-2*) Garland.

— Desegregation of Public Transportation, Facilities, & Programs. LC 91-3631. (Civil Rights, White House & Justice Dept. Ser.: Vol. 8). 248p. 1991. text 29.00 (*0-8240-3376-0*) Garland.

— The Drive to Desegregate Places of Public Accommodation. LC 91-3619. (Civil Rights, White House & Justice Dept. Ser.: Vol. 9). 176p. 1991. text 21.00 (*0-8240-3378-7*) Garland.

— Employment of Blacks by the Federal Government. LC 91-3624. (Civil Rights, White House & Justice Dept. Ser.: Vol. 4). 192p. 1991. text 20.00 (*0-8240-3370-1*) Garland.

— Equal Employment Opportunity. LC 91-3623. (Civil Rights, White House & Justice Dept. Ser.: Vol. 5). 256p. 1991. text 25.00 (*0-8240-3372-8*) Garland.

— Integration of the Armed Forces. LC 91-3625. (Civil Rights, White House & Justice Dept. Ser.: Vol. 3). 496p. 1991. text 41.00 (*0-8240-3369-8*) Garland.

— Justice Department Briefs in Crucial Civil Rights Cases, 1948-1968, 2 vols., Set. LC 91-9326. (Civil Rights, White House & Justice Dept. Ser.: Vol. 18). 1352p. 1992. text 105.00 (*0-8240-3386-8*) Garland.

— Justice Department Civil Rights Policies Prior to 1960: Crucial Documents from the Files of Arthur Brann Caldwell. LC 91-3612. (Civil Rights, White House & Justice Dept. Ser.: Vol. 16). 456p. 1991. text 39.00 (*0-8240-3384-1*) Garland.

— Presidential Committees & White House Conferences. LC 91-3628. (Civil Rights, White House & Justice Dept. Ser.: Vol. 2). 304p. 1991. text 28.00 (*0-8240-3368-X*) Garland.

— Racial Violence & Law Enforcement in the South. LC 91-3628. (Civil Rights, White House & Justice Dept. Ser.: Vol. 10). 544p. 1991. text 56.00 (*0-8240-3379-5*) Garland.

— Securing the Enactment of Civil Rights Legislation: Civil Rights Act of 1964. LC 91-3615. (Civil Rights, White House & Justice Dept. Ser.: Vol. 13). 184p. 1991. text 22.00 (*0-8240-3382-5*) Garland.

— Securing the Enactment of Civil Rights Legislation, 1946-1960. LC 91-3616. (Civil Rights, White House & Justice Dept. Ser.: Vol. 12). 488p. 1991. text 48.00 (*0-8240-3381-7*) Garland.

— Securing the Enactment of Civil Rights Legislation, 1965-1968. LC 91-3614. (Civil Rights, White House & Justice Dept. Ser.: Vol. 14). 464p. 1991. text 40.00 (*0-8240-3383-3*) Garland.

— Urban Race Riots. LC 92-3617. (Civil Rights, White House & Justice Dept. Ser.: Vol. 11). 304p. 1991. 28.00 (*0-8240-3380-9*) Garland.

— Voting Rights. LC 91-3613. (Civil Rights, White House & Justice Dept. Ser.: Vol. 15). 296p. 1991. text 28.00 (*0-8240-3388-4*) Garland.

Belknap, Robert L., ed. Russianness: An Examination of Russian & the West: In Memory of Rufus W. Mathewson. 1989. 29.50 (*0-87501-055-5*) Ardis Pubs.

Belknap, Robert L. & Kuhns, Richard. Tradition & Innovation: General Education & the Reintegration of the University, a Columbia Report. LC 77-3315. 130p. 1977. pap. text 20.00 (*0-231-04323-6*) Col U Pr.

Belknap, W., et al, eds. The Molecular & Cellular Biology of the Potato. 2nd ed. LC 97-179020. (Biotechnology in Agriculture Ser.: No. 12). (Illus.). 288p. 1994. text 105.00 (*0-85198-900-4*) OUP.

Belknap, Waldron P., Jr. American Colonial Painting: Materials for a History. Sellers, Charles C., ed. LC 59-10313. (Illus.). 398p. 1960. text 37.50 (*0-674-02250-5*) Belknap Pr.

— De Peyster Genealogy. LC 56-34875. (Illus.). 125p. 1990. text 10.00 (*0-674-19801-8*) HUP.

Belknapp, Bill, et al. Canyonlands River Guide. LC 96-60227. (Illus.). 1996. 16.95 (*0-916370-11-9*) Westwater.

Bel'kovitch, V. M. & Sh'ekotov, M. N. The Belukha Whale - Belukha: Natural Behavior & Bioacoustics - Povedenie i Bioakustika v Prirode. Recchia, Cheri, ed. Svanidze, Marina A., tr. from RUS. (Illus.). 176p. (Orig.). 1993. pap. 22.00 (*1-880224-07-0*) Woods Hole Ocean.

Bell. Air Pollution & Plant Life. text. write for info. (*0-471-49090-3*); pap. text. write for info. (*0-471-49091-1*) Wiley.

Bell. Atlas of Surgical Orthodontic Corrective Dentistry. 1999. text. write for info. (*0-7216-1487-6*, W B Saunders Co) Harcrt Hlth Sci Grp.

— Boron in Soils & Plants. LC 97-26715. 280p. 1997. text 187.00 (*0-7923-4705-6*) Kluwer Academic.

***Bell.** Colours & Markings Frieze. 2000. pap. 8.95 (*0-85131-590-9*, Pub. by J A Allen) Trafalgar.

Bell. Critical Essays on Kingsley Amis. large type ed. LC 98-35290. (Critical Essays Ser.). 344p. 1998. 49.00 (*0-7838-0039-8*, G K Hall Lrg Type) Mac Lib Ref.

— Data Analysis, Regression & Forecasting. (Cti to Southwestern Ser.). (C). 1994. pap. 31.95 (*1-56527-273-0*) Course Tech.

— Decision Making under Certainty. (Cti to Southwestern Ser.). (C). 1995. pap. 31.95 (*1-56527-274-9*) Course Tech.

— Decision Making under Uncertainty. (Cti To Southwestern Ser.). 1995. pap. 21.95 (*1-56527-275-7*) S-W Pub.

— Degenerate Stochastic. 1995. lib. bdg. 74.95 (*0-582-24689-X*, Pub. by Addison-Wesley) Longman.

— East Moon. 2000. text 22.95 (*0-312-85232-0*) St Martin.

— Eastern Star. 16.95 (*0-685-21937-2*) Wehman.

— Environmental Psychology. 4th ed. (C). 1996. pap. text, teacher ed. 28.00 (*0-15-503245-3*) Harcourt Coll Pubs.

— Environmental Psychology. 5th ed. (C). Date not set. text. write for info. (*0-15-508064-4*) Harcourt Coll Pubs.

***Bell.** Evaluating Psychological Information: Sharpening Your Critical Thinking Skills. 3rd ed. 64p. 1998. pap. text 11.00 (*0-205-28635-6*) Allyn.

Bell. Foreign Exchange Handbook. 1983. lib. bdg. 92.50 (*0-86010-385-4*) Kluwer Academic.

***Bell.** Genetics. (Quick Look Veterinary Ser.). 2000. 23.95 (*1-889325-15-5*, Pub. by Fence Crk Pubng) Blackwell Sci.

— Horse & Pony Breeds Frieze. 2000. pap. 8.95 (*0-85131-591-7*, Pub. by J A Allen) Trafalgar.

— Landslides 6th Edition, Vol. 1. 1992. 158.00 (*90-5410-033-8*) Ashgate Pub Co.

— Landslides 6th Edition, Vol. 2. 1992. 158.00 (*90-5410-034-6*) Ashgate Pub Co.

— Landslides 6th Edition, Vol. 3. 1993. 78.00 (*90-5410-035-4*) Ashgate Pub Co.

Bell. Microeconomics: Price Theory Practice. (C). 1997. text. write for info. (*0-06-501602-5*) Addson-Wesley Educ.

— Modern Drama: Plays, Critics, Theatre. (C). 1994. pap. text, teacher ed. 33.75 (*0-15-502094-3*) Harcourt Coll Pubs.

— Perspectives in Ferrous Metallurgy. 1985. write for info. (*0-08-033422-9*, Pergamon Pr) Elsevier.

— Red Mecury. 1999. text. write for info. (*0-312-16977-9*) St Martin.

Bell & Bradley, eds. United Kingdom National Committee of Comparative Law: Governmental Liability, A Comparative Study, Vol. 13. 294p. 1991. pap. 75.00 (*0-904281-03-5*, Pub. by UK Natl Committee) St Mut.

Bell & Corbett. Little English Handbook. 2nd ed. 288p. (C). 1996. pap. text. write for info. (*0-471-79892-4*) Wiley.

Bell & Gower. Upper Intermediate Matters. 1994. pap. text, student ed. write for info. (*0-582-04664-5*) Addison-Wesley.

— Upper Intermediate Matters: No Key. 1994. pap. text, wbk. ed. write for info. (*0-582-04666-1*, Pub. by Addison-Wesley) Longman.

Bell & Hughes. The Pediatric Anesthesia Handbook. 2nd ed. (Illus.). 720p. (C). (gr. 13). 1996. pap. text 44.95 (*0-8151-0659-9*, 25695) Mosby Inc.

Bell & Roderick. Never Too Late to Learn. 1982. pap. text. write for info. (*0-582-49706-X*, Pub. by Addison-Wesley) Longman.

Bell, jt. auth. see Egenolf.

Bell, jt. auth. see French.

Bell, tr. see Andreas.

Bell, Dale W. Woodstock: An Inside Look at the Movie That Shook up the World & Defined a Generation. LC 99-28969. 250p. 1999. pap. 24.95 (*0-941188-71-X*) M Wiese.

Bell, Jacinta. Exiles, 1. 1999. pap. text 12.95 (*0-9521558-8-5*) Parthian Bks.

Bell, . L. & Machover, Moshe. A Course in Mathematical Logic. xx, 600p. 1977. 114.00 (*0-7204-2844-0*, North Holland) Elsevier.

Bell, Mary-Jean, jt. ed. see Warner, Bonnie.

***Bell, Sherry.** Tinker's Collection. 48p. 2000. 10.95 (*1-57377-091-4*, 0-1988-4-02320-3) Easl Pubns.

Bell, Stacy Jane. Positive Nutrition for HIV Infection & AIDS: A Medically Sound Take Charge Plan to Maintain. 192p. 1996. pap. 12.95 (*0-471-34696-9*) Wiley.

Bell, A. Modern Engine Tuning. LC 97-72302. 1997. 34.95 (*0-85429-978-5*) Haynes Manuals.

— Modern Law of Personal Property in England & Ireland. 1989. 105.00 (*0-406-70100-8*, U.K., MICHIE) LEXIS Pub.

Bell, A., jt. ed. see Lee, W. E.

Bell, A. Craig. Alexandre Dumas: Le Vicomte de Bragelonne (the Man in the Iron Mask) : a Critical Study LC 96-143289. xv, 136p. 1995. write for info. (*0-86303-694-5*) Merlin Bks.

— Brahms: The Vocal Music. LC 94-43514. (Illus.). 264p. 1996. 38.50 (*0-8386-3597-0*) Fairleigh Dickinson.

Bell, A. Craig, tr. & intro. see Dumas, Alexandre.

Bell, A. F. Studies in Portuguese Literature. 1972. 250.00 (*0-87968-243-4*) Gordon Pr.

Bell, A. F., tr. & notes see Vicente, Gil.

Bell, A. Fleming, II. Construction Contracts with North Carolina Local Governments. 3rd ed. LC 96-160796. 69p. (C). 1996. pap. text 12.50 (*1-56011-284-0*, 96.04) Institute Government.

— Ethics, Conflicts & Offices: A Guide for Local Officials. limited ed. LC 97-136579. 227p. 1997. text 20.00 (*1-56011-292-1*) Institute Government.

Bell, A. Fleming, 2nd. Ethics in Public Life--Adapted from Ethics, Conflicts & Offices: A Guide for Local Officials. LC 98-197728. 95p. (C). 1998. pap. text 20.00 (*1-56011-333-2*, 98.13) Institute Government.

Bell, A. Fleming, II. A Model Equipment Lease-Purchase & Security Agreement for North Carolina Local Governments. 81p. (Orig.). (C). 1985. pap. text 12.00 (*1-56011-102-X*, 85.17) Institute Government.

***Bell, A. Fleming, II.** Suggested Rules of Procedure for a City Council. (C). 2000. pap. write for info. (*1-56011-367-7*) Institute Government.

Bell, A. Fleming, II. Suggested Rules of Procedure for Small Local Government Boards. Orig. Title: Suggested Rules of Procedure for Small Governing Boards. 1998. reprint ed. pap. text 8.50 (*1-56011-319-7*) Institute Government.

Bell, A. Fleming, II & Wicker, Warren J., eds. County Government in North Carolina. 4th ed. LC 99-205349. (C). 1998. text 40.00 (*1-56011-345-6*) Institute Government.

Bell, A. G. The Machine Plays Chess. 1978. text 21.00 (*0-08-021221-2*, Pergamon Pr); pap. text 8.95 (*0-08-021222-0*, Pergamon Pr) Elsevier.

Bell, A. Graham. Four-Stroke Performance Tuning. 2nd ed. LC 98-72315. (Illus.). 336p. 1998. 36.95 (*1-85960-435-8*, Pub. by J H Haynes & Co) Motorbooks Intl.

***Bell, A. Graham.** Two-Stroke Performance Tuning. 2nd ed. (Illus.). 272p. 1999. 39.95 (*1-85960-619-9*, 129516AE, Pub. by Haynes Manuals) Motorbooks Intl.

Bell, A. L., ed. Grouting in the Ground. 666p. 1994. 125.00 (*0-7277-1928-9*) Am Soc Civil Eng.

Bell, A. M., jt. auth. see Mallett, A. S.

Bell, Addie. Below the Belt. Costa, Gwen, ed. LC 91-387 2. (Illus.). 1993. 13.95 (*0-87949-360-7*) Ashley Bks.

Bell, Adrian. Corduroy. large type unabridged ed. (Reminiscence Ser.). 274p. 1998. 24.95 (*0-7531-5074-3*, 150743) ISIS Pub.

***Bell, Adrian.** Silver Ley. large type unabridged ed. 1999. 25.95 (*0-7531-5098-0*, 150980, Pub. by ISIS Lrg Prnt) ISIS Pub.

Bell, Adrian & Sigsworth, Alan. The Small Rural Primary School: A Matter of Quality. 225p. 1987. 75.00 (*1-85000-155-3*, Falmer Pr); pap. 37.95 (*1-85000-156-1*, Falmer Pr) Taylor & Francis.

Bell, Adrian D. Plant Form: An Illustrated Guide to Flowering Plant Morphology. (Illus.). 356p. 1991. pap. text 49.95 (*0-19-854219-4*) OUP.

***Bell, Adryan.** Transforming Your Workplace. 96p. 2000. pap. 17.95 (*0-8464-5183-2*) Beekman Pubs.

***Bell, Aili & Koski, Augustus.** Finnish Graded Reader with 14 Cassettes. (Multilingual Books Intensive Cassette Foreign Language Ser.). 740p. 1999. pap. text 179.00 (*1-58214-017-0*) Mltilingl Bks.

Bell, Alan. Sydney Smith. (Illus.). 260p. 1980. text 38.00 (*0-19-812050-8*) OUP.

Bell, Alan P. The Mind & Heart in Human Sexual Behavior: Owning & Sharing Our Personal Truths. LC 97-33435. (Illus.). 408p. 1997. 40.00 (*0-7657-0135-9*) Aronson.

Bell, Albert A. Exploring the New Testament World: An Illustrated Guide to the World of Jesus & the First Christians. LC 98-8168. 1998. pap. 14.99 (*0-7852-1424-0*) Nelson.

Bell, Albert A., Jr. & Allis, James B. Resources in Ancient Philosophy: An Annotated Bibliography of Scholarship in English, 1965-1989. LC 91-39912. 818p. 1991. 95.00 (*0-8108-2520-1*) Scarecrow.

Bell, Alexander G. The Bell Telephone: The Deposition of Alexander Graham Bell in the Suit Brought by the United States to Annul the Bell Patents. LC 74-4665. (Telecommunications Ser.). (Illus.). 480p. 1974. reprint ed. 36.95 (*0-405-06032-7*) Ayer.

Bell, Alexander M. The Principles of Elocution. (Works of Alexander Melville Bell). xvi, 240p. 1985. reprint ed. lib. bdg. 39.00 (*0-932051-80-4*) Rprt Serv.

— Visible Speech the Science of Universal Alphabetics. 1976. reprint ed. 69.00 (*0-403-06591-7*, Regency) Scholarly.

Bell, Alexis T. & Hair, Michael L., eds. Vibrational Spectroscopies for Absorbed Species. LC 80-21181. (ACS Symposium Ser.: No. 137). 1980. 37.95 (*0-8412-0585-X*) Am Chemical.

— Vibrational Spectroscopies for Adsorbed Species. LC 80-21181. (ACS Symposium Ser.: No. 137). (Illus.). 303p. 1980. reprint ed. pap. 94.00 (*0-608-03225-5*, 206374400007) Bks Demand.

Bell, Alexis T. & Hegedus, L. Louis, eds. Catalysis under Transient Conditions. LC 82-20639. (ACS Symposium Ser.: No. 178). 1982. 38.95 (*0-8412-0688-0*) Am Chemical.

— Catalysis under Transient Conditions. LC 81-20639. (ACS Symposium Ser.: No. 178). (Illus.). 317p. reprint ed. pap. 98.30 (*0-608-03244-1*, 206376300007) Bks Demand.

Bell, Alexis T. & Pines, Alexander, eds. NMR Techniques in Catalysis. LC 93-43400. (Chemical Industries Ser.: Vol. 55). (Illus.). 448p. 1994. text 199.00 (*0-8247-9173-8*) Dekker.

Bell, Alexis T. & Shen, Mitchel C., eds. Plasma Polymerization. LC 79-15252. (ACS Symposium Ser.: No. 108). 1979. 43.95 (*0-8412-0510-8*) Am Chemical.

— Plasma Polymerization. LC 79-15252. (ACS Symposium Ser.: Vol. 108). 352p. 1979. reprint ed. pap. 109.20 (*0-608-03086-4*, 206353900007) Bks Demand.

Bell, Alexis T., jt. auth. see Petersen, Eugene E.

Bell, Alison. 50 Nifty Super Scary Crafts & Other Things to Do. LC 96-2983. (Fifty Nifty Super Ser.). (Illus.). 80p. (J). (gr. 3-7). 1996. pap. 6.95 (*1-56565-540-0*, 05400W, Pub. by Lowell Hse Juvenile) NTC Contemp Pub Co.

***Bell, Alison.** Your Beauty, Your Health, Yourself. (Illus.). 144p. (J). 2000. pap. 8.95 (*0-7373-0350-6*, 03506W, Pub. by Lowell Hse Juvenile) NTC Contemp Pub Co.

Bell, Alison. Your Body, Yourself Q & A: Questions & Answers about Your Changing Body. (Teen Body Book Ser.). (Illus.). 192p. (J). (gr. 3-7). 1999. pap. 9.95 (*0-7373-0190-2*, 01902W) NTC Contemp Pub Co.

Bell, Alison & Rooney, Lisa. Your Body, Yourself: A Guide to Your Changing Body. rev. ed. LC 98-141300. (Teen Body Book Ser.). (Illus.). 160p. (J). (gr. 4-8). 1996. pap. 8.95 (*1-56565-532-X*, 05329W, Pub. by Lowell Hse Juvenile) NTC Contemp Pub Co.

Bell, Allan. The Language of News Media. 256p. 1991. pap. 28.95 (*0-631-16435-9*) Blackwell Pubs.

Bell, Allan & Garrett, Peter. Approaches to Media Discourse. LC 97-5253. (Illus.). 304p. (C). 1998. text 62.95 (*0-631-19887-3*); pap. text 28.95 (*0-631-19888-1*) Blackwell Pubs.

Bell, Allan & Holmes, Janet, eds. New Zealand Ways of Speaking English. (Multilingual Matters Ser.: No. 65). 300p. 1990. 99.00 (*1-85359-083-5*, Pub. by Multilingual Matters); pap. 44.95 (*1-85359-082-7*, Pub. by Multilingual Matters) Taylor & Francis.

***Bell, Allan & Kuiper, Koenraad, eds.** New Zealand English. LC 99-42693. (Varieties of English Around the World General Ser.: Vol. 25). 368p. 2000. 75.00 (*1-55619-723-3*) J Benjamins Pubng Co.

Bell, Allison W., jt. auth. see Slack, Nancy G.

Bell, Andreas. Option Valuation in the Presence of Market Imperfections, Vol. 1369. Vol. 5. write for info. (*0-318-69980-X*) P Lang Pubng.

Bell, Anita W., jt. auth. see Bergman, Ronald L.

Bell, Anita W., jt. auth. see Hoffman, Lisa.

Bell, Ann. Dung Fungi: Illustrated Guide to Coprophilous Fungi in New Zealand. (Illus.). 88p. 1983. pap. text, spiral bd. 19.95 (*0-86473-001-2*, Pub. by Victoria Univ Pr) Lubrecht & Cramer.

***Bell, Ann.** Montana. 464p. 2000. pap. 4.97 (*1-57748-794-X*) Barbour Pub.

Bell, Ann. Sanity, Security, Sanctuary: A Physical & Psycho-Spiritual Look at Abortion in Relation to the Wombs of Women & the Story of the Incarnation. Farrell, Helen, ed. (Illus.). 157p. 1999. 36.50 (*1-85776-307-6*) Trans-Atl Phila.

Bell, Anne, jt. auth. see Habenicht, Donna J.

Bell, Anne O., ed. The Diary of Virginia Woolf Vol. 2: Vol. 2, 1920-1924. LC 78-23882. 384p. 1980. pap. 14.00 (*0-15-626037-9*, Harvest Bks) Harcourt.

B

Bell, Anne O., jt. auth. see Woolf, Virginia.

Bell, Anne O., ed. see Woolf, Virginia.

Bell, Anne Olivier, ed. see Woolf, Virginia.

***Bell, Annie.** Annie Bell's Vegetable Book. 256p. 1999. pap. 18.95 (*0-14-025227-4*, Pub. by Pnguin Bks Ltd) Trafalgar.

Bell, Annie. More Taste Than Time. 192p. 1997. pap. 22.95 (*0-09-180677-1*, Pub. by Ebury Pr) Trafalgar.

Bell, Annie A. Record of Marriages in Fayette County: For the Period of Years 1803 to 1851. 138p. 1997. reprint ed. pap. 21.00 (*0-8328-6732-2*) Higginson Bk Co.

— Record of the Pension Abstracts: Revolutionary War Soldiers, War of 1812, & Indian Wars, Who Settled in Warren County. (Illus.). 80p. 1997. reprint ed. pap. 15.00 (*0-8328-6740-3*) Higginson Bk Co.

— Revolutionary War Pensions of Soldiers Who Settled in Fayette County. 121p. 1997. reprint ed. pap. 21.00 (*0-8328-6733-0*) Higginson Bk Co.

Bell, Annie W., compiled by. Marriage Records of Cabell County, 1809-1851. (Illus.). 90p. 1997. reprint ed. pap. 17.50 (*0-8328-6942-2*) Higginson Bk Co.

***Bell, Anthea.** Jack & the Beanstalk: An English Fairy Tale. LC 00-36171. (Illus.). 32p. (J). (gr. k-3). 2000. 15.95 (*0-7358-1374-4*) North-South Bks NYC.

Bell, Anthea. Swan Lake. LC 86-9509. (Illus.). 28p. (J). (gr. 1 up). 1991. pap. 15.95 (*0-88708-028-6*, Picture Book Studio) S&S Childrens.

B

***Bell, Anthea, tr.** The Merry Pranks of Till Eulenspiegel. (Illus.). 32p. (gr. 1-4). 2000. 15.95 (*1-55858-806-X*) North-South Bks NYC.

Bell, Anthea, tr. The Snow Queen. LC 87-1518. (Illus.). 32p. (J). (gr. k-3). 1987. 14.95 (*1-55858-053-0*, Pub. by North-South Bks NYC) Chronicle Bks.

***Bell, Anthea & Blau, Aljoscha.** Jack & the Beanstalk: An English Fairy Tale. LC 00-36171. (Illus.). 32p. (J). (gr. k-3). 2000. pap. 15.88 (*0-7358-1375-2*) North-South Bks NYC.

Bell, Anthea, tr. see Andersen, Hans Christian.

Bell, Anthea, tr. see Bemmann, Hans, ed.

Bell, Anthea, tr. see Brawand, Leo B.

Bell, Anthea, tr. see Brentano, Clemens.

Bell, Anthea, tr. see Drigalski, Dorte V.

Bell, Anthea, tr. see Ende, Michael.

Bell, Anthea, tr. see Fontane, Theodor.

Bell, Anthea, tr. see Grimm, Jacob W. & Grimm, Wilhelm K.

Bell, Anthea, tr. see Grimm, Jacob W., et al.

Bell, Anthea, tr. see Hauff, Wilhelm.

Bell, Anthea, tr. see Pacovska, Kveta.

Bell, Anthea, tr. see Perrault, Charles.

Bell, Anthea, tr. see Pfister, Marcus.

Bell, Anthea, tr. see Sellin, Birgir.

Bell, Anthea, tr. see Sonnleitner, A. T.

Bell, Anthea, tr. see Storm, Theodor.

Bell, Anthea, tr. see Toussaint-Samat, Maguelonne.

Bell, Anthea, tr. see Uderzo & Goscinny, Rene.

Bell, Anthea, tr. see Vainio, Pirkko.

Bell, Anthea, tr. see Velthuijs, Max.

Bell, Art. The Art of Talk. rev. ed. (Illus.). 240p. 1998. 24.95 (*1-879706-77-6*) Paper Chase.

— The Quickening: Today's Trends, Tomorrow's World. 336p. 1997. 24.95 (*1-879706-70-9*) Paper Chase.

— The Quickening: Today's Trends, Tomorrow's World. 336p. 1998. pap. 15.95 (*1-879706-71-7*) Paper Chase.

Bell, Art & Steiger, Brad. The Source: Journey Through the Unexplained. LC 98-67532. 267p. 1999. 24.95 (*1-879706-50-4*) Paper Chase.

***Bell, Art, & Strieber, Whitley.** The Coming Global Superstorm. large type ed. LC 00-27608. (Nonfiction Ser.). 304p. 2000. 30.95 (*0-7838-9034-6*, G K Hall Lrg Type) Mac Lib Ref.

— The Coming Global Superstorm. 2001. reprint ed. 6.99 (*0-671-04191-6*, Pocket Star Bks) PB.

Bell, Art & Strieber, Whitley. The Coming Global Superstorm: And How to Survive It. LC 99-54394. 1999. 23.95 (*0-671-04190-8*, PB Hardcover) PB.

Bell, Art, jt. auth. see Gardner, James.

***Bell, Arthur A.** HVAC Equations, Data, Rules of Thumb. (Illus.). 544p. 2000. 59.95 (*0-07-136129-4*) McGraw-Hill Prof.

Bell, Arthur H. Complete Business Writer's Manual: Model Letters, Memos, Reports & Presentations. 400p. (C). 1991. text 39.95 (*0-13-157538-4*, Busn) P-H.

— Great Jobs Abroad. LC 96-49935. (Illus.). 384p. 1997. pap. 14.95 (*0-07-005839-3*) McGraw.

— NTC's Business Writer's Handbook. 736p. Date not set. pap. 22.95 (*0-8442-5913-6*, VGM Career) NTC Contemp Pub Co.

— NTC's Business Writer's Handbook. LC 94-80055. (Illus.). 736p. 1995. 35.00 (*0-8442-5912-8*, NTC Business Bks) NTC Contemp Pub Co.

— A Pocket Guide Thesaurus. LC 92-9427. (Barron's Pocket Guides Ser.). 1992. vinyl bd. 7.95 (*0-8120-4845-8*) Barron.

— Pocket Guide to Cliches. LC 98-21311. 160p. 1999. pap. 6.95 (*0-7641-0672-4*) Barron.

— A Pocket Guide to Synonyms. (Barron's Pocket Guides Ser.). 1992. vinyl bd. 7.95 (*0-8120-4843-1*) Barron.

— A Way with Words. 1991. 31.95 (*0-87280-121-7*, 3323, Asher-Gallant) Caddylak Systs.

— Writing Effective Letters & Memos. 2nd rev. ed. LC 97-6359. (Barron's Business Success Ser.). (Orig.). 1997. pap. text 6.95 (*0-8120-9824-2*) Barron.

Bell, Arthur H. & Grebanier, Bernard. English Literature: The Beginnings to 1800. 2nd ed. (Barron's College Review Ser.). 450p. (C). 1994. pap. 11.95 (*0-8120-1775-7*) Barron.

— English Literature: 1800-1900. 2nd ed. (Barron's College Review Ser.). (C). 1994. pap. 11.95 (*0-8120-1678-5*) Barron.

Bell, Arthur H. & Smith. Winning with Difficult People. 2nd ed. LC 97-10353. 96p. 1997. pap. text 6.95 (*0-8120-9894-3*) Barron.

Bell, Arthur H. & Smith, Dayle M. Management Communication. 560p. 1998. pap. 58.95 (*0-471-23971-2*) Wiley.

Bell, Arthur H. & Williams, Gary G. Intercultural Business. LC 99-29822. (Barron's Business Success Ser.). 160p. 1999. pap. text 6.95 (*0-7641-1113-2*) Barron.

Bell, Arthur H., et al. American Literature, 1930-Present. LC 94-1568. (Barron's College Review Ser.). 450p. (C). 1994. pap. 11.95 (*0-8120-1836-2*) Barron.

— English Literature 1900-Present. 2nd ed. (Barron's College Review Ser.). (C). 1994. pap. 11.95 (*0-8120-1837-0*) Barron.

— World Literature: Early Origins to 1800. 2nd ed. (Barron's College Review Ser.). 450p. (C). 1994. pap. 11.95 (*0-8120-1811-7*) Barron.

— World Literature: 1800-Present. 2nd ed. (Barron's College Review Ser.). 450p. (C). 1994. pap. 11.95 (*0-8120-1812-5*) Barron.

Bell, Arthur H., ed. see Smith, Dayle M.

Bell, Arthur S., Jr. Peter Charlie: The Cruise of the PC 477. LC 82-71794. (Illus.). 384p. 1982. 14.95 (*0-910355-00-2*) Courtroom Comp.

Bell, Aubrey F. Benito Arias Montano. 1922. pap. 10.00 (*0-87535-009-7*) Hispanic Soc.

— Diogo do Cuoto. (Illus.). 1924. 10.00 (*0-87535-015-1*) Hispanic Soc.

— Fernam Lopez. (Illus.). 1921. 10.00 (*0-87535-006-2*) Hispanic Soc.

— Francisco Sanchez el Brocense. (Illus.). 1925. 10.00 (*0-87535-017-8*) Hispanic Soc.

— Gaspar Correa. (Illus.). 1924. 10.00 (*0-87535-016-X*) Hispanic Soc.

— Juan Gines de Sepulveda. (Illus.). 1925. 10.00 (*0-87535-018-6*) Hispanic Soc.

Bell, August G. Circling Windrock Mountain: Two Hundred Years in Appalachia. LC 98-40113. (Illus.). 336p. 1999. 45.00 (*1-57233-041-4*); pap. 17.50 (*1-57233-038-4*, 9840115) U of Tenn Pr.

Bell, B. House on Punishment Corner. mass mkt. 6.95 (*0-7472-5223-8*, Pub. by Headline Bk Pub) Trafalgar.

— Naked Intent. 1997. mass mkt. 6.95 (*0-7472-5442-7*, Pub. by Headline Bk Pub) Trafalgar.

— Returning to the Casting Couch. mass mkt. 6.95 (*0-7472-4688-2*, Pub. by Headline Bk Pub) Trafalgar.

— Secrets. mass mkt. 6.95 (*0-7472-5224-6*, Pub. by Headline Bk Pub) Trafalgar.

***Bell, Barbara.** Minimus: Starting Out in Latin. (Cambridge Latin Texts Ser.). 80p. (C). 2000. pap., student ed. 17.95 (*0-521-65960-4*) Cambridge U Pr.

— Minimus: Starting Out in Latin. (Cambridge Latin Texts Ser.). 80p. (C). 2000. teacher ed. 59.95 (*0-521-65961-2*) Cambridge U Pr.

— Stacking in Rivertown. 2000. 23.00 (*0-684-87035-5*) Simon & Schuster.

Bell, Barbara, compiled by. An Annotated Guide to Current National Bibliographies. (Government Documents Bibliographies Ser.). 470p. 1986. write for info. (*0-85964-123-6*) Chadwyck-Healey.

Bell, Barbara, jt. auth. see Bright, Vonette.

Bell, Barbara, jt. auth. see Harris, Sara.

Bell, Barbara, ed. see Archambeault, Marci.

Bell, Barbara C. Tools in the Learning Trade. LC 83-15105. 192p. 1984. pap. 13.50 (*0-8108-1743-8*) Scarecrow.

— Tools in the Learning Trade: A Guide to Eight Indispensable Tools for College Students. LC 83-15105. 192p. 1984. text 21.00 (*0-8108-1655-5*) Scarecrow.

Bell, Barney E., ed. see Hash, John A.

***Bell, Becky.** Perfect Slave Abroad. 272p. 1999. pap. 9.95 (*1-901388-47-6*, Pub. by Chimera Pubns) Firebird Dist.

Bell, Benjamin & Redfield, Carol, eds. Authoring Tools for Interactive Learning Environments: A Special Issue of the Journal of the Learning Sciences. (Journal of the Learning Sciences). 153p. 1997. pap. write for info. (*0-8058-9852-2*) L Erlbaum Assocs.

Bell, Bernard. Employment & Wages Annual Averages, 1996. 547p. 1997. per. 46.00 (*0-16-049292-0*) USGPO.

Bell, Bernard I. Crowd Culture. LC 74-117758. (Essay Index Reprint Ser.). 1977. 19.95 (*0-8369-1742-1*) Ayer.

Bell, Bernard I., ed. Affirmations, by a Group of American Anglo-Catholics, Clerical & Lay. LC 68-16906. (Essay Index Reprint Ser.). 1977. 18.95 (*0-8369-0185-1*) Ayer.

***Bell, Bernard J.** Employment & Wages Annual Averages, 1998. 548p. 2000. per. 48.00 (*0-16-059147-3*) USGPO.

— Employment & Wages Annual Averages, 1994. 547p. 1995. per. 39.00 (*0-16-061761-8*) USGPO.

— Employment & Wages Annual Averages, 1997. 549p. 1999. per. 54.00 (*0-16-061773-1*) USGPO.

Bell, Bernard W. The Afro-American Novel & Its Tradition. LC 86-25070. 448p. 1987. pap. 20.95 (*0-87023-688-1*) U of Mass Pr.

***Bell, Bernard W., ed.** Clarence Major & His Art: Portraits of an African American Postmodernist. (Illus.). 360p. 2001. pap. 19.95 (*0-8078-4899-9*); lib. bdg. 59.95 (*0-8078-2586-7*) U of NC Pr.

Bell, Bernard W., et al, eds. W. E. B. Du Bois on Race & Culture: Philosophy, Politics & Poetics. 312p. (C). 1997. pap. 19.99 (*0-415-91557-0*) Routledge.

Bell, Bernard W., et al. Call & Response: The Riverside Anthology of the African American Literary Tradition. Liggins-Hill, Patricia, ed. (C). 1997. text, teacher ed. 11.96 (*0-395-83834-7*) HM.

Bell-Berti, Fredericka & Raphael, Lawrence J., eds. Producing Speech, Contemporary Issues: For Katherine Safford Harris. LC 95-12369. (Modern Acoustics & Signal Processing Ser.). 567p. (C). 1995. 69.95 (*1-56396-286-1*, AIP Pr) Spr-Verlag.

Bell, Betty, jt. auth. see Nutini, Hugo G.

Bell, Betty L. Faces in the Moon. LC 93-42498. (American Indian Literature & Critical Studies Ser.: Vol. 9). 200p. 1995. pap. 10.95 (*0-8061-2774-0*) U of Okla Pr.

Bell, Beverley. Children's Science, Constructivism & Learning in Science. 109p. 1993. pap. 60.00 (*0-7300-1607-2*, ECS 810, Pub. by Deakin Univ) St Mut.

Bell, Beverley, ed. Children's Science: Constructivism & Learning in Science. 109p. 1995. pap. 60.00 (*0-7400-1607-5*, Pub. by Deakin Univ) St Mut.

Bell, Beverly & Gilbert, John. Teacher Development: A Model from Science Education. LC 95-7255. 224p. 1995. 79.95 (*0-7507-0426-8*, Falmer Pr); pap. 27.95 (*0-7507-0427-6*, Falmer Pr) Taylor & Francis.

Bell, Bill. Cat Hiss-tory: A Feline Tour Through the Ages. LC 96-24954. 48p. 1997. 16.00 (*0-517-20046-5*) Random Hse Value.

***Bell, Bill.** One Starry Day in Heaven. LC 98-46437. (Illus.). 48p. (J). (ps-3). 1999. 12.98 (*0-7651-1056-3*) Smithmark.

Bell, Bill D., tr. see Gruen, Anselm.

Bell, Bob. Hunting the Long Tailed Bird. (Illus.). 224p. 1975. 14.95 (*0-88395-027-8*) Freshet Pr.

Bell, Bob, ed. Handloaders Digest 1998: The World's Greatest Handloading Book. 17th ed. LC 62-15069. (Illus.). 480p. 1997. pap. 27.95 (*0-87349-192-0*, HD98) Krause Pubns.

Bell, Bob B. Billy the Kid: The Illustrated Life & Times. (Old West Ser.). (Illus.). 120p. 1992. pap. 24.95 (*0-9639549-0-3*) Honkytonk Sue.

— The Illustrated Life & Times of Billy the Kid. 2nd rev. ed. (Illus.). 192p. 1996. 39.95 (*0-9643343-4-8*); pap. 29.95 (*0-9643343-5-6*) Tri Star-Boze.

— The Illustrated Life & Times of Doc Holliday. 2nd ed. (Illus.). 128p. 1995. 36.95 (*1-887576-01-0*); pap. 26.95 (*1-887576-00-2*) Tri Star-Boze.

— The Illustrated Life & Times of Wyatt Earp. 3rd ed. (Illus.). 144p. 1995. 36.95 (*0-9643343-6-4*); pap. 26.95 (*0-9643343-7-2*) Tri Star-Boze.

— Wyatt Earp: The Illustrated Life & Times. (Old West Ser.). (Illus.). 128p. 1993. pap. 24.95 (*0-9639549-1-1*) Honkytonk Sue.

Bell, Bowyer. The Secret Army: The IRA. 3rd rev. expanded ed. LC 96-3011. 600p. (Orig.). 1997. pap. text 26.95 (*1-56000-901-2*) Transaction Pubs.

Bell, Brad. The Serene Life. unabridged ed. 65p. (Orig.). 1998. pap. 12.95 (*1-892896-71-0*) Buy Books.

Bell, Brenda, ed. see Horton, Myles & Freire, Paulo.

Bell, Brian. Farm Machinery. 4th ed. (Illus.). 352p. 1996. text 44.95 (*0-85236-319-2*, Pub. by Farming Pr) Diamond Farm Bk.

— Farm Workshop. 2nd ed. (Illus.). 224p. 1992. 34.95 (*0-85236-237-4*, Pub. by Farming Pr) Diamond Farm Bk.

— Fifty Years of Farm Machinery. (Illus.). 240p. text 44.95 (*0-85236-263-3*, Pub. by Farming Pr) Diamond Farm Bk.

— Fifty Years of Garden Machinery. (Illus.). 240p. 44.95 (*0-85236-301-X*, Pub. by Farming Pr) Diamond Farm Bk.

Bell, Brian & Cousins, Stewart. Machinery for Horticulture. (Illus.). 304p. 1991. 34.95 (*0-85236-231-5*, Pub. by Farming Pr) Diamond Farm Bk.

Bell, Brian, ed. see Insight Publishing Staff.

Bell, Bruce & Grainger, David A. Basic Operative Dentistry Procedures. LC 72-123419. 419p. reprint ed. pap. 129.90 (*0-8357-3605-9*, 205599700043) Bks Demand.

Bell, Buddy. The Complete Local Church Usher's Handbook. (Illus.). 128p. (Orig.). (C). 1996. pap. 7.99 (*0-89274-793-5*, HH-793) Harrison Hse.

— Greeting 101. LC 99-176796. 112p. 1999. pap. 5.99 (*1-57794-022-9*) Dake Pub.

— The Ministry of Helps Handbook. 128p. (Orig.). 1990. pap. 7.99 (*0-89274-766-8*, HH766) Harrison Hse.

— Ushering 101, 1. 1998. pap. 6.99 (*1-57794-163-2*) Harrison Hse.

Bell, C., tr. see Meyer, Conrad F.

Bell, C. A. English Tibetan Dictionary. (ENG & TIB.). 562p. 1990. reprint ed. 59.95 (*0-8288-9071-4*, F61062) Fr & Eur.

— Grammar of Colloquial Tibetan. 3rd ed. LC 96-138493. 194p. (C). 1996. reprint ed. pap. text 25.00 (*0-7007-0322-5*, Pub. by Curzon Pr Ltd) UH Pr.

Bell, C. A. & Weider, Alan J. Laboratory Aging of Asphalt-Aggregate Mixtures: Field Validation. 204p. (Orig.). (C). 1994. pap. text 15.00 (*0-309-05770-1*, SHRP-A-390) SHRP.

Bell, C. A., et al. Selection of Laboratory Aging Procedures for Asphalt-Aggregate Mixtures. 89p. (Orig.). (C). 1994. pap. text 15.00 (*0-309-05762-0*, SHRP-A-393) SHRP.

***Bell, C. Jeanenne.** Answers to Questions about Old Jewelry: 1840-1950. 5th ed. LC 99-62391. (Illus.). 448p. 2000. pap. 24.95 (*0-87341-731-3*) Krause Pubns.

Bell, C. Jeanenne. Hairwork Jewelry: Identification & Values. LC 98-198502. (Collector's Encyclopedia Ser.). 1998. 24.95 (*1-57432-049-1*, 5046) Collector Bks.

Bell, C. Napier. Tangweera: Life & Adventures among Gentle Savages. (Illus.). 352p. 1989. pap. 14.95 (*0-292-78103-2*) U of Tex Pr.

Bell, C. Ritchie & Lindsey, Anne H. Fall Color & Woodland Harvests: A Guide to the Colorful Fall Leaves, Fruits & Seeds of the Eastern Forests. (Illus.). 192p. (Orig.). 1990. reprint ed. pap. 16.75 (*0-9608688-1-X*) Laurel Hill Pr.

— Fall Color Finder: A Pocket Guide to Autumn Leaves. (Illus.). 64p. (Orig.). 1991. reprint ed. pap. 4.95 (*0-9608688-2-8*, 25,000) Laurel Hill Pr.

Bell, C. Ritchie & Taylor, Bryan J. Florida Wild Flowers & Roadside Plants. xxi, 332p. 1982. reprint ed. pap. 19.95 (*0-9608688-3-6*) Laurel Hill Pr.

— Florida Wild Flowers & Roadside Plants. (Illus.). xxi, 308p. 1982. reprint ed. 24.95 (*0-9608688-0-1*) Laurel Hill Pr.

Bell, C. Ritchie, jt. auth. see Justice, William S.

Bell, C. Ritchie, ed. see Phillips, Harry R.

Bell, Carey, jt. auth. see Horton, Walter.

Bell, Carl I. They Knew Franklin Pierce. 1980. 8.95 (*0-917780-01-9*) April Hill.

Bell, Carla S. Poems with a Message. (Orig.). 1997. pap. write for info. (*1-57553-453-3*) Watermrk Pr.

Bell, Carol, ed. see Pierce, Mark C.

Bell, Carol, tr. see Requena, Yves.

Bell, Carol W. Ohio Guide to Genealogical Sources. 372p. 1993. reprint ed. 30.00 (*0-8063-1228-9*, 397) Genealog Pub.

Bell, Carol W., ed. The Report, Vol. 23. 1983. 5.00 (*0-935057-38-2*) OH Genealogical.

— The Report, Vol. 24. 1984. 3.75 (*0-935057-39-0*) OH Genealogical.

— The Report, Vol. 25. 1985. 5.00 (*0-935057-40-4*) OH Genealogical.

— Report, Vol. 26. 1986. 5.00 (*0-935057-42-0*) OH Genealogical.

— Report, Vol. 27. 1987. 5.00 (*0-935057-66-8*) OH Genealogical.

— Report, Vol. 28. 1988. 5.00 (*0-935057-54-4*) OH Genealogical.

— Report, Vol. 29. 1989. 5.00 (*0-935057-55-2*) OH Genealogical.

— Report, Vol. 30. 1990. 5.00 (*0-935057-59-5*) OH Genealogical.

— Report, Vol. 31. 1991. 5.00 (*0-935057-64-1*) OH Genealogical.

— Report, Vol. 32. 1992. 5.00 (*0-935057-68-4*) OH Genealogical.

Bell, Carolyn, ed. see Marazon, Renee A. & Marazon, David A.

Bell, Caryn C. Revolution, Romanticism, & the Afro-Creole Protest Tradition in Louisiana, 1718-1868. LC 96-35429. 328p. 1996. text 40.00 (*0-8071-2096-0*) La State U Pr.

Bell, Catharine, ed. see Fisher, Lester.

***Bell, Catherine.** Everyday Epicurean. (Illus.). 200p. 2000. pap. 19.95 (*1-58008-225-4*) Ten Speed Pr.

Bell, Catherine. Ritual: Perspectives on the Practice of Religion. LC 96-23945. 368p. 1997. text 60.00 (*0-19-511051-X*) OUP.

— Ritual: Perspectives on the Practices of Religion. LC 96-23945. 368p. 1997. pap. 18.95 (*0-19-511052-8*) OUP.

— Ritual Theory, Ritual Practice. 288p. 1992. pap. text 19.95 (*0-19-507613-3*) OUP.

Bell, Cecil H., jt. auth. see Grady, Richard J.

Bell, Cedric D., ed. Evidence. 402p. 1996. pap. 110.00 (*0-7510-0692-0*, Pub. by HLT Pubns) St Mut.

— Land Law. 394p. 1996. pap. 95.00 (*0-7510-0688-2*, Pub. by HLT Pubns) St Mut.

— Land Law Cases. 380p. 1996. pap. 95.00 (*0-7510-0655-6*, Pub. by HLT Pubns) St Mut.

Bell, Celtic D. Evidence Cases. 300p. 1996. pap. 110.00 (*0-7510-0658-0*, Pub. by HLT Pubns) St Mut.

Bell, Charlene A. Taking Charge: How to Coach Yourself to Quality Living. (Illus.). 242p. (Orig.). 1992. pap. 14.95 (*0-9624320-0-8*) Sunburst IA.

Bell, Charles. History of the Town of Exeter, NH. (Illus.). 557p. 1992. reprint ed. lib. bdg. 56.00 (*0-8328-2505-0*) Higginson Bk Co.

— Portrait of a Dalai Lama: The Life & Times of the Great Thirteenth. (Tibet Book - Yellow Ser.). (Illus.). 464p. 1987. pap. 22.95 (*0-86171-055-X*) Wisdom MA.

— The Religion of Tibet. 1987. reprint ed. 42.50 (*81-7069-002-1*, Pub. by M Manoharial) S Asia.

— The Religion of Tibet. (C). 1994. reprint ed. pap. 16.00 (*81-208-1050-3*, Pub. by Motilal Bnarsidass) S Asia.

— The Religion of Tibet. (Illus.). 235p. 1990. reprint ed. pap. 16.00 (*957-9482-20-9*) Oriental Bk Store.

— Tibet Past & Present. (Illus.). 340p. 1990. reprint ed. 36.50 (*0-317-99944-3*, Pub. by M Manoharial) Coronet Bks.

Bell, Charles, ed. Manual of Colloquial Tibetan. (Illus.). (C). 1979. reprint ed. 180.00 (*0-89771-117-3*, Pub. by Ratna Pustak Bhandar) St Mut.

Bell, Charles A. English-Tibetan Colloquial Dictionary. 1989. 100.00 (*0-7855-0271-8*, Pub. by Ratna Pustak Bhandar) St Mut.

— The People of Tibet. 1980. lib. bdg. 300.00 (*0-87968-481-X*) Krishna Pr.

***Bell, Charles A.** The People of Tibet. 338p. 2000. 34.00 (*81-215-0933-5*, Pub. by Munshiram) Coronet Bks.

Bell, Charles A. The Religion of Tibet. 1975. lib. bdg. 250.00 (*0-87968-482-8*) Krishna Pr.

Bell, Charles A. Tibet: Past & Present. 1975. lib. bdg. 250.00 (*0-87968-483-6*) Krishna Pr.

Bell, Charles Alfred. Grammar of Colloquial Tibetan. LC 98-905012. x, 184 p. 1998. write for info. (*81-206-1325-2*) Asian Educ Servs.

Bell, Charles B. & Miller, Harriett P. A Mysterious Spirit: The Bell Witch of Tennessee. 1972. reprint ed. pap. 9.95 (*0-918450-13-6*) C Elder.

***Bell, Charles E., et al.** Organic Chemistry Laboratory: Standard & Microscale Experiments. 3rd ed. LC 00-30100. (Illus.). 2000. pap. write for info. (*0-03-029272-7*) SCP.

Bell, Charles G. Five Chambered Heart. 84p. 1986. pap. 8.95 (*0-89255-098-8*) Persea Bks.

— The Half Gods. LC 68-23028. 1968. 25.00 (*0-89366-085-X*) Ultramarine Pub.

Bell, Charles G., jt. auth. see Price, Charles M.

Bell, Charles G., jt. ed. see Bradshaw, Ted K.

Bell, Charles H. John Wheelwright His Writings: Including His Fast-Day Sermon 1637 & His Mercurius Americanus, 1645. 253p. 1996. pap. 22.00 (*0-7884-0481-4*, B144) Heritage Bk.

Bell, Charles N. Henry's Journal. 20p. 1982. pap. 3.95 (*0-87770-270-5*) Ye Galleon.

Bell, Chet, jt. auth. see Bell, Jeannette.

Bell, Chip. Customers As Partners: Building Relationships That Last. LC 94-16999. 237p. 1996. reprint ed. pap. 15.95 (*1-881052-78-8*) Berrett-Koehler.

Bell, Chip R. Customers As Partners: Building Relationships That Last. LC 94-16999. (Illus.). 240p. 1994. 24.95 (*1-881052-54-0*) Berrett-Koehler.

— Managers As Mentors: Building Partnerships for Learning. LC 96-7029. 208p. 1998. reprint ed. pap. 16.95 (*1-57675-034-5*) Berrett-Koehler.

Bell, Chip R. & Harari, Oren. Beep! Beep! Competing in the Age of the Road Runner. LC 99-30164. (Illus.). 288p. 2000. 23.95 (*0-446-52353-4*, Pub. by Warner Bks) Little.

***Bell, Chip R. & Harari, Oren.** Beep! Beep! Competing in the Age of the Road Runner. 2001. pap. write for info. (*0-446-67654-3*) Warner Bks.

Bell, Chip R. & Shea, Heather. Dance Lessons: 6 Steps to Great Partnerships in Business & Life. LC 98-27938. (Illus.). 200p. 1998. 24.95 (*1-57675-043-4*) Berrett-Koehler.

Bell, Chip R. & Zemke, Ron. Managing Knock Your Socks off Service. LC 91-48064. (Illus.). 210p. 1999. pap. 17.95 (*0-8144-7784-4*) AMACOM.

Bell, Chip R., jt. auth. see Zemke, Ron.

Bell, Chris. Handbook for ROV Supervisors. (Illus.). 327p. 1997. pap. 162.00 (*1-870945-94-8*) Oilfield Publns.

Bell, Chris, et al. Aspects of Educational & Training Technology, Vol. XXIX. 320p. 1997. 59.95 (*0-7494-1874-5*, Kogan Pg Educ) Stylus Pub VA.

Bell, Chris, jt. auth. see Burn, David.

Bell, Chris, jt. auth. see Cuddy, Beverley.

Bell, Chris, jt. auth. see Harris, Duncan.

Bell, Chris, ed. see Reynolds, Michael.

Bell, Chris A. & Sosnovski, Don. Aging: Binder Evaluation. 81p. (Orig.). (C). 1994. pap. text 15.00 (*0-685-75330-1*, SHRP-A-384) SHRP.

Bell, Christina. The Boy with a Toucan in His Heart. 160p. (J). 1990. 39.00 (*0-85439-397-8*, Pub. by St Paul Pubns) St Mut.

***Bell, Christine.** Peace Agreements & Human Rights. 380p. 2000. text 74.00 (*0-19-829889-7*) OUP.

Bell, Christine. Saint. LC 85-12256. 256p. 1985. 14.95 (*0-910923-21-3*) Pineapple Pr.

Bell, Christine, jt. auth. see Fox, Marie.

Bell, Christine, jt. ed. see Morison, John.

Bell, Christopher, ed. Chemical Factors in Neural Growth, Degeneration & Repair. LC 97-132250. 528p. 1996. 284.50 (*0-444-82529-0*) Elsevier.

— Novel Peripheral Neurotransmitters. (International Encyclopedia of Pharmacology & Therapeutics Ser.: No. 135). (Illus.). 388p. 1991. 127.25 (*0-08-040691-2*, Pub. by PPI) Elsevier.

Bell, Christopher G., jt. auth. see Soltis, Michael J.

Bell, Clair H., jt. auth. see Hager, Georg.

Bell, Clair H., ed. see Fabrizius, Peter.

Bell, Clara, tr. see Balzac, Honore de.

Bell, Clara, tr. see Haeckel, Ernst.

Bell, Clara, tr. see Huysmans, J. K.

Bell, Clara, tr. see Huysmans, Joris K.

Bell, Clara, tr. see Loti-Viaud, Pierre P.

Bell, Clara, tr. see Spitta, Philipp.

Bell, Clare. The Jaguar Princess. 1994. mass mkt. 4.99 (*0-8125-1516-1*) Tor Bks.

Bell, Clare. Ratha's Challenge. LC 94-29209. 256p. (J). (gr. 7 up). 1994. pap. 16.95 (*0-689-50586-8*) McElderry Bks.

Bell, Clarisa. At the Olympics. Kohen, Gabriela, tr. from SPA. (This Is Entertainment Ser.). (Illus.). 24p. (Orig.). (J). (gr. 2-6). 1992. pap. 9.95 (*1-56492-007-0*) Laredo.

— En las Olimpiadas. (This Is Entertainment Ser.). (SPA., Illus.). 24p. (Orig.). (J). (gr. 2-6). 1992. pap. 9.95 (*1-56492-051-8*) Laredo.

— Games People Play. Kohen, Gabriela, tr. from SPA. (This Is Entertainment Ser.). (Illus.). 24p. (J). (gr. 2-6). 1992. lib. bdg. 9.95 (*1-56492-004-6*) Laredo.

— El Teatro: Big Book. (This Is Entertainment Ser.). (SPA., Illus.). 24p. (Orig.). (J). (gr. 2-6). 1992. pap. 19.95 (*1-56492-057-7*) Laredo.

— Vamos a Jugar. (This Is Entertainment Ser.). (SPA., Illus.). 24p. (J). (gr. 2-6). 1992. pap. 9.95 (*1-56492-048-8*) Laredo.

— Vamos a Jugar: Big Book. (This Is Entertainment Ser.). (SPA., Illus.). 24p. (Orig.). (J). (gr. 2-6). 1992. pap. 19.95 (*1-56492-049-6*) Laredo.

Bell, Clarisa, jt. auth. see Kohen, Gabriela.

Bell, Claudia. Inventing New Zealand: Everyday Myths of Pakeha Identity. LC 96-155036. v, 208 p. 1996. write for info. (*0-14-024496-4*) Penguin Putnam.

Bell, Clint C. Maintenance Mechanics Qualification Program. 2nd ed. LC 80-85404. 78p. 1989. reprint ed. pap. 30.00 (*0-608-00685-8*, 203560400096) Bks Demand.

Bell, Clive. Landmarks in Nineteenth Century Painting. LC 67-30197. (Essay Index Reprint Ser.). 1977. 20.95 (*0-8369-0186-X*) Ayer.

— Since Cezanne. (Essay Index Reprint Ser.). 1977. 18.95 (*0-8369-0034-0*) Ayer.

***Bell, Colin.** Scotland's Century. 1999. 35.00 (*0-00-472225-6*, Pub. by HarpC) Trafalgar.

Bell, Colin & Newby, Howard, eds. Sociology of Community: A Collection of Readings. 424p. 1974. 35.00 (*0-7146-2970-7*, Pub. by F Cass Pubs) Intl Spec Bk.

Bell, Coral. Dependent Ally: A Study of Australian Foreign Policy. 2nd ed. 192p. 1994. pap. 24.95 (*1-86373-400-7*, Pub. by Allen & Unwin Pty) Paul & Co Pubs.

— Negotiation from Strength: A Study in the Politics of Power. LC 77-1054. 248p. 1977. reprint ed. lib. bdg. 65.00 (*0-8371-9508-X*, BENS, Greenwood Pr) Greenwood.

— The Reagan Paradox: American Foreign Policy in the 1980s. 192p. 1989. 70.00 (*1-85278-203-X*) E Elgar.

— The Reagan Paradox: U. S. Foreign Policy in the 1980s. 224p. (Orig.). 1989. pap. 14.95 (*0-8135-1474-6*) Rutgers U Pr.

Bell, Corky. Maximum Boost: Designing, Testing, & Installing Turbocharger Systems. LC 97-9087. (Illus.). 256p. 1997. 34.95 (*0-8376-0160-6*) Bentley Pubs.

***Bell, Craig S.** Comprehending Coincidence: Synchronicity & Personal Transformation. 220p. 2000. pap. 18.95 (*0-87785-393-2*, Pub. by Swedenborg) Words Distrib.

Bell, Cressida. Cressida Bell. LC 95-78099. (Illus.). 128p. 1996. 24.95 (*0-8212-2267-8*, Pub. by Bulfinch Pr) Little.

Bell, D., et al. The Lecture Notes on Tropical Medicine. 4th ed. (Lecture Notes Ser.). 320p. 1995. pap. 29.95 (*0-632-03839-X*) Blackwell Sci.

Bell, D. H., ed. Landslides - Glissements de Terrain: Proceedings of the Sixth International Symposium, Christchurch, 10-14.02.1991, 3 vols. (Illus.). 1800p. (C). 1992. text 368.00 (*90-5410-032-X*, Pub. by A A Balkema) Ashgate Pub Co.

Bell, D. J. Planning Corporate Manpower. LC 73-86105. (Manpower Studies Ser.). 191p. reprint ed. pap. 59.30 (*0-608-30410-7*, 201005500071) Bks Demand.

Bell, D. S. & Criddle, Byron. The French Communist Party in the Fifth Republic. LC 93-43411. (Illus.). 306p. 1994. text 59.00 (*0-19-821990-3*, Clarendon Pr) OUP.

Bell, D. S. & Shaw, Eric, eds. The Left in France: Towards the Socialist Republic. 192p. 1983. pap. 57.50 (*0-85124-349-5*, Pub. by Spokesman) Coronet Bks.

Bell, D. Wallace & Hanson, Charles G. Profit Sharing & Profitability: How Profit Sharing Promotes Business Success. 128p. (C). 1987. 108.00 (*1-85091-303-X*) St Mut.

Bell, Dale. Home Care in New York City: Providers, Payers, Clients. (Papers: No. 6). 48p. 1987. 5.00 (*0-934459-11-8*) United Hosp Fund.

Bell, Dana. Airforce Colors, Vol. 3. (Illus.). 96p. (Orig.). 1997. pap. 14.95 (*0-89747-376-0*, 6152) Squad Sig Pubns.

— Colors & Markings of the A-10 Warthog. (Colors & Markings Ser.: Vol. 21). 64p. 1991. pap. 12.95 (*0-8306-3096-1*, 24548) McGraw-Hill Prof.

— USAF Colors & Markings in the 1990s. 144p. 1992. 34.95 (*1-85367-112-6*, 5447) Stackpole.

— USAFI Colors & Markings in the 1990s. LC 93-45331. (Illus.). 178p. 1994. pap. 24.95 (*1-85367-171-1*, 5600) Stackpole.

Bell, Dana, et al. U. S. Air Force Colours. LC 80-503134. 1979. write for info. (*0-85368-484-7*, Pub. by Arms & Armour) Sterling.

Bell, Daniel. Bringing Your Employees into the Business: An Employee Ownership Handbook for Small Business. LC 88-621669. 112p. 1988. 18.95 (*0-933522-18-5*); pap. 9.95 (*0-933522-19-3*) Kent Popular.

— The Coming of Post-Industrial Society: A Venture in Social Forecasting. LC 72-89178. 544p. 1999. pap. 17.50 (*0-465-09713-8*, Pub. by Basic) HarpC.

— Communitarianism & Its Critics. 272p. (C). 1993. pap. text 19.95 (*0-19-827922-1*) OUP.

— The Cultural Contradictions of Capitalism. 20th anniversary ed. LC 96-41616. 400p. 1996. pap. 17.50 (*0-465-01499-2*, Pub. by Basic) HarpC.

***Bell, Daniel.** East Meets West: Human Rights & Democracy in East Asia. LC 99-48077. 344p. 2000. text 65.00 (*0-691-00507-9*, Pub. by Princeton U Pr); pap. text 19.95 (*0-691-00508-7*, Pub. by Princeton U Pr) Cal Prin Full Svc.

Bell, Daniel. The End of Ideology. rev. ed. LC 87-29664. 504p. (Orig.). 1988. reprint ed. 42.00 (*0-674-25229-2*); reprint ed. pap. 18.50 (*0-674-25230-6*) HUP.

***Bell, Daniel.** End of Ideology: On the Exhaustion of Political Ideas in the Fifties. 512p. 2000. pap. 19.95 (*0-674-00426-4*) HUP.

Bell, Daniel. Information Society. Date not set. 19.95 (*0-465-03289-3*, Pub. by Basic) HarpC.

— Marxian Socialism in the United States. LC 67-30481. 228p. reprint ed. pap. 70.70 (*0-608-18439-X*, 203263600080) Bks Demand.

— The Racket-Ridden Longshoreman. (Reprint Series in Social Sciences). (C). 1993. reprint ed. pap. text 5.00 (*0-8290-3813-2*, S-13) Irvington.

— Reforming of General Education. (Foundations of Higher Education Ser.). 2000. write for info. (*1-56000-591-2*) Transaction Pubs.

— The Social Sciences since the Second World War. LC 80-27957. 104p. (C). 1981. reprint ed. 32.95 (*0-87855-426-2*); reprint ed. pap. text 21.95 (*0-87855-872-1*) Transaction Pubs.

— Teletext. 1979. 10.95 (*0-465-08402-8*) Basic.

— The Winding Passage: Sociological Essays & Journeys. 371p. (C). 1991. pap. 24.95 (*0-88738-899-X*) Transaction Pubs.

Bell, Daniel, ed. The Radical Right: The New American Right. enl. rev. ed. LC 78-167309. (Essay Index Reprint Ser.). 1977. reprint ed. 25.95 (*0-8369-2447-9*) Ayer.

***Bell, Daniel, ed.** The Radical Right. 3rd ed. 570p. 2000. pap. 29.95 (*0-7658-0749-1*) Transaction Pubs.

Bell, Daniel & Graubard, Stephen R., eds. Toward the Year 2000: Work in Progress. LC 97-14090. (Illus.). 412p. 1997. pap. text 18.95 (*0-262-52237-3*) MIT Pr.

Bell, Daniel & Kazin, Michael. Marxian Socialism in the United States. 280p. 1996. pap. text 16.95 (*0-8014-8309-3*) Cornell U Pr.

Bell, Daniel A., jt. ed. see Bauer, Joanne R.

Bell, Daniel O. A Pious Bacchanal: Affinities Between the Lives & Works of John Flaxman & Aubrey Beardsley. LC 93-41838. (New Connections Ser.: Vol. 10). 344p. 2000. text 58.95 (*0-8204-2318-1*) P Lang Pubng.

Bell, Darnetta & Bongiorni, Kevin, eds. Cemeteries & Spaces of Death: Inquiries into Their Meaning: Diverse Papers. LC 95-45084. (Illus.). x, 148p. 1996. pap. 13.00 (*1-879378-15-9*) Xenos Riverside.

***Bell, David.** Cybercultures Reader. 2000. pap. 27.95 (*0-415-18379-0*) Routledge.

Bell, David. Distributed Database Systems. LC 91-44177. 410p. (C). 1992. 42.19 (*0-201-54400-8*) Addison-Wesley.

***Bell, David.** Presidential Power in 5th Republic France. 224p. 2000. 65.00 (*1-85973-371-9*, Pub. by Berg Pubs); pap. 19.50 (*1-85973-376-X*, Pub. by Berg Pubs) NYU Pr.

Bell, David. Reason & Passion: A Celebration of the Work of Hanna Segal. LC 97-47599. (Tavistock Clinic Ser.). 304p. (C). 1998. pap. 22.99 (*0-415-92076-0*) Routledge.

— Reason & Passion: A Celebration of the Work of Hanna Segal. LC 97-47599. (Tavistock Clinic Ser.). 304p. (C). 1998. 75.00 (*0-415-92075-2*) Routledge.

— The Roots of Disunity: A Look at Canadian Political Culture. 2nd rev. ed. (Studies in Canadian Politics). (Illus.). 272p. 1992. pap. text 18.95 (*0-19-540858-6*) OUP.

***Bell, David & Binnie, Jon.** The Sexual Citizen. 2000. 59.95 (*0-7456-1653-4*, Pub. by Polity Pr); pap. 24.95 (*0-7456-1654-2*, Pub. by Polity Pr) Blackwell Pubs.

Bell, David & Keil, Roger, eds. Political Ecology: Global & Local. LC 98-13484. 400p. (C). 1998. pap. 32.99 (*0-415-18381-2*) Routledge.

***Bell, David & Kennedy, Barbara M., eds.** The Cybercultures Reader. (Illus.). 792p. 2000. 85.00 (*0-415-18378-2*) Routledge.

Bell, David & Valentine, Gill. Consumption, Space & Identity: Cultural Geographies of Food. LC 96-44153. (Illus.). 256p. (C). 1997. 75.00 (*0-415-13767-5*); pap. 25.99 (*0-415-13768-3*) Routledge.

Bell, David & Valentine, Gill, eds. Mapping Desire: Geographies of Sexualities. LC 94-34825. (Illus.). 500p. (C). (gr. 13). 1995. pap. 25.99 (*0-415-11164-1*, C0058) Routledge.

Bell, David, et al. William Penhallow Henderson: Master Colorist of Santa Fe. LC 84-61888. (Illus.). 108p. (Orig.). 1984. pap. 13.00 (*0-910407-12-6*) Phoenix Art.

Bell, David, jt. ed. see Shaw, Eric.

Bell, David A. Getting the Best Score for Your Film: A Filmmaker's Guide to Music Scoring. LC 94-30604. (Illus.). 130p. (Orig.). 1994. 12.95 (*1-879505-20-7*) Silman James Pr.

— Lawyers & Citizens: The Making of a Political Elite in Old Regime France. (Illus.). 304p. 1994. text 60.00 (*0-19-507670-2*) OUP.

Bell, David A., jt. ed. see Johnson, Daniel M.

Bell, David D. An Index of Authors & Works in Cistercian Libraries in Great Britain. (Cistercian Studies: No. 130). 300p. 1992. 39.95 (*0-87907-530-9*) Cistercian Pubns.

Bell, David E., et al, eds. Decision Making: Descriptive, Normative & Prescriptive Interactions. 633p. 1988. pap. text 42.95 (*0-521-36851-0*) Cambridge U Pr.

Bell, David E. & Reich, Michael R. Health, Nutrition, & Economic Crisis: Approaches to Policy in the Third World. LC 87-30834. 455p. 1987. 65.00 (*0-86569-170-3*, Auburn Hse) Greenwood.

Bell, David E. & Salmon, Walter J. Introduction to Retailing: Test & Cases. LC 95-45167. (SF - Retailing Ser.). 1995. mass mkt. 53.95 (*0-538-86369-2*) S-W Pub.

— Strategic Retailing Management: Text & Cases. 1995. mass mkt. 75.95 (*0-538-84908-8*) S-W Pub.

Bell, David F. Circumstances: Chance in the Literary Text. LC 92-5568. x, 231p. 1993. text 45.00 (*0-8032-1229-1*) U of Nebr Pr.

— Models of Power: Politics & Economics in Zola's "Rougon-Macquart". LC 87-10779. 207p. 1988. reprint ed. pap. 64.20 (*0-608-02140-7*, 206280900003) Bks Demand.

Bell, David H., ed. Volumezero. (Illus.). 76p. (Orig.). 1986. pap. 15.00 (*0-937919-00-4*) RPI Schl Arch.

Bell, David M. The Adventures of Ecomunk: Mr. Beaver Builds a Dam. (Illus.). 68p. (J). (gr. 3-6). 1998. pap. 9.95 (*1-893120-01-5*, EM-01) Glamorgan Bks.

— The Bass' Tale: A Conversational Life History. (Illus.). 70p. (YA). (gr. 8-12). 1998. pap. 9.95 (*1-893120-02-3*, TL-01) Glamorgan Bks.

— Snow Tires for Your Brain: A Layperson's Guide to Using the Old Noggin. 73p. (C). 1998. pap. 9.95 (*1-893120-00-7*, ST-01) Glamorgan Bks.

Bell, David N. A Cloud of Witnesses: An Introductory History of the Development of Christian Doctrine. (Cistercian Studies: No. 109). (Illus.). 225p. 1989. 35.95 (*0-87907-609-7*); pap. 15.95 (*0-87907-709-3*) Cistercian Pubns.

— The Image of Likeness: The Augustinian Spirituality of William of St. Thierry. 1984. 21.95 (*0-87907-878-3*) Cistercian Pubns.

— An Index of Cistercian Authors & Works in Medieval Catalogues in Great Britain, 130. LC 94-21179. (Cistercian Studies). 1994. 42.95 (*0-87907-532-5*) Cistercian Pubns.

— Many Mansions: An Introduction to the Development & Diversity of Medieval Theology. 1996. 34.95 (*0-614-19804-6*) Cistercian Pubns.

— Many Mansions: An Introduction to the Development & Diversity of Medieval Theology. LC 96-213134 (Illus.). 1996. pap. 15.95 (*0-87907-546-5*) Cistercian Pubns.

— What Nuns Read: Books & Libraries in Medieval English Nunneries. LC 94-27837. (Cistercian Studies: No. 158). 1995. 49.95 (*0-87907-558-9*) Cistercian Pubns.

— Wholly Animals: A Book of Beastly Tales. (Cistercian Studies). (Illus.). 300p. 1992. 28.95 (*0-87907-328-4*); pap. 12.95 (*0-87907-628-3*) Cistercian Pubns.

Bell, David N., tr. Mena of Nikiou: The Life of Isaac of Alexandria & the Martyrdom of Saint Marcobius. 1988. 31.95 (*0-317-68104-4*); pap. 12.95 (*0-87907-607-0*) Cistercian Pubns.

Bell, David N., tr. Baldwin of Ford: Spirtual Tractates, 2 vols., Set. 1986. 50.00 (*0-87907-438-8*, CF38); pap. 20.00 (*0-87907-441-8*, CF41) Cistercian Pubns.

— Besa: The Life of Shenoute. (Cistercian Studies: No. 73). 1983. pap. 12.95 (*0-87907-873-1*) Cistercian Pubns.

Bell, David N., ed. see St. Symeon.

Bell, David O. Awesome Chesapeake: A Kid's Guide to the Bay. LC 91-55483. (Illus.). 44p. (J). (gr. 3-8). 1994. 11.95 (*0-87033-457-3*, Tidewtr Pubs) Cornell Maritime.

— Chesapeake Bay Walk. LC 98-216543. (Illus.). 30p. (J). (gr. k-4). 1998. 12.95 (*0-87033-507-3*) Cornell Maritime.

— Dockmanship. LC 91-55483. (Illus.). 104p. 1992. pap. 6.95 (*0-87033-425-5*) Cornell Maritime.

Bell, David R. Core Concepts in Physiology. LC 97-31210. 230p. 1997. pap. 26.00 (*0-316-08868-4*, Little Brwn Med Div) Lppncott W & W.

Bell, David S. Curing Fatigue. 1996. mass mkt. 6.99 (*0-425-14983-8*) Berkley Pub.

— The Doctor's Guide to Chronic Fatigue Syndrome: Understanding, Treating & Living with CFIDS. (Illus.). 256p. 1993. 21.00 (*0-201-62616-0*) Addison-Wesley.

— The Doctor's Guide to Chronic Fatigue Syndrome: Understanding, Treating & Living with CFIDS. 304p. 1995. pap. 13.00 (*0-201-40797-3*) Addison-Wesley.

— The Doctor's Guide to Chronic Fatigue Syndrome: Understanding, Treating, & Living with CFIDS. 275p. 1999. reprint ed. text 21.00 (*0-7881-6289-6*) DIANE Pub.

***Bell, David S.** Parties & Democracy in France: Parties under Presidentialism. (Parties & Democracy Ser.). 256p. 2000. pap. 30.95 (*1-85521-864-X*, Pub. by Ashgate Pub); text 73.95 (*1-85521-861-5*, Pub. by Ashgate Pub) Ashgate Pub Co.

Bell, David S., ed. France. LC 94-48072. (International Library of Politics & Comparative Government). 1995. 199.95 (*1-85521-346-X*, Pub. by Dartmth Pub) Ashgate Pub Co.

— Western European Communists & the Collapse of Communism. LC 92-12214. 1993. 39.50 (*0-85496-806-7*) Berg Pubs.

Bell, David S. & Criddle, Byron. The French Socialist Party: Resurgence & Victory. 2nd ed. (Illus.). 344p. 1988. pap. text 19.95 (*0-19-822870-8*) OUP.

Bell, David S. & Gaffney, John. 1992 & After. Pisani, Edgard, ed. (Journal of Contemporary European Affairs Ser.: No. 1). 330p. 1989. pap. 25.20 (*0-08-037391-7*, Pergamon Pr) Elsevier.

***Bell, David S. & Lord, Christopher.** Transnational Parties in the European Union. LC 97-45893. (Leeds Studies in Democratization). viii, 217p. 1998. 68.95 (*1-84014-401-7*) Ashgate Pub Co.

Bell, David S., et al. A Parents' Guide to CFIDS: How to Be an Advocate for Your Child with Chronic Fatigue Immune Dysfunction Syndrome. LC 98-21756. 162p. 1999. 39.95 (*0-7890-0631-6*, Hawrth Medical); pap. 17.95 (*0-7890-0711-8*, Hawrth Medical) Haworth Pr.

Bell, David V., jt. auth. see Fletcher, Frederick J.

Bell, De Loss E. De Loss Ernest Bell's Treasury of Civil War Humor. LC 98-93584. 250p. 1998. pap. 55.00 (*1-57502-937-5*, P02578) Morris Pubng.

Bell, Deborah, et al, eds. Body & Soul: A Kosher Living Classic. (Illus.). 170p. (Orig.). 1984. reprint ed. 10.00 (*0-8266-0239-8*, Lubavitch Wom Ckbk) Kehot Pubn Soc.

Bell, Debra. Ultimate Guide to Homeschooling. LC 96-38912. 416p. 1997. pap. 19.99 (*0-8499-3988-7*) Tommy Nelson.

***Bell, Debra.** Ultimate Guide to Homeschooling 2001. (Illus.). 2000. pap. text 24.99 (*0-8499-7575-1*) Tommy Nelson.

Bell, Derek. And We Are Not Saved: The Elusive Quest for Racial Justice. 304p. 1989. pap. 14.00 (*0-465-00329-X*, Pub. by Basic) HarpC.

Bell, Derek. Derek Bell: The Mystic Harp. 16.95 (*0-7692-8624-0*) Wrner Bros.

Bell, Derek. Towards Effective Subject Leadership in the Primary School. LC 98-41546. 1999. 90.00 (*0-335-20183-0*) Taylor & Francis.

Bell, Derek & Ritchie, Ron. Towards Effective Subject Leadership in the Primary School. LC 98-41546. (Illus.). 190p. 1999. pap. 25.95 (*0-335-20182-2*) OpUniv Pr.

Bell, Derek, jt. auth. see Hayes, Peter C.

Bell, Derrick A. Afrolantica Legacies. LC 97-35807. 196p. 1997. 24.95 (*0-88378-199-9*); pap. 14.95 (*0-88378-200-6*) Third World.

— The Age of Segregation: Race Relations in the South, 1890-1945, Essays. Haws, Robert J., ed. LC 78-14233. 166p. reprint ed. pap. 51.50 (*0-7837-1399-1*, 204158000021) Bks Demand.

— Civil Rights in Two Thousand Four: Where Will We Be? (Working Papers on Civil Rights). 1988. 2.50 (*0-318-33316-3*, CR2) IPPP.

— Constitutional Conflicts, 2 vols., Pts. I & II. (C). 1997. 60.00 (*0-87084-247-1*) Anderson Pub Co.

— Faces at the Bottom of the Well: The Permanence of Racism. LC 91-59020. 240p. 1993. reprint ed. pap. 12.00 (*0-465-06814-6*, Pub. by Basic) HarpC.

— Gospel Choirs: Psalms of Survival in an Alien Land Called Home. 240p. 1997. pap. 13.00 (*0-465-02413-0*, Pub. by Basic) HarpC.

— Race & Racism. 3rd ed. 976p. 1992. 48.00 (*0-316-08822-6*, Aspen Law & Bus) Aspen Pub.

B

An Asterisk (*) at the beginning of an entry indicates that the title is appearing for the first time.

***Bell, Derrick A.** Race, Racism & American Law. 4th ed. LC 00-20114. 2000. text 65.00 (*0-7355-1202-7*) Panel Pubs.

Bell, Derrick A., ed. Constitutional Conflicts, Pt. I. 608p. (C). 1997. 39.95 (*0-87084-245-5*) Anderson Pub Co.

— Constitutional Conflicts, Pt. II. 1588p. (C). 1997. ring bd. 30.00 (*0-87084-246-3*) Anderson Pub Co.

— Constitutional Conflicts, 2 vols., Pts. I & II. (C). 1997. 47.95 incl. disk (*0-87084-249-8*) Anderson Pub Co.

— Shades of Brown: New Perspectives on School Desegregation. LC 80-21877. 160p. 1980. pap. 49.60 (*0-7837-7449-4*, 204904100010) Bks Demand.

Bell, Desmond, et al. Managing Quality. 236p. 1994. pap. 44.95 (*0-7506-1823-X*) Buttrwrth-Heinemann.

***Bell, Desmond, et al.** Managing Quality. 288p. 2001. pap. 35.95 (*0-7506-4837-6*) Buttrwrth-Heinemann.

Bell, Diana. The Complete Gilbert & Sullivan. (Illus.). 192p. 1998. pap. 25.95 (*1-57715-033-3*) Knckerbocker.

Bell, Diana, jt. tr. see Schreiner, Shelley.

Bell, Diane. An Anthropologist Looks at Australian Society: Professorial Lecture. (C). 1991. pap. 30.00 (*0-7300-1449-5*, Pub. by Deakin Univ) St Mut.

— Daughters of the Dreaming. 2nd ed. LC 93-14760. 342p. 1993. pap. 19.95 (*0-8166-2398-8*) U of Minn Pr.

— Ngarrindjeri Wurruwarrin: A World That Is, Was & Will Be. LC 98-213203. 1999. pap. 27.95 (*1-875559-71-X*, Pub. by SpiniFex Pr) LPC InBook.

Bell, Diane, et al, eds. Gendered Fields: Women, Men & Ethnography. LC 92-18807. 272p. (C). 1993. pap. 25.99 (*0-415-06252-7*, A9603) Routledge.

Bell, Diane & Cahill, Ann J., eds. Aborigines in Australian Society: A Resourceful Book. 220p. (Orig.). (C). 1994. pap. write for info. (*0-9636118-1-X*) Coll Holy Cross.

Bell, Don. I've Been Thinking. LC 91-17223. (Illus.). 112p. (Orig.). 1991. pap. 8.95 (*1-56412-000-7*) Hse Nine Muses.

Bell, Donald H., jt. ed. see Gutman, Herbert G.

Bell, Donna. Countryscapes. 100p. 1992. pap. text 10.50 (*1-56770-249-X*) S Scheewe Pubns.

— The First Waltz. 256p. 1998. pap. 4.99 (*0-8217-5871-3*, Zebra Kensgtn) Kensgtn Pub Corp.

***Bell, Donna.** Heiress to Love. (Zebra Regency Romance Ser.). 256p. 2000. mass mkt. 4.99 (*0-8217-6628-7*, Zebra Kensgtn) Kensgtn Pub Corp.

Bell, Donna. An Improper Pursuit. 224p. 1994. mass mkt. 3.99 (*0-8217-4600-6*, Zebra Kensgtn) Kensgtn Pub Corp.

— Landscapes with Acrylic & Oil. 78p. 1993. pap. 10.50 (*1-56770-282-1*) S Scheewe Pubns.

***Bell, Donna.** Magical Kittens. (Regency Romance Ser.). 2000. mass mkt. 4.99 (*0-8217-6691-0*, Zebra Kensgtn) Kensgtn Pub Corp.

Bell, Donna. Painter to Painter, Vol. 5. (Illus.). 98p. 1992. pap. 10.50 (*1-56770-263-5*) S Scheewe Pubns.

— Sweet Tranquility. 224p. 1997. mass mkt. 4.99 (*0-8217-5544-7*, Zebra Kensgtn) Kensgtn Pub Corp.

— Taste for Love. 256p. 1999. mass mkt. 4.99 (*0-8217-6104-8*) Kensgtn Pub Corp.

***Bell, Donna.** Valentine Kisses. (Regency Romance Ser.). 2000. mass mkt. 4.99 (*0-8217-6464-0*, Zebra Kensgtn) Kensgtn Pub Corp.

Bell, Donna. Words of Love. 1999. mass mkt. 4.99 (*0-8217-6391-1*, Zebra Kensgtn) Kensgtn Pub Corp.

Bell, Doris L. Contemporary Art Trends, 1960-1980: A Guide to Sources. LC 81-5668. 183p. 1981. 21.00 (*0-8108-1445-5*) Scarecrow.

Bell, Doug. Essence of Program Design. LC 97-19665. 200p. (C). 1997. pap. text 19.95 (*0-13-367806-7*) P-H.

— Essence of Programming Using C Plus Plus. LC 96-13458. 208p. (C). 1996. pap. text 19.95 (*0-13-206186-4*) P-H.

***Bell, Doug.** Software Engineering. 3rd ed. LC 99-53633. 2000. pap. 60.00 (*0-201-64856-3*) Addison-Wesley.

Bell, Doug, et al. Software Engineering. 2nd ed. 300p. 1992. pap. 40.00 (*0-13-832536-7*) P-H.

Bell, Douglas. Mojo & the Pickle Jar. 1991. pap. 3.95 (*0-8125-0880-7*, Pub. by Tor Bks) St Martin.

***Bell, Douglas.** Run Over. 256p. 2000. write for info. (*0-679-31024-X*) Random.

Bell, Douglas & Parr, Mike. Java for Students 1.2. 2nd ed. LC 98-39582. (Illus.). 586p. (C). 1998. pap. 62.00 (*0-13-010922-3*) P-H.

Bell, E. Tissue Engineering. 241p. 1993. 75.00 (*0-8176-3687-0*) Birkhauser.

Bell, E. A. & Charlwood, Barry V., eds. Secondary Plant Products. LC 79-16289. (Encyclopedia of Plant Physiology Ser.: Vol. 8). (Illus.). 1980. 248.95 (*0-387-09461-X*) Spr-Verlag.

Bell, E. C. & Whitehead, R. W. Basic Electrical & Electronic Engineering. 4th rev. ed. LC 92-26725. 560p. 1993. 34.95 (*0-632-03493-9*) Blackwell Sci.

— Basic Electrical Engineering & Instrumentation for Engineers. (Illus.). 1977. pap. 29.95 (*0-8464-0175-4*) Beekman Pubs.

Bell, E. T., pseud. Before the Dawn. LC 74-16522. (Science Fiction Ser.). 247p. 1975. reprint ed. 21.95 (*0-405-06314-8*) Ayer.

— The Development of Mathematics. unabridged ed. LC 92-24016. xiii, 637p. 1999. reprint ed. pap. 14.95 (*0-486-27239-7*) Dover.

— Mathematics: Queen & Servant of Science. LC 87-62937. (MAA Spectrum Ser.). 454p. 1987. reprint ed. pap. text 5.00 (*0-88385-447-3*, QAS) Math Assn.

Bell, Edith H. Windham. LC 97-149504. (Images of America Ser.). 1996. pap. 16.99 (*0-7524-0445-8*) Arcadia Publng.

Bell, Edmund H. & Colwell, Mary H. Patterson: James Patterson of Conestoga Manor, & His Descendants. (Illus.). 313p. 1993. reprint ed. pap. 48.50 (*0-8328-3379-7*); reprint ed. lib. bdg. 58.50 (*0-8328-3378-9*) Higginson Bk Co.

Bell, Edward. Hellenic Architecture. LC 73-39657. (Select Bibliographies Reprint Ser.). 1977. reprint ed. 21.95 (*0-8369-9928-2*) Ayer.

— Social Classes & Social Credit in Alberta. 216p. (C). 1994. 60.00 (*0-7735-1168-7*, Pub. by McG-Queens Univ Pr); pap. text 24.95 (*0-7735-1169-5*, Pub. by McG-Queens Univ Pr) CUP Services.

Bell, Edward L. Vestiges of Mortality & Remembrance: A Bibliography on the Historical Archaeology of Cemeteries. 419p. 1994. 55.00 (*0-8108-2893-6*) Scarecrow.

Bell, Elisabeth, tr. see Manara, Milo.

Bell, Elisabeth, tr. see Schuiten, Peeters.

Bell, Elisabeth, tr. see Tardi, Jacques.

Bell, Elizabeth. Kay Boyle: A Study of the Short Fiction. (Twayne's Studies in Short Fiction: No. 34). 190p. (C). 1992. 23.95 (*0-8057-8317-2*) Macmillan.

Bell, Elizabeth, et al, eds. From Mouse to Mermaid: The Politics of Film, Gender, & Culture. LC 94-49374. 272p. 1995. 39.95 (*0-253-32905-1*); pap. 16.95 (*0-253-20978-1*) Ind U Pr.

Bell, Elizabeth, tr. see Pratt, Hugo.

Bell, Elizabeth S. Sisters of the Wind: Voices of Early Women Aviators. (Illus.). 208p. (Orig.). 1994. pap. 14.95 (*0-9623879-4-0*) Trilogy Bks.

Bell, Elouise. Only When I Laugh. LC 90-48786. 136p. (Orig.). 1990. pap. 9.95 (*1-56085-013-2*) Signature Bks.

Bell, Elsa. Counselling in Further & Higher Education. LC 96-481. (Counselling in Context Ser.). 160p. 1996. pap. text 19.95 (*0-335-19167-3*) OpUniv Pr.

Bell, Eric T. The Magic of Numbers. (Illus.). 425p. 1991. reprint ed. pap. 9.95 (*0-486-26788-1*) Dover.

— Men of Mathematics. 608p. 1986. pap. 17.00 (*0-671-62818-6*, Touchstone) S&S Trade Pap.

Bell, Erica, contrib. by. Basic Estate Planning, 1998. LC 99-160010. (New York Practice Skills Course Handbook Ser.). 240 p. 1998. 129.00 (*0-87224-530-6*) PLI.

Bell, Ernest A. Fighting the Traffic in Young Girls: Or, War on the White Slave Traffic. 1975. 250.00 (*0-87968-252-3*) Gordon Pr.

Bell, F. Principles of Mechanics & Biomechanics. (Illus.). 250p. (Orig.). 1998. pap. 41.50 (*1-56593-047-9*, 0295) Singular Publishing.

Bell, F. A. Eastern Star Ritual. pap. 8.50 (*0-911164-08-1*) Powner.

Bell, F. G. Engineering Geology. LC 93-7269. (Illus.). 359p. 1993. pap. 49.95 (*0-632-03223-5*) Blackwell Sci.

***Bell, F. G.** Engineering Properties of Soil & Rocks 4th ed. LC 99-38065. 1999. write for info. (*0-632-05205-8*) Blackwell Sci.

Bell, F. G. Engineering Treatment of Soils. LC 92-40044. (Illus.). 320p. (C). 1993. 70.00 (*0-419-17750-7*, E & FN Spon) Routledge.

— Environmental Geology: Principles & Practice. LC 97-51996. (Illus.). 1998. pap. 67.00 (*0-86542-875-1*) Blackwell Sci.

— Geological Hazards: Their Assessment, Avoidance & Mitigation. LC 98-39190. (Illus.). viii, 648p. (C). 1998. 110.00 (*0-419-16970-9*, B1707) Thomson Learn.

Bell, F. Heward. The Pacific Halibut: The Resource of the Fishery. LC 80-29218. (Illus.). 279p. 1981. pap. 19.95 (*0-88240-141-6*, Alaska NW Bks) Gr Arts Ctr Pub.

Bell-Fialkoff, Andrew. Ethnic Cleansing. 352p. 1999. pap. 16.95 (*0-312-22336-6*) St Martin.

— Role Migrant History Eurasian Step, Vol. 1. LC 99-45059. 1999. text 49.95 (*0-312-21207-0*) St Martin.

Bell, Florian, jt. auth. see Anderson, Duwayne.

Bell, Floy S. The Blessings of Giving. 304p. (YA). 1996. 19.95 (*0-925591-38-6*) Covenant Hse Bks.

Bell, Foster, ed. see Emerson, Vic & Emerson, Pam.

Bell, Frank. Principles of Mechanics & Biomechanics. (Illus.). 224p. 1998. pap. 42.50 (*0-7487-3332-9*, Pub. by S Thornes Pubs) Trans-Atl Phila.

Bell, Frank C. & Stenstrom, William J. An Atlas of the Peripheral Retina. (Illus.). 244p. 1983. text 170.00 (*0-7216-1669-0*, W B Saunders Co) Harcrt Hlth Sci Grp.

Bell, Frank D. Basic Biostatistics: Concepts for the Health Sciences. LC 93-73781. 192p. (C). 1994. text 20.50 (*0-697-14979-X*, WCB McGr Hill) McGrw-H Hghr Educ.

Bell, Frank F. Gladiators of the Glittering Gulches. (Illus.). 163p. (Orig.). 1985. pap. 7.95 (*0-318-04407-2*) Western Horizons Bks.

— The Snow Eagle. (Illus.). 337p. (Orig.). 1990. pap. 8.95 (*0-934959-00-5*) Western Horizons Bks.

Bell, Fred. The Promise. 1992. 15.00 (*0-938294-07-5*) Inner Light.

— Rays of Truth - Crystal of Light: Information & Guidance for the Golden Age. Spinney, Jonathan, ed. (Illus.). 500p. 1999. pap. 27.00 (*1-891850-11-3*) Med Bear.

Bell, Fred G., ed. Ground Engineer's Reference Book. LC 87-5134. (Illus.). 800p. 1987. 335.00 (*0-408-01173-4*) Buttrwrth-Heinemann.

Bell, Fred L. Army Museums West of the Mississippi. LC 97-285. 310p. 1997. pap. 17.95 (*1-55571-395-5*, Hellgate Pr) PSI Resch.

Bell, Frederic. Jenny's Corner. (Illus.). 64p. (J). 1995. pap. 4.95 (*0-374-43744-0*) FS&G.

— Jenny's Corner. (J). (gr. 3-7). 1996. 18.25 (*0-8446-6885-0*) Peter Smith.

— Jenny's Corner. 1995. 10.15 (*0-606-09487-3*, Pub. by Turtleback) Demco.

Bell, Frederic G. Engineering Properties of Soils & Rocks. 3rd ed. LC 91-39429. (Illus.). 353p. 1992. reprint ed. pap. 109.50 (*0-608-04413-X*, 206519400001) Bks Demand.

Bell, G. L. Syria: The Desert & the Sown. 352p. 1984. 250.00 (*1-85077-062-X*, Pub. by Darf Pubs Ltd) St Mut.

Bell, G. M., jt. auth. see Lavis, D. A.

Bell-Gadsby, Cheryl & Siegenberg, Anne L. Reclaiming Herstory: Ericksonian Solution-Focused Therapy for Sexual Abuse. 288p. 1996. text 31.95 (*0-87630-777-2*) Brunner-Mazel.

***Bell-Gam, Ruby A. & Iyam, David Uru.** Nigeria. rev. ed. (World Bibliographical Ser.: Vol. 100). 342p. 1999. 92.00 (*1-85109-327-3*) ABC-CLIO.

Bell, Gary M. A Handlist of British Diplomatic Representatives, 1509-1688. (Royal Historical Society Guides & Handbooks Ser.: No. 16). 314p. (C). 1995. text 59.95 (*0-521-55154-4*) Cambridge U Pr.

Bell, Gavin, jt. auth. see Carey, Rikk.

Bell, Geneva. My Rose: An African American Mother's Story of AIDS. LC 97-3419. 104p. (Orig.). 1997. pap. 12.95 (*0-8298-1160-5*) Pilgrim OH.

Bell, Geoffrey. The Golden Gate & the Silver Screen. LC 81-71875. (Illus.). 192p. 1984. 24.50 (*0-8453-4750-0*, Cornwall Bks) Assoc Univ Prs.

— The Golden Gate & the Silver Screen. LC 81-71875. (Illus.). 192p. 1984. 24.50 (*0-8386-3231-9*) Fairleigh Dickinson.

Bell, George. Writing Effective Sentences. LC 92-22630. 350p. 1992. pap. text 36.00 (*0-205-14037-8*) Allyn.

Bell, George E. Foster Family Ties: A Foster Family History. Cowan, Elisabeth & Bell, Jean P., eds. LC 94-60047. (Illus.). 450p. (C). 1994. text. write for info. (*0-9623275-5-7*) Wayne Ridge.

— The Giermeks in America: The Giermek Family History. 480p. (C). 1992. text 50.00 (*0-9623275-2-2*) Wayne Ridge.

— The Pancios of Galicia: A Pancio Family History. Bell, Jean P. & Ecker, Constance A., eds. (Illus.). 350p. (C). 1993. text. write for info. (*0-9623275-3-0*) Wayne Ridge.

— The Planos from Piedmont: A Plano Family History. Bell, Jean P., ed. & illus. by. LC 94-61997. 450p. (C). 1995. text. write for info. (*0-9623275-4-9*) Wayne Ridge.

— Six Brothers from Hinsdale: The Bell Family History. Bell, Linda V., ed. (Illus.). 350p. (C). 1990. text. write for info. (*0-9623275-1-4*) Wayne Ridge.

— Six Swift Sisters & Related Families Vol. 1: A Swift Family History. Bell, Jean P., ed. LC 96-60261. 600p. 1996. write for info. (*0-9623275-6-5*) Wayne Ridge.

— Thomas Bell - Military Pension Record: The Bell Family History. Bell, Jean P., ed. (Illus.). 200p. (C). 1989. text. write for info. (*0-9623275-0-6*) Wayne Ridge.

Bell, George H. & Rhodes, Diane B. A Guide to the Zoological Literature: The Animal Kingdom. (Illus.). xxiii, 504p. 1994. lib. bdg. 95.00 (*1-56308-082-6*) Libs Unl.

Bell, George I., et al, eds. Theoretical Immunology. LC 77-26655. (Immunology Ser.: No. 8). (Illus.). 660p. reprint ed. pap. 200.00 (*0-7837-3369-0*, 204332700008) Bks Demand.

Bell, George I. & Glasstone, Samuel. Nuclear Reactor Theory. LC 78-22102. 638p. 1979. reprint ed. lib. bdg. 79.50 (*0-88275-790-3*) Krieger.

Bell, George I. & Marr, Thomas G., eds. Computers & DNA. (Santa Fe Institute Ser.). (Illus.). 304p. (C). 1990. pap. 29.95 (*0-201-51561-X*) Addison-Wesley.

Bell, George J. & Guthrie, William. Principles of the Law of Scotland. 6th ed. xxxvi, 1047p. 1998. reprint ed. 220.00 (*1-56169-362-6*) Gaunt.

Bell, George R. North Carolina Real Estate Study & License Preparation Guide. (Illus.). 350p. (Orig.). (C). 1989. pap. 19.95 (*0-9622772-0-7*) Sunshine NC.

Bell, Gerald D. Achievers. LC 73-79581. 200p. 1973. pap. 18.95 (*0-914616-00-5*) Preston-Hill.

Bell, Gertrude. The Hafez Poems of Gertrude Bell: With the Original Persian on the Facing Page. LC 94-7718. (Classics of Persian Literature Ser.: Vol. 1). (ENG & PER., Illus.). 168p. (Orig.). 1994. pap. 15.95 (*0-936347-39-2*) IBEX.

— Teachings of Hafiz. 1979. 19.00 (*0-900860-63-4*, Pub. by Octagon Pr) ISHK.

Bell, Gertrude, tr. Hafez Poems of Gertrude Bell with the Original Persian. 180p. 1996. pap. 15.95 (*0-614-21647-8*, 1396) Kazi Pubns.

Bell, Gertrude L. Syria: The Desert & the Sown. LC 73-6270. (Middle East Ser.). 1979. reprint ed. 35.95 (*0-405-05325-8*) Ayer.

Bell, Gertrude L., jt. auth. see Ramsay, W. M.

Bell, Gilbert T. A Prospect of Sutherland: The Building of a Castle & the Making of a Duchess. LC 96-143384. (Illus.). 234p. pap. 17.95 (*1-874744-25-4*, Pub. by Birlinn Ltd) Dufour.

Bell, Gordon. Pacific Salmon: From Egg to Exit. (Illus.). 128p. (Orig.). 1996. pap. 12.95 (*0-88839-379-2*) Hancock House.

Bell, Gordon H., ed. Educating European Citizens: Citizenship Values & the European Dimension. 160p. 1995. pap. text 29.95 (*1-85346-278-0*, Pub. by David Fulton) Taylor & Francis.

Bell, Gordon H., et al, eds. Action Research, Special Needs & School Development. 204p. 1994. pap. 32.00 (*1-85346-274-8*, Pub. by David Fulton) Taylor & Francis.

Bell, Gordon M., ed. see Metallurgical Society of AIME Staff.

Bell, Gower. Intermediate Matters, Wk. A. 1993. pap. write for info. (*0-582-09265-5*) Addison-Wesley.

— Intermediate Matters, Wk. B. 1993. pap. write for info. (*0-582-09266-3*) Addison-Wesley.

Bell, Graham. Selection: The Mechanism of Evolution. LC 95-17458. 688p. (C). (gr. 13). 1997. write for info. (*0-412-05521-X*) Kluwer Academic.

— Sex & Death in Protozoa: History of an Obsession. (Illus.). 224p. (C). 1989. text 64.95 (*0-521-36141-9*) Cambridge U Pr.

***Bell, Graham & Watson, Ann.** Tastes & Aromas: The Chemical Senses in Science & Industry. 244p. 1999. 59.95 (*0-86840-769-0*, Pub. by New South Wales Univ Pr) Intl Spec Bk.

Bell, H. C., et al. Guide to British West Indian Archive Materials, in London & in the Islands, for the History of the United States. (Carnegie Institute Ser.: Vol. 8). 1926. 40.00 (*0-527-00688-2*) Periodicals Srv.

Bell, H. I. Cults & Creeds in Graeco-Roman Egypt. 1975. pap. 12.50 (*0-89005-088-0*) Ares.

— Egypt from Alexander the Great to the Arab Conquest. xi, 168p. 1980. reprint ed. pap. 15.00 (*0-89005-354-5*) Ares.

Bell, H. Idris. Fragments of an Unknown Gospel & Other Early Christian Papyri. 1981. 250.00 (*0-8490-0188-9*) Gordon Pr.

***Bell, Haddour.** City Visions. 1999. pap. write for info. (*0-582-32741-5*) Addison-Wesley.

Bell, Hannah R. Men's Business, Women's Business: The Spiritual Role of Gender in the World's Oldest Culture. LC 98-30380. (Illus.). 208p. 1998. pap. 14.95 (*0-89281-655-4*) Inner Tradit.

Bell-Hanson, Jeffery. Lullaby for a King. 1.25 (*0-687-50153-9*) Abingdon.

Bell-Hanson, Jeffrey. In This Thy Holy Place. 2.00 (*0-687-06179-2*) Abingdon.

Bell, Harold I. Egypt, from Alexander the Great to the Arab Conquest. LC 77-8057. (Gregynog Lectures for 1946). 168p. 1977. reprint ed. lib. bdg. 38.50 (*0-8371-9093-2*, BEEA, Greenwood Pr) Greenwood.

Bell, Hazel K. Indexing Biographies. 1992. 17.00 (*1-871577-18-7*) Am Soc Index.

Bell, Heather. Frontiers of Medicine in the Anglo-Egyptian Sudan, 1899-1940. LC 98-40976. (Illus.). 278p. 1999. text 78.00 (*0-19-820749-2*) OUP.

Bell, Helen. Idjhil...& the Land Cried for Its Lost Soul. LC 97-105769. 40p. (J). 1995. 19.95 (*1-875560-61-0*) Intl Spec Bk.

Bell, Helena. To Mend a Broken Heart. large type ed. (Linford Romance Library). 272p. 1997. pap. 16.99 (*0-7089-5123-6*, Linford) Ulverscroft.

Bell, Henrietta. The Secret of Chapultepec Castle. 1980. pap. 4.95 (*0-89741-013-0*) Gila River.

Bell, Henry E. The History & Records of the Court of Wards & Liveries. LC 85-81811. (Cambridge Studies in English Legal History). 225p. 1986. reprint ed. 58.00 (*0-912004-38-X*) Gaunt.

Bell, Herbert C. History of Northumberland County, PA. (Illus.). 1256p. 1993. reprint ed. lib. bdg. 119.00 (*0-8328-2847-5*) Higginson Bk Co.

— Washington County, History of Leitersburg District, Washington County, Including Its Original Land Tenure: First Settlement: Material Development; Biographical Sketches, Etc. 331p. 1995. lib. bdg. 39.00 (*0-8328-4693-7*) Higginson Bk Co.

***Bell, Hilari.** Navohar. 336p. 2000. mass mkt. 6.99 (*0-451-45788-9*, ROC) NAL.

Bell, Hilary. Abracadabra Guitar. 80p. (J). (gr. 2-5). 1998. pap. 16.95 (*0-7136-1902-3*, Pub. by A & C Blk) Midpt Trade.

— Wolf Lullaby. 1997. pap. 16.95 (*0-86819-495-6*, Pub. by Currency Pr) Accents Pubns.

Bell, Hobart. Quartet. (C). 1988. pap. 6.00 (*0-9620060-0-9*) Atelier Pr.

Bell, Horace. On the Old West Coast: Being Further Reminiscences of a Ranger. Bartlett, Lanier, ed. LC 76-1242. (Chicano Heritage Ser.). (Illus.). 1977. reprint ed. lib. bdg. 34.95 (*0-405-09485-X*) Ayer.

— Reminiscences of a Ranger: Early Times in Southern California. LC 99-27483. (Western Frontier Library). 528p. 1999. 27.95 (*0-8061-3151-9*) U of Okla Pr.

***Bell, Horace.** Reminiscences of a Ranger: Early Times in Southern California. 2000. pap. 17.95 (*1-55709-500-0*) Applewood.

— Reminiscences of a Ranger Vol. 65: Early Times in Southern California. (Western Frontier Library). 528p. 2000. pap. text 15.95 (*0-8061-3152-7*) U of Okla Pr.

Bell, Howard. More Than a Conqueror: Winning in the Face of Adversity. LC 98-133724. 176p. 1997. pap. 10.99 (*1-56043-302-7*, Treasure Hse) Destiny Image.

Bell, Howard H. Survey of the Negro Convention Movement. LC 74-94129. (American Negro: His History & Literature, Series 3). 1970. reprint ed. 21.95 (*0-405-01915-7*) Ayer.

Bell, Howard H., ed. Minutes of the Proceedings of the National Negro Conventions, 1830-1864. LC 72-105552. (American Negro His History & Literature Ser.: No. 3). 1970. reprint ed. 27.95 (*0-405-01916-5*) Ayer.

Bell, Howard M. Youth Tell Their Story: A Study of the Conditions & Attitudes of Young People in Maryland Between the Ages of 16 & 24. LC 74-1665. (Children & Youth Ser.). 290p. 1974. reprint ed. 26.95 (*0-405-05946-9*) Ayer.

Bell, Hugh M. The Adjustment Inventory. 1979. write for info. (*0-8047-1061-9*) Stanford U Pr.

Bell-Hughes, Janice, ed. see Birts, Donald & Fisher, Joseph.

Bell-Hughes, Janice, ed. see Woolfolk, Thomas, Jr.

Bell, I. E. & Chambers, J. D. Story of Lincoln. (Illus.). 1971. 22.95 (*0-8464-0887-2*) Beekman Pubs.

Bell, Ian. Dreams of Exile: Robert Louis Stevenson, a Biography. LC 93-3792. 320p. 1995. 25.00 (*0-8050-2807-2*); pap. 12.95 (*0-8050-3938-4*, Owl) H Holt & Co.

— Henry Fielding: An Annotated Bibliography. LC 93-34653. (C). 1994. text 56.50 (*0-582-08162-9*) Addison-Wesley.

— Washington Square: Styles of Money. (Masterwork Studies). 1993p. 1993. 23.95 (*0-8057-8359-8*); pap. 13.95 (*0-8057-8596-5*) Macmillan.

An Asterisk (*) at the beginning of an entry indicates that the title is appearing for the first time.

Bell, Ian A. Henry Fielding: Authorship & Authority. (Studies in Eighteenth & Nineteenth Century Literature). 264p. (C). 1994. text 58.66 (*0-582-08169-6*, Pub. by Addison-Wesley) Longman.

— Peripheral Visions: Images of Nationhood in Contemporary British Fiction. 220p. 1996. pap. 24.95 (*0-7083-1260-8*, Pub. by Univ Wales Pr) Paul & Co Pubs.

Bell, Ian F., ed. Henry James: Fiction As History. LC 84-18607. 188p. 1985. 48.00 (*0-389-20515-X*, BNB-08071) B&N Imports.

Bell, Ian F. & Adams, D. K., eds. American Literary Landscapes: The Fiction & the Fact. LC 88-18173. (Critical Studies). 208p. 1989. text 39.95 (*0-312-02421-5*) St Martin.

Bell, Ilona. Elizabethan Women & the Poetry of Courtship. LC 98-3857. (Illus.). 288p. (C). 1999. 59.95 (*0-521-63007-X*) Cambridge U Pr.

Bell, Inge. This Book Is Not Required. 2nd rev. ed. (Illus.). 271p. (C). 1990. pap. text. write for info. (*1-878020-04-8*) Small Pr CA.

Bell, Inge & McGrane, Bernard. The Book Is Not Required. rev. ed. (Illus.). 304p. (C). 1998. pap. text 19.95 (*0-7619-8571-9*) Pine Forge.

— This Book Is Not Required: An Emotional Survival Manual for Students. LC 98-19672. 1998. pap. 28.95 (*0-7619-8572-7*) Sage.

Bell, Iris Y. Los Alamos WAACs-WACs: World War II, 1943-1946. (Illus.). 82p. (Orig.). 1993. 32.50 (*0-9637321-0-2*); pap. 18.50 (*0-9637321-1-0*) I Bell.

Bell, J., ed. see Brady, John.

Bell, J. Bowyer. Back to the Future: The Protestants & a United Ireland. LC 96-201626. 442p. 1997. pap. 16.95 (*1-85371-692-8*) Dufour.

— Dragonwars: Armed Struggle & the Conventions of Modern War. LC 99-20843. 307p. 1999. 39.95 (*1-56000-357-X*) Transaction Pubs.

— The Dynamics of the Armed Struggle. LC 98-10981. 288p. 1998. 57.50 (*0-7146-4865-5*, Pub. by F Cass Pubs); pap. 24.50 (*0-7146-4422-6*, Pub. by F Cass Pubs) Intl Spec Bk.

— The Gun in Politics: An Analysis of Irish Violence 1916-1986. 280p. 1987. 44.95 (*0-88738-126-X*) Transaction Pubs.

— The Gun in Politics: An Analysis of Irish Violence, 1916-1986. 280p. (C). 1991. pap. text 24.95 (*1-56000-566-1*) Transaction Pubs.

***Bell, J. Bowyer.** The IRA 1968-2000: An Analysis of a Secret Army. LC 00-30340. (Series on Political Violence). 420p. 2000. pap. 26.50 (*0-7146-8119-9*, Pub. by F Cass Pubs) Intl Spec Bk.

Bell, J. Bowyer. IRA Tactics & Targets: An Analysis of Tactical Aspects of the Armed Struggle. 117p. (Orig.). 1990. pap. 11.95 (*1-85371-086-5*, Pub. by Poolbeg Pr) Dufour.

— On Revolt: Strategies of National Liberation. LC 75-44026. 300p. 1976. reprint ed. pap. 93.00 (*0-7837-2223-0*, 205731300004) Bks Demand.

— To Play the Game: An Analysis of Sports. 205p. 1986. 39.95 (*0-88738-102-2*) Transaction Pubs.

***Bell, J. Bowyer, ed.** The IRA 1968-2000: An Analysis of a Secret Army. (Cass Ser. on Political Violence). 420p. 2000. 62.50 (*0-7146-5070-6*, Pub. by F Cass Pubs) Intl Spec Bk.

Bell, J. Bowyer, frwd. The Secret Army: The IRA, 1916-1979. rev. ed. LC 89-85273. 481p. 1989. pap. 19.95 (*1-85371-027-X*, Pub. by Poolbeg Pr) Dufour.

Bell, J. Bowyer, intro. Terror Out of Zion: The Fight for Israeli Independence. LC 95-49992. 400p. 1996. pap. text 24.95 (*1-56000-870-9*) Transaction Pubs.

Bell, J. Bowyer & Whaley, Barton. Cheating & Deception. 456p. (C). 1991. pap. 24.95 (*0-88738-868-X*) Transaction Pubs.

Bell, J. Ellis, ed. Spectroscopy in Biochemistry, 2 vols., Vol. 1. 336p. 1981. 129.00 (*0-8493-5551-6*, QP519, CRC Reprint) Franklin.

— Spectroscopy in Biochemistry, 2 vols., Vol. 2. 336p. 1981. 185.00 (*0-8493-5552-4*, QP519, CRC Reprint) Franklin.

Bell, J. G., jt. auth. see Watson, J. S.

Bell, J. J. Courtin' Christina - Wee Macgreegor Enlists. 222p. 1993. pap. 11.95 (*1-874744-10-6*, Pub. by Birlinn Ltd) Dufour.

— Wee Macgreegor - Wee Macgreegor Again. 224p. 1993. pap. 11.95 (*1-874744-09-2*, Pub. by Birlinn Ltd) Dufour.

***Bell, J. L.** The Art of the Intelligible: An Elementary Survey of Mathematics in Its Conceptual Development. LC 99-42469. (Western Ontario Studies in the Philosophy of Science). 260p. 1999. 109.00 (*0-7923-5972-0*) Kluwer Academic.

Bell, J. L. Planet Dexter's Treasure Hunt. 1998. spiral bd. write for info. (*0-201-16542-2*) Addison-Wesley.

— A Primer of Infinitesimal Analysis. LC 97-41877. (Illus.). 136p. (C). 1998. text 29.95 (*0-521-62401-0*) Cambridge U Pr.

Bell, J. L. Soap Science: A Science Book Bubbling with 36 Experiments. (Illus.). 64p. (J). 1993. pap. 10.95 (*1-55074-123-3*) Kids Can Pr.

Bell, J. M. & Mendus, Susan, eds. Philosophy & Medical Welfare. (Royal Institute of Philosophy Lectures: No. 23). 140p. (C). 1989. pap. text 19.95 (*0-521-36856-1*) Cambridge U Pr.

Bell, J. Michael, ed. Won from the Heart. (Illus.). 400p. 1997. 19.95 (*0-9660802-1-1*) Won from the Hrt.

Bell, J. P. Hanover Co. - Quaker Friends of Ye Olden Time, Being in Part a Transcript of the Minute Books of Cedar Creek Meeting, Hanover Co., & the South River Meeting, Campbell Co. (Illus.). 287p. 1997. reprint ed. lib. bdg. 35.00 (*0-8328-6515-X*) Higginson Bk Co.

— Our Quaker Friends of Ye Olden Time. (Illus.). viii, 287p. 1997. reprint ed. pap. 23.50 (*0-7884-0723-6*, B148) Heritage Bk.

Bell, J. Perry. Achieving Success with Integrity. 102p. (Orig.). 1993. pap. 14.95 (*0-9628542-2-0*) Bell Pr.

— Doing Business with Integrity: One Man's Story. 70p. (Orig.). pap. 7.95 (*0-9628542-1-2*) Bell Pr.

— God's Housekeeping: Thoughts on Personal Stewardship. 61p. (Orig.). 1991. pap. 9.95 (*0-9628542-0-4*) Bell Pr.

Bell, J. S. & Engle, George. Cross: Statutory Interpretation. 2nd ed. 195p. 1987. pap. 38.00 (*0-406-57017-5*, U.K., MICHIE) LEXIS Pub.

Bell, Jacob. Profiles in Personality: Personality Enlightenment Which Provokes the Mind & Feelings. 40p. (Orig.). 1988. pap. 9.95 (*0-9621090-0-2*) Bell Pub MA.

Bell, Jade, ed. see Long, Barry.

***Bell, Jadrien.** A. D. 999. 1999. mass mkt. 5.99 (*0-441-00673-6*) Ace Bks.

Bell, James, Jr. A Return to Virtue: Reflections on Living Wisely. 1995. 12.99 (*1-881273-04-0*) Northfield Pub.

Bell, James, Jr., ed. see Gurnall, William.

Bell, James, Jr., ed. see Horton, T. C. & Hurlburt, Charles E.

Bell, James A. Reconstructing Prehistory: Scientific Method in Archaeology. LC 93-25727. 320p. 1994. 69.95 (*1-56639-159-8*); pap. 27.95 (*1-56639-160-1*) Temple U Pr.

Bell, James B. Family History Record Book. LC 81-103290. 269p. 1980. reprint ed. pap. 83.40 (*0-608-00786-2*, 205933500010) Bks Demand.

Bell, James B., jt. auth. see Doane, Gilbert H.

Bell, James B., jt. ed. see Barkdoll, Gerald L.

Bell, James C., Jr. Opening a Highway to the Pacific, 1838-1846. LC 68-56648. (Columbia University. Studies in the Social Sciences: No. 217). reprint ed. 24.50 (*0-404-51217-8*) AMS Pr.

Bell, James H., tr. see Levi-Strauss, Claude.

Bell, James M. Poetical Works. Arnett, Bishop, ed. LC 70-39423. reprint ed. 31.50 (*0-404-00005-3*) AMS Pr.

— Poetical Works of James Madison Bell. LC 78-133148. (Black Heritage Library Collection). 1977. 21.95 (*0-8369-8704-7*) Ayer.

Bell, James M., jt. auth. see Anderson, James A.

***Bell, James S.** Blind Justice. LC 99-40602. 2000. pap. 12.99 (*0-8054-2161-0*) Broadman.

Bell, James S. Circumstantial Evidence. LC 97-3344. 480p. (Orig.). 1997. pap. 13.99 (*0-8054-6359-3*) Broadman.

— Final Witness: A Novel. LC 98-43329. 384p. 1999. pap. 10.99 (*0-8054-1842-3*) Broadman.

Bell, James S., Jr. They Walked with God: Daily Readings from Moody Press Authors. 18.99 (*0-8024-8349-6*, 299) Moody.

Bell, James S. Top Courtroom Performance. LC 88-70834. 80p. (Orig.). 1994. text 85.00 (*0-910355-02-9*) Courtroom Comp.

Bell, James S., Jr., ed. The D. L. Moody Collection: The Highlights of His Writings, Sermons, Anecdotes, & Life Story. 1998. 14.99 (*0-8024-1715-9*) Moody.

Bell, James S., Jr., ed. see Van Dyke, Henry.

Bell, James W. Little Rock Handbook. (Illus.). iv, 88p. (Orig.). 1980. pap. 9.95 (*0-939130-00-9*) J W Bell.

Bell, Janet. Famous Black Quotations. 1995. pap. 15.70 (*0-613-04957-8*) Econo-Clad Bks.

Bell, Janet C. The Soul of Success: Great Business Quotations for African Americans. LC 97-37396. 208p. 1997. 16.95 (*0-471-18022-X*) Wiley.

Bell, Janet C. Victory of the Spirit: Meditations on Black Quotations. LC 95-39709. 176p. (Orig.). 1996. reprint ed. mass mkt. 9.95 (*0-446-67200-9*, Pub. by Warner Bks) Little.

Bell, Janet C., ed. Famous Black Quotations. LC 94-33015. 160p. 1995. reprint ed. mass mkt. 7.99 (*0-446-67150-9*, Pub. by Warner Bks) Little.

Bell, Janet Chatham & Freeman, Lucille Usher. Stretch Your Wings. LC 99-13045. (Illus.). 176p. (YA). (gr. 7-12). 1999. pap. 8.95 (*0-316-03825-3*) Little.

Bell, Janet L. Chronic Physical Illness & Depression among Ethnic Minority Elderly. LC 91-37482. (Studies on the Elderly in America). 168p. 1992. text 25.00 (*0-8153-0513-3*) Garland.

Bell, Jean P., ed. see Bell, George E.

Bell, Jean P., ed. & illus. see Bell, George E.

Bell, Jeanie. Talking about Celia. LC 97-202281. (Black Australian Writers Ser.). 160p. 1997. pap. 24.95 (*0-7022-2833-8*, Pub. by Univ Queensland Pr) Intl Spec Bk.

Bell, Jeannette & Bell, Chet. County Parks of Wisconsin. McBride, Elizabeth, ed. LC 96-61192. (Illus.). 216p. (Orig.). 1996. pap. 16.95 (*0-915024-54-3*) Trails Media.

Bell, Jeffrey. Populism & Elitism: Politics in the Age of Equality. LC 91-47497. 300p. 1992. 21.95 (*0-89526-517-6*) Regnery Pub.

Bell, Jeffrey A. A Problem of Difference: Phenomenology & Poststructuralism. (Toronto Studies in Philosophy). 368p. 1998. text 75.00 (*0-8020-4253-8*) U of Toronto Pr.

— The Problem of Difference: Phenomenology & Poststructuralism. (Toronto Studies in Philosophy). 368p. 1998. pap. text 24.95 (*0-8020-8095-2*) U of Toronto Pr.

Bell, Jennifer. Annie Learns to Ride. (C). 1990. 32.00 (*0-85131-508-9*, Pub. by J A Allen); pap. 24.00 (*0-85131-492-9*, Pub. by J A Allen) Trafalgar.

— Annie Owns a Pony. (C). 1990. 32.00 (*0-85131-524-0*, Pub. by J A Allen) St Mut.

— Annie Owns a Pony. (J). 1990. pap. 24.00 (*0-85131-523-2*, Pub. by J A Allen) Trafalgar.

— Painting & Drawing Horses. 1995. pap. 35.00 (*0-85131-637-9*, Pub. by J A Allen) Trafalgar.

Bell, Jennifer, jt. auth. see Henderson, Carolyn.

Bell, Jerry. Chemical Explorations: A Laboratory Manual for Introductory Chemistry. 400p. (C). 1993. pap. text 37.96 (*0-669-26916-6*); pap. text, teacher ed. 2.66 (*0-669-26917-4*) HM Trade Div.

Bell, Jerry, jt. ed. see Sosa, Maria.

Bell, Jill S. Literacy, Culture & Identity. LC 96-42924. (American University Studies XIV: Vol. 42). 236p. (C). 1998. text 43.95 (*0-8204-3656-9*) P Lang Pubng.

Bell, Jim. Achieving Eco-nomic Security on Spaceship Earth: Using Free-Market-Forces to Save Our Life Support System. 2nd expanded ed. 186, xp. (Orig.). 1995. pap. 14.95 (*0-915841-19-3*) Ecolgcl Life.

— The Complete Idiot's Guide to Prayer. 400p. 1999. pap. text 16.95 (*0-02-863108-0*, Pub. by Macmillan Gen Ref) S&S Trade.

***Bell, Jim.** In the Strength of the Lord: The Life & Teachings of James E. Faust. LC 99-43364. 1999. write for info. (*1-57345-580-6*) Deseret Bk.

Bell, Jim & Campbell, Stan. Bible. LC 98-87593. (Complete Idiot's Guide Ser.). (Illus.). 352p. 1998. pap. 16.95 (*0-02-862728-8*) Macmillan Gen Ref.

Bell, Jim, jt. ed. see Brown, Stephen.

Bell, Joan A., et al. Lovely Lady Dressed in Blue (Bella Dama Vestida en Azul) And the Knights of Our Lady (Los Caballeros de Nuestra Senora) Emmanuelli Klosterman, Carmen A., tr. (Stories of the Faith Ser.). (ENG & SPA., Illus.). 60p. (gr. k-10). 1994. pap. 9.95 (*1-889733-01-6*, 01003) Precious Life Bks.

Bell, Joan K., jt. auth. see Bell, Richard O.

Bell, Joe "Cool Papa" & Pickow, Peter. Improvising Jazz Guitar. (Illus.). 96p. 1987. pap. 16.95 (*0-8256-2348-0*, AM37326) Music Sales.

Bell, Joe D., et al. Principles of Sport Biomechanics. 5th ed. 400p. (C). 1996. pap. text 32.95 (*0-89641-284-9*) American Pr.

Bell, Joe G. Aliens vs. Predator: Prima's Official Strategy Guide. LC 98-65315. 176p. 1999. per. 19.99 (*0-7615-1570-4*) Prima Pub.

Bell, Joe G. Betrayal in Antara: The Official Strategy Guide. LC 96-70078. 384p. 1997. pap., per. 19.99 (*0-7615-0875-9*) Prima Pub.

Bell, Joe G. Command & Conquer: Red Alert Retaliation. (Games Ser.). 96p. 1998. per. 12.99 (*0-7615-1888-6*) Prima Pub.

Bell, Joe G. Command & Conquer: Red Alert Secrets & Solutions - The Unauthorized Edtion. LC 96-67996. 400p. 1997. pap., per. 19.99 (*0-7615-0704-3*) Prima Pub.

Bell, Joe G. Command & Conquered Red Alert-Counterstrike: Unauthorized Secrets & Solutions. LC 97-66165. 144p. 1997. per. 14.99 (*0-7615-1165-2*) Prima Pub.

Bell, Joe G. Heroes of Might Magic II: The Official Strategy Guide. LC 96-69703. 272p. 1996. pap., per. 19.99 (*0-7615-0863-5*) Prima Pub.

Bell, Joe G. Hexen: The Official Strategy Guide (Previously Heretic II) 1996. pap. 19.95 (*0-7615-0388-9*) Prima Pub.

— Lords of Magic: The Official Strategy Guide. LC 97-69338. (Secrets of the Game Ser.). 320p. 1998. per. 19.99 (*0-7615-1147-4*) Prima Pub.

— Mech Warrior 2: The Official Strategy Guide, Vol. 1. 1995. pap. text 19.95 (*1-55958-723-7*) Prima Pub.

— MechWarrior 2: Expansion Pack Secrets & Solutions. 1996. pap. text 12.95 (*0-7615-0578-4*) Prima Pub.

— Myth the Fallen Lords: Unauthorized Secrets & Solutions. LC 97-69251. 224p. 1997. per. 19.99 (*0-7615-1294-7*) Prima Pub.

— Online Games Guide. LC 96-72645. 384p. 1997. per. 19.99 (*0-7615-1065-6*) Prima Pub.

— Unreal Construction Kit: The Official Guide. (Secrets of the Game Ser.). 240p. 1998. per. 19.99 (*0-7615-1092-3*) Prima Pub.

Bell, Joe G., jt. auth. see Harten, Rod.

Bell, Joe G., jt. auth. see Honeywell, Steve.

Bell, Joe Grant. Duke Nukem 3D Construction Kit: Unauthorized. 224p. 1996. pap., per. 19.99 (*0-7615-0710-8*) Prima Pub.

Bell, Joe Grant. Frankenstein: Through the Eyes of the Monster: The Official Strategy Game. 1995. pap. text 19.95 (*0-7615-0096-0*) Prima Pub.

***Bell, Joe Grant.** Half-Life: Prima's Official Strategy Guide. LC 97-75578. 304p. 2000. pap. 19.99 (*0-7615-1360-4*) Prima Pub.

— Half-Life: Prima's Official Strategy Guide. (Value Ser.). 2000. pap. 9.99 (*0-7615-3044-4*) Prima Pub.

Bell, Joe Grant. Mechcommander: Desperate Measure. 1999. pap. 19.99 (*0-7615-2227-1*) Prima Pub.

***Bell, Joe Grant.** MechWarrior 3: Priate's Moon. (Official Strategy Guides Ser.). (Illus.). 288p. (YA). 2000. pap. 14.99 (*0-7615-2731-1*) Prima Pub.

Bell, Joe Grant. MechWarrior III: Prima's Official Strategy Guide. LC 96-67260. 288p. 1999. pap. 19.99 (*0-7615-0390-0*) Prima Pub.

Bell, Joe Grant. MechWarrior II: Mercenaries: The Official Strategy Guide, Vol. 2. LC 96-70240. 216p. 1996. pap., per. 19.99 (*0-7615-0906-2*) Prima Pub.

Bell, Joe Grant. Redjack - Revenge of the Brethren: Prima's Official Strategy Guide. LC 98-67559. (Prima Games Ser.). 240p. 1998. per. 19.99 (*0-7615-1893-2*) Prima Pub.

— Unreal: The Official Strategy Guide. LC 96-71680. 208p. 1998. per. 19.99 (*0-7615-1029-X*) Prima Pub.

Bell, Joe Grant, jt. auth. see Prima Publishing Staff.

Bell, John. Principles of French Law. 578p. 1998. pap. text (*0-19-876395-6*) OUP.

— Single or Joint Venturing? A Comprehensive Approach to Foreign Entry Mode Choice. LC 96-84694. 191p. 1996. 64.95 (*1-85972-383-7*, Pub. by Avebry) Ashgate Pub Co.

Bell, John, ed. Bell's British Theatre, Seventeen Seventy-Six to Seventeen Eighty-One, 21 vols., Set. LC 76-44551. (Illus.). 1977. reprint ed. 1207.50 (*0-404-00800-3*) AMS Pr.

***Bell, John, ed.** Puppets, Masks & Performing Objects. (TDR Book Ser.). (Illus.). 190p. (C). 2000. reprint ed. pap. 19.95 (*0-262-52293-4*) MIT Pr.

Bell, John, ed. Purdue Industrial Waste Conference, 41st: Proceedings. (Illus.). 831p. 1987. boxed set 159.00 (*0-87371-094-0*, L094) Lewis Pubs.

— Selected Plays from Bell's British Theatre, 16 vols., Set. LC 76-44553. (Illus.). reprint ed. 920.00 (*0-404-00840-2*) AMS Pr.

— Supplement to Bell's British Theatre, Farces, 1784, 4 vols., Set. LC 76-44552. (Illus.). 1977. 230.00 (*0-404-00830-5*) AMS Pr.

— Wilfred Owen: Selected Letters. LC 99-179071. (Illus.). 400p. 1998. pap. 19.95 (*0-19-288089-6*) OUP.

Bell, John & Maule, Graham. When Grief Is Raw: Songs for Times of Sorrow & Bereavement. 71p. 1997. pap. text 7.95 (*1-57999-009-6*, G-4829) GIA Pubns.

Bell, John, et al. Principles of French Law. LC 98-12331. 578p. 1998. text 95.00 (*0-19-876394-8*) OUP.

Bell, John, ed. see James, Muriel & Jongeward, Dorothy.

Bell, John A. Opportunities in Machines Shop Trades. (YA). (gr. 8 up). 1990. 13.95 (*0-8442-6147-5*, VGM Career) NTC Contemp Pub Co.

— Opportunities in Machines Shop Trades. (YA). (gr. 8 up). 1993. pap. 10.95 (*0-8442-6148-3*, VGM Career) NTC Contemp Pub Co.

Bell, John B. Northampton County, Virginia, Tithables, 1662-1677. 78p. (Orig.). 1994. pap. 12.00 (*1-55613-893-8*) Heritage Bk.

— Northampton County, Virginia, Tithables, 1720-1769. 411p. (Orig.). 1993. pap. text 28.50 (*1-55613-823-7*) Heritage Bk.

— Northampton County, Virginia, Tithables, 1720-1769. 393p. (Orig.). 1994. pap. text 28.50 (*0-7884-0113-0*) Heritage Bk.

Bell, John D. The Bulgarian Communist Party from Blagoev to Zhivkov. LC 85-17744. (Publication Ser.: No. 320). 202p. (Orig.). 1985. pap. text 9.95 (*0-8179-8202-7*) Hoover Inst Pr.

Bell, John E. Family Therapy. LC 74-22276. 436p. 1995. reprint ed. pap. 60.00 (*1-56821-506-1*) Aronson.

Bell, John I., et al, eds. T Cell Receptor Genes. (Illus.). 514p. 1995. 115.00 (*0-19-262418-0*); pap. text 59.50 (*0-19-262419-9*) OUP.

Bell, John L., Jr. Hard Times: Beginnings of the Great Depression in North Carolina, 1929-1933. (Illus.). xii, 87p. 1982. pap. 5.00 (*0-86526-196-2*) NC Archives.

Bell, John L. Innkeepers & Light Sleepers: Seventeen New Songs for Christmas. 1992. pap. 5.95 (*0-941050-36-X*) GIA Pubns.

Bell, John L. The Last Journey: Reflections for the Time of Grieving. (Illus.). 56p. 1998. 28.95 incl. audio compact disk (*1-57999-040-1*) GIA Pubns.

— On Reflection: Wrestle & Fight & Pray. 116p. 1993. pap. 22.00 (*0-7152-0681-8*, Pub. by St Andrew) St Mut.

— Seven Songs of Mary. 48p. 1998. 6.95 (*1-57999-020-7*) GIA Pubns.

***Bell, John L.** There Is One Among Us: Shorter Songs for Worship. 94p. 1999. pap. 7.95 (*1-57999-051-7*, G-5111) GIA Pubns.

Bell, John L. & Maule, Graham. The Courage to Say No: Twenty-Three Songs for Lent & Easter. 64p. 1996. pap. text 6.95 (*0-941050-53-X*, G-4244) GIA Pubns.

— Love & Anger. 80p. 1998. pap. 8.95 (*1-57999-031-2*, G-4947) GIA Pubns.

Bell, John M., ed. Industrial Waste Conference, Purdue University, Proceedings, 44th. (Illus.). 968p. 1990. boxed set 139.00 (*0-87371-313-3*, L313) Lewis Pubs.

— Proceedings of the Forty-Third Industrial Waste Conference, May 10, 11, 12, 1988, Purdue University. (Illus.). 880p. 1989. boxed set 149.00 (*0-87371-205-6*, L205) Lewis Pubs.

Bell, John P. Crisis in Costa Rica: The 1948 Revolution. LC 77-165920. (Latin American Monographs: No. 24). 206p. reprint ed. pap. 63.90 (*0-608-17916-7*, 202795700057) Bks Demand.

— Modeling the Stripping & Volatilization of Voc in Wastewater Collection & Treatment Systems, Project 91-TFT-1, 1998. LC 98-89662. 1998. write for info. (*0-9662553-6-4*) Wtr Environ Res.

Bell, John S. French Constitutional Law. 392p. 1995. reprint ed. pap. text 38.00 (*0-19-825948-4*) OUP.

— Policy Arguments in Judical Decisions. LC 83-4207. 1985. pap. 19.95 (*0-19-825522-5*) OUP.

— Speakable & Unspeakable in Quantum Mechanics: Collected Papers in Quantum Mechanics. (Illus.). 224p. 1988. pap. text 24.95 (*0-521-36869-3*) Cambridge U Pr.

Bell, John S., jt. auth. see Brown, L. Neville.

Bell, John S., jt. auth. see Eekelaar, John M.

Bell, John T., jt. auth. see Savage, James W.

***Bell, Jon A.** 3D Studio Max R3 F/X & Design. LC 99-43078. 431p. 1999. 49.99 (*1-57610-423-0*) Coriolis Grp.

Bell, Joseph. Sandy of Laguna. (Illus.). 72p. (Orig.). (J). (gr. k-8). 1992. pap. 10.95 (*1-880812-01-0*) S Ink WA.

Bell, Joseph, tr. see Kassem, Abdel-Hakim.

Bell, Joseph D. Industrial Unionism. LC 74-22732. (Labor Movement in Fiction & Non-Fiction Ser.). reprint ed. 34.50 (*0-404-58485-3*) AMS Pr.

Bell, Joseph N. Love Theory in Later Hanbalite Islam. LC 78-5904. 280p. (C). 1979. text 24.50 (*0-87395-244-8*) State U NY Pr.

Bell, Josephine. Death of a Poison-Tongue. large type ed. 1979. 12.00 (*0-7089-0378-9*) Ulverscroft.

— Death on the Reserve. 1997. 19.50 (*0-7540-8500-7*, Black Dagger) Chivers N Amer.

— The Hunter & the Trapped. large type ed. 1991. 27.99 (*0-7089-2475-1*) Ulverscroft.

Bell, Joshua, ed. Mandolin Music in America: Thirty-Eight Hundred Pieces for Mandolin & Where to Find Them. 68p. (Orig.). 1993. pap. 10.00 (*0-9614120-3-8*) Plucked.

Bell, Joyce. The Girl from the Back Streets. 1994. pap. 11.95 (*1-85797-418-2*) Orion Pubng Grp.

— My Rebel Son. 288p. 25.00 (*0-7278-5219-1*) Severn Hse.

— Summer of a Thousand Roses. large type ed. (Linford Romance Library). 272p. 1994. pap. 16.99 (*0-7089-7551-8*) Ulverscroft.

Bell, Judith. Doing Your Research Project: A Guide for First-Time Researchers in Education & Social Science. 3rd ed. LC 99-17596. 256p. 1999. pap. 79.95 (*0-335-20388-4*) Taylor & Francis.

Bell, Judith. So You Want to Get a Degree. 1984. pap. text. write for info. (*0-582-49714-0*, Pub. by Addison-Wesley) Longman.

Bell, Judith, ed. Teachers Talk about Teaching: Coping with Change in Turbulent Times. LC 94-25719. 128p. 1995. pap. 19.95 (*0-335-19174-6*) Open Univ TX.

Bell, Judith & Harrison, Bernard T. Leading People, Learning from People: Lessons from Education Professionals. LC 98-13869. 177p. 1998. 85.00 (*0-335-20075-3*); pap. 27.95 (*0-335-20074-5*) Taylor & Francis.

Bell, Judith, jt. auth. see Ellenberg, Daniel.

Bell, Judith E., et al. The Public Interest in Conversions of Nonprofit Health Charities. LC 98-124762. 60p. 1997. pap. write for info. (*1-887748-15-6*) Milbank Memorial.

Bell, Judy K. Disaster Survival Planning: A Practical Guide for Businesses: Everything You Need to Know to Develop, Implement, & Test Your Own Recovery Plans. (Illus.). 216p. (Orig.). 1991. 19.95 (*0-9630580-0-2*) Disaster Survival.

Bell, Julia B., jt. auth. see Curtin, Michael F.

Bell, Julian. Bonnard. (Color Library). (Illus.). 128p. (C). 1994. pap. 14.95 (*0-7148-3052-6*, Pub. by Phaidon Press) Phaidon Pr.

— What Is Painting? Representation & Modern Art. LC 98-61188. (Illus.). 256p. 1999. pap. 24.95 (*0-500-28101-7*, Pub. by Thames Hudson) Norton.

Bell, Julian, jt. auth. see Hinton, Brian.

Bell, Julian, jt. auth. see Howard, Leland.

Bell, Julie. Hard Curves: The Fantasy Art of Julie Bell. (Illus.). 128p. 1996. reprint ed. pap. 22.95 (*1-56025-131-X*, Thunders Mouth) Avalon NY.

— Soft As Steel: The Fantasy Art of Julie Bell. LC 98-83189. (Illus.). 128p. 1999. pap. 22.95 (*1-56025-191-3*, Thunders Mouth) Avalon NY.

Bell, Julie, jt. auth. see Vallejo, Boris.

Bell, Julie D. Distance Learning: New Technology & New Potential. (State Legislative Reports: Vol. 16, No. 6). 6p. 1991. pap. text 15.00 (*1-55516-305-X*, 7302-1606) Natl Conf State Legis.

Bell, K. & Keller, J., eds. Carbonatite Volcanism: Oldoinyo Lengai & the Petrogenesis of Natrocarbonatites. LC 97-9345. (Illus.). 224p. 1995. 140.95 (*0-387-58299-1*) Spr-Verlag.

Bell-Kanner, Karen. Frontiers: The Life & Times of Bonnie Bird: American Modern Dancer & Dance Educator. (Choreography & Dance Studies). (Illus.). 228p. 1998. pap. text 24.00 (*90-5755-034-2*, Harwood Acad Pubs) Gordon & Breach.

***Bell-Kanner, Karen.** Frontiers: The Life & Times of Bonnie Bird: American Modern Dancer & Dance Educator. (Choreography & Dance Studies). (Illus.). 228p. 1998. text 52.00 (*90-5755-033-4*, Harwood Acad Pubs) Gordon & Breach.

Bell-Kanner, Karen. The Life & Times of Ellen von Frankenberg, Vol. 1. (Choreography & Dance Studies). xvii, 167p. 1991. text 22.00 (*3-7186-5110-6*, Harwood Acad Pubs) Gordon & Breach.

Bell, Karamojo. Wanderings of an Elephant Hunter. 188p. 1988. 29.95 (*0-8464-4969-2*) Beekman Pubs.

Bell, Karen, tr. see Plato.

***Bell, Karen Magnuson.** Fire in Their Eyes: Wildfires & the People Who Fight Them. 1999. 27.12 (*0-8172-3774-7*) Raintree Steck-V.

Bell, Karen N. Strategies for Promoting Health & Assuring Access to Health Care in Child Care Settings. 28p. (Orig.). 1995. pap. 8.00 (*0-926582-14-3*) NCCP.

Bell, Karen N. & Simkin, Linda S. Caring Prescriptions: Comprehensive Health Care Strategies for Young Children in Poverty. LC 92-48194. (Illus.). 96p. (Orig.). 1993. pap. 8.00 (*0-926582-09-7*) NCCP.

Bell, Katherine. Jonathan's Journey. LC 97-62307. 160p. 1998. pap. 9.95 (*1-57921-078-3*, Pub. by WinePress Pub) BookWorld.

Bell, Kathleen, tr. see van Vree, Wilbert.

Bell, Katrina. Engaged to Love. large type ed. (Romance Ser.). 1994. pap. 16.99 (*0-7089-7600-X*, Linford) Ulverscroft.

Bell, Keith. Championship Sports Psychology. LC 89-49136. 200p. 1990. reprint ed. pap. 21.95 (*0-945609-04-3*) Keel Pubns.

— Coaching Excellence. LC 85-51524. 153p. (Orig.). 1989. pap. 19.95 (*0-945609-03-5*) Keel Pubns.

— Psychology for Swimmers. LC 89-49231. (Illus.). 72p. 1980. pap. 11.95 (*0-945609-00-0*) Keel Pubns.

— Stanley Spencer. 408p. 1999. pap. 39.95 (*0-7148-3890-X*) Phaidon Pr.

— Stanley Spencer: A Complete Catalogue of the Paintings. (Illus.). 545p. 1997. 175.00 (*0-7148-2735-5*, Pub. by Phaidon Press) Phaidon Pr.

— What It Takes: The ABC's of Excelling. LC 94-29303. 124p. 1995. 19.95 (*0-945609-22-1*) Keel Pubns.

— Winning Isn't Normal. LC 82-81102. (Illus.). 72p. 1982. pap. 11.95 (*0-945609-01-9*) Keel Pubns.

— You Only Feel Wet When You're Out of the Water: Thoughts on Psychology & Competitive Swimming. LC 91-3321. 130p. (Orig.). 1992. pap. 16.95 (*0-945609-15-9*) Keel Pubns.

Bell, Keith, jt. auth. see Robinson, Duncan.

Bell, Keith F. The Swim to Win Playbook. Neilson, Sandy, ed. LC 97-29459. 256p. 1998. pap., wbk. ed. 29.95 (*0-945609-97-3*) Keel Pubns.

Bell, Ken. The Way We Were. (Illus.). 256p. 1988. 45.00 (*0-8020-3990-1*) U of Toronto Pr.

Bell, L. N. Energetics of the Photosynthesizing Plant Cell. (Soviet Scientific Reviews Supplement Ser., Physicochemical Biology: Vol. 5). xvi, 402p. 1985. text 586.00 (*3-7186-0195-8*) Gordon & Breach.

Bell, L. N. & Gudkov, N. D. Thermodynamics of Light Energy Conversion. (Illus.). xvi, 204p. 1993. pap. 60.00 (*90-5103-081-9*, Pub. by SPB Acad Pub) Balogh.

***Bell, Landon C.** Charles Parish, York County, Virginia: History & Registers: Births, 1648-1789 & Deaths, 1665-1787. 285p. 1999. reprint ed. pap. 25.00 (*0-8063-4844-5*) Clearfield Co.

Bell, Landon C. Charles Parish, York County, Virginia: History & Registers. Births, 1648-1789, Deaths, 1665-1787. 3rd ed. LC 33-27865. xii, 285p. 1996. reprint ed. pap. 15.00 (*0-88490-116-5*) Library of VA.

— Cumberland Parish: Lunenburg County, VA, 1746-1816 Vestry Book, 1746-1816. 633p. 1998. reprint ed. pap. 40.50 (*0-7884-0844-5*, B149) Heritage Bk.

— Lunenburg the Old Free State: A Contribution to the History of Lunenburg County & Southside Virginia, 2 vols., Set. (Illus.). 1267p. 1995. reprint ed. lib. bdg. 132.00 (*0-8328-5132-9*) Higginson Bk Co.

— The Old Free State: A Contribution to the History of Lunenburg County & Southside Virginia, 2 vols. LC 74-5469. (Illus.). 1267p. 1995. reprint ed. pap. 95.00 (*0-8063-0623-8*, 415) Clearfield Co.

— Sunlight on the Southside: Lists of Tithes, Lunenburg County, Virginia 1748-1783. LC 74-5468. (Illus.). 503p. 1998. reprint ed. pap. 37.50 (*0-8063-0622-X*) Clearfield Co.

Bell, Laura S., ed. see Goddard, Larry.

Bell, Laurence, jt. auth. see Flood, Christopher.

Bell, Laurie, ed. Good Girls, Bad Girls. 232p. (Orig.). reprint ed. pap. write for info. (*0-88961-112-2*, Pub. by Womens Pr) LPC InBook.

Bell, Laurie L. Step by Step Phonics: Makes Reading & Writing Easy, Incl. 130p. study guide. rev. ed. LC 94-78951. 67p. 1994. teacher ed. 39.95 incl. audio (*0-9643274-0-6*) Back To The Basics.

— Step-by-Step Phonics Level 2: Makes Reading & Writing Easy. 71p. (Orig.). 1997. pap. text, teacher ed. 29.95 (*0-9643274-3-0*) Back To The Basics.

— Step by Step Phonics Makes Reading & Spelling Easy. 2nd rev. ed. Pack, Sandy, ed. LC 98-92893. Orig. Title: Step by Step Phonics: Makes Reading & Writing Easy. (Illus.). 205p. (J). (gr. 1-3). 1998. pap. 19.95 (*0-9643274-8-1*, BBP19981) Back To The Basics.

Bell, Leland V. Mental & Social Disorder in Sub-Saharan Africa: The Case of Sierra Leone, 1787-1990, 147. LC 91-14922. (Contributions in Afro-American & African Studies: No. 147). 224p. 1991. 57.95 (*0-313-27942-X*, BLQ, Greenwood Pr) Greenwood.

Bell, Leland V., jt. auth. see Tyor, Peter L.

Bell, Leonard. Colonial Constructs: European Images of Maori, 1840-1914. (Illus.). 308p. 45.00 (*1-86940-062-3*, Pub. by Auckland Univ) Paul & Co Pubs.

— Colonial Constructs: European Images of Maori, 1840-1914. (Illus.). 310p. 1992. 49.95 (*0-522-84528-2*, Pub. by Melbourne Univ Pr) Paul & Co Pubs.

***Bell, Leonard N. & Labuza, Theodore P.** Moisture Sorption: Practical Aspects of Isotherm Measurement & Use. 2nd rev. ed. (Illus.). 124p. 2000. 79.00 (*1-891127-18-7*) Eagan Pr.

Bell, Les. Management Skills in Primary Schools. LC 88-31018. (Educational Management Ser.). 304p. reprint ed. pap. 94.30 (*0-608-20316-5*, 207156900002) Bks Demand.

***Bell, Lesley.** Carefully: A Handbook for Home Care Assistants. 144p. 1999. pap. 40.00 (*0-86242-285-X*, Pub. by Age Concern Eng) St Mut.

***Bell, Lesley & Arroba, Tanya.** Staying Sane: Managing the Stress of Caring. 160p. 2000. pap. 40.00 (*0-86242-267-1*, Pub. by Age Concern Eng) St Mut.

Bell, Lewis H., ed. Industrial Noise Control. 2nd expanded rev. ed. (Mechanical Engineering Ser.: Vol. 88). (Illus.). 672p. 1993. text 179.00 (*0-8247-9028-6*) Dekker.

Bell, Lili. The Sea Maidens of Japan. LC 96-16132. (Illus.). 32p. (J). 1997. 14.95 (*1-57102-095-0*, Ideals Child) Hambleton-Hill.

Bell, Lilian A. Papyrus, Tapa, Amate & Rice Paper: Papermaking in Africa, the Pacific, Latin America & Southeast Asia. 4th rev. ed. (Illus.). 146p. (C). 1992. pap. 24.00 (*0-9625076-4-4*) Liliaceae Pr.

— Plant Fibers for Papermaking. (Illus.). 132p. 1995. pap. 21.00 (*0-9625076-5-2*) Liliaceae Pr.

Bell, Linda. Hidden Immigrants: Legacies of Growing up Abroad. LC 96-85041. (West & the Wider World Ser.: Vol. 11). 160p. (Orig.). 1996. pap. 19.95 (0-940121-35-2, P306) Cross Cultural Pubns.

The wife of a retired diplomat raised her children in various assignments around the world. She recounts the problems & pleasures of living a nomad's life, from the perspective of both the children & their parents. Through a series of interviews with children who grew up abroad but are now returned to the United States she addresses issues such as roots, ways to validate the childhood experiences, adjusting to a home country largely unknown, marriage, career choices & the pleasure or pain connected with international moves. She explores with her interviewees the things that helped or hindered their personal growth, as they articulate for the reader the loneliness & isolation, yet strength, that power these "third culture kids." ***Publisher Paid Annotation.***

Bell, Linda A. Rethinking Ethics in the Midst of Violence. LC 93-2697. (New Feminist Perspectives Ser.). 320p. (Orig.). (C). 1993. 71.00 (*0-8476-7844-X*); pap. 26.95 (*0-8476-7845-8*) Rowman.

— Sartre's Ethics of Authenticity. LC 86-19284. 224p. 1982. reprint ed. pap. 69.50 (*0-608-01660-8*, 206231500002) Bks Demand.

Bell, Linda A., ed. Visions of Women. LC 82-4866. (Contemporary Issues in Biomedicine, Ethics, & Society Ser.). 508p. 1983. 49.50 (*0-89603-044-X*); pap. 29.95 (*0-89603-054-7*) Humana.

Bell, Linda A. & Blumenfeld, David, eds. Overcoming Racism & Sexism. 276p. (C). 1995. pap. text 25.95 (*0-8476-8031-2*); lib. bdg. 66.00 (*0-8476-8030-4*) Rowman.

Bell, Linda R. Heartprints. Date not set. write for info. (*0-9625007-1-2*) Windflower TN.

Bell, Linda V., ed. see Bell, George E.

Bell, Lisa. Live Like You Really Mean It! Finding the Miracle in Your Moments. (Illus.). 1999. pap. write for info. (*1-893569-00-4*) Accolade Pub Co.

***Bell, Lisa.** Participassion 101. 2000. write for info. (*1-893569-07-1*) Accolade Pub Co.

— Resilience 101: How to Get Through the Tough Times. 2000. write for info. (*1-893569-05-5*) Accolade Pub Co.

Bell, Lisa. The Zen of Change. (Illus.). 2000. 21.95 (*1-893569-04-7*) Accolade Pub Co.

***Bell, Lisa & Lerner, Beverly.** Prophets of the Obvious: Under Your Nose, in Your Face Life Tactics. (Illus.). 2000. 19.95 (*1-893569-09-8*) Accolade Pub Co.

Bell, Lisa, et al. Asheville: City Business Profiles. LC 96-34985. 1996. pap. write for info. (*1-885352-53-0*) Community Comm.

Bell, Lorna & Seyfer, Eudora. Gentle Yoga. (Illus.). 144p. (Orig.). 1995. pap. 9.95 (*0-89087-636-3*) Celestial Arts.

Bell, Lorna J. The Large Print Book & Its User. LC 80-147607. (Library Association Research Publication: No. 22). (Illus.). 326p. reprint ed. pap. 101.10 (*0-7837-5299-7*, 204505300005) Bks Demand.

Bell, Lou, et al. The Children's Hospital of Philadelphia Guide to Common Childhood Infections. LC 98-18546. 480p. 1998. 29.95 (*0-02-860435-0*) Macmillan.

Bell, Louis, ed. Popular Irish Poetry. (Illus.). 96p. (Orig.). 1995. pap. 7.95 (*0-7171-2270-0*, Pub. by Gill & MacMill) Irish Bks Media.

Bell, Louis M., jt. auth. see Offit, Paul A.

Bell, Louis M., ed. see Schwartz, M. William.

Bell, Louise P. Johnny Tractor & His Pals. 3rd ed. (John Deere Storybook for Little Folks Ser.). (Illus.). iii, 17p. (J). (gr. 2 up). 1997. reprint ed. boxed set 6.95 (*1-887327-15-0*) Ertl Co.

Bell, Lynda. The Lullaby Cherub. (Illus.). 30p. (J). (ps-6). 1994. write for info. (*0-9641771-1-0*) Cherub Prods.

***Bell, Lynda, et al, eds.** Negotiating Culture & Human Rights: Beyond Universalism & Relativism. 364p. 2000. text 40.00 (*0-231-12080-X*); pap. text 19.50 (*0-231-12081-8*) Col U Pr.

Bell, Lynda S. One Industry, Two Chinas. LC 99-10135. (Illus.). 348p. 1999. 49.50 (*0-8047-2998-0*) Stanford U Pr.

Bell, M. Christina Rossetti. LC 74-156294. (English Literature Ser.: No. 33). 1971. reprint ed. lib. bdg. 75.00 (*0-8383-1292-6*) M S G Haskell Hse.

Bell, M. Late Quaternary Environmental Change: Physical & Human Perspectives. 288p. (C). 1996. pap. 77.00 (*0-582-04514-2*) Addison-Wesley.

Bell, M., et al. Quantum Mechanics, High Energy Physics & Accelerators: Selected Papers of John S. Bell. (Series on 20th Century Physics). 1000p. 1995. text 109.00 (*981-02-2115-0*) World Scientific Pub.

Bell, M., jt. ed. see Bonsall, P.

Bell, M., jt. ed. see Newton, P. W.

Bell, Mackenzie. Christina Rossetti: A Biographical & Critical Study. LC 70-148747. reprint ed. 35.00 (*0-404-08724-8*) AMS Pr.

Bell, Madison Smartt. All Souls' Rising. LC 95-12339. 530p. 1995. 25.95 (*0-679-43989-7*); 25.00 (*0-394-18350-9*) Pantheon.

— All Souls' Rising. 544p. 1996. pap. 13.95 (*0-14-025947-3*) Viking Penguin.

— Doctor Sleep. 320p. 1991. 19.95 (*0-15-126100-8*) Harcourt.

***Bell, Madison Smartt.** Master of the Crossroads. 704p. 2000. 30.00 (*0-375-42056-8*) Knopf.

— Narrative Design: Working with Imagination, Craft & Form. 392p. 2000. pap. text 16.95 (*0-393-32021-9*) Norton.

Bell, Madison Smartt. Save Me, Joe Louis. LC 93-233. 1993. 23.95 (*0-15-179432-4*) Harcourt.

Bell, Madison Smartt. Ten Indians. 264p. 1996. 23.00 (*0-679-44246-4*) McKay.

Bell, Madison Smartt. Ten Indians. LC 96-14357. 264p. 1997. pap. 12.95 (*0-14-026846-4*) Viking Penguin.

— The Washington Square Ensemble. 352p. 1984. pap. 11.95 (*0-14-007025-7*, Penguin Bks) Viking Penguin.

— The Year of Silence. 208p. 1989. pap. 12.95 (*0-14-011533-1*, Penguin Bks) Viking Penguin.

***Bell, Madison Smartt & Spires, Elizabeth, eds.** Ploughshares, Winter 1999-00 Vol. 25: Stories & Poems. 238p. 1999. pap. write for info. (*0-933277-27-X*) Ploughshares.

Bell, Madison Smartt, et al. New Millennium Writings: Spring & Summer, 1996. (Illus.). 128p. (Orig.). 1996. pap. 5.95 (*1-888338-01-6*) New Messenger Bks.

Bell, Mae Woods. Bottlenecks Are at the Top: More Wrymes. Ragan, Sam, ed. (Illus.). 110p. (Orig.). 1990. pap. write for info. (*0-938828-04-5*) Falls Tar.

Bell, Major H. On the Old West Coast. 1992. reprint ed. lib. bdg. 75.00 (*0-7812-5007-2*) Rprt Serv.

— Reminiscences of a Ranger. 1992. reprint ed. lib. bdg. 75.00 (*0-7812-5008-0*) Rprt Serv.

Bell, Malcolm. Historic Savannah. 79p. 1977. 12.95 (*0-9610106-3-0*) Historic Sav.

— The Last Goodbye. LC 98-28822. 352p. 1998. 24.95 (*0-312-19310-6*, Thomas Dunne) St Martin.

***Bell, Malcolm.** The Last Goodbye. 352p. 2000. mass mkt. 6.99 (*0-312-95889-7*) St Martin.

Bell, Malcolm, Jr. Major Butler's Legacy: Five Generations of a Slaveholding Family. LC 86-11353. (Illus.). 702p. 1987. 40.00 (*0-8203-0897-8*) U of Ga Pr.

— Major Butler's Legacy: Five Generations of a Slaveholding Family. LC 86-11353. (Brown Thrasher Bks.). (Illus.). 702p. 1989. pap. text 22.95 (*0-8203-1177-4*) U of Ga Pr.

Bell, Malcolm. Sir Edward Burne-Jones: A Record & Review. reprint ed. 37.50 (*0-404-00733-3*) AMS Pr.

Bell, Malcolm & Iseley, N. Jane. Historic Savannah. 6th ed. (Illus.). 79p. reprint ed. pap. 12.95 (*0-9610106-4-9*) Historic Sav.

Bell, Malcolm, et al. Energy Efficiency in Housing. (Urban & Regional Planning & Development Ser.). 192p. 1996. 63.95 (*1-85972-348-9*, Pub. by Avebry) Ashgate Pub Co.

Bell, Malcolm, Jr., ed. see American Academy in Rome Staff.

Bell, Marchella & Belcher, Jwaundace. Finding the 'G' Spot. 300p. 1998. pap. 13.95 (*0-9662377-0-6*) Another Bomb.

***Bell, Margaret.** Child Protection: Families & the Conference Process. LC 99-72841. (Evaluative Research in Social Work Ser.). 258p. 1999. text 69.95 (*1-84014-977-9*, Pub. by Ashgate Pub) Ashgate Pub Co.

Bell, Margaret. A Journey to Ohio in 1810 As Recorded in the Journal of Margaret Van Horn Dwight. (American Biography Ser.). 64p. 1991. reprint ed. lib. bdg. 59.00 (*0-7812-8018-4*) Rprt Serv.

Bell, Margaret, Jr. Margaret Fuller: A Biography. LC 72-164587. (Select Bibliographies Reprint Ser.). 1977. reprint ed. 23.95 (*0-8369-5871-3*) Ayer.

Bell, Margaret E. Watch for a Tall White Sail. 190p. 1992. reprint ed. lib. bdg. 16.95 (*0-89966-912-3*) Buccaneer Bks.

Bell, Marguerite. There Is No Price. (Illus.). 40p. 1996. pap. 4.00 (*1-886467-13-7*) WJM Press.

Bell, Marilyn, ed. see Shakespeare, William.

Bell, Marilyn J., ed. Women As Elders: Images, Visions & Issues. LC 86-25699. (Women & Politics Ser.: Vol. 6, No. 2). 90p. 1987. text 24.95 (*0-86656-621-X*) Haworth Pr.

— Women As Elders: The Feminist Politics of Aging. LC 86-25696. (Women & Politics Ser.; Vol. 6, No. 2). 90p. 1987. reprint ed. pap. 9.95 (*0-918393-34-5*, Harrington Park) Haworth Pr.

Bell, Marion L. Crusade in the City: Revivalism in Nineteenth-Century Philadelphia. (Illus.). 1978. 32.50 (*0-8387-1929-5*) Bucknell U Pr.

Bell, Mark. Aphorism in the Francophone Novel of the Twentieth Century. LC 98-157082. 160p. 1997. 55.00 (*0-7735-1528-3*, Pub. by McG-Queens Univ Pr) CUP Services.

— BBEdit 4 for Macintosh: Visual QuickStart Guide. LC 98-145142. (Illus.). 240p. (C). 1997. pap. text 17.95 (*0-201-69659-2*) Peachpit Pr.

***Bell, Mark.** The Mac OS X Black Book: The Reference Guide for Power Users. (Illus.). 700p. 2000. pap. 49.99 (*1-57610-606-3*) Coriolis Grp.

— The Mac OS X Book: A Beginner's Guide to the Newest Mac OS. (Illus.). 580p. 2000. pap. 39.99 (*1-57610-605-5*) Coriolis Grp.

***Bell, Mark, et al.** Mac OS/X Server Black Book: The System Administrator's Guide to Mac OS/X Server. (Black Book Ser.). (Illus.). 700p. 2000. pap. 49.99 (*1-57610-539-3*) Coriolis Grp.

***Bell, Mark R.** Apocalypse How? Baptists Driving the English Revolution. 256p. 2000. 29.00 (*0-86554-670-3*) Mercer Univ Pr.

Bell, Mark R. Mac OS 8.2 Black Book. LC 98-33996. (Black Book Ser.). (Illus.). 754p. 1998. pap. 49.99 (*1-57610-304-8*) Coriolis Grp.

***Bell, Mark R.** Mac OS 9.1 Book: The Most Up-to-Date Guide to the Newest Features of the Mac OS. (Illus.). 600p. 2000. pap. write for info. (*1-57610-776-0*) Coriolis Grp.

Bell, Mark R. Mac OS 8.5 Book. LC 99-18767. 599p. 1999. pap. text 39.99 (*1-57610-443-5*) Coriolis Grp.

Bell, Mark R., ed. Testament: Transcribed by Mark Russell Bell. LC 96-71184. (Illus.). 1100p. (Orig.). 1997. pap. 21.95 (*0-9654916-0-9*) Oracle Pr CA.

Bell, Martin. Complete Poems. LC 88-51308. 1988. 32.00 (*1-85224-042-3*, Pub. by Bloodaxe Bks); pap. 29.95 (*1-85224-043-1*, Pub. by Bloodaxe Bks) Dufour.

Bell, Martin. In Harm's Way. 288p. 1996. pap. 15.95 (*0-14-025108-1*, Pub. by Pnguin Bks Ltd) Trafalgar.

Bell, Martin. Nenshu & the Tiger: Parables of Life & Death. 112p. 1984. 5.95 (*0-8164-2356-3*) Harper SF.

— The Way of the Wolf. (Epiphany Bks.). 144p. 1983. mass mkt. 6.99 (*0-345-30522-1*) Ballantine Pub Grp.

Bell, Martin & Boardman, John, eds. Past & Present Soil Erosion. (Oxbow Monographs in Archaeology: No. 22). (Illus.). 243p. 1992. pap. 48.00 (*0-946897-46-8*, Pub. by Oxbow Bks) David Brown.

Bell, Martin, ed. & intro. see Hume, David.

Bell, Marvin. Ardor Vol. 2: The Book of the Deadman. (The Book of the Dead Man Ser.). 1997. pap. text 14.00 (*1-55659-081-4*) Copper Canyon.

— Book of the Dead Man. LC 93-43415. 80p. (Orig.). 1994. 22.00 (*1-55659-062-8*); pap. 12.00 (*1-55659-063-6*) Copper Canyon.

— The Escape into You. LC 94-70471. (Classic Contemporaries Ser.). 80p. 1994. reprint ed. pap. 12.95 (*0-88748-203-1*) Carnegie-Mellon.

An Asterisk (*) at the beginning of an entry indicates that the title is appearing for the first time.

— Iris of Creation. LC 90-81355. 140p. (Orig.). 1990. 17.00 (*1-55659-031-8*); pap. 10.00 (*1-55659-032-6*) Copper Canyon.

***Bell, Marvin.** Nightworks: Poems, 1962-2000. 360p. 2000. 28.00 (*1-55659-147-0*) Copper Canyon.

Bell, Marvin. Poetry for a Midsummer's Night: In the Spirit of William Shakespeare's A Midsummer Night's Dream. LC 97-62533. (Illus.). 4p. 1998. 19.50 (*0-9655702-1-5*) Seventy Fourth St.

— Stars Which See, Stars Which Do Not See. 2nd ed. LC 91-72054. (Classic Contemporaries Ser.). 56p. 1992. reprint ed. pap. 12.95 (*0-88748-138-8*) Carnegie-Mellon.

— Wednesday: Selected Poems, 1966-1997. LC 98-166469. 96p. 1998. pap. 14.95 (*1-897648-94-4*, Pub. by Salmon Poetry) Dufour.

Bell, Mary. Just Jerky: The Complete Guide to Making It. Beckmann, Annie, ed. LC 97-149076. (Illus.). 148p. (Orig.). 1996. pap., otabind 14.00 (*0-9653572-0-1*) Dry Store.

— The Long Ride. 250p. 2000. otabind 10.95 (*0-9653572-2-8*) Dry Store.

— Mary Bell's Complete Dehydrator Cookbook. LC 93-38778. 556p. 1994. 15.00 (*0-688-13024-0*, Hearst) Hearst Commns.

Bell, Mary, jt. auth. see Peel, Robin.

***Bell, Mary Reeves.** Checkmate in the Carpathians. (Passport to Danger Ser.: Vol. 4). (Illus.). 208p. (YA). (gr. 7 up). 2000. pap. 5.99 (*1-55661-551-5*) Bethany Hse.

Bell, Mary Reeves. Sagebrush Rebellion, Vol. 2. LC 99-6554. (Passport to Danger Ser.). 208p. 1999. pap. text 5.99 (*1-55661-550-7*) Bethany Hse.

***Bell, Mary Reeves.** Secret of Mezuzah. LC 99-6470. 208p. 1999. pap. text 5.99 (*1-55661-549-3*) Bethany Hse.

***Bell, Mary T.** Cutting Across Time: Logging, Rafting & Milling the Forests of Lake Superior. LC 98-61335. (Illus.). 96p. 1999. 29.95 (*0-931714-84-2*, Pub. by Nodin Pr) Bookmen Inc.

Bell, Mary T. & Lynch, Judith. The Long Ride Cookbook: Lighten Your Load & Take the Stress Out of Wilderness Cooking. (Illus.). 150p. 2000. otabind 14.95 (*0-9653572-3-6*) Dry Store.

Bell, Matthew. Goethe & Naturalistic Anthropology: Man & Other Plants. (Modern Languages & Literature Monographs). 356p. 1994. text 69.00 (*0-19-815894-7*) OUP.

Bell, Maureen. Karuk: The Upriver People. LC 91-29066. (Illus.). 224p. 1990. pap. 8.95 (*0-87961-209-6*) Naturegraph.

Bell, Maureen, et al. Biographical Dictionary of English Women Writers, 1958-1720. (Monograph Ser.). 208p. (C). 1990. 35.00 (*0-8161-1806-X*, Hall Reference) Macmillan.

Bell, Melanie M., ed. Touchtone Telephone - Voice Response Registration: A Guide for Successful Implementation. LC 93-4306. 240p. 1993. 50.00 (*0-929851-15-3*) Am Assn Coll Registrars.

Bell, Melinda. The Night Before Christmas Holiday Crafts & Activity Center. unabridged large type ed. LC 96-79052. 32p. (J). (gr. k-5). 1996. 24.95 incl. cd-rom (*0-9654458-0-1*, Play Again Inter) Bell-Ford Ent.

Bell, Melissa. Cryptych. Strahan, Bradley R., ed. (Illustrated Poetry Chapbook Ser.: No. XIII). (Illus.). 24p. (Orig.). 1994. pap. 5.50 (*0-938872-17-6*) Black Buzzard.

Bell, Meredith M., jt. auth. see Coates, Dennis E.

Bell-Metereau, Rebecca Louise. Hollywood Androgyny. LC 84-16984. 260p. 1985. text 57.50 (*0-231-05834-9*) Col U Pr.

— Hollywood Androgyny. 2nd ed. LC 93-8321. 345p. 1993. pap. 19.00 (*0-231-08467-6*) Col U Pr.

Bell-Metereau, Rebecca Louise, jt. auth. see Frost, Christopher J.

Bell, Michael. F. R. Leavis. (Critics of the Twentieth Century Ser.). 176p. 1988. pap. text 14.95 (*0-415-00898-0*) Routledge.

— F. R. Lewis. LC 88-19908. (Critics of the Twentieth Century Ser.). 168p. reprint ed. pap. 52.10 (*0-608-20317-3*, 207157000002) Bks Demand.

— The Face of Connecticut: People, Geology, & the Land. (Illus.). 196p. 1985. pap. 24.95 (*0-942081-01-3*) CT DEP CGNHS.

— Gabriel Garcia Marquez: Solitude & Solidarity. LC 93-19293. 1993. text 29.95 (*0-312-09988-6*) St Martin.

***Bell, Michael.** The Gardener's Guide to Growing Temperate Bamboos. LC 99-89641. (Illus.). 160p. 2000. 29.95 (*0-88192-445-8*) Timber.

Bell, Michael. Invitation to Environmental Sociology. LC 97-45255. (Sociology for a New Century Ser.). 1998. 29.95 (*0-7619-8509-3*) Pine Forge.

— Literature, Modernism & Myth: Belief & Responsibility in the Twentieth Century. 268p. 1997. text 59.95 (*0-521-58016-1*) Cambridge U Pr.

— Slow Space. LC 98-4583. 512p. 1997. 35.00 (*1-885254-73-3*, Pub. by Monacelli Pr) Penguin Putnam.

— Solarian Chronicles I. 250p. 1993. pap. 8.95 (*0-912526-62-9*) Lib Res.

Bell, Michael, ed. Stanley Saitowitz. (Architecture at Rice Ser.: Vol. 33). (Illus.). 136p. 1996. 27.95 (*1-885232-03-9*) Princeton Arch.

Bell, Michael & Iida, Yasunori. Transportation Network Analysis. LC 96-49966. 226p. 1997. 110.00 (*0-471-96493-X*) Wiley.

Bell, Michael A. & Foster, Susan A., eds. The Evolutionary Biology of the Threespine Stickleback. LC 92-38415. (Illus.). 584p. (C). 1994. text 105.00 (*0-19-857728-1*) OUP.

Bell, Michael D. Development of American Romance: The Sacrifice of Relation. LC 80-12241. 272p. 1981. lib. bdg. 25.00 (*0-226-04211-1*) U Ch Pr.

— The Development of American Romance: The Sacrifice of Relation. LC 80-12241. xiv, 292p. (C). 1984. pap. text 13.50 (*0-226-04213-8*) U Ch Pr.

— The Development of American Romance: The Sacrifice of Relation. LC 80-12241. 305p. reprint ed. pap. 94.60 (*0-608-09384-X*, 205412900004); reprint ed. pap. 94.60 (*0-608-21003-X*, 205453100003) Bks Demand.

— The Problem of American Realism: Studies in the Cultural History of a Literary Idea. LC 92-25231. 256p. (C). 1993. 32.95 (*0-226-04201-4*) U Ch Pr.

— The Problem of American Realism: Studies in the Cultural History of a Literary Idea. x, 256p. 1995. pap. text 15.95 (*0-226-04202-2*) U Ch Pr.

Bell, Michael D., ed. see Brackenridge, Hugh H. & Freneau, Philip.

Bell, Michael D., ed. see Hawthorne, Nathaniel.

Bell, Michael D., ed. see Jewett, Sarah Orne.

***Bell, Michael Davitt.** Culture Genre & Literary Vocations. 2000. lib. bdg. 48.00 (*0-226-04179-4*) U Ch Pr.

Bell, Michael G. H., ed. Transportation Networks, Recent Methodological Advances: Selected Proceedings of the 4th Euro Transportation Meeting. LC 99-209794. 326p. 1999. text 106.50 (*0-08-043052-X*, Pergamon Pr) Elsevier.

***Bell, Michael G. H. & Cassir, Chris.** Reliability of Transport Networks. LC 99-88744. (Traffic Engineering Ser.). 2000. 99.00 (*0-86380-260-5*) Research Studies Pr Ltd.

Bell, Michael J. The World from Brown's Lounge: An Ethnography of Black Middle-Class Play. LC 82-4732. 208p. 1983. text 24.95 (*0-252-00956-8*) U of Ill Pr.

Bell, Michael M. Childerley: The Moral Landscape of a Country Village. LC 93-24209. (Morality & Society Ser.). (Illus.). 292p. 1994. 32.50 (*0-226-04197-2*) U Ch Pr.

— Childerley: The Moral Landscape of a Country Village. LC 93-24209. (Morality & Society Ser.). (Illus.). 292p. 1995. pap. text 17.95 (*0-226-04198-0*) U Ch Pr.

Bell, Michael T. To My Comrades of Life. Gordon, Elissa, ed. (Illus.). 176p. (Orig.). 1995. pap. 10.00 (*0-9643047-9-1*) Cant Miss Pubng.

Bell, Michael W., et al. China at the Threshold of a Market Economy. LC 93-34529. (Occasional Papers: No. 107). 1993. pap. 15.00 (*1-55775-349-0*) Intl Monetary.

Bell, Michele Ashman. An Enduring Love: A Novel. LC 98-41059. 334p. 1998. pap. 13.95 (*1-57734-333-6*, 01113607) Covenant Comms.

***Bell, Michele Ashman.** A Forever Love: A Novel. LC 99-38400. 1999. pap. 13.95 (*1-57734-506-1*, 01114085) Covenant Comms.

Bell, Michele Ashman. An Unexpected Love. LC 98-13773. 1998. pap. 12.95 (*1-57734-243-7*, 01113402) Covenant Comms.

***Bell, Michele Ashman.** Yesterday's Love. LC 99-88761. 2000. 14.95 (*1-57734-602-5*) Covenant Comms.

Bell, Mike, jt. auth. see Blair, Cynthia.

Bell, Millicent. Hawthorne's View of the Artist. LC 62-13566. 214p. (C). 1962. text 24.50 (*0-87395-008-9*) State U NY Pr.

— Meaning in Henry James. 400p. 1991. pap. 20.50 (*0-674-55763-8*) HUP.

— Meaning in Henry James. 400p. (C). 1991. 55.00 (*0-674-55762-X*) HUP.

Bell, Millicent, ed. Cambridge Companion to Edith Wharton. 229p. (C). 1995. text 64.95 (*0-521-45358-5*); pap. text 18.95 (*0-521-48513-4*) Cambridge U Pr.

Bell, Millicent, ed. see Hawthorne, Nathaniel.

Bell, Morris D., jt. ed. see Ciardiello, Jean A.

Bell, Muriel, tr. see Bianco, Lucien.

Bell, N. How to Talk Hoosier. LC 96-150049. (Illus.). 112p. 1996. pap. 7.95 (*1-57166-050-X*) Quixote Pr IA.

— How to Talk Kansan. (Illus.). 111p. 1996. pap. 7.95 (*1-57166-053-4*) Quixote Pr IA.

Bell, N., jt. auth. see Homasson, J. P.

Bell, N., tr. see Von Hohnel, L.

Bell, Nanci. Seeing Stars: Symbol Imagery for Phonemic Awareness, Sight Words & Spelling. LC 98-204444. (Illus.). 302p. 1997. 44.95 (*0-945856-06-7*) Gander Educ.

***Bell, Nanci.** Seeing Stars Decoding Workbook Vol. 2: Who Is Bib? 42p. 1999. pap. text, wbk. ed. 3.95 (*0-945856-15-6*) Gander Educ.

— Seeing Stars Decoding Workbook Vol. 3: Who Is Gus? 42p. 1999. pap. text, wbk. ed. 3.95 (*0-945856-16-4*) Gander Educ.

— Seeing Stars Decoding Workbook Vol. 4: Who Is Poe? 42p. 1999. pap. text, wbk. ed. 3.95 (*0-945856-17-2*) Gander Educ.

— Seeings Stars Decoding Workbook Vol. 1: Who Is Fip? 42p. 1999. pap. text, wbk. ed. 3.95 (*0-945856-14-8*) Gander Educ.

Bell, Nanci. Visualizing & Verbalizing for Language Comprehension & Thinking. 2nd ed. (Illus.). 225p. 1991. lib. bdg. 49.95 (*0-945856-01-6*) Gander Educ.

— Visualizing & Verbalizing Stories. LC 98-204440. 98p. (J). (gr. k-8). 1997. 19.95 (*0-945856-05-9*) Gander Educ.

Bell, Nanci & Lindamood, Phyllis. A Gunny & Ivan Adventure: Ivan King of the Neighborhood. LC 99-177889. 105p. (J). (gr. 4-9). 1997. pap. 6.95 (*0-945856-10-5*) Gander Educ.

— A Gunny & Ivan Adventure Vol. I: Ivan Sleeps Over. LC 98-205401. 59 p. (J). (gr. k-3). 1997. 6.95 (*0-945856-09-1*) Gander Educ.

— Vanilla Vocabulary: Visualized-Verbalized Vocabulary Book - Level II. (Illus.). x, 342p. (J). (gr. 4-7). 1993. pap. 24.95 (*0-945856-03-2*) Gander Educ.

— Vanilla Vocabulary: Visualized-Verbalized Vocubulary Book - Level II, Level I. LC 98-204442. 454p. (J). (gr. k-3). 1997. lib. bdg. 24.95 (*0-945856-08-3*) Gander Educ.

Bell, Nanci, jt. auth. see Turley, Kimberly.

***Bell, Nancy.** Biggie & Meddlesome Mailman. 1999. mass mkt. write for info. (*0-312-97318-7*) St Martin.

Bell, Nancy. Biggie & the Fricasseed Fat. LC 98-23853. 224p. 1998. text 20.95 (*0-312-19238-X*) St Martin.

***Bell, Nancy.** Biggie & the Fricasseed Fat Man. LC 00-42581. 2000. write for info. (*0-7862-2561-0*) Thorndike Pr.

Bell, Nancy. Biggie & the Fricasseed Fatman. 240p. 1999. pap. 5.99 (*0-312-96937-6*, Minotaur) St Martin.

— Biggie & the Mangled Mortician. (Dead Letter Mysteries Ser.). 1998. mass mkt. 5.99 (*0-312-96491-9*) St Martin.

***Bell, Nancy.** Biggie & the Mangled Mortician. LC 00-37747. (Illus.). (J). 2000. pap. write for info. (*0-7862-2562-9*) Thorndike Pr.

Bell, Nancy. Biggie & the Meddlesome Mailman. LC 99-16994. 240p. 1999. text 22.95 (*0-312-20880-4*) St Martin.

***Bell, Nancy.** Biggie & the Meddlesome Mailman. large type ed. LC 00-28644. 287p. 2000. 28.95 (*0-7862-2552-1*) Thorndike Pr.

Bell, Nancy. Biggie & the Poisoned Politician. (Dead Letter Mysteries Ser.). 1997. mass mkt. 5.50 (*0-312-96219-3*) St Martin.

***Bell, Nancy.** Biggie & the Poisoned Politician. large type ed. (Senior Lifestyles Ser.). 257p. 2000. 28.95 (*0-7862-2550-5*) Thorndike Pr.

Bell, Nancy. Something of Value. large type ed. (Linford Romance Library). 272p. 1987. pap. 8.95 (*0-7089-6334-X*, Linford) Ulverscroft.

Bell, Nancy J. & Bell, Robert W., eds. Adolescent Risk Taking. (Illus.). 192p. 1992. text 48.00 (*0-8039-5064-0*); pap. text 24.00 (*0-8039-5065-9*) Sage.

Bell, Nancy J., jt. ed. see Bell, Robert W.

Bell, Nancy N., jt. auth. see Glazer, William M.

Bell, Neal. Cold Sweat. 1988. pap. 5.25 (*0-8222-0227-1*) Dramatists Play.

— On the Bum: or The Next Train Through. 1994. pap. 5.25 (*0-8222-1344-3*) Dramatists Play.

— Operation Midnight Climax. 1982. pap. 5.25 (*0-8222-0862-8*) Dramatists Play.

— Raw Youth: A Play. 53p. 1986. pap. 5.25 (*0-8222-0931-4*) Dramatists Play.

— Ready for the River. 1991. pap. 5.25 (*0-8222-0932-2*) Dramatists Play.

— Sleeping Dogs. 1989. pap. 5.25 (*0-8222-1042-8*) Dramatists Play.

— Two Small Bodies. 1980. pap. 5.25 (*0-8222-1185-8*) Dramatists Play.

Bell, Neill. The Book of Where: Or How to Be Naturally Geographic. (Brown Paper School Bks.). 119p. (YA). (gr. 7 up). 1982. pap. 12.95 (*0-316-08831-5*) Little.

— The Book of Where: Or How to Be Naturally Geographic. (Brown Paper School Bks.). (J). 1982. 18.05 (*0-606-04025-0*, Pub. by Turtleback) Demco.

Bell, Netha. Gun Shootin' Girl Chasin' Whiskey Drinkin' Tales Out of the Land of the Lakes. (Illus.). 176p. 1992. pap. 9.95 (*1-878488-36-8*) Quixote Pr IA.

— Jack King vs. Detective Mackenzie. (Illus.). 172p. (Orig.). 1991. pap. 9.95 (*1-878488-51-7*) Quixote Pr IA.

— Lost & Buried Treasure of the Missouri River. (Illus.). 172p. (Orig.). 1991. pap. 9.95 (*1-878488-57-0*) Quixote Pr IA.

Bell, Netha & Scholl, Gary. Lost & Buried Treasure of the Mississippi River. Carlson, Bruce, ed. (Illus.). 143p. (Orig.). 1991. pap. 9.95 (*1-878488-32-5*) Quixote Pr IA.

Bell, Nica. Directory of Aquaculture in the Northeast. 56p. (Orig.). 1991. pap. 5.00 (*1-56172-003-8*) MIT Sea Grant.

Bell, Nimrod J. Southern Railroad Man: Conductor N. J. Bell's Recollections of the Civil War Era. Ward, James A., ed. LC 93-34199. (Illus.). 232p. (C). 1994. 28.00 (*0-87580-184-6*) N Ill U Pr.

Bell, Nora K., ed. Who Decides? Conflicts of Rights in Health Care. LC 81-83908. (Contemporary Issues in Biomedicine, Ethics, & Society Ser.). 218p. 1982. 44.50 (*0-89603-034-2*) Humana.

Bell, O. W. Devendorf Family. (Illus.). 111p. 1994. reprint ed. pap. 19.50 (*0-8328-4208-7*); reprint ed. lib. bdg. 29.50 (*0-8328-4207-9*) Higginson Bk Co.

Bell, Owain. Stop, Train, Stop! A Thomas the Tank Engine Story. LC 94-15129. (J). (gr. 1 up). 1995. lib. bdg. 11.99 (*0-679-95806-1*) Beginner.

— Stop, Train, Stop! A Thomas the Tank Engine Story. LC 94-15129. (Illus.). (J). (gr. 1 up). 1995. 7.99 (*0-679-85806-7*) Beginner.

Bell, Owain. Thomas the Tank Engine Says Goodnight. (Cuddle Cloth Bks.). 12p. (J). (ps). 1990. 4.99 (*0-679-80791-8*, Pub. by Random Bks Yng Read) Random.

Bell, Owain. Wave Hello to Thomas! A Thomas the Tank Engine Lift-&-Peek-a-Board Book. LC 92-80747. (Lift-&-Peek-A-Board Bks.). 14p. (J). (ps). 1993. 4.99 (*0-679-83877-5*, Pub. by Random Bks Yng Read) Random.

Bell, Owen, jt. auth. see Havel, Geoff.

Bell, P. & Wright, D. Gesteine und Ihre Mineralien Finden und Bestimmen (Rocks & Their Minerals Finding & Recognizing) (Kosmos Naturfuehrer (Nature Guides) Ser.). (GER., Illus.). 192p. 1987. pap. 34.00 (*3-440-05714-3*, Pub. by Franckh-Kosmos) Balogh.

Bell, P. M. France & Britain, 1940-1994: The Long Separation. LC 96-43210. 328p. (C). 1997. pap. 26.73 (*0-582-28920-3*) Longman.

Bell, P. M. France & Britain, 1940-1994: The Long Separation. LC 96-43210. 320p. (C). 1997. 73.00 (*0-582-28921-1*) Longman.

Bell, P. M. France Britain 1900-1940. LC 95-41012. 256p. (C). 1996. pap. text 27.19 (*0-582-22953-7*, Pub. by Addison-Wesley) Longman.

— France Britain 1900 1940. 256p. (C). 1996. text 59.25 (*0-582-22954-5*, Pub. by Addison-Wesley) Longman.

— John Bull & the Bear: British Public Opinion, Foreign Policy & the Soviet Union, 1941-1945. 192p. 1995. text 49.95 (*0-340-53307-2*, Pub. by E A) St Martin.

— John Bull & the Bear: British Public Opinion, Foreign Policy & the Soviet Union, 1941-1945. (Illus.). 192p. 1991. reprint ed. 45.00 (*0-685-49862-X*, A5187, Pub. by E A) Routldge.

— The Origins of the Second World War in Europe. 2nd ed. LC 96-52074. (Origins of Modern Wars Ser.). 1p. (C). 1997. pap. text 22.50 (*0-582-30470-9*) Longman.

Bell, P. R. Arterial Surgery of the Lower Limb. (Illus.). 189p. 1991. text 150.00 (*0-443-03541-5*) Church.

***Bell, Pam.** Love & Sex By the Numbers: A Numerology Guide to Romance. 256p. 2000. pap. 13.00 (*0-380-80840-4*, Quil) HarperTrade.

Bell, Pamela H. & Simon, Jordan. Astronumerology: Your Key to Empowerment Using Stars & Numbers. LC 98-16524. 352p. 1998. pap. 13.00 (*0-380-79466-7*, Avon Bks) Morrow Avon.

Bell, Patricia A., jt. auth. see Turnbull, George I.

Bell, Patricia E. Amor et Amicitia. 80p. (C). 1989. pap. text 11.95 (*0-521-37736-6*) Cambridge U Pr.

Bell, Patricia J. The Prepublishing Handbook: What You Should Know Before You Publish Your First Book. LC 92-72686. 130p. (Orig.). 1992. pap. 12.00 (*0-9618227-2-4*) Cats-paw MN.

— Roughing It Elegantly: A Practical Guide to Canoe Camping. 2nd ed. LC 93-74305. (Illus.). 250p. (Orig.). 1994. pap. 14.95 (*0-9618227-0-8*) Cats-paw MN.

Bell, Patricia J., ed. The Paddler's Planner. 200p. (Orig.). 1989. pap. 7.95 (*0-9618227-3-2*) Cats-paw MN.

Bell, Paul, et al. Nutrition Curriculum: Activities Kit, Level 1, Grades 5-8. (Illus.). 288p. 1986. pap. text 27.95 (*0-87628-617-1*) Ctr Appl Res.

— Nutrition Curriculum: Activities Kit, Level 2, Grades 9-12. (Illus.). 352p. 1986. pap. text 27.95 (*0-87628-618-X*) Ctr Appl Res.

Bell, Paul A. Environmental Psychology. 4th ed. (C). 1996. text 74.00 (*0-15-501496-X*, Pub. by Harcourt Coll Pubs) Harcourt.

Bell, Paul B., Jr., ed. Scanning Electron Microscopy of Cells in Culture. (Illus.). vi, 314p. 1984. reprint ed. pap. 29.00 (*0-931288-31-2*) Scanning Microscopy.

Bell, Paul B. & Simon, Jay, eds. The Law & Business of Licensing: Licensing in the 1990's, 3 vols. LC 90-1961. (IP Ser.). 1990. ring bd. 375.00 (*0-87632-724-2*) West Group.

Bell, Paula R. High Tech Writing: How to Write for the Electronics Industry. LC 85-9498. 233p. 1985. pap. 24.95 (*0-471-81864-X*) Wiley.

Bell, Pauline. The Dead Do Not Praise. large type ed. (Dales Large Print Ser.). 314p. 1997. pap. 18.99 (*1-85389-760-4*, Dales) Ulverscroft.

— Downhill to Death. large type ed. 352p. 1996. 27.99 (*0-7505-0952-X*, Pub. by Mgna Lrg Print) Ulverscroft.

— Feast into Mourning. large type ed. (Dales Large Print Ser.). 3336p. 1998. pap. 19.99 (*1-85389-761-2*, Dales) Ulverscroft.

— A Multitude of Sins. large type ed. (Magna Large Print Ser.). 314p. 1997. 27.99 (*0-7505-1174-5*, Pub. by Mgna Lrg Print) Ulverscroft.

— No Pleasure in Death. large type ed. 369p. 1994. pap. 18.99 (*1-85389-498-2*, Dales) Ulverscroft.

— Sleeping Partners. large type ed. (Magna Large Print Ser.). 375p. 1997. 27.99 (*0-7505-1076-5*) Ulverscroft.

— The Way of a Serpent. large type ed. 336p. 1998. 29.99 (*0-7505-1263-6*) Ulverscroft.

Bell, Pearl T., ed. see Banham, Lorna.

Bell, Pearl T., ed. see Smith, Gloria V.

Bell, Peter. Backgammon: Winning with the Doubling Cube. 200p. 1998. pap. 30.00 (*1-880604-10-8*) Gammon Pr.

— Black & Recovering. 64p. 1993. pap., wbk. ed. 7.75 (*1-56246-079-X*, 6284, HazeldenJohnson Inst) Hazelden.

— Facing My Future. 64p. 1993. pap., wbk. ed. 7.75 (*1-56246-080-3*, 3230, HazeldenJohnson Inst) Hazelden.

— Growing up Black & Proud: A Guide for Teenagers. 128p. 1992. pap. 9.95 (*1-56246-064-1*, 3111, HazeldenJohnson Inst) Hazelden.

— Timber & Iron: Houses in North Queensland Mining Settlements 1861-1920. (Illus.). 1985. 49.95 (*0-7022-1714-X*, Pub. by Univ Queensland Pr) Intl Spec Bk.

Bell, Peter & Bitney, Jim. Growing up Black & Proud: Preventing Alcohol & Other Drug Problems Through Building a Positive Racial Identity: A Curriculum for African-American Youth. LC 92-33124. 1992. pap. 166.95 (*1-56246-063-3*, 3109, HazeldenJohnson Inst) Hazelden.

Bell, Peter, jt. auth. see Anderson, Debra.

Bell, Peter A. & O'Connell, Jeffrey P. Torts & Retorts: The (In)Justice of Accident Law? LC 96-36656. (Contemporary Law Ser.). 288p. 1997. 35.00 (*0-300-06257-5*) Yale U Pr.

Bell, Peter C. Management Science Operations Research: A Strategic Perspective. LC 98-8106. 1998. write for info. (*0-324-00158-4*) Sth-Wstrn College.

— Management Science Operations Research: A Strategic Perspective. 1998. 81.95 (*0-324-00466-4*) Sth-Wstrn College.

Bell, Peter R., et al, eds. Surgical Management of Vascular Disease. (Illus.). 1436p. 1992. text 295.00 (*0-7020-1514-8*, Pub. by W B Saunders) Saunders.

***Bell, Peter R. & Hemsley, Alan R.** Green Plants: Their Origin & Diversity. 2nd ed. (Illus.). 320p. (C). 2000. 74.95 (*0-521-64109-8*); pap. 32.95 (*0-521-64673-1*) Cambridge U Pr.

Bell, Philip & Bell, Roger. Americanization of Australia. LC 99-235577. 282p. 1998. pap. 25.00 (*0-86840-784-4*, Pub. by New South Wales Univ Pr) Intl Spec Bk.

Bell, Philip, jt. ed. see Cloke, Paul.

An Asterisk (*) at the beginning of an entry indicates that the title is appearing for the first time.

Bell, Philip W. Current Cost-Constant Dollar Accounting & Its Uses in the Managerial Decision-Making Process. LC 86-13528. (McQueen Accounting Monograph Ser.: Vol. 3). 73p. (Orig.). 1986. pap. text 10.00 (*0-935951-02-4*) U AR Acc Dept.
— Toward Greater Logic & Utility in Accounting: The Collected Writings of Philip W. Bell. LC 97-33171. (New Works in Accounting History). 488p. 1997. reprint ed. text 127.00 (*0-8153-3039-1*) Garland.

Bell, Philip W., jt. auth. see Edwards, Edgar O.

Bell, Phillip, jt. auth. see Van Leewing, Theo.

Bell, Quentin. The Art Critic & the Art Historian. LC 75-314718. (Leslie Stephen Lecture Ser.: 1973). 34p. reprint ed. pap. 25.00 (*0-8357-5757-9*, 2051369) Bks Demand.
— Bad Art. (Illus.). 320p. 1989. 35.95 (*0-226-04203-0*) U Ch Pr.
— Bloomsbury Recalled. 234p. 1996. 28.00 (*0-231-10564-9*) Col U Pr.
— Bloomsbury Recalled. 1997. pap. 16.00 (*0-231-10565-7*) Col U Pr.
— The Brandon Papers. LC 85-8573. 224p. 1985. 15.95 (*0-685-10655-1*) Harcourt.
— The Brandon Papers. 1986. pap. 5.95 (*0-317-53636-2*) Harcourt.
— Charleston: A Bloomsbury House & Garden. (Illus.). 160p. 1997. 45.00 (*0-8050-5585-1*) H Holt & Co.
— Virginia Woolf: A Biography. LC 73-12870. (Illus.). 530p. (C). 1974. reprint ed. pap. 22.00 (*0-15-693580-5*, Harvest Bks) Harcourt.

Bell, Quentin, jt. frwd. see Collins, Judith.

Bell, R. A., tr. see Gaxotte, Pierre.

Bell, R. C. Board & Table Games from Many Civilizations. LC 79-51819. (Illus.). 448p. 1980. reprint ed. pap. 9.95 (*0-486-23855-5*) Dover.
— Discovering Backgammon. (Handbook Ser.: No. 201). (Illus.). 48p. 1989. pap. 7.50 (*0-85263-474-9*, Pub. by Shire Pubns) Parkwest Pubns.
— Discovering Dice & Dominoes. (Handbook Ser.: No. 255). (Illus.). 48p. 1980. pap. 7.50 (*0-85263-532-X*, Pub. by Shire Pubns) Parkwest Pubns.
— Discovering Mah-Jong. 1989. pap. 25.00 (*0-85263-444-7*, Pub. by Shire Pubns) St Mut.
— Fun at the Lathe. (Illus.). 144p. 1998. 17.95 (*1-86108-057-3*, Pub. by Guild Master) Sterling.
— Mailing & Other Tyneside Pottery. (Album Ser.: No. 170). (Illus.). 32p. 1989. pap. 4.75 (*0-85263-792-6*, Pub. by Shire Pubns) Parkwest Pubns.
— Studies in Romans. 1957. pap. 2.75 (*0-88027-025-X*) Firm Foun Pub.

Bell, R. D. & Scott, F. B. Moths Lepidoptera: Sphingidae, Vol. 5. (Fauna of British India Ser.). (Illus.). xviii, 537p. 1976. reprint ed. 40.00 (*0-88065-056-7*) Scholarly Pubns.

Bell, R. G., jt. auth. see Fontana, Matt.

Bell, R. S., jt. auth. see Coates, F. G.

Bell, R. S., jt. auth. see Coates, T. F.

Bell, R. W., et al, eds. Developmental Psychobiology & Clinical Neuropsychology. (Interfaces in Psychology Ser.: No. 1). 133p. 1984. 24.95 (*0-89672-120-5*); pap. 14.95 (*0-89672-119-1*) Tex Tech Univ Pr.
— Mineral Nutrition of Food Legumes in Thailand, with Particular Reference to Micronutrients. 1990. pap. 60.00 (*1-86320-014-2*, Pub. by ACIAR) St Mut.

Bell, Rachael. A Visit to Italy. LC 99-18085. (A Visit to Ser.). 1999. write for info. (*1-57572-853-2*) Heinemann Lib.

***Bell, Rachel.** Chickens. LC 99-44494. (Farm Animals Ser.). (Illus.). (J). 2000. lib. bdg. write for info. (*1-57572-530-4*) Heinemann Lib.
— Cows. LC 99-42837. (Farm Animals Ser.). (J). 2000. write for info. (*1-57572-529-0*) Heinemann Lib.
— Horses. LC 99-44184. (Farm Animals Ser.). (Illus.). (J). 2000. lib. bdg. write for info. (*1-57572-531-2*) Heinemann Lib.

Bell, Rachel. Ireland. LC 98-37707. (Visit to Ser.). 32p. (J). 1999. lib. bdg. 19.92 (*1-57572-847-8*) Heinemann Lib.

***Bell, Rachel.** Sheep. LC 99-43370. (Farm Animals Ser.). (Illus.). (J). 2000. lib. bdg. write for info. (*1-57572-533-9*) Heinemann Lib.
— Turkeys. LC 99-43372. (Farm Animals Ser.). (Illus.). (J). 2000. lib. bdg. write for info. (*1-57572-534-7*) Heinemann Lib.
— United Kingdom. LC 98-45091. (Visit to Ser.). 32p. (J). 1999. lib. bdg. 19.92 (*1-57572-846-X*) Heinemann Lib.

Bell, Rachel & Peiper, Howard. The A. D. D. & A. D. H. D. Diet. Anderson, Nina, ed. LC 97-66518. 96p. 1997. pap. 9.95 (*1-884820-29-8*) SAFE GOODS.

Bell, Randall. Bell's Guide: The Comprehensive Real Estate Handbook. 2nd ed. LC 97-71983. (Illus.). 538p. 1997. pap. 14.95 (*1-886734-11-9*, 734111) Sequoia Pub Inc.
— Real Estate Damages: An Analysis of Detrimental Conditions. LC 98-52196. 5p. 1999. write for info. (*0-922154-55-4*) Appraisal Inst.

Bell-Ranske, Jutta. Revelation of Man: A Key to Mystic Science (1924) 228p. 1998. reprint ed. pap. 17.95 (*0-7661-0540-7*) Kessinger Pub.

Bell, Ray. Mandolin Scales & Studies. 152p. 1995. spiral bd. 16.95 (*0-7866-0839-0*, 95542) Mel Bay.

Bell, Raymond M. Baskin - Baskins Family, South Carolina - Pennsylvania. 85p. 1997. reprint ed. pap. 16.00 (*0-8328-7407-8*); reprint ed. lib. bdg. 26.00 (*0-8328-7406-X*) Higginson Bk Co.
— Baskins - Baskin Family, Pennsylvania, Virginia, South Carolina. (Illus.). 104p. 1997. reprint ed. pap. 16.50 (*0-8328-7409-4*); reprint ed. lib. bdg. 26.50 (*0-8328-7408-6*) Higginson Bk Co.
— Bell Family of Mifflin County, Pennsylvania: Ancestors & Descendants of John Henderson Bell of Decatur Township. (Illus.). 77p. 1997. reprint ed. pap. 15.00 (*0-8328-7475-2*); reprint ed. lib. bdg. 25.00 (*0-8328-7474-4*) Higginson Bk Co.

Bell, Rebecca S. & Severin, C. Sherman. Profiles Cut from the Wave: CSS Sixth Collection of Poetry. (Collection of National Poetry Ser.). (Illus.). 200p. 1984. pap. 9.95 (*0-942170-06-7*) CSS Pubns.

Bell, Rebecca S. & Severin, C. Sherman, eds. Bittersweet. (Collection of National Poetry Ser.: No. 8). (Illus.). 225p. (Orig.). 1985. pap. 9.95 (*0-317-39877-6*) CSS Pubns.
— I Have Need of the Poets. (Collection of National Poetry Ser.: No. 7). (Illus.). 168p. (Orig.). 1984. pap. 9.95 (*0-942170-07-5*) CSS Pubns.
— The Whisper of Dreams: A Collection of Poetry. (Collection of National Poetry Ser.). (Illus.). 232p. 1982. pap. 9.95 (*0-942170-04-0*) CSS Pubns.

Bell, Reginald. Public School Education of Second-Generation Japanese in California. Daniels, Roger, ed. LC 78-54808. (Asian Experience in North America Ser.). 1979. reprint ed. lib. bdg. 15.95 (*0-405-11264-5*) Ayer.

Bell, Richard & Watt, William M. Introduction to the Qur'an. (Islamic Surveys Ser.). 272p. 1995. pap. 25.00 (*0-7486-0597-5*, Pub. by Edinburgh U Pr) Col U Pr.

Bell, Richard, jt. auth. see Marks, Sandy.

Bell, Richard, jt. auth. see Seow, Jimmy.

Bell, Richard C. & Gillette, M. L. Determining the Equivalent Mass & Dissociation Constant of an Unknown Weak Acid by Titrimetry. Stanitski, C. L., ed. (Modular Laboratory Program in Chemistry Ser.). 16p. (C). 1998. pap. text 1.50 (*0-87540-453-7*, EQUL 453) Chem Educ Res.
— Studying the Rate of the Reaction of Potassium Permanganate & Oxalic Acid. Gillette, M., ed. (Modular Laboratory Program in Chemistry Ser.). 12p. (C). 1998. pap. text 1.50 (*0-87540-505-3*, KINE 505) Chem Educ Res.

Bell, Richard G. Commercial Paper: Suitable for Use with Farnsworth. (Cambridge Ser.). 136p. 1984. pap. text 18.00 (*0-685-54301-3*, Chicago Law Bk) Cambridge Law.
— Decedents' Estates & Trusts: Suitable for Use with Ritchie. (Cambridge Ser.). 470p. 1988. pap. text 21.00 (*0-685-54296-3*, Chicago Law Bk) Cambridge Law.
— Payment Law: Suitable for Use with Whaley. (Cambridge Ser.). 207p. 1995. pap. text 19.00 (*0-685-54297-1*, Chicago Law Bk) Cambridge Law.
— Sales: Suitable for Use with Benfield. (Cambridge Ser.). 221p. 1986. pap. text 14.00 (*0-685-54306-4*, Chicago Law Bk) Cambridge Law.
— Sales: Suitable for Use with Whaley. (Cambridge Ser.). 241p. 1990. pap. text 19.00 (*0-685-54298-X*, Chicago Law Bk) Cambridge Law.
— Secured Transactions: Suitable for Use with Whaley. (Cambridge Ser.). 188p. 1989. pap. text 14.50 (*0-685-54295-5*, Chicago Law Bk) Cambridge Law.

Bell, Richard H. Provoked to Jealousy: The Origin & Purpose of the Jealousy Motif in Romans 9-11. LC 94-212044. (Wissenschaftliche Untersuchungen Zum Neuen Testament Ser.: No. 2, Pt. 63). 493p. (Orig.). 1994. pap. 88.50 (*3-16-146091-X*, Pub. by JCB Mohr) Coronet Bks.
— Simone Weil: The Way of Justice As Compassion. LC 98-17453. (Twentieth-Century Political Thinkers Ser.). 224p. 1998. 58.00 (*0-8476-9079-2*); pap. 19.95 (*0-8476-9080-6*) Rowman.

Bell, Richard H., Jr., et al, eds. Digestive Tract Surgery: A Text & Atlas. LC 95-981. 1,688p. 1995. text 199.00 (*0-397-51344-5*) Lppncott W & W.

Bell, Richard H. & Battin, Barbara, eds. Seeds of the Spirit: Wisdom of the Twentieth Century. LC 94-48631. 200p. (Orig.). 1995. pap. 19.95 (*0-664-25465-9*) Westminster John Knox.

Bell, Richard O. & Bell, Joan K. Auditions & Scenes from Shakespeare. rev. ed. 164p. 1994. reprint ed. pap. 12.95 (*0-933919-27-1*) Theatre Directories.

Bell, Rick, jt. auth. see Polto, Pearl B.

Bell, Riley, et al. Rugby Law: A Plain Language Guide. LC 98-175867. 76 p. 1998. write for info. (*0-7900-0647-2*) Reed Pubng.

Bell, Ritchie, ed. see Crawford, Barrie F.

Bell, Rob, ed. see Bennie, Scott.

Bell, Rob, ed. see Robinson, Andrew.

Bell, Rob, ed. see Shuler, Doug.

Bell, Rob, ed. see Varney, Allen.

Bell, Robbie & Cornelius, Michael. Board Games Round the World: A Resource Book for Mathematical Investigations. (Illus.). 128p. (C). 1989. pap. 20.95 (*0-521-35924-4*) Cambridge U Pr.

Bell, Roberly. Home. (Illus.). 20p. 1995. spiral bd., bds. 30.00 (*0-614-18192-5*) Visual Studies.

Bell, Robert. The Book of Scots-Irish Family Names. LC 88-7452. 286p. 1997. pap. 18.95 (*0-85640-602-3*, Pub. by Blackstaff Pr) Dufour.
— Book of Ulster Surnames. LC 88-7452. 285p. 1988. 26.00 (*0-85640-416-0*, Pub. by Blackstaff Pr) Dufour.
— Book of Ulster Surnames. LC 88-7452. 285p. 1994. pap. 18.95 (*0-85640-405-5*, Pub. by Blackstaff Pr) Dufour.
— Impure Science: Fraud, Compromise & Political Influence in Scientific Research. 320p. 1992. 24.95 (*0-471-52913-3*) Wiley.
— My First Book of Space Coloring & Activity Book. (Illus.). 160p. (J). (gr. 1 up). 1986. pap. 6.95 (*0-671-62407-5*) Litle Simon.
— The Prevention & Treatment of Cancer. 88p. 1996. reprint ed. spiral bd. 10.00 (*0-7873-0089-6*) Hlth Research.
— The Prevention & Treatment of Cancer. 88p. 1996. reprint ed. pap. 8.95 (*1-56459-890-X*) Kessinger Pub.
— PSAT - Preliminary Scholastic Aptitude Test. (Illus.). 750p. 1998. pap. text 15.95 (*0-87891-936-8*) Res & Educ.
— Skill Reinforcers. Buckingham, Anne, ed. (Thinking Skill Library). (Illus.). 104p. (Orig.). (J). (gr. 2-5). 1997. pap., teacher ed. 9.95 (*1-56784-706-4*) Newbridge Educ.

Bell, Robert, ed. Siege of the Castle of Edinburgh. LC 78-39425. (Bannatyne Club, Edinburgh. Publications: No. 23). reprint ed. 22.00 (*0-404-52729-9*) AMS Pr.

Bell, Robert, et al, eds. Troubled Times: Fortnight Magazine & the Troubles in Northern Ireland, 1970-1991. (Illus.). 221p. (Orig.). 1991. pap. 21.00 (*0-85640-462-4*, Pub. by Blackstaff Pr) Dufour.

Bell, Robert & Davis, Anita P. SAT I Reasoning Test. LC 97-68066. (Illus.). 1008p. 2000. pap. text 17.95 (*0-87891-934-1*) Res & Educ.

Bell, Robert & Lockerbie, D. Bruce. In Peril on the Sea: The Story of Ethel Bell & Her Children, Robert & Mary. LC 95-72031. (Jaffray Collection Of Missionary Portraits: No. 14). 1996. pap. 8.99 (*0-87509-642-5*) Chr Pubns.

Bell, Robert & Tight, Malcolm. Open Universities: A British Tradition? LC 92-36208. 1993. 123.00 (*0-335-19126-6*) OpUniv Pr.

Bell, Robert, et al. SAT I Quick Study & Review. LC 97-69911. (Illus.). 300p. 1998. pap. text 10.95 (*0-87891-938-4*) Res & Educ.

Bell, Robert, jt. auth. see Hansen, Rosanna.

Bell, Robert, ed. see Courcelles, M.

Bell, Robert, jt. ed. see Spalek, John M.

Bell, Robert E. The Butterfly Tree. LC 91-15402. (Library of Alabama Classics). 264p. 1991. pap. 14.95 (*0-8173-0560-2*) U of Ala Pr.
— Dictionary of Classical Mythology: Symbols, Attributes, & Associations. LC 81-19141. 390p. 1980. lib. bdg. 60.00 (*0-87436-305-5*) ABC-CLIO.
— Oklahoma Indian Artifacts. Greer, J. K. et al, eds. (Contributions from the Stovall Museum, University of Oklahoma Ser.: No. 4). (Illus.). 114p. (C). 1980. pap. text 6.00 (*1-881346-02-1*) Univ OK Archeol.
— Place Names in Classical Mythology: Greece. LC 88-16870. 350p. 1988. lib. bdg. 60.00 (*0-87436-507-4*) ABC-CLIO.
— Women of Classical Mythology: A Biographical Dictionary. LC 91-26649. (Illus.). 300p. 1991. lib. bdg. 60.00 (*0-87436-581-3*) ABC-CLIO.
— Women of Classical Mythology: A Biographical Dictionary. LC 92-22754. 480p. (C). 1993. pap. 17.95 (*0-19-507977-9*) OUP.

Bell, Robert H. Jocoserious Joyce: The Fate of Folly in "Ulysses" LC 95-36524. (Florida James Joyce Ser.). 248p. (C). 1996. pap. 19.95 (*0-8130-1387-9*) U Press Fla.

Bell, Robert K., Jr. Sample Appraisal Guide: Appraisal Manual. 2nd ed. 162p. 1993. pap. 50.00 (*0-9635502-0-9*) Bels Fl.

Bell, Robert M., et al, eds. Lipid Second Messengers. (Handbook of Lipid Research Ser.: Vol. 8). (Illus.). 330p. 1996. 89.50 (*0-306-45174-3*, Kluwer Plenum) Kluwer Academic.

Bell, Robert M., jt. ed. see Malick, Jeffrey B.

Bell, Robert R. The Philadelphia Lawyer: A History, 1735-1945. LC 91-50194. (Illus.). 328p. 1992. 49.50 (*0-945636-26-1*) Susquehanna U Pr.
— Worlds of Friendship. LC 81-13565. (Sociological Observations Ser.: No. 12). 216p. reprint ed. pap. 67.00 (*0-7837-6583-5*, 204614800011) Bks Demand.

Bell, Robert S. Paul's Letter to the Romans. 1970. pap. 2.75 (*0-88027-036-5*) Firm Foun Pub.

Bell, Robert T. Eleventh Virginia Infantry. (Virginia Regimental Histories Ser.). (Illus.). 103p. 1985. 19.95 (*0-930919-21-1*) H E Howard.

Bell, Robert W. & Bell, Nancy J., eds. Sociobiology & the Social Sciences. LC 89-645312. (Interfaces in Psychology Ser.: No. 3). vi, 130p. (C). 1989. 25.00 (*0-89672-161-2*) Tex Tech Univ Pr.

Bell, Robert W., jt. ed. see Bell, Nancy J.

Bell, Robinette. Violence Against Women in the United States: A Comprehensive Background Paper. 2nd ed. 107p. 1999. reprint ed. pap. text 20.00 (*0-7881-7661-7*) DIANE Pub.

***Bell, Rod, Sr.** The Mantle of the Mountain Man. LC 99-28466. 1999. 15.95 (*1-57924-272-3*) Bob Jones Univ.

***Bell, Roger.** The Haynes Book of Modern Sports Cars. (Illus.). 160p. 2000. 34.95 (*1-85960-676-8*, 130756AE, Pub. by Haynes Manuals) Motorbooks Intl.
— Luke & the Wolf. 40p. 1997. 3.75 (*0-9694127-3-8*) Genl Dist Srvs.

Bell, Roger. Morgans to 1997: A Collectors Guide. (Illus.). 128p. 1997. 27.95 (*1-899870-20-2*, Pub. by Motor Racing) Motorbooks Intl.

Bell, Roger, et al, eds. Assessing Health & Human Services Needs: Concepts, Methods & Applications. LC 81-20249. (Community Psychology Ser.: Vol. VIII). (Illus.). 352p. 1983. 45.95 (*0-89885-057-6*, Kluwer Acad Hman Sci) Kluwer Academic.

Bell, Roger, et al. Negotiating the Pacific Century. LC 96-184999. 324p. 1997. pap. text 29.95 (*1-86448-067-X*, Pub. by Allen & Unwin Pty) Paul & Co Pubs.

Bell, Roger, jt. auth. see Bell, Philip.

Bell, Ron. Disorganized Crime: True Stories of Unlucky Thieves & Stupid Robbers. LC 93-81147. (Illus.). 144p. 1994. pap. 7.95 (*1-56352-126-1*) Longstreet.

Bell, Ronald E. Facilitator Handbook. (Illus.). 27p. 1998. pap. text. write for info. (*1-892664-01-1*) Moves Pubg.
— Semiconductor Business. (Illus.). 37p. (J). 1998. pap. text. write for info. (*1-892664-00-3*) Moves Pubg.

Bell, Ronald E. & Andrews, Mark. Pillar Power. (Illus.). 14p. 1998. pap. text. write for info. (*1-892664-02-X*) Moves Pubg.

Bell, Rosalyn B. Maryland Civil Jury Instructions & Commentary. 1232p. 95.00 (*0-327-01940-9*) LEXIS Pub.

Bell, Rosalyn B. Maryland Civil Jury Instructions & Commentary. 1232p. 1993. 95.00 (*1-55834-056-4*, MICHIE) LEXIS Pub.

***Bell, Rosamund.** Simple Yoga Techniques. LC 99-26094. (Health Factfiles Ser.). 112p. 1999. pap. 12.95 (*0-7370-1606-X*) T-L Custom Pub.

Bell, Rose, jt. ed. see Webb, W. L.

Bell, Rose S. Modern Marriage: How They Keep It Together. LC 90-92119. 93p. (Orig.). 1990. pap. text, per. 10.95 (*0-9614788-3-7*, 333) Tivoli Pub.
— You Can Be Happy. LC 97-60045. 150p. (Orig.). 1997. pap. text 10.95 (*0-9614788-5-3*, 555A) Tivoli Pub.

Bell-Rose, Stephanie, jt. ed. see Bean, Frank D.

Bell, Roseann P., et al. Sturdy Black Bridges: Visions of Black Women in Literature. LC 77-16898. 1979. pap. 7.95 (*0-385-13347-2*, Anchor NY) Doubleday.

Bell, Roselyn, ed. The Hadassah Magazine Jewish Parenting Book. 400p. 1991. pap. 9.95 (*0-380-71366-7*, Avon Bks) Morrow Avon.

Bell, Ross Taylor, jt. auth. see Leonard, Jonathan G.

Bell, Rowen B., jt. auth. see Alperin, J. L.

Bell, Roxana K., jt. auth. see Bell, Trudy E.

Bell, Roy. Biblical Models of Handling Conflict. 115p. 1994. reprint ed. pap. 15.50 (*1-57383-030-5*) Regent College.

Bell, Roy D., jt. auth. see Grenz, Stanley J.

Bell, Rudolf. Party & Faction in American Politics: The House of Representatives, 1789-1801. 32. LC 72-782. (Contributions in American History Ser.: No. 32). 311p. 1974. 59.95 (*0-8371-6356-0*, BPF/, Greenwood Pr) Greenwood.

Bell, Rudolph M. Fate & Honor, Family & Village: Demographic & Cultural Change in Rural Italy since Eighteen Hundred. LC 79-11011. (Illus.). 286p. 1979. 30.00 (*0-226-04208-1*) U Ch Pr.
— Holy Anorexia. LC 85-8460. (Illus.). xii, 248p. 1985. 22.50 (*0-226-04204-9*) U Ch Pr.
— Holy Anorexia. LC 85-8460. (Illus.). xii, 260p. (C). 1987. pap. 15.00 (*0-226-04205-7*) U Ch Pr.
— How to Do It: Guides to Good Living for Renaissance Italians. LC 98-35105. 1999. 25.00 (*0-226-04210-3*) U Ch Pr.

Bell, Rudolph M., jt. auth. see Weinstein, Donald.

Bell, Ruth. Changing Bodies, Changing Live. 3rd ed. LC 97-29249. 398p. 1998. pap. 23.00 (*0-8129-2990-X*, Times Bks) Crown Pub Group.
— Changing Bodies, Changing Lives. Date not set. write for info. (*0-679-45221-4*) McKay.
— Changing Bodies, Changing Lives. rev. ed. (Illus.). 272p. 1988. pap. 12.95 (*0-685-18233-9*) Vin Bks.
— It's Never Too Late to Have a "Wow" Marriage. LC 97-73695. 144p. 1997. pap. 8.99 (*0-88270-741-8*, Logos NJ) Bridge-Logos.

Bell, Ruth, et al. Changing Bodies, Changing Lives: A Book for Teens on Sex & Relationships. (Illus.). 1981. 17.95 (*0-394-50304-X*) Random.

Bell, Ruth, jt. auth. see Eisenhart, Connie.

Bell, Ruth, jt. auth. see Stauros, Sally.

Bell, Ruth E. Sounds of Celebration. LC 98-72702. 150p. 1998. pap. 8.99 (*0-88270-756-6*, Bridge) Bridge-Logos.

Bell, S. R. & Sekar, R., eds. Natural Gas & Alternative Fuels for Engines, Vol. 21. LC 93-74680. 108p. 1994. pap. 35.00 (*0-7918-1185-9*) ASME.

Bell, S. R., et al. Complex Manifolds. (Encyclopaedia of Mathematical Sciences: Vol. 69). x, 310p. 1997. pap. 49.95 (*3-540-62995-5*) Spr-Verlag.

Bell, S. W., et al. Mathematics for Higher National Certificate, Vol. II. 3rd ed. (Illus.). 504p. reprint ed. pap. 143.70 (*0-608-30996-6*, 2050773); reprint ed. pap. 156.30 (*0-608-10686-0*, 2050773) Bks Demand.

Bell, Sadie. Church, the State, & Education in Virginia. LC 78-89148. (American Education: Its Men, Institutions, & Ideas. Series 1). 1977. reprint ed. 47.95 (*0-405-01385-X*) Ayer.

Bell, Sally. Fact-Finding Skills. Sovndal, Jane, ed. (Thinking Skills Library). (Illus.). 110p. (Orig.). (J). (gr. 2-5). 1997. pap., teacher ed. 9.95 (*1-56784-704-8*) Newbridge Educ.
— Time-Saving Tools. Sovndal, Jane, ed. (Thinking Skills Library). (Illus.). 108p. (Orig.). (J). (gr. 2-5). 1997. pap., teacher ed. 9.95 (*1-56784-708-0*) Newbridge Educ.

Bell, Sally C., tr. see Carrion de Fierro, Fanny.

Bell, Sam H. Across the Narrow Sea. 304p. 1987. 21.00 (*0-85640-377-6*, Pub. by Blackstaff Pr) Dufour.
— Across the Narrow Sea. 304p. 1987. pap. 11.95 (*0-85640-378-4*, Pub. by Blackstaff Pr) Dufour.
— December Bride. 300p. 1997. pap. 14.95 (*0-85640-061-0*, Pub. by Blackstaff Pr) Dufour.
— December Bride. 304p. 1992. pap. 11.95 (*1-85158-361-0*, Pub. by Mainstream Pubng) Trafalgar.
— The Hollow Ball. 248p. (Orig.). (YA). (gr. 10-12). 1990. reprint ed. pap. 12.95 (*0-85640-452-7*, Pub. by Blackstaff Pr) Dufour.

Bell, Sam Hanna. Erin's Orange Lily & Summer Loanen & Other Stories. LC 97-135133. 220p. 1997. pap. 15.95 (*0-85640-589-2*, Pub. by Blackstaff Pr) Dufour.

Bell, Samuel H., et al. Federal Civil Procedure & Evidence During Trial - 6th Circuit: Federal Practice Guide. LC 96-76152. (American Inns of Court Ser.). 1200p. 1996. text. write for info. (*0-7620-0060-0*) West Group.

***Bell, Sandra & Coleman, Simon, eds.** The Anthropology of Friendship. 270p. 1999. 65.00 (*1-85973-310-7*, Pub. by Berg Pubs); pap. 19.50 (*1-85973-315-8*, Pub. by Berg Pubs) NYU Pr.

Bell, Sandra, jt. auth. see Cribb, Phillip J.

***Bell, Sarah.** Basketball Saturday. (Illus.). 56p. (J). 2000. pap. 10.00 (*0-8059-4836-8*) Dorrance.

An Asterisk (*) at the beginning of an entry indicates that the title is appearing for the first time.

Bell, Sarah. The British Columbia & Alberta Travel Guide: Guided Outdoor Trips & More, Vol. 1. LC 96-123831. (Illus.). 119p. (Orig.). 1997. pap. 14.95 (*0-919574-97-1*) Gordon Soules Bk.

***Bell, Sarah.** The British Columbia Bed & Breakfast Guide: Also Includes the Banff/Jasper Area. 5th rev. ed. (Illus.). 275p. 2000. pap. 16.95 (*0-919574-78-5*) Gordon Soules Bk.

Bell, Sarah. The British Columbia Bed & Breakfast Guide: Includes the Banff Jasper Area. 1999. pap. text. write for info. (*0-919574-50-5*) Gordon Soules Bk.

— The British Columbia Lodge & Resort Guide: Also Includes the Banff/Jasper Area & the Yukon, Vol. 1. (Illus.). 119p. (Orig.). 1997. pap. 11.95 (*0-919574-80-7*) Gordon Soules Bk.

— The Western Canada Bed & Breakfast Guide: Over 400 B&Bs in British Columbia & Alberta. LC 96-69680. (Illus.). 311p. (Orig.). 1997. pap. 14.95 (*0-919574-05-X*) Gordon Soules Bk.

***Bell, Sarah C.** La Nina: Urban Fairy Tales: Paperdoll. 24p. 1999. pap. 5.00 (*1-887997-15-6*, Pub. by Baksun Bks) SPD-Small Pr Dist.

Bell-Scott, Patricia. Flat-Footed Truths. LC 97-35108. 230p. 1995. 22.00 (*0-8050-4628-3*) H Holt & Co.

— Life Notes. 432p. 1995. pap. 12.00 (*0-393-31206-2*) Norton.

— Truth is Our Only Sword. 1999. pap. write for info. (*0-679-76729-0*) Vin Bks.

Bell-Scott, Patricia & Johnson-Bailey, Juanita. Flat-Footed Truths: Telling Black Women's Lives. (Illus.). 238p. 1999. pap. 12.95 (*0-8050-4629-1*, Pub. by H Holt & Co) VHPS.

Bell-Scott, Patricia, jt. auth. see Consortium for Research on Black Adolescence Staff.

Bell Scott, William. 850 Ornamental Designs from Historic Sources. LC 98-52785. (Pictorial Archive Ser.). (Illus.). 96p. 1999. pap. text 9.95 (*0-486-40465-X*) Dover.

Bell, Shannon. Reading, Writing, & Rewriting the Prostitute Body. LC 93-5447. (Illus.). 240p. 1994. 35.00 (*0-253-31166-7*) Ind U Pr.

— Whore Carnival. 287p. Date not set. 8.00 (*1-57027-022-8*) Autonomedia.

Bell, Sherilyn, jt. auth. see Stewart, Jeff.

Bell, Simon. Elements of Visual Design in the Landscape. (Illus.). 224p. text 76.95 (*0-419-17590-3*, E & FN Spon) Routledge.

— Elements of Visual Design in the Landscape. LC 92-31146. 1992. write for info. (*0-442-31649-6*, E & FN Spon) Routledge.

Bell, Simon. Elements of Visual Design in the Landscape. 224p. (C). (gr. 13). 1996. pap. 34.99 (*0-419-22020-8*) Routledge.

Bell, Simon. Participatory Information Systems: Analysis & Design in Developing Countries. 2nd ed. LC 95-39837. (Studies in Information & Library Management Systems Ser.: Vol. 1). 248p. (C). 1996. 85.00 (*0-415-10603-6*) Routledge.

— Patterns in the Landscape. 1998. 60.00 (*0-419-20340-0*, E & FN Spon) Routledge.

— Recreation for Design. LC 96-71620. (Illus.). 224p. (C). 1997. pap. 70.00 (*0-419-20350-8*, E & FN Spon) Routledge.

Bell, Simon, et al. Who's Had Who? 1990. mass mkt. 9.95 (*0-446-39042-9*, Pub. by Warner Bks) Little.

Bell, Simon, ed. & illus. see Richardson, Ken.

Bell, Stacey J. Positive Nutrition for HIV Infection & AIDS: A Medically Sound Take Charge Plan to Maintain. 192p. 1996. pap. 12.95 (*1-56561-089-X*) Wiley.

Bell, Stacey J., et al. Enteral Nutrition. 1993. text 54.95 (*0-442-01342-6*) Chapman & Hall.

Bell, Stephanie, jt. auth. see Begoun, Paula.

Bell, Stephanie, ed. see Clarke, Marianne.

Bell, Stephanie, ed. see Rosenblum, Joseph.

Bell, Stephen. The Ahab Spirit. 3rd ed. 28p. 1992. reprint ed. pap. 3.50 (*1-891050-05-2*) Key Ministries.

— Australian Manufacturing & the State: The Politics of Industry Policy in the Post-War Era. LC 92-46369. (Illus.). 288p. (C). 1993. pap. write for info. (*0-521-44800-X*) Cambridge U Pr.

— Australian Manufacturing & the State: The Politics of Industry Policy in the Post-War Era. LC 92-46369. (Illus.). 286p. (C). 1993. text 69.95 (*0-521-41628-0*) Cambridge U Pr.

— Breaking Free. 14th rev. ed. 20p. 1980. pap. 2.95 (*1-891050-00-1*) Key Ministries.

— Campanha Gaucha: A Brazilian Ranching System, 1850-1920. LC 98-19120. (Illus.). 304p. 1998. 55.00 (*0-8047-3100-4*) Stanford U Pr.

— Deliverance Workbook. 2nd ed. 27p. 1995. reprint ed. pap. 15.95 (*1-891050-11-7*) Key Ministries.

— El Espiritu de Acab. 2nd ed.Tr. of Ahab Spirit. (ENG & SPA.). 26p. 1993. reprint ed. pap. 3.50 (*1-891050-06-0*) Key Ministries.

— El Espiritu de Jezebel. 2nd rev. ed.Tr. of Jezebel Spirit. (ENG & SPA.). 17p. 1995. pap. 3.50 (*1-891050-08-7*) Key Ministries.

***Bell, Stephen.** Freedom from Fear. Orig. Title: Fear Not. 16p. 1999. pap. 3.50 (*1-891050-15-X*) Key Ministries.

Bell, Stephen. Homes in Zion. vi, 21p. 1995. reprint ed. pap. 6.95 (*1-891050-12-5*) Key Ministries.

— If You Forgive . . . iv, 22p. 1997. pap. 3.95 (*1-891050-14-1*) Key Ministries.

— The Jezebel Spirit. 3rd ed.Tr. of Espiritu de Jezabel. (ENG & SPA.). 16p. 1993. reprint ed. pap. 3.50 (*1-891050-07-9*) Key Ministries.

***Bell, Stephen.** Liberation Totale.Tr. of Breaking Free. (FRE.). 32p. 1999. pap. 2.95 (*1-891050-16-8*) Key Ministries.

Bell, Stephen. Libertad Total. 4th ed.Tr. of Breaking Free. (ENG & SPA.). 21p. 1991. reprint ed. pap. 2.95 (*1-891050-01-X*) Key Ministries.

— No Other Gods. 5th rev. ed. 26p. Date not set. pap. 3.95 (*1-891050-02-8*) Key Ministries.

— No Temas! 2nd rev. ed.Tr. of Fear Not!. (ENG & SPA.). 12p. 1995. pap. 3.50 (*1-891050-04-4*) Key Ministries.

— Rebel, Priest & Prophet: A Biography of Dr. Edward McGlynn. 303p. 1968. 5.00 (*0-911312-28-5*) Schalkenbach.

— Why Cast Out Demons? 12p. 1996. pap. 3.50 (*1-891050-09-5*) Key Ministries.

***Bell, Stephen, ed.** The Unemployment Crisis in Australia: Which Way Out? LC 99-58533. (Illus.). 328p. (C). 2000. text 59.95 (*0-521-64350-3*); pap. text 22.95 (*0-521-64394-5*) Cambridge U Pr.

Bell, Stephen & Head, Brian W., eds. State, Economy & Public Policy in Australia. (Illus.). 400p. 1994. pap. text 38.00 (*0-19-553401-8*) OUP.

Bell, Stephen H., et al. Measuring Employment & Training Program Impacts with Data on Program Applicants. LC 95-37399. 184p. (C). 1995. text 34.00 (*0-88099-158-5*) W E Upjohn.

— Program Applicants As a Comparison Group in Evaluating Training Programs. LC 95-37399. 184p. (C). 1995. pap. text 15.00 (*0-88099-157-7*) W E Upjohn.

Bell, Steve. Back to Your Spiritual Future. 192p. (Orig.). 1993. pap. 8.99 (*1-56476-205-X*, 6-3205, Victor Bks) Chariot Victor.

***Bell, Steve.** If... Bottoms Out. 1998. mass mkt. write for info. (*0-7493-1505-9*) Random House.

Bell, Steve. Stress Control. Scanlon, Kelly, ed. LC 96-68882. (Self-Study Sourcebook Ser.). (Illus.). 149p. 1996. pap. 15.95 (*1-57294-052-2*, 13-0020) SkillPath Pubns.

Bell, Steve & Bell, Valerie. Made to Be Loved: Enjoying Spiritual Intimacy with God & Your Spouse. 192p. 1999. pap. 11.99 (*0-8024-3399-5*) Moody.

Bell, Steve, jt. auth. see Mains, David R.

***Bell, Steven C., ed.** Seven Summits: The Quest to Reach the Highest Point on Every Continent. (Illus.). 144p. 2000. 40.00 (*0-8212-2676-2*) Bulfinch Pr.

Bell, Steven C., jt. auth. see Fragomen, Austin T., Jr.

Bell, Steven C., jt. auth. see Fragomen, Austin T.

Bell, Steven J., jt. auth. see Halperin, Michael.

Bell, Steven J., jt. auth. see Kettell, Brian.

Bell, Steven R. Cauchy Transform, Potential Theory & Conformal Mapping. 160p. 1992. lib. bdg. 69.95 (*0-8493-8270-X*, QA360) CRC Pr.

Bell, Stuart. Ball & Bell on Environmental Law: The Law & Policy Relating to the Protection of the Environment. 4th ed. 570p. 1997. pap. 48.00 (*1-85431-686-9*, Pub. by Blackstone Pr) Gaunt.

— In Search of Revival: A Guide for Everyone Who Wants More. 1998. pap. 10.99 (*0-7684-1001-0*, Revival Pr) Destiny Image.

— Sharing the Wealth: Privatization Through Broad-Based Ownership Strategies. LC 95-13317. (World Bank Discussion Papers: Vol. 285). 40p. 1995. pap. 22.00 (*0-8213-3230-9*, 13230) World Bank.

Bell, Stuart, jt. auth. see Ball, Simon.

***Bell, Stuart R., ed.** Fall Technical Conference of the ASME Internal Combustion Engine Division: Ann Arbor, Michigan, 1999. (ICE Ser.: Vol. 33-1-3). 457p. 1999. 200.00 (*0-7918-1633-8*) ASME.

Bell, Stuart R., ed. Internal Combustion Engine Division Vol. 3: Proceedings: Spring Technical Conference of the ASME Internal Combustion Engine Division, 1998, Fort Lauderdale, FL. LC 98-70886. 380p. 1998. pap. 184.00 (*0-7918-1579-X*) ASME.

Bell, Susan. What Is Auditory Processing? 16p. 1993. pap. 14.95 (*0-937857-45-9*, 1545) Speech Bin.

Bell, Susan, ed. see Yamada, Amy.

Bell, Susan G., ed. Women: From the Greeks to the French Revolution. LC 80-51750. xiv, 313p. 1973. reprint ed. pap. 16.95 (*0-8047-1082-1*) Stanford U Pr.

Bell, Susan G. & Offen, Karen M., eds. Women, the Family, & Freedom: The Debate in Documents, Vol. I, 1750-1880, Vol. I. LC 82-61081. xvi, 561p. 1983. 59.50 (*0-8047-1170-4*); pap. 24.95 (*0-8047-1171-2*) Stanford U Pr.

— Women, the Family, & Freedom: The Debate in Documents, Vol. II, 1880-1950, Vol. II. LC 82-61081. xvi, 474p. 1983. 55.00 (*0-8047-1172-0*); pap. 22.95 (*0-8047-1173-9*) Stanford U Pr.

Bell, Susan G. & Yalom, Marilyn, eds. Revealing Lives: Autobiography, Biography, & Gender. LC 89-26285. (SUNY Series in Feminist Criticism & Theory). 255p. (C). 1990. text 24.50 (*0-7914-0435-8*) State U NY Pr.

Bell, Susan J., compiled by. Full Disclosure: Do You Really Want to Be a Lawyer? 2nd ed. LC 92-12688. (Illus.). 203p. (Orig.). 1992. pap. 13.95 (*1-56079-153-5*) Petersons.

Bell, Susan K., jt. auth. see McKenna, Malcolm C.

Bell, Suzanne, ed. see Ninyerola, Alfonso.

Bell, Suzanne, ed. see Reitz, Ric.

Bell, Suzanne, ed. see Rose, Barbara.

Bell, T. & Mittemeijer, E. J. International Federation for Heat Treatment & Surface Engineering. 240.00 (*1-86125-026-6*) Institute of Management Consultants.

Bell, Tammy L. Preventing Adolescent Relapse, a Guide for Parents, Teachers, & Counselors. 225p. 1990. pap. text 14.00 (*0-8309-0571-5*) Herald Pub Hse.

Bell Telephone Laboratories Technical Staff. A History of Engineering & Science in the Bell System Vol. I: The Early Years, 1875-1925. Fagen, M. D., ed. LC 75-31499. (Illus.). 1087p. reprint ed. pap. 200.00 (*0-608-08066-7*, 206903100001) Bks Demand.

— A History of Engineering & Science in the Bell System Vol. 2: National Service in War & Peace, 1925-1975. Fagen, M. D., ed. LC 75-31499. (Illus.). 773p. reprint ed. pap. 200.00 (*0-608-08067-5*, 206903100002) Bks Demand.

— A History of Engineering & Science in the Bell System Vol. 3: Switching Technology, 1925-1975. Schindler, G. E., Jr., ed. LC 75-31499. (Illus.). 656p. reprint ed. pap. 200.00 (*0-608-08068-3*, 206903100003) Bks Demand.

— A History of Engineering & Science in the Bell System Vol. 4: Physical Sciences, 1925-1980. Millman, S., ed. LC 75-31499. (Illus.). 700p. reprint ed. pap. 200.00 (*0-608-08069-1*, 206903100004) Bks Demand.

— A History of Engineering & Science in the Bell System Vol. 5: Communications Sciences, 1925-1980. Millman, S., ed. LC 75-31499. (Illus.). 543p. reprint ed. pap. 168.40 (*0-608-08070-5*, 206903100005) Bks Demand.

— A History of Engineering & Science in the Bell System Vol. 6: Electronics Technology, 1925-1975. Smits F. M., ed. LC 75-31499. (Illus.). 384p. reprint ed. pap. 119.10 (*0-608-08071-3*, 206903100006) Bks Demand.

— A History of Engineering & Science in the Bell System Vol. 7: Transmission Technology, 1925-1975. O'Neill, E. F., ed. LC 75-31499. (Illus.). 828p. reprint ed. pap. 200.00 (*0-608-08072-1*, 206903100007) Bks Demand.

Bell, Terrel H. The Thirteenth Man: A Reagan Cabinet Memoir. 300p. 1988. 35.00 (*0-02-902351-3*) Free Pr.

Bell, Terrel H., et al. Reclaiming Our Nation at Risk: Lessons Learned - Reforming Our Public Schools. unabridged ed. (Illus.). 600p. (Orig.). 1997. pap. 20.00 (*0-9634636-2-4*) T H Bell.

Bell, Thomas. The Anatomie of Popish Tyrannie. LC 74-28833. (English Experience Ser.: No. 714). 1975. reprint ed. 30.00 (*90-221-0714-0*) Walter J Johnson.

— Out of This Furnace. LC 76-6657. (Illus.). 424p. (C). 1976. reprint ed. pap. 14.95 (*0-8229-5273-4*) U of Pittsburgh Pr.

— Out of This Furnace: Fiftieth Anniversary Edition. LC 91-50105. (Social & Labor History Ser.). (Illus.). 424p. (C). 1991. text 29.95 (*0-8229-3690-9*) U of Pittsburgh Pr.

***Bell, Thomas.** Personal WaterCraft Adventures & Guidebook - Texas. LC 98-96980. (Illus.). 210p. 1999. pap. 23.95 (*0-9668333-0-9*) Life Advents.

Bell, Thomas M. & Gillham, Frederick E. The World of Cotton. (Illus.). 1989. write for info. (*0-318-65483-0*) ContiCotton.

Bell, Tiffany, et al. After Matisse. (Illus.). 64p. 1986. pap. 16.00 (*0-916365-19-0*) Ind Curators.

Bell, Timothy. Bells Alaska TravelGuide. 39th rev. ed. (Illus.). 432p. 1999. pap. text 14.95 (*1-880840-07-3*) Bells AK Trvl.

— Text Compression. (C). 1990. text 57.00 (*0-13-911991-4*) P-H.

Bell, Timothy B. & Wright, Arnold M., eds. Auditing Practice, Research, & Education: A Productive Collaboration. LC 95-24714. 1995. 27.00 (*0-614-08095-9*) Am Inst CPA.

Bell-Tolliver, LaVerne. My Very Own Parent's Training Manual. 36p. 1994. student ed. 9.95 (*0-9642551-0-3*) Empowerment.

— My Very Own Parent's Training Manual Trainer's Guide. 42p. 1994. teacher ed. 9.95 (*0-9642551-1-1*) Empowerment.

***Bell, Tom.** British Hotels, Inns & Other Places. 2nd ed. (Alastair Sawday's Special Places to Stay Ser.). (Illus.). 2001. pap. 19.95 (*0-7627-0771-2*) Globe Pequot.

***Bell, Tom, ed.** British Hotels, Inns & Other Places. LC 99-43788. (Alastair Sawday's Special Places to Stay Ser.). (Illus.). 176p. 2000. 14.95 (*0-7627-0659-7*) Globe Pequot.

Bell, Tom W. & Singleton, Solveig, eds. The Regulators' Revenge: The Future of Telecommunications Deregulation. LC 98-36655. 152p. 1998. 18.95 (*1-882577-68-X*, Pub. by Cato Inst); pap. text 9.95 (*1-882577-69-8*, Pub. by Cato Inst) Natl Bk Netwk.

Bell, Trevor & Plank, Roger. Microcomputers in Civil Engineering. LC 84-17053. (Illus.). 164p. reprint ed. pap. 50.90 (*0-8357-2988-5*, 203925100011) Bks Demand.

Bell, Trudy. Best Bike Rides in the Chesapeake/Allegheny Region: Road Rides for the Serious Cyclist. (Illus.). 288p. 2000. pap. text 13.95 (*0-7627-0485-3*) Globe Pequot.

Bell, Trudy E. Best Bike Rides New York, New Jersey, Pennsylvania: Road Rides for the Serious Cyclist. 2nd ed. LC 99-31194. (Illus.). 288p. 1999. pap. text 13.95 (*0-7627-0475-6*) Globe Pequot.

***Bell, Trudy E.** Engineering Tomorrow. (Illus.). 1999. 49.95 (*0-7803-5360-9*) Inst Electrical.

Bell, Trudy E. The Essential Bicycle Commuter. LC 97-37886. (Illus.). 176p. 1998. pap. 15.95 (*0-07-005503-3*) McGraw.

Bell, Trudy E. & Bell, Roxana K. Bicycling with Children: A Complete How-To Guide. LC 99-6062. (Illus.). 1999. pap. 14.95 (*0-89886-589-1*) Mountaineers.

Bell, Valerie. Getting Out of Your Kids' Faces & into Their Hearts. LC 94-30678. 224p. 1995. pap. 10.99 (*0-310-48451-0*) Zondervan.

— She Can Laugh at the Days to Come: Strengthening the Soul for the Journey Ahead. 208p. 1996. 14.99 (*0-310-20569-7*) Zondervan.

Bell, Valerie, jt. auth. see Bell, Steve.

Bell, Vanessa. Sketches in Pen & Ink: A Bloomsbury Notebook. (Illus.). 214p. 1998. 22.95 (*0-7012-1035-4*, Pub. by Chatto & Windus) Trafalgar.

— Sketches in Pen & Ink: A Bloomsbury Notebook. (Illus.). 214p. 1999. pap. 15.95 (*0-7126-6603-6*, Pub. by Pimlico) Trafalgar.

Bell, Vereen M. Robert Lowell: Nihilist as Hero. 264p. 1983. 36.50 (*0-674-77585-6*) HUP.

Bell, Vikki. Interrogating Incest: Feminism, Foucault, & the Law. LC 93-14810. (Sociology of Law & Crime Ser.). 256p. (C). 1993. pap. 25.99 (*0-415-10104-2*) Routledge.

Bell-Villada, Gene H. Art for Art's Sake & Literary Life: How Politics & Markets Helped Shape the Ideology & Culture of Aestheticism, 1790-1990. LC 95-31648. (Stages Ser.). xi, 342p. 1996. text 50.00 (*0-8032-1260-7*) U of Nebr Pr.

— Art for Art's Sake & Literary Life: How Politics & Markets Helped Shape the Ideology & Culture of Aestheticism, 1790-1990. LC 95-31648. (Stages Ser.). xi, 342p. 1998. pap. 18.95 (*0-8032-6143-8*, Bison Books) U of Nebr Pr.

***Bell-Villada, Gene H.** Borges & His Fiction. LC 99-20938. (Pan American Ser.). 366p. 1999. 45.00 (*0-292-70877-7*) U of Tex Pr.

Bell-Villada, Gene H. Borges & His Fiction: A Guide to His Mind & Art. LC 80-17426. 312p. 1981. reprint ed. pap. 96.80 (*0-7837-9032-5*, 204978300003) Bks Demand.

***Bell-Villada, Gene H.** Borges & His Fiction: A Guide to His Mind & Art. rev. ed. LC 99-20938. (Pan American Ser.). 366p. 1999. pap. 19.95 (*0-292-70878-5*) U of Tex Pr.

Bell-Villada, Gene H. The Carlos Chadwick Mystery: A Novel of College Life & Political Terror. LC 89-85380. 256p. (Orig.). 1990. pap. 9.00 (*0-938513-06-0*) Amador Pubs.

— Garcia Marquez: The Man & His Work. LC 89-16474. xviii, 248p. (C). 1990. pap. 17.95 (*0-8078-4264-8*) U of NC Pr.

— The Pianist Who Liked Ayn Rand: A Novella & 13 Stories. LC 98-71489. 256p. 1999. pap. 14.00 (*0-938513-24-9*) Amador Pubs.

Bell-Villada, Gene H., et al, eds. From Dante to Garcia Marquez: Studies in Romance Literatures & Linguistics. (ENG, FRE & SPA.). xxxi, 411p. 1987. 45.00 (*0-915081-02-4*) Williams Coll.

***Bell, Virginia & Troxell, David.** The Best Friends Staff: Training Ideas for Alzheimer's Programs. 288p. 2000. pap. 32.95 (*1-878812-63-7*, 2637) Hlth Prof Pr.

Bell, Virginia, jt. auth. see Skreczko, Lyn.

Bell, Virginia M. & Troxel, David A. The Best Friends Approach to Alzheimer's Care. LC 96-23307. (Illus.). 272p. (Orig.). 1997. pap. 24.95 (*1-878812-35-1*) Hlth Prof Pr.

Bell, W. C., jt. auth. see Barnes, V. E.

Bell, W. D. Bell of Africa. 165p. 1923. 45.00 (*0-87556-022-9*) Saifer.

Bell, W. D. Bell of Africa. (Illus.). 236p. 1960. pap. text 35.00 (*0-87556-135-7*) Saifer.

— Wanderings of an Elephant Hunter. (Illus.). 185p. 1998. reprint ed. text 25.00 (*0-87556-571-9*) Saifer.

Bell, W. F. Ruin, Redemption, Regeneration. pap. 0.06 (*0-87377-122-2*) GAM Pubns.

Bell, W. Frazier. How to Get the Best Home Loan. 256p. 1992. pap. 19.95 (*0-471-55851-6*) Wiley.

Bell, W. H. Beyond the Northern Lights. (Illus.). 284p. 1998. pap. 23.95 (*0-88839-432-2*) Hancock House.

Bell, W. J. & Adiyodi, K. G. American Cockroach. 1981. 85.00 (*0-412-16140-0*, NO. 6557) Chapman & Hall.

Bell, Walt. Secrets for Small Investors. 1994. pap. 21.95 (*1-880071-30-4*) Simple Sftware.

Bell, Walter. The Easiest Beginning Course on How to Use Your Computer. 1992. pap. 19.95 (*1-880071-14-2*); pap. 24.95 (*1-880071-25-8*) Simple Sftware.

— Easy Instructions for Using Lotus. 1992. pap. 14.95 (*1-880071-18-5*) Simple Sftware.

— Easy Instructions for Using Word Perfect. 1992. pap. 14.95 (*1-880071-23-1*) Simple Sftware.

— Easy Instructions for Using Your Computer. 1991. pap. 14.95 (*1-880071-12-6*) Simple Sftware.

— Easy Instructions for Using Your Computer. (SPA.). 1992. pap. 9.95 (*1-880071-22-3*) Simple Sftware.

— Easy Instructions for Using Your Computer. 1992. 9.95 (*1-880071-24-X*) Simple Sftware.

— Easy Instructions for Using Your Computer. 1994. pap. 14.95 (*1-880071-27-4*) Simple Sftware.

— The Lazy Man's Way to Computers. pap. 24.95 (*1-880071-26-6*) Simple Sftware.

Bell, Walter F. The Philippines in World War II, 1941-1945: A Chronology & Select Annotated Bibliography Of Books & Articles in English, 12. LC 99-30327. 12. 280p. 1999. lib. bdg. 69.50 (*0-313-30614-1*) Greenwood.

Bell, Walter G. Great Fire of London in 1666. LC 70-114464. (Illus.). 387p. 1971. reprint ed. lib. bdg. 49.75 (*0-8371-4774-3*, BEGF, Greenwood Pr) Greenwood.

Bell, Walter G. The Great Plague in London in 1665. LC 75-23682. (Illus.). reprint ed. 47.50 (*0-404-13235-9*) AMS Pr.

Bell, Walter W. WordPerfect Easy Instructions. 1994. pap. text 12.95 (*1-880071-29-0*) Simple Sftware.

Bell, Warren, jt. auth. see Coates, T. F.

***Bell, Wayne.** Ocean Grove. LC 00-102556. (Images of America Ser.). (Illus.). 128p. 2000. pap. 18.99 (*0-7385-0425-4*) Arcadia Publng.

Bell, Wendell. Foundations of Futures Studies Human Science for a New Era Vol. 1: History, Purposes, Knowledge. 390p. 1996. text 39.95 (*1-56000-271-9*) Transaction Pubs.

— Foundations of Futures Studies Human Science for a New Era Vol. 2: Values, Objectivity & the Good Society. 392p. 1996. text 39.95 (*1-56000-281-6*) Transaction Pubs.

— Jamaican Leaders: Political Attitudes in a New Nation. LC 64-19447. (Illus.). 259p. reprint ed. pap. 80.30 (*0-608-17464-5*, 202994500066) Bks Demand.

Bell, Wendell, ed. Democratic Revolution in the West Indies. LC 67-31921. 232p. 1967. 18.95 (*0-87073-018-5*) Schenkman Bks Inc.

Bell, Wendell & Mau, James, eds. Sociology of the Future. LC 72-158565. 464p. 1971. 55.00 (*0-87154-106-8*) Russell Sage.

Bell, Weslea, ed. see McLain, Patrick G., et al.

B

An Asterisk (*) at the beginning of an entry indicates that the title is appearing for the first time.

Bell, Whitfield, ed. see Franklin, Benjamin.

Bell, Whitfield J., Jr. Catalog of Books in the American Philosophical Society Library, 28 vols., Set. LC 70-20392. 1970. lib. bdg. 4875.00 (*0-8371-3266-5*, APB/, Greenwood Pr) Greenwood.

— Catalog of Manuscripts in the American Philosophical Society Library Including the Archival Shelflist, 10 vols. LC 77-297105. 1970. lib. bdg. 2250.00 (*0-8371-4975-4*, AQE/, Greenwood Pr) Greenwood.

— College of Physicians of Philadelphia: A Bicentenial History. LC 87-20570. 326p. 1987. 40.00 (*0-88135-003-6*) Watson Pub Intl.

— The Colonial Physician & Other Essays. LC 75-6652. (Illus.). 236p. 1975. text 16.00 (*0-88202-024-2*, Sci Hist) Watson Pub Intl.

— John Morgan: Continental Doctor. 1965. 12.00 (*0-88135-682-4*) Watson Pub Intl.

— Patriot-Improvers: Biographical Sketches of Members of the American Philosophical Society. LC 97-44313. (Memoirs Ser.: Vol. 226). (Illus.). 530p. 1997. 40.00 (*0-87169-226-0*, M226-bew) Am Philos.

— Towards a National Spirit: Collecting & Publishing in the Early Republic to 1830. 1979. pap. 3.00 (*0-89073-057-1*, 214) Boston Public Lib.

Bell, William. Absolutely Invincible. 2nd unabridged ed. LC 98-224658. 208p. (YA). (gr. 7-11). 1988. pap. 5.99 (*0-7736-7411-X*) STDK.

— Crabbe. 169p. (YA). (gr. 8-12). 1999. mass mkt. 4.95 (*0-7736-7483-7*) STDK.

— Crabbe. unabridged ed. 170p. (J). (gr. 8-12). 1998. pap. 5.99 (*0-7736-7390-3*) Stoddart Publ.

Bell, William. Five Days of the Ghost. unabridged ed. 208p. (Orig.). (J). (gr. 3-6). 1996. mass mkt. 5.95 (*0-7736-7368-7*) STDK.

— Forbidden City. 208p. (YA). 1996. mass mkt. 4.99 (*0-440-22679-1*) BDD Bks Young Read.

— Forbidden City. 208p. 1990. pap. 12.95 (*0-385-25257-9*) Doubleday.

Bell, William. Forbidden City: A Novel of Modern China. 1996. 9.60 (*0-606-04673-9*, Pub. by Turtleback) Demco.

Bell, William. The Golden Disk. (J). 1997. pap. 8.95 (*0-385-25672-8*) Doubleday.

— No Signature. 176p. 1995. mass mkt. 4.99 (*0-7704-2706-5*) Bantam.

— No Signature. 176p. (YA). (gr. 6-10). 1992. text 14.00 (*0-385-25379-6*) Doubleday.

— River My Friend. (Illus.). 32p. (J). (ps-4). 1996. 15.95 (*1-55143-084-3*) Orca Bk Pubs.

— Shakespeare's Puck & His Folkslore, 3 vols. reprint ed. 155.00 (*0-404-00740-6*) AMS Pr.

— Speak to the Earth. 208p. 1996. mass mkt. 4.99 (*0-7704-2724-3*) Bantam.

***Bell, William.** Zack. LC 98-6690. 192p. (YA). (gr. 7). 1999. per. 16.00 (*0-689-82248-0*) S&S Childrens.

Bell, William, ed. Papers Relative to the Regalia of Scotland. LC 71-39426. reprint ed. 42.50 (*0-404-52736-1*) AMS Pr.

***Bell, William Gardner.** Commanding Generals & Chiefs of Staff, 1775-1983: Portraits & Biographical Sketches of the United States Armys Senior Officers. 202p. 1999. boxed set 36.00 (*0-16-049769-8*) USGPO.

Bell, William H. New Concepts in Surgical Correction of Dentofacial Deformities, Vol. 3. (Illus.). 850p. 1985. text 235.00 (*0-7216-1739-5*, W B Saunders Co) Harcrt Hlth Sci Grp.

Bell, William H., et al, eds. Surgical Correction of Dentofacial Deformities, 3 vols., 3. LC 76-27050. (Illus.). 2565p. 1985. 680.00 (*0-7216-1740-9*, W B Saunders Co) Harcrt Hlth Sci Grp.

Bell, William H., et al. Surgical Correction of Dentofacial Deformities, 3 vols., 1. LC 76-27050. 1980. text 235.00 (*0-7216-1675-5*, W B Saunders Co) Harcrt Hlth Sci Grp.

— Surgical Correction of Dentofacial Deformities, 3 vols., 2. LC 76-27050. 1980. text 235.00 (*0-7216-1707-7*, W B Saunders Co) Harcrt Hlth Sci Grp.

Bell, William J. Cockroaches: Behavior, Ecology. (Westview Studies in Insect Biology). (C). 1996. text 59.95 (*0-8133-8819-8*) Westview.

Bell, William R. Antithrombotics. Uprichard, Andrew C. et al, eds. LC 98-29079. (Handbook of Experimental Pharmacology Ser.: Vol. 132). (Illus.). 500p. 1998. 325.00 (*3-540-64691-4*) Spr-Verlag.

Bell, William R., ed. Hematologic & Oncologic Emergencies. 254p. 1993. text 89.95 (*0-443-08871-3*) Church.

Bell, William R., tr. see Virchow, Rudolf L.

Bell, William W. Secrets of a Professional Home Buyer. LC 82-21980. 160p. 1983. pap. 12.95 (*0-930294-00-9*) World Wide OR.

Bell, Zanette, ed. see Junior Auxiliary Staff of Conway.

Bella, A. La, see Bianco, Lucio & La Bella, A., eds.

***Bellaby, Paul.** Sick from Work: The Body in Employment. 252p. 1999. text 65.95 (*0-7546-1041-1*, Pub. by Ashgate Pub) Ashgate Pub Co.

Bellace. Labour Law at the Crossroads: Changing Employment Relationships. LC 96-54218. 1997. 98.00 (*90-411-0366-X*) Kluwer Law Intl.

Bellace, Janice R. & Berkowitz, Alan D. The Landrum-Griffin Act: Twenty Years of Federal Protection of Union Members' Rights. LC 79-2465. (Labor Relations & Public Policy Ser.: No. 19). 383p. reprint ed. pap. 118.80 (*0-8357-3153-7*, 203941600012) Bks Demand.

Bellacera, Carole. Border Crossings. LC 99-20077. 384p. 1999. 24.95 (*0-312-86858-8*, Pub. by Forge NYC) St Martin.

***Bellacera, Carole.** Border Crossings. 448p. 2000. mass mkt. 6.99 (*0-8125-7573-3*, Pub. by Tor Bks) St Martin.

— Spotlight. LC 00-24493. 352p. 2000. 25.95 (*0-312-87451-0*) Forge NYC.

Bellack, A. S. A Clinical Guide for the Treatment of Schizophrenia. LC 88-32137. (Illus.). 344p. (C). 1989. text 59.50 (*0-306-43064-9*, Kluwer Plenum) Kluwer Academic.

Bellack, A. S., et al. International Handbook of Behavior Modification & Therapy: Student Edition. abr. ed. LC 84-226552. (Illus.). 484p. (C). 1985. 49.50 (*0-306-41876-2*, Plenum Trade) Perseus Pubng.

Bellack, A. S., jt. auth. see Hersen, M.

Bellack, A. S., jt. auth. see Morrison, R. L.

Bellack, Alan S., et al, eds. International Handbook of Behavior Modification & Therapy. 2nd ed. (Illus.). 908p. (C). 1989. 130.00 (*0-306-43348-6*, Plenum Trade) Perseus Pubng.

Bellack, Alan S. & Hersen, Michel, eds. Behavioral Assessment: A Practical Handbook. 4th ed. LC 97-27513. 496p. (C). 1998. 61.00 (*0-205-17194-X*) Allyn.

Bellack, Alan S. & Hersen, Michel, eds. Handbook of Behavior Therapy in the Psychiatric Setting. (Critical Issues in Psychiatry Ser.). (Illus.). 672p. (C). 1993. 95.00 (*0-306-44275-2*, Plenum Trade) Perseus Pubng.

Bellack, Alan S., et al. Social Skills Training for Schizophrenia: A Step-by-Step Guide. LC 96-52826. (Treatment Manuals for Practitioners Ser.). 288p. 1997. lib. bdg. 33.50 (*1-57230-177-5*, 0177) Guilford Pubns.

Bellack, Alan S., jt. auth. see Hersen, Michel.

Bellack, Alan S., jt. ed. see Hersen, Michel.

Bellack, Daniel. Conceptual Hierarchies for General Psychologhy. 58p. (C). 1995. text 11.40 (*0-536-58991-7*) Pearson Custom.

Bellack, Janis P. & Edlind, Barbara J. Nursing Assessment & Diagnosis. 2nd ed. (Nursing-Health Science Ser.). 864p. (C). 1992. 54.95 (*0-86720-436-2*) Jones & Bartlett.

Bellack, Leopold. Psychoanalysis As a Science. 208p. (C). 1992. 67.00 (*0-205-13904-3*, Longwood Div) Allyn.

Belladur, Edouard. Dictionnaire de la Reforme. (FRE.). 297p. 1992. pap. 49.95 (*0-7859-7776-7*, 2213030189) Fr & Eur.

Bellafaire, Judith, ed. see Holm, Jeanne M.

Bellafaire, Judith A. Army Nurse Corps: Commemoration of World War 2 Service. 32p. 1994. pap. 1.50 (*0-16-061314-0*) USGPO.

Bellafaire, Judith A. Women's Army Corps: A Commemoration of World War 2 Service. 28p. 1993. pap. 1.50 (*0-16-038207-6*) USGPO.

Bellafaire, Judith L. United States Army & World War 2: Selected Papers from the Army's Commemorative Conferences. (CMH Publication Ser.: No. 68-4). 432p. 1998. pap. 26.00 (*0-16-049589-X*) USGPO.

Bellafiore, Donna R. Straight Talk about Betrayal: A Self-Help Guide for Couples. Heil, Carol, ed. 48p. 1999. per. 5.95 (*0-9668759-0-7*) DRB Alternatives.

Bellafiore, Sharyn. Amos & Abraham. LC 94-33000. (Illus.). 32p. (J). (ps-3). 1994. lib. bdg. 14.95 (*1-56148-139-4*) Good Bks PA.

Bellah. Clinical Health Issues Handbook. 1993. pap. 17.75 (*0-314-02220-1*) West Pub.

Bellah, John L. & Sanow, Edwin J. Dodge, Plymouth & Chrysler Police Cars, 1956-78. LC 94-33836. (Illus.). 224p. 1994. pap. 19.95 (*0-87938-958-3*) MBI Pubg.

Bellah, Karil. Clinical Health Issues Handbook. 2nd ed. LC 98-192974. 189p. 1997. 28.95 (*0-534-53707-3*) Brooks-Cole.

***Bellah, Melanie.** Abby & Her Sisters. (Illus.). 333p. 2000. pap. 14.95 (*0-9669312-1-1*, Pub. by Aten Pr) Bookpeople.

Bellah, Melanie. Tammy: A Biography of a Young Girl. LC 98-94961. (Illus.). xiv, 730p. 1999. pap. 19.95 (*0-9669312-0-3*) Aten Pr.

Bellah, Robert N. Beyond Belief: Essays on Religion in a Post-Traditional World. 320p. 1991. pap. 17.95 (*0-520-07394-0*, Pub. by U CA Pr) Cal Prin Full Svc.

— The Broken Covenant: American Civil Religion in Time of Trial. 1984. 8.95 (*0-8164-2123-4*) Harper SF.

— The Broken Covenant: American Civil Religion in Time of Trial. LC 74-19479. 224p. 1992. pap. text 14.95 (*0-226-04199-9*) U Ch Pr.

— Good Society. 368p. 1992. pap. 13.00 (*0-679-73359-0*) Vin Bks.

— Religious Evolution. (Reprint Series in Sociology). (C). 1993. reprint ed. pap. text 1.90 (*0-8290-2641-X*, S-546) Irvington.

— Tokugawa Religion: The Cultural Roots of Modern Japan. 2nd ed. 272p. 1985. pap. 14.95 (*0-02-902460-9*) Free Pr.

Bellah, Robert N., contrib. by. Sermons That Work: Ten Prize-Winning Sermons. 80p. (Orig.). 1991. pap. 2.95 (*0-88028-124-3*, 1136) Forward Movement.

Bellah, Robert N. & Kawai, Hayao. National Values & International Differences: Moral Visions in Japan & the U. S. (Mansfield American-Pacific Lectures). 140p. 1992. write for info. (*0-9635265-1-0*) U MT Mansfld.

Bellah, Robert N., et al. Habits of the Heart: Individualism & Commitment in American Life. LC 84-16370. 376p. 1985. 48.00 (*0-520-05388-5*, Pub. by U CA Pr) Cal Prin Full Svc.

— Habits of the Heart: Individualism & Commitment in American Life. 376p. (C). 1996. pap. 15.95 (*0-520-20568-5*, Pub. by U CA Pr) Cal Prin Full Svc.

Bellah, Robert N., ed. see Durkheim, Emile.

Bellah, Robert N., jt. ed. see Glock, Charles Y.

Bellahsen, Fabien & Rouche, Daniel. Cold Appetizers. (Eurodelices Ser.). (Illus.). 330p. 1998. 29.95 (*3-8290-1128-8*, 520376) Konemann.

— Desserts. (Eurodelices Ser.). (Illus.). 336p. 1998. 29.95 (*3-8290-1130-X*, 520379) Konemann.

— Fish & Seafood. (Eurodelices Ser.). (Illus.). 336p. 1998. 29.95 (*3-8290-1129-6*, 520378) Konemann.

— Hot Appetizers. (Eurodelices Ser.). (Illus.). 330p. 1998. 29.95 (*3-8290-1127-X*, 520375) Konemann.

— Meat & Poultry. (Eurodelices Ser.). (Illus.). 330p. 1998. 29.95 (*3-8290-1132-6*, 520377) Konemann.

— Pastries. (Eurodelices Ser.). (Illus.). 336p. 1998. 29.95 (*3-8290-1131-8*, 520380) Konemann.

Bellaiche, Andre & Risler, J. J. Sub-Riemannian Geometry. LC 96-35950. (Progress in Mathematics Ser.). 1996. 84.50 (*0-8176-5476-3*) Birkhauser.

Bellaiche, Andre & Risler, J. J., eds. Sub-Riemannian Geometry. LC 96-35950. (Progress In Mathematics Ser.). 404p. 1996. 84.50 (*3-7643-5476-3*) Birkhauser.

Bellaing, Vefa De, see de Bellaing, Vefa.

Bellaire, Marc. Brush Decoration for Ceramics. LC 64-8931. (Ceramics Monthly Handbooks Ser.). (Illus.). 64p. 1964. pap. 7.95 (*0-934706-02-6*) Am Ceramic.

— Underglaze Decoration. (Ceramics Monthly Handbooks Ser.). (Illus.). 64p. 1957. pap. 7.95 (*0-934706-01-8*) Am Ceramic.

Bellairs, George. Death Drops the Pilot. large type ed. 1991. 27.99 (*0-7089-2547-2*) Ulverscroft.

— Death in High Provence. large type ed. 1991. 27.99 (*0-7089-2476-X*) Ulverscroft.

Bellairs, Herbert J. Modern Real Estate Practice in Pennsylvania. 7th ed. 1996. pap. 42.95 (*0-7931-1579-5*, 1510-1707) Dearborn.

***Bellairs, Herbert J., et al.** Modern Real Estate Practice in Pennsylvania. 8th ed. LC 99-45947. 2000. pap. 42.95 (*0-7931-3306-8*, Real Estate Ed) Dearborn.

***Bellairs, John.** The Chessmen of Doom. (John Bellairs Ser.). (Illus.). 160p. (gr. 3-7). 2000. pap. 4.99 (*0-14-130697-1*, PuffinBks) Peng Put Young Read.

Bellairs, John. The Curse of the Blue Figurine. (Skylark Ser.). 208p. (J). (gr. 4-6). 1984. pap. 3.50 (*0-553-15540-7*, RL6IL4 + 15282-3, Skylark BDD) BDD Bks Young Read.

***Bellairs, John.** The Curse of the Blue Figurine. (J). (gr. 4-8). 2000. 19.25 (*0-8446-7138-X*) Peter Smith.

— The Curse of the Blue Figurine. 1996. 9.09 (*0-606-10777-0*, Pub. by Turtleback) Demco.

Bellairs, John. The Curse of the Blue Figurine. (Illus.). 208p. (J). (gr. 3-7). 1996. pap. 4.99 (*0-14-038005-1*) Viking Penguin.

Bellairs, John. The Dark Secret of Weatherend. (Anthony Monday Mystery Ser.). 1997. 9.09 (*0-606-11238-3*, Pub. by Turtleback) Demco.

Bellairs, John. The Doom of the Haunted Opera. (J). 1998. 9.60 (*0-606-13343-7*, Pub. by Turtleback) Demco.

— The Doom of the Haunted Opera. 160p. 1998. pap. 4.50 (*0-14-037657-7*) Viking Penguin.

— The Drum, the Doll & the Zombie. (Johnny Dixon Mystery Ser.). (YA). 1997. 9.09 (*0-606-12683-X*, Pub. by Turtleback) Demco.

— The Drum, the Doll & the Zombie. 160p. (J). (gr. 3-7). 1997. pap. 3.99 (*0-14-037515-5*) Viking Penguin.

— The Eyes of the Killer Robot. (Johnny Dixon Mystery Ser.). 176p. (J). (gr. 3-7). 1998. pap. 4.99 (*0-14-130062-0*, PuffinBks) Peng Put Young Read.

— The Eyes of the Killer Robot. (Johnny Dixon Mystery Ser.). 1998. 10.09 (*0-606-13371-2*, Pub. by Turtleback) Demco.

Bellairs, John. The Face in the Frost. pap. write for info. (*1-58754-105-X*, Pub. by Olmstead Pr) LPC Group.

— The Figure in the Shadows. (J). (gr. 3 up). 1999. 18.75 (*0-8446-7009-X*) Peter Smith.

Bellairs, John. The Figure in the Shadows. (J). 1993. 9.60 (*0-606-05286-0*, Pub. by Turtleback) Demco.

— The Ghost in the Mirror. LC 92-18369. 1994. 9.60 (*0-606-06410-9*, Pub. by Turtleback) Demco.

Bellairs, John. The House with a Clock in Its Walls. 179p. (J). (gr. 4-6). pap. 4.50 (*0-8072-1423-X*) Listening Lib.

Bellairs, John. The House with a Clock in Its Walls. LC 92-26794. (Illus.). 192p. (J). (gr. 3 up). 1993. pap. 4.99 (*0-14-036336-X*, PuffinBks) Peng Put Young Read.

— The House with a Clock in Its Walls. (J). 1994. 19.00 (*0-8446-6758-7*) Peter Smith.

— The House with a Clock in Its Walls. (J). 1993. 9.60 (*0-606-05353-0*, Pub. by Turtleback) Demco.

— The Lamp from the Warlock's Tomb. (Anthony Monday Mystery Ser.). 168p. (J). (gr. 3-7). 1999. pap. 4.99 (*0-14-130077-9*, PuffinBks) Peng Put Young Read.

— The Letter, the Witch & the Ring. LC 92-31361. (Illus.). 208p. (J). (gr. 3 up). 1993. pap. 4.99 (*0-14-036338-6*, PuffinBks) Peng Put Young Read.

Bellairs, John. The Letter, the Witch & the Ring. (J). 1993. 9.09 (*0-606-05424-3*, Pub. by Turtleback) Demco.

Bellairs, John. The Mansion in the Mist. 176p. (YA). (gr. 5 up). 1993. pap. 4.99 (*0-14-034933-2*, PuffinBks) Peng Put Young Read.

— The Mansion in the Mist. (J). 1993. 9.09 (*0-606-05450-2*, Pub. by Turtleback) Demco.

— The Mummy, the Will & the Crypt. 176p. 1985. pap. 3.99 (*0-553-15701-9*) Bantam.

— The Mummy, the Will & the Crypt. LC 83-7223. (Illus.). 176p. (J). (gr. 3-7). 1996. pap. 4.99 (*0-14-038007-8*, PuffinBks) Peng Put Young Read.

— The Mummy, the Will & the Crypt. (J). 1996. 9.09 (*0-606-10883-1*, Pub. by Turtleback) Demco.

***Bellairs, John.** The Revenge of the Wizard's Ghost. (J). (gr. 3 up). 1999. 18.50 (*0-8446-7010-3*) Peter Smith.

Bellairs, John. The Revenge of the Wizard's Ghost. (Johnny Dixon Mystery Ser.). (J). 1997. 9.09 (*0-606-12798-4*, Pub. by Turtleback) Demco.

— The Revenge of the Wizard's Ghost. (Illus.). 160p. (J). (gr. 3-7). 1997. pap. 3.99 (*0-14-038043-4*) Viking Penguin.

Bellairs, John. The Secret of the Underground Room. (J). 1992. 9.09 (*0-606-01744-5*, Pub. by Turtleback) Demco.

Bellairs, John. The Spell of the Sorcerer's Skull. 176p. (J). 1985. pap. 3.99 (*0-553-15726-4*) Bantam.

Bellairs, John. The Spell of the Sorcerer's Skull. (Johnny Dixon Mystery Ser.). 1997. 9.09 (*0-606-11867-5*, Pub. by Turtleback) Demco.

Bellairs, John. The Spell of the Sorcerer's Skull. (Illus.). 160p. (J). (gr. 3-7). 1997. pap. 3.99 (*0-14-038044-2*) Viking Penguin.

— The Treasure of Alpheus Winterborn. LC 96-40082. (Illus.). 192p. (J). 1997. pap. 3.99 (*0-14-038009-4*, PuffinBks) Peng Put Young Read.

Bellairs, John. Treasure of Alpheus Winterborn, an Anthony Monday Mystery. (Anthony Monday Mystery Ser.). (J). 1997. 9.09 (*0-606-12003-3*, Pub. by Turtleback) Demco.

Bellairs, John. The Trolley to Yesterday. LC 88-7113. 192p. (J). (gr. 4-7). 1990. pap. 4.50 (*0-553-15795-7*) Bantam.

— The Trolley to Yesterday. (Johnny Dixon Mystery Ser.). (Illus.). 192p. (J). (gr. 3-7). 1998. pap. 4.99 (*0-14-130092-2*, PuffinBks) Peng Put Young Read.

— The Trolley to Yesterday. (J). 1989. 9.60 (*0-606-04566-X*, Pub. by Turtleback) Demco.

— The Vengeance of the Witch-Finder. (Illus.). 160p. (J). (gr. 3-7). 1995. pap. 4.99 (*0-14-037511-2*, PuffinBks) Peng Put Young Read.

— The Vengeance of the Witch-Finder. (J). 1995. 9.09 (*0-606-08343-X*, Pub. by Turtleback) Demco.

Bellairs, John & Strickland, Brad. The Ghost in the Mirror. 176p. (YA). (gr. 5 up). 1994. pap. 4.99 (*0-14-034934-0*, PuffinBks) Peng Put Young Read.

Bellairs, John, jt. auth. see Strickland, Brad.

Bellairs, R., et al. Formation & Differentiation of Early Embryonic Mesoderm. LC 92-19796. (NATO ASI Ser.: Vol. 231). (Illus.). 350p. (C). 1992. text 105.00 (*0-306-44236-1*, Kluwer Plenum) Kluwer Academic.

Bellairs, Ruth, et al, eds. Somites in Developing Embryos. LC 86-22543. (NATO ASI Series A, Life Sciences: Vol. 118). 330p. 1986. 75.00 (*0-306-42418-5*, Plenum Trade) Perseus Pubng.

Bellairs, Ruth & Osmond, Mark, eds. The Atlas of Chick Development. LC 97-44781. (Illus.). 336p. 1997. text 110.00 (*0-12-084790-6*) Morgan Kaufmann.

Bellais. This Will Be a Picture: The Actor's Guide to Making Movies. 258p. (C). 1997. per. 67.95 (*0-7872-4292-6*, 41429201) Kendall-Hunt.

Bellak, Leopold. Confrontation in Vienna. LC 93-24804. 258p. (Orig.). 1993. pap. 24.95 (*0-918863-05-8*) CPS Inc.

— Crises & Special Problems in Psychoanalysis & Psychotherapy. LC 94-72438. 264p. 1994. pap. text 45.00 (*1-56821-351-4*) Aronson.

— Ego Function Assessment (EFA) A Manual. LC 88-26291. (Orig.). (C). 1989. pap. 10.50 (*0-918863-02-3*) CPS Inc.

— Handbook of Intensive Brief & Emergency Psychotherapy (B. E. P.) LC 83-20947. 170p. (Orig.). 1987. reprint ed. pap. 14.95 (*0-918863-00-7*) CPS Inc.

— Manual for Intensive Brief & Emergency Psychotherapy Manual. LC 87-23865. 50p. (Orig.). 1987. pap. text 9.50 (*0-918863-01-5*) CPS Inc.

— The Porcupine Dilemma. 1970. 10.95 (*0-8065-0223-1*) CPS Inc.

Bellak, Leopold & Abrams, David M. The Thematic Apperception Test, the Children's Apperception Test, & the Senior Apperception Technique in Clinical Use. 6th rev. ed. 492p. (C). 1996. 82.00 (*0-205-18999-7*) Allyn.

Bellak, Leopold & Baker, Samm S. Reading Faces. 1981. 12.45 (*0-03-057869-8*) CPS Inc.

Bellak, Leopold & Barten, Harvey H., eds. Progress in Community Mental Health, Vol. 1. LC 69-15739. 280p. 1969. text 63.00 (*0-8089-0047-1*, 790501, Grune & Strat) Harcrt Hlth Sci Grp.

Bellak, Leopold, et al. Handbook of Intensive Brief & Emergency Psychotherapy. 2nd rev. ed. 257p. 1992. pap. 24.95 (*0-918863-04-X*) CPS Inc.

Bellak, Leopold, jt. ed. see Karasu, Toksoz B.

Bellak, Theodore. Memories of Gliding & Soaring. (Illus.). 214p. (Orig.). 1995. pap. write for info. (*1-57579-004-1*) Pine Hill Pr.

Bellalah, Mondher, jt. auth. see Briys, Eric C.

Bellama, jt. auth. see Umland.

Bellama, J. Michael, jt. auth. see Umland, Jean B.

Bellama, J. Michael, jt. ed. see Brinckman, F. E.

Bellama, J. Michael, jt. ed. see Chvalovsky, Vaclav.

Bellama, Jon M., jt. auth. see Schraml, Jan.

Bellama, Jon M., jt. auth. see Umland, Jean B.

Bellamak, Lu. Non-Judgemental Sacred Dance: Simple Ways to Pray Through Dance. 1984. pap. 3.00 (*0-941500-14-4*) Sharing Co.

Bellamann, Henry. Kings Row. 672p. 1983. pap. 8.95 (*0-88184-059-9*) Carroll & Graf.

Bellamann, Henry & Bellamann, Katherine. Parris Mitchell of Kings Row. Karr, Jay M., ed. & intro. by. (Illus.). 1986. reprint ed. pap. 9.45 (*0-9609926-4-2*) Kingdom Hse.

Bellamann, Katherine, jt. auth. see Bellamann, Henry.

Bellamar, Jeff L. The Bellamar Directory: The A-to-Z Sourcebook for Sports, Fitness, & Active Lifestyles. 247p. 1998. pap. 19.95 (*0-9662684-0-7*) Bellamar Pub.

Bellamy, Amy. Newcomer's Handbook for Seattle. LC 99-234184. 248p. 1998. pap. 14.95 (*0-912301-35-X*) First Bks.

Bellamy, Angela S., jt. ed. see Hill, Bridget T.

Bellamy, Blanche W. & Goodwin, Maud W. Open Sesame! Poetry & Prose for School-Days, 3 Vols. enl. rev. ed. LC 72-451. (Granger Index Reprint Ser.). text 69.95 (*0-8369-9360-8*); 23.95 (*0-8369-6355-5*) Ayer.

Bellamy, C. L., jt. auth. see Evans, Arthur V.

Bellamy, Carol, ed. The State of the World's Children: 1996. (Illus.). 104p. (C). 1996. pap. text 10.95 (*0-19-262747-3*) OUP.

Bellamy, Charles. Experiment in Marriage. LC 77-16040. 320p. 1977. reprint ed. 50.00 (*0-8201-1304-2*) Schol Facsimiles.

Bellamy, Christine & Taylor, John A. Governing in the Information Age. LC 97-23719. 196p. 1998. 99.95 (*0-335-19451-6*); pap. 35.95 (*0-335-19450-8*) OpUniv Pr.

An Asterisk (*) at the beginning of an entry indicates that the title is appearing for the first time.

Bellamy, Christopher. Knights in White Armour: The New Art of War & Peace. (Illus.). 288p. 1998. 35.00 (*0-09-179184-7*, Pub. by Hutchnson) Trafalgar.

Bellamy, D. Richard. 12 Secrets for Manifesting Your Vision, Inspiration & Purpose: How to Make Your Dreams Come True. 217p. 1998. pap. 17.95 (*0-9662306-1-2*) Phi Pub.

Bellamy, David. Blooming Bellany: Herbs & Herbal Healing. (Illus.). 188p. 1994. 26.95 (*0-563-36725-3*, BBC-Parkwest) Parkwest Pubns.

***Bellamy, David.** The Forest. (Our Changing World Ser.). (J). (gr. 1-5). 1999. 7.99 (*0-7112-1385-2*) F Lincoln.

— How Green Are You? (Illus.). (J). (gr. 1 up). 1991. pap. text 7.99 (*0-7112-0679-1*) F Lincoln.

Bellamy, David. Images of the South Wales Mines. (Illus.). 144p. 1997. pap. 22.95 (*0-7509-1569-2*, Pub. by Sutton Pub Ltd) Intl Pubs Mktg.

— Poo, You & the Potoroo's Loo. Balkwill, Fran, ed. (Making Sense of Science Ser.). (Illus.). 32p. (J). 1997. pap. 12.00 (*1-85578-095-X*, Pub. by Portland Pr Ltd) Ashgate Pub Co.

***Bellamy, David.** The River. (Our Changing World Ser.). (J). (gr. 1-5). 1999. 7.99 (*0-7112-1387-9*) F Lincoln.

— The Roadside. (Our Changing World Ser.). (J). (gr. 1-5). 1999. 7.99 (*0-7112-1383-6*) F Lincoln.

— The Rockpool. (Our Changing World Ser.). (J). (gr. 1-5). 1999. 7.99 (*0-7112-1386-0*) F Lincoln.

— Watercolour Landscapes: Everything You Need to Know to Get Started. (Learn to Paint Ser.). (Illus.). 64p. 1999. pap. 15.95 (*0-00-413326-9*, Pub. by HarpC) Trafalgar.

Bellamy, Denis. Aging: A Biomedical Perspective. 418p. 1995. 200.00 (*0-471-92067-3*) Wiley.

Bellamy, Dodie. Feminine Hijinx. 154p. (Orig.). 1990. pap. 5.95 (*0-937815-43-8*) Hanuman Bks.

Bellamy, Dodie & D'Allesandro, Sam. The Letters of Mina Harker. LC 98-12241. (Lingo Magazine Ser.). 221p. 1998. pap. text 13.95 (*1-889097-14-4*) Hard Pr MA.

— Real: The Letters of Mina Harker & Sam D'Allesandro. LC 94-22918. 218p. 1994. pap. 10.95 (*1-883689-16-3*); lib. bdg. 30.95 (*1-883689-17-1*) Talisman Hse.

Bellamy, Donnie D. Light in the Valley: A Pictorial History of the Fort Valley State College since 1895. LC 95-52671. 1996. write for info. (*0-89865-965-5*) Donning Co.

Bellamy, Edward. Apparitions of Things to Come: Edward Bellamy's Tales of Mystery & Imagination. Rosemont, Franklin, ed. 160p. 1990. 25.95 (*0-88286-164-6*); pap. 14.00 (*0-88286-165-4*) C H Kerr.

— The Blindman's World & Other Stories. (Works of Edward Bellamy). 415p. reprint ed. lib. bdg. 79.00 (*0-7812-0948-X*) Rprt Serv.

— Doctor Heidenhoff's Process. LC 72-84878. (BCL Ser. I). 1969. reprint ed. 29.50 (*0-404-00734-1*) AMS Pr.

— Dr. Heidenhoff's Process. (Works of Edward Bellamy). 140p. 1985. reprint ed. lib. bdg. 59.00 (*0-932051-09-X*) Rprt Serv.

— Equality. (BCL Ser. II). (Illus.). 1970. reprint ed. 34.50 (*0-404-00735-X*) AMS Pr.

— Equality. 324p. reprint ed. pap. text 5.95 (*0-8290-2110-8*); reprint ed. lib. bdg. 29.50 (*0-8290-2109-4*) Irvington.

— Equality. (Works of Edward Bellamy). 412p. 1985. reprint ed. lib. bdg. 59.00 (*0-932051-14-6*) Rprt Serv.

— Equality. (Works of Edward Bellamy). 412p. 1992. reprint ed. lib. bdg. 79.00 (*0-7812-0928-5*) Rprt Serv.

— Equality. 2nd ed. 1997. 7.00 (*0-403-00145-5*) Scholarly.

— Looking Backward. White, Frederic R., ed. (University Classics Ser.). Orig. Title: Looking Backward, 2000-1887. 272p. 1979. pap. 12.95 (*0-87532-107-0*) Hendricks House.

— Looking Backward. Tichi, Cecelia, ed. & intro. by. (American Library). Orig. Title: Looking Backward, 2000-1887. 240p. 2000. pap. 11.95 (*0-14-039018-9*) Viking Penguin.

— Looking Backward. Orig. Title: Looking Backward, 2000-1887. 318p. reprint ed. lib. bdg. 24.95 (*0-89190-238-4*, Rivercity Pr) Amereon Ltd.

— Looking Backward. unabridged ed. LC 95-49596. (Thrift Editions Ser.). Orig. Title: Looking Backward, 2000-1887. 160p. 1996. reprint ed. pap. text 2.00 (*0-486-29038-7*) Dover.

***Bellamy, Edward.** Looking Backward: From 2000 to 1887. 220p. 2000. pap. 14.95 (*1-55709-506-X*) Applewood.

— Looking Backward, 2000-1887. 2000. pap. 10.95 (*1-892295-59-8*) Green Integer.

Bellamy, Edward. Looking Backward, 2000-1887. 247p. (C). 1981. pap. 5.00 (*0-07-554374-5*) McGraw.

***Bellamy, Edward.** Looking Backward, 2000-1887. 2000. mass mkt. 5.95 (*0-451-52763-1*, Sig) NAL.

Bellamy, Edward. Looking Backward, 2000-1887. (Modern Library College Editions). 275p. (C). 1982. pap. text 3.75 (*0-685-04266-9*) Random.

— Looking Backward, 2000-1887. Borus, Daniel H., ed. (Bedford Series in History & Culture). 214p. 1995. text 45.00 (*0-312-12244-6*) St Martin.

— Looking Backward, 2000-1887. 1990. reprint ed. lib. bdg. 25.95 (*0-89968-477-7*) Buccaneer Bks.

— Miss Ludington's Sister. LC 71-104414. reprint ed. lib. bdg. 39.50 (*0-8398-0161-0*) Irvington.

— The Religion of Solidarity. (Institute of World Culture Ser.). 132p. 1984. pap. 12.75 (*0-88695-029-5*) Concord Grove.

— Selected Writings on Religion & Society, 11. Schiffman, Joseph, ed. LC 74-40. (American Heritage Ser.: No. 11). 139p. 1974. reprint ed. lib. bdg. 49.50 (*0-8371-7359-0*, BEWR, Greenwood Pr) Greenwood.

— Talks on Nationalism. LC 78-102226. (Select Bibliographies Reprint Ser.). 1977. 21.95 (*0-8369-5111-5*) Ayer.

Bellamy, Elizabeth J. Affective Genealogies: Psychoanalysis, Postmodernism, & the "Jewish Question" after Auschwitz. LC 97-10838. (Texts & Contexts Ser.: Vol. 22). viii, 214p. 1997. text 50.00 (*0-8032-1249-6*) U of Nebr Pr.

— Translations of Power: Narcissism & the Unconscious in Epic History. LC 91-55549. 290p. 1992. pap. text 17.95 (*0-8014-9990-9*) Cornell U Pr.

Bellamy, Elizabeth W. The Four Oaks. (Works of Elizabeth Whitfield Bellamy). 1989. reprint ed. lib. bdg. 90.00 (*0-7812-1946-9*) Rprt Serv.

— The Little Joanna. (Works of Elizabeth Whitfield Bellamy). 1989. reprint ed. lib. bdg. 79.00 (*0-7812-1947-7*) Rprt Serv.

— Old Man Gilbert. (Works of Elizabeth Whitfield Bellamy). 1989. reprint ed. lib. bdg. 79.00 (*0-7812-1948-5*) Rprt Serv.

— Penny Lancaster. (Works of Elizabeth Whitfield Bellamy). 1989. reprint ed. lib. bdg. 79.00 (*0-7812-1949-3*) Rprt Serv.

— The Principle Works of Elizabeth Whitfield Bellamy, Set. 1989. reprint ed. lib. bdg. 63.00 (*0-685-27268-0*) Rprt Serv.

Bellamy, Gail. Design Spirits: Bars, Brewpubs & Techno Clubs. 179p. 1997. pap. 39.95 (*0-614-28154-7*) PBC Intl Inc.

— Design Spirits: Beyond Bars, Clubs & Taverns. (Illus.). 184p. 1995. 42.50 (*0-86636-375-0*) PBC Intl Inc.

Bellamy, J. G. English Criminal Trial, c. 1300-1600. LC 98-166335. 256p. 1998. text 50.00 (*0-8020-4295-3*) U of Toronto Pr.

— The Law of Treason in England in the Later Middle Ages. LC 85-81810. (Cambridge Studies in English Legal History). 284p. 1986. reprint ed. 70.00 (*0-912004-39-8*) Gaunt.

Bellamy, James A., ed. Studies in Near Eastern Culture & History. (Michigan Series on the Middle East: No. 2). 225p. (Orig.). 1990. pap. 17.95 (*0-932098-22-3*) UM Ctr MENAS.

Bellamy, James A., et al, eds. Short Stories, 2 pts., Set. (Contemporary Arabic Readers Ser.: Vol. IV). (ARA.). 1963. 19.95 (*0-916798-14-3*) Intl Bk Ctr.

***Bellamy, James E. C. & Olexson, Dennis W.** Quality Assurance Handbook for Veterinary Laboratories. (Illus.). 106p. 2000. pap. 32.95 (*0-8138-0276-8*) Iowa St U Pr.

Bellamy, James F. Cars Made in Upstate New York. (Illus.). 400p. 1988. text 24.95 (*0-317-91269-0*) Squire Hill Pub.

Bellamy, Joe D. The Frozen Sea. LC 87-31527. 48p. (Orig.). 1988. pap. 5.95 (*0-914061-06-2*) Orchises Pr.

— Literary Luxuries: American Writing at the End of the Millennium. LC 95-20790. 248p. (C). 1995. 29.95 (*0-8262-1029-5*) U of Mo Pr.

— The New Fiction: Interviews with Innovative American Writers. LC 74-14841. 225p. 1974. text 24.95 (*0-252-00430-2*); pap. text 11.95 (*0-252-00555-4*) U of Ill Pr.

— Suzi Sinzinnati. 1989. 18.95 (*0-916366-56-1*, Pub. by Pushcart Pr) Norton.

Bellamy, Joe D., ed. American Poetry Observed: Poets on Their Work. LC 83-6961. (Illus.). 328p. 1984. text 27.50 (*0-252-01042-6*) U of Ill Pr.

— American Poetry Observed: Poets on Their Work. LC 83-6961. (Illus.). 328p. 1988. pap. 12.95 (*0-252-06010-5*) U of Ill Pr.

— New Writers for the Eighties. LC 81-71004. (Fiction International Ser.: No. 13). 282p. (Orig.). 1981. pap. 10.00 (*0-931362-06-7*) Fiction Intl.

Bellamy, Joe D. & Weingarten, Roger, eds. Love Stories-Love Poems. LC 82-84443. 258p. (Orig.). 1982. pap. 12.95 (*0-931362-07-5*) Fiction Intl.

Bellamy, John C. Digital Telephony. 3rd ed. LC 99-34015. (Illus.). 664p. (C). 2000. 95.00 (*0-471-34571-7*) Wiley.

Bellamy, John C. Digital Telephony. 2nd ed. LC 90-37906. (Telecommunications Ser.). 592p. 1991. 89.95 (*0-471-62056-4*) Wiley.

Bellamy, John G. Crime & Public Order in England in the Later Middle Ages. LC 73-163803. (Studies in Social History). 237p. reprint ed. pap. 73.50 (*0-608-12850-3*, 202359300033) Bks Demand.

— The Tudor Law of Treason: An Introduction. LC 79-303364. (Studies in Social History). 305p. reprint ed. pap. 94.60 (*0-608-16882-3*, 205613700050) Bks Demand.

***Bellamy, John S., II.** The Corpse in the Cellar: And Further Tales of Cleveland Woe. LC 99-6828. (Illus.). 256p. 1999. pap. 13.95 (*1-886228-33-7*) Gray & Co Pubs.

Bellamy, John S., II. Maniac in the Bushes: And More Tales of Cleveland Woe. LC 97-33939. (Illus.). 304p. 1997. pap. 13.95 (*1-886228-19-1*) Gray & Co Pubs.

— They Died Crawling . . . And Other Tales of Cleveland Woe: True Stories of the Foulest Crimes & Worst Disasters in Cleveland History. (Illus.). 256p. (Orig.). 1995. pap. 13.95 (*1-886228-03-5*) Gray & Co Pubs.

Bellamy, Joseph. Sin, the Law & the Glory of the Gospel. 274p. 1998. 26.95 (*0-9641803-9-1*) Internat Outreach.

— True Religion Delineated. 388p. 1997. 29.95 (*0-9641803-6-7*) Internat Outreach.

Bellamy, Joyce. Hyde Park for Horsemanship. 155p. 1990. pap. 40.00 (*0-85131-217-9*, Pub. by J A Allen) St Mut.

Bellamy, Joyce M. & Saville, John. Dictionary of Labour Biography, Vol. 10. LC 78-185417. xvii, 272p. 2000. 120.00 (*0-333-38784-8*, Pub. by Macmillan Pr) Kelley.

Bellamy, Joyce M. & Saville, John, eds. Dictionary of Labour Biography, 10 vols., 1. LC 78-185417. 1972. lib. bdg. 75.00 (*0-678-07008-3*) Kelley.

— Dictionary of Labour Biography, 10 vols., 2. LC 78-185417. 1974. lib. bdg. 75.00 (*0-678-07018-0*) Kelley.

— Dictionary of Labour Biography, 10 vols., 3. LC 78-185417. 1976. lib. bdg. 75.00 (*0-333-14415-5*) Kelley.

— Dictionary of Labour Biography, 10 vols., 4. LC 78-185417. 1977. lib. bdg. 75.00 (*0-333-19704-6*) Kelley.

— Dictionary of Labour Biography, 10 vols., 5. LC 78-185417. 1979. lib. bdg. 75.00 (*0-333-22015-3*) Kelley.

— Dictionary of Labour Biography, 10 vols., 6. LC 78-185417. 1982. lib. bdg. 75.00 (*0-333-24095-2*) Kelley.

— Dictionary of Labour Biography, 10 vols., 7. LC 78-185417. 1984. lib. bdg. 75.00 (*0-333-33181-8*) Kelley.

— Dictionary of Labour Biography, 10 vols., 8. LC 78-185417. 1987. lib. bdg. 75.00 (*0-333-38782-1*) Kelley.

— Dictionary of Labour Biography, 10 vols., 9. LC 78-185417. 1993. lib. bdg. 85.00 (*0-333-38783-X*) Kelley.

Bellamy, Katherine. Game, Set & Match. (Scarlet Ser.). (Orig.). 1997. mass mkt. 3.99 (*1-85487-960-X*, Pub. by Scarlet Bks) London Brdge.

Bellamy, Kathryn. Mixed Doubles. (Scarlet Ser.). 1997. mass mkt. 3.99 (*1-85487-988-X*, Pub. by Scarlet Bks) London Brdge.

— Summer of Secrets. (Scarlet Ser.). 1998. mass mkt. 3.99 (*1-85487-885-9*, Pub. by Scarlet Bks) London Brdge.

— Woman Scorned. (Scarlet Ser.). 1998. mass mkt. 3.99 (*1-85487-899-9*, Pub. by Scarlet Bks) London Brdge.

Bellamy, Liz. Commerce, Morality & the Eighteenth-Century Novel. LC 98-199772. 250p. (C). 1998. text 59.95 (*0-521-62224-7*) Cambridge U Pr.

— Jonathan Swift, Gulliver's Travels. LC 92-18096. (Critical Studies of Key Texts). 1992. pap. 12.95 (*0-312-08598-2*); text 35.00 (*0-312-08425-0*) St Martin.

Bellamy, Margot A. & Greenshields, Bruce. Issues in Agricultural Development: Sustainability & Cooperation. (IAAE Occasional Papers: No. 6). 350p. 1992. 38.95 (*1-85521-302-8*, Pub. by Dartmth Pub) Ashgate Pub Co.

Bellamy, Margot A., jt. ed. see Greenshields, Bruce.

Bellamy, Nicholas. Colour Atlas of Clinical Rheumatology. 1985. text 236.50 (*0-85200-761-2*) Kluwer Academic.

— Musculoskeletal Clinical Metrology. 384p. (C). 1993. text 254.00 (*0-7923-8828-3*) Kluwer Academic.

Bellamy, Nicholas, ed. Prognosis in the Rheumatic Diseases. 528p. 1991. text 279.50 (*0-7923-8958-1*) Kluwer Academic.

Bellamy, Paul B. A History of Workmen's Compensation 1898-1915: From Court Room to Board Room. rev. ed. LC 96-28933. (Studies in the History of American Labor). (Illus.). 290p. 1997. text 81.00 (*0-8153-2827-3*) Garland.

Bellamy, Peter. The Artist Project: Portraits of the Real Art World, New York Artists 1981-1990. (Illus.). 256p. 1993. 45.00 (*1-55859-563-5*, Cross Riv Pr) Abbeville Pr.

— The Artist Project: Portraits of the Real Art World, New York Artists 1981-1990. Weber, Marc, ed. 256p. (C). 1991. 65.00 (*0-9625994-1-7*) Independent.

Bellamy, Peter & Chassler, Joseph. Addict's Damn. (Illus.). 220p. 1995. pap. 10.00 (*0-9625994-3-3*) Independent.

Bellamy, Richard. Catch Them after They Fall. Date not set. pap. 8.95 (*1-929293-03-8*) Whole Child Institute.

Bellamy, Richard. Constitutionalism in Transformation: European & Theoretical Perspectives. 248p. (Orig.). (C). 1996. pap. text 28.95 (*0-631-20250-1*) Blackwell Pubs.

— Liberalism & Modern Society: A Historical Argument. LC 92-7406. 330p. 1992. 50.00 (*0-271-00879-2*); pap. 19.95 (*0-271-00880-6*) Pa St U Pr.

— Liberalism & Pluralism: Towards a Politics of Compromise. LC 99-20773. 1999. pap. write for info. (*0-415-19662-0*) Routledge.

***Bellamy, Richard.** Liberalism & Pluralism: Towards Politics of Compromise. LC 99-20773. 240p. (C). 1999. text. write for info. (*0-415-19661-2*) Routledge.

Bellamy, Richard. Modern Italian Social Theory: Ideology & Politics from Pareto to the Present. LC 86-63257. 248p. 1987. 42.50 (*0-8047-1393-6*) Stanford U Pr.

***Bellamy, Richard.** Rethinking Liberalism. LC 99-44170. 224p. 2000. pap. 24.95 (*1-85567-485-8*) P P Pubs.

Bellamy, Richard, ed. Constitutionalism & Democracy: American & European Perspectives. (Avebury Series in Philosophy). 176p. 1996. 70.95 (*1-85972-264-4*, Pub. by Avebry) Ashgate Pub Co.

Bellamy, Richard & Hollis, Martin. Pluralism & Liberal Neutrality. LC 98-20005. 128p. 1999. 49.50 (*0-7146-4916-3*); pap. 24.50 (*0-7146-4470-6*) F Cass Pubs.

Bellamy, Richard & Ross, Angus, eds. A Textual Introduction to Social & Political Theory. LC 95-36976. 350p. (C). 1996. pap. 27.95 (*0-7190-4639-4*) St Martin.

Bellamy, Richard, ed. see Beccaria, Cesare.

Bellamy, Richard, ed. see Gramsci, Antonio.

Bellamy, Robert V., Jr. & Walker, James R. Television & the Remote Control: Grazing on a Vast Wasteland. LC 95-14086. (Communication Ser.). 192p. 1996. lib. bdg. 35.00 (*1-57230-085-X*) Guilford Pubns.

Bellamy, Robert V., jt. ed. see Walker, James R.

***Bellamy, Ronald F.** Textbook of Military Medicine, Warfare, Weaponry & the Casualty Pt. 1: Conventional Warfare, Ballistic, Blast & Burn Injuries. 396p. 2000. boxed set 39.00 (*0-16-059131-7*) USGPO.

Bellamy, Ronald F., jt. ed. see Bowen, Thomas E.

Bellamy, Rufus. Ethnobiology. (C). 1992. 24.00 (*0-907649-57-2*, Pub. by Expedit Advisory Ctr) St Mut.

Bellamy, William D. Full-Scale Ozone Contractor Study. LC 95-179937. (Illus.). 206p. 1995. pap. 81.00 (*0-89867-792-0*, 90668) Am Water Wks Assn.

Bellamy, William D., et al. Integrated Disinfection Design Framework. LC 97-33516. 68p. 1998. write for info. (*0-89867-933-8*, 90739) Am Water Wks Assn.

Bellan Gillen, Patricia. My Signing Book of Numbers. LC 87-28758. (Illus.). 64p. (J). (ps up). 1988. 14.95 (*0-930323-37-8*, Pub. by K Green Pubns) Gallaudet Univ Pr.

***Bellan, Paul M.** Spheromaks. 250p. 1999. 48.00 (*1-86094-141-9*, Pub. by Imperial College) World Scientific Pub.

Bellan, Susan. Small Business & Big Banks. 114p. 29.95 (*1-55028-449-5*, Pub. by J Lorimer) Formac Dist Ltd.

— Small Business & the Big Banks. 114p. pap. 19.95 (*1-55028-448-7*, Pub. by J Lorimer) Formac Dist Ltd.

Bellanca, James. Active Learning Handbook for the Multiple Intelligences Classroom. LC 97-70718. (Illus.). xxx, 464 p. (Orig.). 1997. pap. 29.95 (*1-57517-071-X*, 1466) SkyLght.

— Building a Caring, Cooperative Classroom: Integrating Social Skills Through Language Curriculum. LC 91-62547. 144p. 1991. pap. 21.95 (*0-932935-61-3*) SkyLght.

— The Cooperative Think Tank: Graphic Organizers to Teach Thinking in the Cooperative Classroom. 96p. (Orig.). 1990. pap. text 20.95 (*0-932935-45-1*) SkyLght.

— The Cooperative Think Tank II: Graphic Organizers to Teach Thinking in the Cooperative Classroom. (Illus.). 144p. 1992. pap. text 20.95 (*0-932935-44-3*) SkyLght.

— Keep Them Thinking: A Handbook of Model Lessons, Level 3. (Illus.). 112p. (Orig.). 1990. pap. text 9.95 (*0-932935-06-0*) SkyLght.

Bellanca, James & Fogarty, Robin. Blueprints for Thinking in the Cooperative Classroom. 2nd ed. (Illus.). 382p. 1991. reprint ed. pap. 46.00 (*0-932935-30-3*) SkyLght.

— Catch Them Thinking: A Handbook of Classroom Strategies. (Illus.). 293p. (Orig.). 1986. pap. text 28.95 (*0-932935-02-8*) SkyLght.

Bellanca, James & Fogarty, Robin. Catch Them Thinking: A Handbook of Classroom Strategies. 2nd ed. 293p. (Orig.). 1993. pap. 29.95 (*0-932935-65-6*) SkyLght.

Bellanca, James & Fogarty, Robin. Designing Professional Development for Change: A Systemic Approach. LC 95-75711. 64p. 1995. pap. 11.95 (*0-932935-94-X*) SkyLght.

Bellanca, James & Swartz, Elizabeth, eds. The Challenge of Detracking: A Collection. LC 93-79951. (Illus.). 240p. 1993. pap. text 11.50 (*0-932935-50-8*) SkyLght.

Bellanca, James, et al. Multiple Assessments for Multiple Intelligences. LC 94-75761. 256p. 1994. pap. 35.95 (*0-932935-72-9*, NB1223) SkyLght.

Bellanca, James, jt. auth. see Fogarty, Robin.

Bellanca, James, jt. auth. see Rodriguez, Eleanor R.

Bellanca, James, jt. ed. see Fogarty, Robin.

Bellanca, James A., et al. Multiple Assessments for Multiple Intelligences. 3rd ed. LC 97-75330. xii, 264 p. 1997. write for info. (*1-57517-076-0*) SkyLght.

Bellance, James A. Values & the Search for Self. LC 75-12724. 111p. reprint ed. pap. 34.50 (*0-608-15075-4*, 202592200047) Bks Demand.

Belland, Bruce, et al. When You Feel Like You're Out of Luck. LC 90-92036. Orig. Title: Gimme aelling. (Illus.). 58p. (J). (ps-3). 1991. lib. bdg. 24.95 incl. audio (*1-879209-01-2*) Saundras Story Bks.

Belland, John C., jt. ed. see Hlynka, Denis.

Belland, Kathleen H. & Wells, Mary A., eds. Clinical Nursing Procedures. LC 83-25982. 400p. (C). 1984. pap. text 40.00 (*0-86720-374-9*) Jones & Bartlett.

Bellandi, Robert, ed. see O'Brien & Gere Engineers, Inc. Staff.

Bellange', Deborah & Long, Dani L. Intro to Variable Universal Life Insurance. (Step One Ser.). 106p. spiral bd. 29.95 (*1-57974-034-0*, Pub. by Life Office) PBD Inc.

Bellanger, Maurice G. Adaptive Digital Filters & Signal Analysis. (Electrical Engineering & Electronics Ser.: Vol. 43). (Illus.). 352p. 1987. text 170.00 (*0-8247-7784-0*) Dekker.

***Bellanger, Maurice G.** Digital Processing of Signals. 3rd ed. LC 99-42711. 2000. write for info. (*0-04-719763-3*) Routledge.

— Digital Processing of Signals. 3rd ed. LC 99-42711. 182p. 2000. text 98.00 (*0-471-97673-3*) Wiley.

Bellani, Luigi V. I Libri di Viaggio e le Guide Della Raccolta, 3 vols. (ITA.). 2008p. 1995. reprint ed. 225.00 (*1-888262-77-X*) Martino Pubng.

Bellant, Russ. The Coors Connection: How Coors Family Philanthropy Undermines Democratic Pluralism. (Illus.). 100p. 1990. spiral bd. 7.50 (*0-915987-06-6*) Political Rsch Assocs.

— The Coors Connection: How Coors Family Philanthropy Undermines Democratic Pluralism. (Political Research Associates Bk.). 150p. 1991. 25.00 (*0-89608-417-5*) South End Pr.

— Old Nazis, the New Right & the Reagan Administration: The Role of Domestic Fascist Networks in the Republican Party & Their Effect on U. S. Cold War Politics. 2nd ed. (Illus.). 100p. (Orig.). 1989. spiral bd. 6.50 (*0-915987-05-8*) Political Rsch Assocs.

— Old Nazis, the New Right, & the Republican Party: Domestic Fascist Networks & Their Effect on U. S. Cold War Politics. (Political Research Associates Bk.). 144p. 1991. 25.00 (*0-89608-419-1*); pap. 11.00 (*0-89608-418-3*) South End Pr.

Bellanti, J. A., et al, eds. Neonatal Hematology & Immunology III: Proceedings of the Third Neonatal Hematology & Immunology Symposium, Held in Washington, D. C., U. S. A. on 29 September - 1 October 1996, Vol. 113. LC 97-5558. (International Congress Ser.: Vol. 1131). 262p. 1997. 158.00 (*0-444-82573-8*, Excerpta Medica) Elsevier.

B

An Asterisk (*) at the beginning of an entry indicates that the title is appearing for the first time.

Bellanti, J. A. & Boissel, J. P., eds. Respiratory Immune Defense in Children: Current Knowledge & Possible Therapeutic Interventions. (Journal: Respiration: Vol. 61, Suppl. 1, 1994). (Illus.). iv, 32p. 1994. pap. 15.75 (*3-8055-6077-X*) S Karger.

Bellanti, Joseph A. & Herscowitz, Herbert B., eds. The Reticuloendothelial System Vol. 6: A Comprehensive Treatise: Immunology. LC 79-25933. 370p. 1984. 95.00 (*0-306-41421-X*, Plenum Trade) Perseus Pubng.

Bellanti, Joseph A., et al. Herpesvirus: Recent Studies, 3 vols., Vol. 1. LC 73-13558. 156p. (C). 1974. text 25.50 (*0-8422-7164-3*) Irvington.

Bellanti, Robert, jt. ed. see Georgi, Charlotte.

Bellantoni, Jeff & Woolman, Matt. Type in Motion: Innovations in Digital Graphics. (Illus.). 176p. 1999. 40.00 (*0-8478-2184-6*, Pub. by Rizzoli Intl) St Martin.

Bellantoni, Lisa. Moral Progress: A Process Critique of Mac Intyre. LC 99-30969. (C). 2000. pap. text 15.95 (*0-7914-4444-9*) State U NY Pr.

***Bellantoni, Lisa.** Moral Progress: A Process Critique of Mac Intyre. LC 99-30969. (C). 2000. text 47.50 (*0-7914-4443-0*) State U NY Pr.

Bellantoni, Nicholas F., jt. auth. see Poirier, David A.

Bellany, Ian. A Basis for Arms Control. 155p. 1991. text 61.95 (*1-85521-051-7*, Pub. by Dartmth Pub) Ashgate Pub Co.

Bellany, Ian. The Environment in World Politics: Exploring the Limits. LC 96-38307. 256p. 1997. 80.00 (*1-85898-348-7*) E Elgar.

Bellany, Ian. Reviewing Britain's Defence. (Illus.). 224p. (C). 1994. text 72.95 (*1-85521-462-8*, Pub. by Dartmth Pub) Ashgate Pub Co.

Bellany, Ian, et al, eds. Nuclear Non-Proliferation Treaty. 142p. 1985. 35.00 (*0-7146-3250-3*, Pub. by F Cass Pubs) Intl Spec Bk.

Bellany, Ian & Blacker, Coit D., eds. Antiballistic Missile Defense in the 1980s. 100p. 1983. text 32.50 (*0-7146-3207-4*, Pub. by F Cass Pubs) Intl Spec Bk.

— Verification of Arms Control Agreements. 104p. 1983. 35.00 (*0-7146-3228-7*, Pub. by F Cass Pubs) Intl Spec Bk.

Bellany, Ian & Huxley, Tim. New Conventional Weapons & Western Defense. 1987. 35.00 (*0-7146-3310-0*, Pub. by F Cass Pubs) Intl Spec Bk.

Bellaouar, Abdellatif & Elmasry, Mohamed I. Low-Power Digital VLSI Design: Circuits & Systems. LC 95-16756. (Illus.). 552p. (C). 1995. text 133.00 (*0-7923-9587-5*) Kluwer Academic.

Bellardo. Online Info Retrieval Systems & Services. 256p. 1997. write for info. (*0-12-084795-7*) Acad Pr.

Bellardo, Lewis & Bellardo, Lynn L. A Glossary for Archivists, Manuscript Curators, & Records Managers. (Archival Fundamentals Ser.). 48p. 1992. pap. 27.00 (*0-931828-81-3*) Soc Am Archivists.

Bellardo, Lynn L., jt. auth. see Bellardo, Lewis.

Bellardo, Trudi. Subject Indexing: An Introductory Guide. 1991. student ed. 85.00 (*0-87111-388-0*) SLA.

Bellarmine, Robert. Live Well, Die Holy: The Art of Being a Saint, Now & Forever. rev. ed. Dalton, John, tr. from LAT. LC 98-5912. Orig. Title: De Arte Bene Moriendi (Rome, 1620). 150p. 1998. pap. 12.95 (*0-918477-71-9*) Sophia Inst Pr.

Bellarmine Women's Council Staff. Bellarmine Designers' Show House Cookbook. 322p. 1996. spiral bd. 21.95 (*0-9654529-0-5*, 502-452-8331) Bellarmine CWC.

Bellarosa, James M. A Problem of Plumbing: And Other Stories. LC 89-1544. 128p. (Orig.). 1989. pap. 8.95 (*0-936784-76-8*) J Daniel.

— Virgil Hunter: A Novel. LC 92-39080. 176p. (Orig.). 1993. pap. 9.95 (*1-880284-00-6*) J Daniel.

Bellarts, Larry. Broken Wing II. 2nd rev. ed. LC 99-64186. 102p. 1999. pap. 9.95 (*0-8323-0531-6*) Binford Mort.

Bellarts, Lawrence J. Bird with a Broken Wing: First-Hand Experience of a World War II Fighter Piilot. LC 95-76647. (Illus.). 144p. 1995. pap. 12.95 (*0-8323-0514-6*) Binford Mort.

***Bellas, Bruce.** Naked Heartland: Itinerant Photography of Los Angeles. (Illus.). 2000. 49.95 (*3-925443-88-6*) Janssen.

Bellas, Henry H., jt. auth. see Anderson, Enoch.

Bellas, P. H. Poe - Master of Macabre. (Illus.). 24p. 1996. pap. 7.95 (*0-9670556-0-1*) Xavier Pubg.

Bellas, Ralph A., jt. auth. see Kirk, John W.

Bellaschi, Jules. To Lead & Manage. LC 80-83869. 70p. (Orig.). (C). 1980. pap. 4.95 (*0-9605144-0-6*) MJ Pubns.

Bellasis, Edward. Cherubini: Memorials Illustrative of His Life & Work. LC 70-138497. (Music Ser.). 1971. reprint ed. lib. bdg. 42.50 (*0-306-70071-9*) Da Capo.

— Cherubini: Memorials Illustrative of His Life & Work. (Works of Edward Bellasis). xv, 429p. 1985. reprint ed. lib. bdg. 59.00 (*0-932051-60-X*); reprint ed. lib. bdg. 79.00 (*0-7812-0950-1*) Rprt Serv.

Bellaterra. Encyclopedic Dictionary of Nutrition & Food: Diccionario Enciclopedico de Nutricion y Alimentos. (SPA.). 170p. 1982. pap. 24.95 (*0-8288-1300-0*, S60255) Fr & Eur.

***Bellatti, Robert M. & West, Shari L.** Estate Planning for Farms & Other Qualified Family-Owned Businesses: Under Sections 2032A & 2057. LC 98-88743. 1999. write for info. (*0-7913-3678-6*) Warren Gorham & Lamont.

Bellavance, Diana. Bookkeeping for a Small Business. 6th ed. (Illus.). 24p. 1998. pap. 4.25 (*0-9605276-9-9*) DBA Bks.

Bellavance, Diane. Advertising & Public Relations for a Small Business. 6th ed. LC 94-68753. (Illus.). 100p. (Orig.). 1995. pap. 15.95 (*0-9605276-7-2*) DBA Bks.

— Typing Made Easy: Includes Computer Usage. 8th rev. ed. (Illus.). 20p. (Orig.). 1997. pap. 4.25 (*0-9605276-8-0*, SAN:281-5877) DBA Bks.

Bellavance-Johnson, Marsha. Georgia O'Keeffe in New Mexico: A Guide. (Famous Footsteps Ser.). (Illus.). 32p. (Orig.). 1988. pap. 4.75 (*0-929709-00-4*) Computer Lab.

***Bellavance-Johnson, Marsha.** Georgia O'Keeffe in New Mexico: A Guide. 2nd ed. (Famous Footsteps Ser.). (Illus.). 64p. (Orig.). 1999. pap. 7.95 (*0-929709-14-4*) Computer Lab.

Bellavance-Johnson, Marsha. Marilyn Monroe in Hollywood: A Guide. (Famous Footsteps Ser.). (Illus.). (Orig.). 1992. pap. 4.95 (*0-929709-10-1*) Computer Lab.

— Mark Twain in the U. S. A. Guide. (Famous Footsteps Ser.). (Illus.). (Orig.). 1990. pap. 4.95 (*0-929709-07-1*) Computer Lab.

— Tennessee Williams in Key West & Miami: A Guide. (Famous Footsteps Ser.). (Illus.). (Orig.). 1989. pap. 4.95 (*0-929709-03-9*) Computer Lab.

Bellavance-Johnson, Marsha & Bellavance, Lee. Ernest Hemingway in Idaho: A Guide. 2nd rev. ed. (Famous Footsteps Ser.). (Illus.). (Orig.). 1989. pap. 4.95 (*0-929709-04-7*) Computer Lab.

— Ernest Hemingway in Key West: A Guide. (Famous Footsteps Ser.). (Illus.). 32p. 1987. pap. 4.50 (*0-929709-02-0*) Computer Lab.

— Ernest Hemingway in Key West: A Guide. 2nd ed. (Famous Footsteps Ser.). (Illus.). 64p. 2000. pap. 7.95 (*0-929709-06-3*) Computer Lab.

Bellavance, Lee, jt. auth. see Bellavance-Johnson, Marsha.

Bellavance, Leslie. Analemmic: An Equation of Time. 48p. 1998. boxed set 22.00 (*0-932526-61-6*) Nexus Pr.

Bellavance, Roger, jt. auth. see Bellavance, Tom.

Bellavance, Tom & Bellavance, Roger. Inventing Made Easy: The Entrepreneur's Indispensable Guide to Creating, Patenting & Profiting from Inventions. rev. ed. LC 98-67181. (Illus.). 272p. 1999. pap. 24.95 (*0-9665069-7-9*) Quiet Corner Pr.

Bellavita, Christopher, ed. How Public Organizations Work: Learning from Experience. LC 90-32291. 256p. 1990. 57.95 (*0-275-93387-3*, C3387, Praeger Pubs); pap. 22.95 (*0-275-93391-1*, B3391, Praeger Pubs) Greenwood.

Bellavitis, P. The Unknown Biography of Jesus Christ: A Treasure of Stories about Jesus Christ You Have Never Read! Payne, R. E., ed. (Illus.). 100p. (Orig.). 1997. pap. 5.90 (*1-885308-08-6*) Sr Polit Action.

Bellber, Philip. Cook, Eat, Cha Cha Cha: Festive New World Tapas. LC 96-18698. 1997. pap. 17.95 (*0-8118-1146-8*) Chronicle Bks.

Bellcore & Bell Operating Companies, Technical Per. Telecommunications Transmission Engineering. 3 vols., Set. 3rd ed. LC 90-62180. (Illus.). 824p. (C). 1990. text 399.00 (*1-878108-04-2*) Telcordia Technologies.

— Telecommunications Transmission Engineering, 3 vols., Vol. 1: Principles. 3rd ed. LC 90-62180. (Illus.). 824p. (C). 1990. text 195.00 (*1-878108-01-8*) Telcordia Technologies.

— Telecommunications Transmission Engineering, 3 vols., Vol. 2: Facilities. 3rd ed. LC 90-62180. (Illus.). 824p. (C). 1990. text 195.00 (*1-878108-02-6*) Telcordia Technologies.

— Telecommunications Transmission Engineering, 3 vols., Vol. 3: Networks & Services. 3rd ed. LC 90-62180. (Illus.). 824p. (C). 1990. text 195.00 (*1-878108-03-4*) Telcordia Technologies.

Bellcore Technical Personnel. The Network Management Handbook. (Illus.). 536p. (C). 1990. 495.00 (*1-878108-10-7*) Telcordia Technologies.

— Research on Advanced Television for Broadband ISDN. (Illus.). 239p. (C). 1990. 520.00 (*1-878108-11-5*) Telcordia Technologies.

Belle, Albert. Don't Call Me Joey: The Wit & Wisdom of Albert ("Joey") Belle. (Illus.). 100p. 1998. pap. text 7.95 (*1-55022-349-6*, Pub. by ECW) LPC InBook.

Belle, Barbara. Pixel Helps Pooper Out of a Pickle. (Pixel Ser.: No. 2). (Illus.). 24p. (Orig.). (J). (gr. 1-5). 1995. pap. 3.25 (*0-935163-02-6*) Pixel Prods Pubns.

Belle, Deborah. The After-School Lives of Children: Alone & with Others While Parents Work. LC 99-17931. 200p. 1999. 45.00 (*0-8058-2325-5*) L Erlbaum Assocs.

— Children's Social Networks & Social Supports. LC 88-18704. (Personality Processes Ser.). 384p. 1989. 150.00 (*0-471-62879-4*) Wiley.

Belle, Deborah, ed. Lives in Stress: Women & Depression. LC 81-18379. (Sage Focus Editions Ser.: No. 45). (Illus.). 246p. reprint ed. pap. 76.30 (*0-8357-4737-9*, 203765400009) Bks Demand.

***Belle, Douglas A. Van.** Press Freedom & Global Politics. LC 99-43102. 184p. 2000. 59.95 (*0-275-96790-5*, Praeger Pubs) Greenwood.

Belle, Frances P., tr. see Paz, Ireneo.

Belle Grove Staff. Belle Grove Plantation. pap. 12.95 (*0-9616530-0-0*) Belle Grove Inc.

***Belle Haleine Association Staff.** Purple #05. 496p. 2000. pap. 14.00 (*2-912684-14-5*) Assn Belle.

— Purple Sexe #06. 2000. pap. 14.00 (*2-912684-15-3*) Assn Belle.

***Belle Heleine Association Staff.** Purple, No. 1. 1998. pap. text 14.00 (*2-912684-06-4*, Pub. by Assn Belle) Dist Art Pubs.

— Purple, No. 2. (Illus.). 1998. pap. text 14.00 (*2-912684-07-2*, Pub. by Assn Belle) Dist Art Pubs.

— Purple Sexe, No. 3. 1999. pap. text 12.00 (*2-912684-08-0*, Pub. by Assn Belle) Dist Art Pubs.

Belle-Isle, J. Gerald, jt. auth. see Belleis, L.

***Belle, Joe Grant.** Ace Combat 3 Electrosphere: Prima's Official Strategy Guide. LC 00-10036. (Illus.). 144p. 2000. pap. 14.99 (*0-7615-2792-3*) Prima Pub.

***Belle, John & Leighton, Maxinne R.** Grand Central. LC 98-51419. 192p. 1999. text 39.95 (*0-393-04765-2*) Norton.

Belle, Laval W. Your Gifts Are Not Your Purpose! Leonard, Holli & Hogg, Sharon, eds. 123p. 1998. pap. text 15.00 (*0-9662750-7-1*) Caution Prodns.

Belle, Maureen L. Gaiamancy: Creating Harmonious Environments. Kleiner, Ellen, ed. LC 98-60095. (Illus.). 149p. 1999. pap. 17.00 (*0-9662622-0-4*) White Doe.

Belle, Sarah. Urda. LC 96-90814. (Illus.). 91p. (Orig.). (J). (gr. 4-8). 1996. pap. 12.95 (*0-9655316-0-0*) Urda Pub.

Belle, Tim La, see Reynolds, Larry A. & La Belle, Tim.

Bellear, Lisa. Dreaming in Urban Areas. LC 96-213811. 1996. 18.95 (*0-7022-2856-7*, Pub. by Univ Queensland Pr) Intl Spec Bk.

Bellecci-St. Romain, Lisa. Building Family Faith: Weekly Lectionary-Based Activities, No. 1, Cycle A. LC 93-79278. (Illus.). 112p. (Orig.). 1993. spiral bd. 10.95 (*0-89243-542-9*) Liguori Pubns.

— Building Family Faith: Weekly Lectionary-Based Activities, No. 2, Cycle B. LC 93-79278. (Illus.). 112p. (Orig.). 1993. pap. 10.95 (*0-89243-533-X*) Liguori Pubns.

— Building Family Faith: Weekly Lectionary-Based Activities, No. 3, Cycle C. LC 93-79278. (Illus.). 112p. (Orig.). 1993. spiral bd. 10.95 (*0-89243-543-7*) Liguori Pubns.

— Building Family Faith Through Lent, Cycle B. 48p. 1997. pap. 3.95 (*0-89243-808-8*) Liguori Pubns.

— Building Family Faith Through Lent: Cycle A. LC 95-80170. 48p. 1996. pap. 3.95 (*0-89243-807-X*) Liguori Pubns.

— Building Family Faith Through Lent: Cycle C - Lectionary Based Activities. LC 94-79444. (Illus.). 32p. (Orig.). 1994. pap. 3.95 (*0-89243-772-3*) Liguori Pubns.

Bellecci-St. Romain, Lisa & St. Romain, Philip. Living Together, Loving Together: A Spiritual Guide to Marriage. LC 94-73020. 160p. 1995. pap. 6.95 (*0-89243-788-X*) Liguori Pubns.

Bellecci-St. Romain, Lisa M. Building Family Faith Through Advent: Cycle C. (Illus.). 32p. (Orig.). 1997. pap. 3.95 (*0-7648-0035-3*) Liguori Pubns.

***Bellecci-St. Romain, Lisa M.** Building Family Faith Through Advent Cycle A. (Illus.). 32p. 1998. 3.95 (*0-7648-0034-5*) Liguori Pubns.

Bellefontaine, Jacqueline. Art of Good Food: Potato Fillings. 80p. 1996. 7.98 (*0-7858-0376-9*) Bk Sales Inc.

***Bellefontaine, Jacqueline.** Barbecue & Salads for Summer. (Portable Chef Ser.). (Illus.). 256p. 1999. 7.98 (*0-7651-0875-5*) Smithmark.

— Classic Chinese Recipes. (Classic Cookery Ser.). (Illus.). 256p. 1998. 19.98 (*0-7651-0879-8*) Smithmark.

— Classic Italian Recipes. LC 99-184465. (Classic Cookery Ser.). (Illus.). 256p. 1998. 19.98 (*0-7651-0880-1*) Smithmark.

Bellefontaine, Jacqueline. Great Thai Cookbook. (Illus.). 176p. 1997. 14.99 (*1-85833-334-2*, Pub. by CLib Bks) Whitecap Bks.

— What's Cooking: Barbecue. LC 98-14981. (Illus.). 256p. 1998. 15.98 (*1-57145-149-8*, Thunder Bay) Advantage Pubs.

— What's Cooking: Chocolate. LC 98-21870. (Illus.). 256p. 1998. 15.98 (*1-57145-151-X*, Thunder Bay) Advantage Pubs.

Bellefroid, Jacques & Fuentes, Vilma. Alex Katz: Echoes. Strancel, James, tr. from FRE. (Other Monograph Ser.). (Illus.). 200p. 1992. 39.95 (*1-878552-01-5*) Ptmanteau Pr.

Belleggia, Concetta. I, Jesus. 144p. 1996. pap. 6.95 (*0-8198-3673-7*) Pauline Bks.

Belleggia, Concetta, ed. Real Women: Advice, Commentary & Encouragement for Today's Woman. LC 93-80663. 244p. pap. 12.95 (*0-89870-462-6*) Ignatius Pr.

***Bellegoni, Elvira.** Accounting for the Non-Financial Manager. (Illus.). 128p. 2000. pap. 17.95 (*0-9662542-7-9*) Etta Pub Co.

Bellegoni, Elvira. Bookkeeping & Administration for the Smaller Business. (Illus.). vii, 64p. 1998. pap. 12.95 (*0-9662542-0-1*) Etta Pub Co.

— Love the Least of My Children. (Illus.). 64p. 1999. pap. 12.95 (*0-9662542-4-4*) Etta Pub Co.

— Wanted: A Home, Urgent!!! Very Abused Kitten Needs a Home Desperately. (Illus.). 66p. 1998. pap. 13.95 (*0-9662542-2-8*) Etta Pub Co.

— What Do You Mean I Am 50? (Illus.). 128p. 1999. pap. 14.95 (*0-9662542-5-2*) Etta Pub Co.

***Bellegoni, Elvira, ed.** Desserts: (Simple, Inexpensive, Fast, & Good) (Illus.). 64p. 1999. pap. 11.95 (*0-9662542-1-X*) Etta Pub Co.

Bellegoni, Elvira, jt. auth. see Etta Publishing Staff.

Belleis, L. & Belle-Isle, J. Gerald. General English-French Technical Dictionary: Dictionnaire Technique Generale: Anglais-Francais. 3rd deluxe ed. (ENG & FRE.). 572p. 1983. 175.00 (*0-8288-4728-2*, M6158) Fr & Eur.

Bellem, Robert L. Blue Murder. 158p. 1988. pap. 6.95 (*0-89366-276-3*) Ultramarine Pub.

Bellemain, jt. auth. see Baulac.

Bellemare, P. Dictionnaire des 1000 Trucs. (FRE.). 1998. 36.00 (*0-320-00220-9*) Fr & Eur.

Belleme, Jan, jt. auth. see Belleme, John.

Belleme, John & Belleme, Jan. Cooking with Japanese Foods: A Guide to the Traditional Natural Foods of Japan. (Illus.). 232p. (Orig.). pap. 13.95 (*0-89529-583-0*, Avery) Penguin Putnam.

Bellen, A., et al, eds. Numerical Methods for Ordinary Differential Equations. (Lecture Notes in Mathematics Ser.: Vol. 1386). vii, 136p. 1989. 29.95 (*0-387-51478-3*) Spr-Verlag.

***Bellen, Hugo, ed.** Neurotransmitter Release. LC 99-16240. (Frontiers in Molecular Biology Ser.: No. 23). (Illus.). 458p. 1999. text 120.00 (*0-19-963767-9*) OUP.

— Neurotransmitter Release. LC 99-16240. (Frontiers in Molecular Biology Ser.: Vol. 23). (Illus.). 458p. 1999. pap. text 60.00 (*0-19-963766-0*) OUP.

Bellen, Martine. Places People Dare Not Enter. 67p. (Orig.). 1991. pap. 8.00 (*0-937013-40-4*) Potes Poets.

— Tales of Muraski & Other Poems. (National Poetry Ser.). 91p. 1999. pap. 10.95 (*1-55713-378-6*, Pub. by Sun & Moon CA) SPD-Small Pr Dist.

— Tributes: American Writers on American Writers. Smith, Lee & Morrow, Bradford, eds. (Bi-Annual Volumes of New Writing Ser.: Vol. 29). (Illus.). 360p. (Orig.). 1997. pap. 12.00 (*0-941964-45-0*) Conjunctions.

Bellenden, Jean, jt. auth. see Makgill, Jacques.

Bellenger, Danny N., et al. Qualitative Research in Marketing. LC 76-3765. (American Marketing Association Monograph: No. 3). 86p. reprint ed. pap. 30.00 (*0-608-13400-7*, 202248200027) Bks Demand.

Bellenger, Joseph M., ed. see Maillard, Antoine S.

Bellenger, Sylvain. Views of Some Monuments in Paris at the Time of Louis Philippe. 1998. 120.00 (*2-909838-37-4*, Pub. by A Gourcuff) Antique Collect.

Bellenger, Y., ed. see Ronsard, Pierre De.

***Belleni-Morante, Aldo.** Applied Nonlinear Semigroups. LC 98-22041. (Pure & Applied Mathematics Ser.). 288p. 1998. 99.95 (*0-471-97867-1*) Wiley.

Belleni-Morante, Aldo. A Concise Guide to Semigroups & Evolution Equations. LC 94-7754. (Series on Advances in Mathematics for Applied Sciences). 180p. 1994. text 46.00 (*981-02-1294-1*) World Scientific Pub.

Bellenir, Karen. Diet & Nutrition Sourcebook: Basic Consumer Health Information about Dietary Guidelines... 2nd ed. LC 99-17687. (Health Reference Ser.). 1999. lib. bdg. 78.00 (*0-7808-0228-4*) Omnigraphics Inc.

***Bellenir, Karen, ed.** AIDS Sourcebook. 2nd ed. LC 98-53294. (Health Reference Ser.). (Illus.). 600p. 1999. lib. bdg. 78.00 (*0-7808-0225-X*) Omnigraphics Inc.

— Alcoholism Sourcebook: Basic Consumer Health Information about the Physical & Mental Consequences of Alcohol Abuse... (Health Reference Ser.). 600p. 2000. lib. bdg. 78.00 (*0-7808-0325-6*) Omnigraphics Inc.

— Alzheimer's Disease Sourcebook. 2nd ed. LC 98-51624. (Health Reference Ser.). (Illus.). 600p. 1999. lib. bdg. 78.00 (*0-7808-0223-3*) Omnigraphics Inc.

Bellenir, Karen, ed. Back & Neck Disorders Sourcebook. LC 97-1006. (Health Reference Ser.: Vol. 24). 560p. 1997. 78.00 (*0-7808-0202-0*) Omnigraphics Inc.

***Bellenir, Karen, ed.** Brain Disorders Sourcebook: Basic Consumer Health Information. LC 99-15539. (Health Reference Ser.). 600p. 1999. 78.00 (*0-7808-0229-2*) Omnigraphics Inc.

Bellenir, Karen, ed. Congenital Disorders Sourcebook. LC 97-17092. (Health Reference Ser.: Vol. 29). 1997. lib. bdg. 78.00 (*0-7808-0205-5*) Omnigraphics Inc.

***Bellenir, Karen, ed.** Diabetes Sourcebook. 2nd rev. ed. (Health Reference Ser.). (Illus.). 600p. 1998. lib. bdg. 78.00 (*0-7808-0224-1*) Omnigraphics Inc.

— Digestive Diseases & Disorders Sourcebook. (Health Reference Ser.). (Illus.). 300p. 1999. lib. bdg. 48.00 (*0-7808-0327-2*) Omnigraphics Inc.

— Drug Abuse Sourcebook: Basic Consumer Health Information about Illicit Substances of Abuse & the Diversion of Prescription Medications. (Health Reference Ser.). 600p. 2000. lib. bdg. 78.00 (*0-7808-0242-X*) Omnigraphics Inc.

Bellenir, Karen, ed. Genetic Disorders Sourcebook. (Health Reference Ser.: Vol. 13). 1996. lib. bdg. 78.00 (*0-7808-0034-6*) Omnigraphics Inc.

— Head Trauma Sourcebook. LC 97-1008. (Health Reference Ser.: Vol. 23). 424p. 1997. 78.00 (*0-7808-0208-X*) Omnigraphics Inc.

***Bellenir, Karen, ed.** Heart Diseases & Disorders Sourcebook. 2nd ed. LC 99-58043. (Health Reference Ser.). (Illus.). 750p. 1999. lib. bdg. 78.00 (*0-7808-0238-1*) Omnigraphics Inc.

Bellenir, Karen, ed. Mental Health Disorders Sourcebook. (Health Reference Ser.: Vol. 9). 1995. lib. bdg. 78.00 (*0-7808-0040-0*) Omnigraphics Inc.

***Bellenir, Karen, ed.** Mental Health Disorders Sourcebook. 2nd ed. LC 99-49596. (Health Reference Ser.). (Illus.). 700p. 1999. lib. bdg. 78.00 (*0-7808-0240-3*) Omnigraphics Inc.

Bellenir, Karen, ed. Religious Holidays & Festivals: An Encyclopedic Handbook. 2nd ed. LC 97-24845. 350p. 1997. lib. bdg. 75.00 (*0-7808-0258-6*) Omnigraphics Inc.

— Substance Abuse Sourcebook. LC 96-9511. (Health Reference Ser.: Vol. 14). 1996. lib. bdg. 78.00 (*0-7808-0038-9*) Omnigraphics Inc.

***Bellenir, Karen, ed.** Teen Diet Book. (Teen Health Ser.). (Illus.). 250p. (YA). (gr. 7 up). 2000. lib. bdg. 48.00 (*0-7808-0441-4*) Omnigraphics Inc.

— Teen Mental Health Book. (Illus.). 250p. (YA). (gr. 7 up). 2000. lib. bdg. 48.00 (*0-7808-0442-2*) Omnigraphics Inc.

Bellenir, Karen & Dresser, Peter D., eds. Cardiovascular Diseases & Disorders Sourcebook. LC 95-10583. (Health Reference Ser.: Vol. 5). 683p. 1995. lib. bdg. 78.00 (*0-7808-0032-X*) Omnigraphics Inc.

— Contagious & Non-Contagious Infectious Diseases Sourcebook. (Health Reference Ser.: Vol. 8). 1995. lib. bdg. 78.00 (*0-7808-0075-3*) Omnigraphics Inc.

— Food & Animal Borne Diseases Sourcebook: Basic Information about Diseases That Can Be Spread to Humans Through the Ingestion of Contaminated Food or Water or by Contact with Infected Animals. LC 95-21240. (Health Reference Ser.: Vol. 7). 535p. 1995. 78.00 (*0-7808-0033-8*) Omnigraphics Inc.

Bellenir, Karen, jt. ed. see Dresser, Peter D.

Beller. Transition Metals for Fine Chemical & Organic Synthesis. 1120p. 1998. 595.00 (*3-527-29501-1*) Wiley.

Beller, Andrea H. Small Change: The Economics of Child Support. 1996. pap. text 18.00 (*0-300-06659-7*) Yale U Pr.

Beller, Andrea H. & Graham, John W. Small Change: The Economics of Child Support. LC 92-39623. (Illus.). 392p. 1993. 40.00 (*0-300-05362-2*) Yale U Pr.

Beller, Anthony, ed. Business Law in California. 12th rev. ed. 100p. Date not set. pap. text 14.00 (*0-914504-13-4*) General Educ.
— Business Law in California. 12th rev. ed. (Illus.). 516p. Date not set. text 47.50 (*0-914504-12-6*) General Educ.
Beller, Dan. And the Lord Added to the Church. 1989. pap. 6.95 (*0-911866-08-6*) LifeSprings Res.
— Progress Through Pioneer Evangelism. pap. 2.00 (*0-911866-80-9*) LifeSprings Res.
Beller, Fritz K. & Weir, Robert F., eds. The Beginning of Human Life. LC 93-2827. 416p. (C). 1993. lib. bdg. 160.50 (*0-7923-2165-0*, Pub. by Kluwer Academic) Kluwer Academic.
Beller, George A. Chronic Ischemic Heart Disease. LC 95-1751. (Atlas of Heart Diseases Ser.: Vol. 5). (Illus.). 264p. 1995. text 134.00 (*1-878132-29-6*) Current Med.
— Clinical Nuclear Cardiology. LC 94-25345. (Illus.). 336p. 1995. text 110.00 (*0-7216-3332-3*, W B Saunders Co) Harcrt Hlth Sci Grp.
— Clinical Nuclear Cardiology. 2nd ed. 1999. text. write for info. (*0-7216-7715-0*, W B Saunders Co) Harcrt Hlth Sci Grp.
Beller-Hann, I. A History of Cathay, a Translation & Linguistic Analysis of a Fifteenth-Century Turkic Manuscript. LC 95-69265. (Uralic & Altaic Ser.: Vol. 162). 200p. 1995. 24.90 (*0-933070-37-3*) Res Inst Inner Asian Studies.
***Beller-Hann, Ildiko & Hann, Chris.** Turkish Region: Culture & Civilization on the East Black Sea Coast. (World Anthropology Ser.). 2000. 65.00 (*0-933452-70-5*); pap. 29.95 (*0-933452-71-3*) Schol Am Res.
Beller, Ilex. Life in the Shtetl. Pannell, Alastair D., tr. from FRE. LC 86-19512. (Illus.). 145p. 1986. 49.50 (*0-8419-1095-2*) Holmes & Meier.
Beller, Isi. Sacred Fire. LC 94-9936. 416p. 1994. 21.45 (*1-55970-226-5*, Pub. by Arcade Pub Inc) Time Warner.
Beller, James R. Children's Law Institute LC 98-194848. (Litigation & Administrative Practice Ser.). 352 p. 1998. 129.00 (*0-87224-492-X*) PLI.
— The Soul of St. Louis: A Historical Narrative of Revival in the Gateway City. (Illus.). 300p. 1998. 20.00 (*0-9668766-1-X*) Prairie Fire Pr.
Beller, Jennifer M., jt. auth. see Stoll, Sharon K.
Beller, Mara. Quantum Dialogue: The Making of a Revolution. LC 99-35499. (Science & Its Conceptual Foundations Ser.). 328p. 1999. 35.00 (*0-226-04181-6*) U Ch Pr.
***Beller, Miles.** Dream of Venus (or Living Pictures) (Illus.). 298p. 1999. 24.95 (*0-9663480-0-1*, Pub. by C M Publng) ACCESS Pubs Network.
Beller, Miles, ed. Hey Skinny! Great Advertisements from the Golden Age of Comic Books. LC 94-21428. (Illus.). 96p. 1995. pap. 10.95 (*0-8118-0828-9*) Chronicle Bks.
Beller, Stephen, ed. Rethinking Fin-de-Siecle Vienna, Vol. 2. 2000. 69.95 (*1-57181-139-7*) Berghahn Bks.
Beller, Steven. Francis Joseph. (Profiles in Power Ser.). 224p. (C). 1996. 73.00 (*0-582-06090-7*) Addson-Wesley Educ.
— Francis Joseph. LC 96-19897. (Profiles in Power Ser.). 280p. (C). 1996. pap. 25.66 (*0-582-06089-3*) Longman.
— Vienna & the Jews, 1867-1938: A Cultural History. 281p. (C). 1991. pap. text 22.95 (*0-521-40727-3*) Cambridge U Pr.
***Beller, Susan P.** The Confederate Ladies of Richmond. LC 98-42412. 96p. (YA). (gr. 5-8). 1999. lib. bdg. 25.90 (*0-7613-1470-9*) TFC Bks NY.
Beller, Susan P. Never Were Men So Brave: The Irish Brigade During the Civil War. LC 97-16005. (Illus.). 112p. (YA). (gr. 5-9). 1998. per. 15.00 (*0-689-81406-2*) S&S Childrens.
Beller, Susan P. To Hold This Ground: A Desperate Battle at Gettsburg. LC 94-12775. (Illus.). 96p. (YA). (gr. 4-7). 1995. pap. 15.00 (*0-689-50621-X*) McElderry Bks.
***Beller, Susan Provost.** Billy Yank & Johnny Reb: Soldiering in the Civil War. LC 99-462169. (Illus.). (J). 2000. lib. bdg. write for info. (*0-7613-1869-0*) Millbrook Pr.
— Revolutionary War. LC 00-36019. (Letters From the Home Front Ser.). 2001. lib. bdg. write for info. (*0-7614-1094-5*, Benchmark NY) Marshall Cavendish.
Beller, Susan Provost. Roots for Kids: A Genealogy Guide for Young People. 128p. 1997. pap. 16.95 (*0-8063-1525-3*) Genealog Pub.
Beller, Thomas. Seduction Theory. 208p. 1996. mass mkt. 11.99 (*0-446-67252-1*, Pub. by Warner Bks) Little.
***Beller, Thomas.** The Sleep-Over Artist. LC 00-26111. 256p. 2000. 23.95 (*0-393-04925-6*) Norton.
Beller, Thomas, ed. Personals: Dreams & Nightmares from the Lives of Twenty Young Writers. LC 98-22918. 304p. 1998. pap. 13.00 (*0-395-85796-1*, Mariner Bks) HM.
Beller, Thomas, et al. Open City No. 10: The Editors' Issue. 280p. 1999. pap. 8.00 (*1-890447-21-8*, Pub. by Open City Bks) SPD-Small Pr Dist.
Beller, Thomas, ed. see Berman, David, et al.
Beller, Thomas, ed. see Gaitskill, Mary, et al.
Beller, Thomas, ed. see Lewinsky, Monica S., et al.
Beller, Thomas, ed. see Shapiro, Harvey, et al.
Beller, Thomas, ed. see Wallace, David Foster, et al.
Beller, W., et al, eds. Sustainable Development & Environmental Management of Small Islands. (Man & the Biosphere Ser.: Vol. 5). (Illus.). 420p. 1990. 65.00 (*1-85070-267-5*) Prthnon Pub.
Beller, William S., ed. Puerto Rico & the Sea. Balzac, Irma, tr. (Illus.). 129p. 1974. pap. 5.00 (*0-8477-2301-1*) U of PR Pr.
Beller, Zaret. Nuclear Cardiology: State of the Art & Future Directions. 2nd ed. LC 98-33551. (Illus.). 668p. (C). (gr. 13). 1998. text 129.00 (*0-8151-1740-X*, 30422) Mosby Inc.
Belleroche, J. De, see Coulton, G. R. & De Belleroche, J., eds.
Bellerophon Books Staff. Aces & Airplanes of WW One. (J). (gr. 1-9). 1992. pap. 3.95 (*0-88388-037-7*) Bellerophon Bks.
— Ancient Africa, Vol. 1. (J). (gr. 1-9). 1992. pap. 3.50 (*0-88388-090-3*) Bellerophon Bks.
— Ancient Buildings. (J). (gr. 4-7). 1992. pap. 3.95 (*0-88388-121-7*) Bellerophon Bks.
— Ancient China. (J). (gr. 1-9). 1992. pap. 4.95 (*0-88388-077-6*) Bellerophon Bks.
— Ancient Greece. (J). (gr. 1-9). 1992. pap. 4.95 (*0-88388-000-8*) Bellerophon Bks.
— Ancient Hawaii. (J). (gr. 1-9). 1992. pap. 2.95 (*0-88388-091-1*) Bellerophon Bks.
— Ancient Near East. (J). (gr. 1-9). 1992. pap. 4.95 (*0-88388-002-4*) Bellerophon Bks.
— Ancient Rome. (J). (gr. 1-9). 1992. pap. 4.95 (*0-88388-061-X*) Bellerophon Bks.
— Billy Yank. (J). (gr. 4-7). 1992. pap. 4.95 (*0-88388-155-1*) Bellerophon Bks.
— California Indian Tribes: Northern, Vol. 1. (J). (gr. 1-9). 1995. pap. 3.95 (*0-88388-153-5*) Bellerophon Bks.
— California Indian Tribes: Southern, Vol. 2. (J). (gr. 4-7). 1997. pap. 3.95 (*0-88388-184-5*) Bellerophon Bks.
— French Revolution Paper Dolls. (J). (gr. 1-9). 1993. pap. 5.95 (*0-88388-141-1*) Bellerophon Bks.
— George Caleb Bingham. (J). (gr. 1-9). 1992. pap. 1.95 (*0-88388-151-9*) Bellerophon Bks.
— Giant Poster Book of Ancient Egypt. (J). (gr. k-8). 1995. pap. 5.95 (*0-88388-212-4*) Bellerophon Bks.
— Giant Poster Book of Ancient Mexico. (J). (gr. k-8). 1995. pap. 5.95 (*0-88388-210-8*) Bellerophon Bks.
— Great American Airplanes. (J). (gr. 1-9). 1992. pap. 4.95 (*0-88388-113-6*) Bellerophon Bks.
— Great Indian Chiefs. (J). (gr. 1-9). 1992. pap. 4.95 (*0-88388-033-4*) Bellerophon Bks.
— Henry the Eighth & His Wives. (J). (gr. 1-9). 1992. pap. 4.95 (*0-88388-009-1*) Bellerophon Bks.
— Incas, Aztecs, & Mayas. (J). (gr. 1-9). 1992. pap. 4.95 (*0-88388-010-5*) Bellerophon Bks.
— Infamous Women. (J). (gr. 1-9). 1992. pap. 4.95 (*0-88388-035-0*) Bellerophon Bks.
— Johnny Reb. (J). (gr. 1-9). 1993. pap. 4.95 (*0-88388-180-2*) Bellerophon Bks.
— A Medieval Alphabet. (J). (gr. 1-9). 1992. pap. 4.95 (*0-88388-001-6*) Bellerophon Bks.
— Middle Ages. (J). (gr. 1-9). 1992. pap. 4.95 (*0-88388-007-5*) Bellerophon Bks.
— A Musical Alphabet. (J). (gr. 1-9). 1992. pap. 3.95 (*0-88388-137-3*) Bellerophon Bks.
— The New Testament. (J). (gr. 1-9). 1992. pap. 4.95 (*0-88388-004-0*) Bellerophon Bks.
— Old Testament. (J). (gr. 1-9). 1992. pap. 4.95 (*0-88388-003-2*) Bellerophon Bks.
— Queen Elizabeth the First. (J). (gr. 1-9). 1992. pap. 4.95 (*0-88388-013-X*) Bellerophon Bks.
— Queen Nefertiti. (J). (gr. 1-9). 1992. pap. 3.50 (*0-88388-154-3*) Bellerophon Bks.
— Ramses the Great. (J). (gr. 1-9). 1992. pap. 3.50 (*0-88388-148-9*) Bellerophon Bks.
— Renaissance. (J). (gr. 1-9). 1992. pap. 4.95 (*0-88388-011-3*) Bellerophon Bks.
— Royal Family Paper Dolls. (J). (gr. 1-9). 1992. pap. 4.95 (*0-88388-097-0*) Bellerophon Bks.
— San Diego Mission. (J). (gr. 4-7). 1997. pap. 3.95 (*0-88388-206-X*) Bellerophon Bks.
— Shakespeare. (J). (gr. 1-9). 1992. pap. 4.95 (*0-88388-008-3*) Bellerophon Bks.
— Ships. (J). (gr. 1-9). 1992. pap. 4.95 (*0-88388-016-4*) Bellerophon Bks.
— Story of California, Bk. 1. 1996. pap. text 4.95 (*0-88388-219-1*) Bellerophon Bks.
— Story of California, Bk. 2. 1996. pap. text 4.95 (*0-88388-220-5*) Bellerophon Bks.
— Story of California, Bk. 3. 1996. pap. text 4.95 (*0-88388-215-9*) Bellerophon Bks.
— Story of California, Bk. 4. 1996. pap. text 4.95 (*0-88388-217-5*) Bellerophon Bks.
— Totem Poles. (J). (gr. 1-9). 1992. pap. 5.95 (*0-88388-081-4*) Bellerophon Bks.
— Totem Poles Vol. 3: Kwakiutl. (J). (gr. 4-7). 1996. pap. 5.95 (*0-88388-199-3*) Bellerophon Bks.
— Tournament. (J). (gr. 4-7). 1994. pap. 3.95 (*0-88388-181-0*) Bellerophon Bks.
Bellerophon Books Staff, jt. auth. see Fourth Earl of Chesterfield.
Bellerophon Staff. Paper Soldiers of American Revolution, Vol. 2. (J). (gr. 1-9). 1994. pap. text 3.95 (*0-88388-038-5*) Bellerophon Bks.
Bellerose, R. Philippe. Reinsurance for the Beginner. 4th ed. 190p. pap. 100.00 (*1-85609-106-6*, Pub. by Witherby & Co) St Mut.
Bellerose, R. Phillippe, jt. auth. see Witherby & Co. Ltd. Staff.
Bellerson, Karen J. The Complete & Up -to -Date Fat Book: A Guide to the Fat, Calories, & Fat Percentages in Your Food. 3rd expanded rev. ed. 870p. (Orig.). 1997. mass mkt. 6.95 (*0-89529-738-8*, Avery) Penguin Putnam.
— The Shopper's Guide to Fat in Your Food: A Carry-Along Guide to the Fat, Calories, & Fat Percentages in Brand Name Foods. 96p. mass mkt. 2.50 (*0-89529-610-1*, Avery) Penguin Putnam.
Bellert, I., jt. auth. see Malecki, I.
Bellert, Irena. The Feature System of Quantification in Natural Language. (Groningen-Amsterdam Studies in Semantics: No. 10). ix, 175p. 1989. pap. 44.65 (*90-6765-350-0*) Mouton.
Belles, Dale, jt. auth. see Norvell, Nancy.
***Belles, R. J.** Precursors to Potential Severe Core Damage Accidents: 1996, A Status Report. 296p. 1998. per. 24.00 (*0-16-062880-6*) USGPO.
— Precursors to Potential Severe Core Damage Accidents: 1997 a Status Report. 208p. 1998. per. 17.00 (*0-16-062978-0*) USGPO.
Bellesia, Giovanna, tr. see Maraini, Dacia.
Bellesiles. Pyne U. S. History 97-98. (C). Date not set. pap. text 29.16 (*0-395-88682-1*) HM.
***Bellesiles, Michael A.** Arming America: The Origins of a Naitonal Gun Culture. 640p. 2000. 30.00 (*0-375-40210-1*) Knopf.
Bellesiles, Michael A. Revolutionary Outlaws: Ethan Allen & the Struggle for Independence on the Early American Frontier. 1995. pap. text 18.50 (*0-8139-1603-8*) U Pr of Va.
Bellesiles, Michael A., ed. Lethal Imagination: Violence & Brutality in American History. 485p. 1999. pap. 24.95 (*0-8147-1296-7*) NYU Pr.
***Bellesiles, Michael A., ed.** Lethal Imagination: Violence & Brutality in American History. LC 98-37696. 485p. 1999. text 65.00 (*0-8147-1295-9*) NYU Pr.
Bellessi, Diana & Le Guin, Ursula K. The Twins, the Dream - Las Gemelas, el Sueno: Two Voices - Dos Voces. LC 96-16944. 230p. 1996. pap. 8.95 (*1-55885-179-8*) Arte Publico.
Bellestri, Joseph. Basic Sicilian-English Dictionary. LC 85-73172. 338p. 1985. 20.00 (*0-9615777-0-3*) J Bellestri.
— English-Sicilian Dictionary. 680p. 1988. 25.00 (*0-9615777-1-1*) J Bellestri.
Bellet, D., jt. auth. see Canham, L. T.
Bellet, J. G. The Son of God. pap. 4.25 (*0-88172-169-7*) Believers Bkshelf.
Bellet, Louise P. du, see du Bellet, Louise P.
Bellet, Michel & L'Harmet, Corine. Industry, Space & Competition: The Contribution of Economists of the Past. LC 98-27887. 256p. 1999. 95.00 (*1-85898-856-X*) E Elgar.
Bellet, Roger, ed. see Valles, Jules.
Bellet, Samuel. Clinical Disorders of the Heart Beat. 3rd rev. ed. LC 74-123414. 1327p. reprint ed. pap. 200.00 (*0-608-13290-X*, 205601500044) Bks Demand.
Belletini, G., jt. ed. see Scribano, A.
Bellett, J. G. The Moral Glory of the Lord Jesus Christ. pap. 2.95 (*0-88172-176-X*) Believers Bkshelf.
— Short Meditations, 3 vols., Set. pap. 12.95 (*0-88172-003-8*) Believers Bkshelf.
Belletti, Adriana & Rizzi, Luigi, eds. Parameters & Functional Heads: Essays in Comparative Syntax. (Studies in Comparative Syntax). 312p. 1996. text 65.00 (*0-19-508793-3*); pap. text 39.95 (*0-19-508794-1*) OUP.
***Belleville, Bill.** River of Lakes: A Journey on Florida's St. Johns River. LC 99-33373. 210p. 2000. 24.95 (*0-8203-2156-7*) U of Ga Pr.
Belleville, Linda L. Reflections of Glory: Paul's Polemical Use of the Moses-Doxa Tradition in 2 Corinthians (JSNT Supplement Ser.: Vol. 52). 351p. 1991. 85.00 (*1-85075-265-6*, Pub. by Sheffield Acad) CUP Services.
— Women Leaders & the Church: 3 Crucial Questions. LC 99-51608. (Three Crucial Questions Ser.). 224p. 2000. pap. 13.99 (*0-8010-5351-X*) Baker Bks.
***Belleville, Nyree.** Booking, Promoting & Marketing Your Music: A Complete Guide for Bands & Solo Artists. 200p. 2000. pap. 29.95 (*0-87288-739-1*) Intertec Pub.
Bellevue, Eugene F., ed. see Steele, R. Don.
Bellew, Frank. The Art of Amusing. LC 74-15725. (Popular Culture in America Ser.). (Illus.). 328p. 1975. reprint ed. 28.95 (*0-405-06362-8*) Ayer.
Bellew, H. W. Kashmir & Kashgar: A Narrative of the Journey of the Embassy to Kashgar in 1873-74. 1989. reprint ed. 31.00 (*81-206-0510-1*, Pub. by Asian Educ Servs) S Asia.
Bellew, John C. Shakespeare's Home at New Place. LC 76-113553. reprint ed. 54.50 (*0-404-00736-8*) AMS Pr.
Bellezza, John V., et al. Divine Dyads, Ancient Civilization in Tibet. LC 98-907116. xiv, 497p. 1997. write for info. (*81-86470-19-0*, Pub. by Lib Tibetan W&A) S Asia.
Bellg, Albert, jt. auth. see Rybarczyk, Bruce.
Bellgardt, K. H., jt. auth. see Schhugerl, K.
Belli, Angela & Coulehan, Jack, eds. Blood & Bone: Poems by Physicians. LC 98-7140. 224p. 1998. pap. 17.95 (*0-87745-638-0*); text 29.95 (*0-87745-637-2*) U of Iowa Pr.
Belli, Anna-Maria, ed. Practical Interventional Radiology of the Peripheral Vascular System. 136p. 1994. text 85.00 (*0-340-55865-2*, Pub. by E A) OUP.
Belli, F., et al, eds. Industrial & Engineering Applications of Artificial Intelligence & Expert Systems: 5th International Conference, IEAAIE '92, Paderborn, Germany, June 9-12, 1992: Proceedings. LC 92-16773. (Lecture Notes in Computer Science, Lecture Notes in Artificial Intelligence Ser.: Vol. 604). xv, 702p. 1992. 106.95 (*0-387-55601-X*) Spr-Verlag.
Belli, G., ed. Catalog of the 1995 Venice Biennale. 46th ed. 340p. 1995. pap. 42.00 (*1-56886-018-8*) Marsilio Pubs.
Belli, G. G. The Roman Sonnets. Norse, Harold, tr. LC 60-9955. 1960. pap. 10.00 (*0-912330-72-4*) Jargon Soc.
***Belli, Gabriella.** Deperofuturista. 1999. 50.00 (*88-8118-584-9*) Skira IT.
***Belli, Gariella, ed.** Depero-Futurista. (Illus.). 196p. 1999. 50.00 (*88-8118-487-7*, Pub. by Skira IT) Abbeville Pr.
Belli, Gioconda. From Eve's Rib. White, Steven F., tr. from SPA. LC 93-25956.Tr. of De la Costilla de Eva. 121p. (Orig.). 1989. reprint ed. pap. 9.95 (*1-880684-13-6*) Curbstone.
— The Inhabited Woman. March, Kathleen N., tr. from SPA. LC 94-13983. 412p. 1994. 22.95 (*1-880684-17-9*) Curbstone.
— The Inhabited Woman. 416p. 1995. mass mkt. 14.00 (*0-446-67206-8*, Pub. by Warner Bks) Little.
— Nicaragua Water Fire. (C). 1990. pap. 40.00 (*0-906887-37-2*, Pub. by Greville Pr) St Mut.
Belli, Giuseppe G. Sonnets of Giuseppe Belli. Williams, Miller, tr. from ITA. LC 80-24331. (Illus.). xx, 164p. 1981. text 25.00 (*0-8071-0762-X*) La State U Pr.
Belli, Melvin. Everybody's Guide to the Law: The First Place to Look for the Legal Information You Need Most. LC 87-45254. 672p. 1987. pap. 19.00 (*0-06-272502-5*) HarpC.
Belli, Melvin M., Sr. Modern Damages, 3 vols. 1960. text 67.50 (*0-672-81442-0*, Bobbs) Macmillan.
— Modern Damages, 3 vols. 1966. suppl. ed. write for info. (*0-685-99329-9*, Bobbs) Macmillan.
Belli, Melvin M., Sr. & Krantzler, Mel. Divorcing. 4th ed. 448p. 1990. pap. 16.95 (*0-312-03816-X*) St Martin.
Belli, Melvin M., Sr. & Wilkinson, Allen P. Everybody's Guide to the Law. 640p. 1986. 19.95 (*0-15-142166-8*) Harcourt.
Belli, Melvin M., Sr., jt. auth. see Krantzler, Mel.
Belli, Melvin M., jt. auth. see Moch, Joseph W.
Belli, Pierino. De Re Militari et Bello Tractatus. LC 95-77188. (Classics in International Law Reprint Ser.: No. 18., Vol. 1). 1995. reprint ed. 95.00 (*1-57588-520-4*) W S Hein.
Belli, Pierino. Treatise on Military Matters & Warfare, Vol. 2. LC 95-77297. (Classics in International Law Reprint Ser.: No. 18). 1995. reprint ed. 115.00 (*1-57588-262-0*, 310360) W S Hein.
Bellicha, Georges & Bellicha, Pierre. Dictionnaire Medical. (FRE.). 480p. 1987. pap. 79.95 (*0-7859-7701-5*, 2040163506) Fr & Eur.
Bellicha, Pierre, jt. auth. see Bellicha, Georges.
Bellico, Russell. Sails & Steam in the Mountains: A Maritime & Military History of Lake George & Lake Champlain. 4th ed. LC 92-25010. (Illus.). 400p. 1992. pap. 25.00 (*0-935796-32-0*) Purple Mnt Pr.
***Bellico, Russell P.** Chronicles of Lake Champlain: Journeys in War & Peace. LC 99-23978. (Illus.). 440p. 1999. 75.00 (*0-916346-71-4*); pap. 29.00 (*0-916346-70-6*) Purple Mnt Pr.
Bellico, Russell P. Chronicles of Lake George: Journeys in War & Peace. (Illus.). 415p. 1995. 75.00 (*0-935796-62-2*); pap. 29.00 (*0-935796-63-0*) Purple Mnt Pr.
Bellido, A. G., ed. see Menendez Pidal, Ramon.
Bellido, Antonio Garcia Y, see Garcia y Bellido, Antonio.
***Bellier, Irene & Wilson, Thomas M., eds.** An Anthropology of the European Union: Building, Imagining & Experiencing the New Europe. 224p. 2000. 65.00 (*1-85973-324-7*, Pub. by Berg Pubs); pap. 19.50 (*1-85973-329-8*, Pub. by Berg Pubs) NYU Pr.
Bellier, Marcel, jt. auth. see Gros-Louis, Max.
Bellin, David. The Children's War. LC 79-54050. 1980. 15.95 (*0-935210-00-8*); pap. 8.95 (*0-935210-01-6*) Dundee Pub.
— Software Maintenance: The Small System Management Guide. 176p. 1990. pap. text 30.00 (*0-685-40434-X*) P-H.
Bellin, David & Simone, Susan S. The CRC Card Book. LC 97-8250. 320p. (C). 1997. pap. 34.95 (*0-201-89535-8*) Addison-Wesley.
Bellin, David, ed. see Chapman, Gary.
Bellin, H. & Steinberg, Peter. Dr. Bellin's Beautiful You Book. LC 81-10664. (Illus.). 192p. 1981. 16.95 (*0-685-03838-6*); pap. 7.95 (*0-685-03839-4*) P-H.
Bellin, Harvey F., photos by. Blake & Swedenborg: Opposition Is True Friendship. LC 85-50060. (Illus.). 160p. 1985. pap. 12.95 (*0-87785-127-1*) Swedenborg.
***Bellin, Joshua D.** The Demon of the Continent: Indians & the Shaping of American Literature. LC 00-33799. 2000. pap. write for info. (*0-8122-1748-9*) U of Pa Pr.
Bellin, Mildred G. The Original Jewish Cookbook. 470p. 1984. reprint ed. 17.95 (*0-8197-0058-4*) Bloch.
Bellin, Robert. Comp Defence to 1d4. 2nd ed. 1991. pap. write for info. (*0-08-037151-5*, Pub. by CHES) Macmillan.
Bellin, Robert & Ponzetto, Pietro. Test Your Positional Play. (Illus.). 192p. 1985. pap. 13.95 (*0-02-028090-4*) Macmillan.
Bellina, Joan, jt. auth. see Cronin, Gaynell B.
Bellina, Joseph H. & Bandieramonte, Gaetano. Principles & Practice of Gynecologic Laser Surgery. LC 84-3434. 308p. 1984. 75.00 (*0-306-41543-7*, Plenum Trade) Perseus Pubng.
Bellincioni, Gemma, jt. auth. see Stagno Bellincioni, Bianca.
Bellinetto, Alexandra, tr. see Minnaar, Phillip.
Belling, Andrew. Let's Sing about America. LC 92-763081. (Singalongs Ser.). (Illus.). 32p. (J). (gr. k-2). 1992. pap. text 4.95 (*0-8167-2983-2*) Troll Communs.
***Belling, Detlev.** Legal Protection Against Breaches of Duty on the Part of the German Works Council--Fata Morgana? LC 99-87787. (Potsdamer Rechtswissenschaftliche Reihe Ser.: Bd. 8). x, 96p. 2000. 46.95 (*3-540-66835-7*) Spr-Verlag.
Bellinger, A. R. Syrian Tetradrachmas of Caracalla & Macrinus. 1980. reprint ed. lib. bdg. 30.00 (*0-915262-57-6*) S J Durst.
Bellinger, Alfred R. Catalogue of the Byzantine Coins in the Dumbarton Oaks Collection & in the Whittemore Collection, Vol. 1: Anastasius the First to Maurice, 491-602. Grierson, Philip, ed. LC 92-9036. (Illus.). 490p. 1992. reprint ed. 130.00 (*0-88402-012-6*) Dumbarton Oaks.
— The End of the Seleucids. (Connecticut Academy of Arts & Sciences Ser., Trans.: Vol. 38). 1949. pap. 39.50 (*0-685-22902-5*) Elliots Bks.
— Spires & Poplars. LC 72-144711. (Yale Series of Younger Poets: No. 4). reprint ed. 18.00 (*0-404-53804-5*) AMS Pr.
— Troy the Coins. LC 81-50603. (Illus.). 1979. reprint ed. lib. bdg. 35.00 (*0-915262-32-0*) S J Durst.

An Asterisk (*) at the beginning of an entry indicates that the title is appearing for the first time.

Bellinger, Alfred R. & Bellinger, Charlotte B. Catalogue of the Coins Found at Corinth, 1925, with a Note on the Cleaning of the Coins. (Illus.). 1930. pap. 100.00 (*0-686-51349-5*) Elliots Bks.

***Bellinger, Charles K.** The Genealogy of Violence: Reflections on Creation, Freedom, & Evil. 176p. 2000. text 32.00 (*0-19-513498-2*) OUP.

Bellinger, Charlotte B., jt. auth. see Bellinger, Alfred R.

Bellinger, David, jt. ed. see Needleman, Herbert L.

Bellinger, Elizabeth S., ed. A Costly Obedience: Sermons by Women of Steadfast Spirit. LC 93-45873. 104p. 1994. pap. 14.00 (*0-8170-1205-2*) Judson.

Bellinger, Gerhard. Diccionario Ilustrado de la Biblia. (SPA., Illus.). 664p. 1991. 85.00 (*0-7859-5772-3*) Fr & Eur.

Bellinger, Peter, jt. auth. see Christiansen, Kenneth.

Bellinger, Peter F., jt. auth. see Mari-Mutt, Jose.

Bellinger, W. H., Jr. A Hermeneutic of Curiosity & Readings of Psalm 61. LC 95-6544. (Studies in Old Testament Interpretation: Vol. 1). 1995. text 20.00 (*0-86554-464-6*, MUP-H364) Mercer Univ Pr.

— The Testimony of Poets & Sages: The Psalms & Wisdom Literature. LC 98-16750. (All the Bible Ser.). 112p. 1998. pap. 12.00 (*1-57312-004-9*) Smyth & Helwys.

Bellinger, William H., Jr. Psalms: Reading & Studying the Book of Praises. LC 90-40913. 166p. 1990. pap. 9.95 (*0-943575-35-4*) Hendrickson MA.

Bellinger, William H., jt. ed. see Farmer, William R.

Bellingham, ed. Advanced Medicine. 1975. 32.00 (*0-8464-4455-0*) Beekman Pubs.

Bellingham, Alastair J. Diagnostic Picture Tests in Hematology. 128p. (C). (gr. 13). 1994. pap. text 20.95 (*0-8151-5224-8*, 23041) Mosby Inc.

Bellingham, Alastair J. & Hambly, Henry. Diagnostic Picture Tests in Hematology. LC 94-23606. (Illus.). 118p. 1994. text 15.00 (*0-7234-1936-1*) Mosby Inc.

***Bellingham, Brenda.** Lilly Plays Her Part. (New First Novels Ser.). 64p. 2000. mass mkt. write for info. (*0-88780-500-0*, Pub. by Formac Publ Co) Formac Dist Ltd.

— Lilly to the Rescue. (First Novels). (Illus.). 64p. (J). 1997. bds. 4.95 (*0-88780-387-3*, Pub. by Formac Publ Co) Formac Dist Ltd.

— Lilly's Good Deed. LC 98-95021. (Illus.). 64p. (J). (gr. 1-4). 1998. bds. write for info. (*0-88780-461-6*) FMC.

***Bellingham, Brenda.** Lilly's Good Deed. LC 98-95021. (First Novels Ser.). (Illus.). 64p. (J). (gr. 1-4). 1998. text 3.99 (*0-88780-460-8*, Pub. by Formac Publ Co) Orca Bk Pubs.

***Bellingham, Brenda & Owen, Elizabeth.** Lilly Plays Her Part. 64p. (J). 2000. bds. write for info. (*0-88780-501-9*, Pub. by Formac Publ Co) Formac Dist Ltd.

Bellingham, Bruce. Bellingham by the Bay: Bits, Bites, Adventures in Radio & Real Life. LC 98-29594. 379p. 1998. 19.95 (*1-57178-073-4*) Coun Oak Bks.

Bellingham, Bruce & Evans, Edward G., Jr., eds. Sixteenth-Century Bicinia: A Complete Edition of Munich Bayerische Staatsbibliothek Mus. M5.260. (Recent Researches in Music of the Renaissance Ser.: Vol. RRR16-17). (Illus.). xi, 192p. 1974. pap. 65.00 (*0-89579-050-5*) A-R Eds.

***Bellingham, Dave.** Wizzo Guide Logic Audio Windows 4: How to Turn Your Computer into a Digital Studio. 1999. pap. text 27.90 (*3-927954-47-0*) MM Musik Media.

Bellingham, David. Goddesses Heroes & Shamans: The Young People's Guide to World Mythology. (Illus.). 160p. (J). (gr. 4 up). 1994. 22.95 (*1-85697-999-7*) LKC.

Bellingham, David, et al. Goddesses, Heroes & Shamans: The Young People's Guide to World Mythology. (Illus.). 160p. (J). (gr. 4 up). 1997. pap. 17.95 (*0-7534-5058-5*, Kingfisher) LKC.

— Myths & Legends: Viking, Oriental, Greek. (Illus.). 208p. 1997. 17.98 (*0-7858-0627-X*) Bk Sales Inc.

Bellingham, Linda. Like a TV Hero. 112p. (J). (gr. 3-6). 1991. pap. 5.95 (*0-7736-7315-6*) Stoddart Publ.

Bellinghausen, Patricia, jt. auth. see Ekey, Robert.

Bellingrath, George C. Qualities Associated with Leadership in the Extra-Curricular Activities of the High School. LC 74-176549. (Columbia University. Teachers College. Contributions to Education Ser.: No. 399). reprint ed. 37.50 (*0-404-55399-0*) AMS Pr.

Bellini, Enzo, et al. The Catholic Church Today, 1920-1981. Drury, John, ed. & tr. by. from ITA. (Illustrated History of the Church Ser.). (Illus.). 126p. (YA). (gr. 6-12). 1983. 12.95 (*0-86683-160-6*) Harper SF.

— The Church in Revolutionary Times. Drury, John, ed. & tr. by. from ITA. (Illustrated History of the Church Ser.). (Illus.). 126p. (J). (gr. 6-12). 1981. 12.95 (*0-86683-158-4*) Harper SF.

***Bellini, James L. & Rumrill, Phillip D., Jr.** Research in Rehabilitation Counseling: A Guide to Design, Methodology & Utilization. LC 99-37751. 244p. 1999. 45.95 (*0-398-06993-X*); pap. 32.95 (*0-398-06994-8*) C C Thomas.

Bellini, Paolo, ed. The Illustrated Bartsch Vol. 45: Italian Masters of the Seventeenth Century. 1982. 149.00 (*0-89835-045-X*) Abaris Bks.

— The Illustrated Bartsch Vol. 46: Italian Masters of the Seventeenth Century. (Illus.). 1982. lib. bdg. 149.00 (*0-89835-046-8*) Abaris Bks.

— The Illustrated Bartsch Vol. 46, Commentary: Italian Masters of the Seventeenth Century. 1985. lib. bdg. 149.00 (*0-89835-145-6*) Abaris Bks.

— The Illustrated Bartsch Vol. 47: Italian Masters of the Seventeenth Century. (Illus.). 1983. lib. bdg. 149.00 (*0-89835-047-6*) Abaris Bks.

— The Illustrated Bartsch Vol. 47-1, Commentary: Italian Masters of the Seventeenth Century. 1995. lib. bdg. 149.00 (*0-89835-146-4*) Abaris Bks.

— The Illustrated Bartsch Vol. 47-2: Commentary: Italian Masters of the Seventeenth Century. 1995. lib. bdg. 149.00 (*0-89835-323-8*) Abaris Bks.

Bellini, Paolo & Leach, Mark C., eds. The Illustrated Bartsch Vol. 44: Italian Masters of the Seventeenth Century. (Illus.). 1983. lib. bdg. 149.00 (*0-89835-044-1*) Abaris Bks.

Bellini, Paolo & Wallace, Richard W., eds. The Illustrated Bartsch Vol. 45, Commentary: Italian Masters of the Seventeenth Century. 488p. 1990. lib. bdg. 149.00 (*0-89835-144-8*) Abaris Bks.

Bellini, Paul, jt. auth. see Thompson, Scott.

Bellini, Pietro & Rotelle, John E. Blessed Simon Fidati of Cascia. Fellowes, Audrey, tr. from ITA. LC 88-70284. (Augustinian Ser.: Vol. 13). (Illus.). 112p. 1988. pap. 5.95 (*0-941491-18-8*) Augustinian Pr.

Bellini, Vincenzo. I Puritani Libretto. (ENG & ITA.). 56p. 1986. pap. 4.95 (*0-7935-5397-0*, 50340660) H Leonard.

— Norma in Full Score. 448p. pap. 19.95 (*0-486-27970-7*) Dover.

— Norma Libretto. (ENG & ITA.). 40p. 1986. pap. 4.95 (*0-7935-2774-0*, 50340540) H Leonard.

Bellino, Francis L., et al, eds. Dehydroepiandrosterone (DHEA) & Aging. (Annals of the New York Academy of Sciences Ser.: Vol. 774). 350p. 1996. pap. 95.00 (*1-57331-005-0*) NY Acad Sci.

Bellino, Lydia, jt. auth. see Calkins, Lucy M.

Bellino, Lydia, jt. auth. see McCormick Calkins, Lucy.

***Bellino, O. F. L.** Biology of Menopause. (Serono Symposia USA Ser). (Illus.). 304p. 2000. 140.00 (*0-387-98987-0*) Spr-Verlag.

Bellinzoni, Arthur J., ed. see Massaux, Edouard.

Belliotti, Raymond A. Good Sex: Perspectives on Sexual Ethics. LC 93-9851. 328p. 1993. 35.00 (*0-7006-0604-1*); pap. 16.95 (*0-7006-0605-X*) U Pr of KS.

— Justifying Law: The Debate over Foundations, Goals, & Methods. 301p. (C). 1994. pap. 29.95 (*1-56639-203-9*) Temple U Pr.

— Seeking Identity: Individualism vs. Community in an Ethnic Context. LC 95-31444. 280p. (C). 1995. 35.00 (*0-7006-0729-3*); pap. 17.95 (*0-7006-0730-7*) U Pr of KS.

Belliotti, Raymond Angelo. Stalking Nietzsche, 68. LC 98-8237. (Contributions in Philosophy Ser.: Vol. 68). 200p. 1998. 55.00 (*0-313-30700-8*, Greenwood Pr) Greenwood.

Bellis, Alice O. Doing the Twist to Amazing Grace. LC 98-36256. 128p. 1998. pap. 9.95 (*0-8298-1273-3*) Pilgrim OH.

— Helpmates, Harlots, & Heroes: Women's Stories in the Hebrew Bible. LC 93-31035. 320p. (Orig.). 1994. pap. 22.95 (*0-664-25430-6*) Westminster John Knox.

— The Structure & Composition of Jeremiah 50: 2 - 51: 58. LC 94-13279. (Biblical Press Ser.: Vol. 24). 248p. 1995. 89.95 (*0-7734-2353-2*, Mellen Biblical Pr) E Mellen.

Bellis, Alice O., ed. Many Voices: Multicultural Responses to the Minor Prophets. 116p. (Orig.). (C). 1995. pap. text 23.50 (*0-8191-9837-4*) U Pr of Amer.

— Many Voices: Multicultural Responses to the Minor Prophets. (Illus.). 116p. (Orig.). (C). 1995. lib. bdg. 42.00 (*0-8191-9836-6*) U Pr of Amer.

Bellis Bixel, Patricia. Sailing Ship Elissa. LC 98-2699. (Centennial Series of the Association of Former Students, Texas A&M University: Vol. 76). (Illus.). 144p. 1998. 22.95 (*0-89096-826-8*) Tex A&M Univ Pr.

***Bellis, David D.** Child Welfare: Early Experiences Implementing a Managed Care Approach. (Illus.). 104p. 1999. pap. text 20.00 (*0-7881-8275-7*) DIANE Pub.

Bellis, David D. Foster Care: Implementation of the Multiethnic Placement Act Poses Difficult Challenges. 78p. (C). 1999. pap. text 20.00 (*0-7881-7734-6*) DIANE Pub.

Bellis, David J. Heroin & Politicians: The Failure of Public Policy to Control Addiction in America, 58. LC 80-21373. (Contributions in Political Science Ser.: No. 58). (Illus.). 239p. 1981. 59.95 (*0-313-22557-5*, BHP/, Greenwood Pr) Greenwood.

Bellis, Florence. Gardening & Beyond. (Illus.). 190p. 1986. 14.95 (*0-88192-015-0*) Timber.

Bellis, Jack De, see De Bellis, Jack, compiled by.

Bellis, James. The Place of the Pots in Akan Funerary Custom. LC 82-74220. 59p. (Orig.). 1982. pap. 5.00 (*0-941934-40-3*) Indiana Africa.

Bellis, Peter Damian. One Last Dance with Lawrence Welk & Other Stories. LC 96-70860. 144p. 1996. pap. 9.00 (*0-9654756-0-3*) River Boat Bks.

Bellis, Teri J. Assessment & Management of Central Audiology Processing Disorders: From Science to Practice. (Illus.). 364p. (Orig.). 1996. pap. 55.95 (*1-56593-628-0*, 1302) Thomson Learn.

Bellisco Hernandez. Diccionario de Banca y Bolsa Tomo 2: Espanol-Ingles (Dictionary of Banking & Stock Exchange)Tr. of Dictionary of Banking & Stock Exchange. (SPA.). 165p. 1980. pap. 39.95 (*0-7859-4930-5*) Fr & Eur.

— Spanish-English Dictionary of Banking & Stock Exchange. 163p. pap. 37.50 (*84-85198-05-0*) IBD Ltd.

Bellisco Hernandez, H. English-Spanish Dictionary of Banking & Stock Exchange. 135p. pap. 35.95 (*84-85198-02-6*) IBD Ltd.

Bellisco, Hernandez H. Diccionario de Banca y Bolsa Tomo 1: Ingles-Espanol. (SPA.). 170p. 1977. pap. 39.95 (*0-8288-5311-8*, S50120) Fr & Eur.

Bellisent-Funel, M. C. & Neilson, G. W. The Physics & Chemistry of Aqueous Ionic Solutions. (C). 1987. text 234.00 (*90-277-2534-9*) Kluwer Academic.

Bellisles, Michael. Discussing "The American Promise" A Survival Guide for First-Time Teaching Assistants. 1997. pap. text 6.66 (*0-312-15728-2*) St Martin.

Bellison, Simeon, ed. see Klose, Hyacinthe.

Bellison, Simeon, ed. see Kroepsch, F.

Bellison, Simeon, ed. see Lazarus, H.

Bellissent-Funel, Marie-Claire & Dore, John C., eds. Hydrogen Bond Networks: Proceedings of the NATO Advanced Research Workshop, Cargege, France, August 16-22, 1993. LC 94-13949. (NATO ASI Series C: Mathematical & Physical Sciences: Vol. 435). 564p. (C). 1994. text 336.00 (*0-7923-2884-1*) Kluwer Academic.

Bellissimo, Anthony & Tunks, Eldon. Chronic Pain: The Psychotherapeutic Spectrum. LC 84-9909. 384p. 1984. 89.50 (*0-275-91422-4*, C1422, Praeger Pubs) Greenwood.

Bellissimo, Cinzia C., et al. Benvenuti All' Italiano. (ITA., Illus.). 370p. (J). (gr. 7-9). 1992. pap. text 29.95 (*0-9645107-0-7*) Cima Publ.

***Bellissino, Charles A.** Charles Bellissino's Encyclopedia of Sauces for Your Pasta. LC 98-38705. 304p. 1998. 19.98 (*1-57912-015-6*) Blck Dog & Leventhal.

Bellissino, Charles A. The Encyclopedia of Sauces for Your Food. Packard, Joan, ed. LC 97-211843. (Encyclopedia of Sauces for Your... Ser.: Vol. 2). (Illus.). 500p. 1997. pap. 26.95 (*1-879743-02-7*) M Kimberly Pub.

— The Encyclopedia of Sauces for Your Pasta: The Greatest Collection of Pasta Sauces Ever in One Book. rev. ed. Dedic-Aievoli, Eleanor & Wingate, Enid, eds. LC 94-76781. 560p. (Orig.). 1994. pap. 32.50 (*1-879743-01-9*) M Kimberly Pub.

Belliston, Larry, jt. auth. see Hanks, Kurt.

Belliston, Scott, tr. see Crawford, John L.

***Bellitto, Christopher M.** Lost & Found Catholics: Voices of Vatican II. (Illus.). 96p. 1999. pap. text 7.95 (*0-86716-312-7*, B3127) St Anthony Mess Pr.

— Nicolas de Clamanges: Spirituality, Personal Reform & Pastoral Renewal on the Eve of the Reformations. LC 00-30311. 2001. write for info. (*0-8132-0996-X*) Cath U Pr.

Bellitto, Christopher M. What Every Catholic Should Know about the Millennium. LC 97-74319. 80p. 1998. pap. 3.95 (*0-7648-0146-5*) Liguori Pubns.

Belliveau, G. K. Say to This Mountain: The Life of James T. Jeremiah. LC 99-20813. 1999. 10.99 (*0-87227-201-X*) Reg Baptist.

Belliveau, James E. K Equals X, & Then Some. (Robert Charles Billings Fund Publication Pamphlet Ser.: No. 2). (Illus.). (Orig.). 1965. pap. 1.50 (*0-934552-23-1*) Boston Athenaeum.

Belliveau, Jeannette. An Amateur's Guide to the Planet: 12 Adventure Journeys & Lessons for the Contemporary United States. LC 96-96767. (Illus.). 288p. (Orig.). 1996. pap. 19.95 (*0-9652344-4-4*) Beau Monde.

***Bellizzi, Jamey.** Carols of the British Isles for Acoustic Guitar. 52p. 1998. pap. 17.95 (*0-7866-3466-9*, 95038BCD) Mel Bay.

— Medieval & Renaissance Dance Music for Acoustic Guitar. 96p. 1998. pap. 19.95 incl. audio compact disk (*0-7866-4036-7*, 94847BCD) Mel Bay.

Bellizzi, Jamey, ed. see Scarlatti, Domenico.

Bellizzi, Ralph & Loushine, Robert. A Clinical Atlas of Endodontic Surgery. (Illus.). 135p. 1991. text 59.00 (*0-86715-234-6*) Quint Pub Co.

Bellm, Dan. Buried Treasure. (CSU Poetry Ser.: Vol. LVII). 80p. 1999. 22.50 (*1-880834-47-2*); pap. 12.00 (*1-880834-46-4*) Cleveland St Univ Poetry Ctr.

***Bellm, Dan.** One Hand on the Wheel. (California Poetry Ser.: Vol. 1). 65p. 1999. pap. 12.50 (*0-9666691-0-X*, Pub. by Heyday Bks) SPD-Small Pr Dist.

Bellm, Dan. A Story in a Bottle. Mycue, Edward, ed. (Took Modern Poetry in English Ser.: No. 19). (Illus.). 28p. (Orig.). 1991. pap. 3.00 (*1-879457-22-9*) Norton Coker Pr.

Bellm, Dan & National Center for the Early Childhood Work Force Staff. Making Work Pay in the Child Care Industry: Promising Practices for Improving Compensation. LC 98-169363. 64 p. 1997. write for info. (*1-889956-11-2*) Natl Ctr EC.

Bellm, Dan & Whitebook, Marcy. Taking on Turnover: An Action Guide for Child Care Center Teachers & Directors. 164p. 1998. pap. text, wbk. ed. 19.95 (*1-889956-14-7*) Natl Ctr EC.

Bellm, Dan, et al. Early Childhood Mentoring Curriculum: A Handbook for Mentors. LC 96-48441. 1996. write for info. (*1-889956-00-7*) Natl Ctr EC.

***Bellm, Dan, et al.** Terrain. 72p. 1998. per. 10.00 (*0-917658-30-2*) BPW & P.

Bellm, Dan, ed. see Haack, Peggy.

Bellm, Dan, tr. see Blanco, Alberto.

Bellman, ed. A Short Guide to Writing about Music. LC 99-14759. 174p. (C). 1999. pap. 22.26 (*0-321-01577-0*) Addson-Wesley Educ.

Bellman, Beryl L. Village of Curers & Assassins: On the Production of Fala Kpelle Cosmological Categories. LC 73-76893. (Approaches to Semiotics Ser.: No. 39). 196p. 1975. text 57.70 (*90-279-3042-2*) Mouton.

Bellman, Beryl L. & Jules-Rosette, Bennetta. Paradigm for Looking: Cross Cultural Research with Visual Media. LC 77-15284. (Modern Sociology Ser.). (Illus.). 216p. 1977. text 73.25 (*0-89391-002-3*) Ablx Pub.

Bellman, David, ed. see Pitseolak, Peter.

***Bellman, Geoffrey M.** Beauty of the Beast: Breathing New Life into Organizations. LC 99-58681. 168p. 2000. 27.95 (*1-57675-093-0*, Pub. by Berrett-Koehler) Publishers Group.

Bellman, Geoffrey M. The Consultant's Calling: Bringing Who You Are to What You Do. LC 90-53092. (Management Ser.). 264p. 1990. text 37.95 (*1-55542-253-5*) Jossey-Bass.

— The Consultant's Calling: Bringing Who You Are to What You Do. LC 90-53092. (Management Ser.). 264p. 1992. reprint ed. mass mkt. 20.00 (*1-55542-411-2*) Jossey-Bass.

— Getting Things Done When You Are Not in Charge. LC 92-70094. (Illus.). 292p. 1992. 27.95 (*1-881052-02-8*) Berrett-Koehler.

— Getting Things Done When You Are Not in Charge. LC 93-838. 304p. 1993. per. 12.00 (*0-671-86412-2*, Fireside) S&S Trade Pap.

— Your Signature Path: Gaining New Perspectives on Life & Work. LC 96-31515. 165p. 1996. 24.95 (*1-57675-004-3*) Berrett-Koehler.

Bellman, James F. & Bellman, Kathryn. Antony & Cleopatra Notes. (Cliffs Notes Ser.). 72p. 1981. pap. 4.95 (*0-8220-0002-4*, Cliff) IDG Bks.

Bellman, James F., Jr. & Bellman, Kathryn A. The French Lieutenant's Woman Notes. (Cliffs Notes Ser.). 48p. (YA). (gr. 10-12). 1979. pap. text 4.95 (*0-8220-0499-2*, Cliff) IDG Bks.

Bellman, Jonathan. The Style Hongrois in the Music of Western Europe. LC 93-10150. 224p. (C). 1993. text 45.00 (*1-55553-169-5*) NE U Pr.

Bellman, Jonathan, ed. The Exotic in Western Music. LC 97-16407. 416p. 1997. text 60.00 (*1-55553-320-5*); pap. text 25.00 (*1-55553-319-1*) NE U Pr.

Bellman, Kathryn, jt. auth. see Bellman, James F.

Bellman, Kathryn A., jt. auth. see Bellman, James F., Jr.

Bellman, Kirstie L., jt. ed. see Landauer, Christopher.

***Bellman, Kristie L. & Landauer, Christopher, eds.** Virtual Worlds & Simulation Conference 1998. Vol. 30. 243p. 1998. 50.00 (*1-56555-137-0*) Soc Computer Sim.

Bellman, L., jt. ed. see Manley, K.

Bellman, R., ed. Mathematical Problems in the Biological Sciences: Proceedings. LC 50-1183. (Proceedings of Symposia in Applied Mathematics Ser.: Vol. 14). 250p. 1962. text 34.00 (*0-8218-1314-5*, PSAPM/14) Am Math.

— Stochastic Processes in Mathematical Physics & Engineering: Proceedings. LC 64-18128. (Proceedings of Symposia in Applied Mathematics Ser.: Vol. 16). 318p. 1964. reprint ed. pap. 47.00 (*0-8218-1316-1*, PSAPM/16) Am Math.

Bellman, R. & Wing, G. Milton. An Introduction to Invariant Imbedding. LC 92-29086. (Classics in Applied Mathematics Ser.: No. 8). xvii, 248p. 1992. pap. 33.00 (*0-89871-304-8*) Soc Indus-Appl Math.

Bellman, R., jt. auth. see Beckenbach, Edwin F.

Bellman, R., ed. see Applied Mathematics Symposium Staff.

Bellman, Richard. Introduction to Matrix Analysis. 2nd ed. LC 97-67651. (Classics in Applied Mathematics: No. 19). xxviii, 403p. 1997. pap. 34.00 (*0-89871-399-4*) Soc Indus-Appl Math.

Bellman, Richard & Cooke, Kenneth L. Asymptotic Behavior of Solutions of Differential-Difference Equations. LC 52-42839. (Memoirs Ser.: No. 1/35). 95p. 1959. reprint ed. pap. 24.00 (*0-8218-1235-1*, MEMO/1/35) Am Math.

— Modern Elementary Differential Equations. 2nd rev. ed. LC 94-49360. (Illus.). 240p. 1995. pap. text 8.95 (*0-486-68643-4*) Dover.

Bellman, Richard, ed. see Symposium on Applied Mathematics Staff.

Bellman, Richard E. Invariant Imbedding & Time-Dependent Transport Processes. LC 64-9242. (Modern Analytic & Computational Methods in Science & Mathematics Ser.: Vol. 2). 275p. reprint ed. pap. 85.30 (*0-608-30946-X*, 200764100065) Bks Demand.

— Some Vistas of Modern Mathematics: Dynamic Programming, Invariant Imbedding & the Mathematical Biosciences. LC 68-12974. 151p. reprint ed. pap. 46.90 (*0-608-30434-4*, 200431500041) Bks Demand.

Bellman, Richard Ernest. Eye of the Hurricane: An Autobiography. 344p. (C). 1984. text 47.00 (*9971-966-00-X*); pap. text 24.00 (*9971-966-01-8*) World Scientific Pub.

— Mathematical Methods in Medicine. (Series in Modern Applied Mathematics: Vol. 1). 268p. 1983. text 52.00 (*9971-950-20-0*); pap. text 30.00 (*9971-950-21-9*) World Scientific Pub.

— Selective Computation. (Series in Modern Applied Mathematics: Vol. 4). 250p. (C). 1985. text 46.00 (*9971-966-86-7*) World Scientific Pub.

Bellman, Richard Ernest & Adomian, George. Partial Differential Equations. 312p. 1984. text 154.50 (*90-277-1681-1*) Kluwer Academic.

Bellman, Richard Ernest & Cooke, Kenneth L. Asymptotic Behavior of Solutions of Differential-Difference Equations. LC 52-42839. (American Mathematical Society Ser.: No. 35). 97p. reprint ed. pap. 30.10 (*0-608-09183-9*, 205268700002) Bks Demand.

Bellman, Richard Ernest & Kalaba, Robert. Dynamic Programming & Modern Control. 1966. text 86.00 (*0-12-084856-2*) Acad Pr.

Bellman, Richard Ernest & Roth, R. S. The Laplace Transform. (Series in Modern Applied Mathematics: Vol. 3). 176p. 1984. text 33.00 (*9971-966-73-5*) World Scientific Pub.

— Quasilinearization & the Identification Problem. (Series in Modern Applied Mathematics: Vol. 2). 260p. 1983. text 48.00 (*9971-950-44-8*); pap. text 26.00 (*9971-950-45-6*) World Scientific Pub.

Bellman, Richard Ernest & Roth, Robert S. Methods in Approximation. (Mathematics & Its Applications Ser.). 1986. text 137.50 (*90-277-2188-2*) Kluwer Academic.

Bellman, Richard Ernest & Vasudevan, R. Wave Propagation: An Invariant Imbedding Approach. 1986. text 176.50 (*90-277-1766-4*) Kluwer Academic.

Bellman, Richard Ernest, et al. Mathematical Aspects of Scheduling & Applications. LC 81-15809. (International Series in Modern Applied Mathematics & Computer Science: Vol. 4). (Illus.). 329p. 1982. text 155.00 (*0-08-026477-8*, Pub. by Pergamon Repr) Franklin.

Bellman, Sacha D., jt. auth. see Winternitz, Felix.

Bellman, Steven, jt. auth. see Sann, Alexander.

Bellman, Willard F., ed. Scene Design. (C). 1994. text. write for info. (*0-06-501335-2*) Addison-Wesley.

Bellmann, Klaus, jt. auth. see Hhuttl, R. F.

An Asterisk (*) at the beginning of an entry indicates that the title is appearing for the first time.

Bellmer, Hans & Eluard, Paul. The Doll & the Doll at Play. Bennett, Guy, tr. (Green Integer Bks.: No. 21). 48p. 1999. pap. 10.95 (*1-892295-09-1*, Pub. by Green Integer) Consort Bk Sales.

Bellmon, Henry & Bellmon, Pat C. The Life & Times of Henry Bellmon. LC 91-73539. (Illus.). 381p. 1995. 3.00 (*0-933031-47-5*) Coun Oak Bks.

Bellmon, Pat C., jt. auth. see Bellmon, Henry.

Bello. Elementary Algebra. (Miscellaneous/Catalogs). (C). 1997. pap., student ed. 23.25 (*0-314-20692-2*) Wadsworth Pub.

— Elementary Algebra. 500p. 1997. write for info. (*0-314-20026-6*) West Pub.

— Intermediate Algebra. (Mathematics Ser.). 1997. student ed. 22.25 (*0-314-21016-4*) Wadsworth Pub.

— Intermediate Algebra: A Graphing Approach. (Mathematics Ser.). 1998. student ed. 20.00 (*0-314-20693-0*) Brooks-Cole.

— People & Power in the Pacific: The Struggle for the Post-Cold War Order. LC 92-29810. (Transnational Institute Ser.). 147p. (C). 44.95 (*0-7453-0697-7*, Pub. by Pluto GBR) Stylus Pub VA.

***Bello.** Siamese Tragedy. 29p. 2000. text 65.00 (*1-85649-663-5*, Pub. by Zed Books) St Martin.

Bello, Andres. Selected Writings of Andres Bello. Jaksic, Ivan et al, eds. Lopez-Morillas, Frances, tr. LC 96-44127. (Library of Latin America). 352p. 1997. 30.00 (*0-19-510545-1*) OUP.

Bello, Andres. Selected Writings of Andres Bello. Jaksic, Ivan, ed. Lopez-Morillas, Frances, tr. (Library of Latin America). 368p. 1998. reprint ed. pap. 14.95 (*0-19-510546-X*) OUP.

Bello, Angela A., ed. The Great Chain of Being & Italian Phenomenology. 366p. 1981. lib. bdg. 176.50 (*90-277-1071-6*, D Reidel) Kluwer Academic.

***Bello, Antonio.** Mary: Human & Holy. Duggan, Paul, tr. 96p. 2000. pap. 5.95 (*0-8198-4810-7*) Pauline Bks.

Bello, Emmanuel G., ed. Essays in Honor of Judge Taslim Olawale Elias: Contemporary International Law & African Law, Set, Vols. I & II. 976p. (C). 1992. lib. bdg. 301.50 (*0-7923-1426-3*) Kluwer Academic.

Bello, I. A. The Medieval Islamic Controversy Between Philosophy & Orthodoxy. 187p. 1996. 40.00 (*0-614-21183-2*, 771) Kazi Pubns.

Bello, Ignacio. Elementary Algebra. LC 96-9904. 500p. 1997. mass mkt. 75.95 (*0-314-06857-0*) West Pub.

— Intermediate Algebra. LC 96-9902. 1997. mass mkt. 76.95 (*0-314-06858-9*) West Pub.

— Intermediate Algebra: A Graphing Approach. LC 96-9903. 1997. mass mkt. 76.95 (*0-314-06844-9*) West Pub.

Bello, Ignacio & Britton, Jack R. Topics in Contemporary Mathematics. 5th ed. 896p. (C). 1993. text 64.36 (*0-669-28957-4*); teacher ed. 2.66 (*0-669-28958-2*); student ed. 24.36 (*0-669-28959-0*); student ed. write for info. (*0-669-28960-4*) HM Trade Div.

— Topics in Contemporary Mathematics. 6th ed. 800p. (C). 1997. text 64.36 (*0-669-41784-X*) HM Trade Div.

— Topics in Contemporary Mathematics. 6th ed. (C). 1997. pap. text, student ed. 24.36 (*0-669-41786-6*) HM Trade Div.

Bello, Jane H., ed. see Halsman, Philippe.

Bello, Joan. The Benefits of Marijuana: Physical, Psychological & Spiritual. Mount, Guy, ed. 160p. 1996. per. 12.95 (*0-9604462-9-X*) Sweetlight.

— The Benefits of Marijuana: Physical, Psychological & Spiritual. 2nd rev. unabridged ed. (Illus.). 121p. 1997. pap. 12.95 (*0-9660988-0-3*) Lifeservs Pr.

Bello, Jose M. History of Modern Brazil, 1889 to 1964. Taylor, James L., tr. xix, 362p. 1966. pap. 17.95 (*0-8047-0240-3*) Stanford U Pr.

Bello, Joseph Y. Basic Principles of Teaching. LC LA1631.B44. (Education in Africa Ser.). 183p. reprint ed. pap. 56.80 (*0-8357-5986-5*, 202964300062) Bks Demand.

Bello, Judith H. & Holmer, Alan F. Guide to the United States - Canada Free Trade Agreement. 1379p. 1990. ring bd. 116.00 (*0-13-444209-1*) Aspen Law.

Bello, M. A. Namt: National Advanced Manufacturing Testbed, Toward 21st Century Information-Based Manufacturing. 24p. 1997. pap. 2.50 (*0-16-054726-1*) USGPO.

Bello, Mark & Baum, Michael A. Setting Priorities & Measuring Results at the National Institute of Standards & Technology. 38p. (Orig.). (C). 1995. pap. text 25.00 (*0-7881-2326-2*) DIANE Pub.

Bello, Nino L. The Incredible Book of Vatican Facts & Papal Curiosities: A Treasury of Trivia. LC 97-34251. 256p. (Orig.). 1998. pap. 12.95 (*0-7648-0171-6*) Liguori Pubns.

Bello, Nino Lo, see Lo Bello, Nino.

Bello, Rosario De, see De Bello, Rosario.

Bello, Steve, ed. see Halsman, Philippe.

***Bello, Walden.** Dark Victory. 172p. 1999. 65.00 (*0-7453-1466-X*, Pub. by Pluto GBR) Stylus Pub VA.

Bello, Walden. Siamese Tragedy: Development & Disintegration in Modern Thailand. LC 98-30887. 256p. 1998. pap. 19.95 (*0-935028-74-9*) Inst Food & Develop.

Bello, Walden & Rosenfeld, Stephanie. Dragons in Distress: Asia's Miracle Economies in Crisis. 488p. (Orig.). (C). 1990. pap. 12.95 (*0-935028-55-2*) Inst Food & Develop.

Bello, Walden F., et al. Dark Victory: The U. S., Structural Adjustment, & Global Poverty. LC 93-36220. (Transnational Institute Ser.). 128p. (C). 49.95 (*0-7453-0833-3*, Pub. by Pluto GBR) Stylus Pub VA.

— Dark Victory: The United States & Global Poverty. 160p. (C). 1994. pap. text 14.95 (*0-935028-61-7*) Inst Food & Develop.

Belloc, D. Suzanne. (FRE.). 160p. 1990. pap. 10.95 (*0-7859-2134-6*, 2070382168) Fr & Eur.

Belloc, Denis. Neons. Rodarmor, William, tr. from FRE. 1991. 18.95 (*0-87923-858-5*) Godine.

Belloc, Hilaire. At the Sign of the Lion, & Other Essays. LC 67-22071. (Essay Index Reprint Ser.). 1977. 15.95 (*0-8369-1318-3*) Ayer.

— Avril. (Essay Index Reprint Ser.). 1977. 21.95 (*0-8369-1339-6*) Ayer.

— Cautionary Verses. LC 97-60839. (Public Library Ser.). 192p. 1997. pap. 4.95 (*0-87243-234-3*) Templegate.

— Characters of the Reformation. LC 72-121449. (Essay Index Reprint Ser.). 1977. 26.95 (*0-8369-1696-4*) Ayer.

— Characters of the Reformation: Historical Portraits of the 23 Men & Women & their Place in the Great Religious Revolution of the 16th Century. LC 92-60961. 208p. 1992. reprint ed. pap. 12.00 (*0-89555-466-6*) TAN Bks Pubs.

— The Contrast: Foreign Travelers in America, 1810-1935 Ser. LC 73-13117. 278p. 1974. reprint ed. 24.95 (*0-405-05442-4*) Ayer.

— Conversation with a Cat & Others. LC 69-18920. (Essay Index Reprint Ser.). 1977. 19.95 (*0-8369-0035-9*) Ayer.

— Conversation with an Angel, & Other Essays. LC 68-16907. (Essay Index Reprint Ser.). 1977. reprint ed. 23.95 (*0-8369-0187-8*) Ayer.

— Cranmer. LC 72-4495. (English Biography Ser.: No. 31). 1972. reprint ed. lib. bdg. 75.00 (*0-8383-1610-7*) M S G Haskell Hse.

— The Crisis of Civilization. LC 73-114465. 245p. 1973. reprint ed. lib. bdg. 35.00 (*0-8371-4761-1*, BECC, Greenwood Pr) Greenwood.

— The Crisis of Civilization. LC 92-60965. 208p. 1992. reprint ed. pap. 12.00 (*0-89555-462-3*) TAN Bks Pubs.

— The Crusades: The World's Debate. LC 92-60960. 250p. 1992. reprint ed. pap. 13.50 (*0-89555-467-4*) TAN Bks Pubs.

— Danton: A Study. LC 70-100534. (Illus.). reprint ed. 46.50 (*0-404-00737-6*) AMS Pr.

— Elizabethan Commentary. LC 67-31526. (Studies in Irish Literature: No. 16). 1969. reprint ed. lib. bdg. 75.00 (*0-8383-0707-8*) M S G Haskell Hse.

— Emmanuel Burden, Merchant of Thames St. in the City of London, Exporter of Hardware. LC 75-41024. (BCL Ser. II). reprint ed. 44.50 (*0-404-14642-2*) AMS Pr.

— Essays of a Catholic. LC 67-26713. (Essay Index Reprint Ser.). 1977. 20.95 (*0-8369-0188-6*) Ayer.

— Essays of a Catholic. LC 92-60964. 245p. 1923. reprint ed. pap. 13.00 (*0-89555-463-1*) TAN Bks Pubs.

— Esto Perpetua: Algerian Studies & Impressions. LC 79-95146. (BCL Ser. I). reprint ed. 39.50 (*0-404-00738-4*) AMS Pr.

— Europe & the Faith. LC 92-60963. 191p. 1992. reprint ed. pap. 11.00 (*0-89555-464-X*) TAN Bks Pubs.

— First & Last. LC 68-57302. (Essay Index Reprint Ser.). 1977. 20.95 (*0-8369-0059-6*) Ayer.

***Belloc, Hilaire.** The Girondin. 252p. 2000. pap. 9.95 (*0-594-00189-7*) Eightn Hundrd.

Belloc, Hilaire. Great Heresies. LC 68-16908. (Essay Index Reprint Ser.). 1977. 24.95 (*0-8369-0189-4*) Ayer.

— The Great Heresies. LC 91-66422. 161p. 1993. reprint ed. pap. 9.00 (*0-89555-475-5*) TAN Bks Pubs.

— The Green Overcoat. LC 70-165614. (Select Bibliographies Reprint Ser.). 1977. reprint ed. 21.95 (*0-8369-5921-3*) Ayer.

— Hilaire Belloc: (A Collection of Poems) Thompson, Edward, ed. (Augustan Books of Modern Poetry Ser.). 36p. 1998. reprint ed. 10.00 (*0-89904-734-3*, Silhouette Imprints); reprint ed. pap. 5.00 (*0-89904-735-1*, Silhouette Imprints) Crumb Elbow Pub.

— Hills & the Sea. (Marlboro Travel Ser.). 220p. 1996. pap. 14.95 (*0-8101-6009-9*) Northwestern U Pr.

— Hills & the Sea. LC 71-109709. 314p. 1971. reprint ed. lib. bdg. 38.50 (*0-8371-4200-8*, BEHS, Greenwood Pr) Greenwood.

— How the Reformation Happened. 1990. 18.00 (*0-8446-0483-6*) Peter Smith.

— How the Reformation Happened. LC 92-60962. 180p. 1992. reprint ed. pap. 10.00 (*0-89555-465-8*) TAN Bks Pubs.

— James the Second. LC 73-165615. (Select Bibliographies Reprint Ser.). 1977. reprint ed. 23.95 (*0-8369-5922-1*) Ayer.

— The Jews. 1981. lib. bdg. 250.00 (*0-8490-3220-2*) Gordon Pr.

Belloc, Hilaire. The Jews. unabridged ed. 363p. reprint ed. pap. 12.00 (*0-945001-44-4*) GSG & Assocs.

Belloc, Hilaire. Jim, Who Ran Away from His Nurse, & Was Eaten by a Lion. (Joy Street Bks.). (Illus.). (J). (gr. 2 up). 1987. mass mkt. 4.95 (*0-316-13816-9*) Little.

Belloc, Hilaire. Joan of Arc. 85p. 1997. reprint ed. 16.00 (*0-911845-45-3*) Neumann Pr.

Belloc, Hilaire. Marie Antoinette. LC 70-37871. (Select Bibliographies Reprint Ser.). 1977. reprint ed. 37.95 (*0-8369-6708-9*) Ayer.

— The Mercy of Allah. LC 91-72258. 334p. 1991. reprint ed. pap. 19.00 (*0-87034-100-6*) Fraser Pub Co.

— Miniatures of French History. 300p. 1990. reprint ed. pap. 14.95 (*0-89385-035-7*) Sugden.

— On. LC 68-28742. (Essay Index Reprint Ser.). 1977. 19.95 (*0-8369-0190-8*) Ayer.

— On Anything. LC 79-76893. (Essay Index Reprint Ser.). 1977. 20.95 (*0-8369-0003-0*) Mnemosyne Pub.

— On Everything. LC 70-128208. (Essay Index Reprint Ser.). 1977. 21.95 (*0-8369-1865-7*) Ayer.

— On Nothing & Kindred Subjects. LC 70-104994. (Essay Index Reprint Ser.). 1977. 21.95 (*0-8369-1448-1*) Ayer.

— On Something. LC 68-8437. (Essay Index Reprint Ser.). 1977. reprint ed. 18.95 (*0-8369-0191-6*) Ayer.

— The Path to Rome. LC 87-36772. 267p. 1987. pap. 8.95 (*0-89526-784-5*) Regnery Pub.

— Places. LC 78-117759. (Essay Index Reprint Ser.). 1977. 20.95 (*0-8369-2037-6*) Ayer.

— Robespierre: A Study. LC 72-8441. (Select Bibliographies Reprint Ser.). 1977. reprint ed. 28.95 (*0-8369-6964-2*) Ayer.

— The Servile State. LC 77-2914. 1977. 14.00 (*0-913966-31-2*); pap. 6.00 (*0-913966-32-0*) Liberty Fund.

— Short Talks with the Dead, & Others. LC 67-23175. (Essay Index Reprint Ser.). 1977. 20.95 (*0-8369-0192-4*) Ayer.

— Silence of the Sea. LC 74-107682. (Essay Index Reprint Ser.). 1977. 18.95 (*0-8369-2038-4*) Ayer.

— Survivals & New Arrivals: The Old & New Enemies of the Catholic Church. LC 91-67652. 167p. 1993. pap. 9.00 (*0-89555-454-2*) TAN Bks Pubs.

— This & That & the Other. LC 68-22903. (Essay Index Reprint Ser.). 1977. reprint ed. 23.95 (*0-8369-0193-2*) Ayer.

— Towns of Destiny. LC 72-101273. (BCL Ser. I). (Illus.). reprint ed. 44.50 (*0-404-00745-7*) AMS Pr.

— William the Conqueror. LC 92-60959. 76p. 1992. pap. 7.00 (*0-89555-468-2*) TAN Bks Pubs.

***Belloc, Hilarie.** Songs of Power. LC 99-36645. 208p. (J). (gr. 5-9). 2000. lib. bdg. 16.49 (*0-7868-2487-5*, Pub. by Disney Pr) Little.

Belloc, Hilarie. Songs of Power. LC 99-36645. 224p. (J). (gr. 5-9). 2000. 15.99 (*0-7868-0561-7*) Little.

Bellocq, Pieape. 40 Years of Peb: The Racing World in Sketch & Caricature. (Illus.). 224p. 1995. 59.95 (*0-9648493-0-5*) Daily Racing.

Bellofiore, R. Marxian Economics Vol. II: A Reappraisal - Profits, Prices, & Dynamics. LC 97-17608. 304p. 1998. text 79.95 (*0-312-17665-1*) St Martin.

***Bellofiore, R. & Ferri, Piero.** Financial Fragility & Investment in the Capitalist Economy: The Economic Legacy of Hyman Minsky, Volume II. LC 00-34822. 2000. write for info. (*1-84064-359-5*) E Elgar.

— Financial Keynesianism & Market Instability: The Economic Legacy of Hyman Minsky, Volume I. LC 00-34820. 2000. write for info. (*1-84064-358-7*) E Elgar.

Bellofiore, Riccardo. Marxian Economics Vol. 1: A Reappraisal - Essays on Volume III of Capital; Method, Value, & Money. LC 97-17608. 276p. 1998. text 79.95 (*0-312-17664-3*) St Martin.

Bellofiore, Riccardo, ed. Global Money, Capital Restructuring & the Changing Patterns of Labour. LC 99-14861. 256p. 1999. 85.00 (*1-85898-848-9*) E Elgar.

Belloise, Michael J. Mark & His Friend. LC 94-77012. 269p. 1994. 18.95 (*0-9641541-0-2*) Lieto Pubng.

Belloit, jt. auth. see Radulovich.

Belloli, et al. Johnson, Kaufman, Coate: Partners in the California Style. (Illus.). 144p. 1992. 20.00 (*0-88496-353-5*) Williamson Gallery.

***Belloli, Andrea P.** Exploring World Art. LC 99-26521. (Getty Trust Publications). (Illus.). 120p. (YA). (gr. 5 up). 1999. 24.95 (*0-89236-510-2*, Pub. by J P Getty Trust) OUP.

Belloli, Andrea P. Make Your Own Museum: An Activity Kit for Children. (Getty Trust Publications). (Illus.). 44p. 1999. boxed set 19.95 (*0-89236-297-9*) OUP.

Belloli, Andrea P., jt. ed. see Brougher, Nora H.

Belloli, Andrea P., ed. see Nodal, Al & De Bretteville, Sheila L.

Belloli, G. P., ed. Pediatric Cardiology & Cardiosurgery (Modern Problems in Pediatrics Ser.: Vol. 22). (Illus.). viii, 216p. 1983. pap. 143.50 (*3-8055-3593-7*) S Karger.

Belloli, Jay. Innovations: Contemporary Home Environments. LC 73-93187. (Illus.). 38p. 1973. 6.00 (*0-686-99821-9*) Mus Contemp Art.

— Ron Cooper. (Illus.). 24p. 1973. 6.00 (*0-686-99822-7*) Mus Contemp Art.

Belloli, Jay, ed. Myron Hunt, 1868 to 1952: The Search for a Regional Architecture. LC 84-81891. (California Architecture & Architects Ser.: No. 4). (Illus.). 120p. (Orig.). 1984. pap. 24.50 (*0-912158-90-5*) Hennessey.

***Belloli, Jay, et al.** Radical Past: Contemporary Art & Music in Pasadena, 1960-1974. (Illus.). 144p. 1999. 35.00 (*1-893900-00-2*, Pub. by Armory Ctr Arts) RAM Publications.

Bellomo, Charles & Lynch, John F. Crash, Fire & Rescue Handbook. LC 92-46755. (Training Manual Ser.). 94p. (Orig.). 1982. pap. text 15.50 (*0-89100-250-2*, JS312675) Jeppesen Sanderson.

Bellomo, Manlio. The Common Legal Past of Europe, 1000-1800. Cochrane, Lydia G., tr. from ITA. LC 94-17652. (Studies in Medieval & Early Modern Canon Law). 252p. 1995. 38.95 (*0-8132-0813-0*); pap. 18.95 (*0-8132-0814-9*) Cath U Pr.

***Bellomo, Michael.** Debian GNU/Linux for Dummies. (For Dummies Ser.). (Illus.). 384p. 2000. pap. 24.99 incl. cd-rom (*0-7645-0713-3*) IDG Bks.

— Linux Administration for Dummies. (For Dummies). 408p. 1999. pap. 24.99 incl. cd-rom (*0-7645-0589-0*) IDG Bks.

— Master Red Hat Linux. 612p. 2000. pap. 34.99 incl. cd-rom (*0-7645-3436-X*) IDG Bks.

— Windows 2000 Administration for Dummies. 408p. 2000. pap. 24.99 (*0-7645-0682-X*) IDG Bks.

Bellomo, N., ed. Lecture Notes on the Mathematical Theory of the Boltzmann Equation. LC 95-10544. (Series on Advances in Mathematics for Applied Sciences). 250p. 1995. text 71.00 (*981-02-2166-5*) World Scientific Pub.

Bellomo, N. & Casiati, F., eds. Nonlinear Stochastic Mechanics: IUTAM Symposium, Turin, 1991. LC 92-20009. (International Union of Theoretical & Applied Mechanics Symposia Ser.). xiii, 552p. 1992. 199.95 (*0-387-55545-5*) Spr-Verlag.

Bellomo, N. & Riganti, R., eds. Nonlinear Stochastic Systems in Physics & Mechanics. 260p. 1987. text 49.00 (*9971-5-0249-6*) World Scientific Pub.

***Bellomo, N. & Schiavo, Mauro L.** Lecture Notes on the Mathematical Theory of Generalized Boltzmann Models. LC 99-40190. (Series on Advances in Mathematics for Applied Sciences). 1999. pap. write for info. (*981-02-4078-3*) World Scientific Pub.

Bellomo, N., et al. Mathematical Topics in Nonlinear Kinetic Theory. 240p. 1989. text 61.00 (*9971-5-0702-1*) World Scientific Pub.

— Mathematical Topics in Nonlinear Kinetic Theory II. (Series on Advances in Mathematics for Applied Sciences: Vol. 1). 224p. 1991. text 55.00 (*981-02-0447-7*); pap. text 32.00 (*981-02-0448-5*) World Scientific Pub.

— Nonlinear Stochastic Evolution Problems in Applied Sciences. LC 92-35069. (Mathematics & Its Applications Ser.: Vol. 82). (C). 1992. text 138.00 (*0-7923-2042-5*) Kluwer Academic.

Bellomo, N., jt. ed. see Adam, J. A.

Bellomo, N., ed. see Movchan, A. B. & Movchan, N. V.

Bellomo, Nicola. Modelling Methods & Scientific Computation. 512p. 1994. boxed set 89.95 (*0-8493-8331-5*) CRC Pr.

Bellomo, Nicola, ed. Modeling & Simulation in Science, Engineering & Technology. Date not set. write for info. (*0-614-26638-6*) Birkhauser.

***Bellomo, Nicola & Pulvirenti, M., eds.** Modeling in Applied Sciences: A Kinetic Theory Approach. LC 99-57789. (Modeling & Simulation in Science, Engineering & Technology Ser.). (Illus.). 464p. 1999. 79.95 (*0-8176-4102-5*, Pub. by Birkhauser) Spr-Verlag.

Bellomo, Nicola, et al. Mechanics & Dynamical Systems with Mathematica. LC 99-14394. (Modeling & Simulation in Science, Engineering & Technology Ser.). 400p. (C). 1999. 59.95 (*0-8176-4007-X*) Birkhauser.

Bellomo, Rinaldo & Ronco, C., eds. Acute Renal Failure in the Critically Ill. LC 94-42307. (Update in Intensive Care & Emergency Medicine Ser.: Vol. 20). 1995. 131.00 (*3-540-58401-3*) Spr-Verlag.

Bellomo, Rinaldo, jt. ed. see Ronco, Claudio.

Bellon, Bernard P. Mercedes in Peace & War: German Automobile Workers, 1903-1945. (Illus.). 420p. 1992. pap. text 21.00 (*0-231-06857-3*) Col U Pr.

Bellon, Bertrand & Niosi, Jorge. The Decline of the American Economy. Chodos, Robert, tr. from FRE. 242p. 1988. 45.99 (*0-921689-01-2*, Pub. by Black Rose); pap. 16.99 (*0-921689-00-4*, Pub. by Black Rose) Consort Bk Sales.

Bellon, Eugen. Scattered to All the Winds, 1685-1720: 1685-1720, Migrations of the Dauphine French Hugeunots into Italy, Switzerland, & Germany. Schalliol, Willis L., ed. Gautschi, Erika, tr. from GER. LC 83-70252. Orig. Title: Zerstreut in alle Winde. (Illus.). 267p. (Orig.). 1983. reprint ed. pap. 21.10 (*0-9605732-1-6*) Belle Pubns.

Bellon, Jerry J. Teaching from Research Knowledge. (C). 1991. pap. text 38.20 (*0-675-20639-1*, Merrill Coll) P-H.

Bellon, S. Vic, jt. ed. see Corberan, V. Cortes.

Bellori, Giovanni P. The Lives of Annibale & Agostino Carracci. LC 67-16194. 1968. 28.50 (*0-271-73128-1*) Pa St U Pr.

— Le Vite de Pittori, Scvltori et Architetti Moderni. fac. ed. (Documents of Art & Architectural History Ser. 1: Vol. 4). (ITA., Illus.). 1980. lib. bdg. 50.00 (*0-89371-104-7*) Broude Intl Edns.

Bellori, Giovanni P., jt. auth. see Bartoli, Pietro S.

Bellos, David. Balzac: "Old Goriot" (Landmarks of World Literature Ser.). 124p. 1987. pap. text 11.95 (*0-521-31634-0*) Cambridge U Pr.

— Balzac: "Old Goriot" (Landmarks of World Literature Ser.). 128p. 1987. text 34.95 (*0-521-32799-7*) Cambridge U Pr.

— Georges Perec, a Life in Words: A Biography. 832p. 1993. 45.00 (*0-87923-980-8*) Godine.

***Bellos, David.** Jacques Tati: His Life & Art. (Illus.). 400p. 2000. 40.00 (*1-86046-651-6*) Harvill Press.

Bellos, David, tr. see Ifrah, Georges.

Bellos, David, tr. see Kadare, Ismail.

Bellos, David, tr. see Maspero, Francois.

Bellos, David, tr. see Perec, Georges.

Bellosi, Alida, et al. Interfacial Science in Ceramic Joining: Proceedings of the NATO Advanced Research Workshop on Interfacial Science in Ceramic Joining, Bled, Slovenia, November 12-15, 1997. LC 98-11621. (NATO ASI Ser.). 11p. 1998. write for info. (*0-7923-5221-1*) Kluwer Academic.

Bellosi, Luciano. Cimabue. LC 98-17963. (Illus.). 304p. 1999. 125.00 (*0-7892-0466-5*) Abbeville Pr.

— Duccio: The Maesta. LC 99-70948. (Illus.). 363p. 1999. 120.00 (*0-500-23771-9*, Pub. by Thames Hudson) Norton.

— Giotto. (Grandes Maestros del Arte Ser.). (SPA., Illus.). 80p. pap. 12.99 (*1-878351-28-1*) Riverside NY.

— Giotto: Giotto: Complete Works. rev. ed. LC 98-158566. (Library of Great Masters). (Illus.). 80p. (Orig.). 1982. pap. 12.99 (*1-878351-03-6*) Riverside NY.

Bellot, Hugh H. American History & American Historians. LC 73-19305. (Illus.). 336p. (C). 1974. reprint ed. lib. bdg. 35.00 (*0-8371-7325-6*, BEAH, Greenwood Pr) Greenwood.

Bellot, Hugh H., jt. auth. see Foote, John A.

***Bellot, Hugh H. L.** Temple of the Inner Temple (1914) 242p. 1999. reprint ed. pap. 16.95 (*0-7661-0744-2*) Kessinger Pub.

Bellot, Leland J. William Knox: The Life & Thought of an Eighteenth-Century Imperialist. LC 76-44006. 276p. pap. 85.60 (*0-8357-7725-1*, 203608200002) Bks Demand.

Belloti, Lauren G., jt. auth. see Nogales, Ana.

B

An Asterisk (*) at the beginning of an entry indicates that the title is appearing for the first time.

Bellotti. Proceedings of the Fourth School on Non-Accelerator Particle Astophysics: ICTP, Trieste, Italy, 17-28 July 1995. LC 96-2908. 552p. 1996. write for info. (*981-02-2688-8*) World Scientific Pub.

Bellotti, Bob. The Points Created Pro Basketball Book, 1992-93. 275p. (Orig.). 1992. pap. 15.95 (*0-9621147-3-1*) Night Work Pub.

— The Points Created Pro Basketball Book, 1993-94. 360p. (Orig.). 1993. pap. 15.95 (*0-9621147-4-X*) Night Work Pub.

Bellotti, Laura G., jt. auth. see Levin, Laurie.

Bellotti, Robert. Basketball's Hidden Game: Points Created, Boxscore Defense & Other Revelations. 270p. (Orig.). 1988. pap. 12.95 (*0-9621147-0-7*) Night Work Pub.

Bellotti, Robert S. Bob Bellotti's Basketball Analyst: New Ideas about an Old Game. 275p. (Orig.). 1990. pap. 13.95 (*0-9621147-1-5*) Night Work Pub.

— The Points Created Pro Basketball Book, 1991-92. 350p. (Orig.). 1991. pap. 14.95 (*0-9621147-2-3*) Night Work Pub.

***Bellour, Raymond.** The Analysis of Film. Penley, Constance, ed. LC 99-45486. (Illus.). 352p. 2000. 49.95 (*0-253-33700-3*) Ind U Pr.

Bellour, Raymond & Hanhardt, John G. Eye for I: Video Self-Portraits. LC 90-70089. 48p. 1990. pap. 10.00 (*0-916365-14-X*) Ind Curators.

Bellour, Raymond, ed. see Bronte, Emily Jane.

Bellovin, Steven M., jt. auth. see Cheswick, William.

Bellow, Gary. Law Stories: The Law As Seen from the Outside. 1994. 25.00 (*1-56584-091-7*, Pub. by New Press NY) Norton.

Bellow, Gary & Minow, Martha, eds. Law Stories. LC 96-16551. (Law, Meaning, & Violence Ser.). 248p. (C). 1996. text 37.50 (*0-472-10718-6*, 10718) U of Mich Pr.

— Law Stories. (Law, Meaning, & Violence Ser.). 248p. (C). 1998. pap. text 20.95 (*0-472-08519-0*, 08519) U of Mich Pr.

Bellow, Gary & Moulton, Bea. The Lawyering Process: Ethics & Professional Responsibility. LC 81-67777. (University Casebook Ser.). 460p. 1991. reprint ed. pap. text 18.50 (*0-88277-038-1*) Foundation Pr.

— The Lawyering Process: Negotiation. LC 81-67776. (University Casebook Ser.). 297p. (C). 1988. reprint ed. pap. text 15.25 (*0-88277-039-X*) Foundation Pr.

— The Lawyering Process: Preparing & Presenting the Case. LC 81-67655. (University Casebook Ser.). 516p. (C). 1981. pap. text 18.95 (*0-88277-040-3*) Foundation Pr.

Bellow, Gay & Moulton. The Lawyering Process. 1978. text 38.00 (*0-88277-448-4*) Foundation Pr.

Bellow, Saul. The Actual. LC 96-51173. 112p. 1998. pap. 9.95 (*0-14-027499-5*) Viking Penguin.

— The Adventures of Augie March. 656p. 1995. 20.00 (*0-679-44460-2*) Knopf.

— The Adventures of Augie March. LC 99-205952. 585p. 1999. pap. 14.95 (*0-14-028160-6*) Penguin Putnam.

— The Adventures of Augie March. 544p. 1996. pap. 13.95 (*0-14-018941-6*, Viking) Viking Penguin.

— The Dangling Man. 192p. 1996. pap. 12.95 (*0-14-018935-1*, Penguin Classics) Viking Penguin.

Bellow, Saul. The Dean's December. 346p. 1985. mass mkt. 4.50 (*0-671-60254-3*, WSP) PB.

Bellow, Saul. The Dean's December. LC 80-8705. 312p. 1998. pap. 13.95 (*0-14-018913-0*) Viking Penguin.

— Le Faiseur De Pluie. (FRE.). 480p. 1984. pap. 16.95 (*0-7859-1990-2*, 2070375390) Fr & Eur.

— Henderson the Rain King. 1996. pap. 13.95 (*0-14-018942-4*) Viking Penguin.

— Herzog. (FRE.). 544p. 1986. pap. 16.95 (*0-7859-2040-4*, 2070377512) Fr & Eur.

— Herzog. 352p. 1996. pap. 13.95 (*0-14-018943-2*, Viking) Viking Penguin.

— Him with His Foot in His Mouth: And Other Stories. LC 99-166191. 304p. 1998. pap. 14.95 (*0-14-118023-4*) Viking Penguin.

— Humboldt's Gift. 1996. pap. 14.95 (*0-14-018944-0*) Viking Penguin.

— It All Adds Up: From the Dim Past to the Uncertain Future. 352p. 1995. pap. 12.95 (*0-14-023365-2*, Penguin Bks) Viking Penguin.

— Mr. Sammler's Planet. 352p. 1996. pap. 13.95 (*0-14-018936-X*, Penguin Classics) Viking Penguin.

— More Die of Heartbreak. 336p. 1997. pap. 11.95 (*0-385-31877-4*) Doubleday.

— Mosby's Memoirs & Other Stories. 1996. pap. 11.95 (*0-14-018945-9*) Viking Penguin.

— Ravelstein. LC 99-56336. 240p. 2000. 24.95 (*0-670-84134-X*) Viking Penguin.

— Saul Bellow & the Struggle at the Center. Hollahan, Eugene, ed. LC 91-58150. (Georgia State Literary Studies: No. 12). 1992. 55.00 (*0-404-63212-2*) AMS Pr.

— Seize the Day. LC 96-145374. 144p. 1996. pap. 10.95 (*0-14-018937-8*, Penguin Classics) Viking Penguin.

— Summations. (Chapbooks in Literature Ser.). 29p. 1987. pap. text 5.00 (*0-9614940-9-3*) Bennington Coll.

— A Theft. 1989. pap. 6.95 (*0-318-41472-4*, Penguin Bks) Viking Penguin.

***Bellow, Saul.** To Jerusalem & Back: A Personal Account. LC 99-462349. 260p. 2000. 29.95 (*1-56000-441-X*) Transaction Pubs.

Bellow, Saul. To Jerusalem & Back: A Personal Account. 192p. 1998. pap. 13.95 (*0-14-118075-7*) Viking Penguin.

— The Victim. 288p. 1996. pap. 12.95 (*0-14-018938-6*) Viking Penguin.

***Bellows, Andy Masaki & McDougall, Marina, eds.** Science Is Fiction: The Films of Jean Painleve. LC 99-45932. (Illus.). 224p. 2000. 39.95 (*0-262-02472-1*) MIT Pr.

Bellows, Barbara L. Benevolence among Slaveholders: Assisting the Poor in Charleston, 1670-1860. LC 93-18057. 272p. (C). 1993. text 37.50 (*0-8071-1833-8*) La State U Pr.

Bellows, Barbara L., jt. auth. see Connelly, Thomas L.

Bellows, Cathy. The Grizzly Sisters. LC 90-38787. (Illus.). 32p. (J). (ps-3). 1991. text 14.95 (*0-02-709032-9*, Mac Bks Young Read) S&S Childrens.

Bellows, Dena K. & Lamb, Sandra C. Parties for Home & School: A Piece of Cake. (Illus.). 144p. (J). (ps-4). teacher ed. 8.99 (*0-86653-328-1*, GA647) Good Apple.

Bellows, George. Drawings of George Bellows. Morgan, Charles, ed. (Master Draughtsman Ser.). (Illus.). 48p. 1973. pap. 4.95 (*0-87505-153-7*) Borden.

Bellows, Grace. William Bellows of Gloucester, 1837-1942. (C). 1988. 78.00 (*0-900657-71-5*, Pub. by W Sessions) St Mut.

Bellows, Guy. Chemical Machining. 2nd ed. (Machining Process Ser.: MDC 82-102). (Illus.). 96p. 1982. pap. 12.50 (*0-936974-08-7*) Inst Adv Manuf.

— Low Stress Grinding. (Machining Process Ser.: MDC 83-103). (Illus.). 136p. 1983. pap. 17.50 (*0-936974-09-5*) Inst Adv Manuf.

Bellows, Henry A., tr. from ICE. The Poetic Edda. LC 91-39918. 472p. 1991. reprint ed. lib. bdg. 109.95 (*0-88946-783-8*) E Mellen.

Bellows, Jan. The Practice of Veterinary Dentistry: A Team Effort. LC 98-33711. (Illus.). 216p. (C). 1999. text 64.95 (*0-8138-2617-9*) Iowa St U Pr.

Bellows, Michael D., ed. Asia in the 21st Century: Evolving Strategic Priorities. 265p. (Orig.). (C). 1995. pap. text 45.00 (*0-7881-2352-1*) DIANE Pub.

Bellows, Thomas J. The People's Action Party of Singapore: Emergence of a Dominant Party System. LC 73-114788. (Monographs: No. 14). xii, 195p. 1970. 8.25 (*0-938692-15-1*) Yale U SE Asia.

Bellows, Thomas J., jt. auth. see Winter, Herbert R.

Bellows, Thomas S., jt. auth. see Van Driesche, Roy G.

Bellquist, John E. A Guide to Grammar & Usage for Psychology & Related Fields. 224p. 1993. 59.95 (*0-8058-1394-2*) L Erlbaum Assocs.

— A Guide to Grammar & Usage for Psychology & Related Fields. 224p. 1993. pap. 27.50 (*0-8058-1353-5*) L Erlbaum Assocs.

— A Guide to Grammar & Usage for Psychology & Related Fields. 1994. 12.00 (*1-56321-141-6*); 25.00 (*1-56321-142-4*) L Erlbaum Assocs.

— Strindberg As a Modern Poet: A Critical & Comparative Study. LC 86-4293. (University of California Publications in Modern Philology: No. 117). 201p. 1986. pap. 62.40 (*0-7837-7471-0*, 204919300010) Bks Demand.

Bellringer, Alan W. George Eliot. LC 92-40375. (Modern Novelists Ser.). 176p. 1993. text 24.95 (*0-312-09474-4*) St Martin.

***Bellringer, Paul.** Understanding Problem Gamblers. 220p. 1999. 55.00 (*1-85343-462-0*, Pub. by Free Assoc Bks); pap. 25.00 (*1-85343-463-9*, Pub. by Free Assoc Bks) Intl Spec Bk.

Bellrose, Frank C. Ducks, Geese & Swans of North America. rev. ed. LC 75-33962. (Illus.). 568p. 1981. 49.95 (*0-8117-0535-8*) Stackpole.

Bellrose, Frank C. & Holm, Daniel J. Ecology & Management of the Wood Duck. LC 93-30746. (Illus.). 636p. 1994. 59.95 (*0-8117-0605-2*) Stackpole.

Bellrose, Robert R. Woonsocket. LC 97-191352. (Images of America Ser.). 1997. pap. 16.99 (*0-7524-0585-3*) Arcadia Publng.

Belluardo, J., jt. ed. see Ashraf, Kazi Khaleed.

Bellucci, Elio C. The Hospitality Law Desk Reference. Preston, Jacqueline N., ed. 288p. (Orig.). 1994. pap. text 39.95 (*0-9630523-1-4*) Sternlite Corp.

Belluck, David, jt. auth. see Benjamin, Sally.

***Belluck, David A.** Practical Guide to Understanding, Managing & Reviewing Risk Assessment Reports. (Illus.). 350p. 1999. text 69.95 (*0-8493-4111-6*) CRC Pr.

Bellugi, Ursula, jt. auth. see Klima, Edward S.

Bellunce, Philip R. What Really Matters Is the Heart: A Psychologist Grieves His Mother's Death. (Illus.). 232p. 1998. pap. 20.00 (*0-9661666-0-4*) Bella-Tierra.

***Belluomini, Jenny.** Clean Needle Technique. LC 99-50659. 36p. 1999. pap. write for info. (*0-9673034-0-0*) Complmtry Medcne.

Belluomini, Michele A. Translations from the Dark. LC 93-71697. 58p. (Orig.). 1993. pap. 8.95 (*0-9636617-3-6*) Blue Deer.

Bellury, Phillip R., jt. auth. see Whalen, Charles E., Jr.

Bellush, Bernard. Franklin D. Roosevelt as Governor of New York. LC 68-54257. (Columbia University. Studies in the Social Sciences: No. 585). reprint ed. 20.00 (*0-404-51585-1*) AMS Pr.

Bellush, Bernard, jt. auth. see Bellush, Jewel.

Bellush, Jewel & Bellush, Bernard. Union Power & New York: Victor Gotbaum & District Council 37. LC 84-15926. 474p. 1984. 65.00 (*0-275-91126-8*, C1126, Praeger Pubs) Greenwood.

Bellush, Jewel & Netzer, Dick, eds. Urban Politics, New York Style. LC 89-77913. 480p. (C). (gr. 13). 1990. pap. 35.95 (*0-87332-603-2*) M E Sharpe.

***Bellver, C. G.** Absence & Presence: Spanish Women Poets of the Twenties & Thirties. LC 00-23736. 2000. write for info. (*0-8387-5463-5*) Bucknell U Pr.

Bellville, Cheryl W. The Airplane Book. (Photo Bks.). (Illus.). 48p. (J). (ps-5). 1991. lib. bdg. 22.60 (*0-87614-686-8*, Carolrhoda) Lerner Pub.

— Airplane Book. (J). (ps-5). 1993. pap. 5.95 (*0-87614-618-3*, Carolrhoda) Lerner Pub.

— All Things Bright & Beautiful. 64p. (Orig.). 1984. 7.95 (*0-86683-722-1*, AY8363) Harper SF.

— Flying in a Hot Air Balloon. LC 92-37390. (J). (ps-5). 1993. lib. bdg. 22.60 (*0-87614-750-3*, Carolrhoda) Lerner Pub.

— Rodeo. (Photo Bks.). (Illus.). 32p. (J). (ps-5). 1985. reprint ed. pap. 5.95 (*0-87614-492-X*, Lerner Publctns) Lerner Pub.

Bellville, Cheryl Walsh, jt. auth. see Rendon, Marcie R.

Bellwood, Peter, ed. see Mabbett, Ian & Chandler, David.

Bellwood, Peter S. Prehistory of the Indo-Malaysian Archipelago. 1986. text 125.00 (*0-12-085370-1*) Acad Pr.

— Prehistory of the Indo-Malaysian Archipelago. rev. ed. LC 96-44400. (Illus.). 400p. 1997. text 58.00 (*0-8248-1883-0*); pap. text 32.95 (*0-8248-1907-1*) UH Pr.

Belly, J. M., et al, eds. Measure Theory & Its Applications. (Lecture Notes in Mathematics Ser.: Vol. 1033). 317p. 1983. 42.95 (*0-387-12703-8*) Spr-Verlag.

Belmaker, R. H. & Bannet, J., eds. New Directions in Tardive Dyskinesia Research. (Modern Problems of Pharmacopsychiatry Ser.: Vol. 21). (Illus.). vi, 222p. 1983. 109.75 (*3-8055-3735-2*) S Karger.

Belmaker, Robert H., jt. auth. see George, M. S.

Belman, Dale, et al, eds. Public Sector Employment in a Time of Transition. LC 97-171707. (ILR Press Book - IRRA Research Volume Ser.). 1996. pap. 24.95 (*0-913447-67-6*) Indus Relations Res.

Belmanns, Ronnie, jt. auth. see Hameyer, Kay.

Belmans, R., et al, eds. Vibrations & Audible Noise in Alternating Current Machines. (C). 1988. text 282.00 (*90-247-3732-X*) Kluwer Academic.

Belmans, R., jt. auth. see Nicolet, A.

Belmar, John J. Wisdom Wrapped in Experiences & Labeled Problems: Experiences of a Searching Soul. 200p. 1992. text 19.95 (*0-9632645-0-8*) Sci of Thought.

Belmo. Beatles Sgt. Pepper. (Making of Ser.). 1996. pap. 7.95 (*1-896522-28-9*) CN06.

— Psychedelia. (20th Century Rock & Roll Ser.). 1999. pap. text 13.95 (*1-896522-40-8*) CN06.

Belmont, Eleanor R. The Fabric of Memory. Baxter, Annette K., ed. LC 79-8775. (Signal Lives Ser.). (Illus.). 1980. reprint ed. lib. bdg. 37.95 (*0-405-12824-X*) Ayer.

Belmont Historic District Commission Project Staff. Belmont, Massachusetts: The Architecture & Development of the Town of Homes. (Illus.). 120p. 1984. write for info. (*0-318-57643-0*) Belmont Hist Dist Comm.

Belmont, Jim, et al. Crossroads of the West: A Photographic Look at Fifty Years of Railroading in Utah. LC 98-21849. (Illus.). 160p. 1998. 49.95 (*1-56342-008-2*) Pentrex Media.

Belmont, John S., ed. see Taylor, Walter H.

Belmont, Kathryn. The Fugitive Heart. 1994. per. 3.99 (*0-373-28822-0*) Harlequin Bks.

Belmont, Nicole. Arnold van Gennep: The Creator of French Ethnography. Coltman, Derek, tr. LC 78-8680. 1979. 17.00 (*0-226-04216-2*) U Ch Pr.

— Arnold Van Gennep: The Creator of French Ethnography. Coltman, Derek, tr. LC 78-8680. 173p. Date not set. reprint ed. pap. 53.70 (*0-608-20663-6*, 207210000003) Bks Demand.

Belmont, Perry. American Democrat: The Recollections of Perry Belmont. 2nd ed. LC 42-3269. reprint ed. 32.50 (*0-404-00746-5*) AMS Pr.

— Return to Secret Party Funds. LC 73-19127. (Politics & People Ser.). 258p. 1974. reprint ed. 20.95 (*0-405-05852-7*) Ayer.

Belmonte, C. & Cervero, F., eds. Neurobiology of Nociceptors. (Illus.). 542p. 1996. text 125.00 (*0-19-852334-3*) OUP.

Belmonte, Charles. Understanding the Mass. 1997. pap. 9.95 (*0-933932-89-8*) Scepter Pubs.

Belmonte, Frances R. Women & Health: An Annotated Bibliography. LC 97-22482. (Magill Bibliographies Ser.). 208p. 1997. 35.00 (*0-8108-3385-9*) Scarecrow.

Belmonte, Kevin, ed. see Wilberforce, William.

Belmonte, Matthew. Computer Science, & Why: Science, Language & Literature. 139p. (YA). (gr. 7-12). 1993. pap. 9.99 (*0-89824-530-3*, 5303) Trillium Pr.

Belmonte, Nina, tr. see Janicaud, Dominique.

Belmonte, Thomas. The Broken Fountain. LC 78-32167. 160p. 1980. pap. text 19.00 (*0-231-04543-3*) Col U Pr.

— The Broken Fountain. 2nd ed. 224p. 1989. pap. text 20.00 (*0-231-07059-4*) Col U Pr.

— The Broken Fountain. 2nd enl. ed. 1989. text 52.50 (*0-231-07058-6*) Col U Pr.

Belmonte, Val. Skill Progressions for Player & Coach. Seibel, Darryl, ed. (Illus.). 100p. (Orig.). 1997. pap. 1.00 (*1-890617-01-6*) USA Hockey.

Belmonte, Val & Gregus, Gary. Half Ice Drill Book. Seibel, Darryl, ed. (Illus.). 189p. (Orig.). 1997. pap. 12.95 (*1-890617-00-8*) USA Hockey.

Belmore, Florene, jt. ed. see Young-Ing, Greg.

Belnap, Gillian, ed. The Carnegie Museum of Art Collection Highlights. LC 95-32735. 1995. 45.00 (*0-88039-027-1*) Mus Art Carnegie.

Belnap, Jeffrey. Jose Marti's "Our America" From National to Hemispheric Cultural Studies. LC 98-23367. (New Americanists Ser.). 304p. 1998. pap. 17.95 (*0-8223-2265-X*) Duke.

Belnap, Jeffrey G. & Fernandez, Raul A. Jose Marti's "Our America" LC 98-23367. (New Americanists Ser.). 304p. 1999. 49.95 (*0-8223-2133-5*) Duke.

Belnap, Karma Smith. Not to Worry, Mom, I'm Okay: Lessons in Living from a Beloved Son. LC 96-13841. 1996. pap. 10.95 (*1-55503-931-6*, 01112317) Covenant Comms.

Belnap, Nuel D., Jr., jt. auth. see Anderson, Alan R.

Belnap, Nuel D., jt. auth. see Gupta, Anil.

Belnap, R. Kirk & Haeri, Niloofar. Structuralist Studies in Arabic Linguistics: Charles A. Ferguson's Papers, 1954-1994. LC 97-9136. (Studies in Semitic Languages & Linguistics: No. 24). xii, 276p. 1997. 90.50 (*90-04-10511-5*, NLG119) Brill Academic Pubs.

Belo, Fernando. A Materialist Reading of the Gospel of Mark. O'Connell, Matthew J., tr. from FRE. LC 80-24756.Tr. of Lectero Materialiste de L'evangele de Marc. 384p. (Orig.). reprint ed. pap. 119.10 (*0-8357-2666-5*, 204020200015) Bks Demand.

Belo, Jane. Bali: Rangda & Barong. LC 84-45517. (American Ethnological Society Monographs: No. 16). 1988. reprint ed. 34.50 (*0-404-62915-6*) AMS Pr.

— Bali: Temple Festival. LC 84-45521. (American Ethnological Society Monographs: No. 22). 1988. reprint ed. 34.50 (*0-404-62921-0*) AMS Pr.

— Traditional Balinese Culture: Essays. LC 68-54454. 495p. reprint ed. pap. 153.50 (*0-608-30753-X*, 200611900061) Bks Demand.

Belobaba, Edward P. & Gertner, Eric, eds. Supreme Court Law Review, Vol. 7. 1985. 143.00 (*0-409-86947-3*, MICHIE) LEXIS Pub.

Beloch, Julius. Die Bevolkerung der Griechisch-Romischen Welt. Finley, Moses, ed. LC 79-4962. (Ancient Economic History Ser.). (GER.). 1979. reprint ed. lib. bdg. 48.95 (*0-405-12349-3*) Ayer.

Beloff. Britain & European Union: Dialogue of the Deaf. LC 96-6786. 172p. 1996. text 65.00 (*0-312-16157-3*) St Martin.

— On the Track of Tyranny. Date not set. pap. 12.50 (*0-85303-075-8*, Pub. by M Vallentine & Co) Intl Spec Bk.

Beloff, Gladys, ed. see Beloff, Marvin.

***Beloff, Jim.** Jumpin' Jim's Gone Hawaiian. 88p. 1999. pap. 12.95 (*0-634-00934-6*) H Leonard.

— Jumpin' Jim's '60s Uke-In. 72p. 1999. pap. 12.95 (*0-634-00631-2*) H Leonard.

Beloff, Jim. Jumpin' Jim's Ukulele Favorites. 64p. 1992. pap. 9.95 (*0-7935-2050-9*, 00699377) H Leonard.

— Jumpin' Jim's Ukulele Gems. (Illus.). 72p. 1995. pap. 12.95 (*0-7935-5796-8*) H Leonard.

— Jumpin' Jim's Ukulele Tips & Tunes. 64p. 1994. pap. 9.95 (*0-7935-3377-5*, 00699406) H Leonard.

— The Ukulele: A Visual History. LC 96-44997. (Illus.). 112p. 1997. pap. 24.95 (*0-87930-454-5*) Miller Freeman.

Beloff, John. Parapsychology: A Concise History. 344p. 1997. pap. 18.95 (*0-312-17376-8*) St Martin.

Beloff, John, jt. ed. see Smythies, John R.

Beloff, Marvin. Beyond Is Within. unabridged ed. Beloff, Gladys et al, eds. 1996. spiral bd. 20.00 (*0-9656290-2-3*) Marvs Mike.

— A Family. unabridged ed. Zangari, Rose, ed. 1996. spiral bd. 20.00 (*0-9656290-1-5*) Marvs Mike.

— We'll Build a Museum! unabridged ed. Smith, Jim & Smith, Jackie, eds. 1994. pap. 25.00 (*0-9656290-0-7*) Marvs Mike.

Beloff, Max. The Balance of Power. LC JX1318.B4. (Beatty Memorial Lectures). 83p. reprint ed. pap. 30.00 (*0-7837-1159-X*, 204168800022) Bks Demand.

— Dream of Commonwealth Nineteen Twenty-One to Nineteen Forty-Two. LC 69-11480. (Imperial Sunset Ser.: Vol. 2). (Illus.). 352p. 1989. text 39.50 (*0-911378-92-8*) Sheridan.

— Foreign Policy & the Democratic Process. LC 55-9743. (Albert Shaw Lectures on Diplomatic History). 151p. reprint ed. pap. 46.90 (*0-8357-9272-2*, 201587600001) Bks Demand.

— Foreign Policy & the Democratic Process. LC 76-57665. (Albert Shaw Lectures on Diplomatic History). 134p. 1977. reprint ed. lib. bdg. 35.00 (*0-8371-9463-6*, BEFO, Greenwood Pr) Greenwood.

— An Historian in the Twentieth Century: Chapters in Intellectual Autobiography. LC 92-13127. 192p. (C). 1992. 32.50 (*0-300-05743-1*) Yale U Pr.

— Soviet Policy in the Far East, 1944-1951. LC 75-146852. (Select Bibliographies Reprint Ser.). 1977. reprint ed. 23.95 (*0-8369-5619-2*) Ayer.

— Thomas Jefferson & American Democracy. (History - United States Ser.). 271p. 1993. reprint ed. lib. bdg. 79.00 (*0-7812-4828-0*) Rprt Serv.

— The Tide of Collectivism: Can It Be Turned? LC 79-305904. 23p. 1978. pap. write for info. (*0-85070-623-8*) Conserv Poli Ctr.

— The United States & the Unity of Europe. LC 75-31355. 124p. 1976. reprint ed. lib. bdg. 45.00 (*0-8371-8507-6*, BEUS, Greenwood Pr) Greenwood.

Beloff, Max, ed. Beyond the Soviet Union: The Fragmentation of Power. LC 96-40467. (RISCT Ser.). 304p. 1997. text 78.95 (*1-85521-911-5*, Pub. by Dartmth Pub) Ashgate Pub Co.

Beloff, Max, ed. see Wiener Library Staff.

Beloff, Michael. The Plateglass Universities. LC 70-88559. 208p. 1975. 18.50 (*0-8386-7550-6*) Fairleigh Dickinson.

***Beloff, Michael, et al.** Sports Law. 380p. 1999. 80.00 (*1-84113-073-7*, Pub. by Hart Pub) Intl Spec Bk.

Belofsky, Harold. Plastics Product Design & Process Engineering. LC 94-48205. 552p. 1995. 139.00 (*1-56990-142-2*); pap. 69.00 (*1-56990-179-1*) Hanser-Gardner.

Belohlavek, John M. Let the Eagle Soar! The Foreign Policy of Andrew Jackson. LC 85-1007. 338p. reprint ed. pap. 104.80 (*0-7837-4727-6*, 204438500002) Bks Demand.

Beloin, Edmund & Beloin, Henry. In Any Language: Manuscript Edition. 1953. pap. 13.00 (*0-8222-0559-9*) Dramatists Play.

Beloin, Henry, jt. auth. see Beloin, Edmund.

Beloit, Christian, jt. auth. see Markin, Ed.

Belok, Michael V. & Metos, Thomas H. The University President in Arizona, 1945-1980: An Oral History. LC 89-49146. (Studies in Education: Vol. 7). 296p. 1990. lib. bdg. 89.95 (*0-88946-942-3*) E Mellen.

Belok, Michael V., jt. auth. see Roucek, Joseph S.

Belokolos, E. D., et al. Algebro-Geometrical Approach to Nonlinear Evolution Equations. (Nonlinear Dynamics Ser.). (Illus.). 350p. 1994. 97.95 (*0-387-50265-3*) Spr-Verlag.

Belokrenitsky, Vyacheslav, tr. Capitalism in Pakistan: A History of Socio-Economic Development. (C). 1991. 12.50 (*81-7050-130-X*, Pub. by Patriot Pubs) S Asia.

Belokurov, V. V. & Shirov, D. V. The Theory of Particle Interactions. Millard, P., tr. from RUS. (Translation Ser.). (Illus.). 224p. 1990. 77.00 (*0-88318-715-9*) Am Inst Physics.

Belonax. Food Marketing. 2nd ed. 566p. 1998. pap. text 50.00 (*0-536-01754-9*) Pearson Custom.

***Belongia, Michael T.** Divisia Monetary Aggregates: Right to Theory, Useful in Practice? 1999. text 79.95 (*0-312-22300-5*) St Martin.

Belongia, Michael T., ed. Monetary Policy on the Seventy-Fifth Anniversary of the Federal Reserve System. (C). 1990. lib. bdg. 99.00 (*0-7923-9124-1*) Kluwer Academic.

Belongia, Michael T. & Garfinkel, Michelle R., eds. The Business Cycle: Theories & Evidence, Proceedings of the Sixteenth Annual Economic Policy Conference of the Federal Reserve Bank of St. Louis. LC 92-11616. 240p. (C). 1992. lib. bdg. 85.50 (*0-7923-9239-6*) Kluwer Academic.

Belonick, Steven, ed. A Journey Through Great Lent, Vol. 1. LC 99-206946. 1999. pap. 6.95 (*1-880971-41-0*) Light&Life Pub Co MN.

***Belonogoff, Catherine.** Kaliningrad in Your Pocket No. 3: Svetlogorsk. Kerner, Martin & Lufkens, Matthias, trs. (In Your Pocket Guides Ser.). 47p. 2000. 5.00 (*9986-9115-1-6*) VIYP UAB.

Belonogov, V. A., et al. Eight Papers Translated from the Russian. LC 89-6770. (Translations Ser.: Series 2, Vol. 143). 152p. (Orig.). 1989. text 70.00 (*0-8218-3124-0*, TRANS2/143) Am Math.

***Beloof, Douglas E.** Victims in Criminal Procedure. LC 98-43935. 736p. 1999. 90.00 (*0-89089-673-9*) Carolina Acad Pr.

Belopolskaya, Y. I. & Dalecky, Yu L. Stochastic Equations & Differential Geometry. (C). 1990. text 201.00 (*90-277-2807-0*) Kluwer Academic.

Belore. Lolita, No. 3. (Illus.). 64p. 1997. pap. 9.95 (*1-56163-177-9*, Eurotica) NBM.

— Lolita, Vol. 1. 64p. 1994. pap. 9.95 (*1-56163-116-7*, Eurotica) NBM.

— Lolita, Vol. 2. (SPA.). 64p. 1995. pap. 9.95 (*1-56163-133-7*, Eurotica) NBM.

Belorgey, M., et al. Sediment Transport Mechanisms in Coastal Environments & Rivers. 400p. 1994. text 112.00 (*981-02-1854-0*) World Scientific Pub.

Belosevic, Miodrag. Vital Dye Staining of Giardia & Cryptospridium. LC 97-22877. xvi, 49 p. 1997. pap. write for info. (*0-89867-913-3*, 90733) Am Water Wks Assn.

***Belosevic, Miodrag & AWWA Research Foundation Staff.** Cryptosporidium Parvum Viability Assay. LC 00-42000. 2000. write for info. (*1-58321-029-6*) Am Water Wks Assn.

Belot, Andre. Dictionnaire des Arbres et Arbustes des Jardins. (FRE.). 399p. 1989. 95.00 (*0-7859-8240-X*, 2908041006) Fr & Eur.

Belote, Julianne. The Complete American Housewife, 1787: Being a Collection of the Most Approv'd Recipes of the American Colonies. (Illus.). 183p. 1999. reprint ed. pap. text 10.00 (*0-7881-6023-0*) DIANE Pub.

— Recommended Country Inns: West Coast. 7th ed. (Illus.). 356p. 1999. pap. text 16.95 (*0-7627-0301-6*) Globe Pequot.

Belote, L. The Freshmen Year: Making the Most of College. 2nd ed. 182p. (C). 1998. per. 28.95 (*0-7872-5262-X*) Kendall-Hunt.

Belotserkovskii, O. M., et al, eds. Rarefied Gas Dynamics. 1418p. 1985. 225.00 (*0-306-41932-7*, Plenum Trade) Perseus Pubng.

Belotserkovsky, Sergei M. & Lifanov, Ivan K. Methods of Discrete Vortices. 464p. 1992. boxed set 147.95 (*0-8493-9307-8*, QA925) CRC Pr.

Belott, Peter H. Endocardial Lead Extraction. LC 98-4104. (Illus.). 160p. 1998. pap., teacher ed. 115.00 incl. VHS (*0-87993-671-1*) Futura Pub.

— A Practical Approach to Permanent Pacemaker Implantation, Set. LC 94-39121. (Illus.). 152p. 1996. wbk. ed. 95.00 incl. VHS (*0-87993-594-4*) Futura Pub.

Belotti, Michael, ed. see Buxtehude, Dieterich.

Belous, Richard, jt. auth. see Levitan, Sar A.

Belous, Richard S. Creating a Strong Post-Cold War Economy. 40p. 1990. pap. text 8.00 (*0-89068-104-X*, NPA 247) Natl Planning.

Belous, Richard S., et al, eds. European & American Labor Markets: Different Models & Different Results. 144p. (Orig.). 1992. pap. text 15.00 (*0-89068-112-0*, NPA 257) Natl Planning.

Belous, Richard S. & Hartley, Rebecca S., eds. The Growth of Regional Trading Blocs in the Global Economy. 168p. (Orig.). 1990. pap. text 15.00 (*0-89068-100-7*, NPA 243) Natl Planning.

Belous, Richard S. & Lemco, Jonathan, eds. NAFTA As a Model of Development: The Benefits & Costs of Merging High- & Low-Wage Areas. LC 94-23436. 216p. (C). 1995. text 49.50 (*0-7914-2569-X*); pap. text 19.95 (*0-7914-2570-3*) State U NY Pr.

— NAFTA As a Model of Development: The Benefits & Costs of Merging High & Low Wage Areas. 192p. (Orig.). 1993. pap. text 10.50 (*0-614-03254-7*, NPA 266) Natl Planning.

Belous, Richard S. & McClenahan, Kelly L., eds. Global Corporations & Nation-States: Do Companies or Countries Compete? 105p. (Orig.). 1991. pap. text 15.00 (*0-89068-109-0*, CIR 23 (NPA255)) Natl Planning.

Belous, Richard S. & Symons, Thomas H. Demographic Currents: Trends & Issues That Face the United States, the United Kingdom & Canada. 46p. (Orig.). 1991. pap. text 5.60 (*0-614-03252-0*, NPA 256) Natl Planning.

Belous, Richard S., jt. auth. see Levitan, Sar A.

Belous, Richard S., jt. auth. see Scherer, F. M.

Belous, Richard S., ed. see Goldman, Marshall I., et al.

Belous, Richard S., ed. see Kaufman, Henry, et al.

Belous, Robert, et al, texts. The Sierra Club Guides to the National Parks of the Pacific Northwest & Alaska: The Pacific Northwest & Alaska. rev. ed. LC 95-11449. (Sierra Club Guides to the National Parks Ser.). (Illus.). 400p. 1995. pap. 24.95 (*0-679-76495-X*) Random.

Belousov, L. V. The Dynamic Architecture of a Developing Organism: An Attempt to an Interdisciplinary Approach to the Development of Organisms. LC 98-3387. 1998. 105.00 (*0-7923-5044-8*) Kluwer Academic.

Belousov, S. & Brown, D. Tables of Normalized Associations Legendre Polynomials. LC 62-17650. (Mathematical Tables Ser.: Vol. 18). 1962. 176.00 (*0-08-009723-5*, Pub. by Pergamon Repr) Franklin.

Belousov, V. P. Thermodynamic Properties of Aqueous Solutions of Organic Substances. Bobrov, Nicholas N., tr. from RUS. LC 93-8741.Tr. of Termodinamika Vodnykh Rastvorov Neelektrolitov. (ENG.). 384p. 1993. boxed set 240.00 (*0-8493-9342-6*, QD544) CRC Pr.

Belousov, V. V. Geotectonics. (Illus.). 330p. 1981. 47.95 (*0-387-09173-4*) Spr-Verlag.

Belousov, Yu M., jt. ed. see Smilga, V. P.

Belousova, L. S. & Denisova, L. V. Rare Plants of the World. Sharma, B. R., tr. from RUS. (Illus.). 354p. (C). 1992. text 85.00 (*90-6191-482-5*, Pub. by A A Balkema) Ashgate Pub Co.

Belov, A. Polytechnical Dictionary. 3rd ed. 656p. (C). 1989. 175.00 (*0-7855-6692-9*, Pub. by Collets) St Mut.

***Belov, M. I., et al.** Russians in the Bering Strait 1648-1791. LC 00-90219. (Illus.). 144p. 2000. 19.95 (*0-9626727-2-6*) Whitestone AK.

Belov, Nikolai V. Crystal Chemistry of Large-Cation Silicates. LC 63-17642. 168p. reprint ed. pap. 52.10 (*0-608-10083-8*, 200335700021) Bks Demand.

Belova, Natalia, tr. see Dobychin, Leonid.

Belove, Charles, jt. auth. see Schilling, Donald L.

Beloved Mighty Victory. The I AM Discourses (Original) LC 85-1793. (Saint Germain Ser.: Vol. 9). (Illus.). 528p. 1986. 28.00 (*1-878891-40-5*); pap. 21.00 (*1-878891-41-3*) St Germain Press Inc.

Belovski, Zvi, tr. Shem Mishmuel: Selections on the Weekly Parashah & Festivals. 459p. 1998. 25.95 (*1-56871-141-7*, Pub. by Targum Pr) Feldheim.

***Below, Halina.** Chestnut Dreams. (Illus.). 40p. (J). 2000. 14.95 (*1-55041-545-X*) Fitzhenry & W Ltd.

Below, Halina. The Windy Day. unabridged ed. (Illus.). 32p. (J). (gr. k up). 1996. 16.95 (*1-895555-74-4*) STDK.

Below, Patrick J., et al. The Executive Guide to Strategic Planning. LC 86-27863. (Management Ser.). 159p. 1987. 26.95 (*1-55542-032-X*) Jossey-Bass.

Belowich, Michael. Stratigraphy, Petrology, & Depositional Environments of the Jarvis Creek Coalfield, Alaska. (MIRL Reports: No. 85). 82p. 1988. 8.00 (*0-911043-09-8*) UAKF Min Ind Res Lab.

Belpoliti, Marco, ed. see Levi, Primo.

Belpre, Pura. Firefly Summer. LC 96-15679. 205p. 1996. pap. 9.95 (*1-55885-180-1*, Pinata Bks) Arte Publico.

Belpre, Pura. Firefly Summer. (Illus.). (J). 1996. 13.30 (*0-606-17954-2*) Turtleback.

Belpre, Pura, tr. see Leaf, Munro.

Belpre, Pura, tr. see Leaf, Munro, ed.

Belpulsi, Nathalie B., jt. auth. see Belpulsi, Peter A.

Belpulsi, Peter A. A GI's View of World War II. LC 97-70725. (Illus.). 300p. 1997. 29.95 (*1-882614-20-8*) Globe Pubs.

Belpulsi, Peter A. & Belpulsi, Nathalie B. Shakespeare Yesterday - Today: Student Classic - Julius Caesar. 1990. 23.95 (*0-9623663-3-1*) Globe Pubs.

— Shakespeare Yesterday - Today: Student Classics - Hamlet. 1990. 23.95 (*0-9623663-8-2*) Globe Pubs.

— Shakespeare Yesterday - Today: Student Classics - Macbeth. 1990. 23.95 (*0-9623663-5-8*) Globe Pubs.

— Shakespeare Yesterday - Today: Student Classics - Romeo & Juliet. 1990. 23.95 (*0-9623663-7-4*) Globe Pubs.

Bels, Alberts. The Cage. Kratins, Ojars, tr. from LAV. 149p. 1990. 27.00 (*0-7206-0802-3*, Pub. by P Owen Ltd) Dufour.

Belsare, M. B. An Entymological Gujarati-English Dictionary. 2nd ed. (ENG & GUJ.). 1207p. 1981. 75.00 (*0-8288-1146-6*, M14114) Fr & Eur.

— An Etymological Gujarati English Dictionary. 1220p. 1986. reprint ed. 34.00 (*0-8364-1687-2*, Pub. by Manohar) S Asia.

Belsey, Andrew, jt. ed. see Chadwick, Ruth.

Belsey, Catherine. Critical Practice. (New Accents Ser.). 160p. (C). 1980. pap. 18.99 (*0-415-02563-X*) Routledge.

— Critical Practice. 176p. 1980. pap. 13.95 (*0-416-72950-9*, NO.2021) Routledge.

— Desire: Love Stories in Western Culture. LC 94-14118. (Illus.). 280p. 1994. pap. 28.95 (*0-631-16814-1*) Blackwell Pubs.

— A Feminist Reader. LC 97-12145. 262p. 1997. 75.95 (*1-57718-129-8*) Blackwell Pubs.

— A Feminist Reader. 2nd ed. 262p. 1997. pap. 24.95 (*1-57718-130-1*) Blackwell Pubs.

***Belsey, Catherine.** Shakespeare & the Loss of Eden: The Construction of Family Values in Early Modern Culture. LC 99-31499. (Illus.). 208p. (C). 2000. text 26.00 (*0-8135-2763-5*) Rutgers U Pr.

Belsey, Catherine. The Subject of Tragedy. 288p. (Orig.). 1985. 29.95 (*0-416-32700-1*, 9446); pap. text 13.95 (*0-416-32710-9*, 9447) Routledge.

Belsey, Ronald H., jt. auth. see Skinner, David B.

Belsey, Valerie. The Green Lanes of England. (Illus.). 158p. 1998. pap. 21.95 (*1-870098-69-2*, Pub. by Green Bks) Chelsea Green Pub.

Belsh, Jerry M. & Schiffman, Philip L., eds. Amyotrophic Lateral Sclerosis: Diagnosis & Management for the Clinician. (Illus.). 408p. 1996. 90.00 (*0-87993-628-2*) Futura Pub.

Belshaw. Publishing a Newspaper. (J). (gr. 3-8). 1996. pap. text, wbk. ed. 11.95 (*1-55734-209-1*) Tchr Create Mat.

Belshaw, B. E., tr. see Rijnberk, Adam & De Vries, H. W., eds.

Belshaw, Chris. Osteopathy: Is It for You? (Illus.). 128p. 1993. pap. 11.95 (*0-906540-95-X*, Pub. by Element MA) Penguin Putnam.

Belshaw, Chris & Strutt, Mike. Couples in Crisis: Does Your Relationship Have a Future? 192p. 1996. pap. 12.95 (*0-7063-7467-3*, Pub. by WrLock) Sterling.

Belshaw, George, jt. auth. see Belshaw, Maria Parsons.

Belshaw, George M., ed. Lent with Evelyn Underhill. 2nd ed. LC 89-28659. 112p. 1990. pap. 9.95 (*0-8192-1449-3*) Morehouse Pub.

Belshaw, Maria P. Crossing the Plains to Oregon in 1853. 50p. write for info. (*0-87770-469-4*) Ye Galleon.

***Belshaw, Maria Parsons & Belshaw, George.** Crossing the Plains to Oregon in 1853. LC 00-34963. (Illus.). 2000. pap. write for info. (*0-87770-720-0*) Ye Galleon.

Belshaw, Marjorie. Jumbo Book of Writing Lessons: Intermediate. 304p. (J). (gr. 3-5). 1997. pap. 24.95 (*1-57690-315-X*) Tchr Create Mat.

Belshaw, Patrick. A Kind of Private Magic. LC 95-143853. (Illus.). 239p. 1995. 35.00 (*0-233-98874-2*, Pub. by Andre Deutsch) Trafalgar.

Belshaw, Sheila. Diamonds of the Sun. large type ed. (Linford Romance Library). 240p. 1996. pap. 16.99 (*0-7089-7918-1*) Ulverscroft.

— The Nightingale Will Sing. large type ed. (Linford Romance Library). 272p. 1995. pap. 16.99 (*0-7089-7773-1*, Linford) Ulverscroft.

— Savage Paradise. large type ed. (Linford Romance Library). 304p. 1997. pap. 16.99 (*0-7089-7980-7*, Linford) Ulverscroft.

Belshe, Judy. It's a Freeway Out There! The Parent's Guide to the Film & Commercial Industry. (Illus.). 286p. 1996. spiral bd., wbk. ed. 30.00 (*0-9655530-0-0*) J Belshe.

— The Long Shmooze: Everything the Gate Keepers to Hollywood Don't Have Time to Tell You... Again!! (Illus.). 461p. 1998. spiral bd., wbk. ed. 30.00 (*0-9655530-1-9*) J Belshe.

***Belshe, S. Kimberly, ed.** California Immunization Handbook (1996) A Guide to Implementing the School & Child Care Entry Immunization Requirements of the California School Immunization Law. 5th ed. (Illus.). 43p. 1999. reprint ed. pap. text 20.00 (*0-7881-8555-1*) DIANE Pub.

Belshin, Lee. The Complete Prostate Book: Every Man's Guide. LC 96-18461. 240p. 1996. per. 14.95 (*0-7615-0447-8*) Prima Pub.

Belsinger, Susan. Flowers in the Kitchen. LC 90-56138 (Illus.). 128p. (Orig.). 1991. pap. 14.95 (*0-934026-63-7*) Interweave.

Belsinger, Susan & Dille, Carolyn. The Chile Pepper Book: A Fiesta of Fiery, Flavorful Recipes. Ligon, Linda C., ed. (Illus.). 96p. 1994. pap. 9.95 (*0-934026-93-9*) Interweave.

— The Garlic Book: A Garland of Simple, Savory, Robust Recipes. (Illus.). 72p. (Orig.). 1993. pap. 9.95 (*0-934026-80-7*) Interweave.

— The Greens Book. (Illus.). 112p. 1995. pap. 14.95 (*1-883010-05-5*) Interweave.

Belsinger, Susan, jt. auth. see DeBaggio, Thomas.

Belsinger, Susan, jt. auth. see Dille, Carolyn.

Belsito, Frank. Sleeper Agent in Havana. 160p. (Orig.). 1997. pap. 9.95 (*1-57502-459-4*, P01373) Morris Pubng.

Belsito, Peter. Hardcore California. 128p. 1983. 24.95 (*0-86719-314-X*) Last Gasp.

— Street Art: Punk Poster in San Francisco. 128p. 1982. 9.95 (*0-86719-300-X*) Last Gasp.

Belsky. Psychology of Aging. 3rd ed. LC 98-17981. (Psychology Ser.). 1998. pap. 75.95 (*0-534-35912-4*) Brooks-Cole.

Belsky, Dick. One for the Money. (Academy First Mystery Ser.). 191p. 1985. pap. 5.95 (*0-89733-221-0*) Academy Chi Pubs.

***Belsky, Gary & Gilovich, Thomas.** Why Smart People Make Big Money Mistakes - And How to Correct Them: Lessons from the New Science of Behavioral Economics. 224p. 2000. pap. 12.00 (*0-684-85938-6*, Fireside) S&S Trade Pap.

Belsky, Gary & Gilovick, Thomas. Why Smart People Make Big Money Mistakes & How They Correct Them: Psychology for Financial Success. LC 98-31145. 224p. 1999. 22.50 (*0-684-84493-1*) Simon & Schuster.

Belsky, Janet. Adulthood in America. LC 96-9733. 600p. 1997. mass mkt. 73.95 (*0-314-20189-0*) West Pub.

Belsky, Janet K. Here Tomorrow: Making the Most of Life after Fifty. LC 88-45418. 352p. 1988. 19.95 (*0-8018-3718-9*) Johns Hopkins.

— The Psychology of Aging: Theory, Research & Intervention. 2nd ed. (Psychology Ser.). 460p. (C). 1989. pap. 49.75 (*0-534-12114-4*) Brooks-Cole.

— The Psychology of Aging: Theory, Research & Practice. LC 83-20923. (Psychology Ser.). 550p. (C). 1984. mass mkt. 32.25 (*0-534-02868-3*) Brooks-Cole.

Belsky, Jay, ed. In the Beginning: Readings on Infancy. LC 81-10008. 324p. reprint ed. pap. 100.50 (*0-608-15535-X*, 202971900064) Bks Demand.

Belsky, Jay, et al, eds. The Child in the Family. 288p. 1984. pap. text 14.95 (*0-89859-717-X*) L Erlbaum Assocs.

Belsky, Jay & Nezworski, Teresa, eds. Clinical Implications of Attachments. (Palermo Ser.). 448p. 1988. text 79.95 (*0-89859-778-1*) L Erlbaum Assocs.

Belsky, Jay, et al. The Child in the Family. LC 83-12255. (Illus.). 288p. (C). 1984. pap. text 33.50 (*0-07-554803-8*) McGraw.

— Close Relationships & Socioeconomic Development. Shulman, Shmuel, ed. (Human Development Ser.: Vol. 7). (Illus.). 248p. 1995. text 73.25 (*1-56750-114-1*) Ablx Pub.

Belsky, Judy. Thread of Blue: A Journey Through Loss, Faith & Renewal. 95p. 1992. 12.95 (*0-944070-77-9*) Targum Pr.

Belsky, Nancy A. Building Kites: Flying High with Math. Gideon, Joan, ed. (Math Projects Ser.). (Illus.). 65p. (Orig.). (J). (gr. 5-8). 1994. pap., student ed. 10.95 (*0-86651-918-1*) Seymour Pubns.

Belsky, R. G. Loverboy. LC 96-27120. 1997. mass mkt. 23.00 (*0-380-97439-8*, Avon Bks) Morrow Avon.

— Loverboy. 352p. 1998. mass mkt. 6.50 (*0-380-79068-8*, Avon Bks) Morrow Avon.

— Playing Dead. 345p. 1999. mass mkt. 6.50 (*0-380-79069-6*, Avon Bks) Morrow Avon.

Belsky, Walter & Laufer, Greg. Discovering the Magic of Math: An Upper Elementary & Junior High Teaching Manual. (Illus.). 96p. (Orig.). (C). 1996. pap. text 14.95 (*0-9653980-0-5*) Prism Educ Serv.

Belsley, David A. Conditioning Diagnostics: Collinearity & Weak Data in Regression. LC 90-12574. 396p. 1991. 160.00 (*0-471-52889-7*) Wiley.

Belsley, David A., ed. Computational Techniques for Econometrics & Economic Analysis. LC 93-17956. (Advances in Computational Economics Ser.). 248p. (C). 1993. lib. bdg. 142.00 (*0-7923-2356-4*) Kluwer Academic.

Belsley, David A., et al. Regression Diagnostics: Identifying Influential Data & Sources of Collinearity. LC 79-19876. (Probability & Mathematical Statistics Ser.). 310p. 1980. 165.00 (*0-471-05856-4*) Wiley.

Belsole, Kurt, et al. Word & Spirit No. 14: Aspects of Monasticism in America. (Word & Spirit Ser.: No. 14). 148p. 1992. pap. 8.00 (*0-932506-95-X*) St Bedes Pubns.

Belsole, Robert. Carpal Tunnel Syndrome: A Guide for Patients. Seligson, David, ed. (Orthopedic Ser.). (Illus.). 24p. (Orig.). 1995. pap. 2.95 (*1-885274-08-4*) Health InfoNet Inc.

Belson, David. Speeches for Every Occasion: All the Words You Need. 192p. 1995. pap. 8.95 (*0-8065-1679-8*, Citadel Pr) Carol Pub Group.

— What to Say & How to Say It. 224p. 1985. 4.98 (*0-89009-602-3*) Bk Sales Inc.

— What to Say & How to Say It: For All Occasions. 1961. pap. 8.95 (*0-8065-0891-4*, 98, Citadel Pr) Carol Pub Group.

— What to Say & How to Say It: Model Speeches, Letters & Remarks for Every Occasion. 192p. 1993. pap. 8.95 (*0-8065-1447-7*, Citadel Pr) Carol Pub Group.

Belstein, Roger E. Airlift & Airborne Operations in World War 2. (Illus.). 55p. 1998. pap. 3.25 (*0-16-049673-X*) USGPO.

Belstock, Alan & Smith, Gerald. Consumer Mathematics with Calculator Applications. Gafney, Leo, ed. (gr. 10-12). 1980. text 27.08 (*0-07-004436-8*) McGraw.

Belt, Angela, jt. ed. see Hunter-Cevera, Jennie C.

Belt, Bradley, ed. see Hunt, Alexander T.

Belt, Bradley D. The 21st Century Retirement Security Plan. LC 99-24204. (Panel Report Ser.). 9p. (C). 1999. pap. text 19.95 (*0-89206-353-X*) CSIS.

Belt, Elmer, ed. see Leonardo da Vinci.

Belt, Joe. The Pencil Drawings of Joe Belt. LC 88-25996. 1988. pap. 15.95 (*0-89672-181-7*) Tex Tech Univ Pr.

Belt, Joyce. Create a Christian Christmas Tree: Make Biblical symbols for Your Tree. (Illus.). 64p. 1996. pap. 9.99 (*1-885358-22-9*, DB46501) Rainbow CA.

Belt, Lynda. The Acting Primer: A Course in Making Choices. LC 92-62050. 48p. 1993. pap. 15.95 (*0-9620799-4-4*) Thespis Prodns.

— Improv Game Book Two: A Sourcebook of Games for Improvisation Performance. LC 92-62049. 112p. (C). 1993. pap. 12.95 (*0-9620799-3-6*) Thespis Prodns.

Belt, Lynda & Stockley, Rebecca. Acting Through Improv/Improv Through Theatresports: A Curriculum to Teach Basic Acting Skills & Improvisation. 3rd rev. ed. LC 88-51755. 204p. 1995. pap. 24.95 (*0-9620799-5-2*) Thespis Prodns.

Belt, Lynda D. The Acting Primer: Student Handbook. LC 92-62050. 60p. 1993. pap. 7.95 (*0-9620799-9-5*) Thespis Prodns.

Belt, Philip. The Piano. (New Grove Ser.). 1997. pap. 14.95 (*0-393-30518-X*) Norton.

Belt, Phillip R. The Piano. Sadie, Stanley, ed. (New Grove Musical Instrument Ser.). (Illus.). 1988. 22.50 (*0-393-02553-5*) Norton.

Belt, Sage C., jt. auth. see Bartel, Janice R.

Belt, Sandy. Folk Art Felt: 36 Heartfelt Projects with Creative New Embellishments. LC 96-51831. 128p. 1997. pap. 19.95 (*0-8019-8943-4*) Krause Pubns.

***Belt, Thomas.** Discovery of Stone Implements in Glacial Drift in North America. (LC History-America-E). 22p. 1999. reprint ed. lib. bdg. 69.00 (*0-7812-4308-4*) Rprt Serv.

Belt, Thomas. The Naturalist in Nicaragua. LC 85-8502. (Illus.). xxxvi, 440p. 1985. reprint ed. pap. 15.95 (*0-226-04220-0*) U Ch Pr.

— The Naturalist in Nicaragua. LC 85-8502. (Illus.). xxxvi, 440p. 1985. reprint ed. lib. bdg. 36.00 (*0-226-04219-7*) U Ch Pr.

***Beltane, Jack.** Am I the Matter? A Toyland Tale. 142p. 2000. pap. 8.00 (*1-929309-06-6*) Graveworm Pr.

Beltane, Jack. How to Vanish in America. Date not set. pap. 3.95 (*1-929309-04-X*) Graveworm Pr.

Beltaos, Spyros, ed. River Ice Jams. 390p. 1996. boxed set 58.00 (*0-918334-87-X*, RIJ) WRP.

Belter, Paul A., et al. Bioseparations: Downstream Processing for Biotechnology. 384p. 1988. 99.95 (*0-471-84737-2*) Wiley.

B

Beltethon, Cesar. Johanna's Grave. 76p. 1990. 12.95 (*0-930061-55-1*) Interspace Bks.

Belth, Joseph M. The A. L. Williams Replacement Empire. LC 86-27715. 64p. (Orig.). 1987. pap. 10.00 (*0-941173-00-3*) Insur Forum.

— Life Insurance: A Consumer's Handbook. 2nd ed. LC 84-47705. (Illus.). 240p. 1985. pap. 6.95 (*0-253-20346-5*) Ind U Pr.

— Participating Life Insurance Sold by Stock Companies. (C). 1964. 10.00 (*0-256-00639-3*, Irwn McGrw-H) McGrw-H Hghr Educ.

***Belting, Hans.** Art History After Modernism. 1998. pap. text 19.00 (*0-226-04185-9*); lib. bdg. 65.00 (*0-226-04184-0*) U Ch Pr.

Belting, Hans. The End of the History of Art? Wood, Christopher S., tr. LC 86-24937. xiv, 136p. 1987. 19.95 (*0-226-04217-0*) U Ch Pr.

— The End of the History of Art? Wood, Christopher S., tr. LC 86-24937. 134p. reprint ed. pap. 41.60 (*0-608-08823-4*, 206946200004); reprint ed. pap. 41.30 (*0-608-21004-8*, 205453200003) Bks Demand.

— The Germans & Their Art: A Troublesome Relationship. Kleager, Scott, tr. from ENG. LC 98-4559. (Illus.). 128p. 1998. 20.00 (*0-300-07616-9*) Yale U Pr.

— Likeness & Presence: A History of the Image Before the Era of Art. Jephcott, Edmund, tr. from GER. LC 93-3389.Tr. of Bild und Kult. (Illus.). 676p. 1994. 65.00 (*0-226-04214-6*) U Ch Pr.

— Likeness & Presence: A History of the Image Before the Era of Art. Jephcott, Edmund, tr.Tr. of Bild und Kult. (Illus.). xxiv, 652p. 1996. pap. text 39.95 (*0-226-04215-4*) U Ch Pr.

Belting, Hans, et al. Sigmar Polke: The Three Lies of Painting. (Illus.). 360p. 1997. 75.00 (*3-89322-925-6*) Dist Art Pubs.

Belting, Isabella. Mode und Revolution: Deutschland, 1848/49. (Historische Texte und Studien). (Illus.). 234p. 1997. 70.00 (*3-487-10314-1*) G Olms Pubs.

Belting, Paul E. Development of the Free Public High School in Illinois to 1860. LC 71-89149. (American Education: Its Men, Institutions, & Ideas. Series 1). 1977. reprint ed. 18.95 (*0-405-01386-8*) Ayer.

Beltione, Elizabeth S. Murder among Friends: Violations of Philia in Greek Tragedy. LC 99-13051. 304p. 2000. text 49.95 (*0-19-513149-5*) OUP.

Beltman, Brian W. Dutch Farmer in the Missouri Valley: The Life & Letters of Ulbe Eringa, 1866-1950. LC 95-13565. (Statue of Liberty-Ellis Island Centennial Ser.). (Illus.). 232p. 1996. text 27.95 (*0-252-02195-9*) U of Ill Pr.

Beltman, H. A. Vegetative Strukturen der Parmeliaceae und Ihre Entwicklung. (Bibliotheca Lichenologica Ser.: No. 11). (Illus.). 1978. lib. bdg. 48.00 (*3-7682-1199-1*) Lubrecht & Cramer.

Belton. Ernestine Amanda Members Of The Club Book 3, Vol. 3. LC 97-15546. (Ernestine & Amanda Ser.). 176p. (J). (gr. 4-6). 1998. per. 4.50 (*0-689-81661-8*) S&S Childrens.

— From Miss Ida's Porch. (J). 1998. pap. 5.99 (*0-87628-329-6*) Ctr Appl Res.

— Mckendree. (J). 1999. mass mkt. 16.00 (*0-689-80204-8*) S&S Bks Yung.

Belton, Beth. American Class Society in Numbers. enl. rev. ed. Howard, Bob & Logue, John, eds. LC 79-121955. (Illus.). 112p. 1981. pap. 2.95 (*0-933522-07-X*) Kent Popular.

Belton, Christina, tr. see German National Equestrian Federation Staff.

Belton, D. J., et al, eds. Electronic Packaging Materials Science X Vol. 515: Proceedings Materials Research Society Symposium. 262p. 1998. text 74.00 (*1-55899-421-1*) Materials Res.

Belton, David. Each Night I Die. LC 92-71603. 220p. (Orig.). 1992. pap. 12.95 (*1-878647-07-5*) APU Pub Grp.

Belton, Don, ed. Speak My Name: Black Men on Masculinity & the American Dream. 1997. pap. 16.00 (*0-8070-0937-7*) Beacon Pr.

Belton, Elizabeth, ed. see Misaki, Eri.

Belton, John. American Cinema - American Culture. LC 93-25846. 400p. (C). 1993. pap. 39.69 (*0-07-004466-X*) McGraw.

— Cinema Stylists. LC 82-10793. (Filmmakers Ser.: No. 2). (Illus.). 384p. 1983. 35.00 (*0-8108-1585-0*) Scarecrow.

— Movies & Mass Culture. LC 95-12438. (Depth of Field Ser.). (Illus.). 300p. (C). 1995. text 48.00 (*0-8135-2227-7*); pap. text 18.00 (*0-8135-2228-5*) Rutgers U Pr.

— Widescreen Cinema. (Harvard Film Studies). (Illus.). 288p. 1992. 43.50 (*0-674-95260-X*); pap. 24.50 (*0-674-95261-8*) HUP.

***Belton, John, ed.** Alfred Hitchcock's "Rear Window" LC 99-12160. (Cambridge Film Handbooks Ser.). (Illus.). 192p. (C). 2000. 49.95 (*0-521-56423-9*); pap. 16.95 (*0-521-56453-0*) Cambridge U Pr.

Belton, John, ed. see Rubin, Martin.

Belton, John, ed. see Sikov, Ed.

Belton, John, jt. ed. see Weis, Elisabeth.

Belton, Michael J. S. Cruise to Jupiter: Contributions of the Galileo Imaging Science Team. (Illus.). viii, 718p. 1997. 125.00 (*0-9676875-0-0*) Galileo Image.

— Galileo Mission Extensions: Contributions of the Galileo Imaging Science Team. (Illus.). Date not set. 125.00 (*0-9676875-2-7*) Galileo Image.

— In Orbit at Jupiter: Contributions of the Galileo Imaging Science Team. (Illus.). ix, 837p. 1999. 125.00 (*0-9676875-1-9*) Galileo Image.

Belton, N. R., et al, eds. Brain: Biochemistry & Inherited Metabolic Disease. 128p. 1983. text 107.50 (*0-85200-484-2*) Kluwer Academic.

Belton, N. R. & Toothill, C., eds. Transport & Inherited Disease. 1982. text 183.00 (*0-85200-391-9*) Kluwer Academic.

Belton, Neil. The Good Listener: Helen Bamber, a Life Against Cruelty. LC 98-44755. 320p. 1999. 27.00 (*0-375-40100-8*) Pantheon.

Belton, P. S., ed. Magnetic Resonance in Food Science. 292p. 1995. 129.00 (*0-85404-725-5*) CRC Pr.

***Belton, P. S., et al, eds.** Advances in Magnetic Resonance in Food Science. (Special Publication Ser.: Vol. 231). 24p. 1999. 139.00 (*0-85404-724-7*) Spr-Verlag.

Belton, P. S., et al, eds. Annual Reports on NMR Spectroscopy Vol. 31: Special Edition "Food Science". Vol. 31. (Illus.). 384p. 1995. text 111.00 (*0-12-505331-2*) Acad Pr.

Belton, Robert. Remedies in Employment Discrimination Law. 736p. 1992. boxed set 150.00 (*0-7355-1289-2*) Panel Pubs.

Belton, Robert & Avery, Dianne. Employment Discrimination Law: Cases. 6th ed. LC 98-36909. (Paralegal). 1000p. 1999. text 44.25 (*0-314-06658-6*) West Pub.

Belton, Sandra. Beauty, Her Basket. 1924. write for info. (*0-688-17821-9*, Grenwillow Bks); lib. bdg. write for info. (*0-688-17822-7*, Grenwillow Bks) HarpC Child Bks.

Belton, Sandra. Ernestine & Amanda, Book No. 1. LC 96-11823. Vol. 1. 128p. (J). (gr. 3-7). 1998. per. 3.99 (*0-689-80847-X*) S&S Childrens.

— Ernestine & Amanda, Book No. 2. 1998. per. 3.99 (*0-689-80845-3*) S&S Childrens.

— Ernestine & Amanda, No. 1. 40p. (J). (gr. 3-7). 1996. 16.00 (*0-689-80848-8*) S&S Childrens.

— Ernestine & Amanda, No. 2. LC 96-41443. 176p. (J). (gr. 3-7). 1997. 16.00 (*0-689-80846-1*) S&S Childrens.

— Ernestine & Amanda: Members of the C. L. U. B. LC 97-15546. 160p. (J). (gr. 3-7). 1997. per. 16.00 (*0-689-81611-1*) S&S Childrens.

— From Miss Ida's Porch. (Illus.). 40p. (J). (gr. 2-5). 1998. mass mkt. 5.99 (*0-689-81802-5*) S&S Childrens.

— From Miss Ida's Porch. (J). 1998. 11.44 (*0-606-12940-5*) Turtleback.

— May'naise Sandwiches & Sunshine Tea. LC 93-46781. (Illus.). 32p. (J). (ps-4). 1994. mass mkt. 14.95 (*0-02-709035-3*) S&S Bks Yung.

— McKendree. LC 99-24456. 144p. (YA). (gr. 5-9). 2000. 15.95 (*0-688-15950-8*, Grenwillow Bks) HarpC Child Bks.

— Mysteries on Monroe Street. LC 97-45013. (Ernestine & Amanda Ser.). 153p. (J). (gr. 4-7). 1998. per. 16.00 (*0-689-81612-X*) S&S Childrens.

Belton, Sandra. Pictures for Miss Josie. 1924. write for info. (*0-688-17480-9*, Grenwillow Bks) HarpC Child Bks.

Belton, Sandra. Summer Camp, Ready or Not! (Ernestine & Amanda Ser.). (Illus.). (J). (gr. 3-7). 1997. 16.00 (*0-614-29071-6*) S&S Childrens.

Belton, Sandra & Carpenter, Nancy. Mysteries on Monroe Street. LC 97-45013. (Ernestine & Amanda Ser.: No. 4). 176p. (J). (gr. 4-6). 1999. per. 4.50 (*0-689-81662-6*, 076714004504) Aladdin.

Belton, Teresa, ed. From Arms Race to World Peace. (C). 1989. text 30.00 (*0-902662-91-0*, Pub. by R K Pubns) St Mut.

Belton, Terrence M., jt. auth. see Burghardt, Galen D.

Belton, W. J., contrib. by. Pacific International Conference on Aerospace Science & Technology, 2nd, 1995 & Australian Aeronautical Conference, 6th, 1995. (National Conference Proceedings 95 Ser.: Vol. 1). (Illus.). 982p. 1995. pap. 91.50 (*0-85825-624-X*, Pub. by Inst Engrs Aust-EA Bks) Accents Pubns.

Belton, William, tr. see Sick, Helmut.

Belton, Willie & Cebula, Richard J. Crisis in Commercial Banking. 128p. (C). 1993. pap. text, per. 23.95 (*0-8403-8614-1*, 40861401) Kendall-Hunt.

Beltrametti, E. G. & Levy-Leblond, J. M. Advances in Quantum Phenomena: Proceedings of an International Course Held in Erice, Sicily, February 16-18, 1994. (NATO ASI Ser.: Vol. 347). (Illus.). 388p. (C). 1996. text 138.00 (*0-306-45072-0*, Kluwer Plenum) Kluwer Academic.

Beltrametti, Franco. Another Earthquake. Vangelisti, Paul, tr. 1976. pap. 2.50 (*0-88031-023-5*) Invisible-Red Hill.

Beltrametti, Mauro C. & Sommese, Andrew J. The Adjunction Theory of Complex Projective Varieties Vol. 1. LC 94-27981. (Expositions in Mathematics Ser.: No. 16). 398p. (C). 1995. 89.95 (*3-11-014355-0*) De Gruyter.

Beltrametti, Mauro C., et al. Some Special Properties of the Adjunction Theory for 3-Folds in P p5 s. LC 95-15957. (Memoirs Ser.: No. 554). 63p. 1995. pap. 30.00 (*0-8218-0234-8*, MEMO/116/554) Am Math.

***Beltrami, Arrigio.** Dinosaurs. 1999. pap. text. write for info. (*1-894335-17-1*) TSE Pubg Inc.

— Wild Animals. 1999. pap. text. write for info. (*1-894335-12-0*) Ts Enterprises.

Beltrami, E. J. What Is Random? Discovering Chance & Order in Mathematics & the World. LC 99-18389. 168p. 1999. 21.00 (*0-387-98737-1*, Copernicus) Spr-Verlag.

Beltrami, Edward. Math Modeling in Social & Biomedical Sciences. (C). 1992. 50.00 (*0-86720-292-0*) Jones & Bartlett.

Beltrami, Edward A. Mathematics for Dynamic Modeling. 2nd ed. LC 97-16264. (Illus.). 219p. 1997. text 55.00 (*0-12-085566-6*) Morgan Kaufmann.

***Beltramini, Guido, et al.** Palladio & Northern Europe. (Illus.). 176p. 1999. 45.00 (*88-8118-524-5*, Pub. by Skira IT) Abbeville Pr.

Beltramo, Mario. The Italian Civil Code & Complementary Legislation, 2 vols., Set. LC 91-7912. 1991. ring bd. 275.00 (*0-379-20968-3*) Oceana.

Beltran, Antonio, ed. The Cave of Altamira. LC 99-13832. (Illus.). 180p. 1999. 49.50 (*0-8109-1989-3*, Pub. by Abrams) Time Warner.

Beltran, Bartolome. Guia Practica de La Salud. 1998. pap. 13.95 (*84-7880-763-2*) Planeta.

Beltran, George, ed. see Freemesser, Bernard.

Beltran, Javier. Current Review of Magnetic Resonance Imaging. (Illus.). 416p. 1995. text 99.95 (*1-878132-09-1*) Current Med.

— Current Review of MRI. (Illus.). 400p. 1996. pap. 110.00 (*0-8385-1501-0*, A15014, Apple Lange Med) McGraw.

Beltran, L. Virgilio. Para Atrapar un Foton. (Ciencia para Todos Ser.). (SPA.). pap. 6.99 (*968-16-3579-5*, Pub. by Fondo) Continental Bk.

Beltran, Mary J., jt. auth. see Riley, Mary A.

***Beltran, Rosa.** La Corte de los Ilusos, 1. (Autores Espanoles E Iberoamericanos Ser.). (SPA.). 1998. write for info. (*84-08-02444-2*, Pub. by Planeta Edit) Planeta.

Beltran-Vidal, Daniele, ed. Imaes d'Ernst Junger: Actes due Colloque Organise par le Centre de Recherche sur l'Identite Allemande de l'Universite de Savoie, Chambery (30 et 31 Mars 1995) (FRE.). 176p. 1996. 31.95 (*3-906754-46-4*, Pub. by P Lang) P Lang Pubng.

BeltrandelRio, Hector, tr. see Grin, Oliver D. & Bouwman, Dorothy L.

BeltrandelRio, Marisa, tr. see Grin, Oliver D. & Bouwman, Dorothy L.

Beltrao, Maria D., jt. auth. see Kitchen, K. A.

Beltratti, Andrea. Models of Economic Growth with Environmental Assets. LC 96-14433. (Ecology, Economy & Environment Ser.: Vol. 8). 1996. lib. bdg. 92.50 (*0-7923-4032-9*) Kluwer Academic.

Beltrone, Art, ed. Old Bethpage Village Restoration. (Illus.). 48p. 1990. pap. 3.25 (*0-911357-03-3*) Friends Long Island.

Beltrone, Art & Beltrone, Lee. A Wartime Log. (Illus.). 208p. 1995. 34.95 (*0-943231-90-6*) Howell Pr VA.

Beltrone, Art & Beltrone, Lee. A Wartime Log. 208p. 1997. pap. 80.00 (*1-86227-013-9*, Pub. by Spellmnt Pubs) St Mut.

Beltrone, Lee, jt. auth. see Beltrone, Art.

Beltz. High-Tech Maneuvers: Industrial Policy Lessons from HDTV. 144p. (C). 1991. 29.75 (*0-8447-3767-4*) Am Enterprise.

Beltz, Barbara & Burd, D., eds. Immunocytochemical Techniques: Principles & Practice. (Illus.). 208p. (C). 1989. pap., student ed. 49.95 (*0-86542-065-3*) Blackwell Sci.

Beltz, Bob. Becoming a Man of Prayer: A Seven Week Strategy Based on the Instructions of Jesus. LC 96-22565. 160p. 1996. pap. 10.00 (*0-89109-981-6*, 99816) NavPress.

— Becoming a Man of the Spirit: A Seven-Week Strategy Based on the Ministry of the Holy Spirit. LC 98-51391. 125p. 1999. pap. 9.00 (*1-57683-055-1*) NavPress.

— Daily Disciplines for the Christian Man: Practical Steps to an Empowered Spiritual Life. LC 93-86110. 162p. 1994. pap. 8.00 (*0-89109-765-1*) NavPress.

Beltz, Cynthia A. Borderless Economy: Global Trade Rules & the Internet. 1999. 29.95 (*0-8447-4000-4*); pap. 14.95 (*0-8447-4001-2*) Am Enterprise.

— Financing Entrepreneurs. 150p. (Orig.). 1994. pap. 9.25 (*0-8447-3849-2*, AEI Pr) Am Enterprise.

— The Foreign Investment Debate: Opening Markets Abroad, Closing Markets at Home? LC 95-18045. 200p. 1995. 29.95 (*0-8447-3886-7*, AEI Pr); pap. 14.95 (*0-8447-3887-5*, AEI Pr) Am Enterprise.

Beltz, George F. Memorials of the Most Noble Order of the Garter from Its Foundation to the Present Time. LC 72-178572. reprint ed. 64.50 (*0-404-56527-1*) AMS Pr.

Beltz, Glenn E., et al, eds. Fracture & Ductile vs. Brittle Behavior-Theory, Modelling & Experiment, Vol. 539. LC 99-18998. (Symposium Proceedings Ser.). 334p. 1999. 83.00 (*1-55899-445-9*) Materials Res.

Beltz, Heidi von, see Von Beltz, Heidi.

Beltz, Muriel. Cooking with Natural Foods, No. 1. LC 96-60253. 144p. 1996. reprint ed. spiral bd. 14.95 (*1-57258-110-7*) Teach Servs.

Beltzer, A. I. Acoustics of Solids. ix, 237p. 1988. 104.95 (*0-387-18888-6*) Spr-Verlag.

— Engineering Analysis with Maple/Mathematica. (Illus.). 304p. 1995. text, boxed set 63.00 incl. disk (*0-12-085570-4*) Acad Pr.

— Variational & Finite Element Methods. (Illus.). 240p. 1990. 87.95 (*0-387-51598-4*) Spr-Verlag.

Beltzer, Thomas. Antojitos: Little Cravings. LC 99-25067. 78p. 1999. pap. 14.95 (*0-7734-3117-9*) E Mellen.

Belue, Ted F. The Long Hunt: Death of the Buffalo East of the Mississippi. (Illus.). 288p. 1996. 22.95 (*0-8117-0968-X*) Stackpole.

Belue, Ted F., ed. see Houston, Peter.

Belusevic, Radoje. Neutral Kaons. LC 99-18463. (Tracts in Modern Physics Ser.). 183p. 1999. 119.00 (*3-540-65645-6*) Spr-Verlag.

***Belussi, Fiorenza & Gottardi, Giorgio, eds.** Evolutionary Patterns of Local Industrial Systems. LC 99-75550. 194p. 2000. text 69.95 (*1-84014-520-X*, Pub. by Ashgate Pub) Ashgate Pub Co.

Belval, Norman J., tr. see Massaux, Edouard.

Belvedere, G., ed. Accretion Disks & Magnetic Fields in Astrophysics. (C). 1989. text 171.00 (*0-7923-0295-8*) Kluwer Academic.

Belvedere, G., et al, eds. European Meeting on Solar Physics. LC 94-15101. (Lecture Notes in Physics Ser.: Vol. 432). 1994. 79.95 (*0-387-58041-7*) Spr-Verlag.

Belvin, Betty M. Ray McLain & the National Guard. (Illus.). 214p. 1994. pap. 22.95 (*0-89745-173-2*) Sunflower U Pr.

Belvins, T. F., ed. see Richardson, Robert M.

***Belvisi, M. G. & Mitchell, J. A., eds.** Nitric Oxide in Pulmonary Processes: Role in Physiology & Pathophysiology of Lung Disease. LC 99-36128. (Respiratory Pharmacology & Pharmacotherapy Ser.). (Illus.). 330p. 1999. 119.00 (*3-7643-5718-5*, Pub. by Birkhauser) Spr-Verlag.

Belvoir Publications Staff. The Aviation Consumer Used Aircraft Guide. 3rd exp. ed. (Illus.). 320p. 1989. pap. 27.95 (*0-07-155488-2*) McGraw.

— The Aviation Consumer Used Aircraft Guide. 3rd expanded ed. 1990. pap. 24.95 (*0-8306-2441-4*, 2441) McGraw-Hill Prof.

— Aviation Safety's Flying Circus. 2nd ed. (Illus.). 1989. pap. 14.95 (*0-8306-2421-X*, 2421P) McGraw-Hill Prof.

Belvoir Publications Staff & Thomas, Kas. Aircraft Engine Operating Guide. (Illus.). 224p. 1988. pap. 15.95 (*0-8306-2431-7*, 2431P) McGraw-Hill Prof.

— Lightplane Maintenance: Aircraft Engineer Operating Guide. 224p. 1989. pap. 18.95 (*0-07-155358-4*) McGraw.

Belward, Alan S. & Valenzuela, Carlos R., eds. Remote Sensing & Geographical Information Systems for Resource Management in Developing Countries. (C). 1991. text 237.50 (*0-7923-1268-6*) Kluwer Academic.

Belwin, C. The Complete Christmas Music Collection. Cuellar, Carol, ed. 164p. (Orig.). (YA). 1995. pap. text 16.95 (*0-89724-735-3*, F3350SMA) Wrner Bros.

Belwin Inc. Staff. Complete Rock 'n' Roll Collection: Piano/vocal/chords, Revised Ed. 1998. pap. text 16.95 (*0-7692-2113-0*) Wrner Bros.

Belwood, Jacqueline J. Bats. LC 97-75449. (In Ohio's Backyard Ser.: No. 1). (Illus.). 200p. 1997. ring bd. 12.95 (*0-86727-125-6*) Ohio Bio Survey.

Bely. Petersburg. unabridged ed. (World Classic Literature Ser.). (RUS.). pap. 8.95 (*2-87714-266-3*, Pub. by Bookking Intl) Distribks Inc.

Bely, Andrei. The Christened Chinaman. Beyer, Thomas R., tr. from RUS. LC 91-32723. 187p. (Orig.). 1991. pap. 12.00 (*1-55779-042-6*) Hermitage Pubs.

— Kotik Letaev. Janecek, Gerald J., tr. from RUS. LC 99-19486. (European Classics Ser.). 288p. 1999. pap. 17.95 (*0-8101-1626-X*) Northwestern U Pr.

— Petersburg. Maguire, Robert A. & Malmstad, John E., trs. from RUS. LC 77-74442. 384p. 1979. pap. 15.95 (*0-253-20219-1*, MB 219) Ind U Pr.

— Petersburg. McDuff, David, tr. LC Png UK. 624p. 1996. pap. 15.95 (*0-14-018696-4*, Penguin Classics) Viking Penguin.

***Bely, Andrew.** The Silver Dove. 2000. pap. 17.95 (*0-8101-1757-6*) Northwestern U Pr.

Bely, Andrey. The First Encounter. LC 78-70276. (Illus.). 167p. reprint ed. pap. 51.80 (*0-8357-3691-1*, 203641500003) Bks Demand.

— Gibel' Senatora (Peterburg) Istoricheskaia Drama. Malmstad, John E., ed. & afterword by by. (Modern Russian Literature & Culture, Studies & Texts: Vol. 12). (RUS.). 237p. (Orig.). 1986. pap. 12.00 (*0-933884-52-4*) Berkeley Slavic.

— Korolevna i Rytsari: Skazki. (RUS.). 56p. (C). 1989. reprint ed. pap. 6.50 (*0-933884-69-9*) Berkeley Slavic.

— Posle Razluki: Berlinskii Pesennik. (RUS.). 125p. 1989. reprint ed. pap. 8.00 (*0-933884-74-5*) Berkeley Slavic.

Bely-Dubau, F., ed. Element Abundance Variations in the Sun & Heliosphere: Proceedings of the E2.1 Meeting of COSPAR Scientific Commission E Which Was Held During the 30th COSPAR Scientific Assembly, Hamburg, Germany, 11-21 July, 1994. (Advances in Space Research Ser.: Vol. 15). 102p. 1995. pap. 104.00 (*0-08-042557-7*, Pergamon Pr) Elsevier.

Bely, Pierre Y. & Breckinridge, James B., eds. Space Telescopes & Instruments IV. 370p. 1996. 66.00 (*0-8194-2195-2*) SPIE.

Bely, Pierre Y. & Breckinridge, James B., eds. Space Telescopes & Instruments V. LC 98-227306. (Proceedings of SPIE Ser.: Vol. 3356). 1260p. 1998. 166.00 (*0-8194-2803-5*) SPIE.

Belyaev, A., tr. see Palmov, V.

Belyaev, A. K., tr. see Kolovsky, M. Z., et al.

Belyaev, L. S. Energy Reviews Vol. 5, Pt. 1: Development of System Studies in the Energy Sector of the U. S. S. R. - Taking Uncertainty of Information into Account in Solving, Vol. 5. (Soviet Technology Reviews Ser.: Section A). 92p. 1991. pap. text 94.00 (*3-7186-5162-9*, Harwood Acad Pubs) Gordon & Breach.

Belyaev, S. T. Collective Excitations in Nuclei. x, 74p. 1968. pap. text 58.00 (*0-677-01875-4*) Gordon & Breach.

Belyaev, V. B. Lectures on the Theory of Few-Body Systems. (Nuclear & Particle Physics Ser.). (Illus.). 136p. 1990. 49.95 (*0-387-18587-9*) Spr-Verlag.

Belyaeva, Natasha. Hunger. HIrschman, Jack, tr. from RUS. 1977. pap. 2.50 (*0-317-17250-6*) DAurora Pr.

Belyakov, R. A. & Marmain, Jacques. Mig: Fifty Years of Secret Aircraft Design. LC 93-4526. (Illus.). 479p. 1994. 49.95 (*1-55750-566-7*) Naval Inst Pr.

Belyakov, V. A. Diffraction Optics of Complex-Structured Periodic Media. (Partially Ordered Systems Ser.). (Illus.). 352p. 1992. 119.95 (*0-387-97654-X*) Spr-Verlag.

Belyakov, V. A. & Dmitrienko, V. E. Physics Reviews: Optics of Chiral Liquid Crystals, Vol. 13. Gol'danskii, V. I. et al, eds. (Soviet Scientific Reviews Ser.: Vol. 13, Pt. 1). ii, 222p. 1989. pap. text 249.00 (*3-7186-4950-0*) Gordon & Breach.

Belyakov, Vladimir V. & Raymond, Walter J., eds. Constitution of the Russian Federation: With Commentaries & Interpretations. LC 94-4723. 1994. 35.00 (*1-55618-143-4*); pap. 12.00 (*1-55618-142-6*) Brunswick Pub.

An Asterisk (*) at the beginning of an entry indicates that the title is appearing for the first time.

B

Bemis, J. D. & Bemis, A. A. Watson: History & Genealogy of the Watson Family, Descendants of Matthew Watson Who Came to America in 1718. 163p. 1994. reprint ed. pap. 27.00 (*0-8328-4064-5*); reprint ed. lib. bdg. 37.00 (*0-8328-4063-7*) Higginson Bk Co.

Bemis, Judith & Barrada, Amr. Embracing the Fear: Learning to Manage Anxiety & Panic Attacks. 160p. pap. 10.00 (*0-89486-971-X*, 1510A) Hazelden.

Bemis, Katherine I., jt. auth. see Holtz, Mathilde E.

Bemis, Samuel F. American Foreign Policy & the Blessings of Liberty, & Other Essays. LC 75-11972. 423p. 1975. reprint ed. lib. bdg. 35.00 (*0-8371-8132-1*, BEAF, Greenwood Pr) Greenwood.

— The Diplomacy of the American Revolution. LC 83-12977. 293p. 1983. reprint ed. lib. bdg. 45.50 (*0-313-24173-2*, BEDI, Greenwood Pr) Greenwood.

— Jay's Treaty: A Study in Commerce & Diplomacy. LC 75-11844. (Illus.). 526p. 1975. reprint ed. lib. bdg. 35.00 (*0-8371-8133-X*, BEJT, Greenwood Pr) Greenwood.

— Pinckney's Treaty: America's Advantage from Europe's Distress, 1783-1800. LC 73-8148. (Illus.). 372p. 1973. reprint ed. lib. bdg. 65.00 (*0-8371-6954-2*, BEPT, Greenwood Pr) Greenwood.

Bemis, Stephen E., et al. Job Analysis: An Effective Management Tool. LC 83-18923. 239p. 1988. reprint ed. pap. 74.10 (*0-608-00697-1*, 206146900009) Bks Demand.

Bemis, W. E., jt. auth. see Northcutt, R. G.

Bemiss, Elijah. The Dyer's Companion. LC 73-77377. 312p. 1973. reprint ed. pap. 9.95 (*0-486-20601-7*) Dover.

— Vocabulary Dynamics. 208p. (Orig.). (C). 2000. pap. 17.00 (*0-321-05496-2*) Addson-Wesley Educ.

Bemister, Clara L. Vegetarian Menus: One for Each Day in a Month (185 Recipes) 67p. 1997. pap. 5.00 (*0-89540-280-7*, SB-280) Sun Pub.

Bemister, Margaret. Thirty Indian Legends of Canada. (Illus.). 158p. (J). (gr. 3-7). 1991. pap. 9.95 (*0-88894-025-4*) Publishers Group.

Bemitez, Luis. Seleccion Poetica: Selected Poems. Miranda, Veronica, ed. & tr. by. (Carpeta de Poesia Luz Bilingue Ser.: No. 1). (ENG & SPA.). 40p. (Orig.). 1996. 6.00 (*0-9634009-2-4*) Luz Bilingual.

Bemmann, Hans, ed. The Stone & the Flute. Bell, Anthea, tr. 864p. 1988. pap. 14.95 (*0-14-007445-7*, Penguin Bks) Viking Penguin.

Bemmel, Dolores Van, see Van Bemmel, John & Van Bemmel, Dolores.

Bemmel, J. Van, see Van Bemmel, J., ed.

Bemmel, John Van, see Van Bemmel, John.

Bemmelen, D. J. Van, see Van Bemmelen, D. J.

Bemont, Charles. Simon de Montford, Earl of Leicester, 1208-1265. Jacob, Ernest F., tr. LC 74-9223. (Illus.). 303p. 1974. reprint ed. lib. bdg. 35.00 (*0-8371-7625-5*, BESM, Greenwood Pr) Greenwood.

Bemowski, Karen & Stratton, Brad, eds. 101 Good Ideas: How to Improve Just about Any Process. LC 98-8553. (Illus.). xiv, 284p. 1998. pap. 21.00 (*0-87389-391-3*, H0986) ASQ Qual Pr.

Bempah, Kofi. Crofa: Family Coloring, Photo, & Story Book. (Illus.). (Orig.). (YA). 1995. pap. text 10.00 (*0-9639258-5-7*) N Horizon Pubs.

Bempechat, Janine. Against the Odds: How "At-Risk" Students Exceed Expectations. LC 98-25348. (Education Ser.). 224p. 1998. 32.95 (*0-7879-4385-1*) Jossey-Bass.

***Bempechat, Janine.** Getting Our Kids Back on Track: Educating Children for the Future. 224p. 2000. 25.00 (*0-7879-4991-4*) Jossey-Bass.

Bemporad, Jack & Shevack, Michael. Our Age: The Historic New Era of Christian-Jewish Understanding. (Today's Issues Ser.). 96p. (Orig.). 1996. pap. 6.95 (*1-56548-081-3*) New City.

Bemporad, Jack, jt. auth. see Shevack, Michael.

Bemporad, Jules R. & Herzog, David B., eds. Psychoanalysis & Eating Disorders. 174p. 1989. lib. bdg. 30.00 (*0-89862-388-X*) Guilford Pubns.

Bemrose, Stephen. A New Life of Dante. 224p. 1999. 75.00 (*0-85989-583-1*, Pub. by Univ Exeter Pr); pap. 22.95 (*0-85989-584-X*) Univ Exeter Pr.

Bems, Betsy. The Female Fan Guide to Motorsports. (Illus.). 150p. 1999. pap. 12.95 (*0-9653882-4-7*) BVision Sptsmedia.

Bemtgen, J. M., jt. auth. see Imarisio, G.

Ben Abba, Dor. Hebrew-English, English-Hebrew Dictionary: 35,000 Entries, Transliterated Hebrew Words in English Characters, English Words in Hebrew Characters. (ENG & HEB.). 700p. 1977. 25.50 (*0-87559-211-2*) Shalom.

Ben-Abba, Dov. The Meridian Hebrew-English English-Hebrew Dictionary. 720p. 1994. pap. 18.95 (*0-452-01121-3*, Mer) NAL.

Ben-Aharon, Jesaiah. The New Experience of the Supersensible. 256p. 1995. 39.95 (*0-904693-67-8*, Pub. by Temple Lodge) Anthroposophic.

Ben-Aharon, Moshe, et al. The Many Faces of Judaism: Orthodox, Conservative, Reconstructionist, & Reform. Rossel, Seymour, ed. LC 78-25898. 1979. pap., teacher ed. 14.95 (*0-87441-339-7*) Behrman.

Ben Aharon, Shmuel. Midrash Bet HaShem: The Alphabet. 3rd rev. ed. (Illus.). 22p. 1986. pap. text. write for info. (*0-9616488-1-3*) Alef Bet Comns.

Ben-Akiva, Moshe & Lerman, Steven. Discrete Choice Analysis: Theory & Application to Travel Demand. (Transportation Studies). 384p. (C). 1985. 57.50 (*0-262-02217-6*) MIT Pr.

Ben-Ami, Aharon. Social Change in a Hostile Environment: The Crusador's Kingdom of Jerusalem. LC 68-27412. (Princeton Studies on the Near East). 201p. reprint ed. pap. 62.40 (*0-608-17848-9*, 203263100080) Bks Demand.

Ben-Ami, Issachar. Saint Veneration among the Jews of Morocco. LC 97-15878. (Raphael Patai Series of Jewish Folklore & Anthropology). (Illus.). 384p. 1997. text 49.95 (*0-8143-2198-4*) Wayne St U Pr.

***Ben-Ami, Shlomo, et al.** Ethnic Challenges to the Modern Nation State. LC 99-49537. 2000. text 69.95 (*0-312-23053-2*) St Martin.

***Ben-Amos, Avner.** Funerals, Politics & Memory in Modern France 1789-1996. LC 99-87882. (Illus.). 380p. 2000. text 85.00 (*0-19-820328-4*) OUP.

Ben-Amos, Dan, et al, eds. Mimekor Yisrael: Classical Jewish Folktales. Lask, I. M., tr. LC 88-46028. 560p. 1991. 24.95 (*0-253-31158-6*) Ind U Pr.

— Mimekor Yisreal: Selected Classical Jewish Folktales. Lask, I. M., tr. LC 88-46029. 288p. 1990. 31.95 (*0-253-31156-X*); pap. 13.95 (*0-253-20588-3*, MB 588) Ind U Pr.

Ben-Amos, Dan & Mintz, Jerome R., eds. In Praise of the Baal Shem Tov (Shivhei ha-Besht) The Earliest Collection of Legends about the Founder of Hasidism. LC 93-43456. 384p. 1994. pap. 40.00 (*1-56821-147-3*) Aronson.

Ben-Amos, Dan & Weissberg, Lillian. Cultural Memory & the Construction of Identity. LC 98-24234. 1998. pap. text 27.95 (*0-8143-2753-2*, Great Lks Bks) Wayne St U Pr.

Ben-Amos, Dan, jt. ed. see Noy, Dov.

Ben-Amos, Ilana K. Adolescence & Youth in Early Modern England. LC 93-38314. 320p. 1994. 40.00 (*0-300-05597-8*) Yale U Pr.

***Ben-Amos, Paula G.** Art, Innovation, & Politics in Eighteenth-Century Benin. LC 98-50780. (Illus.). 208p. 1999. text 35.00 (*0-253-33503-5*) Ind U Pr.

Ben-Amotz, Ami, ed. Dunaliella: Physiology, Biochemistry & Biotechnology. 256p. 1992. lib. bdg. 199.00 (*0-8493-6647-X*) CRC Pr.

Ben-Amotz, Noa. Discover Another Nashville: An Updated Essential Guide for Natives & Newcomers with Hundreds of Interesting, Unusual & Alternative Listings. rev. ed. 1996. pap. write for info. (*0-9637105-1-6*) Common Ground.

***Ben-Ari.** ADA for Software Engineers. LC 98-18158. 440p. 1998. pap. text 64.99 incl. cd-rom (*0-471-97912-0*) Wiley.

***Ben Ari.** Mastering Soldiers: Conflict, Emotions & the Enemy in an Israeli Military Unit. 2000. 18.95 (*1-57181-838-3*) Berghahn Bks.

Ben-Ari, Eyal. Body Projects in Japanese Childcare: Culture, Organization & Emotions in a Preschool. 288p. (C). 1997. text 48.00 (*0-7007-0448-5*, Pub. by Curzon Pr Ltd) UH Pr.

— Changing Japanese Suburbia. (Japanese Studies). 250p. 1990. 75.00 (*0-7103-0381-5*, A4533) Routledge.

— Japanese Childcare: An Interpretive Study of Culture & Organization. LC 96-15617. (Japanese Studies). 250p. 1996. 110.00 (*0-7103-0553-2*, Pub. by Kegan Paul Intl) Col U Pr.

— Mastering Soldiers: Conflict, Emotions & the Enemy in an Israeli Military Unit. LC 97-42089. (New Directions in Anthropology Ser.). (Illus.). 157p. 1998. 35.00 (*1-57181-145-1*) Berghahn Bks.

Ben-Ari, Eyal, et al, eds. Unwrapping Japan: Society & Culture in Anthropological Perspective. LC 89-35666. 266p. 1991. pap. text 19.00 (*0-8248-1412-6*) UH Pr.

Ben-Ari, Eyal & Bilu, Yoram, eds. Grasping Land: Space & Place in Contemporary Israeli Discourse & Experience. LC 96-15390. (SUNY Series in Anthropology & Judaic Studies). 160p. (C). 1997. text 54.50 (*0-7914-3217-3*); pap. text 17.95 (*0-7914-3218-1*) State U NY Pr.

Ben-Ari, Eyal, ed. see Eisenstadt, Samuel N.

Ben-Ari, Eyal, jt. ed. see Lomsky-Feder, Edna.

Ben-Ari, M. Principles of Concurrent & Distributed Programming. 2nd ed. 350p. 1990. pap. 64.00 (*0-13-711821-X*) P-H.

Ben-Ari, Monti. Understanding Programming Languages. 376p. 1996. pap. 64.99 (*0-471-95846-8*) Wiley.

Ben-Ari, Yehezkel, ed. Excitatory Amino Acids & Neuronal Plasticity. LC 90-7177. (Advances in Experimental Medicine & Biology Ser.: Vol. 268). (Illus.). 540p. (C). 1990. text 174.00 (*0-306-43534-9*, Kluwer Plenum) Kluwer Academic.

Ben-Ari, Yehezkel, jt. ed. see Schwarcz, Robert.

***Ben-Arieh, Asher & Gal, John, eds.** Into the Promised Land: Issues Facing the Welfare State. LC 00-22342. 240p. 2000. 59.00 (*0-275-96905-3*, C6905, Praeger Pubs) Greenwood.

Ben-Arieh, Y. The Rediscovery of the Holy Land in the Nineteenth Century. 2nd ed. 266p. (C). 1983. text 25.00 (*965-223-326-9*, Pub. by Magnes Pr) Eisenbrauns.

Ben-Arieh, Yehoshua. Jerusalem in the Nineteenth Century. 98p. 1989. pap. 12.00 (*965-05-0051-0*, Pub. by Israel Ministry Def) Gefen Bks.

Ben-Arieh, Yehoshua. The Rediscovery of the Holy Land in the Nineteenth Century. LC 79-67619. (Illus.). 266p. reprint ed. pap. 82.50 (*0-7837-3649-5*, 204352000009) Bks Demand.

Ben-Arieh, Yehoshua & Davis, Moshe, eds. Jerusalem in the Mind of the Western World, 1800-1948. V. LC 96-20171. (With Eyes Toward Zion Ser.: Vol. V). 296p. 1997. 69.50 (*0-275-95405-6*, Praeger Pubs) Greenwood.

Ben-Artzi, M. & Devinatz, A. The Limiting Absorption Principle for Partial Differential Operators. LC 87-1807. (Memoirs of the American Mathematical Society Ser.: Vol. 66/364). 70p. 1987. pap. 16.00 (*0-8218-2426-0*, MEMO/66/364) Am Math.

Ben Artzi-Pelossof, Noa. In the Name of Sorrow & Hope. LC 96-48430. 208p. 1997. pap. 11.00 (*0-8052-1084-9*) Schocken.

Ben-Asher, Joseph & Yaesh, Isaac. Advances in Missile Guidance Theory Vol. 180: Progress in Astronautics & Aeronautics. LC 98-194778. 200p. 1998. 79.95 (*1-56347-275-9*) AIAA.

Ben-Atar, Doron S. & Oberg, Barbara B., eds. Federalists Reconsidered. LC 98-34195. 281p. 1999. text 47.50 (*0-8139-1819-7*) U Pr of Va.

***Ben-Atar, Doron S. & Oberg, Barbara B., eds.** Federalists Reconsidered. LC 98-34195. 310 p. 1999. pap. text 17.50 (*0-8139-1863-4*) U Pr of Va.

Ben-Avner, Yehuda. Vom Orthodoxen Judentum in Deutschland Zwischen Zwei Weltkriegen. (GER.). vi, 100p. 1987. write for info. (*3-487-07969-0*) G Olms Pubs.

***Ben-Avraham, Daniel & Havlin, Shlomo.** Diffusion & Reactions in Fractals & Disordered Systems. (Illus.). 300p. (C). 2000. Price not set. (*0-521-62278-6*) Cambridge U Pr.

Ben Avraham, Eliyahu. Messiah. 32p. 1992. pap. 3.75 (*0-9632485-0-2*) Theiss Pubns.

Ben-Avraham, Zvi, ed. The Evolution of the Pacific Ocean Margins. (Oxford Monographs on Geology & Geophysics: No. 8). (Illus.). 256p. 1989. text 120.00 (*0-19-504301-4*) OUP.

Ben-Bassat, Avraham. Reserve-Currency Diversification & the Substitution Account. LC 84-581. (Studies in International Finance: No. 53). 42p. 1984. pap. text 13.50 (*0-88165-225-3*) Princeton U Int Finan Econ.

***Ben-Bassat, Hedda.** Prophets Without Vision: Subjectivity & the Sacred in Contemporary American Writing. LC 99-54765. 216p. 2000. 38.50 (*0-8387-5433-3*) Bucknell U Pr.

Ben Bassett, M, jt. ed. see Ein-Dor, P.

Ben Chaim, Daphna. Distance in the Theatre: The Aesthetics of Audience Response. LC 83-24231. (Theater & Dramatic Studies: No. 17). 124p. reprint ed. pap. 38.50 (*0-8357-1940-5*, 207065700015) Bks Demand.

Ben-Dak, Joseph, jt. auth. see Azar, Edward E.

Ben-David, Arye. Talmudische Okonomie Band I: Theorie und Praxis der Nationalokonomie Palastinas Zur Zeit der Mischna und Des Thalmuds Aufgrune Talmudischer Quellen. (GER.). xii, 488p. 1973. write for info. (*3-487-04655-5*) G Olms Pubs.

Ben-David, Joseph. Scientific Growth: Essays on the Social Organization & Ethos of Science. (California Studies in the History of Science: No. 8). 576p. 1991. 75.00 (*0-520-06925-0*, Pub. by U CA Pr) Cal Prin Full Svc.

— The Scientist's Role in Society: A Comparative Study with a New Introduction. LC 84-2758. 236p. 1984. reprint ed. pap. text 11.95 (*0-226-04221-9*) U Ch Pr.

— The Scientist's Role in Society: A Comparative Study with a New Introduction. LC 84-2758. 236p. 1984. reprint ed. lib. bdg. 24.00 (*0-226-04227-8*) U Ch Pr.

— The Scientist's Role in Society: A Comparative Study with a New Introduction. LC 84-2758. (Illus.). 235p. Date not set. reprint ed. pap. 72.90 (*0-608-21006-4*, 205453400003) Bks Demand.

— Trends in American Higher Education. LC 78-177370. (Midway Reprint Ser.). xii, 150p. 1981. pap. text 11.00 (*0-226-04225-1*) U Ch Pr.

Ben-David, Joseph & Altbach, Philip G. Centers of Learning: Britain, France, Germany, United States. 240p. (C). 1992. pap. 24.95 (*1-56000-604-8*) Transaction Pubs.

Ben-David, Joseph & Clark, Terry N. Culture & Its Creators. LC 76-610. 336p. 1977. lib. bdg. 36.00 (*0-226-04222-7*) U Ch Pr.

Ben-David, Joseph, ed. see Aron, Raymond.

Ben-David, S., et al, eds. Computational Learning Theory Vol. 120: Third European Conference, EuroCOLT '97, Jerusalem, Israel, March 17-19, 1997, Proceedings. LC 97-6034. (Lecture Notes in Artificial Intelligence Ser.: Vol. 1208). viii, 331p. 1997. pap. 55.00 (*3-540-62685-9*) Spr-Verlag.

Ben-Daya, M., jt. auth. see Raouf, A.

Ben-Dor, G. Shock Wave Reflection Phenomena. (Illus.). 328p. 1991. 109.95 (*0-387-97707-4*) Spr-Verlag.

Ben-Dor, Gabriel. State & Conflict in the Middle East: Emergence of the Post-Colonial State. LC 82-24616. 270p. 1983. 34.95 (*0-275-90946-8*, C0946, Praeger Pubs) Greenwood.

Ben-Dor, Gabriel, jt. ed. see Bengio, Ofra.

***Ben-Dov, Henry.** Of Love & Blood. LC 00-190432. 2000. pap. 18.00 (*0-7388-1704-X*) Xlibris Corp.

— Of Love & Blood: A Novel of Suspense. LC 00-190432. 2000. 25.00 (*0-7388-1703-1*) Xlibris Corp.

Ben-Dov, Meir. Jerusalem Men & Stone. 1987. 24.95 (*0-915361-68-5*) Lambda Pubs.

Ben-Dov, Meir, et al. The Western Wall (Hakotel) (ENG & GER.). 248p. 1995. 19.00 (*965-05-0053-7*, Pub. by Israel Ministry Def) Gefen Bks.

Ben-Dov, Meir, jt. auth. see Rappel, Yoel.

Ben-Dov, Nitza. Agnon's Art of Indirection: Uncovering Latent Content in the Fiction of S. Y. Agnon. LC 93-30732. (Jewish Studies: Vol. 7). x, 167p. 1993. 79.00 (*90-04-09863-1*) Brill Academic Pubs.

Ben-Dov, Yair. A Systematic Catalogue of the Soft Scale Insects (Homoptera: Coccoidea, Coccidae) of the World: With Data on Geographical Distribution, Host Plants, Biology, & Economics Importance. LC 93-9502. (Flora & Fauna Handbook Ser.: No. 9). (Illus.). x, 350p. (Orig.). 1993. pap. 89.95 (*1-877743-13-5*) Sandhill Crane.

Ben-Dov, Yair & Hodgson, Christopher J., eds. Soft Scale Insects: Their Biology, Natural Enemies & Control. LC 97-39995. (World Crop Pests Ser.: Vol. 7B). 442p. 1997. 264.50 (*0-444-82843-5*, SB945, North Holland) Elsevier.

— Soft Scale Insects: Their Biology, Natural Enemies & Control. LC 97-39995. (World Crop Pests Ser.: Vol. 7A). (Illus.). 476p. 1997. 270.00 (*0-444-89303-2*, North Holland) Elsevier.

Ben-Elia, Nahum, ed. Local Government Policy-Making & Management: A Crossnational Perspective. (Orig.). 1993. pap. 15.00 (*0-944285-32-5*) Pol Studies.

— Strategic Changes & Organizational Reorientations in Local Government: A Cross-National Perspective. LC 95-19327. 188p. 1996. text 65.00 (*0-312-12856-8*) St Martin.

Ben Eliezer, Shimon. Destruction & Renewal: The Synagogues of the Jewish Quarter in Jerusalem. 64p. 1973. pap. 13.00 (*965-09-0111-6*, 73811, Pub. by R Mass Ltd) Lambda Pubs.

Ben-Eliezer, Uri. The Making of Israeli Militarism. LC 97-46020. 320p. Date not set. 35.00 (*0-253-33387-3*) Ind U Pr.

Ben-Ephraim, Gavriel. The Moon's Dominion: Narrative Dichotomy & Female Dominance in the First Five Novels of D. H. Lawrence. LC 78-75172. 256p. 1981. 35.00 (*0-8386-2266-6*) Fairleigh Dickinson.

Ben-Ezer, Ehud. Hosni the Dreamer: An Arabian Tale. LC 96-18608. (Illus.). 32p. (J). (ps-3). 1997. 16.00 (*0-374-33340-8*) FS&G.

***Ben-Ezer, Ehud, ed.** Sleepwalkers & Other Stories: The Arab in Hebrew Fiction. LC 98-25852. 184p. 1998. pap. 22.00 (*0-89410-852-2*) L Rienner.

***Ben-Ghiat, Ruth.** Fascist Modernities: Italy, 1922-1945. LC 99-87279. Vol. 42. (Illus.). 334p. 2001. 45.00 (*0-520-22363-2*, Pub. by U CA Pr) Cal Prin Full Svc.

Ben-Gurion, David. Ben-Gurion Looks at the Bible. Kolatch, Jonathan, tr. LC 70-167600. 320p. 1972. 16.95 (*0-8246-0127-0*) Jonathan David.

— My Talks with Arab Leaders. LC 72-94298. 342p. 1973. 30.00 (*0-89388-076-0*) Okpaku Communications.

Ben-Hadd, Betsy, jt. auth. see Hadd, Ooben.

Ben-Haim, Yakov. The Assay of Spacially Random Materials. 1985. text 175.00 (*90-277-2066-5*) Kluwer Academic.

— Robust Reliability in the Mechanical Science. LC 96-13060. 233p. 1996. 74.95 (*3-540-61058-8*) Spr-Verlag.

Ben-Haim, Yakov. Uncertainty: Models & Measures. Natke, H. G., ed. 276p. 1997. pap. 89.95 (*3-527-40104-0*) Wiley.

Ben-Haim, Yakov & Elishakoff, Isaac. Convex Models of Uncertainty in Applied Mechanics. (Studies in Applied Mechanics: No. 25). 222p. 1990. 142.50 (*0-444-88406-8*) Elsevier.

Ben-Horim, Moshe. Essentials of Corporate Finance. 720p. 1987. teacher ed. write for info. (*0-318-61489-8*, H88495); teacher ed. write for info. (*0-318-61490-1*, H88487); student ed. 22.00 (*0-685-17391-7*, H88503); trans. write for info. (*0-318-61491-X*, H12958) P-H.

Ben-Horin, Yoav, jt. ed. see Gordis, David.

Ben-Hur, Ehud & Rosenthal, Ionel, eds. Photomedicine, 3 vols. LC 86-34293. 1987. 361.00 (*0-8493-4673-8*, RM837, CRC Reprint) Franklin.

— Photomedicine, 3 vols., Vol. 1. 224p. 1987. 116.00 (*0-8493-4674-6*, CRC Reprint) Franklin.

— Photomedicine, 3 vols., Vol. 2. 256p. 1987. 125.00 (*0-8493-4675-4*, CRC Reprint) Franklin.

— Photomedicine, 3 vols., Vol. 3. 240p. 1987. 122.00 (*0-8493-4676-2*, CRC Reprint) Franklin.

Ben-Hur, Meir, ed. On Feuerstein's Instrumental Enrichment: A Collection. LC 94-78544. 284p. 1994. pap. 24.95 (*0-932935-76-1*) SkyLght.

Ben-Hur, Raphaella B. Every Individual a King: The Social & Political Thought of Ze'ev Vladimir Jabotinsky. Abramson, Shifa C., tr. from HEB. LC 93-13605.Tr. of Kol Yahid Hu Melekh. 305p. (C). 1993. 39.95 (*0-910250-24-3*) Bnai Brith Intl.

— Every Individual a King: The Social & Political Thought of Ze'ev Vladimir Jabotinsky. Abramson, Shifa C., tr. from HEB. LC 93-13605.Tr. of Kol Yahid Hu Melekh. 305p. (C). 1993. pap. 22.50 (*0-910250-25-1*) Bnai Brith Intl.

Ben-Israel, A. & Gilbert, R. P. Computer-Supported Calculus: With Macsyma Example Sessions, 2 vols. 1000p. 1999. 80.00 (*3-211-82924-5*) Spr-Verlag.

Ben-Israel, Manasseh. The Conciliator: A Reconcilement of the Apparent Contradictions in Holy Scripture. Lindo, Elias H., tr. from SPA. LC 72-83942. (Judaic Studies: No. SHP10). 688p. 1996. reprint ed. 35.00 (*0-87203-115-2*) Hermon.

Ben-Israel, Ruth. International Labour Standards: The Case of Freedom to Strike. 142p. 1988. pap. 54.00 (*90-6544-317-7*) Kluwer Law Intl.

Ben Israel, Yirmeyahu. A People in Bondage. 156p. (YA). (gr. 5 up). 1997. 8.95 (*0-936026-69-3*) R&M Pub Co.

Ben Jacob Ibn Shahin, Nissim. An Elegant Composition Concerning Relief after Adversity. Brinner, William M., tr. from ARA. & intro. by. LC 96-8760. 232p. 1996. pap. 30.00 (*1-56821-984-9*) Aronson.

Ben Jelloun, Tahar. Harrouda. (Folio Ser.: No. 1981). (FRE.). 1988. pap. 8.95 (*2-07-038069-6*) Schoenhof.

— Morocco: Sahara to the Sea. LC 95-1266. (Illus.). 240p. 1995. 60.00 (*0-7892-0030-9*) Abbeville Pr.

— La Priere de l'Absent. 1982. pap. 14.95 (*0-7859-3375-1*) Fr & Eur.

Ben-Jochannan, Josef. We the Black Jews: Witness to the "White Jewish Race" Myth. LC 92-81884. 408p. 1993. reprint ed. pap. 24.95 (*0-933121-40-7*) Black Classic.

Ben-Jochannan, Yosef. Abu Simbel to Ghizeh: A Guide Book & Manual. LC 89-91956. 350p. 1989. pap. 29.00 (*0-933121-27-X*) Black Classic.

— Africa: Mother of Western Civilization. LC 88-72105. 760p. 1988. reprint ed. pap. 34.95 (*0-933121-25-3*) Black Classic.

— Black Man of the Nile & His Family. LC 89-61274. 381p. 1990. pap. 24.95 (*0-933121-26-1*) Black Classic.

— A Chronology of the Bible: Challenge to the Standard Version. 16p. 1995. reprint ed. pap. 4.00 (*0-933121-28-8*) Black Classic.

— Cultural Genocide in the Black & African Studies Curriculum. LC 89-81780. 176p. 1989. pap. 14.95 (*0-938818-19-8*) ECA Assoc.

B

An Asterisk (*) at the beginning of an entry indicates that the title is appearing for the first time.

— From Afrikan Captives to Insane Slaves: The Need for Afrikan History in Solving the "Black" Mental Health Crisis in "America" & the World. LC 92-80732. (Truth & Sanity Reprint Ser.). (Illus.). 224p. 1992. reprint ed. pap. 16.98 (*1-879289-02-4*) Native Sun Pubs.

Ben Joseph, Akiba. Book of Formation (Sepher Yetzirah) Including: The 32 Paths of Wisdom, Their Correspondence with the Hebrew Alphabet & the Tarot Symbols. Stenring, Kurt, tr. 1987. reprint ed. pap. 7.95 (*0-916411-69-9*, Sure Fire) Holmes Pub.

Ben-Joseph, Eli. Aesthetic Persuasion: Henry James, the Jews, & Race. 264p. (Orig.). (C). 1995. pap. text 27.50 (*0-7618-0126-X*); lib. bdg. 59.50 (*0-7618-0125-1*) U Pr of Amer.

Ben-Joseph, Eran, jt. auth. see Southworth, Michael.

ben Joseph, Sa'adia & Linetsky, Michael. A Translation of Saadiah Gaon's Commentary on Creation. LC 99-13644. 232p. 1999. write for info. (*0-7657-6087-8*) Aronson.

Ben-Khayyim, Dov, ed. The Telling: A Loving Hagadah for Passover. 2nd rev. ed. (Illus.). 48p. 1998. reprint ed. pap. 7.00 (*0-9668431-2-6*) O & W Pub.

Ben-Lesser, Jay C. A Foxy Old Woman's Guide to Traveling Alone: Around Town & Around the World. (Illus.). 160p. 1995. pap. 10.95 (*0-89594-789-7*) Crossing Pr.

Ben-Lev, Dina. Broken Helix: Poems by Dinaben-Lev. LC 97-10842. (First Ser.). 80p. 1997. pap. 11.00 (*0-922811-31-8*) Mid-List.

Ben-Lev, Dina. Laura Jensen. LC 97-70325. (Western Writers Ser: Vol. 129). (C). 1997. 4.95 (*0-88430-128-1*) Boise St U W Writ Ser.

Ben-Lev, Dina. Note for a Missing Friend. 28p. (Orig.). 1991. pap. 8.00 (*0-9624178-2-3*, HVWC) Slapering Hol.

— Sober on a Small Plane. 31p. (Orig.). 1995. pap. 6.95 (*0-9636545-5-1*) Wind Pubns.

Ben Maimon, Moses. Eight Chapters of Maimonides on Ethics. (Columbia University. Oriental Studies: No. 7). reprint ed. 37.50 (*0-404-50497-3*) AMS Pr.

Ben Majer, David. They Say It Never Happened. Gorman, Jacqueline L., ed. 340p. 1993. pap. text 30.00 (*0-9639359-6-8*) Koegel Ent.

Ben-Meir, Alon. A Framework for Arab-Israeli Peace. 92p. pap. 7.95 (*0-9638319-0-9*) Robert Pubng.

— The Middle East Imperatives & Choices. LC 75-26110. (Illus.). 1975. 14.95 (*0-915474-01-8*, Effective Learn) Decalogue Bks.

Ben Meir, Dov B. Yitzhak Rabin, 1922-1995. Nijk, Henry & Bagish, Stephen, eds. (Illus.). 191p. 1996. 24.95 (*0-9652606-0-7*) Syndicated Intl.

***Ben-Meir, Ron & Carle, Cliff.** How to Get Free Food in College: The Starving Student's Survival Guide. (Illus.). 96p. (C). 2000. pap. text 7.99 (*1-57644-117-2*) CCC Pubns.

Ben Meir, Samuel. Rabbi Samuel Ben Meir's Commentary on Genesis: An Annotated Translation. Lockshin, Martin I., tr. from HEB. LC 89-33529. 440p. 1989. lib. bdg. 109.95 (*0-88946-256-9*) E Mellen.

Ben-Menachem, E., et al. Antiepileptic Drugs: Pharmacology & Therapeutics. LC 99-10225. 570p. 1999. 399.00 (*3-540-65374-0*) Spr-Verlag.

Ben-Menachem, Mordechai. Managing Software Assets: Software Configuration & the Year 2000. (Slaying the Software Dragon Ser.). 1997. pap. text 39.99 (*1-85032-924-9*) ITCP.

Ben-Menachem, Mordechai & Marliss, Garry. The Year 2000: Turning Y2K to Profit & Advantage. 320p. 1997. pap. 39.99 incl. cd-rom (*1-85032-331-3*) ITCP.

Ben Menachem, Shmuel, ed. see Wahlie, Albert J.

Ben-Menahem, A. & Singh, S. Seismic Waves & Sources. (Illus.). 1000p. 1981. 215.95 (*0-387-90506-5*) Spr-Verlag.

Ben-Menahem, Ari, ed. Vincit Veritas: A Portrait of the Life & Work of Norman Abraham Haskell, 1905-1970. 200p. 1990. 25.00 (*0-87590-762-8*, SP0307628) Am Geophysical.

Ben-Menahem, Ari & Singh, Sarva J. Seismic Waves & Sources. unabridged ed. LC 98-40854. 1136p. 1998. pap. 29.95 (*0-486-40461-7*) Dover.

Ben-Menahem, H. Judicial Deviation in Talmudic Law: Governed by Men, Not by Rules. (Jewish Law in Context Ser.). 168p. 1990. text 116.00 (*3-7186-0509-0*, Harwood Acad Pubs) Gordon & Breach.

Ben-Menahem, Hanina & Hecht, Neil S., eds. Jewish Law in Context Vol. 2: Authority, Process & Method: Studies in Jewish Law. 284p. 1998. text 62.00 (*90-5702-552-3*, ECU79, Harwood Acad Pubs) Gordon & Breach.

Ben-Menashe, Ari. Profits of War: Inside the Secret U.S. Israeli Arms Network. (Illus.). 410p. 1992. 24.95 (*1-879823-01-2*) Sheridan Sq Pr.

Ben-Merre, Diana A. & Murphy, Maureen O., eds. James Joyce & His Contemporaries: A Centenary Tribute, 30. LC 88-32789. (Contributions to the Study of World Literature Ser.: No. 30). 200p. 1989. 62.95 (*0-313-26667-0*, BJJ, Greenwood Pr) Greenwood.

Ben-Moshe, Tuvia. Churchill: Strategy & History. LC 90-26495. 397p. 1991. lib. bdg. 25.00 (*1-55587-142-9*) L Rienner.

Ben, N. Van Der, see Van Der Ben, N.

Ben-Naim, A. Hydrophobic Interactions. LC 79-510. (Illus.). 320p. (C). 1980. text 110.00 (*0-306-40222-X*, Kluwer Plenum) Kluwer Academic.

— Solvation Thermodynamics. LC 87-21738. (Illus.). 260p. (C). 1987. text 85.00 (*0-306-42538-6*, Kluwer Plenum) Kluwer Academic.

— Statistical Thermodynamics for Chemists & Biochemists. (Illus.). 720p. (C). 1991. text 115.00 (*0-306-43848-8*, Kluwer Plenum) Kluwer Academic.

***Ben-Naim, Arieh.** Cooperativity & Regulation in Biochemical Processes. LC 00-21561. 2000. write for info. (*0-306-46331-8*, Kluwer Plenum) Kluwer Academic.

Ben-Natan, Ron. CORBA on the Web. LC 97-48372. 600p. 1998. pap. 44.95 incl. cd-rom (*0-07-006724-4*) McGraw.

Ben-natan, Ron. A Guide to Common Object Request Broker Architecture (CORBA) 1995. pap. 45.00 (*0-07-005427-4*) McGraw.

***Ben-Natan, Ron.** San Francisco Developer's Guide. LC 99-41782. 1999. pap. 49.99 (*0-07-135177-9*) McGraw-Hill HPD.

Ben-Natan, Ron. Web Objects: Designing, Building, & Deploying Object-Oriented Applications for the Web. 1997. pap. text 39.95 (*0-07-006366-4*) McGraw.

— Web Objects: Designing, Building, & Deploying Object-Oriented Applications for the Web. LC 97-70835. (Illus.). 450p. 1997. pap. 39.95 (*0-07-006281-1*) McGraw.

***Ben-Natan, Ron & Sasson, Ori.** IBM WebSphere Starter Kit. (Illus.). 800p. 2000. pap. 69.99 (*0-07-212407-5*) Osborne-McGraw.

Ben-Ner, Avner & Gui, Benedetto, eds. The Nonprofit Sector in the Mixed Economy. LC 93-19165. 288p. (C). 1993. text 52.50 (*0-472-10429-2*, 10429) U of Mich Pr.

Ben-Ner, Avner & Putterman, Louis, eds. Economics, Values, & Organization. LC 97-21733. (Illus.). 552p. (C). 1998. text 85.00 (*0-521-58087-0*) Cambridge U Pr.

***Ben-Ner, Avner & Putterman, Louis, eds.** Economics, Values & Organization. (Illus.). 460p. (C). 2000. pap. 29.95 (*0-521-77411-X*) Cambridge U Pr.

Ben-Ner, Yitzhak. Rustic Sunset & Other Stories. Whitehill, Robert, tr. from HEB. LC 97-14266. 186p. 1998. 32.00 (*0-89410-804-2*, Three Contnts) L Rienner.

Ben-Ner, Yitzhak, et al. Teenage Soldiers-Adult Wars: From the Barracks to the Battlefield. (World Issues Ser.: Vol. 1). (Illus.). (YA). (gr. 7-12). 1991. pap. 8.95 (*0-8239-1305-8*); lib. bdg. 16.95 (*0-8239-1304-X*) Rosen Group.

Ben-Nissan, B., jt. ed. see Sorrell, C. C.

Ben Noah, Joseph, jt. auth. see Khan, Geoffrey.

Ben-o'ni. Out of the Ashes of Casa Blanca. rev. ed. (Illus.). 182p. 1995. text 49.00 (*1-887042-00-8*) Four Wings.

Ben Ouagrham, Sonia, tr. see Abraham-Frois, Gilbert, et al.

Ben-Peretz, Miriam. Learning from Experience: Memory & the Teacher's Account of Teaching. LC 94-17215. (SUNY Series, Teacher Preparation & Development). 176p. (C). 1995. text 49.50 (*0-7914-2303-4*); pap. text 16.95 (*0-7914-2304-2*) State U NY Pr.

— The Teacher-Curriculum Encounter: Freeing Teachers from the Tyranny of Texts. LC 89-28867. (SUNY Series in Curriculum Issues & Inquiries). 152p. (C). 1990. text 74.50 (*0-7914-0375-0*) State U NY Pr.

— The Teacher-Curriculum Encounter: Freeing Teachers from the Tyranny of Texts. LC 89-28867. (SUNY Series in Curriculum Issues & Inquiries). 152p. (C). 1991. pap. text 24.95 (*0-7914-0376-9*) State U NY Pr.

Ben-Peretz, Miriam & Bromme, Rainer, eds. The Nature of Time in Schools: Theoretical Concepts, Practitioner Perceptions. LC 90-36416. 320p. 1990. pap. 99.20 (*0-608-05093-8*, 206564900005) Bks Demand.

— The Nature of Time in Schools: Theoretical Concepts, Practitioner Perceptions. 328p. (C). 1990. text 43.95 (*0-8077-3036-X*); pap. text 22.95 (*0-8077-3035-1*) Tchrs Coll.

Ben-Peretz, Miriam & Schonmann, Shifra. Behind Closed Doors: Teachers & the Role of the Teachers' Lounge. LC 99-15031. 160p. (C). 2000. text 47.50 (*0-7914-4447-3*); pap. text 15.95 (*0-7914-4448-1*) State U NY Pr.

Ben-Po, Joseph. President Trump: A Play about Love, Not a Messy Divorce. Fontaine, Glory, ed. (Illus.). 88p. (Orig.). 1990. pap. 15.95 (*0-9625878-0-X*) White Hse NY.

Ben-Porat, Amir. Between Class & Nation: The Formation of the Jewish Working Class in the Period before Israel's Statehood, 20. LC 85-27281. (Contributions in Labor History Ser.). 255p. 1986. 55.00 (*0-313-25127-4*, BPB/, Greenwood Pr) Greenwood.

— Divided We Stand: Class Structure in Israel from 1948 to the 1980s, 85. LC 89-7493. (Contributions in Sociology Ser.: No. 85). 157p. 1989. 47.95 (*0-313-26402-3*, BDD/, Greenwood Pr) Greenwood.

— The State & Capitalism in Israel, 147. LC 92-42670. (Contributions in Economics & Economic History Ser.: No. 147). 224p. 1993. 62.95 (*0-313-28149-1*, BEZ, Greenwood Pr) Greenwood.

Ben-Porat, Josef. My Odyssey in Mother's Womb. 1979. 6.95 (*0-9603256-0-3*) Brighton House.

Ben Porat, Mordechai. To Baghdad & Back: The Miraculous 2,000 Year Homecoming of the Iraqi Jews. LC 98-19660. 370p. 1998. 29.95 (*965-229-195-1*) Gefen Bks.

Ben-Porath, Yoram, ed. The Israeli Economy: Maturing Through Crises. (Illus.). 432p. 1986. 65.00 (*0-674-46878-3*) HUP.

Ben-Porath, Yossef S. Content Component Scales. Date not set. pap. 6.00 (*0-8166-2503-4*) U of Minn Pr.

Ben-Porath, Yossef S. & Davis, Daniel L. Case Studies for Interpreting the MMPI-A. LC 96-30416. 1996. pap. 25.95 (*0-8166-2729-0*) U of Minn Pr.

Ben-Rafael, Eliezer. Crisis & Transformation: The Kibbutz at Century's End. LC 96-12675. (SUNY Series in Israeli Studies). 282p. (C). 1997. pap. text 21.95 (*0-7914-3226-2*) State U NY Pr.

— Crisis & Transformation: The Kibbutz at Century's End. LC 96-12675. (SUNY Series in Israeli Studies). 282p. (C). 1997. text 65.50 (*0-7914-3225-4*) State U NY Pr.

— The Emergence of Ethnicity: Cultural Groups & Social Conflict in Israel, 7. LC 81-17131. (Contributions in Ethnic Studies: No. 7.). (Illus.). 258p. 1982. 59.95 (*0-313-23088-9*, BRE/, Greenwood Pr) Greenwood.

— Israel-Palestine: A Guerrilla Conflict in International Politics, 161. LC 86-12096. (Contributions in Political Science Ser.: No. 161). 241p. 1987. 62.95 (*0-313-25553-9*, BLR/, Greenwood Pr) Greenwood.

— Status, Power & Conflict in the Kibbutz. 200p. 1988. text 77.95 (*0-566-05506-6*, Pub. by Avebry) Ashgate Pub Co.

Ben-Rafael, Eliezer & Sharot, Stephen. Ethnicity, Religion, & Class in Israeli Society. (Illus.). 297p. (C). 1991. text 69.95 (*0-521-39229-2*) Cambridge U Pr.

Ben-Rafael, Eliezer, jt. ed. see Herzog, Hanna.

Ben-Rafael, Zion, et al, eds. Advances in Assisted Reproductive Technologies. (Illus.). 1094p. (C). 1990. text 270.00 (*0-306-43665-5*, Kluwer Plenum) Kluwer Academic.

***Ben, Rich.** Skunk Works. Janos, Leo, ed. 1998. mass mkt. 13.95 (*0-316-19142-6*, Back Bay) Little.

Ben-Sari, D., et al, eds. Computer Methods in Water Resources: Proceedings of the 2nd International Conference on Computer Methods & Water Resources, 3 vols., No. 2. 350p. 1991. 130.95 (*0-387-53646-9*) Spr-Verlag.

— Computer Methods in Water Resources: Proceedings of the 2nd International Conference on Computer Methods & Water Resources, 3 vols., Two. 390p. 1991. 145.95 (*0-387-53645-0*); 217.95 (*0-387-53647-7*) Spr-Verlag.

— Computer Methods in Water Resources: Proceedings of the 2nd International Conference on Computer Methods & Water Resources, 3 vols., Vol. 2. 1991. 398.00 (*0-685-48734-2*) Spr-Verlag.

Ben-Sasson, Haim H., ed. A History of the Jewish People. (Illus.). 1108p. 1976. pap. text 29.95 (*0-674-39731-2*) HUP.

Ben Sedira, C. Dictionary Arabe to French Algerien. (ARA & FRE.). 608p. 1995. 95.00 (*0-320-00541-0*) Fr & Eur.

Ben-Shahar, Raphael. Wildlife in Southern Africa. (Illus.). 320p. 1999. 19.95 (*3-8290-1446-5*, 521018) Konemann.

Ben-Shakhar, G. & Furedy, J. J. Theories & Applications in the Detection of Deception. xi, 169p. 1989. 79.95 (*0-387-97065-7*) Spr-Verlag.

Ben-Shalom, Ram, jt. auth. see Bahat, Dan.

Ben-Shaul, A., et al. Lasers & Chemical Change. (Chemical Physics Ser.: Vol. 10). (Illus.). 497p. 1981. 80.95 (*0-387-10379-1*) Spr-Verlag.

Ben-Shaul, Israel & Kaiser, Gail. A Paradigm for Decentralized Process Modeling. (International Series in Engineering & Computer Science, Natural Language Processing & Machine Translation: Secs. 337). 301p. (C). 1995. text 119.00 (*0-7923-9631-6*) Kluwer Academic.

Ben-Shaul, Nitzan S. Mythical Expressions of Siege in Israeli Films. LC 97-12630. (Studies in Art & Religious Interpretation: No. 17). 156p. 1997. text 69.95 (*0-7734-8608-9*) E Mellen.

Ben-Shlomo, Yoav, jt. ed. see Kuh, Diana.

Ben Shlomo, Yosef. Lectures on the Philosophy of Spinoza. 124p. 1992. pap. 12.00 (*965-05-0665-9*, Pub. by Israel Ministry Def) Gefen Bks.

— Poetry of Being. 122p. 1990. pap. 12.00 (*965-05-0525-3*, Pub. by Israel Ministry Def) Gefen Bks.

Ben-Sira, Zeev. Immigration, Stress & Readjustment. LC 96-20687. 200p. 1997. 59.95 (*0-275-95632-6*, Praeger Pubs) Greenwood.

— Politics & Primary Medical Care: Dehumanization & Overutilization. 232p. 1988. text 72.95 (*0-566-05566-X*, Pub. by Avebry) Ashgate Pub Co.

— Regression, Stress, & Readjustment in Aging: A Structured, Bio-Psychosocial Perspective on Coping & Professional Support. LC 91-17302. 184p. 1991. 52.95 (*0-275-94078-0*, C4078, Praeger Pubs) Greenwood.

— Zionism at the Close of the Twentieth Century: A Dilemma. LC 93-1285. 132p. 1993. text 69.95 (*0-7734-9291-7*) E Mellen.

Ben-Tor, Amnon, ed. The Archaeology of Ancient Israel. Greenberg, R., tr. (Illus.). 416p. (C). 1992. pap. 30.00 (*0-300-05919-1*) Yale U Pr.

Ben-Tov, Sharona. The Artificial Paradise: Science Fiction & American Reality. LC 95-1033. (Studies in Literature & Science). 216p. 1995. text 37.50 (*0-472-10580-9*, 10580) U of Mich Pr.

Ben-Tovim, Atarah & Boyd, Douglas. The Right Instrument for Your Child: The Key to Unlocking Musical Potential. 144p. 1996. pap. 13.95 (*0-575-05894-3*, Pub. by V Gollancz) Trafalgar.

Ben-Tovin, Atarah. The Flute Book. LC 96-5949. (Illus.). 48p. (J). 1997. 18.95 incl. audio compact disk (*0-8120-8453-5*) Barron.

Ben-Tsur, Chaim. Passover Haggadah: The Original Tradition of the Jews of Yemen. 2nd ed. (Illus.). 120p. 1998. 18.00 (*0-9664128-0-X*) Assoc Jewish Yem.

Ben-Ur, Aviva & Agudas Chassidsi Chabad Staff. The Ladino (Judeo-Spanish) Collection of the Lubavitcher Rebbes: A Descriptive Bibliography. LC 96-36991. 168p. 1997. 49.50 (*0-7618-0601-6*) U Pr of Amer.

Ben-Uri, Galila. Dark Island. LC 93-72271. 172p. (J). (gr. 5-8). 1993. 14.95 (*1-56062-206-7*) CIS Comm.

— The Missing Crown. (Illus.). 223p. (J). (gr. 5-7). 1988. 15.95 (*0-935063-41-2*); pap. 12.95 (*0-935063-42-0*) CIS Comm.

Ben-Uri, Galila. The Mysterious Cargo. (Illus.). 285p. (J). (gr. 5-7). 1989. pap. 14.95 (*1-56062-007-2*) CIS Comm.

Ben-Vri, Galilia. Hijacked. 190p. (J). 1993. 14.95 (*1-56062-143-5*) CIS Comm.

Ben-Yami, M. Fishing with Light. 1978. 50.00 (*0-7855-6928-6*) St Mut.

— Purse Seining Manual. (Illus.). 336p. 1994. 115.00 (*0-85238-193-X*) Blackwell Sci.

***Ben-Yehuda.** Betrayal & Treason. 2000. 49.00 (*0-8133-9776-6*, Pub. by Westview) HarpC.

Ben Yehuda, Ehud. Hebrew-English Dictionary. (HEB & ENG.). 1989. per. 6.99 (*0-671-68862-6*) PB.

Ben-Yehuda, Nachman. Deviance & Moral Boundaries: Witchcraft, the Occult, Science Fiction, Deviant Sciences & Scientists. LC 85-1167. x, 260p. 1985. 25.00 (*0-226-04335-5*) U Ch Pr.

— Deviance & Moral Boundaries: Witchcraft, the Occult, Science Fiction, Deviant Sciences & Scientists. LC 85-1167. x, 260p. (C). 1995. pap. text 12.95 (*0-226-04336-3*) U Ch Pr.

— Deviance & Moral Boundaries: Witchcraft, the Occult, Science Fiction, Deviant Sciences & Scientists. LC 85-1167. 270p. Date not set. reprint ed. pap. 83.70 (*0-608-21007-2*, 205453500003) Bks Demand.

— The Masada Myth: Collective Memory & Mythmaking in Israel. LC 95-13543. 424p. 1995. 60.00 (*0-299-14830-0*); pap. 24.95 (*0-299-14834-3*) U of Wis Pr.

— Political Assassinations by Jews: A Rhetorical Device for Justice. LC 91-36690. (SUNY Series in Deviance & Social Control). 527p. (C). 1992. pap. text 24.95 (*0-7914-1166-4*) State U NY Pr.

— The Politics & Morality of Deviance: Moral Panics, Drug Abuse, Deviant Science, & Reversed Stigmatization. LC 89-4201. (SUNY Series in Deviance & Social Control). 348p. (C). 1989. pap. text 24.95 (*0-7914-0123-5*) State U NY Pr.

Ben-Yehuda, Nachman, jt. auth. see Goode, Erich.

Ben-Yishay, Ari, et al. Fractures & Dislocations: A Manual of Orthopaedic Trauma. (Illus.). 212p. (Orig.). 1994. pap. text. write for info. (*0-9642813-0-9*) Hosp For Joint Diseases.

Ben-Yosef, Andrea L. Solve the Puzzle: Interplay among ADA, FMLA & Workers' Comp. LC 98-7407. 72p. 1998. spiral bd. 47.00 (*0-925773-44-1*) M Lee Smith.

Ben-yu, Guo, jt. ed. see You-lan, Zhu.

Ben-Yusuf, Anna. Edwardian Hats: The Art of Millinery (1909) enl. ed. Shep, R. L., ed. LC 92-93330. (Illus.). 272p. 1992. pap. 24.95 (*0-914046-15-2*) R L Shep.

Ben-Zadok, Efraim, ed. Local Communities & the Israeli Polity: Conflict of Values & Interests. LC 92-40893. (SUNY Series in Israeli Studies). 285p. (C). 1993. pap. text 21.95 (*0-7914-1562-7*) State U NY Pr.

— Local Communities & the Israeli Polity: Conflict of Values & Interests. LC 92-40893. (SUNY Series in Israeli Studies). 285p. (C). 1993. text 64.50 (*0-7914-1561-9*) State U NY Pr.

Ben-Ze'ev, Aaron. The Perceptual System: A Philosophical & Psychological Perspective. LC 92-6211. (American University Studies: Philosophy: Ser. V, Vol. 138). IX, 220p. (Orig.). (C). 1993. pap. text 29.95 (*0-8204-1872-2*) P Lang Pubng.

***Ben-Ze'ev, Aaron.** The Subtlety of Emotions. LC 99-23903. (Illus.). 616p. 2000. 34.95 (*0-262-02463-2*) MIT Pr.

Ben-Ze'ev, Aaron, jt. ed. see Goodman, Robert F.

***Ben-Zeev, Aviv.** The Xenophobe's Guide to the Israelis. (Xenophobe's Guides Ser.). 64p. 2000. pap. 5.95 (*1-902825-34-9*) Oval Bks.

Ben-Zeev, Talia, jt. auth. see Sternberg, Robert.

Ben-Zeev, Talia, jt. ed. see Sternberg, Robert J.

Ben-Zikri, Abdul, jt. auth. see Bresell, Ronald.

Ben-Zion, Barry. Economic Information: Where to Find It. 200p. 1994. write for info. (*0-9640968-0-3*) BZ Pubng.

— Economic Information: Where to Find It. rev. ed. 200p. 1995. write for info. (*0-9640968-1-1*) BZ Pubng.

— Information on the California Economy: Where to Find It. 60p. 1995. write for info. (*0-9640968-5-4*) BZ Pubng.

***Ben Zion, Raphael.** The Anthology of Jewish Mysticism. 2nd ed. Goldman, Bonnie, ed. LC 99-48095. 216p. 2000. pap. 13.95 (*1-880582-47-3*) Judaica Pr.

Ben-Zvi, Abraham. Decade of Transition: Eisenhower, Kennedy, & the Origins of the American-Israeli Alliance. LC 98-5232. 251p. 1998. 47.50 (*0-231-11262-9*); pap. 17.50 (*0-231-11263-7*) Col U Pr.

— The United States & Israel: The Limits of the Special Relationship. LC 92-46441. 312p. 1993. 44.00 (*0-231-08184-7*) Col U Pr.

Ben Zvi, Ehud. A Historical-Critical Study of the Book of Zephaniah. (Beiheft zur Zeitschrift fuer die Alttestamentliche Wissenschaft Ser.: Vol. 198). xii, 389p. (C). 1991. lib. bdg. 113.85 (*3-11-012837-3*) De Gruyter.

Ben-Zvi, Linda. Theater in Israel. LC 95-46189. 480p. (C). 1996. text 52.50 (*0-472-10607-4*, 10607) U of Mich Pr.

Ben-Zvi, Linda, ed. Critical Essays on Susan Glaspell. 368p. 1995. text 49.50 (*0-472-10549-3*, 10549) U of Mich Pr.

Ben-Zvi, Linda, ed. Susan Glaspell: Essays on Her Theater & Fiction. (Illus.). 368p. (C). pap. text. write for info. (*0-472-08438-0*) U of Mich Pr.

Ben-Zvi, Linda, ed. Vital Voices - Anthology of Plays: Twentieth-Century Texts for the Stage by American Women. 448p. (C). Date not set. pap. 15.95 (*0-472-06502-5*, 06502); text 34.50 (*0-472-09502-1*, 09502) U of Mich Pr.

— Women in Beckett: Performance & Critical Perspectives. (Illus.). 280p. 1990. text 37.50 (*0-252-01658-0*) U of Ill Pr.

— Women in Beckett: Performance & Critical Perspectives. (Illus.). 280p. 1992. pap. text 14.95 (*0-252-06256-6*) U of Ill Pr.

Ben-Zvi, Rachel Y. Before Golda - Manya Shochat: A Biography. Shurin, Sandra, tr. from HEB. LC 88-14522. (Illus.). 250p. 1989. reprint ed. 15.00 (*0-930395-07-7*) Biblio NY.

— Before Golda: Manya Shochat: A Biography. Shurin, Sandra, tr. from HEB. LC 88-14522. (Illus.). 250p. (Orig.). 1989. reprint ed. pap. 9.50 (*0-685-23476-2*) Biblio NY.

Benabid, Nadia, tr. see Chraibi, Driss.

Benabid, Nadia, tr. see Laporte, Dominique.

Benabid, Nadia, tr. see Valdes, Zoe.

Benabou, Marcel. Jacob, Menahem, & Mimoun: A Family Epic. Rendall, Steven, tr. from FRE. LC 97-27988. (Stages Ser.). xviii, 224p. 1998. text 35.00 (*0-8032-1285-2*) U of Nebr Pr.

— Why I Have Not Written Any of My Books (Pourquoi Je

B

N'ai Ecrit Aucun de mes Livres) Kornacker, David, tr. LC 95-4887. (French Modernist Library Ser.). xvii, 111p. 1996. text 35.00 (*0-8032-1239-9*, Bison Books) U of Nebr Pr.

— Why I Have Not Written Any of My Books (Pourquoi Je N'ai Ecrit Aucun de mes Livres) Kornacker, David, tr. LC 95-4887. (French Modernist Library Ser.). xvii, 111p. 1998. pap. 10.00 (*0-8032-6139-X*, Bison Books) U of Nebr Pr.

Benac, Henri. Dictionaire des Synonymes: Dictionary of Synonyms.Tr. of Dictionary of Synonyms. (FRE.). 1026p. 1981. 49.95 (*0-8288-1928-9*, M4558) Fr & Eur.

Benac, Henri, ed. see Diderot, Denis.

Benacerraf. Ultrasound in Fetal Syndrome. LC 98-5489. 1998. text 125.00 (*0-443-07968-4*) Church.

Benacerraf, Baruj. From Caracas to Stockholm: The Life of a Noble Laureate. LC 98-23131. (Illus.). 308p. 1998. 32.95 (*1-57392-227-7*) Prometheus Bks.

***Benacerraf, Beryl R., et al.** Ultrasound & Women's Health: March 1998 Syllabus. 2nd ed. (Illus.). 110p. 1998. pap. 68.00 (*1-930047-16-9*, UWH2) Am Inst Ultrasound.

— Update in Ob/Gyn Ultrasound, Vol. II. (Illus.). 116p. 1997. pap. 57.00 (*1-930047-18-5*, UOG2) Am Inst Ultrasound.

Benacerraf, Beryl R., jt. ed. see Hobbins, John C.

Benacerraf, Hilary, ed. see Putnam, Hilary.

Benacka, S. English-Slovak Technical Dictionary. (ENG & SLO.). 1358p. 1980. 95.00 (*0-569-08529-2*) St Mut.

Benacka, S., et al, eds. Weak Superconductivity: Proceedings of the 6th International Symposium. 280p. (C). 1991. text 81.00 (*981-02-0795-6*) World Scientific Pub.

Benacka, S. & Kedro, M., eds. Weak Superconductivity. 290p. (C). 1990. text 175.00 (*0-941743-78-0*) Nova Sci Pubs.

Benade, Arthur H. Fundamentals of Musical Acoustics. 20th ed. 608p. 1990. pap. 16.95 (*0-486-26484-X*) Dover.

— Horns, Strings, & Harmony. LC 78-25707. (Illus.). 271p. 1979. reprint ed. lib. bdg. 35.00 (*0-313-20771-2*, BEHO, Greenwood Pr) Greenwood.

— Horns, Strings, & Harmony. unabridged ed. LC 92-25381. (Illus.). 288p. 1992. reprint ed. pap. text 9.95 (*0-486-27331-8*) Dover.

Benade, Virginia, jt. auth. see Hutchins, Carleen M.

Benadusi, Giovanna. A Provincial Elite in Early Modern Tuscany: Family & Power in the Creation of the State. LC 95-44489. (Studies in Historical & Political Science, 112th Series (1994): Series 114, No. 3). 264p. (C). 1996. text 49.95 (*0-8018-5248-X*) Johns Hopkins.

Benady, Sam. Sherlock Holmes in Gibraltar. (C). 1989. text 40.00 (*0-948466-15-4*, Pub. by Gibraltar Bks) St Mut.

Benady, Tito. The Royal Navy at Gibraltar. (C). 1988. text 105.00 (*0-907771-49-1*, Pub. by Gibraltar Bks) St Mut.

***Benagh, Christine L.** An Englishman in the Courts of the Tsar: The Spiritual Journey of Charles Sydney Gibbes. LC 00-35862. 2000. write for info. (*1-888212-19-5*) Conciliar Pr.

Benagh, Jim. Basketball: Startling Stories Behind the Records. LC 90-22886. (Illus.). 128p. 1992. pap. 5.95 (*0-8069-7291-2*) Sterling.

— Sports Great Herschel Walker. LC 89-28385. (Sports Great Bks.). (Illus.). 64p. (J). (gr. 4-10). 1990. lib. bdg. 17.95 (*0-89490-207-5*) Enslow Pubs.

— Ultimate Sports Trivia Book: The Official Bar Book of Runyon's Saloon. (Illus.). 1991. pap. 8.95 (*0-8065-1273-3*, Citadel Pr) Carol Pub Group.

Benagiano, Giuseppe & Diczfalusy, Egon, eds. Endocrine Mechanisms in Fertility Regulation. fac. ed. LC 79-66514. (Comprehensive Endocrinology Ser.). (Illus.). 366p. pap. 113.50 (*0-7837-7226-2*, 204707200005) Bks Demand.

Benaim de Lasry, Anita. Two Romances: A Study of Medieval Spanish Romances. (Ediciones Criticas Ser.: Vol. 1). 234p. 1982. pap. 12.50 (*0-936388-13-7*) Juan de la Cuesta.

Benaiteau, Claude, tr. see De Gauffecourt, Jean-Vincent C.

Benaka, L., ed. Fish Habitat: Essential Fish Habitat & Rehabilitation. LC 98-88572. (Symposium Ser.: Vol. 22). (Illus.). 477p. 1999. 55.00 (*1-888569-12-3*, 540.22) Am Fisheries Soc.

***Benali, Abdelkader.** Wedding by the Sea. Massotty, Susan, tr. 2000. 23.95 (*1-55970-530-2*, Pub. by Arcade Pub Inc) Time Warner.

Benalla, Abdelaziz, jt. ed. see Gupta, K. C.

Benally, AnCita, jt. auth. see Swisher, Karen Gayton.

Benamara, Abdelkader & Ifeagwu, Sam, eds. OPEC Aid & the Challenge of Development. 160p. 1987. lib. bdg. 55.00 (*0-7099-1969-7*, Pub. by C Helm) Routldge.

Benamati, Dennis C. & Lemelin, Evelina E., compiled by. Publication Opportunities for Law Librarians: An Author's Guide. LC 95-25605. (AALL Publications Ser.: No. 49). xxiv, 318p. 1996. ring bd. 65.00 (*0-8377-9309-2*, Rothman) W S Hein.

Benamati, Dennis C., et al. Criminal Justice Information: How to Find It, How to Use It. LC 97-39576. (Illus.). 248p. 1997. boxed set 59.95 (*0-89774-957-X*) Oryx Pr.

Benamy. Developing Clinical Reasoning. (C). 1998. text 47.00 (*0-12-784591-7*) Acad Pr.

Benamy, Arnon, tr. see Chimenti, Elisa.

Benamy, Avivah & Eliach, Yaffa, eds. Teacher's Guide for Children Who Survived the Holocaust. (Education Ser.). (Illus.). 47p. (Orig.). 1988. pap. text, teacher ed. 4.95 (*0-9609970-6-7*) Mus Jew Heritage.

Benander, Kathryn. Kaleidoscope: Writing, Reading, & Grammar. LC 97-38865. 342p. 1998. pap. text 40.00 (*0-13-530957-3*) P-H.

Benanti, Carol. Real Fossils. Frank, Michael, ed. (Real Collections). (Illus.). 32p. (Orig.). (J). (gr. 3-8). pap. 6.95 (*1-880592-06-1*) Pace Prods.

— There's a Fungus among Us. (Books & Stuff Ser.). (Illus.). 24p. (Orig.). (J). (gr. 3-7). 1996. pap. 8.95 (*0-448-41344-2*, G & D) Peng Put Young Read.

Benanti, Carol & Miller, Ray H. Fun Facts. (About Farm Crops Ser.). (Illus.). iii, 29p. (J). (gr. 2). 1995. boxed set 6.95 (*1-887327-02-9*) Ertl Co.

— Fun Facts. (About Farm Animals Ser.). (Illus.). iii, 29p. (J). (gr. 2 up). 1995. boxed set 6.95 (*1-887327-01-0*) Ertl Co.

Benard, Cheryl. Moghul Buffet. LC 97-49954. 208p. 1998. 22.00 (*0-374-21179-5*) FS&G.

— Moghul Buffet. LC 99-27141. 272p. 2000. pap. 12.00 (*1-56947-179-7*) Soho Press.

***Benard, Cheryl.** Turning on the Girls. 256p. 2001. 23.00 (*0-374-28178-5*) FS&G.

Benard, Cheryl & Khalilzad, Zalmay. The Government of God: Iran's Islamic Republic. LC 83-20880. 232p. 1986. pap. text 21.00 (*0-231-05377-0*) Col U Pr.

Benard, Edmond, jt. ed. see Ryan, John K.

Benard, Elisabeth A. Chinnamasta. LC 94-905052. xiv, 162 p. (C). 1994. 16.00 (*81-208-1065-1*, Pub. by Motilal Bnarsidass) S Asia.

Benard, Elisabeth Anne, jt. ed. see Moon, Beverly Ann.

Benarde, Anita. Games from Many Lands. LC 71-86975. (Illus.). 64p. (J). (gr. 3-7). 1971. lib. bdg. 13.95 (*0-87460-147-9*) Lion Bks.

— Mediterranean Mosaic Designs. (International Design Library). (Illus.). 48p. (Orig.). 1984. pap. 5.95 (*0-88045-049-5*) Stemmer Hse.

— Spanish Ceramic Designs. (International Design Library). (Illus.). 48p. (Orig.). 1984. pap. 5.95 (*0-88045-059-2*) Stemmer Hse.

Benarde, Melvin A. Global Warning ... Global Warming. LC 91-22276. 336p. 1992. 64.95 (*0-471-51323-7*) Wiley.

— Our Precarious Habitat. 2nd rev. ed. (Illus.). 384p. (C). 1973. pap. text 10.50 (*0-393-09372-7*) Norton.

— Our Precarious Habitat. 2nd rev. ed. (Illus.). 384p. 1973. 8.25 (*0-393-06360-7*) Norton.

— Our Precarious Habitat: Fifteen Years Later. LC 88-29158. 656p. 1989. 54.95 (*0-471-61750-4*) Wiley.

Benarde, Melvin A., ed. Asbestos: The Hazardous Fiber. 504p. 1989. lib. bdg. 99.50 (*0-8493-6354-3*, TA55) CRC Pr.

— Disinfection. LC 77-107751. (Illus.). 484p. reprint ed. pap. 150.10 (*0-7837-0753-3*, 204106900019) Bks Demand.

Benardete, M. J., jt. auth. see Flores, Angel.

Benardete, Seth. Herodotean Inquiries. 230p. (C). 1998. 35.00 (*1-890318-32-9*) St Augustines Pr.

— Plato's Sophist: The Being of the Beautiful, Pt. II. LC 85-28861. xx, 200p. 1986. pap. text 18.00 (*0-226-67032-5*) U Ch Pr.

— Plato's Statesman: The Being of the Beautiful, Pt. III. LC 85-28827. xx, 176p. 1986. pap. text 13.95 (*0-226-67033-3*) U Ch Pr.

— Plato's Theatetus, Pt. I. LC 85-28863. xx, 214p. 1986. pap. text 15.50 (*0-226-67031-7*) U Ch Pr.

— The Rhetoric of Morality & Philosophy: Plato's Gorgias & Phaedrus. 215p. 1991. 35.95 (*0-226-04240-5*) U Ch Pr.

— Sacred Transgressions: A Reading of Sophocles' Antigone. LC 98-6763. 168p. 1999. 30.00 (*1-890318-77-9*) St Augustines Pr.

— Socrates' Second Sailing: On Plato's Republic. LC 88-27909. (Illus.). x, 248p. 1992. pap. text 16.95 (*0-226-04244-8*) U Ch Pr.

— Socrates' Second Sailing: On Plato's Republic. LC 88-27909. (Illus.). 248p. 1997. lib. bdg. 36.00 (*0-226-04242-1*) U Ch Pr.

Benardete, Seth, ed. The Bow & the Lyre: A Platonic Reading of the Odyssey. LC 96-32657. 194p. 1996. 31.50 (*0-8476-8367-2*) Rowman.

***Benardete, Seth, et al.** The Argument of the Action: Essays on Greek Poetry & Philosophy. Burger, Ronna & Davis, Michael, eds. LC 99-87699. 408p. 2000. 39.00 (*0-226-04251-0*) U Ch Pr.

Benardete, Seth G., tr. see Aeschylus.

Benardete, Seth G., tr. see Plato.

Benardot, Dan. Nutrition for Serious Athletes. LC 99-46572. 352p. 1999. pap. 16.95 (*0-88011-833-4*) Human Kinetics.

— Sports Nutrition: A Guide for Professionals Working with Active People. 2nd ed. LC 92-49945. 1992. pap. 35.00 (*0-88091-110-7*) Am Dietetic Assn.

Benares, Camden. Common Sense Tarot: A Complete Guide to Tarot Reading As Entertainment. 1992. pap. 9.95 (*0-87877-177-8*) Newcastle Pub.

— Zen Without Zen Masters. LC 85-70387. (Illus.). 128p. 1993. pap. 9.95 (*1-56184-073-4*) New Falcon Pubns.

Benari, Naomi. Inner Rhythm: Dance Training for the Deaf. (Performing Arts Studies Ser). 81p. 1995. text 36.00 (*3-7186-5672-8*, Harwood Acad Pubs); pap. text 26.00 (*3-7186-5673-6*, Harwood Acad Pubs) Gordon & Breach.

— Inner Rhythm: Dance Training for the Deaf. (Performing Arts Studies: Vol. 3). 81p. 1995. pap., text 26.00 incl. vdisk (*3-7186-5675-2*, ECU30, Harwood Acad Pubs); text 27.00 (*3-7186-5611-6*, ECU21, Harwood Acad Pubs); pap. text 12.00 (*3-7186-5612-4*, ECU9, Harwood Acad Pubs) Gordon & Breach.

— Inner Rhythm: Dance Training for the Deaf, Bk. VI. (Performing Arts Studies: Vol. 3). 81p. 1995. text 36.00 incl. vdisk (*3-7186-5674-4*, ECU42, Harwood Acad Pubs) Gordon & Breach.

Benario, Herbert W. Caesaris Augusti Res Gestae et Fragmenta. 2nd rev. ed. LC 89-25021. (Classical Studies: Pedagogy Ser.). (Illus.). 136p. (C). 1990. reprint ed. text 32.50 (*0-8143-2137-2*); reprint ed. pap. text 17.95 (*0-8143-2138-0*) Wayne St U Pr.

— Tacitus Germania: Germany. (Classical Texts Ser.). 128p. 1999. 59.95 (*0-85668-716-2*, Pub. by Aris & Phillips); pap. 22.00 (*0-85668-717-0*, Pub. by Aris & Phillips) David Brown.

Benario, Herbert W., tr. Tacitus' Agricola, Germany, & Dialogue on Orators. rev. ed. LC 90-48807. (Oklahoma Series in Classical Culture: Vol. 8). (Illus.). 160p. 1991. 29.95 (*0-8061-2321-4*) U of Okla Pr.

Benario, Herbert W., jt. ed. see Briggs, Ward W.

Benaron, David, jt. ed. see Sevick-Muraca, Eva.

Benaron, David A., et al, eds. Photon Propagation in Tissues II. (Europto Ser.: Vol. 2925). 312p. 1996. 66.00 (*0-8194-2327-0*) SPIE.

— Photon Propagation in Tissues IV. LC 99-200353. (Europto Ser.: Vol. 3566). 1998. 80.00 (*0-8194-3028-5*) SPIE.

— Photon Propagation in Tissues III. (Europto Ser.: Vol. 3194). 546p. 1998. 107.00 (*0-8194-2626-1*) SPIE.

Benaroya, Haym & Ettouney, Mohammed. Mechanical Vibration: Analysis, Uncertainties, & Control. LC 97-30975. 511p. 1997. 105.00 (*0-13-948373-X*) P-H.

Benaroya, Haym, jt. auth. see Bar-Avi, Patrick.

Benarroch, Eduardo E. Central Autonomic Network: Functional Organization & Clinical Correlations. LC 97-17397. (Illus.). 698p. 1997. 125.00 (*0-87993-673-8*) Futura Pub.

— Medical Neurosciences: An Approach to Anatomy, Pathology, & Physiology by Systems & Levels. 4th ed. LC 98-24218. 19p. 1998. write for info. (*0-7817-1426-5*) Lppncott W & W.

Benary-Isbert, Margot. Dangerous Spring. (YA). (gr. 6-12). 1991. 20.00 (*0-8446-6476-6*) Peter Smith.

— Rowan Farm. (YA). (gr. 5-12). 1991. 20.00 (*0-8446-6475-8*) Peter Smith.

— Under a Changing Moon. LC 97-77063. (Young Adult Bookshelf Ser.). 326p. (YA). (gr. 8 up). 1998. reprint ed. pap. 14.95 (*1-883937-33-7*, 33-7) Bethlehem ND.

Ben'Ary, Ruth. Touch Typing in Ten Lessons. rev. ed. 80p. (Orig.). 1989. pap. 9.95 (*0-399-51529-1*, Perigee Bks) Berkley Pub.

Benassi, August. Technicolor Closure. 11p. 1998. pap. 4.00 (*1-891972-02-2*) Beastkraft Pubg.

Benassy, Jean-Pascal, ed. Macroeconomics & Imperfect Competition. LC 94-44342. (International Library of Critical Writings in Economics: Vol. 46). 544p. 1995. 230.00 (*1-85278-849-6*) E Elgar.

Benat, Chana. They Called Me Frau Anna. LC 90-82060. (C). 1990. 22.95 (*1-56062-029-3*) CIS Comm.

Benat, G. Andrew. Regional Multipliers: A User Handbook for the Regional Input & Output Modeling System (rims 2) 69p. 1997. pap. 6.50 (*0-16-054558-7*) USGPO.

Benatar, Lisa, jt. auth. see Howland, Rebecca.

Benatar, Raquel. Connections 2000: Teacher's Master Set Green Level. (ENG & SPA., Illus.). 12p. (J). (gr. 6-9). 1997. pap., teacher ed. 15.00 (*1-56492-240-5*) Laredo.

— Me, Myself & I: Journal. (Illus.). 24p. (YA). (gr. 3 up). 1997. pap., wbk. ed. 6.95 (*1-56492-146-8*) Laredo.

— My Family: Journal. (Illus.). 24p. (YA). (gr. 3 up). 1997. pap., wbk. ed. 6.95 (*1-56492-179-4*) Laredo.

— Teacher's Masters Set Red Level (3-6) (Connections 2000 Ser.). (SPA., Illus.). 12p. 1997. teacher ed. 15.00 (*1-56492-239-1*) Laredo.

Benatar, Raquel, jt. auth. see Florada, Aida.

Benatar, Stephen. Recovery LC 97-229474. 302p. 1996. write for info. (*0-907123-56-2*) Five Leaves.

Benath, Abdul S. The Mazruiana Collection: A Comprehensive Annotated Bibliography of the Published Works of Ali A. Mazrui, 1962-1997. LC 98-909224. xiii, 348p. 1998. write for info. (*81-207-2119-5*) Sterling Pubs.

Benathen, Isaiah A. Microbiology with Health Care Applications: A Laboratory Manual. (Illus.). 416p. (C). 1993. pap. 32.95 (*0-89863-150-5*) Star Pub CA.

Benatti, Fabio. Deterministic Chaos in Infinite Quantum Systems. (Trieste Notes in Physics Ser.). vi, 225p. 1993. pap. write for info. (*3-540-57017-9*) Spr-Verlag.

— Deterministic Chaos in Infinite Quantum Systems. LC 93-28780. (Trieste Notes in Physics Ser.). 1993. 53.95 (*0-387-57017-9*) Spr-Verlag.

Benaud, Claire-Lise & Bordeianu, Sever. Outsourcing Library Operations in Academic Libraries: An Overview of Issues & Outcomes. LC 98-17118. 215p. 1998. 40.00 (*1-56308-509-7*) Libs Unl.

***Benaud, R.** Anything But. 1998. text 40.00 (*0-340-69648-6*, Pub. by Hodder & Stought Ltd) Trafalgar.

— Appeal of Cricket. 1996. mass mkt. 17.95 (*0-340-63228-3*, Pub. by Hodder & Stought Ltd) Trafalgar.

Benavente, Jacinto. Al Fin, Mujer. 4th ed. (SPA.). 170p. 1981. pap. 12.95 (*0-7859-5155-5*) Fr & Eur.

— Cartas de Mujeres. (SPA.). 144p. 1979. pap. write for info. (*0-7859-5163-6*) Fr & Eur.

— Los Intereses Creados. (Nueva Austral Ser.: No. 133). (SPA.). 1991. pap. text 11.95 (*84-239-1933-1*) Elliots Bks.

— Los Intereses Creados. 3rd ed. 137p. 1987. pap. 9.95 (*0-7859-5150-4*) Fr & Eur.

— Los Intereses Creados - Senora Ama. 1984. pap. 8.95 (*0-7859-5156-3*) Fr & Eur.

— El Principe Que Todo Lo Aprendio en los Libros. (Clasicos Ser.). (SPA.). 72p. 1996. pap. write for info. (*0-929441-39-7*) Pubns Puertorriquenas.

— Principe Que Todo Lo Aprendio en los Libros. 6th ed. 80p. 1983. pap. 8.95 (*0-7859-5208-X*) Fr & Eur.

— Rosas de Otono - Pepa Doncel. (SPA.). 163p. 1968. 9.95 (*0-8288-7029-2*, S8761) Fr & Eur.

— Senora Ama: La Malquerida. Paco, Mariano D., ed. (Nueva Austral Ser.: No. 191). (SPA.). 1991. pap. text 24.95 (*84-239-1991-9*) Elliots Bks.

Benavente, Luis Quinones De, see Quinones De Benavente, Luis.

***Benavides, Adam, Jr.** Archival Investigations for Mission Nuestra Senora de los Dolores de los Ais, San Augustine County, Texas. (Archeology Studies Program: No. 11). (Illus.). 251p. 1998. pap. text. write for info. (*0-9660796-3-9*) TX Dept Transport.

Benavides, Alfredo H., jt. ed. see Padilla, Raymond V.

Benavides, Dalia & Nanez, Lilia. Bilingual Books & More: Cross Curriculum Ideas Using Spanish - English Literature. (Dr. Jac Ser.: Vol. 6). 56p. (Orig.). 1996. pap. text 11.95 (*1-888842-01-6*, 1010) Absey & Co.

Benavides, Gustavo & Daly, M. W., eds. Religion & Political Power. LC 88-24861. 240p. (C). 1989. pap. text 21.95 (*0-7914-0027-1*) State U NY Pr.

Benavides, Magdalena, tr. see Davis, Edward M. & Newcomb, William W., eds.

Benavides, Miguel. The Children of Mariplata: Stories from Costa Rica. LC 91-72159. 55p. 1993. pap. 17.95 (*1-85610-019-7*) Dufour.

Benavides, Rodolfo. Dramaticas Profecias 25 Anos Despues. (SPA.). 1997. pap. 14.98 (*968-13-1240-6*, Pub. by Edit Diana) Libros Fronteras.

— Ejercicios Para Desarrollar Sus Facultades Extrasensoriales. (SPA.). 1997. pap. text 11.98 (*968-13-1941-9*) Libros Fronteras.

Benavides, Rosamel S. Desarrollo y Transformaciones del Cuento Hispanoamericano en el Siglo XIX: Demandas y Expectativas, Vol. 6. (Wor(l)ds of Change Ser.). (SPA.). VIII, 228p. (C). 1996. 48.95 (*0-8204-2509-5*) P Lang Pubng.

Benavides-Vaello, Sandra & Setzler, Heather. Migrant & Seasonal Farmworkers: Health Care Accessibility. (Working Paper Ser.: Vol. 76). 46p. 1994. pap. 5.50 (*0-89940-567-3*) LBJ Sch Pub Aff.

Benavidez, Barbara. My School Years: Kindergarten Through Graduation. (Illus.). (J). (gr. 5-12). 24.95 (*0-9619463-0-X*) Barmarle Pubns.

Benavidez, Max, ed. see Schneider, Jerome.

Benavidez, Roy. Medal of Honor: One Man's Journey from Poverty & Prejudice. 1999. pap. text 16.95 (*1-57488-203-1*) Brasseys.

Benavidez, Roy P., jt. auth. see Craig, John R.

Benavie, Arthur. Deficit Hysteria: A Common Sense Look at America's Rush to Balance the Budget. LC 98-14926. 168p. 1998. 35.00 (*0-275-96308-X*, Praeger Pubs) Greenwood.

Benay, Jeanne. Friedrich Kaiser (1814-1874) & le Theatre Populaire en Autriche au XIXe Siecle, 2 vols., Vol. 14. (Theatrica Ser.: Series 1). (FRE.). 1008p. 1993. 95.95 (*3-906751-06-6*) P Lang Pubng.

***Benay, Jeanne & Ravy, Gilbert, eds.** Ecritures et langages satiriques en Autriche 1914, 1938: Satire in Osterreich 1914, 1938, 10. (Illus.). 495p. 1999. 62.95 (*3-906762-95-5*, Pub. by P Lang) P Lang Pubng.

Benaya, Margaret, tr. see Shamir, Moshe.

Benayoun, Aline. Casablanca Cuisine: French North African Cooking. (Illus.). 192p. 1999. pap. 14.95 (*1-897959-33-8*) IPG Chicago.

Benbassa, Esther. The Jews of France: A History from Antiquity to the Present. LC 99-17461. 270p. 1999. 29.95 (*0-691-05984-5*, Pub. by Princeton U Pr) Cal Prin Full Svc.

Benbassa, Esther, ed. Haim Nahum: A Sephardic Chief Rabbi in Politics, 1892-1923. Kochan, Miriam, tr. from FRE. LC 94-25824. (Judaic Studies). (ENG.). 224p. 1995. pap. text 29.95 (*0-8173-0729-X*) U of Ala Pr.

***Benbassa, Esther & Rodrigue, Aron.** Sephardi Jewry: A History of the Judeo-Spanish Community, 15th to 20th Centuries LC 99-35111. (Jewish Communities in the Modern World Ser.). 352p. 2000. 19.95 (*0-520-21822-1*) U CA Pr.

Benbassa, Esther & Rodrigue, Aron, eds. A Sephardi Life in Southeastern Europe: The Autobiography & Journal of Gabriel Arie, 1863-1939. Todd, Jane Marie, tr. from ENG. LC 97-33415. (Samuel & Althea Stroum Book Ser.). (Illus.). 334p. 1998. pap. 25.00 (*0-295-97674-8*) U of Wash Pr.

Benberry, Cuesta, jt. auth. see Gross, Joyce.

Benberry, Cuesta R., text. Always There: The African-American Presence in American Quilts, 1800-1900. (Illus.). 100p. (Orig.). 1992. pap. 24.95 (*1-880584-02-6*) Kent Qult.

***Benbow, Ann & Malby, Dave.** Science Education for the Beginning Elementary School Teacher. (Education Ser.). 2000. 50.00 (*0-7668-0090-3*) Delmar.

Benbow, Audrey M. Scottish Deerhounds. (KW Ser.). (Illus.). 192p. 1993. text 9.95 (*0-86622-591-9*, KW-217) TFH Pubns.

Benbow, Camilla P. & Lubinski, David. Intellectual Talent: Psychometric & Social Issues. 408p. 1996. pap. text 29.95 (*0-8018-5302-8*) Johns Hopkins.

Benbow, Christopher H., jt. auth. see Benbow, Nancy D.

Benbow, E. W., jt. auth. see Cruickshank, A. H.

Benbow, John & Bridgwater, John. Paste Flow & Extrusion. LC 92-37398. (Advanced Manufacturing Ser.: No. 10). (Illus.). 168p. (C). 1993. text 77.95 (*0-19-856338-8*, Clarendon Pr) OUP.

Benbow, Margaret. Stalking Joy. LC 96-47109. (Walt McDonald First-Book Poetry Ser.). 94p. 1997. 17.95 (*0-89672-375-5*) Tex Tech Univ Pr.

Benbow, Nancy D. & Benbow, Christopher H. Cabins, Cottages & Mansions: Homes of the Presidents of the United States. (Illus.). 234p. (C). 1993. pap. text 25.00 (*0-939631-61-X*) Thomas Publications.

***Benbow, Nanette, et al.** Big Cities Health Inventory 1997: The Health of Urban U. S. A. 3rd ed. (Illus.). 149p. 1999. reprint ed. pap. text 25.00 (*0-7881-8173-4*) DIANE Pub.

***Benbow-Pfalzgraf, Taryn.** American Women Writers: From Colonial Times to the Present: A Critical Reference Guide , 4 vols. 2nd ed. LC 99-43293. 1999. write for info. (*1-55862-433-3*) St James Pr.

Benbow-Pfalzgraf, Taryn, jt. auth. see Pederson, Jay P.

B

Bendall, D. S. Protein Electron Transfer. (Illus.). 304p. (C). 1996. text, teacher ed., student ed. 130.00 (*1-85996-040-5*, Pub. by Bios Sci) Bks Intl VA.

***Bendall, George.** Now the Time! LC 00-103313. 200p. 2000. pap. 15.95 (*0-87516-733-0*) DeVorss.

Bendall, George P. Collected Essays of George Bendall. Bendall, Ann, ed. LC 94-70458. (Mentors of New Thought Ser.). 136p. (Orig.). 1994. pap. 9.95 (*0-87516-669-5*) DeVorss.

— Holy Days & Holidays. LC 95-83031. 144p. (Orig.). 1996. pap. 9.95 (*0-87516-686-5*) DeVorss.

Bendall, George P., ed. see Holmes, Ernest.

Bendall, M. J., jt. auth. see Godwin-Austin, Richard.

Bendall, Molly. Dark Summer. LC 99-10611. (Poetry Ser.). 80p. 1999. 19.95 (*1-881163-29-6*); pap. 11.95 (*1-881163-30-X*) Miami Univ Pr.

Bendall, Pamela & Bendall, Sam. Kids for Sail. (Illus.). 128p. (Orig.). (J). (gr. 4-8). 1990. pap. 6.95 (*0-920501-49-4*) Orca Bk Pubs.

Bendall, Sam, jt. auth. see Bendall, Pamela.

***Bendall, Sarah, et al.** A History of Emmanuel College, Cambridge. LC 99-48203. (Illus.). 727p. 2000. 75.00 (*0-85115-393-3*, Suffolk Records Soc) Boydell & Brewer.

Bendall, Sue, jt. ed. see Ager, Alastair.

Bendaly. Facilitation Skills Training. 1999. 99.95 (*0-07-134734-8*) McGraw.

Bendaly, Leslie. Games Teams Play: Activities & Workouts for Developing Productive Work Teams. 388p. 1996. pap. 24.95 (*0-07-552718-9*) McGraw.

— Games Teams Play: Activities & Workouts For Developing Productive Work Teams. 388p. 1996. 89.95 (*0-07-552719-7*) McGraw.

***Bendaly, Leslie.** More Games Teams Play: Activities & Games for Powering up Your Team's Potential. 400p. 2000. pap. 34.95 (*0-07-560939-8*, Schaums Outline) McGraw-Hill Prof.

— More Games Teams Play: Activities & Games for Powering up Your Team's Potential. (Illus.). 400p. 2000. 99.95 (*0-07-560931-2*, Schaums Outlne) McGraw-Hill Prof.

— Organization 2005: Four Steps Companies Must Take to be Successful in Dynamic Times. Cates, Lori, ed. LC 99-39270. (Illus.). 192p. 1999. pap. 14.95 (*1-57112-102-1*, P1021) Park Ave.

Bendaly, Leslie. Strength in Numbers: Easy Steps to High Performance Teams. rev. ed. (Illus.). 211p. 1999. pap. 18.99 (*0-07-552814-2*) McGraw.

***Bendaly, Leslie.** Winner Instinct: 6 Steps to Success. 2000. 29.95 (*0-00-200009-1*) HarpC.

Bendana, Alejandro. Power Lines: U. S. Domination in the New Global Order. (Voices & Visions Ser.). 320p. 1996. 39.95 (*1-56656-167-1*, Olive Branch Pr); pap. 18.95 (*1-56656-168-X*, Olive Branch Pr) Interlink Pub.

Bendaniel, David J. & Rosenbloom, Arthur H. International Mergers & Acquisitions. (Frontiers in Finance Ser.). 544p. 1997. 79.95 (*0-471-16036-9*) Wiley.

Bendann, Effie. Death Customs: An Analytical Study of Burial Rites. LC 89-63007. xiii, 304p. 1990. reprint ed. lib. bdg. 44.00 (*1-55888-844-6*) Omnigraphics Inc.

Bendat, jt. auth. see Sukiennik.

Bendat, Julius. Nonlinear Systems Techniques & Applications. 2nd ed. LC 97-11446. 474p. 1998. 105.00 (*0-471-16576-X*) Wiley.

Bendat, Julius S. & Piersol, Allan G. Engineering Applications of Correlation & Spectral Analysis. 2nd rev. ed. LC 92-36126. 472p. 1993. 118.00 (*0-471-57055-9*) Wiley.

— Random Data: Analysis & Measurement Procedures. 2nd exp. rev. ed. LC 85-17996. 592p. 1986. 115.00 (*0-471-04000-2*) Wiley.

— Random Data: Analysis & Measurement Procedures. 3rd ed. LC 99-29982. 602p. 2000. 98.95 (*0-471-31733-0*) Wiley.

Bendau, Clifford P. Still Worlds Collide: Philip Wylie & the End of the American Dream. LC 80-10756. (Milford Ser.: Popular Writers of Today: Vol. 30). 63p. 1980. pap. 13.00 (*0-89370-244-7*) Millefleurs.

***Bendavid, Robert.** Abdominal Wall Hernias: Principles & Management. LC 00-20620. (Illus.). 2000. write for info. (*0-387-95004-4*) Spr-Verlag.

Bendavid, Robert, ed. Prostheses & Abdominal Wall Hernias. 500p. 1994. 205.00 (*1-879702-70-3*, R) CRC Pr.

Bendavid-Val, Avron. Regional & Local Economic Analysis for Practitioners. 4th ed. LC 90-41092. 264p. 1991. 59.95 (*0-275-93520-5*, C3520, Praeger Pubs); pap. 24.95 (*0-275-93751-8*, B3751, Praeger Pubs) Greenwood.

Bendavid-Val, Leah. Changing Reality: Recent Soviet Photography. (Illus.). 132p. 1991. 34.95 (*0-912347-76-7*) Fulcrum Pub.

Bendavid-Val, Leah, ed. Propaganda & Dreams: Photographing the 1930s in the U. S. S. R. & U. S. A. (Illus.). 1999. 55.00 (*3-908161-80-0*) Abbeville Pr.

— Realms of the Sea. (Illus.). 1994. 35.00 (*0-87044-855-2*) Natl Geog.

Bendavid-Val, Leah & Heacox, Kim, eds. The Milestones: National Geographic Photographs. LC 99-29397. (Illus.). 336p. 1999. per. 50.00 (*0-7922-7520-9*) Natl Geog.

Bendavid-Val, Leah, ed. see Allen, Thomas B.

Bendavid-Val, Leah, ed. see National Geographic Staff.

Bendazzi, Giannalberto. Cartoons: One Hundred Years of Cinema Animation. Taraboletti-Segre, Anna, tr. from ITA. LC 94-29075. 1995. 89.95 (*0-253-31168-3*); pap. 45.00 (*0-253-20937-4*) Ind U Pr.

***Bende-Nabende, Anthony.** FDI, Regionalism, Government Policy & Endogenous Growth: A Comparative Study of the ASEAN-5 Economics, with Development Policy Implications for the Least Developed Countries. LC 98-74635. 5p. 1999. text 69.95 (*0-7546-1000-4*, Pub. by Ashgate Pub) Ashgate Pub Co.

Bendel, John, compiled by. True Facts. (National Lampoon Ser.). (Illus.). 192p. (Orig.). 1991. pap. 9.95 (*0-8092-4006-8*, 400680, Contemporary Bks) NTC Contemp Pub Co.

Bendel, John & Ward, Jason. National Lampoon Presents True Facts: The Big Book. (Illus.). 272p. 1995. pap. 12.95 (*0-8092-3559-5*) NTC Contemp Pub Co.

Bendel, John & Ward, Jason, compiled by. National Lampoon Presents True Facts: The Big Book. LC 95-23509. 1995. pap. 103.60 (*0-8092-3245-6*) NTC Contemp Pub Co.

Bendel, Peggy, ed. Overline: SEW NEWS Presents Sew Much Better: The Secrets to Sewing Better, Faster & Easier. (Illus.). 208p. (C). 1989. 19.95 (*0-9621148-1-2*) PRMDIA Spcl Intrst.

Bendel-Simso, Paul, jt. auth. see Timpson, William.

Bendel-Simso, Paul, jt. auth. see Timpson, William M.

Bendell, A., ed. Taguchi Methods: Applications in World Industry. (Illus.). 250p. 1989. 89.00 (*0-387-50657-8*) Spr-Verlag.

Bendell, Don. Matched Colts. 1997. mass mkt. 5.99 (*0-451-19128-5*, Sig) NAL.

***Bendell, Don.** War Bonnet. (Historical Fiction Ser.). 320p. 2000. mass mkt. 5.99 (*0-451-19812-3*) NAL.

Bendell, Leonard. Payment in Full: A Guide to Successful Bill Collecting. 176p. 1987. 24.95 (*0-937404-05-5*) Triad Pub FL.

Bendell, Tony & Boulter, Louise. Benchmarking Workout. (Illus.). 250p. (Orig.). 1997. pap. text 25.00 (*0-273-62635-3*) F T P-H.

Bendell, Tony, et al. Benchmarking for Competitive Advantage. 2nd ed. 1997. 72.50 (*0-273-62634-5*, Pub. by Pitman Pub) Trans-Atl Phila.

Bendelow, Gillian & Williams, Simon J. Emotions in Social Life: Critical Themes & Contemporary Issues. LC 97-11499. 368p. (C). 1997. 90.00 (*0-415-13798-5*); pap. 29.99 (*0-415-13799-3*) Routledge.

Bendelow, Gillian, jt. auth. see Williams, Simon J.

Bender, Aimee. The Girl in the Flammable Skirt: Stories. LC 97-44485. 192p. 1998. 21.95 (*0-385-49215-4*) Doubleday.

— The Girl in the Flammable Skirt: Stories. 192p. 1999. pap. 11.95 (*0-385-49216-2*) Doubleday.

***Bender, Aimee.** An Invisible Sign of My Own. LC 99-58948. 240p. 2000. 22.95 (*0-385-49223-5*) Doubleday.

Bender, Amadee. Analysis of Electronic Wire & Cable: Markets & Opportunities. (Illus.). 196p. 1988. pap. text 1800.00 (*1-878218-02-6*) World Info Tech.

— Cable Distribution & Interconnection Systems for Telephone Wire Center Modernization U. S. Markets, Competitors, Customers & Technologies: 1993-1998 Analysis & Forecasts. 250p. 1993. pap. text 2850.00 (*1-878218-40-9*) World Info Tech.

— Competitive Analysis of North American Electrical & Electronic Wire & Cable Manufacturers. 485p. 1988. pap. text 2400.00 (*1-878218-01-8*) World Info Tech.

— Electronic Transformers & Inductors - Opportunities in Magnetics: 1991-1996 Analysis. (Illus.). 340p. 1991. pap. text 1800.00 (*1-878218-22-0*) World Info Tech.

— Hard & Superhard Materials - U. S. Markets, Technologies & Opportunities, 1989-1994 Analysis: Tool Steels - Ceramics - Cemented Carbides - Cubic Boron Nitride - Diamonds - Coatings. (Illus.). 300p. 1989. pap. text 1800.00 (*1-878218-06-9*) World Info Tech.

— Medium & High Voltage Power Cables - North American Markets, Technologies & Opportunities: 1990-1995 Analysis. (Illus.). 200p. 1990. pap. text 1800.00 (*1-878218-13-1*) World Info Tech.

— Piezoelectric Filters: Markets, Applications & Competitors: Quartz Crystal, SAW, Ceramic, Mechanical. (Illus.). 196p. 1988. pap. text 2400.00 (*1-878218-00-X*) World Info Tech.

— U. S. & Canadian Electronic Wire & Cable Manufacturers: 1990 Competitive Analysis. (Illus.). 200p. (Orig.). 1990. pap. 1800.00 (*1-878218-11-5*) World Info Tech.

— U. S. Distribution Channels for Electronic Wire & Cable. 150p. 1989. pap. text 1800.00 (*1-878218-04-2*) World Info Tech.

— U. S. Distribution Channels for Electronic Wire & Cable: 1992-1996 Analysis. 220p. 1993. pap. text 2400.00 (*1-878218-34-4*) World Info Tech.

— U. S. Electrical & Electronic Circuit Breaker & Fuse Markets. (Illus.). 200p. 1989. pap. text 1800.00 (*1-878218-03-4*) World Info Tech.

— U. S. Electrical & Electronic Surge Protection Markets. (Illus.). 225p. 1989. pap. text 1800.00 (*1-878218-05-0*) World Info Tech.

Bender, Amadee & Murawski, Frank. Data & Voice Building Communications Wiring Cable & Apparatus - U. S. Markets, Technologies, & Opportunities: 1997-2002 Analysis & Forecasts. 100p. 1997. pap. text 3900.00 (*1-878218-80-8*) World Info Tech.

— Data & Voice Building Communications Wiring Cable & Apparatus-U. S. Markets, Technologies, & Opportunities: 1996-2000 Analysis & Forecasts. 100p. 1996. pap. text 3900.00 (*1-878218-66-2*) World Info Tech.

— Data & Voice Premises Wiring Systems - U. S. Markets, Technologies, & Opportunities: 1998-2003 Analysis & Forecasts. 100p. 1998. pap. text 3900.00 (*1-878218-93-X*) World Info Tech.

— Local Area Network Cable Cross Connects Outlets Concentrators & Hubs: Markets Technologies, & Opportunities, 1990-1995 Analysis. (Illus.). 200p. 1990. pap. text 1800.00 (*1-878218-10-7*) World Info Tech.

Bender, Amadee, et al. CATV Cable & RF Distribution Products - U. S. Markets, Competitors, & Opportunities, 1995-2000 Analysis & Forecasts. 170p. 1995. pap. text 3490.00 (*1-878218-56-5*) World Info Tech.

— Data & Voice Premises Cabling & Wiring Apparatus - U. S. Markets, Technologies, & Opportunities: 1994-1999 Analysis & Forecasts. 100p. 1994. pap. text 2900.00 (*1-878218-51-4*) World Info Tech.

***Bender, Amadee, et al.** Data & Voice Premises Wiring Systems - U. S. Markets, Technologies & Opportunities: 2000-2005 Analysis & Forecasts. 100p. 2000. pap. text 3900.00 (*1-929904-09-6*) World Info Tech.

Bender, Amadee, et al. Home Wiring Cable & Apparatus - U. S. Markets, Technologies, & Opportunities: 1997-2001 Analysis & Forecasts. 100p. 1997. pap. text 3900.00 (*1-878218-75-1*) World Info Tech.

— LAN Cables & Apparatus - Markets, Technologies & Opportunities: 1992-1996 Analysis. (Illus.). 100p. 1992. pap. text 2400.00 (*1-878218-30-1*) World Info Tech.

— Manufacturers & Distributors of Premises Cabling & Wiring Apparatus, 1993: Strategic Assessment & Competitive Analysis. 100p. 1993. pap. text 2400.00 (*1-878218-41-7*) World Info Tech.

— World Market for Voice & Data Premises: Cabling & Apparatus: 1994-2000. 250p. 1995. pap. text 6900.00 (*1-878218-62-X*) World Info Tech.

Bender, Arnold E. Dictionary of Nutrition & Food Technology. 6th ed. 336p. 1990. text 82.95 (*0-408-03753-9*) Buttrwrth-Heinemann.

Bender, Arnold E. Dictionary of Nutrition & Food Technology. 6th ed. 341p. 1990. 59.95 (*1-85573-365-X*) Technomic.

Bender, Arnold E. & Bender, David A. A Dictionary of Food & Nutrition. (Illus.). 420p. 1995. pap. (*0-19-280006-X*) OUP.

Bender, Arnold E., jt. auth. see Bender, David A.

Bender, B. State & Society: Emergence & Developement of Social Hierarchy & Political Centralization. Gledhill, J. et al, eds. (One World Archaeology Ser.). 368p. (C). 1995. pap. 37.99 (*0-415-12255-4*) Routledge.

Bender, Barbara. Farming in Prehistory: From Hunter-Gatherer to Food-Producer. LC 76-353698. xi, 268p. 1975. 5.50 (*0-212-97003-8*) A & C Blk.

— Stonehenge: Making Space. LC 98-217938. (Materializing Culture Ser.). (Illus.). 256p. 1998. 55.00 (*1-85973-903-2*, Pub. by Berg Pubs); pap. 19.50 (*1-85973-908-3*, Pub. by Berg Pubs) NYU Pr.

Bender, Barbara, ed. Landscape: Politics & Perspectives. LC 92-39620. 352p. 1993. 49.50 (*0-85496-852-0*, Pub. by Berg Pubs); pap. 22.50 (*0-85496-373-1*, Pub. by Berg Pubs) NYU Pr.

Bender, Barbara, ed. see Thomas, Martin.

Bender, Benjamin. Glimpses: Through Holocaust & Liberation. LC 95-4449. (Illus.). 224p. 1995. pap. 15.00 (*1-55643-208-9*) North Atlantic.

Bender, Bert. The Descent of Love: Darwin & the Theory of Sexual Selection in American Fiction, 1871-1926. LC 95-42582. 456p. (C). 1996. text 38.95 (*0-8122-3344-1*) U of Pa Pr.

— Sea-Brothers: The Tradition of American Sea Fiction from Moby-Dick to the Present. LC 88-17321. (Illus.). 282p. (C). 1988. pap. 18.95 (*0-8122-1339-4*) U of Pa Pr.

Bender, Brett. The Coloring Book for the Super-Intelligent. (Illus.). 20p. (Orig.). 1984. pap. write for info. (*0-9615356-0-1*) B Bender.

Bender, Byron W. Spoken Marshallese: An Intensive Language Course with Grammatical Notes & Glossary. (PALI Language Texts, Micronesia Ser.). 464p. (Orig.). 1978. pap. text 17.00 (*0-87022-070-5*) UH Pr.

Bender, C. W. & Swartzendruber, D. B. Bender. Descendants of Daniel Bender. 192p. 1997. reprint ed. pap. 28.50 (*0-8328-7483-3*); reprint ed. lib. bdg. 38.50 (*0-8328-7482-5*) Higginson Bk Co.

***Bender, Carl M. & Orszag, S. A.** Advanced Mathematical Methods for Scientists & Engineers I: Assymptotic Methods & Perturbation Theory. LC 99-44783. (Illus.). 608p. 1999. 69.00 (*0-387-98931-5*) Spr-Verlag.

Bender, Carole, jt. auth. see Gibson, Bob.

Bender, Carrie. Brick Hollow Schoolmarm. LC 98-50568. (Dora's Diary Ser.). (Illus.). 192p. 1999. pap. 8.99 (*0-8361-9095-5*) Herald Pr.

— Chestnut Ridge Acres. LC 97-22082. (Whispering Brook Ser.: Vol. 3). (Illus.). 176p. (Orig.). (J). (gr. 4-8). 1997. pap. 7.99 (*0-8361-9077-7*) Herald Pr.

— A Fruitful Vine. LC 92-36425. (Miriam's Journal Ser.: Vol. 1). 192p. (Orig.). 1996. pap. 7.99 (*0-8361-3613-6*) Herald Pr.

Bender, Carrie. A Golden Sunbeam. LC 96-25796. (Miriam's Journal Ser.: Vol. 5). 192p. 1996. pap. 7.99 (*0-8361-9055-6*) Herald Pr.

— Hemlock Hill Hideaway. LC 99-55154. (Whispering Brook Ser.: Vol. 4). (Illus.). 168p. (J). (gr. 4-8). 2000. pap. 7.99 (*0-8361-9128-5*) Herald Pr.

Bender, Carrie. A Joyous Heart. LC 94-5836. (Miriam's Journal Ser.: Vol. 3). 168p. (Orig.). 1996. pap. 7.99 (*0-8361-3668-3*) Herald Pr.

— Miriam's Cookbook. Meyer, Mary C., ed. LC 97-51939. (Illus.). 112p. 1998. spiral bd. 9.99 (*0-8361-9086-6*) Herald Pr.

— Miriam's Journal Set, 5 bks. 1996. pap. 39.95 (*0-8361-9023-8*) Herald Pr.

— Summerville Days. LC 96-7250. (Whispering Brook Ser.: Vol. 2). (Illus.). 224p. (J). (gr. 4-8). 1996. pap. 7.99 (*0-8361-9040-8*) Herald Pr.

— A Treasured Friendship. LC 95-47390. (Miriam's Journal Ser.: Vol. 4). 160p. (Orig.). 1996. pap. 7.99 (*0-8361-9033-5*) Herald Pr.

***Bender, Carrie.** Whispering Brook Farm. LC 00-25940. (Illus.). (J). 2000. 23.95 (*0-7862-2549-1*) Five Star.

Bender, Carrie. Whispering Brook Farm. LC 94-39706. (Whispering Brook Ser.: Vol. 1). (Illus.). 184p. (J). (gr. 4-6). 1995. pap. 7.99 (*0-8361-9011-4*) Herald Pr.

Bender, Carrie. Whispering Brook Series, 3 vols. (Illus.). 1997. pap. 23.95 (*0-8361-9068-8*) Herald Pr.

Bender, Carrie. A Winding Path. LC 93-44864. (Miriam's Journal Ser.: Vol. 2). 160p. (Orig.). 1996. pap. 7.99 (*0-8361-3656-X*) Herald Pr.

***Bender, Cheryl A.** Our Miracle Baby: Memories & Milestones in the Intensive Care Nursery. (Illus.). 112p. 2000. 32.95 (*0-9673025-2-8*) Wyatt-MacKenzie Pubg.

— Our Miracle Baby Parent Journal. (Illus.). 80p. 2000. 14.95 (*0-9673025-3-6*) Wyatt-MacKenzie Pubg.

Bender, Danene M., ed. Packet for Classroom Teachers about Alternatives to Violence. (Illus.). 108p. 1996. pap. text, teacher ed. 9.95 (*0-9619819-5-4*) Peace Grows.

Bender, Danene M., jt. auth. see Looney, John.

Bender, Danene M., ed. see Looney, John.

Bender, Daniel R., et al. Essays on Audience Perception in Elizabethan & Jacobean Literature. 84p. 1997. pap. 14.95 (*3-7052-0090-9*, Pub. by Poetry Salzburg) Intl Spec Bk.

Bender, David. Computer Law: Evidence & Procedure, 3 vols. 1977. ring bd. 580.00 (*0-8205-1068-8*, 068) Bender.

— Confession of O. J. Simpson: A Work of Fiction. LC 97-177546. 1997. 19.95 (*0-425-16205-2*) Berkley Pub.

Bender, David, jt. auth. see Crosby, David.

Bender, David, jt. auth. see Retton, Mary Lou.

Bender, David, ed. see Fitzgerald, F. Scott.

Bender, David A. Amino Acid Metabolism. 2nd ed. LC 84-26941. (Illus.). 275p. reprint ed. pap. 85.30 (*0-8357-2885-4*, 203912100011) Bks Demand.

— Introduction to Nutrition & Metabolism. 300p. 1997. pap. text 32.95 (*0-7484-0781-2*, Pub. by Tay Francis Ltd) Taylor & Francis.

— Introduction to Nutrition & Metabolism. 2nd ed. 300p. 1997. 85.00 (*0-7484-0782-0*, Pub. by Tay Francis Ltd) Taylor & Francis.

— Nutritional Biochemistry of the Vitamins. (Illus.). 451p. (C). 1992. text 105.00 (*0-521-38144-4*) Cambridge U Pr.

***Bender, David A. & Bender, Arnold E.** Bender's Dictionary of Nutrition & Food Technology. 480p. 1999. text 89.00 (*1-85573-475-3*, Pub. by Woodhead Pubng) Am Educ Systs.

— Bender's Dictionary of Nutrition & Food Technology. 7th ed. LC 99-40222. 1999. write for info. (*0-8493-0018-5*) CRC Pr.

Bender, David A. & Bender, Arnold E. Nutrition: A Reference Handbook. (Illus.). 612p. 1996. text 110.00 (*0-19-262368-0*) OUP.

Bender, David A., jt. auth. see Bender, Arnold E.

Bender, David L., ed. Constructing a Life Philosophy: Opposing Viewpoints. (Opposing Viewpoints Ser.). (Illus.). 264p. (YA). (gr. 10 up). 1993. lib. bdg. 26.20 (*0-89908-198-3*) Greenhaven.

Bender, David R., et al. National Information Policies: Strategies for the Future. LC 92-129033. (SLA Occasional Papers Ser.: No. 2). 70p. reprint ed. pap. 30.00 (*0-608-20000-X*, 207127700010) Bks Demand.

***Bender, Deborah, et al.** Managing Health Services: Cases in Organization Design & Decision Making. LC 99-89904. 2000. write for info. (*1-56793-125-1*) Health Admin Pr.

Bender, Deborah, jt. auth. see Allen, James E.

Bender, Deborah E. & Bean, Cydne. Counseling Skills in Family Planning. 1982. pap., teacher ed. 14.00 (*0-686-47616-6*); pap., student ed. 4.00 (*0-685-55671-9*) Carolina Pop Ctr.

Bender, Donna G. Get a Life! A Friendly Workbook for Planning Your Career. 2nd ed. 212p. 1998. spiral bd. 48.95 (*0-7872-5170-4*, 41517001) Kendall-Hunt.

— Get a Life: A User Friendly Guide to Career Life Planning. 192p. (C). 1994. spiral bd. 34.95 (*0-8403-9201-X*) Kendall-Hunt.

***Bender, Edward A.** Introduction to Mathematical Modeling. 2000. pap. 7.95 (*0-486-41180-X*) Dover.

Bender, Edward A. Mathematical Methods in Artificial Intelligence. LC 95-24708. 664p. 1996. 59.00 (*0-8186-7200-5*, BP07200) IEEE Comp Soc.

Bender, Eileen T. Joyce Carol Oates, Artist in Residence. LC 86-45474. 219p. reprint ed. pap. 67.90 (*0-608-09270-3*, 205407200002) Bks Demand.

Bender, Eileen T., et al, eds. Quick Hits: Successful Strategies by Award Winning Teachers. LC 94-3693. (Illus.). 104p. 1994. pap. text 12.95 (*0-253-20923-4*) Ind U Pr.

***Bender, Elaine.** ACT English Flash 2001. 2nd ed. 162p. 2000. pap. 9.95 (*0-7689-0506-0*) Petersons.

Bender, Elaine. ACT Success. 3rd ed. (Peterson's Test Success Ser.). 352p. 1998. pap. text 14.95 (*0-7689-0013-1*) Petersons.

— Test Yourself English Grammar. (Test Yourself Ser.). 96p. 1996. pap. 9.95 (*0-8442-2357-3*, 23573, NTC Learningworks) NTC Contemp Pub Co.

Bender, Elaine, et al. ACT Success: Complete & Practical Information on the ACT. (Test Success Ser.). 400p. (Orig.). 1996. pap. 24.95 incl. disk (*1-56079-607-3*) Petersons.

***Bender, Elaine, et al.** ACT Success 2001. 3rd ed. 400p. 2000. pap. 16.95 (*0-7689-0406-4*) Petersons.

Bender, Eleanor M., et al, eds. All of Us Are Present: The Stephens College Symposium Women's Education the Future. (C). 1984. pap. 15.00 (*0-916767-01-9*) J M Wood Res.

Bender, Ernest. Urdu: Grammar & Reader. LC 66-20832. (Illus.). 491p. reprint ed. pap. 152.30 (*0-608-11011-6*, 205118500083) Bks Demand.

Bender, Ernest, ed. Indological Studies in Honor of W. Norman Brown. (American Oriental Ser.: Vol. 47). xx, 253p. 1962. 15.00 (*0-940490-47-1*) Am Orient Soc.

Bender, Ernest, ed. The Salibhadra-Dhanna-Carita (The Tale of the Quest for Ultimate Release by Slibhadra & Dhanna) A Work in Old Gujarati. (American Oriental Ser.: Vol. 73). vi, 573p. 1992. 52.00 (*0-940490-73-0*) Am Orient Soc.

Bender, Esther. April Bluebird. LC 95-5297. (Illus.). 32p. (Orig.). (J). (gr. 1-5). 1995. pap. 8.99 (*0-8361-9009-2*) Herald Pr.

An Asterisk (*) at the beginning of an entry indicates that the title is appearing for the first time.

— The Crooked Tree. (Illus.). 32p. (Orig.). (J). (gr. k-5). 1996. pap. 8.99 (*0-8361-9026-2*) Herald Pr.

— A Cry from the Clay. LC 98-45527. (Illus.). 64p. 1999. pap. 12.99 (*0-8361-9100-5*) Herald Pr.

— Katie & the Lemon Tree. LC 94-2581. (Illus.). 88p. (Orig.). (J). (gr. 3-7). 1994. pap. 5.99 (*0-8361-3657-8*) Herald Pr.

— Search for a Fawn. LC 98-22275. (Illus.). 32p. (J). (gr. k-5). 1998. pap. 8.99 (*0-8361-9099-8*) Herald Pr.

— Shadow at Sun Lake. LC 94-33947. 152p. (Orig.). (YA). (gr. 6-10). 1995. pap. 6.99 (*0-8361-9007-6*) Herald Pr.

— Virginia & the Tiny One. LC 98-20317. (Lemon Tree Ser.: Vol. 2). (Illus.). 104p. (J). (gr. 3-7). 1998. pap. 5.99 (*0-8361-9090-4*) Herald Pr.

Bender, Eugene I., jt. auth. see Katz, Alfred H.

Bender, Eugene J. Military Holsters of World War II. (Illus.). 215p. 1998. reprint ed. 45.00 (*1-884849-27-X*) R&R Bks.

Bender, Evelyn. Brazil: Major World Nations. (Major World Nations Ser.). (Illus.). 144p. (YA). (gr. 5 up). 1999. lib. bdg. 19.95 (*0-7910-4758-X*) Chelsea Hse.

Bender, F. Underground Siting of Nuclear Power Plants: Unterirdische Bauweise von Kernkraftwerken. Berichte vom Internationalen Symposium, Hannover, Bundesanstalt Fuer Geowissenschaften und Rohstoffe, 1620. (ENG & GER., Illus.). iv, 412p. 1982. 88.00 (*3-510-65108-1*, Pub. by E Schweizerbartsche) Balogh.

Bender, F., ed. Geo-Resources & Environment: Proceedings of the 4th International Symposium, Hannover, FRG, Federal Institute for Geosciences & Natural Resources, Oct. 16-18, 1985. (Illus.). vi, 144p. 1986. pap. text 45.00 (*3-510-65129-4*, Pub. by E Schweizerbartsche) Balogh.

— The Mineral Resources Potential of the Earth: Proceedings of the 2nd International Symposium, Held in Hannover, Federal Republic of Germany, at the Federal Institute for Geosciences & Mineral Resources, April 18-20, 1979. (Illus.). v, 156p. 1980. pap. text 32.00 (*3-510-65093-X*, Pub. by E Schweizerbartsche) Balogh.

Bender, Filmore E., et al. Optimization for Profit: A Decision Maker's Guide to Linear Programming. LC 91-6615. (Illus.). 540p. 1992. pap. 17.95 (*1-56022-015-5*); lib. bdg. 89.95 (*1-56022-014-7*) Haworth Pr.

Bender, Frederic L. Culture of Extinction. (Religion/Society - Society/Religion Ser.). (C). Date not set. pap. 2.25 (*0-391-03906-7*); text 9.95 (*0-391-03905-9*) Humanities.

Bender, Frederic L., ed. see Marx, Karl & Engels, Friedrich.

Bender, Friedrich. Classic Climbs in the Caucasus. (Illus.). 318p. 1992. 24.95 (*0-89732-116-2*) Menasha Ridge.

— Geologie Von Jordanien. (Beitrage Zur Regionalen Geologie der Erde. Ser.: Vol. 7). (GER., Illus.). xii, 230p. 1968. 93.00 (*3-443-11007-X*, Pub. by Gebruder Borntraeger) Balogh.

— Geology of Burma. (Beitrage Zur Regionalen Geologie der Erde. Ser.: Vol. 16). (GER., Illus.). viii, 293p. 1983. 116.00 (*3-443-11016-9*, Pub. by Gebruder Borntraeger) Balogh.

— Geology of Jordon: Supplementary Edition. (Beitrage Zur Regionalen Geologie der Erde. Ser.: Vol. 7). (Illus.). xi, 196p. 1974. 38.00 (*3-443-11707-4*, Pub. by Gebruder Borntraeger) Balogh.

Bender, Friedrich, ed. The Importance of the Geosciences for the Supply of Mineral Raw Materials: Proceedings of an International Symposium, Held in Hannover, Fed. Rep. of Germany, at the Federal Institute for Geosciences & Mineral Resources, Oct. 25-26, 1976. (Hirt's Stichwortbuecher Ser.). (Illus.). v, 136p. (Orig.). 1977. pap. text 29.00 (*3-510-65079-4*, Pub. by E Schweizerbartsche) Balogh.

— New Paths to Mineral Exploration: Proceedings of the 3rd International Symposium, Hannover, Federal Republic of Germany, at the Federal Institute for Geosciences & Mineral Resources, October 27-29, 1982. (Illus.). v, 169p. (Orig.). 1983. pap. 35.00 (*3-510-65114-6*, Pub. by E Schweizerbartsche) Balogh.

Bender, Friedrich K. & Raza, Hilal A., eds. Geology of Pakistan. LC 95-229261. (Beitrage Zur Regionalen Geologie der Erde. Ser.: Vol. 25). (GER., Illus.). x, 414p. 1995. 146.00 (*3-443-11025-8*, Pub. by Gebruder Borntraeger) Balogh.

Bender, Gary & Johnson, Michael L. Call of the Game: What Really Goes On in the Broadcast Booth. LC 94-26463. (Illus.). 263p. 1994. 19.95 (*1-56625-013-7*) Bonus Books.

Bender, Gerald J., ed. International Affairs in Africa. (Annals Ser.: Vol. 489). 1987. 26.00 (*0-8039-2862-9*); pap. 17.00 (*0-8039-2863-7*) Sage.

Bender, Gordon L., ed. Reference Handbook on the Deserts of North America. LC 80-24791. (Illus.). 594p. 1982. lib. bdg. 145.00 (*0-313-21307-0*, BRD/, Greenwood Pr) Greenwood.

Bender, Gretchen & Druckrey, Timothy, eds. Culture on the Brink: Ideologies of Technology. (Discussions in Contemporary Culture Ser.: Vol. 9). (Illus.). 376p. (Orig.). 1994. pap. 18.95 (*1-56584-496-3*, Pub. by New Press NY) Norton.

***Bender, H. G., et al, eds.** Atlas of Clinical PET in Oncology: PET Versus CT, MRI. 210p. 2000. 145.00 (*3-540-66726-1*) Spr-Verlag.

Bender, Hans. The Mud Sled. Willson, Jeanne, tr. from GER. (Modern German Literature in Translation Ser.). 160p. 1993. 24.95 (*0-911173-04-8*) Dimension Pr.

Bender, Harald. Die Zeit der Bewegung - Strukturdynamik und Transformationsprozesse: Beitrage Zur Theorie Sozialer Bewegungen und Zur Analyse Kollektiven Handelns. (Europaische Hochschulschriften Ser.: Reihe 22, Bd. 301). (GER.). 274p. 1996. 54.95 (*3-631-30053-0*) P Lang Pubng.

Bender, Harold S. Anabaptist Vision. 48p. 1944. pap. 3.99 (*0-8361-1305-5*) Herald Pr.

***Bender, Harold S.** Conrad Grebel. 344p. 1998. pap. 28.00 (*1-57910-157-7*) Wipf & Stock.

Bender, Harold S. & Smith, C. Henry, eds. The Mennonite Encyclopedia, Vol. 1. LC 55-4563. 900p. 1955. 90.00 (*0-8361-1118-4*) Herald Pr.

— The Mennonite Encyclopedia, Vol. 2. LC 55-4563. 912p. 1956. 90.00 (*0-8361-1119-2*) Herald Pr.

— The Mennonite Encyclopedia, Vol. 3. LC 55-4563. 952p. 1957. 90.00 (*0-8361-1120-6*) Herald Pr.

— The Mennonite Encyclopedia, Vol. 4. LC 55-4563. 1184p. 1959. 90.00 (*0-8361-1121-4*) Herald Pr.

Bender, Helmut & Glauberman, George. Local Analysis for the Odd Order Theorem. (London Mathematical Society Lecture Note Ser.: No. 188). 186p. (C). 1995. pap. text 32.95 (*0-521-45716-5*) Cambridge U Pr.

Bender, Henry E., Jr. Uintah Railway: The Gilsonite Route. LC 75-135999. (Illus.). 252p. 1995. 39.95 (*0-911581-36-7*) Heimburger Hse Pub.

Bender, Henry V. A Horace Reader: For Advanced Placement in Latin. (Illus.). 120p. 1998. pap. text 19.95 (*0-941051-67-6*) Focus Pub-R Pullins.

***Bender, Henry V.** Teacher's Manual for a Horace Reader. 1999. pap. 19.95 (*0-941051-68-4*) Focus Pub-R Pullins.

Bender, Henry V., ed. see Catullus, Gaius Valerius.

Bender, Horace, pseud. Letters of Horatio Greenough to His Brother, Henry Greenough. (American Biography Ser.). 250p. 1991. reprint ed. lib. bdg. 69.00 (*0-7812-8156-3*) Rprt Serv.

***Bender, Howard.** Look & Find Casper the Friendly Ghost & the Ghostly Trio. 24p. (J). (gr. 2-7). 1999. pap. 3.95 (*0-8167-6292-9*) Troll Communs.

Bender, Hy. Getting Started with Windows 95. Lombard, Dawn A., ed. 1995. pap. text 36.00 (*0-929321-29-4*) WEKA Pub.

— The Sandman Companion: A Dreamer's Guide to the Award-Winning Comics Series. 304p. 1999. 19.95 (*1-56389-465-3*, Pub. by DC Comics) Time Warner.

Bender, I. B., et al. The Dental Pulp: Biologic Considerations in the Dental Procedures. 3rd ed. LC 65-7149. (Illus.). 358p. 1984. text 45.00 (*0-397-52107-3*, Lippnctt) Lppncott W & W.

Bender, I. B., jt. auth. see Seltzer, Samuel.

***Bender, Ida.** The Dark Abyss of Exile: The Story of Survival. Anderson, Laurel & Wiest, William, trs. 205p. 2000. pap. write for info. (*1-891193-11-2*) ND State Univ.

Bender, J. R., et al. Occupational Exposure, Toxic Properties, & Work Practice Guidelines for Fiber Glass. 48p. 1992. 22.00 (*0-932627-47-1*) Am Indus Hygiene.

Bender, Jack. A Layman's Guide to Installing A Small Business Computer. (Illus.). 128p. 1979. 17.50 (*0-89433-097-7*) Petrocelli.

Bender, James L. NCA Review for the Clinical Laboratory Sciences. 315p. 1985. pap. text 19.50 (*0-316-08889-7*, Little Brwn Med Div) Lppncott W & W.

Bender, Jim. Future Harvest: Pesticide-Free Farming. LC 93-15807. (Our Sustainable Future Ser.). (Illus.). xviii, 159p. (C). 1994. text 35.00 (*0-8032-1233-X*) U of Nebr Pr.

Bender, Jo A. & Budinger, F. C. Favorites from the Lazy Bee: Featuring Americana Basics from the Northwest Mountains. LC 92-97119. (Illus.). 144p. (Orig.). 1992. pap. 9.95 (*1-882584-00-8*) Bender & Assocs.

Bender, John. Imagining the Penitentiary: Fiction & the Architecture of Mind in Eighteenth-Century England. LC 86-25074. (Illus.). 356p. 1989. pap. text 18.95 (*0-226-04229-4*) U Ch Pr.

— Imagining the Penitentiary: Fiction & the Architecture of Mind in Eighteenth-Century England. LC 86-25074. (Illus.). xviii, 356p. 1996. 41.95 (*0-226-04228-6*) U Ch Pr.

Bender, John & Wellbery, David E., eds. Chronotypes: The Construction of Time. 276p. 1991. 42.50 (*0-8047-1910-1*) Stanford U Pr.

— The Ends of Rhetoric: History, Theory, Practice. LC 90-9518. 256p. 1990. 42.50 (*0-8047-1817-2*); pap. 15.95 (*0-8047-1818-0*) Stanford U Pr.

Bender, John, ed. see Fielding, Henry.

Bender, John B. Spenser & Literary Pictorialism. LC 71-166361. 232p. 1972. reprint ed. pap. 72.00 (*0-608-02889-4*, 206395300007) Bks Demand.

Bender, John W., ed. The Current State of the Coherence Theory: Critical Essays on the Epistemic Theories of Keith Lehrer & Lawrence BonJour, with Replies. 304p. (C). 1989. lib. bdg. 138.50 (*0-7923-0220-6*, Pub. by Kluwer Academic) Kluwer Academic.

Bender, John W., jt. auth. see Blocker, H. Gene.

Bender, Judith, et al. Half a Childhood: Quality Programs for Out-of-School Hours. 2nd rev. ed. Orig. Title: Half a Childhood & Time for School-Age Child Care. (Illus.). 250p. (Orig.). 1997. pap. 24.95 (*0-917505-10-7*) School Age.

— Half a Childhood: Time for School-Age Child Care. LC 84-50953. (Illus.). 107p. (Orig.). (C). 1984. pap. 14.95 (*0-917505-01-8*) School Age.

Bender, Karen E. Excel in der Betriebl. (GER.). (C). 1990. text. write for info. (*0-201-56205-7*) Addison-Wesley.

— Introduction to Nutrition & Metabolism. 256p. 1993. 90.00 (*1-85728-078-4*, Pub. by UCL Pr Ltd); pap. 29.50 (*1-85728-079-2*, Pub. by UCL Pr Ltd) Taylor & Francis.

— Learning Disabilities. 3rd ed. LC 97-30427. 512p. 1997. 76.00 (*0-205-27401-3*) P-H.

***Bender, Karen E.** Like Normal People. LC 99-56112. 288p. 2000. 23.00 (*0-395-94515-1*) HM.

Bender, Karen E. Object Oriented Programming. (C). 1990. text. write for info. (*0-201-52310-8*) Addison-Wesley.

Bender, Kathryn N. The Rose of Enchantment. 1996. write for info. (*1-86106-040-8*, Pub. by Minerva Pr) Unity Dist.

Bender, Kenneth J. Psychiatric Medications: A Guide for Mental Health Professionals. (Human Services Guides Ser.: Vol. 61). (Illus.). 120p. (C). 1990. pap. 18.95 (*0-8039-3337-1*) Sage.

Bender, Klaus, ed. Relationes Historicae: Ein Bestandsverzeichnis der Deutschen Messrelationen Von 1583 Bis 1648. (Beitraege zur Kommunikationsgeschichte Ser.: Bd. 2). (GER.). 294p. (C). 1994. lib. bdg. 152.35 (*3-11-014045-4*) De Gruyter.

Bender, Lauretta, ed. see Schilder, Paul.

Bender, Leslie & Braveman, Daan. Power, Privilege & Law. (American Casebook Ser.). 193p. (C). 1994. pap. text. write for info. (*0-314-05931-8*) West Pub.

Bender, Leslie, jt. auth. see Braveman, Daan.

Bender, Lionel. Geography. LC 91-29406. (Picture Pockets Ser.). (Illus.). 96p. (J). (gr. 1-5). 1992. pap. 13.00 (*0-671-75996-5*) S&S Bks Yung.

— Heat & Drought. LC 97-1263. (Living with the Weather Ser.). (J). 1998. 25.69 (*0-8172-5051-4*) Raintree Steck-V.

***Bender, Lionel.** Invention. (Eyewitness Books). (Illus.). (J). (gr. 4-7). 2000. 19.99 (*0-7894-6576-0*) DK Pub Inc.

— Invention. (Eyewitness Books). (J). (gr. 4-7). 2000. 15.95 (*0-7894-5768-7*) DK Pub Inc.

— Miracle of Life: Science Facts. (Illus.). 108p. (YA). 1999. reprint ed. text 25.00 (*0-7881-6832-0*) DIANE Pub.

Bender, Louis W. Spotlight on the Transfer Function: A National Study of State Policies & Practices. 1990. pap. 10.00 (*0-87117-213-5*, 1132) Comm Coll Pr Am Assn Comm Coll.

Bender, Louis W., jt. auth. see Richardson, Richard C., Jr.

Bender, Lovorn. Understanding ADHD. LC 96-23914. 276p. (C). 1996. pap. text 40.00 (*0-13-348731-8*) P-H.

Bender, Lucille. Remembrances of Elvis. 34p. (Orig.). 1996. pap. 9.95 (*1-885206-43-7*) Cader Pubng.

Bender, Lynn-Darrell. Cuba vs. United States: The Politics of Hostility. rev. ed. LC 74-78314. 108p. (C). 198 . 12.50 (*0-913480-51-7*); pap. 5.75 (*0-913480-52-5*) Inter Am U Pr.

— Perspectivas Politicas. rev. ed. LC 83-82307. 167p. 1983. pap. text 6.95 (*0-913480-59-2*) Inter Am U Pr.

— Perspectivas Politicas, Vol. II. LC 79-27350. 115p. 1979. pap. text 4.55 (*0-913480-43-6*) Inter Am U Pr.

— The Politics of Hostility: Castro's Revolution & United States Policy. Zebrowski, John et al, eds. LC 74-78314. (Illus.). 160p. 1974. 7.95 (*0-913480-24-X*) Inter Am U Pr.

Bender, M. C. & Schadeberg, T. C., eds. Nilo-Saharan Proceedings. x, 349p. 1981. pap. 83.10 (*90-70176-26-2*) Mouton.

Bender, M. J. Through the Stalks Exposing. 40p. (Orig.). 1990. pap. 3.00 (*0-685-29033-6*) Landside Pr.

Bender, Margaret O. Le Torneiment Anticrist by Huon de Meri: A Critical Edition. LC 75-33765. (Romance Monographs: No. 17). 1976. 24.00 (*84-399-4702-X*) Romance.

Bender, Mark. Supple Workout: Chest & Shoulders. (Illus.). 80p. 1996. 14.95 (*0-02-861345-7*) Macmillan.

***Bender, Mark.** Trial by Basketball: The Life & Times of Tex Winter. LC 99-59432. (Illus.). 288p. 2000. 22.95 (*1-886110-96-4*) Addax Pubng.

Bender, Max, ed. Interfacial Phenomena in Biological Systems. (Surfactant Science Ser.: Vol. 39). (Illus.) 448p. 1991. text 199.00 (*0-8247-8436-7*) Dekker.

Bender, Michael. All the World's a Stage: A Pop-Up Biography of William Shakespeare. LC 98-52314. (Illus.). 20p. (J). (gr. 2-4). 1999. 14.95 (*0-8118-1147-6*) Chronicle Bks.

***Bender, Michael.** Waiting for Filippo: The Life of Renaissance Architect Filippo Brunelleschi. (Illus.) 22p. (YA). (gr. 6-8). 1999. reprint ed. text 20.00 (*0-7881-6849-5*) DIANE Pub.

Bender, Michael & Baglin, Carol A., eds. Infants & Toddlers: A Resource Guide for Practioners. (Illus.). 204p. (Orig.). (C). 1992. pap. 34.95 (*1-879105-36-5*, 0220) Thomson Learn.

Bender, Michael, et al. Functional Curriculum for Teaching Students with Disabilities Vol. I: Self Care, Motor Skills, Household Management, & Living Skills. 3rd ed. LC 96-138036. (C). 1996. pap. text 31.00 (*0-89079-635-1*, 7631) PRO-ED.

— Functional Curriculum for Teaching Students with Disabilities Vol. II: Nonverbal & Oral Communication. 3rd ed. LC 96-138036. (C). 1996. pap. text 33.00 (*0-89079-636-X*, 7632) PRO-ED.

— Functional Curriculum for Teaching Students with Disabilities Vol. III: Functional Academics. 2nd ed. (C). 1996. pap. text 33.00 (*0-89079-637-8*, 7633) PRO-ED.

— Teaching the Moderately & Severely Handicapped, Vol. II. 2nd ed. LC 84-22861. (Illus.). 352p. 1985. pap. 32.00 (*0-936104-53-8*, 1294) PRO-ED.

— Teaching the Moderately & Severely Handicapped, Vol. III. LC 79-46596. 272p. 1976. pap. text 29.00 (*0-936104-54-6*, 1111) PRO-ED.

Bender, Michael, jt. ed. see Baglin, Carol A.

***Bender, Mike.** The Therapeutic Purposes of Reminiscence. LC 98-61795. 300p. 1999. write for info. (*0-8039-7641-0*) Sage.

Bender, Morris B. Selected Papers of Morris B. Bender: Memorial Volume. fac. ed. Friedland, Robert P., ed. LC 83-2851. (Illus.). 463p. pap. 143.60 (*0-7837-7280-7*, 204702600005) Bks Demand.

Bender, Myron L. Mechanisms of Homogeneous Catalysis from Protons to Proteins. LC 73-153080. 698p. reprint ed. pap. 200.00 (*0-608-10084-6*, 200649000059) Bks Demand.

Bender, Myron L., et al. The Bioorganic Chemistry of Enzymatic Catalysis. LC 83-19857. 312p. 1984. 135.00 (*0-471-05991-9*) Wiley.

Bender, Norman J. Winning the West for Christ: Sheldon Jackson & Presbyterianism on Rocky Mountain Frontier, 1869-1880. 265p. 1996. 40.00 (*0-8263-1670-0*) U of NM Pr.

Bender, P. L., ed. see International Astronomical Union Staff, et al.

Bender, Paula S. How to Keep Your Kids from Driving You Crazy: A Proven Program for Improving Your Child's Behavior & Regaining Control of Your Family. LC 96-20801. 224p. 1996. pap. 14.95 (*0-471-13012-5*) Wiley.

— How to Keep Your Kids from Driving You Crazy: A Proven Program in Improving Your Child's Behavior & Regaining Control of Your Family. LC 96-20801. 210p. 1996. 39.95 (*0-471-16888-2*) Wiley.

***Bender, Paula Stone.** How to Keep Your Teenager from Driving You Crazy: A Proven Program for Enforcing Limits & Restoring Peace to Your Family. LC 00-22656. 224p. 2000. pap. 14.95 (*0-8092-2390-2*, Contemporary Bks) NTC Contemp Pub Co.

Bender, Peter U. Secrets of Power Presentations. rev. ed. (Illus.). 212p. 1995. pap. 12.95 (*1-895565-57-X*) Firefly Bks Ltd.

Bender, Peter U. & Hellman, Eric. Leadership from Within. LC 97-931931. 240p. 1998. pap. 15.95 (*0-7737-5903-4*) Stoddart Publ.

Bender, Philip. New Heaven on a New Earth: Revelation. LC 85-81579. (Faith & Life Bible Studies). 106p. 1985. pap. 1.95 (*0-87303-106-7*) Faith & Life.

B

Bender, R. Launching & Operating Satellites: Legal Issues. LC 97-38209. (Utrecht Studies in Air & Space Law: No. 18). 364p. 1997. 115.00 (*90-411-0507-7*) Kluwer Academic.

Bender, R. James. Postcards of Hitler's Germany, 1923-1936, Vol. 1. LC 98-202382. (Illus.). 368p. 1996. pap. 54.95 (*0-912138-60-2*) Bender Pub CA.

— Postcards of Hitler's Germany 1937-1939, Vol. 2. LC 98-202382. (Illus.). 360p. 1998. 54.95 (*0-912138-61-0*) Bender Pub CA.

— Space Transport Liability: National & International Aspects, Vol. 15. LC 95-23649. (Utrecht Studies in Air & Space Law). 1995. lib. bdg. 151.00 (*90-411-0106-3*, Pub. by M Nijhoff) Kluwer Academic.

Bender, Ralf & Davies, Roger L., eds. New Light on Galaxy Evolution. LC 96-246. 482p. 1996. lib. bdg. 179.00 (*0-7923-3975-4*) Kluwer Academic.

Bender, Renet L., et al. Computer-Assisted Instruction for Students at Risk: A Teachers' Manual. LC 95-36332. 240p. (C). 1996. pap. text 38.00 (*0-205-16062-X*) Allyn.

Bender, Richard W. Herbal Bonsai: Practicing the Art with Fast-Growing Herbs. LC 95-50604. (Illus.). 112p. 1996. pap. 16.95 (*0-8117-2788-2*) Stackpole.

Bender, Robert. The A To Z Beastly Jamboree. LC 94-37189. (Illus.). 32p. (J). (ps-2). 1996. 15.99 (*0-525-67520-5*, Dutton Child) Peng Put Young Read.

— A to Z Beastly Jamboree. 32p. 1999. pap. 5.99 (*0-14-056213-3*, PuffinBks) Peng Put Young Read.

***Bender, Robert.** Lima Beans Would be Illegal: Children's Ideas of a Perfect World. LC 99-32171. (J). 2000. 12.00 (*0-8037-2532-9*, Dial Yng Read) Peng Put Young Read.

— A Little Witch Magic. (J). (gr. 3). 1995. pap. 5.95 (*0-8050-3549-4*) H Holt & Co.

Bender, Robert. A Little Witch Magic. LC 92-4054. (Illus.). 32p. (J). (ps-3). 1995. 14.95 (*0-8050-2126-4*, Bks Young Read) H Holt & Co.

— Most Unusual Lunch. 1999. pap. 4.99 (*0-14-055670-2*) Viking Penguin.

— The Preposterous Rhinoceros: or Alvin's Beastly Birthday. LC 93-14200. (J). 1995. 14.95 (*0-8050-2806-4*) H Holt & Co.

Bender, Robert & Cannoy-Bender, Tammy. Mobil Collectibles: Chasing the Red Horse. LC 98-89679. (Illus.). 160p. 1999. pap. 29.95 (*0-7643-0782-7*) Schiffer.

Bender, Robert A., jt. auth. see Bender, Sara A.

Bender, Roger J. Air Organizations of the Third Reich: The Luft-Waffe. rev. ed. LC 92-83792. (Illus.). 320p. 1993. reprint ed. 39.95 (*0-88740-474-X*) Schiffer.

Bender, Roger J. & Peterson, George A. Hermann Goring from Regiment to Fallschirmpanzerkorps. rev. ed. LC 92-83791. (Illus.). 208p. 1992. reprint ed. 29.95 (*0-88740-473-1*) Schiffer.

Bender, Ross T. Education for Peoplehood: Essays on the Teaching Ministry of the Church. LC 98-118105. (Text Reader Ser.: No. 8). 249p. (Orig.). 1997. pap. 15.00 (*0-936273-25-9*) Inst Mennonite.

Bender, Ross T. & Sell, Alan P., eds. Baptism, Peace & the State in the Reformed & Mennonite Traditions. LC 91-93477. 258p. (C). 1991. 35.00 (*0-88920-204-4*) W Laurier U Pr.

Bender, Ruth. Gentle Relaxing & Strengthening Movements for People with Backproblems, Arthritis & MS. 1983. 1.95 (*0-917434-03-X*) Ruben Pub.

— Yoga Exercises for Every Body. 1975. spiral bd. 9.95 (*0-917434-00-5*) Ruben Pub.

— Yoga Exercises for More Flexible Bodies. (Illus.). 1977. spiral bd. 9.95 (*0-917434-02-1*) Ruben Pub.

Bender, Ruth & Milner, David. Financial Operations. 450p. 1990. pap. 130.00 (*0-85297-383-7*, Pub. by Chartered Bank) St Mut.

Bender, Ruth, jt. auth. see Ward, Keith.

Bender, Sandra G. Recreating Marriage with the Same Old Spouse: A Guide for Couples. LC 98-152427. 144p. 1998. pap., teacher ed. 18.00 (*0-664-25589-2*) Westminster John Knox.

— Recreating Marriage with the Same Old Spouse: A Guide for Couples - Couples Guide. LC 96-52259. 184p. 1997. pap. 15.00 (*0-664-25726-7*) Westminster John Knox.

Bender, Sara A. & Bender, Robert A. We Are One. (Illus.). 97p. (Orig.). 1986. pap. 6.95 (*0-9624630-0-0*) SA & RA Bender.

***Bender, Scott.** Don't Stop the Disco. LC 99-36641. 1999. pap. 8.95 (*0-533-13098-0*) Vantage.

An Asterisk (*) at the beginning of an entry indicates that the title is appearing for the first time.

Bender, Sheila. Sustenance: New & Selected Poems. LC 98-31499. 64p. (Orig.). 1999. pap. 9.95 (*1-56474-300-4*) Fithian Pr.
— Writing Personal Essays: How to Shape Your Life Experiences for the Page. LC 95-2755. 272p. 1995. 17.99 (*0-89879-665-2*, Wrtrs Digest Bks) F & W Pubns Inc.
— Writing Personal Poetry. LC 98-39747. 240p. 1999. pap. 14.99 (*0-89879-813-2*, 10595, Wrtrs Digest Bks) F & W Pubns Inc.
***Bender, Sheila.** A Year in the Life: Journaling for Self-Discovery. 256p. 2000. pap. 14.99 (*0-89879-971-6*, Wrtrs Digest Bks) F & W Pubns Inc.
Bender, Sheila & Killien, Christi. Writing in a New Convertible with the Top Down: A Unique Guide for Writers. rev. ed. LC 97-7219. 160p. 1997. reprint ed. pap. 12.95 (*0-936085-38-X*) Blue Heron OR.
Bender, Skie. A Nice Storm for a New Birth. 80p. 1992. pap. 7.95 (*1-881168-05-0*) Red Danceflr.
Bender, Stephen J., et al. Teaching Health Science: Elementary & Middle School. 4th ed. LC 96-36806. (Health Science Ser.). 512p. 1997. 52.50 (*0-7637-0256-0*) Jones & Bartlett.
Bender, Stephanie. The Power Of Perimenopause. 1999. pap. 12.00 (*0-609-80416-2*) Random Hse Value.
Bender, Stephanie D. & Kelleher, Kathleen. PMS: Women Tell Women How to Control Premenstrual Syndrome. 2nd rev. ed. LC 96-67940. Orig. Title: PMS: A Positive Program to Gain Control. (Illus.). 256p. 1996. pap. 13.95 (*1-57224-052-0*) New Harbinger.
***Bender, Stephen A.** Managing Projects Well. 220p. 1998. pap. 32.95 (*0-7506-4631-4*) Butterworth-Heinemann Ltd.
Bender, Stephen J. & Sorochan, Walter D. Teaching Elementary School Health. 3rd ed. 576p. 1989. 45.00 (*0-86720-411-7*) Jones & Bartlett.
Bender, Stephen J., jt. auth. see Sorochan, Walter D.
Bender, Steve. Callaway Gardens: Legacy of a Dream. Danese, Andrea, ed. LC 96-75430. (Illus.). 144p. 1996. 50.00 (*0-935112-25-1*) Callaway Edns.
Bender, Steve & Dornbush, Magaret. Fax, Modems & Online Services. 1994. pap. text 24.80 (*0-929321-19-7*) WEKA Pub.
Bender, Steve & Rushing, Felder. Passalong Plants. LC 93-7156. (Illus.). xiv, 2p. (C). 1993. 32.50 (*0-8078-2096-2*); pap. 18.95 (*0-8078-4418-7*) U of NC Pr.
Bender, Sue. Everyday Sacred: A Woman's Journey Home. LC 95-14808. (Illus.). 176p. 1995. 24.00 (*0-06-251289-7*, Pub. by Harper SF) HarpC.
— Everyday Sacred: A Woman's Journey Home. LC 95-14808. (Illus.). 176p. 1996. pap. 14.00 (*0-06-251290-0*, Pub. by Harper SF) HarpC.
— Everyday Sacred Journal. 144p. 1997. 18.00 (*0-06-251543-8*, Pub. by Harper SF) HarpC.
— Plain & Simple: A Journey to the Amish. LC 89-45234. 176p. 1989. 21.00 (*0-06-250058-9*) HarperTrade.
— Plain & Simple: A Woman's Journey to the Amish. LC 90-56467. (Illus.). 176p. 1991. reprint ed. pap. 15.00 (*0-06-250186-0*, Pub. by Harper SF) HarpC.
— Plain & Simple Journal: A Journey to the Amish. (Illus.). 144p. 1991. pap. 16.00 (*0-06-250129-1*, Pub. by Harper SF) HarpC.
— Plain & Simple Wisdom. LC 94-38418. 96p. 1995. pap. 9.00 (*0-06-251174-2*, Pub. by Harper SF) HarpC.
Bender, Susan J., jt. ed. see Smith, George S.
Bender, Tamara L., tr. see Vieira, J. L.
Bender Tax Staff. Dictionary of 1040 Deductions. text 56.00 (*0-8205-4039-0*) Bender.
Bender, Texas. Don't Throw in the Trowel: Tips & Quips on Gardening. 128p. 1999. 4.99 (*0-517-20551-3*) Random Hse Value.
Bender, Texas B. Don't Squat with Yer Spurs On! A Cowboy's Guide to Life. LC 92-15213. (Illus.). 144p. 1992. pap. 6.95 (*0-87905-470-0*) Gibbs Smith Pub.
— Don't Squat with Yer Spurs On! II, No. 2. LC 97-6876. (Illus.). 128p. 1997. pap. 6.95 (*0-87905-832-3*) Gibbs Smith Pub.
— Don't Throw in the Trowel: Tips & Quips on Gardening. LC 95-44651. (Illus.). 128p. 1996. pap. 6.95 (*0-87905-735-1*) Gibbs Smith Pub.
— 50 Good Reasons to Be a Cowboy. (Illus.). 112p. 1995. pap. 6.95 (*0-87905-655-X*) Gibbs Smith Pub.
— Horse Sense: Pure & Simple. LC 98-46278. (Illus.). 144p. 1999. pap. 6.95 (*0-87905-886-2*) Gibbs Smith Pub.
— Laughing Stock: A Cow's Guide to Life. LC 93-48165. (Illus.). 112p. 1994. pap. 6.95 (*0-87905-630-4*) Gibbs Smith Pub.
Bender, Texas B. & Montana, Gladiola. A Cynic's Guide to Love. (Illus.). 128p. 1996. pap. 6.95 (*0-87905-696-7*) Gibbs Smith Pub.
— Just One Fool Thing after Another: A Cowfolks' Guide to Romance. LC 93-47139. (Illus.). 144p. 1994. pap. 6.95 (*0-87905-595-2*) Gibbs Smith Pub.
***Bender, Texas Bix.** Don't Dig for Water under the Outhouse: And Other Cowboy Commandments. LC 00-22224. (Illus.). 128p. 2000. pap. 6.95 (*0-87905-977-X*) Gibbs Smith Pub.
Bender, Texas Bix. Wahoo! Cowboys in Love. (Illus.). 64p. 1999. 5.95 (*0-87905-915-X*) Gibbs Smith Pub.
Bender, Thomas. American Academic Culture in Transformation: Fifty Years, Four Disciplines. 370p. 1998. pap. text 16.95 (*0-691-05824-5*, Pub. by Princeton U Pr) Cal Prin Full Svc.
— Community & Social Change in America. LC 82-47981. 176p. (C). 1982. pap. text 13.95 (*0-8018-2924-0*) Johns Hopkins.
— Intellect & Public Life: Essays on the Social History of Academic Intellectuals in the United States. LC 92-11393. 208p. 1992. text 35.00 (*0-8018-4433-9*) Johns Hopkins.
— Intellect & Public Life: Essays on the Social History of Academic Intellectuals in the United States. LC 92-11393. 208p. 1997. reprint ed. pap. text 14.95 (*0-8018-5784-8*) Johns Hopkins.
— Intellectual & Cultural History. 2nd rev. ed. Foner, Eric, ed. (New American History Ser.). 22p. (Orig.). 1997. pap. 5.00 (*0-87229-080-8*) Am Hist Assn.
— New York Intellect: A History of Intellectual Life in New York City from 1750 to the Beginnings of Our Own Time. 448p. 1988. reprint ed. pap. 19.95 (*0-8018-3639-5*) Johns Hopkins.
— Toward an Urban Vision: Ideas & Institutions in Nineteenth-Century America. LC 82-47980. 296p. (Orig.). (C). 1982. pap. text 15.95 (*0-8018-2925-9*) Johns Hopkins.
Bender, Thomas, ed. The Antislavery Debate: Capitalism & Abolitionism As a Problem in Historical Interpretation. LC 91-21075. (C). 1992. 58.00 (*0-520-06639-1*, Pub. by U CA Pr); pap. 17.95 (*0-520-07779-2*, Pub. by U CA Pr) Cal Prin Full Svc.
Bender, Thomas & Schorske, Carl E., eds. Budapest & New York: Studies in Metropolitan Transformation, 1870-1930. (Illus.). 416p. 1994. 39.95 (*0-87154-113-0*) Russell Sage.
Bender, Thomas, ed. see De Tocqueville, Alexis.
Bender, Thomas R., ed. Worker Deaths in Confined Spaces: A Summary of Surveillance Findings & Investigative Case Reports. (Illus.). 273p. (C). 1996. reprint ed. pap. text 35.00 (*0-7881-3183-4*) DIANE Pub.
Bender, Todd & James, Henry. A Concordance to Henry James's The Awkward Age. LC 89-1438. (Concordances to the Works of Henry James: Vol. 5). 400p. 1989. text 30.00 (*0-8240-4437-1*, 869) Garland.
Bender, Todd K. Gerard Manley Hopkins: The Classical Background & Critical Reception of His Work. LC 66-16044. 182p. reprint ed. pap. 56.50 (*0-608-15302-8*, 202923500059) Bks Demand.
Bender, Todd K., ed. Literary Impressionism in Jean Rhys, Ford Madox Ford, Joseph Conrad, & Charlotte Bronte. LC 97-10566. (Origins of Modernism Ser.: Vol. 9). (Illus.). 184p. 1997. text 60.00 (*0-8153-1943-6*, H1887) Garland.
Bender, Todd K. & Higdon, Leon D. A Concordance to Henry James's The Spoils of Poynton. LC 88-12063. (Concordances to the Works of Henry James: Vol. 4). 432p. 1988. text 15.00 (*0-8240-8598-1*, 648) Garland.
Bender, Todd K., et al. A Concordance to Henry James's Turn of the Screw. LC 87-32834. (Concordances to the Works of Henry James: Vol. 3). 264p. 1988. text 15.00 (*0-8240-4147-X*, 828) Garland.
Bender, Todd K., jt. auth. see Foltz, William.
Bender, Todd K., jt. auth. see Johnson, Shirley M.
***Bender, Tom.** Building with the Breath of Life: Working with Chi Energy in Our Homes & Communities. (Illus.). 288p. 2000. pap. 28.00 (*0-9675089-1-6*, 20002) Fire River Pr.
— Silence, Song & Shadows: Our Need for the Sacred in Our Surroundings. (Illus.). 128p. 2000. pap. 27.00 (*0-9675089-0-8*, 20001) Fire River Pr.
Bender, U. Stumbling Heavenward: The Extraordinary Life of an Ordinary Man, Peter Rempel. 1991. pap. text 11.95 (*0-920534-27-9*) Hyperion Pr.
Bender, Urie A., jt. auth. see Redekop, Calvin W.
Bender, Von F., ed. see Weyl, Richard.
Bender, William. Professional Issues in Learning Disabilities: Practical Strategies & Relevant Research Findings. 533p. 1998. text 43.00 (*0-89079-781-1*, 8554) PRO-ED.
Bender, William, et al. Violence Prevention & Reduction in Schools. LC 98-30836. 1999. write for info. (*0-89079-802-8*) PRO-ED.
***Bender, William N.** Learning Disabilities: Characteristics, Identification & Teaching Strategies. 4th ed. 448p. 2000. 71.00 (*0-205-32184-4*) Allyn.
Bender, William N. Teaching Students with Mild Disabilities. LC 95-37933. 384p. 1996. pap. text, teacher ed. 80.00 (*0-13-892720-0*) Allyn.
Bender, William N., ed. Learning Disabilities: Best Practices for Professionals. LC 92-31024. 334p. 1993. 38.00 (*1-56372-058-2*, 6930) PRO-ED.
Bender, William N. & McLaughlin, Phillip J., eds. A. D. D. from A to Z: A Comprehensive Guide to Attention Deficit Disorder. 76p. 1994. pap. text, teacher ed. 195.00 incl. VHS (*1-57035-016-7*, 60KIT) Sopris.
Bender, Wolfgang. Sweet Mother: Modern African Music. Freis, Wolfgang, tr. (Chicago Studies in Ethnomusicology). (Illus.). 248p. 1994. lib. bdg. 45.00 (*0-226-04253-7*) U Ch Pr.
— Sweet Mother: Modern African Music. Freis, Wolfgang, tr. (Chicago Studies in Ethnomusicology). (Illus.). 256p. 1997. pap. 17.95 (*0-226-04254-5*) U Ch Pr.
Benderly, Beryl L. Dancing Without Music. LC 90-41334. 320p. 1980. pap. 15.95 (*0-930323-59-9*) Gallaudet Univ Pr.
Benderly, Beryl L. & Institute of Medicine Staff. In Her Own Right: The Institute of Medicine's Guide to Women's Health Issues. LC 96-26155. 232p. 1997. 29.95 (*0-309-05327-7*) Natl Acad Pr.
Benderly, Beryl L., jt. auth. see Greenspan, Stanley I.
***Benderly, Beryl Lieff.** Jason's Miracle: A Hanukkah Story. LC 99-86328. 120p. (J). (gr. 4-8). 2000. lib. bdg. 14.95 (*0-8075-3781-0*) A Whitman.
Benderly, Jill. Independent Slovenia Origins. 288p. 1996. pap. 19.95 (*0-312-16447-5*) St Martin.
Benderly, Monica. What Shall I Feed the Family Tonight? Short Cuts & Other Ways to Cheat. 107p. 1993. 19.95 (*0-9638157-0-9*) Gourmet Comp.
Bender's Editors. Bender's Forms of Discovery, 34 vols., Set. LC 63-3100. 1963. ring bd. 2330.00 (*0-8205-1103-X*) Bender.
— Bender's Payroll Tax Guide. annuals 1982. write for info. (*0-8205-1539-6*) Bender.
— Benefits Review Board Service: Longshore Reporter, 3 vols. 1974. ring bd. 860.00 (*0-8205-1135-8*) Bender.
— Business Insurance Law & Practice Guide, 4 vols. 1989. ring bd. 435.00 (*0-8205-1591-4*) Bender.
— California Corporations Code with Corporate Securities Rules & Releases. 1972. write for info. (*0-8205-1191-9*) Bender.
— California Forms of Pleading & Practice Annotated, 59 vols. LC 62-52786. (Illus.). 1962. ring bd. 3030.00 (*0-8205-1181-1*) Bender.
— California Incorporation System. 1985. write for info. incl. disk (*0-8205-1638-4*) Bender.
— California Legal Forms: Transaction Guide, 36 vols. 1968. ring bd. 2010.00 (*0-8205-1187-0*) Bender.
— California Points & Authorities, 23 vols. 1965. ring bd. 2010.00 (*0-8205-1186-2*) Bender.
— California Wills & Trust-Forms, 3 vols., \. 1991. ring bd. write for info. (*0-8205-1893-X*) Bender.
— California Wills & Trusts, Vol. 3. 1991. write for info. (*0-8205-1034-3*) Bender.
— Child Custody & Visitation Law & Practice, 4 vols. LC 82-84733. (Illus.). 1983. ring bd. 900.00 (*0-8205-1213-3*) Bender.
— Civil Practice Annual of New York. 1967. ring bd. write for info. (*0-8205-1205-2*) Bender.
— Consolidated Index to Units I-V of Bender's UCC Service, 2 vols. rev. ed. 1981. reprint ed. ring bd. write for info. (*0-8205-1745-3*) Bender.
— Dictionary of 1040 Deductions. 1980. write for info. (*0-8205-3532-X*) Bender.
— Forms of Jury Instruction, 4 vols., Set. 1989. ring bd. 660.00 (*0-8205-1288-5*, 288) Bender.
— Illinois Forms of Jury Instructions, Vol. 3. 1991. 325.00 incl. cd-rom (*0-8205-1699-6*) Bender.
— Medina's Bostwick Practice Manual, 6 vols. 1949. ring bd. 1030.00 (*0-8205-1380-6*) Bender.
— Tax, Estate & Financial Planning for the Elderly-Forms & Practice, Vol. 1. 1991. 210.00 (*0-8205-1774-7*) Bender.
Bender's Editors, ed. Valuation & Distribution of Marital Property, 3 vols. 1984. ring bd. 620.00 (*0-8205-1133-1*) Bender.
Bender's Editors & Abrams, Brenda M. Florida Family Law, 6 vols. LC 86-71657. 1986. ring bd. 530.00 (*0-8205-1513-2*) Bender.
Bender's Editors & Augustine, Don. California Real Estate Law & Practice, 17 vols. 1986. write for info. (*0-318-67983-3*) Bender.
Bender's Editors & Brown, Paul W. Ohio Forms of Pleading & Practice, 18 vols. 1970. ring bd. 2130.00 (*0-8205-1502-7*) Bender.
Bender's Editors & Campbell, Farragher J. Defense of Speeding, Reckless Driving & Vehicular Homicide, 3 vols., Set. LC 84-71307. 1984. ring bd. 455.00 (*0-8205-1104-8*) Bender.
Bender's Editors & Sparber, Byron L. Southeast Transaction Guide, 20 vols. 1976. ring bd. 1340.00 (*0-8205-1632-5*) Bender.
Bender's Editors & Teague, Marvin O. Texas Criminal Practice Guide, 6 vols. 1979. ring bd. 1160.00 (*0-8205-1712-7*) Bender.
Bender's Editors, et al. Bender's Forms for the Consolidated Laws of New York, 54 vols. 1930. 2180.00 (*0-8205-1070-X*) Bender.
— California Products & Liability Actions. 1975. ring bd. 165.00 (*0-8205-1189-7*) Bender.
— California Real Estate Law & Practice, 17 vols. 1973. ring bd. 1830.00 (*0-8205-1271-0*) Bender.
Bender's Editors, jt. auth. see Bongiovanni, Joseph N.
Bender's Editors, jt. auth. see Einhorn, Harold.
Bender's Editors, jt. auth. see Kendrick, John J.
Bender's Editors, jt. auth. see Rohrlich, Chester.
Bender's Editors, jt. auth. see Spires, Jeremiah J.
Benders, Joe. Optional Options: Work Design & Manufacturing Automation. 272p. 1993. 67.95 (*1-85628-490-5*, Pub. by Avebry) Ashgate Pub Co.
Benders, Joe, et al, eds. The Symbiosis of Work & Technology. LC 94-44626. 1995. pap. 49.95 (*0-7484-0317-5*) Taylor & Francis.
Benderskii, A. V., jt. auth. see Benderskii, V. A.
Benderskii, V. A. & Benderskii, A. V. Laser Electrochemistry of Intermediates. LC 95-14176. 336p. 1995. boxed set 244.95 (*0-8493-2865-9*, 2865) CRC Pr.
Benderskii, Victor A., et al. Chemical Dynamics at Low Temperatures. 385p. 1994. 105.00 (*0-471-58585-8*) Wiley.
***Bendersky, Joseph W.** The "Jewish Threat" Anti-Semitic Politics in the American Army. 2000. 30.00 (*0-465-00617-5*, Pub. by Basic) HarpC.
Bendersky, Joseph W. Carl Schmitt, Theorist for the Reich. LC 82-61353. 334p. 1983. reprint ed. pap. 103.60 (*0-608-02515-1*, 206315900004) Bks Demand.
Benderson, Albert E. Critical Approaches to Federico Fellini's Eight & a Half, Vol. 4. LC 74-2078. (Dissertations on Film Ser.). 239p. 1974. 18.95 (*0-405-04877-7*) Ayer.
Benderson, Bruce. Bidgood: James Bidgood. (Illus.). 160p. 1999. 39.99 (*3-8228-7427-2*) Taschen Amer.
— Toward the New Degeneracy Vol. 2: An Essay. 2nd ed. LC 96-61925. (Illus.). 64p. 1998. pap. 10.00 (*0-9646466-3-3*) Edgewise Pr.
— The United Nations of Time Square. LC 87-42542. 24p. 1987. pap. 3.00 (*0-87376-056-5*) Red Dust.
Benderson, Bruce & Sonder, Ben. Evolutionism & Creationism. LC 98-53650. (Impact Ser.). (Illus.). 112p. (YA). (gr. 7 up). 1999. 24.00 (*0-531-11416-3*) Watts.
Benderson, Bruce, tr. see Guyotat, Pierre & Khosla, Maya.
Benderson, Bruce, tr. see Sollers, Philippe.
Bendet, Mayer. Lost & Found Wallet. 1997. 8.95 (*0-932351-37-9*) B P Marketing.
Bendich, A., et al. Antioxidant Nutrients & Immune Functions. LC 89-26570. (Advances in Experimental Medicine & Biology Ser.: No. 262). (Illus.). 184p. (C). 1990. text 75.00 (*0-306-43396-6*, Kluwer Plenum) Kluwer Academic.
Bendich, Adrianne & Butterworth, C. E., eds. Micronutrients in Health & in Disease Prevention. (Illus.). 504p. 1991. text 175.00 (*0-8247-8539-8*) Dekker.
Bendich, Adrianne & Deckelbaum, Richard J., eds. Preventive Nutrition: The Comprehensive Guide for the Health Professionals. LC 96-37937. (Nutrition & Health Ser.). (Illus.). 616p. 1997. 99.50 (*0-89603-351-1*) Humana.
***Bendich, Adrianne & Deckelbaum, Richard J., eds.** Primary & Secondary Preventive Nutrition. (Nutrition & Health Ser.). (Illus.). 500p. 2000. 99.50 (*0-89603-758-4*) Humana.
Bendick, Candy, et al. Harian Creative Awards - I: Featuring the Gospel According to Everyman by Baron Mikan. Barba, Harry, ed. 220p. 1981. lib. bdg. 15.95 (*0-911906-09-6*) Harian Creative Bks.
Bendick, Jeanne. Along Came Galileo. (Illus.). 99p. (J). (gr. 4-8). 1999. pap. 9.95 (*1-893103-01-3*) Beautiful Feet.
— Archimedes & the Door of Science. rev. ed. LC 95-20368. (Living History Library). (Illus.). 143p. (YA). (gr. 5 up). 1995. reprint ed. pap. 11.95 (*1-883937-12-4*, 12-4) Bethlehem ND.
— Artificial Satellites: Helpers in Space. (Early Bird Astronomy Ser.). (Illus.). 32p. (J). (gr. k-2). 1991. pap. 4.95 (*1-878841-56-4*) Millbrook Pr.
— Caves: Underground Worlds. (Illus.). 64p. (J). (gr. 2-4). 1995. 15.95 (*0-8050-2764-5*) H Holt & Co.
— Comets & Meteors: Visitors from Space. (Early Bird Astronomy Ser.). (Illus.). 32p. (J). (gr. k-2). 1991. pap. 4.95 (*1-878841-55-6*); lib. bdg. 19.90 (*1-56294-001-5*) Millbrook Pr.
— Eureka! It's an Automobile! LC 91-34790. (Inventing Ser.). (Illus.). 48p. (J). (gr. 2-6). 1992. pap. 6.95 (*1-56294-700-1*) Millbrook Pr.
— Exploring an Ocean Tide Pool. (J). 1995. pap. 4.95 (*0-8050-3273-8*) H Holt & Co.
— Exploring an Ocean Tide Pool. LC 91-34572. (Illus.). 64p. (J). (gr. 2-4). 1995. 14.95 (*0-8050-2043-8*, Bks Young Read) H Holt & Co.
— Moons & Rings: Companions to the Planets. (Early Bird Astronomy Ser.). (Illus.). 32p. (J). (gr. k-2). 1991. pap. 4.95 (*1-878841-54-8*); lib. bdg. 19.90 (*1-56294-000-7*) Millbrook Pr.
— The Planets: Neighbors in Space. (Early Bird Astronomy Ser.). (Illus.). 32p. (J). (gr. k-2). 1991. pap. 3.80 (*1-878841-51-3*) Millbrook Pr.
— The Planets: Neighbors in Space. (Early Bird Astronomy Ser.). (Illus.). 32p. (J). (gr. k-2). 1991. lib. bdg. 19.90 (*1-878841-03-3*) Millbrook Pr.
— The Stars: Lights in the Night Sky. (Early Bird Astronomy Ser.). (Illus.). 32p. (J). (gr. k-2). 1991. lib. bdg. 19.90 (*1-878841-00-9*) Millbrook Pr.
— The Stars: Lights in the Night Sky. (Early Bird Astronomy Ser.). (Illus.). 32p. (J). (gr. k-2). 1992. pap. 3.80 (*1-878841-48-3*) Millbrook Pr.
— The Sun: Our Very Own Star. (Early Bird Astronomy Ser.). (Illus.). 32p. (J). (gr. k-2). 1991. pap. 4.80 (*1-878841-50-5*); lib. bdg. 19.90 (*1-878841-02-5*) Millbrook Pr.
— The Universe: Think Big! (Early Bird Astronomy Ser.). (Illus.). 32p. (J). (gr. k-2). 1991. lib. bdg. 19.90 (*1-878841-01-7*) Millbrook Pr.
— The Universe: Think Big! (Early Bird Astronomy Ser.). (Illus.). 32p. (J). (gr. k-2). 1992. pap. 3.80 (*1-878841-49-1*) Millbrook Pr.
Bendick, Jeanne & Bendick, Robert. Markets: From Barter to Bar Codes. LC 96-41673. (First Bks.). (Illus.). (J). 1997. lib. bdg. 22.00 (*0-531-20263-1*) Watts.
— Markets: From Barter to Bar Codes. (First Bks.). (J). 1997. pap. text 6.95 (*0-531-15850-0*) Watts.
Bendick, Robert, jt. auth. see Bendick, Jeanne.
Bendickson, Anita, jt. auth. see Brandl, Mary.
Bendig, William, et al. Beatrice Cuming, 1903-1974. (Illus.). 28p. (Orig.). 1990. write for info. (*0-318-66809-2*) Lyman Allyn.
Bendikat, Elfi. Offentliche Nahverkehrspolitik in Berlin und Paris, 1890-1914. 672p. 1998. 186.00 (*3-11-015383-1*) De Gruyter.
Bendikov, Alexander. Potential Theory on Infinite-Dimensional Abelian Groups. LC 95-14980. (Studies in Mathematics: Vol. 21).Tr. of Veroiatnostnaia Teoriia Potentsiala na Beskonechnomernykh Abelevykh Gruppakh. vi, 184p. (C). 1995. lib. bdg. 89.95 (*3-11-014283-X*) De Gruyter.
Bendiksen, Robert, jt. ed. see Fulton, Robert.
Bendikt, George M. & Goodall, Brian L., eds. Metallocene Technology & Modern Catalytic Methods in Commercial Applications. LC 98-89319. 325p. 1999. 160.00 (*1-884207-76-6*) William Andrew.
Bendinelli, Cesare. The Entire Art of Trumpet Playing. Tarr, Edward H., tr. from ITA. & comment by. LC 75-31807. Orig. Title: Volume di Tutta L'Arte della Trombetta. (ENG., Illus.). 20p. 1975. pap. text 5.00 (*0-914282-16-6*) Brass Pr.
Bendinelli, M. & Friedman, H. Coxsackieviruses: A General Update. LC 88-4234. (Infectious Agents & Pathogenesis Ser.). (Illus.). 450p. (C). 1988. text 120.00 (*0-306-42725-7*, Kluwer Plenum) Kluwer Academic.
— Mycobacterium Tuberculosis: Interactions with the Immune System. LC 88-4128. (Infectious Agents & Pathogenesis Ser.). (Illus.). 448p. (C). 1988. text 115.00 (*0-306-42724-9*, Kluwer Plenum) Kluwer Academic.
Bendinelli, M., jt. auth. see Specter, S.
Bendiner, Burton. International Labour Affairs: The World Trade Unions & the Multinational Companies. (Illus.). 216p. 1988. 65.00 (*0-19-827499-8*) OUP.

An Asterisk (*) at the beginning of an entry indicates that the title is appearing for the first time.

Bendiner, Elmer & Bendiner, Jessica. Biographical Dictionary of Medicine. 304p. 1990. 40.00 (*0-8160-1864-2*) Facts on File.

Bendiner, Jessica, jt. auth. see Bendiner, Elmer.

Bendiner, Kenneth. The Art of Ford Madox Brown. LC 96-31023. 1998. 65.00 (*0-271-01656-6*) Pa St U Pr.

— An Introduction to Victorian Painting. LC 84-27038. (Illus.). 208p. 1985. 55.00 (*0-300-03309-5*) Yale U Pr.

***Bending, Lucy.** The Representation of Bodily Pain in Late Nineteenth-Century English Culture. (Oxford English Monographs). (Illus.). 240p. 2000. text 65.00 (*0-19-818717-3*) OUP.

***Bending, N. A. D., et al.** Soil-Forming Materials: Their Use in Land Reclamation. (Illus.). 237p. 1999. 80.00 (*0-11-753489-7*, Pub. by Statnry Office) Balogh.

Bendinger, Bruce H. Copy Workshop Workbook. 2nd ed. LC 91-137828. 396p. (Orig.). (C). 1993. pap. 33.00 (*0-9621415-4-2*, Pub. by Copy Wrkshp) Natl Bk Netwk.

Bendinger, Bruce H., et al. Advertising & the Business of Brands: Class Testing Edition. (Illus.). 650p. (C). 1999. pap. text 35.00 (*1-887229-04-3*) Copy Wrkshp.

***Bendinger, Bruce H., et al.** Advertising & the Business of Brands: 2000 Edition. 650p. (C). 2000. pap. text 50.00 (*1-887229-05-1*) Copy Wrkshp.

Bendinger, Bruce H., jt. auth. see Fortini-Campbell, Lisa.

Bendinger, Bruce H., ed. see Avery, Jim.

Bendinger, Bruce H., ed. see Gossage, Howard L.

Bendini, Silvio A. Christopher Columbus Encyclopedia, Vol. I. 1995. 115.00 (*0-13-142670-2*) P-H.

— Christopher Columbus Encyclopedia, Vol. II. 1995. 115.00 (*0-13-142688-5*) P-H.

— Early Americans Scientific Instruments & Their Makers. rev. ed. (Illus.). 189p. 1986. 51.00 (*0-910845-30-1*, 979) Landmark Ent.

— Ridgefield in Review. (Illus.). 396p. 1994. reprint ed. lib. bdg. 42.50 (*0-8328-4026-2*) Higginson Bk Co.

— Science & Instruments in Seventeenth Century Italy. LC 94-8292. (Collected Studies: No. CS 449). 1994. 124.95 (*0-86078-442-8*, Pub. by Variorum) Ashgate Pub Co.

— Thinkers & Tinkers: Early American Men of Science. (Illus.). 519p. 1983. reprint ed. 30.00 (*0-910845-19-0*, 901) Landmark Ent.

— Thomas Jefferson: Statesman of Science. (Illus.). 604p. 1990. 35.00 (*0-02-897041-1*) Macmillan.

— The Trail of Time: Time Measurement with Incense Clocks in East Asia. (Neeham Research Institute Studies). (Illus.). 366p. (C). 1994. text 130.00 (*0-521-37482-0*) Cambridge U Pr.

Bendini, Silvio A., ed. The Christopher Columbus Encyclopedia, 2 vols., Set. (Illus.). 800p. 1991. 220.00 (*0-13-142662-1*) S&S Trade.

Bendire, Charles E. Life Histories of North American Birds: Their Breeding Habits & Eggs, 2 vols. LC 73-17802. (Natural Sciences in America Ser.). (Illus.). 1042p. 1974. reprint ed. 75.95 (*0-405-05720-2*) Ayer.

Bendis, Brian M. Fire. (Illus.). 120p. 1999. pap. 9.95 (*1-58240-071-7*) Image Comics.

— Fire Complete Graphic Novel. (Illus.). 114p. 1994. 12.95 (*0-941613-61-5*) Stabur Pr.

— Jinx TPB, Vol. 1. (Illus.). 120p. 1997. pap. 9.95 (*1-887279-63-6*) Image Comics.

***Bendis, Brian Michael.** Fortune & Glory: A True Hollywood Comic Book Story. McCrory, K. C. & Rich, Jamie S., eds. (Illus.). 152p. 2000. pap. 14.95 (*1-929998-06-6*) Oni Pr Inc.

Bendit, Laurence J. Mysteries Today & Other Essays. 1994. 5.95 (*0-7229-5024-1*) Theos Pub Hse.

Bendit, Laurence J., jt. auth. see Bendit, Phoebe D.

Bendit, Phoebe D. & Bendit, Laurence J. The Etheric Body of Man: The Bridge of Consciousness. LC 76-46930. 1989. reprint ed. pap. 7.95 (*0-8356-0489-6*, Quest) Theos Pub Hse.

— Our Psychic Sense: A Clairvoyant & a Psychiatrist Explain How it Develops. LC 67-7911. 1967. pap. 5.75 (*0-8356-0034-3*, Quest) Theos Pub Hse.

Benditt, David G. & Benson, D. Woodrow, eds. Cardiac Preexcitation Syndromes. 1986. text 242.00 (*0-89838-771-X*) Kluwer Academic.

Benditt, Theodore M. Rights. LC 81-23448. (Philosophy & Society Ser.). 158p. 1982. text 50.00 (*0-8476-6754-5*) Rowman.

Bendix, Bud, ed. see Hinz, Earl.

Bendix, Deanna M. Diabolical Designs: Paintings, Interiors, & Exhibitions of James McNeill Whistler. LC 94-24957. (Illus.). 360p. 1995. pap. text 34.95 (*1-56098-549-6*) Smithsonian.

BENDIX, J. Introd Compar Government 2000. 24.95 (*0-8133-1749-5*) HarpC.

Bendix, Jane. Chaco: The Anasazi Mystery. LC 97-170923. (Illus.). 125p. (J). (gr. 4-12). 1996. pap. 9.95 (*0-89992-142-6*) Coun India Ed.

— Mi'Ca: Buffalo Hunter. (Illus.). 188p. (J). (gr. 4-12). 1992. 9.95 (*0-89992-131-0*) Coun India Ed.

Bendix, John. Importing Foreign Workers: A Comparison of German & American Policy. (American University Studies: Ser. X, Vol. 26). VIII, 248p. 1990. text 44.95 (*0-8204-1310-0*) P Lang Pubng.

Bendix, Regina. Backstage Domains: Playing "William Tell" in Two Swiss Communities. (Illus.). 319p. 1989. pap. 40.00 (*3-261-03932-9*) P Lang Pubng.

— In Search of Authenticity: The Formation of Folklore Studies. LC 97-11607. 318p. 1997. 55.00 (*0-299-15540-4*); pap. 24.95 (*0-299-15544-7*) U of Wis Pr.

Bendix, Reinhard. Bureaucracy & the Problem of Power. (Reprint Series in Social Sciences). (C). 1993. reprint ed. pap. text 5.00 (*0-8290-4145-1*, S-15) Irvington.

— Embattled Reason, Vol. 1. 2nd rev. ed. 272p. 1986. 39.95 (*0-88738-110-3*) Transaction Pubs.

— Embattled Reason: Essays on Social Knowledge, Vol. 2. 384p. 1989. 44.95 (*0-88738-197-9*) Transaction Pubs.

— Force, Fate & Freedom: On Historical Sociology. 1984. pap. 12.95 (*0-520-06949-8*, Pub. by U CA Pr) Cal Prin Full Svc.

— From Berlin to Berkeley: German-Jewish Identities. LC 85-8578. 320p. (C). 1985. 39.95 (*0-88738-067-0*) Transaction Pubs.

— From Berlin to Berkeley: German Jewish Identities. 314p. (C). 1990. pap. 24.95 (*0-88738-837-X*) Transaction Pubs.

— Higher Civil Servants in American Society, no. 1--1. LC 73-17856. 129p. 1974. reprint ed. lib. bdg. 59.50 (*0-8371-7265-9*, BEHC, Greenwood Pr) Greenwood.

— Kings or People: Power & the Mandate to Rule. 1978. pap. 22.50 (*0-520-04090-2*, Pub. by U CA Pr) Cal Prin Full Svc.

— Max Weber: An Intellectual Portrait. LC 98-26542. (Max Weber Classic Monographs). 1998. write for info. (*0-415-17453-8*) Routledge.

— Max Weber: An Intellectual Portrait. 1978. pap. 19.95 (*0-520-03194-6*, Pub. by U CA Pr) Cal Prin Full Svc.

— Nation-Building & Citizenship: Studies of Our Changing Social Order. enl. ed. 455p. 1996. pap. text 24.95 (*1-56000-890-3*) Transaction Pubs.

— Tradition & Modernity Reconsidered. (Reprint Series in Sociology). (C). 1993. reprint ed. pap. text 4.50 (*0-8290-2693-2*, S-665) Irvington.

— Unsettled Affinities. Von Thadden, Rudolph, ed. LC 92-43184. 302p. (C). 1993. text 44.95 (*1-56000-101-1*) Transaction Pubs.

***Bendix, Reinhard & Guillen, Mauro F.** Work & Authority in Industry. LC 99-87779. 464p. 2000. pap. 29.95 (*0-7658-0668-1*) Transaction Pubs.

Bendix, Reinhard, jt. auth. see Lipset, Seymour M.

Bendix, Sonia. Industrial Relations in South Africa. 3rd ed. LC 97-154383. 752p. 1996. pap. 56.00 (*0-7021-3453-8*, Pub. by Juta & Co) Gaunt.

Bendixen. Critical Essays on Edith Wharton. large type ed. 1998. 47.00 (*0-7838-0048-7*, G K Hall Lrg Type) Mac Lib Ref.

Bendixen, Alfred, ed. The Amber Gods & Other Stories. (American Women Writers Ser.). 300p. (C). 1989. pap. text 15.00 (*0-8135-1401-0*) Rutgers U Pr.

Bendixen, Alfred, ed. see Paulding, James K.

Bendixen, Alfred, jt. ed. see Serafin, Steven.

Bendixen, Henrick, et al, eds. Blood & Blood Products: Safety & Risk. LC 96-70494. 208p. (Orig.). 1996. pap. text 32.00 (*0-309-05583-0*) Natl Acad Pr.

Bendixen, M. A., jt. auth. see Torre, R. L.

Bendixson, Terence. Transport in the 90s - The Shaping of Europe. 64p. (C). 1989. text 130.00 (*0-85406-430-3*, Pub. by Surveyors Pubns) St Mut.

Bendjaballah, Cherif. Introduction to Photon Communication, Vol. VII. Beiglbock, W. et al, eds. (Lecture Notes in Physics Ser.: No. m29). 193p. 1995. 49.95 (*3-540-59166-4*) Spr-Verlag.

Bendjaballah, Cherif, et al, eds. Quantum Aspects of Optical Communications: Proceedings of a Workshop Held at the CNRS Paris, France, 26-28 November 1990. 389p. 1991. 56.95 (*0-387-53862-3*) Spr-Verlag.

Bendl, Joan. Adultodontics: You Are Just the Right Age for Braces. (Illus.). 50p. (Orig.). 1987. lib. bdg. 4.95 (*0-935343-05-9*) Peartree.

Bendl, Kurt. Inside the Internet Reference Guide. (Orig.). 1994. pap. text 9.95 (*0-936767-22-7*) Element K Journals.

Bendler, John T., jt. auth. see LeGrand, Donald G.

Bendon, Chris. Constructions. 130p. 1998. 23.95 (*0-8464-4779-7*) Beekman Pubs.

— Constructions. 130p. (C). 1991. 24.00 (*0-86383-668-2*, Pub. by Gomer Pr) St Mut.

Bendon, Chris. Crossover: A Play on Words or Libretto for an Imaginary Opera. 46p. pap. write for info. (*3-7052-0779-2*, Pub. by Poetry Salzburg) Intl Spec Bk.

— Jewry. 128p. pap. write for info. (*3-7052-0431-9*, Pub. by Poetry Salzburg) Intl Spec Bk.

Bendon, Chris. Novella: A Novel Poem. LC 98-105255. 1997. pap. 14.95 (*3-7052-0086-0*, Pub. by Poetry Salzburg) Intl Spec Bk.

Bendor, S. The Social Structure of Ancient Israel: The Institution of the Family (Beit'ab) from the Settlement to the End of the Monarchy. 1996. pap. write for info. (*0-614-96367-2*, Pub. by Simor Ltd) Eisenbrauns.

***Bendoricchio, G., ed.** Integrated Management of Water Quality. (Water Science & Technology Ser.). 158p. 1999. pap. 163.00 (*0-08-043633-1*, Pergamon Pr) Elsevier.

Bendow, Bernard & Langeler, B. Polariton - Mediated Light Scattering & Electronic Structure of Noble Metals. (Tracts in Modern Physics Ser.: Vol. 82). (Illus.). 1978. 36.95 (*0-387-08814-8*) Spr-Verlag.

Bendrath, Christian. Leibhaftigkeit: Jakob Bohmes Inkarnationsmorphologie. 430p. 1998. 111.00 (*3-11-016237-7*) De Gruyter.

Bendremer, Jutta. Women Surviving the Holocaust: In Spite of the Horror. LC 97-941. (Symposium Ser.). 1997. write for info. (*0-7734-8665-8*) E Mellen.

Bendremer, Jutta T. Women Surviving the Holocaust: In Spite of the Horror. LC 97-941. (Illus.). 1997. write for info. (*0-88946-989-X*) E Mellen.

Bendrick, Barbara J., jt. auth. see Coddington, Dean C.

Bendriem, Bernard & Townsend, David W. The Theory & Practice of 3D PET. LC 98-23005. (Developments in Nuclear Medicine Ser.). 167p. 1998. 78.00 (*0-7923-5108-8*) Kluwer Academic.

Bendroth, Frank. Professional Com Programming with IDL3 MIDL. 500p. 1998. pap. 49.99 (*1-86100-225-4*) Wrox Press.

Bendroth, Margaret L. Fundamentalism & Gender, 1875 to the Present. (Illus.). 192p. 1996. pap. 14.00 (*0-300-06864-6*) Yale U Pr.

Bendroth, Margaret L., jt. ed. see Airhart, Phyllis D.

Bendse, Martin P. & Mota Soares, Carlos A., eds. Topology Design of Structures. (C). 1992. text 293.00 (*0-7923-2055-7*) Kluwer Academic.

Bendsoe, Martin Philip. Optimization of Structural Topology Shape & Material. LC 95-13005. 1995. write for info. (*0-387-59057-9*) Spr-Verlag.

— Optimization of Structural Topology Shape & Material. LC 95-13005. 288p. 1995. 107.95 (*3-540-59057-9*) Spr-Verlag.

Bendt, V. Success with Unit Studies. 1997. pap. 15.00 (*1-880892-44-8*) Com Sense FL.

Bendt, Valerie. Creating Books with Children. 78p. 1993. pap. 18.00 (*1-880892-22-7*) Com Sense FL.

— Frances Study Guide. 1997. 16.00 (*1-880892-65-0*) Com Sense FL.

— How to Create Your Own Unit Study. 116p. 1990. 15.00 (*1-880892-42-1*) Com Sense FL.

***Bendt, Valerie.** Reading Made Easy: A Guide to Teach Your Child to Read. unabridged ed. (Illus.). 512p. 2000. pap. text 36.00 (*1-885814-06-2*) Bendt Fmly.

Bendt, Valerie. Unit Study Idea Book. 105p. 1993. reprint ed. spiral bd. 14.00 (*1-880892-43-X*) Com Sense FL.

Bendtsen, Margit. Sketches & Measurings: Danish Architects in Greece, 1818-1862. (Illus.). 383p. (C). 1993. text 60.00 (*87-7288-500-9*, Pub. by Aarhus Univ Pr) David Brown.

Bendure, Glenda. Lonely Planet Scandinavian & Baltic Europe. 4th ed. (On a Shoestring Ser.). (Illus.). 592p. 1999. pap. text 19.95 (*0-86442-628-3*) Lonely Planet.

Bendure, Glenda & Friary, Ned. Lonely Planet Denmark. 2nd ed. 384p. 1999. pap. 17.95 (*0-86442-609-7*) Lonely Planet.

— Lonely Planet Denmark: Travel Guide. LC 96-223565. (Illus.). 384p. 1996. pap. 17.95 (*0-86442-330-6*) Lonely Planet.

— Lonely Planet Eastern Caribbean. 2nd ed. (Illus.). 560p. 1998. pap. 17.95 (*0-86442-422-1*) Lonely Planet.

— Lonely Planet Hawaii. 4th ed. (Illus.). 608p. 1997. pap. 19.95 (*0-86442-489-2*) Lonely Planet.

— Lonely Planet Honolulu. 2nd ed. (Illus.). 184p. 1997. pap. 12.95 (*0-86442-490-6*) Lonely Planet.

— Lonely Planet Micronesia. 3rd ed. (Illus.). 336p. 1995. pap. 12.95 (*0-86442-310-1*) Lonely Planet.

Bendure, Glenda, et al. Lonely Planet Scandinavian & Baltic Europe. 3rd ed. (Illus.). 576p. 1997. pap. 17.95 (*0-86442-434-5*) Lonely Planet.

Bendure, Glenda, jt. auth. see Friary, Ned.

Bendure, Joan C. The Newfoundland: Companion Dog - Water Dog. (Illus.). 256p. 1994. 25.95 (*0-87605-242-1*) Howell Bks.

Bendure, Zelma & Pfeiffer, Gladys. America's Fabrics: Origin & History, Manufacture, Characteristics & Uses. LC 72-5260. (Technology & Society Ser.). (Illus.). 703p. 1972. reprint ed. 50.95 (*0-405-04685-5*) Ayer.

Bendz, E. P. Joseph Conrad. LC 77-92934. (Studies in Conrad: No. 8). 1970. reprint ed. lib. bdg. 59.95 (*0-8383-0960-7*) M S G Haskell Hse.

Bene. Erasmi Opera Omnia, Vol. 2. x,400p. 1985. 408.50 (*0-444-86878-X*) Elsevier.

Bene. Lambada: Blood Road. pap. 12.95 (*1-56097-240-8*, Pub. by Fantagraph Bks) Seven Hills Bk.

Bene, M. C., et al, eds. IgA Nephropathy: The Twenty-Fifth Year. (Contributions to Nephrology Ser.: Vol. 104). (Illus.). viii, 222p. 1993. 49.75 (*3-8055-5720-5*) S Karger.

Bene, Marie-Christine & Martini, Eric, eds. Immunophenotyping of Blood & Bone Marrow Leukocytes: Application to the Determination of Immune Status & Malignant Haematopathies Analysis. 256p. 1997. text 57.00 (*90-5702-008-4*, Harwood Acad Pubs) Gordon & Breach.

Benecerraf, Paul, tr. see Mehlberg, Henry.

Beneck, John. And Why Did You Come to the Emergency Room? LC 80-20360. 1983. pap. 13.95 (*0-87949-192-2*) Ashley Bks.

Benecke. Mittelhochdeutsches Woerterbuch, 4 vols. (GER.). 1195.00 (*0-7859-7434-2*, 3777604666) Fr & Eur.

— Mittelhochdeutsches Woerterbuch: Index, 4 vols. (GER.). 1990. 995.00 (*0-7859-7433-4*, 3777604674) Fr & Eur.

Benecke, G. F., ed. see Hartmann Von Aue.

Benecke, Josephine, jt. ed. see Schellmann, Jorg.

Benecke, Mary E. Jake's Ladder. Date not set. pap. write for info. (*0-9671698-0-1*) Mary Benecke.

Benedek. Development & Manufacture of Pressure-Sensitive Products. LC 98-38672. (Illus.). 672p. 1998. text 195.00 (*0-8247-0206-9*) Dekker.

Benedek, Dezso. The Songs of the Ancestors: A Comparative Study of Bashic Folklore. (Illus.). 642p. 1991. 55.00 (*957-638-057-X*, ANE008, Pub. by SMC Pub) Antique Collect.

Benedek, Dezso, tr. see Bari, Karoly.

***Benedek, Elek.** Palko the Piper. (J). 1999. pap. text 21.00 (*963-13-4781-8*, Pub. by Corvina Bks) St Mut.

Benedek, Elissa P. & Brown, Catherine F. How to Help Your Child Overcome Your Divorce. 230p. 1995. 23.95 (*0-88048-565-5*, 8565) Am Psychiatric.

— How to Help Your Child Overcome Your Divorce: A Support Guide for Families. LC 98-5011. 336p. 1998. reprint ed. pap. 14.95 (*1-55704-329-9*, Pub. by Newmarket) Norton.

Benedek, Elissa P. & Cornell, Dewey G., eds. Juvenile Homicide. LC 88-7682. (Clinical Practice Ser.: No. 7) 247p. 1989. text 12.95 (*0-88048-145-5*, 8145) Am Psychiatric.

Benedek, Elissa P., jt. auth. see Schetky, Diane H.

Benedek, Emily. Beyond the Four Corners of the World: A Navajo Woman's Journey. LC 98-19793. (Illus.). 376p. 1998. pap. 14.95 (*0-8061-3083-0*) U of Okla Pr.

— On Jewish Identity. 1998. write for info. (*0-8052-4138-8*) Schocken.

— Wind Won't Know Me: A History of the Navajo-Hopi Land Dispute. LC 98-43267. 1999. pap. text 17.95 (*0-8061-3125-X*) U of Okla Pr.

Benedek, G., ed. Surface Properties of Layered Structures. LC 92-26745. (Physics & Chemistry of Materials with Low-Dimensional Structures Ser.: Vol. 16). 352p. (C). 1992. text 226.50 (*0-7923-1961-3*) Kluwer Academic.

Benedek, G., et al, eds. Point & Extended Defects in Semiconductors. (NATO ASI Series B, Physics: Vol. 202). (Illus.). 300p. 1989. 89.50 (*0-306-43336-2*, Plenum Trade) Perseus Pubng.

— Statics & Dynamics of Nonlinear Systems. (Solid-State Sciences Ser.: Vol. 47). (Illus.). 311p. 1983. 75.95 (*0-387-12841-7*) Spr-Verlag.

Benedek, G. & Schneuwly, H., eds. Exotic Atoms in Condensed Matter: Proceedings of the Erice Workshop at the Ettore Majorana Center for Scientific Culture, Erice, Italy, May 19-25, 1990. (Proceedings in Physics Ser.: Vol. 59). (Illus.). 376p. 1992. 97.95 (*0-387-53600-0*) Spr-Verlag.

Benedek, G. & Valbusa, U., eds. Dynamics of Gas-Surface Interaction, Sicily, Italy 1981: Proceedings. (Chemical Physics Ser.: Vol. 21). (Illus.). 282p. 1982. 53.95 (*0-387-11693-1*) Spr-Verlag.

Benedek, G., jt. auth. see Mueller, K. A.

Benedek, G. B. Magnetic Resonance at High Pressure. LC 63-18561. (Interscience Tracts on Physics & Astronomy Ser.: Vol. 24). 109p. reprint ed. pap. 33.80 (*0-608-10048-X*, 205513000008) Bks Demand.

Benedek, G. B. & Villars, F. M. Physics with Illustrative Examples from Medicine & Biology, 2 vols., Vol. 1. 1973. 30.25 (*0-685-00008-7*) Addison-Wesley.

— Physics with Illustrative Examples from Medicine & Biology, 2 vols., Vol. 2. 1974. 30.25 (*0-201-00551-4*) Addison-Wesley.

— Physics with Illustrative Examples from Medicine & Biology, 2 vols., Vol. 3. 1979. 30.25 (*0-685-00009-5*) Addison-Wesley.

— Physics with Illustrative Examples from Medicine & Biology, Vol. 3. 1979. pap. text 32.25 (*0-201-00559-X*) Addison-Wesley.

Benedek, I. Semmelweis Krankheit. 112p. (C). 1983. 24.00 (*963-05-3428-2*, Pub. by Akade Kiado) St Mut.

Benedek, Istran & Heymans, Luc J. Pressure-Sensitive Adhesives & Applications. LC 96-31582. (Illus.). 616p. 1996. text 195.00 (*0-8247-9765-5*) Dekker.

***Benedek, Nelly S. & Rodin, Auguste.** Auguste Rodin: The Burghers of Calais: A Resource for Teachers. LC 99-86926. 2000. write for info. (*0-87099-948-6*) Metro Mus Art.

Benedek, Paul, et al. Developments in Design & Operation of Large Wastewater Treatment Plants: Proceedings of an IAWPRC Workshop Held in Budapest, Hungary, 14-18 September 1987. LC 82-645900. (Water Science & Technology Ser.). (Illus.). 318p. 1988. pap. 114.00 (*0-08-036882-4*, Pergamon Pr) Elsevier.

Benedek, Therese, jt. auth. see Fleming, Joan.

Benedek, Therese, jt. ed. see Anthony, E. James.

***Benedek, Wolfgang, ed.** Development & Developing International & European Law: Essays in Honour of Konrad Ginther on the Occasion of His 65th Birthday Edited by Wolfgang Benedek, Hubert Isak & Renate Kicker. XIV, 799p. 1999. pap. 79.95 (*3-631-34347-7*) P Lang Pubng.

***Benedek, Wolfgang, et al, eds.** Development & Developing International & European: Essays in Honour of Konrad Ginther on the Occasion of His 65th Birthday. LC 99-47878. xiv, 799p. (C). 1999. pap. text 79.95 (*0-8204-4369-7*) P Lang Pubng.

Benedek, Wolfgang, et al, eds. Human Rights in Bosnia & Herzegovina after Dayton: From Theory to Practice. LC 98-30272. 1998. 89.00 (*90-411-1062-3*, Pub. by M Nijhoff) Kluwer Academic.

Benedet, David. Port Arthur Built: An Illustrated History of Port Arthur Shipbuilding. (Great Lakes Marine History Ser.). (Illus.). 148p. 1994. pap. 21.95 (*0-9697778-0-9*, Pub. by RivT) Partners Pubs Grp.

Benedet, Rosalind. Entre Mujeres: Su Recuperacion Fisica y Emocional Despues de la Mastectomia. Casa Hispana Staff, tr. (SPA., Illus.). 92p. 1999. pap. 12.00 (*0-9637917-2-9*) Benedet Pbng.

— Healing: A Woman's Guide to Recovery after Mastectomy. 108p. 1993. pap. 10.00 (*0-9637917-0-2*) Benedet Pbng.

— Healing: A Women's Guide to Lumpectomy & Radiation Therapy. 120p. 1996. pap. 10.00 (*0-9637917-1-0*) Benedet Pbng.

Benedetti, Alessandro. Diaria De Bello Carolino (Diary of the Caroline War 1496) Schullian, Dorothy M., ed. LC 66-21028. (Renaissance Text Ser.: No. 1). x, 276p. 1967. 8.50 (*0-9602696-0-6*) Renaiss Society Am.

Benedetti, Charles Di, see Starr, Jerold M. & Di Benedetti, Charles.

Benedetti, Costantino, et al, eds. Opioid Analgesia: Recent Advances in Systemic Administration. LC 89-24319. (Advances in Pain Research & Therapy Ser.: Vol. 14). 494p. 1990. reprint ed. pap. 153.20 (*0-608-03386-3*, 206408300008) Bks Demand.

— Recent Advances in the Management of Pain. fac. ed. LC 84-15111. (Advances in Pain Research & Therapy Ser.: No. 7). (Illus.). 712p. pap. 200.00 (*0-7837-7510-5*, 204699500005) Bks Demand.

Benedetti, David. Nictitating Membrane. deluxe ed. (Illus.). 64p. 1976. pap. 10.00 (*0-935724-54-0*) Figures.

Benedetti, Gaetano. The Psychotherapy of Schizophrenia. 274p. 1996. pap. 50.00 (*1-56821-756-0*) Aronson.

Benedetti, Gaetano & Furlan, Pier, eds. The Psychotherapy of Schizophrenia: Effective Clinical Approaches - Controversies, Critiques & Recommendations. (Illus.). 429p. 1993. text 39.90 (*0-88937-077-X*) Hogrefe & Huber Pubs.

B

Benedetti, Jean. Stadia, Arenas & Grandstands: Design, Construction & Operation. Thompson, P. et al, eds. 384p. (C). (gr. 13). Date not set. 125.00 (0-419-24040-3, D6657, E & FN Spon) Routledge.
— Stanislavski: A Biography. (Illus.). 320p. 1988. 29.50 (0-87830-984-5, Thtre Arts Bks) Routledge.
— Stanislavski: An Introduction. 79p. 1987. pap. 15.99 (0-87830-578-5, Thtre Arts Bks) Routledge.
Benedetti, Jean, ed. The Moscow Art Theatre Letters. LC 91-19730. (Illus.). 320p. (C). (gr. 13). 1991. 45.00 (0-87830-084-8, A6381, Thtre Arts Bks) Routledge.
Benedetti, Maria. Earth & Spirit: Medicinal Plants & Healing Lore from Puerto Rico. 2nd rev. ed. Orig. Title: Earth & Spirit: Healing Love & More from Puerto Rico. (Illus.). 284p. 1998. pap. 20.00 (0-9633440-1-3) Verde Luz.
— Sembrando y Sanando en Puerto Rico: Tradiciones y Visiones para un Futuro Verde. (SPA., Illus.). 360p. (Orig.). 1996. pap. 23.00 (0-9633440-0-5) Verde Luz.
Benedetti, Mario. Andamios. 1998. pap. 19.95 (968-19-0328-5) Santillana.
— Blood Pact & Other Stories. Alegria, Claribel & Flakoll, Darwin J., eds. LC 96-21343. 214p. 1997. pap. 13.95 (1-880684-39-X) Curbstone.
***Benedetti, Mario.** Cuentos Completos, Benedetti. LC 94-222248. (SPA.). 1998. pap. 25.95 (84-204-8144-0) Santillana.
— Gracias Por el Fuego. (SPA.). 2000. pap. 11.95 (968-19-0492-3) Aguilar.
— La Muerte y Otras Sorpresas. (SPA.). 2000. pap. 9.95 (968-19-0313-7) Aguilar.
— Pedro y el Capitan. (SPA.). 2000. pap. 9.95 (968-19-0495-8) Aguilar.
— La Tregua. (SPA.). 2000. pap. 9.95 (968-19-0488-5) Aguilar.
Benedetti, Mario. La Vida, Ese Parentesis. 1998. pap. text 11.95 (968-19-0446-X) Santillana.
Benedetti, Mario, adapted by. La Muerte y Ostras Sorpresas, Level 4. (Leer en Espanol Ser.). (SPA.). (C). 1998. pap. 6.95 (84-294-3484-4) Santillana.
Benedetti, Paul & Dehart, Nancy, eds. Forward Through the Rearview Mirror: Reflections on & by Marshall Mcluhan. LC 96-78072. (Digital Communications Ser.). 1997. pap. text 25.00 (0-262-52233-0) MIT Pr.
Benedetti, R. & Petronio, C. Lectures on Hyperbolic Geometry. LC 92-20163. (Universitext Ser.). (Illus.). 352p. 1996. 39.00 (0-387-55534-X) Spr-Verlag.
Benedetti, R. & Petronio, Carlo. Branched Standard Spines of 3-Manifolds, Vol. 165. LC 97-7250. (Lecture Notes in Mathematics Ser.). 1997. pap. 27.00 (3-540-62627-1) Spr-Verlag.
Benedetti, Robert. Actor at Work. 7th ed. LC 96-16034. 288p. 1996. 53.00 (0-205-26139-6) Allyn.
***Benedetti, Robert.** Actor at Work. 8th ed. LC 99-56676. 272p. (C). 2000. 51.00 (0-205-31888-6) Allyn.
Benedetti, Robert L. The Actor in You: Sixteen Simple Steps to Understanding the Art of Acting. LC 98-19044. 149p. 1998. pap. text 27.00 (0-205-26999-0) Allyn.
— The Director at Work. (Illus.). 256p. (C). 1984. text 52.00 (0-13-214909-5) P-H.
Benedetti, Robert P. Flammable & Combustible Liquids Code Handbook. 6th ed. LC 97-136867. 510p. 1996. 81.00 (0-87765-408-5, 30HB96) Natl Fire Prot.
Benedetti, Thomas J., jt. auth. see Easterling, Thomas R.
Benedetti, Umberto. An Anthology of Correspondence. 232p. 1991. 30.00 (0-9630506-0-5) U Benedetti.
— Italian Boys at Fort Missoula, 1941-43. LC 91-92245. (Illus.). 136p. 1997. pap. 12.95 (1-57510-035-5) Pictorial Hist.
— Photo Album. 60p. 1993. pap. 10.00 (0-9630506-1-3) U Benedetti.
Benedetto. Journal of Fourier Analysis & Applications. 609p. 1995. per. 84.95 (0-8493-1515-8) CRC Pr.
Benedetto, A. R., et al, eds. Computers in Medical Physics. (American Association of Physicists in Medicine Symposium Ser.: No. 17). 417p. 1990. 75.00 (0-88318-802-3, Pub. by Am Inst Physics) Med Physics Pub.
Benedetto, AmeDeo. Jesus: Man's Star of Hope. (Illus.). 120p. (Orig.). 1989. pap. 5.95 (0-685-28891-9) Star Christ.
Benedetto, Angelo Di, see Di Benedetto, Angelo.
Benedetto, Beverly J., jt. auth. see Benedetto, Richard F.
Benedetto, C. Anthony Di, see Di Benedetto, C. Anthony, ed.
Benedetto, H. Di, see Di Benedetto, H., ed.
Benedetto, J. J., jt. ed. see Cooper, J. M.
Benedetto, John J. Real Variable & Integration. (Illus.). 1976. pap. 49.95 (3-519-02209-5) Adlers Foreign Bks.
Benedetto, John J., ed. Harmonic Analysis & Applications. 368p. 1996. boxed set 84.95 (0-8493-7879-6) CRC Pr.
Benedetto, John J., jt. ed. see Frazier, Michael W.
Benedetto, M. William, jt. auth. see Sutton, David.
Benedetto, Richard F. & Benedetto, Beverly J. Small Business Basics. 352p. (C). 1991. per. 39.95 (0-8403-6387-7) Kendall-Hunt.
Benedetto, Robert. Guide to the Manuscript Collections of the Presbyterian Church, U. S., 17. LC 90-42117. (Bibliographies & Indexes in Religious Studies: No. 17). 584p. 1990. lib. bdg. 115.00 (0-313-27654-4, BGO/, Greenwood Pr) Greenwood.
— Making an Archtop Guitar. (Illus.). 264p. 1996. reprint ed. pap. 39.95 (1-57424-000-5) Centerstream Pub.
— P. T. Forsyth Bibliograph & Index, 27. LC 92-46527. (Bibliographies & Indexes in Religious Studies: No. 27). 192p. 1993. lib. bdg. 69.50 (0-313-28753-8, GR8753, Greenwood Pr) Greenwood.
Benedetto, Robert, ed. Presbyterian Reformers in Central Africa: A Documentary Account of the American Presbyterian Congo Mission & the Human Rights Struggle in the Congo, 1890-1918. Vass, Winifred K., tr. LC 96-46461. 580p. 1996. 156.00 (90-04-10239-6) Brill Academic Pubs.
Benedetto, Robert, et al. Historical Dictionary of Reformed Churches. Woronoff, Jon, ed. & frwd. by. LC 98-50486. (Religions, Philosophies & Movements Ser.: No. 24). 544p. 1999. 79.50 (0-8108-3628-9) Scarecrow.
Benedetto, Robert, ed. see Battles, Ford L.
Benedetto, S. & Biglieri, E. Principles of Digital Transmission with Wireless Applications. LC 98-46066. (Series in Telecommunications). (Illus.). (C). 1999. write for info. (0-306-45753-9, Plenum Trade) Perseus Pubng.
Benedetto, U. Di, see Di Benedetto, U.
Benedi, Claudio F. Human Rights: The Theme of Our Times. 2nd ed. LC 97-2695. 304p. 1997. text 34.95 (1-55778-759-X) Paragon Hse.
Benedick, Richard E. Ozone Diplomacy: New Directions in Safeguarding the Planet. LC 90-20879. (Illus.). 320p. 1991. 35.00 (0-674-65000-X, BENOZO); pap. text 17.95 (0-674-65001-8, BENOZX) HUP.
— Ozone Diplomacy: New Directions in Safeguarding the Planet. LC 97-26498. 512p. 1998. 39.95 (0-674-65002-6); pap. 18.95 (0-674-65003-4) HUP.
Benedickson, J., et al. Canadian North: Source of Wealth or Vanishing Heritage. 1977. pap. 7.40 (0-13-112912-0) P-H.
Benedict. Estimates for Residential/Commercial Supplies. (Construction & Building Trades Ser.). 1994. 22.95 (0-8273-6070-3) Delmar.
— A Principal's Guide to High School Journalism. 2.00 (0-318-19221-7) Quill & Scroll.
Benedict, Alfred P., jt. auth. see Benedict, Nancy E.
Benedict, Arthur H., et al. Composting Municipal Sludge: A Technology Evaluation. LC 87-34746. (Pollution Technology Review Ser.: No. 152). (Illus.). 178p. 1988. 36.00 (0-8155-1162-0) Noyes.
Benedict, Audrey D. A Sierra Club Naturalist's Guide to the Southern Rockies: The Rocky Mountain Regions of Southern Wyoming, Colorado & Northern New Mexico. LC 89-10569. (Naturalist's Guides Ser.). (Illus.). 512p. 1991. pap. 18.00 (0-87156-647-8, Pub. by Sierra) Random.
Benedict, Barbara. Enchantress. 416p. 1996. mass mkt. 4.99 (0-8217-5520-X, Zebra Kensgtn) Kensgtn Pub Corp.
— Every Dream Come True. 384p. 1997. mass mkt. 4.99 (0-8217-5809-8, Zebra Kensgtn) Kensgtn Pub Corp.
— Rings, Roses . . . & Romance. 1997. per. 3.99 (0-373-24104-6, 1-24104-1) Silhouette.
— A Taste of Heaven. 416p. 1993. mass mkt. 4.50 (0-8217-4303-1, Zebra Kensgtn) Kensgtn Pub Corp.
***Benedict, Barbara M.** Curiosity. 2000. 36.00 (0-226-04263-4) U Ch Pr.
Benedict, Barbara M. Framing Feeling: Sentiment & Style in English Prose Fiction, 1745-1800. LC 93-33407. (Studies in the Eighteenth Century: No. 26). 1993. 45.00 (0-404-63526-1) AMS Pr.
— Making the Modern Reader: Cultural Mediation in Early Modern Literary Anthologies. LC 95-53313. 264p. (C). 1996. text 39.50 (0-691-02578-9, Pub. by Princeton U Pr) Cal Prin Full Svc.
— Nevada Statutes, annot. rev. ed. write for info. (0-614-05919-4, MICHIE) LEXIS Pub.
Benedict, Bert & Anderson, Gordon. Estimating for Residential & Commercial Construction. LC 92-40575. 310p. 1993. pap. 71.95 (0-8273-5498-3) Delmar.
Benedict, Bert & Anderson, Gordon. Estimating for Residential & Commercial Construction: Instructor's Guide. 98p. 1994. 14.95 (0-8273-5499-1) Delmar.
Benedict, Bob, et al. Web Authoring Desk Reference. LC 96-79744. 883p. 1997. 49.99 (1-56830-352-1) Hayden.
Benedict, Burnette B. Kinship. Cowden, Frances, ed. (Illus.). 39p. 1995. pap. 6.00 (1-884289-08-8) Grandmother Erth.
Benedict, Burton. The Anthropology of World's Fairs: San Francisco's Panama Pacific International Exposition of 1915. 175p. 1983. 121.95 (0-85967-676-5, Pub. by Scolar Pr); pap. 39.95 (0-85967-677-3, Pub. by Scolar Pr) Ashgate Pub Co.
Benedict, Carl P. A Tenderfoot Kid on Gyp Water. LC 86-6911. (Illus.). xiv, 115p. 1986. reprint ed. pap. 4.95 (0-8032-6079-2, Bison Books) U of Nebr Pr.
Benedict, Carol. Bubonic Plague in Nineteenth-Century China. LC 96-5157. 1996. write for info. (0-8047-2661-2) Stanford U Pr.
Benedict, Clare. Bitter Inheritance. (Scarlet Ser.). 1998. mass mkt. 3.99 (1-85487-951-0, Pub. by Scarlet Bks) London Brdge.
— The Brides of Eden. (Rainbow Romances Ser.). 160p. 1995. 14.95 (0-7090-5514-5, 928) Parkwest Pubns.
— The Brides of Eden. large type ed. (Linford Romance Library). 272p. 1996. pap. 16.99 (0-7089-7900-9) Ulverscroft.
— Desire Unbidden. large type ed. (Dales Large Print Ser.). 228p. 1997. pap. 18.99 (1-85389-779-5, Dales) Ulverscroft.
— Sophie's Wedding. (Scarlet Ser.). 1998. mass mkt. 3.99 (1-85487-882-4, Pub. by Scarlet Bks) London Brdge.
— Tempestuous Shore. large type ed. (Dales Large Print Ser.). (Illus.). 220p. 1996. pap. 18.99 (1-85389-613-6) Ulverscroft.
Benedict, Clare M. St. Sharbel, Mystic of the East. 1990. reprint ed. 11.95 (0-911218-11-4); reprint ed. pap. 5.95 (0-911218-12-2) Ravengate Pr.
Benedict, Dan, ed. see Ekman, Blanche.
Benedict, Daniel. Come to the Waters: Baptism & Our Ministry of Welcoming Seekers & Making Disciples. LC 96-86607. (Christian Initiation Ser.). 160p. 1996. pap. 18.95 (0-88177-179-1, DR179) Discipleship Res.
Benedict, Daniel T., jt. auth. see Miller, Craig K.
Benedict, David. A General History of the Baptist Denomination in America, 2 vols. 1985. reprint ed. 69.00 (0-317-31642-7) Church History.
— General History of the Baptist Denomination in America & Other Parts of the World, 2 vols, Set. LC 73-152974. (Select Bibliographies Reprint Ser.). 1977. reprint ed. 66.95 (0-8369-5726-1) Ayer.
— History of the Donatists. 1985. reprint ed. 21.00 (0-317-31641-9) Church History.
Benedict, Dianne. Shiny Objects. LC 82-10853. (Iowa Short Fiction Award Ser.). 170p. 1982. 5.00 (0-87745-116-8) U of Iowa Pr.
Benedict, Dirk. Confessions of a Kamikaze Cowboy: A True Story of Discovery, Acting, Health, Illness, Recovery, & Life. 2nd ed. LC 90-26196. 240p. 1991. pap. 9.95 (0-89529-479-6, Avery) Penguin Putnam.
***Benedict, Elinor.** All That Divides Us: Poems. LC 00-9804. (May Swenson Poetry Award Ser.). 2000. write for info. (0-87421-333-9) Utah St U Pr.
Benedict, Elinor. Chinavision. Bixby, Robert, ed. 31p. (Orig.). 1995. pap. 6.00 (1-882983-24-6) March Street Pr.
— The Green Heart. 36p. 1994. pap. 5.00 (0-9642298-0-3) IL Writers.
Benedict, Elinor, ed. Passages North Anthology: A Decade of Good Writing. LC 90-5457. 336p. (Orig.). 1989. pap. 11.95 (0-915943-48-4) Milkweed Ed.
Benedict, Elinor & Bixby, Robert. The Tree Between Us. 23p. 1997. pap. 6.00 (1-882983-36-X) March Street Pr.
Benedict, Elizabeth. The Joy of Writing Sex: A Guide for Fiction Writers. LC 96-7333. 160p. 1996. 16.99 (1-884910-21-1, Story Press) F & W Pubns Inc.
Benedict, Ellen M., jt. ed. see Sims, Lynne.
Benedict, Elsie L. & Benedict, Ralph P. Written in 1920. 310p. (Orig.). 1986. 14.95 (0-915659-06-9) Video Athlete.
Benedict, Erastus C. The American Admiralty, Its Jurisdiction & Practice. 650p. 1994. reprint ed. lib. bdg. 69.50 (0-8328-3965-5) Higginson Bk Co.
Benedict, Forest C., et al, eds. Glossary of Compensation Terms. 13p. 1992. 15.00 (1-878240-11-0) Coll & U Personnel.
Benedict, Forest C. & Smith, Cynthia. Supervisor's Guide to Effective Performance Appraisal. 38p. 1992. 15.00 (1-878240-07-2) Coll & U Personnel.
Benedict, Francis G. The Composition of the Atmosphere with Special Reference to Its Oxygen Content. LC 12-23088. (Carnegie Institution of Washington Publication Ser.: Vol. 166). (Illus.). 120p. reprint ed. pap. 37.20 (0-608-06216-2, 206654400008) Bks Demand.
— The Influence of Inanition on Metabolism. LC 08-995. (Carnegie Institution of Washington Publication Ser.: Vol. 77). (Illus.). 550p. reprint ed. pap. 170.50 (0-608-06230-8, 206655900008) Bks Demand.
Benedict, Francis G. & Carpenter, Thorne M. Respiration Calorimeters for Studying the Respiratory Exchange & Energy Transformations of Man. LC 10-9497. (Carnegie Institution of Washington Publication Ser.: Vol. 123). (Illus.). 110p. reprint ed. pap. 34.10 (0-608-06214-6, 206654200008) Bks Demand.
Benedict, Francis G. & Joslin, Elliott P. A Study of Metabolism in Severe Diabetes. LC 13-1475. (Illus.). 143p. reprint ed. pap. 44.40 (0-608-06217-0, 206654600008) Bks Demand.
Benedict, Francis G. & Murschhauser, Hans. Energy Transformations During Horizontal Walking. LC 15-19213. (Carnegie Institution of Washington Publication Ser.: Vol. 231). (Illus.). 100p. reprint ed. pap. 31.00 (0-608-06219-7, 206654800008) Bks Demand.
Benedict, G. G. Vermont in the Civil War, 2 vols., Set. (Illus.). 1428p. 1995. reprint ed. lib. bdg. 147.00 (0-8328-5121-3) Higginson Bk Co.
Benedict, Gary F. Nontraditional Manufacturing Processes. (Manufacturing Engineering & Materials Processing Ser.: Vol. 19). (Illus.). 400p. 1987. text 170.00 (0-8247-7352-7) Dekker.
Benedict, George G. Visions & Verities. LC 57-14845. 222p. 1957. 21.95 (0-87015-077-4) Pacific Bks.
Benedict, Gerald S. The Development & Management of Medical Groups. 149p. (Orig.). 1996. pap. 44.95 (1-56829-049-7, 4856) Med Group Mgmt.
Benedict, Glen E., jt. auth. see Schulz, Wallace W.
Benedict, H. Y. Book of Texas. 1993. reprint ed. lib. bdg. 75.00 (0-7812-5865-0) Rprt Serv.
— Source Book Relative to the History of the University of Texas. 1993. reprint ed. lib. bdg. 75.00 (0-7812-5864-2) Rprt Serv.
Benedict, Helen. Portraits in Print: A Collection of Profiles & the Stories Behind Them. 176p. 1991. text 46.00 (0-231-07226-0) Col U Pr.
— Portraits in Print: A Collection of Profiles & the Stories Behind Them. 176p. 1992. pap. 15.50 (0-231-07227-9) Col U Pr.
— Recovery: How to Survive Sexual Assault for Women, Men, Teenagers, Their Friends & Families. rev. ed. LC 94-15856. 1994. 46.00 (0-231-09674-7); pap. 18.00 (0-231-09675-5) Col U Pr.
— Safe, Strong & Streetwise: The Teenager's Guide to Preventing Sexual Assault. (Joy Street Bks.). (Illus.). 192p. (YA). (gr. 7 up). 1987. pap. 6.95 (0-87113-100-5) Little.
***Benedict, Helen.** The Sailor's Wife. 224p. 2000. pap. 24.00 (1-58195-024-1) Zoland Bks.
Benedict, Helen. Virgin or Vamp: How the Press Covers Sex Crimes. 320p. (C). 1993. reprint ed. pap. 15.95 (0-19-508665-1, 7113) OUP.
Benedict, Henry M. The Genealogy of the Benedicts in America. (Illus.). 494p. 1988. reprint ed. pap. 74.00 (0-8328-0235-2); reprint ed. lib. bdg. 82.00 (0-8328-0234-4) Higginson Bk Co.
Benedict, Howard. NASA: The Endless Journey. 2nd rev. ed. 190p. 1996. reprint ed. 29.95 (0-9610648-7-0) Graphic Hse.
***Benedict, James.** Come Again? Exploring the Hard Sayings of Jesus. (Good Ground Ser.: Vol. 3:2). 43p. 2000. pap. 5.95 (0-87303-375-2) Faith & Life.
— Preach It! Messages of the Bible. (Good Ground Ser.: Vol. 2:1). 41p. 1999. pap. 5.95 (0-87303-359-0) Faith & Life.
Benedict, James S. The Empty Shell: A Collection of Poems & Stories. (Illus.). 226p. 1996. 15.00 (0-9633524-8-2); pap. 10.00 (0-9633524-9-0) JB Press.
— The Phoebe's Nest: An Illustrated Collection of Poems & Stories. (Illus.). 190p. 1998. 15.00 (1-892015-00-5); pap. 10.00 (1-892015-01-3) JB Press.
Benedict, Jan. Cookmark: Cooking Bulk Purchased Grains & Beans. 1995. 1.95 (1-884846-06-8) Colo Whistle.
— Cookmark: Cooking Times & Temperatures. 1994. 1.95 (1-884846-14-9) Colo Whistle.
— Cookmark: Herb & Food Combinations. 1994. 1.95 (1-884846-12-2) Colo Whistle.
— Cookmark: High Altitude Cooking Adjustments, 5000-6000 Ft. 1993. 1.95 (1-884846-00-9) Colo Whistle.
— Cookmark: High Altitude Cooking Adjustments, 6000-9000 Ft. 1993. 1.95 (1-884846-01-7) Colo Whistle.
— Cookmark: Lowfat Substitutions for Healthier Cooking. 1993. 1.95 (1-884846-02-5) Colo Whistle.
— Cookmark: Pressure Cooking Guidelines. 1997. 1.95 (1-884846-07-6) Colo Whistle.
— Cookmark: U. S. - Everyday Kitchen Substitutions. 1995. 1.95 (1-884846-10-6) Colo Whistle.
— Cookmark: U. S. - Metric Conversions. 1993. 1.95 (1-884846-03-3) Colo Whistle.
— Cookmark: Vegetarian Substitutions. 1997. 1.95 (1-884846-09-2) Colo Whistle.
Benedict, Jeanne. The Sophisticated Cookie: Baking with Spirits: The World's Best Cookies Made with Popular Alcoholic Beverages. LC 98-9808. x, 198p. 1998. pap. 14.00 (1-55788-294-0, HP Books) Berkley Pub.
***Benedict, Jeanne.** Sophisticated Entertaining: Spirited Food for Grown-Up Parties. (Illus.). 2000. 24.95 (1-55788-345-9, HP Books) Berkley Pub.
Benedict, Jeff. Mashantucket Pequots. 2000. pap. 15.00 (0-06-093196-5) HarpC.
— Public Heroes, Private Felons: Athletes & Crimes Against Women. LC 97-6528. 224p. 1997. text 32.50 (1-55553-316-7) NE U Pr.
— Public Heroes, Private Felons: Athletes & Crimes Against Women. 1999. pap. text 12.95 (1-55553-382-5) NE U Pr.
***Benedict, Jeff.** Without Reservation: The Making of America's Most Powerful Indian Tribe & Foxwoods the World's Largest Casino. LC 00-24479. 368p. 2000. 26.00 (0-06-019367-0) HarpC.
Benedict, Jeff & Yaeger, Don. Pros & Cons: The Criminals Who Play in the NFL. 432p. 1999. mass mkt. 7.99 (0-446-60747-9, Pub. by Warner Bks) Little.
Benedict, Jeff & Yeager, Don. Pros & Cons: The Criminals Who Play in the NFL. LC 98-28090. 317p. 1998. 24.00 (0-446-52403-4, Pub. by Warner Bks) Little.
Benedict, Jeffrey R. Athletes & Acquaintance Rape. LC 97-45340. (Series on Violence Against Women). 1998. write for info. (0-7619-0966-4); pap. 31.19 (0-7619-0967-2) Sage Pubng.
Benedict, Jeffrey R., jt. ed. see Lapchick, Richard E.
Benedict, John H., et al, eds. Vegetable Oils & Agrichemicals, 4. LC 94-29090. (Cotton Foundation Reference Bks.). 1994. write for info. (0-939809-04-4) Cotton Found.
Benedict, John T. Metrication for the Manager. Boselovic, Len, ed. LC 77-84932. (Illus.). 1977. pap. text 10.00 (0-916148-12-2) Am Natl.
Benedict-Jones, Linda, et al. Pittsburgh Revealed: Photographs since 1850. LC 96-52218. (Illus.). 208p. (Orig.). 1997. pap. 39.95 (0-88039-034-4) Mus Art Carnegie.
Benedict, Julius. Carl Maria Von Weber. LC 74-24040. reprint ed. 38.50 (0-404-12863-7) AMS Pr.
***Benedict, Kate.** Wages of Sin. 256p. 2000. pap. 9.95 (1-901388-53-0, Pub. by Chimera Pubns) Firebird Dist.
Benedict, Kitty. The Fall of the Bastille. (Turning Points in World History Ser.). (Illus.). 64p. (YA). (gr. 7 up). 1991. pap. 7.95 (0-382-24135-5); lib. bdg. 14.95 (0-382-24129-0) Silver Burdett Pr.
Benedict, Kitty & Covington, Karen. The Literary Crowd: Writers, Critics, Scholars, Wits. LC 98-54938. (Illus.). 80p. (gr. 4-7). 2000. lib. bdg. 28.55 (0-8172-5732-2) Raintree Steck-V.
Benedict, Larry & Benedict, Susan. The Video Demo Tape: How to Save Money Making a Tape That Gets You Work. 232p. 1992. pap. 34.95 (0-240-80140-7, Focal) Buttrwrth-Heinemann.
Benedict, Laurel. International Carols for Dulcimer. 32p. 1994. pap. 16.95 incl. audio (0-7866-1142-1, 95309P) Mel Bay.
— International Carols for Dulcimer. (Illus.). 32p. 1994. pap. 7.95 (0-7866-0156-6, 95309) Mel Bay.
Benedict, Linda F., ed. see Qi, Yadong, et al.
Benedict, Lucy. Parents Instruction Destruction Book. 120p. 1993. pap. 6.95 (1-56850-034-3) Chicago Plays.
Benedict, Lyle. Benedict. Story of the Benedicts: Genealogy of the Benedict Family for the Descendants of Ira & Seely Benedict of the 7th Generation in America. (Illus.). 31p. 1997. reprint ed. pap. 6.00 (0-8328-7485-X); reprint ed. lib. bdg. 16.00 (0-8328-7484-1) Higginson Bk Co.
Benedict, M. G., et al. Super-Radiance: Multiatomic Coherent Emission. (Illus.). 376p. 1996. 200.00 (0-7503-0283-6) IOP Pub.
Benedict, Manson, et al. Nuclear Chemical Engineering. 2nd ed. (Illus.). 1024p. (C). 1981. 116.25 (0-07-004531-3) McGraw.

Benedict, Michael, ed. Value: A Journal for Architecture in America Value. (Illus.). 140p. 1997. pap. 22.00 (*0-292-71200-6*) U of Tex Pr.

Benedict, Michael L. The Fruits of Victory: Alternatives in Restoring the Union, 1865-1877. rev. ed. 174p. (C). 1986. reprint ed. pap. text 16.50 (*0-8191-5557-8*) U Pr of Amer.

***Benedict, Michael L.** Twilight Is Dawning: An Anthology of the Later Years. LC 00-28256. 300p. 2000. pap. 19.95 (*1-57249-203-1*, Ragged Edge) White Mane Pub.

Benedict, Michael Les, see Les Benedict, Michael.

Benedict, Michele. Image: Discover & Develop Your Personal Style. (Illus.). 160p. (Orig.). 1987. pap. 17.95 (*0-940277-07-7*) Creative Endeavors Pr.

Benedict, Nancy E. & Benedict, Alfred P. A Handbook of Gemstones & Jewelry. LC 97-200924. (Illus.). ix, 160p. (Orig.). 1996. pap. 18.95 (*0-9652510-0-4*) N & A Benedict.

Benedict, Paul K. Austro-Thai: Language & Culture, with a Glossary of Roots. LC 67-30152. (Monographs). 510p. 1975. 35.00 (*0-87536-323-7*) HRAFP.

Benedict, Paul K. & Bauer, Robert S. Modern Cantonese Phonology. LC 97-8574. (Trends in Linguistics Ser.). 304p. (C). 1997. lib. bdg. 117.05 (*3-11-014893-5*) Mouton.

Benedict, Philip. The Huguenot Population of France, 1600-1685: The Demographic Fate & Customs of a Religious Minority. LC 90-56477. (Transactions Ser.: Vol. 81, Pt. 5). (Illus.). 280p. (Orig.). (C). 1991. pap. 25.00 (*0-87169-815-3*, T815-BEP) Am Philos.

Benedict, Philip, ed. Cities & Social Change in Early Modern France. 224p. 1989. text 55.00 (*0-04-944017-9*) Routledge.

— Cities & Social Change in Early Modern France. 272p. (C). 1992. pap. 27.99 (*0-415-08161-0*, A9406) Routledge.

Benedict, Pinckney. Town Smokes. LC 87-5684. 168p. (Orig.). 1987. pap. 9.95 (*0-86538-058-9*) Ontario Rev NJ.

Benedict, R. L., ed. Anode Resistance Fundamentals & Applications - Classic Papers & Reviews. LC 86-63053. (Illus.). 201p. 1986. pap. 40.00 (*0-915567-25-3*) NACE Intl.

Benedict, Ralph P., jt. auth. see Benedict, Elsie L.

Benedict, Richard. Trashcan Kids. LC 92-19499. 53p. (Orig.). 1992. pap. 11.95 (*0-87120-194-1*, 611-92132) ASCD.

Benedict, Robert. Christmas Carols Easy Piano. 32p. 1987. pap. 5.95 (*0-87166-655-3*, 94261) Mel Bay.

— If Snowmen Could Make Music. 40p. 1993. pap. 5.95 (*0-87166-654-5*, 94263) Mel Bay.

— An Introduction to Boogie, Rock, Blues & Jazz. 48p. 1989. pap. 6.95 (*0-87166-565-4*, 94264) Mel Bay.

— Popular Classics for Easy Piano. 40p. 1989. pap. 5.95 (*0-87166-567-0*, 94265) Mel Bay.

— Sight-Reading for the Classical Guitar: Levels IV-V, Levels IV-V. Stang, Aaron, ed. 64p. (C). 1985. pap. text 12.95 (*0-7692-1285-9*, EL02943) Wrner Bros.

Benedict, Robert P. Fundamentals of Gas Dynamics. LC 83-1273. 44p. (C). 1987. pap. text 8.75 (*0-471-87340-3*) Wiley.

— Fundamentals of Temperature, Pressure & Flow Measurements. 3rd ed. LC 83-23558. 560p. 1984. 175.00 (*0-471-89383-8*) Wiley.

Benedict, Roy G. & McFarlane, James R. Not Only Passengers: How the Electric Railways Carried Freight, Express & Baggage. LC 92-71563. (Bulletin Ser.: No. 129). (Illus.). 128p. 1992. 35.00 (*0-915348-29-2*) Central Electric.

Benedict, Russell. Acts & Laws of the Thirteen Original Colonies & States: Constituting the Extraordinary Collection of Honorary Russell Benedict, Justice of the Supreme Court of New York, 1922. LC 98-20196. 252p. 1998. reprint ed. 85.00 (*1-886363-56-0*) Lawbk Exchange.

Benedict, Ruth. An Anthropologist at Work: Writings of Ruth Benedict. Mead, Margaret, ed. LC 77-3017. (Illus.). 583p. 1977. reprint ed. lib. bdg. 65.00 (*0-8371-9576-4*, BEAW, Greenwood Pr) Greenwood.

— The Chrysanthemum & the Sword: Patterns of Japanese Culture. 324p. 1989. pap. 14.00 (*0-395-50075-3*) HM.

— Continuities & Discontinuities in Cultural Conditioning. (Reprint Series in Social Sciences). (C). 1993. reprint ed. pap. text 5.00 (*0-8290-3844-2*, S-18) Irvington.

— Patterns of Culture. 352p. 1989. reprint ed. pap. 14.00 (*0-395-50088-5*) HM.

— Tales of the Cochiti Indians. 1976. lib. bdg. 59.95 (*0-8490-2729-2*) Gordon Pr.

— Tales of the Cochiti Indians. (Bureau of American Ethnology Bulletins Ser.). 256p. 1995. lib. bdg. 89.00 (*0-7812-4098-0*) Rprt Serv.

— Tales of the Cochiti Indians. LC 81-16426. 270p. reprint ed. pap. 83.70 (*0-608-15776-7*, 203099800073) Bks Demand.

— Tales of the Cochiti Indians. reprint ed. 49.00 (*0-403-03705-0*) Scholarly.

— Zuni Mythology, 2 vols. LC 75-82366. (Columbia Univ. Contributions to Anthropology Ser.: No. 21). 1969. reprint ed. 70.00 (*0-404-50571-6*) AMS Pr.

Benedict, Saint, jt. auth. see Sweetnam, John.

Benedict, Stephen. Public Money & the Muse. 288p. (C). 1991. pap. text 12.50 (*0-393-96135-4*, Norton Paperbks) Norton.

— Public Money & the Muse: Essays on Government Funding for the Arts. 1991. 22.95 (*0-393-03015-6*) Norton.

Benedict, Susan & Carlisle, Lenore, eds. Beyond Words: Picture Books for Older Readers & Writers. LC 92-11964. 144p. (C). 1992. pap. text 21.00 (*0-435-08710-X*, 08710) Heinemann.

Benedict, Susan, jt. auth. see Benedict, Larry.

Benedict, U. 3rd Workshop, Actinides under Pressure. 150p. 1990. text 223.00 (*2-88124-778-4*) Gordon & Breach.

Benedict, William, jt. illus. see Schubert, Leda.

Benedict, William H. New Brunswick in History. 391p. 1993. reprint ed. lib. bdg. 42.50 (*0-8328-2856-4*) Higginson Bk Co.

Benedict, Wolf J. The Effects of Agency Problems on the Financial Behavior, Performance & Efficiency of German Industrial Stock Corporations. LC 99-12893. (European University Studies: Vol.2424). (Illus.). XXX, 411p. 1999. 67.95 (*0-8204-3241-5*) P Lang Pubng.

Benedictine Sisters of Clyde, Missouri Staff. St. Gertrude the Great: Herald of Divine Love. 1994. pap. 1.50 (*0-89555-026-1*) TAN Bks Pubs.

Benedictines of Stanbrook Staff, tr. see St. Teresa of Avila.

***Benedictow.** Black Death. 2000. 65.00 (*0-8133-3376-8*, Pub. by Westview); pap. 20.00 (*0-8133-3386-5*, Pub. by Westview) HarpC.

***Benedictsson, Victoria.** Money. Death, Sarah, tr. from SWE. 186p. 2000. pap. 22.95 (*1-870041-40-2*, Pub. by Norvik Pr) Dufour.

Benedictus. Middle High German Translations of the Regula Sancti Benedicti. Selmer, Carl, ed. & intro. by. (Mediaeval Academy of America Publications: Vol. 17). 1933. 40.00 (*0-527-01689-6*) Periodicals Srv.

Benedicty, Mario & Sledge, Frank R. Discrete Mathematical Structures. 529p. (C). 1987. 1.50 (*0-15-517684-6*) SCP.

***Benedik, Linda & Wirth, Veronica.** Yoga for Equestrians: A New Path to Achieving Union with the Horse. LC 99-87512. 2000. pap. write for info. (*1-57076-136-1*) Trafalgar.

Benedikt, Elliot T. & Halliburton, Robert W., eds. Second AAS Symposium on Physical & Biological Phenomena under Zero G Conditions, Jan. 18, 1963, Los Angeles, CA. LC 57-43769. (Advances in the Astronautical Sciences Ser.: Vol. 14). 382p. 1963. 30.00 (*0-87703-015-4*, Am Astronaut Soc) Univelt Inc.

Benedikt, George M. & Goodall, Brian L., eds. Metallocene Catalyzed Polymers: Materials, Properties, Processing & Markets. (SPE/ PDL Ser.). 400p. 1998. text 160.00 (*1-884207-59-6*) William Andrew.

Benedikt, Michael. Deconstructing the Kimbell. (Illus.). 140p. (Orig.). 1991. pap. 15.95 (*0-930829-16-6*) Lumen Inc.

— For an Architecture of Reality. 74p. (Orig.). 1987. pap. 15.00 (*0-930829-05-0*) Lumen Inc.

Benedikt, Michael. Value. 1997. 40.00 (*0-226-04249-9*) U Ch Pr.

Benedikt, Michael, ed. Buildings & Reality: Architecture in the Age of Information, Vol. 4. (Illus.). 128p. 1988. pap. 22.00 (*0-8478-5484-1*) Ctr for Amer Archit.

Benedikt, Moriz. Anatomical Studies upon Brains of Criminals. Fowler, E. P., tr. from GER. (Historical Foundations of Forensic Psychiatry & Psychology Ser.). (Illus.). 185p. 1980. reprint ed. lib. bdg. 25.00 (*0-306-76071-1*) Da Capo.

Benedikt, Tashcen Verlag, ed. Pablo Picasso I, 6 vols. 1996. pap. 11.99 (*3-8228-8769-2*) Benedikt Taschen.

Benedikt Tashcen Verlag Staff. H.R. Giger Spanish Edition. 1996. pap. 16.99 (*3-8228-9540-7*) Benedikt Taschen.

Benedikter, Franz. The Secrets of Loving Touch. (Illus.). 144p. (Orig.). 1996. pap. 12.95 (*0-941524-90-6*) Lotus Pr.

Benedikto, Ricardo. Dictionary. (TAG & ENG.). 414p. 69.95 (*0-320-03424-0*) Fr & Eur.

Benedikto, Ricardo. English-Tagalog Dictionary. 288p. 1997. 39.95 (*0-7859-9465-3*) Fr & Eur.

***Benediktson, D. Thomas.** Literature & the Visual Arts in Ancient Greece & Rome. LC 99-39788. (Series in Classical Culture). 272p. 2000. 37.95 (*0-8061-3207-8*) U of Okla Pr.

Benediktson, D. Thomas. Propertius: Modernist Poet of Antiquity. LC 88-10115. 176p. (C). 1989. text 26.95 (*0-8093-1453-3*) S Ill U Pr.

Benedini, Marcello, et al, eds. Water Resources Management: Modern Decision Techniques: Selected Papers from the International Symposium on the Application of Systems Analysis to Water Resources Management, Perugia, 1986. (IAHR Proceedings Ser.: No. 4). (Illus.). 155p. (C). 1992. text 123.00 (*90-6191-148-6*, Pub. by A A Balkema) Ashgate Pub Co.

Beneditti, P. G. de, see De Beneditti, P. G., ed.

Beneduce. Tales of the Russian Northwest. LC 99-40002. (J). 2000. 16.00 (*0-689-82113-1*) S&S Childrens.

Beneduce, Ann K. Gulliver's Adventures in Lilliput. 1996. 12.15 (*0-606-11422-X*, Pub. by Turtleback) Demco.

— Jack & the Beanstalk. LC 98-5722. (Illus.). 32p. (J). (gr. k-4). 1999. 15.99 (*0-399-23118-8*, Philomel) Peng Put Young Read.

— A Weekend with Winslow Homer. LC 93-12189. (Illus.). 64p. (J). 1993. 19.95 (*0-8478-1622-2*, Pub. by Rizzoli Intl) St Martin.

— A Weekend with Winslow Homer. 64p. 1996. 9.95 (*0-8478-1919-1*, Pub. by Rizzoli Intl) St Martin.

Beneduce, Ann K., tr. see Skira-Venturi, Rosabianca.

***Beneduce, Ann Keay, et al.** Philipok. LC 99-55298. (Illus.). 32p. (J). (ps-1). 2000. 16.99 (*0-399-23482-9*, Philomel) Peng Put Young Read.

Benefein, Jean, et al. Listen to the Children. LC 86-60493. (Illus.). 55p. 1986. pap. 6.00 (*0-935989-00-5*, NAEYC #304) Natl Assn Child Ed.

Benefiel, Robert. Easy Battles for Lazy Armies. McCanless, William & Dumagaindin, Iris, eds. (Illus.). 130p. 1998. pap. 8.95 (*0-9662437-5-7*) Four AM.

Benefield, Larry D., et al. Treatment Plant Hydraulics for Environmental Engineers. (Illus.). 240p. (C). 1984. text 76.00 (*0-13-930248-4*) P-H.

Benefield, Laurance. My Golf Book. Davis, Marilyn E., ed. & illus. by. 1996. lthr. write for info. (*1-880981-03-3*) A Diff View.

Benefield, Lazelle E. Home Health Care Management. (Illus.). 416p. 1988. text 50.00 (*0-89303-682-X*) P-H.

Benefield, Linda, ed. see Bodie, Idella F.

Benefo, Kofi D. & Schultz, T. Paul. Determinants of Fertility & Child Mortality in Cote d'Ivoire & Ghana. LC 94-4997. (LSMS Working Papers: No. 103). 102p. 1994. pap. 22.00 (*0-8213-2789-5*, 12789) World Bank.

— Determinants of Fertility & Child Mortality in Cote d'Ivoire & Ghana. (FRE.). 104p. 1995. pap. 22.00 (*0-8213-3125-6*, 13125) World Bank.

Benegal, Shyam. Satyajit Ray: A Film. (C). 1988. 14.00 (*81-7046-021-2*, Pub. by Seagull Bks) S Asia.

Benegal, Som. Panorama of Theatre in India. (Illus.). 1968. 69.50 (*0-614-01824-2*) Elliots Bks.

Benegar, Cynthia & McClain, Heidi. Learning in the Mile High City: A Guide to Public & Private Schools in Metro Denver. LC 86-60687. 160p. (Orig.). 1986. pap. 9.95 (*0-9608012-4-3*) Metrosource Pubns.

***Benegar, Dawn M.** 101 Bouncy Bible Rhyme-Time Games for Childrens Ministry: 101 Bible Games That Can Be Used Indoors. 2000. pap. text 16.99 (*0-7644-2217-0*) Group Pub.

Benegar, John. Teaching Writing Skills: A Global Approach. rev. ed. (Illus.). 189p. (Orig.). (gr. 6-12). 1987. pap. 26.95 (*0-943804-31-0*) U of Denver Teach.

Benegar, John, et al. Global Issues in the Middle School. (Illus.). 176p. (Orig.). (J). (gr. 5-8). 1994. pap. 21.95 (*0-89994-377-2*) Soc Sci Ed.

Beneke. Woerterbuch Korrosion: German-English-French-Russian. (FRE, GER & RUS.). 700p. 450.00 (*0-7859-7435-0*, 380272819X) Fr & Eur.

Beneke, C. Deloitte & Touche VAT Handbook. 2nd ed. 1993. pap. write for info. (*0-409-07756-9*, MICHIE) LEXIS Pub.

Beneke, Daphne L. Fifteen Profiles: Distinguished California Modernists. Hall, Doris, ed. LC 98-130454. (Illus.). 96p. (Orig.). 1995. pap. 19.95 (*0-932325-32-7*) Fresno Arts Mus.

Beneke, Everette S. & Rogers, Alvin L. Medical Mycology & Human Mycoses. LC 95-47079. (Illus.). 239p. (C). 1996. 54.95 (*0-89863-175-0*) Star Pub CA.

Beneke, H. Lexikon der Korrosion und des Korrosionsschutzes. (GER.). 389p. 1992. 95.00 (*0-7859-8485-2*, 3802726979) Fr & Eur.

Beneke, Jeff. Build a Kids' Play Yard. Soderstrom, Neil, ed. LC 97-75271. (Illus.). 144p. 1998. pap. 14.95 (*1-58011-001-0*) Creative Homeowner.

— Fences & Gates. Toht, David W., ed. (Easy-Step Ser.). (Illus.). 64p. (Orig.). 1997. pap. text 6.95 (*0-89721-323-8*, Ortho Bks) Meredith Bks.

— Painting. Toht, David W., ed. (Easy-Step Ser.). (Illus.). 64p. (Orig.). 1998. pap. 6.95 (*0-89721-342-4*, 05989, Ortho Bks) Meredith Bks.

— Plumbing. Toht, David W., ed. (Easy-Step Ser.). (Illus.). 64p. (Orig.). 1997. pap. 6.95 (*0-89721-335-1*, 05958, Ortho Bks) Meredith Bks.

— Quick Guide: Stairs & Railings. Bakke, Timothy O. & Ziegner, Rich, eds. LC 96-84681. (Quick Guide Ser.). (Illus.). 80p. (Orig.). 1997. pap. 7.95 (*1-880029-87-X*) Creative Homeowner.

Beneke, Jeff, contrib. by. Plumbing. LC 99-182114. (Easy-Step Ser.). (Illus.). 64p. (Orig.). 1998. pap. 6.95 (*0-8069-7051-0*) Sterling.

Beneke, Jeff & Ross, Douglas. Ortho's All about Home Offices. LC 97-76214. (Illus.). 96p. 1998. pap. 11.95 (*0-89721-416-1*, Ortho Bks) Meredith Bks.

Beneke, Jeff, jt. auth. see Canesso, Claudia.

Beneke, Jurgen, et al. Aspekte Amerikanischer Kultur. (Hildesheimer Beitraege Zu Den Erziehungs und Sozialwissenschaften Ser.: Vol. 31). viii, 190p. 1989. 30.00 (*3-487-09223-9*) G Olms Pubs.

Beneke, Lynda, ed. A Grand Heritage: A Culinary Legacy of Columbus, Mississippi. (Illus.). 370p. 1983. pap. text 14.95 (*0-9612048-0-X*) Heritage Acad.

Beneke, Raymond R. & Winterboer, Ronald D. Linear Programming Applications to Agriculture. LC 72-2298. 252p. 1973. reprint ed. pap. 78.20 (*0-608-00067-1*, 206083300006) Bks Demand.

Beneke, Timothy. Proving Manhood: Reflections on Men & Sexism. 183p. 1997. pap. text 17.95 (*0-520-21266-5*, Pub. by U CA Pr) Cal Prin Full Svc.

— Proving Manhood: Reflections on Men & Sexism. LC 97-1210. 183p. 1997. 48.00 (*0-520-20961-3*, Pub. by U CA Pr) Cal Prin Full Svc.

Beneken, J. E. & Lavelle, S. M., eds. Objective Medical Decision Making: Systems Approach in Acute Disease. (Lecture Notes in Medical Informatics Ser.: Vol. 22). 243p. 1983. 42.95 (*0-387-12671-6*) Spr-Verlag.

Beneken, J. E. & Thevin, V., eds. Advances in Biomedical Engineering: Results of the 4th EC Medical & Health Research Programme (1987-1991) LC 92-75336. (Studies in Health Technology & Informatics: Vol. 7). 374p. (gr. 12). 1993. 130.00 (*90-5199-119-3*, Pub. by IOS Pr) IOS Press.

Beneking, H., jt. ed. see Kallback, B.

Benekohal, Rahim F., ed. Traffic Congestion & Traffic Safety in the 21st Century: Challenges, Innovations, & Opportunities. LC 97-16273. 664p. 1997. 57.00 (*0-7844-0243-4*) Am Soc Civil Eng.

Benekos, Peter J. & Merlo, Alida V., eds. Corrections: Dilemmas & Directions. LC 92-81967. (ACJS - Anderson Monographs). 193p. (C). 1992. pap. 21.95 (*0-87084-235-8*) Anderson Pub Co.

Benekos, Peter J., jt. auth. see Merlo, Alida V.

Benel. Air Traffic. (IJAP Ser.: Vol. 3, No. 4). 1993. 20.00 (*0-8058-9982-0*) L Erlbaum Assocs.

Benello, C. George. From the Ground Up: Essays on Grassroots & Workplace Democracy. Krimerman, Len et al, eds. 251p. write for info. (*1-895431-33-6*); pap. write for info. (*1-895431-32-8*) Black Rose.

— From the Ground Up: Essays on Grassroots & Workplace Democracy. Krimerman, Len et al, eds. 251p. (C). 1992. 30.00 (*0-89608-390-X*); pap. 12.00 (*0-89608-389-6*) South End Pr.

Benello, C. George, et al. Building Sustainable Communities: Tools & Concepts for Self-Reliant Economic Change. 2nd rev. ed. Morehouse, Ward, ed. LC 97-19058. 208p. (Orig.). 1997. 31.50 (*0-942850-37-8*); pap. 16.95 (*0-942850-36-X*) Bootstrap Pr.

Benello, C. George, jt. auth. see Fishman, Walda K.

***Benemann, William, compiled by.** Genre Terms for Law Materials: A Thesaurus. LC 00-27636. (AALL Publications). 31p. 2000. pap. 14.95 (*0-8377-0152-X*, 324510, Rothman) W S Hein.

Benemann, William, ed. A Year of Mud & Gold: San Francisco in Letters & Diaries, 1849-1850. LC 98-55444. (Illus.). 1999. text 29.95 (*0-8032-1293-3*) U of Nebr Pr.

Benemelis, Juan. El Ultimo Comunista. (SPA.). 396p. 1992. pap. write for info. (*0-929441-31-1*) Pubns Puertorriquenas.

Benenate, Becky, ed. see Teresa, Madre.

***Benenberg, Rita.** Rhyme Time Blocks: Applique & Embroidery Patterns. (Illus.). 96p. 2000. pap. 19.95 (*1-57432-752-6*, Am Quilters Soc) Collector Bks.

Benenfeld, Rikki. I Go to School. LC 97-74050. (Illus.). 32p. (J). (ps-k). 1998. 9.95 (*0-922613-82-6*) Hachai Pubng.

Benenson, Abram S. Control of Communicable Diseases Manual. 16th rev. ed. 577p. 1995. pap. 22.00 (*0-87553-222-5*) Am Pub Health.

Benenson, Abram S., ed. Control of Communicable Diseases in Man. 15th ed. 532p. 1990. 15.00 (*0-87553-170-9*) Am Pub Health.

— Control of Communicable Diseases Manual. 16th rev. ed. 577p. 1995. 32.00 (*0-87553-228-4*); 65.00 incl. cd-rom (*0-87553-225-X*) Am Pub Health.

Benenson, Donna. Heirloom Flowers: Old-Fashioned Favorites for Every Garden. (Illus.). 144p. 1999. 27.50 (*1-56799-562-4*, Friedman-Fairfax) M Friedman Pub Grp Inc.

Benenson, Lawrence. The Colin Powell Story. 1996. pap. 4.95 (*0-679-77387-8*) Random.

Benenson, Walter. Lyman Briggs School Physics Laboratory Manual. 188p. 1994. spiral bd. 20.95 (*0-8403-8853-5*) Kendall-Hunt.

Benenzon, Rolando O. Music Therapy, Theory & Manual: Contributions to the Knowledge of Nonverbal Contexts. 2nd ed. LC 96-6334. (Illus.). 296p. 1996. text 59.95 (*0-398-06611-6*); pap. text 44.95 (*0-398-06612-4*) C C Thomas.

Beneri, Marie L. Journey Through Utopia. 338p. 1982. pap. 10.00 (*0-900384-21-2*) Left Bank.

Beneria, Lourdes, ed. Women & Development: The Sexual Division of Labour in Rural Societies. LC 82-606. 278p. 1982. 42.95 (*0-275-90759-7*, C0759, Praeger Pubs) Greenwood.

— Women & Development: The Sexual Division of Labour in Rural Societies. LC 82-606. 278p. 1985. pap. 15.95 (*0-275-91637-5*, B1637, Praeger Pubs) Greenwood.

Beneria, Lourdes & Roldan, Martha. The Crossroads of Class & Gender: Industrial Homework, Subcontracting, & Household Dynamics in Mexico City. LC 86-24901. (Women in Culture & Society Ser.). (Illus.). 216p. (C). 1987. pap. text 19.95 (*0-226-04232-4*); lib. bdg. 42.00 (*0-226-04231-6*) U Ch Pr.

Beneria, Lourdes, ed. see Stimpson, Catharine R.

Benerjee, B. G. Child Development & Socialisation. 156p. 1987. 24.95 (*81-7100-031-2*) Asia Bk Corp.

Benerjee, J. C. Encyclopaedic Dictionary of Psychological Terms. 320p. (C). 1994. pap. 250.00 (*81-85880-28-X*, Pub. by Print Hse) St Mut.

Benerji, S. C. Fundamentals of Ancient Indian Music & Dance. 120p. 1976. 11.95 (*0-318-36326-7*) Asia Bk Corp.

Benes, Edvard. Bohemia's Case for Independence. LC 73-135792. (Eastern Europe Collection). 1971. reprint ed. 12.95 (*0-405-02734-6*) Ayer.

— Masaryk's Path & Legacy: Funeral Oration at the Burial of the President-Liberator, 21 September 1937. LC 77-135793. (Eastern Europe Collection). (Illus.). 1971. reprint ed. 15.95 (*0-405-02735-4*) Ayer.

— Memoirs: From Munich to New War & New Victory. Lias, Godfrey, tr. LC 72-4265. (World Affairs Ser.: National & International Viewpoints). 360p. 1972. reprint ed. 23.95 (*0-405-04561-1*) Ayer.

— My War Memoirs. LC 70-114467. (Illus.). 512p. 1971. reprint ed. lib. bdg. 38.50 (*0-8371-4763-8*, BEMW, Greenwood Pr) Greenwood.

— My War Memories. LC 70-135794. (Eastern Europe Collection). 1971. reprint ed. 30.95 (*0-405-02736-2*) Ayer.

***Benes, Jim.** Chicago Christmas: One Hundred Years of Christmas Wisdom. (Illus.). 298p. 2000. pap. 19.95 (*0-940895-45-5*, Pub. by Cornerstone IL) Midpt Trade.

Benes, Veronica. Lilaveles "A Little Tale" (Illus.). 30p. (J). (ps-4). 1997. 12.97 (*0-9662368-0-7*) V Benes.

Benes, Viktor & Stepan, Josef. Distributions with Given Marginals & Moment Problems. LC 97-16601. 1997. text 154.00 (*0-7923-4573-8*) Kluwer Academic.

Benesch, Friedrich. Energy Crisis. pap. 4.95 (*0-86315-007-1*, 735, Pub. by Floris Bks) Anthroposophic.

Benesch, Friedrich & Wilde, Klaus. Silica, Calcium, & Clay: Processes in Mineral, Plant, Animal, & Man. Breedlove, Charlene, ed. Lauterbach, Eva, tr. LC 95-46337. (Illus.). 1995. pap. 14.95 (*0-935690-05-0*) Schaumburg Pubns.

Benesch, Otto. La Peinture Allemande. (FRE., Illus.). 198p. 1966. lib. bdg. 75.00 (*0-8288-3985-9*) Fr & Eur.

B

An Asterisk (*) at the beginning of an entry indicates that the title is appearing for the first time.

— La Peinture Allemande de Durer a Holbein (Skira) lib. bdg. 50.00 (0-8288-2638-2) Fr & Eur.

Benesch, Sarah, ed. Ending Remediation: Linking ESL & Content in Higher Education. LC 88-50723. 111p. 1988. pap. 14.95 (0-939791-33-1) Tchrs Eng Spkrs.

— ESL in America: Myths & Possibilities. LC 90-43210. 133p. (Orig.). (C). 1990. pap. text 22.00 (0-86709-266-1, 0266, Pub. by Boynton Cook Pubs) Heinemann.

Benesek, Tyne, ed. see Johnson, Laura.

Benesevic, V. Catalogus Codicum Manuscriptorum Graecorum, 2 vols., Set. xxxii, 1008p. 1965. reprint ed. 280.00 incl. 3.5 hd (0-318-70716-0) G Olms Pubs.

Benesh, Bruce K. & Bryant, M. Kevin. Partnership & S Corporation Tax Planning Guide: 1991 Edition. 530p. 1990. pap. text 64.00 (1-878375-16-4) Panel Pubs.

Benesh, Bruce K., et al. Year End Tax Planning for Partnerships & S Corporations: 1992 Edition. 250p. 1991. pap. 59.00 (1-878375-69-5) Panel Pubs.

Benesko, Gary G. Inter-Corporate Business Engineering: Streamlining the Business Cycle from End to End. LC 96-47733. (Illus.). 277p. 1997. 25.00 (1-883872-02-2) Res Triangle.

Benesova. Czech-Italian-Czech Dictionary for Travelers. (CZE & ENG.). 416p. 1983. 13.95 (0-8288-1697-2, M14852) Fr & Eur.

Benest, D. & Froeschle, C., eds. Impacts on Earth. LC 98-3119. (Lecture Notes in Physics: Vol. 505). xvii, 223p. 1998. 68.00 (3-540-64209-9) Spr-Verlag.

Benest, Daniel & Froeschle, Claude, eds. Analysis & Modelling of Discrete Dynamical Systems. (Advances in Discrete Mathematics & Applications Ser.: Vol. 1). 344p. 1998. text 45.00 (90-5699-625-8, ECU58) Gordon & Breach.

***Benest, Frank.** Commit to Learn - Transforming Government from the Inside Out. 100p. 2000. pap. write for info. (1-882403-83-5) The Innovation Grps.

Benest, Frank. Marketing Your Budget: Creative Ways to Engage Citizens in the Bottom Line. Mascenik, William, ed. 125p. 1997. pap. text 38.00 (1-882403-34-7) The Innovation Grps.

— Rightsizing for Local Governments. 94p. 1992. 29.95 (1-882403-04-5) The Innovation Grps.

***Benestad, Finn, ed.** Edvard Grieg: Letters to Colleagues & Friends. Halverson, William H., tr. from NOR. LC 99-74400. (Illus.). xvi, 726p. 2000. 60.00 (0-9645238-2-5) Peer Gynt.

Benestad, J. Brian, ed. see Fortin, Ernest L.

Benestad, J. Brian, ed. & frwd. see Fortin, Ernest L.

Benesty, Jacob, jt. auth. see Gay, Steven L.

Benet, Carol. Sam Shepard on the German Stage: Critics, Politics, Myths. LC 91-18762. (American University Studies: Comparative Literature: Ser. III, Vol. 41). 222p. (C). 1993. text 41.95 (0-8204-1624-X) P Lang Pubng.

Benet, Diana T. Something to Love: Barbara Pym's Novels. LC 85-20976. (Literary Frontiers Ser.: No. 27). 176p. 1986. pap. 14.95 (0-8262-0493-7) U of Mo Pr.

Benet, Diana T. & Lieb, Michael, eds. Literary Milton: Text, Pretext, Context. LC 94-11292. (Duquesne Studies: Language & Literature Ser.: Vol. 16). 274p. (C). 1994. 48.00 (0-8207-0259-5) Duquesne.

Benet, James & Daniels, Arlene K., eds. Education: Straitjacket or Opportunity. LC 78-62887. 199p. 1980. reprint ed. 34.95 (0-87855-298-7) Transaction Pubs.

Benet, Juan. A Meditation. Rabassa, Gregory, tr. from SPA.Tr. of Una Meditacion. 366p. (C). 1983. reprint ed. pap. 8.95 (0-89255-065-1) Persea Bks.

— Return to Region. Rabassa, Gregory, tr. from SPA. LC 84-27467. (Twentieth-Century Continental Fiction Ser.). (Illus.). 320p. 1985. text 52.50 (0-231-05456-4) Col U Pr.

— Return to Region. Rabassa, Gregory, tr. from SPA. LC 84-27467. (Twentieth-Century Continental Fiction Ser.). (Illus.). 320p. 1987. pap. text 19.00 (0-231-05457-2) Col U Pr.

Benet, Juan, adapted by. El Aire de un Crimen, Level 5. (Leer en Espanol Ser.). (SPA.). (C). 1998. pap. 6.95 (84-294-3491-7) Santillana.

Benet, Laura. Famous New England Authors. LC 76-12717. (Illus.). 150p. 1970. 12.95 (0-85699-202-X) Chatham Pr.

— Goods & Chattels. LC 74-142258. (Short Story Index Reprint Ser.). 1977. 19.95 (0-8369-3742-2) Ayer.

Benet, Leslie Z., et al. Pharmacokinetics: A Modern View. Levy, Gerhard & Ferraiolo, B. L., eds. LC 84-15011. 548p. 1984. 95.00 (0-306-41810-X, Plenum Trade) Perseus Pubng.

Benet, Lorenzo, jt. auth. see Hamilton, Scott.

Benet, Lorenzo, jt. auth. see Parker, Star.

Benet McKinney, Mary. Sharing Wisdom. 1986. pap. 9.95 (0-88347-365-8, 661-155 7365) T More.

***Benet, Rosemary, et al.** Johnny Appleseed. LC 99-89391. (Illus.). (J). 2001. write for info. (0-689-82975-2) McElderry Bks.

Benet, Rosemary, jt. auth. see Benet, Stephen Vincent.

Benet, Stephen Vincent. The Devil & Daniel Webster. 12.95 (0-8488-0789-8) Amereon Ltd.

— The Devil & Daniel Webster. 1943. pap. 3.25 (0-8222-0303-0) Dramatists Play.

— Devil & Daniel Webster. Date not set. pap. 9.95 (0-8488-2188-2) Amereon Ltd.

***Benet, Stephen Vincent.** The Devil & Daniel Webster & Other Writings. Ludington, Townsend, ed. & intro. by. LC 99-29999. 400p. 1999. pap. 13.95 (0-14-043740-1, Penguin Classics) Viking Penguin.

Benet, Stephen Vincent. James Shore's Daughter. LC 73-131620. 1934. reprint ed. 39.00 (0-403-00507-8) Scholarly.

— John Brown's Body. 25.95 (0-8488-0916-5) Amereon Ltd.

— John Brown's Body. 1961. pap. 5.25 (0-8222-0594-7) Dramatists Play.

— John Brown's Body. 1982. reprint ed. lib. bdg. 27.95 (0-89966-405-9) Buccaneer Bks.

— John Brown's Body. 340p. 1990. reprint ed. pap. 14.95 (0-929587-26-X, Elephant Paperbacks) I R Dee.

— Johnny Pye. 1994. pap. 6.00 (0-8222-1307-9) Dramatists Play.

— Last Circle. LC 72-10776. (Short Story Index Reprint Ser.). 1977. reprint ed. 23.95 (0-8369-4217-5) Ayer.

— Spanish Bayonet. LC 73-131621. 1926. reprint ed. 29.00 (0-685-27275-3) Scholarly.

— Stephen Vincent Benet's Stories of America. adapted ed. 1971. pap. 5.25 (0-8222-1080-0) Dramatists Play.

— Thirteen O'Clock, Stories of Several Worlds. LC 78-152935. (Short Story Index Reprint Ser.). 1977. reprint ed. 26.95 (0-8369-3793-7) Ayer.

Benet, Stephen Vincent & Benet, Rosemary. A Book of Americans. LC 33-27433. (Illus.). 128p. (J). (gr. 4-6). 1995. pap. 5.95 (0-8050-0297-9, Bks Young Read) H Holt & Co.

Benet, Stephen Vincent, et al. Zero Hour: A Summons to the Free. LC 71-156734. (Essay Index Reprint Ser.). 1977. reprint ed. 20.95 (0-8369-2341-3) Ayer.

Benet, Sula. Song, Dance, & Customs of Peasant Poland. LC 96-13450. 1996. 24.95 (0-7818-0447-7) Hippocrene Bks.

— Song, Dance, & Customs of Peasant Poland. LC 76-44690. reprint ed. 37.50 (0-404-15906-0) AMS Pr.

Benet, William R. First Person Singular. 1988. reprint ed. lib. bdg. 59.00 (0-7812-0375-9) Rprt Serv.

Beneteau, Andre. Etude Sur L'Inspiration et L'Influence De Paul Verlaine. LC 71-94198. (Catholic University of America. Studies in Romance Languages & Literatures: No. 2). (FRE.). reprint ed. 37.50 (0-404-50302-0) AMS Pr.

***Beneti Jornet, Josep M.** Legacy. Zatlin, Phyllis, ed. De Cesaris, Janet, tr. from CAT. LC 99-71172. (Contemporary Spanish Plays Ser.: Vol. 17). (Illus.). xiv, 50p. 2000. pap. 8.00 (1-888463-09-0) Estreno.

Benett, Yves, et al. GNVQ Induction Pack. 250p. 1996. ring bd. 199.00 (0-7494-1852-4, Kogan Pg Educ) Stylus Pub VA.

Benetti, Mara, tr. see Maraini, Dacia.

Benevento, Joe. Holding On. 78p. (Orig.). 1996. pap. 10.00 (0-614-24049-2) Warthog Pr.

Benevidez, Dominque R. A Guide to Understanding Unconscious Mind of a Mother In-Law. 50p. (C). 1995. pap. text 8.00 (0-9648001-0-1) Anaren Pubng.

Benevolo, Leonardo. History of Modern Architecture, 2 vols. Incl. Vol. 1. Tradition of Modern Architecture. 1977. pap. text 23.00 (0-262-52044-3); Vol. 2. Modern Movement. 1977. pap. text 25.00 (0-262-52045-1); 1977. Set pap. text 42.50 (0-262-52046-X) MIT Pr.

Benevot, Maurice, ed. see Cyprian of Carthage, St.

***Benewick, Robert & Donald, Stephanie.** The State of China Atlas. 128p. 1999. pap. 17.95 (0-14-051458-9, Penguin Bks) Viking Penguin.

Benewick, Robert & Green, Philip. The Routledge Dictionary of Twentieth Century Political Thinkers. 2nd ed. LC 97-11585. 296p. (C). 1998. 85.00 (0-415-15881-8); pap. 25.99 (0-415-09623-5) Routledge.

Beney, Peter. Atlanta: A Brave & Beautiful City. LC 94-18398. (Illus.). 144p. 1994. 37.50 (1-56145-098-7); pap. 22.00 (1-56145-095-2) Peachtree Pubs.

— Majesty of Colonial Williamsburg. LC 96-41796. (Illus.). 160p. 1997. 29.95 (0-88289-993-7); pap. text 19.95 (1-56554-249-5) Pelican.

— The Majesty of Colonial Williamsburg. (Majesty Architecture Ser.). 1997. 29.95 (0-614-28059-1) Pelican Publishing Co.

***Beney, Peter.** Majesty of Colonial Williamsburg Postcard Book. 2000. pap. text 9.95 (1-56554-761-6) Pelican.

Beney, Peter. The Majesty of Savannah. LC 92-10968. (Illus.). 96p. 1992. 15.95 (0-88289-906-6) Pelican.

Beney, Peter, photos by. Beautiful Atlanta. (Illus.). 28p. 1995. pap. 8.95 (1-56145-116-9) Peachtree Pubs.

— Beautiful Georgia. (Illus.). 28p. 1995. pap. 8.95 (1-56145-117-7) Peachtree Pubs.

Beney, Peter, photos by. The Majesty of Charleston. LC 93-10099. (Illus.). 96p. 1993. 15.95 (0-88289-955-4) Pelican.

***Beney, Zsuzsa.** Between Words & Silence. 126p. 2000. pap. 16.95 (1-899197-50-8, Pub. by Mares Nest Pub) Dufour.

Benezet, A. Some Historical Account of Guinea. 131p. 1968. reprint ed. 37.50 (0-7146-1888-8, Pub. by F Cass Pubs) Intl Spec Bk.

Benezet, Anthony. Anthony Benezet. LC 77-152916. (Black Heritage Library Collection). 1977. 18.95 (0-8369-8760-8) Ayer.

Benezet, Anthony & Wesley, John. Views of American Slavery. LC 78-82171. (Anti-Slavery Crusade in America Ser.). 1975. reprint ed. 21.95 (0-405-00610-1) Ayer.

Benezet, Louis T. General Education in the Progressive College. LC 70-165704. (American Education Ser, No. 2). 1974. reprint ed. 17.95 (0-405-03693-0) Ayer.

Benezit. Dictionnaire Critique et Documentaire des Peintres, Sculpteurs, Dessinateurs, et Graveurs de Tous les Temps et de Tous les Pays, 10 tomes, Set. (FRE.). 1976. 895.00 (0-8288-5635-4, F1850) Fr & Eur.

— Dictionnaire des Peintres, Sculpteurs, Dessinateurs, Graveurs. (FRE.). 13500p. 1999. 1795.00 (0-320-00675-1) Fr & Eur.

— Dictionnaire des Peintres, Sculpteurs, Dessinateurs, Graveurs. deluxe ed. (FRE.). 13500p. 1999. 4500.00 (0-320-00676-X) Fr & Eur.

Benezit, E. Dictionary of Painters, Sculptors & Graphic Artists, 10 vols., Set. rev. ed. (FRE., Illus.). 1976. 550.00 (2-7000-0149-4) Edns Publisol.

— Dictionnaire des Peintres, Sculpteurs, Dessinateurs et Graveurs: Nouvelle Edition, 10 vols., Set. (FRE.). 7400p. 1976. reprint ed. lib. bdg. 650.00 (2-7000-0157-5, Pub. by Lib Grund) Dealers Choice.

Benezit, Emmanuel. Dictionnaire Critique et Documentaire der Peintres, Sculpteurs, Dessinateurs et Graveurs, 10 vols. (FRE.). 1976. 750.00 (0-8150-0844-9) Wittenborn Art.

***BenEzra, D., ed.** Mediterranean Opthalmological Society Congress - Michaelson Symposium on Ocular Circulation & Neovascularization: VIth Congress, VIth Symposium, Jerusalem, May 2000: Abstracts. (Opthalmologica Ser.: Vol. 214, No. 3 (2000)). (Illus.). 72p. 2000. pap. 25.25 (3-8055-7105-4) S Karger.

— Uveitis Update. LC 99-40686. (Developments in Ophthalmology Ser.: Vol. 31). (Illus.). viii, 190p. 1999. 165.25 (3-8055-6891-6) S Karger.

Benezra, D., et al, eds. Ocular Circulation & Neovascularization. (Documenta Ophthalmologica Proceedings Ser.). (C). 1987. lib. bdg. 285.50 (0-89838-892-9) Kluwer Academic.

Benezra, D., et al. Optimal Use of Sandimmun in Endogenous Uveitis. (Illus.). 30p. 1988. 39.95 (0-387-18878-9) Spr-Verlag.

***BenEzra, David, ed.** Ocular Inflammation: Basic & Clinical Concepts. 512p. 1999. 199.95 (1-85317-507-2, Pub. by Martin Dunitz) Blackwell Sci.

Benezra, Neal. Martin Puryear. LC 91-2366. (Illus.). 160p. 1991. pap. 29.95 (0-86559-092-3) Art Inst Chi.

— Martin Puryear. LC 91-65308. (Illus.). 160p. 1993. pap. 29.95 (0-500-27702-8, Pub. by Thames Hudson) Norton.

— Stephan Balkenhol: Sculptures & Drawings. LC 95-32948. 116p. 1996. 55.00 (3-89322-770-9, Pub. by Edition Cantz) Dist Art Pubs.

Benezra, Neal & Viso, Olga M. Distemper: Dissonant Themes in the Art of the 1990s. (Illus.). 144p. 1996. pap. 32.95 (1-881616-73-8, 620671) Dist Art Pubs.

Benezra, Neal, et al. Bruce Nauman: Exhibition Catalogue. Simon, Joan, ed. LC 94-2902. (Illus.). 232p. (Orig.). 1994. pap. 35.00 (0-935640-42-8) Walker Art Ctr.

— Ed Paschke. LC 89-28252. (Illus.). 156p. 1996. 25.00 (0-86559-084-2) Hudson Hills.

Benezra, Neal D. Regarding Beauty: A View of the Late Twentieth Century. LC 99-14570. 1999. pap. 55.00 (3-89322-782-2) Dr Cantz sche Druckerei GmbH.

Benezra, Neal D., et al. Regarding Beauty: A View of the Late Twentieth Century. LC 99-14570. 1999. write for info. (3-89322-779-2) Dr Cantz sche Druckerei GmbH.

Benfari, Robert. Understanding Your Management Style: Beyond the Meyers-Briggs Type Indicator. 202p. 1991. 25.95 (0-669-24814-2) Jossey-Bass.

***Benfari, Robert C.** Understanding & Changing Your Management Style. LC 99-27759. 282p. 1999. 25.00 (0-7879-0858-4) Jossey-Bass.

***Benfatto, M., et al, eds.** Theory & Computation for Synchrotron Radiation Spectroscopy. LC 00-101911. (AIP Conference Proceedings Ser.: Vol. 514). (Illus.). viii, 164p. 2000. 75.00 (1-56396-936-X, Pub. by Am Inst Physics) Spr-Verlag.

Benfer, Robert A., et al. Expert Systems. (Quantitative Applications in the Social Sciences Ser.: Vol. 77). (Illus.). 96p. 1991. pap. 10.95 (0-8039-4036-X) Sage.

Benfey, Christopher. Degas in New Orleans: Encounters in the Creole World of Kate Chopin & George Washington Cable. LC 97-2817. (Illus.). 294p. 1997. 27.50 (0-679-43562-X) Knopf.

— Emily Dickinson: Lives of a Poet. 1986. 19.95 (0-8076-1150-6); pap. 12.95 (0-8076-1151-4) Braziller.

Benfey, Christopher E. Degas in New Orleans: Encounters in the Creole World of Kate Chopin & George Washington Cable. LC 98-36121. 294p. 1999. pap. 16.95 (0-520-21818-3, Pub. by U CA Pr) Cal Prin Full Svc.

— Emily Dickinson & the Problem of Others. LC 84-2520. 144p. 1984. lib. bdg. 22.50 (0-87023-437-4) U of Mass Pr.

Benfey, Otto Theodor. Friends & the World of Nature. LC 80-82941. 28p. (Orig.). 1980. pap. 4.00 (0-87574-233-5) Pendle Hill.

— From Vital Force to Structural Formulas. (BCHOC Publication: No. 10). (Illus.). 116p. 1964. reprint ed. pap. 18.00 (0-941901-09-2, QD476.B4 1992) Chem Heritage Fnd.

— Introduction to Organic Reaction Mechanisms. LC 80-12301. 224p. 1982. reprint ed. 22.50 (0-89874-173-4) Krieger.

— Kleinere Schriften, 2 vols. in 1. xl, 432p. 1975. reprint ed. 160.00 (3-487-05579-1) G Olms Pubs.

— The Names & Structures of Organic Compounds. LC 82-10012. 228p. (C). 1982. reprint ed. pap. text 18.50 (0-89874-520-9) Krieger.

Benfey, Otto Theodor, ed. Introducing the Chemical Sciences: A CHF Reading List. LC 96-149668. 12p. (Orig.). 1994. pap. 5.00 (0-941901-11-4) Chem Heritage Fnd.

— Kekule Centennial. LC 66-30726. (Advances in Chemistry Ser.: No. 61). 1966. 21.95 (0-8412-0062-9) Am Chemical.

Benfey, Otto Theodor, jt. auth. see Bowden, Mary E.

Benfey, Otto Theodor, tr. see Aftalion, Fred.

Benfey, Otto Theodor, tr. see Watanabe, Masao.

Benfey, Theodore. Sanskrit-English Dictionary. (ENG, GRE, LAT & SAN.). 1145p. 1982. 55.00 (0-8288-1154-7, M14104) Fr & Eur.

Benfield & Alces. Commercial Paper & Alternative Payment Systems. 1987. teacher ed. write for info. (0-8205-0152-2) Bender.

Benfield & Mynster. Business Communication Practice. 90p. (C). 1997. per. 12.95 (0-7872-4434-1, 41443401) Kendall-Hunt.

Benfield, Cynthia M., jt. auth. see Liggett, Twila C.

Benfield, Derek. Running Riot: A Farcical Comedy in Three Acts. LC 86-146867. (Evans Drama Library). 95 p. 1980. write for info. (0-237-49035-8) EVN1 UK.

Benfield, Eric. Purbeck Shop: A Stoneworker's Story of Stone. (C). 1989. 39.00 (1-85455-035-7, Pub. by Ensign Pubns & Print) St Mut.

Benfield, Jack. Benfield Conduit Bending Manual. (Illus.). 109p. (Orig.). 1980. pap. 16.95 (0-87288-510-0) Intertec Pub.

Benfield, Kaid, et al. Once There Were Greenfields: How Urban Sprawl Is Undermining America's Environment, Economy, Social Fabric. LC 99-19928. 1999. pap. 20.00 (1-893340-17-1) Natl Resources Defense Coun.

Benfield, Marion W., Jr. & Hawkland, William D. Sales: Teacher's Manual for Cases & Materials On. 3rd ed. (University Casebook Ser.). 103p. (C). 1992. pap. text. write for info. (1-56662-028-7) Foundation Pr.

— Sales, Cases & Materials On. 3rd ed. (University Casebook Ser.). 605p. 1992. text 36.00 (0-88277-975-3) Foundation Pr.

Benfield, Marion W., Jr., jt. auth. see Alces, Peter A.

Benfield, R. E., et al. Structures & Biological Effects. LC 93-15374. (Structure & Bonding Ser.: Vol. 81). 1993. 119.00 (0-387-56481-0) Spr-Verlag.

Benfield, Steve, jt. ed. see MacDonald, Michael.

Benfield, Warren A. & Dean, James S., Jr. The Art of Double Bass Playing. (Illus.). 40p. 1973. pap. text 8.95 (0-87487-081-X) Summy-Birchard.

Benfold, G. God at Work. 1995. pap. text 4.99 (0-946462-38-0, Pub. by Evangelical Pr) P & R Pubng.

Benforado, Sally. Bring Me a Story. (Mujer Latina Ser.). 66p. 14.95 (0-915745-11-9); pap. 14.95 (0-685-45618-8) Floricanto Pr.

— Bring Me a Story. rev. ed. (J). (gr. 6-10). 14.95 (0-915745-08-9) Floricanto Pr.

***Benford.** Macmillan Compendium of Social Issues. 942p. 1998. 115.00 (0-02-865055-7) Macmillan Gen Ref.

Benford & Ortega. Introductory Sociology: A Reader. (Sociology - Intro Level Ser.). 2001. pap. text 22.00 (0-534-52789-2) Wadsworth Pub.

Benford, Daniel P. Born to Be Lucky: An Autobiography by Daniel P. Benford. LC 94-71594. (Illus.). 300p. 1994. 9.95 (1-882183-34-7) A Page.

Benford Design Group Staff. Small Ships: A Book of Study Plans of Tugs, Freighters, Ferries, Excursion Boats, Trawler Yachts, Houseboats & Fishing Vessels. 3rd ed. 1996. pap. text 25.00 (0-07-006001-0) McGraw.

Benford, Gregory. Across the Sea of Suns. LC 83-17851. 400p. 1984. 25.00 (0-671-44668-1) Ultramarine Pub.

— Against Infinity. 256p. 1998. mass mkt. 5.99 (0-380-79058-0, Eos) Morrow Avon.

— Against Infinity. 1983. 25.00 (0-671-46491-4) Ultramarine Pub.

— Artifact. LC 85-231016. (Illus.). 432p. 1998. reprint ed. mass mkt. 6.99 (0-380-79195-1, Eos) Morrow Avon.

— Cosm. LC 97-29652. 352p. 1998. mass mkt. 23.00 (0-380-97435-5, Eos) Morrow Avon.

— Cosm. LC 97-29652. 384p. 1999. mass mkt. 6.99 (0-380-79052-1, Eos) Morrow Avon.

***Benford, Gregory.** Deep Time: How Humanity Communicates Across Millennia. LC 98-41085. (Illus.). 240p. 1999. 20.00 (0-380-97537-8, Avon Bks) Morrow Avon.

— The Eater. LC 99-57969. 352p. 2000. 24.00 (0-380-97436-3) Morrow Avon.

Benford, Gregory. Foundation's Fear. (Foundation Trilogy Ser.: Vol. 2). 616p. 2000. mass mkt. 6.99 (0-06-105638-3, HarperPrism) HarpC.

***Benford, Gregory.** Human Being. 2001. write for info. (0-380-97716-8, Wm Morrow) Morrow Avon.

Benford, Gregory. Jupiter Project. 208p. (Orig.). 1998. reprint ed. mass mkt. 5.99 (0-380-79057-2, Eos) Morrow Avon.

***Benford, Gregory.** The Martian Race. LC 99-52492. 352p. 1999. 23.95 (0-446-52633-9, Pub. by Warner Bks) Little.

— The Martian Race. 2001. mass mkt. 6.99 (0-446-60890-4, Aspect) Warner Bks.

Benford, Gregory. Matter's End. deluxe limited ed. (Illus.). 84p. 1990. boxed set 115.00 (0-941826-20-1) Cheap St.

***Benford, Gregory.** Nebula Awards Showcase 2000: The Years Best SF & Fantasy Chosen by the Science-Fiction & Fantasy Writers of America. 320p. 2000. 28.00 (0-15-100479-X) Harcourt.

— Nebula Awards Showcase 2000: The Year's Best SF & Fantasy Chosen by the Science-Fiction & Fantasy Writers of America. 320p. 2000. pap. text 14.00 (0-15-600705-3) Harcourt.

Benford, Gregory. Sailing Bright Eternity. 464p. 1996. mass mkt. 5.99 (0-553-57332-2) Bantam.

— Skylife: Visions of Our Homes in Space. LC 99-45540. (J). 2000. pap. write for info. (0-15-600528-X, Harcourt Child Bks) Harcourt.

— Timescape. 512p. 1992. mass mkt. 6.99 (0-553-29709-0) Bantam.

***Benford, Gregory.** Worlds Vast & Various: Stories. 320p. 2000. pap. 13.50 (0-380-79054-8, Avon Bks) Morrow Avon.

Benford, Gregory, ed. Far Futures. 352p. 1997. pap. 15.95 (0-312-86379-9) St Martin.

— The New Hugo Winners, No. 4. 4th ed. 544p. 1997. per. 6.99 (0-671-87852-2) Baen Bks.

Benford, Gregory & Brin, David. Heart of the Comet. 496p. (Orig.). 1987. mass mkt. 6.99 (0-553-25839-7, Spectra) Bantam.

Benford, Gregory & Rotsler, William. Shiva Descending. 400p. 1992. mass mkt. 5.99 (0-8125-1690-7, Pub. by Tor Bks) St Martin.

Benford, Gregory, jt. auth. see Martin, Mark O.

***Benford, Gregory A.** Deep Time: How Humanity Communicates Across Millennia. 2000. pap. 13.00 (0-380-79346-6) Morrow Avon.

An Asterisk (*) at the beginning of an entry indicates that the title is appearing for the first time.

Benford, Harry. Naval Architecture for Non-Naval Architects. (Illus.). 239p. 1991. text 29.50 (*0-939773-08-2*) Soc Naval Arch.
NAVAL ARCHITECTURE FOR NON-NAVAL ARCHITECTS is written in engaging & easily understood terms, this volume concentrates on two aspects of naval architecture: design & analysis. Technical discussions are almost entirely qualitative rather than quantitative & coverage focuses on conventional ships & boats while answering questions about such matters as the proposed vessel's seaworthiness, structural integrity, powering requirements, & functional capability. List $29.50, Members $19.50. The Society of Naval Architects & Marine Engineers, 601 Pavonia Ave., Jersey City, NJ 07306. phone: 201-798-4800. FAX: 201-798-4975. website: http://www.sname.org. *Publisher Paid Annotation.*

— What Every Young Girl Should Know Before She Marries a Naval Architect. 48p. (Orig.). 1985. pap. text 6.00 (*0-931781-01-9*) Jennings Pr.

***Benford, Harry S.** The Gilbert & Sullivan Lexicon. 3rd rev. enl. ed. LC 99-22606. (Illus.). 1999. 25.95 (*0-9667916-1-4*) Queensbury Pr.

Benford, Henry, ed. A Half Century of Maritime Technology: 1943-1993. (Illus.). 616p. 1993. 60.00 (*0-939773-12-0*, HCM) Soc Naval Arch.

Benford, Jay R. Cruising Designs. 4th ed. LC 99-233848. (Illus.). 96p. 1996. pap. 15.95 (*1-888671-00-9*) Tiller.

— Pocket Cruisers & Tabloid Yachts, Vol. 1. rev. ed. LC 99-234170. (Illus.). 96p. 1996. pap. 17.95 (*1-888671-04-1*) Tiller.

— Small Craft Plans. rev. ed. LC 99-234177. (Illus.). 96p. 1997. pap. 17.95 (*1-888671-05-X*) Tiller.

— Small Ship. 4th ed. LC 99-461759. 1997. pap. 25.00 (*1-888671-06-8*) Tiller.

Benford, R. L. Proposal for Gearing Velocity Standard. (Technical Papers: Vol. P109.17). (Illus.). 16p. 1966. pap. text 30.00 (*1-55589-181-0*) AGMA.

Benford, R. L., jt. auth. see Mansfield, D. L.

Benford, S., jt. ed. see Bowers, J.

Benford, Timothy B. World War II Quiz & Fact Book. 1993. 9.98 (*0-88365-826-7*) Galahad Bks.

— World War II Quiz & Fact Book. 1993. 9.98 (*0-88394-086-8*) Promntory Pr.

— WWII Quiz & Fact Book. LC 98-11362. 1999. 7.99 (*0-517-20281-6*) Random Hse Value.

Benford, Tom. Introducing Desktop Video. 350p. 1995. pap. 34.95 incl. cd-rom (*1-55828-415-X*, MIS Pr) IDG Bks.

Benford, Tom. Welcome to . . . CD Rom. 1995. pap. 19.95 (*1-55828-265-3*, MIS Pr) IDG Bks.

— Welcome to PC Sound, Music & MIDI. 1995. pap. 29.95 (*1-55828-316-1*, MIS Pr) IDG Bks.

Beng-Huat Chua. Communitarian Ideology & Democracy. LC 94-39923. (Politics in Asia Ser.). 256p. (C). (gr. 13). 1995. 90.00 (*0-415-12054-3*, C0093) Routledge.

Beng, Tan H., photos by. Tropical Retreats: The Poetics of Place. (Illus.). 288p. 1998. 39.95 (*981-00-8245-2*) Gingko Press.

Beng, Tan H., jt. auth. see Lim, William S.

***Beng, Tan Hock.** Indonesian Accents. 216p. 1999. 39.95 (*0-934590-70-2*) Visual Refer.

Beng, Tan Hock. Tropical Paradises: Lifestyle, Resorts of Asia. 208p. 1999. text 40.00 (*0-8230-5451-9*) Watsn-Guptill.

Benga, Gheorghe. Structure & Properties of Cell Membranes: Molecular Basis of Selected Transport Systems, Vol. II: Molecular Basis of Selected Transport Sys. LC 84-19942. 304p. 1985. 149.00 (*0-8493-5765-9*, QH509, CRC Reprint) Franklin.

— Water Transport in Biological Membranes, Vol. I. 304p. 1988. 135.00 (*0-8493-6082-X*, QH509, CRC Reprint) Franklin.

— Water Transport in Biological Membranes, Vol. II. 304p. 1988. 170.00 (*0-8493-6083-8*, QH509, CRC Reprint) Franklin.

Benga, Gheorghe, ed. Structure & Properties of Cell Membranes: Survey of Molecular Aspects of Membrane Structure & Function, Vol. I. LC 84-19943. 240p. 1985. 138.00 (*0-8493-5764-0*, QH601, CRC Reprint) Franklin.

— Structure & Properties of Cell Membranes: Survey of Molecular Aspects of Membrane Structure & Function, 3 vols., Vol. III: Methodology & Propertiese of Membrane. LC 84-19943. 304p. 1985. 170.00 (*0-8493-5766-7*, QH601, CRC Reprint) Franklin.

Benga, Gheorghe & Tager, J. M., eds. Biomembranes. (Illus.). 235p. 1988. 103.95 (*0-387-18879-7*) Spr-Verlag.

***Benge, Dorothy L. & Sullivan, Laura M., eds.** Los Islenos Cookbook: Canary Island Recipes. LC 99-462379. (Illus.). 460p. 2000. pap. 14.95 (*1-56554-760-8*) Pelican.

Benge, Eugene J. Elements of Modern Management. LC 76-25179. 232p. reprint ed. pap. 72.00 (*0-608-16160-8*, 202358500033) Bks Demand.

Benge, Geoff, jt. auth. see Benge, Janet.

Benge, Geoffrey Francis, jt. auth. see Benge, Janet Hazel.

Benge, Glenn F. Antoine-Louis Barye: Sculptor of Romantic Realism. (Illus.). 210p. 1984. 75.00 (*0-271-00362-6*) A Wofsy Fine Arts.

***Benge, Harvey.** Vital Signs. 2000. 35.00 (*1-899235-47-7*) Dewi Lewis.

***Benge, Janet.** Christian Heroes: Then & Now, 2 vols., Vol. 1-2. 1999. pap. 6.99 (*1-57658-173-X*) YWAM Pub.

Benge, Janet. Christian Heroes: Then & Now, Jim Elliot. 1999. pap. text 8.99 (*1-57658-146-2*) YWAM Pub.

— Corrie Ten Boom: Keeper of the Angel's Den. LC 98-30891. (Christian Heroes Ser.). (gr. 5-9). 1998. pap. text 8.99 (*1-57658-136-5*) YWAM Pub.

***Benge, Janet.** David Livingstone. 1999. pap. text 6.99 (*1-57658-153-5*) YWAM Pub.

Benge, Janet. Eric Liddel: Something Greater Than Gold. LC 98-30892. (Christian Heroes Ser.). (gr. 5-9). 1998. pap. 8.99 (*1-57658-137-3*) YWAM Pub.

***Benge, Janet.** George Mueller. 1999. pap. text 6.99 (*1-57658-145-4*) YWAM Pub.

— Mary Slessor. 1999. pap. text 8.99 (*1-57658-148-9*) YWAM Pub.

Benge, Janet. William Carey: Obliged to Go. LC 98-48980. 1998. 6.99 (*1-57658-147-0*) YWAM Pub.

***Benge, Janet & Benge, Geoff.** Adoniram Judson: Bound for Burma. (Christian Heroes Ser.: Vol. 12). 232p. (YA). (gr. 5 up). 2000. pap. 8.99 (*1-57658-161-6*) YWAM Pub.

Benge, Janet & Benge, Geoff. Amy Carmichael: Rescuer of Precious Gems. LC 98-23396. (Christian Heroes Ser.). 203p. 1998. pap. 8.99 (*1-57658-018-0*) YWAM Pub.

***Benge, Janet & Benge, Geoff.** Cameron Townsend: Good News in Every Language. (Christian Heroes Ser.: Vol. 13). 232p. (YA). (gr. 5 up). 2000. pap. 8.99 (*1-57658-164-0*) YWAM Pub.

Benge, Janet & Benge, Geoff. George Washington Carver, What Do You See? LC 96-15489. (Another Great Achiever Ser.). (Illus.). 48p. (J). (gr. 3). 1997. lib. bdg. 14.95 (*1-57537-102-2*) Advance Pub.

— George Washington Carver, What Do You See? LC 96-15489. (Another Great Achiever Ser.). (Illus.). (J). (gr. 3-6). 1997. 9.95 (*1-57537-101-4*) Advance Pub.

— Gladys Aylward: The Adventure of a Lifetime. LC 98-19368. (Christian Heroes Ser.). 203p. (J). 1998. pap. 8.99 (*1-57658-019-9*) YWAM Pub.

Benge, Janet & Benge, Geoff. Helen Keller--Facing Her Challenges, Challenging the World. (Another Great Achiever Ser.). (Illus.). (J). (gr. 3). 9.95 (*1-57537-107-3*) Advance Pub.

Benge, Janet & Benge, Geoff. Hudson Taylor: Deep in the Heart of China. LC 98-21283. (Christian Heroes Ser.). 205p. (J). (gr. 5-9). 1998. pap. 8.99 (*1-57658-016-4*) YWAM Pub.

— Nate Saint: On a Wing & a Prayer. LC 98-7287. (Christian Heroes Ser.). 201p. (J). 1998. pap. 8.99 (*1-57658-017-2*) YWAM Pub.

Benge, Janet Hazel & Benge, Geoffrey Francis. Helen Keller--Facing Her Challenges, Challenging the World. LC 99-33410. (Another Great Achiever Ser.). (Illus.). 48p. (J). (gr. 3-6). 2000. lib. bdg. 9.95 (*1-57537-105-7*) Advance Pub.

Benge, Ken. The Art of Juggling. LC 77-73876. (Illus.). 144p. 1977. pap. 4.95 (*0-89037-120-2*) Anderson World.

— The Art of Juggling. LC 77-73876. (Illus.). 129p. 1977. reprint ed. pap. 9.95 (*0-917643-01-1*) B Dube.

Benge, Michael & Raleigh, Duane. Rock: Tools & Technique. 2nd ed. LC 95-61192. (Illus.). 128p. (Orig.). 1997. reprint ed. pap. text 11.95 (*1-887216-01-4*, 97004) Elk Mtn Pr.

***Benge, Polly.** Tea for Two: With No Cups. 256p. 2000. pap. 14.95 (*0-9530575-9-3*, Pub. by Travellerseye Ltd) Midpt Trade.

Benge, R. C. Confessions of a Lapsed Librarian. LC 83-20405. 233p. 1984. 26.50 (*0-8108-1676-8*) Scarecrow.

— Technical & Vocational Education in the United Kingdom: A Bibliographical Survey (UNESCO) (Education Studies & Documents: No. 27). 1974. reprint ed. pap. 25.00 (*0-8115-1351-3*) Periodicals Srv.

Benge, Ronald C. Libraries & Cultural Change. LC 71-467778. 278p. reprint ed. pap. 86.20 (*0-7837-5315-2*, 204505400005) Bks Demand.

Benge, Sophie. Private Hong Kong: Where East Meets West. LC 97-21956. (Illus.). 216p. 1997. 50.00 (*0-7892-0342-1*) Abbeville Pr.

— Private Hong Kong: Where East Meets West. (Illus.). 216p. 1999. 17.98 (*0-89660-107-2*, Artabras) Abbeville Pr.

— The Tropical Spa: Asian Secrets of Health, Beauty & Rejuvination. (Illus.). 192p. 1999. pap. 39.95 (*962-593-265-8*) Tuttle Pubng.

***Benge, Sophie & Tettoni, Luca Invernizzi.** Asian Secrets of Health, Beauty, & Relaxation. (Illus.). 128p. 2001. pap. 24.95 (*962-593-854-0*) Tuttle Pubng.

Bengel, Juergen, jt. ed. see Bartsch, Hans H.

Bengel, Wolfgang, et al. Differential Diagnosis of Diseases of the Oral Mucosa. (Illus.). 361p. 1988. text 78.00 (*0-86715-204-4*) Quint Pub Co.

Bengelsdorf, Carollee. The Problem of Democracy in Cuba: Between Vision & Reality. 240p. 1994. pap. text 23.95 (*0-19-509014-4*) OUP.

Bengelsdorf, Winnie. Ethnic Studies in Higher Education. Cordasco, Francesco, ed. LC 77-90407. (Bilingual-Bicultural Education in the U. S. Ser.). 1978. reprint ed. lib. bdg. 28.95 (*0-405-11076-6*) Ayer.

Benger, Wendy. Jobs. (Illus.). 24p. (J). (gr. k-2). 1998. text 4.95 (*1-879835-45-2*, Kaeden) Kaeden Corp.

BenGershom, Ezra. David: Testimony of a Holocaust Survivor. Underwood, J. A., tr. from GER. 320p. 1988. 32.00 (*0-85496-222-0*) Berg Pubs.

Bengesco, G. Voltaire Bibliographie de ses Oeuvres: Paris, 1882-1890, 4 vols. 1974. 280.00 (*0-318-23472-6*) Periodicals Srv.

Bengesser, Gerhard. Wechselbeziehungen zwischen Psychiatrie, Psychologie und Philosophie, Vol. 2. (European University Studies: Ser. 6, Vol. 94). (GER.). 178p. 1982. 26.00 (*3-261-05019-5*) P Lang Pubng.

Bengeyfield, Pete. Mountains & Mesas: The Northern Rockies & the Colorado Plateau. LC 95-48042. (Western Horizons Bks.). (Illus.). 160p. (Orig.). 1996. pap. 17.95 (*0-87358-608-5*) Northland AZ.

Benghiat, Norma, jt. auth. see DeMers, John.

Benghiat, Suzy. Middle Eastern Cooking. 1993. 12.98 (*1-55521-940-3*) Bk Sales Inc.

Bengio, Ofra. Saddam's Word: The Political Discourse in Iraq. LC 97-2308. (Studies in Middle Eastern History). 288p. (C). 1998. text 52.00 (*0-19-511439-6*) OUP.

Bengio, Ofra, ed. Saddam Speaks on the Gulf Crisis: A Collection of Documents. (Contemporary Issues in the Middle East Ser.). 220p. 1992. pap. text 17.95 (*0-8156-7055-9*) Syracuse U Pr.

***Bengio, Ofra & Ben-Dor, Gabriel, eds.** Minorities & the State in the Arab World. LC 98-37994. 224p. 1998. lib. bdg. 49.95 (*1-55587-647-1*) L Rienner.

Bengio, Yoshua. Artificial Neural Networks & Their Application to Sequence Recognition. LC 97-17299. (Illus.). 256p. 1995. mass mkt. 56.95 (*1-85032-170-1*) ITCP.

— Artificial Neural Networks & Their Applications. (C). 1995. mass mkt. 59.95 (*0-412-57170-6*) Chapman & Hall.

Bengisson, Ann M. Managing Mergers & Acquisitions: A European Perspective. 192p. 1992. 63.95 (*0-566-07304-8*, Pub. by Gower) Ashgate Pub Co.

Bengmark, Stig, ed. Progress in Surgery of the Liver Pancreas & Biliary System. (Developments in Surgery Ser.). (C). 1988. text 271.50 (*0-89838-956-9*) Kluwer Academic.

Bengson, Diane. How Weaning Happens. LC 99-61386. (Illus.). 156p. 1999. pap. 10.95 (*0-912500-54-9*) La Leche.
This informative & inspirational publication considers the physical & emotional changes a mother goes through while weaning & further investigates the reasons to wean. Bengson bases her book on the questions & needs of hundreds of mothers she's counseled as an LLL Leader, helping breastfeeding families gently & lovingly complete the nursing relationship. Describes how mothers should determine for themselves when to wean despite socio-cultural & family pressures & provides various methods of weaning that are both gentle & loving. *Publisher Paid Annotation.*

Bengston, Athene, tr. see York, Ute.

Bengston, Betty G. & Hill, Janet S., eds. Classification of Library Materials: Current & Future Potential for Providing Access. 275p. (Orig.). 1990. pap. text 49.95 (*1-55570-027-6*) Neal-Schuman.

Bengston, Bradley P., jt. auth. see Kuz, Julian E.

Bengston, Gary. Kelly, Adam's Secret Dream. 40p. (J). 1991. boxed set 19.95 (*0-9631057-0-1*) Five Corn Danforth.

Bengston, H. Historia de Grecia: Desde Los Comienzos Hasta la Epoca Imperial Romana. (SPA.). 500p. 1993. 150.00 (*84-249-1077-X*) Elliots Bks.

Bengston, Henry. On the Left in America: Memoirs of the Scandinavian-American Labor Movement. Brook, Michael, ed. Westerberg, Kermit B., tr. LC 96-20709. 237p. 1997. pap. 19.95 (*0-8093-2104-1*) S Ill U Pr.

Bengston, Henry. On the Left in America: Memoirs of the Scandinavian-American Labor Movement. Brook, Michael, ed. Westerberg, Kermit B., tr. LC 96-20709. 272p. 1999. 39.95 (*0-8093-2079-7*) S Ill U Pr.

Bengston, John. Silent Echoes, Discovering Early Hollywood Through the Films of Buster Keaton. LC 99-36559. (Illus.). 232p. 1999. pap. 24.95 (*1-891661-06-X*, 106X) Snta Monica.

Bengt-Ake, Lundvall, ed. National Systems of Innovation: Toward a Theory of Innovation & Interactive Learning. LC 92-5781. 1992. text 59.00 (*1-85567-063-1*) St Martin.

Bengt-Pedersen, Carsten, jt. ed. see Thomassen, Niels.

Bengts, jt. auth. see Jeppsson, Bengt.

Bengtson, Athene, ed. see Newhouse, Flower A.

Bengtson, Bradley P., et al. Photographic Atlas of Civil War Injuries: Photographs of Surgical Cases & Specimens. LC 96-75434. (Illus.). 480p. 1996. 125.00 (*0-9635861-8-1*) Med Staff Pr.

— Photographic Atlas of Civil War Injuries: Photographs of Surgical Cases & Specimens. deluxe ed. (Illus.). 480p. 1996. lthr. 200.00 (*0-9653101-0-8*) Med Staff Pr.

Bengtson, Carl R. Zone of Grace. 196p. 1998. pap. 10.95 (*1-57502-680-5*, P01920) Morris Pubng.

Bengtson, David A. & Henshel, Diane S., eds. Environmental Toxicology & Risk Assessment: Biomarkers & Risk Assessment, STP1306. 2nd ed. (Illus.). 475p. 1996. text 91.00 (*0-8031-2031-1*, STP1306) ASTM.

Bengtson, David R. Past Lives of Famous People: Journeys of the Soul. LC 97-9116. 272p. 1997. pap. 15.95 (*1-885394-22-5*) Bluestar Communs.

Bengtson, Glenn D., ed. see Schwartz, L. Dwight.

***Bengtson, Gordon.** A Gentle Journey to Joy. (Illus.). 48p. 1999. pap. 9.95 (*0-9675194-0-3*) Germain Bks.

Bengtson, Melodie N., ed. see Newhouse, Flower A.

Bengtson, Stefan, ed. see Nobel Symposium 84 Staff.

Bengtson, Vern L. The Social Psychology of Aging. LC 73-4918. 1973. pap. 3.50 (*0-672-61339-5*, Bobbs) Macmillan.

Bengtson, Vern L., ed. Adulthood & Aging: Research on Continuities & Discontinuities. (Illus.). 360p. 1996 52.95 (*0-8261-9270-X*) Springer Pub.

Bengtson, Vern L., et al, eds. Adult Intergenerational Relations: Effects of Societal Change. LC 94-17759. (Illus.). 336p. 1994. 42.95 (*0-8261-8560-6*) Springer Pub.

Bengtson, Vern L. & Achenbaum, W. Andrew, eds. The Changing Contract Across Generations. LC 92-39624. (Social Institutions & Social Change Ser.). 329p. 1993. lib. bdg. 49.95 (*0-202-30459-0*) Aldine de Gruyter.

Bengtson, Vern L. & Harootyan, Robert A., eds. Intergenerational Linkages: Hidden Connections in American Society. (Illus.). 352p. 1994. 46.95 (*0-8261-8670-X*) Springer Pub.

Bengtson, Vern L. & Robertson, Joan F., eds. Grandparenthood. LC 85-8337. (Sage Focus Editions Ser.: No. 74). 240p. reprint ed. pap. 74.40 (*0-7837-4567-2*, 204409600003) Bks Demand.

***Bengtson, Vern L. & Schaie, K. Warner, eds.** Handbook of Theories of Aging. LC 98-40529. 536p. 1998. 54.95 (*0-8261-1234-X*) Springer Pub.

Bengtsson, A. B. Does Education Have a Future? (Plan Europe 2000 Ser: No. 10). 1975. pap. text 65.00 (*90-247-1760-4*) Kluwer Academic.

Bengtsson, B. A. The Scythrididae (Lepidoptera) of Northern Europe. (Fauna Entomologica Scandinavica Ser.: No. 13). (Illus.). 138p. 1984. text 35.00 (*90-04-07312-4*) Lubrecht & Cramer.

***Bengtsson, Bengt-Ake.** Growth Hormone. LC 99-19993. (Endocrine Updates Ser.). ix, 359p. 1999. write for info. (*0-7923-8478-4*) Kluwer Academic.

Bengtsson, Finn, et al. Progress in Hepatic Encephalopathy & Metabolic Nitrogen Exchange Proceedings: Seventh International Symposium on Ammonia. (Illus.). 576p. 1991. 324.00 (*0-8493-0180-7*, 180FV, CRC Reprint) Franklin.

Bengtsson, Frans. The Long Ships. 414p. 1992. reprint ed. lib. bdg. 35.95 (*0-89966-934-4*) Buccaneer Bks.

Bengtsson, Gerda. Danish Floral Charted Designs. (Illus.). 48p. 1980. pap. 2.95 (*0-486-23957-8*) Dover.

Bengtsson, L., jt. auth. see Tausk, M.

Bengtsson, Maria. Climates of Competition. (Studies in Global Competition). 288p. 1998. text 37.00 (*90-5702-257-5*, Harwood Acad Pubs) Gordon & Breach.

Bengtsson, R., et al. Nuclear Structure Models. 520p. 1993. text 109.00 (*981-02-1131-7*) World Scientific Pub.

Bengtsson, Tommy, ed. Population, Economy, & Welfare in Sweden. LC 94-33960. 1994. write for info. (*0-387-58423-4*) Spr-Verlag.

— Population, Economy, & Welfare in Sweden. LC 94-33960. (Population Economics Ser.). 1994. 78.95 (*3-540-58423-4*) Spr-Verlag.

Bengtsson, Tommy, et al, eds. Pre-Industrial Population Changes. 420p. 1984. text 77.50 (*91-22-00741-5*) Coronet Bks.

***Bengtsson, Tommy & Saito, Osamu, eds.** Population & Economy: From Hunger to Modern Economic Growth. 450p. 2000. text 95.00 (*0-19-829653-3*) OUP.

***Benguhe, Chris.** Triumphs of the Heart: Miraculous True Stories of the Power of Love. LC 00-29670. 208p. 2000. pap. 12.00 (*0-399-52613-7*, Perigee Bks) Berkley Pub.

Benhabib, Jess, ed. Cycles & Chaos in Economic Equilibrium. (Illus.). 466p. 1992. text 95.00 (*0-691-04249-7*, Pub. by Princeton U Pr) Cal Prin Full Svc.

Benhabib, Seyla. Critique, Norm, & Utopia: A Study of the Foundations of Critical Theory. LC 85-13323. 424p. 1987. pap. text 25.50 (*0-231-06165-X*) Col U Pr.

— The Reluctant Modernism of Hannah Arendt. LC 95-50247. (Modernity & Political Thought Ser.: Vol. 10). 336p. (C). 1996. 48.00 (*0-8039-3816-0*); pap. 22.95 (*0-8039-3817-9*) Sage.

— Situating the Self: Gender, Community, & Postmodernism in Contemporary Ethics. 280p. (C). 1992. pap. 19.99 (*0-415-90547-8*, A6805) Routledge.

Benhabib, Seyla, ed. Democracy & Difference: Contesting Boundaries of the Political. LC 96-2189. 352p. 1996. pap. text 19.95 (*0-691-04478-3*, Pub. by Princeton U Pr) Cal Prin Full Svc.

Benhabib, Seyla, et al, eds. On Max Horkheimer: New Perspectives. (Studies in Contemporary German Social Thought). (Illus.). 533p. 1993. 44.00 (*0-262-02355-5*) MIT Pr.

— On Max Horkheimer: New Perspectives. (Studies in Contemporary German Social Thought). 1995. pap. text 22.00 (*0-262-52207-1*) MIT Pr.

Benhabib, Seyla & Cornell, Drucilla, eds. Feminism As Critique: Essays on the Politics of Gender in Late-Capitalist Societies. LC 87-10939. (Feminist Perspectives Ser.). 193p. 1987. pap. 17.95 (*0-8166-1636-1*) U of Minn Pr.

Benhabib, Seyla & Dallmayr, Fred R., eds. The Communicative Ethics Controversy. 1990. 37.50 (*0-262-02305-9*); pap. text 22.00 (*0-262-52152-0*) MIT Pr.

Benhabib, Seyla, et al. Feminist Contentions: A Philosophical Exchange. LC 94-19436. (Thinking Gender Ser.). 160p. (C). (gr. 13). 1994. pap. 18.99 (*0-415-91086-2*, B4771) Routledge.

Benhabib, Seyla, jt. ed. see D'Entreves, Maurizio P.

Benham, Allen R. English Literature from Widsith to the Death of Chaucer: A Source Book. LC 73-114903. (Select Bibliographies Reprint Ser.). 1977. 35.95 (*0-8369-5307-X*) Ayer.

Benham, Frances & Powell, Ronald R. Success in Answering Reference Questions: Two Studies. LC 86-14629. (Illus.). 313p. 1987. 34.50 (*0-8108-1940-6*) Scarecrow.

Benham, Frederic. Economic Aid to Underdeveloped Countries. LC 85-30594. 121p. 1986. reprint ed. lib. bdg. 55.00 (*0-313-25115-0*, BEEC, Greenwood Pr) Greenwood.

Benham, George C. A Year of Wreck. LC 75-38639. (Black Heritage Library Collection). 1977. reprint ed. 28.95 (*0-8369-8997-X*) Ayer.

B

Benham, Harry C. Elements of Business Statistics: Lecture Notes. 2nd ed. 300p. (C). 1996. spiral bd. 34.95 (*0-7872-2921-0*, 41292101) Kendall-Hunt.

***Benham, Herb.** First Kisses & Other Miracles: Stories form the Porch. 3rd ed. (C). 1999. pap. 12.95 (*0-9677156-0-1*) H Benham.

— Sitting on My Fat Wallet. 1999. pap. 12.95 (*0-9677156-1-X*) H Benham.

Benham, Hervey, jt. auth. see Finch, Roger.

Benham, Hugh. Latin Church Music in England, 1460-1575. LC 79-25063. (Music Reprint Ser.: 1980). (Illus.). 1980. reprint ed. lib. bdg. 35.00 (*0-306-76025-8*) Da Capo.

Benham, Jack L. Camp Bird & the Revenue. (Illus.). 68p. (Orig.). 1979. pap. 3.95 (*0-941026-04-3*) Bear Creek Pub.

— Ouray. (Illus.). 64p. (Orig.). 1976. pap. 3.95 (*0-941026-01-9*) Bear Creek Pub.

— Silverton. rev. ed. (Illus.). 64p. (Orig.). 1981. reprint ed. pap. 3.95 (*0-941026-02-7*) Bear Creek Pub.

Benham, Jack L. & Benham, Sarah, eds. Rocky Mountains Receipts Remedies. rev. ed. (Illus.). 60p. (Orig.). 1966. pap. text 2.95 (*0-941026-08-6*) Bear Creek Pub.

Benham, Jack L., ed. see McLean, Evalyn W. & Sparkes, Boyden.

Benham, Jack L., ed. see Rice, Frank A.

Benham, Jack L., ed. see Rickard, T. A.

Benham, Jack L., ed. & intro. see Jackson, William H. & Holmes, William H.

Benham, Judith L. & Kinstle, James F., eds. Chemical Reactions on Polymers. LC 87-31913. (ACS Symposium Ser.: Vol. 364). 496p. 1988. reprint ed. pap. 153.80 (*0-608-03886-5*, 206433300008) Bks Demand.

Benham, Maenette K. & Heck, Ronald H. Culture & Educational Policy in Hawaii: The Silencing of Native Voices. LC 97-47700. (Sociocultural, Political, & Historical Studies in Education Ser.). 256p. 1998. write for info. (*0-8058-2703-X*); pap. write for info. (*0-8058-2704-8*) L Erlbaum Assocs.

Benham, P. P. Mechanics of Engineering Materials. 2nd ed. 704p. (C). 1996. pap. text 54.95 (*0-582-25164-8*) Addison-Wesley.

Benham, Sarah, jt. ed. see Benham, Jack L.

Benham, William G. The Benham Book of Palmistry: A Practical Treatise on the Laws of Scientific Hand Reading. 688p. (Orig.). 1991. pap. 14.95 (*0-87877-137-9*) Newcastle Pub.

— How to Choose Vocations from the Hand: The Essential Guide for Discovering Your Occupational Personality. (Illus.). 448p. 1995. pap. 14.95 (*0-87877-197-2*, 1-800-932-4809) Newcastle Pub.

— The Laws of Scientific Hand Reading. 635p. 1993. reprint ed. pap. 35.00 (*0-7873-0090-X*) Hlth Research.

— Laws of Scientific Hand Reading: A Practical Treatise on the Art Commonly Called Palmistry (1900) 640p. 1998. reprint ed. pap. 30.00 (*0-7661-0504-0*) Kessinger Pub.

Benhamou, Frederic & Colmerauer, Alan, eds. Constraint Logic Programming: Selected Research. LC 92-38061. (Logic Programming Ser.). (Illus.). 486p. 1993. 60.00 (*0-262-02353-9*) MIT Pr.

Benhamou, J. P., jt. ed. see Okuda, Kunio.

Benhar, O., et al, eds. Theoretical & Experimental Investigations of Hadronic Few-Body Systems. (Few-Body Systems Ser.: Suppl. 1). (Illus.). 640p. 1986. 123.95 (*0-387-81983-5*) Spr-Verlag.

Benhar, O., et al. Electron-Nucleus Scattering: Proceedings of the Workshop. 376p. 1994. text 108.00 (*981-02-1677-7*) World Scientific Pub.

— Neural Networks from Biology to High Energy Physics: Proceedings of the 2nd Workshop. 356p. 1993. text 121.00 (*981-02-1253-4*) World Scientific Pub.

Benharbit, Abdelali, jt. auth. see Al-Moajil, Abdullah H.

Benhart & Scull. Regions of the World Today. 4th ed. 208p. (C). 1998. per. 41.95 (*0-7872-4670-0*, 41467001) Kendall-Hunt.

Benhart, John. The Encyclopedia of Pennsylvania: A Reference Guide to the Keystone State. LC 82-19306. (Encyclopedia of the United States Ser.). (Illus.). 764p. 1984. 89.00 (*0-403-09977-3*) Somerset Pub.

Benhart, John & Scull, C. Rober. Regions of the World Today. 2nd ed. 320p. (C). 1995. per. 26.95 (*0-8403-8329-0*) Kendall-Hunt.

Benhart, John E. & Margin, Alex R., Jr. Wetlands: Science, Politics & Geographic Relationships. LC 95-166703. (Pathways in Geography Ser.: No. 9). (Illus.). 108p. 1994. pap. text 12.00 (*1-884136-01-X*) NCFGE.

Benheim, Els, ed. see Adlerblum, Nima H.

Benhoff, Susan. Capitalization & Punctuation. (Basic Skills Ser.). (Illus.). 32p. (J). (gr. 1). 1997. pap. text 4.95 (*0-88724-403-3*, CD-2103) Carson-Dellos.

— Measurement. (Basic Skills Ser.). (Illus.). 32p. (J). (gr. k-1). 1998. pap. text 4.95 (*0-88724-465-3*, CD-2133) Carson-Dellos.

Beniak, Edouard, jt. auth. see Mougeon, Raymond.

Beniam, Laurence. Issey Miyake. (Illus.). 80p. 1997. 18.95 (*0-7893-0117-2*, Pub. by Universe) St Martin.

Beniaminov, Aleksandr D. Artist Bez Grima: Vospominaniia. LC 95-2549. (RUS., Illus.). 288p. (Orig.). 1995. pap. 14.00 (*1-55779-063-9*) Hermitage Pubs.

Beniashvili, Dzhemali. Experimental Tumors in Monkeys. 176p. 1994. lib. bdg. 139.00 (*0-8493-5383-1*) CRC Pr.

Benice, Daniel D. Brief Calculus & Its Applications, 2 vols. 2nd ed. (C). 1997. text, teacher ed. 11.96 (*0-395-83453-8*) HM.

— Calculus. (C). Date not set. text, teacher ed., suppl. ed. write for info. (*0-395-66107-2*) HM.

— Calculus. (C). 1992. text 77.56 (*0-395-61548-8*) HM.

— Calculus. (C). 1993. pap., teacher ed. 3.96 (*0-395-61550-X*) HM.

— Calculus. (C). 1993. pap., student ed. 13.16 (*0-395-61553-4*) HM.

— Calculus, 2 vols. 2nd ed. LC 96-76865. (C). 1996. text 77.56 (*0-395-77684-8*) HM.

— Calculus Brief, 2 vols. 2nd ed. LC 96-76864. (C). 1996. text 73.56 (*0-395-82464-8*) HM.

Benice, Ronald J. Alaska Tokens. 2nd ed. Schenkman, David E., ed. LC 94-61240. (Illus.). 333p. 1994. 39.95 (*0-918492-10-6*) TAMS.

Benichou, Christian, ed. Practical Guide to Pharmacovigilance: Diagnosis & Reporting of Adverse Drug Reactions. LC 94-6102. 320p. 1994. pap. 148.95 (*0-471-94211-1*) Wiley.

Benichou, Jacques, jt. auth. see Gail, Mitchell H.

Benichou, Paul. The Consecration of the Writer, 1750-1830. Jensen, Mark, tr. LC 98-42381. (European Horizons).Tr. of Sacre de l'Ecrivain, 1750-1830. 1999. text 65.00 (*0-8032-1291-7*); pap. text 25.00 (*0-8032-6152-7*) U of Nebr Pr.

— Morales du Grand Siecle. (Folio Essais Ser.: No. 99). (FRE.). 383p. 1948. pap. 11.95 (*2-07-032473-7*) Schoenhof.

Benichou, Paul, ed. see Hugo, Victor.

Benichoux, R. & Merle, M., eds. European Society for Surgical Research, 21st Congress, Nancy 1986 Abstracts. (Journal: European Surgical Research: Vol. 18, Suppl. 1, 1986). (Illus.). xii, 112p. 1986. pap. 38.50 (*3-8055-4383-2*) S Karger.

Benidickson, Jamie. Environmental Law. (Essentials of Canadian Law Ser.). xvi, 288p. 1997. pap. 30.95 (*1-55221-010-3*, Pub. by Irwin Law) Gaunt.

Benidickson, Jamie. Idleness, Water & a Canoe: Reflections on Paddling for Pleasure. LC 97-160859. (Illus.). 300p. 1997. pap. 17.95 (*0-8020-7910-5*) U of Toronto Pr.

Benidickson, Jamie, jt. auth. see Hodgins, Bruce W.

Benierakis, C. E., et al. Psychoanalysis & the Zest for Living: Reflections & Psychoanalytic Writings in Memory of W. C. M. Scott. Grignon, Michel, ed. (Illus.). 282p. 1998. pap. text 35.95 (*1-883881-27-7*, 27-7) S Freud RT&PF.

Benig, Irving. The Messiah Stones. large type ed. LC 96-11051. 1996. 24.95 (*1-56895-318-6*) Wheeler Pub.

Beniger, James R. The Control Revolution: Technological & Economic Origins of the Information Society. (Illus.). 512p. 1989. reprint ed. pap. 19.50 (*0-674-16986-7*) HUP.

— Trafficking in Drug Users: Professional Exchange Networks in the Control of Deviance. LC 83-5251. (American Sociological Assn. Rose Monographs). 217p. 1984. text 59.95 (*0-521-25753-0*); pap. text 19.95 (*0-521-27680-2*) Cambridge U Pr.

Benigni, Maria L. My Book of Prayers. Lane, Edmund C., tr. (Illus.). 32p. (Orig.). 1995. pap. 3.50 (*0-8189-0678-2*) Alba.

Benigni, Roberto & Cerami, Vicenzo. Life Is Beautiful (La Vita E Bella) A Screenplay. LC 98-43728. (Illus.). 173p. 1998. pap. 10.95 (*0-7868-8469-X*, Pub. by Hyperion) Time Warner.

Benin, Leigh David. The New Labor Radicalism & New York City's Garment Industry: Progressive Labor Insurgents During the 1960s. rev. ed. LC 99-51937. (Studies in the History of American Labor). 336p. 1999. 46.00 (*0-8153-3385-4*) Garland.

Benin, Stephen D. The Footprints of God: Divine Accommodation in Jewish & Christian Thought. LC 90-44127. (SUNY Series in Judaica). 327p. (C). 1993. text 67.50 (*0-7914-0711-X*); pap. text 24.95 (*0-7914-0712-8*) State U NY Pr.

***Bening, V. E.** Asymptotic Theory of Testing Statistical Hypotheses. (Illus.). 294p. 2000. 152.50 (*90-6764-323-8*, Pub. by Uppsala Universitet) Coronet Bks.

***Bening, Lionel & Foster, Harry.** Principles of Verifiable RTL Design - A Functional Coding Style Supporting Verification Processes. 272p. 2000. 98.00 (*0-7923-7788-5*) Kluwer Academic.

Beninger, Gerry, ed. see Floyd, Maita.

Beninger, Toni. SONET Basics. (Illus.). 80p. (Orig.). 1991. pap. 29.95 (*0-917845-15-3*) Intertec IL.

— SS7 Basics. (Illus.). 80p. (Orig.). 1991. pap. 29.95 (*0-917845-16-1*) Intertec IL.

Beninghof, Anne M. Ideas for Inclusion: The Classroom Teacher's Guide to Integrating Students with Severe Disabilities. 158p. 1993. pap. text, teacher ed. 19.95 (*1-57035-003-5*, 53IDEAS) Sopris.

***Beninghof, Anne M.** Making Inclusion Work: Video & Facilitator's Guide. 56p. 1999. 39.50 incl. VHS (*1-57035-206-2*) Sopris.

Beninghof, Anne M. Senseable Strategies: Including Diverse Learners Through Multisensory Strategies. (Illus.). 173p. (J). (ps-6). 1998. pap. 19.95 (*1-57035-160-0*, 53STRAT) Sopris.

Beninghof, Anne M. & Singer, Anne L. Ideas for Inclusion: The School Administrator's Guide. (Illus.). 136p. 1995. pap. text 19.95 (*1-57035-042-6*, 53ADMIN) Sopris.

Benington, George, ed. An Abridged Field Guide to the Maine Writer. 36p. (Orig.). 1984. pap. 2.95 (*0-913341-04-5*) Coyote Love.

Benington, John, jt. auth. see Geddes, Mike.

Benington, Jonathan. Roderic O'Conor: A Biography with a Catalogue of His Work. (Illus.). 248p. (C). 1992. 22.95 (*0-7165-2492-9*, Pub. by Irish Acad Pr) Intl Spec Bk.

Benini, Aldo A. Modern Switzerland. LC 98-14811. (Comparative Society Ser.). 168p. 1998. pap. 13.75 (*0-07-034427-2*) McGraw.

Benini-Horetzky. French-Croatian & Serbian Pocket Dictionary: Francusko-Hrvatski ili Srpski i Hrvatsko ili Srpsko-Francuski Dzepni Rjecni. (FRE & SER.). 328p. 1983. pap. 19.95 (*0-8288-1044-3*, F99500) Fr & Eur.

Benini, Luca & De Michell, Giovanni. Dynamic Power Management: Design Techniques & Cad Tools. LC 97-32140. 248p. 1998. text 105.00 (*0-7923-8086-X*, D Reidel) Kluwer Academic.

Benink, H. A. Financial Integration in Europe. rev. ed. LC 92-16497. (Financial & Monetary Policy Studies: Vol. 24).Tr. of Financi ele Integratie in Europa 1993. 216p. (C). 1992. lib. bdg. 152.50 (*0-7923-1849-8*) Kluwer Academic.

Benink, Harald, ed. Coping with Financial Fragility & Systemic Risk. LC 95-30695. (Financial & Monetary Policy Studies: Vol. 30). 304p. (C). 1996. lib. bdg. 109.00 (*0-7923-9612-X*) Kluwer Academic.

***Benioff, David.** The 25th Hour. 192p. 2001. 24.00 (*0-7867-0772-0*, Pub. by Carroll & Graf) Publishers Group.

Benioff, Ron, ed. see Lee, Jeffrey & Guill, Sandra.

Beniot, P., et al, eds. Les Grottes de Murabba'at: Textes. (Discoveries in the Judaean Desert Ser.: No. II). (Illus.). 320p. 1997. text 105.00 (*0-19-826944-7*) OUP.

— Les Grottes de Murabbat: Planches. (Discoveries in the Judaean Desert Ser.: No. II). (Illus.). 120p. 1997. text 78.00 (*0-19-826945-5*) OUP.

Benirschke, Kurt, ed. Primates. (Illus.). 1120p. 1986. 142.00 (*0-387-96270-0*) Spr-Verlag.

Benirschke, Kurt & Kaufmann, P. Pathology of the Human Placenta. 2nd ed. (Illus.). xiv, 878p. 1992. 218.00 (*0-387-97282-X*) Spr-Verlag.

Benirschke, Kurt & Kaufmann, Peter. Pathology of Human Placenta. 3rd ed. LC 94-25783. (Illus.). 871p. 1995. 179.00 (*0-387-94335-8*) Spr-Verlag.

***Benirschke, Kurt & Kaufmann, Peter.** Pathology of the Human Placenta. 4th ed. LC 99-32440. 944p. 2000. 189.00 (*0-387-98894-7*) Spr-Verlag.

Benirschke, Kurt, jt. auth. see Hsu, T. C.

Benirschke, Max. Color Source Book of Authentic Art Nouveau Designs: 146 Motifs. (Illus.). 32p. 1984. reprint ed. pap. 5.95 (*0-486-24547-0*) Dover.

Benirschke, Rolf. Alive & Kicking! 280p. (Orig.). 1996. pap. 9.95 (*1-885553-40-4*) Firefly Press.

Benis, A. M. Toward Self & Sanity: On the Genetic Origins of the Human Character. LC 84-26313. 528p. 1985. 39.95 (*0-88437-074-7*) Psych Dimensions.

Benis, Leslie. Puli: A Complete & Reliable Handbook. (Illus.). 96p. 1999. 19.95 (*0-7938-0779-4*, RX-129) TFH Pubns.

Benis, Leslie, jt. auth. see Alvi, Dana I.

Benis, Toby R. Romanticism on the Road: The Marginal Gains of Wordsworth's Homeless (Romanticism in Perspective) LC 99-20436. 224p. 1999. text 59.95 (*0-312-22302-1*) St Martin.

Benisch, Mortimer. Menasha: A True East Side Story. (Illus.). 140p. (Orig.). 1990. pap. 8.95 (*0-929256-18-2*) Thundblt Pr NV.

Benisch, Pearl. To Vanquish the Dragon. 1991. 20.95 (*0-87306-570-0*); pap. 16.95 (*0-87306-571-9*) Feldheim.

Benish, Bruce K. & Bryant, M. Kevin. Depreciation Handbook. (Illus.). 1983. ring bd. 180.00 (*0-8205-1713-5*) Bender.

Benish, Gloria D. As God Is My Witness. 118p. (Orig.). 1993. pap. 9.95 (*0-9636100-0-7*) Miracle MT.

— Go Within or Go Without: A Simple Guide to Self Healing. LC 96-94261. (Illus.). 244p. (Orig.). 1996. pap. 12.95 (*0-9636100-2-3*) Miracle MT.

— To Become As Little Children: Fairytales for Adults - for the Child in You. LC 94-91358. (Illus.). 210p. (Orig.). 1994. pap. 16.95 (*0-9636100-1-5*) Miracle MT.

Benison, C. C. Death at Buckingham Palace: Her Majesty Investigates. 288p. 1996. mass mkt. 5.99 (*0-553-57476-0*, Crimeline) Bantam.

— The Death at Sandringham House. (Her Majesty Investigates Ser.). 384p. 1996. mass mkt. 5.99 (*0-553-57477-9*, Crimeline) Bantam.

— Death at Windsor Castle. 400p. 1998. mass mkt. 5.99 (*0-553-57478-7*, Crimeline) Bantam.

Benison, Saul, et al. Walter B. Cannon: The Life & Times of a Young Scientist. LC 86-25951. (Illus.). 528p. 1987. 39.95 (*0-674-94580-8*) Belknap Pr.

Benison, Teresa. The Arrogance of Women. 378p. Date not set. 27.00 (*0-09-179214-2*) Random.

— A Rational Man. 378p. 1997. 26.00 (*0-09-179209-6*, Pub. by Hutchnson) Trafalgar.

Benissad, M. E. Dictionary of Economic, Political & Legal Science. (ARA, ENG & FRE.). 258p. 1983. pap. 49.95 (*0-7859-4862-7*) Fr & Eur.

Beniston, Judith, jt. ed. see Robertson, Ritchie.

Beniston, M. Interactional Between Energy Transformations & Atmospheric Phenomena: A Survey of Recent Research. Pielke, R. A., ed. (C). 1987. text 300.50 (*90-277-2651-5*) Kluwer Academic.

Beniston, M., et al, eds. The Impacts of Climate Change on Forests. LC 98-29447. (Lecture Notes in Earth Sciences Ser.: Vol. 74). (Illus.). xiv, 329p. 1998. pap. 104.00 (*3-540-64681-7*) Spr-Verlag.

***Beniston, Martin.** Environmental Change in Mountains & Uplands. (Key Issues in Environmental Change). 224p. 2000. pap. 29.95 (*0-340-70636-8*, Pub. by E A); text 72.00 (*0-340-70638-4*, Pub. by E A) OUP.

Beniston, Martin. From Turbulence to Climate: Numerical Investigations of the Atmosphere with a Hierarchy of Models. LC 97-31666. (Illus.). 338p. 1998. text 84.95 (*3-540-63495-9*) Spr-Verlag.

Beniston, Martin, ed. Mountain Environments in Changing Climates. LC 93-45308. (Illus.). 464p. (C). 1994. 150.00 (*0-415-10224-3*, B3824) Routledge.

***Benisty, Henri, et al, eds.** Confined Photon Systems: Fundamentals & Applications. LC 99-44340. (Lecture Notes in Physics Ser.: Vol. 531). (Illus.). 493p. 1999. 115.80 (*3-540-66435-1*) Spr-Verlag.

Benita, Simon. Microencapsulation. (Drugs & the Pharmaceutical Sciences Ser.: Vol. 73). (Illus.). 664p. 1996. text 165.00 (*0-8247-9703-5*) Dekker.

***Benita, Simon, ed.** Submicron Emulsions in Drug Targeting & Delivery. (Illus.). 352p. 1999. text 120.00 (*90-5702-349-0*, Harwood Acad Pubs) Gordon & Breach.

Benites, Arlene K. Gypsies - Their Health & Life Events: Index of New Information. 150p. 1998. 47.50 (*0-7883-2028-9*); pap. 44.50 (*0-7883-2029-7*) ABBE Pubs Assn.

Benitez. Reading Tasks Text. Date not set. pap. text. write for info. (*0-582-00512-4*, Pub. by Addison-Wesley) Longman.

Benitez, Ana M. De, see De Benitez, Ana M.

***Benitez, Armando.** Sheer Superstition. 2000. pap. 14.95 (*1-57174-180-1*) N D Walsch.

Benitez, Basave. Mexico Mestizo. (SPA.). pap. 11.99 (*968-16-3715-1*, Pub. by Fondo) Continental Bk.

***Benitez, Carmen L.** What a Difference a Day Makes. Spiller, Linus, ed. 208p. 2000. pap. 15.95 (*0-9679276-0-9*) C L Benitez.

Benitez Claros, Rafael, ed. see Hurtado de Mendoza, Antonio.

Benitez, Fernando. Agua Envenenada (The Poisoned Water) (SPA.). 183p. 1961. pap. 7.99 (*968-16-0635-3*, Pub. by Fondo) Continental Bk.

— Century After Cortes. MacLean, Joan, tr. LC 65-25121. (Illus.). 2000. lib. bdg. 12.50 (*0-226-04230-8*) U Ch Pr.

— Ki, el Drama de un Pueblo. (SPA.). pap. 12.99 (*968-16-1869-6*, Pub. by Fondo) Continental Bk.

— Lazaro Cardenas y la Revolucion I, II, III. (SPA.). pap. 11.99 (*968-16-0457-1*, Pub. by Fondo) Continental Bk.

— La Ruta de Hernan Cortes (The Route of Hernan Cortes) 3rd ed. (SPA.). 308p. 1990. pap. 8.99 (*968-16-0959-X*, Pub. by Fondo) Continental Bk.

Benitez, Helena. Acatos. (Illus.). 204p. 60.00 (*2-940033-57-9*, Pub. by Images) Antique Collect.

Benitez, J. J. Caballo de Troya. 1997. pap. text 12.95 (*84-08-02036-6*) Planeta Edit.

Benitez, J. J. El Arbol y la Serpiente. 1999. pap. text 12.95 (*84-08-02856-1*) Planeta Edit.

— Astronautas de Yave. (SPA., Illus.). 295p. 1998. pap. text 9.95 (*84-08-02274-1*) Planeta Edit.

***Benitez, J. J.** Caballo de Troya 5. (SPA.). 1998. pap. text 12.95 (*84-08-02228-8*) Planeta Edit.

— Caballo de Troya 4. (SPA.). 1997. pap. 12.95 (*84-08-02039-0*) Planeta.

— Caballo de Troya 1. (SPA.). 1999. pap. 12.95 (*84-08-02753-0*) Planeta.

— Caballo de Troya 2. 1997. pap. text 19.98 (*968-406-030-0*) F Planeta.

— Caballo de Troya 2. 1997. pap. text 12.95 (*84-08-02037-4*) Planeta.

Benitez, J. J. Encuentro en Sudafrica. 1999. pap. text 12.95 (*84-08-02854-5*) Planeta Edit.

***Benitez, J. J.** Mis Enigmas Favoritos. (SPA.). 1998. pap. 6.50 (*84-01-46558-3*, Pub. by Plaza) Lectorum Pubns.

Benitez, J. J. El Misterio de la Virgen de Guadalupe. 1995. 22.95 (*84-08-02559-7*) Planeta.

Benitez, J. J., jt. ed. see Jo, Kondo.

Benitez, Jaime. Junto a la Torre. 436p. 1962. 4.00 (*0-8477-2404-2*); pap. 2.00 (*0-8477-2405-0*) U of PR Pr.

— Process Engineering & Design for Air Pollution Control. LC 92-20982. (C). 1992. 63.00 (*0-13-723214-4*) Prntice Hall Bks.

Benitez, Jesus, tr. see Farr, Kenneth H.

Benitez, Jesus, tr. see Farr, Kenneth R.

Benitez, Jesus, tr. see Senior, Clarence.

Benitez, J.J. Caballo De Troya. (SPA.). 1997. pap. text 12.95 (*84-08-02038-2*) Planeta.

***Benitez, Juan Jose.** La Noche Mas Larga. (SPA.). 1999. pap. 14.95 (*84-08-02857-X*) Planeta.

Benitez, Mario A. The Origin of Prejudice in Children. 36p. (Orig.). 1996. pap. 5.95 (*0-9654217-0-8*) Fndtn of Educ Soc.

Benitez, Miena. George Washington Carver, Plant Doctor. (Real Readers Ser.: Level Blue). (Illus.). 32p. (J). (ps-3). 1989. lib. bdg. 21.40 (*0-8172-3522-1*) Raintree Steck-V.

Benitez, Mirna. George Washington Carver, Plant Doctor. (Real Readers Ser.: Level Blue). 32p. (J). 1989. pap. 4.95 (*0-8114-6719-8*) Raintree Steck-V.

— Super Parrot. (Real Reading Ser.: Level Red). (Illus.). 32p. (J). (gr. 1-4). 1989. pap. 4.95 (*0-8114-6704-X*) Raintree Steck-V.

Benitez, Oscar R. Cuasno Concluyo la Guerra. 130p. 1992. pap. 7.95 (*1-881619-02-8*) Edit Encuentro.

— Las Huellas de una Lucha sin Final. (SPA.). 189p. (Orig.). 1986. pap. 10.95 (*0-317-55874-9*) Evergreen Dist.

— Te Canto Mi Corazon. 120p. 1992. pap. 7.95 (*1-881619-01-X*) Edit Encuentro.

— Te Canto Mi Corazon. 6th ed. (SPA.). 120p. 1997. pap. 8.99 (*1-890701-02-5*) La Mancha.

— Treinta Poemas de Amor para Maria. 60p. 1992. pap. 4.95 (*1-881619-03-6*) Edit Encuentro.

— Treinta Poemas de Amor para Maria. 3rd ed. (SPA., Illus.). 62p. 1997. pap. 5.99 (*1-890701-03-3*) La Mancha.

— Versos de Otono. (SPA.). 128p. (Orig.). 1997. pap. 8.99 (*1-890701-00-9*) La Mancha.

Benitez, Rafael G. Anchors: Ethical & Practical Maxims. 88p. 1996. pap. 8.00 (*1-884878-05-9*) Annapol Pubng.

Benitez, Rafael H. La Publicidad en Puerto Rico: Como Fue, Como es, Como se Hace. LC 85-1017. (SPA., Illus.). 275p. 1985. 9.00 (*0-8477-2908-7*) U of PR Pr.

***Benitez-Rojo, Antonio.** La Isla Que se Repite. 2nd ed. (Rama Ser.: Vol. 9). (SPA.). 350p. (C). 1999. pap. 25.00 (*0-910061-37-8*) Ediciones Norte.

Benitez-Rojo, Antonio. The Repeating Island: The Caribbean & the Postmodern Perspective. 2nd ed. Maraniss, James E., tr. LC 96-14685. (Post-Contemporary Interventions Ser.). (SPA.). 376p. 1996. text 59.95 (*0-8223-1860-1*); pap. text 17.95 (*0-8223-1865-2*) Duke.

An Asterisk (*) at the beginning of an entry indicates that the title is appearing for the first time.

— Sea of Lentils. Maraniss, James E., tr. from SPA. LC 90-31381. 204p. 1990. 30.00 (*0-87023-723-3*); pap. 16.95 (*0-87023-754-3*) U of Mass Pr.

***Benitez-Rojo, Antonio.** A View from the Mangrove. Maraniss, James, tr. 256p. 2000. pap. 16.95 (*1-55849-261-5*) U of Mass Pr.

Benitez, Ruben & Smith, Paul C. Hablando seriamente: Textos y pretextos para conversacion y discusion. 2nd ed. LC 95-181576. (SPA., Illus.). 272p. (C). 1994. pap. text 40.00 (*0-13-148172-X*) P-H.

Benitez, Sandra. Bitter Grounds. LC 98-28881. 464p. 1998. pap. 15.00 (*0-312-19541-9*, Picador USA) St Martin.

— Un Lugar Donde Recuerda el Mar: A Place Where the Sea Remembers. 176p. 1996. per. 10.00 (*0-684-82388-8*) Simon & Schuster.

— A Place Where the Sea Remembers. LC 93-25176. 160p. (YA). (gr. 10-12). 1993. 10.00 (*1-56689-011-X*) Coffee Hse.

— A Place Where the Sea Remembers. 176p. 1995. per. 10.00 (*0-671-89267-3*) Simon & Schuster.

***Benitez, Sandra.** The Weight of All Things. LC 99-51759. 256p. 2001. 22.95 (*0-7868-6399-4*, Pub. by Hyperion) Time Warner.

Benitez, Zuleyka. Trouble in Paradise. LC 78-17909. (Lost Roads Ser.: No. 19). (Illus.). 56p. (Orig.). 1980. pap. 9.00 (*0-918786-20-7*) Lost Roads.

Benito, Angel. Diccionario de Ciencias y Tecnicas de Comunicacion Social. (SPA.). 1376p. 1991. 175.00 (*0-7859-5859-2*, 8428513856) Fr & Eur.

Benito Bacho, Jose. Diccionario de la Construccion y Obras Publicas Ingles-Espanol, 2 vols., Set. (ENG & SPA.). 268p. 1975. 95.00 (*0-8288-5811-X*, S50117) Fr & Eur.

— Diccionario de la Construccion y Obras Publicas, Tomo 2: Span. (SPA.). 110p. 1975. 49.95 (*0-8288-5812-8*, S50119) Fr & Eur.

— Diccionario de la Construcion y de Obras Publicas, Tomo 1: Ingles. (SPA.). 168p. 1975. 49.95 (*0-8288-5813-6*, S50118) Fr & Eur.

Benito, G., et al. Palaeohydrology & Environmental Change. LC 98-7027. 368p. 1998. 165.00 (*0-471-98465-5*) Wiley.

Benito, J. Sanchez, et al. Spielend Deutsch Lernen: Interaktive Arbeitsblatter fur Anfanger Bis Fortgeschrittene. (SPA.). 96p. 1996. 29.95 (*3-468-45558-5*); 29.95 (*3-468-49988-4*) Langenscheidt.

Benito, Julio M. Los Prometeos Modernos. (Ciencia para Todos Ser.). (SPA.). pap. 6.99 (*968-16-4212-0*, Pub. by Fondo) Continental Bk.

Benito Mozas, A. Gramatica Practica. (SPA.). 330p. 1992. pap. 18.50 (*84-7640-596-0*, Pub. by Edaf Edit) IBD Ltd.

Benito, Tomas P. Dictionary of Video: English - Spanish. (ENG & SPA.). 96p. 1992. pap. 14.95 (*0-7859-3683-1*, M3151) Fr & Eur.

Benito-Vessels, Carmen. Juan Manuel: Escritura y Recreacion de la Historia. (Spanish Ser.: No. 103). x, 146p. 1994. 25.00 (*1-56954-028-4*) Hispanic Seminary.

Benito-Vessels, Carmen & Zappala, Michael, eds. The Picaresque: A Symposium on the Rogue's Tale. LC 91-51136. 1994. 35.00 (*0-87413-458-7*) U Delaware Pr.

Benito-Vessels, Carmen, jt. ed. see Stone, Marilyn.

Benitone, Troy. Making a Church from Scratch. 1998. pap. 14.95 (*1-885224-18-4*) Bristol Hse.

Benitz, William E. & Tatro, Davis S. The Pediatric Drug Handbook. 3rd ed. LC 95-6862. (Illus.). 688p. (C). (gr. 13). 1995. pap. text 34.95 (*0-8151-0665-3*, 24727) Mosby Inc.

Beniukh, Ksana, jt. auth. see Beniukh, Oleg.

Beniukh, Oleg. Russian-English - English-Russian Standard Dictionary: With Business Terms. rev. ed. 418p. 1997. pap. 18.95 (*0-7818-0280-6*) Hippocrene Bks.

Beniukh, Oleg & Beniukh, Ksana. Russian-English - English-Russian Concise Dictionary. (Concise Dictionaries Ser.). 400p. (Orig.). 1993. pap. 11.95 (*0-7818-0132-X*) Hippocrene Bks.

Benjafield, John G. Cognition. 2nd ed. 500p. (C). 1996. 82.00 (*0-13-398876-7*) P-H.

— A History of Psychology. LC 95-42263. 350p. 1996. 68.00 (*0-205-15403-4*) Allyn.

— Thinking Critically about Research Methods. LC 93-29724. 256p. 1993. pap. 25.00 (*0-205-13917-5*) Allyn.

Benjamin. Architecture on the Surface. 2000. pap. text 47.95 (*0-471-98510-4*) Wiley.

— Briefe. (C). 2000. pap. text 14.95 (*0-226-04238-3*) U Ch Pr.

— Diagnostic Laryngology: Adults & Children. 2nd ed. (Illus.). 192p. 1989. text 152.00 (*0-7216-2838-9*, W B Saunders Co) Harcrt Hlth Sci Grp.

— The Father Who Dwelleth Within. 1979. pap. 2.50 (*0-87516-293-2*) DeVorss.

***Benjamin.** History. 8th ed. 1999. pap. text. write for info. (*0-312-24765-6*) St Martin.

Benjamin. History of Psychology. 2nd ed. 1996. pap., student ed. 52.50 (*0-07-006103-3*) McGraw.

— History of Psychology in Letters. 2nd ed. 2000. text 20.74 (*0-697-20172-4*) McGraw.

***Benjamin.** Musical Structure: Harmony, Form & Counterpoint. 2003. pap. 37.50 (*0-534-55766-X*) Thomson Learn.

Benjamin. Old Testament Story. (Religion Ser.). 1919. mass mkt. 33.95 (*0-534-19188-6*) Wadsworth Pub.

— A Student's Guide to History. 7th ed. LC 97-72369. 200p. 1997. pap. text 19.95 (*0-312-14977-8*) St Martin.

***Benjamin.** Water Chemistry. 2000. 72.00 (*0-07-238390-9*) McGraw.

***Benjamin & Horvit.** Techniques & Materials in Tonal Music. 6th ed. (Music Ser.). 2000. 44.75 (*0-534-51759-5*) Wadsworth Pub.

Benjamin, jt. auth. see Darling.

Benjamin, Francis S. & Toomer, G. J., eds. Campanus of Novara & Medieval Planetary Theory: Theorica Planetarum. LC 78-138057. (Publications in Medieval Science: Vol. 16). (Illus.). 508p. reprint ed. pap. 157.50 (*0-608-20416-1*, 207166900002) Bks Demand.

Benjamin, A. & Hackstaff, L. H. On Free Choice of the Will: Augustine. 208p. (C). 1964. pap. text 8.00 (*0-02-308030-2*, Macmillan Coll) P-H.

Benjamin, A., et al. Surgical Repair & Reconstruction in Rheumatoid Disease. 2nd rev. ed. (Illus.). xviii, 254p. 1993. reprint ed. 247.00 (*0-387-19727-3*) Spr-Verlag.

Benjamin, A. E., jt. ed. see Newcomer, Robert J.

Benjamin, A. H. It Could Have Been Worse. LC 97-29407. (Illus.). 32p. (J). (ps-2). 1998. 14.95 (*1-888444-26-6*, 21024) Little Tiger.

***Benjamin, A. H.** It Could Have Been Worse. (Illus.). 32p. (J). (ps-2). 1999. pap. 5.95 (*1-58431-006-5*, Pub. by Little Tiger) Futech Educ Prods.

— It Could Have Been Worse. (Illus.). (J). 2000. 6.95 (*1-58431-015-4*) Little Tiger.

Benjamin, A. H. Podria Haber Sido Peor. Mlawer, Teresa, tr.Tr. of It Could Have Been Worse. (SPA., Illus.). 32p. (J). (gr. 1-3). 1998. 14.95 (*1-880507-40-4*) Lectorum Pubns.

Benjamin, A. H. & Holstien, Elisabeth. A Duck So Small. LC 97-27876. (Illus.). 32p. (J). (ps-3). 1998. 14.95 (*1-888444-30-4*, 21028) Little Tiger.

***Benjamin, Alan.** Beautiful Blessings. (Precious Moments Ser.). 14p. 2000. 4.99 (*0-307-13470-9*) Gldn Bks Pub Co.

Benjamin, Alan. Busy Bunnies. (Illus.). 16p. (J). (ps up). 1988. pap. 3.95 (*0-671-64807-1*) Litle Simon.

— Christmas Wishes. LC 89-208677. (Chubby Board Bks.). (Illus.). 16p. (J). (ps up). 1989. 3.95 (*0-671-68268-7*) Litle Simon.

— Curious Critters: A Pop-Up Menagerie. (Illus.). (J). (ps-3). 1998. pap. 16.95 (*0-689-81586-7*) S&S Childrens.

— Dear Santa Chubby Board Book. (Illus.). 16p. (J). (ps up). 1993. 3.95 (*0-671-87068-8*) Litle Simon.

— Ducky's Easter Surprise. (Illus.). 16p. (J). (ps up). 1988. pap. 3.95 (*0-671-64808-X*) Litle Simon.

— Halloween Riddles Chubby Board Book. (Illus.). 16p. (J). (ps up). 1993. pap. 3.95 (*0-671-87067-X*) Litle Simon.

— Hallowhat? A Chubby Board Book. (Illus.). 16p. (J). (ps-k). 1992. pap. 3.95 (*0-671-77009-8*) Litle Simon.

— Hanukkah Chubby Board Book. LC 94-163571. (Chubby Board Bks.). (Illus.). 16p. (J). (ps up). 1993. pap. 3.95 (*0-671-87069-6*) Litle Simon.

— Hanukkah with Three Dreidels. (Chubby Board Bks.). (Illus.). (J). (ps-k). 1997. bds. 6.99 (*0-689-80911-5*) S&S Childrens.

— Howl-O-Ween Chubby Board Book. (Illus.). 16p. (J). (ps up). 1993. pap. 3.95 (*0-671-87066-1*) Litle Simon.

— It's Almost Christmas, Rudolph! (Shaped Little Nugget Bks.). 18p. (J). 1998. 3.99 (*0-307-13056-8*, 13056, Goldn Books) Gldn Bks Pub Co.

— Let's Count, Dracula: A Chubby Board Book. (Illus.). 16p. (J). (ps up). 1992. 3.95 (*0-671-77008-X*) Litle Simon.

— Let's Eat: Vamos a Comer. LC 93-151091. (Chubby Board Book in English & Spanish Ser.). (ENG & SPA., Illus.). 16p. (J). (ps-1). 1992. pap. 3.95 (*0-671-76927-8*) Litle Simon.

— Let's Play: Vamos a Jugar. (Chubby Board Book in English & Spanish Ser.). (ENG & SPA., Illus.). 16p. (J). (ps-1). 1992. pap. 4.99 (*0-671-76928-6*) Litle Simon.

— Lift the Flaps... If You Dare. (Flaptime Bks.). 14p. (J). (ps-1). 1998. 6.99 (*0-307-33301-9*, 33301, Goldn Books) Gldn Bks Pub Co.

— Nicaragua: Dynamics of an Unfinished Revolution. 186p. (Orig.). 1989. write for info. (*0-929405-02-1*); pap. 7.95 (*0-929405-03-X*) Walnut Pub.

— A Nickel Buys a Rhyme. LC 92-6475. (Illus.). 40p. (J). (ps up). 1993. 15.00 (*0-688-06698-4*, Wm Morrow) Morrow Avon.

— One Thousand Silly Sandwiches. (Illus.). 18p. (J). (ps up). 1995. 8.95 (*0-671-89830-2*) Litle Simon.

— One Thousand Space Monsters Have Landed. (J). 1980. pap. 4.95 (*0-590-07667-1*) Scholastic Inc.

***Benjamin, Alan.** Peek-a-Boo! I See You. (J). 2001. mass mkt. 4.99 (*0-375-81168-0*, Pub. by Random Bks Yng Read) Random.

Benjamin, Alan. Precious Moments: Little Prayers. LC 97-70653. (Naptime Tales Bks.). (Illus.). 16p. (J). (ps). 1997. bds. 3.99 (*0-307-12829-6*, 12829, Goldn Books) Gldn Bks Pub Co.

— Precious Moments: Little Thank-Yous. LC 97-70280. (Naptime Tales Bks.). (Illus.). 16p. (J). (ps). 1997. bds. 3.99 (*0-307-12831-8*, 12831, Goldn Books) Gldn Bks Pub Co.

— Rat-a-Tat, Pitter Pat. LC 87-568. (Illus.). 40p. (J). (ps). 1987. 11.95 (*0-690-04609-X*) HarpC Child Bks.

— Sandy Paws Is Coming to Town! deluxe ed. LC 97-81056. (Flaptime Bks.). 10p. (J). (ps-1). 1998. 7.99 (*0-307-33101-6*, 33101, Goldn Books) Gldn Bks Pub Co.

— The Slightly Scary Halloween Flap Book. deluxe ed. (Flaptime Bks.). 10p. (J). 1998. 7.99 (*0-307-33100-8*, 33100, Goldn Books) Gldn Bks Pub Co.

— What Color? Que Color? LC 93-151264. (Chubby Board Book in English & Spanish Ser.). (ENG & SPA., Illus.). 16p. (J). (ps-1). 1992. pap. 3.95 (*0-671-76930-8*) Litle Simon.

***Benjamin, Alan.** Winter Wonderland. (Precious Moments Ser.). (Illus.). (J). 2000. 4.99 (*0-307-13473-3*, Goldn Books) Gldn Bks Pub Co.

— Yoo-Hoo! Peek-a-Boo. (J). 2001. mass mkt. 4.99 (*0-375-81167-2*) Random Bks Yng Read.

Benjamin, Alan. Zoo's Who: Babies. (J). 1994. lib. bdg. 3.95 (*0-671-86602-8*) Litle Simon.

— Zoo's Who: Colors. 16p. (J). (ps up). 1994. 3.95 (*0-671-86600-1*) Litle Simon.

Benjamin, Alan, ed. A Treasury of Baby Names. enl. ed. 1983. mass mkt. 5.99 (*0-451-16944-1*, Sig) NAL.

Benjamin, Alan & Appleby, Ellen. One to Ten. 1991. pap. 9.95 (*0-671-74136-5*) S&S Trade.

Benjamin, Alan & Blitzer, Barbara. Mail Order Cat. 1985. 12.95 (*0-671-54619-8*, Fireside) S&S Trade Pap.

Benjamin, Alfred D. The Helping Interview, 3 vols. 3rd ed. LC 80-81650. 208p. (C). 1980. pap. 37.96 (*0-395-29648-X*) HM.

Benjamin, Alfred D. The Helping Interview with Case Illustrations. 3rd ed. LC 86-82663. 304p. (C). 1987. pap. text 37.16 (*0-395-43725-3*) HM.

***Benjamin-Alvarado, Jonathan.** Power to the People: Energy & the Cuban Nuclear Program. LC 99-55074. 192p. 2000. pap. write for info. (*0-415-92438-3*) Routledge.

— Power to the People: Energy & the Cuban Nuclear Program. LC 99-55074. 192p. 2000. 75.00 (*0-415-92437-5*) Routledge.

***Benjamin, Amy.** English Teacher's Guide to Performance Tasks & Rubrics: High School. LC 00-23506. 185p. 2000. pap. 29.95 (*1-883001-93-5*) Eye On Educ.

Benjamin, Amy. Writing in the Content Areas. LC 99-17341. 208p. 1999. pap. 29.95 (*1-883001-77-3*) Eye On Educ.

Benjamin, Andrew. Art, Mimesis & the Avant-Garde: Aspects of a Philosophy of Difference. (Illus.). 320p. (C). 1991. pap. 27.99 (*0-415-06627-1*, A6218) Routledge.

***Benjamin, Andrew.** Philosophy's Literature. 226p. 2000. pap. 29.95 (*1-903083-09-5*, Pub. by Clinamen Pr) Paul & Co Pubs.

Benjamin, Andrew. The Plural Event: Descartes, Hegel, Heidegger. LC 93-16570. 224p. (C). 1993. pap. 27.99 (*0-415-09529-8*, B2461) Routledge.

— The Plural Event: Descartes, Hegel, Heidegger. LC 93-16570. 240p. (C). (gr. 13). 1993. 75.00 (*0-415-09528-X*, B2457) Routledge.

— Present Hope: Philosophy, Architecture, Judaism. LC 97-205268. 192p. (C). 1997. 80.00 (*0-415-13385-8*); pap. 22.99 (*0-415-13386-6*) Routledge.

— Sculpture Art & Design Profile. 96p. 1997. pap. 44.95 (*0-471-97694-6*) Wiley.

— Translation & the Nature of Philosophy: A New Theory of Words. 224p. 1989. 49.95 (*0-415-01059-4*, A3531); pap. 14.95 (*0-415-04485-5*, A3535) Routledge.

— What Is Abstraction? (What Is? Ser.). 69p. 1996. pap. 16.95 (*1-85490-434-5*, Pub. by Wiley) Wiley.

Benjamin, Andrew, ed. Complexity: Architecture/Art/Philosophy. LC 98-116515. (Illus.). 96p. (Orig.). 1995. pap. 35.95 (*1-85490-417-5*) Wiley.

Benjamin, Andrew, ed. Judging Lyotard. LC 91-30983. (Warwick Studies in Philosophy & Literature). 224p. (C). (gr. 13). 1992. pap. 24.99 (*0-415-05257-2*, A7010) Routledge.

— The Problems of Modernity. 224p. 1989. 37.50 (*0-415-01066-7*) Routledge.

Benjamin, Andrew, ed. Sculpture. (Illus.). 96p. (Orig.) 1997. pap. 29.95 (*1-85490-527-9*) Academy Ed UK.

***Benjamin, Andrew & Libeskind, Daniel.** Reiser & Umemoto. 96p. 1998. pap. 39.95 (*0-471-97864-7*) Wiley.

Benjamin, Andrew, jt. auth. see Norris, Christopher.

Benjamin, Andrew, jt. ed. see Fletcher, John.

Benjamin, Andrew, jt. ed. see Osborn, Peter.

***Benjamin, Andrew E.** Architectural Philosophy: Repetition, Function, Alterity. LC 00-38944. 2000. pap. write for info. (*0-485-00605-7*, Pub. by Athlone Pr) Humanities.

Benjamin, Andrew E. Translation & the Nature of Philosophy: A New Theory of Words. LC 88-32296. 199p. reprint ed. pap. 61.70 (*0-608-20318-1*, 207157100002) Bks Demand.

Benjamin, Anna, tr. see Xenophon.

Benjamin, Anne. Decadence in Thirteenth Century Provencal & Hebrew Poetry. 257p. 1987. pap. 39.95 (*0-7734-9211-9*) E Mellen.

— Kidney Failure: Our Success Story. 150p. 1984. 7.50 (*0-86516-050-3*) Bolchazy-Carducci.

— Young Harriet Tubman: Freedom Fighter. LC 91-26404. (Illus.). 32p. (J). (gr. k-2). 1997. pap. 3.50 (*0-8167-2539-X*) Troll Communs.

— Young Harriet Tubman: Freedom Fighter. (Troll First-Start Biography Ser.). (J). 1992. 8.70 (*0-606-02361-5*, Pub. by Turtleback) Demco.

— Young Helen Keller: Woman of Courage. LC 91-26406. (Illus.). 32p. (J). (gr. k-2). 1997. pap. 3.50 (*0-8167-2531-4*) Troll Communs.

— Young Helen Keller: Woman of Courage. (Troll First-Start Biography Ser.). (J). 1992. 8.70 (*0-606-02362-3*, Pub. by Turtleback) Demco.

— Young Pocahontas: Indian Princess. LC 91-32654. (Illus.). 32p. (J). (gr. k-2). 1996. pap. 3.50 (*0-8167-2535-7*) Troll Communs.

— Young Pocahontas: Indian Princess. (Troll First-Start Biography Ser.). (J). 1992. 8.70 (*0-606-02363-1*, Pub. by Turtleback) Demco.

— Young Rosa Parks: A Civil Rights Heroine. LC 95-7599. (Illus.). 32p. (J). (gr. 1-4). 1997. pap. 3.50 (*0-8167-3775-4*) Troll Communs.

— Young Rosa Parks, Civil Rights Heroine. LC 95-7599. (Troll First-Start Biography Ser.). 1996. 8.70 (*0-606-10102-0*, Pub. by Turtleback) Demco.

Benjamin, Anne, ed. see Mandela, Winnie.

Benjamin, Anne M. A History of the Anti-Suffrage Movement in the United States from 1895 to 1920: Women Against Equality. LC 91-40634. 400p. 1992. lib. bdg. 99.95 (*0-7734-9436-7*) E Mellen.

Benjamin, Arthur & Shermer, Michael B. Mathemagics: How to Look Like a Genius Without Really Trying. 228p. 1993. 22.95 (*0-929923-54-5*) Lowell Hse.

— Mathemagics: How to Look Like a Genius Without Really Trying. 2nd rev. ed. 240p. 1998. pap. 18.00 (*0-7373-0008-6*, 00086W) NTC Contemp Pub Co.

— Teach Your Child Math. 3rd ed. (Teach Your Child Ser.). 224p. 1999. pap. 15.95 (*0-7373-0134-1*, 01341W) NTC Contemp Pub Co.

— Teach Your Child Math: Making Math Fun for the Both of You. (Illus.). 168p. (Orig.). 1991. pap. 10.95 (*0-929923-32-4*) Lowell Hse.

Benjamin, Asher. American Builder's Companion: Or, a System of Architecture, Particularly Adapted to the Present Style of Building. (Illus.). 114p. 1969. reprint ed. pap. 10.95 (*0-486-22236-5*) Dover.

— The Architect, or Practical House Carpenter (1844) (Illus.). 192p. 1988. pap. 11.95 (*0-486-25802-5*) Dover.

— Country Builder's Assistant. 64p. 1997. reprint ed. pap. 8.95 (*1-55709-104-8*) Applewood.

— Pattern Books of American Classical Architecture: Practice of Architecture & the Builder's Guide. (Illus.). 475p. 1994. reprint ed. pap. 19.95 (*0-306-80572-3*) Da Capo.

— The Practical House Carpenter. 119p. reprint ed. 49.00 (*0-318-04471-4*) Rprt Serv.

— The Practical House Carpenter: Being a Complete Development of the Grecian Orders of Architecture. 1988. reprint ed. lib. bdg. 39.00 (*0-685-44268-3*) Rprt Serv.

— The Practical House Carpenter: Being a Complete Development of the Grecian Orders of Architecture. 1976. reprint ed. 59.00 (*0-403-06633-6*, Regency) Scholarly.

— The Works of Asher Benjamin: Boston, 1806-1843, 7 vols., Set. Incl. American Builder's Companion, 1806. 158p. 1974. 45.00 (*0-306-71026-9*); Builder's Guide: 1839. 174p. 1974. 47.50 (*0-306-70971-6*); Country Builder's Assistant: 1797. 84p. 1974. 45.00 (*0-306-71027-7*); Elements of Architecture: 1843. 290p. 1974. 47.50 (*0-306-71028-5*); Practical House Carpenter, 1830. 248p. 1974. 45.00 (*0-306-71029-3*); Practice of Architecture, 1833. 236p. 1974. 45.00 (*0-306-71030-7*); Rudiments of Architecture, 1814. 162p. 1974. 45.00 (*0-306-71031-5*); (Architecture & Decorative Art Ser.). 1974. 285.00 (*0-306-71032-3*) Da Capo.

Benjamin, B. General Insurance. (C). 1977. 150.00 (*0-7855-4164-0*, Pub. by Witherby & Co) St Mut.

Benjamin, B. & Pollard, J. H. Analysis of Mortality & Other Acturial Statistics. (C). 1980. 215.00 (*0-7855-4321-X*, Pub. by Witherby & Co) St Mut.

Benjamin, B. S. Statics, Strengths & Structures for Architects. 3rd ed. (Illus.). 332p. (C). 1992. text 50.00 (*0-942387-07-4*) AB Lit Hse.

— Structural Evolution: An Illustrated History. (Illus.). 206p. (C). 1990. 50.00 (*0-942387-05-8*) AB Lit Hse.

Benjamin, B. S., ed. see Dandekar, B. B.

Benjamin, Barbara. A Modern Prayer Guide to St. Teresa of Avila - Interior Castle. LC 91-73654. 52p. 1991. pap. 4.95 (*1-880178-00-1*) Intuitive Discov.

Benjamin, Barbara & Vali, Alexandria D. The Lenten Kitchen. LC 94-33152. 96p. 1995. pap. 6.95 (*0-8091-3542-6*) Paulist Pr.

Benjamin, Barbara, et al. Leadership in the Interactive Age: A Facilitator's Guide. 17p. 1995. 4.95 (*1-880178-06-0*) Intuitive Discov.

— Leadership in the Interactive Age: A Skills Development Workbook. 448p. 1995. 39.95 (*1-880178-05-2*) Intuitive Discov.

Benjamin, Barnard, et al. Pensions: The Problems of Today & Tomorrow. (Studies in Financial Institutions & Markets: No. 4). 272p. text 60.00 (*0-04-332127-5*) Routledge.

Benjamin, Ben E. & Borden, Gale. Listen to Your Pain: The Active Person's Guide to Understanding. LC 82-20066. (Illus.). 1984. pap. 18.95 (*0-14-006687-X*, Penguin Bks) Viking Penguin.

Benjamin, Ben E., jt. ed. see Werner, Ruth.

Benjamin, Bernard. Social & Economic Factors Affecting Morality: Confluence 5. 1965. text 10.00 (*3-11-000279-5*) Mouton.

Benjamin, Bernard & Pollard, J. H. The Analysis of Mortality & Other Actuarial Statistics. 2nd ed. LC HG8781.B38. (Illus.). 480p. reprint ed. pap. 148.80 (*0-608-10635-6*, 207125700009) Bks Demand.

Benjamin, Beth, jt. auth. see Conger, Jay A.

Benjamin, Betsey S. The World of Rozome: Wax-Resist Textiles of Japan. (Illus.). 224p. 1996. 107.00 (*4-7700-1774-X*, Pub. by Kodansha Int) OUP.

Benjamin, Betsy. Dreams & Idle Wishes. 84p. 1991. pap. 12.50 (*0-9634485-0-1*) Mills Hill Pub.

***Benjamin, Bruce.** Endolaryngeal Surgery. (Illus.). 384p. 1998. write for info. (*1-85317-323-1*) Martin Dunitz.

Benjamin, Bruce, et al. A Color Atlas of Otorhinolaryngology. (Illus.). 352p. 1994. text 208.00 (*0-397-51422-0*) Lppncott W & W.

Benjamin, C. Price Guide to the Non-Sports Cards, 1930-1960, No. 2. (Sport Americana Ser.). 448p. 1993. pap. 14.95 (*0-937424-66-8*) Edgewater.

Benjamin, C. H. Resource Guide for Economics of Competition. (Illus.). 100p. (Orig.). pap. text. write for info. (*0-9631679-0-1*) GR Comm Col Edu TC.

Benjamin, Carmen & Butt, John. A New Reference Grammar of Modern Spanish. 2nd ed. (Reference Grammar of Ser.). (Illus.). 536p. 1995. pap. 32.95 (*0-8442-7088-1*, 70881, Natl Textbk Co) NTC Contemp Pub Co.

Benjamin, Carmen, jt. auth. see Butt, John.

Benjamin, Carol Lea. Chosen Puppy: How to Select & Raise a Great Puppy from an Animal Shelter. (Illus.). 96p. 1990. pet. 7.95 (*0-87605-417-3*) Howell Bks.

— Dog Problems. 2nd ed. (Illus.). 224p. 1989. pet. 14.95 (*0-87605-514-5*) Howell Bks.

B

An Asterisk (*) at the beginning of an entry indicates that the title is appearing for the first time.

— Dog Training for Kids. 2nd rev. ed. LC 87-26297. (Illus.). 128p. 1988. 17.95 (0-87605-541-2) Howell Bks.

— Dog Training in Ten Minutes. LC 96-23752. 144p. 1996. 14.95 (0-87605-471-8) Howell Bks.

— The Dog Who Knew Too Much: A Rachel Alexander & Dash Mystery. LC 97-19360. 256p. 1997. 21.95 (0-8027-3312-3) Walker & Co.

— The Dog Who Knew Too Much: A Rachel Alexander & Dash Mystery. 272p. 1998. reprint ed. mass mkt. 5.99 (0-440-22637-6) Dell.

— A Hell of a Dog. LC 98-23138. (Rachel Alexander & Dash Mystery Ser.). 276p. 1998. 22.95 (0-8027-3325-5) Walker & Co.

— A Hell of a Dog: A Rachel Alexander & Dash Mystery. 320p. 1999. mass mkt. 5.99 (0-440-22548-5) Dell.

— Lady Vanishes. LC 99-25682. (Rachel Alexander & Dash Mystery Ser.). 276p. 1999. 23.95 (0-8027-3335-2) Walker & Co.

— Mother Knows Best: The Natural Way to Train Your Dog. LC 84-27871. (Illus.). 256p. 1985. 22.95 (0-87605-666-4) Howell Bks.

— Second-Hand Dog: How to Turn Yours into a First-Rate Pet. LC 88-748. (Illus.). 96p. 1988. per. 6.95 (0-87605-735-0) Howell Bks.

— Surviving Your Dog's Adolescence: A Positive Training Program. LC 93-17879. (Illus.). 224p. 1993. 20.00 (0-87605-742-3) Howell Bks.

— This Dog for Hire: A Rachel Alexander & Dash Mystery. (Rachel Alexander & Dash Mystery Ser.). 304p. 1997. mass mkt. 5.99 (0-440-22520-5) Dell.

— This Dog for Hire: A Rachel Alexander & Dash Mystery. LC 96-26066. (Rachel Alexander & Dash Mystery Ser.). 224p. 1996. 20.95 (0-8027-3292-5) Walker & Co.

— The Wicked Stepdog. 128p. (YA). (gr. 5 up). 1986. mass mkt. 2.50 (0-380-70089-1, Avon Bks) Morrow Avon.

***Benjamin, Carol Lea.** The Wrong Dog. LC 00-34956. (Rachel Alexander & Dash Mystery Ser.). (Illus.). 2000. 23.95 (0-8027-3348-4) Walker & Co.

Benjamin, Carol Lea & Haggerty, Arthur J. Dog Tricks. (Illus.). 120p. 1996. 12.98 (1-884822-46-0) Blck Dog & Leventhal.

Benjamin, Carol Lea, jt. auth. see Haggerty, Arthur J.

Benjamin, Charles & Powell, Charles. Negotiating the 1988 U. S.-Soviet Long-Term Agreements on Grain Purchases. (Pew Case Studies in International Affairs). 1988p. (C). 1988. pap. text 3.50 (1-56927-131-3) Geo U Inst Dplmcy.

Benjamin, Chris, et al, eds. The Bahamas Index & Yearbook: 1992. 250p. 1993. text 100.00 (0-932265-28-6); pap. text 49.95 (0-932265-29-4) White Sound.

Benjamin-Chung, Michele. Math Principles & Practice: Preparing for Health Career Success. LC 98-28717. 176p. 1998. pap. text 33.33 (0-8359-5272-X) P-H.

Benjamin, Claude. Medical Itch. (Illus.). 1964. 11.95 (0-8392-1067-1) Astor-Honor.

Benjamin, Clinton L., et al. Human Biology. LC 95-45014. 1996. write for info. (0-07-022896-5) McGraw.

— Human Biology with Environmental Topic. (C). 1996. pap. text, student ed. 21.25 (0-07-022909-0) McGraw.

— Human Biology with Environmental Topics. LC 95-45015. 688p. (C). 1996. pap. 61.88 (0-07-022907-4) McGraw.

Benjamin, Cynthia. Footprints in the Sand. LC 98-11009. (Hello Reader! Science Ser.: Level 1). (Illus.). 32p. (J). (ps-1). 1999. 3.99 (0-590-44087-X) Scholastic Inc.

— Footprints in the Snow. LC 93-43409. (Hello Reader! Ser.). (Illus.). 32p. (J). (ps-3). 1994. pap. 2.95 (0-590-46663-1, Cartwheel) Scholastic Inc.

Benjamin, Cynthia. Footprints in the Snow. (Hello, Reader! Ser.). 1994. 8.70 (0-606-06982-8, Pub. by Turtleback) Demco.

Benjamin, Cynthia. Footsteps in the Snow, Level 1. LC 93-43409. (Hello Reader! Ser.). (Illus.). (J). (ps-1). 1994. pap. 2.95 (0-590-48296-3) Scholastic Inc.

— I Am a Doctor. (Illus.). 24p. (J). (ps-k). 1994. 6.95 (0-8120-6380-5) Barron.

— I Am a Firefighter. (Illus.). 24p. (J). (ps-k). 1995. 7.95 (0-8120-6538-7) Barron.

— I Am a Forest Ranger. (Illus.). 24p. (J). 1995. 6.95 (0-8120-6463-1) Barron.

— I Am a Pilot. (Illus.). 24p. (J). (ps-k). 1994. 6.95 (0-8120-6407-0) Barron.

— I Am a Police Officer. LC 95-13105. (Illus.). 24p. 1995. 6.95 (0-8120-6438-0) Barron.

— I Am a Zookeeper. (Illus.). 24p. (J). 1995. 6.95 (0-8120-6398-8) Barron.

— I Am an Astronaut. (Illus.). 24p. (J). 1996. 6.95 (0-8120-6539-5) Barron.

— Somos Cuidadores des Zoologico. (SPA., Illus.). 24p. (J). 1995. 6.95 (0-8120-6415-1) Barron.

— Somos Pilotos. (SPA., Illus.). 24p. (J). (ps). 1994. 6.95 (0-8120-6417-8) Barron.

— Tonka Working Hard with the Rescue Helicopter. (Tonka Trucks Storybook Ser.). (Illus.). (J). (ps-2). 1997. pap. 2.99 (0-614-29036-8, Cartwheel) Scholastic Inc.

— What's Going On? LC 98-55129. (Illus.). 32p. (J). (ps-3). 1999. 16.90 (0-7613-2070-9, Copper Beech Bks) Millbrook Pr.

— What's Going On? LC 98-55129. (Real Kids Readers Ser.). (Illus.). 32p. (J). (gr. k-2). 1999. 3.99 (0-7613-2095-4, Copper Beech Bks) Millbrook Pr.

— Working Hard with the Rescue Helicopter. LC 97-177450. (Tonka Trucks Storybook Ser.). (Illus.). 32p. (J). (ps-2). 1997. pap. 2.99 (0-590-13449-3) Scholastic Inc.

— Yo Soy un Medico. (SPA., Illus.). 24p. (J). (ps). 1994. 6.95 (0-8120-6414-3) Barron.

Benjamin, D. Paul, ed. Change of Representation & Inductive Bias. (C). 1989. text 127.50 (0-7923-9055-5) Kluwer Academic.

Benjamin, David. The ITCA Guide to Coaching Winning Tennis. 178p. (C). 1989. pap. text 9.95 (0-13-507054-6) P-H.

— The Joy of Sumo: A Fan's Notes. (Illus.). 256p. (Orig.). 1992. pap. 12.95 (0-8048-1679-4) Tuttle Pubng.

Benjamin, David N., ed. The Home: Words, Interpretations, Meanings & Environment. LC 95-75560. (Ethnoscapes Ser.). 328p. 1995. 91.95 (1-85628-888-9, Pub. by Avebry) Ashgate Pub Co.

Benjamin, Delmar & Wolf, Steve. Gee Bee. LC 93-13065. (Enthusiast Color Ser.). (Illus.). 96p. 1993. pap. 13.95 (0-87938-820-X) MBI Pubg.

Benjamin, Denis R. Mushrooms: Poisons & Panaceas: Health Effects of Mushrooms. LC 94-44126. (Illus.). 416p. 1995. pap. text 59.95 (0-7167-2600-9); pap. text 34.95 (0-7167-2649-1) W H Freeman.

Benjamin, Don C. Deuteronomy & City Life: A Form Criticism of Texts with the Word City ('ir) in Deuteronomy 4: 41 -26: 19. LC 83-3609. (Illus.). 366p. (Orig.). (C). 1983. pap. text 30.00 (0-8191-3139-3) U Pr of Amer.

Benjamin, Don C., jt. auth. see Matthews, Victor H.

Benjamin, Don-Paul. Downhill. (Illus.). 1979. pap. 5.00 (0-932624-01-4) Elevation Pr.

— When You Live Alone: More Things Dedicated Singles Do. (Illus.). (Orig.). 1983. pap. 5.00 (0-932624-06-5) Elevation Pr.

— When You Live Alone: Things Dedicated Singles Do. (Illus.). 1979. pap. 5.00 (0-932624-00-6) Elevation Pr.

Benjamin, E. M. Takedown. LC 99-72400. 205p. (YA). (gr. 9-12). 1999. pap. 9.95 (1-889199-04-4) Banks Channel.

Benjamin, Ed. The Complete Guide to Bicycle Store Operations: With CD Rom Supplement. 200p. 1999. pap. 99.95 incl. cd-rom (0-924272-10-4) Info Net Pub.

Benjamin, Edy L., ed. see Eliseuson, Michael W.

Benjamin, Edy L., ed. see Erman, Robert N.

Benjamin, Eileen, jt. auth. see Trommer, Rosemary Wahtole.

Benjamin, Elsie. Man at Home in the Universe: A Study of the Great Evolutionary Cycle: the "Globes", the "Rounds", "Races", "Root-Races" & "Sub-Races" (Study Ser.: No. 8). 36p. 1981. pap. 5.00 (0-913004-43-X) Point Loma Pub.

— Search & Find: Theosophical Reference Index. Small, W. Emmett & Todd, Helen, eds. (Study Ser.: No. 1). 1978. pap. 7.95 (0-913004-32-4) Point Loma Pub.

— The Stanzas of Dzyan: Notes for Study on Cosmogenesis & Anthropogenesis. (Study Ser.: No. 5). 45p. 1981. pap. 6.00 (0-913004-40-5) Point Loma Pub.

— A Study of the Whole of Man: The Significance of the Seven Principles of Man & the Significance of the Monad. (Study Ser.: No. 6). 41p. 1981. pap. 6.00 (0-913004-41-3) Point Loma Pub.

Benjamin, Ernst, ed. Developing Issues in Academic Freedom. LC 85-644752. (New Directions for Higher Education Ser.: No. HE 88). 110p. (Orig.). 1994. pap. 22.00 (0-7879-9987-3) Jossey-Bass.

Benjamin, Floella. Coming to England. (Illus.). 96p. (J). (gr. 2-4). 1997. pap. 19.95 (1-85793-819-4, Pub. by Pavilion Bks Ltd) Trafalgar.

Benjamin, Francis S., Jr. & Toomer, G. J., eds. Campanus of Novara & Medieval Planetary Theory: "Theorica planetarum" (Medieval Science Publications: No. 16). (Illus.). 508p. 1972. 45.00 (0-299-05960-X) U of Wis Pr.

Benjamin, Fred & Kaplan, Dorothea. Settle It Yourself: Who Needs a Lawyer. 2nd ed. 145p. 1992. pap. 12.95 (0-929387-99-6) Bonus Books.

Benjamin, G. Andrew H., et al. Law & Mental Health Professionals: Washington. 144p. 1998. pap., suppl. ed. 24.95 (1-55798-510-3) Am Psychol.

Benjamin, Gail R. Japanese Lessons: A Year in a Japanese School Through the Eyes of An American Anthropologist & Her Children. LC 96-35698. (Illus.). 304p. (C). 1997. 45.00 (0-8147-1291-6) NYU Pr.

— Japanese Lessons: A Year in a Japanese School Through the Eyes of an American Anthropologist & Her Children. 272p. 1998. reprint ed. pap. 17.95 (0-8147-1334-3) NYU Pr.

Benjamin, Gerald & Brecher, Charles, eds. The Two New Yorks: State-City Relations in the Changing Federal System. LC 88-15778. 560p. 1989. 55.00 (0-87154-107-6) Russell Sage.

Benjamin, Gerald & Dullea, Henrik N., eds. Decision, 1997: Constitutional Change in New York. LC 97-5427. (Illus.). 534p. (Orig.). 1997. pap. 29.95 (0-914341-50-2) Nelson Rockefeller Inst Govt.

Benjamin, Gerald & Malbin, Michael J. Limiting Legislative Terms. 324p. 1992. pap. 23.95 (0-87187-740-6) Congr Quarterly.

Benjamin, Gerald, jt. auth. see Connery, Robert H.

Benjamin, Gerald A. Finding Your Wings: How to Locate Private Investors to Fund Your Venture. LC 95-52272. 288p. 1996. text 34.95 (0-471-14151-8) Wiley.

Benjamin, Gerald A. & Margulis, Joel. Angel Financing: How to Find & Invest Private Equity. LC 99-33743. (Investments Ser.). 336p. 1999. 49.95 (0-471-35085-0) Wiley.

Benjamin, Goodman, jt. auth. see Myra, Anne.

Benjamin, H. Basic Self-Knowledge. 168p. 1980. pap. 8.95 (0-87728-162-9) Weiser.

Benjamin, Harold H. The Wellness Community Guide to Fighting for Recovery from Cancer. expanded rev. ed. LC 95-11417. Orig. Title: From Victim to Victor. 256p. 1995. pap. 13.95 (0-87477-794-1, Tarcher Putnam) Putnam Pub Group.

Benjamin, Harold R., ed. Democracy in the Administration of Higher Education. LC 72-3344. (Essay Index Reprint Ser.). 1977. reprint ed. 18.95 (0-8369-2892-X) Ayer.

Benjamin, Harry. Everyone's Guide to Theosophy. 1969. 10.95 (0-7229-0130-5) Theos Pub Hse.

Benjamin, Henri, jt. auth. see De Rebecque, Constant.

Benjamin, Hugh & Myers, Richard. A Place Like This: Hugh Benjamin's Peter Island. (Illus.). 64p. (Orig.). 1994. pap. 10.95 (0-9639905-3-5) Two Thous-Three Assocs.

Benjamin, Ida. Quality Fat: Quality Gems Within You. 1994. pap. 22.50 (0-9640649-0-1) Ida B Enter.

Benjamin, Ike. Ghetto Supastar. 1998. mass mkt. 6.50 (0-671-02730-1) PB.

Benjamin, Ionie. Black Press in Britain. 144p. 1995. pap. 18.00 (1-85856-028-4, Trentham Bks) Stylus Pub VA.

Benjamin, Israel B. Three Years in America, 1859-1862, 2 vols. Reznikoff, Charles, tr. from GER. LC 74-27962. (Modern Jewish Experience Ser.). 1975. reprint ed. 57.95 (0-405-06693-7) Ayer.

Benjamin, Jack & Cornell, C. A. Probability, Statistics, & Decisions for Civil Engineers. (C). 1960. text 85.00 (0-07-004549-6) McGraw.

Benjamin, Jack, et al. Probability, Statistics & Decisions for Civil Engineers. 2nd ed. 1990. text. write for info. (0-07-004557-7) McGraw.

Benjamin, James. Business & Professional Communication. 2nd ed. (C). 1999. pap. text. write for info. (0-321-00602-X) Addson-Wesley Educ.

— Principles, Elements & Types of Persuasion. LC 96-76311. 352p. (C). 1996. pap. text 49.00 (0-15-502355-1) Harcourt Coll Pubs.

Benjamin, James J. Intermediate Accounting. 1987. teacher ed. write for info. (0-318-61492-8, H89550); teacher ed. write for info. (0-318-61493-6, H89568); teacher ed. write for info. (0-318-61494-4, H05135); student ed. 19.00 (0-685-17392-5, H89576); trans. write for info. (0-318-61495-2, H89592) P-H.

Benjamin, James M., jt. auth. see DeBruyn, Robert L.

Benjamin, Jane. The Motorist's Guide to the Law. 124p. 1993. 40.00 (1-85190-189-2, Pub. by Tolley Pubng) St Mut.

Benjamin, Janice Y., jt. auth. see Block, Barbara.

Benjamin, Janice Y., jt. auth. see Vinitsky, Barbara B.

Benjamin, Jean K., jt. auth. see Roethel, Hans K.

Benjamin, Jeffrey L., jt. compiled by see Kitson, Michael B.

Benjamin, Jerry D. For Freedom: Studies on Galatians. 112p. 1993. pap. text 8.95 (1-881576-13-2) Providence Hse.

Benjamin, Jessica. Bonds of Love: Psychoanalysis, Feminism, & the Problem Domination. 1988. pap. 17.00 (0-394-75730-0) Pantheon.

— Like Subjects, Love Objects: Essays on Recognition & Sexual Difference. LC 95-14346. 250p. 1995. 35.00 (0-300-06419-5) Yale U Pr.

— Like Subjects, Love Objects: Essays on Recognition & Sexual Difference. 250p. 1998. pap. 16.00 (0-300-07430-1) Yale U Pr.

— Shadow of the Other: Intersubjectivity & Gender in Psychoanalysis. LC 97-14660. 149p. (C). 1997. 75.00 (0-415-91236-9) Routledge.

— Shadow of the Other: Intersubjectivity & Gender in Psychoanalysis. 3rd ed. LC 97-14660. 149p. (C). 1997. pap. 19.99 (0-415-91237-7) Routledge.

***Benjamin, Joan, ed.** Great Garden Formulas: The Ultimate Book of Mix-It-Yourself Concoctions for Your Garden. (Illus.). 352p. 2000. pap. 17.95 (0-87596-848-1, Pub. by Rodale Pr Inc) St Martin.

Benjamin, Joan & Ellis, Barbara, eds. Rodale's No-Fail Flower Garden: How to Plan, Plant, & Grow a Beautiful, Easy-Care Garden. (Illus.). 384p. 1996. pap. 15.95 (0-87596-954-2) Rodale Pr Inc.

— Rodale's No-Fail Flower Garden. 1997. pap. 15.95 (0-614-27248-3) Rodale Pr Inc.

Benjamin, Joan, et al. Making Groups Work: Rethinking Practice. LC 98-197584. 208p. 1998. pap. 24.95 (1-86448-304-0, Pub. by Allen & Unwin Pty) Paul & Co Pubs.

Benjamin, Joanna. Benjamin: Global Custody - an English Legal Analysis. 1996. pap. write for info. (0-406-04836-3, BGCE, MICHIE) LEXIS Pub.

Benjamin, Joel, et al, eds. An Anthology of Indo-Caribbean Poetry & Prose. LC 96-209836. 320p. 1998. pap. 24.95 (0-948833-94-7, Pub. by Peepal Tree Pr) Paul & Co Pubs.

Benjamin, John D., ed. Megatrends in Retail Real Estate. LC 95-37846. (Research Issues in Real Estate Ser.: Vol. 3). 392p. (C). 1996. lib. bdg. 144.00 (0-7923-9640-5) Kluwer Academic.

Benjamin, Jules R. The United States & Cuba: Hegemony & Dependent Development, 1880-1934. LC 77-74550. (Pitt Latin American Ser.). 280p. reprint ed. pap. 86.80 (0-7837-2142-0, 204242800004) Bks Demand.

— The United States & the Origins of the Cuban Revolution: An Empire of Liberty in an Age of National Liberation. (Illus.). 241p. 1990. text 47.50 (0-691-07836-X, Pub. by Princeton U Pr); pap. text 17.95 (0-691-02536-3, Pub. by Princeton U Pr) Cal Prin Full Svc.

Benjamin, Kedem. Analysis. (TIME SERIES). text. write for info. (0-471-36355-3) Wiley.

Benjamin, L. Ann & Lord, Jerome E., eds. Family Literacy: Directions in Research & Implications for Practice. 103p. (Orig.). (C). 1996. pap. text 25.00 (0-7881-3034-X) DIANE Pub.

Benjamin, Laura L. One Hundred Years of Progress. Castro, Walter E., ed. (Illus.). 165p. (C). 1989. text 25.00 (0-9624328-0-6) Clemson Univ.

Benjamin, Lewis S. More Stage Favorites of the 18th Century. (Essay Index Reprint Ser.). 1977. 19.95 (0-8369-0194-0) Ayer.

— Stage Favorites of the Eighteenth Century. LC 68-57303. (Essay Index Reprint Ser.). 1977. 20.95 (0-8369-0060-X) Ayer.

— William Makepeace Thackeray: A Biography, 2 vols., Set. (BCL1-PR English Literature Ser.). 1992. reprint ed. lib. bdg. 150.00 (0-7812-7702-7) Rprt Serv.

— William Makepeace Thackeray: A Biography Including Hitherto Uncollected Letters & Speeches & a Bibliography of 1300 Items, 2 vols., Set. LC 15-5841. 1968. reprint ed. 59.00 (0-403-00112-9) Scholarly.

Benjamin, Lewis S. & Hargreaves, Reginald, eds. Great German Short Stories. LC 72-169540. (Short Story Index Reprint Ser.). 1977. reprint ed. 51.95 (0-8369-4001-6) Ayer.

Benjamin, Libby, jt. auth. see Walz, Garry R.

Benjamin, Linda W. Famous Virgin Islanders for Young Readers-Alton A. Adams. Mackay, Marguerite, ed. (Illus.). 32p. (Orig.). 1987. pap. write for info. (0-935357-04-1) CRIC Prod.

***Benjamin, Lois.** Three Black Generations at the Crossroads. LC 99-38053. 2000. pap. write for info. (0-8304-1565-3) Burnham Inc.

Benjamin, Lois, ed. Black Women in the Academy: Promises & Perils. LC 96-47388. 424p. 1997. 49.95 (0-8130-1500-6) U Press Fla.

Benjamin, Lorna S. Interpersonal Diagnosis & Treatment of Personality Disorders. 2nd ed. LC 95-41650. (Diagnosis & Treatment of Mental Disorders Ser.). 431p. 1995. lib. bdg. 45.00 (1-57230-060-4, 0060) Guilford Pubns.

Benjamin, Ludy T., Jr. A History of Psycholgy in Letters. 240p. (C). 1992. text. write for info. (0-697-12980-2) Brown & Benchmark.

— A History of Psychology: Original Sources & Contemporary Research. 576p. (C). 1988. pap. text 37.74 (0-07-004561-5) McGraw.

Benjamin, Ludy T. A History of Psychology: Original Sources & Contemporary Research. 2nd ed. LC 96-20144. 640p. (C). 1996. pap. 56.56 (0-07-005599-8) McGraw.

Benjamin, Ludy T., Jr., ed. American Psychologist Special Issue Vol. 47, No. 2: The History of American Psychology. 263p. 1992. pap. 20.00 (1-55798-170-1) Am Psychol.

Benjamin, Ludy T., et al, eds. Activities Handbook for the Teaching of Psychology, Vol. 4. Vol. 4. 408p. (C). 1999. pap. text 29.95 (1-55798-537-5, 432-1210) Am Psychol.

— Handbook for Teaching Introductory Psychology. 240p. 1985. pap. 27.50 (0-89859-561-4) L Erlbaum Assocs.

Benjamin, Ludy T., Jr. & Lowman, Kathleen D., eds. Activities Handbook for the Teaching of Psychology, Vol. 1. rev. ed. LC 81-1648. Vol. 1. 244p. (Orig.). 1981. pap. 20.00 (0-912704-34-9) Am Psychol.

Benjamin, Ludy T., Jr., et al. Psychology. 3rd ed. 880p. (C). 1993. text 52.00 (0-02-308290-9, Macmillan Coll) P-H.

Benjamin, Marina. Living at the End of the World. LC 99-221970. (Illus.). 300p. 1998. 29.50 (0-330-34203-7, Pub. by Picador) Trans-Atl Phila.

***Benjamin, Marina.** Living at the End of the World: Humanity's Obsession with Its Own Ultimate Demise. 305p. 1999. pap. 17.95 (0-330-34204-5, Pub. by Picador) Trans-Atl Phila.

Benjamin, Marina, ed. A Question of Identity: Women, Science, & Literature. LC 92-38796. (Illus.). 280p. (C). 1993. text 48.00 (0-8135-1982-9); pap. text 20.00 (0-8135-1983-7) Rutgers U Pr.

Benjamin, Mark M. & Li, Chi-Wang. Adsorption & Filtration Studies Using Iron-Oxide-Coated Olivine As a Medium. LC 96-133314. (Illus.). 65p. 1996. pap. 60.00 (0-89867-839-0, 90679) Am Water Wks Assn.

Benjamin, Martin. Splitting the Difference: Compromise & Integrity in Ethics & Politics. LC 89-39224. x, 198p. 1990. 22.50 (0-7006-0414-6); pap. 14.95 (0-7006-0455-3) U Pr of KS.

Benjamin, Martin & Curtis, Joy. Ethics in Nursing. 3rd ed. 264p. 1992. pap. text 26.50 (0-19-506748-7) OUP.

Benjamin, Martin, et al. Swahili Phrasebook. 2nd ed. (Illus.). 240p. 1998. pap. 5.95 (0-86442-509-0) Lonely Planet.

Benjamin, Mary L. Benjamin. Genealogy of the Family of Lt. Samuel Benjamin & Tabitha Livermore, His Wife, Early Settlers of Livermore, Me., with a Record of Their Descent from John Benjamin & John Livermore, the Emigrants, Including Biographical Sketches, Notes & Diary. (Illus.). 92p. 1997. reprint ed. pap. 18.00 (0-8328-7487-6); reprint ed. lib. bdg. 28.00 (0-8328-7486-8) Higginson Bk Co.

Benjamin, McDonald P. Investment Projects in Agriculture: Principles & Case Studies. LC 85-4277. 319p. reprint ed. pap. 98.90 (0-8357-6166-5, 203443900090) Bks Demand.

Benjamin, Medea. Cuba: Talking about Revolution: Conversations with Juan Antonio Blanco. 2nd rev. ed. 128p. 1996. pap. 12.95 (1-875284-97-4) Ocean Pr NJ.

— The Peace Corps & More: 120 Ways to Work, Study & Travel in the Third World. rev. ed. LC 90-27827. 107p. (Orig.). 1991. pap. 6.95 (0-929765-04-4) Seven Locks Pr.

Benjamin, Medea, ed. from SPA. Don't Be Afraid, Gringo: A Honduran Woman Speaks From The Heart: The Story of Elvia Alvarado. LC 88-45725. (Illus.). 208p. 1989. reprint ed. pap. 12.50 (0-06-097205-X, PL 7205, Perennial) HarperTrade.

Benjamin, Medea & Mendonca, Maisa L., eds. Benedita da Silva: An Afro-Brazilian Woman's Story of Politics & Love. LC 97-22158.Tr. of BeneDita. (Illus.). 224p. 1997. pap. 15.95 (0-935028-70-6) Inst Food & Develop.

Benjamin, Medea, jt. ed. see Rosset, Peter.

Benjamin, Michael. Cultural Diversity, Educational Equity, & the Transformation of Higher Education: Group Profiles as a Guide to Policy & Programming. LC 95-26520. 224p. 1996. 59.95 (0-275-95544-3, Praeger Pubs) Greenwood.

Benjamin, Michael J. Crowsongs. LC 97-90404. (Illus.). 55p. 1997. pap. 8.95 (0-533-12390-9) Vantage.

Benjamin, Nancy. Income Distribution & Adjustment in an Agricultural Economy: A General Equilibrium Analysis of Cameroon. LC 97-228149. (Working Papers: No. 41). 37p. (C). 1993. pap. 7.00 (1-56401-141-0) Cornell Food.

An Asterisk (*) at the beginning of an entry indicates that the title is appearing for the first time.

Benjamin, Nancy L. & Honig, Lisa B., eds. The Jewish Home Cookbook. 320p. 1995. 22.95 (*0-9647977-0-4*) WJHC.

Benjamin, Nathan. The Quest for Truth. 262p. (Orig.). 1990. pap. 14.95 (*0-9626412-0-0*, 001) Rose Pub FL.

Benjamin, Nikki. Daddy by Default. (Intimate Moments Ser.: No. 789). 1997. per. 3.99 (*0-373-07789-0*, 1-07789-0) Silhouette.

***Benjamin, Nikki.** Expectant Bride-To-Be. 2001. mass mkt. 4.50 (*0-373-24368-5*, 1-24368-2) Silhouette.

Benjamin, Nikki. The Lady & Alex Payton. (Intimate Moments Ser.). 1996. per. 3.99 (*0-373-07729-7*, 1-07729-6) Silhouette.

— The Major & the Librarian. 1999. per. 4.25 (*0-373-24228-X*, Harlequin) Harlequin Bks.

— My Baby, Your Child. (Special Edition Ser.). 1994. per. 3.50 (*0-373-09880-4*, 5-09880-1) Silhouette.

— On the Whispering Wind. (Family Continuity Program Ser.: No. 23). 1999. per. 4.50 (*0-373-82171-9*, 1-82171-9) Harlequin Bks.

— Only St. Nick Knew. (Special Edition Ser.). 1994. per. 3.50 (*0-373-09928-2*, 1-09928-2) Silhouette.

— Restless Wind. (Intimate Moments Ser.). 1993. per. 3.50 (*0-373-07519-7*, 5-07519-7) Silhouette.

— The Surprise Baby. (Special Edition Ser.). 1998. per. 4.25 (*0-373-24189-5*, 1-24189-2) Silhouette.

— The Wedding Venture. (Intimate Moments Ser.). 1995. per. 3.75 (*0-373-07645-2*, 1-07645-4) Silhouette.

Benjamin, Park. A History of Electricity. LC 74-26249. (History, Philosophy & Sociology of Science Ser.). 1979. reprint ed. 46.95 (*0-405-06579-5*) Ayer.

— Poems of Park Benjamin. LC 70-160914. (Biography Index Reprint Ser.). 1977. reprint ed. 23.95 (*0-8369-8077-8*) Ayer.

Benjamin, Patricia & Lamp, Scott P. Understanding Sports Massage. LC 95-49158. (Illus.). 168p. (Orig.). 1996. pap. text 22.00 (*0-87322-976-2*, BBEN0976) Human Kinetics.

Benjamin, Patricia J., jt. auth. see Tappan, Frances M.

Benjamin, Paul & Thompson, Clive. The Occupational Health & Safety Act: 85 of 1993. 335p. 1994. ring bd. 33.00 (*0-7021-2832-5*, Pub. by Juta & Co); ring bd. 27.50 (*0-7021-3265-9*, Pub. by Juta & Co) Gaunt.

Benjamin, Paul, jt. auth. see Thompson, C.

Benjamin, Peggy H. Years-to-Share. (Illus.). 256p. 1990. pap. 12.50 (*0-9627634-0-3*) P Benjamin.

— Years-to-Share. 2nd ed. (First, Second, Third Paperback Ser.). (Illus.). 256p. 1986. 17.50 (*0-9617063-0-9*) Service Pr.

— Years-to-Share. 2nd ed. (First, Second, Third Paperback Ser.). (Illus.). 256p. 1986. reprint ed. pap. 12.95 (*0-685-38389-X*) Service Pr.

Benjamin, Philip S. The Philadelphia Quakers in the Industrial Age, 1865-1920. LC 76-22967. 301p. 1976. reprint ed. 6.00 (*0-87722-086-7*) Phila Yrly Mtg RSOF.

Benjamin, Rebecca. Passionate Concerto. (Rainbow Romances Ser.). 160p. 1993. 14.95 (*0-7090-4922-6*) Parkwest Pubns.

Benjamin, Richard, photos by. Roger Williams Park: A Gift of Seasons. (Illus.). 96p. 1997. 40.00 (*0-9660760-0-1*) Providence Pks.

Benjamin, Richard K. Introduction & Supplement to Thaxter's Contribution Towards a Monograph of the Laboulbeniacea. 1971. 32.00 (*3-7682-0708-0*) Lubrecht & Cramer.

— The Merosporangiferous Mucorales. (Bibliotheca Mycologica Ser.). (Illus.). 1967. reprint ed. 48.00 (*3-7682-0514-2*) Lubrecht & Cramer.

Benjamin, Robert B. Atlas of Outpatient & Office Surgery. 2nd ed. (Illus.). 290p. 1993. 89.50 (*0-8121-1540-6*) Lppncott W & W.

Benjamin, Robert B., ed. Atlas of Office Surgery, Vol. 1. LC 88-32646. (Illus.). 156p. 1989. reprint ed. pap. 48.40 (*0-7837-2691-0*, 204306900001) Bks Demand.

Benjamin, Robert L. Semantics & Language Analysis. 128p. 1970. pap. text 12.95 (*0-8290-0330-4*) Irvington.

— Semantics & Language Analysis. LC 77-75141. (Speech Communication Ser.). (C). 1970. pap. write for info. (*0-672-61085-X*, SC15, Bobbs) Macmillan.

Benjamin, Robert S., ed. I Am an American, by Famous Naturalized Americans. LC 74-104995. (Essay Index Reprint Ser.). 1977. 19.95 (*0-8369-1449-X*) Ayer.

Benjamin, Rodney. A Serious Influx of Jews: A History of Jewish Welfare in Victoria. 480p. 1998. 48.00 (*1-86448-733-X*, Pub. by Allen & Unwin Pty); pap. 35.00 (*1-86448-732-1*, Pub. by Allen & Unwin Pty) Paul & Co Pubs.

Benjamin, Roger. The Limits of Politics: Collective Goods & Political Change in Post-Industrial Societies. LC 79-19473. (Illus.). 1982. pap. text 7.95 (*0-226-04234-0*) U Ch Pr.

— Matisse's Notes of a Painter: Criticism, Theory, & Context, 1891-1908. LC 86-25056. (Studies in the Fine Arts: Criticism: No. 21). (Illus.). 367p. reprint ed. pap. 113.80 (*0-8357-1743-7*, 207061500005) Bks Demand.

Benjamin, Roger, et al, eds. Balancing State Intervention: The Limits of Transatlantic Markets. LC 94-23389. 288p. 1995. text 55.00 (*0-312-12401-5*) St Martin.

Benjamin, Roger & Elkin, Stephen L., eds. The Democratic State. LC 84-21963. (Studies in Government & Public Policy). viii, 280p. (C). 1985. pap. 14.95 (*0-7006-0262-3*) U Pr of KS.

Benjamin, Roger & Ori, Kan. Tradition & Change in Postindustrial Japan: The Roles of the Political Parties. LC 80-28559. 187p. 1981. 39.95 (*0-275-90583-7*, C0583, Praeger Pubs) Greenwood.

Benjamin, Roger & Yager, Loren. Fairness: The Scylla & Charybdis of U. S.-Japan Relations. LC 93-33575. 86p. 1994. pap. text 15.00 (*0-8330-1465-X*, MR-354-CAPP) Rand Corp.

Benjamin, Roger, et al. The Redesign of Governance in Higher Education. LC 93-5689. 1993. pap. 15.00 (*0-8330-1428-5*, MR-222-LE) Rand Corp.

Benjamin, Roger W. The Limits of Politics: Collective Goods & Political Change in Postindustrial Societies. LC 79-19473. (Illus.). 162p. reprint ed. pap. 50.30 (*0-608-09385-8*, 205413000004); reprint ed. pap. 50.00 (*0-608-21008-0*, 205453600003) Bks Demand.

Benjamin, Roger W., et al. Breaking the Social Contract: The Fiscal Crisis in California Higher Education. LC 98-5917. (Illus.). 31p. 1998. pap. 10.00 (*0-8330-2598-8*, CAE-01-IP) Rand Corp.

Benjamin, Ron & Benjamin, Suzi. Wings of the Morning. 164p. (Orig.). 1993. pap. 7.99 (*0-89228-083-2*) Impact Christian.

Benjamin, Roy. Birdies: How to Tell a Duck Hooker from a Deep-Rough Thrasher. (Illus.). 96p. (Orig.). 1992. pap. write for info. (*0-9633960-0-5*) Golfing Birds Ent.

Benjamin, Ruth. On a Golden Chain. 300p. (C). 1919. pap. 16.95 (*1-56062-081-1*) CIS Comm.

— Selby Printout. 1997. 18.95 (*1-56871-134-4*) Feldheim.

Benjamin, Ruth. Stranger to Her People. LC 93-72273. 207p. (YA). 14.95 (*1-56062-210-5*); pap. 11.95 (*1-56062-231-8*) CIS Comm.

— Yesterday's Child. LC 92-73911. (Illus.). (YA). 16.95 (*1-56062-176-1*); pap. 13.95 (*1-56062-177-X*) CIS Comm.

Benjamin, S. B., jt. ed. see Collen, M. J.

Benjamin, S. G. Our American Artists: With Portraits, Studios & Engravings of Paintings, Repr. of 1879 Ed. LC 75-28870. (Art Experience in Late 19th Century America Ser.: Vol. 6). (Illus.). 1977. lib. bdg. 70.00 (*0-8240-2230-0*) Garland.

— Story of Nation Persia. 330p. 1987. 250.00 (*1-85077-149-9*, Pub. by Darf Pubs Ltd) St Mut.

Benjamin, Sally. A Practical Guide to Understanding, Managing & Reviewing Risk Assessment Reports. ring bd. 69.95 (*1-56670-448-0*) Lewis Pubs.

Benjamin, Sally & Belluck, David. State Groundwater Regulation: Guide to Laws, Standards & Risk Assessment. LC 94-2393. 650p. 1994. 105.00 (*0-87179-795-X*, 0795) BNA Books.

Benjamin, Samuel G. Persia. LC 70-39191. (Select Bibliographies Reprint Ser.). 1977. 24.95 (*0-8369-6793-3*) Ayer.

Benjamin, Samuel G., jt. auth. see Milton, Doris.

Benjamin, Sandra, ed. The World of Benjamin of Tudela: A Medieval Mediterranean Travelogue. LC 94-54882. 1995. 49.50 (*0-8386-3506-7*) Fairleigh Dickinson.

Benjamin, Saragail K. My Dog Ate It. LC 93-25218. 176p. (J). (gr. 4-6). 1994. 14.95 (*0-8234-1047-1*) Holiday.

Benjamin, Scott. Texaco Collector's Guide. LC 97-13149. (Illus.). 128p. 1997. pap. 19.95 (*0-7603-0291-X*) MBI Pubg.

Benjamin, Scott & Henderson, Wayne. Gas Pump Collector's Guide. LC 95-26550. (Illus.). 120p. 1996. pap. 29.95 (*0-7603-0078-X*) MBI Pubg.

— Gasoline Pump Globes: Majors A-P. LC 98-88859. (Illus.). 206p. 1999. pap. 39.95 (*0-7643-0668-5*) Schiffer.

— Gasoline Pump Globes: Majors Q-Z. (Illus.). 256p. 1999. pap. 39.95 (*0-7643-0669-3*) Schiffer.

— Oil Company Logos: Identification Guide. (Illus.). 128p. (Orig.). 1997. pap. 24.95 (*0-9655736-0-5*) PCM Bkshelf.

— Oil Company Signs: A Collector's Guide. LC 95-24759. (Motorbooks International Ser.). (Illus.). 216p. 1995. pap. 14.98 (*0-7603-0073-9*) MBI Pubg.

— Standard Oil: The First 125 Years. (Illus.). 128p. 1996. pap. 19.95 (*0-7603-0086-0*) MBI Pubg.

Benjamin, Scott, jt. auth. see Henderson, Wayne.

Benjamin, Solomon J. Jobs, Land, & Urban Development: The Economic Success of Small Manufacturers in East Delhi, India. LC 90-28671. 172p. 1991. reprint ed. pap. 53.40 (*0-608-02095-8*, 206274800004) Bks Demand.

Benjamin, Stanley B., jt. auth. see DiMarino, Anthony J., Jr.

Benjamin, Stanley B., jt. ed. see DiMarino, Anthony J., Jr.

***Benjamin, Stanley G.** Arizona Sheriff Department Uniform Patches. (Illus.). 10p. 1999. pap. 10.00 (*1-930012-07-1*) Benjamin & Co.

— Benson, Arizona Law Enforcement & History. (Illus.). 44p. 2000. pap. 12.00 (*1-930012-05-5*) Benjamin & Co.

— Bisbee, Arizona Law Enforcement & History. (Illus.). 50p. 2000. pap. write for info. (*1-930012-03-9*) Benjamin & Co.

— Gila Bend, Arizona. (Illus.). 30p. 2000. pap. write for info. (*1-930012-14-4*) Benjamin & Co.

— History of Kearney, Arizona Police Department. (Illus.). 34p. 1998. pap. 10.00 (*1-930012-10-1*) Benjamin & Co.

— History of the Patagonia Marshal's Office: Badges - Patches - Cars & Things. (Illus.). 56p. 1997. pap. 12.00 (*1-930012-12-8*) Benjamin & Co.

— History, Town of Mammoth Police Department. (Illus.). 53p. 1997. pap. 10.00 (*1-930012-11-X*) Benjamin & Co.

— Police Uniform Patches of Central Arizona. (Illus.). 25p. 2000. pap. write for info. (*1-930012-01-2*) Benjamin & Co.

— Police Uniform Patches of Northern Arizona. 25p. 2000. pap. write for info. (*1-930012-02-0*) Benjamin & Co.

— South Tucson, Arizona Police Department, 1936-1998. (Illus.). 104p. 1998. pap. 14.00 (*1-930012-08-X*) Benjamin & Co.

— Southern Arizona City Police Uniform Patches. (Illus.). 33p. 1998. pap. 10.00 (*1-930012-09-8*) Benjamin & Co.

— Southern Arizona City Police Uniform Patches. (Illus.). 33p. 2000. pap. 10.00 (*1-930012-13-6*) Benjamin & Co.

— Tombstone Lawmen, 1880-1999. (Illus.). 53p. 1999. pap. 12.00 (*1-930012-00-4*) Benjamin & Co.

— Tombstone Lawmen, 1880-1999. 2nd rev. ed. (Illus.). 53p. 1999. pap. 12.00 (*1-930012-06-3*) Benjamin & Co.

— Willcox, Arizona Law Enforcement & History. (Illus.). 50p. 2000. pap. write for info. (*1-930012-04-7*) Benjamin & Co.

Benjamin, Starr J., jt. auth. see Jenison, Norma J.

Benjamin, Stephen A. Atlas of Experimentally-Induced Neoplasia in the Beagle Dog. Watson, Charles R & Dagle, Gerald E., eds. LC 96-46999. viii, 172p. 1997. pap. 125.00 (*1-57477-025-X*) Battelle.

Benjamin, Susan. The Public Speaking Handbook. 136p. (Orig.). 1995. pap., teacher ed. 7.95 (*0-673-36153-4*, GoodYrBooks) Addson-Wesley Educ.

— Words at Work. LC 97-18551. 272p. 1997. pap. 13.00 (*0-201-15484-6*) Addison-Wesley.

Benjamin, Susan J., jt. auth. see Collins, Myrtle T.

Benjamin, Susan M. & Sanchez, Susan. Should I Go to the Teacher? Developing a Cooperative Relationship with Your Child's School Community. LC 95-31723. 151p. 1995. pap. 12.00 (*0-435-08126-8*, 08126) Heinemann.

Benjamin, Susan S. An Architectural Album: Chicago's North Shore. rev. ed. LC 91-62211. (Illus.). 208p. 1991. reprint ed. 35.00 (*0-9621602-1-0*) JL Evanston.

Benjamin, Susan S., ed. see Fuller, Cynthia G.

Benjamin, Suzi, jt. auth. see Benjamin, Ron.

Benjamin, T. B. & Benney, D. J. Nonlinear Wave Motion. Newell, A. C., ed. LC 73-19504. (Lectures in Applied Mathematics: Vol. 15). 229p. 1974. text 70.00 (*0-8218-1115-0*, LAM/15) Am Math.

Benjamin, Theresa M. I'd Rather Be Right Than Happy! The Perfect Formula to Failure. 3rd rev. ed. (Orig.). 1996. pap. 18.00 (*1-889943-00-2*) T M Benjamin.

Benjamin, Thomas. Counterpoint in the Style of J. S. Bach. 448p. (C). 1986. 35.00 (*0-02-870280-8*, Schirmer Books) Mac Lib Ref.

— Craft of Modal Counterpoint: A Practical Approach. LC 77-90012. 230p. 1979. 25.00 (*0-02-870480-0*, Schirmer Books) Mac Lib Ref.

— A Little DOS Will Do You. 144p. 1990. pap. 9.95 (*0-931011-29-9*) Grapevine Pubns.

***Benjamin, Thomas.** La Revolucion: Mexico's Great Revolution As Memory, Myth & History. LC F1234.B465 2000. 240p. 2000. 40.00 (*0-292-70880-7*); pap. 18.95 (*0-292-70882-3*) U of Tex Pr.

Benjamin, Thomas. A Rich Land, a Poor People: Politics & Society in Modern Chiapas. 2nd abr. rev. ed. LC 95-41262. (Illus.). 376p. 1996. pap. 22.50 (*0-8263-1713-8*) U of NM Pr.

Benjamin, Thomas, et al. Music for Analysis: Examples from the Common Practice Period & the Twentieth Century. 2nd ed. 418p. (C). 1989. pap. write for info. (*0-534-13428-9*) Wadsworth Pub.

— Music for Analysis: Examples from the Common Practice Period & the Twentieth Century. 3rd ed. 418p. (C). 1991. mass mkt. 41.95 (*0-534-16674-1*) Wadsworth Pub.

— Music for Analysis: Examples from the Common Practice Period & the Twentieth Century. 4th ed. 480p. (C). 1995. spiral bd. 67.95 (*0-534-25506-X*) Wadsworth Pub.

— Techniques & Materials of Tonal Music. 5th ed. LC 97-31386. (Music Ser.). (C). 1997. pap. 72.95 (*0-534-52623-3*) Wadsworth Pub.

— Techniques & Materials of Tonal Music: With an Introduction to Twentieth-Century Techniques. 3rd ed. 280p. (C). 1989. pap. 30.00 (*0-534-13434-3*) Wadsworth Pub.

— Techniques & Materials of Tonal Music: With an Introduction to Twentieth-Century Techniques. 4th ed. 282p. (C). 1991. mass mkt. 43.00 (*0-534-16680-6*) Wadsworth Pub.

Benjamin, Thomas E., et al. Music for Sight Singing. 318p. (C). 1989. pap. 32.95 (*0-534-13416-5*) Wadsworth Pub.

— Music for Sight Singing. 2nd ed. 336p. 1993. 37.50 (*0-534-20823-1*) Wadsworth Pub.

***Benjamin, Thomas E., et al.** Music for Sight Singing. 2nd ed. (Music Ser.). 1999. 40.50 (*0-534-76773-7*) Wadsworth Pub.

Benjamin, Tritobia H. The Life & Art of Lois Mailou Jones. LC 94-18441. (Illus.). 160p. 1994. pap. 25.00 (*0-87654-104-X*) Pomegranate Calif.

Benjamin, Walter. The Arcades Project. Eiland, Howard & McLaughlin, Kevin, trs. from GER. LC 99-27615. 960p. 1999. 39.95 (*0-674-04326-X*) HUP.

— Correspondence of Walter Benjamin. 677p. (C). 199-. 45.00 (*0-226-04237-5*) U Ch Pr.

— Illuminations. LC 68-24382. 1969. reprint ed. pap. 14.00 (*0-8052-0241-2*) Schocken.

— Moscow Diary. Smith, Gary, ed. Sieburth, Richard, tr. LC 86-9964. (Illus.). 160p. 1986. pap. text 9.95 (*0-674-58744-8*) HUP.

— The Origin of German Tragic Drama. 256p. 1998. 22.00 (*1-85984-899-0*, Pub. by Verso) Norton.

— Reflections: Essays, Aphorisms, Autobiographical Writings. Demetz, Peter, ed. Jephcott, Edmund, tr. LC 85-26232. 392p. 1986. reprint ed. pap. 15.00 (*0-8052-0802-X*) Schocken.

— Walter Benjamin: Selected Writings, 1913-1926, Vol. 1. Bullock, Marcus & Jenning, Michael W., eds. (Illus.). 512p. 1996. 35.00 (*0-674-94585-9*) Belknap Pr.

— Walter Benjamin Vol. 2: Selected Writings, 1927-1934. Eiland, Howard & Smith, Gary, eds. (Illus.). 870p. 1999. 37.50 (*0-674-94586-7*) HUP.

Benjamin, Walter, jt. auth. see Adorno, Theodor W.

***Benjamin, Walter W.** The Magical Years: A Boyhood Remembrance. LC 98-87263. 1998. 24.95 (*1-890676-29-2*, Pub. by Beavers Pond) Bookman Bks.

Benjamin, Walter W. War & Reflection. Benson, Douglas, ed. LC 96-70760. (Illus.). 256p. (Orig.). 1996. pap. 12.95 (*0-9640439-1-2*) Red Oak MN.

Benjamin, William J. Borish's Clinical Refraction. Lampert, Richard, ed. LC 96-49871. (Illus.). 960p. (C). 1998. text 150.00 (*0-7216-5688-9*, W B Saunders Co) Harcrt Hlth Sci Grp.

Benjamin, William J., jt. ed. see Rosenblum, William M.

Benjamine, Elbert. Astrological Lore of All Ages. LC 93-10699. 1993. pap. 9.95 (*0-87887-366-X*) Church of Light.

Benjamini, Eli, et al. Immunology: A Short Course. 4th ed. 528p. 2000. pap. 48.50 (*0-471-34890-2*) Wiley.

Benjamins, H. S. Eingeordnete Freiheit: Freiheit und Vorsehung Bei Origenes. (GER.). x, 225p. 1994. 82.50 (*90-04-10117-9*) Brill Academic Pubs.

Benjaminson, Jim. Illustrated Plymouth & Desoto Buyers Guide. LC 96-35797. (Illustrated Buyer's Guide Ser.). (Illus.). 160p. 1996. pap. 17.95 (*0-7603-0107-7*) MBI Pubg.

— Plymouth Commercial Vehicles Photo Archive. (Photo Archive Ser.). (Illus.). 128p. 1999. pap. 29.95 (*1-58388-004-6*, Pub. by Iconografix) Motorbooks Intl.

Benjaminson, Peter. Publish Without Perishing. 144p. 1992. pap. 16.95 (*0-8106-1544-4*) NEA.

— Secret Police: Inside the New York City Department of Investigation. LC 96-24933. 256p. 1997. 22.00 (*1-56980-090-1*) Barricade Bks.

Benjaminson, Peter & Anderson, David. Investigative Reporting. 2nd ed. LC 90-4361. (Illus.). 294p. 1990. reprint ed. pap. 91.20 (*0-608-06861-6*, 206706700009) Bks Demand.

***BenJava, Gustav.** Nikki. LC 00-190327. 318p. 2000. 25.00 (*0-7388-1723-6*); pap. 18.00 (*0-7388-1724-4*) Xlibris Corp.

Benjimen, W., jt. auth. see Lumley, J. S.

Benkadda, S. & Zaslavsky, G. M., eds. Chaos, Kinetics & Nonlinear Dynamics in Fluids & Plasmas: Proceedings of a Workshop Held in Carry-Le Rouet, France, 16-21 June 1997. LC 98-29748. (Lecture Notes in Physics Ser.: Vol. 511). viii, 440p. 1998. 95.00 (*3-540-64635-3*) Spr-Verlag.

Benkadda, S., et al. Transport, Chaos & Plasma Physics. 420p. 1994. text 109.00 (*981-02-1619-X*) World Scientific Pub.

Benkart, G. & Osborn, J., eds. Lie Algebras & Related Topics. LC 90-44712. (Contemporary Mathematics Ser.: Vol. 110). 313p. 1990. pap. 46.00 (*0-8218-5119-5*, CONM/110) Am Math.

Benkart, G. & Osborn, J. M., eds. Line Algebras. (Lecture Notes in Mathematics Ser.: Vol. 1373). v, 145p. 1989. 32.95 (*0-387-51147-4*) Spr-Verlag.

Benkart, G., et al. Stability in Modules for Classical Lie Algebras - A Constructive Approach. LC 90-31825. (Memoirs Ser.: No. 85/430). 165p. 1990. pap. 22.00 (*0-8218-2492-9*, MEMO/85/430) Am Math.

Benkartek, Dietmar. Ein Interpretierendes Worterbuch der Nominalabstrakta Im Narrenschiff Sebastian Brants von Abenteuer Bis Zwietracht. (GER.). 449p. 1996. 63.95 (*3-631-50063-7*) P Lang Pubng.

Benke, Britta. O'Keeffe. 1994. pap. 9.99 (*3-8228-8886-9*) Taschen Amer.

— O'Keeffe. (SPA.). 1996. pap. 9.99 (*3-8228-8825-7*) Taschen Amer.

Benke, Le Etta, jt. auth. see Benke, William.

Benke, Patricia D. Above the Law. 320p. (Orig.). 1997. mass mkt. 5.99 (*0-380-79015-7*, Avon Bks) Morrow Avon.

***Benke, Patricia D.** Cruel Justice. LC 98-94852. 283p. 1999. mass mkt. 6.50 (*0-380-79016-5*, Avon Bks) Morrow Avon.

Benke, Patricia D. False Witness. 1996. mass mkt. 5.99 (*0-380-78184-0*, Avon Bks) Morrow Avon.

— Guilty by Choice. 368p. (Orig.). 1995. mass mkt. 5.50 (*0-380-77566-2*, Avon Bks) Morrow Avon.

Benke, Ralph L., Jr. & Fordhamm. Daceasy Payroll Accounting. (C). 1994. pap. 34.95 (*0-538-83521-4*, AH63AD) S-W Pub.

Benke, Ralph L., jt. auth. see Holt, Robert N.

***Benke, William & Benke, Le Etta.** Church Wake-Up Call: A Ministries Management Approach That is Purpose-Driven & Inter-Generational in Outreach. 141p. (C). 2000. 49.95 (*0-7890-1137-9*); pap. 19.95 (*0-7890-1138-7*) Haworth Pr.

Benke, William & Fowler, John M. All about Real Estate Investing: From the Inside Out. 200p. 1995. per. 19.95 (*1-55738-882-2*, Irwn Prfssnl) McGraw-Hill Prof.

Benkelman, Janna, ed. see Golden, Leora.

Benkendorf, Jayne. 15 Minute Storage Meals: Quick, Healthful Recipes & Food Storage Handbook. (Illus.). 134p. 1999. pap. 12.95 (*0-9651990-2-9*, Pub. by Ludwig Pub OK) Q W Inc.

— The Food Storage Bible. 2nd rev. ed. (Illus.). 368p. 1999. pap. 16.95 (*0-9651990-1-0*, Pub. by Ludwig Pub OK) Q W Inc.

— The No-Cook Cookbook: No Pots & Pans to Scrub! LC 99-64270. 150p. 1999. pap. 14.95 (*0-9651990-3-7*) Ludwig Pub OK.

Benker, Hans. Dictionary of Microcomputers & Applied Mathematics: French-German, German-French. (ENG, FRE & GER.). 188p. 1992. lib. bdg. 95.00 (*0-8288-3831-3*, F104070) Fr & Eur.

***Benker, Hans.** Practical Use of Mathcad: Solving Mathematical Problems with a Computer Algebra System. Rudd, A., tr. from GER. LC 99-33922. xiv, 506p. 1999. 54.00 (*1-85233-166-6*, Pub. by Spr-Verlag) Spr-Verlag.

Benkert, D., et al, eds. Methodology of the Evaluation of Psychotropic Drugs. (Psychopharmacology Ser.: Vol. 8). (Illus.). 200p. 1990. 103.00 (*0-387-52094-5*) Spr-Verlag.

Benkert, Ernst, et al. Francis R. Hewitt: 1936-1992. Hewitt, Karen, ed. (Illus.). 60p. (Orig.). (C). 1994. pap. 25.00 (*0-9641443-0-1*) Inst Prog Painting.

Benkirane, A. Nonlinear Partial Differential Equations. (Pitman Research Notes in Mathematics Ser.). 1996. lib. bdg. 52.95 (*0-582-29213-1*) Longman.

Benkler, Marilyn, ed. see Cefola, Francine R.

Benko, B., jt. auth. see Matejka, D.

Benko, Chris, ed. see Pochiluk, William.

An Asterisk (*) at the beginning of an entry indicates that the title is appearing for the first time.

Benko, Christopher, ed. see Pochiluk, William.

Benko, Ferenc. Geological & Cosmogonic Cycles As Reflected by the New Law of Universal Cyclicity. 400p. (C). 1985. 120.00 (*963-05-3298-0*, Pub. by Akade Kiado) St Mut.

Benko, Georges, ed. Geography, History & Social Sciences. (GeoJournal Library). 276p. (C). 1995. lib. bdg. 161.50 (*0-7923-2543-5*, Pub. by Kluwer Academic) Kluwer Academic.

Benko, Georges & Strohmayer, Ulf. Space & Social Theory: Interpreting Modernity & Postmodernity. LC 96-25628. (Institute of British Geographers Special Publications Ser.). (Illus.). 384p. (Orig.). (C). 1997. text 77.95 (*0-631-19466-5*); pap. text 28.95 (*0-631-19467-3*) Blackwell Pubs.

Benko, James S. Hyec Do: Vital Points for Self-Defense. LC 85-61433. (Illus.). 60p. 1985. pap. 15.00 (*0-937314-09-9*, B-105) ITA Inst.

— I. T. A. TaeKwon-Do Hyungs: Fifth Degree Black Belt Level. (Illus.). 50p. (Orig.). 1987. pap. 25.00 (*0-937314-18-8*, B-111) ITA Inst.

— I. T. A. TaeKwon-Do Hyungs: First Degree Black Belt Level. (Illus.). 70p. (Orig.). 1987. pap. 25.00 (*0-937314-14-5*, B-107) ITA Inst.

— I. T. A. TaeKwon-Do Hyungs: Fourth Degree Black Belt Level. (Illus.). 68p. (Orig.). 1987. pap. 25.00 (*0-937314-17-X*, B-110) ITA Inst.

— I. T. A. TaeKwon-Do Hyungs: Second Degree Black Belt Level. (Illus.). 65p. (Orig.). 1987. pap. 25.00 (*0-937314-15-3*, B-108) ITA Inst.

— I. T. A. TaeKwon-Do Hyungs: Third Degree Black Belt Level. (Illus.). 70p. (Orig.). 1987. pap. 25.00 (*0-937314-16-1*, B-109) ITA Inst.

— International TaeKwon-Do Association Student Manual. (Illus.). 28p. (Orig.). 1985. pap. 11.00 (*0-937314-10-2*, B-106) ITA Inst.

— Korean Cane Techniques: Ji Pang E Sul. LC 95-79348. (Illus.). 118p. 1995. pap. 40.00 (*0-937314-29-3*, B-115) ITA Inst.

— Kwan Jyel Sul: Joint Locks, Holds & Throws for Self-Defense. LC 83-62241. (Illus.). 154p. 1986. pap. 25.00 (*0-937314-08-0*, B-104) ITA Inst.

— Tae Kwon Do Patterns: 1st Degree to 3rd Degree Black Belt. LC 97-73815. (Illus.). 120p. 1997. pap. 45.00 (*0-937314-30-7*, B-117) ITA Inst.

— Tae Kwon Do Patterns: 3rd Degree to 6th Degree Black Belt. LC 97-74609. (Illus.). 156p. 1997. pap. 50.00 (*0-937314-31-5*, B-118) ITA Inst.

— Taekwon-Do Hyungs for Blue & Red Belt Levels. LC 81-82100. (Illus.). 121p. (Orig.). 1981. pap. 15.00 (*0-937314-04-8*, B-103) ITA Inst.

Benko, James S. Taekwon-Do Patterns White Belt to 1st Degree Black Belt. (Illus.). 160p. 1997. pap. 45.00 (*0-937314-28-5*, B-116) ITA Inst.

Benko, Lorand & Imre, Samu, eds. The Hungarian Language. (Janua Linguarum, Ser. Practica: No. 134). (Illus.). 377p. (Orig.). 1972. pap. text 84.65 (*90-279-2075-3*) Mouton.

Benko, Marietta, et al. Space Law in the United Nations. 1985. lib. bdg. 117.00 (*90-247-3157-7*) Kluwer Academic.

Benko, Marietta, jt. auth. see Bockstiegel, Karl-Heinz.

Benko, Marietta, jt. ed. see Bockstiegel, Karl-Heinz.

Benko, Stephen. The Virgin Goddess: Studies in the Pagan & Christian Roots of Mariology. LC 92-44596. (Numen Bookseries (Studies in the History of Religions): No. 59). (Illus.). viii, 296p. 1993. 126.50 (*90-04-09747-3*) Brill Academic Pubs.

Benko, Susana. Vicente Huidobro y el Cubismo (Vincent Huidobro & the Cubism) (SPA.). 225p. 1993. pap. 11.99 (*968-16-4176-0*, Pub. by Fondo) Continental Bk.

Benkov, Keith J. & Winter, Harland S. Managing Your Child's Crohn's Disease & Ulcerative Colitis. 200p. 1995. 21.95 (*1-57101-023-8*) MasterMedia Pub.

Benkovic, Johnette S. The New Age Counterfeit: A Study Guide for Individual or Group Use. LC 95-74824. 96p. 1995. pap. 7.50 (*1-877678-36-8*) Queenship Pub.

Benkovic, Johnnette. Full of Grace: Women & the Abundant Life. LC 97-45997. 1998. pap. text 10.99 (*0-89283-960-0*) Servant.

Benkovic, Stephen J., jt. ed. see Blakley, Raymond L.

Benkovitz, Anne, jt. auth. see Setteducati, Mark.

Benkovitz, Miriam J. Ronald Firbank: A Biography. LC 70-460983. xviii, 300 p. 1970. write for info. (*0-297-00024-1*) Weidenfeld & Nicolson.

Benkovitz, Miriam J., ed. A Bibliography of Ronald Firbank. 2nd ed. 1982. text 59.00 (*0-19-818188-4*) OUP.

Benkovsky, William. Soul Path: A Spiritual Adventure. LC 98-83108. 204p. 1999. 25.00 (*0-7388-0343-X*); pap. 15.00 (*0-7388-0344-8*) Xlibris Corp.

Benkowitz, Joan B., ed. see International Symposium on Solar-Terrestial Physic.

Benkreira, H., ed. Fluid Mixing IV. (Institution of Chemical Engineers Symposium Ser.: No. 121). 464p. 1990. 160.00 (*1-56032-133-4*) Hemisp Pub.

— Thin Film Coating. 218p. 1994. 94.00 (*0-85186-695-6*, Q) CRC Pr.

Benli Gu, jt. ed. see Yu Wei.

Benlliure, Felix, tr. see Hester, H. I.

Benmaman, Virginia. Bilingual Handbook for Public Safety Professionals with Cassette. (ENG & SPA.). 88p. 1995. 29.95 incl. audio (*0-87526-427-1*) Gould.

Benmamoun, Elabbas. The Feature Structure of Functional Categories: A Comparative Study of Arabic Dialects. LC PJ6723.B36 1999. 192p. 2000. text 45.00 (*0-19-511994-0*); pap. text 19.95 (*0-19-511995-9*) OUP.

***Benmamoun, Elabbas, ed.** Perspectives on Arabic Linguistics XIII Vol. XII: Papers from the Twelfth Annual Symposium On Arabic Linguistics, Urbana-Champaign, Illinois, 1998. (Current Issues in Linguistic Theory Ser.: Vol. 190). viii, 204p. 1999. 75.00 (*1-55619-967-8*) J Benjamins Pubng.

***Benmamoun, Elabbas, et al, eds.** Perspective on Arabic Linguistics Vol. XI: Papers from the 11th Annual Symposium on Arabic Linguistics, Atlanta, Georgia, 1997. (Current Issues in Linguistic Theory Ser.: Vol. 167). viii, 231p. 1998. 79.00 (*1-55619-883-3*) J Benjamins Pubng Co.

Benmamoun, Elabbas, jt. ed. see Lappin, Shalom.

Benman, B. E. & Persson, L., eds. Size-Structured Populations: Ecology & Evolution. (Illus.). 310p. 1989. 97.00 (*0-387-50188-6*) Spr-Verlag.

Benmayor, Rina & Skotnes, Andor. International Yearbook of Oral History & Life Stories Vol. 3: Migration & Identity. 234p. 1995. text 59.00 (*0-19-820250-4*) OUP.

Benmayor, Rina, et al. Responses to Poverty among Puerto Rican Women: Identity, Community, & Cultural Citizenship. 118p. 1992. lib. bdg. 10.00 (*1-878483-06-4*) Hunter Coll CEP.

— Stories to Live By: Continuity & Change in Three Generations of Puerto Rican Women. 67p. 1987. lib. bdg. 7.00 (*1-878483-02-1*) Hunter Coll CEP.

Benmayor, Rina, jt. ed. see Flores, William.

Benmenachem, Mordechai. Slaying the Software Dragon: Practice Guide. LC 97-15926. (ITCP-UK Computer Science Ser.). 1997. text 43.99 (*1-85032-326-7*) ITCP.

Benmour, Linda. The Bead Directory: The Most Comprehensive Collection of the Best Bead Sources Available. 6th rev. ed. Firestone, Milton & Scherer, Alice, eds. (Illus.). 278p. 1999. pap. 22.95 (*1-883153-24-7*) B Stone Pr.

— The Book of Bead Tips: One Hundred One of the Best Bead Tips. Scherer, Alice & Firestone, Milton, eds. (Illus.). 132p. (Orig.). 1999. pap. 16.95 (*1-883153-14-X*) B Stone Pr.

— The Buyer's Guide to the Best Beadmakers in America: Color Photoguide to 101 of the Best Contemporary Glass Beadmakers in the U. S. A. Firestone, Milton, ed. (Illus.). 228p. (Orig.). 1999. pap. 24.95 (*1-883153-22-0*) B Stone Pr.

Benmussa, Simone. Benmussa: Three Plays, Includes: Singular Life of Albert Nobbs, Appearances, & Death of Ivan Illich. Wright, Barbara & Watson, Donald, trs. from FRE. (Illus.). 200p. (Orig.). pap. 13.95 (*0-7145-4156-7*) Riverrun NY.

Benn, Alec. Advertising Financial Products & Services: Proven Techniques & Principles for Banks, Investment Firms, Insurance Companies, & Their Agencies. LC 85-24406. (Illus.). 246p. 1986. 65.00 (*0-89930-103-7*, BNH, Quorum Bks) Greenwood.

***Benn, Alec.** The Unseen Wall Street of 1969-1975: And Its Signficance for Today. LC 99-462243. 288p. 2000. 59.95 (*1-56720-333-7*, Q333, Quorum Bks) Greenwood.

Benn, Anna & Bartlett, Rosamund. Literary Russia: A Guide. LC 98-145251. (Illus.). 495p. 1998. pap. 29.50 (*0-333-71197-1*, Pub. by Papermac) Trans-Atl Phila.

Benn, Carl. The Iroquois in the War of 1812. LC 98-227276. (Illus.). 288p. 1998. text 19.95 (*0-8020-4321-6*); pap. text 19.95 (*0-8020-8145-2*) U of Toronto Pr.

Benn, Deborah. How to Maximize Your Wealth Offshore. 1998. 47.95 (*0-7134-8380-6*, Pub. by B T B) Branford.

Benn, Douglas I. & Evans, David J. A. Glaciers & Glaciation. (Arnold Publications). (Illus.). 760p. 1997. text 95.00 (*0-340-65303-5*); pap. text 45.00 (*0-340-58431-9*) OUP.

Benn, Elizabeth, ed. Treasures from the Embroiderers' Guild Collection. (Illus.). 192p. 1995. pap. 19.95 (*0-7153-0372-4*, Pub. by D & C Pub) Sterling.

Benn, Frederick C. Mozart on the Stage. LC 74-24041. reprint ed. 22.50 (*0-404-12864-5*) AMS Pr.

— Mozart on the Stage: Music Book Index. 178p. 1993. reprint ed. lib. bdg. 69.00 (*0-7812-9609-9*) Rprt Serv.

Benn, Gottfried. Poems, 1937-1947. Draghici, Simona, tr. from GER. LC 91-282. 108p. (C). 1991. pap. text 4.95 (*0-943045-06-1*) Plutarch Pr OR.

— Primal Vision. Ashton, E. B., ed. LC 58-13434. 1971. reprint ed. pap. 8.95 (*0-8112-0008-6*, NDP322, Pub. by New Directions) Norton.

— Primal Vision: Selected Writings. Ashton, E. B., ed. Hamburger, Michael & Middleton, Christopher, trs. from GER. 292p. 1985. reprint ed. pap. 18.00 (*0-7145-2529-4*) M Boyars Pubs.

— Prose, Essays, Poems. Becker, Richard & Sander, Volkmar, eds. LC 80-7563. (German Library: Vol. 73). 320p. (C). 1987. 39.50 (*0-8264-0310-7*); pap. 19.95 (*0-8264-0311-5*) Continuum.

— The Voice Behind the Screen. unabridged ed. Draghici, Simona, ed. & tr. by. from GER. LC 96-14104.Tr. of Stimme Hinter dem Vorhang. 56p. 1996. pap. text 4.95 (*0-943045-10-X*) Plutarch Pr OR.

Benn, I. M. & Tucker, R. W. An Introduction to Spinors & Geometry with Applications in Physics. (Illus.). 368p. (C). 1988. pap. 49.00 (*0-85274-261-4*) IOP Pub.

— An Introduction to Spinors & Geometry with Applications in Physics. (Illus.). 368p. 1988. 195.00 (*0-85274-169-3*) IOP Pub.

Benn, J. Miriam. Predicaments of Love. 304p. (C). 59.95 (*0-7453-0528-8*); pap. 24.95 (*0-7453-0529-6*, Pub. by Pluto GBR) Stylus Pub VA.

Benn, M. B. The Drama of Revolt: A Critical Study of Georg Buchner. LC 75-3974. (Anglica Germanica Ser.: No. 2). (Illus.). 329p. 1979. pap. text 25.95 (*0-521-29415-0*) Cambridge U Pr.

Benn, Melissa, et al. The Rape Controversy. (C). 1988. 25.00 (*0-946088-23-3*, Pub. by NCCL) St Mut.

Benn, Melissa, jt. auth. see Sedley, Ann.

***Benn, Nigel.** Dark Destroyer. (Illus.). 2000. 26.00 (*1-85782-308-7*, Pub. by Blake Publng) Seven Hills Bk.

Benn, Nina. How to Live in Heaven on Earth. (Illus.). 72p. 1999. pap. 10.00 (*0-8059-4442-7*) Dorrance.

Benn, Piers. Ethics. 224p. 1998. text 55.00 (*0-7735-1700-6*, Pub. by McG-Queens Univ Pr); pap. text 19.95 (*0-7735-1701-4*, Pub. by McG-Queens Univ Pr) CUP Services.

Benn, R. A. Aids to Microbiology & Infectious Diseases. 208p. (Orig.). 1986. pap. text 22.95 (*0-443-03127-4*) Church.

Benn, Sheila M. Pre-Romantic Attitudes to Landscape in the Writings of Friedrich Schiller. (Quellen und Forschungen zur Sprach und Kulturgeschichte der Germanischen Voelker: Vol. 99-223). xiv, 242p. (C). 1991. lib. bdg. 92.35 (*3-11-012825-X*) De Gruyter.

Benn, Stanley I. A Theory of Freedom. 352p. 1988. text 89.95 (*0-521-34260-0*); pap. text 38.95 (*0-521-34802-1*) Cambridge U Pr.

Benn, Tony. The Sizewell Syndrome: The Links Between Nuclear Power & Nuclear Weapons. 1988. pap. 35.00 (*0-7855-2944-6*) St Mut.

Benn, Tony & Bodington, Joan. Speeches. LC 75-326414. 303p. 1974. write for info. (*0-85124-091-7*) Spkesman.

Benn, Wallace. The Last Word. 1996. 9.99 (*1-85792-079-1*, Pub. by Christian Focus) Spring Arbor Dist.

***Benn, Wallace.** Learning about True Spirituality: Jesus Our Joy. 2000. pap. text 2.99 (*1-85792-443-6*) Christian Focus.

Benna, Theodore. Helping Employees Achieve Retirement Security. (Illus.). 112p. 1996. pap. 16.95 (*1-885123-04-3*) Investors Pr.

Benna, Theodore & Proctor, William. Escaping the Coming Retirement Crisis: How to Secure Your Financial Future. LC 95-21241. 208p. 1995. 24.00 (*0-89109-913-1*) Pinon Press.

Bennabi, Malek. Islam in History & Society. 1988. 12.95 (*0-935782-04-4*) Kazi Pubns.

— The Qur'anic Phenomena. 1988. 9.95 (*0-933511-31-0*) Kazi Pubns.

— The Quranic Phenomenon. 290p. 1996. pap. 10.50 (*0-614-21068-2*, 1051) Kazi Pubns.

Bennack, Virginia M. Smidgen the Miniature Horse. (Illus.). 51p. (Orig.). (J). (gr. k-5). 1996. pap. 4.95 (*0-9655446-0-5*) Aquarita Press.

Bennage, Patricia D., tr. see Aoyama, Shundo.

Bennahum, David. The Beatles: After the Break-Up. LC 95-192717. (In Their Own Words Ser.). (Illus.). 96p. 1992. pap. 15.95 (*0-7119-2558-5*, OP 46424) Omnibus NY.

— Extra Life: Coming of Age in Cyberspace. 256p. 1998. pap. 12.00 (*0-465-01236-1*, Pub. by Basic) HarpC.

Bennahum, David A., ed. Managed Care: Financial, Legal & Ethical Issues. LC 98-50328. (Pilgrim Library of Ethics). 224p. 1999. pap. 23.95 (*0-8298-1274-1*) Pilgrim OH.

Bennahum, David S. Extra Life: Coming of Age in Cyberspace. LC 98-39251. 256p. 1998. 23.00 (*0-465-01235-3*, Pub. by Basic) HarpC.

***Bennahum, Ninotchka D.** Antonia Merce, La Argentina: Flamenco & the Spanish Avant Garde. LC 99-35663. (Illus.). 264p. 2000. 40.00 (*0-8195-6383-8*, Wesleyan Univ Pr) U Pr of New Eng.

Bennani, B. M. A Bowl of Sorrow. 1977. per. 3.00 (*0-912678-36-4*, Greenfld Rev Pr) Greenfld Rev Lit.

Bennani, B. M., tr. Splinters of Bone. LC 74-25797. Orig. Title: Darweesh. 1974. 2.95 (*0-912678-17-8*, Greenfld Rev Pr) Greenfld Rev Lit.

Bennani, Ben, tr. see Darwish, Mahmoud.

Bennardo, Tom, jt. auth. see Stump, Ted M.

Bennassar, Bartholome. Lexico Historico de Espana Moderna y Contemporanea (Siglos XVI-XX) 3rd ed. 224p. 1990. 24.95 (*0-7859-4935-6*) Fr & Eur.

Bennatan, E. M. On Time, Within Budget: Software Project Management Practices & Techniques. 2nd ed. 256p. 1995. pap. 54.99 (*0-471-12811-2*) Wiley.

***Bennatan, E. M.** On Time, Within Budget: Software Project Management Practices & Techniques. 3rd ed. LC 00-27330. 400p. 2000. pap. 54.99 (*0-471-37644-2*) Wiley.

Bennatan, E. M. Software Project Management: A Practitioner's Approach. LC 92-9486. 1992. write for info. (*0-07-707437-8*) McGraw.

— Software Project Management: Practitioner's Approach. 2nd ed. LC 94-5319. 1994. write for info. (*0-07-707648-6*) McGraw.

Bennathan, Esra & Thompson, Louis S. Privitization Problems at Industry Level: Road Haulage in Central Europe. LC 92-33200. (Discussion Papers: No. 182). 64p. 1992. pap. 22.00 (*0-8213-2245-1*, 12245) World Bank.

Bennathan, Marion & Boxall, Marjorie. Effective Intervention in Primary Schools: Nuture Groups. LC 96-222633. 96p. 1996. pap. 22.95 (*1-85346-450-3*, Pub. by David Fulton) Taylor & Francis.

Benne, Kenneth D. Education Professoriate. (Occasional Papers: No. 4). 1974. pap. 10.00 (*0-933669-07-0*) Soc Profs Ed.

— The Task of Post-Contemporary Education: Essays in Behalf of a Human Future. 256p. (C). 1990. pap. text 19.95 (*0-8077-3012-2*) Tchrs Coll.

Benne, Kenneth D. & Tozer, Steven E., eds. Society As Educator in an Age of Transition: Eighty-Sixth Yearbook of the National Society for the Study of Education, Pt. II. xvi, 296p. (C). 1987. 26.00 (*0-226-60145-5*) U Ch Pr.

Benne, Mae. Principles of Children's Services in Public Libraries. LC 90-47427. 332p. 1991. 45.00 (*0-8389-0555-2*) ALA.

Benne, Rob, ed. RNA Editing: The Alteration of Protein Coding Sequences of RNA. LC 93-6500. (Series in Molecular Biology). 200p. 1993. 50.00 (*0-13-782558-7*, Pub. by Tavistock-E Horwood) Routldge.

Benne, Rob, jt. auth. see Grosjean, Henri.

Benne, Robert. The Ethic of Democratic Capitalism: A Moral Reassessment. LC 80-2385. 281p. 1981. reprint ed. pap. 87.20 (*0-608-17185-9*, 202786900056) Bks Demand.

— The Paradoxical Vision: A Public Theology for the Twenty-First Century. LC 94-18251. 256p. 1995. pap. 20.00 (*0-8006-2794-6*, 1-2794, Fortress Pr) Augsburg Fortress.

***Benne, Robert.** Seeing Is Believing: Visions of Life Through Film. LC 98-30924. 1998. write for info. (*0-7618-1268-7*) U Pr of Amer.

Benne, Robert & Hefner, Philip. Defining America: Christian Critique of the American Dream. LC 73-89062. 160p. reprint ed. pap. 49.60 (*0-608-16833-5*, 202694100053) Bks Demand.

Bennecke, Jason. How to Save 42 Percent on a New Computer. Bennecke, Tammy, ed. (Illus.). 128p. (Orig.). 1997. pap. 24.95 (*0-9657715-6-3*) Jaytech.

Bennecke, Tammy, ed. see Bennecke, Jason.

***Bennedetto, Linda Ference.** Finding My Way Back from Fear: A Personal Journal & a Guide to Overcoming Anxiety & Panic Disorders. LC 99-70275. 51p. 1999. pap. 9.95 (*1-928782-01-9*, Strong Bks) Pubg Directions.

Bennee, Archibald John. Regaining Self Control. pap. 8.95 (*1-55517-102-8*) CFI Dist.

Bennefield, David. Straight Talk. 1995. pap. text 5.95 (*0-9645743-0-6*) Franklin Pub.

Bennefield, Robin M., ed. see Johnson, Mary H.

Benneh. New Geography of Ghana. 1988. pap. text. write for info. (*0-582-58532-5*, Pub. by Addison-Wesley) Longman.

Bennell, Alan P., ed. see Brown, Deni.

Bennell, Anthony S. Maratha War Papers of Arthur Wellesley: April to December 1803. 1999. 74.00 (*0-7509-2069-6*) A Sutton.

Bennell, Jennifer. Master Strokes: A Practical Guide to Decorative & Paint Techniques. (Illus.). 160p. 1997. pap. 22.99 (*1-56496-360-8*) Rockport Pubs.

— Master Works: How to Use Paint Finishes to Transform Your Surroundings. (Illus.). 176p. 1994. 29.95 (*1-56496-125-7*) Rockport Pubs.

Bennemann, K. H. Nonlinear Optics in Metals. LC 98-8282. (The International Series of Monographs on Physics: No. 98). (Illus.). 752p. 1999. text 155.00 (*0-19-851893-5*) OUP.

Benner. Assessing Young Children with Special Needs. (Special Education Ser.). 2000. pap. 47.95 (*0-534-34414-3*) Wadsworth Pub.

Benner & Kinsolving, Katherine. Essential Flavors. 304p. 1999. pap. 13.95 (*0-14-024969-9*, Penguin Classics) Viking Penguin.

Benner, jt. auth. see Johnson.

Benner, jt. auth. see Mistovich.

Benner, Alan. Fibre Channel: Gigabit Communications & I/O for Computer Networks. LC 95-38472. 352p. 1995. 70.00 (*0-07-005669-2*) McGraw.

Benner, Allen R., ed. see Homer.

Benner, Bob & Benner, David. Carolina Whitewater: A Canoeist's Guide to the Western Carolinas. rev. ed. LC 84-115920. (Illus.). 262p. 1996. pap. 14.95 (*0-89732-200-2*) Menasha Ridge.

Benner, Bob & McCloud, Tom. A Paddler's Guide to Eastern North Carolina. LC 86-31091. (Illus.). 272p. 1987. pap. 15.95 (*0-89732-041-7*) Menasha Ridge.

Benner, C. S. & Middleton, R. W. Fisheries & Oil Development on the Continental Shelf. LC 91-71563. (Symposium Ser.: No. 11). 172p. 1991. pap. 28.00 (*0-913235-73-3*, 540.11) Am Fisheries Soc.

Benner, Cheryl. An Amish Christmas Coloring Book. (Illus.). (J). (ps-1). 1998. pap. 2.95 (*1-56148-265-X*) Good Bks PA.

Benner, Cheryl A., des. The Country Tea Rose Quilt. (Illus.). 81p. 1993. pap. 12.95 (*1-56148-097-5*) Good Bks PA.

— Garden Sunflower Quilt. LC 95-2504. (Illus.). 108p. 1994. pap. 14.95 (*1-56148-133-5*) Good Bks PA.

Benner, Cheryl A. An Amish Farm Coloring Book. 32p. (Orig.). (J). (ps-1). 1994. pap. 2.95 (*1-56148-120-3*) Good Bks PA.

— An Amish Quilt Coloring Book. 32p. (Orig.). (J). (ps-1). 1994. pap. 2.95 (*1-56148-141-6*) Good Bks PA.

— A Cook's Notebook. (Blank Notebook Ser.). 96p. (Orig.). 1990. pap. 5.95 (*0-934672-92-X*) Good Bks PA.

— A Mother's Notebook: An Illustrated Journal. (Blank Notebook Ser.). 96p. (Orig.). 1990. pap. 5.95 (*0-934672-91-1*) Good Bks PA.

— A Notebook of Memories. (Blank Notebook Ser.). 96p. 1990. pap. 5.95 (*1-56148-004-5*) Good Bks PA.

— Quilter's Notebook Two. (Blank Notebook Ser.). 96p. (Orig.). 1990. pap. 5.95 (*1-56148-005-3*) Good Bks PA.

— Sunny Day Dreams Notebook. 96p. 1990. pap. 5.95 (*0-934672-85-7*) Good Bks PA.

Benner, Cheryl A. & Pellman, Rachel T. The Country Bride Quilt Collection. LC 91-70666. (Country Quilt Ser.). (Illus.). 176p. 1991. pap. 12.95 (*1-56148-015-0*) Good Bks PA.

— The Country Lily Quilt. LC 90-3078. (Illus.). 104p. 1990. pap. 12.95 (*0-934672-88-1*) Good Bks PA.

— The Country Love Quilt. LC 89-23374. 192p. 1989. pap. 12.95 (*0-934672-65-2*) Good Bks PA.

— The Country Paradise Quilt. LC 91-74049. (Illus.). 224p. 1991. pap. 12.95 (*1-56148-050-9*) Good Bks PA.

— Country Quilts for Children. LC 92-16310. (Illus.). 224p. 1992. pap. 12.95 (*1-56148-063-0*) Good Bks PA.

— The Country Songbird Quilt. LC 90-71120. (Illus.). 104p. 1990. pap. 12.95 (*1-56148-006-1*) Good Bks PA.

Benner, David, jt. auth. see Benner, Bob.

Benner, David G. Care of Souls: Revisioning Christian Nurture & Counsel. LC 98-35618. 256p. (C). (gr. 13). 1998. pap. 15.99 (*0-8010-9063-6*) Baker Bks.

An Asterisk (*) at the beginning of an entry indicates that the title is appearing for the first time.

***Benner, David G.** Care of Souls: Revisioning Christian Nurture & Counsel. 252p. 1998. reprint ed. pap. 17.99 (*0-85364-960-X*, Pub. by Paternoster Pub) OM Literature.

Benner, David G. Money Madness & Financial Freedom. (Life Line Ser.). 200p. (Orig.). 1996. pap. write for info. (*1-55059-138-X*) Detselig Ents.

— Strategic Pastoral Counseling: A Short-Term Structured Model. LC 92-17613. 144p. 1992. pap. 9.99 (*0-8010-1027-6*) Baker Bks.

Benner, David G. & Harvey, Robert W. Understanding & Facilitating Forgiveness. LC 96-15340. (Strategic Pastoral Counseling Resources Ser.). 160p. (C). 1996. 14.99 (*0-8010-9019-9*) Baker Bks.

Benner, David G. & Hill, Peter C., eds. Baker Encyclopedia of Psychology & Counseling. 2nd ed. LC 99-21768. (Baker Reference Library Ser.). 1168p. 1999. text 59.99 (*0-8010-2100-6*) Baker Bks.

Benner, David G., jt. auth. see Harvey, Robert W.

Benner, Derek. Learn Archiving & File Compression Programming in Visual C++ 9X. 1998. pap. text 39.95 (*1-55622-599-7*) Wordware Pub.

Benner, Derek A. Learn Graphics File Programming with Delphi 3. LC 97-40626. (Illus.). 400p. 1997. pap. 49.95 (*1-55622-558-X*) Wordware Pub.

Benner, Dietrich & Lenzen, Dieter, eds. Education for the New Europe. LC 95-31517. 192p. (C). 1996. 45.00 (*1-57181-074-9*) Berghahn Bks.

Benner, Dorothy M. Dear Ted - Letters to a Senator. 92p. 1994. pap. 9.75 (*0-9636317-0-5*) Natl Fnd Better Wrld.

Benner, Erica. Really Existing Nationalism: A Post-Communist View from Marx & Engels. 276p. 1996. text 59.00 (*0-19-827959-0*) OUP.

Benner, J. A. Uncle Comanche. LC 95-36530. (Chaparral Books for Young Readers). 174p. (Orig.). (J). (gr. 5-9). 1996. pap. 12.95 (*0-87565-152-6*) Tex Christian.

Benner, Janet. Football: Mysteries Revealed for the Feminine Fan. (Illus.). 144p. (Orig.). 1995. pap. 14.95 (*0-942723-15-5*) Joelle Pub.

— Smoking Cigarettes - The Unfiltered Truth: Understanding Why & How to Quit. LC 87-80270. 144p. (Orig.). 1987. pap. 10.95 (*0-942723-12-0*) Joelle Pub.

***Benner, Joan.** Borderland: A Sequence. 08/1999p. 1999. pap. 30.00 (*1-85072-229-3*, Pub. by W Sessions) St Mut.

Benner, John P., et al, eds. Thermophotovoltaic Generation of Electricity: 3rd NREL Conference. LC 97-74374. (Conference Proceedings: Vol. 401). (Illus.). xxx, 573p. 1997. 140.00 (*1-56396-734-0*, AIP Pr) Spr-Verlag.

Benner, John P., et al. The Second NREL Conference on Thermophotovoltaic Generation of Electricity: Golden, Colorado, July 16-20, 1995. (CP Ser.: No. 358). (Illus.). 544p. 1996. boxed set 140.00 (*1-56396-509-7*) Am Inst Physics.

Benner, Joyce. The Flower Market. 71p. 1995. pap. 10.50 (*1-56770-319-4*) S Scheewe Pubns.

— Kids & Water. 100p. 1991. pap. text 10.50 (*1-56770-234-1*) S Scheewe Pubns.

Benner, Jr., Ludwig, jt. auth. see Hendrick, Kingsley.

Benner, Judith A. Sul Ross: Soldier, Statesman, Educator. LC 82-45891. (Centennial Series of the Association of Former Students: No. 13). (Illus.). 276p. 1983. 29.95 (*0-89096-142-5*) Tex A&M Univ Pr.

Benner, L. Theory for Piano Students, Bk. 1. 56p. 1986. pap. 5.95 (*0-7935-5299-0*, 50330220) H Leonard.

— Theory for Piano Students, Bk. 2. 56p. 1986. pap. 7.95 (*0-7935-5307-5*, 50330270) H Leonard.

— Theory for Piano Students, Bk. 3. 56p. 1986. pap. 6.95 (*0-7935-3817-3*, 50330300) H Leonard.

— Theory for Piano Students, Bk. 5. 56p. 1986. pap. 6.95 (*0-7935-3818-1*, 50331370) H Leonard.

Benner, Ludwig, Jr. Guide 2: Accident Investigation. Brakhage, Cynthia, ed. (Illus.). 114p. (Orig.). 1997. pap. text 18.00 (*0-87939-141-3*, 36010) IFSTA.

— Introduction to Investigation. Brakhage, Cynthia, ed. LC 97-60613. (Illus.). 96p. (Orig.). 1997. pap. text 18.00 (*0-87939-139-1*, 36009) IFSTA.

***Benner, Ludwig, Jr. & Brakhage, Cynthia S.** Fire Investigation. LC 97-60698. (Investigations Ser.). 93p. 1998. 18.00 (*0-87939-143-X*) IFSTA.

Benner, Margaret. Mental Health & Psychiatric Nursing. 3rd ed. LC 96-29146. (Springhouse Notes Ser.). (Illus.). 208p. 1996. 22.95 incl. disk (*0-87434-862-5*) Springhouse Corp.

Benner, Patricia. Breakthroughs in Critical Reading (Text & Exercise Book), Levels 5-8. 1998. text, wbk. ed. 17.25 (*0-8092-0789-3*) NTC Contemp Pub Co.

— Pre-GED Critical Reading Skills. 1987. pap. 10.57 (*0-8092-4844-1*) NTC Contemp Pub Co.

Benner, Patricia, ed. Interpretive Phenomenology: Embodiment, Caring, & Ethics in Nursing. 388p. (C). 1994. text 59.95 (*0-8039-5722-X*); pap. text 26.95 (*0-8039-5723-8*) Sage.

Benner, Patricia, et al. Clinical Wisdom & Interventions in Critical Care: A Thinking-in-Action Approach. Eoyang, Thomas, ed. LC 98-12040. 512p. (C). 1998. pap. text 25.00 (*0-7216-7511-5*, W B Saunders Co) Harcrt Hlth Sci Grp.

— Expertise in Nursing Practice: Caring, Clinical, Judgment & Ethics. (Illus.). 432p. 1995. 46.95 (*0-8261-8700-5*) Springer Pub.

— Knowledge about Care & Caring: State of the Art & Future Developments. Stevenson, Joanne S. & Tripp-Reimer, Toni, eds. 165p. (Orig.). (C). 1990. pap. 14.50 (*1-55810-052-0*, G-177, Am Acad Nursing) Am Nurses Pub.

Benner, Patricia, jt. ed. see Phillips, Susan S.

Benner, Patricia A. Breakthru: Critical Reading Skills. 1989. pap. 10.57 (*0-8092-4238-9*) NTC Contemp Pub Co.

— Critical Reading Exercise Book. 240p. (J). (gr. 5-8). 8.33 (*0-8092-3297-9*) NTC Contemp Pub Co.

Benner, Patricia E. From Novice to Expert: Excellence & Power in Clinical Nursing Practice. 284p. (C). 1984. pap. text 52.00 (*0-201-00299-X*, Health Sci) Addison-Wesley.

— Stress & Satisfaction on the Job: Work Meanings & Coping of Mid-Career Men. LC 84-3252. 203p. 1984. 49.95 (*0-275-91127-6*, C1127, Praeger Pubs) Greenwood.

Benner, Patricia E. & Wrubel, Judith. The Primacy of Caring: Stress & Coping in Health & Illness. 406p. (C). 1989. pap. text 52.00 (*0-201-12002-X*) Addison-Wesley.

Benner, Phylis & Gellert, Sandra. Project Opportunity Pt. A: Curriculum for Training Providers - Mentors & Field Placement Providers - Supervisors. 52p. 1998. ring bd. 150.00 (*1-884093-08-6*) Chldrns Fnd.

Benner, Phylis, et al. Project Opportunity Pt. B: Parent-Education Enhanced Basic Family Child Care Provider Training Course. 276p. 1998. ring bd. 500.00 (*1-884093-09-4*) Chldrns Fnd.

Benner, Richard, jt. auth. see Atnip, Carol.

Benner, S. A., ed. Redesigning the Molecules of Life. (Illus.). vii, 175p. 1988. 51.95 (*0-387-19166-6*) Spr-Verlag.

Benner, Susan. Special Education Issues. LC 97-18651. (C). 1997. 42.95 (*0-534-25230-3*) Wadsworth Pub.

Benner, Susan E. & Leonard, Kathy S., eds. Fire from the Andes: Short Fiction by Women from Bolivia, Ecuador, & Peru. LC 97-4746. (Illus.). 208p. 1998. pap. 19.95 (*0-8263-1825-8*) U of NM Pr.

Benner, Susan M. Assessing Young Children with Special Needs: An Ecological Perspective. 400p. (C). 1992. teacher ed. write for info. (*0-8013-0489-X*, 78322) Longman.

Bennerson, Vivian H. Epheta: Universal Prayers & Thoughts. LC 95-83657. 175p. 1996. pap. 12.95 (*0-614-12679-7*) Brownell & Carroll.

Bennet. Brooking on Building Contracts. 2nd ed. 1980. 69.00 (*0-409-43460-4*, MICHIE) LEXIS Pub.

Bennet, Andrew, et al, eds. Friends in Need: Burden-Sharing in the Gulf War. LC 96-25157. 275p. 1997. text 55.00 (*0-312-15854-8*) St Martin.

Bennet, Anthony J. The American President's Cabinet: From Kennedy to Bush. 250p. 1996. text 49.95 (*0-312-15840-8*) St Martin.

Bennet, Bija. Breathing into Life. 1997. 5.99 (*0-517-18495-8*) Random Hse Value.

Bennet, Bridget, ed. Ripples of Dissent: Women's Stories of Marriage from the 1890s. LC 97-127654. 384p. 1997. 45.00 (*0-460-87777-1*, Pub. by J M Dent & Sons) Trafalgar.

Bennet, C. L. Defining the Manager's Job: The AMA Manual of Position Descriptions. LC 58-14306. (American Management Association Research Study Ser.: No. 33). 447p. reprint ed. pap. 138.60 (*0-608-30182-5*, 205130600094) Bks Demand.

Bennet, Clinton. In Search of Muhammad. LC 98-12243. 256p. 1998. 69.95 (*0-304-33700-5*) Continuum.

— In Search of Muhammad. LC 98-12243. 288p. 1999. pap. 19.95 (*0-304-70401-6*) Continuum.

Bennet, David. Illustrations to the Bible. 18p. (Orig.). (C). 1978. pap. 3.00 (*0-935982-19-1*, SMJ-05) Spertus Coll.

Bennet, Dominic. Managing Foreign Exchange Risk: The Tools & Techniques for Managing Currency Exposure. (Illus.). 280p. (Orig.). 1996. 65.00 (*0-273-61976-4*) F T P H.

Bennet, Doris L. Flight into Infinity. 258p. 1995. write for info. (*1-886134-04-9*) Miraculous Fngerprnt.

Bennet, Doug. Up North: A Guide to Ontario's Wilderness from Blackflies to the Northern Lights. 1997. pap. text 24.99 (*0-7710-1116-4*) McCland & Stewart.

Bennet, Doug. Up North Again: More of Ontarios Wilderness from Pickerel to the Pleiades. LC 96-932520. (Illus.). 1997. pap. text 18.95 (*0-7710-1115-6*) McCland & Stewart.

Bennet, E. A. Meetings with Jung: Conversations Recorded During the Years 1946-1961. LC 81-40459. 214p. 1995. pap. 12.95 (*3-85630-501-7*) Continuum.

— What Jung Really Said. 192p. 1995. pap. 12.95 (*0-8052-1046-6*) Schocken.

Bennet, Gerald J. & Ebrahim, Shah B. The Essentials of Health Care in Old Age. 208p. 1995. pap. text 24.95 (*0-340-61372-6*, Pub. by E A) OUP.

Bennet, H. W. The Gearmotor - A Symbol of Packaged Power. (Technical Papers: Vol. P469.02). (Illus.). 14p. 1949. pap. text 30.00 (*1-55589-435-6*) AGMA.

Bennet, J. E., et al. Catholic Protection of Concrete Bridges: A Manual of Practice. 61p. (C). 1993. pap. text 15.00 (*0-309-05750-7*, SHRP-S-372) SHRP.

Bennet, J. V. Cost-Managerial Accounting: Robotor Inc. Job Order System & Cost Control. 96p. 1985. 19.17 (*0-07-004702-2*) McGraw.

Bennet, Jim. Jim Bennet Rhymes Again: Light Hearted Verse from the Laureate of Atlantic Canada. (Illus.). 108p. 1989. pap. 5.99 (*0-88780-076-9*, Pub. by Formac Publ Co) Formac Dist Ltd.

Bennet, John. Master Skylark. 20.95 (*0-88411-823-1*) Amereon Ltd.

***Bennet, John M., ed.** Loose Watch: A Lost & Found Times Anthology. 205p. 1998. pap. 20.00 (*0-9521256-8-4*, Pub. by Invisible Bks) SPD-Small Pr Dist.

***Bennet, Kim D.** One Lucky Lord. (Wink & a Kiss Ser.). 368p. 2000. mass mkt. 5.50 (*0-505-52363-9*, Love Spell) Dorchester Pub Co.

Bennet, Leonard, et al. Yes Review Workbook, High School Entrance. 1986. pap. 8.95 (*0-87738-026-0*) Youth Ed.

Bennet, M. & Wakeford, R. Selecting Students for Training in Health Care: A Practical Guide to Improving Selection Procedures. (WHO Offset Publications: No. 74). 38p. 1983. 7.00 (*92-4-170074-2*) World Health.

***Bennet, Michael, ed.** The Nature of Cities: Ecocriticism & Urban Environments. LC 99-6284. (Illus.). 312p. 1999. 40.00 (*0-8165-1947-1*) U of Ariz Pr.

Bennet, Paul R. Salt I: Breakthrough or Deadlock? (Pew Case Studies in International Affairs). 59p. (C). 1988. pap. text 3.50 (*1-56927-303-0*) Geo U Inst Dplmcy.

Bennet, Rick. King of a Small World. LC 94-42742. 288p. 1995. 21.45 (*1-55970-284-2*, Pub. by Arcade Pub Inc) Time Warner.

Bennet, Rick. Lost Brother. LC 96-32789. 240p. 1996. 21.45 (*1-55970-367-9*, Pub. by Arcade Pub Inc) Time Warner.

Bennet, Robert A. The Bowl of Baal. 1976. 10.00 (*0-937986-06-2*) D M Grant.

— Thyra: A Romance of the Polar Pit. 258p. 1974. spiral bd. 16.00 (*0-7873-1208-8*) Hlth Research.

— Thyra: A Romance of the Polar Pit. Reginald, R. & Melville, Douglas, eds. LC 77-84199. (Lost Race & Adult Fantasy Ser.). (Illus.). 1978. reprint ed. lib. bdg. 29.95 (*0-405-10957-1*) Ayer.

Bennet, Robert R., jt. auth. see Ferencz, George J.

Bennet, Roger. International Business: Economic, Political, Legal & Cultural Influences. 2nd ed. (Framework Ser.). 416p. (Orig.). 1999. pap. 42.50 (*0-273-63429-1*, Pub. by F T P-H) Trans-Atl Phila.

— Management Research: Guide for the Institutions & Professionals. (Management Development Ser.: No. 20). viii, 245p. 1987. pap. 22.50 (*92-2-103303-1*) Intl Labour Office.

Bennet, S. S. Flora of Hawrah District (West Bengal) 406p. 1979. 250.00 (*0-7855-6639-2*, Pub. by Intl Bk Distr) St Mut.

— Flora of Howrah District (West Bengal) 406p. (C). 1979. text 350.00 (*0-89771-550-0*, Pub. by Intl Bk Distr) St Mut.

Bennet, S. S., ed. An Introduction to Plant Nomenclature. 77p. 1979. 50.00 (*0-7855-3074-6*, Pub. by Intl Bk Distr) St Mut.

Bennet, William. Math Dictionary for Young People. 176p. (YA). (gr. 5 up). 1998. lib. bdg. 19.95 (*0-382-39629-4*) Silver Burdett Pr.

— Teacher's Guide for "The Book of Virtues for Young People" 48p. 1996. pap., teacher ed. 3.95 (*0-382-39002-4*) Silver Burdett Pr.

Bennet, William S., jt. auth. see Dillingham, William P.

Bennetot, Arlette Cotton De, see Cotton de Bennetot, Arlette.

Bennett. Adventure in Music: Opera. 1991. pap. text. write for info. (*0-582-22538-8*, Pub. by Addison-Wesley) Longman.

— Adventures in Music Bk. 3. Date not set. pap. text. write for info. (*0-582-20731-2*, Pub. by Addison-Wesley) Longman.

— Adventures in Music Bk. 4. (J). Date not set. pap. text. write for info. (*0-582-20733-9*, Pub. by Addison-Wesley) Longman.

— Asthma & Eczema. 1998. pap. 11.00 (*0-7225-3145-1*) Thorsons PA.

***Bennett.** Bags of Poems: Family Album. 2000. pap. 6.55 (*0-552-52715-7*, Pub. by Transworld Publishers Ltd) Trafalgar.

Bennett. Basic Weight Training Record. 1995. pap. text 20.00 (*0-205-17371-3*) Allyn.

— Business, Governments & Society. (C). 1998. pap. text. write for info. (*0-201-65674-4*) Addison-Wesley.

— Cardiac Arrhythmias: Practical Notes on Interpretation & Treatment. 5th ed. LC 96-53898. 264p. 1997. pap. text 50.00 (*0-7506-3369-7*) Buttrwrth-Heinemann.

— Carousel Sticker Acitivity Book. pap. 1.00 (*0-486-29888-4*) Dover.

— Cecil Textbook of Medicine. 20th ed. (C). text. write for info. (*0-8089-2155-X*, Grune & Strat) Harcrt Hlth Sci Grp.

— Clay Microstructure. 1986. text 151.50 (*90-277-2263-3*) Kluwer Academic.

— Course Generalized Phrase Structure. (Centre for Computational Linguistics (CCL) Book Ser.). 180p. 1994. pap. 29.95 (*1-85728-217-5*, Pub. by UCL Pr Ltd) Taylor & Francis.

— Criminal Investigation. 4th ed. (Criminal Justice Ser.). 1994. pap., student ed. 17.25 (*0-314-03969-4*) West Pub.

— Criminal Investigations. 4th ed. Date not set. pap. text, teacher ed. write for info. (*0-314-03316-5*) West Pub.

— Ethnobotany of the Suar. LC 99-16043. (Advances in Economic Botany Ser.: Vol. 14). 1999. pap. write for info. (*0-89327-421-6*, AEB14) NY Botanical.

— Festivals. Scholastic, Inc. Staff, ed. 1988. pap. 14.95 (*0-590-70951-8*, Scholastic Hardcover) Scholastic Inc.

— For Power of Communication. 1991. teacher ed. 35.25 (*0-07-004717-0*) McGraw.

— Governing a Crisis. 2nd ed. LC 94-74762. 288p. 1995. pap. text 25.95 (*0-312-11615-2*) St Martin.

— Governing Crisis. 2nd ed. Date not set. pap. text 25.95 (*0-312-14781-3*) St Martin.

— Government Crisis Read White House 96. 2000. pap. text 30.60 (*0-312-14804-6*) St Martin.

— Heavy Duty Truck Technology. 2002. 54.75 (*0-7668-1622-2*) Delmar.

***Bennett.** Heavy Duty Truck Technology. 2002. 12.00 (*0-7668-1623-0*) Delmar.

Bennett. Innovation Concrete Design. (Illus.). 368p. 1997. text. write for info. (*0-419-19710-9*, E & FN Spon) Routledge.

— Introduction to Criminal Justice. (Criminal Justice Ser.). 2002. pap. 32.00 (*0-534-52191-6*) Wadsworth Pub.

— Math Elementary Teaching Activity Approach. 1997. pap., lab manual ed. 57.19 (*0-07-913259-6*) McGraw.

— Math for Elementary Teachers. 5th ed. 2000. 34.50 (*0-07-232653-0*) McGraw.

— Math For Elementary Teachers. 5th ed. 1032p. 2000. 72.50 (*0-07-234681-7*) McGraw.

— Mathematics & Elementary Teaching Concept. 4th ed. 1997. pap. 74.31 (*0-07-561354-9*) McGraw.

— Mathematics Elementary Teaching Concept. 4th ed. 256p. 1998. pap. 20.63 (*0-07-006300-1*) McGraw.

— Medieval Europe. 9th ed. 2001. 25.50 (*0-07-234657-4*) McGraw.

— Medium Heavy Duty Truck Engines, Fuels & Computerized Systems. LC 98-25968. 768p. 1999. text 77.95 (*0-8273-8574-9*) Delmar.

— Medium-Heavy Duty Truck Engines, Fuels, Comp Systems IG. 128p. 1999. text, teacher ed. 33.95 (*0-8273-8575-7*) Delmar.

— Migrating to ATM. (ITCP-UK Computer Science Ser.). 1997. pap. 43.99 (*1-85032-319-4*, VNR) Wiley.

***Bennett.** Mysteries for the New Millennium. 216p. 2000. 25.00 (*0-321-02971-2*) Benjamin-Cummings.

Bennett. Quantitative Reasoning: Mathematics for Citizens in the 21St Century. 128p. (C). 1996. pap. text 26.00 (*0-201-80958-3*) Addison-Wesley.

Bennett. Quantitative Reasoning Preliminary Edition: Mathematics for Citizens in the 21st Century. 1996. teacher ed. 24.00 (*0-201-80959-1*) Addison-Wesley.

Bennett. Skin Flaps. 1998. text. write for info. (*0-7216-3414-1*, W B Saunders Co) Harcrt Hlth Sci Grp.

— Songworks 2: Singing from Sound to Symbol. (Music Ser.). 1998. pap. 46.95 (*0-534-51328-X*) Wadsworth Pub.

— Source Readings for American Government. (C). 1995. pap. text 12.00 (*0-15-502976-2*, Pub. by Harcourt Coll Pubs) Harcourt.

***Bennett.** Supplementing Mathematics: A Quantitative Reasoning Approach. 1998. 93.13 (*0-201-64253-0*) Addison-Wesley.

Bennett. Textbook for Midwives. 13th ed. LC 98-48703. (C). 1999. pap. text 55.95 (*0-443-05586-6*, W B Saunders Co) Harcrt Hlth Sci Grp.

Bennett & Briggs. Using & Understanding Mathematics: A Quantitative Approach Instructor's Guide & Solutions Manual. 256p. 1998. 24.00 (*0-201-59083-2*) Addison-Wesley.

— Using & Understanding Mathematics: A Quantitative Approach Instructor's Testing Manual. 448p. 1998. 24.00 (*0-201-38401-9*) Addison-Wesley.

***Bennett & Haigh.** Breast Disease For Clinicians. 1999. 65.00 (*0-8385-0514-7*) McGraw.

***Bennett & Hess.** Criminal Investigation. 6th ed. 2000. pap. 21.00 (*0-534-57656-7*) Wadsworth Pub.

Bennett, et al. The Apportionment Problem: The Search for the Perfect Democracy. (Hi Map Ser.: No. 8). (Illus.). 60p. pap. text 11.99 (*0-614-05319-6*, HM 5608) COMAP Inc.

— Fair Division. (Hi Map Ser.: No. 9). (Illus.). 60p. pap. text 11.99 (*0-614-05317-X*, HM 5609) COMAP Inc.

— Heavy Duty Truck Systems 3rd ed. 2001. pap. 65.00 (*0-7668-1340-1*) Delmar.

— Local Empower & Business Service: Britain's Experiment with Training & Enterprise Councils. 352p. 1994. 95.00 (*1-85728-144-6*, Pub. by UCL Pr Ltd) Taylor & Francis.

— Military Occupational Analysis: A Special Issue of "Military Psychology", Vol. 8, No. 2, 1996. 1996. pap. 20.00 (*0-8058-9925-1*) L Erlbaum Assocs.

Bennett, jt. auth. see Gershman.

Bennett, jt. auth. see Randall, Peter G.

Bennett, A., et al. Workshops in Cognitive Processes. 2nd ed. 136p. 1982. pap. 10.95 (*0-7100-0932-1*, Routledge Thoemms) Routledge.

Bennett, A., jt. ed. see Kruger, D.

Bennett, A. E. & Sly, Louis J. Blueprint Reading for Welders. 4th ed. 1988. pap. 23.95 (*0-8273-2997-0*) Delmar.

Bennett, A. E. & Sly, Louis J. Blueprint Reading for Welders: Instructor's Guide. 5th ed. 152p. 1993. 17.50 (*0-8273-5580-7*) Delmar.

Bennett, A. G. & Rabbetts, Ronald B. Clinical Visual Optics. 2nd ed. (Illus.). 529p. 1990. 115.00 (*0-7506-0454-9*) Buttrwrth-Heinemann.

Bennett, A. L., ed. see Sappington, Joe.

Bennett, A. LeRoy. Historical Dictionary of the United Nations. LC 95-1505. (International Organizations Ser.: No. 8). (Illus.). 290p. 1995. 52.00 (*0-8108-2992-4*) Scarecrow.

— International Organizations: Principles & Issues. 6th ed. LC 94-35664. 480p. 1994. 52.00 (*0-13-227018-8*) P-H.

Bennett, A. R. The Telephone Systems of the Continent of Europe, 1895, 2 vols. LC 74-4666. (Telecommunications Ser.). 395p. 1974. reprint ed. 40.95 (*0-405-06033-5*) Ayer.

Bennett, Addison C. & Tibbitts, Samuel J. Maximizing Quality Performance in Health Care Facilities. (Health Care Administration Ser.). 267p. 1989. 75.00 (*0-8342-0025-2*) Aspen Pub.

***Bennett, Aileen M.** Cajun & Southern Gluten-Free Delights. 140p. 1999. pap. 14.95 (*0-9665353-1-6*) A&G Pubg.

Bennett, Aileen M. Coping with Celiac, the Great Masquerader. LC 98-93282. 160p. 1998. pap. 12.95 (*0-9665353-0-8*) A&G Pubg.

Bennett, Alan. Alan Bennett: Plays 2, A Kafka's Dick, The Insurance Man, The Old Country, An Englishman Abroad. 1998. pap. 23.99 (*0-571-19442-7*) Faber & Faber.

— Alan Bennett Plays No. 1: Forty Years On; Getting On; Habeas Corpus; & Enjoy. 336p. 1996. pap. 16.95 (*0-571-17745-X*) Faber & Faber.

— London Review of Books. LC 96-48616. 1996. pap. 18.00 (*1-85984-121-X*) Norton.

Bennett, Alan. The Madness of George III. 94p. (Orig.). 1993. pap. 11.95 (*0-571-16749-7*) Faber & Faber.

Bennett, Alan. Madness of King George. 1995. pap. 10.00 (*0-679-76871-8*) Random.

— Talking Heads. (Illus.). 91p. 1992. pap. 10.95 (*0-563-20622-5*, BBC-Parkwest) Parkwest Pubns.

— A Working Life: Child Labour Through the Nineteenth Century. 80p. 1991. pap. 17.95 (*0-946184-66-6*, Pub. by Waterfront Pubns) Maiden Voyage.

B

Bennett, Alan, et al. Mountain Bike! Washington. (Mountain Bike! Ser.). (Illus.). 400p. 1998. pap. 15.95 (*0-89732-280-0*) Menasha Ridge.

Bennett, Alan, jt. auth. see Franks, Norman.

Bennett, Alan D., ed. Journey Through Judaism: The Best of Keeping Posted. LC 90-19938. (YA). (gr. 10 up). 1991. pap. 12.00 (*0-8074-0311-3*, 160500) UAHC.

Bennett, Albert B., Jr. & Nelson, Leonard T. Math: An Informal Approach. 2nd ed. 680p. (C). 1985. text 47.81 (*0-697-06853-6*, WCB McGr Hill) McGrw-H Hghr Educ.

Bennett, Albert B. & Nelson, Leonard T. Mathematics for Elementary Teachers: A Conceptual Approach. 4th ed. LC 97-16757. 1008p. (C). 1997. 65.31 (*0-07-006295-1*) McGraw.

Bennett, Albert B., Jr. & Nelson, Leonard T. Mathematics for Elementary Teachers: An Activity Approach. 3rd ed. 336p. (C). 1992. text 41.88 (*0-697-05917-0*, WCB McGr Hill) McGrw-H Hghr Educ.

Bennett, Albert B. & Nelson, Leonard T. Mathematics for Elementary Teachers: An Activity Approach. 4th ed. LC 97-5914. 1998. write for info. (*0-07-006298-6*) McGraw.

Bennett, Albert B., et al. Looking at Geometry, Unit V. (Math & the Mind's Eye Ser.). (Illus.). 76p. (C). 1987. teacher ed., ring bd. 10.00 (*1-886131-17-1*, ME5) Math Lrning.

— Modeling Integers, Unit VI. (Math & the Mind's Eye Ser.). (Illus.). 31p. (C). 1989. teacher ed., ring bd. 10.00 (*1-886131-18-X*, ME6) Math Lrning.

— Modeling Percentages & Ratios, Unit VII. (Math & the Mind's Eye Ser.). (Illus.). 52p. (C). 1991. teacher ed., ring bd. 10.00 (*1-886131-19-8*, ME7) Math Lrning.

— Modeling Rationals, Unit IV. (Math & the Mind's Eye Ser.). (Illus.). 92p. (C). 1988. teacher ed., ring bd. 10.00 (*1-886131-16-3*, ME4) Math Lrning.

— Modeling Whole Numbers, Unit III. (Math & the Mind's Eye Ser.). (Illus.). 56p. (C). 1988. teacher ed., ring bd. 10.00 (*1-886131-15-5*, ME3) Math Lrning.

— Seeing Mathematical Relationships, Unit 1. (Math & the Mind's Eye Ser.). (Illus.). 29p. (C). 1988. teacher ed., ring bd. 10.00 (*1-886131-13-9*, ME1) Math Lrning.

— Visualizing Number Concepts, Unit II. (Math & the Mind's Eye Ser.). (Illus.). 49p. (C). 1988. teacher ed., ring bd. 10.00 (*1-886131-14-7*, ME2) Math Lrning.

Bennett, Albert B., jt. auth. see Foreman, Linda C.

Bennett, Albert F., jt. ed. see Johnston, Ian A.

Bennett-Alexander, Dawn & Pincus, Laura B. Employment Law for Business. 2nd ed. LC 97-5652. (C). 1997. text. write for info. (*0-256-26684-0*, Irwn Prfssnl) McGraw-Hill Prof.

Bennett-Alexander, Dawn D. Employment Law for Business. 3rd ed. 720p. 2000. 86.25 (*0-07-231403-6*) McGraw.

Bennett-Alexander, Dawn D. & Pincus, Laura B. Employment Law for Business. LC 93-48773. 656p. (C). 1994. text 68.95 (*0-256-12216-4*, Irwn McGrw-H) McGrw-H Hghr Educ.

Bennett, Allegra. Renovating Woman: A Woman's Guide to Home Repair, Maintenance & Finding a Real Man. LC 96-42414. 1997. 22.00 (*0-671-52771-1*) PB.

Bennett, Allen. Corn & Sage. 160p. 1991. pap. 10.98 (*1-880899-00-0*) Melville & Co.

Bennett, Allison. Times Remembered & More Times Remembered: Bethlehem & New Scotland, New York, 2 vols. in 1. (Illus.). 232p. 1997. reprint ed. lib. bdg. 29.00 (*0-8328-7142-7*) Higginson Bk Co.

Bennett, Allison P. The People's Choice: A History of Albany County in Art & Architecture. LC 80-66320. (Illus.). 145p. 1980. pap. 11.95 (*0-89062-124-1*) Albany County.

— The People's Choice: A History of Albany County in Art & Architecture. LC 95-33616. (Illus.). 135p. 1995. reprint ed. pap. 23.00 (*0-935796-66-5*) Purple Mnt Pr.

Bennett, Allison P., jt. auth. see Dunn, Shirley W.

Bennett, Alma. Mary Gordon. 1996. 32.00 (*0-8057-4024-4*, Twyne) Mac Lib Ref.

Bennett, Alva W., ed. Sallust - Index Verborum Sallustianus. xii, 280p. 1969. 65.00 (*0-318-70658-X*) G Olms Pubs.

Bennett, Alva W., ed. see Sallust.

Bennett, Amanda. Baseball: History, Softball, & Legends of the Game. (Unit Study Adventures Ser.). 151p. 1996. pap. text 13.99 (*1-888306-00-9*, Home School Pr) Holly Hall.

— Christmas: History, Prophecy, The Nativity. (Unit Study Adventures Ser.). 111p. 1996. pap. 13.99 (*1-888306-13-0*, Home School Pr) Holly Hall.

— Computers: Technology, Electronics, & Internet. (Unit Study Adventures Ser.). 111p. 1996. pap. 13.99 (*1-888306-05-X*, Home School Pr) Holly Hall.

— Dogs: Fun with Pets, Responsibility, Animal Science. (Unit Study Adventures Ser.: No. 15). (Orig.). (J). (gr. k-12). 1997. pap. 13.99 (*1-888306-27-0*, Home School Pr) Holly Hall.

— Elections: Presidents, Campaigns, & Government. 143p. 1996. pap. text 13.99 (*1-888306-18-1*, Home School Pr) Holly Hall.

— Electricity: Science, Energy, & Inventions. (Unit Study Adventure Ser.). 107p. 1997. pap. 13.99 (*1-888306-06-8*, Home School Pr) Holly Hall.

— Flight. (Unit Study Adventures Ser.). 164p. Date not set. pap. 13.99 (*1-888306-10-6*, Home School Pr) Holly Hall.

— Gardens: History, Gardening & Plant Science. (Unit Study Adventures Ser.). 128p. 1996. pap. text 13.99 (*1-888306-01-7*, Home School Pr) Holly Hall.

— Home: Construction, Architecture & Home Economics. (Unit Study Adventures Ser.). 147p. 1996. pap. 13.99 (*1-888306-07-6*, Home School Pr) Holly Hall.

— Oceans: Sea Life, Exploration, & World Geography. (Unit Study Adventures Ser.). 179p. 1996. pap. 13.99 (*1-888306-08-4*, Home School Pr) Holly Hall.

— Olympics: History, Geography, & Sports. (Unit Study Adventures Ser.). 136p. 1996. pap. text 13.99 (*1-888306-03-3*, Home School Pr) Holly Hall.

— Pioneers: Nature, Life & Times, & American Geography. 141p. 1996. pap. text 13.99 (*1-888306-04-1*, Home School Pr) Holly Hall.

— Space. (Unit Study Adventures Ser.). 164p. Date not set. pap. text 13.99 (*1-888306-09-2*, Home School Pr) Holly Hall.

— Thanksgiving: Prayer, Pilgrims, Native Americans. (Unit Study Adventures Ser.). 95p. 1996. pap. 13.99 (*1-888306-12-2*, Home School Pr) Holly Hall.

— Trains. (Unit Study Adventures Ser.). 120p. 1999. pap. 13.99 (*1-888306-11-4*, Home School Pr) Holly Hall.

— Unit Study Journal: Record Keeping for All Unit Studies. (Unit Study Adventures Ser.). 88p. 1996. pap. text 7.99 (*1-888306-02-5*, Home School Pr) Holly Hall.

Bennett, Amanda & Foley, Terrence B. In Memoriam. LC 97-8972. 1997. pap. 12.00 (*0-684-81902-3*, Fireside) S&S Trade Pap.

Bennett, Amanda, jt. auth. see Garwood, John.

Bennett, Amanda, jt. auth. see Rittenberg, Sidney.

Bennett, Amanda, jt. auth. see Schiller, Lori.

Bennett, Amy, ed. see Oehlbeck, Barbara.

Bennett, Andrea T. & Kessler, James H. Apples, Bubbles, & Crystals: Your Science ABCs. (Illus.). 64p. (J). (ps-2). 1996. pap. 12.95 (*0-07-005827-X*) McGraw-Hill Prof.

— Sunlight, Skycrapers, & Soda Pop: The Wherever-You-Look Science Book. LC 97-23687. (Illus.). 64p. (J). (ps-3). 1997. pap. 12.95 (*0-07-001440-X*, Lrning Triangle) McGraw.

Bennett, Andrew. Condemned to Repetition? The Rise, Fall & Reprise of Soviet-Russian Military Interventionism, 1973-1996. LC 98-46251. (BCSIA Ser.). (Illus.). 250p. 1999. 35.00 (*0-262-02457-8*) MIT Pr.

— Condemned to Repetition? The Rise, Fall & Reprise of Soviet-Russian Military Interventionism, 1973-1996. LC 98-46251. (BCSIA Ser.). (Illus.). 250p. 1999. pap. text 17.50 (*0-262-52257-8*) MIT Pr.

— Keats, Narrative, & Audience: The Posthumous Life of Writing. LC 93-24773. (Studies in Romanticism: No. 6). 266p. (C). 1994. text 59.95 (*0-521-44565-5*) Cambridge U Pr.

***Bennett, Andrew.** Romantic Poets & the Culture of Posterity. LC 98-55152. (Cambridge Studies in Romanticism: No. 35). 275p. (C). 1999. 59.95 (*0-521-64144-6*) Cambridge U Pr.

Bennett, Andrew, ed. Readers & Reading. (Critical Readers Ser.). 288p. (C). 1996. text 66.50 (*0-582-21289-8*, 77028, Pub. by Addison-Wesley) Longman.

— Readers Reading Longman. (Critical Readers Ser.). 288p. (C). 1996. pap. text 30.00 (*0-582-21290-1*, 77027, Pub. by Addison-Wesley) Longman.

***Bennett, Andrew & Royle, Nicholas.** An Introduction to Literature, Criticsm & Theory. 2nd ed. 288p. 1999. pap. text 30.80 (*0-13-010914-2*, Prentice Hall) P-H.

Bennett, Andrew F. Inverse Methods in Physical Oceanography. (Monographs on Mechanics & Applied Mathematics). (Illus.). 364p. (C). 1992. text 74.95 (*0-521-38568-7*) Cambridge U Pr.

***Bennett, Andy.** Popular Music & Youth Culture: Music, Identity & Place. LC 99-16789. 2000. text 59.95 (*0-312-22753-1*) St Martin.

Bennett, Angeline. That Whiff of Sulphur. 64p. (Orig.). 1995. pap. 9.75 (*1-880222-22-1*) Red Apple Pub.

Bennett, Anina. Heartbreakers: Bust Out! (Illus.). 96p. (Orig.). 1997. pap. 9.95 (*1-887279-49-0*) Image Comics.

— Heartbreakers: Super Digest. (Illus.). 104p. 1998. pap. 9.95 (*1-58240-010-5*) Image Comics.

Bennett, Anina, ed. see Baron, Mike & Rude, Steve.

Bennett, Ann, ed. see Kurtz, Don.

Bennett, Ann, ed. see Martinette, Charles G. & Meisel, Louis K.

Bennett, Ann, ed. see Weinberg, Robert.

Bennett, Ann G., ed. see Collins, Max Allan & Elvgren, Drake.

Bennett, Ann G., ed. see Robinson, Frank M.

Bennett, Ann Granning, ed. see Beyer, Chris H.

Bennett, Ann Granning, ed. see Collins, Max Allan.

Bennett, Ann Granning, ed. see Goulart, Ron.

Bennett, Anna, ed. Acts of the Tapestry Symposium. LC 77-91645. (Illus.). 1979. pap. 15.00 (*0-88401-031-7*) Fine Arts Mus.

Bennett, Anna, jt. auth. see Mango, Marlia M.

Bennett, Anna E. Little Witch. LC 52-1374. (Illus.). (J). (gr. 3-5). 1953. lib. bdg. 12.89 (*0-397-30261-4*) HarpC Child Bks.

Bennett, Anna G. & Berson, Ruth. Fans in Fashion. LC 81-65612. (Illus.). 128p. 1981. pap. 15.00 (*0-88401-037-6*) Fine Arts Mus.

Bennett, Anne B. The Management of Philanthropic Funding for Institutional Stabilization: A History of Ford Foundation & New York City Ballet Activities. LC 92-26063. (Non-profit Institutions in America Ser.). 288p. 1992. text 10.00 (*0-8153-0903-1*) Garland.

Bennett, Annie. Madrid. (Blue Guide Ser.). (Illus.). 256p. (Orig.). 1997. pap. 18.95 (*0-393-31345-X*, Norton Paperbks) Norton.

***Bennett, Annie.** Madrid. 2nd ed. (Blue Guide Ser.). (Illus.). (Orig.). 2000. pap. 19.95 (*0-393-32011-1*) Norton.

Bennett, Anthony, jt. auth. see Ramanadham, V. V.

Bennett, Arnold. Anna of Five Towns. Preston, Peter, ed. 304p. 1997. pap. 7.50 (*0-460-87653-8*, Everyman's Classic Lib) Tuttle Pubng.

— Anna of the Five Towns. (Classics Library). 506p. 1998. pap. 3.95 (*1-85326-224-2*, 2242WW, Pub. by Wrdsworth Edits) NTC Contemp Pub Co.

— Anna of the Five Towns. LC 74-5320. (Collected Works of Arnold Bennett: Vol. 1). 1977. reprint ed. 22.95 (*0-518-19082-X*) Ayer.

— Anna of the Five Towns. 281p. 1977. reprint ed. lib. bdg. 13.25 (*0-89966-282-X*) Buccaneer Bks.

— Arnold Bennett. LC 74-5388. (Collected Works of Arnold Bennett: Vol. 2). 1977. reprint ed. 31.95 (*0-518-19083-8*) Ayer.

— The Arnold Bennett Omnibus Book. LC 74-5396. (Collected Works of Arnold Bennett: Vol. 4). 1977. reprint ed. 36.95 (*0-518-19085-4*) Ayer.

— The Author's Craft. LC 74-5396. (Collected Works of Arnold Bennett: Vol. 5). 1977. reprint ed. 21.95 (*0-518-19086-2*) Ayer.

— The Author's Craft & Other Critical Writings of Arnold Bennett. Hynes, Samuel, ed. LC 68-12706. (Regents Critics Ser.). 301p. 1968. reprint ed. pap. 93.40 (*0-7837-0230-2*, 204053800017) Bks Demand.

— Body & Soul. LC 74-5293. (Collected Works of Arnold Bennett: Vol. 6). 1977. reprint ed. 19.95 (*0-518-19087-0*) Ayer.

— The Book of Carlotta. LC 74-6017. (Collected Works of Arnold Bennett: Vol. 7). 1977. reprint ed. 23.95 (*0-518-19088-9*) Ayer.

— Books & Persons. LC 74-546. (Collected Works of Arnold Bennett: Vol. 8). 1977. reprint ed. 26.95 (*0-518-19089-7*) Ayer.

— The Bright Island. LC 74-5327. (Collected Works of Arnold Bennett: Vol. 9). 1977. reprint ed. 18.95 (*0-518-19090-0*) Ayer.

— Buried Alive. LC 74-5327. (Collected Works of Arnold Bennett: Vol. 10). 1977. reprint ed. 28.95 (*0-518-19091-9*) Ayer.

— Buried Alive. (Pocket Classics Ser.). 176p. 1991. reprint ed. pap. 6.95 (*0-7509-0008-3*, Pub. by Sutton Pub Ltd) Intl Pubs Mktg.

— The Card. 23.95 (*0-8488-0736-7*) Amereon Ltd.

— The City of Pleasure. LC 74-5394. (Collected Works of Arnold Bennett: Vol. 11). 1977. reprint ed. 25.95 (*0-518-19092-7*) Ayer.

— Clayhanger. LC 74-5390. (Collected Works of Arnold Bennett: Vol. 12). 1977. reprint ed. 47.95 (*0-518-19093-5*) Ayer.

— The Collected Works of Arnold Bennett, 90 vols, Set. 1976. reprint ed. 1897.50 (*0-8369-7057-8*) Ayer.

— Cupid & Commonsense. LC 74-6015. (Collected Works of Arnold Bennett: Vol. 13). 1977. reprint ed. 20.95 (*0-518-19094-3*) Ayer.

— Denry the Audacious. LC 72-6208. (Collected Works of Arnold Bennett: Vol. 14). 1977. reprint ed. 22.95 (*0-518-19095-1*) Ayer.

— Don Juan De Marana. (Collected Works of Arnold Bennett: Vol. 15). 1977. reprint ed. 22.95 (*0-518-19096-X*) Ayer.

— Fame & Fiction. LC 74-6011. (Collected Works of Arnold Bennett: Vol. 16). 1977. reprint ed. 25.95 (*0-518-19097-8*) Ayer.

— Flora. LC 74-5325. (Collected Works of Arnold Bennett: Vol. 17). 1977. reprint ed. 19.95 (*0-518-19098-6*) Ayer.

— Friendship & Happiness. LC 74-5432. (Collected Works of Arnold Bennett: Vol. 19). 1977. reprint ed. 21.95 (*0-518-19100-1*) Ayer.

— From the Log of the Velsa. LC 74-5317. (Collected Works of Arnold Bennett: Vol. 20). 1977. reprint ed. 34.95 (*0-518-19101-X*) Ayer.

— The Gates of Wrath. LC 74-5322. (Collected Works of Arnold Bennett: Vol. 21). 1977. reprint ed. 23.95 (*0-518-19102-8*) Ayer.

— The Ghost. LC 74-5392. (Collected Works of Arnold Bennett: Vol. 22). 1977. reprint ed. 23.95 (*0-518-19103-6*) Ayer.

— The Glimpse. LC 74-5399. (Collected Works of Arnold Bennett: Vol. 23). 1977. reprint ed. 31.95 (*0-518-19104-4*) Ayer.

— The Grand Babylon Hotel. large type ed. 304p. 1984. 27.99 (*0-7089-8180-1*) Ulverscroft.

— The Grand Babylon Hotel. LC 74-5400. (Collected Works of Arnold Bennett: Vol. 24). 1977. reprint ed. 31.95 (*0-518-19105-2*) Ayer.

— The Grand Babylon Hotel: A Fantasia on Modern Themes. 1971. 27.00 (*0-403-00004-1*) Scholarly.

— The Great Adventure. LC 74-5329. (Collected Works of Arnold Bennett: Vol. 25). 1977. reprint ed. 21.95 (*0-518-19106-0*) Ayer.

— Great Adventure: A Play of Fancy in Four Sets. LC 70-131622. 1970. reprint ed. 16.00 (*0-403-00509-4*) Scholarly.

— A Great Man. LC 74-5321. (Collected Works of Arnold Bennett: Vol. 26). 1977. reprint ed. 22.95 (*0-518-19107-9*) Ayer.

— The Grim Smile of the Five Towns. LC 74-5401. (Collected Works of Arnold Bennett: Vol. 27). 1977. reprint ed. 26.95 (*0-518-19108-7*) Ayer.

— Helen with the High Hand. LC 74-5402. (Collected Works of Arnold Bennett: Vol. 28). 1977. reprint ed. 23.95 (*0-518-19109-5*) Ayer.

— Hilda Lessways. LC 74-5331. (Collected Works of Arnold Bennett: Vol. 29). 1977. reprint ed. 26.95 (*0-518-19110-9*) Ayer.

— The Honeymoon. LC 74-5328. (Collected Works of Arnold Bennett: Vol. 30). 1977. reprint ed. 21.95 (*0-518-19111-7*) Ayer.

— Honeymoon: A Comedy in Three Acts. 1988. reprint ed. lib. bdg. 49.00 (*0-7812-0024-5*) Rprt Serv.

— Honeymoon: A Comedy in Three Acts. LC 74-131623. 1970. reprint ed. 17.00 (*0-403-00510-8*) Scholarly.

— How to Become an Author. 2nd ed. LC 74-5431. (Collected Works of Arnold Bennett: Vol. 31). 1977. reprint ed. 25.95 (*0-518-19112-5*) Ayer.

— How to Live on Twenty-four Hours a Day. LC 74-5288. (Collected Works of Arnold Bennett: Vol. 32). 1977. reprint ed. 22.95 (*0-518-19113-3*) Ayer.

— How to Make the Best of Life. LC 74-5332. (Collected Works of Arnold Bennett: Vol. 33). 1977. reprint ed. 23.95 (*0-518-19114-1*) Ayer.

— Hugo. LC 74-5403. (Collected Works of Arnold Bennett: Vol. 34). 1977. reprint ed. 25.95 (*0-518-19115-X*) Ayer.

— The Human Machine. LC 74-5290. (Collected Works of Arnold Bennett: Vol. 35). 1977. reprint ed. 19.95 (*0-518-19116-8*) Ayer.

— Imperial Palace. LC 74-5409. (Collected Works of Arnold Bennett: Vol. 36). 1977. reprint ed. 47.95 (*0-518-19117-6*) Ayer.

— Journal of Arnold Bennett. (Collected Works of Arnold Bennett: Vol. 38). 1977. 25.95 (*0-518-19119-2*) Ayer.

— Journal of Arnold Bennett, 1896-1910, Pt. 1. LC 74-5371. (Collected Works of Arnold Bennett: Vol. 37). 1977. reprint ed. 36.95 (*0-518-19118-4*) Ayer.

— Journal of Arnold Bennett, 1911-1920, Pt. 2. LC 74-5371. (Collected Works of Arnold Bennett: Vol. 39). 1977. reprint ed. 31.95 (*0-518-19120-6*) Ayer.

— Journal of Arnold Bennett, 1921-1928, Pt. 3. LC 74-5371. (Collected Works of Arnold Bennett: Vol. 40). 1977. reprint ed. 33.95 (*0-518-19121-4*) Ayer.

— Journal of Things New & Old. LC 74-6178. (Collected Works of Arnold Bennett: Vol. 41). 1977. reprint ed. 26.95 (*0-518-19122-2*) Ayer.

— Judith. LC 74-5397. (Collected Works of Arnold Bennett: Vol. 42). 1977. reprint ed. 19.95 (*0-518-19123-0*) Ayer.

— Leonora. LC 74-5379. (Collected Works of Arnold Bennett: Vol. 43). 1977. reprint ed. 22.95 (*0-518-19124-9*) Ayer.

— Liberty! LC 74-5300. (Collected Works of Arnold Bennett: Vol. 44). 1977. reprint ed. 19.95 (*0-518-19125-7*) Ayer.

— Lilian. LC 74-5330. (Collected Works of Arnold Bennett: Vol. 45). 1977. reprint ed. 23.95 (*0-518-19126-5*) Ayer.

— The Lion's Share. LC 74-17027. (Collected Works of Arnold Bennett: Vol. 46). 1977. reprint ed. 34.95 (*0-518-19127-3*) Ayer.

— Literary Taste: How to Form It. LC 74-16487. (Collected Works of Arnold Bennett: Vol. 47). 1977. reprint ed. 22.95 (*0-518-19128-1*) Ayer.

— London Life. LC 74-16480. (Collected Works of Arnold Bennett: Vol. 48). 1977. reprint ed. 22.95 (*0-518-19129-X*) Ayer.

— The Loot of Cities. LC 74-17025. (Collected Works of Arnold Bennett: Vol. 49). 1977. reprint ed. 25.95 (*0-518-19130-3*) Ayer.

— The Loot of the Cities. 1972. 10.00 (*1-880418-08-8*) D M Grant.

— The Love Match. LC 74-16481. (Collected Works of Arnold Bennett: Vol. 50). 1977. reprint ed. 19.95 (*0-518-19131-1*) Ayer.

— A Man from the North. LC 74-17023. (Collected Works of Arnold Bennett: Vol. 51). 1977. reprint ed. 25.95 (*0-518-19132-X*) Ayer.

— Married Life. LC 74-17077. (Collected Works of Arnold Bennett: Vol. 52). 1977. reprint ed. 19.95 (*0-518-19133-8*) Ayer.

— The Matador of the 5 Towns & Other Stories. LC 74-17074. (Collected Works of Arnold Bennett: Vol. 53). 1977. reprint ed. 34.95 (*0-518-19134-6*) Ayer.

— The Matador of the 5 Towns & Other Stories. LC 79-144875. 1971. reprint ed. 25.00 (*0-403-00862-X*) Scholarly.

— Mediterranean Scenes. LC 74-1702. (Collected Works of Arnold Bennett: Vol. 54). 1977. reprint ed. 19.95 (*0-518-19135-4*) Ayer.

— Mental Efficiency & Other Hints to Men & Women. LC 74-17123. (Collected Works of Arnold Bennett: Vol. 55). 1977. reprint ed. 19.95 (*0-518-19136-2*) Ayer.

— Milestones. LC 74-17129. (Collected Works of Arnold Bennett: Vol. 56). 1977. reprint ed. 19.95 (*0-518-19137-0*) Ayer.

— Mr. Prohack: A Comedy in Three Acts. LC 74-17128. (Collected Works of Arnold Bennett: Vol. 58). 1977. reprint ed. 25.95 (*0-518-19138-9*) Ayer.

***Bennett, Arnold.** Murder! 2000. pap. 3.95 (*1-86092-012-8*, Pub. by Travelman Pub) IPG Chicago.

Bennett, Arnold. The Night Visitor & Other Stories. LC 74-17062. (Collected Works of Arnold Bennett: Vol. 59). 1977. reprint ed. 31.95 (*0-518-19140-0*) Ayer.

— The Old Adam. LC 74-17296. (Collected Works of Arnold Bennett: Vol. 60). 1977. reprint ed. 33.95 (*0-518-19141-9*) Ayer.

***Bennett, Arnold.** The Old Wives' Tale. LC 99-41699. 640p. 1999. pap. 9.95 (*0-375-75490-3*) Modern Lib NY.

Bennett, Arnold. The Old Wives' Tale. 624p. 1991. pap. 11.95 (*0-14-018255-1*, Penguin Classics) Viking Penguin.

— The Old Wives' Tale. 622p. 1980. reprint ed. pap. 10.00 (*0-915864-77-0*) Academy Chi Pubs.

— The Old Wives' Tale. LC 74-17060. (Collected Works of Arnold Bennett: Vol. 61). 1977. reprint ed. 47.95 (*0-518-19142-7*) Ayer.

— Our Women. LC 74-17107. (Collected Works of Arnold Bennett: Vol. 62). 1977. reprint ed. 25.95 (*0-518-19143-5*) Ayer.

— Paris Nights & Other Impressions of Places & People. (Collected Works of Arnold Bennett: Vol. 64). (Illus.). 1977. reprint ed. 36.95 (*0-518-19145-1*, 19145) Ayer.

— Piccadilly. LC 74-17299. (Collected Works of Arnold Bennett: Vol. 65). 1977. reprint ed. 22.95 (*0-518-19146-X*) Ayer.

— Polite Farces for the Drawing Room. Date not set. 20.95 (*0-518-19147-8*) NY Times Lib.

— The Pretty Lady. LC 74-17298. (Collected Works of Arnold Bennett: Vol. 67). 1977. reprint ed. 25.95 (*0-518-19148-6*) Ayer.

— Pretty Lady. LC 72-144876. 1971. reprint ed. 18.00 (*0-403-00863-8*) Scholarly.

An Asterisk (*) at the beginning of an entry indicates that the title is appearing for the first time.

— The Price of Love. LC 74-17050. (Collected Works of Arnold Bennett: Vol. 68). 1977. reprint ed. 39.95 (*0-518-19149-4*) Ayer.

— The Reasonable Life. LC 74-16364. (Collected Works of Arnold Bennett: Vol. 69). 1977. reprint ed. 19.95 (*0-518-19150-8*) Ayer.

— The Regent. LC 74-17073. (Collected Works of Arnold Bennett: Vol. 70). 1977. reprint ed. 25.95 (*0-518-19151-6*) Ayer.

— Riceyman Steps. 393p. 1984. reprint ed. pap. 11.95 (*0-89733-093-5*) Academy Chi Pubs.

— The Roll-Call. LC 74-17047. (Collected Works of Arnold Bennett: Vol. 71). 1977. reprint ed. 26.95 (*0-518-19152-4*) Ayer.

— The Savour of Life. LC 74-17048. (Collected Works of Arnold Bennett: Vol. 72). 1977. reprint ed. 26.95 (*0-518-19153-2*) Ayer.

— Self & Self-Management. LC 74-16345. (Collected Works of Arnold Bennett: Vol. 73). 1977. reprint ed. 19.95 (*0-518-19154-0*) Ayer.

— Shelter, Housing, & Homes: A Social Right. LC 95-79357. 193p. 1996. 48.99 (*1-55164-043-0*, Pub. by Black Rose); pap. 19.99 (*1-55164-042-2*, Pub. by Black Rose) Consort Bk Sales.

— The Sinews of War. LC 74-17139. (Collected Works of Arnold Bennett: Vol. 74). 1977. reprint ed. 26.95 (*0-518-19155-9*) Ayer.

— The Statue. LC 74-17141. (Collected Works of Arnold Bennett: Vol. 75). 1977. reprint ed. 22.95 (*0-518-19156-7*) Ayer.

— Stroke of Luck & Dream of Destiny. LC 74-17075. (Collected Works of Arnold Bennett: Vol. 76). 1977. reprint ed. 24.95 (*0-518-19157-5*) Ayer.

— Tales of the Five Towns. LC 74-17131. (Collected Works of Arnold Bennett: Vol. 77). 1977. reprint ed. 23.95 (*0-518-19158-3*) Ayer.

— Teresa of Watling Street. LC 74-17051. (Collected Works of Arnold Bennett: Vol. 78). 1977. reprint ed. 21.95 (*0-518-19159-1*) Ayer.

— These Twain. LC 74-17052. (Collected Works of Arnold Bennett: Vol. 79). 1977. reprint ed. 45.95 (*0-518-19160-5*) Ayer.

— Things That Have Interested Me. LC 74-17049. (First Ser.: Vol. 80). 1977. reprint ed. 30.95 (*0-518-19161-3*, 19161) Ayer.

— Things That Have Interested Me. LC 74-17091. (Second Ser.: Vol. 81). 1977. reprint ed. 26.95 (*0-518-19162-1*) Ayer.

— Things That Have Interested Me. LC 74-17074. (Third Ser.: Vol. 82). 1977. reprint ed. 25.95 (*0-518-19163-X*) Ayer.

— The Title. LC 74-17056. (Collected Works of Arnold Bennett: Vol. 83). 1977. reprint ed. 19.95 (*0-518-19164-8*) Ayer.

— The Truth about an Author. LC 74-17055. (Collected Works of Arnold Bennett: Vol. 84). 1977. reprint ed. 22.95 (*0-518-19165-6*) Ayer.

— The Vanguard. LC 74-17054. (Collected Works of Arnold Bennett: Vol. 85). 1977. reprint ed. 25.95 (*0-518-19166-4*) Ayer.

— What the Public Wants. LC 74-16478. (Collected Works of Arnold Bennett: Vol. 86). 1977. reprint ed. 21.95 (*0-518-19167-2*) Ayer.

— Where Are the Dead? LC 74-17034. (Collected Works of Arnold Bennett: Vol. 87). 1977. reprint ed. 21.95 (*0-518-19168-0*) Ayer.

— Whom God Hath Joined. LC 74-17007. (Collected Works of Arnold Bennett: Vol. 88). 1977. reprint ed. 34.95 (*0-518-19169-9*) Ayer.

— The Woman Who Stole Everything & Other Stories. LC 74-17057. (Collected Works of Arnold Bennett: Vol. 89). 1977. reprint ed. 30.95 (*0-518-19170-2*) Ayer.

— Your United States. LC 74-16408. (Collected Works of Arnold Bennett: Vol. 90). 1977. reprint ed. 22.95 (*0-518-19171-0*) Ayer.

Bennett, Arnold & Knoblauch, Edward. Milestones, a Play in Three Acts. LC 78-131624. 1971. reprint ed. 15.00 (*0-403-00511-6*) Scholarly.

Bennett, Arnold & Knoblock, Edward. Mr. Prohack: A Comedy in Three Acts. Date not set. write for info. (*0-518-19139-7*) NY Times Lib.

Bennett, Arnold, et al. Frank Swinnerton. LC 74-5433. (Collected Works of Arnold Bennett: Vol. 18). 1977. reprint ed. 19.95 (*0-518-19099-4*) Ayer.

Bennett, Arnold, tr. see Dore, Jean.

Bennett, Arnold, tr. see Dumas, Evelyn.

Bennett, Arnold, tr. see Fournier, Louise, et al.

Bennett, Arnold, tr. see Gelinas.

Bennett, Arnold, tr. see Noel, Lise.

Bennett, Arthur, ed. see McCabe, Marsha & Thomas, Joseph D.

Bennett, Arthur G. Valley of Vision. 240p. 1983. reprint ed. pap. 13.99 (*0-85151-228-3*) Banner of Truth.

Bennett, Arthur G. & Rabbetts, Ronald B. Bennett & Rabbetts' Clinical Visual Optics. 3rd ed. LC 97-51177. 450p. 1998. text 120.00 (*0-7506-1817-5*) Buttrwrth-Heinemann.

Bennett, Artie. The Dinosaur Joke Book: A Compendium of Pre-Hysteric Puns. LC 96-37477. 1998. pap. 3.25 (*0-679-88188-3*, Pub. by Random Bks Yng Read) Random.

Bennett, Austin, ed. Optics of Contact Lenses. (C). 1989. 125.00 (*0-900099-22-4*, Pub. by Assn Brit Dispen Opticians) St Mut.

Bennett, B. Build Rabbit Housing. 1983. pap. 2.95 (*0-88266-296-1*, Storey Pub) Storey Bks.

— Education in a Special Hospital. 136p. (C). 1989. 49.00 (*0-7855-6664-3*, Pub. by Univ Nottingham) St Mut.

Bennett, B., jt. ed. see Ogston, Derek.

Bennett, B. Taylor, et al, eds. Nonhuman Primates in Biomedical Research: Diseases. (Illus.). 512p. 1998. 132.00 (*0-12-088665-0*) Acad Pr.

— Nonhuman Primates in Biomedical Research Vol. 1: Biology & Management. (Illus.). 428p. 1995. text 132.00 (*0-12-088661-8*) Acad Pr.

Bennett, B. Taylor, et al. Essentials for Animal Research: A Primer for Research Personnel. 2nd ed. (Illus.). 84p. (C). 1996. reprint ed. pap. text 30.00 (*0-7881-3635-6*) DIANE Pub.

Bennett, B. Taylor, jt. auth. see Fortman, Jeffrey D.

Bennett, Barbara. Comic Visions, Female Voices: Contemporary Women Novelists & Southern Humor. LC 98-20584. (Southern Literary Studies). 144p. 1998. text 27.50 (*0-8071-2288-2*) La State U Pr.

— Forever Eden, No. 15. (Serenade Serenata Ser.). 1985. pap. 2.50 (*0-310-46712-8*, 15530P) Zondervan.

— A Rough Music. large type ed. 428p. 1981. 27.99 (*0-7089-0719-9*) Ulverscroft.

***Bennett, Barbara.** Understanding Jill McCorkle. 2000. 29.95 (*1-57003-350-1*) U of SC Pr.

Bennett, Barbara. Words Take Wing: A Teaching Guide to Creative Writing for Children. LC 82-84013. (Illus.). 194p. 1983. reprint ed. pap. 60.20 (*0-608-00015-9*, 206078100006) Bks Demand.

Bennett, Barbara, jt. auth. see Bennett, Michele.

Bennett, Barbara J. Stonewall Jackson: Lee's Greatest Lieutenant. (History of the Civil War Ser.). (Illus.). 160p. (YA). (gr. 5 up). 1990. pap. 7.95 (*0-382-24048-0*) Silver Burdett Pr.

Bennett, Barbara L., jt. ed. see Wooderson, Dawn C.

Bennett, Barbara R. Emergency Medical Technician & Paramedic Training: Perspectives on Status & Trends. Jacobs, Lenworth M., ed. (Emergency Health Services Review Ser.: Vol. 2, No. 1). 66p. 1983. pap. text 19.95 (*0-917724-51-8*) Haworth Pr.

Bennett, Barrie, et al. Cooperative Learning: Where Heart Meets Mind: An Interactive Resource Book. 345p. 1991. reprint ed. spiral bd. 29.00 (*0-9635240-0-3*) Prof Dev Assocs.

Bennett, Belinda. Law & Medicine. LC 97-157544. 191p. 1997. pap. 33.50 (*0-455-21456-5*, Pub. by LawBk Co) Gaunt.

Bennett, Benjamin. Beyond Theory: Eighteenth-Century German Literature & the Poetics of Irony. LC 92-46530. (Illus.). 376p. (C). 1993. text 49.95 (*0-8014-2841-6*) Cornell U Pr.

— Goethe's Theory of Poetry: Faust & the Regeneration of Language. LC 86-6251. 352p. reprint ed. pap. 109.20 (*0-608-20873-6*, 207197200003) Bks Demand.

— Theater As Problem: Modern Drama & Its Place in Literature. LC 90-55115. 296p. 1990. pap. text 17.95 (*0-8014-9730-2*) Cornell U Pr.

Bennett, Benjamin K. Burgers on the Moon. (Illus.). 10p. (Orig.). (J). 1990. pap. 2.00 (*0-935350-21-7*) Luna Bisonte.

Bennett, Berna. A Gentle Approach to Teaching Children to Swim. (Illus.). 90p. (Orig.). 1997. pap. 12.95 (*0-9658139-0-8*) Berna Bennett.

***Bennett, Bernard.** Mexico from Within, Vol. 1. 260p. 1999. text 26.95 (*0-9673681-0-3*) B Bennett.

Bennett, Beth. Nutrition for Climbers. (How to Rock Climb Ser.). 32p. 1995. pap. 4.95 (*0-934641-76-5*) Falcon Pub Inc.

Bennett, Betty T. Mary Diana Dods: A Gentleman & a Scholar. LC 94-13170. 312p. 1994. reprint ed. pap. 15.95 (*0-8018-4984-5*) Johns Hopkins.

— Mary Wollstonecraft Shelley. 192p. 1998. pap. text 13.95 (*0-8018-5976-X*) Johns Hopkins.

— Mary Wollstonecraft Shelley: An Introduction. LC 98-16237. 192p. 1998. 38.00 (*0-8018-5975-1*) Johns Hopkins.

Bennett, Betty T., ed. The Letters of Mary Wollstonecraft Shelley Vol. III: "What Years I Have Spent" LC 79-24190. 520p. 1988. text 55.00 (*0-8018-2646-2*) Johns Hopkins.

Bennett, Betty T. & Curran, Stuart, eds. Shelley: Poet & Legislator of the World. 304p. 1996. text 48.50 (*0-8018-5175-0*); pap. text 17.95 (*0-8018-5176-9*) Johns Hopkins.

Bennett, Betty T., ed. see Shelley, Mary Wollstonecraft.

Bennett, Beverly. Dinner for Two: A Cookbook for Couples. 196p. 1994. pap. 16.95 (*0-8120-1987-3*) Barron.

Bennett, Beverly & VanVynckt, Virginia. Dictionary of Healthful Food Terms. LC 97-326. (Illus.). 368p. (Orig.). 1997. pap. 8.95 (*0-8120-9751-3*) Barron.

Bennett, Beverly C. The ABC's of Marital Success: A Guidebook for Couples. 76p. 1999. pap. write for info. (*0-9669966-0-7*) Ctr Fam.

Bennett, Bo, jt. auth. see DeVincent-Hayes, Nan.

***Bennett, Bob.** Catching Fundamentals & Techniques. (Illus.). 220p. 2000. pap. 16.95 (*1-57167-321-0*) Coaches Choice.

Bennett, Bob. 101 Pitching Drills. (Illus.). 164p. 2000. pap. 16.95 (*1-57167-318-0*) Coaches Choice.

— Pitching from the Ground Up. 223p. 1997. pap. 20.00 (*1-57167-076-9*) Coaches Choice.

— Rabbits As a Hobby. (Save Our Planet Ser.). (Illus.). 96p. 1991. pap. 8.95 (*0-86622-417-3*, TT003) TFH Pubns.

— Raising Rabbits Successfully. LC 83-27334. (Illus.). 192p. (Orig.). 1984. pap. 9.95 (*0-913589-03-9*) Williamson Pub Co.

— Raising Rabbits the Modern Way. rev. ed. Oxley, Constance, ed. LC 87-45579. (Illus.). 192p. 1988. pap. 12.95 (*0-88266-479-4*, Garden Way Pub) Storey Bks.

***Bennett, Bob.** Storey's Guide to Raising Rabbits: Breeds, Care, Facilities. 288p. 2000. pap. 18.95 (*1-58017-260-1*) Storey Bks.

Bennett, Bobby. Ultimate Soul Music Trivia Book: 501 Questions & Answers about Motown, Rhythm & Blues & More. LC 97-27572. (Illus.). 144p. 1997. pap. text 9.95 (*0-8065-1923-1*, Citadel Pr) Carol Pub Group.

Bennett, Brenda. What's for Dinner? A Guide to Preparing 30 Meals in One Day. (Illus.). vii, 108p. 1996. reprint ed. ring bd. 18.95 (*0-9651526-0-X*, WFD-011) Natural Selections.

Bennett, Brian. Education in a Special Hospital. (C). 1989. 60.00 (*1-85041-025-9*, Pub. by Univ Nottingham) St Mut.

Bennett, Brian & Zellman, Shelley. Autobiography of an Angel. 96p. 1998. pap. 9.95 (*0-9661695-0-6*) Journey Light.

Bennett, Brian A. The Beau Ideal of a Soldier & a Gentleman: The Life of Col. Patrick Henry O'Rorke from Ireland to Gettysburg. LC 96-90224. (Illus.). xvi, 198p. (Orig.). 1996. pap. 22.95 (*0-9651863-0-X*) Triphammer Pubng.

— On a Silver Diamond: The Story of Rochester Community Baseball from 1956-1996. viii, 358p. (Orig.). 1997. pap. 19.95 (*0-9651863-1-8*, 0297-01) Triphammer Pubng.

***Bennett, Brian A.** Sons of Old Monroe: A Regimental History of Patrick O'Rorke's 140th New York Volunteer Infantry. 2nd rev. ed. (Illus.). 718p. 1999. reprint ed. 55.00 (*0-89029-336-8*); reprint ed. pap. 30.00 (*0-89029-334-1*) Morningside Bkshop.

Bennett, Bridget. The Damnation of Harold Frederic: His Lives & Works. LC 96-32953. (Illus.). 332p. 1996. 45.00 (*0-8156-0390-8*, BEDH) Syracuse U Pr.

Bennett, Bridget, jt. ed. see Treglown, Jeremy.

Bennett, Bruce. It's Hard to Get the Angle Right. 34p. 1997. pap. 6.00 (*1-887240-02-0*) GreenTower Pr.

— Navigating the Distances: Poems New & Selected. LC 98-50133. 178p. 1999. 24.95 (*0-914061-79-8*) Orchises Pr.

— Spirit in Exile: Peter Porter & His Poetry. (Illus.). 320p. 1992. text 55.00 (*0-19-554970-8*) OUP.

— Straw into Gold. (CSU Poetry Ser.: No. XVI). 52p. (Orig.). 1984. pap. 4.50 (*0-914946-45-5*) Cleveland St Univ Poetry Ctr.

— Taking Off. LC 91-27165. 96p. (Orig.). 1992. pap. 10.00 (*0-914061-26-7*) Orchises Pr.

Bennett, Bruce, ed. Dorothy Hewett: Selected Critical Essays. LC 95-124224. (Illus.). 294p. 1995. pap. 19.95 (*1-86368-113-2*, Pub. by Fremantle Arts) Intl Spec Bk.

***Bennett, Bruce, ed.** Sincerely Yours, Victor Hammer: Victor Hammer's Letters to Janet Lewis 1945-1948. (Illus.). 64p. 2000. pap. text 15.00 (*1-887196-07-2*) Wells Col Pr.

Bennett, Bruce, et al, eds. Westerly Looks to Asia. pap. 25.00 (*1-86342-169-6*, Pub. by Univ of West Aust Pr) Intl Spec Bk.

Bennett, Bruce & Grono, William. Wide Domain: Western Australian Themes & Images. LC 80-504462. 270 p. 1979. write for info. (*0-207-14018-9*) Angus & Roberts.

Bennett, Bruce & Haskell, Dennis, eds. Myths, Heroes & Anti-Heroes: The Literature of the Asia-Pacific Region. pap. 19.00 (*0-86422-221-1*, Pub. by Univ of West Aust Pr) Intl Spec Bk.

***Bennett, Bruce & Hayes, Susan, eds.** Home & Away: Australian Stories of Belonging & Alienation. 144p. 2000. pap. 19.95 (*1-876268-36-0*, Pub. by Univ of West Aust Pr) Intl Spec Bk.

Bennett, Bruce & Miller, Susan. Daughters of the Sun: Short Stories from Western Australia. LC 94-188222. 1994. pap. 16.95 (*1-875560-26-2*, Pub. by Univ of West Aust Pr) Intl Spec Bk.

Bennett, Bruce & Miller, Susan, eds. Peter Cowan: New Critical Essays. (Orig.). pap. 9.95 (*1-875560-10-6*, Pub. by Univ of West Aust Pr) Intl Spec Bk.

— A Sense of Exile: Essays in the Literature of the Asia-Pacific Region. pap. 12.95 (*0-86422-072-3*, Pub. by Univ of West Aust Pr) Intl Spec Bk.

Bennett, Bruce & Ram, Alur J., eds. Encounters: Selected Indian & Australian Short Stories. 15.00 (*81-7132-008-2*, Pub. by Univ of West Aust Pr) Intl Spec Bk.

Bennett, Bruce & Strauss, Jennifer, eds. The Oxford Literary History of Australia. LC 98-193279. 496p. 1999. 45.00 (*0-19-553737-8*) OUP.

Bennett, Bruce A., ed. Pipeline Infrastructure. (Conference Proceedings Ser.). 536p. 1988. 52.00 (*0-87262-662-8*) Am Soc Civil Eng.

Bennett, Bruce E., et al, eds. Professional Liability & Risk Management. LC 90-1199. 128p. (Orig.). 1990. pap. text 19.95 (*1-55798-101-9*) Am Psychol.

Bennett, Bruce E., et al. Ethics for Psychologists: A Commentary on the APA Ethics Code. LC 94-36224. 254p. (Orig.). 1994. pap. text 24.95 (*1-55798-259-7*, 431-2050) Am Psychol.

Bennett, Bruce W. & Hoyer, Mark C. The New Map Graphics in RSAS 5.0. LC 93-18545. 1993. pap. 9.00 (*0-8330-1337-8*, MR-122-NA) Rand Corp.

Bennett, Bruce W., et al. Future Warfare Scenarios & Asymmetric Threats LC 99-18455. 1999. write for info. (*0-8330-2718-2*) Rand Corp.

— JICM 1.0 Summary. LC 94-19226. 1994. pap. text 13.00 (*0-8330-1551-6*, MR-383-NA) Rand Corp.

— Theater Analysis & Modeling in an Era of Uncertainty: The Present & Future of Warfare. LC 94-4161. 1994. pap. text 13.00 (*0-8330-1511-7*, MR-380-NA) Rand Corp.

— What Are Asymmetric Strategies? 24p. 1999. pap. text 6.00 (*0-8330-2703-4*, DB-246-OSD) Rand Corp.

Bennett, C., et al, eds. Comparative Studies in Adult Education: An Anthology. LC 75-20016. (Occasional Papers: No. 44). 250p. 1975. pap. 9.00 (*0-87060-069-*, OCP 44) Syracuse U Cont Ed.

Bennett, C. E., tr. Odes & Epodes. (Loeb Classical Library: No. 33). 460p. 1927. 18.95 (*0-674-99037-4*) HUP.

Bennett, C. Mehrl & Bennett, John M. Some Blood: Joint Poems. 16p. 1982. pap. 3.00 (*0-935350-07-1*) Luna Bisonte.

— Some Blood: Joint Poems. deluxe limited ed. 16p. 1982. pap. 8.00 (*0-935350-08-X*) Luna Bisonte.

Bennett, C. Mehrl, jt. auth. see Bennett, John M.

Bennett, C. O. & Myers, J. E. Momentum, Heat & Mass Transfer. 3rd ed. (Chemical Engineering Ser.). 848p. (C). 1982. 114.69 (*0-07-004671-9*) McGraw.

Bennett, Carl A. & Franklin, Norman L. Statistical Analysis in Chemistry & the Chemical Industry. LC 54-11428. (Wiley Publications in Statistics Ser.). 724p. reprint ed. pap. 200.00 (*0-608-30024-1*, 205515300008) Bks Demand.

Bennett, Carla. Living in Harmony with Animals. LC 99-58048. 160p. 2000. pap. text 9.95 (*1-57067-085-4*) Book Pub Co.

— Voice & Diction. (C). 1995. 13.11 (*1-56870-167-5*) RonJon Pub.

***Bennett, Carol E.** Jennie's Reprisal. viii, 310p. 2000. per. 16.21 (*0-9679786-0-2*) Chesapeake Moon.

Bennett, Carol S. Economics for Insurance. 108p. (C). 1987. 85.00 (*0-948691-69-7*, Pub. by Witherby & Co) St Mut.

— Economics for Insurance. 112p. (C). 1989. pap. 65.00 (*0-948691-84-0*, Pub. by Witherby & Co) St Mut.

— Insurances of Liability. 130p. (C). 1989. pap. 80.00 (*0-948691-67-0*, Pub. by Witherby & Co) St Mut.

Bennett, Carole L., jt. auth. see Edelson, Norman M.

Bennett, Carolyn. A Thing among Things, an Event among Events: Short Stories. (Illus.). 112p. (Orig.). 1993. pap. 12.00 (*0-913559-23-7*) Birch Brook Pr.

Bennett, Carolyn & Romig, Jack. The Kids' Book of Kaleidoscopes. LC 94-27253. (Illus.). 96p. (YA). (gr. 3 up). 1999. pap. 16.95 (*1-56305-638-0*, 3638) Workman Pub.

Bennett, Cathereen L. Will Rogers: Quotable Cowboy. LC 95-10259. (Illus.). 96p. (J). (gr. 4-6). 1995. lib. bdg. 19.95 (*0-8225-3155-0*, Runestone Pr) Lerner Pub.

— Will Rogers: The Cowboy Who Walked with Kings. 16.95 (*0-88411-848-7*) Amereon Ltd.

***Bennett, Catherine A. & Bennett, Robert T.** Forever Young: How to Get a Life Before It's Over. large type ed. 390p. 1999. pap. 19.95 (*0-9601718-5-1*) Melrose Plantation.

Bennett, Catherine A. & Bennett, Robert T., eds. My Love for Lucy: Real Romance in the 1880s. (Illus.). 250p. 1998. boxed set 100.00 (*0-9601718-4-3*) Melrose Plantation.

Bennett, Catherine A., jt. auth. see Bennett, Robert T.

Bennett, Cathy E. Bennett's Guide to Jury Selection & Trial Dynamics: California Civil Litigation. Hirschhorn, Robert B., ed. 1994. pap. text. write for info. (*0-314-05113-9*) West Pub.

Bennett, Cathy E. & Hirschhorn, Robert B. Bennett's Guide to Jury Selection & Trial Dynamics: California Criminal Litigation. (C). 1994. pap. text. write for info. (*0-314-05114-7*) West Pub.

Bennett, Cathy E. & Mirschhorn, Robert B. Bennett's Guide to Jury Selection & Trial Dynamics in Civil & Criminal Litigation CLE Edition. 220p. (C). 1993. pap. text. write for info. (*0-314-02270-8*) West Pub.

Bennett, Charles. Medical Record Abstraction & Guidelines for Assessing Quality of Care for Hospitalized Patients with AIDS-Related Pneumocystis Carinii Pneumonia. 172p. (Orig.). (C). 1994. pap. text 45.00 (*0-7881-1055-1*) DIANE Pub.

— Twelve on the River St. John. 166p. 1989. 29.95 (*0-8130-0913-8*) U Press Fla.

Bennett, Charles E. Florida's "French" Revolution, 1793-1795. LC 81-7431. x, 218p. 1981. 29.95 (*0-8130-0641-4*) U Press Fla.

— A Latin Grammar. 288p. (C). 1995. reprint ed. pap. text 15.95 (*0-89341-753-X*) Hollowbrook.

Bennett, Charles E. A New Latin Composition. 304p. 1996. reprint ed. pap. 20.00 (*0-86516-345-6*) Bolchazy-Carducci.

Bennett, Charles E. Syntax of Early Latin, 2 vols. in 1. xxi, 409p. 1982. reprint ed. 185.00 (*3-487-01345-2*) G Olms Pubs.

Bennett, Charles E., ed. Cicero - On Old Age-De Senectute: Cicero. (Textbook Ser.). (Illus.). 446p. 1980. pap. text 13.00 (*0-86516-001-5*) Bolchazy-Carducci.

Bennett, Charles E. & Lennon, Donald R. A Quest for Glory: Major General Robert Howe & the American Revolution. LC 91-7825. (Illus.). x, 206p. (C). 1991. 29.95 (*0-8078-1982-4*) U of NC Pr.

— A Quest for Glory: Major General Robert Howe & the American Revolution. LC 91-7825. (Illus.). 219p. reprint ed. pap. 67.90 (*0-608-10493-0*, 207112200009) Bks Demand.

Bennett, Charles E., ed. see Horace.

Bennett, Charles E., ed. see Tacitus, Cornelius.

Bennett, Charles H., ed. see Walpole, Horace.

Bennett, Charles L. & Pajeau, Tammy S. Cancer Policy: Research & Methods. LC 98-22296. (Cancer Treatment & Research Ser.). 200p. 1998. 165.00 (*0-7923-8203-X*) Kluwer Academic.

Bennett, Charles L., jt. ed. see Holt, Stephen S.

Bennett, Cherie. The Accident: Love Hospital. (Hope Hospital Ser.). (J). 1996. 9.05 (*0-606-08965-9*, Pub. by Turtleback) Demco.

Bennett, Cherie. Angel Kisses. (Teen Angels Ser.: No. 3). 160p. (Orig.). (J). 1996. mass mkt. 3.99 (*0-380-78249-9*, Avon Bks) Morrow Avon.

— Bridesmaids. (J). (gr. 6-10). 1996. mass mkt. 3.99 (*0-590-54335-0*) Scholastic Inc.

— Cyra & Rocky. 42p. 1997. pap. 5.50 (*0-87129-745-0*, C97) Dramatic Pub.

***Bennett, Cherie.** Enchanted Hearts: Love Him Forever, No. 6. (Enchanted Hearts Ser.). 176p. 1999. mass mkt. 4.50 (*0-380-80124-8*, Avon Bks) Morrow Avon.

B

— Flirt in the Mirror. Vol. 4. 160p. (YA). (gr. 6-9). 2000. mass mkt. 4.50 (*0-671-03633-5*) S&S Trade.

Bennett, Cherie. Get Well Soon, Little Sister. (Hope Hospital Ser.). 1996. 9.05 (*0-606-09314-1*, Pub. by Turtleback) Demco.

— Get Well Soon, Little Sister: Love Hospital. (Love Hospital Ser.). 160p. (Orig.). (J). (gr. 3-7). 1996. pap. 3.95 (*0-8167-3912-9*, Rainbow NJ) Troll Communs.

— Girls in Boyland. (J). 1997. mass mkt. 4.99 (*0-590-88031-4*) Scholastic Inc.

— Girls in Love. (J). (gr. 7 up). 1996. pap. 4.99 (*0-590-88030-6*) Scholastic Inc.

— Good Girls, Bad Boys. (Trash Ser.). (J). 1997. write for info. (*0-614-29186-0*) Berkley Pub.

*__Bennett, Cherie.__ The Haunted Heart. (Enchanted Hearts Ser.: No. 1). 179p. (YA). (gr. 7-12). 1999. mass mkt. 4.50 (*0-380-80123-X*, Avon Bks) Morrow Avon.

— Heart Trauma. (University Hospital Ser.: Vol. 4). (YA). 2000. mass mkt. 4.50 (*0-425-17404-2*) Berkley Pub.

Bennett, Cherie. Heaven Can Wait. (Teen Angels Ser.: No. 1). (J). (gr. 7). 1996. mass mkt. 3.99 (*0-380-78247-2*, Avon Bks) Morrow Avon.

— Hot Winter Nights. MacDonald, Pat, ed. (Wild Hearts Ser.). 192p. (Orig.). (J). (gr. 3-6). 1994. mass mkt. 3.50 (*0-671-88783-1*, Archway) PB.

— The Initiation. (Hope Hospital Ser.). 160p. (Orig.). (J). (gr. 3-7). 1996. pap. 3.95 (*0-8167-3914-5*) Troll Communs.

— Initiation. (Hope Hospital Ser.). 1996. 9.05 (*0-606-09468-7*, Pub. by Turtleback) Demco.

— John Lennon & Me. 81p. 1996. pap. 5.50 (*0-87129-702-7*, J26) Dramatic Pub.

— Life in the Fat Lane. 272p. (YA). 1999. mass mkt. 4.99 (*0-440-22029-7*) BDD Bks Young Read.

— Life in the Fat Lane. LC 97-24072. 272p. (YA). 1998. 15.95 (*0-385-32274-7*) Delacorte.

*__Bennett, Cherie.__ Love Him Forever. (Illus.). (J). 1999. 9.85 (*0-606-17968-2*) Turtleback.

Bennett, Cherie. Love Never Dies. (Teen Anges Ser.: No. 2). (J). 1996. mass mkt. 3.99 (*0-380-78248-0*, Avon Bks) Morrow Avon.

— Midwest Girls. (Pageant Ser.: No. 2). 167p. (gr. 7-12). 1998. mass mkt. 4.50 (*0-425-16378-4*) Berkley Pub.

— The National Pageant. (Pageant Ser.: No. 5). 176p. (YA). 1998. pap. 4.50 (*0-425-16621-X*, JAM) Berkley Pub.

— Nightmare in Heaven. (Teen Angels Ser.: No. 5). (YA). 1996. mass mkt. 3.99 (*0-380-78578-1*, Avon Bks) Morrow Avon.

*__Bennett, Cherie.__ The Northeast Girls. (Pageant Ser.: No. 3). 183p. (gr. 7-12). 1998. mass mkt. 4.50 (*0-425-16418-7*) Berkley Pub.

Bennett, Cherie. On the Edge. (Wild Hearts Ser.). (J). (gr. 3-6). 1994. pap. 3.50 (*0-671-88781-5*, Archway) PB.

— Passionate Kisses. MacDonald, Pat, ed. (Wild Hearts Ser.). 192p. (Orig.). (J). (gr. 3-6). 1994. mass mkt. 3.50 (*0-671-88782-3*, Archway) PB.

— Samantha Tylers. 1999. pap. 3.50 (*0-14-036504-4*) Viking Penguin.

— Searching for David's Heart. 176p. (gr. 3-7). 1998. pap. text 3.99 (*0-590-30673-1*) Scholastic Inc.

— Southern Girls, Vol. 1. (Pageant Ser.: No. 1). 182p. (gr. 7-12). 1998. mass mkt. 4.50 (*0-425-16377-6*) Berkley Pub.

— Sunset No. 01: Sunset Island. (YA). 1991. pap. 3.99 (*0-425-12969-1*, Splash) Berkley Pub.

— Sunset No. 02: Sunset Kiss. 1991. pap. 3.99 (*0-425-12899-7*, Splash) Berkley Pub.

— Sunset No. 03: Sunset Dreams. 1991. pap. 3.99 (*0-425-13070-3*, Splash) Berkley Pub.

— Sunset No. 04: Sunset Farewell. (YA). 1991. pap. 3.99 (*0-425-12772-9*, Splash) Berkley Pub.

— Sunset No. 05: Sunset Reunion. (J). 1991. pap. 3.99 (*0-425-13318-4*, Splash) Berkley Pub.

— Sunset after Hours. 224p. (Orig.). 1993. mass mkt. 3.50 (*0-425-13666-3*) Berkley Pub.

— Sunset Forever. 208p. 1997. mass mkt. 3.99 (*0-425-15765-2*) Berkley Pub.

— Sunset Heart. 224p. (Orig.). (J). (ps-3). 1994. pap. 3.99 (*0-425-14183-7*, Splash) Berkley Pub.

— Sunset Sensation. 224p. (Orig.). (J). 1994. mass mkt. 3.99 (*0-425-14253-1*) Berkley Pub.

— Sunset Spirit. 224p. (Orig.). (YA). 1995. mass mkt. 3.99 (*0-425-15028-3*) Berkley Pub.

— Sunset Stranger: It's a Strange World. 224p. (Orig.). (YA). 1994. mass mkt. 3.99 (*0-425-14129-2*) Berkley Pub.

— Sunset Surf. (Orig.). 1993. pap. 3.99 (*0-425-13937-9*) Berkley Pub.

— Sunset Tears. 224p. (Orig.). (YA). 1995. mass mkt. 3.99 (*0-425-15027-5*) Berkley Pub.

— Sunset Touch. (YA). 1993. pap. 3.99 (*0-425-13708-2*) Berkley Pub.

— Sunset Wedding. 1993. pap. 3.99 (*0-425-13982-4*) Berkley Pub.

— Sunset Whispers. 224p. (Orig.). (YA). 1992. pap. 3.99 (*0-425-13386-9*) Berkley Pub.

— Sunset Wishes. 224p. (Orig.). 1993. pap. 3.99 (*0-425-13812-7*) Berkley Pub.

— Too Many Boys!, No. 1. (Club Sunset Ser.). 128p. (Orig.). (J). 1994. pap. 3.50 (*0-425-14252-3*) Berkley Pub.

— Trash-Trash: Love, Lies & Video, Sunset Forever. 1997. mass mkt. 71.82 (*0-425-16014-9*) Berkley Pub.

— The Wedding That Almost Wasn't. (J). (gr. 3-7). 1998. mass mkt. 4.50 (*0-590-05959-9*, Apple Paperbacks) Scholastic Inc.

— The West Coast Girls. (Pageant Ser.: No. 4). 1998. mass mkt. 4.50 (*0-425-16501-9*, JAM) Berkley Pub.

— Wild Hearts. MacDonald, Patricia, ed. 208p. (Orig.). (J). (gr. 3-6). 1994. per. 3.50 (*0-671-86513-7*, Archway) PB.

— The Winners on the Road. (Pageant Ser.: No. 6). (YA). 1999. pap. 4.50 (*0-425-16738-0*, JAM) Berkley Pub.

*__Bennett, Cherie.__ Zink. 2001. pap. 4.99 (*0-440-22810-7*) BDD Bks Young Read.

Bennett, Cherie. Zink. LC 99-18165. 243p. (J). (gr. 5-7). 1999. 15.95 (*0-385-32669-6*) Bantam.

— Zink - The Myth, the Legend, the Zebra. 62p. 1998. pap. 5.50 (*0-87129-864-3*, Z12) Dramatic Pub.

— Zink, the Myth, the Legend, the Zebra - Large Cast Version. 72p. 1998. pap. 5.50 (*0-87129-882-1*, Z20) Dramatic Pub.

Bennett, Cherie & Gottesfeld, Jeff. Anne Frank & Me. LC 98-226138. 1997. pap. 5.50 (*0-87129-701-9*, A68) Dramatic Pub.

*__Bennett, Cherie & Gottesfeld, Jeff.__ Condition Critical. (University Hospital Ser.: No. 2). (YA). 1999. mass mkt. 4.50 (*0-425-17256-2*, JAM) Berkley Pub.

— Crisis Point. (University Hospital Ser.: 3). (YA). 2000. mass mkt. 4.50 (*0-425-17338-0*, JAM) Berkley Pub.

Bennett, Cherie & Gottesfeld, Jeff. Dirty Big Secrets. (Trash Ser.: No. 4). 176p. (J). 1997. mass mkt. 3.99 (*0-425-16044-0*) Berkley Pub.

— Good Girls, Bad Guys. (Trash Ser.: No. 3). 176p. 1997. mass mkt. 3.99 (*0-425-15937-X*) Berkley Pub.

— Love, Lies, & Video. (Trash Ser.). (YA). (gr. 7-12). 1997. pap. 3.99 (*0-614-28636-0*) Berkley Pub.

— Love, Lies, & Video. (Trash Ser.: No. 2). 224p. 1997. mass mkt. 3.99 (*0-425-15907-8*) Berkley Pub.

— Rich Girl in the Mirror. (Mirror Image Ser.: Vol. 2). 176p. (YA). 2000. per. 4.50 (*0-671-03631-9*, Archway) PB.

— Star in the Mirror. (Mirror Image Ser.: Vol. 3). 176p. (J). 2000. per. 4.50 (*0-671-03632-7*, Archway) PB.

— Stranger in the Mirror. (Mirror Image Ser.). (YA). (gr. 6-9). 1999. per. 4.50 (*0-671-03630-0*, Archway) PB.

— Teen Angels No. 6: Love Without End. (Teen Angels Ser.: No. 6). 144p. (Orig.). (YA). 1996. mass mkt. 3.99 (*0-380-78579-X*, Avon Bks) Morrow Avon.

— Trash. (Trash Ser.: No. 1). 224p. (YA). 1997. mass mkt. 3.99 (*0-425-15851-9*) Berkley Pub.

— Trash, No. 5. 176p. 1997. mass mkt. 3.99 (*0-425-16087-4*) Berkley Pub.

— Trash, No. 6. 1998. mass mkt. 3.99 (*0-425-16188-9*) Berkley Pub.

*__Bennett, Cherie & Gottesfeld, Jeff.__ University Hospital. (University Hospital Ser.: 1). (YA). 1999. mass mkt. 4.50 (*0-425-17144-2*, JAM) Berkley Pub.

Bennett, Cherrie. Wild Hearts Forever. MacDonald, Patricia, ed. 208p. (Orig.). (J). (gr. 3-6). 1994. mass mkt. 3.50 (*0-671-86515-3*, Archway) PB.

Bennett, Cheryl & Pollock, Geri. Cooking with Tuna. (Illus.). 80p. (Orig.). 1986. pap. write for info. (*0-938927-00-0*) Authors Note.

Bennett, Chris. Land Rover. (Illus.). 128p. 1996. pap. 10.95 (*1-85532-650-7*, Pub. by Ospry) Stackpole.

Bennett, Chris & Ferlie, Ewan. Managing Crisis & Change in Health Care: The Organizational Response to HIV-AIDS. LC 93-50137. 160p. 1994. 133.00 (*0-335-15788-2*); pap. 37.95 (*0-335-15787-4*) OpUniv Pr.

Bennett, Chris, et al. Green Gold the Tree of Life: Marijuana in Magic & Religion. (Illus.). 418p. (Orig.). (C). 1995. pap. text 24.95 (*0-9629872-2-0*) Access Unlmtd.

Bennett, Chris, jt. auth. see Cunnane, Tony.

*__Bennett, Christine I.__ Comprehensive Multiple Education. 4th ed. LC 98-16160. 436p. 1998. pap. text 53.00 (*0-205-28324-1*) Allyn.

Bennett, Christopher. Supercarrier: USS George Washington. LC 96-13068. (Enthusiast Color Ser.). (Illus.). 96p. 1996. pap. 13.95 (*0-7603-0166-2*) MBI Pubg.

— Yugoslavia's Bloody Collapse: Causes, Course & Consequences. 272p. (C). 1995. text 40.00 (*0-8147-1234-7*) NYU Pr.

— Yugoslavia's Bloody Collapse: Causes, Course & Consequences. 272p. (C). 1997. pap. text 17.50 (*0-8147-1288-6*) NYU Pr.

Bennett, Chuck. God in the Corners Vol. 1: Discovering God's Fingerprints in Remote Corners of the World. (Illus.). 96p. 1997. pap. 5.00 (*0-9660334-2-6*) Partners Intl.

— Heroes on the Frontline Vol. 1: Dramatic Stories of God at Work Around Our World. Scanapico, Joey, ed. (Illus.). 78p. 1995. pap. write for info. (*0-9660334-1-8*) Partners Intl.

Bennett, Chuck & Butler, Don. Collecting Football Cards for Fun & Profit: How to Buy, Store & Trade Them - & Keep Track of Their Value As Investments. (Illus.). 158p. (Orig.). 1991. pap. 8.95 (*0-929387-32-5*) Bonus Books.

Bennett, Clarence. Advance & Retreat to Saratoga, 2 vols. in 1. LC 72-8741. (American Revolutionary Ser.). (Illus.). 1979. reprint ed. lib. bdg. 32.00 (*0-8398-0186-6*) Irvington.

*__Bennett, Clayton.__ Montana. (Celebrate the States Ser.). (Illus.). (J). 2001. 35.64 (*0-7614-1068-6*, Benchmark NY) Marshall Cavendish.

Bennett, Clifford. Nursing Home Life: What It Is & What It Could Be. LC 80-52650. (Illus.). 192p. 1980. pap. text 12.00 (*0-913292-19-2*) Tiresias Pr.

Bennett, Clinton. In Search of the Sacred: Anthropology & the Study of Religions. LC 95-38602. 224p. 1996. 110.00 (*0-304-33681-5*); pap. 23.95 (*0-304-33682-3*) Continuum.

Bennett, Colin. What Is Astrology? 124p. 1981. pap. 12.00 (*0-89540-113-4*, SB-113, Sun Bks) Sun Pub.

Bennett, Colin & Sharpley, Robert, eds. Interpolation of Operators. (Pure & Applied Mathematics Ser.: Vol. 133). 469p. 1988. text 124.00 (*0-12-088730-4*) Acad Pr.

Bennett, Colin J. Regulating Privacy: Data Protection & Public Policy in Europe & the United States. LC 91-30559. 288p. 1992. pap. text 19.95 (*0-8014-8010-8*) Cornell U Pr.

Bennett, Colin J. & Grant, Rebecca, eds. Visions of Privacy: Policy Choices for the Digital Age. (Studies in Comparative Political Economy & Public Policy Ser.). (Illus.). 288p. 1998. pap. text 21.95 (*0-8020-8050-2*) U of Toronto Pr.

Bennett, Connie. L' Epouse d'un Autre. (Amours d'Aujourd'Hui Ser.: No. 332). (FRE.). 1999. mass mkt. 5.50 (*0-373-38332-0*, 1-38332-2) Harlequin Bks.

— Fifty Ways to Be Your Lover. (American Romance Ser.). 1994. per. 3.50 (*0-373-16547-1*, 1-16547-1) Harlequin Bks.

— His Brother's Baby: 9 Months Later. 1998. per. 4.25 (*0-373-70796-7*) Harlequin Bks.

— Married to a Stranger. (Superromance Ser.). 1996. per. 3.99 (*0-373-70695-2*, 1-70695-1) Harlequin Bks.

— Single . . . With Children. (Superromance Ser.). 1994. per. 3.50 (*0-373-70586-7*, 1-70586-2) Harlequin Bks.

— Somewhere Out There: Showcase. 1997. per. 3.99 (*0-373-70733-9*, 1-70733-0) Harlequin Bks.

— Suspicions. LC 95-6901. (Intrigue Ser.). 248p. 1995. per. 3.50 (*0-373-22311-0*, 1-22311-4) Harlequin Bks.

— Windstorm. (Men at Work Ser.: Vol. 4). 1998. mass mkt. 4.50 (*0-373-81016-4*, 1-81016-7) Harlequin Bks.

— Windstorm: Women Who Dare. (Superromance Ser.). 1993. mass mkt. 3.50 (*0-373-70562-X*, 1-70562-3) Harlequin Bks.

Bennett, Connie, et al. Indulgence. 368p. (Orig.). 1997. mass mkt. 5.50 (*0-8439-4289-4*, Leisure Bks) Dorchester Pub Co.

Bennett, Crystal M. & Bienkowski, Piotr. Excavations at Tawilan in Southern Jordan. LC 96-143282. (British Academy Monographs in Archaeology: No. 8). (Illus.). 346p. 1996. text 145.00 (*0-19-727007-7*) OUP.

*__Bennett, Curtis D. & Crannell, Annalisa.__ Starting Our Careers: A Collection of Essays & Advice on Professional Development from the Young Mathematicians' Network LC 99-14350. 1999. write for info. (*0-8218-1543-1*) Am Math.

Bennett, Cynthia L. Roadside History of Utah. McKenna, Gwen, ed. LC 99-10612. (Roadside History Ser.). (Illus.). 500p. 1998. pap. 18.00 (*0-87842-383-4*) Mountain Pr.

Bennett, Cynthia T., ed. Medical School Admission Requirements, 1997-98, United States & Canada. 47th ed. xiii, 407p. (Orig.). 1996. pap. 20.00 (*1-57754-000-X*) Assn Am Med Coll.

— Medical School Admission Requirements, 1998-99, United States & Canada. 48th rev. ed. 416p. (C). 1997. pap. 25.00 (*1-57754-003-4*) Assn Am Med Coll.

Bennett, D. Accordion Course Bk. 1: Individual Class Instruction. (Easy Play Ser.). 32p. 1986. pap. 3.95 (*0-7935-5542-6*, 50394290) H Leonard.

— Accordion Course Bk. A: Individual Class Instruction. (Easy Play Ser.). 32p. 1986. pap. 3.95 (*0-7935-5546-9*, 50394270) H Leonard.

— Accordion Course Bk. B: Individual Class Instruction. (Easy Play Ser.). 1986. pap. 3.95 (*0-7935-5565-5*, 50394280) H Leonard.

— Basic Guitar Chords...& More. 48p. 1989. pap. 5.95 (*0-7935-2575-6*, 50480801) H Leonard.

— Conservatory Guitar Method Bk. 1: Basic Guitar Fingerboard Dexterity. 1986. pap. 4.95 (*0-7935-5554-X*, 50394120) H Leonard.

— Dick Bennett Accordion Course Bk. 2: Basic Course for Class or Individual Instruction. (Easy Play Ser.). 32p. 1986. pap. 3.95 (*0-7935-5561-2*, 50394300) H Leonard.

— Guitar for the Small Fry, Bk. 1A. 32p. 1986. pap. 3.95 (*0-7935-2847-X*, 50394150) H Leonard.

— Guitar for the Small Fry, Bk. 1B. 32p. 1986. pap. 3.95 (*0-7935-2848-8*, 50394160) H Leonard.

— Guitar for the Small Fry, Bk. 1C. 32p. 1986. pap. 3.95 (*0-7935-2849-6*, 50394170) H Leonard.

— Holiday Songs for Guitar with Chords for Banjo & Baritone Uke, Ez Lev, Solo, Duet, Trio. 32p. 1986. pap. 3.50 (*0-7935-5557-4*, 50394230) H Leonard.

— Playing the Electric Bass. 40p. 1986. pap. 4.50 (*0-7935-5532-9*, 50394220) H Leonard.

— Primary Guitar Method, Bk. 2. (Easy Play Ser.). 48p. 1986. pap. 4.95 (*0-7935-2851-8*, 50394080) H Leonard.

— Primary Guitar Method, Bk. 3. (Easy Play Ser.). 1986. pap. 4.95 (*0-7935-2852-6*, 50394090) H Leonard.

— Primary Guitar Method Bk. 1: Basic Class or Individual Instruction. (Easy Play Ser.). 48p. 1986. pap. 4.95 (*0-7935-2850-X*, 50394070) H Leonard.

— Primary Guitar Method Bk. 4: Basic Class or Individual Instruction. (Easy Play Ser.). 1986. pap. 4.95 (*0-7935-2853-4*, 50394100) H Leonard.

— Primary Guitar Method Bk. 5: Basic Class or Individual Instruction. (Easy Play Ser.). 1986. pap. 4.95 (*0-7935-2854-2*, 50394110) H Leonard.

— Recorder for Beginners Class or Individual Instruction: For Soprano Alto & Tenor. 32p. 1987. pap. 3.95 (*0-7935-2589-6*, 50489258) H Leonard.

— The Right Stuff for Guitar. 48p. 1988. pap. 4.95 (*0-7935-5519-1*, 50488604) H Leonard.

— Special Guitar Method. 48p. 1992. pap. 4.95 (*0-7935-5527-2*) H Leonard.

— Special Guitar Method. 48p. 1992. pap. 4.95 (*0-7935-5517-5*) H Leonard.

— Special Guitar Method. 40p. 1993. pap. 5.95 (*0-7935-5556-6*) H Leonard.

— Speical Guitar Method. 40p. 1993. pap. 5.95 (*0-7935-5564-7*) H Leonard.

— The Standard Guitar Method, Bk. 1. (Easy Play Ser.). 48p. 1986. pap. 4.95 (*0-7935-2551-9*, 50393970) H Leonard.

— The Standard Guitar Method, Bk. 2. (Easy Play Ser.). 48p. 1986. pap. 4.95 (*0-7935-2583-7*, 50393980) H Leonard.

— The Standard Guitar Method, Bk. 3. (Easy Play Ser.). 48p. 1986. pap. 4.95 (*0-7935-5521-3*, 50393990) H Leonard.

— The Standard Guitar Method, Bk. 4. (Easy Play Ser.). 48p. 1986. pap. 5.95 (*0-7935-5534-5*, 50394000) H Leonard.

— The Standard Guitar Method, Bk. 7. (Easy Play Ser.). 40p. 1986. pap. 5.95 (*0-7935-5563-9*, 50394030) H Leonard.

— The Standard Guitar Method: Beacon, Bk. 5. (Easy Play Ser.). 40p. 1986. pap. 5.95 (*0-7935-5549-3*, 50394010) H Leonard.

— The Standard Guitar Method: Beacon, Bk. 6. (Easy Play Ser.). 40p. 1986. pap. 5.95 (*0-7935-5553-1*, 50394020) H Leonard.

— Standard Guitar Theory Workbook Puzzles Exercises Theory. (Easy Play Ser.). 32p. 1986. pap. 3.50 (*0-7935-5528-0*, 50394060) H Leonard.

— Teach Yourself Piano & Other Keyboard Instruments for Beginners. 48p. 1986. pap. 5.95 (*0-7935-2859-3*, 50394370) H Leonard.

— Tonette a Method for Beginners Also for Song Flute & Flutophone. 32p. 1986. pap. 3.50 (*0-7935-5419-5*, 50502360) H Leonard.

Bennett, D. & Lewis, C., eds. Achieving Competitive Edge, Getting Ahead Through Technology & People: Proceedings of the OMA-U. K. International Conference, 6th. (Illus.). 488p. 1991. 182.95 (*0-387-19702-8*) Spr-Verlag.

Bennett, D. Gordon. Tension Areas of the World. 2nd ed. LC 98-103106. 288p. (C). 1997. per. 70.95 (*0-7872-4328-0*, 41432801) Kendall-Hunt.

— World Population Problems: An Introduction to Population Geography. LC 83-62691. 250p. (C). 1984. pap. text 12.95 (*0-941226-04-2*) Park Pr Co.

*__Bennett, D. Gordon & Hayes, Charles.__ Applied Human Geography. 5th ed. 266p. (C). 1999. per. 41.95 (*0-7872-6408-3*, 41640801) Kendall-Hunt.

Bennett, D. Gordon & Hayes, Charles R. Applied Human Geography. 264p. (C). 1996. pap. text, per. 28.95 (*0-7872-0517-6*) Kendall-Hunt.

Bennett, D. Gordon & Patton, Jeffrey. The United States & Canada: A Systematic Approach. 2nd ed. 200p. 1996. pap. text, per. 42.95 (*0-7872-2633-5*, 41263301) Kendall-Hunt.

Bennett, D. Gordon, ed. see Association of American Geographers Staff.

Bennett, D. J. The Machine Embroidery Handbook: Designing Fabrics with Stitching, Manipulation & Color. Parks, Carol, ed. LC 97-13888. (Illus.). 128p. 1997. 24.95 (*1-887374-45-0*, Pub. by Lark Books) Random.

Bennett, D. M. An Open Letter to Jesus Christ. LC 90-40422. 23p. 1990. reprint ed. pap. 4.00 (*0-911826-44-0*, 5024) Am Atheist.

Bennett, D. M., jt. prod. see Mendum, J. P.

Bennett, D. P. Biology Diagrams, 2 bks. (Illus.). (C). 1988. write for info. (*0-7855-2601-3*); 90.00 (*0-7157-2601-3*); 75.00 (*0-7157-2610-2*) St Mut.

Bennett, D. W. Secrets of Baitfishing. (Illus.). 66p. pap. 3.50 (*0-88839-087-4*) Hancock House.

— Secrets of Bluefishing. (Illus.). 72p. pap. 3.50 (*0-88839-086-6*) Hancock House.

*__Bennett, Damon, ed.__ Retail Consumer Edition of the Marine Appraisal Guide: 2000 Edition. 2000. 34.95 (*1-58033-015-0*) NADA Guides.

Bennett, Damon, ed. Retail Consumer Edition of the N. A. D. A. Marine Appraisal Guide: 1999 Edition. 1680p. 1999. pap. 34.95 (*1-58033-010-X*) NADA Guides.

Bennett, Daniel. Monitor Lizards: Natural History, Biology & Husbandry. (Illus.). 352p. 1997. pap. 49.95 (*3-930612-10-0*, Pub. by Edition Chimaira) Bibliomania.

*__Bennett, Darren.__ Learn to Draw Cats. (Learn to Draw Ser.). (Illus.). 64p. 1999. pap. 14.95 (*0-00-413355-2*, Pub. by HarpC) Trafalgar.

*__Bennett, Darren, et al.__ Drawing Animals: A Step-by-Step Guide to Drawing Success. (Illus.). 192p. 2000. 27.50 (*0-00-413380-3*, Pub. by HarpC) Trafalgar.

Bennett, David. The Creation of Bridges: From Vision to Reality: The Ultimate Challenge of Architecture, Design Fitzhenry & W Ltd & Distance , Vol. 1. 1999. 19.99 (*0-7858-1053-6*) Bk Sales Inc.

— D. L. Moody. LC 94-26318. (Men of Faith Ser.). 128p. 1994. mass mkt. 4.99 (*1-55661-304-0*) Bethany Hse.

— Multicultural States: Rethinking Difference & Identity. LC 98-17304. 320p. (C). 1998. 75.00 (*0-415-12158-2*); pap. 24.99 (*0-415-12159-0*) Routledge.

— One Moo Moo. LC 90-32065. (Illus.). 32p. (J). (ps-2). 1995. 15.95 (*0-8050-1416-0*, Bks Young Read) H Holt & Co.

— Roller Coaster. 1998. 19.99 (*0-7858-0885-X*) Bk Sales Inc.

— A Treasury of Witches & Wizards. LC 95-36026. (Treasury of Stories Ser.). (Illus.). 160p. (J). (ps-4). 1996. pap. 5.95 (*1-85697-678-5*) LKC.

— William Booth. (Men of Faith Ser.). 192p. 1994. mass mkt. 4.99 (*1-55661-307-5*) Bethany Hse.

Bennett, David, ed. The Architecture of Bridge Design. LC 97-138559. 200p. 1997. 92.00 (*0-7277-2529-7*) Am Soc Civil Eng.

Bennett, David & Mascetti, Daniela. Understanding Jewellery. rev. ed. (Illus.). 426p. 1994. 79.50 (*1-85149-205-4*) Antique Collect.

Bennett, David, jt. auth. see Schroeder, Roger.

Bennett, David, jt. auth. see Sylvan, Richard.

Bennett, David C., ed. see Bergman, Gunnar.

Bennett, David H. Cardiac Arrhythmias. 4th ed. LC 93-15125. (Illus.). 224p. 1993. pap. text 55.00 (*0-7506-1638-5*) Buttrwrth-Heinemann.

Bennett, David J. & Forrester, Paul L. Market Focused Production Systems: Design & Implementation. 250p. (C). 1993. pap. 24.95 (*0-13-322157-1*) P-H.

*__Bennett, David W.__ Leadership Images from the New Testament. 192p. 1998. reprint ed. mass mkt. 9.99 (*1-85078-309-8*, Pub. by O M Pubng) OM Literature.

Bennett, De Robigne M. Anthony Comstock: His Career of Cruelty & Crime. LC 73-121102. (Civil Liberties in American History Ser.). 1971. reprint ed. lib. bdg. 22.50 (*0-306-71968-1*) Da Capo.

Bennett, Dean. The Forgotten Nature of New England: A Search for Traces of the Original Wilderness. LC 96-5724. (Illus.). 384p. (Orig.). 1996. pap. 17.95 (*0-89272-374-2*) Down East.

Bennett, Dean B. Allagash, Maine's Wild & Scenic River. LC 94-14451. (Illus.). 112p. 1994. 35.00 (*0-89272-332-7*) Down East.

— Maine's Natural Heritage: Rare Species & Unique Natural Features. LC 86-50855. (Illus.). 285p. 1988. 39.95 (*0-89272-228-2*) Down East.

Bennett, Deb. Conquerors: The Roots of New World Horsemanship. LC 97-77724. (Illus.). 432p. 1998. text 49.95 (*0-9658533-0-6*) Amigo Pubns.

Bennett, Deborah J. Randomness. LC 97-35054. 224p. 1998. 23.95 (*0-674-10745-4*) HUP.

— Randomness. 256p. 1999. pap. 14.00 (*0-674-10746-2*) HUP.

Bennett, Debra K. The Fossil Fauna from Lost & Found Quarries: Hemphillian: Latest Miocene, Wallace County, Kansas. (Occasional Papers: No. 79). 24p. 1979. pap. 1.00 (*0-686-79812-0*) U KS Nat Hist Mus.

Bennett, Deeny, ed. see Marakas, Thalia.

Bennett, Denise. The Color Tree. LC 93-77606. 32p. (J). (gr. 4-5). 1993. 12.95 (*1-880851-07-5*) Greene Bark Pr.

Bennett, Dennis. How to Pray for the Release of the Holy Spirit. LC 85-72459. 119p. 1987. pap. 8.99 (*0-88270-593-8*) Bridge-Logos.

— Nine O'Clock in the Morning: An Episcopal Priest Discovers the Holy Spirit. LC 72-85205. 209p. 1984. pap. 8.99 (*0-88270-629-2*) Bridge-Logos.

***Bennett, Dennis & Bennett, Rita.** El Espiritu Santo y Tu. Gowans, Makiko, ed.Tr. of Holy Spirit & You. (SPA.). 244p. 1999. pap. 7.00 (*0-9673342-0-9*) Sts of Glory.

Bennett, Dennis & Bennett, Rita. The Holy Spirit & You: A Guide to the Spirit-Filled Life. rev. ed. LC 71-140673. 250p. 1971. pap. 10.99 (*0-88270-623-3*) Bridge-Logos.

— Holy Spirit & You (Supplement) A Study Guide to the Spirit-Filled Life. LC 73-75963. 121p. 1973. pap. 4.99 (*0-88270-031-6*) Bridge-Logos.

Bennett, Dennis, jt. auth. see Bennett, Rita.

Bennett, Diane T. & Tarleton, Linda. William Cullen Bryant in Roslyn. LC 78-67782. 164p. 1978. pap. 7.95 (*0-9602242-1-1*) Bryant Library.

Bennett, Dianne. Taxation of Distributions from Qualified Plans. LC 97-162078. (Illus.). 1997. write for info. (*0-13-745092-3*) P-H.

Bennett, Dianne. Taxation of Distributions from Qualified Plans. 2nd ed. LC 97-80919. 1998. write for info. (*0-7913-3383-3*) Warren Gorham & Lamont.

Bennett, Dianne, et al. Taxation of Distributions from Qualified Plans. 1991. text 150.00 (*0-685-69577-8*, TADI) Warren Gorham & Lamont.

Bennett, Dick. Trapshooting Is a Game of Opposites. (Illus.). 132p. (Orig.). Date not set. pap. 19.95 (*0-925012-05-X*) Shotgun Sports.

***Bennett, Donna I.** Jessica's Bear. LC 98-67054. (Illus.). 32p. 1999. pap. 9.95 (*1-878044-57-5*) Mayhaven Pub.

Bennett, Donna I., et al. Elementary Field Experiences: A Handbook with Resources. LC 93-38408. 207p. (C). 1994. mass mkt. 50.95 (*0-8273-5661-7*) Delmar.

Bennett, Dorothy, et al. While Morning Stars Sang. Salisbury, Linda G., ed. LC 91-66376. (Illus.). 104p. (Orig.). 1991. pap. 7.95 (*0-9627974-4-8*) Tabby Hse Bks.

Bennett, Douglas C. Transnational Corporations Versus the State: The Political Economy of the Mexican Auto Industry. Sharpe, Kenneth E., ed. LC 85-42674. 315p. reprint ed. pap. 97.70 (*0-608-06291-X*, 206665300008) Bks Demand.

Bennett, Douglas H., jt. ed. see Watts, Fraser N.

Bennett, Dwight. Crooked River Canyon. large type ed. LC 97-35649. 322p. 1998. lib. bdg. 18.95 (*0-7838-8293-9*, G K Hall Lrg Type) Mac Lib Ref.

***Bennett, Dwight & Lynch, Betsy.** Bits & Bridles: Power Tools for Thinking Riders. LC 00-26336. 192p. 2000. 34.95 (*0-9625898-6-1*, Pub. by EquiMedia) IPG Chicago.

Bennett, E. M. & Trute, Barry, eds. Mental Health Information Systems: Problems & Prospects. LC 83-23683. (Studies in Health & Human Services: Vol. 1). 318p. 1983. 99.95 (*0-88946-125-2*) E Mellen.

Bennett, E. O. Dermatitis in Machinists: Causes & Solutions. LC 92-75660. 240p. 1993. pap. 38.00 (*1-880319-09-8*) Biotech.

— Descendants of Andrew Bird of Colonial Long Island, N. Y. 1999. 59.50 (*0-8328-9777-9*) Higginson Bk Co.

Bennett, Earnest. Hypnotizing Game Who Cross You: It's Really Not a Game. unabridged ed. 456p. 1999. pap. 16.95 (*0-9670248-0-3*) Geo Gor Pub.

Bennett, Ed, et al. The Human Zoo: A Death Row Poetry Collection. LC 97-92556. 140p. 1997. 24.95 (*0-9660602-0-2*); pap. 12.95 (*0-9660602-1-0*); lib. bdg. 24.95 (*0-9660602-2-9*) Poundstone.

Bennett, Edmund. Little Dots & Tiny Specks: Drawings by Edmund Bennett. LC 97-69571. (Illus.). ii, 202p. 1997. 59.00 (*0-9658481-1-6*) S F Reynolds.

— War Babies: Drawings by Edmund Bennett. LC 99-70174. (Illus.). ii, 202p. 1999. 59.00 (*0-9658481-2-4*) S F Reynolds.

Bennett, Edmund H. Farm Law: A Treatise on the Legal Rights & Liabilities of Farmers. 120p. 1996. reprint ed. 32.50 (*0-8377-1981-X*, Rothman) W S Hein.

Bennett, Edmund H., ed. see Indermaur, John.

Bennett, Edna. Popular Jamaican Sayings: Brawta Edition. (Wisdom Ser.). 96p. (Orig.). 1997. pap. 9.95 (*1-885778-18-X*) Seaburn.

Bennett, Edna M. Turquoise & the Indian. rev. ed. LC 66-25963. (Illus.). 152p. 1970. 9.95 (*0-8040-0298-3*) Swallow.

Bennett, Edna M. & Bennett, John F. Turquoise Jewelry of the Indians of the Southwest. (Illus.). 1973. 21.00 (*0-917834-01-1*) Turquoise Bks.

Bennett, Edward. A Treatise Touching the Inconveniences, That the Importation of Tobacco Out of Spaine, Hath Brought into This Land. LC 77-6856. (English Experience Ser.: No. 846). 1977. reprint ed. lib. bdg. 15.00 (*90-221-0846-5*) Walter J Johnson.

Bennett, Edward H., jt. auth. see Burnham, Daniel H.

Bennett, Edward M. Franklin D. Roosevelt & the Search for Security: American-Soviet Relations, 1933-1939. LC 85-10850. (America in the Modern World: Studies in International History). 243p. (C). 1985. 45.00 (*0-8420-2246-5*); pap. text 17.95 (*0-8420-2247-3*) Scholarly Res Inc.

— Franklin D. Roosevelt & the Search for Victory: American-Soviet Relations, 1939-1945. LC 90-8562. (America in the Modern World: Studies in International History). 207p. (C). 1990. 45.00 (*0-8420-2364-X*); pap. text 17.95 (*0-8420-2365-8*) Scholarly Res Inc.

— Social Intervention: Theory & Practice. LC 87-24005. (Studies in Health & Human Services: Vol. 11). (Illus.). 432p. (C). 1987. lib. bdg. 109.95 (*0-88946-136-8*) E Mellen.

Bennett, Edward M., ed. Polycentrism: Growing Dissidence in the Communist Bloc. LC 67-2568. 69p. reprint ed. pap. 30.00 (*0-608-18352-0*, 203303300083) Bks Demand.

Bennett, Edward M. & Tefft, Bruce, eds. Theoretical & Empirical Advances in Community Mental Health. LC 85-21371. (Studies in Health & Human Services: Vol. 5). 280p. 1985. lib. bdg. 89.95 (*0-88946-131-7*) E Mellen.

Bennett, Edward S. Contact Lens Problem Solving. LC 94-19441. (Illus.). 199p. (C). (gr. 13). 1994. pap. text 39.95 (*0-8151-0424-3*, 24262) Mosby Inc.

***Bennett, Edward S. & Henry, Vinita A.** Clinical Manual of Contact Lenses. 2nd ed. LC 99-40672. 639p. 1999. 59.95 (*0-7817-1951-8*) Lppncott W & W.

Bennett, Edward W. German Rearmament & the West, 1932-1933. LC 78-70227. 587p. reprint ed. pap. 182.00 (*0-8357-4673-9*, 203761900008) Bks Demand.

— Germany & the Diplomacy of the Financial Crisis, 1931. LC 62-13261. (Historical Monographs: No. 50). 350p. 1962. 30.00 (*0-674-35250-5*) HUP.

Bennett, Edwin K. A History of the German Novelle. 2nd ed. 331p. reprint ed. pap. 94.40 (*0-608-16412-7*, 2026331) Bks Demand.

Bennett, Elizabeth. Afternoons of a Woman of Leisure. 1993. mass mkt. 5.95 (*1-56201-029-8*, 126) Blue Moon Bks.

— Heart & Soul. 304p. (Orig.). 1994. mass mkt. 4.99 (*0-515-11372-7*, Jove) Berkley Pub.

— Idiots in Paris: Diaries of J. G. Bennett & Elizabeth Bennett, 1949. LC 90-22981. 156p. 1991. pap. 9.95 (*0-87728-724-4*) Weiser.

***Bennett, Elizabeth.** Night Is the Time. 24p. (J). 1999. 1.99 (*0-679-89274-5*, Pub. by Random Bks Yng Read) Random.

— Night Is the Time. 2000. 7.99 (*0-375-90097-7*) Random Hse Chldrns.

Bennett, Elizabeth. Perfect Lies. 400p. 2000. mass mkt. 6.50 (*0-06-101373-0*) HarpC.

Bennett, Elizabeth, jt. ed. see Robinson, John.

Bennett, Elizabeth L., jt. auth. see Robinson, John G.

Bennett, Ellie, et al. The Hands That Made Them: Quilts of Adams County, Pennsylvania. Shetter, Marion, ed. 132p. 1993. pap. 24.95 (*0-9636773-3-0*) Adams Cnty Quilt.

Bennett, Emerson. Mike Fink. LC 75-104415. reprint ed. lib. bdg. 22.50 (*0-8398-0162-9*) Irvington.

— The Prairie Flower: Adventure in the Far West. LC 79-104416. 126p. (C). 1986. reprint ed. pap. text 5.95 (*0-8290-2390-9*); reprint ed. lib. bdg. 22.50 (*0-8398-0163-7*) Irvington.

Bennett, Estelline. Old Deadwood Days. LC 81-14737. (Illus.). xiii, 314p. 1982. reprint ed. pap. 12.95 (*0-8032-6065-2*, Bison Books) U of Nebr Pr.

Bennett, Eva, et al, eds. The Comparative Biochemistry of Parasitic Helminths. 224p. 1988. lib. bdg. 65.00 (*0-7099-5912-5*, Pub. by C Helm) Routldge.

— The Comparative Biochemistry of Parasitic Helminths. 256p. 1989. 65.00 (*0-412-32730-9*) Chapman & Hall.

Bennett, Evan & Somerlott, Robert. The Maya Epic. 135p. 1974. 12.95 (*0-686-27297-8*) U Wisc-River Falls Pr.

Bennett, Evelyn. Frederick Douglass & the War Against Slavery. LC 92-36930. (Gateway Civil Rights Ser.). (Illus.). 32p. (J). (gr. 2-4). 1993. pap. 4.95 (*1-56294-790-7*); lib. bdg. 20.90 (*1-56294-341-3*) Millbrook Pr.

Bennett, F. J., jt. auth. see Byrne, Monica.

Bennett, F. Lawrence. The Management of Engineering: Human, Quality, Organizational, Legal & Ethical Aspects of Professional Practice. LC 95-34032. 496p. 1995. text 95.95 (*0-471-59329-X*) Wiley.

Bennett, F. Lawrence & Machemehi, Jerry L., eds. Civil Engineering in the Arctic Offshore. 1260p. 1985. 108.00 (*0-87262-441-2*) Am Soc Civil Eng.

Bennett, F. Lawrence, jt. auth. see McFadden, Terry T.

Bennett, F. M. Religious Cults Associated with the Amazons. 84p. (C). 1987. reprint ed. lib. bdg. 30.00 (*0-89241-204-6*) Caratzas.

Bennett Financial Advisors Staff. Making Money Last. 320p. 1995. pap. text 21.95 (*0-7872-0962-7*) Kendall-Hunt.

Bennett, Fordyce R. A Reference Guide to the Bible in Emily Dickinson's Poetry. LC 96-42431. 512p. 1996. 55.00 (*0-8108-3247-X*) Scarecrow.

Bennett, Frank. The Illustrated Rules of Basketball. LC 94-1909. (Illustrated Rules of the Game Ser.). (Illus.). 32p. (J). (gr. 1-4). 1995. lib. bdg. 21.27 (*1-884756-08-5*) Davidson Titles.

— The Illustrated Rules of Basketball. LC 94-1909. (Illustrated Sports Ser.). (Illus.). 32p. (J). (gr. 1-4). 1994. pap., per. 6.95 (*1-57102-021-7*, Ideals Child) Hambleton-Hill.

Bennett, Frederick. Computers as Tutors: Solving the Crisis in Education. 232p. (C). 1999. 25.00 (*0-9669583-6-5*) Faben Inc.

Bennett, G. & Moody, M. Wound Care for Health Professionals. (Illus.). 176p. 1995. pap. 44.75 (*1-56593-348-6*, 0672) Singular Publishing.

Bennett, G. G. Complete On-Board Celestial Navigator. (Illus.). 144p. 1998. pap. text 27.95 (*0-07-007110-1*) Intl Marine.

***Bennett, G. H. & Bennett, R.** Survivors: British Merchant Seamen in the Second World War. LC 99-33314. 1999. 45.00 (*1-85285-182-1*) Hambledon Press.

***Bennett, G. H. & Gibson, Marion.** The Later Life of Lord Curzon of Kedleston - Aristocrat, Writer, Politician, Statesman: An Experiment in Political Biography. LC 99-58819. (Studies in British History: Vol. 60). 280p. 2000. text 89.95 (*0-7734-7790-X*) E Mellen.

Bennett, G. M., ed. see Michael, Russ.

Bennett, G. W., jt. ed. see Griffiths, E. C.

Bennett, Gary. Aikido Techniques & Tactics. LC 97-13748. (Martial Arts Ser.). (Illus.). 192p. 1997. pap. 15.95 (*0-88011-598-X*, PBEN0598) Human Kinetics.

***Bennett, Gary & Bennett, Madeline.** The Best Alphabet Book in the Wild West. (Illus.). (J). (ps-2). 1999. 4.95 (*0-916179-96-6*) Ariz Hwy.

— The Best Counting Book in the Wild West. (Illus.). 30p. (J). (ps-2). 2000. 14.95 (*1-893860-13-2*) Ariz Hwy.

Bennett, Gary F., jt. auth. see Peters, Robert W.

Bennett, Gary W. Scams in America: A 40 Billion Dollar a Year Industry. LC 99-90209. 246p. 1999. pap. 24.95 (*0-9670398-0-0*) SN Pr.

Bennett, Gary W., et al. Truman's Scientific Guide to Pest Control Operations. 5th rev. ed. LC 96-80199. (Illus.). 520p. 1997. 74.95 (*0-929870-45-X*) Advanstar Communs.

Bennett-Gates, Dianne, jt. ed. see Zigler, Edward.

Bennett, Gay. A Family in Sri Lanka. LC 85-6891. (Families the World Over Ser.). (Illus.). 32p. (J). (gr. 2-5). 1985. lib. bdg. 18.60 (*0-8225-1661-6*, Lerner Publctns) Lerner Pub.

Bennett, Gaymon, ed. Callings: A Gathering of Autobiographical Stories by Northwest Nazarene College Faculty & Staff. (Illus.). 137p. (Orig.). 1994. pap. 5.00 (*1-880899-01-9*) Melville & Co.

Bennett, Genevieve R., jt. auth. see Morgan, John M., 4th.

Bennett, Geoff. Battle of Jutland. 1999. pap. text 12.99 (*1-84022-204-2*) Wrdsworth Edits.

— Designing TCP-IP Internetworks. (B & F - Computer Science Ser.). 601p. 1995. pap. 54.95 (*0-442-01880-0*, VNR) Wiley.

Bennett, Geoff. Designing TCP/IP Internetworks. (Bancf - Computer Science Ser.). 624p. 1995. 65.00 (*0-471-28643-5*, VNR) Wiley.

Bennett, George. Commissioned to Heal & Other Helpful Essays. (C). 1990. pap. 24.00 (*0-85305-212-3*, Pub. by Arthur James) St Mut.

— Seychelles. LC 93-205226. (World Bibliographical Ser.). 148p. 1993. lib. bdg. 64.00 (*1-85109-182-3*) ABC-CLIO.

Bennett, George, ed. Miracle at Crowhurst. (C). 1990. pap. 40.00 (*0-85305-178-X*, Pub. by Arthur James) St Mut.

Bennett, George, et al. The Historiography of the British Empire- Commonwealth: Trends, Interpretations & Resources. LC 65-15555. 610p. reprint ed. pap. 189.10 (*0-608-12769-8*, 202347200033) Bks Demand.

Bennett, George, ed. see Bennett, J. G.

Bennett, George E. Librarians in Search of Science & Identity: The Elusive Profession. LC 88-14679. 231p. 1988. 29.00 (*0-8108-2075-7*) Scarecrow.

Bennett, George W., intro. Management of Lakes & Ponds. 2nd ed. LC 83-6091. 398p. (C). 1983. reprint ed. text 48.50 (*0-89874-626-4*) Krieger.

Bennett, Gerald A. Treating Drug Abusers: New Directions. 200p. 1989. 49.50 (*0-415-02039-5*, A3461); pap. 15.95 (*0-415-05837-6*, A5206) Routledge.

Bennett, Gerald A. & Kingston, Paul. Elder Abuse: Concepts, Theories & Interventions. LC 93-32199. (Therapy in Practice Ser.). 1993. 47.75 (*1-56593-038-X*, 0432) Singular Publishing.

Bennett, Geraldine M. Jonchen, Son of Cara, Bk. One. LC 95-67934. (Myriadians Ser.). (Illus.). 92p. (YA). (gr. 7 up). 1995. 10.98 (*1-882786-23-8*) New Dawn NY.

— Jonchen, Son of Cara, Ser. (Myriadians Ser.). (Illus.). 1995. pap. write for info. (*1-882786-24-6*) New Dawn NY.

— Katrina & Elishia Learn about Ouija Boards. Shell, Audery & Granger, Debby, eds. LC 94-66954. (Katrina Tells Ser.: Bk. 6). (Illus.). 43p. (Orig.). (J). (gr. 5 up). 1994. pap. 10.79 (*1-882786-04-1*) New Dawn NY.

— Katrina & Elishia Teach about the Aura. Rider, Tracy & Sheil, Audrey, eds. LC 92-83809. (Katrina Tells Ser. Bk. 2). (Illus.). 32p. (J). (gr. 3 up). 1994. pap. 7.98 (*0-9630718-9-0*) New Dawn NY.

— Katrina & Her Friends Learn about Self-Esteem. (Katrina Tells Ser.: Bk. 10). (Illus.). 42p. (Orig.). (YA). (gr. 8 up). 1995. pap. 10.98 (*1-882786-25-4*) New Dawn NY.

— Katrina Helps a Friend Through a Time of Depression Granger, Debby, ed. LC 95-67317. (Katrina Tells Ser.: Bk. 9). (Illus.). 35p. (Orig.). (YA). (gr. 8 up). 1995. pap. 10.98 (*1-882786-29-7*) New Dawn NY.

— Katrina Learns How to Meditate. (Katrina Tells Ser.: Bk. 11). (Illus.). 74p. (Orig.). (YA). (gr. 8 up). 1997. pap. 10.98 (*1-882786-22-X*) New Dawn NY.

— Katrina Tells about Bee Stings. LC 95-67419. (Katrina Tells Ser.: Bk. 7). (Orig.). (J). (gr. k up). 1995. pap. 10.98 (*1-882786-07-6*) New Dawn NY.

— Katrina Tells Jamie about John's Invisible Lesson. rev. ed. Rider, Tracy & Sheil, Audrey, eds. LC 92-83745. (Katrina Tells Ser.: Bk. 1). (Illus.). 32p. (J). (gr. 3 up). 1994. pap. 7.98 (*0-9630718-8-2*) New Dawn NY.

— Katrina Tells of Healing a Kitten. Bk. 8. (J). (gr. k up). pap. write for info. (*0-318-72556-8*) New Dawn NY.

— The Katrina Tells Series. (J). (gr. 3 up). 1994. pap. write for info. (*1-882786-99-8*) New Dawn NY.

— Mickey & Honor. LC 95-67420. (Illus.). 54p. (Orig.). (YA). (gr. 5 up). 1995. pap. 10.98 (*1-882786-21-1*) New Dawn NY.

— Monkey See, Monkey Do. (Katrina Tells Ser.: Bk. 5). (J). (gr. k up). 1995. pap. 10.98 (*1-882786-09-2*) New Dawn NY.

— Opening the Door to Your Inner Self: My Lessons. LC 91-67122. (Illus.). 122p. (Orig.). (J). (gr. 2 up). 1993. pap. 12.98 (*0-9630718-5-8*, 1-87122) New Dawn NY.

— Rebecca Tells of a Miracle of Life: A Special Belief in the Healing Power of Love. Rider, Tracy & Sheil, Audrey, eds. LC 92-83744. (Katrina Tells Ser.: Bk. 3). (Illus.). 42p. (Orig.). (J). (gr. 3-8). 1994. pap. 7.98 (*0-9630718-4-X*) New Dawn NY.

Bennett, Gertrude B. The Heads of Cerberus. Reginald, R. & Melville, Douglas, eds. LC 77-84269. (Lost Race & Adult Fantasy Ser.). (Illus.). 1978. reprint ed. lib. bdg. 23.95 (*0-405-11009-X*) Ayer.

***Bennett, Gillian.** Alas, Poor Ghost! Traditions of Belief in Story & Discourse. LC 99-6558. 240p. 1999. 39.95 (*0-87421-278-2*); pap. 21.95 (*0-87421-277-4*) Utah St U Pr.

Bennett, Gillian, ed. Spoken in Jest. 305p. 1991. 42.50 (*1-85075-257-5*, Pub. by Sheffield Acad) CUP Services.

Bennett, Gillian & Smith, Paul. Contemporary Legend: A Folklore Bibliography. LC 93-15549. (Garland Folklore Bibliographies Ser.: Vol. 18). 368p. 1993. text 20.00 (*0-8240-6103-9*, H1307) Garland.

Bennett, Gillian, ed. see Lindahl, Carl.

Bennett, Gloria. Breaking Through: From Rock to Opera - The Basic Technique of Voice. 120p. 1997. per. 14.95 (*0-7935-7238-X*) H Leonard.

Bennett, Godfrey. Introduction to Mass Communications. 1998. 34.74 (*0-697-37959-0*) McGraw.

***Bennett-Goleman, Tara.** Emotional Alchemy: Transforming Confusion into Clarity. 2001. 24.00 (*0-609-60752-9*) Harmony Bks.

Bennett, Gordon. Yundong: Mass Campaigns in Chinese Communist Leadership. LC 75-620060. (China Research Monographs: No. 12). 133p. 1976. pap. 4.50 (*0-912966-15-7*) IEAS.

Bennett, Gordon, ed. China's Finance & Trade: A Policy Reader. LC 77-99080. 264p. reprint ed. pap. 81.90 (*0-8357-2626-6*, 204011400014) Bks Demand.

Bennett, Gordon D., jt. auth. see Zheng, Chunmiao.

Bennett, Gordon D., jt. ed. see Rosenshein, Joseph.

Bennett, Gordon H., jt. auth. see Marshall, Alejandro.

Bennett, Gordon H., jt. auth. see Pollock, Algernon J.

Bennett, Gordon H., jt. auth. see Voorehoeve, H. C.

Bennett, Gordon H., ed. see Collingwood, Guillermo.

Bennett, Gordon H., ed. see Cutting, Jorge.

Bennett, Gordon H., ed. see Mackintosh, Carlos H.

Bennett, Gordon H., ed. see Rossier, H.

Bennett, Graham. Conserving Europe's Natural Heritage: Towards a European Ecological Network. LC 94-30645. (International Environmental Law & Policy Ser.). 1994. lib. bdg. 104.50 (*1-85966-090-8*) Kluwer Law Intl.

***Bennett, Graham.** Directory of Web Sites. 600p. 1999. lib. bdg. 75.00 (*1-57958-179-X*) Fitzroy Dearborn.

Bennett, Grahame. Factorizing the Classical Inequalities. LC 95-52307. (Memoirs of the American Mathematical Society Ser.: Vol. 576). 130p. 1996. pap. 37.00 (*0-8218-0436-7*, MEMO/120/576) Am Math.

Bennett, Guy. Last Words. (New American Poetry Ser.). 1998. pap. 9.95 (*1-55713-336-0*) Sun & Moon CA.

Bennett, Guy, tr. see Bellmer, Hans & Eluard, Paul.

Bennett, Guy, tr. see Deluy, Henri.

Bennett, Guy, tr. see Giraudon, Liliane.

Bennett, Guy, tr. see Leiris, Michel.

Bennett, Guy, tr. see Paradjanov, Sergei.

Bennett, Guy, tr. & intro. see Steiner, Giuseppe.

Bennett, Gwen P. A Bibliography of Illinois Archaeology. (Scientific Papers: Vol. XXI). xii, 356p. (Orig.). 1985. pap. text 10.00 (*0-89792-105-4*) Ill St Museum.

Bennett, H. Bennett's Cosmetic Formulary. 1993. 90.00 (*0-8206-0340-6*) Chem Pub.

— Chemical Formulary, Vol. 26. 1985. 70.00 (*0-8206-0313-9*) Chem Pub.

— Chemical Formulary, Vol. 27. 1986. 70.00 (*0-8206-0318-X*) Chem Pub.

— Chemical Formulary, Vol. 29. 1990. 70.00 (*0-8206-0338-4*) Chem Pub.

— Chemical Formulary, Vol. 30. 1992. 70.00 (*0-8206-0341-4*) Chem Pub.

— Chemical Formulary, Vol. 31. 1993. 70.00 (*0-8206-0343-0*) Chem Pub.

— Chemical Formulary, Vol. 32. 1994. 70.00 (*0-8206-0345-7*) Chem Pub.

— Chemical Formulary, Vol. 33. 1996. 75.00 (*0-8206-0346-5*) Chem Pub.

— Chemical Formulary Series Vols. 1-35: Cumulative Index. rev. ed. 2000. write for info. (*0-8206-0355-4*) Chem Pub.

— Concise Chemical & Technical Dictionary. 4th ed. 1986. 170.00 (*0-8206-0310-4*) Chem Pub.

— Industrial Waxes. 3rd ed. Fedak, M., ed. (Illus.). (C). 2000. write for info. (*0-8206-0357-0*) Chem Pub.

— Industrial Waxes Vol. 1: Natural Waxes: Synthetic Waxes. 3rd ed. Fedak, M., ed. (Illus.). (C). 2000. write for info. (*0-8206-0358-9*) Chem Pub.

— Industrial Waxes Vol. 2: Compounded Waxes: Technology. 3rd ed. Fedak, M., ed. (Illus.). 2000. write for info. (*0-8206-0359-7*) Chem Pub.

B

Bennett, H., ed. Chemical Formulary, Vol. 23. 1981. 70.00 (*0-8206-0282-5*) Chem Pub.

— Chemical Formulary, Vol. 24. 1982. 70.00 (*0-8206-0291-4*) Chem Pub.

— Chemical Formulary, Vol. 25. 1983. 70.00 (*0-8206-0304-X*) Chem Pub.

— Chemical Formulary, Vol. 34. 1997. 75.00 (*0-8206-0352-X*) Chem Pub.

— Chemical Formulary, Vols. 1-34. Incl. Vol. 1. 1933. 70.00 (*0-8206-0259-0*); Vol. 2. 1935. 70.00 (*0-8206-0260-4*); Vol. 3. 1936. 70.00 (*0-8206-0261-2*); Vol. 4. 1939. 70.00 (*0-8206-0262-0*); Vol. 5. 1941. 70.00 (*0-8206-0263-9*); Vol. 6. 1943. 70.00 (*0-8206-0264-7*); Vol. 7. 1945. 70.00 (*0-8206-0265-5*); Vol. 8. 1948. 70.00 (*0-8206-0266-3*); Vol. 9. 1950. 70.00 (*0-8206-0267-1*); Vol. 10. 1957. 70.00 (*0-8206-0268-X*); Vol. 11. 1961. 70.00 (*0-8206-0269-8*); Vol. 12. 1965. 70.00 (*0-8206-0270-1*); Vol. 13. 1967. 70.00 (*0-8206-0271-X*); Vol. 14. 1968. 70.00 (*0-8206-0272-8*); Vol. 15. 1970. 70.00 (*0-8206-0273-6*); Vol. 16. 1971. 70.00 (*0-8206-0274-4*); Vol. 17. 1973. 70.00 (*0-8206-0275-2*); Vol. 18. 1975. 70.00 (*0-8206-0276-0*); Vol. 19. 1976. 70.00 (*0-8206-0277-9*); Vol. 20. 1977. 70.00 (*0-8206-0278-7*); Vol. 21. 1979. 70.00 (*0-8206-0279-5*); Vol. 22. 1979. 70.00 (*0-8206-0280-9*); write for info. (*0-318-51346-3*) Chem Pub.

— The Chemical Formulary Series, Vol. 28. 450p. 1989. 70.00 (*0-8206-0328-7*) Chem Pub.

— Chemical Formulary Series, Vol. 35. 270p. 2000. 75.00 (*0-8206-0363-5*) Chem Pub.

Bennett, H. E., et al, eds. Reproducibility & Accuracy of Mechanical Tests, STP- 626. (NBS Special Publication Ser.: No. 568). 152p. 1975. pap. 15.00 (*0-8031-0556-8*, STP626) ASTM.

Bennett, H. S. Chaucer & Fifteenth-Century Verse & Prose. (Oxford History of English Literature Ser.: Vol. 2). 356p. 1990. text 60.00 (*0-19-812229-2*) OUP.

— English Books & Readers, 3 vols. 270p. 1969. 150.00 (*0-521-08857-7*) Cambridge U Pr.

— English Books & Readers, 3 vols., Set. 956p. (C). 1990. pap. text 100.00 (*0-521-37991-1*) Cambridge U Pr.

— The Pastons & Their England. LC 90-34447. (Canto Book Ser.). 304p. (C). 1990. pap. 11.95 (*0-521-39826-6*) Cambridge U Pr.

Bennett, Hal Z. Invitation to Success: Conversations with Noble Acton, Master of Individual & Organizational Creativity. 106p. (Orig.). 1997. pap. 9.00 (*0-9656056-2-0*) Tenacity Pr.

— The Lens of Perception. rev. ed. (Field Guides to Inner Resources Ser.). 180p. (Orig.). 1995. pap. 11.95 (*0-89087-723-8*) Celestial Arts.

— Lord of Dark Places. LC 96-60145. 286p. (Orig.). 1997. pap. 13.95 (*1-885983-12-3*) Turtle Point Pr.

— Mind Jogger. LC 85-28943. 144p. (Orig.). 1986. pap. 7.95 (*0-89087-455-7*) Celestial Arts.

— Spirit Circle: A Story of Adventure & Shamanic Revelation. LC 98-67603. 350p. 1998. pap. 18.00 (*0-9656056-3-9*) Tenacity Pr.

— Spirit Guides: What They Are, How to Meet Them & How to Make Use of Them in Every Area of Your Life. 110p. 1997. pap. 9.00 (*0-9656056-4-7*) Tenacity Pr.

— White Mountain Blues: A Good Time Fable Told in the Venerable Tradition of Tall Yarns & Fairy Tales. 134p. 1997. pap. 12.50 (*0-9656056-5-5*) Tenacity Pr.

— Zuni Fetishes: Using Native American Objects for Meditation, Reflection & Insight. LC 92-53210. (Illus.). 192p. 1993. pap. 19.00 (*0-06-250069-4*, Pub. by Harper SF) HarpC.

Bennett, Hal Z., et al, eds. Emerging from Invisibility: A Collection of Literary Pieces by Evolving Writers. annuals 120p. (Orig.). 1997. pap. 11.95 (*0-9656056-0-4*) Tenacity Pr.

Bennett, Hal Z. & Sparrow, Susan J. Follow Your Bliss. 256p. (Orig.). 1990. pap. 8.00 (*0-380-75893-8*, Avon Bks) Morrow Avon.

— Follow Your Bliss. 6th ed. 228p. (Orig.). 1997. reprint ed. pap. 12.95 (*0-9656056-1-2*, FYB2) Tenacity Pr.

Bennett, Hal Z. & Topf, Linda N. You Are Not Your Illness: Seven Principles for Meeting the Challenge of Illness. LC 94-39618. 256p. 1995. per. 12.00 (*0-684-80124-8*, Fireside) S&S Trade Pap.

Bennett, Hal Z., jt. auth. see Grof, Stanislav.

Bennett, Hal Z., ed. see Kiyosaki, Robert T.

Bennett, Hal Z., ed. see Silbey, Uma.

Bennett, Hal Z., ed. see Toms, Michael.

Bennett, Hal Zina. Write from the Heart: Unleashing the Power of Your Creativity. LC 95-18857. 176p. 1995. pap. 12.95 (*1-882591-27-5*) New Wrld Lib.

Bennett, Hank, et al. The Complete Shortwave Listener's Handbook. 3rd ed. (Illus.). 304p. 1986. pap. 17.95 (*0-8306-2655-7*) McGraw-Hill Prof.

Bennett, Harold. Old Wives Tale. 1998. pap. 3.95 (*1-85326-272-2*, Pub. by Wrdsworth Edits) NTC Contemp Pub Co.

Bennett, Harold, ed. see Symposium on Optical Materials for High Power Lase.

Bennett, Harold B. Discovering Genealogical Roots in Suwanee County, Florida (Late 1700's to Early 1900's) ii, 145p. 1997. pap. 16.00 (*0-7884-0731-7*, B155) Heritage Bk.

Bennett, Harold E., et al, eds. Laser-Induced Damage in Optical Materials, 1996, Vol. 2966. 686p. 1997. 116.00 (*0-8194-2370-X*) SPIE.

***Bennett, Harold E. & Dowell, David H., eds.** Free-Electron Laser Challenges II. 202p. 1999. pap. text 72.00 (*0-8194-3084-6*) SPIE.

Bennett, Harold E., jt. ed. see O'Shea, Patrick G.

Bennett, Harold E., ed. see Symposium on Optical Materials for High Power Lase.

Bennett, Harriet H. Auntie's Favorite Short Stories. 32p. 1998. pap. 8.00 (*0-8059-4508-3*) Dorrance.

Bennett, Harris, ed. see Dobson, Charles.

***Bennett, Harry.** The American Presidency, 1945-2000: Illusions of Grandeur. 2000. 27.95 (*0-7509-2277-X*, Pub. by Sutton Publng) Intl Pubs Mktg.

Bennett, Hazel, jt. auth. see Sherlock, Philip M.

Bennett, Heather, ed. see Carlson, David.

Bennett, Helen, jt. auth. see Burnett, Charles J.

Bennett, Helen S. Jack's Amazing Magic Bed. (Illus.). 32p. (J). (gr. 2). 1994. 13.95 (*0-9638747-1-3*); pap. 9.95 (*0-9638747-0-5*) Tomac Pubng.

Bennett, Henry. Ford: We Never Called Him Henry. 1987. reprint ed. pap. 3.95 (*0-8125-9402-9*) Tor Bks.

Bennett, Henry, jt. auth. see Rickard, Philip.

Bennett, Henry H., ed. The County of Ross: A History of Ross County from the Earliest Days...with Biographical Sketches. 736p. 1995. reprint ed. lib. bdg. 75.00 (*0-8328-4615-5*) Higginson Bk Co.

Bennett, Henry S., ed. England from Chaucer to Caxton. LC 77-114904. (Select Bibliographies Reprint Ser.). 1977. 21.95 (*0-8369-5308-8*) Ayer.

***Bennett, Hess.** Criminal Investigation. 6th ed. (Criminal Justice Ser.). 2000. 57.25 (*0-534-57654-0*) Brooks-Cole.

Bennett, Hess. Management & Supervision in Law Enforcement. 3rd ed. 2000. 4975.00 (*0-534-55431-8*) Thomson Learn.

Bennett, Howard F. Precision Power: The First Half Century of Bodine Electric Company. LC 75-41747. (Companies & Men: Business Enterprises in America Ser.). (Illus.). 1976. reprint ed. 37.95 (*0-405-08064-6*) Ayer.

Bennett, Howard N. The Law of Marine Insurance. LC 95-47056. 628p. (C). 1996. text 135.00 (*0-19-825844-5*, Clarendon Pr) OUP.

Bennett, Hugh H. Soil Conservation. LC 74-125731. (American Environmental Studies). 1974. reprint ed. 56.95 (*0-405-02656-0*) Ayer.

Bennett, I. Rugs & Carpets of the World. 352p. 1996. 29.98 (*0-7858-0201-0*) Bk Sales Inc.

Bennett, Ian. Oriental Rugs Vol. 1: Caucasian. (Illus.). 376p. 1981. 89.50 (*0-902028-58-8*) Antique Collect.

Bennett, Irving. Management for the Eyecare Practitioner. LC 92-49731. (Illus.). 220p. 1992. text 84.00 (*0-7506-9319-3*) Buttrwrth-Heinemann.

***Bennett, Isaiah.** Inside Mormonism. 552p. 1999. pap. 19.95 (*1-888992-06-9*) Catholic Answers.

— When Mormons Call: Answering Mormon Missionaries at Your Door. 144p. 1999. pap. 9.95 (*1-888992-07-7*) Catholic Answers.

Bennett, Isobel. The Great Barrier Reef. LC 73-9491. 183p. 1974. write for info. (*0-684-13620-1*) Free Pr.

Bennett, J. A Cup of Starshine: Poems & Pictures for Children. LC 90-47978. (Illus.). 64p. (J). (ps-1). 1991. 16.95 (*0-15-220982-4*, Harcourt Child Bks) Harcourt.

— The Year-Round Gas Barbecue Cookbook. 1993. pap. 12.50 (*0-394-22335-7*) Random.

Bennett, J. A. Managing Tourism Services LC 97-118978. 444p. 1995. write for info. (*0-627-01939-0*) J L Van Schaik.

Bennett, J. A., ed. Langland Piers Plowman. xiv, 259p. 1985. reprint ed. 39.00 (*0-932051-50-2*) Rprt Serv.

Bennett, J. A. & Smithers, G. V., eds. Early Middle English Verse & Prose. 2nd ed. 682p. 1982. pap. text 34.00 (*0-19-871101-8*) OUP.

Bennett, J. C. And Lead Us Not into Temptation: Educators & Interscholastic Football. LC 92-62376. xvi, 125p. 1993. 18.00 (*0-9634751-3-4*) Mencken Mem.

Bennett, J. Claude, jt. auth. see Goldman, Lee.

Bennett, J. Craig, jt. auth. see Boswell, Frank W.

Bennett, J. E., jt. auth. see Kwon-Chung, K. J.

Bennett, J. G. Creation. Blake, A. G., ed. & frwd. by. LC 98-37103. (Studies from the Dramatic Universe). (Illus.). 128p. 1998. reprint ed. pap. 15.00 (*1-881408-08-6*) Bennett Bks.

— Creative Thinking. LC 98-12375. 80p. 1998. reprint ed. pap. 12.00 (*1-881408-07-8*) Bennett Bks.

Bennett, J. G. Deeper Man. LC 94-1586. (Spiritual Classics Editions Ser.). (Illus.). 224p. (Orig.). 1994. reprint ed. pap. 18.00 (*0-9621901-9-5*) Bennett Bks.

Bennett, J. G. Elementary Systematics: A Tool for Understanding Wholes. Seamon, David, ed. 128p. (Orig.). 1993. pap. 13.00 (*0-9621901-7-9*) Bennett Bks.

— Enneagram Studies. LC 82-60166. 144p. 1983. 7.95 (*0-87728-544-6*) Weiser.

— Gurdjieff: A Very Great Enigma. LC 72-91951. 96p. (Orig.). 1973. reprint ed. pap. 6.95 (*0-87728-581-0*) Weiser.

— Gurdjieff: Making a New World. 266p. 1992. reprint ed. pap. 17.95 (*0-9621901-6-0*) Bennett Bks.

— Hazard: The Risk of Realization. rev. ed. LC 90-42534. (Studies from the Dramatic Universe). 128p. 1991. reprint ed. 18.00 (*0-9621901-4-4*); reprint ed. pap. 13.00 (*0-9621901-5-2*) Bennett Bks.

— Intimations: Talks with J. G. Bennett at Beshara. 100p. (Orig.). 1975. pap. 6.50 (*0-904975-02-9*, Pub. by Beshara) New Leaf Dist.

— Is There "Life" on Earth? An Introduction to Gurdjieff. LC 89-38486. 128p. 1989. reprint ed. pap. 13.00 (*0-9621901-1-X*) Bennett Bks.

***Bennett, J. G.** Journeys in Islamic Countries: The Near East Diaries of a Western Seeker. rev. ed. Bennett, George, ed. 272p. 2000. reprint ed. pap. 24.00 (*1-881408-12-4*) Bennett Bks.

— Needs of a New Age Community: Talks on Spiritual Community & Fourth Way Schools. rev. ed. LC 89-18562. 128p. 1990. reprint ed. pap. 13.00 (*0-9621901-2-8*) Bennett Bks.

Bennett, J. G. Sacred Influences: Spiritual Action in Human Life. LC 89-60084. 96p. 1989. reprint ed. pap. 10.00 (*0-9621901-0-1*) Bennett Bks.

— Sex: The Relationship Between Sex & Spiritual Development. 74p. 1981. reprint ed. pap. 7.95 (*0-87728-533-0*) Weiser.

— The Way to Be Free. 208p. 1980. pap. 12.50 (*0-87728-491-1*) Weiser.

— What Are We Living For? LC 91-27795. 124p. 1991. reprint ed. per. 13.00 (*0-9621901-8-7*) Bennett Bks.

Bennett, J. G., et al. The Spiritual Hunger of the Modern Child. Addison, Wendy, ed. LC 87-71204. 220p. 1985. pap. 8.95 (*0-934254-06-0*) Claymont Comm.

Bennett, J. G., tr. see Ouspensky, P. D.

Bennett, J. H. Natural Selection, Heredity & Eugenics. (Illus.). 316p. 1983. text 49.95 (*0-19-858177-7*) OUP.

Bennett, J. H., ed. Statistical Inference & Analysis: Selected Correspondence of R. A. Fisher. (Illus.). 400p. 1990. 90.00 (*0-19-855552-0*) OUP.

Bennett, J. H., ed. see Fisher, R. A.

Bennett, J. M. The Nursery Question. 1991. pap. 5.00 (*0-936128-75-5*) De Young Pr.

Bennett, J. M., ed. Lymphomas, Vol. I. 1981. text 226.00 (*90-247-2479-1*) Kluwer Academic.

Bennett, J. M. & Castles, Alex C. A Source Book of Australian Legal History. x, 299p. 1979. pap. 47.50 (*0-455-19954-X*, Pub. by LawBk Co) Gaunt.

Bennett, J. M. & Mattsson, L. Introduction to Surface Roughness & Scattering. 120p. (Orig.). 1989. pap. text 44.95 (*1-55752-108-5*) Optical Soc.

Bennett, J. P. Introduction to Compiling Techniques: A First Course Using ANSI C, LEX & YACC. (C). 1990. pap. text 43.00 (*0-07-707215-4*) McGraw.

— Introduction to Compiling Techniques: A First Course Using ANSI C, LEX & YACC. 2nd ed. LC 96-31278. (Mcgraw-Hill International Series in Software Engineering). 1996. pap. write for info. (*0-07-709221-X*) McGraw.

Bennett, J. W. Theme of Spenser's "Foure Hymnes" LC 76-100731. 1970. reprint ed. pap. 39.95 (*0-8383-0003-0*) M S G Haskell Hse.

Bennett, J. W. & Ciegler, Alex. Secondary Metabolism & Differentiation in Fungi. (Mycology Ser.: Vol. 5). (Illus.). 504p. 1983. text 225.00 (*0-8247-1819-4*) Dekker.

Bennett, J. W. & Lasure, Linda L., eds. More Gene Manipulations in Fungi. (Illus.). 470p. (C). 1991. text 100.00 (*0-12-088642-1*) Acad Pr.

Bennett, J. W., et al. Intelligence & Cryptanalytic Activities of the Japanese During World War II. 145p. (Orig.). 1986. pap. 28.80 (*0-89412-133-2*) Aegean Park Pr.

Bennett, J. W., ed. see International Conference Radiation Effects in Bree.

Bennett, Jack. The Lieutenant: An Epic Tale of Courage & Endurance on the High Seas LC 78-314502. 130p. 1977. write for info. (*0-207-13395-6*, Pub. by Angus & Roberts) HarpC.

Bennett, Jack. You Can & Should Sell Cars: You Won't Believe How Easy It Is. 3rd rev. ed. (Illus.). 151p. 1998. pap. 19.95 (*0-9625254-1-3*) J B Pub WI.

Bennett, Jack & Schue, Thomas J. Chloride Removal Implementation Guide. 45p. (C). 1993. pap. text 10.00 (*0-309-05606-3*, SHRP-S-347) SHRP.

Bennett, Jack & Turk, Thomas. Criteria for the Catholic Protection of Reinforced Bridge Elements. 14p. (C). 1994. pap. text 5.00 (*0-309-05615-2*, SHRP-S-359) SHRP.

Bennett, Jack A. Chaucer at Oxford & at Cambridge. LC 74-81706. (Illus.). 141p. reprint ed. pap. 43.80 (*0-7837-0533-6*, 204086100019) Bks Demand.

— Middle English Literature. Gray, Douglas, ed. (Oxford History of English Literature Ser.: No. 1). 510p. 1990. reprint ed. pap. text 29.95 (*0-19-811970-4*) OUP.

— Middle English Literature, 1100-1400. Gray, Douglas, ed. (Oxford History of English Literature Ser.: Vol. I). 508p. 1990. text 59.00 (*0-19-812228-4*) OUP.

— Poetry of the Passion: Studies in 12 Centuries of English Verse. 250p. 1984. pap. text 22.50 (*0-19-812832-0*) OUP.

— You Can & Should Sell Cars. (Illus.). 164p. (Orig.). 1989. pap. 14.95 (*0-9625254-0-5*) J B Pub WI.

***Bennett, Jackie.** Cottage Garden Month-by-Month. (Month-by-Month Gardening Ser.). 1999. pap. 14.95 (*0-7153-0829-7*) D & C Pub.

Bennett, Jackie. The Wildlife Garden Month-by-Month. (Illus.). 144p. 1994. 24.95 (*0-7153-0033-4*, Pub. by D & C Pub) Sterling.

— The Wildlife Garden Month-by-Month. (Illus.). 144p. 1997. pap. text 14.95 (*0-7153-0573-5*) Sterling.

Bennett, Jacqui. Man of Chivalry. large type ed. (Linford Romance Library). 304p. 1989. pap. 16.99 (*0-7089-6690-X*, Linford) Ulverscroft.

— Say Goodbye to Yesterday. large type ed. (Linford Romance Library). 1989. pap. 16.99 (*0-7089-6774-4*) Ulverscroft.

***Bennett, James.** Cases in Parkinson's Disease: Interactive CME CD-Rom for Primary Care Physicians. (Illus.). 1999. audio compact disk 99.95 (*1-891524-05-4*) Carden Jennings.

Bennett, James. The Complete Motorcycle Book: A Consumer's Guide. LC 94-20012. (Illus.). 192p. 1995. 27.95 (*0-8160-2899-0*); pap. 14.95 (*0-8160-3181-9*) Facts on File.

— Dakota Dream. LC 93-17854. 144p. (YA). (gr. 7 up). 1995. pap. 3.99 (*0-590-46681-X*, Point) Scholastic Inc.

— Forts & Forays. (American Autobiography Ser.). 85p. 1995. reprint ed. lib. bdg. 69.00 (*0-7812-8458-9*) Rprt Serv.

— I Can Hear the Mourning. LC 89-26680. 208p. (J). (gr. 7 up). 1997. mass mkt. 4.50 (*0-590-16309-4*) Scholastic Inc.

— Oral History & Delinquency: The Rhetoric of Criminology. LC 81-7514. (C). 1981. 32.00 (*0-226-04245-6*) U Ch Pr.

— Oral History & Delinquency: The Rhetoric of Criminology. LC 81-7514. 380p. (C). 1988. pap. text 19.50 (*0-226-04246-4*) U Ch Pr.

— Overland Journey to California. 90p. 1986. 14.95 (*0-87770-391-4*) Ye Galleon.

Bennett, James A. & Botkin, Mark E., eds. The Optimum Shape: Automated Structural Design. (General Motors Research Symposia Ser.). 410p. 1986. 95.00 (*0-306-42419-3*, Plenum Trade) Perseus Pubng.

Bennett, James A. & Foster, Benjamin. The American System of Practical Bookkeeping: Adopted to the Commerce of the United States, 2 vols. LC 75-18457. (History of Accounting Ser.). (Illus.). 1978. reprint ed. 19.95 (*0-405-07541-3*) Ayer.

Bennett, James C. Personal & Professional Keyboarding. 7th ed. (TA - Typing/Keyboarding Ser.). 1995. mass mkt. 41.95 (*0-538-62021-8*) S-W Pub.

— Shedding the Years. 383p. 1996. reprint ed. spiral bd. 22.50 (*0-7873-0091-8*) Hlth Research.

Bennett, James D. & Harrison, Lowell H. Writing History Papers: An Introduction. LC 78-66987. 64p. 1979. pap. text 6.95 (*0-88273-105-X*) Forum Pr IL.

Bennett, James G. My Father's Geisha. Rosenman, Jane, ed. 176p. 1991. reprint ed. pap. 8.00 (*0-671-74000-8*, WSP) PB.

— The Rohna Disaster: World War II's Secret Tragedy. LC 98-89009. 325p. 1998. 25.00 (*0-7388-0183-6*); pap. 15.00 (*0-7388-0184-4*) Xlibris Corp.

Bennett, James R. A Bibliography of Stylistics & Related Criticism, 1967-1983. LC 85-25867. 405p. 1986. lib. bdg. 19.75 (*0-87352-142-0*, T122C) Modern Lang.

— Control of Information in the United States: An Annotated Bibliography of Books. 616p. 1987. lib. bdg. 85.00 (*0-313-28097-5*, BIU/, Greenwood Pr) Greenwood.

— Control of the Media in the United States: An Annotated Bibliography. LC 91-26064. 849p. 1992. text 40.00 (*0-8240-4438-X*, SS458) Garland.

— Political Prisoners & Trials: A Worldwide Annotated Bibliography, 1900-1993. LC 95-6232. 375p. 1995. lib. bdg. 79.50 (*0-7864-0023-4*) McFarland & Co.

Bennett, James T. Fighting Cancer in Comfort: High Overhead at Cancer Society's Colorado Division Shows One Reason Health Dollars Are Scarce. (Issue Papers: No. 4-92). 14p. 1992. pap. text 8.00 (*1-57655-050-8*) Independ Inst.

Bennett, James T. & Dilorenzo, Thomas. Unfair Competition: The Profits of Nonprofits. 232p. 1988. 17.95 (*0-8191-7180-8*) U Pr of Amer.

Bennett, James T. & DiLorenzo, Thomas J. CancerScam: Diversion of Federal Cancer Funds to Politics. LC 97-26547. 175p. 1997. text 32.95 (*1-56000-334-0*) Transaction Pubs.

— Destroying Democracy: How Government Funds Partisan Politics. 561p. 1985. 7.00 (*0-932790-53-4*); pap. 3.00 (*0-932790-54-2*) Cato Inst.

— The Food & Drink Police: America's Nannies, Busybodies, & Petty Tyrants. LC 98-34511. 162p. 1998. 24.95 (*1-56000-385-5*) Transaction Pubs.

***Bennett, James T. & DiLorenzo, Thomas J.** From Pathology to Politics: Public Health in America. 153p. 2000. 29.95 (*0-7658-0023-3*) Transaction Pubs.

Bennett, James T. & DiLorenzo, Thomas J. Official Lies: How Washington Misleads Us. 1992. 19.95 (*0-9632701-0-9*) Groom Bks.

Bennett, James T. & Johnson, Manuel H. Better Government at Half the Price: Private Production of Public Services. LC 80-26361. 117p. 1981. pap. 5.95 (*0-89803-048-X*) Jameson Bks.

— The Political Economy of Federal Government Growth. 148p. 1980. 12.95 (*0-86599-001-8*); pap. 4.95 (*0-86599-002-6*) PERC.

Bennett, James W. Blue Star Rapture. LC 97-15549. 134p. (YA). (gr. 9 up). 1998. per. 16.00 (*0-689-81580-8*, 866194) S&S Childrens.

— Dakota Dream. 1994. 9.09 (*0-606-07407-4*, Pub. by Turtleback) Demco.

— I Can Hear the Mourning Dove. 1990. 9.60 (*0-606-10852-1*, Pub. by Turtleback) Demco.

Bennett, Jane. Thoreau's Nature: Ethics, Politics & the Wild. (Modernity & Political Thought Ser.: Vol. 7). 203p. 1994. 44.00 (*0-8039-3868-3*); pap. 19.95 (*0-8039-3869-1*) Sage.

Bennett, Jane & Chaloupka, William, eds. In the Nature of Things: Language, Politics, & the Environment. LC 92-47101. 292p. (C). 1993. pap. 19.95 (*0-8166-2308-2*) U of Minn Pr.

— In the Nature of Things: Language, Politics & the Environment. LC 92-47101. 292p. (C). 1993. text 49.95 (*0-8166-2307-4*) U of Minn Pr.

***Bennett, Jane, et al.** Watching Wildlife Australia. (Watching Wildlife Ser.). (Illus.). 352p. 2000. pap. 19.95 (*1-86450-032-8*) Lonely Planet.

Bennett, Janet G. The German Shepherd Dog: A Genetic History. (Illus.). 448p. 1992. 49.95 (*0-87605-175-1*) Howell Bks.

— The New Complete German Shepherd Dog. 5th rev. ed. LC 82-1031. (Illus.). 256p. 1982. 25.95 (*0-87605-151-4*) Howell Bks.

Bennett, Janice. Bewitching Kittens. (Zebra Regency Romance Ser.). 256p. 1998. mass mkt. 4.99 (*0-8217-6010-6*, Zebra Kensgtn) Kensgtn Pub Corp.

— Candlelight Wish, 1. (Zebra Regency Romance Ser.). 256p. 1999. mass mkt. 4.99 (*0-8217-6263-X*) Kensgtn Pub Corp.

— The Matchmaking Ghost. (Zebra Romance Ser.). 256p. 1998. pap. 4.99 (*0-8217-5890-X*, Zebra Kensgtn) Kensgtn Pub Corp.

***Bennett, Janice.** Moonlight Wish. (Zebra Regency Romance Ser.). 224p. 2000. mass mkt. 4.99 (*0-8217-6627-9*, Zebra Kensgtn) Kensgtn Pub Corp.

Bennett, Janice. Notorious & Noble, 1. (Zebra Regency Romance Ser.). 288p. 1999. mass mkt. 4.99 (*0-8217-6266-4*) Kensgtn Pub Corp.

An Asterisk (*) at the beginning of an entry indicates that the title is appearing for the first time.

***Bennett, Janice.** Starlight Wish. (Zebra Regency Romance Ser.). 256p. 1999. mass mkt. 4.99 (*0-8217-6417-9*, Zebra Kensgtn) Kensgtn Pub Corp.

Bennett, Janice. Summer Kittens. (Zebra Regency Romance Ser.). 256p. 1999. mass mkt. 4.99 (*0-8217-6230-3*) Kensgtn Pub Corp.

— Tempting Miss. 1989. mass mkt. 3.95 (*0-8217-2849-0*, Zebra Kensgtn) Kensgtn Pub Corp.

***Bennett, Jarratt G.** Maximize Your Inheritance: For Widows, Widowers & Heirs. LC 99-30539. 320p. 1999. pap. 22.95 (*0-7931-3330-0*) Dearborn.

Bennett, Jay. Coverup. 1992. 9.60 (*0-606-12227-3*, Pub. by Turtleback) Demco.

— Coverup. 144p. (YA). 1992. reprint ed. mass mkt. 4.50 (*0-449-70409-2*, Juniper) Fawcett.

— The Dark Corridor. 144p. (YA). (gr. 6 up). 1990. mass mkt. 4.50 (*0-449-70337-1*, Juniper) Fawcett.

— Dark Corridor. 1990. 9.60 (*0-606-01184-6*, Pub. by Turtleback) Demco.

— The Death Ticket. 1985. pap. 2.75 (*0-380-89597-8*, Avon Bks) Morrow Avon.

— The Executioner. LC 81-52413. 176p. (gr. 7-12). 1982. mass mkt. 4.50 (*0-380-79160-9*, Avon Bks) Morrow Avon.

Bennett, Jay. The Haunted One. 1989. 9.09 (*0-606-01186-2*, Pub. by Turtleback) Demco.

Bennett, Jay. I Never Said I Loved You. 128p. 1984. pap. 2.50 (*0-380-86900-4*, Avon Bks) Morrow Avon.

— Masks: A Love Story. LC 79-147396. 121 p. (J). 1971. write for info. (*0-531-01979-9*) Watts.

— Shadows Offstage: A Novel. LC 74-675. 125 p. (J). 1974. write for info. (*0-8407-6385-9*) Nelson Comm.

— Sing Me a Death Song. 144p. (YA). (gr. 7 up). 1991. mass mkt. 4.50 (*0-449-70369-X*, Juniper) Fawcett.

— Sing Me a Death Song. 1991. 9.60 (*0-606-01187-0*, Pub. by Turtleback) Demco.

— Skeleton Man: A Novel. (J). 1988. 9.60 (*0-606-04106-0*, Pub. by Turtleback) Demco.

— Skinhead. 192p. 1992. mass mkt. 4.50 (*0-449-70397-5*, Juniper) Fawcett.

— Skinhead. 1992. 9.60 (*0-606-01188-9*, Pub. by Turtleback) Demco.

Bennett, Jay, ed. Statistics in Sport. LC 98-218571. (An Arnold Publication). (Illus.). 328p. 1998. text 70.00 (*0-340-70072-6*, Pub. by E A) OUP.

Bennett, Jean M. Surface Finish & Its Measurements. 1000p. (Orig.). 1992. text 150.00 (*1-55752-264-2*) Optical Soc.

Bennett, Jeff. The Complete Inflatable Kayaker. (Illus.). 192p. 1995. pap. text 16.95 (*0-07-005428-2*, Ragged Mntain) McGraw-Hill Prof.

***Bennett, Jeff.** The Complete Snowboarder. 2nd ed. (Illus.). 160p. 2000. pap. text 14.95 (*0-07-135787-4*) McGraw.

Bennett, Jeff. The Complete Whitewater Rafter. (Illus.). 192p. 1996. pap. 16.95 (*0-07-005505-X*, Ragged Mntain) McGraw-Hill Prof.

— The Essential Whitewater Kayaker. LC 98-33127. 180p. 1999. pap. 16.95 (*0-07-134327-X*) McGraw.

Bennett, Jeff, ed. Class Five Chronicles: Things Mother Never Told You 'bout Whitewater. (Illus.). 256p. (Orig.). 1992. pap. text 13.95 (*0-9629843-3-7*) Swiftwater Pub.

Bennett, Jeff & Bennett, Tonya. A Guide to the Whitewater Rivers of Washington: 300 Trips for Raft, Kayak & Canoe Throughout the Pacific Northwest. 2nd ed. (Illus.). 352p. 1998. pap. 23.95 (*0-9629843-7-X*) Swiftwater Pub.

***Bennett, Jeff & Donahue, Megan.** The Cosmic Perspective. 1999. pap., teacher ed. 24.00 (*0-8053-8015-9*) Benjamin-Cummings.

Bennett, Jeff & Downey, Scott. The Complete Snowboarder. (Illus.). 144p. 1994. pap. 14.95 (*0-07-005142-9*, Ragged Mntain) McGraw-Hill Prof.

Bennett, Jeffrey O. The Cosmic Perspective. LC 98-48585. 708p. (C). 1998. pap. text 76.00 (*0-201-87878-X*) Addison-Wesley.

***Bennett, Jeffrey O.** Cosmic Perspective: Brief Edition. LC 99-56692. 1999. pap. 62.67 (*0-201-69734-3*) Addison-Wesley.

Bennett, Jeffrey O. & Briggs, William L. Using & Understanding Mathematics: A Quantitative Reasoning Approach. LC 98-3885. 752p. (C). 1998. 81.00 (*0-201-65642-6*) Addison-Wesley.

***Bennett, Jeffrey O., et al.** Statistical Reasoning for Everyday Life. LC 00-32777. 2000. pap. write for info. (*0-201-61488-X*) Addison-Wesley.

Bennett, Jeffrey P. & Phillips, Francine. Breaking the Bonds of Child Abuse: A Guide to Political Action. 196p. 1996. pap. 12.95 (*0-9637698-3-9*) Write Now.

Bennett, Jennifer. The Annual Garden. (Illus.). 176p. 1998. pap. 19.95 (*1-55209-196-1*) Firefly Bks Ltd.

— Dry-Land Gardening: A Xeriscaping Guide for Dry-Summer, Cold-Winter Climates. (Illus.). 176p. 1998. pap. 24.95 (*1-55209-221-6*) Firefly Bks Ltd.

— A Gardener's Guide to Berries. (Illus.). 96p. 1996. pap. text 10.95 (*1-895565-95-2*) Firefly Bks Ltd.

— The Gardener's Guide to Groundcovers. (Illus.). 96p. 1996. pap. text 10.95 (*1-895565-97-9*) Firefly Bks Ltd.

— Lilies of the Hearth: The Historical Relationship Between Women & Plants. (Illus.). 192p. 1991. pap. 14.95 (*0-921820-27-5*) Firefly Bks Ltd.

— The New Northern Gardener. rev. ed. (Illus.). 256p. 1996. pap. 24.95 (*1-55209-012-4*) Firefly Bks Ltd.

— Our Gardens, Ourselves: Reflections on an Ancient Art. (Illus.). 176p. 1994. pap. 14.95 (*0-921820-91-7*) Firefly Bks Ltd.

— The Tomato Handbook: Tips & Tricks for Growing the Best Tomatoes. (Gardener's Guide Ser.: Vol. 6). (Illus.). 96p. 1997. pap. 10.95 (*1-55209-107-4*) Firefly Bks Ltd.

Bennett, Jennifer, ed. see Fisher, Peggy.

Bennett, Jerome V. Budgeting & Forecasting Manual. LC 99-170185. 1998. write for info. (*0-7913-2998-4*) Warren Gorham & Lamont.

Bennett, Jesse Lee. The Diffusion of Science. LC 74-26250. (History, Philosophy & Sociology of Science Ser.). 1975. reprint ed. 19.95 (*0-405-06580-9*) Ayer.

Bennett, Jessica. Innkeepers' Finest Breakfasts. (Illus.). 152p. 1994. pap. text 12.00 (*0-9638785-0-6*) April Haven.

Bennett, Jill. Baa Baa Dead Sheep. 224p. (YA). (gr. 7 up). 1994. pap. 3.50 (*0-590-48507-5*) Scholastic Inc.

— Christmas Poems. (Illus.). 28p. (YA). 2000. 11.95 (*0-19-276222-2*) OUP.

— Jack & the Robbers. LC 98-60511. (Val Biro Bks.). (Illus.). 32p. (J). (gr. 1-3). 1998. pap. 4.99 (*1-887734-45-7*) Star Brght Bks.

— Noisy Poems. (Illus.). 32p. (J). (gr. k-3). 1989. pap. 7.95 (*0-19-278219-3*) OUP.

— Noisy Poems. (J). 1987. 12.15 (*0-606-02125-6*, Pub. by Turtleback) Demco.

— Teeny Tiny. 1998. 10.19 (*0-606-13050-0*, Pub. by Turtleback) Demco.

Bennett, Jill, compiled by. People Poems. (Illus.). 32p. (J). 1992. pap. (*0-19-276110-2*) OUP.

Bennett, Jill, ed. Spooky Poems. (Illus.). 32p. 1990. 14.95 (*0-7737-2350-1*) Genl Dist Srvs.

— Tasty Poems. (Illus.). 32p. (J). 1998. pap. 7.95 (*0-19-276133-1*) OUP.

Bennett, Jim. The Basics of Weight Training. 328p. 1995. pap. text, wbk. ed. 13.00 (*0-205-17364-0*) Allyn.

Bennett, Jim. Bulletproof Offshore Asset Protection: The Money Fortress for the New Millenium. LC 99-90009. (Illus.). 160p. 1999. pap. 24.95 (*0-9669839-0-4*) J Bennett Inst.

— The Calorie Register. 72p. 1991. pap. 7.95 (*1-879031-03-5*) JBBA Pub.

— The Complete Mortocycle Book: A Consumer's Guide. 2nd ed. LC 98-30311. (Illus.). 272p. 1999. 27.95 (*0-8160-3853-8*); pap. 14.95 (*0-8160-3854-6*) Facts on File.

— Weight Training Calorie Register. rev. ed. 96p. 1991. pap. 7.95 (*1-879031-02-7*) JBBA Pub.

— The Weight Training Record. 2nd ed. 208p. 1995. pap., spiral bd. 10.95 (*1-879031-07-8*) JBBA Pub.

— The Weight Training Workbook. 2nd ed. (Weight Training Ser.). (Illus.). 256p. 1995. pap., spiral bd. 12.95 (*1-879031-06-X*) JBBA Pub.

— The Weight Training Workbook: For Women. (Illus.). 256p. (Orig.). 1996. pap., spiral bd. 12.95 (*1-879031-08-6*) JBBA Pub.

Bennett, Jo-Anne. The Complete Year-Round Gas Barbecue Cookbook. LC 94-1652. 218p. 1994. pap. 12.95 (*0-88415-165-4*, 5165) Gulf Pub.

Bennett, Joan S. Reviving Liberty: Radical Christian Humanism in Milton's Great Poems. LC 88-22682. (Illus.). 233p. 1988. 43.00 (*0-674-76697-0*) HUP.

***Bennett, Joe.** Fun Run & Other Oxymorons. 192p. 2000. pap. 12.00 (*0-7432-0511-1*) Simon & Schuster.

Bennett, Joe. Guitar Chords... To Go! 47p. 1999. pap. text 7.95 (*0-7119-7231-1*, AM954240) Music Sales.

— Guitar Riffs... To Go! (Illus.). 47p. 1999. pap. text 7.95 (*0-7119-7232-X*, AM954250) Music Sales.

— Guitar Scales... To Go! (Illus.). 47p. 1999. pap. text 7.95 (*0-7119-7233-8*) Music Sales.

— Guitar Tunings... To Go! (Illus.). 47p. 1999. pap. text 7.95 (*0-7119-7234-6*, AM954272) Music Sales.

***Bennett, Joel.** Time, Intimacy & the Science of Personal Relationships: A Transpersonal Perspective. (A Volume in LEA's Series on Personal Relationships). 272p. 2000. write for info. (*0-8058-3679-9*); pap. write for info. (*0-8058-3680-2*) L Erlbaum Assocs.

Bennett, Joel P. Winning Attorneys' Fees from the U. S. Government. LC 84-4363. 500p. 1984. ring bd. 90.00 (*0-317-00826-9*) NY Law Pub.

***Bennett, John.** Betrayal's Like That. 28p. (C). 2000. pap. 5.00 (*0-912824-41-7*) Vagabond Pr.

Bennett, John. Bodo: Infant of the Aftermath. LC 94-66400. 192p. (Orig.). 1995. pap. 14.95 (*1-882986-17-2*) Smith.

— Construction in the Third Way: Managing Cooperation & Competition in Construction. 384p. 2000. pap. 49.95 (*0-7506-3093-0*, Architectural Pr) Buttrwrth-Heinemann.

— Construction Management & the Chartered Quantity Surveyor. (C). 1986. 45.00 (*0-85406-299-8*, Pub. by Surveyors Pubns) St Mut.

— Crime of the Century. 112p. (Orig.). 1987. pap. 10.00 (*0-915016-37-0*) Second Coming.

— The Doctor to the Dead: Grotesque Legends & Folk Tales of Old Charleston. LC 70-135593. 1982. lib. bdg. 76.50 (*0-8371-5184-8*, AEBDD&, Greenwood Pr) Greenwood.

— The Doctor to the Dead: Grotesque Legends & Folk Tales of Old Charleston. LC 94-35199. 280p. 1995. pap. 9.95 (*1-57003-040-5*) U of SC Pr.

— Karmic Four-Star Buckaroo. 51p. 1997. pap. 8.95 (*0-944754-39-2*) Pudding Hse Pubns.

— Making Little Boxes from Wood. (Illus.). 148p. 1993. pap. 14.95 (*0-946819-39-4*, Pub. by Guild Master) Sterling.

— Master Skylark. (Airmont Classics Ser.). (J). (gr. 5 up). 1965. mass mkt. 1.95 (*0-8049-0092-2*, CL-92) Airmont.

— The Masters of Wisdom: An Esoteric History of the Spiritual Unfolding of Life on This Planet. 192p. 1996. pap. 18.00 (*0-614-21310-X*, 1455) Kazi Pubns.

— The Names We Go By. LC 93-70640. 208p. 1993. pap. 20.00 (*0-913204-29-3*) December Pr.

— The New World Order. LC 91-90037. 88p. 1991. pap. 10.95 (*0-912292-94-6*) Smith.

— Rodeo Town: Interviews. (Illus.). 80p. 1997. pap. 12.00 (*0-912824-38-7*) Vagabond Pr.

— Survival Song: A Journal of Recovery, Pt. 2. 120p. 1985. pap. 10.00 (*0-912824-35-2*) Vagabond Pr.

— Survival Song: A Journal of Recovery, Pt. 3. 120p. 1985. pap. 10.00 (*0-912824-36-0*) Vagabond Pr.

— Tripping in America: A Travel Journal. 160p. 1984. pap. 10.00 (*0-912824-33-6*) Vagabond Pr.

— Whiplash on the Couch. Robertson, Kirk, ed. LC 77-73210. (Orig.). 1979. pap. 3.00 (*0-916918-06-8*) Duck Down.

— The Zoo Manuscript. 1968. 5.00 (*0-686-20739-4*) Sydon.

Bennett, John, ed. The Vagabond Anthology: The Best of Vagabond Magazine. LC 77-90626. 1978. pap. 10.00 (*0-912824-45-X*) Vagabond Pr.

Bennett, John & Stone, Phil. Hikes in the Washington Region, Pt. A: Montgomery & Frederick County in Maryland. LC 86-61526. 112p. 1992. pap. 6.00 (*0-915746-44-1*) Potomac Appalach.

Bennett, John, et al. Ten Eighteenth-Century Voluntaries. Beechey, Gwilym, ed. (Recent Researches in Music of the Baroque Era Ser.: Vol. RRB6). (Illus.). xiii, 97p. 1969. pap. 40.00 (*0-89579-016-5*) A-R Eds.

Bennett, John, jt. auth. see Stone, Phil.

Bennett, John, ed. see Ferlinghetti, Lawrence, et al.

Bennett, John A. Typewriting in a Swimming Pool. (Illus.). 23p. (Orig.). (J). (gr. 2 up). 1995. pap. 2.00 (*0-935350-52-7*) Luna Bisonte.

Bennett, John B. Collegial Professionalism: The Academy, Individualism & the Common Good. LC 97-37069. (Ace/Oryx Series on Higher Education). 208p. 1997. boxed set 32.50 (*1-57356-093-6*) Oryx Pr.

— Rational Thinking: A Study in Basic Logic. 1980. text 35.95 (*0-88229-285-4*) Burnham Inc.

Bennett, John B. & Figuli, David J., eds. Enhancing Departmental Leadership: The Roles of the Chairperson. LC 93-21575. (American Council on Education-Oryx Press Series on Higher Education). (Illus.). 256p. 1990. reprint ed. 27.95 (*0-89774-866-2*) Oryx Pr.

***Bennett, John C.** The History of the Saints: or An Expose of Joe Smith & Mormonism. LC 99-87027. 384p. 2000. 34.95 (*0-252-02589-X*) U of Ill Pr.

Bennett, John C. Orthodontic Treatment Mechanics & the Pre-Adjusted Appliance. (Illus.). 265p. (C). (gr. 13). 1993. text 142.00 (*0-8151-0673-4*, 23026) Mosby Inc.

Bennett, John C., et al. Christian Values & Economic Life. LC 71-99624. (Essay Index Reprint Ser.). 1977. 23.95 (*0-8369-1559-3*) Ayer.

Bennett, John E. Pharmacotherapy & Management of Hypertension. 1994. text 99.00 (*0-443-08896-9*) Church.

Bennett, John E., et al, eds. New Strategies in Fungal Disease. (Frontiers of Infectious Diseases Ser.). (Illus.). 312p. (Orig.). 1992. pap. text 66.95 (*0-443-04684-0*) Church.

Bennett, John F., jt. auth. see Bennett, Edna M.

Bennett, John G. Creative Thinking. 3rd ed. 1989. reprint ed. pap. 10.95 (*0-934254-30-3*) Claymont Comm.

— The Dramatic Universe Vol. 1: The Foundations of Natural Philosophy. (Illus.). 580p. 1997. reprint ed. pap. 34.00 (*1-881408-03-5*) Bennett Bks.

— The Dramatic Universe Vol. 2: The Foundations of Moral Philosophy. (Illus.). 356p. 1997. reprint ed. pap. 34.00 (*1-881408-04-3*) Bennett Bks.

— The Dramatic Universe Vol. 3: Man & His Nature. (Illus.). 315p. 1997. reprint ed. pap. 34.00 (*1-881408-05-1*) Bennett Bks.

— The Dramatic Universe Vol. 4: History. (Illus.). 462p. 1997. reprint ed. pap. 34.00 (*1-881408-06-X*) Bennett Bks.

— Energies: Cosmic, Material, Vital. 3rd ed. 136p. 1989. reprint ed. pap. 11.95 (*0-934254-28-1*) Claymont Comm.

— Foundations of Moral Philosophy, Vol. 2. rev. ed. (Dramatic Universe Ser.). 356p. 1987. 20.00 (*0-934254-17-6*, Pub. by Coombe Springs Pr); pap. 14.95 (*0-934254-16-8*, Pub. by Coombe Springs Pr) Claymont Comm.

— Foundations of Natural Philosophy, Vol. 1. rev. ed. (Dramatic Universe Ser.). 1987. 20.00 (*0-934254-15-X*, Pub. by Coombe Springs Pr); pap. 12.95 (*0-934254-14-1*, Pub. by Coombe Springs Pr) Claymont Comm.

— History, Vol. 1. rev. ed. (Dramatic Universe Ser.). 462p. 1987. 22.00 (*0-934254-21-4*, Pub. by Coombe Springs Pr); pap. 16.95 (*0-934254-20-6*, Pub. by Coombe Springs Pr) Claymont Comm.

— How We Do Things. 3rd ed. 1989. reprint ed. pap. 9.95 (*0-934254-26-5*) Claymont Comm.

— Living in Two Worlds. (Orig.). 1989. pap. 10.95 (*0-934254-31-1*) Claymont Comm.

— Making a Soul: Human Destiny & the Debt of Our Existence. (Spiritual Classics Editions Ser.). 128p. (Orig.). 1995. pap. 14.00 (*1-881408-00-0*) Bennett Bks.

— Man & His Nature, Vol. 3. rev. ed. (Dramatic Universe Ser.). 315p. 1987. 20.00 (*0-934254-19-2*, Pub. by Coombe Springs Pr); pap. 14.95 (*0-934254-18-4*, Pub. by Coombe Springs Pr) Claymont Comm.

— The Masters of Wisdom: An Esoteric History of the Spiritual Unfolding of Life on This Planet. 2nd ed. 192p. 1999. pap. 20.00 (*1-881408-01-9*) Bennett Bks.

***Bennett, John G.** A Spiritual Psychology. LC 99-51419. 200p. 1999. reprint ed. pap. 20.00 (*1-881408-11-6*) Bennett Bks.

Bennett, John G. Talks on Beelzebub's Tales. LC 88-3963. 168p. (Orig.). 1988. pap. 10.00 (*0-87728-680-9*) Weiser.

— Transformation. LC 78-60760. 6.95 (*0-900306-07-6*) Claymont Comm.

— Witness. 1983. 16.95 (*0-934254-24-9*); pap. 8.95 (*0-685-01116-X*) Claymont Comm.

— Witness: The Story of a Search. LC 97-6407. (Spiritual Classics Editions Ser.). (Illus.). 352p. 1997. reprint ed. pap. 20.00 (*1-881408-02-7*) Bennett Bks.

***Bennett, John L.** Leading the Edge of Change: Building Individual & Organizational Capacity for the Evolving Nature of Change. LC 99-68955. 128p. 2000. pap. 11.95 (*0-9678323-0-6*) Paw Print.

Bennett, John M. Ax Tongue. (Illus.). vii, 26p. (Orig.). 1986. pap. 7.98 incl. audio (*0-935350-16-0*) Luna Bisonte.

— Blanksmanship. 21p. (Orig.). 1994. pap. 10.00 incl. audio (*0-935350-49-7*); pap. 6.00 incl. audio (*0-935350-48-9*); pap. 5.00 (*0-935350-47-0*) Luna Bisonte.

— Blind on the Temple. 10p. (Orig.). 1993. pap. 2.50 (*0-935350-46-2*) Luna Bisonte.

— Book Classification. 5p. 1993. pap. 2.00 (*0-935350-43-8*) Luna Bisonte.

— Burning Dog. 24p. 1983. pap. 4.00 (*0-935350-09-8*) Luna Bisonte.

— Burning Dog. deluxe limited ed. 24p. 1983. pap. 9.00 (*0-935350-10-1*) Luna Bisonte.

— Cascade. 1987. pap. 2.00 (*0-935350-68-3*) Luna Bisonte.

— Contents. 1978. pap. 3.00 (*0-935350-69-1*) Luna Bisonte.

— Contents. deluxe ed. 1978. pap. 5.00 (*0-935350-67-5*) Luna Bisonte.

— Fenestration. 10p. (Orig.). 1991. pap. 2.50 (*0-935350-33-0*) Luna Bisonte.

— Image Standards. 1975. pap. 2.50 (*0-935350-72-1*) Luna Bisonte.

— Jerks. 1980. pap. 3.00 (*0-935350-74-8*) Luna Bisonte.

— Jerks. deluxe ed. 1980. pap. 7.00 (*0-935350-73-X*) Luna Bisonte.

— Know Other. (Illus.). 65p. 1998. pap. 10.00 (*1-892280-00-0*) Luna Bisonte.

— Leg. 5p. (Orig.). 1992. pap. 2.00 (*0-935350-76-4*) Luna Bisonte.

***Bennett, John M.** Mailer Leaves Ham. 159p. 1999. pap. 9.95 (*1-880766-19-1*, Pub. by Pantograph Pr) SPD-Small Pr Dist.

Bennett, John M. Meat Dip: Fifteen Labels. 1976. pap. 3.00 (*0-935350-79-9*) Luna Bisonte.

— Meat Watch. 1977. pap. 3.00 (*0-935350-80-2*) Luna Bisonte.

— Meat Watch. deluxe limited ed. 1977. pap. 5.00 (*0-935350-81-0*) Luna Bisonte.

— Milk. 6p. (Orig.). 1990. pap. 2.00 (*0-935350-20-9*) Luna Bisonte.

— Motel Moods. 1980. pap. 2.50 (*0-935350-03-9*) Luna Bisonte.

— Motel Moods. limited ed. 1980. pap. 6.00 (*0-935350-82-9*) Luna Bisonte.

— Nips Poems. (Illus.). 40p. (Orig.). 1980. pap. 3.00 (*0-935350-00-4*) Luna Bisonte.

— Nips Poems. limited ed. (Illus.). 40p. (Orig.). 1980. pap. 6.00 (*0-935350-83-7*) Luna Bisonte.

— Nose Death. 10p. (C). 1984. pap. 2.50 (*0-935350-12-8*) Luna Bisonte.

— Nose Death. deluxe ed. 10p. (C). 1984. pap. 7.50 (*0-935350-13-6*) Luna Bisonte.

— Puking Horse. 1980. pap. 5.00 (*0-935350-04-7*) Luna Bisonte.

— Puking Horse. deluxe limited ed. 1980. pap. 10.00 (*0-935350-86-1*) Luna Bisonte.

— Regression. 1988. pap. 2.00 (*0-935350-18-7*) Luna Bisonte.

— Reversion: Piles of That. (Illus.). 252p. (Orig.). 1994. pap. 30.00 (*0-935350-53-5*) Luna Bisonte.

— Six Portraits. 1975. pap. 2.00 (*0-935350-90-X*) Luna Bisonte.

— Somation. (Illus.). 1992. pap. 2.00 (*0-935350-38-1*) Luna Bisonte.

— Span. 39p. (Orig.). 1990. pap. 3.00 (*0-926935-44-5*) Runaway Spoon.

— Spinal Speech. 46p. 1995. pap. 5.00 (*1-57141-013-9*) Runaway Spoon.

— Stones in the Lake. (Illus.). 20p. (Orig.). 1987. pap. 3.00 (*0-935350-14-4*) Luna Bisonte.

— Swelling. (Illus.). 38p. (Orig.). 1988. pap. 3.00 (*0-926935-05-4*) Runaway Spoon.

— Thirteen Spits. 1986. pap. 2.00 (*0-935350-91-8*) Luna Bisonte.

— Time Release. 1978. pap. 4.00 (*0-935350-92-6*) Luna Bisonte.

— Time Release. deluxe ed. 1978. pap. 5.00 (*0-935350-93-4*) Luna Bisonte.

— Time's Dipstick. 1976. pap. 2.00 (*0-935350-94-2*) Luna Bisonte.

— White Screen, Poetry & Graphics. 1976. pap. 6.00 (*0-935350-95-0*) Luna Bisonte.

Bennett, John M., ed. Controversies in the Management of Lymphomas. (Cancer Treatment & Research Ser.). 1983. text 159.50 (*0-89838-586-5*) Kluwer Academic.

Bennett, John M. & Bennett, C. Mehrl. Applied Appliances. deluxe limited ed. (Orig.). 1981. 5.00 (*0-935350-05-5*) Luna Bisonte.

Bennett, John M. & Berry, Jake. The Lemurs. 10p. 1993. pap. 5.00 incl. audio (*0-935350-40-3*) Luna Bisonte.

Bennett, John M. & Crozier, Robin. Prix Dor. 6p. (Orig.). 1993. pap. 2.00 (*0-935350-85-3*) Luna Bisonte.

Bennett, John M. & Foon, Kenneth A., eds. Immunologic Approaches to the Classification & Management of Lymphomas & Leukemias. (Cancer Treatment & Research Ser.). (C). 1988. text 179.50 (*0-89838-355-2*) Kluwer Academic.

Bennett, John M. & Hallewell, Laurence. Sendero Luminoso in Context: An Annotated Bibliography. LC 98-8382. 320p. 1998. 60.00 (*0-8108-3559-2*) Scarecrow.

Bennett, John M., jt. auth. see Andrews, Bruce.

Bennett, John M., jt. auth. see Bennett, C. Mehrl.

Bennett, John M., jt. auth. see Crozier, Robin.

Bennett, John M., jt. auth. see Mehrl, C.

Bennett, John P. Gymnastics for Everyone. (Physical Education Ser.). 105p. (Orig.). (C). 1995. pap. text 10.95 (*0-89641-236-9*) American Pr.

B

Bennett, John P. & Riemer, Pamela C. Rhythmic Activities & Dance: Dancing for Fun & Fitness. LC 94-38538. (Illus.). 184p. (Orig.). 1995. pap. text 20.00 (*0-87322-718-2*, BBEN0718) Human Kinetics.

Bennett, John P., et al. Teaching Lifelong Leisure Activities. (Illus.). 154p. (C). 1997. pap. text 15.95 (*0-89641-303-9*) American Pr.

Bennett, John R. The Origin of Freemasonry & Knight Templar (1907) 215p. 1996. reprint ed. pap. 17.95 (*1-56459-557-9*) Kessinger Pub.

Bennett, John R., compiled by. Melodiya: A Soviet Russian L. P. Discography, 6. LC 81-4247. (Discographies Ser.: No. 6). (Illus.). 832p. 1981. lib. bdg. 135.00 (*0-313-22596-6*, BME/, Greenwood Pr) Greenwood.

Bennett, John R. & Wimmer, Wilhelm. A Catalogue of Vocal Recordings from the 1898-1926 German Catalogues of the Gramophone Company Limited, Duetsche Grammophon, Vol. 7--7. LC 77-28980. (Voices of the Past Ser.: Vol. 7). 404p. 1978. reprint ed. lib. bdg. 79.50 (*0-313-20236-2*, BECVG) Greenwood.

***Bennett, John Roy, ed.** Jason Mason Middleton-Tapp. (Illus.). 32p. (J). (ps-k). 2000. pap. 10.95 (*1-894222-12-1*) LOB4.

Bennett, John V. & Brachman, Philip S., eds. Hospital Infections. 4th ed. LC 97-28724. (Illus.). 1008p. 1997. text 135.00 (*0-316-08902-8*) Lppncott W & W.

Bennett, John W. Classic Anthropology: Critical Essays: 1944-1996. LC 97-45618. 448p. 1997. text 49.95 (*1-56000-333-2*) Transaction Pubs.

— Highest Traditions: The History of No. 2 Squadron, RAAF. unabridged ed. LC 94-25557. (Illus.). 455p. 1995. 49.95 (*0-644-35230-2*, 9425557, Pub. by AGPS Pr) Intl Spec Bk.

— Human Ecology As Human Behavior: Essay in Environmental & Development Anthropology. expanded ed. LC 95-22325. 368p. (C). 1995. pap. text 24.95 (*1-56000-849-0*) Transaction Pubs.

Bennett, John W. & Ishino, Iwao. Paternalism in the Japanese Economy. LC 72-3538. 307p. 1972. reprint ed. lib. bdg. 65.00 (*0-8371-6424-9*, BEJE, Greenwood Pr) Greenwood.

Bennett, John W. & Kohl, Seena B. Settling the Canadian-American West, 1890-1915: Pioneer Adaptation & Community Building. LC 95-1826. (Illus.). xiii, 297p. 1995. text 55.00 (*0-8032-1254-2*) U of Nebr Pr.

Bennett, John Whitchurch. Ceylon & Its Capabilities: An Account of Its Natural Resources, Indigenous Productions & Commercial Facilities. LC 98-905014. 427, LXXXIV p. 1998. write for info. (*81-206-1168-3*) Asian Educ Servs.

Bennett, Jon. Meeting Needs. 1995. pap. 30.00 (*1-85383-235-9*, Pub. by Escan Pubns) Island Pr.

Bennett, Jonathan. The Act Itself. (Illus.). 248p. 1995. text 42.00 (*0-19-823548-8*) OUP.

— The Act Itself. (Illus.). 248p. 1998. reprint ed. pap. text 19.95 (*0-19-823791-X*) OUP.

— Events & Their Names. LC 88-5261. 254p. (Orig.). (C). 1988. pap. text 16.95 (*0-87220-045-0*); lib. bdg. 37.95 (*0-87220-046-9*) Hackett Pub.

— Linguistic Behavior. LC 89-27985. 320p. (C). 1990. reprint ed. pap. 16.95 (*0-87220-092-2*); reprint ed. lib. bdg. 37.95 (*0-87220-093-0*) Hackett Pub.

— Locke, Berkeley, Hume: Central Themes. 372p. 1971. pap. text 26.00 (*0-19-875016-1*) OUP.

— Rationality: An Essay Towards an Analysis. LC 88-30267. 134p. (C). 1989. reprint ed. pap. 6.95 (*0-87220-066-3*); reprint ed. lib. bdg. 24.95 (*0-87220-067-1*) Hackett Pub.

— A Study of Spinoza's Ethics. LC 83-18568. 406p. (C). 1984. pap. text 16.95 (*0-915145-83-9*); lib. bdg. 37.95 (*0-915145-82-0*) Hackett Pub.

Bennett, Jonathan, ed. see Leibniz, Gottfried Wilhelm.

Bennett, Joseph A. Problems in Descriptive Geometry, Vol. 2. LC QA0501.B4. 61p. reprint ed. pap. 30.00 (*0-608-30416-6*, 200731900063) Bks Demand.

Bennett, Joseph E. Sixguns & Masons. (Illus.). 133p. 1991. 12.00 (*0-935633-12-X*) Anchor Comm.

Bennett, Joseph L. Boilermaker Music Makers: Al Stewart & the Purdue Musical Organizations. LC 86-61175. 182p. 1986. 19.95 (*0-931682-21-5*) Purdue U Pubns.

Bennett, Joseph T., jt. ed. see Dolan, Paul J.

Bennett, Josephine, tr. see Bebey, Francis.

Bennett, Josephine W., ed. see Shakespeare, William.

Bennett, Joshua M. The Gospel of the Great Spirit. LC 89-92667. (Illus.). (gr. 8 up). 1990. text 21.00 (*0-9625910-1-7*) Mornng Star Pub.

— The Writings of the Rabbis & Other Important Discoveries. LC 89-92668. (Illus.). (gr. 8 up). 1990. text 13.00 (*0-9625910-0-9*) Mornng Star Pub.

Bennett, Joy. Another Light. 35p. 1992. pap. write for info. (*0-9632649-0-7*) J Bennett.

— Attractions. 30p. (Orig.). 1992. pap. write for info. (*0-9632649-1-5*) J Bennett.

— Chronos. 20p. (Orig.). 1995. pap. 4.00 (*0-9632649-3-1*) J Bennett.

— Estrous. 60p. (Orig.). 1993. pap. write for info. (*0-9632649-2-3*) J Bennett.

— New Growth. 30p. 1998. pap. 5.00 (*0-9632649-4-X*) J Bennett.

***Bennett, Joy.** Water Wings. 30p. 2000. pap. 5.00 (*0-9632649-5-8*) J Bennett.

Bennett, Joy & Hochmann, Gabriella. Mary McCarthy: An Annotated Bibliography. LC 91-47702. 464p. 1992. text 15.00 (*0-8240-7028-3*, H#1251) Garland.

Bennett, Joyce, ed. see Kitov, Eliyahu, et al.

Bennett, Juda. The Passing Figure: Racial Confusion in Modern American Literature. 2nd ed. (Modern American Literature: Vol. 6). VIII, 142p. (C). 1998. reprint ed. pap. text 24.95 (*0-8204-4265-8*) P Lang Pubng.

Bennett, Judith. Sex Signs. 1990. mass mkt. 6.99 (*0-312-91597-7*) St Martin.

— Sex Signs. rev. ed. LC 96-44813. 368p. 1997. 24.95 (*0-312-15205-1*, Thomas Dunne) St Martin.

Bennett, Judith A. Wealth of the Solomons: A History of a Pacific Archipelago, 1800-1978. LC 86-16080. (Pacific Islands Monographs: No. 3). (Illus.). 544p. 1986. text 38.00 (*0-8248-1078-3*) UH Pr.

Bennett, Judith M. Ale, Beer & Brewsters in England: Women's Work in a Changing World, 1300-1600. LC 96-1271. (Illus.). 280p. 1996. text 49.95 (*0-19-507390-8*) OUP.

***Bennett, Judith M.** Ale, Beer & Brewsters in England, 1300-1600. (Illus.). 280p. 1999. pap. text 19.95 (*0-19-512650-5*) OUP.

Bennett, Judith M. A Medieval Life: Cecilia Penifader of Brigstock c. 1297-1344. LC 98-20580. 192p. 1999. pap. 12.25 (*0-07-290331-7*, McGrw-H College) McGrw-H Hghr Educ.

— Women in the Medieval English Countryside. 338p. (C). 1989. reprint ed. pap. text 23.95 (*0-19-504561-0*) OUP.

— Women in the Medieval English Countryside: Gender & Household in Brigstock Before the Plague. 336p. 1987. text 75.00 (*0-19-504094-5*) OUP.

Bennett, Judith M., ed. Single Women in the European Past - 1250-1800. LC 98-35172. 304p. 1998. 39.95 (*0-8122-3464-2*); pap. 16.50 (*0-8122-1668-7*) U of Pa Pr.

Bennett, Judith M., et al, eds. Sisters & Workers in the Middle Ages. 344p. 1989. pap. 17.50 (*0-226-04248-0*); lib. bdg. 36.00 (*0-226-04247-2*) U Ch Pr.

Bennett, Julian. Trajan, Optimus Princeps: A Life & Times. 1996. 39.95 (*0-253-33216-8*) Ind U Pr.

Bennett, Julienne & Luebbermann, Mimi, eds. Where the Heart Is: A Celebration of Home. LC 94-33971. (Illus.). 224p. (Orig.). 1995. pap. 14.00 (*1-885171-00-5*) Wldcat Canyon.

Bennett, Julienne, jt. auth. see Traeder, Tamara.

Bennett, Julius C. Of Men & Gods. LC 81-82234. 1982. 10.95 (*0-87212-149-6*) Libra.

Bennett, Justian. Trajan: Optimus Princeps: A Life & Times. LC 96-40044. (Roman Imperial Biographies Ser.). 352p. (C). 1997. write for info. (*0-415-16524-5*) Routledge.

Bennett, K. Air Filters: A Selection Guide. 1991. pap. 100.00 (*0-86022-290-X*, Pub. by Build Servs Info Assn) St Mut.

Bennett, K. Efficient Humidification in Buildings. 1995. pap. 100.00 (*0-86022-392-2*, Pub. by Build Servs Info Assn) St Mut.

Bennett, K. D. Evolution & Ecology: The Pace of Life. (Studies in Ecology). (Illus.). 256p. (C). 1996. text 69.95 (*0-521-39028-1*); pap. text 27.95 (*0-521-39921-1*) Cambridge U Pr.

Bennett, K. H. Software Engineering Environments: Research & Practice. (Information Technology Ser.). 1989. text 79.95 (*0-470-21521-6*) P-H.

Bennett, K. M. Humidification in Buildings. (C). 1994. pap. 80.00 (*0-86022-373-6*, Pub. by Build Servs Info Assn) St Mut.

Bennett, Kate. Adult Body Image. (C). 1991. 35.00 (*1-85041-035-6*, Pub. by Univ Nottingham) St Mut.

Bennett, Kathleen P. & LeCompte, Margaret D. The Way Schools Work: A Sociological Analysis of Education. Orig. Title: How Schools Work. 320p. (C). 1995. pap. text 23.95 (*0-685-73079-4*) Longman.

Bennett, Kathryn O. Colonel Sanchez Traditional Foods Cookbook. 113p. (Orig.). Date not set. pap. 9.95 (*0-89708-176-5*) And Bks.

Bennett, Katie B. Charity's Children: The Crowders of West Tennessee, 1772-1920. LC 98-70937. (Illus.). 218p. 1998. pap. 25.00 (*0-9649853-2-2*) R L Bennett.

— Soaking the Yule Log: Biographical Sketches of the Brown, Cheshier, Sain & Allied Families, 1749-1995. 542p. 1995. text 42.00 (*0-9649853-1-4*) R L Bennett.

Bennett, Kay D. Big Book of Indian Beadwork Designs. LC 98-52998. (Illus.). 64p. 1999. pap. 6.95 (*0-486-40283-5*) Dover.

Bennett, Kenneth A. A Field Guide for Human Skeletal Identification. 2nd ed. LC 93-14458. (Illus.). 124p. (C). 1993. spiral bd. 36.95 (*0-398-05884-9*) C C Thomas.

— The Indians of Point of Pines, Arizona: A Comparative Study of Their Physical Characteristics. LC 72-76616. (Anthropological Papers of the University of Arizona: No. 23). 83p. reprint ed. pap. 30.00 (*0-608-12775-2*, 202431600037) Bks Demand.

Bennett, Keree M. B. & Castiello, Umberto, eds. Insights into the Reach to Grasp Movement. LC 93-47507. (Advances in Psychology Ser.). 418p. 1994. 152.50 (*0-444-89931-6*, North Holland) Elsevier.

Bennett, Kevin, ed. see Ippongi, Bang.

Bennett, Kevin, tr. see Aro, Hiroshi.

Bennett, Kevin, tr. see Takachiho, Haruka.

Bennett, Kim D., et al, eds. Fiber Optic Sensors V, Vol. 2895. 598p. 1996. 102.00 (*0-8194-2296-7*) SPIE.

***Bennett, Kimberly A.** Jane Rochester. 256p. 2000. pap. 13.95 (*0-595-09184-9*, Writers Showcase) iUniversecom.

Bennett, L. Managing the Business Environment. (Illus.). 400p. 1997. mass mkt. 29.95 (*0-412-62920-8*) Chapman & Hall.

Bennett, L. A. & Ames, G. M. The American Experience with Alcohol: Contrasting Cultural Perspectives. LC 85-9302. (Illus.). 514p. (C). 1985. 102.00 (*0-306-41945-9*, Plenum Trade) Perseus Pubng.

Bennett, L. Don. The Philosophy of Numbers: Their Tone & Colors. 168p. 1996. reprint ed. pap. 13.95 (*1-56459-652-4*) Kessinger Pub.

Bennett, L. H., et al, eds. High Temperature Superconductors: Magnetic Interactions. 440p. (C). 1989. pap. 48.00 (*9971-5-0825-7*); text 125.00 (*9971-5-0820-6*) World Scientific Pub.

Bennett, L. H. & Waber, J. T., eds. Energy Bands in Metals & Alloys. LC 67-29668. (Metallurgical Society Conference Ser.: Vol. 45). 203p. reprint ed. pap. 63.00 (*0-608-11361-1*, 200153300079) Bks Demand.

Bennett, L. H. & Watson, R. E. Magnetic Multilayers. 300p. 1994. text 99.00 (*981-02-1767-6*) World Scientific Pub.

Bennett, L. H., ed. see Metallurgical Society of AIME Staff.

Bennett, Lance W. & Feldman, Martha S. Reconstructing Reality in the Courtroom: Justice & Judgment in American Culture. LC 81-5125. (Crime, Law & Deviance Ser.). 213p. 1981. reprint ed. pap. 66.10 (*0-7837-9213-1*, 204996300004) Bks Demand.

Bennett, LaRon D., Sr. The Million Man March: The Untold Story. Garcia, Katie, ed. LC 97-126601. 128p. (Orig.). 1996. pap. 10.95 (*0-9653831-0-5*) BHse Publng.

Bennett, Larry. Fragments of Cities: The New American Downtowns & Neighborhoods. LC 90-7434. (Urban Life & Landscape Ser.). 208p. 1990. text 42.50 (*0-8142-0524-0*) Ohio St U Pr.

— Multiprotocol Network Management: A Practical Guide to NetView for AIX. 288p. 1996. pap. 45.00 (*0-07-709122-1*) McGraw.

— Neighborhood Politics: Chicago & Sheffield. LC 97-17787. (Illus.). 288p. 1997. text 50.00 (*0-8153-2112-0*) Garland.

— Neighborhood Politics: Chicago & Sheffield. LC 97-17787. (Illus.). 288p. 1997. pap. text 21.95 (*0-8153-2113-9*) Garland.

Bennett, Larry, jt. ed. see Edsforth, Ronald W.

Bennett, Larry J., jt. auth. see Tyrrell, William B.

Bennett, Laura. Making Labour Law in Australia: Industrial Relations, Politics & Law. 1994. pap. write for info. (*0-455-21212-0*, Pub. by LawBk Co) Gaunt.

Bennett, Laura G. By All That Is Sacred. 400p. 1991. mass mkt. 4.99 (*0-380-76320-6*, Avon Bks) Morrow Avon.

Bennett, Lawrence A. Counseling in Correctional Environments. LC 77-21269. (New Vistas in Counseling Ser.: Vol. VI). 94p. 1978. 24.95 (*0-87705-319-7*, Kluwer Acad Hman Sci) Kluwer Academic.

Bennett, Legro. Life Is Change: Poems by Legro Bennett. 65p. 1995. mass mkt. 13.30 (*0-9644321-4-5*) Camel Dung Writ.

Bennett, Legro, jt. auth. see Clutter, Christopher L.

Bennett, Leonard S., et al. Preparation for Civil Service. 1980. pap. 4.95 (*0-87738-019-8*) Youth Ed.

— Review Workbook for Adult Education in Mathematics & English. 1980. pap. 7.50 (*0-87738-001-5*) Youth Ed.

***Bennett, Lerone, Jr.** Before the Mayflower: A History of Black America. LC 00-36530. (Illus.). 2000. write for info. (*0-87485-091-6*) Johnson Chicago.

Bennett, Lerone, Jr. Before the Mayflower: A History of Black America. 6th rev. ed. 720p. 1993. pap. 16.95 (*0-14-017822-8*, Penguin Bks) Viking Penguin.

— Forced into Glory: Abraham Lincoln's White Dream. LC 99-49496. 1999. 35.00 (*0-87485-085-1*) Johnson Chicago.

— Great Moments in Black History: Wade in the Water. LC 00-22120. 2000. 19.95 (*0-87485-078-9*) Johnson Chicago.

— Pioneers in Protest. LC 68-55366. 267p. 1968. 10.95 (*0-87485-026-6*) Johnson Chicago.

— The Shaping of Black America. LC 74-20659. 365p. 1975. 19.95 (*0-87485-071-1*) Johnson Chicago.

— The Shaping of Black America: The Struggles & Triumphs of African Americans, 1619-1990s. 368p. 1993. pap. 14.95 (*0-14-017568-7*, Penguin Bks) Viking Penguin.

— What Manner of Man? A Biography of Martin Luther King Jr, 1929-1968. LC 83-189238. (Illus.). 251p. 1968. 19.95 (*0-87485-027-4*) Johnson Chicago.

Bennett, Lerone, Jr., jt. auth. see Johnson, John H.

Bennett, Lerone, Jr., jt. auth. see Johnson, John J.

Bennett, Lerone, Jr., ed. see Ebony Editors.

Bennett, Linda. Managing the Business Environment. 380p. 1997. pap. 18.99 (*1-86152-176-6*) Thomson Learn.

Bennett, Linda A. Personal Choice in Ethnic Identity Maintenance: Serbs, Croats & Slovenes in Washington, D. C. LC 77-93261. 230p. 1978. pap. 10.00 (*0-918660-06-8*) Ragusan Pr.

Bennett, Linda L. Symbolic State Politics: Education Funding in Ohio, 1970-1980. LC 83-48760. (American University Studies: Political Science: Ser. X, Vol. 1). 164p. (C). 1983. pap. text 17.35 (*0-8204-0052-1*) P Lang Pubng.

Bennett, Linda L. & Bennett, Stephen E. Living with Leviathan: Americans Coming to Terms with Big Government. LC 90-39015. (Studies in Government & Public Policy). xvii, 192p. 1990. 29.95 (*0-7006-0432-4*); pap. 14.95 (*0-7006-0433-2*) U Pr of KS.

Bennett, Lisa. Beat the System! 1200 Tips for Coming Out on Top in Every Deal & Transaction. Bredenberg, Jeff, ed. LC 97-549. 544p. 1997. 27.95 (*0-87596-388-9*) Rodale Pr Inc.

Bennett, Liza. Madison Avenue Murder. 224p. (Orig.). 1989. spiral bd. 3.50 (*0-373-26016-4*) Harlequin Bks.

— Seventh Avenue Murder. 1990. mass mkt. 3.50 (*0-373-26041-5*) Harlequin Bks.

Bennett, Logan J. Training Grouse & Woodcock Dogs. (Illus.). 146p. 1989. reprint ed. 24.95 (*0-936075-17-1*) Gunnerman Pr.

Bennett, Lori J. Plug in the Sun. (J). (gr. 1-8). 1992. pap. 12.95 (*1-878347-20-9*) NL Assocs.

Bennett, Louise B., jt. auth. see Baum, Richard.

Bennett, Lydia. Deep Waters. 352p. 1995. 27.00 (*0-340-60073-X*, Pub. by Hodder & Stought Ltd) Trafalgar.

Bennett, Lydia & Miller, David. Health Workers & AIDS: Research, Intervention & Current Issues in Burnout & Response. LC 96-139391. 419p. 1995. text 60.00 (*3-7186-5659-0*, Harwood Acad Pubs) Gordon & Breach.

Bennett, Lydia, et al. Health Workers & AIDS: Research, Intervention & Current Issues in Burnout & Response. LC 96-139391. 419p. 1995. pap. text 30.00 (*3-7186-5660-4*, Harwood Acad Pubs) Gordon & Breach.

Bennett, Lynn & Goldberg, Mike. Providing Enterprise Development & Financial Services to Women: A Decade of Bank Experience in Asia. LC 93-21457. (Asia Technical Department Ser.: Vol. 236). 70p. 1993. pap. 22.00 (*0-8213-2682-1*, 12682) World Bank.

Bennett, M. Agincourt 1415. (Campaign Ser.: No. 9). (Illus.). 96p. pap. 14.95 (*1-85532-132-7*, 9508, Pub. by Ospry) Stackpole.

— Rolls-Royce: The History of the Car. LC 96-75167. (Illus.). 160p. 1996. 39.95 (*0-85429-972-6*, Pub. by GT Foulis) Haynes Manuals.

— Rolls-Royce & Bentley. (Illus.). 160p. 1998. 50.95 (*1-85960-441-2*, Pub. by J H Haynes & Co) Motorbooks Intl.

— Scottish Customs: From the Cradle to the Grave. 1992. 22.95 (*0-7486-6118-2*, Pub. by Polygon) Subterranean Co.

Bennett, M., et al. Handbook of Obstetrics & Gynecology. 4th ed. 496p. 1995. pap. text 24.99 (*0-412-58530-8*, Pub. by E A) OUP.

Bennett, M., jt. auth. see Gaskell, R. M.

Bennett, M. D., jt. auth. see Ryder, G. H.

Bennett, M. D., jt. ed. see Brandham, P. E.

Bennett, M. J. The Four Powers of Communication. (C). 1991. pap. text 25.50 (*0-07-557113-7*) McGraw.

Bennett, M. J. & Lorimer, G. W., eds. Microscopy of Oxidation: Proceedings of the International Conference Held at the University of Cambridge, UK. 428p. 1991. pap. 130.00 (*0-901462-90-X*, Pub. by Inst Materials) Ashgate Pub Co.

Bennett, M. J., jt. ed. see Newcomb, S. B.

Bennett, M. K. Affine & Projective Geometry. LC 94-44365. 248p. 1995. 94.95 (*0-471-11315-8*) Wiley.

— The World's Food: A Study of the Interrelations of World Populations, National Diets & Food Potentials. LC 75-26295. (World Food Supply Ser.). (Illus.). 1976. reprint ed. 25.95 (*0-405-07768-8*) Ayer.

Bennett, M. R., et al, eds. Geology on Your Doorstep: The Role of Urban Geology in Earth Heritage Conservation. (Illus.). 288p. 1996. 64.00 (*1-897799-54-3*, 351, Pub. by Geol Soc Pub Hse) AAPG.

Bennett, Madeline. Sudden Endings: Wife Rejection in Happy Marriages. 1991. 22.00 (*0-668-09428-1*, Arco) Macmillan Gen Ref.

Bennett, Madeline, jt. auth. see Bennett, Gary.

Bennett, Marcia J. Shadow Singer. 256p. (Orig.). 1984. mass mkt. 3.95 (*0-345-31776-9*, Ballantine) Ballantine Pub Grp.

Bennett, Mardi. Images of Long Ago: Photos, Postcards & "Pen Pictures from the Garden of the World": Los Gatos, Saratoga & Monte Sereno. 54p. (Orig.). 1987. pap. 10.98 (*0-9632682-0-1*) Marben Assocs.

Bennett, Mardi, ed. see Council History Task Force Staff & Sturrock, James P.

Bennett, Margaret. Biking for Grown Ups. 249p. reprint ed. 8.95 (*0-686-35966-6*) Sugarfree.

— Cross-Country Skiing for the Fun of It. 206p. reprint ed. 8.95 (*0-686-35965-8*) Sugarfree.

— Oatmeal & the Catechism: Scottish Gaelic Settlers in Quebec. 330p. 1998. pap. 66.00 (*0-85976-461-3*, Pub. by J Donald) St Mut.

— Oatmeal & the Catechism: Scottish Gaelic Settlers in Quebec. (Illus.). 352p. 1998. 65.00 (*0-7735-1810-X*) McG-Queens Univ Pr.

Bennett, Margie, jt. auth. see Wigginton, Eliot.

Bennett, Margo E. & Lumbert, David E. A. S. C. Tattoo Directory, 1996. (Illus.). 256p. (Orig.). 1996. pap. 15.95 (*1-887080-02-3*) Action Publ.

— A. S. C. Tattoo Directory, 1997. (Illus.). 288p. 1997. pap., per. 15.95 (*1-887080-03-1*) Action Publ.

— A. S. C. Tattoo Directory, 1999. (Illus.). 452p. 1999. pap. 15.95 (*1-887080-07-4*) Action Publ.

— A. S. C. Tattoo Directory, 1998. (Illus.). 358p. 1998. pap. 15.95 (*1-887080-04-X*) Action Publ.

***Bennett, Margo E. & Lumbert, David E.** A. S. C. Tattoo Directory, 2000: Tattoo Artists, Tattoo Studios, Conventions, Schools, Museums, Body Piercing, Henna, Vendors, Permanent Cosmetics - Worldwide. 7th ed. (Illus.). 552p. 2000. pap. 18.95 (*1-887080-09-0*) Action Pub.

— A. S. C. Tattoo Directory, 2001: Tattoo Artists, Tattoo Studios, Conventions, Schools, Museums, Body Piercing, Henna, Vendors & Permanent Cosmetics Worldwide. 8th ed. (Illus.). 662p. 2001. pap. 18.95 (*1-887080-10-4*) Action Pub.

Bennett, Margo E., jt. auth. see Lumbert, David E.

Bennett, Margot. The Man Who Didn't Fly. 200p. 1994. 19.50 (*0-7451-8624-6*, Black Dagger) Chivers N Amer.

Bennett, Marian. God Made Kittens. (Happy Day Bks.). (Illus.). 24p. (J). (ps). 1994. pap. 1.99 (*0-7847-0268-3*, 04218) Standard Pub.

***Bennett, Marian.** God Made Puppies. Derico, Laura, ed. (Illus.). 24p. (J). (ps-2). 2000. pap. 1.99 (*0-7847-1186-0*, 04336) Standard Pub.

Bennett, Marian. God Made Puppies. Beegle, Shirley, ed. (Happy Day Bks.). (Illus.). 24p. (J). (ps-3). 1994. reprint ed. pap. 1.99 (*0-7847-0256-X*, 04206) Standard Pub.

Bennett, Marian, ed. Growing in God's Love. (Children's Bible Study Ser.). (Illus.). 320p. (Orig.). (J). 1997. pap., teacher ed. 26.99 (*0-7847-0624-7*, 42036) Standard Pub.

Bennett, Marilyn. Texas Coastal Bend: A Visitor's Guide. (Illus.). 192p. (Orig.). 1992. pap. 12.95 (*0-89015-834-7*) Sunbelt Media.

***Bennett, Mark.** Developmental Psychology. LC 99-29808. 338p. 1999. 54.95 (*0-86377-577-2*) L Erlbaum Assocs.

An Asterisk (*) at the beginning of an entry indicates that the title is appearing for the first time.

— Developmental Psychology: Achievements & Prospects LC 99-29808. 1999. write for info. (*0-86377-578-0*, Pub. by Psychol Pr) Taylor & Francis.

Bennett, Mark. How to Live a Sitcom Life: A Guide to T. V. Etiquette. (Illus.). 240p. 1998. 23.95 (*1-57500-058-X*, Pub. by TV Bks) HarpC.

***Bennett, Mark.** TV Sets: Fantasy Blueprints of Classic TV Homes. (Illus.). 144p. 2000. 14.98 (*1-57912-107-1*, 81107) Blck Dog & Leventhal.

Bennett, Mark. TV Sets: Fantasy Blueprints of Classic TV Homes. LC 98-134899. 144p. 1999. pap. 14.95 (*1-57500-017-2*, Pub. by TV Bks) HarpC.

Bennett, Mark, ed. The Development of Social Cognition: The Child as Psychologist. LC 92-48513. 210p. 1993. pap. text 19.95 (*0-89862-597-1*) Guilford Pubns.

Bennett, Mark, jt. auth. see Hermann, Michele G.

Bennett, Mark W., et al. Employment Relationships: Law & Practice. LC 98-16007. 1000p. 1998. ring bd. 179.00 (*1-56706-376-4*, 63764) Aspen Law.

Bennett, Marnie. Colorado Event Sites & Services, Vol. 1. rev. ed. (Illus.). ii, 134p. (Orig.). 1996. pap. 24.00 (*0-9652394-0-3*) Event Lib.

Bennett, Martha. Home by Suppertime. (Illus.). 180p. 1991. 17.00 (*0-9630366-0-2*) Sweet Watermelon.

Bennett, Martin. Rolls-Royce & Bentley: The Crewe Years. (Illus.). 384p. 1995. 100.00 (*0-85429-908-4*, Pub. by J H Haynes & Co) Motorbooks Intl.

***Bennett, Martin.** Rolls-Royce & Bentley: The Crewe Years. 2nd ed. (Illus.). 368p. 1999. 100.00 (*1-85960-643-1*) Haynes Manuals.

Bennett, Martin, as told by. West African Trickster Tales. (Myths & Legends Ser.). (Illus.). 128p. (YA). (gr. 5-12). 1994. pap. 12.95 (*0-19-274172-1*) OUP.

Bennett, Martyn. Civil Wars Experienced: Britain & Ireland, 1638-1661. LC 99-33248. 224p. 1999. pap. 22.99 (*0-415-15902-4*) Routledge.

***Bennett, Martyn.** Civil Wars Experienced: Britain & Ireland, 1638-1661. LC 99-33248. 224p. (C). 2000. text 75.00 (*0-415-15901-6*) Routledge.

Bennett, Martyn. The Civil Wars in Britain & Ireland, 1638-1651. (Illus.). 384p. (C). 1996. 66.95 (*0-631-19154-2*); pap. 30.95 (*0-631-19155-0*) Blackwell Pubs.

— The Civil Wars, 1637-1653. Briggs, Asa, ed. LC 99-170513. (Pocket Histories Ser.). 128p. 1998. pap. 9.95 (*0-7509-1912-4*, Pub. by Sutton Pub Ltd) Intl Pubs Mktg.

— England Civl War Seminar. LC 94-46858. (Seminar Studies in History). 148p. (C). 1995. pap. text 14.06 (*0-582-35392-0*, Pub. by Addison-Wesley) Longman.

***Bennett, Martyn.** Historical Dictionary of the British & Irish Civil Wars, 1637-1660. Woronoff, Jon, ed. & frwd. by. LC 99-26024. (Historical Dictionaries of War, Revolution & Civil Unrest Ser.: No. 14). (Illus.). 352p. 1999. 65.00 (*0-8108-3661-0*) Scarecrow.

— Oliver Cromwell: A Biographical Companion. 2002. lib. bdg. 45.00 (*1-57607-145-6*) ABC-CLIO.

Bennett, Mary. Artists of the Pre-Raphaelite Circle: The First Generation. (Illus.). 240p. (C). 1988. pap. 45.00 (*0-85331-539-6*, Pub. by Lund Humphries) Antique Collect.

— An Iowa Album: A Photographic History, 1860-1920. LC 90-35493. (Bur Oak Original Ser.). (Illus.). 344p. 1990. 32.95 (*0-87745-253-9*) U of Iowa Pr.

Bennett, Mary & Juhl, Paul C. Iowa Stereographs: Three-Dimensional Visions of the Past. LC 97-24362. (Bur Oak Original Ser.). (Illus.). 392p. 1997. 34.95 (*0-87745-606-2*) U of Iowa Pr.

Bennett, Mary C. Commentary to the US-Netherlands Tax Convention. LC 94-15760. 1994. 185.00 (*90-6544-893-4*) Kluwer Law Intl.

Bennett, Mary J., jt. auth. see Simm, Betty B.

Bennett, Mary K. & Palmquist, Judy. Soft & Easy Exercise for Everyone: Recommended for Fibromyalgia & Osteoporosis. unabridged ed. (Illus.). 160p. (Orig.). 1997. pap. 19.95 (*0-9658619-0-2*) Fitness Is Busn.

Bennett, Mathew & Doyle, P., eds. Issues in Environmental Geology. 448p. 1998. 115.00 (*1-86239-014-2*, Pub. by Geol Soc Pub Hse) AAPG.

Bennett, Matthew. The Baby Journal. (Illus.). 36p. 1993. pap. 10.00 (*0-88166-200-3*) Meadowbrook.

— The Baby Journal. (Illus.). 1993. 10.00 (*0-671-86777-6*) S&S Trade.

— Lifestyles of the Trim & Healthy. (Illus.). 60p. 1994. pap. 5.95 (*0-9629502-9-7*) Conceivable Concepts.

— The Maternal Journal. (Illus.). 28p. 1992. pap. 10.00 (*0-88166-185-6*) Meadowbrook.

***Bennett, Matthew.** The Maternal Journal: Your Personal Pregnancy Guide. (Illus.). 28p. 1999. per. 10.00 (*0-671-31798-9*) S&S Trade.

Bennett, Matthew. Oracle Websystem 2.0 Unleashed. 600p. Date not set. pap. text 49.99 incl. cd-rom (*1-57521-179-3*) Sams.

— Tales of the East, Vol. 1. Dulfon, Alan & Richards, Roy, eds. (Illus.). 166p. (Orig.). 1994. pap. 9.95 (*1-884295-00-2*) Ananta Prnting.

Bennett, Matthew & Doyle, Peter. Environmental Geology: Geology & the Human Environment. LC 97-15135. 512p. 1998. pap. 44.95 (*0-471-97459-5*) Wiley.

Bennett, Matthew, jt. auth. see Doyle, Peter.

Bennett, Matthew, jt. auth. see Hooper, Nicholas.

Bennett, Matthew, jt. auth. see Hughes, Dewi.

Bennett, Matthew, jt. auth. see Parker, Don.

Bennett, Matthew, jt. ed. see Doyle, Peter.

Bennett, Matthew R. & Glasser, Neil F. Glacial Geology: Ice Sheets & Landforms. LC 95-46353. 376p. 1996. pap. 59.95 (*0-471-96345-3*) Wiley.

***Bennett, Maureen A.** Oliver & Audrey's Big Sand Box. (Oliver & Audrey Otter's Adventures Presents Ser.: Vol. 2). (Illus.). 46p. (J). (ps-6). 1998. pap. 14.95 (*1-929914-02-4*, Ruf-Fur Pubns) Megaverse.

— Oliver & Audrey's First Adventure. (Oliver & Audrey Otter's Adventures Presents Ser.: Vol. 1). (Illus.). 58p. (J). (ps-6). 1998. pap. 14.95 (*1-929914-01-6*, Ruf-Fur Pubns) Megaverse.

— The Wolf & the Whitetail. (Illus.). 72p. (YA). (gr. 7-12). 1999. pap. 5.95 (*1-929914-00-8*, Ruf-Fur Pubns) Megaverse.

Bennett, Max R. The Idea of Consciousness: Synapses & the Mind. 224p. 1997. text 48.00 (*90-5702-202-8*, Harwood Acad Pubs); pap. text 22.00 (*90-5702-203-6*, Harwood Acad Pubs) Gordon & Breach.

Bennett, Merit. Law & the Heart: A Practical Guide for Successful Lawyer/Client Relationships. 3rd rev. ed. LC 96-77235. 168p. 1996. pap. 14.95 (*1-57282-000-4*, D20004) Message NM.

Bennett, Michael. The Asbestos Racket. Arnold, Ron, ed. xii, 241p. 1991. pap. 9.95 (*0-939571-11-0*) Free Enter Pr.

— The Battle of Bosworth. 199p. 1993. pap. 19.95 (*0-312-10320-4*) St Martin.

***Bennett, Michael.** The Battle of Bosworth. 320p. 2000. pap. 16.95 (*0-7509-2461-6*) Sutton Publng.

Bennett, Michael. Discovering & Restoring Antique Furniture: A Practical Illustrated Guide for the Buyer & Restorer of Period Antique Furniture. (Illus.). 160p. 1996. pap. 19.95 (*0-304-34740-X*, Pub. by Cassell) Sterling.

— The Flaxseed Revolution: Nature's Source of Omega-3, Lignans & Fiber. LC 97-97083. (Illus.). 96p. 1998. pap. 11.95 (*1-891410-01-6*) Optimal HealthSpan.

— Richard II & the Revolution of 1339. 1999. 35.00 (*0-7509-2283-4*) Sutton Pub Ltd.

— Wild Yam - Nature's Source of Phytohormones. LC 97-92632. (Illus.). xii, 76p. 1997. pap. text 9.95 (*1-891410-00-8*) Optimal HealthSpan.

***Bennett, Michael & Dickerson, Vanessa D., eds.** Recovering the Black Female Body: Self-Representations by African American Women. LC 00-27657. (Illus.). 304p. (C). 2000. text 52.00 (*0-8135-2838-0*); pap. text 22.00 (*0-8135-2839-9*) Rutgers U Pr.

***Bennett, Michael & Teague, David, eds.** The Nature of Cities: Ecocriticism & Urban Environments. LC 99-6284. (Illus.). 312p. 1999. pap. 19.95 (*0-8165-1949-8*) U of Ariz Pr.

Bennett, Michael, et al. Elementary Algebra. (Illus.). 400p. 1985. pap. text 48.95 (*0-912675-12-8*); pap. text. write for info. (*0-912675-13-6*) Ardsley.

Bennett, Michael D. Hear It? I: (Musical Storms-Musical Battles) 20p. 1982. pap. 12.95 (*0-934019-05-3*) Memphis Musicraft.

— Hear It? II: (Classical Ensembles - Off-Beat Solo Insts.) 24p. 1982. pap. 12.95 (*0-934019-07-X*) Memphis Musicraft.

— Surviving in General Music I. 97p. (Orig.). 1979. pap. 9.95 (*0-934019-00-2*) Memphis Musicraft.

Bennett, Michael D., ed. see High, Linda R. & Kindt, Carol L.

Bennett, Michael D., ed. see Parker, Lisa A.

Bennett, Michael J. Belted Heroes & Bound Women: The Myth of the Homeric Warrior King. LC 96-30604. (Greek Studies: Interdisciplinary Approaches). 256p. (C). 1997. pap. text 22.25 (*0-8226-3061-3*); lib. bdg. 57.50 (*0-8226-3060-5*) Rowman.

— When Dreams Came True: The GI Bill & the Making of Modern America. 352p. 1996. 27.95 (*1-57488-041-1*) Brasseys.

***Bennett, Michael J.** When Dreams Come True: The GI Bill & the Making of Modern America. (Illus.). 1999. pap. 19.95 (*1-57488-218-X*) Brasseys.

Bennett, Michael J., ed. Ultrasound in Perinatal Care. LC 83-21632. (Wiley Series on Perinatal Practice: No. 1). (Illus.). 199p. reprint ed. pap. 61.70 (*0-8357-4546-5*, 203744500008) Bks Demand.

Bennett, Michael V., ed. Synaptic Transmission & Neuronal Interaction. fac. ed. LC 73-83886. (Society of General Physiologists Ser.: No. 28). (Illus.). 400p. pap. 124.00 (*0-7837-7532-6*, 204697200005) Bks Demand.

Bennett, Michael V. & Spray, David C., eds. Gap Junctions. LC 85-11329. 412p. 1985. 70.00 (*0-87969-187-5*) Cold Spring Harbor.

Bennett, Michele & Bennett, Barbara. Twenty-Two Texas Women: Strong, Tough & Independent. LC 95-37373. (Illus.). 120p. (J). (gr. 6-9). 1996. 14.95 (*1-57168-062-4*, Eakin Pr) Sunbelt Media.

Bennett, Michelle. Rejoice, O My Soul: Resources for a Self-Directed Retreat. LC 93-2303. 96p. 1993. pap. 9.95 (*0-8091-3408-X*) Paulist Pr.

Bennett, Mike. A Cordwainer Smith Checklist. (Booklet Ser.: No. 37). 28p. 1991. pap. text 3.00 (*0-936055-49-9*) C Drumm Bks.

Bennett, Mildred. The Autobiography of Mildred Bennett, the Early Years: The Winter Is Past. (Mellen Lives Ser.: Vol. 4). 150p. 1989. 69.95 (*0-88946-218-6*) E Mellen.

Bennett, Mildred R. Vanity Fair Notes. (Cliffs Notes Ser.). 80p. 1964. pap. 4.95 (*0-8220-1320-7*) IDG Bks.

— The World of Willa Cather. LC 94-44205. (Illus.). xvi, 304p. 1995. pap. 16.00 (*0-8032-5013-4*, Bison Books) U of Nebr Pr.

Bennett, Millard & Corrigan, John D. Successful Communications & Effective Speaking. 1976. pap. 4.95 (*0-13-860437-1*, Reward) P-H.

Bennett, Milly. On Her Own: Journalistic Adventures from San Francisco to the Chinese Revolution, 1917-1927. Grunfeld, A. Tom, ed. LC 92-39241. 384p. (gr. 13). 1993. text 66.95 (*0-87332-523-0*, East Gate Bk); pap. text 26.95 (*1-56324-182-X*, East Gate Bk) M E Sharpe.

Bennett, Milton J., ed. Basic Concepts of Intercultural Communication: Selected Readings. LC 98-15278. 270p. 1998. pap. text 22.95 (*1-877864-62-5*) Intercult Pr.

Bennett, Milton J., jt. auth. see Stewart, Edward C.

Bennett, Myra. Our Ancestors & Us. LC 98-72265. 1998. pap. 36.99 (*0-9666972-0-0*, OAAU-1) Intl Pub & Dist.

Bennett, N., et al. Teaching Through Play: Teachers Thinking & Classroom Practice. LC 96-19875. 160p. 1996. pap. 23.95 (*0-335-19732-9*) OpUniv Pr.

Bennett, Nancy & Bennett, Pearl. My ABC Book. (Illus.). 54p. (J). (ps-1). 1988. student ed. 12.00 (*0-9622242-0-0*) Red Baron Pub Co.

Bennett, Neil, jt. auth. see Li, Jiali.

Bennett, Neville. Managing Learning in the Primary Classroom. 32p. 1992. pap. 6.00 (*0-948080-74-4*, Trentham Bks) Stylus Pub VA.

***Bennett, Neville, et al.** Asian Students in New Zealand. LC 98-234172. 1998. write for info. (*0-908935-30-7*) Vict U Well IPS.

Bennett, Neville S. Teaching Styles & Pupil Progress. 203p. 1976. 26.95 (*0-674-87095-6*) HUP.

Bennett, Neville S. & Carre, Clive. Learning to Teach. LC 92-37257. 256p. (C). 1993. pap. 22.99 (*0-415-08310-9*, B0733) Routledge.

Bennett, Neville S., et al. The Quality of Pupil Learning Experiences. 272p. (C). 1984. 59.95 (*0-86377-010-X*) L Erlbaum Assocs.

***Bennett, Neville S., et al.** Skills Development in Higher Education & Employment LC 99-40907. 2000. pap. 37.95 (*0-335-20335-3*) Taylor & Francis.

Bennett, Neville S., jt. auth. see Dunne, Elizabeth.

***Bennett, Nicholas, ed.** The Register of Henry Burghersh, Bishop of Lincoln, 1320-1342: Institutions to Benefices in the Archdeaconries of Lincoln, Stow & Leicester. (Publications of the Lincoln Record Society: Vol. 0267-2634). 240p. 1999. 55.00 (*0-901503-64-9*, Lincoln Record Soc) Boydell & Brewer.

Bennett, Nigel. Managing Professional Teachers. 208p. 1996. text 29.95 (*1-85396-269-4*, Pub. by P Chapman) Taylor & Francis.

Bennett, Nigel & Elrod, P. N. Keeper of the King. LC 96-36663. 384p. 1997. 21.00 (*0-671-87759-3*, Starline NY) Baen Bks.

— Keeper of the King. 1998. per. 6.99 (*0-671-87862-X*) PB.

***Bennett, Nigel C. & Faulkes, Christopher G.** African Mole-Rats: Ecology & Eusociality. (Illus.). 287p. (C). 2000. 59.95 (*0-521-77199-4*) Cambridge U Pr.

***Bennett, Noel.** Genuine Navajo Rug: How to Tell. 2nd rev. ed. (Wild & Woolly West Ser.: No. 39). (Illus.). 36p. 2000. pap. 3.95 (*0-86541-054-2*) Filter.

Bennett, Noel. Navajo Weaving Way: The Path from Fleece to Rug. LC 97-11687. (Illus.). 160p. 1997. pap. text 19.95 (*1-883010-30-6*) Interweave.

Bennett, Noel, ed. see Bighorse, Tiana.

Bennett, Norman R. Africa & Europe from Roman Times to National Independence. 2nd ed. 160p. 1984. 34.95 (*0-8419-0900-8*, Africana); pap. 16.95 (*0-8419-0901-6*, Africana) Holmes & Meier.

— Arab Versus European: Diplomacy & War in Nineteenth-Century East Central Africa. 350p. 1986. 49.50 (*0-8419-0861-3*, Africana) Holmes & Meier.

Bennett, Norman R., ed. Discovering the African Past: Essays in Honor of Daniel F. McCall. (Boston University Papers on Africa: No. VIII). 150p. (Orig.). 1987. pap. 11.00 (*0-915118-14-9*) Boston U African.

Bennett, Olivia. A Family in Egypt. LC 84-19468. (Families the World Over Ser.). (Illus.). 32p. (J). (gr. 2-5). 1985. lib. bdg. 18.60 (*0-8225-1652-7*, Lerner Publctns) Lerner Pub.

***Bennett, Oscar H.** The Colored Garden. LC 99-56321. 264p. 2000. pap. 12.50 (*0-9659701-9-1*) Laughing Owl.

— The Colored Garden. (Illus.). 2000. pap. text. write for info. (*0-9659701-7-5*) Laughing Owl.

Bennett, P. Psychology & Health Promotion. LC 97-9042. 1997. pap. 28.95 (*0-335-19765-5*) OpUniv Pr.

Bennett, P. D., et al, eds. Aqueous Batteries. LC 97-137470. (Proceedings Ser.: Vol. 96-16). (Illus.). 248p. 1997. 54.00 (*1-56677-166-8*) Electrochem Soc.

Bennett, P. D. & Sakai, T. Hydrogen & Metal Hydride Batteries. (Proceedings Ser.: Vol. 94-27). 456p. 1995. 61.00 (*1-56677-086-6*) Electrochem Soc.

Bennett, P. D., et al. Marketing. 800p. (C). 1987. text 69.25 (*0-07-004721-9*) McGraw.

Bennett, P. R. & Moore, G. E. Molecular Biology for Obstetricians & Gynecologists. (Illus.). 192p. 1991. 75.00 (*0-632-02744-4*) Blackwell Sci.

***Bennett, Pam Johnson.** Litterbox Training: And Other Feline Hygiene Etiquette. (Laugh Your Way Through... Ser.). 1999. pap. text. write for info. (*1-889540-54-4*) Bowtie Press.

Bennett, Pamela J., ed. Progress after Statehood: A Book of Readings. 570p. 1974. 9.95 (*1-885323-26-3*); pap. 4.95 (*1-885323-27-1*) IN Hist Bureau.

Bennett, Patricia, jt. ed. see Jones, Donald G.

Bennett, Patrick. Rough & Rowdy Ways: The Life & Hard Times of Edward Anderson. LC 88-1151. (Tarleton State University Southwestern Studies in the Humanities: No. 4). (Illus.). 208p. 1988. 19.95 (*0-89096-352-5*) Tex A&M Univ Pr.

— Talking with Texas Writers: Twelve Interviews. LC 80-5516. (Illus.). 320p. 1980. 22.95 (*0-89096-099-2*) Tex A&M Univ Pr.

Bennett, Patrick R. Comparative Semitic Linguistics A Manual. LC 98-17772. 292p. 1998. pap. text 29.95 (*1-57506-021-3*) Eisenbrauns.

Bennett, Paul. Appalachian Mettle. LC 97-68167. 190p. 1997. pap. 15.95 (*1-886028-27-3*) Savage Pr.

— Breathing Well. LC 96-53555. (Bodyworks Ser.). (J). 1997. lib. bdg. 16.95 (*0-382-39777-0*) Silver Press.

— Breathing Well. LC 96-53555. (Bodyworks Ser.). (J). (gr. 2-5). 1997. pap. 5.95 (*0-382-39778-9*) Silver Press.

***Bennett, Paul.** Catching A Meal. (Illus.). 32p. (ps-4). 1999. 21.40 (*0-8172-5252-5*) Raintree Steck-V.

Bennett, Paul. Changing Shape. 1994. 21.39 (*0-8172-4894-3*) Raintree Steck-V.

— Earthquake. LC 98-39023. (World Reacts Ser.). (Illus.). 32p. (YA). (gr. 3 up). 1999. lib. bdg. 21.30 (*1-887068-44-9*) Smart Apple.

— Eating Healthy. LC 96-38127. (Bodyworks Ser.). (J). 1997. pap. 5.95 (*0-382-39780-0*) Silver Burdett Pr.

— Escaping from Enemies. (Nature's Secrets Ser.). (Illus.). 32p. (J). (gr. 1-5). 1995. lib. bdg. 21.40 (*1-56847-358-3*) Raintree Steck-V.

— The Eye of Reason. 1976. pap. 6.00 (*0-686-34441-3*) Orchard.

— Famine. LC 98-39025. (World Reacts Ser.). (Illus.). 32p. (YA). (gr. 3 up). 1999. lib. bdg. 21.30 (*1-887068-88-0*) Smart Apple.

— Flood. LC 98-31310. (World Reacts Ser.). (Illus.). 32p. (YA). (gr. 3 up). 1999. lib. bdg. 21.30 (*1-887068-89-9*) Smart Apple.

***Bennett, Paul.** Garden Lover's Guide to the Midwest. LC 99-50000. (Illus.). 192p. 2000. pap. 21.95 (*1-56898-165-1*) Princeton Arch.

Bennett, Paul. The Garden Lover's Guide to the Northeast. LC 98-53015. (Garden Lover's Guides Ser.). (Illus.). 150p. 1999. pap. 21.95 (*1-56898-163-5*) Princeton Arch.

***Bennett, Paul.** The Garden Lover's Guide to the South. (Garden Lover's Guide to the United States Ser.). (Illus.). 192p. 2000. pap. 21.95 (*1-56898-164-3*) Princeton Arch.

Bennett, Paul. Healthy Eating. (Bodyworks Ser.). 1997. 16.95 (*0-382-39779-7*) Silver Burdett Pr.

— Hibernation. (Nature's Secrets Ser.). (Illus.). 32p. (J). (gr. 1-5). 1994. lib. bdg. 21.40 (*0-8172-5251-7*) Raintree Steck-V.

***Bennett, Paul.** Introduction to Clinical Health Psychology. LC 00-37365. 2000. pap. write for info. (*0-335-20497-X*) Taylor & Francis.

Bennett, Paul. Keeping Clean. (Nature's Secrets Ser.). (Illus.). 32p. (J). (gr. 1-5). 1995. lib. bdg. 21.40 (*1-56847-359-1*) Raintree Steck-V.

— Keeping Fit. LC 96-45466. (Bodyworks Ser.). (J). 1997. pap. 5.95 (*0-382-39782-7*, Silver Pr NJ); lib. bdg. 12.95 (*0-382-39781-9*, Silver Pr NJ) Silver Burdett Pr.

— Living Things. 1975. pap. 6.00 (*0-686-18089-5*) Orchard.

— Migration. (Nature's Secrets Ser.). (Illus.). 32p. (J). (gr. 1-5). 1994. lib. bdg. 21.40 (*1-56847-209-9*) Raintree Steck-V.

— My Brain & Senses. LC 97-6028. (Bodyworks Ser.). (J). 1997. lib. bdg. 16.95 (*0-382-39783-5*) Silver Burdett Pr.

— My Brain & Senses. LC 97-6028. (Bodyworks Ser.). (J). (gr. 2-5). 1997. pap. 5.95 (*0-382-39784-3*) Silver Burdett Pr.

— Pollinating a Flower. (Nature's Secrets Ser.). (Illus.). 32p. (J). (gr. 1-5). 1994. lib. bdg. 21.40 (*1-56847-206-4*) Raintree Steck-V.

— Strange Affinity. 1975. pap. 6.00 (*0-318-04215-0*) Orchard.

— The Sun & What It Says Endlessly. 32p. 1995. pap. 7.95 (*0-944754-29-5*) Pudding Hse Pubns.

***Bennett, Paul.** Tale of a Waggish Dog: Max. LC 98-67051. 192p. 1999. pap. 12.95 (*1-878044-64-8*) Mayhaven Pub.

Bennett, Paul. War. LC 98-39021. (World Reacts Ser.). (Illus.). 32p. (YA). (gr. 3 up). 1999. lib. bdg. 21.30 (*1-887068-90-2*) Smart Apple.

— What Was It Like Before Electricity? LC 94-28575. (Read All about It Ser.). (Illus.). 32p. (J). 1995. lib. bdg. 5.00 (*0-8114-5734-6*) Raintree Steck-V.

Bennett, Paul & Murphy, Simon. Psychology & Health Promotion. LC 97-9042. 1997. 96.00 (*0-335-19766-3*) OpUniv Pr.

Bennett, Paul, et al. Current Developments in Health Psychology. 352p. 1990. text 95.00 (*3-7186-5064-9*, Harwood Acad Pubs) Gordon & Breach.

— Raising a Family. (Nature's Secrets Ser.). (Illus.). 32p. (J). (gr. 1-5). 1995. lib. bdg. 21.40 (*1-56847-361-3*) Raintree Steck-V.

Bennett, Paul A., ed. Books & Printing: A Treasury for Typophiles. LC 90-1009. (Illus.). 436p. 29.95 (*0-913720-72-0*) Beil.

***Bennett, Paul A., ed.** Books & Printing: A Treasury for Typophiles. LC 90-1009. (Illus.). 417p. 2000. pap. 19.95 (*1-929490-03-8*) Beil.

Bennett, Paul E. Advanced Circuit Analysis. (Illus.). 304p. (C). 1995. 79.95 (*0-15-501843-4*) OUP.

— Advanced Circuit Analysis. 685p. (C). 1992. text. write for info. (*0-318-69070-5*) SCP.

— Sardine Carriers & Seiners of the Maine Coast. LC 92-90763. (Illus.). 70p. 1992. 23.95 (*0-9632725-0-0*) P E Bennett.

Bennett, Paul J. Conference under the Tamarind Tree: Three Essays in Burmese History. LC 77-137999. (Monographs: No. 15). viii, 153p. 1971. 8.25 (*0-938692-14-3*) Yale U SE Asia.

— How to Build the Bootstrap Dinghy. 44p. 1999. pap. 15.00 (*0-9664280-1-3*) Shstrng Pubng.

Bennett, Paul P. & Clark, Velma R. The Art of Hungarian Cooking. 2nd rev. ed. (Illus.). 225p. 1997. pap. 11.95 (*0-7818-0586-4*) Hippocrene Bks.

Bennett, Paul R. Russian Negotiating Strategy: Analytic Case Studies from Salt & Start. 1997. lib. bdg. 65.00 (*1-56072-455-2*, Nova Kroshka Bks) Nova Sci Pubs.

— SALT II & the Soviet First-Strike Threat. (Pew Case Studies in International Affairs). 50p. (C). 1993. pap. text 3.50 (*1-56927-330-8*) Geo U Inst Dplmcy.

— The Soviet Union & Arms Control: Negotiating Strategy & Tactics. LC 89-8627. 201p. 1989. 57.95 (*0-275-93168-4*, C3168, Praeger Pubs) Greenwood.

***Bennett, Paul W.** Flying, a Look Back: A Chronicle of American Aviation over the Past 60 Years. LC 99-65853. (Illus.). 320p. 1999. 29.95 (*0-9674216-0-8*) Capitana.

Bennett, Paula. Emily Dickinson: Woman Poet. LC 90-70742. (Illus.). 237p. (C). 1991. pap. text 14.95 (*0-87745-310-1*) U of Iowa Pr.

Bennett, Paula & Rosario, Vernon, 2nd, eds. Solitary Pleasures: The Historical, Literary & Artistic Discourses of Autoeroticism. LC 95-22216. 288p. (C). (gr. 13). 1995. 80.00 (*0-415-91173-7*, C0240) Routledge.

Bennett, Paula & Rosario, Vernon A., 2nd, eds. Solitary Pleasures: The Historical, Literary & Artistic Discourses of Autoeroticism. LC 95-22216. 288p. (C). (gr. 13). 1995. pap. 20.99 (*0-415-91174-5*, C0243) Routledge.

Bennett, Paula B., ed. Nineteenth Century American Women Poets: An Anthology. LC 97-6863. (Blackwell Anthologies Ser.). 640p. 1997. 83.95 (*0-631-20398-2*); pap. 34.95 (*0-631-20399-0*) Blackwell Pubs.

Bennett, Pearl. My 1-2-3 Book. (Illus.). 12p. (Orig.). (J). (ps-1). 1990. student ed. 4.00 (*0-9622242-1-9*) Red Baron Pub Co.

Bennett, Pearl, jt. auth. see Bennett, Nancy.

Bennett, Peggy D. & Bartholomew, Douglas R. Songworks Vol. I: Singing in the Education of Children. LC 96-31776. (Music Ser.). (C). 1996. 60.95 (*0-534-51327-1*) Wadsworth Pub.

Bennett, Perry, et al. Thresholds No. 8: Viewing Culture. Bratton, Benjamin et al, eds. (Illus.). 124p. 1994. pap. 10.00 (*1-892751-02-X*) Thresholds.

Bennett, Peter. AMA Dictionary of Marketing Terms. 2nd ed. (Illus.). 898p. 1995. 39.95 (*0-8442-3598-9*, NTC Business Bks) NTC Contemp Pub Co.

— Path of Grace: Social Organization & Temple Worship in a Vaishnava Sect. (C). 1993. 24.00 (*81-7075-024-5*, Pub. by Hindustan) S Asia.

B

Bennett, Peter, ed. Good Clinical Practice & Ethics in European Drug Research. 1994. 49.95 (*0-86197-121-3*, Pub. by Bath Univ Pr) Intl Spec Bk.

— Plasmids. (C). 1997. text. write for info. (*0-582-10125-5*, Pub. by Addison-Wesley) Longman.

Bennett, Peter & Barrie, Steven. The 7-Day Detox Miracle: Restore Your Mind & Body's Natural Vitality with This Safe & Effective Life-Enhancing Program. 304p. 1998. per. 15.95 (*0-7615-1422-8*) Prima Pub.

Bennett, Peter & Calman, Kenneth, eds. Risk Communication & Public Health. LC 99-10437. (Illus.). 320p. 1999. text 42.50 (*0-19-263037-7*) OUP.

Bennett, Peter B., et al, eds. High Pressure Biology & Medicine: Essays Presented to the Fifth International Meeting on High Pressure Biology. LC 98-18397. 418p. 1998. 75.00 (*1-58046-033-X*) Univ Rochester Pr.

Bennett, Peter B. & Elliott, David H. The Physiology & Medicine of Diving. (Illus.). 613p. (C). 1993. pap. 84.00 (*0-941332-02-0*, D088) Best Pub Co.

Bennett, Peter B. & Elliott, David H., eds. The Physiology & Medicine of Diving. 4th ed. (Illus.). 624p. 1993. text 147.00 (*0-7020-1589-X*, Pub. by W B Saunders) Saunders.

Bennett, Peter B. & Marquis, Robert E., eds. Basic & Applied High Pressure Biology. LC 93-31570. (Illus.). 480p. (C). 1994. 75.00 (*1-878822-25-X*) Univ Rochester Pr.

Bennett, Peter G. Analysing Conflict & Its Resolution: Some Mathematical Contributions. (Institute of Mathematics & Its Applications Conference Series, New Ser.: New Series 8). (Illus.). 360p. 1987. text 65.00 (*0-19-853611-9*) OUP.

Bennett, Phil. Safety Aspects of Computer Control. 272p. 1993. text 135.00 (*0-7506-1102-2*) Buttrwrth-Heinemann.

Bennett, Philip & Runnalls, Graham, eds. The Editor & the Text. 224p. 1991. 45.00 (*0-7486-0154-6*, EU-1546, Pub. by Edinburgh U Pr) Col U Pr.

Bennett, Philip, tr. see Zumthor, Paul.

Bennett, Philip E., jt. ed. see Van Emden, Wolfgang.

Bennett, Phillip. Let Yourself Be Loved. LC 97-21394. (Illumination Bks.). 96p. (Orig.). 1997. pap. 5.95 (*0-8091-3736-4*, 3736-4) Paulist Pr.

Bennett, Phyllis. Our Perfect Example: Following God's Ways. (Knowing God Ser.). 64p. 1994. 5.99 (*0-310-48331-X*) Zondervan.

— Our Wise Counselor: Seeking God's Guidance. (Knowing God Ser.). 64p. 1994. 5.99 (*0-310-48311-5*) Zondervan.

Bennett, R. The Choral Singer's Handbook. 144p. 1984. per. 6.95 (*0-88188-468-5*, 8606) H Leonard.

— Form & Design. (Cambridge Assignments in Music Ser.). (Illus.). 72p. 1981. pap. text 10.95 (*0-521-29812-1*) Cambridge U Pr.

Bennett, R., jt. auth. see Bennett, G. H.

***Bennett, R. A.** Death Called at Night. large type ed. 304p. 1999. pap. 18.99 (*0-7089-5478-2*, Linford) Ulverscroft.

Bennett, R. A. Food for Faith. 1996. 7.99 (*1-85792-243-3*, Pub. by Christian Focus) Spring Arbor Dist.

— A Short Walk to Death. large type ed. 250p. 1996. pap. 18.99 (*1-85389-588-1*, Dales) Ulverscroft.

***Bennett, R. A.** Silence of Guilt. large type ed. 272p. 1999. pap. 18.99 (*0-7089-5604-1*, Linford) Ulverscroft.

Bennett, R. F., tr. see Tellenbach, Gerd.

Bennett, R. H., et al, eds. Microstructure of Fine-Grained Sediments: From Mud to Shale. (Frontiers of Sedimentary Geology Ser.). (Illus.). 624p. 1990. 190.00 (*0-387-97339-7*) Spr-Verlag.

Bennett, R. J. The Finance of Cities in West Germany. (Illus.). 62p. 1983. pap. 22.00 (*0-08-031462-7*, Pergamon Pr) Elsevier.

Bennett, R. J., ed. Decentralization, Local Governments & Markets: Towards a Post-Welfare Agenda. (Illus.). 432p. 1990. 79.00 (*0-19-828687-2*) OUP.

Bennett, R. J., jt. auth. see Wilson, Alan G.

Bennett, R. W. Eastman: The Puritan Ancestors in America of Georgia Ann Eastman (Mrs Wm Morris Bennett), b. Savannah, Ga., 1839 . . . d. Jacksonville, Fla., 1921. 132p. 1997. reprint ed. pap. 21.00 (*0-8328-8414-6*); reprint ed. lib. bdg. 31.00 (*0-8328-8413-8*) Higginson Bk Co.

***Bennett, Rab.** Under the Shadow of the Swastika: The Moral Dilemmas of Resistance & Collaboration in Hitler's Tyranny. LC 99-22569. 1999. text 40.00 (*0-8147-9860-8*) NYU Pr.

Bennett, Ralph. Scaffolder's Handbook: Design & Safety Standards for Stationary Scaffolds. 1993. 69.95 (*0-07-004736-7*) McGraw.

— Settlements in the Americas: Cross-Cultural Perspectives. LC 90-50411. (Illus.). 296p. 1993. 45.00 (*0-87413-411-0*) U Delaware Pr.

Bennett, Ralph F. Intelligence Investigations: How Ultra Changed History. LC 96-31397. (Studies in Intelligence Ser.). 216p. 1996. 47.50 (*0-7146-4742-X*, Pub. by F Cass Pubs); pap. 24.50 (*0-7146-4300-9*, Pub. by F Cass Pubs) Intl Spec Bk.

Bennett, Ralph K., jt. auth. see Pilon, Juliana G.

Bennett, Randall. Total 1-2-3. 1920. 34.75 (*0-13-925280-0*) P-H.

— The White Mountains. LC 95-172248. (Images of America Ser.). 1994. pap. 14.99 (*0-7524-0077-0*) Arcadia Publng.

Bennett, Randall H. A Fifield Genealogy: Some Descendants of William Fifield of Ipswich & Newbury, Massachusetts, & Hampton, New Hampshire. 200p. (Orig.). 1989. pap. text. write for info. (*0-9622736-0-0*) R H Bennett.

— Oxford County, Maine: A Guide to Its Historic Architecture. LC 84-62624. (Illus.). xxiv, 564p. (Orig.). 1987. pap. 18.00 (*0-9614460-0-5*) Oxford Co Hist.

Bennett, Randall H., ed. see Shirrefs, Herbert P.

Bennett, Randy & Ward, William C., eds. Construction Versus Choice in Cognitive Measurement: Issues in Constructed Response, Performance Testing, & Portfolio Assessment. 344p. 1993. text 69.95 (*0-8058-0964-3*) L Erlbaum Assocs.

Bennett, Randy E. & Maher, Charles A., eds. Emerging Perspectives on Assessment of Exceptional Children. LC 86-3128. (Special Services in the Schools Ser.: Vol. 2, Nos. 2 & 3). 193p. 1986. text 39.95 (*0-86656-410-1*) Haworth Pr.

— Microcomputers & Exceptional Children. LC 84-10784. (Special Services in the Schools Ser.: Vol. 1, No. 1). 113p. (C). 1984. text 39.95 (*0-86656-297-4*); pap. text 19.95 (*0-86656-440-3*) Haworth Pr.

Bennett, Randy E., jt. auth. see Maher, Charles A.

Bennett, Rebecca. Circle of Fire. large type ed. (Romance Ser.). 288p. 1994. pap. 16.99 (*0-7089-7538-0*) Ulverscroft.

— Echoes from the Sea. large type ed. (Rainbow Romances Ser.). 160p. 1994. pap. 14.95 (*0-7090-5399-1*, 917, Linford) Ulverscroft.

— Echoes from the Sea. large type ed. (Linford Romance Library). 240p. 1995. pap. 16.99 (*0-7089-7784-7*, Linford) Ulverscroft.

***Bennett, Rebecca.** Fate Holds My Destiny. large type ed. 248p. 1999. pap. 18.99 (*0-7089-5574-6*, Linford) Ulverscroft.

— Fiery Assignment. large type ed. 288p. 2000. pap. 18.99 (*0-7089-5647-5*, Linford) Ulverscroft.

Bennett, Rebecca. Rivals in Love. large type ed. (Linford Romance Library). 320p. 1995. pap. 16.99 (*0-7089-7672-7*, Linford) Ulverscroft.

— Veil of Guilt. large type ed. (Linford Romance Library). 240p. 1992. pap. 16.99 (*0-7089-7197-0*, Linford) Ulverscroft.

— Vision of Love. (Rainbow Romances Ser.: No. 898). 160p. 1994. 14.95 (*0-7090-4970-6*) Parkwest Pubns.

— Vision of Love. large type ed. LC 93-48429. 173p. 1994. lib. bdg. 16.95 (*0-8161-5953-X*, G K Hall Lrg Type) Mac Lib Ref.

***Bennett, Rebecca & Erin, Charles A., eds.** HIV & AIDS Testing, Screening, & Confidentiality: Ethics, Law, & Social Policy. (Issues in Biomedical Ethics Ser.). 302p. 1999. text 45.00 (*0-19-823801-0*) OUP.

Bennett, Reginald. The Mountains Look Down: A History of Chichester, a Company Town in the Catskills. Mosher, Howard Frank, ed. LC 99-12854. (Illus.). 151p. 1999. pap. 15.00 (*0-916346-69-2*) Purple Mnt Pr.

Bennett, Rejena. A Journal: From Survivor to Survivor/Your Journey of Conquest. LC 95-81115. 66p. (Orig.). (YA). (gr. 10-12). 1995. pap. 6.95 (*0-9649853-0-6*) R L Bennett.

***Bennett, Richard.** The Black & Tans. 232p. 2000. pap. 70.00 (*1-86227-098-8*, Pub. by Spellmnt Pubs) St Mut.

Bennett, Richard. Your Quest for God. 1996. 3.99 (*1-85792-216-6*, Pub. by Christian Focus) Spring Arbor Dist.

Bennett, Richard & Buckingham, Martin, eds. Far from Rome, Near to God. 362p. 1997. pap. 11.95 (*0-85151-733-1*) Banner of Truth.

Bennett, Richard A. Food for Faith: A Biblical Manual - Guidelines for a Consistent & Living Fellowship. 2nd rev. ed. LC 98-67798. 160p. 1998. pap. 9.95 (*1-57736-112-1*) Providence Hse.

— Food for Faith: A Biblical Manual, Guidelines for a Consistent & Living Fellowship with God. rev. ed. LC 94-60509. (Illus.). 128p. 1994. pap. 4.95 (*1-884704-00-X*) Trumpet Hse.

— Your Quest for God. 1998. pap. 9.95 (*1-57736-114-8*) Providence Hse.

— Your Quest for God: A Tool for Evangelism. 4th rev. ed. LC 98-67799. 160p. 1998. pap. 9.95 (*1-57736-113-X*) Providence Hse.

Bennett, Richard C. Second Opinion: A Holistic Approach to Treating Adults with A. D. D. 110p. 1994. pap. text 19.95 (*1-885988-00-1*) Add Resources.

Bennett, Richard D., jt. auth. see Hall, James W.

***Bennett, Richard E.** The Exodus As Reformation. (Leonard J. Arrington Mormon History Lecture Ser.: No. 3). 40p. 1998. pap. 5.95 (*0-87421-251-0*) Utah St U Pr.

Bennett, Richard E. We'll Find the Place: The Mormon Exodus, 1846-1848. LC 97-26740. xix, 428p. 1997. 19.95 (*1-57345-286-6*) Deseret Bk.

Bennett, Richard E., jt. ed. see McKee, David L.

Bennett, Richard M. The Truth Set Us Free: 20 Nuns Tell Their Story. LC 97-61892. 256p. 1997. pap. 12.95 (*1-57921-067-8*) WinePress Pub.

Bennett, Richard M., jt. auth. see Hicks, Granville.

Bennett, Richard R., ed. Police at Work: Policy Issues & Analysis. LC 82-23126. (Perspectives in Criminal Justice Ser.: No. 5). 168p. reprint ed. pap. 52.10 (*0-8357-8469-X*, 203473700091) Bks Demand.

***Bennett, Richard V.** Perseverance Pass. LC 99-97512. 2000. 24.95 (*0-533-13421-8*) Vantage.

***Bennett, Rick.** Destroying Angel: Air Aria from "Opera of the Blades" Gottlieb, Mark, tr. LC 00-103789. 432p. 2000. 30.00 (*0-9701026-1-5*) Gurus.

Bennett, Rita. To Heaven & Back: True Stories of Those Who Have Made the Journey. LC 97-14381. 208p. 1997. pap. 10.99 (*0-310-21078-X*) Zondervan.

Bennett, Rita. You Can Be Emotionally Free. LC 81-2117. 254p. 1998. reprint ed. pap. 10.99 (*0-88270-748-5*) Bridge-Logos.

Bennett, Rita & Bennett, Dennis. Trinidad del Hombre. Carrodeguas, andy, ed. Lievano, M. Francisco, tr. from SPA. Orig. Title: Trinity of Man. 224p. 1982. mass mkt. 4.50 (*0-8297-1298-4*) Vida Pubs.

Bennett, Rita, jt. auth. see Bennett, Dennis.

Bennett, Robert. The Official "Cooking Hot & Spicy Food with Beer" Cookbook. (Illus.). 82p. 1993. pap. 9.95 (*0-9638956-0-5*); disk 9.95 (*0-9638956-1-3*) R Bennett.

— Quotations from the Poems & Songs of Robert Burns. 42p. 1986. 25.00 (*0-7855-2033-3*, Pub. by Saltire Soc) St Mut.

— Raising Rabbits the Modern Way. LC 75-31601. (Illus.). 156p. 1983. pap. 9.95 (*0-88266-067-5*, Garden Way Pub) Storey Bks.

— Sun Angles for Design. LC 78-103157. 1978. pap. 20.00 (*0-9601718-1-9*) Melrose Plantation.

— Wrath of John Steinbeck. 1972. 59.95 (*0-8490-1337-2*) Gordon Pr.

— Wrath of John Steinbeck. LC 74-34402. (Studies in Fiction: No. 34). 1970. reprint ed. lib. bdg. 75.00 (*0-8383-0347-1*) M S G Haskell Hse.

***Bennett, Robert & Dodd, Christopher J., eds.** Investigating the Impact of the Year 2000 Problem: The United States Senate Special Committee on the Year 2000 Technology Problem. (Illus.). 163p. 1999. pap. text 35.00 (*0-7881-8168-8*) DIANE Pub.

Bennett, Robert A. The Bohemians: American Adventures from Bret Harte's Overland Monthly. 365p. 1987. pap. 10.95 (*0-936546-11-5*) Pioneer Pr Bks.

— Walla Walla: A Nice Place to Raise a Family, 1920 -1954. 200p. 1987. 24.95 (*0-936546-13-1*); pap. 16.95 (*0-936546-12-3*) Pioneer Pr Bks.

— Walla Walla: A Town Built to Be a City, 1900-1919. 232p. 1982. 21.95 (*0-936546-06-9*); pap. 14.95 (*0-936546-07-7*) Pioneer Pr Bks.

— Walla Walla: Portrait of a Western Town, 1804-1898. 180p. 1980. 21.95 (*0-936546-01-8*); pap. 14.95 (*0-936546-00-X*) Pioneer Pr Bks.

Bennett, Robert A., ed. A Small World of Our Own: Authentic Pioneer Stories of the Pacific Northwest from the Old Settlers Contest of 1892. 382p. 1985. pap. 10.95 (*0-936546-10-7*) Pioneer Pr Bks.

— We'll All Go Home in the Spring: Personal Accounts & Adventures As Told by the Pioneers of the West. LC 83-63182. 382p. 1984. pap. 10.95 (*0-936546-08-5*) Pioneer Pr Bks.

Bennett, Robert A. & Edwards, O. C. The Bible for Today's Church. (Church's Teaching Ser.: Vol. 2). 320p. 1982. 6.20 (*0-8164-0419-4*) Harper SF.

***Bennett, Robert B.** Romance & Reformation: The Erasmian Spirit of Shakespeare's "Measure for Measure" LC 99-39897. 192p. 2000. 36.00 (*0-87413-671-7*) U Delaware Pr.

Bennett, Robert E. Courtroom Procedures for Court Reporters: Syllabus. 1977. pap. text 7.95 (*0-89420-031-3*, 456010); audio 42.30 (*0-89420-137-9*, 456000) Natl Book.

***Bennett, Robert F.** Sandpounders: An Interpretation of the History of the United States Life-Saving Service, Based on Its Annual Reports for the Years 1870 Through 1914. 197p. 1999. per. 18.00 (*0-16-049749-3*) USGPO.

Bennett, Robert F. & Dodd, Christopher J. Senate Special Report on Y2K. 272p. 1999. pap. 9.99 (*0-7852-6851-0*) Nelson.

Bennett, Robert J. Central Grants to Local Governments: The Political & Economic Impact of the Rate Support Grant in England & Wales. LC 82-4378. (Cambridge Geographical Studies: No. 17). 365p. reprint ed. pap. 104.10 (*0-608-17573-0*, 2030581) Bks Demand.

Bennett, Robert J. & Chorley, R. J. Environmental Systems: Philosophy, Analysis, & Control. LC 78-55535. 636p. 1978. reprint ed. pap. 197.20 (*0-608-03313-8*, 206402500008) Bks Demand.

Bennett, Robert J. & Krebs, Gunter, eds. Local Business Taxes in Britain & Germany. 348p. 1988. 79.00 (*3-7890-1536-9*, Pub. by Nomos Verlags) Intl Bk Import.

Bennett, Robert J. & McCoshan, Andrew. Enterprise & Human Development: Local Capacity Building. 352p. 1993. 88.00 (*1-85396-212-0*, Pub. by P Chapman) Taylor & Francis.

Bennett, Robert L. Career Planning Guide for Earning & Learning. (Illus.). 60p. (Orig.). (C). 1982. pap. 3.50 (*0-936148-02-0*) Action Link.

— Earning & Learning. LC 80-65003. (Illus.). 256p. (Orig.). (C). 1980. pap. 7.95 (*0-936148-01-2*) Action Link.

Bennett, Robert L. & Bergmann, Barbara R. A Microsimulated Transactions Model of the United States Economy. LC 85-45049. 165p. reprint ed. pap. 51.20 (*0-7837-2193-5*, 204253100004) Bks Demand.

Bennett, Robert T. & Bennett, Catherine A. How to Get a Life: Turn Burnout & Blues into Bliss. large type ed. 360p. 1998. pap. 19.95 (*0-9601718-7-8*) Melrose Plantation.

— Retirement Handbook: A Complete Guide to Enjoying Life. 2nd large type rev. ed. 720p. 1998. ring bd. 49.95 (*0-9601718-3-5*) Melrose Plantation.

— Retirement Handbook: A Complete Guide to Enjoying Life. 3rd large type rev. ed. 360p. 1999. pap. 19.95 (*0-9601718-6-X*) Melrose Plantation.

— The Retirement Handbook: 1998 Edition. large type ed. LC 97-92557. (Retirement Handbook Ser.: No. 1). 720p. 1997. ring bd. 49.95 (*0-9601718-2-7*) Melrose Plantation.

Bennett, Robert T., jt. auth. see Bennett, Catherine A.

Bennett, Robert T., jt. ed. see Bennett, Catherine A.

***Bennett, Robin.** The Practical Guide to the Genetic Family History. LC 98-37273. 251p. 1999. pap. 49.95 (*0-471-25154-2*) Wiley.

Bennett, Rodney. The First Steps in Speech Training. 1973. text 1.50 (*0-686-09393-3*) Expression.

***Bennett, Roger.** Corporate Strategy. 2nd ed. (Frameworks Ser.). 416p. (Orig.). 1999. pap. 42.50 (*0-273-63430-5*, Pub. by F T P-H) Trans-Atl Phila.

Bennett, Roger. Corporate Strategy & Business Planning. 320p. (Orig.). 1995. pap. 44.50 (*0-273-63416-X*, Pub. by Pitman Pub) Trans-Atl Phila.

— Employee Relations. 2nd ed. vi, 295p. 1997. pap. 44.50 (*0-7121-1071-2*, Pub. by Pitman Pub) Trans-Atl Phila.

— Getting Started in Export. (Small Business Ser.). 1995. pap. 15.95 (*0-7494-1558-4*) Kogan Page Ltd.

— Heavenly Highway Hymns. 1996. 9.99 (*0-8341-9526-7*) Lillenas.

— International Marketing. 1997. pap. text 30.00 (*0-7494-1337-9*) Kogan Page Ltd.

— International Marketing: Strategy, Planning, Market Entry & Implementation. 2nd ed. 400p. 1998. pap. 30.00 (*0-7494-2272-6*) Kogan Page Ltd.

— Management. 3rd ed. 404p. 1997. pap. 47.50 (*0-7121-1068-2*, Pub. by Pitman Pub) Trans-Atl Phila.

— Organisational Behaviour. 3rd ed. 310p. 1994. pap. 44.50 (*0-273-63424-0*, Pub. by Pitman Pub) St Mut.

Bennett, Roger & Prescott, Kate. European Business: An Issue-Based Approach. 2nd ed. 1996. pap. 42.50 (*0-7121-1059-3*, Pub. by Pitman Pub) St Mut.

Bennett, Roger, jt. auth. see Graham, H. T.

Bennett, Roger, ed. see Donne, John.

Bennett, Roger, ed. see Pont, Tony.

Bennett, Ronan. The Catastrophist. LC 99-26906. 336p. 1999. 23.50 (*0-684-86334-0*) S&S Trade.

***Bennett, Ronan.** The Catastrophist: A Novel. 336p. 2000. pap. 13.00 (*0-684-87036-3*) Scribner.

Bennett, Ross, ed. Visiting Our Past: America's Historylands. rev. ed. (Illus.). 400p. 1986. 27.95 (*0-87044-647-9*) Natl Geog.

Bennett, Roy. Music Dictionary. 414p. (C). 1996. pap. 23.95 (*0-521-56930-3*) Cambridge U Pr.

— Opera. (Illus.). 48p. (C). 1996. pap. 10.95 (*0-521-56935-4*) Cambridge U Pr.

Bennett, Russell H. Quest for Ore. fac. ed. LC 63-14391. (Illus.). 422p. 1963. reprint ed. pap. 130.90 (*0-7837-7843-0*, 204760200007) Bks Demand.

Bennett, Ruth. 1997 AEE Energy & Environment Industry Survey. LC 97-188601. 424p. (C). 1997. pap. text 95.00 (*0-13-762155-8*) P-H.

Bennett, Ruth, et al, eds. Coordinated Service Delivery Systems for the Elderly: New Approaches for Care & Referral in New York State. LC 83-13041. (Advanced Models & Practice in Aged Care Ser.: No. 2). 198p. 1984. text 39.95 (*0-86656-157-9*) Haworth Pr.

Bennett, Ruth & Fairmont Press Staff. AEE Energy & Environmental Industry Survey '96. 134p. (C). 1996. pap. text 95.00 (*0-13-264508-4*) P-H.

Bennett, Ruth, jt. auth. see Bennett, Steve.

Bennett, Ruth M. 1995 AEE Energy & Environmental Industry Survey. LC 95-60080. 128p. 1995. pap. 200.00 (*0-88173-220-6*) Fairmont Pr.

Bennett, Ruth M., ed. Energy & Environmental Industry Survey, 1997. LC 97-188601. 344p. 1997. pap. 105.00 (*0-88173-281-8*) Fairmont Pr.

Bennett, S. History of Control Engineering, 1800-1930. (Control Engineering Ser.: No. 8). (Illus.). 224p. 1986. reprint ed. pap. 39.00 (*0-86341-047-2*, CE008) INSPEC Inc.

— A History of Control Engineering, 1930-1955. (Control Engineering Ser.: No. 47). xii, 252p. 1993. pap. 48.00 (*0-86341-299-8*, CE047Z); boxed set 85.00 (*0-86341-280-7*, CE047) INSPEC Inc.

Bennett, S., ed. Optics Eighty-Four, Vol. 32, No. 2. (Journal of Modern Optics Ser.). 1985. 55.00 (*0-85066-956-1*) Taylor & Francis.

Bennett, S. & Virk, G. S., eds. Computer Control of Real-Time Processes. (Control Engineering Ser.: No. 41). 1990. 95.00 (*0-86341-220-3*, CE041) INSPEC Inc.

Bennett, S. A. How to Write for Comic Books! (World of Cartooning Ser.). (Illus.). 64p. 1992. 16.95 (*0-944099-22-X*) Comic Art.

— A Parent's Guide to . . . the World of Comic Books. (World of Cartooning Ser.). (Illus.). 64p. 16.95 (*0-944099-23-8*) Comic Art.

Bennett, S. A., ed. see Barry, Bill.

Bennett, S. A., ed. see Doyle, Arthur Conan.

Bennett, S. A., ed. see Singer, Bob.

Bennett, S. A., ed. see Stoker, Bram.

An Asterisk (*) at the beginning of an entry indicates that the title is appearing for the first time.

Bennett, S. B. Bennett, Bently & Beers Families (Of N. Y.) (Illus.). 50p. 1997. reprint ed. pap. 10.00 (*0-8328-7493-0*); reprint ed. lib. bdg. 20.00 (*0-8328-7492-2*) Higginson Bk Co.

Bennett, S. Christopher. Pterosaurs: The Flying Reptiles. LC 93-29845. (Prehistoric Life Ser.). (Illus.). 64p. (J). (gr. 5-7). 1995. lib. bdg. 24.00 (*0-531-11181-4*) Watts.

Bennett, S. G., jt. auth. see Pratt, K. J.

***Bennett, S. W. & O'Neale, K., eds.** Progressive Development of Practical Skills in Chemistry: A Guide to Early-Undergraduate Experimental Work. 186p. 1999. pap. 29.95 (*0-85404-950-9*, Pub. by Royal Soc Chem) Spr-Verlag.

Bennett, Sally. Sixty Is Just Extreme Middle Age: And Other Absurdities. (Illus.). 64p. (Orig.). 1993. pap. text 6.95 (*0-9636600-0-4*) Twiga Pub.

Bennett, Sandy & Sullivan, Tom J. Wildflower Safaris by Car: A Unique Guide to Minnesota's North Shore & the Superior National Forest. Bissell, Beryl S., ed. (Illus.). 149p. 1999. 19.95 (*0-9671442-0-5*) Arctic Riviera.

Bennett, Sanford. Old Age: Its Cause & Prevention. 394p. 1996. reprint ed. spiral bd. 26.00 (*0-7873-0092-6*) Hlth Research.

Bennett, Sara, et al. Private Health Providers in Developing Countries: Serving the Public Interest? LC 97-6650. 1997. write for info. (*1-85649-495-0*); pap. 25.00 (*1-85649-496-9*) Humanities.

Bennett, Sarah L. The Mountain Biker's Guide to New Mexico. LC 93-46387. (Mountain Bike Ser.). 245p. (Orig.). 1994. pap. 14.95 (*1-56044-219-0*) Falcon Pub Inc.

— Mountain Biking Arizona. LC 97-1713. (America by Mountain Bike Ser.). (Illus.). 229p. 1996. pap. 12.95 (*1-56044-431-2*) Falcon Pub Inc.

***Bennett, Saul.** Harpo Marx at Prayer. 2000. pap. text 14.00 (*0-9662299-6-7*) Archer Books.

Bennett, Saul. Jesus Matinees: And Other Poems. 30p. 1998. pap. 7.95 (*0-944754-52-X*) Pudding Hse Pubns.

— New Fields & Other Stones: On a Child's Death. LC 98-70021. 97p. 1998. 19.95 (*0-9662299-0-8*) Archer Books.

Bennett, Saxon. Both Sides. LC 98-46300. 192p. 1999. pap. 11.95 (*1-56280-236-4*) Naiad Pr.

— Old Ties. LC 96-39471. 208p. (Orig.). 1997. pap. 11.95 (*1-56280-159-7*) Naiad Pr.

— A Question of Love. LC 97-40428. 240p. 1998. pap. 11.95 (*1-56280-205-4*) Naiad Pr.

***Bennett, Saxon.** Sweet Fire. 2000. pap. 11.95 (*0-9677753-5-3*) Bella Bks.

Bennett, Saxon. The Wish List. 224p. 1996. pap. 10.95 (*1-56280-125-2*) Naiad Pr.

Bennett, Scott. Public Affairs Research Methods: A Quantitative Introduction. LC 96-26631. 392p. 1996. text 99.95 (*0-7734-8770-0*) E Mellen.

— The Quantitative Approach in Political Science: An Introduction. 376p. 1986. lib. bdg. 99.95 (*0-88946-205-4*) E Mellen.

— Winning & Losing: Australian National Elections. LC 96-216333. 160p. 1996. pap. 24.95 (*0-522-84506-1*, Pub. by Melbourne Univ Pr) Paul & Co Pubs.

Bennett, Scott, ed. Technology & Work in Canada. LC 90-31082. (Canadian Studies: Vol. 8). 324p. 1990. lib. bdg. 99.95 (*0-88946-213-5*) E Mellen.

Bennett, Scotty. Bob Marley. LC 99-203417. 1998. text 9.95 (*0-312-17937-5*) St Martin.

Bennett, Shari, jt. auth. see Bean, Barbara.

***Bennett, Simone.** Drummers. (Nick Hern Bks.). 2000. pap. 14.95 (*1-85459-457-5*) Theatre Comm.

Bennett, Siy, et al. Blueprint Reading for Welders. 6th ed. LC 98-24070. 384p. 1998. 46.95 (*0-7668-0852-1*) Delmar.

Bennett, Sophie, tr. see Barakat, Hoda.

Bennett, Sophie, tr. see Zayyat, Latifa.

Bennett, Stephanie. Strip Search: Revealing Today's Best College Cartoonists. LC 98-88678. 1999. pap. text 9.95 (*0-8362-8343-0*) Andrews & McMeel.

Bennett, Stephanie & Hall, Amy. Postcards from the '80s: 80 Lists to Remember. LC 98-53692. 1999. 10.95 (*0-8362-9270-7*) Andrews & McMeel.

Bennett, Stephen. Fast Guide to Emagic Logic. 1999. pap. text 22.95 (*1-870775-55-4*) Cimothas Pub.

Bennett, Stephen E. Apathy in America, 1960-1984: Causes & Consequences of Citizen Political Indifference. 208p. (C). 1986. text 39.50 (*0-941320-39-1*) Transnatl Pubs.

Bennett, Stephen E., jt. auth. see Bennett, Linda L.

Bennett, Stephen E., jt. ed. see Craig, Stephen C.

Bennett, Stephen J., jt. auth. see Frangos, Stephen J.

Bennett, Stephen R., ed. see Aro, Hiroshi.

Bennett, Stephen R., ed. see Hirano, Toshihiro.

Bennett, Stephen R., ed. see Ippongi, Bang.

Bennett, Stephen R., ed. see Kirano, Toshihiro.

Bennett, Stephen R., IV, ed. see Takachiho, Haruka.

Bennett, Steve. The Plugged-In Parent: What You Should Know about Kids, Computers, & Technology. LC 98-9514. 1998. pap. 15.00 (*0-8129-6378-4*) Random.

Bennett, Steve & Bennett, Ruth. Parenting in the Electronic Age: What Every Parent Needs to Know about Safe, Sensible, Purposeful Computing. 1997. 22.00 (*0-679-44856-X*) Random.

— Three Hundred Sixty-Five Outdoor Activities You Can Do with Your Child. 480p. 1993. pap. 6.95 (*1-55850-260-2*) Adams Media.

— 365 TV-Free Activities You Can Do with Your Child. 2nd ed. (Illus.). 480p. 1996. pap. 7.95 (*1-55850-585-7*) Adams Media.

Bennett, Steve J. The Portable Businessaurus: A Treasury of Insight, Wit & Wisdom from Tomorrow's Captians of Industry. (Illus.). 96p. 1998. pap. 7.95 (*1-886284-29-6*, Pub. by Chandler Hse) Natl Bk Netwk.

Bennett, Steven J. & Wallace, Thomas F. World Class Manufacturing. LC 93-60672. 350p. 1994. 81.00 (*0-939246-42-2*) Wiley.

Bennett, Stuart. Real Time Computer Control: An Introduction. 2nd ed. 432p. 1994. pap. 82.00 (*0-13-764176-1*) P-H.

***Bennett, Sue.** Women & Gardens, 1590s-1990s. (Illus.). 176p. 2000. 30.00 (*1-85514-288-0*, Pub. by Natl Port Gall) Antique Collect.

Bennett, Sue, jt. auth. see Runnings, John.

Bennett, Susan. Neurological Disabilities: Assessment & Treatment. LC 97-52018. 400p. 1998. text 39.95 (*0-397-55151-7*) Lppncott W & W.

— Performing Nostalgia: Shifting Shakespeare & the Contemporary Past. LC 95-8574. 208p. (C). 1995. pap. 25.99 (*0-415-07326-X*) Routledge.

— Performing Nostalgia: Shifting Shakespeare & the Contemporary Past. LC 95-8574. 208p. (C). (gr. 13). 1995. 90.00 (*0-415-07325-1*) Routledge.

— Theatre Audiences: A Theory of Production & Reception. 2nd ed. LC 97-11461. 264p. (C). 1997. 75.00 (*0-415-15722-6*); pap. 24.99 (*0-415-15723-4*) Routledge.

Bennett, Susan, jt. auth. see Collie, Michael.

Bennett, Susan, tr. see Heym, Georg.

Bennett, Suzanne, jt. auth. see Peterson, Jane T.

Bennett, Swannee. The Likeness Trade: Portrait Painting in Arkansas, 1780-1900. (Illus.). 20p. (Orig.). 1996. pap. write for info. (*0-9651500-0-3*) AR Territorial.

Bennett, Swannee & Worthen, William B. Arkansas Made: A Survey of the Decorative, Mechanical, & Fine Arts Produced in Arkansas, 1819-1870, Vol. II. LC 89-20508. 229p. 1991. pap. 40.00 (*1-55728-184-X*); text 55.00 (*1-55728-183-1*) U of Ark Pr.

Bennett, T., jt. auth. see Gass, Tyler E.

Bennett, T. J., et al, eds. Emerging Technologies: Proceedings of the ASME International Mechanical Engineering Congress & Exposition, San Francisco, CA, 1995. LC 95-81281. (1995 ASME International Mechanical Engineering Congress & Exposition Ser.). 104p. 1995. 48.00 (*0-7918-1745-8*, I00386) ASME.

Bennett, T. J., jt. ed. see Lee, Y. C.

Bennett, T. L. The Neuropsychology of Epilepsy. (Critical Issues in Neuropsychology Ser.). (Illus.). 336p. (C). 1992. text 54.50 (*0-306-43948-4*, Kluwer Plenum) Kluwer Academic.

Bennett, T. W. Human Rights & African Customary Law. LC 96-172966. 174p. 1995. pap. 36.50 (*0-7021-3544-5*, Pub. by Juta & Co) Gaunt.

***Bennett, T. W.** Human Rights & African Customary Law. 215p. 2000. pap. 41.00 (*0-7021-5095-9*, Pub. by Juta & Co) Gaunt.

Bennett, T. W. Sourcebook of African Customary Law for Southern Africa. 462p. 1991. pap. 40.00 (*0-7021-2546-6*, Pub. by Juta & Co) Gaunt.

Bennett, T. W., et al, eds. Acta Juridica. 1992. write for info. (*0-7021-2919-4*, Pub. by Juta & Co) Gaunt.

Bennett-Talbot, Betty. Games on Horseback. LC 98-55400. 144p. 1999. pap. 19.95 (*1-58017-134-6*) Storey Bks.

Bennett, Terry. Korea: Caught in Time. LC 98-191905. (Illus.). 160p. 1998. 37.50 (*1-85964-109-1*, Pub. by Garnet-Ithaca) LPC InBook.

Bennett, Terry. The Man Who Once Was & Now Is. pap. write for info. (*0-9667720-1-6*) Emmanuel Found.

Bennett, Terry & Gardiner, Sheila. Nervous Control of Blood Vessels. (Autonomic Nervous System Ser.). 592p. 1996. text 90.00 (*3-7186-5139-4*, Harwood Acad Pubs) Gordon & Breach.

Bennett, Terry, jt. intro. see Cortazzi, Hugh.

Bennett, Tess, et al. Developing Individualized Family Support Plans. 240p. 1990. pap. text 24.95 (*0-914797-69-7*) Brookline Bks.

Bennett, Thomas G. A Health Program for the Children of a County. LC 77-176555. (Columbia University. Teachers College. Contributions to Education Ser.: No. 584). reprint ed. 37.50 (*0-404-55584-5*) AMS Pr.

Bennett, Thomas L., ed. Readings in the Psychology of Perception. 179p. (C). 1971. pap. text 11.95 (*0-8422-0160-2*) Irvington.

— Readings in the Psychology of Perception. 2nd ed. 1973. pap. text 9.95 (*0-685-48425-4*, 0-8422-0325) Irvington.

Bennett, Thomas L. & Raymond, Michael J., eds. Mild Brain Injury: A Special Issue of "Applied Neuropsychology" 83p. 1997. pap. write for info. (*0-8058-9868-9*) L Erlbaum Assocs.

Bennett, Thomas R. Learning to Be Human in A Push-Button World. LC 70-146631. 96p. 1971. write for info. (*0-377-91101-1*) Friendship Pr.

***Bennett, Tina K.** Feng Shui Candle Lighting. 206p. 1999. pap. 18.99 (*0-9621143-0-8*, 2500, Pub. by T Ketch-Bennett) New Leaf Dist.

Bennett, Tom. State of the Great Lakes: 1997 Annual Report. Waszak, Martha, ed. (Illus.). 44p. (C). 1999. pap. text 15.00 (*0-7881-4358-1*) DIANE Pub.

Bennett, Tony. Formalism & Marxism. (New Accents Ser.). 1979. pap. 12.95 (*0-416-70880-3*, NO. 2047) Routledge.

— Good Life: The Autobiography of Tony Bennett. 1998. 25.00 (*0-684-85872-X*) S&S Trade.

— Outside Literature. 320p. (C). 1990. pap. 24.99 (*0-415-01094-2*, A4848) Routledge.

— Show & Tell. LC 94-12936. (Culture Ser.). (Illus.). 320p. (C). (gr. 13). 1995. pap. 24.99 (*0-415-05388-9*, C0144) Routledge.

— Tony Bennett: What My Heart Has Seen. LC 96-7913. (Illus.). 151p. 1996. 40.00 (*0-8478-1972-8*, Pub. by Rizzoli Intl) St Martin.

Bennett, Tony, et al, eds. Rock & Popular Music: Politics, Policies, Institutions. LC 93-20233. (Culture Ser.). (C). 1993. pap. write for info. (*0-415-06362-0*) Routledge.

— Rock & Popular Music: Politics, Policies, Institutions. LC 93-20233. (Culture Ser.). 320p. (C). 1993. pap. 25.99 (*0-415-06369-8*) Routledge.

Bennett, Tony & Friedwald, Will. The Good Life: An Autobiography of Tony Bennett. (Illus.). 384p. 1998. 25.00 (*0-671-02469-8*) PB.

Bennett, Tony & Woollacott, Janet. Bond & Beyond: The Political Career of a Popular Hero. 256p. 1986. pap. 13.95 (*0-416-01361-9*, 9887); text 35.00 (*0-416-01351-1*, 9901) Routledge.

***Bennett, Tony, et al.** Accounting for Tastes: Australian Everyday Cultures. LC 99-31121. (Illus.). 320p. 1999. 64.95 (*0-521-63234-X*); pap. 24.95 (*0-521-63504-7*) Cambridge U Pr.

Bennett, Tony, et al. Popular Culture & Social Relations. 224p. 1986. pap. 34.95 (*0-335-15107-8*) OpUniv Pr.

Bennett, Tonya, jt. auth. see Bennett, Jeff.

Bennett, Trevor & Wright, Richard T. Burglars on Burglary: Prevention & the Offender. LC 84-13575. 197p. 1984. text 61.95 (*0-566-00756-8*) Ashgate Pub Co.

Bennett, Trevor, jt. auth. see Graham, John.

Bennett, Trevor, jt. auth. see Taylor, Bruce.

Bennett, Trude, jt. auth. see Braveman, Paula.

Bennett, Trude, jt. auth. see Hill, Ian T.

Bennett, V. Ruth & Brown, Linda K., eds. Myles Textbook for Midwives. 12th ed. LC 93-3748. 876p. 1993. pap. text 55.95 (*0-443-04581-X*) Church.

Bennett, Valerie P., jt. auth. see Perlmutter, Amos.

Bennett, Vicki. Mirrors. 119p. (C). 1990. pap. 60.00 (*0-86439-146-3*, Pub. by Boolarong Pubns) St Mut.

Bennett, Vicki A. Keeper of the Fire. 144p. 1998. pap. 16.50 (*0-9668529-0-7*) Earthlght.

***Bennett, Virginia.** A UFO Primer. (Fringe Ser.: Vol. 1). (Illus.). 96p. 2000. pap. 7.95 (*1-57951-020-5*, Pub. by Ronin Pub) Publishers Group.

Bennett, Virginia, tr. see Landa, L. N.

Bennett, Vivienne. The Politics of Water: Urban Protest, Gender, & Power in Monterrey, Mexico. (Latin American Ser.). (Illus.). 256p. (C). 1995. text 39.95 (*0-8229-3908-8*) U of Pittsburgh Pr.

— The Politics of Water: Urban Protest, Gender & Power in Monterrey, Mexico. (Latin American Ser.). 256p. 1995. pap. 19.95 (*0-8229-5616-0*) U of Pittsburgh Pr.

Bennett, W., ed. see Stevenson, David, et al.

Bennett, W. C., et al. Anti-Maud: By a Poet of the People. Fredeman, William E. et al, eds. (Victorian Muse Ser.). 307p. 1986. lib. bdg. 20.00 (*0-8240-8623-6*) Garland.

Bennett, W. J., Jr. & Blakely, Jeffrey A. The Persian Period (Stratum V) LC 80-21724. (Joint Archaeological Expedition to Tell el-Hesi Ser.: No. 3). (Illus.). xxvii, 483p. 1990. text 95.00 (*0-931464-54-4*) Eisenbrauns.

Bennett, W. J., Jr., jt. auth. see Blakely, Jeffrey A.

Bennett, W. Lance. News: The Politics of Illusion. 3rd ed. LC 95-3575. (700 (College) Ser.). 256p. (C). 1995. pap. 45.00 (*0-8013-1167-5*, 79661) Longman.

***Bennett, W. Lance.** News: The Politics of Illusion. 4th ed. 304p. 2000. pap. 39.00 (*0-8013-1921-8*) Longman.

Bennett, W. Lance. News: Politics Illusion. 2nd ed. 216p. (C). 1989. pap. text 28.50 (*0-582-28664-6*, 71683) Addison-Wesley.

***Bennett, W. Lance & Entman, Robert M., eds.** Mediated Politics: Communication in the Future of Democracy. (Communication, Society & Politics Ser.). (Illus.). 472p. 2000. write for info. (*0-521-78356-9*); pap. write for info. (*0-521-78976-1*) Cambridge U Pr.

Bennett, W. Lance & Paletz, David L., eds. Taken by Storm: The Media, Public Opinion, & U. S. Foreign Policy in the Gulf War. LC 93-45527. 341p. 1994. pap. 15.95 (*0-226-04259-6*) U Ch Pr.

— Taken by Storm: The Media, Public Opinion, & U. S. Foreign Policy in the Gulf War. LC 93-45527. 341p. 1997. lib. bdg. 40.00 (*0-226-04258-8*) U Ch Pr.

Bennett, W. Lance, jt. auth. see Asard, Erik.

Bennett, W. M., jt. ed. see Wolfson, Marsha.

Bennett, W. Scott. Control & Measurement of Unintentional Electromagnetic Radiation. LC 96-34315. 260p. 1997. 59.95 (*0-471-17564-1*) Wiley.

Bennett, W. W. The Great Revival in the Southern Armies. 1992. 23.99 (*0-87377-996-7*) GAM Pubns.

Bennett, Wayne. Criminal Investigation. 5th ed. 1998. student ed. 18.75 (*0-534-53533-X*) Brooks-Cole

Bennett, Wayne W. & Hess, Karen. Management & Supervision in Law Enforcement. 2nd ed. LC 95-37730. 650p. (C). 1996. 83.95 (*0-314-06751-5*) West Pub.

Bennett, Wayne W. & Hess, Karen M. Criminal Investigation. 4th ed. Jucha, ed. LC 93-45031. 650p. (C). 1994. text 56.00 (*0-314-02862-5*) West Pub.

— Criminal Investigation. 5th ed. LC 97-34881. 700p. (C). 1997. 79.95 (*0-534-53532-1*) Wadsworth Pub.

— Management & Supervision in Law Enforcement. Jucha, ed. 645p. (C). 1992. text 54.75 (*0-314-91105-7*) West Pub.

Bennett, Wendell C. & D'Harnoncourt, Rene. Ancient Art of the Andes. LC 54-6135. (Museum of Modern Art Publications in Reprint). (Illus.). reprint ed. 27.00 (*0-405-01521-6*) Ayer.

Bennett, Whitman. A Practical Guide to American 19th Century Color Plate Books, Set only. 162p. 1996. reprint ed. 45.00 (*1-888262-14-1*) Martino Pubng.

Bennett, Wilhelmine. Habits - A Journal: One Womans Struggle Against Religious Persecution. 145p. 1998. pap. 12.50 (*1-57502-892-1*, PO2453) Morris Pubng.

Bennett, Will. Zero. Owen, Maureen, ed. LC 83-539. 1984. pap. 6.00 (*0-916382-31-1*) Telephone Bks.

***Bennett, William.** Absent Minded Beggars: The Volunteers in the Boer War. 1999. write for info. (*0-85052-685-X*) Pen & Sword Bks Ltd.

Bennett, William. Adventures from the Book of Virtues: Compassion: Zach Lends a Hand. LC 96-19824. 24p. (ps-2). 1996. pap. 3.25 (*0-689-81049-0*) S&S Childrens.

— Adventures from the Book of Virtues: Courage: Annie's Race, No. 2. LC 96-19825. 24p. (J). (ps-2). 1996. 3.25 (*0-689-81048-2*) S&S Childrens.

— Adventures from the Book of Virtues: Responsibility: Annie Shows Off. LC 96-25853. 24p. (ps-2). 1996. pap. 3.25 (*0-689-81050-4*) S&S Childrens.

Bennett, William & Christensen, James, eds. Advanced ChemTech Handbook of Combinatorial & Solid Phase Organic Chemistry: A Comprehensive Guide to Principles, Products & Protocols. (Illus.). 400p. 1998. pap. 25.00 (*0-9665883-0-4*) Advanced Chem.

Bennett, William & Smale, Gerald G., eds. Community Social Work in Scotland. (Pictures of Practice Ser.: Vol. 1). (C). 1989. 65.00 (*0-7855-0090-1*, Pub. by Natl Inst Soc Work) St Mut.

Bennett, William & Smale, Gerald G., trs. Community Social Work in Scotland Vol. 1: Pictures of Practice. (C). 1989. pap. 30.00 (*0-902789-61-9*, Pub. by Natl Inst Soc Work) St Mut.

Bennett, William A. Beagle Training Basics. Luther, Luana, ed. LC 94-74083. (Illus.). 172p. 1995. pap. 21.95 (*0-944875-33-5*) Doral Pub.

***Bennett, William D.** North Carolina Genealogical Society Journal, 1975-1984--Consolidated. LC 97-228519. 600p. 1999. pap. 45.00 (*0-8063-4711-2*) Clearfield Co.

***Bennett, William Doub.** Currituck County (North Carolina) Eighteenth Century Tax & Militia Records. 114p. 2000. reprint ed. pap. 26.50 (*0-8063-4987-5*, Pub. by Clearfield Co) ACCESS Pubs Network.

Bennett, William F. The Athlete in You: A Sportsmedicine Self-Care Guide. 200p. (Orig.). 1997. pap. 12.95 (*0-9647700-3-2*) Capital Com Inc.

Bennett, William F., ed. Nutrient Deficiencies & Toxicities in Crop Plants. LC 93-71744. (Illus.). 202p. 1993. 69.00 (*0-89054-151-5*) Am Phytopathol Soc.

Bennett, William F., et al, eds. Modern Grain Sorghum Production. LC 89-13470. (Illus.). 178p. (C). 1990. text 32.95 (*0-8138-1121-X*) Iowa St U Pr.

Bennett, William F., et al. Modern Grain Sorghum Production: Student Study Guide. LC 89-13470. (Illus.). 56p. 1990. reprint ed. pap., student ed. 30.00 (*0-608-06885-3*, 206709300009) Bks Demand.

Bennett, William H. Beginning Debate. (Illus.). iii, 114p. (Orig.). (YA). (gr. 7-12). 1995. pap. text 19.95 (*1-889510-21-1*) Chmpionship Debate.

Bennett, William H. An Introduction to the Gothic Language. Lehmann, Winfred P., ed. LC 79-87574. (Introductions to Older Languages Ser.: No. 2). xvii, 190p. 1980. lib. bdg. 32.00 (*0-87352-290-7*, Z1010) Modern Lang.

Bennett, William H. Lincoln Douglas: The Text. iii,60,xivp. (Orig.). (YA). (gr. 7-12). 1989. pap. text 19.95 (*1-889510-24-6*) Chmpionship Debate.

Bennett, William H. Mock Trial Teacher's Guide. (Illus.). 92p. 1998. pap. text 12.00 (*1-889510-38-6*) Chmpionship Debate.

— The Really Big Theory Block Book. (Illus.). vi, 277p. (Orig.). (YA). (gr. 7-12). 1995. pap. text 47.00 (*1-889510-02-5*) Chmpionship Debate.

— Varsity Debate: Experiences in Advanced Debate Theory & Practice. iv, 244p. (Orig.). (YA). (gr. 7-12). 1996. text 39.00 (*1-889510-22-X*) Chmpionship Debate.

Bennett, William H. Varsity Debate: Experiences in Advanced Debate Theory & Practice. iv, 244p. (Orig.). (YA). (gr. 7-12). 1996. pap. text 29.00 (*1-889510-23-8*) Chmpionship Debate.

Bennett, William H., ed. Advanced Value Debate: Lincoln Douglas & C.E.D.A. Issues. 2nd rev. ed. xi, 336p. 1996. pap. text 48.00 (*1-889510-09-2*) Chmpionship Debate.

— Debate Judging. ii, 62p. (Orig.). 1981. pap. text 19.00 (*1-889510-03-3*) Chmpionship Debate.

Bennett, William H. & Archuleta, Hank. Techniques of Flowsheeting. 34p. (Orig.). (YA). (gr. 7-12). 1990. pap. text 5.00 (*1-889510-28-9*) Chmpionship Debate.

Bennett, William H. & Gonsalves, Teresa A. The Really Big L. D. Block Book, Vol. 1. (Illus.). v, 274p. (Orig.). (YA). (gr. 7-12). 1989. pap. text 47.00 (*1-889510-08-4*) Chmpionship Debate.

Bennett, William H. & Rosenberg, James. The How To's of Library Research. (Illus.). 80p. (Orig.). (YA). (gr. 7-12). 1995. pap. text 19.95 (*1-889510-27-0*) Chmpionship Debate.

Bennett, William H. & Schnippel, Greg. The Kritik. 110p. (Orig.). (YA). (gr. 7-12). 1996. pap. text 39.00 (*1-889510-00-9*) Chmpionship Debate.

Bennett, William H., et al. Beginning Debate Teacher's Guide. ii, 80p. (Orig.). 1996. pap. text 24.00 (*1-889510-05-X*) Chmpionship Debate.

Bennett, William H., et al. Successful Speech. Bailey, Michelle et al, eds. (Illus.). v, 151p. (Orig.). (YA). (gr. 7-12). 1995. 39.00 (*1-889510-13-0*); pap. text 29.00 (*1-889510-14-9*) Chmpionship Debate.

Bennett, William H., et al. Successful Speech: Teacher's Guide. Bailey, Michelle et al, eds. (Illus.). vi, 261p. (Orig.). 1995. pap. text, teacher ed. 45.00 (*1-889510-12-2*) Chmpionship Debate.

Bennett, William H., jt. auth. see Jones, Bob, Jr.

Bennett, William H., jt. auth. see Winn, Mary.

Bennett, William I., et al, eds. Your Good Health: How to Stay Well, & What to Do When You're Not. LC 87-19671. (Illus.). 520p. 1987. text 39.00 (*0-674-96631-7*) HUP.

Bennett, William I., et al. Your Good Health: How to Stay Well, & What to Do When You're Not. Johnson, Timothy & Goldfinger, Stephen E., eds. (Illus.). 520p. 1989. pap. text 15.95 (*0-674-96632-5*) HUP.

Bennett, William J. The Book of Virtues. (J). (ps-2). 1996. pap. 12.95 (*0-689-81240-X*) S&S Childrens.

— The Book of Virtues. 832p. 1996. per. 16.00 (*0-684-83577-0*) S&S Trade.

— Book of Virtues, Vol. 2, set. abr. ed. 1994. audio 25.00 (*0-671-50557-2*, 102602, Pub. by S&S Audio) Lndmrk Audiobks.

B

— The Book of Virtues: A Treasury of the World's Great Moral Stories. (Illus.). 672p. 1993. 29.50 (*0-671-68306-3*) S&S Trade.

— Book of Virtues: Honesty: Zach's Tall Tale. LC 96-19823. 24p. (J). (ps-2). 1996. pap. 3.25 (*0-689-80902-6*) S&S Bks Yung.

— The Book of Virtues for Young People: A Treasury of Great Moral Stories. LC 96-53584. 384p. (J). (gr. 5 up). 1997. per. 17.00 (*0-689-81613-8*) S&S Trade.

— The Children's Book of America. LC 98-15491. (Illus.). 112p. (J). 1998. 21.00 (*0-684-84930-5*) S&S Trade.

***Bennett, William J.** Children's Book of Faith. (Illus.). (J). 2000. 24.95 (*0-385-32771-4*) Doubleday.

Bennett, William J. Children's Book of Heroes 1998. 1997. pap. 10.95 (*0-684-83959-8*) S&S Trade.

— A Curriculum for American Students: James Madison Elementary School. 61p. (Orig.). (C). 1993. pap. text 25.00 (*0-7881-0020-3*) DIANE Pub.

— The De-Valuing of America. 272p. 1994. 17.99 (*1-56179-224-1*) Focus Family.

— The De-Valuing of America. 1995. pap. 12.99 (*1-56179-360-4*) Focus Family.

— The Death of Outrage: Bill Clinton & the Assault on American Ideals. LC 99-461904. 128p. 1998. 20.00 (*0-684-81372-6*) Free Pr.

***Bennett, William J.** The Death of Outrage: Bill Clinton & the Assault on American Ideals. LC 99-461904. 160p. 1999. pap. 12.00 (*0-684-86403-7*) S&S Trade.

Bennett, William J. The Death of Outrage: Bill Clinton & the Assault on American Ideals. large type ed. LC 98-44916. 1999. 30.00 (*0-7838-0441-5*, G K Hall Lrg Type) Mac Lib Ref.

— The Devaluing of America: The Fight for Our Culture & Our Children. 272p. 1992. 20.00 (*0-671-68305-5*) S&S Trade.

— The Devaluing of America: The Fight for Our Culture & Our Children. 272p. 1994. pap. 12.00 (*0-671-79719-0*) S&S Trade.

— First Lessons: A Report on Elementary Education in America. 83p. (Orig.). 1996. pap. text 20.00 (*0-7881-2793-4*) DIANE Pub.

— Index of Leading Cultural Indicators. 144p. 1994. pap. 8.95 (*0-671-88326-7*, Touchstone) S&S Trade Pap.

***Bennett, William J.** The Index of Leading Cultural Indicators: American Society at the End of the Twentieth Century. rev. expanded ed. LC 99-42788. 272p. 1999. pap. 10.95 (*1-57856-344-5*) Waterbrook Pr.

— Index of Leading Cultural Indicators American Society at the End of the 20th Century. LC 99-42788. 272p. 1999. pap. 10.95 (*0-385-49912-4*) Doubleday.

Bennett, William J. The Index of Leading Cultural Indicators, 1994. 138p. 1993. pap. 8.95 (*0-685-65180-0*) Heritage Found.

— The Moral Compass. 825p. 1996. per. 16.00 (*0-684-83578-9*) S&S Trade.

***Bennett, William J.** Our Country's Founders: Words of Advice from the Founders in Stories, Letters, Poems & Speeches. 1998. 17.00 (*0-8054-1600-5*) Broadman.

Bennett, William J. Our Sacred Honor: Words of Advice from the Founders in Stories, Letters, Poems & Speeches. LC 97-33047. (Illus.). 384p. 1997. 24.50 (*0-684-84138-X*) S&S Trade.

— The Spirit of America: Words of Advice from the Founders in Stories, Letters, Poems & Speeches. 1998. pap. 14.00 (*0-684-84794-9*, Touchstone) S&S Trade Pap.

— Virtues Collection, 2 vol., Set. 1996. pap. text, per., boxed set 32.00 (*0-684-00457-7*, Touchstone) S&S Trade Pap.

Bennett, William J., ed. The Book of Virtues for Young People: A Treasury of Great Moral Stories. (Illus.). 384p. (YA). (gr. 5 up). 1995. lib. bdg. 16.95 (*0-382-24923-2*) Silver Burdett Pr.

***Bennett, William J., ed.** The Children's Book of America. (Illus.). 114p. (J). (gr. 4-6). 2000. reprint ed. 21.00 (*0-7881-9358-9*) DIANE Pub.

Bennett, William J., ed. The Children's Book of Heroes. LC 96-47191. (Illus.). 110p. (J). (ps-3). 1997. 21.00 (*0-684-83445-6*, Scribner Pap Fic) S&S Trade Pap.

— The Children's Book of Virtues. LC 95-17867. (Illus.). 111p. (J). (ps-3). 1995. 21.00 (*0-684-81353-X*) S&S Trade.

— The Country's Founders: A Book of Advice for Young People. LC 98-6592. 296p. (YA). (gr. 7). 1998. per. 17.00 (*0-689-82106-9*) S&S Childrens.

— The Moral Compass: Stories for a Life's Journey. 824p. 1999. text 30.00 (*0-7881-6168-7*) DIANE Pub.

— Our Sacred Honor: Words of Advice from the Founders in Stories, Letters, Poems, & Speeches. LC 97-29467. (Illus.). 320p. 1997. 14.99 (*0-8054-0153-9*) Broadman.

***Bennett, William J., ed.** Our Sacred Honor: Words of Advice from the Founders in Stories, Letters, Poems & Speeches. 430p. 2000. reprint ed. text 25.00 (*0-7881-6487-2*) DIANE Pub.

Bennett, William J., ed. The Moral Compass: Stories for a Life's Journey. LC 95-4783. 608p. 1995. 29.50 (*0-684-80313-5*) S&S Trade.

***Bennett, William J., et al.** The Educated Child: A Parent's Guide from Preschool Through Eighth Grade. LC 99-40335. 688p. 1999. 30.00 (*0-684-83349-2*) Free Pr.

— The Educated Child: A Parent's Guide from Preschool Through Eighth Grade. 2000. pap. 16.00 (*0-684-87272-2*, Touchstone) S&S Trade Pap.

Bennett, William J., et al. Values & Public Policy. (C). 1988. pap. text 9.95 (*1-55872-000-6*) Fam Res Council.

Bennett, William M., ed. Drugs & Renal Disease. 2nd ed. (Monographs in Clinical Pharmacology: Vol. 2). (Illus.). 205p. 1986. text 44.00 (*0-443-08403-3*) Church.

— Nephrotoxicity of Clinically Relevant Drugs. (Journal: Mineral & Electrolyte Metabolism Ser.: Vol. 2, No. 4, 1994). (Illus.). 76p. 1994. pap. 41.75 (*3-8055-6091-5*) S Karger.

Bennett, William M. & McCarron, David A., eds. Pharmacotherapy of Renal Disease & Hypertension. fac. ed. LC 87-11649. (Contemporary Issues in Nephrology Ser.: No. 17). (Illus.). 429p. 1987. reprint ed. pap. 133.00 (*0-7837-7896-1*, 204765200008) Bks Demand.

Bennett, William P. First Baby in Camp. (Shorey Historical Ser.). 68p. reprint ed. pap. 10.00 (*0-8466-0161-3*, S161) Shoreys Bkstore.

Bennett, William R., Jr. Health & Low-Frequency Electromagnetic Fields. LC 93-40340. (Illus.). 208p. (C). 1994. 30.00 (*0-300-05763-6*) Yale U Pr.

Bennett, William S. Visualizing Software: A Graphic Notation for Analysis, Design, & Discussion. (Illus.). 208p. 1992. text 110.00 (*0-8247-8714-5*) Dekker.

Bennett, William S., ed. WEESKA Microcomputers Hardware - Software Design: A Step-by-Step Example. 2nd ed. (What Every Engineer Should Know Ser.: Vol. 27). (Illus.). 272p. 1990. text 65.00 (*0-8247-8193-7*) Dekker.

Bennett, William T. Book of Virtues for Young People. (YA). 1996. pap. 9.99 (*0-689-81037-7*) S&S Childrens.

Bennett, Winnie. Double Inheritance. 206p. mass mkt. 4.99 (*1-55197-026-0*) Picasso Publ.

Bennette, Hermand. Ain't No Help on the Way. 76p. 1990. 10.00 (*0-8187-0121-8*) Harlo Press.

Bennetts, John R. Far Away in Australia. 1981. 20.00 (*0-7223-1411-6*, Pub. by A H S Ltd) St Mut.

Bennetts, Pamela. Beau Barron's Lady. large type ed. 1994. 27.99 (*0-7089-3181-2*) Ulverscroft.

***Bennetts, Pamela.** The De Montfort Legacy. large type ed. 448p. 1999. 31.99 (*0-7505-1342-X*, Pub. by Mgna Lrg Print) Ulverscroft.

Bennetts, Pamela. Lady of the Masque. large type ed. 336p. 1994. 27.99 (*0-7089-3127-8*) Ulverscroft.

— The Loving Highwayman. large type ed. (Ulverscroft). 336p. 1994. 27.99 (*0-7089-3035-2*) Ulverscroft.

— Lucy's Cottage. large type ed. (Linford Romance Library). 336p. 1998. pap. 17.99 (*0-7089-5227-5*, Linford) Ulverscroft.

— Mid-Summer Morning. large type ed. (Large Print Ser.). 352p. 1994. 27.99 (*0-7089-3000-X*) Ulverscroft.

***Bennetts, Pamela.** One Dark Night. 232p. 2000. 31.99 (*0-7089-4213-X*) Ulverscroft.

Bennetts, Pamela. Regency Rogue. large type ed. (Dales Large Print Ser.). 288p. 1998. pap. 19.99 (*1-85389-793-0*, Dales) Ulverscroft.

Bennetts, Pamela. Richard & the Knights of God LC 77-3682. 512p. (J). 1977. write for info. (*0-89340-069-6*) Chivers N Amer.

Bennetts, Pamela. Ruby. large type ed. 352p. 1994. 27.99 (*0-7089-3071-9*) Ulverscroft.

Benneville, James S. De, see De Benneville, James S.

Benney, D., et al. A Symposium to Honor C. C. Lin. 452p. 1988. text 102.00 (*9971-5-0245-3*) World Scientific Pub.

Benney, D. J., jt. auth. see Benjamin, T. B.

Benney, Lona, et al, eds. The Color of Fashion. LC 92-14676. (Illus.). 256p. 1992. 65.00 (*1-55670-311-2*) Stewart Tabori & Chang.

***Bennhold-Thomsen, Veronik.** Subsistence Perspective. 2000. pap. 25.00 (*1-85649-776-3*) Zed Books.

***Bennholdt, Veronik.** Subsistence Perspective. LC 99-52073. 246p. 2000. text 65.00 (*1-85649-775-5*) Zed Books.

Benni. Terra! 1985. pap. 6.95 (*0-07-545204-9*) McGraw.

Bennich-Bjorkman, Li. Organising Innovation Research: The Inner Life of University. LC 97-27903. (Issues in Higher Education Ser.). 250p. 1997. 85.00 (*0-08-043072-4*, Pergamon Pr) Elsevier.

***Bennick, Ann.** Active Filing for Business Records. 1999. pap. write for info. (*0-933887-85-X*) ARMA Intl.

Bennie, D. Season in Hell. 1997. text 35.00 (*1-85158-904-X*, Pub. by Mainstream Pubng) Trafalgar.

Bennie, David. Not Playing for Celtic. (Illus.). 224p. 1996. 29.95 (*1-85158-757-8*, Pub. by Mainstream Pubng) Trafalgar.

Bennie, Frances. Learning Centers: Development & Operation. LC 76-58528. 340p. 1977. 39.95 (*0-87778-097-8*) Educ Tech Pubns.

Bennie, Lynn G. How Scotland Votes. LC 96-52828. 1997. pap. 24.95 (*0-7190-4511-8*) St Martin.

Bennie, Lynn G., et al. How Scotland Votes: Scottish Parties & Elections. LC 96-52828. (Political Analyses Ser.). 1997. text 79.95 (*0-7190-4510-X*, Pub. by Manchester Univ Pr) St Martin.

***Bennie, Michael.** Mastering Business English: How to Sharpen up Your Communication Skills at Work. 4th ed. (Illus.). 208p. (Orig.). 1998. pap. 19.95 (*1-85703-376-0*) How To Bks.

Bennie, Scott. Classic Enemies. Bell, Rob et al, eds. (Champions Ser.). (Illus.). 112p. (Orig.). (C). 1989. pap. 13.00 (*1-55806-044-8*, 403) Hero Games.

Bennigsen, Alexandre & Lemercier-Quelquejay, Chantal. Les Mouvements Nationaux Chez les Musulmans de Russie, 2 tomes. Incl. No. 3. "Sultangalievisme" au Tatarstan. 1960. pap. 38.25 Tome II. Presse et le Mouvement National Chez les Musulmans De Russie Avant 1920. (Illus.). 1964. pap. 31.60 (*90-279-6244-8*); (Move with Me Ser.). Set pap. 38.25 (*0-685-03444-5*) Mouton.

Bennike, Pia. Palaeopathology of Danish Skeletons: A Comparative Study of Demography, Disease, & Injury. (Illus.). 272p. (Orig.). 1985. pap. text 58.50 (*87-500-2571-6*) Coronet Bks.

Bennin, Bruce, et al. Histologic Diagnosis of Inflammatory Skin Diseases: An Algorithmic Method Based on Pattern Analysis. 2nd ed. LC 96-29038. (Illus.). 950p. 1997. 250.00 (*0-683-30376-7*) Lppncott W & W.

Benning, A. H. Community Industries of the Shakers: A New Look. Emerich, A. D., ed. (Illus.). 48p. 1983. pap. 8.00 (*0-317-00714-9*) Shaker Her Soc.

Benning, B., jt. auth. see Lester, L.

Benning, Brannon P., jt. auth. see Bittker, Boris I.

Benning, Forbes, ed. see Gauthier, Mark.

Benning, Lee E. Oh, Fudge! A Celebration of America's Favorite Candy. 320p. 1995. pap. 12.95 (*0-8050-2546-4*) H Holt & Co.

— Oh Fudge! A Celebration of America's Favorite Traditional Candy. LC 89-27487. 256p. 1995. 19.95 (*0-8050-1196-X*) H Holt & Co.

Benning, M. A., ed. Flammability & Sensitivity of Materials in Oxygen-Enriched Atmospheres STP 910, Vol. 2. LC 82-73766. (Special Technical Publication Ser.). (Illus.). 245p. 1986. text 56.00 (*0-8031-0474-X*, STP910) ASTM.

Benninga. Corporate Finance. 2nd ed. 1998. 59.25 (*0-07-230102-3*) McGraw.

Benninga, H. A History of Lactic Acid Making: A Chapter in the History of Biotechnology. (C). 1990. text 155.00 (*0-7923-0625-2*) Kluwer Academic.

Benninga, Jacques, ed. Moral, Character, & Civic Education in the Elementary School. 304p. (C). 1991. text 49.00 (*0-8077-3056-4*) Tchrs Coll.

— Moral, Character & Civic Education in the Elementary School. 304p. (C). 1991. pap. text 24.95 (*0-8077-3055-6*) Tchrs Coll.

Benninga, Simon. Financial Modeling. LC 97-21780. (Illus.). 400p. 1997. 49.50 (*0-262-02437-3*) MIT Pr.

***Benninga, Simon.** Financial Modeling. 2nd ed. LC 00-35473. (Illus.). 596p. 2000. 59.95 (*0-262-02482-9*) MIT Pr.

Benninga, Simon. Numerical Techniques in Finance. 256p. (Orig.). 1989. pap. text 26.00 (*0-262-52141-5*) MIT Pr.

— Numerical Techniques in Finance. 256p. (Orig.). 1989. 42.00 (*0-262-02286-9*) MIT Pr.

Benninger, Gerry, ed. see Floyd, Maita.

Benninger, Martin. Landwirtschaft - Umwelt - Sozialismus: Das Agrarpolitische Instrument "Bewirtschaftungsvereinbarung" in den Neuen Landern der Bundesrepublik Deutschland. (GER., Illus.). 243p. 1996. 44.95 (*3-631-30983-X*) P Lang Pubng.

Benninger, Michael, et al, eds. Vocal Arts Medicine: The Care & Prevention of Professional Voice Disorders. LC 93-5013. (Illus.). 374p. 1993. text 69.00 (*0-86577-439-0*) Thieme Med Pubs.

Benninger, Stephen J., jt. auth. see Earley, David B.

***Benningfield, Phillip.** Colorado Bouldering. LC 99-71072. (Illus.). 384p. 1999. pap. 28.00 (*1-892540-00-2*) Sharp End.

— Mountain Biking Colorado's Western Slope. LC 00-131518. (Illus.). 112p. 2000. pap. 9.95 (*1-892540-11-8*) Sharp End.

Benninghove, A., ed. see International Conference on Secondary Ion Mass Spe.

Benninghoven, A. Ion Formation from Organic Solids (IFOS IV) Mass Spectrometry of Involatile Material: Proceedings of the Fourth International Conference, Munster, Federal Republic of Germany, September 21-23, 1987. LC 89-14765. (Illus.). 167p. reprint ed. pap. 51.80 (*0-608-00195-3*, 206097800006) Bks Demand.

Benninghoven, A., ed. Ion Formation from Organic Solids: Proceedings, Muenster, FRG, 1982. (Chemical Physics Ser.: Vol. 25). (Illus.). 269p. 1983. 59.95 (*0-387-12244-3*) Spr-Verlag.

Benninghoven, A., et al, eds. Secondary Ion Mass Spectrometry: SIMS-II. LC 79-23997. (Chemical Physics Ser.: Vol. 9). (Illus.). 298p. 1979. 51.00 (*3-540-09843-7*) Spr-Verlag.

— Secondary Ion Mass Spectrometry SIMS III: Proceedings. (Chemical Physics Ser.: Vol. 19). (Illus.). 444p. 1982. 64.95 (*0-387-11372-X*) Spr-Verlag.

Benninghoven, A., et al. Secondary Ion Mass Spectrometry: Basic Concepts, Instrumental Aspects, Applications & Trends. LC 86-11014. (Monographs on Analytical Chemistry & Its Applications). 1264p. 1987. 385.00 (*0-471-01056-1*) Wiley.

— Secondary Ion Mass Spectrometry: Sims IX. 1008p. 1994. 650.00 (*0-471-94218-9*) Wiley.

Benninghoven, A., ed. see International Conference on Secondary Ion Mass Spectrometry Staff.

Benningsen, Alexandre A. & Wimbush, Enders S. Muslim National Communism in the Soviet Union: A Revolutionary Strategy for the Colonial World. LC 78-8608. xxii, 304p. 1980. pap. text 7.95 (*0-226-04236-7*, P915) U Ch Pr.

Bennington, Allen, jt. auth. see Kennedy, Lona B.

Bennington, Geoff, tr. see Lyotard, Jean-Francois.

***Bennington, Geoffrey.** Interrupting Derrida. LC 99-56919. (Warwick Studies in European Philosophy Ser.). 256p. 2000. write for info. (*0-415-22426-8*) Routledge.

— Interrupting Derrida. LC 99-56919. (Warwick Studies in European Philosophy Ser.). 256p. (C). 2000. pap. write for info. (*0-415-22427-6*) Routledge.

Bennington, Geoffrey. Jacques Derrida. 1999. pap. 20.00 (*0-226-04262-6*) U Ch Pr.

— Legislations: The Politics of Deconstruction. LC 93-46858. 256p. (C). 1994. pap. 20.00 (*0-86091-668-5*, Pub. by Verso) Norton.

Bennington, Geoffrey & Derrida, Jacques. Jacques Derrida. LC 92-11186. (Religion & Postmodernism Ser.). (Illus.). 428p. (C). 1993. 27.50 (*0-226-04261-8*) U Ch Pr.

Bennington, Geoffrey, tr. see Derrida, Jacques.

Bennington, Geoffrey, tr. see Lyotard, Jean-Francois.

Bennington, J., jt. auth. see Harrop-Griffiths, Hilton.

Bennington, Jane, jt. auth. see Harrop-Griffiths, Hilton.

Bennington, Richard R. Furniture Marketing: From Product Development to Distribution. (Illus.). 310p. (C). 1984. pap. 45.00 (*0-87005-491-0*) Fairchild.

— Furniture Retailing in the United States. LC 95-45289. (Illus.). 63p. 1995. spiral bd. 450.00 (*0-921577-56-7*) AKTRIN.

— Furniture Wholesaling in the United States. LC 94-10998. 50p. 1994. spiral bd. 450.00 (*0-921577-43-5*) AKTRIN.

Bennington, Robert & Christie, Cort W. 1-800-AWAY-IRS: The Answer to a Nations Plea. 2nd ed. 192p. 1998. reprint ed. pap. 12.95 (*1-882180-99-2*) Griffin CA.

Bennington Slaughter Associates Staff, ed. Portraits Period. (Illus.). 88p. 1990. per. write for info. (*0-9627710-0-7*) Prtrt Brkrs of Amer.

Bennink, H. J., jt. ed. see Out, H. J.

***Bennion.** Introduction to Foods. 1999. pap. text 68.00 (*0-13-014233-6*) P-H.

Bennion. Introductory Foods. 11th ed. LC 99-31240. (Illus.). 730p. 1999. 75.00 (*0-13-923988-X*) P-H.

Bennion, ed. Clinical Nutrition. (C). 1978. text. write for info. (*0-321-01537-1*) Addson-Wesley Educ.

Bennion, F. A. Bennion: Statutory Interpretation. 3rd ed. 1997. write for info. (*0-406-02126-0*, BSI3, MICHIE) LEXIS Pub.

Bennion, Francis A. The Constitutional Law of Ghana. LC 63-3133. (Butterworth's African Law Ser.: No. 5). 563p. reprint ed. pap. 174.60 (*0-608-13607-7*, 205125900093) Bks Demand.

Bennion, Harden. Bennion Family of Utah, Vol. I. (Illus.). 241p. 1997. reprint ed. pap. 36.50 (*0-8328-7495-7*); reprint ed. lib. bdg. 46.50 (*0-8328-7494-9*) Higginson Bk Co.

Bennion, Janet. Women of Principle: Female Networking in Contemporary Mormon Polygyny. (Illus.). 192p. 1998. 29.95 (*0-19-512070-1*) OUP.

***Bennion, John.** The Burial Pool. LC 99-53298. 2000. pap. write for info. (*1-56085-140-6*) Signature Bks.

Bennion, Junius L., jt. auth. see Schneider, Edward W.

***Bennion, Lowell & Rohde, Jerry.** Traveling the Trinity Highway. (Illus.). 256p. 2000. pap. 19.95 (*0-9640261-2-0*) MtnHome Bks.

Bennion, Lowell C., jt. auth. see Peterson, Gary B.

Bennion, Lowell L. How Can I Help? Final Selections by the Legendary Writer, Teacher & Humanitarian. LC 96-12054. 190p. 1996. 13.95 (*1-56236-229-1*, Pub. by Aspen Bks) Origin Bk Sales.

Bennion, Sherilyn C. Equal to the Occasion: Women Editors of the Nineteenth-Century West. LC 90-39025. (Wilbur S. Shepperson Series in History & Humanities). (Illus.). 248p. 1990. 24.95 (*0-87417-163-6*) U of Nev Pr.

Bennis, Benjamin J., pseud. Colorado Restaurants & Recipes: From Small Towns. (Illus.). 340p. 1995. otabind 16.00 (*0-9629799-2-9*) Small Town.

— Colorado Restaurants off the Beaten Path: With Recipes. LC 99-178852. (Illus.). 320p. 1998. otabind 19.00 (*0-9629799-3-7*) Small Town.

Bennis, Charles W. Illinois Zup & I. 80p. 1991. lib. bdg. write for info. (*0-9631317-0-2*) C W Bennis.

Bennis, Hans. Gaps & Dummies. 2nd ed. (Linguistic Models Ser.). xii, 338p. 1987. reprint ed. pap. 69.00 (*3-11-013276-1*) Mouton.

Bennis, Hans & Van Kemenade, Ans. Linguistics in the Netherlands, 1989. (AVT Publications). x, 194p. (Orig.). (C). 1989. pap. 42.90 (*90-6765-420-5*) Mouton.

***Bennis, Phyllis.** Calling the Shots: How Washington Dominates Today's UN. 2000. pap. 18.95 (*1-56656-353-4*) Interlink Pub.

Bennis, Phyllis & Moushabeck, Michel, eds. Altered States: A Reader in the New World Order. LC 93-4299. 540p. 1993. 39.95 (*1-56656-115-9*, Olive Branch Pr) Interlink Pub.

— Beyond the Storm: A Gulf Crisis Reader. LC 91-22095. (Illus.). 448p. (C). 1991. pap. 14.95 (*0-940793-82-2*, Olive Branch Pr) Interlink Pub.

Bennis, Warren. Managing People Is Like Herding Cats: Warren Bennis on Leadership. LC 96-61955. 239p. 1997. 24.95 (*0-9634917-5-X*) Exec Excell.

— Managing People Is Like Herding Cats: Warren Bennis on Leadership. 240p. 1999. pap. 12.00 (*1-890009-61-X*) Exec Excell.

— Why Leaders Can't Lead. 1997. mass mkt. 20.00 (*0-7879-0943-2*) Jossey-Bass.

Bennis, Warren & Biederman, Patricia W. Organizing Genius. 256p. 1998. pap. 13.00 (*0-201-33989-7*) Addison-Wesley.

Bennis, Warren & Goldsmith, Joan. Learning to Lead: A Workbook on Becoming a Leader. 2nd ed. LC 97-17568. 208p. 1997. pap. 15.00 (*0-201-31140-2*) Addison-Wesley.

Bennis, Warren & Mische, Michael. 21st Century Organization. 128p. 1997. mass mkt. 16.50 (*0-7879-0939-4*) Jossey-Bass.

Bennis, Warren, jt. auth. see Heenan, David A.

Bennis, Warren G. Beyond Bureaucracy: Essays on the Development & Evolution of Human Organization. LC 92-41386. (Management Ser.). 284p. 1993. pap. 27.00 (*1-55542-522-4*) Jossey-Bass.

***Bennis, Warren G.** Managing the Dream: Reflections on Leadership & Change. 256p. 2000. pap. text 15.00 (*0-7382-0332-7*) Perseus Pubng.

Bennis, Warren G. Old Dogs Can (And Must) Learn New Tricks: More Warren Bennis on Leadership & Change. 1999. write for info. (*1-890009-34-2*) Exec Excell.

— On Becoming a Leader. 1990. pap. 12.95 (*0-201-55087-3*) Addison-Wesley.

— Reinventing Leadership: Strategies to Empower the Organization. 208p. 1997. pap. 14.00 (*0-688-15126-4*, Quil) HarperTrade.

— Why Leaders Can't Lead: The Unconscious Conspiracy Continues. LC 88-46091. (Management Ser.). 192p. 1989. text 30.00 (*1-55542-152-0*) Jossey-Bass.

Bennis, Warren G., ed. American Bureaucracy. (Society Bks.). 187p. 1970. reprint ed. 32.95 (*0-87855-053-4*); reprint ed. pap. text 19.95 (*0-87855-546-3*) Transaction Pubs.

An Asterisk (*) at the beginning of an entry indicates that the title is appearing for the first time.

Bennis, Warren G., pref. Leaders on Leadership: Interviews with Top Executives. LC 91-40754. (Harvard Business Review Book Ser.). 288p. 1992. 29.95 (*0-87584-307-7*) Harvard Busn.

Bennis, Warren G. & Goldsmith, Joan. Learning to Lead: A Workbook on Becoming a Leader. LC 94-2182. 1994. pap. 19.95 (*0-201-56310-X*) Addison-Wesley.

Bennis, Warren G. & Nana, Burt. Leaders: Strategies for Taking Charge. 2nd ed. LC 96-47290. 235p. 1997. pap. 14.00 (*0-88730-839-2*, HarpBusn) HarpInfo.

Bennis, Warren G. & Nanus, Burt. Leaders: The Strategies for Taking Charge. LC 85-48323. 256p. 1986. reprint ed. pap. 13.00 (*0-06-091336-3*, PL1336, Perennial) HarperTrade.

Bennis, Warren G. & Slater, Phillip E. The Temporary Society. rev. ed. (Business & Management Ser.). 176p. 1998. mass mkt. 20.00 (*0-7879-4331-2*) Jossey-Bass.

Bennis, Warren G., et al. Beyond Leadership: Balancing Economics, Ethics & Ecology. 2nd ed. LC 96-5381. (Developmental Management Ser.). 1996. pap. 28.95 (*1-55786-960-X*) Blackwell Pubs.

Bennis, Warren G., jt. auth. see Mitroff, Ian I.

***Bennison, Charles E., et al.** In Praise of Congregations: Leadership in the Local Church Today. LC 98-27147. 1999. 14.95 (*1-56101-151-7*) Cowley Pubns.

Bennison, G. M. & Moseley, K. A. Introduction to Geological Structures & Maps. 6th ed. (Arnold Publications). (Illus.). 144p. 1997. pap. text 16.95 (*0-340-69240-5*) OUP.

Bennison, George M. An Introduction to Geological Structures & Maps. 5th ed. (Illus.). 80p. 1990. pap. text 9.95 (*0-340-51760-3*, A4123, Pub. by E A) Routldge.

Bennison, R. L. The Impact of Town Centre Shopping Schemes in Britain: Their Impact on Traditional Retail Environments. (Progress in Planning Ser.: Vol. 14, Part 1). (Illus.). 104p. 1980. pap. 16.25 (*0-08-026789-0*, Pergamon Pr) Elsevier.

Bennitt, Mark, ed. History of the Louisiana Purchase Exposition. LC 75-22801. (America in Two Centuries Ser.). (Illus.). 1976. reprint ed. 95.95 (*0-405-07673-8*) Ayer.

Bennitt, Roger. Borrowing Money: A Reference Book of Math, Stats & Info. 9th ed. 132p. 1998. pap. 15.00 (*1-56150-224-3*) Intl Wealth.

— Borrowing Money: A Reference Book of Math, Strategies, & Information. 8th ed. 132p. 1996. pap. 15.00 (*1-56150-174-3*) Intl Wealth.

— Borrowing Money: A Reference Book of Math, Strategies & Information. 10th ed. 132p. 1999. pap. 15.00 (*1-56150-275-8*) Intl Wealth.

***Bennitt, Roger.** Borrowing Money: A Reference Book of Math, Strategies & Information. 11th ed. 132p. 2000. pap. 15.00 (*1-56150-335-5*) Intl Wealth.

Bennitt, Roger S. Fianance Guide with Formulated Solutions for Excel: Managing Finance for Business, Non-Profit & Government Entities. (Illus.). 300p. 2000. pap. 99.00 (*0-9630468-3-7*) Finance Guide Pub.

— The Financial Decision Maker's Manual: Professional Edition. 745p. (Orig.). 1993. pap. 24.00 (*0-9630468-0-2*) Finance Guide Pub.

***Benno, Mark.** Email Collaboration: Netscape Communicator 4.7. (Recipes4Success Ser.). (Illus.). 2000. 69.95 (*0-9673308-7-4*) Tech Learning Inc.

Benno, Thoma. El Mejor de Somos Cubanos. 1998. pap. text 7.95 (*3-86187-102-5*) Bookazine Co Inc.

Benno, Thoma. Postcardbook #1: With 30 Postcards. (Illus.). 1997. pap. 7.95 (*3-86187-108-4*) B Gmunder.

— Somos Cubanos. 1998. pap. text 39.95 (*3-86187-115-7*) B Gmunder.

Bennof, Richard. Selected Data on Federal Support to Universities & Colleges: Fiscal Year, 1993. (Illus.). 42p. (C). 1998. reprint ed. pap. text 20.00 (*0-7881-3139-7*) DIANE Pub.

Benns, F. Lee. The American Struggle for the British West India Carrying-Trade 1815-1830. LC 68-55479. (Reprints of Economic Classics Ser.). 207p. 1972. reprint ed. lib. bdg. 35.00 (*0-678-00793-4*) Kelley.

Bennum, Mervyn, jt. ed. see Newitt, Malyn D. D.

Benny, Daniel J. Private Investigators Desk Reference. 40p. 1993. spiral bd. 15.00 (*1-928987-59-1*) Intl Fdtn Protect.

Benny, Jack & Benny, Joan. Sunday Nights At Seven: The Jack Benny Story. (Illus.). 1991. mass mkt. 8.99 (*0-446-39321-5*) Warner Bks.

Benny, Joan, jt. auth. see Benny, Jack.

Benny, Louis M., ed. see McGrath, James.

Benny, Norman, tr. see Simenon, Georges.

Bennyhoff, James & Elsasser, Albert. Sonoma Mission: Historical & Archaeological Study of Primary Construction, 1923-1913. (University of California Archaeological Survey, Department of Anthropology, Berkeley CA Ser.: No. 27). (Illus.). 100p. (C). 1954. reprint ed. pap. text 11.25 (*1-55567-630-8*) Coyote Press.

Bennyhoff, James A. An Appraisal of the Archaeological Resources of Yosemite National Park. fac. ed. (Reports of the University of California Archaeological Survey: No. 34). (Illus.). 104p. 1956. reprint ed. pap. 11.56 (*1-55567-352-X*) Coyote Press.

— Californian Fish Spears & Harpoons. fac. ed. Gifford, Edward W. et al, eds. (University of California Publications: No. 9:4). (Illus.). 47p. (C). 1950. reprint ed. pap. 5.31 (*1-55567-097-0*) Coyote Press.

Bennyhoff, James A. & Fredrickson, David A. Toward a New Taxonomic Framework for Central California Archaeology: Essays. Hughes, Richard E., ed. (Contributions of the University of California Archaeological Research Facility Ser.: No. 52). 128p. 1994. pap. 14.00 (*1-882744-02-0*) U CA Arch Res Fac.

Beno, Mike, ed. The Christmases We Used to Know. LC 96-67060. 164p. 1996. 14.95 (*0-89821-160-3*, 20407) Reiman Pubns.

— Forks in the Road. LC 97-75525. (Illus.). 164p. 1998. 16.95 (*0-89821-217-0*) Reiman Pubns.

— Overheard at the Country Cafe. LC 98-67163. 178p. 1998. 15.99 (*0-89821-238-3*) Reiman Pubns.

— Tough Times, Strong Women. LC 97-65761. 164p. 1997. 14.95 (*0-89821-203-0*, 24496) Reiman Pubns.

— When Families Made Memories Together. LC 94-66341. 164p. 1994. 14.95 (*0-89821-124-7*, 19503) Reiman Pubns.

***Beno, Mike, ed.** When the Banks Closed, We Opened Our Hearts. LC 98-68486. (Illus.). 164p. 1999. 19.99 (*0-89821-257-X*) Reiman Pubns.

Beno, Mike, ed. see Holmes, Cora.

Beno, Mike, ed. see Reiman Publications Staff.

Benoff, David S. The General Radiotelephone Operators Study Guide for Avionics Technicians. 208p. (C). 1996. pap. text 24.95 (*0-88487-210-6*, JS312670) Jeppesen Sanderson.

Benois, Alexandre. Reminiscences of the Russian Ballet. Britnieva, Mary, tr. LC 77-7791. (Series in Dance). (Illus.). 1977. reprint ed. lib. bdg. 45.00 (*0-306-77426-7*) Da Capo.

Benoist, Alain De, see De Benoist, Alain.

Benoist, Luc. The Esoteric Path: An Introduction to the Hermetic Tradition. (Illus.). 128p. (Orig.). 1986. pap. 12.95 (*1-85274-043-4*) Sterling.

Benoist-Mechin, Jacques. History of the German Army since the Armistice. Taylor, E. R., tr. from FRE. 345p. 1988. reprint ed. 45.00 (*0-86527-373-1*) Fertig.

Benoit, jt. auth. see Hausman.

Benoit, jt. auth. see O'Donnell.

Benoit, Alphonse. St. Gregoire de Nazianze. vi, 788p. 1973. reprint ed. 200.00 (*3-487-04695-4*) G Olms Pubs.

Benoit, Andre & Munier, Charles. Le Bapteme dans l'Eglise Ancienne. (Traditio Christiana Ser.: Vol. 9). (FRE.). 374p. 1994. 117.95 (*3-906752-42-9*, Pub. by P Lang) P Lang Pubng.

— Die Taufe in der Alten Kirche. (Traditio Christiana Ser.: Bd. 9). (GER.). 374p. 1994. 117.95 (*3-906752-43-7*, Pub. by P Lang) P Lang Pubng.

***Benoit, Bertrand.** Social-Nationalism: An Anatomy of French Euroscepticism. LC 97-37027. 188p. 1998. text 72.95 (*1-84014-015-1*, Pub. by Ashgate Pub) Ashgate Pub Co.

Benoit, Cecil R. When Love Is Not Enough: A Childs View of Parenting. 1990. pap. 12.95 (*0-939298-77-5*) J M Pr.

Benoit, D., et al, eds. Microbeam & Nanobeam Analysis. (Illus.). 560p. 1996. pap. 219.50 (*3-211-82874-5*) Spr-Verlag.

Benoit, David. Fourteen Things Witches Hope Parents Never Find Out, 2 cass. (Illus.). 1994. audio 19.95 (*1-879366-76-2*) Hearthstone OK.

— Fourteen Things Witches Hope Parents Never Find Out. (Illus.). 167p. 1994. pap. 10.95 (*1-879366-75-4*) Hearthstone OK.

— Who's Watching the Playpen? LC 96-210204. 195p. 1995. pap. 11.95 (*1-57558-000-4*) Hearthstone OK.

Benoit, David & Graff, Charles G. Theft by Deception. (Illus.). 12p. (Orig.). (YA). (gr. 7 up). 1987. pap. text 1.50 (*0-923105-08-5*) Glory Ministries.

Benoit, David & Wilmington, Harold L. The Battleplan for the Battlefield. (Illus.). 146p. 1990. student ed. 49.95 (*0-923105-12-3*) Glory Ministries.

***Benoit-Dusausoy, Annick & Fontaine, Guy.** History of European Literature. 2nd ed. LC 99-31445. 720p. 1999. 125.00 (*0-415-17334-5*) Routledge.

Benoit, E., ed. Dynamic Bifurcations: Proceedings of a Conference Held in Luminy, France, March 5-10, 1990. (Lecture Notes in Mathematics Ser.: Vol. 1493). vii, 219p. 1991. 41.95 (*0-387-54900-5*) Spr-Verlag.

Benoit, Emile. Progress & Survival: An Essay on the Future of Mankind. Gohn, Jack B., ed. LC 80-14423. 130p. 1980. 47.95 (*0-275-90452-0*, C0452, Praeger Pubs) Greenwood.

Benoit-Guilbot, Odile. Long Term Unemployment. 1994. 18.00 (*1-85567-212-X*) St Martin.

Benoit-Guilbot, Odile & Gallie, Duncan, eds. Long-Term Unemployment. LC 94-13741. (Social Change in Western Europe Ser.). 182p. 1994. 45.00 (*1-85567-248-0*) St Martin.

Benoit, Henry C., jt. auth. see Higgins, Julia S.

Benoit, Herve. Digital Television: MPEG- 2 & Principles of the DVB System. LC 97-190819. 200p. 1997. pap. 59.95 (*0-471-23810-4*) Wiley.

***Benoit, Herve.** Satellite Television. 164p. 1999. pap. 31.95 (*0-471-35824-X*, Wiley Heyden) Wiley.

Benoit, Hubert. Supreme Doctrine: Psychological Studies in Zen Thought. 2nd ed. LC 96-125851. 234p. 1995. pap. 19.95 (*1-898723-14-1*, Pub. by Sussex Acad Pr) Intl Spec Bk.

— Zen & the Psychology of Transformation: The Supreme Doctrine. rev. ed. 264p. 1990. pap. 12.95 (*0-89281-272-9*) Inner Tradit.

Benoit, J. C., ed. see International Congress of Psychotherapy Staff.

Benoit, J. Pierre. U. S. Interest Rates & the Interest Rate Dilemma for the Developing World. LC 85-12348. (Illus.). 248p. 1986. 59.95 (*0-89930-131-2*, BIR/, Quorum Bks) Greenwood.

***Benoit, Jean & Lutenegger, A. J.** National Geotechnical Experimentation Sites. LC 00-22935. (Geotechnical Special Publications). 2000. write for info. (*0-7844-0484-4*) Am Soc Civil Eng.

Benoit, Jean-Claude, et al. Dictionnaire Clinique des Therapies Familiales Systemiques. (FRE.). 1988. write for info. (*0-7859-7935-2*, 2-7101-0694-9) Fr & Eur.

Benoit, John, jt. auth. see Perkins, Ken.

Benoit-Levy, Jean. Art of the Motion Picture. LC 70-112568. (Literature of Cinema Ser.). 1977. reprint ed. 18.95 (*0-405-01603-4*) Ayer.

Benoit, Marcelle. Dictionnaire de la Musique en France aux XVIIe et XVIIIe Siecles. (FRE.). 1992. 235.00 (*0-7859-7775-9*, 2213028249) Fr & Eur.

Benoit, Margaret. A Case of Reel Murder. (Crime Files Ser.). 112p. (YA). (gr. 5 up). 1997. text 10.95 (*0-07-006391-5*, Lrning Triangle); pap. text 5.95 (*0-07-006392-3*, Lrning Triangle) McGraw.

— Death of a Road Scholar. (Crime Files Ser.). 112p. (YA). (gr. 5 up). 1997. text 10.95 (*0-07-006393-1*, Lrning Triangle); pap. text 5.95 (*0-07-006394-X*, Lrning Triangle) McGraw.

— Who Framed Art Decco? LC 97-43018. (Illus.). 112p. (YA). (gr. 5 up). 1997. text 10.95 (*0-07-006309-5*) McGraw.

— Who Framed Art Decco? LC 97-43018. (Illus.). 145p. (YA). (gr. 5 up). 1997. pap. 4.95 (*0-07-006274-9*) McGraw.

— Who Killed Olive Souffle? (Illus.). 144p. (YA). (gr. 5-9). 1997. pap. 4.95 (*0-07-006275-7*) McGraw.

Benoit, Michelle, jt. auth. see Pitre, Glen.

Benoit, Monette, The A. D. A., Civil Rights, Affirmative Action, Business, Convention Handbook for Reporters & Captioners. (Handbooks for Reporters Ser.: No. 3). 350p. 1995. pap. text 26.95 (*1-881149-07-2*) CRRB.

— CSR, RPR, RMR, Written Knowledge Test, Court Reporter Reference Textbook. 5th rev. ed. (Court Reporter Reference Bks.: No. 1). 300p. 1992. pap. text 29.95 (*1-881149-00-5*) CRRB.

— CSR, RPR, RMR Written Knowledge Test Court Reporter Reference Workbook. (Court Reporter Reference Bks.: No. 2). 1995. pap. text, wbk. ed. 20.95 (*1-881149-01-3*) CRRB.

— The Environment, Sciences, Weather, Geology Handbook for Reporters & Captioners. (Handbooks for Reporters Ser.: No. 2). Orig. Title: Weather, Physical Sciences, Geology Handbook. 1994. pap. text 26.95 (*1-881149-06-4*) CRRB.

— The Politics, Elections, Government, Military, Criminal Handbook for Reporters & Captioners. (Handbooks for Reporters Ser.: No. 4). 255p. 1995. pap. text 26.95 (*1-881149-08-0*) CRRB.

— Q & A Popcorn Dictation, 180 WPM. (Q & A Popcorn Ser.: Vol. III). 1997. pap. 22.95 (*1-881149-15-3*) CRRB.

— Q & A Popcorn Dictation, 225 WPM. (Q & A Popcorn Ser.). (Orig.). 1993. pap. 22.95 (*1-881149-03-X*) CRRB.

— Q & A Popcorn Dictation, 200 WPM. (Q & A Popcorn Ser.: Vol. II). (Orig.). 1996. pap. 22.95 (*1-881149-39-9*) CRRB.

— REAL-TIME Vocabulary Workbook. (Court Reporter Reference Bks.: No. 3). 1993. pap. text 20.95 (*1-881149-02-1*) CRRB.

— The Sports, Olympics, Security, Terrorism Handbook for Reporters & Captioners. (Handbooks for Reporters Ser.: No. 1). Orig. Title: The Sports Handbook for Reporters & Captioners. 1994. pap. text 28.95 (*1-881149-05-6*) CRRB.

— The Universal Religions, Ethics, & Philosophy Handbook for Reporters & Captioners. (Handbooks for Reporters Ser.: No. 5). 340p. 1997. pap. text 26.95 (*1-881149-12-9*) CRRB.

Benoit, Monette, jt. auth. see Adams, Carol.

Benoit, Monette, ed. see Edmondson, Stephen.

Benoit, Pamela J. Telling the Success Story: Acclaiming & Disclaiming Discourse. LC 96-47391. (SUNY Series in Speech Communication). 207p. (C). 1997. pap. text 12.95 (*0-7914-3318-8*) State U NY Pr.

— Telling the Success Story: Acclaiming & Disclaiming Discourse. LC 96-47391. (SUNY Series in Speech Communication). 207p. (C). 1997. text 39.50 (*0-7914-3317-X*) State U NY Pr.

Benoit, Philippe. Project Finance at the World Bank: An Overview of Policies & Instruments. LC 95-48254. (Technical Papers: No. 312). 124p. 1996. pap. 22.00 (*0-8213-3521-9*, 13521) World Bank.

Benoit, R. L., jt. auth. see Frumer, Louis R.

***Benoit, Ray & Vomvoris, George.** Satan's Den. LC 00-190839. 160p. 2000. 25.00 (*0-7388-1866-6*); pap. 18.00 (*0-7388-1867-4*) Xlibris Corp.

— Six Men. LC 99-91909. 153p. 2000. 25.00 (*0-7388-1214-5*); pap. 18.00 (*0-7388-1215-3*) Xlibris Corp.

***Benoit, Robert.** Imperial Calcasieu, Louisiana. (Images of America Ser.). (Illus.). 128p. 2000. pap. 18.99 (*0-7385-0581-1*) Arcadia Publng.

Benoit-Rohmer, Florence, ed. The Minority Question in Europe: Texts & Commentary. LC 97-175949. 180p. 1996. pap. 15.00 (*92-871-2932-0*, Pub. by Council of Europe) Manhattan Pub Co.

Benoit, Susannah. I Am Vietnamese American. LC 97-2582. (Our American Family Ser.). (J). (gr. k-3). 1997. lib. bdg. 15.93 (*0-8239-5009-3*, PowerKids) Rosen Group.

Benoit-Wagner. Le Francais Actif Cassette, No. 2B. 72p. wbk. ed. 10.95 (*0-88729-811-7*) Langenscheidt.

Benoit, William L. Accounts, Excuses, & Apologies: A Theory of Image Restoration Discourse. LC 94-31901. (SUNY Series in Communication Studies). 197p. (C). 1994. pap. text 14.95 (*0-7914-2186-4*) State U NY Pr.

— Seeing Spots: A Functional Analysis of Presidential Television Advertisements, 1952-1996. LC 98-56624. (Praeger Series in Political Communication). 256p. 1999. 59.95 (*0-275-96645-3*, Praeger Pubs) Greenwood.

Benoit, William L., et al, eds. Readings in Argumentation. LC 92-9887. (Studies in Argumentation in Pragmatics & Discourse Analysis: Vol. 11). xii, 813p. 1992. lib. bdg. 244.65 (*3-11-013576-0*) Mouton.

***Benoit, William L. & Blaney, Joseph R.** Campaign '96: A Functional Analysis of Acclaiming, Attacking & Defending. LC 98-15646. (Praeger Series in Political Communication). 288p. 1998. 59.95 (*0-275-96361-6*, Praeger Pubs) Greenwood.

Benoit, William L. & Wells, William T. Candidates in Conflict: Persuasive Attack & Defense in the 1992 Presidential Debates. LC 96-16792. (Studies in Rhetoric & Communication). 272p. (Orig.). 1996. pap. text 24.95 (*0-8173-0868-7*) U of Ala Pr.

Benoit, William L., jt. auth. see Blaney, Joseph L.

Benokraitis. Family Fueds. LC 99-44976. 386p. 1999. pap. text 29.40 (*0-13-912460-8*) P-H.

— Marriages & Families. 3rd ed. 1998. pap. text, student ed. 19.00 (*0-13-922197-2*) P-H.

Benokraitis, Ben, jt. auth. see Stull, Andrew T.

***Benokraitis, Nijole V.** Contemporary Ethnic Families in the United States: Characteristics, Variations, & Dynamics. 400p. 2001. pap. text 44.00 (*0-13-089326-9*, Prentice Hall) P-H.

Benokraitis, Nijole V. Marriages & Families. 2nd ed. 1996. pap. text, student ed. 22.00 (*0-13-209529-7*) P-H.

— Marriages & Families: Changes, Choices, & Constraints. 3rd ed. LC 98-5440. 603p. (C). 1998. 74.67 (*0-13-915935-5*) P-H.

— Subtle Sexism: Current Practices & Prospects for Change. LC 96-35662. 400p. 1997. 56.00 (*0-7619-0385-2*); pap. 26.95 (*0-7619-0386-0*) Sage.

Benokraitis, Nijole V. & Feagin, Joe R. Modern Sexism: Blatant, Subtle & Covert Discrimination. 2nd ed. LC 94-22624. 240p. 1994. pap. text 34.67 (*0-13-588617-1*) P-H.

Benokraitis, Nijole V., jt. auth. see Macionis, John J.

Benoliel, Bernard & Parry, C. Hubert. Parry Before Jerusalem: Studies of His Life & Music with Excerpts from His Published Writings. LC 96-32134. (Illus.). 275p. 1997. text 87.95 (*0-85967-927-6*, Pub. by Scolar Pr) Ashgate Pub Co.

B

Benoliel, Doug. Northwest Foraging: Wild Edibles of the Pacific Northwest. (Illus.). 1974. pap. 12.95 (*0-913140-13-9*) Signpost Bk Pub.

Benoliel, Jeanne Q., ed. Death Education for the Health Professional. LC 81-20153. (Death Education, Aging & Health Care Ser.). (Illus.). 118p. 1982. text 60.95 (*0-89116-248-8*) Hemisp Pub.

Benolkin, Michael, ed. Kaman HH-43 Huskie Modeler's Quick Reference Manual. 19p. 1998. pap. 15.00 (*1-891344-06-4*, 8001) TacAir Pubns.

Benolkin, Michael C. Air Intelligence - Small Scale Aircraft Modelers Guide 1999. rev. ed. 1999. pap. 18.95 (*1-891344-12-9*, 2008) TacAir Pubns.

— Air Intelligence Large Scale Modelers Guide, 2000-2001. rev. ed. (Air Intelligence Ser.). 2000. pap. 18.95 (*1-891344-11-0*, 2007) TacAir Pubns.

— Air Intelligence Small Scale Modelers Guide, 2000-2001. (Air Intelligence Ser.). 2000. pap. write for info. (*1-891344-13-7*, 3001) TacAir Pubns.

Benolkin, Michael C., ed. Air Intelligence - 1/48 Aircraft Modeler's Guide 1999. rev. ed. 1999. pap. 29.95 (*1-891344-10-2*, 2006) TacAir Pubns.

— Air Intelligence - 1/72 Aircraft Modelers Guide 1999. rev. ed. 199p. 1999. pap. 29.95 (*1-891344-09-9*, 2005) TacAir Pubns.

— Army Intelligence - Armor Modeler's Guide, 1999. 1999. pap. write for info. (*1-891344-14-5*) TacAir Pubns.

— Auto Modeler's Guide, 1999. 1999. pap. write for info. (*1-891344-16-1*) TacAir Pubns.

— Naval Intelligence - Ship Modeler's Guide, 1999. 1999. pap. write for info. (*1-891344-15-3*) TacAir Pubns.

— Space & SciFi Modeler's Guide, 1999. 1999. pap. write for info. (*1-891344-17-X*) TacAir Pubns.

Benor, Daniel, et al. Agricultural Extension: The Training & Visit System. 95p. 1984. pap. text 22.00 (*0-8213-0140-3*, 10140) World Bank.

Benor, Ehud. Worship of the Heart: A Study of Maimonides' Philosophy of Religion. LC 94-39855. (SUNY Series in Jewish Philosophy). 262p. (C). 1995. pap. text 19.95 (*0-7914-2636-X*) State U NY Pr.

Benos. Current Topics in Membranes, Vol. 4. 380p. (C). 1999. 99.95 (*0-12-153347-6*) Acad Pr.

Benos, Dale J. Amiloride-Sensitive Sodium Channels. (Current Topics in Membranes Ser.). (Illus.). 380p. 1999. pap. 64.95 (*0-12-089030-5*) Acad Pr.

Benoschofsky, Ilona & Scheiber, Alexander. Jewish Museum of Budapest. 242p. (C). 1989. text 210.00 (*0-569-09192-6*, Pub. by Collets) St Mut.

***Benoschofsky, Ilona & Scheiber, Sandor.** The Jewish Museum of Budapest. 244p. 1999. 32.00 (*963-13-4075-9*, Pub. by Corvina Bks) St Mut.

Benoun, Victor. Your Castle, No Hassle: How to Buy a House, Find a Good Mortgage... & Keep Your Sense of Humor. 340p. 1999. pap. 17.95 (*1-56343-176-9*, Pub. by Silver Lake) Natl Bk Netwk.

Benoussan, Alain. Stochastic Control of Partially Observable Systems. 360p. (C). 1992. text 89.95 (*0-521-35403-X*) Cambridge U Pr.

Benoussan, Alain & Lions, J. L., eds. Analysis & Optimization of Systems. (Lecture Notes in Control & Information Sciences: Vol. 111). (Illus.). 1175p. 1988. 174.95 (*0-387-19237-9*) Spr-Verlag.

— Analysis & Optimization of Systems, Versailles, France, 1982: Proceedings. (Lecture Notes in Control & Information Sciences: Vol. 44). (Illus.). 987p. 1982. 94.95 (*0-387-12089-0*) Spr-Verlag.

— International Symposium on Systems Optimization & Analysis. (Lecture Notes in Control & Information Sciences: Vol. 14). (Illus.). 1979. 28.95 (*0-387-09447-4*) Spr-Verlag.

Benoussan, Alain & Verjus, J. P., eds. Future Tendencies in Computer Science, Control & Applied Mathematics: International Conference on the Occasion of the 25th Anniversary of INRIA: Paris, France, December 1992: Proceedings. LC 92-41021. (Lecture Notes in Computer Science Ser.: Vol. 653). 1992. 57.95 (*0-387-56320-2*) Spr-Verlag.

Benoussan, Alain, et al. Representation & Control of Infinite Dimensional Systems, Vol. 2. (Systems & Control: Foundations & Applications Ser.). 343p. 1993. 92.00 (*0-8176-3642-0*) Birkhauser.

Benovic, Jeffrey L. Regulation of G Protein Coupled Receptor Function & Expression. LC 99-30367. 301p. 1999. 149.95 (*0-471-25277-8*) Wiley.

— Regulation of G Protein Coupled Receptor Function & Expression. LC 99-30367. 320p. 2000. lib. bdg. 56.95 (*0-471-25269-7*) Wiley.

Benowitz, June M. Encyclopedia of American Women & Religion. LC 98-25706. (Illus.). 480p. 1998. lib. bdg. 75.00 (*0-87436-887-1*) ABC-CLIO.

Benowitz, Neal L., ed. Nicotine Safety & Toxicity. LC 97-46155. (Illus.). 224p. 1998. text 59.50 (*0-19-511496-5*) OUP.

Benowitz, Stephen I. Cancer. LC 98-36123. (Diseases & People Ser.). 128p. (YA). (gr. 6 up). 1999. lib. bdg. 20.95 (*0-7660-1181-X*) Enslow Pubs.

Benoyendranath, Banerjea. The Practice of Freedom. 1983. 9.00 (*0-8364-0918-3*, Pub. by Minerva) S Asia.

Benrey, Janet, jt. auth. see Benrey, Ron.

***Benrey, Ron & Benrey, Janet.** Little White Lies. 2001. pap. 12.99 (*0-8054-2371-0*) Broadman.

***BenRoy, Rocco.** How to Make Your Kitchen Your Pharmacy. 20p. (C). 1999. pap. 2.95 (*0-9672359-1-X*) Eternal Way.

Benrubi, Guy I., ed. Obstetric & Gynecologic Emergencies. (Illus.). 464p. 1993. text 73.00 (*0-397-51352-6*) Lppncott W & W.

— Obstetric Emergencies. (Illus.). 216p. 1989. text 66.00 (*0-443-08614-1*) Church.

Benrud, Eleanor M. The Last Sibling: A North Dakota Memoir. LC 90-70816. (Illus.). 93p. (Orig.). 1990. pap. 12.95 (*1-878815-00-8*) Reflected Images.

Bens, A. Active English: Pronunciation & Speech. 1977. pap. text 20.25 (*0-13-003392-8*) P-H.

Bens, Elsa De, see De Bens, Elsa, ed.

Bens, Ingrid. Facilitating with Ease! Goldman, Michael, ed. 190p. (Orig.). 1997. pap. text 39.00 (*1-890416-00-2*) Participative Dyn.

***Bens, Ingrid.** Facilitating with Ease! A Step-by-Step Guidebook with Customizable Worksheets on CD-ROM. LC 99-45515. 224p. 2000. pap., wbk. ed. 44.95 incl. cd-rom (*0-7879-5194-3*, Pfffr & Co) Jossey-Bass.

Bens, Ingrid. Facilitation at a Glance. Goldman, Michael, ed. 173p. 1999. spiral bd. 6.95 (*1-890416-05-3*) Participative Dyn.

— Team Launch! Team Leader's Manual. Goldman, Michael, ed. 172p. 1997. spiral bd. 24.00 (*1-890416-01-0*) Participative Dyn.

— Team Launch! Team Member's Manual. Goldman, Michael, ed. 102p. 1997. spiral bd. 12.00 (*1-890416-02-9*) Participative Dyn.

— Teams in Trouble. Goldman, Michael, ed. 180p. (Orig.). 1997. pap. text 39.00 (*1-890416-03-7*) Participative Dyn.

Bens, Paul G., Jr., jt. auth. see Kanner, Ellie.

Bens, Robert A. God Is Not a Stranger. LC 97-167791. (Illus.). vii, 70p. (Orig.). 1996. pap. 8.95 (*0-9655976-0-1*) Metaphys Inst.

Bensahel, Daniel C., ed. Optical Properties of Low Dimensional Silicon Structures: Proceedings of the NATO Advanced Research Workshop, Meylan, France, March 1-3, 1993. (NATO Advanced Science Institutes Series C: Mathematical & Physical Sciences). 254p. (C). 1993. text 174.50 (*0-7923-2446-3*) Kluwer Academic.

Bensaia, Andreea. Guide to International Schools: 1994-1995 Edition. 2nd rev. ed. (Illus.). 294p. 1994. pap. 19.00 (*0-935016-25-2*, Pub. by Zinn Pub Grp) Empire Pub Srvs.

Bensalem Association of Women Writers Staff. The Book of the Living Dead. Everett, Joann M., ed. (Illus.). 59p. (Orig.). 1985. pap. 10.00 (*0-930069-05-6*) Jasmine Pr.

— Icicle Carnival. Zettlemoyer, Ron, ed. (Illus.). 59p. (Orig.). 1984. pap. 5.00 (*0-930069-02-1*) Jasmine Pr.

— She Is Me. Stets, Susan S., ed. (Illus.). 68p. (Orig.). 1986. pap. 5.95 (*0-930069-08-0*) Jasmine Pr.

Bensande-Vincent, Bernadette, jt. ed. see Lundgren, Anders.

Bensari, D., et al, eds. Computational Water Resources. LC 91-76271. (Computational Methods in Water Resources Ser.). 330p. 1991. pap. 98.00 (*1-56252-086-5*) Computational Mech MA.

Bensaude-Vincent, Bernadette & Abbri, Ferdinando, eds. Lavoisier in European Context: Negotiating a New Language for Chemistry. LC 95-384. 303p. 1995. 45.95 (*0-88135-189-X*, Sci Hist) Watson Pub Intl.

Bensaude-Vincent, Bernadette & Stengers, Isabelle. A History of Chemistry. Van Dam, Deborah, tr. (Illus.). 288p. 1996. 37.50 (*0-674-39659-6*) HUP.

***Bensberg, Gabriele.** Die Laxdoela saga im Spiegel christlich mittelalterlicher Tradition. 2000. 47.95 (*3-631-36009-6*) P Lang Pubng.

Bensch, E., et al. Russian, English & German Dictionary of Shipbuilding & Fishing Industry: Schiffbau-Schiffahrt Fischereittechnik: Russisch-English-Deutsch. (ENG, GER & RUS.). 784p. 1981. 125.00 (*0-8288-4677-4*, M12665) Fr & Eur.

Bensch, Erhard, jt. auth. see Dipl-Ling, V.

Bensch, Stephen P. Barcelona & Its Rulers, 1096-1291. (Cambridge Studies in Medieval Life & Thought: No. 26). (Illus.). 477p. (C). 1995. text 74.95 (*0-521-43511-0*) Cambridge U Pr.

Benschoten, Elizabeth Van, see Van Benschoten, Elizabeth.

***Benscoter, Dee.** Spell Well! 40 Quick, Fun-Filled Ways to Help Kids of All Learning Styles Master Their Spelling. (Illus.). 64p. 2000. pap. text 10.95 (*0-439-18519-X*) Scholastic Inc.

Bense, Judith A. Archaelogy of Colonial Pensacola. LC 98-52079. (Ripley P. Bullen Series). (Illus.). 320p. 1999. 49.95 (*0-8130-1661-4*) U Press Fla.

— Archaeology of the Southeastern United States: Paleoindian to World War I. (Illus.). 388p. 1994. text 89.95 (*0-12-089060-7*); pap. text 39.95 (*0-12-089061-5*) Acad Pr.

Bense, Max, et al. Jan Peter Tripp, Ein 17. Januar. (GER., Illus.). 88p. 1986. 60.00 (*3-925782-06-0*) Die Gal Verlag.

Bense, Walter E., tr. see Troeltsch, Ernst.

Bensel, E. Ven-Ten. King Arthur. LC 68-791. 1970. reprint ed. lib. bdg. 75.00 (*0-8383-0693-4*) M S G Haskell Hse.

Bensel-Meyers. Rhetoric for Academic Reasoning. 448p. (C). 1997. pap. text, teacher ed. 47.00 (*0-06-040627-5*) Addson-Wesley Educ.

***Bensel-Meyers, ed.** New Students Guide Research Unthinkable. 2nd ed. 168p. 1998. pap. text 12.70 (*0-536-01816-2*) P-H.

Bensel, Richard. Sectionalism & American Political Development, 1880-1980. LC 84-40145. (Illus.). 520p. (C). 1984. reprint ed. text 35.00 (*0-299-09830-3*) U of Wis Pr.

Bensel, Richard F. Yankee Leviathan: The Origins of Central State Authority in America, 1859-1877. (Illus.). 464p. (C). 1991. text 69.95 (*0-521-39136-9*); pap. text 24.95 (*0-521-39817-7*) Cambridge U Pr.

***Bensel, Richard Franklin.** The Political Economy of American Industrialization, 1877 - 1900. (Illus.). 512p. 2001. write for info. (*0-521-77233-8*); pap. write for info. (*0-521-77604-X*) Cambridge U Pr.

Benseler, David, jt. ed. see Moore, Suzanne.

***Benseler, David P.** Teaching German in Twentieth-Century America. (Monatshefte Occasional Volumes Ser.: Vol. 15). (GER & ENG.). 2000. 24.95 (*0-299-16830-1*) U of Wis Pr.

Benseler, David P., et al, eds. Teaching German in America: Prolegomena to a History. LC 88-2957. (Monatshefte Occasional Volumes Ser.: Vol. 7). (Illus.). 320p. reprint ed. pap. 99.20 (*0-608-09845-0*, 206923300003) Bks Demand.

Bensen, Clark H. Congressional Districts, 103rd Congress: Map Supplement to District-Level Returns, Vol. 1. 110p. 1993. spiral bd. 25.00 (*1-57708-022-X*, PER-93-1B) Polidata.

— Congressional Districts, 103rd Congress No. 1: District-Level Returns for Congress & President for the 1992 General Election. (Illus.). 240p. 1993. spiral bd. 47.00 (*1-57708-021-1*, PER-93-1A) Polidata.

***Bensen, Clark H.** Demographic Abstract, Any County, Connecticut: Towns, Cities & Places, 1990 Census Edition. (Illus.). 80p. 1999. ring bd. 55.00 (*1-57708-366-0*, DOX-CT) Polidata.

— Demographic Abstract, Any County, Delaware: County Subdivisions, 1990 Census Edition. (Illus.). 80p. 1999. ring bd. 65.00 (*1-57708-382-2*, DOX-DE) Polidata.

— Demographic Abstract, Any County, Florida: County Subdivisions & Places, 1990 Census Edition. (Illus.). 80p. 1999. ring bd. 65.00 (*1-57708-389-X*, DOX-FL) Polidata.

— Demographic Abstract, Any County, Georgia: County Subdivisions & Places, 1990 Census Edition. (Illus.). 80p. 1999. ring bd. 65.00 (*1-57708-388-1*, DOX-GA) Polidata.

— Demographic Abstract, Any County, Illinois: Townships & Places, 1990 Census Edition. (Illus.). 80p. 1999. ring bd. 65.00 (*1-57708-372-5*, DOX-IL) Polidata.

— Demographic Abstract, Any County, Indiana: Townships & Places, 1990 Census Edition. (Illus.). 80p. 1999. ring bd. 65.00 (*1-57708-371-7*, DOX-IN) Polidata.

— Demographic Abstract, Any County, Iowa: Townships & Places, 1990 Census Edition. (Illus.). 80p. 1999. ring bd. 65.00 (*1-57708-376-8*, DOX-IA) Polidata.

— Demographic Abstract, Any County, Kentucky: County Subdivisions & Places, 1990 Census Edition. (Illus.). 80p. 1999. ring bd. 65.00 (*1-57708-390-3*, DOX-KY) Polidata.

— Demographic Abstract, Any County, Maine: Towns, Cities & Places, 1990 Census Edition. (Illus.). 80p. 1999. ring bd. 55.00 (*1-57708-361-X*, DOX-ME) Polidata.

— Demographic Abstract, Any County, Maryland: County Subdivisions, 1990 Census Edition. (Illus.). 80p. 1999. ring bd. 65.00 (*1-57708-383-0*, DOX-MD) Polidata.

— Demographic Abstract, Any County, Massachusetts: Towns, Cities & Places, 1990 Census Edition. (Illus.). 80p. 1999. ring bd. 55.00 (*1-57708-364-4*, DOX-MA) Polidata.

— Demographic Abstract, Any County, Michigan: Townships & Places, 1990 Census Edition. (Illus.). 80p. 1999. ring bd. 65.00 (*1-57708-373-3*, DOX-MI) Polidata.

— Demographic Abstract, Any County, Minnesota: Townships & Places, 1990 Census Edition. (Illus.). 80p. 1999. ring bd. 65.00 (*1-57708-375-X*, DOX-MN) Polidata.

— Demographic Abstract, Any County, Missouri: Townships & Places, 1990 Census Ediitoin. (Illus.). 80p. 1999. ring bd. 65.00 (*1-57708-377-6*) Polidata.

— Demographic Abstract, Any County, New Hampshire: Towns, Cities & Places, 1990 Census Edition. (Illus.). 80p. 1999. ring bd. 55.00 (*1-57708-362-8*, DOX-NH) Polidata.

— Demographic Abstract, Any County, New Jersey: Municipalities & Places, 1990 Census Edition. (Illus.). 80p. 1999. ring bd. 65.00 (*1-57708-368-7*, DOX-NJ) Polidata.

— Demographic Abstract, Any County, New York: Towns, Cities & Places, 1990 Census Edition. (Illus.). 80p. 1999. ring bd. 65.00 (*1-57708-367-9*, DOX-NY) Polidata.

— Demographic Abstract, Any County, North Carolina: Townships & Places, 1990 Census Edition. (Illus.). 80p. 1999. ring bd. 65.00 (*1-57708-386-5*, DOX-NC) Polidata.

— Demographic Abstract, Any County, Ohio: Townships & Places. (Illus.). 80p. 1999. ring bd. 65.00 (*1-57708-370-9*, DOX-OH) Polidata.

— Demographic Abstract, Any County, Pennsylvania: Townships & Places, 1990 Census Edition. (Illus.). 80p. 1999. ring bd. 65.00 (*1-57708-369-5*, DOX-PA) Polidata.

— Demographic Abstract, Any County, Rhode Island: Towns, Cities & Places, 1990 Census Edition. (Illus.). 80p. 1999. ring bd. 55.00 (*1-57708-365-2*, DOX-RI) Polidata.

— Demographic Abstract, Any County, South Carolina: County Subdivisions & Places, 1990 Census Edition. (Illus.). 80p. 1999. ring bd. 65.00 (*1-57708-387-3*, DOX-SC) Polidata.

— Demographic Abstract, Any County, Tennessee: County Subdivisions & Places, 1990 Census Edition. (Illus.). 80p. 1999. ring bd. 65.00 (*1-57708-391-1*, DOX-TN) Polidata.

— Demographic Abstract, Any County, Vermont: Towns, Cities & Places, 1990 Census Edition. (Illus.). 80p. 1999. ring bd. 55.00 (*1-57708-363-6*, DOX-VT) Polidata.

— Demographic Abstract, Any County, Virginia: County Subdivisions & Places. (Illus.). 80p. 1999. ring bd. 65.00 (*1-57708-384-9*, DOX-VA) Polidata.

— Demographic Abstract, Any County, West Virginia: County Subdivisions, 1990 Census Edition. (Illus.). 80p. 1999. ring bd. 65.00 (*1-57708-385-7*, DOX-WV) Polidata.

— Demographic Abstract, Any County, Wisconsin: Towns, Cities & Places, 1990 Census Edition. (Illus.). 80p. 1999. ring bd. 65.00 (*1-57708-374-1*, DOX-WI) Polidata.

Bensen, Clark H. Demographic Atlas of Connecticut: Towns, Cities & Places 1990 Census Edition. (Demographic Guides Ser.: Vol. 10). (Illus.). 140p. 1998. lib. bdg. 64.00 (*1-57708-109-9*, DOM-09-96Z) Polidata.

— Demographic Atlas of Delaware: County Subdivisions & Places, 1990 Census Edition. (Demographic Guides Ser.: Vol. 44). (Illus.). 84p. 1998. lib. bdg. 59.00 (*1-57708-110-2*, DOM-10-962) Polidata.

— Demographic Atlas of Florida: County Subdivisions & Places, 1990 Census Edition. (Demographic Guides Ser.: Vol. 46). (Illus.). 670p. 1998. lib. bdg. 110.00 (*1-57708-112-9*, DOM-12-962) Polidata.

— Demographic Atlas of Georgia: County Subdivisions & Places, 1990 Census Edition. (Demographic Guides Ser.: Vol. 48). (Illus.). 1342p. 1998. lib. bdg. 148.00 (*1-57708-113-7*, DOM-13-962) Polidata.

— Demographic Atlas of Illinois: Townships & Places, 1990 Census Edition. (Demographic Guides Ser.: Vol. 24). (Illus.). 1002p. 1998. lib. bdg. 130.00 (*1-57708-117-X*, DOM-17-96Z) Polidata.

— Demographic Atlas of Indiana: Townships & Places, 1990 Census Edition. (Demographic Guides Ser.: Vol. 26). (Illus.). 824p. 1998. lib. bdg. 121.00 (*1-57708-118-8*, DOM-18-96Z) Polidata.

— Demographic Atlas of Iowa: Townships & Places, 1990 Census Edition. (Demographic Guides Ser.: Vol. 50). (Illus.). 862p. 1998. lib. bdg. 125.00 (*1-57708-119-6*, DOM-19-962) Polidata.

— Demographic Atlas of Kentucky: County Subdivisions & Places, 1990 Census Edition. (Demographic Guides Ser.: Vol. 36). (Illus.). 1048p. 1998. lib. bdg. 132.00 (*1-57708-121-8*, DOM-21-96Z) Polidata.

— Demographic Atlas of Maine: Towns, Cities & Places, 1990 Census Edition. (Demographic Guides Ser.: Vol. 14). (Illus.). 202p. 1998. lib. bdg. 69.00 (*1-57708-123-4*, DOM-23-96Z) Polidata.

— Demographic Atlas of Maryland: County Subdivision & Places, 1990 Census Edition. (Demographic Guides Ser.: Vol. 52). (Illus.). 292p. 1998. lib. bdg. 77.00 (*1-57708-124-2*, DOM-24-962) Polidata.

— Demographic Atlas of Massachusetts: Towns, Cities & Places, 1990 Census Edition. (Demographic Guides Ser.: Vol. 12). (Illus.). 218p. 1998. lib. bdg. 71.00 (*1-57708-125-0*, DOM-25-96Z) Polidata.

— Demographic Atlas of Michigan: Townships & Places 1990 Census Edition. (Demographic Guides Ser.: Vol. 28). (Illus.). 758p. 1998. lib. bdg. 118.00 (*1-57708-126-9*, DOM-26-96Z) Polidata.

— Demographic Atlas of Minnesota: Townships & Places, 1990 Census Edition. (Demographic Guides Ser.: Vol. 32). (Illus.). 766p. 1998. lib. bdg. 120.00 (*1-57708-127-7*, DOM-27-96Z) Polidata.

— Demographic Atlas of Missouri: Townships & Places, 1990 Census Edition. (Demographic Guides Ser.: Vol. 34). (Illus.). 1036p. 1998. lib. bdg. 132.00 (*1-57708-129-3*, DOM-29-96Z) Polidata.

— Demographic Atlas of New Hampshire: Towns, Cities & Places, 1990 Census Edition. (Demographic Guides Ser.: Vol. 16). (Illus.). 148p. 1998. lib. bdg. 65.00 (*1-57708-133-1*, DOM-33-96Z) Polidata.

— Demographic Atlas of New Jersey: Municipalities & Places, 1990 Census Edition. (Demographic Guides Ser.: Vol. 18). (Illus.). 260p. 1998. lib. bdg. 74.00 (*1-57708-134-X*, DOM-34-96Z) Polidata.

— Demographic Atlas of New York: Towns, Cities & Places (1990 Census Edition) (Polidata Demographic Guides Ser.: Vol. 8). (Illus.). 590p. 1998. lib. bdg. 109.00 (*1-57708-136-6*, DOM36-94Z) Polidata.

— Demographic Atlas of North Carolina: Townships & Places 1990, Census Edition. (Demographic Guides Ser.: Vol. 38). (Illus.). 990p. 1998. lib. bdg. 129.00 (*1-57708-137-4*, DOM-37-96Z) Polidata.

— Demographic Atlas of Ohio: Townships & Places, 1990 Census Edition. (Demographic Guides Ser.: Vol. 2). (Illus.). 774p. 1998. lib. bdg. 122.00 (*1-57708-139-0*, DOM94-39-Z) Polidata.

— Demographic Atlas of Pennsylvania: Townships & Places, 1990 Census Edition. (Demographic Guides Ser.: Vol. 30). (Illus.). 762p. 1998. lib. bdg. 118.00 (*1-57708-142-0*, DOM-42-96Z) Polidata.

— Demographic Atlas of Rhode Island: Towns, Cities & Places, 1990 Census Edition. (Demographic Guides Ser.: Vol. 20). (Illus.). 98p. 1998. lib. bdg. 60.00 (*1-57708-144-7*, DOM-44-96Z) Polidata.

— Demographic Atlas of South Carolina: County Subdivisions & Places, 1990 Census Edition. (Demographic Guides Ser.: Vol. 54). (Illus.). 450p. 1998. lib. bdg. 91.00 (*1-57708-145-5*, DOM-45-962) Polidata.

— Demographic Atlas of Tennessee: County Sub Divisions & Places, 1990 Census Edition. (Demographic Guides Ser.: Vol. 40). (Illus.). 842p. 1998. lib. bdg. 122.00 (*1-57708-147-1*, DOM-47-96Z) Polidata.

— Demographic Atlas of Vermont: Towns, Cities & Places, 1990 Census Edition. (Illus.). 176p. 1998. lib. bdg. 67.00 (*1-57708-150-1*) Polidata.

— Demographic Atlas of Virginia: County Subdivisions & Places, 1990 Census Edition. (Demographic Guides Ser.: Vol. 42). (Illus.). 1014p. 1998. lib. bdg. 130.00 (*1-57708-151-X*, DOM-51-96Z) Polidata.

— Demographic Atlas of West Virginia: County Subdivision & Places, 1990 Census Edition. (Demographic Guides Ser.: Vol. 56). (Illus.). 508p. 1998. lib. bdg. 96.00 (*1-57708-154-4*, DOM-54-962) Polidata.

— Demographic Atlas of Wisconsin: Towns, Cities & Places, 1990 Census Edition. (Demographic Guides Ser.: Vol. 58). (Illus.). 646p. 1998. lib. bdg. 109.00 (*1-57708-155-2*, DOM-55-962) Polidata.

— Demographic Base Maps, Area/Markets By State. (Reference Maps: Vol. 1). 394p. 1997. ring bd. 64.00 (*1-57708-081-5*) Polidata.

— Demographic Guide to Connecticut: Towns, Cities & Places 1990 Census Edition. (Demographic Guides Ser.: Vol. 9). (Illus.). 302p. 1998. lib. bdg. 78.00 (*1-57708-309-1*, DOG-09-96Z) Polidata.

— Demographic Guide to Delaware: County Subdivisions & Places, 1990 Census Edition. (Demographic Guides Ser.: Vol. 43). (Illus.). 200p. 1998. lib. bdg. 69.00 (*1-57708-310-5*, DOG-10-962) Polidata.

— Demographic Guide to Florida: County Subdivisions & Places, 1990 Census Edition. (Demographic Guides Ser.: Vol. 45). (Illus.). 491p. 1998. lib. bdg. 95.00 (*1-57708-312-1*, DOG-12-962) Polidata.

— Demographic Guide to Georgia: County Subdivisions & Places, 1990 Census Edition. (Demographic Guides Ser.: Vol. 47). (Illus.). 529p. 1998. lib. bdg. 108.00 (*1-57708-313-X*, DOG-13-962) Polidata.

— Demographic Guide to Illinois: Townships & Places 1990 Census Edition. (Demographic Guides Ser.: Vol. 23). (Illus.). 890p. 1998. lib. bdg. 124.00 (*1-57708-317-2*, DOG-17-96Z) Polidata.

— Demographic Guide to Indiana: Townships & Places, 1990 Census Edition. (Demographic Guides Ser.: Vol. 25). (Illus.). 768p. 1998. lib. bdg. 120.00 (*1-57708-318-0*, DOG-18-96Z) Polidata.

— Demographic Guide to Iowa: Townships & Places, 1990 Census Edition. (Demographic Guides Ser.: Vol. 49). (Illus.). 768p. 1998. lib. bdg. 120.00 (*1-57708-319-9*, DOG-19-962) Polidata.

— Demographic Guide to Kentucky: County Subdivisions & Places, 1990 Census Edition. (Demographic Guides Ser.: Vol. 35). (Illus.). 442p. 1998. lib. bdg. 91.00 (*1-57708-321-0*, DOG-21-96Z) Polidata.

— Demographic Guide to Maine: Towns, Cities & Places 1990, Census Edition. (Demographic Guides Ser.: Vol. 13). (Illus.). 424p. 1998. lib. bdg. 89.00 (*1-57708-323-7*, DOG-23-96Z) Polidata.

— Demographic Guide to Maryland: County Subdivisions & Places, 1990 Census Edition. (Demographic Guides Ser.: Vol. 51). (Illus.). 351p. 1998. lib. bdg. 82.00 (*1-57708-324-5*, DOG-24-962) Polidata.

— Demographic Guide to Massachusetts: Towns, Cities & Places, 1990 Census Edition. (Demographic Guides Ser.: Vol. 11). (Illus.). 402p. 1998. lib. bdg. 87.00 (*1-57708-325-3*, DOG-25-96Z) Polidata.

— Demographic Guide to Michigan: Townships & Places, 1990 Census Edition. (Demographic Guides Ser.: Vol. 27). (Illus.). 842p. 1998. lib. bdg. 122.00 (*1-57708-326-1*, DOG-26-96Z) Polidata.

— Demographic Guide to Minnesota: Townships & Places, 1990 Census Edition. (Demographic Guides Ser.: Vol. 31). (Illus.). 768p. 1998. lib. bdg. 120.00 (*1-57708-327-X*, DOG-27-96Z) Polidata.

— Demographic Guide to Missouri: Townships & Places, 1990 Census Edition. (Demographic Guides Ser.: Vol. 33). (Illus.). 874p. 1998. lib. bdg. 123.00 (*1-57708-329-6*, DOG-29-96Z) Polidata.

— Demographic Guide to New Hampshire: Towns, Cities & Places, 1990 Census Edition. (Demographic Guides Ser.: Vol. 15). (Illus.). 318p. 1998. lib. bdg. 80.00 (*1-57708-333-4*, DOG-33-96Z) Polidata.

— Demographic Guide to New Jersey: Municipalities & Places, 1990 Census Edition. (Demographic Guides Ser.: Vol. 17). (Illus.). 480p. 1998. lib. bdg. 94.00 (*1-57708-334-2*, DOG-34-96Z) Polidata.

— Demographic Guide to New York: Towns, Cities & Places, (1990 Census Edition) (Polidata Demographic Guides Ser.: Vol. 7). (Illus.). 734p. 1998. lib. bdg. 116.00 (*1-57708-336-9*, DOG36-94Z) Polidata.

— Demographic Guide to North Carolina: Townships & Places, 1990 Census Edition. (Demographic Guides Ser.: Vol. 37). (Illus.). 768p. 1998. lib. bdg. 120.00 (*1-57708-337-7*, DOG-37-96Z) Polidata.

— Demographic Guide to Ohio: Townships & Places, 1990

An Asterisk (*) at the beginning of an entry indicates that the title is appearing for the first time.

Census Edition. LC 96-194745. (Demographic Guides Ser.: Vol. 1). (Illus.). 766p. 1998. lib. bdg. 120.00 (*1-57708-339-3*, DOG94-39-Z) Polidata.

— Demographic Guide to Pennsylvania: Townships & Places, 1990 Census Edition. (Demographic Guides Ser.: Vol. 29). (Illus.). 872p. 1998. lib. bdg. 123.00 (*1-57708-342-3*, DOG-42-96Z) Polidata.

— Demographic Guide to Rhode Island: Towns, Cities & Places, 1990 Census Edition. (Demographic Guides Ser.: Vol. 19). (Illus.). 232p. 1998. lib. bdg. 72.00 (*1-57708-344-X*, DOG-44-96Z) Polidata.

— Demographic Guide to South Carolina: County Subdivisions & Places, 1990 Census Edition. (Demographic Guides Ser.: Vol. 53). (Illus.). 354p. 1998. lib. bdg. 87.00 (*1-57708-345-8*, DOG-45-962) Polidata.

— Demographic Guide to Tennessee: County Subdivisions & Places, 1990 Census Edition. (Demographic Guides Ser.: Vol. 39). (Illus.). 411p. 1998. lib. bdg. 98.00 (*1-57708-347-4*, DOG-47-96Z) Polidata.

— Demographic Guide to the United States: Districts of the 105th Congress, 1990 Census Edition. (Demographic Guides: Vol. 43). 956p. 1998. lib. bdg. 121.00 (*1-57708-359-8*) Polidata.

— Demographic Guide to Vermont: Towns, Cities & Places, 1990 Census Edition. (Demographic Guides: Vol. 21). 326p. 1998. lib. bdg. 80.00 (*1-57708-350-4*) Polidata.

— Demographic Guide to Virginia: County Subdivisions & Places, 1990 Census Edition. (Demographic Guides Ser.: Vol. 41). (Illus.). 413p. 1998. lib. bdg. 91.00 (*1-57708-351-2*, DOG-51-96Z) Polidata.

— Demographic Guide to West Virginia: County Subdivisions & Places, 1990 Census Edition. (Demographic Guides Ser.: Vol. 55). (Illus.). 330p. 1998. lib. bdg. 82.00 (*1-57708-354-7*, DOG-54-962) Polidata.

— Demographic Guide to Wisconsin: Towns, Cities & Places, 1990 Census Edition. (Demographic Guides Ser.: Vol. 57). (Illus.). 768p. 1998. lib. bdg. 120.00 (*1-57708-355-5*, DOG-55-962) Polidata.

***Bensen, Clark H.** Demographic to & Atlas of Connecticut: Towns, Cities & Places, 1990 Census Omnibus. (Demographic Guides Ser.: Vol. 106). (Illus.). 442p. 1998. lib. bdg. 102.00 (*1-57708-303-2*, DOB-09-99) Polidata.

— Demographic to & Atlas of Delaware: County Subdivisions & Places, 1990 Census Omnibus. (Demographic Guides Ser.: Vol. 108). (Illus.). 284p. 2000. lib. bdg. 87.00 (*1-57708-314-8*, DOB-10-99) Polidata.

— Demographic to & Atlas of Maine: Towns, Cities & Places, 1990 Census Omnibus. (Demographic Guides Ser.: Vol. 101). (Illus.). 626p. 1998. lib. bdg. 111.00 (*1-57708-103-X*, DOB-23-99) Polidata.

— Demographic to & Atlas of Maryland: County Subdivisions & Places, 1990 Census Omnibus. (Demographic Guides Ser.: Vol. 109). (Illus.). 642p. 2000. lib. bdg. 112.00 (*1-57708-343-1*, DOB-24-99) Polidata.

— Demographic to & Atlas of Massachusetts: Towns, Cities & Places, 1990 Census Omnibus. (Demographic Guides Ser.: Vol. 104). (Illus.). 620p. 1998. lib. bdg. 111.00 (*1-57708-143-9*, DOB-25-99) Polidata.

— Demographic to & Atlas of New Hampshire: Towns, Cities & Places, 1990 Census Omnibus. (Demographic Guides Ser.: Vol. 102). (Illus.). 464p. 1998. lib. bdg. 103.00 (*1-57708-107-2*, DOB-33-99) Polidata.

— Demographic to & Atlas of New Jersey: Municipalities & Places, 1990 Census Omnibus. (Demographic Guides Ser.: Vol. 107). (Illus.). 740p. 1998. lib. bdg. 117.00 (*1-57708-307-5*, DOB-34-99) Polidata.

— Demographic to & Atlas of Rhode Island: Towns, Cities & Places, 1990 Census Omnibus. (Demographic Guides Ser.: Vol. 105). (Illus.). 330p. 1998. lib. bdg. 92.00 (*1-57708-152-8*, DOB-44-99) Polidata.

— Demographic to & Atlas of Vermont: Towns, Cities & Places, 1990 Census Omnibus. (Demographic Guides Ser.: Vol. 103). (Illus.). 502p. 1998. lib. bdg. 105.00 (*1-57708-114-5*, DOB-50-99) Polidata.

— Demographic to & Atlas of West Virginia: County Subdivisions & Places, 1990 Census Omnibus. (Demographic Guides Ser.: Vol. 110). (Illus.). 858p. 2000. lib. bdg. 123.00 (*1-57708-352-0*, DOB-54-99) Polidata.

— Eleciton History for Maine: Counties & Media Markets. (Election Histories Ser.: Vol. 9). 266p. 1999. lib. bdg. 93.00 (*1-57708-823-9*, EHC-ME) Polidata.

Bensen, Clark H. Election History for Illinois: Counties & Media Markets. (Election Histories Ser.: Vol. 1). 842p. 1997. lib. bdg. 123.00 (*1-57708-817-4*) Polidata.

***Bensen, Clark H.** Election History for Mississippi: Counties & Media Markets. (Election Histories Ser.: Vol. 7). 764p. 1999. lib. bdg. 118.00 (*1-57708-828-X*, EHC-MS) Polidata.

— Election History for Nevada: Counties & Media Markets. (Election Histories Ser.: Vol. 5). 368p. 1999. lib. bdg. 98.00 (*1-57708-832-8*, EHC-NV) Polidata.

— Election History for New York: Counties & Media Markets. (Election Histories Ser.: Vol. 3). 736p. 1999. lib. bdg. 117.00 (*1-57708-836-0*, EHC-NY) Polidata.

Bensen, Clark H. Election History for Ohio: Counties & Media Markets. (Election Histories Ser.: Vol. 2). 758p. 1998. lib. bdg. 121.00 (*1-57708-839-5*) Polidata.

***Bensen, Clark H.** Election History for South Carolina: Counties & Media Markets. (Election Histories Ser.: Vol. 6). 562p. 1999. lib. bdg. 108.00 (*1-57708-845-X*, EHC-SC) Polidata.

— Election History for Vermont: Counties & Media Markets. (Election Histories Ser.: Vol. 4). 390p. 1999. lib. bdg. 99.00 (*1-57708-850-6*, EHC-VT) Polidata.

— Election Yearbook for Illinois: Counties. (Election Yearbooks: Vol. 4). 200p. 1999. ring bd. 50.00 (*1-57708-717-8*, EYC-IL) Polidata.

— Election Yearbook for New York: Counties. (Election Yearbooks: Vol. 1). 200p. 1999. ring bd. 50.00 (*1-57708-736-4*, EYC-NY) Polidata.

— Election Yearbook for Ohio: Counties. (Election Yearbooks: Vol. 5). 200p. 1999. ring bd. 50.00 (*1-57708-739-9*, EYC-OH) Polidata.

— Election Yearbook for Tennessee: Counties. (Election Yearbooks: Vol. 3). 200p. 1999. ring bd. 50.00 (*1-57708-747-X*, EYC-TN) Polidata.

— Election Yearbook for Vermont: Counties & Selected Towns (Cities) (Election Yearbooks: Vol. 2). 200p. 1999. ring bd. 50.00 (*1-57708-750-X*, EYC-VT) Polidata.

— Population Estimates, 1998: States & Counties, as of July 1, 1998. 592p. 1999. ring bd. 98.00 (*1-57708-613-9*, BEC-98) Polidata.

— Population Estimates, 1999: States & Counties, as of July 1, 1999. 592p. 2000. ring bd. 98.00 (*1-57708-614-7*, BEC-99) Polidata.

Bensen, Clark H. Presidential Election, 1996 Vol. 1: States of Counties, Nov. 5, 1996 General Election, 3 vols. (Election Reports). (Illus.). 640p. 1997. lib. bdg. 112.00 (*1-57708-911-1*, ERA-999-96Z) Polidata.

— Presidential Election, 1996 Vol. 2: Districts of the 105th Congress, Nov. 5, 1999 General Election, 3 vols. (Election Reports: Vol. 4). 500p. 1997. lib. bdg. 100.00 (*1-57708-913-8*, ERC-999-96Z) Polidata.

— Presidential Election, 1996 Vol. 3: Statistical Areas & Markets, Nov. 5, 1996 General Election, 3 vols. (Election Reports: Vol. 5). 500p. 1997. lib. bdg. 115.00 (*1-57708-915-4*, ERE-999-96Z) Polidata.

— Roster of the Vermont Legislature, 1966-1990. (Illus.). x, 408p. 1989. spiral bd. 65.00 (*1-57708-031-9*, PMR-VT-90) Polidata.

Bensen, D. R. Death in the Hills. Grad, Doug, ed. (Tracker Ser.: No. 3). 256p. (Orig.). 1992. pap. 3.50 (*0-671-73836-4*) PB.

Bensen, D. R., ed. see Mowrey, Daniel B.

Bensen, D. R., ed. see Wodehouse, P. G.

Bensen, David W. & Sparrow, Arnold H., eds. Survival of Food Crops & Livestock in the Event of Nuclear War: Proceedings. LC 77-170334. (AEC Symposium Ser.). 762p. 1971. 26.75 (*0-87079-219-9*, CONF-700909); fiche 9.00 (*0-87079-220-2*, CONF-700909) DOE.

Bensen, Don, ed. see Broekstra, Robbert.

Bensen, Don R., ed. see Bland, Jeffrey S.

Bensen, Don R., ed. see Braverman, Eric R.

Bensen, Don R., ed. see Buchman, Dian Dincin.

Bensen, Don R., ed. see Callinan, Paul.

Bensen, Don R., ed. see Crayhon, Robert.

Bensen, Don R., ed. see Friedrich, Joan A. & Wade, Carlson.

Bensen, Don R., ed. see Hoffer, Abram & Walker, Morton.

Bensen, Don R., ed. see Lien, Eric J. & Li, Wen Y.

Bensen, Don R., ed. see Mindell, Earl L.

Bensen, Don R., ed. see Mindell, Earl L. & Hopkins, Virginia L.

Bensen, Joe. Pony Bob's Daring Ride: A Pony Express Adventure. LC 94-46348. (Highlights from American History Ser.). (Illus.). 32p. (J). 1995. pap. 5.95 (*1-56044-263-8*) Falcon Pub Inc.

— Souvenirs from High Places: A History of Mountaineering Photography. LC 98-231243. (Illus.). 144p. 1998. 35.00 (*0-89886-598-0*) Mountaineers.

Bensen, Joe, jt. auth. see Green, Randall.

Bensen, Maxine, ed. From Pittsburgh to the Rocky Mountains: Major Stephen Long's Expedition, 1819-1820. LC 88-16369. (Fulcrum's American History Ser.). (Illus.). 438p. 1988. 20.00 (*1-55591-022-X*) Fulcrum Pub.

Bensen, Robert. Scripture of Venus. (Illus.). 60p. (C). 1999. 50.00 (*0-934714-03-7*); pap. 10.00 (*0-934714-04-5*) Swamp Pr.

Bensen, Robert, ed. see Bertagnolli, Leslie.

Bensen, Robert, ed. see Johnston, William L.

Bensen, Rosie. Fessic the Eddy School Cat. (Illus.). iii, 24p. 1999. pap. 5.95 (*0-9668325-0-7*) R Bensen.

Bensen, William & Bensen, Wynn. Conquering Rheumatoid Arthritis. LC 98-206414. 90 p. 1996. pap. 9.95 (*0-9697781-8-X*, Empowering Pr) Decker.

Bensen, Wynn, jt. auth. see Bensen, William.

Benser, Caroline C. Egon Wellesz, 1885-1974: Chronicle of a Twentieth-Century Musician. LC 84-47786. (American University Studies: History: Ser. IX, Vol. 8). XXI, 407p. (C). 1985. text 50.00 (*0-8204-0138-2*) P Lang Pubng.

Benser, Caroline C. & Urrows, David F. Randall Thompson: A Bio-Bibliography. 38. LC 90-29279. (Bio-Bibliographies in Music Ser.: No. 38). 248p. 1991. lib. bdg. 55.00 (*0-313-25521-0*, BRO, Greenwood Pr) Greenwood.

BenShea, Noah. Great Jewish Quotes: Five Thousand Years of Truth & Humor from the Bible to George Burns. 144p. (Orig.). 1993. pap. 7.00 (*0-345-38345-1*) Ballantine Pub Grp.

— Jacob the Baker. 128p. 1990. pap. 10.00 (*0-345-36662-X*) Ballantine Pub Grp.

— Jacob's Journey: Wisdom to Find the Way, Strength to Carry on. 144p. 1992. pap. 9.00 (*0-345-37799-0*) Ballantine Pub Grp.

Benshea, Noah. Jacob's Ladder. 192p. 1998. pap. 11.00 (*0-345-40438-6*) Ballantine Pub Grp.

***BenShea, Noah.** What Every Principal Would Like to Say... And What to Say Next Time: Quotations for Leading, Learning & Living. LC 99-50417. 159p. 2000. pap. 24.95 (*0-7619-7606-X*); lib. bdg. 55.95 (*0-7619-7605-1*) Corwin Pr.

Benshoff. Substance Abuse & Rehabilitation. LC 99-50374. (Counseling Ser.). 384p. 1999. pap. 52.95 (*0-534-34223-X*) Brooks-Cole.

Benshoff, Harry M. Monsters in the Closet: Homosexuality & the Horror Film. (Illus.). 304p. 1997. pap. 18.95 (*0-7190-4473-1*) St Martin.

Bensidoun, Sylvain. Le Dymamisme de la Vallee du Zeravson (Uzbekistan-USSR) Bruchey, Stuart, ed. LC 80-2795. (Dissertations in European Economic History Ser.).Tr. of Dynamic Valley of Zeravsan (Uzbekistan-USSR). (Illus.). 1981. lib. bdg. 34.95 (*0-405-13979-9*) Ayer.

***Bensignor, Rick.** New Thinking in Technical Analysis: Trading Models from the Masters. (Professional Library). 2000. 55.00 (*1-57660-049-1*) Bloomberg NJ.

Bensimon, Estela M. & Neumann, Anna. Redesigning Collegiate Leadership: Teams & Teamwork in Higher Education. 200p. 1994. reprint ed. pap. text 15.95 (*0-8018-4956-X*) Johns Hopkins.

Bensimon, Estela M., et al. On Assuming a College or University Presidency: Lessons & Advice from the Field. 80p. 1989. pap. 10.00 (*1-56377-001-6*, NO3901) Am Assn Higher Ed.

Bensimon, Estela M., jt. auth. see Tierney, William G.

Bensing, Kay, ed. see Johnston-Rowbotham, Leah.

Bensinger, Charles. Designing the New World: A Map for Change. West, Ann, ed. (Illus.). 264p. (Orig.). 1996. pap. 14.95 (*0-931294-02-9*) Timewindow Pubns.

— Psyearth Quest: A Prophetic Novel. LC 98-13071. 240p. 1998. pap. 15.00 (*1-879181-53-3*) Bear & Co.

Bensinger, Gad J. Festschrift for Sarah B. Schaar. 150p. 1987. 9.50 (*0-933757-15-8*) Ill Academy.

— A Graphic Overview of the Organization & Process of the Criminal Justice System in Chicago & Cook County, 2 vols., Set. 2nd rev. ed. (Illus.). (C). 1985. spiral bd. 15.00 (*0-942854-08-X*) Loyola U Crim.

— A Graphic Overview of the Organization & Process of the Criminal Justice System in Chicago & Cook County, Vol. 1. rev. ed. (Illus.). 101p. (C). 1985. pap. write for info. (*0-942854-06-3*); pap. write for info. (*0-942854-07-1*) Loyola U Crim.

— Justice in Israel: The Criminal Justice System. 3rd rev. ed. (Illus.). 131p. 1998. pap. 14.95 (*0-942511-79-4*) OICJ.

Bensinger, Gad J., ed. Annals of the Illinois Academy of Criminology, 1950-1991, 5 vols. 1900p. write for info. (*0-933757-01-8*); write for info. (*0-933757-02-6*) write for info. (*0-933757-03-4*); write for info. (*0-933757-04-2*); write for info. (*0-933757-05-0*) Ill Academy.

— Annals of the Illinois Academy of Criminology, 1950-1991, 5 vols., Set. 1900p. 450.00 (*0-933757-00-X*) Ill Academy.

— Critical Issues in Criminal Justice: Proceedings of the Illinois Academy of Criminology, 1985-1986 Program. 55p. (C). 1988. pap. text 8.00 (*0-933757-17-4*) Ill Academy.

***Bensinger, Gad J., ed.** The Illinois Academy of Criminology the First Fifty Years: An Anthology. (Illus.). 117p. (C). 2000. pap. text 20.00 (*0-933757-24-7*) Ill Academy.

Bensinger, Gad J. & Lurigio, Arthur J. Sex Offenders: A Challenge for Community Corrections. 65p. (Orig.). 1996. pap. 10.00 (*0-942854-21-7*) Loyola U Crim.

***Bensinger, Gad J. & Lurigio, Arthur J., eds.** The Female Offender. 55p. (C). 2000. pap. text 10.00 (*0-942854-22-5*) Ill Academy.

Bensinger, Gad J. & Lurigio, Arthur J., eds. Gangs & Community Corrections. 58p. (C). lib. bdg. 10.00 (*0-942854-18-7*) Loyola U Crim.

Bensinger, Gad J. & Rowe, Cyprian, eds. Law Enforcement & AIDS: Questions of Justice & Care. 58p. 1988. pap. text 7.00 (*0-942854-13-6*) Loyola U Crim.

Bensinger, Gad J., jt. ed. see Lurigio, Arthur J.

Bensinger, Lenore, jt. auth. see Mast, Edward.

Bension, Shmuel. New York Production Manual, 1979-80: The Producer's Masterguide for Motion Picture, Television, Commercials & Videotape Industries. LC 79-644582. 600p. 1979. pap. 35.00 (*0-935744-00-2*) Prod Mstrguide.

— The Producer's Master-Guide, 1983: The International Production Manual for Motion Picture, Television, Commercials, Cable & Videotape Industries in the United States & Canada. 3rd ed. LC 83-641703. 624p. (Orig.). (C). 1982. pap. 58.00 (*0-935744-02-9*) Prod Mstrguide.

— The Producer's Masterguide, 1986: The International Production Manual for Motion Picture, Broadcast Television, Commercials, Cable & Videotape Industries in the United States, Canada, the United Kingdom, Ireland, The Caribbean Islands & Bermuda. 6th ed. LC 83-641703. 600p. (Orig.). 1986. pap. 69.95 (*0-935744-05-3*) Prod Mstrguide.

— The Producer's Masterguide, 1987: The International Production Manual for Motion Picture, Broadcast Television, Commercials, Cable & Videotape Industries Throughout the United States, Canada, the United Kingdom, The Caribbean Islands & Bermuda, Ireland & New Zealand. 7th ed. LC 83-641703. 600p. 1987. 79.95 (*0-935744-06-1*) Prod Mstrguide.

— The Producer's Masterguide, 1988: The International Production Manual for Motion Picture, Broadcast Television, Commercials, Cable & Videotape Industries Throughout the United States, Canada, the United Kingdom, the Caribbean Islands & Bermuda, Israel, Australia & New Zealand. 8th ed. LC 83-641703. 500p. 1988. 79.95 (*0-935744-07-X*) Prod Mstrguide.

— The Producer's Masterguide, 1989: The International Production Manual for Motion Picture, Broadcast Television, Commercials, Cable & Videotape Industries Throughout the United States, Canada, the United Kingdom, the Caribbean Islands & Bermuda, Israel, Australia & New Zealand. 9th ed. LC 83-641703. 500p. 1989. 89.95 (*0-935744-08-8*) Prod Mstrguide.

— The Producer's Masterguide, 1984: The International Production Manual for Motion Picture, Television, Commercials, Cable & Videotape Industries in the United States, Canada & the United Kingdom. 4th ed. LC 83-641703. 770p. 1985. pap. 69.95 (*0-935744-03-7*) Prod Mstrguide.

— The Producer's Masterguide, 1985: The International Production Manual for Motion Picture, Television, Commercials, Cable & Videotape Industries in the United States, Canada & the United Kingdom. 5th ed. LC 83-641703. 700p. (Orig.). 1985. pap. 69.95 (*0-935744-04-5*) Prod Mstrguide.

— Producer's Masterguide, 1997/1998: The International Production Manual for Motion Picture, Broadcast-Television, Commercials, Cable, & Videotape Industries Throughout the U. S., Canada, the U. K., the Caribbean Islands, Mexico, Israel, Australia, & New Zealand, Europe, South America, & the Far East. 500p. 1997. pap. 125.00 (*0-935744-16-9*) Prod Mstrguide.

— The Producer's Masterguide, 1996: The International Production Manual for Motion Picture, Broadcast-Television, Commercials, Cable, & Videotape Industries Throughout the U. S., Canada, the U. K., the Caribbean Islands, Mexico, Israel, Australia, & New Zealand, Europe, South America, & the Far East. 15th ed. 500p. 1996. pap. 125.00 (*0-935744-15-0*) Prod Mstrguide.

— The Producer's Masterguide, 1995: The International Production Manual for Motion Picture, Broadcast Television, Commercials, Cable & Videotape Industries Throughout the U. S., Canada, U. K., Caribbean Islands, Bermuda, Israel, Australia, New Zealand, Austria, Norway, Philippines & Mexico. 14th ed. 400p. 1995. pap. 120.00 (*0-935744-13-4*) Prod Mstrguide.

— The Producer's Masterguide, 1990: The International Production Manual for Motion Picture, Broadcast Television, Commercials, Cable & Videotape Industries Throughout the United States, Canada, the United Kingdom, the Caribbean Islands & Bermuda, Israel, Australia & New Zealand, Austria & Mexico. 10th ed. LC 83-641703. 500p. 1990. 98.95 (*0-935744-09-6*) Prod Mstrguide.

— The Producer's Masterguide, 1991: The International Production Manual for Motion Picture, Broadcast Television, Commercials, Cable & Videotape Industries Throughout the United States, Canada, the United Kingdom, the Caribbean Islands & Bermuda, Israel, Australia & New Zealand, Austria & Mexico. 11th ed. LC 83-641703. 500p. 1991. 98.95 (*0-935744-10-X*) Prod Mstrguide.

— The Producer's Masterguide, 1992: The International Production Manual for Motion Picture, Broadcast Television, Commercials, Cable & Videotape Industries Throughout the United States, Canada, the United Kingdom, the Caribbean Islands & Bermuda, Israel, Australia & New Zealand, Austria, Philippines & Mexico. 12th ed. 400p. 1992. pap. 98.95 (*0-935744-11-8*) Prod Mstrguide.

— The Producer's Masterguide, 1993/94: The International Production Manual for Motion Picture, Broadcast Television, Commercials, Cable & Videotape Industries Throughout the United States, Canada, the United Kingdom, the Caribbean Islands, Israel, Europe, Australia, Austria, Japan, Philippines, & Mexico. 13th ed. 400p. 1993. pap. 115.00 (*0-935744-12-6*) Prod Mstrguide.

— Producer's Masterguide, 2000: The International Production Manual for Motion Picture, Broadcast-Television, Feature Films, Commercials, Cable, & Videotape Industries Throughout the U. S., Canada, the United Kingdom, the Caribbean Islands, Mexico, Israel, Australia, New Zealand, Europe, South America, the Far East & Africa. 18th ed. LC 83-641703. 500p. 2000. pap. 125.00 (*0-935744-17-7*) Prod Mstrguide.

Bension, Shmuel, ed. New York Production Manual, 1981: The Producer's Masterguide for Motion Picture, Television, Commercials & Videotape Industries. 2nd ed. 1100p. 1981. pap. 58.00 (*0-935744-01-0*) Prod Mstrguide.

Benski, Claude, et al. The Mars Effect: A French Test of over 1,000 Sports Champions. LC 95-44463. 157p. 1996. pap. 21.00 (*0-87975-988-7*) Prometheus Bks.

Benskin, E. Extermination of Forests. 200p. 1985. pap. 175.00 (*0-7855-0354-4*, Pub. by Intl Bks & Periodicals) St Mut.

Benskin, Jan, jt. auth. see Dehn, Bonnie.

Benskina, Orelia. In Retrospect. 1986. 25.00 (*0-946270-34-1*, Pub. by Pentland Pr) St Mut.

Bensko, John. Green Soldiers. LC 80-26052. (Yale Series of Younger Poets: No. 76). 78p. 1981. reprint ed. pap. 30.00 (*0-7837-4554-0*, 208034500005) Bks Demand.

***Bensko, John.** The Iron City. LC 99-50618. 2000. pap. 14.95 (*0-252-06871-8*) U of Ill Pr.

Bensko, John. The Waterman's Children. LC 93-32434. 104p. 1994. pap. 10.95 (*0-87023-902-3*); lib. bdg. 20.00 (*0-87023-901-5*) U of Mass Pr.

***Bensky, Alan.** Short-Range Wireless Communication: Fundamentals of RF System Design & Application. (Demystified Ser.). (Illus.). 274p. 2000. pap. 49.95 (*1-878707-53-1*, Pub. by LLH Tech Pub) IPG Chicago.

Bensky, Dan & Barolet, Randall. Chinese Herbal Medicine: Formulas & Strategies. LC 89-81674. (Illus.). 592p. (C). 1990. text 85.00 (*0-939616-10-6*) Eastland.

Bensky, Dan, ed. see Shanghai College of Traditional Chinese Medicine S.

Bensky, Lynda & Shawn, Wendy. The Concerned Parents Guide to L. A. County Schools. 212p. 1990. pap. text 13.95 (*0-9626059-0-5*) Castbusters.

Bensley. Critical Thinking in Psychology: A Unified Skills Approach. LC 97-21646. (Psychology Ser.). (C). 1997. pap. 25.95 (*0-534-25620-1*) Wadsworth Pub.

B

Bensley, Benjamin A. Practical Anatomy of the Rabbit: An Elementary Laboratory Textbook in Mammalian Anatomy. 8th ed. Craigie, E. Horne, ed. LC 68-9247. 405p. reprint ed. pap. 125.60 (*0-7837-0029-6*, 203401500016) Bks Demand.

Bensley, Connie. Central Reservations: New & Selected Poems. 126p. (Orig.). 1990. pap. 18.95 (*1-85224-128-4*, Pub. by Bloodaxe Bks) Dufour.

— Choosing to be a Swan: New Poems. 64p. 1995. pap. 15.95 (*1-85224-314-7*, Pub. by Bloodaxe Bks) Dufour.

Bensley, Loren B., Jr. & Bensley, Robert J. Coordinating School-Based Sex & HIV/AIDS Education Programs. LC 97-93192. 90p. 1997. pap. 15.00 (*0-9655436-1-7*) Balance Grp.

— Implementing & Evaluating Sex & HIV/AIDS Education Programs in Michigan Schools. LC 96-79436. 96p. 1996. pap. 12.50 (*0-9655436-0-9*) Balance Grp.

Bensley, Robert J. & Brookins-Fisher, Jodi, eds. Community Health Education Methods: A Practitioner's Guide. LC 97-72291. 300p. 1997. pap. 29.95 (*0-9655436-2-5*) Balance Grp.

Bensley, Robert J., jt. auth. see Bensley, Loren B., Jr.

Bensmaia, Reda. The Barthes Effect: The Essay As Reflective Text. Fedkiew, Pat, tr. from FRE. (Theory & History of Literature Ser.: Vol. 54). xxxi, 152p. (Orig.). 1987. pap. 12.95 (*0-8166-1379-6*) U of Minn Pr.

— Years of Passages. 1995. pap. 21.95 (*0-8166-2393-7*) U of Minn Pr.

Bensman, Bobbi. Bouldering with Bobbi Bensman. LC 97-25955. (Illus.). 96p. 1999. pap. 15.95 (*0-8117-2677-0*) Stackpole.

Bensman, Bobbi & Boga, Steve. Bouldering with Bobbi Bensman. LC 97-25955. (Climbing Specialists Ser.). (Illus.). 96p. 1998. pap. 14.95 (*0-8117-2734-3*) Stackpole.

Bensman, David. The Practice of Solidarity: American Hat Finishers in the Nineteenth Century. LC 83-6592. (Working Class in American History Ser.). (Illus.). 264p. 1985. text 27.50 (*0-252-01093-0*) U of Ill Pr.

Bensman, Joseph, et al, eds. Politics, Character, & Culture: Perspectives from Hans Gerth, 41. LC 81-13426. (Contributions in Sociology Ser.: No. 41). 290p. 1982. 65.00 (*0-313-22863-9*, VSP/, Greenwood Pr) Greenwood.

Bensman, Joseph & Lilienfeld, Robert. Between Public & Private: The Lost Boundaries of the Self. LC 78-24751. 1979. pap. 12.95 (*0-02-902680-6*) Free Pr.

— Craft & Consciousness: Occupational Technique & the Development of World Images. 2nd ed. (Communication & Social Order Ser.). 419p. 1991. pap. text 33.95 (*0-202-30385-3*); lib. bdg. 59.95 (*0-202-30384-5*) Aldine de Gruyter.

Bensman, Joseph, jt. auth. see Vidich, Arthur J.

***Bensman, Marvin R.** The Beginning of Broadcast Regulation in the Twentieth Century. LC 99-56536. 280p. 2000. per. 35.00 (*0-7864-0737-9*) McFarland & Co.

Benso, Harold J. & Talaro, Kathleen P. Human Anatomy Laboratory Textbook. 5th ed. 368p. (C). 1995. text 38.50 (*0-697-21928-3*, WCB McGr Hill) McGrw-H Hghr Educ.

***Benso, Silvia.** The Face of Things: A Different Side of Ethics. (C). 2000. pap. text (*0-7914-4574-7*) State U NY Pr.

— The Face of Things: A Different Side of Ethics. (C). 2000. text 57.50 (*0-7914-4573-9*) State U NY Pr.

Benson. British Coalminers in the 19th Century. 288p. 1993. 61.95 (*0-7512-0196-0*) Ashgate Pub Co.

Benson. Firm for Life. 1997. 23.00 (*0-593-90174-6*) Bantam.

— Healthcare Computing. 1995. pap. text 29.00 (*0-582-22978-2*, Pub. by Addison-Wesley) Longman.

— Medical Informatics. 1994. pap. text. write for info. (*0-582-08271-4*, Pub. by Addison-Wesley) Longman.

— Microbiology. 8th ed. 2001. lab manual ed. 42.74 (*0-07-231888-0*); lab manual ed. 37.00 (*0-07-231889-9*) McGraw.

— Retailing Industry. 1350p. 2000. text 475.00 (*1-86064-348-5*, Pub. by I B T) St Martin.

— Texas Politics. (C). 1996. pap. text, teacher ed. 42.00 (*0-15-503540-1*) Harcourt Coll Pubs.

— University Physics. rev. ed. 420p. 1996. pap. 36.95 (*0-471-14604-8*) Wiley.

***Benson.** Wallace Stegner a Study of the Short Fiction. LC 98-27650. 1998. 29.00 (*0-8057-1669-6*, Twyne) Mac Lib Ref.

***Benson & Cullen.** White Collar Offender. 200p. 2000. text 45.00 (*0-8133-2493-9*) Westview.

Benson & Horwood, William. Toad Triumphant. 288p. 1998. pap. 11.95 (*0-312-18304-6*) St Martin.

Benson & Talaro. Human Anatomy. 4th ed. 1993. lab manual ed. 80.00 (*0-697-15021-6*, WCB McGr Hill) McGrw-H Hghr Educ.

Benson & Talero. Human Anatomy. 5th ed. 1995. text, teacher ed., lab manual ed. 15.93 (*0-697-21929-1*, WCB McGr Hill) McGrw-H Hghr Educ.

Benson, et al. Anat. Physiology Inter. History. 5th ed. 1994. 53.74 incl. sl. (*0-697-26055-0*, WCB McGr Hill) McGrw-H Hghr Educ.

Benson, jt. auth. see Prescott.

Benson, jt. auth. see Steinbacker.

Benson, A. & Hedin, Allan. Swedes in America, 1638-1938. LC 73-98681. (American History & Americana Ser.: No. 47). 1969. reprint ed. lib. bdg. 75.00 (*0-8383-0326-9*) M S G Haskell Hse.

Benson, A. C., ed. Cambridge Essays on Education. 232p. 1977. 18.95 (*0-8369-0273-4*) Ayer.

Benson, A. T. Important Events of the Century: 1786-1876. 400p. 1993. pap. 35.00 (*0-87556-757-6*) Saifer.

Benson, Adolph B. Farm, Forge & Philosophy: Chapters of a Swedish Immigrant's Life. 1961. 1.00 (*0-318-03684-3*) Swedish-Am.

— Sweden & the American Revolution. 1926. 30.00 (*0-686-17387-2*) R S Barnes.

— Swedes in America, 1638-1938. (History - United States Ser.). 614p. 1993. reprint ed. lib. bdg. 109.00 (*0-7812-4869-8*) Rprt Serv.

Benson, Adolph B., tr. see Almqvist, Carl Jonas Love.

***Benson, Al.** Gastrointestinal Oncology. LC 98-22563. (Cancer Treatment & Research Ser.). 17p. 1998. write for info. (*0-7923-8205-6*) Kluwer Academic.

Benson, Al. Vortex of Fear. 436p. (Orig.). 19.95 (*1-880396-43-2*, JP9643-2) Jalmar Pr.

— Vortex of Fear. LC 93-38346. (Orig.). 1994. 24.95 (*0-913969-60-5*) Univ Pub Assocs.

Benson, Alie H., jt. auth. see Harrel, Irene B.

Benson, Allan L. Nikola Tesla, Dreamer: His Three-Day Trip to Europe & His Scheme to Split the Earth. 29p. 1996. reprint ed. spiral bd. 8.00 (*0-7873-0093-4*) Hlth Research.

Benson, Allen C. Neal Schuman Complete Internet Companion for Librarians. LC 97-29536. (Netguides Ser.). 513p. 1997. 65.00 (*1-55570-317-8*) Neal-Schuman.

— Securing PCs & Data in Libraries & Schools: A Handbook with Menuing, Anti-Virus, & Other Protective Software. LC 98-9355. 250p. 1998. pap. 125.00 (*1-55570-321-6*) Neal-Schuman.

Benson, Allen C. & Fodemski, Linda. Connecting Kids & the Internet: A Handbook for Librarians, Teachers, & Parents. (Illus.). 382p. (Orig.). 1996. pap. 45.00 (*1-55570-244-9*) Neal-Schuman.

***Benson, Allen C. & Fodemski, Linda.** Connecting Kids & the Internet: A Handbook for Librarians, Teachers & Parents. 2nd rev. ed. LC 99-16424. 382p. 1999. pap. 49.95 (*1-55570-348-8*) Neal-Schuman.

***Benson, Andrew D.** The True Origins of Christianity & the Bible. rev. ed. 358p. 1999. pap. text 25.00 (*1-929372-00-0*) Prudent Pubg Co.

***Benson, Angela.** Awakening Mercy. LC 00-26866. (Heartquest Ser.). 2000. 9.99 (*0-8423-1939-5*) Tyndale Hse.

Benson, Angela. Bands of Gold. 352p. 1994. mass mkt. 4.99 (*0-7860-0072-4*, Pinncle Kensgtn) Kensgtn Pub Corp.

— Between the Lines. 342p. 1996. pap. 4.99 (*0-7860-0267-0*) Kensgtn Pub Corp.

— A Family Wedding. 1997. per. 3.99 (*0-373-24085-6*, 1-24085-2) Silhouette.

— For All Time. 304p. 1995. mass mkt. 4.99 (*0-7860-0171-2*, Pinncle Kensgtn) Kensgtn Pub Corp.

— The Nicest Guy in America. 352p. 1997. mass mkt. 4.99 (*0-7860-0443-6*, Pinncle Kensgtn) Kensgtn Pub Corp.

— The Nicest Guy in America. large type ed. LC 98-3737. 1998. 23.95 (*0-7862-1461-9*) Thorndike Pr.

— Second Chance Dad: Christmas Arch. (Special Edition Ser.: No. 1146). 1997. per. 3.99 (*0-373-24146-1*, 1-24146-2) Harlequin Bks.

***Benson, Angela.** Telling the Tale: The African-American Fiction Writer's Guide. 224p. 2000. pap. 12.00 (*0-425-17054-3*) Berkley Pub.

Benson, Angela. The Way Home. 304p. 1997. mass mkt. 4.99 (*0-7860-0373-1*, Pinncle Kensgtn) Kensgtn Pub Corp.

Benson, Ann. Beadweaving: New Needle Techniques & Original Designs. LC 93-12799. (Illus.). 144p. 1993. 27.95 (*0-8069-0400-3*, Chapelle) Sterling.

— Beadweaving: New Needle Techniques & Original Designs. (Illus.). 320p. 1996. pap. 14.95 (*0-8069-0401-1*) Sterling.

— Beadwork Basics. (Illus.). 128p. 1995. pap. 14.95 (*0-8069-0878-5*, Chapelle) Sterling.

— The Burning Road. LC 98-27783. 480p. 1999. 23.95 (*0-385-33289-0*) Delacorte.

***Benson, Ann.** The Burning Road. 2000. mass mkt. 6.50 (*0-440-22591-4*) Dell.

Benson, Ann. The Plague Tales. 688p. 1998. mass mkt. 6.50 (*0-440-22510-8*) Dell.

— Two-Hour Beaded Projects: More Than 200 Designs. (Illus.). 128p. 1997. pap. text 14.95 (*0-8069-4271-1*, Chapelle) Sterling.

Benson, Ann, jt. auth. see Allsop, Terry.

Benson, Ann, ed. see Allsop, Terry.

Benson, Ann G., et al. To Know for Real: Royce S. Pitkin & Goddard College. LC 87-15562. (Illus.). 288p. 2000. 25.00 (*0-912362-20-0*) Adamant Pr.

Benson, Anna & Warburton, Neil. Looms & Weaving. (Album Ser.: Vol. 154). (Illus.). 32p. 4.75 (*0-85263-753-5*, Pub. by Shire Pubns) Lubrecht & Cramer.

Benson, Anna, jt. auth. see Benson, Cynthia.

Benson, Anna, jt. auth. see Knopp, Fay H.

Benson, Anna B. Solo Dolci: The Italian Dessert Cookbook. LC 96-19362. (Illus.). 208p. 1996. 19.95 (*1-56474-185-0*) Fithian Pr.

***Benson, April L.** I Shop, Therefore I Am: Compulsive Buying & the Search for Self. LC RC569.5.S56I12 2000. 2000. 55.00 (*0-7657-0242-8*) Aronson.

Benson, Arlene. The Noontide Sun: The Field Journals of the Rev. Stephen Bowers, LC 97-29865. (Anthropological Papers: Vol. 44). (Illus.). 301p. 1997. pap. 27.50 (*0-87919-136-8*) Ballena Pr.

— The Noontide Sun: The Field Journals of the Rev. Stephen Bowers, Pionner Archaeologist. LC 97-29865. (Anthropological Papers: Vol. 44). (Illus.). 301p. 1997. 36.00 (*0-87919-135-X*) Ballena Pr.

Benson, Arthur C. Alfred Tennyson. LC 69-13820. 243p. 1969. reprint ed. lib. bdg. 35.00 (*0-8371-1071-8*, BENA, Greenwood Pr) Greenwood.

— Alfred Tennyson. (BCL1-PR English Literature Ser.). 243p. 1992. reprint ed. lib. bdg. 79.00 (*0-7812-7693-4*) Rprt Serv.

— At Large. LC 73-128209. (Essay Index Reprint Ser.). 1977. 26.95 (*0-8369-1941-6*) Ayer.

— Child of the Dawn: A Journey from Death to Rebirth. LC 94-19524. 1994. reprint ed. 16.95 (*1-885018-02-9*); reprint ed. pap. 9.95 (*1-885018-03-7*) Logo Press.

— Edward Fitzgerald. 1988. reprint ed. lib. bdg. 49.00 (*0-7812-0085-7*) Rprt Serv.

— Edward Fitzgerald. LC 71-131625. 1970. reprint ed. 10.00 (*0-403-00512-4*) Scholarly.

— Escape, & Other Essays. LC 74-152157. (Essay Index Reprint Ser.). 1977. reprint ed. 23.95 (*0-8369-2345-6*) Ayer.

— From a College Window. (BCL1-PR English Literature Ser.). 250p. 1992. reprint ed. lib. bdg. 79.00 (*0-7812-7436-2*) Rprt Serv.

— Paul the Minstrel & Other Stories. LC 70-106247. (Short Story Index Reprint Ser.). 1977. 26.95 (*0-8369-3283-8*) Ayer.

— Rossetti. (BCL1-PR English Literature Ser.). 238p. 1992. reprint ed. lib. bdg. 79.00 (*0-7812-7630-6*) Rprt Serv.

— Ruskin: A Study in Personality. (BCL1-PR English Literature Ser.). 323p. 1992. reprint ed. lib. bdg. 89.00 (*0-7812-7637-3*) Rprt Serv.

— Tennyson. 4th ed. LC 76-137369. (Select Bibliographies Reprint Ser.). 1977. reprint ed. 18.95 (*0-8369-5570-6*) Ayer.

— Walter Pater. (BCL1-PR English Literature Ser.). 226p. 1992. reprint ed. lib. bdg. 79.00 (*0-7812-7612-8*) Rprt Serv.

Benson, B. J. & Herbort, Diane. Gardening with Ribbons. 36p. 1994. pap. text 15.95 (*0-9629056-0-7*) Quilters Res.

Benson, Barbara. Latrobe & Rominson, the Engineer As Agent of Technological Transfer: The Engineer As Agent of Technological Transfer. (Illus.). 72p. 1975. pap. 1.25 (*0-914650-07-6*) Hagley Museum.

Benson, Barbara & Barnett, Susan. Student-Led Conferencing Using Showcase Portfolios. LC 98-25475. (1-Off Ser.). (Illus.). 160p. 1998. pap. 27.95 (*0-8039-6766-7*) Corwin Pr.

Benson, Barbara E. Logs & Lumber: The Development of Lumbering in Michigan's Lower Peninsula, 1837-1870. (Illus.). 1989. 25.00 (*0-916699-14-5*) CMU Clarke Hist Lib.

Benson, Barbara E., et al. An Anthology of Delaware Papermaking. (Illus.). 96p. 1991. 195.00 (*0-938768-26-3*) Oak Knoll.

Benson, Barry W. & Boege, Steven. Handbook of Good Laboratory Practice. 448p. 1998. text 100.00 (*1-56032-573-9*) Hemisp Pub.

Benson, Benjamin A. Parenthood Is Your Greatest Achievement: An Interactive Family, Education & Genealogical Resource Book & Diary. 140p. 1993. 12.95 (*0-9637122-0-9*) Partners Educ.

Benson, Betty L. Nature's Melody: A Guide to Georgia Wildflowers. Patrick, Thomas S., ed. LC 82-74400. (Illus.). 226p. (Orig.). 1994. pap. 25.00 (*0-9612486-1-0*) Garden GA.

Benson, Beverly, jt. auth. see Byrd, Patricia.

***Benson, Bob, Sr. & Benson, Michael W.** Disciplines for the Inner Life. 2000. reprint ed. pap. 20.00 (*0-9677725-0-8*) Deeper Life Pr.

Benson, Bob, jt. auth. see Dean Fry, Karen.

Benson, Bobbi L. & Burnes, Jennifer J. Crossing Colorado: Adventures on Colorado's Scenic & Historic Byways. (Colorado Source Travel Book Ser.). 300p. 1998. pap. text 17.95 (*0-9637238-0-4*) Benson Barnes Pub.

Benson, Bonnie, jt. auth. see McNeill, Beth.

Benson, Brooke, ed. see Lahr Schier, Mary.

Benson, Brooke, ed. see Pearlstein, Mitchell B. & Meeks, Annette.

Benson, Bruce, jt. auth. see Greenhut, M. L.

Benson, Bruce L. The Enterprise of Law: Justice Without the State. 400p. 1990. 39.95 (*0-936488-29-8*); pap. 14.95 (*0-936488-30-1*) PRIPP.

— Privatization in Criminal Justice. 68p. 1996. pap. 7.95 (*0-945999-54-2*, 1008) Independent Inst.

— To Serve & Protect: Privatization & Community in Criminal Justice. LC 98-19688. (Political Economy of the Austrian School Ser.). 416p. 1998. text 37.50 (*0-8147-1327-0*) NYU Pr.

— Toxic Torts by Government. (Independent Policy Reports). 59p. (Orig.). 1996. pap. 6.95 (*0-945999-53-4*) Independent Inst.

Benson, Bruce L. & Rasmussen, David W. Illicit Drugs & Crime. (Independent Policy Reports). 67p. (Orig.). 1996. pap. 7.95 (*0-945999-46-1*) Independent Inst.

Benson, Bruce L., jt. auth. see Brakel, Samuel J.

Benson, Bruce L., jt. auth. see Rasmussen, David W.

Benson, C. David, ed. Critical Essays on Chaucer's Troilus & Criseyde & His Major Early Poems. 256p. 1991. text 65.00 (*0-8020-5006-9*); pap. text 18.95 (*0-8020-6937-1*) U of Toronto Pr.

Benson, C. David & Blanchfield, Lynne S. The Manuscripts of "Piers Plowman" The B-Version. LC 97-28792. (Illus.). 352p. 1997. 110.00 (*0-85991-501-8*, DS Brewer) Boydell & Brewer.

Benson, C. H. Arte de Ensenar. Villalobos, Fernando P., tr. from ENG. (Curso para Maestros Cristianos Ser.: No. 5).Tr. of Art of Teaching. (SPA.). 128p. 1971. pap. 7.99 (*0-89922-016-9*) Caribe Betania.

— Conozcamos al Alumno. Villalobos, Fernando P., tr. from ENG. (Curso para Maestros Cristianos Ser.: No. 4).Tr. of Understanding Children & Youth. (SPA.). 128p. 1972. pap. 7.99 (*0-89922-014-2*) Caribe Betania.

Benson, C. H. Escuela Dominical en Accion. Villalobos, Fernando P., tr. from ENG. (Curso para Maestros Cristianos Ser.: No. 6).Tr. of Church at Study Sunday School Ministry. (SPA.). 122p. 1972. pap. 7.99 (*0-89922-018-5*) Caribe Betania.

Benson, C. H. Poesia y Profecia del Antiquo Testamento. Villalobos, Fernando P., tr. from ENG. (Curso para Maestros Cristianos Ser.: No. 2).Tr. of Broadening Your Biblical Horizon. (SPA.). 122p. 1972. pap. 7.99 (*0-89922-010-X*) Caribe Betania.

Benson, C. T., jt. auth. see Grove, Larry C.

Benson, Carmen. Seven Splendid Moments. 96p. 1974. mass mkt. 5.99 (*0-88368-054-8*) Whitaker Hse.

Benson, Carol, ed. see Dyer, M. Phillip.

Benson, Carolyn V. The Outlet Shopper: A Guide to Factory Outlet Shopping in Pennsylvania, Maryland, Virginia & the District of Columbia. 2nd ed. Modrak, Nancy C., ed. (Illus.). 192p. 1990. pap. 9.95 (*0-915168-20-0*) Wash Bk Trad.

Benson, Charles J., jt. auth. see Bates, John H.

Benson, Charles S. & Hodgkinson, Harold L. Implementing the Learning Society: New Strategies for Financing Social Objectives. LC 73-21072. 167p. reprint ed. pap. 51.80 (*0-608-14786-9*, 202565000045) Bks Demand.

Benson, Charlotte & Clay, Edward. The Impact of Drought on Sub-Saharan African Economies: A Preliminary Examination. LC 97-52167. (Technical Paper Ser.: No. 401). 92p. 1998. pap. 22.00 (*0-8213-4180-4*, 14180) World Bank.

***Benson, Chris & Christian, Scott, eds.** Writing for the Community: Models, Methods & Motives. LC 99-59241. 2000. pap. text. write for info. (*1-893056-05-8*) Calendar Islands.

Benson, Chris, jt. auth. see Howard, Tharon.

***Benson, Clarence H.** Teaching Science & Design & Technology in The Early Years. 1999. pap. text 27.95 (*1-85346-547-X*) David Fulton.

Benson, Clarence H. Teaching Techniques. rev. ed. LC 84-129711. 96p. 1983. pap. text 9.95 (*0-910566-05-4*) Evang Trg Assn.

— The Triune God. rev. ed. 96p. 1970. pap. text 9.95 (*0-910566-09-7*) Evang Trg Assn.

Benson, Clarence H., jt. auth. see Schultz, Samuel J.

Benson, Clark & Gordon, Alex. College: Your Complete Guide to the Best Five Years of Your Life. Kallenberg, Gregory, ed. (Illus.). 148p. (Orig.). 1994. pap. 14.95 (*0-88092-080-7*) Picket Fence.

Benson, Constance A., jt. ed. see Korvick, Joyce A.

Benson, Constance L. God & Caesar: Troeltsch's Social Teaching As Legitimation. 324p. 1998. 44.95 (*1-56000-384-7*) Transaction Pubs.

Benson, Craig H. Risk-Based Corrective Action & Brownfields Restorations. LC 98-33992. (Geotechnical Special Publication Ser.). 312p. 1998. 45.00 (*0-7844-0389-9*) Am Soc Civil Eng.

Benson, Cynda L. Early American Illuminated Manuscripts from the Ephrata Cloiser. 24p. 1994. pap. 6.00 (*0-87391-046-X*) Smith Coll Mus Art.

— 101 Visions: Centurions. Brairton, Betsey, ed. (Illus.). 40p. 1997. pap. write for info. (*0-9654682-1-6*) Savannah Coll.

Benson, Cynda L. & Sallee, Katherine. Icons of the Century: Jacob Lawrence. Van Baron, Judith & Brairton, Betsey, eds. (Illus.). 26p. 1998. 12.00 (*0-9654682-4-0*) Savannah Coll.

Benson, Cynthia & Benson, Anna. Firm for Life. (Illus.). 240p. 1998. reprint ed. pap. 13.00 (*0-7679-0175-4*) Broadway BDD.

Benson, D. Representation & Cohomology Vol. 1: Basic Representative Theory of Finite Groups & Associative Algebras, Vol. 1. (Studies in Advanced Mathematics: No. 30). 384p. (C). 1998. reprint ed. pap. text 29.95 (*0-521-63653-1*) Cambridge U Pr.

— Representation & Cohomology Vol. 2: Cohomology of Groups & Modules. (Studies in Advanced Mathematics: No. 31). 288p. (C). 1998. reprint ed. pap. text 29.95 (*0-521-63652-3*) Cambridge U Pr.

Benson, D. & Cohen, F. Mapping Class Groups of Low Genus & Their Cohomology. LC 90-26421. (Memoirs Ser.: Vol. 90/443). 104p. 1991. pap. 21.00 (*0-8218-2506-2*, MEMO/90/443) Am Math.

Benson, D., jt. auth. see Townes, P.

Benson, D. F. & Ardila, Alfredo. Aphasia: A Clinical Perspective. (Illus.). 456p. (C). 1996. text 52.50 (*0-19-508934-0*) OUP.

Benson, D. Frank. The Neurology of Thinking. LC 93-6521. (Illus.). 328p. (C). 1994. text 59.50 (*0-19-505882-8*) OUP.

Benson, D. Frank & Zaidel, Eran, eds. The Dual Brain: Hemispheric Specialization in Humans. LC 85-24955. 430p. 1985. lib. bdg. 55.00 (*0-89862-643-9*) Guilford Pubns.

Benson, D. Frank, jt. auth. see Cummings, Jeffrey L.

Benson, D. J. Modular Representation Theory: New Trends & Methods. (Lecture Notes in Mathematics Ser.: Vol. 1081). xi, 231p. 1984. 37.95 (*0-387-13389-5*) Spr-Verlag.

— Polynomial Invariant of Finite Groups. (London Mathematical Society Lecture Note Ser.: No. 190). 1993. pap. write for info. (*0-521-45866-8*) Cambridge U Pr.

— Representations & Cohomology Vol. 1: Basic Representative Theory of Finite Groups & Associative Algebra, Vol. I. (Studies in Advanced Mathematics: No. 30). 356p. (C). 1991. text 54.95 (*0-521-36134-6*) Cambridge U Pr.

Benson, D. J. & Asaro, R. A., eds. Advanced Computational Methods for Material Modeling. LC 93-73602. (PVP Ser., Vol. 268; AMD Ser.: Vol. 180). 243p. pap. 65.00 (*0-7918-1251-0*) ASME.

Benson, D. M., jt. ed. see Campbell, C. L.

Benson, D. R. The Renegade, No. 4. Grad, Doug, ed. (Tracker Ser.). 224p. (Orig.). 1992. pap. 3.50 (*0-671-73837-2*) PB.

Benson, D. Woodrow, jt. ed. see Benditt, David G.

Benson, Dale S. Measuring Outcomes in Ambulatory Care. LC 92-49961. 192p. (Orig.). 1992. pap. 49.95 (*1-55648-094-6*, 169106) AHPI.

Benson, Dale S. & Miller, Jane A. AmbuQual II: An Ambulatory Quality Assessment & Quality Management System. 2nd ed. (AmbuQual Ser.). 345p. 1993. pap. 148.00 (*0-9603164-8-5*) Clarian Hlth.

— Quality Assessment for Primary Care Centers. 3rd rev. ed. (Quality Primary Care Ser.). 1993. pap. 28.00 (*0-9603164-9-3*) Clarian Hlth.

Benson, Dale S. & Van Osdol, William R. Quality Audit Systems for Primary Care Centers. 3rd rev. ed. (Quality Primary Care Ser.). x, 451p. 1993. pap. 85.00 (*1-884742-01-7*) Clarian Hlth.

***Benson, Dan.** New Retirement: How to Secure Finanical Freedom & Live Out Your Dreams. 210p. 2000. pap. 14.99 (*0-8499-4248-9*) Word Pub.

— Retirement Alternative. LC 99-39399. 225p. 1999. pap. 19.99 (*0-8499-3772-8*) Word Pub.

Benson, Dan. 21 Days to Financial Freedom: A Proven Plan for Beginning New Habits. (Twenty-One Days Ser.). 144p. 1998. pap. 6.99 (*0-310-21751-2*) Zondervan.

Benson, Dan, ed. see DeMoss, Robert G., Jr.

Benson, Dan, ed. see Jantz, Gregory.

Benson, Dan, ed. see Temple, Todd.

Benson, Dan, ed. see Yorkey, Mike.

Benson, Daryl, photos by. Alberta: A Collection of 22 Postcards. (Illus.). 22p. 1999. pap. 6.95 (*1-55105-175-3*) Lone Pine.

— Rocky Mountains: A Collection of 22 Postcards (Canada) (Illus.). 22p. 1999. pap. 6.95 (*1-55105-187-7*) Lone Pine.

— Rocky Mountains: A Collection of 22 Postcards (U. S.) (Illus.). 22p. 1999. pap. 6.95 (*1-55105-189-3*) Lone Pine.

***Benson, Daryl & Wilson, Dale.** Guide to Photographing the Canadian Landscape. (Illus.). 152p. 2000. pap. text 29.95 (*0-9684576-0-6*) Photosecrets.

Benson, David. Easy Pic'n: A Beginner's Guide to Using PIC16/17 Microcontrollers from Square 1. (Illus.). 148p. (Orig.). 1996. pap. 29.95 (*0-9654162-0-8*) Sq One Elect.

— PIC'n Techniques Vol. 1: PIC Microcontroller Applications Guide. (Illus.). 275p. 1999. pap. 34.95 (*0-9654162-3-2*) Sq One Elect.

— PIC'n up the Pace Vol. 1: An Intermediate Guide to Using PIC16/17 Microcontrollers from Square 1. (Illus.). 272p. 1997. pap. 34.95 (*0-9654162-1-6*) Sq One Elect.

Benson, David F. Aphasia, Alexia, & Agraphia. LC 79-17205. (Clinical Neurology & Neurosurgery Monographs: No. 1). (Illus.). 223p. 1979. reprint ed. pap. 69.20 (*0-7837-6266-6*, 204597800010) Bks Demand.

Benson, Delwin E., et al. Wildlife Stewardship & Recreation on Private Lands. Winn, Judy F., ed. LC 98-47136. (Agriculture Ser.: Vol. 1). (Illus.). 224p. 1999. 29.95 (*0-89096-872-1*) Tex A&M Univ Pr.

Benson, Dennis C. Dennis Benson's Creative Bible Studies: Matthew-Acts: 401 Experiences to Help Youth Crawl Inside the Scriptures. (Illus.). 654p. 1985. pap. 21.99 (*0-931529-01-8*) Group Pub.

***Benson, Dennis K.** Return on Inves$tment: Guidelines to Determine Workforce Development Impact. 2nd ed. 148p. 1999. pap. 75.00 (*0-931405-01-7*) Approp Solutions.

Benson, Dennis K. Return on Inve$tment: Guidelines to Determine Workforce Development Impact. 58p. (Orig.). 1996. pap. 75.00 (*0-931405-00-9*) Approp Solutions.

Benson, Diana, jt. auth. see Benson, Jerry.

Benson, Don & Whitehead, Geoffrey. Transport & Distribution. 345p. (C). 1989. 100.00 (*0-7855-6113-7*, Pub. by Inst Pur & Supply) St Mut.

Benson, Donald C. The Moment of Proof: Mathematical Ephiphanies. LC 97-52139. (Illus.). 352p. 1999. 30.00 (*0-19-511721-2*) OUP.

***Benson, Donald C.** The Moment of Proof: Mathematical Epiphanies. (Illus.). 352p. 2000. pap. 17.95 (*0-19-513919-4*) OUP.

Benson, Douglas & Hughes, John A. The Perspective of Ethnomethodology. LC 82-10113. 213p. reprint ed. pap. 66.10 (*0-8357-6584-9*, 203597900097) Bks Demand.

Benson, Douglas, ed. see Benjamin, Walter W.

Benson, Douglas, ed. see Hill, Stan.

Benson, E. F. Charlotte Bronte. LC 70-173101. (Illus.). 1977. reprint ed. 25.95 (*0-405-08262-2*) Ayer.

— Colin. 1994. pap. 12.95 (*1-873741-15-4*) LPC InBook.

— Colin, II. 1995. pap. 13.95 (*1-873741-20-0*) LPC InBook.

— The Collected Ghost Stories of E. F. Benson. Dalby, Richard, ed. 624p. 1996. pap. 14.95 (*0-7867-0365-2*) Carroll & Graf.

— Desirable Residences & Other Stories. 304p. 1992. pap. 12.95 (*0-19-282977-7*) OUP.

— Lucia in London. LC 98-37616. 232p. 1999. pap. 11.95 (*1-55921-277-2*) Moyer Bell.

— Lucia's Progress. LC 98-53775. 234p. 2000. pap. 11.95 (*1-55921-233-0*) Moyer Bell.

— Mapp & Lucia. LC 98-52500. 234p. 2000. pap. 12.95 (*1-55921-232-2*) Moyer Bell.

***Benson, E. F.** Mapp & Lucia. (Humour Classics). 2000. 14.95 (*1-85375-390-4*, Pub. by Prion) Trafalgar.

Benson, E. F. Miss Mapp. LC 98-37623. 232p. 1999. pap. 11.95 (*1-55921-275-6*) Moyer Bell.

***Benson, E. F.** Miss Mapp, Set. unabridged ed. 1999. 41.95 incl. audio (*1-55685-587-7*) Audio Bk Con.

— The Passenger. Adrian, Jack, ed. xx, 160p. 1999. 39.00 (*1-899562-81-8*) Ash-Tree.

Benson, E. F. Queen Lucia. LC 97-41891. 176p. 1998. pap. 10.95 (*1-55921-252-7*) Moyer Bell.

***Benson, E. F.** Queen Lucia, Set. unabridged ed. (C). 1998. 41.95 incl. audio (*1-55685-584-2*) Audio Bk Con.

Benson, E. F. Raven's Brood. 1993. reprint ed. pap. 14.95 (*1-873741-09-X*, Pub. by Millvres Bks) LPC InBook.

***Benson, E. F.** The Terror by Night. Adrian, Jack, ed. (Collected Spook Stories Ser.: Vol. 1). xviii, 170p. 1998. 38.50 (*1-899562-55-9*) Ash-Tree.

— Trouble for Lucia. 232p. 2000. pap. 11.95 (*1-55921-281-0*) Moyer Bell.

Benson, E. F. Trouble for Lucia. 1992. reprint ed. lib. bdg. 18.95 (*0-89966-960-3*) Buccaneer Bks.

Benson, E. F. & Dalby, Richard. The Collected Ghost Stories of E. F. Benson. LC 95-202712. 624 p. 1992. write for info. (*1-85487-110-2*) ROB1.

Benson, E. F., ed. see James, Henry.

***Benson, Edmund F. & Benson, Susan.** Anti Graffiti Week: Teacher's Manual. (Illus.). 1999. pap. text, teacher ed. 25.00 (*1-58614-010-8*) Arise Found.

— Arise Basic Health 101: Health & Hygiene Instructor's Manual. (Illus.). 32p. 1996. pap. text, teacher ed. write for info. (*1-58614-030-2*) Arise Found.

— Arise Basic Health 101: Health & Hygiene Learner's Workbook. (Illus.). 64p. (J). (gr. 3-4). 1996. pap. text, wbk. ed. 12.95 (*1-58614-031-0*) Arise Found.

— Arise Basic Health 101: Nutrition & Exercise Instructor's Manual. (Illus.). 32p. 1996. pap. text, teacher ed. write for info. (*1-58614-032-9*) Arise Found.

— Arise Basic Health 101: Nutrition & Exercise Learner's Workbook. (Illus.). 64p. (gr. 3-4). 1996. pap. text, wbk. ed. 12.95 (*1-58614-033-7*) Arise Found.

— Arise Basic Health 101: Quiz Booklet. (Illus.). 24p. (J). (gr. 3-4). 1996. pap. text 7.49 (*1-58614-034-5*) Arise Found.

— Arise Best Citizen Middle School Edition: Instructor's Manual. (Illus.). 1999. pap. text, teacher ed. write for info. (*1-58614-003-5*) Arise Found.

— Arise Best Citizen Middle School Edition: Learner's Workbook. (Illus.). (gr. 3-4). 1999. pap. text, wbk. ed. write for info. (*1-58614-004-3*) Arise Found.

— Arise Brain Food: Being Safe. (Illus.). 71p. (J). (gr. 3-4). 1996. pap. text 29.95 (*1-58614-038-8*) Arise Found.

— Arise Brain Food: Creating a Positive Outlook. (Illus.). 65p. (J). (gr. 3-4). 1996. pap. text 29.95 (*1-58614-036-1*) Arise Found.

— Arise Brain Food: More Secrets of Success. (Illus.). 89p. (J). (gr. 3-4). 1996. pap. text 29.95 (*1-58614-039-6*) Arise Found.

— Arise Brain Food: Peaceful Living. (Illus.). 85p. (J). (gr. 3-4). 1996. pap. text 29.95 (*1-58614-035-3*) Arise Found.

— Arise Brain Food: Supercharging Your System. (Illus.). 88p. (J). (gr. 3-4). 1996. pap. text 29.95 (*1-58614-037-X*) Arise Found.

— Arise Brain Food: The Right Stuff. (Illus.). 78p. (J). (gr. 3-4). 1996. pap. text 29.95 (*1-58614-040-X*) Arise Found.

— Arise Brain Food Bonus Book: Money Matters. (Illus.). 31p. (J). (gr. 3-4). 1996. pap. text 9.95 (*1-58614-041-8*) Arise Found.

— Arise Fatherhood: Instructor's Manual. (Illus.). 32p. 1999. pap. text, teacher ed. write for info. (*1-58614-056-6*) Arise Found.

— Arise Fatherhood: Learner's Workbook. (Illus.). 64p. (J). (gr. 3-4). 1999. pap. text, wbk. ed. 12.95 (*1-58614-057-4*) Arise Found.

— Arise Law Enforcement: Instructor's Manual. (Illus.). 32p. 1999. pap. text, teacher ed. write for info. (*1-58614-005-1*) Arise Found.

— Arise Law Enforcement: Learner's Workbook. (Illus.). 64p. (J). (gr. 3-4). 1999. pap. text, wbk. ed. write for info. (*1-58614-006-X*) Arise Found.

— Arise Parenting 101: Building a Family Instructor's Manual. (Illus.). 32p. 1999. pap. text, teacher ed. write for info. (*1-58614-068-X*) Arise Found.

— Arise Parenting 101: Building a Family Learner's Workbook. (Illus.). 64p. (gr. 3-4). 1999. pap. text, wbk. ed. 12.95 (*1-58614-069-8*) Arise Found.

— Arise Parenting 101: Keeping Kids Safe at Home Instructors's Manual. (Illus.). 32p. 1999. pap. text, teacher ed. write for info. (*1-58614-058-2*) Arise Found.

— Arise Parenting 101: Keeping Kids Safe at Home Learner's Workbook. (Illus.). 64p. (J). (gr. 3-4). 1999. pap. text, wbk. ed. 12.95 (*1-58614-059-0*) Arise Found.

— Arise Parenting 101: Keeping Kids Safe Outside Instructor's Manual. (Illus.). 32p. 1999. pap. text, teacher ed. write for info. (*1-58614-060-4*) Arise Found.

— Arise Parenting 101: Keeping Kids Safe Outside Learner's Workbook. (Illus.). 64p. (J). (gr. 3-4). 1999. pap. text, wbk. ed. 12.95 (*1-58614-061-2*) Arise Found.

— Arise Parenting 101: Quiz Booklet. (Illus.). 36p. (J). (gr. 3-4). 1999. pap. text 7.49 (*1-58614-070-1*) Arise Found.

— Arise Parenting 101: Raising an Emotionally Healthy Child Instructor's Manual. (Illus.). 32p. 1999. pap., teacher ed. write for info. (*1-58614-066-3*) Arise Found.

— Arise Parenting 101: Raising an Emotionally Healthy Child Learner's Workbook. (Illus.). 64p. (J). (gr. 3-4). 1999. pap. text, wbk. ed. 12.95 (*1-58614-067-1*) Arise Found.

— Arise Parenting 101: Your Child's Mental Development Instructor's Manual. (Illus.). 32p. 1999. pap. text, teacher ed. write for info. (*1-58614-062-0*) Arise Found.

— Arise Parenting 101: Your Child's Mental Development Learner's Workbook. (Illus.). 64p. 1999. pap. text, wbk. ed. 12.95 (*1-58614-063-9*) Arise Found.

— Arise Parenting 101: Your Child's Physical Development Instructor's Manual. (Illus.). 32p. 1999. pap. text, teacher ed. write for info. (*1-58614-064-7*) Arise Found.

— Arise Parenting 101: Your Child's Physical Development Learner's Workbook. (Illus.). 64p. 1999. pap. text, wbk. ed. 12.95 (*1-58614-065-5*) Arise Found.

— Arise Playlets. (Illus.). (J). (gr. 3-4). 1999. pap. text. write for info. (*1-58614-103-1*) Arise Found.

— Burn Awareness Week: Teacher's Manual. (Illus.). 1999. pap. text, teacher ed. 25.00 (*1-58614-013-2*) Arise Found.

— Character & Ethics Manual. (Illus.). 136p. (J). (gr. 3-4). 1999. pap. text 32.95 (*1-58614-073-6*) Arise Found.

— A Day in the Life of a Dropout. (Illus.). 36p. (J). (gr. 3-4). 1999. pap. text 9.95 (*1-58614-086-8*) Arise Found.

— 83 Activities for Taneka's Urban Life Tales. (Illus.). 52p. (J). (gr. 3-4). 1999. pap. text 7.95 (*1-58614-100-7*) Arise Found.

— Electrical Safety Week: Teacher's Manual. (Illus.). 1999. pap. text, teacher ed. 25.00 (*1-58614-008-6*) Arise Found.

— Four Wheel Drive for the Mind: Learning Strategies & Time Management Instructor's Manual. (Illus.). 32p. 1996. pap. text, teacher ed. write for info. (*1-58614-025-6*) Arise Found.

— Four Wheel Drive for the Mind: Learning Strategies & Time Management Learner's Workbook. (Illus.). 64p. (J). (gr. 3-4). 1996. pap. text, wbk. ed. 12.95 (*1-58614-026-4*) Arise Found.

— Four Wheel Drive for the Mind: Networking, Jobs & Money Instructor's Manual. (Illus.). 32p. 1996. pap. text, teacher ed. write for info. (*1-58614-027-2*) Arise Found.

— Four Wheel Drive for the Mind: Networking, Jobs & Money Learner's Workbook. (Illus.). 64p. (J). (gr. 3-4). 1996. pap. text, wbk. ed. 12.95 (*1-58614-028-0*) Arise Found.

— Four Wheel Drive for the Mind: Quiz Booklet. (Illus.). 28p. (gr. 3-4). 1996. pap. text 7.49 (*1-58614-029-9*) Arise Found.

— Four Wheel Drive for the Mind: Self-Esteem Instructor's Manual. (Illus.). 32p. 1996. pap. text, teacher ed. write for info. (*1-58614-023-X*) Arise Found.

— Four Wheel Drive for the Mind: Self-Esteem Learner's Workbook. (Illus.). 64p. (J). (gr. 3-4). 1996. pap. text, wbk. ed. 12.95 (*1-58614-024-8*) Arise Found.

— Hacia una Mentalidad Mas Dinamica: Autoestima Cuaderno del Participante. (SPA., Illus.). 64p. (gr. 3-4). 1999. pap. text 12.95 (*1-58614-084-1*) Arise Found.

— Hacia una Mentalidad Mas Dinamica: Autoestima Manual del Instructor. (SPA., Illus.). 32p. 1999. pap. text, teacher ed. write for info. (*1-58614-083-3*) Arise Found.

— Hacia una Mentalidad Mas Dinamica Cuaderno de Pruebas. (SPA., Illus.). 28p. (J). (gr. 3-4). 1999. pap. text 7.49 (*1-58614-085-X*) Arise Found.

— I Forgive You Because It's Good for Me. (Illus.). 42p. (J). (gr. 3-4). 1996. pap. text 9.95 (*1-58614-098-1*) Arise Found.

— If I Could Start Life Over... (Illus.). 16p. (J). (gr. 3-4). 1999. pap. text 2.95 (*1-58614-087-6*) Arise Found.

— An Indoor Environmental Audit in the Form of a Flip Chart. (Illus.). 11p. 1996. pap. text. write for info. (*1-58614-101-5*) Arise Found.

— Kids Need to Know. (Illus.). 16p. (J). (gr. 3-4). 1999. pap. text 2.95 (*1-58614-093-0*) Arise Found.

— Lead Awareness Week: Teacher's Manual. (Illus.). 1999. pap. text, teacher ed. 25.00 (*1-58614-012-4*) Arise Found.

— Little by Little Art Book. (Illus.). (J). (gr. 3-4). 1999. pap. text 9.99 (*1-58614-002-7*) Arise Found.

— Little by Little Manual. (Illus.). (J). (gr. 3-4). 1994. pap. text 64.95 (*1-58614-000-0*) Arise Found.

— Little by Little Puppet Plays. (Illus.). (J). (gr. 3-4). 1999. pap. text 7.49 (*1-58614-001-9*) Arise Found.

— Mama Said. (Illus.). 16p. (J). (gr. 3-4). 1999. pap. text 2.95 (*1-58614-095-7*) Arise Found.

— Una Obra en Marcha: El Manejo de la Ira Cuaderno del Participante. (SPA., Illus.). 64p. (J). (gr. 3-4). 1999. pap. text 12.95 (*1-58614-079-5*) Arise Found.

— Una Obra en Marcha: El Manejo de la Ira Manual del Instructor. (SPA., Illus.). 32p. 1999. pap. text, teacher ed. write for info. (*1-58614-078-7*) Arise Found.

— Una Obra en Marcha: Violencia & Conflicto Cuaderno del Participante. (SPA., Illus.). 64p. (gr. 3-4). 1999. pap. 12.95 (*1-58614-081-7*) Arise Found.

— Una Obra en Marcha: Violencia & Conflicto Manual del Instructor. (SPA., Illus.). 32p. 1999. pap. text, teacher ed. write for info. (*1-58614-080-9*) Arise Found.

— Una Obra en Marcha Cuaderno de Pruebas. (SPA., Illus.). 32p. (J). (gr. 3-4). 1999. pap. text 7.49 (*1-58614-082-5*) Arise Found.

— Parents Need to Know. (Illus.). 1999. pap. text 2.95 (*1-58614-094-9*) Arise Found.

— Poison Prevention Week: Teacher's Manual. (Illus.). 1999. pap. text, teacher ed. 25.00 (*1-58614-009-4*) Arise Found.

— Rescue Me! Mother Earth Calls 911: The Basics Instructor's Manual. (Illus.). 32p. 1999. pap. text, teacher ed. write for info. (*1-58614-074-4*) Arise Found.

— Rescue Me! Mother Earth Calls 911: The Basics Learner's Workbook. (Illus.). 64p. (J). (gr. 3-4). 1999. pap. text, wbk. ed. 12.95 (*1-58614-075-2*) Arise Found.

— Rescue Me! Mother Earth Calls 911: What's Hurting Me Instructor's Manual. (Illus.). 32p. 1999. pap. text, teacher ed. write for info. (*1-58614-076-0*) Arise Found.

— Rescue Me! Mother Earth Calls 911: What's Hurting Me Learner's Workbook. (Illus.). 64p. (J). (gr. 3-4). 1999. pap. text, wbk. ed. 12.95 (*1-58614-077-9*) Arise Found.

— So You're Thinking of Dropping Out of School: Instructor's Manual. (Illus.). 32p. 1999. pap. text, teacher ed. write for info. (*1-58614-071-X*) Arise Found.

— So You're Thinking of Dropping Out of School: Learner's Workbook. (Illus.). 48p. 1999. pap. text, teacher ed 19.95 (*1-58614-072-8*) Arise Found.

— Sprouts - A Teenage Parenting Program: Building a Family Instructor's Manual. (Illus.). 31p. 1997. pap. text, teacher ed. write for info. (*1-58614-052-3*) Arise Found.

— Sprouts - A Teenage Parenting Program: Building a Family Learner's Workbook. (Illus.). 88p. (J). (gr. 3-4). 1997. pap. text, wbk. ed. 14.95 (*1-58614-053-1*) Arise Found.

— Sprouts - A Teenage Parenting Program: Emotional Development Instructor's Manual. (Illus.). 28p. 1997. pap. text, teacher ed. write for info. (*1-58614-046-9*) Arise Found.

— Sprouts - A Teenage Parenting Program: Emotional Development Learner's Workbook. (Illus.). 69p. (J). (gr. 3-4). 1997. pap. text, wbk. ed. 13.95 (*1-58614-047-7*) Arise Found.

— Sprouts - A Teenage Parenting Program: Keeping Your Child Safe Instructor's Manual. (Illus.). 70p. 1997. pap. text, teacher ed. write for info. (*1-58614-050-7*) Arise Found.

— Sprouts - A Teenage Parenting Program: Keeping Your Child Safe Learner's Workbook. (Illus.). 128p. (J). (gr. 3-4). 1997. pap. text, wbk. ed. 16.95 (*1-58614-051-5*) Arise Found.

— Sprouts - A Teenage Parenting Program: Mental Development Instructor's Manual. (Illus.). 21p. 1997. pap. text, teacher ed. write for info. (*1-58614-048-5*) Arise Found.

— Sprouts - A Teenage Parenting Program: Mental Development Learner's Workbook. (Illus.). 49p. (J). (gr. 3-4). 1997. pap. text, wbk. ed. 10.95 (*1-58614-049-3*) Arise Found.

— Sprouts - A Teenage Parenting Program: Physical Development Instructor's Manual. (Illus.). 29p. 1997. pap. text, teacher ed. write for info. (*1-58614-044-2*) Arise Found.

— Sprouts - A Teenage Parenting Program: Physical Development Learner's Workbook. (Illus.). 72p. (J). (gr. 3-4). 1997. pap. text, wbk. ed. 15.95 (*1-58614-045-0*) Arise Found.

— Sprouts - A Teenage Parenting Program: Prenatal, Delivery & Postpartum Instructor's Manual. (Illus.). 34p. 1997. pap. text, teacher ed. write for info. (*1-58614-042-6*) Arise Found.

— Sprouts - A Teenage Parenting Program: Prenatal, Postpartum & Delivery Learner's Workbook. (Illus.). 93p. (J). (gr. 3-4). 1997. pap. text, wbk. ed. 15.95 (*1-58614-043-4*) Arise Found.

— Sprouts - A Teenage Parenting Program: Teen Pregnancy Instructor's Manual. (Illus.). 17p. 1997. pap. text, teacher ed. write for info. (*1-58614-054-X*) Arise Found.

— Sprouts - A Teenage Parenting Program: Teen Pregnancy Learner's Workbook. (Illus.). 37p. (J). (gr. 3-4). 1997. pap. text, wbk. ed. 9.95 (*1-58614-055-8*) Arise Found.

— Stranger Safety Week: Teacher's Manual. (Illus.). 1999. pap. text, teacher ed. 25.00 (*1-58614-011-6*) Arise Found.

— Success Log. (Illus.). 36p. (J). (gr. 3-4). 1996. pap. text 9.95 (*1-58614-097-3*) Arise Found.

— Success Week Teacher's Manual. (Illus.). 1999. pap. text, teacher ed. 25.00 (*1-58614-007-8*) Arise Found.

— 31 of Taneka's Urban Life Tales. (Illus.). 56p. (J). (gr. 3-4). 1999. pap. text 9.95 (*1-58614-099-X*) Arise Found.

— Trapped. (Illus.). 16p. (J). (gr. 3-4). 1999. pap. text 2.95 (*1-58614-096-5*) Arise Found.

— 20 More Ways to Tell If You Are Successful. (Illus.). 16p. (J). (gr. 3-4). 1999. pap. text 2.95 (*1-58614-089-2*) Arise Found.

— 20 Tips for Avoiding Guilt. (Illus.). 16p. (J). (gr. 3-4). 1999. pap. text 2.95 (*1-58614-090-6*) Arise Found.

— 20 Tips for Conquering Fear. (Illus.). 16p. (J). (gr. 3-4). 1999. pap. text 2.95 (*1-58614-092-2*) Arise Found.

— 20 Tips for Controlling Worry. (Illus.). 16p. (J). (gr. 3-4). 1999. pap. text 2.95 (*1-58614-091-4*) Arise Found.

— 20 Ways to Tell If You Are Successful. (Illus.). 16p. (gr. 3-4). 1999. pap. text 2.95 (*1-58614-088-4*) Arise Found.

— Water Is Precious Flip Chart. (Illus.). 22p. 1996. pap. text. write for info. (*1-58614-102-3*) Arise Found.

— Work in Progress: Anger Management Instructor's Manual. (Illus.). 32p. 1996. pap. text, teacher ed. write for info. (*1-58614-014-0*) Arise Found.

— Work in Progress: Anger Management Learner's Workbook. (Illus.). 64p. (J). (gr. 3-4). 1996. pap. text, wbk. ed. 12.95 (*1-58614-015-9*) Arise Found.

— Work in Progress: Domestic & Sexual Abuse Instructor's Manual. (Illus.). 32p. 1999. pap. text, teacher ed. write for info. (*1-58614-018-3*) Arise Found.

— Work in Progress: Domestic & Sexual Abuse Learner's Workbook. (Illus.). 64p. (J). (gr. 3-4). 1996. pap. text, wbk. ed. 12.95 (*1-58614-019-1*) Arise Found.

— Work in Progress: Quiz Booklet. (Illus.). 32p. (J). (gr. 3-4). 1996. pap. text 7.49 (*1-58614-022-1*) Arise Found.

— Work in Progress: Substance Abuse & Guns Instructor's Manual. (Illus.). 32p. 1996. pap. text, teacher ed. write for info. (*1-58614-016-7*) Arise Found.

— Work in Progress: Substance Abuse & Guns Learner's Workbook. (Illus.). 64p. (J). (gr. 3-4). 1996. pap. text, wbk. ed. 12.95 (*1-58614-017-5*) Arise Found.

— Work in Progress: Violence & Conflict Instructor's Manual. (Illus.). 32p. 1996. pap. text, teacher ed. write for info. (*1-58614-020-5*) Arise Found.

— Work in Progress: Violence & Conflict Learner's Workbook. (Illus.). 64p. (J). (gr. 3-4). 1996. pap. text, wbk. ed. 12.95 (*1-58614-021-3*) Arise Found.

Benson, Edward, tr. see Schlesinger, Roger, ed.

Benson, Edward F. The Blotting Book. LC 75-32734. (Literature of Mystery & Detection Ser.). 1976. reprint ed. 23.95 (*0-405-07864-1*) Ayer.

— Freaks of Mayfair. LC 77-150536. (Short Story Index Reprint Ser.). (Illus.). 1977. reprint ed. 19.95 (*0-8369-3833-X*) Ayer.

— Spook Stories. Reginald, R. & Menville, Douglas A., eds. LC 75-46252. (Supernatural & Occult Fiction Ser.). 1976. reprint ed. lib. bdg. 23.95 (*0-405-08112-X*) Ayer.

Benson, Egbert. Vindication of the Captors of Major Andre. (American Revolutionary Ser.). reprint ed. lib. bdg. 32.50 (*0-8398-0187-4*) Irvington.

Benson, Eileen, ed. see Taetzsch, Lyn.

B

Benson, Elizabeth P. Animal Ancient World. (Illus.). 0.00 (*0-691-03596-2*) Princeton U Pr.

Benson, Elizabeth P. Birds & Beasts of Ancient Latin America. LC 97-2976. (Illus.). 184p. 1997. 39.95 (*0-8130-1518-9*) U Press Fla.

— An Olmec Figure at Dumbarton Oaks. LC 70-184640. (Studies in Pre-Columbian Art & Archaeology: No. 8). (Illus.). 95p. 1971. pap. 6.00 (*0-88402-035-5*) Dumbarton Oaks.

Benson, Elizabeth P., ed. Death & the Afterlife in Pre-Columbian America: A Conference at Dumbarton Oaks, October 27, 1973. LC 74-22694. (Illus.). 196p. 1975. 18.00 (*0-88402-062-2*) Dumbarton Oaks.

— Dumbarton Oaks Conference on Chavin, October 26 & 27, 1968. LC 73-153502. (Illus.). 124p. 1971. 15.00 (*0-88402-037-1*) Dumbarton Oaks.

— Mesoamerican Sites & World-Views: Conference at Dumbarton Oaks, October 16 & 17, 1976. LC 79-92647. (Illus.). 256p. 1981. 24.00 (*0-88402-097-5*) Dumbarton Oaks.

— Mesoamerican Writing Systems: A Conference at Dumbarton Oaks, October 30 & 31, 1971. LC 73-93086. (Illus.). 226p. 1973. 24.00 (*0-88402-048-7*) Dumbarton Oaks.

— The Olmec & Their Neighbors: Essays in Memory of Matthew W. Stirling. LC 79-49262. (Illus.). 346p. 1981. 30.00 (*0-88402-098-3*) Dumbarton Oaks.

— Pre-Columbian Metallurgy of South America, Proceedings: A Conference at Dumbarton Oaks, October 18 & 19, 1975. LC 79-49261. (Illus.). 107p. 1979. 24.00 (*0-88402-094-0*) Dumbarton Oaks.

— Sea in the Pre-Columbian World: Conference at Dumbarton Oaks, October 26 & 27, 1974. LC 76-58217. (Illus.). 188p. 1977. 18.00 (*0-88402-071-1*) Dumbarton Oaks.

Benson, Elizabeth P. & Fuente, Beatriz de la, eds. Olmec Art of Ancient Mexico. (Illus.). 400p. 1996. 80.00 (*0-8109-6328-0*, Pub. by Abrams) Time Warner.

Benson, Elizabeth P. & Griffin, Gillett G., eds. Maya Iconography. LC 87-26372. (Illus.). 395p. reprint ed. pap. 122.50 (*0-608-06307-X*, 206666900008) Bks Demand.

Benson, Elizabeth P., jt. auth. see Coe, Michael D.

Benson, Elizabeth P., ed. see Dumbarton Oaks Collection Staff.

Benson, Elizabeth P., jt. ed. see Roberston, Merle G.

Benson, Ellis S., et al. Career Guide in Pathology. LC 97-42841. 1997. 20.00 (*0-89189-428-4*) Am Soc Clinical.

***Benson, Ellis S., et al.** Career Guide in Pathology. LC 97-42841. 1999. write for info. (*0-89189-418-7*) Am Soc Clinical.

Benson, Ellis S., jt. ed. see Stefanini, Mario.

Benson, Eugene & Conolly, L. W., eds. The Oxford Companion to Canadian Theater. (Illus.). 680p. 1990. 59.00 (*0-19-540672-9*) OUP.

Benson, Eugene & Conolly, Leonard, eds. Encyclopedia of Post-Colonial Literatures in English, 2 vols., Set. LC 94-235480. 1874p. (C). 1994. text, boxed set 305.00 (*0-415-05199-1*) Routledge.

Benson, Eugene & Toye, William, eds. Oxford Companion to Canadian Literature. 2nd ed. LC PR9180.2.O94 1997. 1168p. 1998. 65.00 (*0-19-541167-6*) OUP.

Benson, Evelyn, jt. ed. see Benson, Morton.

Benson, Ezra Taft. Beware of Pride & the Book of Mormon: Keystone of Our Religion. LC 97-78184. 39 p. 1998. write for info. (*0-87579-881-0*) Deseret Bk.

— An Enemy Hath Done This. 1969. pap. 10.95 (*0-88494-184-1*) Bookcraft Inc.

— Farmers at the Crossroads. 1956. 8.95 (*0-8159-5501-4*) Devin.

— Farmers at the Crossroads. LC 82-997. (Illus.). 107p. 1982. reprint ed. lib. bdg. 57.50 (*0-313-23484-1*, BENF, Greenwood Pr) Greenwood.

— Missionaries to Match Our Message. 1990. pap. 5.95 (*0-88494-779-3*) Bookcraft Inc.

— The Proper Role of Government. 32p. 1975. reprint ed. pap. 2.50 (*0-89036-122-3*) Liahona Pub Trust.

— The Teachings of Ezra Taft Benson. 1988. 24.95 (*0-88494-639-8*) Bookcraft Inc.

— A Witness & a Warning. LC 88-70533. ix, 86p. 1988. 12.95 (*0-87579-153-0*) Deseret Bk.

Benson, F. A., ed. Millimeter & Submillimeter Waves. LC 77-489384. (Illus.). 579p. reprint ed. pap. 179.50 (*0-608-14721-4*, 202572300046) Bks Demand.

***Benson, Floyd & Robinson, Maxx.** How to Get Even Without Going to Jail. unabridged ed. LC 99-74583. (Illus.). 160p. 2000. per. 19.95 (*1-891014-09-9*) Cardinal Books.

Benson, Floyd, ed. see Benson, Fred.

Benson, Frank. Summer, 1909. (Fine Art Jigsaw Puzzles Ser.). 1989. 9.95 (*0-934967-46-6*) Battle Rd Pr.

Benson, Fred. It's Their Culture, Stupid! Dis'ing Racial Differences. Benson, Floyd, ed. (Illus.). 320p. 1998. 24.95 (*1-891014-04-8*); pap. 19.95 (*1-891014-05-6*) Cardinal Books.

Benson, G. Jazz Etudes over Classic Jazz Changes. 72p. 1997. pap. 14.95 (*0-7935-8512-0*) H Leonard.

Benson, G. C. The New Centralization: A Study of Intergovernmental Relationships in the U. S. LC 77-74928. (American Federalism-the Urban Dimension Ser.). 1978. reprint ed. lib. bdg. 19.95 (*0-405-10477-4*) Ayer.

Benson, Gary. The Art of Railroad Photography. Emmerich, Michael, ed. (Illus.). 148p. (Orig.). 1992. 39.95 (*0-89024-133-3*, 01055) Kalmbach.

Benson, Gary J. Rolling Thunder: A Portrait of North American Railroading. 1991. 49.95 (*0-393-02907-7*) Norton.

Benson, Gary J. & Maggitti, Phil. In the Irons: Show Jumping, Dressage, & Eventing in North America. LC 94-12282. (Illus.). 192p. 1994. pap. 50.00 (*0-87605-967-1*) Howell Bks.

Benson, George. The Best of George Benson. (Piano-Vocal-Guitar Ser.). 80p. 1994. per. 14.95 (*0-7935-2395-8*) H Leonard.

— The Silent Self: A Journal of Spiritual Discovery. 86p. (Orig.). 1992. pap. 3.95 (*0-88028-133-2*, 1175) Forward Movement.

— Then Joy Breaks Through. 1998. pap. 6.95 (*0-88028-202-9*, 1486) Forward Movement.

Benson, Gordon, Jr., ed. Poul Anderson - Myth-Maker & Wonder-Weaver: An Interim Bibliography (1947-1985) 4th ed. 46p. 1982. pap. 3.50 (*0-912613-03-3*) Galactic Central.

Benson, Gordon, Jr., jt. ed. see Utter, Virgil.

Benson, H. W. Democratic Rights for Union Members: A Guide to Internal Union Democracy. 245p. 1979. 9.00 (*0-9602244-1-6*) Assn Union Demo.

Benson, Harold. Anatomy & Physiology Laboratory Textbook, Intermediate Version, Fetal Pig. 3rd ed. LC 95-60467. 541p. (C). 1995. text 52.92 (*0-697-21930-5*, WCB McGr Hill) McGraw-H Hghr Educ.

Benson, Harold E. Benson. Narrative History of the Family of Caleb Ellis Benson & Alice Anzanette Hatch, 1603-1924. 103p. 1997. reprint ed. pap. 16.50 (*0-8328-7499-X*); reprint ed. lib. bdg. 26.50 (*0-8328-7498-1*) Higginson Bk Co.

Benson, Harold J. Microbiological Applications. 7th ed. 480p. (C). 1997. text 41.00 (*0-697-34139-9*, WCB McGr Hill) McGraw-H Hghr Educ.

— Microbiological Applications: A Laboratory Manual in General Microbiology. 5th ed. 384p. (C). 1990. text. write for info. (*0-697-05762-3*, WCB McGr Hill) McGrw-H Hghr Educ.

— Microbiological Applications: A Laboratory Manual in General Microbiology. 7th ed. 1997. pap. text, lab manual ed. 31.00 (*0-697-34140-2*) McGraw.

— Microbiological Applications: Short. 4th ed. 368p. (C). 1985. spiral bd. write for info. (*0-697-00306-X*, WCB McGr Hill) McGrw-H Hghr Educ.

Benson, Harold J. & Talaro, Kathleen P. Human Anatomy Laboratory Textbook. 4th ed. 368p. (C). 1992. text. write for info. (*0-697-15020-8*, WCB McGr Hill) McGrw-H Hghr Educ.

Benson, Harold J., et al. Anatomy & Physiology. 5th ed. 1992. text, teacher ed. 18.75 (*0-697-08692-5*) McGraw.

— Anatomy & Physiology. 6th ed. 1994. text, teacher ed., lab manual ed. 10.93 (*0-697-16015-7*) McGraw.

— Anatomy & Physiology: Complete Version, Lab Manual. 6th ed. 664p. (C). 1994. text 44.00 (*0-697-16016-5*, WCB McGr Hill) McGrw-H Hghr Educ.

— Anatomy & Physiology Intermediate. 4th ed. 1995. text, teacher ed., lab manual ed. 7.81 (*0-697-21931-3*, WCB McGr Hill) McGrw-H Hghr Educ.

— Anatomy & Physiology Lab Text: Intermediate Version - Fetal Pig. 2nd ed. 514p. (C). 1992. text. write for info. (*0-697-15018-6*) Brown & Benchmark.

— Anatomy & Physiology Laboratory Textbook: Intermediate Version. 4th ed. 552p. (C). 1995. text 47.00 (*0-697-21932-1*, WCB McGr Hill) McGrw-H Hghr Educ.

— Anatomy & Physiology Laboratory Textbook, Complete Version. 5th ed. 640p. (C). 1991. text. write for info. (*0-697-08691-7*, WCB McGr Hill) McGrw-H Hghr Educ.

— Anatomy & Physiology Laboratory Textbook, Complete Version. 5th ed. 640p. (C). 1992. text. write for info. (*0-697-08689-5*, WCB McGr Hill) McGrw-H Hghr Educ.

— Anatomy & Physiology Laboratory Textbook, Short Version. 6th ed. 512p. (C). 1994. text, spiral bd. 38.50 (*0-697-16014-9*, WCB McGr Hill) McGrw-H Hghr Educ.

Benson, Harris. University Physics, 2 vols., Vol. 2. rev. ed. LC 95-41514. 1008p. 1995. pap. 96.95 (*0-471-00689-0*) Wiley.

— University Physics, 2 vols., Vol. 2. rev. ed. 1008p. 1996. text 111.95 (*0-471-15264-1*) Wiley.

— University Physics, Spreadsheets. 114p. 1991. pap. 28.95 (*0-471-53954-6*) Wiley.

Benson, Harry. The Beatles: In the Beginning. (Illus.). 128p. 1993. 15.95 (*0-87663-642-3*, Pub. by Universe) St Martin.

— The Beatles: Now & Then. (Illus.). 128p. 1998. pap. 19.95 (*0-7893-0220-9*, Pub. by Universe) St Martin.

— First Familes - An Intimate Portrait from the Kennedys to the Clintons. LC 97-1418. 128p. 1997. 29.95 (*0-8212-2360-7*, Pub. by Bulfinch Pr) Little.

***Benson, Harry.** First Families: An Intimate Portrait from the Kennedys to the Clintons. (Illus.). 128p. 2000. 30.00 (*0-7881-9400-3*) DIANE Pub.

Benson, Harry. First Families: An Intimate Portrait from the Kennedys to the Clintons. 1997. 29.95 (*0-614-28245-4*) Little.

Benson, Hazel B. Behavior Modification & the Child: An Annotated Bibliography, 3. LC 79-7358. (Contemporary Problems of Childhood Ser.: No. 3). 398p. 1979. lib. bdg. 55.00 (*0-313-21489-1*, BBM/, Greenwood Pr) Greenwood.

Benson, Hazel B., compiled by. The Dying Child: An Annotated Bibliography, 6. LC 88-11008. (Contemporary Problems of Childhood Ser.: No. 6). 291p. 1988. lib. bdg. 65.00 (*0-313-24708-0*, BDY/, Greenwood Pr) Greenwood.

Benson, Henry C. & Sperry, Phillip A. Life among the Choctaws. 324p. 1994. reprint ed. 36.95 (*1-56869-055-X*); reprint ed. pap. 21.95 (*1-56869-056-8*) Oldbuck Pr.

***Benson, Herbert.** The Relaxation Response. 240p. 2000. reprint ed. pap. 12.50 (*0-380-81595-8*, Avon Bks) Morrow Avon.

Benson, Herbert. Timeless Healing. LC 96-49270. 352p. 1997. per. 13.00 (*0-684-83146-5*) S&S Trade.

— Timeless Healing: The Power & Biology of Belief. 352p. 1996. 24.00 (*0-684-81441-2*) S&S Trade.

Benson, Herbert & Klipper, Miriam Z. The Relaxation Response. (Illus.). 256p. 2000. mass mkt. 6.99 (*0-380-00676-6*, HarpTorch) Morrow Avon.

Benson, Herbert & Proctor, William. Your Maximum Mind. 272p. 1989. mass mkt. 5.50 (*0-380-70664-4*, Avon Bks) Morrow Avon.

Benson, Herbert & Stark, Marg. Timeless Healing: The Power & Biology of Belief. 350p. 1998. text 24.00 (*0-7881-5775-2*) DIANE Pub.

— Timeless Healing: The Power & Biology of Belief. large type ed. LC 96-2763. 1996. 24.95 (*1-56895-366-6*, Compass) Wheeler Pub.

Benson, Herman. Democratic Rights in Federal Employee Unions: A Ramble Through the Law's Bureaucratic Maze. 1995. pap. 3.00 (*0-614-29599-8*) Assn Union Demo.

— How to Get an Honest Union Election. 1987. pap. 4.00 (*0-9602244-4-0*) Assn Union Demo.

Benson, Herman, et al, eds. Union Democracy in the Construction Trades. 33p. 1985. pap. 3.00 (*0-9602244-2-4*) Assn Union Demo.

Benson, Hugh H. Socratic Wisdom: The Model of Knowledge in Plato's Early Dialogues. LC 98-50103. 304p. 2000. text 55.00 (*0-19-512918-0*) OUP.

Benson, Hugh H., ed. Essays on the Philosophy of Socrates. 384p. (C). 1992. pap. text 24.95 (*0-19-506757-6*) OUP.

Benson, Ivor. The Siege of South Africa: What the Press Doesn't Tell You. 1986. lib. bdg. 79.50 (*0-8490-3820-0*) Gordon Pr.

Benson, Ivor. The Zionist Factor: The Jewish Impact on 20th Century History. unabridged ed. 205p. 1986. reprint ed. pap. 15.00 (*0-945001-63-0*) GSG & Assocs.

Benson, J., et al. North Eastern Accelerator Personnel: Symposium of '91, 25th. 436p. 1992. text 109.00 (*981-02-1108-2*) World Scientific Pub.

Benson, J., jt. ed. see Smith, K.

Benson, J. Ernest. Theory & Design of Loudspeaker Enclosures. rev. ed. LC 97-164532. (Illus.). 244p. 1996. reprint ed. pap. 24.95 (*0-7906-1093-0*) Prompt Publns.

Benson, J. L. The Necropolis of Kalorizki. (Studies in Mediterranean Archaeology: Vol. XXXVI). (Illus.). 170p. 1973. pap. 52.50 (*91-85058-55-6*) P Astroms.

Benson, J. L., jt. auth. see Schaus, Gerald P.

Benson, J. L., jt. auth. see Stillwell, Agnes N.

Benson, J. L., tr. see Kantorowicz, Gertrud.

Benson, J. Thomas, ed. Female Pelvic Floor Disorders: Investigation & Management. (Illus.). 750p. (C). 1992. 109.00 (*0-393-71013-0*) Norton.

Benson, J. Thomas, jt. ed. see Stenchever, Morton A.

Benson, Jack L. Horse, Bird & Man: The Origins of Greek Painting. LC 70-95787. (Illus.). 253p. reprint ed. pap. 78.50 (*0-608-11321-2*, 202213300024) Bks Demand.

Benson, Jackson. Wallace Stegner: His Life & Work. 1997. pap. 16.95 (*0-14-024796-3*) Viking Penguin.

Benson, Jackson J. Hemingway: The Writer's Art of Self-Defense. LC 70-77139. 212p. reprint ed. pap. 65.80 (*0-608-18639-2*, 205584200039) Bks Demand.

— Looking for Steinbeck's Ghost. LC 88-40205. (Illus.). 224p. 1988. 27.95 (*0-8061-2155-6*) U of Okla Pr.

— The True Adventures of John Steinbeck, Writer: A Biography. (Illus.). 1120p. 1990. reprint ed. pap. 22.00 (*0-14-014417-X*, Penguin Bks) Viking Penguin.

Benson, Jackson J., ed. New Critical Approaches to the Short Stories of Ernest Hemingway. LC 90-3463. 528p. (C). 1991. text 64.95 (*0-8223-1065-1*); pap. text 24.95 (*0-8223-1067-8*) Duke.

— The Short Novels of John Steinbeck: Critical Essays. LC 89-27255. 360p. (Orig.). (C). 1990. pap. text 23.95 (*0-8223-0994-7*) Duke.

Benson, Jackson J., jt. ed. see Astro, Richard.

Benson, Jackson L. The Short Stories of Ernest Hemingway: Critical Essays. LC 74-75815. xv, 375p. 1975. reprint ed. pap. text 20.95 (*0-8223-0386-8*) Duke.

Benson, James, et al, eds. Systemic Perspectives on Discourse, Vol. 1. LC 84-28466. (Advances in Discourse Processes Ser.: Vol. 15). 400p. 1985. text 78.50 (*0-89391-193-3*) Ablx Pub.

Benson, James & Greaves, William. Systemic Perspectives on Discourse, Vol. 2. Freedle, Roy O., ed. LC 84-28466. (Advances in Discourse Processes Ser.: Vol. 16). 308p. 1985. text 78.50 (*0-89391-202-6*) Ablx Pub.

Benson, James A., jt. ed. see Weinberg, Bella H.

Benson, James D., et al, eds. Systemic Functional Approaches to Discourse: Selected Papers from the 12th International Systemic Workshop. LC 87-31461. (Advances in Discourse Processes Ser.: Vol. 26). 384p. 1988. text 78.50 (*0-89391-403-7*) Ablx Pub.

Benson, James K. Irish & German Families & the Economic Development of Midwestern Cities, 1860-1895. LC 90-41582. (European Immigrants & American Society Ser.). 420p. 1990. reprint ed. text 25.00 (*0-8240-7422-X*) Garland.

Benson, James S., ed. Dental Amalgam: A Scientific Review & Recommended Public Health Service Strategy for Research Education & Regulation. 183p. 1999. reprint ed. pap. text 30.00 (*0-7881-8056-8*) DIANE Pub.

Benson, James W. Patanjali's Remarks on Anga. (Oxford University South Asian Studies Ser.). 260p. 1990. 16.95 (*0-19-562022-4*) OUP.

Benson, Janie, et al. Meeting Women's Needs for Post-Abortion Family Planning: Framing the Questions. (Issues in Abortion Care Ser.).Tr. of Cubriendo las Necesidades de las Mujeres en Cuanto a la Planificacion Familiar Post-Aborto. 69p. 1992. pap. 6.00 (*1-882220-01-3*) IPAS.

***Benson, Jarlath F.** Working More Creatively with Groups. 2nd ed. LC 00-32300. 2000. pap. write for info. (*0-415-23038-1*) Routledge.

Benson, Jeffrey, jt. auth. see Poliner, Rachel A.

***Benson, Jerry & Benson, Diana.** How to Witness to a Mormon. 2000. pap. 15.00 (*0-8024-6439-4*) Moody.

***Benson, Jessica.** Lord Stanhope's Proposal. (Regency Romance Ser.). 2000. mass mkt. 4.99 (*0-8217-6537-X*, Zebra Kensgtn) Kensgtn Pub Corp.

Benson, Jim. America's Private Land: A Geography of Hope. rev. ed. (Illus.). 80p. (C). 1998. pap. text 25.00 (*0-7881-7092-9*) DIANE Pub.

— Of Marriage & Piracy: 25 Poems. LC 99-25056. 72p. 1999. pap. text 14.95 (*0-7734-3115-2*) E Mellen.

— USAF for the 21st Century: Super Wing: Total Force Integration. (Illus.). 128p. 1996. pap. 21.95 (*1-85532-617-5*, Pub. by Ospry) Motorbooks Intl.

Benson, Jim, jt. auth. see Okagaki, Alan.

Benson, Jim, jt. auth. see Skelton, Scott.

Benson, Jo. Infertility & IVF. 1997. pap. text 15.95 (*1-85727-093-2*, Pub. by Scarlet Pr) LPC InBook.

— Love, Labour & Loss: Stillbirth & Neonatal Death. 192p. 1996. pap. text 17.95 (*1-85727-063-0*, Pub. by Scarlet Pr) LPC InBook.

Benson, Jodie. Gordon's Print Price Annual, 1998. 2016p. 1998. 175.00 (*0-931036-04-6*) Gordon s Art.

Benson, Jodie L. Gordon's Photography Price Annual International, 1998. annuals 302p. 1998. 85.00 (*0-931036-54-2*) Gordon s Art.

***Benson, Jodie L., ed.** Gordon's Photography Price Annual International, 1999. 432p. 1999. 95.00 (*0-931036-55-0*) Gordon s Art.

— Gordon's Print Price Annual, 1999. 2016p. 1999. 245.00 (*0-931036-17-8*) Gordon s Art.

— Gordon's Print Price Annual, 1999: Supplement to Gordon's Print Price Annual, 1999. 894p. 1999. ring bd. 95.00 (*0-931036-18-6*) Gordon s Art.

— Lawrence's Dealer Print Prices Annual, 1999. 1086p. 1999. 145.00 (*0-931036-77-1*) Gordon s Art.

Benson, Jodie L., ed. Lawrence's Dealer Print Prices Annual, 1998. annuals 1086p. 1998. 145.00 (*0-931036-76-3*) Gordon s Art.

Benson, Joe. Illustrated Alfa Romeo Buyer's Guide. 2nd ed. LC 92-10165. (MBI Illustrated Buyer's Guide Ser.). (Illus.). 176p. 1992. pap. 17.95 (*0-87938-633-9*) MBI Pubg.

— Scenic Driving Utah. (Illus.). 248p. (Orig.). 1996. pap. 14.95 (*1-56044-486-X*) Falcon Pub Inc.

— The Traveler's Guide to the Pony Express Trail. LC 95-8232. (Illus.). 140p. 1995. pap. 12.95 (*1-56044-233-6*) Falcon Pub Inc.

— Uncle Joe's Record Guide: Eric Clapton, Jimi Hendrix, The Who. 288p. 1988. pap. 9.95 (*0-943031-03-6*) J Benson Unlimit.

— Uncle Joe's Record Guide: Hard Rock, the First Two Generations. 320p. 1988. pap. 9.95 (*0-943031-04-4*) J Benson Unlimit.

— Uncle Joe's Record Guide: Progressive Rock. (Illus.). 320p. (Orig.). 1989. pap. 9.95 (*0-943031-11-7*) J Benson Unlimit.

— Uncle Joe's Record Guide: The Beatles. 124p. 1990. pap. 9.95 (*0-943031-13-3*) J Benson Unlimit.

— Uncle Joe's Record Guide: The Rolling Stones. 124p. 1987. pap. 9.95 (*0-943031-02-8*) J Benson Unlimit.

Benson, Joel D. Cooperation to Competition: English Perspective & Policy on Anglo-Dutch Economic Relations During the Reign of James I. LC 89-13034. (American University Studies: History: Ser. IX, Vol. 81). XIV, 272p. 1990. text 49.95 (*0-8204-1147-7*) P Lang Pubng.

***Benson, John.** At o Z Scouting Guide, 2000-2001. 1999. pap. 24.95 (*1-880876-87-6*) Diamond Lib.

— Benson's Guide to Baseball on the Internet. 2000. pap. 19.95 (*1-880876-89-2*) Diamond Lib.

Benson, John. Entrepreneurism in Canada: A History of "Penny Capitalists" LC 91-4497. (Canadian Studies: Vol. 12). 184p. 1991. lib. bdg. 79.95 (*0-88946-260-7*) E Mellen.

***Benson, John.** Future Stars: The Rookies of 2000-2001. 1999. pap. 19.95 (*1-880876-84-1*) Diamond Lib.

Benson, John. Prime Time: The Middle Aged in Twentieth-Century Britain. LC 97-20597. 1997. text. write for info. (*0-582-25658-5*, Pub. by Addison-Wesley) Longman.

— Prime Time: The Middle Aged in Twentieth-Century Britain. LC 97-20597. (C). 1998. pap. text 20.63 (*0-582-25657-7*, Pub. by Addison-Wesley) Longman.

— Rise Consumer Society Britain 1880-1980. LC 93-41571. (Themes in British Social History Ser.). (C). 1995. pap. text 33.60 (*0-582-07288-3*) Addison-Wesley.

— Rise Consumer Socty Brit. LC 93-41571. (Themes in British Social History Ser.). (C). 1994. text 56.50 (*0-582-07289-1*, Pub. by Addison-Wesley) Longman.

***Benson, John.** Rotisserie Baseball Annual, 2000. 1999. pap. 22.95 (*1-880876-88-4*) Diamond Lib.

Benson, John. The Working Class in Britain, 1850-1939. (Themes in British Social History Ser.). 240p. (C). 1990. text 39.75 (*0-582-05316-1*, 78286) Longman.

Benson, John & Blengino, Tony, eds. Future Stars: The Rookies of 1999-2000. 288p. 1998. pap. 19.95 (*1-880876-18-3*) Diamond Lib.

Benson, John & DelVecchio, Douglas A., eds. Rotisserie Baseball Annual 1999. annuals (Rotisserie League Baseball Ser.). 336p. 1998. pap. text 22.95 (*1-880876-22-1*) Diamond Lib.

An Asterisk (*) at the beginning of an entry indicates that the title is appearing for the first time.

Benson, John & Moyer, Steve, eds. The Baseball Player Guide A to Z, 1999. (Baseball Player Guide A to Z Ser.). 352p. 1998. pap. 24.95 (*1-880876-83-3*) Diamond Lib.

Benson, John & Neville, Robert G., eds. Studies in the Yorkshire Coal Industry. LC 76-11778. xii, 180p. 1976. lib. bdg. 35.00 (*0-678-06793-7*) Kelley.

Benson, John & Shaw, Gareth. The Evolution of Retail Systems, 1800-1914. (Illus.). 206p. 1992. text 54.00 (*0-7185-1335-5*, Pub. by Leicester U Pr) Cassell & Continuum.

Benson, John, jt. auth. see Rowley, Chris.

Benson, John A., ed. see Institute of Medicine Staff.

Benson, John C. & Baron, Randall. Rotisserie Baseball: Playing for Blood, Vol. 2. 200p. 1994. pap. 12.95 (*0-910791-87-2*) Diamond Lib.

Benson, John C. & Baron, Randall, eds. Rotisserie Baseball: Playing for Fun, Vol. 1. 200p. 1994. pap. 12.95 (*0-910791-86-4*) Diamond Lib.

***Benson, John L.** The Soul: How to Guide to Eternity. 100p. 1999. pap. 14.95 (*0-9634173-7-1*) Hugos Pr.

Benson, John R., Jr. TGF Beta & Cancer. LC 98-42195. (Medical Intelligence Unit Ser.: No. 7). 171p. 1998. 99.00 (*1-57059-539-9*) Landes Bioscience.

Benson, Judi & Falk, Agneta, eds. The Long Pale Corridor: Contemporary Poems of Bereavement. 320p. 1996. pap. 18.95 (*1-85224-317-1*, Pub. by Bloodaxe Bks) Dufour.

***Benson, Judith.** Butterfly Gardens. (Illus.). (J). 1999. 2.00 (*1-895836-73-5*, Tesseract) Bk Collective.

***Benson, Judith & McCrae, Lori M.** Butterfly Gardens. 70p. (J). (gr. 2-4). 1999. pap. 5.95 (*1-895836-71-9*, Tesseract) Bk Collective.

Benson, Karen, jt. auth. see Benson, Robert.

Benson, Kathleen & Haskins, James. Space Challenger: The Story of Guion Bluford. LC 84-4251. (Trailblazers Ser.). (Illus.). 64p. (J). (gr. 4-7). 1984. lib. bdg. 16.95 (*0-87614-259-5*, Carolrhoda) Lerner Pub.

Benson, Kathleen, jt. auth. see Haskins, James.

Benson, Kathleen, jt. auth. see Haskins, James.

Benson, Kathleen, jt. auth. see Haskins, James S.

Benson, Kathleen, jt. auth. see Haskins, Jim.

***Benson, Kathlene.** Preventing Falls in the Elderly. (Illus.). 77p. 2000. pap. 29.95 (*1-888343-28-1*) Hartman Pub.

Benson, Kathlene, jt. auth. see Fuzy, Jetta.

Benson, Kathryn C., ed. San Diego Firefighters Centennial Cookbook. (Illus.). 184p. (Orig.). (C). 1989. pap. 8.00 (*0-9622550-0-9*) SDFDCCC.

Benson, Keith R., jt. auth. see Jacques, Roger.

***Benson, Kelly.** FCTE Earth Science. abr. ed. Wynne, Sharon, ed. (Praxis Ser.). (Illus.). 100p. (C). 2000. spiral bd. 22.50 (*1-58197-069-2*) XAM.

***Benson, Kelly, et al.** FTCE General Science. Wynne, Sharon, ed. (Praxis Ser.). (C). 2000. per. 22.50 (*1-58197-077-3*) XAM.

— PRAXIS Subject Area Assessment General Science. (Praxis Ser.). (C). 2000. spiral bd. 22.50 (*1-58197-054-4*) XAM.

Benson, Larry D. King Arthur's Death: The Middle English 'stanzaic Morte Arthur' & 'alliterative Morte Arthur' LC 73-13545. (Library of Literature). 1974. pap. text 8.35 (*0-672-61010-8*, Bobbs) Macmillan.

Benson, Larry D., ed. King Arthur's Death: The Middle English Stanzaic Morte Arthur & Alliterative Morte Arthur. rev. ed. LC 94-26544. (Teams Middle English Text Ser.). 1994. pap. 13.00 (*1-879288-38-9*) Medieval Inst.

— The Learned & the Lewed: Studies in Chaucer & Medieval Literature. LC 74-78719. (English Studies: No. 5). 448p. 1974. pap. 9.95 (*0-674-51888-8*) HUP.

— The Wisdom of Poetry: Essays in Early English Literature in Honor of Morton W. Bloomfield. 1982. pap. 13.95 (*0-918720-16-8*); boxed set 22.95 (*0-918720-15-X*) Medieval Inst.

Benson, Larry D., ed. see Chaucer, Geoffrey.

Benson, Laura Lee. This is Our Earth. 1994. 12.15 (*0-606-07121-0*, Pub. by Turtleback) Demco.

Benson, Laura Lee. This Is Our Earth. LC 93-11936. (Illus.). 32p. (J). (ps-3). 1997. reprint ed. 15.95 (*0-88106-839-X*); reprint ed. pap. 6.95 (*0-88106-838-1*) Charlesbridge Pub.

— Washington, D. C. A Scrapbook. LC 98-53799. (Illus.). 32p. (J). (gr. 2-6). 1999. pap. 6.95 (*0-88106-063-1*) Charlesbridge Pub.

***Benson, Laura Lee.** Washington, D. C. A Scrapbook. LC 98-53799. (Illus.). 32p. (J). (gr. 2-6). 1999. 15.95 (*0-88106-064-X*) Charlesbridge Pub.

Benson, Laura Lee & Zirkel, Robert. Organic Dairy Farming: Kickapoo Organic Resource Network. LC 95-67281. (Illus.). 87p. (Orig.). pap. 6.00 (*0-9637982-1-9*) Orang-Utan Pr.

Benson, Lawrence R. Acquisition Management in the United States Air Force & Its Predecessors. 64p. 1997. pap. 4.25 (*0-16-061370-1*) USGPO.

Benson, Lee. The Best of Benson: A 20-Year Anthology of Sports Writing. LC 98-29420. 1998. pap. 14.95 (*1-57345-417-6*, Shadow Mount) Deseret Bk.

— Blind Trust: The True Story of Enid Greene & Joe Waldholtz. LC 97-76917. (Illus.). 368p. 1997. 15.95 (*1-888106-97-2*) Agreka Bks.

— The Concept of Jacksonian Democracy: New York As a Test Case. LC 61-6286. 367p. reprint ed. pap. 113.80 (*0-608-06402-5*, 206676300008) Bks Demand.

Benson, Lee, jt. auth. see Coonradt, Charles A.

Benson, Lee, jt. auth. see Edwards, LaVell.

Benson, Leon & Visotsky, Jeffrey. Orthopedic Pearls. LC 99-14699. (Illus.). 402p. (C). 1999. pap. text 21.95 (*0-8036-0185-9*) Davis Co.

Benson, Lewis. Catholic Quakerism: A Vision for All Men. 108p. 1968. pap. text 9.00 (*0-941308-03-0*) Phila Yrly Mtg RSOF.

Benson, Linda. The Ili Rebellion: The Moslem Challenge to Chinese Authority in Xingjiang, 1944-1949. LC 89-37237. 306p. (gr. 13). 1990. text 80.95 (*0-87332-509-5*, East Gate Bk) M E Sharpe.

Benson, Linda & Svanberg, Ingvar. China's Last Nomads: The History & Culture of China's Kazaks. LC 97-45582. (Studies on Modern China). 270p. (gr. 13). 1998. pap. text 27.95 (*1-56324-782-8*, East Gate Bk) M E Sharpe.

— China's Last Nomads: The History & Culture of China's Kazaks. LC 97-45582. (Studies on Modern China). (Illus.). 270p. (gr. 13). 1998. text 71.95 (*1-56324-781-X*, East Gate Bk) M E Sharpe.

Benson, Linda & Svanberg, Ingvar, eds. The Kazaks of China: Essays on an Ethnic Minority. (Studia Multiethnica Upsaliensia: No. 5). (Illus.). 250p. (Orig.). 1988. pap. 46.50 (*91-554-2255-1*, Pub. by Uppsala Univ Acta Univ Upsaliensis) Coronet Bks.

Benson, Lyman D. The Cacti of the United States & Canada. LC 73-80617. (Illus.). xii, 1104p. 1982. 125.00 (*0-8047-0863-0*) Stanford U Pr.

— The Native Cacti of California. 1969. 10.95 (*0-8047-0696-4*) Stanford U Pr.

— The Native Cacti of California. LC 69-13176. (Illus.). xii, 243p. 1969. pap. 22.50 (*0-8047-1526-2*) Stanford U Pr.

Benson, M. English-Serbocroatian Dictionary. 2nd rev. ed. 722p. (C). 1986. 150.00 (*0-7855-6487-X*, Pub. by Collets) St Mut.

— Serbocroatian-English Dictionary. 2nd rev. ed. 769p. (C). 1986. 160.00 (*0-7855-6691-0*, Pub. by Collets) St Mut.

Benson, M. D., jt. ed. see Kisilevsky, R.

Benson, M. Wayne, jt. auth. see Hoskins, Bob.

Benson, Margie. The Awesome Almanac: Wisconsin. LC 92-74706. 1993. 18.43 (*0-606-09026-6*, Pub. by Turtleback) Demco.

Benson, Margie & Jacobsen, Nancy. Awesome Almanacs: Wisconsin. (J). (gr. 4-12). 1993. pap. 12.95 (*1-880190-02-8*) B&B Pub.

Benson, Marius. Now Is the Time: A Personal Account of South Africa's Historic Transition from Apartheid to Democracy. LC 95-103688. 156p. 1994. write for info. (*0-7333-0357-9*) ABC Ent.

Benson, Marjorie. The Awesome Almanac: Ohio. LC 92-74711. 1995. 20.10 (*0-606-09024-X*, Pub. by Turtleback) Demco.

— Yellowstone. LC 94-34461. (Wonders of the World Ser.). (Illus.). 64p. (J). 1995. lib. bdg. 25.64 (*0-8114-6365-6*) Raintree Steck-V.

Benson, Martin, jt. auth. see Gimmy, Arthur E.

Benson, Mary. Athol Fugard & Barney Simon: Bare Stage, a Few Props, Great Theatre. LC 97-172948. 184p. 1999. pap. 14.95 (*0-86975-506-4*, Pub. by Ravan Pr) Ohio U Pr.

— A Far Cry: The Making of a South African. (Ravan Writers Ser.). (Illus.). 264p. (Orig.). 1995. pap. text 12.95 (*0-86975-486-6*, Pub. by Ravan Pr) Ohio U Pr.

— Nelson Mandela: The Man & the Movement. 1994. pap. 215.40 (*0-393-31275-5*) Norton.

— Nelson Mandela: The Man & the Movement. 2nd ed. 1994. pap. 10.95 (*0-393-31281-X*, Norton Paperbks) Norton.

Benson, Mary, ed. see Mandela, Winnie.

Benson, Mary S. Women in Eighteenth-Century America: A Study of Opinion & Social Usage. LC 75-41025. (BCL Ser. II). 1976. reprint ed. 39.50 (*0-404-51405-7*) AMS Pr.

Benson, Maxine. Martha Maxwell, Rocky Mountain Naturalist. LC 86-6936. (Women in the West Ser.). (Illus.). 335p. 1986. text 50.00 (*0-8032-1192-9*, Bison Books) U of Nebr Pr.

— Martha Maxwell, Rocky Mountain Naturalist. LC 86-6936. (Women in the West Ser.). (Illus.). 335p. 1999. pap. 15.95 (*0-8032-6155-1*, Bison Books) U of Nebr Pr.

— One Thousand One Colorado Place Names. LC 94-13556. (Illus.). 230p. 1994. 25.00 (*0-7006-0632-7*); pap. 11.95 (*0-7006-0633-5*) U Pr of KS.

Benson, Michael. Ballparks of North America: A Comprehensive Historical Reference to Baseball Grounds, Yards, & Stadiums, 1845 to Present. LC 89-45007. (Illus.). 505p. 1989. lib. bdg. 45.00 (*0-89950-367-5*) McFarland & Co.

***Benson, Michael.** Blackjack Strategy. 2000. pap. 14.95 (*1-58574-026-8*) Lyons Pr.

— Convertibles: Sun, Wind & Speed. 1998. pap. text 10.98 (*1-57717-040-7*) Todtri Prods.

Benson, Michael. Crashes & Collisions. LC 97-690. (Race Car Legends Ser.). (Illus.). 64p. (J). (gr. 3 up). 1997. 15.95 (*0-7910-4435-1*) Chelsea Hse.

— Dale Earnhardt. LC 95-18224. (Race Car Legends Ser.). 64p. (J). (gr. 3 up). 1996. lib. bdg. 15.95 (*0-7910-3180-2*) Chelsea Hse.

***Benson, Michael.** Dale Earnhardt. (Race Car Legends Ser.). (Illus.). 64p. (J). (gr. 4-7). 1999. pap. text 8.95 (*0-7910-5756-9*) Chelsea Hse.

— Essential Bowling. LC 99-42539. 1999. pap. 12.95 (*1-55821-968-4*) Lyons Pr.

— Gloria Estefan. LC 99-36262. (A&E Biography Ser.). (Illus.). 128p. (YA). (gr. 4-7). 2000. pap. 7.95 (*0-8225-9692-X*, Lerner Publctns) Lerner Pub.

— Gloria Estefan. LC 99-36262. (A&E Biography Ser.). (Illus.). 128p. (YA). (gr. 6-9). 2000. 25.26 (*0-8225-4982-4*, Lerner Publctns) Lerner Pub.

— Hardcore. (Premiere Wrestling Ringside Special Ser.: No. 7). 2000. pap. 4.99 (*0-88013-028-8*, Pub. by Starlog Grp Inc) Kable News Co Inc.

Benson, Michael. Muscle Cars: Thunder & Greased Lightening. 1998. pap. text 10.98 (*1-57717-008-3*) Todtri Prods.

— Pregnancy Myths: What Not to Expect When You're Expecting. 156p. 1995. pap. 9.95 (*1-56924-822-2*) Marlowe & Co.

— Women in Racing. LC 97-14226. (Race Car Legends Ser.). (Illus.). 64p. (J). (gr. 3 up). 1997. 15.95 (*0-7910-4432-7*) Chelsea Hse.

Benson, Michael, ed. Civil War Tech Journal, No. 5. (Starlog Movie Ser.). (Illus.). (YA). 1999. pap. 5.99 (*0-934551-54-5*) Starlog Grp Inc.

***Benson, Michael, ed.** Premier Wrestling Ringside No. 6: Hardcore. 2000. pap. 3.99 (*0-88013-015-6*, Pub. by Starlog Grp Inc) Kable News Co Inc.

— Raw vs. Nitro. (TV Wrestlers Ser.: No. 43). 2000. pap. 6.99 (*0-88013-020-2*, Pub. by Starlog Grp Inc) Kable News Co Inc.

— Raw vs. Nitro. (TV Wrestlers Ser.: No. 47). 2000. pap. write for info. (*0-88013-022-9*, Pub. by Starlog Grp Inc) Kable News Co Inc.

Benson, Michael, ed. Starlog Celebrity Series Presents No. 6: Baseball Superstars. 1998. pap. 4.99 (*0-934551-51-0*) Starlog Grp Inc.

***Benson, Michael, ed.** Starlog Movie Hits #7 Vol. V: Civil War Untold Stories. 1999. pap. 5.99 (*0-934551-9?-2*, Pub. by Starlog Grp Inc) Kable News Co Inc.

— Starlog Movie Hits Presents No. 8 Vol. VI: Vietnam Untold Stories. 2000. pap. 5.99 (*0-88013-005-9*, Pub. by Starlog Grp Inc) Kable News Co Inc.

Benson, Michael, ed. Starlog's 100 Years of Automobiles. (Illus.). 1999. pap. 9.99 (*0-934551-78-2*, Pub. by Starlog Grp Inc) Kable News Co Inc.

— Starlog's 100 Years of Baseball. (Illus.). 1999. pap. 9.99 (*0-934551-77-4*, Pub. by Starlog Grp Inc) Kable News Co Inc.

***Benson, Michael, ed.** Superstar Wrestlers Presents Ultimate Wrestling, No. 4. 2000. pap. 4.99 (*0-88013-000-8*, Pub. by Starlog Grp Inc) Kable News Co Inc.

— Superstar Wrestlers Presents Ultimate Wrestling, No. 5. 2000. pap. 4.99 (*0-88013-001-6*, Pub. by Starlog Grp Inc) Kable News Co Inc.

— Superstar Wrestling Presents Ultimate Wrestling, No. 3. 1999. pap. 4.99 (*0-934551-99-5*, Pub. by Starlog Grp Inc) Kable News Co Inc.

Benson, Michael, ed. TV Wrestlers - Bad Dudes, Vol. 42. 2000. pap. 6.99 (*0-934551-87-1*, Pub. by Starlog Grp Inc) Kable News Co Inc.

— TV Wrestlers - Beauties of Wrestling, Vol. 40. 1999. pap. 6.99 (*0-934551-85-5*, Pub. by Starlog Grp Inc) Kable News Co Inc.

***Benson, Michael, ed.** TV Wrestlers - Raw vs. Nitro, Vol. 39. 1999. pap. 6.99 (*0-934551-84-7*, Pub. by Starlog Grp Inc) Kable News Co Inc.

Benson, Michael, ed. TV Wrestlers - Raw vs. Nitro, Vol. 41. 1999. pap. 6.99 (*0-934551-86-3*, Pub. by Starlog Grp Inc) Kable News Co Inc.

— TV Wrestlers Presents No. 3: Beauties of Wrestling. 1999. pap. 4.99 (*0-934551-62-6*) Starlog Grp Inc.

— TV Wrestlers Presents No. 4: Goldberg vs. Austin. 1998. pap. 4.99 (*0-934551-59-6*) Starlog Grp Inc.

— Vietnam the Untold Stories. (Five Star Publications Presents). (YA). 1998. pap. 5.99 (*0-934551-53-7*) Starlog Grp Inc.

— Vietnam Untold Stories. (Starlog Movie Ser.: Vol. IV, No. 7). 1999. pap. 5.99 (*0-934551-82-0*) Starlog Grp Inc.

***Benson, Michael, ed.** Wrestlemania. (TV Wrestlers Ser.: No. 45). 2000. pap. 6.99 (*0-88013-021-0*, Pub. by Starlog Grp Inc) Kable News Co Inc.

Benson, Michael, jt. ed. see Napolitano, George.

Benson, Michael D. Birth Day! The Last 24 Hours of Pregnancy. 144p. 1994. pap. 10.95 (*1-56924-952-0*) Marlowe & Co.

— Coping with Birth Control. (Coping Skills Library). 128p. (J). 1998. reprint ed. pap. 6.95 (*1-56838-217-0*) Hazelden.

— Gynecologic Pearls. 2nd ed. LC 99-55261. (Illus.). 304p. 2000. pap. text 19.95 (*0-8036-0502-1*) Davis Co.

***Benson, Michael D.** Obstetrical Pearls: A Practical Guide for the Efficient Resident. 3rd ed. LC 99-24043. 226p. (Orig.). 1999. pap. 19.99 (*0-8036-0432-7*) Davis Co.

Benson, Michael D. Pregnancy Myths: An Obstetrician Demystifies Pregnancy from Conception to Birth. LC 98-28523. 352p. 1998. pap. 14.95 (*1-56924-695-5*) Marlowe & Co.

Benson, Michael J. Travelers Pocket Guide: A Guide to Security & Travel Tips. 74p. 1998. pap. 9.95 (*0-9664177-0-4*) Brtsh Bobby.

Benson, Michael K. Children's Orthopaedics & Fractures. 1994. text 139.00 (*0-443-04372-8*) Church.

Benson, Michael L. & Cullen, Francis T. Combating Corporate Crime: Local Prosecutors at Work. LC 97-45999. (Series on White-Collar & Organized Crime). (Illus.). 312p. 1998. text 55.00 (*1-55553-353-1*); pap. text 22.50 (*1-55553-352-3*) NE U Pr.

Benson, Michael T. Harry S. Truman & the Founding of Israel. LC 96-54017. 240p. 1997. 59.95 (*0-275-95807-8*, E814, Praeger Pubs) Greenwood.

Benson, Michael W., jt. auth. see Benson, Bob, Sr.

Benson, Morton. Dictionary of Russian Personal Names: With a Revised Guide to Stress & Morphology. (Illus.). 188p. (C). 1992. text 59.95 (*0-521-41165-3*) Cambridge U Pr.

— English-Serbocroatian Dictionary. (CRO, ENG & SER.). 669p. 1981. 95.00 (*0-7859-0815-3*, M9635) Fr & Eur.

— An English-Serbocroatian Serbocroatian-English Dictionary. 344p. 1982. 75.00 (*0-7855-0992-5*) St Mut.

— Serbocroatian-English Dictionary. 2nd rev. ed. (ENG & SER.). 844p. 1990. 125.00 (*0-8288-0499-0*, M9630) Fr & Eur.

— Standard English-Serbo-Croatian, Serbo-Croatian-English Dictionary: A Dictionary of Bosnian, Croatian, & Serbian Standards. LC 98-20575. (CRO, ENG & SER.). 800p. (C). 1998. text 85.00 (*0-521-64209-4*); pap. text 39.95 (*0-521-64553-0*) Cambridge U Pr.

Benson, Morton, ed. English-SerboCroatian Dictionary. 3rd ed. 774p. (C). 1990. text 89.95 (*0-521-38496-6*) Cambridge U Pr.

Benson, Morton & Benson, Evelyn, eds. Russian-English Dictionary of Verbal Collocations (REDVC) LC 92-34482. xviii, 269p. 1993. 47.00 (*1-55619-483-8*); pap. 23.95 (*1-55619-484-6*) J Benjamins Pubng Co.

Benson, Morton & Sljivic-Simsic, Biljana, eds. SerboCroatian-English Dictionary. 3rd ed. 837p. (C). 1990. text 89.95 (*0-521-38495-8*) Cambridge U Pr.

Benson, Morton, et al. The BBI Dictionary of English Word Combinations. 2nd rev. ed. LC 97-34474. xl, 386p. 1997. pap. 19.95 (*1-55619-521-4*); lib. bdg. 38.00 (*1-55619-520-6*) J Benjamins Pubng Co.

— Lexicographic Description of English. LC 86-17506. (Studies in Language Companion: No. 14). xiii, 275p. 1986. 81.00 (*90-272-3014-5*) J Benjamins Pubng Co.

— Using the BBI Combinatory Dictionary of English: A Workbook with Exercises. x, 58p. (Orig.). 1991. pap. text 6.95 (*1-55619-094-8*) J Benjamins Pubng Co.

Benson, Morton, et al. Using the BBI Combinatory Dictionary of English: A Workbook with Exercises--Together with the BBI. 1991. 43.00 (*1-55619-528-1*); pap. 25.00 (*1-55619-529-X*) J Benjamins Pubng Co.

Benson, Nettie L. The Provincial Deputation in Mexico: Harbinger of Provincial Autonomy, Independence, & Federalism. LC 91-43937. (Institute of Latin American Studies Special Publication). (Illus.). 239p. 1992. text 35.00 (*0-292-76531-2*) U of Tex Pr.

Benson, Nettie L., tr. & intro. see Ramos-Arizpe, Miguel.

Benson, Nicholas. Rats' Tales: The Staffordshire Regiment at War in the Gulf. (Illus.). 164p. 1993. 30.00 (*1-85753-060-8*, Pub. by Brasseys) Brasseys.

***Benson, Nigel.** Introducing Psychology. (Illus.). 176p. 2000. pap. 10.95 (*1-84046-004-0*, Pub. by Totem Bks) Natl Bk Netwk.

Benson, Norma, jt. auth. see Zauner, Christian.

Benson, Oscar H., jt. auth. see Tod, Osma G.

Benson, P. F., ed. Screening & Management of Potentially Treatable Genetic Metabolic Disorders. 176p. 1984. text 164.50 (*0-85200-784-1*) Kluwer Academic.

Benson, Pamela, ed. see Chaucer, Geoffrey.

Benson, Pamela J. The Invention of the Renaissance Woman: The Challenge of Female Independence in the Literature & Thought of Italy & England. 384p. 1992. text 50.00 (*0-271-00812-1*); pap. text 17.95 (*0-271-00814-8*) Pa St U Pr.

Benson, Patrick. Robin Hood. LC 89-33419. 80p. (J). (gr. 4-6). 1995. 12.95 (*0-8050-1206-0*, Bks Young Read) H Holt & Co.

Benson, Patrick, jt. auth. see Hoban, Russell.

Benson, Paul, ed. Anthropology & Literature. (Illus.). 336p. (C). 1993. text 44.95 (*0-252-01944-X*); pap. text 18.95 (*0-252-06261-2*) U of Ill Pr.

Benson, Paul & Otis, Pauletta. The Politics of American Government: Test Item File. 2nd ed. 1997. 33.32 (*0-312-15316-3*) St Martin.

Benson, Paul, et al. Lone Star Politics. 144p. (C). 1997. pap. text, student ed. 19.50 (*0-15-503544-4*) Harcourt Coll Pubs.

— Long Star Politics. LC 96-76366. 400p. (C). 1996. pap. text 41.50 (*0-15-503538-X*, Pub. by Harcourt Coll Pubs) Harcourt.

Benson, Peggy. Listening for a God Who Whispers: A Woman's Discovery of Quiet Understanding. Date not set. reprint ed. pap. write for info. (*0-9677725-1-6*) Deeper Life Pr.

Benson, Peggy, jt. auth. see Gaither, Gloria.

Benson, Peter J. Comprehensive English-Esperanto Dictionary. LC 94-61165. 607p. 1995. pap. 20.00 (*0-939785-03-X*, CEED02); text 27.00 (*0-939785-02-1*, CEED01) Esperanto League North Am.

Benson, Peter L. All Kids Are Our Kids. LC 97-21092. Orig. Title: Creating Healthy Communities. 320p. 1997. 24.95 (*0-7879-1068-6*) Jossey-Bass.

Benson, Peter L. All Kids Are Our Kids: What Communities Must Do to Raise Caring & Responsible Children & Adolescents. 304p. 1997. 24.95 (*1-57482-300-0*) Search Inst.

Benson, Peter L. The Troubled Journey: A Portrait of 6th-12th Grade Youth. 92p. 1993. pap. 10.00 (*1-57482-308-6*) Search Inst.

Benson, Peter L. & Guerra, Michael J. Sharing the Faith: The Beliefs & Values of Catholic High School Teachers. 85p. 1985. 6.00 (*0-318-18578-4*) Natl Cath Educ.

Benson, Peter L. & Hill, Dorothy. Religion on Capitol Hill: Myths & Realities. LC 86-16434. (Illus.). 237p. 1986. pap. text 23.95 (*0-19-504168-2*) OUP.

Benson, Peter L. & Roehlkepartain, Eugene C. Beyond Leaf Raking: Learning to Serve/Serving to Learn. 123p. 1993. pap. 13.95 (*1-57482-122-9*) Abingdon.

Benson, Peter L., et al. A Fragile Foundation: The State of Developmental Assets among American Youth. LC 99-12993. 172p. 1998. pap. 17.95 (*1-57482-352-3*) Search Inst.

— Growing up Adopted: A Portrait of Adolescents & Their Families. 128p. 1994. pap. 7.95 (*1-57482-324-8*) Search Inst.

— Starting Out Right: Development Assets for Children. LC 98-201791. 116p. 1997. pap. 14.95 (*1-57482-364-7*) Search Inst.

Benson, Peter L., et al. Starting Out Right Report Highlights: Developmental Assets for Children. 1997. pap. 9.95 (*1-57482-363-9*) Search Inst.

Benson, Peter L., et al. What Kids Need to Succeed: Proven, Practical Ways to Raise Good Kids. expanded rev. ed. LC 98-9850. 256p. 1998. pap. text 5.99 (*1-57542-030-9*) Free Spirit Pub.

Benson, Peter L., et al. What Kids Need to Succeed: Proven, Practical Ways to Raise Good Kids. rev. ed. Date not set. pap. 5.99 (*1-57482-337-X*) Free Spirit Pub.

B

Benson, Peter L., et al. What Teens Need to Succeed: Proven, Practical Ways to Shape Your Own Future. LC 98-6036. 272p. (YA). (gr. 6 up). 1998. pap. 14.95 (*1-57542-027-9*) Free Spirit Pub.

Benson, Peter L., jt. auth. see Roehlkepartain, Eugene C.

Benson, Philip F. & Fensom, Anthony H. Genetic Biochemical Disorders. (Oxford Monographs on Medical Genetics: No. 2). (Illus.). 600p. 1986. 110.00 (*0-19-261193-3*) OUP.

— Genetic Biochemical Disorders. (Oxford Monographs on Medical Genetics: No. 2). (Illus.). 600p. 1986. pap. 59.50 (*0-19-261642-0*) OUP.

Benson, Philippa, et al. Technical Writing: What It Is & How to Do It. LC 99-38274. (Illus.). 208p. 2000. pap. 16.00 (*1-57685-267-9*) LrningExprss.

Benson, Priscilla J., ed. Proceedings of the 1993 Undergraduate Symposium on Research in Astronomy. 118p. (C). 1994. pap. text. write for info. (*1-882334-03-5*) Keck NE Astron.

— Proceedings of the 1996 Undergraduate Symposium on Research in Astronomy. (Orig.). (C). 1996. pap. text. write for info. (*1-882334-06-X*) Keck NE Astron.

Benson, R. J. Wear Studies of Fine Pitch Gear Materials. (Technical Papers: Vol. P249.06). (Illus.). 44p. 1957. pap. text 30.00 (*1-55589-348-1*) AGMA.

Benson, Ragnar. Acquiring New ID: How to Easily Use the Latest Computer Technology to Drop Out, Start Over, & Get on with Your Life. (Illus.). 152p. 1996. pap. 20.00 (*0-87364-894-3*) Paladin Pr.

— Action Careers: Employment in the High-Risk Job Market. 360p. reprint ed. pap. 9.95 (*0-8065-1079-X*, Citadel Pr) Carol Pub Group.

— David's Tool Kit: A Citizen's Guide to Taking Out Big Brother's Heavy Weapons. LC 96-79748. (Illus.). 217p. (Orig.). 1996. pap. 16.95 (*1-55950-143-X*, 32060) Loompanics.

— Do-It-Yourself Medicine: How to Find & Use the Most Effective Antibiotics, Painkillers, Anesthetics, & Other Miracle Drugs...Without Costly Doctors' Prescriptions or Hospitals. LC 98-103946. (Illus.). 113p. 1997. pap. 20.00 (*0-87364-918-4*) Paladin Pr.

— The Greatest Explosions in History: The Fire, Flash & Fury of Natural & Man-Made Disasters. (Illus.). 192p. 1991. pap. 7.95 (*0-8065-1278-4*, Citadel Pr) Carol Pub Group.

— Home-Built Claymore Mines: A Blueprint for Survival. (Illus.). 64p. 1993. pap. 12.00 (*0-87364-726-2*) Paladin Pr.

— Homemade C-4: A Recipe for Survival. (Illus.). 56p. 1990. pap. 14.00 (*0-87364-558-8*) Paladin Pr.

— Homemade Grenade Launchers: Constructing the Ultimate Hobby Weapon. (Illus.). 144p. 1991. 16.00 (*0-87364-626-6*) Paladin Pr.

— Live off the Land in the City & Country. (Illus.). 272p. 1981. 29.95 (*0-87364-200-7*) Paladin Pr.

— Mantrapping. (Illus.). 88p. 1981. pap. 15.00 (*0-87364-215-5*) Paladin Pr.

— The Modern Survival Retreat: A New & Vital Approach to Retreat Theory & Practice. LC 98-209848. (Illus.). 120p. 1998. pap. 15.00 (*0-87364-980-X*) Paladin Pr.

— Modern Weapons Caching: A Down-to-Earth Approach to Beating the Government Gun Grab. (Illus.). 104p. 1990. pap. 15.00 (*0-87364-583-9*) Paladin Pr.

— The Most Dangerous Game: Advanced Mantrapping Techniques. (Illus.). 120p. 1986. pap. 16.00 (*0-87364-356-9*) Paladin Pr.

— Ragnar's Action Encyclopedia, 2 vols., Vol. 2. rev. ed. LC 95-151723. (Illus.). 248p. 1999. pap. 40.00 (*0-87364-926-5*) Paladin Pr.

— Ragnar's Action Encyclopedia of Practical Knowledge & Proven Techniques: A Do-It-Yourself Guide, 2 vols., Vol. 1. rev. ed. LC 95-151723. (Illus.). 344p. 1999. pap. 35.00 (*0-87364-801-3*) Paladin Pr.

— Ragnar's Guide to the Underground Economy. (Illus.). 160p. 1999. pap. 18.00 (*1-58160-011-9*) Paladin Pr.

— Ragnar's Ten Best Traps & a Few Others That Are Damn Good, Too. (Illus.). 136p. 1985. pap. 16.00 (*0-87364-328-3*) Paladin Pr.

***Benson, Ragnar.** Ragnar's Urban Survival: A Hard-Times Guide to Staying Alive in the City. (Illus.). 220p. 2000. pap. 20.00 (*1-58160-059-3*) Paladin Pr.

Benson, Ragnar. Survival Poaching. (Illus.). 250p. 1980. text 29.95 (*0-87364-183-3*) Paladin Pr.

— The Survival Retreat: A Total Plan for Retreat Defense. (Illus.). 136p. 1983. pap. 12.00 (*0-87364-275-9*) Paladin Pr.

— Survivalist's Medicine Chest. (Illus.). 80p. 1982. pap. 14.00 (*0-87364-256-2*) Paladin Pr.

— Switchblade: The Ace of Blades. (Illus.). 104p. 1989. pap. 15.00 (*0-87364-500-6*) Paladin Pr.

Benson, Ralph C. & Pernoll, Martin L. Benson & Pernoll's Handbook of Obstetrics & Gynecology. 9th ed. (Illus.). 832p. 1993. pap. text 35.00 (*0-07-105405-7*) McGraw-Hill HPD.

Benson, Ray. Learn Western Swing Guitar. (Homespun Tapes Ser.). 1996. VHS 39.95 (*0-7935-6865-X*) H Leonard.

***Benson, Raymond.** Doubleshot: The New James Bond Adventure. LC 00-23224. 272p. 2000. 23.95 (*0-399-14614-8*) Putnam Pub Group.

Benson, Raymond. The Facts of Death. 1999. reprint ed. mass mkt. 6.99 (*0-515-12550-4*, Jove) Berkley Pub.

***Benson, Raymond.** The Facts of Death: The New James Bond Adventure. LC 97-52926. 288p. 1998. 23.95 (*0-399-14405-6*, G P Putnam) Peng Put Young Read.

— High Time to Kill. (James Bond Adventures Ser.). 304p. 2000. mass mkt. 6.99 (*0-515-12833-3*, Jove) Berkley Pub.

Benson, Raymond. High Time to Kill: James Bond New Bond Adventure. LC 98-54718. 272p. 1999. 23.95 (*0-399-14500-1*, G P Putnam) Peng Put Young Read.

***Benson, Raymond.** High Time to Kill: New Bond Adventure. LC PS3552.E547666H54. 2000. 28.95 (*0-7862-2338-3*) Thorndike Pr.

Benson, Raymond. Tomorrow Never Dies. (James Bond Ser.). 1997. mass mkt. 6.99 (*1-57297-345-5*) Blvd Books.

***Benson, Raymond.** The World Is Not Enough. 1999. mass mkt. 6.99 (*0-425-17350-X*) Blvd Books.

Benson, Raymond. Zero Minus Ten. 1998. reprint ed. mass mkt. 6.99 (*0-515-12336-6*, Jove) Berkley Pub.

Benson, Richard. Geophysical Techniques for Waste Detection. 1998. write for info. (*0-87371-118-1*, L118) Lewis Pubs.

***Benson, Richard.** A Yale Album: The Third Century. (Illus.). 192p. 2000. 39.95 (*0-300-08723-3*) Yale U Pr.

Benson, Richard, photos by. Lay This Laurel. limited ed. LC 73-84997. (Illus.). 80p. 1973. 60.00 (*0-87130-036-2*) Eakins.

Benson, Richard & Mariners' Museum (Newport News, Va.) Staff. A Maritime Album: 100 Photographs & Their Stories. LC 97-22154. (Illus.). 245p. 1997. pap. 24.95 (*0-917376-48-X*) Mariners Mus.

Benson, Richard, jt. auth. see Szarkowski, John.

Benson, Richard E., jt. ed. see Brossi, Arnold.

Benson, Richard V. Secrets of Successful Direct Mail. (Illus.). 208p. 1994. 29.95 (*0-8442-3178-9*, NTC Business Bks) NTC Contemp Pub Co.

— Secrets of Successful Direct Mail. (Illus.). 208p. 1994. pap. 16.95 (*0-8442-3294-7*, NTC Business Bks) NTC Contemp Pub Co.

Benson, Rita. Alligator Mouse & Other Disasters. LC 93-18052. (Illus.). (J). 1994. write for info. (*0-383-03674-7*) SRA McGraw.

— Looking after the Babysitter. LC 93-26221. (Voyages Ser.). (Illus.). (J). 1994. 4.25 (*0-383-03760-3*) SRA McGraw.

— Rosa's Diary. LC 93-28972. (Voyages Ser.). (Illus.). (J). 1994. 4.25 (*0-383-03772-7*) SRA McGraw.

— What Angela Needs. LC 92-34266. (Voyages Ser.). (Illus.). (J). 1993. 14.00 (*0-383-03666-6*) SRA McGraw.

Benson, Rita, ed. see Debussy, Claude.

Benson, Robert. Between the Dreaming & the Coming True: The Road Home to God. LC 96-1455. 1996. pap. 10.00 (*0-06-060900-1*) Harper SF.

***Benson, Robert.** Between the Dreaming & the Coming True: The Road Home to God. 2001. pap. 12.95 (*1-58542-088-3*, Tarcher Putnam) Putnam Pub Group.

— By What Authority. 252p. 2000. pap. 9.95 (*0-594-00282-6*) Eightn Hundrd.

— Challenging Corporate Rule: The Petition to Revoke Unocal's Charter as a Guide to Citizen Action. 170p. 2000. pap. 9.95 (*1-891843-04-4*) Apex Pr.

Benson, Robert. Living Prayer. LC 98-15290. 224p. 1998. 21.95 (*0-87477-920-0*, Tarcher Putnam) Putnam Pub Group.

— Living Prayer. LC 99-20278. 224p. 1999. reprint ed. pap. 12.00 (*0-87477-967-7*, Tarcher Putnam) Putnam Pub Group.

***Benson, Robert.** The Queen's Tragedy. 252p. 2000. pap. 9.95 (*0-594-00033-5*) Eightn Hundrd.

— Venite: A Book of Daily Prayer. LC 99-46211. 263p. 2000. 24.95 (*1-58542-013-1*, Tarcher Putnam) Putnam Pub Group.

Benson, Robert & Benson, Karen. Favorite Texas Birds, Vol. I: Their Songs & Calls, Vol. 1. (Louise Lindsey Merrick Natural Environment Ser.: No. 14). 1993. audio 10.95 (*0-89096-550-1*) Tex St Hist Assn.

Benson, Robert A. Essays on Architecture in the Midwest. LC 92-37812. 168p. 1992. pap. 20.00 (*0-9630969-1-5*) Interalia Des.

Benson, Robert B. Mark of the Beast, Six Six Six. 132p. (Orig.). 1993. pap. 7.50 (*0-9616327-0-4*) Brandt Bks.

— The Wizard of Bergen. (Wolfgang Brandt Ser.). 125p. (Orig.). (YA). (gr. 7-12). 1987. pap. 7.50 (*0-9616327-1-2*) Brandt Bks.

Benson, Robert E., et al. How to Prepare for, Take & Use a Deposition. 444p. 1990. ring bd. 89.98 (*0-938065-49-1*) James Pub Santa Ana.

Benson, Robert G. & Naylor, Eric W. Essays in Honor of Edward B. King. (Illus.). 258p. (Orig.). 1991. pap. 25.00 (*0-918769-30-2*) Univ South Pr.

Benson, Robert H. Book of Essays. LC 68-54325. (Essay Index Reprint Ser.). 1977. reprint ed. 19.95 (*0-8369-0195-9*) Ayer.

— Lord of the World. LC 74-15951. (Science Fiction Ser.). 352p. 1975. reprint ed. 32.95 (*0-405-06277-X*) Ayer.

***Benson, Robert H.** Lord of the World. unabridged ed. LC 99-47255. (Catholic Writers Ser.). 384p. 2000. reprint ed. pap. 22.00 (*1-890318-38-8*, Pub. by St Augustines Pr) Chicago Distribution Ctr.

Benson, Robert H. The Necromancers. LC 75-36826. (Occult Ser.). 1976. reprint ed. 26.95 (*0-405-07939-7*) Ayer.

— Papers of a Pariah. LC 67-23176. (Essay Index Reprint Ser.). 1977. 19.95 (*0-8369-0196-7*) Ayer.

Benson, Robert L. The Bishop-Elect: A Study in Medieval Ecclesiastical Office. LC 65-17130. 460p. reprint ed. pap. 142.60 (*0-8357-7276-4*, 201053500068) Bks Demand.

Benson, Robert L. & Constable, Giles, eds. Renaissance & Renewal in the Twelfth Century. (Medieval Academy Reprints for Teaching Ser.: No. 26). 848p. 1991. reprint ed. pap. text 27.50 (*0-8020-6850-2*) U of Toronto Pr.

Benson, Robert L., jt. auth. see Warner, Michael.

Benson, Ron. Beginnings: Teaching & Learning in the Kindergarten. LC 93-20194. 155p. 1993. pap. text 21.95 (*1-878450-54-9*, 503) R Owen Pubs.

— Kit Renderings. LC 97-129064. (Illus.). 80p. (Orig.). 1996. 9.95 (*0-89024-273-9*, 12169) Kalmbach.

Benson, Rowland S. Advanced Engineering Thermodynamics. 2nd ed. 1977. 158.00 (*0-08-020719-7*, Pub. by Pergamon Repr) Franklin.

Benson, Roy. The Runners' Coach. 128p. 1994. 12.95 (*0-915297-13-2*) Cedarwinds.

Benson, S. V., jt. ed. see Neil, G. R.

Benson, Sally. Meet Me in St. Louis. 1978. pap. 5.50 (*0-87129-246-7*, M24) Dramatic Pub.

Benson, Sally, jt. ed. see Frankenberger, W. T.

Benson, Sally B. Child Play & Playthings: Index of New Information with Authors & Subjects. LC 92-54215. 180p. 1992. 44.50 (*1-55914-582-X*); pap. 39.50 (*1-55914-583-8*) ABBE Pubs Assn.

Benson, Seymour. Florida Family Law: A Common Sense Approach. rev. ed. Campaigne, Carol, ed. LC 95-78179. 2500p. 1995. text. write for info. (*0-7620-0024-4*) West Group.

Benson, Shirley, tr. see Khrushchev, Sergei N.

Benson, Sidney W. The Foundations of Chemical Kinetics. LC 80-16099. 742p. 1982. reprint ed. lib. bdg. 69.50 (*0-89874-194-7*) Krieger.

— Thermochemical Kinetics. 2nd ed. 336p. 1976. 129.95 (*0-471-06781-4*) Wiley.

Benson, Sonia. Asian American Reference Library: Cumulative Index. LC 98-130239. 32 p. 1997. write for info. (*0-7876-1883-7*, UXL) Gale.

— Hispanic American Reference Library: Cumulative Index LC 98-163518. 31 p. 1997. write for info. (*0-7876-1882-9*, UXL) Gale.

Benson, Sonia, ed. see Sylvester, Theodore L.

Benson, Sonja, jt. auth. see Gafner, George.

Benson, Stella. The Far-Away Bride. LC 77-138606. 354p. 1972. reprint ed. lib. bdg. 69.50 (*0-8371-5714-5*, BEFB, Greenwood Pr) Greenwood.

***Benson, Stella.** The Healing Musician: A Guide to Playing Healing Music at the Bedside. (Illus.). 202p. 1999. pap. 29.00 (*0-9675453-0-7*) NewGrail.

Benson, Stephen. Creative Sugarpaste: Basic Techniques. (Sugarcraft Skills Ser.). 1994. pap. text 11.95 (*1-85391-350-2*) Merehurst Ltd.

Benson, Steve. Blue Book. (Illus.). 223p. (Orig.). 1988. pap. 12.50 (*0-935724-34-6*) Figures.

— Evanly Days. 140p. 1988. pap. 9.95 (*0-938448-28-5*, Phoenix Map Svce) Wide World Maps.

— Reverse Order. 92p. (Orig.). 1989. pap. 9.00 (*0-937013-25-0*) Potes Poets.

***Benson, Steve.** Roaring Spring. 52p. 1998. pap. 9.95 (*84-87467-31-8*, Pub. by Zasterle Pr) SPD-Small Pr Dist.

Benson, Steve & Keane, Bill. Where Do You Draw the Line? Lessner, Richard, ed. (Illus.). 170p. 1992. pap. 10.95 (*0-938448-72-2*) Wide World Maps.

Benson, Steve D. Press Brake Technology: A Guide to Precision Sheet Metal Bending. LC 96-70755. (Illus.). 212p. 1997. 48.00 (*0-87263-483-3*, 2545) SME.

Benson, Steven. From Soup to Nuts: Finding & Keeping Healthcare Employees. rev. ed. 1999. 21.50 (*0-929442-40-7*, 2147PP) Prof Prnting & Pub.

Benson, Steven V. A Personal Orientation Manual for the NHA. 175p. (Orig.). (C). 1991. pap. text 32.00 (*1-877735-30-2*, 2175PP) Prof Prnting & Pub.

***Benson, Susan.** Pioneers of the Soil: California Farmers Cultivating a Healthier Future. 2000. pap. text 16.95 (*0-935028-77-3*) Inst Food & Develop.

Benson, Susan, jt. auth. see Benson, Edmund F.

Benson, Susan, ed. see El Shazly, Saad.

Benson, Susan P. Counter Cultures: Saleswomen, Managers, & Customers in American Department Stores, 1890-1940. LC 85-21012. (Working Class in American History Ser.). (Illus.). 344p. 1986. text 27.50 (*0-252-01252-6*) U of Ill Pr.

— Counter Cultures: Saleswomen, Managers, & Customers in American Department Stores, 1890-1940. LC 85-21012. (Working Class in American History Ser.). (Illus.). 344p. 1988. pap. text 17.95 (*0-252-06013-X*) U of Ill Pr.

Benson, Susan P., et al, eds. Presenting the Past: Essays on History & the Public. (Critical Perspectives on the Past Ser.). (Illus.). 448p. 1986. pap. 22.95 (*0-87722-413-7*) Temple U Pr.

Benson, Susan W., ed. Berry Benson's Civil War Book: Memoirs of a Confederate Scout & Sharpshooter. LC 92-27349. (Illus.). 215p. 1993. 19.95 (*0-8203-1487-0*) U of Ga Pr.

Benson, Ted. Inside Your Shortwave Radio. 90p. 1992. pap. 14.95 (*0-936653-40-X*) Tiare Pubns.

***Benson, Ted.** One Track Mind: Photographic Essays on Western Railroading. (Illus.). 176p. 2000. 45.00 (*1-55046-273-3*) Boston Mills.

Benson, Tedd. The Timber-Frame Home: Design, Construction & Finishing. 2nd ed. LC 96-44276. 1997. 34.95 (*1-56158-129-1*, 070260) Taunton.

***Benson, Tedd.** Timberframe: The Art & Craft of the Post & Beam Home. LC 99-31212. 240p. 1999. write for info. (*1-56158-281-6*) Taunton.

Benson, Tedd & Gruber, James. Building the Timber Frame House: The Revival of a Forgotten Craft. (Illus.). 220p. 1981. per. 20.00 (*0-684-17286-0*, Scribners Ref) Mac Lib Ref.

Benson, Thomas, ed. see Purcell, William M.

Benson, Thomas W., ed. American Rhetoric: Context & Criticism. LC 88-29689. 432p. (C). 1989. 41.95 (*0-8093-1509-2*) S Ill U Pr.

— Landmark Essays on Rhetorical Criticism. (Landmark Essays Ser.: Vol. 5). 264p. (C). 1993. pap. text 22.50 (*1-880393-08-5*, Hermagoras) L Erlbaum Assocs.

— Rhetoric & Political Culture in Nineteenth-Century America. (Rhetoric & Public Affairs Ser.: No. 6). 215p. 1997. 31.95 (*0-87013-468-X*) Mich St U Pr.

Benson, Thomas W. & Prosser, Michael H., eds. Readings in Classical Rhetoric. xii, 341p. (C). 1988. reprint ed. pap. text 24.50 (*0-9611800-3-X*, Hermagoras) L Erlbaum Assocs.

Benson, Thomas W., jt. auth. see Anderson, Carolyn.

Benson, Thomas W., ed. see Hauser, Gerard A.

Benson, Thomas W., jt. ed. see Hogan, J. Michael.

Benson, Thomas W., ed. see Marback, Richard.

Benson, Thomas W., ed. see Watson, Martha.

Benson, Thomas W., ed. see White, Eugene E.

Benson, Thomas W., ed. see Xing Lu.

Benson, Timothy O. Raoul Hausmann & Berlin Dada. LC 86-28049. (Studies in the Fine Arts: The Avant-Garde: No. 55). 298p. reprint ed. pap. 92.40 (*0-8357-2050-0*, 207069200004) Bks Demand.

Benson, Toni. Cemetery Records of Van Buren County, Michigan: Paw Paw Township, Vol. 1. (Illus.). 225p. 1993. pap. 20.00 (*0-9620998-3-X*) F-Ami-Lee.

— Source Check: A Research Checklist for United States Genealogical Research. 25p. 1995. pap. 7.00 (*0-9620998-5-6*) F-Ami-Lee.

— Van Buren County Poorhouse/Infirmary Records, 2 vols., Set. 500p. 1995. pap. 25.00 (*0-9620998-4-8*) F-Ami-Lee.

Benson, Toni, intro. Van Buren County Plat Book, Michigan: Completely Indexed - Circa, 1933. rev. ed. (C). 1988. pap. 10.00 (*0-9620998-0-5*) F-Ami-Lee.

Benson, Tony & Ray, Irv. Run with the Best: A Coach'e Guide to Training Middle & Long Distance Running Based on the Cerutty & Lydiard Models. (Illus.). 128p. 1998. pap. 16.95 (*0-911521-53-4*) Tafnews.

Benson, Tracy, jt. auth. see Scheetz, Mary.

Benson, Trevor M., jt. auth. see Anastasovski, Petar K.

Benson, Valerie. Nurses Never Cry. large type ed. (Dales Large Print Ser.). 282p. 1995. pap. 18.99 (*1-85389-550-4*, Dales) Ulverscroft.

Benson, Vern. Don't Resist Cigarettes: A Mathematician's System to Solve the Smoking Problem. (Illus.). 100p. (Orig.). 1994. pap. 14.95 (*0-9635792-5-8*) First Data Pubs.

Benson, Veronica. Current Estimates from the National Health Interview Survey, 1993. 225p. 1995. per. 16.00 (*0-16-061433-3*) USGPO.

— Current Estimates from the National Health Interview Survey, 1995. 438p. 1998. per. 34.00 (*0-16-061498-8*) USGPO.

***Benson, Vicki & Cummins, Carrice.** The Power of Retelling: Developmental Steps for Building Comprehension. LC 00-31989. 2000. spiral bd. write for info. (*0-322-01541-3*) Wright Group.

***Benson, Victoria Harnish & Lejnieks, Vincent Arturs.** To No Man's Glory: A Child's Journey from Holocaust to Healing. 200p. 2000. pap. 14.95 (*0-9676566-0-5*) Silver Dove.

Benson-Von der Ohe, Elizabeth. First & Second Marriages. LC 86-18220. 229p. 1987. 55.00 (*0-275-92401-7*, C2401, Praeger Pubs) Greenwood.

Benson-Von der Ohe, Elizabeth E. & Mason, Valmari M. An Annoted Bibliography of U. S. Scholarship on the History of the Family. LC 85-48008. (Studies in Social History: No. 6). 1986. 45.00 (*0-404-61606-2*) AMS Pr.

Benson, Warren S., jt. auth. see Gangel, Kenneth O.

Benson, William, jt. auth. see Schlenk, Daniel.

Benson, William E. Retinal Detachment: Diagnosis & Management. 2nd ed. LC 65-10911. (Illus.). 224p. 1988. text 68.25 (*0-397-50926-X*, Lippnctt) Lppncott W & W.

Benson, William E., et al. Current Techniques in Opthalmic Laser Surgery. 2nd ed. (Illus.). 224p. 1995. text 139.95 (*1-878132-57-1*) Current Med.

Benson, William E., jt. auth. see Regillo, Carl D.

Benson, William H. & Jacoby, Oswald. Magic Cubes: New Recreations, 2 pts., Set. (Illus.). 96p. (Orig.). 1982. pap. 5.95 (*0-486-24140-8*) Dover.

Benson, William H., jt. auth. see Jacoby, Oswald.

Bensoussan. Vital Meridian. 1996. text 33.95 (*0-443-04255-1*, W B Saunders Co) Harcrt Hlth Sci Grp.

Bensoussan, A. & Lions, J. L., eds. Analysis & Optimization of Systems. (Lecture Notes in Control & Information Sciences: Vol. 83). xiv, 901p. 1986. 126.95 (*0-387-16729-3*) Spr-Verlag.

Bensoussan, A., ed. see International Conference on Analysis & Optimizatio.

Bensoussan, Alain, et al. Representation & Control of Infinite Dimensional Systems, Vol. 1. LC 92-10323. (Systems & Control: Foundations & Applications Ser.). (Illus.). 320p. 1992. 86.50 (*0-8176-3641-2*) Birkhauser.

Benstock, Bernard. Critical Essays on James Joyce's "Ulysses" (Critical Essays on British Literature Ser.). 344p. 1989. 48.00 (*0-8161-8766-5*, G K Hall & Co) Mac Lib Ref.

— Narrative Con-Texts in Dubliners. LC 93-3377. 170p. 1993. text 34.95 (*0-252-02058-8*) U of Ill Pr.

— Sean O'Casey. LC 72-124101. (Irish Writers Ser.). 123p. 1975. 8.50 (*0-8387-7748-1*); pap. 1.95 (*0-8387-7618-3*) Bucknell U Pr.

Benstock, Bernard, ed. Critical Essays on James Joyce. (Critical Essays on American Literature Ser.). 248p. (C). 1985. 48.00 (*0-8161-8751-7*, G K Hall & Co) Mac Lib Ref.

— James Joyce: The Augmented Ninth. 384p. 1988. 39.95 (*0-8156-2446-8*) Syracuse U Pr.

— The Seventh of Joyce. LC 81-47775. 281p. (Orig.). reprint ed. pap. 87.20 (*0-7837-1745-8*, 205727900024) Bks Demand.

Benstock, Bernard & Staley, Thomas F., eds. British Mystery Writers, 1860-1919. (Dictionary of Literary Biography Ser.: Vol. 70). 400p. 1988. text 155.00 (*0-8103-1748-6*) Gale.

— British Mystery Writers, 1920-1939. (Dictionary of Literary Biography Ser.: Vol. 77). 414p. 1988. text 155.00 (*0-8103-4555-2*, 006545-M99348) Gale.

Benstock, Bernard, jt. auth. see Benstock, Shari.

An Asterisk (*) at the beginning of an entry indicates that the title is appearing for the first time.

Benstock, Bernard, jt. ed. see Bushrui, Suheil Badi.

Benstock, Bernard, jt. ed. see Staley, Thomas F.

Benstock, Seymour L., ed. Johann Sebastian: A Tercentenary Celebration, 19. LC 90-32455. (Contributions to the Study of Music & Dance Ser.: No. 19). 176p. 1992. 47.95 (*0-313-27441-X*, BJA, Greenwood Pr) Greenwood.

Benstock, Shari. Textualizing the Feminine: On the Limits of Genre. LC 91-2516. (Project for Discourse & Theory Ser.: Vol. 7). (Illus.). 288p. 1991. 29.95 (*0-8061-2358-3*); pap. 14.95 (*0-8061-2383-4*) U of Okla Pr.

— Women of the Left Bank: Paris, 1900-1940. (Illus.). 566p. (Orig.). (C). 1986. 32.95 (*0-292-79029-5*) U of Tex Pr.

— Women of the Left Bank: Paris, 1900-1940. (Illus.). 566p. (Orig.). (C). 1986. pap. 19.95 (*0-292-79040-6*) U of Tex Pr.

Benstock, Shari, ed. Feminist Issues in Literary Scholarship. LC 85-45984. 252p. 1987. pap. 6.25 (*0-253-20414-3*, MB 414) Ind U Pr.

— The Private Self: Theory & Practice of Women's Autobiographical Writings. LC 88-1282. vii, 319p. (C). 1988. 49.95 (*0-8078-1791-0*) U of NC Pr.

Benstock, Shari & Benstock, Bernard. Who's He When He's at Home: A James Joyce Directory. LC 79-17947. 251p. reprint ed. pap. 77.90 (*0-7837-5731-X*, 204539200006) Bks Demand.

***Benstock, Shari & Ferriss, Suzanne, eds.** Footnotes: On Shoes. LC 00-34204. (Illus.). 288p. 2001. 52.00 (*0-8135-2870-4*); pap. 24.00 (*0-8135-2871-2*) Rutgers U Pr.

Benstock, Shari & Ferriss, Suzanne, eds. On Fashion. LC 93-13886. (Illus.). 320p. (C). 1994. text 45.00 (*0-8135-2032-0*); pap. text 19.00 (*0-8135-2033-9*) Rutgers U Pr.

Benstock, Shari & Grossman, Barbara. No Gifts from Chance: A Biography of Edith Wharton. LC 93-33704. (Illus.). 544p. 1994. 28.00 (*0-684-19276-4*, Scribners Ref) Mac Lib Ref.

Benstock, Shari, ed. see Wharton, Edith.

Benston, George J. The Anti-Redlining Rules: An Analysis of the Federal Home Loan Bank Board's Proposed Nondiscrimination Requirements. (LEC Occasional Paper). 1978. pap. text 2.50 (*0-916770-06-0*) Law & Econ U Miami.

— Conglomerate Mergers: Causes, Consequences, & Remedies. LC 80-12017. (AEI Studies: No. 270). (Illus.). 84p. reprint ed. pap. 30.00 (*0-8357-4452-3*, 203729000008) Bks Demand.

***Benston, George J.** Regulating Financial Markets: A Critique & Some Proposals. LC 99-35733. 1999. pap. text 16.95 (*0-8447-4124-8*, AEI Pr) Am Enterprise.

Benston, George J. Regulating Financial Markets: A Critique & Some Proposals. (Hobart Papers: No. 135). 130p. 1998. pap. 29.50 (*0-255-36415-6*, Pub. by Inst Economic Affairs) Coronet Bks.

— The Separation of Commercial & Investment Banking: The Glass-Steagall Act Revisited & Reconsidered. 276p. 1990. 55.00 (*0-19-520830-7*) OUP.

Benston, George J., et al. Perspectives on Safe & Sound Banking: Past, Present, & Future. 352p. 1986. 44.00 (*0-262-02246-X*) MIT Pr.

***Benston, Kimberly W.** Performing Blackness: Enactments of African-American Modernism. LC 99-54173. 336p. 2000. pap. 24.99 (*0-415-00949-9*) Routledge.

— Performing Blackness: Enactments of African-American Modernism. LC 99-54173. 336p. (C). 2000. text 75.00 (*0-415-00948-0*) Routledge.

Benston, Kimberly W. Speaking for You: The Vision of Ralph Ellison. 438p. 1988. 29.95 (*0-88258-169-4*) Howard U Pr.

Benston, Kimberly W., ed. Speaking for You - PA: The Vision of Ralph Ellison. 2nd ed. LC 87-17019. 448p. (C). 1990. reprint ed. pap. 17.95 (*0-88258-005-1*) Howard U Pr.

Bensusan, Pierre. Guitar Book of Pierre Bensusan. 188p. 1987. per. 19.95 (*0-88188-620-3*, 00699072) H Leonard.

***Bensusan, Pierre.** Pierre Bensusan Presents Dadgad Guitar. 80p. 2000. pap. 22.95 (*0-7866-5770-7*, 99238BCD) Mel Bay.

Bensussan, G., jt. auth. see Labica, G.

Bensussen, Rusty. Shortcuts to a Perfect Sewing Pattern. LC 88-30833. (Illus.). 160p. (Orig.). 1993. pap. 12.95 (*0-8069-6822-2*) Sterling.

Bent, Alfred E., jt. auth. see Ostergard, Donald R.

Bent, Alfred E., jt. ed. see Ostergard, Donald R.

Bent, Allen H. Allen: Walter Allen of Newbury, Massachusetts & Some Descendants, 1640. 66p. 1994. reprint ed. pap. 13.00 (*0-8328-4174-9*) Higginson Bk Co.

— The Bent Family in America: A Genealogy of the Descendants of John Bent Who Settled in Sudbury, Mass. in 1638. (Illus.). 313p. 1988. reprint ed. pap. 49.50 (*0-8328-0241-7*); reprint ed. lib. bdg. 59.50 (*0-8328-0240-9*) Higginson Bk Co.

— Bibliography of the White Mountains. rev. ed. Hanrahan, Jack, ed. LC 79-179457. (Bibliographies of New Hampshire History Ser.). 134p. 1972. reprint ed. pap. 9.50 (*0-912274-11-5*, 1239) Picton Pr.

Bent, Arthur C. Life Histories of 50 Familiar North American Birds. Newforth, Patricia, ed. & selected by by. LC 95-26797. 1996. write for info. (*0-253-33051-3*); pap. write for info. (*0-253-21063-1*) Ind U Pr.

— Life Histories of North American Gallinaceous Birds. (Illus.). 1963. pap. 10.95 (*0-486-21028-6*) Dover.

— Life Histories of North American Marsh Birds. (Illus.). 1963. pap. 13.95 (*0-486-21082-0*) Dover.

— Life Histories of North American Petrels & Pelicans & Their Allies. (Illus.). xiv, 335p. 1987. reprint ed. pap. 11.95 (*0-486-25525-5*) Dover.

— Life Histories of North American Wagtails, Shrikes, Vireos & Their Allies. (Illus.). 1965. pap. 11.95 (*0-486-21085-5*) Dover.

— Life Histories of North American Wild Fowl. 685p. 1987. reprint ed. pap. 15.95 (*0-486-25422-4*) Dover.

— Life Histories of North American Woodpeckers: Deluxe Edition. LC 91-48014. (Illus.). 286p. 1992. 29.95 (*0-253-31160-8*) Ind U Pr.

Bent, Charles, ed. History of Whiteside County, IL. 536p. 1993. reprint ed. lib. bdg. 56.00 (*0-8328-3444-0*) Higginson Bk Co.

Bent, Christine. The New York Times Book of World War I. 1980. 18.95 (*0-405-13465-7*) Ayer.

Bent, Christine, jt. auth. see Keylin, Arleen.

Bent, Gilbert O. Bent. "Who Begot Thee?" - Some Genealogical & Historical Notes Made in an Effort to Trace the American Progenitors of One Individual Living in America in 1903. (Illus.). 78p. 1997. reprint ed. pap. 15.50 (*0-8328-7501-5*); reprint ed. lib. bdg. 25.50 (*0-8328-7500-7*) Higginson Bk Co.

Bent, Ian D. Analysis. Sadie, Stanley, ed. (Grove Handbooks in Music Ser.). (C). 1987. 55.75 (*0-393-02447-4*) Norton.

Bent, Ian D., ed. Music Analysis in the Nineteenth Century, Vol. 1. LC 93-12313. (Cambridge Readings in the Literature of Music Ser.: No. 1). 391p. (C). 1994. text 80.00 (*0-521-25969-X*) Cambridge U Pr.

— Music Analysis in the Nineteenth Century Vol. 2: Hermeneutic Approaches. (Cambridge Readings in the Literature of Music Ser.). 319p. (C). 1994. text 69.95 (*0-521-46183-9*) Cambridge U Pr.

— Music Theory in the Age of Romanticism. 255p. (C). 1996. text 64.95 (*0-521-55102-1*) Cambridge U Pr.

Bent, James A. Applied Cost & Schedule Control. LC 82-5077. (Cost Engineering Ser.: Vol. 3). (Illus.). 430p. reprint ed. pap. 133.30 (*0-608-08913-3*, 206954800005) Bks Demand.

Bent, James A. & Humphreys, Kenneth K., eds. Effective Project Management Through Applied Cost & Schedule Control. (Cost Engineering Ser.: Vol. 26). (Illus.). 464p. 1996. text 110.00 (*0-8247-9715-9*) Dekker.

Bent, James A. & Thumann, Albert. Project Management for Engineering & Construction. 2nd ed. LC 93-29879. 1993. write for info. (*0-88173-182-X*) Fairmont Pr.

Bent, James T. The Ruined Cities of Mashonaland. LC 70-161256. (Black Heritage Library Collection). 1977. reprint ed. 32.95 (*0-8369-8528-1*) Ayer.

Bent, Judith. Dear Friend: Thomas Garrett & William Still, Collaborators on the Underground Railroad. (YA). (gr. 10 up). 1997. 15.99 (*0-614-25381-0*, Dutton Child) Peng Put Young Read.

Bent, Margaret, ed. Oxford, Bodleian Library, MS.Canon.Misc. 213. fac. ed. (Late Medieval & Early Renaissance Music in Facsimile Ser.). (Illus.). 376p. 1995. lib. bdg. 175.00 (*0-226-23706-0*) U Ch Pr.

Bent, Margaret & Wathey, Andrew, eds. Fauvel Studies: Allegory, Chronicle, Music, & Image in Paris, Bibliotheque Nationale MS Francais 146. LC 97-12910. (Illus.). 686p. 1998. text 170.00 (*0-19-816579-X*) OUP.

Bent, Margaret, ed. see Rossini, Gioachino.

Bent, Margaret, tr. see Kirkendale, Warren.

Bent, Martin, ed. Livestock Productivity Enhancers: An Economic Assessment. (Illus.). 176p. 1993. text 65.00 (*0-85198-800-8*) OUP.

Bent, Mary J., et al, eds. Allegheny General: Portrait of an Urban Medical Center. 1991. 40.00 (*0-9628790-0-2*) Allegheny Health.

Bent, Nancy. Beyond M S: It's All in the Image. 281p. 1995. 25.00 (*0-913412-76-7*) Brandon Hse.

Bent, Robert D., ed. Pion Production & Absorption in Nuclei, 1981: Indiana University Cyclatron Facility. LC 82-70678. (AIP Conference Proceedings Ser.: No. 79). 432p. 1982. lib. bdg. 36.00 (*0-88318-178-9*) Am Inst Physics.

Bent, Robert F. Forgiving Your Parents. 1990. mass mkt. 8.95 (*0-446-39142-5*, Pub. by Warner Bks) Little.

***Bent, Ruth.** Llama Hiking with Katie. 28p. (J). (gr. 1-3). 2000. pap. 8.00 (*0-615-11191-2*) Sijama.

Bent, Sandy L., ed. see Bent, Wayne C.

Bent, Silas. Justice Oliver Wendell Holmes: A Biography. 402p. 1996. 98.00 (*1-56169-197-6*) Gaunt.

— Justice Oliver Wendell Holmes: A Biography. LC 75-98636. (BCL Ser. I). (Illus.). 1969. reprint ed. 47.50 (*0-404-00751-1*) AMS Pr.

— Newspaper Crusaders. LC 77-90609. (Essay Index Reprint Ser.). 1977. 21.95 (*0-8369-1245-4*) Ayer.

Bent, Simon. Sugar, Sugar. 104p. 1999. pap. 10.95 (*1-84002-033-4*) Theatre Comm.

— Three Plays. (Oberon Bks.). 312p. 1997. pap. 18.95 (*1-870259-64-5*) Theatre Comm.

Bent, Susan, ed. Back in Town: An Anthology of Chico Poets. LC 80-23860. (Illus.). 158p. 1980. pap. text 7.95 (*0-918606-02-0*) Heidelberg Graph.

Bent, Timothy, tr. Henry Miller: The Paris Years. LC 94-39261. 240p. 1996. pap. 13.45 (*1-55970-347-4*, Pub. by Arcade Pub Inc) Time Warner.

Bent, Timothy, ed. see Reverdy, Pierre.

Bent, Timothy, tr. see Brassai.

Bent, TImothy, tr. see Mitterrand, Francois & Wiesel, Elie.

Bent, Wayne C. His Only Gift: A Testimony. Bent, Sandy L., ed. LC 87-82269. 192p. 1988. pap. 4.95 (*0-9619431-0-6*) LifeSupports.

Bentahila, Abdelali. Language Attitudes among Arabic-French Bilinguals in Morocco. 182p. 1983. 53.00 (*0-905028-15-5*, Pub. by Multilingual Matters) Taylor & Francis.

***Bentall, Mark, et al.** ATM & Internet Protocol: A Convergence of Technologies. LC 98-175529. 192p. 1998. pap. 49.95 (*0-471-31427-7*) Wiley.

***Bentall, Peter, et al.** Employment-Intensive Infrastructure Programmes: Capacity Building for Contracting in the Construction Sector. 238p. 1999. pap. 23.95 (*92-2-111581-X*, Pub. by ILO) ILO Pubns Ctr.

Bentall, Richard, jt. auth. see Slade, Peter D.

Bente, F. Historical Introduction to the Book of Concord. 266p. 1965. pap. 18.00 (*0-570-03262-8*, 15-1926) Concordia.

Bente, Thomas O. Spanish Conversation & Composition. 274p. (C). 1976. 50.94 (*0-07-004808-8*) McGraw.

Benteen, John. The Bronco Trail: Sundance. large type ed. (Linford Western Library). 1991. pap. 16.99 (*0-7089-7121-0*) Ulverscroft.

— Fargo. large type ed. (Linford Western Library). 304p. 1992. pap. 16.99 (*0-7089-7297-7*) Ulverscroft.

— Fargo: Dakota Badlands. large type ed. (Linford Western Library). 272p. 1992. pap. 16.99 (*0-7089-7169-5*) Ulverscroft.

— Fargo: The Sharpshooters. large type ed. (Linford Western Library). 224p. 1985. pap. 16.99 (*0-7089-6081-2*) Ulverscroft.

— Fargo: Valley of the Skulls. large type ed. (Linford Western Library). 240p. 1991. pap. 16.99 (*0-7089-7033-8*) Ulverscroft.

— Sundance: Dead Man's Canyon - Bring Me His Scalp. large type ed. 1984. 15.95 (*0-7089-1153-6*) Ulverscroft.

— Sundance: Death in the Lava. large type ed. (Linford Western Library). 240p. 1985. pap. 16.99 (*0-7089-6082-0*) Ulverscroft.

— Sundance: Overkill. large type ed. (Linford Western Library). 240p. 1985. pap. 16.99 (*0-7089-6074-X*) Ulverscroft.

— Sundance: Silent Enemy. large type ed. (Linford Western Library). 256p. 1985. pap. 16.99 (*0-7089-6078-2*) Ulverscroft.

— Sundance: The Pistoleros. large type ed. (Linford Western Library). 272p. 1993. pap. 16.99 (*0-7089-7309-4*, Linford) Ulverscroft.

— Sundance: The Wild Stallions. large type ed. (Linford Western Library). 272p. 1992. pap. 16.99 (*0-7089-7181-4*) Ulverscroft.

— The Trail Ends at Hell. large type ed. 1991. pap. 16.99 (*0-7089-6957-7*) Ulverscroft.

— Wolf's Head. large type ed. (Linford Western Library). 272p. 1994. pap. 16.99 (*0-7089-7573-9*) Ulverscroft.

Benteftifa, M. Hafed, jt. auth. see Kurz, Ludwik.

Bentel, Gunilla C. Radiation Therapy Planning. 2nd ed. LC 95-16244. 592p. 1995. text 68.00 (*0-07-005115-1*) McGraw-Hill HPD.

Bentel, Gunilla C., et al. Treatment Planning & Dose Calculation & Treatment Planning in Radiation Oncology. (Illus.). 265p. 1982. text 54.00 (*0-08-027176-6*, H230, Pergamon Pr); pap. text 24.00 (*0-08-027175-8*, Pergamon Pr) Elsevier.

— Treatment Planning & Dose Calculation in Radiation Oncology. 4th ed. 352p. 1991. text 42.00 (*0-07-105246-1*) McGraw-Hill HPD.

Bentel, Gunilla Carleson. Patient Positioning & Immobilization in Radiation Therapy. LC 98-26930. 211p. 1998. pap. 45.00 (*0-07-134158-7*) McGraw.

Bentele, Max. Engine Revolutions: The Autobiography of Max Bentele. 296p. 1991. 19.00 (*1-56091-081-X*, R-109) Soc Auto Engineers.

Bentele, Ursula & Cary, Eve. Appellate Advocacy: Principles & Practice. 3rd ed. 410p. (C). 1998. pap. 34.95 (*0-87084-220-X*) Anderson Pub Co.

Benthall, A. P. The Trees of Calcutta & Its Neighbourhood. 515p. (C). 1988. 90.00 (*0-7855-3233-1*, Pub. by Scientific) St Mut.

Benthall, Jonathan. Disasters, Relief & the Media. 300p. 1994. text 19.95 (*1-85043-737-8*, Pub. by I B T) St Martin.

Benthall, Joseph L. Archeological Investigation of the Shannon Site, Montgomery County, Virginia. (Publication Ser.: No. 32). xi, 152p. 1969. pap. 7.55 (*0-88490-063-0*) Library of VA.

Bentham, Antigone V. Greece: The All-in-One Travel & Language Guide. LC 98-4811. (Get Around in . . . Ser.). (GRE., Illus.). 128p. 1998. pap. 8.95 (*0-8442-0155-3*, 01553, Passprt Bks); pap. 19.95 incl. audio (*0-8442-0188-X*, 0188X, Passprt Bks) NTC Contemp Pub Co.

Bentham, Frederick. Art of Stage Lighting. 3rd ed. (Illus.). 1976. 24.95 (*0-87830-009-0*, Thtre Arts Bks) Routledge.

Bentham, G. The Botany of the Voyage of H. M. S. Sulphur, under the Command of Captain Sir Edward Belcher 1832-42. (Illus.). 1968. 160.00 (*3-7682-0542-8*) Lubrecht & Cramer.

Bentham, G. Genera Plantarum, Vols. 1-3. 4277p. (C). 1979. reprint ed. pap. 3000.00 (*81-7089-010-1*, Pub. by Intl Bk Distr) St Mut.

— General Plantarum, Vol. 1. xv, 1040p. (C). 1990. reprint ed. write for info. (*0-7855-2573-4*, Pub. by Intl Bk Distr) St Mut.

— General Plantarum, Vol. 2. ix, 1258p. (C). 1990. reprint ed. write for info. (*0-318-63730-8*, Pub. by Intl Bk Distr) St Mut.

— General Plantarum, Vol. 3. viii, 1279p. (C). 1990. reprint ed. write for info. (*0-7855-2575-0*, Pub. by Intl Bk Distr) St Mut.

Bentham, G. Plantae Hartwegianae: Plantas Hartwegianas Imprimis Mexicanas Adjectis Nonullis Grahamianis Enumerat Novasque Describit. 1971. reprint ed. 96.00 (*3-7682-0673-4*) Lubrecht & Cramer.

Bentham, G. & Hooker, J. D. Supplemental Papers to Bentham & Hooker's Genera Plantarum. 1971. reprint ed. 175.00 (*3-7682-0706-4*) Lubrecht & Cramer.

Bentham, G. & Mueller, F. von. Flora Austaliensis: Description of the Plants of the Australian Territory. 4289p. 1966. reprint ed. lib. bdg. 250.00 (*90-6123-010-1*) Lubrecht & Cramer.

Bentham, Jeremy. Bentham's Theory of Fictions. LC 75-41026. reprint ed. 24.50 (*0-404-14508-6*) AMS Pr.

— Chrestomathia. Smith, M. J. & Burston, W. H., eds. (Collected Works of Jeremy Bentham). (Illus.). 452p. 1984. text 95.00 (*0-19-822610-1*) OUP.

***Bentham, Jeremy.** The Collected Works of Jeremy Bentham Correspondence, Volume 11: January 1822 To June 18. Fuller, Catherine & Rosen, F., eds. (Illus.). 510p. 2000. text 110.00 (*0-19-820866-9*) OUP.

Bentham, Jeremy. Colonies, Commerce, & Constitutional Law: Rid Yourselves of Ultramaria & Other Writings on Spain & Spanish America. Schofield, Philip & Rosen, F., eds. 534p. 1996. text 110.00 (*0-19-822612-8*) OUP.

— The Correspondence of Jeremy Bentham. Incl. Vol. 4. October 1788-1797. 506p. (C). 1981. text 120.00 (*0-485-13204-4*, Pub. by Athlone Pr); Vol. 5. October 1788-1797. 403p. (C). 1981. text 120.00 (*0-485-13205-2*, Pub. by Athlone Pr); write for info. (*0-318-58059-4*, Pub. by Athlone Pr) Humanities.

Bentham, Jeremy. The Correspondence of Jeremy Bentham: January 1817 to June 1820, Vol. 9. Conway, Stephen, ed. (Collected Works of Jeremy Bentham). 542p. 1990. text 115.00 (*0-19-822616-0*) OUP.

Bentham, Jeremy. The Correspondence of Jeremy Bentham Vol. 6: January 1798 to December 1801. Dinwiddy, John R., ed. (Collected Works of Jeremy Bentham). 526p. 1984. text 85.00 (*0-19-822613-6*) OUP.

— The Correspondence of Jeremy Bentham Vol. 7: January 1802 to December 1808. Dinwiddy, John R., ed. (Collected Works of Jeremy Bentham). (Illus.). 634p. 1988. text 119.00 (*0-19-822614-4*) OUP.

— The Correspondence of Jeremy Bentham Vol. 8: January 1809 to December 1816. Conway, Stephen, ed. (Collected Works of Jeremy Bentham). 626p. 1988. text 125.00 (*0-19-822615-2*) OUP.

— Deontology: A Table of the Springs of Action on Utilitarianism. Goldworth, Amnon, ed. Incl. Table of the Springs of Action & the Article on Utilitarianism. 1983. (Collected Works of Jeremy Bentnam). (Illus.). 430p. 1983. Set text 110.00 (*0-19-822609-8*) OUP.

— First Principles Preparatory to Constitutional Code. Schofield, Philip, ed. (Collected Works of Jeremy Bentham). 400p. 1989. text 110.00 (*0-19-822747-7*) OUP.

— A Fragment on Government. Montague, Francis C., ed. LC 80-10507. 241p. 1980. reprint ed. lib. bdg. 38.50 (*0-313-22323-8*, BEFG, Greenwood Pr) Greenwood.

— An Introduction to the Principles of Morals & Legislation. Lafleur, J., ed. (Library of Classics: No. 6). 432p. 1970. pap. 14.95 (*0-02-841200-1*) Hafner.

— Justice & Codification Petitions: Being Forms Proposed for Signature by All Persons Whose Desire It Is to See Justice No Longer Sold, Delayed or Denied & to Obtain a Possibility of That Knowledge of the Law, in Proportion to the Want of Which They Are Subjected to Unjust Punishments & Deprived of the Benefit of Their Rights. 382p. 1992. reprint ed. 47.50 (*0-8377-1920-8*, Rothman) W S Hein.

— Legislator of the World: Writings in Codification, Law & Education. Schofield, Philip & Harris, Jonathan, eds. LC 99-198145. (The Collection Works of Jeremy Bentham). 508p. 1999. text 110.00 (*0-19-820747-6*) OUP.

— Limits of Jurisprudence Defined: Being Part Two of an Introduction to the Principles of Morals & Legislation. LC 71-100143. (Illus.). 358p. 1970. reprint ed. lib. bdg. 35.00 (*0-8371-3249-5*, BEJU, Greenwood Pr) Greenwood.

— Official Aptitude Maximized, Expense Minimized. Schofield, Philip, ed. 556p. 1993. text 85.00 (*0-19-820403-5*) OUP.

— Plan of Parliamentary Reform, in the Form of a Catechism, with Reasons for Each Article. LC 75-41027. (BCL Ser. II). reprint ed. 39.50 (*0-404-14777-1*) AMS Pr.

— Political Tactics. Pease-Watkin, Catherine, ed. 308p. 1999. text 90.00 (*0-19-820772-7*) OUP.

— Principles of Morals & Legislation. LC 88-60151. (Great Books in Philosophy). 354p. (C). 1988. pap. 8.95 (*0-87975-434-6*) Prometheus Bks.

— Rationale of Judicial Evidence, Specially Applied to English Practice from the Manuscripts of Jeremy Bentham: Specially Applied to English Practice, 5 vols. 1995. reprint ed. 350.00 (*0-8377-1979-8*, Rothman) W S Hein.

— Securities Against Misrule & Other Constitutional Writings for Tripoli & Greece. Schofield, Philip, ed. (Collected Works of Jeremy Bentham). 378p. 1991. text 110.00 (*0-19-822725-6*) OUP.

***Bentham, Jeremy.** TCP/IP Lean: Creating Web Servers for Embedded Systems. 400p. 2000. pap. 44.95 incl. cd-rom (*1-929629-11-7*, Pub. by C M P Books) Publishers Group.

***Bentham, Jeremy.** The Theory of Legislation, 2 vol. 548p. 1999. reprint ed. 165.00 (*1-56169-467-3*) Gaunt.

Bentham, Jeremy. The Theory of Legislation. (Illus.). iii, 555p. 1987. reprint ed. 75.00 (*0-8377-1947-X*, Rothman) W S Hein.

Bentham, Jeremy & Hart, H. L. A. An Introduction to the Principles of Morals & Legislation. 2nd ed. Burns, J. H. & Hart, H. L., eds. LC 96-136001. (Illus.). 456p. (C). 1996. pap. text 35.00 (*0-19-820516-3*) OUP.

Bentham, Johan Van, see Van Bentham, Johan.

Bentham, Peggy. VDU Terminal Sickness: Computer Health Risks & How to Protect Yourself. 2nd ed. (Orig.). 1996. pap. text 18.95 (*1-897766-21-1*, Pub. by Jon Carpenter) Paul & Co Pubs.

Benthe, Arnold. As I Remember. Sobieszek, Robert A. & Bunnell, Peter C., eds. LC 76-24684. (Sources of Modern Photography Ser.). (Illus.). 1979. reprint ed. lib. bdg. 35.95 (*0-405-09660-7*) Ayer.

Bentheim, Tienke Van, see Van Bentheim, Tieneke.

An Asterisk (*) at the beginning of an entry indicates that the title is appearing for the first time.

Benthem, J. V. The Logic of Time. 1982. text 135.00 (*90-277-1421-5*) Kluwer Academic.

Benthem, J. Van, see Van Benthem, J.

Benthem, Johan F. Van, see Van Benthem, Johan F., ed.

Benthem, Johan Van, see Van Benthem, Johan.

Benthem, John Van, see Van Benthem, John.

Benthic, Arch E. The Id of the Squid. LC 79-129864. 120p. 4.95 (*0-685-01167-4*) Compass VA.

Benthien, Brenda, tr. see Arnheim, Rudolf.

Benthuysen, A. S. Van, see Van Benthuysen, A. S.

Benti, Wynne. Favorite Dog Hikes in & Around Los Angeles. 112p. 1995. mass mkt. 10.95 (*0-9647530-0-6*) Spotted Dog CA.

Benti, Wynne, jt. auth. see Wheelock, Walt.

Benti, Wynne, ed. see Adams, Ansel.

Benti, Wynne, ed. see Butchart, Harvey.

Benti, Wynne, ed. see Clyde, Norman.

Bentil, Kweku K. Construction Project Administration. (C). 2001. 60.00 (*0-13-377920-3*, Macmillan Coll) P-H.

— Fundamentals of the Construction Process. 450p. 1989. 69.95 (*0-87629-138-8*, 67260) R S Means.

Bentinck-Smith, William. Building a Great Library: The Coolidge Years at Harvard. (Illus.). 301p. 1976. 20.00 (*0-674-08578-7*) HUP.

Bentinck-Smith, William, ed. The Harvard Book. enl. rev. ed. LC 81-20078. 546p. 1982. 44.00 (*0-674-37301-4*) HUP.

B

Bentivegna, Joseph F. The Neglected & Abused: A Physician's Year in Haiti. (Illus.). 180p. (Orig.). (C). 1990. pap. 12.95 (*0-9626001-0-5*) Michelle Pub.

— When to Refuse Treatment: A Practical Guide for Dying in Peace. (Illus.). 190p. (Orig.). (C). 1992. 13.95 (*0-9626001-1-3*) Michelle Pub.

Bentivegna, Vincenzo, et al, eds. Evaluation of the Built Environment for Sustainability. LC 97-65934. (Illus.). 592p. (C). (gr. 13). 1998. 100.00 (*0-419-21990-0*, D5585, E & FN Spon) Routledge.

Bentivengo, Edmund, ed. see Gilligan, David.

Bentivoglio & Zoccoli, Franca. Women Artists of Italian Futurism: Almost Lost to History. LC 94-73077. (Illus.). 1998. text 35.00 (*1-877675-26-1*); pap. text 25.00 (*1-877675-18-0*) Midmarch Arts.

Bentkover, Judith D., et al. Benefits Assessment. 1985. text 126.50 (*90-277-2022-3*) Kluwer Academic.

***Bentkus, V., et al.** Limit Theorems of Probability Theory. Prokhorov, Yu V., ed. Seckler, B. D., tr. from RUS. 320p. 1999. 104.00 (*3-540-57045-4*) Spr-Verlag.

Bentle, Jane, ed. see Reynolds, Annie & Gordon, Albert.

Bentle, Jane, ed. see Reynolds, Annie & Phillips, Thomas Bruce.

Bentler, Peter M., jt. auth. see Newcomb, Michael D.

Bentley. Christianity. 1988. pap. text. write for info. (*0-582-22342-3*) Addison-Wesley.

— Civiliation: Global History, Vol. 1. 1995. student ed. 19.95 (*0-07-004931-9*) McGraw.

— Civilization: Global History. 1995. teacher ed. 19.95 (*0-07-004933-5*) McGraw.

— Civilization: Global History, Vol. 2. 1995. student ed. 19.95 (*0-07-004932-7*) McGraw.

Bentley. Explorers, Guides & Trappers. (J). 1995. 16.98 (*0-8050-4011-0*) H Holt & Co.

— Improving the Rider's Position. (Threshold Picture Guide Ser.: No. 32). (Illus.). 1994. pap. 12.00 (*1-872082-65-3*) Half Halt Pr.

— Life & Teaching of Jesus. Date not set. pap. text. write for info. (*0-582-34312-7*, Pub. by Addison-Wesley) Longman.

— Luke. 1991. pap. text. write for info. (*0-582-03579-1*, Pub. by Addison-Wesley) Longman.

— Marrow of Tradition. 2001. pap. write for info. (*0-312-19406-4*) St Martin.

— Passing on the Truth. 1997. pap. 15.99 (*0-85234-389-2*, Pub. by Evangelical Pr) P & R Pubng.

Bentley. Primary Design Technology in Practice. Date not set. pap. text. write for info. (*0-582-05700-0*, Pub. by Addison-Wesley) Longman.

Bentley. Psychology. 4th ed. 320p. (C). 1992. pap. text, student ed., wbk. ed. 18.80 (*0-13-735176-3*) P-H.

— Science Teaching Methods for Elementary School. LC 99-41930. 1999. pap. 73.95 (*0-534-12912-9*) Brooks-Cole.

— Step by Step Massage for Head. 144p. 1999. text 16.95 (*0-312-24720-6*) St Martin.

***Bentley.** Traditions & Encounters, Vol. VII. 271p. 1999. pap., student ed. 18.11 (*0-07-005361-8*) McGraw.

Bentley, jt. auth. see Pearce.

Bentley, Amy. Eating for Victory: Food Rationing & the Politics of Domesticity. LC 97-45471. 312p. 1998. text 44.95 (*0-252-02419-2*); text 19.95 (*0-252-06727-4*) U of Ill Pr.

Bentley, Anne. Data Administration: A Data Naming Primer Guideline & a Data Naming Practictioner's Guide. (Illus.). 45p. (Orig.). 1995. pap. text 20.00 (*0-7881-2327-0*) DIANE Pub.

Bentley, Arthur F. Inquiry into Inquiries: Essays in Social Theory. Ratner, Sidney, ed. LC 75-31655. 365p. 1975. reprint ed. lib. bdg. 69.50 (*0-8371-8463-0*, BEII, Greenwood Pr) Greenwood.

— The Process of Government: A Study of Social Pressures. rev. ed. 520p. (C). 1994. pap. 24.95 (*1-56000-778-8*) Transaction Pubs.

Bentley, Arthur F., jt. auth. see Dewey, John.

Bentley, Barbara & Elias, Thomas S., eds. Biology of Nectaries. LC 82-4200. (Illus.). 336p. 1983. text 69.00 (*0-231-04446-1*) Col U Pr.

Bentley, Beth. Little Fires. LC 98-109798. (Local International Ser.). 128p. 1998. pap. 15.95 (*1-885942-04-4*) Cune.

Bentley, Beth, ed. see Hall, Hazel.

Bentley, Bill. Math Games & Activities for the Primary Grades. 64p. (J). (gr. k-2). 8.99 (*0-86653-883-6*, FE0883) Fearon Teacher Aids.

Bentley, Brian S. Hit Me Once, Hit Me Twice: A Story about Domestic Violence. LC 98-207137. 240p. 1998. pap. 12.95 (*1-890632-01-5*) Cool Jack Pub.

— One Time: The Story of a South Central Los Angeles Police Officer. 235p. (Orig.). 1997. pap. 14.95 (*1-890632-00-7*) Cool Jack Pub.

Bentley, C. R., et al, eds. Contributions to Antarctic Research, Vol. I. (Antarctic Research Ser.: Vol. 50). 101p. 1990. 30.00 (*0-87590-760-1*, AR0507601) Am Geophysical.

Bentley, Carlota, ed. see Cornelius, Edwin T.

***Bentley, Chantelle, ed.** Poet's Market: 1,800 Places to Publish Your Poetry. 608p. 2000. pap. 23.99 (*0-89879-981-3*) F & W Pubns Inc.

— 2000 Poet's Market: 1,800 Places to Publish Your Poetry. 608p. 1999. pap. 23.99 (*0-89879-915-5*, 10613, Wrtrs Digest Bks) F & W Pubns Inc.

Bentley, Cheryl. Guide to the Palace Hotels of India. 1992. pap. text 13.95 (*1-55650-538-8*) Hunter NJ.

Bentley, Chris. Brushing the Teeth of Elvis' Monkey: And Other True Stories from the Ozarks. 192p. (Orig.). 1996. pap. 9.95 (*0-9650541-0-1*) Offspring Bks.

Bentley, Colin. Computer Project Management. LC QA0076.9.M3B. (Computing Sciences Ser.). 120p. reprint ed. pap. 37.20 (*0-7837-4015-8*, 204384500011) Bks Demand.

— Prince No. 2: A Practical Guide. LC 97-168234. 350p. 1997. pap. text 44.95 (*0-7506-3240-2*) Buttrwrth-Heinemann.

Bentley, Colin & Rudman, Bernadette. SSADM: Using SSADM in a Prince Environment. LC 95-205104. (Computer Weekly Professional Ser.). (Illus.). 240p. reprint ed. pap. 74.40 (*0-608-09700-4*, 206986600007) Bks Demand.

***Bentley-Cranch, Dana.** Edward VII: Image of an Era, 1841-1910. 160p. 1999. reprint ed. pap. text 17.00 (*0-7881-6795-2*) DIANE Pub.

Bentley, Cynthia & Fleming, Charles, Jr. Never Boil Your Alarm Clock. 289p. 1990. write for info. (*0-9632511-0-4*) Chase Pubs.

Bentley, D. J. English Criminal Justice in the Nineteenth Century. LC 98-3533. 1998. 60.00 (*1-85285-135-X*) Hambledon Press.

Bentley, D. J., ed. see Keir, David L. & Lawson, Frederick H.

Bentley, D. M. Mimic Fires: Accounts of Early Long Poems on Canada. 368p. (C). 1994. 60.00 (*0-7735-1200-4*, Pub. by McG-Queens Univ Pr) CUP Services.

Bentley, Darlee M. Medical Prescriptions--Abuse, Choices, Control, Evaluation, Habits, Generics & Computerization: Index of New Information with Authors, Subjects, & Bibliography. LC 96-12514. 1996. 47.50 (*0-7883-0820-3*); pap. 44.50 (*0-7883-0821-1*) ABBE Pubs Assn.

***Bentley, David Simmons.** The 99 Beautiful Names of God: For All the People of the Book. LC 99-42624. 112p. 1999. pap. 11.99 (*0-87808-299-9*) William Carey Lib.

***Bentley, Dawn.** The Big Race Playset: A Pop-Up Race Track with 2 Wind-Up Race Cars. (Illus.). (J). 1999. 24.95 (*1-58117-038-6*) Intervisual Bks.

Bentley, Dawn. Calico Kitty: Cuddly Cloth Board Book. (Illus.). 8p. (J). 1999. bds. 9.95 (*1-58117-043-2*, Piggy Toes Pr) Intervisual Bks.

— Cat Nap: An Interactive Lift-the Flap, Pop-Up, Counting Book. (Illus.). 10p. (J). 1999. 9.95 (*1-58117-033-5*, Pub. by Intervisual Bks) Andrews & McMeel.

— The Fairytale Village: Pop-Up Playset. 1996. 35.90 (*0-446-16340-6*, Pub. by Warner Bks) Little.

— Fuzzy Bear: A Getting Dressed Book. (Illus.). 10p. (J). (gr. 2 up). 1998. 10.95 (*1-58117-011-4*, Piggy Toes Pr) Intervisual Bks.

***Bentley, Dawn.** Icky Sticky Anteater. (Illus.). 18p. (J). 2000. 9.95 (*1-58117-079-3*, Piggy Toes Pr) Intervisual Bks.

Bentley, Dawn. I'm a Pink Piggy: A Baby Buddy Book. LC 99-161326. (Baby Buddy Bks.: No. 4). (Illus.). 8p. (J). (ps up). 1998. bds. 4.95 (*1-888443-70-7*, Piggy Toes Pr) Intervisual Bks.

***Bentley, Dawn.** Jay Jay the Jet Plane's Shapes. (Peek-A-Boo Board Bks.). (Illus.). 12p. (J). 2000. bds. 6.95 (*1-58117-101-3*, Piggy Toes Pr) Intervisual Bks.

Bentley, Dawn. Little Lost Duck: A Baby Buddy Book. LC 98-233142. (Baby Buddy Bks.). (Illus.). 12p. (J). (ps up). 1998. bds. 4.95 (*1-888443-72-3*, Piggy Toes Pr) Intervisual Bks.

***Bentley, Dawn.** Mommy, Is That You? A Move & Play Book. (Move & Play Bks.). (Illus.). 10p. (J). 2000. 6.95 (*1-58117-073-4*, Piggy Toes Pr) Intervisual Bks.

Bentley, Dawn. My First Flashlight: A Book & Flashlight. LC 97-180869. (Illus.). 14p. (J). (ps). 1997. 12.95 (*0-590-10099-8*, Cartwheel) Scholastic Inc.

— My Make Believe Briefcase. (What's Inside? Bks.). (Illus.). (J). (ps-2). 1997. 9.99 (*0-614-28725-1*) NAL.

— My Make Believe Purse. (What's Inside? Bks.). (Illus.). (J). (ps-2). 1997. 9.99 (*0-614-28724-3*) NAL.

— Patchwork Puppies: Cuddly Cloth Board Book. (Illus.). 8p. (J). 1999. 9.95 (*1-58117-044-0*, Piggy Toes Pr) Intervisual Bks.

— Santa's Surprise: A Pop-Up Story Box. (Illus.). 12p. (J). (gr. 2 up). 1998. 12.95 (*1-58117-018-1*, Pub. by Intervisual Bks) Andrews & McMeel.

— Take a Bow, Cow: Hand Puppet & Story Book. (Read-Along Pals Ser.). (Illus.). 10p. (J). (gr. 2 up). 1998. bds. 9.95 (*1-888443-63-4*, Piggy Toes Pr) Intervisual Bks.

— Time to Eat! A Shake-n-Move Book about Colors. LC 99-474911. (Shake-N-Move Ser.). (Illus.). 12p. (J). (ps-k). 1999. 5.99 (*0-689-81408-9*) Litle Simon.

— Time to Play! A Shake-n-Move Book about Opposites. LC 99-162737. (Shake-N-Move Ser.). (Illus.). 12p. (J). (ps-k). 1999. 5.99 (*0-689-81407-0*) Litle Simon.

— Who Say's Moo? A Baby Buddy Book, 4 vols. LC 98-233141. (Baby Buddy Bks.). (Illus.). 12p. (J). 1998. 4.95 (*1-888443-73-1*, Piggy Toes Pr) Intervisual Bks.

***Bentley, Dawn, ed.** Where's Daddy? A Move & Play Book. (Move & Play Bks.). (Illus.). 10p. (J). 2000. 6.95 (*1-58117-074-2*, Piggy Toes Pr) Intervisual Bks.

Bentley, Dawn, jt. auth. see Dodds, Siobhan.

Bentley, Dawn, jt. auth. see Hatfield, Jerry.

Bentley, Dawn, jt. auth. see Welply, Michael.

Bentley, Debbie. Baptism & Communion. (Basic Christian Doctrine Ser.: No. 3). 5p. (Orig.). (YA). 1995. pap. 1.00 (*1-885090-02-1*) Cosecha Latina.

— Baptism of the Holy Spirit. (Basic Christian Doctrine Ser.: No. 4). 8p. (Orig.). (YA). 1995. pap. 1.00 (*1-885090-03-X*) Cosecha Latina.

— Discipleship: Learning to Walk with Jesus. (Basic Christian Doctrine Ser.: No. 2). 11p. (Orig.). (YA). 1995. pap. 1.00 (*1-885090-01-3*) Cosecha Latina.

— Divine Healing. (Basic Christian Doctrine Ser.: No. 8). 14p. (Orig.). (YA). 1995. pap. 1.00 (*1-885090-07-2*) Cosecha Latina.

— Eternal Life & Christ's Second Coming. (Basic Christian Doctrine Ser.: No. 10). 7p. (Orig.). (YA). 1995. pap. 1.00 (*1-885090-09-9*) Cosecha Latina.

— Faith. (Basic Christian Doctrine Ser.: No. 7). 10p. (Orig.). (YA). 1995. pap. 1.00 (*1-885090-06-4*) Cosecha Latina.

— The Fruit of the Spirit. (Basic Christian Doctrine Ser.: No. 5). 7p. (Orig.). (YA). 1995. pap. 1.00 (*1-885090-04-8*) Cosecha Latina.

— The Gifts of the Spirit. (Basic Christian Doctrine Ser.: No. 6). 10p. (YA). 1995. pap. 1.00 (*1-885090-05-6*) Cosecha Latina.

— Prayer & Intercession. (Basic Christian Doctrine Ser.: No. 9). 16p. (Orig.). (YA). 1995. pap. 1.00 (*1-885090-08-0*) Cosecha Latina.

— Salvation. (Basic Christian Doctrine Ser.: No. 1). 6p. (Orig.). (YA). 1995. pap. 1.00 (*1-885090-00-5*) Cosecha Latina.

Bentley, Delia, jt. ed. see Smith, John Charles.

Bentley, Di & Watts, Mike. Communicating in School Science. 224p. 1992. 95.00 (*1-85000-642-3*, Falmer Pr); pap. 32.95 (*1-85000-643-1*, Falmer Pr) Taylor & Francis.

— Learning & Teaching in School Sciences: Practical Alternatives. 192p. 1989. 110.00 (*0-335-09514-3*); pap. 33.95 (*0-335-09513-5*) OpUniv Pr.

— Primary Science & Technology: Practical Alternatives. LC 93-10657. 224p. 1994. 103.95 (*0-335-19029-4*); pap. 31.95 (*0-335-19028-6*) OpUniv Pr.

Bentley, Diana, et al. The Really Practical Guides: Primary English. (Illus.). 256p. 1999. pap. 30.00 (*0-7487-2937-2*, Pub. by S Thornes Pubs) Trans-Atl Phila.

***Bentley, Donald, et al.** Pediatric Gastroenterology & Clinical Nutrition. (Illus.). 304p. 2000. text 165.00 (*0-19-262808-9*) OUP.

Bentley, E. C. Trent's Last Case. Date not set. lib. bdg. 21.95 (*0-8488-2177-7*) Amereon Ltd.

— Trent's Last Case. 1976. lib. bdg. 29.95 (*0-89968-165-4*, Lghtyr Pr) Buccaneer Bks.

— Trent's Last Case. 256p. 1991. mass mkt. 4.95 (*0-88184-770-4*) Carroll & Graf.

— Trent's Last Case. LC 96-53232. (Mystery Classics Ser.). (Illus.). 192p. 1997. reprint ed. pap. text 2.00 (*0-486-29687-3*) Dover.

— Woman in Black. 1976. lib. bdg. 13.95 (*0-89968-166-2*, Lghtyr Pr) Buccaneer Bks.

Bentley, E. C. & Allen, H. Warner. Trent's Own Case. 324p. 1988. reprint ed. mass mkt. 3.95 (*0-88184-349-0*) Carroll & Graf.

Bentley, Earl, jt. auth. see Nichols, Christopher P.

Bentley, Elizabeth P. The Genealogist's Address Book. 3rd ed. 653p. 1995. pap. 34.95 (*0-8063-1455-9*) Genealog Pub.

— The Genealogist's Address Book. 4th ed. 842p. 1999. reprint ed. pap. 39.95 (*0-8063-1580-6*) Genealog Pub.

***Bentley, Elizabeth P.** Index to the 1850 Census of Pennsylvania: Berks County, Bucks County, Lancaster County, Luzerne & Wyoming Counties, Northampton County, 5 vols. in 1. 542p. 1998. reprint ed. pap. 38.50 (*0-8063-4759-7*, 9306) Clearfield Co.

Bentley, Elizabeth P. Index to the 1800 Census of Massachusetts. LC 78-58855. 305p. 1999. pap. 26.50 (*0-8063-0817-6*, Pub. by Clearfield Co) ACCESS Pubs Network.

— Index to the 1800 Census of North Carolina. 270p. 1997. reprint ed. pap. 26.50 (*0-8063-0751-X*, 435) Clearfield Co.

— Index to the 1810 Census of North Carolina. 282p. 2000. reprint ed. pap. 27.50 (*0-8063-0788-9*, 440, Pub. by Clearfield Co) ACCESS Pubs Network.

— Index to the 1820 Census of Tennessee. 287p. 1999. reprint ed. pap. 26.50 (*0-8063-0946-6*, 468, Pub. by Clearfield Co) ACCESS Pubs Network.

— Passenger Arrivals at the Port of New York, 1820-1829. LC 98-75654. 1491p. 1999. 95.00 (*0-8063-1610-1*) Genealog Pub.

Bentley, Elizabeth Petty. County Courthouse Book. 2nd ed. LC 95-79104. 405p. 1996. pap. 34.95 (*0-8063-1485-0*) Genealog Pub.

— Directory of Family Associations. 3rd ed. 355p. 1996. pap. 34.95 (*0-8063-1523-7*) Genealog Pub.

***Bentley, Elizabeth Petty.** Passenger Arrivals at the Port of New York, 1820-1829. 2000. 85.00 (*0-8063-1625-X*) Genealog Pub.

Bentley, Eljee, et al, contrib. by. We Baptists. LC 99-70372. 96p. 1999. pap. 11.95 (*1-57736-143-1*) Providence Hse.

Bentley, Emily, et al. Law & Mental Health Professionals: Alabama. LC 98-41032. 309p. 1999. 59.95 (*1-55798-512-X*) Am Psychol.

Bentley, Eric. Bentley on Brecht. (Illus.). 416p. 1999. pap. 18.95 (*1-55783-331-1*) Applause Theatre Bk Pubs.

— The Cult of the Superman. Orig. Title: A Century of Hero Worship. 1990. 16.50 (*0-8446-0486-0*) Peter Smith.

— In Search of Theatre. (Illus.). 424p. 1992. reprint ed. pap. 18.95 (*1-55783-111-4*) Applause Theatre Bk Pubs.

— The Kleist Variations: Based on Plays by Heinrich von Kleist. rev. ed. LC 89-39410. 224p. 1990. pap. 18.95 (*0-8093-1629-3*) S Ill U Pr.

— The Life of the Drama. 384p. 1991. reprint ed. pap. 12.95 (*1-55783-110-6*) Applause Theatre Bk Pubs.

— Modern Theatre, 6 Vols, 2. 1990. 23.00 (*0-8446-1655-9*) Peter Smith.

— Modern Theatre, 6 Vols, 3. 1990. 23.00 (*0-8446-1656-7*) Peter Smith.

— Modern Theatre, 6 Vols, 4. 1990. 23.00 (*0-8446-1657-5*) Peter Smith.

— Modern Theatre, 6 Vols, 5. 1990. 23.00 (*0-8446-1658-3*) Peter Smith.

— Modern Theatre, 6 Vols, 6. 1990. 23.00 (*0-8446-1659-1*) Peter Smith.

— Modern Theatre, 6 Vols, Vol. 1. 1990. 23.00 (*0-8446-1654-0*) Peter Smith.

— Modern Theatre, Vols. 1-6. 1990. 138.00 (*0-8446-1653-2*) Peter Smith.

— Rallying Cries: Three Plays. 235p. 1987. reprint ed. pap. 12.95 (*0-8101-0743-0*) Northwestern U Pr.

— Thinking about the Playwright. 364p. 1987. pap. 15.95 (*0-8101-0733-3*) Northwestern U Pr.

***Bentley, Eric.** What Is Theatre? Incorporating "The Dramatic Event" & Other Reviews, 1944-1967. rev. ed. LC 99-87399. 512p. 2000. pap. 16.00 (*0-8090-9695-1*) Hill & Wang.

Bentley, Eric, ed. Life Is a Dream & Other Spanish Classics. Campbell, Roy, tr. from SPA. LC 85-15671. (Eric Bentley's Dramatic Repertoire Ser.). 304p. 1985. pap. 24.95 (*1-55783-005-3*) Applause Theatre Bk Pubs.

— Life Is a Dream & Other Spanish Classics. Campbell, Roy, tr. 1989. pap. 10.95 (*1-55783-006-1*) Applause Theatre Bk Pubs.

— The Misanthrope & Other French Classics. (Eric Bentley's Dramatic Repertoire Ser.). 330p. 1986. pap. 10.95 (*0-936839-19-8*) Applause Theatre Bk Pubs.

— The Servant of Two Masters & Other Italian Classics. (Eric Bentley's Dramatic Repertoire Ser.). (ITA.). 272p. 1986. pap. 10.95 (*0-936839-20-1*) Applause Theatre Bk Pubs.

— The Theory of the Modern Stage. 496p. 1997. pap. text 16.95 (*1-55783-279-X*) Applause Theatre Bk Pubs.

Bentley, Eric, ed. from GER. Before Brecht: Four German Plays. LC 85-15623. (Eric Bentley's Dramatic Repertoire Ser.). (Illus.). 272p. 1985. 24.95 (*1-55783-009-6*); pap. 8.95 (*1-55783-010-X*) Applause Theatre Bk Pubs.

Bentley, Eric & Robinson, Earl, eds. The Brecht-Eisler Song Book. 192p. 1997. pap. 19.95 (*0-8256-0168-1*, OK 62281) Music Sales.

Bentley, Eric, jt. auth. see Brecht, Bertolt.

Bentley, Eric, ed. see Brecht, Bertolt.

Bentley, Eric, ed. see Shaw, George Bernard.

Bentley, Eric, ed. & tr. see Brecht, Bertolt.

Bentley, Eric, tr. see Brecht, Bertolt.

Bentley, Eric, tr. see Chekhov, Anton.

Bentley, Eric, tr. see Pirandello, Luigi.

Bentley, Eric, tr. & adapted by see Brecht, Bertolt.

Bentley, Eric, tr. & intro. see Brecht, Bertolt.

Bentley, Eric, tr. & intro. see Gogol, Nikolai Vasilevich.

Bentley, Eric, tr. & intro. see Wedekind, Frank.

***Bentley, Evie.** Awareness: Biorhythms, Sleep & Dreaming. LC 99-30613. 1999. pap. write for info. (*0-415-18873-3*) Routledge.

— Awareness: Biorhythms, Sleep & Dreaming. LC 99-30613. (Modular Psychology Ser.). 176p. (C). 1999. text. write for info. (*0-415-18872-5*) Routledge.

Bentley, G., ed. Medicinal Plants, Set, Vols. 1-4. 1982. reprint ed. 1000.00 (*81-7089-002-0*, Pub. by Intl Bk Distr) St Mut.

Bentley, G. Carter, jt. ed. see Carey, Peter B.

Bentley, G. E., Jr. Blake Books Supplement: A Bibliography of Publications & Discoveries about William Blake, 1971-1992. LC 93-43095. (Illus.). 768p. (C). 1995. text 150.00 (*0-19-812354-X*, Clarendon Pr) OUP.

— The Blake Collection of Mrs. Landon K. Thorne. LC 71-179936. (Illus.). 68p. 1971. pap. 10.00 (*0-87598-034-1*) Pierpont Morgan.

Bentley, G. E., ed. Editing Eighteenth-Century Novels: Papers on Fielding, Lesage, Richardson, Sterne, & Smollett, Given at the Conference on Editorial Problems, University of Toronto, November, 1973. (Conference on Editorial Problems Ser.: No. 9). 1987. 42.50 (*0-404-63659-4*) AMS Pr.

Bentley, G. E., Jr., ed. see Cumberland, George.

Bentley, Geoffrey & Conly, Maurice, eds. Portrait of an Air Force: The Royal New Zealand Air Force 1937-1987. 212p. (C). 1988. 95.00 (*1-86934-010-8*, Pub. by Grantham Hse) St Mut.

Bentley, George, jt. ed. see Duthie, Robert.

Bentley, George R. The Episcopal Diocese of Florida: 1892-1975. (Illus.). 328p. 1989. 39.95 (*0-8130-0932-4*) U Press Fla.

Bentley, Gerald, Jr. The Jacobean & Caroline Stage. Incl. Vol. 6-7. Theatres, Appendixes to Vol. 6 & General Index: The Jacobean & Caroline Stage. 718p. 1968. text 89.00 (*0-19-811626-8*); write for info. (*0-318-54850-X*) OUP.

An Asterisk (*) at the beginning of an entry indicates that the title is appearing for the first time.

Bentley, Gerald E., Jr. Blake Records Supplement: Being New Materials Relating to the Life of William Blake Discovered since the Publication of Blake Records (1969) (Illus.). 200p. (C). 1988. text 75.00 (*0-19-812853-3*) OUP.

Bentley, Gerald E. The Professions of Dramatist & Player in Shakespeare's Time, 1590-1642. LC 83-43059. 658p. reprint ed. pap. 200.00 (*0-7837-4327-0*, 204403100012) Bks Demand.

Bentley, Gerald E., Jr. Shakespeare: A Biographical Handbook. LC 85-27246. 256p. 1986. reprint ed. lib. bdg. 52.50 (*0-313-25042-1*, BESH, Greenwood Pr) Greenwood.

Bentley, Gerald E. Shakespeare & His Theatre. LC 64-11350. 136p. reprint ed. pap. 42.20 (*0-608-18283-4*, 203152700075) Bks Demand.

— Shakespeare & Jonson: Their Reputations in the Seventeenth Century Compared. LC PR2959.B4. 350p. Date not set. reprint ed. pap. 108.50 (*0-608-21009-9*, 205453700003) Bks Demand.

Bentley, Gerald E., Jr., ed. Seventeenth-Century Stage. LC 68-26759. (Patterns of Literary Criticism Ser.). 1968. lib. bdg. 20.00 (*0-226-04308-8*) U Ch Pr.

— William Blake: The Critical Heritage. (Critical Heritage Ser.). (Illus.). 320p. 1975. 69.50 (*0-7100-8234-7*, Routledge Thoemms) Routledge.

Bentley, Gerald E. & Nurmi, Martin K. A Blake Bibliography: Annotated Lists of Works, Studies, & Blakeana. LC 64-19946. 411p. reprint ed. pap. 127.50 (*0-8357-7310-8*, 200100500053) Bks Demand.

Bentley, Gerald E., Jr., et al. Essays on the Blake Followers. LC 83-12789. (Illus.). 101p. (C). 1983. pap. 4.95 (*0-87328-080-6*) Huntington Lib.

Bentley, Gerald E., jt. auth. see Millett, Fred B.

Bentley, Gerald E., Jr., ed. see Shakespeare, William.

Bentley, Greg W. Shakespeare & the New Disease: The Dramatic Function of Syphilis in "Troilus & Cressida," "Measure for Measure," & "Timon of Athens" (American University Studies: English Language & Literature: Ser. IV, Vol. 85). 252p. (C). 1989. text 36.95 (*0-8204-0817-4*) P Lang Pubng.

Bentley, H. Wilder. The Art of Laurence Rickett Williams: An Appreciation. LC N 6512.W5B4. 42p. reprint ed. pap. 30.00 (*0-8357-5763-3*, 205002900057) Bks Demand.

Bentley, Harry C. Bibliography of Works on Accounting by American Authors. 197p. 1998. reprint ed. 150.00 (*1-57898-077-1*) Martino Pubng.

Bentley, Heather A. & Bentley, Neil R. The Irregular Verb Book: Fun Activities for Serious Students. (Illus.). 40p. 1997. wbk. ed. 19.99 (*0-9661726-0-4*) Watermark Pub.

***Bentley, Ian.** Responsive Environments. 192p. 2001. 47.95 (*0-7506-4768-X*) Buttrwrth-Heinemann.

Bentley, Ian. Urban Transformations: Power, People & Urban Design. LC 98-39830. 1999. write for info. (*0-415-12823-4*) Routledge.

***Bentley, J., et al, eds.** Advances in Materials Problem Solving with the Electron Microscope Vol. 589: Materials Research Society Symposium Proceedings. 2000. text 93.00 (*1-55899-497-1*) Materials Res.

Bentley, J. D., jt. auth. see Houseman, R. E.

Bentley, J. P. An Introduction to Reliability & Quality Engineering. (C). 1993. pap. text 43.95 (*0-582-08970-0*, Pub. by Addison-Wesley) Longman.

Bentley, James. Blue Guide: Western Germany. 2nd ed. 1995. pap. 21.95 (*0-393-31196-1*, Norton Paperbks) Norton.

— East of the City: The London Docklands Story. (Illus.). 224p. 1998. 40.00 (*1-86205-057-0*, Pub. by Pavilion Bks Ltd) Trafalgar.

— Fort Towns of France: The Bastides of the Dordogne & Aquitaine. (Illus.). 244p. 1993. 29.95 (*1-85043-608-8*, Pub. by I B T) St Martin.

— Life & Food in the Dordogne. LC 87-20396. 184p. 1987. 18.95 (*0-941533-04-2*, NAB) I R Dee.

— The Most Beautiful Villages of Brittany. LC 98-61828. (Illus.). 208p. 1999. 40.00 (*0-500-01935-5*, Pub. by Thames Hudson) Norton.

— The Most Beautiful Villages of Burgundy. LC 98-60038. (Illus.). 224p. 1998. 40.00 (*0-500-01862-6*, Pub. by Thames Hudson) Norton.

— The Most Beautiful Villages of England. LC 98-61184. (Most Beautiful Villages Ser.). (Illus.). 208p. 1999. 40.00 (*0-500-01905-3*, Pub. by Thames Hudson) Norton.

— The Most Beautiful Villages of the Dordogne: France's Hidden Treasure. LC 96-60055. (Illus.). 224p. 1996. 40.00 (*0-500-54201-5*, Pub. by Thames Hudson) Norton.

— Munich & Bavaria. (Illustrated Travel Guides from Thomas Cook Ser.). (Illus.). 192p. 1994. pap. 12.95 (*0-8442-9062-9*, Passprt Bks) NTC Contemp Pub Co.

— Munich & Bavaria. 2nd ed. (Illus.). 192p. 1997. pap. 14.95 (*0-8442-4839-8*) NTC Contemp Pub Co.

— To Live in France. LC 97-60323. (Illus.). 224p. 1997. 45.00 (*0-500-01796-4*, Pub. by Thames Hudson) Norton.

Bentley, James H. Electrical Engineering Sample Exam: For the Professional Engineer's Exam. 2nd ed. (Illus.). 90p. 1998. pap. 23.50 (*1-57645-035-X*, 35X) Engineering.

— A Programmed Review for Electrical Engineering: For the Professional Engineer's Exam. 3rd ed. (Illus.). 238p. 1999. pap. 44.50 (*1-57645-034-1*, 341) Engineering.

Bentley, James R., jt. auth. see Dorman, John F.

Bentley, Jeffery W. Today There Is No Misery: The Ethnography of Farming in Northwest Portugal. LC 91-24390. (Arizona Studies in Human Ecology). (Illus.). 177p. 1992. 33.50 (*0-8165-1244-2*) U of Ariz Pr.

Bentley, Jerome T. The Effects of Standard Oil's Vertical Integration into Transportation on the Structure & Performance of the American Petroleum Industry, 1872-1884. Bruchey, Stuart, ed. LC 78-22660. (Energy in the American Economy Ser.). (Illus.). 1979. lib. bdg. 17.95 (*0-405-11964-X*) Ayer.

Bentley, Jerry H. Humanists & Holy Writ: New Testament Scholarship in the Renaissance. LC 83-42547. 260p. reprint ed. pap. 80.60 (*0-7837-1429-7*, 204178400023) Bks Demand.

— Old World Encounters: Cross-Cultural Contacts & Exchanges in Pre-Modern Times. (Illus.). 240p. (C). 1993. pap. text 21.95 (*0-19-507640-0*) OUP.

— Politics & Culture in Renaissance Naples. LC 87-945511. 342p. reprint ed. pap. 106.10 (*0-608-06392-4*, 206675300008) Bks Demand.

— Shapes of World History in Twentieth-Century Scholarship. Adas, Michael, ed. (Essays on Global & Comparative History Ser.). 34p. 1995. reprint ed. pap. 6.00 (*0-87229-076-X*) Am Hist Assn.

— Traditions & Encounters: A Global Perspective on the Past. 1999. 38.00 (*0-07-236229-4*) McGraw.

Bentley, Jerry H. & Ziegler, Herbert F. Tranditions & Encounters: A Global Perspective on the Past. LC 99-13503. 1999. 48.00 (*0-07-004923-8*) McGraw.

Bentley, Joan & Hobbs, Linda. How to Do Science Experiments with Children. (Illus.). 224p. (J). (gr. 1-3). 1994. pap. text, teacher ed. 24.95 (*1-55799-337-8*, EMC 846) Evan-Moor Edu Pubs.

Bentley, Joan, et al. Simple Science Experiments. (Science Ser.). (Illus.). 32p. (J). (gr. 2-3). Date not set. pap., wbk. ed. 2.50 (*1-58610-121-8*) Learn Horizon.

Bentley, John. Egypt Guide. 448p. 1998. pap. text 17.95 (*1-883323-71-1*) Open Rd Pub.

***Bentley, John.** Vermont Guide. 336p. 2000. 16.95 (*1-892975-20-3*) Open Rd Pub.

Bentley, John P. Introduction to Reliability & Quality Engineering. 2nd ed. LC 98-34263. 256p. (C). 1998. pap. text 59.95 (*0-201-33132-2*) Addison-Wesley.

Bentley, Jon L. More Programming Pearls: Confessions of a Coder. (Illus.). 224p. (C). 1988. pap. text 20.95 (*0-201-11889-0*) Addison-Wesley.

Bentley, Joni. Riding Success Without Stress, Vol. 1. 1997. 57.00 (*0-85131-701-4*, Pub. by J A Allen) Trafalgar.

Bentley, Joseph. Everything Electrical. pap. 6.95 (*0-931841-06-2*) Satchells Pub.

Bentley, Joseph, jt. auth. see Brooker, Jewel S.

Bentley, Judith. Brides, Midwives & Widows. (Settling the West Ser.). (Illus.). 96p. (J). (gr. 5-8). 1995. lib. bdg. 20.40 (*0-8050-2994-X*) TFC Bks NY.

***Bentley, Judith.** Dear Friend. 144p. 1999. pap. write for info. (*0-14-038344-1*) Viking Penguin.

Bentley, Judith. Dear Friend: Thomas Garrett & William Still, Collaborators on the Underground Railroad. LC 96-27989. (Illus.). 128p. (J). 1997. 15.99 (*0-525-65156-X*) NAL.

— Explorers, Trappers & Guides. (Settling the West Ser.). (Illus.). 96p. (J). (gr. 5-8). 1995. lib. bdg. 16.98 (*0-8050-2995-8*) H Holt & Co.

— Fidel Castro. (In Focus Biographies Ser.). 128p. (J). (gr. 4-7). 1991. pap. 7.95 (*0-671-70199-1*, Julian Messner) Silver Burdett Pr.

— Fidel Castro. (In Focus Biographies Ser.). 128p. (YA). (gr. 4-7). 1991. lib. bdg. 13.95 (*0-671-70198-3*, Julian Messner) Silver Burdett Pr.

Bentley, Karen. Ashleigh's Farewell. (Thoroughbred Ser.). 1996. 9.09 (*0-606-10342-2*, Pub. by Turtleback) Demco.

— Ashleigh's Hope. (Thoroughbred Super Edition Ser.). 1996. 9.09 (*0-606-10343-0*, Pub. by Turtleback) Demco.

— Glory in Danger. (Thoroughbred Ser.). 1996. 9.09 (*0-606-10341-4*, Pub. by Turtleback) Demco.

Bentley, Karen. Glory's Triumph. (Thoroughbred Ser.). (J). 1996. 9.09 (*0-606-08643-9*, Pub. by Turtleback) Demco.

Bentley, Karen. The Unsers. LC 95-18676. (Race Car Legends Ser.). 64p. (J). (gr. 3 up). 1996. lib. bdg. 15.95 (*0-7910-3186-1*) Chelsea Hse.

***Bentley, Karen Anne.** Stop Out-of-Control Eating: Create Strength Through Inner Peace. LC 99-66600. (Big Heart Way Ser.). 144p. 1999. pap. 15.95 (*0-9666967-1-9*) Big Heart Bks.

***Bentley, Kassandra.** Getting Started in Online Day Trading. (Getting Started In Ser.). 224p. 2000. pap. 18.95 (*0-471-38017-2*) Wiley.

Bentley, Kassandra, jt. auth. see Brown, David L.

Bentley, Kenneth W. Isoquinoline Alkaloids. (Chemistry & Biochemistry of Organic Natural Products Ser.). 476p. 1998. text 117.00 (*90-5702-229-X*, Harwood Acad Pubs) Gordon & Breach.

***Bentley, Kevin, ed.** Sailor: Vintage Photos of a Masculine Icon. (Illus.). 112p. 2000. 24.95 (*1-57178-094-7*) Coun Oak Bks.

Bentley, Kia J. & Walsh, Joseph. Social Work & Psychotropic Medicine. (Social Work Ser.). 1995. mass mkt. 41.00 (*0-534-34101-2*) Brooks-Cole.

***Bentley, Kia J. & Walsh, Joseph.** Social Work & Psychotropic Medicine. 2nd ed. (Social Work Ser.). 2000. 28.25 (*0-534-36542-6*) Brooks-Cole.

Bentley, Kia J. & Walsh, Joseph. The Social Worker & Psychotropic Medication: Toward Effective Collaboration with Mental Health Clients, Families, & Providers. LC 95-35303. 230p. 1995. 44.95 (*0-534-34004-0*) Brooks-Cole.

Bentley, Lemuel E. African in America. LC 76-20830. (Illus.). 72p. 1976. 5.00 (*0-686-27414-8*) Du Sable Mus.

Bentley, Linda H. & Kiesl, Jennifer J., eds. Investment Statistics Locator. expanded rev. ed. LC 94-39014. 304p. 1994. 69.95 (*0-89774-781-X*) Oryx Pr.

Bentley, Lonnie, jt. auth. see Whitten, Jeffrey L.

Bentley, M. Shining in the Darkness. 1998. pap. text 11.99 (*0-85234-403-1*) P & R Pubng.

Bentley, M. E., jt. auth. see Bassett, R. L.

Bentley, Michael. Balancing the Books: Micah & Nehemiah. 1994. pap. text 8.99 (*0-85234-324-8*, Pub. by Evangelical Pr) P & R Pubng.

— Building for God's Glory (Haggai & Zechariah) 1989. pap. 11.99 (*0-85234-259-4*, Pub. by Evangelical Pr) P & R Pubng.

— Living for Christ (One & Two Peter) 1990. pap. 11.99 (*0-85234-279-9*, Pub. by Evangelical Pr) P & R Pubng.

— Modern Historiography: An Introduction. LC 98-39503. xii, 182 p. 1999. pap. 16.99 (*0-415-20267-1*) Routledge.

***Bentley, Michael.** Politics Without Democracy, 1815-1914: Perception & Preoccupation in British Government. LC 99-26095. (Classic Histories of England Ser.). (Illus.). 352p. 1999. pap. text 32.95 (*0-631-21813-0*) Blackwell Pubs.

Bentley, Michael. Politics Without Democracy, 1815-1914: Perception & Preoccupation in British Government. 2nd ed. LC 99-26095. (Classic Histories of England Ser.). (Illus.). 352p. 1999. text 64.95 (*0-631-21812-2*) Blackwell Pubs.

— Saving a Fallen World. 1992. pap. 14.99 (*0-85234-300-0*, Pub. by Evangelical Pr) P & R Pubng.

— Science Smart Junior, Vol. 2. (Princeton Review Ser.). 1999. pap. 10.00 (*0-679-77538-2*) Random.

***Bentley, Michael.** Travelling Homeward. 1999. pap. text 16.99 (*0-85234-429-5*) Evangelical Pr.

Bentley, Michael, ed. Companion to Historiography. LC 97-202105. 856p. (C). 1997. 165.00 (*0-415-03084-6*, D2242) Routledge.

— Public & Private Doctrine: Essays in British History Presented to Maurice Cowling. LC 92-32135. 369p. (C). 1993. text 69.95 (*0-521-40013-9*) Cambridge U Pr.

Bentley, Michael B. Power Macintosh Programmer's Guide: A Road Map to Native PowerPC Application Development. 1995. pap. 28.95 (*0-201-40789-2*) Addison-Wesley.

***Bentley, Nancy.** Young Journalist's Book: How to Write & Produce Your Own Newspaper. (Illus.). 64p. (J). (gr. 3-6). 2000. pap. text 8.95 (*0-7613-1377-X*, Copper Beech Bks) Millbrook Pr.

Bentley, Nancy & Guthrie, Donna. Putting on a Play: The Young Playwright's Guide to Scripting, Directing, & Performing. LC 95-47543. (Illus.). 64p. (J). (gr. 2-4). 1996. lib. bdg. 22.40 (*0-7613-0011-2*) Millbrook Pr.

***Bentley, Nancy & Guthrie, Donna.** The Young Journalist's Book: How to Write & Produce Your Own Newspaper. LC 97-43692. (Illus.). 64p. (J). (gr. 3-6). 1998. lib. bdg. 23.40 (*0-7613-0360-X*) Millbrook Pr.

Bentley, Nancy & Guthrie, Donna. The Young Producer's Video Book: How to Write, Shoot & Direct Your Own Videos. (Illus.). 64p. (J). (gr. 3-6). 1995. pap. 7.95 (*1-56294-688-9*) Millbrook Pr.

Bentley, Nancy, et al. The Young Producer's Video Book: How to Write, Shoot & Direct Your Own Videos. LC 94-48300. (Illus.). 64p. (J). (gr. 3-6). 1995. lib. bdg. 21.90 (*1-56294-566-1*) Millbrook Pr.

Bentley, Neil R., jt. auth. see Bentley, Heather A.

Bentley, Nelson. Collected Shorter Poems. 192p. (Orig.). 1988. pap. 10.00 (*0-944920-01-2*) Bellowing Ark Pr.

— The Flying Oyster: The Collected Apocalypses of Nelson Bentley. 120p. (Orig.). 1997. pap. 20.00 (*0-944920-26-8*) Bellowing Ark Pr.

Bentley, Nicholas. Paybed. 1977. 12.00 (*0-233-96845-8*) Transatl Arts.

Bentley, Nicole, ed. see Owens, Janette.

Bentley, Nicole, ed. see Willis, Jack.

Bentley, P. The Brontes. LC 75-30922. (Studies in the Brontes: No. 64). 1975. lib. bdg. 75.00 (*0-8383-2095-1*) M S G Haskell Hse.

Bentley, P. E. English Regional Novel. (Studies in Fiction: No. 34). (C). 1970. reprint ed. pap. 22.95 (*0-8383-0107-X*) M S G Haskell Hse.

Bentley, P. H., ed. Recent Advances in the Chemistry of Beta-Lactam Antibiotics: 4th International Symposium, 1988. 368p. 1989. 109.00 (*0-85186-816-9*, R6816) CRC Pr.

Bentley, P. H. & O'Hanlon, P. J., eds. Anti-Infectives: Recent Advances in Chemistry & Structure Activity Relationships. (Special Publication Ser.: No. 198). xii, 338p. 1997. 174.00 (*0-85404-707-7*) Am Chemical.

Bentley, P. J. Comparative Vertebrate Endocrinology. 3rd ed. LC 97-27048. (Illus.). 546p. (C). 1998. text 110.00 (*0-521-62002-3*); pap. text 44.95 (*0-521-62998-5*) Cambridge U Pr.

— Elements of Pharmacology: A Primer on Drug Action. LC 80-26624. (Illus.). 168p. 1981. pap. text 19.95 (*0-521-28074-5*) Cambridge U Pr.

Bentley, Paul. Ted Hughes. LC 97-20600. (Studies in Twentieth-Century Literature). (C). 1998. text 61.00 (*0-582-22776-3*) Longman.

***Bentley, Pauline.** Cavalier's Masque. large type ed. 368p. 2000. 20.99 (*1-85389-989-5*, Pub. by Dales Lrg Prnt) Ulverscroft.

Bentley, Pauline. Marriage Rites. large type ed. 350p. 1995. 23.99 (*0-263-14424-0*, Pub. by Mills & Boon) Ulverscroft.

— Penruthin's Wife. large type ed. 350p. 1996. 23.99 (*0-263-14523-9*, Pub. by Mills & Boon) Ulverscroft.

— Shadow of Pengarron. large type ed. (Dales Large Print Ser.). 388p. 1996. pap. 18.99 (*1-85389-649-7*, Dales) Ulverscroft.

— Song of Wychaven. large type ed. (Dales Large Print Ser.). 400p. 1998. pap. 19.99 (*1-85389-832-5*, Dales) Ulverscroft.

Bentley, Peter. The Book of Dream Symbols. (Illus.). 48p. 1995. 7.95 (*0-8118-0664-2*) Chronicle Bks.

— The Book of Love Symbols. (Illus.). 48p. 1995. 7.95 (*0-8118-0689-8*) Chronicle Bks.

Bentley, Peter, ed. see Porter, J. R.

***Bentley, Peter J.** Evolutionary Design by Computers. 2nd ed. (Illus.). 650p. 1999. 69.95 incl. cd-rom (*1-55860-605-X*, Pub. by Morgan Kaufmann) Harcourt.

Bentley, Phyllis. The Brontes. LC 85-51359. (Literary Lives Ser.). (Illus.). 144p. 1998. pap. 12.95 (*0-500-26016-8*, Pub. by Thames Hudson) Norton.

Bentley, Phyllis, compiled by. The Brontes. 39.00 (*1-56696-114-9*) Jackdaw.

Bentley, R. Medicinal Plants, Vols. 1-4. 1999. reprint ed. pap. 1400.00 (*81-7089-167-1*, Pub. by Intl Bk Distr) St Mut.

Bentley, R. & Triman, H. Medicinal Plants, Set, Vols. 1-4. 1400p. (C). 1981. 700.00 (*0-7855-7512-X*) St Mut.

Bentley, R. D. & Mariska, J. T., eds. Magnetic Reconnection in the Solar Atmosphere, Vol. 111. (ASP Conference Series Proceedings). 436p. 1996. 52.00 (*1-886733-31-7*) Astron Soc Pacific.

Bentley, Ray. Building Godly Character. Smith, Chuck, ed. (Calvary Basics Ser.). 84p. 1995. pap. 3.50 (*0-936728-59-0*) Word for Today.

— Tender Mercies: Applying God's Mercy to Your Life. Gillespie, Jennie, ed. (Illus.). 96p. (Orig.). 1993. pap. 4.95 (*0-9638878-0-7*) In The Word.

— Think on These Things: Attitudes for Successful Living. Gillespie, Jennie, ed. (Illus.). 136p. 1996. 9.95 (*0-9638878-1-5*) In The Word.

Bentley, Richard. The Correspondence, 2 vols. in 1. Wordsworth, C., ed. (Anglistica & Americana Ser.: No. 93). xxxii, 838p. 1977. reprint ed. 185.00 incl. 3.5 hd (*3-487-06320-4*) G Olms Pubs.

— Novels from Richard Bentley's Standard Novels Series, 12 vols. reprint ed. write for info. (*0-404-54400-2*) AMS Pr.

— Works, 3 vols. Dyce, Alexander, ed. LC 66-6448. reprint ed. 275.00 (*0-404-00760-0*) AMS Pr.

— The Works. xxxii, 1378p. 1971. reprint ed. 305.00 (*3-487-04071-9*) G Olms Pubs.

B

Bentley, Richard, et al, eds. Groupware & the World Wide Web. LC 97-8245. 1997. text 77.00 (*0-7923-4534-7*) Kluwer Academic.

Bentley, Richard & Coles, Alex, eds. De-, Dis-, Ex- Vol. 1: Ex-Cavating Modernism. LC 97-213592. (Illus.). 124p. 1997. pap. 15.95 (*1-901033-05-8*, Pub. by Black Dog Pubg) RAM Publications.

Bentley, Richard, ed. see Milton, John.

Bentley, Richard P. Thermal Efficiency Construction. 1988. pap. 15.75 (*0-9600902-0-7*) R P Bentley.

Bentley, Robert, Inc. Staff. Audi Fox Service Manual, 1973-1979. LC 79-53187. (Illus.). 562p. 1979. pap. 39.95 (*0-8376-0097-9*) Bentley Pubs.

— Austin-Healey 100-4 Drivers. 1994. 25.00 (*0-8376-0572-5*) Bentley Pubs.

— Austin-Healey 100-6 Drivers. (Illus.). 74p. 1994. 25.00 (*0-8376-0573-3*) Bentley Pubs.

— BMW 3-Series Service Manual, 1984-1990. (Illus.). 528p. (Orig.). 1990. pap. 49.95 (*0-8376-0325-0*) Bentley Pubs.

— Jaguar MK 10 & 420g, 1961-69. (Illus.). 364p. 1994. 90.00 (*0-8376-0577-6*) Bentley Pubs.

— Jaguar XJ6 Series 1, 1968-72. (Illus.). 186p. 1994. 50.00 (*0-8376-0578-4*) Bentley Pubs.

— Jaguar XJ6 Series 2, 1972-79. (Illus.). 400p. 1994. 90.00 (*0-8376-0579-2*) Bentley Pubs.

— Jaguar XK 150 Drivers Handbook. (Illus.). 84p. 1994. pap. 35.00 (*0-8376-0582-2*) Bentley Pubs.

— Jaguar XK 140 Drivers Handbook. (Illus.). 72p. 1994. pap. 35.00 (*0-8376-0581-4*) Bentley Pubs.

— Jaguar XK 120 Drivers Handbook. (Illus.). 72p. 1994. pap. 35.00 (*0-8376-0580-6*) Bentley Pubs.

— MG Midget 1500 Worksh., 1975-79. (Illus.). 384p. 1994. 40.00 (*0-8376-0596-2*) Bentley Pubs.

— MG Midget TD Drivers Handbook. (Illus.). 74p. 1994. pap. 16.00 (*0-8376-0584-9*) Bentley Pubs.

— MG Midget TF & TF 1500 Driver. (Illus.). 64p. 1994. pap. 16.00 (*0-8376-0583-0*) Bentley Pubs.

— MGA 1500 Driver's Handbook, 1960. (Illus.). 64p. 1994. pap. 16.00 (*0-8376-0589-X*) Bentley Pubs.

— MGB Driver's Handbook U. S., 1975. (Illus.). 100p. 1994. pap. 16.00 (*0-8376-0588-1*) Bentley Pubs.

— MGB Driver's Handbook U. S., 1972. (Illus.). 76p. 1994. pap. 16.00 (*0-8376-0592-X*) Bentley Pubs.

— MGB Tourer & GT Drive Handbook. (Illus.). 62p. 1994. pap. 16.00 (*0-8376-0586-5*); pap. 16.00 (*0-8376-0587-3*) Bentley Pubs.

— MGB Tourer & GT Driver's Handbook (1969) (Illus.). 76p. 1994. pap. 16.00 (*0-8376-0591-1*) Bentley Pubs.

— Saab 900 Eight Valve Official Service Manual, 1981-1988. (Illus.). 560p. 1992. 54.95 (*0-8376-0310-2*) Bentley Pubs.

— SAAB 900, 16 Valve Official Service manual, 1985-1993. (Illus.). 622p. 1993. pap. 54.95 (*0-8376-0313-7*) Bentley Pubs.

— Tourer & GT Drive Handbook, 68. (Illus.). 62p. 1994. pap. 16.00 (*0-8376-0585-7*) Bentley Pubs.

— Toyota Celica, 1978-1984: Service Manual. (Illus.). 584p. (Orig.). 1984. pap. 26.50 (*0-8376-0256-4*) Bentley Pubs.

— Toyota Corolla, 1980-1983: Service Manual 1.8 Models. LC 83-62734. (Illus.). 640p. (Orig.). 1984. pap. 29.95 (*0-8376-0246-7*) Bentley Pubs.

— Toyota Corolla, 1980-1981: 1.8 Service Manual. 1981. 1.95 (*0-8376-0245-9*) Bentley Pubs.

— Toyota Corolla, 1973-1979: 1600 Service Manual. LC 79-53189. (Illus.). (Orig.). 1979. pap. 29.95 (*0-8376-0242-4*) Bentley Pubs.

— Triumph Spitfire 1500, 1975-1980. 1994. 50.00 (*0-8376-0555-5*) Bentley Pubs.

— Triumph Spitfire Mark IV Workshop Manual: 1971 to 1974. (Illus.). 216p. 1994. 45.00 (*0-8376-0593-8*) Bentley Pubs.

— Triumph TR2 & TR3 Service Instruction Manual: 1954 to 1961. 1994. 45.00 (*0-8376-0594-6*) Bentley Pubs.

— Volkswagen Dasher Service Manual, 1974-1981, Including Diesel. rev. ed. LC 81-66944. (Illus.). 692p. (Orig.). 1981. pap. 44.95 (*0-8376-0083-9*) Bentley Pubs.

— Volkswagen GTI Golf-Jetta Service Manual, 1985-1992. (Illus.). 840p. 1990. pap. 49.95 (*0-8376-0342-0*) Bentley Pubs.

— Volkswagen Passat: Service Maual 1990, 1991, 1992, 1993 - 4-Cylinder Gasoline Models Including Gl & Wagon. LC 96-36416. (Illus.). 582p. 1996. pap. 54.95 (*0-8376-0378-1*) Bentley Pubs.

— Volkswagen Rabbit, Jetta Diesel Service Manual: 1977-84 Diesel Models, Including Pickup Truck & Turbo-Diesel. 4th rev. ed. LC 84-70138. (Illus.). 624p. (Orig.). 1984. pap. 39.95 (*0-8376-0184-3*) Bentley Pubs.
— Volkswagen Rabbit, Scirocco, Jetta Service Manual: 1980-1984 Gasoline Models, Including Pickup Truck, Convertible, & GTI. LC 84-70139. (Illus.). 720p. (Orig.). 1984. pap. 39.95 (*0-8376-0183-5*) Bentley Pubs.
— Volkswagen Rabbit, Scirocco Service Manual, Gasoline Models, 1975-1979. rev. ed. LC 79-57170. (Illus.). 628p. (Orig.). 1986. pap. 39.95 (*0-8376-0107-X*) Bentley Pubs.
— Volkswagon Jetta, Golf, GTI, Cabrio Service Manual: Including Jetta III & Golf III, 1993, 1994, 1995, 1996, 1997. LC 97-99. (Illus.). 742p. 1999. pap. 59.95 (*0-8376-0365-X*) Bentley Pubs.
Bentley, Robert, Inc. Staff & Audi of America, Inc. Staff. Audi 80, 90, Coupe Quattro: Official Factory Repair Manual 1988, 1989, 1990, 1991, 1992, Including 80 Quattro, 90 Quattro & 20-Valve Models. LC 96-16851. (Illus.). 1861p. 1996. 144.95 (*0-8376-0368-4*) Bentley Pubs.
Bentley, Robert, Inc. Staff & British Leyland Motors Staff. Austin-Healey 3000 MK 1 & 2 Drivers Handbook (1959-1963) Bk. 1. (Illus.). 65p. 1994. 25.00 (*0-8376-0574-1*) Bentley Pubs.
Bentley, Robert, Inc. Staff & Jaguar Cars Ltd. Staff. The Jaguar S-Type, 3.4 & 3.8 Litre, Workshop Manual, 1963-1966. (Illus.). 566p. 1994. 90.00 (*0-8376-0576-8*) Bentley Pubs.
Bentley, Robert L. Dangerous Games: The True Story of a Convicted Murderer on Death Row Who Changed His Sex & Won Her Freedom. LC 92-39499. 1993. 19.95 (*1-55972-180-4*, Birch Ln Pr) Carol Pub Group.
Bentley, Ross. Speed Secrets: Professional Race Driving Techniques. LC 98-7282. 160p. 1998. pap. 15.95 (*0-7603-0518-8*) MBI Pubg.
***Bentley, Ross & Langford, Ronn.** Inner Speed Secrets. LC 99-59983. (Illus.). 160p. 2000. pap. 15.95 (*0-7603-0834-9*, Pub. by MBI Pubg) Motorbooks Intl.
Bentley, Roy. Any One Man: Poems. (Midwest Writers Ser.). 124p. (Orig.). (C). 1992. 18.95 (*0-933087-24-1*); pap. 8.95 (*0-933087-23-3*) Bottom Dog Pr.
Bentley, Roy. Boy in Boat. 1986. lib. bdg. 15.95 (*0-8173-0290-5*) University of London IRS.
Bentley, Roy, et al. Three by Three: Bloom Blood, after Uelsmann, the Edge of Heaven. Smith, Larry, ed. (Ohio Writers Ser.: Nos. 9, 10 & 11). (Illus.). 108p. (Orig.). 1988. pap. 7.95 (*0-933087-11-X*) Bottom Dog Pr.
Bentley, S. P., ed. Engineering Geology of Waste Disposal. (Geological Society Engineering Geology Special Publication Ser.: No. 11). (Illus.). viii, 576p. 1995. 148.00 (*1-897799-46-2*, 346, Pub. by Geol Soc Pub Hse) AAPG.
Bentley, Scott. Ground Air. 1994. 6.00 (*1-882022-23-8*) O Bks.
Bentley, Sean. Grace & Desolution. 32p. 1996. pap. 9.95 (*1-885942-00-1*) Cune.
***Bentley, Stanley L.** Native Orchids of the Southern Appalachian Mountains. LC 99-87675. (Illus.). 272p. 2000. 39.95 (*0-8078-2563-8*); pap. 24.95 (*0-8078-4872-7*) U of NC Pr.
Bentley, Sudjai N. Oriental Cooking in the Adirondacks. LC 92-90200. 1992. pap. 10.00 (*0-9600902-1-5*) R P Bentley.
Bentley, Susan A. Acrylic Painter's Reference Book. 3rd ed. (Illus.). 112p. 1989. pap. 13.95 (*0-941284-65-4*) J Shaw Studio.
***Bentley-Taylor, David.** Josephus: A Unique Witness; Independent Evidence Confirming the New Testament Story. 2000. pap. 9.99 (*1-85792-499-1*) Christian Focus.
Bentley, Thomas Roy, jt. auth. see Mandel, Eli.
Bentley, Tom. Learning Beyond the Classroom. LC 98-19892. 208p. (C). (gr. 13). 1998. pap. 24.99 (*0-415-18259-X*, D5920) Routledge.
Bentley, Toni & Kirstein, Lincoln. Costumes by Karinska. LC 95-7407. (Illus.). 192p. 1995. 60.00 (*0-8109-3516-3*, Pub. by Abrams) Time Warner.
Bentley, Trevor. Facilitation: Providing Opportunities for Learning. LC 93-31420. (Training Ser.). 152p. 1994. pap. 29.95 (*0-07-707684-2*) McGraw.
— Information Systems Strategies for Business. 1998. pap. text 30.00 (*0-7494-2681-0*) Kogan Page Ltd.
— Managing Information: Avoiding Overload. (CIMA Business Skills Ser.). 164p. 1998. pap. 30.00 (*0-7494-2682-9*) Kogan Page Ltd.
Bentley, Trevor J. Bridging the Performance Gap. LC 96-8725. 250p. 1996. text 69.95 (*0-566-07760-4*, Pub. by Gower) Ashgate Pub Co.
— Sharpen Your Skills in Motivating People to Perform. LC 96-9742. 1998. pap. 19.95 (*0-07-709072-1*) McGraw.
Bentley, Trevor J. & Clayton, Susan. Profiting from Diversity. LC 97-42339. 192p. 1998. 69.95 (*0-566-07931-3*, Pub. by Gower) Ashgate Pub Co.
Bentley, V., et al, eds. Major Chemical Companies of the World, 1999, 2 vols., Set. 2020p. 1999. pap. 855.00 (*1-86099-135-1*, Pub. by G & W) Am Educ Systs.
— Major Energy Companies of the World, 1999. 300p. 1999. pap. 855.00 (*1-86099-136-X*) Am Educ Systs.
— Major Food & Drink Companies of the World, 1999. 2315p. 1999. pap. 855.00 (*1-86099-138-6*) Am Educ Systs.
— Major Telecommunications Companies of the World, 1999. 1999. pap. 855.00 (*1-86099-139-4*) Am Educ Systs.
Bentley, Vicci. Forever Young. 1999. pap. text 18.95 (*1-85868-253-3*, Pub. by Carlton Bks Ltd) Natl Bk Netwk.
Bentley, Victor. Possessing Truth in Balance & Anatomy of a Backslider. LC 89-8945. 128p. (Orig.). (YA). 1989. pap. 2.99 (*0-932581-48-X*) Word Aflame.
***Bentley, W. A.** Snowflakes in Photographs. LC 00-38336. (Illus.). 2000. pap. 9.95 (*0-486-41253-9*) Dover.
Bentley, W. A. & Humphreys, W. J. Snow Crystals. (Illus.). 226p. 1962. pap. 17.95 (*0-486-20287-9*) Dover.
— Snow Crystals. (Illus.). (J). (gr. 5 up). 1990. 30.25 (*0-8446-1660-5*) Peter Smith.
Bentley, William. The Diary of Rev. William Bentley: 1784-1819, Vols. 2 & 4. 1990. 37.00 (*0-8446-1071-2*) Peter Smith.
Bentley, William, jt. auth. see Gelbard, Martin K.
Bentley, William G. Indoor & Outdoor Games. (J). (gr. k-6). 1966. pap. 7.99 (*0-8224-3910-7*) Fearon Teacher Aids.
Bentley, William K. & Corbett, James M. Prison Slang: Words & Expressions Depicting Life Behind Bars. LC 91-52763. 128p. 1992. lib. bdg. 28.50 (*0-89950-646-1*) McFarland & Co.
Bentley, William R. & Gowen, Marcia M., eds. Forest Resources & Wood-Based Biomass Energy As Rural Development Assets. (C). 1994. text 24.00 (*81-204-0923-X*, Pub. by Oxford IBH) S Asia.
— Forest Resources & Wood-Based Biomass Energy As Rural Development Assets. (Illus.). 376p. 1994. text 35.00 (*1-886106-06-1*) Science Pubs.
Bently, Arnold. Musical Ability in Children & Its Measurement. 1966. 9.95 (*0-8079-0187-3*) October.
Bently, L., jt. auth. see Howells, G. W.
Bently, Lionel. Law & the Senses: Sensational Jurisprudence. LC 96-8272. (Law & Social Theory Ser.). 272p. 1996. 64.95 (*0-7453-1069-9*, Pub. by Pluto GBR) Stylus Pub VA.
Bently, Lionel & Flynn, Leo. Law & the Senses: Perception & Regulation. 272p. 1996. pap. 21.95 (*0-7453-1068-0*, Pub. by Pluto GBR) Stylus Pub VA.
Bently, Lionel, jt. auth. see Sherman, Brad.
Bently, Peter, ed. The Dictionary of World Myth. LC 94-44700. 240p. 1995. 26.95 (*0-8160-3300-5*) Facts on File.
— The Dictionary of World Myth. LC 94-44700. (Illus.). 240p. 1995. pap. 17.95 (*0-8160-3325-0*) Facts on File.
Bento, Kenny, jt. auth. see Schell, Wanda.
Bento, M. C. & Bertolami, O. Classical & Quantum Gravity: Proceedings of the 1st Iberian Meeting on Gravity. 356p. 1993. text 109.00 (*981-02-1369-7*) World Scientific Pub.
Bentolila, Alain, ed. Dictionnaire Elementaire Creole Haitien-Francais. (FRE.). 1976. write for info. (*0-7859-7787-2*, 2218036002) Fr & Eur.
Bentolila, Alain, ed. see Nougayrol, Pierre, et al.
Benton. Acquiring a World View. (C). 2001. pap. text. write for info. (*0-15-507951-4*) Harcourt Coll Pubs.
— Arts & Culture. 216p. (C). 1998. pap. text, student ed. 15.00 (*0-13-084149-8*) P-H.
— Elements in Plane Surveying. 1991. teacher ed. 26.25 (*0-07-004885-1*) McGraw.
Benton, ed. Products Liability: Prevention & Defense. 1993. write for info. (*1-56257-341-1*, MICHIE) LEXIS Pub.
Benton & Diyanni. Arts & Culture. (C). 1998. pap. text, student ed. write for info. (*0-13-082401-1*) P-H.
— Arts & Culture, Vol. 2. 1998. pap. text, student ed. 13.33 (*0-13-863812-8*) P-H.
— Arts Combination & Music 98-99. 1999. 55.33 (*0-13-012292-0*) P-H.
***Benton, Wilson.** Everything You Wanted to Know about Predestinatin, but Was Afraid to Ask. (Truth for Life Ser.). 20p. 2000. 5.95 (*1-884416-33-0*, Reformed Acad Pr) A Press.
Benton, A. H. Indian Moral Instruction & Caste Problems. 121p. 1978. 14.95 (*0-318-36810-2*) Asia Bk Corp.
Benton, Allen H. Fleas of Medical & Veterinary Importance. (Illus.). 12p. 1985. pap. 0.90 (*0-942788-13-3*) Iris Visual.
— An Illustrated Key to the Fleas of the Eastern United States. (Marginal Media Bioguide Ser.: No. 3). (Illus.). 34p. (Orig.). 1983. 2.00 (*0-942788-09-5*) Iris Visual.
— Light & Natural. (Illus.). 184p. (Orig.). 1992. pap. 9.00 (*0-942788-20-6*) Iris Visual.
— Wild Worlds. (Illus.). viii, 222p. (Orig.). 1988. pap. 8.95 (*0-942788-16-8*) Iris Visual.
Benton, Allen H. & Bunting, Richard L. Young People's Nature Guide. (Illus.). 177p. (J). (gr. 2-4). 1978. pap. text 3.00 (*0-942788-05-2*); 6.00 (*0-942788-06-0*) Iris Visual.
Benton, Allen H., see Fitzwarren, Albert E., pseud.
Benton, Amanda. Silent Stranger. 160p. 1998. pap. 3.99 (*0-380-79222-2*, Avon Bks) Morrow Avon.
Benton, Arthur, jt. auth. see Riva, Daria.
Benton, Arthur L. Contributions to Neuropsychological Assessment: Judgment of Line Orientation. 1985. text 19.95 (*0-19-503324-8*) OUP.
Benton, Arthur L. Contributions to Neuropsychological Assessment: Tests: 6: Judgement of Line Orientation. 1983. text 85.00 (*0-19-503323-X*) OUP.
Benton, Arthur L. Studies in Neuropsychology: Selected Papers of Arthur Benton. Spreen, Otfried & Costa, Louis, eds. (Illus.). 320p. 1985. text 47.50 (*0-19-503636-0*) OUP.
Benton, Arthur L., et al. Contribution to Neuropsychological Assessment: A Clinical Manual. 2nd ed. (Illus.). 176p. 1994. pap. text 32.50 (*0-19-509179-5*) OUP.
***Benton, Arthur Lester.** Exploring the History of Neuropsychology: Selected Papers. LC 99-88047. 352p. 2000. text 65.00 (*0-19-513808-2*) OUP.
Benton-Banai, Edward. The Mishomis Book: The Voice of the Ojibway. unabridged ed. LC 80-138057. (Illus.). 114p. 1988. pap. 19.95 (*1-893487-00-8*) Indian Country.
Benton, Barbara, ed. Soldiers for Peace. (Illus.). 272p. 1996. 29.95 (*0-8160-3509-1*) Facts on File.
— Soldiers for Peace. (Illus.). 272p. 1996. pap. 14.95 (*0-8160-3510-5*) Facts on File.
Benton-Borghi, Beatrice H., et al. Best Friends: Teacher & Parent Guide. LC 96-92559. (Illus.). 60p. 1996. teacher ed., wbk. ed. 19.95 (*1-888927-25-9*, BFG) Open Minds.
— Down the Aisle: Teacher & Parent Guide. LC 96-92557. (Illus.). 60p. 1996. pap., teacher ed. 19.95 (*1-888927-27-5*, DTAG) Open Minds.
— A Thousand Lights: Teacher & Parent Guide. LC 96-92556. (Illus.). 60p. 1996. pap., teacher ed. 19.95 (*1-888927-28-3*, ATLG) Open Minds.
— Whoa, Nellie! Parent & Teacher Guide. LC 96-92558. (Illus.). 60p. 1996. pap., teacher ed. 19.95 (*1-888927-26-7*, WNG) Open Minds.
Benton-Borghi, Beatrice Hope & Cloern, Margaret, eds. Best Friends Journal. LC 97-68929. (Illus.). 84p. (YA). (gr. 3-10). 1997. spiral bd. 14.95 (*1-888927-50-X*) Open Minds.
— Down the Aisle Journal. LC 97-68931. (Illus.). 84p. (YA). (gr. 3-10). 1997. spiral bd. 14.95 (*1-888927-52-6*) Open Minds.
— A Thousand Lights Journal. LC 97-68932. (Illus.). 84p. (YA). (gr. 3-10). 1997. spiral bd. 14.95 (*1-888927-53-4*) Open Minds.
— Whoa, Nellie! Journal. LC 97-68930. (Illus.). 84p. (YA). (gr. 3-10). 1997. spiral bd. 14.95 (*1-888927-51-8*) Open Minds.
Benton, Bruce, jt. auth. see Kim, Aehyung.
Benton Calhoun, Keith. Four Hundred Hours: A Father's Journal of His Daughter's Kidnap & Murder. 250p. 1999. 22.95 (*0-9663078-2-8*) Graystone Pub Co.
***Benton, Charles.** Guide to International Photographic Competitions. LC 99-72180. (Illus.). 96p. 1999. pap. 29.95 (*0-936262-88-5*) Amherst Media.
Benton, Charles & Kaye, Richard, eds. How to Comply with OSHA in the Construction Industry. 1995. ring bd. 149.00 (*0-929321-27-8*) WEKA Pub.
Benton, Charles E. Benton. Caleb Benton & Sarah Bishop, Their Ancestors & Descendants. (Illus.). 92p. 1997. reprint ed. pap. 18.00 (*0-8328-7507-4*); reprint ed. lib. bdg. 28.00 (*0-8328-7506-6*) Higginson Bk Co.
Benton, Christine, compiled by. A Mother's Book of Poems. LC 94-29325. 160p. 1994. 12.00 (*0-8092-3525-0*) NTC Contemp Pub Co.
— One Hundred & One Poems of Romance. LC 92-15046. (Illus.). 144p. 1992. 12.00 (*0-8092-3929-9*, 392990, Contemporary Bks) NTC Contemp Pub Co.
Benton, Christine M., jt. auth. see Barkley, Russell A.
Benton, Corrine. The Return to the Promised Land. 32p. 1995. pap., per. 6.00 (*0-8059-3637-8*) Dorrance.
Benton Count Historical Society Staff, compiled by. Last Census of Benton Co. Prior to the Civil War. 132p. (Orig.). 1992. pap. 10.00 (*0-938041-08-8*) Arc Pr AR.
***Benton, D. A.** How to Act Like a CEO: 11 Rules for Getting to the Top & Staying There. 2000. 19.95 (*0-07-135998-2*) McGraw.
Benton, D. A. Lions Don't Need to Roar: Using the Leadership Power of Personal Presence to Stand Out, Fit in & Move Ahead. 272p. 1993. reprint ed. mass mkt. 13.99 (*0-446-39499-8*, Pub. by Warner Bks) Little.
— The $100,000 Club: How to Make a Six-Figure Income. 304p. pap. write for info. (*0-446-67514-8*) Warner Bks.
— The $100,000 Club: How to Make a Six-Figure Income. LC 97-29934. 304p. 1998. 25.00 (*0-446-52083-7*, Pub. by Warner Bks) Little.
***Benton, D. A.** The $100,000 Club: How to Make a Six-Figure Income. 320p. 2000. mass mkt. 7.50 (*0-446-60825-4*) Warner Bks.
— Secrets of a CEO Coach: Your Personal Training Guide to Thinking Like a Leader & Acting Like a CEO. (Illus.). 224p. 2000. pap. 12.95 (*0-07-136075-1*) McGraw.
— Secrets of a CEO Coach: Your Personal Training Guide to Thinking Like a Leader & Acting Like a CEO. LC 98-51527. 211p. 1999. 21.95 (*0-07-007108-X*) Osborne-McGraw.
Benton, D. Dean. Mosquito Park Secrets: How to Live Outrageously Happy & Healthy. 96p. 1998. pap. 9.95 (*0-9664821-0-7*) Spring Daisy.
Benton, David. Food for Thought. 1996. pap. 13.95 (*0-14-025223-1*, Pub. by Pnguin Bks Ltd) Trafalgar.
Benton, Debra A. How to Think Like a CEO: The 22 Vital Traits You Need to Be the Person at the Top. 480p. 1999. mass mkt. 14.99 (*0-446-67307-2*, Pub. by Warner Bks) Little.
Benton, Donald S. Federal Banking Laws. rev. ed. 1152p. 1990. 145.00 (*0-7913-0714-X*) Warren Gorham & Lamont.
— Federal Banking Laws, No. 1. 1152p. 1991. suppl. ed. 52.50 (*0-7913-0024-2*) Warren Gorham & Lamont.
Benton, Donald S., jt. ed. see Douglas, James A.
Benton, Douglas. Applied Human Relations: An Organizational & Skill Development Approach. 6th ed. LC 97-12993. 579p. (C). 1997. pap. text 61.00 (*0-13-755919-4*) P-H.
Benton, E. V., et al, eds. Nuclear Track Registration: Proceedings of the Pacific Northwest Conference, 5th, Hanford Engineering Development Laboratory, Westinghouse Hanford Company, Richland, WA, July 28-29, 1982. 96p. 1983. pap. 61.00 (*0-08-030274-2*, Pergamon Pr) Elsevier.
Benton, Eva. Chosen for a Purpose. 280p. (Orig.). 1996. pap. 11.99 (*1-889389-03-X*) End-Time Wave.
Benton, Everett C. A History of Guildhall, VT. (Illus.). 270p. 1993. reprint ed. lib. bdg. 32.50 (*0-8328-3181-6*) Higginson Bk Co.
Benton, Frances. The Making of a Baltimore Album Quilt. (Illus.). 64p. 1995. 16.95 (*1-881320-45-6*, Black Belt) Black Belt Communs.
Benton, Frank. Cowboy Life on the Sidetrack. Myers, James E., ed. 120p. 1986. reprint ed. pap. 7.95 (*0-942936-04-3*) Lincoln-Herndon Pr.
Benton, Gregor. China's Urban Revolutionaries: Explorations in the History of Chinese Trotskyism, 1921-1952. LC 95-22300. 304p. (C). 1996. pap. 19.95 (*0-391-03947-4*); text 55.00 (*0-391-03921-0*) Humanities.
— Chinese in Europe. Picke, Frank N., ed. LC 97-9663. 276p. 1998. text 75.00 (*0-312-17526-4*) St Martin.
— Mountain Fires: The Red Army's Three-Year War in South China, 1934-1938. (Philip E. Lilienthal Bks.). (C). 1992. 85.00 (*0-520-04158-5*, Pub. by U CA Pr) Cal Prin Full Svc.
***Benton, Gregor.** New Fourth Army: Communist Resistance along the Yangtze & the Huai, 1938-1941. LC 99-10875. 800p. 1999. 80.00 (*0-520-21992-9*, Pub. by U CA Pr) Cal Prin Full Svc.
Benton, Gregor, ed. from CHI. An Oppositionist for Life: Memoirs of the Chinese Revolutionary Zheng Chaolin. LC 95-42652. (Historical Memories Ser.). (C). 1997. text 49.95 (*0-391-03966-0*) Humanities.
— An Oppositionist for Life: Memoirs of the Chinese Revolutionary Zheng Chaolin. LC 95-42652. (Historical Memories Ser.). (Illus.). 344p. (C). 1997. pap. 18.50 (*0-391-03967-9*) Humanities.
Benton, Gregor & Hunter, Alan. Wild Lily, Prairie Fire: China's Road to Democracy, Yan'an to Tian'anmen, 1942-1989. LC 95-5200. 400p. 1995. text 60.00 (*0-691-04359-0*, Pub. by Princeton U Pr) Cal Prin Full Svc.
Benton, Gregor & Hunter, Alan, eds. Wild Lily, Prairie Fire: China's Road to Democracy, Yan'an to Tian'anmen, 1942-1989. LC 95-5200. 400p. 1995. pap. text 20.95 (*0-691-04358-2*, Pub. by Princeton U Pr) Cal Prin Full Svc.
Benton, Gregor, tr. see Chen, Duxiu.
Benton, Gregor, tr. see Marx, Karl.
Benton, Holley. The Geese & the Tortoise & Other Stories. 32p. (J). (gr. 3-5). 1995. 14.99 (*0-9639913-1-0*) Tata Pubng.
Benton, Hope. Best Friends. LC 96-92563. (Illus.). 109p. (J). (gr. 3-8). 1996. 14.95 (*1-888927-00-3*, BFB); pap. 4.50 (*1-888927-78-X*, BFB) Open Minds.
— Down the Aisle. LC 96-92561. (Illus.). (J). (gr. 3-8). 1996. 14.95 (*1-888927-02-X*, DTAB); pap. 14.95 (*1-888927-80-1*, DTAB) Open Minds.
— A Thousand Lights. LC 96-92560. (Illus.). 95p. (J). (gr. 3-8). 1996. 14.95 (*1-888927-03-8*, ATLB); pap. 4.50 (*1-888927-81-X*, ATLB) Open Minds.
— Whoa, Nellie! LC 96-92562. (Illus.). 102p. (J). (gr. 3-8). 1996. 14.95 (*1-888927-01-1*, WNB); pap. 4.50 (*1-888927-79-8*, WNB) Open Minds.
Benton, J., et al, eds. Diagnostic Techniques for Semiconductor Materials & Devices. LC 92-70113. (Proceedings Ser.: Vol. 92-2). 292p. 1992. 36.00 (*1-56677-001-7*) Electrochem Soc.
Benton, J. Edwin & Morgan, David R., eds. Intergovernmental Relations & Public Policy, 156. LC 86-3155. (Contributions in Political Science Ser.: No. 56). 232p. 1986. 59.95 (*0-313-25443-5*, BIL/, Greenwood Pr) Greenwood.
Benton, J. Edwin, jt. ed. see Morgan, David.
***Benton, Janet.** Agrarian Reform in Theory & Practice: A Study of the Lake Titicaca Region of Bolivia. LC 99-76346. 207p. 1999. text 61.95 (*1-85972-696-8*, Pub. by Ashgate Pub) Ashgate Pub Co.
Benton, Janet. Vitamin A: Everything You Need to Know. LC 98-36550. 1998. pap. 10.95 (*1-882606-44-2*) Peoples Med Soc.
Benton, Janetta R. Holy Terrors: Gargoyles on Medieval Buildings. LC 96-36002. (Illus.). 140p. 1997. 29.95 (*0-7892-0182-8*) Abbeville Pr.
— The Medieval Menagerie: Animals in the Art of the Middle Ages. LC 92-15412. (Illus.). 192p. 1992. 14.98 (*1-55859-133-8*) Abbeville Pr.
Benton, Janetta Rebold. Arts & Culture: An Introduction to the Humanities. 1998. pap. text 59.00 (*0-13-083911-6*) P-H.
***Benton, Janetta Rebold.** Arts & Culture: An Introduction to the Humanities. LC 97-17901. (Illus.). 464p. 1998. pap. text 55.00 (*0-13-083909-4*) P-H.
Benton, Janetta Rebold & Diyanni. Arts & Culture: An Introduction to the Humanities, Vol. II. 2nd ed. Vol. 2. 1998. pap. text 58.00 (*0-13-083900-0*) P-H.
Benton, Jeffrey. The Very Worst Road: Travellers' Accounts of Crossing Alabama's Old Creek Indian Territory, 1820-1847. LC 98-42155. 1998. 12.95 (*0-945477-13-9*) Hist Chattahoochee.
Benton, Jeffrey C. The Air Force Officer's Guide. (Illus.). 368p. 1996. pap. 19.95 (*0-8117-2655-X*) Stackpole.
— The Air Force Officer's Guide. 32nd ed. 1999. pap. text 19.95 (*0-8117-2656-8*) Stackpole.
***Benton, Jeffrey C.** They Served Here: Thirty-Three Maxwell Men. (Illus.). 78p. 1999. pap. 12.00 (*1-58566-074-4*) Air Univ.
Benton, Jill. Naomi Mitchison: A Biography. (Illus.). 216p. 1992. pap. text 15.00 (*0-04-440862-5*) NYU Pr.
Benton, Joanna. Keeping Close. (Orig.). 1983. pap. 10.00 (*0-8065-0839-6*, Citadel Pr) Carol Pub Group.
Benton, John. Carmen, No. 1. 192p. (Orig.). (YA). (gr. 7-12). 1990. reprint ed. mass mkt. 3.50 (*0-8007-8159-7*) J Benton Bks.
— Christians In a Consumer Culture: Escaping the Cult of Choice Invading Your Life. 175p. 1999. pap. 9.99 (*1-85792-484-3*) Christian Focus.
— Coming to Faith in Christ. 15p. 1977. pap. 1.25 (*0-85151-252-6*) Banner of Truth.
— Debbie. 192p. (Orig.). (J). (gr. 7-12). 1980. pap. 3.50 (*0-8007-8398-0*) J Benton Bks.
— How Can a God of Love Send People to Hell? 1985. pap. 3.99 (*0-85234-216-0*, Pub. by Evangelical Pr) P & R Pubng.
— Jackie. 192p. (Orig.). (J). (gr. 7-12). 1981. pap. 3.50 (*0-8007-8406-5*) J Benton Bks.
— Kari. 192p. (J). (gr. 7-12). 1984. pap. 3.50 (*0-8007-8491-X*) J Benton Bks.
— Lefty. 192p. (Orig.). (J). (gr. 7-12). 1981. pap. 3.50 (*0-8007-8401-4*) J Benton Bks.

An Asterisk (*) at the beginning of an entry indicates that the title is appearing for the first time.

— Looking for the Answer. 1983. pap. 2.99 (*0-85234-202-0*, Pub. by Evangelical Pr) P & R Pubng.
— Lori, No. 3. 176p. (Orig.). (YA). (gr. 7-12). 1990. reprint ed. mass mkt. 3.50 (*0-8007-8385-9*) J Benton Bks.
— Losing Touch with the Living God (Malachi) (Welwyn Commentary Ser.). 1985. pap. 8.99 (*0-85234-212-8*, Pub. by Evangelical Pr) P & R Pubng.
— New Hope Series, 10 bks., Set. 2004p. (J). (gr. 3-12). 35.00 (*0-9635411-1-0*) J Benton Bks.
— One Lady at a Time. 126p. 1993. pap. text 3.50 (*0-9635411-0-2*) J Benton Bks.
— One World, One Way. 1992. pap. 4.99 (*0-85234-294-2*, Pub. by Evangelical Pr) P & R Pubng.
— Patti, No. 2. 192p. (Orig.). (YA). (gr. 7-12). 1990. reprint ed. mass mkt. 3.50 (*0-8007-8346-8*) J Benton Bks.
— Sheila. 192p. (J). (gr. 7-12). 1982. pap. 3.50 (*0-8007-8419-7*) J Benton Bks.
***Benton, John.** Slandering the Angels. 1999. pap. 11.99 (*0-85234-424-4*) Evangelical Pr.
Benton, John. Straightening Out the Self. 1997. pap. text 11.99 (*0-85234-384-1*, Pub. by Evangelical Pr) P & R Pubng.
— Tasha. 176p. (Orig.). (J). 1994. pap. 3.50 (*0-9635411-2-9*) J Benton Bks.
— Terri. 192p. (J). (gr. 7-12). 1981. pap. 3.50 (*0-8007-8408-1*) J Benton Bks.
Benton, John & Peet, John. God's Riches. 64p. 1992. student ed. 11.99 (*0-85151-601-7*) Banner of Truth.
Benton, John F. Culture, Power & Personality in Medieval France. Bisson, Thomas N., ed. 544p. 1991. 70.00 (*1-85285-030-2*) Hambledon Press.
Benton, John F., ed. Self & Society in Medieval France: The Memories of Abbot Guibert of Nogent. (Medieval Academy Reprints for Teaching Ser.). 260p. (C). 1984. reprint ed. pap. text 12.95 (*0-8020-6550-3*) U of Toronto Pr.
Benton, John H. Benton. David Benton, Jr. & Saral Bingham, Their Ancestors & Descendants & Other Ancestral Lines. (Illus.). 88p. 1997. reprint ed. pap. 17.00 (*0-8328-7505-8*); reprint ed. lib. bdg. 27.00 (*0-8328-7504-X*) Higginson Bk Co.
Benton, Josephine M. Martha & Mary: A Woman's Relationship to Her Home. (C). 1947. pap. 4.00 (*0-87574-036-7*) Pendle Hill.
Benton, Josiah H., Jr. A Notable Libel Case: The Criminal Prosecution of Theodore Lyman Jr. by Daniel Webster in the Supreme Judicial Court of Massachusetts November Term, 1828. (Illus.). 1985. reprint ed. lib. bdg. 20.00 (*0-8377-0347-6*, Rothman) W S Hein.
— Samuel Blade Benton, His Ancestors & Descendants, 1620-1901. (Illus.). 366p. 1988. reprint ed. pap. 55.00 (*0-8328-0243-3*); reprint ed. lib. bdg. 63.00 (*0-8328-0242-5*) Higginson Bk Co.
Benton, Josiah H. Warning Out in New England. LC 70-137370. (Select Bibliographies Reprint Ser.). 1977. 16.95 (*0-8369-5571-4*) Ayer.
— Warning Out in New England, 1656-1817. 131p. 1995. reprint ed. pap. 17.50 (*0-8328-4492-6*); reprint ed. pap. 17.50 (*0-8328-4610-4*); reprint ed. lib. bdg. 27.50 (*0-8328-4491-8*); reprint ed. lib. bdg. 27.50 (*0-8328-4609-0*) Higginson Bk Co.
Benton, Jude. The Poet from Prison. 32p. (Orig.). 1994. pap. 6.00 (*1-878149-27-X*) Counterpoint Pub.
Benton, Judee K. Developing Skills for International Trade: A Practical Guide for Export Training. 2nd ed. 230p. 1992. pap. text. write for info. (*1-884023-50-9*) Team Exports.
— Developing Skills for International Trade: A Practical Guide for Export Training & Skills Workbook & Answer Book. 2nd ed. 230p. 1992. pap. text. write for info. (*1-884023-52-5*) Team Exports.
— Developing Skills for International Trade: Skills Workbook & Answer Book. 2nd ed. 166p. 1992. pap., wbk. ed. write for info. (*1-884023-51-7*) Team Exports.
***Benton, Karla.** Nurse in Love. 336p. 1999. 20.99 (*1-85389-954-2*) Ulverscroft.
***Benton, Kenneth.** Greek Fire. large type ed. LC 99-52470. (Nightingale Ser.). 2000. pap. 20.95 (*0-7838-8864-3*, G K Hall Lrg Type) Mac Lib Ref.
— Red Hen Conspiracy. 336p. 1999. 20.99 (*1-85389-986-0*) Ulverscroft.
— A Single Monstrous Act. large type ed. 416p. 1998. pap. 17.99 (*0-7089-5336-0*) Ulverscroft.
Benton, Kenneth. Sole Agent. large type ed. (Dales Large Print Ser.). 368p. 1998. pap. 19.99 (*1-85389-812-0*, Dales) Ulverscroft.
— Time for Murder. large type ed. 352p. 1998. pap. 17.99 (*0-7089-5396-4*, Linford) Ulverscroft.
***Benton, Kenneth.** Twenty-Fourth Level. large type ed. 352p. 1999. pap. 20.99 (*1-85389-909-7*) Ulverscroft.
Benton, Kitty. Easy Guide to Serging Fine Fabrics. LC 96-2941. (Sewing Companion Library). (Illus.). 112p. 1997. pap. 17.95 (*1-56158-090-2*, 070214) Taunton.
Benton, Lauren A. Invisible Factories: The Informal Economy & Industrial Development in Spain. LC 89-4543. (SUNY Series in the Anthropology of Work). 231p. (C). 1990. pap. text 24.95 (*0-7914-0224-X*) State U NY Pr.
Benton, Linda. I See Patterns, Vol. 3706. (Emergent Reader Bks.). (Illus.). 8p. (J). (gr. k-2). 1995. pap. 1.75 (*0-916119-97-1*) Creat Teach Pr.
— I See Patterns, Vol. 3763. (Emergent Reader Big Bks.). (Illus.). 8p. (J). (gr. k-2). 1996. pap. 8.98 (*1-57471-101-6*) Creat Teach Pr.
Benton, Linda, et al. Math Resource Guide, Vol. 3499. Corker, Jeanne & Williams, Rozanne L., eds. (Learn to Read Resource Guide Ser.). (Illus.). 80p. 1996. pap. text 25.98 (*1-57471-146-6*, 3499) Creat Teach Pr.
Benton, Lisa. The Presidio: From Army Post to National Park. LC 97-51930. (Illus.). 288p. 1998. text 29.95 (*1-55553-335-3*) NE U Pr.
Benton, Lisa & Short, John R., eds. Environmental Discourse & Practice. LC 98-34506. 320p. 1999. 59.95 (*0-631-21113-6*); pap. 26.95 (*0-631-21114-4*) Blackwell Pubs.
***Benton, Lisa M. & Short, John R., eds.** Environmental Discourses: A Reader. LC 99-17019. 448p. 1999. 59.95 (*0-631-21636-7*) Blackwell Pubs.
— Environmental Discourses: A Reader. 448p. 2000. pap. 26.95 (*0-631-21637-5*) Blackwell Pubs.
Benton, M. J. Dinosaurs. LC 97-51121. (Illus.). 63p. (J). (gr. 3-7). 1998. 16.95 (*0-7534-5131-X*) LKC.
Benton, M. J., jt. auth. see Haslam, Andrew.
Benton, Major T., jt. auth. see Yoder, Susan.
Benton, Mathew. Introduction to Composite Materials. LC 98-88638. 54p. 1997. pap. write for info. (*0-9668123-4-4*) Mission Pr.
***Benton, Megan.** In Beauty & the Book: Fine Editions & Cultural Distinction in America. LC 99-38198. (Illus.). 336p. 2000. 30.00 (*0-300-08213-4*) Yale U Pr.
Benton, Megan L., jt. ed. see Gutjahr, Paul C.
***Benton, Michael.** Encyclopedia of Awesome Dinosaurs. (Illus.). 2000. 15.95 (*0-7613-0846-6*, Copper Beech Bks) Millbrook Pr.
— Studies in the Spectator Role: Literature, Painting & Pedagogy. LC 99-41947. 224p. 2000. pap. write for info. (*0-415-20828-9*) Routledge.
***Benton, Michael, et al, eds.** The Age of Dinosaurs in Russia & Mongolia. LC 99-16743. (Illus.). 550p. 2000. 110.00 (*0-521-55476-4*) Cambridge U Pr.
Benton, Michael J. Dinosaur & Other Prehistoric Animal Factfinder. LC 92-53119. (Illus.). 256p. (J). (gr. 4-8). 1993. pap. 14.95 (*1-85697-802-8*, Kingfisher) LKC.
— The Dinosaur Encyclopedia. Barish, Wendy, ed. (Illus.). 192p. (J). (gr. 4 up). 1984. pap. 7.95 (*0-671-51046-0*) S&S Bks Yung.
— Dinosaurios y Otros Animales Prehistoricos-Dinosaurs & Other Prehistoric Animals Factfinder: Y Otros Animales Prehistoricos (Dinosaurs & Other Prehistoric Animals Factfinder) Ignacio de la Pena, Luis, tr. (SPA., Illus.). 256p. (J). (gr. 4-6). 1995. pap. 12.95 (*1-85697-542-8*) LKC.
— Dinosaurs. LC 93-19072. (Picturepedia Ser.). (Illus.). (J). (gr. 3-7). 1993. 12.95 (*1-56458-382-1*) DK Pub Inc.
— Dinosaurs. LC 94-9362. (First Facts Ser.). (Illus.). 128p. (J). (ps-3). 1994. pap. 7.95 (*1-85697-524-X*) LKC.
— Dinosaurs. LC 90-30837. (Picture Pockets Ser.). (Illus.). 96p. (J). (gr. 1-5). 1992. mass mkt. 8.00 (*0-671-75999-X*) S&S Bks Yung.
— Historical Atlas of the Dinosaurs. 144p. 1997. pap. 16.95 (*0-14-051336-1*) Viking Penguin.
— The Penguin Historical Atlas of the Dinosaurs. 144p. 1996. pap. 16.95 (*0-614-19893-3*) Viking Penguin.
— Vertebrate Palaeontology. 246p. (C). 1990. pap. text 24.95 (*0-04-566002-6*) Routledge.
Benton, Mike. The Complete Guide to Computer Camps & Workshops. LC 83-15578. 208p. 1984. pap. write for info. (*0-672-52796-0*) Macmillan.
— Dinosaurs Existed? LC 94-16252. (How Do We Know? Ser.). (Illus.). 48p. (J). (gr. 4-8). 1995. lib. bdg. 24.26 (*0-8114-3878-3*) Raintree Steck-V.
Benton, Mike & Firefly, Rufus T. White Trash Gardening. LC 95-45772. (Illus.). 160p. (Orig.). 1996. pap. 14.95 (*0-87833-907-8*) Taylor Pub.
Benton, Nathaniel S. History of Herkemer County, N.Y. 497p. 1993. reprint ed. lib. bdg. 52.00 (*0-8328-3074-7*) Higginson Bk Co.
Benton, P. A. Languages & Peoples of Bornu, 2 vols., Vol. 1. 2nd ed. 304p. 1968. 65.00 (*0-7146-1635-4*, Pub. by F Cass Pubs) Intl Spec Bk.
— Languages & Peoples of Bornu, 2 vols., Vol. 2. 2nd ed. 373p. 1968. 45.00 (*0-7146-1626-5*, Pub. by F Cass Pubs) Intl Spec Bk.
— Sultanate of Bornu. Shultze, A., tr. 401p. 1968. reprint ed. 55.00 (*0-7146-1717-2*, Pub. by F Cass Pubs) Intl Spec Bk.
***Benton, Peter.** Special Needs & the Beginning Teacher. 2000. pap. 24.95 (*0-304-70674-4*) Continuum.
Benton, Peter, et al. A Fourth Poetry Book. 128p. (J). (gr. 5-7). 1987. pap. 8.95 (*0-19-918151-9*) OUP.
Benton-Powers, Susan & Paterson, Lee T. Sexual Harassment: What You Need to Know. LC 94-68537. (Fifty-Minute Ser.). 106p. (Orig.). 1992. pap. 15.95 (*1-56052-312-3*) Crisp Pubns.
Benton, Richard. Bedlam Patterns: Love & the Idea of Madness in Poe's Fiction. 1979. pap. 2.75 (*0-910556-13-X*) Enoch Pratt.
Benton, Richard A. Pangasinan Dictionary. LC 75-152456. (Hawaii University, Honolulu, Pacific & Asian Linguistics Institute Ser.). 329p. reprint ed. pap. 102.00 (*0-608-11014-0*, 200797500068) Bks Demand.
— Pangasinan Reference Grammar. McKaughan, Howard P., ed. LC 72-152458. (PALI Language Texts: Philippines Ser.). 286p. (C). reprint ed. 88.70 (*0-8357-9826-7*, 201721300004) Bks Demand.
— Spoken Pangasinan. LC 79-152457. (University of Hawaii, Honolulu. Pacific & Asian Linguistics Institute Ser.). 729p. reprint ed. pap. 200.00 (*0-608-11023-X*, 201721400004) Bks Demand.
Benton, Rita. The Elf of Discontent & Other Plays. LC 79-50017. (One-Act Plays in Reprint Ser.). 1980. reprint ed. 28.00 (*0-8486-2041-0*) Roth Pub Inc.
Benton, Robert. Basic Structural Detailing. LC 88-34168. 298p. 1989. reprint ed. pap. 92.40 (*0-608-03607-2*, 206443000009) Bks Demand.
Benton, Robert J. Kant's "Second Critique" & the Problem of Transcendental Arguments. 1978. pap. text 81.00 (*90-247-2055-9*) Kluwer Academic.
Benton, Russell E. & St. Paul University Press. Emma Naea Rooke, 1836-1885: Beloved Queen of Hawaii. (Illus.). 76p. 1988. lib. bdg. 49.95 (*0-88946-039-6*) E Mellen.
Benton, Scott, jt. auth. see Laasch, Jack.
* **Benton, Sharan A.** Wisdom Keepers: A Resource for Faith Sharing among Seniors. 128p. 2000. pap. 8.95 (*0-88489-626-9*) St Marys.
***Benton, Stephen A.** Saint-Frances Guide to Outpatient Medicine. LC 99-24904. 550p. 1999. 19.95 (*0-683-30187-X*) Lppncott W & W.
— Selected Papers on Three-Dimensional Displays. LC 00-34436. (Milestone Ser.). 2000. write for info. (*0-8194-3893-6*) SPIE.
***Benton, Stephen A., ed.** Practical Holography XIII. 264p. 1999. pap. text 72.00 (*0-8194-3108-7*) SPIE.
Benton, Stephen A., ed. Practical Holography XII, Vol. 3293. 276p. 1998. 69.00 (*0-8194-2733-0*) SPIE.
Benton, Stephen A. & Trout, T. John, eds. Practical Holography XI & Holographic Materials III, Vol. 3011. LC 97-175316. 378p. 1997. 69.00 (*0-8194-2422-6*) SPIE.
Benton, Ted. Natural Relations? Ecology, Animal Rights & Social Justice. 280p. (C). 1993. pap. 19.00 (*0-86091-590-5*, A9732, Pub. by Verso) Norton.
— Philosophy & the New Right. (Pluto Perspectives Ser.). (C). 1996. text 45.00 (*0-7453-0503-2*); pap. text 15.95 (*0-7453-0504-0*) Westview.
Benton, Ted, ed. The Greening of Marxism. LC 96-3419. (Democracy & Ecology Ser.). 1996. pap. text 18.95 (*1-57230-119-8*, 0119); lib. bdg. 42.95 (*1-57230-118-X*, 0118) Guilford Pubns.
Benton, Ted, jt. ed. see Redclift, Michael.
Benton, Thomas. Bank of the United States. 1972. 59.95 (*0-87968-701-0*) Gordon Pr.
— Uncle Jeb & the Spirit. 1997. 15.95 (*1-57980-000-9* BUNCLE) Claitors.
Benton, Thomas H. An Artist in America. 4th rev. ed. LC 82-20279. (Illus.). 418p. 1983. pap. 24.95 (*0-8262-0399-X*) U of Mo Pr.
— Speech of Mr. Benton of Missouri on the Oregon Question Delivered in the Senate of the United States, May 22, 25, 28, 1846. LC 98-15111. 98p. 1998. pap. 19.95 (*0-87770-610-7*) Ye Galleon.
***Benton, Thomas H.** Speech of Mr. Benton of Missouri on the Oregon Question Delivered in the Senate of the United States, May, 22, 25, 28, 1846. LC 98-15111. 98p. 1998. pap. 14.95 (*0-87770-639-5*) Ye Galleon.
Benton, Thomas H., ed. Abridgement of the Debates of Congress, 16 vols. reprint ed. lib. bdg. 2880.00 (*0-404-00770-8*) AMS Pr.
Benton, Virginia P. This Faith, What Is It? A Seed Measure of the Substance of God. LC 97-77661. (Illus.). 117p. 1997. pap. 9.99 (*0-9661855-0-1*) Bendita Casa.
Benton, Walter. This Is My Beloved. 1949. 20.00 (*0-394-40458-0*) Knopf.
Benton, Wilbourn E., ed. 1787: Drafting the U. S. Constitution, 2 vols., Set. LC 84-40563. 1598p. 1986. 89.50 (*0-89096-217-0*) Tex A&M Univ Pr.
Benton, Wilbourn E. & Grimm, George, eds. Nuremberg: German Views of the War Trials. LC 55-5739. 240p. reprint ed. pap. 74.40 (*0-8357-8976-4*, 203341000036) Bks Demand.
Benton, William. Marmalade. LC 97-74601. (Illus.). 52p. 1997. pap. 11.95 (*0-9660170-0-5*) G Adams Gal.
***Benton, William, et al.** Signs in the Heavens: A Message for Our Time. (Illus.). 224p. 2000. pap. 18.00 (*1-888604-12-3*) SunShine CO.
Benton, William, ed. & intro. see Bishop, Elizabeth.
Benton, William A. Whig Loyalism: An Aspect of Political Ideology in the American Revolutionary Era. LC 69-19433. 231p. 1975. 32.50 (*0-8386-7338-4*) Fairleigh Dickinson.
Benton, William G. Where the Water Hits the Wheel: Fifteen Sermons on the Great Beliefs of the Christian Faith. LC 93-3849. 136p. 1993. pap. 11.00 (*1-880837-34-X*) Smyth & Helwys.
Benton, William, Museum of Art Staff. Bulletin, Vol. 1, No. 1. 28p. 1972. write for info. (*0-918386-07-1*) W Benton Mus.
— Bulletin, Vol. 1, No. 2. 24p. 1973. 1.00 (*0-918386-10-1*) W Benton Mus.
— Bulletin, Vol. 1, No. 3. 32p. 1974. 1.00 (*0-918386-14-4*) W Benton Mus.
— Bulletin, Vol. 1, No. 4. 38p. 1976. 1.00 (*0-918386-19-5*) W Benton Mus.
— Bulletin, Vol. 1, No. 5. 48p. 1977. 1.00 (*0-918386-24-1*) W Benton Mus.
— Bulletin, Vol. 1, No. 6. 32p. 1978. 1.00 (*0-918386-25-X*) W Benton Mus.
— Bulletin, Vol. 1, No. 7. 31p. 1979. 1.00 (*0-918386-30-6*) W Benton Mus.
Bentor, Y. K., ed. Marine Phosphorites. (Special Publications: N0. 29). 247p. 1980. 33.50 (*0-918985-09-9*) SEPM.
Bentor, Yael. Consecration of Images & Stupas in Indo-Tibetan Tantric Buddhism. LC 96-33876. (Brill's Indological Library: No. 11). xxii, 416p. 1996. 165.50 (*90-04-10541-7*) Brill Academic Pubs.
Bentosino, Harmony, ed. see Emmons, T. Louis.
***Bentov, Itzhak.** Brief Tour of Higher Consciousness: A Cosmic Book on the Mechanics of Creation. 2nd ed. LC 00-24448. (Illus.). 144p. 2000. pap. text 12.95 (*0-89281-814-X*, Destiny Bks) Inner Tradit.
Bentov, Itzhak. Stalking the Wild Pendulum: On the Mechanics of Consciousness. 208p. 1988. pap. 12.95 (*0-89281-202-8*, Destiny Bks) Inner Tradit.
Bentovim, Arnon. Trauma-Organized Systems: Physical & Sexual Abuse in Families. rev. ed. 148p. 1992. pap. text 23.00 (*1-85575-012-0*, Pub. by H Karnac Bks Ltd) Other Pr LLC.
Bentsen, Steve, ed. see Seale, Jan E.
Bentsen, William, ed. Appeals & ISAF Cases. (Illus.). 200p. 1998. pap. text 25.00 (*1-882502-53-1*) US Sail Assn.
Bentson, George J., et al. Discrimination in Financial Services: A Special Issue of the Journal of Financial Services Research. LC 97-9972. 1997. lib. bdg. 131.00 (*0-7923-9885-8*) Kluwer Academic.
Bentson, Marilyn & Mitchell, Elisabeth. Talk Time Handbook: Conversations Sessions for Volunteer Facilitators & Limited English Speaking Participants. (Illus.). 105p. 1998. reprint ed. pap. text 20.00 (*0-7881-4223-2*) DIANE Pub.
Bentson, Randolph. Inside Linux: A Look at Operating System Development. 275p. (Orig.). (C). 1996. pap. 22.00 (*0-916151-89-1*) Specialized Sys.
***Bentsur, Eytan.** Making Peace: A First Hand Account of the Arab-Israeli Peace Process. 2000. write for info. (*0-275-96876-6*, Praeger Pubs) Greenwood.
Bentur, A., et al. Steel Corrosion in Concrete: Fundamentals & Civil Engineering Practice. LC 98-150903. (Illus.). 208p. (C). 1998. 100.00 (*0-419-22530-7*, E & FN Spon) Routledge.
Bentur, Mindess. Fibre-Reinforced Cementitious Composites. 1990. mass mkt. 191.50 (*1-85166-393-2*) Elsevier.
Bentwich, Norman D. Solomon Schechter. 1964. 6.00 (*0-8381-3105-0*) USCJE.
Bentz, Audrey A. Am I Fun to Live With? 1993. pap. 6.95 (*1-55673-590-1*, 7989) CSS OH.
Bentz, Dale M. Reflections on a Lifetime. 128p. 1991. pap. 9.95 (*0-944266-12-6*) Maecenas Pr.
Bentz, Edna M. If I Can You Can Decipher Germanic Record. (DAN, GER & LAT.). 85p. 1982. spiral bd. 16.50 (*0-9615420-0-4*) E M Bentz.
Bentz, Joe, ed. Viral Fusion Mechanisms. 544p. 1992. lib. bdg. 249.00 (*0-8493-5606-7*, QR454) CRC Pr.
Bentz, John D. Descendants of Martin Benz-Dorothea Schmeller. (Illus.). 310p. 1983. pap. 15.00 (*0-9612438-0-5*) J D Bentz.
Bentz, Joseph. A Son Comes Home. LC 99-6412. 320p. 1999. pap. text 10.99 (*0-7642-2207-4*) Bethany Hse.
— Song of Fire. 448p. (Orig.). 1995. pap. 12.99 (*0-7852-7882-6*) Nelson.
Bentz, Michael L., ed. Pediatric Plastic Surgery. LC 96-53379. 1099p. (C). 1999. 295.00 (*0-8385-7820-9*, A-7820-2, Apple Lange Med) McGraw.
Bentz, Rick & Allison, Christine. Street Smarts for Kids: What Parents Must Know to Keep Their Children Safe. LC 99-24417. 1999. pap. 10.95 (*0-449-91237-X*) Ballantine Pub Grp.
Bentz, Robert J. Opportunity Is Calling Vol. 1: How to Start Your Own Successful 900 Number. (Orig.). 1993. pap. 29.95 (*0-9637758-5-5*) ATS Pubng.
Bentz, Suzzane, ed. see Weston, Victoria.
Bentz, Valerie M. Becoming Mature: Childhood Ghosts & Spirits in Adult Life. (Communication & Social Order Ser.). 296p. 1989. pap. text 28.95 (*0-202-30359-4*); lib. bdg. 51.95 (*0-202-30358-6*) Aldine de Gruyter.
Bentz, Valerie M. & Mayes, Philip E., eds. Women's Power & Roles As Portrayed in Visual Images of Women in the Arts & Mass Media. LC 93-5817. (Illus.). 240p. 1993. text 89.95 (*0-7734-9329-8*) E Mellen.
Bentz, Valerie M. & Shapiro, Jeremy J. Mindful Inquiry in Social Research. LC 98-19720. 216p. 1998. 56.00 (*0-7619-0408-5*); pap. write for info. (*0-7619-0409-3*) Sage.
Bentz, William F., jt. ed. see Sterling, Robert R.
Bentzen. Seeing Young Children. 4th ed. (Early Childhood Education Ser.). (C). 2000. pap. 35.95 (*0-7668-1102-6*) Delmar.
Bentzen, Warren R. Seeing Young Children. 3rd ed. (Early Childhood Education Ser.). 1997. 10.50 (*0-8273-7666-9*) Delmar.
— Seeing Young Children: A Guide for Observing & Recording Behavior. LC 85-1564. 272p. (C). 1985. pap. 27.00 (*0-8273-2329-8*) Delmar.
— Seeing Young Children: A Guide to Observing & Recording Behavior. 2nd ed. 269p. 1991. pap. 28.50 (*0-8273-4477-5*) Delmar.
— Seeing Young Children: A Guide to Observing & Recording Behavior. 2nd ed. 269p. 1991. pap., teacher ed. 9.50 (*0-8273-4478-3*) Delmar.
— Seeing Young Children: A Guide to Observing & Recording Behavior. 3rd ed. (Illus.). 384p. (C). 1996. mass mkt. 40.95 (*0-8273-7665-0*) Delmar.
Bentzon. The Condition of Woman in the United States: A Traveller's Notes. Alger, Abby L., tr. 285p. 1977. 18.95 (*0-8369-2638-2*) Ayer.
***Benua, Laura.** Phonological Relations Between Words. LC 00-37123. (Outstanding Dissertations in Linguistics Ser.). 2000. write for info. (*0-8153-3810-4*) Garland.
Benuigui, L. Gilles, jt. auth. see Chakrabarti, Bikas K.
Benum, Sara H., jt. auth. see Bland, Jeffrey S.
Benum, Sara H., ed. see Bland, Jeffrey S.
Benumof, Jonathan L. Anesthesia & Uncommon Diseases. 4th ed. Day, Lesley, ed. LC 97-28926. (Illus.). 672p. 1997. text 95.00 (*0-7216-8673-7*, W B Saunders Co) Harcrt Hlth Sci Grp.
— Anesthesia for Thoracic Surgery. 2nd ed. LC 93-42770. (Illus.). 1994. text 115.00 (*0-7216-4467-8*, W B Saunders Co) Harcrt Hlth Sci Grp.
— Clinical Procedures in Anesthesia & Intensive Care. (Illus.). 992p. 1992. text 158.00 (*0-397-50950-2*) Lppncott W & W.
Benumof, Jonathan L., ed. Airway Management: Principles & Practice. (Illus.). 952p. (C). (gr. 13). 1995. text 150.00 (*0-8151-0625-4*, 24614) Mosby Inc.
Benumof, Jonathan L. & Saidman, Lawrence J. Anesthesia & Perioperative Complications. (Illus.). 704p. (C). (gr. 13). 1991. text 120.00 (*0-8016-0586-5*, 00586) Mosby Inc.

B

Benumof, Jonathan L. & Saidman, Lawrence J., eds. Anesthesia & Perioperative Complications. 2nd ed. LC 99-22920. (Illus.). 640p. 1999. text 129.00 (0-8151-2619-0, 31640) Mosby Inc.

***Benun, Llise.** Self-Promotion Online. (Illus.). 144p. 2000. pap. 29.99 (1-58180-069-X, North Lght Bks) F & W Pubns Inc.

Benur, Daniel. Science Validates Spiritual Healing. (Healing Research Ser.). (Illus.). 350p. 1997. write for info. (1-886785-11-2) Vision Pub.

Benus, Jacob M., et al. Self-Employment Programs: A New Reemployment Strategy, Final Report on the UI Self-Employment Demonstration. (Illus.). 220p. (C). 1997. reprint ed. pap. text 40.00 (0-7881-4574-6) DIANE Pub.

Benuska, Lee, ed. Loma Prieta Earthquake of October 17, 1989, Reconnaissance Report. (Illus.). 450p. 1990. pap. 30.00 (0-943198-71-2, 90-01) Earthquake Eng.

Benuzzi, A. & Zaldivar, J. M., eds. Safety of Chemical Batch Reactors & Storage Tanks. (C). 1991. text 208.50 (0-7923-1233-3) Kluwer Academic.

Benuzzi, Felice. No Picnic on Mount Kenya. LC 98-70651. (Adventure Library: No. 16). (Illus.). 240p. 1998. reprint ed. lib. bdg. 32.50 (1-885283-15-6) Advent Library.

***Benuzzi, Felice.** No Picnic on Mount Kenya. LC 98-50951 . (Illus.). 240p. 1998. reprint ed. pap. 14.95 (1-55821-876-9) Lyons Pr.

Benvenga, Nancy. Healing the Wounds of Emotional Abuse: The Journey Worth the Risk. LC 95-72648. 96p. (Orig.). 1996. pap. 6.95 (1-878718-30-4, Resurrection Pr) Catholic Bk Pub.

— The Lector's Ministry: Your Guide to Proclaiming the Word. (RVC Liturgical Ser.). 48p. (Orig.). 1990. pap. 3.95 (0-9623410-8-8, Resurrection Pr) Catholic Bk Pub.

Benvenga, Nancy, ed. The Great Seasons: Your Guide to Celebrating. (RVC Liturgical Ser.). 48p. (Orig.). 1990. pap. 3.95 (0-9623410-4-5, Resurrection Pr) Catholic Bk Pub.

— The Liturgy of the Hours: Your Guide to Praying at Home & in Your Parish Community. (RVC Liturgical Ser.). 48p. (Orig.). 1990. pap. 3.95 (0-9623410-7-X, Resurrection Pr) Catholic Bk Pub.

— Our Liturgy: Your Guide to the Basics. LC 89-92734. (RVC Liturgical Ser.). 64p. (Orig.). 1990. pap. 4.25 (0-9623410-1-0, Resurrection Pr) Catholic Bk Pub.

Benvenga, Nancy, ed. see Torrell, Dolores L.

Benveniste, A., et al. Stochastic Approximations & Adaptive Algorithms. Balakrishnan, A. V. et al, eds. Wilson, S. S., tr. from FRE. (Applications of Mathematics Ser.: Vol. 22). (Illus.). xi, 365p. 1990. 98.95 (0-387-52894-6) Spr-Verlag.

Benveniste, Albert & Hoetis, Themistocles, eds. Zero: A Review of Literature & Art, Nos. 1[00ad]7. (Avant Garde Magazines Ser.). 1974. reprint ed. 28.95 (0-405-01753-7) Ayer.

Benveniste, Asa. Invisible Ink. 16p. (Orig.). 1990. pap. text 4.00 (0-935162-09-7) Singing Horse.

— Throw Out the Lifeline, Lay Out the Course: Poems 1965-1985. 144p. 1983. pap. 17.95 (0-85646-098-2, Pub. by Anvil Press) Dufour.

Benveniste, Debra. Diagnosis & Treatment of Sociopaths & Clients with Sociopathic Traits. LC 95-72227. 208p. 1996. text 49.95 (1-57224-047-4) New Harbinger.

Benveniste, Emile. Problemes de Linguistique Generale. (Tel Ser.). (FRE.). 356p. 1966. pap. 17.95 (2-07-029338-6) Schoenhof.

— Problemes de Linguistique Generale. (Tel Ser.). (FRE.). 286p. 1974. pap. 15.95 (2-07-020420-0) Schoenhof.

— Problems in General Linguistics. (Miami Linguistics Ser.: No. 8). 317p. 1973. pap. 25.00 (0-87024-310-1) U of Miami Pr.

Benveniste, Etty N., jt. ed. see Ransohoff, Richard M.

Benveniste, Guy. Bureaucracy. pap. write for info. (0-87835-059-4) Thomson Learn.

Benveniste, Guy. Mastering the Politics of Planning: Crafting Credible Plans & Policies That Make a Difference. LC 89-8189. (Public Administration-Management Ser.). 336p. 1989. 33.95 (1-55542-167-9) Jossey-Bass.

— Professionalizing the Organization: Reducing Bureaucracy to Enhance Effectiveness. LC 86-27567. (Jossey-Bass Management Ser.). 316p. reprint ed. pap. 98.00 (0-7837-6532-0, 204564400007) Bks Demand.

— The Twenty-First Century Organization: Analyzing Current Trends, Imagining the Future. LC 93-35549. (Public Administration Series, Nonprofit Sector Series, & Management Ser.). 336p. 1994. 33.95 (1-55542-626-3) Jossey-Bass.

Benvenisti, Eyal. The International Law of Occupation. LC 92-15185. 248p. (C). 1993. text 39.50 (0-691-05666-8, Pub. by Princeton U Pr) Cal Prin Full Svc.

Benvenisti, Meron. City of Stone: The Hidden History of Jerusalem. LC 96-14965. (Illus.). 283p. 1996. 35.00 (0-520-20521-9, Pub. by U CA Pr) Cal Prin Full Svc.

— City of Stone: The Hidden History of Jerusalem. (Illus.). 283p. 1998. pap. 16.95 (0-520-20768-8, Pub. by U CA Pr) Cal Prin Full Svc.

— Intimate Enemies: Jews & Arabs in a Shared Land. LC 95-1933. (Illus.). 250p. 1995. 30.00 (0-520-08567-1, Pub. by U CA Pr) Cal Prin Full Svc.

— Jerusalem, the Torn City. LC 76-12226. 439p. 1976. reprint ed. pap. 136.10 (0-7837-2978-2, 205747600006) Bks Demand.

— Sacred Landscape: The Buried History of the Holy Land Since 1948. Kaufman-Lacusta, Maxine, tr. from HEB. LC 99-37874. 417p. 2000. 35.00 (0-520-21154-5, Pub. by U CA Pr) Cal Prin Full Svc.

Benvenisty, David. Shmuel Bet. (Illus.). 63p. pap. 3.25 (965-17-0059-9, 14-524) Board Jewish Educ.

Benvenuto, Bice. Concerning the Rites of Psychoanalysis: or The Villa of the Mysteries. LC 95-118277. 261p. (C). 1994. pap. 19.99 (0-415-91256-3, B7265) Routledge.

— Concerning the Rites of Psychoanalysis: or The Villa of the Mysteries. 261p. (C). (gr. 13). 1994. 70.00 (0-415-91255-5, B7261) Routledge.

Benvenuto, Bice & Kennedy, Roger G. The Works of Jacques Lacan: An Introduction. LC 86-3847. 237p. 1986. 27.50 (0-685-13555-1); pap. 12.95 (0-685-13556-X) St Martin.

Benvenuto, Darrell, ed. see Carspecken, Margaret.

Benvenuto, E. An Introduction to the History of Structural Mechanics Pt. I: Statics & Resistance of Solids. 280p. 1990. 79.95 (0-387-96227-1) Spr-Verlag.

— An Introduction to the History of Structural Mechanics Pt. II: Vaulted Structures & Elastic Systems. (Illus.). 232p. 1990. 79.95 (0-387-97187-4) Spr-Verlag.

Benvenuto, Richard. Amy Lowell. (Twayne's United States Authors Ser.). 189p. 1985. 22.95 (0-8057-7436-X, Twayne) Mac Lib Ref.

— Emily Bronte. (English Authors Ser.: No. 326). 160p. (C). 1982. 28.95 (0-8057-6813-0) Macmillan.

***Benvie, Niall.** The Art of Nature Photography: Perfect Your Pictures In-Camera & In-Computer. (Illus.). 160p. 2000. pap. 24.95 (0-8174-3311-2) Watsn-Guptill.

***Benvie, Sam.** The Encyclopedia of North American Trees. (Illus.). 304p. 2000. 35.00 (1-55209-408-1) Firefly Bks Ltd.

Benvie, Sam, jt. auth. see Noordhuis, Klaas T.

Benvie, Sam, jt. ed. see Van der Horst, Arend.

Benward. Advanced Sight Seeing & Ear Training. 1989. teacher ed. 30.62 (0-697-03869-6) McGraw.

— Ear Training. 6th ed. 256p. 1999. pap. 43.75 (0-07-228770-5) McGraw.

— Introduction to Ear Training & Sights. 2nd ed. 1992. teacher ed. 14.06 (0-697-10643-8) McGraw.

— Practical Beginning Theory. 8th ed. 1999. 31.00 (0-07-234797-X) McGraw.

Benward & Kolosick. Ear Training Technique. 5th ed. 1995. teacher ed. 29.37 (0-697-28785-8, WCB McGr Hill) McGrw-H Hghr Educ.

Benward, Bruce. Advanced Sightsinging & Ear Training: Strategies & Applications. 192p. (C). 1989. text. write for info. (0-697-03868-8) Brown & Benchmark.

— Music in Theory & Practice, Vol. 1. 5th ed. 432p. (C). 1993. spiral bd. write for info. (0-318-69096-9) Brown & Benchmark.

Benward, Bruce & Carr. Sightsinging Complete. 6th ed. 320p. 1998. pap. text 46.56 (0-697-34395-2) McGraw.

Benward, Bruce & Carr, Maureen A. Sightsinging Complete. 5th ed. 336p. (C). 1991. text. write for info. (0-697-05845-X) Brown & Benchmark.

Benward, Bruce & Jackson. Practical Beginning Theory: A Fundamentals Worktext. 8th ed. 336p. 1999. pap. 38.75 (0-697-34397-9) McGraw.

Benward, Bruce & Jackson, Barbara. Practical Beginning Theory. 7th ed. 1992. teacher ed. 14.68 (0-697-10636-5, WCB McGr Hill) McGrw-H Hghr Educ.

Benward, Bruce & Jackson, Barbara S. Practical Beginning Theory. 7th ed. (C). 1991. audio. write for info. (0-697-10637-3) Brown & Benchmark.

— Practical Beginning Theory: A Fundamentals Worktext. 7th ed. 320p. (C). 1991. text. write for info. (0-697-10635-7) Brown & Benchmark.

Benward, Bruce & Kolosick, J. Timmothy. Ear Training: A Technique for Listening. 5th ed. 250p. (C). 1995. spiral bd. write for info. (0-697-25837-8) Brown & Benchmark.

Benward, Bruce & White, Gary. Music in Theory & Practice, Vol. I. 6th ed. 1997. teacher ed. 12.81 (0-697-28787-4, WCB McGr Hill) McGrw-H Hghr Educ.

— Music in Theory & Practice, Vol. II. 6th ed. 1998. teacher ed. write for info. (0-697-32875-9, WCB McGr Hill) McGrw-H Hghr Educ.

Benward, Bruce & White, Gary C. Music in Theory & Practice. 6th ed. 288p. (C). 1996. text, wbk. ed. 21.87 (0-697-28789-0) Brown & Benchmark.

— Music in Theory & Practice, 2. 6th ed. LC 96-83191. 416p. (C). 1997. text. write for info. (0-697-32874-0, WCB McGr Hill) McGrw-H Hghr Educ.

— Music in Theory & Practice, 2. 6th ed. 288p. (C). 1997. text, student ed. 21.87 (0-697-32876-7, WCB McGr Hill) McGrw-H Hghr Educ.

— Music in Theory & Practice, I. 5th ed. 288p. (C). 1992. text 26.87 (0-697-12532-7) Brown & Benchmark.

— Music in Theory & Practice, Vols. I-II. 5th ed. 256p. (C). 1992. text 26.87 (0-697-12528-9) Brown & Benchmark.

Benward, Bruce, et al. Introduction to Sightsinging & Ear Training. 2nd ed. 304p. (C). 1992. text. write for info. (0-697-10642-X) Brown & Benchmark.

Benward, Bruce, jt. auth. see White, Gary C.

Benward-Kolosick. Ear Training Technique Course. 5th ed. 1995. (0-697-33311-6, WCB McGr Hill) McGrw-H Hghr Educ.

Benware, Paul N. Lucas. (Comentario Biblico Portavoz Ser.). Orig. Title: Luke (Everyman's Bible Commentary). (SPA.). 152p. 1994. pap. 6.99 (0-8254-1059-2, Edit Portavoz) Kregel.

— Luke: Gospel of the Son of Man. (Everyman's Bible Commentaries Ser.). pap. 9.99 (0-8024-2074-5, 484) Moody.

— Panorama del Antiguo Testamento. (Comentario Biblico Portavoz Ser.). Orig. Title: Survey of the Old Testament (Everyman's Bible Commentary). (SPA.). 280p. 1994. pap. 8.99 (0-8254-1060-6, Edit Portavoz) Kregel.

— Panorama del Nuevo Testamento. (Comentario Biblico Portavoz Ser.). Orig. Title: Survey of the New Testament (Everyman's Bible Commentary). (SPA.). 304p. 1993. pap. 8.99 (0-8254-1061-4, Edit Portavoz) Kregel.

— Survey of New Testament. 144p. (C). 1994. pap. text, student ed., spiral bd. 19.95 (0-7872-0313-0) Kendall-Hunt.

— A Survey of the New Testament. (Everyman's Bible Commentaries Ser.). pap. 12.99 (0-8024-2092-3, 482) Moody.

— A Survey of the Old Testament. expanded rev. ed. (Everyman's Bible Commentaries Ser.). pap. 12.99 (0-8024-2093-1, 458) Moody.

— Understanding End Times Prophecy: A Comprehensive Approach. pap. 15.99 (0-8024-9077-8, 310) Moody.

Benware, Paul N. & Harris, Brian. Leaders in the Making: A Workbook for Discovering & Developing Church Leaders. wbk. ed. 12.99 (0-8024-4928-X, 201) Moody.

Benware, W. A. Workbook in Historical Phonology: Sound Change, Internal Reconstruction, Comparative Reconstruction. 112p. (C). 1997. pap. 19.50 (0-7618-0885-X) U Pr of Amer.

Benware, Wilbur A. Phonetics & Phonology of Modern German: An Introduction. LC 85-7683. 191p. (Orig.). 1986. reprint ed. pap. 59.30 (0-7837-9388-X, 206013300005) Bks Demand.

Benwell, Deirdre A., jt. ed. see Repacholi, Michael H.

Benwell-Morison, jt. auth. see Suess.

Benwell-Morison, D. A., jt. ed. see Seuss, Michael J.

Beny, Roloff, photos by. People: Legends in Life & Art. LC 95-60280. (Illus.). 208p. 1995. 50.00 (0-500-97426-8, Pub. by Thames Hudson) Norton.

Benya, Rosemarie & Muller, Kurt E. Children & Languages: Research, Practice & Rationale for the Early Grades. 241p. 1987. 15.00 (0-944675-37-9); pap. 10.00 (0-614-03012-9) Amer Forum.

Benyamini, Amiran. Patent Infringement in the European Community. LC 93-2935. (IIC Studies Ser.: Vol. 13). 433p. 1993. pap. 199.00 (3-527-28530-X, Wiley-VCH) Wiley.

Benyamini, Yoav & Lindenstrauss, Joram. Geometric Nonlinear Functional Analysis. LC 99-17734. (Colloquium Publications). 488p. 1999. write for info. (0-8218-0835-4) Am Math.

Benyei, Candace R. Understanding Clergy Misconduct in Religious Systems: Scapegoating, Family Secrets & the Abuse of Power. LC 97-37001. 204p. 1998. 29.95 (0-7890-0451-8); pap. 19.95 (0-7890-0452-6) Haworth Pr.

***Benyei, Tamas.** Acts of Attention: Figure & Narrative in Postwar British Novels. (Debrecener Studien zur Literatur Ser.). 231p. 1999. pap. 37.95 (3-631-35295-6) P Lang Pubng.

— Acts of Attention: Figure & Narrative in Postwar British Novels. LC 99-51957. (Debrecener Studien zur Literatur: Vol. 6). 231p. (C). 1999. pap. text 37.95 (0-8204-4366-2) P Lang Pubng.

Benymon-Davies, P. Information Systems Failure & How to Avoid Them. (Financial Times Management Briefings Ser.). 1997. pap. 94.50 (0-273-63213-2, Pub. by F T P-H) Trans-Atl Phila.

Benyo Press Staff. Advanced Indoor Exercise. (Runner's World Ser.). 1982. pap. 9.95 (0-02-499460-X, Macmillan Coll) P-H.

— Indoor Exercise. (Runner's World Ser.). 1978. pap. 16.95 (0-02-499540-1, Macmillan Coll) P-H.

— Indoor Exercise. (Runner's World Ser.). 1982. pap. 9.95 (0-02-499530-4, Macmillan Coll) P-H.

Benyo, Rich & Provost, Rhoda. Runner's World Advanced Indoor Exercise Book. 1981. spiral bd. 11.95 (0-89037-167-9) Anderson World.

Benyo, Rich & Provost, Rhoda. Runner's World Indoor Exercise Book. 200p. spiral bd. 11.95 (0-89037-190-3) Anderson World.

Benyo, Richard. How to Make a Marathon Event. 1992. pap. 13.95 (0-679-73930-0) Random.

— Return to Running. LC 78-55787. (Illus.). 235p. 1978. pap. 3.95 (0-89037-128-8) Anderson World.

— Running Past 50. LC 97-52054. (Ageless Athlete Ser.). (Illus.). 256p. 1998. pap. 16.95 (0-88011-705-2, PBEN0705) Human Kinetics.

Benyo, Richard, jt. auth. see Herrin, Kym.

Benyo, Richard, jt. auth. see LaLanne, Elaine.

Benyon, D. R. & Skidmore, Steve, eds. Automating Systems Development. LC 88-17827. (Illus.). 516p. 1988. 110.00 (0-306-42931-4, Plenum Trade) Perseus Pubng.

Benyon, David. Information & Data Modelling. 2nd ed. LC 96-42413. (Information Systems Ser.). 1996. pap., student ed. 45.31 (0-07-709241-4) McGraw.

Benyon, David & Palanque, Philippe, eds. Critical Issues in User Interface Systems Engineering. LC 95-32280. (Applied Computing Ser.). (Illus.). 294p. 1996. pap. 69.00 (3-540-19964-0) Spr-Verlag.

Benyon, David, et al. Conceptual Modeling for User Interface Development. LC 98-51145. 188p. 1998. pap. 59.95 (1-85233-009-0) Spr-Verlag.

Benyon, David, jt. auth. see Sutcliffe, Alistair.

Benyon, E. D. Master Fard Muhammad: Detroit History. Cuba, Prince, ed. 19p. (Orig.). 1990. pap. 3.95 (1-56411-109-1) Untd Bros & Sis.

Benyosef, Simcha H. Living the Kabbalah: A Guide to the Sabbath & the Festivals in the Teachings of Rabbi Moshe Luria. LC 99-11840. 240p. 1999. 29.95 (0-8264-1149-5) Continuum.

Benyuch, Oleg. Ukrainian-English - English-Ukrainian Standard Dictionary. (Hippocrene Standard Dictionaries Ser.). (ENG & UKR.). 590p. (Orig.). 1995. pap. 24.95 (0-7818-0374-8) Hippocrene Bks.

— Ukrainian-English Standard Dictionary (With Complete Phonetics) (Standard Dictionaries Ser.). 286p. (Orig.). 1994. pap. 14.95 (0-7818-0189-3) Hippocrene Bks.

— Ukrainian Phrasebook & Dictionary. 205p. (Orig.). 1993. pap. 11.95 (0-7818-0188-5); audio 12.95 (0-7818-0191-5) Hippocrene Bks.

Benyukh, Oleg, ed. English-Russian Comprehensive Dictionary. (Comprehensive Dictionaries Ser.). (ENG & RUS.). 800p. 1996. reprint ed. pap. 35.00 (0-7818-0442-6) Hippocrene Bks.

— Russian-English Comprehensive Dictionary, Vol. 2. LC 96-54645. (ENG & RUS.). 800p. 1996. 60.00 (0-7818-0506-6) Hippocrene Bks.

Benyukh, Oleg P., ed. Russian-English Comprehensive Dictionary. LC 96-54645. (ENG & RUS.). 800p. 1997. pap. 35.00 (0-7818-0560-0) Hippocrene Bks.

Benyus, Janine M. Biomimicry: Innovation Inspired by Nature. LC 96-52336. 288p. 1997. 25.00 (0-688-13691-5, Wm Morrow) Morrow Avon.

***Benyus, Janine M.** Biomimicry: Innovation Inspired by Nature. 320p. 1998. reprint ed. pap. 13.00 (0-688-16099-9, Quil) HarperTrade.

Benyus, Janine M. The Field Guide to Wildlife Habitats of the Eastern United States. 336p. 1989. per. 16.00 (0-671-65908-1) S&S Trade Pap.

— Secret Language & Remarkable Behavior of Animals. LC 98-28743. 448p. 1998. 15.98 (1-57912-036-9) Blck Dog & Leventhal.

Benz. Grammar Dimensions. 2nd ed. (College ESL Ser.: Bk. 2). (J). 1997. pap., wbk. ed. 13.95 (0-8384-4003-7) Heinle & Heinle.

— Molecular Medicine: Clinical Implications. 1993. 55.00 (0-397-44610-1) Lppncott W & W.

***Benz, Arnold O.** The Future of the Universe: Chance, Chaos, God? LC 99-56794. 176p. 2000. 24.95 (0-8264-1220-3) Continuum.

Benz, Arnold O. Plasma Astrophysics: Kinetic Processes in Solar & Stellar Coronae. LC 93-24191. (Astrophysics & Space Science Library). 320p. (C). 1993. lib. bdg. 137.00 (0-7923-2429-3) Kluwer Academic.

Benz, Arnold O., ed. Radio Continua During Solar Flares: Selected Contributions to the Workshop Held at Duino, Italy, May 1985. 1986. lib. bdg. 152.00 (90-277-2291-9) Kluwer Academic.

Benz, Arnold O., et al, eds. Coronal Magnetic Energy Releases: Proceedings of the CESRA Workshop Held in Caputh - Potsdam, Germany, 16-20 May 1994. LC 95-12156. (Lecture Notes in Physics Ser.: Vol. 444). x, 293p. 1995. 72.95 (3-540-59109-5) Spr-Verlag.

Benz, Arthur & Goetz, Klaus H., eds. A New German Public Sector? Reform, Adaptation & Stability. (Association for the Study of German Politics Ser.). 250p. 1996. text 77.95 (1-85521-710-4, Pub. by Dartmth Pub) Ashgate Pub Co.

Benz-Bohm, G., jt. auth. see Ebel, Klaus-Dietrich.

Benz, Carolyn, jt. auth. see Newman, Isadore.

Benz, Carolyn R., jt. auth. see Newman, Isadore.

Benz, Charmaine M., jt. ed. see MacDowell, Marsha.

***Benz, Cheryl & Dworak, Kara.** Tapestry Listening & Speaking 1. LC 99-88144. 2000. 25.95 (0-8384-0009-4) Heinle & Heinle.

Benz, Christopher C., ed. Oncogenes. (Cancer Treatment & Research Ser.). (C). 1989. text 217.50 (0-7923-0237-0) Kluwer Academic.

Benz, Christopher C. & Liu, Edison T., eds. Cancer Oncogenes & Tumor Suppressor Genes in Human Malignancies. LC 92-49212. (Cancer Treatment & Research Ser.: Vol. CTAR 63). (C). 1993. text 254.00 (0-7923-1960-5) Kluwer Academic.

Benz, Christopher J. How to Use Ami Pro 4.0: Make Ami Pro Work for You. 1995. pap. text 17.95 (1-56276-244-3, Ziff-Davis Pr) Que.

— MS Publisher for Windows 95 for Dummies. 352p. 1996. pap. 19.99 (0-7645-0016-3) IDG Bks.

Benz, Ernest. Fertility, Wealth & Politics in Three Southwest German Villages, 1650-1900. LC 99-22627. (Studies in Central European Histories). 1999. write for info. (0-391-04093-6) Humanities.

— The Mystical Sources of German Romantic Philosophy. Reynolds, Blair et al, trs. from FRE. LC 83-21154. (Pittsburgh Theological Monographs, New Ser.: No. 6). vi, 133p. 1983. pap. 10.00 (0-915138-50-6) Pickwick.

Benz, Ernst. A Theology of Electricity: On the Encounter & Dialogue Between Theology & the Natural Sciences in the Seventeenth & Eighteenth Centuries. Taraba, Wolfgang, tr. (Princeton Theological Monographs: No. 19). xix, 108p. (Orig.). 1990. pap. 19.95 (0-915138-92-1) Pickwick.

Benz, George W. & Collins, David E., eds. Aquatic Fauna in Peril: The Southeastern Perspective. LC 97-12587. (Illus.). 600p. 1997. write for info. (0-9654841-0-6) Lenz Design GA.

Benz, Lina. Eduard Sueskind (1807-1874) Pfarrer, Volksmann, Visionaer. (Europaeische Hochschulschriften Ser.: Reihe 3, Band 668). (GER., Illus.). 826p. 1998. pap. 114.95 (3-631-48566-2) P Lang Pubng.

Benz, Maudy. Oh, Jackie: A Novel. LC 97-50370. 224p. 1998. 19.95 (1-885266-59-6) Story Line.

— Oh, Jackie: A Novel. LC 99-461934. 208p. 1999. reprint ed. pap. 12.95 (0-425-17044-6) Berkley Pub.

Benz, Michael R. & Lindstrom, Lauren E. Building School-to-Work Programs: Strategies for Youth with Special Needs. LC 96-35179. 1997. pap. text 26.00 (0-89079-712-9, 8282) PRO-ED.

Benz, Michael R., jt. auth. see Blalock, Ginger.

Benz, Reinhold. Facebuilding: The Daily Five-Minute Program for a Beautiful Wrinkle Free Face. LC 90-24302. (Illus.). 64p. 1991. pap. 10.95 (0-8069-8339-6) Sterling.

Benz, Stephen, jt. ed. see Carey-Webb, Allen.

Benz, Stephen C. Guatemalan Journey. LC 95-11138. (Illus.). (C). 1996. pap. 14.95 (0-292-70840-8); text 35.00 (0-292-70839-4) U of Tex Pr.

Benz, Stephen M. & American Society Of Civil Engineers Staff. The Project Manager's CADD Survival Guide. LC 97-16679. 184p. 1997. 22.00 (0-7844-0247-7) Am Soc Civil Eng.

Benz, Steve. Green Dreams: Travels in Central America. 220p. 1998. pap. 12.95 (*0-86442-523-6*) Lonely Planet.
Benz, Willi. The Art of Suiseki: Classic Japanese Stone Gardening. LC 98-53453. (Illus.). 192p. 1998. 29.95 (*0-8069-6315-8*) Sterling.
Benz, Wolfgang. DTV Woerterbuch Zeitgeschichte. (GER.). 29.95 (*0-7859-7436-9*, 3423032952) Fr & Eur.
— The Holocaust. LC 98-30726. 1999. pap. 14.50 (*0-231-11215-7*) Col U Pr.
— The Holocaust: A German Historian Examines the Genocide. Sydenham-Kwiet, Jane, tr. from GER. LC 98-30726. 176p. 1999. 22.00 (*0-231-11214-9*) Col U Pr.
Benz, Wolfgang, ed. Die Vertreibung der Deutschen aus dem Osten: Ursachen, Ereignisse, Folgen. (GER.). 1995. pap. 15.25 (*3-596-12784-X*, Pub. by Fischer Tasch) Intl Bk Import.
Benz, Wolfgang, et al, eds. Jews in the Weimar Republic. (Schriftenreihe Wissenschaftlicher Abhandlungen des Leo Baeck Instituts Ser.: No. 57). (ENG & GER.). 288p. 1998. 79.50 (*3-16-146873-2*, Pub. by JCB Mohr) Coronet Bks.
— Der Nationalsozialismus. Studien zur Ideologie und Herrschaft. (GER.). 272p. 1993. pap. 22.50 (*3-596-11984-7*, Pub. by Fischer Tasch) Intl Bk Import.
Benz, Wolfgang & Pehle, Walter H., eds. Encyclopedia of German Resistance to the Nazi Movement. LC 96-20003. 360p. 1996. 39.50 (*0-8264-0945-8*) Continuum.
— Lexikon des deutschen Widerstandes. (GER.). 432p. 1994. 43.25 (*3-10-005702-3*, Pub. by S Fischer) Intl Bk Import.
Benza, Joseph F., Jr. & Zumwalde, Ralph D. Preventing AIDS.. A Practical Guide for Everyone. 85p. (Orig.). 1987. 18.95 (*0-9617818-0-7*); pap. text 9.95 (*0-317-55082-9*) Jalsco Inc.
Benzar, Brian J. & Benzar, Kitty B. Alpine Loop Scenic Backcountry Byway. (Back Roads of the San Juan Mountains Ser.). (Illus.). 32p. 1994. pap. 4.95 (*1-928759-00-9*) Backcountry CO.
— Ophir-Imogene Loop & Yankee Boy Basin. (Back Roads of the San Juan Mountains Ser.). (Illus.). 32p. 1995. pap. 4.95 (*1-928759-01-7*) Backcountry CO.
— San Juan Skyway. (Back Roads of the San Juan Mountains Ser.). (Illus.). 32p. 1997. pap. 4.95 (*1-928759-02-5*) Backcountry CO.
Benzar, Kitty B., jt. auth. see Benzar, Brian J.
Benze, James G., Jr. Presidential Power & Management Techniques: The Carter & Reagan Administrations in Historical Perspective, 175. LC 87-233. (Contributions in Political Science Ser.: No. 175). 171p. 1987. 49.95 (*0-313-25601-2*, BZP/) Greenwood.
Benzecri, J. P. & Gopalan, eds. Correspondence Analysis Handbook. (Statistics: Textbooks & Monographs: Vol. 125). (Illus.). 688p. 1992. text 185.00 (*0-8247-8437-5*) Dekker.
Benzel. Spine Surgery: Complication Avoidance & Management. LC 98-25169. (C). 1998. text 325.00 (*0-443-07540-9*, B2227) Church.
Benzel, Dave, jt. auth. see Favret, Ben.
Benzel, David. Psyching for Slalom: An Illustrated Guide to the Mind & Muscle of the Complete Skier. Robertson, Jo, ed. (Illus.). 127p. (Orig.) (YA). 1989. pap. 15.95 (*0-944406-05-X*) World Pub FL.
Benzel, Edward & Waxman, Stephen G. Diseases of the Spine & Spinal Cord. LC 99-26448. (Contemporary Neurology Ser.: 58). (Illus.). 432p. 2000. text 120.00 (*0-19-512968-7*) OUP.
Benzel, Edward C. Biomechanics of Spine Stabilization: Principles & Clinical Practice. 278p. 1994. text 89.00 (*0-07-005091-0*) McGraw-Hill HPD.
Benzel, Edward C. & Stillerman, Charles B., eds. The Thoracic Spine. LC 98-30127. (Illus.). 654p. 1998. 165.00 (*0-942219-75-9*) Quality Med Pub.
Benzel, Edward C., jt. auth. see Wild, Gaynor C.
Benzel, Edward C., jt. ed. see Rengachary, Setti S.
Benzel, Edward C., jt. ed. see Selman, Warren R.
Benzel, Edward C., jt. ed. see Zdeblick, Thomas A.
Benzel, Katherine F. The Room in Context: Design Without Boundaries. LC 97-14909. (Illus.). 388p. 1997. 59.95 (*0-07-005956-X*) McGraw.
Benzel, Kathryn N. & De La Vars, Lauren P., eds. Images of the Self As Female: The Achievement of Women Artists in Re-Envisioning Feminine Identity. LC 90-34981. (Women's Studies: Vol. 4). (Illus.). 344p. 1992. lib. bdg. 99.95 (*0-88946-122-8*) E Mellen.
Benzel, Rick. Making Money in a Health Service Business on Your Home-Based PC. 2nd ed. LC 96-29742. (Illus.). 316p. 1997. pap. text 34.95 incl. cd-rom (*0-07-913139-5*) McGraw.
Benzel, Rick & Sheehy-Hussey, Katherine. Legal & Paralegal Services on Your Home-Based PC: Entrepreneurial PC Series. LC 93-48742. 1994. pap. 16.95 (*0-07-005109-7*, Windcrest) TAB Bks.
Benzi, R., et al, eds. Turbulence in Spatially Extended Systems. 315p. (C). 1993. lib. bdg. 165.00 (*1-56072-120-0*) Nova Sci Pubs.
Benzi, Roberto, ed. Advances in Turbulence V: Proceedings of the Fifth European Turbulence Conference, Siena, Italy, 5-8 July 1994. LC 95-10903. (Fluid Mechanics & Its Applications Ser.: Vol. 24). 612p. 1995. text 293.00 (*0-7923-3032-3*) Kluwer Academic.
Benzian, Julius, jt. ed. see Steinschneider, Moritz.
Benzie, Alex. Years Midnight. 576p. 1996. pap. 15.95 (*0-14-025130-8*, Pub. by Pnguin Bks Ltd) Trafalgar.
Benzie, David, jt. ed. see Wright, June L.
Benzie, J. A. H., et al. Allozyme Electrophoretic Methods for Analysisng Genetic Variation in Giant Clams. 1993. pap. 42.00 (*1-86320-074-6*, Pub. by ACIAR) St Mut.
Benzie, William. Dr. F. J. Furnivall: A Victorian Scholar Adventurer. LC 83-12095. 320p. 1983. 29.95 (*0-937664-57-X*) Pilgrim Bks OK.
Benziger, I. Katherine. Falsification of Type. 115p. (Orig.). 1995. pap. text 25.00 (*1-880931-05-2*) KBA Pub.
Benziger, I. Katherine & Sohn, Anne. The Art of Using Your Whole Brain. 3rd rev. ed. (Illus.). 304p. (Orig.). (YA). 1995. pap. 20.00 (*1-880931-06-0*) KBA Pub.
Benziger, John. The Corpuscles: Adventurers in Inner Space. LC 88-92390. (Illus.). 64p. (J). (gr. k-6). 1989. 11.95 (*0-9620961-0-5*) Corpuscles Intergalactica.
— The Corpuscles Meet the Virus Invaders. LC 90-80327. (Illus.). 30p. (J). (gr. 3-6). 1990. 14.95 (*0-9620961-1-3*) Corpuscles Intergalactica.
Benziger, Katherine. The BTSA User Manual. 108p. (Orig.). 1994. pap. text 25.00 (*1-880931-04-4*) KBA Pub.
— Developing Positive Self Esteem: A Self Help Workbook. 51p. (Orig.). (YA). 1990. pap. text, wbk. ed. 15.00 (*1-880931-01-X*) KBA Pub.
— Overcoming Depression: A Self-Help Workbook. 60p. (Orig.). (YA). 1992. pap. text 15.00 (*1-880931-02-8*) KBA Pub.
— Physiological & Psychophysiological Bases for Jungian Concepts: An Annotated Bibliography. (Illus.). 45p. 1996. pap. 15.00 (*1-880931-08-7*) KBA Pub.
Benziger, Marieli & Reberdy, Janet. August Benziger: International Portrait Painter. LC 93-19230. (Illus.). 360p. 1993. 29.95 (*1-55612-614-X*, LL1614) Sheed & Ward WI.
*__Benziger, Marquerite.__ Austria Nazified: Years of Terror, 1938-1955. (Illus.). 72p. 1999. pap. 8.00 (*0-8059-4783-3*) Dorrance.
Benziger Staff. Kitchen Table Gospel: An Adventure in Family Catechesis : General Overview, Cycle B. LC 97-162734. 288 p. 1996. write for info. (*0-02-651083-9*, Benzger Pub) Glencoe.
Benziger, Theodore H., ed. Temperature, 2 pts. Incl. Pt. 1. Arts & Concept. 1977. 66.00 (*0-12-786141-6*); Pt. 2. Thermal Homeostasis. 1977. 73.00 (*0-12-786142-4*); (Benchmark Papers in Human Physiology: Vols. 9 & 10). 1977. write for info. (*0-318-50376-X*) Acad Pr.
Benziman, Uzi. Sharon: An Israeli Caesar. LC 85-13461. 276p. 1985. 17.95 (*0-915361-23-X*) Lambda Pubs.
*__Benzing, David H.__ Bromeliaceae: Profile of an Adaptive Radiation. (Illus.). 688p. (C). 2000. 110.00 (*0-521-43031-3*) Cambridge U Pr.
Benzing, David H. Vascular Epiphytes: General Biology & Related Biota. (Cambridge Tropical Biology Ser.). (Illus.). 372p. (C). 1990. text 80.00 (*0-521-26630-0*) Cambridge U Pr.
Benzinger, Immanuel. Hebraische Archaologie. (Angelos-Lehrubucher Ser.: Bd. 1). xxiv, 437p. 1974. reprint ed. 150.00 (*3-487-05165-6*) G Olms Pubs.

***Benzinger, John C. Many Rooms: Classic Religious Themes in Literature. 235p. 2000. pap. 19.95 (*0-940121-54-9*, Pub. by Cross Cultural Pubns) BookWorld.**
This is an anthology of religious works by Anthony Burgess, Albert Camus, Stephen Crane, Jean Giano, Herman Hesse, C.S. Lewis, Joyce Carol Oates, N. Scott Peck, Chaim Potok, William Saroyan, Alexander Solzhenitsyn, John Steinbeck, John Updike & Alice Walker. Selected & introduced by Reverend John Bensinger, a theologian, chaplain & teacher for over thirty years. *Publisher Paid Annotation.*

Benzinger, Maurice. Wacky Wisdom: How To Do Hundreds of Unusual Things. LC 96-35262. 256p. 1997. 7.99 (*0-517-14939-7*) Random Hse Value.
Benzle, Robin C. Cooking with Humor: A Unique Recipe Collection. LC 91-90952. 160p. 1991. pap. 15.00 (*0-9629398-4-6*) VanTine Pub.
— The Ziggy Cookbook: Great Food from Mom's Diner. LC 93-60839. (Illus.). 254p. (Orig.). 1993. pap. 16.00 (*0-9629398-2-X*) VanTine Pub.
Benzley, Steven E., jt. ed. see Rybicki, Edmund F.
Benzola, Edward J. & Beach, Neva. Temporary Child: A Foster Care Survivor's Story. LC 93-84352. 144p. 1993. 18.95 (*1-883359-02-3*); pap. 12.95 (*1-883359-03-1*) Real People CA.
*__Benzon.__ Beethoven's Anvil. 2000. pap. 15.00 (*0-465-01544-1*, Pub. by Basic) HarpC.
Benzon. Learning How to Learn 92+ 1992. pap., student ed. 18.50 (*0-03-054932-9*) H Holt & Co.
Benzon, Honorio, et al. Essentials of Pain Medicine & Regional Anesthesia. Ross, Allan, ed. LC 98-24849. 495p. (C). 1999. pap. text. write for info. (*0-443-06509-8*) Church.
Benzon, William, jt. auth. see Friedhoff, Richard M.
Benzoni, Juliette. Marianne & the Lords of the East LC 76-365189. 242 p. 1975. write for info. (*0-434-06609-5*) Buttrwrth-Heinemann.
Benzoni, Peter. Beyond the Mine - The Pete Benzoni Story. LC 97-68168. (Illus.). 427p. 1997. 24.95 (*1-886028-28-1*) Savage Pr.
Benzwie, Teresa. A Moving Experience: Dance for Lovers of Children & the Child Within. (Illus.). 224p. 1988. pap. 29.00 (*0-913705-25-X*) Zephyr Pr AZ.
Beocoff, Terri A. Insider's Guide to Book Publishing: How to Develop & Sell Books by Understanding the Publishin. 1999. pap. text. write for info. (*0-945213-35-2*) Rudi Pub.
Beolchi, L. & Kuhn, M. H. Medical Imaging. LC 94-73420. (Studies in Health Technology & Informatics: Vol. 19). 225p. (gr. 12). 1995. 103.00 (*90-5199-210-6*) IOS Press.
Beolchi, L., jt. auth. see DeMaeseneer, J.
Beolco, Angelo. The Veteran & Weasel: Two One Act Renaissance Plays, Vol. 17. Ferguson, Ronnie, tr. from ITA. (Studies in Italian Culture). 152p. (C). 1995. text 46.95 (*0-8204-2700-4*) P Lang Pubng.
Beon, Yves. Planet Dora: A Memoir of the Holocaust & the Birth of the Space Age. 288p. 1998. pap. 20.00 (*0-8133-3492-6*, Pub. by Westview) HarpC.
Beonar, R. Craig, ed. see Marmo, Brent.
Beongcheon Yu, tr. & intro. see Natsume Soseki, pseud.
Beothy, Erzebet. Die Bezeichnungen Fur Himmelsrichtungen in Den Finnisch Ugrischen Sprachen. LC 67-63037. (Uralic & Altaic Ser.: Vol. 84). 241p. 1967. pap. text 14.00 (*0-87750-033-9*) Res Inst Inner Asian Studies.
Beotra, B. R. The Immoral Traffic (Prevention) Act 1956 with States Rules. 4th ed. (C). 1988. 175.00 (*0-7855-4797-5*) St Mut.
— Law of Cinematograph, Cine Workers & Videos, Etc. (C). 1990. 175.00 (*0-89771-187-4*) St Mut.
— Powers & Duties of Magistrates. (C). 1990. 175.00 (*0-89771-188-2*) St Mut.
Beougher, Pamela D., ed. see Liotti, Robert C.
Beougher, Sharon & Dorsett, Mary. Women & Evangelism: An Evangelistic Lifestyle from a Woman's Perspective. (Illus.). 292p. 1994. pap. 41.95 incl. audio (*1-879089-16-5*); lab manual ed. 10.95 (*1-879089-15-7*) B Graham Ctr.
Beougher, Timothy K. & Reed, Alvin, eds. Evangelism for a Changing World. 296p. 1995. pap. 14.99 (*0-87788-240-1*, H Shaw Pubs) Waterbrook Pr.
Beougher, Timothy K., ed. & pref. see Baxter, Richard.
Beowulf. Beowulf. Collins, Rowland L., ed. LC 64-10837. (Midland Bk.: MB-73). 127p. reprint ed. pap. 39.40 (*0-8357-7134-2*, 205549300023) Bks Demand.
— Beowulf. Gordon, R. K., tr. 64p. 1992. reprint ed. pap. 1.00 (*0-486-27264-8*) Dover.
— Beowulf, A New Verse Translation for Fireside & Classroom. (BCL1-PR English Literature Ser.). 153p. 1992. reprint ed. lib. bdg. 69.00 (*0-7812-7160-6*) Rprt Serv.
— Beowulf, with the Finnsburg Fragment. Wyatt, A. J., ed. LC 52-46501. 295p. reprint ed. pap. 84.10 (*0-8357-7135-0*, 2026355) Bks Demand.
— Beowulf, with the Finnsburg Fragment. (BCL1-PR English Literature Ser.). 257p. 1992. reprint ed. lib. bdg. 79.00 (*0-7812-7159-2*) Rprt Serv.
Beozzo, Oscar, jt. ed. see Wilford, Felix.
Bephage. Social Sciences Applied to Nursing. 2000. pap. text 30.00 (*0-443-05719-2*, W B Saunders Co) Harcrt Hlth Sci Grp.
Bepko, Claudia. The Heart's Progress: A Memoir. LC 96-32570. 227p. 1998. pap. 12.95 (*0-14-024366-6*) Viking Penguin.
Bepko, Claudia, ed. Feminism & Addiction. LC 91-38268. (Journal of Feminist Family Therapy). 256p. 1992. lib. bdg. 49.95 (*1-56024-220-5*) Haworth Pr.
Bepko, Claudia, ed. Feminism & Addiction. LC 91-38268. (Journal of Feminist Family Therapy). 256p. 1992. pap. text 19.95 (*1-56024-221-3*) Haworth Pr.
Bepko, Claudia & Krestan, Jo-Ann. The Responsibility Trap: A Blueprint for Treating the Alcoholic Family. 320p. (C). 1985. 35.00 (*0-02-902880-9*) Free Pr.
— Too Good For Her Own Good: Breaking Free from the Burden of Female Responsibility. LC 89-46071. 272p. 1991. pap. 13.00 (*0-06-092081-5*, Perennial) HarperTrade.
*__Bepler, Laurie & Bepler, Virginia.__ The Road North: Rte 7 from Norwalk to Canaan. (Images of America Ser.). 128p. 1999. pap. 18.99 (*0-7385-0256-1*) Arcadia Publng.
Bepler, Virginia, jt. auth. see Bepler, Laurie.
Beppler, Virginia, et al. Wilton in the Golden Age of Postcards. (Images of America Ser.). 1997. pap. 16.99 (*0-7524-0866-6*) Arcadia Publng.
Bepsiktepe, Pshukrhu T., et al. Environmental Degradation of the Black Sea: Challenges & Remedies. LC 99-21106. (Nato Science Series. Partnership Sub-Series Environmental Security, 2). 1999. write for info. (*0-7923-5675-6*) Kluwer Academic.
Bequaert, Joseph C. & Miller, Walter B. The Mollusks of the Arid Southwest, with an Arizona Check List. LC 72-187825. 287p. reprint ed. pap. 89.00 (*0-608-15790-4*, 202737900055) Bks Demand.
Bequai, August. How to Prevent Computer Crime: A Guide for Managers. LC 83-6952. 328p. reprint ed. pap. 101.70 (*0-7837-3517-0*, 205785100008) Bks Demand.
Bequele, A. & Boyden, J. Combating Child Labour. xiii, 226p. 1988. 36.00 (*92-2-106388-7*) Intl Labour Office.
Bequele, Assefa & Boyden, Jo, eds. Combating Child Labour. rev. ed. xiii, 226p. (Orig.). 1995. reprint ed. pap. 27.00 (*92-2-106389-5*) Intl Labour Office.
Bequele, Assefa & Myers, W. E. First Things First in Child Labour: Eliminating Work Detrimental to Children. LC 96-117515. 136p. 1995. pap. 18.00 (*92-2-109197-X*) Intl Labour Office.
Bequer, Gustavo A. Leyendas. Lopez, Estrada F., ed. (Nueva Austral Ser.: No. 36). (SPA.). 1991. pap. text 24.95 (*84-239-1836-X*) Elliots Bks.
— Rimas y Declaraciones Poeticas. Lopez, Estrada F., ed. (Nueva Austral Ser.: No. 6). (SPA.). 1991. pap. text 11.95 (*84-239-1806-8*) Elliots Bks.
Bequette, Jim. Historic Founding of Cape Girardeau, Missouri LC 97-93532. 40p. 1997. write for info. (*0-9658043-0-5*) J Bequette.
Bequette, Jim, ed. Skeeter: Hoglegs, Hipshots, & Jalapenos: Selected Works of Skeeter Skelton, Vol. II. 2nd ed. (Illus.). 288p. 1991. 19.95 (*0-9621148-6-3*) PRMDIA Spcl Intrst.
Bequette, Jim, ed. see Skelton, Skeeter.
Bequette, Wayne B. Process Dynamics: Modeling, Analysis & Simulation. LC 97-36052. 640p. (C). 1998. lab manual ed. 99.00 (*0-13-206889-3*) P-H.
Bequist, Thomas H. Pocket Atlas of MRI Body Anatomy. 2nd ed. LC 95-17885. (Illus.). 104p. 1995. pap. text 16.95 (*0-7817-0336-0*) Lppncott W & W.
Ber, Leonid & Gazella, Karolyn A. Activate Your Immune System: Natural Substance Provides Ultimate Support. (Illus.). 93p. 1998. pap. 7.95 (*1-890694-11-8*) IMPAKT Communs.
Ber Levin, Sholom. Toldos Avrohom Chaim.Tr. of Biography of Avrohom Chaim. (HEB.). 142p. 1998. 15.00 (*0-8266-2000-0*) Kehot Pubn Soc.
Ber of Bolechow. The Memoirs of Ber of Bolechow (1723-1805) LC 73-2186. (Jewish People; History, Religion, Literature Ser.). 1973. reprint ed. 21.95 (*0-405-05252-9*) Ayer.
Bera, W., et al. The Use of Victim-Offender Communication in the Treatment of Sexual Abuse: Three Intervention Models. 112p. (Orig.). 1990. pap. 17.50 (*1-884444-29-6*) Safer Soc.
Berabe, Jan Christian, ed. see Patterson, Susan.
Berachos, Sheva. Sason V'Simchah. 18.99 (*0-89906-648-8*, U-SAVH); pap. 15.99 (*0-89906-649-6*, U-SAVP) Mesorah Pubns.
Berachya & Gollancz, Hermann. The Ethical Treatises of Berachya, Son of Rabbi Natronai Ha-Nakdan. LC 73-2187. (Jewish People; History, Religion, Literature Ser.). 1973. reprint ed. 41.95 (*0-405-05253-7*) Ayer.
*__Beracs, Jozsef & Chikan, Attila, eds.__ Managing Business in Hungary: An International Perspective: Transition, Competitiveness & Economic Growth. LC 99-227257. 506p. 1999. 78.00 (*963-05-7598-1*, Pub. by Akade Kiado) Intl Spec Bk.
Beral, Valerie, et al, eds. Childhood Cancer & Nuclear Installations. 496p. 1993. pap. text 61.00 (*0-7279-0815-4*, Pub. by BMJ Pub) Login Brothers Bk Co.
Beral, Valerig, et al, eds. Cancer, HIV & AIDS. (Cancer Surveys Ser.: Vol. 10). (Illus.). 250p. (C). 1991. text 60.00 (*0-87969-362-2*) Cold Spring Harbor.
Beran. Instructors Manual to Accompany General Chemistry Principles. 184p. 1994. pap. text 24.95 (*0-471-00775-7*) Wiley.
— Last Partrician. 1999. pap. 14.95 (*0-312-20659-3*) St Martin.
— Outline to Accompany Atkins. (C). 1990. 12.00 (*0-7167-2116-3*) W H Freeman.
Beran, et al. Variations in the Global Water Budget. 1983. text 220.00 (*90-277-1364-2*) Kluwer Academic.
Beran, Carol. Living over the Abyss: Margaret Atwood's Life Before Man. (Canadian Fiction Studies: Vol. 23). (Illus.). 99p. (C). 1993. pap. 14.95 (*1-55022-125-6*, Pub. by ECW) Genl Dist Srvs.
Beran, George W. Handbook in Zoonoses: Viral Zoonoses, Sect B: Vol. 1. 544p. 1981. 287.00 (*0-8493-2911-6*, RC113, CRC Reprint) Franklin.
— Handbook of Zoonoses: Bacteria, Sect. A. 2nd ed. 560p. 1994. boxed set 294.95 (*0-8493-3205-2*) CRC Pr.
— Handbook of Zoonoses: Viruses, Sect. B. 2nd ed. 608p. 1994. boxed set 294.95 (*0-8493-3206-0*) CRC Pr.
Beran, George W., ed. Handbook in Zoonoses: Viral Zoonoses, Sect. B: Vol. 2. 528p. 1981. 275.00 (*0-8493-2912-4*, RC113, CRC Reprint) Franklin.
Beran, George W., jt. auth. see Steele, J.
Beran, Harry. Betel-Chewing Equipment of East New Guinea. (Ethnography Ser.: No. 8). (Illus.). 72p. 1989. pap. 10.50 (*0-85263-969-4*, Pub. by Shire Pubns) Parkwest Pubns.
Beran, J. A. Chemistry in the Laboratory: A Study of Chemical & Physical Changes. 2nd ed. 416p. 1995. pap. 58.95 (*0-471-10952-5*) Wiley.
*__Beran, J. A.__ Laboratory Manual for Principles of General Chemistry. 6th ed. LC 99-32790. 480p. 1999. pap. 58.95 (*0-471-31452-8*) Wiley.
Beran, Jan. From Six-on-Six to Full Court Press: A Century of Iowa Girls' Basketball. LC 93-5448. (Illus.). 240p. 1993. 24.95 (*0-8138-2369-2*) Iowa St U Pr.
— Statistical Methods for Long-Memory Processes. LC 94-14144. 1994. write for info. (*0-412-98681-7*) Chapman & Hall.
Beran, Ladislav. Orthomodular Lattices. 1985. text 220.00 (*90-277-1715-X*) Kluwer Academic.
Beran, Mark J. & Parrent, George B. Theory of Partial Coherence. LC QC0670.B46. 207p. reprint ed. pap. 64.20 (*0-608-30861-7*, 201013700068) Bks Demand.
Beran, Max A. Carbon Sequestration in the Biosphere: Processes & Prospects. LC 95-31118. (NATO ASI Ser.: Vol. 33). 320p. 1995. 185.95 (*3-540-60190-2*) Spr-Verlag.
Beran, Michael Knox. The Last Patrician: Bobby Kennedy & the End of the American Aristocracy. LC 98-10200. (Illus.). 288p. 1998. text 23.95 (*0-312-18625-8*) St Martin.
Beran, Nancy J. & Toomey, Beverly G., eds. Mentally Ill Offenders & the Criminal Justice System: Issues in Forensic Services. LC 78-19782. 193p. 1979. 57.95 (*0-275-90330-3*, C0330, Praeger Pubs) Greenwood.
Beran, R. G., jt. ed. see Pachlatko.
Beran, Roy. Neurology for General Practitioners. (Illus.). 224p. 1996. text 50.00 (*0-07-470205-X*) McGraw-Hill HPD.
Beran, Roy G. & Carmi, Amnon, eds. Epilepsy & Law. ii, 266p. 1998. pap. 40.00 (*965-7077-01-X*, 324080) W S Hein.
Beranbaum, Rose L. The Cake Bible. LC 88-1369. (Illus.). 420p. 1988. 30.00 (*0-688-04402-6*, Wm Morrow) Morrow Avon.
— The Pie & Pastry Bible. (Illus.). 512p. 1998. 35.00 (*0-684-81348-3*) Scribner.
— Rose's Christmas Cookies. LC 90-6505. (Illus.). 272p. 1998. 22.00 (*0-688-10136-4*, Wm Morrow) Morrow Avon.
Beranbaum, Rose L. Rose's X-Mas Cookies. 1924. pap. write for info. (*0-688-16375-0*, Hearst) Hearst Commns.
Beranek, Leo L. Acoustical Measurements. rev. ed. LC 88-82582. 841p. 1989. 46.00 (*0-88318-590-3*) Acoustical Soc Am.

B

An Asterisk (*) at the beginning of an entry indicates that the title is appearing for the first time.

— Acoustics. LC 86-70671. 492p. 1986. 33.00 (*0-88318-494-X*) Acoustical Soc Am.
— Concert & Opera Halls: How They Sound. LC 95-35793. (Illus.). 643p. 1996. 49.95 (*1-56396-530-5*) Acoustical Soc Am.
— Noise Reduction. LC 91-61139. 776p. 1991. reprint ed. 34.95 (*0-932146-58-9*) Peninsula CA.
Beranek, Leo L., ed. Noise & Vibration Control. rev. ed. LC 89-80604. (Illus.). 672p. 1989. reprint ed. 38.00 (*0-9622072-0-9*) INCE NY.
Beranek, Leo L. & Ver, I. L., eds. Noise & Vibration Control Engineering: Principles & Applications. LC 92-11347. 816p. 1992. 190.00 (*0-471-61751-2*) Wiley.
Beranger, C., jt. auth. see Jarrige, R.
Beranger, G., et al. The Book of Steel. 192.00 (*1-898298-38-6*) Spr-Verlag.
Beranger, Gabriel. Beranger's Antique Buildings of Ireland. Harbison, Peter, ed. LC 99-175904. (Illus.). 240p. 1998. boxed set 55.00 (*1-85182-426-X*, Pub. by Four Cts Pr) Intl Spec Bk.
— Beranger's Antique Buildings of Ireland. limited ed. Harbison, Peter, ed. LC 99-175904. (Illus.). 240p. 1998. pap. 24.95 (*1-85182-427-8*, Pub. by Four Cts Pr) Intl Spec Bk.
Beranger, Gabriel, et al. Beranger's Views of Ireland. LC 91-206973. 111 p. 1991. write for info. (*0-901714-94-1*) Royal Irish Acad.
Berard & Marthaler, L., eds. New Catholic Encyclopedia, Vol. XVIII, Supplement 1978-1988. (Illus.). 599p. 1989. 74.50 (*0-685-26975-2*) J Heraty Assocs.
Berard, ed. see Balzac, Honore de.
Berard, A., ed. Documents d'Etudes Sociales sur l'Anarchie. (History of Political Violence Ser.). (FRE.). 1985. reprint ed. lib. bdg. 40.00 (*0-527-41197-3*) Periodicals Srv.
Berard, Barbara, ed. see Bannister, Hank & Crane, Tim.
Berard, Edward V. Project Management Handbook for Object-Oriented Software Development. (C). 2001. 36.75 (*0-13-138611-5*, Macmillan Coll) P-H.
Berard, Evelyne. Tempo, No. 1. (FRE., Illus.). 223p. 1996. pap. text 23.95 (*2-278-04423-0*, Pub. by Edns Didier) Hatier Pub.
— Tempo, No. 2. (FRE., Illus.). 1997. pap. text 24.95 (*2-278-04427-3*, Pub. by Edns Didier) Hatier Pub.
Berard, Jean-Baptiste. L' Art du chant. fac. ed. (Monuments of Music & Music Literature in Facsimile Ser., Series I: Vol. 75). 1967. lib. bdg. 37.50 (*0-8450-2275-X*) Broude.
***Berard, Jim.** The Flying Cat & Other Amazing Stories of the Washington Monument. (Illus.). 144p. 2000. pap. write for info. (*1-889324-20-5*) EPM Pubns.
Berard, Michael F. & Wilder, D. R. Fundamentals of Phase Equilibria in Ceramic Systems. (Illus.). 231p. (C). 1990. text 55.00 (*1-878907-00-X*, RAN) TechBooks.
Berard, Michael F., jt. auth. see Jones, John T.
Berard, P. H. Spectral Geometry: Direct & Inverse Problems. (Lecture Notes in Mathematics Ser.: Vol. 1207). xiv, 272p. 1986. pap. 33.80 (*0-387-16788-9*) Spr-Verlag.
Berard, Samuel J. Principles of Machine Design. LC 55-6078. 546p. reprint ed. pap. 169.30 (*0-608-11699-8*, 201244700081) Bks Demand.
Berardesca, Enzo, et al, eds. Bioengineering of the Skin: Cutaneous Blood Flow & Erythema. (Dermatology: Clinical & Basic Science Ser.). 320p. 1994. boxed set 157.95 (*0-8493-8371-4*) CRC Pr.
Berardi, Gigi M. World Food, Population & Development. LC 85-14398. (Illus.). 368p. (C). 1986. pap. 29.00 (*0-8476-7456-8*, R7456) Rowman.
Berardi, Lucy K. Mission Write. (Illus.). (Orig.). (J). (gr. 7-8). 1978. pap. 1.80 (*0-915441-00-4*); pap., student ed. 1.80 (*0-915441-01-2*); student ed. 1.00 (*0-915441-04-7*); 15.00 (*0-915441-02-0*); 15.00 (*0-915441-03-9*); 1.00 (*0-915441-05-5*); 1.00 (*0-915441-06-3*); 15.00 (*0-915441-07-1*) Mission Write.
Berardi, Marianne. Under the Influence: The Students of Thomas Hart Benton. (Illus.). 150p. (Orig.). 1993. pap. write for info. (*0-9615372-2-1*) Albrecht Art Mus.
Berardi, Patricia. And the Lord Said... Triumph Over Tragedy. 214p. (Orig.). 1991. pap. 5.95 (*1-879946-77-7*) Key Pub & Print.
Berardi, Patricia, ed. see Hicks, Chuck.
Berardi, Stefano & Coppo, Mario. Types for Proofs & Programs: International Workshop Types '95, Torino, Italy, June 5-8, 1995 Selected Papers, Vol. 115. LC 96-43300. (Lecture Notes on Computer Science Ser.). x, 296p. 1996. 56.00 (*3-540-61780-9*) Spr-Verlag.
Berardo, Felix F., ed. Middle & Late Life Transitions. LC 82-61685. (Annals of the American Academy of Political & Social Science Ser.: Vol. 464). 1982. 26.00 (*0-8039-1932-8*); pap. 17.00 (*0-8039-1933-6*) Sage.
Berardy, Paxton & Knappman, Edward W. Best Educational Internet Sites for Social Studies Students. LC 98-84258. viii, 190 p. 1998. write for info. (*1-57163-900-4*) Sofsource.
Beratan, Kathi K., ed. Reconstructing the History of Basin & Range Extension Using Sedimentology & Stratigraphy. (Special Papers: No. 303). (Illus.). 212p. 1996. pap. 78.50 (*0-8137-2303-5*) Geol Soc.
***Beratung, Projektgruppe Wissenschaftliche.** Organisationslernen Durch Wissensmanagement. (Illus.). 184p. 1999. 34.00 (*3-631-35029-5*) P Lang Pubng.
Beratz, Gottlieb. The German Colonies on the Lower Volga: Their Origin & Early Development. Giesinger, Adam, ed. Reeves-Marquardt, Dona B. et al, trs. LC 91-21746. 370p. 1991. 25.00 (*0-914222-20-1*) Am Hist Soc Ger.
Beraud, Henri. Twelve Portraits of the French Revolution. Boyd, M., tr. LC 68-16909. (Essay Index Reprint Ser.). 1977. 20.95 (*0-8369-0197-5*) Ayer.
Berbar, Halim. Vietnam Postwar. (Illus.). 202p. 1995. 55.00 (*983-9808-34-6*, Pub. by Delta Edits) Weatherhill.
Berbari, E., jt. ed. see El-Sharkaway, M.
***Berbari, Edward J. & Steinberg, Jonathan S.** A Practical Guide to the Use of the High-Resolution Electrocardiogram. LC 99-52567. (Illus.). 192p. 1999. 52.00 (*0-87993-445-X*) Futura Pub.
Berbau, Jean. Aprendizaje y Formacion: Una Pedagogia. (SPA.). pap. 9.99 (*968-16-2869-1*, Pub. by Fondo) Continental Bk.
Berbenliev, P. Architectural Heritage on the Lands of Bulgaria. 320p. (C). 1988. text 300.00 (*0-569-09175-6*, Pub. by Collets) St Mut.
Berber, R. D. & Kravaris, Costas. Nonlinear Model Based Process Control. LC 98-29495. (Applied Sciences Ser.). 1998. 399.00 (*0-7923-5220-3*) Kluwer Academic.
Berber, Rivdan, ed. Methods of Model Based Process Control. LC 95-17072. (NATO ASI Ser.; Series E, Applied Sciences: Vol. 293). 1995. text 386.50 (*0-7923-3524-4*) Kluwer Academic.
Berberabe, Patricia A. An Easy Way to Understand the Holy Bible: A Spiritual Interpretation of the Old & New Testaments. 247p. 1996. pap. 6.00 (*0-9649173-0-0*) P A Berberabe.
— An Easy Way to Understand the Holy Bible on the Ten Commandments: A Spiritual Interpretations. 80p. Date not set. pap. 10.00 (*0-9649173-1-9*) P A Berberabe.
Berberi, D. Vest Pocket Arabic. 210p. 1996. pap. 6.50 (*0-614-21659-1*, 1285) Kazi Pubns.
Berberi, Dilaver. Traveler's Italian Dictionary. 1993. pap. 5.95 (*0-8050-2911-7*) H Holt & Co.
— Traveler's Italian Dictionary: English-Italian, Italian-English. rev. ed. LC 93-19015. 1993. pap. 6.95 (*0-8327-0724-4*) Cortina.
— Vest Pocket Arabic. LC 89-15367. (ARA & ENG.). 1975. pap. 5.95 (*0-8489-5109-3*) Inst Lang Study.
Berberi, Dilaver, ed. see Laita, Luis M. & Gil de Montes, Carmen.
Berberi, Dilaver, ed. see Zotter, Josefa.
Berberian, Bernard. The Armenian Directory Yellow Pages: Uniarts Advertising Company. 500p. 1994. 8.00 (*1-885179-15-4*) Uniarts.
***Berberian, Houri.** Love of Freedom Has No Fatherland: The Politicization of Armenians & the Iranian Constitutiona. 216p. 2000. pap. 30.00 (*0-8133-3817-4*) Westview.
Berberian, S. K. Baer-Rings. LC 72-189105. (Grundlehren der Mathematischen Wissenschaften Ser.: Vol. 195). 315p. 1972. 68.95 (*0-387-05751-X*) Spr-Verlag.
— Lectures in Functional Analysis & Operator Theory. (Graduate Texts in Mathematics Ser.: Vol. 15). 370p. 1988. 60.95 (*0-387-90080-2*) Spr-Verlag.
Berberian, S. K., tr. see Dixmier, J.
Berberian, Schahan. Fifty Songs. 224p. (Orig.). 1983. pap. 10.00 (*0-934728-08-9*) D O A C.
Berberian, Sterling K. A First Course in Real Analysis. LC 93-46020. (Undergraduate Texts in Mathematics Ser.). (Illus.). 237p. 1994. 43.95 (*0-387-94217-3*) Spr-Verlag.
— Fundamentals of Real Analysis. LC 98-13045. (Universitext Ser.). 1998. pap. 54.95 (*0-387-98480-1*) Spr-Verlag.
— Introduction to Hilbert Space. 2nd ed. vi, 206p. (C). 1991. text 16.95 (*0-8284-0287-6*, 287) Chelsea Pub.
Berberich, Chris, jt. auth. see Lang, Greg.
Berberick, Nancy. StormBlade. LC 87-50059. (DragonLance Heroes Trilogy: Vol. 2). (Illus.). 392p. (Orig.). 1988. pap. 5.99 (*0-88038-597-9*, Pub. by TSR Inc) Random.
***Berberick, Nancy V.** Dalamar the Dark. (DragonLance Classics Ser.). 320p. 2000. mass mkt. 5.99 (*0-7869-1565-X*) TSR Inc.
***Berberick, Nancy Varian, et al.** Bertrem's Guide to the Age of Mortals: Everyday Life in Krynn of the Fifth Age. 320p. 2000. mass mkt. 6.99 (*0-7869-1437-8*) Wizards Coast.
Berberoglu, Berch. Class, State & Development in India. (Illus.). 330p. (C). 1992. text 36.00 (*0-8039-9401-X*) Sage.
— Class Structure & Social Transformation. LC 94-12352. 144p. 1994. 49.95 (*0-275-94924-9*, Praeger Pubs) Greenwood.
— Classical & Contemporary Social Theory: A Critical Perspective. LC 92-76215. 166p. (Orig.). 1993. text 34.95 (*1-882289-07-2*); pap. text 16.95 (*1-882289-06-4*) Gen Hall.
— Critical Perspectives in Sociology: A Reader. 2nd ed. 320p. 1993. per. 34.95 (*0-8403-8468-8*, 40846801) Kendall-Hunt.
— The Internationalization of Capital: Imperialism & Capitalist Development on a World Scale. LC 86-25259. 245p. 1987. 57.95 (*0-275-92169-7*, C2169, Praeger Pubs) Greenwood.
— Political Sociology: A Comparative Historical Approach. LC 90-80204. (Illus.). 200p. (Orig.). 1990. text 35.95 (*0-930390-09-1*); pap. text 18.95 (*0-930390-08-3*) Gen Hall.
— Turmoil in the Middle East: Imperialism, War & Political Instability. LC 99-13221. 176p. (C). 1999. text 49.50 (*0-7914-4411-2*); pap. text 16.95 (*0-7914-4412-0*) State U NY Pr.
Berberoglu, Berch, ed. The National Question: Nationalism, Ethnic Conflict, & Self-Determination in the Twentieth Century. LC 95-11672. (Orig.). (C). 1995. pap. text 24.95 (*1-56639-343-4*) Temple U Pr.
— The National Question: Nationalism, Ethnic Conflict, & Self-Determination in the Twentieth Century. LC 95-11672. 327p. (Orig.). (C). 1995. lib. bdg. 69.95 (*1-56639-342-6*) Temple U Pr.
— Power & Stability in the Middle East. LC 89-8966. 288p. (C). 1989. pap. 19.95 (*0-86232-809-8*, Pub. by Zed Books); text 55.00 (*0-86232-808-X*, Pub. by Zed Books) St Martin.
Berberova, Nina. Aleksandr Blok: A Life. Marsack, Robyn, tr. from FRE. LC 96-17053. 144p. 1996. 22.50 (*0-8076-1408-4*) Braziller.
— Biiankurskie Prazdniki I Drugie Rasskazy. (RUS.). 260p. 1989. pap. 22.00 (*0-89830-032-0*) Russica Pubs.
***Berberova, Nina.** The Book of Happiness. Schwartz, Marian, tr. from RUS. LC 98-44261. Orig. Title: Kniga Schast'ia. 205p. 1999. 23.95 (*0-8112-1401-X*, Pub. by New Directions) Norton.
Berberova, Nina. Cape of Storms. Schwartz, Marian, tr. from RUS. LC 99-41309. 256p. 1999. 23.95 (*0-8112-1416-8*, Pub. by New Directions) Norton.
— Kursiv Moi, 2 vols. LC 82-61509. (RUS., Illus.). 720p. (Orig.). 1983. write for info. (*0-89830-080-0*) Russica Pubs.
— Kursiv Moi, 2 vols., 1. LC 82-61509. (RUS., Illus.). 720p. (Orig.). 1983. write for info. (*0-89830-079-7*); write for info. (*0-89830-066-5*) Russica Pubs.
— Kursiv Moi, 2 vols., 2. LC 82-61509. (RUS., Illus.). 720p. (Orig.). 1983. write for info. (*0-89830-067-3*) Russica Pubs.
— Kursiv Moi, 2 vols., Set. LC 82-61509. (RUS., Illus.). 720p. (Orig.). 1983. 48.00 (*0-89830-078-9*); pap. 36.00 (*0-89830-065-7*) Russica Pubs.
— The Ladies from St. Petersburg: Three Novellas. Schwartz, Marian, tr. LC 98-18968. (RUS.). 192p. 1998. 19.95 (*0-8112-1377-3*, Pub. by New Directions) Norton.
***Berberova, Nina.** The Ladies from St. Petersburg: Three Novellas. Schwartz, Marian, tr. from RUS. 2000. pap. 12.95 (*0-8112-1436-2*, Pub. by New Directions) Norton.
Berberova, Nina. Liudi i Lozhi: Russkie Masony XX Stoletiia. LC 85-61638. (RUS.). 300p. (Orig.). 1987. 48.50 (*0-89830-098-3*) Russica Pubs.
— Stikhi: Nineteen Twenty-One to Nineteen Eighty-Three. LC 84-60081. (Russica Poetry Ser.: No. 4). (RUS.). 120p. (Orig.). 1984. pap. 18.50 (*0-89830-072-X*) Russica Pubs.
— Zheleznaia Zhenshchina. LC 80-54020. (RUS.). 400p. (Orig.). 1981. 30.00 (*0-89830-131-9*) Russica Pubs.
Berberova, Nina, ed. see Tolstoy, Leo.
Berbig, Roland, ed. Theodor Fontane und Friedrich Eggers Briefwechsel: Mit Fontanes Briefen an Karl Eggers und der Korrespodenz von Friedrich Eggers an Emilie Fontane. (Schriften der Theodor Fontane-Gesellschaft Ser.). (GER.). 480p. (C). 1997. lib. bdg. 156.00 (*3-11-014987-7*) De Gruyter.
Berbiguier, B. 18 Exercises or Etudes for the Flute. 28p. 1986. pap. 5.95 (*0-7935-5404-7*, 50259650) H Leonard.
***Berbon, P. B., et al, eds.** Superplasticity--Current Status & Future Potential Vol. 601: Materials Research Society Symposium Proceedings. LC 00-25161. (Symposium Proceedings Ser.). 374p. 2000. text 90.00 (*1-55899-509-9*) Materials Res.
Berc, Shelley. The Shape of Wilderness. LC 95-31068. 300p. (Orig.). 1995. pap. 12.95 (*1-56689-036-5*) Coffee Hse.
— Thomas Hardy's Tess of the d'Urbervilles. (Barron's Book Notes Ser.). (C). 1984. pap. 2.50 (*0-8120-3445-7*) Barron.
Bercaw, Edna C. Halmoni's Day. LC 98-47169. 2000. 15.99 (*0-8037-2444-6*, Dial Yng Read) Peng Put Young Read.
Bercaw, Mary K. Melville's Sources. 213p. 1987. 44.95 (*0-8101-0734-1*) Northwestern U Pr.
***Bercaw, Nancy.** Gender & the Southern Body Politic. LC 99-51779. (Chancellor's Symposium Ser.). 280p. 2000. text 35.00 (*1-57806-257-8*) U Pr of Miss.
***Berce-Bratko, Branka.** Can Small Urban Communities Survive? Culturological Analysis in Urban Rehabilitation: Cases in Slovenia & Scotland. (Contemporary Trends in European Social Sciences Ser.). 300p. 2000. text 74.95 (*1-84014-157-3*, Pub. by Ashgate Pub) Ashgate Pub Co.
Berce, Yves-Marie. The Birth of Absolutism: A History of France, 1598-1661. Rex, Richard, tr. LC 95-31745. 272p. 1995. text 49.95 (*0-312-15800-9*) St Martin.
— Croquants et Nu-Pieds. (FRE.). 303p. 1990. pap. 12.95 (*0-7859-1678-4*, 2070326268) Fr & Eur.
— History of Peasant Revolts: The Social Origins of Rebellion in Early Modern France. Whitmore, Amanda, tr. from FRE. LC 90-53182. 400p. 1990. reprint ed. 59.95 (*0-8014-2544-1*); reprint ed. pap. text 21.95 (*0-8014-9775-2*) Cornell U Pr.
Berceli, T. Nonlinear Active Microwave Circuits. 1987. pap. 130.00 (*963-05-4303-6*, Pub. by Akade Kiado) St Mut.
Berceo. Milagros de Nuestra Senora. (SPA.). 148p. 1966. 9.95 (*0-8288-7025-X*, S3346) Fr & Eur.
— Signos Que Apareceran. (SPA.). 308p. 1980. 16.75 (*0-8288-7010-1*, S37437) Fr & Eur.
Berceo, Bonzalo. Vida de San Millan de la Cogolla Obias Completas II. rev. ed. Dutton, Brian, ed. (Monagrafias A Ser.: Vol. IV). (SPA.). 296p. (C). 1967. pap. 51.00 (*0-7293-0192-3*, Pub. by Tamesis Bks Ltd) Boydell & Brewer.
Berceo, Gonzalo. La Vida de Santo Domingo de Silos: Estudio y Edicion Critica. Dutton, Brian, ed. (Monagrafias A Ser.: Vol. LXXIV). (SPA.). 293p. (Orig.). (C). 1978. pap. 51.00 (*0-7293-0067-6*, Pub. by Tamesis Bks Ltd) Boydell & Brewer.
Berceo, Gonzalo D. Milagros de Nuestra Senora. Cacho Blecva, Juan M., ed. (Nueva Austral Ser.: No. 103). (SPA.). 1991. pap. text 14.95 (*84-239-1903-X*) Elliots Bks.
Berceo, Gonzalo De, see De Berceo, Gonzalo.
Berces, Gonzalo D. La Vida de Santo Domingo de Silos: Poema de Santa Orio. Ruffinatto, Aldo, ed. (Nueva Austral Ser.: No. 262). (SPA.). 1993. pap. text. write for info. (*84-239-7262-3*) Elliots Bks.
***Berch, Bettina.** The Woman Behind the Lens: The Life & Work of Frances Benjamin Johnston, 1864-1952. LC 00-22173. (Illus.). 212p. 2000. 65.00 (*0-8139-1938-X*); pap. 24.95 (*0-8139-2009-4*) U Pr of Va.
Berch, Michael A., et al. Introduction to Legal Method & Process. 2nd ed. (American Casebook Ser.). 585p. (C). 1992. 57.50 (*0-314-00412-2*) West Pub.
— Introduction to Legal Method & Process Cases & Materials, Teacher's Manual to Accompany. 2nd ed. (American Casebook Ser.). 100p. (C). 1992. pap. text. write for info. (*0-314-01376-8*) West Pub.
Berchem, Denis Van, see Van Berchem, Denis.
Berchem-Simon, Odette. Ergonomics Action in Mining the Results of the 5th ECSC Programme. 316p. 1994. 45.00 (*92-826-5090-1*, CE-NA-14831-2AC, Pub. by Comm Europ Commun) Bernan Associates.
Bercholz, Samuel & Kohn, Sherab C., eds. Entering the Stream: An Introduction to the Buddha & His Teachings. LC 93-31453. (Illus.). 352p. (Orig.). 1994. pap. 18.00 (*0-87773-981-1*, Pub. by Shambhala Pubns) Random.
Bercht, Fatima, et al. Contemporary Art from Chile. Fox, Geoffrey et al, trs. from ENG. (Illus.). 64p. (Orig.). 1991. 12.00 (*1-879128-02-0*) Americas Soc.
Bercht, Fatima, ed. see Alegria, Ricardo E., et al.
Berchtold, R., ed. see Paquet, K. J., et al.
Berci, George & Cuschieri, Alfred. Bile Ducts & Bile Duct Stones. Bralow, Lisette, ed. 320p. 1996. text 110.00 (*0-7216-1488-4*, W B Saunders Co) Harcrt Hlth Sci Grp.
Bercik, Elaine V. Thorns among the Sagebrush. 189p. 1984. 7.95 (*0-89697-161-9*) Intl Univ Pr.
Bercik, Janet & Blair-Larson, Susan M. Joining Forces to Guide the New Teacher. 1993. ring bd. 19.95 (*0-89420-280-4*, 343530) Natl Book.
— Joining Forces to Guide the New Teacher: Mentor Edition. 1993. teacher ed., ring bd. 22.50 (*0-89420-300-2*, 343535) Natl Book.
Bercik, Janet T. Student Teaching Guidebook. 131p. (C). 1990. ring bd. 24.90 (*0-89420-269-3*, 343550) Natl Book.
Berck, Eva. Yonder the Bridge: The Story of an Impossible Courtship. Alberts, Robert C., ed. 496p. 1991. 19.95 (*0-9629937-0-0*); pap. 11.95 (*0-9629937-1-9*) Somerset PA.
Berck, Judith. No Place to Be: Voices of Homeless Children. (Illus.). 144p. (J). (gr. 5 up). 1992. 17.00 (*0-395-53350-3*) HM.
Berck, Peter & Bigman, David, eds. Food Security & Food Inventories in Developing Countries. (Illus.). 400p. 1993. text 90.00 (*0-85198-810-5*) OUP.
Berck, Peter & Sydsaeter, K. Economists' Mathematical Manual. x, 166p. 1991. 32.00 (*0-387-54370-8*) Spr-Verlag.
Berck, Peter & Sydsaeter, Knut. Economists' Mathematical Manual. 2nd ed. LC 92-46065. (Illus.). 166p. 1994. 29.95 (*0-387-56374-1*) Spr-Verlag.
Bercken, William Van den, see Van den Bercken, William.
***Berckhan, Barbara, et al.** Public & Professional Speaking: A Confident Approach for Women. 180p. 1999. pap. 22.50 (*1-85343-473-6*, Pub. by Free Assoc Bks) Intl Spec Bk.
Berckhemer, H. & Hsu, K. J., eds. Alpine-Mediterranean Geodynamics. (Geodynamics Ser.: Vol. 7). 216p. 1982. 22.00 (*0-87590-503-X*) Am Geophysical.
Berckman, Evelyn. The Beckoning Dream. 20.95 (*0-88411-269-1*) Amereon Ltd.
— The Evil of Time. 20.95 (*0-88411-270-5*) Amereon Ltd.
— The Heir of Starvelings. 21.95 (*0-88411-271-3*) Amereon Ltd.
— The Hovering Darkness. 20.95 (*0-88411-272-1*) Amereon Ltd.
— Lament for Four Brides. 20.95 (*0-88411-273-X*) Amereon Ltd.
— Strange Bedfellows. 20.95 (*0-88411-274-8*) Amereon Ltd.
Bercoff, R. Perez, ed. The Molecular Basis of Viral Replication. LC 87-15226. (NATO ASI Series A, Life Sciences: Vol. 136). (Illus.). 594p. 1987. 135.00 (*0-306-42619-6*, Plenum Trade) Perseus Pubng.
Bercot, David, ed. A Dictionary of Early Christian Beliefs. LC 98-8259. 704p. 1998. 34.95 (*1-56563-357-1*) Hendrickson MA.
Bercot, David W. Common Sense: A New Approach to Understanding Scripture. LC 92-80133. 180p. (Orig.). 1992. pap. 7.95 (*0-924722-06-1*) Scroll Pub.
— Let Me Die in Ireland: The True Story of Patrick. LC 99-210833. 1999. pap. text 8.95 (*0-924722-08-8*) Scroll Pub.
— Will the Real Heretics Please Stand Up: A New Look at Today's Evangelical Church in the Light of Early Christianity. 192p. (Orig.). 1989. pap. 7.95 (*0-924722-00-2*) Scroll Pub.
Bercovici, Eric. Tread Lightly My Dear. 1990. 17.95 (*1-55972-027-1*, Birch Ln Pr) Carol Pub Group.
Bercovici, H. Operator Theory & Arithmetic in H: Infinity Sign. LC 88-10344. (Mathematical Surveys & Monographs: Vol. 26). 275p. 1988. text 82.00 (*0-8218-1528-8*, SURV/26) Am Math.
Bercovici, H. & Foias, C. I., eds. Nonselfadjoint Operator Algebras, Operator Theory, & Related Topics: The Carl M. Pearcy Anniversary Volume. (Operator Theory Ser.: Vol. 104). 224p. 1998. 89.50 (*3-7643-5954-4*) Spr-Verlag.
Bercovici, H., et al. Dual Algebras with Applications to Invariant Subspaces & Dilation Theory. LC 84-24528. (CBMS Regional Conference Series in Mathematics: No. 56). 108p. 1985. pap. 24.00 (*0-8218-0706-4*, CBMS/56) Am Math.
Bercovici, Konrad. Volga Boatman. LC 72-131628. 1970. reprint ed. 15.00 (*0-403-00515-9*) Scholarly.
Bercovitch, Jacob, ed. ANZUS in Crisis: Alliance Management in International Affairs. LC 87-26856. 240p. 1988. text 55.00 (*0-312-01223-3*) St Martin.
— Resolving International Conflicts: The Theory & Practice of Mediation. 1995. pap. 19.95 (*1-55587-601-3*) L Rienner.
Bercovitch, Sacvan. American Jeremiad. LC 78-53283. 254p. 1980. pap. 19.95 (*0-299-07354-8*) U of Wis Pr.
— The Cambridge History of American Literature Vol. 1: 1590-1820. 842p. 1997. pap. text 28.95 (*0-521-58571-6*) Cambridge U Pr.

— The Office of the Scarlet Letter. LC 90-25796. (Parallax). 200p. 1991. text 40.00 (*0-8018-4203-4*) Johns Hopkins.

— The Office of "The Scarlet Letter" (Parallax: Re-Visions of Culture & Society Ser.). 200p. 1993. reprint ed. pap. text 14.95 (*0-8018-4584-X*) Johns Hopkins.

— The Puritan Origins of the American Self. LC 74-29713. 260p. 1977. write for info. (*0-300-01754-5*); pap. 18.00 (*0-300-02117-8*) Yale U Pr.

— The Puritan Origins of the American Self. LC 74-29713. 260p. reprint ed. pap. 80.60 (*0-8357-8753-2*, 203366900087) Bks Demand.

— The Rites of Assent. 384p. (C). (gr. 13). 1992. 75.00 (*0-415-90014-X*, 1182); pap. 24.99 (*0-415-90015-8*, 1187) Routledge.

Bercovitch, Sacvan, ed. The American Puritan Imagination: Essays in Revaluation. LC 73-94136. 273p. reprint ed. pap. 77.90 (*0-8357-5393-X*, 2027269) Bks Demand.

— The Cambridge History of American Literature: Prose Writing - 1820-1865, Vol. 2. 907p. (C). 1995. text 80.00 (*0-521-30106-8*) Cambridge U Pr.

— The Cambridge History of American Literature Vol. 8: Poetry & Criticism, 1940-1995. 557p. (C). 1996. text 69.95 (*0-521-49733-7*) Cambridge U Pr.

— Library of American Puritan Writings: The Seventeenth Century, 27 vols., Set. Incl. Vol. 1. Election Day Sermons: Massachusetts. LC 84-45975. lib. bdg. 76.50 (*0-404-60801-9*); Vol. 2. Election Day Sermons: Plymouth & Connecticut. LC 84-45975. 76.50 (*0-404-60802-7*); Vol. 3. Fast Day Sermons. LC 84-45975. 76.50 (*0-404-60803-5*); Vol. 4. Sermons on Conduct & Manners. LC 84-45975. 76.50 (*0-404-60804-3*); Vol. 5. Execution Sermons. LC 84-45975. 76.50 (*0-404-60805-1*); Vol. 6. Aspects of Puritan Religious Thought. LC 84-45975. Vol. 7. Puritan Personal Writings: Diaries. LC 84-45975. Vol. 8. Puritan Personal Writings: Autobiographies & Other Writings. LC 84-45975. 240p. Vol. 9. Histories & Narratives. LC 84-45975. 76.50 (*0-404-60809-4*); Vol. 10. Tracts Against New England. LC 84-45975. 76.50 (*0-404-60810-8*); Vol. 11. Orthodox Evangelist. Norton, John. LC 84-45975. Vol. 12. John Cotton: The New England Way. LC 84-45975. 76.50 (*0-404-60812-4*); Vol. 13. John Cotton: The Way of Faith. LC 84-45975. 76.50 (*0-404-60813-2*); Vol. 14. John Cotton: The End of the World. LC 84-45975. 76.50 (*0-404-60814-0*); Vol. 15. Thomas Hooker: The Soules Preparation for Christ. LC 84-45975. Vol. 16. Thomas Hooker: The Soules Humiliation. LC 84-45975. Vol. 17. Thomas Hooker: The Soules Implantation. LC 84-45975. Vol. 18. Thomas Hooker: The Soules Exaltation. LC 84-45975. Vol. 19. Richard Mather: Life, Journal & Selected Writings. LC 84-45975. 76.50 (*0-404-60819-1*); Vol. 20. Increase Mather: Jeremiads. LC 84-45975. 76.50 (*0-404-60820-5*); Vol. 21. Increase Mather: Doctrine. LC 84-45975. 76.50 (*0-404-60821-3*); Vol. 22. Increase Mather: Two Tracts. LC 84-45975. 76.50 (*0-404-60822-1*); Vol. 23. Cotton Mather: Historical Writings. LC 84-45975. 76.50 (*0-404-60823-X*); Vol. 24. Cotton Mather: Apocalyptic Writings. LC 84-45975. 76.50 (*0-404-60824-8*); Vol. 25. Cotton Mather: Sermons on Church & State. LC 84-45975. 76.50 (*0-404-60825-6*); Vol. 26. Samuel Willard: Selected Sermons. LC 84-45975. 76.50 (*0-404-60826-4*); Vol. 27. Vision of New England: Selected Writings. Bercovitch, Sacvan. LC 84-45975. 76.50 (*0-404-60827-2*); LC 84-45975. (American Puritan Writings Ser.). 1938. reprint ed. write for info. (*0-404-60800-0*) AMS Pr.

***Bercovitch, Sacvan, ed.** Prose Writing, 1940-1990. (Cambridge History of American Literature Ser.). 800p. (C). 1999. 85.00 (*0-521-49732-9*) Cambridge U Pr.

Bercovitch, Sacvan, ed. Reconstructing American Literary History. (English Studies: No. 13). 384p. 1985. 20.00 (*0-674-75085-3*) HUP.

— Reconstructing American Literary History. (English Studies: No. 13). 384p. 1986. pap. 9.95 (*0-674-75086-1*) HUP.

Bercovitch, Sacvan & Patell, Cyrus R., eds. The Cambridge History of American Literature, Vol. 1, 1590-1820. LC 92-42479. 845p. (C). 1994. text 85.00 (*0-521-30105-X*) Cambridge U Pr.

Bercovitch, Sacvan, ed. see West, Nathanael.

Bercovitch, Vi. Mirror, Mirror: Terse Verse for Seasoned Citizens. (Illus.). 66p. pap. (*0-9695180-5-6*) Shloreline.

Bercovitz, Alan. The Financial Freedom Course. 200p. 1985. ring bd. 29.50 (*0-916735-00-1*) New Venture.

Bercow, Larry, photos by. Two of a Kind: Dogs That Look Like Their Owners. LC 99-11793. (Illus.). 96p. 1999. mass mkt. 9.99 (*0-446-67479-6*, Pub. by Warner Bks) Little.

Bercu, B. B., jt. ed. see Stabler, B.

Bercu, Barry B., ed. Basic & Clinical Aspects of Growth Hormone. LC 88-12527. (Serono Symposia U. S. A. Ser.). (Illus.). 392p. 1988. 110.00 (*0-306-42921-7*, Plenum Trade) Perseus Pubng.

Bercu, Barry B. & Shulman, D. I., eds. Advances in Perinatal Thyroidology. (Advances in Experimental Medicine & Biology Ser.: Vol. 299). (Illus.). 280p. (C). 1991. text 107.00 (*0-306-44006-7*, Kluwer Plenum) Kluwer Academic.

Bercu, Barry B. & Walker, R. F., eds. Growth Hormone Secretagogues. LC 96-632. (Proceedings of the Serono Symposia U. S. A. Ser.). (Illus.). 488p. 1996. 135.00 (*0-387-94707-8*) Spr-Verlag.

Bercu, Barry B. & Walker, Richard F. Growth Hormone Secretagogues in Clinical Practice. LC 98-13319. (Illus.). 504p. 1998. text 195.00 (*0-8247-9832-5*) Dekker.

Bercu, Barry B. & Walker, Richard F., eds. Growth Hormone Two: Basic & Clinical Aspects. LC 93-28882. 1994. 142.00 (*0-387-94133-9*) Spr-Verlag.

Bercu, Barry B., jt. ed. see Pomerance, H. H.

***Bercuson, David.** Blood on the Hills: The Canadian Army in the Korean War. 269p. 1999. text 35.00 (*0-8020-0980-8*) U of Toronto Pr.

Bercuson, David. Canada & the Birth of Israel: A Study in Canadian Foreign Policy. LC DS0063.2.C. 302p. reprint ed. pap. 93.70 (*0-7837-1045-3*, 204135700020) Bks Demand.

— Confrontation at Winnipeg: Labour, Industrial Relations & the General Strike. rev. ed. 240p. (C). 1990. reprint ed. pap. text 24.95 (*0-7735-0794-9*, Pub. by McG-Queens Univ Pr) CUP Services.

— Maple Leaf Against the Axis: Canada's Second World War. 336p. 1998. pap. 21.95 (*0-7737-5952-2*) Stoddart Publ.

— Significant Incident: Canada's Army, the Airborne, & the Murder in Somalia. LC 97-127975. 256p. 1997. 26.95 (*0-7710-1113-X*) McCland & Stewart.

— True Patriot: A Biography of Brooke Claxton. (Illus.). 360p. 1993. text 35.00 (*0-8020-2984-1*) U of Toronto Pr.

Bercuson, David & Granatstein, Jack L. Dictionary of Canadian Military History. 228p. (C). 1994. pap. (*0-19-541107-2*) OUP.

Bercuson, David & Wise, S. F., eds. The Valour & the Horror Revisited. 192p. 1994. 60.00 (*0-7735-1259-4*, Pub. by McG-Queens Univ Pr); pap. 22.95 (*0-7735-1271-3*, Pub. by McG-Queens Univ Pr) CUP Services.

Bercuson, David, et al. Colonies: Canada to 1867. (C). 1992. pap. text 33.25 (*0-07-551013-8*) McGraw.

Bercuson, David, ed. see Joint Atlantic Canada-Western Canadian Studies Con.

Bercuson, Kenneth, et al. Singapore: A Case Study in Rapid Development. (Occasional Paper Ser.: No. 119). 75p. 1995. pap. 15.00 (*1-55775-463-2*) Intl Monetary.

Bercusson, Brian. European Labor Law. LC 97-108264. 430p. 1995. pap. text 75.00 (*0-406-04595-X*, MICHIE) LEXIS Pub.

Berczi, Istvan, ed. Pituitary Function & Immunity. 336p. 1986. lib. bdg. 248.00 (*0-8493-6107-9*, QR182) CRC Pr.

Berczi, Istvan & Kovacs, Kalman, eds. Hormones & Immunity. 1987. text 242.50 (*0-85200-848-1*) Kluwer Academic.

Berczi, Istvan & Szelenyi, Judith, eds. Advances in Psychoneuroimmunology. LC 94-47537. (Hans Selye Symposia on Neuroendocrinology & Stress Ser.: Vol. 3). 390p. 1995. text 110.00 (*0-306-44883-1*, Kluwer Plenum) Kluwer Academic.

Berczyk, Cheryl. Consider This. (Illus.). 127p. (Orig.). 1992. pap. 9.95 (*0-926301-10-1*) IP Inc MN.

Berczynski, Thomas, tr. see Olesha, IUrii Karlovich.

Berd, Malcolm, jt. ed. see Boehm, Erika.

Berda, Marty & Blaisdell, Mary J. Science Projects for All Students. LC 97-35540. (Illus.). 288p. (J). (gr. 4-7). 1997. ring bd. 165.00 (*0-8160-3569-5*) Facts on File.

***Berdahl, Daphne.** Altering States: Ethnographies of Transition in Eastern Europe & the Former Soviet Union. LC 00-20478. 264p. (C). 2000. text 59.50 (*0-472-11058-6*, 11058); pap. text 24.95 (*0-472-08617-0*, 08617) U of Mich Pr.

Berdahl, Daphne. Where the World Ended: Re-Unification & Identity in the German Borderland. LC 98-7099. 307p. 1999. 16.95 (*0-520-21477-3*, Pub. by U CA Pr) Cal Prin Full Svc.

***Berdahl, Daphne.** Where the World Ended: Transition & Identity in the German Borderland. LC 98-7099. 1999. 45.00 (*0-520-21476-5*, Pub. by U CA Pr) Cal Prin Full Svc.

Berdahl, Robert M. The Politics of the Prussian Nobility: The Development of a Conservative Ideology, 1770-1848. LC 88-17616. 398p. reprint ed. pap. 123.40 (*0-608-06303-7*, 206666500008) Bks Demand.

Berdahl, Robert O. British Universities & the State. Metzger, Walter P., ed. LC 76-55198. (Academic Profession Ser.). 1977. reprint ed. lib. bdg. 21.95 (*0-405-10029-9*) Ayer.

Berdal. U. S., Norway & the Cold War 1954-1960. LC 96-22554. 250p. 1997. text 49.95 (*0-312-16281-2*) St Martin.

***Berdal, Mats & Malone, David M., eds.** Greed & Grievance: Economic Agendas in Civil War. LC 99-86829. 256p. 2000. pap. 17.95 (*1-55587-868-7*) L Rienner.

— Greed & Grievance: Economic Agendas in Civil War. LC 99-86829. 256p. 2000. 49.95 (*1-55587-892-X*) L Rienner.

Berdal, Mats R. Demobilization & Deintegration after Civil Wars. (Adelphi Papers: No. 303). 88p. 1996. pap. text 26.00 (*0-19-828026-2*) OUP.

Berdan. The Web of Culture: An Introduction to Cultural Anthropology. (Anthropology Ser.). 2001. pap. 42.00 (*0-534-57438-6*) Wadsworth Pub.

Berdan, David. ExpressCheck Version Five. 256p. 1994. 39.95 (*0-614-04243-7*) Expressware.

— ExpressGraph: Version One. 92p. 1986. student ed. 29.95 (*1-878012-02-9*) Expressware.

Berdan, David & McGinnis, Ken. File Express 5.1: Database Management Software. (Illus.). 425p. 1992. 99.00 incl. disk (*1-878012-06-1*) Expressware.

Berdan, F., jt. comment see De Durand-Forest, J.

Berdan, Frances F. Aztecs. (Indians of North America Ser.). (J). 1989. 15.05 (*0-606-04027-7*, Pub. by Turtleback) Demco.

— The Aztecs of Central Mexico: An Imperial Society. 224p. (C). 1982. pap. text 23.50 (*0-03-055736-4*) Harcourt Coll Pubs.

Berdan, Frances F. & Anawalt, Patricia R. Codex Mendoza, 3 vols., Vol. Set. LC 91-15397. (C). 1992. boxed set 555.00 (*0-520-06234-5*, Pub. by U CA Pr) Cal Prin Full Svc.

— The Essential Codex Mendoza. LC 96-19507. (Illus.). 415p. 1997. pap. 42.50 (*0-520-20454-9*, Pub. by U CA Pr) Cal Prin Full Svc.

Berdan, Frances F. & Barber, Russell J. Spanish Thread on Indian Looms: Mexican Folk Costumes. Correa, Rafael E., tr. (ENG & SPA., Illus.). 112p. 1988. per. 17.00 (*0-945486-04-9*) CSU SBRVFAM.

Berdan, Frances F., et al. Aztec Imperial Strategies. LC 94-42796. (Illus.). 390p. 1996. 60.00 (*0-88402-211-0*, Dumbarton Rsch Lib) Dumbarton Oaks.

Berdan, Frances F., jt. auth. see Barber, Russell J.

Berdan, Yuriy. S Tochki Zreniya Torshera: Micronovels & Short Stories. Kolker, Yuri, ed. LC 98-60408. (RUS., Illus.). 220p. 1998. pap. 12.00 (*1-885563-09-4*) VIA Press MD.

Berdanier, Carolyn D. Advanced Nutrition: Macronutrients. LC 94-11519. (Modern Nutrition Ser.). (Illus.). 304p. 1994. boxed set 104.95 (*0-8493-8500-8*, 8500) CRC Pr.

***Berdanier, Carolyn D.** Advanced Nutrition: Macronutrients. 2nd ed. (Modern Nutrition Ser.). 392p. (C). 2000. ring bd. 99.95 (*0-8493-8735-3*) CRC Pr.

Berdanier, Carolyn D. Advanced Nutrition: Micronutrients. (Modern Nutrition Ser.). 256p. (C). 1997. boxed set 94.95 (*0-8493-2664-8*) CRC Pr.

— Handbook of Nutrition & Food. 1999. 114.95 (*0-8493-2705-9*) CRC Pr.

Berdanier, Carolyn D., ed. Nutrients & Gene Expression: Clinical Aspects. LC 96-14781. (Modern Nutrition Ser.). 240p. 1996. boxed set 139.95 (*0-8493-9485-6*) CRC Pr.

Berdanier, Carolyn D. & Hargrove, James L., eds. Nutrition & Gene Expression. 592p. 1992. lib. bdg. 169.00 (*0-8493-6961-4*, QP144) CRC Pr.

Berdanier, Carolyn D., jt. auth. see Hargrove, James L.

***Berdayes, Vicente W. & Murphy, John, eds.** Computers, Human Interaction & Organizations: Critical Issues. LC 99-59851. 264p. 2000. 65.00 (*0-275-96385-3*, Praeger Pubs) Greenwood.

Berde, E., et al, eds. Neurohypophysial Hormones & Similar Polypeptides. (Handbook of Experimental Pharmacology Ser.: Vol. 23). (Illus.). 1968. 184.00 (*0-387-04149-4*) Spr-Verlag.

Berdecio, Robert, ed. see Posada, Jose G.

Berden, J. H., et al, eds. Gesellschaft Fur Nephrologie: Deutsche Arbeitsgemeinschaft Fur Klinische Nephrologie, Nederlandse Vereniging Voor Nefrologie: Joint Scientific Meeting, Aachen, September 1997: Invited Papers. (Kidney & Blood Pressure Research Ser.: Vol. 20, No. 3, 1997). (Illus.). 74p. 1997. pap. 55.75 (*3-8055-6568-2*) S Karger.

Berden, John M. & Forthergill, John. Fourteen Stories from One Plot, Based on "Mr Fothergill's Plot. 1977. 23.95 (*0-8369-4262-0*, 6064) Ayer.

Berdes, Celia, et al, eds. Geragogics: European Research in Gerontological Education & Educational Gerontology. LC 92-40000. (Gerontology & Geriatrics Education Ser.: Vol. 13, Nos. 1 & 2). (Illus.). 180p. 1993. 39.95 (*1-56024-397-X*) Haworth Pr.

Berdes, George R. Friendly Adversaries: The Press & Government. LC 79-84597. 196p. 1969. reprint ed. pap. 60.80 (*0-608-04193-9*, 206492800011) Bks Demand.

Berdes, Jane L., ed. see Sirmen, Maddalena L.

Berdiaev, Nicolas. Leontiev. (Russian Ser.: Vol. 15). 1958. reprint ed. pap. 25.00 (*0-87569-004-1*) Academic Intl.

Berdiaev, Nikolai, et al. Vekhi (Landmarks) Shatz, Marshall S., ed. & tr. by. from RUS. Zimmerman, Judith E., tr. from RUS. LC 94-26039. 224p. (C). (gr. 13). 1994. pap. text 34.95 (*1-56324-391-1*) M E Sharpe.

— Vekhi (Landmarks) Zimmerman, Judith E., tr. from RUS. LC 94-26039. 224p. (C). (gr. 13). 1994. text 75.95 (*1-56324-390-3*) M E Sharpe.

Berdiaev, Nikolai A. The Beginning & the End. French, Reginald M., tr. from RUS. LC 76-6083. 256p. 1975. reprint ed. lib. bdg. 65.00 (*0-8371-8837-7*, BEBE, Greenwood Pr) Greenwood.

— The Russian Idea. French, Reginald M., tr. LC 78-32021. 255p. 1979. reprint ed. lib. bdg. 65.00 (*0-313-20968-5*, BERN, Greenwood Pr) Greenwood.

— Solitude & Society. Reavey, George, tr. from RUS. LC 70-98211. 207p. 1976. reprint ed. lib. bdg. 35.00 (*0-8371-3250-9*, BESS, Greenwood Pr) Greenwood.

Berdichevsky, V., et al, eds. Homogenization. LC 99-24583. (Advances in Mathematics for Applied Sciences Ser.). 420p. 1998. text 54.00 (*981-02-3096-6*) World Scientific Pub.

Berdichevsky, Victor L. Thermodynam Chaos. 1997. lib. bdg. 60.00 (*0-582-08734-1*, Pub. by Addison-Wesley) Longman.

Berdichewsky, Bernardo, ed. Anthropology & Social Change in Rural Areas: The Impact of Agrarian Reform upon Local Communities. (World Anthropology Ser.). (Illus.). xviii, 564p. 1979. text 75.40 (*90-279-7810-7*) Mouton.

Berdicio, Marion D., tr. see Frank, Andre G.

Berdine, William C. Good Ol' Stumptoe U. LC 96-95188. 256p. (Orig.). 1996. pap. 11.00 (*0-9631802-2-3*) Berdine.

— It Takes a Funny Man . . . (The Best of Bill Berdine) LC 94-96825. 256p. 1995. 15.00 (*0-9631802-1-5*) Berdine.

— My Granddaddy Was a Ramblin' Man. LC 97-94443. 264p. 1997. 20.00 (*0-9631802-3-1*) Berdine.

— The Untheory of Evolution: And Other Scientific Studies Including Hunting, Fishing & Sex. LC 91-90760. 243p. 1992. 19.95 (*0-9631802-0-7*) Berdine.

Berdine, William H., jt. auth. see Blackhurst, A. Edward.

Berding, Andrew. The Making of Foreign Policy. LC 66-14226. (U. S. A. Survey Ser.). 102p. 1966. 4.95 (*0-87107-002-2*) Potomac.

Berdini, Paolo. The Religious Art of Jacopo Bassano: Painting As Visual Exegesis. (Cambridge Studies in New Art History & Criticism). (Illus.). 230p. 1997. text 64.95 (*0-521-56170-1*) Cambridge U Pr.

Berdjis, Nassim W. Imagery in Vladimir Nabokov's Last Russian Novel, Dar: The Gift, & Other Prose Works of the 1930s. LC 95-42207. (Mainzer Studien zur Amerikanistik Ser.: Bd. 31). (Illus.). 396p. 1995. pap. 63.95 (*0-8204-2931-7*, 68665) P Lang Pubng.

Berdoe, Edward. Browning & the Christian Faith. LC 79-130244. (Studies in Browning: No. 4). 1970. reprint ed. lib. bdg. 75.00 (*0-8383-1134-2*) M S G Haskell Hse.

— Browning's Message to His Time. LC 73-16003. (Studies in Browning: No. 4). 1974. reprint ed. lib. bdg. 75.00 (*0-8383-1724-3*) M S G Haskell Hse.

***Berdoll, Linda. The Bar Sinister: Pride & Prejudice Continues. LC 99-91196. 468p. 1999. pap. 18.50 (*0-9674817-0-8*) Well There.**

The Bar Sinister is an affectionate, if tongue in cheek furthering of Jane Austen's Pride & Prejudice. Although the story is rather epic in scope, thanks to a playful tweaking of the language, it never falls narrowly into the category off drama. Indeed, the author has sought to have fun with not only the language but Austen's characters as well, taking them (often quite explicitly) where no one else has dared. Not surprisingly, this audacity has incited no little outraged swooning amongst Jane Austen purists. (To any possible affronted souls we extend our sincere apologies & gently discourage purchase of this book.) But those readers who like their stories vivid, lovers earthy & comedic adventures hilarious have embraced The Bar Sinister wholeheartedly.To make up your own mind, The Bar Sinister is available in national bookstores for $18.50. But it can be purchased by credit card & at the discounted price of $15.00 at our website www.thebarsinister.com. *Publisher Paid Annotation.*

Berdt, Dennys De, see De Berdt, Dennys.

Berdugo, A., et al. Ositos Nada Mas - Primarily Bears. (ENG & SPA.). 159p. (J). (gr. k-6). 1992. 16.95 (*1-881431-30-4*, 1432) AIMS Educ Fnd.

Berdy, Janos. Handbook Antibiotic Compounds. (CRC Handbook of Antibiotic Compounds Ser.: Vol. 5). 576p. 1981. 307.00 (*0-8493-3456-X*, QV350, CRC Reprint) Franklin.

— Handbook of Antibiotic Compounds, Vol. XIV, Pt. 1. 464p. 1987. lib. bdg. 200.00 (*0-8493-3435-7*) CRC Pr.

— Handbook of Antibiotic Compounds, Vol. XIV, Pt. 2. 344p. 1987. lib. bdg. 200.00 (*0-8493-3436-5*) CRC Pr.

— Handbook of Antibiotic Compounds: Antibiotics from Higher Forms of Life: Higher Plants, Vol. VIII, Pt. II. 448p. 1982. 244.00 (*0-8493-3460-8*, QV250, CRC Reprint) Franklin.

— Handbook on Antibiotic Compounds, Vol. XIII, Pt. 1. 344p. 1987. lib. bdg. 225.00 (*0-8493-3431-4*) CRC Pr.

— Handbook on Antibiotic Compounds, Vol. XIII, Pt. 2. 416p. 1987. lib. bdg. 225.00 (*0-8493-3432-2*) CRC Pr.

— Handbook on Antibiotic Compounds, Vol. XIII, Pt. 3. 376p. 1987. lib. bdg. 225.00 (*0-8493-3433-0*) CRC Pr.

Berdy, Janos, ed. Handbook Antibiotic Compounds, Vol. XI, Pt. I. 704p. 1985. lib. bdg. 271.00 (*0-8493-3463-2*, QV250, CRC Reprint) Franklin.

— Handbook Antibiotic Compounds, Vol. XI, Pt. II. 408p. 1985. lib. bdg. 242.00 (*0-8493-3464-0*, CRC Reprint) Franklin.

— Handbook of Antibiotic Compounds, Vol. 7. (Miscellaneous Antibiotics with Unknown Chemical Structure Ser.). 272p. 1981. 153.00 (*0-8493-3458-6*, QV250, CRC Reprint) Franklin.

— Handbook of Antibiotic Compounds, Vol. X. 560p. 1982. 308.00 (*0-8493-3462-4*, QV250, CRC Reprint) Franklin.

— Handbook of Antibiotic Compounds, Vol. XII. 720p. 1985. lib. bdg. 271.00 (*0-8493-3465-9*, QV250) CRC Pr.

— Handbook of Antibiotic Compounds, Vols. I-IV. Incl. Vol. I. Carbohydrate Antibiotics. 472p. 1980. 255.00 (*0-8493-3451-9*, QV350, CRC Reprint); Vol. II. Macrocyclic Lactone (Lactam) Antibiotics. 552p. 1980. 299.00 (*0-8493-3452-7*, QV350, CRC Reprint); Vol. III. Quinone & Similar Antibiotics. 440p. 1980. 240.00 (*0-8493-3453-5*, QV350, CRC Reprint); Vol. IV, Pt. 1. Amino Acid & Peptide Antibiotics. 576p. 1980. 312.00 (*0-8493-3454-3*, CRC Reprint); Vol. IV, Pt. 2. Peptolide & Macromolecular Antibiotics. 376p. 1980. 205.00 (*0-8493-3455-1*, CRC Reprint); 1980. write for info. (*0-318-51461-3*) CRC Pr.

— Handbook of Antibiotic Compounds: Alicyclic, Aromatic & Aliphatic Antibiotics, Vol. 6. (CRC Handbook of Antibiotic Compounds Ser.). 384p. 1981. 260.00 (*0-8493-3457-8*, QV250, CRC Reprint) Franklin.

— Handbook of Antibiotic Compounds: Antibiotics from Higher Forms of Life: Higher Plants, Vol. VIII, Pt. I. 424p. 1982. 234.00 (*0-8493-3459-4*, QV250, CRC Reprint) Franklin.

— Handbook of Antibiotic Compounds: Antibiotics from Higher Forms of Life: Lichens, Algae, & Animal Organisms, Vol. IX. (CRC Handbook of Antibiotic Compounds Ser.). 248p. 1982. 137.00 (*0-8493-3461-6*, QV250, CRC Reprint) Franklin.

Berdy, Janos, et al, eds. Handbook of Antibiotic Compounds, 2 vols., Vol. XIII, Pts. 1-3: Microbial Metabolites. 1072p. 1987. 585.00 (*0-685-18934-1*) CRC Pr.

— Handbook of Antibiotic Compounds, Vol. XIV, Pts. 1-2. 720p. 1987. 330.00 (*0-8493-3434-9*, RS431) CRC Pr.

B

— Handbook of Antibiotic Compounds: Vol. XIII: Microbial Metabolites, Pts. 1, 2, 3, 3 vols. 1987. 485.00 (*0-8493-3430-6*, RS431) CRC Pr.

Berdy, Janos & Aszalos, A. Handbook of Antibiotic Compounds, 14 bks., Set. 1980. reprint ed. 3553.00 (*0-8493-3450-0*, CRC Reprint) Franklin.

Berdyaev, Nicolas. Bourgeois Mind, & Other Essays. LC 67-22072. (Essay Index Reprint Ser.). 1977. 22.95 (*0-8369-0198-3*) Ayer.

— Freedom & the Spirit. LC 72-2567. (Select Bibliographies Reprint Ser.). 1980. reprint ed. 35.95 (*0-8369-6848-4*) Ayer.

— Origin of Russian Communism. 192p. 1960. pap. text 16.95 (*0-472-06034-1*, 06034, Ann Arbor Bks) U of Mich Pr.

Berdyaev, Nikolai A. The Russian Idea. French, R. M., tr. from RUS. Orig. Title: Russkaya Ideya. 280p. 1992. reprint ed. 26.95 (*0-940262-54-1*, Lindisfarne); reprint ed. pap. 16.95 (*0-940262-49-5*, Lindisfarne) Anthroposophic.

Bereano, Philip L. Technology As a Social & Political Phenomenon. LC 76-18723. 554p. reprint ed. pap. 171.80 (*0-608-15684-1*, 203200400077) Bks Demand.

Bereavement Publishing Inc. Staff. Food for the Soul: A " Best of Bereavement" Poetry Collection. (Illus.). 80p. (Orig.). 1996. pap. 9.95 (*0-9627165-1-0*, 1160) Bereavement Pub.

Berebgarius, Turonensis. De Sacra Coena Adversus Lanfrancum Liber Posterior: E Codice Guelferbytano Primum Ediderunt A. F. et F. Th. Vischer. (Berengarii Turonensis Quae Supersunt Tam Edita Quam Inedita Ser.: No. 1). (GER.). vi, 302p. 1975. reprint ed. write for info. (*3-487-05898-7*) G Olms Pubs.

***Berebitsky, Julie.** Like Our Very Own: Adoption & the Changing Culture of Motherhood, 1851-1950. 2001. 34.95 (*0-7006-1051-0*) U Pr of KS.

Berebitsky, William. A Very Long Weekend: The National Guard in Korea, 1950-1953. LC 96-34615. (Illus.). 295p. 1996. 29.95 (*1-57249-022-5*) White Mane Pub.

Berebom, Joshua & Nagarkatte, Umesh. Prealgebra. 670p. (C). 1991. pap. text 71.50 (*0-15-571043-5*) SCP.

Berechman, Joseph. Public Transit Economics & Deregulation Policy. LC 92-41258. (Studies in Regional Science & Urban Economics: Vol. 23). (Illus.). 360p. 1993. 133.50 (*0-444-89275-3*, North Holland) Elsevier.

Berechman, Joseph, et al, eds. Transport & Land Use. LC 96-32420. (Modern Classics in Regional Science Ser.: No. 2). 736p. 1996. 270.00 (*1-85898-109-3*) E Elgar.

Berechman, Joseph, jt. auth. see Banister, David.

Berechman, Joseph, jt. ed. see Banister, David.

Bereciartu, Gurutz J. Decline of the Nation-State. Douglass, William A., tr. LC 94-9097. (Ethnonationalism in Comparative Perspective Ser.). 248p. 1994. text 32.95 (*0-87417-238-1*) U of Nev Pr.

Berecz, Janos. 1956 Counter-Revolution in Hungary: Words & Weapons. rev. ed. Butykai, Istvan, tr. from HUN. 223p. (C). 1986. 45.00 (*963-05-4370-2*, Pub. by Akade Kiado) St Mut.

Berecz, John M. All the Presidents Women: An Examination of Sexual Styles from Presidents Truman to Clinton. (Illus.). 350p. 1999. pap. 18.95 (*0-89334-289-0*) Humanics Ltd.

— Beyond Shame & Pain: Forgiving Yourself & Others. LC 97-29449. 196p. 1998. pap. 16.75 (*0-7880-1183-9*) CSS OH.

— Sexual Styles. Walker, Christopher, ed. LC 98-86001. (Illus.). 298p. 1998. lib. bdg. 28.95 (*0-89334-287-4*, Humanics Trade) Humanics Ltd.

— Understanding Tourette Syndrome, Obsessive-Compulsive Disorder & Related Problems: A Developmental & Catastrophe Theory Perspective. LC 91-4824. (Illus.). 366p. 1991. 44.95 (*0-8261-7390-X*) Springer Pub.

Berecz, Victor G., Jr. The Pioneer Period of Hungarian Airmail. (Illus.). 244p. (Orig.). 1996. pap. 10.00 (*0-939429-16-0*) Am Air Mail.

Bereczki, Gabor, jt. auth. see Vikar, Laszlo.

Bereczki, Gabor, jt. ed. see Vikar, Laszlo.

Bereczky, M. C. Advances in Protozoological Research: Proceedings of the 1st International Conference of Hungary on Protozoology & Memorial Session for Jozsef Gelei, 1885-1952. 549p. (C). 1986. 174.00 (*963-05-4437-7*, Pub. by Akade Kiado) St Mut.

Bereday, George Z. Universities for All. LC 72-11624. (Jossey-Bass Higher Education Ser.). 175p. reprint ed. pap. 54.30 (*0-608-17088-7*, 202774600056) Bks Demand.

Bereday, George Z. & Lauwerys, Joseph A., eds. Yearbook of Education, 1958: The Secondary School Curriculum. LC 73-38704. (Essay Index Reprint Ser.). 1977. reprint ed. 35.95 (*0-8369-2680-3*) Ayer.

— Yearbook of Education, 1959: Higher Education. LC 73-38704. (Essay Index Reprint Ser.). 1977. reprint ed. 31.95 (*0-8369-2681-1*) Ayer.

— Yearbook of Education, 1957: Education & Philosophy. LC 73-38704. (Essay Index Reprint Ser.). 1977. reprint ed. 24.95 (*0-8369-2679-X*) Ayer.

Bereday, George Z. & Pennar, Jaan, eds. The Politics of Soviet Education. LC 75-28662. 217p. 1976. reprint ed. lib. bdg. 75.00 (*0-8371-8477-0*, BEPS, Greenwood Pr) Greenwood.

Bereday, George Z. & Volpicelli, Luigi, eds. Public Education in America: A New Interpretation of Purpose & Practice. LC 77-23510. 212p. 1977. reprint ed. lib. bdg. 59.50 (*0-8371-9702-3*, BEPU, Greenwood Pr) Greenwood.

Beredene, Jocelyn. What Difference Did the Deed of Christ Make? 27p. 1979. reprint ed. pap. 2.95 (*0-88010-103-2*) Anthroposophic.

Beredon, Juliet. Chinese New Year Festivals. (Illus.). 29p. reprint ed. pap. 19.50 (*0-89346-860-6*) Heian Intl.

Beregi, Edit, ed. Centenarians in Hungary. (Interdisciplinary Topics in Gerontology Ser.: Vol. 27). (Illus.). xii, 210p. 1990. 146.25 (*3-8055-5204-1*) S Karger.

Beregi, Edit, et al. Renal Biopsy in Glomerular Diseases. 334p. (C). 1978. 110.00 (*963-05-1356-0*) St Mut.

Beregovaia, N. A., et al. Contributions to the Archaeology of the Soviet Union: With Special Emphasis on Central Asia, the Caucasus & Armenia, Set. Field, Henry, ed. Klein, Richard G. et al, trs. LC 67-79842. (Harvard University. Peabody Museum of Archaeology & Ethnology. Antiquities of the New World Ser.: Vol. 3, No. 1). lib. bdg. 47.50 (*0-404-52644-6*) AMS Pr.

Beregovoy, G. T., ed. see Murashkevich, A. M. & Novichkov, N. N.

Bereishith-Shemoth, jt. auth. see Swift, Dayan M.

Bereiter, Carl & Scardamalia, Marlene, eds. The Psychology of Written Composition. 389p. (C). 1987. text 89.95 (*0-89859-647-5*) L Erlbaum Assocs.

— The Psychology of Written Composition. 389p. (C). 1987. pap. text 45.00 (*0-8058-0038-7*) L Erlbaum Assocs.

Bereiter, Carl, jt. auth. see Anderson, Valerie.

Bereiter-Hahn, J., et al, eds. Biology of the Integument: Vertebrates. (Biology of the Integument Ser.: Vol. 2). (Illus.). 870p. 1986. 361.95 (*0-387-13244-9*) Spr-Verlag.

— Cytomechanics. (Illus.). 310p. 1987. 133.95 (*0-387-18123-7*) Spr-Verlag.

Bereiter, Susan R. & Miller, Steven M. Troubleshooting & Human Factors in Automated Manufacturing Systems. LC 88-38248. (Illus.). 310p. 1989. 48.00 (*0-8155-1187-6*) Noyes.

Berek, Jonathan S. & Hacker, Neville F. Practical Gynecologic Oncology. 2nd ed. 721p. 1994. text 90.00 (*0-614-32078-X*) Lppncott W & W.

— Practical Gynecologic Oncology. 2nd ed. (Illus.). 608p. 1994. 94.00 (*0-683-00597-9*) Lppncott W & W.

Berek, Jonathan S. & Hacker, Neville F. Practical Gynecologic Oncology. 3rd ed. 752p. text 129.00 (*0-683-30719-3*) Lppncott W & W.

Berek, Jonathan S., et al. Novak's Gynecology. 12th ed. LC 96-16316. (Illus.). 1360p. 1996. 95.00 (*0-683-00593-6*) Lppncott W & W.

Berek, M., jt. auth. see Rinne, F.

Berelson, Bernard. The Great Debate on Population Policy: An Instructive Entertainment. LC 75-22229. 32p. (Orig.). 1975. pap. text 2.95 (*0-87834-050-5*) Population Coun.

Berelson, Bernard & Ansheim, Lester. The Library's Public: A Report of the Public Library Inquiry. LC 75-31430. 174p. 1976. reprint ed. lib. bdg. 38.50 (*0-8371-8499-1*, BELP, Greenwood Pr) Greenwood.

Berelson, Bernard R., et al. Voting: A Study of Opinion Formation in a Presidential Campaign. LC 54-11205. (Midway Reprint Ser.). (Illus.). 416p. 1986. pap. text 30.00 (*0-226-04350-9*) U Ch Pr.

Bereman. Compensation Decision Making. (C). 1996. pap. 29.50 (*0-15-504473-7*, Pub. by Harcourt Coll Pubs) Harcourt.

— Compensation Decision Making. 2nd ed. (C). 1998. text 19.00 (*0-03-024613-X*) Harcourt Coll Pubs.

Beren, Joel, ed. see De Berardinis, Olivia.

Beren, Peter, jt. auth. see Bunnin, Brad.

Berenay, Alix. A Frog Prince. 32p. (J). (gr. 2-4). 1995. 14.95 (*0-8050-0426-2*, Bks Young Read) H Holt & Co.

Berenbaum, Howard, ed. see Goddard, Perilou.

Berenbaum, Linda B. The Gothic Imagination: Expansion in Gothic Literature & Art. LC 80-67035. (Illus.). 140p. 1982. 28.50 (*0-8386-3068-5*) Fairleigh Dickinson.

Berenbaum, May R. Bugs in the System. 400p. 1996. pap. 15.00 (*0-201-40824-4*) Addison-Wesley.

— Bugs in the System: Insects & Their Impact on Human Affairs. 377p. 1995. 25.00 (*0-201-62499-0*) Addison-Wesley.

***Berenbaum, May R.** Buzzwords: A Scientist Muses on Sex, Bugs & Rock 'n' Roll. 180p. 1999. pap. 18.00 (*0-309-06835-5*) Natl Acad Pr.

Berenbaum, May R. Ninety-Nine Gnats, Nits, & Nibblers. LC 88-15420. (Illus.). 288p. 1989. 15.95 (*0-252-06027-X*) U of Ill Pr.

— Ninety-Nine More Maggots, Mites, & Munchers. LC 92-34639. (Illus.). 288p. 1993. 15.95 (*0-252-06322-8*); text 37.95 (*0-252-02016-2*) U of Ill Pr.

Berenbaum, May R., et al, eds. Annual Review of Entomology 1999, Vol. 44. 635p. 1999. 120.00 (*0-8243-0144-7*) Annual Reviews.

Berenbaum, May R., jt. ed. see Rosenthal, Gerald A.

Berenbaum, Michael. After Tragedy & Triumph: Modern Jewish Thought & the American Experience. 228p. (C). 1990. 47.95 (*0-521-38057-X*) Cambridge U Pr.

— Elie Wiesel: God, the Holocaust, & the Children of Israel. LC 94-1009. Orig. Title: Vision of the World. 1994. 15.95 (*0-87441-556-X*) Behrman.

— A Mosaic of Victims: Non-Jews Persecuted & Murdered by the Nazis. 320p. (Orig.). (C). 1990. text 45.00 (*0-8147-1131-6*) NYU Pr.

— A Mosaic of Victims: Non-Jews Persecuted & Murdered by the Nazis. 244p. (Orig.). (C). 1992. pap. text 18.50 (*0-8147-1175-8*) NYU Pr.

— The World Must Know: A History of the Holocaust As Told in the United States Holocaust Memorial Museum. LC 92-32813. (Illus.). 240p. 1993. pap. 23.00 (*0-316-09134-0*) Little.

Berenbaum, Michael, ed. Witness to the Holocaust: An Illustrated Documentary History of the Holocaust as Told in the Words of its Victims, Perpetrators & Bystanders. LC 96-22595. (Illus.). 400p. 1997. 32.50 (*0-06-270108-8*, Harper Ref) HarpC.

Berenbaum, Michael & Peck, Abraham J., eds. The Holocaust & History: The Known, the Unknown, the Disputed, & the Reexamined. LC 97-40030. 1024p. Date not set. 65.00 (*0-253-33374-1*) Ind U Pr.

Berenbaum, Michael, jt. ed. see Roth, John K.

Berenbaum, Sheri A., ed. Gonadal Hormones & Sex Differences in Behavior: A Special Issue of Developmental Neuropsychology. 297p. 1998. pap. write for info. (*0-8058-9834-4*) L Erlbaum Assocs.

Berenbaum, Stanford P., jt. auth. see Ettinger, David A.

Berenbeim, Ronald E. Corporate Ethics. (Report: No. 900). (Illus.). viii, 31p. (Orig.). 1987. pap. text 60.00 (*0-8237-0343-6*) Conference Bd.

Berenbein, Boris A. Pseudocarcinoma of the Skin. Tatarchenko, V. E., tr. from RUS. LC 84-24988. (Illus.). 277p. 1985. reprint ed. pap. 85.90 (*0-608-05419-4*, 206588800006) Bks Demand.

Berenberg, Samuel R. Brain: Fetal & Infant. 1978. text 155.50 (*90-247-2022-2*) Kluwer Academic.

Berenberg, Samuel R., ed. see International Children's Center Conference Staff.

Berenblatt, Alena J., jt. auth. see Berenblatt, Maida.

Berenblatt, Maida & Berenblatt, Alena J. Changeweavers: A Pathway to Spiritual Renewal. 200p. 1996. pap. 10.95 (*1-55874-398-7*, 3987) Health Comm.

— Make an Appointment with Yourself: Simple Steps to Positive Self-Esteem. LC 94-31966. 120p. (Orig.). 1994. pap. 7.95 (*1-55874-319-7*, 3197) Health Comm.

Berenblum, Isaac. Man Against Cancer: The Story of Cancer Research. LC 52-13023. 196p. reprint ed. pap. 60.80 (*0-608-30502-2*, 200383000037) Bks Demand.

Berenbom. Prealgebra. (C). 1990. pap. text, student ed. 24.50 (*0-15-571044-3*) Harcourt Coll Pubs.

— Prealgebra. (C). 1991. pap. text, teacher ed. 11.75 (*0-15-571045-1*) Harcourt Coll Pubs.

Berenbon, Howard. Harness Handicapping the Computer Way. LC 95-68651. 70p. 1995. pap. 19.95 (*0-9646207-1-5*) Soft Exchange.

— Mostly BASIC: Applications for Your IBM-PC, 2 Vols., Bk. 1. 1983. write for info. (*0-672-22076-8*, 22093) Macmillan.

— Mostly BASIC: Applications for Your IBM-PC, 2 Vols., Bk. 2. 1983. write for info. (*0-672-22093-8*) Macmillan.

— Thoroughbred Handicapping the Computer Way. LC 95-68650. 65p. 1995. pap. 19.95 (*0-9646207-0-7*) Soft Exchange.

Berend-Corinth, Charlotte & Hernad, Beatrice. Lovis Corinth: The Paintings - Catalogue Raisonne. 2nd rev. ed. (GER., Illus.). 960p. 1992. boxed set 275.00 (*1-55660-197-2*) A Wofsy Fine Arts.

Berend, Denyse. Sylloge Nummorum Graecorum: The Collection of the American Numismatic Society: Sicily 3: Syracuse - Siceliotes, Pt. 5. (Illus.). 108p. 1988. pap. 75.00 (*0-89722-224-5*) Am Numismatic.

Berend, Ivan T. Capital Intensity & Development Policy. 265p. (C). 1985. 110.00 (*963-05-3930-6*, Pub. by Akade Kiado) St Mut.

***Berend, Ivan T.** Central & Eastern Europe, 1944-1993: Detour from the Periphery to the Periphery. (Studies in Modern Economic History: Vol. 1). 432p. 1999. pap. write for info. (*0-521-66352-0*) Cambridge U Pr.

Berend, Ivan T. Central & Eastern Europe 1944-1993: Detour from the Periphery to the Periphery. (Cambridge Studies in Modern Economic History: No. 1). 432p. (C). 1996. text 64.95 (*0-521-55066-1*) Cambridge U Pr.

— Decades of Crisis: Central & Eastern Europe Before World War II. LC 97-39432. 485p. 1998. 40.00 (*0-520-20617-7*, Pub. by U CA Pr) Cal Prin Full Svc.

Berend, T. I., ed. History As a Discipline-Scholarly & Scholastic. 1980. pap. 50.00 (*963-05-2592-5*, Pub. by Akade Kiado) St Mut.

Berend, T. I. & Ranki, Gyorgy. East Central Europe in the 19th & 20th Centuries. 164p. (C). 1977. 65.00 (*963-05-1309-9*, Pub. by Akade Kiado) St Mut.

— Underdevelopment & Economic Growth: Studies in Hungarian Social & Economic History. 300p. 1979. 75.00 (*0-7855-2766-4*, Pub. by Akade Kiado) St Mut.

— Underdevelopment & Economic Growth Studies in Hungarian Social & Economic History. 300p. (C). 1979. 75.00 (*963-05-1754-X*, Pub. by Akade Kiado) St Mut.

Berendes, J., tr. Dioskurides (Codex Neapolitanus, Biblioteca Nazionale, Ms. Ex Vindob. Gr. 1) De Materia Medica. fac. ed. (Codices Selecti Ser.: Vol. LXXXVIII). (GER.). 344p. 1988. lthr. 5017.00 (*3-201-01417-6*, Pub. by Akademische Druck-und) Balogh.

Berendes, Julius. Die Pharmacie Bei Den Alten Culturvolkern. xxii, 528p. 1989. reprint ed. 120.00 (*3-487-00902-1*) G Olms Pubs.

Berendes, Mary. Australia. LC 97-40650. (Illus.). 32p. (J). 1998. lib. bdg. 22.79 (*1-56766-513-6*) Childs World.

— Beluga Whales. LC 97-33251. (Illus.). 32p. (J). 1998. lib. bdg. 22.79 (*1-56766-489-X*) Childs World.

— Deer. LC 99-33999. (Illus.). 32p. (J). (gr. 3-5). 1999. lib. bdg. 22.79 (*1-56766-586-1*) Childs World.

— Ferrets. LC 97-35223. (Illus.). 32p. (J). 1998. lib. bdg. 22.79 (*1-56766-477-6*) Childs World.

— Germany. LC 98-43001. (Illus.). 32p. 1999. lib. bdg. 22.79 (*1-56766-598-5*) Childs World.

— Italy. LC 98-43003. (Illus.). 32p. (J). 1999. lib. bdg. 22.79 (*1-56766-581-0*) Childs World.

— Jamaica. LC 97-49952. (Illus.). 32p. (J). 1998. lib. bdg. 22.79 (*1-56766-515-2*) Childs World.

— Mexico. LC 96-30665. (Countries Ser.). (Illus.). 32p. (J). (gr. 2-6). 1997. lib. bdg. 22.79 (*1-56766-372-9*) Childs World.

— Piranhas. LC 97-31355. (Illus.). 32p. (J). 1998. lib. bdg. 22.79 (*1-56766-493-8*) Childs World.

***Berendes, Mary.** Saint Patrick's Day Shamrocks. LC 98-56521. (Illus.). 32p. 1999. lib. bdg. 22.79 (*1-56766-643-4*) Childs World.

Berendes, Mary. Spain. LC 97-43665. (Illus.). 32p. (J). 1998. lib. bdg. 22.79 (*1-56766-518-7*) Childs World.

— Wombats. LC 97-33249. (Nature Books Ser.). (Illus.). 32p. (J). (gr. 2-6). 1998. lib. bdg. 22.79 (*1-56766-482-2*) Childs World.

***Berends, Mark.** Assessing the Progress of New American Schools: A Status Report. LC 99-44907. (Illus.). xvi, 42p. (C). 1999. pap. 7.50 (*0-8330-2761-1*, MR-1085-EDU) Rand Corp.

Berends, Nancy L., jt. auth. see Patzelt, Lawrence H.

Berends, Polly. Whole Child, Whole Parent. 4th ed. LC 97-9532. 400p. 1997. pap. 17.00 (*0-06-092818-2*, Perennial) HarperTrade.

Berends, Polly B. The Case of the Elevator Duck. (Stepping Stone Bks.). (J). 1990. 9.19 (*0-606-04181-8*, Pub. by Turtleback) Demco.

— The Case of the Elevator Duck. LC 88-23971. (Stepping Stone Bks). (Illus.). 64p. (J). (ps-3). 1989. reprint ed. pap. 3.99 (*0-394-82646-9*, Pub. by Random Bks Yng Read) Random.

— Gently Lead: How to Teach Your Children about God While Finding Out for Yourself. LC 97-49001. 192p. 1998. pap. 14.95 (*0-8245-1733-4*, Crsrd) Crossroad NY.

— Whole Child-Whole Parent. LC 81-48029. (Illus.). 384p. (Orig.). 1987. pap. 16.00 (*0-06-091427-0*, PL1427, Perennial) HarperTrade.

Berends, Polly Berrien. I Heard Said the Bird. (Picture Puffin Ser.). (J). (ps-1). 1998. pap. 5.99 (*0-14-056426-8*, PuffinBks) Peng Put Young Read.

Berendsen, B. S. Regional Models of Trade & Development. (Studies in Development & Planning: Vol. 7). 1978. lib. bdg. 78.50 (*90-207-0753-1*) Kluwer Academic.

Berendsohn, Walter. The Arboreal Vegetation of the Laderas de la Laguna, a Neotropical Forest Fragment in El Salvador, C. A. A. Computer-Aided Study. (Dissertationes Botanicae Ser.: Band 165). (Illus.). vi, 194p. 1991. pap. 48.00 (*3-443-64077-X*, Pub. by Gebruder Borntraeger) Balogh.

Berendt, Gerald E., et al. Contract Law & Practice. 1484p. (C). 1998. 59.95 (*0-87084-173-4*) Anderson Pub Co.

Berendt, Joachim-Ernst. The Jazz Book: From Ragtime to Fusion & Beyond. rev. ed. LC 92-17412. 560p. 1997. pap. 19.95 (*1-55652-098-0*) Chicago Review.

— The Jazz Book: From Ragtime to Fusion & Beyond. 6th rev. ed. LC 92-17412. 560p. 1992. 29.00 (*1-55652-099-9*, Lawrence Hill) Chicago Review.

— The Third Ear: On Listening to the World. 89p. (Orig.). 1995. pap. 13.95 (*0-8050-2007-1*, Owl) H Holt & Co.

— The World Is Sound - Nada Brahma: Music & the Landscape of Consciousness. 240p. 1991. reprint ed. pap. 14.95 (*0-89281-318-0*, Destiny Bks) Inner Tradit.

Berendt, Joachim-Ernst & Capra, Fritjof. Nada Brahma: The World Is Sound. 240p. 1987. 16.95 (*0-89281-168-4*, Destiny Bks) Inner Tradit.

Berendt, John. Midnight in the Garden of Good & Evil. 35.00 (*0-679-44944-2*) Discovery.

— Midnight in the Garden of Good & Evil. 1998. 25.00 (*0-676-54681-1*) Random.

— Midnight in the Garden of Good & Evil: A Savannah Story. LC 93-3955. 400p. 1994. 25.00 (*0-679-42922-0*) Random.

— Midnight in the Garden of Good & Evil: A Savannah Story. 386p. 1999. pap. 12.00 (*0-679-75152-1*) Vintage Publng.

— Midnight in the Garden of Good & Evil: A Savannah Story. large type ed. 400p. 1995. pap. 20.00 (*0-679-76283-3*) Random Hse Lrg Prnt.

***Berendt, John.** Minuit Dans Le Jardin Du Bien Et Du Mal. 4th ed. 1998. pap. 12.95 (*2-266-07518-7*) Distribks Inc.

Berendt, Robert J. & Taft, J. Richard. How to Rate Your Development Office: A Fund Raising Primer for the Chief Executive. LC 83-50709. 88p. 1983. 23.95 (*0-914756-54-0*, 600017) Taft Group.

Berendzen, Richard. Man Discovers the Galaxies. LC 84-1770. 1984. pap. text 21.00 (*0-231-05827-6*) Col U Pr.

— Man Discovers the Galaxies. 1976. text 15.95 (*0-07-004845-2*) McGraw.

Berenfeld, Boris, jt. auth. see Schrum, Lynne.

Berengario, et al. Saint Clare of the Cross of Montefalco. LC 98-19222. 1998. pap. 8.95 (*1-889542-06-7*) Augustinian Pr.

Berengarten, Sidney, et al. The Columbia University School of Social Work: A History of Social Pioneering. LC 86-73108. (Illus.). 64p. (Orig.). 1987. pap. text 7.50 (*0-941547-00-0*) Columbia Social Work.

— The Columbia University School of Social Work: A History of Social Pioneering, Monograph 2. LC 87-34216. (Illus.). 56p. (Orig.). 1988. pap. text 7.50 (*0-941547-01-9*) Columbia Social Work.

— The Columbia University School of Social Work: A History of Social Pioneering, Monograph 3. (Illus.). 28p. (Orig.). 1991. pap. text 4.00 (*0-941547-02-7*) Columbia Social Work.

— The Columbia University School of Social Work: A History of Social Pioneering, Monograph 5. 38p. (Orig.). 1993. pap. text 4.00 (*0-941547-04-3*) Columbia Social Work.

— The Columbia University School of Social Work, No. 4: A History of Social Pioneering Monograph. 35p. (Orig.). 1992. pap. text 4.00 (*0-941547-03-5*) Columbia Social Work.

***Berengaut, Julian.** The Baltic Countries: From Economic Stabilization to Eu Accession. LC 99-169057. (Occasional Papers). ix, 78 p. 1998. write for info. (*1-55775-738-0*) Intl Monetary.

Berenger-Feraud, Laurent J. Les Peuplades de la Senegambie: Histoire, Ethnographie, Moeurs et Coutumes, Legendes, etc. (B. E. Ser.: No. 169). (FRE.). 1879. 50.00 (*0-8115-3081-7*) Periodicals Srv.

— Recueil de Contes Populaires de la Senegambie. (B. E. Ser.: No. 38). (FRE.). 1885. 30.00 (*0-8115-2989-4*) Periodicals Srv.

Berenger, Jean. A History of Habsburg Empire, 1700-1918. LC 93-7777. (Illus.). 342p. (C). 1997. pap. text 23.44 (*0-582-09007-5*, Pub. by Addison-Wesley) Longman.

An Asterisk (*) at the beginning of an entry indicates that the title is appearing for the first time.

— A History of the Habsburg Empire, 1700-1918. 352p. (C). 1997. text 60.00 (*0-582-09008-3*, Pub. by Addison-Wesley) Longman.

— A History of the Habsburg Empire, 1273-1700. Simpson, C. A., tr. from FRE. LC 93-7777.Tr. of Histoire de l'Empire Habsbourg. 496p. (C). 1994. text 79.50 (*0-582-09009-1*, 76253, Pub. by Addison-Wesley); pap. text 42.19 (*0-582-09010-5*, Pub. by Addison-Wesley) Longman.

Berenholtz, Richard, photos by. Panoramic New York. LC 93-11114. (Illus.). 1993. text 35.00 (*0-86565-146-9*) Vendome.

Berens, Carol. Hotel Bars & Lobbies. (Illus.). 229p. 1996. 59.95 (*0-07-005828-8*) McGraw.

Berens, Christa K., et al, eds. The Bahamas Index & Yearbook, 1996, No. 11. 250p. 1997. text 100.00 (*0-932265-43-X*); pap. text 49.95 (*0-932265-44-8*) White Sound.

Berens de Haan, Barthold. Critical Dictionary of Psychology: Dictionnaire Critique De Psychiatrie. (FRE.). 304p. 1986. 39.95 (*0-8288-1788-X*, M2335) Fr & Eur.

Berens, Debbie, jt. auth. see Marek, Annemarie.

Berens, Gayle L., contrib. by. The Directory of Real Estate Development & Related Education Programs. 6th ed. 140p. 1996. pap. text 19.95 (*0-87420-787-8*, D95) Urban Land.

Berens, Gayle L., et al. Urban Parks & Open Spaces. LC 97-61903. 1997. pap. write for info. (*0-87420-809-2*, U10) Urban Land.

Berens, H. Training of the Left Hand Opus 89: 49 Exercises 25 Piano Studies. 32p. 1986. pap. 7.95 (*0-7935-5224-9*) H Leonard.

Berens, John F., ed. Criminal Justice Documents: A Selective, Annotated Bibliography of U. S. Government Publications since 1975, 7. LC 87-158. (Bibliographies & Indexes in Law & Political Science Ser.: No. 7). 251p. 1987. lib. bdg. 75.00 (*0-313-25183-5*, BCS/) Greenwood.

Berens, Linda, jt. auth. see Isachsen, Olaf.

***Berens, Linda V.** Dynamics of Personality Type: Understanding & Applying Jung's Cognitive Processes. (Understanding Yourself & Others Ser.). (Illus.). 42p. 1999. 7.95 (*0-9664624-5-9*) Telos Pubns.

— Understanding Yourself & Others: An Introduction to Temperament. 44p. 2000. 5.95 (*0-9664624-4-0*) Telos Pubns.

***Berens, Linda V. & Nardi, Dario.** The 16 Personality Types: Descriptions for Self-Discovery. (Understanding Yourself & Other Ser.). (Illus.). 52p. 1999. 6.95 (*0-9664624-7-5*, 201) Telos Pubns.

Berens, Robert J. Citizen Soldier: The Fighting Style of Brigadier General Edward W. Bird. LC 95-8424. 1995. write for info. (*0-9635812-7-9*) Sigler Print.

***Berens, Robert J.** Limbo on the Yalu & Beyond: The Ted Sprouse Story. 2000. pap. 11.95 (*0-941072-35-5*) Southern Herit.

Berenschot, B. V. Evaluation of Software Packages for Production Control. 500p. 1989. 475.00 (*0-948577-38-X*, Pub. by Elsvr Adv Tech) Elsevier.

Berensohn, Paul S. Finding One's Way with Clay: 25th Anniversary Edition. 25th rev. ed. LC 98-126333. (Illus.). 165p. 1997. pap. 26.50 (*0-9657773-0-8*, FOW) Clay Biscuit Bks TX.

Berenson & Levine. Business Statis. 1998. pap. text, student ed. 25.33 (*0-13-761339-3*) P-H.

— Statistics Manager Using Microsoft Excel. 2nd ed. 1115p. (C). 1999. 97.33 (*0-13-020312-2*) P-H.

Berenson, et al. Basic Business Statistics: Concepts & Applications. 7th ed. LC 98-38873. 1114p. 1998. 97.33 (*0-13-795618-5*) P-H.

Berenson, Bernard. Aesthetics & History. LC 52-1732. 242p. reprint ed. pap. 75.10 (*0-8357-5218-6*, 201298400083) Bks Demand.

— Aesthetics & History. LC 52-1732. 242p. 1955. reprint ed. 49.00 (*0-403-03882-0*) Somerset Pub.

— Sketch for Self-Portrait. 144p. 1999. reprint ed. text 12.00 (*0-7881-6279-9*) DIANE Pub.

— Studies in Medieval Painting. LC 73-153884. (Graphic Art Ser.). (Illus.). 148p. 1975. reprint ed. pap. 5.95 (*0-306-80010-1*); reprint ed. lib. bdg. 39.50 (*0-306-70292-4*) Da Capo.

Berenson, Bernard, ed. see Mariano, Nicky.

Berenson, Bernhard. The Florentin Painters of the Renaissance. 20.00 (*0-8196-2018-1*) Biblo.

Berenson, Edward. Populist Religion & Left-Wing Politics in France, 1830-1852. LC 83-42548. 333p. 1984. reprint ed. pap. 103.30 (*0-7837-9297-2*, 206003600004) Bks Demand.

— The Trial of Madame Caillaux. LC 91-2689. (Illus.). 296p. 1992. 45.00 (*0-520-07347-9*, Pub. by U CA Pr); pap. 16.95 (*0-520-08428-4*, Pub. by U CA Pr) Cal Prin Full Svc.

Berenson, F. M. Understanding Persons: Personal & Impersonal Relationships. LC 91-35953. 226p. 1991. reprint ed. lib. bdg. 89.95 (*0-7734-9848-6*) E Mellen.

Berenson, Gerald S. Introduction of Comprehensive Health Promotion for Elementary Schools: The Health Ahead/Heart Smart Program. LC 98-91057. 1998. pap. 19.95 (*0-533-12554-5*) Vantage.

Berenson, Gerald S., ed. Causation of Cardiovascular Risk Factors in Children: Perspectives on Cardiovascular Risk in Early Life. LC 85-19592. (Illus.). 428p. reprint ed. pap. 132.70 (*0-608-09630-X*, 205440600007) Bks Demand.

Berenson, James R., ed. Biology & Management of Multiple Myeloma. (Current Clinical Oncology Ser.). 400p. 2000. 125.00 (*0-89603-706-1*) Humana.

Berenson, Jan. Will Power! A Biography of Will Smith. (J). 1997. 9.09 (*0-606-12099-8*, Pub. by Turtleback) Demco.

— Will Power: A Will Smith Biography. 144p. (J). 1997. per. 3.99 (*0-671-88784-X*, Archway) PB.

Berenson, Kathryn. Quilts of Provence: The Art & Craft of French Quiltmaking. (Illus.). 192p. 1995. 45.00 (*0-8050-4639-9*) H Holt & Co.

Berenson, Laurien. Deep Cover. 384p. 1994. mass mkt. 4.50 (*0-8217-4692-8*, Zebra Kensgtn) Kensgtn Pub Corp.

— Dog Eat Dog: A Melanie Travis Mystery. 336p. 1997. mass mkt. 5.99 (*1-57566-227-2*, Knsington) Kensgtn Pub Corp.

— Hair of the Dog: A Melanie Travis Mystery. LC 97-71647. 320p. 1997. 18.95 (*1-57566-222-1*, Knsington) Kensgtn Pub Corp.

— Hair of the Dog: A Melanie Travis Mystery. (Melanie Travis Mystery Ser.). 336p. 1998. mass mkt. 5.99 (*1-57566-356-2*) Kensgtn Pub Corp.

***Berenson, Laurien.** Hush Puppy. 304p. 1999. 20.00 (*1-57566-469-0*, Knsington) Kensgtn Pub Corp.

— Hush Puppy. (Melanie Travis Mystery Ser.). 2000. mass mkt. 5.99 (*1-57566-600-6*, Knsington) Kensgtn Pub Corp.

Berenson, Laurien. A Pedigree to Die For: A Melanie Travis Mystery. 288p. 1996. mass mkt. 4.99 (*1-57566-003-2*) Kensgtn Pub Corp.

— A Pedigree to Die For: A Melanie Travis Mystery. 288p. 1997. pap. 9.95 (*1-57566-125-X*, Knsington) Kensgtn Pub Corp.

— A Pedigree to Die For: A Melanie Travis Mystery, 1. 1999. mass mkt. 5.99 (*1-57566-374-0*) Kensgtn Pub Corp.

— A Pedigree to Die For: A Melanie Travis Mystery. 1996. pap. 4.99 (*0-8217-5227-8*) NAL.

— Underdog: A Melanie Travis Mystery. 320p. 1996. 18.95 (*1-57566-011-3*) Kensgtn Pub Corp.

— Underdog: A Melanie Travis Mystery. 336p. 1996. mass mkt. 4.99 (*1-57566-108-X*, Knsington) Kensgtn Pub Corp.

— Underdog: A Melanie Travis Mystery. 1996. pap. 16.95 (*0-8217-5224-3*) NAL.

***Berenson, Laurien.** Unleashed. (Melanie Travis Mystery Ser.). 2000. 20.00 (*1-57566-596-4*, Knsington) Kensgtn Pub Corp.

Berenson, Laurien. Watchdog. LC 98-65623. (Melanie Travis Mystery Ser.: No. 5). 314p. (YA). (gr. 10 up). 1998. 20.00 (*1-57566-350-3*) Kensgtn Pub Corp.

***Berenson, Laurien.** Watchdog. (Melanie Travis Mystery Ser.). 1999. pap. 5.99 (*1-57566-472-0*, Knsington) Kensgtn Pub Corp.

Berenson, Mark & Levine, David M. Business Statistics: A First Course. LC 97-50037. 554p. 1998. text 63.00 (*0-13-744178-9*) P-H.

Berenson, Mark L. & Levine, David M. Basic Business Statistics: Concepts & Applications. 2nd ed. (Illus.). 752p. (C). 1983. student ed. 10.95 (*0-685-06112-4*) P-H.

***Berenson, Marvin H. & Edgar, Roberta.** Think Yourself Smokeless Vol. 2: Empowering Your Mind to Control Your Behavior & Stop Smoking Forever. LC 00-190832. 210p. 2000. pap. 34.95 (*0-9700885-0-7*) Crescndo Pub CA.

Berenson, Michael A., jt. auth. see Barron, Paul.

Berenson, Paul. Understand & Treat Alcoholism. Date not set. 19.95 (*0-465-08875-9*, Pub. by Basic) HarpC.

***Berenson-Perkins, Janet.** Kabbalah Decoder. LC 00-24426. (Illus.). 144p. 2000. 21.95 (*0-7641-5262-9*) Barron.

***Berenson, Rhoda.** Lori: My Daughter's Political Imprisonment in Peru. (Illus.). 208p. 2000. (*1-893956-06-7*) Context Bks.

Berenson, Robert A., jt. auth. see Zelman, Walter A.

Berenstain, Jan & Berenstain, Stan. The Berenstain Bears & the Love Match. LC 97-38410. (Berenstain Bears Big Chapter Bks.). (J). (gr. 4-7). 1998. pap. 3.99 (*0-679-88942-6*) Random.

— The Berenstain Bears at the Teen Rock Cafe. LC 96-1854. (Berenstain Bears Big Chapter Bks.). (Illus.). 104p. (J). (gr. 2-6). 1996. pap. 3.99 (*0-679-87570-0*) Random.

— The Berenstain Bears at the Teen Rock Cafe. LC 96-1854. (Berenstain Bears Big Chapter Bks.). (Illus.). (J). (gr. 4-7). 1996. lib. bdg. 11.99 (*0-679-97570-5*) Random.

Berenstain, Jan & Berenstain, Stan. The Berenstain Bears at the Teen Rock Cafe. (Berenstain Bears Big Chapter Bks.). (J). (gr. 2-6). 1996. 8.60 (*0-606-10753-3*, Pub. by Turtleback) Demco.

Berenstain, Jan & Berenstain, Stan. The Berenstain Bears Go Up & Down. LC 98-29757. (Early Step into Reading Ser.). (Illus.). 32p. (J). (ps-3). 1999. pap. 3.99 (*0-679-88720-2*) Random.

— Los Osos Scouts Berenstain enla Cueva del Murcielago Gigante. (Berenstain Bear Scouts Ser.).Tr. of Berenstain Bear Scouts & the Giant Bat Cave. (SPA.). 64p. (J). (gr. 3-6). 1995. pap. 2.99 (*0-590-59749-3*) Scholastic Inc.

Berenstain, Jan, jt. see Berenstain, Stan.

Berenstain, Jan, jt. auth. see Berenstain, Stan.

***Berenstain, Stan.** Bbears Dollars & Sense. (J). 2001. mass mkt. 3.25 (*0-375-81124-9*, Pub. by Random Bks Yng Read) Random.

Berenstain, Stan. Bears Scouts. (SPA.). (J). 1997. mass mkt. 3.50 (*0-590-94478-9*, Apple Paperbacks) Scholastic Inc.

— Berenstain Activity Book. (J). (gr. 2-5). 1997. pap. write for info. (*0-590-06706-0*) Scholastic Inc.

***Berenstain, Stan.** Berenstain Bears & Baby Makes Five. (Berenstain Bears Ser.). (Illus.). (J). 2000. 8.70 (*0-606-18485-6*) Turtleback.

— Berenstain Bears & Mama's New Job. (Illus.). (J). 1999. pap. 10.25 (*0-88103-144-5*) Econo-Clad Bks.

— Berenstain Bears & No Guns Allowed. (Berenstain Bears Big Chapter Bks.). (Illus.). (J). 2000. 9.34 (*0-606-18486-4*) Turtleback.

— Berenstain Bears & the Big Blooper. (Berenstain Bears First Time Bks.). (Illus.). (J). 2000. 8.99 (*0-679-98962-5*) Random Bks Yng Read.

— The Berenstain Bears & the Big Question. 24p. (J). (ps-3). 1999. pap. 3.25 (*0-679-88961-2*) Random House.

— Berenstain Bears & the Great Ant Attack. (Berenstain Bears Big Chapter Bks.). (Illus.). (J). 2000. 9.34 (*0-606-18487-2*) Turtleback.

Berenstain, Stan. Berenstain Bears & The Phantom of the Gymnasium. (Illus.). (J). 2000. pap. 3.99 (*0-679-88949-3*, Pub. by Random Bks Yng Read) Random.

***Berenstain, Stan.** The Berenstain Bears & Too Much Junk Food. (Illus.). (J). 1999. pap. 10.25 (*0-8085-3551-X*) Econo-Clad Bks.

— Berenstain Bears Don't Pollute. (Illus.). (J). 1999. pap. 10.25 (*0-8335-6545-1*) Econo-Clad Bks.

— Berenstain Bears Go in & Out. (Early Step into Reading Ser.). (Illus.). (J). 2000. 9.44 (*0-606-18488-0*) Turtleback.

Berenstain, Stan. The Berenstain Bears Learn about Strangers. LC 84-43157. (Berenstain Bears First Time Bks.). (Illus.). 32p. (J). (ps-3). 1985. lib. bdg. 8.99 (*0-394-97334-8*, Pub. by Random Bks Yng Read) Random.

— The Berenstain Bears Meet Santa Bear. LC 84-4829. (Berenstain Bears First Time Bks.). (Illus.). 30p. (J). (ps-1). 1984. pap. 3.25 (*0-394-86880-3*, Pub. by Random Bks Yng Read) Random.

***Berenstain, Stan.** Big Bear, Small Bear. (J). 1998. 9.19 (*0-606-13953-2*, Pub. by Turtleback) Demco.

Berenstain, Stan. By the Sea. 1998. 9.19 (*0-606-13954-0*, Pub. by Turtleback) Demco.

— A Cub's Garden of Verses. 2001. 6.99 (*0-375-80205-3*) Random.

— El Robot Chiflado.Tr. of Run Amuck Robot. 1997. 8.60 (*0-606-11576-5*, Pub. by Turtleback) Demco.

Berenstain, Stan & Berenstain, Jan. The Bear Detectives: The Case of the Missing Pumpkin. LC 75-1603. (I Can Read It All By Myself: Beginner Books). (Illus.). 48p. (J). (ps-3). 1975. 7.99 (*0-394-83127-6*) Beginner.

— The Bear Detectives: The Case of the Missing Pumpkin. LC 75-1603. (I Can Read It All By Myself: Beginner Books). (Illus.). 48p. (J). (ps-3). 1975. lib. bdg. 11.99 (*0-394-93127-0*) Beginner.

— Bear Scouts. LC 67-21919. (I Can Read It All By Myself: Beginner Books). (Illus.). 72p. (J). (ps-3). 1967. 7.99 (*0-394-80046-X*) Beginner.

— Bears in the Night. LC 74-158386. (Bright & Early Bks.). (Illus.). 35p. (J). (ps-3). 1971. lib. bdg. 11.99 (*0-394-92286-7*, Pub. by Random Bks Yng Read) Random.

— Bears in the Night. (Bright & Early Bks.). (Illus.). (J). (ps-3). 1971. 7.99 (*0-394-82286-2*, Pub. by Random Bks Yng Read) Random.

— Bears on Wheels. LC 72-77840. (Bright & Early Bks.). (Illus.). (J). (ps-3). 1969. 7.99 (*0-394-80967-X*, Pub. by Random Bks Yng Read); lib. bdg. 9.99 (*0-394-90967-4*, Pub. by Random Bks Yng Read) Random.

— The Bears' Picnic. LC 66-10156. (I Can Read It All By Myself: Beginner Books). (Illus.). 72p. (J). (ps-3). 1966. 7.99 (*0-394-80041-9*) Beginner.

Berenstain, Stan & Berenstain, Jan. The Bears' Picnic. (I Can Read It All By Myself: Beginner Books). (J). (ps-3). 1911. audio 49.32 (*0-394-12834-6*) McKay.

Berenstain, Stan & Berenstain, Jan. Bears' Vacation. LC 68-28460. (I Can Read It All By Myself: Beginner Books). (Illus.). 72p. (J). (ps-3). 1968. 7.99 (*0-394-80052-4*) Beginner.

— El Bebe de los Osos Berenstain: (The Berenstain Bears' New Baby) De Cuenca, Pilar & Alvarez, Ines, trs. from ENG. LC 81-12193. (Bilingual Picturebacks Ser.). (SPA., Illus.). 32p. (Orig.). (J). (ps-3). 1982. pap. 3.25 (*0-394-85144-7*, Pub. by Random Bks Yng Read) Random.

***Berenstain, Stan & Berenstain, Jan.** Berenstain Baby Bears - It's Bathtime. (Illus.). 5p. (J). (ps). 2000. 4.99 (*0-375-80480-3*) Random Bks Yng Read.

Berenstain, Stan & Berenstain, Jan. Berenstain Bear Scouts. (J). 1995. pap. 71.76 (*0-590-59726-4*) Scholastic Inc.

— The Berenstain Bear Scouts & the Coughing Catfish. LC 96-232912. (Berenstain Bear Scouts Ser.). (Illus.). 32p. (J). (gr. 4-7). 1998. pap. 3.50 (*0-590-60384-1*) Scholastic Inc.

Berenstain, Stan & Berenstain, Jan. The Berenstain Bear Scouts & the Coughing Catfish. (Berenstain Bear Scouts Ser.). (J). (gr. 3-6). 1996. 8.09 (*0-606-09065-7*, Pub. by Turtleback) Demco.

Berenstain, Stan & Berenstain, Jan. Berenstain Bear Scouts & the Evil Eye. (Berenstain Bear Scouts Ser.). (J). (gr. 2-5). 1998. pap. 3.99 (*0-590-94488-6*, Little Apple) Scholastic Inc.

***Berenstain, Stan & Berenstain, Jan.** Berenstain Bear Scouts & the Evil Eye. (Berenstain Bear Scouts Ser.). (J). (gr. 3-6). 1998. 9.09 (*0-606-13190-6*, Pub. by Turtleback) Demco.

Berenstain, Stan & Berenstain, Jan. The Berenstain Bear Scouts & the Humongous Pumpkin. (Berenstain Bear Scouts Ser.). (Illus.). 64p. (J). (gr. 4-7). 1995. pap. 2.99 (*0-590-60380-9*) Scholastic Inc.

— The Berenstain Bear Scouts & the Humongous Pumpkin. LC 97-135056. (Berenstain Bear Scouts Ser.). 32p. (J). (gr. 2-5). 1996. pap. text 3.50 (*0-590-60386-8*) Scholastic Inc.

— The Berenstain Bear Scouts & the Humongous Pumpkin. (Berenstain Bear Scouts Ser.). (J). (gr. 3-6). 1995. 8.60 (*0-606-07276-4*, Pub. by Turtleback) Demco.

— The Berenstain Bear Scouts & the Ice Monster. (Berenstain Bear Scouts Ser.). (Illus.). 32p. (J). (gr. 2-5). 1997. pap. 3.50 (*0-590-94479-7*, Little Apple) Scholastic Inc.

Berenstain, Stan & Berenstain, Jan. The Berenstain Bear Scouts & the Ice Monster. (Berenstain Bear Scouts Ser.). (J). (gr. 3-6). 1997. 8.60 (*0-606-12627-9*, Pub. by Turtleback) Demco.

Berenstain, Stan & Berenstain, Jan. Berenstain Bear Scouts & the Magic Crystal Caper. (Berenstain Bear Scouts Ser.). (Illus.). (J). (gr. 3-6). 1997. pap. 2.99 (*0-614-29029-5*, Little Apple) Scholastic Inc.

— Berenstain Bear Scouts & the Magic Crystal Caper. (Berenstain Bear Scouts Ser.). 32p. (J). (gr. 2-5). 1997. pap. text 3.50 (*0-590-94475-4*, Little Apple) Scholastic Inc.

Berenstain, Stan & Berenstain, Jan. Berenstain Bear Scouts & the Magic Crystal Caper. (Berenstain Bear Scouts Ser.). (J). (gr. 3-6). 1997. 8.60 (*0-606-11107-7*, Pub. by Turtleback) Demco.

Berenstain, Stan & Berenstain, Jan. The Berenstain Bear Scouts & the Missing Merit Badges. LC 97-50466. (Berenstain Bear Scouts Ser.). (Illus.). 32p. (J). (gr. k-2). 1998. pap. 3.50 (*0-590-56390-4*, Pub. by Scholastic Inc) Penguin Putnam.

— The Berenstain Bear Scouts & the Missing Merit Badges. (Berenstain Bear Scouts Ser.). (J). (gr. 3-6). 1998. 8.70 (*0-606-13191-4*, Pub. by Turtleback) Demco.

— Berenstain Bear Scouts & the Really Big Disaster. (Berenstain Bear Scouts Ser.). (Illus.). 32p. (J). (gr. 2-5). 1998. pap. text 3.50 (*0-590-94481-9*, Little Apple) Scholastic Inc.

***Berenstain, Stan & Berenstain, Jan.** Berenstain Bear Scouts & the Really Big Disaster. (Berenstain Bear Scouts Ser.). (J). (gr. 3-6). 1998. 8.60 (*0-606-13192-2*, Pub. by Turtleback) Demco.

Berenstain, Stan & Berenstain, Jan. Berenstain Bear Scouts & the Ripoff Queen. (Berenstain Bear Scouts Ser.). (Illus.). 112p. (J). (gr. 2-5). 1998. pap. text 3.99 (*0-590-94493-2*) Scholastic Inc.

— Berenstain Bear Scouts & the Run-Amuck Robot. LC 98-172308. (Berenstain Bear Scouts Ser.). (Illus.). 32p. (J). (gr. 2-5). 1997. pap. 3.50 (*0-590-94477-0*, Little Apple) Scholastic Inc.

— Berenstain Bear Scouts & the Run-Amuck Robot. (Berenstain Bear Scouts Ser.). (J). (gr. 3-6). 1997. 8.60 (*0-606-11108-5*, Pub. by Turtleback) Demco.

— Berenstain Bear Scouts & the Sci-Fi Pizza. (Berenstain Bear Scouts Ser.). (J). (gr. 3-6). 1997. 8.09 (*0-606-11109-3*, Pub. by Turtleback) Demco.

— The Berenstain Bear Scouts & the Sci-Fi Pizza. LC 97-135054. (Berenstain Bear Scouts Ser.). (J). (gr. 4-7). 1996. pap. text 2.99 (*0-590-60385-X*) Scholastic Inc.

— The Berenstain Bear Scouts & the Search for Naughty Ned. LC 97-50471. (Berenstain Bear Scouts Ser.). (Illus.). 32p. (J). (gr. k-2). 1998. pap. 3.50 (*0-590-56509-5*, Pub. by Scholastic Inc) Penguin Putnam.

— The Berenstain Bear Scouts & the Search for Naughty Ned. (Berenstain Bear Scouts Ser.). (J). (gr. 3-6). 1998. 8.70 (*0-606-13193-0*, Pub. by Turtleback) Demco.

Berenstain, Stan & Berenstain, Jan. The Berenstain Bear Scouts & the Sinister Smoke Ring. (Berenstain Bear Scouts Ser.). (Illus.). (J). (gr. 3-6). 1997. write for info. (*0-614-29603-X*) Scholastic Inc.

Berenstain, Stan & Berenstain, Jan. The Berenstain Bear Scouts & the Sinister Smoke Ring. LC 97-135055. (Berenstain Bear Scouts Ser.). 32p. (J). (gr. 3-6). 1997. mass mkt. 3.50 (*0-590-94473-8*) Scholastic Inc.

— The Berenstain Bear Scouts & the Sinister Smoke Ring. (Berenstain Bear Scouts Ser.). (Illus.). (J). (gr. 3-6). 1997. pap. 2.99 (*0-614-29028-7*, Little Apple) Scholastic Inc.

— Berenstain Bear Scouts & the Sinister Smoke Ring. (Berenstain Bear Scouts Ser.). (J). (gr. 3-6). 1997. 8.60 (*0-606-11110-7*, Pub. by Turtleback) Demco.

— The Berenstain Bear Scouts & the Stinky Milk Mystery. LC 98-41400. (Berenstain Bear Scouts Ser.). (Illus.). 32p. (J). (gr. k-2). 1999. pap. 3,50 (*0-590-56524-9*, Cartwheel) Scholastic Inc.

— Berenstain Bear Scouts & the Terrible Talking Termite. (Berenstain Bear Scouts Ser.). (Illus.). (J). (gr. 4-7). 1996. pap. 2.99 (*0-590-60383-3*) Scholastic Inc.

Berenstain, Stan & Berenstain, Jan. Berenstain Bear Scouts & the Terrible Talking Termite. (Berenstain Bear Scouts Ser.). (J). (gr. 3-6). 1996. 8.09 (*0-606-09066-5*, Pub. by Turtleback) Demco.

Berenstain, Stan & Berenstain, Jan. The Berenstain Bear Scouts & the White-Water Mystery. LC 98-36419. (Merit Badge Mystery Ser.). (J). 1999. 3.50 (*0-590-56522-2*) Scholastic Inc.

— Berenstain Bear Scouts Ghost Versus Ghost. (Berenstain Bear Scouts Ser.). (J). (gr. 3-6). 1996. 8.09 (*0-606-11111-5*, Pub. by Turtleback) Demco.

— Berenstain Bear Scouts in Giant Bat Cave. (Berenstain Bear Scouts Ser.). (J). (gr. 3-6). 1995. 8.60 (*0-606-07277-2*, Pub. by Turtleback) Demco.

— The Berenstain Bear Scouts in Giant Bat Cave. LC 95-229190. (Berenstain Bear Scouts Ser.). 64p. (J). (gr. 4-7). 1995. pap. 2.99 (*0-590-60379-5*) Scholastic Inc.

— Berenstain Bear Scouts Meet Bigpaw. (Berenstain Bear Scouts Ser.). 32p. (J). (gr. 2-5). 1996. pap. 3.50 (*0-590-60381-7*) Scholastic Inc.

— Berenstain Bear Scouts Meet Bigpaw. (Berenstain Bear Scouts Ser.). (J). (gr. 3-6). 1995. 8.09 (*0-606-08488-6*, Pub. by Turtleback) Demco.

— Berenstain Bear Scouts Save That Backscratcher. (Berenstain Bear Scouts Ser.). (Illus.). (J). (gr. 4-7). 1996. pap. 2.99 (*0-590-60382-5*) Scholastic Inc.

Berenstain, Stan & Berenstain, Jan. Berenstain Bear Scouts Save That Backscratcher. (Berenstain Bear Scouts Ser.). (J). (gr. 3-6). 1996. 8.09 (*0-606-09067-3*, Pub. by Turtleback) Demco.

Berenstain, Stan & Berenstain, Jan. The Berenstain Bear Scouts Scream Their Heads Off. LC 98-171519. (Berenstain Bear Scouts Ser.). 32p. (J). (gr. 3-6). 1998. pap. text 3.50 (*0-590-94484-3*, Little Apple) Scholastic Inc.

B

An Asterisk (*) at the beginning of an entry indicates that the title is appearing for the first time.

— The Berenstain Bear Scouts Scream Their Heads Off. (Berenstain Bear Scouts Ser.). (J). (gr. 3-6). 1998. 8.60 (0-606-13194-9, Pub. by Turtleback) Demco.

— The Berenstain Bears, 7 vols., Set. (Early Childhood First Bks.). (Illus.). (J). (ps-2). Date not set. lib. bdg. 97.65 (1-56674-942-5) Forest Hse.

— Berenstain Bears: A Visit to the Big City. (Magic Touch Talking Bks.). (Illus.). 22p. (J). (ps-2). 1996. 19.99 (1-888208-08-2) Hasbro.

— Berenstain Bears: A Visit to the Big Museum. (Magic Touch Talking Bks.). (Illus.). 22p. (J). (ps-2). 1996. 19.99 (1-888208-09-0) Hasbro.

— The Berenstain Bears: Family Tree House. (Pop-Up Sound-Up Bks.). 2p. (J). (ps-2). 1993. write for info. (1-883366-06-2) YES Ent.

— The Berenstain Bears: No Girls Allowed. LC 85-18246. (Berenstain Bears First Time Bks.). (Illus.). 32p. (J). (gr. k-2). 1986. pap. 3.25 (0-394-87331-9, Pub. by Random Bks Yng Read); lib. bdg. 8.99 (0-394-97331-3, Pub. by Random Bks Yng Read) Random.

— The Berenstain Bears: No Girls Allowed. (Berenstain Bears First Time Bks.). (J). (gr. k-2). 1986. 8.20 (0-606-01993-6, Pub. by Turtleback) Demco.

***Berenstain, Stan & Berenstain, Jan.** Berenstain Bears: There's Gold in Them. (J). 2000. lib. bdg. 11.99 (0-679-98951-X, Pub. by Random Bks Yng Read) Random.

— Berenstain Bears: There's Gold in Them. (Illus.). (J). 2000. pap. 3.99 (0-679-88951-5, Pub. by Random Bks Yng Read) Random.

Berenstain, Stan & Berenstain, Jan. Berenstain Bears: When I Grow Up. (Magic Touch Talking Bks.). (Illus.). 22p. (J). (ps-2). 1996. 19.99 (1-888208-10-4) Hasbro.

— The Berenstain Bears Vol. 7: Back to School. large type ed. (Early Childhood First Bks.). (Illus.). 24p. (J). (ps-2). 1998. lib. bdg. 13.95 (1-56674-213-7) Forest Hse.

— The Berenstain Bears Vol. 7: Bedtime Story. large type ed. (Early Childhood First Bks.). (Illus.). 24p. (J). (ps-2). 1998. lib. bdg. 13.95 (1-56674-214-5) Forest Hse.

— The Berenstain Bears Vol. 7: Get the Grouchies. large type ed. (Early Childhood First Bks.). (Illus.). 24p. (J). (ps-2). 1998. lib. bdg. 13.95 (1-56674-253-6) Forest Hse.

— The Berenstain Bears Vol. 7: Help Around the House. large type ed. (Early Childhood First Bks.). (Illus.). 24p. (J). (ps-2). 1998. lib. bdg. 13.95 (1-56674-215-3) Forest Hse.

— The Berenstain Bears Vol. 7: Hold Hands at the Big Mall. large type ed. (Early Childhood First Bks.). (Illus.). 24p. (J). (ps-2). 1998. lib. bdg. 13.95 (1-56674-216-1) Forest Hse.

— The Berenstain Bears Vol. 7: On the Road. large type ed. (Early Childhood First Bks.). (Illus.). 24p. (J). (ps-2). 1998. lib. bdg. 13.95 (1-56674-217-X) Forest Hse.

— The Berenstain Bears Vol. 7: Say Please & Thank You. large type ed. (Early Childhood First Bks.). (Illus.). 24p. (J). (ps-2). 1998. lib. bdg. 13.95 (1-56674-218-8) Forest Hse.

— The Berenstain Bears Accept No Substitutes. LC 93-8869. (Berenstain Bears Big Chapter Bks.). (Illus.). 98p. (J). (gr. 4-7). 1993. pap. 3.50 (0-679-84035-4, Pub. by Random Bks Yng Read) Random.

— The Berenstain Bears & Baby Makes Five. LC 99-30687. (First Time Books). (Illus.). 32p. (J). (ps-1). 2000. lib. bdg. 8.99 (0-679-98960-9, Pub. by Random Bks Yng Read) Random.

***Berenstain, Stan & Berenstain, Jan.** The Berenstain Bears & Baby Makes Five. LC 99-30687. (First Time Books). (Illus.). 32p. (J). (ps-1). 2000. pap. 3.25 (0-679-88960-4, Pub. by Random Bks Yng Read) Random.

Berenstain, Stan & Berenstain, Jan. The Berenstain Bears & Mama's New Job. LC 84-4787. (Berenstain Bears First Time Bks.). (Illus.). 32p. (J). (ps-3). 1984. pap. 3.25 (0-394-86881-1, Pub. by Random Bks Yng Read) Random.

— The Berenstain Bears & Queenie's Crazy Crush. LC 97-15587. (Berenstain Bears Big Chapter Bks.). (Illus.). 112p. (J). (gr. 2-6). 1997. pap. 3.99 (0-679-88745-8, Pub. by Random Bks Yng Read) Random.

— The Berenstain Bears & Queenie's Crazy Crush. LC 97-15587. (Berenstain Bears Big Chapter Bks.). (J). (gr. 2-6). 1997. lib. bdg. 11.99 (0-679-98745-2, Pub. by Random Bks Yng Read) Random.

— The Berenstain Bears & Queenie's Crazy Crush. (Berenstain Bears Big Chapter Bks.). (J). (gr. 2-6). 1997. 9.09 (0-606-12628-7, Pub. by Turtleback) Demco.

— The Berenstain Bears & the Bad Dream. LC 87-27295. (Berenstain Bears First Time Bks.). (Illus.). 32p. (J). (gr. k-2). 1988. lib. bdg. 6.99 (0-394-97341-0, Pub. by Random Bks Yng Read) Random.

— The Berenstain Bears & the Bad Dream. LC 87-27295. (Berenstain Bears First Time Bks.). (Illus.). 32p. (J). (ps-3). 1988. pap. 3.25 (0-394-87341-6, Pub. by Random Bks Yng Read) Random.

— The Berenstain Bears & the Bad Dream. LC 87-27295. (Berenstain Bears First Time Bks.). 32p. (J). (gr. k-2). 1988. 8.45 (0-606-03730-6, Pub. by Turtleback) Demco.

— The Berenstain Bears & the Bad Habit. LC 86-3205. (Berenstain Bears First Time Bks.). (Illus.). 32p. (J). (ps-3). 1987. pap. 3.25 (0-394-87340-8, Pub. by Random Bks Yng Read) Random.

— The Berenstain Bears & the Bad Habit. (Berenstain Bears First Time Bks.). (J). (gr. k-2). 1986. 8.45 (0-606-00616-8, Pub. by Turtleback) Demco.

Berenstain, Stan & Berenstain, Jan. The Berenstain Bears & the Bermuda Triangle. LC 96-25935. (Berenstain Bears Big Chapter Bks.). (Illus.). 102p. (J). (gr. 2-6). 1997. pap. 3.99 (0-679-87649-9) Random.

Berenstain, Stan & Berenstain, Jan. The Berenstain Bears & the Bermuda Triangle. (Berenstain Bears Big Chapter Bks.). (J). (gr. 2-6). 1997. 8.60 (0-606-11112-3, Pub. by Turtleback) Demco.

***Berenstain, Stan & Berenstain, Jan.** The Berenstain Bears & the Big Date. (Berenstain Bears Big Chapter Bks.). (J). (gr. 2-6). 1998. 9.09 (0-606-13951-6, Pub. by Turtleback) Demco.

Berenstain, Stan & Berenstain, Jan. The Berenstain Bears & the Big Date. LC 97-23457. (Berenstain Bears Big Chapter Bks.). (J). (gr. 1-7). 1998. pap. 3.99 (0-679-88941-8) Vin Bks.

— The Berenstain Bears & the Big Date. LC 97-23457. (Berenstain Bears Big Chapter Bks.). (J). (gr. 3-5). 1998. lib. bdg. 11.99 (0-679-98941-2) Vin Bks.

***Berenstain, Stan & Berenstain, Jan.** The Berenstain Bears & the Big Question. (J). 1999. lib. bdg. 8.99 (0-679-98961-7, Pub. by Random Bks Yng Read) Random.

Berenstain, Stan & Berenstain, Jan. The Berenstain Bears & the Big Road Race. LC 87-4581. (Berenstain Bears First Time Readers Ser.). (Illus.). 32p. (J). (ps-3). 1987. pap. 3.25 (0-394-89134-1, Pub. by Random Bks Yng Read) Random.

— The Berenstain Bears & the Big Road Race. (Berenstain Bears First Time Readers Ser.). 32p. (J). (ps-3). 1987. 8.45 (0-606-00617-6, Pub. by Turtleback) Demco.

— Berenstain Bears & the Birds & the Bees. (J). 1999. pap. 3.25 (0-679-88958-2) Random.

— Berenstain Bears & the Birds & the Bees. (Berenstain Bears First Time Bks.). (Illus.). 24p. (J). (gr. k-3). 2000. lib. bdg. 8.99 (0-679-98959-5) Random.

— The Berenstain Bears & the Blame Game. LC 97-6750. (Berenstain Bears First Time Bks.). (J). (ps-1). 1997. lib. bdg. 8.99 (0-679-98743-6, Pub. by Random Bks Yng Read) Random.

— The Berenstain Bears & the Blame Game. LC 97-6750. (Berenstain Bears First Time Bks.). (Illus.). 34p. (J). (ps-1). 1997. 3.25 (0-679-88743-1, Pub. by Random Bks Yng Read) Random.

— The Berenstain Bears & the Blame Game. (Berenstain Bears First Time Bks.). (J). (gr. k-2). 1997. 8.45 (0-606-12629-5, Pub. by Turtleback) Demco.

— The Berenstain Bears & the Bully. LC 92-45875. (Berenstain Bears First Time Bks.). (Illus.). 32p. (J). (ps-3). 1993. pap. 3.25 (0-679-84805-3, Pub. by Random Bks Yng Read) Random.

— The Berenstain Bears & the Bully. (Berenstain Bears First Time Bks.). (J). (gr. k-2). 1993. 8.45 (0-606-05754-4, Pub. by Turtleback) Demco.

— The Berenstain Bears & the Double Dare. LC 87-27296. (Berenstain Bears First Time Bks.). (Illus.). 32p. (J). (ps-3). 1988. pap. 3.25 (0-394-89748-X, Pub. by Random Bks Yng Read) Random.

— The Berenstain Bears & the Double Dare. LC 87-27296. (Berenstain Bears First Time Bks.). (Illus.). 32p. (J). (gr. k-2). 1988. 8.45 (0-606-03729-2, Pub. by Turtleback) Demco.

— The Berenstain Bears & the Dress Code. LC 94-19826. (Berenstain Bears Big Chapter Bks.). (Illus.). 103p. (J). (gr. 4-7). 1994. pap. 3.50 (0-679-86665-5, Pub. by Random Bks Yng Read); lib. bdg. 11.99 (0-679-96665-X, Pub. by Random Bks Yng Read) Random.

— The Berenstain Bears & the Drug Free Zone. LC 92-31604. (Berenstain Bears Big Chapter Bks.). (Illus.). 100p. (J). (gr. 4-7). 1993. pap. 3.50 (0-679-83612-8, Pub. by Random Bks Yng Read) Random.

— The Berenstain Bears & the Drug Free Zone. LC 92-31604. (Berenstain Bears Big Chapter Bks.). (Illus.). 100p. (J). (ps-3). 1993. lib. bdg. 11.99 (0-679-93612-2, Pub. by Random Bks Yng Read) Random.

— The Berenstain Bears & the Escape of the Bogg Brothers. LC 98-54963. (Step into Reading Ser.: A Step 1 Book). (J). 2000. lib. bdg. 11.99 (0-679-99228-6) Random.

***Berenstain, Stan & Berenstain, Jan.** The Berenstain Bears & the Escape of the Bogg Brothers. LC 98-54963. (Step into Reading Ser.: A Step 3 Book). (Illus.). (J). 2000. pap. 3.99 (0-679-89228-1, Pub. by Random Bks Yng Read) Random.

Berenstain, Stan & Berenstain, Jan. The Berenstain Bears & the G-Rex Bones. (Berenstain Bears Big Chapter Bks.). (J). (gr. 2-5). 1999. lib. bdg. 11.99 (0-679-98945-5) Random.

— The Berenstain Bears & the G-Rex Bones. (Berenstain Bears Big Chapter Bks.). (J). (gr. 2-6). 2001. lib. bdg. 11.99 (0-679-98949-8) Random.

— The Berenstain Bears & the G-Rex Bones. LC 98-36353. (Berenstain Bears Big Chapter Bks.). (J). (gr. 2-6). 1999. pap. 3.99 (0-679-88945-0) Random Hse Chldrns.

— The Berenstain Bears & the Galloping Ghost. LC 94-2772. (Berenstain Bears Big Chapter Bks.). (Illus.). 104p. (J). (ps-3). 1994. pap. 3.50 (0-679-85815-6, Pub. by Random Bks Yng Read) Random.

— The Berenstain Bears & the Galloping Ghost. (Berenstain Bears Big Chapter Bks.). (Illus.). 104p. (J). (gr. 2-6). 1994. lib. bdg. 11.99 (0-679-95815-0, Pub. by Random Bks Yng Read) Random.

— The Berenstain Bears & the Ghost of the Auto Graveyard. (Berenstain Bears Big Chapter Bks.). (Illus.). (J). (gr. 2-6). 1997. pap. 3.50 (0-614-28938-6) Random Bks Yng Read.

— The Berenstain Bears & the Ghost of the Auto Graveyard. LC 96-52537. (Berenstain Bears Big Chapter Bks.). (Illus.). 102p. (J). (gr. 2-5). 1997. pap. 3.50 (0-679-87651-0, Pub. by Random Bks Yng Read) Random.

— The Berenstain Bears & the Ghost of the Auto Graveyard. LC 96-52537. (Berenstain Bears Big Chapter Bks.). (J). (gr. 2-6). 1997. lib. bdg. 11.99 (0-679-97651-5, Pub. by Random Bks Yng Read) Random.

— The Berenstain Bears & the Ghost of the Auto Graveyard. (Berenstain Bears Big Chapter Bks.). (J). (gr. 2-6). 1997. 8.60 (0-606-11113-1, Pub. by Turtleback) Demco.

— The Berenstain Bears & the Ghost of the Forest. LC 88-42586. (Berenstain Bears First Time Readers Ser.). (Illus.). 30p. (J). (ps-3). 1988. pap. 3.25 (0-394-80565-8, Pub. by Random Bks Yng Read) Random.

Berenstain, Stan & Berenstain, Jan. The Berenstain Bears & the Ghost of the Forest. (Berenstain Bears First Time Readers Ser.). 30p. (J). (ps-3). 1988. 8.45 (0-606-03984-8, Pub. by Turtleback) Demco.

Berenstain, Stan & Berenstain, Jan. The Berenstain Bears & the Giddy Grandma. (Berenstain Bears Big Chapter Bks.). (Illus.). 93p. (J). (gr. 2-6). 1994. pap. 3.50 (0-679-85814-8, Pub. by Random Bks Yng Read) Random.

Berenstain, Stan & Berenstain, Jan. The Berenstain Bears & the Giddy Grandma. LC 94-11469. (Berenstain Bears Big Chapter Bks.). (Illus.). 93p. (J). (gr. 4-7). 1994. lib. bdg. 11.99 (0-679-95814-2, Pub. by Random Bks Yng Read) Random.

— The Berenstain Bears & the Great Ant Attack. (Berenstain Bears Big Chapter Bks.). (Illus.). 112p. (J). (gr. 3-7). 2000. pap. 3.99 (0-679-88950-7) Random.

— The Berenstain Bears & the Great Ant Attack. (Berenstain Bears Big Chapter Bks.). (Illus.). 112p. (J). (gr. 3-7). 2000. lib. bdg. 11.99 (0-679-98950-1, Pub. by Random Bks Yng Read) Random.

Berenstain, Stan & Berenstain, Jan. The Berenstain Bears & the Green-Eyed Monster. LC 93-50109. (Berenstain Bears First Time Bks.). (Illus.). (J). (gr. k-2). 1995. lib. bdg. 8.99 (0-679-96434-7, Pub. by Random Bks Yng Read) Random.

— The Berenstain Bears & the Green-Eyed Monster. LC 93-50109. (Berenstain Bears First Time Bks.). (Illus.). (J). (ps-3). 1995. pap. 3.25 (0-679-86434-2, Pub. by Random Bks Yng Read) Random.

— The Berenstain Bears & the Green-Eyed Monster. (Berenstain Bears First Time Bks.). (J). (gr. k-2). 1995. 8.45 (0-606-07278-0, Pub. by Turtleback) Demco.

— The Berenstain Bears & the Haunted Hayride. LC 96-52541. (Berenstain Bears Big Chapter Bks.). (Illus.). 112p. (J). (gr. 2-6). 1997. pap. 3.99 (0-679-87650-2, Pub. by Random Bks Yng Read) Random.

— The Berenstain Bears & the Haunted Hayride. (Berenstain Bears Big Chapter Bks.). (J). (gr. 2-6). 1997. 9.09 (0-606-12630-9, Pub. by Turtleback) Demco.

— The Berenstain Bears & the Haunted Hayride. LC 96-52541. (Berenstain Bears Big Chapter Bks.). (J). (gr. 2-6). 1997. lib. bdg. 11.99 (0-679-97650-7) Vin Bks.

— The Berenstain Bears & the Homework Hassle. LC 97-6753. (Berenstain Bears First Time Bks.). (Illus.). 32p. (J). (ps-1). 1997. pap. 3.25 (0-679-88744-X, Pub. by Random Bks Yng Read) Random.

— The Berenstain Bears & the Homework Hassle. LC 97-6753. (Berenstain Bears First Time Bks.). (J). (ps-1). 1997. lib. bdg. 8.99 (0-679-98744-4, Pub. by Random Bks Yng Read) Random.

— The Berenstain Bears & the Homework Hassle. (Berenstain Bears First Time Bks.). (J). (gr. k-2). 1997. 8.70 (0-606-12631-7) Turtleback.

— The Berenstain Bears & the In-Crowd. LC 88-32095. (Berenstain Bears First Time Bks.). (Illus.). 32p. (J). (ps-3). 1989. pap. 3.25 (0-394-83013-X, Pub. by Random Bks Yng Read) Random.

— The Berenstain Bears & the In-Crowd. (Berenstain Bears First Time Bks.). 32p. (J). (gr. k-2). 1989. 8.45 (0-606-04168-0, Pub. by Turtleback) Demco.

— The Berenstain Bears & the Love Match. LC 97-38410. (Berenstain Bears Big Chapter Bks.). (J). (gr. 3-5). 1998. lib. bdg. 11.99 (0-679-98942-0, Pub. by Random Bks Yng Read) Random.

***Berenstain, Stan & Berenstain, Jan.** The Berenstain Bears & the Love Match. (Berenstain Bears Big Chapter Bks.). (J). (gr. 2-6). 1998. 9.09 (0-606-13952-4, Pub. by Turtleback) Demco.

Berenstain, Stan & Berenstain, Jan. The Berenstain Bears & the Messy Room. Lerner, Sharon, ed. LC 82-18612. (Berenstain Bears First Time Bks.). (Illus.). 32p. (J). (ps-3). 1983. pap. 3.25 (0-394-85639-2, Pub. by Random Bks Yng Read) Random.

— The Berenstain Bears & the Messy Room. Lerner, Sharon, ed. (Berenstain Bears First Time Bks.). (Illus.). 32p. (J). (gr. k-2). 1983. lib. bdg. 5.99 (0-394-95639-7, Pub. by Random Bks Yng Read) Random.

— The Berenstain Bears & the Messy Room. (Berenstain Bears First Time Bks.). (Illus.). 32p. (J). (gr. k-3). 1998. pap., wbk. ed. 3.99 (0-679-88773-3, Pub. by Random Bks Yng Read) Random.

— The Berenstain Bears & the Messy Room. (Berenstain Bears First Time Bks.). 32p. (J). (gr. k-2). 1983. 8.45 (0-606-01640-6, Pub. by Turtleback) Demco.

— The Berenstain Bears & the Messy Room First Time Workbook. (Berenstain Bears First Time Bks.). (Illus.). 32p. (J). (gr. k-3). 1998. pap. 3.99 (0-679-88774-1, Pub. by Random Bks Yng Read) Random.

— The Berenstain Bears & the Missing Dinosaur Bone. LC 79-3458. (I Can Read It All By Myself: Beginner Books). (Illus.). 48p. (J). (ps-3). 1980. 7.99 (0-394-84447-5); lib. bdg. 11.99 (0-394-94447-X) Beginner.

— The Berenstain Bears & the Missing Honey. LC 87-4549. (Berenstain Bears First Time Readers Ser.). (Illus.). 32p. (J). (ps-3). 1987. pap. 3.25 (0-394-89133-3, Pub. by Random Bks Yng Read) Random.

— The Berenstain Bears & the Missing Honey. (Berenstain Bears First Time Readers Ser.). 32p. (J). (ps-3). 1987. 8.45 (0-606-00611-7, Pub. by Turtleback) Demco.

***Berenstain, Stan & Berenstain, Jan.** The Berenstain Bears & the Missing Watermelon Money. LC 98-54970. (Step into Reading Ser.: A Step 2 Book). (J). (gr. 1-3). 2000. pap. 20.01 (0-679-89230-3) Random.

Berenstain, Stan & Berenstain, Jan. The Berenstain Bears & the Missing Watermelon Money. LC 98-54970. (Step into Reading Ser.: A Step 2 Book). (J). (gr. 1-3). 2001. lib. bdg. 16.01 (0-679-99230-8) Random Bks Yng Read.

— The Berenstain Bears & the Nerdy Nephew. LC 92-32564. (Berenstain Bears Big Chapter Bks.). (Illus.). 98p. (J). (gr. 2-6). 1993. pap. 3.50 (0-679-83610-1, Pub. by Random Bks Yng Read) Random.

— The Berenstain Bears & the New Girl in Town. LC 92-32570. (Berenstain Bears Big Chapter Bks.). (Illus.). 101p. (J). (gr. 4-7). 1993. pap. 3.50 (0-679-83613-6, Pub. by Random Bks Yng Read) Random.

— The Berenstain Bears & the Perfect Crime (Almost) LC 98-10031. (Berenstain Bears Big Chapter Bks.). 112p. (J). (gr. k-3). 1998. pap. 3.99 (0-679-88943-4) Random.

— The Berenstain Bears & the Perfect Crime (Almost) LC 98-10031. (Berenstain Bears Big Chapter Bks.). (J). (gr. 2-6). 1998. lib. bdg. 11.99 (0-679-98943-9, Pub. by Random Bks Yng Read) Random.

— The Berenstain Bears & the Prize Pumpkin. LC 90-32865. (Berenstain Bears First Time Bks.). (Illus.). 32p. (J). (ps-3). 1990. pap. 3.25 (0-679-80847-7, Pub. by Random Bks Yng Read); lib. bdg. 5.99 (0-679-90847-1, Pub. by Random Bks Yng Read) Random.

— The Berenstain Bears & the Red-Handed Thief. LC 93-8870. (Berenstain Bears Big Chapter Bks.). (Illus.). 102p. (J). (gr. 2-6). 1993. pap. 3.50 (0-679-84033-8, Pub. by Random Bks Yng Read) Random.

— Berenstain Bears & the Scavenger Hunt. (J). 1997. pap. 5.99 (0-679-87325-2) Random Bks Yng Read.

— The Berenstain Bears & the School Scandal Sheet. (Berenstain Bears Big Chapter Bks.). (Illus.). 103p. (J). (gr. 2-6). 1994. pap. 3.50 (0-679-85812-1, Pub. by Random Bks Yng Read) Random.

— The Berenstain Bears & the Showdown at Chainsaw Gap. (Berenstain Bears Big Chapter Bks.). (J). (gr. 2-4). 1995. 8.60 (0-606-08489-4, Pub. by Turtleback) Demco.

— The Berenstain Bears & the Sitter. LC 81-50046. (Berenstain Bears First Time Bks.). (Illus.). 32p. (J). (ps-3). 1981. pap. 3.25 (0-394-84837-3, Pub. by Random Bks Yng Read) Random.

— The Berenstain Bears & the Sitter. (Berenstain Bears First Time Bks.). (J). (gr. k-2). 1981. 8.45 (0-606-00389-4, Pub. by Turtleback) Demco.

— The Berenstain Bears & the Slumber Party. LC 89-35223. (Berenstain Bears First Time Bks.). (Illus.). 32p. (J). (ps-3). 1990. pap. 3.25 (0-679-80419-6, Pub. by Random Bks Yng Read) Random.

— The Berenstain Bears & the Spooky Old Tree. LC 77-93771. (Bright & Early Bks.). (Illus.). (J). (ps-3). 1978. 7.99 (0-394-83910-2, Pub. by Random Bks Yng Read); lib. bdg. 11.99 (0-394-93910-7, Pub. by Random Bks Yng Read) Random.

— The Berenstain Bears & the Tic-Tac-Toe Mystery. LC 98-54971. (Step into Reading Ser.: A Step 2 Book). (J). (gr. 1-3). 2001. lib. bdg. 11.99 (0-679-99229-4) Random.

— The Berenstain Bears & the Trouble with Friends. LC 85-30165. (Berenstain Bears First Time Bks.). (Illus.). 32p. (J). (ps-3). 1987. pap. 3.25 (0-394-87339-4, Pub. by Random Bks Yng Read) Random.

— The Berenstain Bears & the Trouble with Grownups. LC 91-27430. (Berenstain Bears First Time Bks.). (Illus.). 32p. (J). (ps-3). 1992. pap. 3.25 (0-679-83000-6, Pub. by Random Bks Yng Read) Random.

— The Berenstain Bears & the Trouble with Grownups. (Berenstain Bears First Time Bks.). (J). (gr. k-2). 1992. 8.45 (0-606-01494-2, Pub. by Turtleback) Demco.

— The Berenstain Bears & the Truth. LC 83-3304. (Berenstain Bears First Time Bks.). (Illus.). 32p. (J). (ps-3). 1988. pap. 3.25 (0-394-85640-6, Pub. by Random Bks Yng Read) Random.

— The Berenstain Bears & the Truth. (Berenstain Bears First Time Bks.). 32p. (J). (gr. k-2). 1983. 8.45 (0-606-02779-3, Pub. by Turtleback) Demco.

— The Berenstain Bears & the Week at Grandma's. LC 85-25743. (Berenstain Bears First Time Bks.). (Illus.). 32p. (J). (gr. k-2). 1986. lib. bdg. 5.99 (0-394-97335-6, Pub. by Random Bks Yng Read) Random.

— The Berenstain Bears & the Week at Grandma's. LC 85-25743. (Berenstain Bears First Time Bks.). (Illus.). 32p. (J). (ps-3). 1986. pap. 3.25 (0-394-87335-1, Pub. by Random Bks Yng Read) Random.

— The Berenstain Bears & the Week at Grandma's. (Berenstain Bears First Time Bks.). 32p. (J). (gr. k-2). 1986. 8.45 (0-606-00629-X, Pub. by Turtleback) Demco.

— The Berenstain Bears & the Wheelchair Commando. LC 93-8871. (Berenstain Bears Big Chapter Bks.). (Illus.). 102p. (J). (gr. 4-7). 1993. pap. 3.50 (0-679-84034-6, Pub. by Random Bks Yng Read) Random.

— The Berenstain Bears & Too Much Birthday. LC 85-14529. (Berenstain Bears First Time Bks.). (Illus.). 32p. (J). (ps-3). 1986. pap. 3.25 (0-394-87332-7, Pub. by Random Bks Yng Read) Random.

Berenstain, Stan & Berenstain, Jan. The Berenstain Bears & Too Much Birthday. (Berenstain Bears First Time Bks.). 32p. (J). (gr. k-2). 1986. 8.45 (0-606-01992-8, Pub. by Turtleback) Demco.

Berenstain, Stan & Berenstain, Jan. The Berenstain Bears & Too Much Junk Food. (Berenstain Bears First Time Bks.). (J). (ps up). 1986. 7.95 incl. audio (0-394-88008-0) Random.

— The Berenstain Bears & Too Much Junk Food. Lerner, Sharon, ed. LC 84-40393. (Berenstain Bears First Time Bks.). (Illus.). 32p. (J). (gr. k-2). 1985. lib. bdg. 6.99 (0-394-97217-1, Pub. by Random Bks Yng Read) Random.

— The Berenstain Bears & Too Much Junk Food. Lerner, Sharon, ed. LC 84-40393. (Berenstain Bears First Time Bks.). (Illus.). 30p. (J). (ps-3). 1985. pap. 3.25 (0-394-87217-7, Pub. by Random Bks Yng Read) Random.

— The Berenstain Bears & Too Much Junk Food. LC 84-40393. (Berenstain Bears First Time Bks.). 30p. (J). (gr. k-2). 1985. 8.45 (0-606-03420-X, Pub. by Turtleback) Demco.

— The Berenstain Bears & Too Much Pressure. LC 92-6544.

B

(Berenstain Bears First Time Bks.). (Illus.). 32p. (J). (ps-3). 1992. pap. 3.25 (*0-679-83671-3*, Pub. by Random Bks Yng Read) Random.

Berenstain, Stan & Berenstain, Jan. The Berenstain Bears & Too Much Pressure. (Berenstain Bears First Time Bks.). (J). (gr. k-2). 1992. 8.45 (*0-606-02314-3*, Pub. by Turtleback) Demco.

Berenstain, Stan & Berenstain, Jan. The Berenstain Bears & Too Much Teasing. LC 95-1634. (Berenstain Bears First Time Bks.). (Illus.). (J). (ps-3). 1995. pap. 3.25 (*0-679-87706-1*) Random.

— The Berenstain Bears & Too Much Teasing. LC 95-1634. (Berenstain Bears First Time Bks.). (Illus.). 101p. (J). (ps-3). 1995. lib. bdg. 8.99 (*0-679-97706-6*) Random.

— The Berenstain Bears & Too Much Teasing. (Berenstain Bears First Time Bks.). (J). (gr. k-2). 1995. 8.45 (*0-606-08490-8*, Pub. by Turtleback) Demco.

— The Berenstain Bears & Too Much TV. LC 83-22887. (Berenstain Bears First Time Bks.). (Illus.). 32p. (J). (ps-3). 1984. pap. 3.25 (*0-394-86570-7*, Pub. by Random Bks Yng Read) Random.

— The Berenstain Bears & Too Much TV. (Berenstain Bears First Time Bks.). (Illus.). (J). (ps-1). 1989. 7.95 incl. audio (*0-394-82894-1*, Pub. by Random Bks Yng Read) Random.

Berenstain, Stan & Berenstain, Jan. The Berenstain Bears & Too Much TV. (Berenstain Bears First Time Bks.). 32p. (J). (gr. k-2). 1984. 8.45 (*0-606-03165-0*, Pub. by Turtleback) Demco.

Berenstain, Stan & Berenstain, Jan. The Berenstain Bears & Too Much Vacation. LC 88-32094. (Berenstain Bears First Time Bks.). (Illus.). 32p. (J). (ps-3). 1989. pap. 3.25 (*0-394-83014-8*, Pub. by Random Bks Yng Read) Random.

— The Berenstain Bears & Too Much Vacation. (Berenstain Bears First Time Bks.). 32p. (J). (gr. k-2). 1989. 8.45 (*0-606-04169-9*, Pub. by Turtleback) Demco.

— The Berenstain Bears Are a Family. LC 95-73053. (Berenstain Bears Toddler Bks.). 23p. (J). (ps-3). 1996. 3.99 (*0-679-88185-9*, Pub. by Random Bks Yng Read) Random.

— The Berenstain Bears at Camp Crush. LC 94-15995. (Berenstain Bears Big Chapter Bks.). (Illus.). 112p. (J). (gr. 2-6). 1994. pap. 3.50 (*0-679-86028-2*, Pub. by Random Bks Yng Read) Random.

— The Berenstain Bears at Camp Crush. LC 94-15995. (Berenstain Bears Big Chapter Bks.). (Illus.). 112p. (J). (ps-3). 1994. lib. bdg. 11.99 (*0-679-96028-7*, Pub. by Random Bks Yng Read) Random.

— The Berenstain Bears at the Mansion. (J). 1997. lib. bdg. 11.99 (*0-679-98156-X*, Pub. by Random Bks Yng Read) Random.

— Berenstain Bears' Bad Habit. (J). 1987. pap. text 1.95 (*0-394-89341-7*) Random.

— The Berenstain Bears Big Bear, Small Bear. LC 97-36284. (Early Step into Reading Ser.). (J). (ps-k). 1998. pap. 3.99 (*0-679-88717-2*) Random.

— The Berenstain Bears Big Bear, Small Bear. LC 97-36284. (Early Step into Reading Ser.). (J). (ps-k). 1998. lib. bdg. 11.99 (*0-679-98717-7*, Pub. by Random Bks Yng Read) Random.

— The Berenstain Bears' Big Book of Science & Nature. (J). 1997. pap. 12.99 (*0-679-88652-4*, Pub. by Random Bks Yng Read) Random.

— The Berenstain Bears Blaze a Trail. LC 87-4552. (Berenstain Bears First Time Readers Ser.). (Illus.). 32p. (J). (ps-3). 1987. pap. 3.25 (*0-394-89132-5*, Pub. by Random Bks Yng Read) Random.

— The Berenstain Bears Blaze a Trail. (Berenstain Bears First Time Readers Ser.). 32p. (J). (gr. k-3). 1987. 8.45 (*0-606-00619-2*, Pub. by Turtleback) Demco.

— The Berenstain Bears Bunny Hop, 2. (Coloring Bks.). (J). 1999. pap. 1.99 (*0-679-89474-8*, Pub. by Random Bks Yng Read) Random.

— The Berenstain Bears by the Sea. LC 97-36285. (Step into Reading Ser.: A Step 1 Book). (Illus.). 30p. (J). (ps-3). 1998. pap. 3.99 (*0-679-88719-9*) Random.

— The Berenstain Bears by the Sea. LC 97-36284. (Step into Reading Ser.: A Step 1 Book). (J). (gr. k-3). 1998. lib. bdg. 11.99 (*0-679-98719-3*, Pub. by Random Bks Yng Read) Random.

— The Berenstain Bears Catch the Bus. LC 98-29760. (Step into Reading Ser.: A Step 1 Book). (Illus.). 32p. (J). (ps-3). 1999. pap. 3.99 (*0-679-89227-3*) Random Hse Chldrns.

— The Berenstain Bears Catch the Bus. LC 98-29760. (Step into Reading Ser.: A Step 1 Book). (Illus.). 32p. (J). (gr. k-3). 1999. lib. bdg. 11.99 (*0-679-99227-8*) Random Hse Chldrns.

— The Berenstain Bears' Christmas Tree. large type ed. LC 80-5087. (Illus.). 32p. (J). (ps-2). 1980. 14.00 (*0-394-84566-8*, Pub. by Random Bks Yng Read) Random.

— The Berenstain Bears' Comic Valentine. large type ed. LC 97-2076. (Illus.). 48p. (J). (ps-3). 1998. 10.95 (*0-590-94729-X*) Scholastic Inc.

— The Berenstain Bears Cook it! Breakfast for Mama! (Berenstain Bears First Time Do It Bks.). (J). (ps-3). 1996. pap. 3.25 (*0-614-15728-5*) Random.

— The Berenstain Bears Cook it! Breakfast for Mama! LC 95-46648. (Berenstain Bears First Time Do It Bks.). (Illus.). 24p. (J). (ps-3). 1996. pap. 3.25 (*0-679-87316-3*) Random.

— The Berenstain Bears Cook it! Breakfast for Mama! (Berenstain Bears First Time Do It Bks.). (Illus.). (J). (ps-3). 1996. lib. bdg. 8.99 (*0-679-97316-8*) Random.

— The Berenstain Bears Cook it! Breakfast for Mama! (Berenstain Bears First Time Do It Bks.). (J). (ps-3). 1996. 8.45 (*0-606-09068-1*, Pub. by Turtleback) Demco.

— The Berenstain Bears Count Their Blessings. LC 95-1629. (Berenstain Bears First Time Bks.). (Illus.). 32p. (J). (ps-3). 1995. pap. 3.25 (*0-679-87707-X*) Random.

— The Berenstain Bears Count Their Blessings. LC 95-1629. (Berenstain Bears First Time Bks.). (Illus.). (J). (gr. k-2). 1995. lib. bdg. 8.99 (*0-679-97707-4*) Random.

— The Berenstain Bears Count Their Blessings. (Berenstain Bears First Time Bks.). (J). (gr. k-2). 1995. 8.45 (*0-606-08491-6*, Pub. by Turtleback) Demco.

***Berenstain, Stan & Berenstain, Jan.** Berenstain Bears Dollars & Sense. 2000. pap. 3.25 (*0-679-88962-0*, Pub. by Random Bks Yng Read) Random.

Berenstain, Stan & Berenstain, Jan. The Berenstain Bears Don't Pollute (Anymore) LC 91-9147. (Berenstain Bears First Time Bks.). (Illus.). 32p. (J). (ps-1). 1991. pap. 3.25 (*0-679-82351-4*, Pub. by Random Bks Yng Read) Random.

— The Berenstain Bears Don't Pollute (Anymore) LC 91-9147. (Berenstain Bears First Time Bks.). (Illus.). 32p. (J). (ps-3). 1991. lib. bdg. 8.99 (*0-679-92351-9*, Pub. by Random Bks Yng Read) Random.

— The Berenstain Bears Draw-It: Drawing Lessons from Stan & Jan. (Berenstain Bears First Time Do It Bks.). (Illus.). (J). (ps-3). 1996. pap. 3.25 (*0-679-87314-7*) Random.

— The Berenstain Bears Draw-It: Drawing Lessons from Stan & Jan. (Berenstain Bears First Time Do It Bks.). (Illus.). (J). (ps-3). 1996. lib. bdg. 8.99 (*0-679-97314-1*) Random.

Berenstain, Stan & Berenstain, Jan. The Berenstain Bears Draw-It: Drawing Lessons from Stan & Jan. (Berenstain Bears First Time Do It Bks.). (J). (ps-3). 1996. 8.45 (*0-606-10754-1*, Pub. by Turtleback) Demco.

Berenstain, Stan & Berenstain, Jan. The Berenstain Bears' Easter Surprise. large type ed. LC 97-33301. (Illus.). 48p. (J). (ps-3). 1998. 10.95 (*0-590-94730-3*) Scholastic Inc.

— The Berenstain Bears Fly-It: Up, Up & Away. LC 96-32906. (Berenstain Bears First Time Do It Bks.). (Illus.). 23p. (J). (ps-3). 1996. pap. 3.25 (*0-679-87317-1*) Random.

— The Berenstain Bears Fly It: Up, Up, & Away. (Berenstain Bears First Time Do It Bks.). (J). (ps-3). 1996. 8.45 (*0-606-10755-X*, Pub. by Turtleback) Demco.

— The Berenstain Bears Forget Their Manners. LC 84-43156. (Berenstain Bears First Time Bks.). (Illus.). 32p. (J). (ps-3). 1985. pap. 3.25 (*0-394-87333-5*, Pub. by Random Bks Yng Read) Random.

— The Berenstain Bears Forget Their Manners. (Berenstain Bears First Time Bks.). (Illus.). (J). (gr. k-2). 1986. pap. 7.95 incl. audio (*0-394-88343-8*, Pub. by Random Bks Yng Read) Random.

— The Berenstain Bears Forget Their Manners. (Berenstain Bears First Time Bks.). 32p. (J). (gr. k-2). 1985. 8.45 (*0-606-00260-X*, Pub. by Turtleback) Demco.

— The Berenstain Bears' Four Seasons. LC 95-73052. (Berenstain Bears Toddler Bks.). 23p. (J). (ps-3). 1996. 3.99 (*0-679-88182-4*, Pub. by Random Bks Yng Read) Random.

— The Berenstain Bears Get in a Fight. (Berenstain Bears First Time Bks.). (J). (gr. k-2). 1995. 14.50 (*1-57135-122-1*) Living Bks.

— The Berenstain Bears Get in a Fight. (Berenstain Bears First Time Bks.). (J). (gr. k-2). 1995. pap. 39.95 (*1-57135-126-4*); lib. bdg. 99.95 (*1-57135-127-2*) Living Bks.

— The Berenstain Bears Get in a Fight. LC 81-15866. (Berenstain Bears First Time Bks.). (Illus.). 32p. (J). (gr. k-2). 1982. pap. 3.25 (*0-394-85132-3*, Pub. by Random Bks Yng Read) Random.

— The Berenstain Bears Get in a Fight. (Berenstain Bears First Time Bks.). (J). (gr. k-2). 1982. 8.45 (*0-606-00390-8*, Pub. by Turtleback) Demco.

— The Berenstain Bears Get Stage Fright. LC 85-25716. (Berenstain Bears First Time Bks.). (Illus.). 32p. (J). (ps-3). 1986. pap. 3.25 (*0-394-87337-8*, Pub. by Random Bks Yng Read) Random.

— The Berenstain Bears Get Stage Fright. (Berenstain Bears First Time Bks.). 32p. (J). (gr. k-2). 1986. 8.45 (*0-606-00620-6*, Pub. by Turtleback) Demco.

— The Berenstain Bears Get the Don't Haftas. LC 98-65546. (Jellybean Bks.). (J). (ps-3). 1998. lib. bdg. 7.99 (*0-679-99236-7*, Pub. by Random Bks Yng Read) Random.

— The Berenstain Bears Get the Don't Haftas, No. 2. LC 98-65546. (Jellybean Bks.). 24p. (J). (ps-3). 1998. 1.99 (*0-679-89236-2*, Pub. by Random Bks Yng Read) Random.

— The Berenstain Bears Get the Gimmies. LC 88-42587. (Berenstain Bears First Time Bks.). (Illus.). 32p. (J). (gr. k-2). 1988. lib. bdg. 8.99 (*0-394-90566-0*, Pub. by Random Bks Yng Read) Random.

— The Berenstain Bears Get the Gimmies. LC 88-42587. (Berenstain Bears First Time Bks.). (Illus.). 32p. (J). (ps-3). 1988. pap. 3.25 (*0-394-80566-6*, Pub. by Random Bks Yng Read) Random.

— The Berenstain Bears Get the Gimmies. (Berenstain Bears First Time Bks.). (Illus.). 32p. (J). (gr. k-3). 1998. pap., wbk. ed. 3.99 (*0-679-88772-5*, Pub. by Random Bks Yng Read) Random.

— The Berenstain Bears Get the Gimmies. LC 88-42587. (Berenstain Bears First Time Bks.). 32p. (J). (gr. k-2). 1988. 8.45 (*0-606-03731-4*, Pub. by Turtleback) Demco.

— The Berenstain Bears Get the Gimmies. (Berenstain Bears First Time Bks.). (Illus.). 32p. (J). (gr. k-2). 1990. reprint ed. audio. write for info. (*0-318-66803-3*) Random Bks Yng Read.

— The Berenstain Bears Get the Gimmies. LC 88-42587. (Berenstain Bears First Time Bks.). (Illus.). 32p. (J). (ps-1). 1990. reprint ed. 7.95 incl. audio (*0-679-80313-0*, Pub. by Random Bks Yng Read) Random.

— The Berenstain Bears Get the Noisies. (Jellybean Bks.). (J). (ps-3). 1999. lib. bdg. 7.99 (*0-679-99266-9*) Random.

— The Berenstain Bears Get the Noisies. LC 98-66290. (Jellybean Bks.). (Illus.). 24p. (J). (ps-3). 1999. 1.99 (*0-679-89266-4*, Pub. by Random Bks Yng Read) Random.

***Berenstain, Stan & Berenstain, Jan.** The Berenstain Bears Get the Scaredies. (Jellybean Bks.). (Illus.). 24p. (J). (ps-3). 1999. lib. bdg. 7.99 (*0-679-99323-1*, Pub. by Random Bks Yng Read) Random.

— The Berenstain Bears Get the Scaredies, Bk. 4. (Jellybean Bks.). (Illus.). 24p. (J). (ps-k). 1999. pap. 1.99 (*0-679-89323-7*, Pub. by Random Bks Yng Read) Random.

Berenstain, Stan & Berenstain, Jan. The Berenstain Bears Get the Screamies. LC 98-65547. (Jellybean Bks.). (J). (ps-3). 1998. lib. bdg. 7.99 (*0-679-99235-9*, Pub. by Random Bks Yng Read) Random.

— The Berenstain Bears Get the Screamies. LC 98-65547. (Jellybean Bks.). (Illus.). 24p. (J). (ps-3). 1998. 1.99 (*0-679-89235-4*, Pub. by Random Bks Yng Read) Random.

***Berenstain, Stan & Berenstain, Jan.** Berenstain Bears Get the Twitchies. (Jellybean Books Just for Preschoolers). (Illus.). 24p. (J). (ps). 2000. 2.99 (*0-375-80127-8*, Pub. by Random Bks Yng Read) Random.

Berenstain, Stan & Berenstain, Jan. The Berenstain Bears Get Their Kicks. (Berenstain Bears First Time Bks.). (J). (gr. k-2). 1998. 8.45 (*0-606-13955-9*, Pub. by Turtleback) Demco.

— The Berenstain Bears Get Their Kicks, No. 3. LC 97-76109. (Berenstain Bears First Time Bks.). (Illus.). 32p. (J). (gr. k-3). 1998. pap. 3.25 (*0-679-88955-8*, Pub. by Random Bks Yng Read) Random.

— The Berenstain Bears Get Their Kicks, No. 3. LC 97-76109. (Berenstain Bears First Time Bks.: Vol. 3). (J). (ps-3). 1998. lib. bdg. 8.99 (*0-679-98955-2*, Pub. by Random Bks Yng Read) Random.

— The Berenstain Bears Go Hollywood. LC 99-24466. (Illus.). 112p. (J). (gr. 3-5). 1999. pap. 3.99 (*0-679-88948-5*) Random.

***Berenstain, Stan & Berenstain, Jan.** The Berenstain Bears Go Hollywood. Vol. 30. (Illus.). 112p. (ps-3). 1999. lib. bdg. 11.99 (*0-679-98948-X*) Random.

Berenstain, Stan & Berenstain, Jan. The Berenstain Bears Go In & Out. LC 98-29756. (Illus.). 32p. (J). (ps-3). 1999. pap. 3.99 (*0-679-89225-7*, Pub. by Random Bks Yng Read) Random.

— The Berenstain Bears Go In & Out. 5th ed. LC 98-29756. 32p. (J). 1999. lib. bdg. 11.99 (*0-679-99225-1*, Pub. by Random Bks Yng Read) Random.

— The Berenstain Bears Go Out for the Team. LC 85-30164. (Berenstain Bears First Time Bks.). (Illus.). 32p. (J). (ps-3). 1987. pap. 3.25 (*0-394-87338-6*, Pub. by Random Bks Yng Read) Random.

— The Berenstain Bears Go Out for the Team. LC 85-30164. (Berenstain Bears First Time Bks.). (Illus.). 32p. (J). (gr. k-2). 1991. 7.95 incl. audio (*0-679-81495-7*, Pub. by Random Bks Yng Read) Random.

— The Berenstain Bears Go Platinum. LC 98-17760. (Berenstain Bears Big Chapter Bks.). 106p. (J). (gr. k-3). 1998. pap. 3.99 (*0-679-88944-2*, Pub. by Random Bks Yng Read) Random.

— The Berenstain Bears Go Platinum. LC 98-17760. (Berenstain Bears Big Chapter Bks.). (Illus.). 112p. (J). (gr. k-3). 1998. lib. bdg. 11.99 (*0-679-98944-7*, Pub. by Random Bks Yng Read) Random.

— The Berenstain Bears Go to Camp. LC 81-15864. (Berenstain Bears First Time Bks.). (Illus.). 32p. (J). (ps-3). 1982. pap. 3.25 (*0-394-85131-5*, Pub. by Random Bks Yng Read) Random.

— The Berenstain Bears Go to Camp. (Berenstain Bears First Time Bks.). (J). (gr. k-2). 1982. 8.45 (*0-606-00392-4*, Pub. by Turtleback) Demco.

— The Berenstain Bears Go to School. LC 77-79853. (Berenstain Bears First Time Bks.). (Illus.). (J). (gr. k-2). 1978. lib. bdg. 5.99 (*0-394-93736-8*, Pub. by Random Bks Yng Read) Random.

— The Berenstain Bears Go to School. LC 77-79853. (Berenstain Bears First Time Bks.). (Illus.). 32p. (J). (ps-3). 1978. pap. 3.25 (*0-394-83736-3*, Pub. by Random Bks Yng Read) Random.

— The Berenstain Bears Go to School. (Berenstain Bears First Time Bks.). (Illus.). (J). (gr. k-2). 1987. 8.45 (*0-606-01481-0*, Pub. by Turtleback) Demco.

— The Berenstain Bears Go to the Doctor. (Berenstain Bears First Time Bks.). (J). (gr. k-2). 1985. pap. 7.95 incl. audio (*0-394-87663-6*) Random.

— The Berenstain Bears Go to the Doctor. LC 81-50043. (Berenstain Bears First Time Bks.). (Illus.). 32p. (J). (gr. k-2). 1981. lib. bdg. 5.99 (*0-394-94835-1*, Pub. by Random Bks Yng Read) Random.

— The Berenstain Bears Go to the Doctor. LC 81-50043. (Berenstain Bears First Time Bks.). (Illus.). 32p. (J). (ps-3). 1981. pap. 3.25 (*0-394-84835-7*, Pub. by Random Bks Yng Read) Random.

— The Berenstain Bears Go to the Doctor. (Berenstain Bears First Time Bks.). (J). (gr. k-2). 1981. 8.45 (*0-606-00393-2*, Pub. by Turtleback) Demco.

— The Berenstain Bears Go Up & Down. LC 98-29757 (Early Step into Reading Ser.). (Illus.). 32p. (J). (ps-3). 1999. lib. bdg. 11.99 (*0-679-98720-7*, Pub. by Random Bks Yng Read) Random.

— The Berenstain Bears Grow it! Mother Nature Has Such a Green Thumb! (Berenstain Bears First Time Do It Bks.). (J). (ps-3). 1996. 3.25 (*0-614-15729-3*) Random.

— The Berenstain Bears Grow it! Mother Nature Has Such a Green Thumb! LC 96-1842. (Berenstain Bears First Time Do It Bks.). (Illus.). 24p. (J). (ps-3). 1996. pap. 3.25 (*0-679-87315-5*) Random.

— The Berenstain Bears Grow it! Mother Nature Has Such a Green Thumb! LC 96-1842. (Berenstain Bears First Time Do It Bks.). (Illus.). (J). (ps-3). 1996. lib. bdg. 8.99 (*0-679-97315-X*) Random.

— The Berenstain Bears Grow it! Mother Nature Has Such a Green Thumb! (Berenstain Bears First Time Do It Bks.). (J). (ps-3). 1996. 8.45 (*0-606-09069-X*, Pub. by Turtleback) Demco.

— The Berenstain Bears' Home Sweet Tree. LC 97-187902. (Illus.). (J). 1997. 11.99 (*0-679-87328-7*, Pub. by Random Bks Yng Read) Random.

— The Berenstain Bears in Big Bear City. (Illus.). (J). 1996. 4.99 (*0-679-87324-4*, Pub. by Random Bks Yng Read) Random.

— The Berenstain Bears in Maniac Mansion. LC 96-5452. (Berenstain Bears Big Chapter Bks.). (Illus.). (J). (gr. 2-6). 1996. lib. bdg. write for info. (*0-614-14028-5*) Random.

— The Berenstain Bears in Maniac Mansion. LC 96-5452. (Berenstain Bears Big Chapter Bks.). (J). (gr. 2-6). 1996. pap. 3.50 (*0-679-88156-5*, Pub. by Random Bks Yng Read) Random.

— The Berenstain Bears in Maniac Mansion. (Berenstain Bears Big Chapter Bks.). (J). (gr. 2-6). 1996. 8.60 (*0-606-10756-8*, Pub. by Turtleback) Demco.

— The Berenstain Bears in the Dark. (Berenstain Bears First Time Bks.). (J). (gr. k-2). 1996. 23.75 (*1-57135-200-7*) Living Bks.

— The Berenstain Bears in the Dark. (Berenstain Bears First Time Bks.). 32p. (J). (gr. k-2). 1997. cd-rom 49.95 (*1-57135-204-X*) Living Bks.

— The Berenstain Bears in the Dark. LC 82-5395. (Berenstain Bears First Time Bks.). 32p. (J). (ps-3). 1982. pap. 3.25 (*0-394-85443-8*, Pub. by Random Bks Yng Read) Random.

Berenstain, Stan & Berenstain, Jan. The Berenstain Bears in the Dark. (Berenstain Bears First Time Bks.). 32p. (J). (gr. k-2). 1982. 8.45 (*0-606-00394-0*, Pub. by Turtleback) Demco.

Berenstain, Stan & Berenstain, Jan. The Berenstain Bears in the Freaky Funhouse. LC 94-47956. (Berenstain Bears Big Chapter Bks.). (Illus.). 103p. (J). (gr. 4-7). 1995. pap. 3.99 (*0-679-87244-2*) Random.

— The Berenstain Bears in the Freaky Funhouse. (Berenstain Bears Big Chapter Bks.). (J). (gr. 2-6). 1995. 8.60 (*0-606-07279-9*, Pub. by Turtleback) Demco.

— The Berenstain Bears in the House of Mirrors. LC 98-18937. (Early Step into Reading Ser.). (Illus.). (J). (gr. k-3). 1999. pap. 3.99 (*0-679-89226-5*) Random.

— The Berenstain Bears in the House of Mirrors. LC 98-18937. (Early Step into Reading Ser.). (J). (gr. k-3). 1999. lib. bdg. 11.99 (*0-679-99226-X*) Random.

— The Berenstain Bears in the Wax Museum. LC 99-12686. (J). 1999. lib. bdg. 11.99 (*0-679-98947-1*, Pub. by Random Bks Yng Read) Random.

***Berenstain, Stan & Berenstain, Jan.** The Berenstain Bears in the Wax Museum. LC 99-12686. (J). 1999. pap. 3.99 (*0-679-88947-7*, Pub. by Random Bks Yng Read) Random.

Berenstain, Stan & Berenstain, Jan. The Berenstain Bears Learn about Strangers. LC 84-43157. (Berenstain Bears First Time Bks.). (Illus.). 32p. (J). (ps-3). 1985. pap. 3.25 (*0-394-87334-3*, Pub. by Random Bks Yng Read) Random.

— The Berenstain Bears Learn about Strangers. (Berenstain Bears First Time Bks.). 32p. (J). (gr. k-2). 1985. 8.45 (*0-606-00259-6*, Pub. by Turtleback) Demco.

— The Berenstain Bears Learn About Strangers. (Berenstain Bears First Time Bks.). (Illus.). 32p. (J). (ps-1). 1986. pap. 7.95 incl. audio (*0-394-88346-2*, Pub. by Random Bks Yng Read) Random.

— The Berenstain Bears Lend a Helping Hand. LC 98-7367. (Berenstain Bears First Time Bks.). (Illus.). 32p. (J). (gr. k-3). 1998. pap. 3.25 (*0-679-88956-6*) Random.

— The Berenstain Bears Lend a Helping Hand, No. 4. LC 98-7367. (Berenstain Bears First Time Bks.). (Illus.). 32p. (J). (gr. k-3). 1998. lib. bdg. 8.99 (*0-679-98956-0*, Pub. by Random Bks Yng Read) Random.

— The Berenstain Bears Lost in Cyberspace. LC 98-46400. (Berenstain Bears Big Chapter Bks.). (J). (gr. 2-4). 1999. pap. 3.99 (*0-679-88946-9*) Random.

— The Berenstain Bears Lost in Cyberspace. LC 98-46400. (Berenstain Bears Big Chapter Bks.). (J). (gr. 3-5). 1999. lib. bdg. 11.99 (*0-679-98946-3*) Random.

— The Berenstain Bears' Mad, Mad, Mad Toy Craze. LC 98-36353. (Berenstain Bears First Time Bks.). (J). (gr. k-2). 1999. lib. bdg. 8.99 (*0-679-98958-7*) Random.

— The Berenstain Bears' Media Madness. LC 94-40741. (Berenstain Bears Big Chapter Bks.). (Illus.). 100p. (J). (gr. 4-7). 1995. pap. 3.99 (*0-679-86664-7*) Random.

— The Berenstain Bears' Media Madness. (Berenstain Bears Big Chapter Bks.). (J). (gr. 2-6). 1995. 8.60 (*0-606-07280-2*, Pub. by Turtleback) Demco.

— The Berenstain Bears Meet Santa Bear. (Berenstain Bears First Time Bks.). (J). (gr. k-2). 1984. 8.45 (*0-606-12632-5*, Pub. by Turtleback) Demco.

— The Berenstain Bears' Moving Day. LC 81-50044. (Berenstain Bears First Time Bks.). (Illus.). 32p. (J). (gr. k-2). 1981. lib. bdg. 5.99 (*0-394-94838-6*, Pub. by Random Bks Yng Read) Random.

Berenstain, Stan & Berenstain, Jan. The Berenstain Bears' Moving Day. LC 81-50044. (Berenstain Bears First Time Bks.). (Illus.). 32p. (J). (gr. k-2). 1981. pap. 3.25 (*0-394-84838-1*, Pub. by Random Bks Yng Read) Random.

— The Berenstain Bears' Moving Day. (Berenstain Bears First Time Bks.). (J). (gr. k-2). 1981. 8.45 (*0-606-00395-9*, Pub. by Turtleback) Demco.

Berenstain, Stan & Berenstain, Jan. The Berenstain Bears' New Baby. LC 74-2535. (Berenstain Bears First Time Bks.). (Illus.). 32p. (J). (ps-3). 1974. pap. 3.25 (*0-394-82908-5*, Pub. by Random Bks Yng Read) Random.

— The Berenstain Bears' New Baby. (Berenstain Bears First Time Bks.). (Illus.). (J). (gr. k-2). 1974. 8.45 (*0-606-01483-7*, Pub. by Turtleback) Demco.

B

— Berenstain Bears' New Clothes. (J). 1997. pap. 5.99 (*0-679-87326-0*, Pub. by Random Bks Yng Read) Random.

— The Berenstain Bears' New Neighbors. LC 93-47145. (Berenstain Bears First Time Bks.). (Illus.). 32p. (J). (ps-1). 1994. pap. 3.25 (*0-679-86435-0*, Pub. by Random Bks Yng Read) Random.

— The Berenstain Bears' New Neighbors. LC 93-47145. (Berenstain Bears First Time Bks.). (Illus.). 32p. (J). (ps-3). 1994. lib. bdg. 8.99 (*0-679-96435-5*, Pub. by Random Bks Yng Read) Random.

Berenstain, Stan & Berenstain, Jan. The Berenstain Bears' New Neighbors. (Berenstain Bears First Time Bks.). (J). (gr. k-2). 1994. 8.45 (*0-606-06227-0*, Pub. by Turtleback) Demco.

Berenstain, Stan & Berenstain, Jan. The Berenstain Bears' Nursery Tales. LC 73-1901. (Berenstain Bears First Time Bks.). (Illus.). 32p. (J). (ps-3). 1973. pap. 3.25 (*0-394-82665-5*, Pub. by Random Bks Yng Read) Random.

— The Berenstain Bears' Nursery Tales. (Berenstain Bears First Time Bks.). (J). (gr. k-2). 1973. 8.45 (*0-606-01484-5*, Pub. by Turtleback) Demco.

— The Berenstain Bears on the Job. LC 87-9739. (Berenstain Bears First Time Readers Ser.). (Illus.). 32p. (J). (ps-3). 1987. pap. 3.25 (*0-394-89131-7*, Pub. by Random Bks Yng Read) Random.

— The Berenstain Bears on the Job. (Berenstain Bears First Time Readers Ser.). 32p. (J). (ps-3). 1987. 8.45 (*0-606-00625-7*, Pub. by Turtleback) Demco.

— The Berenstain Bears on the Moon. LC 84-20428. (Bright & Early Bks.). (Illus.). 38p. (J). (ps-3). 1985. 7.99 (*0-394-87180-4*, Pub. by Random Bks Yng Read) Random.

***Berenstain, Stan & Berenstain, Jan.** Berenstain Bears Phenom in the Family. LC 99-52550. (Berenstain Bears Big Chapter Bks.). (Illus.). (J). 2000. lib. bdg. 11.99 (*0-679-98952-8*, Pub. by Random Bks Yng Read) Random.

Berenstain, Stan & Berenstain, Jan. The Berenstain Bears Play Ball. large type ed. LC 97-15200. (Illus.). 48p. (J). (ps-3). 1998. 10.95 (*0-590-94732-X*) Scholastic Inc.

— The Berenstain Bears Ready, Get Set, Go! LC 88-42589. (Berenstain Bears First Time Readers Ser.). (Illus.). 32p. (J). (ps-3). 1988. pap. 3.25 (*0-394-80564-X*, Pub. by Random Bks Yng Read) Random.

Berenstain, Stan & Berenstain, Jan. The Berenstain Bears Ready, Get Set, Go! (Berenstain Bears First Time Readers Ser.). (J). (ps-3). 1988. 8.45 (*0-606-03985-6*, Pub. by Turtleback) Demco.

Berenstain, Stan & Berenstain, Jan. The Berenstain Bears Ride the Thunderbolt. LC 97-36292. (Early Step into Reading Ser.). (J). (ps-k). 1998. pap. 3.99 (*0-679-88718-0*) Random.

— The Berenstain Bears Ride the Thunderbolt. LC 97-36292. (Early Step into Reading Ser.). (J). (ps-3). 1998. lib. bdg. 11.99 (*0-679-98718-5*, Pub. by Random Bks Yng Read) Random.

— The Berenstain Bears Ride the Thunderbolt. (Early Step into Reading Ser.). (J). (ps-k). 1998. 9.19 (*0-606-13956-7*, Pub. by Turtleback) Demco.

— The Berenstain Bears Say Goodnight. LC 95-73054. (Berenstain Bears Toddler Bks.). 23p. (J). (ps-3). 1996. 3.99 (*0-679-88183-2*) McKay.

— The Berenstain Bears' Science Fair. LC 76-8121. (Bear Facts Library). (Illus.). 72p. (J). (ps-4). 1984. pap. 7.99 (*0-394-86603-7*, Pub. by Random Bks Yng Read) Random.

Berenstain, Stan & Berenstain, Jan. The Berenstain Bears' Science Fair. (Bear Facts Library). (J). 1977. 13.19 (*0-606-03166-9*, Pub. by Turtleback) Demco.

Berenstain, Stan & Berenstain, Jan. The Berenstain Bears' Take-Along Library. Incl. Berenstain Bears & the Messy Room. (Illus.). 32p. (J). (gr. k-2). 1985. Berenstain Bears & the Sitter. (Illus.). 32p. (J). (gr. k-2). 1985. Berenstain Bears & Too Much TV. (Illus.). 32p. (J). (gr. k-2). 1985. Berenstain Bears in the Dark. (Illus.). 32p. (J). (gr. k-2). 1985. Berenstain Bears Visit the Dentist. (Illus.). 32p. (J). (gr. k-2). 1985. (Illus.). (J). (ps-3). 1985. 11.50 (*0-394-87615-6*) Random Bks Yng Read.

— The Berenstain Bears' Thanksgiving. large type ed. LC 96-38775. (Illus.). 48p. (J). (ps-3). 1997. 10.95 (*0-590-94731-1*) Scholastic Inc.

— The Berenstain Bears' That Stump Must Go! LC 97-40641. (Beginner Bks.). (Illus.). 48p. (J). (gr. k-3). 2000. lib. bdg. 11.99 (*0-679-98963-3*, Pub. by Random Bks Yng Read) Random.

— The Berenstain Bears, the Birds & the Bees & the Bears. (J). 1999. write for info. (*0-679-88971-X*) Random.

***Berenstain, Stan & Berenstain, Jan.** The Berenstain Bears, the Birds & the Bees & the Bears. LC 98-46396. (Berenstain Bears First Time Bks.). (Illus.). 24p. (J). (gr. k-3). 1999. pap. 3.25 (*0-679-88959-0*, Pub. by Random Bks Yng Read) Random.

Berenstain, Stan & Berenstain, Jan. The Berenstain Bears the Whole Year Through: With Earthsaver Tips & Things to Do for Each & Every Month of the Year. LC 96-38778. (J). (gr. 2-5). 1997. write for info. (*0-590-94462-2*) Scholastic Inc.

— The Berenstain Bears Think of Those in Need. LC 98-54215. (J). 1999. pap. 3.25 (*0-679-88957-4*) Random.

— The Berenstain Bears Think of Those in Need. LC 98-54215. (Illus.). 24p. (J). (gr. k-3). 1999. lib. bdg. 8.99 (*0-679-98957-9*) Random.

— The Berenstain Bears Trick or Treat. LC 89-30884. (Berenstain Bears First Time Bks.). (Illus.). 32p. (J). (ps-3). 1989. pap. 3.25 (*0-679-80091-3*, Pub. by Random Bks Yng Read) Random.

— The Berenstain Bears' Trouble at School. LC 86-4999. (Berenstain Bears First Time Bks.). (Illus.). 32p. (J). (ps-3). 1987. pap. 3.25 (*0-394-87336-X*, Pub. by Random Bks Yng Read) Random.

— The Berenstain Bears' Trouble at School. (Berenstain Bears First Time Bks.). 32p. (J). (gr. k-2). 1986. 8.45 (*0-606-00626-5*, Pub. by Turtleback) Demco.

— The Berenstain Bears' Trouble with Money. LC 83-3305. (Berenstain Bears First Time Bks.). (Illus.). 32p. (J). (ps-3). 1983. pap. 3.25 (*0-394-85917-0*, Pub. by Random Bks Yng Read) Random.

— The Berenstain Bears' Trouble with Money. (Berenstain Bears First Time Bks.). 32p. (J). (gr. k-2). 1998. pap., wbk. ed. 3.99 (*0-679-88775-X*, Pub. by Random Bks Yng Read) Random.

— The Berenstain Bears' Trouble with Money. (Berenstain Bears First Time Bks.). 32p. (J). (gr. k-2). 1983. 8.45 (*0-606-02777-7*, Pub. by Turtleback) Demco.

— The Berenstain Bears' Trouble with Pets. LC 90-32956. (Berenstain Bears First Time Bks.). (Illus.). 32p. (J). (ps-3). 1990. pap. 3.25 (*0-679-80848-5*, Pub. by Random Bks Yng Read) Random.

— The Berenstain Bears' Trouble with Pets. (Berenstain Bears First Time Bks.). (J). (gr. k-2). 1990. 8.45 (*0-606-04615-1*, Pub. by Turtleback) Demco.

— The Berenstain Bears Visit the Dentist. LC 81-50045. (Berenstain Bears First Time Bks.). (Illus.). 32p. (J). (ps-3). 1981. pap. 3.25 (*0-394-84836-5*, Pub. by Random Bks Yng Read) Random.

— The Berenstain Bears Visit the Dentist. LC 81-50045. (Berenstain Bears First Time Bks.). (Illus.). 32p. (J). (ps-3). 1981. lib. bdg. 5.99 (*0-394-94836-X*, Pub. by Random Bks Yng Read) Random.

— The Berenstain Bears Visit the Dentist. (Berenstain Bears First Time Bks.). (J). (gr. k-2). 1981. 8.45 (*0-606-00396-7*, Pub. by Turtleback) Demco.

— The Berenstain Bears Yike! Yike! Where's My Trike? (Illus.). (J). 1996. 4.99 (*0-679-87577-8*, Pub. by Random Bks Yng Read) Random.

— Berenstain's A Book. LC 97-6783. (Bright & Early Bks.). (J). (ps-1). 1997. lib. bdg. 11.99 (*0-679-98705-3*, Pub. by Random Bks Yng Read) Random.

— Berenstain's A Book. LC 97-6783. (Bright & Early Bks.). (J). (ps-3). 1997. 7.99 (*0-679-88705-9*, Pub. by Random Bks Yng Read) Random.

— The Berenstains' B Book. LC PZ7.B4483Bg 1997. (Bright & Early Bks.). (Illus.). (J). (ps-3). 1971. lib. bdg. 11.99 (*0-394-92324-3*, Pub. by Random Bks Yng Read) Random.

— The Berenstains' B Book. (Bright & Early Bks.). (Illus.). 36p. (J). (ps-1). 1971. 7.99 (*0-394-82324-9*, Pub. by Random Bks Yng Read) Random.

— Berenstains' C Book. LC 97-10120. (Bright & Early Bks.). (J). (ps-1). 1997. lib. bdg. 11.99 (*0-679-98834-3*, Pub. by Random Bks Yng Read) Random.

— Berensteins' C book. LC 97-10120. (Bright & Early Bks.). (Illus.). (J). 1997. 7.99 (*0-679-88834-9*, Pub. by Random Bks Yng Read) Random.

— The Berstain Bears Fly it. (Illus.). (J). 1996. lib. bdg. 8.99 (*0-679-97317-6*) Random.

— The Berstain Bears' Spring Fling, 1. (Coloring Bks.). (J). 1999. pap. 1.99 (*0-679-89473-X*, Pub. by Random Bks Yng Read) Random.

— Big Honey Hunt. LC 62-15115. (I Can Read It All By Myself: Beginner Books). (Illus.). 64p. (J). (ps-3). 1962. 7.99 (*0-394-80028-1*) Beginner.

— Bike Lesson. LC 64-11460. (I Can Read It All by Myself: Beginner Books). (Illus.). 64p. (J). (ps-3). 1964. lib. bdg. 11.99 (*0-394-90036-7*, Pub. by Random Bks Yng Read) Random.

— Bike Lesson. LC 64-11460. (I Can Read It All by Myself: Beginner Books). (Illus.). 64p. (J). (ps-3). 1966. 7.99 (*0-394-80036-2*, Pub. by Random Bks Yng Read) Random.

— The Day of the Dinosaur. LC 87-9828. (Berenstain Bears First Time Readers Ser.). (Illus.). 32p. (J). (ps-3). 1987. pap. 3.25 (*0-394-89130-9*, Pub. by Random Bks Yng Read) Random.

— The Day of the Dinosaur. (Berenstain Bears First Time Readers Ser.). 32p. (J). (ps-3). 1987. 8.45 (*0-606-01344-X*, Pub. by Turtleback) Demco.

— Eager Beavers: The Berenstain Bears. (Comes to Life Bks.). 16p. (J). (ps-2). 1993. write for info. (*1-883366-02-X*) YES Ent.

— Eager Beavers: The Berenstain Bears. (Comes to Life Bks.). 16p. (J). (ps-2). 1994. write for info. (*1-883366-73-9*) YES Ent.

— En de Bezige Bevers: The Berenstain Bears. DigiPro Staff, tr. from ENG. (Comes to Life Bks.).Tr. of Eager Beavers. (DUT.). 16p. (J). (ps-2). 1994. write for info. (*1-883366-89-5*) YES Ent.

— En De Geheimzinnige Getallen: The Berenstain Bears. DigiPro Staff, tr. from ENG. (Comes to Life Bks.).Tr. of Mysterious Numbers. (DUT.). 16p. (J). (ps-2). 1994. write for info. (*1-883366-90-9*) YES Ent.

— Et les Castors Consciencieux: The Berenstain Bears. DigiPro Staff, tr. from ENG. (Comes to Life Bks.).Tr. of Eager Beavers. (FRE.). 16p. (J). (ps-2). 1994. write for info. (*1-883366-64-X*) YES Ent.

— Et les Nombres Mysterieux: The Berenstain Bears. DigiPro Staff, tr. from ENG. (Comes to Life Bks.).Tr. of Mysterious Numbers. (FRE.). 16p. (J). (ps-2). 1994. write for info. (*1-883366-65-8*) YES Ent.

— Hat, New Hat. (Bright & Early Bks.: No. 9). (Illus.). (J). (ps-1). 1970. lib. bdg. 11.99 (*0-394-90669-1*, Pub. by Random Bks Yng Read) Random.

— He Bear, She Bear. LC 74-5518. (Bright & Early Bks.). (Illus.). 48p. (J). (ps-3). 1974. 7.99 (*0-394-82997-2*, Pub. by Random Bks Yng Read) Random.

— He Bear, She Bear. (Bright & Early Bks.). (Illus.). 24p. (J). (ps-3). 1999. 4.99 (*0-679-89426-8*, Pub. by Random Bks Yng Read) Random.

— Home Sweet Tree: The Berenstain Bears. (Play Along Ser.). 16p. (J). (ps-2). 1995. write for info. (*1-57234-061-4*) YES Ent.

— Inside, Outside, Upside Down. LC 96-70731. (Bright & Early Bks.). (J). (ps-3). 1997. 4.99 (*0-679-88632-X*) Random.

***Berenstain, Stan & Berenstain, Jan.** Inside, Outside, Upside Down. (Bright & Early Bks.). (J). (ps-3). 2000. 7.99 (*0-375-80253-3*) Random.

Berenstain, Stan & Berenstain, Jan. Inside, Outside, Upside Down. LC 68-28465. (Bright & Early Bks.). (Illus.). (J). (ps-1). 1968. 7.99 (*0-394-81142-9*, Pub. by Random Bks Yng Read) Random.

— Inside, Outside, Upside Down. LC 68-28465. (Bright & Early Bks.). (Illus.). (J). (ps-3). 1968. lib. bdg. 11.99 (*0-394-91142-3*, Pub. by Random Bks Yng Read) Random.

— Life with Pa Pa: The Berenstain Bears. (Comes to Life Bks.). 16p. (J). (ps-2). 1993. write for info. (*1-883366-01-1*) YES Ent.

— Me First, Me First. (Board Bks.). 7p. (J). 1999. pap. 3.99 (*0-679-89332-6*, Pub. by Random Bks Yng Read) Random.

— My New Bed: From Crib to Bed. 2nd ed. (Berenstain Bears Baby Board Books Ser.). (J). (ps). 1999. pap. 3.99 (*0-679-89333-4*, Pub. by Random Bks Yng Read) Random.

— My Everyday Book, Vol. 6. 7p. 2000. pap. 4.99 (*0-679-89337-7*) Random.

— My Potty & I: A Friend In Need. 4th ed. (Berenstain Bears Baby Board Books Ser.). (Illus.). 7p. (J). (ps). 1999. pap. 3.99 (*0-679-89335-0*, Pub. by Random Bks Yng Read) Random.

— My Trusty Car Seat: Buckle Up For Safety. 3rd ed. (Berenstain Bears Baby Board Books Ser.). (J). (ps). 1999. pap. 3.99 (*0-679-89334-2*, Pub. by Random Bks Yng Read) Random.

— Mysterious Numbers: The Berenstain Bears. (Comic Tale Easy Reader Ser.). 16p. (J). (ps-2). 1993. write for info. (*1-883366-00-3*) YES Ent.

— Mysterious Numbers: The Berenstain Bears. (Comes to Life Bks.). 16p. (J). (ps-2). 1994. write for info. (*1-883366-74-7*) YES Ent.

— Not So Buried Treasure: The Berenstain Bears. (Comes to Life Bks.). 16p. (J). (ps-2). 1995. write for info. (*1-57234-057-6*) YES Ent.

— Old Hat, New Hat. (Bright & Early Bks.). (Illus.). (J). (ps-3). 1970. 7.99 (*0-394-80669-7*, Pub. by Random Bks Yng Read) Random.

— Old Hat, New Hat. LC 96-70730. (Bright & Early Bks.). (J). (ps-3). 1997. 4.99 (*0-679-88630-3*, Pub. by Random Bks Yng Read) Random.

— Los Osos Berenstain & el Cuarto Desordenado. Guibert, Rita, tr. from ENG. LC 91-50191. (Berenstain Bears First Time Bks.).Tr. of Berenstain Bears & the Messy Room. (SPA., Illus.). 32p. (J). (ps-3). 1992. pap. 3.25 (*0-679-83470-2*, Pub. by Random Bks Yng Read) Random.

— Los Osos Berenstain & la Ninera. Guibert, Rita, tr. from ENG. LC 92-46719. (Berenstain Bears First Time Bks.).Tr. of Berenstain Bears & the Sitter. (SPA., Illus.). 32p. (J). (ps-3). 1993. pap. 3.25 (*0-679-84746-4*, Pub. by Random Bks Yng Read) Random.

— Los Osos Berenstain & las Paleas Entre Amigos. Guibert, Rita, tr. from ENG. LC 92-14807. (Berenstain Bears First Time Bks.).Tr. of Berenstain Bears & the Trouble with Friends. (SPA., Illus.). 32p. (J). (gr. k-2). 1993. pap. 3.25 (*0-679-84006-0*, Pub. by Random Bks Yng Read) Random.

— Los Osos Berenstain Dia de Mudanza. Guibert, Rita, tr. from ENG. LC 93-37312. (Berenstain Bears First Time Bks.). Orig. Title: Berenstain Bears' Moving Day. (SPA., Illus.). 32p. (J). (gr. k-2). 1994. pap. 3.25 (*0-679-85430-4*, Pub. by Random Bks Yng Read) Random.

— Los Osos Berenstain en la Oscuridad. Guibert, Rita, tr. from ENG. LC 91-51092. (Berenstain Bears First Time Bks.).Tr. of Berenstain Bears In The Dark. (SPA., Illus.). 32p. (J). (ps-3). 1992. pap. 3.25 (*0-679-83471-0*, Pub. by Random Bks Yng Read) Random.

— Los Osos Berenstain, No Se Permiten Ninas. LC 93-29904. (Berenstain Bears First Time Bks.).Tr. of Berenstain Bears, No Girls Allowed. (SPA.). 32p. (J). (gr. k-2). 1994. pap. 3.25 (*0-679-85431-2*, Pub. by Random Bks Yng Read) Random.

— Los Osos Berenstain y Demasiada Fiesta. Guibert, Rita, tr. from ENG. LC 92-45874. (Berenstain Bears First Time Bks.).Tr. of Berenstain Bears & Too Much Birthday. (SPA., Illus.). 32p. (J). (ps-3). 1993. pap. 3.25 (*0-679-84745-6*, Pub. by Random Bks Yng Read) Random.

— Los Osos Scouts Berenstain & el Complot de la Gran Calabaza. (Berenstain Bear Scouts Ser.).Tr. of Berenstain Bear Scouts & the Humongous Pumpkin. (SPA.). 64p. (J). (gr. 3-6). 1995. pap. 2.99 (*0-590-59750-7*) Scholastic Inc.

***Berenstain, Stan & Berenstain, Jan.** Los Osos Scouts Berenstain Gritan de Terror. (Berenstain Bear Scouts Ser.).Tr. of Berenstain Bear Scouts Scream Their Heads Off. (SPA.). (J). (gr. 3-6). 1998. 8.60 (*0-606-13580-4*, Pub. by Turtleback) Demco.

Berenstain, Stan & Berenstain, Jan. Los Osos Scouts Berenstain Salvan a Rascaespaldas. (Berenstain Bear Scouts Ser.).Tr. of Berenstain Bear Scouts Save that Backscratcher. (SPA., Illus.). (J). (gr. 4-7). 1996. mass mkt. 2.99 (*0-590-69766-8*) Scholastic Inc.

— Los Osos Scouts Berenstain Salvan a Rascaespaldas. (Berenstain Bear Scouts Ser.).Tr. of Berenstain Bear Scouts Save that Backscratcher. (SPA.). (J). (gr. 3-6). 1996. 8.19 (*0-606-09575-6*, Pub. by Turtleback) Demco.

— Los Osos Scouts Berenstain Se Encuentran Con Patagrande. (Berenstain Bear Scouts Ser.).Tr. of Berenstain Bear Scouts Meet BigPaw. (SPA.). (J). (gr. 3-6). 1996. pap. 2.99 (*0-590-67664-4*) Scholastic Inc.

Berenstain, Stan & Berenstain, Jan. Los Osos Scouts Berenstain Se Encuentran Con Patagrande. (Berenstain Bear Scouts Ser.).Tr. of Berenstain Bear Scouts Meet BigPaw. (SPA.). (J). (gr. 3-6). 1995. 8.09 (*0-606-08563-7*, Pub. by Turtleback) Demco.

Berenstain, Stan & Berenstain, Jan. Los Osos Scouts Berenstain y el Bagre Que Tose. (Berenstain Bear Scouts Ser.).Tr. of Berenstain Bear Scouts & the Coughing Catfish. (SPA.). (J). (gr. 3-6). 1996. pap. text 2.99 (*0-590-87729-1*) Scholastic Inc.

— Los Osos Scouts Berenstain y el Bagre Que Tose. (Berenstain Bear Scouts Ser.).Tr. of Berenstain Bear Scouts & the Coughing Catfish. (SPA.). (J). (gr. 3-6). 1996. 8.09 (*0-606-09719-8*, Pub. by Turtleback) Demco.

— Los Osos Scouts Berenstain y El Complot de La Gran Calabaza. (Berenstain Bear Scouts Ser.).Tr. of Berenstain Bear Scouts & the Humongous Pumpkin. (SPA.). (J). (gr. 3-6). 1995. 8.09 (*0-606-07805-3*, Pub. by Turtleback) Demco.

— Los Osos Scouts Berenstain y el Desastre Colosal. (Berenstain Bear Scouts Ser.).Tr. of Berenstain Bear Scouts & the Really Big Disaster. (SPA.). (J). (gr. 3-6). 1998. pap. text 3.50 (*0-590-94482-7*, Little Apple) Scholastic Inc.

***Berenstain, Stan & Berenstain, Jan.** Los Osos Scouts Berenstain y el Desastre Colosal, 1. (Berenstain Bear Scouts Ser.).Tr. of Berenstain Bear Scouts & the Really Big Disaster. (SPA.). (J). (gr. 3-6). 1998. 8.60 (*0-606-13581-2*, Pub. by Turtleback) Demco.

Berenstain, Stan & Berenstain, Jan. Los Osos Scouts Berenstain y el Monstruo De Hielo. (Berenstain Bear Scouts Ser.).Tr. of Berenstain Bear Scouts & the Ice Monster. (SPA.). (J). (gr. 3-6). 1997. pap. text 3.50 (*0-590-94480-0*) Scholastic Inc.

Berenstain, Stan & Berenstain, Jan. Los Osos Scouts Berenstain y el Monstruo De Hielo. (Berenstain Bear Scouts Ser.).Tr. of Berenstain Bear Scouts & the Ice Monster. (SPA.). (J). (gr. 3-6). 1997. 8.60 (*0-606-12760-7*, Pub. by Turtleback) Demco.

Berenstain, Stan & Berenstain, Jan. Los Osos Scouts Berenstain y la Bola de Cristal Magica. (Berenstain Bear Scouts Ser.).Tr. of Berenstain Bear Scouts & the Magic Crystal Ball. (SPA.). (J). (gr. 3-6). 1997. pap. text 3.50 (*0-590-94476-2*) Scholastic Inc.

— Los Osos Scouts Berenstain y la Bola de Cristal Magica. (Berenstain Bear Scouts Ser.).Tr. of Berenstain Bear Scouts & the Magic Crystal Ball. (SPA.). (J). (gr. 3-6). 1997. 8.60 (*0-606-11577-3*, Pub. by Turtleback) Demco.

— Los Osos Scouts Berenstain y la Guerra de los Fantasmas. (Berenstain Bear Scouts Ser.).Tr. of Berenstain Bear Scouts & the War of the Ghosts. (SPA.). (J). (gr. 3-6). 1996. pap. text 2.99 (*0-590-93381-7*) Scholastic Inc.

— Los Osos Scouts Berenstain y la Guerra de los Fantasmas. (Berenstain Bear Scouts Ser.).Tr. of Berenstain Bear Scouts & the War of the Ghosts. (SPA.). (J). (gr. 3-6). 1996. 8.09 (*0-606-10480-1*, Pub. by Turtleback) Demco.

— Los Osos Scouts Berenstain y la Pizza Voladora. (Berenstain Bear Scouts Ser.).Tr. of Berenstain Bear Scouts & the Sci-Fi Pizza. (SPA.). (J). (gr. 3-6). 1996. 8.09 (*0-606-10481-X*, Pub. by Turtleback) Demco.

— Los Osos Scouts Berenstain y la Terrible Termita Habladora. (Berenstain Bear Scouts Ser.).Tr. of Berenstain Bear Scouts & the Terrible Talking Termite. (SPA.). (J). (gr. 3-6). 1996. mass mkt. 2.99 (*0-590-73850-X*) Scholastic Inc.

Berenstain, Stan & Berenstain, Jan. Los Osos Scouts Berenstain y la Terrible Termita Habladora. (Berenstain Bear Scouts Ser.).Tr. of Berenstain Bear Scouts & the Terrible Talking Termite. (SPA.). (J). (gr. 3-6). 1996. 8.09 (*0-606-09576-4*, Pub. by Turtleback) Demco.

Berenstain, Stan & Berenstain, Jan. Los Osos Scouts Berenstain y los Siniestros Anillos de Humo. (Berenstain Bear Scouts Ser.).Tr. of Berenstain Bear Scouts & the Sinister Smoke Rings. (SPA.). (J). (gr. 3-6). 1997. pap. 3.50 (*0-590-94474-6*) Scholastic Inc.

— Los Osos Scouts Berenstain y los Siniestros Anillos de Humo. (Berenstain Bear Scouts Ser.).Tr. of Berenstain Bear Scouts & the Sinister Smoke Rings. (SPA., Illus.). (J). (gr. 3-6). 1997. pap. 3.50 (*0-614-29041-4*) Scholastic Inc.

— Los Osos Scouts Berenstain y los Siniestros Anillos de Humo. (Berenstain Bear Scouts Ser.).Tr. of Berenstain Bear Scouts & the Sinister Smoke Rings. (J). (gr. 3-6). 1997. 8.70 (*0-606-11578-1*, Pub. by Turtleback) Demco.

— Pacifier Days: A Fond Farewell, Vol. 5. LC 98-73132. (Berenstain Bears Baby Board Books Ser.). (Illus.). 14p. (J). (ps). 1999. pap. 4.99 (*0-679-89336-9*) Random.

***Berenstain, Stan & Berenstain, Jan.** Say Night Night. (Berenstain Bears Big Chapter Bks.). (Illus.). 5p. (J). 2000. 4.99 (*0-375-80521-4*) Random House.

Berenstain, Stan & Berenstain, Jan. That Stump Must Go! LC 97-40641. (Beginner Bks.). (Illus.). 48p. (J). (gr. k-3). 2000. 7.99 (*0-679-88963-9*, Pub. by Random Bks Yng Read) Random.

— Y Los Castores Trabajadores: The Berenstain Bears. DigiPro Staff, tr. from ENG. (Comes to Life Bks.).Tr. of Eager Beavers. (SPA.). 16p. (J). (ps-2). 1994. write for info. (*1-57234-007-X*) YES Ent.

***Berenstain, Stan & Jan.** Berenstain Bears & No Guns Allowed. LC 99-47879. (Illus.). 112p. (J). (gr. 3-5). 2000. pap. 3.99 (*0-679-88953-1*, Pub. by Random Bks Yng Read) Random.

— Berenstain Bears & No Guns Allowed. LC 99-47879. (Illus.). 112p. (J). (gr. 3-5). 2001. lib. bdg. 11.99 (*0-679-98953-6*, Pub. by Random Bks Yng Read) Random.

Berenstain, Stan & Koontz, Dean. The Berenstain Bears & the Spooky Old Tree. (Bright & Early Bks.). (J). (ps-3). 1978. 18.66 incl. audio (*0-394-00940-1*) Random.

An Asterisk (*) at the beginning of an entry indicates that the title is appearing for the first time.

Berenstain, Stan, et al. Comes to Life StoryPlayer & the Berenstain Bears & les Nombres Mysterieux. DigiPro Staff, tr. from ENG. (Comes to Life Bks.). (FRE.). 16p. (J). (ps-2). 1994. write for info. (*1-57234-002-9*) YES Ent.

Berenstain, Stan, jt. auth. see Berenstain, Jan.

Berenstain, Stan, jt. auth. see Cole, Joanna.

Berenstain, Stan, jt. auth. see McMillan, Bruce.

Berenstein, A. & Lasjaunias, P. Surgical Neuroangiography, Vol. 3. (Illus.). 420p. 1997. 225.00 (*0-387-17501-6*) Spr-Verlag.

— Surgical Neuroangiography Vol. 4: Endocascular Treatment of Cerebral Problems, Vol. 4. (Illus.). 425p. 1993. 215.00 (*0-387-17500-8*) Spr-Verlag.

— Surgical Neuroangiography Vol. 5: Endocascular Treatment of Spine & Spinal Cord. (Illus.). 320p. 1994. 215.00 (*0-387-55043-7*) Spr-Verlag.

Berenstein, A., jt. auth. see Kupersmith, M. J.

Berenstein, A., jt. auth. see Lasjaunias, P.

Berenstein, Alejandro, jt. auth. see Lasjaunias, Pierre.

Berenstein, C. A., et al. Integral Geometry, Radon Transforms & Complex Analysis: Lectures Given at the First Session of the Centro Internazionale Matematico Estivo (C. I. M. E.) Held in Venezia, Italy, June 3-12, 1996, Vol. 168. Tarabusi, E. Casadio et al, eds. LC 98-13003. (Lecture Notes in Mathematics: Vol. 1684). vii, 145p. 1998. 33.00 (*3-540-64207-2*) Spr-Verlag.

Berenstein, Carl & Woodward, Bob. The Final Days. 480p. 1994. pap. 14.00 (*0-671-89440-4*) S&S Trade.

Berenstein, Carlos A., ed. Complex Analysis I. (Lecture Notes in Mathematics Ser.: Vol. 1275). xv, 331p. 1987. 47.95 (*0-387-18356-6*) Spr-Verlag.

— Complex Analysis II. (Lecture Notes in Mathematics Ser.: Vol. 1276). ix, 320p. 1987. 47.95 (*0-387-18357-4*) Spr-Verlag.

— Complex Analysis III. (Lecture Notes in Mathematics Ser.: Vol. 1277). x, 350p. 1987. pap. 47.90 (*0-387-18355-8*) Spr-Verlag.

Berenstein, Carlos A. & Gay, R. Complex Variables: An Introduction. Ewing, J. H. et al, eds. LC 97-209660. (Graduate Texts in Mathematics Ser.: Vol. 125). (Illus.). 664p. 1997. 64.95 (*0-387-97349-4*) Spr-Verlag.

Berenstein, Carlos A. & Gay, Roger. Complex Analysis & Special Topics in Harmonic Analysis. LC 94-41894. (Illus.). 528p. 1995. 86.95 (*0-387-94411-7*) Spr-Verlag.

Berenstein, Carlos A., et al. Residue Currents & Bezout Identities. LC 93-30493. 172p. 1993. 49.50 (*0-8176-2945-9*) Birkhauser.

Berenstein, Frederick. Lost Boys: Reflections on Psychoanalysis & Countertransference. 120p. (C). 1995. 20.00 (*0-393-70188-3*) Norton.

Berenstein, Rhona J. Attack of the Leading Ladies: Gender, Sexuality & Spectatorship in Classic Horror Cinema. (Film & Culture Ser.). (Illus.). 274p. 1996. 47.50 (*0-231-08462-5*); pap. 18.50 (*0-231-08463-3*) Col U Pr.

Berent, Irwin, jt. auth. see Evans, Rod L.

Berent, Irwin M. & Evans, Rod. The Dictionary of Highly Unusual Words. LC 97-114965. 144p. (Orig.). 1997. mass mkt. 5.50 (*0-425-15606-0*) Berkley Pub.

Berent, Irwin M. & Evans, Rod L. The Right Words: The Three Hundred-Fifty Best Things to Say to Get Along with People. 112p. (Orig.). 1992. mass mkt. 4.99 (*0-446-36358-8*, Pub. by Warner Bks) Little.

— Weird Words. 256p. (Orig.). 1995. mass mkt. 5.99 (*0-425-14404-6*) Berkley Pub.

Berent, Irwin M., jt. auth. see Evans, Rod L.

Berent, Irwin M., jt. auth. see Zubatsky, David S.

Berent, Irwin M., jt. ed. see Evans, Rod L.

Berent, Jonathan & Lemley, Amy. Beyond Shyness: How to Conquer Social Anxieties. 288p. 1994. per. 12.00 (*0-671-88525-1*) S&S Trade Pap.

Berent, Mark. Eagle Station. 1993. mass mkt. 5.99 (*0-515-11208-9*, Jove) Berkley Pub.

— Phantom Leader. 448p. 1992. mass mkt. 5.99 (*0-515-10785-9*, Jove) Berkley Pub.

— Rolling Thunder. 1989. mass mkt. 6.50 (*0-515-10190-7*, Jove) Berkley Pub.

— Steel Tiger. 1990. pap. 5.99 (*0-515-10467-1*, Jove) Berkley Pub.

— Storm Flight. 512p. 1994. reprint ed. pap. text 5.99 (*0-515-11432-4*, Jove) Berkley Pub.

Berent, Stanley, jt. ed. see Sackellares, J. Chris.

Berentes, Drew. Apple LOGO: A Complete, Illustrated Handbook. (Illus.). 406p. (Orig.). 1984. 18.95 (*0-8306-0751-X*) McGraw-Hill Prof.

Berentsen, William H., ed. Contemporary Europe: A Geographical Analysis. 7th ed. LC 96-37342. 688p. 1997. text 87.95 (*0-471-58336-7*) Wiley.

Berentzen, Sigurd. Children Constructing Their Social World. (Bergen Studies in Social Anthropology: No. 36). 170p. 1986. pap. text 13.95 (*0-936508-67-1*, Pub. by Bergen Univ Dept Social Anthro) MBIPubg.

Bereny, Justin A. Electric Transportation: Survey & Directory of Emerging Technologies (2000) (Illus.). 425p. 2000. pap. 195.00 (*0-89934-315-5*, BT-64); lib. bdg. 255.00 (*0-89934-316-3*, BT-964) Bus Tech Bks.

— Survey of the Emerging Solar Energy Industry: 1977 Edition. De Winter, Francis, ed. (Illus.). 405p. 1977. reprint ed. lib. bdg. 155.00 (*0-89934-212-4*, BT920) Bus Tech Bks.

Bereny, Justin A., ed. Battery Performance, Research & Development. (Electric Vehicle Information Ser.: Vol. 1, Pts. A-C). (Illus.). 206p. 1996. lib. bdg. 155.00 (*0-89934-240-X*, BT927) Bus Tech Bks.

— Battery Performance, Research & Development: Part A: NAVSEA Battery Document; Part B: Advanced Battery Systems: R & D Program Plan; Part C: Performance & Availability of Batteries for EV's: a Report of the Battery Technical Advisory Panel. (Electric Vehicle Information Ser.: Vol 1, Pts. A-C). (Illus.). 206p. 1996. pap. 105.00 (*0-89934-239-6*, BT027) Bus Tech Bks.

Bereny, Justin A., jt. auth. see Howell, Yvonne.

Berenyi, D., et al, eds. High-Energy Ion-Atom Collisions: Proceedings of the 4th Workshop on High-Energy Ion-Atom Collision Processes, Held at Debrecen, Hungary, 17-19 September 1990. (Lecture Notes in Physics Ser.: Vol. 376). ix, 364p. 1991. 56.95 (*0-387-53738-4*) Spr-Verlag.

Berenyi, D. & Hock, G. High-Energy Ion-Atom Collisions. 308p. 1985. 350.00 (*0-569-08859-3*, Pub. by Collets) St Mut.

— High Energy Ion-Atom Collisions, No. 2. 306p. (C). 1985. 350.00 (*0-685-46639-6*, Pub. by Collets) St Mut.

— High Energy Ion-Atom Collisions, Vol. 2. 308p. (C). 1985. 108.00 (*963-05-4091-6*, Pub. by Akade Kiado) St Mut.

Berenyi, D. & Hock, G., eds. High-Energy Ion-Atom Collisions. (Lecture Notes in Physics Ser.: Vol. 294). 540p. 1988. 70.95 (*0-387-18732-4*) Spr-Verlag.

Berenyi, Gabor, jt. auth. see Nemes, Livia.

Berenzy. What's the Matter Sammy? (J). 1999. text 15.95 (*0-8050-4024-2*) St Martin.

Berenzy, Alix. The Frog Prince. (J). 1991. 11.15 (*0-606-00449-1*, Pub. by Turtleback) Demco.

— Puss in Boots. (J). 1995. 14.95 (*0-8050-1284-2*) H Holt & Co.

— Rapunzel. 32p. 1998. pap. 6.95 (*0-8050-5793-5*) H Holt & Co.

Berenzy, Alix. A Frog Prince. LC 88-29628. 32p. (J). (ps up). 1995. pap. 5.95 (*0-8050-1848-4*, Owlet BYR) H Holt & Co.

Berenzy, Alix. Rapunzel. 32p. (J). (ps-2). 1995. 15.95 (*0-8050-1283-4*) H Holt & Co.

***Beres, Cynthia Breslin.** Longhouse. LC 00-27815. (Native American Homes Ser.). (Illus.). 2000. write for info. (*1-55916-247-3*) Rourke Bk Co.

Beres, Louis R. Apocalypse: Nuclear Catastrophe in World Politics. LC 80-13541. (Illus.). (C). 1980. lib. bdg. 24.00 (*0-226-04360-6*) U Ch Pr.

— Apocalypse: Nuclear Catastrophe in World Politics. LC 80-13541. (Illus.). (C). 1982. pap. text 9.95 (*0-226-04361-4*) U Ch Pr.

— Apocalypse: Nuclear Catastrophe in World Politics. LC 80-13541. 331p. reprint ed. pap. 102.70 (*0-608-08827-7*, 206946600004); reprint ed. pap. 102.70 (*0-608-20664-4*, 207210100003) Bks Demand.

— Nuclear Strategy & World Order: The U. S. Imperative. 52p. 1982. pap. 14.95 (*0-911646-12-4*) Transaction Pubs.

Beres, Louis R. & Targ, Harry R. Constructing Alternative World Futures: Reordering the Planet. LC 76-54678. 264p. 1977. 22.95 (*0-87073-566-7*); pap. 13.95 (*0-87073-567-5*) Schenkman Bks Inc.

Beres, Nancy, et al, eds. Island of Rivers: An Anthology Celebrating Fifty Years of Olympic National Park. (Illus.). 178p. (Orig.). 1988. pap. text 8.95 (*0-914019-18-X*) NW Interpretive.

***Beres, Samantha.** Grade Boosters Bk. 2: Questions & Answers. (Grade Boosters Ser.). (Illus.). 64p. (J). (gr. 1). 1999. pap. 5.95 (*0-7373-0200-3*, 02003w) NTC Contemp Pub Co.

Beres, Samantha. 101 Things Every Kid Should Know About Science. LC 97-49847. (Illus.). 96p. (J). (gr. 2-5). 1998. 14.95 (*1-56565-956-2*) Lowell Hse Juvenile.

— 101 Things Every Kid Should Know About Science. LC 97-49847. (Illus.). 96p. (J). (gr. 3-7). 1998. pap. 9.95 (*1-56565-916-3*, 09163W, Pub. by Lowell Hse Juvenile) NTC Contemp Pub Co.

— 101 Things Every Kid Should Know about the Human Body. LC 99-30621. (Illus.). 112p. (J). (gr. 3-6). 2000. 14.95 (*0-7373-0329-8*, 03298W, Pub. by Lowell Hse) NTC Contemp Pub Co.

— 101 Things Every Kid Should Know about the Human Body. LC 99-30621. (Illus.). 112p. (J). (gr. 3-7). 2000. pap. 9.95 (*0-7373-0222-4*, 02224W) NTC Contemp Pub Co.

Berescik, Susan, ed. see Barth, Shannon.

Beresford. Shiatsu Theory & Practice. 1996. text 67.00 (*0-443-04941-6*, W B Saunders Co) Harcrt Hlth Sci Grp.

Beresford, Brian, tr. see Rabten, Geshe & Dhargyey, Geshe.

Beresford, D. R., et al. Accounting for Income Taxes: A Review of Alternatives. LC 83-81594. (Financial Accounting Standards Board Research Report Ser.). (Illus.). 156p. (Orig.). 1983. pap. 6.00 (*0-910065-18-7*) Finan Acct Found.

Beresford, David. Ten Men Dead: The Story of the 1981 Irish Hunger Strike. 352p. 1997. pap. text 12.00 (*0-87113-702-X*, Atlntc Mnthly) Grove-Atltic.

Beresford, H. Richard. Neurology & the Law: Private Litigation & the Public Policy. LC 97-34794. (Contemporary Neurology Ser.: No. 51). (Illus.). 208p. (C). 1998. text 89.00 (*0-8036-0168-9*) OUP.

Beresford Hartwell, Geoffrey M., ed. see Chartered Institute of Arbitrators (Great Britain).

Beresford, J. D. H. G. Wells. LC 72-2072. (English Literature Ser.: No. 33). 1972. reprint ed. lib. bdg. 59.00 (*0-8383-1467-8*) M S G Haskell Hse.

— The Wonder. LC 99-35542. (Bison Frontiers of Imagination Ser.). 303p. 1999. pap. 13.00 (*0-8032-6162-4*) U of Nebr Pr.

Beresford, John. Collecting Information for School Improvement: Model Questionnaires & Research Instruments. 1998. pap. 39.95 (*1-85346-556-9*, Pub. by David Fulton) Taylor & Francis.

Beresford, John, ed. James Woodforde: The Diary of a Country Parson, 1758-1802. 622p. (Orig.). 1996. pap. 16.95 (*1-85311-138-4*, Pub. by Canterbury Press Norwich) Morehouse Pub.

Beresford, John C., jt. ed. see Ellis, Diane C.

Beresford, John D. Gossip of the Seventeenth & Eighteenth Centuries. LC 68-29191. (Essay Index Reprint Ser.). 1977. reprint ed. 19.95 (*0-8369-0199-1*) Ayer.

— The Hampdenshire Wonder. LC 74-15952. (Science Fiction Ser.). 304p. 1975. reprint ed. 25.95 (*0-405-06278-8*) Ayer.

— Mister Du Quesne, & Other Essays. LC 68-24845. (Essay Index Reprint Ser.). 1977. 19.95 (*0-8369-0200-9*) Ayer.

— Nineteen Impressions. LC 71-103492. (Short Story Index Reprint Ser.). 1977. 19.95 (*0-8369-3234-X*) Ayer.

— Storm & Peace. LC 67-28744. (Essay Index Reprint Ser.). 1977. 19.95 (*0-8369-0201-7*) Ayer.

Beresford, Jon & Owen, Maureen, eds. Marrow Stromal Cell Culture. LC 97-30196. (Handbooks in Practical Animal Cell Biology). (Illus.). 166p. (C). 1998. text 64.95 (*0-521-58021-8*); pap. text 24.95 (*0-521-58978-9*) Cambridge U Pr.

Beresford-Kroeger, Diana. Bioplanning a North Temperate Garden. 256p. 1996. pap. 34.95 (*1-55082-152-0*, Pub. by Quarry Pr) LPC InBook.

Beresford, Larry. The Hospice Handbook: A Complete Guide. LC 92-32814. 165p. 1993. pap. 14.95 (*0-316-09138-3*, Back Bay) Little.

— Under a Gibbous Moon: The Adventures of Mr. Funky. LC 96-78883. 82p. 1996. per. 10.00 (*0-9636156-1-0*) Broken Shadow.

Beresford, M. Gogol's Government Inspector: Critical Study. (Critical Studies in Russian Literature Ser.). 1997. pap. 16.95 (*1-85399-439-1*, Pub. by Brist Class Pr) Focus Pub-R Pullins.

Beresford, M., ed. Tolstoy: The Death of Ivan Ilyich (Smert' Ivana Il'icha) (Bristol Russian Texts Ser.). (RUS.). 1992. pap. 18.95 (*1-85399-359-X*, Pub. by Brist Class Pr) Focus Pub-R Pullins.

Beresford, M., ed. see Gogol, Nikolai Vasilevich.

Beresford, M. W. History on the Ground: Six Studies in Maps & Landscapes. LC 79-27733. 256p. 1971. write for info. (*0-416-15130-2*) Routledge.

— Time & Place. 420p. (C). 1985. 60.00 (*0-907628-39-7*) Hambledon Press.

Beresford, M. W. & Hurst, John G. Deserted Medieval Villages: Studies. LC 72-879113. xviii, 340 p. 1971. write for info. (*0-7188-1373-1*) Lutterwrth.

Beresford, Maurice. History on the Ground. LC 99-161738. (Illus.). 256p. 1998. pap. 29.95 (*0-7509-1884-5*, Pub. by Sutton Pub Ltd) Intl Pubs Mktg.

— The Lost Villages of England. LC 99-202683. (History Handbooks Ser.). (Illus.). 448p. 1998. pap. 29.95 (*0-7509-1848-9*, Pub. by Sutton Pub Ltd) Intl Pubs Mktg.

Beresford, Melanie. Vietnam. (Marxist Regimes Ser.). 262p. 1988. text 49.00 (*0-685-61126-4*) St Martin.

— Vietnam. (Marxist Regimes Ser.). 220p. 1988. 47.50 (*0-86187-448-X*); text 17.50 (*0-86187-449-8*) St Martin.

Beresford, Melanie, jt. auth. see Phong, Dang.

Beresford, Peter & Harding, Tessa, eds. A Challenge to Change: Practical Experiences of Building User-Led Service. 211p. 1993. pap. 17.95 (*0-902789-85-6*, Pub. by Natl Inst Soc Work) St Mut.

Beresford, Peter & Trevillion, Steven. Developing Skills for Community Care. 176p. 1995. pap. 28.95 (*1-85742-237-6*) Ashgate Pub Co.

Beresford, Peter & Turner, Michael. It's Our Welfare: Report of the Citizens Commission on the Future of the Welfare State. 190p. 1996. pap. 48.00 (*1-899942-17-3*, Pub. by Natl Inst Soc Work) St Mut.

Beresford, Peter, jt. auth. see Harding, Tessa.

Beresford, Peter, jt. ed. see Trevillion, Steven.

***Beresford, Quentin.** Governments, Markets & Globalisation: Australian Public Policy in Context. 272p. 2000. pap. 29.95 (*1-86508-169-8*, Pub. by Allen & Unwin Pty) Paul & Co Pubs.

Beresford, Quentin & Omaji, Paul. Our State of Mind: Racial Planning & the Stolen Generations. 296p. 1998. pap. 19.95 (*1-86368-235-X*, Pub. by Fremantle Arts) Intl Spec Bk.

Beresford, Richard. A Dance to the Music of Time by Nicolas Poussin. LC 95-212358. (Illus.). 80p. 1995. pap. 21.95 (*0-900785-46-2*, Pub. by Wallace Collect) Antique Collect.

Beresford, S. Motor Neurone Disease (Amyotrophic Lateral Sclerosis) 196p. 1995. pap. 41.50 (*1-56593-318-4*, 0648) Singular Publishing.

Beresford, Steven M. Improve Your Vision Without Glasses or Contact Lenses. LC 96-22038. 128p. 1996. per. 10.00 (*0-684-81438-2*) S&S Trade.

Beresford, Thomas P. & Gomberg, Edith S., eds. Alcohol & Aging. (Illus.). 360p. 1995. text 65.00 (*0-19-508090-4*) OUP.

Beresford, Thomas P., jt. ed. see Hall, R. C.

Beresford, Titan. Cinderella. 4th ed. (Illus.). 1998. reprint ed. mass mkt. 6.95 (*1-56333-606-5*) Masquerade.

Beresford, Titian. Chidewell House & Other Stories. 1997. mass mkt. 6.95 (*1-56333-554-9*) Masquerade.

— Judith Boston. 3rd ed. 1997. reprint ed. mass mkt. 6.50 (*1-56333-525-5*) Masquerade.

Beresin, V., ed. see Markov, M. A.

Beresnev, L. A., et al. Ferroelectric Liquid Crystals. 152p. 1988. pap. text 128.00 (*2-88124-245-6*) Gordon & Breach.

Beresniak, A. Dictionnaire Raisonne des Termes d'Entreprises du Medicaments. (FRE.). 1998. 95.00 (*0-320-00267-5*) Fr & Eur.

Beresniak, Daniel. Symbols of Freemasonry. (Illus.). 123p. 1998. 45.00 (*2-84323-033-0*, Pub. by Rizzoli Intl) St Martin.

Beressem, Hanjo, jt. auth. see Lang, Susan.

Berest, Boris P., ed. see Strogat, Lew, pseud.

Berest, P., jt. ed. see Vouille, G.

Berestetskii, V. B. & Landau, L. D. Quantum Electrodynamics, Vol. 4. 2nd ed. 667p. 1982. pap. text 66.95 (*0-7506-3371-9*) Buttrwrth-Heinemann.

Berestizhevsky, Samuel, jt. auth. see Kolosova, Tanya.

Berestycki, Henri. Variational Methods. (Progress in Nonlinear Differential Equations & Their Applications Ser.). 1990. 96.50 (*0-8176-3452-5*) Birkhauser.

Berestycki, Henri & Larrouturou, Bernard. Mathematical Modelling of Planar Flame Propagation. LC 93-4716. (Pitman Monographs & Surveys in Pure & Applied Mathematics). 1996. pap. write for info. (*0-582-03332-2*) Longman.

Berets, Chuck, jt. auth. see Kyle, Carolyn.

Beretta, Alan, jt. ed. see Alderson, J. Charles.

Beretta, Giordano B., ed. Color Imaging Vol. 3018: Device-Independent Color, Color Hard Copy, & Graphic Arts II. LC 97-175340. 432p. 1997. 89.00 (*0-8194-2429-3*) SPIE.

Beretta, Giordano B. & Eschbach, Reiner, eds. Color Imaging. 568p. pap. text 111.00 (*0-8194-3119-2*) SPIE.

Beretta, Giordano B. & Eschbach, Reiner, eds. Color Imaging Vol. 3300: Device-Independent Color, Color Hardcopy & Graphic Arts III. LC 98-175580. 428p. 1998. 89.00 (*0-8194-2740-3*) SPIE.

Beretta, Ilva. The World's a Garden: Garden Poetry of the English Renaissance. (Studia Anglistica Upsaliensia Ser.: No. 84). 208p. (Orig.). 1993. pap. 42.50 (*91-554-3155-0*) Coronet Bks.

Beretta, Marco. The Enlightenment of Matter: The Definition of Chemistry from Agricola to Lavoisier. LC 93-8797. (Uppsala Studies in Ancient Mediterranean & Near Eastern Civilizations: No. 15). (Illus.). xvi, 396p. (C). 1993. 49.95 (*0-88135-152-0*, Sci Hist) Watson Pub Intl.

— A History of Non-Printed Science: A Select Catalogue of the Waller Collection. (Acta Bibliothecae R. Universitatis Upsaliensis Ser.: No. 31). (Illus.). 199p. (Orig.). 1993. pap. 47.50 (*91-554-3070-8*, Pub. by Uppsala Universitet) Coronet Bks.

Beretta, Marco & Angsmyr, Tore. Sidereus Nuncius & Stella Polaris: The Scientific Relations Between Italy & Sweden in Early Modern History. LC 96-38088. (Uppsala Studies in the History of Science). 168p. 1997. 39.95 (*0-88135-188-1*) Watson Pub Intl.

***Bereuter, Doug, ed.** Aid Activities in Asia & the Central Asian Republics: Congressional Hearing. 91p. (C). 1999. reprint ed. pap. text 20.00 (*0-7881-8440-7*) DIANE Pub.

— Challenges in U. S.-Asian Policy: Congressional Hearing. 251p. 2000. pap. text 40.00 (*0-7881-8641-8*) DIANE Pub.

Bereuter, Doug, ed. Crisis in the Taiwan Strait: Implications for U. S. Foreign Policy. 104p. (C). 1998. pap. text 25.00 (*0-7881-7085-6*) DIANE Pub.

***Bereuter, Doug, ed.** Democratic Continuity & Change in South Asia: Congressional Hearing. 75p. (C). 1999. reprint ed. pap. text 20.00 (*0-7881-8439-3*) DIANE Pub.

— Hong Kong's Reversion to the People's Republic of China: Congressional Hearing. 124p. (C). 1999. reprint ed. pap. text 25.00 (*0-7881-8438-5*) DIANE Pub.

— India - Pakistan Nuclear Proliferation: Congressional Hearing. 78p. (C). 1999. reprint ed. pap. text 20.00 (*0-7881-8436-9*) DIANE Pub.

Bereuter, Doug, ed. Nuclear Issues in the South Pacific: Hearing Before the Committee on International Relations, U. S. House of Representatives. (Illus.). 152p. 1998. reprint ed. pap. text 30.00 (*0-7881-4227-5*) DIANE Pub.

Berey, David, ed. Barron's Regents Exams & Answers: Earth Science. rev. ed. LC 57-58736. 300p. (YA). (gr. 10-12). 1996. pap. text 5.95 (*0-8120-3165-2*) Barron.

Berezanski, I. & Kaliuzhny, I. Harmonic Analysis in Hypercomplex Systems. LC 98-14437. (Mathematics & Its Applications Ser.). 483p. 1998. write for info. (*0-7923-5029-4*) Kluwer Academic.

Berezanskii, I. Makarovich, et al. Functional Analysis, Vol. 1. Malyshev, Peter V., tr. from RUS. LC 96-6354. (Operator Theory, Advances & Applications Ser.: Vols. 85 & 86). 1996. write for info. (*0-8176-5344-9*) Birkhauser.

— Functional Analysis, Vol. 2. Malyshev, Peter V., tr. from RUS. LC 96-6354. (Operator Theory, Advances & Applications Ser.: Vols. 85 & 86). 1996. write for info. (*0-8176-5345-7*) Birkhauser.

Berezanskii, Ju. M., et al. Expansions in Eigenfunctions of Selfadjoint Operators. LC 67-22347. (Translations of Mathematical Monographs: Vol. 17). 809p. 1968. text 92.00 (*0-8218-1567-9*, MMONO/17) Am Math.

— Nine Papers on Functional Analysis. (Translations Ser.: Series 2, Vol. 93). 253p. 1970. 44.00 (*0-8218-1793-0*, TRANS2/93) Am Math.

— Twelve Papers on Analysis & Applied Mathematics. (Translations Ser.: Series 2, Vol. 35). 363p. 1964. 42.00 (*0-8218-1735-3*, TRANS2/35) Am Math.

Berezanskii, Yu. Selfadjoint Operators in Spaces of Functions of Infinitely Many Variables. McFaden, H. H., tr. LC 85-30841. (Translations of Mathematical Monographs: Vol. 63). 438p. 1986. text 136.00 (*0-8218-4515-2*, MMONO/63) Am Math.

Berezansky, Y. M. & Kondratiev, Y. G. Spectral Methods in Infinite-Dimensional Analysis, 2 vols. (Mathematical Physics & Applied Mathematics Ser.: Vol. 12). 572p. 1995. lib. bdg. 495.00 (*0-7923-2849-3*) Kluwer Academic.

Berezansky, Y. M., et al. Functional Analysis, Vol. I. (Operator Theory, Advances & Applications Ser.: Vol. 85). 448p. 1996. 170.50 (*3-7643-5344-9*) Birkhauser.

— Functional Analysis, Vol. II. (Operator Theory, Advances & Applications Ser.: Vol. 86). 312p. 1996. 142.00 (*3-7643-5345-7*) Birkhauser.

Berezhkov, Valentin M. At Stalin's Side: His Interpreter's Memoirs from the October Revolution to the Fall of the Dictator's Empire. Mikheyev, Sergei M., tr. from RUS. LC 94-19044. (Illus.). 320p. 1994. 22.50 (*1-55972-212-6*, Birch Ln Pr) Carol Pub Group.

B

An Asterisk (*) at the beginning of an entry indicates that the title is appearing for the first time.

Berezhnoi, A. N. & Semenov, A. V. Binary Diffusion Coefficients of Liquid Vapors in Gases. Shakhlevich, Kirill, tr. from RUS. LC 96-45117. 200p. 1997. 88.50 (*1-56700-078-9*) Begell Hse.

Berezhnoi, Anatolii I. Glass-Ceramics & Photo-Sitalls. LC 69-12509. 464p. reprint ed. pap. 143.90 (*0-608-16592-1*, 202629700049) Bks Demand.

Berezin, Boris D. Coordination Compounds of Porphyrins & Phthalocyanines. Vopian, V. G., tr. LC 80-40958. (Illus.). 300p. reprint ed. pap. 93.00 (*0-608-17658-3*, 203037100069) Bks Demand.

Berezin, F. A. & Kirillov, A. A. Introduction to Superanalysis. 1987. text 294.00 (*90-277-1668-4*) Kluwer Academic.

Berezin, F. A. & Shubin, M. A. The Schrodinger Equation. (C). 1991. text 385.50 (*0-7923-1218-X*) Kluwer Academic.

Berezin, F. A., et al. Eight Papers on Differential Equations & Functional Analysis. (Translations Ser.: Series 2, Vol. 56). 295p. 1966. 51.00 (*0-8218-1756-6*, TRANS2/56) Am Math.

Berezin, I. & Denisiv, E. Oxidation of Cyclohexane. LC 66-12651. 1966. 140.00 (*0-08-011378-8*, Pub. by Pergamon Repr) Franklin.

Berezin, I. & Zhidkov, N. Computing Methods, Vol. 2. LC 61-11157. 1965. 300.00 (*0-08-010011-2*, Pub. by Pergamon Repr) Franklin.

Berezin, Josh. Getting into Yale: How One Student Wrote This Book & Got into the School of His Dreams. LC 97-39252. 224p. (J). 1998. pap. 13.45 (*0-7868-8302-2*, Pub. by Hyperion) Time Warner.

Berezin, Mabel. Making the Fascist Self: The Political Culture of Interwar Italy. LC 96-53410. (Wilder House Series in Politics, History, & Culture). (Illus.). 296p. 1996. pap. text 18.95 (*0-8014-8420-0*) Cornell U Pr.

— Making the Fascist Self: The Political Culture of Interwar Italy. LC 96-53410. (Wilder House Series in Politics, History, & Culture). (Illus.). 296p. 1997. text 45.00 (*0-8014-3202-2*) Cornell U Pr.

Berezin, Martin A. & Cath, Stanley H., eds. Geriatric Psychiatry: Grief, Loss & Emotional Disorders in the Aging Process. 380p. 1965. 55.00 (*0-8236-2120-0*) Intl Univs Pr.

Berezin, V. Moscow Metro: Photoguide. (Illus.). 234p. (C). 1989. 100.00 (*0-569-08961-1*, Pub. by Collets) St Mut.

Berezin, Yu A. Modelling Non-Linear Wave Processes. Yuzina, L. Ya, tr. from RUS. 189p. 1987. lib. bdg. 155.00 (*90-6764-075-1*, Pub. by VSP) Coronet Bks.

Berezina, N. M. & Kaushanskii, D. A. Presowing Irradiation of Plant Seeds. 2nd enl. rev. ed. Dhote, A. K., tr. (Russian Translation Ser.: No. 70). (Illus.). 294p. (C). 1989. text 110.00 (*90-6191-946-0*, Pub. by A A Balkema) Ashgate Pub Co.

Berezina, N. M. & Kaushanski, D. A. Presowing Irradiation of Plant Seeds. (C). 1989. 37.50 (*81-7087-041-0*, Pub. by Oxford IBH) S Asia.

Berezinskii, V. S., et al. Astrophysics of Cosmic Rays. Reinders, L. J., tr. from RUS. xii, 534p. 1990. 213.00 (*0-444-88641-9*, North Holland) Elsevier.

Berezkin, V. G. Gas-Liquid Solid Chromatography. (Chromatographic Science Ser.: Vol. 56). (Illus.). 256p. 1991. text 155.00 (*0-8247-8425-1*) Dekker.

Berezkin, V. G. & de Zeeuw, J. Capillary Gas Adsorption Chromatography. 1998. 105.00 (*3-527-29675-1*) Wiley.

Berezkin, V. G. & Drugov, Yu S. Gas Chromatography in Air Pollution Analysis. (Journal of Chromatography Library: No. 49). 212p. 1991. 184.00 (*0-444-98732-0*) Elsevier.

Berezney, Ronald & Jeon, Kwang W., eds. Nuclear Matrix: Structural & Functional Organization, Vols. 162A & 162B. LC 97-135683. (Illus.). 1047p. 1997. pap. text 69.00 (*0-12-384620-X*) Morgan Kaufmann.

Berezovenko, Yu F. New English-Russian Dictionary of Legal Terms. (ENG & RUS.). 308p. 1993. 95.00 (*0-7859-9083-6*) Fr & Eur.

Berfenstam, Ragnar & William-Olsson, Inger. Early Child Care in Sweden, Vol. 2. (International Monographs on Early Child Care). xii, 156p. 1973. text 117.00 (*0-677-04890-4*) Gordon & Breach.

Berg. Advanced Java Development for the Enterprise. LC 98-18367. 608p. (C). 1998. 49.95 incl. cd-rom (*0-13-080461-4*, Prentice Hall) P-H.

— Family Practice Two Thousand. (Illus.). 550p. 2000. text 66.95 (*0-8151-6858-6*, 31731) Mosby Inc.

— Family Practice Two Thousand & One. 2001. 66.95 (*0-8151-2035-4*, 31732) Mosby Inc.

— Family Practice Two Thousand & Two. 2002. 66.95 (*0-8151-2037-0*, 31733) Mosby Inc.

— Gustave Flaubert. LC 96-39866. 1997. 32.00 (*0-8057-8295-8*, Twyne) Mac Lib Ref.

— International Migration, Immobility . . . LC 97-202469. 1997. 55.00 (*1-85973-971-7*, Pub. by Berg Pubs) NYU Pr.

— Introduction to Botany. 1996. text 6.40 (*0-03-020908-0*) Harcourt Coll Pubs.

— Introduction to Botany. LC 96-70013. (C). 1996. text 76.00 (*0-03-075453-4*) Harcourt Coll Pubs.

— Introduction to Criminal Justice. (Criminal Justice Ser.). 2001. pap. 48.00 (*0-534-55611-6*) Wadsworth Pub.

*__Berg.__ Introduction to Criminal Justice. 2001. pap., student ed. 15.00 (*0-534-55613-2*) Wadsworth Pub.

Berg. Literature Francaise, Vol. I. (C). 1996. text 64.50 (*0-03-072392-2*) Harcourt Coll Pubs.

— Litterature Francaise, Vol. 1. (FRE.). (C). 1994. text 64.50 (*0-03-039849-5*) Harcourt Coll Pubs.

— Miracles, Mysteries, & Prayer I: Kabbalah. (RUS.). 224p. 1997. pap. 11.95 (*0-924457-93-7*) Res Ctr Kabbalah.

— Miracles, Mysteries, & Prayer II: Kabbalah. (RUS., Illus.). 224p. 1997. pap. 11.95 (*0-924457-94-5*) Res Ctr Kabbalah.

— 1998 Year Book of Family Practice. (Illus.). 472p. 1998. text 66.95 (*0-8151-9629-6*, 24966) Mosby Inc.

— Parlons Affaires. (C). 1998. text 53.00 (*0-03-022528-0*, Pub. by Harcourt Coll Pubs) Harcourt.

— War & Memory in the 20th Century. LC 98-120916. 1997. 55.00 (*1-85973-194-5*, Pub. by Berg Pubs) NYU Pr.

Berg & Bergveld, P. Sensor Technology in the Netherlands: State of the Art. LC 98-14436. (Mesa Monographs). 325p. 1998. write for info. (*0-7923-5010-3*) Kluwer Academic.

Berg & Clifford. Consumers & Luxury, 1650-1850. 256p. 1999. pap. 29.95 (*0-7190-5274-2*); text 79.95 (*0-7190-5273-4*) Manchester Univ Pr.

Berg & Rice. Ergonomics in Clinical Practice: Prevention & Rehabilitation. LC 97-34808. 369p. 1998. text 47.50 (*0-7506-9714-8*) Buttrwrth-Heinemann.

Berg, Christopher. Mastering Guitar Technique: Process & Essence. 144p. 1997. 19.95 (*0-7866-2373-X*, 96216) Mel Bay.

Berg, A., ed. Application of Remote Sensing to Agricultural Production Forecasting: Proceedings of a Seminar Held at the Joint Research Centre of the Commission of the European Communities, Ispra, Italy. 272p. (C). 1981. 155.00 (*90-6191-089-7*, Pub. by A A Balkema) Ashgate Pub Co.

Berg, A. J. Van Den, see Van Den Berg, A. J.

Berg, A. Scott. Goldwyn: A Biography. LC 98-28688. 592p. 1998. pap. 16.00 (*1-57322-723-4*, Riverhd Trade) Berkley Pub.

— Lindbergh. (Illus.). 1999. pap. 16.00 (*0-425-17041-1*) Berkley Pub.

*__Berg, A. Scott.__ Lindbergh. LC 98-18548. (Illus.). 628p. 1998. 30.00 (*0-399-14449-8*) Putnam Pub Group.

Berg, A. Scott. Max Perkins. 1989. pap. 6.95 (*0-671-68174-5*, WSP) PB.

— Max Perkins: Editor of Genius. LC 96-52584. 512p. 1997. pap. 15.00 (*1-57322-621-1*, Riverhd Trade) Berkley Pub.

*__Berg, A. van den, et al.__ Micro Total Analysis Systems 2000: Proceedings of the [MU] TAS 2000 Symposium, Held in Enschede, the Netherlands, 14-18 May 2000. LC 00-31324. 2000. write for info. (*0-7923-6387-6*) Kluwer Academic.

Berg, Adriane G. Financial Planning for Couples: How to Work Together to Build Security & Success. 2nd ed. LC 93-15467. 256p. 2000. reprint ed. pap. 16.95 (*1-55704-376-0*, Pub. by Newmarket) Norton.

— Gifting to People You Love: The Complete Family Guide to Making Gifts, Bequests & Investments for Children. LC 96-21567. 208p. 1996. 24.95 (*1-55704-273-X*, Pub. by Newmarket) Norton.

— How to Stop Fighting about Money & Make Some. 256p. 1989. mass mkt. 4.50 (*0-380-70775-6*, Avon Bks) Morrow Avon.

— Keys to Avoiding Probate & Reducing Estate Taxes. (Barron's Business Keys Ser.). 160p. (Orig.). 1992. pap. text 4.95 (*0-8120-4668-4*) Barron.

— Making up for Lost Time. 272p. 1995. reprint ed. mass mkt. 5.99 (*0-380-72490-1*, Avon Bks) Morrow Avon.

— Your Wealth-Building Years: Financial Planning for 18- to 35-Year Olds. 4th ed. LC 94-29154. 272p. 2000. reprint ed. pap. 16.95 (*1-55704-375-2*) Newmarket.

Berg, Adriane G. & Bochner, Arthur Berg. The Totally Awesome Business Book for Kids: With Twenty Super Businesses You Can Start Right Now. LC 95-7688. (Illus.). 160p. (YA). 1995. pap. 10.95 (*1-55704-226-8*, Pub. by Newmarket) Norton.

— Totally Awesome Money Book for Kids (& Their Parents) LC 93-35812. (Illus.). 145p. (J). (gr. 4-12). 1993. pap. 10.95 (*1-55704-176-8*, Pub. by Newmarket) Norton.

Berg, Alan. The Nutrition Factor: Its Role in National Development. LC 73-1081. 290p. 1973. pap. 16.95 (*0-8157-0913-7*) Brookings.

Berg, Alban. Wozzeck. John, Nicholas, ed. Blocknel, Eric & Hartfold, Vicki, trs. LC 90-44450. (English National Opera Guide Series: Bilingual Libretto, Articles: No. 42). (Illus.). (Orig.). 1991. pap. 9.95 (*0-7145-4201-6*) Riverrun NY.

Berg, Albert J. Van Den, see Van Den Berg, Albert J., ed.

Berg, Albert Jan van den, see van den Berg, Albert Jan, ed.

Berg, Albert M., jt. auth. see Segal, David.

Berg, Alfred O. 1997 Year Book of Family Practice. (Illus.). 592p. (C). (gr. 13). 1997. text 66.95 (*0-8151-9628-8*, 24965) Mosby Inc.

Berg, Alfred O., jt. auth. see Stool, Sylvan E.

Berg, Alice, et al. Celebrate! with Little Quilts. LC 95-35157. 1995. pap. 22.95 (*1-56477-108-3*, B227) Martingale & Co.

— Little Quilts All Through the House. Reikes, Ursula G., ed. LC 93-2611. (Illus.). 80p. 1993. pap. 21.95 (*1-56477-033-8*, B163) Martingale & Co.

— Living with Little Quilts. White, Janet, ed. LC 97-16865. (Illus.). 64p. 1997. 16.95 (*1-56477-192-X*, B306) Martingale & Co.

Berg, Arnoud Van Den, see Van Den Berg, Arnoud.

Berg, Art E. Finding Peace in Troubled Waters: Ten Life Preservers for When Your Ship Springs a Leak. LC 95-24242. xii, 114p. 1995. 12.95 (*1-57345-047-2*) Deseret Bk.

— Finding Peace in Troubled Waters: Ten Life Preservers for When Your Ship Springs a Leak. 2nd ed. LC 97-45964. 1998. pap. 12.95 (*1-57345-310-2*, Shadow Mount) Deseret Bk.

— Some Miracles Take Time: A Love Story, a Tragedy, a Triumph. 180p. 1990. pap. 14.95 (*1-883437-00-8*) Invictus Comm.

Berg, Astrid. Career Metamorphosis: Career Development Through Self Understanding. LC 90-92027. 1990. pap. 19.95 (*0-9627862-7-6*) Sefa Bks.

— Creatavision: Instructor-Counselor Resource Book. 64p. student ed. 10.00 (*0-9627862-6-8*) Sefa Bks.

— Finding the Work You Love: A Woman's Career Guide. LC 93-28936. (Illus.). 154p. (Orig.). (C). 1994. pap. 15.95 (*0-89390-269-1*) Resource Pubns.

Berg, B., et al, eds. Lattice Higgs Workshop. 300p. 1988. text 77.00 (*9971-5-0686-6*) World Scientific Pub.

Berg, Barbara A. What to Do When Life Is Driving You Crazy! LC 96-93010. (Illus.). 251p. 1997. pap. 14.95 (*0-9654014-0-5*) Creat Options.

*__Berg, Barbara J.__ The Women's Movement Today: A Hot Issue. LC 98-50274. (Hot Issues Ser.). (Illus.). 64p. (gr. 6 up). 2000. lib. bdg. 19.95 (*0-7660-1200-X*) Enslow Pubs.

*__Berg, Bruce L.__ Policing in Modern Society. LC 98-48869. 480p. 1999. pap. 44.95 (*0-7506-9867-5*) Buttrwrth-Heinemann.

Berg, Bruce L. Qualitative Research Methods for the Social Sciences. 3rd ed. LC 96-49934. 290p. 1997. pap. 40.00 (*0-205-26475-1*) Allyn.

*__Berg, Bruce L. & Horgan, John J.__ Criminal Investigation. 3rd ed. 1999. teacher ed. 16.65 (*0-02-800929-0*) Glencoe.

Berg, Bruce L. & Horgan, John J. Criminal Investigation. 3rd ed. LC 97-13607. 1997. 48.95 (*0-02-800928-2*) Macmillan.

Berg, Bruce L., jt. auth. see Mutchnick, Robert J.

*__Berg, Bruce Lawrence.__ Qualitative Research Methods for the Social Sciences. 4th ed. LC 00-23770. 336p. 2000. pap. 40.00 (*0-205-31847-9*) Allyn.

Berg, Bruce O. Child Neurology: A Clinical Manual. LC 84-80920. (Illus.). 316p. 1986. pap. text 19.95 (*0-930010-05-1*) Jones Med.

— Child Neurology: A Clinical Manual. 2nd ed. (Illus.). 450p. 1994. text 58.00 (*0-397-51328-3*) Lppncott W & W.

Berg, Bruce O., ed. Principles of Child Neurology. (Illus.). 1500p. 1996. text 135.00 (*0-07-005193-3*) McGraw-Hill HPD.

Berg, Bryan. Classroom Close-Ups: A Guide to Using Video Technology in the Classroom. 80p. 1995. teacher ed. 9.99 (*0-614-16917-8*, GA1538) Good Apple.

Berg, C. & Forst, G. Potential Theory on Locally Compact Abelian Groups. (Ergebnisse der Mathematik und Ihrer Grenzgebiete Ser.: Vol. 87). 240p. 1975. 59.95 (*0-387-07249-7*) Spr-Verlag.

Berg, C., et al. Harmonic Analysis on Semigroups: Theory of Positive Definite & Related Functions. (Graduate Texts in Mathematics Ser.: Vol. 100). (Illus.). 335p. 1984. 54.95 (*0-387-90925-7*) Spr-Verlag.

Berg, C. C. & Rosselli, P. F. Flora of Ecuador No. 27A: Cecropiaceae. (Opera Botanica Series B). 107p. 1993. pap. 57.00 (*87-88702-68-5*, Pub. by Coun Nordic Pubs) Balogh.

Berg, C. C. & Wiebes, J. T. African Fig Trees & Fig Wasps. (Verhandelingen der Koninklijke Nederlandse Akademie van Wetenschappen, Afd. Natuurkunde Ser.: No. 89). 298p. pap. 84.50 (*0-444-85741-9*) Elsevier.

Berg, Carl J. Culture of Marine Invertebrates. 1983. 55.00 (*0-87933-105-4*) Jones & Bartlett.

Berg, Carl J., Jr., jt. auth. see Orr, Katherine S.

*__Berg, Carol.__ Transformation. 2000. mass mkt. 6.99 (*0-451-45795-1*, ROC) NAL.

Berg, Cees C. Moraceae, Olmedieae, Brosimeae. LC 70-130519. (Flora Neotropica Monographs: No. 7). (Illus.). 228p. 1985. reprint ed. pap. 18.00 (*0-89327-264-7*) NY Botanical.

Berg, Cees C., et al. Cecropiaceae: Coussapoa & Pourouma, with an Introduction to the Family. (Flora Neotropica Monographs: No. 51). (Illus.). 208p. 1990. pap. text 41.50 (*0-89327-352-X*) NY Botanical.

Berg, Charles M. An Investigation of the Motives for & Realization of Music to Accompany the American Silent Film, 1896-1927. Lowett, Garth E., ed. LC 75-21428. (Dissertations on Film Ser.). 1976. lib. bdg. 20.95 (*0-405-07531-6*) Ayer.

Berg, Charles R. Cinema of Solitude: A Critical Study of Mexican Film, 1967-1983. LC 92-7492. (Film Studies). (Illus.). 264p. (C). 1992. text 35.00 (*0-292-70791-6*) U of Tex Pr.

Berg, Charles R., jt. auth. see Mora, Pat.

Berg, Christian, et al, eds. The Turn of the Century (Le Tournant du Siecle) Modernism & Modernity in Literature & the Arts - Le Modernisme et la Modernite dans la Litterature et les Arts, No. 3. LC 94-13181. (FRE.). 670p. (C). 1994. lib. bdg. 164.60 (*3-11-014018-7*) De Gruyter.

Berg, Christian, ed. see Huysmans, J. K.

Berg, Claude. The Theory of Graphs & Its Applications. Doig, Alison, tr. from FRE. LC 81-23719. 247p. 1982. reprint ed. lib. bdg. 59.75 (*0-313-23351-9*, BETG, Greenwood Pr) Greenwood.

Berg, Clayton L., Jr. & Pretiz, Paul E. Spontaneous Combustion: Grass Roots Christianity, Latin American Style. LC 95-49639. 1996. pap. 9.95 (*0-87808-265-4*) William Carey Lib.

*__Berg, Clifford J.__ Advanced Java 2 Development for Enterprise Applications. 2nd ed. 812p. (C). 2000. pap. text 49.99 (*0-13-084875-1*, Pub. by P-H) S&S Trade.

Berg, Clifford J. Remote System Administration. (C). 1999. 39.99 (*0-13-022299-2*) P-H.

Berg, Clifford J. & Digital Focus Staff. Java FAQs. (C). 2001. pap. 26.95 (*0-13-272980-6*) P-H.

*__Berg, Colin.__ Feather & Stone: Songs of T'ai Chi Ch'uan. (Illus.). 80p. 1999. pap. 10.00 (*0-9676465-0-2*) Tadpole Bks.

— Leaving No Track: A View of T'ai Chi Ch'uan. (Illus.). 112p. 1999. pap. 19.95 (*0-9676465-1-0*) Tadpole Bks.

Berg Collection Staff, ed. see Woolf, Virginia.

*__Berg, Constance.__ Lectionary Tales for the Pulpit. LC 98-9783. (Series II). 148p. 1999. pap. 13.50 (*0-7880-1370-X*) CSS OH.

— Lectionary Tales for the Pulpit: Series III, Cycle C. 154p. 2000. pap. 13.95 (*0-7880-1707-1*); disk 13.95 (*0-7880-1708-X*) CSS OH.

Berg, Cori, jt. auth. see Bishop, Debbie.

Berg-Cross, Linda. Basic Concepts in Family Therapy: An Introductory Text. LC 86-22774. 399p. 1987. text 29.95 (*0-86656-565-5*) Haworth Pr.

*__Berg-Cross, Linda.__ Basic Concepts in Family Therapy: An Introductory Text. 2nd ed. LC 99-54668. (Illus.). 616p. (C). 1999. pap. 59.95 (*0-7890-0941-2*) Haworth Pr.

— Basic Concepts in Family Therapy: An Introductory Text. 2nd ed. LC 99-54668. (Illus.). 616p. (C). 2000. 89.95 (*0-7890-0646-4*) Haworth Pr.

Berg-Cross, Linda. Couples Therapy. LC 96-35621. 488p. 1997. 59.95 (*0-8039-7128-1*); pap. 27.95 (*0-8039-7129-X*) Sage.

Berg, Cynthia A., jt. ed. see Sternberg, Robert J.

Berg, Dale. The Resident's Quick Reference to Internal Medicine. (Illus.). 210p. 1990. spiral bd. 21.95 (*0-397-51083-7*) Lppncott W & W.

*__Berg, Dale D.__ Advanced Clinical Skills & Physical Diagnosis. LC 98-27856. (Illus.). 471p. 1998. pap. 39.95 (*0-86542-544-2*) Blackwell Sci.

Berg, Dale D. Handbook of Primary Care Medicine. (Illus.). 812p. 1993. spiral bd. 31.95 (*0-397-51213-9*) Lppncott W & W.

— Handbook of Primary Care Medicine. 2nd ed. LC 97-48991. 760p. 1998. pap. text 31.00 (*0-7817-1431-1*) Lppncott W & W.

Berg, Daniel. Creating Business Applications Using Parallel Technology. 416p. 1996. pap. text 34.99 (*0-471-14282-4*) Wiley.

— Long Island Shore Diver: A Diver's Guide to Long Island's Beach Dives. 2nd ed. (Illus.). 100p. 1992. pap. text. write for info. (*0-9616167-7-6*) Aqua Explorers.

— Shipwreck Diving: A Complete Diver's Handbook to Mastering the Skills of Wreck Diving. (Illus.). 88p. (Orig.). 1991. pap. 12.95 (*0-9616167-5-X*) Aqua Explorers.

— Shore Diver: A Diver's Guide to Long Island Beach Sites. (Illus.). 96p. (Orig.). 1987. pap. 12.95 (*0-9616167-1-7*) Aqua Explorers.

— Wreck Diving Manual. (Specialty Diver Ser.). 88p. 1995. pap. text. write for info. (*1-880229-23-4*) Concept Sys.

— Wreck Valley Vol. 2: A Record of Shipwrecks off Long Island's South Shore & New Jersey. 2nd ed. (Illus.). 200p. (Orig.). 1990. pap. 18.95 (*0-9616167-3-3*) Aqua Explorers.

Berg, Daniel & Berg, Denise. Bermuda Shipwrecks: A Vacationing Diver's Guide to Bermuda's Shipwrecks. (Illus.). 64p. (Orig.). 1990. pap. 12.95 (*0-9616167-4-1*) Aqua Explorers.

— Florida Shipwrecks: The Diver's Guide to Shipwrecks Around the State of Florida & the Florida Keys. (Illus.). 180p. (Orig.). 1991. pap. 19.95 (*0-9616167-6-8*) Aqua Explorers.

— New Jersey Beach Diver: A Diver's Guide to New Jersey Beach Dives. (Illus.). 100p. pap. text. write for info. (*0-9616167-8-4*) Aqua Explorers.

— Tropical Shipwrecks: A Vacationing Divers Guide to the Bahamas & Caribbean. (Illus.). 160p. (Orig.). (YA). 1989. pap. text 12.95 (*0-9616167-2-5*) Aqua Explorers.

Berg, Daniel, jt. auth. see Alef, Edward R.

Berg, Daniel, jt. auth. see Lewis, Bil.

Berg, Daniel J. & Fritzinger, J. Steven. Advanced Techniques for Java Developers. 2nd rev. ed. LC 98-41506. 528p. 1999. pap. 49.99 incl. cd-rom (*0-471-32718-2*) Wiley.

Berg, Daniel J., jt. auth. see Lewis, Bil.

Berg, Dave. Dave Berg: Our Sick World. (Illus.). 192p. 1980. mass mkt. 1.75 (*0-446-94404-1*, Pub. by Warner Bks) Little.

— Dave Berg Looks at Living. (Illus.). 192p. (Orig.). (J). 1980. mass mkt. 1.75 (*0-446-94400-9*, Pub. by Warner Bks) Little.

— Dave Berg Looks at People. (Illus.). 192p. (Orig.). (J). 1978. mass mkt. 1.50 (*0-446-88901-6*, Pub. by Warner Bks) Little.

— Dave Berg Looks at the Neighborhood. (Illus.). 192p. 1990. mass mkt. 3.50 (*0-446-35558-5*, Pub. by Warner Bks) Little.

— Dave Berg Looks at Things. (Illus.). 192p. (J). 1985. mass mkt. 2.50 (*0-446-32827-8*, Pub. by Warner Bks) Little.

Berg, David N. & Smith, Kenwyn K., eds. The Self in Social Inquiry: Researching Methods. LC 88-11320. 400p. 1988. pap. 124.00 (*0-608-04805-4*, 205258200004) Bks Demand.

Berg, David N., jt. auth. see Smith, Kenwyn K.

*__Berg, David R. & Ferrier, Grant.__ The U. S. Environmental Industry: Meeting the Challenge: U. S. Industry Faces the 21st Century. Paugh, Jon, ed. (Illus.). 190p. (C). 2000. reprint ed. pap. text 35.00 (*0-7881-8401-6*) DIANE Pub.

Berg, Deena, tr. see Plautus & Terence.

Berg, Denise, jt. auth. see Berg, Daniel.

Berg, Donald J. American Country Building Design: Rediscovered Plans for 19th Century Farmhouses, Cottages, Landscapes, Barns, Carriage Houses & Outbuildings. LC 97-22143. (Illus.). 160p. 1997. 14.95 (*0-8069-9674-9*) Sterling.

*__Berg, Donald J.__ Carriage Barns: Scources of Building Plans, Kits, Products & Services to Help You Create a New Garage, Workshop, Stable, Backyard Office, Studio or Live-In with Old-Style Charm. (Illus.). 96p. 1999. pap. 9.95 (*0-9663075-3-4*, BB04) D J Berg.

Berg, Donald J. Modern American Dwellings, 1897. (Yesterday's Home Ser.). (Illus.). 96p. (Orig.). 1984. reprint ed. pap. 9.00 (*0-937214-09-4*) Antiquity Re.

— Suburban & Country Homes, 1893. (Yesterday's Home Ser.). (Illus.). 80p. (Orig.). 1985. reprint ed. pap. 8.00 (*0-937214-10-8*) Antiquity Re.

Berg, Donald J., ed. The Backroad Home: Simply Country Designs of Cottages, Cabins, Barns, Stables, Garages, & Garden Sheds, with Sources for Blueprints, Kits, Building Accessories, Catalogs, & Guide Books. (Illus.). 96p. 1999. pap. 9.95 (*0-9663075-2-6*, BB03) D J Berg.
— Barns & Backbuildings: Designs for Barns, Carriage Houses, Stables, Garages & Sheds. LC 98-70418. (Illus.). 96p. 1998. pap. 9.95 (*0-9663075-0-X*, BB01) D J Berg.
— How to Build in the Country: Good Advice from the Past on How to Choose a Site, Plan, Design, Build, Decorate & Landscape Your Country Home. 3rd rev. ed. LC 98-93982. (Illus.). 128p. 1999. pap. 12.95 (*0-9663075-1-8*, BB02) D J Berg.
— Shoppell's Modern Houses, 1887. (Yesterday's Home Ser.). (Illus.). 48p. (Orig.). 1983. pap. 6.00 (*0-937214-06-X*) Antiquity Re.

Berg, Donna L. A Guide to the Oxford English Dictionary. 2nd ed. (Illus.). 224p. 1993. 22.00 (*0-19-869179-3*) OUP.

Berg, Douglas E. & Howe, Martha M., eds. Mobile DNA. (Illus.). 990p. 1989. 89.00 (*1-55581-005-5*) ASM Pr.

Berg, Edward Vander, see Vander Berg, Edward.

Berg, Elizabeth. Durable Goods. 208p. 1997. mass mkt. 6.99 (*0-380-72884-2*, Avon Bks) Morrow Avon.

***Berg, Elizabeth.** Durable Goods. 208p. 1999. pap. 12.50 (*0-380-72308-5*, Avon Bks) Morrow Avon.
— Durable Goods. large type ed. LC 00-31751. 187p. 2000. lib. bdg. 25.95 (*1-58547-049-X*) Ctr Point Pubg.

Berg, Elizabeth. Escaping Into the Open: The Art of Writing True. LC 99-11192. 240p. 1999. 23.00 (*0-06-019179-1*) HarpC.
— The Joy School. 224p. 1998. pap. 11.95 (*0-345-42309-7*) Ballantine Pub Grp.
— Joy School. large type ed. LC 97-34311. (Wheeler Large Print Book Ser.). 1997. 24.95 (*1-56895-488-3*) Wheeler Pub.

***Berg, Elizabeth.** Open House: A Novel. LC 99-54258. 256p. 2000. 23.95 (*0-375-50100-2*) Random.

Berg, Elizabeth. The Pull of the Moon. 271p. 1997. mass mkt. 6.50 (*0-515-12089-8*, Jove) Berkley Pub.

***Berg, Elizabeth.** Pull of the Moon. 2000. pap. 12.95 (*0-425-17648-7*) Berkley Pub.

Berg, Elizabeth. The Pull of the Moon. large type ed. 1996. 22.95 (*0-7862-0816-3*) Thorndike Pr.
— Range of Motion. 1996. mass mkt. 6.50 (*0-515-11978-4*, Jove) Berkley Pub.

***Berg, Elizabeth.** Range of Motion. 2000. pap. 12.95 (*0-425-16876-X*) Berkley Pub.

Berg, Elizabeth. Range of Motion. large type ed. (Americana Series). 1996. 22.95 (*0-7862-0613-6*) Thorndike Pr.
— Senegal, 6 vols. , Set. LC 98-7790. (Cultures of the World Ser.). 128p. (J). 1999. lib. bdg. 35.64 (*0-7614-0872-X*) Marshall Cavendish.
— Talk Before Sleep. 224p. 1997. pap. 11.95 (*0-385-31878-2*) Doubleday.

***Berg, Elizabeth.** Until the Real Thing Comes Along. 288p. 2000. pap. 14.00 (*0-345-43739-X*) Ballantine Pub Grp.

Berg, Elizabeth. Until the Real Thing Comes Along. LC 97-25206. 272p. 1999. 23.00 (*0-679-45722-4*) Random.

***Berg, Elizabeth.** Until the Real Thing Comes Along. large type ed. LC 99-27782. 1999. 26.95 (*1-56895-764-5*) Wheeler Pub.

Berg, Elizabeth. What We Keep. (Ballantine Reader's Circle Ser.). 272p. 1999. pap. 12.00 (*0-345-42329-1*) Ballantine Pub Grp.
— What We Keep. LC 97-42070. 288p. 1998. 23.00 (*0-375-50099-5*) Random.
— What We Keep. LC 98-35886. 1998. 25.95 (*1-56895-661-4*, Compass) Wheeler Pub.

***Berg, Elizabeth.** You Gotta Have Heart: The Art of Writing True. 240p. 2000. pap. 12.00 (*0-06-092929-4*, Perennial) HarperTrade.

Berg, Eric. Baby Makes Four. LC 93-8909. (J). 1993. 10.00 (*1-56071-327-5*) ETR Assocs.
— Bernie's Safe Ideas. LC 93-8905. (J). 1993. 10.00 (*1-56071-324-0*) ETR Assocs.
— Five Special Senses. LC 93-8906. (J). 1993. 10.00 (*1-56071-328-3*) ETR Assocs.
— The Pink Medicine Lesson. LC 93-8908. (J). (gr. 4 up). 1993. 10.00 (*1-56071-326-7*) ETR Assocs.
— Try It, You'll Like It! LC 93-8907. (J). 1993. 10.00 (*1-56071-325-9*) ETR Assocs.

Berg, Frances M. Afraid to Eat: Children & Teens in Weight Crisis. 2nd rev. ed. 320p. 1997. 24.95 (*0-918532-53-1*, Hlthy Weight Jrnl); pap. 17.95 (*0-918532-52-3*, Hlthy Weight Jrnl) Hlthy Wght Network.

Berg, Frances M. Afraid to Eat Series, 2 vols. Incl. Afraid to Eat: Helping Children & Teens in Today's Weight Crisis. 3rd ed. 2000. 27.95 (*0-918532-56-6*); Children & Teens Afraid to Eat: Helping Youth in Today's Weight-Obsessed World. 3rd ed. 352p. 2000. pap. 19.95 (*0-918532-55-8*); Women Afraid to Eat: Breaking Free in Today's Weight-Obsessed World. (Illus.). 384p. 2000. pap. 17.95 (*0-918532-62-0*); Women Afraid to Eat: Breaking Free in Today's Weight-Obsessed World. 384p. 2000. 24.95 (*0-918532-63-9*); write for info. (*0-918532-70-1*); pap. write for info. (*0-918532-69-8*) Hlthy Wght Network.

Berg, Frances M. Ethnic Heritage in North Dakota. (Illus.). 176p. 1983. pap. 17.95 (*0-918532-14-0*, Flyng Diamond) Hlthy Wght Network.
— North Dakota: Land of Changing Seasons. LC 76-45874. (Old West Region Ser.: Vol. 1). (Illus.). 176p. 1977. 28.95 (*0-918532-01-9*, Flyng Diamond); pap. 17.95 (*0-918532-02-7*, Flyng Diamond) Hlthy Wght Network.

Berg, Frederick S. Acoustics & Sound Systems in Schools. LC 93-16561. (Illus.). 267p. (Orig.). (C). 1993. pap. text 49.95 (*1-56593-079-7*, 0384) Thomson Learn.
— Listening & Speech Package: LAS-PAC, 2 vols. Incl. Vol. 2. Speech Workbook. 304p. 1978. text 60.50 (*0-8089-1129-5*, 790552, W B Saunders Co); 1978. 88.00 (*0-685-62780-2*, Grune & Strat) Harcrt Hlth Sci Grp.

Berg, G., et al, eds. Differential Equations: Proceedings of the International Conference, 1977. 198p. 1977. pap. text 43.50 (*91-554-0698-X*) Coronet Bks.

Berg, G. P. Van Den, see Olivier, P. A. & Van Den Berg, G. P.

Berg, G. V., et al. Earthquake in Romania, March 4, 1977. 39p. 1980. pap. 12.00 (*0-685-14398-8*) Earthquake Eng.

Berg, G. Van Den, see Van Den Berg, G.

Berg, Gary & Gafney, Leo. Using Calculators for Business Problems. 3rd ed. 276p. 1993. teacher ed. 8.00 (*1-56118-578-7*); pap. text 18.95 (*1-56118-577-9*) Paradigm MN.

Berg, George L., Jr., ed. The Great American Priorities. 382p. (Orig.). (C). 1992. pap. text 34.50 (*0-8191-8841-7*); lib. bdg. 67.50 (*0-8191-8840-9*) U Pr of Amer.

Berg, Gerald. Methods for Recovering Viruses from the Environment. LC 87-10069. 280p. 1987. 141.00 (*0-8493-6246-6*, QR385, CRC Reprint) Franklin.

Berg, Gerald, ed. Viral Pollution of the Environment. 248p. 1983. 144.00 (*0-8493-6245-8*, TD427, CRC Reprint) Franklin.

Berg, Gertrude. Molly & Me. 22.95 (*0-88411-098-2*) Amereon Ltd.
— Molly Goldberg's Cookbook. 1994. lib. bdg. 24.95 (*1-56849-508-0*) Buccaneer Bks.

***Berg, Gertrude & Waldo, Myra.** The Molly Goldberg Jewish Cookbook. (Illus.). 320p. 1999. pap. 12.95 (*0-9669833-0-0*) Ivyland Bks.

Berg, Ginny C., ed. Indianapolis Memories: Festivals Cookbook. (TravelCookbooks Ser.: No. 1). (Illus.). 64p. 1997. 12.00 (*0-89730-231-1*) R J Berg.

Berg, Glenn. MCSE Training Guide: WIndows NT Essentials. 2nd ed. LC 98-86317. (Training Guides). 1998. 49.99 (*1-56205-919-X*) New Riders Pub.

***Berg, Glenn.** Network+ Exam Fast Track. (Fast Track (Hal Leonard) Ser.). (Illus.). 351p. 1999. pap. 29.99 (*0-7357-0904-1*) New Riders Pub.

Berg, Goran & Hammar, Mats, eds. Modern Management of the Menopause: A Perspective for the 21st Century. LC 94-1746. (International Congress, Symposium & Seminar Ser.: Vol. 8). 626p. 1994. 75.00 (*1-85070-544-5*) Prthnon Pub.

Berg, Gosta, jt. auth. see Arwidsson, Greta.

Berg, H. C., jt. ed. see Plafker, George.

Berg, H. K. & Giloi, Wolfgang K., eds. The Use of Formal Specification of Software. (Informatik-Fachberichte Ser.: Vol. 36). 388p. 1981. 38.00 (*0-387-10442-9*) Spr-Verlag.

Berg, Hans, jt. auth. see Berg, Karin.

Berg, Harry D., ed. see National Council for the Social Studies Staff.

***Berg, Herbert.** The Development of Exegesis in Early Islam: The Authenticity of Muslim Literature from the Formative Period. 288p. 2000. 80.00 (*0-7007-1224-0*, Pub. by Curzon Pr Ltd) Paul & Co Pubs.

Berg, Howard C. Random Walks in Biology. rev. ed. LC 93-12708. 190p. (C). 1993. pap. text 16.95 (*0-691-00064-6*, Pub. by Princeton U Pr) Cal Prin Full Svc.

Berg, Howard S. Super Reading Secrets. 256p. (Orig.). 1992. mass mkt. 5.99 (*0-446-36299-9*, Pub. by Warner Bks) Little.

Berg, Howard S. & Conyers, Marcus A. Speed Reading the Easy Way. 300p. 1998. pap. 12.95 (*0-8120-9852-8*, 835984) Barron.

Berg, I., jt. auth. see Kalleberg, A. L.

Berg, Ian & Nursten, Jean, eds. Unwillingly to School. 4th ed. 336p. 1996. pap. 38.50 (*0-88048-648-1*) Am Psychiatric.

Berg, Ian, et al. Off School, in Court: An Experimental & Psychiatric Investigation of Severe School Attendance Problems. (Research in Criminology Ser.). (Illus.). 160p. 1988. 112.00 (*0-387-96744-3*) Spr-Verlag.

Berg, Ian, jt. ed. see Hersov, Lionel A.

Berg, Insoo. Building Solutions: A Substance Abuse Treatment Manual. LC 97-18361. 185p. 1997. pap. 25.00 (*0-393-70251-0*) Norton.
— Building Solutions in Child Protective Services. (Professional Bks.). 240p. 1999. 30.00 (*0-393-70310-X*) Norton.

Berg, Insoo K. Family Based Service: Solutions-Focused Approach. 169p. 1992. pap. text. write for info. (*0-9633113-6-0*) Brief Fam Ther Ctr.
— Family-Based Services: A Solution-Focused Approach. 192p. (C). 1994. 27.00 (*0-393-70162-X*) Norton.
— Solution Focusd Therapy Working. (C). 2000. VHS 95.00 (*0-205-31545-3*) Allyn.

Berg, Insoo K. & Miller, Scott D. Working with the Problem Drinker: A Solution-Focused Approach. 220p. (C). 1992. 27.00 (*0-393-70134-4*) Norton.

Berg, Insoo K., jt. auth. see Miller, Scott D.

Berg, Irwin A., ed. Response Set in Personality Assessment. LC 66-28342. 1967. 42.75 (*0-202-25019-9*) Irvington.

Berg, Irwin A. & Pennington, L. A., eds. Introduction to Clinical Psychology. LC 66-20081. (Illus.). 773p. reprint ed. 200.00 (*0-8357-9914-X*, 201246700081) Bks Demand.

Berg, Isabelle. A Cat of Many Tales: From the Journals of "Ice" Berg: . . . A Real Cool Sophisticat. (Illus.). 176p. 1998. 21.95 (*0-9646803-8-6*) Plant Speak Prods.

Berg, Ivar, jt. ed. see Murphey, Murray G.

Berg, J. C. Van Den, see Van Den Berg, J. C., ed.

Berg, J. Gary. Managing Compensation. LC 76-9809. 256p. reprint ed. pap. 79.40 (*0-608-12153-3*, 202391000034) Bks Demand.

Berg, J. H., jt. auth. see Derlega, V. J.

Berg, J. M., et al, eds. Alzheimer's Disease, Down Syndrome, & Their Relationship. LC 93-28474. (Illus.). 320p. 1994. text 110.00 (*0-19-262382-6*) OUP.

Berg, J. R. & Huston, C. K. Gas Chromatography Science & Technology. (Chromotographic Science Ser.). Date not set. write for info. (*0-8247-9447-8*) Dekker.

Berg, J. Van Den, see Van den Berg, J., ed.

Berg, James A. Principes Fondamentaux de la Vie Chretienne. Bernard, Hautz, ed.Tr. of Basics for Believers. (FRE.). 1987. pap. 1.95 (*0-89084-393-7*, 031948) Bob Jones Univ.

***Berg, James J. & Freeman, Chris, eds.** The Isherwood Century: Essays on the Life & Work of Christopher Isherwood. (Illus.). 296p. 2000. 34.95 (*0-299-16700-3*) U of Wis Pr.

Berg, Jan, ed. Bernard Bolzano: Theory of Science. Terrell, B., tr. from GER. LC 72-92524. (Synthese Historical Library: No. 5). Orig. Title: Wissenschaftslehre. 4 4p. 1973. text 206.50 (*90-277-0248-9*, D Reidel) Kluwer Academic.
— Nordic Security in the 1990's: Options in the Changing Europe. LC 92-11703. (C). 1992. text 59.00 (*0-86187-080-8*) St Martin.

Berg, Jan, jt. auth. see Wagner-Doebler, Roland.

Berg, Jean H., jt. auth. see Stauffer, Russell G.

Berg, Jeff & Burgess, Jim. The Debt-Free Church: Moving Toward Financial Freedom While Growing Your Ministry. LC 96-207819. pap. 10.99 (*0-8024-2286-1*, 125) Moody.

Berg, Jeremy, jt. auth. see Lippard, Stephen J.

Berg, Jerome S. On the Short Waves, 1923-1945: Broadcast Listening in the Pioneer Days of Radio. (Illus.). 280p. 1999. boxed set 42.50 (*0-7864-0506-6*) McFarland & Co.

Berg, Jim. Changed into His Image: God's Plan for Transforming Your Life. LC 98-52722. 384p. 1999. pap. 15.95 (*1-57924-205-7*) Bob Jones Univ.

***Berg, Jim.** Taking Time to Change: An Interactive Study Guide for Changed into His Image. (Illus.). 2000. write for info. (*1-57924-271-5*) Bob Jones Univ.

***Berg, Jim & Nyberg, Tim.** The Jumbo Book of Duct Tape. (Illus.). 464p. 2000. pap. 9.95 (*0-7611-2110-2*) Workman Pub.

Berg, Jimmy. Von der RingstraBe zur 72nd Street. Jimmy Bergs Chansons aus dem Wien der dreiBiger Jahre und dem New Yorker Exil, Vol. 17. Jarka, Horst, ed. (Austrian Culture Ser.). (Illus.). XI, 318p. (C). 1996. 59.95 (*0-8204-2694-6*) P Lang Pubng.

Berg, Jo. Recipes for Fun! What to Do When There's Nothing to Do. 80p. (YA). 1996. 6.95 (*1-888827-16-5*) Castlemoyle Bks.

***Berg, Johanna.** Songbird. LC 99-48423. 67p. (J). 1999. 6.49 (*1-57924-297-9*) Bob Jones Univ.

Berg, John C. Wettability. LC 93-12059. (Surfactant Science Ser.: Vol. 49). (Illus.). 552p. 1993. text 250.00 (*0-8247-9046-4*) Dekker.

Berg, Joseph M., ed. Science & Service in Mental Retardation: Proceedings of the Seventh Congress of the International Association for the Scientific Study of Mental Deficiency. 512p. 1986. text 47.50 (*0-416-40650-5*, 1042) Routledge.

Berg, Joseph M., jt. ed. see Hicks, E. K.

Berg, Julie. Beverly Cleary. LC 93-12958. (Young at Heart Ser.). (Illus.). 32p. (YA). (gr. 4 up). 1993. lib. bdg. 4.98 (*1-56239-222-0*) ABDO Pub Co.
— E. B. White. LC 94-5307. 1994. pap. 4.95 (*1-56239-367-7*) ABDO Pub Co.
— E. B. White. LC 94-5307. (Illus.). 32p. 1994. lib. bdg. 14.98 (*1-56239-356-1*) ABDO Pub Co.

***Berg, Julie.** Friendship A Record Book About the ABC's of Friendship. 1999. 20.00 (*1-57977-148-3*) Havoc Pub.

Berg, Julie. H. A. Rey. LC 94-32229. (Tribute to the Young at Heart Ser.). (Illus.). (J). (gr. 3-4). 1994. pap. 4.95 (*1-56239-368-5*); lib. bdg. 14.98 (*1-56239-357-X*) ABDO Pub Co.
— John Steptoe. LC 94-3391. (Tribute to the Young at Heart). (J). 1994. pap. 4.95 (*1-56239-370-7*) ABDO Pub Co.

Berg, Julie. John Steptoe. LC 94-3391. (Tribute to the Young at Heart). (Illus.). 32p. (J). 1994. lib. bdg. 14.98 (*1-56239-359-6*) ABDO Pub Co.

Berg, Julie. Maurice Sendak. LC 93-15738. (Young at Heart Ser.). (J). 1993. pap. 4.95 (*1-56239-365-0*) ABDO Pub Co.
— Maurice Sendak. LC 93-15738. (Young at Heart Ser.). (Illus.). 32p. (J). 1993. lib. bdg. 14.98 (*1-56239-225-5*) ABDO Pub Co.
— Richard Scarry. LC 94-3392. (Tribute to the Young at Heart). 1994. pap. 4.95 (*1-56239-369-3*) ABDO Pub Co.
— Richard Scarry. LC 94-3392. (Tribute to the Young at Heart). (Illus.). 32p. (J). 1994. lib. bdg. 14.98 (*1-56239-358-8*) ABDO Pub Co.

***Berg, Julie.** School Days: A Record Book from Preschool to Sixth Grade. 1999. 20.00 (*1-57977-149-1*) Havoc Pub.

Berg, Julie. Stan & Jan Barenstain. LC 93-12959. (Young at Heart Ser.). (Illus.). 32p. (J). 1993. lib. bdg. 14.98 (*1-56239-224-7*) ABDO Pub Co.
— Tomie de Paola. LC 93-12960. (Young at Heart Ser.). (Illus.). (J). 1993. pap. 4.95 (*1-56239-363-4*); lib. bdg. 14.98 (*1-56239-223-9*) ABDO Pub Co.

Berg, Julie, jt. auth. see Kallen, Stuart A.

Berg, Julie, jt. auth. see Nielsen, Shelly.

Berg, Julie, ed. see Bickman, Connie.

Berg, Julie, ed. see Child, Elizabeth.

Berg, Julie, ed. see Kallen, Stuart A.

Berg, Julie, ed. see Nielsen, Shelly.

Berg, Julie, ed. see Wheeler, Jill C.

Berg, Kabbalist P. & Berg, Phillip S. Immortality Now! Ancient Lessons for Eternal Life. 250p. 1997. 22.95 (*1-55874-533-5*) Health Comm.

Berg, Kare. Die Zeit des Jahwisten: Ein Beitrag zur Datierung Jahwistischer Vatertexte. (Beiheft zur Zeitschrift fuer die Alttestamentliche Wissenschaft Ser.: Band). xi, 329p. (C). 1990. lib. bdg. 113.85 (*3-11-011892-0*) De Gruyter.

Berg, Kare, et al, eds. Genetic Approaches of Coronary Heart Disease & Hypertension. (Illus.). 150p. 1991. 109.00 (*0-387-54476-3*) Spr-Verlag.
— Genetic Approaches to Noncummunicable Diseases. 160p. 1995. 86.95 (*3-540-60289-5*) Spr-Verlag.
— Human Gene Mapping 6, Oslo 1981. (Journal: Cytogenetics & Cell Genetics: Vol. 32, No. 1-4). (Illus.). viii, 320p. 1982. pap. 94.00 (*3-8055-3559-7*) S Karger.

Berg, Karen, jt. auth. see Gilma, Andrew.

Berg, Karin & Berg, Hans. Greenland Through the Year. LC 72-90689. (Illus.). 24p. (J). (gr. k-4). 1973. 11.95 (*0-87592-023-3*) Scroll Pr.

Berg, Karl & Godwin, George. The Sadist, an Account of the Crimes of a Serial Killer, Together with Peter Kurten, a Study in Sadism. LC 90-6953. (Criminology, Law Enforcement, & Social Problems Ser.: No. 144). (Illus.). 352p. (C). 1998. 35.00 (*0-87585-144-4*) Patterson Smith.

Berg, Karsten & Breitkreuz, Christoph. Mesozoische Plutone in der Nordchilenischen Kuestenkordillere: Petrogenese, Geochronologie, Geochemie und Geodynamik Mantelbetonten Magmatite. (Geotektonische Forschungen Ser.: Vol. 66). (GER.). 107p. 1983. 57.00 (*3-510-50032-6*, Pub. by E Schweizerbartsche) Balogh.

B

Berg, Ken. Maud Hart Lovelace. LC 94-3389. (Tribute to the Young at Heart). (Illus.). 32p. (J). 1994. pap. 4.95 (*1-56239-372-3*) ABDO Pub Co.
— Maud Hart Lovelace. LC 94-3389. (Tribute to the Young at Heart). (Illus.). 32p. (J). 1994. lib. bdg. 14.98 (*1-56239-361-8*) ABDO Pub Co.

Berg, Kent Van Den, see Van Den Berg, Kent.

Berg, Kevin A. Jibberish & Rhyme. (Illus.). 104p. (J). (gr. k-6). 1993. lib. bdg. 15.95 (*0-9636795-0-3*) Child Tech Bks.

Berg, Kris. Bass Lines in Minutes. (Illus.). 40p. (Orig.). (C). pap. 7.95 (*1-56516-035-5*) H Leonard.

Berg, Kris & Latin, Richard. Essentials of Modern Research Methods. LC 93-44092. 288p. 1994. 72.00 (*0-13-644014-2*) P-H.

Berg, Kristi K., ed. see Leigh, Carole.

Berg, Kristian, et al, eds. Photochemotherapy: Photodynamic Therapy & Other Modalities III. LC 98-164537. (Europto Ser.: Vol. 3191). 380p. 1997. 107.00 (*0-8194-2623-7*) SPIE.

Berg, Kristian, jt. ed. see Ehrenberg, Benjamin.

Berg, Laurel L. The Coggeshall Ladies: Civil War Heroines. LC 92-91008. (Orig.). Date not set. pap. 10.95 (*0-614-30106-8*) Poko Press.

Berg, Leif. Bringing Cases Before the European Commission & Court of Human Rights LC 98-202028. vii, 161p. 1997. write for info. (*952-12-0030-8*, Pub. by Abo Akademi) Women Ink.

Berg, Leila. Flickerbook. 260p. 1998. 22.95 (*1-86207-004-0*, Pub. by Granta) Midpt Trade.

***Berg, Leila.** The God Stories: A Celebration of Legends. 254p. 2000. 24.95 (*0-7112-1315-1*, Pub. by F Lincoln) Antique Collect.

Berg, Leila. Reading & Loving. 1976. 19.95 (*0-7100-8475-7*, Routledge Thoemms); pap. 11.95 (*0-7100-8476-5*, Routledge Thoemms) Routledge.

Berg, Leo Van Den, see Van Den Berg, Leo.

Berg, Leo Van Der, see Van Der Berg, Leo.

Berg, Lisa E., jt. ed. see Kreilkamp, Ann.

Berg, Lois A. An Eritrean Family. LC 95-46970. (Journey Between Two Worlds Ser.). (J). 1996. lib. bdg. 22.60 (*0-8225-3405-3*, Lerner Publctns) Lerner Pub.
— An Eritrean Family. (Illus.). 56p. (gr. 3-6). 1997. pap. 8.95 (*0-8225-9755-1*, First Ave Edns) Lerner Pub.

Berg, Maggie. Jane Eyre: Portrait of a Life. LC 87-14877. (Twayne's Masterworks Ser.: Vol. 10). 144p. 1987. pap. 18.00 (*0-8057-8010-6*) Macmillan.
— Wuthering Heights. LC 96-31198. 1996. 29.00 (*0-8057-8051-3*, Twyne); per. 14.95 (*0-8057-8101-3*, Twyne) Mac Lib Ref.

Berg, Manfred & Cocks, Geoffrey, eds. Medicine & Modernity: Public Health & Medical Care in Nineteenth-& Twentieth-Century Germany. LC 96-15487. (Publications of the German Historical Institute, Washington, D.C.). 249p. 1997. text 64.95 (*0-521-56411-5*) Cambridge U Pr.

Berg, Marc. Rationalizing Medical Work: Decision-Support Techniques & Medical Practices. LC 96-2928. (Inside Technology Ser.). 250p. 1997. 35.00 (*0-262-02417-9*) MIT Pr.

Berg, Marc & Mol, Annemarie. Differences in Medicine: Unraveling Practices, Techniques & Bodies. LC 97-37836. (Body, Commodity, Text Ser.). 1998. write for info. (*0-8223-2162-9*) Duke.

Berg, Marc & Mol, Annemarie, eds. Differences in Medicine: Unraveling Practices, Techniques & Bodies. LC 97-37836. (Body, Commodity, Text Ser.). 272p. 1998. pap. 17.95 (*0-8223-2174-2*) Duke.

Berg, Marjorie R., et al. Ambulatory Prenatal Nursing Care: Practice Standards for Positive Pregnancy Outcomes. LC 85-27649. 224p. 1986. pap. 29.95 (*0-8261-5330-5*) Springer Pub.

Berg, Mark de. Computational Geometry: Algorithms & Applications. LC 97-18880. 350p. 1997. 32.95 (*3-540-61270-X*) Spr-Verlag.
— Ray Shooting, Depth Orders & Hidden Surface Removal. (Lecture Notes in Computer Science Ser.: Vol. 703). x, 201p. 1993. pap. write for info. (*3-540-57020-9*) Spr-Verlag.
— Ray Shooting, Depth Orders & Hidden Surface Removal. (Lecture Notes in Computer Science Ser.). x, 201p. 1993. 39.95 (*0-387-57020-9*) Spr-Verlag.

***Berg, Mark de, et al.** Computational Geometry: Algorithms & Applications. 2nd rev. ed. LC 99-89215. xii, 369p. 2000. 34.95 (*3-540-65620-0*) Spr-Verlag.

Berg, Mark R., et al. Jobs & Energy in Michigan: The Next Twenty Years. LC 80-24884. 210p. reprint ed. pap. 65.10 (*0-7837-5262-8*, 204500000005) Bks Demand.

Berg, Martha. Test Questions the Brain. 2nd ed. 1993. 16.00 (*0-7167-2514-2*) W H Freeman.

Berg, Mary G., tr. see Agosin, Marjorie.

Berg, Mary G., tr. see Demitropulos, Libertad.

Berg, Mary G., tr. see Riesco, Laura.

Berg, Matthew Paul, ed. see Kreisky, Bruno.

Berg, Maxine. The Age of Manufactures, 1700-1820: Industry, Innovation, & Work in Britain. 2nd ed. LC 93-23364. (Illus.). 304p. (C). 1994. pap. 27.99 (*0-415-06935-1*, A7862) Routledge.

— A Woman in History: Eileen Power, 1889-1940. (Illus.). 308p. (C). 1996. text 69.95 (*0-521-40278-6*); pap. text 26.95 (*0-521-56852-8*) Cambridge U Pr.

Berg, Maxine, ed. Political Economy in the 20th Century. 192p. 1989. lib. bdg. 45.00 (*0-389-20896-5*, N8452) B&N Imports.

Berg, Maxine & Bruland, Kristine, eds. Technological Revolutions in Europe: Historical Perspectives. LC 97-50056. 336p. 1998. 90.00 (*1-85898-681-8*) E Elgar.

***Berg, Michael C.** The Fourier-Analytic Proof of Quadratic Reciprocity. LC 99-52756. 128p. 2000. text 69.95 (*0-471-35830-4*, Wiley-Interscience) Wiley.

Berg, Michel, jt. auth. see Ketonen, Leena.

Berg, Miguel & Pretiz, Pablo. Mensajeros de Esperanza (The Gospel People) (SPA.). 125p. 1994. write for info. (*1-56063-776-5*) Editorial Unilit.

Berg, Mike & Pretiz, Paul. The Gospel People. 156p. 1992. pap. 2.95 (*0-912552-77-8*) MARC.

Berg, N., jt. auth. see Levine, C.

Berg, N. Edward. The New Era of Electronic Composition. LC 79-92190. 188p. reprint ed. pap. 58.30 (*0-7837-0361-9*, 204068300018) Bks Demand.

Berg, Nancy E. Exile from Exile: Israeli Writers from Iraq. LC 95-44136. (SUNY Series in Israeli Studies). 205p. (C). 1996. text 57.50 (*0-7914-2979-2*); pap. text 18.95 (*0-7914-2980-6*) State U NY Pr.

Berg, Niki, photos by. Wholly Cow. (Illus.). 96p. 1988. 27.50 (*0-89659-816-0*) Abbeville Pr.

Berg, Norman. Regret to Inform You: Experiences of Families Who Lost a Family Member in Vietnam. LC 99-37716. 154p. 1999. 16.95 (*1-55571-509-5*) PSI Resch.

Berg, Norman G., ed. see Fink, H. & Mullenix, L.

Berg, Norman G., ed. see Schultz, N. & Sirico, L.

Berg, Norman J. & Pellegrino, John M., eds. Acousto-Optic Signal Processing: Theory & Implementation. 2nd ed. LC 95-41066. (Optical Engineering Ser.: Vol. 51). (Illus.). 600p. 1995. text 180.00 (*0-8247-8925-3*, TA1770) Dekker.

Berg, O., et al. Spread Spectrum in Mobile Communication. (Telecommunications Ser.: No. 40). 480p. 1998. 89.00 (*0-85296-935-X*, TE040) INSPEC Inc.

Berg, Oona Van Den, see Van Den Berg, Oona.

Berg, Orville R. & Woolverton, Donald G., eds. Seismic Stratigraphy No. II: An Integrated Approach to Hydrocarbon Exploration. LC 85-18652. (American Association of Petroleum Geologists. Memoir Ser.: No. 39). (Illus.). 422p. 1985. reprint ed. pap. 130.90 (*0-608-02744-8*, 206340900006) Bks Demand.

Berg, Oyvind. Totschweigetaktiken. Barnett, Anthony, tr. from GER. 64p. (Orig.). 1991. pap. 9.00 (*0-907954-14-6*, Pub. by Allardyce Barnett) SPD-Small Pr Dist.

Berg, P. A., et al, eds. Autoimmune Liver Disease. (Falk Symposium Ser.). 128p. 1998. text 80.00 (*0-7923-8730-9*) Kluwer Academic.

Berg, P. A. & Leuschner, U., eds. Bile Acids & Immunology: Proceedings of the 86th Falk Symposium Held in Basel, Switzerland, October 17-18, 1995. LC 96-17379. (Basel Liver Week Ser.: Pt. I). 1996. text 132.50 (*0-7923-8700-7*) Kluwer Academic.

Berg, P. J. Van Den, see Van Den Berg, P. J., ed.

Berg, P. M. Van Den, see Fokkema, J. T. & Van Den Berg, P. M.

Berg, P. M. Van Den, see Blok, H. & Van Den Berg, P. M.

Berg, P. M. Van Den, see Van Den Berg, P. M.

***Berg, Patti.** Bride for a Night. LC 99-96451. 384p. 2000. mass mkt. 5.99 (*0-380-80736-X*, Avon Bks) Morrow Avon.

Berg, Patti. If I Can't Have You. 384p. 1998. mass mkt. 5.99 (*0-380-79554-X*, Avon Bks) Morrow Avon.

— Looking for a Hero. 384p. 1998. mass mkt. 5.99 (*0-380-79555-8*, Avon Bks) Morrow Avon.

— Till the End of Time. 384p. 1997. mass mkt. 5.99 (*0-380-78339-8*, Avon Bks) Morrow Avon.

***Berg, Patti.** Wife for a Day. 384p. 1999. mass mkt. 5.99 (*0-380-80735-1*, Avon Bks) Morrow Avon.

Berg, Patti. Wishes Come True. 384p. (Orig.). 1996. mass mkt. 5.99 (*0-380-78338-X*, Avon Bks) Morrow Avon.

Berg, Paul & McGregor, James L. Elementary Partial Differential Equations. (C). 1988. text 61.74 (*0-07-004850-9*) McGraw.

Berg, Paul & Singer, Maxine. Dealing with Genes: The Language of Heredity. LC 01-75179. (Illus.). 269p. (C). 1992. text 38.00 (*0-935702-69-5*) Univ Sci Bks.

Berg, Paul, jt. auth. see Singer, Maxine.

Berg, Paul K. Nineteenth Century Photographic Cases & Wall Frames. unabridged ed. LC 95-94712. (Illus.). x, 418p. 1995. pap. 52.00 (*0-9659670-0-X*) P K Berg.

Berg, Peter. Discovering Your Life-Place: A First Bioregional Workbook. 26p. 1995. 10.00 (*0-937102-03-2*) Planet Drum Books.

***Berg, Peter.** Dispatches from Ecuador. (Illus.). 36p. 1999. 3.00 (*0-937102-05-9*) Planet Drum Books.

Berg, Peter, ed. Reinhabiting a Separate Country: A Bioregional Anthology of Northern California. (Illus.). 220p. (Orig.). 1978. pap. 7.00 (*0-937102-00-8*) Planet Drum Books.

Berg, Philip S. Gift of the Bible. (FRE.). 160p. 1994. pap. 10.95 (*0-924457-08-2*) Res Ctr Kabbalah.

— The Kabbalah Connection. 224p. (C). 1983. 12.95 (*0-943688-02-7*); pap. 11.95 (*0-943688-03-5*) Res Ctr Kabbalah.

— The Kabbalah Connection. (SPA.). 256p. 1989. 12.95 (*0-943688-86-8*); pap. 12.95 (*0-943688-87-6*) Res Ctr Kabbalah.

— The Kabbalah Connection. (HEB.). 224p. 1993. pap. 11.95 (*0-924457-47-3*) Res Ctr Kabbalah.

— Kabbalah for the Layman, Vol. I. (SPA.). 224p. 1986. 12.95 (*0-943688-43-4*); pap. 11.95 (*0-943688-44-2*) Res Ctr Kabbalah.

— Kabbalah for the Layman, Vol. I. (HEB.). 160p. 1987. 12.95 (*0-943688-24-8*); 12.95 (*0-943688-47-7*); pap. 10.95 (*0-943688-23-X*); pap. 11.95 (*0-943688-48-5*) Res Ctr Kabbalah.

— Kabbalah for the Layman, Vol. I. (RUS.). 224p. 1988. pap. 12.95 (*0-943688-74-4*); pap. 12.95 (*0-943688-73-6*) Res Ctr Kabbalah.

— Kabbalah for the Layman, Vol. I. (GER.). 224p. 1988. 12.95 (*0-943688-75-2*); pap. 11.95 (*0-943688-76-0*) Res Ctr Kabbalah.

— Kabbalah for the Layman, Vol. I. (POR.). 256p. 1989. 12.95 (*0-924457-36-8*); 12.95 (*0-924457-38-4*); pap. 12.95 (*0-924457-37-6*) Res Ctr Kabbalah.

— Kabbalah for the Layman, Vol. I. (PER.). 224p. 1990. 12.95 (*0-943688-77-9*); pap. 14.95 (*0-943688-78-7*) Res Ctr Kabbalah.

— Kabbalah for the Layman, Vol. II. (Mandarin Ser.). (CHI.). 256p. 1991. 12.95 (*0-924457-40-6*) Res Ctr Kabbalah.

— Kabbalah for the Layman, Vol. III. (Mandarin Ser.). (CHI.). 256p. 1992. 13.95 (*0-924457-42-2*) Res Ctr Kabbalah.

— Kabbalah for the Layman, Vol. 3. (HEB., Illus.). 256p. 1997. pap. 10.95 (*0-924457-23-6*) Res Ctr Kabbalah.

— Kabbalah for the Layman I. 224p. 1982. 12.95 (*0-943688-00-0*); pap. 11.95 (*0-943688-01-9*) Res Ctr Kabbalah.

— Kabbalah for the Layman I. (ITA.). 224p. 1992. pap. 10.95 (*0-924457-32-5*) Res Ctr Kabbalah.

— Kabbalah for the Layman III. 256p. 1988. 13.95 (*0-943688-69-8*); pap. 12.95 (*0-943688-70-1*) Res Ctr Kabbalah.

— Kabbalah for the Layman III. (HEB.). 192p. 1989. 13.95 (*0-924457-22-8*); 13.95 (*0-924457-26-0*); pap. 12.95 (*0-924457-27-9*) Res Ctr Kabbalah.

— Kabbalah for the Layman III. (SPA.). 256p. 1991. 13.95 (*0-924457-24-4*); pap. 12.95 (*0-924457-25-2*) Res Ctr Kabbalah.

— Kabbalah for the Layman II. 224p. 1988. 12.95 (*0-943688-82-5*); pap. 11.95 (*0-943688-83-3*) Res Ctr Kabbalah.

— Kabbalah for the Layman II. (HEB.). 224p. 1989. 12.95 (*0-924457-04-X*); 12.95 (*0-924457-18-X*); 12.95 (*0-924457-20-1*); pap. 11.95 (*0-924457-05-8*); pap. 11.95 (*0-924457-19-8*); pap. 12.95 (*0-924457-21-X*) Res Ctr Kabbalah.

— Kabbalah for the Layman II. (ITA.). 224p. 1992. pap. 11.95 (*0-924457-33-3*) Res Ctr Kabbalah.

— Miracles, Mysteries & Prayer I. (ENG.). 12p. 1993. pap. 11.95 (*0-924457-83-X*); pap. 11.95 (*0-924457-84-8*); pap. 11.95 (*0-924457-85-6*); pap. 11.95 (*0-924457-88-0*) Res Ctr Kabbalah.

— Miracles, Mysteries & Prayer II. (ENG.). 12p. 1993. pap. 11.95 (*0-924457-90-2*); pap. 11.95 (*0-924457-86-4*); pap. 11.95 (*0-924457-87-2*); pap. 11.95 (*0-924457-89-9*) Res Ctr Kabbalah.

— Power of Aleph Beth, Vol. I. (FRE.). 288p. 1989. 14.95 (*0-924457-28-7*); 14.95 (*0-943688-94-9*); 14.95 (*0-924457-67-8*); pap. 13.95 (*0-924457-29-5*); pap. 12.95 (*0-943688-95-7*); pap. 12.95 (*0-924457-68-6*) Res Ctr Kabbalah.

— Power of Aleph Beth, Vol. II. (SPA.). 256p. 1989. 12.95 (*0-943688-96-5*); 12.95 (*0-924457-69-4*); pap. 12.95 (*0-943688-97-3*); pap. 12.95 (*0-924457-70-8*) Res Ctr Kabbalah.

— Power of Aleph Beth, Vol. II. (FRE.). 224p. 1990. 12.95 (*0-924457-30-9*); pap. 11.95 (*0-924457-31-7*) Res Ctr Kabbalah.

— Power of the Aleph Beth, Vol. 1. 288p. 1988. 14.95 (*0-943688-11-6*); pap. 13.95 (*0-943688-10-8*) Res Ctr Kabbalah.

— Power of the Aleph Beth, Vol. II. 224p. 1988. 12.95 (*0-943688-56-6*); pap. 11.95 (*0-943688-57-4*) Res Ctr Kabbalah.

— The Star Connection. (ITA.). 256p. 1994. pap. 13.95 (*0-924457-65-1*) Res Ctr Kabbalah.

— The Star Connection. rev. ed. 224p. 1992. 14.95 (*0-318-70374-2*); pap. 12.95 (*0-318-70375-0*); pap. 12.95 (*0-318-70376-9*); pap. 12.95 (*0-318-70377-7*); pap. 12.95 (*0-318-70378-5*); pap. 15.95 (*0-318-70379-3*); pap. 14.95 (*0-924457-11-2*) Res Ctr Kabbalah.

— Ten Luminous Emmanations, Vol. I. (SPA.). 224p. (C). pap. write for info. (*0-943688-14-0*) Res Ctr Kabbalah.

— Ten Luminous Emmanations, Vol. II. (SPA.). 224p. (C). pap. write for info. (*0-943688-15-9*) Res Ctr Kabbalah.

— Time Zones: Your Key to Control. 256p. 1990. 13.95 (*0-924457-00-7*); pap. 12.95 (*0-924457-01-5*) Res Ctr Kabbalah.

— Time Zones: Your Key to Control. (SPA.). 256p. 1991. 13.95 (*0-924457-59-7*); 13.95 (*0-924457-54-6*); pap. 12.95 (*0-924457-60-0*); pap. 12.95 (*0-924457-55-4*); pap. 13.95 (*0-924457-74-0*) Res Ctr Kabbalah.

— Time Zones: Your Key to Control. (HEB.). 256p. 1994. pap. 11.95 (*0-924457-76-7*) Res Ctr Kabbalah.

— To the Power of One. 256p. 1991. 15.95 (*0-924457-02-3*); pap. 14.95 (*0-924457-03-1*) Res Ctr Kabbalah.

— To the Power of One. (SPA.). 13p. 1992. pap. 14.95 (*0-924457-64-3*) Res Ctr Kabbalah.

— To the Power of One. (FRE.). 13p. 1994. pap. 14.95 (*0-924457-63-5*); pap. 12.95 (*0-924457-71-6*) Res Ctr Kabbalah.

— Wheels of a Soul. (HEB.). 160p. 1986. 13.95 (*0-943688-41-8*); pap. 11.95 (*0-943688-42-6*) Res Ctr Kabbalah.

— Wheels of a Soul. (FRE.). 288p. 1987. 13.95 (*0-943688-71-X*); 13.95 (*0-943688-45-0*); pap. 13.95 (*0-943688-46-9*); pap. 13.95 (*0-943688-72-8*) Res Ctr Kabbalah.

— Wheels of a Soul. (PER.). 256p. 1989. 13.95 (*0-924457-16-3*); 14.95 (*0-924457-06-6*); pap. 13.95 (*0-924457-17-1*); pap. 13.95 (*0-924457-07-4*) Res Ctr Kabbalah.

— Wheels of a Soul. (Mandarin Ser.). (CHI.). 288p. 1992. 13.95 (*0-924457-44-9*); pap. 11.95 (*0-924457-45-7*); pap. 11.95 (*0-318-70264-9*) Res Ctr Kabbalah.

— Wheels of a Soul. rev. ed. 224p. 1991. 13.95 (*0-318-70381-5*) Res Ctr Kabbalah.

— The Zohar: Parshat Pinhas I. (SPA.). 256p. 1992. pap. 12.95 (*0-924457-78-3*) Res Ctr Kabbalah.

— The Zohar: Parshat Pinhas II. (SPA.). 288p. 1993. pap. 12.95 (*0-924457-80-5*) Res Ctr Kabbalah.

— The Zohar: Parshat Pinhas III. (SPA.). 256p. 1993. pap. 12.95 (*0-924457-82-1*) Res Ctr Kabbalah.

Berg, Philip S., tr. from ARC. The Zohar: Parashat Pinhas, Vol. II. 256p. 1987. 13.95 (*0-943688-52-3*); pap. 12.95 (*0-943688-53-1*) Res Ctr Kabbalah.

— The Zohar: Parashat Pinhas, Vol. III. 256p. 1988. 13.95 (*0-943688-54-X*); pap. 12.95 (*0-943688-55-8*) Res Ctr Kabbalah.

— Zohar: Parshat Pinhas, Vol. I. 288p. 1986. 14.95 (*0-943688-50-7*); pap. 13.95 (*0-943688-51-5*) Res Ctr Kabbalah.

Berg, Philip S. & Brandwein, Yehuda. Wheels of a Soul on Tape, 3 vols., 3. 850p. 1973. 13.95 incl. audio (*0-924457-53-8*) Res Ctr Kabbalah.

Berg, Philip S., ed. see Ashlag, Yehuda R.

Berg, Philip S., ed. see Kahana, S. Z.

Berg, Phillip S., jt. auth. see Berg, Kabbalist P.

Berg, R. J. La Querelle des Critiques en France a la Fin de XIXe Siecle. (American University Studies: Romance Languages & Literature: Ser. II, Vol. 151). VII, 201p. 1990. 43.95 (*0-8204-1342-9*) P Lang Pubng.

Berg, R. J. & Leroy, Fabrice. La Grammaire a l'Oeuvre, Tome II. 5th ed. (FRE.). 752p. (C). 1996. wbk. ed., lab manual ed. 35.50 (*0-03-072398-1*) Harcourt Coll Pubs.

Berg, Ragnar, jt. auth. see Hauser, Gayelord.

Berg, Richard. Depression & the Integrated Life. LC 81-7976. 184p. 1981. pap. 9.95 (*0-8189-0412-7*) Alba.

Berg, Richard, jt. ed. see Rowe, John C.

Berg, Richard A., et al. Screening for Brain Impairment: A Manual for Mental Health Practice. 2nd ed. 264p. 1994. 33.95 (*0-8261-5741-6*) Springer Pub.

Berg, Richard E. & Stork, David G. The Physics of Sound. 2nd ed. LC 94-20877. 416p. (C). 1994. 76.00 (*0-13-183047-3*) P-H.

Berg, Richard L. & Wright, Edmund, eds. Frost Action & Its Control. 145p. 1984. 20.00 (*0-87262-395-5*) Am Soc Civil Eng.

Berg, Rick, jt. ed. see James, David E.

***Berg, Robert.** The Writings of John. (Spiritual Discovery Ser.). 126p. 2000. pap. 9.95 (*0-88243-231-1*, 02-0231); pap. 4.95 (*0-88243-131-5*, 02-0131) Gospel Pub.

Berg, Robert C. Group Counseling: Concepts & Procedures. 3rd ed. LC 98-42714. 200p. 1998. pap. text 24.95 (*1-56032-662-X*) Hemisp Pub.

Berg, Robert C. & Johnson, James A., eds. Group Counseling: A Sourcebook of Theory & Practice. 1975. 18.95 (*0-405-18853-6*, 113) Ayer.

Berg, Robert C., et al. Group Counseling: Concepts & Procedures. 3rd ed. LC 98-20909. 457p. 1998. pap. 34.95 (*1-56032-663-8*) Hemisp Pub.

Berg, Robert J. & Whitaker, Jennifer S., eds. Strategies for African Development. (Illus.). 280p. 1986. pap. 24.95 (*0-520-05782-1*, Pub. by U CA Pr) Cal Prin Full Svc.

Berg, Robert L., ed. see Institute of Medicine Staff.

Berg, Robert L., jt. ed. see Johansen, Robert T.

Berg, Robin. World War II Envelope Art of Cecile Cowdery. (Illus.). 80p. 1992. pap. 20.00 (*0-910667-22-5*) USM.

Berg, Roger. Profitable Portrait Photography. LC 97-75208. (Illus.). 128p. 1998. pap. 29.95 (*0-936262-65-6*) Amherst Media.

***Berg, Ron.** Northwoods Fish Cookery. LC 99-50532. 2000. pap. 16.95 (*0-8166-3583-8*) U of Minn Pr.

Berg, Ron, et al. The Gunflint Lodge Cookbook: Elegant Northwoods Dining. LC 97-14009. 1997. pap. 17.95 (*0-8166-2831-9*) U of Minn Pr.

***Berg, Rona.** Beauty, the New Basics. (Illus.). 512p. 2001. pap. 22.95 (*0-7611-0186-1*) Workman Pub.

Berg, Rosalie, et al. Programs for Spouses of Foreign Students. 25p. 1986. 12.00 (*0-912207-28-0*) NAFSA Washington.

Berg, Sara J. Van den, see Van den Berg, Sara J.

***Berg-Schlosser, Dirk.** Conditions of Democracy in Europe. LC 99-50144. 2000. text 79.95 (*0-312-22843-0*) St Martin.

Berg-Schlosser, Dirk & Rytlewski, Ralf, eds. Political Culture in Germany. LC 92-12880. 1993. text 49.95 (*0-312-08530-3*) St Martin.

Berg-Schlosser, Dirk & Siegler, Rainer. Political Stability & Development: A Comparative Analysis of Kenya, Tanzania, & Uganda. LC 90-8249. 226p. 1990. lib. bdg. 40.00 (*1-55587-165-8*) L Rienner.

Berg, Shelley C. Le Sacre du Printemps: Seven Productions from Nijinsky to Martha Graham. LC 87-29421. (Theater & Dramatic Studies: No. 48). (Illus.). 217p. reprint ed. pap. 67.30 (*0-8357-1842-5*, 207059100004) Bks Demand.

Berg, Shirley T. Robert Hardin & Descendants. 300p. (Orig.). 1996. pap. 20.00 (*1-57798-002-6*, 0026) BerryPatch.

Berg, Sjef Van Den, see Watt, James H. & Van Den Berg, Sjef.

Berg-Sobre, Judith. Bartolome de Cardenas, "El Bermejo" Itinerant Painter in the Crown of Aragon. LC 96-46068. (Iberian Studies in History, Literature & Culture). (Illus.). 320p. 1997. pap. 49.95 (*1-57309-062-X*, Cath Scholar Pr) Intl Scholars.

— Bartolome de Cardenas, "El Bermejo" Itinerant Painter in the Crown of Aragon. LC 96-46068. (Iberian Studies in History, Literature & Culture). (Illus.). 320p. 1997. 69.95 (*1-57309-063-8*, Cath Scholar Pr) Intl Scholars.

— Bartolome de Cardenas "El Bermejo" Pintor Errante en la Corona de Aragon. Danieri, Silvia S., tr. (SPA., Illus.). 320p. 1997. 69.95 (*1-57309-138-3*, Cath Scholar Pr); pap. 49.95 (*1-57309-137-5*, Cath Scholar Pr) Intl Scholars.

***Berg, Stacie Zoe.** Living with Breast Cancer. 400p. 1999. pap. 15.95 (*0-02-863491-8*) Macmillan.

***Berg, Stephen.** Body Electric: 25 Years of America's Best Poetry from the American Poetry Review. LC 99-55513. 512p. 2000. 35.00 (*0-393-04826-8*) Norton.

Berg, Stephen. Crow with No Mouth: Ikkyu Fifteenth Century Zen Master. LC 88-63223. 80p. (Orig.). 1989. pap. 10.00 (*1-55659-022-9*) Copper Canyon.

— Daughters: Poems by Stephen Berg. LC 77-134465. 1971. pap. 6.55 (*0-672-61153-8*, Bobbs) Macmillan.

***Berg, Stephen.** Footnotes to an Unfinished Poem. LC 00-21880. 2000. pap. write for info. (*0-914061-82-8*) Orchises Pr.

— Halo. 64p. 2000. 19.95 (*1-878818-79-1*, Pub. by Sheep Meadow) U Pr of New Eng.

Berg, Stephen. In It. Poems. LC 85-28842. 88p. (Orig.). 1986. 9.95 (*0-252-01235-6*) U of Ill Pr.

— New & Selected Poems. LC 91-72065. 200p. (Orig.). 1992. 21.00 (*1-55659-044-X*); pap. 12.00 (*1-55659-043-1*) Copper Canyon.

— Oblivion: Poems. 152p. 1995. 12.95 (*0-252-06457-7*) U of Ill Pr.

***Berg, Stephen.** Porno Diva/Numero Uno: An Anonymous Confession. (Profile Ser.). 88p. 2000. pap. 12.95 (*1-889097-39-X*) Hard Pr MA.

Berg, Stephen. Shaving. LC 96-61434. 128p. 1998. 23.95 (*1-884800-17-3*); pap. 12.95 (*1-884800-14-9*) Four Way Bks.

— Steel Cricket: Versions, 1958-1997. LC 97-4653. 240p. 1997. pap. text 16.00 (*1-55659-075-X*) Copper Canyon.

— With Akhmatova at the Black Gates: Variations. Poems. LC 80-14469. 86p. 1981. 14.95 (*0-252-00833-2*) U of Ill Pr.

Berg, Stephen & Mezey, Robert, eds. The New Naked Poetry: Recent American Poetry in Open Forms. LC 75-12999. 1976. pap. write for info. (*0-672-61354-9*) Macmillan.

Berg, Stephen, tr. see Sojun, Ikkyu.

Berg, Stephen, tr. see Sophocles.

Berg, Steven L. Song of a Simple, Separate Person: A Learning Styles Workbook. (Illus.). (Orig.). (C). 1995. pap. 10.00 (*0-9642273-0-4*) Back Porch Pr.

— Spirituality & Addiction: A Bibliography. xiii, 82p. (Orig.). (C). 1993. pap. 12.00 (*1-877686-06-9*) Bishop Bks.

Berg, Steven L., ed. Alcoholism & Recovery: A Manual for Pastoral Ministry. 200p. (Orig.). 1989. pap. 8.95 (*0-685-27224-9*) Guest Hse Inc.

— A Guide to Michigan Quilt Collections. (Illus.). (Orig.). 1994. pap. 7.00 (*0-9642273-1-2*) Back Porch Pr.

— Jewish Alcoholism & Drug Addiction: An Annotated Bibliography, 5. LC 93-21634. (Bibliographies & Indexes in Ethnic Studies: No. 5). 184p. 1993. lib. bdg. 65.00 (*0-313-27603-X*, Greenwood Pr) Greenwood.

Berg, Susan, jt. auth. see For Women Editors.

Berg, Susan, jt. ed. see Prevention Health Books Staff.

Berg, Susan G. & Prevention Health Books Staff. Food Smart: Savory Strategies to Defy Disease. LC 97-35545. (Women's Edge Health Enhancement Guides). 1998. write for info. (*0-87596-481-8*) Rodale Pr Inc.

***Berg, Susan G. & Prevention Health Books for Women Staff.** Women's Health Today 1999: 60 Minutes to a New You LC 99-183105. xi 307 p. 1999. write for info. (*1-57954-055-4*) Rodale Pr Inc.

Berg, Sven D. & Hassell, George. The Geddy Foundry. LC 91-19034. (Colonial Williamsburg Historic Trades Book). (Illus.). 60p. (Orig.). 1992. pap. 5.99 (*0-87935-086-5*) Colonial Williamsburg.

Berg, Temma F., et al, eds. Engendering the Word: Feminist Essays in Psychosexual Poetics. LC 88-4881. 320p. 1989. text 29.95 (*0-252-01555-X*); pap. text 15.95 (*0-252-06016-4*) U of Ill Pr.

Berg, Thomas. Linguistic Structure & Change: An Explanation from Language Processing. (Illus.). 350p. 1998. text 95.00 (*0-19-823672-7*) OUP.

Berg, Thomas C. The State & Religion in a Nutshell. LC 97-51739. (Paralegal). 292p. (C). 1998. pap. text 13.50 (*0-314-22663-X*) West Pub.

Berg, Toni. Breastfeeding: Something Special for Mother & Baby. rev. ed. (Illus.). 26p. 1992. reprint ed. pap. 2.95 (*0-945886-10-1*) New Futures.

Berg, Vibeke. Yoga During Pregnancy. 1983. 6.95 (*0-671-45987-2*, Fireside) S&S Trade Pap.

— Yoga in Pregnancy. 135p. 1983. 12.95 (*0-940500-24-8*, Pub. by D B Taraporevala) Asia Bk Corp.

Berg, Viola Jacobson. Pathways for the Poet. 130p. 1999. pap. write for info. (*1-889732-18-4*) Word-For-Word.

An Asterisk (*) at the beginning of an entry indicates that the title is appearing for the first time.

Berg, W. & Martin, L. Emile Zola. (Twayne's World Authors Ser.). 160p. 1992. 32.00 (*0-8057-8271-0*) Macmillan.

Berg, Warren G. Historical Dictionary of Malta. LC 95-10312. (European Historical Dictionaries Ser.: No. 10). 190p. 1995. 42.00 (*0-8108-3018-3*) Scarecrow.

Berg-Weger, Marla. Daughters Caring for Elderly Parents: Relationship Between Stress & Choice. rev. ed. LC 96-821. (Studies on the Elderly in America). (Illus.). 172p. 1996. text 20.00 (*0-8153-2401-4*) Garland.

***Berg-Weger, Marla & Birkenmaier, Julie.** The Practicum Companion for Social Work: Integrating Class & Field Work. LC 99-16837. 305p. (C). 1999. pap. text 36.00 (*0-321-04519-X*) Addson-Wesley Educ.

Berg, William J. The Visual Novel: Emile Zola & the Art of His Times. 304p. 1992. 45.00 (*0-271-00826-1*) Pa St U Pr.

Berg, William J., et al. Saint Oedipus: Psychocritical Approaches to Flaubert's Art. LC 81-17441. 312p. 1982. text 47.50 (*0-8014-1383-4*) Cornell U Pr.

Berg, William J., tr. see Bertin, Jacques.

Berg, William M. & Boguslaw, Robert. Communication & Community: An Approach to Social Psychology. (Illus.). 400p. (C). 1985. text 42.60 (*0-13-153818-7*) P-H.

Berga, Gilda, jt. auth. see Berger, Melvin.

Berga, L., ed. Dam Safety: Proceedings of an International Symposium on New Trends Guidelines on Dam Safety, Barcelona, 17-19 June 1998, 2 vols. (Illus.). 1616p. (C). 1998. text 156.00 (*90-5410-974-2*, Pub. by A A Balkema) Ashgate Pub Co.

Berga, Tatjana. Latvian Collections: Anglo-Saxon & Later British Coins. (Sylloge of Coins of the British Isles, Vol 45; British Academy Ser.). (Illus.). 88p. 1997. text 80.00 (*0-19-726163-9*) OUP.

Bergad, Laird W. Coffee & the Growth of Agrarian Capitalism in Nineteenth-Century Puerto Rico. LC 82-61354. 271p. reprint ed. pap. 84.10 (*0-7837-0082-2*, 204034300016) Bks Demand.

— Cuban Rural Society in the Nineteenth Century: The Social & Economic History of Monoculture in Matanzas. LC 89-36040. 449p. reprint ed. pap. 139.20 (*0-608-02946-7*, 206401200008) Bks Demand.

***Bergad, Laird W.** Slavery & the Demographic & Economic History of Minas Gerais, Brazil, 1720-1888. LC 98-50559. (Latin American Studies: Vol. 85). (Illus.). 400p. (C). 1999. 54.95 (*0-521-65266-9*) Cambridge U Pr.

Bergad, Laird W., et al. The Cuban Slave Market, 1790-1880. (Cambridge Latin American Studies: No. 79). (Illus.). 272p. (C). 1995. text 74.95 (*0-521-48059-0*) Cambridge U Pr.

Bergad, Ruth. Early Childhood Units for Music. (Illus.). 144p. 1995. pap., teacher ed. 12.95 (*1-55734-205-9*, TCM205) Tchr Create Mat.

— Ears for Little Gleaners. unabridged ed. (Children's Heritage Ser.). (Illus.). 95p. (J). (gr. 4-6). 1996. pap. 5.50 (*1-58339-129-0*, D29) Triangle Press.

Bergadano, Francesco & DeRaedt, Luc, eds. Machine Learning: EMCL-94. LC 94-8266. (Lecture Notes in Computer Science, Lecture Notes in Artificial Intelligence Ser.: Vol. 784). 1994. write for info. (*3-540-57868-4*) Spr-Verlag.

Bergadano, Francesco & Gunetti, Daniele. Inductive Logic Programming: From Machine Learning to Software Engineering. LC 95-14956. (Logic Programming Ser.). 1995. 40.00 (*0-262-02393-8*) MIT Pr.

Bergadano, Francesco & Raedt, Luc, eds. Machine Learning: EMCL-94. LC 94-8266. (Lecture Notes in Computer Science, Lecture Notes in Artificial Intelligence Ser.: Vol. 784). 1994. 61.95 (*0-387-57868-4*) Spr-Verlag.

Bergado, D. T., et al. Improvement Techniques of Soft Ground in Subsiding & Lowland Environment. (Illus.). 232p. (C). 1994. text 85.00 (*90-5410-144-X*, Pub. by A A Balkema) Ashgate Pub Co.

— Improving Techniques of Soft Ground in Subsiding & Lowland Environment. (Illus.). 222p. (C). 1994. pap. 45.00 (*90-5410-153-9*, Pub. by A A Balkema) Ashgate Pub Co.

— Soft Ground Improvement in Lowland Environment. 440p. 1996. pap. 52.00 (*0-7844-0151-9*) Am Soc Civil Eng.

Bergado, D. T., jt. auth. see Chandra, S.

Bergaigne, Abel. Vedic Religion. Paranjpe, V. G., tr. 1978. 55.00 (*0-89684-006-9*, Pub. by Motilal Bnarsidass) S Asia.

Bergal, David & Schmid, Hillel, eds. Organizational Change & Development in Human Service Organizations: Administration in Social Work, Vol. 16, Nos. 3/4. LC 92-41586. (Illus.). 223p. 1993. lib. bdg. 49.95 (*1-56024-373-2*) Haworth Pr.

Bergala, Alain. Magnum Cinema: Photographs from 50 Years of Movie-Making. (Illus.). 360p. (C). 1995. 69.95 (*0-7148-3375-4*, Pub. by Phaidon Press) Phaidon Pr.

— Magnum Cinema: Photographs from 50 Years of Movie-Making. (Illus.). 360p. 1998. pap. 29.95 (*0-7148-3772-5*, Pub. by Phaidon Press) Phaidon Pr.

Bergalli, Roberto & Sumner, Colin. Social Control & Political Order: European Perspectives at the End of the Century. LC 96-68422. 176p. 1996. 69.95 (*0-8039-7558-9*); pap. 24.95 (*0-8039-7559-7*) Sage.

Bergamar, Kate. Discovering Hill Figures. 1989. pap. 25.00 (*0-85263-798-5*, Pub. by Shire Pubns) St Mut.

***Bergamar, Kate.** Discovering Hill Figures. (Illus.). 96p. 1999. pap. 9.50 (*0-7478-0345-5*, Pub. by Shire Pubns) Parkwest Pubns.

Bergamin, Jose. Beltenebros: De la Naturaleza y Figuracion Fronteriza De la Poesia. 77p. (C). 1969. 3.75 (*0-8477-3112-X*); pap. 3.00 (*0-8477-3113-8*) U of PR Pr.

— Poems of Jose Bergamin (1896-1983) Echoes of a Distant Sea. Garrison, David, tr. from SPA. LC 91-4715. (Hispanic Literature Ser.: Vol. 12). (ENG & SPA., Illus.). 114p. 1991. lib. bdg. 59.95 (*0-7734-9778-1*) E Mellen.

Bergamini, Andrea. Beethoven & the Classical Age. (Masters of Music Ser.). (Illus.). 64p. (YA). (gr. 6 up). 1999. 14.95 (*0-7641-5133-9*) Barron.

***Bergamini, Andrea.** History of Rock Music. (Masters of Music Ser.). 64p. (J). 2000. pap. 14.95 (*0-7641-5137-1*) Barron.

— Music of the World. 64p. 1999. 14.95 (*0-7641-5135-5*) Barron.

Bergamot, Stella, jt. auth. see Markley, Elaine.

Bergan, Bill, ed. Championship Drills for Basketball Vols. 1-4: Offensive Drills, 4 bks., Set. 64p. (Orig.). 1980. pap. 25.95 (*0-932741-98-3*) Championship Bks & Vid Prodns.

— Championship Drills for Football Vols. 1-4: Offensive Drills, 4 bks., Set. 64p. 1982. pap. 25.95 (*1-56404-000-3*) Championship Bks & Vid Prodns.

Bergan, Francis. The History of the New York Court of Appeals, 1847-1932. LC 84-16960. 368p. 1985. text 69.00 (*0-231-05950-7*) Col U Pr.

Bergan, Helen J. Climbing Kilimanjaro: An African Odyssey. LC 99-94331. (Illus.). 168p. 1999. pap. 14.95 (*0-9615277-4-9*) BioGuide Pr.

— Where the Information Is: A Guide to Electronic Research for Nonprofit Organizations. LC 96-96139. (Illus.). 257p. (Orig.). 1996. pap. 29.95 (*0-9615277-2-2*) BioGuide Pr.

— Where the Money Is: A Fund Raiser's Guide to the Rich. 2nd enl. rev. ed. LC 91-76590. (Illus.). 257p. (Orig.). 1992. pap. 29.95 (*0-9615277-6-5*) BioGuide Pr.

***Bergan, J. J. & Ballard, J., eds.** Chronic Venous Insufficiency: Diagnosis & Treatment. LC 99-22604. xii, 204p. 2000. 265.00 (*1-85233-172-0*, Pub. by Spr-Verlag) Spr-Verlag.

Bergan, J. R. & Kratochwill, Thomas R. Behavioral Consultation & Therapy. (Applied Clinical Psychology Ser.). (Illus.). 526p. (C). 1989. 85.00 (*0-306-43345-1*, Plen Insight) Perseus Pubng.

Bergan, J. R., jt. auth. see Kratochwill, Thomas R.

Bergan, Jack R., jt. auth. see Feld, Jason K.

Bergan, Jacqueline Syrup & Schwan, S. Marie. Birth. (Take & Receive Ser.). (Illus.). 168p. 1985. pap. 6.95 (*0-88489-170-4*) St Marys.

— Forgiveness. (Take & Receive Ser.). 184p. 1985. pap. 6.95 (*0-88489-169-0*) St Marys.

— Freedom. (Take & Receive Ser.). 180p. 1988. pap. 6.95 (*0-88489-172-0*) St Marys.

— Love. (Take & Receive Ser.). 144p. 1985. pap. 6.95 (*0-88489-168-2*) St Marys.

— Praying with Ignatius of Loyola. Koch, Carl, ed. (Companions for the Journey Ser.). (Illus.). 120p. 1991. pap. 8.95 (*0-88489-263-8*) St Marys.

— Surrender. (Take & Receive Ser.). 168p. 1986. pap. 6.95 (*0-88489-171-2*) St Marys.

— Taste & See: Prayer Services for Gatherings of Faith. Koch, Carl, ed. 112p. 1996. pap. 7.95 (*0-88489-377-4*); spiral bd. 9.95 (*0-88489-391-X*) St Marys.

Bergan, John & Guzzetta, Vincent. U. S. Sailing & Yachting First Aid. 485p. 1992. pap. 15.00 (*1-882502-04-3*) US Sail Assn.

Bergan, John J. Aortic Surgery. 1989. text 165.00 (*0-7216-2914-8*, W B Saunders Co) Harcrt Hlth Sci Grp.

— Venous Disorders. (Vademecum Ser.). 2000. spiral bd. 45.00 (*1-57059-528-3*) Landes Bioscience.

Bergan, John J., jt. ed. see AbuRahma, Ali F.

Bergan, John J., jt. ed. see Gloviczki, Peter.

Bergan, John J., jt. ed. see Goldman, Mitchel P.

Bergan, John J., ed. see Symposium on Venous Problems (1976: Northwestern U.

Bergan, John R., et al. The Classroom Activity Library. (Illus.). 188p. (Orig.). 1994. pap. 24.95 (*1-888639-00-8*, CAL) Assessmnt Tech.

— Times for Learning. (Illus.). 237p. (Orig.). 1994. pap. 21.95 (*1-888639-01-6*, TFL) Assessmnt Tech.

Bergan, John R., jt. auth. see Feld, Jason K.

Bergan, Pal & Wik, Audun. RW8 Manual: Tips & Tricks for 8-Way Sequential Freefall Skydiving. 96p. (Orig.). 1990. pap. text 14.95 (*0-9607814-6-3*) AeroGraphics.

***Bergan, Ronald.** Coen Brothers. (Illus.). 272p. 2000. pap. text 14.95 (*1-56025-254-5*, Thunders Mouth) Avalon NY.

Bergan, Ronald. Francis Ford Coppola--Close Up: The Making of His Movies. (Directors Close Up Ser.). (Illus.). 144p. 1998. pap. 13.95 (*1-56025-194-8*, Thunders Mouth) Avalon NY.

— The Great Theatres of London. (Illus.). 200p. 1997. 24.95 (*1-85375-057-3*, Pub. by Prion) Trafalgar.

— Jean Renoir: Projections of Paradise. (Illus.). 378p. 1995. pap. 14.95 (*0-87951-608-9*, Pub. by Overlook Pr) Penguin Putnam.

— Katharine Hepburn: An Independent Woman. LC 95-83505. (Illus.). 192p. 1996. 27.45 (*1-55970-351-2*, Pub. by Arcade Pub Inc) Time Warner.

— Sergei Eisenstein: A Life in Conflict. LC 98-31822. (Illus.). 248p. 1999. 29.95 (*0-87951-924-X*, Pub. by Overlook Pr) Penguin Putnam.

Bergan, T., jt. auth. see Norris, John R.

Bergan, Tom, ed. Urinary Tract Infections. LC 97-2774. (Infectiology Ser.: Vol. 1, 1997). (Illus.). 142p. 1997. 97.50 (*3-8055-6440-6*) S Karger.

Bergant, Dianne. The Earth Is the Lord's: The Bible, Ecology, & Worship. LC 98-5538. (American Essays in Liturgy Ser.). 72p. 1998. pap. 6.95 (*0-8146-2528-2*) Liturgical Pr.

— Introduction to the Bible. (Collegeville Bible Commentary - Old Testament Ser.: Vol. 1). 72p. 1985. pap. 4.95 (*0-8146-1369-1*, Liturg Pr Bks) Liturgical Pr.

— Israel's Wisdom Literature: A Liberation-Critical Reading of the Old Testament, 4 vols., Vol. 1. Laffey, Aliee L., ed. LC 97-203. 224p. 1997. pap. 20.00 (*0-8006-2875-6*, Fortress Pr) Augsburg Fortress.

— Song of Songs: The Love Poetry of Scripture. (Spiritual Commentaries on the New Testament Ser.). 152p. 1998. pap. 9.95 (*1-56548-100-3*) New City.

Bergant, Dianne, ed. The Collegeville Commentary: Old Testament Series, 25 vols. pap. 111.50 (*0-8146-1394-2*, Liturg Pr Bks) Liturgical Pr.

***Bergant, Dianne & Fragomeni, Richard N.** Preaching the New Lectionary, Year C. 456p. 2000. pap. 29.95 (*0-8146-2474-X*) Liturgical Pr.

Bergant, Dianne & Fragomeni, Richard N. Preaching the New Lectionary, Year B Edition. LC 99-16138. 440p. (C). 1999. pap. 29.95 (*0-8146-2473-1*) Liturgical Pr.

Bergant, Dianne & Karris, Robert J., eds. Collegeville Bible Commentary. 1344p. 1989. 69.95 (*0-8146-1484-1*) Liturgical Pr.

— The Collegeville Bible Commentary: New Testament, NAB. LC 92-23578. 464p. 1992. pap. 16.95 (*0-8146-2211-9*) Liturgical Pr.

— The Collegeville Bible Commentary: Old Testament, NAB. LC 92-23578. 880p. 1992. pap. 24.95 (*0-8146-2210-0*) Liturgical Pr.

Bergant, Dianne, ed. see Ellis, Peter F.

Bergant, Dianne, ed. see Perelmuter, Hayim G., et al.

Bergant, Dianne, ed. see Rybolt, John E.

Bergant, Dianne, ed. see Spilly, Alphonse.

Bergant, Kathleen A. Communication Skills for Cosmotologists. 1992. pap. 19.95 (*1-56253-087-9*) Milady Pub.

Bergantino, David. Deadly Disguise: Freddy Krueger's Tales of Terror. (New Elm Street Novel Ser.: No. 6). (Orig.). (YA). 1995. mass mkt. 3.99 (*0-8125-5195-8*, Pub. by Tor Bks) St Martin.

— Help Wanted No. 5: Freddy Kreuger's Tales of Terror. (New Elm Street Novel Ser.: No. 5). (Orig.). (YA). (gr. 6 up). 1995. 3.99 (*0-8125-5193-1*, Pub. by Tor Bks) St Martin.

— Wes Craven's New Nightmare: The Real Story. 224p. 1994. mass mkt. 4.99 (*0-8125-5166-4*, Pub. by Tor Bks) St Martin.

Bergantino, David. Why I Quit the Babysitters Club. (Bone Chillers Ser.). 1997. 9.09 (*0-606-11152-2*, Pub. by Turtleback) Demco.

Bergantino, David. Zorro & the Dragon Riders. 224p. 1999. mass mkt. 5.99 (*0-8125-6768-4*) Forge Pr.

Bergantino, David & Richards, Bruce. Twice Burned No. 4: Freddy Krueger's Tales of Terror, 6. (New Elm Street Novel Ser.: No. 4). (Orig.). (YA). (gr. 6 up). 1995. 3.99 (*0-8125-5192-3*, Pub. by Tor Bks) St Martin.

— Virtual Terror No. 3: Freddy Krueger's Tales of Terror. (New Elm Street Novel Ser.: No. 3). 160p. (Orig.). (YA). (gr. 6 up). 1995. 3.99 (*0-8125-5190-7*, Pub. by Tor Bks) St Martin.

Bergantino, Len. Making an Impact in Therapy: How the Master Clinicians Intervene. LC 93-38140. 300p. 1994. pap. 50.00 (*1-56821-162-7*) Aronson.

— Psychotherapy Insight & Style: The Existential Moment. LC 86-71119. 288p. 1986. 45.00 (*0-87668-906-3*) Aronson.

Bergau, Nancy, jt. auth. see Soedharno, R.

***Bergaud, Bernard.** Dictionary of Pharmacoepidemiology. (Illus.). 250p. 2000. text 99.95 (*0-471-80361-8*) Wiley.

Bergbower, Cornelius. Sparkling Plug Collectors Guide, Vol. 1. (Illus.). 96p. (Orig.). 1986. pap. 9.95 (*0-9616653-0-0*) C Bergbower.

Bergbreiter, D. E. & Martin, R., eds. Functional Polymers. (Illus.). 224p. 1989. 79.50 (*0-306-43203-X*, Plenum Trade) Perseus Pubng.

Bergdall, Terry D. Methods for Active Participation: Experiences in Rural Development from East to Central Africa. (Illus.). 222p. 1994. pap. text 29.95 (*0-19-572785-1*) OUP.

***Bergdoll, Barry.** European Architecture 1750-1890. (Oxford History of Art Ser.). (Illus.). 288p. 2000. pap. 17.95 (*0-19-284222-6*) OUP.

Bergdoll, Barry. Leon Vaudoyer: Historicism in the Age of Industry. (Architectural History Foundation Ser.). (Illus.). 416p. 1994. 65.00 (*0-262-02380-6*) MIT Pr.

Bergdoll, Barry, et al. Mastering McKim's Plan: Columbia's First Century on Morningside Heights. LC 97-74871. (Illus.). 249p. (C). 1997. 50.00 (*1-884919-05-7*); pap. 35.00 (*1-884919-04-9*) Wallach Art Gallery.

Bergdoll, Merlin S. & Chesney, P. Joan. Toxic Shock Syndrome. (Illus.). 248p. 1990. boxed set 139.00 (*0-8493-6671-2*, R) CRC Pr.

Berge. Modeling for Synthesis. (Current Issues in Electronic Modeling (CIEM) Ser.). Date not set. lib. bdg. write for info. (*0-7923-9877-7*) Kluwer Academic.

Berge, Ann F. La, see La Berge, Ann F.

***Berge, Bjorn.** Ecology of Building Materials. (Illus.). 464p. 2000. pap. 94.95 (*0-7506-3394-8*, Architectural Pr) Buttrwrth-Heinemann.

***Berge, Britt-Marie & Ve, Hildur.** Action Research for Gender Equity. LC 99-16161. (Feminist Educational Thinking Ser.). 1999. 27.95 (*0-335-20022-2*) OpUniv Pr.

Berge, C. Graphs. rev. ed. (Mathematical Library: Vol. 6). xiv,414p. 1985. 138.00 (*0-444-87603-0*) Elsevier.

— Hypergraphs: Combinatorics of Finite Sets. (Mathematical Library: No. 45). 256p. 1989. 122.50 (*0-444-87489-5*, North Holland) Elsevier.

Berge, Carol. Secrets, Gossip & Slander. 234p. (Orig.). 1984. pap. 9.95 (*0-918408-20-2*) Ishmael Reed.

— Zebras, or, Contour Lines. LC 91-68421. 320p. (Orig.). 1991. pap. 20.00 (*0-916185-01-X*) Ctr Pr NM.

Berge, Carol, ed. see Crews, Judson.

Berge, Carol, ed. see Sagan, Miriam.

Berge, Claude. Topological Spaces: Including a Treatment of Mutli-Valued Functions, Vector Spaces & Convexity. Patterson, E. M., tr. (Illus.). 284p. 1997. reprint ed. pap. text 8.95 (*0-486-69653-7*) Dover.

Berge, Erling. Law & the Governance of Renewable Resources. LC 98-26344. 1998. pap. 29.95 (*1-55815-504-X*) ICS Pr.

Berge, George W. The Free Pass Bribery System: Showing How the Railroads, Through the Free Pass Bribery System, Procure the Government Away from the People. LC 73-19128. (Politics & People Ser.). (Illus.). 338p. 1974. reprint ed. 25.95 (*0-405-05853-5*) Ayer.

Berge, H. C. Ten, see Ten Berge, H. C.

Berge Henegouwen, G. P. Van, see Van Berge Henegouwen, G. P., ed.

Berge, James. Automating the Welding Process. LC 93-27580. 220p. 1994. 42.95 (*0-8311-3051-2*) Indus Pr.

Berge, Jean-Michel. Hardware - Software Codesign & Co-Verification. LC 96-52088. (Current Issues in Electronic Modeling Ser.). 188p. (C). 1996. lib. bdg. 110.00 (*0-7923-9689-8*) Kluwer Academic.

— Meta-Modeling: Performance & Information Modeling, 2 vols., Set. LC 96-18914. (Current Issues in Electronic Modeling Ser.). 152p. (C). 1996. lib. bdg. 115.00 (*0-614-18916-0*, D Reidel) Kluwer Academic.

— Meta-Modeling: Performance & Information Modeling, Set, Issues 5-8. LC 96-41149. (Current Issues in Electronic Modeling Ser.). 176p. (C). 1996. text 318.00 (*0-7923-9690-1*) Kluwer Academic.

— VHDL, 1992: The New Features of the VHDL Hardware Description Language. 232p. (C). 1993. text 131.50 (*0-7923-9356-2*) Kluwer Academic.

Berge, Jean-Michel, ed. Current Issues in Electronic Modeling, Issues 9-12. LC 97-16151. 168p. (C). 1997. text 432.00 (*0-7923-9878-5*) Kluwer Academic.

— Modeling in Analog Design. (Current Issue in Electronic Modeling CIEM Ser.). 176p. (C). 1995. text 120.50 (*0-7923-9569-7*) Kluwer Academic.

— Object-Oriented Modeling. LC 96-41149. (Current Issues in Electronic Modeling Ser.). 168p. (C). 1996. lib. bdg. 125.00 (*0-7923-9688-X*) Kluwer Academic.

Berge, Jean-Michel, et al, eds. Hardware Component Modeling. LC 96-10839. (Current Issues in Electronic Modeling (CIEM) Ser.: Vol. 5). 155p. (C). 1996. lib. bdg. 99.50 (*0-7923-9686-3*) Kluwer Academic.

— Model Generation in Electronic Design. LC 95-11943. (Current Issues in Electronic Modeling CIEM Ser.: Vol. 1). 168p. (C). 1995. text 120.50 (*0-7923-9568-9*) Kluwer Academic.

— Multimedia Database Management Systems. (Kluwer International Series in Engineering & Computer Science). 216p. (C). 1997. lib. bdg. 270.00 (*0-7923-9874-2*) Kluwer Academic.

Berge, Jean-Michel, et al. Meta-Modeling: Performance & Information Modeling. Daniel, Barbara, ed. LC 96-18914. (Current Issues in Electronic Modeling Ser.). (C). 1996. lib. bdg. 115.00 (*0-7923-9687-1*, D Reidel) Kluwer Academic.

— VHDL Designer's Reference. LC 92-10613. 480p. (C). 1992. text 230.00 (*0-7923-1756-4*) Kluwer Academic.

Berge, Joerg Vanden. Golf: The Practice Book, Vol. 1. (Illus.). 170p. 1999. spiral bd. 14.95 (*3-8290-1381-7*, 520736) Konemann.

— Golf: The Practice Book: Trouble Shots, Vol. 2. (Illus.). 170p. 1999. spiral bd. 14.95 (*3-8290-2797-4*, 521041) Konemann.

Berge, Pierre. Yves Saint Laurent. (Illus.). 80p. 1997. 18.95 (*0-7893-0067-2*, Pub. by Universe) St Martin.

Berge, Pierre & Cox, Madison. Majorelle: An Artist in Morocco. LC 99-30840. (Small Books of Great Gardens Ser.). 79p. 1999. text 18.95 (*0-86565-210-4*) Vendome.

Berge, Pierre, et al. Order Within Chaos: Towards a Deterministic Approach to Turbulence. LC 86-9097. 380p. 1987. reprint ed. 175.00 (*0-471-84967-7*) Wiley.

***Berge, Wendell.** Cartels: Challenge to a Free World. (Business Classics Ser.). 266p. 2000. pap. 34.95 (*1-58798-013-4*) Beard Bks.

Berge, Zane & Collins, Marie. Computer-Mediated Communications & the Online Classroom: Higher Education, Vol. 2. LC 94-23868. (Communication Series: Communication Pedagogy & Practice Subseries). 224p. 1994. pap. text 22.95 (*1-881303-11-X*) Hampton Pr NJ.

— Computer-Mediated Communications & the Online Classroom Vol. 1: Overview & Perspectives. LC 94-23868. (Communication Series: Communication Pedagogy & Practice Subseries). 256p. 1994. text 52.50 (*1-881303-08-X*); pap. text 22.95 (*1-881303-09-8*) Hampton Pr NJ.

— Computer-Mediated Communications & the Online Classroom Vol. 2: Higher Education. LC 94-23868. (Communication Series). 224p. 1994. text 47.50 (*1-881303-10-1*) Hampton Pr NJ.

Berge, Zane & Collins, Mauri. Computer - Mediated Communication & the Online Classroom Vol. 3: Distance Education. Phillips, Gerald M., ed. (Communication Series: Communication Pedagogy & Practice Subseries). 272p. (C). 1994. text 55.00 (*1-881303-12-8*); pap. text 22.95 (*1-881303-13-6*) Hampton Pr NJ.

Berge, Zane & Collins, Mauri L., eds. Wired Together Vol. 1: The Online Classroom in K-12: Perspectives & Instructional Design. LC 97-22976. (Illus.). 272p. (C). 1997. pap. text 22.95 (*1-57273-087-0*) Hampton Pr NJ.

— Wired Together Vol. 1: The Online Classroom in K-12: Perspectives & Instructional Design. LC 97-22976. (Illus.). 280p. (C). 1997. text 55.00 (*1-57273-086-2*) Hampton Pr NJ.

— Wired Together Vol. 2: The Online Classroom in K-12: Case Studies. LC 97-22976. (Illus.). 240p. (C). 1997. text 49.50 (*1-57273-088-9*); pap. text 21.95 (*1-57273-089-7*) Hampton Pr NJ.

B

An Asterisk (*) at the beginning of an entry indicates that the title is appearing for the first time.

— Wired Together Vol. 3: The Online Classroom in K-12: Teacher Education & Professional Development. LC 97-22976. 224p. (C). 1997. text 45.00 (*1-57273-090-0*); pap. text 21.95 (*1-57273-091-9*) Hampton Pr NJ.

— Wired Together Vol. 4: The Online Classroom in K-12: Writing, Reading & Language Acquisition. 272p. (C). 1997. text 55.00 (*1-57273-092-7*) Hampton Pr NJ.

Berge, Zane & Collins, Mauri L., eds. Wired Together Vol. 4: The Online Classroom in K-12: Writing, Reading & Language Acquisition. 272p. (C). 1997. pap. text 22.95 (*1-57273-093-5*) Hampton Pr NJ.

Berge, Zane L. Distance Training: How Innovative Organizations Are Using Technology to Maximize Learning & Meet Business Objectives. Schreiber, Deborah A., ed. LC 98-40416. (Business & Management Ser.). xliii, 441p. 1998. 34.95 (*0-7879-4313-4*) Jossey-Bass.

***Berge, Zane L.** Sustaining Distance Training: Integrating Learning Technologies Into the Fabric of the Enterprise. 2000. 36.95 (*0-7879-5331-8*) Jossey-Bass.

Bergee, C. Jaye. Interior Design Law & Business Practices. 232p. 1994. 80.00 (*0-471-58342-1*) Wiley.

Bergee, Jean-Michel. High-Level System Modeling: Specification Languages. Levia, Oz et al, eds. (Current Issues in Electronic Modeling CIEM Ser.: Vol. 3). 176p. (C). 1995. text 120.50 (*0-7923-9632-4*) Kluwer Academic.

Bergee, Lee K. Guest of the Emperor: The Personal Story of Ex-POW Frank O. Promnitz, USMC. LC 87-81073. 1988. lib. bdg. 19.95 (*0-9620719-0-0*) Four Freedoms Pr.

Bergeijk, Herman & Hauptmann, Deborah. Notations. LC 98-220735. (Illus.). 224p. 1998. pap. 30.00 (*90-5662-072-X*, Pub. by NAi Uitgevers) Dist Art Pubs.

Bergeijk, Peter A. van. Economic Diplomacy, Trade & Commercial Policy: Positive & Negative Sanctions in a New World Order. LC 94-6035. 208p. 1994. 90.00 (*1-85278-893-3*) E Elgar.

Bergeijk, Peter A. Van, see Van Bergeijk, Peter A.

Bergel, Alice R., jt. ed. see Bergel, Kurt.

Bergel, Alice R., ed. & tr. see Schweitzer, Albert, et al.

***Bergel, Colin.** Mail by the Pail. (Illus.). 32p. 2000. 16.95 (*0-8143-2890-3*, Great Lks Bks) Wayne St U Pr.

— Mail by the Pail. LC 00-9687. (Illus.). (J). 2000. pap. write for info. (*0-8143-2891-1*) Wayne St U Pr.

Bergel, Gary P. When You Were Formed in Secret - Abortion in America. 9th rev. ed. (Illus.). 32p. 1998. pap. 1.00 (*0-9662714-0-8*) IFA.

Bergel, Kurt, ed. Ferdinand von Saar: Zehn Studien. LC 94-49203. (Studies in Austrian Literature, Culture, & Thought). 221p. 1995. 33.00 (*1-57241-004-3*) Ariadne CA.

Bergel, Kurt & Bergel, Alice R., eds. Albert Schweitzer & Alice Ehlers: A Friendship in Letters. 132p. (C). 1991. lib. bdg. 39.00 (*0-8191-8327-X*) U Pr of Amer.

Bergel, Kurt, ed. & tr. see Schweitzer, Albert, et al.

Bergel, Kurt, tr. see Von Saar, Ferdinand.

Bergel, Thomas, jt. auth. see Blewitt, Mary.

Bergeles, G., jt. ed. see Rodi, Wolfgang.

***Bergelson, David.** Descent. Sherman, Joseph, tr. from YID. LC 99-36857. (Texts & Translations Ser.). 240p. 1999. pap. 9.95 (*0-87352-788-7*) Modern Lang.

— The Stories of David Bergelson: Yiddish Short Fiction from Russia. Werman, Golda, ed. & tr. by. LC 96-1795. (Judaic Traditions in Literature, Music, & Art Ser.). 160p. 1996. text 39.95 (*0-8156-2712-2*, WESD) Syracuse U Pr.

Bergelson, V., et al, eds. Convergence in Ergodic Theory & Probability. LC 96-21518. (Ohio State University Mathematical Research Institute Publications: Vol. 5). xi, 445p. (C). 1996. lib. bdg. 98.95 (*3-11-014219-8*, 100/96) De Gruyter.

***Bergelson, V. & McCutcheon, Randall.** An Ergodic LP Polynomial Szemerbedi Theorem. LC 00-36258. 2000. write for info. (*0-8218-2657-3*) Am Math.

Bergeman, C. S. Aging: Genetic & Environmental Influences. LC 97-4592. (Individual Differences & Development Ser.). 160p. 1997. 31.00 (*0-8039-7377-2*); pap. 13.99 (*0-8039-7378-0*) Sage.

Bergeman, George W. & Scott, James P. TUTOR WBK APP 20/20 STATISTICS. 208p. (C). 1986. pap. text 21.00 (*0-03-002867-1*) SCP.

Bergemann, Verna E., jt. auth. see Reed, Arthea J.

Bergen. Found American Publication Education. 3rd ed. 1999. text 32.00 (*0-07-235739-8*) McGraw.

— Mike Lawrence's Workbook on the Two-over-One System. LC 90-159351. 189p. 1987. pap. 11.95 (*0-939460-35-1*) Devyn Pr.

***Bergen.** Power Systems Analysis. 2nd ed. LC 99-20875. 619p. 1999. 105.00 (*0-13-691990-1*) P-H.

Bergen. Ultimate Rugrats Trivia Sticker Book. (Rugrats Ser.). (J). Date not set. pap. 5.99 (*0-689-82892-6*) S&S Childrens.

Bergen, Abe. Living the Beatitudes. (Fast Lane Bible Studies Ser.). (Illus.). 76p. (J). (gr. 7-9). 1994. pap. 12.95 (*0-87303-211-X*) Faith & Life.

Bergen, Adrienne F., et al. Positioning for Function: The Wheelchair & Other Assistive Technologies. (Illus.). (Orig.). (C). 1990. pap. text 49.95 (*0-911681-04-3*) Valhalla Rehab.

Bergen, Bernard J. The Banality of Evil: Hannah Arendt & "The Final Solution" LC 98-4044. 208p. 1998. 58.00 (*0-8476-9209-4*); pap. 22.95 (*0-8476-9210-8*) Rowman.

— Illumination by Darkness: Freud & the Social Bond. LC 91-33002. (Reshaping of Psychoanalysis: From Sigmund Freud to Ernest Becker Ser.: Vol. 1). 148p. (C). 1992. text 39.95 (*0-8204-1759-9*) P Lang Pubng.

Bergen, Bernard J., jt. auth. see Arney, William R.

Bergen, Bernard J., jt. auth. see Rosenberg, Stanley D.

Bergen, Bernice B. Sarasota Times Past: A Reflective Collection of the Florida Gulf Coast. (Illus.). 192p. 1993. pap. 19.95 (*0-9633461-3-X*) Valiant Pr.

Bergen, Betsy M. Human Sexuality. 5th ed. (C). 1995. pap. text, student ed. 26.25 (*0-673-99073-7*) Addson-Wesley Educ.

Bergen, Brooksie & Bergen, John. Carefree Canoeing in Florida. LC 97-5439. (Illus.). 162p. 1997. pap. 16.95 (*0-88415-171-9*, 5171) Gulf Pub.

Bergen, Doris. Assessment Methods for Infants & Toddlers: Transdisciplinary Team Approaches. LC 94-12519. (Early Childhood Education Ser.). 336p. 1994. 52.00 (*0-8077-3380-6*) Tchrs Coll.

— Assessment Methods for Infants & Toddlers: Transdisciplinary Team Approaches. LC 94-12519. (Early Childhood Education Ser.). 336p. (C). 1994. pap. text 25.95 (*0-8077-3379-2*) Tchrs Coll.

— Play As a Medium for Learning & Development. LC 98-17376. 144p. 1998. reprint ed. pap. text 18.00 (*0-87173-142-8*) ACEI.

Bergen, Doris, jt. ed. see Fromberg, Doris P.

Bergen, Doris L. Twisted Cross: The German Christian Movement in the Third Reich. LC 95-17954. (Illus.). 370p. (C). 1996. pap. text 19.95 (*0-8078-4560-4*); lib. bdg. 49.95 (*0-8078-2253-1*) U of NC Pr.

Bergen, Edgar. How to Become a Ventriloquist. 20.95 (*0-88411-824-X*) Amereon Ltd.

***Bergen, Edgar.** How to Become a Ventriloquist. LC 99-54545. 2000. pap. 3.95 (*0-486-41086-2*) Dover.

Bergen, Fanny D., ed. Animal & Plant Lore, Collected from the Oral Tradition of English Speaking Folk. LC 99-4363. (AFS Memoirs Ser.). 1972. reprint ed. 30.00 (*0-527-01059-6*) Periodicals Srv.

— Current Superstitions, Collected from the Oral Tradition of English Speaking Folk. LC 04-4052. (AFS Memoirs Ser.: Vol. 4). 1972. reprint ed. 30.00 (*0-527-01056-1*) Periodicals Srv.

***Bergen, Glenn.** MCSE Upgrading from NT 4 to 2000 Exam Prep. (Exam Prep Ser.). 700p. 2000. pap. 49.99 (*1-57610-691-8*) Coriolis Grp.

Bergen, Henry, ed. Lydgate's Fall of Princes, Pt. I. (EETS, ES Ser.: Vol. 121). 1969. reprint ed. 30.00 (*0-8115-3413-8*) Periodicals Srv.

— Lydgate's Fall of Princes, Pt. II. (EETS, ES Ser.: Vol. 122). 1969. reprint ed. 30.00 (*0-8115-3414-6*) Periodicals Srv.

— Lydgate's Fall of Princes, Pt. III. (EETS, ES Ser.: Vol. 123). 1969. reprint ed. 30.00 (*0-8115-3415-4*) Periodicals Srv.

— Lydgate's Fall of Princes, Pt. IV. (EETS, ES Ser.: Vol. 124). 1969. reprint ed. 30.00 (*0-8115-3416-2*) Periodicals Srv.

— Lydgate's Fall of Princes, Vol. I. (EETS Extra Ser.: Vol. 121). 1967. reprint ed. 30.00 (*0-19-722572-1*, Pub. by EETS) Boydell & Brewer.

— Lydgate's Fall of Princes, Vol. II. (EETS Extra Ser.: Vol. 122). 1967. reprint ed. 30.00 (*0-19-722573-X*, Pub. by EETS) Boydell & Brewer.

— Lydgate's Fall of Princes, Vol. III. (EETS Extra Ser.: Vol. 123). 1967. reprint ed. 30.00 (*0-19-722574-8*, Pub. by EETS) Boydell & Brewer.

— Lydgate's Fall of Princes, Vol. IV. (EETS Extra Ser.: Vol. 124). 1967. reprint ed. 30.00 (*0-19-722575-6*, Pub. by EETS) Boydell & Brewer.

Bergen, Henry, ed. see Lydgate, John.

Bergen, Jeffrey & Montgomery, Susan, eds. Advances in Hopf Algebras. LC 94-804. (Lecture Notes in Pure & Applied Mathematics Ser.: Vol. 158). (Illus.). 344p. 1994. pap. text 145.00 (*0-8247-9065-0*) Dekker.

Bergen, Jeremy, jt. auth. see Enns, Aiden S.

Bergen, John, jt. auth. see Bergen, Brooksie.

Bergen, John J., ed. Spanish in the United States: Sociolinguistic Issues. LC 90-32166. (Illus.). 179p. 1990. reprint ed. pap. 55.50 (*0-608-04092-4*, 206482400011) Bks Demand.

Bergen, John J. & Bills, Garland D., eds. Spanish & Portuguese in Social Context. LC 83-9076. 124p. (Orig.). reprint ed. pap. 38.50 (*0-7837-6306-9*, 204602100010) Bks Demand.

Bergen, Lara. Discover the United States of America: State Stats, Fun Facts & a Puzzle of the 50 States. (Puzzlebook Ser.). (Illus.). 52p. (J). (gr. 2-7). 1999. 14.99 (*1-58476-000-1*) Innovative Kids.

— Find Your Way to the Lost World: Jurassic Park. LC 96-80492. (Lost World). (Illus.). 64p. (Orig.). (J). (gr. 1-6). 1997. pap. 4.95 (*0-448-41574-7*, G & D) Peng Put Young Read.

***Bergen, Lara.** Into the Woods. (Illus.). (J). 2000. 9.34 (*0-606-18779-0*) Turtleback.

Bergen, Lara. The Rat Pack: Rizzo's Countdown Adenture. LC 97-72240. (Muppet Books Ser.). (Illus.). 24p. (J). 1997. 4.95 (*0-448-41561-5*, G & D) Peng Put Young Read.

— Sleepover. LC 96-153867. (J). 1996. pap. 7.00 (*0-448-41332-9*, G & D) Peng Put Young Read.

***Bergen, Lara.** X-Men. (Illus.). (J). (ps-3). 2000. pap. 4.99 (*0-440-41712-0*, YB BDD) BDD Bks Young Read.

Bergen, Lara, adapted by. Washington Irving's Rip Van Winkle, Level 2. LC 96-24335. (All Aboard Reading Ser.). (Illus.). 48p. (J). (gr. 1-3). 1997. pap. 3.95 (*0-448-41136-9*, G & D) Peng Put Young Read.

Bergen, Lara R. Bead It! A Complete Jewelry Kit. (Books & Stuff Ser.). (Illus.). 24p. (J). (gr. 3 up). 1994. pap. 14.95 (*0-448-40499-0*, G & D) Peng Put Young Read.

— Sleepover! For the Coolest Night of Your Life. (Books & Stuff Ser.). (Illus.). 32p. (J). (gr. 1 up). 1996. pap. text 9.95 (*0-448-40956-9*, G & D) Peng Put Young Read.

— Stuck on the Presidents. (Books & Stuff Ser.). (Illus.). 48p. (Orig.). (J). (gr. 2 up). 1997. pap. 7.95 (*0-448-41284-5*, G & D) Peng Put Young Read.

***Bergen, Lara Rice.** Into the Woods. (Back to Sherwood Ser.: 1). 176p. (J). (gr. 4-7). 2000. pap. 3.99 (*0-440-22853-0*, LLL BDD) BDD Bks Young Read.

— Mystery Men. LC 99-24492. 1999. pap. 4.99 (*0-440-41574-8*) Dell.

— The Trouble with Brenan. (Back to Sherwood Ser.: 2). (J). (gr. 4-7). 2000. pap. 3.99 (*0-440-22856-5*, LLL BDD) BDD Bks Young Read.

— Trouble with Brenan. (Illus.). (J). 2000. 9.34 (*0-606-18780-4*) Turtleback.

***Bergen, Lara Rice, contrib. by.** Lewis & Clark. LC 99-55477. (Explorers & Exploration Ser.). 48p. (J). 2000. 22.83 (*0-7398-1486-9*) Raintree Steck-V.

— Triceratops. LC 99-55479. (Prehistoric Creatures Then & Now Ser.). 32p. (J). 2000. lib. bdg. 22.03 (*0-7398-0103-1*) Raintree Steck-V.

Bergen, Laura R., et al. Balto: All Aboard Reading. LC 95-38057. 32p. (J). (ps-1). Date not set. pap. write for info. (*0-448-41115-6*, G & D) Peng Put Young Read.

Bergen, Linda Van, see Hogg, Richard & Van Bergen, Linda, eds.

Bergen, M. Betsy. S.g. Individual,marriage & The Family. 8th ed. (Sociology-Upper Level). 253p. (C). 1993. mass mkt., student ed. 12.00 (*0-534-19730-2*) Wadsworth Pub.

Bergen, M. Van, see Van Bergen, M.

***Bergen, Marja.** Riding the Roller Coaster: Living with Mood Disorders. 160p. 1999. pap. 14.95 (*1-896836-31-3*) NStone Publ.

Bergen, Martha, ed. Ezra & Nehemiah. 6th ed. LC 98-48093. 1999. pap. text 5.95 (*0-8054-9194-5*) Broadman.

Bergen, Marty. Better Bidding with Bergen, Vol. I: Uncontested Auctions. LC 86-159457. 199p. 1986. pap. 11.95 (*0-939460-32-7*, 1701) Devyn Pr.

— Better Bidding with Bergen, Vol. II: Competitive Auctions. LC 86-159457. 149p. 1986. pap. 9.95 (*0-939460-33-5*, 1702) Devyn Pr.

— Better Bidding with Bergen: Competitive Bidding, Fit Bids & More. 1998. pap. 9.95 (*0-910791-78-3*) Devyn Pr.

— Everyone's Guide to the New Convention Card. 152p. 1994. pap. 9.95 (*0-9634715-3-8*) L Cohen NJ.

***Bergen, Marty.** More Points Schmoints. 224p. 1999. 19.95 (*0-9637533-5-5*) Bergen Bks.

Bergen, Marty. Points Schmoints: Bergen's Winning Bridge Secrets. 224p. 1995. 19.95 (*0-9637533-2-0*) Bergen Bks.

— Points Schmoints: Bergen's Winning Bridge Secrets. Ohtaka, Kassie, tr. (ENG & JPN.). 215p. 1997. 26.50 (*0-9658055-0-6*) Knockout Bks.

— Why Play Bridge. 1999. pap. 14.95 (*0-670-86416-1*) Viking Penguin.

Bergen, Michael. How to Have Fun at Work: The Complete Employee Recreation-Services Handbook. 1989. pap. 89.50 (*0-614-05758-2*) Abbott Langer Assocs.

Bergen, Philip. Index to SABR Publications, Nineteen Eighty-Seven. 60p. 1987. pap. 3.00 (*0-910137-28-5*) Soc Am Baseball Res.

— Old Boston in Early Photograph. 18th ed. (Illus.). 128p. 1990. pap. 11.95 (*0-486-26184-0*) Dover.

Bergen, Raquel K. Issues in Intimate Violence. LC 97-45324. 314p. 1998. write for info. (*0-7619-0935-4*); pap. write for info. (*0-7619-0936-2*) Sage Pubng.

— Wife Rape: Understanding the Response of Survivors & Service Providers. LC 96-4426. (Sage Series on Violence Against Women: Vol. 2). 208p. (C). 1996. 42.00 (*0-8039-7240-7*); pap. 18.95 (*0-8039-7241-5*) Sage.

Bergen, Robert, ed. Biblical Hebrew & Discourse Linguistics. LC 94-68219. 560p. 1994. pap. text 40.00 (*1-55671-007-0*) S I L Intl.

Bergen, Robert D. First & Second Samuel. LC 98-18014. (Shepherd's Notes Ser.). 1998. 5.95 (*0-8054-9063-9*) Broadman.

— 1, 2 Samuel. LC 96-41891. (New American Commentary Ser.). 1996. 29.99 (*0-8054-0107-5*) Broadman.

Bergen, T., jt. ed. see Norris, John R.

Bergen, Teunis G. The Bergen Family: The Descendants of Hans Hansen Bergen of New York & Brooklyn, with Notes on Other Long Island Families. (Illus.). 658p. 1988. reprint ed. pap. 83.50 (*0-8328-0245-X*); reprint ed. lib. bdg. 93.50 (*0-8328-0244-1*) Higginson Bk Co.

— Register of the Early Settlers of Kings County, Long Island, N. Y. From Its First Settlement by Europeans to 1700. 452p. 1997. reprint ed. pap. 36.00 (*0-8063-4743-0*, 9121) Clearfield Co.

Bergen, Wesley J. Elisha & the End of Prophetism. (JSOTS Ser.: Vol. 286). 220p. 1999. 60.00 (*1-85075-949-9*, Pub. by Sheffield Acad) CUP Services.

Bergendahl, M. H., jt. auth. see Koschmann, A. H.

Bergendoff, Conrad. The Church of Sweden on the Delaware, 1638-1831. LC 87-71046. (Augustana Historical Society Publicatios: No. 37). 38p. 1988. pap. 5.00 (*0-910184-37-2*) Augustana.

— A History of the Augustana Library. LC 90-83651. 48p. 1990. pap. 5.00 (*0-910184-39-9*) Augustana.

— One Hundred Years of Oratorio at Augustana: A History of the Handel Oratorio Society, 1881-1980. LC 81-52434. (Augustana Historical Society Publications: No. 29). 54p. 1981. 7.50 (*0-910184-00-3*); pap. 5.00 (*0-910184-29-1*) Augustana.

Bergendoff, Conrad, ed. Letters from Andover to Hogarp, Sweden, 1858-1898. LC 88-80478. (Augustana College Library Occasional Papers, Wallin Lecture: No. 17). 53p. 1988. pap. 4.00 (*0-910182-44-2*) Augustana Coll.

Bergendoff, Conrad & Lehman, Helmut T., eds. Luther's Works: Church & Ministry II, Vol. 40. LC 55-9893. 432p. 1958. 30.00 (*0-8006-0340-0*, 1-340, Fortress Pr) Augsburg Fortress.

Bergendoff, Conrad & Van Doren, Mark. Perspective in American Education, & Doctors & Masters. (Augustana College Library Occasional Papers, Wallin Lecture: No. 7). 20p. 1961. pap. 1.00 (*0-910182-28-0*) Augustana Coll.

Bergendoff, Conrad, tr. see Mauritzson, Jules.

Bergendoff, Conrad J. Olavus Petri & the Ecclesiastical Transformation in Sweden (1521-1552) A Study in the Swedish Reformation. LC 83-45600. reprint ed. 32.50 (*0-404-19868-6*) AMS Pr.

Bergendoff, Marlowe, ed. see Gipple, Pat & Clemens, Matthew.

Bergener, Manfred, et al, eds. Aging, Health, & Healing. LC 94-23930. (Illus.). 648p. 1995. 79.00 (*0-8261-8620-3*) Springer Pub.

— Challenges in Aging. (Sandoz Lectures in Gerontology). (Illus.). 304p. 1991. text 99.95 (*0-12-090163-3*) Acad Pr.

Bergener, Manfred & Finkel, Sanford I., eds. Treating Alzheimer's & Other Dementias: Recent Research Advances. LC 94-45399. 1995. 61.95 (*0-8261-8930-X*) Springer Pub.

Bergenfeld, Nathan. Life Spirals. Jaffe, Louise, ed. (Illus.). 48p. 1987. write for info. (*0-9618733-0-2*) N Bergenfeld.

Bergengren, Ralph W. Perfect Gentleman. LC 67-23177. (Essay Index Reprint Ser.). 1977. 12.95 (*0-8369-0202-5*) Ayer.

— The Seven Ages of Man. 108p. 1977. 13.95 (*0-8369-0203-3*) Ayer.

Bergenholtz, Christina, ed. see Fotiades, Valla D.

Bergenholtz, Henning. Madagassisch-Deutsch Woerterbuch. (GER.). 656p. 1991. 135.00 (*0-7859-8555-7*, 3924690626) Fr & Eur.

Bergenholtz, Henning, et al, eds. Wegweiser Durch die Grammatik von Heinrich Bauer: Verzeichnisse und Erlauterungen. (GER.). (C). 1991. lib. bdg. 220.00 (*3-11-012577-3*) De Gruyter.

Bergenholtz, Henning & Tarp, Sven, eds. Manual of Specialised Lexicography: The Preparation of Specialised Dictionaires. LC 95-19988. (Benjamins Translation Library: No. 12). 256p. 1995. 50.00 (*1-55619-693-8*) J Benjamins Pubng Co.

Bergenn, Victor, jt. ed. see Dalton, Thomas.

Bergens. Prevert. (Classiques du XXe Siecle Ser.). pap. 9.95 (*0-685-37054-2*, F119340) Fr & Eur.

— Raymond Queneau. 34.50 (*0-685-37074-7*) Fr & Eur.

Bergenstahl, B., jt. ed. see Dickinson, E.

***Bergenthal, Kathrin.** Studien Zum Mini-boom der Nueva Narrativa Chilena: Literatur Im Neoliberalismus. 301p. 1999. 51.95 (*3-631-33612-8*) P Lang Pubng.

Bergentz, S. E. & Bergqvist, D. Iatrogenic Vascular Injuries. (Illus.). 210p. 1989. 93.95 (*0-387-50308-0*) Spr-Verlag.

Bergeon, Richard, jt. auth. see De Jager, Peter.

Berger. Childhood & Adolescence. 5th ed. 2000. teacher ed. 82.00 (*1-57259-727-5*); student ed. 13.00 (*1-57259-725-9*) Worth.

— Clinical Neurooncology, 2 vols. 2000. text. write for info. (*0-7216-8148-4*, W B Saunders Co) Harcrt Hlth Sci Grp.

— The Compensation Handbook. 4th ed. LC 99-47477. 646p. 1999. 89.95 (*0-07-134309-1*) McGraw.

— The Developing Person Through Childhood. 2000. 39.00 (*1-57259-427-6*) Worth.

— The Developing Person Through Childhood & Adolescence. LC 99-64435. 2000. 47.00 (*1-57259-417-9*) Worth.

***Berger.** The Developing Person through the Life Span. 5th ed. LC 99-87969. 2000. pap. text. write for info. (*1-57259-429-2*) Worth.

— Developing Person Through the Lifespan. 5th ed. 2000. pap. text, student ed. write for info. (*1-57259-944-8*) Worth.

Berger. A Fortunate Man. 1982. 6.95 (*0-07-544872-6*) McGraw.

— Fundamentals of Nursing: Instructors Manual with Disk. 250p. 1998. write for info. incl. disk (*0-8385-2640-3*, A2640-9) Appleton & Lange.

— Human Behavior: A Perspective for the Helping Professions 5th ed. (C). 2000. pap. text. write for info. (*0-8013-3038-6*) Addison-Wesley.

— Land Transformation. 1424p. 1993. 57.00 (*0-316-09278-9*, Aspen Law & Bus) Aspen Pub.

— Probability & Statistics. 3rd ed. 1997. 22.00 (*0-07-303744-3*) McGraw.

— The Sense of Sight. 1986. 10.95 (*0-07-544931-5*) McGraw.

— Statistics, Business & Economics. 2nd ed. 676p. (C). 1998. pap. text 52.75 (*0-536-01448-5*) Pearson Custom.

***Berger.** Your Official Grown-Ups Guide to AOL & the Internet. LC 99-51485. (Aol Press). 456p. 2000. pap. 19.99 (*0-7645-3417-3*) IDG Bks.

***Berger & Maurer.** Experimental Design for Management. 2001. pap. 60.00 (*0-534-35822-5*) Thomson Learn.

***Berger & Williams.** Fundamentals of Nursing: Media Edition. 2nd ed. 2000. pap. write for info. incl. disk (*0-13-054947-9*) P-H.

Berger & Wint, eds. New Concepts for Coating Protection of Steel Structures - STP 841. 135p. 1985. 28.00 (*0-8031-0236-4*, STP841) ASTM.

Berger, jt. auth. see Caprio.

Berger, jt. auth. see Roberts.

Berger, jt. auth. see Weinstein.

Berger, Alison J. Jesus, Teach Me to Pray; A Catholic Child's Prayerbook. 1999. 9.95 (*0-89622-967-X*) Twenty-Third.

***Berger, Leslie.** Gangs & Crime. (Crime, Justice & Punishment Ser.). 2000. 19.95 (*0-7910-5767-4*) Chelsea Hse.

An Asterisk (*) at the beginning of an entry indicates that the title is appearing for the first time.

Berger, Leslie B. Incest, Work, & Women: Understanding the Consequences of Incest on Women's Careers, Work, & Dreams. LC 98-22657. 234p. 1998. 49.95 (*0-398-06882-8*); pap. 35.95 (*0-398-06883-6*) C C Thomas.

Berger & Associates Cost Consultants, Inc. Staff. Berger Building & Design Cost File, 1982: General Construction Trades, Vol. I. LC 82-70008. (Illus.). 477p. (C). 1982. pap., per. 34.50 (*0-942564-00-6*) Building Cost File.

— Berger Building & Design Cost File, 1982: Mechanical, Electrical Trades, Vol. 2. LC 82-70008. (Illus.). 207p. (C). 1982. pap., per. 24.50 (*0-942564-01-4*) Building Cost File.

— The Berger Building & Design Cost File, 1983: General Construction Trades, Vol. 1. LC 83-70008. 477p. 1983. pap. 36.75 (*0-942564-02-2*) Building Cost File.

— The Berger Building & Design Cost File, 1983: Mechanical, Electrical Trades, Vol. 2. LC 83-70008. 207p. 1983. pap. 26.45 (*0-942564-04-9*) Building Cost File.

— Berger Building & Design Cost File, 1984: Mechanical, Electrical Trades, Vol. 2. LC 84-70008. (Illus.). 300p. 1984. pap. 32.50 (*0-942564-05-7*) Building Cost File.

Berger, A., ed. The Big Bang & George Lemaitre. 1984. text 192.50 (*90-277-1848-2*) Kluwer Academic.

— Dupuytren's Disease: Pathobiochemistry & Clinical Management. LC 93-34322. 1994. 123.00 (*0-387-57239-2*) Spr-Verlag.

— The Evangelical Hamburger: Essays on Commonplace Aspects of American Culture & Society. (C). 1970. pap. text 15.95 (*0-686-79906-2*) Irvington.

Berger, A., et al, eds. Understanding Climate Changes, IUGG 7. (Geophysical Monograph Ser.: Vol. 52). 188p. 1989. 26.00 (*0-87590-457-2*) Am Geophysical.

Berger, A. J., jt. auth. see Kear, Janet.

Berger, A. L., et al, eds. Climate & Geo-Sciences. (C). 1989. pap. text 148.50 (*0-7923-0412-8*); lib. bdg. 234.00 (*0-7923-0404-7*) Kluwer Academic.

Berger, Adam, et al, eds. Homes for the Homeless: A Handbook for Action. LC 90-81010. 260p. 1990. 24.95 (*0-89089-394-2*); pap. 14.95 (*0-89089-393-4*) Carolina Acad Pr.

Berger, Adriana, jt. auth. see Allen, Douglas.

Berger, Alan. Non-Ferrous Metals - World Markets & Opportunities Vol. 1: 1997-2002 Analysis & Forecasts. 100p. 1997. pap. text 2400.00 (*1-878218-84-0*) World Info Tech.

— Non-Ferrous Metals - World Markets & Opportunities Vol. 2: 1997-2002 Analysis & Forecasts. 61p. 1998. pap. text 3900.00 (*1-878218-92-1*) World Info Tech.

Berger, Alan A. Witness to the Sacred: Mystical Tales of Primitive Hasidism. (Illus.). (C). 1977. pap. text 4.00 (*0-914914-10-3*) New Horizons.

Berger, Alan L. Children of Job: American Second-Generation Witnesses to the Holocaust. LC 96-26918. (SUNY Series in Modern Jewish Literature & Culture Ser.). 241p. (C). 1997. pap. text 19.95 (*0-7914-3358-7*) State U NY Pr.

— Children of Job: American Second-Generation Witnesses to the Holocaust. LC 96-26918. (SUNY Series in Modern Jewish Literature & Culture Ser.). 241p. (C). 1997. text 59.50 (*0-7914-3357-9*) State U NY Pr.

— Crisis & Covenant: The Holocaust in American Jewish Fiction. LC 84-26813. (SUNY Series in Modern Jewish Literature & Culture). 234p. (C). 1985. text 65.50 (*0-88706-085-4*); pap. text 21.95 (*0-88706-086-2*) State U NY Pr.

Berger, Alan L., ed. Bearing Witness to the Holocaust, 1939-1989. LC 91-28678. (Symposium Ser.: Vol. 31). (Illus.). 376p. 1991. lib. bdg. 99.95 (*0-7734-9644-0*) E Mellen.

— Judaism in the Modern World. 304p. (C). 1994. text 50.00 (*0-8147-1212-6*); pap. text 19.50 (*0-8147-1223-1*) NYU Pr.

Berger, Alan L., jt. auth. see Patterson, David.

Berger, Albert I. The Magic That Works: John W. Campbell & the American Response to Technology. Burgess, Mary A., ed. LC 84-373. (Milford Series: Popular Writers of Today: Popular Writers of Today: Vol. 46). 232p. 1993. pap. 25.00 (*0-89370-275-7*, 10404305) Millefleurs.

Berger, Albert J., jt. auth. see Hlastala, Michael P.

Berger, Allen. Handbook for Preparing for an International Reading Association (IRA)/ National Council for Accreditation of Teacher Education (NCATE) Program Review in Reading. LC 98-43236. 56p. 1998. pap. 10.95 (*0-87207-200-2*, 200) Intl Reading.

***Berger, Allen & Shafran, Elizabeth A.** Teens for Literacy: Promoting Reading & Writing in Schools & Communities. 96p. 1999. pap. 14.95 (*0-87207-255-X*, 255) Intl Reading.

Berger, Amelie, ed. Twice Humanity: Implications for Local & Global Resource Use. 187p. 1998. pap. 24.95 (*91-7106-415-X*) Almqvist Wiksell.

***Berger, Amy.** The Twenty Year Itch: Confessions of a Corporate Warrior. (Illus.). 225p. 1998. pap. 12.00 (*0-9665915-0-X*) Motivat Magic.

Berger, Andre L., ed. Climatic Variations & Variability: Facts & Theories. xxvi, 771p. 1981. text 249.00 (*90-277-1300-6*) Kluwer Academic.

Berger, Andrew J. Bird Life in Hawaii. 2nd ed. (Illus.). 72p. 1993. pap. 6.95 (*0-89610-282-3*, 24525-000) Island Heritage.

— Hawaiian Birdlife. 2nd rev. ed. LC 80-26332. (Illus.). 278p. 1983. 34.95 (*0-8248-0742-1*) UH Pr.

Berger, Andrew J., jt. auth. see Van Tyne, Josselyn.

Berger, Ann. Handbook of Supportive Oncology. 650p. 1996. pap. text 34.95 (*0-397-51560-X*) Lppncott W & W.

— Teaching the Literacy Hour in an Inclusive Classroom: Supporting Pupils with Learning Difficulties, Vol. 1. (Resource Materials for Teachers Ser.). 1999. pap. 26.95 (*1-85346-630-1*) David Fulton.

Berger, Ann, et al. Principles & Practice of Supportive Oncology. LC 97-41365. 800p. 1997. text 85.00 (*0-397-51559-6*) Lppncott W & W.

Berger, Anna B., tr. see Leroi-Gourham, Andre.

Berger, Anna M. Mensuration & Proportion Signs: Origins & Evolution. LC 92-12195. (Oxford Monographs on Music). (Illus.). 284p. 1993. text 65.00 (*0-19-816230-8*, Clarendon Pr) OUP.

Berger, Anthony R. & Iams, William J., eds. Geoindicators: Assessing Rapid Environmental Change in Earth Systems. LC 99-227731. (Illus.). 478p. 1996. text 99.00 (*90-5410-631-X*, Pub. by A A Balkema) Ashgate Pub Co.

Berger, Arnold E., ed. Orendel: Ein Deutsches Spielmannsgedicht. (GER.). cxxxiv, 191p. (C). 1974. reprint ed. text 84.60 (*3-11-003399-2*) De Gruyter.

Berger, Arthur & Berger, Joyce. Reincarnation: Fact or Fable?: An Examination of the Case for & Against. 1992. pap. 15.95 (*1-85538-111-7*, Pub. by Aqrn Pr) HarpC.

Berger, Arthur A. Agit-Pop: Political Culture & Communication Theory. 254p. 1989. 34.95 (*0-88738-315-7*) Transaction Pubs.

— An Anatomy of Humor. LC 92-18197. 246p. (C). 1993. text 34.95 (*1-56000-086-4*) Transaction Pubs.

— An Anatomy of Humor. 192p. 1998. pap. 22.95 (*0-7658-0494-8*) Transaction Pubs.

— The Art of Comedy Writing. LC 97-6163. 147p. 1997. text 29.95 (*1-56000-324-3*) Transaction Pubs.

— Blind Men & Elephants: Perspectives on Humor. 200p. (C). 1994. 34.95 (*1-56000-185-2*) Transaction Pubs.

— Cultural Criticism: A Primer of Key Concepts. (Foundations of Popular Culture Ser.: Vol. 4). 220p. 1994. 42.00 (*0-8039-5733-5*); pap. 18.95 (*0-8039-5734-3*) Sage.

— Essentials of Mass Communication Theory. LC 95-11882. 215p. (C). 1995. 42.00 (*0-8039-7356-X*); pap. 17.95 (*0-8039-7357-8*) Sage.

— Improving Writing Skills: Memos, Letters, Reports, & Proposals. (Survival Skills for Scholars Ser.: Vol. 9). 128p. (C). 1993. text 37.00 (*0-8039-4822-0*); pap. text 16.50 (*0-8039-4823-9*) Sage.

— Li'l Abner: A Study of American Satire. LC 94-17079. (Studies in Popular Culture). (Illus.). 191p. 1994. reprint ed. text 30.00 (*0-87805-712-9*); reprint ed. pap. text 14.95 (*0-87805-713-7*) U Pr of Miss.

— Manufacturing Desire: Media, Popular Culture, & Everyday Life. 287p. (C). 1996. text 34.95 (*1-56000-226-3*) Transaction Pubs.

— Media Analysis Techniques. (CommText Ser.: Vol. 10). 180p. (C). 1991. text 42.00 (*0-8039-4361-X*); pap. text 18.95 (*0-8039-4362-8*) Sage.

— Media Analysis Techniques. 2nd ed. LC 98-8876. 220p. 1998. 46.00 (*0-7619-1453-6*); pap. 21.95 (*0-7619-1454-4*) Sage.

— Media Research Techniques. (Illus.). 160p. 1991. 42.00 (*0-8039-4179-X*); pap. 18.95 (*0-8039-4180-3*) Sage.

— Media Research Techniques. 2nd ed. LC 97-45406. 175p. 1998. write for info. (*0-7619-1536-2*); pap. write for info. (*0-7619-1537-0*) Sage.

— Narratives in Popular Culture, Media, & Everyday Life. LC 96-25182. 138p. 1996. 44.00 (*0-7619-0344-5*); pap. 18.95 (*0-7619-0345-3*) Sage.

— Popular Culture Genres: Theories & Texts. (Foundations of Popular Culture Ser.: Vol. 2). 160p. (C). 1992. text 42.00 (*0-8039-4725-9*); pap. text 18.95 (*0-8039-4726-7*) Sage.

— The Postmodern Presence: Readings on Postmodernism in American Culture & Society. LC 97-45393. 320p. 1998. 62.00 (*0-7619-8979-X*); pap. 24.95 (*0-7619-8980-3*) AltaMira Pr.

Berger, Arthur A. Postmortem for a Postmodernist. LC 97-4893. 176p. 1997. 18.95 (*0-7619-8911-0*); pap. 54.00 (*0-7619-8910-2*) AltaMira Pr.

Berger, Arthur A. Reading Matter: Multidisciplinary Perspectives on Material Culture. 145p. (C). 1991. text 32.95 (*0-88738-435-8*) Transaction Pubs.

— Scripts: Writing for Radio & Television. (Illus.). 160p. (C). 1990. 45.00 (*0-8039-3761-X*); pap. 19.95 (*0-8039-3762-8*) Sage.

— Seeing Is Believing: An Introduction to Visual Communication. LC 97-10862. xiv, 210p. 1997. pap. text 28.95 (*1-55934-909-3*, 1909) Mayfield Pub.

— Signs in Contemporary Culture: An Introduction to Semiotics. 2nd rev. ed. 255p. 1998. pap. text 19.95 (*1-879215-37-3*) Sheffield WI.

— Television As an Instrument of Terror. LC 78-55942. 214p. 1979. 21.95 (*0-87855-708-3*) Transaction Pubs.

— Television in Society. 224p. 1986. 34.95 (*0-88738-109-X*) Transaction Pubs.

Berger, Arthur A., ed. Film in Society. LC 78-55943. 151p. 1980. 24.95 (*0-87855-245-6*) Transaction Pubs.

Berger, Arthur A., et al, eds. Perspectives on Death & Dying: Cross-Cultural & Multi-Disciplinary Views. LC 88-63424. 270p. 1989. pap. text 22.95 (*0-914783-27-0*) Charles.

***Berger, Arthur Asa.** Ads, Fads, & Consumer Culture: Advertising's Impact on American Character & Culture. 160p. 2000. 59.00 (*0-7425-0030-6*) Rowman.

— Ads, Fads, & Consumer Culture: Advertising's Impact on American Character & Society. 160p. 2000. pap. 16.95 (*0-7425-0031-4*) Rowman.

— Murder Ad Nauseam: A Solomon Hunter Mystery. 128p. 2000. pap. 18.00 (*0-7388-2067-9*) Xlibris Corp.

Berger, Arthur S. Dying & Death in Law & Medicine: A Forensic Primer for Health & Legal Professionals. LC 92-18875. 240p. 1992. 59.95 (*0-275-93928-6*, C3928, Praeger Pubs) Greenwood.

— When Life Ends: Legal Overviews, Medicolegal Forms & Hospital Policies. LC 94-43173. 208p. 1995. 62.95 (*0-275-94620-7*, Praeger Pubs) Greenwood.

Berger, Arthur S. & Berger, Joyce. Encyclopedia of Parapsychology & Psychical Research. 554p. 1994. 45.00 (*1-56924-996-2*) Marlowe & Co.

— Fear of the Unknown: Enlightened Aid-in-Dying. LC 94-37740. 176p. 1995. 59.95 (*0-275-94683-5*, Praeger Pubs) Greenwood.

Berger, Arthur S. & Berger, Joyce, eds. To Die Or Not to Die? Cross-disciplinary, Cultural & Legal Perspectives on the Right to Choose Death. LC 90-34370. 208p. 1990. 55.00 (*0-275-93585-X*, C3585, Praeger Pubs) Greenwood.

Berger, B. Michael, ed. see Berger, Graenum.

Berger, Barbara. Animalia. LC 82-9521. (Illus.). 64p. (J). (gr. 2-6). 1999. pap. 14.95 (*0-89087-508-1*) Celestial Arts.

— Animalia. 1999. pap. text 7.95 (*1-58246-012-4*) Tricycle Pr.

***Berger, Barbara H.** The Road to Power: Fast Food for the Soul. 144p. 2000. pap. 13.95 (*0-9651576-4-4*) Heart Link.

Berger, Barbara H. The Donkey's Dream. LC 84-18905. (Illus.). 32p. (J). (ps-3). 1985. 15.95 (*0-399-21233-7*, Philomel) Peng Put Young Read.

— Grandfather Twilight. (Illus.). 32p. (J). (ps-3). 1984. 16.95 (*0-399-20996-4*, Philomel) Peng Put Young Read.

— Gwinna. LC 88-30676. (Illus.). 128p. (J). 1990. 22.95 (*0-399-21738-X*, Philomel) Peng Put Young Read.

— The Jewel Heart. LC 94-5691. (Illus.). 32p. (J). (ps-3). 1994. 15.95 (*0-399-22681-8*, Philomel) Peng Put Young Read.

— The Jewel Heart. (Illus.). 32p. (J). (ps-3). 1998. pap. 5.99 (*0-698-11634-8*, PapStar) Peng Put Young Read.

***Berger, Barbara H.** Jewel Heart. 1998. 11.19 (*0-606-13537-5*, Pub. by Turtleback) Demco.

Berger, Barbara H. A Lot of Otters. LC 95-50532. (Illus.). 32p. (J). (gr. k-1). 1997. 16.99 (*0-399-22910-8*, Philomel) Peng Put Young Read.

— When the Sun Rose. LC 86-2484. (Illus.). 32p. (J). (ps-2). 1986. 14.95 (*0-399-21360-0*, Philomel) Peng Put Young Read.

— When the Sun Rose. LC 86-2484. (Illus.). 32p. (J). (ps-3). 1997. pap. 5.95 (*0-698-11434-5*, PapStar) Peng Put Young Read.

Berger, Barbara Helen. Angels on a Pin. LC 98-6942. (Illus.). 40p. (J). (ps-1). 2000. 16.99 (*0-399-23247-8*, Philomel) Peng Put Young Read.

***Berger, Barbara Helen.** The Donkey's Dream. 32p. (J). (ps-3). 1999. pap. 5.99 (*0-698-11605-4*, PuffinBks) Peng Put Young Read.

— Grandfather Twilight. 32p. (J). (gr. k). 1999. 6.99 (*0-399-23421-7*) Peng Put Young Read.

Berger, Barbara Helen. Grandfather Twilight. LC 83-19490. (J). 1984. 11:15 (*0-606-03986-4*, Pub. by Turtleback) Demco.

***Berger, Barbara Helen.** A Lot of Otters. (Picture Puffin Ser.). (Illus.). 32p. (J). (ps-1). 2000. pap. 6.99 (*0-698-11863-4*, PuffinBks) Peng Put Young Read.

Berger, Barbara J., jt. auth. see Chernecky, Cynthia C.

Berger, Bennett M. An Essay on Culture: Symbolic Structure & Social Structure. LC 94-33086. 207p. 1995. pap. 17.95 (*0-520-20017-9*, Pub. by U CA Pr) Cal Prin Full Svc.

Berger, Bennett M., ed. Authors of Their Own Lives: Intellectual Autobiographies by Twenty American Sociologists. 503p. 1990. 50.00 (*0-520-06555-7*, Pub. by U CA Pr) Cal Prin Full Svc.

— Authors of Their Own Lives: Intellectual Autobiographies by Twenty American Sociologists. 1992. pap. 19.95 (*0-520-06556-5*, Pub. by U CA Pr) Cal Prin Full Svc.

Berger, Bernard B., ed. Control of Organic Substances in Water & Wastewater. LC 86-31141. (Pollution Technology Review Ser.: No. 140). (Illus.). 459p. 1987. 45.00 (*0-8155-1118-3*) Noyes.

Berger, Bill, jt. ed. see Gibson, Gary.

Berger, Bill D. & Anderson, Kenneth E. Modern Petroleum: A Basic Primer of the Industry. 3rd ed. LC 92-26928. 537p. 1992. 64.95 (*0-87814-386-6*, P4481) PennWell Bks.

***Berger, Bill D. & Anderson, Kenneth E.** Petroleo Moderno: Un Manual Basico de la Industria. 537p. 1999. 64.95 (*0-87814-755-1*) PennWell Bks.

***Berger, Bob.** How to Prepare for the SAT9 5th Grade. (Illus.). 115p. (J). (gr. 5-7). 1999. 19.95 (*1-930288-00-X*) Carney Ed Serv.

Berger, Brigitte. Child Care & Mediating Structures: A Conference. Callahan, Sidney, ed. LC 79-17710. (AEI Symposia Ser.: No. 796). 96p. reprint ed. pap. 30.00 (*0-8357-4448-5*, 203728500008) Bks Demand.

— Culture of Entrepreneurship. 242p. 1991. 29.95 (*1-55815-159-1*) ICS Pr.

Berger, Bruce. Almost an Island: Travels in Baja California. LC 98-9012. 240p. 1998. 39.95 (*0-8165-1901-3*); pap. 17.95 (*0-8165-1902-1*) U of Ariz Pr.

— A Dazzle of Hummingbirds. Leon, Vicki, ed. LC 94-30869. (Close up: A Focus on Nature Ser.). (Illus.). 40p. (Orig.). (YA). (gr. 5 up). 1994. pap. 7.95 (*0-382-24894-5*); lib. bdg. 14.95 (*0-382-24893-7*) Silver Burdett Pr.

— Facing the Music. 90p. 1995. pap. 10.00 (*1-881090-14-0*) Confluence Pr.

— The Telling Distance: Conversations with the American Desert. LC 89-33144. (Illus.). 243p. 1990. 19.95 (*0-932576-74-5*) Breitenbush Bks.

— The Telling Distance: Conversations with the American Desert. LC 96-44304. 1997. pap. 19.95 (*0-8165-1677-4*) U of Ariz Pr.

— There Was a River. 198p. (Orig.). 1994. 42.00 (*0-8165-1469-0*); pap. 17.95 (*0-8165-1493-3*) U of Ariz Pr.

Berger, Byron R., ed. Advances in Research on Mineral Resources, 1994. (Illus.). 77p. (C). 1995. pap. text 45.00 (*0-7881-1932-X*) DIANE Pub.

Berger, Candyce. Restructuring & Resizing: Strategies for Social Work & Other Human Services Administrators in Health Care. LC 92-33264. (Illus.). 84p. (Orig.). 1993. pap. 57.00 (*0-87258-626-X*, 187150) Am Hospital.

Berger, Carl. Honour & the Search for Influence: A History of the Royal Society of Canada, 1882-1994. (Illus.). 160p. 1996. text 45.00 (*0-8020-0794-5*); pap. text 14.95 (*0-8020-7153-8*) U of Toronto Pr.

— The Korea Knot, a Military-Political History. rev. ed. LC 86-22767. 255p. 1986. reprint ed. lib. bdg. 79.50 (*0-313-25281-5*, BEKK, Greenwood Pr) Greenwood.

— Science, God, & Nature in Victorian Canada. LC QH0021.C3B47. (Joanne Goodman Lectures: No. 1982). (Illus.). 112p. reprint ed. pap. 34.80 (*0-8357-3631-8*, 203635900003) Bks Demand.

— The Sense of Power: Studies in the Ideas of Canadian Imperialism, 1867-1914. LC 79-470040. 289p. reprint ed. pap. 89.60 (*0-8357-6356-0*, 203571000096) Bks Demand.

— The Writing of Canadian History: Aspects of English-Canadian Historical Writing 1900-1970. 1977. pap. 6.95 (*0-19-540280-4*) OUP.

— The Writing of Canadian History: Aspects of English-Canadian Historical Writing 1900-1970. 2nd ed. 376p. 1986. text 35.00 (*0-8020-2546-3*); pap. text 20.95 (*0-8020-6568-6*) U of Toronto Pr.

Berger, Carl, ed. Approaches to Canadian History. LC 23-16213. (Canadian Historical Readings Ser.: No. 1). 1967. pap. text 10.95 (*0-8020-1459-3*) U of Toronto Pr.

— The United States Air Force in Southeast Asia, 1961-73: An Illustrated Account. 381p. 1984. write for info. (*0-912799-16-1*) AFH & MP.

Berger, Cathy. Op Den Graeff - Updegrove: Indexes & Pedigrees of Known Descendants of Herman Op Den Graeff. Jones, Iris C., ed. 87p. (Orig.). 1991. pap. text 12.00 (*0-9620067-2-6*) Links Geneal Pubns.

Berger, Charles. Forms of Farewell: The Late Poetry of Wallace Stevens. LC 84-40489. 216p. 1985. reprint ed. pap. 67.00 (*0-608-01904-6*, 206255600003) Bks Demand.

Berger, Charles, jt. ed. see Lehman, David.

Berger, Charles R. Communication & Social Influence Processes. 1995. pap. 17.95 (*0-87013-487-6*) Mich St U Pr.

— Planning Strategic Interaction. LC 96-54036. (LEA's Communication Ser.). 184p. 1997. 39.95 (*0-8058-2308-5*) L Erlbaum Assocs.

Berger, Charles R. & Chaffee, Steven H., eds. Handbook of Communication Science. 928p. 1987. text 79.95 (*0-8039-2199-3*) Sage.

Berger, Charles R., jt. ed. see Roloff, Michael E.

Berger, Charryl, et al, eds. Environmentally Concious Design & Manufacturing Vol. 2: Recent Advances. 478p. (Orig.). (C). 1994. write for info. (*0-614-16444-3*) TSI Pr.

Berger, Claire & Anton, Klaus, eds. Supercritical Fluid Chromatography with Packed Colums. LC 97-34426. (Chromatographic Science Ser.). (Illus.). 472p. 1997. text 185.00 (*0-8247-0013-9*) Dekker.

Berger, Curtis J. Land Ownership & Use. 3rd ed. LC 81-86687. 1983. 56.00 (*0-316-09154-5*, Aspen Law & Bus) Aspen Pub.

— Supplement to Land Ownership '89. 1989. 11.50 (*0-316-09148-0*, Aspen Law & Bus) Aspen Pub.

Berger, Curtis J. & Johnstone, Quintin. Land Transfer & Finance: Cases & Materials. 4th ed. 1424p. 1993. boxed set 60.00 (*0-7355-0622-1*, 06221) Panel Pubs.

Berger, Curtis J. & Weidenbeck, Peter J., Jr. Partnership Taxation, Teacher's Manual to Accompany Cases & Materials. (American Casebook Ser.). 167p. (C). 1989. pap. text. write for info. (*0-314-67336-9*) West Pub.

Berger, Curtis J. & Wiedenbeck, Peter J. Case & Materials on Partnership Taxation, 1991 Supplement. (American Casebook Ser.). 118p. (C). 1991. pap. 14.50 (*0-314-89930-8*) West Pub.

— Partnership Taxation, Cases & Materials. (American Casebook Ser.). 788p. (C). 1988. 50.50 (*0-314-48238-5*) West Pub.

Berger, Curtis J. & Williams, Joan. Property: Land Ownership & Use. 4th ed. 1300p. 1997. teacher ed., boxed set 60.00 (*1-56706-509-0*, 65090) Panel Pubs.

Berger, D., jt. auth. see Bergeron, Caroline.

Berger, D., tr. see Mechnikov, et al.

Berger, Dale E., et al, eds. Application of Cognitive Psychology: Problem Solving, Education & Computing. 264p. (C). 1986. text 49.95 (*0-89859-710-2*) L Erlbaum Assocs.

Berger, David. Alcoholism for Beginners. (Illus.). 176p. 1994. pap. 9.95 (*0-86316-163-4*) Writers & Readers.

— The Jewish-Christian Debate in the High Middle Ages: A Critical Edition of the Nizzahon Vetus. LC 95-48485. 606p. 1996. pap. 50.00 (*1-56821-919-9*) Aronson.

— The Legacy of Jewish Migration, 1881: And Its Impact. (Social Science Monographs). 189p. 1983. text 61.00 (*0-88033-026-0*, Pub. by East Eur Monographs) Col U Pr.

— Teach Yourself Director 6 in 21 Days. 400p. 1997. 39.99 (*1-56830-409-9*) Hayden.

Berger, David, ed. History & Hate: The Dimensions of Antisemitism. 138p. 1997. pap. 19.95 (*0-8276-0636-2*) JPS Phila.

Berger, David, et al, eds. The M. D. Anderson Surgical Oncology Handbook. LC 94-3421. 464p. 1994. pap. text 36.95 (*0-316-56431-1*, Little Brwn Med Div) Lppncott W & W.

B

An Asterisk (*) at the beginning of an entry indicates that the title is appearing for the first time.

Berger, David, jt. auth. see Hinton, Milt.

Berger, David, ed. see Gerhard, Johann.

Berger, David, tr. see Moll, Albert.

Berger, David A. The Cheapest Way to Make Phone Calls, Send Faxes or Use the Internet. 130p. 1995. pap. 9.95 (*0-9649653-0-5*) Value Added Serv.

Berger, David G., jt. auth. see Hinton, Milt.

Berger, David J., jt. auth. see Bagley, Constance E.

Berger, David L. Industrial Security. LC 79-628. 360p. 1980. 36.95 (*0-913708-32-1*) Buttrwrth-Heinemann.

— Industrial Security. 2nd ed. LC 98-48867. 336p. 1999. write for info. (*0-7506-7139-4*) Buttrwrth-Heinemann.

Berger, David O., ed. see Gerhard, Johann.

Berger, Deborah, jt. auth. see Berger, Richard.

Berger, Diane. The Bathroom. LC 96-12130. (Illus.). 144p. 1996. 29.95 (*0-7892-0086-4*) Abbeville Pr.

— The Dining Room. (Illus.). 144p. 1993. 29.95 (*1-55859-555-4*) Abbeville Pr.

— We Heard the Angels of Madness: A Family Guide to Coping with Manic Depression. 308p. 1992. pap. 11.95 (*0-688-11615-9*, Quil) HarperTrade.

Berger, Dominique & Merieux, Regine. Cadences, No. 1. (FRE.). 224p. 1994. pap. text 18.95 (*2-278-04319-6*, Pub. by Edns Didier) Hatier Pub.

— Cadences, No. 2. (FRE.). 223p. 1995. pap. text 19.95 (*2-278-04322-6*, Pub. by Edns Didier) Hatier Pub.

Berger, Donald. Quality Hill. (Lost Roads Ser.: No. 39). 64p. (Orig.). 1993. pap. 9.95 (*0-918786-44-4*) Lost Roads.

Berger, Donna, jt. auth. see O'Keefe, Edward.

Berger, Donna S., jt. auth. see O'Keefe, Edward.

Berger, E. L. Research Directions for the Decade: 1990 Summer Study on High Energy Physics. 1000p. 1992. text 178.00 (*981-02-0931-2*) World Scientific Pub.

Berger, E. Roy & Mittiga, Linda. Common Bonds: Reflections of a Cancer Doctor. LC 94-24684. 246p. 1994. 24.95 (*1-883257-07-7*) Hlth Edu Lit.

Berger, E. Roy, jt. auth. see Lewis, James, Jr.

Berger, Edward. Basically Speaking: An Oral History of George Duvivier. LC 93-28497. (Studies in Jazz: No. 17). (Illus.). 514p. 1993. 62.50 (*0-8108-2691-7*) Scarecrow.

Berger, Edward, ed. Intellectual Property Primary Law Sourcebook: Statutes & Regulations. 1011p. 1998. 60.00 (*0-8205-3053-0*, 1063) Bender.

Berger, Edward, et al, eds. Annual Review of Jazz Studies Vol. 1: 1982. 178p. 1982. pap. 18.50 (*0-8108-2295-4*) Scarecrow.

— Annual Review of Jazz Studies Vol. 2: 1983. 224p. 1983. pap. 18.50 (*0-8108-2296-2*) Scarecrow.

— Annual Review of Jazz Studies Vol. 4: 1988. 224p. 1988. pap. 21.00 (*0-8108-2298-9*) Scarecrow.

— Annual Review of Jazz Studies Vol. 5: 1991. LC 82-644466. (Illus.). 274p. 1991. 31.00 (*0-8108-2478-7*) Scarecrow.

— Annual Review of Jazz Studies, 1993, Vol. 6. (Illus.). 308p. 1993. 41.50 (*0-8108-2727-1*) Scarecrow.

— Annual Review of Jazz Studies, 1994-1997. (Studies in Jazz: No. 7). (Illus.). 296p. 1996. 39.00 (*0-8108-3122-8*) Scarecrow.

Berger, Edward, jt. auth. see Reig, Teddy.

Berger, Eileen. A Family for Andi. (Love Inspired Ser.: No. 57). 1999. mass mkt. 4.50 (*0-373-87057-4*, 1-87057-5) Harlequin Bks.

Berger, Elena L. Labour, Race & Colonial Rule: The Copperbelt from 1924 to Independence. (Oxford Studies in African Affairs). 1974. text 55.00 (*0-19-821690-4*) OUP.

Berger, Elmer. Peace for Palestine: First Lost Opportunity. LC 92-45726. 304p. (C). 1993. 49.95 (*0-8130-1207-4*) U Press Fla.

Berger, Elmer, jt. auth. see Tack, Deane A.

Berger, Eric G. & Roth, Jurgen. The Golgi Apparatus. LC 97-28601. 1997. write for info. (*0-8176-5692-8*) Birkhauser.

Berger, Eric G. & Roth, Jurgen, eds. The Golgi Apparatus. LC 97-28601. ix, 306p. 1997. 98.50 (*3-7643-5692-8*) Birkhauser.

Berger, Esther M. Moneysmart Divorce: What Women Need to Know about Money & Divorce. 240p. 1996. 22.00 (*0-684-81165-0*) S&S Trade.

Berger, Esther M. & Hasbun, Connie C. Money Smart: Secrets Women Always Wanted to Know about Money. LC 93-2694. 304p. 1993. 22.00 (*0-671-76061-0*) S&S Trade.

Berger, Eugenia Hepworth. Parents As Partners in Education: Families & Schools Working Together. 5th ed. LC 99-18773. (Illus.). 563p. (C). 1999. pap. text 40.00 (*0-13-099654-8*) P-H.

Berger, Eunice, jt. auth. see Berger, Jack.

Berger, Ewald. Ornamental Coffers: Eight Centuries of European Craftsmanship. 1999. 110.00 (*3-925369-83-X*) Arnoldsche Art Pubs.

Berger, Florence & Ferguson, Dennis H. Inn-Ovation: Creativity Techniques for Hospitality Managers. LC 90-12328. 144p. 1990. 59.95 (*0-471-52774-2*) Wiley.

Berger, Frances De T. Mierda. 1990. pap. 9.95 (*0-452-26424-3*, Plume) Dutton Plume.

Berger, Frances de T. & Eversz, Kim W. Mas Mierda! More of the Real You Were Never Taught in School. LC 94-25530. (Illus.). 1995. pap. 8.95 (*0-452-27185-1*, Plume) Dutton Plume.

Berger, Friederike, et al, eds. Symbolae Berolinenses fur Dieter Harlfinger. (GER.). vi, 457p. 1993. pap. 108.00 (*90-256-1047-1*, Pub. by AM Hakkert) BookLink Distributors.

Berger, G., et al, eds. Second Trimester Abortion. 1981. text 162.50 (*90-247-2487-2*) Kluwer Academic.

Berger, Gabriella E. Menopause & Culture. LC 98-46899. 1999. write for info. (*0-7453-1488-0*) Pluto GBR.

Berger, Gary S. & Westrom, Lars V., eds. Pelvic Inflammatory Disease. LC 92-9149. (Illus.). 219p. 1992. reprint ed. pap. 67.90 (*0-608-05834-3*, 205979900007) Bks Demand.

Berger, Gary S., et al. The Couple's Guide to Fertility: Updated with the Newest Scientific Techniques That Can Help You Have a Baby. rev. ed. LC 94-17765. 480p. 1994. pap. 16.95 (*0-385-47124-6*) Doubleday.

Berger, Georg. Die Beratenden Psychiater des Deutschen Heeres 1939 bis 1945. (GER., Illus.). 328p. 1998. 51.95 (*3-631-33296-3*) P Lang Pubng.

Berger, George N. Car Maintenance Reminder & Record Book. 70p. 1990. pap., vinyl bd. 5.95 (*0-9626720-0-9*) Value Maintenance.

Berger, Geri. Little Lost Lamb. 1981. pap. 2.50 (*0-8198-4415-2*) Pauline Bks.

Berger, Gilda. African Savannah. (Smart Science Ser.). (Illus.). 16p. (J). (gr. 2-5). Date not set. pap. 5.95 (*1-58273-500-X*) Newbridge Educ.

Berger, Gilda. Alcoholism & the Family. LC 93-10898. (Changing Family Ser.). (Illus.). 128p. (YA). (gr. 7-12). 1993. lib. bdg. 24.00 (*0-531-12548-3*) Watts.

— Celebrate! Stories of the Jewish Holidays. LC 97-40150. (Illus.). 128p. (J). (ps-3). 1998. 17.95 (*0-590-93503-8*, Pub. by Scholastic) Scholastic Inc.

Berger, Gilda. The Coral Reef. (Smart Science Ser.). (Illus.). 16p. (J). (gr. 2-5). Date not set. pap. 5.95 (*1-58273-501-8*) Newbridge Educ.

Berger, Gilda. Crack: The New Drug Epidemic. (Impact Bks.). (Illus.). 128p. (YA). (gr. 7-12). 1994. lib. bdg. 24.00 (*0-531-11188-1*) Watts.

Berger, Gilda. The Desert. (Smart Science Ser.). (Illus.). 16p. (J). (gr. 2-5). Date not set. pap. 5.95 (*1-58273-502-6*) Newbridge Educ.

— Dinosaurs. (Smart Science Ser.). (Illus.). 16p. (J). (gr. 2-5). Date not set. pap. 5.95 (*1-58273-503-4*) Newbridge Educ.

— Electricity. (Smart Science Ser.). (Illus.). 16p. (J). (gr. 2-5). Date not set. pap. 5.95 (*1-58273-504-2*) Newbridge Educ.

Berger, Gilda. Joey's Story: Straight Talk about Drugs. (YA). 1992. pap. 4.80 (*0-395-63559-4*) HM.

— Joey's Story: Straight Talk about Drugs. (Get Real! Ser.). (Illus.). 64p. (YA). (gr. 7 up). 1991. lib. bdg. 18.90 (*1-56294-003-1*) Millbrook Pr.

Berger, Gilda. Matter. (Smart Science Ser.). (Illus.). 16p. (J). (gr. 2-5). Date not set. pap. 5.95 (*1-58273-506-9*) Newbridge Educ.

Berger, Gilda. Meg's Story: Straight Talk about Drugs. (YA). 1992. pap. 4.80 (*0-395-63557-8*) HM.

— Meg's Story: Straight Talk about Drugs. LC 91-21515. (Get Real! Ser.). (Illus.). 64p. (YA). (gr. 7 up). 1992. pap. 4.95 (*1-56294-804-0*) Millbrook Pr.

— Meg's Story: Straight Talk about Drugs. (Get Real! Ser.). (J). 1992. 10.15 (*0-606-02741-6*, Pub. by Turtleback) Demco.

Berger, Gilda. The Ocean. (Smart Science Ser.). (Illus.). 16p. (J). (gr. 2-5). Date not set. pap. 5.95 (*1-58273-507-7*) Newbridge Educ.

Berger, Gilda. Patty's Story: Straight Talk about Drugs. (YA). 1992. pap. 4.80 (*0-395-63558-6*) HM.

Berger, Gilda. Planets. (Smart Science Ser.). (Illus.). 16p. (J). (gr. 2-5). Date not set. pap. 5.95 (*1-58273-508-5*) Newbridge Educ.

— Polar Regions. (Smart Science Ser.). (Illus.). 16p. (J). (gr. 2-5). Date not set. pap. 5.95 (*1-58273-509-3*) Newbridge Educ.

Berger, Gilda. Premenstrual Syndrome: A Guide for Young Women. 3rd rev. ed. LC 91-34647. (Illus.). 96p. (YA). (gr. 7-12). 1991. pap. 7.95 (*0-89793-088-6*) Hunter Hse.

Berger, Gilda. Rain Forest. (Smart Science Ser.). (Illus.). 16p. (J). (gr. 2-5). Date not set. pap. 5.95 (*1-58273-510-7*) Newbridge Educ.

— The Restless Earth. (Smart Science Ser.). (Illus.). 16p. (J). (gr. 2-5). Date not set. pap. 5.95 (*1-58273-511-5*) Newbridge Educ.

— Rocks. (Smart Science Ser.). (Illus.). 16p. (J). (gr. 2-5). Date not set. pap. 5.95 (*1-58273-512-3*) Newbridge Educ.

— Sound. (Smart Science Ser.). (Illus.). 16p. (J). (gr. 2-5). Date not set. pap. 5.95 (*1-58273-513-1*) Newbridge Educ.

— Weather. (Smart Science Ser.). (Illus.). 16p. (J). (gr. 2-5). Date not set. pap. 5.95 (*1-58273-514-X*) Newbridge Educ.

***Berger, Gilda & Berger, Melvin.** Why Don't Haircuts Hurt? Questions & Answers about the Human Body. LC 97-45874. (Question & Answer Ser.). (Illus.). 48p. (J). (gr. 2-4). 1999. pap. 5.95 (*0-439-08569-1*, Pub. by Scholastic Inc) Penguin Putnam.

Berger, Gilda, jt. auth. see Berger, Melvin.

Berger, Gordon M., ed. & tr. see Munemitsu, Mutsu.

Berger, Gordon Mark. Parties Out of Power in Japan, 1931-1941. LC 76-3243. 432p. reprint ed. pap. 123.20 (*0-8357-3429-3*, 2039687) Bks Demand.

Berger, Graenum. A Not So Silent Envoy: A Biography of Ambassador Samuel David Berger. LC 92-76083. (Illus.). 225p. 1992. pap. 13.50 (*0-9635641-0-2*) J W B Hampton.

— Rescue the Ethiopian Jews! A Memoir, 1955-1995. Berger, B. Michael, ed. LC 97-93722. 236p. 1997. pap. 19.95 (*0-9635641-1-0*) J W B Hampton.

Berger, Guy. Social Structure & Rural Development in the Third World. (Illus.). 168p. (C). 1992. text 54.95 (*0-521-39258-6*) Cambridge U Pr.

***Berger, Guy & Schiffer, Nancy N.** Pueblo & Navajo Contemporary Pottery & Directory of Artists. LC 99-88913. (Illus.). 192p. 1999. pap. 29.95 (*0-7643-1024-0*) Schiffer.

Berger, H., ed. Non-Destructive Testing Standards: A Review - STP 624. 338p. 1977. 33.75 (*0-8031-0196-1*, STP624) ASTM.

***Berger, Hans.** Automating with Simatic. 250p. 2000. 55.00 (*3-89578-133-9*) Publicis.

— Automating with Step 7 in LAD & FDB: Sigmatic S7-300/400 Programmable Controllers. 338p. 2000. 64.95 (*3-89578-131-2*) Wiley.

— Automating with Step 7 in STL & SCL: Simatic S7-300/400 Programmable Controllers. (Illus.). 436p. 2000. 79.95 (*3-89578-140-1*) Wiley.

— Automating with STEP 7 in STL: SIMATIC S7-300/400 Programmable Controllers. LC 99-198019. 310p. 1998. 95.00 incl. disk (*3-89578-093-6*, Pub. by Publicis) IBD Ltd.

Berger, Hans G., ed. see McKenzie, E. D.

Berger, Harald, et al, eds. Verborum Amor: Studien zur Geschichte & Kunst der Deutschen Sprache Festschrift fur Stefan Sonderegger zum 65. Geburstag. (GER.). xiv, 830p. (C). 1992. lib. bdg. 284.65 (*3-11-011682-0*) De Gruyter.

***Berger, Harold & Iddings, Frank.** Neutron Radiography. (Illus.). 80p. 1998. pap. 75.00 (*1-890596-10-8*, NTIAC-SR-98-01) TX Res Inst.

Berger, Harold & Jones, Thomas, contrib. by. Nondestructive Inspection of Composite Materials. (Illus.). 389p. 1995. ring bd. 149.95 (*1-56676-339-8*) Technomic.

Berger, Harold & Mordfin, Leonard, eds. Nondestructive Testing Standards - Present & Future. LC 92-20433. (STP Ser.: Vol. 1151). (Illus.). 250p. 1992. text 77.00 (*0-8031-1487-7*, STP1151) ASTM.

Berger, Harris M. Metal, Rock, & Jazz: Perception & the Phenomenology of Musical Experience. LC 98-43706. (Music Culture Ser.). (Illus.). 350p. 1999. pap. 22.95 (*0-8195-6376-5*, Wesleyan Univ Pr); text 50.00 (*0-8195-6371-4*, Wesleyan Univ Pr) U Pr of New Eng.

***Berger, Harry.** The Absence of Grace: Sprezzatura & Suspicion in Two Renaissance Courtesy Books. LC 00-22874. 2001. pap. write for info. (*0-8047-3905-6*) Stanford U Pr.

— Dialogical Warfare. 0.00 (*0-691-06845-3*) Princeton U Pr.

***Berger, Harry, Jr.** Fictions of the Pose: Rembrandt Against the Italian Renaissance. LC 99-39775. 656p. 1999. 85.00 (*0-8047-3323-6*) Stanford U Pr.

***Berger, Harry.** Fictions of the Pose: Rembrandt Against the Italian Renaissance. LC 99-39775. 656p. 1999. pap. text 39.95 (*0-8047-3324-4*) Stanford U Pr.

Berger, Harry, Jr. Imaginary Audition: Shakespeare on Stage & Page. 1989. 45.00 (*0-520-06558-1*, Pub. by U CA Pr) Cal Prin Full Svc.

— Imaginary Audition: Shakespeare on Stage & Page. 193p. 1990. pap. 18.95 (*0-520-07306-1*, Pub. by U CA Pr) Cal Prin Full Svc.

— Making Trifles of Terrors: Redistributing Complicities in Shakespeare. Erickson, Peter, ed. & intro. by. LC 96-17085. 1997. write for info. (*0-8047-2732-5*); pap. 19.95 (*0-8047-2852-6*) Stanford U Pr.

— Revisionary Play: Studies in the Spenserian Dynamics. 494p. 1988. pap. 18.95 (*0-520-07180-8*, Pub. by U CA Pr) Cal Prin Full Svc.

— Second World & Green World: Studies in Renaissance Fiction-Making. (Illus.). 542p. 1988. pap. 22.50 (*0-520-07181-6*, Pub. by U CA Pr) Cal Prin Full Svc.

Berger, Harvey, ed. see Tan, Richard & Warnke, Cheryl.

Berger, Helen, jt. auth. see Sefkow, Paula.

Berger, Helen A. A Community of Witches: Contemporary Neo-Paganism & Witchcraft in the United States. LC 98-19677. (Studies in Comparative Religion). (Illus.). 250p. 1999. text 24.95 (*1-57003-246-7*) U of SC Pr.

Berger, Helmut. Mongraph of the Oxytrichidae (Ciliophore, Hypotrichia) LC 99-30413. (Monographiae Biologicae). 1999. write for info. (*0-7923-5795-7*) Kluwer Academic.

Berger, Henry W., ed. A William Appleman Williams Reader: Selections from His Major Historical Writings. LC 92-17013. 416p. 1992. text 35.00 (*1-56663-008-8*); pap. text 16.95 (*1-56663-002-9*, Elephant Paperbacks) I R Dee.

Berger, Heribert, ed. Vitamins & Minerals in Pregnancy & Lactation. LC 88-3221. (Nestle Nutrition Workshop Ser.: Vol. 16). 478p. 1988. reprint ed. pap. 148.20 (*0-608-04717-1*, 206543800004) Bks Demand.

Berger, Horst. Light Structures, Structures of Light: The Art & Engineering of Tensile Architecture. (Illus.). 208p. 1996. 60.00 (*3-7643-5352-X*, Pub. by Birkhauser) Princeton Arch.

Berger, Howard. On the Road: An Inside View of Life with a NHL Team. (Illus.). 256p. 1995. pap. 14.95 (*1-895629-51-9*) Warwick Publ.

— On the Road - Again. (Illus.). 256p. 1999. pap. 15.95 (*1-894020-62-6*, Pub. by Warwick Publ) Firefly Bks Ltd.

Berger, I. K. Everybody's Guide to Paradise. 204p. 1986. pap. 45.00 (*0-7212-0776-6*, Pub. by Regency Pr GBR) St Mut.

Berger, Iris. Threads of Solidarity: Women in South African Industry, 1900-1980. LC 91-23112. (Illus.). 384p. 1992. text 45.00 (*0-253-31173-X*); pap. text 8.95 (*0-253-20700-2*) Ind U Pr.

Berger, Iris & Robertson, Claire C., eds. Women & Class in Africa. LC 85-17568. 300p. (C). 1986. 55.00 (*0-8419-0979-2*) Holmes & Meier.

Berger, Iris, et al. Women in Sub-Saharan Africa. LC 98-53906. (Restoring Women to History Ser.). (Illus.). 168p. 1999. text 35.00 (*0-253-33476-4*) Ind U Pr.

***Berger, Iris, et al.** Women in Sub-Saharan Africa. LC 98-53906. (Restoring Women to History Ser.). (Illus.). 168p. 1999. pap. 12.95 (*0-253-21309-6*) Ind U Pr.

Berger, Iris, jt. ed. see Robertson, Claire C.

Berger, J. O. Statistical Decision Theory & Bayesian Analysis. 2nd ed. (Series in Statistics). (Illus.). xvi, 617p. 1997. 64.95 (*0-387-96098-8*) Spr-Verlag.

— Statistical Decision Theory & Bayesian Analysis. 3rd ed. (Series in Statistics). (Illus.). xvi, 617p. 1993. write for info. (*3-540-96098-8*) Spr-Verlag.

Berger, J. O., et al, eds. Bayesian Robustness. LC 96-77159. (Lecture Notes - Monograph Ser.: No. 29). (Illus.). 360p. 1997. pap. 49.00 (*0-940600-41-2*) Inst Math.

Berger, J. O., jt. auth. see Gupta, Shanti S.

Berger, J. O., ed. see Arnold, Barry C., et al.

Berger, J. O., ed. see Bolfarine, H. & Zacks, S.

Berger, J. O., ed. see Brockwell, P. J., et al.

Berger, J. O., ed. see Choi, B. K.

Berger, J. O., ed. see Gabler, S.

Berger, J. O., jt. ed. see Gupta, Shanti S.

Berger, J. O., ed. see Iida, K. & Fienberg, Stephen E.

Berger, J. O., ed. see Le Cam, Lucien M. & Lo Yang, G.

Berger, J. O., ed. see Salsburg, D. & Fienberg, Stephen E.

Berger, J. O., ed. see Schmitz, Norbert, et al.

Berger, J. O., ed. see Tanner, Martin A.

Berger, J. O., ed. see Wright, T.

Berger, J. R. & Tewary, V. K., eds. Green's Functions & Boundary Element Analysis for Modeling of Mechanical Behavior of Advanced Materials. (Illus.). 166p. (C). 1998. pap. text 35.00 (*0-7881-4818-4*) DIANE Pub.

Berger, Jack & Berger, Eunice. Inside America: The Great American Industrial Tour Guide. 2nd rev. ed. (Illus.). 363p. (Orig.). 1997. pap. 21.95 (*0-9655306-1-2*) Heritage Pub MA.

***Berger Jackson, Margaret.** Hildegard of Bingen: On Natural Philosophy & Medicine. LC 99-19615. (Library of Medieval Women: Vol. 1369-9652). 192p. 1999. pap. 19.95 (*0-85991-551-4*) Boydell & Brewer.

Berger, Jacqueline. The Mythologies of Danger. 86p. 1998. 24.00 (*1-878325-18-3*); pap. 11.00 (*1-878325-19-1*) Bluestem Press.

Berger, James. After the End: Representations of Post-Apocalypse LC 98-40328. 1999. 18.95 (*0-8166-2933-1*); write for info. (*0-8166-2932-3*) U of Minn Pr.

Berger, James O. & Wolpert, Robert L. The Likelihood Principle. LC 84-48467. (IMS Lecture Notes - Monographs: Vol. 6). 206p. 1984. pap. 25.00 (*0-940600-06-4*) Inst Math.

***Berger, Janice & Hall, Harry.** Emotional Fitness: Discovering Our Natural Healing Power. 256p. 2000. pap. 22.95 (*0-13-018182-X*) P-H.

Berger, Jason. A New Deal for the World: Eleanor Roosevelt & American Foreign Policy, 1920-1962. 240p. 1981. text 63.00 (*0-930888-07-3*, SSM1) Col U Pr.

Berger, Jeanette K., jt. auth. see Berger, Stephen S.

Berger, Jeffrey W., et al. Age-Related Macular Degeneration. LC 98-39679. 1998. 175.00 (*0-323-00200-5*) Mosby Inc.

Berger, Jerry A., contrib. by. Chromatic Abstractions: Paintings & Sculpture by Ida Kohlmeyer. (Illus.). 32p. (Orig.). (C). 1996. pap. 5.00 (*0-934306-13-3*) Springfield.

— Contemporary Masterworks in Clay from the San Angelo Museum of Fine Arts. (Illus.). 16p. (Orig.). (C). 1996. pap. 3.00 (*0-934306-14-1*) Springfield.

Berger, Jerry A. & Schlier, Deborah J. Watercolor U. S. A., 1996. (Illus.). 24p. (Orig.). 1996. pap. 5.00 (*0-934306-12-5*) Springfield.

Berger, Jerry A. & Shapiro, Michael E. Watercolor U. S. A., 1998. (Illus.). 24p. 1998. pap. 5.00 (*0-934306-19-2*) Springfield.

Berger, Jerry A., jt. contrib. by see Kiehl, David.

Berger, Joan. The Outer Space Tracing Fun Book. 32p. (J). (ps-3). 1992. pap. 1.95 (*0-590-45133-2*) Scholastic Inc.

Berger, Joan, et al. Wacky Animals Tracing Fun. 32p. (J). (ps-3). 1994. pap. 1.95 (*0-590-48125-8*) Scholastic Inc.

Berger, Joel. Wild Horses of the Great Basin: Social Competition & Population Size. LC 85-8604. (Wildlife Behavior & Ecology Ser.). (Illus.). 348p. Date not set. reprint ed. pap. 107.90 (*0-608-20665-2*, 207210200003) Bks Demand.

— Wild Horses of the Great Basin: Social Competiton & Population Size. LC 85-8604. (Wildlife Behavior & Ecology Ser.). (Illus.). 348p. 1986. lib. bdg. 33.00 (*0-226-04367-3*) U Ch Pr.

Berger, Joel & Cunningham, Carol. Mating, Conservation, & Bison. LC 93-46571. (Methods & Cases in Conservation Science Ser.). 1994. 34.50 (*0-231-08456-0*) Col U Pr.

Berger, Joel, jt. auth. see Cunningham, Carol.

Berger, Joerg. The Dialect of Holy Island: Anglo-Saxon Language & Literature. (European University Studies: Ser. 14, Vol. 83). 172p. 1980. pap. 29.00 (*3-261-04784-4*) P Lang Pubng.

Berger, John. About Looking. 1992. 24.50 (*0-8446-6635-1*) Peter Smith.

— About Looking. LC 91-50099. (Vintage International Ser.). (Illus.). 224p. 1992. pap. 13.00 (*0-679-73655-7*) Vin Bks.

— And Our Faces, My Heart, Brief As Photos. LC 91-50221. (Vintage International Ser.). 112p. 1992. pap. 10.00 (*0-679-73656-5*) Vin Bks.

— Another Way of Telling. 1995. pap. 19.00 (*0-679-73724-3*) Vin Bks.

— Art & Revolution: Ernst Neizvestny & the Role of the Artist in the U. S. S. R. LC 97-8130. 191p. 1998. pap. 13.00 (*0-679-73727-8*) Vin Bks.

— Charging Ahead: The Business of Renewable Energy & What it Means for America. LC 96-50885. (Illus.). 399p. 1997. 30.00 (*0-8050-3771-3*) H Holt & Co.

— Corker's Freedom. 288p. 1981. 5.95 (*0-906495-08-3*); pap. 5.95 (*0-904613-40-2*) Writers & Readers.

— Corkers Freedom. 1995. pap. 11.00 (*0-679-75513-6*) Vin Bks.

— The Foot of Clive. 160p. 1981. 12.95 (*0-906495-09-1*); pap. 4.95 (*0-904613-88-7*) Writers & Readers.

An Asterisk (*) at the beginning of an entry indicates that the title is appearing for the first time.

— Fortunate Man: The Story of a Country Doctor. 1997. pap. 13.00 (*0-679-73726-X*) Vin Bks.

— G. A Novel. LC 91-50094. (Vintage International Ser.). 336p. 1992. pap. 15.00 (*0-679-73654-9*) Vin Bks.

***Berger, John.** Isabelle: Oranges for the Son of Alexander Levy. 2000. pap. 12.99 (*1-900850-33-8*) Arcadia Bks.

Berger, John. Keeping a Rendezvous. LC 92-50073. 1992. pap. 15.00 (*0-679-73714-6*) Vin Bks.

***Berger, John.** King. 2000. pap. 12.00 (*0-375-70534-1*, Pub. by Knopf) Random House.

Berger, John. King: A Street Story. LC 98-44838. 192p. 1999. 20.00 (*0-375-40556-9*) Pantheon.

— Lilac & Flag. LC 92-50076. 1992. pap. 12.00 (*0-679-73719-7*) Vin Bks.

***Berger, John.** Once in Europa. (Illus.). 2000. 27.50 (*1-58234-070-6*) Bloomsbury Pubg.

Berger, John. Once in Europa. LC 92-50075. 1992. pap. 14.00 (*0-679-73716-2*) Vin Bks.

— A Painter of Our Time. 1996. pap. 12.00 (*0-679-73723-5*) Vin Bks.

— A Painter of Our Time. 192p. 1981. 11.95 (*0-904613-12-7*); pap. 4.95 (*0-904613-13-5*) Writers & Readers.

— Permanent Red: Essays in Seeing. 223p. 1981. 12.95 (*0-906495-07-5*) Writers & Readers.

— Permanent Red: Essays in Seeing. (Illus.). 224p. 1981. pap. 6.95 (*0-904613-92-5*) Writers & Readers.

— Photocopies. LC 96-11650. 192p. 1996. 2.99 (*0-679-43525-5*) Pantheon.

— Photocopies. 1998. pap. 12.00 (*0-679-75517-9*) Vin Bks.

— Photocopies. aut. ed. 1996. 22.00 (*0-676-52053-7*) Random.

— Pig Earth. LC 92-50074. 1992. pap. 12.00 (*0-679-73715-4*) Vin Bks.

— The Sense of Sight. 1992. 22.50 (*0-8446-6612-2*) Peter Smith.

— The Sense of Sight: Writings. LC 93-13120. 1993. reprint ed. pap. 15.00 (*0-679-73722-7*) Vin Bks.

— A Seventh Man. 1981. pap. 6.95 (*0-906495-90-3*) Writers & Readers.

— Silence, Please: Stories after the Works of Juan Munoz. 144p. 1996. 27.50 (*3-931141-21-7*, Pub. by Scalo Pubs) Dist Art Pubs.

— The Success & Failure of Picasso. LC 93-13121. 1993. reprint ed. pap. 15.00 (*0-679-73725-1*) Vin Bks.

— To the Wedding. 1996. pap. 12.00 (*0-679-76777-0*) Random.

— Ways of Seeing. 1999. pap. write for info. (*0-14-013515-4*) P-H.

— Ways of Seeing. 1990. 24.25 (*0-8446-6175-9*) Peter Smith.

— Wet Rocks Seen from Above. (Illus.). 48p. 1996. 32.95 (*3-9520497-3-5*, Pub. by Memory-Cage) Dist Art Pubs.

Berger, John, ed. Environmental Restoration: Science & Strategies for Restoring the Earth. LC 89-26719. (Illus.). 398p. 1990. text 27.00 (*0-933280-94-7*); pap. text 15.95 (*0-933280-93-9*) Island Pr.

Berger, John, frwd. Maritne Franck: One Day to the Next. LC 98-86913. (Illus.). 168p. 1999. 45.00 (*0-89381-845-3*) Aperture.

Berger, John & Andreadakis, Katya B. Titian: Nymph & Shepherd. (Illus.). 120p. 1996. 25.00 (*3-7913-1672-9*, Pub. by Prestel) te Neues.

Berger, John & Bielski, Nella. Isabelle. LC 97-154900. 64p. 1998. pap. 19.95 (*1-900850-07-9*) Dufour.

Berger, John & Tanner, Alain. Jonah Who Will Be Twenty-Five in the Year Two-Thousand. Palmer, Michael, tr. from FRE.Tr. of Jonas qui aura 25 ans en l'An 2000. (Illus.). 176p. (Orig.). 1983. 20.00 (*0-913028-97-5*); pap. 9.95 (*0-913028-98-3*) North Atlantic.

Berger, John, ed. see Witkin, Jane, et al.

***Berger, John E.** Ten Hits, One Run, Nine Errors: Gospel Sermons for Sundays after Pentecost (Last Third), Cycle C. LC 00-35802. 62p. 2000. pap. 7.50 (*0-7880-1740-3*); disk 7.50 (*0-7880-1741-1*) CSS OH.

***Berger, John J.** Beating the Heat: Why & How We Must Combat Global Warming. (Illus.). 128p. 2000. pap. 10.00 (*1-893163-05-9*, Pub. by Berkeley Hills) Publishers Group.

Berger, John J. Charging Ahead: The Business of Renewable Energy & What It Means for America. LC 98-15166. (Illus.). 416p. 1998. 18.95 (*0-520-21614-8*, Pub. by U CA Pr) Cal Prin Full Svc.

— Understanding Forests. LC 97-45867. (Sierra Club Guides). 1998. pap. 16.00 (*0-87156-420-3*, Pub. by Sierra) Random.

Berger, John R. Green's Functions & Boundary Element Analysis for Modeling of Mechanical Behavior of Advanced Materials. 172p. 1997. per. 16.00 (*0-16-054491-2*) USGPO.

Berger, Jonathan & Sinton, John W. Water, Earth, & Fire: Land Use & Environmental Planning in the New Jersey Pine Barrens. LC 84-47963. (Illus.). 248p. 1985. reprint ed. pap. 76.90 (*0-608-05925-0*, 206626100008) Bks Demand.

Berger, Joseph. The Young Scientists: America's Future & the Winning of the Westinghouse. LC 93-25339. 243p. 1993. 21.95 (*0-201-63255-1*) Addison-Wesley.

Berger, Joseph, et al, eds. Sociological Theories in Progress: New Formulations. (Illus.). 416p. (C). 1989. text 44.00 (*0-8039-3525-0*) Sage.

Berger, Joseph & Zelditch, Morris. Status, Power, & Legitimacy: Strategies & Theories. LC 98-13610. 390p. 1997. text 49.95 (*1-56000-343-X*) Transaction Pubs.

Berger, Joseph & Zelditch, Morris, Jr., eds. Status, Rewards & Influence. LC 84-47979. (Jossey-Bass Social & Behavioral Science Ser.). 513p. reprint ed. pap. 159.10 (*0-8357-4966-5*, 203789900009) Bks Demand.

— Theoretical Research Programs: Studies in the Growth of Theory. LC 93-12907. 502p. (C). 1993. 57.50 (*0-8047-2230-7*) Stanford U Pr.

Berger, Joseph, et al. Types of Formalization in Small-Group Research. LC 79-27703. (Illus.). 159p. 1980. reprint ed. lib. bdg. 55.00 (*0-313-22328-9*, BETF, Greenwood Pr) Greenwood.

Berger, Joseph, ed. see Conner, Thomas L. & Fisek, M. Hamit.

Berger, Joseph C. & Castorina, Edward P. A Manager's Guide to Environmental Compliance. 164p. 1994. pap. 75.00 (*0-923606-07-6*) Amer CC Pubs.

Berger, Joseph R. & Levy, Robert, eds. AIDS & the Nervous System. 2nd ed. LC 96-2020. 624p. 1996. text 121.00 (*0-7817-0309-3*) Lppncott W & W.

Berger, Joseph R., jt. auth. see Caprio, Frank.

Berger, Joseph R., jt. auth. see Caprio, Frank S.

Berger, Joyce, jt. auth. see Berger, Arthur.

Berger, Joyce, jt. auth. see Berger, Arthur S.

Berger, Joyce, jt. ed. see Berger, Arthur S.

Berger, Judith. Herbal Rituals. LC 98-34277. 256p. 1998. text 23.95 (*0-312-19281-9*) St Martin.

— Herbal Rituals. 256p. 1999. pap. 12.95 (*0-312-24301-4*) St Martin.

***Berger, Julian.** The Gaia Atlas of First Peoples: A Future for the Indigenous World. (Illus.). 191p. 1999. reprint ed. text 25.00 (*0-7881-6413-9*) DIANE Pub.

Berger, K., ed. see Motter & Dupre.

Berger, Karen. Advanced Backpacking. LC 97-43849. (Trailside Series Guide). (Illus.). 192p. 1998. pap. 17.95 (*0-393-31769-2*) Norton.

— Backpacker's Everyday Wisdom: 1001 Expert Tips for Hikers. LC 97-25591. (Illus.). 208p. 1997. pap. 16.95 (*0-89886-523-9*) Mountaineers.

— Fundamentals of Nursing. 2nd ed. LC 97-37909. 1998. pap. text 63.95 (*0-8385-2594-6*) Appleton & Lange.

— Hiking & Backpacking: A Complete Guide. LC 95-5528. (Trailside Series Guide). (Illus.). 224p. 1995. pap. 18.95 (*0-393-31334-4*) Norton.

— Trailside Guide to Scuba Diving. LC 99-88409. 224p. 1999. pap. 18.95 (*0-393-31944-X*) Norton.

Berger, Karen, ed. Tell Me, Dark. (Illus.). 80p. 1998. mass mkt. 14.95 (*1-56389-088-7*, Pub. by DC Comics) Time Warner.

Berger, Karen & Bostwick, John, III. What Women Need to Know about Breast Self-Examination. (Illus.). 8p. 1995. pap. 1.95 (*0-942219-99-6*) Quality Med Pub.

— What Women Want to Know about Breast Implants. 2nd ed. (Illus.). 57p. 1998. pap. 6.00 (*1-57626-105-0*) Quality Med Pub.

— A Woman's Decision: Breast Care, Treatment & Reconstruction. 3rd ed. LC 98-38011. (Illus.). 680p. 1998. pap. 18.50 (*1-57626-080-1*, QMP) Quality Med Pub.

— A Woman's Decision: Breast Care, Treatment & Reconstruction Third Edition. 3rd ed. LC 98-41310. 592p. 1998. pap. 18.95 (*0-312-18229-5*, Pub. by Tor Bks) St Martin.

***Berger, Karen & Smith, Daniel R.** Pacific Crest Trail: A Hiker's Companion. (Illus.). 2000. pap. 18.95 (*0-88150-431-9*, Pub. by Countryman) Norton.

Berger, Karen & Smith, Daniel R. Where the Waters Divide: A 3,000-Mile Trek Along America's Continental Divide. LC 97-23823. (Illus.). 356p. 1997. reprint ed. pap. 17.95 (*0-88150-403-3*, Pub. by Countryman) Norton.

Berger, Karen, ed. see Delano, Jamie.

Berger, Karen, ed. see DeMatteis, J. M.

Berger, Karen, ed. see Ennis, Garth.

Berger, Karen, ed. see Fowler, Christopher.

Berger, Karen, ed. see Gaiman, Neil.

Berger, Karen, ed. see Lunch, Lydia.

Berger, Karen, ed. see Morrison, Grant.

Berger, Karen J. & Williams, Marilyn A. Fundamentals of Nursing: Collaborating for Optimal Health. (Illus.). 1632p. (C). 1992. pap. text 59.95 (*0-8385-1213-5*, A1213-6) Appleton & Lange.

Berger, Karen Templeton. All She Wants. (Scarlet Ser.). 1998. mass mkt. 3.99 (*1-85487-546-9*, Pub. by Scarlet Bks) London Brdge.

Berger, Karl. Mycological Dictionary. 2nd ed. (CZE, ENG, FRE, GER & LAT.). 432p. 1980. 125.00 (*0-8288-0068-5*, M15339) Fr & Eur.

— Mycological Dictionary in Eight Languages: German, English, French, Spanish, Latin, Czech, Polish, Russian. 2nd rev. ed. (Illus.). 432p. 1980. lib. bdg. 80.00 (*3-437-20220-0*) Lubrecht & Cramer.

— Schiller, Sein Leben, und Seine Werke, Set, Vols. 1 & 2. rev. ed. LC 70-178909. (BCL Ser. I). (Illus.). reprint ed. 165.00 (*0-404-00790-2*) AMS Pr.

Berger, Karol. Theories of Chromatic & Enharmonic Music in Late Sixteenth Century Italy. Buelow, George, ed. LC 79-24734. (Studies in Musicology: No. 10). 187p. 1980. reprint ed. pap. 58.00 (*0-8357-1065-3*, 207003700063) Bks Demand.

***Berger, Karol.** A Theory of Art. LC 98-47060. 304p. 1999. 35.00 (*0-19-512860-5*) OUP.

Berger, Kathleen S. The Developing Person Through Childhood & Adolescence. 2nd ed. 627p. (C). 1986. text 41.95 (*0-87901-241-2*) Worth.

— The Developing Person Through Childhood & Adolescence. 2nd ed. 627p. (C). 1986. 9.95 (*0-87901-242-0*) Worth.

— The Developing Person Through Childhood & Adolescence. 3rd ed. 580p. 1991. text 54.95 (*0-87901-476-8*) Worth.

— The Developing Person Through Childhood & Adolescence. 3rd ed. 580p. 1991. pap. text, student ed. 13.95 (*0-87901-477-6*) Worth.

— The Developing Person Through Childhood & Adolescence. 4th ed. 736p. 1995. text 49.60 (*1-57259-002-5*) Worth.

— The Developing Person Through Childhood & Adolescence. 4th ed. 288p. 1995. pap. text, student ed. 12.80 (*1-57259-009-2*) Worth.

— The Developing Person Through the Life Span. 1997. pap. text, student ed. 12.40 (*1-57259-225-7*) Worth.

— The Developing Person Through the Life Span. 2nd ed. 622p. (C). 1988. text 54.95 (*0-87901-381-8*) Worth.

— The Developing Person Through the Life Span. 2nd ed. 622p. (C). 1988. 9.95 (*0-87901-382-6*) Worth.

— The Developing Person Through the Life Span. 3rd ed. LC 93-60514. 691p. 1993. text 46.80 (*0-87901-59-2*); pap. text, student ed. 12.40 (*0-87901-680-9*) Worth.

— The Developing Person Through the Life Span. 4th ed. LC 96-60598. 1997. text 50.80 (*1-57259-106-4*) Worth.

— The Developing Person Through the Life Span. 4th ed. 864p. 1998. write for info. (*1-57259-199-4*) Worth.

Berger, Kathleen S. & Thompson, Ross A. The Developing Person Through Childhood. 624p. 1995. pap. text 41.40 (*1-57259-016-5*) Worth.

***Berger, Kathy L.** The Hailey & Max Stories. Wise, Noreen, ed. (Book-a-Day Collection). 48p. (YA). (ps up). 2000. pap. 6.95 (*1-58584-415-2*) Huckleberry CT.

Berger, Kenneth W., ed. Asian Resources in the Southeastern United States: Archival & Manuscript Resources on China & Japan in North Carolina. (Occasional Papers: No. 1). 73p. (Orig.). 1985. pap. 10.00 (*0-941481-01-8*) SE Conf Assn Asian Studies.

— Asian Resources in the Southeastern United States: Archival & Manuscript Resources on East Asia in Georgia. (Occasional Papers: No. 2). 58p. (Orig.). 1985. pap. 10.00 (*0-941481-02-6*) SE Conf Assn Asian Studies.

— Asian Studies in the Southeast: A Twenty-Five Year Retrospective. LC 86-31351. (Occasional Papers: No. 2). x, 78p. (Orig.). 1987. pap. 10.00 (*0-941481-04-2*) SE Conf Assn Asian Studies.

Berger-Kiss, Andres. Children of the Dawn. unabridged ed. Perry, Carla, ed. LC 98-74313. 204p. 1999. pap. 12.95 (*1-892076-06-3*) Dancing Moon.

— Voices from the Earth (Voces de la Tierra) A Bilingual Anthology of Poetry. unabridged ed. (ENG & SPA., Illus.). 203p. 1996. 14.95 (*958-648-105-0*) Partners-West.

Berger, Klaus. Die Amen-Worte Jesu: Eine Untersuchung zum Problem der Legitimation in Apokalyptischer Rede. (Beiheft zur Zeitschrift fuer die Neuetestamentliche Wissenschaft Ser.: No. 39). (AMH & GER.). (C). 1970. 60.00 (*3-11-006445-6*) De Gruyter.

— The Truth under Lock & Key: Jesus & the Dead Sea Scrolls. Currie, James S., tr. from GER. LC 94-33665.Tr. of Qumran und Jesus. 128p. (Orig.). 1995. pap. 15.95 (*0-664-25547-7*) Westminster John Knox.

Berger, Klaus, ed. see Geiger, Moritz.

Berger, Klaus P. Formalisierte Oder "Schleichende" Kodifizierung des Transnationalen Wirtschaftsrechts: Zu Den Methodischen und Praktischen Grundlagen der Lex Mercatoria. lvi, 294p. 1996. write for info. (*3-11-015044-1*) De Gruyter.

— International Economic Arbitration. 1993. lib. bdg. 216.00 (*90-6544-672-9*) Kluwer Academic.

Berger, Klaus P. & Center for Transnational Law Staff. The Creeping Codification of the Lex Mercatoria. 1998. 108.00 (*90-411-1094-1*) Kluwer Law Intl.

Berger, L. I. Semiconductor Materials. LC 96-41739. (Illus.). 496p. 1996. boxed set 129.95 (*0-8493-8912-7*) CRC Pr.

Berger, Lance A. & Sikora, Martin J. The Change Management Handbook: A Road Map to Corporate Transformation. LC 93-2553. 516p. 1993. 80.00 (*1-55623-975-0*, Irwn McGrw-H) McGrw-H Hgnr Educ.

Berger, Lance A., et al. Deengineering the Corporation: Leading Growth from Within. LC 97-95281. 160p. 1998. 12.00 (*0-9662333-0-1*) Haverford Busn.

Berger, Lance A., jt. auth. see Rock, Milton L.

Berger, Larry. Up Your Score: The Underground Guide to the SAT. LC 98-195950. 288p. 1998. pap. 9.95 (*0-7611-1135-2*) Workman Pub.

***Berger, Larry.** Up Your Score: The Underground Guide to the SAT 2001-2002. (Illus.). 288p. 2000. pap. 13.95 (*0-7611-1988-4*) Workman Pub.

Berger, Larry & Harris, Lynn. Tray Gourmet: Be Your Own Chef in the College Cafeteria. LC 91-75630. (Illus.). 192p. 1992. 10.95 (*0-9627403-2-2*) Lake Isle Pr.

Berger, Larry, et al. Up Your Score: The Underground Guide to the SAT, 1997-1998 Edition. LC 96-17390. (Illus.). 288p. 1996. pap. 8.95 (*0-7611-0483-6*, 10483) Workman Pub.

Berger, Laura S., ed. Twentieth-Century Young Adult Writers. LC 93-42870. (Twentieth-Century Writers Ser.). 830p. 1993. 140.00 (*1-55862-202-0*) St James Pr.

Berger, Lawrence A., et al. Cycles & Crises in Property-Casualty Insurance: Causes & Implications for Public Policy. (Illus.). 412p. (C). 1991. 150.00 (*0-89382-180-2*) Nat Assn Insurance.

Berger, Lawrence R. The Green Lantern: A Guide for Achieving the American Dream. 2nd large type rev. ed. 54p. 1995. mass mkt. 8.00 (*0-9673741-0-3*) L B & Assocs.

— Instant Poetry (Just Add Words) 2nd rev. ed. 54p. 1999. mass mkt. 9.50 (*0-9673741-1-1*) L B & Assocs.

Berger, Lawrence R. & Mohan, Dinesh, eds. Injury Control: A Global View. (Illus.). 292p. (C). 1996. text 39.50 (*0-19-563680-5*) OUP.

Berger, Leon. The Essentials for Starting a Mail-Order Medical-Ostomy Supply Business: The Story of a Pioneer Mail-Order Medical-Ostomy Supply Business. LC 91-72051. 96p. (Orig.). 1991. pap. 12.95 (*0-9629534-0-7*) Career Pubs.

***Berger, Leon.** Globo Sapiens: Fiction for a Business Class Lounge. 220p. 1999. pap. 21.95 (*1-55022-390-9*, Pub. by ECW) LPC InBook.

Berger, Lisa. Feathering Your Nest: The Retirement Planner IDS Financial Library. LC 92-50928. (Illus.). 512p. 1993. pap. 13.95 (*1-56305-296-2*, 3296) Workman Pub.

Berger, Lisa, jt. auth. see Rosen, Robert H.

Berger, Lou, jt. auth. see Stiles, Norman.

Berger, Louis S. Introductory Statistics: A New Approach for Behavioral Science Students. LC 79-2484. 407p. 1981. 60.00 (*0-8236-2775-6*) Intl Univs Pr.

— Psychoanalytic Theory & Clinical Relevance: What Makes a Theory Consequential for Practice? 213p. 1985. 29.95 (*0-88163-042-X*) Analytic Pr.

— Substance Abuse as Symptom: A Psychoanalytic Critique of Treatment Approaches & the Cultural Beliefs That Sustain Them. 372p. 1991. text 45.00 (*0-88163-102-7*) Analytic Pr.

Berger, Lutz. Geschieden Von Allem AuBer Gott: Sufik und Welt Bei Abu cAbd Ar-Rahman As-Sulami. (Arabistische Texte und Studien: Vol. 12). (GER.). 220p. 1998. write for info. (*3-487-10650-7*) G Olms Pubs.

Berger, M. Geometry I. LC 94-242207. (Universitext Ser.). (Illus.). xiii, 427p. 1994. 62.95 (*0-387-11658-3*) Spr-Verlag.

— Geometry II. Cole, M. & Levy, S., trs. (Universitext Ser.). (Illus.). 406p. 1996. pap. 59.95 (*0-387-17015-4*) Spr-Verlag.

— Mathematics of Nonlinear Science. LC 90-574. (Contemporary Mathematics Ser.: Vol. 108). 153p. 1990. pap. 33.00 (*0-8218-5114-4*, CONM/108) Am Math.

Berger, M., et al, eds. Antiepileptic Drugs in Psychiatry. (Journal: Neuropsychobiology: Vol. 27, No. 3, 1993). (Illus.). 76p. 1993. pap. 58.50 (*3-8055-5839-2*) S Karger.

Berger, M. & Gostiaux, B. Differential Geometry-Manifolds, Curves & Surfaces. (Graduate Tests in Mathematics Ser.: Vol. 115). 480p. 1987. 65.95 (*0-387-96626-9*) Spr-Verlag.

Berger, M., et al. Problems in Geometry. (Problem Books in Mathematics). (Illus.). 184p. 1984. 59.95 (*0-387-90971-0*) Spr-Verlag.

Berger, M., ed. see Adams, D. R. & Hedberg, L. J.

Berger, M., ed. see Berline, N., et al.

Berger, M., ed. see Buhlmann, H.

Berger, M., ed. see Conway, J. H. & Sloane, N. J.

Berger, M., ed. see Figotin, A.

Berger, M., ed. see Hewitt, E. & Ross, K. A.

Berger, M., ed. see Kashiwara, Masaki & Schapira, P.

Berger, M., ed. see Orlik, P. P. & Terao, H.

Berger, M., ed. see Pommerenke, C.

Berger, M. A. & Fienberg, Stephen E. An Introduction to Probability & Stochastic Processes. Olkin, Ingram, ed. (Texts in Statistics Ser.). (Illus.). 208p. 1992. 58.95 (*0-387-97784-8*) Spr-Verlag.

Berger, M. S. Mathematical Structures of Nonlinear Science. (C). 1990. text 226.50 (*0-7923-0728-3*) Kluwer Academic.

Berger, Manfred, et al. German Election Panel Study, 1972. 1974. write for info. (*0-89138-108-2*) ICPSR.

Berger, Marc A. & Sloan, Alan D. A Method of Generalized Characteristics. LC 82-8741. (Memoirs of the American Mathematical Society Ser.: No. 38/266). 35p. 1982. pap. 16.00 (*0-8218-2266-7*, MEMO/38/266) Am Math.

Berger, Margaret A., jt. auth. see Weinstein, Jack B.

Berger, Marguerite & Buvinic, Mayra, eds. Women's Ventures: Assistance to the Informal Sector in Latin America. fac. ed. LC 89-39190. (Kumarian Press Library of Management for Development). 288p. 1989. pap. 89.30 (*0-7837-7585-7*, 204733800007) Bks Demand.

Berger, Marie-H., jt. auth. see Bunsell, A. R.

Berger, Marie-Odile. Icaos '96 - Images, Wavelets & PDEs: Proceedings of the 12th International Conference on Analysis & Optimization of Systems, Paris, June 26-28, 1996. LC 96-26595. (Lecture Notes in Control & Information Sciences: Vol. 219). 400p. 1996. pap. 63.00 (*3-540-76076-8*) Spr-Verlag.

Berger, Marilyn J. Trial Advocacy. 928p. 1989. 48.00 (*0-316-09165-0*, Aspen Law & Bus) Aspen Pub.

Berger, Marilyn J., et al. Pretrial Advocacy: Planning, Analysis, & Strategy. 752p. 1988. teacher ed. write for info. (*0-316-09164-2*, 91642) Aspen Law.

— Pretrial Advocacy: Planning, Analysis & Strategy. 752p. 1988. pap. text 50.00 (*0-316-09162-6*, Aspen Law & Bus) Aspen Pub.

— Trial Advocacy: Planning, Analysis, & Strategy. 928p. 1989. teacher ed. write for info. (*0-316-09166-9*, 91669) Aspen Law.

Berger, Mark T. Under Northern Eyes: Latin American Studies & U. S. Hegemony in the Americas, 1898-1990. LC 94-44645. (Caribbean & Latin American Studies). 1995. text 35.00 (*0-253-31172-1*) Ind U Pr.

Berger, Mark T. & Borer, Douglas A. The Rise of East Asia: Critical Visions of the Pacific Century. LC 96-43154. 344p. (C). 1997. pap. 25.99 (*0-415-16168-1*) Routledge.

— The Rise of East Asia: Critical Visions of the Pacific Century. LC 96-43154. 344p. (C). 1997. 85.00 (*0-415-16167-3*) Routledge.

Berger, Marshal D. Vest Pocket Russian. LC 89-15396. (ENG & RUS.). 1989. pap. 5.95 (*0-8489-5105-0*) Inst Lang Study.

***Berger, Martin A.** Man Made: Thomas Eakins & the Construction of Gilded Age Manhood. LC 00-22764. (Men & Masculinity Ser.: Vol. 6). (Illus.). 181p. 2000. pap. 19.95 (*0-520-22209-1*, Pub. by U CA Pr) Cal Prin Full Svc.

— Man Made: Thomas Eakins & the Construction of Gilded-Age Manhood. LC 00-22764. (Men & Masculinity Ser.: Vol. 6). (Illus.). 181p. 2000. 50.00 (*0-520-22208-3*) U CA Pr.

B

An Asterisk (*) at the beginning of an entry indicates that the title is appearing for the first time.

Berger, Marvin. Doppler Echocardiography in Heart Disease. fac. ed. LC 86-32787. (Basic & Clinical Cardiology Ser.: No. 10). 383p. 1987. reprint ed. pap. 118.80 (*0-7837-8332-9*, 204911900010) Bks Demand.

Berger, Mary I. Speak Standard, Too: Add Mainstream American English to Your Talking Style. 150p. 1997. pap. 20.00 (*0-9630778-0-5*) Orchrd Bks IL.

A nonjudgmental program for acquiring & teaching oral/written standard American English pronunciation & grammar, for speakers of nonstandard English dialects such as Black English, Brooklynese or other regional & foreign accents. It is a student text, teacher resource or self-help program. The author is a speech-language pathologist & college instructor who has worked with nonstandard English-speaking students & adults for 25 years. She uses the BI-DIALECTIC method that encourages acquisition of standard English in addition to, not instead of, a primary style; students learn to "switch" situationally from one dialect to the other. The book emphasizes that nonstandard dialects are different, not deficient; it contrasts speech equivalencies rather than corrections; instructors are encouraged to respect dialectic differences & not to teach in terms of right & wrong. The book has over 180 lessons on pronunciation & grammar & some linguistic information on the derivation of dialects. The program is used nationally in a variety of settings. A H.S. English Chair says, "It's an excellent book...invaluable in helping students to master standard English;" a Univ. Speech Dept. Chair writes that it's "...easy to apply, respectful, practical, motivating & user-friendly...I highly recommend it...;" & from HEARSAY, a speech journal: "Here is a needed, well-written, well-organized book for anyone trying to add standard English to his/her speaking repertoire. I endorse it whole-heartedly!" Call or write for info. or to order: ORCHARD BOOKS, INC., 2222 N. Orchard St., Chicago, IL 60614, 800-528-5244; FAX (312) 528-9481.
Publisher Paid Annotation.

— Speak Standard, Too: Add Mainstream American English to Your Talking Style. Set. 150p. 1991. 50.00 incl. audio (*0-9630778-2-1*) Orchrd Bks IL.

–Teach Standard, Too: Teach Oral & Written Standard English as a Second Dialect to English-Speaking Students. 2nd large type ed. Oberman, Bonnie, ed. 520p. (Orig.). (C). 1997. reprint ed. pap., teacher ed. 60.00 (*0-9630778-3-X*) Orchrd Bks IL.

A teacher's manual that teaches oral & written standard English grammar & pronunciation to nonstandard English speaking &/or foreign language background students (K-12). The author is a speech-language pathologist & college instructor who has taught standard English acquisition for 25 years, & emphasizes that children must SPEAK standard English before they can read, write or take tests in it. Contains SCHOOLTALK/FRIENDTALK - 95 scripted lessons that teach SYSTEMATIC acquisition of standard English for school. Introductory unit demonstrates that nonstandard dialects & their speakers are DIFFERENT, NOT DEFICIENT, following units teach more than 120 standard grammar & pronunciations features such as ED-ENDINGS, S-ENDINGS, AM/IS/ARE/WAS/WERE, ASK & (TH). Lesson plans, teacher scripts, games, songs, skits, drills teach students to: identify their own nonstandard speech rules; contrast them with equivalent standard rules; practice/master/monitor standard rules; practice new rules in writing & reading. Extensive appendix has progress chart & scripts for teacher-parent meetings, home practice & teaching older students. Used & praised nationally by educators: Los Angles teacher: "A MOST NECESSARY, USEFUL & USER-FRIENDLY MANUAL - CHILDREN LOVE THE LESSONS & LEARN!" Univ. of Tenn. Professor: "I AM IN AWE OF ITS COMPREHENSIVENESS; A SUPERLATIVE JOB; I SHALL BE A HUMAN COMMERCIAL FOR IT." Contact Orchard Books, Inc., 2222 N. Orchard St., Chicago, IL 60614. 800-528-5244, FAX: 773-528-9481. (Refer to SPEAK STANDARD, TOO annotation). ***Publisher Paid Annotation.***

Berger, Mary J. Jesus Lives in Us: Activity Book. 96p. (J). (gr. 5). pap. 2.50 (*0-8198-3931-0*) Pauline Bks.

Berger, Mary J. & Heffernan, Mary A. Jesus Is Forever: Project Book. 87p. (J). (gr. 8). pap. 2.25 (*0-8198-3946-9*) Pauline Bks.

Berger, Mary J., jt. auth. see Dalton, Denise.

Berger, Mary J., jt. auth. see Parise, Michael.

Berger, Mary J., tr. see Martini, Carlo M.

***Berger, Maurice.** Adrian Piper A Retrospective, 1965-2000. 200p. 1999. pap. text 25.00 (*1-890761-02-8*) Univ MD Fine Arts.

Berger, Maurice. Ciphers of Identity. LC 95-73788. 44p. 1994. 20.00 (*0-9624565-4-3*) Univ MD Fine Arts.

— Crisis of Criticism. 192p. 1998. pap. 17.95 (*1-56584-417-3*, Pub. by New Press NY) Norton.

— Environmental Terror. LC 91-67647. 33p. 1991. pap. 10.00 (*0-9624565-2-7*) Univ MD Fine Arts.

— Minimal Politics. (Illus.). 200p. 1997. pap. 14.95 (*1-890761-00-1*) Dist Art Pubs.

— No Doubt: African-American Art of the 90s. (Illus.). 28p. (Orig.). 1996. spiral bd. 12.00 (*1-888332-02-6*) Aldrich Mus.

Berger, Maurice. White Lies: Race & the Myths of Whiteness. LC 98-73832. 224p. 1999. 23.00 (*0-374-28949-2*) FS&G.

***Berger, Maurice.** White Lies: Race & the Myths of Whiteness. LC 98-73832. 224p. 2000. pap. 14.00 (*0-374-52715-6*) FS&G.

***Berger, Maurice, ed.** Modern Art & Society: An Anthology of Social & Multicultural Readings. (Illus.). 310p. 2000. reprint ed. pap. text 17.00 (*0-7881-6967-X*) DIANE Pub.

Berger, Maurice, et al, eds. Constructing Masculinity. LC 95-22214. 320p. (C). (gr. 13). 1995. 80.00 (*0-415-91052-8*, B4487); pap. 24.99 (*0-415-91053-6*, B4491) Routledge.

Berger, Maurice & Isaak, Jo A. Nancy Spero & Leon Golub: Notes in Time. 48p. 20.00 (*0-9624565-6-X*) Univ MD Fine Arts.

Berger, Maurice, et al. The Theater of Refusal: Black Art & Mainstream Criticism. (Illus.). 88p. (Orig.). 1993. pap. 16.50 (*1-884355-00-5*) U CA Fine Arts.

Berger, Mel. Cross Cultural Team Building: Guidelines for More Effective Communication & Negotiation. LC 96-19791. (Mcgraw-Hill Training Ser.). 1996. pap. write for info. (*0-07-707919-1*) McGraw.

Berger, Melvin. All about Electricity: A Do-It-Yourself Science Book. 32p. (J). (ps-5). 1995. pap. 3.95 (*0-590-48077-4*) Scholastic Inc.

— All about Light: A Do-It-Yourself Science Book. 32p. (J). (ps-3). 1995. pap. 3.95 (*0-590-48076-6*) Scholastic Inc.

— All about Magnifying Glasses. 32p. (J). (ps-3). 1993. pap. 4.95 (*0-590-45510-9*) Scholastic Inc.

— All about Seeds: A Hands-on Science Book. 32p. (J). (ps-3). 1992. pap. 2.95 (*0-590-44909-5*) Scholastic Inc.

— All about Sound. LC 94-218339. (Do-It-Yourself Science Ser.). 32p. (J). (ps-3). 1994. pap. 3.95 (*0-590-46760-3*) Scholastic Inc.

— All about Water. (Do-It-Yourself Science Ser.). 32p. (J). (ps-3). 1994. pap. 3.95 (*0-590-46761-1*) Scholastic Inc.

— Amazing Sharks. Reed, Janet, ed. (Ranger Rick Science Spectacular Ser.). 16p. (J). (gr. 2-4). 1995. pap. 16.95 (*1-56784-213-5*) Newbridge Educ.

— Amazing Sharks: Student Book. Reed, Janet, ed. (Ranger Rick Science Spectacular Ser.). (Illus.). 16p. (Orig.). (J). (gr. 2-4). 1996. pap. 3.95 (*1-56784-238-0*) Newbridge Educ.

— Amazing Sharks: Theme Pack. Reed, Janet, ed. (Ranger Rick Science Spectacular Ser.). (Illus.). (Orig.). (J). (gr. 2-4). 1995. pap. 36.90 (*1-56784-270-4*) Newbridge Educ.

— Amazing Water. Evento, Susan, ed. (Early Science Big Bks.). (Illus.). 16p. (Orig.). (J). (ps-2). 1995. pap. 16.95 (*1-56784-104-X*) Newbridge Educ.

— Amazing Water: Mini Book. Evento, Susan, ed. (Early Science Big Bks.). (Illus.). 16p. (Orig.). (J). (ps-2). 1995. pap. 3.95 (*1-56784-129-5*) Newbridge Educ.

— Amazing Water Theme Pack. Evento, Susan, ed. (Macmillan Early Science Big Bks.). (Illus.). (J). (ps-2). 1995. pap. 49.95 (*1-56784-186-4*) Newbridge Educ.

— Animal Senses. Lunis, Natalie, ed. (Ranger Rick Science Spectacular Ser.). 16p. (J). (gr. 2-4). 1995. pap. 16.95 (*1-56784-215-1*) Newbridge Educ.

— Animal Senses: Student Book. Lunis, Natalie, ed. (Ranger Rick Science Spectacular Ser.). (Illus.). 16p. (Orig.). (J). (gr. 2-4). 1996. pap. 3.95 (*1-56784-240-2*) Newbridge Educ.

— Animal Senses: Theme Pack. Lunis, Natalie, ed. (Ranger Rick Science Spectacular Ser.). (Illus.). (Orig.). (J). (gr. 2-4). 1996. pap. 36.90 (*1-56784-267-4*) Newbridge Educ.

— Animals & Their Babies. Lunis, Natalie, ed. (Early Science Big Bks.). (Illus.). 16p. (J). (ps-2). 1993. pap. 16.95 (*1-56784-005-1*) Newbridge Educ.

— Animals & Their Babies: Mini Book. Lunis, Natalie, ed. (Early Science Big Bks.). (Illus.). 16p. (J). (ps-2). 1993. pap. 3.95 (*1-56784-030-2*) Newbridge Educ.

— Animals & Their Babies Theme Pack. Evento, Susan, ed. (Macmillan Early Science Big Bks.). (Illus.). (J). (ps-2). 1995. pap. 49.95 (*1-56784-137-6*) Newbridge Educ.

— Animals in Danger. Lunis, Natalie, ed. (Ranger Rick Science Spectacular Ser.). 16p. (J). (gr. 2-4). 1993. pap. 16.95 (*1-56784-202-X*) Newbridge Educ.

— Animals in Danger: Student Book. Lunis, Natalie, ed. (Ranger Rick Science Spectacular Ser.). (Illus.). 16p. (Orig.). (J). (gr. 2-4). 1996. pap. 3.95 (*1-56784-227-5*) Newbridge Educ.

— Animals in Danger: Theme Pack. Lunis, Natalie, ed. (Ranger Rick Science Spectacular Ser.). (Illus.). (Orig.). (J). (gr. 2-4). 1996. pap. 36.90 (*1-56784-272-0*) Newbridge Educ.

— Animals in Hiding. Lunis, Natalie, ed. (Early Science Big Bks.). (Illus.). 16p. (J). (ps-2). 1993. pap. 16.95 (*1-56784-010-8*) Newbridge Educ.

— Animals in Hiding: Mini Book. Lunis, Natalie, ed. (Early Science Big Bks.). (Illus.). 16p. (J). (ps-2). 1994. pap. 3.95 (*1-56784-035-3*) Newbridge Educ.

— Animals in Hiding Theme Pack. Evento, Susan, ed. (Macmillan Early Science Big Bks.). (Illus.). (J). (ps-2). 1995. pap. 49.95 (*1-56784-142-2*) Newbridge Educ.

— An Apple a Day. Trumbauer, Lisa, ed. (Early Science Big Bks.). (Illus.). 16p. (J). (ps-2). 1993. pap. 16.95 (*1-56784-011-6*) Newbridge Educ.

— An Apple a Day: Mini Book. Trumbauer, Lisa, ed. (Early Science Big Bks.). 16p. (J). (ps-2). 1995. pap. 3.95 (*1-56784-036-1*) Newbridge Educ.

— An Apple a Day Theme Pack. Evento, Susan, ed. (Macmillan Early Science Big Bks.). (Illus.). (J). (ps-2). 1995. pap. 49.95 (*1-56784-143-0*) Newbridge Educ.

— As Big As a Whale. Lunis, Natalie, ed. (Ranger Rick Science Spectacular Ser.). 16p. (J). (gr. 2-4). 1993. pap. 16.95 (*1-56784-201-1*) Newbridge Educ.

— As Big As a Whale: Student Book. Lunis, Natalie, ed. (Ranger Rick Science Spectacular Ser.). (Illus.). 16p. (Orig.). (J). (gr. 2-4). 1996. pap. 3.95 (*1-56784-226-7*) Newbridge Educ.

— As Big As a Whale: Theme Pack. Lunis, Natalie, ed. (Ranger Rick Science Spectacular Ser.). (Illus.). (J). (gr. 2-4). 1996. pap. 36.90 (*1-56784-273-9*) Newbridge Educ.

— The Big Bears. Trumbauer, Lisa, ed. (Early Science Big Bks.). (Illus.). 16p. (J). (ps-2). 1994. pap. 16.95 (*1-56784-015-9*) Newbridge Educ.

— The Big Bears: Mini Book. Trumbauer, Lisa, ed. (Early Science Big Bks.). 16p. (J). (ps-2). 1995. pap. 3.95 (*1-56784-042-6*) Newbridge Educ.

— The Big Bears Theme Pack. Evento, Susan, ed. (Macmillan Early Science Big Bks.). (Illus.). (J). (ps-2). 1995. pap. 49.95 (*1-56784-147-3*) Newbridge Educ.

***Berger, Melvin.** Billions of Bugs: A Book about Insects. LC 99-41768. (Hello Reader! Ser.). (Illus.). 40p. (J). (gr. 1-3). 2000. 3.99 (*0-439-08748-1*) Scholastic Inc.

Berger, Melvin. Bubbles, Bubbles, Everywhere Theme Pack. Evento, Susan, ed. (Macmillan Early Science Big Bks.). (Illus.). (J). (ps-2). 1995. pap. 49.95 (*1-56784-149-X*) Newbridge Educ.

— Busy As a Bee. Evento, Susan, ed. (Early Science Big Bks.). (Illus.). 16p. (Orig.). (J). (ps-2). 1995. pap. 16.95 (*1-56784-101-5*) Newbridge Educ.

— Busy As a Bee: Mini Book. Evento, Susan, ed. (Early Science Big Bks.). (Illus.). 16p. (Orig.). (J). (ps-2). 1995. pap. 3.95 (*1-56784-126-0*) Newbridge Educ.

— Busy As a Bee: Theme Pack. Evento, Susan, ed. (Macmillan Early Science Big Bks.). (Illus.). (J). (ps-2). 1995. pap. 49.95 (*1-56784-183-X*) Newbridge Educ.

— A Butterfly Is Born. Trumbauer, Lisa, ed. (Early Science Big Bks.). (Illus.). 16p. (J). (ps-2). 1993. pap. 16.95 (*1-56784-012-4*) Newbridge Educ.

— A Butterfly is Born: Mini Book. Trumbauer, Lisa, ed. (Early Science Big Bks.). 16p. (J). (ps-2). 1995. pap. 3.95 (*1-56784-037-X*) Newbridge Educ.

— A Butterfly is Born Theme Pack. Evento, Susan, ed. (Macmillan Early Science Big Bks.). (Illus.). (J). (ps-2). 1995. pap. 49.95 (*1-56784-144-9*) Newbridge Educ.

***Berger, Melvin.** Buzz! A Book about Insects. (Hello, Reader! Ser.). (Illus.). (J). 2000. 9.44 (*0-606-18521-6*) Turtleback.

Berger, Melvin. Call of the Wolves. Reed, Janet, ed. (Ranger Rick Science Spectacular Ser.). 16p. (Orig.). (J). (gr. 2-4). 1995. pap. 16.95 (*1-56784-216-X*) Newbridge Educ.

— Call of the Wolves: Student Book. Reed, Janet, ed. (Ranger Rick Science Spectacular Ser.). (Illus.). 16p. (Orig.). (J). (gr. 2-4). 1996. pap. 3.95 (*1-56784-241-0*) Newbridge Educ.

— Call of the Wolves: Theme Pack. Reed, Janet, ed. (Ranger Rick Science Spectacular Ser.). (Illus.). (J). (gr. 2-4). Date not set. pap. 36.90 (*1-56784-271-2*) Newbridge Educ.

— Can Kids Save the Earth? Evento, Susan, ed. (Ranger Rick Science Spectacular Ser.). 16p. (J). (gr. 2-4). 1994. pap. 16.95 (*1-56784-209-7*) Newbridge Educ.

— Can Kids Save the Earth? Student Book. Evento, Susan, ed. (Ranger Rick Science Spectacular Ser.). (Illus.). 16p. (Orig.). (J). (gr. 2-4). 1996. pap. 3.95 (*1-56784-234-8*) Newbridge Educ.

— Can Kids Save the Earth? Theme Pack. Evento, Susan, ed. (Ranger Rick Science Spectacular Ser.). (Illus.). (Orig.). (J). (gr. 2-4). 1996. pap. 36.90 (*1-56784-274-7*) Newbridge Educ.

— Chirping Crickets. LC 96-51661. (Let's-Read-&-Find-Out Science Ser.). (Illus.). 32p. (J). (gr. k-4). 1998. 15.95 (*0-06-024961-7*); lib. bdg. 15.89 (*0-06-024962-5*) HarpC.

— Chirping Crickets. (Let's Read-&-Find-Out Science Ser.). (J). 1998. 10.15 (*0-606-13270-8*, Pub. by Turtleback) Demco.

— Chirping Crickets, Stage 2. LC 96-51661. (Let's-Read-&-Find-Out Science Bks.). (Illus.). 32p. (J). (gr. k-4). 1998. pap. 4.95 (*0-06-445180-1*) HarpC Child Bks.

— Chomp! A Book about Sharks. LC 98-22215. (Hello Readers! Ser.). (Illus.). 40p. (J). (gr. 1-3). 1999. 3.99 (*0-590-52298-1*) Scholastic Inc.

— Complete Program. Evento, Susan, ed. (Macmillan Early Science Big Bks.). (Illus.). (J). (ps-2). 1995. pap. write for info. (*1-56784-188-0*) Newbridge Educ.

— Computers Answers Question & Answer Book. (J). 1985. 11.50 (*0-690-04479-8*) HarpC Child Bks.

— Computers in Your Life. (J). (gr. 5 up). 1981. 12.95 (*0-690-04100-4*) HarpC Child Bks.

— Computers in Your Life. LC 80-2452. (Trophy Nonfiction Bk.). (Illus.). 128p. (J). (gr. 5-8). 1984. pap. 4.95 (*0-06-446001-0*, HarpTrophy) HarpC Child Bks.

— Consumer Protection Labs. LC 75-6686. (Scientists at Work Ser.). (Illus.). (J). (gr. 2-4). 1950. lib. bdg. 11.89 (*0-381-99622-0*) HarpC Child Bks.

— Creatures That Glow: A Book about Bioluminescent Animals. (Illus.). (J). 1996. pap. 5.99 (*0-590-58108-2*) Scholastic Inc.

— Creatures That Glow: A Book about Bioluminescent Animals. 1996. 11.19 (*0-606-09170-X*, Pub. by Turtleback) Demco.

— Digging for Dinosaurs. Evento, Susan, ed. (Ranger Rick Science Spectacular Ser.). 16p. (J). (gr. 2-4). 1994. pap. 16.95 (*1-56784-205-4*) Newbridge Educ.

— Digging for Dinosaurs: Student Book. Evento, Susan, ed. (Ranger Rick Science Spectacular Ser.). (Illus.). 16p. (Orig.). (J). (gr. 2-4). 1996. pap. 3.95 (*1-56784-230-5*) Newbridge Educ.

— Digging for Dinosaurs: Theme Pack. Evento, Susan, ed. (Ranger Rick Science Spectacular Ser.). (Illus.). (Orig.). (J). (gr. 2-4). 1996. pap. 36.90 (*1-56784-277-1*) Newbridge Educ.

— Dinosaurs. (Stranger Than Fiction Ser.). 128p. (J). 1990. pap. 2.95 (*0-380-76052-5*, Avon Bks) Morrow Avon.

— Discovering Jupiter: The Amazing Collision in Space. LC 96-165061. (Illus.). 55p. (J). (ps-3). 1995. pap. 4.95 (*0-590-48824-4*) Scholastic Inc.

— Discovering Mars: The Amazing Story of the Red Planet. LC 94-123286. 56p. (J). (gr. 4-7). 1992. pap. 3.95 (*0-590-45221-5*) Scholastic Inc.

— Discovery Readers, 12 vols. 1999. 191.40 (*0-7910-5075-0*) Chelsea Hse.

— Disease Detectives. LC 77-26589. (Scientists at Work Ser.). (Illus.). (J). (gr. 4 up). 1978. lib. bdg. 12.89 (*0-690-03908-5*) HarpC Child Bks.

***Berger, Melvin.** Dive! A Book of Deep-Sea Creatures. LC 99-42690. (Hello Reader! Ser.). (Illus.). 40p. (J). (ps-3). 2000. 3.99 (*0-439-08747-3*) Scholastic Inc.

— Dive! A Book of Deep Sea Creatures. (Illus.). (J). 2000. 9.44 (*0-606-18536-4*) Turtleback.

Berger, Melvin. Don't Believe It. (Illus.). 64p. (J). (gr. 2-5). 1998. pap. 4.99 (*0-590-68852-9*) Scholastic Inc.

***Berger, Melvin.** Don't Believe It! Fibs & Facts about Animals. 1998. 10.09 (*0-606-13339-9*, Pub. by Turtleback) Demco.

Berger, Melvin. Early Science Big Book Collection. Evento, Susan, ed. (Macmillan Early Science Big Bks.). (Illus.). (J). (ps-2). 1995. pap. write for info. (*1-56784-189-9*) Newbridge Educ.

— Early Science Big Books, 6 units, Set. Evento, Susan & Trumbauer, Lisa, eds. (J). (ps-2). 1995. pap. 89.00 (*1-56784-829-X*); pap. 326.00 (*1-56784-832-X*); pap. 178.00 (*1-56784-833-8*) Newbridge Educ.

— Early Science Big Books, 72 bks., Set. Evento, Susan & Trumbauer, Lisa, eds. (Illus.). (J). (ps-2). 1995. pap., student ed. 178.00 (*1-56784-825-7*) Newbridge Educ.

— Earth & Beyond Big Books Set. Evento, Susan, ed. (Macmillan Early Science Big Bks.). (Illus.). (J). (ps-2). 1995. pap. write for info. (*1-56784-168-6*) Newbridge Educ.

— Earth & Beyond Set. Evento, Susan, ed. (Macmillan Early Science Big Bks.). (Illus.). (J). (ps-2). 1995. pap. write for info. (*1-56784-167-8*) Newbridge Educ.

— Exploring the Mind & Brain. LC 82-45582. (Scientists at Work Ser.). (Illus.). 128p. (J). (gr. 5 up). 1983. 11.95 (*0-690-04251-5*); lib. bdg. 12.89 (*0-690-04252-3*) HarpC Child Bks.

— Flies Taste with Their Feet: Weird Facts about Insects. (Strange World Ser.). (J). (gr. 2-5). 1997. pap. text 2.99 (*0-590-93994-7*) Scholastic Inc.

— Food & Nutrition Big Books Set. Evento, Susan, ed. (Macmillan Early Science Big Bks.). (Illus.). (J). (ps-2). 1995. pap. write for info. (*1-56784-174-0*) Newbridge Educ.

— Food & Nutrition Set. Evento, Susan, ed. (Macmillan Early Science Big Bks.). (Illus.). (J). (ps-2). 1995. pap. write for info. (*1-56784-173-2*) Newbridge Educ.

— The Four Seasons. Evento, Susan, ed. (Early Science Big Bks.). (Illus.). 16p. (Orig.). (J). (ps-2). 1995. pap. 16.95 (*1-56784-100-7*) Newbridge Educ.

— The Four Seasons: Mini Book. Evento, Susan, ed. (Early Science Big Bks.). (Illus.). 16p. (Orig.). (J). (ps-2). 1995. pap. 3.95 (*1-56784-125-2*) Newbridge Educ.

— The Four Seasons Theme Pack. Evento, Susan, ed. (Macmillan Early Science Big Bks.). (Illus.). (J). (ps-2). 1995. pap. 49.95 (*1-56784-182-1*) Newbridge Educ.

— From Peanuts to Peanut Butter. Lunis, Natalie, ed. (Early Science Big Bks.). (Illus.). 16p. (J). (ps-2). 1992. pap. 16.95 (*1-56784-001-9*) Newbridge Educ.

— From Peanuts to Peanut Butter: Mini Book. Lunis, Natalie, ed. (Early Science Big Bks.). (Illus.). 16p. (J). (ps-2). 1993. pap. 3.95 (*1-56784-026-4*) Newbridge Educ.

— From Peanuts to Peanut Butter Theme Pack. Evento, Susan, ed. (Macmillan Early Science Big Bks.). (Illus.). (J). (ps-2). 1995. pap. 49.95 (*1-56784-133-3*) Newbridge Educ.

— Germs Make Me Sick! LC 84-45334. (Let's-Read-&-Find-Out-Science Bks.). (Illus.). 32p. (J). (ps-3). 1985. lib. bdg. 14.89 (*0-690-04429-1*) HarpC Child Bks.

— Germs Make Me Sick! (Let's-Read-And-Find-Out Science. Stage 2 Ser.). (J). 1995. 10.15 (*0-606-08439-8*, Pub. by Turtleback) Demco.

— Germs Make Me Sick! rev. ed. LC 93-27059. (Let's-Read-&-Find-Out Science Bks.). (Illus.). 32p. (J). (ps-3). 1995. 15.95 (*0-06-024249-3*); pap. 4.95 (*0-06-445154-2*, HarpTrophy); lib. bdg. 15.89 (*0-06-024250-7*) HarpC Child Bks.

— Growing Pumpkins. Trumbauer, Lisa, ed. (Early Science Big Bks.). (Illus.). 16p. (J). (ps-2). 1994. pap. 16.95 (*1-56784-018-3*) Newbridge Educ.

An Asterisk (*) at the beginning of an entry indicates that the title is appearing for the first time.

— Growing Pumpkins: Mini Book. Trumbauer, Lisa, ed. (Early Science Big Bks.). 16p. (J). (ps-2). 1995. pap. 3.95 (*1-56784-043-4*) Newbridge Educ.

— Growing Pumpkins Theme Pack. Evento, Susan, ed. (Macmillan Early Science Big Bks.). (Illus.). (J). (ps-2). 1995. pap. 49.95 (*1-56784-175-9*) Newbridge Educ.

— Growl! A Book about Bears. LC 98-22212. (Hello Readers! Ser.). (Illus.). 40p. (J). (gr. 1-3). 1998. 3.99 (*0-590-63266-3*) Scholastic Inc.

— How Do Animals Sleep? Evento, Susan, ed. (Ranger Rick Science Spectacular Ser.). 16p. (J). (gr. 2-4). 1996. pap. 16.95 (*1-56784-219-4*) Newbridge Educ.

— How Do Animals Sleep? Student Book. Evento, Susan, ed. (Ranger Rick Science Spectacular Ser.). (Illus.). 16p. (Orig.). (J). (gr. 2-4). 1996. pap. 3.95 (*1-56784-244-5*) Newbridge Educ.

— How Do Animals Sleep? Theme Pack. Evento, Susan, ed. (Ranger Rick Science Spectacular Ser.). (Illus.). (Orig.). (J). (gr. 2-4). 1996. pap. 36.90 (*1-56784-269-0*) Newbridge Educ.

— How Life Began. 1990. 14.95 (*0-385-44529-6*) Doubleday.

— The Human Body. Evento, Susan, ed. (Early Science Big Bks.). 16p. (Orig.). (J). (ps-2). 1996. pap. 16.95 (*1-56784-315-8*) Newbridge Educ.

— The Human Body: Mini Book. Evento, Susan, ed. (Early Science Big Bks.). 16p. (Orig.). (J). (ps-2). 1996. pap. 3.95 (*1-56784-340-9*) Newbridge Educ.

— Hundred & One Nature Jokes. 96p. (J). (gr. 4-6). 1994. pap. 1.95 (*0-590-47763-3*) Scholastic Inc.

— Insect Lives. Schaffer, Donna, ed. (Ranger Rick Science Spectacular Ser.). 16p. (J). (gr. 2-4). 1996. pap. 16.95 (*1-56784-220-8*) Newbridge Educ.

— Insect Lives: Student Book. (Ranger Rick Science Spectacular Ser.). (Illus.). 16p. (Orig.). (J). (gr. 2-4). 1996. pap. 3.95 (*1-56784-245-3*) Newbridge Educ.

— Kids for the Earth. Trumbauer, Lisa, ed. (Early Science Big Bks.). (Illus.). 16p. (J). (ps-2). 1994. pap. 16.95 (*1-56784-020-5*) Newbridge Educ.

— Kids for the Earth: Mini Book. Trumbauer, Lisa, ed. (Early Science Big Bks.). 16p. (J). (ps-2). 1995. pap. 3.95 (*1-56784-045-0*) Newbridge Educ.

— Kids for the Earth Theme Pack. Evento, Susan, ed. (Macmillan Early Science Big Bks.). (Illus.). (J). (ps-2). 1995. pap. 49.95 (*1-56784-177-5*) Newbridge Educ.

— Leaping Frogs. Trumbauer, Lisa, ed. (Early Science Big Bks.). (Illus.). 16p. (J). (ps-2). 1995. pap. 16.95 (*1-56784-023-X*) Newbridge Educ.

— Leaping Frogs Theme Pack. Evento, Susan, ed. (Macmillan Early Science Big Bks.). (Illus.). (J). (ps-2). 1995. pap. 49.95 (*1-56784-180-5*) Newbridge Educ.

— Life Cycles Big Books Set. Evento, Susan, ed. (Macmillan Early Science Big Bks.). (Illus.). (J). (ps-2). 1995. pap. write for info. (*1-56784-172-4*) Newbridge Educ.

— Life Cycles Set. Evento, Susan, ed. (Macmillan Early Science Big Bks.). (Illus.). (J). (ps-2). 1995. pap. write for info. (*1-56784-171-6*) Newbridge Educ.

— Life in a Coral Reef. Lunis, Natalie, ed. (Ranger Rick Science Spectacular Ser.). 16p. (J). (gr. 2-4). 1994. pap. 16.95 (*1-56784-204-6*) Newbridge Educ.

— Life in a Coral Reef: Student Book. Lunis, Natalie, ed. (Ranger Rick Science Spectacular Ser.). (Illus.). 16p. (Orig.). (J). (gr. 2-4). 1996. pap. 3.95 (*1-56784-229-1*) Newbridge Educ.

— Life in a Coral Reef: Theme Pack. Lunis, Natalie, ed. (Ranger Rick Science Spectacular Ser.). (Illus.). (Orig.). (J). (gr. 2-4). 1996. pap. 36.90 (*1-56784-263-1*) Newbridge Educ.

— Life in a Tree: Mini Book. Evento, Susan, ed. (Early Science Mini Bks.). 16p. (Orig.). (J). (ps-2). 1996. pap. 3.95 (*1-56784-338-7*) Newbridge Educ.

— Life in the Desert. Schaffer, Donna, ed. (Rnager Rick Science Spectacular Ser.). (Illus.). 16p. (Orig.). (J). (gr. 2-4). 1996. pap. 16.95 (*1-56784-217-8*) Newbridge Educ.

— Life in the Desert: Student Book. Schaffer, Donna, ed. (Ranger Rick Science Spectacular Ser.). (Illus.). 16p. (Orig.). (J). (gr. 2-4). 1996. pap. 3.95 (*1-56784-242-9*) Newbridge Educ.

— Life in the Desert: Theme Pack. Schaffer, Donna, ed. (Ranger Rick Science Spectacular Ser.). (Illus.). (Orig.). (J). 1996. pap. 36.90 (*1-56784-264-X*) Newbridge Educ.

— Life in the Polar Regions. Lunis, Natalie, ed. (Ranger Rick Science Spectacular Ser.). 16p. (J). (gr. 2-4). 1994. pap. 16.95 (*1-56784-210-0*) Newbridge Educ.

— Life in the Polar Regions: Student Book. Lunis, Natalie, ed. (Ranger Rick Science Spectacular Ser.). (Illus.). 16p. (Orig.). (J). (gr. 2-4). 1996. pap. 3.95 (*1-56784-235-6*) Newbridge Educ.

— Life in the Polar Regions: Theme Pack. Lunis, Natalie, ed. (Ranger Rick Science Spectacular Ser.). (Illus.). (Orig.). (J). (gr. 2-4). 1996. pap. 36.90 (*1-56784-265-8*) Newbridge Educ.

— Life in the Rain Forest. Lunis, Natalie, ed. (Ranger Rick Science Spectacular Ser.). 16p. (J). (gr. 2-4). 1993. pap. 16.95 (*1-56784-200-3*) Newbridge Educ.

— Life in the Rain Forest: Student Book. Lunis, Natalie, ed. (Ranger Rick Science Spectacular Ser.). (Illus.). 16p. (Orig.). (J). (gr. 2-4). 1996. pap. 3.95 (*1-56784-225-9*) Newbridge Educ.

— Life in the Rain Forest: Theme Pack. Lunis, Natalie, ed. (Ranger Rick Science Spectacular Ser.). (Illus.). (Orig.). (J). (gr. 2-4). 1996. pap. 36.90 (*1-56784-266-6*) Newbridge Educ.

— Life in the Sea. Trumbauer, Lisa, ed. (Early Science Big Bks.). (Illus.). 16p. (J). (ps-2). 1993. pap. 16.95 (*1-56784-013-2*) Newbridge Educ.

— Life in the Sea Theme Pack. Evento, Susan, ed. (Macmillan Early Science Big Bks.). (Illus.). (J). (ps-2). 1995. pap. 49.95 (*1-56784-145-7*) Newbridge Educ.

— Life on the African Savannah. Lunis, Natalie, ed. (Ranger Rick Science Spectacular Ser.). 16p. (J). (gr. 2-4). 1995. pap. 16.95 (*1-56784-214-3*) Newbridge Educ.

— Life on the African Savannah: Student Book. Lunis, Natalie, ed. (Ranger Rick Science Spectacular Ser.). (Illus.). 16p. (Orig.). (J). (gr. 2-4). 1996. pap. 3.95 (*1-56784-239-9*) Newbridge Educ.

— Life on the African Savannah: Theme Pack. Lunis, Natalie, ed. (Ranger Rick Science Spectacular Ser.). (Illus.). (Orig.). (J). (gr. 2-4). 1996. pap. 36.90 (*1-56784-262-3*) Newbridge Educ.

— Light. Evento, Susan, ed. (Early Science Big Bks.). (Illus.). 16p. (Orig.). (J). (ps-2). 1995. pap. 16.95 (*1-56784-105-8*) Newbridge Educ.

— Light: Mini Book. Evento, Susan, ed. (Early Science Big Bks.). (Illus.). 16p. (Orig.). (J). (ps-2). 1995. pap. 3.95 (*1-56784-130-9*) Newbridge Educ.

— Light Theme Pack. Evento, Susan, ed. (Macmillan Early Science Big Bks.). (Illus.). (J). (ps-2). 1995. pap. 49.95 (*1-56784-187-2*) Newbridge Educ.

Berger, Melvin. Look Out for Turtles! LC 90-36894. (Trophy Let's-Read-&-Find-Out Bk., Stage 2). (Illus.). 32p. (J). (gr. k-4). 1996. pap. 4.95 (*0-06-445156-9*, HarpTrophy) HarpC Child Bks.

Berger, Melvin. Look Out for Turtles! LC 90-36894. (Let's-Read-&-Find-Out Science Bks.: Stage 2). (Illus.). 32p. (J). (ps-3). 2000. lib. bdg. 15.89 (*0-06-022540-8*) HarpC Child Bks.

— Look Out for Turtles! (Let's Read-&-Find-Out Science Ser.). 1992. 10.15 (*0-606-09572-1*, Pub. by Turtleback) Demco.

— Looking at the Planets: A Book about the Solar System. (Illus.). 32p. (J). (gr. 1-3). 1995. pap. 5.95 (*0-590-20300-2*) Scholastic Inc.

— Looking at the Planets: A Book about the Solar System. 1995. 11.15 (*0-606-07804-5*, Pub. by Turtleback) Demco.

— Macmillan Early Science Big Books, 4 vols., Set. (Illus.). (J). (ps-2). 1995. pap. write for info. (*1-56784-645-9*) Newbridge Educ.

— Make Mine Ice Cream. Lunis, Natalie, ed. (Early Science Big Bks.). (Illus.). 16p. (J). (ps-2). 1993. pap. 16.95 (*1-56784-007-8*) Newbridge Educ.

— Make Mine Ice Cream: Mini Book. Lunis, Natalie, ed. (Early Science Big Bks.). (Illus.). 16p. (J). (ps-2). 1993. pap. 3.95 (*1-56784-032-9*) Newbridge Educ.

— Make Mine Ice Cream Theme Pack. Evento, Susan, ed. (Macmillan Early Science Big Bks.). (Illus.). (J). (ps-2). 1995. pap. 49.95 (*1-56784-139-2*) Newbridge Educ.

— Medical Center Lab. LC 76-12964. (Scientists at Work Ser.). (Illus.). (J). (gr. 3 up). 1936. lib. bdg. 11.89 (*0-381-99602-6*) HarpC Child Bks.

— The Mighty Ocean. Weidenman, Lauren, ed. (Ranger Rick Science Spectacular Ser.). (Illus.). 16p. (Orig.). (J). (gr. 2-4). 1996. pap. 16.95 (*1-56784-218-6*) Newbridge Educ.

— The Mighty Ocean: Student Book. Weidenman, Lauren, ed. (Ranger Rick Science Spectacular Ser.). (Illus.). 16p. (Orig.). (J). (gr. 2-4). 1996. pap. 3.95 (*1-56784-243-7*) Newbridge Educ.

— The Mighty Ocean: Theme Pack. Weidenman, Lauren, ed. (Ranger Rick Science Spectacular Ser.). (Illus.). (Orig.). (J). (gr. 2-4). 1996. pap. 36.90 (*1-56784-278-X*) Newbridge Educ.

— Mind Control. LC 82-46004. 128p. (J). (gr. 5 up). 1985. 12.89 (*0-690-04348-1*) HarpC Child Bks.

— Monsters. (Stranger Than Fiction Ser.). 128p. (J). 1991. pap. 2.95 (*0-380-76053-3*, Avon Bks) Morrow Avon.

— The Mystery of Magnets. Trumbauer, Lisa, ed. (Early Science Big Bks.). (Illus.). 16p. (J). (ps-2). 1995. pap. 16.95 (*1-56784-022-1*) Newbridge Educ.

— The Mystery of Magnets: Mini Book. Trumbauer, Lisa, ed. (Early Science Big Bks.). 16p. (J). (ps-2). 1995. pap. 3.95 (*1-56784-047-7*) Newbridge Educ.

— The Mystery of Magnets Theme Pack. Evento, Susan, ed. (Macmillan Early Science Big Bks.). (Illus.). (J). (ps-2). 1995. pap. 49.95 (*1-56784-179-1*) Newbridge Educ.

— The Native American Told Us So: Student Book. Lunis, Natalie, ed. (Ranger Rick Science Spectacular Ser.). (Illus.). 16p. (Orig.). (J). (gr. 2-4). 1996. pap. 3.95 (*1-56784-236-4*) Newbridge Educ.

— The Native Americans Told Us So. Lunis, Natalie, ed. (Ranger Rick Science Spectacular Ser.). 16p. (J). (gr. 2-4). 1994. pap. 16.95 (*1-56784-211-9*) Newbridge Educ.

— The Native Americans Told Us So: Thee Pack. Lunis, Natalie, ed. (Ranger Rick Science Spectacular Ser.). (Illus.). (Orig.). (J). (gr. 2-4). 1996. pap. 36.90 (*1-56784-275-5*) Newbridge Educ.

— The New Earth Book: Our Changing Planet. LC 79-7828. (Illus.). 128p. (J). (gr. 5 up). 1980. 12.95 (*0-690-00735-3*) HarpC Child Bks.

— Oil Spill! LC 92-34779. (Illus.). 32p. (J). (gr. k-4). 1994. pap. 4.95 (*0-06-445121-6*, HarpTrophy) HarpC Child Bks.

— Oil Spill! LC 92-34779. (Let's-Read-&-Find-Out Science Bks.: Stage 2). (Illus.). 32p. (J). (gr. k-4). 1994. 15.00 (*0-06-022909-8*) HarpC Child Bks.

Berger, Melvin. Oil Spill! (Let's-Read-And-Find-Out Science. Stage 2 Ser.). 1994. 10.15 (*0-606-06631-4*, Pub. by Turtleback) Demco.

Berger, Melvin. One Hundred & One Spooky Halloween Jokes. 96p. (J). (gr. 4-6). 1993. pap. 1.95 (*0-590-47143-0*) Scholastic Inc.

— One Hundred & One Wacky State Jokes. 96p. (J). (gr. 4-6). 1991. pap. 1.95 (*0-590-44487-5*) Scholastic Inc.

— One Hundred One President Jokes. 96p. (J). (gr. 4-6). 1990. pap. 1.95 (*0-590-43166-8*) Scholastic Inc.

— One Hundred One Wacky Camping Jokes. 96p. (gr. 4-6). 1992. pap. 2.99 (*0-590-45773-X*) Scholastic Inc.

— 101 Wacky Camping Jokes. (J). 1992. 8.09 (*0-606-01768-2*, Pub. by Turtleback) Demco.

— 101 Wacky State Jokes. (J). 1991. 7.05 (*0-606-01772-0*, Pub. by Turtleback) Demco.

— Out in Space. Evento, Susan, ed. (Early Science Big Bks.). (Illus.). 16p. (Orig.). (J). (ps-2). 1995. pap. 16.95 (*1-56784-102-3*) Newbridge Educ.

— Out in Space: Mini Book. Evento, Susan, ed. (Early Science Big Bks.). (Illus.). 16p. (Orig.). (J). (ps-2). 1995. pap. 3.95 (*1-56784-127-9*) Newbridge Educ.

— Out in Space Theme Pack. Evento, Susan, ed. (Macmillan Early Science Big Bks.). (Illus.). (J). (ps-2). 1995 pap. 49.95 (*1-56784-184-8*) Newbridge Educ.

— Outdoor Science Adventures. 112p. (J). (gr. 4-7). 1994. pap. 2.95 (*0-590-46855-3*) Scholastic Inc.

— Pasta, Please! Trumbauer, Lisa, ed. (Early Science Big Bks.). (Illus.). 16p. (J). (ps-2). 1994. pap. 16.95 (*1-56784-021-3*) Newbridge Educ.

— Pasta, Please! Mini Book. Trumbauer, Lisa, ed. (Early Science Big Bks.). 16p. (J). (ps-2). 1996. pap. 3.95 (*1-56784-046-9*) Newbridge Educ.

— Pasta, Please! Theme Pack. Evento, Susan, ed. (Macmillan Early Science Big Bks.). (Illus.). (J). (ps-2). 1995 pap. 49.95 (*1-56784-178-3*) Newbridge Educ.

— Physical Science Big Books Set. Evento, Susan, ed. (Macmillan Early Science Big Bks.). (Illus.). (J). (ps-2). 1995. pap. write for info. (*1-56784-166-X*) Newbridge Educ.

— Physical Science Set. Evento, Susan, ed. (Macmillan Early Science Big Bks.). (Illus.). (J). (ps-2). 1995. pap. write for info. (*1-56784-165-1*) Newbridge Educ.

— Plants. Evento, Susan, ed. (Macmillan Early Science Big Bks.). (Illus.). (J). (ps-2). 1995. pap. write for info. (*1-56784-164-3*) Newbridge Educ.

— Plants Set. Evento, Susan, ed. (Macmillan Early Science Big Bks.). (Illus.). (J). (ps-2). 1995. pap. write for info. (*1-56784-163-5*) Newbridge Educ.

— Ranger Rick Big Books, 12 units, Set. Lunis, Natalie & Schaffer, Donna, eds. (J). (gr. 2-4). 1995. pap. 173.00 (*1-56784-831-1*) Newbridge Educ.

— Ranger Rick Big Books, 6 units, Set, Version II. Lunis, Natalie & Schaffer, Donna, eds. (J). (gr. 2-4). 1995. pap. 89.00 (*1-56784-830-3*) Newbridge Educ.

— Ranger Rick Science Spectacular, 4 vols., Set. (Illus.). (J). (gr. 2-4). 1995. pap. write for info. (*1-56784-646-7*) Newbridge Educ.

— The Restless Earth. Evento, Susan, ed. (Ranger Rick Science Spectacular Ser.). 16p. (J). (gr. 2-4). 1995. pap. 16.95 (*1-56784-212-7*) Newbridge Educ.

— The Restless Earth: Student Book. Evento, Susan, ed. (Ranger Rick Science Spectacular Ser.). (Illus.). 16p. (Orig.). (J). (gr. 2-4). 1996. pap. 3.95 (*1-56784-237-2*) Newbridge Educ.

— The Restless Earth: Theme Pack. Evento, Susan, ed. (Ranger Rick Science Spectacular Ser.). (Illus.). (Orig.). (J). (gr. 2-4). 1996. pap. 36.90 (*1-56784-280-1*) Newbridge Educ.

***Berger, Melvin.** Scholastic Science Dictionary. LC 99-87883. (Illus.). 224p. (J). (gr. 4). 2000. 19.95 (*0-590-31321-5*) Scholastic Inc.

Berger, Melvin. See, Hear, Touch, Taste, Smell. Lunis, Natalie, ed. (Early Science Big Bks.). (Illus.). 16p. (J). (ps-2). 1993. pap. 16.95 (*1-56784-009-4*) Newbridge Educ.

— See, Hear, Touch, Taste, Smell: Mini Book. Lunis, Natalie, ed. (Early Science Big Bks.). (Illus.). 16p. (J). (ps-2). 1994. pap. 3.95 (*1-56784-034-5*) Newbridge Educ.

— See, Hear, Touch, Taste, Smell Theme Pack. Evento, Susan, ed. (Macmillan Early Science Big Bks.). (Illus.). (J). (ps-2). 1995. pap. 49.95 (*1-56784-141-4*) Newbridge Educ.

— Seeds Get Around. Lunis, Natalie, ed. (Early Science Big Bks.). (Illus.). 16p. (J). (ps-2). 1993. pap. 16.95 (*1-56784-006-X*) Newbridge Educ.

— Seeds Get Around Theme Pack. Evento, Susan, ed. (Macmillan Early Science Big Bks.). (Illus.). (J). (ps-2). 1995. pap. 49.95 (*1-56784-138-4*) Newbridge Educ.

— Simple Machines. Evento, Susan, ed. (Early Science Big Bks.). (Illus.). 16p. (Orig.). (J). (ps-2). 1995. pap. 16.95 (*1-56784-103-1*) Newbridge Educ.

— Simple Machines: Mini Book. Evento, Susan, ed. (Early Science Big Bks.). (Illus.). 16p. (Orig.). (J). (ps-2). 1995. pap. 3.95 (*1-56784-128-7*) Newbridge Educ.

— Simple Machines Theme Pack. Evento, Susan, ed. (Macmillan Early Science Big Bks.). (Illus.). (J) (ps-2). 1995. pap. 49.95 (*1-56784-185-6*) Newbridge Educ.

Berger, Melvin. Spinning Spiders. (Let's-Read-&-Find-Out Science Bks.: Vol. 2). 40p. (J). (gr. k-4). Date not set. lib. bdg. 15.89 (*0-06-028697-0*) HarpC Child Bks.

Berger, Melvin. Spinning Spiders. (Illus.). 40p. (J). (gr. k-4). Date not set. 15.95 (*0-06-028696-2*); pap. 4.95 (*0-06-445207-7*, HarpTrophy) HarpC Child Bks.

— Squirrels All Year Long. (Early Science Big Bks.) (Illus.). 16p. (J). (ps-2). 1992. pap. 16.95 (*1-56784-003-5*) Newbridge Educ.

— Squirrels All Year Long: Mini Books. Lunis, Natalie, ed. (Early Science Big Bks.). (Illus.). 16p. (J). (ps-2). 1993. pap. 3.95 (*1-56784-028-0*) Newbridge Educ.

— Squirrels All Year Round Theme Pack. Evento, Susan, ed. (Macmillan Early Science Big Bks.). (Illus.). (J) (ps-2). 1995. pap. 49.95 (*1-56784-135-X*) Newbridge Educ.

— The Story of Folk Music. LC 76-18159. (Illus.). (J). (gr. 6 up). 1976. lib. bdg. 29.95 (*0-87599-215-3*) S G Phillips.

— Strange World: Frogs. (J). 1997. mass mkt. 2.99 (*0-590-93778-2*) Scholastic Inc.

— Stranger Than Fiction: Killer Bugs. 128p. (Orig.). (J). 1990. pap. 3.50 (*0-380-76036-3*, Avon Bks) Morrow Avon.

— Stranger Than Fiction: Sea Monsters. 96p. (J). 1991. pap. 2.95 (*0-380-76054-1*, Avon Bks) Morrow Avon.

— Student Book Classroom Library. Evento, Susan, ed. (Macmillan Early Science Big Bks.). (Illus.). (J). (ps-2). 1995. pap. write for info. (*1-56784-190-2*) Newbridge Educ.

— Student Book Starter Set. Evento, Susan, ed. (Macmillan Early Science Big Bks.). (Illus.). (J). (ps-2). 1995. pap. write for info. (*1-56784-191-0*) Newbridge Educ.

— Switch On, Switch Off. LC 88-17638. (Let's-Read-&-Find-Out Science Bks.). (Illus.). 32p. (J). (gr. k-3). 1989. 13.95 (*0-690-04784-3*); lib. bdg. 15.89 (*0-690-04786-X*) HarpC Child Bks.

Berger, Melvin. Switch On, Switch Off. (Let's Read-&-Find-Out Science Ser.). (YA). 1989. 10.15 (*0-606-04822-7*, Pub. by Turtleback) Demco.

Berger, Melvin. Switch On Switch Off. LC 88-17638. (Trophy Let's-Read-&-Find-Out Bk.). (Illus.). 32p. (J). (ps-3). 1990. pap. 4.95 (*0-06-445097-X*, HarpTrophy) HarpC Child Bks.

— Telephones, Televisions, & Toilets: How They Work & What Can Go Wrong. (Discovery Readers Ser.). (J). 1993. 9.70 (*0-606-05663-7*, Pub. by Turtleback) Demco.

— Those Fabulous Frogs. Reed, Janet, ed. (Ranger Rick Science Spectacular Ser.). 16p. (J). (gr. 2-4). 1994. pap. 16.95 (*1-56784-208-9*) Newbridge Educ.

— Those Fabulous Frogs. Reed, Janet, ed. (Ranger Rick Science Spectacular Ser.). (Illus.). 16p. (J). (gr. 2-4). 1996. pap., student ed. 3.95 (*1-56784-233-X*) Newbridge Educ.

— Those Fabulous Frogs: Theme Pack. Reed, Janet, ed. (Ranger Rick Science Spectacular Ser.). (Illus.). (Orig.). (J). (gr. 2-4). 1996. pap. 36.90 (*1-56784-268-2*) Newbridge Educ.

— Tornadoes Can Make It Rain Crabs: Weird Facts about Natural Disasters. (Strange World Ser.). (J). (gr. 2-5). 1997. pap. text 2.99 (*0-590-93995-5*) Scholastic Inc.

— A Tour of the Planets. Lunis, Natalie, ed. (Ranger Rick Science Spectacular Ser.). 16p. (J). (gr. 2-4). 1994. pap. 16.95 (*1-56784-207-0*) Newbridge Educ.

— A Tour of the Planets: Student Book. Lunis, Natalie, ed. (Ranger Rick Science Spectacular Ser.). (Illus.). 16p. (Orig.). (J). (gr. 2-4). 1996. pap. write for info. (*1-56784-232-1*) Newbridge Educ.

— A Tour of the Planets: Theme Pack. Lunis, Natalie, ed. (Ranger Rick Science Spectacular Ser.). (Illus.). (Orig.). (J). (gr. 2-4). 1996. pap. 36.90 (*1-56784-279-8*) Newbridge Educ.

— The Vegetable Garden. Evento, Susan, ed. (Early Science Big Bks.). (Illus.). 16p. (J). (ps-2). 1995. pap. 16.95 (*1-56784-024-8*) Newbridge Educ.

— The Vegetable Garden: Mini Book. Evento, Susan, ed. (Early Science Big Bks.). 16p. (J). (ps-2). 1995. pap. 3.95 (*1-56784-049-3*) Newbridge Educ.

— The Vegetable Garden Theme Pack. Evento, Susan, ed. (Macmillan Early Science Big Bks.). (Illus.). (J). (ps-2). 1995. pap. 49.95 (*1-56784-181-3*) Newbridge Educ.

— The Web of Life. Lunis, Natalie, ed. (Ranger Rick Science Spectacular Ser.). 16p. (J). (gr. 2-4). 1994. pap. 16.95 (*1-56784-206-2*) Newbridge Educ.

— The Web of Life: Student Book. Lunis, Natalie, ed. (Ranger Rick Science Spectacular Ser.). (Illus.). 16p. (Orig.). (J). (gr. 2-4). 1996. pap. 3.95 (*1-56784-231-3*) Newbridge Educ.

— The Web of Life: Theme Pack. Lunis, Natalie, ed. (Ranger Rick Science Spectacular Ser.). (Illus.). (Orig.). (J). (gr. 2-4). 1996. pap. 36.90 (*1-56784-276-3*) Newbridge Educ.

— A Whale is Not a Fish & Other Animal Mix-Ups. 1995. 10.19 (*0-606-10040-7*, Pub. by Turtleback) Demco.

— Where Are the Stars During the Day? A Book about Stars. (Discovery Readers Ser.). (J). 1993. 9.70 (*0-606-05699-8*, Pub. by Turtleback) Demco.

Berger, Melvin. Where Did Your Family Come From? A Book about Immigrants. (Discovery Readers Ser.). (J). 1993. 9.70 (*0-606-05700-5*, Pub. by Turtleback) Demco.

Berger, Melvin. Where Do the Animals Live? Trumbauer, Lisa, ed. (Early Science Big Bks.). (Illus.). 16p. (J). (ps-2). 1994. pap. 14.95 (*1-56784-019-1*) Newbridge Educ.

— Where Do the Animals Live? Mini Book. Trumbauer, Lisa, ed. (Early Science Big Bks.). 16p. (J). (ps-2). 1995. pap. 3.95 (*1-56784-044-2*) Newbridge Educ.

— Where Do the Animals Live? Theme Pack. Evento, Susan, ed. (Macmillan Early Science Big Bks.). (Illus.). (J). (ps-2). 1995. pap. 49.95 (*1-56784-176-7*) Newbridge Educ.

— Where Does All the Garbage Go? Lunis, Natalie, ed. (Early Science Big Bks.). (Illus.). 16p. (J). (ps-2). 1992. pap. 16.95 (*1-56784-002-7*) Newbridge Educ.

— Where Does All the Garbage Go? Mini Book. Lunis, Natalie, ed. (Early Science Big Bks.). (Illus.). 16p. (J). (ps-2). 1993. pap. 3.95 (*1-56784-027-2*) Newbridge Educ.

— Where Does All the Garbage Go? Theme Pack. Evento, Susan, ed. (Macmillan Early Science Big Bks.). (Illus.). (J) (ps-2). 1995. pap. 49.95 (*1-56784-134-1*) Newbridge Educ.

— Who Cares about the Weather? Lunis, Natalie, ed. (Early Science Big Bks.). (Illus.). 16p. (J). (ps-2). 1992. pap. 16.95 (*1-56784-004-3*) Newbridge Educ.

— Who Cares about the Weather? Mini Book. Lunis, Natalie, ed. (Early Science Big Bks.). (Illus.). 16p. (J). (ps-2). 1993. pap. 3.95 (*1-56784-029-9*) Newbridge Educ.

— Who Cares about the Weather Theme Pack. Evento, Susan, ed. (Macmillan Early Science Big Bks.). (Illus.). (J). (ps-2). 1995. pap. 49.95 (*1-56784-136-8*) Newbridge Educ.

— Whole World in Your Hands: Looking at Maps. (Discovery Readers Ser.). (J). 1993. 9.70 (*0-606-05703-X*, Pub. by Turtleback) Demco.

— Why I Cough, Sneeze, Shiver, Hiccup. (J). 1983. 12.95 (*0-690-04253-1*) HarpC Child Bks.

B

***Berger, Melvin.** Why I Sneeze, Shiver, Hiccup, & Yawn. LC 98-55542. (Let's-Read-&-Find-Out Science Bks.). (Illus.). 40p. (J). (gr. k-4). 2000. 15.95 (*0-06-028144-8*); lib. bdg. 15.89 (*0-06-028143-X*) HarpC Child Bks.

Berger, Melvin. Wild Weather. Lunis, Natalie, ed. (Ranger Rick Science Spectacular Ser.). 16p. (J). (gr. 2-4). 1993. pap. 16.95 (*1-56784-203-8*) Newbridge Educ.

— Wild Weather: Student Book. Lunis, Natalie, ed. (Ranger Rick Science Spectacular Ser.). (Illus.). 16p. (Orig.). (J). (gr. 2-4). 1996. pap. 3.95 (*1-56784-228-3*) Newbridge Educ.

— Wild Weather: Theme Pack. Lunis, Natalie, ed. (Ranger Rick Science Spectacular Ser.). (Illus.). (Orig.). (J). (gr. 2-4). 1996. pap. 36.90 (*1-56784-281-X*) Newbridge Educ.

— World of Animals Big Books Set. Evento, Susan, ed. (Macmillan Early Science Big Bks.). (Illus.). (J). (ps-2). 1995. pap. write for info. (*1-56784-170-8*) Newbridge Educ.

— World of Animals Set. Evento, Susan, ed. (Macmillan Early Science Big Bks.). (Illus.). (J). (ps-2). 1995. pap. write for info. (*1-56784-169-4*) Newbridge Educ.

— The World of Ants. Lunis, Natalie, ed. (Early Science Big Bks.). (Illus.). 16p. (J). (ps-2). 1993. pap. 16.95 (*1-56784-008-6*) Newbridge Educ.

— The World of Ants: Mini Books. Lunis, Natalie, ed. (Early Science Big Bks.). (Illus.). 16p. (J). (ps-2). 1993. pap. 3.95 (*1-56784-033-7*) Newbridge Educ.

— The World of Ants: Theme Pack. Evento, Susan, ed. (Macmillan Early Science Big Bks.). (Illus.). (J). (ps-2). 1995. pap. 49.95 (*1-56784-140-6*) Newbridge Educ.

— The World of Dance. LC 78-14498. (Illus.). (YA). (gr. 7 up). 1978. 29.95 (*0-87599-221-8*) S G Phillips.

— The World of Dinosaurs. Trumbauer, Lisa, ed. (Early Science Big Bks.). (Illus.). 16p. (J). (ps-2). 1994. pap. 16.95 (*1-56784-016-7*) Newbridge Educ.

— The World of Dinosaurs: Mini Book. Trumbauer, Lisa, ed. (Early Science Big Bks.). (Illus.). 16p. (J). (ps-2). 1995. pap. 3.95 (*1-56784-040-X*) Newbridge Educ.

— The World of Dinosaurs Theme Pack. Evento, Susan, ed. (Macmillan Early Science Big Bks.). (Illus.). (J). (ps-2). 1995. pap. 49.95 (*1-56784-148-1*) Newbridge Educ.

— You Are What You Eat. Trumbauer, Lisa, ed. (Early Science Big Bks.). (Illus.). 16p. (J). (ps-2). 1994. pap. 16.95 (*1-56784-014-0*) Newbridge Educ.

— You Are What You Eat Theme Pack. Evento, Susan, ed. (Macmillan Early Science Big Bks.). (Illus.). (J). (ps-2). 1995. pap. 49.95 (*1-56784-146-5*) Newbridge Educ.

Berger, Melvin & Berga, Gilda. What Do Animals Do in Winter? How Animals Survive the Cold. LC 98-26954. (Discovery Readers Ser.). (Illus.). 48p. (J). (gr. k up). 1999. lib. bdg. 15.95 (*0-7910-5070-X*) Chelsea Hse.

Berger, Melvin & Berger, Gilda. Baboons Waited on Tables in Ancient Egypt: Weird Facts about Ancient Civilizations. (Strange World Ser.). (Illus.). (J). (gr. 2-5). 1997. pap. 2.99 (*0-614-29019-8*) Scholastic Inc.

***Berger, Melvin & Berger, Gilda.** Brrr! A Book about Polar Animals. LC 00-20823. (Hello Reader! Science Ser.). (Illus.). 40p. (J). (gr. 1-3). 2000. pap. 3.99 (*0-439-20165-9*) Scholastic Inc.

Berger, Melvin & Berger, Gilda. Can It Rain Cats & Dogs? Questions & Answers about Weather. LC 98-3042. (Illus.). 48p. (J). 1999. pap. 5.95 (*0-590-13090-0*) Scholastic Inc.

***Berger, Melvin & Berger, Gilda.** Can It Rain Cats & Dogs? Questions & Answers about Weather. LC 98-3042. (Question & Answer Ser.). (Illus.). 48p. (J). (gr. 2-4). 1999. 12.95 (*0-590-13083-8*, Pub. by Scholastic Inc); pap. 5.95 (*0-439-08573-X*, Pub. by Scholastic Inc) Penguin Putnam.

Berger, Melvin & Berger, Gilda. Did Dinosaurs Live in Your Backyard? LC 97-30263. (Scholastic Question & Answer Ser.). (J). 1999. 5.95 (*0-590-13085-4*) Scholastic Inc.

— Did Dinosaurs Live in Your Backyard? Questions & Answers about Dinosaurs. LC 97-30263. (Question & Answer Ser.). (Illus.). 48p. (J). (gr. 2-4). 1999. pap. 5.95 (*0-439-08568-3*, Pub. by Scholastic Inc) Penguin Putnam.

***Berger, Melvin & Berger, Gilda.** Did Dinosaurs Live in Your Backyard? Questions & Answers about Dinosaurs. LC 97-30263. (Question & Answer Ser.). (Illus.). 48p. (J). (gr. 2-4). 1999. 12.95 (*0-590-13078-1*, Pub. by Scholastic Inc) Penguin Putnam.

— Do All Spiders Spin Webs? Questions & Answers about Spiders. (Question & Answer Ser.). (Illus.). 48p. (J). (gr. 4-7). 2000. pap. text 5.95 (*0-439-14881-2*) Scholastic Inc.

— Do All Spiders Spin Webs? Questions & Answers about Spiders. LC 99-42738. (Question & Answer Ser.). (Illus.). 48p. (J). (gr. 4-7). 2000. 14.95 (*0-439-09586-7*) Scholastic Inc.

Berger, Melvin & Berger, Gilda. Do Stars Have Points. LC 97-36005. (Scholastic Question & Answer Ser.). (J). 1998. pap. 5.95 (*0-590-13087-0*) Scholastic Inc.

— Do Stars Have Points? Questions & Answers about Stars & Planets. LC 97-36005. (Question & Answer Ser.). (Illus.). 48p. (J). (gr. 2-4). 1999. 12.95 (*0-590-13080-3*, Pub. by Scholastic Inc); pap. 5.95 (*0-439-08570-5*, Pub. by Scholastic Inc) Penguin Putnam.

***Berger, Melvin & Berger, Gilda.** Do Tarantulas Have Teeth? Questions & Answers about Poisonous Creatures. (Question & Answer Ser.). (Illus.). 48p. (J). (gr. 4-7). 2000. pap. 5.95 (*0-439-14877-4*) Scholastic Inc.

— Do Tarantulas Have Teeth? Questions & Answers about Poisonous Creatures. LC 99-17402. (Question & Answer Ser.). (Illus.). 48p. (J). (gr. 4-7). 2000. 14.95 (*0-439-09578-6*) Scholastic Inc.

— Do Tornadoes Really Twist? Questions & Answers about Tornadoes & Hurricanes. LC 99-24946. (Scholastic Question & Answer Ser.). Date not set. 10.01 (*0-439-09585-9*) Scholastic Inc.

— Do Tornadoes Really Twist? Questions & Answers about Tornadoes & Hurricanes. LC 99-24946. (Question & Answer Ser.). (Illus.). 48p. (J). (gr. 2-4). 2000. 14.95 (*0-439-09584-0*) Scholastic Inc.

— Do Tornadoes Really Twist? Questions & Answers about Tornadoes & Hurricanes. LC 99-2496. (Question & Answer Ser.). (Illus.). 48p. (J). (gr. 2-4). 2000. 5.95 (*0-439-14880-4*) Scholastic Inc.

Berger, Melvin & Berger, Gilda. Do Whales Have Belly Buttons? LC 98-13430. (Illus.). (J). 1998. write for info. (*0-590-13088-9*) Scholastic Inc.

***Berger, Melvin & Berger, Gilda.** Do Whales Have Belly Buttons? Questions & Answers about Whales & Dolphins. LC 98-13430. (Question & Answer Ser.). (Illus.). 48p. (J). (gr. 2-4). 1999. 12.95 (*0-590-13081-1*, Pub. by Scholastic Inc); pap. 5.95 (*0-439-08571-3*, Pub. by Scholastic Inc) Penguin Putnam.

Berger, Melvin & Berger, Gilda. Frogs Swallow with Their Eyes: Weird Facts about Reptiles & Amphibians. (Strange World Ser.). (Illus.). (J). (gr. 2-5). 1997. pap. 2.99 (*0-614-29018-X*) Scholastic Inc.

— How Do Airplanes Fly? A Book about Airplanes. (Discovery Readers Ser.). (Illus.). 48p. (J). (gr. 1 up). 1998. lib. bdg. 15.95 (*0-7910-5064-5*) Chelsea Hse.

— How Do Airplanes Fly? A Book about Airplanes. LC 95-38469. (Discovery Readers Ser.). (Illus.). 48p. (J). (gr. k-4). 1996. pap. 4.50 (*1-57102-044-6*, Ideals Child) Hambleton-Hill.

— How Do Flies Walk Upside Down? LC 98-18457. (J). 1999. 5.95 (*0-590-13089-7*) Scholastic Inc.

***Berger, Melvin & Berger, Gilda.** How Do Flies Walk Upside Down? Questions & Answers about Insects. LC 98-18457. (Question & Answer Ser.). (Illus.). 48p. (J). (gr. 2-4). 1999. 12.95 (*0-590-13082-X*, Pub. by Scholastic Inc); pap. 5.95 (*0-439-08572-1*, Pub. by Scholastic Inc) Penguin Putnam.

Berger, Melvin & Berger, Gilda. How's the Weather? A Look at Weather & How It Changes. LC 98-21539. (Discovery Readers Ser.). (Illus.). 48p. (J). (gr. k up). 1999. lib. bdg. 15.95 (*0-7910-5067-X*) Chelsea Hse.

— How's the Weather? A Look at Weather & How It Changes. LC 93-16686. (Discovery Readers Ser.). (Illus.). 48p. (J). (gr. k-4). 1993. pap., per. 4.50 (*0-8249-8599-0*, Ideals Child) Hambleton-Hill.

— Life in the Rainforest: Plants, Animals, & People. LC 98-21542. (Discovery Readers Ser.). (Illus.). 48p. (J). (gr. k up). 1999. lib. bdg. 15.95 (*0-7910-5068-8*) Chelsea Hse.

— Life in the Rainforest: Plants, Animals, & People. LC 94-6006. (Discovery Readers Ser.). (Illus.). 48p. (J). (gr. k-4). 1994. pap., per. 4.50 (*1-57102-007-1*, Ideals Child) Hambleton-Hill.

— Round & Round the Money Goes: What Money Is & How We Use It. LC 98-7509. (Discovery Readers Ser.). (Illus.). 48p. (J). (gr. k up). 1999. lib. bdg. 15.95 (*0-7910-5066-1*) Chelsea Hse.

— Round & Round the Money Goes: What Money Is & How We Use It. LC 93-14770. (Discovery Readers Ser.). (Illus.). 48p. (J). (gr. k-4). 1993. pap., per. 4.50 (*0-8249-8598-2*, Ideals Child) Hambleton-Hill.

***Berger, Melvin & Berger, Gilda.** Screech! A Book about Bats. (Hello Reader! Science Ser.). (Illus.). 40p. (J). (gr. 1-3). 2000. pap. 3.99 (*0-439-20164-0*) Scholastic Inc.

Berger, Melvin & Berger, Gilda. Telephones, Televisions, & Toilets: How They Work - And What Can Go Wrong. (Discovery Readers Ser.). (Illus.). 48p. (J). (gr. k up). 1999. lib. bdg. 15.95 (*0-7910-5065-3*) Chelsea Hse.

— Telephones, Televisions, & Toilets: How They Work & What Can Go Wrong. LC 92-18198. (Discovery Readers Ser.). (Illus.). 48p. (J). (gr. k-4). 1993. pap., per. 4.50 (*0-8249-8608-3*, Ideals Child) Hambleton-Hill.

— Water, Water Everywhere: A Book about the Water Cycle. Tull, Bobbi, ed. LC 98-26955. (Discovery Readers Ser.). (Illus.). 48p. (J). (gr. k up). 1999. lib. bdg. 15.95 (*0-7910-5069-6*) Chelsea Hse.

— Water, Water Everywhere: A Book about the Water Cycle. LC 95-16024. (Discovery Readers Ser.). (Illus.). 48p. (J). (gr. k-4). 1995. pap., per. 4.50 (*1-57102-042-X*, Ideals Child) Hambleton-Hill.

— What Do Animals Do in Winter? How Animals Survive the Cold. LC 95-10419. (Discovery Readers Ser.). (Illus.). 48p. (J). (gr. k-4). 1995. pap., per. 4.50 (*1-57102-041-1*, Ideals Child) Hambleton-Hill.

***Berger, Melvin & Berger, Gilda.** What Makes an Ocean Wave? Questions & Answers about Oceans. LC 99-41771. (Scholastic Question & Answer Ser.). (J). 2001. pap. 4.99 (*0-439-09589-1*) Scholastic Inc.

Berger, Melvin & Berger, Gilda. Where Are the Stars During the Day? A Book about Stars. LC 98-28660. (Discovery Readers Ser.). (Illus.). 48p. (J). (gr. k up). 1999. lib. bdg. 15.95 (*0-7910-5071-8*) Chelsea Hse.

— Where Are the Stars During the Day? A Book about Stars. LC 92-18200. (Discovery Readers Ser.). (Illus.). 48p. (J). (gr. k-4). 1993. pap., per. 4.50 (*0-8249-8607-5*, Ideals Child) Hambleton-Hill.

— Where Did Your Family Come From? A Book about Immigrants. LC 98-23870. (Discovery Readers Ser.). (Illus.). 48p. (J). (gr. k up). 1999. lib. bdg. 15.95 (*0-7910-5063-7*) Chelsea Hse.

— Where Did Your Family Come From? A Book about Immigrants. LC 92-28626. (Discovery Readers Ser.). (Illus.). 48p. (J). (gr. k-4). 1993. pap., per. 4.50 (*0-8249-8610-5*, Ideals Child) Hambleton-Hill.

— Where Does the Mail Go? LC 98-28449. (Discovery Readers Ser.). (Illus.). 48p. (J). (gr. k up). 1999. lib. bdg. 15.95 (*0-7910-5072-6*) Chelsea Hse.

— Where Does the Mail Go? A Book about the Postal System. LC 94-6254. (Discovery Readers Ser.). (Illus.). 48p. (J). (gr. k-4). 1994. pap., per. 4.50 (*1-57102-006-3*, Ideals Child) Hambleton-Hill.

— The Whole World in Your Hands: Looking at Maps. LC 98-26981. (Discovery Readers Ser.). (Illus.). 48p. (J). (gr. k up). 1999. lib. bdg. 15.95 (*0-7910-5073-4*) Chelsea Hse.

— The Whole World in Your Hands: Looking at Maps. LC 92-18199. (Discovery Readers Ser.). (Illus.). 48p. (J). (gr. k-4). 1993. pap., per. 4.50 (*0-8249-8609-1*, Ideals Child) Hambleton-Hill.

— Why Did the Dinosaurs Disappear? The Great Dinosaur Mystery. LC 98-26208. (Discovery Readers Ser.). (Illus.). 48p. (YA). (gr. k up). 1999. lib. bdg. 15.95 (*0-7910-5074-2*) Chelsea Hse.

Berger, Melvin & Berger, Gilda. Why Did the Dinosaurs Disappear? The Great Dinosaur Mystery. LC 94-29806. (Discovery Readers Ser.). (Illus.). 48p. (J). (gr. k-4). 1995. mass mkt. 4.50 (*1-57102-026-8*, Ideals Child) Hambleton-Hill.

— Why Do Volcanoes Blow Their Tops? Questions & Answers about Volcanoes & Earthquakes. LC 99-19392. (Question & Answer Ser.). (Illus.). 48p. (J). (gr. 2-4). 2000. 14.95 (*0-439-09580-8*) Scholastic Inc.

— Why Do Volcanoes Blow Their Tops? Questions & Answers about Volcanoes & Earthquakes. LC 99-19392. (Question & Answer Ser.). (Illus.). 48p. (J). (gr. 2-4). 2000. 5.95 (*0-439-14878-2*) Scholastic Inc.

Berger, Melvin & Berger, Gilda. Why Don't Haircuts Hurt? Questions & Answers about the Human Body. LC 97-45874. (Question & Answer Ser.). (Illus.). 48p. (J). (gr. 2-4). 1999. 12.95 (*0-590-13079-X*, Pub. by Scholastic Inc) Penguin Putnam.

— Why Don't Haircuts Hurt? Questions & Answers about Your Body. LC 97-45874. (Question & Answer Ser.). (J). 1998. pap. write for info. (*0-590-13086-2*) Scholastic Inc.

Berger, Melvin & Kuhn, Dwight. Bubbles, Bubbles, Everywhere. Trumbauer, Lisa, ed. (Early Science Big Bks.). (Illus.). 16p. (J). (ps-2). 1994. pap. 16.95 (*1-56784-017-5*) Newbridge Educ.

— Bubbles, Bubbles, Everywhere: Mini Book. Trumbauer, Lisa, ed. (Early Science Big Bks.). 16p. (J). (ps-2). 1996. pap. 3.95 (*1-56784-041-8*) Newbridge Educ.

Berger, Melvin & Meisel, Paul. Why I Sneeze, Shiver, Hiccup, & Yawn. LC 98-55542. (Let's-Read-&-Find-Out Science Bks.). (Illus.). 40p. (J). (gr. k-4). 2000. pap. 4.95 (*0-06-445193-3*) HarpC Child Bks.

***Berger, Melvin H., et al.** Can You Hear a Shout in Space? Questions & Answers about Space Exploration. LC 99-13212. (Question & Answer Ser.). (J). 2000. pap. write for info. (*0-439-09583-2*) Scholastic Inc.

— Do All Spiders Spin Webs? Questions & Answers about Spiders. LC 99-42738. (Question & Answer Ser.). (Illus.). (J). 2000. pap. write for info. (*0-439-09587-5*) Scholastic Inc.

— Do Penguins Get Frostbite? Questions & Answers about Polar Animals. LC 00-25257. (Question & Answer Ser.). (Illus.). (J). 2000. pap. write for info. (*0-439-19377-X*) Scholastic Inc.

Berger, Melvin H., et al. Do Tarantulas Have Teeth? Questions & Answers About Poisonous Creatures. LC 99-17402. (Scholastic Question & Answer Ser.). 1999. write for info. (*0-439-09579-4*) Scholastic Inc.

***Berger, Melvin H., et al.** How Do Bats See in the Dark? Questions & Answers about Night Creatures. LC 00-23930. (Question & Answer Ser.). (Illus.). (J). 2000. pap. write for info. (*0-439-19375-3*) Scholastic Inc.

Berger, Melvin H., et al. Leaping Frogs: Mini Book. Trumbauer, Lisa, ed. (Early Science Big Bks.). 16p. (J). (ps-2). 1995. pap. 3.95 (*1-56784-048-5*) Newbridge Educ.

***Berger, Melvin H., et al.** What Do Sharks Eat for Dinner? Questions & Answers about Sharks. LC 99-59899. (Question & Answer Ser.). (Illus.). (J). 2000. pap. write for info. (*0-439-19373-7*) Scholastic Inc.

— Why Do Volcanoes Blow Their Tops? Questions & Answers about Volcanoes & Earthquakes. LC 99-19392. (Question & Answer Ser.). 1999. write for info. (*0-439-09581-6*) Scholastic Inc.

— Why Do Wolves Howl? Questions & Answers about Wolves. LC 00-37160. (Scholastic Question & Answer Ser.). (Illus.). (J). 2000. write for info. (*0-439-19379-6*) Scholastic Inc.

Berger, MelvinH., jt. auth. see Berger, Gilda.

Berger, Melvin H. A Whale Is Not a Fish & Other Animal Mix-Ups. LC 95-236670. (J). 1995. pap. 4.99 (*0-590-47477-4*) Scholastic Inc.

Berger, Melvin H. & Peck, Marshall, III. A Whale Is Not a Fish & Other Animal Mix-Ups. (FRE., Illus.). 64p. (J). pap. 6.99 (*0-590-16026-5*) Scholastic Inc.

Berger, Melvyn S. Nonlinearity & Functional Analysis. 1977. text 99.00 (*0-12-090350-4*) Acad Pr.

Berger, Merrill, jt. auth. see Segaller, Stephen.

Berger, Meyer. The Eight Million: Journal of a New York Correspondent. LC 82-22212. (Morningside Bk.). (Illus.). 1983. reprint ed. pap. text 22.00 (*0-231-05711-3*) Col U Pr.

— Story of the New York Times: The First Hundred Years, 1851-1951. LC 75-122933. (American Journalists Ser.). 1971. reprint ed. 21.95 (*0-405-01652-2*) Ayer.

Berger, Meyer, jt. auth. see Keller, James G.

Berger, Michael & Jurkovic, Gregory J. Practicing Family Therapy in Diverse Settings. LC 94-70555. 396p. 1994. pap. 50.00 (*1-56821-238-0*) Aronson.

***Berger, Michael & Thoreau, Henry David.** Thoreau's Late Career & "The Dispersion of Seeds" (Studies in American & English Literature). 256p. 2000. write for info. (*1-57113-168-X*, Pub. by Camden Hse) Boydell & Brewer.

Berger, Michael, et al. Practicing Family Therapy in Diverse Settings. LC 83-49256. (Jossey-Bass Social & Behavioral Science Ser.). 396p. reprint ed. pap. 122.80 (*0-8357-4817-0*, 203775400009) Bks Demand.

Berger, Michael R. How to Be A "WISE" guy (or gal) large type ed. LC 98-96289. (Illus.). 240p. (Orig.). 1998. pap. write for info. (*0-9664887-0-9*) WiseGuy Pubns.

Berger, Michael S. Rabbinic Authority. 240p. 1998. text 45.00 (*0-19-512269-0*) OUP.

Berger, Milton M. Working with People Called Patients. LC 76-46483. 176p. 1984. pap. text 23.95 (*0-87630-126-X*) Brunner-Mazel.

Berger, Milton M., ed. Women Beyond Freud: New Concepts of Feminine Psychology. 224p. 1993. text 34.95 (*0-87630-709-8*) Brunner-Mazel.

Berger, Mira, ed. see Nevo, Denise.

Berger, Mitchel S. & Wilson, Byron. The Gilomas. Zorab, Richard, ed. LC 95-42774. (Illus.). xxii, 796p. (C). 1998. text 235.00 (*0-7216-4825-8*, W B Saunders Co) Harcrt Hlth Sci Grp.

Berger, Moise E. & Perschbacher, Rex R. Guide to California Evidence, 2 vols. 410p. 1990. suppl. ed. 57.50 (*0-685-66648-4*, MICHIE) LEXIS Pub.

— Guide to California Evidence, 2 vols. 410p. 1991. suppl. ed. 43.50 (*0-685-66649-2*, MICHIE) LEXIS Pub.

— Guide to California Evidence, 2 vols. 410p. 1992. suppl. ed. 45.50 (*0-685-70881-0*, MICHIE) LEXIS Pub.

Berger, Morris I. The Settlement, the Immigrant & the Public School: A Study of the Influence of the Settlement Movement & the New Migration Upon Public Education, 1890-1924. Cordasco, Francesco, ed. LC 80-841. (American Ethnic Groups Ser.). 1981. lib. bdg. 24.95 (*0-405-13405-3*) Ayer.

Berger, Morroe. Military Elite & Social Change: Egypt since Napoleon. LC DT0100.B38. (Research Monograph: Center for International Studies, Woodrow Wilson School of Public & International Affairs: No. 6). 39p. reprint ed. pap. 30.00 (*0-608-14267-0*, 201572500097) Bks Demand.

— Real & Imagined Worlds: The Novel & Social Science. 320p. 1977. 37.95 (*0-674-74941-3*) HUP.

Berger, Morroe, et al. Benny Carter: A Life in American Music, 2 vols. LC 82-10634. (Studies in Jazz: No. 1). 877p. 1982. 65.00 (*0-8108-1580-X*) Scarecrow.

Berger, Morroe, jt. auth. see De Stael, Germaine.

***Berger Morse, Margaret.** Choices. LC 98-90306. 1999. 13.95 (*0-533-12782-3*) Vantage.

Berger, Murray H., ed. see Lewis, Barry.

Berger, Nancy O., jt. auth. see Marquardt, Michael J.

Berger, Natalia. Jews & Medicine: Religion, Culture, Science. LC 97-26717. (Illus.). 275p. 1997. 50.00 (*0-8276-0644-3*) JPS Phila.

Berger, Nomi. My Brother Peter: Murder or Suicide? 288p. 1998. pap. text 16.99 (*1-55207-010-7*, Pub. by R Davies Pub) Genl Dist Srvs.

Berger, P. William Blake: Poet & Mystic. LC 67-31287. (Studies in Blake: No. 3). 1969. reprint ed. lib. bdg. 75.00 (*0-8383-0778-7*) M S G Haskell Hse.

Berger, Pam. Internet for Active Learners: Curriculum-Based Strategies for K.12. LC 98-23102. xiv, 189 p. 1998. 35.00 (*0-8389-3487-0*) ALA.

Berger, Pam & Kinnell, Susan. CD-ROM for Schools: The Definitive Handbook. LC 95-121192. 274p. 1994. pap. 29.95 (*0-910965-13-7*) Info Today Inc.

Berger, Patricia & Bartholomew, Terese T. Mongolia: The Legacy of Chinggis Khan. LC 95-15198. 339p. 1995. pap. 35.00 (*0-614-09404-6*) Asian Art Mus.

Berger, Patricia & Casler, Jennifer R. Tomb Treasures from China: The Buried Art of Ancient Xi'an. LC 94-27657. 80p. 1994. pap. 15.00 (*0-912804-30-0*) Kimbell Art.

Berger, Paul. Seattle Subtext. LC 83-26047. (Illus.). 52p. 1984. pap. 15.00 (*0-941104-09-5*) Real Comet.

— Seattle Subtext. (Artists' Books Ser.). 52p. 1984. 30.00 (*0-89822-037-8*) Visual Studies.

Berger, Paul & Guthmiller, Carol M. You Can Do It! 55 Thoughts, Feelings & Solutions on How I Cope With My Stroke to Help You with Your Stroke or Brain Injury. 16p. 1998. pap. 3.00 (*0-9668378-0-0*, 5599801) Positive Power.

Berger, Paul & Mensh, Stephanie. How to Conquer the World with One Hand...And An Attitude. LC 99-60113. 220p. 1999. pap. 14.00 (*0-9668378-1-9*, No. 0299001) Positive Power.

Berger, Paul, jt. auth. see Roberts, Mary L.

Berger, Paul D., et al, eds. Pesticide Formulations & Application Systems. (Special Technical Publication Ser.: Vol. 13, No. STP 1183). (Illus.). 420p. 1993. text 61.00 (*0-8031-1888-0*, STP1183) ASTM.

Berger, Paul D., jt. auth. see Roberts, Mary L.

***Berger, Paul E. & Mensh, Stephanie.** You Can Do It! 105 Thoughts, Feelings & Solutions to Inspire You. rev. ed. 32p. 2000. pap. 5.00 (*0-9668378-2-7*) Positive Power.

Berger, Paul S. & Siegel, Mayer. Pensions & Employee Benefits under the 1982 Tax Act: Coping with the Greatest Changes Since ERISA. (Illus.). 1982. write for info. (*0-318-57052-1*) Harcourt.

Berger, Pearl, tr. see Avivi, Yosef.

Berger, Peter L. A Far Glory: The Quest for Faith in an Age of Credulity. LC 92-24946. 232p. 1992. text 27.95 (*0-02-902930-9*) Free Pr.

— Invitation to Sociology: A Humanistic Perspective. LC 63-8758. 208p. 1963. pap. 10.95 (*0-385-06529-9*) Doubleday.

— The Precarious Vision. LC 76-1981. 238p. 1976. reprint ed. lib. bdg. 69.50 (*0-8371-8657-9*, BEPV, Greenwood Pr) Greenwood.

— Redeeming Laughter: The Comic Dimension of Human Experience. LC 97-12095. xvii, 215p. (C). 1997. lib. bdg. 23.95 (*3-11-015562-1*) De Gruyter.

— Sacred Canopy: Elements of a Sociological Theory of Religion. LC 67-19805. 240p. 1990. reprint ed. pap. 10.95 (*0-385-07305-4*, Anchor NY) Doubleday.

An Asterisk (*) at the beginning of an entry indicates that the title is appearing for the first time.

Berger, Peter L., ed. Capitalism & Equality in America: Modern Capitalism, Vol. 1. LC 86-24739. (Illus.). 325p. 1987. lib. bdg. 29.95 (*0-8191-5572-1*) U Pr of Amer.

— Capitalism & Equality in America: Modern Capitalism, Vol. 1. LC 86-24739. (Illus.). 325p. 1987. pap. 17.95 (*0-8191-5573-X*) U Pr of Amer.

— Capitalism & Equality in the Third World: Modern Capitalism, Vol. II. LC 86-24749. (Illus.). 375p. 1987. pap. 17.95 (*0-8191-5575-6*) U Pr of Amer.

— The Capitalist Spirit: Toward a Religious Ethic of Wealth Creation. 180p. 1990. 21.95 (*1-55815-112-5*) ICS Pr.

— The Desecularization of the World: Resurgent Religion & World Politics. LC 99-32103. 144p. 1999. pap. 17.00 (*0-8028-4691-2*) Eerdmans.

— Institutions of Democracy & Development. LC 93-16001. (Sequoia Seminar Publication). 1993. 34.95 (*1-55815-072-2*) ICS Pr.

***Berger, Peter L., ed.** The Limits of Social Cohesion: Conflict & Mediation in Pluralist Societies: A Report of the Bertelsmann Foundation to the Club of Rome. 416p. 1999. pap. text 26.00 (*0-8133-6719-0*, Pub. by Westview) HarpC.

Berger, Peter L. & Hsiao, Hsin-Huang, eds. In Search of an East Asian Development Model. 352p. 1987. 39.95 (*0-88738-149-9*) Transaction Pubs.

— In Search of an East Asian Development Model. 352p. 1999. pap. 24.95 (*0-88738-686-5*) Transaction Pubs.

Berger, Peter L. & Luckmann, Thomas. Social Construction of Reality: A Treatise in the Sociology of Knowledge. LC 66-14925. 240p. 1967. pap. 11.95 (*0-385-05898-5*, Anchor NY) Doubleday.

— Social Construction of Reality: A Treatise in the Sociology of Knowledge. LC 66-14925. reprint ed. write for info. (*0-89197-578-0*) Irvington.

Berger, Peter L. & Neuhaus, Richard J. To Empower People: From State to Civil Society. 20th anniversary ed. Novak, Michael, ed. 100p. 1996. 24.95 (*0-8447-3944-8*) Am Enterprise.

Berger, Peter L., et al. Aspiring to Freedom: Commentaries on John Paul II's Encyclical "The Social Concerns of the Church" Myers, Kenneth A., ed. LC 88-16563. 183p. reprint ed. pap. 56.80 (*0-7837-0522-0*, 204084600018) Bks Demand.

Berger, Peter L., jt. ed. see Bernstein, Ann.

Berger, Peter W. & Dunahoo, Kermit L. Iowa Legal Forms: Criminal Law, 1983-1993. (Iowa Legal Forms Ser.). 200p. ring bd. 60.00 incl. disk (*0-86678-192-7*, 81007-10, MICHIE); ring bd. 85.00 incl. disk (*0-685-49474-8*, MICHIE); suppl. ed. 40.00 (*0-86678-035-1*, MICHIE) LEXIS Pub.

Berger, Petra. Feltcraft: Making Dolls, Gifts & Toys. Orig. Title: Spelen Met Vilt. (Illus.). 88p. (J). (gr. 2-6). 1994. pap. 12.95 (*0-86315-190-6*, 24312, Pub. by Floris Bks) Gryphon Hse.

Berger, Phil. Blood Season: Mike Tyson & the World of Boxing. 2nd ed. LC 89-3158. (Illus.). 346p. 1996. pap. 13.95 (*1-56858-069-X*) FWEW.

***Berger, Phil.** Forever Showtime: The Checkered Life of Pistol Pete Maravich. LC 99-42597. 248p. 1999. 23.95 (*0-87833-237-5*) Taylor Pub.

— The Last Laugh. 2000. 17.95 (*0-8154-1096-4*) Cooper Sq.

Berger, Phil. Mickey Mantle. LC 98-20175. (Illus.). 192p. 1998. 20.00 (*0-517-20099-6*) Random Hse Value.

— The Miracle on 33rd Street: The New York Knickerbockers' Championship Season, 1969-70. LC 93-39326. (Illus.). 258p. 1994. pap. 14.95 (*1-56858-008-8*) FWEW.

— Punch Lines: Berger on Boxing. LC 92-38537. (Illus.). 328p. 1993. 24.95 (*0-941423-93-X*) FWEW.

Berger, Phil & Jacob, Craig. Twisted Genius: Confessions of a 10 Million Dollar Scam Man. LC 95-13291. (Illus.). 206p. 1995. 19.95 (*1-56858-044-4*) FWEW.

Berger, Phil, jt. auth. see Holmes, Larry.

Berger, Phil, jt. auth. see Olajide, Michael, Jr.

Berger-Prossdorf, Tamara. Die Funktion der Heilsarmeegeistichen in Den Draman Brechts. LC 91-43585. (American University Studies: Germanic Languages & Literature Ser.: Ser. I, Vol. 97). XI, 244p. (C). 1993. text 42.95 (*0-8204-1798-X*) P Lang Pubng.

Berger, R. G. Aroma Biotechnology. (Illus.). 169p. 1995. 159.95 (*3-540-58606-7*) Spr-Verlag.

Berger, R. G., jt. ed. see Schieper, T.

Berger, R. W. & Hart, T. H. Statistical Process Control: A Guide for Implementation. (Quality & Reliability Ser.: Vol. 8). (Illus.). 80p. 1986. text 35.00 (*0-8247-7625-9*) Dekker.

Berger, Rachel. Malaysia's Forests: A Resource Without a Future? 216p. (C). 1991. text 125.00 (*0-906527-32-5*, Pub. by Surrey Beatty & Sons) St Mut.

Berger, Rainer, jt. auth. see Nicholson, H. B.

Berger, Raoul. Congress vs. the Supreme Court. LC 75-75426. 440p. 1969. 41.00 (*0-674-16210-2*) HUP.

— Death Penalties: The Supreme Court's Obstacle Course. 252p. 1982. 29.95 (*0-674-19426-8*) HUP.

— Executive Privilege: A Constitutional Myth. LC 73-93837. (Studies in Legal History). 384p. 1974. 42.50 (*0-674-27425-3*) HUP.

— Federalism: The Founders' Design. LC 86-40524. 224p. 1987. 24.95 (*0-8061-2059-2*) U of Okla Pr.

— Government by Judiciary: The Transformation of the Fourteenth Amendment. 384p. 1977. 34.50 (*0-674-35795-7*) HUP.

— Government by Judiciary: The Transformation of the Fourteenth Amendment. 2nd rev. ed. LC 96-16162. 540p. 1997. 19.50 (*0-86597-143-9*); pap. 9.50 (*0-86597-144-7*) Liberty Fund.

— Impeachment: The Constitutional Problems. LC 72-75428. (Studies in Legal History). 359p. 1974. pap. 18.00 (*0-674-44476-0*) HUP.

— Impeachment: The Constitutional Problems, Enlarged Edition. 1999. pap. 18.00 (*0-674-44478-7*) HUP.

Berger, Raymond M. Gay & Gray: The Older Homosexual Man. 2nd ed. LC 95-23223. (Illus.). 333p. 1995. pap. 14.95 (*1-56023-875-5*); text 39.95 (*1-56024-986-2*) Haworth Pr.

Berger, Raymond M. & Patchner, Michael A. Implementing the Research Plan: A Guide for the Helping Professions. (Human Services Guides Ser.: Vol. 51). 106p. (C). 1989. pap. text 18.95 (*0-8039-3034-8*) Sage.

— Planning for Research: A Guide for the Helping Professions. (Human Services Guides Ser.: Vol. 50). 160p. (C). 1988. pap. text 18.95 (*0-8039-3033-X*) Sage.

— Planning for Research: A Guide for the Helping Professions. LC 87-17535. (Sage Human Services Guides Ser.: Vol. 50). 160p. reprint ed. pap. 49.60 (*0-608-09791-8*, 206996500007) Bks Demand.

Berger, Raymond M., et al. Implementing the Research Plan: A Guide for the Helping Professions. LC 87-15371. (Sage Human Services Guide Ser.: Vol. 51). (Illus.). 176p. reprint ed. pap. 54.60 (*0-608-09785-3*, 206995900007) Bks Demand.

Berger, Regina, jt. auth. see Karlin, Muriel S.

Berger, Rene & Eby, Lloyd, eds. Art & Technology. LC 85-21552. (Illus.). 422p. 1986. 29.95 (*0-89226-029-7*) Paragon Hse.

Berger, Richard & Berger, Deborah. Biopotency: Your Guide to Problem-Free Sexual Fulfillment. 272p. 1990. mass mkt. 4.95 (*0-380-70816-7*, Avon Bks) Morrow Avon.

Berger, Richard A. Applied Exercise Physiology. LC 81-2322. 301p. reprint ed. pap. 93.40 (*0-8357-5677-7*, 205656700074) Bks Demand.

Berger, Richie E. & Lane, Frederick S., 3rd. Vermont Jury Instructions. 400p. 1993. ring bd. 85.00 (*1-56257-293-8*, MICHIE) LEXIS Pub.

Berger, Rita, jt. auth. see Berger, Thomas.

Berger, Robert. Undecidability of the Domino Problem. LC 52-42839. (Memoirs Ser.: No. 1/66). 72p. 1966. pap. 16.00 (*0-8218-1266-1*, MEMO/1/66) Am Math.

— World of Dress Daggers. (Illus.). 296p. (C). 1995. 39.95 (*0-941540-22-7*) Blacksmith Corp.

Berger, Robert & Conser, Anne. The Last Remaining Seats: Movie Palaces of Tinseltown. LC 97-7138. (Illus.). 136p. (Orig.). 1997. pap. 32.00 (*0-9643119-6-8*) Balcony Pr.

Berger, Robert A. Songwriting: A Structured Approach. LC 83-70101. (Illus.). 108p. (Orig.). 1983. pap. 8.95 (*0-911999-00-0*) Beer Flat.

Berger, Robert C., ed. see Hermans, Maurice-Auguste, et al.

Berger, Robert J. Know Your Broomhandle Mauser Pistols. LC 85-16805. (Illus.). 86p. 1994. pap. 12.95 (*0-941540-09-X*, 1005) Blacksmith Corp.

— Know Your Czechoslovakian Pistols. LC 89-18451. (Know Your Gun Ser.). (Illus.). 86p. 1994. pap. 12.95 (*0-941540-17-0*, 1007) Blacksmith Corp.

Berger, Robert J., et al. Experiment in a Juvenile Court: A Study of a Program of Volunteers Working with Juvenile Probationers. LC 75-620133. (Illus.). 492p. reprint ed. pap. 152.60 (*0-7837-5263-6*, 204500100005) Bks Demand.

Berger, Robert W. In the Garden of the Sun King: Studies on the Park of Versailles under Louis XIV. LC 85-1603. (Illus.). 220p. 1985. 35.00 (*0-88402-141-6*) Dumbarton Oaks.

— The Palace of the Sun: The Louvre of Louis the Fourteenth. (Illus.). 336p. (C). 1993. 75.00 (*0-271-00847-4*) Pa St U Pr.

— Public Access to Art in Paris: A Documentary History from the Middle Ages to 1800. LC 97-48464. 1362p. 1999. 75.00 (*0-271-01749-X*) Pa St U Pr.

— A Royal Passion: Louis XIV As Patron of Architecture. (Illus.). 224p. (C). 1994. text 64.95 (*0-521-44029-7*) Cambridge U Pr.

— A Royal Passion: Louis XIV As Patron of Architecture. (Illus.). 224p. 1997. pap. text 23.95 (*0-521-58644-5*) Cambridge U Pr.

Berger, Roberto I., tr. Spanish for Law Enforcement Officers. 16p. 1993. pap. 2.00 (*1-884493-02-5*) Pocket Pr.

Berger, Roger W., jt. ed. see Pyzdek, Thomas.

Berger, Ron, jt. ed. see Searles, Patricia.

Berger, Ronald J., ed. The Sociology of Juvenile Delinquency. 2nd ed. LC 95-9129. (Criminal Justice). 1996. pap. text 55.95 (*0-8304-1416-9*) Thomson Learn.

Berger, Ronald J., et al. Feminism & Pornography. LC 90-24125. 192p. 1991. 52.95 (*0-275-93819-0*, C3819, Praeger Pubs) Greenwood.

Berger, Ronald M. The Most Necessary Luxuries: The Mercers' Company of Coventry, 1550-1680. (Illus.). 328p. (C). 1993. 60.00 (*0-271-00867-9*) Pa St U Pr.

Berger, Roni. Stepfamilies: A Multi-Dimensional Perspective. LC 98-6171. 274p. 1998. lib. bdg. 49.95 (*0-7890-0280-9*) Haworth Pr.

— Stepfamilies: A Multi-Dimensional Perspective. LC 98-6171. 252p. 1998. pap. text 29.95 (*0-7890-0281-7*) Haworth Pr.

***Berger, Rony.** Preventive Approaches to Couples Therapy. LC 99-14074. 1999. text 39.95 (*0-87630-876-0*) Brunner-Mazel.

Berger, Roy, jt. auth. see Lewis, James, Jr.

Berger, Ruth. Medical Intuition: How to Combine Inner Resources with Modern Medicine. LC 95-19107. (Illus.). 160p. (Orig.). 1995. pap. 9.95 (*0-87728-851-8*) Weiser.

— The Secret Is in the Rainbow: Aura Interrelationships. LC 86-50045. 128p. 1986. reprint ed. pap. 7.95 (*0-87728-638-8*) Weiser.

Berger, S., et al. Isotope Effects in NMR Spectroscopy. (NMR-Basic Principles & Progress Ser.: Vol. 22). (Illus.). 160p. 1990. 55.95 (*0-387-51286-1*) Spr-Verlag.

Berger, S. A., et al. Introduction to Bioengineering. (Illus.). 540p. 1996. text 95.00 (*0-19-856516-X*) OUP.

Berger, S. A., ed. see Lewis, E. R.

Berger, Samantha. The Boat Book. LC 98-53312. (Science Emergent Readers Ser.). 1999. pap. 10.01 (*0-439-08125-4*) Scholastic Inc.

— Electricity. LC 98-53314. 1999. pap. 10.01 (*0-439-08122-X*) Scholastic Inc.

— Games. LC 98-53542. 1998. pap. 2.50 (*0-439-04566-5*) Scholastic Inc.

***Berger, Samantha.** Honk! Toot! Beep! LC 00-35781. (My First Hello Reader Ser.). (Illus.). (J). 2000. pap. write for info. (*0-439-21037-2*) Scholastic Inc.

Berger, Samantha. In the Air. LC 98-53311. 1999. pap. 10.01 (*0-439-08124-6*) Scholastic Inc.

— Light. LC 98-53310. 1999. pap. 10.01 (*0-439-08120-3*) Scholastic Inc.

***Berger, Samantha.** Then & Now. LC 98-45004. (J). 1998. pap. 3.25 (*0-439-04602-5*) Scholastic Inc.

Berger, Samantha & Chanko, Pamela. Big & Little. LC 98-54207. (Learning Center Emergent Readers Ser.). 1998. 2.50 (*0-439-04597-5*) Scholastic Inc.

— Festivals. LC 98-41002. 1998. 2.50 (*0-439-04561-4*) Scholastic Inc.

— School. LC 99-26319. (Social Studies Emergent Readers Ser.). (J). 1999. 10.01 (*0-439-04553-3*) Scholastic Inc.

Berger, Samantha & Chessen, Betsey. Apples. LC 98-53547. 1998. 2.50 (*0-439-04592-4*) Scholastic Inc.

Berger, Samantha & Moreton, Daniel. Celebrations. LC 98-50496. (Social Studies Emergent Readers Ser.). (J). 1999. 2.50 (*0-439-04557-6*) Scholastic Inc.

— Patterns. LC 98-54212. (Learning Center Emergent Readers Ser.). 1998. 2.50 (*0-439-04599-1*) Scholastic Inc.

***Berger, Samantha, et al.** It's Spring! LC 99-41765. Hello Reader! Ser.). (Illus.). (J). 2000. pap. write for info. (*0-439-08754-6*) Scholastic Inc.

Berger, Samantha, jt. auth. see Canizares, Susan.

Berger, Samantha, jt. auth. see Chessen, Betsey.

Berger, Samantha, jt. auth. see Moreton, Daniel.

Berger, Samuel. L' Histoire de la Vulgate Pendant les Premiers Siecles du Moyen Age. xxiv, 443p. 1976. reprint ed. 80.00 (*3-487-06109-0*) G Olms Pubs.

Berger, Sandra Carroll. What's Noteworthy on School Reform. 46p. 1994. pap. 3.25 (*0-16-063565-9*) USGPO.

Berger, Sandra L. College Planning for Gifted Students. 2nd rev. ed. LC 94-2386. 1998. pap. text 24.00 (*0-86586-312-1*, P330R) Coun Exc Child.

Berger, Sandy. How to Have a Meaningful Relationship with Your Computer. LC 97-65715. (Illus.). 250p. 1997. pap. 18.95 (*1-887472-36-3*) Sunstar Pubng.

Berger, Schaufel. Construction Equipment Managment. LC 98-38289. 357p. 1998. 77.00 (*0-13-716267-7*) P-H.

Berger-Schunn, Anni. Practical Color Measurement: A Primer for the Beginner, a Reminder for the Expert. Saltzman, Max, tr. from GER. 192p. 1994. 79.95 (*0-471-00417-0*) Wiley.

Berger, Sid. Anatomy of a Literary Hoax. 20p. 1995. pap. 35.00 (*0-938768-49-2*) Oak Knoll.

Berger, Sidney. Bird Boy: A Full-Length Drama. (Illus.). 36p. 1988. pap. 4.00 (*0-88680-295-4*) I E Clark.

— Rapunzel: From the Brothers Grimm. (Illus.). 32p. (J). (ps up). 1991. pap. 3.50 (*0-88680-359-4*) I E Clark.

Berger, Sidney & Landes, Rob. Little Red Riding Hood: A Musical. 1996. pap. 3.50 (*1-57514-197-3*, 0097) Encore Perform Pub.

— The Magic Machine: A Musical. 38p. (J). 1995. pap. 4.00 (*1-57514-147-7*, 0087) Encore Perform Pub.

— Wonderboy! (J). (gr. 3-9). 1996. pap. 3.50 (*1-57514-160-4*, 0088) Encore Perform Pub.

Berger, Sidney, ed. see Everson, William.

Berger, Sidney, jt. ed. see Luere, Jeane.

Berger, Sidney E. The Design of Bibliographies: Observations, References & Examples, 6. LC 91-34485. (Bibliographies & Indexes in Library & Information Science: No. 6). 224p. 1992. lib. bdg. 85.00 (*0-313-28425-3*, BGV, Greenwood Pr) Greenwood.

Berger, Sidney E., ed. see Twain, Mark, pseud.

Berger, Sidney L. The Little Match Girl: The Musical. (Illus.). 32p. (Orig.). (J). (gr. 4 up). 1985. pap. 4.00 (*0-88680-230-X*) I E Clark.

***Berger, Simon.** International Joint Ventures. (Management Briefings Ser.). (Illus.). 1999. pap. 167.50 (*0-273-64508-0*, Pub. by F T P-H) Trans-Atl Phila.

Berger, Stefan. The British Labour Party & the German Social Democrats, 1900-1931. (Historical Monographs). 316p. 1995. text 58.00 (*0-19-820500-7*) OUP.

— The Search for Normality: National Identity & Historical Consciousness in Germany since 1800. LC 96-53355. 320p. 1997. 59.95 (*1-57181-863-4*) Berghahn Bks.

***Berger, Stefan.** Social Democracy in Nineteenth & Twentieth Century Germany. LC 99-22334. (Themes in Modern German History Ser.). 288p. 1999. pap. 27.53 (*0-582-29814-8*) Longman.

— Social Democracy in Nineteenth & Twentieth Century Germany. LC 99-22334. (Themes in Modern German History Ser.). 288p. (C). 1999. 79.95 (*0-582-29815-6*) Longman.

Berger, Stefan & Broughton, David, eds. The Force of Labour: The Western European Labour Movement & the Working Class in the Twentieth Century. 320p. 1995. 60.00 (*0-85496-381-2*, Pub. by Berg Pubs); pap. 19.50 (*1-85973-023-X*, Pub. by Berg Pubs) NYU Pr.

Berger, Stefan & Smith, Angel, eds. Nationalism, Labour & Ethnicity 1870-1939. 256p. 1999. 79.96 (*0-7190-5052-9*, Pub. by Manchester Univ Pr) St Martin.

Berger, Stefan, et al. NMR Spectroscopy of the Non-Metallic Elements. Becconsall, Jack, tr. LC 96-15919. 1098p. 1997. 485.00 (*0-471-96763-7*) Wiley.

— Writing National Histories: Western Europe since 1800. LC 98-21825. 1999. 85.00 (*0-415-16426-5*); pap. 27.99 (*0-415-16427-3*) Routledge.

Berger, Stephen A. Natural Causes: Death & Disease for the Serious Consumer. 398p. 1992. 19.95 (*965-229-056-4*, Pub. by Gefen Pub Hse) Gefen Bks.

Berger, Stephen A., compiled by. The Infectious Diseases of Israel. 192p. 1992. 19.95 (*965-229-073-4*, Pub. by Gefen Pub Hse) Gefen Bks.

Berger, Stephen D. The Development of Legitimating Ideas: Intellectuals & Politicians in Post-War Western Germany. LC 91-22959. (Harvard Studies in Sociology). 293p. 1991. text 20.00 (*0-8240-8309-1*) Garland.

Berger, Stephen L., jt. auth. see Castleman, Barry I.

Berger, Stephen S. & Berger, Jeanette K. A Tooth Fairy Tale. LC 96-83330. (Illus.). 32p. (Orig.). (J). (ps-3). 1996. pap. 9.95 (*0-9651089-9-6*) Dragon Breath.

Berger, Steven H. Establishing a Forensic Psychiatric Practice: A Practical Guide. LC 97-10232. 160p. 1997. 29.00 (*0-393-70252-9*) Norton.

Berger, Steven J. The Expectant Father. LC 93-36432. 96p. 1994. pap. 7.95 (*0-942963-40-7*) Distinctive Pub.

Berger, Steven N., et al. Bankruptcy Law & Procedure: A Guide for Paralegals, 2, Vol. 2. 3rd ed. 896p. 1999. boxed set 145.00 (*0-471-05123-3*) Wiley.

Berger, Stuart M. Forever Young: Twenty Years Younger in 20 Weeks. 272p. 1990. mass mkt. 4.95 (*0-380-70696-2*, Avon Bks) Morrow Avon.

— How to Be Your Own Nutritionist. 384p. 1988. mass mkt. 6.99 (*0-380-70318-1*, Avon Bks) Morrow Avon.

— What Your Doctor Didn't Learn in Medical School . . . & What You Can Do About It! 352p. 1989. reprint ed. mass mkt. 4.95 (*0-380-70319-X*, Avon Bks) Morrow Avon.

Berger, Sue, et al. Element of the Week. (Illus.). (Orig.). 1989. pap. text 10.50 (*1-877991-00-7*, AP1832) Flinn Scientific.

Berger, Suzanne. Peasants Against Politics: Rural Organization in Brittany, 1911-1967. LC 73-174541. (Center for International Affairs Ser.). (Illus.). 312p. 1972. 41.00 (*0-674-65925-2*) HUP.

Berger, Suzanne & Dore, Ronald, eds. The National Diversity & Global Capitalism. (Studies in Political Economy). (Illus.). 376p. 1996. pap. text 17.95 (*0-8014-8319-0*) Cornell U Pr.

Berger, Suzanne & Lester, Richard K., eds. Made by Hong Kong. LC 97-189765. (Illus.). 392p. (C). 1997. text 32.00 (*0-19-590358-7*) OUP.

Berger, Suzanne & Piore, Michael J. Dualism & Discontinuity in Industrial Societies. LC 79-25172. (Illus.). 176p. 1980. text 64.95 (*0-521-23134-5*) Cambridge U Pr.

Berger, Suzanne E. Legacies. LC 84-70353. 72p. 1984. 6.95 (*0-914086-48-0*); pap. 3.95 (*0-914086-49-9*) Alice James Bks.

— These Rooms. Norris, Joan & Peich, Michael, eds. LC 79-83711. 1979. 12.00 (*0-915778-38-6*); pap. 6.00 (*0-915778-39-4*) Penmaen Pr.

Berger, Sven. Die Treuhaenderische Verwaltung des Vermoegens der Parteien und Massenorganisationen der DDR: Gesetzgeberischer Auftrag und Verwaltungspraktische Umsetzung. (Europaeische Hochschulschriften Ser.: Reihe 2, Band 2388). (GER., Illus.). XVII, 225p. 1998. pap. 45.95 (*3-631-33410-9*) P Lang Pubng.

Berger, Teresa. Theology in Hymns: Reflections on the "Collection of Hymns for the Use of the People Called Methodists (1780)" (Kingswood Ser.). 224p. (Orig.). 1995. pap. 14.95 (*0-687-00281-8*) Abingdon.

— Women's Ways of Worship: Gender Analysis & Liturgical History. LC 98-34348. 180p. 1999. pap. 21.95 (*0-8146-6173-4*) Liturgical Pr.

Berger, Terry. I Have Feelings. LC 70-147123. (Illus.). 32p. (J). (ps-3). 1971. 18.95 (*0-87705-021-X*, Kluwer Acad Hman Sci); pap. 10.95 (*0-89885-342-7*, Kluwer Acad Hman Sci) Kluwer Academic.

— I Have Feelings Too. LC 79-15863. 32p. (J). (ps-3). 1979. 16.95 (*0-87705-441-X*, Kluwer Acad Hman Sci) Kluwer Academic.

— Lucky. LC 73-16817. (Lead-off Bks.). 48p. (J). (ps-3). 1976. 6.95 (*0-87955-110-0*); write for info. (*0-87955-710-9*) O'Hara.

Berger, Terry & Reid, Robert. Bed & Breakfast Southeastern States. (Bed & Breakfast Ser.). 128p. 1990. pap. 13.95 (*0-13-068180-6*, P-H Travel) Prntice Hall Bks.

Berger, Terry W. Lives Plucked from a Discarded Address Book, 1965-1995. 200p. 1996. 15.00 (*0-9652366-0-9*) TWB.

Berger, Thomas. The Christmas Craft Book. Lawson, Polly, tr. (Illus.). 86p. (J). 1990. reprint ed. pap. 12.95 (*0-86315-110-8*, Pub. by Floris Bks) Gryphon Hse.

— Granted Wishes. deluxe ed. 30p. 1984. 50.00 (*0-935716-33-5*) Lord John.

— The Harvest Craft Book. (Illus.). 88p. 1997. pap. 12.95 (*0-86315-147-7*, 1614, Pub. by Floris Bks) Anthroposophic.

— The Houseguest. 1988. 16.95 (*0-316-09163-4*) Little.

— Killing Time. 1990. pap. 9.95 (*0-316-09147-2*) Little.

— Little Big Man. 30.95 (*0-8488-0429-5*) Amereon Ltd.

— Little Big Man. 480p. 1989. pap. 13.95 (*0-385-29829-3*, Delta Trade) Dell.

— The Little Troll. Lawson, Polly, tr. (GER., Illus.). 32p. (J). (gr. k-3). 1992. 14.95 (*0-86315-112-4*, Pub. by Floris Bks) Gryphon Hse.

— The Mouse & the Potato. Lawson, Polly, tr. (DUT., Illus.). 32p. (J). (ps-2). 1990. reprint ed. 14.95 (*0-86315-103-5*, Pub. by Floris Bks) Gryphon Hse.

***Berger, Thomas.** Neighbors. 288p. 2000. pap. 13.00 (*1-58195-023-3*) Zoland Bks.

B

Berger, Thomas. The Return of Little Big Man: A Novel. LC 98-26862. 448p. (gr. 8). 1999. 25.00 (*0-316-09844-2*) Little.

***Berger, Thomas.** The Return of Little Big Man: A Novel. 448p. 2000. pap. 13.95 (*0-316-09117-0*, Back Bay) Little.

Berger, Thomas. The Return of Little Big Man: A Novel. large type ed. LC 99-18830. 695p. 1999. write for info. (*0-7838-8600-4*) Mac Lib Ref.

— Stan Bolivan & the Dragon. (J). pap. 17.95 (*0-86315-152-3*, 1585, Pub. by Floris Bks) Anthroposophic.

— The Tree That Grew Through the Roof. (Illus.). 20p. (J). (ps-1). 1995. 14.95 (*0-86315-213-9*, 26013, Pub. by Floris Bks) Gryphon Hse.

Berger, Thomas & Berger, Rita. Easter Craft Book. 12.95 (*0-86315-161-2*, 713, Pub. by Floris Bks) Anthroposophic.

Berger, Thomas L., et al. An Index of Characters in Early Modern English Drama: Printed Plays, 1500-1660. rev. ed. LC 97-43341. 300p. (C). 1998. 69.95 (*0-521-62149-6*) Cambridge U Pr.

Berger, Thomas L., jt. auth. see Maguire, Laurie E.

Berger, Thomas L., jt. ed. see Gossett, Susanne.

Berger, Thomas L., ed. see Shakespeare, William.

Berger, Thomas R. Long & Terrible Shadow: White Values & Native Rights in the Americas Since 1492. 2nd ed. 183p. 1999. pap. text 17.95 (*0-295-97807-4*) U of Wash Pr.

— Village Journey: The Report of the Alaska Native Review Commission. rev. ed. 204p. 1995. pap. 10.95 (*0-8090-1579-X*) Hill & Wang.

Berger, Thomas R., et al. The Arctic: Choices for Peace & Security--A Public Inquiry. 240p. (Orig.). 1989. pap. 14.95 (*0-919574-82-3*) Gordon Soules Bk.

Berger, Thomas U. Cultures of Antimilitarism: National Security in Germany & Japan. LC 97-48479. 272p. 1998. text 38.00 (*0-8018-5820-8*) Johns Hopkins.

Berger, Timothy, et al. Manual of Therapy for Skin Diseases. 349p. 1990. pap. text 35.00 (*0-443-08477-7*) Church.

Berger, Toby, jt. ed. see Zhongxing Ye.

***Berger, Todd R.** Love of Goldens: The Ultimate Tribute to Golden Retrievers. LC 99-88399. (PetLife Library). (Illus.). 160p. 2000. pap. 19.95 (*0-89658-469-0*) Voyageur Pr.

— Love of Labs: The Ultimate Tribute to Labrador Retrievers. LC 99-86897. (PetLife Library). (Illus.). 160p. 2000. pap. 19.95 (*0-89658-468-2*) Voyageur Pr.

— Love of Spaniels: The Ultimate Tribute to Cockers, Springers & Other Great Spaniels. (PetLife Library). (Illus.). 160p. 2000. 29.95 (*0-89658-453-4*) Voyageur Pr.

Berger, Todd R. Majestic Elk. LC 98-11499. (Illus.). 160p. 1998. 35.00 (*0-89658-384-8*) Voyageur Pr.

***Berger, Todd R., ed.** Labs Afield: The Ultimate Tribute to the World's Greatest Retriever. LC 00-36506. (PetLife Library). (Illus.). 160p. 2000. 29.95 (*0-89658-489-5*) Voyageur Pr.

Berger, Todd R., ed. Love of Dogs: The Ultimate Tribute to Our Best Friend. LC 98-37543. (PetLife Library). (Illus.). 160p. 1999. 29.95 (*0-89658-412-7*) Voyageur Pr.

— Love of German Shepherds: The Ultimate Tribute. LC 99-13245. (PetLife Library). (Illus.). 160p. 1999. 29.95 (*0-89658-446-1*) Voyageur Pr.

— Love of Goldens. LC 98-17603. (Petlife Library). (Illus.). 160p. 1998. 29.95 (*0-89658-385-6*) Voyageur Pr.

Berger, Todd R., jt. ed. see Dregni, Michael.

Berger, Tom, ed. see Peterson, Edith.

***Berger, U. & Schwichtenberg, H., eds.** Computational Logic. LC 99-13850. (NATO ASI Ser.: Vol. 165). 460p. 1998. 119.00 (*3-540-64589-6*) Spr-Verlag.

Berger, Vance, jt. auth. see Research & Education Association Staff.

Berger, W. H., et al, eds. The South Atlantic Vol. X: Present & Past Circulation. LC 96-50016. (Illus.). 644p. 1997. 133.00 (*3-540-62079-6*) Spr-Verlag.

Berger, W. H. & Labeyrie, L. D., eds. Abrupt Climatic Change - Evidence & Implications. (C). 1987. text 161.50 (*90-277-2604-3*) Kluwer Academic.

Berger, W. H., jt. auth. see Seibold, E.

Berger, Walter A. & Snyder, George M. Freshly Remember'd. (Illus.). 233p. (Orig.). 1993. pap. 20.00 (*0-9639330-0-0*) Schneider-McGuirk.

Berger, William. Wagner Without Fear: Learning to Love - And Even Enjoy - Opera's Most Demanding Genius. LC 98-19825. 464p. pap. 15.00 (*0-375-70054-4*) Vin Bks.

***Berger, William E.** Allergies & Asthma for Dummies. (For Dummies Ser.). 384p. 2000. pap. 19.99 (*0-7645-5218-X*) IDG Bks.

***Berger, Williams.** Verdi with a Vengeance: An Energetic Guide to the Life & Complete Works of the King of Opera. 2000. pap. 15.00 (*0-375-70518-X*) Vin Bks.

Berger, Zeev. Satellite Hydrocarbon Exploration: Interpretation & Integration Techniques. LC 94-8948. (Illus.). xi, 319p. 1994. 111.95 (*0-387-57348-8*) Spr-Verlag.

Bergera, Gary J., ed. Line upon Line: Essays on Mormon Doctrine. LC 88-30867. (Essays on Mormonism Ser.: No. 1). 198p. 1989. pap. 14.95 (*0-941214-69-9*) Signature Bks.

Bergera, Gary J., ed. see Roberts, Brigham H.

Bergera, Gary J., ed. see Ruess, Everett.

Bergera, Janet. Vital Signs: A Mission of the Heart. LC 95-1145. (J). 1995. pap. 9.95 (*1-55503-773-9*, 01111817) Covenant Comms.

Bergerac. First Book of American Folk Songs. 48p. (J). 1998. pap. 3.50 (*0-486-28885-4*) Dover.

— My First Book of Christmas Songs. (Illus.). 1997. pap. 3.50 (*0-486-29718-7*) Dover.

***Bergerac.** My First Book of Classical Music: 20 Themes by Beethoven, Mozart, Chopin & Other Great Composers. (J). 2000. pap. 3.95 (*0-486-41092-7*) Dover.

Bergerac, ed. My First Book of Irish Songs & Celtic Dances: 21 Favorite Pieces in Easy Piano Arrangements. (Illus.). 48p. 1998. pap. 3.95 (*0-486-40405-6*) Dover.

Bergerac, Olivia de, see De Bergerac, Olivia.

Bergere, Anne. German Names. LC 94-94186. (Illus.). 380p. (Orig.). 1994. pap. 19.95 (*0-9640850-0-3*) Asgard Pubng.

***Bergere, Lee & Hilton-Barber, Brett.** In the Footsteps of Eve: The Mystery of Human Origins. LC 00-28071. (Illus.). 304p. 2000. per. 26.00 (*0-7922-7682-5*, Pub. by Natl Geog) S&S Trade.

Bergere, Marie-Claire. Sun Yat-Sen. Lloyd, Janet, tr. from FRE. LC 97-35504. (Illus.). 480p. 1998. 45.00 (*0-8047-3170-5*) Stanford U Pr.

***Bergere, Marie-Claire.** Sun Yat-Sen. 2000. pap. text 24.95 (*0-8047-4011-9*) Stanford U Pr.

Bergere, R., et al. Intermediate Energy Nuclear Physics: Proceedings of the 4th Course of the Intermediate School of Intermediate Energy Nuclear Physics. 450p. 1984. 81.00 (*9971-950-22-7*) World Scientific Pub.

Bergeret, L. F. The Preventive Obstacle, or Conjugal Onanism. De Marmon, P., tr. from FRE. LC 73-20616. (Sex, Marriage & Society Ser.). 192p. 1974. reprint ed. 20.95 (*0-405-05794-6*) Ayer.

Bergerhof, Kurt, et al. Die Elfenbeininschriften und S-Texte aus Ugarit. (Alter Orient und Altes Testament Ser.: Vol. 13). (GER.). 185p. 1976. pap. text 12.00 (*3-7887-0493-4*) NeukirchenerV.

Bergero, Adriana J. El Debate Politico Vol. 8: Modernidad, Poder y Disidencia En Yo el Supremo De Augusto Roa Bastos. (Wor(l)ds of Change Ser.). (SPA.). X, 285p. (C). 1995. text 57.95 (*0-8204-2583-4*) P Lang Pubng.

Bergeron. First Responder. 4th ed. 1995. pap., wbk. ed. 25.67 (*0-8359-4969-9*) P-H.

— First Responder. 5th ed. 1998. pap., wbk. ed. 25.67 (*0-8359-5266-5*) P-H.

Bergeron & Bizjak. First Responder. 5th ed. 1998. pap., teacher ed. 36.80 (*0-8359-5273-8*) P-H.

Bergeron & Bizjak, Gloria J. First Responder. 4th ed. 1995. pap., teacher ed. 36.80 (*0-8359-4967-2*) P-H.

Bergeron, et al. First Responder. 5th ed. LC 98-8032. 576p. 1998. pap. text 49.00 (*0-8359-5186-3*) P-H.

Bergeron, Arthur W., Jr. Confederate Mobile. 271p. 1998. text 35.00 (*0-7881-5464-8*) DIANE Pub.

Bergeron, Arthur W. Confederate Mobile. LC 91-15776. 283p. reprint ed. pap. 87.80 (*0-608-08721-1*, 206928900003) Bks Demand.

***Bergeron, Arthur W., Jr.** Confederate Moble. LC 99-87925. (Illus.). 296p. 2000. pap. 16.95 (*0-8071-2573-3*) La State U Pr.

Bergeron, Arthur W., Jr. Guide to Louisiana Confederate Military Units, 1861-1865. LC 88-29214. 229p. 1996. pap. 12.95 (*0-8071-2102-9*) La State U Pr.

Bergeron, Arthur W., Jr., ed. Civil War Reminiscences of Major Silas T. Grisamore, C. S. A. LC 92-37038. (Illus.). 240p. 1993. 24.95 (*0-8071-1817-6*) La State U Pr.

Bergeron, Bette S. & Rudenga, Liz. Journeying: Integrating Literacy Learning in Grades K to 3. 208p. 1999. teacher ed., spiral bd. 29.95 (*1-58108-035-2*) Pencil Point.

***Bergeron, Bryan.** Eternal E-Customer: How Emotionally Intelligent Interfaces Can Create Long-Lasting Customer Relations. 2001. 27.95 (*0-07-136479-X*) McGraw.

***Bergeron, Caroline & Berger, D.** Bind Your Own Book (Adult) 2000. (*0-9679662-6-4*) Hardbound.

— Bind Your Own Book (Children's) 25p. 2000. (*0-9679662-0-5*) Hardbound.

Bergeron, Clifton G. & Risbud, Subhash H., eds. Introduction to Phase Equilibria in Ceramics. 158p. 1984. 42.00 (*0-916094-58-8*, PHINTR) Am Ceramic.

Bergeron, David M. King James & Letters of Homoerotic Desire. LC 98-48368. (Illus.). 260p. 1999. text 24.95 (*0-87745-669-0*) U of Iowa Pr.

***Bergeron, David M.** Practicing Renaissance Scholarship: Plays & Pageants, Patrons & Politics. LC 99-50701. (Medieval & Renaissance Literary Studies). (Illus.). 240p. 2000. text 55.00 (*0-8207-0313-3*) Duquesne.

Bergeron, David M., ed. Reading & Writing in Shakespeare. LC 95-24193. (Illus.). 288p. 1996. 42.50 (*0-87413-557-5*) U Delaware Pr.

Bergeron, David M. & Atkins, Douglas G. Shakespeare & Deconstruction. 2nd ed. (American University Studies: English Language & Literature: Ser. IV, Vol. 57). VIII, 283p. (C). 1991. text 44.00 (*0-8204-0530-2*) P Lang Pubng.

Bergeron, David M. & De Sousa, Geraldo U. Shakespeare: A Study & Research Guide. 3rd rev. ed. LC 94-37236. viii, 208p. (Orig.). 1995. pap. 14.95 (*0-7006-0693-9*) U Pr of KS.

— Shakespeare: A Study & Research Guide. 3rd rev. ed. LC 94-37236. viii, 208p. (Orig.). 1995. 29.95 (*0-7006-0692-0*) U Pr of KS.

Bergeron, F., et al. Combinatorial Species & Tree-Like Structures. Readdy, Margaret, tr. from FRE. LC 96-46136. (Encyclopedia of Mathematics & Its Applications Ser.: Vol. 67). (Illus.). 478p. (C). 1997. text 80.00 (*0-521-57323-8*) Cambridge U Pr.

Bergeron, J. The Early Universe with the VLT: Proceedings of the ESO Workshop, Held at Garching, Germany, 1-4 April 1996. LC 96-53244. (ESO Astrophysics Symposia Ser.). 1997. 38.00 (*3-540-62414-7*) Spr-Verlag.

Bergeron, J., ed. see VLT Opening Symposium Staff.

Bergeron, J. David. First Responder. 2nd ed. (Illus.). 416p. 1987. pap. text 17.00 (*0-89303-683-8*) P-H.

Bergeron, J. David & Bizjak, Gloria J. First Responder. 4th ed. LC 95-11230. 544p. 1995. pap. 40.00 (*0-8359-4964-8*) P-H.

Bergeron, Jacqueline, ed. Highlights of Astronomy Vol. 9: As Presented at the XXI General Assembly of the IAU, Buenos Aires. 776p. (C). 1992. pap. text 137.50 (*0-7923-1916-8*); lib. bdg. 275.00 (*0-7923-1915-X*) Kluwer Academic.

— Reports on Astronomy. LC 93-50750. (Transactions of the International Astronomical Union Ser.: Vol. 22A). 616p. 1994. lib. bdg. 200.50 (*0-7923-2709-8*) Kluwer Academic.

— Transactions of the International Astronomical Union: Proceedings of the 21st General Assembly, Buenos Aires, 1991, Vol. XXI B. LC 92-25559. 952p. 1992. lib. bdg. 306.00 (*0-7923-1914-1*) Kluwer Academic.

Bergeron, James H., jt. ed. see Fitzpatrick, Peter.

***Bergeron, Janick.** Writing Testbenches: Functional Verification of HDL Models. LC 99-89335. 2000. write for info. (*0-7923-7766-4*) Kluwer Academic.

Bergeron, Johanne & Heft, L. Rhododendron und Immergruene Laubgehoelze (Rhododendrons & Evergreen Shrubs) 3rd ed. (GER., Illus.). 272p. 1991. 86.00 (*3-8001-6366-7*, Pub. by Eugen Ulmer) Balogh.

Bergeron, Katherine. Decedent Enchantments: The Revival of Gregorian Chant at Solesmes. LC 97-24120. (California Studies in 19th Century Music). (Illus.). 196p. 1998. 35.00 (*0-520-21008-5*, Pub. by U CA Pr) Cal Prin Full Svc.

Bergeron, Katherine & Bohlman, Philip V., eds. Disciplining Music: Musicology & Its Canons. LC 91-37836. (Illus.). 233p. 1992. 29.50 (*0-226-04368-1*) U Ch Pr.

— Disciplining Music: Musicology & Its Canons. (Illus.). xii, 220p. 1996. pap. text 15.95 (*0-226-04370-3*) U Ch Pr.

***Bergeron, Ken.** Professional Vegetarian Cooking. LC 98-47051. 448p. 1999. 44.95 (*0-471-29235-4*) Wiley.

Bergeron, L. Dictionnaire de la Langue Quebecoise.Tr. of Dictionary of Quebecoise. (FRE.). 574p. 1980. pap. 125.00 (*0-8288-1092-3*, M9360) Fr & Eur.

Bergeron, Leandre. Why There Must Be a Revolution in Quebec. (Illus.). 144p. 1978. pap. 4.95 (*0-919600-16-6*, Pub. by NC Ltd) U of Toronto Pr.

Bergeron, Louis. France under Napoleon. Palmer, Robert R., tr. from FRE. LC 81-47115. (Illus.). 240p. 1981. pap. text 18.95 (*0-691-00789-6*, Pub. by Princeton U Pr) Cal Prin Full Svc.

***Bergeron, Louis & Maiullari-Pontois, Maria Teresa.** Industry, Architecture & Engineering: American Ingenuity, 1750-1950. (Illus.). 288p. 2000. 65.00 (*0-8109-3473-6*, Pub. by Abrams) Time Warner.

Bergeron, Louis J. Water Hammer in Hydraulics & Wave Surges in Electricity. LC TC0160.B443. 337p. reprint ed. pap. 104.50 (*0-608-11480-4*, 201158800080) Bks Demand.

Bergeron, Lyle E. Cajun Humor, Little. 2nd ed. (Illus.). 35p. (Orig.). 1993. pap. text 6.95 (*0-9636785-0-7*) L E Bergeron.

***Bergeron, Marcel.** Riemannian Geometry During the Second Half of the Twentieth Century. LC 99-32803. (University Lecture Ser.). 182p. 1999. write for info. (*0-8218-2052-4*) Am Math.

Bergeron, Marcel & Nerou, Jean-Pierre. English - French Vocabulary of Optical Electronics. (ENG & FRE.). 86p. 1992. pap. 39.95 (*0-8288-9411-6*) Fr & Eur.

Bergeron, Marilyn. A Community Affair: Solving the Problem of Teen Pregnancy & Disease. 128p. (Orig.). 1996. pap. 10.00 (*1-883893-68-2*) WinePress Pub.

Bergeron, Michel, jt. auth. see Lacinski, Paul.

Bergeron, Paul H. Antebellum Politics in Tennessee. LC 82-40170. 244p. 1982. 29.00 (*0-8131-1469-1*) U Pr of Ky.

— Paths of the Past: Tennessee, 1770-1970. LC 79-14896. (Tennessee Three Star Ser.). (Illus.). 136p. 1979. pap. 7.00 (*0-87049-274-8*) U of Tenn Pr.

— The Presidency of James K. Polk. LC 87-2174. (American Presidency Ser.). xvi, 312p. 1987. 29.95 (*0-7006-0319-0*) U Pr of KS.

Bergeron, Paul H., ed. The Papers of Andrew Johnson Vol. 15: Volume 15 September 1868 April 1869. LC 67-25733. (Illus.). 688p. 1998. text 60.00 (*1-57233-028-7*) U of Tenn Pr.

***Bergeron, Paul H., ed.** The Papers of Andrew Johnson Vol. 16: May 1896 - July 1875. LC 67-25733. (Illus.). 840p. (C). 2000. text 60.00 (*1-57233-091-0*, Pub. by U of Tenn Pr) U Ch Pr.

Bergeron, Paul H., ed. The Papers of Andrew Johnson, April-August 1868 Vol. 14. LC 67-25733. (Illus.). 624p. (C). 1997. text 60.00 (*0-87049-991-2*) U of Tenn Pr.

— The Papers of Andrew Johnson, August 1866-January 1867, Vol. 11. LC 67-25733. (Illus.). 800p. (C). 1994. text 60.00 (*0-87049-828-2*) U of Tenn Pr.

— The Papers of Andrew Johnson, February-August, 1867, Vol. 12. LC 67-25733. 592p. 1995. text 60.00 (*0-87049-896-7*) U of Tenn Pr.

— The Papers of Andrew Johnson, February-July, 1866, Vol. 10. LC 67-25733. (Illus.). 832p. 1992. text 60.00 (*0-87049-764-2*) U of Tenn Pr.

— The Papers of Andrew Johnson, May-August 1865, Vol. 8. LC 67-25733. (Papers of Andrew Johnson Ser.). 762p. 1990. text 60.00 (*0-87049-613-1*) U of Tenn Pr.

— The Papers of Andrew Johnson, September 1865-January 1866, Vol. 9. LC 67-25733. (Illus.). 712p. 1991. text 60.00 (*0-87049-689-1*) U of Tenn Pr.

— The Papers of Andrew Johnson, September 1867-March 1868, Vol. 13. LC 67-25733. 768p. (C). 1997. text 60.00 (*0-87049-946-7*) U of Tenn Pr.

Bergeron, Paul H., et al. Tennesseans & Their History. LC 99-6126. (Illus.). 496p. 1999. 30.00 (*1-57233-055-4*, Pub. by U of Tenn Pr) U Ch Pr.

— Tennesseans & Their History. LC 99-6126. (Illus.). 496p. 1999. pap. 15.00 (*1-57233-056-2*, Pub. by U of Tenn Pr) U Ch Pr.

Bergeron, Peter, jt. auth. see Kwon, Charles.

Bergeron, Raymond J. Development of Iron Chelators for Clinical Use. 432p. 1993. boxed set 187.95 (*0-8493-8679-9*, RM666) CRC Pr.

Bergerot, Franck & Merlin, Arnaud. The Story of Jazz: Bop & Beyond. De Jager, Marjolijn, tr. (Discoveries Ser.). (Illus.). 160p. 1993. pap. 12.95 (*0-8109-2876-0*, Pub. by Abrams) Time Warner.

Bergersen, Ben. CTT All-in-One Certification Exam Guide. LC 99-54055. (All-in-One Certification Ser.). 500p. 1999. write for info. (*0-07-135630-4*) Osborne-McGraw.

***Bergersen, Ben.** i-Net+ & All-In-One Certification Exam Guide. 750p. 2000. pap. 54.99 (*0-07-212265-X*) McGraw-Hill Prof.

Bergersen, Ben, jt. auth. see Groth, David.

Bergersen, Birger & Plischke, Michael. Equilibrium Statistical Physics. 450p. 1994. pap. text 44.00 (*981-02-1642-4*) World Scientific Pub.

Bergersen, Birger, jt. auth. see Pliscke, Micheal.

Bergersen, E. P., jt. auth. see Nesler, T. P.

Bergersen, F. J., ed. Methods for Evaluating Biological Nitrogen Fixation. LC 79-41785. 712p. reprint ed. pap. 200.00 (*0-8357-2768-8*, 203989300014) Bks Demand.

Bergerson, Betty & Comty, Christina M. Continuous Ambulatory Peritoneal Dialysis (CAPD) 210p. 1983. ring bd. 30.00 (*1-56488-008-7*) Dialyrn.

Bergerson, Birger & Plischke, Michael. Equilibrium Statistical Physics. 2nd ed. 450p. 1994. text 90.00 (*981-02-1641-6*) World Scientific Pub.

Bergerson, Frederic A. The Army Gets an Air Force: Tactics of Insurgent Bureaucratic Politics. LC 79-18191. (Illus.). 232p. reprint ed. pap. 72.00 (*0-7837-4260-6*, 204395200012) Bks Demand.

Bergerson, Howard W. Palindromes & Anagrams. 192p. (Orig.). 1973. pap. 5.95 (*0-486-20664-5*) Dover.

Bergerson, Michael, ed. see International Congress of Nephrology Staff.

Bergerson, Peter J., ed. Teaching Public Policy: Theory, Research, & Practice, 268. LC 90-43371. (Contributions in Political Science Ser.: No. 268). 240p. 1991. 59.95 (*0-313-27636-6*, BTD/, Greenwood Pr) Greenwood.

— Teaching Public Policy & Administration. (Orig.). 1989. pap. 15.00 (*0-944285-09-0*) Pol Studies.

Bergerud. Word & Information Processing: Concepts of Office Automation. 4th ed. 1988. text 35.90 (*0-471-60909-9*) P-H.

***Bergerud & Busche.** Microsoft Windows 2000 Beginning Course. 2000. pap. 19.95 (*0-538-72417-X*) Thomson Learn.

— Microsoft Windows 2000 Comprehensive. (Computer Applications Ser.). (C). 2000. pap., wbk. ed. 9.95 (*0-538-72404-8*) Sth-Wstrn College.

Bergerud & Busche. Microsoft Windows 98: Complete Course. (Computer Applications Ser.). 1998. mass mkt. 35.25 (*0-538-72119-7*) S-W Pub.

***Bergerud & Busche.** Microsoft Windows 98: Quicktorial. 1998. pap. 22.95 (*0-538-72062-X*); pap. 16.75 (*0-538-72064-6*) Thomson Learn.

— MS Windows 2000 Comprehensive Crs. (C). 2000. pap. 54.95 (*0-538-72400-5*) Sth-Wstrn College.

Bergerud, Arthur T. & Gratson, Michael W., eds. Adaptive Strategies & Population Ecology of Northern Grouse, Vol. II, Theory & Synthesis. LC 86-19248. (Illus.). 396p. 1988. pap. 24.95 (*0-8166-1471-7*) U of Minn Pr.

Bergerud, Eric. Touched with Fire: The Land War in the South Pacific. (Illus.). 566p. 1996. 34.95 (*0-614-19994-8*) Viking Penguin.

Bergerud, Eric M. Fire in the Sky: The Air War in the South Pacific. LC 99-40472. (Illus.). 608p. 2000. text 35.00 (*0-8133-2985-X*, Pub. by Westview) HarpC.

— Red Thunder, Tropic Lightning: The World of a Combat Division in Vietnam. (Illus.). 352p. 1994. pap. 13.95 (*0-14-023545-0*, Penguin Bks) Viking Penguin.

— Touched with Fire: The Land War in the South Pacific. (Illus.). 608p. 1997. pap. 14.95 (*0-14-024696-7*) Penguin Putnam.

Bergerud, Marly. Microsoft Windows 3.1: Concepts & Applications. (DF - Computer Applications Ser.). (C). 1993. mass mkt. 41.95 (*0-538-70713-5*) S-W Pub.

— Windows 95 Complete Course. LC 96-3914. (Computer Applications Ser.). 1996. mass mkt. 48.95 (*0-538-71377-1*) S-W Pub.

— Windows 95 Quick Course. (DF - Computer Applications Ser.). 248p. 1996. mass mkt. 22.95 (*0-538-64113-4*) S-W Pub.

— Windows 3.1, Easy Reference Guide. (DF - Computer Applications Ser.). 1994. mass mkt. 9.95 (*0-538-63384-0*) S-W Pub.

Bergerud, Marly & Busche, Don. Understanding Microcomputers & Applications Software. (DF - Computer Applications Ser.). (C). 15.95 (*0-538-70653-8*); 15.95 (*0-538-70654-6*) S-W Pub.

Bergerud, Marly, jt. auth. see Busche, Don.

Bergerud, Marly K. & Busche, Don. Windows 3.1: Quick Start. LC 92-46644. (Quick Start Ser.). (C). 1993. mass mkt. 19.95 (*0-538-71086-1*) S-W Pub.

Bergerud, Marly K. & Gonzalez, Jean. Understanding Word & Information Processing: A Study Guide & Projects Manual. 125p. (C). 1984. pap. text 17.50 (*0-471-80173-9*) P-H.

Bergerud, Marly K. & Keller, Thomas. Computers for Managing Information. LC 87-20979. 1988. pap. text 6.85 (*0-471-60157-8*) P-H.

Berges, Darlene & Berges, John. The Daily Seven Ray Energy Journal. (Illus.). 129p. 1996. wbk. ed. 14.95 (*0-9641549-1-9*) Planetwrk Pr.

***Berges, John.** Hidden Foundations of the Great Invocation. LC 00-191188. (Illus.). xv, 255p. 2000. pap. 21.95 (*0-9641549-3-5*) Planetwrk Pr.

An Asterisk (*) at the beginning of an entry indicates that the title is appearing for the first time.

Berges, John. Sacred Vessel of the Mysteries: The Great Invocation, Word of Power, Gift of Love. LC 98-132190. (Illus.). 493p. 1997. pap. 21.95 (*0-9641549-2-7*) Planetwrk Pr.

— Seven Ray Energy Cards: An Intuitive Tool for Working with the Seven Rays. 138p. 1994. spiral bd. 31.95 (*0-9641549-0-0*) Planetwrk Pr.

Berges, John, jt. auth. see Berges, Darlene.

Berges, Judith A. Reflections. Schreiber, Hans-Martin, tr. (ENG & GER., Illus.). (Orig.). 1993. pap. 18.95 (*0-685-75403-0*); pap. 18.95 (*0-9637411-0-1*) Berges Tours.

Berges, Marcelo S. Diccionario del Negocio Inmobiliario.Tr. of Dictionary of Real Estate Terms. (SPA.). 240p. 1997. pap. text 24.95 (*0-7931-2149-3*, 1913-4301) Dearborn.

Bergesen, Albert, ed. Crises in the World-System. LC 82-21474. (Political Economy of the World-System Annuals Ser.: No. 6). 311p. reprint ed. pap. 96.50 (*0-8357-8470-3*, 203473800091) Bks Demand.

Bergesen, Albert, jt. ed. see Boswell, Terry.

***Bergesen, Albert J.** God in the Movies. (Illus.). 152p. 2000. 29.95 (*0-7658-0020-9*) Transaction Pubs.

Bergesen, Chris, ed. International Directory of Electric Power Producers & Distributors. 9th ed. 800p. 1998. 345.00 (*0-614-10165-4*) Utility Data Inst.

Bergesen, Chris, ed. see Utility Data Institute Staff.

Bergesen, Helge O., et al, eds. Green Globe Yearbook 1992. (Illus.). 304p. 1992. 49.95 (*0-19-823322-1*) OUP.

Bergesen, Helge O. & Parmann, Georg, eds. Green Globe Yearbook 1994: International Co-operation on Environment & Development. (Illus.). 354p. 1994. 49.95 (*0-19-823324-8*) OUP.

Bergesen, Helge O., et al. Implementing the European CO2 Commitment: A Joint Policy Proposal. 50p. (C). 1995. pap. 10.95 (*0-905031-91-1*) Brookings.

Bergeson, Kenneth L., jt. ed. see Inyang, Hilary I.

***Bergeson, Lynn L.** Basic Books: Fifra. LC 00-42148. 2000. write for info. (*1-57073-834-3*) Amer Bar Assn.

Bergeson, Sandra, jt. auth. see Balsamo, Larry.

Bergessen, Albert. The Sacred & the Subversive: Political Witch-Hunts as National Rituals. LC 84-61370. (Society for Scientific Study of Religion Monographs: No. 4). 1984. pap. 5.50 (*0-932566-03-0*) Soc Sci Stud Rel.

Bergessen, Helge O. & Parmann, Georg, eds. Green Globe Yearbook 1995: Yearbook of International Co-Operation on Environment & Development. (Illus.). 320p. 1995. text 49.95 (*0-19-823325-6*) OUP.

Bergeth, R. Twelve Secrets for Cashing Out: How to Sell Your Company for the Most Profit. 336p. (C). 1994. text 45.00 (*0-13-176454-3*) P-H.

Bergethon, Bjonnar, jt. auth. see Nye, Robert E.

Bergethon, Bjornar, et al. Musical Growth in the Elementary School. 6th ed. LC 96-75034. 448p. (C). 1996. pap. text 51.50 (*0-15-501648-2*, Pub. by Harcourt Coll Pubs) Harcourt.

Bergethon, P. R. The Physical Basis of Biochemistry: The Foundations of Molecular Biophysics. LC 97-26975. (Illus.). 650p. 1998. text 69.95 (*0-387-98262-0*) Spr-Verlag.

Bergethon, P. R. & Simons, E. R., eds. Biophysical Chemistry. (Illus.). xiv, 340p. 1989. 69.95 (*0-387-97053-3*, 3010) Spr-Verlag.

***Bergethon, Peter R.** The Atmosphere: An Ocean of Air, Student Science Journal. (Illus.). 156p. (YA). (gr. 6-8). 1999. pap. text. write for info. (*1-58447-065-8*) Symmetry Lrng.

— The Atmosphere: An Ocean of Air, Teacher Manual. (Illus.). vi, 156p. 1999. pap. text, teacher ed. write for info. (*1-58447-064-X*) Symmetry Lrng.

— Atoms & Elements Pt. I: An Introduction to Chemistry, Student Science Journal. (Illus.). 58p. (YA). (gr. 5-8). 2000. pap. text. write for info. (*1-58447-055-0*) Symmetry Lrng.

— Atoms & Elements Pt. I: An Introduction to Chemistry, Teacher Manual. (Illus.). x, 58p. 2000. pap. text, teacher ed. write for info. (*1-58447-054-2*) Symmetry Lrng.

— Atoms & Elements Pt. II: Exploring the Particulate Model of Matter, Student Science Journal. (Illus.). 105p. 2000. pap. text. write for info. (*1-58447-075-5*) Symmetry Lrng.

— Atoms & Elements Pt. II: Exploring the Particulate Model of Matter, Teacher Manual. (Illus.). x, 105p. 2000. pap. text, teacher ed. write for info. (*1-58447-074-7*) Symmetry Lrng.

— Describing My World: Student Science Journal. (Illus.). 139p. (J). (gr. 1-3). 2000. pap. text. write for info. (*1-58447-003-8*) Symmetry Lrng.

— Describing My World: Teacher Manual. (Illus.). 139p. 2000. pap. text, teacher ed. write for info. (*1-58447-002-X*) Symmetry Lrng.

— The Electric World: An Introduction to Electricity, Student Science Journal. (Illus.). 84p. (J). (gr. 4-6). 1999. pap. text. write for info. (*1-58447-013-5*) Symmetry Lrng.

— The Electric World: An Introduction to Electricity, Teacher Manual. (Illus.). x, 84p. 1999. pap. text, teacher ed. write for info. (*1-58447-012-7*) Symmetry Lrng.

— Exploring My World: Marty's Miraculous Monday. (Illus.). 73p. (J). (gr. k-1). 1999. pap. text. write for info. (*1-58447-001-1*) Symmetry Lrng.

— The Journey Begins. (Illus.). 35p. 1999. pap. text. write for info. (*1-58447-026-7*) Symmetry Lrng.

— Learning the Language of Patterns: A Teacher's Guided Tour. (Illus.). 149p. 1999. spiral bd. write for info. (*1-58447-029-1*) Symmetry Lrng.

— Learning the Language of Patterns: Student Science Journal. (Illus.). 74p. (YA). (gr. 4-9). 1999. pap. text. write for info. (*1-58447-030-5*) Symmetry Lrng.

— Learning the Language of Patterns: Teacher Manual. (Illus.). xvi, 74p. 1999. teacher ed., spiral bd. write for info. (*1-58447-031-3*) Symmetry Lrng.

— Learning the Language of Patterns: The Overview. (Illus.). 19p. 1999. pap. text. write for info. (*1-58447-028-3*) Symmetry Lrng.

— Magnets & Magnetism: Student Science Journal. (Illus.). 96p. (J). (gr. 4-6). 1999. pap. text. write for info. (*1-58447-015-1*) Symmetry Lrng.

— Magnets & Magnetism: Teacher Manual. (Illus.). xix, 96p. 1999. pap. text, teacher ed. write for info. (*1-58447-014-3*) Symmetry Lrng.

— Marty's Miraculous Monday. (Illus.). 36p. (J). (gr. k-4). 1999. pap. write for info. (*1-58447-004-6*) Symmetry Lrng.

— Marty's Miraculous Monday Reader. (Illus.). (J). (gr. k-3). Date not set. pap. text. write for info. (*1-58447-011-9*) Symmetry Lrng.

— Measuring My World: Student Science Journal. (Illus.). Date not set. pap. text. write for info. (*1-58447-006-2*) Symmetry Lrng.

— Measuring My World: Teacher Manual. (Illus.). Date not set. pap. text, teacher ed. write for info. (*1-58447-005-4*) Symmetry Lrng.

— The Microscope: Technology, Lenses & Light, Student Science Journal. (Illus.). 137p. (YA). (gr. 6-8). 2000. pap. text. write for info. (*1-58447-047-X*) Symmetry Lrng.

— The Microscope: Technology, Lenses & Light, Teacher Manual. (Illus.). xxiv, 137p. 2000. pap. text, teacher ed. write for info. (*1-58447-046-1*) Symmetry Lrng.

— The Mystery of the Electric Lemon: An Introduction to Electrochemistry, Student Science Journal. (Illus.). 47p. (YA). (gr. 6-9). 1999. pap. text. write for info. (*1-58447-059-3*) Symmetry Lrng.

— The Mystery of the Electric Lemon: An Introduction to Electrochemistry, Teacher Manual. (Illus.). 47p. 1999. pap. text, teacher ed. write for info. (*1-58447-058-5*) Symmetry Lrng.

— Sparks to Circuits - Electricity: Models & Mechanisms, Student Science Journal. (Illus.). 80p. (YA). (gr. 6-8). 1999. pap. text. write for info. (*1-58447-019-4*) Symmetry Lrng.

— Sparks to Circuits - Electricity: Models & Mechanisms, Teachers Manual. (Illus.). 80p. 1999. pap. text, teacher ed. write for info. (*1-58447-018-6*) Symmetry Lrng.

— Understanding My World: Student Science Journal. (Illus.). Date not set. pap. text. write for info. (*1-58447-008-9*) Symmetry Lrng.

— Understanding My World: Teachers Manual. (Illus.). Date not set. pap. text, teacher ed. write for info. (*1-58447-007-0*) Symmetry Lrng.

— The World of Gravity: Student Science Manual. (Illus.). 75p. (J). (gr. 5-7). 1999. pap. text, student ed. write for info. (*1-58447-033-X*) Symmetry Lrng.

— The World of Gravity: Teacher Manual. (Illus.). 75p. 1999. pap. text, teacher ed. write for info. (*1-58447-032-1*) Symmetry Lrng.

Bergevin, Yves, ed. Health Technology Assessment: A Needs-Based Approach. LC 97-700149. xviii, 156p. 1996. pap. 20.00 (*0-88936-752-3*, Pub. by IDRC Bks) Stylus Pub VA.

Bergey, Alyce. David & Jonathan: 1 Samuel 18-20. (Arch Bks.). (Illus.). 24p. (J). (gr. k-4). 1987. pap. 1.99 (*0-570-09006-7*, 59-1434) Concordia.

— The Fishermen's Surprise: John 21; Luke 5:1-11. (Arch Bks.). (Illus.). 1970. 1.99 (*0-570-06028-1*, 59-1139) Concordia.

— The World God Made: The Story of Creation. (Arch Bks.). (J). (ps-3). 1970. pap. 1.99 (*0-570-06011-7*, 59-1114) Concordia.

Bergey, Mary T. & Miller, Leroy. A Symphony of Frogs: An Autobiography. LC 97-35965. 1997. write for info. (*1-57864-016-4*); pap. write for info. (*1-57864-018-0*) Donning Co.

Bergez. The Craft of Editing. (Freshman English/Advanced Writing Ser.). 1909. mass mkt. 35.95 (*0-534-19914-3*) Wadsworth Pub.

Bergez, John, ed. Hands-On History: Projects & Activities to Accompany Lean John, California's Horseback Hero. 48p. (J). (gr. 3-6). 1998. pap. 7.95 (*0-933818-66-1*) Ghost Town.

— Hands-On History: Projects & Activities to Accompany Otters, Octopuses, & Odd Creatures of the Deep. (History & Happenings of California Ser.). 48p. (J). (gr. 3-6). 1992. pap. 7.95 (*0-933818-61-0*) Ghost Town.

— Hands-On History: Projects & Activities to Accompany Tales & Treasures of California's Missions. (History & Happenings of California Ser.). 56p. (J). (gr. 3-6). 1993. pap. 8.95 (*0-933818-64-5*) Ghost Town.

— Hands-On History: Projects & Activities to Accompany Tales & Treasures of the California Gold Rush. (History & Happenings of California Ser.). 64p. (J). (gr. 3-6). 1995. pap. 8.95 (*0-933818-65-3*) Ghost Town.

Bergez, John, ed. see Delmar, Charles O.

Bergez, John, ed. see Livermore, Donald R.

Bergez, John, ed. see Reinstedt, Randall A.

Bergfalk, Bradley J. & Koptak, Paul E., eds. To Hear & Obey. 184p. 1997. pap. 15.95 (*0-910452-83-0*) Covenant.

Bergfeld, John A., jt. ed. see Pearl, Arthur J.

Bergfeld, Rainer. Diccionario Riodeuro: Biologia. 3rd ed. (SPA.). 244p. 1982. pap. 39.95 (*0-7859-5070-2*) Fr & Eur.

— Herder Lexicon of Biology: Herder Lexikon, Biologie. 7th ed. (GER.). 237p. 1984. 35.00 (*0-8288-1220-9*, M7453) Fr & Eur.

Bergfeld, Wilma F. & Masline, Shelagh R. A Woman Doctor's Guide to Skin Care: Essential Facts & Up-to-the-Minute Information on Keeping Skin Healthy at Any Age. LC 95-1576. (Illus.). 224p. (J). 1996. pap. 9.70 (*0-7868-8100-3*, Pub. by Hyperion) Time Warner.

Bergfeldt, Inga. Scandinavian Cross Stitch on Linen & Cotton. Malmberg, Lars & Bress, Seymour, trs. from SWE. 64p. 1989. 19.95 (*0-9623468-0-2*); pap. 14.95 (*0-9623468-1-0*) Stellar Pub Hse.

Bergflexner, Stuart, et al, eds. Oxford Amer.dictionary. 832p. 1980. pap. 12.50 (*0-380-51052-9*, Avon Bks) Morrow Avon.

— Oxford Amer.dictionary. 832p. 1982. mass mkt. 4.99 (*0-380-60772-7*, Avon Bks) Morrow Avon.

Bergfors, Judith L. Call It Universe. (Illus.). 72p. (Orig.). 1992. pap. 19.95 (*0-9634630-0-4*) Winston Pubns.

Bergfors, Terese M., ed. Protein Crystallization: Techniques, Strategies & Tips. LC 98-75232. (Illus.). 250p. (C). 1999. lab manual ed. 69.95 (*0-9636817-5-3*) Intl Univ Line.

Berggoetz, Glen, jt. auth. see Moyer, Alan.

Berggreen, Brit & Marinatos, Nanno, eds. Greece & Gender. (Papers from the Norwegian Institute at Athens: No. 2). (Illus.). 184p. (Orig.). 1995. pap. 32.50 (*82-91626-00-6*, Pub. by P Astroms) Coronet Bks.

Berggren, Christian. Alternatives to Lean Production: Work Organization in the Swedish Auto Industry. 2nd ed. LC 92-20986. (Cornell International Industrial & Labor Relations Reports: No. 22). 312p. 1993. pap. text 23.95 (*0-87546-317-7*, ILR Press) Cornell U Pr.

Berggren, Christian & Nomura, Masami. The Resilience of Corporate Japan: Competitive Strategies & Personnel Practices in a New Low-Growth Era. LC 97-196510. 208p. 1997. pap. 26.95 (*1-85396-309-7*, Pub. by P Chapman) Taylor & Francis.

Berggren, Dick. Stock Car Racing. (Illus.). 80p. 1995. 9.98 (*0-8317-7731-1*) Smithmark.

Berggren, Don. The Magnificent Metric System: A Magical Guide to the Marvels of Metrics. LC 76-40527. (Illus.). (Orig.). 1976. 2.95 (*0-912800-34-8*) Woodbridge Pr.

Berggren, Eric & Berggren, Kristina. San Giovenale Vol. I, Fasc. 5: The Necropoleis of Porzarago, Grotte Tufarina & Montevangone. (Acta Instituti Romani Regni Sueciae, Series in 4 Degrees: Vol. XXVI:I,5). (Illus.). 195p. 1972. pap. 32.50 (*91-7042-000-9*, Pub. by P Astroms) Coronet Bks.

— San Giovenale Vol. II, Fasc. 2: Excavations in Area B, 1957-1960. (Acta Instituti Romani Regni Sueciae, Series in 4 Degrees: Vol. XXVI:II,2). (Illus.). 97p. 1981. pap. 59.50 (*91-7042-078-5*, Pub. by P Astroms) Coronet Bks.

Berggren, J. L. Episodes in the Mathematics of Medieval Islam. (Illus.). 200p. 1986. 65.95 (*0-387-96318-9*) Spr-Verlag.

***Berggren, J. Lennart.** Ptolemy's Geography: An Annotated Translation of the Theoretical Chapters. (Illus.). 232p. 2000. 39.50 (*0-691-01042-0*) Princeton U Pr.

Berggren, Karen. Circle of Shamans: Healing Through Ecstacy, Rhythm, & Myth. LC 97-44362. 192p. 1997. pap. 12.95 (*0-89281-622-8*) Inner Tradit.

Berggren, Kristina, jt. auth. see Berggren, Eric.

***Berggren, Lennart, et al.** PI: A Source Book. 2nd ed. LC 99-46584. 752p. 1999. 64.95 (*0-387-98946-3*) Spr-Verlag.

Berggren, Ruth, ed. see Wilde, Oscar.

Berggren, William A., jt. auth. see Haq, Bilal U.

Berggren, William A., jt. auth. see Prothero, Donald R.

Bergh, B. O., jt. auth. see Kalloo, G.

Bergh, G. C. Van Den, see Van Den Bergh, G. C.

Bergh, Huub Van den, see Rijlaarsdam, Gert & Van den Bergh, Huub, eds.

Bergh, Jeroen C. Van Den, see Van Den Bergh, Jeroen C.

Bergh, Jeroen C. Van den, see Van den Bergh, Jeroen C., ed.

Bergh, Jeroen C. Van Den, see Van Den Bergh, Jeroen C., ed.

Bergh, Jeroen C. Van den, see Van den Bergh, Jeroen C.

Bergh, M. Van Den, see Reiten, I. & Van Den Bergh, M.

Bergh, Nan Van Den, see Van Den Bergh, Nan, ed.

Bergh, Peter. The Art of Ogden M. Pleissner. LC 84-47649. (Illus.). 110p. 1984. 50.00 (*0-87923-530-6*) Shelburne.

— The Art of Ogden M. Pleissner. 1984. reprint ed. write for info. (*0-939384-22-1*) Shelburne.

Bergh, Peter, jt. auth. see Rabbitt, John T.

Bergh, Peter A., jt. auth. see Rabbit, John T.

Bergh, Peter A., jt. auth. see Rabbitt, John T.

Bergh, Rene. Dressmaker's Handbook: A Complete Guide to Techniques & Materials. 160p. 1999. 29.95 (*1-85368-710-3*) New Holland.

— Make Your Own Patterns: An Easy Step-by-Step Guide to Making over 60 Patterns. (Illus.). 128p. 1997. pap. 17.95 (*1-85368-702-2*, Pub. by New5 Holland) Sterling.

Bergh, Rene, jt. auth. see Coetzee, Karen.

Bergh, Roger Van Den, see Van Den Bergh, Roger.

Bergh, Roger Van Den, see Faure, Michael.

Bergh, Roger Van Den, see Deketelaere, Kurt & Faure, Michael, eds.

Berghahn, Klaus, ed. The German-Jewish Dialogue Reconsidered: A Symposium in Honor of George L. Mosse. (German Life & Civilization Ser.: Vol. 20). VIII, 299p. (C). 1996. text 53.95 (*0-8204-3107-9*) P Lang Pubng.

Berghahn, Marion. Continental Britons: German Jewish Refugees from Nazi Germany. 1988. pap. 14.95 (*0-85496-157-7*) St Martin.

Berghahn, Volker R. Germany & the Approach of War in 1914. 2nd ed. LC 93-7850. 1993. text 39.95 (*0-312-09993-2*) St Martin.

— Germany & the Approach of War in 1914. 2nd ed. 290p. 1993. pap. 30.95 (*0-312-10076-0*) St Martin.

— Imperial Germany, 1871-1914: Economy, Society, Culture & Politics. LC 94-20683. 380p. (C). 1994. text 59.95 (*1-57181-013-7*); pap. text 17.95 (*1-57181-014-5*) Berghahn Bks.

— Modern Germany: Society, Economy & Politics in the Twentieth Century. 2nd ed. (Illus.). 336p. 1987. 69.95 (*0-521-34505-7*); pap. text 19.95 (*0-521-34748-3*) Cambridge U Pr.

Berghahn, Volker R., ed. Quest for Economic Empire: The European Strategies of German Big Business in the Twentieth Century. LC 95-38477. 240p. 1996. pap. 22.50 (*1-57181-931-2*) Berghahn Bks.

— Quest for Economic Empire: The European Strategies of German Big Business in the Twentieth Century. rev. ed. LC 95-38477. 240p. (C). 1996. 59.95 (*1-57181-027-7*) Berghahn Bks.

Berghahn, Volker R. & Karsten, Detlev. Industrial Relations in West Germany. LC 87-9395. 261p. 1987. pap. 16.50 (*0-907582-71-0*) Berg Pubs.

Berghahn, Volker R. & Schissler, Hanna, eds. Perceptions of History: An Analysis of School Textbooks. LC 87-15845. 181p. 1988. 19.50 (*0-85496-526-2*) Berg Pubs.

Berghahn, Volker R., tr. see Born, Karl E.

Berghahn, Volker R., tr. see Broszat, Martin.

Berghahn, Volker R., tr. see Hoffmann, Hilmar.

Berghahn, Volker R., tr. see Von Meding, Dorothee.

Berghammer, Gretta & Caspers, Rod. Broken Hearts. 1984. pap. 5.50 (*0-87129-142-8*, B70) Dramatic Pub.

Berghammer, Gretta, jt. ed. see Jennings, Coleman A.

Berghammer, R., et al, eds. Graph-Theoretic Concepts in Computer Science: Seventeenth International Workshop, WG '91 Fischbachau, Germany, June 17-19, 1991 Proceedings. (Lecture Notes in Computer Science Ser.: Vol. 570). viii, 253p. 1992. 43.00 (*0-387-55121-2*) Spr-Verlag.

Berghammer, R. & Lakhnech, Y., eds. Tool Support for System Specification, Development & Verification. (Advances in Computing Science Ser.). 230p. 1999. 49.95 (*3-211-83282-3*) Spr-Verlag.

Berghan, Connie, jt. auth. see Chaney, Rose.

Berghaus, G., et al, eds. DNA-Technology & Its Forensic Application: Proceedings of an International Symposium Cologne, September 13-14, 1990. (Illus.). 224p. 1991. pap. 111.00 (*0-387-54035-0*) Spr-Verlag.

Berghaus, Gunter. Facism & Theatre: Comparative Studies on the Aesthetics & Politics of Performance in Europe, 1925-1945. LC 95-20516. (Illus.). 304p. 1996. 59.95 (*1-57181-877-4*); pap. 24.50 (*1-57181-901-0*) Berghahn Bks.

— Futurism & Politics: Between Anarchist Rebellion & Fascist Reaction, 1909-1944. LC 95-38491. 256p. 1996. pap. 59.95 (*1-57181-867-7*) Berghahn Bks.

— Italian Futurist Theatre, 1909-1944. (Illus.). 610p. 1998. text 120.00 (*0-19-815898-X*) OUP.

Berghaus, Gunter, ed. Theatre & Film in Exile: German Artists in Great Britain, 1933-1945. LC 89-116. (Illus.). 304p. 1990. 19.95 (*0-85496-025-2*) Berg Pubs.

Berghaus, Nona. First Run WordPerfect 6. 1993. 16.00 (*1-56529-429-7*) Que.

Berghaus, U., jt. auth. see Hensen, Friedhelm.

Berghe, Christian L. Van Den, see Van den Berghe, Christian L.

Berghe, G. Van den, see Van den Berghe, G.

Berghe, Guido V. Political Rights for European Citizens. 256p. (Orig.). 1982. text 79.95 (*0-566-00524-7*) Ashgate Pub Co.

Berghe, J. P. Van den, see Van den Berghe, J. P.

Berghe, L. Van Den, see Van den Berghe, L.

Berghe, Lutgart Van Den, see Van Den Berghe, Lutgart, ed.

Berghe, Pierre L. Van Den, see Van Den Berghe, Pierre L.

Berghe, Wouter Van den, see Van den Berghe, Wouter.

Bergheim, Laura. An American Festival of World Capitals: From Garlic Queens to Cherry Parades. LC 96-27814. 299p. 1997. pap. 14.95 (*0-471-14350-2*) Wiley.

Bergheim, Laura A. The Look It up Guide to Washington Libraries & Archives. LC 95-41198. 377p. 1995. lib. bdg. 55.00 (*0-933833-35-0*) Beacham Pub Corp.

Berghel, Hal, jt. ed. see Eberlein, Gerald L.

Bergher, Karen. Opening Doors to College Success. 288p. (C). 1992. pap. text 29.95 (*0-8403-8122-0*) Kendall-Hunt.

Berghese, C. G. & Thanzawna, R. L. History of the Mizos. (C). 1997. 46.00 (*81-259-0308-9*, Pub. by Vikas) S Asia.

Berghman, G., jt. auth. see WIllems, M.

Berghman, J., et al. Social Security Taxation & Europe. 89p. 1993. pap. 33.00 (*90-6215-349-6*, Pub. by Maklu Uitgev) Gaunt.

Berghman, Jos & Cantillon, Bea. The European Face of Social Security: Essays in Honour of Heran Deleeck. 448p. 1993. 72.95 (*1-85628-603-7*, Pub. by Avebry) Ashgate Pub Co.

Berghmans, Francis, jt. ed. see Taylor, Edward W.

Berghoef, Gerard & DeKoster, Lester. The Believer's Handbook. LC 82-72686. 295p. 1982. 18.95 (*0-934874-03-4*) Chr Lib Pr.

— The Deacon's Handbook. 269p. 1980. 18.95 (*0-934874-01-8*) Chr Lib Pr.

— The Elders Handbook. LC 79-54143. 303p. (C). 1979. 18.95 (*0-934874-00-X*) Chr Lib Pr.

— The Great Divide: Christianity or Evolution. 176p. 1988. 8.95 (*0-934874-07-7*) Chr Lib Pr.

— The Great Divide: Christianity or Evolution? 184p. 1989. reprint ed. pap. 8.99 (*0-85151-558-4*) Banner of Truth.

— Liberation Theology: The Church's Future Shock. 197p. 1984. 15.95 (*0-934874-06-9*) Chr Lib Pr.

Berghof, Oliver, ed. see Forster, George.

Berghofer, Renate. Analytik und Isolierung Phenolischer Inhaltsstoffe Von Hypericum Perforatum L. Aus Anbau und Wildvorkommen und Vergleich Mit Anderen Heimischen Hypericum Arten. (Dissertationes Botanicae Ser.: Band 106). (GER., Illus.). vii, 178p. 1987. pap. 48.00 (*3-443-64018-4*, Pub. by Gebruder Borntraeger) Balogh.

An Asterisk (*) at the beginning of an entry indicates that the title is appearing for the first time.

B

B

*Berghoff, Beth, et al. Beyond Reading & Writing: Inquiry, Curriculum & Multiple Ways of Knowing. LC 99-87800. (Illus.). 2000. pap. write for info. (0-8141-2341-4, 23414) NCTE.

Bergholm, Fredrik. MOSES Handbook: Model for Stimulating the Economy of Sweden. (Industrial Institute for Economic & Social Research Report Ser.: No. 35). 213p. (Orig.). 1989. pap. 85.00 (91-7204-319-9) Coronet Bks.

Bergholz, Fred W. The Partition of the Steppe: The Struggle of the Russians, Manchus, & the Zunghar Mongols for Empire in Central Asia, 1619-1758: a Study in Power Politics. LC 92-35176. (American University Studies: History: Ser. IX, Vol. 109). VII, 522p. (C). 1993. text 79.95 (0-8204-1575-8) P Lang Pubng.

Bergholz, Thomas. Der Aufbau des Lukanischen Doppelwerkes: Untersuchungen zum Formalliterarischen Charakter von Lukas-Evangelium und Apostelgeschichte. (Europaische Hochschulschriften Ser.: Reihe 23, Bd. 545). (GER.). 156p. 1995. 28.95 (3-631-49209-X) P Lang Pubng.

Berghout, E. W. & Remenyi, D. S., eds. The Fourth European Conference on the Evaluation of Information Technology: October 30-31, 1997 Delft, The Netherlands. (Illus.). 220p. 1997. pap. 57.50 (90-407-1546-7, Pub. by Delft U Pr) Coronet Bks.

*Berghuis, David J. & Jongsma, Arthur E., eds. The Severe & Persistent Mental Illness Treatment Planner. (Practice Planners Ser.). 224p. 2000. pap. 175.00 incl. disk (0-471-35962-9) Wiley.

Berghuis, Paul, et al. Respiration. (Biophysical Measurement Ser.). (Illus.). 170p. (Orig.). (C). 1992. 28.00 (0-9627449-3-X) SpaceLabs.

Bergie, Sigrid. Turning out the Lights. 87p. 1988. pap. 6.00 (0-89823-111-6) New Rivers Pr.

Bergie, Sigrid, ed. Where Laugh Touches Tears. (Illus.). 165p. (Orig.). 1991. pap. 8.00 (0-927663-17-1) COMPAS.

Bergiel, jt. auth. see Walters.

Bergier, Jacques. L' Homme Eternal. (Embellissement De la Vie Ser.: Vol. I). (FRE.). 1973. pap. 11.95 (0-7859-1738-1, 2070363562) Fr & Eur.

— La Matin des Magiciens. (FRE.). 640p. 1972. pap. 13.95 (0-7859-1701-2, 2070361292) Fr & Eur.

Bergier, Jacques, jt. auth. see Pauwels, Louis.

Bergier, Jean-Francois. Pour une Historire des Alpes, Moyen Age et Temps Modernes. LC 97-40359. (Variorum Collected Studies Ser.: Vol. 587). 350p. 1998. text 109.95 (0-86078-653-6, Pub. by Ashgate Pub) Ashgate Pub Co.

Bergier, Nicolas. Historie des Grands Chemins de l'Empire Romain. 937p. reprint ed. write for info. (0-318-71319-5) G Olms Pubs.

Bergin. Handbook of Psychotherapy 5th ed. pap. text. write for info. (0-471-37755-4) Wiley.

Bergin, A. & Haward, M. Japan's Tuna Industry: A Setting Sun or New Dawn. 157p. (C). 1995. lib. bdg. 125.00 (1-56072-241-X) Nova Sci Pubs.

Bergin, Allen E. & Garfield, Sol L., eds. Handbook of Psychotherapy & Behavior Change. 4th ed. 880p. 1993. text 122.95 (0-471-54513-9) Wiley.

— Handbook of Psychotherapy & Behavior Change. 4th ed. 1994. pap. text 21.95 (0-471-01023-5) Wiley.

Bergin, Allen E., jt. auth. see Richards, P. Scott.

Bergin, Allen E., jt. ed. see Richards, P. Scott.

*Bergin, Bonnie & McNally, Robert Aquinas. Understanding "Dog Mind" Bonnie Bergin's Guide to Bringing Out the Best in Your Dog. (Illus.). 288p. 2000. pap. 14.95 (0-316-09124-3) Little.

Bergin, Edward, ed. The Definitive Guide to Underground Humor: Quaint Quotes about Death, Funny Funeral Home Stories & Hilarious Headstone Epitaphs. 2nd rev. ed. LC 95-74710. (Illus.). 96p. (Orig.). 1996. pap. 8.95 (0-9648442-8-1) Offbeat Pubng.

Bergin, Edward J. A Star to Steer Her By: A Self-Teaching Guide to Offshore Navigation. LC 83-71313. 216p. 1983. pap. 18.50 (0-87033-309-7) Cornell Maritime.

Bergin, Eilis, jt. auth. see Fitzgerald, Eddie.

Bergin, Feryl J. You . . . And Being a Student: Motivational Study Activities. rev. ed. (Illus.). 112p. 1995. student ed., per. 9.95 (0-936955-01-5) Eminent Pubn.

— You . . . And Being a Success: Motivational Speaking Communication Skills. (Illus.). 112p. (Orig.). (YA). (gr. 6-12). 1994. pap., student ed., per. 9.95 (0-936955-04-X) Eminent Pubn.

— You . . . And Being a Teenager: Motivational Activities for Teens. rev. ed. (Illus.). 112p. (YA). (gr. 6-12). 1991. pap., per. 9.95 (0-936955-00-7) Eminent Pubn.

— You . . . And Being a Winner: Motivational Writing Communication Skills. (Illus.). 112p. (Orig.). (YA). (gr. 6-12). 1994. pap., student ed., per. 9.95 (0-936955-03-1) Eminent Pubn.

— You . . . And Being an Achiever: Motivational Activities in Functional Writing. (Illus.). 112p. (YA). (gr. 6-12). 1996. pap. text 9.95 (0-936955-06-6) Eminent Pubn.

— You . . . And Being an Adventurer: Motivational Exercises in Creative Writing. (Illus.). 112p. (YA). (gr. 6-12). 1998. pap. 9.95 (0-936955-07-4) Eminent Pubn.

— You . . . And Being an Explorer: Motivational Self-Awareness Activities. (Illus.). 112p. (Orig.). (YA). (gr. 6-12). 1991. pap., student ed., per. 9.95 (0-936955-05-8) Eminent Pubn.

— You...& Being a Worker: Motivational Work Activities. (Illus.). 112p. (Orig.). (YA). (gr. 6-12). 1991. pap., student ed., per. 9.95 (0-936955-02-3) Eminent Pubn.

Bergin, Francis. Successful Presentations. LC 95-167116. 94p. 1995. pap. 39.00 (0-13-434143-0) P-H.

Bergin, J. Rise of Richelieu. LC 97-4354. 282p. 1997. text 24.95 (0-7190-5238-6, Pub. by Manchester Univ Pr) St Martin.

Bergin, James D. Medicine Recall. LC 97-11939. (Recall Ser.). 901p. 1997. pap. 28.00 (0-683-18098-3) Lppncott W & W.

*Bergin, James J. & Freeman, Chris. The Isherwood Century: Essays on the Life & Work of Christopher Isherwood. LC 99-6742. 1999. pap. write for info. (0-299-16704-6) U of Wis Pr.

Bergin, James J. & Holmes, Geraldine C. Continuing Medical Education in the Community Hospital. LC 79-55326. (Illus.). 112p. 1979. text 22.00 (0-935466-00-2); pap. text 16.00 (0-935466-01-0) Pierson Pubs.

Bergin, Joe. Cardinal De La Rochefoucauld: Leadership & Reform in the French Church. LC 87-14255. 288p. (C). 1988. 45.00 (0-300-04104-7) Yale U Pr.

— Data Structure Programming: With the Standard Template Library in C++ Gries, D. & Schneider, F. B., eds. LC 97-45234. (Undergraduate Texts in Computer Science Ser.). 330p. 1998. text 49.95 (0-387-94920-8) Spr-Verlag.

Bergin, John. From Inside. (Illus.). 288p. 1993. pap. 24.95 (0-87816-239-9) Kitchen Sink.

Bergin, John & O'Barr, James, eds. Bonesaw. (Illus.). 144p. (Orig.). 1993. pap. 14.95 (1-879450-62-3) Kitchen Sink.

Bergin, Joseph. Cardinal de la Rochefoucauld: Leadership & Reform in the French Church. LC 87-14255. 310p. 1987. reprint ed. pap. 96.10 (0-608-07570-1, 208026100004) Bks Demand.

— Cardinal Richelieu: Power & the Pursuit of Wealth. 1990. pap. 20.00 (0-300-04860-2) Yale U Pr.

— Data Abstraction: The Object-Oriented Approach Using C++, Macintosh Set. (C). 1994. text 64.74 (0-07-911692-2) McGraw.

— The Making of the French Episcopate, 1589-1661. LC 96-18336. 752p. 1996. 57.00 (0-300-06751-8) Yale U Pr.

Bergin, Joseph & Brockliss, Laurence, eds. Richelieu & His Age. LC 92-35777. (Illus.). 312p. (C). 1992. text 79.00 (0-19-820231-8, Clarendon Pr) OUP.

Bergin, Joseph, et al. Karel ++ A Gentle Introduction to the Art of Object-Oriented Programming. LC 96-35741. 208p. 1996. pap. 30.95 (0-471-13809-6) Wiley.

Bergin, Kathleen A. An Evaluation of the Devouge Spring East Sites, 4-SBr-4451 & 4-SBr-4561, Fort Irwin, San Bernardino County, California. fac. ed. (Fort Irwin Archaeology Project, Research Reports: No. 8). (Illus.). 119p. (C). 1984. reprint ed. pap. text 13.13 (1-55567-532-8) Coyote Press.

— An Evaluation of the Fourteen Metates Site, SBr-4458, Fort Irwin, San Bernardino County, California. fac. ed. (Fort Irwin Archaeology Project, Research Reports: No. 4). (Illus.). 115p. 1982. reprint ed. pap. text 13.13 (1-55567-526-3) Coyote Press.

Bergin, Kathleen A. & Ferraro, D. D. Interim Analysis Report: Data Recovery of Bow Willow Wash South. fac. ed. (Fort Irwin Archaeology Project, Research Reports: No. 20). (Illus.). 204p. 1987. reprint ed. pap. text 21.88 (1-55567-546-8) Coyote Press.

Bergin, Kathleen A. & Warren, C. N. A Research Design for the Data Recovery of Bow Willow Wash South (Site 4-SBr-4204), a Pavement Quarry Within Fort Irwin, San Bernardino County, California. fac. ed. (Fort Irwin Archaeology Project, Research Reports: No. 9). (Illus.). 118p. 1983. reprint ed. pap. text 13.13 (1-55567-533-6) Coyote Press.

Bergin, Kathleen A., et al. The Data Recovery of Three Sites in Bow Willow Wash South: The Fieldwork Phase, Fort Irwin, San Bernardino County, California. fac. ed. (Fort Irwin Archaeology Project, Research Reports: No. 14). (Illus.). 344p. 1985. reprint ed. pap. text 36.25 (1-55567-540-9) Coyote Press.

Bergin, Mark. Castle. LC 99-14186. 1999. 26.00 (0-531-14571-9) Watts.

— Castles. 1999. pap. text 9.95 (0-531-15421-1) Watts.

— Space Shuttle. LC 99-15239. (Fast Forward Ser.). 1999. 26.00 (0-531-14573-5); pap. text 9.95 (0-531-15423-8) Watts.

— Wonders of the World. LC 99-15238. (Fast Forward Ser.). 1999. 26.00 (0-531-14574-3) Watts.

— The Wonders of the World. (Fast Forward Ser.). 1999. pap. text 9.95 (0-531-15424-6) Watts.

Bergin, Mark, jt. auth. see MacDonald, Fiona.

Bergin, Mark, jt. auth. see Steedman, Scott.

Bergin, Mary & Gethers, Judy. Spago Chocolate. LC 98-27258. 237p. 1999. 29.95 (0-679-44833-0) Random House.

Bergin, Paul. A History of the Worcester District Medical Society. 200p. 1994. pap. 15.00 (0-9641948-0-5) Worcest Dist Med Soc.

Bergin, Paul R. Voting by Institutional Investors on Corporate Governance Issues in the 1988 Proxy Season. 139p. (Orig.). 1988. pap. 25.00 (0-931035-30-9) IRRC Inc DC.

Bergin, Thomas, ed. Computer-Aided Software Engineering: Issues & Trends for the 1990s & Beyond. LC 91-76951. 550p. 1993. text 55.95 (1-878289-15-2) Idea Group Pub.

Bergin, Thomas F. & Haskell, Paul G. Estates in Land & Future Interests. 2nd ed. LC 84-13695. (University Textbook Ser.). 259p. (C). 1991. reprint ed. text 22.75 (0-88277-184-1) Foundation Pr.

Bergin, Thomas G. Anthology of the Provencal Troubadours, 2 vols., 1. LC 72-91287. (Yale Romanic Studies, Second Ser.: No. 23). (Illus.). 300p. (C). reprint ed. pap. 93.00 (0-8357-9077-0, 201680200001) Bks Demand.

— Anthology of the Provencal Troubadours, 2 vols., 2. LC 72-91287. (Yale Romanic Studies, Second Ser.: No. 23). (Illus.). 251p. (C). reprint ed. pap. 77.90 (0-608-16128-4, 201680200002) Bks Demand.

— Dante. LC 76-10974. (Illus.). 326p. 1976. reprint ed. lib. bdg. 65.00 (0-8371-7973-4, BEDA, Greenwood Pr) Greenwood.

— Under Scorpio. LC 82-19377. 39p. 1982. pap. 2.95 (0-933760-02-7) Solaris Pr.

Bergin, Thomas G., ed. see Petrarca, Francesco.

Bergin, Thomas G., ed. & tr. see Dante Alighieri.

Bergin, Thomas G., ed. & tr. see Machiavelli, Niccolo.

Bergin, Thomas G., tr. see Petrarca, Francesco.

Bergin, Thomas G., tr. see Vico, Giambattista.

Bergin, Thomas G., tr. & anno. see Petrarca, Francesco.

Bergin, Thomas J. & Gibson, Richard G. History of Programming Languages. Gordon, Peter S., ed. LC 95-33539. 864p. (C). 1996. 57.95 (0-201-89502-1) Addison-Wesley.

Bergin, Thomas J., jt. auth. see Lefter, James.

Bergis, K. Kleines Diabetes-Lexikon. (GER.). 225p. 1988. 49.95 (0-7859-8271-X, 3110116200) Fr & Eur.

Bergjan, Silke-Petra. Theodoret von Cyrus und der Neunizaenismus: Aspekte der Altkirchlichen Trinitaetslehre. (Arbeiten zur Kirchengeschichte Ser.: No. 60). (GER.). x, 246p. 1993. lib. bdg. 113.85 (3-11-013955-3) De Gruyter.

Bergland, Brita. The Poet at Its Desk. 1987. pap. 8.00 (0-942433-12-2) Awede Pr.

— The Rebirth of the Older Child: Poems. (Poetry Ser.). 64p. 1993. pap. 8.00 (0-930901-85-1) Burning Deck.

— The Rebirth of the Older Child: Poems. limited ed. (Poetry Ser.). 64p. 1993. pap. 15.00 (0-930901-86-X) Burning Deck.

Bergland, Eric O. & Marr, Jerry. Prehistoric Life on the Olympic Peninsula: The First Inhabitants of a Great American Wilderness. (Illus.). 88p. (Orig.). 1988. pap. text 8.95 (0-685-34733-8) NW Interpretive.

Bergland, Martha. A Farm under a Lake. LC 89-2062. 208p. 1989. 17.95 (1-55597-119-9) Graywolf.

— Idle Curiosity. LC 96-78744. 225p. 1997. 22.95 (1-55597-257-8) Graywolf.

*Bergland, Renee L. The National Uncanny: Indian Ghosts & American Subjects. LC 99-35382. (Reencounters with Colonialism Ser.). 211p. 2000. 40.00 (0-87451-943-8); pap. 19.95 (0-87451-944-6) U Pr of New Eng.

Berglas, S. The Success Syndrome: Hitting Bottom When You Reach the Top. (Illus.). 312p. (C). 1986. 24.50 (0-306-42349-9, Plenum Trade) Perseus Pubng.

Berglas, Steven & Baumeister, Roy F. Your Own Worst Enemy: Understanding the Paradox of Self-Defeating Behavior. LC 92-53238. 208p. 1994. reprint ed. pap. 11.00 (0-465-09341-8) Basic.

Bergler, Edmund. Conflict in Marriage: The Unhappy Undivorced. 226p. (C). 1992. reprint ed. pap. 24.95 (0-8236-8025-8) Intl Univs Pr.

— Curable & Incurable Neurotics: Problems of "Neurotic" vs. "Malignant" Psychic Masochism. LC 93-18828. 510p. 1993. reprint ed. 70.00 (0-8236-1092-6) Intl Univs Pr.

— Divorce Won't Help: xlvi, 240p. 1994. reprint ed. pap. 24.95 (0-8236-8032-0) Intl Univs Pr.

— Fashion & the Unconscious. 330p. (C). 1992. reprint ed. pap. 24.95 (0-8236-8046-0) Intl Univs Pr.

— Money & Emotional Conflicts. LC 84-22390. xiii, 269p. 1985. 40.00 (0-8236-3445-0, 03445) Intl Univs Pr.

— Principles of Self-Damage. LC 92-1423. 506p. (C). 1992. reprint ed. 70.00 (0-8236-4315-8) Intl Univs Pr.

— Psychology of Gambling. LC 84-22381. 254p. 1985. 37.50 (0-8236-5570-9) Intl Univs Pr.

— The Revolt of the Middle-Aged Man. LC 84-22396. xxiv, 312p. 1985. 45.00 (0-8236-5830-9, 05830) Intl Univs Pr.

— The Superego: Unconscious Conscience - The Key to the Theory & Therapy of Neurosis. LC 88-13652. 372p. 1989. 55.00 (0-8236-6252-7) Intl Univs Pr.

— The Talent for Stupidity: The Psychology of the Bungler, the Incompetent, & the Ineffectual. LC 97-9002. 250p. 1998. 37.50 (0-8236-6345-0) Intl Univs Pr.

— The Writer & Psychoanalysis. 2nd ed. 320p. (C). 1992. reprint ed. pap. 24.95 (0-8236-8330-3) Intl Univs Pr.

Bergler, Reinhold. Man & Cat: The Benefits of Cat Ownership. (Illus.). 120p. 1991. 42.95 (0-632-03157-3) Blackwell Sci.

Bergles, Arthur E., ed. Heat Transfer in Electronic & Microelectronic Equipment. (Proceedings of the International Center for Heat & Mass Transfer Ser.). (Illus.). 1100p. 1990. 220.00 (0-89116-277-1) Hemisp Pub.

Bergles, Arthur E. & Ishigai, Seiken. Two Phase Flow Dynamics & Reactor Safety. 1981. text 110.00 (0-07-004904-1) McGraw.

Bergles, Arthur E. & Webb, R. L., eds. Augmentation of Convective Heat & Mass Transfer. LC 75-143215. 168p. reprint ed. pap. 52.10 (0-8357-5882-6, 201585600097) Bks Demand.

Bergles, Arthur E., et al. Process, Enhanced & Multiphase Heat Transfer: A Festschrift for A. E. Bergles. LC 96-36955. 1996. write for info. (1-56700-079-7) Begell Hse.

Bergles, Arthur E., ed. see Alifanov, O. M.

Berglie, Carole, jt. auth. see Geffen, Alice M.

Berglind, Hans. Towards an Action Theory for Social Work Five Essays. 104p. (Orig.). 1988. pap. 32.50 (91-22-01236-2) Coronet Bks.

*Bergling, C. M. & Bergling, J. M. Art Monograms & Lettering: 100th Anniversary Collector's Edition. 21st deluxe ed. LC 99-76683. (Encyclopedias of Technical Art Bks.: Vol. I). (Illus.). 114p. 2000. text 64.95 (0-9677808-1-0) Bergling Prodns.

Bergling, C. M., jt. auth. see Bergling, J. M.

*Bergling, J. M. & Bergling, C. M. Art Alphabets & Lettering: 100th Anniversary Collector's Edition. 10th deluxe ed. LC 99-76681. (Encyclopedias of Technical Art Bks.: Vol. II). (Illus.). 112p. 2000. text 64.95 (0-9677808-2-9) Bergling Prodns.

— Heraldic Designs & Engravings; Heraldic Dictionary of Terms: 100th Anniversary Collector's Edition. 4th deluxe ed. LC 99-80154. (Encyclopedias of Technical Art Bks.: Vol. IV). (Illus.). 96p. 2000. text 64.95 (0-9677808-4-5) Bergling Prodns.

— Ornamental Designs & Illustrations: 100th Anniversary Collector's Edition. 5th deluxe ed. LC 99-76682. (Encyclopedias of Technical Art Bks.: Vol. III). (Illus.). 110p. 2000. text 64.95 (0-9677808-3-7) Bergling Prodns.

*Bergling, J. M., et al. Encyclopedias of Technical Art Books: 100th Anniversary Collector's Edition, 4 vols. deluxe ed. (Illus.). 2000. text 275.00 (0-9677808-0-2) Bergling Prodns.

Bergling, J. M., jt. auth. see Bergling, C. M.

Bergling, John M. Art Alphabets & Lettering. 9th ed. LC 67-29582. 1995. 24.95 (0-910222-01-0) Gem City Coll.

— Art Monograms & Lettering. 20th ed. LC 63-22577. 1992. 24.95 (0-910222-02-9) Gem City Coll.

— Heraldic Designs & Engravings Manual. rev. ed. LC 66-25383. (Illus.). 1994. 24.95 (0-910222-04-5) Gem City Coll.

— Heraldic Designs for Artists & Craftspeople. LC 96-49780. (Illus.). 1997. pap. 7.95 (0-486-29663-6) Dover.

— Ornamental Designs & Illustrations. 4th ed. LC 63-22578. 1992. 24.95 (0-910222-05-3) Gem City Coll.

*Berglof, Eric. Stuck in Transit: Rethinking Russian Economic Reform. 2000. pap. text 22.50 (1-898128-44-8) Ctr Econ Policy Res.

Berglof, Erik. Corporate Control & Capital Structure: Essays on Property Rights & Financial Contracts. 193p. (Orig.). 1991. pap. 97.50 (91-971005-6-0) Coronet Bks.

Berglund, Abraham. United States Steel Corporation: A Study of the Growth & Influence of Combination in the Iron & Steel Industry. LC 72-76677. (Columbia University. Studies in the Social Sciences: No. 73). 1968. reprint ed. 39.50 (0-404-51073-6) AMS Pr.

Berglund, Abraham & Wright, Phillip G. Tariff on Iron & Steel. (Brookings Institution Reprint Ser.). reprint ed. lib. bdg. 36.50 (0-697-00151-2) Irvington.

Berglund, Anders R. & Zakharov, Vasilii V. The Novgorod Mint During the Swedish Occupation, 1611-1617. (Illus.). v, 56p. (Orig.). 1983. pap. 13.00 (0-912671-03-3) Russian Numis.

Berglund, Anna, tr. see Chapel of the Air Ministries Staff.

Berglund, Axel-Ivar. Zulu Thought-Patterns & Symbolism. LC 89-11039. (Illus.). 402p. 1989. 39.95 (0-253-31175-6); pap. 9.95 (0-253-21205-7) Ind U Pr.

Berglund, Bjorn E., et al. Palaeoecological Events During the Last 15,000 Years: Regional Synthesis of Palaeoecological Studies in Lakes & Mires in Europe. 784p. 1996. 300.00 (0-471-95840-9, VS00) Wiley.

Berglund, Brad. Worship at Calvary: Your Guide to Meaningful & Effective Worship. (Illus.). 1997. pap., wbk. ed. 9.95 (0-9639671-2-6) Access Pubng.

Berglund, Brita. Gambia. 101p. 1975. write for info. (91-7106-096-0, Pub. by Nordic Africa) Transaction Pubs.

Berglund, Catherine Anne. Ethics for Health Care. LC 99-206857. (Illus.). 240p. 1999. pap. text 39.95 (0-19-554172-3) OUP.

Berglund, Daniel R., jt. auth. see Coburn, Christopher M.

Berglund, Edward P., ed. see Lumley, Brian, et al.

Berglund, Eeva. Knowing Nature, Knowing Science: An Ethnography of Local Environmental Activism. 250p. 1998. 55.00 (1-874267-34-0, Pub. by White Horse Pr) Paul & Co Pubs.

Berglund, Fredrik. 150 Years of Amalgam. 66p. 1995. 20.00 (0-941011-14-3, B54) Bio-Probe.

Berglund, Gosta W. Mental Growth: A Study of Changes in Test Ability Between the Ages of Nine & Sixteen Years. (Studia Scientiae Paedagogicae Upsaliensia: No. 6). 1965. pap. 79.50 (0-317-27518-6) Elliots Bks.

Berglund, Gregory. Bombay: The Black Pages. LC 94-900288. (C). 1994. 6.50 (81-7223-118-0, Pub. by Indus Pub) S Asia.

Berglund, J. F., et al. A Compact Right Topological Semigroups & Generalizations of Almost Periodicity. (Lecture Notes in Mathematics Ser.: Vol. 663). (Illus.). 1978. 35.95 (0-387-08919-5) Spr-Verlag.

Berglund, Lars. The Secret of Luo Shu: Numerology in Chinese Art & Architecture. (Illus.). 402p. (Orig.). 1990. pap. 115.00 (91-628-0068-X) Coronet Bks.

— A Selection of Paintings by Cui Zifan: A Contemporary Master of the People's Republic of China. unabridged ed. (Illus.). 69p. 1995. pap. 19.95 (1-877921-14-9) Pacific Asia.

Berglund, Lee. Wheat Belt Route: Wichita Northwestern: The Story of a Dust Bowl Railroad. 92p. 1998. pap. 22.95 (0-942035-45-3) South Platte.

Berglund, Mary C. Gather the Children: Cycle C Celebrating the Word with Ideas, Activities, Prayer & Projects. 1988. pap. 20.95 (1-56929-025-3, Pastoral Press) OR Catholic.

— Gather the Children, Cycle A: Celebrating the Word with Ideas, Activities, Prayer & Projects. 240p. 1989. pap. 20.95 (1-56929-061-X, Pastoral Press) OR Catholic.

— Gather the Children, Cycle B: Celebrating the Word with Ideas, Activities, Prayer & Projects. 137p. 1988. pap. 15.95 (1-56929-012-1, Pastoral Press) OR Catholic.

*Berglund, Mary Hanley. Otis Orchards the First Fifty Years. 266p. 1998. reprint ed. pap. 15.95 (0-87770-683-2) Ye Galleon.

Berglund, Rita. An Alphabet about Kids with Cancer. (Illus.). 89p. (J). 1994. 19.95 (0-9629365-3-7) Childrens Lgcy.

Berglund, S., et al, eds. Utilisation of Sewage Sludge on Land: Rates of Application & Long-Term Effects of Metals. 1983. text 148.50 (90-277-1701-X) Kluwer Academic.

Berglund, Sten, et al, eds. The Handbook of Political Change in Eastern Europe. LC 98-27169. 400p. 1998. 100.00 (1-85898-840-3) E Elgar.

An Asterisk (*) at the beginning of an entry indicates that the title is appearing for the first time.

Berglund, Sten & Aarebrot, Frank H. The Political History of Eastern Europe in the Twentieth Century: The Struggle Between Democracy & Dictatorship. LC 96-41938. (Studies of Communism in Transition). 208p. 1997. 70.00 (*1-85898-478-5*) E Elgar.

Bergman. Electronic Architectures for Digital Processing. 350p. 1993. 52.00 (*0-13-248287-8*) P-H.

— Ferrous & Non-Ferrous Alloys: Proceedings of the Metallurgical Society of Canada. 1990. 38.00 (*0-08-040429-4*, Pergamon Pr) Elsevier.

***Bergman.** Image Databases. 350p. (C). 2000. write for info. (*0-471-32116-8*) Wiley.

Bergman & Gittins, John C. Statistical Methods for Pharmaceutical Research Planning. (Statistics: Textbooks & Monographs). (Illus.). 272p. 1985. text 135.00 (*0-8247-7146-X*) Dekker.

Bergman & Renwick. Introduction to Geography. 2nd ed. LC 98-20383. 553p. 1998. pap. text 73.33 (*0-13-907452-X*) P-H.

***Bergman & Renwick.** Introduction to Geography: People, Places, & Environment. 1999. suppl. ed. write for info. (*0-13-018814-X*) P-H.

Bergman & Roth. New York Real Property Forms, 9 vols. 1948. ring bd. 1220.00 (*0-8205-1140-4*) Bender.

Bergman, Abby B. Learning Center Activities for the Full-Day Kindergarten. 288p. (C). 1990. pap. text 27.95 (*0-87628-512-4*) P-H.

— A Survival Kit for the Elementary School Principal: With over 150 Reproducible Forms, Checklists & Letters. LC 98-27033. (Illus.). 446p. (C). 1998. spiral bd. 37.95 (*0-13-745985-8*) P-H.

Bergman, Abby B., et al. The Complete School-Age Child Care Resource Kit: Practical Guidelines, Materials, & Activities for Implementing a Quality SACC Program. LC 94-44935. 349p. 1995. spiral bd. 27.95 (*0-87628-268-0*) Ctr Appl Res.

Bergman, Abby B., jt. auth. see Jacobson, Willard J.

Bergman, Abraham & Choate, Judith. Why Did My Baby Die? The Phenomenon of Sudden Infant Death Syndrome & How to Cope with It. LC 73-92794. 1975. 20.00 (*0-89388-146-5*) Okpaku Communications.

Bergman, Abraham B. The "Discovery" of Sudden Infant Death Syndrome: Lessons in the Practice of Political Medicine. LC 87-34542. 257p. 1988. pap. 12.50 (*0-295-96601-7*) U of Wash Pr.

— The Discovery of Sudden Infant Death Syndrome: Lessons in the Practice of Political Medicine. LC 85-30778. (Illus.). 254p. 1986. 75.00 (*0-275-92059-3*, C2059, Praeger Pubs) Greenwood.

***Bergman, Abraham B.** 20 Common Problems in Pediatrics. (Illus.). 528p. 2000. Price not set. (*0-07-134901-4*) McGraw.

Bergman, Abraham B., ed. Political Approaches to Injury Control at the State Level. LC 91-40227. 128p. 1992. pap. text 9.95 (*0-295-97176-2*) U of Wash Pr.

***Bergman, Alan.** Alan & Marilyn Bergman. 2000. pap. 10.95 (*0-7692-8676-X*) Wrner Bros.

Bergman, Andrew. We're in the Money: Depression America & Its Films. (Illus.). 224p. 1992. reprint ed. pap. text 12.95 (*0-929587-85-5*, Elephant Paperbacks) I R Dee.

Bergman-Angstadt, B.J. Fabulous Florida. Fones, Mardy, ed. LC 98-76473. 128p. 1999. pap. 6.95 (*1-887654-28-3*) Premium Pr TN.

Bergman, Ann. Out & About Seattle with Kids: The Ultimate Family Guide for Fun & Learning. 2nd ed. 1998. pap. text 14.95 (*0-9614626-9-8*) NW Parent Pub.

Bergman, Ann & Carroll, Coleen. Out & about Seattle with Kids. (Illus.). 213p. 1993. pap. 12.95 (*0-9614626-3-9*) NW Parent Pub.

Bergman, Ann & Williamson, Rosi. Going Places: Family Getaways in the Pacific Northwest. (Illus.). 374p. 1995. pap. 14.95 (*0-9614626-5-5*) NW Parent Pub.

***Bergman, Ann, et al.** Going Places. 4th rev. ed. 580p. 1999. pap. 19.95 (*0-9614626-8-X*) NW Parent Pub.

Bergman, Anni. Ours, Yours, Mine: Mutuality & the Emergence of the Separate Self. LC 98-21039. 1998. 45.00 (*1-56821-374-3*) Aronson.

Bergman, Avraham Y. The Torah Commanded: A Glimpse of Essence. LC 98-90021. 1998. 21.95 (*0-533-12682-7*) Vantage.

Bergman, Barbara. New Mexico Objections at Trial. 190p. 1992. pap. 39.50 (*0-614-05924-0*, MICHIE) LEXIS Pub.

Bergman, Barbara E., jt. auth. see Hollander, Nancy.

Bergman, Barbara S. Worm Dissection Explained. 22p. (YA). (gr. 10 up). 1988. pap., wbk. ed. 7.00 (*0-8064-1209-7*, B18) Bergwall.

Bergman, Bella. Hebrew: A Language Course (Shalav Bet), Level 2. Band, Ora, ed. (Illus.). 243p. (C). 1983. pap. text 12.95 (*0-87441-360-5*) Behrman.

Bergman, Bo & Klefsjo, Bengt. Quality: From Customer Needs to Customer Satisfaction. LC 94-7346. 478p. (C). 1994. pap. 44.69 (*0-07-709016-0*) McGraw.

Bergman, Bruce J. Bergman on NY Mortgage Foreclosures, 3 vols. 1990. ring bd. 235.00 (*0-8205-1461-6*) Bender.

Bergman, Bruce J., et al. Occupational Compensation Survey Pts. II & III: Pay Comparisons, 1992, Locality Pay, 1992. (Illus.). 171p. (Orig.). (C). 1996. pap. text 50.00 (*0-7881-3550-3*) DIANE Pub.

Bergman, C. H., et al, eds. Algebraic Logic & Universal Algebra in Computer Science: Conference, Ames, Iowa, U. S. A., June 1-4, 1988 Proceedings. (Lecture Notes in Computer Science Ser.: Vol. 425). xii, 292p. 1990. 46.95 (*0-387-97288-9*) Spr-Verlag.

Bergman, Carol. Searching for Fritzi. (Illus.). 130p. 1999. pap. 10.00 (*0-9673134-0-6*) Mediacs.

— Sidney Poitier: Actor. Huggins, Nathan I., ed. (Black Americans of Achievement Ser.). (Illus.). 124p. (Orig.). (YA). (gr. 5 up). 1989. pap. 8.95 (*0-7910-0209-8*) Chelsea Hse.

***Bergman, Charles.** Orion's Legacy: A Cultural History of Man As Hunter. 359p. 2000. reprint ed. pap. text 14.00 (*0-7881-6981-5*) DIANE Pub.

Bergman, Clifford, tr. see Lenz, Martin.

Bergman, Clifford, tr. see Reeders, Jacques W. & Rosenbusch, Gerd.

Bergman, Clifford, tr. see Reif, Emil, et al.

Bergman, David. Gaiety Transfigured: Gay Self-Representation in American Literature. LC 91-50321. (Wisconsin Project on American Writers Ser.). 240p. (C). 1993. reprint ed. pap. 14.95 (*0-299-13054-1*) U of Wis Pr.

— Heroic Measures. LC 97-52322. 96p. 1998. pap. 14.00 (*0-8142-0784-7*, BERHEX); text 35.00 (*0-8142-0783-9*, BERHEO) Ohio St U Pr.

— Men on Men 7: Best New Gay Fiction. LC 98-19321. 368p. 1998. pap. 13.95 (*0-452-27734-5*, Plume) Dutton Plume.

— The Story: Readers & Writers of Fiction. 640p. (C). 1988. teacher ed. write for info. (*0-318-62762-0*) Macmillan.

Bergman, David, ed. Camp Grounds: Style & Homosexuality. LC 93-8818. (Illus.). 312p. (Orig.). 1993. 45.00 (*0-87023-877-9*); pap. 17.95 (*0-87023-878-7*) U of Mass Pr.

— Men on Men Five: Best New Gay Fiction. 352p. 1994. pap. 13.95 (*0-452-27244-0*, Plume) Dutton Plume.

— Men on Men 6: Best New Gay Fiction. 352p. 1996. pap. 12.95 (*0-452-27708-6*, Plume) Dutton Plume.

Bergman, David & Epstein, Daniel M. The Health Guide to Literature. 2nd ed. LC 86-81266. 1472p. (C). 1990. teacher ed. 2.66 (*0-669-13002-8*); audio 2.66 (*0-669-13004-4*) HM Trade Div.

— The Health Guide to Poetry. LC 82-81623. 493p. (C). 1983. pap. text 32.76 (*0-669-05111-X*); teacher ed. 2.66 (*0-669-05877-7*) HM Trade Div.

— The Heath Guide to Literature. 1543p. (C). 1992. teacher ed. 2.66 (*0-669-20593-1*) HM Trade Div.

Bergman, David, ed. see Ashbery, John.

Bergman, David F. & Tek, M. Rasin. Retrograde Condensation in Natural Gas Pipelines. LC 75-32098. 512p. reprint ed. pap. 158.80 (*0-8357-8306-5*, 203396100087) Bks Demand.

***Bergman, Deborah.** Knitting Goddess. 176p. 2000. 17.95 (*0-7868-6611-X*, Pub. by Disney Pr) Time Warner.

— Knitting Goddess. 2001. pap. 12.95 (*0-7868-8530-0*, Pub. by Disney Pr) Time Warner.

Bergman, Denise, ed. City River of Voices. (Illus.). 91p. (Orig.). 1992. pap. 9.95 (*0-931122-68-6*) West End.

Bergman, Donna. Kids Go! Seattle: A Fun-Packed, Fact-Filled, Travel & Activity Book. LC 96-2386. (Illus.). 144p. (J). (gr. 4-7). 1996. pap. 7.95 (*1-56261-307-3*, J Muir) Avalon Travel.

Bergman, Edward F. Human Geography: Cultures, Connections & Landscapes. LC 94-17511. 532p. 1994. 74.67 (*0-13-121278-8*) P-H.

— Woodlawn Remembers: Cemetery of American History. 1988. pap. 24.95 (*0-932052-68-1*) North Country.

***Bergman, Eric.** Information Design - For Information Appliances & Interactive Consumer Devices. Neilsen, Jakob et al, eds. (Interactive Consumer Technologies Ser.). 375p. (C). 1999. pap. text 44.95 (*1-55860-600-9*) Morgan Kaufmann.

Bergman, Eugene, jt. auth. see Bragg, Bernard.

Bergman, Eugene, jt. ed. see Batson, Trenton W.

Bergman, Eugene, jt. ed. see Batson, Trent.

***Bergman, Eva & Hansson, Lars-Anders.** Lake Ringsjhon. LC 99-43424. (Developments in Hydrobiology Ser.). 1999. write for info. (*0-7923-5955-0*) Kluwer Academic.

Bergman, Gary F., jt. auth. see Taylor, Ross L.

Bergman, George M. An Invitation to General Algebra & Universal Constructions. (Illus.). 398p. (C). 1998. pap. text 45.00 (*0-9655211-4-1*) H Helson.

Bergman, George M. & Hausknecht, Adam O. Cogroups & Co-Rings in Categories of Associative Rings. LC 96-147. (Mathematical Surveys & Monographs: Vol. 45). 388p. 1996. text 79.00 (*0-8218-0495-2*, SURV/45) Am Math.

Bergman, Gunnar. Corrosion of Plastics & Rubber in Process Equipment: Experiences from the Pulp & Paper Industry. Bennett, David C. & Sharp, W. B., eds. Marton, Joseph, tr. from SWE. LC 95-7651. (Illus.). 182p. 1995. 90.00 (*0-89852-273-0*, 0101R206) TAPPI.

Bergman, H., ed. Ureter. (Illus.). 780p. 1981. 250.00 (*0-387-90561-8*) Spr-Verlag.

Bergman, Harold L., ed. see Society of Environmental Toxicology & Chemistry (S.

Bergman, Helen, jt. ed. see Harris, Maxine.

Bergman, Herbert, ed. see Whitman, Walt.

Bergman, Hjalmar. Four Plays: Markurells of Wadkoping, the Baron's Will, Swedenhielms, Mr. Sleeman Is Coming. Johnson, Walter, ed. LC 68-11037. (American-Scandinavian Foundation Scandinavian Studies). (Illus.). 310p. 1968. 25.00 (*0-295-97884-8*) U of Wash Pr.

— Jac the Clown. Weiss, Hanna K., tr. & intro. by. LC 95-43117. (SCAN Ser.). xx, 220p. 1996. 55.00 (*1-57113-041-1*) Camden Hse.

Bergman, Ingmar. The Best Intentions. 304p. 1993. 22.45 (*1-55970-207-9*, Pub. by Arcade Pub Inc) Time Warner.

— The Best Intentions. Tate, Joan, tr. from SWE. LC 94-54828. 304p. 1994. pap. 11.45 (*1-55970-249-4*, Pub. by Arcade Pub Inc) Time Warner.

— Images: My Life in Film. Ruuth, Marianne, tr. from SWE. LC 94-4759. (Illus.). 416p. 1994. 27.45 (*1-55970-186-2*, Pub. by Arcade Pub Inc) Time Warner.

— Images: My Life in Film. Ruuth, Marianne, tr. from SWE. LC 94-4759. (Illus.). 416p. 1995. pap. 17.45 (*1-55970-293-1*, Pub. by Arcade Pub Inc) Time Warner.

— Laterna Magica. (FRE.). 380p. 1991. pap. 14.95 (*0-7859-2158-3*, 2070383385) Fr & Eur.

— Persona & Shame. Bradfield, Keith, tr. from SWE. 192p. 1989. 12.95 (*0-7145-0756-3*) M Boyars Pubs.

— Private Confessions. LC 96-41618. 160p. 1996. 19.45 (*1-55970-364-4*, Pub. by Arcade Pub Inc) Time Warner.

— Private Confessions. Tate, Joan, tr. from SWE. LC 96-41618. 176p. 1997. pap. 11.45 (*1-55970-395-4*, Pub. by Arcade Pub Inc) Time Warner.

— A Project for the Theatre. Marker, Frederick J. & Marker, Lise-Lone, eds. 192p. 1987. pap. text 11.95 (*0-8044-6040-X*) F Ungar Bks.

— Sunday's Children. Tate, Joan, tr. from SWE. LC 93-40096. 160p. 1995. pap. 9.70 (*1-55970-292-3*, Pub. by Arcade Pub Inc) Time Warner.

— Sunday's Children: A Novel. Tate, Joan, tr. from SWE. LC 93-40096. 160p. 1994. 16.45 (*1-55970-244-3*, Pub by Arcade Pub Inc) Time Warner.

— Talking with Ingmar Bergman. Jones, G. William, ed. LC 83-9692. (Illus.). 132p. 1983. 24.95 (*0-87074-187-X*); pap. 12.50 (*0-87074-191-8*) SMU Press.

Bergman, Irwin. Jackie Robinson: Baseball Pioneer. LC 93-25170. (Junior Black Americans of Achievement Ser.). (Illus.). 76p. (J). (gr. 4-7). 1993. lib. bdg. 14.95 (*0-7910-1771-0*) Chelsea Hse.

Bergman, J. & Van Der. Heterocycles in Bio-Organic Chemistry. 1991. 132.00 (*0-85186-877-0*) CRC Pr.

***Bergman, J. Peter.** Counterpoints. vi, 50p. 1999. pap. 11.95 (*0-9677919-0-1*, Digital Hand Pr) Meaning & Form.

Bergman, James, ed. Spit Tobacco & Youth. (Illus.). 71p. 1998. pap. text 20.00 (*0-7881-7173-9*) DIANE Pub.

Bergman, Jay. Vera Zasulich: A Biography. LC 82-80927. 280p. 1983. 42.50 (*0-8047-1156-9*) Stanford U Pr.

Bergman, Jed I., et al. Managing Change in the Non-Profit Sector: Lessons from the Evolution of Five Independent Research Libraries. LC 95-4705. (Nonprofit Sector Ser.). 285p. 1996. text 32.95 (*0-7879-0138-5*) Jossey-Bass.

Bergman, Jerry. Blood Transfusions: A History & Evaluation of the Religions, Biblical & Medical Objections. 220p. (Orig.). (C). 1994. pap. 9.95 (*1-883858-27-5*) Witness CA.

— The Theocratic War Doctrine: Why Jehovah's Witnesses Lie in Court. 70p. 1998. pap. 3.95 (*1-883858-62-3*) Witness CA.

Bergman, Jerry, compiled by. Jehovah's Witnesses: A Comprehensive & Selectively Annotated Bibliography, 48. LC 98-37845. (Bibliographies & Indexes in Religious Studies: Vol. 48). 368p. 1999. lib. bdg 69.50 (*0-313-30510-2*, Greenwood Pr) Greenwood.

Bergman, Jerry & Howe, George. Vestigial Organs Are Fully Functional: A History & Evaluation of the Vestigial Organ Origins Concept. Williams, Emmett L., ed. (Creation Research Society Monographs: No. 4). (Illus.). 97p. (Orig.). 1990. pap. text 11.00 (*0-940384-09-4*) Creation Research.

Bergman, Jerry R. Jehovah's Witnesses & the Problem of Mental Illness. 1992. pap. 12.95 (*1-883858-13-5*) Witness CA.

Bergman, Joel S. Fishing for Barracuda: Pragmatics of Brief Systemic Therapy. 1985. 19.95 (*0-393-70005-4*) Norton.

***Bergman, John F.** The History of Reedley's Railroads, 1888-2000. LC 99-67101. (Illus.). v, 52p. (C). 1999. pap. 20.00 (*0-9675018-0-6*) Reedley Hist.

Bergman, John F. Sunset Railway: To the Midway-Sunset Fields. (Illus.). 110p. 1995. 24.95 (*0-943500-14-1*) Kern Historical.

Bergman, Judith. Holistic Health: High Level Wellness & Menopause. pap. 6.95 (*1-884570-13-5*) Research Triangle.

Bergman, Julie. Los Angeles Fires of the Heart. (Illus.). 80p. (Orig.). 1995. pap. 14.00 (*0-9644458-5-9*) Undercover Bks.

***Bergman, Katherine M. & Snedden, John W., eds.** Isolated Shallow Marine Sand Bodies: Sequence Stratigraphic Analysis & Sedimentologic Interpretation. (Special Publications: Vol. 64). (Illus.). 362p. 1999. 120.00 (*1-56576-057-3*) SEPM.

Bergman, Kristen. South Florida Retirement & Relocation Guide. large type ed. (Retirement & Relocation Guides Ser.). (Illus.). 350p. Date not set. pap. 24.95 (*1-56559-104-6*) HGI-Over Fifty.

Bergman, L., et al. Energy & Economic Adjustment. 248p. (Orig.). 1983. pap. text 70.00 (*91-7204-186-2*) Coronet Bks.

Bergman, L. A., jt. auth. see Tan, C. A.

Bergman, L. A., jt. ed. see Tzou, H. S.

Bergman, Lars, ed. Environmental Toxicology, Economics & Institutions: The Atrazine Case Study. LC 94-22251. (Economy & Environment Ser.). 192p. 1994. lib. bdg. 106.00 (*0-7923-2986-4*) Kluwer Academic.

Bergman, Lars, et al. Telecommunications: Competition & Regulation in European Network Industries Monitoring European Deregulation, 1998. 150p. 1998. pap. 25.00 (*1-898128-37-5*, Pub. by Ctr Econ Policy Res) Brookings.

Bergman, Lars R., et al, eds. Developmental Science & the Holistic Approach. LC 99-55359. 424p. 1999. write for info. (*0-8058-3374-9*) L Erlbaum Assocs.

Bergman, Lars R., jt. ed. see Magnusson, David.

Bergman, Lee, jt. auth. see Daly, James.

Bergman, Lee, jt. auth. see Daly, James A.

Bergman, Lincoln, jt. auth. see Kopp, Jaine.

Bergman, Lincoln, ed. see Agler, Leigh.

Bergman, Lincoln, ed. see Ahouse, Jeremy J. & Barber, Jacqueline.

Bergman, Lincoln, ed. see Barber, Jacqueline.

Bergman, Lincoln, ed. see Barber, Jacqueline & Willard, Carolyn.

Bergman, Lincoln, ed. see Barber, Jacqueline, et al.

Bergman, Lincoln, ed. see Barrett, Katharine.

Bergman, Lincoln, ed. see Barrett, Katharine & Willard, Carolyn.

Bergman, Lincoln, ed. see Barrett, Katharine, et al.

Bergman, Lincoln, ed. see Barrett, Katherine.

Bergman, Lincoln, ed. see Barrett, Katherine & Sneider, Cary I.

Bergman, Lincoln, ed. see Barrett, Katherine, et al.

Bergman, Lincoln, ed. see Beals, Kevin & Willard, Carolyn.

Bergman, Lincoln, ed. see Brady, Susan & Willard, Carolyn.

Bergman, Lincoln, ed. see Braxton, Beverly, et al.

Bergman, Lincoln, ed. see Cuomo, Celia.

Bergman, Lincoln, ed. see Echols, Jean C.

Bergman, Lincoln, ed. see Echols, Jean C., et al.

Bergman, Lincoln, ed. see Gonsalves, Philip & Kopp, Jaine.

Bergman, Lincoln, ed. see Goodman, Jan M.

Bergman, Lincoln, ed. see Goodman, Jan M. & Kopp, Jaine.

Bergman, Lincoln, ed. see Goodman, Jan, et al.

Bergman, Lincoln, ed. see Gould, Alan.

Bergman, Lincoln, ed. see Hocking, Colin, et al.

Bergman, Lincoln, ed. see Jagoda, Susan, et al.

Bergman, Lincoln, ed. see Kopp, Jaine.

Bergman, Lincoln, ed. see Kopp, Jaine & Hosoume, Kimi.

Bergman, Lincoln, ed. see Lowell, Laura & Willard, Carolyn.

Bergman, Lincoln, ed. see Sneider, Cary.

Bergman, Lincoln, ed. see Sneider, Cary I.

Bergman, Lincoln, ed. see Sneider, Cary I. & Gould, Alan.

Bergman, Lincoln, ed. see Sneider, Cary I., et al.

Bergman, Lincoln, ed. see Sneider, Cary & Barber, Jacqueline.

Bergman, Lincoln, ed. see Stage, Elizabeth, et al.

Bergman, Lincoln, ed. see Strang, Craig, et al.

Bergman, Lincoln, ed. see Sutter, Debra, et al.

Bergman, Lincoln, ed. see Tilley, Rebecca & Willard, Carolyn.

Bergman, Louis A. Proverb Wit & Widom. 560p. 1997. pap. 16.95 (*0-399-52273-5*, Perigee Bks) Berkley Pub.

***Bergman, Mara.** Bears, Bears Everywhere! (Illus.). 32p. (J). 1999. pap. 6.95 (*0-7641-0931-6*) Barron.

Bergman, Margareta. Mirror, Mirror. Ralston, Veronica, tr. from SWE. LC 98-230638. 256p. 1998. 29.95 (*0-7206-1046-X*, Pub. by P Owen Ltd) Dufour.

Bergman, Marvin, ed. Iowa History Reader. 468p. 1996. text 27.95 (*0-8138-2177-0*) Iowa St U Pr.

Bergman, Marvin, jt. ed. see Stromquist, Shelton.

Bergman, Meir. Shaarei Orah: Commentary on the Weekly Sidrah. 1997. 22.95 (*0-87306-855-6*) Feldheim.

Bergman, Michael & Sicard, Gregorio A., eds. Surgical Management of the Diabetic Patient. LC 90-9064. 425p. 1991. reprint ed. pap. 131.80 (*0-608-03387-1*, 206408400008) Bks Demand.

Bergman, Ozer, ed. see Kramer, Chaim.

Bergman, Ozer, ed. see Nachman.

Bergman, Ozer, ed. see Rabbe Nachman.

Bergman, Ozer, ed. see Rabbi Nachman of Breslov.

Bergman, Ozer, ed. see Starett, Yehoshua.

Bergman, Ozer, ed. & tr. see Rabbi Nachman of Breslov.

Bergman, Paul. The Deposition Handbook. LC 99-28350. 384p. 1999. pap. 29.95 (*0-87337-538-6*) Nolo com.

— Trial Advocacy in a Nutshell. 3rd ed. LC 97-33632. (Nutshell Ser.). 353p. (C). 1997. pap. 21.50 (*0-314-21200-0*) West Pub.

Bergman, Paul & Asimow, Michael R. Reel Justice: The Courtroom Goes to the Movies. LC 95-44217. (Illus.). 288p. (Orig.). 1996. pap. 14.95 (*0-8362-1035-2*) Andrews & McMeel.

Bergman, Paul & Berman-Barrett, Sara J. The Criminal Law Handbook: Know Your Rights, Survive the System. 2nd ed. LC 98-19201. 512p. 1999. 24.95 (*0-87337-489-4*) Nolo com.

— Represent Yourself in Court: How to Prepare & Try a Winning Case. 2nd ed. LC 97-14437. 1995. pap. text 29.95 (*0-87337-402-9*) Nolo com.

Bergman, Paul, jt. auth. see Binder, David A.

Bergman, Paul, jt. ed. see Conklin, David.

Bergman, Paul Bruce. Transcript Exercises for Learning Evidence. 274p. (C). 1992. pap. 22.50 (*0-314-01143-9*) West Pub.

— Transcript Exercises for Learning Evidence, Teacher's Manual to Accompany. 20p. (C). 1992. pap. text. write for info. (*0-314-01307-5*) West Pub.

— Trial Advocacy in a Nutshell. 2nd ed. (Nutshell Ser.). 354p. (C). 1989. reprint ed. pap. text 16.00 (*0-314-66493-9*) West Pub.

Bergman, Phyllis, ed. see Fontainne, L. Manonne.

Bergman, R. K., jt. auth. see Munoz, John J.

Bergman, R. N., ed. see Cobelli, C.

Bergman, Ray. Around the Majors in Sixty Days: My Baseball Dream. Hettler, Judith, ed. LC 97-220817. (Illus.). 160p. 1997. pap. 14.97 (*0-9658970-0-1*); pap. 12.97 (*0-9658970-1-X*) R Bergman.

***Bergman, Ray.** Trout. (Illus.). 512p. 2000. pap. 29.95 (*1-58667-014-X*, Pub. by Derrydale Pr) Natl Bk Netwk.

Bergman, Rebecca, ed. Nursing Research for Nursing Practice: An International Perspective. 250p. 1990. pap. 37.50 (*0-412-33500-X*, A4439) Chapman & Hall.

***Bergman, Rhona.** The Idea of Gould. (Illus.). 226p. 1999. pap. write for info. (*0-9673367-0-8*) Lev Pub.

Bergman, Richard N. & Lovejoy, Jennifer C., eds. Minimal Model Approach & Determinants of Glucose Tolerance. LC 97-18553. (Pennington Center Nutrition Ser.: Vol. 7). 424p. 1997. text 90.00 (*0-8071-2238-6*) La State U Pr.

Bergman, Robert. A Kind of Rapture. LC 98-16456. (Illus.). 120p. 1998. 45.00 (*0-679-44257-X*) Pantheon.

B

An Asterisk (*) at the beginning of an entry indicates that the title is appearing for the first time.

Bergman, Robert E. & Moore, Thomas V. Managing Interactive Video-Multimedia Projects. LC 89-77528. (Illus.). 240p. (Orig.). (C). 1990. pap. 44.95 (*0-87778-209-1*) Educ Tech Pubns.

Bergman, Robert P. The Salerno Ivories: Ars Sacra from Medieval Amalfi. LC 79-22616. (Illus.). 268p. 1981. 50.00 (*0-674-78528-2*) HUP.

Bergman, Robert P. & Zafran, Eric M. Splendor of the Popes: Treasures from the Sistine Chapel & the Vatican Museums & Library. (Illus.). 50p. (Orig.). 1989. pap. text 12.00 (*0-911886-37-0*) Walters Art.

Bergman, Robert P., et al. Vatican Treasures: Early Christian, Renaissance & Baroque Art from the Papal Collections. (Illus.). 111p. 1999. text 30.00 (*0-7881-6104-0*) DIANE Pub.

Bergman, Roland W. Amazon Economics: The Simplicity of Shipibo Indian Wealth. LC 80-20198. (Dellplain Latin American Studies: No. 6). 271p. reprint ed. pap. 84.10 (*0-8357-5340-9*, 202259500028) Bks Demand.

Bergman, Ronald A., et al. Histology. (Illus.). 384p. 1996. text 31.95 (*0-7216-3089-8*, W B Saunders Co) Harcrt Hlth Sci Grp.

Bergman, Ronald A., jt. auth. see Afifi, Adel K.

Bergman, Ronald A., jt. auth. see Tountas, Chris P.

Bergman, Ronald L. & Bell, Anita W. Emotional Fitness Conditioning: An Action Plan for Lifelong Emotional Health. LC 97-52655. 256p. 1998. pap. 14.00 (*0-399-52435-5*, Perigee Bks) Berkley Pub.

Bergman, S. C., jt. auth. see Mitchell, R. H.

Bergman, Samuel & Bruckner, Steven. Introduction to Computers & Computer Programming. LC 72-140834. (C). 1972. text. write for info. (*0-201-00552-2*) Addison-Wesley.

Bergman, Shmuel H. Dialogical Philosophy from Kierkegaard to Buber. Gerstein, Arnold A., tr. from HEB. LC 90-38138. (SUNY Series in Jewish Philosophy). 257p. (C). 1991. text 24.50 (*0-7914-0623-7*) State U NY Pr.

Bergman, Simchah, tr. see Rabbi Nachman of Breslov.

***Bergman, Stefan.** Big Foot: A Complete Guide. (Illus.). 1998. pap. text 19.95 (*3-89124-497-5*) Meyer & Meyer.

Bergman, Stefan. The Kernel Function & Conformal Mapping. rev. ed. LC 68-58995. (Mathematical Surveys & Monographs: No. 5). 257p. 1950. reprint ed. pap. 45.00 (*0-8218-1505-9*, SURV/5) Am Math.

Bergman, Susan. Anonymity: The Secret Life of an American Family. LC 93-27136. 198p. 1994. 20.00 (*0-374-25407-9*) FS&G.

Bergman, Susan. Buried Life. text. write for info. (*0-374-11737-3*) VHPS.

Bergman, Susan, ed. Martyrs: Contemporary Writers on Modern Lives of Faith. LC 96-14863. 1996. pap. 11.00 (*0-06-061121-9*) Harper SF.

— Martyrs: Contemporary Writers on Modern Lives of Faith. LC 97-466393. 334p. 1998. reprint ed. pap. 15.00 (*1-57075-161-7*) Orbis Bks.

Bergman, T. Dissertation on Elective Attractions. 400p. 1970. reprint ed. 37.50 (*0-7146-1592-7*, Pub. by F Cass Pubs) Intl Spec Bk.

Bergman, T., et al, eds. Proceedings of the 32nd National Heat Transfer Conference, Baltimore, Maryland, August 8-12, 1997, Vol. 9. (HTD Ser.: Vol. 347). 340p. 1997. 100.00 (*0-7918-1814-4*, H01095) ASME Pr.

Bergman, T. O., ed. Chemical Lectures of H. T. Scheffer. Schufle, J. A., tr. LC 92-8726. (Chemists & Chemistry Ser.: Vol. 14). 560p. (C). 1992. lib. bdg. 321.50 (*0-7923-1760-2*) Kluwer Academic.

Bergman, Tamar. Along the Tracks. Swirsky, Michael, tr. LC 90-27521. 256p. (J). (gr. 6-9). 1991. 16.00 (*0-395-55328-8*, Sandpiper) HM.

— Along the Tracks. Swirsky, Michael, tr. from HEB. LC 90-27521. 245p. (J). (gr. 5-9). 1995. pap. 6.95 (*0-395-74513-6*, Sandpiper) HM.

— Along the Tracks. (YA). (gr. 6-9). 1991. 11.05 (*0-606-08688-9*, Pub. by Turtleback) Demco.

Bergman-Taney, Janet, jt. auth. see Clark, Kenneth.

Bergman, Thomas. Don't Turn Away, 2 bks. Inc. One Day at a Time: Children Living with Leukemia. LC 88-42972. (Illus.). 48p. (J). (gr. 4-5). 1989. lib. bdg. 19.93 (*1-55532-913-6*); Precious Time: Children Living with Muscular Dystrophy. LC 96-5726. 48p. (J). (gr. 4 up). 1996. lib. bdg. 19.93 (*0-8368-1597-1*); (J). 1993. Set lib. bdg. 45.20 (*0-8368-1706-0*) Gareth Stevens Inc.

***Bergman, Thomas.** Seeing in Special Ways: Children Living with Blindness. (Illus.). 54p. (YA). 2000. text 20.00 (*0-7881-9062-8*) DIANE Pub.

Bergman, Tom, jt. auth. see Scott, Greg.

Bergman, Torbern. Bergman's Thunderstorm Lecture. Schufle, Joseph A., tr. from GER. (Illus.). 130p. (C). 1993. 35.00 (*0-945407-08-4*) Meadow Pr NM.

Bergman, Torbern O. Physical & Chemical Essays, 3 vols. 1979. lib. bdg. 350.00 (*0-8490-2438-2*) Gordon Pr.

***Bergman, Torbjorn & Damgaard, Erik, eds.** Delegation & Accountability in European Integration: The Nordic Parliamentary Democracies & the European Union. LC 00-20072. (Library of Legislative Studies). 180p. 2000. 57.50 (*0-7146-5066-8*, Pub. by F Cass Pubs); pap. 24.50 (*0-7146-8115-6*, Pub. by F Cass Pubs) Intl Spec Bk.

Bergman, Tzvi. Gateway to the Talmud: The History of the Development of the Jewish Talmud. Arem, T. Z., ed. Kasnett, R. N., tr. from HEB. (ArtScroll Mesorah Ser.). 160p. 1985. 17.99 (*0-89906-208-3*); pap. 14.99 (*0-89906-209-1*) Mesorah Pubns.

Bergman, U., et al. Studies in Drug Utilization: Methods & Applications. (WHO Regional Publications, European Ser.: No. 8). 185p. 1979. 20.00 (*92-9020-108-8*, 1310008) World Health.

Bergman-Ungar, Robert, ed. see Artist Consortium Staff.

Bergman, Werner & Heller, Wilfried. Angular Light Scattering Maxima & Minima in Monodisperse & Heterodisperse Systems of Spheres. LC 77-6931. (Illus.). 362p. reprint ed. pap. 112.30 (*0-8357-9828-3*, 201366000087) Bks Demand.

Bergmann. Child Care Problem. 1999. text. write for info. (*0-312-21149-X*) St Martin.

— Chiropractic Techniques. 2nd ed. 1998. text 125.00 (*0-443-07633-2*, W B Saunders Co) Harcrt Hlth Sci Grp.

Bergmann. Compensation Decision Making. 3rd ed. LC 97-68472. (C). 1997. text 85.50 (*0-03-024634-2*, Pub. by Harcourt Coll Pubs) Harcourt.

***Bergmann, Horst, et al.** Everyone a Leader: A Grassroots Model for the New Workplace. LC 98-49084. 244p. 1999. 24.95 (*0-471-19763-7*) Wiley.

***Bergmann, Barbara R. & Bush, Jim.** Is Social Security Broke? A Cartoon Guide to the Issues. (Illus.). 120p. (C). 2000. pap. 15.95 (*0-472-06743-5*, 06743); text 29.95 (*0-472-09743-1*, 09743) U of Mich Pr.

Bergmann, Barbara R. The Economic Emergence of Women. pap. write for info. (*0-312-23243-8*) St Martin.

— The Economic Emergence of Women. 1999. text. write for info. (*0-312-21941-5*) St Martin.

Bergmann, Barbara R. In Defense of Affirmative Action. 224p. 1997. pap. 13.00 (*0-465-09834-7*, Pub. by Basic) HarpC.

Bergmann, Barbara R. Saving Our Children from Poverty: What the United States Can Learn from France. 184p. (C). 1996. text 34.95 (*0-87154-114-9*) Russell Sage.

***Bergmann, Barbara R.** Saving Our Children from Poverty: What the United States Can Learn from France. 184p. 1999. pap. 14.95 (*0-87154-115-7*) Russell Sage.

Bergmann, Barbara R., jt. auth. see Bennett, Robert L.

***Bergmann, Bettina.** Art of Ancient Spectacle. (Illus.). 384p. 2000. 50.00 (*0-300-07733-5*) Yale U Pr.

Bergmann, E. D. & Pullmann, B., eds. Chemical & Biochemical Reactivity, April, 1973. (Jerusalem Symposia on Quantum Chemistry & Biochemistry Ser.: No. 6). 1975. text 248.50 (*90-277-0554-2*) Kluwer Academic.

Bergmann, Elizabeth & Colton, Elizabeth O. Connecting to Creativity: Ten Keys to Unlocking Your Creative Potential. 1999. pap. text 15.95 (*1-892123-09-6*) Capital VA.

Bergmann, Emilie L. Art Inscribed: Essays on Ekphrasis in Spanish Golden Age Poetry. LC 79-966. (Studies in Romance Languages: No. 35). (Illus.). 362p. 1979. 20.00 (*0-674-04805-9*) HUP.

Bergmann, Emilie L. & Smith, Paul J., eds. Entiendes? Queer Readings, Hispanic Writings. LC 94-40313. (Series Q). (ENG & SPA., Illus.). 480p. 1995. text 54.95 (*0-8223-1600-5*); pap. text 19.95 (*0-8223-1615-3*) Duke.

Bergmann, Ernst & Pullman, Bernard, eds. Molecular & Quantum Pharmacology. LC 74-83002. (Jerusalem Symposia on Quantum Chemistry & Biochemistry Ser.: No. 7). 522p. 1975. text 261.50 (*90-277-0525-9*) Kluwer Academic.

Bergmann, Ernst R. Von, see Von Bergmann, Ernst R.

Bergmann, Frank, ed. Upstate Literature: Essays in Memory of Thomas F. O'Donnell. LC 84-26853. (New York State Bks.). 256p. 1985. pap. text 19.95 (*0-8156-2331-3*) Syracuse U Pr.

Bergmann, Frank, ed. see Adams, Samuel H.

Bergmann, Frank, ed. see Edmonds, Walter D.

Bergmann, Fredrick L., jt. ed. see Pedicord, Harry W.

Bergmann, Frithjof. On Being Free. LC 77-89760. 1988. pap. text 15.00 (*0-268-01493-0*) U of Notre Dame Pr.

Bergmann, Gudrun. The Viking Cards Deck/Book Set. (Illus.). 148p. 1997. pap. 19.95 (*0-88079-239-6*, VKS99) US Games Syst.

Bergmann, Gustav. Logic & Reality. LC 64-10261. 365p. reprint ed. pap. 113.20 (*0-608-10119-2*, 200423400039) Bks Demand.

— Meaning & Existence. LC 60-5036. 286p. (Orig.). reprint ed. pap. 88.70 (*0-608-09846-9*, 206923400003) Bks Demand.

— The Metaphysics of Logical Positivism. LC 77-28139. 340p. 1978. reprint ed. lib. bdg. 35.00 (*0-313-20235-4*, BEML, Greenwood Pr) Greenwood.

— New Foundations of Ontology. Heald, William, ed. LC 91-31693. 488p. (C). 1992. text 55.00 (*0-299-13130-0*) U of Wis Pr.

— Realism: A Critique of Brentano & Meinong. LC 67-12003. 468p. reprint ed. pap. 145.10 (*0-608-09847-7*, 206923500003) Bks Demand.

***Bergmann, H.** Radioactive Isotopes in Clinical Medicine & Research XXIII: Proceedings of the 23rd International Badgastein Symposium. LC 98-43515. 1999. write for info. (*0-8176-5967-6*) Birkhauser.

Bergmann, H., et al, eds. Radioactive Isotopes in Clinical Medicine & Research. LC 94-42695. (Advances in Pharmacological Sciences Ser.). 480p. 1995. 109.00 (*0-8176-5082-2*) Birkhauser.

— Radioactive Isotopes in Clinical Medicine & Research: Proceedings of the 22nd Badgastein Symposium. LC 96-39717. (Advances in Pharmacological Sciences Ser.: Vol. XXIV). 528p. 1997. 155.00 (*3-7643-5645-6*) Spr-Verlag.

Bergmann, H. & Kroiss, A. Radioactive Isotopes in Clinical Medicine & Research: Proceedings of the 22nd Badgastein Symposium. LC 96-39717. (Advances in Pharmacological Sciences Ser.). 1997. write for info. (*0-8176-5645-6*) Birkhauser.

Bergmann, H., et al. Radioactive Isotopes in Clinical Medicine & Research: Proceedings of the 23rd International Badgastein Symposium. LC 98-43515. 600p. 1998. 159.00 (*3-7643-5967-6*) Birkhauser.

Bergmann, H., jt. ed. see Sinzinger, Helmet F.

Bergmann, Hans. God in the Street: New York Writing from the Penny Press to Melville. LC 95-6624. (Illus.). (C). 1995. pap. text 22.95 (*1-56639-358-2*); lib. bdg. 69.95 (*1-56639-357-4*) Temple U Pr.

Bergmann, Heinz. Lexikon der Videotechnik. (GER.). 144p. 1992. 39.95 (*0-7859-8478-X*, 3800717735) Fr & Eur.

Bergmann, Joachim. Die Schaubuhne - Die Weltbuhne, 1905-1933, 3 vols. 1200p. 1991. lib. bdg. 375.00 (*3-598-10831-1*) K G Saur Verlag.

Bergmann, Jorg R. Discreet Indiscretions: The Social Organization of Gossip. Bednarz, John, Jr., tr. from GER. LC 93-4263. (Communication & Social Order Ser.).Tr. of Klatsch. 224p. 1993. pap. text 26.95 (*0-202-30468-X*); lib. bdg. 48.95 (*0-202-30467-1*) Aldine de Gruyter.

Bergmann, Jorg R. & Linell, Per, eds. Morality in Discourse: A Special Double Issue of Research on Language & Social Interaction. 200p. 1999. pap. 39.50 (*0-8058-9811-5*) L Erlbaum Assocs.

Bergmann, Kenneth J., jt. ed. see Yahr, Melvin D.

Bergmann, L. & Mitrou, Paris S., eds. Cytokines in Cancer Therapy. (Beitraege Zur Onkologie, Contributions to Oncology Ser.: Vol. 46). (Illus.). x, 392p. 1994. 121.75 (*3-8055-5809-0*) S Karger.

Bergmann, Leola N. Music Master of the Middle West: The Story of F. Melius Christiansen & the St. Olaf Choir. 2nd ed. LC 68-16222. (Music Ser.). 1968. reprint ed. 32.50 (*0-306-71057-9*) Da Capo.

Bergmann, Ludwig & Schaefer, Clemens. Constituents of Matter: Atoms, Molecules, Nuclei & Particles. LC 97-26728. 950p. (C). 1997. text 95.00 (*3-11-013990-1*) De Gruyter.

— Optics. LC 99-22303. 1400p. 1999. 99.95 (*3-11-014318-6*) De Gruyter.

***Bergmann, Maria V.** What I Heard in the Silence: Role Reversal, Trauma & Creativity in the Lives of Women. LC 00-39572. 2000. write for info. (*0-8236-6842-8*) Intl Univs Pr.

Bergmann, Marilyn A., jt. auth. see Bergmann, Thomas J.

***Bergmann, Martin S.** The Hartmann Era. LC 99-89140. 2000. 60.00 (*1-892746-22-0*) Other Pr LLC.

Bergmann, Martin S. In the Shadow of Moloch. 328p. 1992. text 49.50 (*0-231-07248-1*) Col U Pr.

Bergmann, Martin S. & Hartman, Frank R., eds. The Evolution of Psychoanalytic Technique. 520p. 1990. text 76.00 (*0-231-07420-4*); pap. text 25.50 (*0-231-07421-2*) Col U Pr.

Bergmann, Martin S. & Jucovy, Milton E., eds. Generations of the Holocaust. 360p. 1991. text 70.00 (*0-231-07422-0*) Col U Pr.

Bergmann, Merrie, et al. The Logic Book. 2nd ed. 480p. (C). 1990. text 49.00 (*0-07-909524-0*) McGraw.

— The Logic Book. 3rd ed. LC 96-22699. 1996. text. write for info. (*0-07-006059-2*) McGraw.

***Bergmann, P. G., et al, eds.** Classical & Quantum Nonlocality. (Science & Culture Ser.). 256p. 2000. 68.00 (*981-02-4296-4*) World Scientific Pub.

Bergmann, Peter & De Sabbata, Venzo, eds. Topological Properties & Global Structure of Space Time. (NATO ASI Series B, Physics: Vol. 138). 280p. 1986. 69.50 (*0-306-42367-7*, Plenum Trade) Perseus Pubng.

Bergmann, Peter G. Introduction to the Theory of Relativity. 307p. (C). 1976. reprint ed. pap. 8.95 (*0-486-63282-2*) Dover.

— Riddle of Gravitation. LC 68-11537. 270p. 1977. text 25.00 (*0-684-15378-5*) S&S Trade.

— The Riddle of Gravitation. rev. ed. LC 92-22218. (Illus.). xxii, 234p. 1993. reprint ed. pap. text 8.95 (*0-486-27378-4*) Dover.

Bergmann, Peter G., et al, eds. Spin in Gravity: Is It Possible to Give an Experimental Basis to Torsion?: International School of Cosmology & Gravitation XV Course Erice, Italy 13 - 20 May 1997. (Science & Culture Ser.). 270p. 1998. 58.00 (*981-02-3459-7*) World Scientific Pub.

***Bergmann, R., et al.** Developing Industrial Case-Based Reasoning Applications: The INRECA Methodology. LC 99-35155. (Lecture Notes in Artificial Intelligence Ser.: Vol. 1612). xx, 188p. 1999. pap. 45.00 (*3-540-66182-4*) Spr-Verlag.

Bergmann, Ralph & Kott, Alexander, eds. Integrating Planning, Scheduling, & Execution in Dynamic & Uncertain Environments: Papers from the 1998 AIPS Workshop. (Technical Reports). (Illus.). 151p. 1998. spiral bd. 25.00 (*1-57735-055-3*) AAAI Pr.

Bergmann, Rolf. Verzeichnis der althochdeutschen und altsaechsischen Glossenhandschriften: Mit Bibliographie der Glosseneditionen, der Handschriftenbeschreibungen und der Dialektbestimmungen. LC 72-76056. (Arbeiten zur Fruehmittelalterforschung Ser.: Vol. 6). (GER.). (C). 1973. 79.25 (*3-11-003713-0*) De Gruyter.

Bergmann, Seth D. Compiler Design: Theory, Tools, & Examples. 320p. (C). 1994. text 52.50 (*0-697-17086-1*, WCB McGr Hill) McGrw-H Hghr Educ.

Bergmann, Sherrel & Rudman, Gerald J. Decision-Making Skills for Middle School Students. 64p. 1985. pap. 8.95 (*0-8106-1528-2*) NEA.

Bergmann, Theodor, et al, eds. Bukharin in Retrospect. LC 93-28403. (Socialism & Social Movements Ser.). 256p. (C). (gr. 13). 1994. text 70.95 (*0-87332-691-1*) M E Sharpe.

Bergmann, Thesi & Freud, Anna. Children in the Hospital. LC 65-28803. 162p. 1966. 27.50 (*0-8236-0800-X*) Intl Univs Pr.

— Children in the Hospital. LC 65-28803. 162p. 1974. pap. 24.95 (*0-8236-8017-7*, 020800) Intl Univs Pr.

Bergmann, Thomas F. & Davis, P. Thomas. Distractive Joint Manipulation. LC 96-40215. (Illus.). 304p. (C). (gr. 13). 1997. text 82.00 (*0-8151-0900-8*, 28148) Mosby Inc.

Bergmann, Thomas F., et al. Chiropractic Technique: Principles & Procedures. (Illus.). 816p. 1993. text 182.00 (*0-443-08752-0*) Church.

Bergmann, Thomas J. & Bergmann, Marilyn A. Instructor's Manual with Test Items to Accompany Hills - Bergmann - Scarpello, Compensation Decision Making. 2nd ed. 230p. (C). 1994. text 33.75 (*0-03-033059-9*) Dryden Pr.

Bergmann, Werner, ed. Error Without Trial: Current Research on Antisemitism. (Psychological Research on Antisemitism Ser.). 546p. (C). 1987. text 157.70 (*3-11-010775-9*) De Gruyter.

Bergmann, Werner & Erb, Rainer. Anti-Semitism in Germany. 1996. 44.95 (*0-614-95762-1*) Transaction Pubs.

— Anti-Semitism in Germany: The Post-Nazi Epoch From 1945-1995. LC 96-36347. 293p. 1997. text 39.95 (*1-56000-270-0*) Transaction Pubs.

Bergmans, Bernhard. Inside Information & Securities Trading: A Legal & Economic Analysis of the Foundations of Liability in the U. S. A. & European Community. 256p. (C). 1991. lib. bdg. 117.00 (*1-85333-569-X*, Pub. by Graham & Trotman) Kluwer Academic.

Bergmans, Jan W. Digital Baseband Transmission & Recording. LC 96-40958. 652p. (C). 1996. text 148.50 (*0-7923-9775-4*) Kluwer Academic.

***Bergmark, A. & Klingemann, H., eds.** Drug Treatment Systems in an International Perspective. (European Addiction Research Ser.: Vol. 5, No. 3). (Illus.). 58p. 1999. pap. 25.25 (*3-8055-6966-1*) S Karger.

Bergmark, Janet. In the Presence of Aliens: A Personal Experience of Dual Consciousness. LC 97-25807. 224p. (Orig.). 1999. pap. 12.95 (*1-56718-063-9*) Llewellyn Pubns.

Bergmark, Jean B., jt. auth. see Spritzer, Lorraine N.

Bergmeier, H. J. P. & Lotz, Rainer E. Hitler's Airwaves: The Inside Story of Nazi Radio Broadcasting & Propaganda Swing. LC 96-36617. 352p. 1997. 42.00 (*0-300-06709-7*) Yale U Pr.

Bergmeister, Manfred, jt. auth. see Pracht, Klaus.

Bergmeyer. Methods of Enzymatic Analysis: Cumulated Subject Index. 3rd ed. (Bergmeyer Methods of Enzymatic Analysis Ser.). 91p. 1987. 105.00 (*3-527-26053-6*) Wiley.

Bergmeyer, H. C., ed. Amtogens & Antibodies 2, Vol. 11, Antigens and Antibodies 2. 3rd ed. 509p. 1986. 310.00 (*3-527-26051-X*, Wiley-VCH) Wiley.

Bergmeyer, Hans U. Metabolites 3: Lipids, Amino Acids & Related Compounds, Vol. 8, Metabolites 3: Lipids, Amino Acids and Rel. 3rd ed. LC 84-105641. (Illus.). 629p. 1985. 320.00 (*3-527-26048-X*, Wiley-VCH) Wiley.

— Proteins & Peptides Hormones, Vol. 9, Proteins and Peptides. 3rd ed. 572p. 1985. 320.00 (*3-527-26049-8*, Wiley-VCH) Wiley.

Bergmeyer, Hans U., ed. Antigens & Antibodies 1, Vol. 10, Antigens and Antibodies 1. 3rd ed. LC 84-105641. 509p. 1986. 310.00 (*3-527-26050-1*, Wiley-VCH) Wiley.

— Drugs & Pesticides, Vol. 12, Drugs and Pesticides. 3rd ed. LC 84-105641. 499p. 1986. 320.00 (*3-527-26052-8*, Wiley-VCH) Wiley.

— Enzymes 1: Oxidoreductases & Transferases, Vol. 3, Enzymes 1: Oxidoreductases, Transferases. 3rd ed. LC 84-105641. 606p. 1983. 305.00 (*3-527-26043-9*, Wiley-VCH) Wiley.

— Enzymes 3: Peptidases, Proteinases & Their Inhibitors, Vol. 5, Enzymes 3: Peptidases, Proteinases and The. 3rd ed. LC 84-105641. 598p. 1984. 320.00 (*3-527-26045-5*, Wiley-VCH) Wiley.

— Enzymes 2: Esterases, Glycosidases, Lyases & Ligases, Vol. 4, Enzymes 2: Esterases, Glycosidases, Lyases. 3rd ed. LC 84-105641. 426p. 1984. 320.00 (*3-527-26044-7*, Wiley-VCH) Wiley.

— Fundamentals, Vol. 1, Fundamentals. 3rd ed. LC 84-105641. 574p. 1983. 278.00 (*3-527-26041-2*, Wiley-VCH) Wiley.

— Metabolites 2: Tri- & Dicarboxylic Acids, Purines, Pyrimidines & Derivatives, Coenzymes & Inorganic Compounds, Vol. 7, Metabolites 2: Tri- and Dicarboxylic Acids. 3rd ed. 642p. 1985. 325.00 (*3-527-26047-1*, Wiley-VCH) Wiley.

Bergmeyer, Hans U., ed. Methods of Enzymatic Analysis: Cumulated Subject Index. 3rd ed. LC 84-105641. 90p. 1987. 80.00 (*0-89573-243-2*, Wiley-VCH) Wiley.

Bergmeyer, Hans U., ed. Methods of Enzymatic Analysis: Metabolites 1 - Carbohydrates, Vol. 6, Metabolites 1: Carbohydrates. 3rd ed. 701p. 1984. 320.00 (*3-527-26046-3*, Wiley-VCH) Wiley.

Bergmeyer, Hans U., ed. Samples, Reagents & Assessment of Results, Vol. 2, Samples, Reagents, Assessment of Results. 3rd ed. LC 84-105641. 539p. 1983. 320.00 (*3-527-26042-0*, Wiley-VCH) Wiley.

Bergna, Horacio E., ed. The Colloid Chemistry of Silica: Developed from a Symposium Sponsored by the Division of Colloid & Surface Chemistry at the 200th National Meeting of the American Chemistry Society, Washington, DC, August 26-31, 1990. LC 93-11456. (Advances in Chemistry Ser.: No. 234). (Illus.). 718p. 1994. text 145.00 (*0-8412-2103-0*, Pub. by Am Chemical) OUP.

Bergnano, Enrico, ed. see Hernandez, Orlando.

Bergner, Daniel. God of the Rodeo: The Quest For Redemption in Louisiana's Angola Prison. LC 98-18485. 304p. 1998. 24.00 (*0-609-60105-9*) Crown Pub Group.

— God of the Rodeo: The Quest for Redemption in Louisiana's Angola Prison. 1999. pap. 13.95 (*0-345-43553-2*, Ballantine) Ballantine Pub Grp.

Bergner, Erik E., et al, eds. Compartments, Pools & Spaces in Medical Physiology: Proceedings. LC 67-61865. (AEC Symposium Ser.). 600p. 1967. pap. 21.00 (*0-87079-167-2*, CONF-661010); fiche 9.00 (*0-87079-168-0*, CONF-661010) DOE.

An Asterisk (*) at the beginning of an entry indicates that the title is appearing for the first time.

Bergner, Hans & Hoffman, Leonard. Bioenergetik Landwirtschaftlicher Nutztiere. (GER.). 384p. 1996. text 98.00 (*3-7186-5809-7*, Harwood Acad Pubs) Gordon & Breach.

Bergner, Heinz, selected by. English Short Stories of the Nineteenth Century. (Olms Studien: No. 16). xxiii, 486p. 1969. 19.37 (*0-685-66463-5*) G Olms Pubs.

Bergner, Jeffrey T. The Origin of Formalism in Social Science. LC 80-17484. 160p. 1981. 19.50 (*0-226-04362-2*) U Ch Pr.

— The Origin of Formalism in Social Science. LC 80-17484. 174p. reprint ed. pap. 54.00 (*0-608-09386-6*, 205413100004); reprint ed. pap. 53.70 (*0-608-21010-2*, 2054538) Bks Demand.

Bergner, Jeffrey T., jt. ed. see Bader, William B.

Bergner, Klaus-Dieter. Natur und Technik in der Literatur des Fruhen Expressionismus. (Europaische Hochschulschriften Ser.: Reihe 1, Bd. 1679). 348p. 1998. pap. 51.95 (*3-631-33328-5*) P Lang Pubng.

Bergner, Lawrence, ed. see Eisenberg, Mickey S.

Bergner, Mario. Setting Love in Order: Hope & Healing for the Homosexual. LC 94-40047. 208p. (Orig.). (YA). (gr. 10). 1995. pap. 11.99 (*0-8010-5186-X*, Hamewith MI) Baker Bks.

Bergner, Paul. The Healing Power of Echinacea, Goldenseal & Other Immune System Herbs. LC 97-400. 336p. 1997. per. 15.00 (*0-7615-0809-0*) Prima Pub.

— The Healing Power of Garlic: The Enlightened Person's Guide to Nature's Most Medicinal Plant. LC 95-30728. 304p. 1995. pap. text 15.95 (*0-7615-0098-7*) Prima Pub.

***Bergner, Paul.** The Healing Power of Garlic: The Enlightened Person's Guide to Nature's Most Versatile Medicinal Plant. 289p. 1999. reprint ed. pap. text 17.00 (*0-7881-6735-9*) DIANE Pub.

Bergner, Paul. The Healing Power of Ginseng & the Tonic Herbs: The Enlightened Person's Guide. (Healing Power Ser.). (Illus.). 288p. 1996. per. 14.95 (*0-7615-0472-9*) Prima Pub.

— Healing Power of Minerals, Special Nutrients, & Trace Elements. LC 97-20545. 320p. 1997. per. 15.00 (*0-7615-1021-4*) Prima Pub.

Bergner, Paul. Poder Cuartivo del Ajo. (SPA.). 1997. pap. text 7.98 (*970-643-033-4*) Selector.

***Bergner, Paul & Hufford, David J.** Country Doctor's Book of Folk Remedies & Healing Wisdom LC 99-208065. 384p. 1998. write for info. (*0-7853-2831-9*) Pubns Intl Ltd.

Bergner, Raymond M. Pathological Self-Criticism: Assessment & Treatment. (Series in Social/Clinical Psychology). 220p. 1995. 39.50 (*0-306-44961-7*, Kluwer Plenum) Kluwer Academic.

Bergner, Raymond M., ed. Studies in Psychopathology: The Descriptive Psychology Approach. 256p. (C). 1993. pap. 19.95 (*0-9625661-3-6*) Descriptive Psych Pr.

Bergner, Raymond M., jt. ed. see Jeffrey, H. Joel.

Bergner, Raymond M., jt. ed. see Roberts, Mary K.

***Bergner, Reinhard.** Die Berthold-Otto-Schulen In Magdeburg: Ein Vergessenes Kapitel Reformpadagogischer Schulgeschichte Von 1920 Bis 1950. (GER., Illus.). 444p. 1999. 68.00 (*3-631-32381-6*) P Lang Pubng.

Bergner, W., jt. auth. see Kircher, R.

Bergnian, Bo. Knifemaking: A Complete Guide to Crafting Knives, Handles, & Sheaths. Doran, Laura D., ed. Matteson, Edith, tr. from SWE. LC 97-23536. Orig. Title: Knivar & Kniva Pa Mitt Satt. (Illus.). 152p. 1997. pap. 18.95 (*1-887374-37-X*, Pub. by Lark Books) Random.

Bergo, Bettina. Levinas Between Ethics & Politics: For the Beauty that Adorns the Earth. LC 99-24358. (Phaenomenologica Ser.). 1999. write for info. (*0-7923-5694-2*) Kluwer Academic.

Bergo, Bettina, tr. see Levinas, Emmanuel.

Bergoffen, Debra B. The Philosophy of Simone de Beauvoir: Gendered Phenomenologies, Erotic Generosities. LC 97-1516. (SUNY Series in Feminist Philosophy). 250p. (C). 1996. text 54.50 (*0-7914-3151-7*); pap. text 17.95 (*0-7914-3152-5*) State U NY Pr.

Bergogne-Berezin, E., et al, eds. Acinetobacter: Microbiology, Epidemiology, Infections, Management. LC 95-30812. 288p. 1995. boxed set 189.95 (*0-8493-9223-3*, 4833) CRC Pr.

***Bergoin, Catherine.** Decorating Porcelain: The American Technique. (Illus.). 80p. 2000. pap. 19.95 (*0-233-99548-X*, Pub. by Andre Deutsch) Trafalgar.

— Porcelain Painting: The Latest Technique. (Illus.). 80p. 2000. pap. 19.95 (*0-233-99547-1*, Pub. by Andre Deutsch) Trafalgar.

Bergold, Ralph. Der Glaube Vor Dem Anspruch der Wissenschaft: Der Dialog Zwischen Naturwissenschaft und Theologie Am Beispiel Von Schopfungsglaube und Evolutionstheorie. (Europaische Hochschulschriften Ser.: Reihe 23, Bd. 437). (GER., Illus.). VII, 345p. 1991. 62.80 (*3-631-44200-9*) P Lang Pubng.

Bergold, Roger. Roger Bergolds Dairy Wine Companion Vol. 1: A Term a Day Wine Calendar. Winfield, Ann, ed. (Illus.). 320p. (Orig.). 1996. 12.95 (*1-889841-04-8*) Chapel Hill.

Bergon, Frank. Shoshone Mike. (Western Literature Ser.). 304p. 1994. pap. 13.00 (*0-87417-244-6*) U of Nev Pr.

— Stephen Crane's Artistry. LC 75-19159. 190p. reprint ed. pap. 58.90 (*0-608-18780-1*, 202982400065) Bks Demand.

— The Temptations of St. Ed & Brother S. Frank Bergon. LC 93-17053. (Western Literature Ser.). 320p. 1993. 22.00 (*0-87417-226-8*) U of Nev Pr.

— Wild Game. LC 94-41278. (Western Literature Ser.). 336p. 1995. 22.00 (*0-87417-257-8*) U of Nev Pr.

— The Wilderness Reader. LC 94-31862. 384p. (Orig.). 1994. pap. 15.95 (*0-87417-250-0*) U of Nev Pr.

Bergon, Frank, ed. The Journals of Lewis & Clark. (Illus.). 560p. 1989. pap. 14.95 (*0-14-025217-7*, Penguin Bks) Viking Penguin.

Bergonzi. Poetry, 1870-1914. 1983. pap. text. write for info. (*0-582-35147-2*, Pub. by Addison-Wesley) Longman.

Bergonzi, Benet. Old Gramophones & Other Talking Machines. 1989. pap. 4.75 (*0-7478-0104-5*, Pub. by Shire Pubns) St Mut.

Bergonzi, Bernard. David Lodge. (Writers & Their Work Ser.). 95p. (Orig.). 1996. pap. text 15.00 (*0-7463-0755-1*, Pub. by Northcote House) U Pr of Miss.

— Exploding English: Criticism, Theory, Culture. 256p. 1991. reprint ed. pap. 24.95 (*0-19-811261-0*) OUP.

— Heroes' Twilight. enl. rev. ed. 240p. 1996. pap. 24.95 (*1-85754-135-9*, Pub. by Carcanet Pr) Paul & Co Pubs.

— T. S. Eliot Four Quartets. LC 71-438030. (Casebook Ser.). 269p. 1969. write for info. (*0-333-09144-2*) Macmillan.

***Bergonzi, Bernard.** War Poets & Other Subjects. LC 99-65142. 211p. 2000. 78.95 (*0-7546-0036-X*) Ashgate Pub Co.

Bergonzi, Bernard. Wartime & Aftermath: English Literature & Its Background, 1939-60. LC 92-26593. 240p. 1993. pap. 15.95 (*0-19-289222-3*) OUP.

Bergonzi, Bernard, ed. see Gissing, George R.

Bergonzi, Louis & Smith, Julia. Effects of Arts Education on Participation in the Arts. LC 96-7843. (National Endowment for the Arts Research Division Report Ser.: No. 36). 77p. 1996. pap. 11.95 (*0-929765-47-8*) Seven Locks Pr.

***Bergos, Joan.** Gaudi: The Man & His Work. (Illus.). 320p. 1999. 75.00 (*0-8212-2627-4*, Pub. by Bulfinch Pr) Little.

Bergquist, Anders, ed. see Simonetti, Manlio.

Bergquist, Carl. Build Your Own Test Equipment. (Illus.). 267p. 1998. pap. 29.95 (*0-7906-1130-9*) Prompt Publns.

***Bergquist, Carl.** Laser Design Toolkit. LC 98-68718. 223p. 1999. pap. 29.95 (*0-7906-1183-X*) Prompt Publns.

Bergquist, Carl. The Video Hacker's Handbook. LC 97-68181. (Illus.). 336p. 1997. pap. 29.95 (*0-7906-1126-0*) Prompt Publns.

***Bergquist, Carl J.** Howard W. Sams Ham Radio Operator's Guide. 320p. 1999. pap. 29.95 (*0-7906-1195-3*) Prompt Publns.

— Telephone Projects. LC 98-67314. 1998. pap. text 29.95 (*0-7906-1168-6*) Prompt Publns.

Bergquist, Charles. Labor & the Course of American Democracy: U. S. History in Latin American Perspective. LC 96-48532. (C). 1996. pap. 22.00 (*1-85984-126-0*, Pub. by Verso) Norton.

Bergquist, Charles, ed. Labor in the Capitalist World-Economy. LC 83-27015. (Political Economy of the World-System Annuals Ser.: No. 7). (Illus.). 312p. reprint ed. pap. 96.80 (*0-8357-8471-1*, 203473900091) Bks Demand.

Bergquist, Charles, ed. see Sanchez, George J. & Sanchez, Gonzalo J.

Bergquist, Charles W. Coffee & Conflict in Colombia 1886-1910. LC 78-59581. xiv, 277p. 1986. reprint ed. pap. text 19.95 (*0-8223-0735-9*) Duke.

— Labor in Latin America: Comparative Essays on Chile, Argentina, Venezuela & Colombia. LC 84-51648. (Illus.). 414p. reprint ed. pap. 30.00 (*0-608-20215-0*, 207146900012) Bks Demand.

Bergquist, Craig & Lucke, Peggy. How to Plan & Build Bookcases, Cabinets & Shelves. Shakery, Karen, ed. LC 86-72432. (Illus.). 96p. 1987. pap. 9.95 (*0-89721-088-3*) Meredith Bks.

Bergquist, Gilbert T. Florida Assessment of Coastal Trends (1997) (Illus.). 214p. (C). 1999. pap. text 50.00 (*0-7881-7656-0*) DIANE Pub.

Bergquist, Gilbert T., jt. ed. see Baudot, Jacques.

Bergquist, J. Gordon. Minnetaka Indian Boy. (Illus.). 150p. (Orig.). 1985. pap. text 9.75 (*0-9615483-0-4*) Bergquist Pub.

***Bergquist, Kathie.** Ricky Martin. (Illus.). 1999. pap. 12.95 (*0-8230-8407-8*, Billboard Bks) Watsn-Guptill.

***Bergquist, Lars.** Swedenborg's Dream Diary. Hallengren, Anders, tr. from SWE. (Swedenborg Studies: Vol. 11). 230p. 2000. 24.95 (*0-87785-198-0*, Pub. by Swedenborg) Words Distrib.

Bergquist, Lizbeth S. Investment Sales Compliance for Financial Institutions: Banking & Securities Laws & Regulations, Identifying & Managing Compliance Risks & Disclosure Regulations. LC 96-44033. 288p. (C). 1996. text 125.00 (*0-7863-0963-6*, Irwn McGrw-H) McGrw-H Hghr Educ.

Bergquist, Lois M. Changing Patterns of Infectious Disease. LC 84-3957. 295p. reprint ed. pap. 91.50 (*0-7837-2692-9*, 204307000006) Bks Demand.

Bergquist, Lois M. & Pogosian, Barbara. Microbiology: Principles & Health Science Applications. LC 99-40813. (Illus.). 590p. 2000. pap. text. write for info. (*0-7216-7663-4*, W B Saunders Co) Harcrt Hlth Sci Grp.

Bergquist, Peter, ed. Orlando di Lasso Studies. LC 98-11734. (Genres in American Cinema Ser.). (Illus.). 275p. (C). 1999. text 64.95 (*0-521-59387-5*) Cambridge U Pr.

Bergquist, Peter, ed. see Di Lasso, Orlando.

Bergquist, Ronald E. The Role of Airpower in the Iran-Iraq War. 108p. 1988. pap. 3.75 (*1-58566-023-X*) Air Univ.

Bergquist, William H. The Postmodern Organization: Mastering the Art of Irreversible Change. LC 92-43606. (Management Ser.). 299p. 1993. text 32.95 (*1-55542-533-X*) Jossey-Bass.

Bergquist, William H. & Phillips, Steven R. A Handbook for Faculty Development. Incl. Vol. 2. LC 80-69254. 1977. pap. 11.00 (*0-937012-09-2*); Vol. 3. LC 80-69254. 1981. pap. 11.00 (*0-937012-11-4*); LC 2 vols.. 15.00 (*0-614-30389-3*) Coun Indep Colleges.

Bergquist, William H., et al. Building Strategic Relationships: How to Extend Your Organization's Reach Through Partnerships, Alliances, & Joint Ventures. (Management Ser.). 272p. 1995. text 32.95 (*0-7879-0092-3*) Jossey-Bass.

Bergquist, William H., et al. Stroke Survivors. LC 94-11647. (Health-Management Ser.). 279p. 1994. pap. 25.00 (*1-55542-669-7*) Jossey-Bass.

***Bergqvist, Christina, ed.** Equal Democracies? Gender & Politics in the Nordic Countries. 328p. (C). 1999. 37.00 (*82-00-12799-0*, Pub. by Scand Univ Pr) IBD Ltd.

Bergqvist, D., jt. auth. see Bergentz, S. E.

Bergqvist, David. Postoperative Thromboembolism: Frequency, Etiology, Prophylaxis. (Illus.). 248p. 1983. 71.95 (*0-387-12062-9*) Spr-Verlag.

Bergreen, Gary. Coping with Study Strategies. rev. ed. (Coping Ser.). (YA). (gr. 7-12). 1990. lib. bdg. 17.95 (*0-8239-1140-3*) Rosen Group.

Bergreen, Laurence. As Thousands Cheer: The Life of Irving Berlin. (Illus.). 704p. 1996. reprint ed. pap. 18.95 (*0-306-80675-4*) Da Capo.

— Capone: The Man & the Era. (Illus.). 720p. 1994. 30.00 (*0-671-74456-9*) S&S Trade.

— Capone: The Man & the Era. 704p. 1996. per. 18.00 (*0-684-82447-7*, Touchstone) S&S Trade Pap.

— Louis Armstrong: An Extravagant Life. 592p. 1998. pap. 16.00 (*0-7679-0156-8*) Broadway BDD.

***Bergreen, Lawrence.** Voyage to Mars: NASA's Search for Life Beyond Earth. 384p. 2000. 24.95 (*1-57322-156-X*, Riverhead Books) Putnam Pub Group.

Bergren, Anne B., ed. see McDonald, Julie.

Bergren, Kris, jt. auth. see Collins, David R.

Bergren, Lisa T. Firestorm. LC 96-219786. 273p. 1996. pap. 9.99 (*0-88070-953-7*, Palisades OR) Multnomah Pubs.

— Refuge. 336p. 1994. pap. 9.99 (*0-88070-875-1*, Palisades OR) Multnomah Pubs.

— Treasure. large type ed. LC 96-51930. 1997. 22.95 (*0-7838-8066-9*, G K Hall Lrg Type) Mac Lib Ref.

Bergren, Lisa T., et al. A Mother's Love. LC 97-480. 286p. 1997. pap. 9.99 (*1-57673-106-5*, Palisades OR) Multnomah Pubs.

— Silver Bells. LC 97-18326. 256p. 1997. pap. 9.99 (*1-57673-119-7*, Palisades OR) Multnomah Pubs.

***Bergren, Lisa Tawn.** The Bridge. 240p. 2000. 14.95 (*1-57856-272-4*) Waterbrook Pr.

— The Captain's Bride. LC 99-161347. (Northern Lights Ser.: Bk. 1). 400p. 1998. pap. 10.95 (*1-57856-013-6*) Waterbrook Pr.

Bergren, Lisa Tawn. Chosen. 292p. 1996. pap. 9.99 (*0-88070-768-2*, Palisades OR) Multnomah Pubs

— Deep Harbor. (Northern Lights Ser.: Vol. 2). 384p. 1999. pap. 10.95 (*1-57856-045-4*) Waterbrook Pr.

***Bergren, Lisa Tawn.** God Gave Us You. (Illus.). 40p. (J). (ps-2). 2000. 9.95 (*1-57856-323-2*) Waterbrook Pr.

— Midnight Sun. LC 99-89444. (Northern Lights Ser.: Vol. 3). 384p. 2000. pap. 10.95 (*1-57856-113-2*) Waterbrook Pr.

Bergren, Melissa. Big, Big Trucks. Hoffman, Joan, ed. (Start to Read! Ser.). (Illus.). 32p. (J). (ps-2). 1994. pap. 3.99 (*0-88743-431-2*, 06083) Sch Zone Pub Co.

Bergren, Theodore A. Sixth Ezra: The Text & Origin. 296p. (C). 1998. text 52.00 (*0-19-511201-6*) OUP.

***Bergren, Theodore A. & Stone, Michael E., eds.** Biblical Figures Outside the Bible. LC 98-39935. 448p. 1998. 35.00 (*1-56338-247-4*) TPI PA.

Bergrun, Norman R. Ringmakers of Saturn. 1986. 80.00 (*0-7855-2134-8*, Pub. by Pentland Pr) St Mut.

— Ringmakers of Saturn. Ross, Meg, ed. LC 86-81530. (Illus.). 128p. 1986. 80.00 (*0-946270-33-3*, Pub. by Pentland Pr) Trafalgar.

Bergsen, David. Murder Crosses the Equator: A Father Jack Carthier Mystery. 1999. pap. text 10.95 (*1-891874-03-9*) Recover Comns.

Bergslad, Knut, ed. Niigugis Maqaxtazaqangis: Atkan Historical Traditions. 2nd ed. 114p. 1979. pap. 4.00 (*0-933769-16-4*) Alaska Native.

Bergsland, David. Digital Drawing: Print & Web Graphics Using Freehand. LC 99-39005. 350p. (C). 1999. pap. 41.95 (*0-7668-1639-7*) Delmar.

— Printing in a Digital World. (Graphic Communications Ser.). 512p. 1996. mass mkt. 55.95 (*0-8273-7283-9*) Delmar.

— Printing in a Digital World - IRK. 112p. 1996. 19.95 (*0-8273-7480-1*) Delmar.

***Bergsland, David.** Publishing with Indesign. (Student Material TV Ser.). 352p. (C). 2000. pap. 39.95 (*0-7668-2001-7*) Thomson Learn.

Bergsland, Knut. Aleut Grammar: Unangam Tunuganaan Achixaasix. LC 97-38814. (Research Paper Ser.). 1997. pap. 33.00 (*1-55500-064-9*) Alaska Native.

Bergsland, Knut, compiled by. Aleut Dictionary, Unangam Tunudgusiiian Unabridged Lexicon of the Aleutian, Pribilof & Commander Islands Aleut Language. LC 92-44852. xlvi, 739p. 1994. pap. 37.50 (*1-55500-047-9*) Alaska Native.

Bergsland, Knut, ed. Ancient Aleut Personal Names, Kadaangim Asangin/Asangis: Materials from the Billings Expedition, 1790-1792. LC 98-196503. 170p. 1998. pap. 16.00 (*1-55500-065-7*) Alaska Native.

Bergsland, Knut & Dirks, Moses, eds. Unangam Ungiikangin Kayux Tunusangin: Aleut Tales & Narratives, 1909-1910. (Illus.). 729p. 1990. pap. text 29.00 (*1-55500-036-3*) Alaska Native.

Bergsma, Daniel. Cancer & Genetics. (Alan R. Liss Ser.: Vol 12, No. 1). 1976. 28.00 (*0-686-18077-1*) March of Dimes.

Bergsma, Daniel, ed. Congenital Malformations in Singletons: Epidemiologic Survey. LC 74-79906. (March of Dimes Ser.: Vol. 10, No. 11). 1976. 12.50 (*0-686-14567-4*) March of Dimes.

— Cytogenetics, Environmental Malformation Syndromes. LC 76-20510. (Alan R. Liss Ser.: Vol 12, No. 5). 1976. 42.00 (*0-686-18079-8*) March of Dimes.

— Developmental Disabilities: Psychologic & Social Implications. LC 76-44446. (Alan R. Liss Ser.: Vol. 12, No. 4). 1976. 25.00 (*0-686-18080-1*) March of Dimes.

— Disorders of Connective Tissue. LC 75-17345. (March of Dimes Ser.: Vol. 11, No. 6). 1976. 16.95 (*0-686-14574-7*) March of Dimes.

— Embryology & Pathogenesis & Prenatal Diagnosis. (Alan R. Liss Ser.: Vol. 13, No 3d). 1977. 42.00 (*0-686-23120-1*) March of Dimes.

— Ethical Issues Arising in the Genetic Counseling Relationship. LC 78-70429. (National Foundation Ser.: Vol. 14, No. 9). 1978. write for info. (*0-686-23952-0*) March of Dimes.

— Ethical, Social & Legal Dimensions of Screening for Human Genetic Disease. (March of Dimes Ser.: Vol. 10, No. 6). 1974. 13.95 (*0-686-10018-2*) March of Dimes.

— The Eye & Inborn Errors of Metabolism. LC 76-12112. (Alan R. Liss Ser.: Vol. 12, No. 3). 1976. 83.00 (*0-686-18081-X*) March of Dimes.

— Genetic Effects on Aging. (Alan R. Liss Ser.: Vol. 14, No. 1). 1978. 70.00 (*0-686-10130-8*) March of Dimes.

— Genetic Forms of Hypogonadism. LC 75-8432. (Symposia Ser.: Vol. 11, No. 4). 1976. 13.95 (*0-686-14572-0*) March of Dimes.

— Genetics & Cytogenetics. (March of Dimes Ser.: Vol. 10, No. 9). 1974. 12.95 (*0-686-10016-6*) March of Dimes.

— Growth Problems & Clinical Advances. LC 76-21714. (Alan R. Liss Ser.: Vol. 12, No. 6). 1976. 42.00 (*0-686-18083-6*) March of Dimes.

— Human Gene Mapping, Winnipeg, August 1977: Winnipeg Conference, 4th International Workshop. (Human Gene Mapping Ser.: No. 4). (Illus.). 1979. pap. 71.50 (*3-8055-3052-8*) S Karger.

— Infant at Risk. (March of Dimes Ser.: Vol. 10, No. 2). 1974. 11.50 (*0-686-10021-2*) March of Dimes.

— International Workshop on Human Gene Mapping: Proceedings, New Haven Conference. (March of Dimes Ser.: Vol. 10, No. 3). 1974. 13.50 (*0-686-10020-4*) March of Dimes.

— Iron Metabolism & Thalassemia. LC 76-25835. (Alan R. Liss Ser.: Vol 12, No. 8). 1976. 31.00 (*0-686-18085-2*) March of Dimes.

— Limb Malformations. (Symposia Ser.: Vol. 10, No. 5). 1974. 15.00 (*0-686-10019-0*) March of Dimes.

— Malformation Syndromes. (March of Dimes Ser.: Vol. 10, No. 7). 1974. 12.95 (*0-686-10017-4*) March of Dimes.

— Medical Genetics Today: Papers Presented at the Johns Hopkins Hospital, Baltimore, Maryland, June 15 & 16, 1972. LC 78-78434. (Birth Defects, Original Article Ser.: Vol. 10, no. 10). 314p. reprint ed. pap. 97.40 (*0-608-13625-5*, 202073600018) Bks Demand.

— The Molecular Basis of Cell-Cell Interaction. (Alan R. Liss Ser.: Vol. 14, No. 2). 1978. 80.00 (*0-686-10131-6*) March of Dimes.

— Morphogenesis & Malformation of Face & Brain. LC 75-24570. (Alan R. Liss Ser.: Vol. 11, No. 7). 1976. 43.00 (*0-686-14575-5*) March of Dimes.

— Morphogenesis & Malformation of the Genital System, Vol. 13, No. 2. LC 77-535. (Alan R. Liss Ser.). 1977. 25.00 (*0-686-20483-2*) March of Dimes.

— Morphogenesis & Malformation of the Limb, Vol. 13, No. 1. LC 76-55004. (Alan R. Liss Ser.). 1977. 49.00 (*0-686-20484-0*) March of Dimes.

— Natural History of Specific Birth Defects. (Alan R. Liss Ser.: Vol. 13, No. 3c). 1977. 42.00 (*0-686-23122-8*) March of Dimes.

— New Chromosomal & Malformation Syndromes. LC 75-16885. (March of Dimes Ser.: Vol. 11, No.5). 1976. 16.95 (*0-686-14573-9*) March of Dimes.

— Normal Values for Selected Physical Parameters: An Aid to Syndrome Delineation. LC 75-25485. (National Foundation Ser.: Vol. 10, No. 13). 1974. write for info. (*0-686-18086-0*) March of Dimes.

— Numerical Taxonomy of Birth Defects & Polygenic Disorders. (Alan R. Liss Ser.: Vol. 13, No. 3a). 1977. 28.00 (*0-686-23124-4*) March of Dimes.

— Skeletal Dysplasias. (March of Dimes Ser.: Vol. 10, No. 8). 1974. 12.95 (*0-686-10015-8*) March of Dimes.

— Trends in Teaching Genetics. (Alan R. Liss Ser.: Vol. 13, No. 6). 1977. 23.00 (*0-686-23125-2*) March of Dimes.

— Urinary System & Others, Pt. 16. (Alan R. Liss Ser.: Vol. 10, No. 4). 1974. 48.00 (*0-686-23126-0*) March of Dimes.

— Urinary System Malformations in Children. (Alan R. Liss Ser.: Vol. 13, No. 5). 1977. 70.00 (*0-686-23127-9*) March of Dimes.

— X-Linked Mental Retardation & Verbal Disability. (March of Dimes Ser.: Vol. 10, No. 1). 1974. 11.50 (*0-686-10022-0*) March of Dimes.

Bergsma, Daniel & Goldstein, Allan, eds. Neurochemical & Immunologic Components in Schizophrenia. (Alan R. Liss Ser.: Vol. 14, No. 5). 1978. 64.00 (*0-685-03293-0*) March of Dimes.

Bergsma, Daniel & Kargar, S., eds. Human Gene Mapping III, Vol 12, No. 7. LC 76-2955. 1976. write for info. (*0-686-18084-4*) March of Dimes.

Bergsma, Daniel & Summitt, Robert L., eds. Cell Surface Factors, Immune Deficiencies, Twin Studies. (Alan R. Liss Ser.: Vol. 14, No 6A). 1978. 34.00 (*0-686-23949-0*) March of Dimes.

Bergsma, Daniel, ed. see Baltimore Conference Staff.

Bergsma, Daniel, ed. see Birth Defects Annual Conference Staff.

Bergsma, Daniel, jt. ed. see Myrianthopoulos, Ntinos C.

Bergsma, Daniel, jt. ed. see Rosenquist, Glenn C.

Bergsma, Daniel, ed. see Rotterdam Conference Staff.

Bergsma, Daniel, jt. ed. see Summit, Robert.

B

An Asterisk (*) at the beginning of an entry indicates that the title is appearing for the first time.

Bergsma, Jody, et al. Dragon. LC 99-25689. (Illus.). 32p. (J). (ps up). 1999. 15.95 (*0-935699-17-1*) Illum Arts. In this dramatic new fairy tale, a gentle prince & an angry, fire-breathing dragon are born on the same day & share a unique destiny. Bergsma's illustrations capture the riveting excitement of the dragon's world & the whimsical charm of a Celtic kingdom. Here animals talk, dragons fly & kings must be made. "Children of all ages will love Dragon. Jody Bergsma's powerful watercolors are a perfect match for her delightful new fairy tale, in which children see that they can turn even the fiercest enemy into a friend." Jack Canfield, Co-Author, Chicken Soup for the Kid's Soul. *Publisher Paid Annotation.*

Bergsma, Jurrit. Bergsma Doctors & Patients. LC 96-53893. 200p. 1997. pap. text 37.00 (*0-7923-4395-6*) Kluwer Academic.

***Bergsma, Jurrit & Thomasma, David C.** Autonomy & Clinical Medicine - Renewing the Health Professional Relation with the Patient. 224p. 2000. 96.00 (*0-7923-6207-1*) Kluwer Academic.

Bergsma, Otto K. Three Dimensional Simulation of Fabric Draping: Development & Application. (Illus.). xvi, 137p. (Orig.). 1996. pap. 52.50 (*90-407-1351-0*, Pub. by Delft U Pr) Coronet Bks.

Bergsman, Michael, ed. see Werner, Jeffrey & Mustain, Chris.

Bergsman, Paul. Controlling the World with Your PC. LC 94-75298. (Illus.). 268p. 1994. pap. 35.00 (*1-878707-15-9*) LLH Tech Pub.

Bergsmo, Morten, ed. Studying the Writings of Shoghi Effendi. 216p. (Orig.). 1991. pap. 15.95 (*0-85398-336-4*) G Ronald Pub.

Bergson, Abram. Essays in Normative Economics. LC 66-13177. (Illus.). 266p. 1966. reprint ed. pap. 82.50 (*0-7837-1671-0*, 205720300024) Bks Demand.

— Productivity & the Social System - The U. S. S. R. & the West. LC 77-15493. 288p. 1978. 37.95 (*0-674-71165-3*) HUP.

Bergson, Abram. Soviet National Income & Product in 1937. LC 75-104222. 156p. 1970. reprint ed. lib. bdg. 59.50 (*0-8371-3332-7*, BESO, Greenwood Pr) Greenwood.

Bergson, Abram. Structure of Soviet Wages: A Study in Socialist Economics. LC 44-1242. (Economic Studies: No. 76). 271p. 1944. 20.00 (*0-674-84480-7*) HUP.

— Welfare, Planning, & Employment: Selected Essays in Economic Theory. 288p. 1982. 39.50 (*0-262-02175-7*) MIT Pr.

Bergson, Abram & Levine, Herbert S., eds. The Soviet Economy Towards the Year 2000. 496p. (Orig.). (C). 1985. text 55.00 (*0-04-335045-3*); pap. text 24.95 (*0-04-335053-4*) Routledge.

Bergson, Anika. Zone Therapy. 1989. mass mkt. 3.95 (*1-55817-208-4*, Pinncle Kensgtn) Kensgtn Pub Corp.

Bergson, Henri. Creative Evolution. Mitchell, Arthur, tr. from FRE. LC 97-46431. 1998. pap. 12.95 (*0-486-40036-0*) Dover.

— Creative Evolution. Mitchell, Arthur, tr. LC 74-28524. 453p. 1975. reprint ed. lib. bdg. 65.00 (*0-8371-7917-3*, BECEV, Greenwood Pr) Greenwood.

— Creative Evolution. Mitchell, Arthur, tr. LC 83-19859. 460p. 1984. reprint ed. pap. text 29.00 (*0-8191-3553-4*) U Pr of Amer.

— Creative Mind. Andison, Mabelle L., tr. LC 68-19264. 307p. 1968. reprint ed. lib. bdg. 65.00 (*0-8371-0310-X*, BECM, Greenwood Pr) Greenwood.

***Bergson, Henri.** The Creative Mind: An Introduction to Metaphysics. 254p. 1999. reprint ed. 28.95 (*0-7351-0072-1*) Replica Bks.

Bergson, Henri. Les Deux Sources de la Morale et de la Religion. (FRE.). 1976. pap. 20.95 (*0-8288-9077-3*) Fr & Eur.

***Bergson, Henri.** Duration & Simultaneity: Bergson & the Einsteinian Universe. Jacobson, Leon, tr. 224p. 2000. pap. 35.00 (*1-903083-01-X*, Pub. by Clinamen Pr) Paul & Co Pubs.

Bergson, Henri. Duree et Simultaneite. (FRE.). 1968. pap. 35.95 (*0-8288-9072-2*) Fr & Eur.

— Ecrits et Paroles. (FRE.). 1959. pap. 34.95 (*0-8288-9073-0*) Fr & Eur.

— L' Energie Spirituelle. (FRE.). pap. 18.95 (*0-8288-9075-7*, 2130430341) Fr & Eur.

— Essai sur les Donnees Immediates de la Conscience. (FRE.). pap. 18.95 (*0-8288-9074-9*, 2130419593) Fr & Eur.

— L' Evolution Creatrice. (FRE.). 24.95 (*0-8288-9076-5*, 2130426948) Fr & Eur.

— An Introduction to Metaphysics. Hulme, T. E., tr. from FRE. LC 99-28080. 64p. (C). 1999. reprint ed. pap. text 6.95 (*0-87220-474-X*); reprint ed. lib. bdg. 29.95 (*0-87220-475-8*) Hackett Pub.

— Introduction to Metaphysics. 98p. 1998. reprint ed. pap. 16.95 (*0-7661-0213-0*) Kessinger Pub.

— Laughter: An Essay on the Meaning of the Comic. Brereton, Cloudesley & Rothwell, Fred, trs. (Green Integer Bks.: No. 14). 184p. 1999. reprint ed. pap. 11.95 (*1-892295-02-4*, Pub. by Green Integer) Consort Bk Sales.

— Matiere et Memoire: Essai sur la Relation du Corps a l'Esprit. 3rd ed. (FRE.). 1990. pap. 18.95 (*0-7859-3013-2*) Fr & Eur.

— Matter & Memory. Paul, N. M. & Palmer, W. S., trs. from FRE. LC 87-37124. 284p. 1988. 28.95 (*0-942299-04-3*); pap. 14.95 (*0-942299-05-1*) Zone Bks.

— Memoire et Vie. (FRE.). 1975. pap. 24.95 (*0-8288-9078-1*) Fr & Eur.

— Mind-Energy, Lectures & Essays. Carr, H. Wildon, tr. from FRE. LC 74-28922. 262p. 1975. reprint ed. lib. bdg. 59.50 (*0-8371-7931-9*, BEEN, Greenwood Pr) Greenwood.

— Oeuvres. 125.00 (*0-685-37204-9*) Fr & Eur.

— La Pensee et la Mouvant. 4th ed. (FRE.). 1993. pap. 28.95 (*0-7859-3447-2*) Fr & Eur.

— La Pensee et le Mouvement. 39.95 (*0-685-37210-3*) Fr & Eur.

— Le Rire: Essai sur la Signification du Comique. 6th ed. (FRE.). 1991. pap. 15.95 (*0-7859-3017-5*) Fr & Eur.

— Time & Free Will: An Essay on the Immediate Data of Consciousness. 277p. 1996. reprint ed. pap. 24.95 (*1-56459-593-5*) Kessinger Pub.

— The Two Sources of Morality & Religion. Audra, R. Ashley et al, trs. from FRE. LC 77-89762. 1977. pap. text 16.50 (*0-268-01835-9*) U of Notre Dame Pr.

— The Two Sources of Morality & Religion. LC 74-10373. 308p. 1975. reprint ed. lib. bdg. 38.50 (*0-8371-7679-4*, BETS, Greenwood Pr) Greenwood.

Bergson, Henry. Laughter. 1996. 26.00 (*0-8446-1666-4*) Peter Smith.

Bergson, Peter A. Spaces for Children: Learning-Play Structures for Home & School. (Illus.). 55p. (Orig.). 1984. pap. 8.00 (*0-9606434-1-9*) Open Connections.

Bergson, Peter A., jt. auth. see Shilcock, Susan D.

Bergsson, Gudbergur. The Swan. Scudder, Bernard, tr. LC 97-179778. 152p. 1998. 14.95 (*1-899197-35-4*) Dufour.

Bergstein, jt. auth. see O'Brien.

***Bergstein, Mary & Nanni.** The Sculpture of Nanni Di Banco. LC 99-47383. 2000. text 79.50 (*0-691-00982-1*, Pub. by Princeton U Pr) Cal Prin Full Svc.

***Bergstein, Mary, et al.** Image & Enterprise: The Photographs of Adolphe Braun. 159p. 1999. pap. 29.95 (*0-911517-66-9*) Thames Hudson.

Bergstein, Mary, ed. see Bright, Deborah, et al.

Bergstein, Mickey. Penn State Sports Stories & More. Hope, John, ed. LC 98-65584. (Illus.). xvi, 300p. 1998. pap. 19.95 (*1-879441-45-4*) RB Bks.

Bergsten, C. Fred. America in the World Economy: A Strategy for the 1990s. LC 88-39852. 218p. (Orig.). (C). 1988. pap. 13.95 (*0-88132-082-X*) Inst Intl Eco.

— Approaches to Greater Flexibility of Exchange Rates: The Burgenstock Papers, Arranged by C. Fred Bergsten, George N. Halm, Fritz Machlup, Robert V. Roosa. Halm, George N., ed. LC 78-111633. 450p. 1970. reprint ed. pap. 139.50 (*0-7837-9377-4*, 206012100004) Bks Demand.

— Dilemmas of the Dollar: The Economics & Politics of United States International Monetary Policy. 2nd rev. ed. LC 96-7104. 614p. (C). (gr. 13). 1996. pap. text 51.95 (*0-87332-600-8*) M E Sharpe.

— The Korea-United States Economic Relationship. LC 96-51871. 1997. pap. 15.00 (*0-88132-240-7*) Inst Intl Eco.

— El Sistema Monetario Internacional en los Proximos Veinticinco Anos: Simposio Celebrado en la Universidad de Basilea con Ocasion de las Bodas de Plata de las Conferencias Per Jacobsson, 12 de Junio de 1988. LC HG3881.B4648. (Conferencia Per Jacobsson Ser.: Vol. 1988). (SPA.). 62p. reprint ed. pap. 30.00 (*0-608-08779-3*, 206941800004) Bks Demand.

— Whither APEC? Progress to Date & the Agenda for the Future. LC 97-19897. 1997. pap. 16.95 (*0-88132-248-2*) Inst Intl Eco.

Bergsten, C. Fred, ed. Pacific Dynamism & the International Economic System. LC 92-37824. (Illus.). 402p. (Orig.). (C). 1993. pap. text 25.00 (*0-88132-196-6*) Inst Intl Eco.

Bergsten, C. Fred & Cline, William R. Trade Policy of the 1980's. LC 82-18746. (Policy Analyses in International Economics Ser.: No. 3). 84p. reprint ed. pap. 30.00 (*0-608-12189-4*, 202479300038) Bks Demand.

— The United States-Japan Economic Problem. 2nd ed. LC 86-83417. (Policy Analyses in International Economics Ser.: No. 13). 182p. reprint ed. pap. 56.50 (*0-7837-6142-2*, 204349900009) Bks Demand.

Bergsten, C. Fred & Henning, C. Randall. Global Economic Leadership & the Group of Seven. LC 95-17295. 192p. (C). 1996. pap. 25.00 (*0-88132-218-0*) Inst Intl Eco. Sluggish global growth, frequent currency crises & huge trade imbalances all reveal the failure of the Group Seven industrial nations to provide effective leadership of the world economy. The G-7 has played this role in the past & must do so again to assure global prosperity. Part of the G-7's decline is due to continuing policy differences among the United States. Germany & Japan The bigger problem, however, is a new "consensus for the inaction "based on fears of trying to counter the huge flows of international private capital, the existence of large budget deficits & the resistance of central banks to coordination by anyone. The study offers a comprehensive analysis of all these changes in the world economy & reaches optimistic reading of the prospects for effective G-7 leadership. It proposes an action program that includes reforming the exchange rate regime, instituting an early warning system to prevent new monetary crises, augmenting the resources of the IMF to deal with private capital flows & institutional reform of the G-7 itself. *Publisher Paid Annotation.*

Bergsten, C. Fred & Krause, Lawrence B., eds. World Politics & International Economics. LC 75-15684. 373p. reprint ed. pap. 115.70 (*0-608-12092-8*, 202412800035) Bks Demand.

Bergsten, C. Fred & Noland, Marcus. Reconcilable Differences? United States - Japan Economic Conflict. LC 93-13689. 271p. 1993. pap. 19.95 (*0-88132-129-X*) Inst Intl Eco.

Bergsten, C. Fred, et al. American Multinationals & American Interests. LC 77-91786. 549p. reprint ed. pap. 170.20 (*0-8357-5381-6*, 203000500067) Bks Demand.

–Avoiding the Apocalypse: Economics of Korean Unification: The Future of the Two Koreas. 350p. 2000. pap. 22.00 (*0-88132-278-4*) Inst Intl Eco. On the Korean peninsula one of the greatest success stories of the post-war era confronts a famine-ridden & possibly nuclear-armed - totalitarian state. The stakes are extradorinarily high for both North & South Korea & for countries such as the United States that have a direct stake in these affairs. This book examines the situation in the two Koreas in terms of three crises: the nuclear confrontation between the United State & North Korea, the North Korean famine & the South Korean financial crisis. Out of these, the future of the peninsula is then explored under three alternative scenarios: successful reform in North Korea, collapse & absorption (as happened in Germany) & "muddling through" in which North Korea, supported by foreign powers makes ad hoc, regime-preserving reforms that fall short of fundamental transformation. *Publisher Paid Annotation.*

— Conditions for Partnership in International Economic Management. (Triangle Papers: No. 32). 1986. pap. 6.00 (*0-930503-01-5*) Trilateral Comm.

— From Rambouillet to Versailles: A Symposium. LC 82-23424. (Essays in International Finance Ser.: No. 149). 48p. 1982. pap. text 10.00 (*0-88165-056-0*) Princeton U Int Finan Econ.

— The International Monetary System: The Next Twenty-Five Years - Symposium at Basle University to Commemorate Twenty-Five Years of Per Jacobsson Lectures, June 12, 1988. LC HG3881.B4648. (Per Jacobsson Lecture Ser.: Vol. 1988). 57p. reprint ed. pap. 30.00 (*0-608-08777-7*, 206941600004) Bks Demand.

— The Reform of International Institutions. (Triangle Papers: No. 11). 1976. pap. 15.00 (*0-318-02786-0*); pap. 6.00 (*0-930503-52-X*) Trilateral Comm.

— Le Systeme Monetaire International: Les Vingt-Cinq Prochaines Annees: Symposium Organise a l'Universite de Basle en l'Honneur du Vingt-Cinquieme Anniversaire des Conferences Per Jacobsson, 12 Juin 1988. LC HG3881.B4658. (Conferences Per Jacobsson Ser.: Vol. 1988). (FRE.). 66p. reprint ed. pap. 30.00 (*0-608-08778-5*, 206941700004) Bks Demand.

Bergsten, Eric. International Commercial Arbitration, 5 vols. LC 74-17320. 1980. ring bd. 650.00 (*0-379-00266-3*) Oceana.

Bergsten, Eric E. International Commercial Arbitration: Pacific Rim, Vol. 1. LC 97-39949. 1997. ring bd. 180.00 (*0-379-10157-2*) Oceana.

Bergsten, Gunilla U. Thomas Mann's "Doctor Faustus" The Sources & Structure of the Novel. LC 69-14483. 254p. reprint ed. pap. 78.80 (*0-608-14353-7*, 202003100016) Bks Demand.

Bergsten, Martha C. The State of the Child in Pennsylvania: A 1999 Guide to Child Well Being in Pennsylvania. 4th ed. Steketee, Martha W. & McCormick, M. Diane, eds. 324p. 1999. pap. 33.00 (*0-9645008-4-1*) PA Ptnership.

Bergsten, Martha C. & Steketee, Martha W. The State of the Child in Pennsylvania: A 1997 Guide to Child Well-Being in Pennsylvania Counties. 3rd ed. (Fact Book Ser.). 256p. 1997. pap. 29.00 (*0-9645008-3-3*) PA Ptnership.

Bergstra, J. A. & Feijs, Loe M., eds. Algebraic Methods II: Theory, Tools & Applications. (Lecture Notes in Computer Science Ser.: Vol. 490). vi, 434p. 1991. 44.95 (*0-387-53912-3*) Spr-Verlag.

Bergstra, J. A., jt. ed. see Wirsing, M.

Bergstralh, Jay T., et al, eds. Uranus. LC 90-21185. (Space Science Ser.). 1076p. (YA). 1991. 84.00 (*0-8165-1208-6*) U of Ariz Pr.

Bergstrand, Bengt-Goran & Oldberg, Ingmar, eds. Stability in Central Europe: Weakening & Strengthening Factors. (Illus.). 157p. (C). 1996. reprint ed. pap. text 35.00 (*0-7881-3052-8*) DIANE Pub.

Bergstrand, Jeffrey H. NYT Going Global: 25 Keys to International Operations. Redburn, Tom, ed. LC 99-27693. 104p. 1999. pap. 12.95 (*0-86730-779-X*) Lebhar Friedman.

Bergstrand, Jeffrey H., ed. see Cosimano, T. F., et al.

Bergstrand, Simon & Rigas, Doganis. The Impact of Soviet Shipping. (Illus.). 220p. 1987. text 70.00 (*0-04-338143-X*) Routledge.

Bergstrasser, Gotthelf & Daniels, Peter T. Introduction to the Semitic Languages: Text Specimens & Grammatical Sketches. rev. ed. LC 82-11588. xxiii, 276p. (C). 1995. reprint ed. pap. text 47.50 (*0-931464-17-X*) Eisenbrauns.

Bergstrasser, Ludwig. Der Politische Katholizismus. (Deutsche Staatsgedanke Ser.: Bd. III, 1,2). (GER.). 700p. 1976. reprint ed. write for info. (*3-487-05897-9*) G Olms Pubs.

Bergstresser, Ralph. Dr. Nikola Tesla: The Forgotten Super Man of Our Industrial Age. 16p. 1996. reprint ed. spiral bd. 8.00 (*0-7873-0094-2*) Hlth Research.

Bergstrom. English-Swedish, Swedish-English Dictionary. (ENG & SWE.). 744p. 1993. 26.95 (*0-7859-7461-X*, 9127715159) Fr & Eur.

— Experm Economics. 2nd ed. 1999. 17.00 (*0-07-236932-9*) McGraw.

Bergstrom, Abram R., et al, eds. Stability & Inflation: A Volume of Essays to Honour the Memory of A. W. H. Phillips. LC 77-4420. (Illus.). 341p. reprint ed. pap. 105.80 (*0-8357-4318-7*, 203711700007) Bks Demand.

Bergstrom, Alan J., ed. see Linn, Carl E.

Bergstrom, Bengt. Theories of Stress & Performance: A Short Overview. 40p. (Orig.). (C). 1992. pap. text 20.00 (*1-56806-046-7*) DIANE Pub.

***Bergstrom, Christer & Mikhailov, Andrey.** Operation Barbarossa, 1941. (Black Cross/Red Star Ser.: Vol. I). (Illus.). 3340p. 2000. 39.95 (*0-935553-48-7*, Pub. by Pacifica Military) Motorbooks Intl.

Bergstrom, Corinne. Losing Your Best Friend. LC 79-20622. (Illus.). 32p. (J). (ps-3). 1980. 16.95 (*0-87705-471-1*, Kluwer Acad Hman Sci) Kluwer Academic.

Bergstrom, Elaine. Blood Alone. 336p. 1994. mass mkt. 4.99 (*0-441-00088-6*) Ace Bks.

***Bergstrom, Elaine.** Blood to Blood. 2000. mass mkt. 5.99 (*0-441-00774-0*) Ace Bks.

Bergstrom, Elaine. The Door Through Washington Square. 1998. mass mkt. 6.99 (*0-441-00544-6*) Ace Bks.

***Bergstrom, Elaine.** Mina. 2000. mass mkt. 5.99 (*0-441-00662-0*) Ace Bks.

Bergstrom, Elaine. Shattered Glass. 384p. 1994. reprint ed. mass mkt. 4.99 (*0-441-00067-3*) Ace Bks.

Bergstrom, G., jt. auth. see Svanborg, A.

Bergstrom, Gunnel, jt. ed. see Englund, Claes.

Bergstrom, Heidi, et al, contrib. by. Vocational Education & Training in Finland. LC 98-125532. 1997. 25.00 (*92-828-1912-4*, HX-06-97-577ENC, Pub. by Comm Europ Commun) Bernan Associates.

Bergstrom, I., et al, eds. Nobel Symposium, '91: Trapped Charged Particles & Related Fundamental Physics, Lysekil, Sweden 18 - 26 August 1994. 400p. 1996. text 98.00 (*981-02-2481-8*, Po-P2952) World Scientific Pub.

Bergstrom, Inger. Grammatical Correctness & Communicative Ability: A Performance Analysis of the Written & Spoken English of Swedish Learners. (Umea Studies in the Humanities: No. 81). 223p. (Orig.). 1987. pap. text 36.50 (*91-7174-285-9*) Coronet Bks.

Bergstrom, Ingvar. Dutch Still-Life Painting in the Seventeenth Century. LC 81-81718. (Illus.). xxxii, 330p. 1982. reprint ed. lib. bdg. 60.00 (*0-87817-279-3*) Hacker.

Bergstrom, Janet. Cinema & Psychoanalysis: Parallel Histories. LC 98-18190. 1999. 45.00 (*0-520-20747-5*, Pub. by U CA Pr) Cal Prin Full Svc.

— Cinema & Psychoanalysis: Parallel Histories. LC 98-18190. 305p. 1999. 17.95 (*0-520-20748-3*, Pub. by U CA Pr) Cal Prin Full Svc.

Bergstrom, Joan M. The Best Summer Ever: A Parents' Guide. LC 94-42376. 112p. (J). (gr. 1-7). 1995. pap. 9.95 (*1-883672-22-8*) Tricycle Pr.

Bergstrom, K. G. An Odyssey to Freedom: Four Themes in Colin Wilson's Novels. 160p. (Orig.). 1983. pap. text 30.00 (*91-554-1405-2*) Coronet Bks.

Bergstrom, Ken, et al. Mentoring: A Resource & Training Guide for Educators. 400p. (C). 1993. 98.00 (*1-878234-06-4*) Reg Lab Educ IOT NE Isls.

Bergstrom, Kim, jt. auth. see Bergstrom, Leslie.

***Bergstrom, L.** Cosmology & Particle Astrophysics. LC 99-193517. 356p. 1999. pap. 64.95 (*0-471-97042-5*) Wiley.

Bergstrom, L. The Moonshell. large type ed. (Orig.). 1990. pap. 16.99 (*0-7089-6914-3*, Linford) Ulverscroft.

***Bergstrom, L. & Goobar, Ariel.** Cosmology & Particle Astrophysics. LC 99-193517. (Wiley-Praxis Series in Astronomy & Astrophysics). (Illus.). 356p. 1999. write for info. (*0-471-97041-7*) Wiley.

Bergstrom, L. & Kirchmann, H., eds. Carbon & Nutrient Dynamics in Natural & Agricultural Tropical Ecosystems. (A CAB International Publication). (Illus.). 336p. 1998. text 90.00 (*0-85199-218-8*) OUP.

Bergstrom, L., jt. ed. see Clarholm, M.

Bergstrom, Len V., jt. ed. see Rosenberg, Marie B.

Bergstrom, Lennourt, jt. ed. see Pugh, Robert J.

Bergstrom, Leslie. Scenic San Diego. (Illus.). 68p. 1990. pap. 4.95 (*0-9612668-4-8*) Talk Town.

— Trips on Wheels. (Illus.). 128p. 1985. pap. 8.50 (*0-9612668-1-3*) Talk Town.

Bergstrom, Leslie & Bergstrom, Kim. Trips on Twos. (Illus.). 72p. 1987. pap. 4.95 (*0-9612668-2-1*) Talk Town.

Bergstrom, Louise. Midsummer Bride. 1980. pap. 1.50 (*0-373-58014-2*) Harlequin Bks.

Bergstrom, M. Swedish/English-English/Swedish Dictionary. (ENG & SWE.). 1993. 40.50 (*0-7859-9737-7*) Fr & Eur.

Bergstrom, M., et al. Swedish-English - English-Swedish Dictionary. 744p. 1993. 40.50 (*91-27-71515-9*, Pub. by Natur och Kulturs) IBD Ltd.

Bergstrom, Nancy. Pressure Ulcer Treatment 15: Reference for Clinicians. 27p. 1994. pap. 32.00 (*0-16-061538-0*) USGPO.

Bergstrom, Nancy. Treatment of Pressure Ulcers: Clinical Prctice Guideline. (Illus.). 154p. (C). 1997. reprint ed. pap. text 40.00 (*0-7881-2418-8*) DIANE Pub.

Bergstrom, Nancy. Treatment of Pressure Ulcers 15: Clinical Practice. 164p. 1995. per. 7.00 (*0-16-061537-2*) USGPO.

Bergstrom, Randolph E. Courting Danger: Injury & Law in New York City, 1870-1910. LC 92-52744. 232p. (C). 1992. text 39.95 (0-8014-2607-3) Cornell U Pr.

*Bergstrom, Stefan. Between Real & Unreal: A Thematic Study of E.T.A. Hoffmann's "Die Serapionsbruder" LC 98-30525. (Studies on Themes & Motifs in Literature: Vol. 49). 152p. (C). 2000. 40.95 (0-8204-4275-5) P Lang Pubng.

Bergstrom, Stig M., ed. see Geological Society of America Conodont Biostratigr.

*Bergstrom, Ted & Varian, Hal R. Workouts in Intermediate Microeconomics. 1999. pap. 17.00 (0-393-97371-9) Norton.

*Bergstrom, Theodore C. & Miller, John H. Experiments with Economic Principles: Microeconomics. 2nd ed. LC 99-35213. (Illus.). 2000. write for info. (0-07-229518-X) McGrw-H Hghr Educ.

Bergstrom, Villy, ed. Government & Growth. LC HD87.G69 1997. (FIEF Studies in Labor Markets & Economic Policy: No. 6). (Illus.). 274p. 1998. text 67.00 (0-19-829037-3) OUP.

Bergstrom, Villy & Vredin, Anders, eds. Measuring & Interpreting Business Cycles. LC 94-13283. (FIEF Studies in Labor Markets & Economic Policy). (Illus.). 282p. 1995. text 55.00 (0-19-828859-X, Clarendon Pr) OUP.

Bergsund, Marika F., jt. auth. see Dwyer, John P.

Bergt, Caolyn S. & Rathmann, Rodney L., eds. Integrating the Faith: Teacher's Guide, Preschool-Kindergarten. LC 97-202911. 1997. per. 17.95 (0-570-09807-6, 22-2721) Concordia.

Bergt, Carolyn. Savior Is Here - Listen & Cheer: Christmas. 1997. pap. text 22.00 (0-570-05519-9, 54-0075) Concordia.

*Bergt, Carolyn. The Savior Is Here! Listen & Cheer. (Small Big Bks.). (Illus.). 16p. (J). (ps-3). 1998. pap. 2.49 (0-570-05541-5, 54-0078GJ) Concordia.

— Something Wonderful. LC 99-182982. (Small Big Bks.). (Illus.). 16p. (J). (ps-1). 1998. pap. 2.49 (0-570-05542-3, 54-0079GJ) Concordia.

— What Does This Mean? (Illus.). (J). 1999. pap. 2.49 (0-570-05546-6) Concordia.

Bergt, Carolyn & Mitter, Kathy. The Adventures of Martin Luther. 16p. pap. 2.49 (0-570-00661-9) Concordia.

Bergt, Carolyn S. & Rathmann, Rodney L., eds. Integrating the Faith Vol. 2: Teacher's Guide, Grades 1 & 2. LC 97-202911. 1997. per. 17.95 (0-570-09808-4, 22-2722) Concordia.

— Integrating the Faith Vol. 3: Teacher's Guide, Grades 3 & 4. LC 97-202911. 1997. per. 17.95 (0-570-09809-2, 22-2723) Concordia.

— Integrating the Faith Vol. 4: Teacher's Guide, Grades 5 & 6. LC 97-202911. 1997. per. 17.95 (0-570-09810-6, 22-2724) Concordia.

— Integrating the Faith Vol. 5: Teacher's Guide, Grades 7 & 8. LC 97-202911. 1997. per. 17.95 (0-570-09811-4, 22-2725) Concordia.

— Integrating the Faith Vol. 6: Administrator's Guide. LC 97-202911. 1997. per. 17.95 (0-570-09812-2, 22-2726) Concordia.

Bergter, Annette. Das Kapitel Inna-Wa-Ahawatuha Aus Dem "Manhag Assalik" des Grammatikers Abu Hayyan Al-Garnati (1256-1344) (Arabistische Texte und Studien: Vol. 2). 201p. 1988. 35.00 (3-487-09019-8) G Olms Pubs.

Bergthold, Judith C. Prehistoric Settlement & Trade Models in the Santa Clara Valley, California. x, 328p. (C). 1985. reprint ed. pap. text 35.63 (1-55567-017-2) Coyote Press.

Bergthold, Linda A. Purchasing Power in Health: Business, the State, & Health Care Politics. LC 89-37778. 264p. (C). 1990. text 40.00 (0-8135-1487-8) Rutgers U Pr.

Bergtsson, L., et al, eds. Dynamic Meteorology: Data Assimilation Methods (Proceedings) (Applied Mathematical Sciences Ser.: Vol. 36). (Illus.). 330p. 1981. 72.95 (0-387-90632-0) Spr-Verlag.

Berguer, Ramon & Bauer, Raymond B., eds. Vertebrobasilar Arterial Occlusive Disease: Medical & Surgical Management. LC 83-22900. 352p. 1984. reprint ed. pap. 109.20 (0-608-00432-4, 206114700007) Bks Demand.

Berguer, Ramon & Caplan, Louis R. Vertebrobasilar Arterial Disease. (Illus.). 299p. 1992. 75.00 (0-942219-22-8) Quality Med Pub.

Berguer, Ramon & Kieffer, Edouard. Surgery of the Arteries to the Head. (Illus.). 236p. 1992. 198.00 (0-387-97748-1) Spr-Verlag.

Berguer, Ramon & Weiss, Harold, eds. The Carotid & the Eye. LC 85-6336. 223p. 1985. 49.95 (0-275-91332-5, C1332, Praeger Pubs) Greenwood.

Berguer, Ramon, jt. ed. see Branchereau, Alain.

Bergum, Gerald E., ed. Applications of Fibonacci Numbers: Proceedings of the Fifth International Conference on Fibonacci Numbers & Their Applications, Held at the University of St. Andrews, Scotland, July 20-24, 1992, Vol. 5. (DIVS-Diverse Ser.). 660p. (C). 1993. text 285.50 (0-7923-2491-9) Kluwer Academic.

— Applications of Fibonacci Numbers Vol. 6: Proceedings of 'The Sixth International Research Conference on Fibonacci Numbers & Their Applications,' Washington State University, Pullman, WA, USA, July 18-22, 1994. 560p. (C). 1996. text 254.00 (0-7923-3956-8) Kluwer Academic.

Bergum, Gerald E., et al, eds. Applications of Fibonacci Numbers, Vol. 3. (C). 1989. text 207.50 (0-7923-0523-X) Kluwer Academic.

— Applications of Fibonacci Numbers, Vol. 4. (C). 1991. text 175.00 (0-7923-1309-7) Kluwer Academic.

— Fibonacci Numbers & Their Applications. 1986. text 166.50 (90-277-2234-X) Kluwer Academic.

Bergum, Steve, jt. auth. see Blanchette, John.

Bergum, Vangie. A Child on Her Mind: The Experience of Becoming a Mother. LC 96-9032. 208p. 1997. 59.95 (0-89789-446-4, Bergin & Garvey); pap. 18.95 (0-89789-447-2, Bergin & Garvey) Greenwood.

*Bergunder, Michael. Die Sudindische Pfingstbewegung im 20. Jahrhundert: Eine Historische und Systematische Untersuchung. XIV, 382p. 1999. 56.95 (3-631-33771-X) P Lang Pubng.

Berguson, Johnny. The Comprehensive Guide to Cassette Ministry. 258p. 19.97 incl. audio (1-883906-12-1) Kingdom Prods.

Bergvall, Ake. The Enabling of Judgment: Sir Philip Sidney & the Education of the Reader. (Studia Anglistica Upsaliensia Ser.: No. 70). 137p. (Orig.). 1989. pap. 37.50 (91-554-2353-1) Coronet Bks.

Bergvall, Caroline, tr. see Brossard, Nicole.

Bergvall, Victioria L., et al. Rethinking Language & Gender Research: Theory & Practice. LC 96-20024. (Real Language Ser.). 1996. pap. text 28.88 (0-582-26573-8) Longman.

Bergveld, P. Electromedical Instrumentation: A Guide for Medical Personnel. LC 77-85711. (Techniques of Measurement in Medicine Ser.: No. 2). 144p. reprint ed. pap. 41.10 (0-608-16416-X, 2026332) Bks Demand.

Bergveld, P., jt. auth. see Berg.

Bergwall. AutoCAD Release 10. (CAD/CAM Ser.). 1990. 350.00 (0-8273-4168-7, VNR) Wiley.

— Parallel Circuits. (Electronic Technology Ser.). 1991. 95.00 (0-8273-4818-5, VNR) Wiley.

— Series - Parallel Circuits. (Electronic Technology Ser.). 1991. 95.00 (0-8273-4819-3, VNR) Wiley.

— Symbols, Diagrams & Circuits. (Electronic Technology Ser.). 1991. 85.00 (0-8273-4808-8, VNR) Wiley.

Bergwall, Bruce, et al, adapted by. Basic Electricity: Direct Current. (Illus.). 34p. (YA). (gr. 10 up). 1987. pap., wbk. ed. 7.00 (0-614-22217-6, E12) Bergwall.

Bergwall, David F., jt. ed. see Rosoff, Arnold J.

Bergwall Productions Staff. A47 Automotive Test Equipment Package. 405.00 (0-8064-1487-1, Pub. by Delmar) Thomson Learn.

— C50 Mentoring Explained Package. 791.95 (0-8064-1602-5, Pub. by Delmar) Thomson Learn.

— DF52 Basic ARC Welding Software. 473.95 (0-8064-1367-0, Pub. by Delmar) Thomson Learn.

— First Step for Autocad R14 Packages (10 Tips & Lesson Set) 1425.95 (0-8064-1654-8, Pub. by Delmar) Thomson Learn.

— F52 Basic Welding Package. 473.95 (0-8064-1362-X, Pub. by Delmar) Thomson Learn.

— W29 Compound Miter Saw. 140.95 (0-8064-1726-9, Pub. by Delmar) Thomson Learn.

Bergwall Productions Staff & Collins, Paula. E41 Troubleshooting PC Hardware Package. 480.00 (0-8064-1625-4, Pub. by Delmar) Thomson Learn.

Bergwall Productions Staff & Young, Kasey. DA41 Basic Automotive Jobs Software. 485.00 (0-8064-1646-7, Pub. by Delmar) Thomson Learn.

— F53 Tig Welding Series Package. 473.95 (0-8064-1592-4, Pub. by Delmar) Thomson Learn.

Berhardt, R. Encyclopedia of Public International Law. 2000. 462.50 (0-444-86248-X) Elsevier.

Berhaut, M. Caillebotte: The Impressionist. (Rhythem & Color Two Ser.). 1970. 9.95 (0-8288-9517-1) Fr & Eur.

Berheide, Catherine W., jt. ed. see Chow, Esther N.

Berhens, D., ed. see Eckermann, Reiner, et al.

Berhold, Marvin. Decision Systems Restructure Management. LC 96-90898. Date not set. pap. 19.95 (0-9655134-7-5) Tridec.

Berhow, Mark A., et al. Citrus Limonoids: Functional Chemicals in Agriculture & Foods. (ACS Symposium Ser.: No. 758). 100.00 (0-8412-3651-8, Pub. by Am Chemical) OUP.

Beri, B. P. Law of Marriage & Divorce in India. 750p. (C). 1989. 300.00 (0-7855-1411-2) St Mut.

Beri, B. P., ed. Commentaries on Dowry Prohibition Act, 1961: Together with Guroodas Banerjee's Tagore Law Lectures on Law of Streedhan, 1988 with Supplement. (C). 1990. 90.00 (0-7855-5582-X) St Mut.

Beri, Christine. The Classic Art of Viennese Pastry: From Strudel to Sachetorte - More Than 100 Traditional Recipes. LC 97-17964. (Culinary Arts Ser.). (Illus.). 350p. (C). 1998. 39.95 (0-442-02302-2, VNR) Wiley.

Beri, K. K. History & Culture of South East Asia (Modern) (C). 1994. write for info. (81-207-1650-7) Sterling Pubs.

Berik, Gunser. Women Carpet Weavers in Rural Turkey: Patterns of Employment, Earnings & Status. (Women, Work & Development Ser.: No. 15). xiii, 112p. (Orig.). 1987. pap. 18.00 (92-2-106004-7) Intl Labour Office.

Berindei, Mihnea & Veinstein, Gilles. L' Empire Ottoman et les Pays Roumains, 1544-1545: Etude et Document. Pritsak, Omeljan & Guillou, Andre, eds. LC 87-81953. (Studies in Ottoman Documents Pertaining to the Ukraine & the Black Sea Countries). (Illus.). 375p. 1988. pap. text 34.00 (0-916458-23-7) Harvard Ukrainian.

Bering, Henrik. Helmut Kohl: The Man Who Reunited Germany, Rebuilt Europe, & Thwarted the Soviet Empire. LC 99-19324. 262p. 1999. 27.95 (0-89526-325-4, Pub. by Regnery Pub) Natl Bk Netwk.

— Outpost Berlin: The History of the American Military Forces in Berlin, 1945-1994. LC 95-11172. (Illus.). 200p. 1995. pap. 16.95 (1-883695-07-4) Edition Q.

Bering, Rudiger. Musicals. (Crash Course Ser.). (Illus.). 192p. 1998. pap. 13.95 (0-7641-0436-5) Barron.

Beringer, J. A. Hans Thoma: Complete Etchings. rev. ed. (ENG & GER., Illus.). 304p. 1991. 150.00 (1-55660-076-3) A Wofsy Fine Arts.

Beringer, Richard E. Historical Analysis: Contemporary Approaches to Clio's Craft. LC 84-23368. 338p. (C). 1986. reprint ed. 31.50 (0-89874-751-1) Krieger.

Beringer, Richard E., et al. The Elements of Confederate Defeat: Nationalism, War Aims, & Religion. LC 88-17311. 272p. 1989. 15.00 (0-8203-1076-X) U of Ga Pr.

— Why the South Lost the Civil War. LC 85-8638. (History Book Club Selection). (Illus.). 608p. (C). 1986. text 34.95 (0-8203-0815-3) U of Ga Pr.

— Why the South Lost the Civil War. LC 85-8638. (Brown Thrasher Bks.). (Illus.). 608p. (C). 1991. pap. 24.95 (0-8203-1396-3) U of Ga Pr.

Beringer, Richard E., jt. auth. see Alexander, Thomas B.

Beringer, Robert A. Bright Intervals: 40 Brief Worship Services & Meditations for Any Occasion. LC 98-49322. 132p. 1999. pap. 12.50 (0-7880-1337-8) CSS OH.

— Turning Points: Sermons for Lent & Easter. LC 94-33074. 86p. (Orig.). 1995. pap. 9.50 (0-7880-0283-X) CSS OH.

Beringer, Theodore, jt. auth. see Borysenko, Myrin.

Berins, Jane & Samuels, Madilyn. New Orleans Q & A: Trivial Questions, Terrific Answers. (Illus.). 96p. (Orig.). 1985. pap. 5.95 (0-9614929-0-2) Royale LA.

Berinstain, Valerie. Great Carpets of the World. LC 96-16065. (Illus.). 360p. 1996. text 85.00 (0-86565-980-X) Vendome.

— India & the Mughal Dynasty. LC 97-42423. (Discoveries Ser.). (Illus.). 160p. 1998. pap. 12.95 (0-8109-2856-6, Pub. by Abrams) Time Warner.

Berinstein, Eduardo H., tr. see McLaughlin, Karen A. & Brilliant, Kelly J.

*Berinstein, Paula. Alternative Energy: An Essential Reference. (Illus.). 208p. 2000. pap. 59.95 (1-57356-248-3) Oryx Pr.

Berinstein, Paula. Finding Images Online: Online User's Guide to Image Searching in Cyberspace. Feldman, Susan E., ed. LC 96-230467. (Cyber Age Bks.). (Illus.). 357p. (Orig.). 1996. pap. 29.95 (0-910965-21-8) Info Today Inc.

— Finding Statistics Online: How to Locate the Elusive Numbers You Need. Bjorner, Susanne, ed. LC 98-22165. (Illus.). 320p. 1998. pap. 29.95 (0-910965-25-0) Info Today Inc.

Berio, Luciano, et al. Luciano Berio: Two Interviews. Osmond-Smith, David, ed. & tr. by. from ITA. LC 84-12346. (Illus.). 192p. 1989. reprint ed. pap. 12.95 (0-7145-2898-6) M Boyars Pubs.

Beriozkin, V. Artists of the Bolshoi Theatre. 176p. 1976. 60.00 (0-569-08360-5) St Mut.

Beriozkina, Patricia, tr. see Polivanov, Konstantin, ed.

Beris, Antony N. & Edwards, Brian J. The Thermodynamics of Flowing Systems: With Internal Microstructure. (Oxford Engineering Science Ser.: No. 36). (Illus.). 704p. (C). 1994. text 140.00 (0-19-507694-X, 3804) OUP.

Beris, Sandra, ed. see Van Osdol, Louise.

Berisford, Julie, ed. see Carroll, Bradley W. & Ostlie, Dale A.

Berish. Amazing Stories Level 3. LC 98-71985. 1998. pap. 16.17 (0-395-94913-0) HM.

Berish & Thibaudeau. English Fast Forward, Bk. 1. (Illus.). 156p. 1995. pap. text, student ed. 20.40 (0-13-359811-X) P-H.

— English Fast Forward 2, Bk. 2. (C). 1995. text, student ed. 20.40 (0-13-513731-4, Prentice Hall) P-H.

— Grammar Connections, Bk. 1. (Illus.). 2000. pap. text, student ed., wbk. ed. 24.80 (0-13-310939-9) P-H.

Berish, L. English Fast Forward Student, Bk. 3. 1995. pap. text, student ed. 20.40 (0-13-398314-5) P-H.

Berish, Lynda & Thibaudeau, Sandra. Canadian English Made Easy, Bk. 1. 164p. 1994. pap. text 29.95 (0-13-305251-6) P-H.

— Canadian English Made Easy, Bk. 2. 160p. 1994. pap. text 29.95 (0-13-305269-9) P-H.

Berish, Lynda & Thibaudeau, Sandra. Grammar Connections, Bk. 2. (Illus.). 246p. 1995. 23.60 (0-13-333288-8) P-H.

— Grammar Connections, Bk. 3. (Illus.). 246p. 1996. 23.60 (0-13-333304-3) P-H.

Berisha, Milazim. Escape from Kosovo: One Family's Desperate Attempt to Avoid the Slaughter. Humphrey, Linda, ed. 176p. 1999. pap. 19.95 (1-878398 09-1, Blue Note Bks) Blue Note Pubns.

Beriss, Sandra, ed. see Van Osdol, L. Louise.

Beristain, Helena. Dictionary of Rhetoric & Poetry: Diccionario de Retorica & Poetica. (ENG & SPA.). 500p. 1985. 29.95 (0-8288-2030-9, F79510) Fr & Eur.

Beritashvili, Ivan S. Vertebrate Memory: Characteristics & Origin. Barlow, John S., tr. LC 74-157930. (Illus.). 157p. 1971. reprint ed. pap. 48.70 (0-608-05488-7, 206595700006) Bks Demand.

Berjeron-Oliver, Sherry & Oliver, Bruce. Working Without Pain: Eliminate Repetitive Strain Injuries with Alexander Technique. LC 96-68768. (Illus.). 124p. 1997. pap. 18.95 (0-9651047-0-2) Pac Inst Alexdr.

Berk. Child Development. 5th ed. LC 99-21227. 776p. (C). 1999. 82.00 (0-205-28634-8, Macmillan Coll) P-H.

*Berk. Data Analysis with Microsoft Excel. (Business Statistics Ser.). 2000. pap. 36.95 (0-534-36278-8) PWS Pubs.

— Development Through the Lifespan. 2nd ed. 2000. pap. 22.67 (0-205-32143-7) Allyn.

— Development Through the Lifespan: Observation Guide. 2nd ed. 2000. pap. 2.00 (0-205-32162-3) Allyn.

Berk. Development Thru Life & Practice. 1998. text 56.25 (0-205-28956-8) Allyn.

— Infants & Children: Prenatal. 3rd ed. LC 98-203228. 624p. 1998. pap. text 62.00 (0-205-28670-4, Longwood Div) Allyn.

— Infants, Children & Adolescents. 3rd ed. 1998. pap. text, student ed. 22.00 (0-205-28669-0, Longwood Div) Allyn.

— Infants, Children & Adolscents. 3rd ed. LC 98-25280. 736p. 1998. 81.00 (0-205-28504-X) Allyn.

Berk. Introduction to Statistics with Systat. LC 97-209841. 376p. (C). 1997. pap. 58.00 incl. disk (0-13-903329-7) P-H.

Berk. Landscapes of Development: An Anthology of Readings. LC 98-28398. (Education Ser.). 1998. pap. 38.95 (0-534-54378-2) Wadsworth Pub.

— Observation Guide Children Development. 5th ed. 1999. pap. text 1.50 (0-205-30275-0) Allyn.

Berk, jt. auth. see Johnson.

Berk, A., et al. Water Shortage: Lessons in Conservation from the Great California Drought, 1976-77. 220p. 1984. reprint ed. lib. bdg. 47.50 (0-8191-4092-9) U Pr of Amer.

Berk, Ann. Laugh Lines. 240p. 1990. mass mkt. 4.50 (0-380-70891-4, Avon Bks) Morrow Avon.

Berk, Carole A., jt. auth. see Morrill, Penny C.

Berk, Cybele & Bozdemir, Michel. Dictionnaire Francais-Turc. (FRE.). 1991. write for info. (0-7859-8207-8, 2-901795-42-0) Fr & Eur.

Berk, Diane. Preparing for Your Interview: Getting the Job You Want. Brett, Elaine, ed. LC 89-82098. (Fifty-Minute Ser.). 62p. (Orig.). 1990. pap. 10.95 (1-56052-033-7) Crisp Pubns.

Berk, Eta F. & Allardyce, Gilbert. Chosen: A Holocaust Memoir - The Eta Fuchs Berk Story. 140p. 1992. pap. 7.95 (0-86492-131-4, Pub. by Goose Ln Edits) Genl Dist Srvs.

Berk, Frank, jt. auth. see Berk, William A.

Berk, Fred & Venable, Lucy. Holiday in Israel. LC 78-111026. (Illus.). 70p. (Orig.). (C). 1977. pap. text 19.95 (0-932582-08-7, Pub. by Dance Notation); audio 15.00 (0-685-08560-0) Dance Notation.

— Ten Folk Dances in Labanotation. i, 32p. (C). 1959. audio 15.00 (0-685-08568-6) Dance Notation.

— Ten Folk Dances in Labanotation. (Illus.). 32p. (C). 1959. pap. text 7.95 (0-932582-09-5, Pub. by Dance Notation) Princeton Bk Co.

Berk, Gerald. Alternative Tracks: The Constitution of American Industrial Order, 1865-1917. (Series in Constitutional Thought). 243p. 1997. reprint ed. pap. text 15.95 (0-8018-5636-1) Johns Hopkins.

Berk, Gregory C., jt. auth. see Ertel, Mike.

Berk, Helene. Be Lean, Healthy, Energetic! Medical Health Planner for a Metabolic Makeover. 1999. pap. 30.58 (0-9663748-6-X, Pub. by Health Commit) ACCESS Pubs Network.

— Metabolicmakeover: A 52 Week Health & Fitness Planner To Guide You In Balancing Blood Sugars, Mo, 1. 2nd ed. 1998. pap. text. write for info. (0-9663748-0-0) Health Commit.

Berk, Hulda G. Early Childhood Education: An Introduction. LC 87-33400. (Illus.). 169p. (C). 1988. pap. text 23.95 (0-87975-422-2) Prometheus Bks.

Berk, Ilhan. History of a Face. Barkan, Stanley H., ed. Halman, Talat S., tr. (Review Turkish Writers Chapbook Ser.: No. 3).Tr. of Turkish & Eng.. 48p. 1991. 15.00 (0-89304-285-4); 15.00 (0-685-26680-X); pap. 5.00 (0-89304-286-2) Cross-Cultrl NY.

Berk, J. L. & Sampliner, J. E., eds. Handbuch der Intensivmedizin. 3rd enl. rev. ed. (Illus.). xiv, 650p. 1986. pap. 77.50 (3-8055-3766-2) S Karger.

Berk, James I. & Sampliner, James F. Handbook of Critical Care. 2nd ed. 1982. 39.50 (0-316-09171-5, Little Brwn Med Div) Lppncott W & W.

Berk, Jeremiah E. Consumer Bankruptcy. 200p. 1988. pap. text 60.00 (0-942954-21-1) NYS Bar.

*Berk, Joe & Berk, Susan. Quality Management for the Technology Sector. LC 00-22363. 208p. 2000. pap. 34.95 (0-7506-7316-8) Buttrwrth-Heinemann.

Berk, Jon & Jainchill, Michael C. Connecticut Law of Uninsured & Underinsured Motorist Coverage. 437p. 1993. text 145.00 (1-878698-22-2) Atlantic Law.

— 1997 Supplement to Connecticut Law of Uninsured & Underinsured Motorist Coverage. 304p. 1998. pap. 64.00 (1-878698-45-1) Atlantic Law.

— 1996 Supplement to Connecticut Law of Uninsured & Underinsured Motorist Coverage. 249p. 1996. pap. 62.00 (1-878698-37-0) Atlantic Law.

*Berk, Jon & Jainchill, Michael C. Two Thousand Supplement to Conneticut Law of Uninsured & Underinsured Motorist Coverage. 2nd ed. 83p. 2000. 53.00 (1-878698-59-1) Atlantic Law.

Berk, Jon & Jaindell, Michael C. 1995 Supplement to Connecticut Law of Uninsured & Underinsured Motorist Coverage. 146p. 1995. pap. 56.00 (1-878698-32-X) Atlantic Law.

*Berk, Jon & Jainehill, Michael C. Connecticut Law of Uninsured & Underinsured Motorist Coverage. 2nd ed. LC 99-228173. 623p. 1999. 165.00 (1-878698-53-2) Atlantic Law.

Berk, Joseph. The Gatling Gun: 19th Century Machine Gun to 21st Century Vulcan. (Illus.). 136p. 1991. text 29.95 (0-87364-644-4) Paladin Pr.

Berk, Joseph & Berk, Susan. Handbook for First Time Managers. 192p. 1998. 12.95 (0-8069-0678-2) Sterling.

Berk, Judy, ed. see Morong, Bill.

Berk, Karen, ed. see Zagat Publishers Staff.

Berk, Kenneth, jt. auth. see Carey, Patrick.

Berk, Krista J. & Tobey, Stephen R. Board Practices: The Structure & Compensation of Boards Directors at S&P 500 Companies for 1996. 2nd ed. Sacks, Michael & Singer, Jim, eds. (Illus.). 54p. 1996. 95.00 (1-879775-46-8) IRRC Inc DC.

Berk, Laura E. Child Development. 5th ed. 1999. pap. text, student ed. 17.00 (0-205-30272-6) Allyn.

— Development Through the Lifespan. LC 97-45631. 752p. 1997. 82.00 (0-205-14684-8) P-H.

— Development Through the Lifespan: Instructor's Resource Manual. 576p. (C). 1997. text, teacher ed. write for info. (0-205-27939-2, T7939-6) Allyn.

— Infants & Children: Prenatal Through Middle Childhood Observation Guide (Chronological), Observation Guide. 2nd ed. 1996. write for info. (*0-205-17427-2*, H7427-1) Allyn.

Berk, Laura E. & Winsler, Adam. Scaffolding Children's Learning: Vygotsky & Early Childhood Education. LC 95-69457. (Illus.). 182p. (Orig.). 1995. pap. text 8.00 (*0-935989-68-4*, 146) Natl Assn Child Ed.

Berk, Laura E., jt. ed. see Diaz, Rafael M.

Berk, Lynn M. English Syntax: From Word to Discourse. LC 98-23348. 336p. (C). 1999. text 58.00 (*0-19-512352-2*); pap. text 24.95 (*0-19-512353-0*) OUP.

Berk, Lynn V. Testing & Remediating Auditory Processing TRAP. 112p. 1997. 35.00 (*0-937857-76-9*, 1233) Speech Bin.

Berk, Marjorie. The Programmer's COBOL: A Complete Reference. LC 70-20656. xxviii, 320 p. 1970. write for info. (*0-07-004895-9*) McGraw.

Berk, Meridith & Vavrus, Toni. Great Book of School Jokes. (Illus.). 96p. (Orig.). (J). 1995. pap. 4.95 (*0-8069-0783-5*) Sterling.

Berk, Michael D. & Zipser, Dean J. California Lis Pendens Practice: 8/97 Update. Chapin, John K., ed. LC 94-71649. 210p. 1997. ring bd. 32.00 (*0-7626-0138-8*, RE-32173) Cont Ed Bar-CA.

— California Lis Pendens Practice: 9/99 Update. 2nd ed. Briggs, Donald R., ed. LC 94-71649. 114p. 1999. ring bd. 38.00 (*0-7626-0360-7*, RE-32174) Cont Ed Bar-CA.

Berk, Paul, jt. ed. see Conard, James.

Berk, Paul D., et al, eds. Hans Popper: A Tribute. LC 91-27884. 207p. 1992. reprint ed. pap. 64.20 (*0-608-03388-X*, 206408500008) Bks Demand.

Berk, Paul D., jt. ed. see Tavoloni, Nicola.

Berk, Philip. Thank You for Sharing. LC 94-7451. 254p. 1996. pap. 12.95 (*1-885487-11-8*) Brownell & Carroll.

Berk, Richard A. & Rossi, Peter H. Thinking about Program Evaluation. (Illus.). 128p. (C). 1990. text 42.00 (*0-8039-3704-0*); pap. text 17.95 (*0-8039-3705-9*) Sage.

— Thinking about Program Evaluation. 2nd ed. LC 98-25412. 128p. 1998. 52.00 (*0-7619-1764-0*) Sage.

— Thinking About Program Evaluation. 2nd ed. LC 98-25412. viii, 128 p. 1999. write for info. (*0-7619-1765-9*) Sage.

Berk, Richard A., jt. auth. see Rossi, Peter H.

Berk, Robert. Starting, Managing, & Promoting the Small Library. LC 89-10704. 160p. (gr. 13). 1990. text 70.95 (*0-87332-576-1*) M E Sharpe.

***Berk, Ronald A.** Professors Are from Mars Students Are from Snickers. 1998. pap. 19.95 (*0-912150-52-1*) Atwood Pub LLC.

Berk, Ronald A., ed. Handbook of Methods for Detecting Test Bias. LC 81-48190. (Illus.). 335p. 1982. reprint ed. pap. 103.90 (*0-608-05927-7*, 206623000008) Bks Demand.

— Performance Assessment: Methods & Applications. LC 86-2947. (Illus.). 560p. 1986. reprint ed. pap. 173.60 (*0-608-05926-9*, 206626200008) Bks Demand.

Berk, Ronald A., ed. see Johns Hopkins University National Symposium on Edu.

Berk, S. F. The Gender Factory: The Apportionment of Work in American Households. LC 84-24861. (Illus.). 262p. (C). 1985. 52.50 (*0-306-41795-2*, Plenum Trade) Perseus Pubng.

***Berk, S. L. & Davis, William R.** Medicine: Pretest Self-Assessment & Review. 9th ed. LC 00-35562. (Illus.). 190p. 2000. write for info. (*0-07-135960-5*) McGraw.

Berk, S. L., jt. ed. see Verghese, Abraham.

Berk, Sally A. Martini Book: How to Fashion & Savor the Perfect Drink. 192p. 1997. 10.98 (*1-884822-98-3*) Blck Dog & Leventhal.

Berk, Sally A. New, New York Bartender's Guide. 256p. 1997. 10.98 (*1-57912-005-9*) Blck Dog & Leventhal.

***Berk, Sally Ann.** The Big Little Book of Jewish Wit & Wisdom. LC 00-30356. (Illus.). 320p. 2000. 10.98 (*1-57912-146-2*) Blck Dog & Leventhal.

Berk, Sally Ann. California Health Bar Drink Guide. (Illus.). 224p. 9.98 (*1-884822-27-4*) Blck Dog & Leventhal.

Berk, Sally Ann. Farmer's Market Guide & Cookbook. (Illus.). 256p. 1996. 9.98 (*1-884822-36-3*) Blck Dog & Leventhal.

Berk, Sally Ann. Naturalist's Herb Guide. 248p. 1996. 9.98 (*1-884822-52-5*) Blck Dog & Leventhal.

— Tomart's Encyclopedia of Action Figures: The 1001 Most Popular Collectibles of All Time. LC 98-9452. (Illus.). 320p. 2000. 14.98 (*1-57912-009-1*) Blck Dog & Leventhal.

Berk, Sally Ann, jt. auth. see Wakeman, James.

Berk, Sarah F., ed. Women & Household Labor. LC 79-23003. (Sage Yearbooks in Women's Policy Studies: No. 5). (Illus.). 295p. reprint ed. pap. 91.50 (*0-8357-8472-X*, 203474000091) Bks Demand.

Berk-Seligson, Susan. The Bilingual Courtroom: Court Interpreters in the Judicial Process. (Language & Legal Discourse Ser.). (Illus.). 312p. 1997. lib. bdg. 60.00 (*0-226-04371-1*) U Ch Pr.

— The Bilingual Courtroom: Court Interpreters in the Judicial Process. (Language & Legal Discourse Ser.). (Illus.). 312p. 1998. pap. text 24.00 (*0-226-04373-8*) U Ch Pr.

Berk, Sharon G. Wastewater Organisms: A Color Atlas. LC 00-48. (Illus.). 48p. 1993. lib. bdg. 99.95 (*0-87371-623-X*, L623) Lewis Pubs.

***Berk, Sheryl.** Blind Date. 2000. mass mkt. write for info. (*0-06-103069-4*) HarpC.

Berk, Sheryl. The Ultimate Prom Guide. LC 98-73500. (Illus.). 101p. (Orig.) (YA). (gr. 8-12). 1999. pap. 8.95 (*0-06-107155-2*) HarpC Child Bks.

Berk, Stephen E. A Time to Heal: John Perkins, Community Development & Racial Reconciliation. LC 97-11672. (Illus.). 448p. (Orig.). 1997. pap. 17.99 (*0-8010-5756-6*) Baker Bks.

Berk, Stephen M. Year of Crisis, Year of Hope: Russian Jewry & the Pogroms of 1881-1882, 11. LC 84-25216. (Contributions in Ethnic Studies: No. 11). 231p. 1985. 62.95 (*0-313-24609-2*, BPG/, Greenwood Pr) Greenwood.

Berk, Steven, ed. Medicine: Pre-Test Self-Assessment & Review. 8th ed. LC 97-18093. (Pretest Clinical Science Ser.). (Illus.). 200p. 1997. pap. text 18.95 (*0-07-052527-7*) McGraw-Hill HPD.

Berk, Susan & Bloom, Jill. Uncommon Boston: A Guide to Hidden Spaces & Special Places. LC 86-20684. 224p. 1987. pap. 7.95 (*0-201-10662-0*) Addison-Wesley.

Berk, Susan, jt. auth. see Berk, Joe.

Berk, Susan, jt. auth. see Berk, Joseph.

Berk, William. Chinese Healing Arts: Internal Kung Fu. Berk, William R., ed. Dudgeon, John, tr. LC 86-50612. 209p. (Orig.). 1986. reprint ed. pap. 9.95 (*0-86568-083-3*, 222) Unique Pubns.

Berk, William A. Detroit Receiving Hospital Emergency Medicine Handbook. 3rd ed. 204p. 1995. pap. text 10.95 (*1-882663-01-2*) Plymouth VT.

***Berk, William A., ed.** Detroit Receiving Hospital Emergency Medicine Handbook. 4th rev. ed. 250p. 2000. pap. 14.95 (*1-882663-49-7*) Plymouth VT.

Berk, William A. & Berk, Frank. Guide to Airport Airplanes: An Illustrated Handbook Allowing Rapid Identification of Airlines Flown by Major Airlines. 2nd ed. LC 97-127981. (Illus.). 168p. (YA). 1996. pap. 14.95 (*1-882663-10-1*) Plymouth VT.

Berk, William R., ed. see Berk, William.

Berka, J. C., jt. auth. see Herpy, M.

Berka, Karel. Measurement: Its Concepts, Theories & Problems. 256p. 1982. text 171.00 (*90-277-1416-9*, D Reidel) Kluwer Academic.

Berka, Randy, jt. ed. see Leong, Sally A.

***Berka, Walter, et al, eds.** Autonomy in Education. (Yearbook of the European Association for Education Law & Policy Ser.: Vol. 3). 480p. 2000. text 156.00 (*90-411-1311-8*) Kluwer Law Intl.

Berkan, Riza C. & Trubatch, Sheldon. Fuzzy System Design Principles: Building Fuzzy If-Then Rule Bases. LC 97-3658. 520p. 1997. 89.95 (*0-7803-1151-5*, PC5622) Inst Electrical.

Berkan, William A. Child Abuse & Neglect Prevention: A Resource & Planning Guide. 140p. (Orig.). (J). (gr. k-12). 1993. pap. text 21.00 (*1-57337-043-6*) WI Dept Pub Instruct.

Berkan, William A., jt. auth. see Deaton, Robert L.

Berkane, Maia, ed. Latent Variable Modeling & Applications to Causality. LC 96-40195. (Lectures Notes in Statistics Ser.: Vol. 120). 281p. 1997. pap. 44.95 (*0-387-94917-8*) Spr-Verlag.

Berke. Berke's 20 Questions for the Writer. 6th ed. (C). 1998. pap. text 33.75 (*0-15-503719-6*) Harcourt Coll Pubs.

— Twenty Questions for the Writer. 6th ed. (C). 1994. pap. text, teacher ed. 33.75 (*0-15-500858-7*) Harcourt Coll Pubs.

Berke, jt. auth. see Gioello, Debbie Ann.

Berke, Conrad. Entrepreneur Magazine: Successful Advertising for Small Businesses. LC 96-531. 199p. 1996. pap. 19.95 (*0-471-14083-X*) Wiley.

Berke, Deborah & Harris, Steven, eds. Architecture of the Everyday. LC 97-20294. (Illus.). 224p. (Orig.). 1997. pap. 19.95 (*1-56898-114-7*) Princeton Arch.

Berke, Diane. The Gentle Smile: Practicing Oneness in Daily Life. 144p. (Orig.). 1995. pap. 12.95 (*0-8245-1499-8*) Crossroad NY.

— Love Always Answers: Walking the Path of a Course in Miracles. 176p. (Orig.). 1994. pap. 11.95 (*0-8245-1432-7*) Crossroad NY.

Berke, Jacqueline. Twenty Questions for the Writer. 6th ed. LC 94-76735. (C). 1994. pap. text 41.50 (*0-15-500857-9*, Pub. by Harcourt Coll Pubs) Harcourt.

— Twenty Questions for the Writer: A Rhetoric with Readings. 5th ed. 722p. (C). 1990. pap. text 3.50 (*0-15-592406-0*) Harcourt Coll Pubs.

Berke, Joel S., et al. Politicians, Judges & City Schools: Reforming School Finance in New York. LC 84-60265. 228p. 1985. 34.00 (*0-87154-108-4*) Russell Sage.

Berke, Joseph H. Even Paranoids Have Enemies: New Perspectives on Paranoia & Persecution. LC 97-26882. 248p. (C). 1998. 80.00 (*0-415-15557-6*); pap. 25.99 (*0-415-15558-4*) Routledge.

Berke, Judith. Acting Problems. 32p. 1993. pap. 6.00 (*1-878851-02-0*) Silverfish Rev Pr.

Berke, Lori, jt. auth. see Sagel, Gail.

Berke, Martin C. Motorcycle Journeys Through New England: You Don't Have to Get Lost to Find the Good Roads. 2nd ed. (Motorcycle Journeys Ser.). (Illus.). 224p. 1994. pap., per. 19.95 (*0-9621834-8-2*) Whitehorse NH.

— Motorcycle Journeys Through the Southwest. LC 95-229145. (Motorcycle Journeys Ser.). (Illus.). 432p. 1994. pap. 19.95 (*0-9621834-9-0*) Whitehorse NH.

Berke, Melvyn & Grant, Joanne. Games Divorced People Play. (Illus.). 264p. 1986. 12.95 (*0-13-346205-6*, Busn) P-H.

Berke, Michael. Selling Equipment Leasing. LC 93-49660. 350p. 1994. 59.95 (*0-8144-5122-5*) AMACOM.

Berke, Neal S., et al, eds. Corrosion Rates of Steel in Concrete. LC 90-509. (Special Technical Publication (STP) Ser.: No. 1065). (Illus.). 200p. 1990. text 39.00 (*0-8031-1458-3*, STP1065) ASTM.

— Techniques to Assess the Corrosion Activity of Steel Reinforced Concrete Structures, STP1276. 2nd ed. LC 96-35303. (Illus.). 200p. 1996. pap. text 39.00 (*0-8031-2009-5*, STP1276) ASTM.

Berke, Philip R. & Beatley, Timothy. After the Hurricane: Linking Recovery to Sustainable Development in the Caribbean. LC 97-115. 240p. 1997. text 49.95 (*0-8018-5624-8*) Johns Hopkins.

— Planning for Earthquakes: Risk, Politics, & Policy. (Illus.). 240p. 1992. text 40.00 (*0-8018-4255-7*) Johns Hopkins.

Berke, Thomas. Workbook for Inorganic, Organic, & Biological Chemistry. 416p. (C). 1992. spiral bd. 49.95 (*0-8403-8070-4*, 40807001) Kendall-Hunt.

Berkebile, Don H., ed. American Carriages, Sleighs, Sulkies & Carts. LC 76-17222. (Pictorial Archive Ser.). (Illus.). 168p. 1977. pap. 9.95 (*0-486-23328-6*) Dover.

Berkebile, Donald H. Carriage Terminology: An Historical Dictionary. LC 77-118. (Smithsonian Institution Press Publication: No. 6028). 487p. reprint ed. pap. 151.00 (*0-608-17751-2*, 205646500069) Bks Demand.

Berkebile, Donald H., ed. Horse Drawn Commercial Vehicles: 200 Illustrations of Nineteenth-Century Stagecoaches, Delivery Wagons, Fire Engines, etc. (Illus.). 160p. 1989. pap. 12.95 (*0-486-26020-8*) Dover.

Berkel, Bob & Kornbluth, Alfred. Electronic Surveillance Countermeasures. LC 94-92459. (CCS SecuritySource Library: Vol. II). (Illus.). 900p. 1995. 300.00 (*1-884674-02-X*) CCS Security.

Berkel, Bob & Rapaport, Lowell. Covert Audio Interception. LC 93-91000. (CCS SecuritySource Library: Vol. 1). (Illus.). 720p. 1994. 300.00 (*1-884674-01-1*) CCS Security.

Berkel, Bob, et al. The SecuritySource Library, 12 vols., Set, Vols. I-XII. LC 98-7459. (Illus.). lib. bdg. write for info. (*1-884674-00-3*) CCS Security.

Berkel, Bob, ed. see Lavas, Ray.

Berkel, Bob, ed. see Prentiss, Lee.

Berkel, Boyce N. How to Prevent Home Accidents & Handle Emergencies Effectively. LC 79-55195. (Illus.). 1979. pap. 7.50 (*0-9603184-0-2*) B Berkel.

Berkel, Kees Van, see Van Berkel, Kees.

Berkel, Klaas Van, see Van Berkel, Klaas.

Berkeley, A. E. & Barnes, Ann, eds. Labor Relations in Hospitals & Health Care Facilities: Proceedings of a Conference Presented by the American Arbitration Association & the Federal Mediation & Conciliation Service, 1975. LC 75-45236. 110p. reprint ed. pap. 34.10 (*0-608-12567-9*, 202397200035) Bks Demand.

Berkeley, Adrian. The Focal Guide to Photography & the Law. LC 94-106239. 167p. reprint ed. pap. 51.80 (*0-608-06252-9*, 206658100008) Bks Demand.

Berkeley, Anthony. Jumping Jenny. 1997. 19.50 (*0-7451-8701-3*, Black Dagger) Chivers N Amer.

— Not to Be Taken. 224p. 1995. 19.50 (*0-7451-8658-0*, Black Dagger) Chivers N Amer.

Berkeley, Arthur E., jt. auth. see Colosi, Thomas R.

Berkeley, Arthur E., jt. auth. see McDermott, E. Patrick.

Berkeley, Bernard. Floors: Selection & Maintenance. LC 68-23014. (American Library Association LTP Publication Ser.: No. 13). 326p. reprint ed. pap. 101.10 (*0-608-13221-7*, 202419600035) Bks Demand.

Berkeley, Bill. Fire in Their Wake: The Methods Behind Africa's Madness. 1999. write for info. (*0-201-31137-2*) Addison-Wesley.

***Berkeley, Bill.** The Graves Are Not Yet Full: Race Tribe, & Power at the Heart of Africa. 364p. 2000. 27.50 (*0-465-00641-8*, Pub. by Basic) HarpC.

Berkeley, Bud. Foreskin: A Closer Look. LC 93-10531. (Illus.). 207p. (Orig.). 1993. pap. 9.95 (*1-55583-212-1*) Alyson Pubns.

Berkeley, David S. Blood Will Tell in Shakespeare's Plays. (Graduate Studies: No. 28). 107p. (C). 1984. 35.00 (*0-89672-118-3*) Players Pr.

Berkeley, Dorothy S., jt. auth. see Berkeley, Edmund.

Berkeley, Dorothy S., jt. ed. see Berkeley, Edmund.

Berkeley, Edmund & Berkeley, Dorothy S. George William Featherstonhaugh: The First U. S. Government Geologist. LC 87-5006. (History of American Science & Technology Ser.). 376p. 1988. text 42.50 (*0-8173-0365-0*) U of Ala Pr.

— The Life & Travels of John Bartram: From Lake Ontario to the River St. John. LC 81-4083. (Illus.). xv, 376p. 1990. pap. 18.95 (*0-8130-0995-2*) U Press Fla.

— The Life & Travels of John Bartram: From Lake Ontario to the River St. John. LC 81-4083. (Florida State University Bks.). 392p. reprint ed. pap. 121.60 (*0-8357-6925-9*, 203798400009) Bks Demand.

Berkeley, Edmund & Berkeley, Dorothy S., eds. The Correspondence of John Bartram, 1734-1777. (Illus.). 784p. 1992. 85.00 (*0-8130-1123-X*) U Press Fla.

Berkeley, Edmund, jt. auth. see Smith-Berkeley, Dorothy.

Berkeley, Elizabeth M., ed. see James, Henry, et al.

Berkeley, Elizabeth M., ed. see James, William.

Berkeley, Elizabeth M., jt. ed. see Skrupskelis, Ignas K.

Berkeley, Ellen P. Maverick Cats: Encounters with Feral Cats. LC 87-60370. (Illus.). 144p. 1987. reprint ed. pap. 12.95 (*0-933050-45-3*) New Eng Pr VT.

Berkeley, Ellen P. & McQuaid, Matilda, eds. Architecture: A Place for Women. LC 88-29299. (Illus.). 256p. (C). 1989. pap. text 19.95 (*0-87474-231-5*) Smithsonian.

***Berkeley, Ellen Perry, ed.** At Grandmother's Table: Women Write about Food Life & the Enduring Bond Between Grandmothers & Granddaughters. (Illus.). 288p. 2000. 24.95 (*1-57749-096-7*) Fairview Press.

Berkeley, G. De Motu & the Analyst: A Modern Edition, with Introductions & Commentary. Jesseph, Douglas M., ed. & tr. by. (New Synthese Historical Library). 244p. (C). 1991. text 146.50 (*0-7923-1520-0*) Kluwer Academic.

Berkeley, George. George Berkeley Alciphron in Focus. Berman, David, ed. LC 92-10796. (Philosophers in Focus Ser.). 256p. (C). 1993. pap. 27.99 (*0-415-06373-6*, A9932) Routledge.

— Maxims Concerning Patriotism (Berkeley) McCormick, Malachi, ed. 24p. 1985. 7.00 (*0-943984-22-X*) Stone St Pr.

— Philosophical Works: Including the Works on Vision. Ayers, M. R., ed. 358p. 1993. pap. 8.95 (*0-460-87343-1*, Everyman's Classic Lib) Tuttle Pubng.

— Philosophical Writings. Jessop, T. E., ed. LC 69-13823. 278p. 1969. reprint ed. lib. bdg. 65.00 (*0-8371-1056-4*, BEPW, Greenwood Pr) Greenwood.

— Principles of Human Knowledge & Three Dialogues. Robinson, Howard, ed. (Oxford World's Classics Ser.). 278p. 1999. pap. 9.95 (*0-19-283549-1*) OUP.

— Principles of Human Knowledge & Three Dialogues Between Hylas & Philonius. Woolhouse, Roger, ed. & intro. by. 224p. 1988. pap. 10.95 (*0-14-043293-0*, Penguin Classics) Viking Penguin.

— The Principles of Human Knowledge & Three Dialogues Between Hylas & Philonous. 1990. 16.50 (*0-8446-5833-2*) Peter Smith.

— Selections from Berkeley. LC 72-4216. (Select Bibliographies Reprint Ser.). 1977. reprint ed. 24.95 (*0-8369-6873-5*) Ayer.

— Three Dialogues Between Hylas & Philonous. Perry, John, ed. LC 94-70214. 138p. (C). 1994. pap. text 5.95 (*0-941736-05-9*) Arete Pr.

— Three Dialogues Between Hylas & Philonous. Adams, Robert M., ed. LC 79-65276. (HPC Classics Ser.). 138p. (C). 1979. pap. text 4.95 (*0-915144-61-1*); lib. bdg. 21.95 (*0-915144-62-X*) Hackett Pub.

— Three Dialogues Between Hylas & Philonous. LC 88-61327. (Great Books in Philosophy). 110p. (C). 1988. pap. 4.95 (*0-87975-499-0*) Prometheus Bks.

— Three Dialogues between Hylas & Philonous. Dancy, Jonathan, ed. (Oxford Philosophical Texts Ser.). 192p. (C). 1998. pap. text 11.95 (*0-19-875149-4*) OUP.

— A Treatise Concerning the Principles of Human Knowledge. Winkler, Kenneth, ed. & intro. by. LC 82-2876. (HPC Classics Ser.). 156p. (C). 1982. pap. text 5.95 (*0-915145-39-1*); lib. bdg. 21.95 (*0-915145-40-5*) Hackett Pub.

— A Treatise Concerning the Principles of Human Knowledge. Dancy, Jonathan, ed. (Oxford Philosophical Texts Ser.). 244p. (C). 1998. pap. text 11.95 (*0-19-875161-3*) OUP.

— A Treatise Concerning the Principles of Human Knowledge. Dancy, Jonathan, ed. (Oxford Philosophical Texts Ser.). 244p. (C). 1998. text 29.95 (*0-19-875160-5*) OUP.

— A Treatise Concerning the Principles of Human Knowledge: Three Dialogues Between Hylas & Philonous. 288p. (C). 1985. pap. 8.00 (*0-87548-446-8*) Open Court.

— The Works of George Berkeley, Bishop of Cloyne, 9 vols. Luce, A. A. & Jessop, Thomas E., eds. 1990. reprint ed. pap. 770.00 (*0-8115-0322-4*) Periodicals Srv.

Berkeley, George. The Works of George Berkeley, Bishop of Cloyne: (Macintosh) Jessop, T. E. & Luce, A. A., eds. (Past Masters Ser.). (C). write for info. (*1-57085-045-3*) Intelex.

Berkeley, George. Works on Vision. Turbayne, Colin M., ed. LC 62-11787. (Orig.). 1963. 6.60 (*0-672-51033-2*, Bobbs); pap. 4.35 (*0-672-60267-9*, LLA83, Bobbs) Macmillan.

— Works on Vision, 83. Turbayne, Colin M., ed. LC 81-7160. (Library of Liberal Arts: No. 83). 158p. (Orig.). 1981. reprint ed. lib. bdg. 49.75 (*0-313-23186-9*, BEWV, Greenwood Pr) Greenwood.

Berkeley, George, et al. British Imperialism: Three Documents. (Research Library of Colonial Americana). 1972. 25.95 (*0-405-03330-3*, 11657) Ayer.

Berkeley, Heather, et al, eds. Children's Rights: Legal & Educational Issues. LC 80-454939. (Ontario Institute for Studies in Education, Symposium Ser.: No. 9). 181p. pap. 56.20 (*0-608-14874-1*, 202614600048) Bks Demand.

Berkeley Holistic Health Center Staff, compiled by. Holistic Health Lifebook. LC 81-2846. (Illus.). 430p. 1981. pap. 12.95 (*0-915904-53-5*) And-Or Bks.

Berkeley, James P. Knowing the Old Testament. 171p. 1954. pap. 12.00 (*0-8170-0088-7*) Judson.

Berkeley, Jill B. CGL Reporter: Binder 10. 322p. 1998. 416.00 (*1-886813-37-X*) Intl Risk Mgt.

***Berkeley, Jill B.** CGL Reporter: Binder 12. 324p. 2000. write for info. (*1-886813-50-7*) Intl Risk Mgt.

— CGL Reporter: Fall 1999. 11th ed. 600p. (C). 1999. 416.00 (*1-886813-45-0*) Intl Risk Mgt.

Berkeley, Kathleen. Like a Plague of Locusts: From an Antebellum Town to a New South City, Memphis, Tennessee, 1850-1880. LC 91-12700. (Dissertations in Nineteenth-Century American Political & Social History). 400p. 1991. 82.00 (*0-8240-8193-5*) Garland.

— The Women's Liberation Movement in America. LC 99-25007. (Guides to Historic Events of the Twentieth Century Ser.). 256p. 1999. 39.95 (*0-313-29875-0*, GR9875, Greenwood Pr) Greenwood.

***Berkeley, Laura.** The Keeper of Wisdom. (Illus.). 32p. (J). (ps-7). 2000. 15.95 (*1-84148-203-X*) Barefoot Bks NY.

Berkeley, Laura. The Seeds Of Peace. (Illus.). 32p. (J). (gr. k-7). 1999. 15.95 (*1-84148-007-X*) Barefoot Bks NY.

***Berkeley, Laura.** The Spirit of the Massai Man. 32p. (J). (gr. 3-6). 2000. 16.95 (*1-902283-74-0*) Barefoot Bks NY.

Berkeley, M. J. Observations, Botanical & Physiological on the Potato Murrain. (Phytopathological Classics Ser.). 108p. 1948. 22.00 (*0-89054-009-8*) Am Phytopathol Soc.

An Asterisk (*) at the beginning of an entry indicates that the title is appearing for the first time.

Berkeley, M. J. & Broome, C. E. Notices of British Fungi: Eighteen Forty-One to Eighteen Forty-Five, 35 papers bd. in 1 vol., Vol. 1. 1967. 120.00 (*3-7682-0456-1*) Lubrecht & Cramer.

Berkeley Macintosh Users Group Staff. Zen & the Art of Resource Editing. 1995. pap. 20.00 (*1-879791-00-5*) BMUG.

Berkeley Poets Cooperative Staff, ed. Berkeley Poets Cooperative Anthology, 1970-1980. 256p. 1980. pap. 12.95 (*0-917658-12-4*) BPW & P.

Berkeley, Robert J., ed. see Crockett, Laura.

Berkeley, Roy. A Spy's London: A Walk Book of One Hundred Thirty-Six Sites in Central London Relating to Spies, Spycatchers, & Subversives from More Than a Century of London's Secret History. (Illus.). 192p. 1994. pap. 16.95 (*0-85052-113-0*, Pub. by Leo Cooper) Trans-Atl Phila.

Berkeley, Sabina, ed. & tr. see Schieder, Theodor.

Berkeley, Sara. Home Movie Nights. 62p. 1989. pap. 9.95 (*1-85186-050-9*) Dufour.

— Penn. 48p. 1989. pap. 9.95 (*1-85186-013-4*) Dufour.

***Berkeley, Sara.** Shadowing Hannah. 2000. pap. 15.95 (*1-902602-04-8*, Pub. by New Island Books) Dufour.

Berkeley, Sara. The Swimmer in the Deep Blue Dream. 156p. 1989. pap. 12.95 (*1-85186-092-4*) Dufour.

Berkeley, Sara, et al. Facts about Water: New & Selected Poems. 96p. 1995. pap. 15.95 (*1-85224-292-2*, Pub. by Bloodaxe Bks) Dufour.

Berkeley, Selma G. & Jackson, Barbara E. Your Career As a Medical Secretary Transcriber. LC 74-34233. (Wiley Biomedical-Health Publication Ser.). 208p. reprint ed. pap. 64.50 (*0-608-13695-6*, 205508800008) Bks Demand.

Berkeley Seminar on Federalism (1st, 1987) Staff. Perspectives on Federalism: Papers from the First Berkeley Seminar on Federalism. Scheiber, Harry N., ed. LC 87-2618. 193p. reprint ed. pap. 59.90 (*0-608-20125-1*, 207139700011) Bks Demand.

Berkeley Seminar on Federalism (3rd, 1988) Staff. Power Divided: Essays on the Theory & Practice of Federalism: Papers from the Third Berkeley Seminar on Federalism. Scheiber, Harry N. et al, eds. LC 89-15593. 179p. reprint ed. pap. 55.50 (*0-608-20121-9*, 207139300011) Bks Demand.

Berkeley Seminar on Federalism (4th, 1992) Staff. North American & Comparative Federalism: Essays for the 1990s. Scheiber, Harry N., ed. LC 91-47941. 110p. reprint ed. pap. 34.10 (*0-608-20128-6*, 207140000011) Bks Demand.

Berkeley, Theodore, tr. from LAT. Guerric of Igny Liturgical Sermons, 2 vols. (Cistercian Fathers Ser.: No. 8 & No. 32). 378p. 1971. 15.00 (*0-87907-400-0*) Cistercian Pubns.

Berkeley, Theodore, tr. see Clement, Olivier.

Berkeley Travel Staff. Fodor's Campground Vacations. Date not set. pap. 17.00 (*0-679-02994-X*) Fodors Travel.

Berkeley Warner Community Center Youth. Express Yourself: Works by Tomorrow's Leaders. 40p. (YA). (gr. 6-12). 1996. pap. text 5.00 (*1-887012-01-X*) Hanovr Pr.

Berkell, Dianne E., ed. Autism: Identification, Education, & Treatment. 328p. 1992. pap. 34.50 (*0-8058-0897-3*); text 69.95 (*0-8058-0896-5*) L Erlbaum Assocs.

Berkely. Software Development Project & Management. 1990. boxed set. write for info. (*0-318-68272-9*) P-H.

Berkely, Jon. A Little Book of Irish Sayings. (Little Irish Book Ser.). 60p. 1995. 9.95 (*0-86281-517-7*, Pub. by Appletree Pr) Irish Bks Media.

Berkemeier, Anne. Kognitive Prozesse Beim Zewitschrifterwerb: Zweitalphabetisierung Griechisch-Deutsch-Bilingualer Kinder im Deutschen. (Arbeiten zur Sprachanalyse Ser.: No. 29). (Illus.). 374p. 1997. 63.95 (*3-631-31714-X*) P Lang Pubng.

Berkemeyer, Kathy M. Learning Corel Office 7. Gaines, Ayana, ed. LC 97-190254. (Learning Series Texts). (Illus.). 1997. pap. 27.00 (*1-56243-334-2*, Z-12) DDC Pub.

— Learning Corel WordPerfect 7. Gaines, Ayana, ed. LC 97-208368. (Learning Series Texts). (Illus.). (Orig.). 1997. pap. text 27.00 (*1-56243-432-2*, Z-16) DDC Pub.

— Quick Reference Guide for Quicken 4 for Windows. LC 95-125665. 1995. pap. 12.00 (*1-56243-242-7*, G7) DDC Pub.

— Quick Reference Guide for WordPerfect 6.1 for Windows. 1996. 15.00 (*1-56243-306-7*, W19HC); pap. 12.00 (*1-56243-257-5*, W19) DDC Pub.

Berkemeyer, Kathy M., ed. see Brown, Margaret.

Berkemeyer, Kathy M., ed. see Gosselin, Don.

Berkemeyer, Kathy M., ed. see Greenberg, Seth.

Berkemeyer, Kathy M., ed. see Heartland, Amanda.

Berkenbosch, Frank, jt. ed. see Rothwell, Nancy J.

Berkenholz, Robet J., et al. Effective Adult Learning. LC 98-72262. 1999. 43.75 (*0-8134-3160-3*) Interstate.

Berkenkamp, Lauri, jt. auth. see Schenck, Deborah.

Berkenkotter, Carol & Huckin, Thomas N. Genre Knowledge in Disciplinary Communication: Cognition - Culture - Power. 216p. 1995. pap. 27.50 (*0-8058-1612-7*); text 45.00 (*0-8058-1611-9*) L Erlbaum Assocs.

Berkenmeyer, Wilhelm C. Albany Protocol, 1731-1750. LC 92-80057. (Illus.). 704p. 1992. reprint ed. 49.50 (*0-89725-077-X*, 1364) Picton Pr.

Berkery, Michael J. & Bolek, Raymond W. Touche Ross Guide to Selecting a Small Business Computer. LC 84-26528. 337p. 1985. pap. 19.95 (*0-13-925744-6*) P-H.

Berkery, Peter M. Making Health Care Reform Work: How the New Law Affects You & Your Employer. pap. 9.95 (*0-7863-0344-1*, Irwn Prfssnl) McGraw-Hill Prof.

Berkery, Peter M., Jr. The 1993 Tax Act, National Association of Manufacturers Edition: How the New Legislation Can Pay Off for You. 1993. text 10.95 (*0-7863-0289-5*, Irwn Prfssnl) McGraw-Hill Prof.

— Personal Financial Planning for Gays & Lesbians: Our Guide to Prudent Decision Making. 336p. 1996. text 24.95 (*0-7863-0482-0*, Irwn Prfssnl) McGraw-Hill Prof.

Berkes, Fikret. Common Property Resources: Ecology & Community Based Sustainable Development. 302p. (C). 1991. pap. 475.00 (*81-7089-140-X*, Pub. by Intl Bk Distr) St Mut.

— Common Property Resources: Ecology of Community Based Sustainable Development. 320p. 1989. 59.50 (*1-85293-080-2*) St Martin.

— Sacred Ecology: Traditional Ecological Knowledge & Resource Management. LC 98-43381. 1999. 75.00 (*1-56032-694-8*); pap. 25.95 (*1-56032-695-6*) Hemisp Pub.

Berkes, Fikret, et al, eds. Linking Social & Ecological Systems: Management Practices & Social Mechanisms for Building Resilience. (Illus.). 476p. (C). 1998. text 80.00 (*0-521-59140-6*) Cambridge U Pr.

***Berkes, Fikret & Folke, Carl, eds.** Linking Social & Ecological Systems: Management Practices & Social Mechanisms for Building Resilience. (Illus.). 459p. (C). 2000. pap. 31.95 (*0-521-78562-6*) Cambridge U Pr.

Berkes, Niyazi. Development of Secularism in Turkey. LC 99-200292. 537p. (C). 1998. 75.00 (*0-415-91983-5*); pap. 22.99 (*0-415-91982-7*) Routledge.

Berkes, Niyazi, ed. & tr. see Gokalp, Ziya.

Berkett, Lorraine P. Management Guide for Low-Input Sustainable Apple Production. (Illus.). 54p. (Orig.). (C). 1994. pap. text 30.00 (*0-7881-0754-2*) DIANE Pub.

Berkewicz, Ulla. Angels Are Black & White. Willson, A. Leslie, tr. from GER. iv, 214p. 1997. 35.00 (*1-57113-112-4*) Camden Hse.

— Josef Is Dying. Williams, Gerald, tr. from GER. Orig. Title: Josef Stribt. 99p. (Orig.). 1992. pap. 11.00 (*0-942996-15-1*) Post Apollo Pr.

Berkey, Barry R. & Berkey, Velma. Decoy & Wildfowl Art Trivia. 131p. (Orig.). 1989. pap. text 15.50 (*0-9606930-1-7*) V A Berkey.

Berkey, Brian F. The Keys to Tulsa. Rosenman, Jane, ed. LC 90-26403. 416p. 1991. reprint ed. mass mkt. 12.00 (*0-671-70727-2*, WSP) PB.

Berkey, Curtis, jt. auth. see Kickingbird, Lynn.

Berkey, Dennis D. Applied Calculus. 3rd ed. LC 93-86829. (C). 1994. text 91.00 (*0-03-076173-5*); pap. text, suppl. ed. write for info. (*0-03-098106-9*) Harcourt Coll Pubs.

— Applied Calculus/Calculus for Management. 3rd ed. (C). 1994. pap. text, teacher ed. 32.00 (*0-03-076174-3*) Harcourt Coll Pubs.

— Applied Calculus/Calculus for Management: Test Bank. 3rd ed. (C). 1993. pap. text, teacher ed., suppl. ed. 37.50 (*0-03-076176-X*, Pub. by Harcourt Coll Pubs) Harcourt.

— Biology Applications. 2nd ed. (C). 1993. pap. text, suppl. ed. 10.00 (*0-03-097206-X*) Harcourt Coll Pubs.

— Calculus. 3rd ed. (C). 1992. pap. text, teacher ed., suppl. ed. 40.50 (*0-03-073361-8*, Pub. by Harcourt Coll Pubs) Harcourt.

— Calculus, Vol. I. 3rd ed. (C). 1992. pap. text, teacher ed. 50.25 (*0-03-051023-6*) Harcourt Coll Pubs.

— Calculus, Vol. 2. 3rd ed. (C). 1992. pap. text, teacher ed. 50.25 (*0-03-094347-7*) Harcourt Coll Pubs.

— Calculus & Mathematics Manual. 3rd ed. (C). 1992. pap. text 24.50 (*0-03-076154-9*) Harcourt Coll Pubs.

— Calculus for Management. 2nd ed. (C). 1990. pap. text, teacher ed. 34.00 (*0-03-032774-1*) Harcourt Coll Pubs.

— Calculus for Management, Social, & Life Sciences. 3rd ed. LC 93-86618. (C). 1993. text 90.50 (*0-03-076163-8*) Harcourt Coll Pubs.

— Calculus for Management, Social & Life Sciences. 3rd ed. (C). 1994. pap. text. write for info. (*0-03-003554-6*); pap. text, suppl. ed. write for info. (*0-03-098103-4*) Harcourt Coll Pubs.

— Derive Manual Calculus. 3rd ed. (C). 1992. pap. text 21.00 (*0-03-076156-5*) Harcourt Coll Pubs.

— SSM VOL I CALCULUS 3ED+, Vol. I. 3rd ed. (C). 1992. pap. text, student ed. 28.50 (*0-03-049507-5*) Harcourt Coll Pubs.

— ST SOL MAN CALC/MANAGEMENT 3E. 3rd ed. (C). 1994. pap. text, student ed. 26.50 (*0-03-076168-9*) Harcourt Coll Pubs.

— STD SOL MNL APPLIED CALCULUS3E. 3rd ed. (C). 1994. pap. text, student ed. 24.00 (*0-03-076178-6*) Harcourt Coll Pubs.

Berkey, Dennis D. & Blanchard, Paul. Calculus. 3rd ed. 1200p. (C). 1992. teacher ed. write for info. (*0-03-076153-0*) SCP.

— CALCULUS OF ONE VARIABLE 3E. 3rd ed. 1200p. (C). 1992. text 82.00 (*0-03-076514-5*) SCP.

— CALCULUS 3RD EDITION. 3rd ed. 1200p. (C). 1992. text 112.50 (*0-03-046927-9*) SCP.

Berkey, Geri A. Easy in Reading. (Illus.). 66p. 1978. teacher ed. 6.95 (*1-878669-27-3*, 6073) Crea Tea Assocs.

Berkey, Jim, jt. auth. see Tracy, Jack.

Berkey, John C., ed. see Browning, Robert.

Berkey, John C., ed. see Dreiser, Theodore.

Berkey, Jonathan. The Transmission of Knowledge in Medieval Cairo: A Social History of Islamic Education. (Near East Studies). 244p. 1992. text 47.50 (*0-691-03191-6*, Pub. by Princeton U Pr) Cal Prin Full Svc.

Berkey, Robert F. & Edwards, Sarah A., eds. Christology in Dialogue. LC 92-47004. 400p. (Orig.). (C). 1993. pap. 24.95 (*0-8298-0956-2*) Pilgrim OH.

Berkey, Velma, jt. auth. see Berkey, Barry R.

Berkheiser, Samuel W., Jr. Fetid Barite Occurrences, Western Berks County, Pennsylvania. (Mineral Resource Reports: No. 84). (Illus.). 43p. 1984. pap. 6.25 (*0-8182-0053-7*) Commonweal PA.

— High-Purity Silica Occurrences in Pennsylvania. (Mineral Resource Reports: No. 88). (Illus.). 67p. 1985. pap. 7.85 (*0-8182-0071-5*) Commonweal PA.

— Reconnaissance Survey of Potential Carbonate Whiting Sources in Pennsylvania. (Mineral Resource Reports: No. 83). (Illus.). 53p. (Orig.). 1983. pap. 4.45 (*0-8182-0024-3*) Commonweal PA.

Berkhof, Hendrikus. Christ & the Powers. 2nd rev. ed. LC 62-13713. 80p. 1977. pap. 5.99 (*0-8361-1820-0*) Herald Pr.

***Berkhof, Hendrikus.** Christian Faith: An Introduction to the Study of the Faith. 594p. 1999. pap. 45.00 (*1-57910-266-2*) Wipf & Stock.

Berkhof, Hendrikus. Cristo y Los Poderes. (SPA.). 85p. 1985. pap. 5.50 (*0-939125-01-3*) CRC Wrld Lit.

— Two Hundred Years of Theology: Report of a Personal Journey. fac. ed. Vriend, John, tr. LC 89-11786. 336p. 1989. reprint ed. pap. 104.20 (*0-7837-7945-3*, 204770100008) Bks Demand.

Berkhof, Louis. Historia de las Doctrinas Cristianas.Tr. of History of Christian Doctrines. 360p. 1995. reprint ed. pap. 8.50 (*0-85151-716-1*) Banner of Truth.

— The History of Christian Doctrine. 1978. 29.99 (*0-85151-005-1*) Banner of Truth.

— Introduccion a la Teologia Sistematica. (SPA.). 225p. 1988. 12.00 (*0-939125-02-1*) CRC Wrld Lit.

— Manual de Doctrina Cristiana. 4th ed. (SPA.). 296p. 1991. pap. 12.00 (*0-939125-03-X*) CRC Wrld Lit.

— Manual of Christian Doctrine. 1939. pap. 18.00 (*0-8028-1647-9*) Eerdmans.

— Principios de Interpretacion Biblica. rev. ed. (SPA.). 175p. 1990. pap. 8.50 (*0-939125-04-8*) CRC Wrld Lit.

— Sumario de Doctrina Cristiana. 5th ed. Vila, David, tr. from ENG.Tr. of Summary of Christian Doctrine. (SPA.). 240p. 1986. pap. 8.50 (*0-939125-05-6*) CRC Wrld Lit.

— Summary of Christian Doctrine. 184p. 1997. pap. 7.99 (*0-85151-055-8*) Banner of Truth.

— Summary of Christian Doctrine. 1938. pap. 14.00 (*0-8028-1513-8*) Eerdmans.

— Systematic Theology. LC 96-32290. 989p. 1996. 45.00 (*0-8028-3820-0*) Eerdmans.

— Systematic Theology. 784p. 1998. reprint ed. 29.99 (*0-85151-056-6*) Banner of Truth.

— Teologia Sistematica. 8th ed. (SPA.). 935p. 1993. 32.00 (*0-939125-06-4*) CRC Wrld Lit.

Berkhof, Louis & Van Til, Cornelius. Foundations of Christian Education: Addresses to Christian Teachers. LC 89-39157. 140p. 1989. reprint ed. pap. 9.99 (*0-87552-114-2*, Pub. by Evangelical Pr) P & R Pubng.

Berkhofer, Robert, ed. see Baker, M. Joyce.

Berkhofer, Robert, ed. see Biemer, Linda B.

Berkhofer, Robert, ed. see Friedman, Jean E.

Berkhofer, Robert, ed. see Goodwin, Everett C.

Berkhofer, Robert, ed. see Gragg, Larry D.

Berkhofer, Robert, ed. see Hast, Adele.

Berkhofer, Robert, ed. see Rotella, Elyce J.

Berkhofer, Robert, ed. see Stuart, Paul.

Berkhofer, Robert F., Jr. Beyond the Great Story: History As Text & Discourse. LC 95-2005. (Illus.). 392p. (C). 1995. text 43.00 (*0-674-06907-2*) Belknap Pr.

— Beyond the Great Story: History As Text & Discourse. (Illus.). 400p. 1997. reprint ed. pap. 18.95 (*0-674-06908-0*) HUP.

— Salvation & the Savage: An Analysis of Protestant Missions & American Indian Response, 1787-1862. LC 77-22857. 186p. 1977. reprint ed. lib. bdg. 65.00 (*0-8371-9745-7*, BESSA, Greenwood Pr) Greenwood.

— The White Man's Indian: Images of the American Indian from Columbus to the Present. LC 78-11047. (Illus.). 1979. pap. 8.76 (*0-394-72794-0*, V-794) Vin Bks.

Berkhout, A. J. Applied Seismic Wave Theory. (Advances in Seismic Wave Theory Ser.: Vol. 1). 380p. 1987. 141.50 (*0-444-42898-4*) Elsevier.

— Seismic Migration: Imaging of Acoustic Energy by Wave Field Extrapolation, Part A: Theoretical Aspects. (Developments in Solid Earth Geophysics Ser.: No. 14A). xx,446p. 1985. 184.50 (*0-444-42547-0*) Elsevier.

Berkhout, A. J., jt. auth. see Wapenaar, C. P.

Berkhout, Carl. Cynewulf: Basic Readings. Bjork, Robert E., ed. LC 96-5754. (Basic Readings in Anglo-Saxon England Ser.: No. 4). (Illus.). 392p. 1996. text 50.00 (*0-8153-1758-1*, H1869) Garland.

Berkhout, Carl, et al, eds. Old English Prose. (Basic Readings on Anglo-Saxon England Ser.). 300p. Date not set. text 40.00 (*0-8153-0305-X*) Garland.

Berkhout, Carl & Szarmach, Paul. The Archaeology of Anglo-Saxon England. Karkov, Catherine E. & Trahern, Joseph B., Jr., eds. LC 99-30865. (Basic Readings in Anglo-Saxon England Ser.: Vol. 7). 512p. 1999. text 85.00 (*0-8153-2916-4*, H2086) Garland.

Berkhout, Carl T. & Russell, Jeffrey B. Medieval Heresies: A Bibliography, 1960-1979. xvi, 201p. pap. 22.86 (*0-88844-360-9*) Brill Academic Pubs.

Berkhout, Marco. Integrated Audio Amplifiers in BCD Technology. LC 97-29157. (The Kluwer International Series in Engineering & Computer Science: No. 418). 224p. 1997. text 126.50 (*0-7923-8003-7*) Kluwer Academic.

***Berkhout, Monique & Robinson, Francesca.** Madame Joy: The Story of Human Drug Use & the Politics of Its Regulation. 2000. pap. 12.95 (*0-7322-6506-1*) HarpC.

Berkhuijsen, Elly M., ed. see International Astronomical Union Staff.

Berkin. Making America, Vol. 1. (C). Date not set. pap. text 48.36 (*0-395-50252-7*) HM.

— Making America, Vol. 2. (C). Date not set. pap. text 48.36 (*0-395-50253-5*) HM.

— Making America Complete. (C). Date not set. text 63.16 (*0-395-50251-9*) HM.

Berkin, Carol. First Generations: Women in Colonial America. 256p. 1997. pap. text 12.00 (*0-8090-1606-0*) Hill & Wang.

— Making America. (C). 1995. pap. text, student ed. 19.56 (*0-395-50249-7*) HM.

— Making America. (C). 1995. pap., teacher ed., suppl. ed. 11.96 (*0-395-71438-9*) HM.

— Making America, No. 2. (C). 1995. pap. text, student ed. 19.56 (*0-395-50250-0*) HM.

— Making America Complete. (C). 1996. pap. text 39.16 (*0-395-77442-X*) HM.

— Women of America. (C). 1995. pap. text 38.76 (*0-395-74155-6*) HM.

— Women's Voices, Women's Lives: Documents in Early American History. 1998. pap. text 16.95 (*1-55553-350-7*) NE U Pr.

Berkin, Carol & Horowitz, Leslie, eds. Women's Voices, Women's Lives: Documents in Early American History. LC 98-11255. 224p. 1998. text 45.00 (*1-55553-351-5*) NE U Pr.

Berkin, Carol, et al. Making America: A History of the United States, Vol. I. annot. ed. (C). 1994. text, teacher ed. 49.56 (*0-395-71883-X*) HM.

— Making America: A History of the United States, Vol. II. annot. ed. (C). 1994. text, teacher ed. 49.56 (*0-395-71884-8*) HM.

— Making America: A History of the United States, Brief Edition. (C). 1996. text, teacher ed. 11.96 (*0-395-83776-6*); pap. text 27.96 (*0-395-83645-X*) HM.

— Making America: A History of the United States, Brief Edition. annot. ed. (C). 1996. text, teacher ed. 40.36 (*0-395-83846-0*) HM.

— Making America: A History of the United States, Brief Edition, Vol. I. (C). 1996. pap. text, student ed. 19.56 (*0-395-83777-4*) HM.

— Making America: A History of the United States, Brief Edition, Vol. II. (C). 1997. pap. text, student ed. 19.56 (*0-395-83778-2*) HM.

— Making America: A History of the United States Since 1865 : Brief Edition. 384p. (C). 1996. pap. text 27.96 (*0-395-83646-8*) HM.

— Making America Vol. I: A History of the United States: To 1877. 500p. (C). 1994. pap. text 48.36 (*0-395-71880-5*) HM.

— Making America Vol. B: A History of the United States, Since 1865. 600p. (C). 1994. pap. text 48.36 (*0-395-71881-3*) HM.

Berkin, Carol R. & Lovett, Clara M., eds. Women, War & Revolution. LC 79-26450. 310p. (C). 1980. 36.95 (*0-8419-0502-9*) Holmes & Meier.

Berkin, Carol R., et al. History: CUNY Panel: Rethinking the Disciplines, Vol. 8D. (Women in the Curriculum Ser.). 65p. 1997. pap. 10.00 (*1-885303-12-2*) Towson St Univ.

***Berkin, Ephim.** Medications without Prescriptions. Chernayakhovskaya, leonora, ed. (RUS., Illus.). 224p. 2000. pap. 12.00 (*1-893552-07-1*) Mir Collection.

Berkin, Sarah C., jt. auth. see Schon, Isabel.

Berkkowitz, Carol. Pediatrics: A Primary Care Approach. 2nd ed. LC 99-49760. (Text & Review Ser.). (Illus.). 525p. 2000. pap. text. write for info. (*0-7216-8183-2*, W B Saunders Co) Harcrt Hlth Sci Grp.

***Berkland, Ted.** We Are Guests: Reflections from Crex Meadows. unabridged ed. (Illus.). 96p. 1999. pap. 10.00 (*0-9671140-0-4*) Pine Cone Pubns.

Berkley. Super Horoscope: Taurus, 1997. 1996. mass mkt. 6.99 (*0-425-15349-5*) Berkley Pub.

— Super Horoscopes Aquarius 2000. 1999. pap. text 7.99 (*0-425-16885-9*) Berkley Pub.

— Super Horoscopes Aries 2000. 1999. pap. text 7.99 (*0-425-16878-6*) Berkley Pub.

— Super Horoscopes Cancer 2000. 1999. pap. text 7.99 (*0-425-16881-6*) Berkley Pub.

— Super Horoscopes Capricorn 2000. 1999. pap. text 7.99 (*0-425-16888-3*) Berkley Pub.

— Super Horoscopes Gemini 2000. 1999. pap. text 7.99 (*0-425-16879-4*) Berkley Pub.

— Super Horoscopes Leo 2000. 1999. pap. text 7.99 (*0-425-16882-4*) Berkley Pub.

— Super Horoscopes Libra 2000. 1999. pap. text 7.99 (*0-425-16884-0*) Berkley Pub.

— Super Horoscopes Pisces 2000. 1999. pap. text 7.99 (*0-425-16887-5*) Berkley Pub.

— Super Horoscopes Sagittarius 2000. 1999. pap. text 7.99 (*0-425-16889-1*) Berkley Pub.

— Super Horoscopes Scorpio 2000. 1999. pap. text 7.99 (*0-425-16886-7*) Berkley Pub.

— Super Horoscopes Tarus 2000. 1999. pap. text 7.99 (*0-425-16880-8*) Berkley Pub.

— Super Horoscopes Virgo 2000. 1999. pap. text 7.99 (*0-425-16883-2*) Berkley Pub.

Berkley, Ethel S. Big & Little, Up & Down. LC 84-46016. (Young Scott Bks.). (Illus.). (J). 1950. 11.95 (*0-201-09111-9*) HarpC Child Bks.

Berkley, George E. The Craft of Public Administration. 8th ed. LC 99-18621. 432p. 1999. pap. 49.00 (*0-697-38590-6*) McGraw.

— The Filenes. Caso, Adolph, ed. LC 98-16772. 1998. pap. 18.95 (*0-8283-2035-7*) Branden Bks.

— Hitler's Gift: The Story of Theriesendsadt. (Illus.). 400p. 1993. 22.95 (*0-8283-1954-5*) Branden Bks.

— Jews. Caso, Adolph, ed. LC 96-47021. 460p. 1997. pap. 17.95 (*0-8283-2027-6*) Branden Bks.

— Vienna & Its Jews: The Tragedy of Success, 1880s-1980s. LC 88-1521. 460p. 1988. 24.95 (*0-8191-6816-5*) Madison Bks UPA.

Berkley, George E. & Rouse, John, Jr. The Craft of Public Administration. 6th ed. 448p. (C). 1993. text. write for info. (*0-697-12705-2*) Brown & Benchmark.

— The Craft of Public Administration. 7th ed. LC 96-84167. 448p. (C). 1996. text. write for info. (*0-697-23758-3*) Brown & Benchmark.

— The Craft of Public Administration. 7th ed. 464p. (C). 1997. pap., per. write for info. (*0-07-114033-6*) McGraw.

Berkley, Gerald W., jt. auth. see Flynt, Wayne.

B

An Asterisk (*) at the beginning of an entry indicates that the title is appearing for the first time.

Berkley, Henry J. A Treatise on Mental Diseases. Grob, Gerald N., ed. LC 78-22549. (Historical Issues in Mental Health Ser.). (Illus.). 1980. reprint ed. lib. bdg. 50.95 (*0-405-11903-8*) Ayer.

***Berkley, James D.** The Dynamics of Church Finance. Wiersbe, Warren W., ed. (Ministry Dynamics for a New Century Ser.). 160p. (gr. 13 up). 2000. pap. 10.99 (*0-8010-9105-5*) Baker Bks.

Berkley, James D., ed. Leadership Handbook of Management & Administration. 544p. 1997. pap. 19.99 (*0-8010-9040-7*) Baker Bks.

— Leadership Handbook of Outreach & Care. 528p. 1997. pap. text 19.99 (*0-8010-9042-3*, Leadership Hand) Baker Bks.

— Leadership Handbook of Preaching & Worship. 544p. 1997. pap. text 19.99 (*0-8010-9041-5*, LEADERSHIP HAND) Baker Bks.

— The Leadership Handbook Series. 1616p. 1997. pap. 49.95 (*0-8010-9049-0*) Baker Bks.

Berkley, Mark A. & Stebbins, William C., eds. Comparative Perception, 2 vols., Vol. 2. 1010p. 1990. 329.95 (*0-471-52428-X*) Wiley.

Berkley Publishing Staff. Aquarius. (Berkley Super Horoscopes Ser.). 256p. 1997. pap. 6.99 (*0-425-15896-9*) Berkley Pub.

— Aries. (Berkley Super Horoscopes Ser.). 256p. (Orig.). 1997. pap. 6.99 (*0-425-15886-1*) Berkley Pub.

— Cancer. (Berkley Super Horoscopes Ser.). 256p. 1996. pap. 6.99 (*0-425-15889-6*) Berkley Pub.

— Capricorn. (Berkley Super Horoscopes Ser.). 256p. 1997. pap. 6.99 (*0-425-15895-0*) Berkley Pub.

— Leo '98. (Berkley Super Horoscopes Ser.). 256p. 1997. pap. 6.99 (*0-425-15890-X*) Berkley Pub.

— Libra '98. (Berkley Super Horoscopes Ser.). 256p. 1997. pap. 6.99 (*0-425-15892-6*) Berkley Pub.

— 1998 Super Horoscopes: Pisces. (Berkley Super Horoscopes Ser.). 256p. 1997. pap. 6.99 (*0-425-15897-7*) Berkley Pub.

— Riverside Webster's II Dictionary: Student Edition. 1996. mass mkt. 6.50 (*0-425-15489-0*) Berkley Pub.

— Riverside Webster's II Dictionary. 1996. 11.60 (*0-606-02685-1*, Pub. by Turtleback) Demco.

— Taurus. (Berkley Super Horoscopes Ser.). 256p. 1997. pap. 6.99 (*0-425-15887-X*) Berkley Pub.

— Virgo. (Berkley Super Horoscopes Ser.). 256p. 1997. pap. 6.99 (*0-425-15891-8*) Berkley Pub.

Berkley Publishing Staff, jt. auth. see Houghton Mifflin Company Staff.

Berkley, Robert. Berries: A Cookbook. (Illus.). 120p. 1990. per. 16.95 (*0-671-69019-1*, Fireside) S&S Trade Pap.

— Health Food Book. (Runner's World Ser.). 1982. pap. 9.95 (*0-02-499520-7*, Macmillan Coll) P-H.

— Peppers: A Cookbook. (Illus.). 120p. (Orig.). 1992. per. 17.00 (*0-671-74598-0*, Fireside) S&S Trade Pap.

Berkley, Susan. Speak to Influence: How to Unlock the Hidden Power of Your Voice. LC 98-96218. 192p. 1999. pap. 14.95 (*0-9664302-1-2*) Cmpbll Hall.

Berkley, Theodore, tr. from LAT. Guerric of Igny Liturgical Sermons, 2 vols, 1. (Cistercian Fathers Ser.: No. 8 & No. 32). 378p. 1971. 7.95 (*0-87907-408-6*, Cistercian Pubns.

***Berkley, Timothy W.** From a Broken Covenant to Circumcision of the Heart: Pauline Intertextual Exegesis in Romans 2:17-29. LC 99-87044. (Dissertation Ser.: Vol. 175). x, 260p. 2000. 45.00 (*0-88414-015-6*) Soc Biblical Lit.

Berkman. Consumer Behavior. 2nd ed. (SWC-Marketing Ser.). 1981. teacher ed. write for info. (*0-534-01633-2*) Wadsworth Pub.

— Retail Management. 1988. 45.00 (*0-07-557642-2*) McGraw.

***Berkman, Alan & Bakalar, Nicholas.** Hepatitis A to G: The Facts You Need to Know about All Forms of This Dangerous Disease. 2000. mass mkt. 6.99 (*0-446-60832-7*) Warner Bks.

Berkman, Alexander. The Anti-Climax. 1972. 59.95 (*0-87968-647-2*) Gordon Pr.

***Berkman, Alexander.** Prison Memoirs of an Anarchist. LC 99-15897. 260p. 1999. reprint ed. pap. 14.95 (*0-940322-34-X*, Pub. by NY Rev Bks) Micpt Trade.

Berkman, Alexander. The Russian Tragedy. Nowlin, William G., Jr., ed. 1979. 11.25 (*0-932366-03-1*); pap. 4.50 (*0-932366-02-3*) Black Thorn Bks.

— The Russian Tragedy. 112p. 1976. reprint ed. write for info. (*0-919618-40-5*); reprint ed. pap. write for info. (*0-919618-39-1*) Black Rose.

— The Russian Tragedy. 96p. 1988. reprint ed. pap. 9.95 (*0-948984-00-7*, Pub. by Phoenix Pr) AK Pr Dist.

— The Russian Tragedy: Comprising, the Russian Tragedy, the Russian Revolution & the Communist Party, the Kronstadt Rebellion. LC DK0265.B465.. 136p. 1976. reprint ed. pap. 42.20 (*0-608-00453-7*, 206127200007) Bks Demand.

— What Is Communist Anarchism? 118p. 1992. reprint ed. pap. 9.95 (*0-948984-11-2*, Pub. by Phoenix Pr) AK Pr Dist.

Berkman, Alexander & Newell, Peter. ABC of Anarchism. 3rd ed. 112p. 1980. pap. 5.00 (*0-900384-03-4*) Left Bank.

Berkman, Alexander, ed. see De Cleyre, Voltairine.

Berkman, Harold W. & Gilson, Christopher C. Consumer Behavior, 2nd. 2nd ed. LC 80-29645. (SWC-Marketing). 483p. (C). 1981. mass mkt. 29.75 (*0-534-00957-3*) PWS Pubs.

Berkman, Harold W., et al. Consumer Behavior. LC 96-45180. 1996. write for info. (*0-8442-3674-8*) NTC Contemp Pub Co.

Berkman, James L. The Ballad of "Big George" Foreman: The Patriot, Vol. 8. 4p. (Orig.). 1993. pap. 10.00 (*0-943662-14-1*, 3-686-021) Runaway Pubns

— The Ballad of "Big George" Foreman II: The Patriot. (Patriot Ser.: Vol. 9). 4p. (Orig.). 1995. pap. 10.00 (*0-943662-15-X*, 3-686-021) Runaway Pubns.

— The Ballad of Big Mac. 4p. 1998. pap. 10.00 (*0-943662-16-8*) Runaway Pubns.

— The Ballads. (Illus.). 40p. (Orig.). 1984. pap. 10.00 (*0-943662-04-4*, 164-356) Runaway Pubns.

— But Jesus. (Patriot Ser.: Vol. 7, No. 1). (Orig.). 1990. pap. 10.00 (*0-943662-13-3*, 2-870-544) Runaway Pubns.

***Berkman, James L.** The Collected Works. 120p. 2000. 15.00 (*0-943662-17-6*) Runaway Pubns.

Berkman, James L. Fistfighter II: The Patriot, Vol. 6, No. 2. (Illus.). (Orig.). 1989. pap. 10.00 (*0-943662-11-7*, 2-663-920) Runaway Pubns.

— The Patriot, Vol. 1, No. 1. LC 01-464941. (Illus.). (Orig.). 1984. pap. 10.00 (*0-943662-05-2*) Runaway Pubns.

— The Patriot, Vol. 3, No. 1. (Illus.). (Orig.). 1986. pap. 10.00 (*0-943662-07-9*, 256-649) Runaway Pubns.

— The Patriot, Vol. 4-No. 1. (Illus.). (Orig.). 1987. pap. 10.00 (*0-943662-08-7*, 2-098-376) Runaway Pubns.

— The Patriot, Vol. 5, No. 1. LC 02-348479. (Orig.). 1988. pap. 10.00 (*0-943662-09-5*) Runaway Pubns.

— The Patriot, Vol. 6, No. 1. LC 02-600. (Orig.). 1989. pap. 10.00 (*0-943662-10-9*, 02-600919) Runaway Pubns.

— The Patriot: The Scripturion, Vol. 2, No. 1. (Orig.). 1985. pap. text 10.00 (*0-943662-06-0*, 1-751-040) Runaway Pubns.

— Shoot Out. 32p. (Orig.). 1983. pap. 10.00 (*0-943662-02-8*, 1-166-723) Runaway Pubns.

— Track o' the Bear. (Patriot Ser.: Vol. 6, No. 3). (Illus.). (Orig.). 1989. pap. 10.00 (*0-943662-12-5*, 2-766-522) Runaway Pubns.

Berkman, Joanna. Fodor's Fun in Rio LC 86-218147. 156 p. 1986. write for info. (*0-340-40053-6*) Church.

Berkman, Joyce A. The Healing Imagination of Olive Schreiner: Beyond South African Colonialism. LC 88-38518. (Illus.). 330p. 1989. 35.00 (*0-87023-676-8*) U of Mass Pr.

— The Healing Imagination of Olive Schreiner: Beyond South African Colonialism. LC 88-38518. (Illus.). 336p. 1993. pap. 19.95 (*0-87023-836-1*) U of Mass Pr.

Berkman, Lisa F. & Kawachi, Ichiro, eds. Social Epidemiology. LC 99-29249. (Illus.). 416p. 2000. text 65.00 (*0-19-508331-8*) OUP.

Berkman, Marsha L. & Starkman, Elaine M., eds. Here I Am: Contemporary Jewish Stories from Around the World. LC 98-14407. 480p. 1998. pap. 24.95 (*0-8276-0654-0*) JPS Phila.

Berkman, Michael B. The State Roots of National Politics: Congress & the Tax Agenda, 1978-1986. LC 93-16227. (Policy & Institutional Studies). 216p. (C). 1993. pap. 15.95 (*0-8229-5508-3*); text 49.95 (*0-8229-3761-1*) U of Pittsburgh Pr.

***Berkman, Robert I.** Find It Fast: How to Uncover Expert Information on Any Subject in Print or Online. 5th ed. 368p. 2000. pap. 15.00 (*0-06-273747-3*, HarpRes) HarpInfo.

Berkman, Robert I. Find It Fast Fourth Edition: How to Uncover Expert Information on Any Subject--In Print or Online. 4th ed. LC 96-52526. 352p. 1997. pap. 14.00 (*0-06-273473-3*) HarpC.

Berkman, Robert I. How to Find Market Research Online LC 99-181981. 1996. write for info. (*1-56241-536-0*) FIND-SVP.

— The Scholar's Guide to Research in the Digital Age: How to Make the Most of the Internet, Digital Libraries, E-journals, & More. 230p. 1999. text 55.00 (*0-8147-1341-6*); pap. text 18.50 (*0-8147-1342-4*) NYU Pr.

Berkman, Sue. Everything Your HMO Doesn't Want You to Know: A Survival Guide. 1997. pap. 8.95 (*0-614-27369-2*) Villard Books.

Berkman, Sue, ed. see Connolly, John J.

Berkman, Sylvia. Blackberry Wilderness. LC 79-116939. (Short Story Index Reprint Ser.). 1977. 20.95 (*0-8369-3441-5*) Ayer.

Berkman, Ted. Around the World in 80 Years: Newsrooms, Sound Stages, Private Encounters & Public Affairs. LC 98-17479. (Illus.). 357p. 1998. 27.95 (*0-9627896-1-5*) Manifest Pubns.

Berkmeyer, Kathy M., ed. see Toliver, Pamela R.

Berkmoes, Ryan V. Lonely Planet Chicago. LC 99-230673. (Illus.). 256p. 1998. pap. 15.95 (*0-86442-549-X*) Lonely Planet.

***Berkmoes, Ryan V.** Lonely Planet Moscow. (Travel Guides Ser.). (Illus.). 224p. 2000. pap. text 15.95 (*1-86450-054-9*) Lonely Planet.

Berkmuller, Klaus. Environmental Education about the Rain Forest. (Illus.). 222p. 1992. 27.00 (*2-8317-0098-1*, Pub. by IUCN) Island Pr.

Berkner, Dimity S. & Sellen, Betty-Carol, eds. New Options for Librarians: Finding a Job in a Related Field. LC 83-22143. 300p. 1984. 39.95 (*0-918212-73-1*) Neal-Schuman.

Berkner, Lutz. Access to Postsecondary Education for the 1992 High School Graduates. LC 98-108601. 116p. 1997. per. 10.00 (*0-16-049287-4*) USGPO.

Berkner, Lutz & Malizio, Andrew G. Student Financing of Undergraduate Education, 1995-96: With an Essay on Student Loans. LC 98-224785. (Education Department Publication Ser.: No. NCES 98-076). (Illus.). 234p. 1998. pap. 18.00 (*0-16-049810-4*) USGPO.

Berkner, Lutz K. Descriptive Summary of 1989-90 Beginning Postsecondary Students: 5 Years Later, with an Essay on Postsecondary Persistence & Attainment. 286p. 1996. pap. 17.00 (*0-16-048643-2*) USGPO.

Berkner, Will P. The Great Mural. LC 93-74847. 1994. pap. 7.95 (*1-55673-825-0*, 7995, Fairway Pr) CSS OH.

Berko. Business Communicating. LC 95-73247. 1996. pap. text 51.95 (*0-312-13395-2*) St Martin.

— Communicating, 6 vols. (C). Date not set. pap., teacher ed., suppl. ed. 39.16 (*0-395-71669-1*) HM.

— Communicating, 5 vols. 5th ed. (C). Date not set. pap. text, teacher ed., suppl. ed. write for info. (*0-395-60769-8*) HM.

— Communicating Activities, 6 vols. (C). Date not set. pap. 19.96 (*0-395-72501-1*) HM.

— Connecting. (C). 1994. pap. text, teacher ed. 34.00 (*0-15-501590-7*) Harcourt Coll Pubs.

— Connecting. 2nd ed. LC 96-75216. (C). 1996. pap. text 56.00 (*0-15-503227-5*) Harcourt.

— Connecting. 2nd ed. (C). 1996. pap. text, teacher ed. 28.00 (*0-15-505307-8*) Harcourt Coll Pubs.

Berko, Ferenc, photos by. 60 Years of Photography the Discovering Eye. (Illus.). 128p. 1995. 45.00 (*3-905514-39-7*, Pub. by Edit Stemmle) Dist Art Pubs.

Berko, Glea. Psycholinguistics. 2nd ed. (C). 1997. pap. text, teacher ed. 28.00 (*0-15-504107-X*) Harcourt.

— Psycholinguistics. 2nd ed. (C). 1997. text 71.00 (*0-15-504106-1*) Harcourt.

Berko, Gleason. The Development of Language. 4th ed. LC 96-27292. 504p. 1996. 64.00 (*0-205-19885-6*) Allyn.

Berko Gleason, Jean. The Development of Language. 4th ed. (C). 1997. teacher ed. write for info. (*0-205-26334-8*, T6334-1) Allyn.

Berko, Robert L. Complete Guide to Federal & State Benefits for Veterans, Their Families & Survivors. 10th ed. 192p. (Orig.). 1987. pap. 9.00 (*0-934873-05-4*) Consumer Ed Res.

— Complete Guide to Federal & State Benefits for Veterans, Their Families & Survivors. 11th ed. (Illus.). (Orig.). 1989. write for info. (*0-934873-12-7*) Consumer Ed Res.

— Consumers Guide to Social Security Benefits: How to Get Everything You Are Entitled to under the Latest Laws. LC 86-23933. 144p. 1987. 9.00 (*0-934873-04-6*) Consumer Ed Res.

— Guide to Salt Content of Your Foods: Including a Listing of over 1,000 Brand-Named & Basic Foods: With Recipes for Cooking Without a Salt Shaker. LC 83-72862. (Illus.). 80p. 1983. 5.00 (*0-317-57938-X*) Consumer Ed Res.

— Homeowners & Renters Guide to the Language of Real Estate, Banking, Law & Building. 1986. write for info. (*0-318-61888-5*) Consumer Ed Res.

— How to Find People with Information from Public Records. 1995. write for info. (*0-934873-20-8*) Consumer Ed Res.

— 1995 Complete Guide to Federal & State Benefits for Veterans, their Families & Survivors. LC 94-31413. 240p. pap. 34.72 (*0-934873-16-X*) Consumer Ed Res.

— Parenting: Nurturing a Baby into a Well-Adjusted Teenager. 72p. write for info. (*0-318-61889-3*) Consumer Ed Res.

— Small Home Repairs Made Easy. write for info. (*0-318-61890-7*) Consumer Ed Res.

— Using Public Records to Find & Investigate Anyone. LC 96-72172. 1997. 36.04 (*0-934873-21-6*) Consumer Ed Res.

— Using Public Records to Find or Investigate Anyone. 210p. 1997. pap. 25.00 (*0-614-23615-0*) Consumer Ed Res.

— Where to Get Grants & Loans to Repair & Remodel Your Home. LC 96-72227. 1997. pap. 29.10 (*0-934873-24-0*) Consumer Ed Res.

Berko, Robert L. & Jarvie, Frank. Vital Information for My Heirs. 96p. pap. write for info. (*0-934873-18-6*) Consumer Ed Res.

Berko, Robert L. & Spiegel, Monroe. Consumer's Guide to Home Repair Grants & Loans. LC 86-70756. 1986. 6.00 (*0-685-18142-1*) Consumer Ed Res.

Berko, Robert L., jt. auth. see Consumer Guide Editors.

Berko, Roy M. Communicating. 7th ed. LC 97-72443. 1997. pap. text 32.67 (*0-395-86887-4*) HM.

Berko, Roy M., et al. Basic-ly Communicating: An Activity Approach. 2nd ed. 312p. (C). 1988. text. write for info. (*0-697-04072-0*) Brown & Benchmark.

Berkoben, L. D. Coleridge's Decline As a Poet. (Studies in English Literature: No. 98). 171p. (Orig.). 1975. pap. text 36.95 (*90-279-3226-3*) Mouton.

***Berkoff, Frances, et al.** Power Eating: How to Play Hard & Eat Smart for the Time of Your Life. rev. ed. LC TX361.A8B47. (Illus.). 240p. 2000. pap. 17.95 (*1-55263-111-7*, Pub. by Key Porter) Firefly Bks Ltd.

***Berkoff, Nancy.** Vegan in Volume: Vegan Quantity Recipes for Every Occasion. Wasserman, Debra, ed. (Illus.). 272p. 2000. pap. 19.95 (*0-931411-21-1*) Vegetarian Resc.

Berkoff, Nancy & Collins, Elizabeth. Echinacea & Immunity: Everything You Need to Know about. LC 98-43578. (Natural Pharmacist Ser.). (Illus.). 160p. 2000. pap. 6.99 (*0-7615-1558-5*) Prima Pub.

Berkoff, Steven. Acapulco. 51p. 1987. pap. 10.00 (*0-929741-01-3*) Playsmith.

— Actor. 5p. 1994. 10.00 (*0-929741-00-5*) Playsmith.

— Brighton Beach Scumbags. 25p. 1994. pap. 10.00 (*0-929741-02-1*) Playsmith.

Berkoff, Steven. The Collected Plays, Vol. 1. 400p. 1995. pap. 15.95 (*0-571-16903-1*) Faber & Faber.

Berkoff, Steven. Dahling You Were Mahvelois. 31p. 1994. pap. 10.00 (*0-929741-03-X*) Playsmith.

— Decadence. 21p. 1989. pap. 10.00 (*0-929741-04-8*) Playsmith.

— Dog. 5p. 1994. pap. 10.00 (*0-929741-05-6*) Playsmith.

— East. 21p. pap. 10.00 (*0-929741-06-4*) Playsmith.

Berkoff, Steven. Graft: Tales of an Actor. LC 98-208914. 144p. 1999. 25.00 (*1-84002-040-7*, Pub. by Theatre Comm) Consort Bk Sales.

***Berkoff, Steven.** Graft: Tales of an Actor. (Oberon Bks.). 2000. pap. 12.95 (*1-84002-038-5*) Theatre Comm.

— Harry's Christmas. 11p. 1994. pap. 10.00 (*0-929741-07-2*) Playsmith.

Berkoff, Steven. I Am Hamlet. LC 89-77130. 224p. 1990. pap. 10.95 (*0-8021-3224-3*, Grove) Grove-Atltc.

Berkoff, Steven. Kvetch. 33p. 1986. pap. 10.00 (*0-929741-08-0*) Playsmith.

— Lunch. 15p. 1985. pap. 10.00 (*0-929741-09-9*) Playsmith.

— Massage. 10.00 (*0-929741-10-2*) Playsmith.

— Richard II in New York. (Oberon Bks.). 160p. 2000. pap. 15.95 (*1-84002-057-1*) Theatre Comm.

— Sink the Belgrano! 27p. pap. 10.00 (*0-929741-11-0*) Playsmith.

Berkoff, Steven. Theatre of Steven Berkoff. 176p. (C). 1992. pap. 25.00 (*0-413-67340-5*, A0691) Heinemann.

— Theatre of Steven Berkoff. 1992. 25.00 (*0-413-66150-4*, A0626, Methuen Drama) Methn.

Berkom, Bev Ulsrud van. Ancient Scandinavian Designs. 2nd ed. (International Design Library). (Illus.). 48p. 1985. pap. 6.95 (*0-88045-073-8*, Intl Design) Stemmer Hse.

Berkooz, M. Nuzi Dialect of Akkadian: Orthography & Phonology. (LD Ser.: No. 23). 1937. pap. 25.00 (*0-527-00769-2*) Periodicals Srv.

Berkov, Robert. Strong Man of China. LC 70-124225. (Select Bibliographies Reprint Ser.). (Illus.). 1977. 21.95 (*0-8369-5413-0*) Ayer.

Berkove, Lawrence I. Dan De Quille. (Western Writers Ser: VBol. 136). pap. 5.95 (*0-88430-135-4*) Boise St U W Writ Ser.

Berkove, Lawrence I. Ethical Records of Twain & the Circle of Sagebrush Journalists. (Quarry Farm Papers: Vol. 5). 27p. 1994. pap. 5.00 (*1-880817-07-1*) EC Ctr Mark T Stu.

Berkove, Lawrence I., ed. The Fighting Horse of the Stanislaus: Stories & Essays by Dan De Quille. LC 90-10751. (Illus.). 283p. 1990. pap. 16.95 (*0-87745-299-7*) U of Iowa Pr.

Berkove, Lawrence I., ed. see Bierce, Ambrose.

Berkove, Lawrence I., ed. see De Quille, Dan.

Berkovic. Genetics of Focal Epilepsies. Date not set. 96.00 (*0-86196-569-8*, Pub. by J Libbey Med) Bks Intl VA.

***Berkovic, Sally.** Straight Talk: My Dilemma as an Orthodox Jewish Woman. LC 99-26775. 254p. 1999. 25.00 (*0-88125-661-7*) Ktav.

Berkovich, Felix. Jewish Chess Masters on Stamps. LC 99-87524. (Illus.). 176p. 2000. boxed set 40.00 (*0-7864-0683-6*) McFarland & Co.

Berkovich, IA. G., et al. Characters of Finite Groups. Shumyatsky, P. & Zobina, V., trs. from RUS. LC 97-39813. (Translations of Mathematical Monographs Ser.). 382p. 1997. text 129.00 (*0-8218-4606-X*) Am Math.

Berkovich, V. Spectral Theory & Analytic Geometry over Non-Archimedean Fields. LC 90-830. (Mathematical Surveys & Monographs: Vol. 33). 169p. 1990. text 55.00 (*0-8218-1534-2*, SURV/33) Am Math.

Berkovich, Ya G. & Zhmud', E. M. Characters of Finite Groups, Pt. 2. LC 97-39813. (Translations of Mathematical Monographs: Vol. 181). 332p. 1998. 115.00 (*0-8218-0532-0*) Am Math.

Berkovitch, Israel. Energy Sources & Policy: An Overview & Guide to the Literature. (Keynote Ser.). 186p. 1996. pap. 55.00 (*0-7123-0805-9*, Pub. by SRIS) L Erlbaum Assocs.

***Berkovitch, Nitza.** From Motherhood to Citizenship: Women's Rights & International Organizations. LC 98-45776. 1999. 34.95 (*0-8018-6028-8*) Johns Hopkins.

Berkovits, Eliezer. Faith after the Holocaust. 1973. pap. 11.95 (*0-87068-193-1*) Ktav.

— The Jewish Woman in Time & Torah. 1990. 19.95 (*0-88125-311-1*) Ktav.

— Major Themes in Modern Philosophies of Judaism. 1974. 25.00 (*0-87068-264-4*) Ktav.

— Not in Heaven: The Nature & Function of Halakha. LC 82-23255. 131p. 1983. pap. 11.95 (*0-88125-003-1*) Ktav.

Berkovits, Masha, jt. auth. see Langer, Elky.

Berkovitz, B. K. Anatomia Oral. 2nd ed. (C). 1996. text 88.40 (*84-8174-139-6*) Mosby Inc.

Berkovitz, B. K. Oral Anatomy 3. 3rd ed. 2001. text 79.95 (*0-323-00873-9*) Mosby Inc.

Berkovitz, B. K., et al, eds. The Periodontal Ligament in Health & Disease. (Illus.). 472p. 1982. 203.00 (*0-08-024412-2*, Pub. by Pergamon Repr) Franklin.

Berkovitz, B. K. & Moxham, B. J. Oral Anatomy, Embryology & Histology. LC 94-46127. (Self-Assessment Picture Tests in Dentistry Ser.). 144p. (C). (gr. 13). 1994. text 25.50 (*0-7234-2007-6*) Mosby Inc.

Berkovitz, B. K., et al. Color Atlas & Textbook of Oral Anatomy, Histology, & Embryology. 2nd rev. ed. LC 92-12712. (Illus.). 328p. (C). (gr. 13). 1992. text 73.00 (*0-8151-0697-1*, 21901) Mosby Inc.

Berkovitz, Jay R. The Shaping of a Jewish Identity in Nineteenth-Century France. LC 89-16507. 308p. (C). 1989. 34.95 (*0-8143-2011-2*) Wayne St U Pr.

— The Shaping of a Jewish Identity in Nineteenth-Century France. 308p. 1995. reprint ed. pap. text 16.95 (*0-8143-2012-0*) Wayne St U Pr.

Berkovitz, Philip. Blended Beauty. (Illus.). 160p. 1995. 24.95 (*0-89815-742-0*) Ten Speed Pr.

Berkovski, Boris M., ed. Magnetic Fluids & Applications Handbook. (UNESCO Series of Learning Materials). 1996. write for info. (*1-56700-053-3*) Begell Hse.

Berkovsky, Boris M., ed. Magnetic Fluids & Applications Handbook & Database. 851p. 1996. 165.00 (*1-56700-062-2*) Begell Hse.

Berkovsky, Boris M. & Krakov, M. S. Thermomechanics of Magnetic Fluids, Vol. 2. (Thermal Physics Ser.: Vol. 2, Pt. 1). iv, 102p. 1989. pap. text 117.00 (*3-7186-4812-1*) Gordon & Breach.

Berkow, jt. auth. see Rich.

Berkow, Daniel N., jt. auth. see Page, Richard C.

An Asterisk (*) at the beginning of an entry indicates that the title is appearing for the first time.

***Berkow, Ira.** Court Vision: Unexpected Views on the Lure of Basketball. LC 99-45201. 288p. 2000. 24.00 (*0-688-16842-6*, Wm Morrow) Morrow Avon.

Berkow, Ira. Hank Greenberg: Hall-of-Fame Slugger. LC 90-43005. (Illus.). 108p. (J). (gr. 3-7). 1991. 13.95 (*0-8276-0376-2*) JPS Phila.

Berkow, Ira, jt. auth. see Mason, Jackie.

***Berkow, Ita G.** Edward Hopper, 1. 1998. 10.98 (*1-880908-48-4*) Todtri Prods.

Berkow, Joseph W. Fluorescein & Indocyanine Green Angiography: Technique & Interpretation. 2nd ed. LC 97-19753. (Ophthalmology Monographs). 1997. write for info. (*1-56055-044-9*) Am Acad Ophthal.

Berkow, Joseph W., et al. Fluorescein Angiography: A Guide to the Interpretation of Fluorescein Angiograms. 2nd ed. (Illus.). 160p. 1984. 25.00 (*0-317-94076-7*) Am Acad Ophthal.

Berkow, Robert. Manuel Merck de Diagnostic et Therapeutic. (FRE.). 1988. lib. bdg. 195.00 (*0-8288-3829-1*, F120190) Fr & Eur.

— The Merck Manual of Medical Information: Home Edition. 1648p. 1999. per. 7.99 (*0-671-02727-1*) PB.

Berkow, Robert, ed. Merck Manual: Arabic Language Edition. (ARA.). Date not set. 150.00 (*0-7859-9677-X*) Fr & Eur.

— Merck Manual: Chinese Language Edition. (CHI.). Date not set. 150.00 (*0-7859-9676-1*) Fr & Eur.

— Merck Manual: Czech Language Edition. (CZE.). Date not set. 150.00 (*0-7859-9680-X*) Fr & Eur.

— Merck Manual: French Language Edition. (FRE.). Date not set. 225.00 (*0-7859-9675-3*) Fr & Eur.

— Merck Manual: German Language Edition. (GER.). Date not set. 195.00 (*0-7859-9674-5*) Fr & Eur.

— Merck Manual: Hungarian Language Edition. (HUN.). Date not set. 150.00 (*0-7859-9669-9*) Fr & Eur.

— Merck Manual: Italian Language Edition. (ITA.). Date not set. 150.00 (*0-7859-9672-9*) Fr & Eur.

— Merck Manual: Japanese Language Edition. (JPN.). Date not set. 295.00 (*0-7859-9681-8*) Fr & Eur.

— Merck Manual: Polish Language Edition. (POL.). Date not set. 150.00 (*0-7859-9670-2*) Fr & Eur.

Berkow, Robert, et al, eds. The Merck Manual: Centennial Edition. 17th ed. (Merck Manual of Diagnosis & Therapy Ser.). (Illus.). 1999. 35.00 (*0-911910-10-7*) Merck.

— The Merck Manual of Geriatrics. 2nd ed. LC 96-168522. 1995. 25.00 (*0-911910-66-2*) Merck.

Berkow, Robert, ed. see McGraw-Hill Book Company Staff.

Berkow, Robert, ed. see Merck & Co., Inc. Staff.

***Berkow, Robert.** The Merck Manual of Medical Information. 1536p. 2000. pap. 19.95 (*0-671-02726-3*) PB.

***Berkowitch, John E.** Trends in Japanese Textile Technology. 112p. (C). 2000. pap. text 30.00 (*0-7881-8938-7*) DIANE Pub.

Berkowitz. American Drama 20th Century. (C). 1992. pap. text 45.50 (*0-582-01602-9*) Longman.

— Business Week Edition. 6th ed. 1999. 72.50 (*0-07-234292-7*) McGraw.

— Marketing. 5th ed. 1996. 69.25 (*0-256-22074-3*) McGraw.

***Berkowitz.** Marketing. 6th ed. LC 99-30269. 1999. 65.25 (*0-07-365645-3*) McGraw.

Berkowitz. Marketing Preview. 5th ed. 1996. 37.50 (*0-256-22890-6*) McGraw.

— Pediatrics: A Primary Care Approach. (C). text. write for info. (*0-8089-2074-X*, Grune & Strat); text. write for info. (*0-8089-2118-5*, Grune & Strat) Harcrt Hlth Sci Grp.

Berkowitz, A. "Don't Do What I Did!" A Sure-Fire Step-by-Step to Fulfilling Relationships. 180p. 1998. pap. 39.95 (*0-7021-4537-8*, Pub. by Juta & Co) Intl Spec Bk.

Berkowitz, Alan. A Guide to the Bright Angel Trail. Priehs, T. J., ed. 1979. pap. 2.95 (*0-938216-09-0*) GCA.

— A Guide to the North Kaibab Trail. Priehs, T. J., ed. 1980. pap. 2.95 (*0-938216-10-4*) GCA.

Berkowitz, Alan D. & Miscimarra, Philip A. The NLRB & Secondary Boycotts: Supplement 1981-1998. (Labor Relations & Public Policy Ser.: Vol. 4). 200p. 1998. 25.00 (*1-891496-06-9*) J M Olin.

Berkowitz, Alan D., jt. auth. see Bellace, Janice R.

***Berkowitz, Alan J.** Patterns of Disengagement: The Practice & Portrayal of Reclusion in Early Medieval China. LC 99-57586. 1999. 55.00 (*0-8047-3603-0*) Stanford U Pr.

Berkowitz, Allan & Moskovitz, Patti, eds. Embracing the Covenant: Converts to Judaism Talk about Why & How. LC 96-5159. 192p. 1996. pap. 15.95 (*1-879045-50-8*) Jewish Lights.

Berkowitz, Ariel & Berkowitz, D'vorah. Take Hold: Embracing Our Divine Inheritance in Israel. (Illus.). 336p. 1998. pap. 16.95 (*1-892124-01-7*) First Fruits CO.

Berkowitz, B. J., ed. see Metallurgical Society of AIME Staff.

Berkowitz, Bernard. Statistics for Poets. (Illus.). 123p. 1991. pap. text 19.95 (*0-9668784-0-X*) Pangloss Press.

Berkowitz, Bernard, jt. auth. see Newman, Mildred.

Berkowitz, Bob. His Secret Life. LC 97-2258. 272p. 1997. 22.50 (*0-684-81103-0*) S&S Trade.

— His Secret Life: Male Sexual Fantasies. 1998. per. 6.50 (*0-671-02608-9*) PB.

Berkowitz, Bob & Gittines, Roger. What Men Won't Tell You but Women Need to Know. 192p. 1991. mass mkt. 5.99 (*0-380-71364-0*, Avon Bks) Morrow Avon.

Berkowitz, Bruce D. Strategic Intelligence for American National Security. 264p. 1989. pap. text 17.95 (*0-691-02339-5*, Pub. by Princeton U Pr) Cal Prin Full Svc.

***Berkowitz, Bruce D. & Goodman, Allan E.** Best Truth: Intelligence in the Information Age. LC 99-39390. (Illus.). 193p. 2000. 22.50 (*0-300-08011-5*) Yale U Pr.

Berkowitz, Bruce D., jt. auth. see Goodman, Allan E.

Berkowitz, Bruce D., ed. see Darling, Arthur B.

Berkowitz, Carol D. Pediatrics: A Primary Care Approach. (C). 1996. pap. text 18.00 (*0-8089-1975-X*, Grune & Strat) Harcrt Hlth Sci Grp.

— Pediatrics: A Primary Care Approach. Schmitt, Bill, ed. LC 95-23414. (Saunders Text & Review Ser.). (Illus.). 525p. 1996. pap. text 33.95 (*0-7216-5623-4*, W B Saunders Co) Harcrt Hlth Sci Grp.

Berkowitz, Daniel A., ed. Social Meanings of News: A Text-Reader. LC 96-51208. 400p. (C). 1997. 62.00 (*0-7619-0075-6*, 00756); pap. 29.95 (*0-7619-0076-4*, 00764) Sage.

Berkowitz, David & Soyer, Dolores. Behind the Gold Curtain: Fifty Years in the Metropolitan Opera Orchestra. LC 95-76145. (Illus.). 190p. 1995. 22.95 (*0-913559-29-6*) Birch Brook Pr.

Berkowitz, David S. John Selden's Formative Years: Politics & Society in Early Seventeenth-Century England. LC 86-83051. (Illus.). 376p. 1988. 50.00 (*0-918016-91-6*) Folger Bks.

Berkowitz, David S., ed. see Morison, Richard.

Berkowitz, D'vorah, jt. auth. see Berkowitz, Ariel.

Berkowitz, Edward D. America's Welfare State: From Roosevelt to Reagan. LC 90-46424. (American Moment Ser.). 224p. 1991. text 38.95 (*0-8018-4127-5*) Johns Hopkins.

— Mr. Social Security: The Life of Wilbur J. Cohen. LC 94-39964. (Illus.). 416p. 1995. 34.95 (*0-7006-0707-2*) U Pr of KS.

— Rehabilitation: The Federal Government's Response to Disability, 1935 to 1954. Phillips, William R. & Rosenberg, Janet, eds. LC 79-6896. (Physically Handicapped in Society Ser.). 1980. lib. bdg. 36.95 (*0-405-13107-0*) Ayer.

***Berkowitz, Edward D.** To Improve Human Health: A History of the Institute of Medicine. LC 98-40289. 1998. 40.00 (*0-309-06188-1*) Natl Acad Pr.

Berkowitz, Edward D., ed. Social Security after Fifty: Successes & Failures, 5. LC 86-19383. (Studies in Social Welfare Policies & Programs: No. 5). 176p. 1987. 45.00 (*0-313-25542-3*, BZS/, Greenwood Pr) Greenwood.

Berkowitz, Edward D. & McQuaid, Kim. Creating the Welfare State: The Political Economy of Twentieth Century Reform. LC 79-22524. 204p. 1980. lib. bdg. 34.95 (*0-275-90453-9*, C0453, Praeger Pubs) Greenwood.

— Creating the Welfare State: The Political Economy of Twentieth-Century Reform. rev. ed. LC 91-41034. 250p. 1992. pap. 14.95 (*0-7006-0528-2*) U Pr of KS.

— Creating the Welfare State: The Political Economy of Twentieth-Century Reform. 2nd enl. rev. ed. LC 87-25871. 258p. 1988. 62.95 (*0-275-92747-4*, C2747, Praeger Pubs) Greenwood.

Berkowitz, Edward D., jt. auth. see Kingson, Eric R.

Berkowitz, Edward D., ed. see Institute of Medicine Staff.

Berkowitz, Eric & Kerin, Roger. Marketing (Canadian) 344p. (C). 1991. student ed., per. 19.95 (*0-256-10229-5*, Irwn McGrw-H) McGrw-H Hghr Educ.

Berkowitz, Eric & Pol, Louis G. Healthcare Marketing Research. LC 96-38962. 264p. (C). 1996. text 45.00 (*1-55738-642-0*, Irwn Prfssnl) McGraw-Hill Prof.

***Berkowitz, Eric, et al.** Marketing. 6th ed. 350p. (C). 1999. pap., student ed. 28.75 (*0-07-365817-0*) McGrw-H Hghr Educ.

Berkowitz, Eric N. Essentials of Health Care Marketing. LC 95-40372. 350p. 1995. 50.00 (*0-8342-0687-0*) Aspen Pub.

Berkowitz, Eric N., et al. Marketing. 5th ed. LC 96-21378. 752p. (C). 1996. text 68.95 (*0-256-18968-4*, Irwn McGrw-H) McGrw-H Hghr Educ.

— Marketing: Wall Street Journal Readings. 4th ed. (C). 1999. text, student ed. 73.95 (*0-256-18179-9*, Irwn McGrw-H) McGrw-H Hghr Educ.

— Marketing, Canadian. 2nd ed. 800p. (C). 1995. text 48.95 (*0-256-12088-9*, Irwn McGrw-H) McGrw-H Hghr Educ.

— Marketing CPS - Textmaps: A Chapter-by-Chapter Guide for Exploring Main Ideas & Terms in Marketing. 4th rev. ed. (C). 1995. 14.00 (*0-256-19139-5*, Irwn McGrw-H) McGrw-H Hghr Educ.

— Marketing Study Guide. 5th ed. 344p. (C). 1996. text 26.25 (*0-256-21971-0*, Irwn McGrw-H) McGrw-H Hghr Educ.

Berkowitz, Eric N., jt. auth. see Hillestad, Steven G.

***Berkowitz, George & Doerfer, Jane.** The Legal Seafoods Cookbook. 1999. 26.00 (*0-8446-7018-9*) Peter Smith.

Berkowitz, George & Doerfer, Jane. The Legal Seafoods Cookbook: Simply Perfect Recipes from Boston's Favorite Seafood Restaurant. LC 87-8922. (Illus.). 192p. 1988. pap. 15.95 (*0-385-23183-0*) Doubleday.

Berkowitz, Gerald, jt. auth. see Neimark, Paul.

Berkowitz, Gerald M. American Drama of the Twentieth Century. LC 92-9396. (Literature in English Ser.). 312p. (C). 1995. pap. 51.00 (*0-582-01601-0*, 79343) Addison-Wesley.

Berkowitz, Gerald M. New Broadways: Theatre Across America: Approaching a New Millennium. 2000. pap. 19.95 (*1-55783-412-1*) Applause Theatre Bk Pubs.

— New Broadways: Theatre Across America Approaching a New Millennium. rev. ed. LC 96-37922. 320p. 1997. 24.95 (*1-55783-257-9*) Applause Theatre Bk Pubs.

***Berkowitz, Henry.** Amphibians & Reptiles. rev. ed. Lampert, Erv, ed. (Educational Coloring Bks.). (Illus.). 32p. (J). (gr. 1-4). 1999. reprint ed. pap. 3.95 (*0-932855-49-0*) Winner Enter.

Berkowitz, Henry. The Dinosaurs. Lampert, Erv, ed. (Educational Coloring Bks.). (Illus.). 32p. (J). (gr 1-4). 1996. pap. 3.95 (*0-932855-47-4*) Winner Enter.

— Dolphins & Whales. Lampert, Erv, ed. (Educational Coloring Bks.). (Illus.). 32p. (J). (gr. 1-4). 1996. pap. 3.95 (*0-932855-48-2*) Winner Enter.

— Fish Facts & Fancies. Lampert, Erv, ed. (Educational Coloring Bks.). (Illus.). 32p. (J). (gr. 1-4). 1996. pap. 3.95 (*0-932855-46-6*) Winner Enter.

Berkowitz, Howard C. Designing Architectures for Routing & Switching: Reengineering Your Network Structure. LC 98-84330. 1998. pap. 45.00 (*1-57870-059-0*) Macmillan Tech.

— Designing Routing & Switching Architectures for Enterprise Networks. (Network Architecture & Development Ser.). 1999. 45.00 (*1-57870-060-4*) New Riders Pub.

***Berkowitz, Howard C.** WAN Survival Guide: Strategies for VPNs & Multi-Service Networks. (Networking Council Ser.). 512p. 2000. pap. 49.99 (*0-471-38428-3*) Wiley.

Berkowitz, Howard L., jt. ed. see Levitan, Stephan J.

Berkowitz, Jane. Kansas City Coffee House Cookbook. (Illus.). 96p. (Orig.). 1996. pap. 9.95 (*1-878686-27-5*) Pig Out Pubns.

Berkowitz, Jeff. Fractal Cosmos: The Art of Mathematical Design. LC 97-65899. (Illus.). 212p. (Orig.). 1998. pap. 29.95 (*1-56937-064-8*) Amber Lotus.

Berkowitz, Joan B., et al, eds. Marine Electrochemistry. LC 73-75170. (Illus.). 414p. reprint ed. pap. 128.40 (*0-608-10962-2*, 205044500081) Bks Demand.

Berkowitz, Joan B., ed. see Energy Storage Symposium Staff, et al.

***Berkowitz, Julie S.** Adorn the Halls: History of the Art Collection of Thomas Jefferson University. Clendenin, Malcolm, ed. (Illus.). 720p. 1999. write for info (*0-9674384-1-1*) Thom Jeff Univ.

Berkowitz, Lawrence B., jt. auth. see Lee, Franklyn E.

Berkowitz, Leonard. Advances in Experimental Social Psychology, Vol. 19. (Serial Publication Ser.). 1985. pap. 24.95 (*0-12-000010-5*) Acad Pr.

— Aggression: Its Causes, Consequences, & Control. 1992. pap. 33.50 (*0-07-004883-5*) McGraw.

— Aggression: Its Causes, Consequences, & Control. LC 92-31862. 496p. 1993. text 59.95 (*1-56639-035-8*) Temple U Pr.

— Aggression: Its Causes, Consequences & Control. LC 92-33589. (Series in Social Psychology). 512p. (C). 1992. pap. text 39.69 (*0-07-004874-6*) McGraw.

***Berkowitz, Leonard.** Causes & Consequences of Feelings. (Studies in Emotion & Social Interaction). (Illus.). 256p. 2000. 64.95 (*0-521-63325-7*); pap. 19.95 (*0-521-63363-X*) Cambridge U Pr.

Berkowitz, Leonard, ed. Advances in Experimental Social Psychology, Vol. 12. (Serial Publication Ser.). 1979. text 116.00 (*0-12-015212-6*); lib. bdg. 55.00 (*0-12-015282-7*) Acad Pr.

— Advances in Experimental Social Psychology, Vol. 13. (Serial Publication Ser.). 1980. text 116.00 (*0-12-015213-4*) Acad Pr.

— Advances in Experimental Social Psychology, Vol. 14. (Serial Publication Ser.). 1981. text 116.00 (*0-12-015214-2*) Acad Pr.

— Advances in Experimental Social Psychology, Vol. 15. (Serial Publication Ser.). 270p. 1982. text 116.00 (*0-12-015215-0*) Acad Pr.

— Advances in Experimental Social Psychology, Vol. 16. (Serial Publication Ser.). 1984. text 116.00 (*0-12-015216-9*) Acad Pr.

— Advances in Experimental Social Psychology, Vol. 17. (Serial Publication Ser.). 1984. text 116.00 (*0-12-015217-7*) Acad Pr.

— Advances in Experimental Social Psychology, Vol. 18. LC 64-23452. (Serial Publication Ser.). 1984. text 116.00 (*0-12-015218-5*) Acad Pr.

— Advances in Experimental Social Psychology, Vol. 20. (Serial Publication Ser.). 351p. 1987. text 110.00 (*0-12-015220-7*) Acad Pr.

— Advances in Experimental Social Psychology, Vol. 22. (Serial Publication Ser.). 364p. 1989. text 101.00 (*0-12-015222-3*) Acad Pr.

Berkowitz, Linda. Little Bird & Moon Sandwich. LC 97-24270. 32p. (J). 1998. lib. bdg. 17.99 (*0-517-70962-7*, Pub. by Crown Bks Yng Read) Random.

— Little Bird & the Moon Sandwich. LC 97-24270. 32p. (J). 1998. 16.00 (*0-517-70961-9*, Pub. by Crown Bks Yng Read) Random.

Berkowitz, Luci & Brunner, Theodore F., eds. Lucilius: Index Lucilianus. xiv, 171p. 1968. 40.00 (*0-318-71974-6*) G Olms Pubs.

— Persius Flaccus, Aulus: Index Verborum Quae in Saturis Auli Persi Flacci Reperiuntur. xvi, 160p. 1967. 50.00 (*0-318-71969-X*) G Olms Pubs.

Berkowitz, Luci & Squitier, Karl A., eds. Thesaurus Linguae Graecae: Canon of Greek Authors & Works. 3rd ed. (Illus.). 536p. 1990. text 55.00 (*0-19-506037-7*) OUP.

Berkowitz, Luci, ed. see Arnobius.

Berkowitz, Luci, ed. see Persius.

Berkowitz, Luci, ed. see Sophocles.

Berkowitz, Marvin W. & Oser, Fritz K., eds. Moral Education: Theory & Applications. 472p. (C). 1985. text 89.95 (*0-89859-557-6*) L Erlbaum Assocs.

***Berkowitz, Michael.** The Jewish Self-Image in the West. LC 99-41831. (Illus.). 192p. 2000. text 35.00 (*0-8147-9861-6*) NYU Pr.

Berkowitz, Michael. Western Jewry & the Zionist Project, 1914-1933. LC 96-13024. (Illus.). 321p. (C). 1996. text 59.95 (*0-521-47087-0*) Cambridge U Pr.

— Zionist Culture & West European Jewry Before the First World War. LC 96-33936. 1996. reprint ed. pap. 18.95 (*0-8078-4605-8*) U of NC Pr.

Berkowitz, Mina, jt. auth. see Crowl, Thomas K.

Berkowitz, Monroe, et al, eds. Economic Consequences of Traumatic Spinal Cord Injury. 212p. 1992. pap. 79.95 (*0-939957-44-2*) Demos Medical.

Berkowitz, Monroe & Burton, John F., Jr. Permanent Disability Benefits in Workers' Compensation. LC 87-22874. 440p. 1987. text 36.00 (*0-88099-051-1*); pap. text 18.00 (*0-88099-050-3*) W E Upjohn.

Berkowitz, Monroe & Hill, M. Anne, eds. Disability & the Labor Market: Economic Problems, Policies & Programs. 2nd ed. 336p. 1989. pap. text 16.95 (*0-87546-153-0*, ILR Press) Cornell U Pr.

Berkowitz, Monroe, et al. Forging Linkages: Modifying Disability Benefit Programs to Encourage Employment: Reporting on Projects in Belgium, France, Netherlands, Federal Republic of Germany, Israel & Sweden. (Illus.). 200p. (Orig.). 1989. pap. text 10.00 (*0-685-31959-8*) Rehab Intl.

— Spinal Cord Injury: An Analysis of Medical & Social Costs. LC 98-4054. 200p. 1998. 89.95 (*1-888799-17-X*) Demos Medical.

Berkowitz, Monroe, jt. ed. see Hunt, H. Allan.

Berkowitz, Neal. Learn Microsoft Access Programming for the Advanced User. 1998. pap. text 39.95 (*1-55622-589-X*) Wordware Pub.

***Berkowitz, Neal & Bean, Deborah.** Learn ACT! 2000 for the Advanced User. (Illus.). 400p. (C). 2000. pap. 39.95 (*1-55622-744-2*) Wordware Pub.

Berkowitz, Neal, jt. auth. see Bean, Deborah.

Berkowitz, Norbert. Fossil Hydrocarbons: Chemistry & Technology. LC 97-23439. (Illus.). 351p. 1997. text 89.00 (*0-12-091090-X*) Morgan Kaufmann.

Berkowitz, Paul. U. S. Rangers: The Law of the Land. 480p. 1994. pap. text 24.08 (*1-56226-203-3*) CAT Pub.

Berkowitz, Peter. Nietzsche: The Ethics of an Immoralist. LC 94-34119. 336p. 1995. text 41.00 (*0-674-62442-4*, BERNIE) HUP.

— Nietzsche: The Ethics of an Immoralist. 336p. 1996. pap. 17.50 (*0-674-62443-2*) HUP.

***Berkowitz, Peter.** Virtue & the Making of Modern Liberalism. LC 98-34871. (New Forum Bks.). 1999. 27.95 (*0-691-01688-7*, Pub. by Princeton U Pr) Cal Prin Full Svc.

Berkowitz, Raymond S. Modern Radar: Analysis, Evaluation & System Design. LC 65-21446. 676p. reprint ed. pap. 200.00 (*0-608-10286-5*, 201741100007) Bks Demand.

Berkowitz, Richard. Handbook for Prescribing Medications. 2nd ed. 422p. 1986. pap. text 34.95 (*0-316-09199-5*, Little Brwn Med Div) Lppncott W & W.

Berkowitz, Richard L., et al, eds. Obstetric Ultrasonography: Gynecologic Oncology. fac. ed. LC 88-18141. (Contemporary Issues in Obstetrics & Gynecology Ser.: No. 3). (Illus.). 260p. 1988. reprint ed. pap. 80.60 (*0-7837-7890-2*, 204764600007) Bks Demand.

Berkowitz, Richard L., et al. Handbook for Prescribing Medications During Pregnancy. 2nd ed. 1986. pap. text 6.50 (*0-685-03072-5*, Little Brwn Med Div) Lppncott W & W.

Berkowitz, Robert, jt. auth. see Eisenberg, Michael B.

Berkowitz, Robert E., jt. auth. see Eisenberg, Michael.

Berkowitz, Robert E., jt. auth. see Eisenberg, Michael B.

Berkowitz, Samuel. Cleft Lip & Palate: Perspectives in Management with an Introduction to Craniofacial Anomalies, Vols. 1 & 2. (Illus.). 904p. 1996. pap. 390.00 (*1-56593-590-X*, 1206) Thomson Learn.

— The Cleft Palate Story. LC 94-7902. (Illus.). 240p. (Orig.). 1994. pap. 24.00 (*0-86715-259-1*) Quint Pub Co.

— The Cleft Palate Story. 240p. (Orig.). 1994. 29.95 (*1-56593-745-7*, 1448) Singular Publishing.

Berkowitz, Sol. A New Approach to Sight-Singing. 4th ed. (C). 1997. pap. text 36.00 (*0-393-96908-8*) Norton.

— New Approaches to Sight Singing. 4th ed. (C). 1998. pap. text 45.00 (*0-393-97271-2*) Norton.

Berkowitz, Stephen A., et al. The Investment Performance of Corporate Pension Plans: Why They Do Not Beat the Market Regularly. LC 87-19030. 143p. 1988. 59.95 (*0-89930-224-6*, LPN/, Quorum Bks) Greenwood.

Berkowitz, Stephen D., jt. auth. see Wellman, Barry.

Berkowitz, Steve. Introduction to Structural Analysis. 2nd ed. (C). Date not set. pap. 55.00 (*0-8133-1784-3*) Westview.

— Introduction to Structural Analysis. 2nd ed. (C). 1998. pap. text 17.95 (*0-8133-1785-1*) Westview.

Berkowitz, Steven, ed. A Critical Edition of George Buchanan's Baptistes & of Its Anonymous Seventeenth-Century Translation Tyrannicall-Government Anatomized. rev. ed. LC 91-34201. (Renaissance Imagination Ser.). (Illus.). 624p. 1992. text 20.00 (*0-8153-0450-1*) Garland.

Berkowitz, William. Dialogues in Judaism: Jewish Dilemmas Defined, Debated, & Explored. LC 91-8732. 552p. 1991. 50.00 (*0-87668-654-4*) Aronson.

— Local Heroes. LC 86-46364. 350p. 1987. pap. 16.95 (*0-669-15830-5*) Lxngtn Bks.

Berkowitz, Yizchak, jt. auth. see Finkelman, Shimon.

Berks, John, tr. see Faure, Christine.

Berksen, Barbara. Island of the Blue Dolphins: A Study Guide. (Novel-Ties Ser.). (J). (gr. 4-6). 1984. pap. text, teacher ed., student ed. 15.95 (*0-88122-088-4*) Lrn Links.

***Berkshire Reference Works Staff.** Encyclopedia of Millennialism & Millennial Movements. Landes, Richard A., ed. LC 99-52373. (Religion & Society Ser.). (Illus.). 480p. 2000. text 125.00 (*0-415-92246-1*) Routledge.

B

An Asterisk (*) at the beginning of an entry indicates that the title is appearing for the first time.

Berkshire Reference Works Staff. International Encyclopedia for Women & Sports, 3 vols. 1999. 325.00 (0-02-864954-0) Mac Lib Ref.

— International Encyclopedia for Women & Sports, Vol. 1. 1999. 110.00 (0-02-864951-6) Mac Lib Ref.

— International Encyclopedia for Women & Sports, Vol. 2. 1999. 110.00 (0-02-864952-4) Mac Lib Ref.

— International Encyclopedia for Women & Sports, Vol. 3. 1999. 110.00 (0-02-864953-2) Mac Lib Ref.

Berkson, Bill. Blue Is the Hero. 1976. pap. 4.00 (0-917824-02-4) L Pubns.

— Blue Is the Hero. 1976. 7.50 (0-685-79245-5); pap. 4.00 (0-685-79247-1) L Pubns.

— Blue Is the Hero. deluxe ed. 1976. 15.00 (0-685-79246-3) L Pubns.

— Lush Life. Elmslie, Kenward, ed. LC 84-51752. 52p. (Orig.). 1985. pap. 6.00 (0-915990-26-1) Z Pr.

***Berkson, Bill.** Serenade: Poems & Prose 1975, 1989. LC 99-89811. (Illus.). 125p. 2000. pap. 14.00 (1-58195-016-0, Pub. by Zoland Bks) SPD-Small Pr Dist.

Berkson, Bill. Start Over. (Desert Island Chapbook Ser.). 32p. 1983. pap. 3.50 (0-939180-24-3) Tombouctou.

***Berkson, Bill, text.** Elaine de Kooning: Portraits. (Illus.). 20p. 1999. pap. 15.00 (1-58821-035-9) Salander OReilly.

Berkson, Bill & Shaw, Reesey. Table Tops: Morandi's Still Lifes to Mapplethorpe's Flower Studies. LC 97-67206. (Illus.). 51p. 1997. pap. 25.00 (1-885088-07-8) CA Ctr Arts.

Berkson, Bill, jt. auth. see Doty, Robert M.

Berkson, Bill, jt. auth. see Waldman, Anne.

Berkson, Burt. Alpha-Lipoic Acid Breakthrough. LC 98-33577. 224p. 1998. per. 14.00 (0-7615-1457-0) Prima Pub.

— Frequently Asked Questions All about B Vitamins. (FAQs All about Health Ser.). 1998. mass mkt. 2.99 (0-89529-908-9, Avery) Penguin Putnam.

***Berkson, Burt, et al.** Syndrome X: The Complete Nutritional Program to Prevent & Reverse Insulin Resistance. LC 99-49639. (Illus.). 288p. 1999. text 24.95 (0-471-35835-5) Wiley.

Berkson, Carmel. The Divine & Demonaic: Mahisa's Heroic Struggle with Durga. LC 95-911640. (Illus.). 352p. 1995. text 29.95 (0-19-563555-8) OUP.

— Elephanta: The Cave of Shiva. LC 82-20525 (Illus.). 132p. reprint ed. pap. 41.00 (0-608-06417-3, 206663000008) Bks Demand.

***Berkson, Carmel, photos by.** Elephants: The Cave of Shiva. 1999. pap. 300.00 (81-208-1284-0, Pub. by Motilal Bnarsidass) St Mut.

***Berkson, D. Lindsey.** Healthy Digestion the Natural Way: Preventing & Healing Heartburn, Constipation, Gas, Diarrhea, Inflammatory Bowel & Gallbladder Diseases, Ulcers, Irritable Bowel Syndrome, Food Allergies & More. LC 99-32330. (Illus.). 256p. 2000. pap. 16.95 (0-471-34962-3) Wiley.

— Hormone Deception: How & Why we Need to Protect Ourselves from Hormone Deception. LC 99-52831. 407p. 2000. 24.95 (0-8092-2538-7, 253870, Contemporary Bks) NTC Contemp Pub Co.

Berkson, Devaki. The Foot Book: A Holistic Guide to Foot Care Using Reflexology, Massage, Diet, Exercise, & Visualization. LC 91-58520. (Illus.). 224p. 1992. reprint ed. pap. 11.50 (0-06-092296-6, Perennial) HarperTrade.

Berkson, Dorothy, ed. see Stowe, Harriet Beecher.

Berkson, Gershon. Children with Handicaps: A Review of Behavioral Research. 464p. 1993. text 99.95 (0-89859-987-3) L Erlbaum Assocs.

Berkson, Isaac B. The Ideal & the Community: A Philosophy of Education. LC 70-115977. 302p. 1970. reprint ed. lib. bdg. 65.00 (0-8371-3056-5, EEIC, Greenwood Pr) Greenwood.

— Theories of Americanization: A Critical Study. LC 77-87743. (American Education: Its Men, Institutions, & Ideas. Series 1). 1975. reprint ed. 18.95 (0-405-01387-6) Ayer.

Berkson, Jacob B. A Canary's Tale Vol. I & II: The Final Battle, Politics, Poisons, & Pollution vs. the Environment & the Public Health - The Odyssey (Vol. I) & Research, References & Resources (Vol. II), 2 in 1. (Illus.). 480p. 1996. 19.95 (0-9655358-0-0) Canarys Tale.

Berkson, Jonathon M., jt. ed. see Akal, Tuncay.

Berkson, Lindsey. Nature's Way to a Trouble Free Digestion. LC 96-52366. 320p. 1997. pap. text 13.95 (0-13-258724-6) P-H.

***Berkson, Marc & VanDusen, Susan.** The Synagogue: House of the Jewish People. LC 99-11858. (Illus.). 96p. (gr. 3-5). 1999. pap. 5.95 (0-87441-664-7) Behrman.

Berkstresser, Gordon, et al, eds. Automation in the Textile Industry: From Fibers to Apparel. 1995. 72.00 (1-870812-68-9, Pub. by Textile Inst) St Mut.

Berktay, Fatmagul. Women & Religion. 240p. 1997. 52.99 (1-55164-103-8, Pub. by Black Rose) Consort Bk Sales.

— Women & Religion. 240p. 1998. pap. 23.99 (1-55164-102-X, Pub. by Black Rose) Consort Bk Sales.

Berktay, Halil & Faroqhi, Suraiya, eds. New Approaches to the State & Peasant in Ottoman History. 282p. 1992. text 49.50 (0-7146-3468-9, Pub. by F Cass Pubs) Intl Spec Bk.

Berktold, Jennifer, et al. Subsequent Educational Attainment of High School Dropouts. LC 98-184952. xi, 67 p. 1998. write for info. (0-16-049600-4) USGPO.

***Berkus, Barry A.** Architecture Art Parallels Connections. (Illus.). 224p. 2000. 45.00 (1-86470-084-X, Pub. by Images) Antique Collect.

— Architecture/Art/Parallels/Connections. (Illus.). 208p. 2000. 40.00 (0-8230-0293-4) Watsn-Guptill.

Berkus, Rusty. Appearances: Clearings Through the Masks of Our Existence. (Illus.). 64p. (Orig.). 1984. pap. 19.95 (0-9609888-1-5) Red Rose Pr.

— Consciousness of Deserving. (Illus.). 1992. pap. 19.95 (0-9609888-7-4) Red Rose Pr.

— In Celebration of Friendship. (Illus.). 64p. (Orig.). 1990. pap. 19.95 (0-9609888-8-2) Red Rose Pr.

— Life Is a Gift. (Illus.). 64p. (Orig.). 1982. pap. 19.95 (0-9609888-0-7) Red Rose Pr.

— Nell the Nebbish: (The True Adventures of a Mensch in Hiding) Allison, Alida, ed. (Illus.). 64p. (Orig.). 1988. pap. 7.95 (0-9609888-4-X) Red Rose Pr.

— Soulprints. (Illus.). 64p. (Orig.). 1988. pap. 19.95 (0-9609888-3-1) Red Rose Pr.

— To Heal Again: Toward Serenity & the Resolution of Grief. (Illus.). 64p. (Orig.). 1996. pap. 19.95 (0-9609888-2-3) Red Rose Pr.

— Your Path to Spiritual Starhood: Empowering Your Sacred Self. 64p. (Orig.). 1998. pap. 11.95 (1-889891-97-5) Red Rose Pr.

Berkvam, Michael L. Liberty, Equality . . . or Death: The French Revolution, 1789-1794. (Illus.). 141p. 1989. pap. 10.00 (1-879598-10-8) IN Univ Lilly Library.

Berkvens-Stevelinck, Christiane, et al, eds. The Emergence of Tolerance in the Dutch Republic. LC 97-7074. (Studies in the History of Christian Thought, 0081-8607: No. 76). (ENG & FRE.). 288p. 1997. 108.00 (90-04-10768-1) Brill Academic Pubs.

— Le Magasin de l'Univers - The Dutch Republic As the Centre of the European Book Trade. (Brill's Studies in Intellectual History: Vol. 31). (ENG & FRE., Illus.). x, 319p. 1991. 107.00 (90-04-09493-8) Brill Academic Pubs.

Berkvens-Stevelinck, Christiane & Nieuweboer, Adele. Catalogue des Manuscrits de la Collection Prosper-Marchand. (Codices Manuscripti Ser.: No. XXVI). (FRE., Illus.). x, 214p. 1988. pap. 78.50 (90-04-08618-8) Brill Academic Pubs.

Berky, Andrew S., ed. Challenge to American Life. LC 76-134052. (Essay Index Reprint Ser.). 1977. 17.95 (0-8369-2143-7) Ayer.

Berky, Andrew S., tr. see Sommer, Fedor.

Berky, George J., et al. Western Myth: Twentieth Century Update, the Aspen Art Museum, February 11 to April 11, 1993. LC 92-75716. 22p. 1993. write for info. (0-934324-18-2) Aspen Art Mus.

Berl, Christine. The Classic Art of Viennese Pastry: From Strudel to Sachertorte--More Than 100 Traditional Recipes. 277p. 1997. 39.95 (0-471-29202-8, VNR) Wiley.

Berl, Emmanuel. Sylvia. (FRE.). 1972. pap. 10.95 (0-7859-1718-7, 2070362655) Fr & Eur.

Berl, Fred. Social Change & Social Work Practice: Writings of Fred Berl. 243p. (C). 1988. 24.95 (0-9620785-0-6) D Berl.

Berl, W. G. & Powell, W. R. Efficient Comfort Conditioning: The Heating & Cooling of Buildings. (AAAS Selected Symposium; 27 Ser.). 1979. 31.50 (0-89158-290-8) Westview.

Berlack, Ronald. Software Configuration Managem. LC 91-33348. (Series in Software Engineering Practice). 352p. 1991. 79.99 (0-471-53049-2) Wiley.

Berlage. OSF Motif. (C). 1990. text. write for info. (0-201-55906-4) Addison-Wesley.

Berlage, Brian. Adventures in Growing up: I Really Do Love My Brothers. (Illus.). (Orig.). 1994. pap. 12.95 (0-9644367-0-1) Brian Berlage.

Berlage, Gai. Understanding Social Issues: Critical Thinking & Analysis. 5th ed. LC 98-14649. 176p. (C). 1998. pap. 25.00 (0-205-27613-X) P-H.

Berlage, Gai I. Women in Baseball: The Forgotten History. LC 93-25049. 224p. 1994. 22.50 (0-275-94735-1, C4735, Praeger Pubs) Greenwood.

Berlage, Gai I. & Egelman, William. Understanding Social Issues: Sociological Fact Finding. 2nd ed. 150p. 1990. pap. text. write for info. (0-205-12255-8, H22551) Allyn.

Berlage, Hendrik P. Hendrik Petrus Berlage: Thoughts on Style, 1886-1909. Whyte, Iain B. & De Wit, Wim, trs. LC 95-14641. (Texts & Documents Ser.). 348p. 1996. pap. 45.00 (0-89236-334-7, Pub. by J P Getty Trust) OUP.

Berlage, Lodewijk & Stokke, Olav S., eds. Evaluating Development Assistance: Approaches & Methods. LC 92-13087. (EADI Book Ser.: Vol. 14). 214p. 1992. 42.50 (0-7146-3479-4, Pub. by F Cass Pubs) Intl Spec Bk.

Berlak, Ann & Berlak, Harold. Dilemmas of Schooling. 1989. pap. 15.95 (0-416-74140-1, 3566) Routledge.

Berlak, Harold, et al. Toward a New Science of Educational Testing & Assessment. LC 90-28708. (SUNY Series, Teacher Preparation & Development). (Illus.). 235p. (C). 1992. text 59.50 (0-7914-0877-9); pap. text 19.95 (0-7914-0878-7) State U NY Pr.

Berlak, Harold, jt. auth. see Berlak, Ann.

Berland. Technoscience. 1997. pap. 19.50 (0-85315-825-8, Pub. by Lawrence & Wishart) NYU Pr.

Berland, Alwyn. Light in August: A Study in Black & White. (Masterwork Studies). 136p. 1992. pap. 13.95 (0-8057-8100-5, 95, Twyne) Mac Lib Ref.

— Light in August: A Study in Black & White. (Masterwork Studies: No. 95). 136p. 1992. 29.00 (0-8057-8050-5, Twyne) Mac Lib Ref.

Berland, Dinah, ed. see Moll, Gary & Young, Stanley.

Berland, Jody & Hornstein, Shelley, eds. Capital Culture: A Reader on Modernist Legacies, State Institutions, (Illus.). 286p. 2000. 65.00 (0-7735-1725-1, Pub. by McG-Queens Univ Pr) CUP Services.

Berland, Joseph C. No Five Fingers Are Alike: Cognitive Amplifiers in Social Context. LC 81-7154. (Illus.). 257p. 1982. 47.95 (0-674-62540-4) HUP.

Berland, Nancy. Glass Slippers. 1996. mass mkt. 4.99 (0-7860-0239-5, Pinncle Kensgtn) Kensgtn Pub Corp.

— Island Fever. (Lucky in Love Ser.: No. 24). 320p. 1993. mass mkt. 3.50 (0-8217-4083-0, Zebra Kensgtn) Kensgtn Pub Corp.

Berland, Terry. Breaking into Commercials. LC 97-11782. 352p. 1997. pap. 12.95 (0-452-27770-1, Plume) Dutton Plume.

Berland, Warren. Out of the Box for Life. 240p. 2000. pap. 13.00 (0-06-093051-9) HarpC.

— Out of the Box for Life: (Being Free Is Just a Choice) LC 98-31562. 240p. 1999. 23.95 (0-06-019100-7) HarpC.

Berlandier, Jean L. The Indians of Texas in Eighteen Thirty. Leclerq, Patricia R., tr. LC 69-13118. (Smithsonian Publication: No. 4745). (Illus.). 263p. reprint ed. pap. 81.60 (0-608-18402-0, 203069700070) Bks Demand.

Berlandier, Jean L., et al. Journey to Mexico During the Years, 1826-1834, 2 vols. Ohlendorf, Sheila M. & Bigelow, Josette, eds. LC 80-51995. 305p. 1981. boxed set 75.00 (0-87611-044-8) Tex St Hist Assn.

Berlanstein, Lenard R. The Barristers of Toulouse in the Eighteenth Century (1740-1793) LC 75-9784. (Johns Hopkins University Studies in Historical & Political Science: 93d Ser., No. 1). (Illus.). 223p. reprint ed. pap. 69.20 (0-8357-6839-2, 203552700095) Bks Demand.

— Big Business & Industrial Conflict in Nineteenth-Century France: A Social History of the Parisian Gas Company. LC 90-47352. (Illus.). 352p. 1991. 55.00 (0-520-07234-0, Pub. by U CA Pr) Cal Prin Full Svc.

Berlanstein, Leonard R. The Working People of Paris, 1817-1914. LC 84-47951. (Johns Hopkins University Studies in Historical & Political Science: Vol. 2). 293p. 1984. reprint ed. pap. 90.90 (0-608-03652-8, 206447800009) Bks Demand.

Berlanstein, Leonard R., ed. The Industrial Revolution & Work in Nineteenth Century Europe. LC 91-45629. (Rewriting Histories Ser.). 208p. (C). 1992. pap. 24.99 (0-415-07053-8, A6568) Routledge.

— Rethinking Labor History: Essays on Discourse & Class Analysis. LC 92-24297. (Illus.). 248p. (C). 1993. text 39.95 (0-252-01975-X); pap. text 14.95 (0-252-06279-5) U of Ill Pr.

Berlant, Lauren. The Anatomy of National Fantasy: Hawthorne, Utopia, & Everyday Life. 248p. 1994. lib. bdg. 32.00 (0-226-04376-2) U Ch Pr.

— The Anatomy of National Fantasy: Hawthorne, Utopia & Everyday Life. 278p. 1996. pap. text 17.95 (0-226-04377-0) U Ch Pr.

***Berlant, Lauren & Duggan, Lisa, eds.** Our Monica, Ourselves: The Clinton Affair & the National Interest. 2001. 55.00 (0-8147-9865-9); pap. 18.95 (0-8147-9864-0) NYU Pr.

Berlant, Lauren G. The Anatomy of National Fantasy: Hawthorne, Utopia & Everyday Life. LC 90-26907. 277p. Date not set. reprint ed. pap. 85.90 (0-608-21011-0, 205453900003) Bks Demand.

— The Queen of America Goes to Washington City: Essays on Sex & Citizenship. LC 96-35146. (Series Q). (Illus.). 336p. 1997. pap. 16.95 (0-8223-1924-1); lib. bdg. 49.95 (0-8223-1931-4) Duke.

***Berlant, Lauren Gail.** Intimacy. 1999. pap. text 25.00 (0-226-38443-8); lib. bdg. 45.00 (0-226-38441-1) U Ch Pr.

Berlant, Lauren Gail, jt. auth. see Letinsky, Laura.

Berlay, Louise. The Magic of the Mind: How to Do What You Want with Your Life. 1983. reprint ed. pap. 10.00 (0-9617296-0-0) Berle Bks.

Berle, A. A., Jr., et al. America's Recovery Program. Wilcox, Clair et al, eds. LC 76-104990. (Essay Index Reprint Ser.). 1977. 23.95 (0-8369-1591-7) Ayer.

Berle, A. Lynn. Water Aerobics. 2nd ed. 128p. (C). 1996. per. 23.95 (0-7872-2166-X, 41216601) Kendall-Hunt.

Berle, Adolf A. Latin America: Diplomacy & Reality. LC 81-3818. (Council on Foreign Relations Ser.), 144p. 1981. reprint ed. lib. bdg. 55.00 (0-313-22970-8, BELAM, Greenwood Pr) Greenwood.

Berle, Adolf A., Jr. Studies in the Law of Corporation Finance. LC 95-77926. (Business Enterprises Reprint Ser.). xvii, 199p. 1995. reprint ed. 55.00 (0-89941-975-5, 308840) W S Hein.

Berle, Adolf A. & Means, Gardiner C. The Modern Corporation & Private Property. 426p. (C). 1991. pap. 29.95 (0-88738-887-6) Transaction Pubs.

Berle, Adolf A., Jr. & Means, Gardiner C. The Modern Corporation & Private Property. LC 38-11139. (Business Enterprises Reprint Ser.). xiii, 396p. 1982. reprint ed. lib. bdg. 52.50 (0-89941-183-5, 302080) W S Hein.

Berle, Arnie. Arnie Berle's Complete Handbook for Jazz Improvisation. 1972. pap. 16.95 (0-8256-2805-9, AM26626) Music Sales.

— Bebop & Swing Classics for Sax. 1997. 9.95 (0-8256-1584-4, AM 940324) Music Sales.

— Chords & Progressions for Jazz & Popular Guitar. LC 87-111844. (Illus.). 128p. 1986. pap. 19.95 (0-8256-1056-7, AM 61565) Omnibus NY.

Berle, Arnie. Encyclopedia of Scales, Modes & Melodic Patterns: Beginning-Intermediate Level. 96p. 1997. pap. 12.95 (0-7866-1791-8, 95736) Mel Bay.

Berle, Arnie. Fretboard Basics. 96p. 1993. spiral bd. 12.95 (1-56222-429-8, 94671) Mel Bay.

— How to Create & Develop a Jazz Sax Solo. 88p. 1983. pap. 9.95 (1-56222-088-8, 94528) Mel Bay.

— How to Play Bass Guitar. (Illus.). 80p. 1980. pap. 11.95 (0-8256-2397-9, AM35171, Amsco Music) Music Sales.

— Improvisation for the Contemporary Musician. 72p. 1998. pap. text 14.95 (0-8256-1642-5, AM945329) Music Sales.

— Jazz Saxophone Licks, Phrases & Patterns. 88p. 1987. spiral bd. 10.95 (1-56222-089-6, 94529) Mel Bay.

— New Guitar Techniques for Sightreading. Stang, Aaron, ed. 104p. (Orig.). (YA). 1991. pap. text 12.95 (0-89898-583-8, F3141GTX) Wrner Bros.

— Patterns, Scales & Modes for Jazz Guitar. 1994. 21.95 (0-8256-2552-1, AM71382) Omnibus NY.

— Theory & Harmony for the Contemporary Musician. LC 96-199102. (Illus.). 112p. (Orig.). 1996. pap. 16.95 (0-8256-1499-6, AM931360) Omnibus NY.

— Understanding Chord Progressions for Guitar. (Illus.). 64p. (Orig.). 1996. pap. 5.95 (0-8256-1488-0, AM 931250, Amsco Music) Music Sales.

Berle, Arnie & Galbo, Mark. Beginning Fingerstyle Blues Guitar. (Illus.). 96p. 1996. pap. 19.95 (0-8256-2556-4, AM 71390) Music Sales.

Berle, Beatrice B. Eighty Puerto Rican Families in New York City: Health & Disease Studied in Context. LC 74-14221. (Puerto Rican Experience Ser.). (Illus.). 356p. 1975. reprint ed. 29.95 (0-405-06211-7) Ayer.

Berle-Carman, Mary, et al. Three Out of Four Like Spaghetti: Data & Fractions. Brennan, Ann Marie et al, eds. (Investigations in Number, Data, & Space Ser.). (Illus.). 79p. (Orig.). 1994. pap., teacher ed. 22.95 (0-86651-818-5, DS21256) Seymour Pubns.

— Three Out of Four Like Spaghetti: Data & Fractions. rev. ed. Anderson, Catherine & Cory, Beverly, eds. LC 97-196096. (Investigations in Number, Data, & Space Ser.). (Illus.). 81p. (Orig.). (YA). (gr. 4 up). 1997. pap. text 22.95 (1-57232-753-7, 47000) Seymour Pubns.

Berle-Carman, Mary, jt. auth. see Battista, Michael T.

Berle-Carmen, Mary, jt. auth. see Tierney, Cornelia.

Berle, Gustav & Kirschner, Paul. The Instant Business Plan: Twelve Quick & Easy Steps to a Successful Business. (Illus.). 250p. 1997. pap. 14.95 (0-940673-71-1) Puma Pub Co.

— The Internation Instant Business Plan: Twelve Quick & Easy Steps to a Successful Business. 200p. (Orig.). 1996. pap. 19.95 (0-940673-81-9) Puma Pub Co.

Berle, Gustav, jt. auth. see Alarid, William M.

Berle, Lina W. George Eliot & Thomas Hardy. 1968. 6.50 (0-685-26778-4) Bookfinger.

Berle, Milton. Milton Berle's Private Joke File. 672p. 1992. pap. 21.00 (0-517-58716-5, Crown) Crown Pub Group.

Berle, Milton. More of the Best of Milton Berle's Private Joke File. 553p. 1996. 12.98 (0-7858-0719-5) Castle Bks.

Berle, Milton. More of the Best of Milton Berle's Private Joke File. Rosen, Milt, ed. 560p. 1994. reprint ed. pap. 15.00 (0-380-71953-3, Avon Bks) Morrow Avon.

Berle, William & Lewis, Brad. My Father, Uncle Miltie. 1999. 22.00 (1-56980-149-5) Barricade Bks.

Berleant, Arnold. The Aesthetics of Environment. 256p. (C). 1992. 44.95 (0-87722-993-7) Temple U Pr.

— The Aesthetics of Environment. 256p. (C). 1995. pap. 22.95 (1-56639-334-5) Temple U Pr.

— Art & Engagement. 288p. 1991. 59.95 (0-87722-797-7) Temple U Pr.

— Art & Engagement. 288p. 1993. pap. 22.95 (1-56639-084-2) Temple U Pr.

— Living in the Landscape: Toward an Aesthetics of Environment. LC 96-29328. 176p. 1997. 25.00 (0-7006-0811-7) U Pr of KS.

Berleant, R. Montserrat. LC 92-146793. (World Bibliographical Ser.). 131p. 1991. lib. bdg. 55.00 (1-85109-154-8) ABC-CLIO.

Berleant-Schiller, Riva, et al. Antigua & Barbuda, Vol. 182. (World Bibliographical Ser.). 252p. 1995. lib. bdg. 67.00 (1-85109-228-5) ABC-CLIO.

***Berlekamp, Elwyn.** The Dots-&-Boxes Game: Sophisticated Child's Play. (Illus.). 120p. 2000. pap. 15.00 (1-56881-129-2) AK Peters.

Berlekamp, Elwyn R. Algebraic Coding Theory. rev. ed. 474p. 1984. reprint ed. pap. 42.80 (0-89412-063-8) Aegean Park Pr.

— Key Papers in the Development of Coding Theory. 296p. 1974. 79.95 (0-87942-031-6, PC00323) Inst Electrical.

Berlekamp, Elwyn R. & Rodgers, Tom, eds. The Mathemagician & Pied Puzzler: A Collection in Tribute to Martin Gardner. LC 98-51744. (Illus.). 266p. 1999. 34.00 (1-56881-075-X) AK Peters.

Berlekamp, Elwyn R. & Wolfe, David. Mathematical Go: Chilling Gets the Last Point. LC 93-46609. (Illus.). 256p. 1994. 39.00 (1-56881-032-6) AK Peters.

Berlekamp, Elwyn R., et al. Winning Ways, Vol. 2. LC 81-66678. 1982. text 117.00 (0-12-091152-3) Acad Pr.

— Winning Ways: For Your Mathematical Plays, 2 vols., Vol. 2, Games in Particular. LC 81-66678. 1982. pap. text 69.00 (0-12-091102-7) Acad Pr.

Berlemont, A., jt. auth. see Gouesbet, G.

Berler, Alexander. New Towns in Israel. 384p. 1970. boxed set 39.95 (0-87855-174-3) Transaction Pubs.

Berler, Beatrice. The Conquest of Mexico: A Modern Rendering of William H. Prescott's History. LC 88-70846. (Illus.). 145p. 1988. pap. text 10.95 (0-931722-70-5) Corona Pub.

Berler, Beatrice, tr. see Portillo y Pacheco, Jose L.

Berler, E., jt. auth. see Edelstein, B. A.

Berler, Ron, ed. see Wilson, Glenn, et al.

Berler, Ruzena. Cattle Car to Kazakhstan: A Woman Doctor's Triumph of Courage in World War II. LC 98-90364. 1999. 21.95 (0-533-12781-5) Vantage.

Berlescu, Elena. Encyclopedic Medical Dictionary of Balneoclimatology: Dictionar Enciclopedi Medical de Balneoclimatologie. 1982. write for info. (0-8288-1887-8, M15840) Fr & Eur.

Berlese, A. N. Icones Fungorum Omnium Hucusque Cognitorum: Ad Usum Sylloges Saccardianae Accomodatae, 4 vols. 1968. pap. 300.00 (3-7682-0575-4) Lubrecht & Cramer.

Berlet, Anthony C., jt. auth. see Kozin, Scott H.

Berlet, Chip. Clouds Blur the Rainbow: The Other Side of the New Alliance Party. 15p. (Orig.). 1987. spiral bd. 3.50 (0-915987-03-1) Political Rsch Assocs.

***Berlet, Chip & Lyons, Matthew N.** Right Wing Populism in America: Too Close for Comfort. (Critical Perspectives Ser.). 2000. lib. bdg. 38.95 (1-57230-568-1, C0568) Guilford Pubns.

An Asterisk (*) at the beginning of an entry indicates that the title is appearing for the first time.

— Right Wing Populism in America: Too Close for Comfort. (Illus.). 400p. 2000. pap. 19.95 (*1-57230-562-2*) Guilford Pubns.

Berlet, Chip, ed. see Lyons, Matthew N., et al.

Berlet, Chip, ed. see Pharr, Suzanne, et al.

Berleth, Richard. Mary Patten's Voyage. Mathews, Judith, ed. LC 93-45919. (Illus.). 40p. (J). (gr. 3-6). 1994. lib. bdg. 14.95 (*0-8075-4987-8*) A Whitman.

— Samuel's Choice. Mathews, Judith, ed. LC 89-77186. (Illus.). 40p. (J). (gr. 3-6). 1990. lib. bdg. 14.95 (*0-8075-7218-7*) A Whitman.

Berleth, Richard J. The Orphan Stone; The Minnesinger Dream of Reich, 15. LC 89-17238. 288p. 1990. 62.95 (*0-313-26856-8*, BOA/, Greenwood Pr) Greenwood.

Berleur, J., et al, eds. Landscapes for an Information Society. 528p. 1991. 64.95 (*0-387-97453-9*) Spr-Verlag.

Berlev, Oleg, jt. auth. see Hodjash, Svetlana.

Berlew, David, et al. The Effective Uses of Power & Authority. 1979. text 10.00 (*0-07-004907-6*) McGraw.

***Berley, Marc.** After the Heavenly Tune: English Poetry & the Aspiration to Song. LC 00-8592. 300p. 2000. text 59.00 (*0-8207-0316-8*) Duquesne.

Berley, Marc, jt. ed. see Wienir, David.

***Berley, Peter.** The Modern Vegetarian Kitchen. (Illus.). 352p. 2000. 35.00 (*0-06-039295-9*) HarpC.

Berliant, Adam. The Used Car Reliability & Safety Guide. 2nd ed. 384p. 1997. pap. 14.99 (*1-55870-438-8*, Betrwy Bks) F & W Pubns Inc.

Berlichingen, Gotz V. Lebens-Beschreibung. xvi, 334p. 1977. reprint ed. 80.00 (*3-487-06112-0*) G Olms Pubs.

***Berlie, Jean.** Macao 2000. LC 99-44985. 256p. 2000. text 35.00 (*0-19-592074-0*) OUP.

Berlien, H. P. & Schmittenbecher, P. P. Laser Surgery in Children. LC 97-18416. 1997. text. write for info. (*3-540-62633-6*) Spr-Verlag.

Berlien, H. P. & Schmittenbecher, P. P., eds. Manual of Internal Fixation in Small Animals. 2nd enl. rev. ed. LC 97-20200. (Illus.). 450p. 1997. write for info. (*3-540-63000-7*) Spr-Verlag.

***Berlin.** Genetics & Hearing Loss. 140p. 2000. pap. 71.95 (*0-7693-0103-7*) Singular Publishing.

— Hair Cell Micromechanics & Hearing. 2000. pap. 57.50 (*0-7693-0125-8*, Pub. by Singular Publishing) Thomson Learn.

Berlin & Pentney. Human Rights & Freedoms in Canada: Cases, Notes & Materials. 750p. 1987. pap. 65.00 (*0-409-81308-7*, MICHIE) LEXIS Pub.

Berlin, A. Enmerkar & Ensuhkesdanna: A Sumerian Narrative Poem. (Occasional Publications of the Babylonian Fund: No. 2). (Illus.). xi, 102p. 1979. 15.00 (*0-934718-29-6*) U Museum Pubns.

Berlin, A., ed. Assessment of Toxic Agents at the Workplace. 660p. 1983. text 376.50 (*0-89838-613-6*) Kluwer Academic.

Berlin, A., et al, eds. Immunotoxicology. (Developments in Hematology & Immunology Ser.). 1987. text 300.50 (*0-89838-843-0*) Kluwer Academic.

Berlin, A., et al. The Use of Biological Specimens for the Assessment of Human Exposure to Environmental Pollutants. 1979. text 148.50 (*90-247-2168-7*) Kluwer Academic.

Berlin, A. A., et al. Principles of Polymer Composites. (Polymers, Properties & Applications Ser.: Vol. 10). (Illus.). 150p. 1985. 141.95 (*0-387-15051-X*) Spr-Verlag.

***Berlin, Adam.** Headlock. 276p. 2000. 21.95 (*1-56512-266-6*, 72266) Algonquin Bks.

Berlin, Adele. Biblical Poetry Through Medieval Jewish Eyes. LC 90-26773. (Indiana Studies in Biblical Literature). 228p. 1991. 14.95 (*0-253-31176-4*) Ind U Pr.

— The Dynamics of Biblical Parallelism. LC 84-48250. 191p. reprint ed. pap. 59.30 (*0-608-09271-1*, 205407300002) Bks Demand.

***Berlin, Adele.** Esther. (Bible Commentary Ser.). 2001. 34.95 (*0-8276-0699-0*) JPS Phila.

Berlin, Adele. Poetics & Interpretation of Biblical Narrative. LC 94-4841. 180p. 1994. pap. 15.95 (*1-57506-002-7*) Eisenbrauns.

— Zephaniah: A New Translation with Introduction & Commentary. LC 93-37736. (Anchor Bible Ser.: Vol. 25A). 192p. 1994. 29.00 (*0-385-26631-6*) Doubleday.

Berlin, Adele & Cooperman, Bernard D., eds. Religion & Politics in the Ancient Near East. (Studies & Texts in Jewish History & Culture: No. 1). 1996. boxed set 25.00 (*1-883053-24-2*) Univ Pr MD.

Berlin, Adele, et al. Introduction to Hebrew Poetry, Job, Psalms, & 1 & 2 Maccabees. (New Interpreter's Bible: Vol. 4). 1100p. 1996. 65.00 (*0-687-27817-1*) Abingdon.

Berlin, Alexandre A. & Minsker, Karl S. Fast Polymerization Processes. (Polymer Science & Engineering Monographs). 110p. 1996. pap. text 20.00 (*2-88449-191-0*) Gordon & Breach.

Berlin, Alexandre A., jt. auth. see Minsker, Karl S.

Berlin, Andrea & Slane, Kathleen W. Tel Anafa II Pt. I: The Hellenistic & Roman Pottery: The Plain Wares - The Fine Wares. Herbert, Sharon C., ed. (JRA Supplementary Ser.: Vol. 10, Pt. 2). (Illus.). 592p. 1997. 89.50 (*1-887829-98-9*) Jour Roman Arch.

Berlin, Berry. The American Trojan Horse: U. S. Television Confronts Canadian Economic & Cultural Nationalism, 22. LC 90-3338. (Contributions to the Study of Mass Media & Communications Ser.: No. 22). 128p. 1990. 49.95 (*0-313-27508-4*, BAX, Greenwood Pr) Greenwood.

Berlin, Brent. Ethnobiological Classification: Principles of Categorization of Plants & Animals in Traditional Societies. (Illus.). 326p. 1992. text 60.00 (*0-691-09469-1*, Pub. by Princeton U Pr) Cal Prin Full Svc.

— Tzeltal Numerical Classifiers: A Study in Ethnographic Semantics. (Janua Linguarum, Ser. Practica: No. 70). (Orig.). 1968. pap. text 73.85 (*3-11-000011-3*) Mouton.

Berlin, Brent & Kay, Paul. Basic Color Terms: Their Universality & Evolution. LC 99-12619. (David Hume Ser.). 200p. (C). 1999. reprint ed. pap. text 22.95 (*1-57586-162-3*) CSLI.

Berlin, Brent, jt. auth. see Berlin, Elois A.

Berlin, Carol Young. What Grows Here? Mountain Gardening in Northern California. 4th ed. (Illus.). 200p. 1996. pap. 22.95 (*0-9638514-0-3*) C Y Berlin.

***Berlin Center Historical Society Staff.** Berlin Center, Ohio. (Images of America Ser.). (Illus.). 128p. 2000. pap. 18.99 (*0-7385-0709-1*) Arcadia Publng.

Berlin, Charles. Catalog of the Yiddish Collection: Harvard College Library, 3 vols. 1265p. 1993. lib. bdg. 665.00 (*3-598-41242-8*) K G Saur Verlag.

— Index to Festschriften in Jewish Studies. (C). 1971. 50.00 (*0-87068-133-8*) Ktav.

— Studies in Jewish Bibliography, History & Literature: In Honor of I. Edward Kiev. (C). 1971. 50.00 (*0-87068-143-5*) Ktav.

Berlin, Charles I. Hair Cells & Hearing Aids. LC 95-34353. (Illus.). 160p. 1995. pap. 55.00 (*1-56593-403-2*, 0867) Thomson Learn.

— Neurotransmission & Hearing Loss: Basic Science, Diagnosis & Management. LC 97-937. (Illus.). 184p. (Orig.). 1997. 55.00 (*1-56593-834-8*, 1630) Thomson Learn.

— Otoacoustic Emissions: Basic Science & Clinical Applications. LC 97-50307. (Illus.). 124p. 1998. pap. 55.00 (*1-56593-975-1*, 1930) Thomson Learn.

***Berlin, Charles I., ed.** The Efferent Auditory System: Basic Science & Clinical Applications. LC 99-22667. 16p. 1999. pap. 57.50 (*0-7693-0013-8*) Thomson Learn.

Berlin, Daniel, et al. CGI Programming Unleashed. 648p. 1996. 49.99 (*1-57521-151-3*) Sams.

Berlin, Delia. Training Captive Bred Parrots. (Illus.). 128p. 1996. 23.95 (*0-7938-2184-3*, TS242) TFH Pubns.

Berlin, Donna, ed. SSMILes: School Science & Mathematics Integrated Lessons. (Classroom Activities Ser.: No. C4). 191p. (Orig.). (J). (gr. 2-10). 1997. pap. 18.00 (*0-912047-11-9*) Sch Sci Math.

Berlin, Donna F. A Bibliography of Integrated Science & Mathematics Teaching & Learning Literature. (Topics for Teachers Ser.). 64p. (Orig.). (C). 1991. pap. text 7.50 (*0-912047-10-0*) Sch Sci Math.

Berlin, Ed I. Free at Last. 572p. 1997. 10.98 (*0-7858-0804-3*) Bk Sales Inc.

Berlin, Edward A. King of Ragtime: Scott Joplin & His Era. (Illus.). 352p. 1995. pap. 13.95 (*0-19-810408-1*) OUP.

— King of Ragtime: Scott Joplin & His Era. (Illus.). 352p. 1996. pap. 14.95 (*0-19-510108-1*) OUP.

— Ragtime: A Musical & Cultural History. LC 78-51759. 1980. pap. 14.95 (*0-520-05219-6*, Pub. by U CA Pr) Cal Prin Full Svc.

— Reflections & Research on Ragtime. LC 86-81842. (I.S.A.M. Monographs: No. 24). (Illus.). 112p. 1987. pap. 10.00 (*0-914678-27-2*) Inst Am Music.

Berlin, Elois A. & Berlin, Brent. Medical Ethnobiology of the Highland Maya of Chiapas, Mexico: The Gastrointestinal Diseases. 352p. 1996. text 85.00 (*0-691-03741-8*, Pub. by Princeton U Pr) Cal Prin Full Svc.

Berlin, G. Lennis. Earthquakes & the Urban Environment, 3 Vols., Vol. 1. 224p. 1980. 123.00 (*0-8493-5173-1*, QE539, CRC Reprint) Franklin.

— Earthquakes & the Urban Environment, 3 Vols., Vol. 2. 192p. 1980. 110.00 (*0-8493-5174-X*, CRC Reprint) Franklin.

— Earthquakes & the Urban Environment, 3 Vols., Vol. 3. 288p. 1980. 99.00 (*0-8493-5175-8*, CRC Reprint) Franklin.

Berlin, George L. Defending the Faith: Nineteenth-Century American Jewish Writing on Christianity & Jesus. LC 88-15440. (SUNY Series in Religious Studies). 288p. (C). 1989. pap. text 21.95 (*0-88706-921-5*) State U NY Pr.

Berlin, Graydon L., jt. auth. see Avery, Thomas E.

Berlin, Helene, ed. see Anderson, Jerry D.

Berlin, Helene, ed. see Brown, Donald R. & Mathews, Wendell G.

Berlin, Helene, ed. see Messner, Stephen D., et al.

Berlin, Herausgegeben von der, see von der Berlin, Herausgegeben.

Berlin, Howard M. BRS-Seven: The Phase-Locked Loop with Experiments. LC 78-6535. 1978. pap. text 10.95 (*0-89704-017-1*) E&L Instru.

***Berlin, Howard M.** The Charlie Chan Film Encyclopedia. LC 99-56163. (Illus.). 368p. 2000. lib. bdg. 55.00 (*0-7864-0709-3*) McFarland & Co.

— The Coins & Banknotes of Palestine under the British Mandate, 1927-1947. (Illus.). 128p. 2000. 45.00 (*0-7864-0879-0*) McFarland & Co.

— The Illustrated Electronics Dictionary. 256p. (C). 1990. 36.40 (*0-675-20451-8*, Merrill Coll) P-H.

Berlin, Howard M. TRS-1 555 Timer Applications Source Book with Experiments. Larsen, David G., ed. (Bugbook Reference Ser.). 1976. pap. text 8.00 (*0-89704-011-2*) E&L Instru.

Berlin, Howard M. & Getz, Frank C. Fundamentals of Operational Amplifiers & Linear Integrated Circuits. (C). 1990. text 54.00 (*0-675-21002-X*, Merrill Coll) P-H.

Berlin, Howard M. & Getz, Frank C., Jr. Principles of Electronic Instrumentation & Measurement. 512p. (C). 1990. pap. text, lab manual ed. 25.80 (*0-675-20450-X*, Merrill Coll) P-H.

Berlin, Howard M., jt. auth. see Stone, Robert T.

Berlin, Ira. Families & Freedom: A Documentary History of African American Kinship in the Civil War Era. LC 96-24826. (Illus.). 304p. 1997. 25.00 (*1-56584-026-7*, Pub. by New Press NY) Norton.

***Berlin, Ira.** Many Thousands Gone: The First Two Centuries of Slavery in North America. LC 98-15336. (Illus.). 497p. 1998. 29.95 (*0-674-81092-9*) Belknap Pr.

— Many Thousands Gone: The First Two Centuries of Slavery in North America. 2000. pap. 16.95 (*0-674-00211-3*) HUP.

Berlin, Ira. Remembering Slavery: Teaching Supplement. 48p. 1998. pap. 49.95 (*1-56584-489-0*) New Press NY.

— Slaves Without Masters: The Free Negro in the Antebellum South. LC 92-1631. 448p. 1992. pap. 14.95 (*1-56584-028-3*, Pub. by New Press NY) Norton.

Berlin, Ira, et al, eds. Free at Last: A Documentary History of Slavery, Freedom, & the Civil War. LC 92-53726. (Illus.). 608p. 1992. 27.50 (*1-56584-015-1*, Pub. by New Press NY) Norton.

— Free at Last: A Documentary History of Slavery, Freedom, & the Civil War. 1993. pap. 15.95 (*1-56584-120-4*, Pub. by New Press NY) Norton.

— Freedom, a Documentary History of Emancipation 1861-1867 Series I, Vol. 1: The Destruction of Slavery. 896p. 1986. text 80.00 (*0-521-22979-0*) Cambridge U Pr.

— Freedom, a Documentary History of Emancipation 1861-1867 Series I, Vol. 2: The Wartime Genesis of Free Labor - The Upper South. (Illus.). 814p. (C). 1993. text 95.00 (*0-521-41742-2*) Cambridge U Pr.

— Freedom, a Documentary History of Emancipation 1861-1867 Series I, Vol. 3: The Wartime Genesis of Free Labor: The Lower South. (Illus.). 975p. (C). 199 . text 80.00 (*0-521-39493-7*) Cambridge U Pr.

— Freedom, a Documentary History of Emancipation 1861-1867, Series II: The Black Military Experience. LC 82-4446. 784p. 1983. text 80.00 (*0-521-22984-7*) Cambridge U Pr.

— Freedom's Soldiers: The Black Military Experience in the Civil War. LC 98-149583. (Illus.). 208p. (C). 1998. text 49.95 (*0-521-63258-7*); pap. text 14.95 (*0-521-63449-0*) Cambridge U Pr.

— Remembering Slavery: African Americans Talk about Their Personal Experiences of Slavery & Emancipation, 2 cass. (Illus.). 352p. 1998. boxed set 49.95 incl. audio (*1-56584-425-4*, Pub. by New Press NY) Norton.

Berlin, Ira & Hoffman, Ronald, eds. Slavery & Freedom in the Age of the American Revolution. LC 86-11232. (Blacks in the New World Ser.). (Illus.). 352p. 1986. pap. text 12.95 (*0-252-01363-8*) U of Ill Pr.

Berlin, Ira & Morgan, Philip D., eds. Cultivation & Culture: Labor & the Shaping of Slave Life in the Americas. LC 92-31010. (Carter G. Woodson Institute Series in Black Studies). 388p. (C). 1993. text 49.50 (*0-8139-1421-3*) U Pr of Va.

— The Slaves' Economy: Independent Production by Slaves in the Americas. 213p. 1995. pap. 26.50 (*0-7146-4172-3*, Pub. by F Cass Pubs) Intl Spec Bk.

Berlin, Ira & Rowland, Leslie. Families in Freedom: A Documentary History of African American Kinship in the Civil War Era. 1996. 25.00 (*0-614-96809-7*) New Press NY.

Berlin, Ira & Rowland, Leslie S., eds. Families & Freedom: A Documentary History of African-American Kinship in the Civil War Era. (Illus.). 288p. 1998. pap. 16.95 (*1-56584-440-8*, 800.233.4830, Pub. by New Press NY) Norton.

***Berlin, Ira, et al.** Remembering Slavery: African Americans Talk about Their Personal Experiences of Slavery & Emancipation. (Illus.). 2000. pap. 16.95 (*1-56584-587-0*, Pub. by New Press NY) Norton.

Berlin, Ira, et al. Slaves No More: Three Essays on Emancipation & the Civil War. (Illus.). 265p. (C). 1992. pap. 15.95 (*0-521-43692-3*); text 59.95 (*0-521-43102-6*) Cambridge U Pr.

Berlin, Ira, jt. intro. see Starobin, Robert S.

Berlin, Irving. All by Myself. (Piano-Vocal-Guitar Ser.). 6p. 1990. per. 3.95 (*0-7935-9068-X*) H Leonard.

— Berlin Irving Piano Solos. 64p. 1991. pap. 10.95 (*0-7935-0709-X*, 00290345) H Leonard.

Berlin, Irving. Easter Parade. 32p. 15.95 (*0-06-029125-7*); pap. 5.95 (*0-06-443720-5*); lib. bdg. 15.89 (*0-06-029126-5*) HarpC.

— Irving Berlin: Ballads. LC 94-704223. 104p. 1991. per. 12.95 (*0-7935-0378-7*) H Leonard.

— Irving Berlin: Ragtime & Early Songs. LC 94-704224. 96p. (Orig.). 1991. per. 10.95 (*0-7935-0377-9*) H Leonard.

Berlin, Irving. Irving Berlin Pt. 1: Early Songs, 1907-1911. Hamm, Charles, ed. LC 94-24904. (Music of the U. S. A. - Recent Researches in American Music Ser.: Vol. MUSA 2). (Illus.). liii, 247p. 1994. pap. 125.00 (*0-89579-305-9*) A-R Eds.

— Irving Berlin Pt. 2: Early Songs, 1907-1914. Hamm, Charles, ed. (Music of the U. S. A. - Recent Researches in American Music Ser.: Vol. MU2B (A21)MUSA2). (Illus.). xiv, 359p. 1994. pap. 155.00 (*0-89579-340-7*) A-R Eds.

— Irving Berlin Collection, Vol. 306. 176p. 1991. per. 14.95 (*0-7935-0440-6*, 00102147) H Leonard.

— Irving Berlin Favorites - Easy Organ Adventure #9. 48p. 1982. pap. 5.95 (*0-7935-6661-4*) H Leonard.

— The Irving Berlin Treasure Clarinet. 32p. 1996. pap. 5.95 (*0-7935-7069-7*) H Leonard.

— The Irving Berlin Treasure Trumpet. 32p. 1996. pap. 5.95 (*0-7935-7072-7*) H Leonard.

— The Irving Berlin Treasury Alto Sax. 32p. 1996. pap. 5.95 (*0-7935-7070-0*) H Leonard.

— The Irving Berlin Treasury Flute. 32p. 1996. pap. 5.95 (*0-7935-7062-X*) H Leonard.

— The Irving Berlin Treasury Trombone. 32p. 1996. pap. 5.95 (*0-7935-7074-3*) H Leonard.

— Louisiana Purchase: Vocal Selections. 40p. 1997. pap. 8.95 (*0-7935-7351-3*) H Leonard.

Berlin, Irving. White Christmas. 32p. 16.95 (*0-06-029123-0*); pap. 5.95 (*0-06-443719-1*); lib. bdg. 16.89 (*0-06-029124-9*) HarpC.

Berlin, Irving N., ed. Bibliography of Child Psychiatry & Child Mental Health: With a Selected List of Films. LC 74-11813. 508p. 1976. 44.95 (*0-87705-244-1*, Kluwer Acad Hman Sci) Kluwer Academic.

Berlin, Isaiah. Against the Current: Essays in the History of Ideas. Hardy, Henry, ed. 410p. 1998. pap. 19.95 (*0-7126-6690-7*, Pub. by Pimlico) Trafalgar.

— Concepts & Categories: Philosophical Essays. 1999. pap. text 14.95 (*0-691-00234-7*, Pub. by Princeton U Pr) Cal Prin Full Svc.

— First & the Last. LC 99-26531. 141p. 1999. 19.95 (*0-940322-09-9*) NY Rev Bks.

— Four Essays on Liberty. 288p. 1990. pap. text 14.95 (*0-19-281034-0*) OUP.

— The Hedgehog & the Fox: An Essay on Tolstoy's View of History. 96p. 1993. reprint ed. pap. 6.95 (*1-56663-019-3*, Elephant Paperbacks) I R Dee.

— Karl Marx: His Life & Environment. 4th ed. 256p. 1996. pap. 14.95 (*0-19-510326-2*) OUP.

— Personal Impressions. LC 99-490994. (Illus.). 288p. 1998. pap. 19.95 (*0-7126-6601-X*, Pub. by Pimlico) Trafalgar.

***Berlin, Isaiah.** The Power of Ideas. Hardy, Henry, ed. 2000. 24.95 (*0-691-05018-X*) Princeton U Pr.

Berlin, Isaiah. The Proper Study of Mankind: An Anthology of Essays. Hardy, Henry & Hausheer, Roger, eds. LC 97-43470. 672p. 1998. 35.00 (*0-374-23750-6*) FS&G.

***Berlin, Isaiah.** The Proper Study of Mankind: An Anthology of Essays. Hardy, Henry & Hausheer, Roger, eds. 672p. 2000. pap. 16.00 (*0-374-52717-2*) FS&G.

Berlin, Isaiah. Russian Thinkers. 1992. 24.75 (*0-8446-6604-1*) Peter Smith.

— Russian Thinkers. 336p. 1979. pap. 13.95 (*0-14-013625-8*, Viking) Viking Penguin.

— The Sense of Reality: Studies in Ideas & Their History. Hardy, Henry, ed. LC 96-39829. 304p. 1997. 25.00 (*0-374-26092-3*) FS&G.

— A Sense of Reality: Studies in Ideas & Their History. Hardy, Henry, ed. 304p. 1998. pap. 13.00 (*0-374-52569-2*) FS&G.

***Berlin, Isaiah.** Three Critics of the Enlightenment: Vico, Hamann, Herder. LC 00-27419. (Illus.). 2000. 45.00 (*0-691-05726-5*, Pub. by Princeton U Pr); pap. 16.95 (*0-691-05727-3*, Pub. by Princeton U Pr) Cal Prin Full Svc.

Berlin, Isaiah, ed. The Age of Enlightenment. LC 72-117760. (Essay Index Reprint Ser.). 1980. 19.95 (*0-8369-1822-3*) Ayer.

— The Age of Enlightenment: The Eighteenth Century Philosophers. (Orig.). 1984. pap. 12.95 (*0-452-00904-9*, Mer) NAL.

Berlin, Isaiah & Hardy, Henry. The Crooked Timber of Humanity: Chapters in the History of Ideas. LC 97-34247. 288p. 1998. pap. text 14.95 (*0-691-05838-5*, Pub. by Princeton U Pr) Cal Prin Full Svc.

— The Roots of Romanticism. LC 98-41657. 160p. 1999. 24.95 (*0-691-00713-6*, Pub. by Princeton U Pr) Cal Prin Full Svc.

***Berlin, Isaiah, et al.** The Guest from the Future: Anna Akhmatova & Isaiah Berlin. Wood, Antony, tr. from GER. LC 99-32516. (Illus.). 250p. 1999. text 25.00 (*0-374-16727-3*) FS&G.

Berlin, Isaiah, tr. see Turgenev, Ivan Sergeevich.

Berlin, Isaiah, tr. see Turgenev, Ivan Sergeevich & Pritchett, V. S.

Berlin, Isaiah, tr. see Venturi, Franco.

Berlin, Isaiah, tr. & intro. see Turgenev, Ivan Sergeevich.

Berlin, James, Sr. Cup'igtat Laanguaruntenka. large type ed.Tr. of My Yup'ik Eskimo Toys. (ESK., Illus.). 12p. (J). (gr. k-3). 1999. pap. text 17.00 (*1-58084-112-0*) Lower Kuskokwim.

***Berlin, James, Sr.** My Yupik Eskimo Toys. large type ed. (Illus.). 12p. (J). (gr. k-3). 1999. pap. text 17.00 (*1-58084-074-4*) Lower Kuskokwim.

— Yugtaat Naanguat. large type ed.Tr. of My Yup'ik Eskimo Toys. (ESK., Illus.). 12p. (J). (gr. k-3). 1999. pap. text 17.00 (*1-58084-075-2*) Lower Kuskokwim.

Berlin, James A. Rhetoric & Reality: Writing Instruction in American Colleges, 1900-1985. LC 86-20428. (Studies in Writing & Rhetoric). 236p. 1987. pap. text 14.95 (*0-8093-1360-X*) S Ill U Pr.

— Writing Instruction in Nineteenth-Century American Colleges. LC 83-20116. (Studies in Writing & Rhetoric). 128p. (Orig.). 1984. pap. 14.95 (*0-8093-1166-6*) S Ill U Pr.

Berlin, James A. & Vivion, Michael J., eds. Cultural Studies in the English Classroom. LC 93-7509. 326p. (C). 1993. pap. text 29.00 (*0-86709-320-X*, 0320, Pub. by Boynton Cook Pubs) Heinemann.

Berlin, Jean V., ed. A Confederate Nurse: The Diary of Ada W. Bacot 1860-1863. LC 93-30098. 220p. 1994. 24.95 (*0-87249-970-7*) U of SC Pr.

***Berlin, Jean V., ed.** A Confederate Nurse: The Diary of Ada W. Bacot, 1860-1863. 212p. 2000. pap. 12.95 (*1-57003-386-2*) U of SC Pr.

Berlin, Jean V., ed. see Sherman, William T.

Berlin, Jeffrey B., et al, eds. Turn-of-the-Century Vienna & Its Legacy: Essays in Honor of Donald G. Daviau. 546p. 1993. text 49.50 (*0-929497-74-0*) Ariadne CA.

Berlin, Jeffrey B. & Lawson, Richard H., eds. Approaches to Teaching Mann's "Death in Venice" & Other Short Fiction. LC 92-16888. (Approaches to Teaching World Literature Ser.: No. 43). x, 199p. 1992. pap. 18.00 (*0-87352-710-0*, AP43P); lib. bdg. 37.50 (*0-87352-709-7*, AP43C) Modern Lang.

***Berlin, Joey.** Toxic Fame: Celebrities Speak on Stardom. 534p. 2000. reprint ed. pap. text 20.00 (*0-7881-9037-7*) DIANE Pub.

Berlin, Joyce E., jt. ed. see Erhardt, Carl L.

B

An Asterisk (*) at the beginning of an entry indicates that the title is appearing for the first time.

Berlin, K. Darrell, jt. auth. see Butler, George B.

Berlin, K. Darrell, jt. ed. see McEwen, W. E.

Berlin, L., jt. auth. see Smith, A. B.

Berlin, Leonard, et al. Malpractice Issues in Radiology. LC 98-6639. (Illus.). 154p. 1998. write for info. (*1-890705-00-4*) Am Roentgen.

Berlin, Louis, jt. auth. see Smith, Alexander B.

Berlin, Lucia. Homesick: New & Selected Stories. LC 90-20297. 280p. 1990. 25.00 (*0-87685-816-7*); pap. 25.00 (*0-87685-815-9*) Black Sparrow.

— Safe & Sound. 104p. 1989. pap. 9.00 (*0-918395-10-0*) Poltroon Pr.

— So Long: Stories 1987-1992. LC 93-6659. 214p. (C). 1993. 25.00 (*0-87685-894-9*); pap. 13.00 (*0-87685-893-0*) Black Sparrow.

— So Long: Stories 1987-1992. deluxe ed. LC 93-6659. 214p. (C). 1993. 30.00 (*0-87685-895-7*) Black Sparrow.

— Where I Live Now: Stories, 1993-1998. LC 99-13108. 185p. 1999. 25.00 (*1-57423-092-1*) Black Sparrow.

— Where I Live Now: Stories, 1993-1998. LC 99-13108. 240p. 1999. pap. 15.00 (*1-57423-091-3*) Black Sparrow.

— Where I Live Now: Stories, 1993-1998. limited ed. LC 99-13108. 185p. 1999. 35.00 (*1-57423-093-X*) Black Sparrow.

Berlin, Lucia, ed. see Hawkins, Bobbie L.

Berlin, Normand. The Base String: The Underworld in Elizabethan Drama. 224p. 1975. 26.50 (*0-8386-6753-8*) Fairleigh Dickinson.

— O'Neill's Shakespeare. (Theater: Theory - Text - Performance Ser.). 280p. (C). 1993. text 47.50 (*0-472-10469-1*, 10469) U of Mich Pr.

— The Secret Cause: A Discussion of Tragedy. LC 81-4089. 208p. 1983. pap. text 16.95 (*0-87023-398-X*) U of Mass Pr.

Berlin, Pamela S., et al. A Missouri Playwrights' Anthology of Prize-Winning Plays. Knittel, Robert E., ed. LC 81-82168. 383p. (Orig.). 1981. pap. 8.95 (*0-933038-01-1*) Grass Hooper Pr.

Berlin, Patricia G. Great Impressions: The Art & Technique of Rubber Stamping. 90p. 1998. pap. 19.95 (*1-886388-01-6*) Flower Valley Pr.

Berlin, Peter. The Geostationary Applications Satellite. (Illus.). 232p. 1988. text 74.95 (*0-521-33525-6*) Cambridge U Pr.

***Berlin, Peter.** The Xenophobe's Guide to the Swedes. (Xenophobe's Guides Ser.). 64p. 1999. pap. 5.95 (*1-902825-44-6*) Oval Bks.

Berlin, Rena J., et al. Mystery in Room 11. 178p. 1994. wbk. ed. 29.95 (*1-888528-00-1*) Res Develop.

Berlin, Rick, jt. auth. see Hawks, Robb.

Berlin, Robert E. Radioactive Waste Management. LC 88-17359. 444p. 1989. 215.00 (*0-471-85792-0*) Wiley.

Berlin Staff. Berlin Electronic Devices. 5th ed. LC 98-28800. 1998. pap. text, lab manual ed. 36.80 (*0-13-080023-6*) P-H.

Berlin, Susan. Ways We Live: Exploring Community. LC 97-221043. (Illus.). 176p. (Orig.). 1997. pap. 16.95 (*0-86571-363-4*) New Soc Pubs.

Berlin, Wade, ed. see Heath, Maya.

Berlin, William S. On the Edge of Politics: The Roots of Jewish Political Thought in America. 14. LC 78-4018. (Contributions in Political Science Ser.: No. 14). 206p. 1979. 55.00 (*0-313-20422-5*, BEP/, Greenwood Pr) Greenwood.

Berlin, Wissenschaftliche K. Zu, see Von Der Societat, Herausgeben & Zu Berlin, Wissenschaftliche K.

Berlind, tr. see Vas, Istvan.

Berlind, Bruce, tr. Birds & Other Relations: Selected Poetry of Dezso Tandori. 112p. 1986. pap. 9.95 (*0-691-01433-7*, Pub. by Princeton U Pr); text 30.00 (*0-691-06685-X*, Pub. by Princeton U Pr) Cal Prin Full Svc.

Berlind, Bruce, tr. see Oravecz, Imre.

Berlind, Bruce, tr. see Orban, Otto.

Berlind, Robert, jt. contrib. by see Bruhn, Thomas P.

Berline, Byron. Byron Berline/Jumpin the Strings. 48p. 1996. pap. 24.95 incl. audio compact disk (*0-7866-1767-5*); pap. 9.95 (*0-7866-1765-9*, 95720) Mel Bay.

Berline, Byron. Fiddling Through the Years, Vol. 1. (Illus.). 76p. 1990. pap. 17.95 incl. audio (*0-931759-45-5*) Centerstream Pub.

Berline, N., et al. Heat Kernels & Dirac Operators. 2nd ed. Berger, M. et al, eds. (Grundlehren der Mathematischen Wissenschaften Ser.: Vol. 298). 369p. 1996. 98.00 (*0-387-53340-0*) Spr-Verlag.

Berliner. Conducting Symphonies. 1985. 14.95 (*0-13-166786-6*); 21.95 (*0-13-166794-7*) P-H.

Berliner, Abraham. Aus dem Leben der Deutschen Juden im Mittelalter. Katz, Steven, ed. LC 79-7127. (Jewish Philosophy, Mysticism & History of Ideas Ser.). 1980. reprint ed. lib. bdg. 17.95 (*0-405-12241-1*) Ayer.

— Gesammelte Schriften, Band 1. (GER.). vi, 239p. 1988. reprint ed. write for info. (*3-487-07938-0*) G Olms Pubs.

— Geschichte der Juden in Rom von der Altesten Zeit bis zur Gegenwart, 2 vols. in 1. xxvi, 484p. 1987. reprint ed. 105.00 (*3-487-07956-9*) G Olms Pubs.

Berliner, Barbara & Corey, Melinda. The Book of Answers: The New York Public Library Telephone Reference Service's Most Unusual & Entertaining Questions. 320p. 1992. per. 11.00 (*0-671-75192-7*, Fireside) S&S Trade Pap.

Berliner, Barbara, et al. The Book of Answers: The New York Public Library Telephone Reference Service's Most Unusual & Entertaining Questions. 228p. 1990. 21.45 (*0-13-957432-8*) P-H.

Berliner, David. The Manufactured Crisis. (C). 1995. pap. text. write for info. (*0-8013-1671-5*) Addison-Wesley.

Berliner, David C. & Biddle, Bruce J. The Manufactured Crisis: Myths, Fraud & the Attack on America's Public Schools. LC 95-3271. 432p. 1995. 25.00 (*0-201-40957-7*) Addison-Wesley.

Berliner, David C. & Casanova, Ursula. Putting Research to Work in Your School. LC 96-76991. 246p. (Orig.). 1996. pap. 32.95 (*1-57517-064-7*, 1448) SkyLght.

Berliner, David C., et al. The Manufactured Crisis: Myths, Fraud & the Attack on America's Public Schools. 432p. 1996. pap. 16.00 (*0-201-44196-9*) Addison-Wesley.

Berliner, David C., jt. auth. see Cage, N. L.

Berliner, David C., jt. auth. see Fisher, Charles W.

Berliner, David C., jt. auth. see Gage, Nathaniel L.

Berliner, David C., ed. see Review of Research in Education Staff.

Berliner, Don. Aviation: Reaching for the Sky. LC 96-4940. (Innovators Ser.). (Illus.). 144p. (YA). (gr. 5-12). 1997. lib. bdg. 19.95 (*1-881508-33-1*) Oliver Pr MN.

— Before the Wright Brothers. (Space & Aviation Ser.). (Illus.). 72p. (J). (gr. 5 up). 1990. lib. bdg. 22.60 (*0-8225-1588-1*, Lerner Publctns) Lerner Pub.

— Living in Space. LC 92-24847. (Space & Aviation Ser.). (Illus.). 72p. (YA). (gr. 6-9). 1993. lib. bdg. 22.60 (*0-8225-1599-7*, Lerner Publctns) Lerner Pub.

***Berliner, Don.** The Paris Air Show. (Illus.). 156p. 2000. pap. 29.95 (*0-7603-0728-8*, 129830AP, Pub. by MBI Pubg) Motorbooks Intl.

— UFO Briefing Document. Strieber, Whitley, ed. 288p. 2000. mass mkt. 6.99 (*0-440-23638-X*) Dell.

Berliner, Don. Want a Job? Get Some Experience. Want Experience? Get a Job. LC 78-18304. 192p. reprint ed. pap. 59.60 (*0-608-12854-6*, 202358900033) Bks Demand.

Berliner, Don, jt. auth. see Friedman, Stanton.

Berliner, Franz. Wildebeest. LC 90-82449. (Illus.). 32p. (J). (ps-3). 1991. 13.95 (*0-8249-8488-9*, Ideals Child) Hambleton-Hill.

***Berliner, Hans.** System: A World Champion's Approach to Chess. (Illus.). 1999. pap. text. write for info. (*1-901983-10-2*, Pub. by Gambit) BHB Intl.

Berliner, Helen. Enlightened by Design. LC 98-31178. (Illus.). 256p. 1999. pap. 22.95 (*1-57062-334-1*, Pub. by Shambhala Pubns) Random.

Berliner, Howard. A System of Scientific Medicine. 180p. 1985. 29.95 (*0-422-79520-8*, 9822, Pub. by Tavistock); pap. 13.95 (*0-422-79530-5*, 9829, Pub. by Tavistock) Routldge.

Berliner, Isaac & Rivera, Diego. City of Palaces. limited ed. (Illus.). 144p. 1996. 49.95 (*0-9649634-0-X*) Jacoby Pr.

Berliner, Jan & Statman, Jan B. Battered Woman's Survival Guide: Breaking the Cycle. rev. ed. 168p. 1995. 18.95 (*0-87833-890-X*); pap. text 9.95 (*0-87833-889-6*) Taylor Pub.

Berliner, Janet. Children of the Dusk. Bk. 3. (Madagascar Manifesto Ser.). 1997. mass mkt. 5.99 (*1-56504-932-2*, Borealis) White Wolf.

Berliner, Janet, ed. Desire Burn. 272p. 1995. pap. 9.95 (*0-7867-0259-1*) Carroll & Graf.

Berliner, Janet & Guthridge, George. Child of the Journey. (Madagascar Manifesto Ser.: Bk. II). 1996. pap. 5.99 (*1-56504-942-X*, Borealis) White Wolf.

— Child of the Light. (Madagascar Manifesto Ser.: Bk. 1). (Illus.). 440p. (Orig.). 1996. pap. 5.99 (*1-56504-931-4*, 12100, Borealis) White Wolf.

Berliner, Janet, jt. ed. see Beagle, Peter S.

Berliner, Janet, ed. see Oates, Joyce Carol, et al.

Berliner, Joseph S. The Economics of the Good Society: The Variety of Economic Arrangements. LC 98-52530. 400p. 1999. 74.95 (*0-631-20828-3*); pap. 34.95 (*0-631-20829-1*) Blackwell Pubs.

— Factory & Manager in the U. S. S. R. LC 57-9068. (Russian Research Center Studies: No. 27). 406p. reprint ed. pap. 125.90 (*0-7837-4099-9*, 205792200011) Bks Demand.

— Soviet Industry from Stalin to Gorbachev: Essays on Management & Innovation. LC 87-47839. (Cornell Studies in Soviet History & Science). 288p. 1988. 45.00 (*0-8014-2170-5*) Cornell U Pr.

Berliner, L. J. Biological Magnetic Resonance Vol. 14: Spin Labeling: The Next Millennium. (Illus.). 354p. (C). 1998. text 125.00 (*0-306-45644-3*, Kluwer Plenum) Kluwer Academic.

— Thrombin: Structure & Function. (Illus.). 354p. (C). 1992. text 115.00 (*0-306-43991-3*, Kluwer Plenum) Kluwer Academic.

Berliner, L. J. & Reuben, J. Biological Magnetic Resonance, Vol. 9. (Illus.). 264p. (C). 1990. text 114.00 (*0-306-43341-9*, Kluwer Plenum) Kluwer Academic.

— Biological Magnetic Resonance Vol. 10: Carbohydrates & Nucleic Acids. (Illus.). 304p. (C). 1992. text 95.00 (*0-306-44060-1*, Kluwer Plenum) Kluwer Academic.

— Biological Magnetic Resonance Vol. 11: In Vivo Spectroscopy. (Illus.). 348p. (C). 1992. text 110.00 (*0-306-44276-0*, Kluwer Plenum) Kluwer Academic.

— Biological Magnetic Resonance Vol. 12: NMR of Paramagnetic Molecules. (Illus.). 454p. (C). 1993. text 120.00 (*0-306-44387-2*, Kluwer Plenum) Kluwer Academic.

— Biological Magnetic Resonance Vol. 13: EMR of Paramagnetic Molecules. (Illus.). 414p. (C). 1993. text 120.00 (*0-306-44397-X*, Kluwer Plenum) Kluwer Academic.

— Spin Labeling: Theory & Applications, Vol. 8. (Biological Magnetic Resonance Ser.: Vol. 8). (Illus.). 670p. (C). 1989. text 145.00 (*0-306-43072-X*, Kluwer Plenum) Kluwer Academic.

Berliner, L. J., jt. auth. see Krishna, N. R.

***Berliner, L. Mark, et al, eds.** Studies in Atmospheric Sciences. LC 99-52678. (Lecture Notes in Statistics Ser.: Vol. 144). 208p. 2000. pap. 44.95 (*0-387-98757-6*) Spr-Verlag.

Berliner, Larry & Berliner, Susan. ReWriter, Bk. I. (Illus.). 38p. (Orig.). (J). (gr. 5-8). 1985. pap. text 17.95 (*0-913935-28-X*) ERA-CCR.

— ReWriter, Bk. II. (Illus.). 38p. (Orig.). (J). (gr. 6-9). 1985. pap. text 17.95 (*0-913935-29-8*) ERA-CCR.

Berliner, Lawrence J. & Reuben, Jacques, eds. Biological Magnetic Resonance, Vol. 3. LC 78-16035. 288p. 1981. 85.00 (*0-306-40612-8*, Plenum Trade) Perseus Pubng.

— Biological Magnetic Resonance, Vol. 4. LC 78-16035. 360p. 1982. 85.00 (*0-306-40968-2*, Plenum Trade) Perseus Pubng.

— Biological Magnetic Resonance, Vol. 5. LC 78-16035. 322p. 1983. 85.00 (*0-306-41293-4*, Plenum Trade) Perseus Pubng.

— Biological Magnetic Resonance, Vol. 6. LC 78-16035. 318p. 1984. 85.00 (*0-306-41683-2*, Plenum Trade) Perseus Pubng.

— Biological Magnetic Resonance, Vol. 7. LC 78-16035. 334p. 1987. 85.00 (*0-306-42455-X*, Plenum Trade) Perseus Pubng.

Berliner, Lawrence J. & Robitaille, P.-M., eds. Biological Magnetic Resonance, Vol. 15. (Illus.). 255p. (C). 1999. text 125.00 (*0-306-45886-1*, Kluwer Plenum) Kluwer Academic.

Berliner, Lawrence J., jt. ed. see Krishna, N. R.

Berliner, Louise. Texas Guinan, Queen of the Night Clubs. LC 92-1720. (Illus.). 253p. 1993. 24.95 (*0-292-78111-3*) U of Tex Pr.

Berliner, Marilyn J. & Lindberg, Jan F. Acoustic Particle Velocity Sensors: Design, Performance & Applications. (AIP Press Conference Proceedings Ser.: No. 368). (Illus.). 464p. 1996. 140.00 (*1-56396-549-6*, AIP Pr) Spr-Verlag.

Berliner, Michael S., ed. see Rand, Ayn.

Berliner, Nancy. Beyond the Screen: Chinese Furniture of the 16th & 17th Centuries. LC 96-75974. 1996. 50.00 (*0-87846-434-4*) Mus Fine Arts Boston.

Berliner, Nancy & Dantzler, Lea, eds. Cincinnati Days in History: A Bicentennial Almanac. (Illus.). 224p. (Orig.). 1988. pap. 9.00 (*0-933002-04-1*) Cin Post.

Berliner, Nancy & Handler, Sarah. Friends of the House: Furniture from China's Towns & Villages. 1996. 50.00 (*0-88389-134-4*, PEMP214) Peabody Essex Mus.

Berliner, Paul. The Soul of Mbira: Music & Traditions of the Shona People of Zimbabwe. LC 76-24578. (Perspectives on Southern Africa Ser.: No. 26). (Illus.). 332p. reprint ed. pap. 103.00 (*0-7837-4761-6*, 204450800003) Bks Demand.

Berliner, Paul F. The Soul of Mbira: Music & Traditions of the Shona People of Zimbabwe. LC 92-41356. (Illus.). xxii, 334p. (C). 1993. pap. 17.00 (*0-226-04379-7*) U Ch Pr.

— Thinking in Jazz: The Infinite Art of Improvisation. LC 93-34660. (Chicago Studies in Ethnomusicology). (Illus.). 904p. (C). 1994. pap. 29.95 (*0-226-04381-9*) U Ch Pr.

— Thinking in Jazz: The Infinite Art of Improvisation. LC 93-34660. (Chicago Studies in Ethnomusicology). (Illus.). 672p. (C). 1995. lib. bdg. 85.00 (*0-226-04380-0*) U Ch Pr.

Berliner, Robert W., jt. ed. see Orloff, Jack.

Berliner, Susan, jt. auth. see Berliner, Larry.

Berliner, Terry, jt. auth. see Diamond, David.

Berlinerblau, Jacques. Heresy in the University: The Black Athena Controversy & the Responsibilities of American Intellectuals. LC 98-8499. 304p. (C). 1999. text 50.00 (*0-8135-2587-X*); pap. text 20.00 (*0-8135-2588-8*) Rutgers U Pr.

— The Vow & the 'Popular Religious Groups' of Ancient Israel: A Philological & Sociological Inquiry. (Journal for the Study of the Old Testament Supplement Ser.: No. 210). 219p. 1996. 60.00 (*1-85075-578-7*, Pub. by Sheffield Acad) CUP Services.

Berling, David, jt. auth. see Biekert, Russell.

Berling, Judith A. A Pilgrim in Chinese Culture: Negotiating Religious Diversity. LC 97-30863. (Faith Meets Faith Ser.). 160p. (Orig.). 1997. pap. 18.00 (*1-57075-152-8*) Orbis Bks.

Berlinger, B. Evoloid - A New Concept in High Ratio Gearing. (Technical Papers: Vol. P109.37). (Illus.). 9p. 1975. pap. text 30.00 (*1-55589-369-4*) AGMA.

Berlinger, Eli. Basic Structures. Date not set. pap. text, teacher ed. 21.95 (*0-314-96597-1*) West Pub.

— Strictly Structured BASIC. LC 85-21489. (Illus.). 372p. (C). 1986. pap. text 48.00 (*0-314-93152-X*) West Pub.

— Strictly Structured VAX BASIC. 451p. (C). 1988. mass mkt. 48.00 (*0-314-64977-8*) West Pub.

— Turbo Pascal. Date not set. pap. text, teacher ed. write for info. (*0-314-70742-5*) West Pub.

Berlinger, Eli & Zirkel, Gene. Turbo Pascal. Ricci, ed. 490p. (C). 1990. pap. text 50.75 (*0-314-66781-4*) West Pub.

Berlinghoff, William P. & Washburn, Robert. The Mathematics of the Elementary Grades. (Illus.). 602p. 1990. text 48.95 (*0-912675-80-2*); pap. text, teacher ed. write for info. (*0-912675-81-0*) Ardsley.

Berlinghoff, William P., et al. A Mathematics Sampler: Topics for the Liberal Arts. 4th rev. ed. (Illus.). 592p. (C). 1996. text 53.95 (*1-880157-23-3*, 7-23-3) Ardsley.

Berlingieri, Francesco. Berlingieri on Arrest of Ships: A Commentary on the 1952 Arrest Convention. 248p. 1992. 130.00 (*1-85044-465-X*) LLP.

— Time-Barred Actions. 2nd ed. (International Maritime Law Ser.). 256p. 1993. boxed set 110.00 (*1-85044-525-7*) LLP.

Berlinquette, Esther R. A Metaphysical Spiritual Development Course. Rizer, Arden C., Jr., ed. (Illus.). 36p. 1998. 10.25 (*0-939795-48-5*) Amer Spirit.

Berlins, Marcel & Dyer, C. Law Machine. annuals 4th ed. 1994. pap. 15.95 (*0-14-023478-0*, Pub. by Pnguin Bks Ltd) Trafalgar.

Berlinski, Allen, ed. see Foster, Linda N.

Berlinski, Allen, ed. see Leo, Kathleen R.

Berlinski, Allen, ed. see Richmond, Steve.

Berlinski, David. The Advent of the Algorithm: The Idea That Rules the World. LC 98-43755. 368p. (C). 2000. 28.00 (*0-15-100338-6*) Harcourt.

***Berlinski, David.** Newton's Gift: How Sir Isaac Newton Unlocked the System of the World. 2000. 24.00 (*0-684-84392-7*) Free Pr.

Berlinski, David. A Tour of the Calculus. 1997. pap. 14.00 (*0-679-74788-5*); pap. 14.00 (*0-676-52041-3*) Vin Bks.

Berlinsky, Ellen B., jt. auth. see Schine, Gary L.

***Berliocchi, Luigi.** The Orchid in Lore & Legend. Griffiths, Mark, ed. (Illus.). 224p. 2000. 29.95 (*0-88192-491-1*) Timber.

Berlioz, Hector. The Art of Music & Other Essays: (A Travers Chants) Csicsery-Ronay, Elizabeth, ed. & tr. by. LC 93-3752. (Illus.). 1994. 29.95 (*0-253-31164-0*) Ind U Pr.

— Conductor, the Theory of His Art. 2002. 25.00 (*0-403-00247-8*) Scholarly.

— Conductor, the Theory of His Art. (Works of Hector Berlioz). reprint ed. lib. bdg. 59.00 (*0-7812-0737-1*) Rprt Serv.

***Berlioz, Hector.** A Critical Study of Beethoven's Nine Symphonies. Evans, Edwin, tr. from FRE. 200p. 2000. reprint ed. pap. 15.00 (*0-252-06942-0*) U of Ill Pr.

— A Critical Study of Beethoven's Nine Symphonies: With "A Few Words on His Trios & Sonatas": A Criticism of "Fidelio" & an Introductory Essay on Music LC 90-34891. 1990. 39.00 (*1-878592-13-0*) Native Amer Bk Pubs.

Berlioz, Hector. Critical Study of Beethoven's Nine Symphonies with a Few Words on His Trios & Sonatas. 1988. reprint ed. lib. bdg. 59.00 (*0-7812-0736-3*) Rprt Serv.

— A Critical Study of Beethoven's Nine Symphonies with a Few Words on His Trios & Sonatas, a Criticism of His Fidelio, & an Introductory Essay on Music. 165p. 1958. reprint ed. 49.00 (*0-403-01508-1*) Scholarly.

***Berlioz, Hector.** La Damnation de Faust: Dramatic Legend in Full Score. 1998. pap. 24.95 (*0-486-40169-3*) Dover.

— L 'Enfance du Christ, Op. 25, in Full Score: Sacred Trilogy for Solo Voices, Chorus & Orchestra. 1999. pap. text 15.95 (*0-486-40852-3*) Dover.

Berlioz, Hector. Evenings with the Orchestra. LC 98-54094. 1999. pap. 16.00 (*0-226-04374-6*) U Ch Pr.

— Gluck & His Operas. Evans, Edwin, tr. LC 73-7695. (Illus.). 167p. 1973. reprint ed. lib. bdg. 35.00 (*0-8371-6938-0*, BEGO, Greenwood Pr) Greenwood.

— Gluck & the Opera. 1988. reprint ed. lib. bdg. 75.00 (*0-7812-0474-7*) Rprt Serv.

— The Life, As Written by Himself in His Letters & Memoirs. Boult, Katharine F., tr. from FRE. LC 74-24042. reprint ed. 37.50 (*0-404-12865-3*) AMS Pr.

— Memoirs. (Illus.). 547p. 1966. pap. 13.95 (*0-486-21563-6*) Dover.

— Memoirs of Hector Berlioz from 1803 to 1865. (Music Book Index Ser.). 533p. 1992. reprint ed. lib. bdg. 99.00 (*0-7812-9478-9*) Rprt Serv.

— Mozart, Weber & Wagner. 1988. reprint ed. lib. bdg. 49.00 (*0-7812-0566-2*) Rprt Serv.

— Mozart, Weber & Wagner. 1976. reprint ed. lib. bdg. 59.00 (*0-403-08963-8*) Scholarly.

— New Letters of Berlioz, 1830-1868. Barzun, Jacques, tr. & intro. by. LC 75-100144. 322p. 1974. reprint ed. lib. bdg. 35.00 (*0-8371-3251-7*, BENL, Greenwood Pr) Greenwood.

— Requiem Mass & Te Deum in Full Score. 304p. 1996. pap. 17.95 (*0-486-29091-3*) Dover.

— Roman Carnival & Other Overtures in Full Score. 192p. 1995. pap. 12.95 (*0-486-28750-5*) Dover.

— Symphonie Fantastique. Cone, Edward T., ed. (Critical Scores Ser.). (C). 1971. pap. text 16.00 (*0-393-09926-1*) Norton.

— Symphonie Fantastique OP 14. 1998. pap. text 4.95 (*0-486-29890-6*, 741725Q) Dover.

— Symphony Fantastique & Harold in Italy in Full Score. (Music Scores & Music to Play Ser.). 320p. 1984. reprint ed. pap. 14.95 (*0-486-24657-4*) Dover.

— A Treatise on Modern Instrumentation & Orchestration. 1976. 69.00 (*0-403-06679-4*, Regency) Scholarly.

— A Treatise on Modern Instrumentation & Orchestration. 1988. reprint ed. lib. bdg. 79.00 (*0-7812-0266-3*) Rprt Serv.

— Les Troyens Libretto Custom for Metropolitan Opera. 56p. 1993. pap. 2.46 (*0-7935-2978-6*) H Leonard.

Berlioz, Hector & Strauss, Richard. Treatise on Instrumentation. (Illus.). 432p. 1991. reprint ed. pap. 19.95 (*0-486-26903-5*) Dover.

Berlis, Angela & Klaus-Dieter, Gerth, eds. Christus Spes: Liturgie und Glaube Im Okumenischen Kontext Festschrift Fur Bischof Sigisbert Kraft unter Mitarbeit von Paul Berbers und Thaddaus A. Schnitker. (GER., Illus.). XXVI, 351p. 1994. 33.95 (*3-631-46621-8*) P Lang Pubng.

Berlit, Peter. Memorix Neurology. (Memorix Ser.). (Illus.). 304p. 1996. pap. text 16.95 (*0-412-56070-4*, Pub. by E A) OUP.

— Vasculitis, Rheumatic Disease, & the Nervous System. Moore, Patricia, ed. LC 92-48500. 1992. 35.00 (*0-387-54853-X*) Spr-Verlag.

Berlitz. Berlitz Junior Spanish. (SPA., Illus.). (J). (ps-2). 1989. bds. 19.95 incl. audio (*0-689-71317-7*) Aladdin.

— Teddy Berlitz French II. 1996. pap. 19.95 incl. audio (*0-689-71817-9*) Aladdin.

Berlitz, Charles. Atlantis: The Eighth Continent. 256p. 1985. mass mkt. 5.99 (*0-449-20742-0*, Crest) Fawcett.

— Bermuda Triangle. 272p. 1978. mass mkt. 5.99 (*0-380-00465-8*, Avon Bks) Morrow Avon.

B

An Asterisk (*) at the beginning of an entry indicates that the title is appearing for the first time.

— Charles Berlitz's World of Strange Phenomena. 368p. 1990. mass mkt. 5.99 (*0-449-21825-2*, Crest) Fawcett.
— French Step-by-Step. LC 89-25104. 308p. (YA). (gr. 10). 1989. pap. 11.99 (*0-922066-33-7*) Wynwood.
— German Step-by-Step. LC 90-32659. 336p. 1990. pap. 11.99 (*0-922066-43-4*) Wynwood.
— Ingles Step-by-Step. LC 90-32678. 272p. (gr. 10). 1990. pap. 11.99 (*0-922066-44-2*) Wynwood.
— Italian Step-by-Step. LC 90-12128. 384p. (gr. 10). 1989. pap. 11.99 (*0-922066-42-6*) Wynwood.
— Passport to Italian. rev. ed. 240p. 1979. mass mkt. 6.99 (*0-451-16764-3*, Sig) NAL.
— Passport to Russian. (ENG & RUS.). 208p. (Orig.). 1992. mass mkt. 6.99 (*0-451-17200-0*, Sig) NAL.
— Passport to Spanish. rev. ed. 240p. 1993. mass mkt. 6.99 (*0-451-17831-9*, Sig) NAL.
— Spanish Step-by-Step. LC 89-25106. 348p. (YA). (gr. 10). 1990. pap. 11.99 (*0-922066-28-0*) Wynwood.
— Your Passport to Arabic. 256p. 1999. pap. 5.99 (*0-451-18165-4*, Sig) NAL.

Berlitz, Charles & Moore, William I. The Roswell Incident: The Classic Study of UFO Contact. 192p. 1990. mass mkt. 5.99 (*0-425-12602-1*) Berkley Pub.

Berlitz, Charles & Moore, William L. The Roswell Incident: The Classic Study of UFO Contact. (Illus.). 192p. 1997. 6.98 (*1-56731-132-6*, MJF Bks) Fine Comms.

Berlitz Editors. African Phrase Book. (AFA., Illus.). 192p. 1996. pap. text 8.95 (*2-8315-5184-6*) Berlitz.
— Algarve Pocket Guide, 1998. rev. ed. (Pocket Guides Ser.). (Illus.). 1998. pap. 8.95 (*2-8315-6284-8*) Berlitz.
— Amsterdam Pocket Guide. rev. ed. (Illus.). 144p. 1998. pap. 8.95 (*2-8315-6286-4*) Berlitz.
— Arabic Cassette Pack. unabridged ed. 1998. pap. 18.95 incl. audio (*2-8315-6269-4*) Berlitz.
— Arabic Phrase Book. rev. ed. (Phrase Bks.). (ENG & ARA., Illus.). 192p. 1998. pap. text 7.95 (*2-8315-6264-3*) Berlitz.
— Australia Pocket Guide. rev. ed. (Illus.). 192p. 1998. pap. 10.95 (*2-8315-6521-9*) Berlitz.
— Bali & Lombok Pocket Guide. (Illus.). 192p. 1997. pap. 8.95 (*2-8315-6288-0*) Berlitz.
— Barcelona Guia Turistica. rev. ed. (Pocket Guides Ser.). (SPA., Illus.). 144p. 1998. pap. 8.95 (*2-8315-7000-X*) Berlitz.

***Berlitz Editors.** Barcelona Pocket Guide. (Pocket Guides Ser.). (Illus.). 144p. 2000. pap. 8.95 (*2-8315-7686-5*) Berlitz.

Berlitz Editors. Basic Japanese. unabridged ed. (Illus.). 192p. pap. 34.95 incl. audio (*2-8315-6246-5*) Berlitz.
— Berlin Pocket Guide. rev. ed. LC 99-215111. (Pocket Guides Ser.). (Illus.). 144p. 1998. pap. 8.95 (*2-8315-6413-1*) Berlitz.
— Berlitz Business French Phrase Book. (FRE.). 192p. 1996. pap. 8.95 (*2-8315-5159-5*) Berlitz.
— Berlitz Business German Phrase Book. (GER.). 192p. 1996. pap. 8.95 (*2-8315-5160-9*) Berlitz.
— Berlitz Business Italian Phrase Book. (ITA.). 192p. 1996. pap. 8.95 (*2-8315-5161-7*) Berlitz.
— Berlitz Business Spanish Phrase Book. (SPA.). 192p. 1996. pap. 8.95 (*2-8315-5162-5*) Berlitz.
— Berlitz Business Travel Guide to Europe. expanded rev. ed. (Illus.). 432p. 1998. pap. 8.95 (*2-8315-7009-3*) Berlitz.
— Berlitz European Menu Reader. (Illus.). 336p. 1998. pap. 8.95 (*2-8315-6245-7*) Berlitz.
— Berlitz Guide to Travel Photography. (Illus.). 144p. 1996. pap. text 9.95 (*2-8315-5702-X*) Berlitz.
— Berlitz Russian Workbook. (Berlitz Basic Ser.). (RUS.). 128p. 1998. pap. text, wbk. ed. 12.95 (*2-8315-6589-8*) Berlitz.
— Berlitz Travel Guide: Bermuda. 1982. pap. write for info. (*0-686-96940-5*) Macmillan.

***Berlitz Editors.** Boston Pocket Guide. LC 99-222006. (Pocket Guides Ser.). (Illus.). 144p. 2000. pap. 8.95 (*2-8315-7687-3*) Berlitz.

Berlitz Editors. Brussels Pocket Guide. rev. ed. (Pocket Guides Ser.). (Illus.). 144p. 1998. pap. 8.95 (*2-8315-6291-0*) Berlitz.
— Budapest Pocket Guide, 1999. rev. ed. (Pocket Guides Ser.). (Illus.). 144p. 1999. pap. 8.95 (*2-8315-6955-9*) Berlitz.

***Berlitz Editors.** California Guia Turistica. (Pocket Guides Ser.). (SPA., Illus.). 144p. 1998. pap. 8.95 (*2-8315-6566-9*) Berlitz.
— California Pocket Guide. (Illus.). 144p. 2000. 8.95 (*2-8315-7689-X*) Berlitz.

Berlitz Editors. Canada Pocket Guide, 1998. rev. ed. (Pocket Guides Ser.). (Illus.). 256p. 1998. pap. 10.95 (*2-8315-6292-9*) Berlitz.

***Berlitz Editors.** Canary Islands Pocket Guide. (Illus.). 192p. 2000. pap. 8.95 (*2-8315-7690-3*) Berlitz.
— Cancun & Cozumel Pocket Guide. (Illus.). 144p. 2000. 8.95 (*2-8315-7691-1*) Berlitz.

Berlitz Editors. Channel Islands Pocket Guide 1998. rev. ed. (Pocket Guides Ser.). (Illus.). 1998. pap. 8.95 (*2-8315-6294-5*) Berlitz.
— Chinese-Cantonese Cassette Pack. unabridged rev. ed. 1998. pap. 18.95 incl. audio (*2-8315-6271-6*) Berlitz.
— Chinese-Cantonese Phrase Book. (Illus.). 192p. 1998. pap. 7.95 (*2-8315-6266-X*) Berlitz.
— Chinese-Mandarin Cassette Pack. unabridged ed. 1998. pap. 18.95 incl. audio (*2-8315-6270-8*) Berlitz.
— Chinese-Mandarin Phrase Book. (Illus.). 192p. 1998. pap. 7.95 (*2-8315-6265-1*) Berlitz.

***Berlitz Editors.** Costa del Sol Pocket Guide. (Illus.). 192p. 2000. pap. 8.95 (*2-8315-7692-X*) Berlitz.

Berlitz Editors. Costa Rica Pocket Guide. (Pocket Guides Ser.). (Illus.). 144p. 1999. pap. 8.95 (*2-8315-7007-7*) Berlitz.
— Crete Pocket Guide: 1998. rev. ed. LC 99-475486. (Pocket Guides Ser.). (Illus.). 1998. pap. 8.95 (*2-8315-6420-4*) Berlitz.

***Berlitz Editors.** Cuba Pocket Guide. (Illus.). 192p. 2000. pap. 8.95 (*2-8315-7693-8*) Berlitz.
— Cyprus Pocket Guide. (Pocket Guides Ser.). (Illus.). 2000. pap. 8.95 (*2-8315-7167-7*) Berlitz.

Berlitz Editors. Czech Republic Pocket Guide. (Pocket Guides Ser.). (Illus.). 192p. 1996. pap. 8.95 (*2-8315-5969-3*) Berlitz.

***Berlitz Editors.** Danish Cassette Pack. unabridged ed. (Cassette Pack Ser.). 192p. 2000. 18.95 incl. audio (*2-8315-7741-1*) Berlitz.

Berlitz Editors. Danish/English Dictionary. (ENG & DAN.). 368p. 1998. pap. 7.95 (*2-8315-6305-4*) Berlitz.
— Dutch/English Dictionary. (ENG & DUT.). 368p. 1998. pap. 7.95 (*2-8315-6306-2*) Berlitz.
— Eastern European Cassette Pack. (Cassette Pack Ser.). (Illus.). 192p. 1995. 21.95 incl. audio (*2-8315-1539-4*) Berlitz.
— Egypt Pocket Guide, 1998. rev. ed. (Pocket Guides Ser.). (Illus.). 144p. 1998. pap. 8.95 (*2-8315-6300-3*) Berlitz.

***Berlitz Editors.** English Today (Spanish), Set. (Today Ser.). (ENG & SPA., Illus.). 1998. pap., student ed., boxed set 59.95 incl. audio (*2-8315-6199-X*) Berlitz.

Berlitz Editors. Essential French. (Essentials Ser.). (Illus.). 296p. 1996. pap. text 10.95 (*2-8315-5715-1*) Berlitz.
— Essential German. (Essentials Ser.). (GER., Illus.). 428p. 1996. pap. text 10.95 (*2-8315-5716-X*) Berlitz.
— Essential Italian. (Essentials Ser.). (ITA., Illus.). 296p. 1996. pap. text 10.95 (*2-8315-5717-8*) Berlitz.
— Essential Japanese. (Berlitz Essentials Ser.). (JAV., Illus.). 296p. 1997. pap. text 10.95 (*2-8315-6234-1*) Berlitz.
— Essential Russian. (Berlitz Essentials Ser.). (RUS.). 296p. 1997. pap. text 10.95 (*2-8315-6235-X*) Berlitz.
— Essential Spanish. (Essentials Ser.). (SPA., Illus.). 272p. 1996. pap. text 10.95 (*2-8315-5718-6*) Berlitz.
— Finnish/English Dictionary. (FIN & ENG.). 368p. 1998. pap. 7.95 (*2-8315-6309-7*) Berlitz.
— The Five Crayons French. (Berlitz Kids Ser.). (FRE & ENG., Illus.). 64p. (J). (gr. k-4). 1998. pap. 16.95 incl. audio (*2-8315-6534-0*) Berlitz.

***Berlitz Editors.** Florence Pocket Guide. (Illus.). 192p. 2000. pap. 8.95 (*2-8315-7696-2*) Berlitz.
— Florida Pocket Guide. (Illus.). 144p. 2000. pap. 8.95 (*2-8315-7710-1*) Berlitz.

Berlitz Editors. France Pocket Guide, 1998. rev. ed. (Pocket Guides Ser.). (Illus.). 256p. 1998. pap. 10.95 (*2-8315-6416-6*) Berlitz.
— French Cassette Pack. unabridged rev. ed. 1998. pap. 17.95 incl. audio (*2-8315-6330-5*) Berlitz.
— French Grammar Handbook. rev. ed. (FRE., Illus.). 239p. 1998. pap. 10.95 (*2-8315-6387-9*) Berlitz.
— French Phrase Book. rev. ed. (Berlitz Phrase Books & Dictionary Ser.). (FRE., Illus.). 192p. 1998. pap. text 7.95 (*2-8315-6239-2*) Berlitz.

***Berlitz Editors.** French Think & Talk. unabridged ed. (Think & Talk Ser.). (Illus.). 1998. 149.95 incl. audio, cd-rom (*2-8315-6181-7*) Berlitz.
— French Today, 4 cass. (Today Ser.). (FRE., Illus.). 1998. pap., student ed., boxed set 59.95 incl. audio (*2-8315-6195-7*) Berlitz.

Berlitz Editors. French Verb Handbook. rev. ed. (FRE., Illus.). 210p. 1998. pap. 10.95 (*2-8315-6388-7*) Berlitz.
— French Vocabulary Handbook. (FRE., Illus.). 256p. 1998. pap. 10.95 (*2-8315-6389-5*) Berlitz.
— French/English Dictionary. (FRE & ENG.). 368p. 1998. pap. 7.95 (*2-8315-6379-8*) Berlitz.
— German Grammar Handbook. rev. ed. (GER., Illus.). 262p. 1998. pap. 10.95 (*2-8315-6390-9*) Berlitz.
— German Phrase Book. rev. ed. (Berlitz Phrase Book & Dictionary Ser.). (GER., Illus.). 192p. 1998. pap. text 7.95 (*2-8315-6240-6*) Berlitz.

***Berlitz Editors.** German Think & Talk. unabridged ed. (Think & Talk Ser.). (Illus.). 1998. 149.95 incl. audio, cd-rom (*2-8315-6182-5*) Berlitz.
— German Today, 4 cass. (Today Ser.). (GER., Illus.). 1998. student ed., boxed set 59.95 incl. audio (*2-8315-6196-5*) Berlitz.

Berlitz Editors. German Verb Handbook. (GER., Illus.). 289p. 1998. pap. 10.95 (*2-8315-6391-7*) Berlitz.
— German Vocabulary Handbook. (GER., Illus.). 256p. 1998. pap. 10.95 (*2-8315-6392-5*) Berlitz.
— German/English Dictionary. (ENG & GER.). 368p. 1998. pap. 7.95 (*2-8315-6380-1*) Berlitz.
— Greek Cassette Pack. rev. ed. 1999. pap. 18.95 incl. audio (*2-8315-6532-4*) Berlitz.
— Greek CD Pack. (Compact Disc Ser.). (GRE.). 192p. 1994. 18.95 incl. audio compact disk (*2-8315-1497-5*) Berlitz.

***Berlitz Editors.** Greek Islands Pocket Guide. (Illus.). 192p. 2000. pap. 8.95 (*2-8315-7169-3*) Berlitz.

Berlitz Editors. Hawaii Pocket Guide, 1998. rev. ed. (Pocket Guides Ser.). (Illus.). 144p. 1998. pap. 8.95 (*2-8315-6304-6*) Berlitz.
— Hong Kong Pocket Guide. rev. ed. LC 99-222940. (Illus.). 192p. 1998. pap. 8.95 (*2-8315-6324-0*) Berlitz.

***Berlitz Editors.** Hungarian Cassette Pack. (Cassettepaks Ser.). (HUN., Illus.). 192p. 2000. 18.95 (*2-8315-7743-8*) Berlitz.
— Hungarian Phrase Book. (Phrase Bks.). (Illus.). 192p. 2000. pap. 8.95 (*2-8315-7735-7*) Berlitz.
— Ibiza & Formentera Pocket Guide. rev. ed. (Illus.). 144p. 2000. 8.95 (*2-8315-6967-2*) Berlitz.

Berlitz Editors. Indonesia Pocket Guide. (Pocket Guides Ser.). (Illus.). 192p. 1993. pap. 10.95 (*2-8315-2223-4*) Berlitz.
— Intermediate French Workbook, 1998, Level II. (Workbook Ser.). (FRE., Illus.). 208p. 1998. pap. text, wbk. ed. 12.95 (*2-8315-6010-1*) Berlitz.
— Intermediate Spanish Workbook 1998, Level II. (Workbook Ser.). (SPA., Illus.). 208p. 1998. pap. text, wbk. ed. 12.95 (*2-8315-6008-X*) Berlitz.
— Ireland Pocket Guide. rev. ed. LC 99-222942. (Illus.). 192p. 1998. pap. 8.95 (*2-8315-6325-9*) Berlitz.
— Istanbul & the Aegean Coast Pocket Guide. rev. ed. (Pocket Guides Ser.). (Illus.). 144p. 1999. pap. 8.95 (*2-8315-6972-9*) Berlitz.
— Italian-English Dictionary. (ITA & ENG.). 368p. 1998. pap. 7.95 (*2-8315-6381-X*) Berlitz.
— Italian Grammar Handbook. (ITA., Illus.). 256p. 1998. pap. 10.95 (*2-8315-6393-3*) Berlitz.
— Italian Phrase Book. rev. ed. (Berlitz Phrase Book & Dictionary Ser.). (ITA., Illus.). 192p. 1998. pap. text 7.95 (*2-8315-6241-4*) Berlitz.

***Berlitz Editors.** Italian Think & Talk. (Think & Talk Ser.). (Illus.). 1998. 149.95 incl. audio, cd-rom (*2-8315-6183-3*) Berlitz.
— Italian Today. (Today Ser.). (ITA., Illus.). 1998. student ed., boxed set 59.95 incl. audio (*2-8315-6197-3*) Berlitz.

Berlitz Editors. Italian Verb Handbook. rev. ed. (ITA., Illus.). 256p. 1998. pap. 10.95 (*2-8315-6394-1*) Berlitz.
— Italian Vocabulary Handbook. rev. ed. (ITA., Illus.). 256p. 1998. pap. 10.95 (*2-8315-6395-X*) Berlitz.
— Italy Pocket Guide. rev. ed. (Illus.). 192p. 1998. pap. 10.95 (*2-8315-6308-9*) Berlitz.
— Japanese Cassette Pack. rev. ed. (Cassettepack Ser.). 1998. pap. 18.95 incl. audio (*2-8315-6272-4*) Berlitz.
— Japanese Phrase Book. (JPN., Illus.). 224p. 1998. pap. 7.95 (*2-8315-6267-8*) Berlitz.
— Kenya Pocket Guide. LC 96-227426. (Berlitz Travellers Guide Ser.). (Illus.). 144p. 1994. pap. 8.95 (*2-8315-2652-3*) Berlitz.
— Korean Cassette Pack. rev. ed. (Cassettepack Ser.). 1998. pap. 18.95 incl. audio (*2-8315-6273-2*) Berlitz.
— Korean Phrase Book. (KOR., Illus.). 192p. 1998. pap. 7.95 (*2-8315-6268-6*) Berlitz.
— Latin American Spanish Phrase Book. 2nd rev. ed. (Berlitz Phrase Book & Dictionary Ser.). (SPA., Illus.). 224p. 1998. pap. 7.95 (*2-8315-6242-2*) Berlitz.
— Lisbon Pocket Guide 1998. rev. ed. (Pocket Guides Ser.). (Illus.). 144p. 1998. pap. 8.95 (*2-8315-6559-6*) Berlitz.

***Berlitz Editors.** London Pocket Guide. (Illus.). 144p. 2000. pap. 8.95 (*2-8315-7698-9*) Berlitz.

Berlitz Editors. Madeira Pocket Guide, 1998. rev. ed. (Pocket Guides Ser.). (Illus.). 1998. pap. 8.95 (*2-8315-6472-7*) Berlitz.

***Berlitz Editors.** Madrid Pocket Guide. rev. ed. (Illus.). 144p. 2000. pap. 8.95 (*2-8315-7700-4*) Berlitz.
— Mallorca & Menorca Pocket Guide. (Illus.). 192p. 2000. pap. 8.95 (*2-8315-7168-5*) Berlitz.

Berlitz Editors. Malta Pocket Guide, 1998. rev. ed. (Pocket Guides Ser.). (Illus.). 136p. 1998. pap. 8.95 (*2-8315-6313-5*) Berlitz.
— Miami Pocket Guide, 1998. rev. ed. (Pocket Guides Ser.). (Illus.). 144p. 1998. pap. 8.95 (*2-8315-6975-3*) Berlitz.
— Munich Pocket Guide. rev. ed. (Pocket Guides Ser.). (Illus.). 144p. 1999. pap. 8.95 (*2-8315-6988-5*) Berlitz.
— Naples & Amalfi Coast Pocket Guide, 1998. rev. ed. (Pocket Guides Ser.). (Illus.). 128p. 1998. pap. 8.95 (*2-8315-6418-2*) Berlitz.

***Berlitz Editors.** New Orleans Pocket Guide. (Pocket Guides Ser.). (Illus.). 144p. 2000. pap. 8.95 (*2-8315-7702-0*) Berlitz.
— New York Pocket Guide. (Pocket Guides Ser.). (Illus.). 144p. 2000. pap. 8.95 (*2-8315-7170-7*) Berlitz.
— Norwegian Cassette Packs. (NOR.). 192p. 2000. 18.95 (*2-8315-7744-6*) Berlitz.
— Norwegian Phrase Book. (Illus.). 192p. 2000. pap. 7.95 (*2-8315-7736-5*) Berlitz.

Berlitz Editors. Norwegian/English Dictionary. (NOR & ENG.). 368p. 1998. pap. 7.95 (*2-8315-6382-8*) Berlitz.
— Nueva York Guia Turistica. (Pocket Guides Ser.). (SPA., Illus.). 144p. 1998. pap. 8.95 (*2-8315-6562-6*) Berlitz.
— 1,000 Palabras en Ingles. (ENG & SPA., Illus.). 64p. 1998. pap. 12.95 (*2-8315-6553-7*) Berlitz.
— Paris Guia Turistica, 1998. rev. ed. (Pocket Guides Ser.). (SPA., Illus.). 144p. 1998. pap. 8.95 (*2-8315-6563-4*) Berlitz.

***Berlitz Editors.** Paris Pocket Guide. (Pocket Guides Ser.). (Illus.). 144p. 2000. pap. 8.95 (*2-8315-7703-9*) Berlitz.

Berlitz Editors. Portugal Pocket Guide, 1998. rev. ed. (Pocket Guides Ser.). (Illus.). 144p. 1998. pap. 10.95 (*2-8315-6316-X*) Berlitz.
— Portuguese Cassette Pack. (CD Pack Ser.). (POR., Illus.). 1999. pap. 19.95 incl. audio, cd-rom (*2-8315-6346-1*) Berlitz.
— Portuguese Cassette Pack. rev. ed. (Cassettepack Ser.). 1998. pap. 17.95 incl. audio (*2-8315-6334-8*) Berlitz.

***Berlitz Editors.** Portuguese Phrase Book. rev. ed. (Berlitz Phrase Book & Dictionary Ser.). (POR., Illus.). 192p. 1998. pap. text 7.95 (*2-8315-6243-0*) Berlitz.

Berlitz Editors. Portuguese/English Dictionary. 368p. 1998. pap. 7.95 (*2-8315-6383-6*) Berlitz.
— Prague Pocket Guide. rev. ed. (Illus.). 144p. 1998. pap. 8.95 (*2-8315-6317-8*) Berlitz.
— Rhodes Pocket Guide, 1998. rev. ed. (Pocket Guides Ser.). (Illus.). 1998. pap. 8.95 (*2-8315-6520-0*) Berlitz.

***Berlitz Editors.** Romanian Cassette Pack. (Cassette Pack Ser.). (RUM., Illus.). 192p. 2000. 18.95 (*2-8315-7745-4*) Berlitz.
— Rome Pocket Guide. (Illus.). 144p. 2000. pap. 8.95 (*2-8315-7705-5*) Berlitz.

Berlitz Editors. Russian: Think & Talk. (Think & Talk Language Courses Ser.). (RUS., Illus.). 1994. pap., wbk. ed. 149.95 incl. audio (*2-8315-1675-7*) Berlitz.
— Russian Cassette Pack. rev. ed. 1999. pap. 18.95 incl. audio (*2-8315-6533-2*) Berlitz.
— Russian Phrase Book. (RUS., Illus.). 192p. 1998. pap. 7.95 (*2-8315-6238-4*) Berlitz.

***Berlitz Editors.** San Francisco Pocket Guide. LC 99-226249. (Pocket Guides Ser.). (Illus.). 144p. 2000. pap. 8.95 (*2-8315-7706-3*) Berlitz.

Berlitz Editors. Singapore Pocket Guide. rev. ed. (Pocket Guides Ser.). (Illus.). 136p. 1998. pap. 8.95 (*2-8315-6320-8*) Berlitz.
— South Africa Pocket Guide. rev. ed. (Pocket Guides Ser.). (Illus.). 144p. 1998. pap. 8.95 (*2-8315-6321-6*) Berlitz.
— Southern Caribbean Pocket Guide. rev. ed. (Illus.). 192p. 1998. pap. 8.95 (*2-8315-6322-4*) Berlitz.
— Spanish Grammar Handbook. rev. ed. (SPA., Illus.). 262p. 1998. pap. 10.95 (*2-8315-6396-8*) Berlitz.
— Spanish Phrase Book. rev. ed. (Berlitz Phrase Book & Dictionary Ser.). (SPA., Illus.). 224p. 1998. pap. 7.95 (*2-8315-6244-9*) Berlitz.

***Berlitz Editors.** Spanish Think & Talk. (Think & Talk Ser.). (Illus.). 1998. 225.00 incl. audio, cd-rom (*2-8315-6184-1*) Berlitz.
— Spanish Today. (Today Ser.). (SPA., Illus.). 1998. pap., student ed., boxed set 59.95 incl. audio (*2-8315-6198-1*) Berlitz.

Berlitz Editors. Spanish Verb Handbook. (SPA., Illus.). 231p. 1998. pap. 10.95 (*2-8315-6397-6*) Berlitz.
— Spanish Vocabulary Handbook. rev. ed. (SPA., Illus.). 256p. 1998. pap. 10.95 (*2-8315-6398-4*) Berlitz.
— Spanish/English Dictionary. (SPA & ENG.). 368p. 1998. pap. 7.95 (*2-8315-6384-4*) Berlitz.
— Swedish-English Dictionary. (SWE & ENG.). 368p. 1998. pap. 7.95 (*2-8315-6385-2*) Berlitz.

***Berlitz Editors.** Thai Phrase Book. (Phrase Bk.). (Illus.). 192p. 2000. pap. 8.95 (*2-8315-7739-X*) Berlitz.

Berlitz Editors. Thailand Pocket Guide, 1998. rev. ed. (Pocket Guides Ser.). (Illus.). 144p. 1998. pap. 8.95 (*2-8315-6358-5*) Berlitz.

***Berlitz Editors.** Toronto Pocket Guide. rev. ed. (Pocket Guides Ser.). (Illus.). 144p. 1998. pap. 8.95 (*2-8315-7707-1*) Berlitz.

Berlitz Editors. Turkish/English Dictionary. (TUR & ENG.). 368p. 1998. pap. 7.95 (*2-8315-6386-0*) Berlitz.
— U. S. A. Pocket Guide. rev. ed. (Pocket Guides Ser.). (Illus.). 256p. 1998. pap. 10.95 (*2-8315-6362-3*) Berlitz.

***Berlitz Editors.** Venice Pocket Guide. (Illus.). 144p. 2000. pap. 8.95 (*2-8315-7708-X*) Berlitz.
— Vienna Pocket Guide. (Pocket Guides Ser.). (Illus.). 144p. 2000. pap. 8.95 (*2-8315-7709-8*) Berlitz.
— Walt Disney World & Orlando Pocket Guide. (Illus.). 144p. 2000. pap. 8.95 (*2-8315-7171-5*) Berlitz.

Berlitz Editors. Walt Disney World Pocket Guide: Spanish ed. (Pocket Guides Ser.). (SPA., Illus.). 144p. 1998. pap. 8.95 (*2-8315-7005-0*) Berlitz.

Berlitz Editors, ed. Basic English for Spanish Workbook. (ENG & SPA.). 128p. 1998. pap., wbk. ed. 12.95 (*2-8315-6352-6*) Berlitz.
— Basic French Workbook. (FRE.). 128p. 1998. pap., wbk. ed. 12.95 (*2-8315-6348-8*) Berlitz.
— Basic German Workbook. (GER.). 128p. 1998. pap., wbk. ed. 12.95 (*2-8315-6349-6*) Berlitz.
— Basic Italian Workbook. (ITA.). 128p. 1998. pap., wbk. ed. 12.95 (*2-8315-6350-X*) Berlitz.
— Basic Japanese Workbook. (Berlitz Basic Ser.). (JPN.). 128p. 1998. pap. text, wbk. ed. 12.95 (*2-8315-6588-X*) Berlitz.
— Basic Spanish Workbook. (SPA.). 128p. 1998. pap., wbk. ed. 12.95 (*2-8315-6351-8*) Berlitz.

Berlitz Editors, jt. auth. see Berlitz Editors Staff.

Berlitz Editors Staff. Berlitz Japanese CD Pack. rev. ed. (CD Pack Ser.). (JPN., Illus.). 1999. pap. 19.95 incl. audio (*2-8315-6282-1*) Berlitz.

Berlitz Editors Staff & Berlitz Editors. Berlitz Basic Italian. (Basic Ser.). (ENG & ITA., Illus.). 192p. 1994. student ed. 29.95 incl. audio (*2-8315-1239-5*) Berlitz.
— Dutch Cassette Pack. unabridged ed. (Cassettepaks Ser.). (DUT.). 192p. 1993. 18.95 incl. audio (*2-8315-6950-8*) Berlitz.

Berlitz Editors Staff & Berlitz Staff. Japanese Think & Talk. (Think & Talk Ser.). (JPN.). 1992. wbk. ed. 149.95 incl. audio (*2-8315-1654-4*) Berlitz.

Berlitz Kids Editors. The Five Crayons English for Spanish. LC 99-182771. (Berlitz Kids Ser.). (Illus.). 64p. (J). (gr. k-4). 1998. pap. 16.95 incl. audio (*2-8315-6546-4*, Berlitz Kids) Berlitz.
— The Five Crayons German. (Berlitz Kids Ser.). (GER & ENG., Illus.). 64p. (J). (gr. k-4). 1998. pap. 16.95 incl. audio (*2-8315-6537-5*, Berlitz Kids) Berlitz.
— The Five Crayons Italian. (Berlitz Kids Ser.). (ITA & ENG., Illus.). 64p. (J). (gr. k-4). 1998. pap. 16.95 incl. audio (*2-8315-6540-5*, Berlitz Kids) Berlitz.
— The Five Crayons Spanish. LC 98-24048. (Berlitz Kids Ser.). (SPA & ENG., Illus.). 64p. (J). (gr. k-4). 1998. pap. 16.95 incl. audio (*2-8315-6543-X*, Berlitz Kids) Berlitz.
— French Language Pack, 1998. (Language Pack Ser.). (Illus.). (J). (ps-4). 1998. pap. 24.95 (*2-8315-6225-2*, Berlitz Kids) Berlitz.
— German Language Pack, 1998. (Language Pack Ser.). (Illus.). (J). (ps-4). 1998. pap. 24.95 (*2-8315-6227-9*, Berlitz Kids) Berlitz.
— Italian Language Pack. (Language Pack Ser.). (Illus.). (J). (ps-4). 1998. pap. 24.95 (*2-8315-6226-0*, Berlitz Kids) Berlitz.
— The Missing Cat: English-Spanish. (Berlitz Kids Ser.). (ENG & SPA., Illus.). 64p. (J). (gr. k-4). pap. text 16.95 incl. audio (*2-8315-5710-0*) Berlitz.
— The Missing Cat: French-English. (Berlitz Kids Ser.). (ENG & FRE., Illus.). 64p. (J). (gr. k-4). 1996. pap. text 16.95 incl. audio (*2-8315-5711-9*) Berlitz.
— The Missing Cat: German-English. (Berlitz Kids Ser.). (ENG & GER., Illus.). 64p. (J). (gr. k-4). 1996. pap. text 16.95 incl. audio (*2-8315-5712-7*) Berlitz.

B

— The Missing Cat: Italian-English. (Berlitz Kids Ser.). (ENG & ITA., Illus.). 64p. (J). (gr. k-4). 1996. pap. text 16.95 incl. audio (*2-8315-5713-5*) Berlitz.

— The Missing Cat: Spanish-English. (Berlitz Kids Ser.). (ENG & SPA., Illus.). 64p. (J). (gr. k-4). 1996. pap. text 16.95 incl. audio (*2-8315-5714-3*) Berlitz.

— 1,000 French Words. LC 98-196846. (ENG & FRE., Illus.). 64p. 1998. pap. 12.95 (*2-8315-6549-9*, Berlitz Kids) Berlitz.

— 1,000 German Words. LC 98-196843. (ENG & GER., Illus.). 64p. 1998. pap. 12.95 (*2-8315-6550-2*, Berlitz Kids) Berlitz.

— 1,000 Italian Words. (ENG & ITA., Illus.). 64p. 1998. pap. 12.95 (*2-8315-6551-0*, Berlitz Kids) Berlitz.

— 1,000 Spanish Words. LC 98-18960. (SPA & ENG., Illus.). 64p. 1998. pap. 12.95 (*2-8315-6552-9*, Berlitz Kids) Berlitz.

— Picture Dictionary English/Spanish. (Berlitz Kids Ser.). (SPA., Illus.). 128p. 1998. pap. text 16.95 (*2-8315-6253-8*) Berlitz.

— Picture Dictionary French/English. LC 98-221215. (Berlitz Kids Ser.). (FRE., Illus.). 128p. 1998. pap text 16.95 (*2-8315-6254-6*) Berlitz.

— Picture Dictionary German/English. LC 98-221213. (Berlitz Kids Ser.). (GER., Illus.). 128p. 1998. pap. text 16.95 (*2-8315-6255-4*) Berlitz.

— Picture Dictionary Italian/English. (Berlitz Kids Ser.). (ITA., Illus.). 128p. 1998. pap. text 16.95 (*2-8315-6256-2*) Berlitz.

— Picture Dictionary Spanish/English. LC 97-36273. (Berlitz Kids Ser.). (SPA., Illus.). 128p. 1998. pap text 16.95 (*2-8315-6257-0*) Berlitz.

— Spanish Language Pack, 1998. (Language Pack Ser.). (Illus.). (J). (ps-4). 1998. pap. 24.95 (*2-8315-6224-4*, Berlitz Kids) Berlitz.

— A Visit to Grandma: English-Spanish. LC 99-182783. (Adventures with Nicholas Ser.). (SPA., Illus.). 64p. (J). (gr. 4-9). 1997. pap. text 16.95 incl. audio (*2-8315-6248-1*) Berlitz.

— A Visit to Grandma: French-English. (Adventures with Nicholas Ser.). (FRE & ENG., Illus.). 64p. (J). (gr. 4-9). pap. text 16.95 incl. audio (*2-8315-6249-X*) Berlitz.

— A Visit to Grandma: German-English. (Adventures with Nicholas Ser.). (GER & ENG., Illus.). 64p. (J). (gr. 4-9). pap. text 16.95 incl. audio (*2-8315-6250-3*) Berlitz.

— A Visit to Grandma: Italian-English. (Adventures with Nicholas Ser.). (ITA & ENG., Illus.). 64p. (J). (gr. 4-9). pap. text 16.95 incl. audio (*2-8315-6251-1*) Berlitz.

— A Visit to Grandma: Spanish-English. (Adventures with Nicholas Ser.). (SPA & ENG., Illus.). 64p. (J). (gr. 4-9). pap. text 16.95 incl. audio (*2-8315-6252-X*) Berlitz.

***Berlitz Publishing Staff.** Bahamas Pocket Guide. (Berlitz Pocket Guide Ser.). (SPA.). 144p. 1999. pap. 8.95 (*2-8315-7267-3*) Berlitz.

— Beijing Pocket Guide. rev. ed. (Berlitz Pocket Guide Ser.). (Illus.). 144p. 2000. pap. 8.95 (*2-8315-7126-X*, Pub. by Berlitz) Globe Pequot.

— Berlitz Business English. 2000. pap. 34.95 (*2-8315-7314-9*) Berlitz.

— Berlitz French/English Reference Dictionary. (Bilingual Reference Dictionaries). (FRE & ENG.). 692p. 2000. pap. 14.95 (*2-8315-7122-7*) Berlitz.

— Berlitz German/English Reference Dictionary. (Bilingual Reference Dictionaries). (ENG & GER.). 692p. 2000. pap. 14.95 (*2-8315-7123-5*) Berlitz.

— Berlitz Spanish/English Reference Dictionary. (Bilingual Reference Dictionaries). 692p. 2000. pap. 14.95 (*2-8315-7125-1*) Berlitz.

— Bermuda Pocket Guide. (Berlitz Pocket Guide Ser.). 144p. 1999. pap. 8.95 (*2-8315-7213-4*) Berlitz.

— Bermuda Pocket Guide. rev. ed. (Berlitz Pocket Guide Ser.). (SPA.). 144p. 1999. pap. 8.95 (*2-8315-7268-1*) Berlitz.

— Bruges Ghent Pocket Guide. (Berlitz Pocket Guide Ser.). 144p. 1999. pap. 8.95 (*2-8315-7214-2*) Berlitz.

— Buenos Aires Pocket Guide. (Berlitz Pocket Guide Ser.). 144p. 1999. pap. 8.95 (*2-8315-7127-8*, Pub. by Berlitz); pap. 8.95 (*2-8315-7269-X*) Berlitz.

— Cape Town. (Pocket Guides Ser.). 2000. pap. 8.95 (*2-8315-6983-4*) Berlitz.

— Chicago. (Pocket Guide Ser.). (Illus.). 144p. 1999. pap. 8.95 (*2-8315-7132-4*) Berlitz.

— Chicago Pocket Guide: Spanish ed. (Berlitz Pocket Guide Ser.). 1999. pap. 8.95 (*2-8315-7270-3*) Berlitz.

— China. (Berlitz Pocket Guide Ser.). 256p. 1999. pap. 10.95 (*2-8315-7049-2*) Berlitz.

— Costa Dorada & Tarragona. (Berlitz Pocket Guide Ser.). 144p. 1999. pap. 8.95 (*2-8315-6964-8*) Berlitz.

— Dublin. (Pocket Guides Ser.). (Illus.). 144p. 2000. pap. 8.95 (*2-8315-7694-6*) Berlitz.

— Edinburgh Pocket Guide. (Pocket Guides Ser.). (Illus.). 144p. 2000. pap. 8.95 (*2-8315-7695-4*) Berlitz.

— French West Indies Pocket Guide. rev. ed. (Berlitz Pocket Guide Ser.). 144p. 1999. pap. 8.95 (*2-8315-7216-9*, Pub. by Berlitz) Globe Pequot.

— Jamaica Pocket Guide. (Berlitz Pocket Guide Ser.). (SPA.). 144p. 1999. pap. 8.95 (*2-8315-7272-X*) Berlitz.

Berlitz Publishing Staff. Jamaica Pocket Guide. (Berlitz Pocket Guide Ser.). (Illus.). 144p. 1999. pap. 8.95 (*2-8315-7218-5*) Berlitz.

***Berlitz Publishing Staff.** Japan Pocket Guide. (Berlitz Pocket Guide Ser.). 256p. 1999. pap. 10.95 (*2-8315-7219-3*) Berlitz.

— Jerusalem. (Pocket Guide Ser.). (Illus.). 1999. pap. 8.95 (*2-8315-7172-3*) Berlitz.

— Lake District. (Pocket Guides Ser.). 1999 pap. text 8.95 (*2-8315-7173-1*) Berlitz.

— Las Vegas: Pocket Guide. (Pocket Guides Ser.). (Illus.). 1999. pap. 8.95 (*2-8315-7142-1*) Berlitz.

— Las Vegas Pocket Guide: Spanish ed. (Berlitz Pocket Guide Ser.). 1999. pap. 8.95 (*2-8315-7273-8*) Berlitz.

— Latin-American Spanish Reference Dictionary. (Bilingual Reference Dictionaries). (SPA & ENG.). 692p. 2000. pap. text 14.95 (*2-8315-7330-0*, Pub. by Berlitz) Globe Pequot.

— Mexico Pocket Guide. (Berlitz Pocket Guide Ser.). 256p. 1999. pap. 10.95 (*2-8315-7221-5*) Berlitz.

— Mexico Pocket Guide. rev. ed. (Berlitz Pocket Guide Ser.). (SPA.). 256p. 1999. pap. 8.95 (*2-8315-7275-4*) Berlitz.

— Miami. (Pocket Guide Ser.). (SPA., Illus.). 1999. pap. 8.95 (*2-8315-7035-2*) Berlitz.

— Morocco Pocket Guide. (Berlitz Pocket Guide Ser.). 144p. 1999. pap. 8.95 (*2-8315-7222-3*) Berlitz.

— Nepal Pocket Guide. rev. ed. (Berlitz Pocket Guide Ser.). 144p. 1999. pap. 8.95 (*2-8315-7223-1*, Pub. by Berlitz) Globe Pequot.

— New Zealand Pocket Guide. (Berlitz Pocket Guide Ser.). (Illus.). 144p. 1999. pap. 8.95 (*2-8315-7224-X*) Berlitz.

— Puerto Rico Pocket Guide. (Berlitz Pocket Guide Ser.). (SPA.). 144p. 1999. pap. 8.95 (*2-8315-7277-0*) Berlitz.

— Puerto Rico Pocket Guide. (Berlitz Pocket Guide Ser.). 144p. 1999. pap. 8.95 (*2-8315-7225-8*) Berlitz.

— Rio de Janeiro Pocket Guide. (Berlitz Pocket Guide Ser.). 144p. 1999. pap. 8.95 (*2-8315-7155-3*) Berlitz.

— Rio de Janeiro Pocket Guide: Spanish ed. (Berlitz Pocket Guide Ser.). (SPA.). 144p. 1999. pap. 8.95 (*2-8315-7278-9*) Berlitz.

— Switzerland: Pocket Guide. (Illus.). 1999. pap. text 10.95 (*2-8315-7159-6*) Berlitz.

— Tokyo Pocket Guide. rev. ed. (Berlitz Pocket Guide Ser.). 144p. 1999. pap. 8.95 (*2-8315-7226-6*) Berlitz.

Berlitz Publishing Staff. Turkey Pocket Guide. (Pocket Guide Ser.). 1998. pap. 10.95 (*2-8315-6361-5*) Berlitz.

***Berlitz Publishing Staff.** Vancouver. (Pocket Guides Ser.). (Illus.). 1999. pap. text 8.95 (*2-8315-7163-4*) Berlitz.

— Virgin Islands Pocket Guide. (Berlitz Pocket Guide Ser.). (SPA.). 144p. 1999. pap. 8.95 (*2-8315-7279-7*) Berlitz.

— Virgin Islands Pocket Guide. rev. ed. (Berlitz Pocket Guide Ser.). 144p. 1999. pap. 8.95 (*2-8315-7227-4*) Berlitz.

***Berlitz Publishing Staff, ed.** Algarve. (Pocket Guides Ser.). (Illus.). 2001. pap. 8.95 (*2-8315-7684-9*) Berlitz.

— Brazilian-Portuguese English Dictionary. (POR & ENG.). 2000. pap. 7.95 (*2-8315-6263-5*) Berlitz.

— Brussels. (Pocket Guides Ser.). (Illus.). 2001. pap. 8.95 (*2-8315-7688-1*) Berlitz.

— Corfu. (Pocket Guides Ser.). (Illus.). 136p. 2000. pap. 8.95 (*2-8315-7166-9*) Berlitz.

— Corsica. (Pocket Guides Ser.). (Illus.). 2001. pap. 8.95 (*2-8315-6985-0*) Berlitz.

Berlitz Publishing Staff, ed. Czech Phrase Book. (Phrase Book & Dictionary Ser.). (CZE., Illus.). 192p. 1999. pap. 8.95 (*2-8315-6925-7*) Berlitz.

***Berlitz Publishing Staff, ed.** Dictionary of American English. 592p. 1999. pap. 24.95 (*2-8315-7328-9*, Pub. by Berlitz) Globe Pequot.

— European Phrase Book. (Phrase Bks.). 2000. pap. 8.95 (*2-8315-7740-3*) Berlitz.

— French. (Revised Basic Ser.). (FRE & ENG.). 2000. pap. 49.95 (*2-8315-7724-1*) Berlitz.

— Indonesian Phrase Book. (Phrase Bks.). (Illus.). 2000. pap. 8.95 (*2-8315-7092-1*) Berlitz.

— Lisbon. (Pocket Guides Ser.). (Illus.). 2001. pap. 8.95 (*2-8315-7697-0*) Berlitz.

— Madeira. (Pocket Guides Ser.). (Illus.). 2001. pap. 8.95 (*2-8315-7699-7*) Berlitz.

— Malta. (Pocket Guides Ser.). (Illus.). 2001. pap. 8.95 (*2-8315-7701-2*) Berlitz.

— Puerto Vallarta & Acapulco. (Pocket Guides Ser.). (Illus.). 2000. pap. 8.95 (*2-8315-6984-2*) Berlitz.

— Romanian Phrase Book. (Phrase Bks.). 2000. pap. 8.95 (*2-8315-7737-3*) Berlitz.

— Spanish. (Revised Basic Ser.). (SPA & ENG.). 2000. pap. 49.95 (*2-8315-7723-3*) Berlitz.

— Washington, D. C. (SPA.). 144p. 1999. pap. 8.95 (*2-8315-7280-0*) Berlitz.

Berlitz Staff. Berlitz European. (CD Pack Ser.). 192p. 1992. pap. 23.95 incl. audio compact disk (*2-8315-1543-2*) Berlitz.

Berlitz Staff. Berlitz Greek for Your Trip. 1987. 15.00 (*0-8161-8965-X*, Hall Reference) Macmillan.

— Berlitz Scandinavian Phrase Book. (Illus.). 192p. 1995. pap. 8.95 (*2-8315-5123-4*) Begos & Rosenberg.

— Berlitz Spanish for Your Trip. 1987. text 15.00 (*0-8161-8961-7*, Hall Reference) Macmillan.

— Costa Rica Pocket Guide: Spanish ed. 1999. pap. text 8.95 (*2-8315-7271-1*) Berlitz.

***Berlitz Staff.** Danish: Phrase Book & Dictionary. (Phrase Bks.). (Illus.). 192p. 2000. pap. 7.95 (*2-8315-7732-2*) Berlitz.

— East European: Phrase Book & Dictionary. LC 73-20997. (Phrase Bk.). (Illus.). 192p. 2000. pap. 8.95 (*2-8315-7733-0*) Berlitz.

— Finnish Phrase Book. LC 75-11284. 192p. 2000. 8.95 (*2-8315-7734-9*) Berlitz.

— German for Dummies. 432p. 2000. pap. 24.99 incl. cd-rom (*0-7645-5195-7*) IDG Bks.

— Italian for Dummies. 432p. 2000. pap. 24.99 incl. cd-rom (*0-7645-5196-5*) IDG Bks.

Berlitz Staff. Los Angeles Pocket Guide: Spanish ed. 1999. pap. text 8.95 (*2-8315-7274-6*) Berlitz.

— Montreal Pocket Guide. rev. ed. (Berlitz Pocket Guide Ser.). 1998. pap. 8.95 (*2-8315-6981-8*) Berlitz.

***Berlitz Staff.** Scandinavian: Phrase Book & Dictionary. 192p. 2000. pap. 8.95 (*2-8315-7738-1*) Berlitz.

— Swahili. (Cassette Pack Ser.). (SWA., Illus.). 192p. 1995. 16.95 incl. audio (*2-8315-1391-X*) Berlitz.

— Swahili: Phrase Book & Dictionary. 192p. 2000. pap. 8.95 (*2-8315-6205-8*) Berlitz.

— Thai Cassette Pack. (Cassette Pack Ser.). (THA., Illus.). 192p. 2000. 18.95 (*2-8315-7747-0*) Berlitz.

Berlitz Staff, contrib. by. Scandinavian Cassette Pack. 192p. 1993. pap. 21.95 incl. audio (*2-8315-5135-8*) Berlitz.

Berlitz Staff & Vedral, Joyce L. The Berlitz Self-Teacher: French. 300p. 1987. pap. 12.95 (*0-399-51323-X*, Perigee Bks) Berkley Pub.

— The Berlitz Self-Teacher: German. 300p. 1987. pap. 12.95 (*0-399-51322-1*, Perigee Bks) Berkley Pub.

— The Berlitz Self-Teacher: Italian. 324p. 1987. pap. 12.95 (*0-399-51325-6*, Perigee Bks) Berkley Pub.

— The Berlitz Self-Teacher: Spanish. 300p. 1987. pap. 12.95 (*0-399-51324-8*, Perigee Bks) Berkley Pub.

Berlitz Staff, jt. auth. see Berlitz Editors Staff.

Berlitz Staff, tr. see DiFiore, Dante.

Berlo, Janet Catherine. Native North American Art. LC 99-177938. (Illus.). 302p. 1998. 39.95 (*0-19-284266-8*) OUP.

***Berlo, Janet Catherine.** Quilting Lessons: Notes from the Scrap Bag of a Writer & Quilter. (Illus.). 2001. 20.00 (*0-8032-1318-2*) U of Nebr Pr.

— Spirit Beings & Sun Dancers: Black Hawk's Vision of the Lakota World. (Illus.). 2000. 60.00 (*0-8076-1465-3*) Braziller.

Berlo, Janet Catherine, ed. Art, Ideology, & the City of Teotihuacan: A Symposium at Dumbarton Oaks, 8th & 9th October 1988. LC 92-8244. (Illus.). 452p. 1992. 38.00 (*0-88402-205-6*, Dumbarton Rsch Lib) Dumbarton Oaks.

— The Early Years of Native American Art History: The Politics of Scholarship & Collecting. LC 92-8955. (McLellan Bks.). (Illus.). 256p. 1992. 30.00 (*0-295-97202-5*) U of Wash Pr.

— Plains Indian Drawings, 1865-1935: Pages from a Visual History. LC 96-5517. (Illus.). 240p. 1996. 60.00 (*0-8109-3742-5*, Pub. by Abrams) Time Warner.

— Plains Indian Drawings, 1865-1935: Pages from a Visual History. LC 96-5517. (Illus.). 1996. pap. write for info. (*1-885444-02-8*) Am Fed Arts.

Berlo, Janet Catherine & Phillips, Ruth. Native North American Art. LC 99-177938. (Oxford History of Art Ser.). (Illus.). 302p. 1998. pap. 16.95 (*0-19-284218-8*) OUP.

Berlo, Janet Catherine & Wilson, Lee Anne. Arts of Africa, Oceania, & the Americas: Selected Readings. LC 91-45137. 392p. (C). 1992. pap. text 49.00 (*0-13-756230-6*) P-H.

Berlo, Janet Catherine, jt. ed. see Diehl, Richard A.

Berlocher, Stewart H., jt. ed. see Howard, Daniel J.

***Berlot, G. & Delooz, H.** Trauma Operative Procedures. LC 99-32479. (Topics in Anaesthesia & Critical Care Ser.). 1999. write for info. (*88-470-0045-9*, Pub. by Spr-Verlag) Spr-Verlag.

Berlow, Alan. Dead Seasons. 1998. pap. 14.00 (*0-679-74789-3*) Vin Bks.

Berlow, Harry, jt. auth. see Sheer, Anita.

Berlow, Lawrence H. Medical Ethics: A Reference Handbook. (Contemporary Ethical Issues Ser.). (Illus.). 256p. 1997. 39.50 (*0-87436-930-4*, FN-1718) ABC-CLIO.

***Berlow, Lawrence H.** Reference Guide to Famous Engineering Landmarks. (Illus.). 275p. 1999. lib. bdg. 75.00 (*1-57958-092-0*) Fitzroy Dearborn.

Berlow, Lawrence H. The Reference Guide to the World's Famous Landmarks: Bridges, Tunnels, Dams, Roads, & Other Structures. LC 97-36051. (Illus.). 272p. 1997. boxed set 65.00 (*0-89774-966-9*) Oryx Pr.

— Sports Ethics: A Reference Handbook. (Contemporary World Issues Ser.). 204p. (YA). (gr. 7 up). 1994. lib. bdg. 39.50 (*0-87436-769-7*) ABC-CLIO.

Berlowe, Burt, jt. auth. see Cress, Joseph N.

Berlowitz, Leslie C., jt. ed. see Beard, Rick.

Berlowitz, Marvin J. & Chapman, Frank E., Jr., eds. The United States Educational System: Marxist Approaches. LC 80-12394. (Studies in Marxism: Vol. 6). 221p. 1980. pap. 7.50 (*0-930656-11-3*) MEP Pubns.

Berlowitz, Marvin J. & Edari, Ronald S., eds. Racism & the Denial of Human Rights: Beyond Ethnicity. LC 83-26796. (Studies in Marxism: Vol. 13). 136p. 1984. 17.95 (*0-930656-33-4*) MEP Pubns.

Berlowitz, Marvin J., ed. see Aptheker, Herbert.

Berlyand, M. E. Prediction & Regulation of Air Pollution: Revised & Updated Version of the Russian Edition. (Atmospheric Sciences Library). 320p. 1991. lib. bdg. 141.50 (*0-7923-1000-4*) Kluwer Academic.

Berlye, Milton. Your Career in the World of Work. LC 75-12236. 1975. pap. write for info. (*0-672-97534-3*) Macmillan.

Berlyn, G. P. Botanical Microtechnique & Cytochemistry. 326p. 1997. pap. 500.00 (*81-7089-243-0*, Pub. by Intl Bk Distr) St Mut.

Berlyn, Graeme P. & Miksche, Jerome P. Botanical Microtechnique & Cytochemistry. LC 75-34090. (Illus.). 326p. (C). 1976. text 41.95 (*0-8138-0220-2*) Iowa St U Pr.

— Botanical Microtechnique & Cytochemistry. LC 75-34090. (Illus.). 334p. 1976. reprint ed. pap. 103.60 (*0-608-00151-1*, 206093200006) Bks Demand.

Berlyn, Patricia, jt. auth. see Bakon, Shimon.

Berlyne, D. E., ed. Studies in the New Experimental Aesthetics. LC 74-13600. 348p. reprint ed. 107.90 (*0-8357-9148-3*, 205070400082) Bks Demand.

Berlyne, G. H., ed. Reprinted Selected Top Articles Published, 1976-1977. (Karger Highlights, Nephrology One Ser.). (Illus.). 1978. pap. 13.25 (*3-8055-2938-4*) S Karger.

Berlyne, Geoffrey M., ed. The Kidney Today: Selected Topics in Renal Science. (Contributions to Nephrology Ser.: Vol. 100). (Illus.). viii, 296p. 1992. 49.75 (*3-8055-5555-5*) S Karger.

Berlyne, Geoffrey M., ed. see Congress on Toxic Nephropathies, 6th, Parma, June.

Berlyne, Geoffrey M., ed. see International Symposium on Parathyroid in Uremia Staff.

Berman. Approach Democracy. 2nd ed. 192p. 1998. pap. text, student ed. 22.00 (*0-13-080393-6*) P-H.

***Berman.** Astronomy for the Underpaid. 2000. pap. text. write for info. (*0-7167-3500-8*) W H Freeman.

Berman. Color Atlas Basic Histology. 2nd rev. ed. LC 97-223478. (Illus.). 356p. (C). 1997. spiral bd. 44.95 (*0-8385-1435-9*, A-1435-5, Apple Lange Med) McGraw.

***Berman.** The Cream of the Cosmos. 2000. pap. text. write for info. (*0-7167-3498-2*) W H Freeman.

Berman. Get Acquainted with Jesus. 1997. pap., teacher ed. 5.95 (*0-687-98075-5*) Abingdon.

***Berman.** How to Build a Universe. 2000. pap. text. write for info. (*0-7167-3497-4*) W H Freeman.

Berman. The Listening System. 1999. 13.00 (*0-07-232871-1*) McGraw.

Berman. Marketing Channels Text & Software. 1997. text 65.00 (*0-471-25507-6*) Wiley.

Berman. Portraits of American Cape Cod. (Illus.). 1998. 15.99 (*0-89009-881-6*) Bk Sales Inc.

— State & Local Politics. 7th ed. 1993. pap. text, teacher ed. 16.56 (*0-697-13970-0*) McGraw.

***Berman.** Urban Astronomy. 2000. pap. text. write for info. (*0-7167-3499-0*) W H Freeman.

Berman. The Video Listening System. 1999. 16.00 (*0-07-232872-X*) McGraw.

— Winning Words. (C). 1994. pap. text 17.00 (*0-15-599701-7*, Pub. by Harcourt Coll Pubs) Harcourt.

Berman & Greiner. The Nature & Functions of Law. 4th ed. 1980. text 31.50 (*0-88277-495-6*) Foundation Pr.

Berman & Slobin, Dan I., eds. The Acquisition of Hebrew: The Crosslinguistic Study of Language Acquisition. (Crosslinguistic Study of Language Acquisition Ser.). 144p. 1986. pap. 17.50 (*0-89859-842-7*) L Erlbaum Assocs.

Berman, jt. auth. see Barnet.

Berman, jt. auth. see Evans.

Berman, A. Islamic Coins of the Collection of the Institute of Islamic Art. (Illus.). 1976. pap. 50.00 (*1-886720-05-3*) S J Durst.

— Vintage Style: Buying & Wearing Classic Vintage Clothes. (Illus.). 288p. 2000. 40.00 (*0-06-019475-8*) HarpC.

Berman, A. Michael. Data Structures via C++ Objects by Evolution. LC 96-42323. (Illus.). 496p. (C). 1997. text 62.95 (*0-19-510843-4*) OUP.

Berman, Aaron. Forestville Tales: International Folk Stories. LC 76-56544. (Illus.). 71p. (J). (gr. k-12). 1993. pap. text 7.50 (*1-882483-28-6*) Alta Bk Ctr.

— Nazism, the Jews & American Zionism, 1933-1988. rev. ed. LC 90-11942. (Illus.). 240p. (C). 1992. pap. 16.95 (*0-8143-2232-8*) Wayne St U Pr.

Berman, Aaron, ed. see Olshtain, Elite, et al.

Berman, Abraham & Plemmons, Robert J. Nonnegative Matrices in the Mathematical Sciences. LC 94-37449. (Classics in Applied Mathematics Ser.: Vol. 9). xx, 340p. 1994. pap. 30.00 (*0-89871-321-8*) Soc Indus-Appl Math.

Berman, Abraham, et al. Nonnegative Matrices in Dynamic Systems. LC 88-33934. 192p. 1989. 160.00 (*0-471-62074-2*) Wiley.

***Berman, Alan.** The Complete Book of Floors. (Illus.). 192p. 2000. pap. 29.95 (*0-7112-1612-6*, Pub. by F Lincoln) Antique Collect.

Berman, Alan. Floor Magic. LC 96-29864. 1997. pap. 29.95 (*0-679-75892-5*) Pantheon.

Berman, Alan J. & Feder, Irwin. Basic Business Communication: Writing Your Way to a Successful Career. LC 78-62046. 240p. 1978. pap. text 7.00 (*0-918618-11-8*) Pella Pub.

Berman, Alan L., ed. Suicide Prevention: Case Consultations. LC 89-26342. (Death & Suicide Ser.: Vol. 10). 176p. 1990. 29.95 (*0-8261-7120-6*) Springer Pub.

Berman, Alan L. & Jobes, David A. Adolescent Suicide: Assessment & Intervention. 277p. 1991. 24.95 (*1-55798-107-8*); pap. text 19.95 (*1-55798-114-0*) Am Psychol.

***Berman, Alex & Flannery, Michael.** American Botanico-Medical Movements: Vox Populi. 2000. 69.95 (*0-7890-0899-8*); pap. 24.95 (*0-7890-1235-9*) Haworth Pr.

Berman, Alex, ed. see Design Engineering Technical Conference (1977: Chi.

Berman, Alice. Skater's Edge Sourcebook: Ice Skating Resource Guide. 2nd rev. ed. LC 97-62435. (Illus.). 456p. (Orig.). 1998. pap. 39.95 (*0-9643027-1-3*) Skaters Edge.

The SKATER'S EDGE SOURCEBOOK is a comprehensive resource book & rink directory for the sport of ice skating. The second edition (1998) is 70

bigger than the first, & includes: (1) COMPANIES - 620 companies listed by name, then cross-referenced by services provided ⊞; (2) RINKS - profiles of more than 1100 skating rinks in the U.S. ⊞; (3) BOOKS - more than 1200 skating books dating back to 1792; (4) VIDEOS - over 190 skating videos & where to find them. Other sections include associations, boots & blades, champions, fan clubs, federations, training centers, summer skating schools & more. New chapters on adult skaters, hockey, precision & speedskating. Also included are articles on GUIDE TO FITTING SKATES, SKATE BOOTS, GUIDE TO BLADES, LACING SKATES, CHOOSING A PRO, CHOOSING A SUMMER SCHOOL & more.

B

Berman, Allen G. Papal Coins. (Illus.). 255p. 1991. 59.50 (*0-915018-43-8*) Attic Bks.

— Papal Numismatic History: The Emancipation of the Papal State. 2nd ed. (Illus.). 165p. 1991. pap. 29.50 (*0-915018-44-6*) Attic Bks.

— Warman's Coins & Paper Money: A Value & Identification Guide. LC 99-62390. 256p. 1999. pap. 19.95 (*0-87341-741-0*) Krause Pubns.

Berman, Antoine. The Experience of the Foreign: Culture & Translation in Romantic Germany. Heyvaert, S., tr. from FRE. LC 90-28938. (SUNY Series, Intersections: Philosophy & Critical Theory). 261p. (C). 1992. text 64.50 (*0-7914-0875-2*); pap. text 21.95 (*0-7914-0876-0*) State U NY Pr.

Berman, Armand. Vacuum Engineering Calculations, Formulas, & Solved Exercises. (Illus.). 257p. 1992. text 88.00 (*0-12-092455-2*) Acad Pr.

Berman, Art. From the New Criticism to Deconstruction: The Reception of Structuralism & Post-Structuralism. LC 87-27230. 344p. 1988. text 32.50 (*0-252-01508-8*); pap. text 15.95 (*0-252-06002-4*) U of Ill Pr.

— Preface to Modernism. LC 93-36653. 360p. 1994. text 39.95 (*0-252-02103-7*); pap. text 15.95 (*0-252-06391-0*) U of Ill Pr.

Berman, Arthur L. The Second Comings. LC 99-90484. 365p. 1999. 25.00 (*0-7388-0412-6*); pap. 15.00 (*0-7388-0413-4*) Xlibris Corp.

Berman, Audrey, jt. auth. see Haft, Timothy D.

Berman, Avis. James McNeill Whistler. LC 93-9453. (First Impressions Ser.). (Illus.). 92p. (J). 1993. 19.95 (*0-8109-3968-1*, Pub. by Abrams) Time Warner.

— Poetry of Sight. 2000. write for info. (*0-517-70567-2*) Random.

Berman, Avis & Agee, William C. Jacob Kainen: Essays. LC 93-8196. 1993. 40.00 (*0-937311-07-3*) Natl Mus Amer Art.

Berman, Barbara, ed. Library of Congress Subject Headings in Philosophy: A Thesaurus. 550p. 1999. 65.00 (*0-912632-64-X*) Philos Document.

Berman, Barbara & Friederwitzer, Fredda J. Active Math: Mathematics Activities for the Primary Years. 120p. (C). 1991. teacher ed. 50.00 (*1-880744-04-X*) Educ Support.

— Mathematics Through Measurement, Pt. I. rev. ed. (Project S.I.T.E. Ser.). 63p. (C). 1983. pap. text 15.00 (*1-880744-02-3*) Educ Support.

— Mathematics Through Measurement, Pt. II. rev. ed. 48p. (C). 1983. pap. text 15.00 (*1-880744-03-1*) Educ Support.

— Measurement in the Elementary School: Workbook Manual for Teachers. rev. ed. (Project S.I.T.E. Ser.). 102p. (C). 1991. student ed. 15.00 (*1-880744-00-7*) Educ Support.

— Trainer's Manual: Project S.I.T.E.: Training Skills Handbook. rev. ed. 126p. (C). 1991. pap. text 25.00 (*0-685-51624-5*) Educ Support.

Berman, Barbara, jt. auth. see Friederwitzer, Fredda J.

Berman-Barrett, Sara J., jt. auth. see Bergman, Paul.

Berman, Barry. Marketing Channels. LC 95-36680. 736p. 1995. text 93.95 (*0-471-57748-0*) Wiley.

Berman, Barry & Evans, Joel R. Retail Management: A Strategic Approach. 7th ed. LC 97-38137. 768p. 1997. 97.00 (*0-13-613829-2*) P-H.

***Berman, Barry & Evans, Joel R.** Retail Management: A Strategic Approach. 8th ed. 746p. 2000. 86.67 (*0-13-026334-6*) P-H.

Berman, Barry, jt. auth. see Evans, Joel R.

Berman, Barry, ed. see American Marketing Association Staff.

Berman, Bary, jt. auth. see Evans, Joel.

Berman, Ben. The Dictionary of Business & Credit Terms. Andover, James J., ed. LC 82-14231. 208p. 1983. 3.00 (*0-934914-45-1*) NACM.

***Berman, Beverley C.** Moodles. 176p. 2000. pap. 14.95 (*1-58244-074-3*) Rutledge Bks.

Berman, Bob. Cosmic Adventure: A Renegade Astronomer's Guide to Our World & Beyond. LC 98-17819. (Illus.). 224p. 1998. 25.00 (*0-688-14495-0*, Wm Morrow) Morrow Avon.

***Berman, Bob.** Cosmic Adventure: Other Secrets Beyond the Night Sky. LC 98-17819. (Illus.). 272p. 2000. pap. 13.00 (*0-688-17218-0*, Quil) HarperTrade.

Berman, Bob. Secrets of the Night Sky: The Most Amazing Things in the Universe You Can See with the Naked Eye. LC 95-46182. (Illus.). 336p. 1996. pap. 16.00 (*0-06-097687-X*) HarpC.

***Berman, Boris.** Notes from the Pianist's Bench. LC 00-36514. (Illus.). 288p. 2000. 30.00 (*0-300-08375-0*) Yale U Pr.

***Berman, Brian & Thomadsen, Bruce.** Study Guide for Radiation Oncology Physics Board Exams. (Illus.). 75p. 2000. pap. text 29.95 (*0-944838-94-4*) Med Physics Pub.

Berman, Bruce. Journey of the Dolphin King. LC 98-87028. 192p. 1999. pap. 11.95 (*1-56315-178-2*) SterlingHse.

Berman, Bruce & Lonsdale, John. Unhappy Valley: Clan, Class, & State in Colonial Kenya. LC 91-28362. (Eastern African Studies). 528p. (Orig.). (C). 1991. text 50.00 (*0-8214-1016-4*) Ohio U Pr.

— Unhappy Valley: Clan, Class, & State in Colonial Kenya, 1. LC 91-28362. (Eastern African Studies). 521p. (Orig.). (C). 1992. pap. text 19.95 (*0-8214-1017-2*) Ohio U Pr.

— Unhappy Valley: Clan, Class, & State in Colonial Kenya, 2. LC 91-28362. (Eastern African Studies). 521p. (Orig.). (C). 1992. pap. text 19.95 (*0-8214-1025-3*) Ohio U Pr.

Berman, Bruce, ed. see Euromoney Books Staff.

Berman, Bruce J. Control & Crisis in Colonial Kenya: The Dialectic of Domination. LC 89-72154. (Eastern African Studies). 495p. 1990. text 44.95 (*0-8214-0965-4*) Ohio U Pr.

— Florida Civil Procedure LC 98-172373. (West's Florida Practice Ser.). xxxi, 820 p. 1998. write for info. (*0-314-23219-2*) West Pub.

Berman, Bruce J. & Leys, Colin T., eds. African Capitalists in African Development. LC 93-28585. 288p. 1993. lib. bdg. 55.00 (*1-55587-417-7*) L Rienner.

***Berman, Carol.** Overcoming Stress in the Workplace. 260p. 2000. 29.95 (*0-8290-5212-7*) Ardent Media.

Berman, Carol. Overcoming Stress in the Workplace. 275p. Date not set. write for info. (*0-8290-2634-7*) Irvington.

— Sidney Poitier: First Black Male Academy Award Winner. 1990. pap. 3.95 (*0-87067-566-4*) Holloway.

***Berman, Chere.** Chords: Sounds of a Journey. (Illus.). 84p. 2000. pap. 34.95 (*0-9700371-0-4*, 09700301) C Berman.

Berman, Christine & Fromer, Jacki. Meals Without Squeals: Child Care Feeding Guide & Cookbook. 2nd rev. ed. LC 97-29116. (Illus.). 288p. 1997. pap. 16.95 (*0-923521-39-9*) Bull Pub.

— Teaching Children about Food: A Teaching & Activities Guide. (Illus.). 96p. 1991. pap. 10.95 (*0-923521-15-1*) Bull Pub.

Berman, Claire. Caring for Yourself While Caring for Your Aging Parents: How to Help, How to Survive. LC 95-32613. 88p. 1995. 22.50 (*0-8050-3734-9*); pap. 12.95 (*0-8050-4109-5*, Owl) H Holt & Co.

***Berman, Claire.** Caring for Yourself While Caring for Your Aging Parents: How to Help, How to Survive. 255p. 2000. reprint ed. text 22.00 (*0-7881-6982-3*) DIANE Pub.

Berman, Claire. Great City for Kids: A Parent's Guide to a Child's New York. LC 69-13086. (Illus.). 1969. 5.95 (*0-672-50690-4*, Bobbs); pap. 3.95 (*0-672-50691-2*, Bobbs) Macmillan.

— Making It As a Stepparent. LC 85-45177. 224p. 1986. reprint ed. pap. 12.00 (*0-06-097019-7*, PL 7019, Perennial) HarperTrade.

— What Am I Doing in a Step-Family? (Illus.). 48p. (J). (gr. 2 up). 1982. 12.00 (*0-8184-0325-X*) Carol Pub Group.

— What Am I Doing in a Stepfamily? (Where Did I Come From Ser.). (Illus.). (J). (gr. k-7). 1992. pap. 8.95 (*0-8184-0563-5*, L Stuart) Carol Pub Group.

Berman, Claire, jt. auth. see Elgart, Arty.

Berman, Claudia. School Around Us: 25 Years. LC 94-93849. (Illus.). 195p. (Orig.). 1994. pap. text 18.95 (*0-9643758-0-X*) Schl Around Us.

Berman, Claudia G., et al. Oncologic Imaging: A Clinical Perspective. LC 96-32622. (Illus.). 700p. 1997. text 95.00 (*0-07-005114-3*) McGraw-Hill HPD.

Berman, Colette & Miller, Yosef, eds. The Beautiful People of the Book: A Tribute to Ethopian Jews in Israel. 1988. 35.00 (*965-222-112-0*) Millhouse Pubs.

***Berman, Constance H.** The Cistercian Evolution. LC 99-48399. (Middle Ages Ser.). 1999. 59.95 (*0-8122-3534-7*) U of Pa Pr.

Berman, Constance H. Medieval Agriculture, the Southern French Countryside & the Early Cistercians: A Study of Forty-Three Monasteries. LC 84-71079. (Transactions Ser.: Vol. 76, Pt. 5). 179p. 1986. pap. 15.00 (*0-87169-765-3*, T765-BEC) Am Philos.

— Medieval Agriculture, the Southern French Countryside & the Early Cistercians: A Study of Forty-Three Monasteries. LC 84-71079. (American Philosophical Society, Transactions Ser.: Vol. 76). (Illus.). 193p. reprint ed. pap. 59.90 (*0-7837-4331-9*, 204404200012) Bks Demand.

Berman, Constance H. & Connell, Charles W., eds. World of Medieval Women. 163p. (Orig.). 1985. pap. 12.95 (*0-937058-22-X*) West Va U Pr.

Berman, D. L., et al. Nineteen Papers on Statistics & Probability. LC 61-9803. (Selected Translations on Mathematical Statistics & Probability Ser.: Vol. 5). 380p. 1965. 42.00 (*0-8218-1455-9*, STAPRO/5) Am Math.

Berman, Daniel, jt. ed. see Navarro, Vicente.

Berman, Daniel M. & O'Connor. Who Owns the Sun? People, Politics, & the Struggle for a Solar Economy. 356p. 1997. pap. 17.95 (*1-890132-08-X*) Chelsea Green Pub.

Berman, Daniel M. & O'Connor, John T. Who Owns the Sun? People, Politics & the Struggle for a Solar Economy. LC 96-43593. 331p. 1996. 24.95 (*0-930031-86-5*) Chelsea Green Pub.

Berman, Daniel S. Clinical Gated Cardiac SPECT. Germano, Guido, ed. LC 99-19070. (Illus.). 387p. 1999. 125.00 (*0-87993-432-8*) Futura Pub.

Berman, Davaid R. State & Local Politics. 8th ed. 72p. (C). 1996. pap. text, teacher ed. 1.95 (*0-7656-0007-2*) M E Sharpe.

Berman, David. Actual Air. LC 99-63712. 106p. 1999. pap. 12.95 (*1-890447-04-8*, 5) Open City Bks.

— George Berkeley: Idealism & the Man. (Illus.). 241p. 1996. pap. text 19.95 (*0-19-826467-4*) OUP.

— A History of Atheism in Britain: From Hobbes to Russell. 288p. 1988. lib. bdg. 72.50 (*0-7099-3271-5*, Pub. by C Helm) Routldge.

— State & Local Politics. 9th ed. LC 99-20509. 512p. 1999. pap. text 39.95 (*0-7656-0421-3*) M E Sharpe.

Berman, David, ed. Atheism in Britain: A Collection of Key Works, 5 vols., Set. 1996. 495.00 (*1-85506-474-X*) Bks Intl VA.

Berman, David, et al. Open City Vol. 7: The Rubbed Away Girl. Beller, Thomas & Pinchdeck, Daniel, eds. 1999. pap. text 8.00 (*1-890447-18-8*) Open City Bks.

Berman, David, ed. see Berkeley, George.

Berman, David, ed. see Drury, M. O.

Berman, David, ed. see Schopenhauer, Arthur.

Berman, David R. Arizona Politics & Government. LC 98-13653. (Politics & Governments of the American States Ser.). (Illus.). xxviii, 257p. 1998. pap. 22.00 (*0-8032-6146-2*) U of Nebr Pr.

— Arizona Politics & Government: The Quest for Autonomy, Democracy, & Development. LC 98-13653. (Politics & Governments of the American States Ser.). 1998. text 45.00 (*0-8032-1288-7*) U of Nebr Pr.

— Reformers, Corporations, & the Electorate: An Analysis of Arizona's Age of Reform. (Illus.). 304p. 1992. 35.00 (*0-87081-249-1*) Univ Pr Colo.

— State & Local Politics. 7th ed. 464p. (C). 1993. text. write for info. (*0-697-12696-X*) Brown & Benchmark.

— State & Local Politics. 8th ed. LC 96-19264. 460p. (C). (gr. 13). 1996. pap. text 43.95 (*1-56324-767-4*) M E Sharpe.

Berman, David R., ed. County Governments in an Era of Change, 314. LC 92-30013. (Contributions in Political Science Ser.: No. 314). 192p. 1993. 45.00 (*0-313-27824-5*, BNG/, Greenwood Pr) Greenwood.

Berman, Dorothy M., jt. auth. see Matthews, Joseph L.

Berman, E. R. Biochemistry of the Eye. LC 90-14353. (Perspectives in Vision Research Ser.). (Illus.). 492p. (C). 1991. text 115.00 (*0-306-43633-7*, Kluwer Plenum) Kluwer Academic.

Berman, Edgar. In Africa with Schweitzer. 300p. 1986. 21.95 (*0-88282-025-7*) New Horizon NJ.

Berman, Edward. Labor Disputes & the President of the United States. LC 75-76691. (Columbia University. Studies in the Social Sciences: No. 249). reprint ed. 27.50 (*0-404-51249-6*) AMS Pr.

Berman, Edward H. African Reactions to Missionary Education. LC 74-22497. (Publications of the Center for Education in Africa). 255p. reprint ed. pap. 79.10 (*0-8357-5240-2*, 203013700067) Bks Demand.

Berman, Eileen L. Downsized-A Unique Approach to Rebuilding Your Life. LC 98-38875. 1998. 18.95 (*0-89806-211-X*) Eng Mgmt Pr.

— You're Fired! A Unique Approach to Rebuilding Your Life. LC 98-11416. (Illus.). 96p. 1998. pap. 19.95 (*0-89806-183-0*, UFIRED) Eng Mgmt Pr.

Berman, Eleanor. Away for the Weekend: Great Getaways Less Than 200 Miles from New York City for Every Season of the Year. 5th rev. ed. LC 96-54054. 1997. pap. 16.00 (*0-609-80020-2*) Random Hse Value.

— Away for the Weekend: Mid-Atlantic States. LC 98-46375. 1999. pap. 16.00 (*0-609-80400-6*) Random Hse Value.

— Away for the Weekend: Midwest. LC 99-17595. 1999. pap. 16.00 (*0-609-80401-4*) Crown.

***Berman, Eleanor.** Away for the Weekend? New York. 6th rev. ed. LC 00-21192. (Illus.). 304p. 2000. pap. 16.00 (*0-609-80596-7*, Three Riv Pr) Crown Pub Group.

Berman, Eleanor. Away for the Weekend: New York with Kids. 1995. pap. 16.00 (*0-517-88279-5*, Crown) Crown Pub Group.

— Away for the Weekend: Northern California. LC 98-38222. 1999. pap. 16.00 (*0-609-80374-3*) Random Hse Value.

— Away for the Weekend: Northern California. rev. ed. LC 95-30648. 288p. 1996. pap. 16.00 (*0-517-88519-0*) Crown Pub Group.

— Away for the Weekend: 52 Great Getaways in Connecticut & Maine. 5th ed. LC 97-44622. 1998. pap. 16.00 (*0-609-80169-4*, Crown) Crown Pub Group.

— Away for the Weekend, Mid-Atlantic: Great Getaways Within 250 Miles of Washington, D.C., in Delaware, Maryland, Virginia, West Virginia, Pennsylvania, New Jersey. 3rd rev. ed. LC 96-4201. 288p. 1996. pap. 17.00 (*0-517-88678-2*) Crown Pub Group.

— Grandparenting ABCs: A Beginner's Handbook. LC 97-52657. 208p. 1998. pap. 13.00 (*0-399-52436-3*, Perigee Bks) Berkley Pub.

— The Laboratory Practice of Clinical Toxicology. LC 95-48096. (Illus.). 220p. 1996. pap. 38.95 (*0-398-06582-9*); text 56.95 (*0-398-06581-0*) C C Thomas.

— Mid-West. (52 Weekend & Day Trips Ser.). 1996. pap. 16.00 (*0-614-12770-X*) Crown Pub Group.

— New York. LC 92-53471. (Eyewitness Travel Guides Ser.). (Illus.). 432p. 1993. pap. 24.95 (*1-56458-184-5*) DK Pub Inc.

— New York Neighborhoods: A Food Lovers Walking, Eating & Shopping Guide to Ethnic Enclaves in New York's Five Boroughs. LC 99-22940. (Illus.). 256p. 1999. pap. 14.95 (*0-7627-0442-X*) Globe Pequot.

— Northeast. (52 Weekend & Day Trips Ser.). 1996. pap. 16.00 (*0-614-12771-8*) Crown Pub Group.

***Berman, Eleanor.** Recommended Bed & Breakfasts New England. 2nd ed. LC 99-37609. (Illus.). 336p. 1999. pap. text 16.95 (*0-7627-0550-7*) Globe Pequot.

Berman, Eleanor. Toxic Metals & Their Analysis. LC 79-41781. (Heyden International Topics in Science Ser.). (Illus.). 303p. reprint ed. pap. 94.00 (*0-608-15579-9*, 202964100062) Bks Demand.

— Traveling Solo: Advise & Ideas for More Than 250 Great Vacations. 2nd ed. LC 98-54364. (Illus.). 320p. 1999. pap. text 16.95 (*0-7627-0418-7*) Globe Pequot.

Berman, Ellen. Eyewitness Guide to New York: Spanish Edition. (SPA.). 432p. 1994. 59.95 (*0-7859-9940-2*) Fr & Eur.

Berman, Emanuel, ed. Essential Papers on Literature & Psychoanalysis. (Essential Papers in Psychoanalysis). 550p. (C). 1993. text 75.00 (*0-8147-1184-7*); pap. text 27.50 (*0-8147-1185-5*) NYU Pr.

Berman, Esme. Berman's Art & Artisits of South Africa. (Illus.). 545p. 1999. 58.95 (*1-86812-345-6*) Menasha Ridge.

— Painting in South Africa. 500p. 1999. 20.95 (*1-86812-479-7*) Menasha Ridge.

Berman, Eugene. Eugene Berman. Levy, Julien, ed. LC 73-160915. (Biography Index Reprint Ser.). 1977. reprint ed. 33.95 (*0-8369-8078-6*) Ayer.

Berman, Evan M. Productivity in Public & Non-Profit Organizations. LC 97-33869. 1998. write for info. (*0-7619-1030-1*); pap. write for info. (*0-7619-1031-X*) Sage.

Berman, Evan M., et al, eds. The Ethics Edge. LC 98-12422. (Practical Management Ser.). 248p. 1998. pap. 23.95 (*0-87326-161-5*, 42330) Intl City-Cnty Mgt.

Berman, Evan M., jt. auth. see Kearney, Richard C.

Berman, Fran. Trash to Cash: How Businesses Can Save Money & Increase Profits. 260p. 1996. lib. bdg. 29.95 (*1-884015-96-4*) St Lucie Pr.

Berman, Garry. Best of the Britcoms: From Fawlty Towers to Absolutely Fabulous. LC 99-35301. 1999. pap. write for info. (*0-87833-160-3*) Taylor Pub.

Berman, Gennady P., et al. Crossover-Time in Quantum Boson & Spin Systems. LC 94-19412. (Lecture Notes in Physics, New Series M, Monographs: Vol. 21). 1994. 54.95 (*0-387-58011-5*) Spr-Verlag.

— Introduction to Quantum Computers. LC 98-23218. (Illus.). 200p. 1998. 32.00 (*981-02-3490-2*) World Scientific Pub.

Berman, George, et al. French Law: Constitution & Selective Legislation. 1982. ring bd. 145.00 (*0-929179-00-5*) Juris Pubng.

Berman, Gerald & Brown, D. Collection of Problems on a Course of Mathematical Analysis. LC 63-11927. (International Series of Monographs on Pure & Applied Mathematics: Vol. 64). 1965. 259.00 (*0-08-013502-1*, Pub. by Pergamon Repr) Franklin.

Berman, Gold & West, PC Kamberg Staff. Massachusetts Collections Manual. 250p. 1991. ring bd. 95.00 (*0-614-05895-3*, MICHIE) LEXIS Pub.

Berman, Hannah. Melutovna: A Novel. LC 74-27963. (Modern Jewish Experience Ser.). 1975. reprint ed. 33.95 (*0-405-06694-5*) Ayer.

Berman, Harold. Bronzes: Sculptors & Founders, 1800-1930, Index. LC 94-23075. 1994. 20.00 (*0-88740-704-8*) Schiffer.

— Bronzes: Sculptors & Founders, 1800-1930, Vol. I. LC 94-23075. (Illus.). 224p. 1994. 79.95 (*0-88740-700-5*) Schiffer.

— Bronzes: Sculptors & Founders, 1800-1930, Vol. II. LC 94-23075. (Illus.). 272p. 1994. 79.95 (*0-88740-701-3*) Schiffer.

— Bronzes: Sculptors & Founders, 1800-1930, Vol. III. LC 94-23075. (Illus.). 320p. 1995. 79.95 (*0-88740-702-1*) Schiffer.

— Bronzes: Sculptors & Founders, 1800-1930, Vol. IV. LC 94-23075. (Illus.). 400p. 1995. 79.95 (*0-88740-703-X*) Schiffer.

— Encyclopedia of Bronzes, Sculptors & Founders, 1800-1930, 4 vols., Set. (Illus.). 1988. 295.00 (*0-318-37094-8*) Edns Publisol.

Berman, Harold, tr. see Sachs, Abraham S.

Berman, Harold J. Justice in the U. S. S. R: An Interpretation of the Soviet Law. rev. ed. LC 63-15045. (Russian Research Center Studies: No. 3). 460p. 1963. pap. 31.00 (*0-674-49151-3*) HUP.

— Law & Revolution: The Formation of the Western Legal Tradition. 672p. 1985. pap. 22.95 (*0-674-51776-8*) HUP.

— Russians in Focus. LC 71-90610. (Essay Index Reprint Ser.). 1977. 23.95 (*0-8369-1391-4*) Ayer.

Berman, Harold J., tr. Soviet Criminal Law & Procedure, the RSFSR Codes. 2nd ed. LC 72-81269. (Russian Research Center Studies: No. 50). 408p. 1972. 44.00 (*0-674-82636-1*) HUP.

Berman, Harold J., et al. The Nature & Functions of Law. 5th ed. LC 95-47047. (Paralegal). 853p. 1996. text 45.95 (*1-56662-238-7*) Foundation Pr.

Berman, Harry J. Interpreting the Aging Self: Personal Journals of Later Life. LC 94-23168. (Illus.). 248p. 1994. 35.95 (*0-8261-8060-4*) Springer Pub.

Berman, Harvey W. & Saylor, Larry J., eds. Litigating the Commercial Case. LC 91-78182. 460p. 1992. 115.00 (*0-685-65663-2*, 92-020) U MI Law CLE.

Berman, Helen. Ad Sales Vol. 1: Winning Secrets of the Magazine Pros. 448p. 1996. 69.95 (*0-9649716-1-5*) Berman Pubng.

— Ad Sales Vol. 2: Winning Secrets of the Magazine Pros. 400p. 1996. 69.95 (*0-9649716-2-3*) Berman Pubng.

— Ad Sales Vols. 1 & 2: Winning Secrets of the Magazine Pros, 2 vols., Set. 960p. 1996. 119.95 (*0-9649716-0-7*) Berman Pubng.

Berman, I., ed. see Explosive Metalworking Techniques Seminar Staff.

***Berman, Ilan.** Partnership in Transition: U. S. - Israel Strategic Cooperation Beyond the Cold War. Colbert, James, ed. 81p. 2000. pap. 14.95 (*0-9644523-5-9*) Jewish Inst Nat Secur.

Berman, Irene B., tr. see Ibsen, Henrik.

Berman, Irwin, jt. auth. see Milikowski, Clara.

Berman, Irwin, ed. see American Society of Mechanical Engineers Staff.

Berman, J-P., et al. Dictionnaire de l'Anglais Economique et Commercial: Dictionary of Commercial & Economic English. (ENG & FRE.). 412p. 1980. pap. 22.95 (*0-8288-1254-3*, M4800) Fr & Eur.

Berman, Jay S. Police Administration & Progressive Reform: Theodore Roosevelt as Police Commissioner of New York, 19. LC 87-8651. (Contributions in Criminology & Penology Ser.: No. 19). 167p. 1987. 49.95 (*0-313-25554-7*, BMO/, Greenwood Pr) Greenwood.

Berman, Jeffrey. Diaries to an English Professor: Pain & Growth in the Classroom. LC 94-10564. 304p. (C). 1994. pap. 18.95 (*0-87023-928-7*) U of Mass Pr.

— Diaries to an English Professor: Pain & Growth in the Classroom. 304p. (C). 1995. lib. bdg. 45.00 (*0-87023-927-9*) U of Mass Pr.

— Narcissism & the Novel. 320p. (C). 1990. text 50.00 (*0-8147-1132-4*) NYU Pr.

— Narcissism & the Novel. 350p. (C). 1992. pap. text 19.50 (*0-8147-1171-5*) NYU Pr.

— Surviving Literary Suicide. LC 98-32202. 304p. 1999. 60.00 (*1-55849-195-3*); pap. 18.95 (*1-55849-211-9*) U of Mass Pr.

Berman, Jeffrey A. Competence-Based Employment Interviewing. LC 96-54287. 184p. 1997. 59.95 (*1-56720-050-8*, Quorum Bks) Greenwood.

Berman, Jeffrey B., jt. auth. see Crump, David.

Berman, Jeffrey M., jt. ed. see Hall, J. K.

Berman, Jennifer. Adult Children of Normal Parents. Tobias, Eric, ed. (Illus.). 80p. (Orig.). 1994. pap. 8.00 (*0-671-86489-0*) PB.

— Glorafilla Needle-Point Collection: With 25 Complete Projects. (Illus.). 200p. 1997. pap. 19.95 (*0-7153-0683-9*) Sterling.

***Berman, Jennifer.** Why Dogs Are Better Than Kids. LC 00-30453. (Illus.). 80p. 2000. pap. 7.95 (*0-7407-0987-9*) Andrews & McMeel.

Berman, Jennifer. Why Dogs Are Better Than Men. Tobias, Eric, ed. (Illus.). 80p. (Orig.). 1993. pap. 10.00 (*0-671-86488-2*) PB.

***Berman, Jennifer & Berman, Laura.** For Women Only: A Revolutionary Guide for Women to Overcoming Sexual Dysfunction & Reclaiming Your Sex Life. (Illus.). 320p. 2001. text 25.00 (*0-8050-6405-2*) H Holt & Co.

Berman, Jill. Forest Service: Distribution of Timber Sales Receipts, Fiscal Years 1995 Through 1997. (Illus.). 48p. (C). 1999. pap. text 20.00 (*0-7881-7815-6*) DIANE Pub.

Berman, Jill, ed. see Schopenhauer, Arthur.

Berman, Joan. Ethnography & Folklore of the Indians of Northwestern California No. 5: A Literature Review & Annotated Bibliography. Breschini, Gary S. & Haversat, Trudy, eds. (Archives of California Prehistory Ser.: No. 5). 122p. (Orig.). 1986. pap. 13.75 (*1-55567-029-6*) Coyote Press.

***Berman, Joel A.** Comprehensive Breast Care: Surviving Breast Cancer. Caso, Adolph, ed. (Illus.). 380p. 2000. pap. 19.95 (*0-8283-2057-8*) Branden Bks.

Berman, John J., ed. see Nebraska Symposium on Motivation Staff.

Berman, Jude & Crisp, Alan. The Healing Zone: The Work of Jean Vaziri. 233p. (Orig.). 1997. pap. 12.95 (*0-9605022-4-6*) Pathwys Pr CA.

Berman, Jude, et al. Study Guide to the American Psychiatric Press Textbook of Neuropsychiatry. 3rd ed. 256p. 1997. pap. text, student ed. 26.00 (*0-88048-804-2*, 8804) Am Psychiatric.

— Study Guide to the American Psychiatric Press Textbook of Psychiatry. 2nd ed. LC RC0454.A419. 258p. (Orig.). reprint ed. pap. 80.00 (*0-608-20027-1*, 207129900010) Bks Demand.

Berman, Judith, et al. Study Guide to the American Psychiatric Press Textbook of Consultation-Liaison Psychiatry. LC 98-53143. 226p. 1999. 25.00 (*0-88048-805-0*) Am Psychiatric.

Berman, Judith, jt. auth. see Polit, Denise F.

Berman, Karen. American Indian Traditions & Ceremonies. (Illus.). 128p. 1998. text 45.00 (*0-7881-5725-6*) DIANE Pub.

Berman, Ken & Paul, Jerome. Fundamentals of Sequential & Parallel Algorithms. (Computer Science Ser.). 800p. 1996. mass mkt. 82.95 (*0-534-94674-7*) PWS Pubs.

Berman, Laine A. Speaking Through the Silence: Narratives, Social Conventions, & Power in Java. LC 97-29990. (Oxford Studies in Anthropological Linguistics: No. 19). (Illus.). 276p. 1998. text 65.00 (*0-19-510888-4*) OUP.

Berman, Larry. Approaching Democracy. 1995. pap. text, teacher ed. write for info. (*0-13-507377-4*) Allyn.

— Approaching Democracy. 1996. pap. text, teacher ed. write for info. (*0-13-507393-6*) Allyn.

Berman, Larry. Approaching Democracy. 2nd ed. LC 98-30844. 687p. 1998. pap. text 57.33 (*0-13-793902-7*) P-H.

— Lyndon Johnson's War: The Road to Stalemate in Vietnam. 1991. pap. 9.95 (*0-393-30778-6*) Norton.

— Planning a Tragedy: The Americanization of the War in Vietnam. 224p. 1983. reprint ed. pap. 9.95 (*0-393-95326-2*) Norton.

Berman, Larry, et al. Approaching Democracy. LC 95-36407. 647p. 1995. text 65.00 (*0-13-033457-X*) P-H.

Berman, Laura, jt. auth. see Berman, Jennifer.

Berman, Laurel, et al. Water Quality: Urban Runoff Solutions. (Special Repors: No. 61). 32p. (Orig.). 1991. pap. text 35.00 (*0-917084-18-7*) Am Public Works.

Berman, Laurence D. The Musical Image: A Theory of Content, 30. LC 92-32210. (Contributions to the Study of Music & Dance Ser.: No. 30). 408p. 1993. 65.00 (*0-313-28434-2*, BLI, Greenwood Pr) Greenwood.

Berman, Lawrence M. & Letellier, Bernadette. Pharaohs: Treasures of Egyptian Art from the Louvre. LC 95-45358. (Illus.). 1996. write for info. (*0-940717-31-X*); pap. write for info. (*0-940717-32-8*) Cleveland Mus Art.

Berman, Lawrence V., et al, eds. Essays in Medieval Judaism: Study of Judaism. 35.00 (*0-87068-486-8*) Ktav.

Berman, Lea. Face Time. 288p. 2000. 24.00 (*0-06-039201-0*, ReganBks) HarperTrade.

***Berman, Leonard H.** Consider My Servant. LC 00-190421. 2000. 25.00 (*0-7388-1679-5*); pap. 18.00 (*0-7388-1680-9*) Xlibris Corp.

Berman, Leslie & Wood, Heather, eds. Grass Roots International Folk Resource Directory. 2nd rev. ed. 232p. 1987. pap. 12.95 (*0-9614589-1-7*) Grass Roots Productions.

— Grass Roots International Folk Resource Directory 1985. (Illus.). 200p. 1985. pap. text 12.95 (*0-9614589-0-9*) Grass Roots Productions.

Berman, Linda. Behind the Eight Ball. 1992. pap. 11.95 (*0-13-117581-5*) P-H.

— The Goodbye Painting. LC 81-20217. (Illus.). 32p. (J). (ps-3). 1982. 16.95 (*0-89885-074-6*, Kluwer Acad Hman Sci) Kluwer Academic.

Berman, Linda & Penix, Sherry. San Deigo Activity & Coloring Book. 2nd ed. 14.95 (*0-9670612-6-1*) Sher-A-Craft.

Berman, Lonny E. & Arthur, John R., eds. Optics for High-Brightness Synchrotron Radiation Beamlines II, Vol. 2856. 368p. 1996. 66.00 (*0-8194-2244-4*) SPIE.

Berman, Lorna & St. David's University Press Staff. Images & Impressions of Old Age in the Great Works of Western Literature (700 B.C. to 1900 A.D.) An Analytical Compendium. LC 87-9697. 400p. 1987. text 99.95 (*0-88946-037-X*) E Mellen.

Berman, Lorna, jt. auth. see Sobkowska-Ashcroft, Irina.

Berman, Louis A. The Akedah: The Binding of Isaac. LC 97-5627. (Illus.). xx, 259p. 1997. 40.00 (*1-56821-899-0*) Aronson.

— Practical Idioms - Using Phrasal Verbs in Everyday Contexts: Intermediate Through Advanced. (Illus.). 192p. 1994. pap. 12.95 (*0-8442-0672-5*, 06725, Natl Textbk Co) NTC Contemp Pub Co.

— Vegetarianism & the Jewish Tradition. LC 81-11729. 120p. 1982. 19.95 (*0-87068-756-5*) Ktav.

Berman, Louise M., et al. Toward Curriculum for Being: Voices of Educators. LC 90-40121. (SUNY Series in Curriculum Issues & Inquiries). 205p. (C). 1991. text 21.50 (*0-7914-0630-X*) State U NY Pr.

Berman, Lynn, ed. see Orent, Tom.

Berman, M. B., et al. The Independent European Force: Costs of Independence. LC 93-3583. 1993. pap. text 9.00 (*0-8330-1365-3*, MR-178-AF/A/OSD) Rand Corp.

Berman, Madeline C. Connections... LC 99-18944. 72p. 1999. pap. text 14.95 (*0-7734-3105-5*) E Mellen.

Berman, Maggie, jt. auth. see Anderson, Dan.

Berman, Mark L., ed. Motivation & Learning: Applying Contingency Management Techniques. LC 70-160894. 222p. 1972. pap. 24.95 (*0-87778-023-4*) Educ Tech Pubns.

***Berman, Marshall.** Adventures in Marxism. LC 99-34646. 1999. 25.00 (*1-85984-734-X*, Pub. by Verso) Norton.

— Adventures in Marxism. 288p. 2000. pap. 17.00 (*1-85984-309-3*, Pub. by Verso) Norton.

Berman, Marshall. All That Is Solid Melts into Air: The Experience of Modernity. 384p. 1988. pap. 13.95 (*0-14-010962-5*, Penguin Bks) Viking Penguin.

— All That Is Solid Melts into the Air: The Experience of Modernity. 1990. 24.75 (*0-8446-6681-5*) Peter Smith.

Berman, Martha. Dancing on Sand. (Indiana Short Fiction Contest Ser.: No. 1). 104p. 1987. pap. 5.95 (*1-880649-20-9*) Writ Ctr Pr.

— Fielding's Scandinavia. Knoles, Kathy, ed. (Travel Guides Ser.). (Illus.). 580p. (Orig.). 1995. pap. 16.95 (*1-56952-049-6*) Fielding Wrldwide.

***Berman, Matt.** Childrens Book Awards, 99. annuals 1999. 19.50 (*1-56308-771-5*) Libs Unl.

Berman, Matt. What Else Should I Read? Guiding Kids to Good Books, Vol. 1. LC 95-16213. xxi, 211p. 1995. pap. text 24.50 (*1-56308-241-1*) Libs Unl.

— What Else Should I Read? Guiding Kids to Good Books, Vol. 2. 200p. 1996. pap. text 24.00 (*1-56308-419-8*) Libs Unl.

Berman, Matt & Dupuy, Marigny J. Children's Book Awards Annual, 1998. 188p. 1998. pap. 18.50 (*1-56308-649-2*) Teacher Ideas Pr.

Berman, Maxine. The Only Boobs in the House Are Men. LC 94-21814. 140p. (Orig.). 1994. pap. 9.95 (*1-879094-34-7*) Momentum Bks.

Berman, Melanie. Building Jewish Life Prayers & Blessings Activity Book. (Building Jewish Life Ser.). (Illus.). 32p. (Orig.). (J). (gr. k-2). 1991. pap. text 1.95 (*0-933873-66-2*) Torah Aura.

— Sharing Passover: A Guide to Celebration with Your Kids. 38p. 1994. pap. 3.95 (*1-884857-03-5*) Sisu Home Enter.

Berman, Melanie & Grishaver, Joel Lurie. My Weekly Sidra. (Illus.). 192p. (gr. k-3). 1988. pap. 8.50 (*0-933873-21-2*) Torah Aura.

***Berman, Michael.** Interactions Access: Integrated Skills. (C). 2000. pap., teacher ed. 28.75 (*0-07-233049-X*) McGrw-H Hghr Educ.

— Interactions One: Integrated Skills. (C). 2000. pap., teacher ed. 28.75 (*0-07-233051-1*) McGrw-H Hghr Educ.

— Interactions Two: Integrated Skills. (C). 2000. pap., teacher ed. 28.75 (*0-07-233054-6*) McGrw-H Hghr Educ.

Berman, Michael. A Multiple Intelligences Road to an ELT Classroom. 200p. 1998. pap. 35.00 (*1-899836-23-3*, Pub. by Crown Hse) LPC Group.

***Berman, Michael & Brown, David.** The Power of Metaphor: Story Telling & Guided Journeys for Trainers & Therapists. 160p. 2000. pap. 19.95 (*1-899836-43-8*, Pub. by Crown Hse) LPC Group.

Berman, Michael, tr. see Varela-Cid, Eduardo.

***Berman, Michael R., ed.** Parenthood Lost: Healing the Pain after Miscarriage, Stillbirth & Infant Death. LC 00-29257. 224p. 2000. 24.95 (*0-89789-614-9*, Bergin & Garvey) Greenwood.

Berman, Mimi C. & Cohen, Harris L. Obstetrics & Gynecology. 2nd ed. LC 96-39954. (Diagnostic Medical Sonography Ser.). 732p. 1997. text 105.00 (*0-397-55261-0*, Lippnctt) Lppncott W & W.

Berman, Morris. Coming to Our Senses: Body & Spirit in the Hidden History of the West. LC 98-60423. (Illus.). 425p. 1998. reprint ed. pap. 18.95 (*0-9664168-3-X*) Seattle Writers.

— The Reenchantment of the World. LC 81-67178. (Illus.). 368p. 1981. pap. text 18.95 (*0-8014-9225-4*) Cornell U Pr.

— Social Change & Scientific Organization: The Royal Institution, 1799-1844. LC 77-79702. (Illus.). 249p. 1978. 45.00 (*0-8014-1093-2*) Cornell U Pr.

***Berman, Morris.** The Twilight of American Culture. 224p. 2000. 24.95 (*0-393-04879-9*) Norton.

Berman, Morris. Wandering God: A Study in Nomadic Spirituality. LC 99-26802. (C). 2000. text 73.50 (*0-7914-4441-4*); pap. text 24.95 (*0-7914-4442-2*) State U NY Pr.

Berman, Myron. The Attitude of American Jewry Towards East European Jewish Immigration, 1881-1914. Cordasco, Francesco, ed. LC 80-842. (American Ethnic Groups Ser.). 1981. lib. bdg. 60.95 (*0-405-13406-1*) Ayer.

— The Last of the Jews? LC 98-38466. 1998. write for info. (*0-7618-1247-4*) U Pr of Amer.

Berman, Nancy L. The Thrift Shop Maniac's Guide: To the Delaware Valley & the Universe, Vol. II, 1993-1994. 128p. 1993. pap. 9.95 (*0-9639533-0-3*) Thrift Shop.

Berman, O., jt. auth. see Ahituv, N.

Berman, Patricia G. Edvard Munch: Mirror Reflections. LC 86-70376. (Illus.). 122p. 1986. pap. 12.95 (*0-943411-10-6*) Norton Gal Art.

— Modern Hieroglyphs: Gestural Drawing & the European Vanguard, 1900-1918. (Illus.). 128p. 1995. pap. text 29.95 (*1-881894-06-1*) WC Davis Mus & Cult.

Berman, Patricia G., et al. Munch & Women: Image & Myth. LC 96-29322. 1997. 24.95 (*0-88397-121-6*) Art Srvc Intl.

Berman, Paul. Blacks & Jews: Alliances & Arguments. 1996. pap. 12.95 (*0-614-12882-X*) OUP.

— Democracy's Trombones: Essays on the Modern History of Rebellion. 1994. 24.95 (*0-15-133792-6*); pap. 12.95 (*0-15-600110-1*) Harcourt.

Berman, Paul. School Reform & Student Diversity. 296p. 1997. pap. 17.00 (*0-16-048883-4*) USGPO.

Berman, Paul. A Tale of Two Utopias: The Political Journey of the Generation of 1968. 352p. 1997. pap. 13.00 (*0-393-31675-0*) Norton.

***Berman, Paul & RPP International Staff.** The State of Charter Schools: Third-Year Report. LC 99-224170. (Illus.). 62p. 1999. pap. write for info. (*0-16-050048-6*) USGPO.

Berman, Paul, et al. National Study of Charter Schools: Second-Year Report, 1998. LC 98-214737. (Education Department Publication SAI 98 Ser.: Vol. 3033). (Illus.). 130p. 1998. pap. 12.00 (*0-16-049752-3*) USGPO.

Berman, Paul R., ed. Atom Interferometry. LC 96-9899. (Illus.). 478p. 1996. text 125.00 (*0-12-092460-9*) Morgan Kaufmann.

— Cavity Quantum Electrodynamics. (Advances in Atomic, Molecular & Optical Physics Ser.: Supplement 2). (Illus.). 464p. 1993. text 111.00 (*0-12-092245-2*) Acad Pr.

Berman, Pearl. Therapeutic Exercises for Victimized & Neglected Girls: Applications for Individual, Family, & Group Psychotherapy. LC 94-15881. 178p. (Orig.). 1994. pap. 28.95 (*1-56887-003-5*, TEVBP, Prof Resc Pr) Pro Resource.

Berman, Pearl S. Case Conceptualization & Treatment Planning: Exercises for Integrating Theory with Clinical Practice. LC 96-51275. 272p. 1997. 52.00 (*0-7619-0214-7*); pap. 24.95 (*0-7619-0215-5*) Sage.

Berman, Peter & Khan, M. E., eds. Paying for India's Health Care. LC 92-48184. (Illus.). 326p. 1993. 38.00 (*0-8039-9463-X*) Sage.

Berman, Peter A., ed. Health Sector Reform in Developing Countries: Making Health Development Sustainable. LC 95-20671. (Series on Population & International Health). 416p. 1996. pap. 15.00 (*0-674-38525-X*) HUP.

Berman, Phil. Catamaran Racing from Start to Finish. (Illus.). 1989. pap. 19.95 (*0-393-30602-X*) Norton.

***Berman, Phil.** Catamaran Sailing. 2nd ed. LC 98-54158. 224p. 1999. pap. 21.95 (*0-393-31880-X*) Norton.

Berman, Philip. On Faith. 1999. write for info. (*0-671-00161-2*) S&S Trade.

— On Faith. 1999. pap. write for info. (*0-671-00162-0*) S&S Trade.

Berman, Philip L. The Journey Home. 1998. per. 14.00 (*0-671-50237-9*, PB Trade Paper) PB.

Berman, Phillip, jt. auth. see Goodall, Jane.

Berman, Phillip L. & Goldman, Connie. The Ageless Spirit. 272p. 1992. pap. 9.00 (*0-345-36956-4*) Ballantine Pub Grp.

Berman, Phillip L., jt. auth. see Goodall, Jane.

Berman, Phyllis O. & Waskow, Arthur O. Tales of Tikkun: New Jewish Stories to Heal the Wounded World. LC 96-32547. 156p. 1996. pap. 14.95 (*1-56821-991-1*) Aronson.

Berman, Phyllis W. & Pedersen, Frank A., eds. Men's Transitions to Parenthood: Longitudinal Studies of Early Family Experience. LC 86-29165. 264p. 1987. 49.95 (*0-89859-814-1*) L Erlbaum Assocs.

Berman Press. Southern African Customs Union (SACU) 1998 Edition. (FRE.). 1999. pap. text 50.00 (*0-89059-128-8*) Bernan Pr.

— Trade Policy Review Nigeria, 1998. 1999. 50.00 (*0-89059-110-5*) Bernan Pr.

— The Definitive Series for Country-Specific Trade Policy Information. (SPA.). 1999. pap. 45.00 (*0-89059-131-8*); pap. text 45.00 (*0-89059-130-X*) Bernan Pr.

— Trade Policy Review Argentina. (SPA.). 1999. pap. text 50.00 (*0-89059-141-5*) Bernan Pr.

— Trade Policy Review Argentina, 1998. (FRE.). 1999. pap. text 50.00 (*0-89059-140-7*) Bernan Pr.

— Trade Policy Review Australia. (FRE.). 1999. 50.00 (*0-89059-132-6*); pap. text 50.00 (*0-89059-133-4*) Bernan Pr.

— Trade Policy Review Australia, 1998. 1998. 50.00 (*0-89059-111-3*) Bernan Pr.

— Trade Policy Review Canada: 1998 Edition. 285p. 1999. 50.00 (*0-89059-122-9*) Bernan Pr.

— Trade Policy Review Guinea. 1999. 50.00 (*0-89059-117-2*) Bernan Pr.

— Trade Policy Review Hong Kong: 1998 Edition. 244p. 1999. 50.00 (*0-89059-121-0*) Bernan Pr.

— Trade Policy Review Hungary. (SPA.). 1999. pap. text 50.00 (*0-89059-135-0*) Bernan Pr.

— Trade Policy Review Hungary: 1998 Edition. (FRE.). 1999. pap. text 50.00 (*0-89059-134-2*) Bernan Pr.

— Trade Policy Review India: 1998 Edition. (FRE.). 1999. pap. text 50.00 (*0-89059-124-5*) Bernan Pr.

— Trade Policy Review Indonesia, 1998. 270p. 1999. 50.00 (*0-89059-118-0*) Bernan Pr.

— Trade Policy Review Japan, 1998. (FRE.). 1999. pap. text 50.00 (*0-89059-126-1*) Bernan Pr.

— Trade Policy Review Solomon Islands. (SPA.). 1999. pap. text 50.00 (*0-89059-143-1*) Bernan Pr.

— Trade Policy Review Solomon Islands: 1998 Edition. (FRE.). 1999. pap. text 50.00 (*0-89059-142-3*) Bernan Pr.

— Trade Policy Review Turkey: 1998 Edition. 1999. 50.00 (*0-89059-119-9*) Bernan Pr.

***Berman Press.** Trade Policy Review Uruguay, 1998. 1999. 50.00 (*0-89059-120-2*) Bernan Pr.

Berman Press Staff. Southern African Customs Union (SACU) (SPA.). 1999. pap. text 50.00 (*0-89059-129-6*) Bernan Pr.

— Trade Policy Review - Jamaica. (FRE.). 1999. 50.00 (*0-89059-136-9*, BWTO/1369); 50.00 (*0-89059-137-7*, BWTO/1377) Bernan Pr.

— Trade Policy Review - Jamaica, 1998. 1999. 50.00 (*0-89059-113-X*, BWTO-113X) Bernan Pr.

— Trade Policy Review Argentina. 310p. 1999. 50.00 (*0-89059-115-6*) Bernan Pr.

— Trade Policy Review Burkina Faso & Mali. 1999. 50.00 (*0-89059-114-8*) Bernan Pr.

— Trade Policy Review Canada. (SPA.). 1999. pap. text 50.00 (*0-89059-155-5*) Bernan Pr.

— Trade Policy Review Canada: 1998 Edition. (FRE.). 1999. pap. text 50.00 (*0-89059-154-7*) Bernan Pr.

— Trade Policy Review Guinea. (FRE.). 1999. pap. text 50.00 (*0-89059-144-X*) Bernan Pr.

— Trade Policy Review Hong Kong. (FRE.). 1999. pap. text 50.00 (*0-89059-152-0*); pap. text 50.00 (*0-89059-153-9*) Bernan Pr.

— Trade Policy Review Hungary, 1998. 181p. 1999. 50.00 (*0-89059-112-1*) Bernan Pr.

— Trade Policy Review Indonesia. (FRE.). 1999. pap. text 50.00 (*0-89059-146-6*); pap. text 50.00 (*0-89059-147-4*) Bernan Pr.

— Trade Policy Review Solomon Islands: 1998 Edition. 149p. 1999. 50.00 (*0-89059-116-4*) Bernan Pr.

— Trade Policy Review Turkey. (FRE.). 1999. pap. text 50.00 (*0-89059-148-2*); pap. text 50.00 (*0-89059-149-0*) Bernan Pr.

— Trade Policy Review Uruguay. (FRE.). 1999. pap. text 50.00 (*0-89059-150-4*); pap. text 50.00 (*0-89059-151-2*) Bernan Pr.

Berman, Richard. Hostile Witness. 304p. (Orig.). 1996. mass mkt. 5.99 (*0-380-77813-0*, Avon Bks) Morrow Avon.

— Unjust Death. 352p. (Orig.). 1995. mass mkt. 5.50 (*0-380-77812-2*, Avon Bks) Morrow Avon.

Berman, Richard, jt. auth. see Groff, David.

Berman, Richard L. & McBride, Deborah. Natural Washington: A Nature-Lover's Guide to Parks, Wildlife Refuges, Trails, Gardens, Zoos, Forests, Aquariums & Arboreums Within a Day's Trip of the Nation's Capital. 4th rev. ed. LC 98-38069. (Illus.). 352p. 1999. pap. 14.95 (*1-889324-15-9*, EPM) Howell Pr VA.

Berman, Rick, et al, contrib. by. Star Trek First Contact: A Novel by J. M. Dillard Based on the Film Star Trek Generations II. (Illus.). 256p. 1996. 27.00 (*0-614-19273-0*) PB.

Berman, Rick, jt. auth. see Dillard, J. M.

Berman, Robert. Globali: Learn Geography with Amazing Associations. 3rd ed. 12p. 1996. write for info. (*0-9679067-0-9*) Globali Inter.

Berman, Robert, tr. see Andronikashvili, E. L.

Berman, Robert A. Fade In: The Screenwriting Process. 2nd rev. ed. LC 96-29509. 400p. 1997. 24.95 (*0-941188-58-2*, 30rls) M Wiese.

Berman, Robert M. More Than Survival: One Man's Plan to Move Mississippi Forward. LC 88-90829. 256p. (Orig.). 1988. pap. 9.95 (*0-937552-25-9*, QRP Bks) Quail Ridge.

Berman, Robert P. Soviet Air Power in Transition. LC 77-86493. (Studies in Defense Policy). 82p. 1978. pap. 7.95 (*0-8157-0923-4*) Brookings.

Berman, Robert P. & Baker, John C. Soviet Strategic Forces: Requirements & Responses. LC 82-70889. (Studies in Defense Policy). 171p. 1982. 26.95 (*0-8157-0926-9*); pap. 9.95 (*0-8157-0925-0*) Brookings.

Berman, Ronald. Advertising & Social Change. LC 81-14326. (Sage Commtext Ser.: No. 8). 159p. 1981. reprint ed. pap. 49.30 (*0-608-01082-0*, 205939100001) Bks Demand.

An Asterisk (*) at the beginning of an entry indicates that the title is appearing for the first time.

— Culture & Politics. 182p. (C). 1984. lib. bdg. 30.00 (*0-8191-3706-5*) U Pr of Amer.

***Berman, Ronald.** Fitzgerald, Hemingway & the Twenties. 2000. 29.95 (*0-8173-1057-6*) U of Ala Pr.

Berman, Ronald. The Great Gatsby & Fitzgerald's World of Ideas. LC 96-45287. 264p. 1997. text 29.95 (*0-8173-0869-5*) U of Ala Pr.

— The Great Gatsby & Modern Times. LC 93-10601. 176p. 1994. text 24.95 (*0-252-02045-6*) U of Ill Pr.

— The Great Gatsby & Modern Times. 208p. 1996. 12.95 (*0-252-06589-1*) U of Ill Pr.

Berman, Ronald, ed. Solzhenitsyn at Harvard: The Address, Twelve Early Responses, & Six Later Reflections. LC 79-26033. 160p. 1980. pap. 9.95 (*0-89633-023-0*) Ethics & Public Policy.

Berman, Ronald, jt. ed. see Smith, Ralph A.

Berman, Russell. Paul von Hindenburg. (World Leaders Past & Present Ser.). (Illus.). 120p. (YA). (gr. 5 up). 1987. lib. bdg. 19.95 (*0-87754-532-4*) Chelsea Hse.

Berman, Russell A. Between Fontane & Tucholsky: Literary Criticism & the Public Sphere in Imperial Germany. LC 83-9371. (New York University Ottendorfer Ser.: Vol. 17). 176p. (Orig.). (C). 1983. pap. text 18.40 (*0-8204-0012-2*) P Lang Pubng.

— Cultural Studies of Modern Germany: History, Representation, & Nationhood. LC 93-9987. 240p. (Orig.). (C). 1993. pap. 16.95 (*0-299-14014-8*) U of Wis Pr.

— Enlightenment or Empire: Colonial Discourse in German Culture. LC 97-32628. (Modern German Culture & Literature Ser.). xi, 272p. 1998. text 50.00 (*0-8032-1284-4*) U of Nebr Pr.

— Modern Culture & Critical Theory: Art, Politics, & the Legacy of the Frankfurt School. LC 89-40249. 286p. (Orig.). (C). 1989. pap. text 18.95 (*0-299-12084-8*) U of Wis Pr.

— The Rise of the Modern German Novel: Crisis & Charisma. LC 85-24770. (Central Asian Studies). 352p. 1986. 43.00 (*0-674-77165-6*) HUP.

Berman, Ruth. American Bison. (Nature Watch Bks.). (Illus.). (J). (gr. 2-5). 1992. lib. bdg. 19.93 (*0-87614-697-3*, Carolrhoda) Lerner Pub.

— Ants. LC 95-15123. (Early Bird Nature Bks.). (Illus.). (J). (gr. 1-3). 1996. lib. bdg. 19.93 (*0-8225-3012-0*, Lerner Publctns) Lerner Pub.

— Climbing Tree Frogs. LC 98-2679. (Pull Ahead Bks.). (Illus.). (J). 1998. pap. 5.95 (*0-8225-3611-0*) Lerner Pub.

— Climbing Tree Frogs. LC 98-2679. (Pull Ahead Bks.). (Illus.). (J). (gr. k-2). 1998. 19.93 (*0-8225-3605-6*) Lerner Pub.

— My Pet Dog. LC 98-50709. (All about Pets Ser.). (Illus.). 64p. (J). (gr. 3-6). 2000. 22.60 (*0-8225-2259-4*, Lerner Publctns) Lerner Pub.

— Peacocks. LC 95-12204. (Early Bird Nature Bks.). (Illus.). 47p. (J). (gr. 2-5). 1996. lib. bdg. 19.95 (*0-8225-3009-0*, Lerner Publctns) Lerner Pub.

— Sharks. LC 94-21468. (Illus.). 48p. (J). Date not set. pap. 7.95 (*0-87614-897-6*, Carolrhoda) Lerner Pub.

— Sharks. LC 94-21468. (Nature Watch Bks.). (Illus.). 47p. (J). (gr. 3-5). 1995. lib. bdg. 14.95 (*0-87614-870-4*, Carolrhoda) Lerner Pub.

— Spinning Spiders. LC 98-3348. (Pull Ahead Books Ser.). (J). 1998. pap. 5.95 (*0-8225-3610-2*) Lerner Pub.

— Spinning Spiders. LC 98-3348. (Pull Ahead Books Ser.). (J). (gr. k-2). 1998. 19.93 (*0-8225-3604-8*) Lerner Pub.

— Squeaking Bats. LC 97-38702. (Pull Ahead Bks.). (J). 1998. pap. 5.95 (*0-8225-3608-0*) Lerner Pub.

— Squeaking Bats. LC 97-38702. (Pull Ahead Bks.). (J). (gr. k-2). 1998. lib. bdg. 21.27 (*0-8225-3602-1*) Lerner Pub.

— Watchful Wolves. LC 97-38027. (Pull Ahead Bks.). (Illus.). (J). 1998. pap. 5.95 (*0-8225-3606-4*) Lerner Pub.

— Watchful Wolves. LC 97-38027. (Pull Ahead Bks.). (Illus.). 32p. (J). (ps-2). 1998. lib. bdg. 21.27 (*0-8225-3600-5*) Lerner Pub.

***Berman, Ruth, ed.** Guys & Their Dogs. LC 99-37646. (Illus.). 80p. 1999. 18.95 (*1-889540-45-5*) Bowtie Press.

Berman, Ruth & Litoff, Judy B. Dear Poppa: The World War II Berman Family Letters. LC 97-6447. 317p. 1997. 29.95 (*0-87351-357-6*); pap. 15.95 (*0-87351-358-4*) Minn Hist.

Berman, Ruth & Nature's Images Staff. Buzzing Rattlesnakes. LC 97-46564. (Pull Ahead Bks.). (J). 1998. pap. 5.95 (*0-8225-3609-9*) Lerner Pub.

***Berman, Ruth & Nature's Images Staff.** Buzzing Rattlesnakes. LC 97-46564. (Pull Ahead Bks.). (Illus.). 32p. (J). (gr. k-2). 1998. 21.27 (*0-8225-3603-X*) Lerner Pub.

Berman, Ruth & Stone, Lynn M. Fishing Bears. LC 97-38112. 1998. pap. 5.95 (*0-8225-3607-2*) Lerner Pub.

— Fishing Bears. LC 97-38112. (Illus.). 32p. (J). (ps-2). 1998. lib. bdg. 21.27 (*0-8225-3601-3*) Lerner Pub.

Berman, Ruth A. & Slobin, Dan I. Relating Events in Narrative: A Crosslinguistic Developmental Study. LC 93-39190. 768p. 1994. text 125.00 (*0-8058-1435-3*) L Erlbaum Assocs.

Berman, S. D., et al, trs. Thirteen Papers Translated from the Russian. LC 89-15010. (Translations Ser.: Series 2, Vol. 144). 140p. 1989. 70.00 (*0-8218-3125-9*, TRANS2/144) Am Math.

Berman, S. D., et al. Nine Papers on Logic & Group Theory. LC 51-5559. (Translations Ser.: Series 2, Vol. 64). 256p. 1967. 47.00 (*0-8218-1764-7*, TRANS2/64) Am Math.

Berman, Sabina. Bubbeh. Labinger, Andrea G., tr. from SPA. LC 98-5560. (Discoveries Ser.). 96p. 1998. pap. 12.95 (*0-935480-93-5*) Lat Am Lit Rev Pr.

Berman, Salee & Berman, Victor. The Birth Center: An Approach to the Birth Experience. 1985. 17.45 (*0-671-60733-2*) S&S Trade.

Berman, Sally. Catch Them Thinking in Science: A Handbook of Classroom Strategies. LC 93-78421. (Illus.). 110p. (Orig.). 1993. pap. 26.95 (*0-932935-55-9*) SkyLght.

— Making Choice Theory Work in the Quality Classroom. 110p. 1997. pap. 25.95 (*1-57517-040-X*) SkyLght.

— A Multiple Intelligences Road to a Quality Classroom. LC 95-79276. (Illus.). 104p. (Orig.). 1995. pap. 24.95 (*1-57517-005-1*, 1346) SkyLght.

— Project Learning for the Multiple Intelligences Classroom. LC 97-77116. 159p. 1997. pap. 32.95 (*1-57517-077-9*) SkyLght.

***Berman, Sally & Schumer, Sue.** Service Learning for the Multiple Intelligences Classroom. LC 98-61155. xi, 186 p. 1999. write for info. (*1-57517-120-1*) SkyLght.

Berman, Sanford. How to Lessen Misunderstandings. LC 72-75525. 29p. 1972. pap. text 5.95 (*0-918970-12-1*) Intl Gen Semantics.

— Prejudices & Antipathies: A Tract on the LC Subject Heads Concerning People. LC 92-50944. 229p. 1993. pap. 24.95 (*0-89950-828-6*) McFarland & Co.

— Understanding & Being Understood. LC 72-75526. 77p. 1972. pap. text 9.95 (*0-918970-13-X*) Intl Gen Semantics.

Berman, Sanford, ed. Subject Cataloging: Critiques & Innovations. LC 84-10554. (Technical Services Quarterly Ser.: Vol. 2, Nos. 1-2ca). 224p. 1985. text 49.95 (*0-86656-265-6*) Haworth Pr.

Berman, Sanford & Danky, James P. Alternative Library Literature, 1996/1997: A Biennial Anthology. (Illus.). 280p. 1998. pap. 35.00 (*0-7864-0493-0*) McFarland & Co.

Berman, Sanford & Danky, James P., eds. Alternative Library Literature, 1992-1993: A Biennial Anthology. LC 84-646841. (Illus.). 383p. 1994. pap. 35.00 (*0-89950-970-3*) McFarland & Co.

Berman, Sanford & Danky, James P., eds. Alternative Library Literature, 1994-1995: A Biennial Anthology. LC 84-646841. (Illus.). 333p. 1996. pap. 35.00 (*0-7864-0239-3*) McFarland & Co.

Berman, Sanford I., ed. Logic & General Semantics: Writings of Oliver L. Reiser & Others. LC 88-83271. 1989. 42.95 (*0-685-54382-X*); pap. 19.95 (*0-918970-36-9*) Intl Gen Semantics.

Berman, Sanford I., ed. see Lee, Irving J.

Berman, Saul, ed. see Shak, Nieson N.

Berman, Scot A. Learning Talmud: A Guide to Talmud Terminology & Rashi Commentary. LC 96-39697. 1997. pap. 25.00 (*0-7657-5958-6*) Aronson.

Berman, Scott, et al, eds. Comprehensive Textbook of Vascular Access. (Illus.). 300p. 2000. text 85.00 (*1-57626-000-3*) Quality Med Pub.

Berman, Sheldon. Children's Social Consciousness & the Development of Social Responsibility. LC 96-14444. (SUNY Series, Democracy & Education). 254p. (C). 1997. text 54.50 (*0-7914-3197-5*); pap. text 19.95 (*0-7914-3198-3*) State U NY Pr.

— Investing with Pentablocks. 1997. pap. text 10.95 (*1-57452-023-7*) Cuisenaire.

— Making History: A Social Studies Curriculum in the Participation Series. 90p. (Orig.). 1984. pap. 19.00 (*0-614-18084-8*) Eductrs Soc Respons.

— Teaching Mathematics with Pentablocks. 112p. 1997. pap. text 12.95 (*1-57452-024-5*) Cuisenaire.

Berman, Sheldon & LaFarge, Phyllis, eds. Promising Practices in Teaching Social Responsibility. LC 92-11632. (SUNY Series, Democracy & Education). 267p. (C). 1993. text 64.50 (*0-7914-1397-7*) State U NY Pr.

Berman, Sheldon, jt. ed. see La Farge, Phyllis.

Berman, Sheri. Social Democratic Moment: Ideas & Politics in the Making of Interwar Europe. 320p. 1999. text 45.00 (*0-674-44261-X*) HUP.

Berman, Sonia. The Crossing - Adano to Catonsville: Leland Hayward's Producing Career. LC 94-2325. (Illus.). 338p. 1995. 60.50 (*0-8108-2848-0*) Scarecrow.

Berman, Stephen. On the Semantics of Wh-Clauses. LC 93-46330. 200p. 1994. text 15.00 (*0-8153-1742-5*) Garland.

— Pediatric Decision Making. 3rd ed. (Illus.). 704p. (C). (gr. 13). 1996. text 76.95 (*0-8151-0715-3*, 27677) Mosby Inc.

Berman, Steve W. A Tarnished Hero: A Sam Sharpstein Novel. LC 87-92175. 1989. 17.95 (*0-87212-214-X*) Libra.

Berman, Susan. Fly Away Home. 1996. mass mkt. 5.99 (*0-380-78179-4*, Avon Bks) Morrow Avon.

— Lady Las Vegas: The Inside Story Behind America's Neon Oasis. (Illus.). 224p. 1997. 29.95 (*1-57500-020-2*, Pub. by TV Bks) HarpC.

***Berman, Susan.** Lady Las Vegas: The Inside Story Behind America's Neon Oasis. (Illus.). 223p. 2000. reprint ed. text 30.00 (*0-7881-9265-5*) DIANE Pub.

Berman, Susan. Spiderweb. 320p. 1997. mass mkt. 5.99 (*0-380-78180-8*, Avon Bks) Morrow Avon.

Berman, T., et al, eds. The Daily Growth Cycle of Phytoplankton: Proceedings of the Fifth International Workshop of the Group for Aquatic Primary Productivity, Held at Breukelen, The Netherlands, 20-28 April 1990. LC 92-24985. (Developments in Hydrobiology Ser.: No. 76). 210p. (C). 1992. text 189.00 (*0-7923-1907-9*) Kluwer Academic.

Berman, Tom, jt. ed. see Witzel, Karl-Paul.

Berman, Victor, jt. auth. see Berman, Salee.

Berman, Wallace, contrib. by. Wallace Berman: A Retrospective. LC 78-70599. (Illus.). 118p. 1978. pap. 22.50 (*0-911291-03-2*, Pub. by Fellows Cont Art) RAM Publications.

Berman, William. How to Dissect. 240p. (Orig.). 1985. per. 12.00 (*0-671-76342-3*) S&S Trade Pap.

Berman, William C. America's Right Turn: From Nixon to Bush. LC 93-38003. (American Moment Ser.). 1994. pap. 14.95 (*0-8018-4826-1*); text 38.95 (*0-8018-4825-3*) Johns Hopkins.

— America's Right Turn: From Nixon to Clinton. 2nd ed. LC 97-43685. (The American Moment Ser.). 232p. 1998. text 38.95 (*0-8018-5871-2*); pap. text 14.95 (*0-8018-5872-0*) Johns Hopkins.

— The Politics of Civil Rights in the Truman Administration. LC 70-114736. 273p. 1970. reprint ed. pap. 84.70 (*0-608-04445-8*, 206497700012) Bks Demand.

— William Fulbright & the Vietnam War. LC 87-22500. 245p. reprint ed. pap. 76.00 (*0-608-10525-2*, 207114500009) Bks Demand.

Berman, William H., jt. ed. see Austad, Carol S.

Berman, William H., jt. ed. see Sperling, Michael B.

Berman, Yaakov. Teen Health the Natural Way: How to Successfully Control:Acne, Obesity, Allergies, PMS, & More. (Illus.). 176p. (YA). (gr. 7-11). 1995. pap. 10.95 (*0-943706-52-1*) Pitspopany.

Berman, Yitzhak, jt. auth. see Phillips, David.

Bermann, C., et al, eds. Biomechanics: Basic & Applied Research. (Developments in Biomechanics Ser.). (C). 1987. text 417.00 (*0-89838-961-5*) Kluwer Academic.

Bermann, Diane E., jt. auth. see Kovich, Karen M.

Bermann, Eric. Scapegoat: The Impact of Death-Fear on an American Family. LC 73-80573. 371p. 1973. reprint ed. pap. 115.10 (*0-7837-4712-8*, 205906400003) Bks Demand.

Bermann, George A. European Community Law: Selected Documents: Including European Union Materials, 1998 Edition LC 97-225126. (American Casebook Ser.). ix, 734 p. 1997. pap. 28.00 (*0-314-22808-X*) West Pub.

Bermann, George A., et al. Cases & Materials on European Community Law. (American Casebook Ser.). 1218p. (C). 1993. 16.00 (*0-314-06628-4*) West Pub.

— Course Materials on the Law of European Economic Community. (American Casebook Ser.). 1200p. (C). 1993. 68.50 (*0-314-01170-6*) West Pub.

— European Community Law: Selected Documents. (American Casebook Ser.). 687p. 1993. pap. 22.00 (*0-314-01529-9*) West Pub.

— European Economic Community Law Cases & Materials. large type ed. (American Casebook Ser.). 400p. (C). 1998. pap. 20.50 (*0-314-22853-5*) West Pub.

Bermann, Georgina. Estimation & Inference in Bivariate & Multivariate Ordinal Probit Models. 138p. (Orig.). 1993. pap. 36.00 (*91-554-3162-3*) Coronet Bks.

Bermann, Karl. Under the Big Stick: Nicaragua & the United States since 1848. LC 86-1767. 339p. (Orig.). 1986. pap. 12.00 (*0-89608-323-3*); boxed set 25.00 (*0-89608-324-1*) Compita Pub.

Bermann, Karl, ed. & tr. see Sandino, Augusto C., et al.

Bermann, Marc. Lukurmata: Household Archaeology in Prehispanic Bolivia. LC 93-23366. 328p. 1994. text 65.00 (*0-691-03359-5*, Pub. by Princeton U Pr) Cal Prin Full Svc.

Bermann, Richard A. Home from the Sea: Robert Louis Stevenson in Samoa. Hapgood, Elizabeth, tr. from GER. 288p. 1987. reprint ed. mass mkt. 5.95 (*0-935180-29-X*) Mutual Pub HI.

— The Mahdi of Allah: The Story of the Dervish, Mohammed Ahmed. John, Robin, tr. LC 80-1935. reprint ed. 36.00 (*0-404-18955-5*) AMS Pr.

Bermann, Sandra, tr. see Manzoni, Alessandro.

Bermann, Sandra L. The Sonnet over Time: A Study in the Sonnets of Petrarch, Shakespeare, & Baudelaire. LC 87-87220. (Studies in Comparative Literature: No. 63). ix, 174p. (C). 1988. 37.50 (*0-8078-7063-3*) U of NC Pr.

Bermant, A. & Brown, D. Course of Mathematical Analysis, Pt. 1. LC 62-9695. (International Series of Monographs on Pure & Applied Mathematics: Vol. 44). 1963. 225.00 (*0-08-010013-9*, Pub. by Pergamon Repr) Franklin.

— Course of Mathematical Analysis, Pt. II. LC 62-9695. (On Pure & Applied Mathematics Ser.). 1963. 174.00 (*0-08-009817-7*, Pub. by Pergamon Repr) Franklin.

Bermant, A. & Sneddon, Ian N. Course of Mathematical Analysis, Pt. 1. LC 62-9695. (International Series of Monographs on Pure & Applied Mathematics: No. 44). 1963. 225.00 (*0-08-013471-8*, Pub. by Pergamon Repr) Franklin.

***Bermant, Chaim.** Genesis: A Latvian Childhood. (Illus.). 188p. 1999. text 28.95 (*1-86105-175-1*) Robson.

Bermant, Charles. Planning & Managing Effective E-Mail Applications. LC 95-50848. 214p. 1996. pap. 265.00 (*1-56607-960-8*) Comput Tech Res.

— 32-Bit Operating Systems: Upgrading the Desktop. LC 95-2241. (Illus.). 170p. 1995. pap. 275.00 (*1-56607-043-0*) Comput Tech Res.

— Windows 95 Migration Strategies. LC 95-35591. (Illus.). 180p. 1995. pap. 260.00 (*1-56607-957-8*) Comput Tech Res.

Bermant, Gordon, et al. Chapter 11 Venue Choices by Large Public Companies: Report to the Committee on the Administration of the Bankruptcy System. (Illus.). 72p. (C). 1999. pap. text 20.00 (*0-7881-4363-8*) DIANE Pub.

***Bermbudez-Otero, Ricardo.** Generative Theory & Corpus Studies: A Dialogue from 10 I CEHL. LC 00-30389. (Topics in English Linguistics Ser.). 2000. write for info. (*3-11-016687-9*) Mouton.

Berme, Necip, et al, eds. Biomechanics of Normal & Pathological Human Articulating Joints. (NATO Advanced Science Institutes Series C: Mathematical & Physical Sciences). 1985. text 184.00 (*90-247-3164-X*) Kluwer Academic.

Bermejo, Ana, tr. see Vasquez, Juan J., ed.

Bermejo, F. J., jt. ed. see Pesquera, L.

Bermel, Derek. Carnaval Noir Piano Solo. 8p. 1997. pap. 4.95 (*0-7935-8923-1*) H Leonard.

Bermel, Albert. Comic Agony: Mixed Impressions in the Modern Theater. 223p. 1993. 35.00 (*0-8101-1071-7*) Northwestern U Pr.

— Comic Agony: Mixed Impressions in the Modern Theatre. 223p. 1996. pap. text 15.95 (*0-8101-1410-0*) Northwestern U Pr.

— Contradictory Characters: An Interpretation of the Modern Theatre. LC 96-4838. (Illus.). 298p. 1996. reprint ed. pap. 15.95 (*0-8101-1441-0*) Northwestern U Pr.

— Farce: A History from Aristophanes to Woody Allen. LC 89-21846. 464p. (C). 1990. pap. 21.95 (*0-8093-1645-5*) S Ill U Pr.

— Moliere's Theatrical Bounty: A New View of the Plays. LC 89-5982. (Illus.). 300p. (C). 1990. 36.95 (*0-8093-1550-5*); pap. 21.95 (*0-8093-1551-3*) S Ill U Pr.

***Bermel, Albert.** Shakespeare at the Moment: Playing the Comedies. LC 99-44251. 342p. 2000. pap. 21.95 (*0-325-00205-3*) Heinemann.

— Shakespeare at the Moment: Playing the Comedies as they Happen. LC 99-44251. 2000. text 40.00 (*0-325-00206-1*) Heinemann.

Bermel, Albert, ed. from FRE. A Dozen French Farces from the 15th to the 20th Centuries. LC 97-3325. 416p. (Orig.). 1997. pap. 18.95 (*0-87910-092-3*) Limelight Edns.

Bermel, Albert, ed. & tr. see Gozzi, Carlo.

Bermel, Albert, tr. see Moliere.

Bermel, Albert, tr. & intro. see Moliere.

Bermel, Neil. Context & the Lexicon in the Development of Russian Aspect. LC 97-18525. (University of California Publications in Linguistics). 1997. pap. 50.00 (*0-520-09812-9*, Pub. by U CA Pr) Cal Prin Full Svc.

Bermel, Neil, tr. see Fischerova, Daniela.

Bermel, Neil, tr. see Kohout, Pavel.

Bermelin, I. & Wolter, A. The New Parakeet Handbook. 1986. pap. 9.95 (*0-8120-2985-2*) Barron.

Bermeo, Nancy, ed. Liberalization & Democratization: Change in the Soviet Union & Eastern Europe. 200p. 1992. pap. text 14.95 (*0-8018-4418-5*) Johns Hopkins.

***Bermeo, Nancy & Nord, Philip, eds.** Civil Society Before Democracy: Lessons from Nineteenth-Century Europe. 320p. 2000. 69.00 (*0-8476-9549-2*) Rowman.

— Civil Society Before Democracy: Lessons from Nineteenth-Century Europe. 320p. 2000. pap. 26.95 (*0-8476-9550-6*) Rowman.

***Bermeo, Nancy G., ed.** Unemployment in Southern Europe. LC 99-58701. 264p. 2000. 57.50 (*0-7146-4935-X*, Pub. by F Cass Pubs); pap. 24.50 (*0-7146-4495-1*, Pub. by F Cass Pubs) Intl Spec Bk.

Bermerjo, Luis M. Towards Christian Reunion: Vatican I: Obstacles & Opportunities. 320p. 1987. reprint ed. pap. text 27.00 (*0-8191-6474-7*) U Pr of Amer.

***Bermingham, Alan, et al.** Multiskilling for Television Production. 368p. 2000. pap. 56.95 (*0-240-51557-9*, Focal) Buttrwrth-Heinemann.

Bermingham, Alan, et al. The Video Studio: A Media Manual. 3rd rev. ed. LC 94-3408. (Media Manuals Ser.). 192p. 1994. pap. 29.95 (*0-240-51392-4*, Focal) Buttrwrth-Heinemann.

Bermingham, Ann. Landscape & Ideology: The English Rustic Tradition, 1740-1860. LC 85-24509. (Illus.). 400p. 1986. 60.00 (*0-520-05287-0*, Pub. by U CA Pr) Cal Prin Full Svc.

***Bermingham, Ann.** Learning to Draw: Studies in the Cultural History of a Polite & Useful Art. LC 99-59794. (Illus.). 304p. 2000. 75.00 (*0-300-08039-5*) Yale U Pr.

Bermingham, Ann & Brewer, John, eds. Consumption of Culture, 1600-1800: Image Object Text. (Consumption & Culture in the 17th & 18th Century Ser.). (Illus.). 660p. (C). 1997. pap. 55.00 (*0-415-15997-0*) Routledge.

Bermingham, Peter. American Art in the Barbizon Mood. LC 74-26664. (Illus.). 192p. reprint ed. pap. 59.60 (*0-8357-5354-9*, 201137200075) Bks Demand.

— Tucson's Early Moderns, 1945-1965. LC 98-61210. 1998. write for info. (*1-891800-08-6*) U of Ariz Pr.

Bermingham, Peter, jt. auth. see National Museum of American Art Staff.

Bermond, J. C. & Raynal, Michel, eds. Distributed Algorithms. (Lecture Notes in Computer Science Ser.: Vol. 392). vi, 315p. 1989. 40.00 (*0-387-51687-5*, 3543) Spr-Verlag.

Bermont, Hubert. How to Become a Successful Consultant in Your Own Field. 3rd ed. 224p. 1995. pap. 12.95 (*1-55958-695-8*) Prima Pub.

— How to Become a Successful Consultant in Your Own Field. 3rd ed. 224p. 2000. pap. 14.00 (*0-7615-1100-8*) Prima Pub.

— How to Become a Successful Consultant in Your Own Field. 3rd enl. rev. ed. 232p. 1991. 21.95 (*1-55958-119-0*) Prima Pub.

Bermont, John. How to Europe: The Complete Travelers Handbook. 2nd ed. LC 85-124822. (Illus.). 502p. 1987. pap. 9.95 (*0-940792-41-9*) Murphy & Broad.

— How to Europe: The Complete Traveler's Handbook. 3rd ed. 1992. pap. 17.95 (*0-940792-60-5*) Murphy & Broad.

Bermudez, A., ed. Optimal Control of Systems Governed by Partial Differential Equations. (Lecture Notes in Control & Information Sciences: Vol. 114). (Illus.). 331p. 1989. 71.95 (*0-387-50495-8*) Spr-Verlag.

Bermudez, Andrea B. Doing Our Homework: How Schools Can Engage Hispanic Communities. LC 94-21398. 92p. (Orig.). 1993. pap. 12.00 (*1-880785-11-0*) ERIC-CRESS.

— Influence of the Institution of Free Learning on Spanish Education. LC 76-51193. (Coleccion de Estudios Hispanicos - Hispanic Studies Collection). 1978. pap. 10.00 (*0-89729-190-5*) Ediciones.

Bermudez, Fernando. Death & Resurrection in Guatemala. Barr, Robert R., tr. from SPA. LC 85-48305.Tr. of Cristo Muere y Resucita en Guatemala. 96p. (Orig.). reprint ed. pap. 30.00 (*0-8357-2667-3*, 204020300015) Bks Demand.

B

An Asterisk (*) at the beginning of an entry indicates that the title is appearing for the first time.

Bermudez-Gallegos, Marta. Poder y transgresion: Peru, Metafora e Historia. (SPA.). 196p. (Orig.). 1996. pap. text 26.00 (*0-9640795-5-0*) Latinoam Edit.

— Poesia, Sociedad y Cultura: Dialogos y Retratos Del Peru Colonial. 189p. 49.50 (*0-916379-99-X*) Scripta.

Bermudez, Jose L. The Paradox of Self-Consciousness. LC 97-40757. (Representation & Mind Ser.). (Illus.). 236p. 1998. 30.00 (*0-262-02441-1*, Bradford Bks) MIT Pr.

Bermudez, Jose L., et al, eds. The Body & the Self. LC 94-33975. 1995. 40.00 (*0-262-02386-5*, Bradford Bks) MIT Pr.

— The Body & the Self. (Illus.). 384p. 1998. reprint ed. pap. text 19.50 (*0-262-52248-9*, Bradford Bks) MIT Pr.

***Bermudez, Jose Luis.** The Paradox of Self-Consciousness. LC 97-40757. (Representation & Mind Ser.). (Illus.). 360p. 2000. reprint ed. pap. 18.00 (*0-262-52277-2*) MIT Pr.

***Bermudez, Joseph.** Armed Forces for North Korea. 2000. text. write for info. (*1-86064-500-3*, Pub. by I B T) St Martin.

***Bermudez, Joseph S., Jr.** The Armed Forces of North Korea. 1999. text 22.50 (*1-86064-486-4*, Pub. by I B T) St Martin.

Bermudez, Joseph S., Jr. North Korean Special Forces. 2nd ed. LC 97-36345. (Special Warfare Ser.). (Illus.). 320p. 1997. 39.95 (*1-55750-066-5*) Naval Inst Pr.

Bermudez, Manuel, jt. auth. see King, Kim.

Bermudez, Maria T. Mexican Family Favorites Cook Book. LC 83-11692. 144p. 1983. ring bd. 6.95 (*0-914846-17-5*) Golden West Pub.

***Bermudez-Onopa, R. David.** The Foam Ship LC 99-164804. 92p. 1998. write for info. (*1-881713-50-4*) Pubns Puertorriquenas.

Bermudez, Pedro R. & Cruz, Barbara C. Latin America & the Caribbean from a Global Perspective: A Resource Guide for Teachers. 174p. (C). 1991. teacher ed., ring bd. 21.00 (*1-879862-00-X*) FL Intl U Latin.

Bern, Annie. The Lonesome Run. 192p. 1998. pap. 15.95 (*1-58244-006-9*) Rutledge Bks.

Bern, Arthur La, see La Bern, Arthur.

Bern, Jay. A Long Way. LC 98-65641. 310p. 1998. pap. 18.95 (*1-57197-121-1*) Pentland Pr.

Bern, Murray M. & Frigoletto, Fredric D., eds. Hematologic Disorders in Maternal-Fetal Medicine. LC 89-12460. 706p. 1990. 329.95 (*0-471-56213-0*) Wiley.

Bern, Ron & Luftglass, Manny. Gone Fishin' The 100 Best Spots in New York. LC 99-25679. (Illus.). 176p. 1999. pap. 16.00 (*0-8135-2745-7*) Rutgers U Pr.

Bern, Ron, jt. auth. see Luftglass, Manny.

***Berna, G. A.** Frapcon-3: Computer Code for Calculation of Steady-state, Thermal-Mechanical Behavior of Oxide Fuel Rods for High Burnup. 118p. 1998. per. 9.50 (*0-16-062883-0*) USGPO.

Berna, Henri. Dictionnaire Technique et Administratif de la Navigation Interieure. (FRE.). 393p. 1977. 125.00 (*0-8288-5395-9*, M6030) Fr & Eur.

Bernabe, ed. Poetarum Epicorum Graecorum, Pt. I. rev. ed. (GRE.). 1996. 69.50 (*3-8154-1706-6*, T1706, Pub. by B G Teubner) U of Mich Pr.

Bernabe, Albertus, ed. Nicandrus: Nicandri Colophonii Carminum Index et Concordantia. write for info. (*0-318-71954-1*) G Olms Pubs.

— Orphei Hymni - Orphei Hymnorum Concordantia. (Alpha-Omega, Reihe A Ser.: Bd. LXXXIV). (GER.). 184p. 1988. 55.00 (*3-487-07872-4*) G Olms Pubs.

Bernabe, Albertus, ed. see Nicandrus.

Bernabe, Emma, et al. Ilokano Lessons. McKaughan, Howard P., ed. LC 76-152459. (PALI Language Texts: Philippines Ser.). 471p. reprint ed. pap. 146.10 (*0-8357-9823-2*, 201721500004) Bks Demand.

Bernabe, Jan, jt. ed. see Dubin, Cindy.

Bernabe, Jan, jt. ed. see Schaeffer, Mary S.

Bernabe, Jan C., jt. ed. see Horner, Chris.

Bernabe, Jan C., ed. see Schaeffer, Mary L.

Bernabe, Jan Christian, ed. see Henry, Sherrye.

Bernabe, Jan Christian, ed. see Isom-Rodiguez, Lisa.

Bernabe, Rafael. Respuestas Al Colonialismo en la Politica Puertorriquena, 1899-1929. LC 96-85393. 320p. 1996. pap. 12.25 (*0-929157-40-0*) Ediciones Huracan.

Bernabei, R. & Tao, C. The Dark Side of the Universe - Experimental Efforts & Theoretical Framework: Proceedings of the International Workshop. 316p. 1994. text 95.00 (*981-02-1600-9*) World Scientific Pub.

Bernabei, R. W., jt. ed. see Bernabei, S.

Bernabei, S. & Bernabei, R. W., eds. Applications of Radio-Frequency Power to Plasmas: Seventh Topical Conference. LC 87-71812. (Conference Proceeding Ser.: No. 159). 496p. 1987. lib. bdg. 70.00 (*0-88318-359-5*) Am Inst Physics.

***Bernabei, Stefano & Paoletti, Franco, eds.** Radio Frequency Power in Plasmas: 13th Topical Conference. (Conference Proceedings Ser.: Vol. 485). (Illus.). 516p. 1999. 125.00 (*1-56396-861-4*, Pub. by Am Inst Physics) Spr-Verlag.

Bernabeu, J., et al, eds. CP Non-Conservation & B Physics. 360p. (C). 1989. text 113.00 (*9971-5-0747-1*) World Scientific Pub.

Bernabo, Lawrance M., jt. ed. see Lucaites, John L.

Bernabo, M. & Picchi, Fernando. Grande Dizionario di Marina: Inglese-Italiano, Italiano-Inglese. (ENG & ITA.). 963p. 1970. 125.00 (*0-8288-6538-8*, M9298) Fr & Eur.

***Bernabo, Massimo.** Pseudepigraphical Images in Early Art, Vol. 6. (Dead Sea Scrolls & Christian Origins Library). (Illus.). 1999. pap. text. write for info. (*0-941037-85-1*) D & F Scott.

Bernacca, Pier L., ed. see Ruffini, Remo.

Bernacchi, Louis, ed. To the South Polar Regions. 346p. 1998. pap. 210.00 (*1-85297-035-9*, Pub. by Archival Facs) St Mut.

Bernacchi, Richard L. Chapter Fourteen '91. rev. ed. 1991. 60.00 (*0-316-09252-5*, Aspen Law & Bus) Aspen Pub.

— Computer Law, 2 vols., 1. 1986. 165.00 (*0-316-09201-0*, Aspen Law & Bus) Aspen Pub.

— Computer Law, 2 vols., 2. 1986. 165.00 (*0-316-09202-9*, Aspen Law & Bus) Aspen Pub.

Bernacchi, Richard L., et al. Bernacchi on Computer Law: A Guide to the Legal & Management Aspects of Computer Technology, 2 vols. 1056p. 1986. 295.00 (*0-316-09203-7*, Aspen Law & Bus) Aspen Pub.

Bernache, Carolyn. Gateway to Achievement in the Content Areas: Essential Language, Concepts, & Skills. 1994. pap., teacher ed. 21.12 (*0-8442-0719-5*); pap., student ed. 9.47 (*0-8442-0718-7*) NTC Contemp Pub Co.

Bernacki, Ludwik. T. Dramat i Muzyka za Stanislawa Augusta, 2 vols., Set. (Illus.). reprint ed. 150.00 (*0-318-23359-2*) Szwede Slavic.

Bernacsek, G. M., jt. auth. see Bossche, J. P.

***Bernad, Denes.** Rumanian Air Force: The Prime Decade, 1938-1947. (Foreign Air Forces Ser.: Vol. 6080). (Illus.). 80p. 1999. pap. 11.95 (*0-89747-402-3*) Squad Sig Pubns.

Bernad, Miguel A. The Inverted Pyramid & Other "Political" Reflections. vii, 82p. (Orig.). (C). 1992. pap. 7.50 (*971-10-0454-2*, Pub. by New Day Pub) Cellar.

Bernad, Peter G. Closed-Head Injury: A Clinical Source Book. 400p. 1994. 95.00 (*1-55834-155-2*, 60573-10, MICHIE) LEXIS Pub.

— Closed-Head Injury: A Clinical Source Book. 2nd ed. LC 98-86445. 475p. 1998. 100.00 (*0-327-00276-X*, 6057311) LEXIS Pub.

***Bernad, Peter G.** Closed-Head Injury: A Clinical Source Book, 1999 Supplement, Pocketpart. 63p. 1999. write for info. (*0-327-01667-1*, 6057412) LEXIS Pub.

Bernad, Peter G. Neurotoxicology: A Clinical Source Book. LC 98-85162. 1998. text 105.00 (*0-327-00132-1*, 66067-10) LEXIS Pub.

— Neurotoxicology: A Clinical Sourcebook, 1999 Supplement. 72p. 1999. write for info. (*0-327-01487-3*, 6606610) LEXIS Pub.

Bernadac, Marie-Laure. Louise Bourgeois. (Illus.). 192p. 1996. 35.00 (*2-08-013600-3*, Pub. by Flammarion) Abbeville Pr.

Bernadac, Marie-Laure & Du Bouchet, Paule. Picasso: Master of the New Idea. Lovelace, Carey, tr. (Discoveries Ser.). (Illus.). 200p. 1993. pap. 12.95 (*0-8109-2802-7*, Pub. by Abrams) Time Warner.

Bernadac, Marie-Laure, et al. Picasso Museum, Paris: The Masterpieces. 2nd ed. (Illus.). 224p. 1991. 45.00 (*3-7913-1118-2*, Pub. by Prestel) te Neues.

Bernadac, Marie-Laure, ed. see Bourgeois, Louise.

Bernaden, John A., jt. auth. see Williams, Anna F.

Bernades, P., jt. ed. see Roze, C.

***Bernadi, C., et al.** Spectral Methods for Axisymmetric Domains. (Series in Applied Mathmatics). 358p. 1999. pap. 71.00 (*2-84299-070-6*) ESME.

Bernadine. The Stealing. (C). 1993. pap. text 17.25 (*0-07-005154-2*) McGraw.

Bernading, Margaret B. Exploring Pragmatic Language: Games for Practice. (Illus.). 46p. 1991. 79.00 (*0-7616-7761-5*) Commun Skill.

Bernado, Jordi. Good News. (Illus.). 216p. 1999. 39.95 (*84-89698-98-8*) Actar.

Bernado, Jordi & Prat, Ramon, photos by. Berlin Bis. (Illus.). 200p. 1999. 25.00 (*84-89698-42-2*, 910681, Pub. by Actar) Dist Art Pubs.

Bernado, Jordi, ed. see Goldbeck, Eugene O.

Bernadot, Dan. Four Steps to Less Fat & Better Nutrition: A Rational Approach to Weight Loss. (Illus.). 127p. (Orig.). (YA). (gr. 9-12). 1983. pap. 6.95 (*0-936007-19-2*, 2550) Meridian Educ.

Bernadou, J. B., tr. see Makarov, S. O.

Bernadou, M. Finite Element Methods for Thin Shell Problems. 376p. 1996. 155.00 (*0-471-95647-3*) Wiley.

Bernahl, Susan, ed. see Hamilton, James.

Bernahl, Susan, ed. see Hamilton, James & Trantmann, Ted.

Bernal, Deborah, et al. Vital Signs: Working Doctors Tell the Real Story Behind Medical School & Practice. LC 94-28687. 219p. 1994. pap. 12.95 (*1-56079-376-7*) Petersons.

Bernal, Dick. America Spiritually Mapped. 173p. (Orig.). 1994. pap. 9.95 (*1-884920-02-0*) Jubilee Christian Ctr.

— Diary of a Reluctant Recruit. 182p. 1988. pap. 6.95 (*0-88144-127-9*) Christian Pub.

— Don't Stop, Go Ahead. Montgomery, Dan & Montgomery, Katie, eds. LC 98-127053. 240p. (Orig.). 1996. pap. text 10.00 (*1-884920-10-1*) Jubilee Christian Ctr.

— Kingdom Journey. Montgomery, Dan & Montgomery, Katie, eds. 174p. (Orig.). 1996. pap. 10.00 (*1-884920-06-3*) Jubilee Christian Ctr.

— Removing the "Ites" from Your Promised Land. 82p. (Orig.). 1995. pap. 5.95 (*1-884920-03-9*) Jubilee Christian Ctr.

— Storming Hell's Brazen Gates. 96p. 1988. pap. 4.95 (*0-88144-124-4*) Christian Pub.

— When Lucifer & Jezebel Join Your Church. 97p. (Orig.). 1994. pap. 6.95 (*1-884920-00-4*) Jubilee Christian Ctr.

Bernal, Dick & Kenoly, Ron. Lifting Him Up: How You Can Experience Spirit-Led Praise & Worship. LC 95-68302. 1995. pap. 8.99 (*0-88419-403-5*) Creation House.

Bernal, Dionisio, jt. auth. see Leet, Kenneth M.

Bernal, Guillermo & Rodriguez, Wanda C. Clasificacion Diagnostica en Puerto Rico. (SPA.). 68p. 1992. pap. write for info. (*0-929441-26-5*) Pubns Puertorriquenas.

Bernal, J. D. Science in History, 4 vols. Incl. Vol. 2. Scientific & Industrial Revolution. 1971. pap. text 16.50 (*0-262-52021-4*); 1971. Set pap. 40.00 (*0-262-52082-6*) MIT Pr.

Bernal, J. E. Human Immunogenetics: Principles & Clinical Applications. Roberts, D. F., tr. LC 86-5677. 220p. 1986. 99.95 (*0-85066-355-5*); pap. 44.95 (*0-85066-334-2*) Taylor & Francis.

Bernal, Luis L., ed. see Cho, David Y.

Bernal, Mairym Cruz, tr. see Varela, Maria Elena Cruz.

Bernal, Marie L., ed. see American Association of Law Libraries Staff.

Bernal, Martha E. & Knight, George P., eds. Ethnic Identity: Formation & Transmission among Hispanics & Other Minorities. LC 91-46990. (SUNY Series, United States Hispanic Studies). (Illus.). 331p. (C). 1993. pap. text 24.95 (*0-7914-1302-0*) State U NY Pr.

Bernal, Martin. Black Athena Vol. 1: The Afroasiatic Roots of Classical Civilization: The Fabrication of Ancient Greece, 1785-1985. 575p. 1987. pap. text 18.95 (*0-8135-1277-8*) Rutgers U Pr.

— Black Athena Vol. II: The Archaeological & Documentary Evidence. (Illus.). 750p. (C). 1991. pap. 19.95 (*0-8135-1584-X*) Rutgers U Pr.

— Cadmean Letters: The Transmission of the Alphabet to the Aegean & Further West Before 1400 B.C. LC 90-2977. xiii, 156p. 1990. text 27.50 (*0-931464-47-1*) Eisenbrauns.

Bernal, Peggy P. The Huntington Library, Art Collections & Botanical Gardens: A Visitor's Guide. LC 92-25873. (Illus.). 64p. 1993. pap. 16.95 (*0-87328-134-9*) Huntington Lib.

Bernal, Peggy P., ed. see Houk, Walter.

Bernal, Penny, jt. auth. see Hewitt, Lonnie B.

Bernal Pinilla, Luis D. Anacaona y las Tormentas (Anacaona & the Tempest) (SPA.). 182p. (YA). 1994. pap. 6.99 (*968-16-4269-4*, Pub. by Fondo) Continental Bk.

— La Batalla de la Luna Rosada (The Battle of the Pink Moon) (SPA., Illus.). 64p. (YA). 1991. pap. 5.99 (*968-16-3658-9*, Pub. by Fondo) Continental Bk.

Bernal, Richard. Jack & the Beanstalk. (Children's Classics Ser.). 32p. (J). 1991. 6.95 (*0-8362-4903-8*) Andrews & McMeel.

— Peter & the Wolf. 32p. (J). (ps-3). 1992. 6.95 (*0-8362-4921-6*) Andrews & McMeel.

Bernal, Richard, jt. auth. see Murphy, Elspeth Campbell.

Bernal, Salvador. Alvaro del Portillo. 288p. 1999. pap. 13.95 (*1-889334-18-9*) Scepter Pubs.

Bernal, Samuel D. Drug Resistance in Oncology. LC 97-22375. (Basic & Clinical Oncology Ser.: Vol. 13). (Illus.). 416p. 1997. text 165.00 (*0-8247-9295-5*) Dekker.

Bernal, Samuel D. & Hesketh, Paul J., eds. Lung Cancer Differentiation: Implications for Diagnosis & Treatment. (Lung Biology in Health & Disease Ser.: Vol. 58). (Illus.). 496p. 1992. text 230.00 (*0-8247-8638-6*) Dekker.

Bernal, Victoria. Cultivating Workers. 1991. text 52.50 (*0-231-07172-8*) Col U Pr.

Bernaldo De Quiros, C. Modern Theories of Criminality. De Salvio, Alfonso, tr. from SPA. (Modern Criminal Science Ser.: Vol. 1). xxvii, 249p. 1987. reprint ed. 39.00 (*0-8377-2511-9*, Rothman) W S Hein.

Bernall, Carmen, tr. see Powers, Marshall K.

***Bernall, Cassie.** She Said "Yes!" 2000. pap. 8.50 (*5-550-02141-2*) Nairi.

***Bernall, Misty.** She Said Yes: The Unlikely Martydom of Cassie Bernall. (Illus.). 176p. 2000. 5.99 (*0-7434-0052-6*) PB.

— She Said Yes: The Unlikely Martyrdom of Cassie Bernall. LC 99-39752. (Illus.). 140p. (YA). 1999. 17.00 (*0-87486-987-0*, Pub. by Plough) Spring Arbor Dist.

— She Said Yes: The Unlikely Martyrdom of Cassie Bernall. 1999. 17.00 (*0-8499-1645-3*) Word Pub.

Bernan Press Editors, ed. Cumulated Index to the Public Papers of President Bush. LC 95-193850. 275p. 1995. lib. bdg. 65.00 (*0-89059-028-1*) Bernan Pr.

— Cumulated Index to the Public Papers of President Reagan. LC 95-193835. 307p. 1995. lib. bdg. 75.00 (*0-89059-027-3*) Bernan Pr.

Bernan Press Staff. Education Statistics of the United States 1999. (Bernan Press U. S. Databook Ser.). 657p. 1999. pap. 74.00 (*0-89059-066-4*) Bernan Pr.

— North American Industry Classification System: United States, 1997. LC 19-981000. 1200p. 1998. 32.50 (*0-89059-097-4*) Bernan Pr.

— North American Industry Classification System United States 1997. 1247p. 1998. pap. text 28.50 (*0-89059-098-2*) Bernan Pr.

— Statistical Abstract of the United States 1997: The National Data Book. 1996. 42.00 (*0-89059-068-0*) Bernan Pr.

***Bernan Press Staff.** Statistical Abstract of US: Library Edition, 1999. 119th large type ed. (Statistical Abstract of the United State Ser.). 1000p. 1999. 55.00 (*0-89059-226-8*) Bernan Pr.

Bernan Press Staff. Trade Policy Review - Trinidad & Tobago. (SPA.). 1999. 50.00 (*0-89059-173-3*, BWTO/1733) Bernan Pr.

— Trade Policy Review - Trinidad & Tobago. 1999. 50.00 (*0-89059-171-7*, BWTO/1717) Bernan Pr.

— Trade Policy Review - Trinidad & Tobago, 1998. (FRE.). 1999. 50.00 (*0-89059-172-5*, BWTO/1725) Bernan Pr.

— WTO Dispute Settlement Decisions Reporter, Vol. 3. (Illus.). 1998. boxed set 90.00 (*0-89059-162-8*) Bernan Pr.

***Bernan Press Staff & World Trade Organization Staff.** Bolivia. (Trade Policy Review Ser.). 1999. 50.00 (*0-89059-197-0*) Bernan Pr.

— Egypt. (Trade Policy Review Ser.). 1999. 50.00 (*0-89059-196-2*) Bernan Pr.

— Israel. (Trade Policy Review Ser.). 2000. 50.00 (*0-89059-199-7*) Bernan Pr.

— Nicaragua. (Trade Policy Review Ser.). 2000. 50.00 (*0-89059-201-2*) Bernan Pr.

— Papa New Guinea. (Trade Policy Review Ser.). 2000. 50.00 (*0-89059-203-9*) Bernan Pr.

— Philippines. (Trade Policy Review Ser.). 2000. 50.00 (*0-89059-200-4*) Bernan Pr.

— Romania. (Trade Policy Review Ser.). 2000. 50.00 (*0-89059-202-0*) Bernan Pr.

— Southern African Customs Union: Botswana. (Trade Policy Review Ser.: Vol. 2). 1999. 50.00 (*0-89059-205-5*) Bernan Pr.

— Southern African Customs Union: Lesotho. (Trade Policy Review Ser.: Vol. 3). 1999. 50.00 (*0-89059-206-3*) Bernan Pr.

— Southern African Customs Union: Namibia. (Trade Policy Review Ser.: Vol. 4). 1999. 50.00 (*0-89059-207-1*) Bernan Pr.

— Southern African Customs Unions: Swaziland. (Trade Policy Review Ser.: Vol. 5). 1999. 50.00 (*0-89059-208-X*) Bernan Pr.

— Thailand. (Trade Policy Review Ser.). 2000. 50.00 (*0-89059-204-7*) Bernan Pr.

— Togo 1999. (Trade Policy Review Ser.). 1999. 50.00 (*0-89059-194-6*) Bernan Pr.

— United States, 1999. (Trade Policy Review Ser.). 1999. 50.00 (*0-89059-198-9*) Bernan Pr.

***Bernan Press Staff & WTO Staff.** World Trade Organization Basic Instruments & Selected Documents, 3. 1999. 55.00 (*0-89059-193-8*, Pub. by Wrld Trade) Bernan Associates.

— World Trade Organization Basic Instruments & Selected Documents, Vol. 1. 1999. 55.00 (*0-89059-191-1*, Pub. by Bernan Pr) Bernan Associates.

— World Trade Organization Basic Instruments & Selected Documents, Vol. 2. 1999. 55.00 (*0-89059-192-X*, Pub. by Bernan Pr) Bernan Associates.

Bernan Press Staff, jt. auth. see Gaquin, Deirdre A.

Bernan Press Staff, jt. auth. see Kurian, George Thomas.

Bernan Press Staff, jt. auth. see Patton, James J.

Bernan Press Staff, jt. auth. see U. S. Department of Commerce, Economics & Statisti.

Bernan Press Staff, jt. auth. see U. S. Postal Service Staff.

Bernand, Carmen. Descubrimiento, Conquista y Colonizacion de America a Quinientos Anos (Discovery, Conquest & Colonization of America after 500 Years) (SPA.). 1994. pap. 14.99 (*968-16-4291-0*, Pub. by Fondo) Continental Bk.

— Dias Aciagos Para Paucar Guaman (Fateful Days for Paucar Guaman) (SPA., Illus.). 108p. (YA). 1993. pap. 6.99 (*968-16-4041-1*, Pub. by Fondo) Continental Bk.

— Historia del Nuevo Mundo. (SPA.). pap. 22.99 (*968-16-4017-9*, Pub. by Fondo) Continental Bk.

— The Incas: People of the Sun. (Discoveries Ser.). (Illus.). 192p. 1994. pap. 12.95 (*0-8109-2894-9*, Pub. by Abrams) Time Warner.

Bernanke. Principles of Macroeconomics. 2000. 41.00 (*0-07-228967-8*); student ed. 12.74 (*0-07-228968-6*) McGraw.

***Bernanke.** Principles of Microeconomics. 2000. 66.50 (*0-07-021991-5*, McGrw-H College) McGrw-H Hghr Educ.

Bernanke, Ben, jt. auth. see Abel, Andy.

***Bernanke, Ben S.** Essays on the Great Depression. 2000. 29.95 (*0-691-01698-4*, Pub. by Princeton U Pr) Cal Prin Full Svc.

— Macroeconomics. 3rd ed. 1998. 92.00 (*0-201-44132-2*) Addison-Wesley.

Bernanke, Ben S. & Rotemberg, Julio, eds. NBER Macroeconomics Annual, 1995. (NBER Macroeconomics Annual Ser.). (Illus.). 300p. (C). 1996. pap. text 20.00 (*0-262-52205-5*) MIT Pr.

— NBER Macroeconomics Annual, 1996. (Illus.). 300p. (C). 1996. 40.00 (*0-262-02414-4*); pap. text 22.00 (*0-262-52222-5*) MIT Pr.

— NBER Macroeconomics Annual, 1997. (Illus.). 300p. 1997. pap. text 20.00 (*0-262-52242-X*) MIT Pr.

— NBER Macroeconomics Annual, 1998. (Illus.). 300p. 1999. 45.00 (*0-262-02455-1*) MIT Pr.

— NBER Macroeconomics Annual 1998. (Illus.). 300p. 1999. pap. text 25.00 (*0-262-52256-X*) MIT Pr.

***Bernanke, Ben S. & Rotemberg, Julio, eds.** NBER Macroeconomics Annual 1999. (Illus.). 300p. 2000. 50.00 (*0-262-02476-4*); pap. 25.00 (*0-262-52271-3*) MIT Pr.

Bernanke, Ben S., et al. Inflation Targeting: Lessons from the International Experience. LC 98-39632. 304p. 1998. text 24.95 (*0-691-05955-1*, Pub. by Princeton U Pr) Cal Prin Full Svc.

Bernanke, Ben S., jt. auth. see Abel, Andrew.

Bernanos, Georges. Le Crepuscule des Vieux: Essai. (FRE.). 368p. 1956. 55.00 (*0-7859-1103-0*, 2070206491) Fr & Eur.

— Un Crime. 8.95 (*0-7859-0635-5*, F87830) Fr & Eur.

— Dialogue des Carmelites. (Coll. Le Livre de Vie). (FRE.). pap. 10.95 (*0-8288-9079-X*, F87641) Fr & Eur.

— The Diary of a Country Priest. 304p. 1984. pap. 10.95 (*0-88184-013-0*) Carroll & Graf.

— Essais et Ecrits de Combat. Bridel et al, eds. (Pleiade Ser.). (FRE.). 77.95 (*2-07-010654-3*) Schoenhof.

— Essais et Ecrits de Combat, Vol. 1. Esteve, Francoise, ed. (FRE.). 1988. lib. bdg. 125.00 (*0-7859-3810-9*) Fr & Eur.

— Francais, Si Vous Saviez (1945-1948) 9.95 (*0-7859-0633-9*, F87670) Fr & Eur.

— La France contre les Robots. (FRE.). 284p. 1970. pap. 10.95 (*0-7859-4886-4*) Fr & Eur.

— La Grande Peur des Bien-Pensants. pap. 9.95 (*0-685-23915-2*) Fr & Eur.

— Les Grands Cimetieres Sous La Lune. 1962. 14.95 (*0-7859-0598-7*, F87710) Fr & Eur.

An Asterisk (*) at the beginning of an entry indicates that the title is appearing for the first time.

— The Heroic Face of Innocence: Three Stories. Morris, Pamela & Batchelor, R., trs. from FRE. LC 98-50872. 150p. 1999. pap. 13.00 (0-8028-4565-7) Eerdmans.

***Bernanos, Georges.** The Impostor. Whitehouse, J. C., tr. from FRE. LC 98-35947. 208p. 1999. pap. 20.00 (0-8032-6153-5); text 45.00 (0-8032-1290-9) U of Nebr Pr.

Bernanos, Georges. Imposture. 1958. 15.95 (0-685-11248-9, F87720); pap. 9.95 (0-7859-0783-1, F87720) Fr & Eur.

— Jeanne, Relapse et Sainte. 16.95 (0-685-37219-7) Fr & Eur.

— Joie. (FRE.). 1956. 15.95 (0-685-11278-0, F87741); pap. 13.95 (0-8288-9080-3) Fr & Eur.

— Journal d'Un Cure de Campagne. 1955. 8.95 (0-7859-0601-0, FC1884) Fr & Eur.

— Last Essays. LC 68-23409. 263p. 1968. reprint ed. lib. bdg. 38.50 (0-8371-0019-4, BELE, Greenwood Pr) Greenwood.

— Lettre aux Anglais: Essai. pap. 12.95 (0-685-37221-9, F87770) Fr & Eur.

— La Liberte, Pourquoi Faire? Essai. pap. 8.95 (0-685-37222-7, F87780) Fr & Eur.

— Un Mauvais Reve. (FRE.). 1988. pap. 10.95 (0-7859-3218-6, 2266022776) Fr & Eur.

— Mr. Ouine. (Illus.). 288p. 1999. pap. 17.95 (0-525-24492-1, Dutt) Dutton Plume.

— Monsieur Ouine. 1960. 8.95 (0-7859-0923-0, F87790) Fr & Eur.

— Monsieur Ouine. Bush, William S., tr. from FRE. & intro. by. LC 99-39572. 256p. 2000. pap. 20.00 (0-8032-6161-6, Bison Books) U of Nebr Pr.

***Bernanos, Georges.** Monsieur Ouine. Bush, William S., tr. & intro. by. LC 99-39572. 256p. 2000. 40.00 (0-8032-1304-2, Bison Books) U of Nebr Pr.

Bernanos, Georges. Nous Autres Francais: Essai. pap. 38.95 (0-685-37223-5, F87800) Fr & Eur.

— Nouvelle Histoire de Mouchette. 1960. 8.95 (0-7859-0604-5, F87810) Fr & Eur.

— Scandale de la Verite. (FRE.). 1984. pap. 19.95 (0-7859-2696-8) Fr & Eur.

— Sous le Soleil de Satan. 1957. 11.95 (0-7859-0610-X, F87820) Fr & Eur.

***Bernanos, Georges.** Under Satan's Sun. Whitehouse, J. C., tr. 288p. 2001. pap. 20.00 (0-8032-6180-2, Bison Books); text 50.00 (0-8032-1306-9) U of Nebr Pr.

Bernanos, Georges, et al. Oeuvres Romanesques Completes. Picon et al, eds. 1962. 75.00 (0-7859-0606-1, F87590) Fr & Eur.

Bernanos, Michel. The Other Side of the Mountain. Halperin, Elaine P., tr. from FRE. LC 90-46018. 107p. 1990. reprint ed. 18.95 (0-87797-180-3) Cherokee.

Bernard. Bernard of Clairvaux: Sermons for the Summer Seasons, Liturgical Sermons 3. Kienzle, Beverly, tr. from LAT. (Cistercian Fathers Ser.: No. 53). 256p. 1991. pap. 13.95 (0-87907-453-1) Cistercian Pubns.

— Bruno Requiem for Marilyn. 1999. text 29.95 (0-312-08150-2) St Martin.

— Eternally Yours. 1999. mass mkt. 4.99 (0-7860-0197-6, Pinncle Kensgtn) Kensgtn Pub Corp.

— Health Psychology. (C). 1993. pap. text, teacher ed. 35.00 (0-03-098881-0) Harcourt Coll Pubs.

— How to Mix One Hundred Cocktails: An Ideal Book for Any Bar. 96p. 1995. pap. 4.95 (0-572-00184-3, Pub. by Foulsham UK) Assoc Pubs Grp.

— The Mommy Guide for Toddlers. 1996. pap. write for info. (0-8092-3366-5) NTC Contemp Pub Co.

— Teaching Early Childhood Math. (C). 2001. pap. text 39.00 (0-15-500871-4) Harcourt Coll Pubs.

— Turbulent Flow. 300p. (C). 2000. text 74.95 (0-471-33219-4) Wiley.

Bernard, et al, eds. Chameleon, 1984-1995: An Anthology of Student Writing. 93p. (YA). (gr. 9-12). 1995. pap. 10.00 (0-944920-17-9) Bellowing Ark Pr.

Bernard & O'Brien, Maureen M. Bernard of Clairvaux: The Parables & the Sentences LC 90-29021. (Cistercian Fathers Ser.). (ENG.). 1999. write for info. (0-87907-755-7) Cistercian Pubns.

Bernard, A. J., et al, eds. Leucocyte Typing. (Illus.). 820p. 1984. 139.00 (0-387-12056-4) Spr-Verlag.

Bernard, Alan. Kalahari Bushmen. LC 93-32423. (Threatened Cultures Ser.). (Illus.). 48p. (YA). (gr. 6-10). 1994. lib. bdg. 24.26 (1-56847-160-2) Raintree Steck-V.

Bernard, Amanda, ed. see Lehning, Percy B.

Bernard, Andre. Now All We Need Is a Title: Famous Book Titles & How They Got That Way. 128p. 1996. pap. 11.00 (0-393-31436-7, Norton Paperbks) Norton.

Bernard, Andre, ed. Rotten Rejections. 1990. 12.50 (0-916366-57-X, Pub. by Pushcart Pr) Norton.

Bernard, Andre, jt. ed. see Fadiman, Clifton.

Bernard, Andre, jt. ed. see Henderson, Bill.

Bernard, April. Blackbird Bye Bye. 1989. 16.95 (0-318-41456-2) Random.

— Lives of the Women Poets. Date not set. write for info. (0-393-03840-8) Norton.

— Psalms: Poems. 72p. 1995. pap. 9.00 (0-393-31304-2) Norton.

***Bernard, Artis.** The Boy on Drums & His Sister on the Cymbals. 2000. pap. 10.00 (0-9679581-0-5) Inleaf Pr.

Bernard, B. A. & Shroot, B., eds. From Molecular Biology to Therapeutics. (Pharmacology & the Skin Ser.: Vol. 5). (Illus.). viii, 196p. 1993. 216.75 (3-8055-5776-0) S Karger.

Bernard, B. De, see Pecile, A. & De Bernard, B., eds.

Bernard, Barbara & Long, Scott M. Burning Roses. 284p. 1996. 21.99 (0-9648592-3-8) Serenity LA.

Bernard, Barry, ed. see Miller, Judy.

Bernard, Barry, ed. see Miller, Judy A.

***Bernard, Betty.** One of These Mornings. 224p. 1999. pap. 13.95 (0-88739-275-X) Creat Arts Bk.

Bernard, Bob, ed. Nexis (R) Product Guide, 4 vols. 1992. write for info. (0-318-72162-7); write for info. (0-318-72163-5); write for info. (0-318-72164-3); write for info. (0-318-72165-1) LEXIS-NEXIS.

— Nexis (R) Product Guide, 4 vols., Set. 1992. 65.00 (0-926578-09-X) LEXIS-NEXIS.

Bernard, Bruce. The Impressionist. (Illus.). 272p. 1994. write for info. (1-57215-010-6) World Pubns.

— Vincent by Himself. 1995. 32.98 (0-7858-0428-5) Bk Sales Inc.

Bernard, Bruce, ed. Century: One Hundred Years of Human Progress, Regression, Suffering & Hope. 1120p. 1999. 49.95 (0-7148-3848-9) Phaidon Pr.

Bernard, Bruce & Bresson, Henri C. Humanity & Inhumanity: The Photographic Journey of George Rodger. (Illus.). 320p. (C). 1994. text 69.95 (0-7148-3165-4, Pub. by Phaidon Press) Phaidon Pr.

***Bernard, Bruce D.** Selecting the Form of Business Entity: Analyzing LLCs & Other Choices. Sigmund, Thomas J., ed. 258p. 2000. pap. 49.95 (0-9664544-1-3) OSBACLE Institute.

Bernard, Bruce R. Selecting the Right Form of Business: The Comprehensive Decision-Making Guide for the Business Advisor. 384p. 1996. 55.00 (0-7863-1056-1, Irwn Prfssnl) McGraw-Hill Prof.

Bernard, Bruno. Bernard of Hollywood Pin-Ups: Guide to Pin-Up Photography. (Illus.). 170p. 1999. 19.99 (3-8228-7172-9) Taschen Amer.

Bernard, C. & Huette, C. Illustrated Manual of Operative Surgery & Surgical Anatomy. (American Civil War Medical Ser.: No. 7). (Illus.). 513p. 1991. reprint ed. 125.00 (0-930405-42-0) Norman SF.

***Bernard, Charles L., compiled by.** Cemetery Directory of Vernon County, Missouri. 2nd rev. ed. 230p. 1999. pap. 30.00 (1-893046-00-1, Bushwacker Mus) Vernon Cty Hist Soc.

Bernard, Christian. So Mote It Be! 172p. (Orig.). 1995. pap. text 12.95 (0-9526420-0-X, 510214) GLELJ AMORC.

Bernard, Christine, ed. see Elder, Gladys.

Bernard, Christopher. The Dilettante of Cruelty: Deserts. unabridged ed. (Cimarron Poetry Ser.). 45p. (Orig.). 1997. pap. 5.00 (0-9653587-2-0) Meridien Pr.

Bernard, Christopher, ed. see James, Randall E.

Bernard, Cicero H., jt. auth. see Epp, Chirold D.

Bernard, Claude. Experimental Medicine. 2nd ed. LC 99-25208. 226p. 1999. write for info. (0-7658-0615-0) Transaction Pubs.

— Introduction to the Study of Experimental Medicine. Greene, Henry C., tr. 226p. (C). 1957. pap. 7.95 (0-486-20400-6) Dover.

Bernard, Claude, jt. auth. see Descotes, Jacques.

Bernard, Craig D., jt. auth. see Austin, Douglas V.

Bernard, Daniel. Praying up a Storm. 112p. (Orig.). 1997. pap. 7.00 (1-57892-050-7, Pastors In Print) Prayer Pt Pr.

Bernard, Daniel G. Bringing Home the Bride. 238p. 1995. mass mkt. 5.99 (0-88368-371-7) Whitaker Hse.

Bernard, David. Essentials of Holiness. 32p. (Orig.). 1989. pap. 3.99 (0-932581-55-2) Word Aflame.

— Essentials of Oneness Theology. (Illus.). 32p. (Orig.). 1985. pap. 3.99 (0-912315-89-X) Word Aflame.

— God's Infallible Word: The Inspiration, Canon & Text of the Bible. LC 92-20682. 232p. (Orig.). 1992. pap. 8.99 (1-56722-001-0) Word Aflame.

— History of Christian Doctrine Vol. 3: The Twentieth Century, A. D. 1900-2000. 254p. 1999. pap. 10.99 (1-56722-221-8) Word Aflame.

— In the Name of Jesus. LC 91-38203. 96p. (Orig.). 1992. pap. 5.99 (0-932581-95-1) Word Aflame.

— Light on Masonry. 560p. 1993. reprint ed. pap. 33.00 (1-56459-361-4) Kessinger Pub.

— The Oneness of God & a Study Guide for the Oneness of God. 504p. 1998. 19.99 (1-56722-220-X) Word Aflame.

Bernard, David & Bernard, Loretta. En Busca de la Santidad (In Search of Holiness) (SPA.). 304p. 1998. pap. 9.99 (1-56722-219-6) Word Aflame.

Bernard, David, ed. see Kays, William M. & London, A. L.

Bernard, David, ed. see Nation, Edna.

Bernard, David K. Doctrinas Esenciales de la Biblia: Essential Doctrines of the Bible. (SPA.). 32p. (Orig.). 1994. pap. 3.99 (1-56722-021-5) Word Aflame.

— Escenciales del Nuevo Nacimiento. Orig. Title: Essentials of the New Birth. (SPA.). 42p. (Orig.). 1991. pap. 3.99 (0-932581-94-3) Word Aflame.

— Essential Doctrines of the Bible. 32p. (Orig.). 1988. pap. 3.99 (0-932581-28-5) Word Aflame.

— Essentials of the New Birth. (Illus.). 40p. (Orig.). 1987. pap. 3.99 (0-932581-21-8) Word Aflame.

— A Handbook of Basic Doctrines: A Compilation of Scripture References. LC 88-19948. (Illus.). 112p. (Orig.). 1988. pap. 5.99 (0-932581-37-4) Word Aflame.

— A History of Christian Doctrine, Vol. I. LC 95-31170. 352p. 1995. pap. 9.99 (1-56722-036-3) Word Aflame.

— A History of Christian Doctrine Vol. 2: The Reformation to the Holiness Movement, A. D. 1500-1900. LC 95-31170. 336p. 1996. pap. 9.99 (1-56722-187-4) Word Aflame.

— Manual de Doctrinas Basicas: Una Compilacion de Referencias Biblicas. Medina, Grover J., tr. (SPA.). 112p. (Orig.). 1996. mass mkt. 5.99 (1-56722-141-6) Word Aflame.

— The Message of Colossians & Philemon. LC 90-37051. (Illus.). 186p. (Orig.). 1990. pap. 8.99 (0-932581-70-6) Word Aflame.

— The Message of Romans. LC 87-14747. (Illus.). 340p. (Orig.). 1987. pap. 9.99 (0-932581-18-8) Word Aflame.

— The New Birth. LC 85-106418. 346p. (Orig.). 1984. pap. 9.99 (0-912315-77-6) Word Aflame.

***Bernard, David K.** The New Birth & Study Guide for the New Birth. 506p. 1999. 19.99 (1-56722-238-2) Word Aflame.

Bernard, David K. Oneness & Trinity, A. D. 100-300: The Doctrine of God in Ancient Christian Writings. LC 90-29268. 200p. (Orig.). 1991. pap. 7.99 (0-932581-81-1) Word Aflame.

— The Oneness of God. LC 86-19051. 326p. (Orig.). 1983. pap. 9.99 (0-912315-12-1) Word Aflame.

— The Oneness View of Jesus Christ. LC 94-4416. 176p. (Orig.). 1994. pap. 7.99 (1-56722-020-7) Word Aflame.

— Practical Holiness: A Second Look. LC 86-11976. 336p. (Orig.). 1985. pap. 9.99 (0-912315-91-1) Word Aflame.

— Spiritual Gifts. LC 97-33496. 240p. 1997. pap. 8.99 (1-56722-204-8) Word Aflame.

— The Trinitarian Controversy in the Fourth Century. LC 93-16363. 80p. (Orig.). 1993. pap. 5.99 (1-56722-009-6) Word Aflame.

— Understanding the Articles of Faith: An Examination of United Pentecostal Beliefs. LC 99-216474. 48p. 1998. pap. 3.99 (1-56722-212-9) Word Aflame.

— La Unidad de Dios. Nix, Kelley, tr. from ENG.Tr. of Oneness of God. (SPA.). 343p. (Orig.). 1996. pap. 9.99 (1-56722-186-6) Word Aflame.

Bernard, David K. & Stegall, Neil. A Study Guide for the Oneness of God. 114p. (Orig.). (C). 1989. pap. 7.99 (0-932581-59-5) Word Aflame.

Bernard, David K., jt. auth. see Bernard, Loretta A.

Bernard, David K., jt. auth. see Stegall, Neil.

Bernard, David K., ed. see Ellis, Oma & Smelser, Georgia.

Bernard, David K., ed. see Hall, J. L.

Bernard, David K., jt. ed. see Hall, J. L.

Bernard, Denes. Heinkel He112 in Action. (Aircraft in Action Ser.). (Illus.). 50p. 1996. pap. 9.95 (0-89747-352-3) Squad Sig Pubns.

Bernard, Diane. Eternally Yours. 304p. 1996. mass mkt. 4.99 (0-8217-5368-1, Zebra Kensgtn) Kensgtn Pub Corp.

— Renaissance Man. 304p. 1997. mass mkt. 4.99 (0-8217-5628-1, Zebra Kensgtn) Kensgtn Pub Corp.

Bernard, Donald R. Life & Times of John Manjiro. (C). 1992. text 29.68 (0-07-004947-5) McGraw.

Bernard-Donals, Michael. The Practice of Theory: Rhetoric, Knowledge, & Pedagogy in the Academy. LC 97-8796. (Literature, Culture, Theory Ser.: Vol. 26). 256p. (C). 1998. pap. 19.95 (0-521-59506-1); text 59.95 (0-521-59433-2) Cambridge U Pr.

Bernard-Donals, Michael F. & Glejzer, Richard R., eds. Rhetoric in an Antifoundational World: Language, Culture, & Pedagogy. LC 97-19675. 448p. 1998. 35.00 (0-300-07022-5) Yale U Pr.

Bernard, E. N., ed. Tsunami Hazard: A Practical Guide for Tsunami Hazard Reduction. (C). 1991. lib. bdg. 13.50 (0-7923-1174-4) Kluwer Academic.

Bernard, Elaine. Technological Change & Skills Development. 162p. (C). 1991. 60.00 (0-7300-1251-4, Pub. by Deakin Univ) St Mut.

Bernard, Elizabeth. How to Kiss a Guy. (Love Stories Ser.). 192p. (YA). (gr. 7-12). 1995. mass mkt. 4.50 (0-553-56662-8) Bantam.

Bernard, Elton D. The Korean Frontier: A Story of Pentecostal Revival. LC 88-31274. (Illus.). 240p. (Orig.). 1989. pap. 4.99 (0-932581-43-9) Word Aflame.

Bernard, Ernest S., jt. auth. see Bird, Isabella Lucy.

Bernard, Eunice C. Honey Bee Milly: Honey Bee - Apis Mellifera. LC 93-73420. (Illus.). 70p. (Orig.). (J). (gr. 4 up). 1994. pap. 17.00 (0-9629950-5-3) Ashbrook Pub.

Bernard, Eunice J. I - the Real You. LC 96-85920. 61p. (Orig.). (J). (gr. 4 up). 1996. pap. 13.00 (0-9629950-7-X) Ashbrook Pub.

— Pregnancy - The Time to Develop the Child's Awareness. 15p. (Orig.). 1997. pap. text 5.00 (0-9629950-8-8) Ashbrook Pub.

Bernard, F. R., et al. A Catalogue of the Living Marine Bivalve Molluscs of China. 160p. (Orig.). 1993. pap. 39.50 (962-209-324-8, Pub. by HK Univ Pr) Cornet Bks.

Bernard, Felix. Elements de Paleontologie. Gould, Stephen Jay, ed. LC 79-8325. (History of Paleontology Ser.). (FRE., Illus.). 1980. reprint ed. lib. bdg. 107.95 (0-405-12705-7) Ayer.

Bernard, Felix, jt. auth. see King-Smith, Dick.

Bernard, Franz & Bauer, Hans. Kooperatives Lernen in der Berufsschule: Abschlubericht des Modellversuches. (GER., Illus.). 304p. 1997. 54.95 (3-631-31542-2, P Lang Pubng.

***Bernard, Fred.** The Yellow Train. LC 99-45318. (Illus.). 2000. 17.95 (1-56846-128-3, Creative Eds) Creative Co.

***Bernard, G. W.** Power & Politics in Tudor England. LC 00-34848. 2000. write for info. (0-7546-0245-1, Pub. by Ashgate Pub) Ashgate Pub Co.

Bernard, George. Inside the National Enquirer: Confessions of an Undercover Reporter. Hammond, Debbie, ed. LC 76-44613. 1977. 22.95 (0-87949-089-6) Ashley Bks.

— Principia Economica. (C). 1989. lib. bdg. 182.50 (0-7923-0186-2) Kluwer Academic.

Bernard, George, jt. auth. see Coldrey, Jennifer.

Bernard, Graham. Why You Are Who You Are: A Conversation with Richard. 208p. (Orig.). 1985. pap. 9.95 (0-89281-100-5, Destiny Bks) Inner Tradit.

Bernard, H. A., et al. Recent Sediments of Southeast Texas - A Field Guide to the Brazos Alluvial & Deltaic Plains & the Galveston Barrier Island Complex. (Guidebook Ser.: GB 11). 132p. 1970. reprint ed. pap. 7.00 (0-686-29319-3) Bur Econ Geology.

Bernard, H. Russell. Research Methods in Anthropology: Qualitative & Quantitative Approaches. 2nd ed. 536p. (C). 1994. 69.00 (0-8039-5244-9); pap. 32.00 (0-8039-5245-7) AltaMira Pr.

Bernard, H. Russell, ed. Handbook of Methods in Cultural Anthropology. LC 98-25423. (Illus.). 816p. (C). 1998. 89.95 (0-7619-9151-4) AltaMira Pr.

Bernard, Harold S. & MacKenzie, K. Roy, eds. Basics of Group Psychotherapy. LC 94-16964. 224p. 1994. lib. bdg. 31.00 (0-89862-117-8) Guilford Pubns.

Bernard, Harold W, Jr. Global Warming Unchecked: Signs to Watch For. LC 92-41065. (Illus.). 200p. 1993. 32.50 (0-253-31178-0); pap. text 14.95 (0-253-20819-X) Ind U Pr.

Bernard, Harry. Le Roman Regionaliste aux Etats-Unis, 1913-1940. (BCL1-PS American Literature Ser.). 387p. 1993. reprint ed. lib. bdg. 89.00 (0-7812-6589-4) Rprt Serv.

Bernard, Harvey R. & Pedraza, Jesus S. Native Ethnography: A Mexican Indian Describes His Culture. LC 88-18628. (Illus.). 649p. 1989. pap. 200.00 (0-608-05177-2, 205259800001) Bks Demand.

Bernard, Hautz, ed. see Berg, James A.

Bernard, Heald T. Time's Winged Chariot. 136p. 1985. 55.00 (0-907033-26-1) St Mut.

Bernard, Helene. Great Women Initiates or the Feminine Mystic. Ziebel, Michelle, tr. from FRE. LC 84-50133. (Illus.). 151p. (Orig.). 1984. pap. 9.95 (0-912057-36-X, 501930) GLELJ AMORC.

Bernard, Ian. Film & Television Acting: From Stage to Screen. 2nd ed. LC 97-24630. 176p. 1998. pap. 19.95 (0-240-80301-9, Focal) Buttrwrth-Heinemann.

***Bernard, Ian.** Writing Humor: Giving the Comedic Touch to All Forms of Writing. 185p. 2000. pap. 14.95 (0-88496-445-0) Capra Pr.

Bernard, Ida M. I Am a Living Miracle: An Autobiography. 1995. 15.95 (0-533-08867-4) Vantage.

Bernard, J., ed. Technical Advances in Biofilm Reactors. (Water Science & Technology Ser.: No. 22). (Illus.). 510p. 1990. pap. 203.00 (0-08-040170-8, Pergamon Pr) Elsevier.

Bernard, J. G. Experimental Investigation & Numerical Modelling of Cyclones for Application at High Temperatures. 240p. (Orig.). 1992. pap. 57.50 (90-6275-807-X, Pub. by Delft U Pr) Coronet Bks.

Bernard, J. H. St. John, Vols. 1 & 2: Critical & Exegetical Commentary, Vols. 1 & 2. Driver, Samuel R. et al, eds. write for info. (0-318-50940-7, Pub. by T & T Clark) Bks Intl VA.

— St. John, Vols. 1 & 2: Critical & Exegetical Commentary, Vols. 1 & 2. Driver, Samuel R. et al, eds. (International Critical Commentary Ser.). 456p. 1993. 39.95 (0-567-05025-4, Pub. by T & T Clark) Bks Intl VA.

— St. John, Vols. 1 & 2: Critical & Exegetical Commentary, Vols. 1 & 2. Driver, Samuel R. et al, eds. (International Critical Commentary Ser.). 480p. 1994. 39.95 (0-567-05024-6, Pub. by T & T Clark) Bks Intl VA.

Bernard, J. H., tr. see Kant, Immanuel.

Bernard, J. W., jt. auth. see Gunkler, A. A.

Bernard, Jacqueline. Journey Toward Freedom: The Story of Sojourner Truth. LC 90-34481. 270p. 1990. 35.00 (1-55861-023-5) Feminist Pr.

— Journey Toward Freedom: The Story of Sojourner Truth. LC 90-34481. (Illus.). 272p. 1990. pap. 14.95 (1-55861-024-3) Feminist Pr.

Bernard, James, jt. auth. see Marsh, Dave.

Bernard, Jami. Chick Flicks: Movie Lover's Guide to the Movies Women Love. (Illus.). 240p. 1996. pap. text 16.95 (0-8065-1836-7, Citadel Pr) Carol Pub Group.

— First Films: Illustrious, Obscure, & Embarrassing Movie Debuts. LC 92-37571. 1993. 15.95 (0-8065-1402-7, Citadel Pr) Carol Pub Group.

— Total Exposure: The Movie Buff's Guide to Celebrity Nude Scenes. (Illus.). 288p. 1995. pap. 17.95 (0-8065-1619-4, Citadel Pr) Carol Pub Group.

— Total Exposure: The Movie Buff's Guide to Celebrity Nude Scenes. rev. ed. LC 99-11927. (Illus.). 320p. 1999. pap. 18.95 (0-8065-2079-5, Citadel Pr) Carol Pub Group.

Bernard, Jan S. & Schneider, Miriam. The True Work of Dying: A Practical & Compassionate Guide to Easing the Dying Process. LC 96-33886. 256p. 1996. mass mkt. 22.00 (0-380-97329-4, Avon Bks) Morrow Avon.

Bernard, Jan S., jt. auth. see Schneider, Miriam.

Bernard, Janine & Hackney, Harold L. Untying the Knot: A Guide to Civilized Divorce. 204p. (Orig.). 1983. 7.95 (0-86683-800-7) Harper SF.

Bernard, Janine M. & Goodyear, Rodney K. Fundamentals of Clinical Supervision. 2nd ed. LC 97-31203. 354p. (C). 1997. 59.00 (0-205-17531-7, H75310) Allyn.

Bernard, Jean-Jacques. Nationale Six. Kroff, Alexander Y. & Bottke, Karl G., eds. (FRE., Illus.). (Orig.). 1961. pap. text 12.95 (0-89197-312-5) Irvington.

Bernard, Jean-Louis. Dictionnaire de l'Insolite et du Fantastique. (FRE.). 356p. 1974. 24.95 (0-8288-6013-0, M6608) Fr & Eur.

Bernard, Jeff, et al, eds. Semiotics with "Symbolicity" 1990: Proceedings of the Fifteenth Annual Meeting of the Semiotic Society of America. 704p. (Orig.). (C). 1993. lib. bdg. 95.00 (0-8191-8868-9) U Pr of Amer.

Bernard, Jessie. The Female World from a Global Perspective. LC 86-45475. 303p. reprint ed. pap. 94.00 (0-8357-3945-7, 205704000004) Bks Demand.

— The Future of Marriage. LC 82-6991. 384p. 1982. pap. 19.00 (0-300-02853-9, Y-441) Yale U Pr.

— Women, Wives, Mothers: Values & Options. LC 74-18210. 286p. 1975. pap. text 26.95 (0-202-30281-4) Aldine de Gruyter.

Bernard, Jessie, jt. ed. see Broderick, Carlfred B.

Bernard, Joel. Authority, Autonomy & Radical Commitment: Stephen & Abby Kelley Foster. 39p. 1981. pap. 6.00 (0-912296-50-X) Am Antiquarian.

An Asterisk (*) at the beginning of an entry indicates that the title is appearing for the first time.

— The Transit of "Small, Merry" Anglo-American Culture: Sir John BarleyCorne & Sir Richard Rum (& Captain Whiskey) 57p. 1990. pap. 8.00 (*0-944026-24-9*) Am Antiquarian.

Bernard, John. Retrospections of America, 1797-1811. Matthews, Brander & Hutton, Laurence, eds. LC 73-83401. 392p. 1972. 26.95 (*0-405-08263-0*, Pub. by Blom Pubns) Ayer.

Bernard, John, ed. Retrospections of America, 1797-1811. 380p. 1987. reprint ed. pap. 19.50 (*1-55613-020-1*) Heritage Bk.

Bernard, John A. & Washio, Tasahi. Expert Systems Applications Within the Nuclear Industry. 275p. 1989. 39.00 (*0-89448-034-0*, 300024) Am Nuclear Soc.

Bernard, John D. & Alessi, Paul T., eds. Vergil at Two Thousand: Commemorative Essays on the Poet & His Influence. LC 85-48005. (Ars Poetica Ser.: No. 3). 1986. 39.50 (*0-404-62503-7*) AMS Pr.

Bernard, John W. CIM in the Process Industries. LC 88-35771. (Illus.). 224p. reprint ed. pap. 69.50 (*0-608-20291-6*, 207155000001) Bks Demand.

Bernard, Jonathan W. The Music of Edgard Varese. LC 86-22431. (Composers of the Twentieth Century Ser.). 296p. reprint ed. pap. 91.80 (*0-7837-3281-3*, 205768300006) Bks Demand.

Bernard, Jonathan W., ed. Elliott Carter: Collected Essays & Lectures, 1937-1995. LC 96-26355. (Eastman Studies in Music: No. 7). 389p. 1998. pap. 24.95 (*1-58046-025-9*) Univ Rochester Pr.

Bernard, Josef. The Electronic Project Builder's Reference: Designing & Modifying Circuits. (Illus.). 208p. 1989. 22.95 (*0-8306-9260-6*); pap. 14.95 (*0-8306-3260-3*) McGraw-Hill Prof.

Bernard, Julia & Bernard, Nicholas. New Decorator. LC 98-47710. (Illus.). 10p. 1999. 24.95 (*0-7894-4121-7*) DK Pub Inc.

***Bernard, Kathleen, et al, eds.** The Bahamas Index & Yearbook 1999. 234p. 2000. pap. text 49.95 (*0-932265-58-8*) White Sound.

— The Bahamas Index & Yearbook 1999, Vol. 14. 234p. 2000. text 100.00 (*0-932265-57-X*) White Sound.

Bernard, Kenneth. The Baboon in the Nightclub. LC 93-79280. (Illus.). 72p. (Orig.). 1994. pap. 8.95 (*1-878580-54-X*) Asylum Arts.

— Clown at Wall: A Kenneth Bernard Reader. (Occasional Book Ser.). (Illus.). (Orig.). 1997. pap. 16.00 (*0-913057-48-7*) Confront Mag Pr.

— Curse of Fool: Three Plays. LC 91-76942. (Illus.). 150p. (Orig.). 1992. 17.95 (*1-878580-49-3*); pap. 8.95 (*1-878580-48-5*) Asylum Arts.

— From the District File. 128p. 1992. 18.95 (*0-932511-52-X*); pap. 8.95 (*0-932511-53-8*) Fiction Coll.

— How We Danced While We Burned Followed by La Justice, or the Cock That Crew. LC 90-80159. 136p. (Orig.). 1990. pap. 7.95 (*1-878580-23-X*) Asylum Arts.

— The Qui Parle Play & Poems. 160p. 1999. pap. 12.00 (*1-878580-64-7*) Asylum Arts.

Bernard, Kenneth J. & Wellenzohn, Henry J. Foundations of Mathematics. (Illus.). 274p. (Orig.). (C). 1997. pap. text 44.95 (*0-943202-60-4*) H & H Pub.

Bernard L. Madison for the Committee on the Mathem. A Challenge of Numbers: People in the Mathematical Sciences. 136p. 1990. pap. text 9.95 (*0-309-04190-2*) Natl Acad Pr.

Bernard, Larry & Krupat, Edward. Health Psychology. (Illus.). 600p. (C). 1994. text 74.00 (*0-03-074417-2*, Pub. by Harcourt Coll Pubs) Harcourt.

Bernard le Bovier de Fontenelle. Conversations on the Plurality of Worlds. Hargreaves, H. A., tr. LC 90-31220. 132p. 1990. 40.00 (*0-520-06361-9*, Pub. by U CA Pr); pap. 14.95 (*0-520-07171-9*, Pub. by U CA Pr) Cal Prin Full Svc.

Bernard, Leo & O'Neill, Angus, eds. Antiquarian Books: A Companion for Booksellers, Librarians & Collectors. LC 94-2436. (Illus.). 480p. (C). 1994. text 84.95 (*0-8122-3268-2*) U of Pa Pr.

Bernard, Leonard. Idget the Midget. LC 97-49607. (J). 1998. write for info. (*0-9634661-5-1*) Bernard Bks.

— Itza: The Boy Who Rode a Jaguar. LC 97-48308. (J). 1998. 16.95 (*0-9634661-1-9*) Bernard Bks.

— Pelican Paradise. LC 97-48299. (J). 1998. write for info. (*0-9634661-3-5*) Bernard Bks.

Bernard, Levine, ed. The Dissolving Image: The Spiritual-Esthetic Development of W. B. Yeats. LC 70-86953. 181p. reprint ed. pap. 56.20 (*0-7837-3815-3*, 204363500010) Bks Demand.

Bernard, Loretta, jt. auth. see Bernard, David.

Bernard, Loretta A. & Bernard, David K. In Search of Holiness. LC 88-10767. 288p. (Orig.). 1981. pap. 9.99 (*0-912315-40-7*) Word Aflame.

Bernard, Louise. Descriptive & Visual Dictionary of Historical Collections. 2nd ed. LC 98-177422. (Illus.). 281p. 1997. pap. 45.95 (*0-660-14801-3*, Pub. by Canadian Govt Pub) Accents Pubns.

Bernard, Luther L. Instinct: A Study in Social Psychology. Coser, Lewis A. & Powell, Walter W., eds. LC 79-6984. (Perennial Works in Sociology). (Illus.). 1980. reprint ed. lib. bdg. 46.95 (*0-405-12084-2*) Ayer.

Bernard, M. My First Mass Book. (J). (ps-3). Date not set. pap. text 1.95 (*0-88271-165-2*) Regina Pr.

Bernard, M. E. Rational-Emotive Therapy with Children & Adolescents. 2nd ed. 352p. 1994. 45.00 (*0-471-57670-0*) Wiley.

— Using Rational-Emotive Therapy Effectively: A Practitioner's Guide. (Illus.). 366p. (C). 1991. 102.00 (*0-306-43754-6*, Plenum Trade) Perseus Pubng.

Bernard, M. E. Using Rational-Emotive Therapy Effectively: A Practitioner's Guide. (Illus.). 366p. (C). 1991. pap. 42.50 (*0-306-43755-4*, Plenum Trade) Perseus Pubng.

Bernard, M. E., jt. auth. see Ellis, A.

Bernard, Marc. Pareils a des Enfants. (FRE.). 1979. pap. 11.95 (*0-7859-1887-6*, 2070371034) Fr & Eur.

Bernard, Marc, ed. see Zola, Emile.

Bernard, Margie. Daughter of Derry. (C). 1988. text 21.50 (*0-7453-0411-7*) Westview.

Bernard, Marie. The Art of Graphology. LC 85-51385. (Illus.). x, 416p. 1985. pap. 45.00 (*0-87875-304-4*) Whitston Pub.

Bernard, Marie. Conversations of the Saints. LC 98-37432. 160p. 1999. pap. text 12.95 (*0-7648-0386-7*) Liguori Pubns.

— Sexual Deviations as Seen in Handwriting. LC 90-70215. (Illus.). xvi, 408p. 1990. 49.50 (*0-87875-360-5*) Whitston Pub.

Bernard, Mary. Sappho: A New Translation. 124p. 1958. pap. 10.95 (*0-520-01117-1*, Pub. by U CA Pr) Cal Prin Full Svc.

Bernard, Melanie, et al. American Medical Association Family Cookbook: Good Food That's Good for You. (Illus.). 528p. 1999. pap. 16.00 (*0-671-53668-0*, PB Trade Paper) PB.

Bernard, Melanie, ed. see Noble & Associates - Tyson Foods, Inc. Staff.

Bernard, Michael. Staying Rational in an Irrational World: Albert Ellis & Rational Emotive Therapy. 288p. 1991. pap. 9.95 (*0-8184-0559-7*, L Stuart) Carol Pub Group.

Bernard, Michael & DiGuiseppe, Raymond, eds. Rational Emotive Consultation in Applied Settings. (School Psychology Ser.). 224p. 1993. text 49.95 (*0-8058-0578-8*) L Erlbaum Assocs.

Bernard, Michael & Schneider, Mark, eds. Land Policy. (Orig.). 1984. pap. 15.00 (*0-918592-70-4*) Pol Studies.

Bernard, Michael, jt. auth. see Gillet, Susan.

Bernard, Michael, tr. see Halter, Marek.

Bernard, Michael E. Taking the Stress Out of Teaching. 19.95 (*0-85924-918-2*, B114) Inst Rational-Emotive.

— You Can Do It! How to Boost Your Child's Achievement in School. LC 96-48245. 384p. 1997. mass mkt. 12.99 (*0-446-67193-2*, Pub. by Warner Bks) Little.

Bernard, Michael E., jt. ed. see Wolfe, Janet L.

Bernard, Michael M. Constitutions, Taxation & Land Policy, 2 vols., Vol. 1. LC 78-24792. 176p. reprint ed. pap. 54.60 (*0-7837-5715-8*, 204542400001) Bks Demand.

— Constitutions, Taxation & Land Policy, 2 vols., Vol. 2. LC 78-24792. 141p. reprint ed. pap. 43.80 (*0-7837-5716-6*, 204542400002) Bks Demand.

***Bernard, Miriam.** Promoting Health in Old Age: Critical Issues in Self Health Care. LC 99-42447. (Rethinking Ageing Ser.). 2000. pap. 29.95 (*0-335-19247-5*) OpUniv Pr.

Bernard, Mitchell, et al. The Rights of Single People. (ACLU Ser.). 124p. (Orig.). 1985. pap. 6.95 (*0-8093-9956-3*) S Ill U Pr.

Bernard, Neuhaus Von, see Von Bernard, Neuhaus.

Bernard, Nicholas, jt. auth. see Bernard, Julia.

Bernard of Clairvaux. Bernard of Clairvaux: Parables (Parabolae) Casey, Michael, tr. from LAT. (Cistercian Studies: No. 55A).Tr. of Parabolae Sancti Bernardi. (Illus.). 112p. 1997. write for info. (*0-87907-155-9*) Cistercian Pubns.

— Bernard of Clairvaux: Sermons for the Summer Seasons, Liturgical Sermons 3. Kienzle, Beverly, tr. from LAT. (Cistercian Fathers Ser.: No. 53). 256p. 1991. 25.95 (*0-87907-153-2*) Cistercian Pubns.

— Bernard of Clairvaux: Sermons on the Song of Songs, Vol. IV. Edmonds, Irene & Leclercq, Jean, trs. (Cistercian Fathers Ser.: No. 40). 1980. pap. 7.00 (*0-87907-740-9*) Cistercian Pubns.

— Bernard of Clairvaux on the Song of Songs, Vol. II. Walsh, Kilian, tr. (Cistercian Fathers Ser.: No. 7). 1976. pap. 7.00 (*0-87907-707-7*) Cistercian Pubns.

— Cistercians & Cluniacs: Apologia to Abbot William. 1986. pap. 5.00 (*0-87907-102-8*) Cistercian Pubns.

— Letters. James, Bruno S., tr. LC 78-63344. (Crusades & Military Orders Ser.: Second Series). reprint ed. 82.50 (*0-404-17004-8*) AMS Pr.

— The Life & Death of Saint Malachy the Irishman. (Cistercian Fathers Ser.: No. 10). 170p. 7.95 (*0-87907-910-X*) Cistercian Pubns.

— On Loving God: Selections from Sermons by St. Bernard of Clairvaux. Martin, Hugh, ed. LC 79-8706. (Treasury of Christian Bks.). 125p. 1981. reprint ed. lib. bdg. 49.50 (*0-313-20787-9*, BEOL, Greenwood Pr) Greenwood.

— Sermons on the Song of Songs, Vol. 1. (Cistercian Fathers Ser.: No. 4). 1971. pap. 7.00 (*0-87907-704-2*) Cistercian Pubns.

— Treatises I: Apologia, Precept & Dispensation. (Cistercian Fathers Ser.: No. 1). 190p. 7.95 (*0-87907-101-X*) Cistercian Pubns.

— Your Angels Guard My Steps: A 40-Day Journey in the Company of Bernard of Clairvaux. Hazard, David, ed. (Rekindling the Inner Fire Ser.: Vol. 10). 16p. (Orig.). 1998. pap. 8.99 (*1-55661-723-2*) Bethany Hse.

Bernard of Clairvaux & Amadeus of Lausanne. Magnificat: Homilies in Praise of the Blessed Virgin Mary. (Cistercian Fathers Ser.: No. 18). 1993. pap. 7.95 (*0-87907-148-6*) Cistercian Pubns.

Bernard of Cluny. Scorn for the World: Bernard of Cluny's de Contemptu Mundi: The Latin Text with English Translation. Pepin, Ronald E., ed. & tr. by. (Medieval Texts & Studies: No. 8). 189p. 1991. 39.95 (*0-937191-35-3*) Mich St U Pr.

Bernard, Oliver. Getting over It: An Autobiography. 159p. 1992. 33.00 (*0-7206-0865-1*, Pub. by P Owen Ltd) Dufour.

Bernard, Oliver, tr. & intro. see Apollinaire, Guillaume.

Bernard, Oliver, tr. & intro. see Rimbaud, Arthur.

Bernard, P. Planning in Soviet Union. LC 66-14654. 1966. 146.00 (*0-08-013503-X*, Pub. by Pergamon Repr) Franklin.

Bernard, P. & Dubeif, H. The Decline of the Third Republic, 1914-1938. (Cambridge History of Modern France Ser.: No. 5). 384p. 1988. pap. text 22.95 (*0-521-35854-X*) Cambridge U Pr.

Bernard, P., jt. ed. see Basar, Tamer S.

Bernard, P., ed. see Bertoin, J., et al.

Bernard, P., ed. see Gine, E., et al.

Bernard, Pam. My Own Hundred Doors. Rogers, Bertha, ed. (Poetry Award Ser.). 60p. (Orig.). 1996. pap. 10.95 (*0-9646844-4-6*) Bright Hill.

Bernard, Patricia. The Outcast. 304p. (YA). (gr. 7-12). 1998. pap. 7.95 (*0-7322-5768-9*) HarpC.

— The Punisher. 1999. pap. 7.95 (*0-7322-5775-1*) Colns.

— Rule Changer. (Outcast Trilogy Ser.: No. 3). 1999. pap. 7.95 (*0-7322-5907-X*, Pub. by HarpC) Consort Bk Sales.

Bernard, Paul P. From the Enlightenment to the Police State: The Public Life of Johann Anton Pergen. 264p. 1991. text 35.95 (*0-252-01745-5*) U of Ill Pr.

— Integrated Inventory Management. LC 98-35369. 511p. 1999. 74.95 (*0-471-32513-9*) Wiley.

Bernard, Paul P. The Limits of Enlightenment: Joseph II & the Law. LC 79-12030. 160p. 1979. text 19.95 (*0-252-00735-2*) U of Ill Pr.

— Rush to the Alps. (East European Monographs: No. 37). 228p. 1978. text 46.00 (*0-914710-30-3*, Pub. by East Eur Monographs) Col U Pr.

Bernard, Pierre R. The Resurrection of the Lord: Mystery of Faith. Manning, Francis V., tr. from FRE. LC 96-785. 144p. (Orig.). 1996. pap. 7.95 (*0-8189-0741-X*) Alba.

Bernard, R. Rain Forest. 80p. (J). 1997. pap. 12.95 (*0-590-59919-4*) Scholastic Inc.

Bernard, R., tr. see Zoghby, Elias.

Bernard, Raymond. Agharta, the Subterranean World. 59p. 1996. reprint ed. spiral bd. 12.00 (*0-7873-0099-3*) Hlth Research.

— Flying Saucers from the Earth's Interior. 85p. 1993. reprint ed. spiral bd. 12.50 (*0-7873-0098-5*) Hlth Research.

— The Great Secret Count St. Germain. 2nd ed. 91p. 1993. reprint ed. pap. 14.00 (*0-7873-0095-0*) Hlth Research.

— Herbal Elixirs of Life. 31p. 1996. reprint ed. spiral bd. 8.50 (*0-7873-0096-9*) Hlth Research.

— The Hollow Earth. (Illus.). 1969. pap. 7.95 (*0-8065-0546-X*, Citadel Pr) Carol Pub Group.

— The Hollow Earth. 134p. 1996. reprint ed. pap. 17.50 (*0-7873-0097-7*) Hlth Research.

— The Hollow Earth: The Greatest Geographical Discovery in History. 256p. 1991. pap. 7.95 (*0-8216-2507-1*, Carol Paperbacks) Carol Pub Group.

— Prenatal Origin of Genius. 75p. 1996. reprint ed. spiral bd. 12.00 (*0-7873-1215-0*) Hlth Research.

Bernard, Raymond W. Apollonius the Nazarene: Mystery Man of the Bible. (Essene-Jesus-Apollonius Ser.: Vol. 3). 57p. 1996. reprint ed. spiral bd. 11.00 (*0-7873-1211-8*) Hlth Research.

— Are Chemicals in Drinking Water Menacing Your Health? 26p. 1996. reprint ed. spiral bd. 8.00 (*0-7873-1115-4*) Hlth Research.

— Are the New Super Sprays Endangering Your Health? 48p. 1996. reprint ed. spiral bd. 8.50 (*0-7873-1142-1*) Hlth Research.

— Are You Being Poisoned by the Foods You Are Eating? 1996. reprint ed. spiral bd. 8.00 (*0-7873-1118-9*) Hlth Research.

— Constipation. 51p. 1996. reprint ed. spiral bd. 9.50 (*0-7873-1217-7*) Hlth Research.

— Creation of the Superman. 75p. 1996. reprint ed. spiral bd. 12.00 (*0-7873-1003-4*) Hlth Research.

— Danger We All Face: The Radioactive Peril. rev. ed. 62p. 1996. reprint ed. spiral bd. 9.00 (*0-7873-1159-6*) Hlth Research.

— Dead Sea Scrolls & the Life of the Ancient Essene. (Essene-Jesus-Apollonius Ser.: Vol. 1). 29p. 1996. reprint ed. spiral bd. 10.50 (*0-7873-1209-6*) Hlth Research.

— Escape from Destruction: How to Survive in the Atomic Age. 35p. 1994. reprint ed. spiral bd. 8.00 (*0-7873-1158-8*) Hlth Research.

— From Chrishna to Christ. 148p. (Orig.). 1996. reprint ed. spiral bd. 15.50 (*0-7873-1212-6*) Hlth Research.

— Meat-Eating: A Cause of Disease. 1996. spiral bd. 10.00 (*0-7873-1007-7*) Hlth Research.

— The Mysteries of Human Reproduction. 126p. 1994. reprint ed. spiral bd. 14.50 (*0-7873-1157-X*) Hlth Research.

— Newest Discoveries in Nutrition. 1996. spiral bd. 10.00 (*0-7873-1012-3*) Hlth Research.

— Nutritional Methods of Blood Regeneration. 1996. spiral bd. 14.00 (*0-7873-1011-5*) Hlth Research.

— Nutritional Methods of Intestinal Regeneration, Pts. I & II. 1996. spiral bd. 14.00 (*0-7873-1010-7*) Hlth Research.

— Nutritional Sex Control & Rejuvenation. 1996. spiral bd. 10.50 (*0-7873-1009-3*) Hlth Research.

— Organic Foods for Health. 1996. spiral bd. 9.00 (*0-7873-1008-5*) Hlth Research.

— The Organic Revolution in Nutrition: The Future of Vitamins, Natural Versus Synthetic. 20p. 1996. reprint ed. spiral bd. 9.00 (*0-7873-1213-4*) Hlth Research.

— Organic Way to Health, Pt. III. (Science of Organic Dietetics Ser.). 1996. spiral bd. 9.00 (*0-7873-0995-8*) Hlth Research.

— Organic Way to Health Pt. 1: Nutritional Value of Organic Foods & Sea Vegetation. (Science of Organic Dietetics Ser.). 1996. spiral bd. 9.00 (*0-7873-0997-4*) Hlth Research.

— Organic Way to Health Pt. 2: Seed Protein vs. Animal Proteins. (Science of Organic Dietetics Ser.). 1996. spiral bd. 9.00 (*0-7873-0996-6*) Hlth Research.

— Organic Way to Health Pt. 4: Latest Advances in Nutrition from the New Organic Viewpoint. (Science of Organic Dietetics Ser.). 1996. spiral bd. 11.00 (*0-7873-0994-X*) Hlth Research.

— The Physiological Enigma of Woman: The Mystery of Menstruation. 183p. 1996. reprint ed. spiral bd. 16.00 (*0-7873-1214-2*) Hlth Research.

— Pythagoras, the Immortal Sage. 69p. 1958. reprint ed. spiral bd. 11.00 (*0-7873-0101-9*) Hlth Research.

— The Revolt Against Chemicals. (Science of Organic Dietetics Ser.). 86p. 1996. reprint ed. spiral bd. 10.00 (*0-7873-1027-1*) Hlth Research.

— Science Discovers the Physiological Value of Continence. 46p. 1994. reprint ed. spiral bd. 9.00 (*0-7873-1025-5*) Hlth Research.

— Science of Regeneration: Physiological Methods of Male & Female Regeneration, Pts. I & II. 44p. 1996. spiral bd. 12.50 (*0-7873-1216-9*) Hlth Research.

— The Secret Life of Jesus the Essene. (Essene-Jesus-Apollonius Ser.: Vol. 2). 56p. 1997. reprint ed. spiral bd. 9.00 (*0-7873-1210-X*) Hlth Research.

— The Secret of Rejuvenation: Professor Brown Sequard's Great Discovery. 1996. spiral bd. 10.00 (*0-7873-0998-2*) Hlth Research.

— The Serpent Fire: Awakening Kundalini. 98p. (Orig.). 1996. reprint ed. spiral bd. 15.00 (*0-7873-1056-5*) Hlth Research.

— Super Foods from Super Soil. 1996. spiral bd. 9.50 (*0-7873-0993-1*) Hlth Research.

— Super-Health Thru Organic Super-Food. 163p. 1994. reprint ed. spiral bd. 16.50 (*0-7873-1127-8*) Hlth Research.

Bernard, Raymond W. & Pfeiffer, Enrenfried E. Shall We Eat Bread? Is Wheat a Healthful Food? 29p. 1994. reprint ed. spiral bd. 9.50 (*0-7873-1057-3*) Hlth Research.

Bernard, Raymond W., ed. see Morgan, Sampson.

Bernard, Reams, ed. see Brigham, William.

Bernard, Rein. Iskry (The Sparks) I Pelena Upala S Nashikh Glaz (As If a Veil Have Fallen from Our Eye) LC 96-11037. (RUS.). 248p. 1996. 24.95 (*1-55779-087-6*); pap. 15.00 (*1-55779-090-6*) Hermitage Pubs.

Bernard, Richard. Isle of Man: or The Legal Proceeding in Man-Shire Against Sinne. LC 76-57356. (English Experience Ser.: No. 775). 1977. reprint ed. lib. bdg. 45.00 (*90-221-0775-2*) Walter J Johnson.

Bernard, Richard, et al. A Gift in Trust Wilmington Friends School. A Celebration of Our First 250 Years. 1998. text 55.00 (*0-9664011-0-7*) Wlmngton Frnds Schl.

Bernard, Richard M. The Melting Pot & the Altar: Marital Assimilation in Early Twentieth-Century Wisconsin. LC 80-16287. 190p. reprint ed. pap. 58.90 (*0-7837-2977-4*, 205747700006) Bks Demand.

Bernard, Richard M., ed. Snowbelt Cities: Metropolitan Politics in the Northeast & Midwest since World War II. LC 89-19931. 284p. 1990. 35.00 (*0-253-31177-2*) Ind U Pr.

Bernard, Robert W., ed. Surgical Restoration of the Aging Face. (Illus.). 333p. 1996. text 115.00 (*0-7506-9438-6*) Buttrwrth-Heinemann.

Bernard, Robin. Bats. 32p. 1998. pap. 8.95 (*0-590-10617-1*) Scholastic Inc.

— The Bug Book. (Illus.). (J). 1994. pap. 10.95 (*0-590-49743-X*) Scholastic Inc.

— Deserts. (J). 1996. pap. 10.95 (*0-590-49801-0*) Scholastic Inc.

— Insects. LC 98-49827. 1999. 7.95 (*0-7922-9431-9*) Natl Geog.

***Bernard, Robin.** Insects. LC 98-49827. 1999. pap. 12.95 (*0-7922-9425-4*) Natl Geog.

Bernard, Robin. Interactive Animal Kit: Bears. 1996. pap. 10.95 (*0-590-67479-X*) Scholastic Inc.

— Juma & the Honey-Guide: An African Tale. LC 95-20007. (Illus.). 32p. (J). (gr. 1-3). 1996. 13.95 (*0-382-39163-2*); pap. 5.95 (*0-382-39164-0*); lib. bdg. 15.95 (*0-382-39162-4*) Silver Burdett Pr.

— Penguins: A Theme Unit Developed in Cooperation with P.R.B.O. Biological Research. 1994. pap. 10.95 (*0-590-49639-5*) Scholastic Inc.

***Bernard, Robin.** Quickart Crayon Projects: 25 Instant Activities That Bring Out The Creativity in Every Child. (Illus.). 64p. 1999. pap. 10.95 (*0-590-98339-3*) Scholastic Inc.

Bernard, Robin. Tree for All Seasons. LC 98-32435. 1999. write for info. (*0-7922-9427-0*); pap. write for info. (*0-7922-9435-1*) Natl Geog.

Bernard, Ryan. The Corporate Intranet. 2nd ed. 464p. 1997. pap. 29.99 (*0-471-24775-8*) Wiley.

Bernard, Shane K. Swamp Pop: Cajun & Creole Rhythm & Blues. LC 95-53231. (American Made Music Ser.). (Illus.). 232p. (C). 1996. 50.00 (*0-87805-875-3*); cd-rom 16.00 (*0-87805-896-6*) U Pr of Miss.

Bernard-Shaw, Mary. Archaeological Investigations at Los Morteros, AA:12:57 (ASM), Locus 1, in the Northern Tucson Basin. (Technical Reports: No. 87-8). (Illus.). 103p. 1987. pap. 8.00 (*1-886398-00-3*) Desert Archaeol.

— Archaeological Investigations at the Lonetree Site, AA:12:120 (ASM), in the Northern Tucson Basin. (Technical Reports: No. 90-1). (Illus.). 294p. (Orig.). 1990. pap. 12.00 (*1-886398-03-8*) Desert Archaeol.

— Archaeological Investigations at the Redtail Site, AA:12:149 (ASM) in the Northern Tucson Basin. (Technical Reports: No. 89-8). (Illus.). 289p. (Orig.). 1989. pap. 12.00 (*1-886398-02-X*) Desert Archaeol.

An Asterisk (*) at the beginning of an entry indicates that the title is appearing for the first time.

Bernard-Shaw, Mary & Huntington, Frederick W. Rincon Phase Seasonal Occupation in the Northern Tucson Basin. (Technical Reports: No. 90-2). (Illus.). 290p. (Orig.). 1990. pap. 12.00 (1-886398-04-6) Desert Archaeol.

Bernard, Shulamit L. Racial Differences in Perceptions of Access to Health Care among the Elderly. rev. ed. LC 96-39994. (Studies on the Elderly in America). (Illus.). 183p. 1997. text 58.00 (0-8153-2646-7) Garland.

Bernard, Sidney. Metamorphosis of Peace: Essays & Poems. 25p. 1984. pap. 3.50 (0-933292-13-9) Arts End.

Bernard, Stanley, et al. Map & Track: State Initiatives to Encourage Responsible Fatherhood. LC 97-24729. 80p. 1997. pap. 19.95 (0-926582-22-4) NCCP.

— Map & Track: State Initiatives to Encourage Responsible Fatherhood, 1999 Edition. LC 99-32963. 200p. 1999. pap. 19.95 (0-926582-24-0) NCCP.

Bernard, Stephane. The Franco-Moroccan Conflict, 1943-1956. LC 67-24490. 716p. reprint ed. pap. 200.00 (0-8357-8720-6, 203367200087) Bks Demand.

Bernard, Susan. The Mommy Guide. 416p. 1994. pap. 16.95 (0-8092-3797-0, 379700, Contemporary Bks) NTC Contemp Pub Co.

***Bernard, Susan & Yager, Cary O.** The Mommy & Daddy Guide to Kindergarten: Real-Life Advice & Tips from Parents & Other Experts. LC 00-31411. 224p. 2000. pap. 14.95 (0-8092-2547-6, Contemporary Bks) NTC Contemp Pub Co.

Bernard, Susan A. The Fortuneflower. LC 95-76914. (Illus.). 137p. (Orig.). 1995. pap. 20.00 (0-9629950-6-1) Ashbrook Pub.

Bernard, Ted & Young, Jora. The Ecology of Hope: Communities Collaborate for Sustainability. LC 98-117507. (Illus.). 192p. (Orig.). 1996. pap. 16.95 (0-86571-355-3) New Soc Pubs.

Bernard, Theod. Hindu Philosophy. (C). 1996. pap. 10.00 (81-208-1372-3, Pub. by Motilal Bnarsidass) S Asia.

Bernard, Thierry M., ed. Advanced Focal Plane Arrays & Electronic Cameras. (Europto Ser.: Vol. 2950). 342p. 1996. 66.00 (0-8194-2354-8) SPIE.

— Advanced Focal Plane Arrays & Electronic Cameras II. LC 99-200310. (Europto Ser.: Vol. 3410). 246p. 1998. 59.00 (0-8194-2862-0) SPIE.

Bernard, Thomas. The Consensus-Conflict Debate: Form & Content in Social Theories. LC 83-2032. 264p. 1983. text 64.50 (0-231-05670-2) Col U Pr.

— The New School: 1809 Edition. Stern, Jeffrey, ed. & intro. by. (Classics in Education Ser.). 120p. 1996. reprint ed. 65.00 (1-85506-271-2) Bks Intl VA.

Bernard, Thomas J. The Cycle of Juvenile Justice. (Illus.). 208p. (C). 1991. pap. text 21.95 (0-19-507183-2) OUP.

Bernard, Thomas J., ed. see Hassine, Victor, et al.

Bernard, Tristan. Dictionnaire Humoristique de A a Z. Drachline, Pierre, ed. (FRE.). 1993. write for info. (0-7859-8125-X, 2-86274-287-2) Fr & Eur.

***Bernard, Virginia.** Eliza & the Sacred Mountain. (Illus.). 128p. (J). (gr. 4-8). 2000. pap. 7.95 (1-893577-05-8, Pub. by Four Corners Pubg) Seven Hills Bk.

Bernard, Virginia. Eliza down Under: Going to Sydney. (Illus.). 96p. 2000. pap. 7.95 (1-893577-02-3) Four Corners Pubg.

Bernard, W. B., jt. auth. see Johnson, T. W.

Bernard Westcott, Nadine. I Know an Old Lady Who Swallowed a Fly. 1988. 12.15 (0-606-13506-5, Pub. by Turtleback) Demco.

Bernard, Y. & Colli, J. C. Economic & Finance Dictionary French-English-German-Spanish. 6th ed. 1515p. 1996. 145.00 (2-02-030086-9, Pub. by Editions Seuil) IBD Ltd.

Bernard, Yolande & Janowski, Samek. Vocabulary of Government Finance Management. 2nd ed. (FRE & ENG., Illus.). 580p. 1997. pap. 52.95 (0-660-60198-2, Pub. by Canadian Govt Pub) Accents Pubns.

Bernard, Yves. Dictionary of Economics & Finance: English, French, German & Spanish. 4th ed. (ENG, FRE, GER & SPA.). 1996. 225.00 (0-7859-9476-9) Fr & Eur.

— International Economic & Financial Dictionary, English, French, German, Spanish. 6th ed. (ENG, FRE, GER & SPA.). 1511p. 1994. 195.00 (0-7859-9937-X) Fr & Eur.

Bernard, Yves & Colli, Jean-Claude. Economics & Finance Dictionaries: Dictionnaire Economique et Financier. 1200p. 1989. 195.00 (0-8288-1262-4, M4643) Fr & Eur.

***Bernard, Yves & Colli, Jean-Claude.** International Economic & Financial Dictionary: A Multi-Lingual Guide to the European Community, 1993. Moyer, Darienne, tr. (ENG, FRE, GER & SPA.). 468p. 2000. reprint ed. pap. text 25.00 (0-7881-6948-3) DIANE Pub.

Bernard, Yves & Colli, Jean-Claude. Vocabulaire Economique et Financier: Coll. Points Economie. 6th ed. (FRE.). 634p. 1990. pap. 14.95 (0-7859-4807-4, M6031) Fr & Eur.

— Vocabulario Economico y Financiero. (SPA.). 488p. 1981. pap. 36.00 (0-7859-4916-X) Fr & Eur.

Bernard, Yves, et al. Dictionary of Economics & Finance: Diccionario Economico y Financiero. 3rd ed. (ENG & SPA.). 1341p. 1981. 150.00 (0-8288-1287-X, S33136) Fr & Eur.

Bernardelli, C., jt. auth. see Levialdi, Stefano.

Bernardelli, J., jt. auth. see Bankowski, Z.

Bernardes, Jon. Family Studies: An Introduction. LC 96-47497. 256p. (C). 1997. 80.00 (0-415-16468-0); pap. 22.99 (0-415-16469-9) Routledge.

Bernardez, Aurora, ed. see Cortazar, Julio.

Bernardez-Clark, Eliana De, see Georgiou, George & De Bernardez-Clark, Eliana, eds.

***Bernardez, Manucia.** Space Songs for Children: Fun Songs & Activities about Outer Space. (Illus.). 100p. 1999. pap. 17.95 (0-936823-19-4) Pearce Evetts.

Bernardi. Tax in North Africa. 1994. pap. text 50.00 (90-6544-779-2) Kluwer Academic.

***Bernardi, Adria.** The Day Laid on the Altar. LC 00-23151. 224p. 2000. 24.95 (1-58465-044-3) U Pr of New Eng.

Bernardi, Adria. Houses with Names: The Italian Immigrants of Highwood, Illinois. (Illus.). 304p. 1990. 25.95 (0-252-01581-9) U of Ill Pr.

***Bernardi, Adria.** In the Gathering Woods. 142p. 2000. 22.50 (0-8229-4131-7) U of Pittsburgh Pr.

***Bernardi, Adria, et al.** The Thing about Love Is... 304p. 1999. pap. 15.95 (0-9673109-0-3) Polyphony Pr.

Bernardi, Bernardo. The Mugwe, a Failing Prophet: A Study of a Religious & Public Dignitary of the Meru of Kenya. LC 59-3468. 227p. reprint ed. pap. 70.40 (0-608-13443-0, 202278500029) Bks Demand.

Bernardi, Bernardo, ed. The Concept & Dynamics of Culture. (World Anthropology Ser.). xii, 630p. 1977. 78.50 (90-279-7939-1) Mouton.

***Bernardi, C., et al.** Spectral Methods for Axisymmetric Domains. (Series in Applied Mathmatics). 358p. 1999. 90.00 (2-84299-071-4, Pub. by ESME) Elsevier.

Bernardi, Christine & Maday, Yvon, eds. Analysis, Algorithms & Applications of Spectral & High Order Methods for Partial Differential Equations: Selected Papers from the International Conference on Spectral & High Order Methods (ICOSAHOM '92) Le Corum, Montpellier, France, 22-26 June 1992. LC 94-22802. 520p. 1994. 266.00 (0-444-89564-7) Elsevier.

Bernardi, Daniel. Star Trek & History: Race-Ing Toward a White Future. LC 97-17665. 1998. 48.00 (0-8135-2465-2); pap. 17.00 (0-8135-2466-0) Rutgers U Pr.

Bernardi, Daniel, ed. The Birth of Whiteness: Race & the Emergence of United States Cinema. LC 95-52727. (Illus.). 350p. (C). 1996. text 50.00 (0-8135-2275-7); pap. text 18.95 (0-8135-2276-5) Rutgers U Pr.

Bernardi, Dominic Di, see Hyvernaud, Georges.

Bernardi, Dominic Di, see Roubaud, Jacques.

Bernardi, Dominic Di, see Hyvernaud, Georges.

Bernardi, Dominic Di, see Hyvernaud, Georges & Di Bernardi, Dominic.

Bernardi, Dominic Di, see Roubaud, Jacques.

Bernardi, Dominic Di, see Hyvernaud, Georges.

Bernardi, Dominic Di, see Roubaud, Jacques.

Bernardi, Dominic Di, see Roubaud, Jacques & Di Bernardi, Dominic.

Bernardi, Dominic Di, see Roubaud, Jacques.

Bernardi, Dominic Di, see Roubaud, Jacques & Di Bernardi, Dominic.

Bernardi, Francesco & Rivail, Jean-Louis, eds. Computational Chemistry: F.E.C.S. Conference. (AIP Conference Proceedings Ser.: No. 330). (Illus.). 900p. 1995. text 165.00 (1-56396-457-0) Am Inst Physics.

Bernardi, G., ed. The Basal Ganglia 3. (Advances in Behavioral Biology Ser.: Vol. 39). (Illus.). 793p. (C). 1991. text 198.00 (0-306-43720-1, Kluwer Plenum) Kluwer Academic.

Bernardi, G., jt. ed. see Mooney, Harold A.

Bernardi, Janet, jt. auth. see Mahedy, William.

Bernardi, Philip. Improvisation Starters: A Collection of Nine Hundred Improvisation Situations for the Theater. 160p. 1992. pap. 12.99 (1-55870-233-4, Betrwy Bks) F & W Pubns Inc.

Bernardi, Philip & Havens, Diane. Twice upon a Time. LC 95-15994. (Illus.). 24p. (J). 1995. pap. 6.00 (0-88734-425-9) Players Pr.

Bernardi, Roy & Wilson, Fred. Greater Syracuse: Center of an Empire. LC 98-34565. (Urban Tapestry Ser.). (Illus.). 250p. 1998. 44.95 (1-881096-64-5) Towery Pub.

Bernardi, S. D. Bibliography of Schlicht Functions. 363p. 1982. 15.00 (0-936166-09-6) Polygonal Pub.

Bernardin. Practical Considerations of RF. text. write for info. (0-471-49183-7) Wiley.

Bernardin, Claude & Stanton, Tom. Rocket Man: Elton John from A-Z. LC 96-22900. 280p. 1996. pap. 19.95 (0-275-95698-9, Praeger Pubs) Greenwood.

— Rocket Man: The Encyclopedia of Elton John. LC 95-9938. 280p. 1995. lib. bdg. 39.95 (0-313-29700-2, Greenwood Pr) Greenwood.

Bernardin, H. John. Human Resources Management: An Experimental Approach. (C). 1993. text 58.00 (0-07-004916-5) McGraw.

— Women in the Work Force. LC 82-13170. 242p. 1982. 55.00 (0-275-90761-9, C0761, Praeger Pubs) Greenwood.

Bernardin, James. Giants! Stories from around the World. abr. ed. LC 94-37086. 80p. (J). (gr. 3-7). 1995. 17.00 (0-15-200883-7, Harcourt Child Bks) Harcourt.

Bernardin, John H. & Russell, Joyce E. Human Resource Management: An Experiential Approach. 2nd ed. LC 97-32386. 704p. 1997. pap. 63.75 (0-07-005846-6) McGraw.

Bernardin, Joseph Buchanan. Introduction to the Episcopal Church. rev. ed. 140p. 1990. pap. 9.95 (0-8192-1231-8) Morehouse Pub.

Bernardin, Joseph Louis. A Blessing to Each Other: Cardinal Joseph Bernardin & Jewish-Catholic Dialogue. LC 96-79340. 200p. 1996. pap. 18.00 (1-56854-104-X, BERNAR) Liturgy Tr Pubns.

***Bernardin, Joseph Louis.** El Don de la Paz. 1999. 21.95 (84-08-02411-6) Planeta Edit.

Bernardin, Joseph Louis. The Gift of Peace: Personal Reflections. LC 98-28019. 176p. 1998. pap. 11.00 (0-385-49434-3) Doubleday.

— The Gift of Peace: Personal Reflections. LC 96-50335. 156p. 1997. 17.95 (0-8294-0955-6) Loyola Pr.

— The Gift of Peace: Personal Reflections. large type ed. LC 97-43528. 224p. 1998. pap. 13.95 (0-8027-2725-5) Walker & Co.

— Growing in Wisdom, Age & Grace: A Guide for Parents in the Religious Education of Their Children. rev. ed. (Illus.). 104p. 1996. pap. 12.00 (0-8215-3309-6) Sadlier.

— Guia para la Asamblea. Huck, Gabe, ed. (Basics of Ministry Ser.: No. 3). Orig. Title: Our Communion, Our Peace, Our Promise. (ENG & SPA., Illus.). 58p. 1997. pap. 5.00 (1-56854-215-1, SGUIDE) Liturgy Tr Pubns.

— Guide for the Assembly. rev. ed. Huck, Gabe, ed. LC 97-8275. (Basics of Ministry Ser.: No. 2). Orig. Title: Our Communion, Our Peace, Our Promise. (Illus.). 64p. (Orig.). 1997. pap. 5.00 (1-56854-214-3, EGUIDE) Liturgy Tr Pubns.

— A Moral Vision for America. Langan, John P., ed. LC 97-37973. 176p. 1998. 45.00 (0-87840-675-1) Georgetown U Pr.

***Bernardin, Joseph Louis.** Selected Works of Joseph Cardinal Bernardin Vol. 1: Homilies & Teaching Documents. Spilly, Alphonse P., ed. LC 99-39499. 680p. 2000. 34.95 (0-8146-2583-5) Liturgical Pr.

— Selected Works of Joseph Cardinal Bernardin Vol. 2: Church & Society. Spilly, Alphonse P., ed. 688p. 2000. 34.95 (0-8146-2584-3) Liturgical Pr.

Bernardin, Joseph Louis. The Word of Cardinal Bernardin. LC 96-52982. vi, 226p. (Orig.). 1996. pap. 14.95 (1-57703-000-1) CMS.

Bernardin, Joseph Louis, et al. Consistent Ethic of Life. Fuechtmann, Thomas G., ed. LC 88-61497. vi, 258p. (Orig.). 1988. pap. 12.95 (1-55612-120-2) Sheed & Ward WI.

Bernardin, Joseph Louis, jt. auth. see Reese, Thomas J.

Bernardin, Tom. The Ellis Island Immigrant Cookbook. 272p. 1997. spiral bd. 17.95 (0-9629198-3-7) T Bernardin.

Bernardin, Tom, jt. auth. see Patraker, Deborah M.

***Bernardini, Alberto, ed.** Seismic Damage to Masonry Buildings: Proceedings of the International Workshop, Padova, Italy, 25-27 June, 1998. (Illus.). 265p. 1999. text 88.00 (90-5809-115-5) A A Balkema.

Bernardini, C., et al. Thinking Physics for Teaching: Proceedings of an International Conference on Thinking Science for Teaching: The Case of Physics Held in Rome, Italy, September 22-27, 1994. (Illus.). 464p. (C). 1996. 125.00 (0-306-45192-1, Plenum Trade) Perseus Pubng.

***Bernardini, G., et al, eds.** Atlas of Xenopus Development. LC 99-18460. (Illus.). 100p. 1999. 92.00 (88-470-0036-X, Pub. by Spr-Verlag) Spr-Verlag.

***Bernardini, Paolo & Fiering, Norman, eds.** The Jews & the Expansion of Europe to the West, 1400-1800. LC 99-44924. (European Expansion & Global Interaction Ser.: Vol. 2). 544p. 2000. 49.95 (1-57181-153-2) Berghahn Bks.

Bernardini, Piero. The Italian Law on Arbitration: English Text & Notes. LC 98-21732. (Arbitration Legislation Ser.). (DUT & ENG.). 140p. 1998. 54.00 (90-411-1030-5) Kluwer Law Intl.

Bernardini, Robert. Christmas All Over. LC 96-20080. (Illus.). 32p. (J). (gr. 1-4). 1996. 14.95 (1-56554-205-3) Pelican.

— Santa's Christmas Surprise. LC 94-12716. (Illus.). 32p. (J). (ps-3). 1994. 14.95 (1-56554-089-1) Pelican.

— Southern Love for Christmas. LC 93-1248. (Illus.). 32p. (J). (gr. 4-7). 1993. reprint ed. text 14.95 (0-88289-974-0) Pelican.

— A Southern Time Christmas. LC 91-12467. (Illus.). 32p. (J). (gr. 4-7). 1991. reprint ed. text 14.95 (0-88289-828-0) Pelican.

Bernardino, Adriana. Telecommuting: The Employer's & Employee's Decision-Making Process. rev. ed. LC 96-36710. (Studies on Industrial Productivity). (Illus.). 178p. 1996. text 51.00 (0-8153-2723-4) Garland.

Bernardino de Sahagun, Fray. Primeros Memoriales. LC 96-45377. (Civilization of the American Indian Ser.: Vol. 200, Pt. 1). 192p. 1993. pap. 170.00 (0-8061-1678-9) U of Okla Pr.

— Primeros Memoriales, Vol. 200. Sullivan, Thelma D., tr. LC 96-45377. (Civilization of the American Indian Ser.: Vol. 200, Pt. II). (Illus.). 352p. 1997. 75.00 (0-8061-2909-3) U of Okla Pr.

Bernardino, Valerie, ed. see Beachum, Millie.

Bernardo, Aldo S. Francesco Petrarca, Citizen of the World. LC 79-13968. 315p. (C). 1980. pap. text 19.95 (0-87395-392-4) State U NY Pr.

— Petrarch, Laura & the Triumphs. LC 74-22084. 234p. (C). 1974. text 19.50 (0-87395-289-8, PSU1, Pub. by State U NY Pr) Pegasus Pr.

Bernardo, Aldo S. & Levin, Saul, eds. The Classics in the Middle Ages. (Medieval & Renaissance Texts & Studies: Vol. 69). 432p. 1990. 25.00 (0-86698-078-4, MR69) MRTS.

Bernardo, Aldo S. & Pellegrini, Anthony L., eds. Dante, Petrarch, Boccaccio: Studies in the Italian Trecento in Honor of Charles S. Singleton. LC 83-717. (Medieval & Renaissance Texts & Studies: Vol. 22). (Illus.). 430p. 1983. 36.00 (0-86698-061-X, MR22) MRTS.

Bernardo, Aldo S., tr. see Petrarca, Francesco.

Bernardo, Anilu. Fitting In. LC 96-15676. 200p. (J). (gr. 7 up). 1996. pap. 9.95 (1-55885-173-9, Pinata Bks) Arte Publico.

— Fitting In. 1996. 13.05 (0-606-13390-9, Pub. by Turtleback) Demco.

— Jumping off to Freedom. LC 95-37667. 198p. (YA). (gr. 6-12). 1996. pap. 9.95 (1-55885-088-0, Pinata Bks) Arte Publico.

— Jumping Off to Freedom. 1996. 13.05 (0-606-13547-2, Pub. by Turtleback) Demco.

— Loves Me, Loves Me Not. 169p. (J). (gr. 6-12). 1998. pap. 9.95 (1-55885-259-X, Pinata Bks) Arte Publico.

Bernardo, Barbara. Paralegal: An Insider's Guide to One of the Fastest-Growing Careers. 3rd ed. LC 98-126339. (Peterson's Guides Ser.). 224p. 1997. pap. text 16.95 (1-56079-894-7) Petersons.

— Paralegal: An Insider's Guide to One of the Fastest-Growing Occupations of the 1990s. 2nd ed. LC 92-45649. 224p. 1993. pap. 11.95 (1-56079-242-5) Petersons.

Bernardo, C. Joseph & Bacon, Eugene H. American Military Policy. LC 74-9697. 548p. 1974. reprint ed. lib. bdg. 79.50 (0-8371-7615-8, BEMP, Greenwood Pr) Greenwood.

Bernardo, Connie, ed. see Gallant, JD & RV Consumer Group Staff.

Bernardo, Francis C. Through Mary's Eyes: Reflections of Her Life & Times. LC 97-25008. 80p. (Orig.). 1997. pap. 6.95 (0-8091-3745-3, 3745-3) Paulist Pr.

Bernardo, J. M., et al, eds. Bayesian Statistics Vol. 5: Proceedings of the Fifth Valencia International Meeting. LC 96-13440. (Illus.). 824p. 1996. text 115.00 (0-19-852356-4, Clarendon Pr) OUP.

***Bernardo, Jose M., et al, eds.** Bayesian Statistics 6: Proceedings of the Sixth Valencia International Meeting. (Illus.). 880p. 1999. text 140.00 (0-19-850485-3) OUP.

Bernardo, Jose M. & Smith, Adrian F. Bayesian Theory. LC 93-37554. (Probability & Mathematical Statistics Ser.). 604p. 1994. 215.00 (0-471-92416-4) Wiley.

***Bernardo, Jose R.** The Secret of the Bulls. 299p. 1999. reprint ed. text 22.00 (0-7881-6598-4) DIANE Pub.

Bernardo, Jose R. Silent Wing. LC 98-10521. 240p. (YA). 1998. 23.00 (0-684-84389-7) S&S Trade.

— Silent Wing. large type ed. LC 98-48558. (Thorndike Basic Ser.). 1999. 26.95 (0-7862-1757-X) Thorndike Pr.

Bernardo, Jose Raul. The Secret of the Bulls: Reading Group Guide. 1997. pap. write for info. (0-684-00255-8, Scribner Pap Fic) S&S Trade Pap.

Bernardo, Joseph, ed. see Resetarits, William J.

Bernardo, Karen, jt. auth. see Curtin, Lawrence.

Bernardo, Karen, ed. see Mirra, Gerald B.

Bernardo, Lisa Marie. Pediatric Emergency Nursing Procedures. (Nursing-Health Science Ser.). 1992. pap. text 42.50 (0-86720-330-7) Jones & Bartlett.

Bernardo, Mark A. De, see De Bernardo, Mark A.

Bernardo, Stephanie. The Ethnic Almanac. LC 80-18776. 1981. pap. 10.95 (0-385-14144-0) Doubleday.

Bernardoni, Gus. Golf God's Way. LC 77-80414. (Illus.). 256p. reprint ed. pap. 11.95 (0-9629952-0-7) Bernardoni Ent.

Bernardr, B., ed. Poisonous Plants of All Countries, 1923. (C). 1923. 170.00 (0-7855-2284-0, Pub. by Scientific) St Mut.

Bernards, Monique. Changing Traditions: Al-Mubarrad's Refutation of Sibawayh & the Subsequent Reception of the Kitab. LC 97-8571. (Studies in Semitic Languages & Linguistics: Vol. 23). (Illus.). 352p. 1996. 97.50 (90-04-10595-6) Brill Academic Pubs.

Bernards, Neal. Big Blue: The Kentucky Wildcats Story. LC 98-38328. (College Sports Today Ser.). (Illus.). 32p. (YA). (gr. 4 up). 1999. lib. bdg. 21.30 (0-88682-992-5, Creat Educ) Creative Co.

— Elections: Locating the Author's Main Idea. LC 92-21793. (Opposing Viewpoints Juniors Ser.). (Illus.). 36p. (J). (gr. 4-7). 1992. lib. bdg. 16.20 (1-56510-022-0) Greenhaven.

— Garnet & Gold: The Florida State Seminoles Story. LC 98-46471. (Illus.). 32p. (YA). (gr. 4 up). 1999. lib. bdg. 21.30 (0-88682-977-1, Creat Educ) Creative Co.

— Gun Control. LC 91-15561. (Overview Ser.). (Illus.). 112p. (YA). (gr. 5-8). 1991. lib. bdg. 22.45 (1-56006-127-8) Lucent Bks.

— Maize & Blue: The Michigan Wolverines Story. LC 98-30934. (College Sports Today Ser.). (Illus.). 32p. (YA). (gr. 4 up). 1999. lib. bdg. 21.30 (0-88682-979-8, Creat Educ) Creative Co.

— Mir Space Station. LC 98-18246. (Above & Beyond Ser.). (Illus.). 32p. (YA). (gr. 4 up). 2000. lib. bdg. 21.30 (1-58340-049-4) Smart Apple.

— The Palestinian Conflict: Identifying Propaganda Techniques. LC 90-37741. (Opposing Viewpoints Juniors Ser.). (Illus.). 36p. (J). (gr. 3-6). 1990. lib. bdg. 16.20 (0-89908-602-0) Greenhaven.

Bernards, Neal. Population: Detecting Bias. LC 92-17419. (Opposing Viewpoints Juniors Ser.). (Illus.). 36p. (J). (gr. 4-7). 1992. lib. bdg. 16.20 (0-89908-622-5) Greenhaven.

Bernards, Neal. The War on Drugs: Examining Cause & Effect Relationships. LC 91-22021. (Opposing Viewpoints Juniors Ser.). (Illus.). 36p. (J). (gr. 4-7). 1991. lib. bdg. 16.20 (0-89908-612-8) Greenhaven.

Bernards, Neal & Szumski, Bonnie. Prisons: Detecting Bias. LC 90-45284. (Opposing Viewpoints Juniors Ser.). (Illus.). 36p. (J). (gr. 3-6). 1990. lib. bdg. 16.20 (0-89908-604-7) Greenhaven.

Bernardus Guidonis. Manuel de l'Inquisiteur, 2 vols. in 1. Mollat, G., ed. LC 78-63183. (Heresies of the Early Christian & Medieval Era Ser.: Second Ser.). reprint ed. 79.50 (0-404-16199-5) AMS Pr.

Bernardy, Catherine J. Fuel. LC 98-6291. (Let's Investigate Ser.). 32p. (J). (gr. 1-4). 1998. lib. bdg. 19.95 (0-88682-989-5, Creat Educ) Creative Co.

***Bernardy, Catherine J.** Sojourner Truth: Abolitionist & Women's Rights Activist. LC 00-9279. (Historical American Biographies Ser.). 2001. write for info. (0-7660-1257-3) Enslow Pubs.

Bernardy, Catherine J., et al. Let's Investigate, 12 Vol. (Illus.). 384p. (J). 167.40 (0-88682-667-5) Creative Co.

Bernareggi, Adriano. Les Papes. (FRE., Illus.). 95p. 1940. lib. bdg. 8.95 (0-8288-3998-0) Fr & Eur.

Bernaschek, G., et al. Endosonography in Obstetrics & Gynecology. (Illus.). 192p. 1990. 181.00 (0-387-50328-5) Spr-Verlag.

Bernaschoni, John R. Guide to Antiques & Fine Arts. (Reference Library). 1998. pap. 6.95 (1-85326-343-5, 3435WW, Pub. by Wrdsworth Edits) NTC Contemp Pub Co.

Bernasconi, Maurizio & Tenucci, Marco. Extreme Rafting. (Extreme Sports Ser.). (Illus.). 128p. 1998. pap. 22.50 (0-7893-0221-7, Pub. by Universe) St Martin.

B

An Asterisk (*) at the beginning of an entry indicates that the title is appearing for the first time.

Bernasconi, Robert. Heidegger in Question: The Art of Existing. LC 92-23831. (Philosophy & Literary Theory Ser.). (Illus.). 288p. (C). 1993. text 45.00 (0-391-03761-7) Humanities.

— Heidegger in Question: The Art of Existing. LC 92-23831. (Philosophy & Literary Theory Ser.). 288p. (C). 1996. pap. 18.50 (0-391-03963-6) Humanities.

***Bernasconi, Robert, ed.** Race. 2001. 62.95 (0-631-20782-1); pap. 27.95 (0-631-20783-X) Blackwell Pubs.

Bernasconi, Robert & Critchley, Simon, eds. Re-Reading Levinas. LC 90-41833. (Studies in Continental Thought). 270p. 1991. 39.95 (0-253-31179-9); pap. 15.95 (0-253-20624-3) Ind U Pr.

***Bernasconi, Robert & Lott, Tommy Lee, eds.** The Idea of Race. LC 99-52338. 256p. (C). 2000. pap. 10.95 (0-87220-458-8); lib. bdg. 34.95 (0-87220-459-6) Hackett Pub.

Bernasconi, Robert, ed. see Gadamer, Hans-Georg.

Bernasconi, Robert, jt. ed. see Wood, David.

Bernasconi, S., jt. ed. see Attansio, A.

Bernasconi, Stefano M. Geochemical & Microbial Controls on Dolomite Formation in Anoxic Environments - A Case Study from the Middle Triassic: Ticino, Switzerland. (Contributions to Sedimentology Ser.: No. 19). (Illus.). vi, 109p. 1994. pap. 44.00 (3-510-57019-7, Pub. by E Schweizerbartsche) Balogh.

Bernasek, S. Heterogeneous Reaction Dynamics. 1995. 55.00 (0-89573-742-6, Wiley-VCH) Wiley.

Bernasek, S. Heterogeneous Reaction Dynamics. 158p. 1995. 89.95 (0-471-18547-7) Wiley.

Bernat, Ivan, ed. Iron Metabolism. Gosztonyi, Eva, tr. from HUN. 416p. 1983. 85.00 (0-306-30829-0, Plenum Trade) Perseus Pubng.

Bernat, James L. Ethical Issues in Neurology. LC 94-19096. 364p. 1994. text 63.00 (0-7506-9501-3) Buttrwrth-Heinemann.

Bernat, James L. & Vincent, Frederick M. Neurology: Problems in Primary Care. 2nd ed. Karaffa, Melanie C., ed. LC 92-6786. (Problems in Primary Care Ser.). (Illus.). 900p. 1993. pap. text 49.95 (1-878487-85-X, 5855M) Practice Mgmt Info.

Bernat, Robin. Waiting: Eleven Poems of Love & Anticipation. LC 97-92330. (Illus.). (Orig.). 1997. pap. 10.00 (0-9659336-0-1) Circle B Pr.

Bernat, Tivadar. An Economic Geography of Hungary. 2nd ed. Compton, P. A. & Vegas, I., trs. 473p. (C). 1989. 171.00 (963-05-4990-5, Pub. by Akade Kiado) St Mut.

Bernatchez, David. Poems of Fear & Delight. 36p. 1994. pap. 5.00 (0-9626735-9-5) Rabeth Pub Co.

Bernatchez, Yvon, jt. auth. see Fleury, Claude.

Bernath. Cactus Col. Bk. 1998. pap. 2.95 (0-486-24097-5) Dover.

— Trees of the Northeast. 1950. pap. text 2.95 (0-486-23734-6) Dover.

Bernath, Gary. Blue Poetry. 2nd ed. Ewen, David, ed. (Illus.). 64p. 1997. reprint ed. pap. 7.00 (1-889436-00-3) Ewen Prime.

Bernath, Jeno. Poppy: The Genus Papaver. (Medicinal & Aromatic Plants-Industrial Profiles Ser.). 360p. 1998. text 100.00 (90-5702-271-0, Harwood Acad Pubs) Gordon & Breach.

Bernath, Joseph. Pirket Ovous: Beir Yehuda. 2nd ed. write for info. (1-879515-00-8) Beir Yehuda.

***Bernath, Maja.** Parents Book for Your Baby's First Year. (Orig.). 1999. pap. 5.98 (0-345-43638-5, Ballantine) Ballantine Pub Grp.

Bernath, Peter F. Spectra of Atoms & Molecules. (Illus.). 416p. (C). 1995. text 67.95 (0-19-507598-6) OUP.

Bernath, Stefen. Floral Borders on Layout Grids. 1988. pap. text 20.80 (0-486-26535-8) Dover.

— Garden Flowers-Coloring Book. (J). 1978. pap. 2.95 (0-486-23142-9) Dover.

— Ready-to-Use Floral Borders on Layout Grids. (Clip Art Ser.). (Illus.). 64p. 1988. text 5.95 (0-486-25562-X) Dover.

— Ready-to-Use Floral Spot Illustrations. (Clip Art Ser.). (Illus.). 64p. 1989. pap. 5.95 (0-486-26064-X) Dover.

— Tropical Fish - Coloring Book. (J). 1978. pap. 2.95 (0-486-23620-X) Dover.

Bernath, Stuart L. Squall Across the Atlantic: American Civil War Prize Cases & Diplomacy. LC 76-79042. 239p. reprint ed. pap. 74.10 (0-608-15835-6, 203142500074) Bks Demand.

Bernatowicz, Elizabeth C., jt. auth. see Holman, Susan R.

Bernatzik, Hugo A. Akha & Miao: Problems of Applied Ethnography in Farther India. LC 73-114702. (Monographs). 780p. 1970. 30.00 (0-87536-027-0) HRAFP.

Bernatzky, A. Tree Ecology & Preservation. (Developments in Agricultural & Managed-Forest Ecology Ser.: Vol. 2). viii,358p. 1978. 157.50 (0-444-41606-4) Elsevier.

Bernau, George. Candle in the Wind. 544p. 1992. mass mkt. 5.99 (0-446-36128-3, Pub. by Warner Bks) Little.

— Promises to Keep. 1989. mass mkt. 5.95 (0-446-35605-0, Pub. by Warner Bks) Little.

***Bernau, Katharina.** Die Voraussetzungen Und Umfang Der Haftung Des Patentlizenznehmers Nach Deutschem Und Us-Amerikanischem Recht. XLII, 478p. 1999. 73.95 (3-631-31719-0) P Lang Pubng.

Bernauer, James W. Michel Foucault's Force of Flight: Toward an Ethics for Thought. LC 89-31526. (Contemporary Studies in Philosophy & the Human Sciences). 280p. (C). 1992. reprint ed. pap. 17.50 (0-391-03740-4) Humanities.

Bernauer, James W. & Rasmussen, David, eds. The Final Foucault. 176p. (Orig.). 1988. pap. text 13.50 (0-262-52132-6) MIT Pr.

Bernauer, Markus, ed. see Alexis, Willibald.

Bernauer, Thomas. The Chemistry of Regime Formation. LC 93-20003. 479p. 1993. 72.95 (1-85521-349-4, Pub. by Dartmth Pub) Ashgate Pub Co.

Bernauer, Thomas, et al, eds. The Politics of Postive Incentives in Arms Control. LC 98-58082. (Studies in International Relations). 202p. 1999. 34.95 (1-57003-301-3) U of SC Pr.

Bernauer, Thomas, jt. auth. see Singh, Jasjit.

Bernauer, Wolfgang, et al, eds. Cicatrising Conjunctivitis. LC 97-28508. (Developments in Ophthalmology Ser.: Vol. 28, 1997). (Illus.). xvi, 266p. 1997. 248.00 (3-8055-6443-0) S Karger.

Bernay, Toni & Cantor, Dorothy W., eds. The Psychology of Today's Woman. LC 89-31197. 400p. 1989. pap. text 15.95 (0-674-72109-8) HUP.

— The Psychology of Today's Woman: New Psychoanalytic Visions. 377p. (C). 1986. text 45.00 (0-88163-036-5) Analytic Pr.

Bernays, Anne. Professor Romeo. LC 96-29913. (Hardscrabble Bks.). 287p. 1997. reprint ed. pap. 14.95 (0-87451-809-1) U Pr of New Eng.

— What If? Writing Exercises for Fiction Writers. 3rd ed. (C). 1999. pap. text Price not set. (0-321-02686-1) Addison-Wesley.

Bernays, Anne & Painter, Pamela. What If: Writing Exercises for Fiction Writers. LC 89-46518. 256p. 1991. reprint ed. pap. 13.00 (0-06-272006-6, Harper Ref) HarpC.

— What If? Writing Exercises for Fiction Writers. rev. ed. LC 94-9793. 400p. (C). 1997. pap. 25.66 (0-673-99002-8) Addson-Wesley Educ.

Bernays, Anne, jt. auth. see Kaplan, Justin.

Bernays, Edward L. The Later Years: Public Relations Insights, 1956-1986. Swift, Paul, ed. (C). 1986. 9.95 (0-9617642-0-1) H Penn Hudson.

Bernays, Elizabeth A. Insect-Plant Interactions, Vol. III. 200p. 1991. 139.95 (0-8493-4123-X, QL496) CRC Pr.

— Insect-Plant Interactions, Vol. 4. 256p. 1992. boxed set 145.95 (0-8493-4124-8, QL496) CRC Pr.

Bernays, Elizabeth A., ed. Insect-Plant Interactions, I. 168p. 1989. 133.00 (0-8493-4121-3, SB) CRC Pr.

— Insect-Plant Interactions, Vol. V. 256p. 1993. lib. bdg. 195.95 (0-8493-4125-6) CRC Pr.

Bernays, Jacob. Gesammelte Abhandlungen, 2 vols., Set. xxx, 752p. 1971. reprint ed. 160.00 (0-318-70718-7) G Olms Pubs.

— Grundzuge der Verlorenen Abhandlung des Aristoteles Uber Wirkung der Tragodie. (GER.). xi, 70p. 1970. reprint ed. 20.00 (0-318-70875-2) G Olms Pubs.

— Theophrastos' Schrift Uber Frommigkeit. Mit Bemerkungen Zu Porphyrios' Schrift Uber Enthaltsamkeit. iv, 192p. 1979. reprint ed. 50.00 (3-487-06826-5) G Olms Pubs.

Bernays, Paul. Axiomatic Set Theory. 234p. 1991. pap. 8.95 (0-486-66637-9) Dover.

Bernazzani, William P. Defer Payment - Let the Next Generation Pay. LC 80-13862. 1981. 21.95 (0-87949-145-0) Ashley Bks.

Bernbach, Jeffrey M. Job Discrimination II: How to Fight, How to Win. rev. ed. LC 98-65504. 192p. 1998. pap. 15.00 (0-9653753-1-5) R&R Writers.

Bernbaum, Daniel & Hansen, Frederikke, texts. Out of the North: Contemporary Art from Denmark & Sweden. (Illus.). 144p. 1999. pap. 30.00 (3-89322-509-9) Edition Cantz.

Bernbaum, Edwin. Sacred Mountains of the World. LC 90-8038. 1990. 50.00 (0-87156-712-1, Pub. by Sierra) Random.

— Sacred Mountains of the World. LC 97-35987. 317p. 1998. pap. 29.95 (0-520-21422-6, Pub. by U CA Pr) Cal Prin Full Svc.

— Sacred Mountains of the World. LC 90-8038. (Illus.). 320p. 1992. reprint ed. pap. 25.00 (0-87156-508-0, Pub. by Sierra) Random.

Bernbaum, Ernest. The Drama of Sensibility: A Sketch of the History of English Comedy & Domestic Tragedy. 1990. 16.50 (0-8446-1074-7) Peter Smith.

— The Mary Carleton Narratives, 1663-73. LC 76-164588. (Select Bibliographies Reprint Ser.). 1977. reprint ed. 17.95 (0-8369-5872-1) Ayer.

***Bernbom, Gerry.** Knowledge Management & the Information Revolution in Higher Education, Vol. 3. (Educause Leadership Strategies Ser.). 2000. pap. 16.95 (0-7879-5011-4) Jossey-Bass.

Bernd, A., et al. Cell & Tissue Culture Models in Dermatological Research. LC 92-36359. 1993. 172.00 (0-387-55972-8) Spr-Verlag.

Bernd, Clifford A. Franz Grillparzer's "Der Arme Spielmann" New Directions in Criticism. LC 86-71136. (GERM Ser.: Vol. 25). (Illus.). x, 392p. 1988. 45.00 (0-938100-43-2) Camden Hse.

— Poetic Realism in Scandinavia & Central Europe, 1820-1895. (GERM Ser.). xvi, 243p. 1995. 65.00 (1-57113-010-1) Camden Hse.

— Theodor Storm's Craft of Fiction: The Torment of a Narrator. LC 67-64644. (North Carolina. University. Studies in the Germanic Languages & Literatures: No. 43). reprint ed. 34.00 (0-404-50943-6) AMS Pr.

Bernd, Clifford A., et al, eds. Goethe Proceedings: Essays Commemorating the Goethe Sesquicentennial. LC 83-72540. (GERM Ser.: Vol. 12). (Illus.). 190p. 1984. 39.95 (0-938100-28-9) Camden Hse.

— Romanticism & Beyond: A Festschrift for John F. Fetzer. (California Studies in German & European Romanticism & in the Age of Goethe: Vol. 2). VIII, 280p. (C). 1996. 55.95 (0-8204-3006-4) P Lang Pubng.

***Bernd, Ed, Jr.** Jose Silva's Ultramind ESP System: Think Your Way to Success. 224p. 2000. pap. 13.99 (1-56414-451-8) Career Pr Inc.

Bernd, Ed, Jr. Relax, It's Good for You. 2.95 (0-913343-35-8) Inst Psych Inc.

Bernd, Ed, Jr., jt. auth. see Silva, Jose.

Bernd, Joseph L., jt. ed. see Herndon, James F.

Berndes, Katherine R. How to Become a Better Consumer: Seven Steps in the Buying Process. (Illus.). 136p. 1988. pap. 12.95 (0-9600962-0-5) Displays Sch.

— How to Write a Personal Narrative: Five Steps in the Writing Process. (Illus.). 65p. 1988. pap. 7.95 (0-9600962-2-1) Displays Sch.

— How to Write Your Autobiography: Writing & Organizational Skills. (Illus.). 258p. (J). (gr. 5-12). 1997. pap. 23.95 (0-9600962-6-4) Displays Sch.

Bernds, Edward. Mr. Bernds Goes to Hollywood: My Early Life & Career in Sound Recording at Columbia with Frank Capra & Others. LC 98-47142. (Filmmakers Ser.: No. 65). (Illus.). 312p. 1999. 45.00 (0-8108-3602-5) Scarecrow.

Berndt. Child Development. 2nd ed. 1996. 13.75 (0-697-27550-7, WCB McGr Hill) McGrw-H Hghr Educ.

— Information Technology & Productivity. 160p. 1995. pap. text 226.00 (3-7186-5787-2, Harwood Acad Pubs) Gordon & Breach.

— Uniform Pharmaceutical Pricing: An Economic Analysis. 50p. (Orig.). 1994. pap. 9.95 (0-8447-7028-0) Am Enterprise.

Berndt, B. C. Ramanujan's Notebooks, Pt. IV. 432p. 1993. 107.95 (0-387-94109-6) Spr-Verlag.

Berndt, Bruce C. Ramanujan's Notebooks. 2nd ed. (Illus.). xiii, 510p. 1997. 98.95 (0-387-97503-9) Spr-Verlag.

— Ramanujan's Notebooks, Pt. 1. (Illus.). 430p. 1985. 107.95 (0-387-96110-0) Spr-Verlag.

— Ramanujan's Notebooks, Pt. 2. (Illus.). xi, 359p. 1988. 107.95 (0-387-96794-X) Spr-Verlag.

— Ramanujan's Notebooks, Pt. V. 600p. 1997. 97.95 (0-387-94941-0) Spr-Verlag.

Berndt, Bruce C., et al. Analytic Number Theory. (Progress in Mathematics Ser.: Vol. 85). 558p. 1990. 67.00 (0-8176-3481-9) Birkhauser.

— Chapter Nine of Ramanujan's Second Notebook: Infinite Series Identities, Transformations, & Evaluations. LC 83-11803. (Contemporary Mathematics Ser.: No. 23). 83p. 1983. pap. 25.00 (0-8218-5024-5, CONM/23) Am Math.

— Gauss & Jacobi Sums. LC 97-44440. (Canadian Mathematical Society Series & Advanced Texts). 600p. 1998. 89.95 (0-471-12807-4, Wiley-Interscience) Wiley.

— Ramanujan: Letters & Commentary. LC 95-5254. (History of Mathematics Ser.: No. 9). 347p. 1995. text 59.00 (0-8218-0287-9, HMATH/9) Am Math.

Berndt, C. C. & Sampath, S., eds. 1995 Advances in Thermal Spray Science & Technology: Proceedings of the 8th National Thermal Spray Conference. LC 95-211747. 774p. 1995. 108.00 (0-87170-541-9, 6537) ASM.

Berndt, Catherine H. Pheasant & Kingfisher: An Aboriginal Tale - Originally Told by Nganalgindja in the Gunwinggu Language. LC 94-29581. (Illus.). 24p. (J). (gr. 1-5). 1994. pap. 4.95 (1-879531-64-X); lib. bdg. 9.95 (1-879531-65-8) Mondo Pubng.

Berndt, Catherine H., jt. auth. see Berndt, Ronald M.

***Berndt, Chard.** Biblical Classification of Life: A Framework & Reference for Authentic Biblical Biology. LC 00-90430. (Illus.). 192p. 2000. pap. 24.95 (0-9677850-0-6, BCL-P) Elihu Pub.

Berndt, Christopher C., et al. Thermal Spray: A United Forum for Scientific & Technological Advances: Proceedings of the United Thermal Spray Conference, 15-18 September 1997, Indianapolis, Indiana. LC 97-42824. 1020p. 1997. 155.00 (0-87170-618-0, 6635) ASM.

Berndt, Christopher C. & Bernecki, Thomas F., eds. Thermal Spray Coatings: Research, Design & Applications. LC 93-71173. 691p. 1993. 98.00 (0-87170-470-6, 6339) ASM.

Berndt, Ernst R. Practice of Econometrics. LC 96-21200. (Illus.). 720p. (C). 1991. text 45.25 (0-201-17628-9) Addison-Wesley.

— Practice of Econometrics. (Illus.). 222p. (C). 1994. pap. text 26.73 (0-201-17629-7) Addison-Wesley.

Berndt, Ernst R. The Practice of Econometrics: Classic & Contemporary. 702p. 1996. 98.00 (0-201-49900-2) Addison-Wesley.

— The Practice of Econometrics: Classic & Contemporary. LC 96-21200. (Illus.). (C). 1996. text. write for info. (0-201-51488-5) Addison-Wesley.

Berndt, Ernst R. The Practice of Econometrics: Classic & Contemporary. 2nd ed. (C). 1998. text. write for info. (0-201-82393-4) Addison-Wesley.

Berndt, Ernst R. & Triplett, Jack E., eds. Fifty Years of Economic Measurement: The Jubilee of the Conference on Research in Income & Wealth. LC 90-19371. (National Bureau of Economic Research Studies in Income & Wealth: Vol. 54). (Illus.). x, 464p. 1991. pap. text 26.00 (0-226-04385-1) U Ch Pr.

— Fifty Years of Economic Measurement: The Jubilee of the Conference on Research in Income & Wealth. LC 90-19371. (National Bureau of Economic Research Studies in Income & Wealth: Vol. 54). (Illus.). 392p. 1992. lib. bdg. 65.00 (0-226-04384-3) U Ch Pr.

Berndt, Harry E. New Rulers in the Ghetto: The Community Development Corporation & Urban Poverty, 28. LC 76-47888. (Contributions in Afro-American & African Studies: No. 28). (Illus.). 161p. 1977. 47.95 (0-8371-9399-0, BNL/, Greenwood Pr) Greenwood.

Berndt, Hendrick. The TINA Book: A Co-Operative Solution for a Competitive World. LC 98-40035. 1998. write for info. (0-13-095400-4) P-H.

Berndt, J., jt. auth. see Yasui, E.

Berndt, Jodie, jt. auth. see Blue, Ron.

Berndt, Judy. Rural Sociology: A Bibliography of Bibliographies. LC 85-26070. 185p. 1986. 21.00 (0-8108-1860-4) Scarecrow.

Berndt, Jurgen, et al. Generalized Heisenberg Groups & Damek-Ricci Harmonic Spaces. LC 95-1415. (Lecture Notes in Mathematics Ser.: Vol. 1598). 125p. 1995. 27.00 (0-387-59001-3) Spr-Verlag.

***Berndt, Michael C.** Platelets, Thrombosis & the Vessel Wall. (Advances in Vascular Biology Ser.: Vol. 6). 356p. 1999. text 90.00 (90-5702-369-5, Harwood Acad Pubs) Gordon & Breach.

Berndt, R. & Schmidt, R. Elements of the Representation Theory of the Jacobi Group. (Progress in Mathematics Ser.: Vol. 163). 232p. 1998. 69.95 (3-7643-5922-6) Birkhauser.

***Berndt, Rita Sloan.** Quantitative Production Analysis. 1999. pap. text. write for info. (0-86377-769-4) L Erlbaum Assocs.

Berndt, Robert J. Your Lasa Apso. LC 74-77246. 160 p. 1974. write for info. (0-87714-028-6) Denlingers.

***Berndt, Rolf.** An Introduction to Sympletic Geometry. LC 00-33139. (Graduate Studies in Mathematics: Vol. 26). 224p. 2000. 36.00 (0-8218-2056-7) Am Math.

Berndt, Rolf & Schmidt, Ralf. Elements of the Representation Theory of the Jacobi Group. LC 98-18101. (Progress in Mathematics Ser.). 1998. 69.95 (0-8176-5922-6) Birkhauser.

***Berndt, Ronald.** Aboriginal Australian Art. 1999. pap. 29.95 (1-876334-02-9) Sterling.

Berndt, Ronald M. Love Songs of Arnhem Land. LC 77-83828. (Illus.). 274p. reprint ed. pap. 85.00 (0-608-09387-4, 205413200004); reprint ed. pap. 84.40 (0-608-21012-9, 2054540) Bks Demand.

— The Sacred Site: the Western Arnhem Land Example. LC 71-857385. (Australian Aboriginal Studies Ser.). vi, 63p. 1969. write for info. (0-85575-005-7) AIB & TSIS.

Berndt, Ronald M. & Berndt, Catherine H. The Speaking Land: Myth & Story in Aboriginal Australia. LC 94-15525. (Illus.). 468p. 1994. pap. 16.95 (0-89281-518-3) Inner Tradit.

Berndt, Thomas J. American Tanks of WWII. (Enthusiast Color Ser.). (Illus.). 96p. 1994. pap. 13.95 (0-87938-930-3) MBI Pubg.

— Child Development. 3rd ed. 1999. 56.50 (0-697-38193-5) McGraw.

— Standard Catalog of U. S. Military Vehicles, 1940-1965. LC 92-72123. (Illus.). 272p. 1993. 29.95 (0-87341-223-0, MV01) Krause Pubns.

Berndt, Thomas J. Child Development. 800p. (C). 1994. text. write for info. (0-697-27399-7) Brown & Benchmark.

— Child Development. 2nd ed. LC 96-86612. 800p. (C). 1996. text 48.00 (0-697-27549-3) Brown & Benchmark.

— Child Development. 2nd ed. LC 96-86612. 768p. (C). 1996. text, boxed set. write for info. (0-697-35967-0) Brown & Benchmark.

— Child Development. 2nd ed. 768p. (C). 1997. pap. text. write for info. (0-07-114908-2) McGraw.

Berndt, Thomas J. & Ladd, Gary W., eds. Peer Relationships in Child Development. LC 88-5779. (Personality Processes Ser.). 434p. 1989. 175.00 (0-471-85131-0) Wiley.

Berndt, Thomas J. & Perry, Bridgett T. Child Development: Student Study Guide. 2nd ed. 272p. (C). 1996. text, student ed. 16.25 (0-697-27551-5) Brown & Benchmark.

Berndt, Thomas J., jt. ed. see Wentzel, Kathryn R.

Berndt, William O., jt. ed. see Haley, Thomas J.

Berndt, William O., jt. ed. see Hayes, A. W.

Berndtson, Arthur. Power, Form & Mind. LC 80-65658. 296p. 1981. 38.50 (0-8387-5010-9) Bucknell U Pr.

Berndtsson, Mikael & Hansson, Jorgen. Active & Real-Time Database Systems (ARTDB-95) Proceedings of the First International Workshop on Active & Real-Time Database Systems: Skovde, Sweden, 9-11 June 1995. (Workshops in Computing Ser.). 267p. 1996. pap. 69.00 (3-540-19983-7) Spr-Verlag.

***Berne, Betsy.** Bad Timing. 2001. 22.95 (0-679-46318-6) Random.

Berne, Bruce J., ed. Statistical Mechanics, 2 pts. Incl. Equilibrium Techniques. LC 76-46977. 242p. 1977. (0-306-33505-0, Kluwer Plenum); Time-Dependent Processes. LC 76-46977. 362p. 1977. 89.50 (0-306-33506-9, Kluwer Plenum); LC 76-46977. (Modern Theoretical Chemistry Ser.: Vols. 5 & 6). (Illus.). 1977. write for info. (0-318-55337-6, Plenum Trade) Perseus Pubng.

Berne, Bruce J., et al, eds. Classical & Quantum Dynamics in Condensed Phase Simulations: Proceedings of the International School of Physics Lerici, Italy 7 - 18 July 1997. 820p. 1998. 128.00 (981-02-3498-8) World Scientific Pub.

Berne, Bruce J., jt. auth. see Pecora.

Berne, Doreen S., ed. see DiCandia, Thomas A.

Berne, Eric. Games People Play. 1996. pap. 10.00 (0-345-41003-3) Ballantine Pub Grp.

Berne, Eric. Que Dice Usted Despues de Decir Hola? 1997. pap. text 18.98 (968-419-610-5) Grijalbo Edit.

Berne, Francois & Cordonnier, J. Industrial Water Treatment: Refining Petrochemicals & Gas Processing Techniques. LC 94-23572. (Illus.). 248p. 1995. 69.00 (0-88415-908-6, 5908) Gulf Pub.

— Industrial Water Treatment, Refining, Petrochemicals, & Gas Processing Techniques. 1994. 340.00 (0-7855-2707-9, Pub. by Edits Technip) Enfield Pubs NH.

Berne, Francois & Cordonnier, Jean. Industrial Water Treatment Refining Petrochemicals & Gas Processing Techniques. (Illus.). 264p. (C). 1995. 360.00 (2-7108-0673-8, Pub. by Edits Technip) Enfield Pubs NH.

Berne, Jennifer, jt. auth. see Willey, R. J.

An Asterisk (*) at the beginning of an entry indicates that the title is appearing for the first time.

***Berne, Katrina.** Chronic Fatigue Syndrome, Fibromyalgia & Other Invisible Illnesses: A Comprehensive & Compassionate Guide. 3rd rev. ed. (Illus.). 352p. 2000. pap. 15.95 (*0-89793-280-3*, Pub. by Hunter Hse) Publishers Group.

Berne, Katrina. Running on Empty: The Complete Guide to Chronic Fatigue Syndrome. 2nd ed. LC 95-44914. (Illus.). 336p. 1995. 24.95 (*0-89793-192-0*); pap. 14.95 (*0-89793-191-2*) Hunter Hse.

***Berne, Martine.** A Perfect Rogue. 2000. mass mkt. 5.99 (*0-8217-6848-4*, Zebra Kensgtn) Kensgtn Pub Corp.
— Prize. 2000. mass mkt. 4.99 (*0-8217-6477-2*, Zebra Kensgtn) Kensgtn Pub Corp.

Berne, Patricia H. & Savary, Louis M. Building Self-Esteem in Children. expanded ed. 192p. 1996. pap. 15.95 (*0-8245-1549-8*) Crossroad NY.

***Berne, Robert, ed.** Principles of Physiology. 3rd ed. LC 99-19992. 1999. text 54.00 (*0-323-00813-5*) Harcourt.

Berne, Robert, et al, eds. Outcome Equity in Education. LC 94-31096. (Yearbook of the American Education Finance Association Ser.: Vol. 15). (Illus.). 288p. 1994. 54.95 (*0-8039-6160-X*) Corwin Pr.

Berne, Robert & Stiefel, Leanna. The Measurement of Equity in School Finance: Conceptual, Methodological & Empirical Dimensions. LC 83-24394. (Illus.). 317p. reprint ed. pap. 98.30 (*0-7837-4784-5*, 204454000003) Bks Demand.

Berne, Robert, jt. auth. see Jacobson, Stephen L.

Berne, Robert M., ed. Handbook of Physiology: Section 2, The Cardiovascular System, Vol. I: The Heart. (American Physiological Society Book). (Illus.). 978p. 1988. text 160.00 (*0-19-520663-0*) OUP.

Berne, Robert M., et al, eds. Annual Review of Physiology, Vol. 45. LC 39-15404. (Illus.). 1983. text 42.00 (*0-8243-0345-8*) Annual Reviews.
— Annual Review of Physiology, Vol. 46. LC 39-15404. (Illus.). 1984. text 42.00 (*0-8243-0346-6*) Annual Reviews.
— Annual Review of Physiology, Vol. 47. LC 39-15404. (Illus.). (C). 1985. text 42.00 (*0-8243-0347-4*) Annual Reviews.
— Annual Review of Physiology, Vol. 48. LC 39-15404. (Illus.). 1986. text 42.00 (*0-8243-0348-2*) Annual Reviews.
— Annual Review of Physiology, Vol. 49. LC 39-15404. (Illus.). 1987. text 42.00 (*0-8243-0349-0*) Annual Reviews.
— Annual Review of Physiology, Vol. 50. LC 39-15404. (Illus.). 1988. text 42.00 (*0-8243-0350-4*) Annual Reviews.
— The Regulatory Function of Adenosine. 1983. text 249.50 (*90-247-2779-0*) Kluwer Academic.

Berne, Robert M. & Edelman, I. S., eds. Annual Review of Physiology, Vol. 42. LC 39-15404. (Illus.). 1980. 42.00 (*0-8243-0342-3*) Annual Reviews.

Berne, Robert M. & Levy. Physiology. 4th ed. LC 97-38215. (Illus.). 1232p. (C). (gr. 13). 1998. text 60.00 (*0-8151-0952-0*, 31012) Mosby Inc.
— Principles of Physiology. 2nd ed. (Illus.). 816p. (C). (gr. 13). 1995. pap. text 53.00 (*0-8151-0523-1*, 24422) Mosby Inc.

Berne, Robert M. & Levy, Mathew N. Cardiovascular Physiology. 7th ed. LC 96-28899. (Illus.). 336p. (C). (gr. 13). 1996. pap. text 35.95 (*0-8151-0901-6*, 28159) Mosby Inc.

***Berne, Robert M. & Levy, Matthew N.** Cardiovascular Physiology. 8th ed. LC 00-32430. (Illus.). 2000. write for info. (*0-323-01127-6*) Mosby Inc.

Berne, Robert M. & Levy, Matthew N., eds. Case Studies in Psychology. (Illus.). 224p. (C). (gr. 13). 1994. pap. text 20.00 (*0-8151-0544-4*, 24349) Mosby Inc.

Berne, Samuel A. Creating Your Personal Vision: A Mind-Body Guide for Better Eyesight - Natural Vision Improvement: Holistic Healing. LC 94-72147. (Illus.). 170p. (Orig.). 1994. pap. 15.95 (*0-9641599-3-7*) Color Stone.

Berne, Stanley. Alphabet Soup: An Orderly Collection of Disorderly Thought. Scharf, Albert, ed. (Illus.). 240p. 1994. 22.00 (*0-913844-20-9*); pap. 13.95 (*0-913844-21-7*) Danrus Pubs.

Berne, Stanley. At One with Birds: Empire, America, a Prose Sequence. pap. 10.95 (*0-913844-25-X*) Risng Tide NM.

Berne, Stanley. The Dialogues. LC 62-7479. (Illus.). 108p. 1962. pap. 100.00 (*0-913844-15-2*) Am Canadian.
— Future Language: How English Will Shift into Its Next Phase. LC 75-36891. (Archives of Post-Modern Literature Ser.). 1976. pap. 22.50 (*0-913844-02-0*) Am Canadian.
— Gravity Drag: The Chance Texts. (Samizdat Ser.). (Illus.). 40p. 1999. pap. 8.95 (*0-913844-23-3*) Risng Tide NM.
— The Great American Empire. LC 81-85003. (Archives of Post-Modern Literature Ser.). (Illus.). 1982. 25.00 (*0-913844-13-6*) Am Canadian.
— The Great American Empire. LC 81-85003. (Archives of Post-Modern Literature Ser.). (Illus.). 1982. pap. 25.00 (*0-913844-11-X*) Am Canadian.
— The Multiple Modern Gods & Other Stories. LC 64-21952. (Illus.). 1964. pap. 22.50 (*0-913844-05-5*) Am Canadian.
— The New Rubaiyat of Stanley Berne, Vol. 1. LC 73-77094. (Archives of Post-Modern Literature Ser.). 111p. 1973. pap. 25.00 (*0-913844-00-4*) Am Canadian.

***Berne, Stanley.** Swimming to Significance: "Open-Structure" - A New Era in Written English. (Codex Title Ser.: No. 2). (Illus.). 84p. 1999. pap. 9.95 (*0-913844-24-1*) Risng Tide NM.

Berne, Stanley. To Hell with Optimism!! A Slash & Burn Satire. (Illus.). 197p. 1997. pap. 12.95 (*0-913844-22-5*) Risng Tide NM.
— The Unconscious Victorious & Other Stories: The New English Structure. LC 69-20442. (Archives of Post-Modern Literature Ser.). (Illus.). 1969. pap. 20.00 (*0-913844-04-7*) Am Canadian.

Berne, Stanley & Zekowski, Arlene. Every Person's Little Book of P-L-U-T-O-N-I-U-M: All You Need to Know to Stay Alive in the Nuclear Age. (Illus.). 168p. 1992. pap. 12.95 (*0-913844-19-5*) Risng Tide NM.

Berne, Stanley, et al. Yefief 2: Health & Human Rights (A View along the Running Edge) limited ed. Racuya-Robbins, Ann, ed. Weinberger, Eliot & Morales, Harry, trs. (Illus.). 160p. 1995. pap. 24.95 (*1-884434-01-0*) Images For Media.

Berne, Stanley, jt. auth. see Zekowski, Arlene.

Berne, Suzanne. A Crime in the Neighborhood. LC 96-47654. 294p. 1997. 17.95 (*1-56512-165-1*, 72165) Algonquin Bks.
— A Crime in the Neighborhood. 1998. pap. write for info. (*0-8050-5852-4*, Owl) H Holt & Co.
— A Crime in the Neighborhood. LC 98-14098. 285p. 1998. pap. 11.00 (*0-8050-5580-0*, Owl) H Holt & Co.

Bernecka-Urban, K. M. Russian Historical Reader with Exercises. (ENG & RUS., Illus.). 138p. (Orig.). (C). 1996. pap. text 39.95 (*1-890086-00-2*) Global Pr MN.

***Bernecker, Sven & Dretske, Fred I., eds.** Knowledge: Readings in Contemporary Epistemology. LC 99-89740. (Illus.). 600p. (C). 2000. pap. text 32.95 (*0-19-875261-X*) OUP.

Bernecker, Walther & Tobler, Hans W., eds. Development & Underdevelopment in America: Contrasts of Economic Growth in North & Latin America in Historical Perspective. LC 93-11856. (Studies in North America: No. 8). iv, 335p. (C). 1993. lib. bdg. 120.00 (*3-11-013519-8*) De Gruyter.

Bernecki, Thomas F., ed. Thermal Spray Research & Applications: Proceedings of the Third National Thermal Spray Conference Held May 20-25, 1990, in Long Beach, CA. LC 91-70802. (Illus.). 808p. 1991. reprint ed. pap. 200.00 (*0-608-02629-8*, 206328700004) Bks Demand.

Bernecki, Thomas F., jt. ed. see Berndt, Christopher C.

Berneking, Nancy J. & Joern, Pamela C., eds. Re-Membering & Re-Imagining. LC 95-16811. (Illus.). 264p. (Orig.). 1995. pap. 15.95 (*0-8298-1074-9*) Pilgrim OH.

***Bernell, Bonnie.** Bountiful Women: Stop "Weighting" & Live Your Life. 2000. pap. 15.95 (*1-885171-47-1*) Wldcat Canyon.

Bernelle, Agnes. The Fun Palace: An Autobiography. LC 96-230863. 250p. 1997. pap. 21.00 (*1-874675-28-7*) Dufour.

Bernelle, Agnes, ed. Decantations in Honour of Maurice Craig. 1996. 69.95 (*0-946640-64-5*, Pub. by Lilliput Pr) Irish Bks Media.

Bernem, T. Wirtschaftenglisch - Worterbuch. (ENG & GER.). 350p. 1990. lib. bdg. 95.00 (*0-8288-3848-8*) Fr & Eur.

Bernen, Robert, jt. auth. see Bernen, Satia.

Bernen, Satia & Bernen, Robert. Myth & Religion in European Painting, 1270-1700: The Stories As the Artists Knew Them. LC 73-162220. 280p. 1973. write for info. (*0-09-458650-0*) Constable & Co.

Berner. Writing Literary Features. (Communication Textbook-McCombs Sub-Series). 115p. (Orig.). (C). 1988. pap. text 14.95 (*0-8058-0279-7*) L Erlbaum Assocs.

Berner, Andrew. Time Management in the Small Library. 1988. student ed. 85.00 (*0-87111-392-9*) SLA.

Berner, Andrew & St. Clair, Guy. The Best of OPL, II: Selected Readings from the One-Person Library, 1990-1994. LC 95-53102. 350p. 1996. 36.00 (*0-87111-438-0*) SLA.

Berner, B., jt. auth. see Kydonieus, Agis F.

Berner, Boel, ed. Gendered Practices: Feminist Studies of Technology & Society. 287p. 1997. pap. 52.50 (*91-22-01747-X*, Pub. by Almqvist Wiksell) Coronet Bks.

Berner, Brad K. The Spanish-American War: A Historical Dictionary. LC 98-21102. (Historical Dictionaries of War, Revolution, & Civil Unrest Ser.). 248p. 1998. 85.00 (*0-8108-3490-1*) Scarecrow.

Berner, Bret & Dinh, Steven M. Electronically Controlled Drug Delivery. LC 98-15824. (Illus.). 272p. 1998. lib. bdg. 129.95 (*0-8493-7681-5*) CRC Pr.

Berner, Bret, ed. see Kydonieus, Agis F.

Berner, Carl W. At Home Away: Devotions for Students. LC 96-14010. 128p. (C). 1996. pap. 6.99 (*0-570-04856-7*, 12-3292) Concordia.

Berner, Carroll A., ed. see Worthen, Frederick Dustin.

Berner, E. S., et al, eds. Clinical Decision Support Systems: Theory & Practice. LC 98-21883. (Health Informatics Ser.). (Illus.). 264p. 1998. 49.00 (*0-387-98575-1*) Spr-Verlag.

Berner, Elizabeth K. & Berner, Robert A. Global Environment: Water, Air & Geochemical Cycles. LC 95-25174. 376p. 1995. pap. text 73.00 (*0-13-301169-0*) P-H.
— The Global Water Cycle: Geochemistry & Environment. (Illus.). 480p. 1987. text 55.00 (*0-13-357195-5*) P-H.

Berner, Erhard. Defending a Place in the City: Localities & the Struggle for Urban Land in Metro Manila. LC 98-947586. 264p. 1998. pap. text 24.00 (*971-550-270-9*) UH Pr.

Berner, J. Kevin & Daula, Thomas V. Armed Forces Guide to Personal Financial Planning. 3rd ed. 416p. 1994. pap. 22.95 (*0-8117-2501-4*) Stackpole.

Berner, Jeff. The Joy of Working from Home: Making a Life While Making a Living. LC 94-19624. (Illus.). 240p. (Orig.). 1994. pap. 12.95 (*1-881052-46-X*) Berrett-Koehler.

Berner, Lewis & Pescador, Manuel L. The Mayflies of Florida. rev. ed. LC 87-16005. (Illus.). 431p. 1988. 49.95 (*0-8130-0845-X*) U Press Fla.

Berner, Loretta. Rancho los Cerritos. (Illus.). 1975. pap. 4.50 (*0-916552-01-2*) Acoma Bks.
— A Step Back in Time. (Illus.). 72p. 1990. pap. 11.00 (*0-9610250-4-2*) Hist Soc of Long Bch.

Berner, Loretta, ed. Earthquake '33. (Illus.). 64p. 1981. pap. 11.00 (*0-614-29736-2*) Hist Soc of Long Bch.
— The Pike on the Silverstrand. (Illus.). 72p. 1982. pap. 11.00 (*0-9610250-3-4*) Hist Soc of Long Bch.

Berner, Loretta, et al. Shades of the Past. LC 95-76271. (Illus.). 67p. (Orig.). 1995. pap. 11.00 (*0-9610250-5-0*) Hist Soc of Long Bch.

Berner, Maureen, jt. ed. see Galbraith, James K.

Berner, Orjan. Soviet Policies Toward the Nordic Countries. LC 86-9087. 206p. (Orig.). 1986. pap. 22.50 (*0-8191-5382-6*); lib. bdg. 44.50 (*0-8191-5381-8*) U Pr of Amer.

Berner, P., et al, eds. Current Perspectives in Lithium Prophylaxis. (Bibliotheca Psychiatrica Ser.: Vol. 161). (Illus.). viii, 248p. 1981. pap. 76.75 (*3-8055-1753-X*) S Karger.

Berner, P. & Diehl, L. W., eds. The Treatment of Complicated Epilepsies in Adults. (Bibliotheca Psychiatrica Ser.: No. 158). (Illus.). 1978. 50.50 (*3-8055-2814-0*) S Karger.

Berner, P. & Gabriel, E., eds. Affect & Emotion Journal: Psychopathology, Vol. 21, No. 2-3, 1988. (Illus.). 92p. 1989. pap. 64.50 (*3-8055-5005-7*) S Karger.

Berner, P., et al. Diagnostic Criteria for Functional Psychoses. 2nd ed. 284p. (C). 1992. text 95.00 (*0-521-42315-5*) Cambridge U Pr.

Berner, P., ed. see Zapotoczky, H. G.

Berner, R. Thomas. The Literature of Journalism: Text & Context. LC 98-21190. 288p. 1999. pap. text 24.95 (*1-891136-00-3*) Strata Pub Co.
— Parents Whose Parents Were Divorced. LC 91-6813. (Illus.). 164p. 1992. pap. 19.95 (*1-56024-139-X*); lib. bdg. 39.95 (*1-56024-138-1*) Haworth Pr.

Berner, Richard C. Seattle Vol. 1: From Boomtown, Urban Turbulence, to Restoration. LC 91-74159. (Seattle in the Twentieth Century Ser.: Vol. 1). (Illus.). 398p. (Orig.). 1991. pap. 24.95 (*0-9629889-0-1*) Charles Pr.
— Seattle, 1921-1940: From Boom to Bust. (Seattle in the Twentieth Century Ser.: Vol. 2). 576p. (Orig.). 1992. pap. 25.95 (*0-9629889-1-X*) Charles Pr.
— Seattle Transformed Vol. 3: World War II to Cold War. (Illus.). 330p. (Orig.). Date not set. pap. write for info. (*0-9629889-2-8*, Pub. by Charles Pr) Partners-West.

Berner, Robert A. Early Diagenesis: A Theoretical Approach. LC 80-7510. (Geochemistry Ser.: No. 1). (Illus.). 256p. 1980. pap. text 39.50 (*0-691-08260-X*, Pub. by Princeton U Pr) Cal Prin Full Svc.

Berner, Robert A., jt. auth. see Berner, Elizabeth K.

***Berner, Robert L.** Defining American Indian Literature: One Nation Divisible. LC 99-26137. 164p. 1999. text 79.95 (*0-7734-8039-0*) E Mellen.

Berner, Robert L. The Rule of Four: Four Essays on the Principle of Quaternity. (Studies on Themes & Motifs in Literature: Vol. 21). XII, 153p. (C). 1996. text 39.95 (*0-8204-2840-X*) P Lang Pubng.

Berner, Ronald M. Temple Arts of Kerala: A South Indian Tradition. 272p. 1985. 100.00 (*0-317-52158-6*, Pub. by S Chand & Co) St Mut.

Berner, Steven M. Macbeth. (Quick Study Shakespeare Ser.). 4p. pap. 3.95 (*1-57222-261-1*) Barcharts.
— Romeo & Juliet. (Quick Study Shakespeare Ser.). 4p. pap. 3.95 (*1-57222-262-X*) Barcharts.

Berner, Tamar. Ultrastructure of Microalgae. 320p. 1993. lib. bdg. 229.00 (*0-8493-6323-3*, QK568) CRC Pr.

Berner, Thomas R. Writing Literary Features. (Communication Textbook-McCombs Sub-Series). 115p. (C). 1988. text 29.95 (*0-8058-0278-9*) L Erlbaum Assocs.

***Berner, Tom.** Brooklyn Navy Yard. (Images of America Ser.). 128p. 1999. pap. 18.99 (*0-7524-0860-7*) Arcadia Publng.

Berneri, Marie L. Journey Through Utopia. LC 71-93316. (Essay Index Reprint Ser.). 1977. 31.95 (*0-8369-1392-2*) Ayer.
— Neither East nor West: Selected Writings, 1939-1948. (Centenary Ser.). (Illus.). 192p. (Orig.). 1988. pap. 8.75 (*0-900384-42-5*) Left Bank.

Berners. First Childhood. 288p. 1998. pap. 14.95 (*1-885983-31-X*) Turtle Point Pr.

Berners, E. D., jt. auth. see Ferguson, S. M.

Berners-Lee, Tim. Weaving the Web: The Original Design & Ultimate Destiny of the World Wide Web by Its Inventor. LC 99-27665. 226p. 2000. pap. 15.00 (*0-06-251587-X*, HarpBusn) HarpInfo.

Berners-Lee, Tim & Fischetti, Mark. Weaving the Web: The Original Design & Ultimate Destiny of the World Wide Web by Its Inventor. LC 99-27665. 240p. 1999. 26.00 (*0-06-251586-1*, Pub. by Harper SF) HarpC.

***Berners-Lee, Tim & Fischetti, Mark.** Weaving the Web: The Original Design & Ultimate Destiny of the World Wide Web by its Inventor, Set. 1999. audio 18.00 (*0-694-52125-6*) HarperAudio.

Bernes, Claes & Grundsten, Claes. The Environment. (National Atlas of Sweden Ser.). (Illus.). 1992. 108.00 (*91-87760-10-X*) Coronet Bks.

Bernet, Charles. Dictionnaire du Francais Parle. (FRE.). 1989. lib. bdg. 69.95 (*0-8288-2496-7*) Fr & Eur.

Bernet De Rodrigues, Josefina, jt. auth. see Rodrigues, Louis J.

Bernet, Elizabeth. Wings of Love. (J). 1998. 11.95 (*0-671-75203-0*); pap. 8.00 (*0-671-76959-6*) S&S Bks Yung.

Bernet, Gerard E., ed. see Burnett, G.

Bernet, Rudolf, et al. An Introduction to Husserlian Phenomenology. (Studies in Phenomenology & Existential Philosophy). (Orig.). 1993. 49.95 (*0-8101-1005-9*); pap. 19.95 (*0-8101-1030-X*) Northwestern U Pr.

***Bernet, Thomas.** L'Ironie d'Alberto Savino a la Croisee des Discours. (Publications Universitaires Europeennes). 246p. 1999. 41.95 (*3-906763-75-7*, Pub. by P Lang) P Lang Pubng.

Bernet, William, jt. auth. see Meeks, John E.

Bernett. The Louis Armstrong Companion. 1998. pap. 15.00 (*0-02-864718-1*) Mac Lib Ref.

***Bernett, Dick.** Without Rhyme & Reason: Contemporary Poems of Urban America. (Illus.). 60p. 1999. pap. 20.00 (*0-9674029-0-5*) Fall Back Baby.

Bernett, Donna L. A Study of Fashion Interest & Clothing Selection Motives. Lee, Don Y., ed. 180p. 1992. lib. bdg. 39.00 (*0-685-60787-9*) Eastern Pr.

Bernewitz, Fred von, see Geissman, Grant & von Bernewitz, Fred.

***Berney, Charlotte.** Fundamentals of Hawaiian Mysticism. LC 99-88516. (Fundamentals of Ser.). 160p. 2000. pap. 12.95 (*1-58091-026-2*, Pub. by Crossing Pr) Publishers Group.

Berney, Charlotte, jt. auth. see Duncan, A.

Berney, Kate, ed. Contemporary Dramatists. 5th ed. 843p. 1993. 140.00 (*1-55862-185-7*) St James Pr.

Berney, Kate & Templeton, N. G., eds. Contemporary American Dramatists. LC 94-11448. 768p. 1994. 60.00 (*1-55862-214-4*) St James Pr.
— Contemporary British Dramatists. LC 94-13899. (Contemporary Literature Ser.). 768p. 1994. 60.00 (*1-55862-213-6*) St James Pr.
— Contemporary Women Dramatists. LC 94-13898. (Contemporary Literature Ser.). 335p. 1994. 50.00 (*1-55862-212-8*) St James Pr.

Berney, Louis. The Road to Bobby Joe: And Other Stories. 1991. 18.95 (*0-15-177870-1*) Harcourt.

Berney, Mary F. & Ayers, Jerry B., eds. Evaluating Preparation Programs for School Leaders & Teachers in Specialty Areas. (C). 1990. lib. bdg. 73.50 (*0-7923-9079-2*) Kluwer Academic.

Berney, Mary F., jt. ed. see Ayers, Jerry B.

Berney, Paul R. & Kusel, Jimie. Financial Accounting: Text & Cases. LC 91-57946. 530p. 1992. 35.95 (*0-87393-141-6*) Dame Pubns.

Berney, R. E. My Strange Cyberlife. 126p. 1998. pap. 11.95 (*1-892896-33-8*) Buy Books.

Berney, Sarah J. Cat by the Tail. (Sabrina, the Teenage Witch Ser.: No. 7). 96p. (J). (gr. 2-4). 1999. pap. 3.99 (*0-671-02383-7*) PB.

Berney, William, jt. auth. see Richardson, Howard.

Bernfeld, Betsy. Offender Rehabilitation in Pra. 2000. pap. text. write for info. (*0-471-72026-7*) Wiley.

Bernfeld, Ellen & Bryant, Anne. Songs for Dogs (& the People Who Love Them) (Illus.). 48p. (Orig.). 1995. pap. write for info. (*0-9648762-2-1*) Gloryvision.
— Songs for Dogs (& the People Who Love Them) abr. ed. (Illus.). 28p. (Orig.). 1995. pap. write for info. (*0-9648762-4-8*) Gloryvision.

Bernfeld, Ellen, jt. auth. see Bryant, Anne.

Bernfeld, Lisa I., ed. Public Relations for the Franchisee: How to Create Your Own Publicity. 144p. 1990. pap. text 17.00 (*0-9636466-0-5*) LIBooks.

Bernfeld, P. Biogenesis of Natural Compounds. 2nd rev. ed. LC 62-21549. 1967. 531.00 (*0-08-011962-X*, Pub. by Pergamon Repr) Franklin.

Bernfield, Lynne. When You Can You Will: Why You Can't Always Do What You Want to Do & What to Do about It. 240p. 1994. pap. 10.00 (*0-425-14375-9*) Berkley Pub.
— When You Can You Will: Why You Can't Always Do What You Want to Do...& What to Do about It. 224p. 1992. 21.95 (*1-56565-008-5*) Lowell Hse.

Bernfield, Merton, ed. Molecular Basis of Morphogenesis. 276p. 1993. 199.95 (*0-471-30515-4*) Wiley.

***Bernhagen, Stephanie.** Take Back Your Life! Travel Full-Time in an RV. LC 00-102625. 380p. 2000. pap. 19.95 (*0-9700263-0-7*, Pub. by Bern-Colns) BookMasters.

Bernhard. Rain Forest Coloring Book. (Illus.). (J). pap. 2.95 (*0-486-40112-X*) Dover.
— Wetlands Plants & Animals Coloring Book. (Illus.). (J). pap. 2.95 (*0-486-27749-6*) Dover.

Bernhard & Walsh, Michelle. Leadership: The Key to Professionalization of Nursing. 3rd ed. LC 94-241837. (Illus.). 223p. (C). (gr. 13). 1994. pap. text 35.00 (*0-8151-0526-6*, 24347) Mosby Inc.

Bernhard, Albert & Jayasumana, Anura P. FDDI & FDDI II Vol. I & II: Architecture, Protocols & Performance. LC 93-42249. 1993. 83.00 (*0-89006-633-7*) Artech Hse.

Bernhard, Annika. State Birds & Flowers Coloring Book. (Illus.). 48p. (J). (gr. k-3). 1990. pap. 2.95 (*0-486-26456-4*) Dover.

Bernhard, Armin. Der Bildungsprozefs in Einer Epoche der Ambivalenz: Studien zur Bildungsgeschichte in der Asthetik des Widerstands. (GER.). 1996. 44.95 (*3-631-49526-9*) P Lang Pubng.

***Bernhard, Armin.** Demokratische Reformpadagogik und die Vision Von der Neuen Erziehung: Sozialgeschichtliche und Bildungstheoretische Analysen Zur Entschiedenen Schulreform. 316p. 1999. 45.95 (*3-631-32860-5*) P Lang Pubng.

Bernhard, Bob. Professional's Book of Gerbils. (Illus.). 160p. 1993. 17.95 (*0-86622-669-9*, TS-120) TFH Pubns.

Bernhard, Brendan. Pizarro, Orellana, & the Exploration of the Amazon. Goetzmann, William H., ed. (World Explorers Ser.). (Illus.). 120p. (YA). (gr. 5 up). 1991. lib. bdg. 19.95 (*0-7910-1305-7*) Chelsea Hse.

B

An Asterisk (*) at the beginning of an entry indicates that the title is appearing for the first time.

Bernhard, C. G., et al, eds. Science, Technology & Society in the Time of Alfred Nobel: Proceedings of a Nobel Symposium 52 Held at Bjorkborn, Karlskoga, Sweden, August 17-22, 1981. LC 82-11254. (Illus.). 440p. 1982. 197.00 (0-08-027939-2, Pub. by Pergamon Repr) Franklin.

***Bernhard, Durga.** Earth, Sky, Wet, Dry: A Book of Opposites. LC 99-23084. 40p. (J). (gr. k-4). 2000. lib. bdg. 17.99 (0-531-33213-6) Orchard Bks Watts.

— Earth, Sky, Wet, Dry: A Book of Opposites. LC 99-23084. (Illus.). 40p. (J). (gr. k-4). 2000. 16.95 (0-531-30213-X) Orchard Bks Watts.

Bernhard, Emery. Eagles: Lions of the Sky. LC 93-1833. (Illus.). 32p. (J). (gr. k-3). 1994. lib. bdg. 15.95 (0-8234-1105-2) Holiday.

— Happy New Year! (Illus.). 32p. (J). (gr. 1-4). 1996. 15.99 (0-525-67532-9, Dutton Child) Peng Put Young Read.

— Prairie Dogs. LC 96-22849. (Illus.). 40p. (J). (ps-3). 1997. 15.00 (0-15-201286-9) Harcourt.

— A Ride on Mother's Back: A Day of Baby-Carrying Around the World. LC 95-41483. (Illus.). 40p. (J). 1996. 16.00 (0-15-200870-5) Harcourt.

— Time to Play: Children's Games Around the World. LC 97-30435. (Illus.). (J). 1999. 14.99 (0-525-67553-1, Dutton Child) Peng Put Young Read.

— The Way of the Willow Branch. LC 95-9977. (Illus.). 32p. (J). (ps-3). 1996. 15.00 (0-15-200844-6) Harcourt.

Bernhard, Ernest C. Computer Aided Engineering Of. 1985. 46.95 (0-02-948590-8) Free Pr.

Bernhard, F., jt. auth. see Decker, H.

Bernhard, Fabian, ed. see Glanville, Joseph.

Bernhard, Fred & Clapp, Steve. Widening the Welcome of Your Church: Biblical Hospitality & the Vital Congregation. 144p. 1996. pap. 14.00 (0-9637206-9-4) LifeQuest IN.

Bernhard, Gwyn K. Gwyn Karon Bernhard's Kids' Talk: Kids' Talk in the Classroom Workbook, No. 1. 125p. (J). (gr. 5-9). 1989. 85.00 (1-877819-04-2) Kids Talk CT.

Bernhard, Hans-Joachim & Smith, Duncan. Remembering Rostock, 1972-1990: The Ahrenshoop Symposium of the Brown-Rostock Exchange Program, March, 1989. 156p. (C). 1991. lib. bdg. 39.50 (0-8191-8370-9) U Pr of Amer.

Bernhard, J. Gary. Primates in the Classroom: An Evolutionary Perspective on Children's Education. LC 87-19153. 216p. (Orig.). (C). 1988. pap. text 16.95 (0-87023-610-5) U of Mass Pr.

Bernhard, J. Gary & Glantz, Kalman. Staying Human in the Organization: Our Biological Heritage & the Workplace. LC 92-892. (Human Evolution, Behavior & Intelligence Ser.). 176p. 1992. 52.95 (0-275-94295-3, C4295, Praeger Pubs) Greenwood.

Bernhard, James. Black Video. 200p. 1997. pap. write for info. (1-891239-02-3) Primeval Pr.

— Lmno P. 95p. (Orig.). 1995. pap. 10.00 (0-944920-20-9) Bellowing Ark Pr.

— The Night Watchman. 180p. 1997. pap. write for info. (1-891239-00-7) Primeval Pr.

Bernhard, Jeffrey D. Itch: Mechanisms & Management of Pruritus. (Illus.). 480p. 1993. pap. text 52.00 (0-07-004935-1) McGraw-Hill HPD.

Bernhard, Julia, jt. auth. see Alt, Arthur T.

Bernhard, Kathleen. Work with Your Disability. pap. 12.95 (0-9666480-0-5) DrKathleen.

Bernhard, Keith & Merritt, Cathleen. Getting Started with the Claris Works Database. 48p. (Orig.). 1993. pap. 19.95 incl. disk (0-9620807-5-6) Natl AppleWrks.

Bernhard, Keith, jt. auth. see Merritt, Cathlee M.

Bernhard, Keith, jt. ed. see Merritt, Cathleen.

Bernhard, M., et al, eds. The Importance of Chemical Speciation in Environmental Processes. (Dahlem Workshop Reports: Vol. 33). (Illus.). 700p. 1987. 232.95 (0-387-15362-4) Spr-Verlag.

Bernhard, Michael & Breatnach, Padraig A. Die Regensburger Schottenlegende - Libellus de Fundacione Ecclesie Consecratj Petri. (GER.). x, 324p. 1977. 68.00 (3-615-00160-5, Pub. by Weidmann) Lubrecht & Cramer.

Bernhard, Michael H. The Origins of Democratization in Poland: Workers, Intellectuals, & Oppositional Politics, 1976-1980. 400p. (C). 1993. pap. 21.00 (0-231-08093-X) Col U Pr.

Bernhard, Michael H. & Szlajfer, Henryk, eds. From the Polish Underground: Selections from Krytyka, 1978-1993. Slaijfer, Chmielewska, tr. LC 94-18841. 496p. 1995. 80.00 (0-271-01400-8); pap. 22.50 (0-271-01401-6) Pa St U Pr.

***Bernhard, Nancy.** Best of Baby Boomer Trivia. LC 99-93937. 1999. pap. 10.95 (0-533-13198-7) Vantage.

Bernhard, Nancy E. U. S. Television News & Cold War Propaganda, 1947-1960. LC 98-24721. (Cambridge Studies in the History of Mass Communications). (Illus.). 256p. (C). 1999. 59.95 (0-521-59415-4) Cambridge U Pr.

Bernhard, P., jt. auth. see Basar, Tamer S.

Bernhard, Pierre, jt. auth. see Basar, Tamer S.

Bernhard, Pierre, jt. ed. see Siguerdidjane, H. B.

Bernhard, Robert J. & Bolton, Stuart, eds. Proceedings of the International Conference on Noise Control Engineering Held July 10-12, 1995 Newport Beach, CA, U. S. A., Set, Vols. 1 & 2. (Inter-Noise Ser.). lvi, 1450p. 150.00 (0-931784-32-8) Noise Control.

Bernhard, Ruth, photos by. Ruth Bernhard: The Gift of the Commonplace. LC 95-62339. (Lux Ser.: Vol. IV). (Illus.). 48p. 1998. 40.00 (0-9630393-4-2) Ctr for Photo.

***Bernhard, Sandra.** May I Kiss You On The Lips, Miss Sandra. LC 98-47725. 256p. 1998. 24.00 (0-688-16471-4, Wm Morrow) Morrow Avon.

— May I Kiss You On The Lips, Miss Sandra. 224p. 1999. pap. 14.00 (0-688-17163-X, Wm Morrow) Morrow Avon.

Bernhard, Sandy & Ela, Thomas. The House Journal: A Resource to Evaluate & Document the History, Alterations, & Records of Your House & Property. LC 93-17385. (Illus.). 112p. 1993. 15.95 (0-89133-235-9) Wiley.

Bernhard, Thomas. Concrete. McLintock, David, tr. LC 86-1285. vi, 160p. 1986. pap. 14.00 (0-226-04398-3) U Ch Pr.

— Correction. Wilkins, Sophie, tr. LC 89-27656. (Phoenix Fiction Ser.). viii, 282p. 1990. pap. 15.95 (0-226-04393-2) U Ch Pr.

— Extinction. McClintock, David, tr. LC 96-23209. 336p. 1996. pap. 14.95 (0-226-04383-5) U Ch Pr.

— Gargoyles. Winston, Richard & Winston, Clara, trs. LC 85-23223. vi, 214p. 1986. pap. 15.00 (0-226-04399-1) U Ch Pr.

— Histrionics: Three Plays. Northcott, Kenneth J., tr. LC 89-20198. 292p. 1990. pap. 14.95 (0-226-04395-9); lib. bdg. 51.00 (0-226-04394-0) U Ch Pr.

— The Lime Works. Wilkins, Sophia, tr. LC 86-1287. (Illus.). vi, 248p. 1986. pap. 16.95 (0-226-04397-5) U Ch Pr.

— The Loser. Dawson, Jack, tr. 200p. 1996. pap. 13.95 (0-226-04388-6) U Ch Pr.

— Maitres Anciens. (FRE.). 253p. 1991. pap. 10.95 (0-7859-2165-6, 2070383903) Fr & Eur.

— Old Masters: A Comedy. Osers, Ewald, tr. LC 92-18986. (Phoenix Fiction Ser.). iv, 160p. 1992. pap. 12.95 (0-226-04391-6) U Ch Pr.

— On the Mountain. Stockman, Russell, tr. from GER. LC 91-61533. 128p. 1993. pap. 10.95 (0-910395-76-4) Marlboro Pr.

***Bernhard, Thomas.** Three Novellas. 2000. 25.00 (0-226-04432-7) U Ch Pr.

Bernhard, Thomas. The Voice Imitator. Northcott, Kenneth J., tr. LC 97-14412. 112p. 1997. 17.95 (0-226-04401-7) U Ch Pr.

— Voice Imitator. 1998. pap. 10.00 (0-226-04402-5) U Ch Pr.

— Wittgenstein's Nephew: A Friendship. McLintock, David, tr. LC 89-27716. (Phoenix Fiction Ser.). vi, 108p. 1990. pap. 10.00 (0-226-04392-4) U Ch Pr.

— Woodcutters. McLintock, David, tr. from GER. LC 88-26076. iv, 186p. 1989. pap. 13.95 (0-226-04396-7) U Ch Pr.

— Yes. Osers, Ewald, tr. from GER. LC 92-17921. (Phoenix Fiction Ser.). iv, 140p. 1992. pap. 11.95 (0-226-04390-8) U Ch Pr.

Bernhard, Victor M. & Towne, Jonathan B., eds. Complications in Vascular Surgery. 522p. 1991. 89.00 (0-942219-20-1) Quality Med Pub.

Bernhard, Virginia. A Durable Fire. 528p. 1991. mass mkt. 4.95 (0-380-70873-6, Avon Bks) Morrow Avon.

— Ima Hogg: The Governor's Daughter. (Illus.). 160p. 1996. pap. text 13.95 (1-881089-91-6) Brandywine Press.

***Bernhard, Virginia.** Slaves & Slaveholders in Bermuda, 1616-1782. LC 99-34249. 336p. 1999. 37.50 (0-8262-1227-1) U of Mo Pr.

Bernhard, Virginia, ed. Hidden Histories of Women in the New South. 264p. 1994. 34.95 (0-8262-0958-0) U of Mo Pr.

Bernhard, Virginia, et al, eds. Southern Women: Histories & Identities. 240p. 1993. text 34.95 (0-8262-0868-1) U of Mo Pr.

Bernhard, Virginia & Fox-Genovese, Elizabeth, eds. Birth of American Feminism: The Seneca Falls Woman's Rights Convention of 1848. (Illus.). 240p. (C). 1995. pap. text 13.95 (1-881089-34-7) Brandywine Press.

Bernhard, Winfred E. Fisher Ames, Federalist & Statesman, 1758-1808. LC 65-23142. (Illus.). 386p. reprint ed. pap. 119.70 (0-8357-3917-1, 203665200004) Bks Demand.

Bernhard, Yetta. How to Be Somebody. 1975. pap. 9.95 (0-930017-01-3) Sci & Behavior.

— Self-Care In & Out of Bed. 1975. pap. 12.00 (0-930017-00-5) Sci & Behavior.

Bernhardi, Charlotte, ed. see Von Krusenstern, Adam J.

Bernhardi Trow, Katherine. Habits of Mind: The Experimental College Program at Berkeley. LC 98-6238. (Illus.). 483p. 1998. pap. 19.95 (0-87772-380-X) UCB IGS.

Bernhardsen, Tor. Geographic Information Systems: An Introduction. 2nd ed. LC 98-38195. 392p. 1999. 59.95 (0-471-32192-3) Wiley.

Bernhardson, Wayne. Lonely Planet Argentina, Uruguay & Paraguay. 3rd ed. 768p. 1999. pap. 21.95 (0-86442-641-0) Lonely Planet.

— Lonely Planet Argentina, Uruguay & Paraguay: Travel Guide. 2nd ed. (Illus.). 768p. 1996. pap. 19.95 (0-86442-336-5) Lonely Planet.

— Lonely Planet Baja, California. 4th ed. (Illus.). 328p. 1998. pap. 16.95 (0-86442-445-0) Lonely Planet.

— Lonely Planet Buenos Aires. 2nd ed. 160p. 1999. pap. 12.95 (0-86442-643-7) Lonely Planet.

— Lonely Planet Chile & Easter Island. 4th ed. (Illus.). 452p. 1997. pap. 19.95 (0-86442-421-3) Lonely Planet.

— Lonely Planet Chile & Easter Island Travel Atlas: With Travel Information & Roadtesting. (Lonely Planet Ser.). 1997. pap. text 14.95 (0-86442-517-1) Lonely Planet.

Bernhardt, Barbara, et al, eds. Proceedings of the UBC International Conference on Phonological Acquisition. (Illus.). 292p. (C). 1996. pap. 25.00 (1-57473-009-6); lib. bdg. 54.00 (1-57473-109-2) Cascadilla Pr.

Bernhardt, Barbara A. The Marfan Syndrome: A Booklet for Teachers. 1992. pap. text 3.00 (0-918335-07-8) Natl Marfan Foun.

Bernhardt, Barbara A., et al. The Marfan Syndrome: A Booklet for Teenagers. (Illus.). 20p. (YA). 1988. pap. 3.00 (0-918335-03-5) Natl Marfan Foun.

Bernhardt, Barbara H. & Stemberger, Joseph P. Workbook in Nonlinear Phonology for Clinical Application. LC 98-50043. 1999. 35.00 (0-89079-810-9) PRO-ED.

Bernhardt, Barbara H. & Sternberger, Joseph P., eds. Handbook of Phonological Development: From the Perspective of Constraint-Based Nonlinear Phonology. LC 97-80298. (Illus.). 793p. (C). 1997. text 149.95 (0-12-092830-2) Morgan Kaufmann.

Bernhardt, Christoph. Bauplatz GroB-Berlin. 400p. 1997. text 124.00 (3-11-015382-3) De Gruyter.

Bernhardt, Clyde E. I Remember: Eighty Years of Black Entertainment, Big Bands, & the Blues. LC 85-26355. (Illus.). 290p. (Orig.). 1986. pap. text 19.95 (0-8122-1223-1) U of Pa Pr.

Bernhardt, David K., ed. Being a Parent: Unchanging Values in a Changing World. LC 74-484635. 202p. reprint ed. pap. 62.70 (0-8357-7117-2, 202359400033) Bks Demand.

Bernhardt, Debra, et al. Working Womenroots: An Oral History Primer. 2nd ed. 33p. 1980. pap. 5.00 (0-87736-342-0) U of Mich Inst Labor.

***Bernhardt, Debra E. & Bernstein, Rachel.** Ordinary People, Extraordinary Lives: A Pictorial History of Working People in New York City. LC 99-50742. (Illus.). 221p. 2000. 34.95 (0-8147-9866-7) NYU Pr.

***Bernhardt, Dee, et al.** Good News, Day by Day: Bible Reflections for Teens. 384p. (YA). 2000. pap. 10.95 (0-88489-601-3) St Marys.

Bernhardt, Donna B., ed. Recreation for the Disabled Child. LC 84-19330. (Physical & Occupational Therapy in Pediatrics Ser.: Vol. 4, No. 3). 110p. 1985. text 39.95 (0-86656-263-X) Haworth Pr.

— Sports Physical Therapy. (Clinics in Physical Therapy Ser.: Vol. 10). (Illus.). 223p. (C). 1986. text 49.95 (0-443-08444-0) Church.

Bernhardt, Edythe. ABCs of Thinking with Caldecott Books. (Illus.). 124p. 1988. pap. 12.95 (0-913839-70-1, BL178) Pieces of Lrning.

Bernhardt, Elizabeth B. Reading Development in a Second Language: Theoretical, Empirical & Classroom Perspectives. DiPietro, Robert J., ed. (Second Language Learning Ser.: Vol. 1). 272p. (C). 1991. pap. 39.50 (0-89391-734-6); text 73.25 (0-89391-675-7) Ablx Pub.

Bernhardt, Elizabeth B., ed. Life in Language Immersion Classrooms. LC 92-15152. (Multilingual Matters Ser.: No. 86). 1992. 74.95 (1-85359-151-3, Pub. by Multilingual Matters); pap. 29.95 (1-85359-150-5, Pub. by Multilingual Matters) Taylor & Francis.

Bernhardt, Eva D. Goethe's "Romische Elegien" The Lover & the Poet. Mommsen, Katharina, ed. (Germanic Studies in America: Vol. 59). (Illus.). 218p. 1990. 17.00 (3-261-04218-4) P Lang Pubng.

Bernhardt, Gale. The Female Cyclist: Gearing up a Level. LC 99-18666. (Ultimate Training Series From Velo Press). (Illus.). 240p. (Orig.). 1999. pap. 16.95 (1-884737-58-7) VeloPress.

***Bernhardt, Gale.** Training Plans for Multisport Athletes. LC 00-32075. (Ultimate Training Ser.). 2000. 16.95 (1-884737-82-X) VeloPress.

Bernhardt, H., jt. ed. see Ives, K. J.

Bernhardt, H. J., jt. ed. see Ives, K. J.

Bernhardt, John W. Itinerant Kingship & Royal Monasteries in Early Medieval Germany, c. 936-1075. LC 92-34399. (Cambridge Studies in Medieval Life & Thought: No. 4). 398p. (C). 1993. text 74.95 (0-521-39489-9) Cambridge U Pr.

Bernhardt, Joshua. The Alaskan Engineering Commission: Its History, Activities & Organization. LC 72-3017. (Brookings Institution. Institute for Government Research. Service Monographs of the U. S. Government: No. 4). reprint ed. 24.50 (0-404-57104-2) AMS Pr.

— The Interstate Commerce Commission: Its History, Activities & Organization. LC 72-3036. (Brookings Institution. Institute for Government Research. Service Monographs of the U. S. Government: No. 18). reprint ed. 25.00 (0-404-57118-2) AMS Pr.

— The Railroad Labor Board: Its History, Activities & Organization. LC 72-3037. (Brookings Institution. Institute for Government Research. Service Monographs of the U. S. Government: No. 19). reprint ed. 21.50 (0-404-57119-0) AMS Pr.

— The Tariff Commission: Its History, Activities & Organization. LC 72-3018. (Brookings Institution. Institute for Government Research. Service Monographs of the U. S. Government: No. 5). reprint ed. 21.50 (0-404-57105-0) AMS Pr.

Bernhardt-Kabisch, Ernest. Robert Southey. Bowman, Sylvia E., ed. (Twayne's English Authors Ser.). 200p. (C). 1977. lib. bdg. 20.95 (0-8057-6692-8) Irvington.

Bernhardt, Karl A. & Davis, Graeme. The Word Order of Old High German. LC 97-46077. (Studies in German Language & Literature: Vol. 19). 140p. 1997. text 69.95 (0-7734-8463-9) E Mellen.

Bernhardt, Karl-Georg. Untersuchungen Zur Besiedlung und Dynamik der Vegetation Von Sand- und Schlickpionierstandorten. (Dissertationes Botanicae Ser.: Band 202). (Illus.). vi, 223p. 1993. pap. 65.00 (3-443-64114-8, Pub. by Gebruder Borntraeger) Balogh.

— Untersuchungen Zur Biologie der Begleitflora Mediterraner Wein- und Getreidekulturen Im Westlichen Sizilien: Begleitflora Mediterraner Wein und Getreidekulturen im Westlichen Sizilien. (Dissertationes Botanicae Ser.: Band 103). (Illus.). iv, 138p. 1987. pap. 36.00 (3-443-64015-X, Pub. by Gebruder Borntraeger) Balogh.

***Bernhardt, Karl-Heinz.** Goldfish & Fancy Goldfish. (Aqualog Special Ser.: Vol. 8). (Illus.). 48p. 1998. 25.00 (3-931702-45-6, Pub. by Verlag ACS) Hollywood.

Bernhardt, Kathryn. Rents, Taxes, & Peasant Resistance: The Lower Yangzi Region, 1840-1950. (Illus.). 344p. (C). 1992. 45.00 (0-8047-1880-6) Stanford U Pr.

***Bernhardt, Kathryn.** Women & Property in China: 960-1949. LC 99-27947. 1999. 45.00 (0-8047-3526-3) Stanford U Pr.

Bernhardt, Kathryn & Huang, Philip C., eds. Civil Law in Qing & Republican China. LC 94-11687. (Law, Society, & Culture in China Ser.). xiv, 340p. 1994. 47.50 (0-8047-2274-9) Stanford U Pr.

Bernhardt, Kenneth L. CPS Cases in Marketing Management Select Material. 6th ed. 160p. (C). 1995. 21.95 (0-256-21179-5, Irwn McGrw-H) McGrw-H Hghr Educ.

Bernhardt, Kenneth L. & Kinnear, Thomas. Cases in Marketing Management. 7th ed. LC 96-37108. 736p. (C). 1996. text 70.65 (0-256-20464-0, Irwn McGrw-H) McGrw-H Hghr Educ.

— Cases in Marketing Management: Select Material. 6th ed. 128p. (C). 1995. text 17.95 (0-256-20950-2, Irwn McGrw-H) McGrw-H Hghr Educ.

Bernhardt, Kenneth L. & Kinnear, Thomas C. Cases in Marketing Management. 6th ed. LC 93-5594. (Marketing Ser.). 768p. (C). 1993. text 70.65 (0-256-12246-6, Irwn McGrw-H) McGrw-H Hghr Educ.

Bernhardt, Kenneth L., et al. Cases in Marketing Management & Marketing. 6th ed. (C). 1994. text 74.00 (0-256-18520-4, Irwn McGrw-H) McGrw-H Hghr Educ.

Bernhardt, L. Jerry, Jr. & McHaney, Larry J. Student Space Simulation. 256p. 1990. pap. 19.95 (0-8273-4191-1) Delmar.

Bernhardt, Lysiane S. Sarah Bernhardt, My Grandmother. Holland, Vyvyan, tr. LC 79-8054. reprint ed. 26.50 (0-404-18365-4) AMS Pr.

Bernhardt, M. & Curtis, J. . . . And a 10-Foot Pole. (Rolemaster Standard System Ser.). (Illus.). 1999. 20.00 (1-55806-370-6, 5703) Iron Crown Ent Inc.

***Bernhardt, Marcia.** Barns, Farms & Yarns: In Iron County, Michigan. LC 99-76133. (Illus.). iv, 120p. 1999. pap. 25.00 (0-9677230-0-0) Iron County.

Bernhardt, Mike. Voices of the Grieving Heart. LC 94-68210. 144p. 1994. pap. 11.95 (0-9642810-0-7) Cypress Point.

Bernhardt, P. A., et al, eds. Space Plasma Physics: Proceedings of the Topical Meeting of the COSPAR Interdisciplinary Scientific Commission D (Meetings D5 & D7) of the COSPAR 29th Plenary Meeting Held in Washington, D. C., U. S. A., 28 August-5 September, 1992. (Advances in Space Research Ser.: Vol. 13/10). 350p. 1993. pap. 210.50 (0-08-042342-6, Pergamon Pr) Elsevier.

Bernhardt, Partrick. Mantra Voyage: Le Son Comme Moyen de Realisation de Soi. (FRE.). 1998. 21.95 (2-89466-020-0) Edns Roseau.

Bernhardt, Peter. The Rose's Kiss: A Natural History of Flowers. LC 99-21386. 250p. 1999. text 24.95 (1-55963-564-9, Shearwater Bks) Island Pr.

Bernhardt, R. Encyclopedia of Disputes Instalment 12: Geographic Issues. 430p. 1990. 196.00 (0-444-86243-9, North Holland) Elsevier.

— Encyclopedia of Public International Law. 1999. 462.50 (0-444-86247-1) Elsevier.

— Encyclopedia of Public International Law: Consolidated Edition, 5 vols. 1992. 2486.00 (0-7204-0131-3, Pergamon Pr) Elsevier.

— Encyclopedia of Public International Law Consolidated Edition, Vol. 1 (A-D) LC 95-159566. 1992. 475.00 (0-444-86244-7, North Holland) Elsevier.

— Encyclopedia of Public International Law Consolidated Edition, Vol. 2 (E-I) 1995. 462.50 (0-444-86245-5, North Holland) Elsevier.

— Encyclopedia of Public International Law Consolidated Edition, Vol. 3 (J-P) LC 95-159566. 1998. write for info. (0-444-86246-3, North Holland) Elsevier.

Bernhardt, R., ed. Interim Measures Indicated by International Courts. (Beitrage Zur Auslandischen Offentlichen Rectund V: Vol. 117). 308p. 1995. 69.00 (0-387-58270-3) Spr-Verlag.

Bernhardt, R., et al. Digest of the Decisions of the International Court of Justice, 1976-1985. (Fontes Iuris Gentium Ser.: Vol. 7). 768p. 1990. 283.95 (0-387-51726-X, 3606) Spr-Verlag.

Bernhardt, R., ed. see International Symposium on the Judicial Settlement.

Bernhardt, R., ed. see Wolfrum, Rudiger.

Bernhardt, Regis, et al, eds. Curriculum Leadership: Rethinking Schools for the 21st Century. LC 97-52261. 320p. (C). 1998. text 65.00 (1-57273-149-4); pap. text 26.50 (1-57273-150-8) Hampton Pr NJ.

Bernhardt, Roger. California Mortgage & Deed of Trust Practice. 2nd ed. Scott, Craig H., ed. LC 89-83396. (Illus.). 579p. 1990. text 115.00 (0-88124-177-6, RE-31340) Cont Ed Bar-CA.

***Bernhardt, Roger.** California Mortgage & Deed of Trust Practice, 2 vols. 3rd ed. Blanchette, Janis L. et al, eds. LC 00-102304. 812p. 2000. 179.00 (0-7626-0396-8, RE-33110) Cont Ed Bar-CA.

Bernhardt, Roger. California Real Estate Finance. 3rd ed. LC 95-83226. 520p. 1996. lib. bdg. 60.00 (0-89089-677-1) Carolina Acad Pr.

— California Real Estate Law. LC 67-5714. 1992. 60.00 (0-317-03214-3) West Group.

— Property: Cases & Statutes. LC 99-202244. (American Casebook Ser). 969p. 1999. 44.25 (0-314-23232-X) West Pub.

Bernhardt, Roger & Hoban, Thomas. Federal Real Estate Law Deskbook. 1360p. (Orig.). 1994. 95.00 (0-7913-2308-0) Warren Gorham & Lamont.

***Bernhardt, Roger & Tour-Sarkissian, Christine.** Bernhardt's California Real Estate Cases, 2000. Chapin, John K. & Briggs, Donald R., eds. LC 00-102936. 714p. 2000. 95.00 (0-7626-0408-5, RE-33200) Cont Ed Bar-CA.

Bernhardt, Roger H. Property. 2nd ed. 388p. (C). 1991. pap., text, pap. text 24.50 (0-314-86227-7) West Pub.

— Real Property in a Nutshell. 3rd ed. LC 93-24677. (Nutshell Ser.). 475p. 1993. pap. 21.00 (0-314-02436-0) West Pub.

***Bernhardt, Roger H.** Real Property in a Nutshell. 4th ed. (Nutshell Ser.). 1999. pap. 23.00 (*0-314-23806-9*) West Pub.

Bernhardt, Roger H. & Burkhart, Ann M. Property. 3rd ed. LC 97-35462. (Black Letter Ser.). 403p. (C). 1997. pap., suppl. ed. 24.50 incl. disk (*0-314-22795-4*) West Pub.

Bernhardt, Sarah. The Art of the Theatre. Stenning, H. J., tr. LC 70-82819. 1972. 20.95 (*0-405-08264-9*, Pub. by Blom Pubns) Ayer.

— Memories of My Life. LC 68-56475. (Illus.). 1972. reprint ed. 30.95 (*0-405-08265-7*, Pub. by Blom Pubns) Ayer.

— My Double Life: The Memoirs of Sarah Bernhardt. Tietze Larson, Victoria, tr. from FRE. LC 98-30036. (SUNY Series, Women Writers in Translation). 352p. (C). 1999. pap. text 24.95 (*0-7914-4054-0*) State U NY Pr.

— My Double Life: The Memoirs of Sarah Bernhardt. Tietze Larson, Victoria, tr. from FRE. LC 98-30036. (SUNY Series, Women Writers in Translation). 352p. (C). 1999. text 73.50 (*0-7914-4053-2*) State U NY Pr.

Bernhardt, Stephen A., jt. auth. see Smith, Edward L.

Bernhardt, Stephen A., jt. ed. see Garay, Mary S.

Bernhardt, Susanne, tr. see Lukacs, Georg.

Bernhardt, Ursula. Die Funktion der Kataloge in Ovids Exilpoesie. (Altertumswissenschaftliche Texte und Studien: Bd. 15). (GER.). xiv, 447p. 1986. 70.00 (*3-487-07759-0*) G Olms Pubs.

Bernhardt, Victoria L. Data Analysis for Comprehensive Schoolwide Improvement. LC 98-9736. 300p. 1998. pap. 29.95 (*1-883001-57-9*) Eye On Educ.

***Bernhardt, Victoria L.** Designing & Using Databases. LC 00-23823. (Illus.). 2000. write for info. (*1-883001-95-1*) Eye On Educ.

Bernhardt, Victoria L. The School Portfolio: A Comprehensive Framework for School Improvement. 2nd ed. LC 98-41529. 270p. 1999. pap. 29.95 (*1-883001-64-1*) Eye On Educ.

***Bernhardt, Victoria L., et al.** The Example School Portfolio: A Companion to the School Portfolio. LC 99-56802. (Illus.). 250p. 2000. pap. text 29.95 (*1-883001-92-7*) Eye On Educ.

Bernhardt, William. Blind Justice. (Southwest Mysteries Ser.). 1992. mass mkt. 5.99 (*0-345-37483-5*) Ballantine Pub Grp.

— Blind Justice. large type ed. 1993. 80.95 (*0-7862-9989-4*, G K Hall Lrg Type) Mac Lib Ref.

***Bernhardt, William.** The Code of Buddyhood. 342p. 1999. pap. 15.95 (*0-9673131-2-0*) HAWK Pubng Grp.

Bernhardt, William. Cruel Justice. LC 95-14697. 1997. mass mkt. 5.99 (*0-345-40803-9*) Ballantine Pub Grp.

— Cruel Justice. large type ed. LC 96-7168. 1996. pap. 22.95 (*1-56895-323-2*) Wheeler Pub.

— Dark Justice. LC 98-28182. 400p. 1999. 22.50 (*0-345-40738-5*) Ballantine Pub Grp.

***Bernhardt, William.** Dark Justice. 1999. mass mkt. 6.99 (*0-345-43476-5*) Ballantine Pub Grp.

Bernhardt, William. Deadly Justice. LC 93-90073. 306p. 1993. mass mkt. 5.99 (*0-345-38027-4*) Ballantine Pub Grp.

— Deadly Justice. large type ed. 1994. 65.95 (*0-7862-9988-6*, G K Hall Lrg Type) Mac Lib Ref.

— Double Jeopardy. 1996. mass mkt. 5.99 (*0-345-39784-3*) Ballantine Pub Grp.

— Double Jeopardy. large type ed. (Niagara Large Print Ser.). 431p. 1996. 27.99 (*0-7089-5828-1*) Ulverscroft.

— Extreme Justice. LC 98-96399. (Ben Kincaid). 376p. 1999. mass mkt. 6.99 (*0-345-42481-6*) Ballantine Pub Grp.

— The Midnight Before Christmas: A Holiday Thriller. LC 98-20329. (The/Ben Kincaid "Justice" Ser.). 1998. 14.95 (*0-345-42810-2*) Ballantine Pub Grp.

— The Midnight Before Christmas: A Holiday Thriller. 1999. mass mkt. 5.99 (*0-345-42811-0*) Ballantine Pub Grp.

— Naked Justice. 1998. mass mkt. 6.99 (*0-449-00087-7*, GM) Fawcett.

— Naked Justice. large type ed. (Niagara Large Print Ser.). 688p. 1997. 29.50 (*0-7089-5879-6*) Ulverscroft.

— Perfect Justice. 1995. mass mkt. 5.99 (*0-345-39133-0*) Hse Collectbls.

— Primary Justice. 1992. mass mkt. 5.99 (*0-345-37479-7*) Ballantine Pub Grp.

***Bernhardt, William.** Primary Justice. LC 98-42592. 1998. 20.95 (*0-7862-1659-X*) Five Star.

— Silent Justice. LC 99-53224. 400p. 2000. 23.00 (*0-345-42812-9*) Ballantine Pub Grp.

Bernhardt, William, ed. Legal Briefs: Stories by Today's Best Thriller Writers. 352p. 1999. mass mkt. 6.99 (*0-440-22571-X*) Dell.

Bernhei, Phillip. In Doras Freud Hysteria. 1991. pap. 20.50 (*0-231-06907-3*) Col U Pr.

Bernheim. Ruth Rendell. 1998. 22.95 (*0-8057-4625-0*, Twyne) Mac Lib Ref.

Bernheim, Alfred L. The Business of the Theatre. LC 64-14693. 1972. 24.95 (*0-405-08266-5*, Pub. by Blom Pubns) Ayer.

Bernheim, B. Douglas. Saving for Prosperity: The U. S. Saving Rate. 112p. 1990. 18.95 (*0-87078-312-2*); pap. 8.95 (*0-87078-313-0*) Century Foundation.

Bernheim, B. Douglas & Shoven, John B., eds. National Saving & Economic Performance. (Illus.). 396p. 1991. 54.95 (*0-226-04404-1*) U Ch Pr.

Bernheim, David. Defense of Narcotic Cases, 3 vols. 1972. ring bd. 590.00 (*0-8205-1249-4*) Bender.

***Bernheim, Douglas.** Esplanner 2000. 2000. pap. 49.95 (*0-262-52292-6*) MIT Pr.

Bernheim, Gotthardt D. History of the German Settlements & of the Lutheran Church in North & South Carolina. 557p. 1996. reprint ed. pap. 40.00 (*0-8063-8001-2*, 475) Clearfield Co.

Bernheim, Hippolyte. Bernheim's New Studies in Hypnotism. Sandor, Richard S., tr. from GER. (Illus.). xix, 407p. (C). 1980. 60.00 (*0-8236-0496-9*) Intl Univs Pr.

Bernheim, Hippolyte. Suggestive Therapeutics. 440p. 100.00 (*1-85506-673-4*) Thoemmes Pr.

Bernheim, Kayla F. The Lanahan Cases & Readings in Abnormal Behavior. 379p. (Orig.). (C). 1997. pap. text 26.25 (*0-9652687-0-5*) Lanahan Pubs.

Bernheim, Kayla F. & Lehman, Anthony. Working with Families of the Mentally Ill. LC 85-18754. 1985. 22.95 (*0-393-70009-7*) Norton.

Bernheim, Kayla F. & Lewine, Richard R. Schizophrenia: Symptoms, Causes, Treatments. (Illus.). (C). 1979. pap. text. write for info. (*0-393-09017-5*) Norton.

Bernheim, Kayla F., et al. The Lanahan Cases in Developmental Psychopathology. 195p. (Orig.). (C). 1999. pap. text 18.75 (*0-9652687-5-6*) Lanahan Pubs.

Bernheim, Pierre-Antoine. James, Brother of Jesus. 1997. pap. 27.00 (*0-334-02695-4*) TPI PA.

Bernheimer, Alan. Cafe Isotope. 1980. per. 7.50 (*0-935724-00-1*) Figures.

Bernheimer, Charles. Figures of Ill Repute: Representing Prostitution in Nineteenth-Century France. LC 96-53654. (Illus.). 329p. 1997. pap. text 17.95 (*0-8223-1947-0*) Duke.

— Figures of Ill Repute: Representing Prostitution in Nineteenth-Century France. LC 89-1993. (Illus.). 352p. 1989. 41.50 (*0-674-30115-3*) HUP.

— Flaubert & Kafka: Studies in Psychopoetic Structure. LC 82-1842. 280p. 1982. 45.00 (*0-300-02633-1*) Yale U Pr.

Bernheimer, Charles, ed. Comparative Literature in the Age of Multiculturalism. LC 94-29219. (Parallax). 232p. 1994. text 39.95 (*0-8018-5004-5*); pap. text 14.95 (*0-8018-5005-3*) Johns Hopkins.

Bernheimer, Charles & Kahane, Claire. In Dora's Case. 2nd ed. 1990. pap. text 19.50 (*0-231-07221-X*) Col U Pr.

Bernheimer, Charles L. Rainbow Bridge: Circling Navajo Mountain & Explorations in the "Badlands" of Southern Utah & Northern Arizona. (CAS Reprint Ser.). (Illus.). 239p. 1999. reprint ed. mass mkt. 20.00 (*0-932752-09-8*) Ctr Anthrop Studies.

Bernheimer, Kate, ed. Mirror, Mirror, on the Wall: Women Writers Explore the Fairy Tales That Have Changed Their Lives. LC 97-42242. 368p. 1998. pap. 14.00 (*0-385-48681-2*, Anchor NY) Doubleday.

Bernheimer, Kathryn. The 50 Funniest Movies of All Time: A Critic's Ranking. LC 98-53838. (Illus.). 224p. 1999. pap. 16.95 (*0-8065-2091-4*, Citadel Pr) Carol Pub Group.

— 50 Greatest Jewish Movies: A Critic's Ranking of the Very Best. LC 97-47098. (Illus.). 240p. 1998. 19.95 (*1-55972-457-9*, Birch Ln Pr) Carol Pub Group.

Bernheimer, Paul. The HubBub Guide to Cycling. iii, 127p. 1997. spiral bd. 14.95 (*0-9659097-0-0*) DBLpromotions.

Bernheimer, Richard. The Nature of Representation: A Phenomenological Inquiry. Janson, H. W., ed. LC 61-8057. 263p. reprint ed. pap. 81.60 (*0-608-11852-4*, 205026300058) Bks Demand.

Bernholc, J., et al, eds. Impurities, Defects & Diffusion in Semiconductors Vol. 163: Bulk & Layered Structures. 1050p. 1990. text 17.50 (*1-55899-051-8*) Materials Res.

Bernholz, Jean F. & Sumner, Patricia H. Success in Reading & Writing. 2nd ed. (Illus.). 288p. 1991. 27.95 (*0-673-36005-9*, GoodYrBooks) Addson-Wesley Educ.

Bernholz, Jean F., jt. auth. see Sumner, Patricia H.

Bernholz, P., et al, eds. Political Competition, Innovation & Growth: A Historical Analysis. LC 98-27595. viii, 308p. 1998. 92.00 (*3-540-64680-9*) Spr-Verlag.

Bernholz, Peter. Flexible Exchange Rates in Historical Perspective. LC 82-6167. (Studies in International Finance: No. 49). 48p. 1982. pap. text 13.50 (*0-88165-220-2*) Princeton U Int Finan Econ.

— The International Game of Power: Past, Present & Future. (New Babylon Studies in the Social Sciences: No. 42). (Illus.). x, 232p. 1985. 75.40 (*0-89925-033-5*) Mouton.

Bernholz, Peter & Radnitzky, Gerard, eds. Das Okonomische Weltbild: Beitrage zu einer Neuen Politischen Okonomie. (International Carl Menger Library). (GER.). 350p. (C). 1991. 59.00 (*3-88405-072-9*) Philosophia Pr.

Bernicer, G., jt. auth. see Lord, E.

Bernick, Michael. Urban Illusions: New Approaches to Inner City Unemployment. LC 87-7208. 253p. 1987. 59.95 (*0-275-92804-7*, C2804, Praeger Pubs) Greenwood.

Bernick, Michael S. & Cervero, Robert B. Transit Villages in the 21st Century. LC 96-34617. (Illus.). 387p. 1996. 42.95 (*0-07-005475-4*) McGraw.

Bernidake-Aldous, Eleftheria A. Blindness in a Culture of Light: Especially the Case of Oedipus at Colonus of Sophocles. LC 89-12752. (American University Studies: Classical Languages & Literature: Ser. XVII, Vol. 8). XIV, 243p. 1990. text 40.50 (*0-8204-1024-1*) P Lang Pubng.

***Bernido, C. C., et al, eds.** Mathematical Methods of Quantum Physics: 2nd Jagna International Workshop: Essays in Honor of Professor Hiroshi Ezawa. 362p. 1999. text 120.00 (*90-5699-211-2*) Gordon & Breach.

Bernie, Barbara. Chinese Medicine: The Complete Guide to Acupuncture, Chinese Herbal Medicine, Food Cures, & Preventive Care. Gao, Duo, ed. (Illus.). 1998. pap. 22.95 (*1-56025-176-X*, Thunders Mouth) Avalon NY.

Bernie, Shirley A., jt. auth. see Sansom-Flood, Renee.

Bernier, Charles L. & Yerkey, A. Neil. Cogent Communication: Overcoming Reading Overload, 26. LC 78-73794. (Contributions in Librarianship & Information Science Ser.: No. 26). (Illus.). 280p. 1979. 59.95 (*0-313-20893-X*, BEC/) Greenwood.

Bernier, Donald R., et al. Nuclear Medicine: Technology & Techniques. 4th ed. LC 97-6999. (Illus.). 544p. (C). (gr. 13). 1997. text 91.00 (*0-8151-1991-7*, 30346) Mosby Inc.

Bernier, Donald R., jt. auth. see Wells, L. David.

Bernier, Evariste. Baxter Bear & Moses Moose. LC 90-61408. (Illus.). 48p. (J). (gr. 1-3). 1990. pap. text 8.95 (*0-89272-413-7*) Down East.

Bernier, Francois. Travels in the Mogul Empire, AD 1656-1668. 1996. 44.00 (*81-206-1169-1*, Pub. by Asian Educ Servs) S Asia.

— Travels in the Mogul Empire, AD 1656-1668. 1989. reprint ed. 18.00 (*81-85395-12-8*, Pub. by Low Price) S Asia.

— Travels in the Mogul Empire, AD 1656-1668. 2nd ed. Constable, Archibald, tr. (Illus.). 500p. reprint ed. text 47.50 (*0-685-13398-2*) Coronet Bks.

Bernier, Georges, ed. The Physiology of Flowering, 3 vols., III. 288p. 1985. 162.00 (*0-8493-5711-X*, CRC Reprint) Franklin.

— The Physiology of Flowering, 3 vols., Vol. I. 168p. 1981. 95.00 (*0-8493-5709-8*, QK830, CRC Reprint) Franklin.

— The Physiology of Flowering, 3 vols., Vol. II. 248p. 1981. 139.00 (*0-8493-5710-1*, CRC Reprint) Franklin.

Bernier, Georges, jt. ed. see Lord, Elizabeth M.

Bernier, Gerald & Salee, Daniel. The Shaping of Quebec Politics & Society: Colonialism, Power, & the Transition to Capitalism in the 19th Century. 250p. 1992. 75.00 (*0-8448-1697-3*, Crane Russak) Taylor & Francis.

***Bernier-Grand, Carmen T.** In The Shade Of The Nispero Tr. 2001. pap. 4.50 (*0-440-41660-4*) BDD Bks Young Read.

Bernier-Grand, Carmen T. In the Shade of the Nispero Tree. LC 98-41160. 192p. (J). (gr. 3-7). 1999. 15.95 (*0-531-30154-0*); lib. bdg. 16.99 (*0-531-33154-7*) Orchard Bks Watts.

— Juan Bobo: Four Folktales from Puerto Rico. (I Can Read Bks.). (J). (gr. 2-4). 1995. 8.95 (*0-606-08435-5*, Pub. by Turtleback) Demco.

— Poet & Politician of Puerto Rico: Don Luis Munoz Marin. LC 94-21985. (Illus.). 128p. (J). (gr. 4 up). 1995. 15.95 (*0-531-06887-0*); lib. bdg. 16.99 (*0-531-08737-9*) Orchard Bks Watts.

Bernier, Ivan, jt. ed. see Beck, Stanley M.

Bernier, J. J., et al. Traite de Gastro-Enterologie, 2 vols. (FRE., Illus.). 1600p. 1984. 295.00 (*2-257-10431-5*) S M P F Inc.

Bernier, Jacques, jt. auth. see Roland, Charles G.

***Bernier, Julie.** The Athletic Training Quick Reference Dictionary. 350p. (C). 2000. pap. text 20.00 (*1-55642-461-2*) SLACK Inc.

Bernier, Julie, jt. auth. see Levy, Linda.

Bernier, Olivier. Words of Fire, Deeds of Blood: The Mob, the Monarchy & the French Revolution. (Illus.). 384p. 1989. 21.95 (*0-316-09206-1*) Little.

***Bernier, P., et al, eds.** Advances in Synthetic Metals: Twenty Years of Progress in Science & Technology. 452p. 1999. 198.00 (*0-444-72003-0*); 761.50 (*0-444-72005-7*) Elsevier.

Bernier, P., et al. Chemical Physics of Intercalation 2. LC 93-17706. (NATO ASI Ser.: Vol. 305). (Illus.). 414p. (C). 1993. text 129.50 (*0-306-44482-8*, Kluwer Plenum) Kluwer Academic.

Bernier, Patrick, et al, eds. Science & Technology of Fullerene Materials. (MRS Symposium Proceedings Ser.: Vol. 359). 583p. 1995. 70.00 (*1-55899-260-X*) Materials Res.

Bernier, Patrick & Lefrant, Serge. Le Carbone Dans Tous Ses Etats. (Illus.). 584p. 1997. text 148.00 (*90-5699-056-X*, Harwood Acad Pubs) Gordon & Breach.

Bernier, Patrick & Lefrant, Serge. Le Carbone Dans Tous Ses Etats. (Illus.). 584p. 1997. pap. text 45.00 (*90-5699-057-8*) Gordon & Breach.

Bernier, Paul. Eucharist: Celebrating Its Rhythms in Our Lives. LC 92-75342. 160p. 1993. pap. 7.95 (*0-87793-505-X*) Ave Maria.

— Ministry in the Church: A Historical & Pastoral Approach. LC 92-64051. 336p. (Orig.). 1992. pap. 16.95 (*0-89622-536-4*) Twenty-Third.

Bernier, Rene, jt. auth. see Dorosh, Paul.

Bernier, Rene, jt. auth. see Sahn, David E.

Bernier, Richard G. The Deer Trackers: The Allure & Adventures Surrounding Big Whitetails We Have Trailed - And the Lessons They Have Taught Us. Greeley, Martin, ed. LC 99-95208. (Illus.). xx, 275p. 1999. 49.95 (*0-9673085-0-X*); pap. 19.95 (*0-9673085-1-8*) Big Whitetail.

Bernier, Robert. The Pro Golf Teaching Manual. pap. 2.95 (*0-89741-008-4*) Gila River.

Bernier, Ronald M. Himalayan Architecture. LC 95-35280. (Illus.). 208p. 1997. 55.00 (*0-8386-3602-0*) Fairleigh Dickinson.

— Temple Arts of Kerala: A South Indian Tradition. (Illus.). 258p. 1982. 99.00 (*0-940500-79-5*) Asia Bk Corp.

— The Temples of Nepal. 204p. 1985. 45.00 (*0-317-52159-4*, Pub. by S Chand & Co) St Mut.

— The Temples of Nepal: An Introductory Survey. (Illus.). 247p. 1970. text 27.50 (*0-685-43589-X*) Coronet Bks.

Bernier, Rosamond. Sculpture in Ceramic by Miro & Artigas: With 2 Original Lithographs by Joan Miro. 28p. 1956. pap. 250.00 (*0-8150-0027-8*) Wittenborn Art.

Bernier, Serge. French Canadians & Bilingualism in the Canadian Armed Forces: 1969-1987 Official Languages: National Defense's Response to the Federal Policy, Vol. II. (Illus.). 843p. (Orig.). 1994. pap. 71.50 (*0-660-13616-3*, Pub. by Canadian Govt Pub) Accents Pubns.

Bernieri, Frank J., jt. auth. see Hall, Judith A.

Bernig, Jorg. Eingekesselt: Die Schlacht um Stalingrad im Deutschsprachigen Roman Nach 1945. LC 96-42506. (German Life & Civilization Ser.: Vol. 23). (GER.). XIV, 376p. (C). 1997. text 58.95 (*0-8204-3667-4*) P Lang Pubng.

***Bernik, V. I. & Dodson, M. M.** Metric Diophantine Approximation on Manifolds. (Cambridge Tracts in Mathematics Ser.: No. 137). 192p. (C). 2000. 44.95 (*0-521-43275-8*) Cambridge U Pr.

***Bernikow, Louise.** Bark If You Love Me: A Woman-Meets-Dog Story. 208p. 2000. 18.95 (*1-56512-258-5*) Algonquin Bks.

Bernikow, Louise & National Women's History Project Staff. The American Women's Almanac: A Celebration of Women from Colonial Times to the Present. LC 96-50917. 400p. 1997. pap. 29.95 (*0-425-15686-9*) Berkley Pub.

— The American Women's Almanac: An Inspiring & Irreverent Women's History. LC 96-50917. 400p. (Orig.). 1997. pap. 16.95 (*0-425-15616-8*) Berkley Pub.

Bernincasa, Janis, ed. I Walked the Road Again: Great Stories from the Catskill Mountains. LC 94-18146. (Illus.). 192p. 1994. pap. 14.50 (*0-935796-53-3*) Purple Mnt Pr.

Berning, Bill & Berning, Jan. Scales: A Collector's Guide. LC 98-89617. (Illus.). 160p. 1999. pap. 29.95 (*0-7643-0778-9*) Schiffer.

Berning, Jacqueline & Steen, Suzanne N. Sports Nutrition for the '90s: The Health Professional's Handbook. rev. ed. 300p. 1991. 64.00 (*0-8342-0216-6*) Aspen Pub.

Berning, Jacqueline R. & Steen, Suzanne N. Nutrition for Sport & Exercise. 2nd ed. LC 98-11758. 300p. 1998. 52.00 (*0-8342-0882-2*) Aspen Pub.

Berning, Jan, jt. auth. see Berning, Bill.

Berninger, Virginia W., ed. The Varieties of Orthographic Knowledge. LC 94-30307. 1994. lib. bdg. write for info. (*0-7923-3081-1*) Kluwer Academic.

— The Varieties of Orthographic Knowledge, Vol. 1. LC 94-30307. 1994. lib. bdg. 148.00 (*0-7923-3080-3*) Kluwer Academic.

— The Varieties of Orthographic Knowledge Vol. II: Relationships to Phonology, Reading, & Writing. (Neuropsychology & Cognition Ser.). 428p. (C). 1995. lib. bdg. 136.00 (*0-7923-3641-0*) Kluwer Academic.

Berninghaus, S. & Seifert-Vogt, H. G. International Migration under Incomplete Information: A Microeconomic Approach. (Studies in International Economics & Institutions). (Illus.). viii, 115p. 1991. 62.95 (*0-387-54091-1*) Spr-Verlag.

Berninghausen, John & Huters, Ted. Revolutionary Literature in China: An Anthology. LC 76-51581. 109p. reprint ed. pap. 33.80 (*0-608-14592-0*, 202481400038) Bks Demand.

Berninghausen, Jutta & Kerstan, Birget. Forging New Paths: Feminist Social Methodology & Rural Women in Java. LC 92-28910. 256p. (C). 1992. text 25.00 (*1-85649-072-6*, Pub. by Zed Books) St Martin.

Bernini, Gian Lorenzo. The Impresario. 2nd ed. Beecher, Donald & Ciavolella, Massimo, eds. & trs. by. 68p. 1985. pap. 6.95 (*0-919473-49-0*, PDH44, Pub. by Dovehouse) Sterling.

Bernini, Giuliano & Ramat, Paolo. Negative Sentences in the Languages of Europe: A Typological Approach. LC 96-15690. (Empirical Approaches to Language Typology Ser.: Vol. 16). xii, 274p. (C). 1996. lib. bdg. 94.80 (*3-11-014064-0*) Mouton.

Bernini, P. M., jt. auth. see Saunders, R. L.

Bernink, Mieke, jt. ed. see Cook, Pam.

Bernitsas, Michael M. & Guha-Thakurta, S. Program HYDCYL: A Database for Calculation of Hydrodynamic Loading of Circular Cylinders. LC VM0605.. (University of Michigan, Dept. of Naval Architecture & Marine Engineering, Report Ser.: No. 267). 41p. reprint ed. pap. 30.00 (*0-608-12942-9*, 202468200038) Bks Demand.

Bernitsas, Michael M. & Kekridis, Nikos S. Nonlinear Simulation of Time Dependent Towing of Ocean Vehicles. LC VM0521.. (University of Michigan, Dept. of Naval Architecture & Marine Engineering, Report Ser.: No. 283). 59p. reprint ed. pap. 30.00 (*0-608-14585-8*, 202482400038) Bks Demand.

Bernitsas, Michael M., et al. Parametric Analysis of Static 2-Dimensional Riser Behavior. LC VM0605.. (University of Michigan, Dept. of Naval Architecture & Marine Engineering, Report Ser.: No. 287). 154p. reprint ed. pap. 47.80 (*0-608-12937-2*, 202468600038) Bks Demand.

Bernitsas, Michael M., jt. auth. see Imron, A.

Bernitsas, Michael M., jt. auth. see Kokarakis, J. E.

Bernitsas, Michael M., jt. auth. see Kokkinis, Theodore.

Bernknopf, Jeff. A Practical Guide to Fourth Generation Programming Languages. (Illus.). 320p. 1989. text 39.95 (*0-07-004960-2*) McGraw.

Bernknopf, Richard L., ed. Domestic Coal Distribution: An Interregional Programming Model for the U. S. Coal Industry. LC 85-5792. (Contemporary Studies in Energy Analysis & Policy: Vol. 5). 230p. 1986. 73.25 (*0-89232-431-7*) Jai Pr.

Bernknopf, Richard L., et al. Societal Value of Geologic Maps. (Illus.). 53p. (Orig.). (C). 1994. pap. text 35.00 (*0-7881-0728-3*) DIANE Pub.

Bernkopf, Michael. Science of Galileo, Level 3. McConochie, Jean A., ed. (Regents Readers Ser.). (Illus.). 80p. 1983. pap. text 2.50 (*0-88345-457-2*, 21092) Prentice ESL.

Bernlef, J. Driftwood House: Poems. Rollins, Scott, tr. from DUT. 44p. 1992. 28.00 (*0-930126-40-8*) Typographeum.

Bernlohr, David A. & Banaszak, Leonard. Lipid Binding Proteins Within Molecular & Cellular Biochemistry. LC 98-28801. (Developments in Molecular & Cellular Biochemistry Ser.). 1998. write for info. (*0-7923-8223-4*) Kluwer Academic.

Bernofsky, Susan, tr. see Von Rezzori, Gregor.

Bernofsky, Susan, tr. see Walser, Robert.

Bernor, Raymond I., ed. see Dixon, Dougal.

B

Bernor, Raymond L., et al, eds. The Evolution of Western Eurasion Neogene Mammal Faunas. LC 96-11747. 528p. 1996. 150.00 (*0-231-08246-0*) Col U Pr.

Bernor, Raymond L., ed. see Parker, Steve.

Bernos de Gasztold, Carmen. Prayers from the Ark. (FRE.). (J). (gr. 3-8). 29.95 (*0-685-11511-9*) Fr & Eur.

— Prayers from the Ark. 1976. pap. 11.95 (*0-14-058677-6*) NAL.

— Prayers from the Ark: Selected Poems. (J). 1995. 11.19 (*0-606-08589-0*, Pub. by Turtleback) Demco.

Bernoskie, Robert D. Food for Thought: Tasteful Trivia for Beginning & Seasoned Food Lovers. LC 90-92166. (Illus.). 192p. (Orig.). 1991. pap. 8.45 (*0-9628283-0-0*) Orig Traveling Chef.

Bernoskie, Robert D., ed. Butter in the Bard: Reading Between the Viands of Wm. Shakespeare. LC 91-90346. (Illus.). 184p. (Orig.). 1992. pap. 15.95 (*0-9628283-1-9*) Orig Traveling Chef.

— Cooking with Shakespeare: Chefspearean & Pan-Cultural Cuisine. LC 91-66176. (Illus.). 1991. pap. 18.95 (*0-9628283-2-7*) Orig Traveling Chef.

Bernot, Denise. Dictionnaire Birman-Francais. (FRE.). 324p. 1993. pap. 65.00 (*0-7859-5665-4*, 2877230465) Fr & Eur.

Bernot, Denise & Blancart. Nouville: Un Village Francais. (Ordres Sociaux Ser). 464p. 1996. pap. text 71.00 (*2-88449-058-2*) Gordon & Breach.

B

Bernotas, Adolphe, et al. 30 Bicycle Tours in New Hampshire: A Guide to Selected Backcountry Roads through the Granite State. 3rd rev. ed. LC 91-7546. (Bicycle Tours Ser.). 240p. 1991. pap. 13.00 (*0-88150-192-1*, Pub. by Countryman) Norton.

Bernotas, Bob. Amiri Baraka: Poet & Playwright. Huggins, Nathan I., ed. (Black Americans of Achievement Ser.). (Illus.). 124p. (YA). (gr. 5 up). 1991. lib. bdg. 19.95 (*0-7910-1117-8*) Chelsea Hse.

— Jim Thorpe: Sac & Fox Athlete. (Illus.). 116p. (YA). (gr. 5 up). 1993. lib. bdg. 19.95 (*0-7910-1722-2*) Chelsea Hse.

— Jim Thorpe: Sac & Fox Athlete. (North American Indians of Achievement Ser.). 1992. 14.15 (*0-606-07742-1*, Pub. by Turtleback) Demco.

— Nothing to Prove: The Jim Abbott Story. Urda, John, ed. (Illus.). 192p. (YA). 1995. 18.00 (*1-56836-064-9*) Kodansha.

— Sitting Bull, Chief of the Sioux. (North American Indians of Achievement Ser.). (J). 1992. 13.15 (*0-606-08168-2*) Turtleback.

Bernoth, E., et al. Gynaekologie. (Illus.). 656p. 1984. 180.00 (*3-8055-3861-8*) S Karger.

Bernoth, Eva Maria, ed. Furunculosis. 576p. 1997. text 135.00 (*0-12-093040-4*) Acad Pr.

Bernoulli, Carl A. Die Heiligen der Merowinger. (GER.). xvi, 336p. 1981. reprint ed. write for info. (*3-487-07065-0*) G Olms Pubs.

Bernoulli, Jakob. Die Gesammelten Werke Vol. 3: Wahrscheinlichkeitsrechnung. (GER., Illus.). 594p. 1975. 105.95 (*3-7643-0713-7*) Birkhauser.

Bernoulli, Jakob, ed. Der Briefwechsel von Johann Bernoulli, Vol. I. (GER.). 531p. 1980. 118.00 (*0-8176-0027-2*) Birkhauser.

Bernoulli, Johann J. Griechische Ikonographie Mit Ausschlub Alexanders und der Diadochen, 3 vols., Set. (GER.). xxx, 612p. 1969. reprint ed. 240.00 (*0-318-70876-0*) G Olms Pubs.

— Romische Ikonographie, 4 vols. xlviii, 1284p. 1969. reprint ed. 465.00 (*0-318-71075-7*) G Olms Pubs.

***Bernreuter, D. L.** Investigation of Techniques for the Development of Seismic Design Basis Using the Probabilistic Seismic Hazard Analysis. 167p. 1998. per. 15.00 (*0-16-062909-8*) USGPO.

Bernreuter, Robert G. The Personality Inventory. 1986. write for info. (*0-8047-1065-1*) Stanford U Pr.

Bernreuther, A., et al. Analysis of Chiral Organic Molecules: Methodology & Applications. xvii, 331p. (C). 1995. lib. bdg. 108.00 (*3-11-013659-7*) De Gruyter.

Berns. After the People Vote: A Guide to the Electoral College. enl. rev. ed. 50p. (C). 1992. pap. 7.95 (*0-8447-3802-6*) Am Enterprise.

— Child, Family, Community. 3rd ed. 1996. 63.00 (*0-15-504471-0*, Pub. by Harcourt Coll Pubs) Harcourt.

— Child, Family, School, Community. 4th ed. (C). 1996. pap. text, student ed. 25.00 (*0-15-504014-6*, Pub. by Harcourt Coll Pubs) Harcourt.

***Berns, Betsy.** The Female Fan Guide to Pro Football. 4th ed. (Illus.). 150p. 1999. pap. 12.95 (*0-9653882-3-9*) BVision Sptsmedia.

Berns, Fred. Sell Yourself: 501 Ways to Get Them to Buy from You. 226p. 1998. pap. 21.95 (*1-890777-01-3*) Select Pr.

Berns, Gabriel, ed. & tr. see Alberti, Rafael.

Berns, Gisela N. Greek Antiquity in Schiller's Wallenstein. LC 85-1112. (Germanic Languages & Literatures Ser.: No. 104). xii, 154p. 1985. 27.50 (*0-8078-8105-8*) U of NC Pr.

— Greek Antiquity in Schiller's Wallenstein. LC 85-1112. (University in North Carolina Studies in the Germanic Languages & Literatures: Vol. 104). 166p. reprint ed. pap. 51.50 (*0-608-08617-7*, 206914000003) Bks Demand.

***Berns, Henry.** 3D Scroll Saw Patterns & Techniques. (Illus.). 92p. 1998. pap. 12.95 (*1-56523-090-6*) Fox Chapel Pub.

***Berns, J. B.** Urban Rebounding: An Exercise for the New Millennium. (Illus.). 174p. 2000. pap. 16.95 (*0-9647265-2-1*) KE Pub.

Berns, J. B., jt. auth. see Van Leuvensteijn, J. A.

Berns, Jeffrey S., jt. ed. see Kimmel, Paul L.

***Berns, Jennifer & Mittermann, Lauren.** Moments of Grace: Our Time with Jason Petry Berns. 72p. 1998. pap. 7.95 (*0-9638558-1-6*) Maple Grove.

***Berns, Joan F. & Schnipper, Hester H.** Woman to Woman: The First Essential Step for Women Newly Diagnosed with Breast Cancer. LC 99-29595. 160p. 1999. pap. 12.00 (*0-380-80632-0*, Avon Bks) Morrow Avon.

Berns, Joel M. Understanding Impacted Wisdom Teeth. 2nd ed. LC 98-6116. (Illus.). 32p. 1998. pap. 26.00 (*0-86715-240-0*) Quint Pub Co.

— Understanding Periodontal Diseases. rev. ed. LC 92-37495. (Illus.). 74p. 1993. pap. 26.00 (*0-86715-239-7*) Quint Pub Co.

— Why Replace a Missing Back Tooth? 2nd ed. LC 93-21223. (Illus.). 24p. 1994. pap. 20.00 (*0-86715-231-1*) Quint Pub Co.

— Why Root Canal Therapy? 2nd ed. LC 93-36688. (Illus.). 61p. (Orig.). 1993. pap. 28.00 (*0-86715-284-2*) Quint Pub Co.

Berns, Kenneth I. The Parvoviruses. (Viruses Ser.). (Illus.). 424p. (C). 1984. text 115.00 (*0-306-41412-0*, Kluwer Plenum) Kluwer Academic.

Berns, Kenneth I., et al, eds. Current Topics in Microbiology & Immunology Vol. 218: Adeno-Associated Virus (AAV) Vectors in Gene Therapy. 258p. 1996. 138.00 (*3-540-61076-6*) Spr-Verlag.

Berns, Kenneth I. & Whitley, R. W., eds. Latency by Herpes Simplex Viruses: Journal: Intervirology, 1991, Vol. 32, No. 2. (Illus.). 52p. 1991. pap. 37.50 (*3-8055-5362-5*) S Karger.

Berns, Kenneth I., ed. see Institute of Medicine Staff.

Berns Lewis, Mary. In Delaware... Dancing with the Sun. LC 99-90381. (Illus.). 160p. 1999. write for info. (*0-9671275-0-5*) NorthStar Studio.

Berns, M. Contexts of Competence: Social & Cultural Considerations in Communicative Language Teaching. (Topics in Language & Linguistics Ser.). (Illus.). 196p. (C). 1990. 47.50 (*0-306-43469-5*, Plenum Trade) Perseus Pubng.

Berns, Margie, jt. auth. see Savignon, Sandra J.

Berns, Marla C. Ceramic Gestures: New Vessels by Magdalene Odundo. LC 95-21504. (Illus.). 1995. pap. 18.00 (*0-942006-28-3*) U of CA Art.

Berns, Marla C., ed. The Furniture of R. M. Schindler. LC 96-44736. (Illus.). 176p. (Orig.). 1997. pap. 25.00 (*0-942006-30-5*) U of CA Art.

Berns, Marla C. & Hudson, Barbara R. The Essential Gourd: Its Art & History in Northeastern Nigeria. LC 85-48263. (UCLA Museum of Cultural History Ser.). (Illus.). 192p. (Orig.). 1986. pap. 25.00 (*0-930741-08-0*) UCLA Fowler Mus.

Berns, Marla C. & Moir, Alfred. Thomas Pierson: A Tribute to Two Colleagues. (Illus.). 12p. 1993. pap. 3.00 (*0-942006-64-X*) U of CA Art.

Berns, Roberta M. Child, Family & Community. 4th ed. (C). 1996. pap. text, teacher ed. 28.00 (*0-15-503167-8*) Harcourt.

— Child, Family, Community. 3rd ed. (C). 1993. pap. text, teacher ed. 4.75 (*0-03-072383-3*) Harcourt Coll Pubs.

— Child, Family, Community: Socialization & Support. 2nd ed. (Illus.). 592p. (C). 1989. teacher ed. write for info. (*0-03-028588-7*) Harcourt Coll Pubs.

— Child, Family, School & Community: Socialization & Support. 4th ed. LC 96-75815. 650p. (C). 1996. text 69.50 (*0-15-501981-3*, Pub. by Harcourt Coll Pubs) Harcourt.

— Topical Child Development. LC 90-20927. 608p. (C). 1994. mass mkt. 55.50 (*0-8273-5727-3*) Delmar.

***Berns, Roy S.** Billmeyer & Saltzman Principles of Color Technology. 3rd ed. LC 99-45534. 304p. 2000. text 99.95 (*0-471-19459-X*, Wiley-Interscience) Wiley.

Berns, Sandra. Company Law & Governance: An Australian Perspective. 558p. 1998. pap. text (*0-19-553795-5*) OUP.

— Concise Jurisprudence. (Concise Ser.). 180p. 1993. pap. 30.00 (*1-86287-109-4*, Pub. by Federation Pr) Gaunt.

— To Speak as a Judge: Difference, Voice & Power. LC 98-46596. (Applied Legal Philosophy Ser.). 14p. (C). 1999. text 87.95 (*1-84014-742-3*, Pub. by Ashgate Pub) Ashgate Pub Co.

Berns, Tony. The Creative Home Financing Manual. large type ed. 131p. (Orig.). (C). 1998. pap. text, spiral bd. 29.95 (*0-9662335-7-3*) Info Res Pubs.

Berns, Walter. The First Amendment & the Future of American Democracy. LC 85-5495. 266p. (C). 1985. reprint ed. pap. 8.95 (*0-89526-820-5*) Regnery Pub.

— For Capital Punishment: Crime & the Morality of the Death Penalty. 226p. (C). 1991. reprint ed. pap. text 24.00 (*0-8191-8150-1*) U Pr of Amer.

— Taking the Constitution Seriously. 288p. (C). 1992. pap. text 17.95 (*0-8191-7970-1*) U Pr of Amer.

Bernsdorf, Wilhelm & Knospe, Horst, eds. International Lexicon of Sociology, 2 vols., Set. 1986. 175.00 (*3-432-82652-4*) Transaction Pubs.

— International Lexicon of Sociology, 2 vols., Vol. 2: 1969-1984. 963p. 1986. write for info. (*3-432-90702-8*) Transaction Pubs.

Bernsdorff, Hans, jt. auth. see Classen, Carl J.

Bernsen, Jens. Why Design? (C). 1989. pap. text 35.00 (*0-85072-227-6*) St Mut.

Bernsen, Jens & Lerstrom, Kirsten. The Design-Based Enterprise. 136p. (C). 1988. text 100.00 (*0-85072-231-4*) St Mut.

Bernsen, Niels Ole. Heidegger's Theory of Intentionality. (Odense University Studies in Philosophy: No. 6). 276p. (Orig.). 1986. pap. 42.00 (*87-7492-587-3*, Pub. by Odense Universitets Forlag) Coronet Bks.

— Knowledge: A Treatise on Our Cognitive Situation. (Odense Studies in Philosophy: No. 3). 686p. (Orig.). 1978. pap. 53.50 (*87-7492-260-2*, Pub. by Odense Universitets Forlag) Coronet Bks.

Bernsen, Nielsole O., et al. Designing Interactive Speech Systems: From First Ideas to User Testing. LC 97-46543. x, 270p. 1998. pap. 99.00 (*3-540-76048-2*) Spr-Verlag.

Bernsheim, Hermit, et al, eds. The Man Behind the Camera. LC 76-24683. (Sources of Modern Photography Ser.). (Illus.). 1979. reprint ed. lib. bdg. 15.95 (*0-405-09655-0*) Ayer.

Bernson, Carol, jt. auth. see Karnbach, James.

Bernspang, Birgitta, tr. see Fisher, Anne G.

Bernst, jt. auth. see Bernstein.

***Bernstam, Michael S. & Rabushka, Alvin.** Fixing Russia's Banks: A Proposal for Growth. LC 98-22972. (Publication Ser.: No. 449). 114p. 1998. pap. 16.95 (*0-8179-9572-2*) Hoover Inst Pr.

Bernstam, Victor A. Handbook of Gene Level Diagnostics in Clinical Practice. 672p. 1992. lib. bdg. 125.00 (*0-8493-6824-3*, RB155) CRC Pr.

— Pocket Guide to Gene Level Diagnostics in Clinical Practice. 560p. 1992. lib. bdg. 69.95 (*0-8493-4485-9*, RB155) CRC Pr.

Bernstein. Beat the Millennium Crash. LC 99-22517. 256p. 1999. pap. text 25.00 (*0-7352-0119-6*) PH Pr.

— Early European History. 2nd ed. 1998. 36.74 (*0-07-154053-9*) McGraw.

***Bernstein.** Emotional Vampires. 256p. 2000. 19.95 (*0-07-135259-7*) McGraw.

Bernstein. Financial Statement Analysis. 6th ed. 1998. 60.00 (*0-07-134528-0*) McGraw.

— Finanical Statement Analysis. 7th ed. 2000. 70.25 (*0-07-232113-X*) McGraw.

***Bernstein.** How the Features Markets Work. 2nd ed. 2000. pap. 20.00 (*0-13-030961-3*) P-H.

Bernstein. Law Office Computer Literacy. (Paralegal Ser.). (C). 2001. pap. 24.75 (*0-8273-8146-8*) Delmar.

— Learning Disorders in Children. 1998. 28.00 (*1-56593-178-5*) Thomson Learn.

***Bernstein.** Neuro-Oncology: The Essentials. (Illus.). 736p. 1999. 149.00 (*0-86577-880-9*) Thieme Med Pubs.

— Polymorphism in Molecular Crystal. text. write for info. (*0-471-48972-7*) Wiley.

— Ready-to-use Phonics Activities for Irregular Vowel Combinations, Diphthongs Andr-Controlled Vowels. 1999. pap. 5.95 (*0-87628-504-3*) Ctr Appl Res.

Bernstein. Trading International Futures Markets. 1999. pap. text. write for info. (*0-7352-0087-4*) P-H.

— Understanding Risk. 1995. 24.95 (*0-02-903032-3*) S&S Trade.

Bernstein & Bernst. Biology. 1995. teacher ed. 19.68 (*0-697-10151-7*) McGraw.

Bernstein & Picker. Introduction to Music. LC 98-219313. 700p. (C). 1998. pap. text 38.00 (*0-536-01274-1*) Pearson Custom.

Bernstein, jt. auth. see Zyskind.

***Bernstein, Marc D.** Hurricane at Biak: MacArthur Against the Japanese, May-August 1944. LC 00-190572. 2000. 25.00 (*0-7388-1840-2*); pap. 18.00 (*0-7388-1841-0*) Xlibris Corp.

Bernstein, A., et al, eds. Chiral Dynamics: Theory & Experiment: Proceedings of the Workshop Held in Mainz, Germany, September 1-5, 1997. LC 98-29747. (Lecture Notes in Physics Ser.: Vol. 513). xi, 394p. 1998. 86.00 (*3-540-64716-3*) Spr-Verlag.

Bernstein, Al D. Victims of Mental, Political & Spiritual Adultery: A Psychology of Religion & a Philosophy of Politics in a Dramatic Novel Based on Fact. 434p. 1991. pap. 20.00 (*0-9611682-1-8*) Rel Psych.

Bernstein, Alan & Freiermuth, Donna. The Practice Builder: Complete Marketing Library of $1,000,000 Strategies. 400p. 1992. text 69.95 (*0-13-678798-3*) P-H.

Bernstein, Alan, tr. see Myrdal, Jan.

Bernstein, Alan B. The Emergency Public Relations Manual. 3rd ed. (Illus.). 234p. 1987. reprint ed. ring bd. 149.00 (*0-9611824-2-3*) PASE.

— The Emergency Public Relations Manual. 3rd ed. (Illus.). 234p. 1988. reprint ed. per. 99.95 (*0-9611824-3-1*) PASE.

Bernstein, Alan E. The Formation of Hell: Death & Retribution in the Ancient & Early Christian Worlds. 416p. 1993. text 45.00 (*0-8014-2893-9*) Cornell U Pr.

— The Formation of Hell: Death & Retribution in the Ancient & Early Christian Worlds. 416p. 1996. pap. text 17.95 (*0-8014-8131-7*) Cornell U Pr.

Bernstein, Albert J. Dinosaur Brains. 1996. pap. 11.00 (*0-345-41021-1*) Ballantine Pub Grp.

Bernstein, Albert J. & Rozen, Sydney C. Dinosaur Brains: Dealing with All Those Impossible People at Work. LC 88-22336. 272p. 1989. 29.95 (*0-471-61808-X*) Wiley.

Bernstein, Alison R. American Indians & World War II: Toward a New Era in Indian Affairs. LC 90-50682. 288p. 1991. 23.95 (*0-8061-2330-3*) U of Okla Pr.

***Bernstein, Alison R.** American Indians & World War II Toward a New Era in Indian Affairs. 264p. 1999. pap. text 12.95 (*0-8061-3184-5*) U of Okla Pr.

Bernstein, Alison R., jt. auth. see Smith, Virginia B.

Bernstein, Allen. Tax Guide for College Teachers, 1985. 400p. 1984. pap. 18.95 (*0-916018-27-X*) Acad Info Serv.

— Tax Guide for College Teachers, 1986. 416p. 1985. pap. 19.95 (*0-916018-30-X*) Acad Info Serv.

— Tax Guide for College Teachers, 1988. 21.95 (*0-916018-36-9*) Acad Info Serv.

Bernstein, Alvin H., ed. see Polybius.

Bernstein, Alvin H., jt. ed. see Tanham, George K.

Bernstein, Amy L. Baltimore, 1797-1997: Bringing Our Heritage into the 21st Century. LC 97-66361. (Illus.). 224p. 1997. 34.95 (*1-882933-17-6*) Cherbo Pub Grp.

Bernstein, Andrew D., photos by. NBA Hoop Shots: Classic Moments from a Super Era. (Illus.). 144p. (Orig.). 1996. 34.95 (*0-942627-24-5*); pap. 21.95 (*0-942627-23-7*) Woodford Pubng.

Bernstein, Andy. The Pharmer's Almanac: The Unofficial Guide to Phish. LC 98-220842. 272p. 1998. pap. text 15.95 (*0-425-16356-3*) Berkley Pub.

Bernstein, Andy, et al, eds. The Pharmeis Almanac Vol. 4: The Unofficial Guide to Phish. (Pharmer's Almanac Ser.). (Illus.). 276p. 1997. pap. 15.95 (*1-890200-03-4*) Melting Media.

Bernstein, Anita, ed. Products Liability Anthology. LC 94-45933. 257p. 1995. pap. 29.95 (*0-87084-704-X*) Anderson Pub Co.

***Bernstein, Ann & Berger, Peter L., eds.** Business & Democracy: Cohabitation Or Contradiction. 224p. 2000. reprint ed. pap. 28.95 (*0-8264-4765-1*) Continuum.

Bernstein, Ann & Weiner, Myron. Migration & Refugee Policies: An Overview. LC 98-36010. 1999. write for info. (*1-85567-505-6*, Pub. by P P Pubs) CRC Pr.

Bernstein, Anne. Daria's Diary. 1998. per. 12.00 (*0-671-01709-8*) PB.

Bernstein, Anne C. Flight of the Stork: What Children Think (And When) about Sex & Family Building. rev. ed. LC 94-21672. 288p. 1994. reprint ed. pap. 14.00 (*0-944934-09-9*) Perspect Indiana.

— Yours, Mine, & Ours: How Families Change When Remarried Parents Have a Child Together. 1990. pap. 10.95 (*0-393-30668-2*) Norton.

Bernstein, Anne E. & Warner, Gloria M. Women Treating Women: Case Material from Women Treated by Female Psychoanalysts. LC 84-8996. xv, 310p. (C). 1985. 45.00 (*0-8236-6863-0*, 06863) Intl Univs Pr.

Bernstein, Arlene. Growing Season: A Healing Journey into the Heart of Nature. LC 95-12583. 192p. (Orig.). 1995. pap. 11.95 (*1-885171-10-2*) Wldcat Canyon.

Bernstein, Arnie. Hollywood on Lake Michigan: 100 Years of Chicago & the Movies. LC 98-85568. (Illus.). 364p. 1998. pap. 15.00 (*0-9642426-2-1*) Lake Claremont.

Bernstein, Aron M. & Holstein, Barry R., eds. Chiral Dynamics: Theory & Experiment: Proceedings of the Workshop Held at MIT, Cambridge, MA, U. S. A., 25-29 July 1994. (Lecture Notes in Physics Ser.: Vol. 452). 351p. 1995. 92.95 (*3-540-59279-2*) Spr-Verlag.

Bernstein, Art. Best Hikes of the Marble Mountains & Russian Wilderness Areas, California: A Hiking Guide to the Northernmost California. (Illus.). 260p. 1996. pap. 16.00 (*1-879415-18-6*) Mtn n Air Bks.

— Best Hikes of the Trinity Alps: A Guide to Hiking Trails & Lakes. LC 93-22446. (Illus.). 254p. (Orig.). 1993. pap. 17.00 (*1-879415-05-4*) Mtn n Air Bks.

— Ninety Best Day-Hikes: Southwest Oregon & Far Northern California. 192p. (Orig.). 1994. pap. text 12.95 (*0-9617525-7-2*) Cloudcap Bks.

Bernstein, Art & Jackman, Andrew. Portland Hikes: The Best Day-Hikes in Oregon & Washington Within 100 Miles. 2nd ed. LC 97-38136. (Illus.). 320p. 1998. pap. 18.00 (*1-879415-22-4*) Mtn n Air Bks.

Bernstein, Barbara. Lost & Found: A Closer Look at Dying. 128p. (Orig.). 1994. pap. 9.95 (*0-87516-663-6*) DeVorss.

Bernstein, Barbara, jt. auth. see Tibbetts, John.

***Bernstein, Barton E. & Hartsell, Thomas L.** The Portable Ethicist: An A-Z Guide to Responsible Practice. 288p. 2000. pap. 39.95 (*0-471-38265-5*) Wiley.

Bernstein, Barton E. & Hartsell, Thomas L. The Portable Lawyer for Mental Health Professionals: An A-Z Guide to Protecting Your Clients, Your Practice & Yourself. LC 98-10048. 288p. 1998. pap. 39.95 (*0-471-24869-X*) Wiley.

***Bernstein, Basil.** Pedagogy, Symbolic Control & Identity. LC 99-87951. 256p. 2000. pap. 23.95 (*0-8476-9576-X*); text 65.00 (*0-8476-9575-1*) Rowman.

Bernstein, Basil & Brannen, Julia, eds. Children, Research & Policy. 192p. 1996. 79.95 (*0-7484-0405-8*); pap. 27.95 (*0-7484-0406-6*) Taylor & Francis.

Bernstein, Bernard. Sanctification & the Art of Silversmithing: Processes & Techniques; a Handbook for Museums. 40p. 1994. write for info. (*0-9640234-8-2*) Judaica Museum.

Bernstein, Blanche. The Pattern of Consumer Debt, 1935-36: A Statistical Analysis. (Financial Research Program II: Studies in Consumer Installment Financing: No. 6). 256p. 1940. reprint ed. 66.60 (*0-87014-465-0*) Natl Bur Econ Res.

— Saving a Generation: A Twentieth Century Fund Paper. 63p. (Orig.). (C). 1986. pap. text 7.50 (*0-87078-206-1*) Century Foundation.

Bernstein, Bob. Cooperative Learning in Math. 112p. teacher ed. 12.99 (*0-86653-716-3*, GA1433) Good Apple.

— Friday Afternoon Fun. (Illus.). 64p. (J). (gr. 2-6). 1984. student ed. 8.99 (*0-86653-206-4*, GA 558) Good Apple.

— Math Drillsters. (Illus.). 224p. 1992. 16.99 (*0-86653-660-4*, GA1392) Good Apple.

— Math Thinking Motivators. 96p. (J). (gr. 2-7). 1988. student ed. 11.99 (*0-86653-431-8*, GA1049) Good Apple.

— Mathemactivities. 112p. (J). (gr. 2-7). 1991. 12.99 (*0-86653-617-5*, GA1336) Good Apple.

— The Mathmaker. 112p. teacher ed. 12.99 (*0-86653-741-4*, GA1456) Good Apple.

— Monday Morning Magic. 64p. (J). (gr. k-6). 1982. 7.99 (*0-86653-080-0*, GA 425) Good Apple.

— Numbers Count. 96p. (J). (gr. 2-7). 1990. 11.99 (*0-86653-542-X*, GA1151) Good Apple.

— Thinking Numbers. 96p. (J). (gr. 2-7). 1989. 9.99 (*0-86653-506-3*, GA1094) Good Apple.

Bernstein, Bonnie. Day By Day. 2nd ed. (J). (gr. k-6). 1989. pap. 17.99 (*0-8224-4253-1*) Fearon Teacher Aids.

Bernstein, Bonnie & Blair, Leigh. Native American Crafts Workshop. LC 81-82041. (Crafts Workshop Ser.). (J). (gr. 3-8). 1982. pap. 11.99 (*0-8224-9784-0*) Fearon Teacher Aids.

***Bernstein, Bruce & Rushing, W. Jackson.** Modern by Tradition: American Indian Painting in the Studio Style. (Illus.). 176p. 1999. pap. 29.95 (*0-89013-291-7*) Museum NM Pr.

An Asterisk (*) at the beginning of an entry indicates that the title is appearing for the first time.

Bernstein, Bruce & Rushing, W. Jackson. Modern by Tradition: American Indian Painting in the Studio Style. (Illus.). 120p. 1999. pap. 29.95 (*0-89013-286-0*, Pub. by Museum NM Pr) U of NM Pr.

Bernstein, Bruce, ed. see Tryk, Sheila.

Bernstein, Burton J. Plane Crazy: A Celebration of Flying. (Illus.). 192p. 1985. 16.95 (*0-685-11128-8*) HM.

Bernstein, Carl & Politi, Marco. His Holiness: John Paul II & the Hidden History of Our Time. (Illus.). 608p. 1997. pap. 14.95 (*0-14-026691-7*) Viking Penguin.

Bernstein, Carl & Woodward, Bob. All the President's Men. 1994. reprint ed. lib. bdg. 29.95 (*1-56849-568-4*) Buccaneer Bks.

Bernstein, Carl, jt. auth. see Woodward, Bob.

Bernstein, Carol, et al. On Call Psychiatry. Schmitt, William, ed. LC 96-42344. (Illus.). 272p. 1997. pap. text 21.95 (*0-7216-6526-8*, W B Saunders Co) Harcrt Hlth Sci Grp.

Bernstein, Carol, jt. auth. see Bertherat, Therese.

Bernstein, Carol L. The Celebration of Scandal: Toward the Sublime in Victorian Urban Fiction. 256p. 1991. 35.00 (*0-271-00718-4*) Pa St U Pr.

Bernstein, Carole. Familiar. LC 97-9733. 1997. 20.00 (*1-882413-37-7*); pap. 12.00 (*1-882413-36-9*) Hanging Loose.

Bernstein, Charles. Controlling Interests. 2nd ed. (Roof Bks.). 88p. 1985. pap. text 60.00 (*0-937804-03-7*) Segue NYC.

— Great Restaurant Innovators. 1981. pap. 25.95 (*0-86730-239-9*) Lebhar Friedman.

— Islets - Irritations. (Roof Bks.). 101p. 1992. reprint ed. pap. 9.95 (*0-937804-47-9*) Segue NYC.

— Little Orphan Anagram. (Illus.). 40p. 1997. 1500.00 (*1-887123-14-8*) Granary Bks.

— Log Rhythms. (Illus.). 24p. 1998. pap. 35.00 (*1-887123-25-3*) Granary Bks.

— My Way: Speeches & Poems. LC 98-30345. 321p. 1999. pap. 18.00 (*0-226-04410-6*); lib. bdg. 46.00 (*0-226-04409-2*) U Ch Pr.

— Nude Formalism: With Susan Bee. 20p. 1989. pap. 5.00 (*1-55713-092-2*) Sun & Moon CA.

— The Occurrence of Tune. (Segue Bks.). (Illus.). 24p. (Orig.). 1983. pap. text 60.00 (*0-937804-08-8*) Segue NYC.

— A Poetics. 240p. (C). 1992. 44.50 (*0-674-67854-0*); pap. 17.95 (*0-674-67857-5*) HUP.

— Rough Trades. (Sun & Moon Classics Ser.: No. 14). 106p. 1989. pap. 10.95 (*1-55713-080-9*) Sun & Moon CA.

— Senses of Responsibility. 28p. 1990. pap. 4.00 (*0-945926-16-2*) Paradigm RI.

— The Sophist. 179p. 1987. 16.95 (*0-940650-78-9*); pap. 11.95 (*0-940650-79-7*) Sun & Moon CA.

— The Sophist. deluxe ed. 180p. 1987. 30.00 (*0-940650-80-0*) Sun & Moon CA.

— Stigma. 1981. pap. 3.00 (*0-930794-49-4*) Station Hill Pr.

Bernstein, Charles, ed. Close Listening: Poetry & th Performed Word. LC 97-32636. (Illus.). 400p. 1998. pap. 19.95 (*0-19-510992-9*) OUP.

— Close Listening: Poetry & the Performed Word. LC 97-32636. (Illus.). 400p. 1998. text 60.00 (*0-19-510991-0*) OUP.

Bernstein, Charles, ed. Live at the Ear. Date not set. write for info. (*0-614-30092-4*) DILLON ELEMENOPE.

Bernstein, Charles, ed. Live at the Ear. 32p. (C). 1994. 15.95 incl. audio compact disk (*1-885905-36-X*, 5-7777-2) DILLON ELEMENOPE.

— 99 Poets/1999: An International Poetics Symposium: An International Poetics Symposium. Vol. 26, No. 1. 260p. 1999. pap. text 12.00 (*0-8223-6467-0*) Duke.

Bernstein, Charles & Cadiot, Olivier. Red, Green & Black. 48p. (Orig.). 1990. pap. 8.00 (*0-937013-34-X*) Potes Poets.

Bernstein, Charles & Paul, Ronald N. Winning the Chain Restaurant Game: Eight Key Strategies. 285p. 1994. 59.95 (*0-471-30545-6*) Wiley.

Bernstein, Charles, et al. Perception. Wellman, Don, ed. Guss, David M., tr. (Toward a New Poetics Ser.: Vol. 2). (Illus.). 224p. 1982. pap. 6.95 (*0-942030-02-8*) O ARS.

Bernstein, Charles B. The Rothschilds of Nordstetten: Their History & Genealogy. (Illus.). 280p. 1989. pap. 30.00 (*0-9622737-0-8*) C B Bernstein.

Bernstein, Charles B., jt. auth. see Rosenstein, Neil.

Bernstein, Cynthia G., ed. The Text & Beyond: Essays in Literary Linguistics. LC 93-29447. 552p. (C). 1997. pap. text 29.95 (*0-8173-0699-4*) U of Ala Pr.

Bernstein, Cynthia G., et al. Language Variety in the South Revisited. LC 96-29636. 328p. 1994. text 49.95 (*0-8173-0882-2*) U of Ala Pr.

Bernstein, D. L. Existence Theorems in Partial Differential Equations. (Annals of Mathematics Studies: No. 23). 1950. 25.00 (*0-527-02739-1*) Periodicals Srv.

Bernstein, Dan, ed. Nebraska Symposium on Motivation, 1997 Vol. 45: Gender & Motivation. 256p. 1999. text 45.00 (*0-8032-1300-X*) U of Nebr Pr.

Bernstein, Daniel & Shelov, Steven P. Pediatrics. (Illus.). 456p. 1996. pap. 37.95 (*0-683-00640-1*) Lppncott W & W.

Bernstein, Daniel, ed. see Smith, Jeannette.

Bernstein, Daniel J. Using Motif with C++ (Advances in Object Technology: No. 5). 392p. (C). 1996. per. 39.95 (*0-13-207390-0*) Cambridge U Pr.

Bernstein, Daniel J., ed. see Nebraska Symposium on Motivation Staff.

Bernstein, Daryl. Better Than a Lemonade Stand: Small Business Ideas for Kids. LC 92-15226. (Kid's Books by Kids Ser.). (Illus.). 176p. (J). (gr. 2-10). 1992. 14.95 (*1-885223-15-3*) Beyond Words Pub.

— Better Than a Lemonade Stand: Small Business Ideas for Kids. LC 92-15226. (Kids Books by Kids Ser.). (Illus.). 150p. (YA). (gr. 2-10). 1992. pap. 7.95 (*0-941831-75-2*) Beyond Words Pub.

— Kids Can Succeed! Fifty-One Tips for Real Life from One Kid to Another. (Illus.). 216p. (Orig.). (J). (gr. 3-7). 1993. pap. 5.95 (*1-55850-285-8*) Adams Media.

Bernstein, Daryl & Hammond, Joe. Venture Adventure: Strategies for Thriving in the Jungle of Entrepreneurship. LC 94-44135. (Illus.). 200p. (C). 1996. 18.95 (*1-885223-11-0*) Beyond Words Pub.

— The Venture Adventure: Strategies for Thriving in the Jungle of Entrepreneurship. LC 94-44135. (Illus.). 224p. (C). 1996. pap. 12.95 (*1-885223-09-9*) Beyond Words Pub.

Bernstein, David. Advertising Outdoors. (Illus.). 240p. 1997. 75.00 (*0-7148-3635-4*, Pub. by Phaidon Press) Phaidon Pr.

— Apples of Gold. 1997. pap. 6.95 (*0-914131-91-5*, A080) Torah Umesorah.

— Parshas Beshalach. (Chumash Study Aid Ser.). (ENG & HEB., Illus.). 192p. (J). (gr. 5-8). 1991. pap. text 8.00 (*0-914131-96-6*, A148) Torah Umesorah.

— Parshas Mishpatim. (Chumash StudyAid Ser.). (Illus.). 177p. 1997. pap., wbk. ed. 8.00 (*0-914131-89-3*, A150) Torah Umesorah.

Bernstein, David, ed. Cooperative Business Ventures Between U. S. Companies & Russian Defense Enterprises. LC 97-203068. 321p. 1997. pap. 15.00 (*0-935371-45-1*) CFISAC.

— Defense Industry Restructuring in Russia: Case Studies & Analysis. 223p. 1994. pap. 15.00 (*0-935371-34-6*) CFISAC.

Bernstein, David E. & De Medina, Maria D., eds. Hepatitis Viruses. 7th rev. ed. (Illus.). 79p. 1998. pap. text 25.00 (*1-879772-11-6*) Health Studies.

Bernstein, David H. & Practising Law Institute Staff. Protecting Your Intellectual Property Assets. LC 98-182398. (Patents, Copyrights, Trademarks, & Literary Property Course Handbook Ser.). 560 p. 1998. 129.00 (*0-87224-477-6*) PLI.

Bernstein, David J. The Mystery of the Bayeux Tapestry. LC 86-30864. (Illus.). 272p. 1987. 29.95 (*0-226-04400-9*) U Ch Pr.

Bernstein, David W., jt. ed. see Hatch, Christopher.

Bernstein, Deborah. The Struggle for Equality: Urban Women Workers in Prestate Israeli Society. LC 86-8203. 219p. 1986. 57.95 (*0-275-92139-5*, C2139, Praeger Pubs) Greenwood.

Bernstein, Deborah S. Constructing Boundaries: Jewish & Arab Workers in Mandatory Palestine. LC 99-37759. (C). 2000. text 71.50 (*0-7914-4539-9*); pap. text 23.95 (*0-7914-4540-2*) State U NY Pr.

Bernstein, Deborah S., ed. Pioneers & Homemakers: Jewish Women in Pre-State Israel. LC 91-21247. 312p. 1992. text 21.50 (*0-7914-0905-8*) State U NY Pr.

Bernstein, Deena K. & Tiegerman, Ellenmorris. Language & Communication Disorders in Children. 4th ed. LC 96-48262. 544p. 1997. 72.00 (*0-205-19894-5*) Allyn.

Bernstein, Dennis & Kean, Leslie. Henry Hyde's Moral Universe: Where More Than Space & Time Are Warped. LC 99-24681. 192p. 1999. pap. 9.00 (*1-56751-166-X*); lib. bdg. 29.95 (*1-56751-167-8*) Common Courage.

Bernstein, Doris. Female Identity Conflict in Clinical Practice. Freedman, Norbert & Distler, Betsy, eds. LC 92-48974. 216p. 1993. 40.00 (*0-87668-502-5*) Aronson.

***Bernstein, Douglas A., et al.** New Directions in Progressive Relaxation Training: A Guidebook for Helping Professionals. LC 99-43100. 176p. 2000. write for info. (*0-275-96318-7*, Praeger Pubs); pap. write for info. (*0-275-96837-5*, Praeger Pubs) Greenwood.

Bernstein, Douglas A. Psychiatry Exam, 3 vols. (C). Date not set. text 65.96 (*0-395-69045-5*) HM.

— Psychology, 4 vols. (C). Date not set. write for info. (*0-395-78965-6*) HM.

— Psychology, 3 vols. (C). 1993. pap., teacher ed., suppl. ed. 6.76 (*0-395-69047-1*) HM.

— Psychology, 3 vols. (C). 1993. pap., teacher ed. 6.76 (*0-395-69046-3*) HM.

— Psychology, 3 vols. 3rd ed. LC 93-78678. (C). 1993. text 65.96 (*0-395-64955-2*) HM.

— Psychology, 3 vols. 3rd ed. (C). 1993. pap. text, student ed. 20.36 (*0-395-67540-5*) HM.

— Psychology: Testbank, 4 vols. 4th ed. (C). 1996. pap. text, suppl. ed. 11.96 (*0-395-82882-1*) HM.

Bernstein, Douglas A., et al. Psychology. 784p. (C). 1987. write for info. (*0-318-61892-3*) HM.

— Psychology, 4 vols. 4th ed. LC 96-76573. 627p. (C). 1996. text 68.36 (*0-395-77071-8*) HM.

— Psychology, 4 vols. 4th ed. (C). 1996. text, teacher ed. 11.96 (*0-395-77985-5*) HM.

— Psychology, 4 vols. 4th annot. ed. (C). 1996. text, teacher ed. 69.56 (*0-395-77983-9*) HM.

Bernstein, E. F., ed. Amaurosis Fugax. (Illus.). 480p. 1988. 99.00 (*0-387-96601-3*) Spr-Verlag.

Bernstein, Eckhard, ed. see Steen, Charlie R.

***Bernstein, Eduard.** Cromwell & Communism: Socialism & Democracy in the Great English Revolution. 288p. 2000. reprint ed. pap. 34.00 (*0-85124-630-3*, Pub. by Spkesman) Coronet Bks.

Bernstein, Eduard. My Years of Exile: Reminiscences of a Socialist. Miall, Bernard, tr. from GER. LC 86-1865.Tr. of Vo-ker zu Hause. 287p. 1986. reprint ed. lib. bdg. 65.00 (*0-313-25114-2*, BMYY, Greenwood Pr) Greenwood.

— The Preconditions of Socialism. Tudor, Henry, ed. & tr. by. LC 92-23175. (Cambridge Texts in the History of Political Thought Ser.). 265p. (C). 1993. text 59.95 (*0-521-39121-0*); pap. text 19.95 (*0-521-39808-8*) Cambridge U Pr.

— Selected Writings of Eduard Bernstein, 1900-1921. Steger, Manfred, ed. & tr. by. LC 95-30963. 240p. (C). 1996. text 49.95 (*0-391-03919-9*) Humanities.

Bernstein, Edward. Ferdinand Lassalle As a Social Reformer. Aveling, Eleanor, tr. from GER. LC 74-131631. 1970. reprint ed. 12.00 (*0-403-00514-3*) Scholarly.

Bernstein, Edward & Bernstein, Judith. Case Studies in Emergency Medicine & the Health of the Public. LC 96-1930. (Medical Ser.). 352p. 1996. pap. 56.00 (*0-7637-0029-0*) Jones & Bartlett.

Bernstein, Eleanor. Disciples at the Crossroads: Perspectives on Worship & Church Leadership. 168p. (Orig.). 1993. pap. text 10.95 (*0-8146-2146-5*) Liturgical Pr.

Bernstein, Eleanor & Brooks-Leonard, John, eds. Children in the Assembly of the Church. LC 92-36339. 80p. 1993. pap. 8.95 (*0-929650-66-2*, ND/CA) Liturgy Tr Pubns.

Bernstein, Eleanor & Connell, Martin, eds. The Changing Face of the Church. LC 98-35452. (Notre Dame Conference Ser.: Vol. 4). 246p. 1998. pap. 16.00 (*1-56854-259-3*, FACE) Liturgy Tr Pubns.

— Traditions & Transitions. LC 98-3182. (Notre Dame Conference Ser.: Vol. 3). 304p. 1998. pap. 16.00 (*1-56854-024-8*) Liturgy Tr Pubns.

Bernstein, Elinor, jt. auth. see Womack, Morris M.

Bernstein, Ellen, ed. Ecology & the Jewish Spirit: Where Nature & the Sacred Meet. LC 97-35828. 288p. 1998. 23.95 (*1-879045-88-5*) Jewish Lights.

***Bernstein, Ellen, ed.** Ecology & the Jewish Spirit: Where Nature & the Sacred Meet. 288p. 2000. pap. 16.95 (*1-58023-082-2*) Jewish Lights.

Bernstein, Ellen & Fink, Dan. Let the Earth Teach You Torah. (Illus.). 184p. (Orig.). 1992. teacher ed. 22.50 (*0-9632848-1-9*) Shomrei Adamah.

Bernstein, Ellen, ed. see Lewis, Joe.

Bernstein, Elliot R., ed. Chemical Reactions in Clusters. (Topics in Physical Chemistry Ser.). (Illus.). 272p. (C). 1996. text 90.00 (*0-19-509004-7*) OUP.

Bernstein, Eugene F., ed. Vascular Diagnosis. 4th ed. LC 93-4086. (Illus.). 1058p. (C). (gr. 13). 1993. text 258.00 (*0-8016-6557-4*, 06557) Mosby Inc.

Bernstein, Frances. Classical Living: Ancient Rituals & Rhythms for Hearth & Home. LC 99-55433. 256p. 2000. 24.00 (*0-06-251624-8*) Harper SF.

***Bernstein, Frances.** Classical Living: Reconnecting with the Rituals for Ancient Rome. LC 99-55433. 2000. 13.00 (*0-06-251625-6*) Harper SF.

Bernstein, Fred, jt. auth. see Phillips, Debora.

Bernstein, Gail L. Haruko's World: A Japanese Farm Woman & Her Community. LC 82-61783. (Illus.). xviii, 199p. 1983. 37.50 (*0-8047-1174-7*); pap. 12.95 (*0-8047-1287-5*) Stanford U Pr.

— Japanese Marxist: A Portrait of Kawakami Hajime, 1879-1946. (East Asian Monographs: No. 152). 240p. 1990. pap. 20.00 (*0-674-47194-6*) HUP.

Bernstein, Gail L., ed. Recreating Japanese Women, 1600-1945. LC 90-11194. (Illus.). 352p. 1991. pap. 18.95 (*0-520-07017-8*, Pub. by U CA Pr) Cal Prin Full Svc.

***Bernstein, Gail S.** Human Services?...That Must Be So Rewarding: A Practical Guide for Professional Development. 2nd ed. 1999. pap. text 23.95 (*1-878812-49-1*) Hlth Prof Pr.

Bernstein, Gail S. Human Services?...That Must Be So Rewarding: A Practical Guide for Professional Development. 2nd ed. LC 98-36525. 1998. pap 23.50 (*1-55766-332-7*) P H Brookes.

Bernstein, Gary. The Glamorous World of People Photography. LC 97-28338. (Illus.). 160p. 1997. 54.95 (*0-9658571-1-5*) Marathon NE.

— Portrait Hollywood: Gary Bernstein's Classic Celebrity Photographs. Rochmis, Jon, ed. LC 94-60747. (Illus.). 144p. 1994. 34.95 (*0-942627-02-4*) Woodford Pubng.

Bernstein, George B. A Fifteen-Year Forecast of Information-Processing Technology. LC 77-128581. 187p. 1969. 19.00 (*0-403-04486-3*) Scholarly.

Bernstein, George L. Liberalism & Liberal Politics in Edwardian England. 256p. (C). 1986. pap. text 18.95 (*0-04-942199-9*) Routledge.

Bernstein, H., jt. auth. see Gavriljuk, V. G.

Bernstein, Harry. The Brazilian Diamond in Contracts, Contraband & Capital. LC 87-25336. (Illus.). 170p. (Orig.). 1988. pap. text 20.00 (*0-8191-6532-8*); lib. bdg. 41.50 (*0-8191-6531-X*) U Pr of Amer.

— The Lord Mayor of Lisbon: The Portuguese Tribune of the People & His 24 Guilds. (Atlantic Studies on Society in Change: No. 57). 208p. (C). 1989. lib. bdg. 41.50 (*0-8191-7235-9*) U Pr of Amer.

Bernstein, Harry, ed. see Dean, Douglas.

Bernstein, Harvey M. & Lemer, Andrew C. Solving the Innovation Puzzle. 136p. 1996. pap. 23.00 (*0-7844-0023-7*) Am Soc Civil Eng.

Bernstein, Haskell E. Being Human: The Art of Feeling Alive. 224p. 1990. pap. 23.95 (*0-685-47895-5*) Gardner Pr.

Bernstein, Henrietta. The Ark of the Covenant, the Holy Grail: Message for the New Millennium. LC 98-72809. (Illus.). 272p. 1999. pap. 21.95 (*0-87516-722-5*) DeVorss.

— Cabalah Primer: Introduction to English-Hebrew Cabalah. 192p. 1984. pap. 12.95 (*0-87516-526-5*) DeVorss.

Bernstein, Henrietta, jt. auth. see Ransom, Victoria.

Bernstein, Henry, ed. The Agrarian Question in South Africa. 180p. (Orig.). (C). 1996. 42.00 (*0-7146-4737-3*, Pub. by F Cass Pubs); pap. 22.00 (*0-7146-4292-4*, Pub. by F Cass Pubs) Intl Spec Bk.

Bernstein, Henry, et al, eds. The Journal of Peasant Studies: A Twenty Volume Index, 1973-1993. LC 94-11290. 133p. 1994. 55.00 (*0-7146-4591-5*, Pub. by F Cass Pubs) Intl Spec Bk.

Bernstein, Henry & Campbell, Bonnie K., eds. Contradictions of Accumulation in Africa: Studies in Economy & State. LC 84-11640. (Sage Series on African Modernization & Development: No. 10). 312p. 1985. reprint ed. pap. 96.80 (*0-608-01120-7*, 205942400001) Bks Demand.

Bernstein, Henry, ed. see Byres, T. J., et al.

Bernstein, Henry, jt. ed. see Johnson, Hazel.

Bernstein, Herbert & Lookofsky, Joseph M. Understanding the CISG in Europe. LC 96-6526. 219p. 1997. pap. 70.00 (*90-411-0951-X*) Kluwer Law Intl.

Bernstein, Herbert J., jt. auth. see Fortun, Mike.

Bernstein, Herman. Celebrities of Our Time. LC 68-8438. (Essay Index Reprint Ser.). 1977. 20.95 (*0-8369-0204-1*) Ayer.

Bernstein, Howard. On Leave with Norgood. Iddings, Kathleen, ed. LC 86-63864. 72p. (Orig.). 1989. pap. text, per. 9.95 (*0-931289-00-9*) San Diego Poet Pr.

Bernstein, Howard, jt. auth. see Cohen, Smadar.

Bernstein, I. A., ed. Biochemical Responses to Environmental Stress. LC 79-151618. (Illus.). 165p. 1971. reprint ed. pap. 51.20 (*0-608-05479-8*, 202187000026) Bks Demand.

— Processes in Cutaneous Epidermal Differentiation. LC 87-10327. 400p. 1987. 105.00 (*0-275-92406-8*, C2406, Praeger Pubs) Greenwood.

Bernstein, I. A. & Seiji, M., eds. Biochemistry of Normal & Abnormal Epidermal Differentiation. (Current Problems in Dermatology Ser.: Vol. 10). (Illus.). x, 442p. 1981. pap. 118.50 (*3-8055-1915-X*) S Karger.

Bernstein, I. A., jt. ed. see Seigi, M. S.

***Bernstein, I. Leonard.** Asthma in the Workplace. 2nd rev. expanded ed. LC 99-29230. (Illus.). 768p. 1999. text 225.00 (*0-8247-1963-8*) Dekker.

Bernstein, I. Leonard, et al. Asthma in the Workplace. (Illus.). 688p. 1993. text 230.00 (*0-8247-8799-4*) Dekker.

Bernstein, I. Leonard, jt. auth. see Weiner, Murray.

Bernstein, I. M., ed. see American Society for Metals Staff.

Bernstein, I. M., ed. see International Conference on Effect of Hydrogen on.

Bernstein, Ignaz. Katalog Dziext Tresci Przyslowiowej Skladajacych Biblioteke Ignacego Bernsteina, 2 vols. reprint ed. suppl. ed. write for info. (*0-318-71738-7*) G Olms Pubs.

Bernstein, Ilene N., ed. Validity Issues in Evaluative Research. LC 75-32373. (Sage Contemporary Social Science Issues Ser.: No. 23). 134p. reprint ed. pap. 41.60 (*0-608-14202-6*, 202187000026) Bks Demand.

Bernstein, Ilene N. & Freeman, Howard E. Academic & Entrepreneurial Research: The Consequences of Diversity in Federal Evaluation Studies. LC 74-83208. 108p. 1975. text 25.00 (*0-87154-109-2*) Russell Sage.

Bernstein, Ira. Appalachian Clogging & Flatfooting Steps. (Illus.). 170p. 1992. student ed., spiral bd. 19.95 (*1-880160-00-5*) I Bernstein.

Bernstein, Ira H. & Havig, Paul. Computer Literacy: Getting the Most from Your PC. LC 98-25450. 426p. 1998. 69.00 (*0-7619-1138-3*); pap. 34.95 (*0-7619-1139-1*) Sage.

Bernstein, Ira H., jt. auth. see Nunnally, Jim C.

Bernstein, Irving. Guns or Butter: The Presidency of Lyndon Johnson. (Illus.). 656p. 1996. text 45.00 (*0-19-506312-0*) OUP.

— Living UJA History. LC 97-37382. 1997. 34.95 (*0-8276-0648-6*) JPS Phila.

— The New Deal Collective Bargaining Policy. LC 75-8997. (FDR & the Era of the New Deal Ser.). xi, 178p. 1975. reprint ed. lib. bdg. 27.50 (*0-306-70703-9*) Da Capo.

Bernstein, Iver. The New York City Draft Riots: Their Significance for American Society & Politics in the Age of the Civil War. (Illus.). 384p. 1991. reprint ed. pap. text 24.95 (*0-19-507130-1*) OUP.

Bernstein, J. A Theory for Everything: Essays & Short Fiction. LC 96-1553. 320p. 1996. 25.00 (*0-387-94700-0*) Spr-Verlag.

***Bernstein, J.** The Wildest Dreams of Key: A Profile of Nepal. 1998. pap. 68.00 (*0-7855-7659-2*) St Mut.

Bernstein, J., et al, eds. Technology & Infertility: Clinical Psychosocial, Legal, & Ethical Aspects. (Illus.). 440p. 1993. 89.00 (*0-387-97793-7*) Spr-Verlag.

Bernstein, J., ed. see American Association of Anatomists, Cajal Club Mee.

Bernstein, J., jt. ed. see Rosenberg, H. S.

Bernstein, J. B., jt. ed. see Donnelly, Karen J.

Bernstein, J. H., et al. Applied Multivariate Analysis. (Illus.). 510p. 1988. 96.95 (*0-387-96542-4*) Spr-Verlag.

Bernstein, J. I. Research & Development, Tax Incentives, & the Structure of Production & Financing. LC 86-94275. (Ontario Economic Council Research Studies: No. 31). viii, 108p. 1986. pap. text 11.95 (*0-8020-6629-1*) U of Toronto Pr.

Bernstein, J. J. Neural Prostheses: Materials, Physiology & Histopathology of Electrical Stimulation of the Nervous System. (Journal: Brains, Behavior & Evolution: Vol. 14, No. 1-2). (Illus.). 1977. 64.50 (*3-8055-2640-7*) S Karger.

Bernstein, J. M. The Fate of Art: Aesthetic Alienation from Kant to Derrida & Adorno. (Literature & Philosophy Ser.). 310p. 1992. text 50.00 (*0-271-00838-5*); pap. text 17.95 (*0-271-00839-3*) Pa St U Pr.

— Recovering Ethical Life: Jurgen Habermas & the Future of Critical Theory. LC 94-12152. 304p. (C). 1995. pap. 24.99 (*0-415-11783-6*, B4759) Routledge.

Bernstein, J. M. & Van Cauwenberge, P., eds. Immunomodulation in Respiratory Infection. (Journal: Respiration: Vol. 59, Suppl. 3, 1992). (Illus.). iv, 32p. 1992. pap. 15.75 (*3-8055-5672-1*) S Karger.

Bernstein, J. M., ed. see Adorno, Theodor W.

Bernstein, J. S. Benjamin James. LC 78-110707. (Twayne's World Authors Ser.). 1985. lib. bdg. 20.95 (*0-8057-2464-8*) Irvington.

Bernstein, J. S., tr. see Cela, Camilo Jose.

B

An Asterisk (*) at the beginning of an entry indicates that the title is appearing for the first time.

Bernstein, J. S., tr. see Garcia Marquez, Gabriel.

Bernstein, J. S., tr. see Rubert de Ventos, Xavier.

Bernstein, Jack. The Guide to Selling Advertising Space. 2nd ed. 224p. 1990. pap. 37.50 (*0-9616226-1-X*) JB & Me.

— The Menu. 96p. (Orig.). 1993. pap. 22.50 (*0-9616226-8-7*) JB & Me.

— The Perfect Media Kit. 125p. (Orig.). 1991. pap. 17.50 (*0-9616226-4-4*) JB & Me.

— Resume Writing, Interviewing & Roleplaying Skills for Salespeople Looking for New Jobs. 64p. (Orig.). 1993. 12.50 (*0-9616226-5-2*) JB & Me.

— TQS: Total Quality Sales. 224p. (Orig.). 1997. pap. 29.95 (*0-9616226-7-9*) JB & Me.

Bernstein, Jack, ed. Flat Panel Display Manufacturing Related Equipment & Materials. 158p. 1999. 945.00 (*1-884730-15-9*, Interlingua) JB & Me.

— Nikkei Microdevices: 1998 Flat Panel Display Yearbook. (Illus.). 218p. 1998. 495.00 (*1-884730-13-2*, Interlingua) JB & Me.

— Nikkei Microdevices 1999 Flat Panel Display Yearbook. (Illus.). 220p. 1999. 995.00 (*1-884730-16-7*, Interlingua) JB & Me.

— The Present State & Future Prospect of the Liquid Crystal-Related Market. 1998. 945.00 (*1-884730-17-5*, Interlingua) JB & Me.

***Bernstein, Jacob.** Seasonality: Systems, Strategies & Signals. LC 97-38741. (Wiley Trader's Exchange Ser.). 240p. 1998. 55.00 (*0-471-16811-4*) Wiley.

Bernstein, Jacob I. Cycles of Profit: How to See Beyond Short Term Stock Market Volatility to Predictable Trends & Major Market Opportunities. LC 91-58512. 304p. 1991. 29.95 (*0-88730-471-0*, HarpBusn) HarpInfo.

— Cyclic Analysis in Futures Trading: Systems, Methods, & Procedures. LC 87-26350. 295p. 1988. 99.95 (*0-471-01185-1*) Wiley.

— How the Futures Markets Work. (C). 1989. pap. text 17.95 (*0-13-407222-7*) NY Inst Finance.

— How to Profit in Precious Metals. LC 84-19561. 240p. 1985. reprint ed. pap. 74.40 (*0-7837-2838-7*, 205763400006) Bks Demand.

— The Investor's Quotient: The Psychology of Successful Investing in Commodities & Stocks. 2nd ed. LC 93-18785. 304p. 1993. 49.95 (*0-471-55876-1*) Wiley.

— Jake Bernstein's New Guide to Investing in Metals. LC 90-20035. 257p. 1991. 34.95 (*0-471-51251-6*) Wiley.

— Jake Bernstein's Seasonal Futures Spreads: High-Probability Seasonal Spreads for Futures Trader. LC 89-36416. 296p. 1990. 110.00 (*0-471-50214-6*) Wiley.

— New Facts on Futures: Insights & Strategies for Winning in the Futures Markets. rev. ed. 325p. 1992. 24.95 (*1-55738-422-3*, Irwn Prfssnl) McGraw-Hill Prof.

— The New Prosperity: Investment Opportunities in Long-Wave Economic Cycles. 1988. 19.95 (*0-317-03945-8*) NY Inst Finance.

— Short-Term Futures Trading: Systems, Strategies & Techniques for the Day- Trader. 300p. 1992. pap. 32.50 (*1-55738-474-6*, 474, Irwn Prfssnl) McGraw-Hill Prof.

— Timing Signals in the Futures Market: The Trader's Definitive Guide to Buy-Sell Indicators. 1990. 45.00 (*1-55738-155-0*, Irwn Prfssnl) McGraw-Hill Prof.

— Why Traders Lose, How Traders Win: Timing Futures Trades with Daily Market Sentiment. 250p. 1992. 37.50 (*1-55738-252-2*, Irwn Prfssnl) McGraw-Hill Prof.

***Bernstein, Jake.** Beat the Millennium Crash: How to Profit the Coming Financial Crisis. 2000. pap. 14.00 (*0-7352-0155-2*) PH Pr.

Bernstein, Jake. The Compleat Day Trader: Trading Systems, Strategies, Timing Indicators, & Analytical Methods. LC 94-41343. (Illus.). 227p. 1995. 39.95 (*0-07-009251-6*) McGraw.

— The Compleat Day Trader II. LC 98-5656. (Illus.). 232p. 1998. 39.95 (*0-07-094501-2*) McGraw.

***Bernstein, Jake.** Compleat Guide to Day Trading Stocks. (Compleat Day Trader Ser.). (Illus.). 312p. 2000. 39.95 (*0-07-136125-1*) McGraw.

— How the Futures Markets Work. 2nd ed. LC 00-23837. (Illus.). 352p. 2000. pap. 20.00 (*0-7352-0129-3*) PH Pr.

— Investor's Quotient: The Psychology of Successful Investing in Commodities & Stocks. 2nd ed. 304p. 2000. pap. 18.95 (*0-471-38362-7*) Wiley.

— Strategies for the Electronic Futures Trader. LC 99-53047. 256p. 1999. pap. 39.95 (*0-07-135232-5*) McGraw.

— Trading the International Future Markets: The Markets, the Systems & the Strategies for Achieving the Trader's "Edge" (Illus.). 352p. 2000. 50.00 (*0-7352-0136-6*) PH Pr.

***Bernstein, Jane.** Bereft: A Sister's Story. LC 99-48798. 240p. 2000. 22.00 (*0-86547-586-5*) N Point Pr.

Bernstein, Jane. Loving Rachel. 1994. pap. text 15.00 (*0-941038-01-7*) Coyne & Chenoweth.

Bernstein, Jane A. Music Printing in Renaissance Venice: The Scotto Press (1539-1572) (Illus.). 1200p. 1998. 175.00 (*0-19-510231-2*) OUP.

Bernstein, Jane A., ed. Chansons Published by Jacques Moderne: La Parangon des Chansons. Cinquiesme Livre Contenant XXVIII Chansons. . . (Lyons, 1539) & Le Parangon des Chansons. Sixiesme Livre Contenant XXV Chansons Nouvelles. . . (Lyons, 1540) LC 93-20011. (Sixteenth-Century Chanson Ser.: Vol. 26). 228p. 1993. text 88.00 (*0-8240-3125-3*) Garland.

— Chansons Published by Jacques Moderne: Le Parangon des Chansons, Neufuiesme Livre Contenant XXXI Chansons, Lyons, 1541 & Le Parangon des Chansons, Dixiesme Livre Contenant XXX Chansons, Lyons, 1543. LC 93-20270. (Sixteenth-Century Chanson Ser.: Vol. 28). 224p. 1993. text 88.00 (*0-8240-3127-X*) Garland.

— Chansons Published by Jacques Moderne: Le Parangon des Chansons, Septiesme Livre Contenant XXVII Chansons, Lyons, 1540 & Le Parangon des Chansons, Huytiesme Livre Contenant XXX Chansons, Lyons, 1541. LC 93-21825. (Sixteenth-Century Chanson Ser.: Vol. 27). 232p. 1993. text 88.00 (*0-8240-3126-1*) Garland.

— Chansons Published by Jacques Moderne le Parangon des Chansons Tiers Livre Contentant XXVI Chansons . . . (Lyons, 1538) & Le Parangon des Chansons Quart Livre Contenant XXII Chansons a Deux et Troys Parties (Lyons, 1539) LC 93-20010. (Sixteenth Century Chanson Ser.: Vol. 25). 192p. 1993. text 79.00 (*0-8240-3124-5*) Garland.

— Claude le Jeune: Complete Unpublished Chansons. LC 89-752930. (Sixteenth Century Chanson Ser.: Vol. 16). 248p. 1989. text 30.00 (*0-8240-3115-6*) Garland.

— De Bussy, Entraigues, Antoine de Fevin, Fourmentin, Mathieu Gascongne, Robert Godard, Nicholas Grouzy, Antoine De Hauville, Jean Herissant, Nicolle Des Cellier De Hesdin, Jacotin, Jacquet. LC 94-947. (Sixteenth-Century Chanson Ser.: No. 10). 288p. 1994. reprint ed. text 95.00 (*0-8240-3109-1*) Garland.

— Fabrice Marin Caietain: Airs mis en musique a quatre parties par Fabrice Marin Caietain sur les poesies de P. de Ronsard, & autres excelens poetes. LC 94-45716. (The Sixteenth-Century Chanson Ser.: Vol. 4). 256p. 1995. text 105.00 (*0-8240-3103-2*) Garland.

— Francois Regnard, Jean Richafort, Rogier Pathie, Luigi Rouince, Jean Rousee. LC 91-754795. (Sixteenth Century Chanson Ser.: Vol. 21). 248p. 1992. text 94.00 (*0-8240-3120-2*) Garland.

— French Chansons of the Sixteenth Century. LC 84-43062. (Illus.). 224p. (C). 1985. 30.00 (*0-271-00397-9*) Pa St U Pr.

— Lambert de Beaulieu, Benedictus Appenzeller, Bercoy, Besancourt, Boyvin, Briault, Pierre Cadeac, Chevalier, Ciron, Severin Cornet, Thomas Crecquillon, Pierre de la Rue, De la Font, Desbordes, Jacques de Buisson, Estienne Du. LC 94-946. (Sixteenth-Century Chanson Ser.: No. 9). 280p. 1994. reprint ed. text 105.00 (*0-8240-3108-3*) Garland.

— Nicolas Millot, Merchandy, Nicolas de Marle, Thomas Champion (Mithou), Pierre Moulu, Jean Mouton, Pagnier, Hilaire Penet, Claude Petit Jehan. LC 90-755315. (Sixteenth Century Chanson Ser.: Vol. 19). 280p. 1991. 90.00 (*0-8240-3118-0*) Garland.

— Orlande de Lassus: Chansons 107-145. LC 87-750544. (Sixteenth-Century Chanson Ser.: Vol. 14). 202p. 1988. text 30.00 (*0-8240-3113-X*) Garland.

— Orlande de Lassus: Chansons 34-71. LC 87-750544. (Sixteenth-Century Chanson Ser.: Vol. 11). 208p. 1987. text 30.00 (*0-8240-3110-5*) Garland.

— Orlande de Lassus: Chansons 34-71. LC 87-750544. (Sixteenth-Century Chanson Ser.: Vol. 12). 208p. 1988. text 30.00 (*0-8240-3111-3*) Garland.

— Le Parangon des Chansons (Premier Livre) (Lyons (1538)) & Le Parangon des Chansons. Second Livre Contenant XXXI Chansons (Lyons, 1540) LC 92-777218. (Sixteenth-Century Chanson Ser.: Vol. 24). 232p. 1993. text 88.00 (*0-8240-3123-7*) Garland.

— Pierre Clereau: Odes de Pierre de Ronsard. LC 88-752951. (16th Century Chanson Ser.: Vol. 7). 184p. 1989. text 30.00 (*0-8240-3106-7*) Garland.

— Pierre Santerre, the Complete Chansons: Alessandro Striggio, Touteau, Phillipe Verdelot, Johannes Verius, Antoine de Villers. LC 92-750047. (Sixteenth-Century Chanson Ser.: Vol. 22). 160p. 1992. text 72.00 (*0-8240-3121-0*) Garland.

— Premier Livre de Chanson a Deux Parties (Paris, 1758) LC 92-753535. (Sixteenth Century Chanson Ser.: Vol. 15). 264p. 1992. text 94.00 (*0-8240-3114-8*) Garland.

— Second Livre d'Airs Des Plus Excelants Musiciens De Nostre Tems: Reduiz a Quatre Parties. Par M. Di. Le Blanc (Paris, 1579) Airs De Court. Mis En Musique a 4. E 5. Parties. De Plusieurs Autheurs (Paris, 1597) LC 95-5010. (Sixteenth-Century Chanson Ser.: Vol. 3). 208p. 1995. text 94.00 (*0-8240-3102-4*) Garland.

Bernstein, Janis D. Alternative Approaches to Pollution Control & Waste Management: Regulatory & Economic Instruments. LC 93-16297. (Urban Management Ser.: No. 3). 80p. 1993. pap. 22.00 (*0-8213-2344-X*, 12344) World Bank.

— Land Use Considerations in Urban Environmental Management. LC 93-40298. (Urban Management Program Ser.: No. 12). 110p. 1994. pap. 22.00 (*0-8213-2723-2*, 12723) World Bank.

Bernstein, Jared. Low-Wage Labor Market Indicators by City & State: The Constraints Facing Welfare Reform. (Illus.). 100p. (C). 1998. pap. text 20.00 (*0-7881-7516-5*) DIANE Pub.

Bernstein, Jared, jt. auth. see Mishel, Lawrence.

Bernstein, Jared, jt. auth. see Mishel, Lawrence R.

Bernstein, Jay, et al, eds. Urinary Tract Pathology: An Illustrated Practical Guide to Diagnosis. LC 91-4872. (Illus.). 264p. 1992. reprint ed. pap. 81.90 (*0-608-04727-9*, 206544800004) Bks Demand.

Bernstein, Jay, jt. ed. see Gardner, Kenneth D., Jr.

Bernstein, Jay H. Spirits Captured in Stone: Shamanism & Traditional Medicine among the Taman of Borneo. LC 96-43233. 220p. 1996. pap. text 17.95 (*1-55587-692-7*, 876927); lib. bdg. 49.95 (*1-55587-691-9*, 876919) L Rienner.

Bernstein, Jay M., ed. The Frankfurt School: Critical Assessments, 6 vols., Set. LC 94-22726. (Illus.). 2496p. (C). (gr. 13). 1994. 985.00 (*0-415-05859-7*, B4159) Routledge.

Bernstein, Jeremy. Albert Einstein: And the Frontiers of Physics. (Oxford Scientists Ser.). (Illus.). 192p. (YA). (gr. 7 up). 1996. 22.00 (*0-19-509275-9*) OUP.

— Albert Einstein: And the Frontiers of Physics. (Oxford Portraits in Science Ser.). (Illus.). 192p. (YA). (gr. 7 up). 1997. pap. 12.95 (*0-19-512029-9*) OUP.

Bernstein, Jeremy. Cranks, Quarks, & the Cosmos: Writings on Science. LC 97-19450. 1997. write for info. (*0-19-288043-8*) OUP.

— Dawning of the Raj: The Life & Trials of Warren Hastings. LC 99-88030. (Illus.). 352p. 2000. 28.95 (*1-56663-281-1*, Pub. by I R Dee) Natl Bk Netwk.

Bernstein, Jeremy. Hitler's Uranium Club: The Secret Recordings at Farm Hall. (Illus.). 464p. 1995. 34.95 (*1-56396-258-6*) Am Inst Physics.

— In the Himalayas: Journeys Through Nepal, Tibet, & Bhutan. rev. ed. (Illus.). 336p. 1996. pap. 16.95 (*1-55821-443-7*, 14437) Lyons Pr.

— Introduction to Cosmology. 224p. (C). 1997. pap. 24.95 (*0-13-905548-7*) P-H.

— Kinetic Theory in the Expanding Universe. (Cambridge Monographs on Mathematical Physics). 160p. 1988. text 52.95 (*0-521-36050-1*) Cambridge U Pr.

— The Life It Brings: One Physicist's Beginnings. (Illus.). 1987. 16.45 (*0-89919-470-2*, Pub. by Ticknor & Fields) HM.

— Quantum Profiles. 166p. (C). 1991. text 29.95 (*0-691-08725-3*, Pub. by Princeton U Pr) Cal Prin Full Svc.

Bernstein, Jeremy & Feinberg, Gerald. Cosmological Constants: Papers In Modern Cosmology. LC 86-2220. 352p. 1986. text 68.50 (*0-231-06376-8*) Col U Pr.

— Cosmological Constants: Papers In Modern Cosmology. LC 86-2220. 352p. 1989. pap. text 30.50 (*0-231-06377-6*) Col U Pr.

***Bernstein, Jeremy & Fishbane, Paul M.** Modern Physics. LC 99-86230. 624p. 2000. 89.33 (*0-13-955311-8*) P-H.

Bernstein, Jerrold G. Handbook of Drug Therapy in Psychiatry. 3rd ed. LC 95-17730. 576p. (C). (gr. 13). 1995. text 49.95 (*0-8016-8101-4*) Mosby Multi-Media.

Bernstein, Joanne E. Taking Off: Travel Tips for a Carefree Trip. LC 85-45171. (Illus.). 224p. (J). (gr. 7 up). 1986. lib. bdg. 12.89 (*0-397-32107-4*) HarpC Child Bks.

— Taking Off: Travel Tips for a Carefree Trip. LC 85-45440. (Trophy Nonfiction Bk.). (Illus.). 224p. (YA). (gr. 7 up). 1986. pap. 3.95 (*0-06-446047-9*, HarpTrophy) HarpC Child Bks.

Bernstein, Joel & Bryant, Tom. A Taste of Texas Ranching: Cowboys & Cooks. (Illus.). 256p. (Orig.). 1995. pap. 18.95 (*0-89672-348-8*) Tex Tech Univ Pr.

Bernstein, Joel, jt. auth. see Bryant, Tom.

Bernstein, Joel M., et al, eds. Immunologic Diseases of the Ear. LC 97-42727. (Annals of the New York Academy of Sciences Ser.: Vol. 830). 376p. 1997. 120.00 (*1-57331-100-6*) NY Acad Sci.

Bernstein, Joel M. & Ogra, Pearay L., eds. Immunology of the Ear. LC 85-42511. (Illus.). 533p. 1987. reprint ed. pap. 165.30 (*0-608-05835-1*, 205980100007) Bks Demand.

Bernstein, Joel M., ed. see New York Academy of Sciences Staff.

Bernstein, John A. Nietzsche's Moral Philosophy. LC 85-46001. 216p. 1987. 36.50 (*0-8386-3283-1*) Fairleigh Dickinson.

— Progress & the Quest for Meaning: A Philosophical & Historical Inquiry. LC 92-52717. 224p. 1993. 36.50 (*0-8386-3503-2*) Fairleigh Dickinson.

— Shaftsbury, Rousseau & Kant: An Introduction to the Conflict Between Aesthetic & Moral Values in Modern Thought. LC 78-75190. 192p. 1980. 29.50 (*0-8386-2351-4*) Fairleigh Dickinson.

Bernstein, Jon. Pretty in Pink: The Golden Age of Teenage Movies. LC 96-44748. (Illus.). 224p. 1997. pap. 14.95 (*0-312-15194-2*) St Martin.

Bernstein, Jordana S., jt. auth. see Meador, Daniel J.

Bernstein, Joseph & Lunts, Valery. Equivalent Sheaves & Functors. LC 94-16027. (Lecture Notes in Mathematics Ser.: No. 1578). 1994. 29.95 (*0-387-58071-9*) Spr-Verlag.

Bernstein, Judith, jt. auth. see Bernstein, Edward.

Bernstein, Judith, jt. auth. see Lewis, Judith A.

Bernstein, Judith H., jt. ed. see Shuval, Judith T.

Bernstein, Judith R. When the Bough Breaks: Forever after the Death of a Son or Daughter. 1998. pap. text 10.95 (*0-8362-5282-9*) Andrews & McMeel.

***Bernstein, Julianne & Mozes, Deborah B., eds.** Voices from Ariel: Ten-Minute Plays Reflecting the Jewish Experience. 95p. 1999. pap. 5.60 (*0-87129-895-3*) Dramatic Pub.

Bernstein, Ken, jt. auth. see Collom, Jack.

Bernstein, Ken, jt. auth. see Hoff, Paul S.

Bernstein, Kerry. High Speed CMOS Design Styles. LC 98-28409. 1998. write for info. (*0-7923-8220-X*) Kluwer Academic.

Bernstein, L. The Modified Algorithm of Jacobi-Perron. LC 52-42839. (Memoirs of the American Mathematical Society Ser.: No. 67). 44p. 1966. pap. 16.00 (*0-8218-1267-X*, MEMO/1/67C) Am Math.

Bernstein, L., jt. auth. see Wong, Harry.

Bernstein, L. B. Deutsch-Russisches Worterbuch fur Wasserbau. deluxe ed. (GER & RUS.). 579p. 1961. 39.95 (*0-8288-6814-X*, M9100) Fr & Eur.

Bernstein, Laura, ed. Wealth Angles. 238p. 1991. 29.00 (*0-945332-28-9*) Agora Inc MD.

Bernstein, Laurie A. Sonia's Daughters: Prostitutes & Their Regulation in Imperial Russia. LC 94-41271. 357p. 1995. 50.00 (*0-520-08916-2*, Pub. by U CA Pr) Cal Prin Full Svc.

***Bernstein, Lawrence & Yuhas, C. M.** Basic Concepts for Managing Telecommunications Networks: Copper to Sand to Glass to Air. LC 99-42730. (Publishers Network & Systems Management Ser.). 1999. write for info. (*0-306-46237-0*, Kluwer Plenum) Kluwer Academic.

Bernstein, Lawrence F., ed. La Couronne et Fleur des Chansons a Troys, 2 vols. (Masters & Monuments of the Renaissance Ser.: Vol. 3). (Illus.). 1980. pap. 150.00 (*0-8450-7303-6*) Broude.

Bernstein, Lenny, jt. auth. see Carver, Reginald.

Bernstein, Leonard. Leonard Bernstein: The Harvard Years (1935-39) 1999. 30.00 (*0-9648083-4-X*) Eos Music.

— One Hand One Heart: From West Side Story Piano & Violin. 6p. 1986. pap. 3.95 (*0-7935-5319-9*, 50287990) H Leonard.

— Somewhere: From West Side Story for Vocal & Piano. 6p. 1986. pap. 3.95 (*0-7935-5324-5*, 50288050) H Leonard.

— The Unanswered Question: Six Talks at Harvard. (Charles Eliot Norton Lectures). 438p. 1976. boxed set 30.00 incl. lp (*0-674-81065-1*) HUP.

— The Unanswered Question: Six Talks at Harvard. (Charles Eliot Norton Lectures). 438p. 1981. pap. text 20.50 (*0-674-92001-5*) HUP.

— West Side Story: Choral Selection. 32p. 1986. pap. 2.50 (*0-7935-5497-7*, 50307850) H Leonard.

— West Side Story: Easy Piano Selections. 20p. 1986. pap. 4.95 (*0-7935-2009-6*, 50329750) H Leonard.

— West Side Story: Orchestra Set/Full Score/Parts. 1986. pap. text 75.00 (*0-7935-4873-X*, 50343100) H Leonard.

— West Side Story: Piano. 12p. 1986. pap. 5.95 (*0-7935-5006-8*, 50288290) H Leonard.

Bernstein, Leonard S. Official Gd Wine Snb. LC 81-18707. 180p. 1982. pap. 10.95 (*0-688-01605-7*, Quil) HarperTrade.

Bernstein, Leopold & Wild, John J. Financial Statement Analysis: Theory, Application, & Interpretation. 6th ed. 1997. pap. 89.69 (*0-256-26736-7*) McGraw.

Bernstein, Leopold A. Analysis of Financial Statements. 4th ed. LC 93-1209. 432p. 1993. text 60.00 (*1-55623-930-0*, Irwn Prfssnl) McGraw-Hill Prof.

— Financial Statement Analysis: Theory, Application & Interpretation. 5th ed. LC 92-25686. 1024p. (C). 1992. text 75.50 (*0-256-10223-6*, Irwn McGrw-H) McGrw-H Hghr Educ.

Bernstein, Leopold A. & Maksy, Mostafa M. Cases in Financial Statement Reporting & Analysis. (C). 1985. pap. text 36.95 (*0-256-03316-1*, Irwn McGrw-H) McGrw-H Hghr Educ.

Bernstein, Leopold A. & Wild, John J. Analysis of Financial Statements. 5th ed. LC 98-56045. (Illus.). 529p. 1999. 60.00 (*0-07-094504-7*) McGraw.

— Financial Statement Analysis: Theory, Application & Interpretation. 6th ed. LC 97-5129. 768p. (C). 1997. 62.36 (*0-256-16704-4*, Irwn Prfssnl) McGraw-Hill Prof.

Bernstein, Leopold A., jt. auth. see Engler, Calvin.

Bernstein, Lewis. Concurrency in Programming & Database Systems. (Computer Science-Math Ser.). 1993. 56.25 (*0-86720-205-X*) Jones & Bartlett.

Bernstein, Leyna. Best Practices: The Model Employee Handbook for California Nonprofits. LC 98-228299. (Jossey-Bass Nonprofit & Public Management Ser.). 112p. 1998. pap. 49.95 (*0-7879-4574-9*) Jossey-Bass.

Bernstein, Linda R. The Family Vacation Health & Safety Guide. (Orig.). pap. 4.99 (*0-425-14732-0*) Berkley Pub.

— The Family Vacation Health & Safety Guide. 304p. (Orig.). 1995. pap. text 4.99 (*0-425-14297-3*) Berkley Pub.

Bernstein, Lisa. The Transparent Body. LC 88-10656. (Wesleyan New Poets Ser.). 64p. 1989. pap. 12.95 (*0-8195-1163-3*, Wesleyan Univ Pr) U Pr of New Eng.

Bernstein, Louis & Garibaldi, Louis E. Reflections on an Aquarium. Barr, Vilma, ed. LC 92-70602. (Illus.). 96p. (Orig.). 1992. 26.95 (*0-9632150-0-0*) Drum Comns.

— Reflections on an Aquarium. Barr, Vilma, ed. LC 92-70602. (Illus.). 96p. (Orig.). (YA). 1992. pap. text 16.95 (*0-9632150-1-9*) Drum Comns.

Bernstein, Malcolm E., et al. Strategic Sales Development: A Consultative Selling Process, 2 vols. 1986. write for info. (*0-318-59344-0*) Human Equat.

Bernstein, Marcelle. Salka. large type ed. 576p. 1987. 11.50 (*0-7089-8385-5*, Charnwood) Ulverscroft.

Bernstein, Margery. My Brother, the Pest. LC 98-35822. (Real Kids Readers Ser.). (Illus.). 32p. (J). (gr. k-2). 1999. pap. 3.99 (*0-7613-2080-6*, Copper Beech Bks); lib. bdg. 16.90 (*0-7613-2055-5*, Copper Beech Bks) Millbrook Pr.

— Stop That Noise! LC 98-38107. (Real Kids Readers Ser.). (Illus.). 48p. (J). (gr. 1-3). 1999. pap. 3.99 (*0-7613-2085-7*, Copper Beech Bks); lib. bdg. 17.90 (*0-7613-2060-1*, Copper Beech Bks) Millbrook Pr.

— That Cat! LC 98-10045. (Real Kids Readers Ser.). (Illus.). 32p. (J). (gr. k-2). 1998. pap. 3.99 (*0-7613-2044-X*); lib. bdg. 16.90 (*0-7613-2019-9*) Millbrook Pr.

Bernstein, Margery. That's Hard, That's Easy. LC 97-31373. (Real Kids Readers Ser.). (Illus.). 32p. (J). (gr. k-2). 1998. pap. 3.99 (*0-7613-2032-6*) Millbrook Pr.

***Bernstein, Margery.** That's Hard, That's Easy. LC 97-31373. (Real Kids Readers Ser.). (Illus.). 32p. (J). (gr. k-2). 1998. lib. bdg. 16.90 (*0-7613-2007-5*) Millbrook Pr.

Bernstein, Mark. Grand Eccentrics: Turning the Century: Dayton & the Inventing of America. LC 96-68626. (Illus.). 288p. 1996. pap. 19.95 (*1-882203-13-5*) Orange Frazer.

***Bernstein, Mark.** New Bremen 2000. 96p. 2000. 20.00 (*1-882203-66-6*) Orange Frazer.

Bernstein, Mark, jt. auth. see Harden, Mike.

Bernstein, Mark D. New Bremen. LC 98-4943. (Illus.). 163p. 1998. 19.95 (*1-882203-54-2*) Orange Frazer.

Bernstein, Mark H. Fatalism. LC 91-27879. 177p. 1992. reprint ed. pap. 54.90 (*0-608-03487-8*, 206420200008) Bks Demand.

— On Moral Considerability: An Essay on who Morally Matters. 208p. 1998. text 35.00 (*0-19-512391-3*) OUP.

Bernstein, Mark L. & Cottone, James A. Forensic Odontology. 1999. 79.95 (*0-8493-9525-9*) CRC Pr.

Bernstein, Martin, jt. auth. see Creamer, Daniel.

Bernstein, Martin D. & Yoder, Lloyd W. Power Boilers. LC 98-43261. 282p. 1997. 59.95 (*0-7918-0056-3*, 800563) ASME Pr.

An Asterisk (*) at the beginning of an entry indicates that the title is appearing for the first time.

Bernstein, Martin D., ed. see National Congress on Pressure Vessels & Piping Staff.

Bernstein, Marver H. The Job of the Federal Executive. LC 86-18289. 256p. 1986. lib. bdg. 69.50 (*0-313-25273-4*, BEJFE, Greenwood Pr) Greenwood.

— Regulating Business by Independent Commission. LC 77-2985. 306p. 1977. reprint ed. lib. bdg. 45.00 (*0-8371-9563-2*, BERB, Greenwood Pr) Greenwood.

Bernstein, Matthew. Controlling Hollywood: Censorship/regulation in the Studio Era. LC 99-14093. (Depth of Field Ser.). 308p. 1999. pap. 19.00 (*0-8135-2707-4*) Rutgers U Pr.

— Walter Wanger, Hollywood Independent. 1994. 45.00 (*0-520-08127-7*, Pub. by U CA Pr) Cal Prin Full Svc.

***Bernstein, Matthew.** Walter Wanger, Hollywood Independent. LC 99-88848. (Commerce & Mass Culture Ser.). 2000. 19.95 (*0-8166-3548-X*) U of Minn Pr.

***Bernstein, Matthew, ed.** Controlling Hollywood: Censorship & Regulation in the Studio Era. LC 99-14093. (Depth of Field Ser.). (Illus.). 308p. 1999. text. write for info. (*0-8135-2706-6*) Rutgers U Pr.

Bernstein, Matthew & Studlar, Gaylyn, eds. Visions of the East: Orientalism in Film. LC 96-18112. (Illus.). 325p. (C). 1997. text 50.00 (*0-8135-2294-3*); pap. text 18.95 (*0-8135-2295-1*) Rutgers U Pr.

Bernstein, Matthew, jt. auth. see Studlar, Gaylyn.

Bernstein, Melvin H. Art & Design at Alfred: A Chronicle of a Ceramics College. LC 84-46094. (Illus.). 288p. 1986. 36.50 (*0-87982-515-4*) Art Alliance.

Bernstein, Melvin H., ed. see Chapman, John J.

Bernstein, Melvin H., jt. ed. see Hoy, John C.

Bernstein, Melvin H., ed. see Rush, James.

Bernstein, Michael & Wolosoff, Lester. Raising Capital: The Grant Thornton Guide for Entrepreneurs. 1996. text 15.12 (*0-7863-1195-9*, Irwn McGrw-H) McGrw-H Hghr Educ.

Bernstein, Michael A. Foregone Conclusions: Against Apocalyptic History. LC 93-39502. (Contraversions Ser.: Vol. 4). 1994. 27.50 (*0-520-08785-2*, Pub. by U CA Pr) Cal Prin Full Svc.

— The Great Depression: Delayed Recovery & Economic Change in America, 1929-1939. (Studies in Economic History & Policy: The United States in the Twentieth Century). (Illus.). 288p. (C). 1989. pap. text 20.95 (*0-521-37985-7*) Cambridge U Pr.

— Prima Della Rivoluzione. LC 83-83108. (Poets Ser.). 65p. 1984. 25.00 (*0-915032-41-4*); pap. 11.95 (*0-915032-16-3*) Natl Poet Foun.

— The Tale of the Tribe: Ezra Pound & the Modern Verse Epic. LC 80-129. 335p. reprint ed. pap. 103.90 (*0-7837-4325-4*, 204402900012) Bks Demand.

Bernstein, Michael A. & Adler, David E., eds. Understanding American Economic Decline: A Structural & Institutional Approach. 425p. (C). 1994. text 64.95 (*0-521-45063-2*); pap. text 20.95 (*0-521-45679-7*) Cambridge U Pr.

Bernstein, Michael C. & Wolosoff, Lester. Raising Capital: The Grant Thornton LLP Guide for Entrepreneurs. 171p. 1995. text 50.00 (*0-7863-0150-3*, Irwn Prfssnl) McGraw-Hill Prof.

Bernstein, Michel. Rock-a-Bye Lambie Pie. LC 95-128303. (Illus.). 32p. 1994. 6.95 (*0-8362-4727-2*) Andrews & McMeel.

Bernstein, Michele Root, see Bernstein, Robert & Root Bernstein, Michele.

Bernstein, Morey. The Search for Bridey Murphy. Date not set. lib. bdg. 22.95 (*0-8488-1955-1*) Amereon Ltd.

Bernstein, N. Coordination & Regulation of Movements. LC 66-25078. 1967. 95.00 (*0-08-011940-9*, Pub. by Pergamon Repr) Franklin.

Bernstein, Neil I. Chef Neil's International Vegetarian Cookbook: Healthy Food That Tastes Great. 64p. 1995. 5.00 (*1-57067-008-0*) Book Pub Co.

— Treating the Unmanageable Adolescent: A Guide to Oppositional Defiant & Conduct Disorders. LC 96-15620. 368p. 1997. 40.00 (*1-56821-630-0*) Aronson.

Bernstein, Nicolai A. & Latash, Mark L. Dexterity & Its Development. Turvey, Michael T., ed. (Resources for Ecological Psychology Ser.). 480p. 1995. text 99.95 (*0-8058-1646-1*) L Erlbaum Assocs.

Bernstein, Nina. Wilder. 1997. write for info. (*0-679-43979-X*) Pantheon.

— Wilder. 1998. pap. write for info. (*0-679-75834-8*) Vin Bks.

Bernstein, Norman & Sussex, James N., eds. Handbook of Psychiatric Consultation with Children & Youth. LC 84-3376. 416p. 1984. text 44.95 (*0-88331-148-8*) R B Luce.

Bernstein, Norman R. Emotional Care of the Facially Burned & Disfigured. 1976. pap. 16.50 (*0-316-09193-6*, Little Brwn Med Div) Lppncott W & W.

Bernstein, Norman R., et al. Coping Strategies for Burn Survivors & Their Families. LC 87-7339. (Illus.). 159p. 1988. 55.00 (*0-275-92407-6*, C2407, Praeger Pubs) Greenwood.

Bernstein, Patricia. Having a Baby: Moms Tell Their Stories. Peters, Sally, ed. 336p. (Orig.). 1993. per. 10.00 (*0-671-72614-5*) PB.

Bernstein, Paul. American Work Values: Their Origin & Development. LC 96-21982. (SUNY Series in the Sociology of Work). 368p. (C). 1997. pap. text 19.95 (*0-7914-3216-5*) State U NY Pr.

— Computers for Lawyers. 297p. 1992. pap. 50.00 (*0-941916-64-2*) West Group.

Bernstein, Paul. Computers for Lawyers: A Complete Guide to Law Office Automation. 2nd ed. LC 97-68085. write for info. (*0-8366-9006-0*) West Group.

Bernstein, Paul. Computers for Lawyers Vol. II: Comprehensive Guide to Automating Your Law Firm. Kruvant, Cathy, ed. (Orig.). 1995. pap. write for info. (*0-941916-71-5*) West Group.

Bernstein, Paul & Green, Robert W. History of Civilization to Sixteen Forty-Eight. (Quality Paperback Ser.: No. 64). 355p. (Orig.). 1976. reprint ed. pap. 12.95 (*0-8226-0064-1*) Littlefield.

Bernstein, Paula. The Statistical Handbook on Technology. LC 99-41232. (Statistical Handbook Ser.). (Illus.). 277p. 1999. 65.00 (*1-57356-208-4*) Oryx Pr.

Bernstein, Peter L. Against the Gods: The Remarkable Story of Risk. 400p. 1998. pap. 14.95 (*0-471-29563-9*) Wiley.

Bernstein, Peter L. Against the Gods: The Remarkable Story of Risk. LC 96-33861. 400p. 1996. 29.95 (*0-471-12104-5*) Wiley.

— Capital Ideas: The Improbable Origins of Modern Wall Street. 340p. 1993. per. 14.95 (*0-02-903012-9*) Free Pr.

— The Portable MBA in Investment. LC 95-18969. (Portable MBA Ser.). 448p. 1995. 34.95 (*0-471-10661-5*) Wiley.

***Bernstein, Peter L.** The Power of Gold: The History of an Obsession. 432p. 2000. 27.95 (*0-471-25210-7*) Wiley.

Bernstein, Peter L. & Damodaran, Aswarth. Investment Management. LC 97-43844. 480p. 1998. 49.95 (*0-471-19716-5*) Wiley.

— Investment Management. LC 97-43844. 480p. 1998. pap. 39.95 (*0-471-19715-7*) Wiley.

Bernstein, Peter L. & Fabozzi, Frank J. Streetwise: The Best of the Journal of Portfolio Management. LC 97-15849. 325p. 1997. text 69.50 (*0-691-01129-X*, Pub. by Princeton U Pr) Cal Prin Full Svc.

— Streetwise: The Best of the Journal of Portfolio Management. LC 97-15849. 325p. 1998. pap. text 24.95 (*0-691-01128-1*, Pub. by Princeton U Pr) Cal Prin Full Svc.

Bernstein, Philip S. Best Practices of Effective Nonprofit Organizations: A Practitioner's Guide. LC 97-618. 186p. 1997. 29.95 (*0-87954-755-3*) Foundation Ctr.

— What the Jews Believe. LC 77-28446. (Illus.). 100p. 1978. reprint ed. lib. bdg. 35.00 (*0-313-20228-1*, BEWJ, Greenwood Pr) Greenwood.

Bernstein, Phillip A. & Newcomer, Eric. Principles of Transaction Processing. LC 96-47916. 364p. (Orig.). 1998. text 44.95 (*1-55860-415-4*) Morgan Kaufmann.

Bernstein, Phyllis, et al. Financial Planning for CPAs. 8th ed. LC 99-23515. 464p. 1999. pap. 149.00 incl. cd-rom (*0-471-32359-4*) Wiley.

Bernstein, R. B., ed. Atom-Molecule Collision Theory: Guide for the Experimentalist. LC 78-27380. (Physics of Atoms & Molecules Ser.). (Illus.). 1979. 155.00 (*0-306-40121-5*, Plenum Trade) Perseus Pubng.

Bernstein, Rachel, jt. auth. see Bernhardt, Debra E.

Bernstein, Ralph L. & Rosenberg, Andrew D. Manual of Orthopedic Anesthesia & Related Pain Syndromes. (Illus.). 496p. (Orig.). 1993. pap. text 72.00 (*0-443-08843-8*) Church.

Bernstein, Rebecca Sample. Addy's Cookbook: A Peek at Dining in the Past with Meals You Can Cook Today. LC 94-25071. (American Girls Collection). (Illus.). 48p. (YA). (gr. 2 up). 1994. pap. 5.95 (*1-56247-123-6*) Pleasant Co.

Bernstein, Rebecca Sample, jt. auth. see Evert, Jodi.

Bernstein, Rebecca Sample, jt. contrib. by see Salisbury, Mark.

Bernstein, Richard. Dictatorship of Virtue: How the Battle Over Multiculturalism is Reshaping Our Schools, Our Country, & Our Lives. LC 96-110831. 384p. 1995. pap. 14.00 (*0-679-76398-8*) Random.

— Fragile Glory: A Portrait of France & the French. 368p. 1991. pap. 14.95 (*0-452-26678-5*, Plume) Dutton Plume.

— The Road of Great Events. 1999. 0.00 (*0-375-40009-5*); pap. write for info. (*0-679-78157-9*) Knopf.

— Style Investing: Unique Insight into Equity Management. LC 94-35163. 256p. 1995. 60.00 (*0-471-03570-X*) Wiley.

Bernstein, Richard & Agel, Jerome. The Congress. LC 88-21025. (Into the Third Century Ser.). (YA). (gr. 7 up). 1989. 12.95 (*0-8027-6832-6*); lib. bdg. 13.85 (*0-8027-6833-4*) Walker & Co.

— The Supreme Court. LC 88-21027. (Into the Third Century Ser.). (YA). (gr. 7 up). 1989. lib. bdg. 13.85 (*0-8027-6835-0*) Walker & Co.

***Bernstein, Richard & Association for Investment Management and Research.** Asian Equity Investing: Proceedings of the AIMR Seminar "Advances in Asian Equity Management: Style Investing" October 28-29, 1997, Singapore. LC 99-208075. (Illus.). 1998. write for info. (*0-935015-20-5*) Inst Charter Finan Analysts.

Bernstein, Richard & Munro, Ross H. The Coming Conflict with China. 1998. pap. 13.00 (*0-679-77662-1*) Vin Bks.

Bernstein, Richard B. & Agel, Jerome. Amending America: If We Love the Constitution So Much, Why Do We Keep Trying to Change It? 416p. 1995. pap. 17.95 (*0-7006-0715-3*) U Pr of KS.

— The Presidency. LC 88-21026. (Into the Third Century Ser.). (YA). (gr. 7 up). 1989. 12.95 (*0-8027-6829-6*); lib. bdg. 13.85 (*0-8027-6831-8*) Walker & Co.

— The Supreme Court. LC 88-21027. (Into the Third Century Ser.). (YA). (gr. 7 up). 1989. 12.95 (*0-8027-6834-2*) Walker & Co.

Bernstein, Richard B. & Rice, Kym S. Are We to Be a Nation? The Making of the Constitution. LC 86-19590. (Illus.). 356p. 1987. pap. text 17.50 (*0-674-04476-2*) HUP.

Bernstein, Richard B., jt. ed. see Schechter, Stephen L.

Bernstein, Richard J. Beyond Objectivism & Relativism: Science, Hermeneutics, & Praxis. LC 83-12439. 320p. (Orig.). 1983. pap. 18.95 (*0-8122-1165-0*) U of Pa Pr.

— Freud & the Legacy of Moses. LC 98-14400. (Cambridge Studies in Religion & Critical Thought: No. 4). 168p. (C). 1998. text 59.95 (*0-521-63096-7*); pap. text 18.95 (*0-521-63877-1*) Cambridge U Pr.

— Hannah Arendt & the Jewish Question. (Illus.). 255p. (C). 1996. 35.00 (*0-262-02406-3*); pap. text 18.00 (*0-262-52214-4*) MIT Pr.

— The New Constellation: The Ethical-Political Horizons of Modernity - Postmodernity. (Illus.). 360p. 1992. pap. text 22.00 (*0-262-52166-0*) MIT Pr.

— Philosophical Profiles: Essays in a Pragmatic Mode. LC 85-16431. 328p. (C). 1986. 41.95 (*0-8122-7995-5*) U of Pa Pr.

— The Restructuring of Social & Political Theory. LC 76-12544. 310p. (C). 1978. pap. 17.95 (*0-8122-7742-2*) U of Pa Pr.

Bernstein, Richard J., ed. Perspectives on Peirce: Critical Essays on Charles Sanders Peirce. LC 80-13703. 148p. 1980. reprint ed. lib. bdg. 38.50 (*0-313-22414-5*, BEPP, Greenwood Pr) Greenwood.

***Bernstein, Richard K.** Dr. Bernsteins Diabetes Solution 2000. pap. write for info. (*0-316-09391-2*, Back Bay) Little.

Bernstein, Richard K. & Aubert, Timothy J. Dr. Bernstein's Diabetes Solution: A Complete Guide to Achieving Normal Blood Sugars. LC 96-37900. (Illus.). 416p. (gr. 8). 1997. 24.95 (*0-316-09344-0*) Little.

Bernstein, Richard W., ed. Habermas & Modernity. 240p. (Orig.). 1985. 25.00 (*0-262-02227-3*); pap. text 15.00 (*0-262-52102-4*) MIT Pr.

Bernstein, Robert & Root Bernstein, Michele. Honey, Mud, Maggots & Other Medical Marvels: The Science Behind Folk Remedies & Old Wives' Tales. 288p. 1998. pap. 13.00 (*0-395-92492-8*) HM.

Bernstein, Robert & Worth, Richard. Divorced Dad's Handbook: One-Hundred Questions & Answers for Men to Have a Fullfilling Relationship with Their Children Following a Divorce. 176p. 1995. pap. 12.95 (*0-933025-40-8*) Blue Bird Pub.

Bernstein, Robert A. Straight Parents, Gay Children: Inspiring Families to Live Honestly & with Greater Understanding. 2nd ed. LC 98-56506. 224p. 1999. pap. 13.95 (*1-56025-229-4*, Thunders Mouth) Avalon NY.

Bernstein, Robert A. & Dyer, James A. An Introduction to Political Science Methods. 3rd ed. 348p. (C). 1991. pap. text 41.20 (*0-13-489071-X*) P-H.

Bernstein, Robert L., et al. Book Publishing in the U. S. S. R. Reports of the Delegations of U. S. Book Publishers Visiting the U. S. S. R., 1962 & 1970. 2nd enl. ed. LC 76-37283. 182p. 1971. pap. 12.50 (*0-674-07874-8*) HUP.

Bernstein, Robert M., jt. auth. see Rassman, William R.

Bernstein, Roberta. Ellsworth Kelly: At Right Angles, 1964-1966. (Illus.). 28p. 1991. pap. 8.00 (*1-880641-00-3*) M Leavin Gal.

— Jasper Johns. Broude, Norma, ed. (Rizzoli Art Ser.). (Illus.). 24p. (Orig.). 1993. pap. 7.95 (*0-8478-1576-1*, Pub. by Rizzoli Intl) St Martin.

— Jasper Johns' Paintings & Sculptures, 1954-1974: "The Changing Focus of the Eye" Foster, Stephen, ed. LC 85-998. (Studies in the Fine Arts: The Avant-Garde: No. 46). 271p. reprint ed. pap. 84.10 (*0-8357-1601-5*, 207062700009) Bks Demand.

Bernstein, Robin. Terrible, Terrible! A Folktale Retold. LC 98-11484. (Illus.). 32p. (J). (ps-5). 1998. pap. 6.95 (*1-58013-017-8*) Kar-Ben.

— Terrible, Terrible! A Folktale Retold. LC 98-11484. (Illus.). 32p. (J). (gr. k-5). 1998. 15.95 (*1-58013-016-X*) Kar-Ben.

Bernstein, Robin F. & Moore, Cathy. A Journal for Healing: Writing Through Pain & Illness. 208p. 1996. pap. 18.95 (*0-385-48184-5*, Main St Bks) Doubleday.

— Letters for Tomorrow: A Journal for Expectant Moms & Dads. LC 94-9466. 160p. 1995. pap. 20.00 (*0-385-47515-2*) Doubleday.

Bernstein, Robin F., jt. auth. see Moore, Cathy.

Bernstein, Ron, et al. The Entrepreneur's Guide to Equity Compensation. 2nd rev. ed. 80p. 1998. pap. 35.00 (*0-9664077-1-7*) Found Enter Dev.

Bernstein, Rosella. Phonics Activities for Reading Success. LC 98-145250. (Illus.). 320p. 1997. pap. text 24.95 (*0-87628-564-7*) Ctr Appl Res.

— Sound Out! Ready-to-Use Phonics Activities for Special Children. LC 93-17470. (Illus.). 320p. 1993. pap. text 28.95 (*0-87628-867-0*) Ctr Appl Res.

Bernstein, Ross. Fifty Years - Fifty Heroes Vol. 1: A Celebration of Minnesota Sports. (Illus.). 128p. 1997. 19.95 (*0-9634871-1-6*) Bernstein Ent.

***Bernstein, Ross.** Frozen Memories: Celebrating a Century of Minnesota Hockey. LC 99-67416. (Illus.). 176p. 1999. 22.95 (*0-931714-82-6*, Pub. by Nodin Pr) Bookmen Inc.

— Gary Payton: Star Guard. LC 99-31675. (Sports Reports Ser.). (Illus.). 104p. (gr. 4-10). 2000. lib. bdg. 20.95 (*0-7660-1330-8*) Enslow Pubs.

Bernstein, Ross. Gopher Hockey by the Hockey Gopher. Gilbert, John, ed. (Illus.). 238p. (Orig.). 1992. pap. 13.95 (*0-9634871-0-8*) Bernstein Ent.

Bernstein, Ruth A. & Bernstein, Stephen. Biology. LC 94-77923. 720p. (C). 1995. text 40.00 (*0-697-15105-0*, WCB McGr Hill) McGrw-H Hghr Educ.

— Biology. 720p. (C). 1995. boxed set. write for info. (*0-697-04456-4*, WCB McGr Hill) McGrw-H Hghr Educ.

— Biology. 720p. (C). 1995. text, student ed. 20.00 (*0-697-10149-5*, WCB McGr Hill) McGrw-H Hghr Educ.

— Biology. 728p. (C). 1997. per. write for info. (*0-07-114894-9*, WCB McGr Hill) McGrw-H Hghr Educ.

Bernstein, Ruth A., et al. Biology. 256p. (C). 1996. text, lab manual ed. 23.00 (*0-697-10150-9*, WCB McGr Hill) McGrw-H Hghr Educ.

Bernstein, S. Birds Bk. 1: Piano Solo. 16p. 1986. pap. 4.95 (*0-7935-3877-7*) H Leonard.

— Birds Bk. 2: Piano Solo. 1986. pap. 5.95 (*0-7935-3587-9*) H Leonard.

— Fantasy on Theme by Francisco: Piano Solo. 8p. 1995. pap. 5.95 (*0-7935-4303-7*, 50482378) H Leonard.

— Musiphysicality for Piano. 72p. 1991. pap. 9.95 (*0-7935-0609-3*) H Leonard.

— Twenty Lessons in Keyboard Choreography. 200p. 1991. pap. 18.95 (*0-7935-0372-8*) H Leonard.

Bernstein, S. J., tr. see Garcia Marquez, Gabriel.

Bernstein, Sam. Ritual & Belief: Chinese Jade & Related Arts, Vol. 3. (Illus.). 108p. 1994. 65.00 (*0-9638932-0-3*) S Bernstein & Co.

Bernstein, Samuel. Essays in Political & Intellectual History. LC 73-86729. (Essay Index Reprint Ser.). 1977. 20.95 (*0-8369-1171-7*) Ayer.

— The First International in America. LC 62-52478. vii, 312p. 1965. 45.00 (*0-678-00102-2*) Kelley.

Bernstein, Sanford I., jt. auth. see Zyskind, Judith W.

Bernstein, Sara. Hand Clap: "Miss Mary Mack" & Forty-Two Other Handclapping Games for Kids. LC 94-24752. (Illus.). 128p. 1994. pap. 6.95 (*1-55850-426-5*) Adams Media.

Bernstein, Sara T. The Seamstress: A Memoir of Survival. LC 97-9461. (Illus.). 320p. 1997. 25.95 (*0-399-14322-X*, G P Putnam) Peng Put Young Read.

Bernstein, Sara Tuvel. The Seamstress: A Memoir of Survival. 384p. 1999. reprint ed. pap. 13.00 (*0-425-16630-9*) Berkley Pub.

Bernstein, Saul. The Orthodox Union Story: A Centenary Portrayal. 400p. 1997. pap. 40.00 (*0-7657-9953-7*) Aronson.

Bernstein, Saul, ed. Jubilee - Our First Forty Years: Kew Gardens Synagogue Adath Yeshurun. (Illus.). 192p. 1990. lib. bdg. 20.00 (*0-9626356-0-X*) Kew Gar Syn Adath Yes.

Bernstein, Serge & Poussin, Charles D. Approximation, 2 Vols. in 1. LC 69-16996. 19.95 (*0-8284-0198-5*) Chelsea Pub.

***Bernstein, Serge & Rioux, Jean-Pierre.** The Pompidou Years, 1969-1974. Woodall, Christopher, tr. (Cambridge History of Modern France Ser.: No. 9). (Illus.). 296p. (C). 2000. text 59.95 (*0-521-58061-7*) Cambridge U Pr.

Bernstein, Seymour. With Your Own Two Hands: Self-Discovery Through Music. 320p. 1995. pap. 12.95 (*0-7935-5712-7*) H Leonard.

Bernstein, Seymour F. New York Tax Handbook. 480p. 1988. 19.50 (*0-13-620469-4*) P-H.

— New York Tax Handbook. 400p. 1988. 18.95 (*0-13-620485-6*, Busn) P-H.

— New York Tax Handbook, 1984. 436p. 1984. 11.00 (*0-686-89040-X*, 62061-7) P-H.

— New York Tax Handbook, 1985. write for info. (*0-318-58208-2*) P-H.

Bernstein, Sharon C. A Family That Fights. Levine, Abby, ed. LC 90-29889. (Illus.). 32p. (J). (gr. k-4). 1991. lib. bdg. 13.95 (*0-8075-2248-1*) A Whitman.

Bernstein, Sidney & Hall, Irwin. Criminal Defense Techniques, 10 vols. 1969. ring bd. 1900.00 (*0-8205-1202-8*) Bender.

Bernstein, Sidney, ed. see Mason, James.

***Bernstein, Stan.** The State of World Population: Six Billion: A Time for Choices. Marshall, Alex, ed. (Illus.). 76p. (C). 2000. pap. text 20.00 (*0-7881-8983-2*) DIANE Pub.

Bernstein, Stanley & King, Lawrence P. Collier Bankruptcy Compensation Guide. 1988. 225.00 (*0-8205-1536-1*) Bender.

Bernstein, Stephen. Alasdair Gray LC 99-12237. 1999. write for info. (*0-8387-5414-7*) Bucknell U Pr.

— Two Thousand Solved Problems in Statistics: A Workbook for Writers, Form C. LC 99-38347. (Schaum's Solved Problems Ser.). 354p. (C). 1998. pap. 15.95 (*0-07-005023-6*) McGraw.

Bernstein, Stephen, jt. auth. see Bernstein, Ruth A.

***Bernstein, Steve.** There's a Book in There Somewhere: Insignificant Events of My Life. unabridged ed. Axelson-Berry, Kitty, ed. (Illus.). 118p. 1999. 24.95 (*0-9662602-3-6*) Modern Memoirs.

Bernstein, Steven. Film Production. 2nd rev. ed. (Illus.). 216p. 1994. pap. 42.95 (*0-240-51343-6*, Focal) Buttrwrth-Heinemann.

Bernstein, Steven, et al, eds. Hysterectomy: Clinical Recommendations & Indications for Use. LC 97-47170. 1997. pap. 15.00 (*0-8330-2574-0*) Rand Corp.

Bernstein, Steven, et al. Hysterectomy: A Review of the Literature on Indications, Effectiveness, & Risks. LC 95-48361. 1997. pap. 15.00 (*0-8330-2347-0*) Rand Corp.

Bernstein, Steven J. I Am Secretly an Important Man. (Illus.). 132p. 1995. 12.95 (*0-9638594-1-2*) Zero Hour.

— More Noise, Please! 2nd ed. LC 95-81515. (Illus.). 192p. (Orig.). 1996. pap. 8.00 (*0-939306-09-3*) Left Bank.

Bernstein, Steven J., et al. Hysterectomy: Ratings of Appropriateness. LC 97-32738. (Illus.). 137p. 1997. pap. 15.00 (*0-8330-2571-6*, MR-592/3) Rand Corp.

Bernstein, Stuart A. Road to Naka-Ima: A Man's Journey to a New Civilization. LC 96-128920. (Sounds of a New Order Ser.). 240p. (Orig.). 1995. pap. 19.00 (*0-9648834-0-6*) Cassiquiare.

Bernstein, Susan. Virtuosity of the Nineteenth Century: Performing Music & Language in Heine, Liszt & Baudelaire. LC 98-8654. 344p. 1998. 55.00 (*0-8047-3279-5*); pap. 19.95 (*0-8047-3505-0*) Stanford U Pr.

Bernstein, Susan D. Confessional Subjects: Revelations of Gender & Power in Victorian Literature & Culture. LC 96-23854. 232p. (C). (gr. 13). 1997. 45.00 (*0-8078-2313-9*); pap. 17.95 (*0-8078-4624-4*) U of NC Pr.

Bernstein, Susan N. Teaching Real Writing 3: Background Readings. 192p. 1998. pap. text 0.01 (*0-312-15445-3*) St Martin.

B

An Asterisk (*) at the beginning of an entry indicates that the title is appearing for the first time.

Bernstein, Susan R. Managing Contracted Services: Administrating Ethical & Political Issues in Nonprofit Agencies. 230p. 1991. 59.95 (*0-87722-808-6*); pap. 22.95 (*0-87722-809-4*) Temple U Pr.

Bernstein, Terry, et al. Internet Security for Business. 452p. 1996. pap. 34.95 (*0-471-13752-9*) Wiley.

Bernstein, Theodore M. Bernstein's Reverse Dictionary. 1999. lib. bdg. 27.95 (*1-56723-153-5*) Yestermorrow.

— The Careful Writer: A Modern Guide to English Usage. LC 65-12404. 490p. (C). 1977. pap. 16.95 (*0-689-70555-7*, 233) Atheneum Yung Read.

Bernstein, Thomas P. Muted Differences: The Negotiations to Normalize U. S. - Chinese Relations. (Pew Case Studies in International Affairs). 69p. (C). 1995. pap. text 3.50 (*1-56927-426-6*) Geo U Inst Dplmcy.

— Up to the Mountains & down to the Villages: The Transfer of Youth from Urban to Rural China. LC 77-76291. (Illus.). 371p. 1977. 50.00 (*0-300-02135-6*) Yale U Pr.

Bernstein, Tracey. Why I Love This Guy. 96p. 1995. mass mkt. 4.99 (*0-8217-0108-8*, Zebra Kensgtn); mass mkt. 4.99 (*0-7860-0108-9*, Pinncle Kensgtn) Kensgtn Pub Corp.

Bernstein, Tree. Journal of the Lingering Fall. (Illus.). 28p. (Orig.). 1994. pap. 4.95 (*1-880743-05-1*) Dead Metaphor.

Bernstein, Victor H. The Holocaust: Final Judgement. rev. ed. LC 79-55440. 304p. 1980. 9.95 (*0-672-52624-7*, Bobbs) Macmillan.

Bernstein, Vivian. American Government: Freedom, Rights, Responsibilities. 1997. teacher ed. 6.30 (*0-8114-7794-0*) Raintree Steck-V.

— America's History Bk. 1: Land of Liberty. 1997. pap., student ed. 14.07 (*0-8172-6334-9*) Raintree Steck-V.

— America's History Bk. 2: Land of Liberty. 1997. pap., student ed. 14.07 (*0-8172-6335-7*) Raintree Steck-V.

— America's History Bks. 1 & 2: Land of Liberty. 1997. teacher ed. 7.35 (*0-8172-6338-1*); pap., teacher ed. 7.35 (*0-8172-6336-5*) Raintree Steck-V.

— America's History Bks. 1 & 2: Land of Liberty. LC 97-184483. (J). 1997. student ed. 28.59 (*0-8172-6337-3*) Raintree Steck-V.

— America's Story. 1997. student ed. 24.99 (*0-8114-2793-5*) Raintree Steck-V.

— America's Story Bk. 1: Before 1865. 1997. pap., student ed. 12.60 (*0-8114-2791-9*) Raintree Steck-V.

— America's Story Bk. 2: After 1865. 1997. pap., student ed. 12.60 (*0-8114-2792-7*) Raintree Steck-V.

— Decisions for Health. 1997. teacher ed. 5.95 (*0-8114-7790-8*); pap., teacher ed. 5.95 (*0-8114-3302-1*); teacher ed., ring bd. 84.75 (*0-8114-7789-4*) Raintree Steck-V.

— Decisions for Health, Bk. 1. 1997. pap., student ed. 11.28 (*0-8114-3300-5*) Raintree Steck-V.

— Decisions for Health, Bk. 2. 1997. pap., student ed. 11.28 (*0-8114-3301-3*) Raintree Steck-V.

— Decisions for Health: The Complete Edition. LC 96-104148. 1997. student ed. 24.99 (*0-8114-7788-6*) Raintree Steck-V.

— Personal Health. (Life Skills for Today's World Ser.). 1997. pap., student ed. 9.32 (*0-8114-1915-0*) Raintree Steck-V.

— World Geography & You. (Illus.). 1997. student ed. 25.39 (*0-8172-6829-4*) Raintree Steck-V.

— World Geography & You, Bk. 1. (Illus.). 1997. pap., student ed. 12.67 (*0-8172-6827-8*) Raintree Steck-V.

— World Geography & You, Bk. 2. (Illus.). 1997. pap., student ed. 12.67 (*0-8172-6828-6*) Raintree Steck-V.

— World History & You. (Illus.). 1997. student ed. 25.45 (*0-8172-6328-4*) Raintree Steck-V.

— World History & You, Bk. 1. (Illus.). 1997. pap., student ed. 12.67 (*0-8172-6325-X*) Raintree Steck-V.

— World History & You, Bk. 2. (Illus.). 1997. pap., student ed. 12.67 (*0-8172-6326-8*) Raintree Steck-V.

— World History & You, Bks. 1 & 2. (Illus.). 1997. pap., teacher ed. 7.35 (*0-8172-6327-6*) Raintree Steck-V.

— The World of Work. (Life Skills for Today's World Ser.). 1997. pap., student ed. 9.32 (*0-8114-1913-4*) Raintree Steck-V.

— Your Own Home. (Life Skills for Today's World Ser.). 1997. pap., student ed. 9.32 (*0-8114-1914-2*) Raintree Steck-V.

***Bernstein, Walter.** Inside Out: A Memoir of the Blacklist. 320p. 2000. pap. text 16.00 (*0-306-80936-2*, Pub. by Da Capo) HarpC.

***Bernstein, William.** Intelligent Asset Allocator: How to Build Your Portfolio to Maximize Returns & Minimize Risks. (Illus.). 224p. 2000. 29.95 (*0-07-136236-3*) McGraw.

Bernstel, Janet Bighan, jt. auth. see Heady, Christy.

Bernstengel, Olaf. Sachsisches Wandermarionettetheater. (Illus.). 96p. 1995. pap. text 9.00 (*3-364-00316-5*) Gordon & Breach.

Bernstine, Alvin C. As for Me & My House: Some Redemptive Words for the Black Family. LC 94-10332. 1994. 8.95 (*0-910683-24-7*) Townsnd-Pr.

— How to Develop a Department of Christian Education within the Local Baptist Church: A Congregational-Enablement Model. LC 95-5623. 1995. write for info. (*0-910683-31-X*) Townsnd-Pr.

Bernstine, Karen J., ed. Church & Family Together: A Congregational Manual for Black Family Ministry. 72p. 1996. pap. 12.00 (*0-8170-1243-5*) Judson.

Bernstine, Richard L., jt. ed. see Thompson, Horace E.

Bernstock, Judith E. Joan Mitchell. LC 87-35376. (Illus.). 228p. 1988. 35.00 (*0-933920-82-2*, Pub. by Hudson Hills) Natl Bk Netwk.

— Under the Spell of Orpheus: The Persistence of a Myth in Twentieth-Century Art. (Illus.). 272p. (C). 1991. 36.95 (*0-8093-1659-5*) S Ill U Pr.

Bernstock, Peter. Ace's Exambusters Algebra I Study. 2nd ed. Burchard, Elizabeth R., ed. (Exambusters Ser.). 384p. (YA). (gr. 7 up). 2000. reprint ed. pap. 10.95 (*1-881374-92-0*, Exambusters) Ace Acad.

Bernstock, Peter N. Handbook for Microcomputer Technicians. 451p. 1993. pap. 34.95 (*0-471-56043-X*) Wiley.

Bernt, Joseph, jt. ed. see Greenwald, Marilyn.

Bernthal, John E., et al, eds. Child Phonology: Characteristics, Assessment & Intervention with Special Populations. LC 94-31616. (Current Therapy of Communication Disorders Ser.). (Illus.). 256p. 1994. 49.00 (*0-86577-502-8*) Thieme Med Pubs.

Bernthal, John E. & Bankson, Nicholas W. Articulation & Phonological Disorders. 4th ed. LC 97-13185. 432p. 1997. 72.00 (*0-205-19693-4*) P-H.

Bernthal, Mark. La Banda de Barney Y Babybop: La Alegria de Comparti. (SPA., Illus.). 32p. (J). 1997. pap. text 2.95 (*1-57064-169-2*, Barney Publ) Lyrick Pub.

— Barney & BJ Go to the Police Station. LC 97-72911. (Barney's Go to Ser.). (Illus.). 24p. (J). (ps-k). 1998. pap. 3.25 (*1-57064-238-9*) Lyrick Pub.

— Barney Goes to the Fair. Davis, Guy, ed. (Barney's Go to Ser.). 24p. (J). (ps-k). 2000. pap. 3.25 (*1-57064-721-6*, Barney Publ) Lyrick Pub.

— Barney Van a la Granja. LC 97-76177. (Barney's Go to Ser.). (SPA.). (J). (ps-3). 1998. pap. text 3.25 (*1-57064-418-7*) Lyrick Pub.

— Barney's Book of Shapes. LC 97-75563. (Barney Ser.). (Illus.). 22p. (J). (ps-k). 1998. bds. 5.95 (*1-57064-242-7*) Lyrick Pub.

— Barney's Trick Or Treat. LC 97-70877. (Barney Ser.). (Illus.). 24p. (J). (ps-k). 1997. pap. text 3.25 (*1-57064-178-1*, Barney Publ) Lyrick Pub.

— Barney's 12 Days of Christmas. LC 98-65337. (Barney Ser.). 26p. (J). (ps-k). 1998. bds. 13.95 (*1-57064-241-9*) Lyrick Pub.

***Bernthal, Mark.** Barney's 12 Days of Christmas. LC 98-65337. (Barney Ser.). (Illus.). 24p. (J). (ps-3). 2000. 9.95 (*1-57064-835-2*) Lyrick Pub.

Bernthal, Mark. La Gran Aventura de Barney. LC 97-76176. (Barney Ser.). (SPA.). (J). (ps-3). 1998. pap. 3.25 (*1-57064-419-5*) Lyrick Pub.

Bernthal, Mark S. Baby Bop Goes to School. Dowdy, Linda C., ed. LC 93-74290. (Barney Ser.). (Illus.). 24p. (J). (ps-k). 1994. 4.95 (*1-57064-020-3*) Lyrick Pub.

— Baby Bop's ABC Book. Hartley, Linda, ed. LC 93-77869. (Barney Ser.). (Illus.). 26p. (J). (ps-k). 1993. pap. 3.25 (*1-57064-008-4*, Barney Publ) Lyrick Pub.

— Barney & Baby Bop Go to School. Larsen, Margie, ed. LC 93-74290. (Barney's Go to Ser.). (Illus.). 24p. (J). (ps-3). 1996. pap. 3.25 (*1-57064-075-0*) Lyrick Pub.

— Barney & Baby Bop Go to the Library. LC 98-65559. (Barney's Go to Ser.). (Illus.). 24p. (J). (ps-k). 1999. pap. 3.25 (*1-57064-447-0*, Barney Publ) Lyrick Pub.

— Barney & BJ Go to the Fire Station. Larsen, Margie, ed. LC 95-79189. (Barney's Go to Ser.). (Illus.). 24p. (J). (ps-3). 1996. pap. 3.25 (*1-57064-072-6*) Lyrick Pub.

— Barney Goes to the Farm. LC 97-74901. (Barney's Go to Ser.). (Illus.). 24p. (J). (ps-k). 1998. pap. text 3.25 (*1-57064-261-3*) Lyrick Pub.

— Barney y BJ Van a la Estacion de Bomberos. LC 96-86718. (Barney Go to Ser.). (SPA., Illus.). 24p. (J). (ps-k). 1997. pap. text 2.95 (*1-57064-167-6*, Barney Publ) Lyrick Pub.

— Barney's Adventure Hunt. LC 97-74902. (Barney Ser.). (Illus.). 18p. (J). (ps-k). 1998. 5.95 (*1-57064-263-X*) Lyrick Pub.

— Barney's Big Balloon. LC 95-75347. (Barney's Beginnings Ser.). (Illus.). 24p. (Orig.). (J). (ps-k). 1995. pap. 3.25 (*1-57064-044-0*) Lyrick Pub.

— Barney's Christmas Surprise. LC 96-83768. (Barney Ser.). (Illus.). 24p. (J). (ps-k). 1997. reprint ed. pap. 12.99 (*1-57064-131-5*, Barney Publ) Lyrick Pub.

— Barney's Great Adventure. (Barney Ser.). 24p. (J). (ps-k). 1998. pap. text 3.25 (*1-57064-262-1*) Lyrick Pub.

— Barney's Great Adventure Book & Tape. (Barney Ser.). (Illus.). 24p. (J). (ps-k). 1998. pap. 6.95 (*1-57064-249-4*) Lyrick Pub.

— Barney's Number Friends. Larsen, Margie, ed. LC 95-83156. (Barney Ser.). (Illus.). 24p. (J). (ps-k). 1996. bds. 5.95 (*1-57064-079-3*) Lyrick Pub.

— Francesco's Easter Surprise. 24p. (J). 1998. pap. text 2.95 (*1-57064-264-8*) Lyrick Pub.

— Francesco's Friends. 24p. (J). 1998. pap. text 2.95 (*1-57064-265-6*) Lyrick Pub.

— El Gran Globo de Barney: Una Aventura de Escondidillas. (SPA., Illus.). 24p. (J). 1997. pap. text 2.95 (*1-57064-168-4*, Barney Publ) Lyrick Pub.

Bernthal, Mark S. & Wormser, Deborah. Barney's Storybook Treasury. LC 98-66950. (Barney Ser.). (Illus.). 176p. (J). (ps-k). 1999. 10.95 (*1-57064-579-5*, Barney Publ) Lyrick Pub.

Bernthal, Mark S., jt. auth. see Barney Publishing Staff.

Bernthal, Ron. Saturday Night in Havana. 96p. 1992. pap. 9.95 (*0-9631682-1-5*) Mariposa Pr.

Bernton, Hal, et al. The Forbidden Fuel: Power Alcohol in the Twentieth Century. LC 81-85112. (Illus.). 312p. 1982. 29.95 (*0-941726-00-2*) Boyd Griffin.

Berntsen, Arnstein. Norway: Eighteen Seventy-Seven to Eighteen Seventy-Eight Issue Ore Denominations, Shaded Posthorn. Richter, Jared H., ed. Steen, Gunnar, tr. from NOR. (Illus.). 58p. (Orig.). 1984. pap. text 5.00 (*0-936493-03-8*) Scand Philatelic.

***Berntsen, Carl A.** A History of Medical Care in New York City: The Principal Founders of Cornell University Medical College with Articles on the Development of Medical Education & Care in the U. S. Stanbury, Elise B., ed. 323p. 1998. text 100.00 (*0-9668386-0-2*) E B Stanbury.

Berntsen, Maxine, jt. ed. see Zelliot, Eleanor.

Bernucci, Leopoldo M. Historia de un Malentendido: Un Estudio Transtextual de La Guerra del Fin del Mundo de Mario Vargas Llosa. (University of Texas Studies in Contemporary Spanish-American Fiction: Vol. 5). XVIII, 242p. (C). 1989. text 42.95 (*0-8204-0974-X*) P Lang Pubng.

Bernus, Ed., jt. auth. see Ag Sidiyene, Ehya.

Bernus, P., et al, eds. Handbook on Architectures of Information Systems. LC 98-26194. (International Handbooks on Information Systems Ser.). (Illus.). x, 834p. 1998. 189.00 (*3-540-64453-9*) Spr-Verlag.

Bernus-Taylor, Marthe, jt. auth. see Caubet, Annie.

Bernuy, J. Noriega, ed. Pichka Harawikuna: Five Quechua Poets. Ahern, Maureen, tr. LC 98-37802. (ENG, QUE & SPA.). 160p. 1998. pap. 14.95 (*0-935480-98-6*) Lat Am Lit Rev Pr.

Bernzweig, Eli P. By Accident, Not Design: The Case for Comprehensive Injury Reparations. LC 80-20815. 221p. 1980. 57.95 (*0-275-91686-3*, C1686, Praeger Pubs) Greenwood.

— The Nurse's Liability for Malpractice: A Programmed Course. 6th ed. LC 95-30160. (Illus.). 496p. (C). (gr. 13). 1995. pap. text 37.00 (*0-8151-0702-1*, 26104) Mosby Inc.

Bero-Johnson, Jamie & Johnson, Jamie. Purinton Pottery. LC 97-66896. (Schiffer Book for Collectors Ser.). (Illus.). 224p. 1997. pap. 29.95 (*0-7643-0290-6*) Schiffer.

Beroaldo, Filippo. Filippo Beroaldo the Elder, Annotationes Centum: Critical Edition with Commentary. Ciapponi, Lucia A., ed. (Medieval & Renaissance Texts & Studies: Vol. 131). 192p. 1995. 28.00 (*0-86698-138-1*, MR131) MRTS.

Beroff, Art & Moyers, Dwayne. Where's the Money? Sure Fire Financing Solutions for Your Small Business. LC 98-51284. (Illus.). 350p. 1999. pap. 19.95 (*1-891984-03-9*) Entrepreneur.

***Berofsky, Adrienne.** The Disney Bakery. LC 00-100797. (Illus.). 64p. (YA). (gr. 3 up). 2000. 14.99 (*0-7868-5312-3*) Disney Pr.

Berofsky, Adrienne. Disney Bakery Cookbook. 64p. (J). (gr. 1-5). 2000. 14.99 (*0-7868-3246-0*, Pub. by Disney Pr) Little.

— Disney's Cooking with Mickey & Friends. 96p. (YA). (gr. 3 up). 1999. 9.99 (*0-7868-3230-4*, Pub. by Disney Pr) Time Warner.

Berofsky, Bernard. Freedom from Necessity: The Metaphysical Basis of Responsibility. 224p. 1988. text 27.50 (*0-7102-0998-3*, Routledge Thoemms) Routledge.

— Liberation from Self: A Theory of Personal Autonomy. 284p. (C). 1995. text 69.95 (*0-521-48045-0*) Cambridge U Pr.

Beroggi, Giampiero E. Decision Modeling in Policy Management: An Introduction to the Analytic Concepts. LC 98-42966. xxiv, 349p. 1999. write for info. (*0-7923-8331-1*) Kluwer Academic.

***Beroggi, Giampiero E.** Safety Concepts in Land Use Engineering: The Case of Underground Infrastructures. (Research in Progress in systmes Engineering: 02). (Illus.). 100p. 1999. pap. 22.50 (*90-407-1810-5*, Pub. by Delft U Pr) Coronet Bks.

Beroggi, Giampiero E. & Wallace, William A. Operational Risk Management: The Integration of Decision, Communications & Multimedia Technologies. LC 98-23721. 1998. 125.00 (*0-7923-8178-5*) Kluwer Academic.

Beroggi, Giampiero E. & Wallace, William A., eds. Computer Supported Risk Management. LC 95-3067. (Topics in Safety Risk Reliability & Quality Ser.: Vol. 4). 384p. (C). 1995. text 206.00 (*0-7923-3372-1*) Kluwer Academic.

Berolzheimer, jt. auth. see Decker.

Berolzheimer, Alan R., jt. auth. see Decker, Douglas A.

Berolzheimer, Alan R., ed. see Webster, Daniel.

Berolzheimer, Fritz. World's Legal Philosophies. (Modern Legal Philosophy Ser.: Vol. 2). lv, 490p. 1998. reprint ed. 165.00 (*1-56169-381-2*) Gaunt.

Berolzheimer, Ruth, jt. ed. see Culinary Arts Institute Staff.

Beronius, George, ed. see Allen, Dodie & Andre, Bruce.

Berosh, Craig, jt. ed. see Whitmire, Robin M.

Beroul. The Romance of Tristan. Fredrick, Alan S., tr. (Classics Ser.). 176p. 1978. pap. 10.95 (*0-14-044230-8*, Penguin Classics) Viking Penguin.

Beroza, Morton, ed. Pest Management, Insect Sex Attractants & Other Behavior-Controlling Chemicals. LC 76-1873. (ACS Symposium Ser.: Vol. 23). 200p. 1976. reprint ed. pap. 62.00 (*0-608-03553-X*, 206427200008) Bks Demand.

— Pest Management with Insect Sex Attractants. LC 76-1873. (ACS Symposium Ser.: No. 23). 1976. 27.95 (*0-8412-0308-3*) Am Chemical.

Beroza, Morton, jt. auth. see Leonhardt, Barbara A.

Beroza, Morton, jt. ed. see Kydonieus, Agis F.

Berq, Richard A., jt. auth. see Franzen, Michael D.

Berque, Jacques. Arab Rebirth: Pain & Ecstasy. Hoare, Quintin, tr. from FRE. Orig. Title: Les Arabes. 138p. (Orig.). 1984. pap. 10.95 (*0-86356-015-6*) Evergreen Dist.

— Arab Rebirth: Pain & Ecstasy. Hoare, Quintin, tr. from FRE. Orig. Title: Les Arabes. 138p. (Orig.). 1984. 21.00 (*0-86356-105-5*, Pub. by Saqi) Intl Spec Bk.

Berquirt, Cindy. Minnesota State Government Spending. (Illus.). 20p. 1996. pap. 3.00 (*1-877889-14-8*) League Wmn Voters MN.

Berquist, Andrew, jt. auth. see Berquist, Kim.

Berquist, Carl, jt. auth. see Reeder, Curt.

Berquist, Charlene. Public Speaking Workbook. 224p. (C). 1995. spiral bd. 21.95 (*0-7872-1351-9*, 41135101) Kendall-Hunt.

***Berquist, Gilbert T., ed.** Florida Assessment of Coastal Trends (1995) (Illus.). 245p. 1999. reprint ed. pap. text 30.00 (*0-7881-7680-3*) DIANE Pub.

Berquist, Goodwin F., jt. ed. see Nelson, Sylvia.

Berquist, Jon L. Ancient Wine, New Wineskins: The Lord's Supper in Old Testament Perspective. 184p. (Orig.). 1991. pap. 13.95 (*0-8272-0019-6*) Chalice Pr.

***Berquist, Jon L.** Incarnation. LC 99-50543. (Understanding Biblical Themes Ser.). 168p. 2000. pap. 16.99 (*0-8272-3825-8*) Chalice Pr.

Berquist, Jon L. Judaism in Persia's Shadow: A Social & Historical Approach. LC 95-20934. 288p. 1995. 23.00 (*0-8006-2845-4*, 1-2845) Augsburg Fortress.

— Reclaiming Her Story: The Witness of Women in the Old Testament. 184p. (Orig.). 1992. pap. 14.99 (*0-8272-3212-8*) Chalice Pr.

— Surprises by the River: The Prophecy of Ezekiel. 168p. (Orig.). 1993. pap. 11.99 (*0-8272-3432-5*) Chalice Pr.

Berquist, Kim & Berquist, Andrew. Managing Information Highways: The Prism Book: Principles, Methods, & Case Studies for Designing Telecommunications Management Systems. LC 96-48513. (Lecture Notes in Computer Science Ser.: Vol. 1164). 417p. 1996. 68.00 (*3-540-62008-7*) Spr-Verlag.

Berquist, Laura. Designing Your Own Classical Curriculum. 3rd ed. LC 97-73398. 265p. 1998. pap. 14.95 (*0-89870-660-2*) Ignatius Pr.

— Harp & Laurel Wreath: Poetry & Dictation for the Classical Curriculum. LC 98-73638. 1999. pap. text 19.95 (*0-89870-716-1*) Ignatius Pr.

Berquist, Paul. Saguaro Cactus. LC 96-37097. (Habitats Ser.). (J). (gr. 2-5). 1997. lib. bdg. 24.00 (*0-516-20713-X*) Childrens.

— Saguaro Cactus. (Habitats Ser.). 1997. pap. 6.95 (*0-516-26065-0*) Childrens.

Berquist, Thomas H. Imaging of Orthopedic Trauma & Surgery. (Illus.). 799p. 1986. text 220.00 (*0-7216-1102-8*, W B Saunders Co) Harcrt Hlth Sci Grp.

Berquist, Thomas H. MRI of the Musculoskeletal System. 4th ed. 670p. text 170.00 (*0-7817-2574-7*) Lppncott W & W.

Berquist, Thomas H. Pocket Atlas of MRI Musculoskeletal Anatomy. LC 95-16479. (Illus.). 96p. 1995. pap. text 16.95 (*0-7817-0337-9*) Lppncott W & W.

***Berquist, Thomas H.** Radiology of the Foot & Ankle. 2nd ed. LC 99-30529. 602p. 1999. text 160.00 (*0-7817-2009-5*) Lppncott W & W.

Berquist, Thomas H., ed. Imaging Atlas of Orthopedic Appliances & Prostheses. LC 94-20580. (Illus.). 1008p. 1994. text 215.00 (*0-7817-0222-4*) Lppncott W & W.

— Imaging of Orthopedic Trauma. 2nd ed. 928p. 1991. text 159.00 (*0-88167-805-8*) Lppncott W & W.

— MRI of the Musculoskeletal System. 3rd ed. LC 95-31754. (Illus.). 864p. 1995. text 170.00 (*0-7817-0310-7*) Lppncott W & W.

— Radiology of the Foot & Ankle. (Illus.). 528p. 1989. text 179.00 (*0-88167-445-1*) Lppncott W & W.

Berquo, Elza & Xenos, Peter, eds. Family Systems & Cultural Change. LC 92-12428. (International Studies in Demography). (Illus.). 240p. 1993. text 59.00 (*0-19-828384-9*, Clarendon Pr) OUP.

Berr, B. Jubilations in Style: Late Intermediate Piano Solos. 24p. 1993. pap. 6.95 (*0-7935-2538-1*, 00290432) H Leonard.

Berr, Frieder, et al, eds. Future Perspectives in Gastroenterology: International Congress, Leipzig, June 1996. (Digestion Ser.: Vol. 58, Suppl. 1, 1997). iv, 116p. 1997. pap. 50.50 (*3-8055-6503-8*) S Karger.

Berra, P. Bruce, jt. ed. see Chen, C. Y.

Berra, P. Bruce, jt. ed. see Choudhary, Alok N.

Berra, P. Bruce, jt. ed. see Hariri, Salim.

Berra, Tim M. Evolution & the Myth of Creationism: A Basic Guide to the Facts in the Evolution Debate. LC 89-51484. (Illus.). 220p. 1990. pap. 9.95 (*0-8047-1770-2*) Stanford U Pr.

— A Natural History of Australia. LC 97-42820. (Illus.). 256p. (C). 1998. text 44.95 (*0-12-093155-9*) Morgan Kaufmann.

Berra, Yogi. The Yogi Book: I Really Didn't Say Everything I Said! LC 97-52802. (Illus.). 127p. 1998. pap. 7.95 (*0-7611-1090-9*) Workman Pub.

***Berra, Yogi.** The Yogi Book: I Really Didn't Say Everything I Said! (Illus.). 128p. 1999. 12.95 (*0-7611-1568-4*) Workman Pub.

Berra, Yogi & Horton, Tom. Yogi: It Ain't Over. (Illus.). 336p. 1997. mass mkt. 5.99 (*0-06-100012-4*, Harp PBks) HarpC.

***Berra, "Yogi" (Lawerence).** Yogi Berra's Baseball Book: The Game & How to Play It. Ross, Sayre, ed. (Illus.). 80p. 1999. pap. 10.95 (*0-87460-393-5*) Lion Bks.

Berrada, Mohamet. The Game of Forgetting. Boullata, Issa, tr. from ARA. (Modern Middle Eastern Literature in Translation Ser.). 150p. (Orig.). 1996. pap. 10.95 (*0-292-70845-9*) U of Tex Pr.

Berrang, George. Personal Inventory/Medical Alert Kit. 2nd rev. ed. i, 10p. 1997. ring bd. 29.95 (*0-9663990-0-5*) Ancora Pubns.

Berrange, Jevan P. The Geology of Southern Guyana, South America. 112p. 1978. 40.00 (*0-11-880771-4*, Pub. by Statnry Office) Balogh.

Berre, Aline Le, see Le Berre, Aline.

Berre, Francois Le, see Le Berre, Francois.

Berreby, David. Members Only. 2000. write for info. (*0-316-09030-1*) Little.

Berrell, Daniel J. Inside Nature's Pyramid. iv, 214p. 1998. pap. 10.95 (*0-9663897-0-0*) Barry Publ.

Berreman, Gerald D. Hindus of the Himalayas: Ethnography & Change. 2nd ed. (Illus.). 498p. 1997. pap. 15.95 (*0-19-564108-6*) OUP.

An Asterisk (*) at the beginning of an entry indicates that the title is appearing for the first time.

Berreman, J. V. Tribal Distribution in Oregon. LC 37-20181. (American Anthropological Association Memoirs Ser.). 1974. reprint ed. pap. 25.00 (*0-527-00546-0*) Periodicals Srv.

Berren, Michael R., jt. ed. see Beutler, Larry E.

Berrens, L. The Chemistry of Atopic Allergens. (Monographs in Allergy: Vol. 7). 1971. 81.00 (*3-8055-1150-7*) S Karger.

Berrens, Lubertus. Science Friction: Grins & Groans among the Titles of Scientific Studies. LC 95-4088. (Illus.). 92p. 1995. pap. 19.50 (*0-88937-146-6*) Hogrefe & Huber Pubs.

Berrenson, Marc. Bodily Harm. 224p. (Orig.). 1992. mass mkt. 4.50 (*0-380-76613-2*, Avon Bks) Morrow Avon.

— Kill All the Lawyers? 320p. 1994. mass mkt. 4.50 (*0-8217-4714-2*, Zebra Kensgtn) Kensgtn Pub Corp.

— L. A. Snitch. 256p. (Orig.). 1991. pap. 3.95 (*0-380-76324-9*, Avon Bks) Morrow Avon.

— Special Circumstances. 272p. (Orig.). 1991. pap. 3.50 (*0-380-76077-0*, Avon Bks) Morrow Avon.

— Transformation. 352p. 1993. mass mkt. 4.50 (*0-8217-4294-9*, Zebra Kensgtn) Kensgtn Pub Corp.

Berres, et al. The Deep Sea Adventure Series: Low Vocabulary, High Interest Level. large type ed. Incl. Danger Below. (*0-89064-093-9*); Frogmen in Action. 10.00 (*0-89064-248-6*); Pearl Divers. 10.00 (*0-89064-092-0*); Pearl Sic. Rocket Divers. (*0-89064-095-5*); Sea Hunt. Date not set. (*0-89064-249-4*); Submarine Rescue. 10.00 (*0-89064-250-8*); Treasure under the Sea. 10.00 (*0-89064-091-2*); Whale Hunt. 10.00 (*0-89064-094-7*); (J). (gr. 3-9). reprint ed. write for info. (*0-318-66042-3*) NAVH.

— Rocket Divers. (Deep Sea Adventure Ser.). 10.00 (*0-614-30521-7*) NAVH.

— Sea Hunt. (Deep Sea Adventure Ser.). 10.00 (*0-614-30522-5*) NAVH.

Berres, Michael, et al, eds. Creating Tomorrow's Schools Today: Stories of Inclusion, Change, & Renewal. LC 96-9093. (Special Education Ser.: Vol. 17). 216p. (C). 1996. text 46.00 (*0-8077-3550-7*); pap. text 21.95 (*0-8077-3549-3*) Tchrs Coll.

Berresford-Ellis, Peter. The Celtic Empire: The First Millennium of Celtic History c.1000 BC to 51 AD. LC 91-70474. (Illus.). 256p. 1991. 34.95 (*0-89089-457-4*) Carolina Acad Pr.

Beresford, Geoffrey. Applied Calculus. (C). 1996. pap., student ed. 17.16 (*0-395-74628-0*) HM.

— Applied Calculus. (C). 1996. pap. text, student ed. 22.36 (*0-395-74626-4*) HM.

— Applied Calculus. (C). 1996. pap., teacher ed., suppl. ed. 11.96 (*0-395-74627-2*) HM.

— Brief Applied Calculus. 608p. (C). 1996. text 73.56 (*0-395-70824-9*) HM.

Berressem, Hanjo. Lines of Desire: Reading Gombrowicz's Fiction with Lacan. LC 97-53227. 340p. 1998. 79.95 (*0-8101-1309-0*) Northwestern U Pr.

— Pynchon's Poetics: Interfacing Theory & Text. 288p. (C). 1993. text 37.50 (*0-252-01919-9*); pap. text 15.95 (*0-252-06248-5*) U of Ill Pr.

Berressem, Hanjo & Herzogenrath, Bernd, contrib. by. Near Encounters: Festschrift for Richard Martin. LC 96-150033. xiii, 310p. 1995. 57.95 (*3-631-48552-2*) P Lang Pubng.

Berret, Anthony J. Mark Twain & Shakespeare: A Cultural Legacy. 218p. (C). 1993. lib. bdg. 48.00 (*0-8191-9220-1*) U Pr of Amer.

***Bereteaga, Choly.** Nueva Cocina para la Mujer. (SPA.). 1999. pap. 21.50 (*84-241-2256-9*) Everest SP.

Bereth, David, ed. American Paintings: 1830-1915. LC 82-61415. (Illus.). 40p. (Orig.). 1982. pap. 3.00 (*0-940784-03-3*) Miami Univ Art.

— Harvey Breverman: Draftsman-Painter. LC 87-61749. (Works from 1977-1987 Ser.). (Illus.). 30p. (Orig.). 1987. pap. 10.00 (*0-940784-10-6*) Miami Univ Art.

Berrett, A. M., tr. see Chaliand, Gerard.

Berrett, A. M., tr. see Chaliand, Gerard & Rageau, Jean-Pierre.

Berrett, A. M., tr. see Gadant, Monique, ed.

Berrett, A. M., tr. see Mahjoub, Azzam, ed.

Berrett, A. M., tr. see Mince, Juliette.

Berrett, Jean, ed. The Head Nurse: Her Leadership Role. 468p. (C). 1987. 125.00 (*81-7002-054-9*, Pub. by Himalayan Bks) St Mut.

Berrett, Joshua & Bourgois, Louis G. The Musical World of J. J. Johnson. LC 99-10077. (Studies in Jazz: No. 35). (Illus.). 464p. 1999. text 65.00 (*0-8108-3648-3*) Scarecrow.

Berrett, LaMar C. & Ogden, D. Kelly. Discovering the World of the Bible. 1996. pap. 24.95 (*0-910523-52-5*) Grandin Bk Co.

Berrett, Lisa. Peekin Through the Past: Easy Scrapbook Pages. (Illus.). 40p. 1997. 8.99 (*1-58050-073-0*, 40-6117) Provo Craft.

— Peekin' Through the Past - Summer Fun. 1998. pap. 8.99 (*1-58050-050-1*, 40-6181) Provo Craft.

— Peekin Through the Past "Seasonal Ideas" 44p. 1997. 8.99 (*1-58050-022-6*, 40-6151) Provo Craft.

— Reekin Through the Past "Baby Days" (Illus.). 40p. 1997. 8.99 (*1-58050-021-8*, 40-6150) Provo Craft.

Berrett, Paul, tr. see Arias, Juan.

Berrettini, jt. auth. see Nurnberger, John I.

Berrey, Henry, jt. auth. see Olsen, Maryann.

Berri. Te-in Giro Per La Letteratura. (College Italian). (ITA.). (C). 1995. pap., teacher ed. 39.95 (*0-8384-4969-7*) Heinle & Heinle.

Berri, Kenneth, jt. auth. see Giansiracusa, Elizabeth.

Berrian, Brenda. Bibliography of African Women Writers & Journalists. LC 84-52276. (Illus.). 1985. 15.00 (*0-89410-226-5*, Three Contnts) L Rienner.

Berrian, Brenda & Broek, Aart. Bibliography of Women Writers from the Caribbean: 1831-1986. LC 86-51311. 361p. 1989. pap. 20.00 (*0-89410-601-5*, Three Contnts) L Rienner.

***Berrian, Brenda F.** Awakening Spaces. LC 99-55026. (Studies in Ethnomusicology). (Illus.). 216p. 1999. pap. text 16.00 (*0-226-04456-4*) U Ch Pr.

— Awakening Spaces: French Caribbean Popular Song, Music, & Culture. LC 99-55026. 1999. lib. bdg. 40.00 (*0-226-04455-6*) U Ch Pr.

Berriault, Gina. Afterwards: A Novel. LC 97-47736. 160p. Date not set. pap. 12.50 (*1-887178-74-0*, Pub. by Counterpt DC) HarpC.

***Berriault, Gina.** Great Petrowski: An Illustrated Fable. LC 99-87232. (Illus.). 96p. 2000. text 16.00 (*1-58243-074-8*, Pub. by Counterpt DC) HarpC.

Berriault, Gina. The Lights of Earth. LC 97-25630. 176p. 1997. pap. 12.50 (*1-887178-53-8*, Pub. by Counterpt DC) HarpC.

— The Son. 160p. Date not set. pap. 12.50 (*1-887178-75-9*, Pub. by Counterpt DC) HarpC.

— Women in Their Beds: New & Selected Stories. 352p. 1997. pap. text 17.95 (*1-887178-38-4*, Pub. by Counterpt DC) HarpC.

Berrichon, Paterne. La Vie de Jean-Arthur Rimbaud. LC 77-10252. (Symbolists Ser.). (FRE.). reprint ed. 49.50 (*0-404-16307-6*) AMS Pr.

Berrichon, Paterne, ed. see Rimbaud, Jean N.

***Berrick, A. J. & Keating, M. E.** Categories & Modules with K-Theory in View. LC 99-25756. (Cambridge Studies in Advanced Mathematics: Vol. 67). (Illus.). 360p. (C). 2000. 54.95 (*0-521-63276-5*) Cambridge U Pr.

— An Introduction to Rings & Modules: With K-Theory in View. LC 98-49424. (Cambridge Studies in Advanced Mathematics: No. 65). (Illus.). 288p. (C). 2000. 54.95 (*0-521-63274-9*) Cambridge U Pr.

Berrick, A. Jon, et al, eds. Geometry from the Pacific Rim: Proceedings of the Pacific Rim Geometry Conference Held at National University of Singapore, Republic of Singapore, December 12-17, 1994. LC 97-10529. ix, 431p. (C). 1997. text 158.95 (*3-11-014792-0*) De Gruyter.

Berrick, Jill D. Faces of Poverty: Portraits of Women & Children on Welfare. 224p. 1997. pap. 13.95 (*0-19-511375-6*) OUP.

Berrick, Jill D. & Gilbert, Neil. With the Best of Intentions: The Child Sexual Abuse Prevention Movement. LC 91-24680. 211p. 1991. lib. bdg. 30.00 (*0-89862-564-5*) Guilford Pubns.

Berrick, Jill D., et al. The Tender Years: Toward Developmentally-Sensitive Child Welfare Services for Very Young Children. (Child Welfare Ser.). (Illus.). 224p. (C). 1998. text 50.00 (*0-19-511452-3*); pap. text 21.95 (*0-19-511453-1*) OUP.

Berrick, Stephan. Crabs of Cape Cod. (Natural History Ser.: No. 3). (Illus.). 80p. 1986. pap. 6.95 (*0-916275-01-9*) Cape Cod Mus Nat His.

Berridale-Johnson, Michelle, jt. auth. see Jacobs, Gill.

***Berridge.** Touch & Go. 2000. pap. 9.95 (*0-552-99648-3*, Pub. by Transworld Publishers Ltd) Trafalgar.

Berridge, Celia. Hannah's New Boots. LC 92-14124. (Illus.). 24p. (J). (ps-1). 1993. 10.95 (*0-590-45888-4*) Scholastic Inc.

Berridge, David. Foster Care: A Research Review. LC 99-175613. 1997. write for info. (*0-11-321911-3*) Statnry Office.

Berridge, David & Brodie, Isabelle. Children's Home Revisited. LC 98-151324. 200p. 1998. pap. 28.95 (*1-85302-565-8*, Pub. by Jessica Kingsley) Taylor & Francis.

Berridge, David, et al. Social Work & Assessment with Adolescents. 334p. 1996. pap. 38.50 (*1-874579-56-3*, Pub. by Natl Childrens Bur) Paul & Co Pubs.

Berridge, David, jt. auth. see Grimshaw, Roger.

Berridge, David, jt. auth. see Smith, Peter M.

Berridge, Edward. The Lives of the Saints. 160p. 1995. pap. 14.95 (*0-7022-2749-8*, Pub. by Univ Queensland Pr) Intl Spec Bk.

***Berridge, Geoffrey, et al.** A Dictionary of Diplomacy. LC 00-40511. 2000. write for info. (*0-333-76496-X*, Pub. by Macmillan) St Martin.

Berridge, Geoffrey R. The Politics of the South Africa Run: European Shipping & Pretoria. LC 87-1600. (Illus.). 268p. 1987. 59.00 (*0-19-827484-X*) OUP.

— South Africa, the Colonial Powers & "African Defence" The Rise & Fall of the White Entente, 1948-60. LC 92-18426. 1993. text 59.95 (*0-312-08592-3*) St Martin.

Berridge, John C. Techniques for the Automated Optimization of HPLC Separations. fac. ed. LC 85-12485. (Illus.). 215p. 1985. pap. 66.70 (*0-7837-7664-0*, 204741700007) Bks Demand.

Berridge, Mary, photos by. A Positive Life: Portraits of Women Living with HIV. LC 96-72481. (Illus.). 128p. 1997. 27.50 (*0-7624-0198-2*) Running Pr.

Berridge, Mavis E., ed. see International Symposium on Adapted Physical Activi.

***Berridge, N. G.** Geology of the Grantham District. (British Geological Survey Ser.). (Illus.). ix, 133p. 1999. 90.00 (*0-11-884530-6*, Pub. by Statnry Office) Balogh.

Berridge, Virginia. AIDS in the U. K. The Making of a Policy, 1981-1994. LC 95-38985. (Illus.). 404p. (C). 1996. text 80.00 (*0-19-820472-8*); pap. text 24.95 (*0-19-820473-6*) OUP.

— Health & Society in Britain since 1939. LC 98-43280. (New Studies in Economic & Social History: No. 38). (Illus.). 110p. (C). 1999. pap. 13.95 (*0-521-57641-5*); text 39.95 (*0-521-57230-4*) Cambridge U Pr.

— Opium & the People: Opiate Use & Policy in 19th- & Early 20th-Century Britain. rev. ed. 370p. 1998. 65.00 (*1-85343-413-2*, Pub. by Free Assoc Bks); pap. 25.00 (*1-85343-414-0*, Pub. by Free Assoc Bks) NYU Pr.

Berridge, William A., et al. Purchasing Power of the Consumer: A Statistical Index. LC 75-39232. (Getting & Spending: The Consumer's Dilemma Ser.). (Illus.). 1976. reprint ed. 29.95 (*0-405-08009-3*) Ayer.

Berrie. Tropical Plant Science. 1988. pap. text. write for info. (*0-582-64705-3*, Pub. by Addison-Wesley) Longman.

Berrie, Barbara H., et al. Conservation Research 1996/1997. LC 72-600309. (Studies in the History of Art Ser.: Vol. 57). (Illus.). 194p. 1997. pap. 35.00 (*0-89468-264-4*) Natl Gallery Art.

Berrie, T. W. Electricity Economics & Planning. (Power Ser.: No. 16). 312p. 1992. text 85.00 (*0-86341-282-3*) INSPEC Inc.

Berriedale-Johnson, Michele. Diabetic Cookbook. 1998. pap. text 12.95 (*1-85967-669-3*, Lorenz Bks) Anness Pub.

Berriedale-Johnson, Michelle. Low-Salt Cookbook. (Healthy Eating Library). 1999. pap. 12.95 (*0-7548-0184-5*, Lorenz Bks) Anness Pub.

— The Victorian Cookbook. LC 89-7598. (Illus.). 160p. 1989. 24.95 (*0-940793-38-5*) Interlink Pub.

Berrien, Allen. The Boat Doctor. LC 98-30010. (Boating Magazine Book Ser.). (Illus.). 144p. 1998. pap. 16.95 (*0-07-006667-1*) Intl Marine.

— Hearst Marine Books Practical Small Powerboat Maintenance. LC 94-22837. (Illus.). 1995. pap. 15.00 (*0-688-13172-7*, Wm Morrow) Morrow Avon.

Berrien, Kenneth, jt. ed. see Indik, Bernard P.

Berrien, William, jt. auth. see De Moraes, Borba.

Berrier, Mark D., Jr. The Bible for Busy People. LC 93-36082. 130p. (Orig.). 1993. pap. 8.95 (*1-55622-032-4*, Seaside Pr) Wordware Pub.

Berrigan, Anselm. Integrity & Dramatic Life. 64p. 1999. pap. 10.00 (*1-890311-05-7*, Pub. by Edge Bks) SPD-Small Pr Dist.

— They Beat Me over the Head with a Sack. 14p. 1998. 5.00 (*1-890311-03-0*) Edge Bks.

Berrigan, Daniel. And the Risen Bread: Selected & New Poems, 1957-1997. LC 98-12691. xx, 417p. 1998. 37.50 (*0-8232-1821-X*); pap. 17.95 (*0-8232-1822-8*) Fordham.

— Beside the Sea of Glass: The Song of the Lamb. (Classic Prayer Ser.). (Illus.). 112p. 1984. 4.95 (*0-8164-2174-9*) Harper SF.

— Block Island. 100p. 1984. pap. 14.95 (*0-87775-176-5*) Unicorn Pr.

***Berrigan, Daniel.** The Bride: Images of the Church. LC 99-55608. (Illus.). 128p. 2000. pap. 22.00 (*1-57075-305-9*) Orbis Bks.

Berrigan, Daniel. Daniel: Under the Siege of the Divine. LC 98-14517. (Illus.). 231p. 1998. 15.00 (*0-87486-952-8*) Plough.

— Ezekiel: Vision in the Dust. LC 97-24654. (Illus.). 144p. (Orig.). 1997. pap. 16.00 (*1-57075-135-8*) Orbis Bks.

— Homage to Gerard Manley Hopkins. 60p. pap. 9.95 (*1-879175-13-4*) Fortkamp.

— Isaiah: Spirit of Courage, Gift of Tears. 160p. 1996. 20.00 (*0-8006-2998-1*, 1-2998, Fortress Pr) Augsburg Fortress.

— Jeremiah: The World, the Wound of God. LC 98-27712. 160p. 1998. 18.00 (*0-8006-3138-2*, 1-3138) Augsburg Fortress.

***Berrigan, Daniel.** Job: And Death No Dominion. 256p. 2000. 24.95 (*1-58051-074-4*) Sheed & Ward WI.

Berrigan, Daniel. May All Creatures Live. (Illus.). 105p. 1984. 100.00 (*0-933861-05-2*) H Berliner.

— Minor Prophets, Major Themes. 400p. 1995. pap. 19.95 (*1-879175-17-7*) Fortkamp.

— The Nightmare of God. LC 81-51877. (Sunburst Originals Ser.: No. 9). (Illus.). 144p. (Orig.). 1983. pap. 6.00 (*0-934648-08-5*) Sunburst Pr.

— Prison Poems. LC 73-76683. 124p. 1982. pap. 14.95 (*0-87775-149-8*) Unicorn Pr.

— Sorrow Built a Bridge: Friendship & AIDS. 231p. (Orig.). 1989. pap. 14.95 (*1-879175-04-5*) Fortkamp.

— Tulips in the Prison Yard. 80p. pap. 9.95 (*1-873790-24-4*) Fortkamp.

— Uncommon Prayer: A Book of Psalms. rev. ed. LC 98-36585. (Illus.). 160p. 1998. pap. 14.00 (*1-57075-193-5*) Orbis Bks.

— We Die Before We Live: Talking with the Very Ill. 160p. 1984. 11.95 (*0-8164-0462-3*) Harper SF.

— Whereon to Stand: The Acts of the Apostles & Ourselves. 300p. (Orig.). (C). 1991. pap. 17.95 (*1-879175-08-8*) Fortkamp.

Berrigan, Daniel, et al. The Time's Discipline: The Eight Beatitudes & Nuclear Resistance. (Illus.). 286p. (Orig.). 1989. pap. 14.95 (*1-879175-02-9*) Fortkamp.

Berrigan, Daniel, jt. auth. see Hanh, Thich Nhat.

Berrigan, Edmund. Disarming Matter. 82p. 1999. pap. 12.50 (*0-9669430-0-7*, Pub. by Owl Pr CA) SPD-Small Pr Dist.

Berrigan, Joseph R., Jr., jt. auth. see White, D. S.

Berrigan, Joseph R., ed. & tr. see Patavino, Rolandino.

Berrigan, Joseph R., tr. see Aesop.

***Berrigan, Philip & Crane, Susan.** Disciples & Dissidents: The Prison Writings of the Prince of Peace Plowshares. Wilcox, Fred, ed. 200p. 2000. 25.95 (*1-884540-52-X*) Haleys.

Berrigan, Philip & Wilcox, Fred A. Fighting the Lamb's War: The Autobiography of Philip Berrigan. LC 96-7940. 232p. 1996. pap. 15.00 (*1-56751-100-7*); lib. bdg. 29.95 (*1-56751-101-5*) Common Courage.

Berrigan, Sandy. Summer Sleeper. 43p. 1981. pap. 4.00 (*0-916382-24-9*) Telephone Bks.

Berrigan, Ted. A Certain Slant of Sunlight. LC 88-90556. 112p. 1988. pap. 9.00 (*0-929022-00-9*) O Bks.

— Red Wagon. LC 76-26054. 1976. 7.95 (*0-916328-05-8*); pap. 3.00 (*0-916328-01-5*) Yellow Pr.

— Red Wagon. deluxe ed. LC 76-26054. 1976. 15.00 (*0-685-93040-8*) Yellow Pr.

***Berrigan, Ted.** The Sonnets. LC 00-27865. 2000. 16.00 (*0-14-058927-9*, Penguin Bks) Viking Penguin.

Berrigan, Ted. Talking in Tranquility: Interviews with Ted Berrigan. Scalapino, Leslie, ed. LC 91-71934. 208p. (C). 1991. pap. text 10.50 (*0-939691-05-1*) Avenue B.

— Talking in Tranquility: Interviews with Ted Berrigan. LC 91-71934. 208p. 1991. 10.50 (*0-614-00634-1*) O Bks.

— Train Ride. 48p. (Orig.). 1978. pap. 6.00 (*0-931428-21-1*) Vehicle Edns.

Berrill, Deborah & Tarr, Marcia, eds. Perspectives on Written Argument. LC 96-24443. (Written Language Ser.). 288p. (Orig.). (C). 1996. text 62.50 (*1-57273-038-2*); pap. text 26.50 (*1-57273-039-0*) Hampton Pr NJ.

Berrill, Deborah, jt. auth. see Berrill, Michael.

Berrill, Jack. The Best of Gil Thorp, Vol. 2. Shaughnessy, Matt, ed. (Illus.). 256p. (Orig.). 1988. pap. 16.95 (*0-930099-03-6*) Take Five Pubs.

— Best of Gil Thorp Vol. 3, Vol. 3. 256p. 1989. pap. 19.95 (*0-930099-04-4*) Take Five Pubs.

— Fired Up! A Gil Thorp Collection. (Illus.). 300p. (Orig.). 1998. write for info. (*0-930099-13-3*); pap. 29.95 (*0-930099-12-5*) Take Five Pubs.

— Rockin' the Armory: A Gil Thorp Collection. 256p. 1995. pap. 19.95 (*0-930099-10-9*) Take Five Pubs.

— Sheesh: A Gil Thorp Collection. 256p. 1991. pap. 19.95 (*0-930099-07-9*) Take Five Pubs.

— Victory in the Valley: A Gil Thorp Collection. (Illus.). 256p. (Orig.). 1997. pap. 21.95 (*0-930099-11-7*) Take Five Pubs.

— Waxing Nostalgic: A Gil Thorp Collection. 256p. 1993. pap. 19.95 (*0-930099-09-5*) Take Five Pubs.

Berrill, Jacquelyn, jt. auth. see Berrill, N. J.

Berrill, Kevin T., jt. auth. see Herek, Gregory M.

Berrill, Michael. The Plundered Seas. LC 97-6192. 1997. 22.50 (*0-87156-945-0*, Pub. by Sierra) Random.

Berrill, Michael & Berrill, Deborah. A Sierra Club Naturalist's Guide to the North Atlantic Coast: Cape Cod to Newfoundland. LC 80-23086. (Naturalist's Guides Ser.). (Illus.). 512p. 1982. pap. 16.00 (*0-87156-243-X*, Pub. by Sierra) Random.

Berrill, N. J. & Berrill, Jacquelyn. One Thousand & One Questions Answered about the Seashore. LC 76-12889. (One Thousand & One Questions Ser.). (Illus.). 305p. 1976. reprint ed. pap. 8.95 (*0-486-23366-9*) Dover.

Berrill, Philip. Everyone's Guide to Oil Painting. 64p. 1996. pap. text 5.95 (*1-85304-832-1*, Pub. by Ravette Bks) Assoc Pubs Grp.

— Everyone's Guide to Pastel Painting. 64p. 1996. pap. text 5.95 (*1-85304-831-3*, Pub. by Ravette Bks) Assoc Pubs Grp.

— Everyone's Guide to Sketching. 64p. 1996. pap. text 5.95 (*1-85304-829-1*, Pub. by Ravette Bks) Assoc Pubs Grp.

— Everyone's Guide to Watercolor Painting. 64p. 1996. pap. text 5.95 (*1-85304-830-5*, Pub. by Ravette Bks) Assoc Pubs Grp.

Berriman, A. E., Jr., et al. Industrial Administration: A Series of Lectures. Chandler, Alfred D., ed. LC 79-7546. (History of Management Thought & Practice Ser.). 1980. reprint ed. lib. bdg. 23.95 (*0-405-12330-2*) Ayer.

Berriman, Algernon E. Historical Meteorology. LC 70-91753. 224p. 1970. reprint ed. lib. bdg. 35.00 (*0-8371-2424-7*, BEHM, Greenwood Pr) Greenwood.

Berrin, Kathleen, ed. The Spirit of Ancient Peru: Treasures from the Musco Arqueologico Rafael Larco Herrera. LC 97-60322. (Illus.). 216p. 1997. 45.00 (*0-500-01802-2*, Pub. by Thames Hudson) Norton.

Berrin, Kathleen & Seligman, Thomas K. The Bay Area Collects: Art from Africa, Oceania, & the Americas. LC 82-71433. (Illus.). 112p. 1982. pap. 7.95 (*0-88401-040-6*) Fine Arts Mus.

Berrin, Kathleen, jt. auth. see Siroto, Leon.

Berrin, Susan, Celebrating the New Moon: A Rosh Chodesh Anthology. 376p. 1998. pap. 44.00 (*0-7657-6022-3*) Aronson.

***Berrin, Susan.** Living Words: Best High Holiday Sermons of 5759. 1999. pap. 14.95 (*0-9664306-1-1*) JFL Bks.

Berrin, Susan, ed. A Heart of Wisdom: Making the Jewish Journey from Midlife through the Elder Years. LC 97-25581. 384p. 1997. 24.95 (*1-879045-73-7*) Jewish Lights.

— A Heart of Wisdom: Making the Jewish Journey from Midlife through the Elder Years. LC 97-25581. 384p. 1999. pap. 18.95 (*1-58023-051-2*) Jewish Lights.

Berring, Robert, jt. ed. see Woxland, Thomas.

Berring, Robert C. Finding the Law. 10th ed. (American Casebook Ser.). 331p. (C). 1995. pap. text 21.00 (*0-314-06084-7*) West Pub.

***Berring, Robert C.** Finding the Law. 11th ed. 1999. pap. 25.50 (*0-314-23216-8*) West Pub.

***Berring, Robert C., intro.** Bluebook: A Sixty-Five Year Retrospective with Introduction by Robert Berring. LC 98-87425. 1998. 195.00 (*1-57588-525-5*) W S Hein.

Berring, Robert C., jt. auth. see Olson, Kent C.

Berringer, Jan, jt. auth. see Lindsay, Art.

Berrington, Hugh, ed. Britain in the Nineties: The Politics of Paradox. LC 98-16038. 240p. 1998. 54.50 (*0-7146-4880-9*, Pub. by F Cass Pubs); pap. 22.50 (*0-7146-4434-X*, Pub. by F Cass Pubs) Intl Spec Bk.

Berrington, Hugh B., ed. Change in British Politics. (Illus.). 248p. 1984. 32.50 (*0-7146-3243-0*, BHA-03243, Pub. by F Cass Pubs) Intl Spec Bk.

Berrington, K. A., jt. ed. see Burke, P. G.

Berrington, Patricia. The Famous Rose Callahan. LC 97-91989. 485p. 1997. lthr. 27.95 (*0-9658379-0-4*) Silver Rose Prodns.

***Berrino, F., et al, eds.** Eurocare 2: Survival of Cancer Patients in Europe in the Late Eighties. (IARC Scientific Publications: 151). 450p. 2000. pap. text 69.00 (*92-832-2151-6*) OUP.

Berrino, F., ed. see International Agency for Research on Cancer Staff.

B

An Asterisk (*) at the beginning of an entry indicates that the title is appearing for the first time.

Berrios, Angel. Biologia Animal: Manual de Laboratorio. 195p. (C). 1994. 24.95 (*1-881375-19-6*) Libreria Univ.

Berrios, Angel, jt. auth. see De Figueroa, Yesmin A.

Berrios, German E. The History of Mental Symptoms: Descriptive Psychopathology since the Nineteenth Century. (Illus.). 581p. (C). 1996. text 180.00 (*0-521-43135-2*); pap. text 69.95 (*0-521-43736-9*) Cambridge U Pr.

Berrios, German E. & Freeman, Hugh, eds. 150 Years of British Psychiatry Vol. II: The Aftermath. LC 96-209910. 650p. 1996. 90.00 (*0-485-11506-9*, Pub. by Athlone Pr) Humanities.

— One Hundred Fifty Years of British Psychiatry, 1841-1991. LC RC0450.G7A15. 480p. 1991. reprint ed. pap. 148.80 (*0-608-01822-8*, 206247100003) Bks Demand.

***Berrios, German E. & Hodges, John R., eds.** Memory Disorders in Psychiatric Practice. (Illus.). 512p. (C). 2000. pap. 64.95 (*0-521-57671-7*) Cambridge U Pr.

***Berrios, German E. & Porter, Roy.** A History of Clinical Psychiatry: The Origin & History of Psychiatric Disorders. LC 98-52022. 15p. 1999. pap. 39.95 (*0-485-24211-7*, Pub. by Athlone Pr) Transaction Pubs.

Berrios, German E. & Porter, Roy, eds. The History of Clinical Psychiatry: The Origin & History of Psychiatric Diseases. 480p. (C). 1995. text 65.00 (*0-8147-1259-2*) NYU Pr.

Berrios, J., jt. auth. see Sahai, H.

Berrios, Luz, tr. see Arnold, Johann C.

Berrios, Miquel, ed. Methods in Cell Biology Vol. 53: Nuclear Structure & Function. (Illus.). 625p. 1997. pap. 64.95 (*0-12-093170-2*); text 99.95 (*0-12-564155-9*) Morgan Kaufmann.

Berrios-Ortiz, A. & Selandev, R. B. Skeletal Musculature in Larval Phases of the Beetle Epicauta Segmenta, (Coleoptera, Meloidae) (Entomologica Ser.: Vol. 16). (Illus.). 1979. text 85.50 (*90-6193-126-6*) Kluwer Academic.

Berrios-Ortiz, Luis. Abastos de Alimentos Para el Hogar. LC 82-2773. (Illus.). ix, 119p. (Orig.). (C). 1982. pap. 5.00 (*0-8477-2778-5*) U of PR Pr.

***Berrios, Ruben.** Contracting for Development: The Role of For-profit Contractors in U.S. Foreign Development Assistance. LC 99-34114. 184p. 2000. 55.00 (*0-275-96633-X*) Greenwood.

Berris, Anthony, tr. see Lavie, Peretz.

Berris, Anthony, tr. see Oved, Yaacov.

Berrisford, Carl T., tr. see Bartra, Roger.

Berrisford, Julia, ed. see Gould, Harvey & Tobochnik, Jan.

Berrisford, Julia, ed. see Minitab Inc. Staff.

Berrisford, Julia, ed. see Morgan, Larry A.

Berrisford, Julia, ed. see Triola, Mario F.

Berrisford, Julia, ed. see Weiss, Neil A.

Berrisford, Julie, ed. see Knight, Randall D.

Berrisford, Julie, ed. see Morrison, David & Owen, Tobias C.

Berrisford, Julie, ed. see Weiss, Neil A.

Berrisford, Julie, ed. see Young, Hugh D. & Freedman.

***Berrizbeitia, Anita & Pollak, Linda.** Inside Outside: Between Architecture & Landscape. 192p. 1999. 50.00 (*1-56496-631-3*, Pub. by Rockport Pubs) F & W Pubns Inc.

Berrnard, Thomas N., jt. auth. see Kirkaldy-Willis, William H.

***Berrner, Karina.** Brush Strokes: A Personal Journey to Peace of Mind. Jacobs, Pamela D. & Murray, Maggie, eds. LC 99-67462. (Illus.). 148p. 2000. pap. 11.95 (*1-885003-28-5*, Pub. by R D Reed Pubs) Midpt Trade.

Berroeta, Isabelle. Indigo Blue. 72p. (C). 1989. 40.00 (*0-7212-0764-2*, Pub. by Regency Pr GBR) St Mut.

Berrol, Selma C. East Side - East End: Eastern European Jews in London & New York, 1870-1920. LC 93-34037. 176p. 1994. 52.95 (*0-275-94772-6*, Praeger Pubs) Greenwood.

— The Empire City: New York & Its People, 1624-1995. LC 96-27455. 200p. 1997. 49.95 (*0-275-95795-0*, Praeger Pubs) Greenwood.

***Berrol, Selma C.** The Empire City: New York & its People, 1624-1996. LC 96-27455. 200p. 2000. pap. 22.95 (*0-275-96935-5*, Praeger Pubs) Greenwood.

Berrol, Selma C. Getting Down to Business: Baruch College in the City of New York, 1847-1987. 32. LC 88-25065. (Contributions to the Study of Education Ser.: No. 32). 568p. 1989. 65.00 (*0-313-26401-5*, BGD/, Greenwood Pr) Greenwood.

— Growing up in America: Immigrant Children in America, Then & Now. LC 94-24563. (History of American Childhood Ser.). 1995. 33.00 (*0-8057-4103-8*, Twyne); pap. 20.00 (*0-8057-4104-6*, Twyne) Mac Lib Ref.

— Immigrants at School: New York City, Eighteen Ninety-Eight to Nineteen Fourteen. Cordasco, Francesco, ed. LC 77-90872. (Bilingual-Bicultural Education in the U. S. Ser.). 1978. lib. bdg. 44.95 (*0-405-11077-4*) Ayer.

— Julia Richman: A Notable Woman. LC 91-58936. (Illus.). 160p. 1993. 29.50 (*0-944190-12-X*) Balch IES Pr.

Berrones, Sofia. Youth Ministry . . . Finding Your Way: Catholic Youth Ministry, Youth Ministry Training. (Illus.). 56p. (Orig.). 1987. pap. text. write for info. (*0-942417-00-3*) Mission Catechists.

Berrong, Richard M. Every Man for Himself: Social Order & Its Dissolution in Rabelais. (Stanford French & Italian Studies: Vol. 38). 160p. 1985. pap. 56.50 (*0-915838-56-7*) Anma Libri.

— Grammar & Translation for the Italian Libretto. 330p. (Orig.). 1996. pap. 24.95 (*1-885064-02-0*) Excalibur Pub.

— Rabelais & Bakhtin: Popular Culture in "Gargantua & Pantagruel" LC 85-21773. xiv, 156p. 1986. text 45.00 (*0-8032-1191-0*) U of Nebr Pr.

Berrong, Richard M., ed. The Politics of Opera in Turn-of-the-Century Italy: As Seen Through the Letters of Alfredo Catalani. LC 92-40031. (Studies in the History & Interpretation of Music: Vol. 38). 160p. 1993. text 69.95 (*0-7734-9230-5*) E Mellen.

Berrueto, Eliseo M. El Presidencialismo Mexicano (The Mexican Presidentialism) (SPA.). 299p. 1996. pap. 14.99 (*968-16-4967-2*, Pub. by Fondo) Continental Bk.

Berry. Activities for Database Pathways Series. 1997. pap. 13.95 (*0-538-72031-X*) Thomson Learn.

— Activities for Integrated Software: Pathways Series. 1997. pap. 13.95 (*0-538-72033-6*) Thomson Learn.

— Activities for Prsnt Graphics: Pathways Series. 1997. pap. 13.95 (*0-538-72032-8*) Thomson Learn.

— Activities for Spreadsheet Pathways Series. 1997. pap. 13.95 (*0-538-72030-1*) Thomson Learn.

— Activities for Word Processing: Pathways Series. 1997. pap. 13.95 (*0-538-72029-8*) Thomson Learn.

Berry. Building Better Computer Skills. 1997. pap. 20.95 (*0-538-71824-2*) S-W Pub.

— The Environmental Law & Compliance Handbook. 700p. 2000. 89.95 (*0-07-134094-7*) McGraw-Hill Prof.

— Introduction to Astronomical Image Processing. 1991. pap. 29.95 (*0-943396-32-8*) Willmann-Bell.

— Introduction to Non-Linear Systems. (Mathematics Ser.). 224p. 1997. pap. text 15.95 (*0-340-67700-7*, VNR) Wiley.

— Managing Investments. (C). 1990. pap. text, teacher ed. 27.50 (*0-03-022039-4*) Harcourt Coll Pubs.

— Managing Investments. 2nd ed. (C). 1996. pap. text. write for info. (*0-03-075486-0*) Harcourt Coll Pubs.

— Mastering Data Mining. 240p. (C). 1999. pap. 44.99 (*0-471-33123-6*) Wiley.

— Mathematical Modelling Methodology, Models & Micros. (Mathematics & Its Applications Ser.). 350p. 1986. text 97.95 (*0-470-20717-5*) P-H.

***Berry.** Pathways: Internet Projects. 2000. pap. 17.95 (*0-538-72430-7*) Sth-Wstrn College.

— Pathways: Internet Projects, Core. (Computer Applications Ser.). 2000. pap., student ed. 21.95 (*0-538-72423-4*) Sth-Wstrn College.

Berry. Statistics: A Bayestian Perspective. (Statistics Ser.). 1995. pap., teacher ed. 54.50 (*0-534-23473-9*) PWS Pubs.

Berry & Lindgren. Statistics: Theory & Methods. 2nd ed. 1995. mass mkt. 28.00 (*0-534-50480-9*) Brooks-Cole.

Berry & Stickel. Leadership for Collaborative Schools. 140p. (C). 1997. per. 23.95 (*0-7872-3941-0*, 41394101) Kendall-Hunt.

Berry, et al. APL & Insight. (Orig.). 1978. pap. 6.50 (*0-917326-08-3*) APL Pr.

Berry, Elanor. Mcarandy Was Hanged Under Tyburn Tree. LC 98-105686. 254p. 1997. 0.00 (*0-7223-3120-7*) A H Stockwell.

Berry, James W., et al. Chemical Villains: A Biology of Pollution. LC 73-11099. vii, 189p. 1974. write for info. (*0-8016-0663-2*) Mosby Inc.

Berry, A. J., et al, eds. Management & Control Theory. LC 97-45889. (History of Management Thought Ser.). 497p. 1998. text 179.95 (*1-84014-013-5*, Pub. by Ashgate Pub) Ashgate Pub Co.

Berry, Adrian. Galileo & the Dolphins: Amazing but True Stories from Science. LC 97-1012. (Illus.). 288p. 1997. 19.95 (*0-471-18365-2*) Wiley.

— Life in the Coming Millennium. LC 99-11772. 1999. 7.99 (*0-517-20374-X*) Random Hse Value.

Berry, Adrian, ed. The Book of Scientific Anecdotes. LC 92-44255. (Illus.). 239p. (C). 1993. reprint ed. 34.95 (*0-87975-806-6*); reprint ed. pap. 16.95 (*0-87975-836-8*) Prometheus Bks.

***Berry, Aidan.** Financial Accounting. 2nd ed. (ITBP Acquisitions Ser.). 1999. pap. 21.99 (*1-86152-479-X*) Thomson Learn.

Berry, Aidan. Financial Accounting: An Introduction. (Illus.). 136p. 1995. pap. text, teacher ed. 43.00 (*0-412-54580-2*, Chap & Hall NY) Chapman & Hall.

Berry, Aidan & Jarvis, Robin. Accounting in a Business Context: Teachers' Guide. 2nd ed. 208p. (C). (gr. 13). 1994. pap. text 52.00 (*0-412-58750-5*, Chap & Hall NY) Chapman & Hall.

Berry, Aidan, et al. Bank Lending: Beyond the Theory. LC 93-18868. 1993. write for info. (*0-412-47310-0*) Chapman & Hall.

Berry, Aiden & Jarvis, Robin. Accounting in a Business Context. 3rd ed. 448p. 1997. pap. 20.99 (*1-86152-090-5*) Thomson Learn.

Berry, Alana. Go Bananas! Cookbook. (Illus.). 102p. 1992. pap. 7.95 (*0-9634985-7-6*) Runaway Pr.

— Go Bananas! Cookbook. (Illus.). 128p. 1995. 10.95 (*0-9634985-8-4*) Runaway Pr.

— Know Your Spices: An Alphabetical Guide to Your Spice Rack. (Illus.). 64p. 1995. 4.95 (*0-9634985-6-8*) Runaway Pr.

Berry, Albert. Essays on Industrialization in Colombia. LC 83-5175. 329p. (C). 1983. 37.95 (*0-87918-053-6*) ASU Lat Am St.

Berry, Albert, ed. Poverty, Economic Reform, & Income Distribution in Latin America. LC 97-22276. (Critical Perspectives LA Ser.). 278p. 1998. lib. bdg. 58.00 (*1-55587-746-X*) L Rienner.

Berry, Albert R. & Cline, William R. Agrarian Structure & Productivity in Developing Countries. LC 78-20524. 1979. text 45.00 (*0-8018-2190-8*) Johns Hopkins.

***Berry, Alice Fiola.** The Charm of Catastrophe: A Study of Rabelais's Quart Livre. 168p. 2001. pap. text 30.00 (*0-8078-9271-8*) U of NC Pr.

***Berry, Andrew.** Biodiversity & Climate Change: Conservation in the Face of Uncertainty. (Illus.). 32p. 2000. pap. write for info. (*1-930465-08-4*) Ctr Biodiv & Conserv.

Berry, Arnold & Brasfield, Barry. Anesthesiology. (House Officer Ser.). (Illus.). 512p. 1995. pap. text 21.95 (*0-683-01018-2*) Lppncott W & W.

Berry, Arthur. The Little Gold-Mine. 1990. 45.00 (*0-9511427-7-1*, Pub. by Bullfinch Pubns) St Mut.

Berry, B. W., et al. Meat Freezing: A Source Book. (Developments in Food Science Ser.: No. 20). viii,386p. 1989. 218.50 (*0-444-87463-1*) Elsevier.

Berry, Barbara S. Mama's Garden. (Illus.). 195p. 1998. 25.00 (*1-887905-10-3*) Pkway Pubs.

Berry, Benny J. Gambling's Greatest Secrets Revealed. 102p. 1997. per. 29.95 (*0-9642984-0-6*) Prosper Pubg.

Berry, Bertice. Bertice: The World According to Me. 288p. 1996. 20.50 (*0-684-81457-9*) S&S Trade.

— Bertice: The World According to Me. LC 96-54610. 256p. 1997. per. 11.00 (*0-684-83140-6*, Fireside) S&S Trade Pap.

***Berry, Bertice.** The Haunting of Hip Hop. 2001. 21.95 (*0-385-49845-4*) Doubleday.

— Redemption Song. LC 99-55781. 181p. 2000. 19.95 (*0-385-49844-6*) Doubleday.

Berry, Bertice. You Still Ghetto. LC 98-170602. 128p. 1997. pap. 7.95 (*0-312-18236-8*) St Martin.

Berry, Bertice & Coker, Joan. Sckraight from the Ghetto: You Know You're Ghetto If . . . LC 96-37232. 1996. pap. 8.95 (*0-312-15448-8*) St Martin.

Berry, Bertrice. Daily Ghetto Medowtations: Affirmations for the Ghetto in You. 1999. pap. 9.95 (*1-890194-04-2*) Pines One.

Berry, Bob. Carving & Painting Trout. (Illus.). 96p. 1998. pap. 19.95 (*0-8117-2702-5*) Stackpole.

— Fish Carving: An Introduction: 2nd Revised ed. LC 98-45189. 1999. pap. 19.95 (*0-8117-2767-X*) Stackpole.

Berry, Bonnie. Social Rage: Emotion & Cultural Conflict. LC 99-15566. (Sociology/Psychology/Reference Ser.). 296p. 1999. 65.00 (*0-8153-3089-8*, SS1187) Garland.

Berry, Boyd M. Process of Speech: Puritan Religious Writing & Paradise Lost. LC 75-36933. 320p. reprint ed. pap. 99.20 (*0-608-14661-7*, 202583000046) Bks Demand.

Berry-Bravo, Judy. Texts & Contexts in Idea Vilarino's Poetry. LC 93-86774. (Illus.). 270p. (C). 1994. 32.00 (*0-938972-21-9*) Spanish Lit Pubns.

***Berry, Brian J. L.** John Littleton of Accomack County, Virginia, His Family & Descendants. 94p. 2000. 28.00 (*0-7404-0564-0*); pap. 18.00 (*0-7404-0565-9*) Higginson Bk Co.

Berry, Brian J. L. Long-Wave Rhythms in Economic Development & Political Behavior. LC 90-4586. (Illus.). 280p. 1991. text 49.50 (*0-8018-4035-X*) Johns Hopkins.

— Parks. Rufus Parks Pedigree: 17 Centuries of One Family's Ancestry. (Illus.). 166p. 1995. reprint ed. pap. 29.00 (*0-8328-4884-0*); reprint ed. lib. bdg. 39.00 (*0-8328-4883-2*) Higginson Bk Co.

— Shapley. The Shapleigh, Shapley & Shappley Families: A Comprehensive Genealogy, 1635-1993. (Illus.). 534p. 1995. reprint ed. pap. 79.50 (*0-8328-4890-5*); reprint ed. lib. bdg. 89.50 (*0-8328-4889-1*) Higginson Bk Co.

— Shapley. Westward, the American Shapleys: The Family & Descendants of David Shapley, a 17th-Century Marblehead (MA.), with Pedigrees of Spouses...& English Ancestry & American Descent of Five Additional Shapley Immigrants. (Illus.). 466p. 1995. reprint ed. pap. 69.50 (*0-8328-4888-3*); reprint ed. lib. bdg. 79.50 (*0-8328-4887-5*) Higginson Bk Co.

— Sisson. Yankee Heritage: A Sisson Ancestry (with 257 Connecting Lines) (Illus.). 549p. 1995. reprint ed. pap. 83.00 (*0-8328-4892-1*); reprint ed. lib. bdg. 93.00 (*0-8328-4891-3*) Higginson Bk Co.

Berry, Brian J. L., ed. City Classification Handbook: Methods & Application. LC 71-171911. (Wiley Series in Urban Research). 406p. reprint ed. pap. 125.90 (*0-608-10318-7*, 202250000027) Bks Demand.

— The Nature of Change in Geographical Ideas. LC 75-39294. (Perspectives in Geography Ser.: Vol. 3). (Illus.). 167p. 1978. pap. 12.50 (*0-87580-525-6*) N Ill U Pr.

— The Nature of Change in Geographical Ideas, vol. 3. LC 75-39294. (Perspectives in Geography Ser.: Vol. 3). (Illus.). 167p. 1978. 28.00 (*0-87580-063-7*) N Ill U Pr.

— Urbanization & Counterurbanization. LC 76-15864. (Urban Affairs Annual Reviews Ser.: No. 11). (Illus.). 334p. reprint ed. pap. 103.60 (*0-8357-4736-0*, 203765300009) Bks Demand.

Berry, Brian J. L. & Bruzewicz, Andrew J. Land Use, Urban Form & Environmental Quality. LC 73-87830. (University of Chicago, Department of Geography, Research Paper Ser.: No. 155). 466p. 1974. reprint ed. pap. 144.50 (*0-608-02246-2*, 206288700004) Bks Demand.

Berry, Brian J. L. & Conkling, Edgar C. Global Economy in Transition. 2nd ed. LC 96-28138. 498p. (C). 1996. 82.67 (*0-13-505264-5*) P-H.

Berry, Brian J. L., et al. Essays on Geography & Economic Development. Ginsburg, Norton, ed. LC 60-2105. (University of Chicago, Department of Geography, Research Paper Ser.: No. 62). 195p. reprint ed. pap. 60.50 (*0-7837-0384-8*, 204070400018) Bks Demand.

— The Impact of Urban Renewal on Small Business: The Hyde Park-Kenwood Case. LC 68-9490. (Illus.). 284p. reprint ed. pap. 88.10 (*0-608-06203-0*, AU00492000008) Bks Demand.

— The Rhythms of American Politics. LC 98-23407. 176p. (C). 1998. 49.00 (*0-7618-1153-2*); pap. 27.50 (*0-7618-1154-0*) U Pr of Amer.

Berry, Brian J. L., jt. auth. see Cohen, Yehoshua S.

Berry, Buford, jt. auth. see Burke, Frank M.

***Berry, Burton Y.** Romanian Diaries, 1944-1947. Bodeu, Cornelia, ed. 720p. 2000. 49.95 (*973-9432-07-7*, Pub. by Ctr Romanian Studies) Intl Spec Bk.

Berry, C. J. First Steps in Winemaking. 240p. pap. 12.95 (*0-900841-83-4*) G W Kent.

Berry, C. J. First Steps in Winemaking. 9th ed. (Illus.). 238p. 1996. pap. 22.50 (*1-85486-139-5*) Nexus Special Interests.

— Home Brewed Beers & Stouts: How to Brew Superb Ales, Beers, Lagers & Stouts from Kits, Malt, Malt Extract & Dried Malt Extract. 6th ed. (Illus.). 155p. (Orig.). 1995. pap. 18.95 (*1-85486-123-9*) Nexus Special Interests.

— One Hundred Thirty Winemaking Recipes. 128p. (Orig.). 1993. reprint ed. pap. 10.95 (*0-9619072-5-8*) G W Kent.

Berry, C. L., ed. Paediatric Pathology. (Illus.). 710p. 1985. 115.00 (*0-387-10507-7*) Spr-Verlag.

— Paediatric Pathology. 2nd ed. (Illus.). 750p. 1989. 266.00 (*0-387-19536-X*) Spr-Verlag.

— The Pathology of Devices. LC 93-32868. (Current Topics in Pathology Ser.: Vol. 86). 1994. 237.00 (*0-387-54393-7*) Spr-Verlag.

Berry, C. L. & Pratt, J., eds. Transplantation Pathology: A Guide for Practicing Pathologists. (Current Topics in Pathology Ser.: No. 92). (Illus.). 240p. 1998. 155.00 (*3-540-64096-7*) Spr-Verlag.

Berry-Caban, Cristobal S. Hispanics in Wisconsin: A Bibliography of Resource Materials. LC 81-5308. 258p. 1981. pap. 12.95 (*0-87020-209-X*) State Hist Soc Wis.

Berry, Carla F. & Mindes, Gayle. Planning a Theme-Based Curriculum: Goals, Themes, Activities, & Planning Guides for 4's & 5's. (Illus.). 160p. (Orig.). 1992. pap. 12.95 (*0-673-46409-1*, GoodYrBooks) Addson-Wesley Educ.

Berry, Carmen R. Daddies & Daughters. 288p. 1999. pap. 10.00 (*0-684-84993-3*) S&S Trade Pap.

Berry, Carmen R. Girlfriends: Invisible Bonds, Enduring Ties. LC 95-36542. 240p. 1998. 20.00 (*1-885171-20-X*) Wldcat Canyon.

— Women's Rites: Rituals Shared by Girlfriends. 1998. 4.95 (*0-8362-5422-8*) Andrews & McMeel.

— Your Body Never Lies. 218p. (Orig.). 1994. 21.95 (*1-879290-02-2*); pap. 12.95 (*1-879290-03-0*) PageMill Pr.

Berry, Carmen R. & Baker, Mark W. Who's to Blame? How to Deal with a Victim Without Becoming One Yourself. 240p. (Orig.). 1996. pap. 14.00 (*0-89109-915-8*) Pinon Press.

Berry, Carmen R. & Traeder, Tamara. Girlfriends Are Forever. 1998. 4.95 (*0-8362-5420-1*) Andrews & McMeel.

— Girlfriends for Life: Friendships Worth Keeping Forever. LC 99-12220. (Illus.). 224p. 1999. pap. 13.95 (*1-885171-32-3*) Wldcat Canyon.

— The Girlfriends Keepsake Book: The Story of Our Friendship. LC 96-29374. (Illus.). 72p. 1996. 19.95 (*1-885171-13-7*) Wldcat Canyon.

— Girlfriends Talk about Men: Sharing Secrets for a Great Relationship. LC 97-29944. 384p. (Orig.). 1997. pap. 14.95 (*1-885171-21-8*) Wldcat Canyon.

Berry, Carmen R., jt. auth. see Traeder, Tamara.

Berry, Carmen Renee. Coming Home to Your Body: 365 Simple Ways to Nourish Yourself Inside & Out. LC 96-18632. 416p. 1996. pap. 14.95 (*1-879290-07-3*) PageMill Pr.

— Girlfriends Are Forever, 1. 1998. 10.95 (*0-8362-5488-0*) Andrews & McMeel.

— Is Your Body Trying to Tell You Something? Why It Is Wise to Listen to Your Body & How Massage & Body Work Can Help. LC 96-43499. 216p. (Orig.). 1997. pap. 14.95 (*1-879290-11-1*) PageMill Pr.

Berry, Carmen Renee & Barrington, Lynn. Daddies & Daughters. LC 98-17972. 281p. (YA). 1998. 20.00 (*0-684-84992-5*) S&S Trade.

Berry, Carmen Renee & Traeder, Tamara. Girlfriends. large type ed. 1999. 26.95 (*0-7862-1969-6*) Mac Lib Ref.

***Berry, Carmen Renee & Traeder, Tamara.** A Girlfriends Gift: Reflections on the Extraordinary Bonds of Friendship. (Illus.). 192p. 2000. 13.95 (*1-885171-43-9*) Wldcat Canyon.

Berry, Carole. The Death of a Dancing Fool. LC 95-21057. 272p. (Orig.). 1996. pap. 21.95 (*0-425-15143-3*, Prime Crime) Berkley Pub.

— The Death of a Dancing Fool. (Orig.). 1996. mass mkt. 5.99 (*0-425-15513-7*) Berkley Pub.

— The Death of a Difficult Woman. 272p. 1995. pap. 4.99 (*0-425-15008-9*, Prime Crime) Berkley Pub.

— The Death of a Dimpled Darling. 1997. mass mkt. 5.99 (*0-425-16097-1*, Prime Crime) Berkley Pub.

— Death of a Downsizer. (Bonnie Indermill Ser.). 260p. 1999. mass mkt. 5.99 (*0-425-16614-7*, Prime Crime) Berkley Pub.

— The Letter of the Law: Bonnie Indermill Mystery. 1995. mass mkt. 4.99 (*0-425-15105-0*) Berkley Pub.

Berry, Carole C. Effective Appellate Advocacy: Brief Writing & Oral Argument. LC 98-11516. (American Casebook Ser.). 300p. 1998. pap. 36.50 (*0-314-21170-5*) West Pub.

***Berry, Chad.** Southern Migrants, Northern Exiles. LC 99-6511. 2000. 21.95 (*0-252-06841-6*) U of Ill Pr.

Berry, Charlene. Cajun Heat. (Indigo Love Stories Ser.). 1999. pap. 8.95 (*1-885478-59-3*, Pub. by Genesis Press) BookWorld.

— Love's Deceptions. 1996. pap. 10.95 (*1-885478-11-9*) Genesis Press.

Berry, Charles A. The Secret of Vatican Hill. (Illus.). 296p. (Orig.). 1987. pap. 10.00 (*0-943625-00-9*) Allen & Nurri.

Berry, Charles R. The Reform in Oaxaca, 1856-76: A Microhistory of the Liberal Revolution. LC 80-15378. (Illus.). 302p. reprint ed. pap. 93.70 (*0-8357-3788-8*, 203651900003) Bks Demand.

Berry, Chris, ed. Perspectives on Chinese Cinema. enl. rev. ed. (Illus.). 244p. 1991. reprint ed. pap. 21.95 (*0-85170-272-4*, Pub. by British Film Inst) Ind U Pr.

Berry, Chris, tr. see Ding, Xiaoqi.

An Asterisk (*) at the beginning of an entry indicates that the title is appearing for the first time.

Berry, Christopher. Social Theory of the Scottish Enlightenment. LC 98-115302. 224p. 1997. pap. 25.00 (*0-7486-0864-8*, Pub. by Edinburgh U Pr) Col U Pr.

Berry, Christopher & Bailey, Edward. Bankruptcy - Law & Practice. 1987. 128.00 (*0-406-52610-9*, U.K., MICHIE) LEXIS Pub.

Berry, Christopher J. Hume, Hegel & Human Nature. 239p. 1982. lib. bdg. 135.00 (*90-247-2682-4*, Pub. by M Nijhoff) Kluwer Academic.

Berry, Christopher S., et al. Wisconsin Business Corporation Law. 980p. 1992. 125.00 (*0-945574-52-5*) State Bar WI.

Berry, Cicely. The Actor & the Text. rev. ed. LC 92-25204. (Acting Ser.). 288p. 1992. pap. 16.95 (*1-55783-138-6*) Applause Theatre Bk Pubs.

— Voice & the Actor. 160p. 1991. pap. 9.95 (*0-02-041555-9*) Macmillan.

— Your Voice & How to Use It: The Classical Guide to Speaking with Confidence. 160p. 1995. pap. 10.95 (*0-86369-826-3*, Pub. by Virgin Bks) London Brdge.

Berry, Cindy, contrib. by. Hymns with a Classical Touch. 48p. 1988. 9.99 (*0-8341-9224-1*, MB-596) Lillenas.

Berry, Clifford R. & Daniel, Gregory B., eds. Handbook of Veterinary Nuclear Medicine. (Illus.). 184p. (Orig.). 1996. pap. text 35.00 (*0-9651794-0-0*) N C State Univ.

Berry, Colin L., ed. Paediatric Pathology. 3rd ed. LC 95-33587. 960p. 1995. 214.00 (*3-540-19936-5*) Spr-Verlag.

Berry, Connie, ed. see Lambert, Lee R. & Lambert, Erin.

Berry, D., et al. The Preservation of Open Space in the New Jersey Pinelands. (Discussion Papers: No. 73). 1974. pap. 10.00 (*1-55869-098-0*) Regional Sci Res Inst.

Berry, D., jt. ed. see Halloran, M. E.

Berry, D. H., ed. see Cicero, Marcus Tullius.

Berry, D. K. & Alberta Staff. Alberta's Arctic Grayling Management & Recovery Plan. viii, 27 p. 1998. (*0-7785-0149-3*) APAB.

Berry, D. R., et al, eds. Yeast Biotechnology. (Illus.). 512p. 1987. text 125.00 (*0-04-574042-9*) Routledge.

Berry, D'Anna, ed. Housing, Husbandry & Welfare of Sheep & Goats: Bibliography. Jan. 1985-April 1994. 84p. (Orig.). 1997. pap. text 30.00 (*0-7881-4029-9*) DIANE Pub.

Berry, D'Anna J., et al. Information Resources for Reptiles, Amphibians, Fish, & Cephalopods Used in Biomedical Research. (Illus.). 87p. (Orig.). (C). 1994. pap. text 35.00 (*0-7881-0400-4*) DIANE Pub.

Berry, David. The Creative Vision of Guillaume Apollinaire: A Study in Imagination. (Stanford French & Italian Studies: Vol. 25). vi, 165p. 1982. pap. 56.50 (*0-915838-14-1*) Anma Libri.

— Environmental Protection & Collective Action: The Case of Urban Open Space. (Discussion Papers: No. 61). 1973. pap. 10.00 (*1-55869-040-9*) Regional Sci Res Inst.

— G. R. Point. 1979. pap. 5.25 (*0-8222-0467-3*) Dramatists Play.

— Idling of Farmland in the Philadelphia Region, 1930 to 1970. (Discussion Papers: No. 88). 1976. pap. 10.00 (*1-55869-052-2*) Regional Sci Res Inst.

— Landscape Aesthetics & Environment Planning: A Critique of Underlying Premises. (Discussion Papers: No. 85). 1975. pap. 10.00 (*1-55869-067-0*) Regional Sci Res Inst.

***Berry, David.** Media Ethics: Practices & Representations. 320p. 1999. pap. 32.95 (*0-7506-4162-2*, Focal) Buttrwrth-Heinemann.

Berry, David. Open Space Values: A Household Survey of Two Philadelphia Parks. (Discussion Papers: No. 76). 1974. pap. 10.00 (*1-55869-087-5*) Regional Sci Res Inst.

— The Whales of August. 1984. pap. 5.25 (*0-8222-1234-X*) Dramatists Play.

***Berry, David, ed.** Ethics & Media Culture: Practices & Representations. 350p. 1999. pap. text 32.95 (*0-240-51603-6*, Focal) Buttrwrth-Heinemann.

Berry, David & Coughlin, Robert E. Land & Landscape in the Philadelphia Region, 2025. (Discussion Papers: No. 95). 1977. pap. 10.00 (*1-55869-065-4*) Regional Sci Res Inst.

Berry, David & Horrocks, Simon, eds. David Lloyd George: The Movie Mystery. LC 99-159506. (Illus.). 224p. 1999. pap. 16.95 (*0-7083-1371-X*, Pub. by Univ Wales Pr) Paul & Co Pubs.

Berry, David & Nourse, Jonathan. Practical Earth Science Exercises. 88p. (C). 1996. pap. text, per. 23.95 (*0-7872-2853-2*, 41285301) Kendall-Hunt.

Berry, David & Steiker, Gene. The Concept of Justice in Regional Planning: Some Policy Implications. (Discussion Papers: No. 69). 1973. pap. 10.00 (*1-55869-016-6*) Regional Sci Res Inst.

— An Economic Analysis of Transfer of Development Rights. (Discussion Papers: No. 81). 1975. pap. 10.00 (*1-55869-032-8*) Regional Sci Res Inst.

— Landscape, Image & Design: A Survey of Open Space Planners. (Discussion Papers: No. 77). 1974. pap. 10.00 (*1-55869-068-9*) Regional Sci Res Inst.

Berry, David, et al. The Farmer's Response to Urbanization: A Study of the Middle Atlantic States. (Discussion Papers: No. 92). 1976. pap. 10.00 (*1-55869-047-6*) Regional Sci Res Inst.

Berry, David, jt. auth. see Berry, Ellen.

Berry, David A., jt. auth. see Berry, Ellen T.

Berry, David C. Divorce Boxing: Poems. LC 98-14841. 1998. 24.00 (*0-910055-43-2*); pap. 14.00 (*0-910055-44-0*) East Wash Univ.

Berry, David E., jt. ed. see Beaulieu, Joyce E.

Berry, David R. Chimney Tops. (Illus.). 32p. (J). (gr. 2-5). 1995. 10.95 (*0-9644826-0-6*) Craiger Assoc.

Berry, Dawn B. The Divorce Sourcebook. LC 95-34272. 324p. 1995. 25.00 (*1-56565-335-1*) Lowell Hse.

— The Divorce Sourcebook. 2nd rev. ed. 336p. 1998. pap. 17.00 (*0-7373-0023-X*, 0023XW) NTC Contemp Pub Co.

— The Divorce Sourcebook: Everything You Need to Know. 324p. 1996. pap. 16.00 (*1-56565-474-9*) Lowell Hse.

— Domestic Violence Sourcebook. 252p. 1996. pap. 16.00 (*1-56565-441-2*) Lowell Hse.

— Domestic Violence Sourcebook. 2nd ed. 288p. 1998. pap. 16.00 (*1-56565-873-6*, 08736W, Pub. by Lowell Hse) NTC Contemp Pub Co.

— Equal Compensation for Women. 288p. 1995. pap. 15.00 (*1-56565-217-7*) Lowell Hse.

— The Estate Planning Sourcebook. LC 99-17385. 256p. 1999. pap. 17.95 (*0-7373-0076-0*, 00760W) NTC Contemp Pub Co.

— The 50 Most Influential Women in Law. (Illus.). 368p. 1996. 30.00 (*1-56565-469-2*) Lowell Hse.

Berry, Dawn Bradley. The Divorce Recovery Sourcebook. 304p. 1998. pap. 17.00 (*0-7373-0002-7*, 00027W) NTC Contemp Pub Co.

***Berry, Dawn Bradley.** The Domestic Violence Sourcebook. 3rd ed. 288p. 2000. pap. 16.95 (*0-7373-0419-7*, 04197W, Pub. by Lowell Hse) NTC Contemp Pub Co.

Berry, Diane. Let's Get Moving - Movement in the Classroom: Video Manual. 3rd ed. (Illus.). 22p. (C). 1994. pap. text 5.00 (*1-878631-19-5*) S Kovalik.

Berry, Diane & Hart, Anna. Expert Systems: Human Issues. (ITCP-UK Computer Science Ser.). (C). 1990. mass mkt. 56.95 (*0-412-37790-X*) Chapman & Hall.

Berry, Dianne & Hart, Anna. Expert Systems: Human Issues. 250p. 1990. 35.00 (*0-262-02307-5*) MIT Pr.

Berry, Dianne C., ed. How Implicit Is Implicit Learning? LC 97-37706. (Debates in Psychology). (Illus.). 254p. 1998. pap. text 35.00 (*0-19-852351-3*) OUP.

— How Implicit Is Implicit Learning? Debates in Psychology. LC 97-37706. (Debates in Psychology). (Illus.). 254p. 1998. text 85.00 (*0-19-852352-1*) OUP.

Berry, Dick. Forecasting Sales with the Personal Computer: Guidelines for Marketing & Sales Managers. LC 87-7284. 222p. 1988. 55.00 (*0-89930-329-3*, BYF/, Quorum Bks) Greenwood.

— Managing Service for Results. LC 83-12821. (Illus.). 287p. 1983. reprint ed. pap. 89.00 (*0-7837-9044-9*, 204979500003) Bks Demand.

Berry, Don. Don Berry Short Stories. 44p. (Orig.). 1994. pap. 4.95 (*0-9636614-1-8*) Alder Pr OR.

Berry, Don. Here Comes the Show! (Illus.). 64p. (Orig.). (J). (gr. 3-4). 1997. pap. 22.00 (*0-9635348-1-5*) Everett Pub Lib.

Berry, Don. A Majority of Scoundrels. LC 61-10198. 1990. reprint ed. pap. 7.95 (*0-89174-028-7*) Comstock Edns.

— To Build a Ship. LC 60-5835. 1977. reprint ed. pap. 3.95 (*0-89174-029-5*) Comstock Edns.

— Trask. LC 60-5835. 376p. 1976. reprint ed. pap. 3.95 (*0-89174-001-5*) Comstock Edns.

— Women of Hawaii. (Illus.). 84p. (Orig.). 1986. pap. 17.95 (*0-916947-04-1*) Winn Bks.

Berry, Donald A. Modern Statistics. 2nd ed. (Statistics Ser.). 1995. pap., student ed. 17.95 (*0-534-50481-7*) Wadsworth Pub.

— Statistical Methodology in the Pharmaceutical Sciences. (Statistics: Textbooks & Monographs: Vol. 104). (Illus.). 600p. 1989. text 195.00 (*0-8247-8117-1*) Dekker.

— Statistics: A Bayesian Perspective. (C). 1995. pap. 83.95 (*0-534-23472-0*) Wadsworth Pub.

Berry, Donald A., et al, eds. Bayesian Analysis in Statistics & Econometrics: Essayss in Honor of Arnold Zellner. LC 95-22393. (Probability & Mathematical Ser.). 608p. 1995. 155.00 (*0-471-11856-7*, Wiley-Interscience) Wiley.

Berry, Donald A. & Lindgren, Bernard W. Statistics: Theory & Methods. 2nd ed. LC 95-30979. (C). 1995. pap. 101.95 (*0-534-50479-5*) PWS Pubs.

Berry, Donald A. & Stangl, Dalene K., eds. Bayesian Biostatistics. (Statistics: Textbooks & Monographs: Vol. 151). (Illus.). 696p. 1996. text 180.00 (*0-8247-9334-X*) Dekker.

***Berry, Donald K.** Introduction to Wisdom & Poetry of the Old Testament. 1999. pap. 24.99 (*0-8054-1999-3*) Broadman.

Berry, Donald K. The Psalms & Their Readers: Interpretive Strategies for Psalm 18. (JSOT Supplement Ser.: No. 153). 160p. 1993. 52.50 (*1-85075-399-7*, Pub. by Sheffield Acad) CUP Services.

Berry, Donald L. An Inquiry into the Nature & Usefullness of a Perspectival Approach to the Study of Religion: Disestablishing the Christian Paradigm. LC 90-27905. (Studies in the Theory of Religion: Vol. 1). 156p. 1991. lib. bdg. 69.95 (*0-88946-222-4*) E Mellen.

— Traveler's Advisory. LC 90-6095. (Poetry Ser.: Vol. 9). 68p. 1990. lib. bdg. 24.95 (*0-88946-879-6*) E Mellen.

Berry, Donald L. & Lindgren, Bernard W. Statistics: Theory & Methods. LC 89-48611. (Statistics). 650p. (C). 1990. pap. 47.75 (*0-534-09942-4*) Wadsworth Pub.

Berry, Donna, et al. Activities for Empowerment. 1994. ring bd. 139.95 (*0-87425-964-9*) HRD Press.

— Fifty Activities for Coaching - Mentoring. 1993. ring bd. 139.95 (*0-87425-218-0*) HRD Press.

Berry, Dorothea M. A Bibliographic Guide to Educational Research. 3rd ed. LC 90-48184. 508p. 1990. 55.00 (*0-8108-2343-8*) Scarecrow.

Berry, Edmund G. Emerson's Plutarch. LC 80-2525. reprint ed. 37.00 (*0-404-19250-5*) AMS Pr.

Berry, Edward. The Making of Sir Philip Sidney. (Illus.). 256p. 1998. text 45.00 (*0-8020-4288-0*) U of Toronto Pr.

Berry, Edward, jt. ed. see Woodbridge, Linda.

Berry, Eileen. Roses on Baker Street. LC 97-47278. (Illus.). 48p. (J). 1998. pap. 5.49 (*0-89084-934-X*) Bob Jones Univ.

Berry, Eleanor. The Most Singular Adventures of Eddie Vernon LC 99-182302. 278p. 1998. write for info. (*0-7223-3232-7*, Pub. by A H S Ltd) St Mut.

***Berry, Eleanor.** The Rendon Boy to the Grave is Gone: (The Book Which Nearly Killed Its Author & Near the End, Turned Her Tongue Black) LC 99-488212. 445p. 1999. write for info. (*0-7223-3273-4*, Pub. by A H S Ltd) St Mut.

Berry, Eliot. A Poetry of Force & Darkness: The Fiction of John Hawkes. LC 79-282. (Milford Ser.: Popular Writers of Today: Vol. 22). 64p. 1979. pap. 13.00 (*0-89370-232-3*) Millefleurs.

Berry, Elizabeth. Elizabeth Berg's Magic Beans. 1998. write for info. (*0-609-60115-6*) C Potter.

— The Writing on the Walls. (C). 1989. 45.00 (*0-9505159-2-2*, Pub. by Saltire Soc) St Mut.

Berry, Elizabeth, jt. auth. see Berry, William D.

Berry, Ellen. Gifts That Make a Difference: How to Buy Hundreds of Great Gifts Sold through Non-Profits. LC 92-71865. (Illus.). 264p. (Orig.). 1995. pap. 7.95 (*0-9633126-6-9*) Foxglove Pub.

— Gifts That Save the Animals: 1001 Great Gifts Sold by Nonprofits That Protect Animals. LC 95-60918. (Illus.). 320p. 1995. pap. 9.95 (*0-9633126-4-2*) Foxglove Pub.

Berry, Ellen & Berry, David. Our Quaker Ancestors: Finding Them in Quaker Records. 136p. 1996. reprint ed. 19.95 (*0-8063-1190-8*, 483) Genealog Pub.

Berry, Ellen E. Curved Thought & Textual Wandering: Gertrude Stein's Postmodernism. 216p. (C). 1992. text 42.50 (*0-472-10300-8*, 10300) U of Mich Pr.

***Berry, Ellen E.** Transcultural Experiments: Russian & American Models of Creative Communication. LC 99-14323. 338p. 1999. text 49.95 (*0-312-21808-7*) St Martin.

Berry, Ellen E., ed. Postcommunism & the Body Politic: Genders 22. 380p. (C). 1995. text 55.00 (*0-8147-1247-9*); pap. text 19.50 (*0-8147-1248-7*) NYU Pr.

Berry, Ellen E. & Miller-Pogacar, Anesa, eds. Re-Entering the Sign: Articulating New Russian Culture. LC 94-41428. 376p. 1995. pap. text 21.95 (*0-472-08277-9*, 08277) U of Mich Pr.

— Re-Entering the Sign: Perspectives on New Russian Culture. LC 94-41428. 376p. 1995. text 52.50 (*0-472-10301-6*, 10301) U of Mich Pr.

Berry, Ellen T. & Berry, David A. Early Ohio Settlers: Purchasers of Land in Southwestern Ohio, 1800-1840, Vol. II. (Illus.). 372p. 1993. reprint ed. 30.00 (*0-8063-1162-2*, 481) Genealog Pub.

Berry, Erick. The Land & People of Finland. rev. ed. LC 78-37246. (Portraits of the Nations Ser.). (Illus.). (J). (gr. 5-9). 1972. lib. bdg. 11.89 (*0-397-31255-5*) HarpC Child Bks.

— The Land & People of Iceland. rev. ed. LC 72-1569. (Portraits of the Nations Ser.). (Illus.). (J). (gr. 5-9). 1972. lib. bdg. 11.89 (*0-397-31401-9*) HarpC Child Bks.

Berry, F. Clifton, Jr. Inventing the Future: How Science & Technology Transform Our World. 192p. 1992. 24.95 (*0-02-881029-5*, 4107M) Brasseys.

***Berry, F. Clifton, Jr.** Milestones of the First Century of Flight. 2000. 34.95 (*1-57488-311-9*) Brasseys.

Berry, F. Clifton, Jr., et al, eds. Spies, Black Ties & Mango Pies: Stories & Recipes from CIA Families All over the World. LC 97-21347. 208p. 1997. pap. 19.95 (*1-885352-80-8*) Community Comm.

Berry, F. J., jt. ed. see Dickson, D. P.

Berry, Fabio, tr. see Tafuri, Manfredo, ed.

Berry, Faith. Langston Hughes: Before & Beyond Harlem. 384p. 1992. pap. 15.95 (*0-8065-1307-1*, Citadel Pr) Carol Pub Group.

Berry, Faith, ed. From Bondage to Liberation: Writings by & about Afro-Americans from 1700 to the Present. LC 78-20931. 400p. (C). 1999. 27.95 (*0-8264-0567-3*) Continuum.

— Good Morning Revolution: Selected Poetry & Prose of Langston Hughes. 224p. 1992. pap. 9.95 (*0-8065-1308-X*, Citadel Pr) Carol Pub Group.

— A Scholar's Conscience: Selected Writings of J. Saunders Redding, 1942-1977. 248p. 1992. pap. text 19.95 (*0-8131-0806-3*) U Pr of Ky.

Berry, Faith, ed. see Redding, J. Saunders.

Berry, Fred, Jr. Holy Man, Holy War. LC 97-4779. 184p. 1997. pap. 9.95 (*1-885373-10-4*) Emerald Ink.

Berry, Fred & Kress, W. John. Heliconia: An Identification Guide. LC 90-9867. (Illus.). 344p. (C). 1991. pap. 24.95 (*1-56098-007-9*) Smithsonian.

Berry, Fred & Novak, John. The History of Arkansas. rev. ed. LC 85-63312. (Illus.). 296p. (J). (ps-8). 1997. 30.00 (*0-914546-61-9*) Rose Pub.

Berry, Frederic A. Anesthetic Management of Difficult & Routine Pediatric Patients. 2nd ed. (Illus.). 457p. 1990. text 72.00 (*0-443-08678-8*) Church.

Berry, Frederic A., ed. Anesthetic Management of Difficult & Routine Pediatric Patients. LC 85-25468. (Illus.). 476p. reprint ed. pap. 147.60 (*0-8357-3069-7*, 203932500012) Bks Demand.

Berry, Frederick A. & Steward, David J., eds. Pediatrics for the Anesthesiologist. (Illus.). 400p. 1993. text 72.00 (*0-443-08930-2*) Church.

Berry, G. Medieval English Jetons. 1974. 15.00 (*0-685-51549-4*) S J Durst.

Berry, G., jt. auth. see Armitage, P.

Berry, Gail. Little Fox & the Golden Hawk. (Illus.). 32p. (J). (gr. 1-9). 1991. 9.50 (*0-912411-36-8*) Open Horizons.

Berry, Garvin, jt. auth. see Chapman, Betty.

Berry, Gaynor. First Five Hundred Words. (Nine Hundred Thirty-Three Ser.). 28p. (J). 1993. pap. 3.50 (*0-7214-1520-2*, Ladybrd) Penguin Putnam.

— First Picture Dictionary. (Nine Hundred Thirty-Three Ser.). 26p. (J). 1993. pap. 3.50 (*0-7214-1519-9*, Ladybrd) Penguin Putnam.

— First Words for Me. (Nine Hundred Thirty-Three Ser.). 26p. (J). 1993. pap. 3.50 (*0-7214-1522-9*, Ladybrd) Penguin Putnam.

Berry, Gene D. Hydrogen as a Transportation Fuel: Costs & Benefits. (Hydrogen Fuel Information Ser.: Vol. V). (Illus.). 115p. 1997. lib. bdg. 135.00 (*0-89934-327-9*, BT972) Bus Tech Bks.

Berry, George. Seventeenth Century England: Traders & Their Tokens. (Illus.). 168p. 1988. lib. bdg. 42.00 (*1-85264-003-0*) S J Durst.

Berry, George R. A Dictionary of New Testament Greek Synonyms. 1979. pap. 4.95 (*0-310-21161-1*) Zondervan.

Berry, George Ricker. The Interlinear Greek-English New Testament. 1967. 34.99 (*0-310-21170-0*, 9216) Zondervan.

— The Interlinear Greek-English New Testament. 800p. 1993. 39.99 (*0-310-39380-9*) Zondervan.

***Berry, Glen.** Kulshan.com's Guide to Whatcom County. Brierly, Ken, ed. 160p. 1999. pap. 9.95 (*0-9674389-0-X*) Berry Intl Inc.

Berry, Gordon L. & Asamen, Joy K., eds. Children & Television: Images in a Changing Socio-Cultural World. (Illus.). 320p. (C). 1993. text 55.00 (*0-8039-4699-6*); pap. text 26.00 (*0-8039-4700-3*) Sage.

Berry, Gordon L., jt. ed. see Asamen, Joy K.

Berry, Graham, jt. auth. see Kennerly, Byron.

Berry, H. Jehovahs Witnesses. 1988. pap. text 1.35 (*0-8474-0818-3*) Back to Bible.

— Masons. 1990. pap. text 1.35 (*0-8474-0828-0*) Back to Bible.

— Mormons. 1988. pap. text 1.35 (*0-8474-0820-5*) Back to Bible.

— Roman Catholics. 1988. pap. text 1.35 (*0-8474-0821-3*) Back to Bible.

— Seventh-Day Adventists. 1988. pap. text 1.35 (*0-8474-0816-7*) Back to Bible.

Berry, H. & Jawad, Asm. Rheumatology. 1985. text 73.50 (*0-85200-900-3*) Kluwer Academic.

Berry, Harold J. New Age Movement. 1996. pap. 1.35 (*0-8474-0827-2*) Back to Bible.

— The Truth Twisters. LC 98-130875. (Illus.). 361p. 1987. pap. 12.99 (*0-8474-1212-1*) Back to Bible.

Berry, Harold J. What They Believe, 7 vols. 1989. pap. 7.99 (*0-8474-1811-1*) Loizeaux.

Berry, Harrison M., Jr. Radiologic Anatomy of the Jaws. LC 82-60263. (Illus.). 144p. (Orig.). 1982. pap. text 29.95 (*0-8122-1130-8*) U of Pa Pr.

Berry, Harrison M., Jr., ed. Emergency Physician's Guide to Dental Care. LC 83-3455. 154p. 1983. reprint ed. pap. 47.80 (*0-608-03563-7*, 205964700009) Bks Demand.

Berry, Henry. Semper Fi, Mac: Living Memories of the U. S. Marines in World War II. LC 96-32779. 384p. 1996. pap. 13.00 (*0-688-14956-1*, Wm Morrow) Morrow Avon.

Berry, Herb. The Lure of Fishing. (Illus.). 154p. (Orig.). 1988. write for info. (*0-9620934-3-2*); pap. 14.95 (*0-9620934-0-8*); lib. bdg. 19.95 (*0-9620934-1-6*) XLN Pubs.

Berry, Herbert. The Boar's Head Playhouse. LC 84-48448. (Illus.). 240p. 1986. 45.00 (*0-918016-81-9*) Folger Bks.

— The Noble Science: A Study & Transcription of Sloane Ms. 2530, Papers of the Masters of Defence of London, Temp. Henry VIII to 1590. LC 91-50103. (Illus.). 152p. 1991. 32.50 (*0-87413-441-2*) U Delaware Pr.

— Shakespeare's Playhouses. LC 85-48061. (Studies in the Renaissance: No.19). (Illus.). 1987. 34.50 (*0-404-62289-5*) AMS Pr.

Berry, Herbert, ed. The First Public Playhouse: The Theatre in Shoreditch, 1576-1598. LC 79-321991. 151p. reprint ed. pap. 46.90 (*0-7837-1041-0*, 204135200020) Bks Demand.

Berry, Herbert & Berry, Lila S. Business Mathematics. 480p. (C). 1992. text 45.00 (*0-697-15357-6*, WCB McGr Hill) McGrw-H Hghr Educ.

— Business Mathematics in a Changing World. 64p. (C). 1991. text, student ed. 9.38 (*0-697-14643-X*, WCB McGr Hill) McGrw-H Hghr Educ.

Berry, Holly. Old MacDonald Had a Farm. LC 93-41328. 32p. (J). (ps-2). 1994. lib. bdg. 14.88 (*1-55858-282-7*, Pub. by North-South Bks NYC) Chronicle Bks.

— Old MacDonald Had a Farm. LC 93-41328. 32p. (J). (ps-2). 1997. pap. 6.95 (*1-55858-703-9*, Pub. by North-South Bks NYC) Chronicle Bks.

Berry-Houston. Psychology at Work. 2nd ed. LC 97-13527. 592p. 1997. 64.69 (*0-697-20173-2*) McGraw.

— Psychology at Work. 3rd ed. 2000. 43.00 (*0-697-36182-9*) McGraw.

Berry, Ian. Living Apart: South Africa under Apartheid. LC 96-173007. 288p. 1996. 69.95 (*0-7148-3523-4*, Pub. by Phaidon Press) Phaidon Pr.

Berry, Ira A. & Nash, Robert A. Pharmaceutical Process Validation. 2nd ed. (Drugs & the Pharmaceutical Sciences Ser.: Vol. 57). (Illus.). 648p. 1993. text 150.00 (*0-8247-8777-3*) Dekker.

Berry, Ira R. & Harpaz, Daniel, eds. Validation of Bulk Pharmaceutical Chemicals. LC 97-2463. (Illus.). 350p. 1997. 229.00 (*1-57491-042-6*) Interpharm.

Berry, Iris. Two Blocks East of Vine. LC 97-130532. (Illus.). 108p. (Orig.). 1994. pap. 11.00 (*1-884615-00-7*) Incommcdo San Diego.

Berry, J. Mathematical Modelling. (Plastics Ser.). 1995. pap. 17.95 (*0-340-61404-8*, VNR) Wiley.

Berry, J., et al, eds. Indigenous Cognition: Functioning in Cultural Context. 1988. lib. bdg. 162.50 (*90-247-3671-4*) Kluwer Academic.

Berry, J., et al. Introductory Mathematics Through Science Applications. (Illus.). 576p. 1989. pap. text 47.95 (*0-521-28446-5*) Cambridge U Pr.

— Mathematics: A Second Start. 1995. write for info. (*0-13-149857-6*) Prntice Hall Bks.

Berry, J., jt. auth. see Sveshnikov, A. G.

Berry, J., jt. auth. see Timan, A.

Berry, J. Bill, ed. Home Ground: Southern Autobiography. 216p. 1992. text 29.95 (*0-8262-0813-4*) U of Mo Pr.

B

Berry, J. Duncan, tr. see Giedion, Sigfried.

Berry, J. S., et al, eds. Teaching & Applying Mathematical Modelling. LC 84-4561. (Mathematics & Its Applications Ser.: 1-176). 491p. 1984. text 96.95 (*0-470-20079-0*) P-H.

Berry, J. W., et al, eds. Health & Cross-Cultural Psychology: Toward Applications. LC 87-23515. (Cross-Cultural Research & Methodology Ser.: No. 10). (Illus.). 336p. 1988. reprint ed. pap. 104.20 (*0-608-01148-7*, 205944800001) Bks Demand.

Berry, J. W. & Laponce, J. A., eds. Ethnicity & Culture in Canada: The Research Landscape. LC 93-94628. 579p. 1993. text 65.00 (*0-8020-2897-7*); pap. text 30.00 (*0-8020-7759-5*) U of Toronto Pr.

Berry, Jack, tr. West African Folktales. 229p. (Orig.). 1991. 29.95 (*0-8101-0979-4*); pap. 14.95 (*0-8101-0993-X*) Northwestern U Pr.

Berry, Jack F. Unjustified Damnation. LC 98-85653. 462p. 1998. pap. 24.95 (*0-9664385-3-1*) Jim Jac.

Berry, Jake. Brambu Drezi. 70p. 1994. pap. 7.00 (*0-926935-94-1*) Runaway Spoon.

— Brambu Drezi, Bk. 2. (Illus.). 66p. 1998. pap. 9.95 (*1-880766-18-3*) Pantograph Pr.

— Drafts of the Sorcery. 37p. 1998. 7.00 (*0-937013-81-1*) Potes Poets.

— Equations. (Illus.). 43p. (Orig.). 1992. pap. 3.00 (*0-926935-63-1*) Runaway Spoon.

— Ex Tracx Ions: Prescinded Vocabulates. 17p. 1989. pap. text 0.50 (*0-944215-05-X*) Ninth St Lab.

— Species of Abandoned Light. 80p. (Orig.). 1995. pap. 8.95 (*1-880766-09-4*) Pantograph Pr.

Berry, Jake, jt. auth. see Arguelles, Ivan.

Berry, Jake, jt. auth. see Bennett, John M.

Berry, Jake, jt. auth. see Haggland, S. Gustav.

Berry, Jake, ed. see MisKowski, Mike & Foley, Jack.

Berry, James. Celebration Song. (Illus.). 32p. (J). (ps-3). 1994. pap. 14.00 (*0-671-89446-3*) S&S Bks Yung.

Berry, James. Hot Earth Cold Earth. 160p. 1996. pap. 18.95 (*1-85224-330-9*, Pub. by Seren Bks) Dufour.

— International Directory of Hemp Products & Suppliers. LC 96-94235. 144p. 1996. pap. 29.95 (*1-57282-005-5*, 020055) Message NM.

— Rough Sketch Beginning. LC 95-15471. (Illus.). 32p. (J). (gr. 4 up). 1996. 18.00 (*0-15-200112-3*) Harcourt.

— Tales of the West of Ireland. LC 67-15940. 218p. 1989. reprint ed. pap. 14.95 (*0-85105-502-8*, Pub. by Smyth) Dufour.

— A Thief in the Village. LC 87-24695. 1990. pap. 4.99 (*0-14-034357-1*, PuffinBks) Peng Put Young Read.

Berry, James, compiled by. Classic Poems to Read Aloud. (Illus.). 256p. (J). (gr. 2 up). 1995. 18.95 (*1-85697-987-3*) LKC.

— Classic Poems to Read Aloud. (Illus.). 256p. (J). (gr. 2 up). 1997. pap. 8.95 (*0-7534-5069-0*, Kingfisher) LKC.

Berry, James, ed. News for Babylon: The Chatto Book of Westindian-British Poetry. 1998. pap. 22.95 (*1-85224-379-1*, Pub. by Bloodaxe Bks) Dufour.

Berry, James & Mcgreal, Stanley, eds. European Cities, Planning Systems & Property Markets. (Illus.). 448p. (C). 1994. 85.00 (*0-419-18940-8*, E & FN Spon) Routledge.

Berry, James F., jt. auth. see Dennison, Mark S.

Berry, James R. Ajeemah & His Son. LC 92-6615. (Willa Perlman Bks.). 96p. (YA). (gr. 7 up). 1994. mass mkt. 4.95 (*0-06-440523-0*, HarpTrophy) HarpC Child Bks.

Berry, James R. Ajeemah & His Son. (J). 1994. 9.70 (*0-606-05726-9*, Pub. by Turtleback) Demco.

Berry, James R. Don't Leave an Elephant to Go & Chase a Bird. LC 94-24317. (Illus.). 1996. 15.00 (*0-671-89021-2*) S&S Bks Yung.

— Don't Leave an Elephant to Go & Chase a Bird. (Illus.). 32p. (J). (ps-3). 1996. 16.00 (*0-689-80464-4*) S&S Childrens.

— Everywhere Faces Everywhere. LC 96-30301. (Illus.). 80p. (J). (gr. 5-9). 1997. 16.00 (*0-689-80996-4*) S&S Childrens.

— First Palm Trees. (J). 1997. 15.00 (*0-671-89200-2*) S&S Bks Yung.

— First Palm Trees. LC 96-24618. (Illus.). 40p. (J). (ps-3). 1997. 17.00 (*0-689-81060-1*) S&S Childrens.

— Isn't My Name Magical? Sister & Brother Poems. LC 97-24627. (Illus.). 32p. (YA). (gr. k-5). 1999. mass mkt. 16.00 (*0-689-80013-4*) S&S Bks Yung.

— Magicians of Erianne. LC 85-45833. 256p. (YA). (gr. 7 up). 1988. 13.95 (*0-06-020556-3*) HarpC Child Bks.

Berry, Jan & Weidland, Rodney. Art of Preserving. LC 96-29491. (Illus.). 160p. (Orig.). 1997. pap. 17.95 (*0-89815-895-8*) Ten Speed Pr.

Berry, Jason. The Spirit of Black Hawk: A Mystery of Africans & Indians. LC 95-20270. (Illus.). 128p. 1995. 20.00 (*0-87805-806-0*) U Pr of Miss.

Berry, Jason, et al. Up from the Cradle of Jazz: New Orleans Music since World War II. (Illus.). 299p. 1992. reprint ed. pap. 16.95 (*0-306-80493-X*) Da Capo.

Berry, Jason, jt. auth. see Gould, Philip.

Berry, Jeff. Cities of Darkness: DC/New Orleans, Vol. 3. 1998. pap. text 16.00 (*1-56504-235-2*) White Wolf.

Berry, Jeff & Kaye, Annene. Beachbum Berry's Grog Log. Pape, Craig, ed. (Illus.). 96p. 1998. pap. 9.95 (*0-943151-20-1*) Slave Labor Bks.

Berry, Jeffrey M. The Interest Group Society. 2nd ed. (C). 1989. pap. text 22.00 (*0-673-39889-7*) Addson-Wesley Educ.

— Interest Group Society. 3rd ed. LC 96-2313. 267p. (C). 1997. pap. 38.00 (*0-673-52511-2*) Addson-Wesley Educ.

— Lobbying for the People: The Political Behavior of Public Interest Groups. LC 77-71973. 344p. reprint ed. pap. 106.70 (*0-608-06428-9*, 206664100008) Bks Demand.

***Berry, Jeffrey M.** The New Liberalism: The Rising Power of Citizen Groups. LC 98-40248. 4p. 1999. 24.95 (*0-8157-0908-0*) Brookings.

Berry, Jeffrey M., et al. Rebirth of Urban Democracy. 326p. 1993. 42.95 (*0-8157-0928-5*) Brookings.

Berry, Jerome T. Marriages of Phelps County Missouri Bk. 1: 28 Mar 1867-12 May 1881. 47p. 1944. pap. write for info. (*1-893474-12-7*) Phelps Cnty Gene.

Berry, Jill S., ed. see Graves, Frederick.

Berry, Jim, et al, contrib. by. Birds: An Explore Your World Handbook. LC 99-24585. (Illus.). 192p. (YA). 1999. pap. 13.95 (*1-56331-800-8*) Discovery.

Berry, Jim, et al, eds. Urban Regeneration: Property Investment & Development. LC 92-36203. (Illus.). 352p. (C). 1993. 85.00 (*0-419-18310-8*, E & FN Spon) Routledge.

***Berry, Jim & McGreal, Stanley.** Cities of Pacific Rim: Planning Systems & Property Markets. LC 99-19782. 384p. (C). 1999. text. write for info. (*0-419-24280-5*) Routledge.

Berry, Jo. Beloved Unbeliever: A Woman's Workshop. (Woman's Workshop Ser.). 176p. (Orig.). 1985. 5.95 (*0-310-42661-8*, 11219P) Zondervan.

— Beloved Unbeliever: Loving Your Husband into the Faith. 169p. (Orig.). 1981. pap. 10.99 (*0-310-42621-9*, 11215P) Zondervan.

— Making Your Life a Ministry: The Priscilla Principle. 176p. 1984. pap. 6.95 (*0-310-42631-6*, 11218P) Zondervan.

Berry, Jo, ed. The Goodspeed Biographical & Historical Memoirs of Faulkner County. (Illus.). 52p. (Orig.). 1996. pap. 10.00 (*1-57798-000-X*, 000X) BerryPatch.

— The Goodspeed Biographical & Historical Memoirs of Garland County. (Illus.). 57p. (Orig.). 1996. pap. 6.00 (*1-57798-009-3*, 0093) BerryPatch.

— The Goodspeed Biographical & Historical Memoirs of Grant County. (Illus.). 47p. (Orig.). 1996. pap. 6.00 (*1-57798-006-9*, 0069) BerryPatch.

— The Goodspeed Biographical & Historical Memoirs of Hot Spring County. (Illus.). 52p. (Orig.). 1996. pap. 10.00 (*1-57798-001-8*, 0018) BerryPatch.

— The Goodspeed Biographical & Historical Memoirs of Jefferson County. (Illus.). 105p. (Orig.). 1996. pap. 8.00 (*1-57798-007-7*, 0077) BerryPatch.

— The Goodspeed Biographical & Historical Memoirs of Lonoke County. (Illus.). 89p. (Orig.). 1996. pap. 8.00 (*1-57798-005-0*, 0050) BerryPatch.

— The Goodspeed Biographical & Historical Memoirs of Perry County. (Illus.). 44p. (Orig.). 1996. pap. 6.00 (*1-57798-008-5*, 0085) BerryPatch.

— The Goodspeed Biographical & Historical Memoirs of Pulaski County. (Illus.). 189p. (Orig.). 1996. pap. 10.00 (*1-57798-004-2*, 0042) BerryPatch.

— The Goodspeed Biographical & Historical Memoirs of Saline County. (Illus.). 105p. (Orig.). 1996. pap. 8.00 (*1-57798-003-4*, 0034) BerryPatch.

Berry, Joanne, jt. auth. see Laurence, Ray.

Berry, John. The Leonardo DiCaprio Album. (Illus.). 80p. 1997. pap. 15.95 (*0-85965-242-4*, Pub. by Plexus) Publishers Group.

***Berry, John, et al, eds.** Dictionary of Mathematics. 260p. 1999. 40.00 (*1-57958-157-9*) Fitzroy Dearborn.

Berry, John R. Good Words for New Christians. (Orig.). (J). (gr. 6-12). 1987. pap. 2.95 (*0-9616900-0-3*) J R Berry.

Berry, John S. Mathematical Modeling Courses. (Mathematics & Its Applications Ser.). 340p. 1987. text 104.00 (*0-470-20836-8*) P-H.

Berry, John W., et al, eds. Handbook of Cross-Cultural Psychology: Basic Processes & Human Development, Vol. 2. 2nd ed. 439p. (C). 1997. 61.00 (*0-205-16075-1*) Allyn.

Berry, John W., et al, eds. Handbook of Cross-Cultural Psychology Vol. 1: Theory & Method, Vol. 1. 2nd ed. LC 96-16261. Vol. 1. 406p. (C). 1996. 61.00 (*0-205-16074-3*) Allyn.

Berry, John W., et al, eds. Handbook of Cross-Cultural Psychology Vol. 3: Social Behavior & Applications. 2nd rev. ed. 544p. (C). 1997. 61.00 (*0-205-16076-X*) Allyn.

Berry, John W., et al. Cross-Cultural Psychology: Research & Applications. (Illus.). 475p. (C). 1992. pap. text 36.95 (*0-521-37761-7*) Cambridge U Pr.

Berry, John W., jt. auth. see Kim, Uichol.

Berry, John W., jt. ed. see Irvine, Sidney H.

Berry, John W., jt. ed. see Lonner, Walter J.

Berry, Jon, jt. auth. see Guber, Selina S.

Berry, Jonathan, ed. Diamond Dust. (Illus.). vii, 121p. (Orig.). 1991. pap. 9.95 (*1-879479-00-1*) ICE WA.

Berry, Jonathan, ed. see Divinsky, Nathan.

Berry, Jonathan, ed. see Fauber, Richard E.

Berry, Jonathan, ed. see Pliester, Leon.

Berry, Jonathan, ed. see Seirawan, Yasser & Minev, Nikolay.

Berry, Jonathan, ed. see Seirawan, Yasser & Tisdall, Jonathan.

Berry, Jonathan, ed. see Seirawan, Yasser, et al.

Berry, Joseph A., jt. ed. see Lucas, William J.

Berry, Joseph K. Beyond Mapping: Concepts, Algorithms, & Issues in GIS. LC 92-42643. (Illus.). 266p. 1993. pap. 32.95 (*0-9625063-6-2*) GIS World Bks.

— Beyond Mapping: Concepts, Algorithms & Issues in GIS. 246p. 1996. pap. text 32.95 (*0-470-23676-0*) Halsted Pr.

— Beyond Mapping: Concepts, Algorithms & Issues in GIS & GCON, Version 1.1 Set. 246p. 1996. pap. text 39.95 (*0-470-23695-7*) Halsted Pr.

— Spatial Reasoning for Effective GIS. (Illus.). 224p. (Orig.). 1995. pap. text 32.95 (*1-882610-14-8*) GIS World Bks.

— Spatial Reasoning for Effective GIS. 208p. (Orig.). 1996. pap. text 32.50 (*0-470-23633-7*) Halsted Pr.

Berry, Joseph P. Minutemen News. unabridged ed. 326p. (Orig.). 1997. pap. 19.00 (*0-9657898-0-2*) Legend Bks.

***Berry, Joy.** Bad Habits: Get over It! rev. ed. (Winning Skills Ser.: Vol. 6). (Illus.). 48p. (YA). (gr. 7-12). 2000. pap. 2.95 (*1-58634-165-0*) Goldstar.

— Being Good: A Social Skills Book About. rev. ed. (Living Skills Ser.: Vol. 6). (Illus.). 48p. (J). (gr. 1-7). 2000. pap. 4.95 (*1-58634-115-4*) Goldstar.

— Being in Public: A Good Manners Book About. rev. ed. (Living Skills Ser.: Vol. 8). (Illus.). 48p. (J). (gr. 1-7). 2000. pap. 4.95 (*1-58634-123-5*) Goldstar.

— Being Prepared: A Safety Book About. rev. ed. (Living Skills Ser.: Vol. 2). (Illus.). 48p. (J). (gr. 1-7). 2000. pap. 4.95 (*1-58634-099-9*) Goldstar.

— Cleaning Your Room: A Fun & Easy Book About. rev. ed. (Living Skills Ser.: Vol. 2). (Illus.). 48p. (J). (gr. 1-7). 2000. pap. 4.95 (*1-58634-133-2*) Goldstar.

— Criticism - Rejection: Get over It! rev. ed. (Winning Skills Ser.: Vol. 3). (Illus.). 48p. (YA). (gr. 7-12). 2000. pap. 2.95 (*1-58634-162-6*) Goldstar.

— Death: Good Answers to Tough Questions About. rev. ed. (Good Answers to Tough Questions Ser.: Vol. 16). (Illus.). 48p. (J). 2000. pap. 4.95 (*1-58634-226-6*, 01-0901-16) Goldstar.

— Disasters: Good Answers to Tough Questions About. rev. ed. (Good Answers to Tough Questions Ser.: Vol. 14). (Illus.). 48p. (J). 1999. pap. 4.95 (*1-58634-224-X*, 01-0901-14) Goldstar.

— Divorce: Good Answers to Tough Questions About. rev. ed. (Good Answers to Tough Questions Ser.: Vol. 5). (Illus.). 48p. (J). 2000. pap. 4.95 (*1-58634-215-0*, 01-0901-05) Goldstar.

— Earning an Allowance: A Kid's Money Book About. rev. ed. (Living Skills Ser.: Vol. 1). (Illus.). 48p. (J). (gr. 1-7). 2000. pap. 4.95 (*1-58634-140-5*) Goldstar.

— Eating: A Good Manners Book About. rev. ed. (Living Skills Ser.: Vol. 2). (Illus.). 48p. (J). (gr. 1-7). 2000. pap. 4.95 (*1-58634-117-0*) Goldstar.

— Eating Disorders: Good Answers to Tough Questions About. rev. ed. (Good Answers to Tough Questions Ser.: Vol. 7). (Illus.). 48p. (J). 2000. pap. 4.95 (*1-58634-217-7*, 01-0901-07) Goldstar.

— Fear: Get over It! rev. ed. (Winning Skills Ser.: Vol. 1). (Illus.). 48p. (YA). (gr. 7-12). 2000. pap. 2.95 (*1-58634-160-X*) Goldstar.

— From Humans to Superstars: The Human Race Club Gets a New Name. (Superstar Kids' Club Short Stories Ser.). (Illus.). 48p. (J). (gr. 2-6). 1999. pap. 3.95 (*1-58634-251-7*) Goldstar.

— Let's Talk about Accepting "No" An Early Social Skills Book. rev. ed. (Let's Talk about Ser.: Vol. 5). (Illus.). 36p. (J). (ps-3). 2000. pap. 3.95 (*1-58634-058-1*) Goldstar.

— Let's Talk About Being Fair: An Early Social Skills Book. (Let's Talk about Ser.: Vol. 6). 36p. (J). (ps-2). 2000. 3.95 (*1-58634-059-X*) Goldstar.

— Let's Talk about Being Good: An Early Social Skills Book. rev. ed. (Let's Talk about Ser.: Vol. 4). (Illus.). 36p. (J). (ps-2). 1999. pap. 3.95 (*1-58634-057-3*, 01-0204-04) Goldstar.

— Let's Talk about Being Patient: An Early Social Skills Book. rev. ed. (Let's Talk about Ser.: Vol. 2). (Illus.). 36p. (J). (ps-2). 1999. pap. 3.95 (*1-58634-055-7*, 01-0204-02) Goldstar.

— Let's Talk about Feeling Defeated: A Personal Feelings Book. rev. ed. (Let's Talk about Ser. : Vol. 4). (Illus.). 36p. (J). (ps-2). 2000. pap. 3.95 (*1-58634-035-2*) Goldstar.

— Let's Talk about Feeling Disappointed: An Interpersonal Feelings Book. rev. ed. (Let's Talk about Ser.: Vol. 4). (Illus.). 36p. (J). (ps-2). 1999. pap. 3.95 (*1-58634-043-3*, 01-0202-04) Goldstar.

— Let's Talk about Feeling Embarrassed: An Interpersonal Feelings Book. rev. ed. (Let's Talk about Ser.: Vol. 1). (Illus.). 36p. (J). (ps-2). 2000. pap. 3.95 (*1-58634-040-9*) Goldstar.

— Let's Talk about Feeling Frustrated: A Personal Feelings Book. rev. ed. (Let's Talk about Ser.: Vol. 3). (Illus.). 36p. (J). (ps-2). 1999. pap. 3.95 (*1-58634-034-4*, 01-0201-03) Goldstar.

— Let's Talk about Feeling Inferior: An Interpersonal Feelings Book. rev. ed. (Let's Talk about Ser.: Vol. 2). (Illus.). 36p. (J). (ps-3). 2000. pap. 3.95 (*1-58634-041-7*) Goldstar.

— Let's Talk about Feeling Jealous: An Interpersonal Feelings Book. rev. ed. (Let's Talk about Ser.: Vol. 3). (Illus.). 36p. (J). (ps-2). 1999. pap. 3.95 (*1-58634-042-5*, 01-0202-03) Goldstar.

— Let's Talk about Feeling Worried: A Personal Feelings Book. rev. ed. (Let's Talk about Ser. : Vol. 2). (Illus.). 36p. (J). (ps-3). 2000. pap. 3.95 (*1-58634-033-6*) Goldstar.

— Let's Talk about Playing with Others: An Early Social Skills Book. rev. ed. (Let's Talk about Ser.: Vol. 7). (Illus.). 36p. (J). (ps-2). 1999. pap. 3.95 (*1-58634-060-3*, 01-0204-07) Goldstar.

— One Leg at a Time: A Short Story about Human Similarities. (Superstar Kids' Club Short Stories Ser.: Vol. 1). (Illus.). 48p. (J). (gr. 2-6). 1999. pap. 3.95 (*1-58634-252-5*) Goldstar.

— Rude People: Get over It! rev. ed. (Winning Skills Ser.: Vol. 4). (Illus.). 48p. (YA). (gr. 5-12). 2000. pap. 2.95 (*1-58634-163-4*) Goldstar.

— Stress: Get over It! rev. ed. (Winning Skills Ser.: Vol. 2). (Illus.). 48p. (YA). (gr. 7-12). 2000. pap. 2.95 (*1-58634-161-8*) Goldstar.

— Substance Abuse: Good Answers to Tough Questions About. rev. ed. (Good Answers to Tough Questions Ser.: Vol. 8). (Illus.). 48p. (J). 2000. pap. 4.95 (*1-58634-218-5*, 01-0901-08) Goldstar.

— Teach Me about Bathtime: A Special Times Book. rev. ed. (Teach Me about Ser. : Vol. 2). (Illus.). 32p. (J). 1999. bds. 5.95 (*1-58634-001-8*, 01-0101-02) Goldstar.

— Teach Me about Bedtime: A Special Times Book. rev. ed. (Teach Me about Ser.: Vol. 3). (Illus.). 32p. (J). 1999. bds. 5.95 (*1-58634-002-6*, 01-0101-03) Goldstar.

— Teach Me about Crying: A Safe & Sound Book. rev. ed. (Teach Me about Ser.: Vol. 2). (Illus.). 32p. (J). 1999. bds. 5.95 (*1-58634-009-3*, 01-0103-02) Goldstar.

— Teach Me about Mealtime: A Special Times Book. rev. ed. (Teach Me about Ser. : Vol. 1). (Illus.). 32p. (J). 1999. pap. 5.95 (*1-58634-000-X*, 01-0101-01) Goldstar.

— Teach Me about Potty Training: A Growing up Book. rev. ed. (Teach Me about Ser.: Vol. 2). (Illus.). 32p. (J). 1999. bds. 5.95 (*1-58634-005-0*, 01-0102-02) Goldstar.

— Teach Me about Separation: A Growing up Book. rev. ed. (Teach Me about Ser.: Vol. 4). (Illus.). 32p. (J). 1999. bds. 5.95 (*1-58634-007-7*, 01-0102-04) Goldstar.

— Tough Situations: Get over It! rev. ed. (Winning Skills Ser.: Vol. 5). (Illus.). 48p. (YA). (gr. 7-12). 2000. pap. 2.95 (*1-58634-164-2*) Goldstar.

— Trauma: Good Answers to Tough Questions About. rev. ed. (Good Answers to Tough Questions Ser.: Vol. 12). (Illus.). 48p. (J). 2000. pap. 4.95 (*1-58634-222-3*, 01-0901-12) Goldstar.

Berry, Joy W. Every Kid's Guide to Saving the Earth. LC 92-38724. (Environmental Bks.). (Illus.). 64p. (J). (gr. 1-6). 1992. lib. bdg. 16.95 (*1-878363-72-7*) Forest Hse.

— Every Kid's Guide to Saving the Earth. (Illus.). 64p. (J). (gr. 1-5). 1993. pap. 6.95 (*0-8249-8554-0*, Ideals Child) Hambleton-Hill.

— Let's Talk about Being Helpful. (J). (ps-3). 1996. pap. text 3.50 (*0-590-62385-0*) Scholastic Inc.

— Let's Talk about Feeling Afraid. (Let's Talk About Ser.). (Illus.). (J). (ps-1). 1996. pap. 3.50 (*0-614-15764-1*) Scholastic Inc.

Berry, Joy W. Let's Talk about Feeling Afraid. (J). (ps-3). 1996. pap. text 3.50 (*0-590-62384-2*) Scholastic Inc.

Berry, Joy W. Let's Talk about Feeling Angry. LC 96-147738. (J). (ps-1). 1996. pap. text 3.50 (*0-590-62386-9*) Scholastic Inc.

— Let's Talk about Feeling Sad. (ps-3). 1996. pap. text 3.50 (*0-590-62387-7*) Scholastic Inc.

— Let's Talk about Needing Attention. LC 96-201787. (J). (ps-3). 1996. pap. text 3.50 (*0-590-62424-5*) Scholastic Inc.

— Let's Talk about Saying No. (Illus.). (J). (ps-1). 1996. pap. 3.50 (*0-614-15765-X*) Scholastic Inc.

— Let's Talk about Saying No. LC 96-134281. (Illus.). (J). (ps-3). 1996. pap. text 3.50 (*0-590-62425-3*) Scholastic Inc.

— Parenting Matters. Gouch, Annette, ed. LC 90-26140. 250p. (Orig.). 1991. pap. 19.95 (*0-929635-05-1*) Cole Pub Co Inc.

Berry, Joy W., et al. Rhythm & Movement: 160 Experiences for Children, Including Patterns to Use with Sticks, Cups, Balls, Rags, Hoops & Rope. LC 77-89556. (Can Make & Do Bks.). (Illus.). 176p. 1977. write for info. (*0-8499-8107-7*) Word Pub.

Berry, Joy Wilt. Let's Talk about Being Helpful. 1996. 8.70 (*0-606-09544-6*, Pub. by Turtleback) Demco.

Berry, Joy Wilt. Let's Talk about Feeling Angry. 1995. 8.70 (*0-606-09546-2*, Pub. by Turtleback) Demco.

Berry, Joy Wilt. Let's Talk about Feeling Sad. 1996. 8.70 (*0-606-09547-0*, Pub. by Turtleback) Demco.

— Let's Talk about Needing Attention. 1996. 9.19 (*0-606-09548-9*, Pub. by Turtleback) Demco.

— Let's Talk about Saying No. LC 96-134281. 1996. 8.70 (*0-606-09549-7*, Pub. by Turtleback) Demco.

Berry, Joyce K. & Gordon, John C., eds. Environmental Leadership: Developing Skills & Styles. LC 93-6542. 1993. text 50.00 (*1-55963-243-7*); pap. text 24.00 (*1-55963-244-5*) Island Pr.

Berry, Judy O. & Hardman, Michael L. Lifespan Perspectives on the Family & Disability. 48p. (C). 1997. pap. text, teacher ed. write for info. (*0-205-27397-1*, T7397-7) Allyn.

Berry, Judy V. & Hardman, Michael L. Lifespan Perspectives on the Family & Disability. LC 97-16309. 288p. 1997. pap. text 56.00 (*0-205-19395-1*) Allyn.

Berry, Julie. Worn Thresholds. LC 95-190495. 112p. 1995. pap. 11.95 (*0-919626-75-0*, Pub. by Brick Bks) Genl Dist Srvs.

***Berry, Kathleen S.** The Dramatic Arts & Cultural Studies: Educating Against the Grain. LC 99-49314. (Critical Education Practice Ser.: No. 21). 200p. 1999. pap. 24.95 (*0-8153-3727-2*, SS0861) Garland.

Berry, Kathleen S., jt. auth. see Kincheloe, Joe.

Berry, Kathryn E., ed. see Presley, Deni.

Berry, Ken. Cambodia: From Red to Blue: Australia's Initiate for Peace. LC 98-200332. 200p. 1998. pap. 24.95 (*1-86373-980-7*, Pub. by Allen & Unwin Pty) Paul & Co Pubs.

— Tele Operating System: CD: Console Display. 1989. pap. 40.00 (*0-317-93703-0*) Crosby Assocs.

— Tele Operating System: FS: File System. 1989. pap. 40.00 (*0-317-93704-9*) Crosby Assocs.

— Tele Operating System: SK: System Kernel. (Orig.). 1989. pap. 50.00 (*0-317-93705-7*) Crosby Assocs.

— Tele Operating System: XS: Index System. 1989. pap. 50.00 (*0-317-93706-5*) Crosby Assocs.

Berry, Kevin. Charlotte Bronte at the Seaside. (C). 1989. text 45.00 (*0-948929-39-1*) St Mut.

Berry, L., jt. auth. see Lewis, L. A.

Berry, Lamar D. The Power of Internal Marketing: Building a Values-Based Corporate Culture. (Illus.). 140p. 1996. 22.00 (*1-888042-07-9*) Good Readng.

Berry, Laura. The Child, the State & the Victorian Novel. LC 99-35304. (Victorian Literature & Culture Ser.). 2000. 32.50 (*0-8139-1909-6*) U Pr of Va.

Berry, LaVerle, ed. see Federal Research Division, Library of Congress Sta.

Berry, LaVerle, jt. ed. see Ofcansky, Thomas P.

Berry, Leonard & Kates, Robert W., eds. Making the Most of the Least: Alternative Ways to Development. LC 79-11619. 282p. 1980. 44.95 (*0-8419-0434-0*) Holmes & Meier.

B

An Asterisk (*) at the beginning of an entry indicates that the title is appearing for the first time.

— Into All the World. (Christian Day School Ser.). (J). (gr. 4). 1992. 16.50 (0-87813-925-7) Christian Light.

Berry, Ron. History is What You Live. 149p. 1998. pap. 25.95 (0-8464-4910-2) Beekman Pubs.

— Peregrine Watching. 97p. 1987. pap. 11.95 (0-8464-4638-3) Beekman Pubs.

— Peregrine Watching. 97p. (C). 1987. pap. 30.00 (0-86383-362-4, Pub. by Gomer Pr) St Mut.

— This Bygone. 205p. 1996. 26.95 (0-8464-4625-1) Beekman Pubs.

***Berry, Ron.** What Nerds Don't Want You to Know! (Nerds' Secrets Ser.). (Illus.). 40p. (YA). 2000. 12.99 (1-891100-72-6, Pub. by Smart Kids Publ) Penton Overseas.

***Berry, Ron & Norris, Annette.** I Hate Homework! Organizer. (Nerds' Secrets Ser.). (Illus.). 40p. (YA). 2000. 12.99 (1-891100-73-4, Pub. by Smart Kids Publ) Penton Overseas.

***Berry, Ron & Sharp, Chris.** It's Bedtime. (It's Time to... Ser.). (Illus.). 16p. (J). (ps-k). 2000. bds. 6.95 (1-891100-61-0, Pub. by Smart Kids Publ) Penton Overseas.

— It's Meal Time. (It's Time to... Ser.). (Illus.). 16p. (J). (ps). 2000. bds. 6.95 (1-891100-62-9, Pub. by Smart Kids Publ) Penton Overseas.

— It's Potty Time for Boys. (It's Time to... Ser.). (Illus.). 16p. (J). (ps-k). 2000. bds. 6.95 (1-891100-60-2, Pub. by Smart Kids Publ) Penton Overseas.

— It's Potty Time for Girls. (It's Time to... Ser.). (Illus.). 16p. (J). (ps-k). 2000. bds. 6.95 (1-891100-59-9, Pub. by Smart Kids Publ) Penton Overseas.

Berry, Ron, et al. Crassy the Crude Beastie: A Beastie Book about Good Manners. (Good Behavior Builders Ser.). (Illus.). 161p. (J). (ps-1). 1996. 5.95 (1-883761-03-4) Fmly Life Prods.

— Fritter the Wasteful Beastie: A Beastie Book about Conserving Resources. (Good Behavior Builders Ser.). (Illus.). 161p. (J). 1993. 5.95 (1-883761-02-6) Fmly Life Prods.

— Glumby the Grumbler: A Beastie Book about Being Grateful. (Good Behavior Builders Ser.). (Illus.). 161p. (J). (ps-1). 1993. 5.95 (1-883761-00-X) Fmly Life Prods.

— Hogger the Hoarding Beastie: A Beastie Book about Sharing. (Good Behavior Builders Ser.). (Illus.). 161p. (J). (ps-1). 1993. 5.95 (1-883761-01-8) Fmly Life Prods.

— Moogie the Messy Beastie: A Beastie Book about Being Neat. (Good Behavior Builders Ser.). (Illus.). 161p. (J). (ps-1). 1993. 5.95 (1-883761-05-0) Fmly Life Prods.

— Scrappy the Squabbler: A Beastie Book about Getting along with Others. (Good Behavior Builders Ser.). (Illus.). 161p. (J). (ps-1). 1993. 5.95 (1-883761-04-2) Fmly Life Prods.

Berry, Ron, jt. auth. see Duey, Kathleen.

***Berry, Ruth.** Freud. (Guides for Beginners - Great Lives Ser.). 2000. pap. 11.95 (0-340-78012-6, Pub. by Headway) Trafalgar.

— Jung. (Guides for Beginners - Great Lives Ser.). 2000. pap. 11.95 (0-340-78055-X, Pub. by Headway) Trafalgar.

— Working with Dreams: How to Understand Your Dreams & Use Them for Personal & Creative Development. 144p. 2000. pap. 14.95 (1-85703-381-7, Pub. by How To Bks) Midpt Trade.

Berry, Rynn. Famous Vegetarians & Their Favorite Recipes. 1987. pap. 12.95 (0-915572-68-0) Panjandrum.

— Famous Vegetarians & Their Favorite Recipes: Lives & Lore from Buddha to the Beatles. rev. ed. (Illus.). 268p. 1999. reprint ed. pap. 15.95 (0-9626169-1-5) Pythago Bks.

— Food for the Gods: Vegetarianism & the World's Religions. LC 97-29810. (Illus.). 392p. 1998. pap. 19.95 (0-9626169-2-3) Pythago Bks.

— The New Vegetarians. (Illus.). 192p. 1989. pap. 10.95 (0-9626169-0-7) Pythago Bks.

Berry, S. L. Indianapolis. (Illus.). 60p. (J). (gr. 3 up). 1990. write for info. (0-685-33006-0, Mac Bks Young Read) S&S Childrens.

— Indianapolis. (Downtown America Ser.). (Illus.). 60p. (J). (gr. 3 up). 1990. lib. bdg. 13.95 (0-87518-426-X, Dillon Silver Burdett) Silver Burdett Pr.

***Berry, S. Torriano.** 50 Most Influential Black Films Movies That Changed the Way We See America. LC 99-45316. 1999. pap. text 15.95 (0-8065-2133-3) Carol Pub Group.

Berry, Sandra H., et al. Measuring Patient Reported Health Status in Advanced HIV Disease: HIV-PARSE Survey Instrument. LC 94-32313. 1994. pap. 9.00 (0-8330-1584-2, MR-342-NIAID) Rand Corp.

***Berry, Sandra K.** Unique Sense of Mind. LC 98-90058. 1999. pap. 8.95 (0-533-12694-0) Vantage.

Berry, Sara. No Condition Is Permanent: The Social Dynamics of Agrarian Change in Sub-Saharan Africa. LC 93-7102. (Illus.). 288p. (C). 1993. pap. 22.95 (0-299-13934-4) U of Wis Pr.

***Berry, Sara S.** Chiefs Know Their Boundaries: Essays on Property, Power & the Past in Asante, 1896-1996. LC 00-35036. (Social History of Africa Ser.). 2000. write for info. (0-325-07003-2); lib. bdg. write for info. (0-325-07002-4) Greenwood.

***Berry, Sarah.** Screen Style: Fashion & Femininity in 1930s Hollywood. LC 99-40065. (Commerce & Mass Culture Ser.). 2000. write for info. (0-8166-3313-4) U of Minn Pr.

— Screen Style: Fashion & Feminity in 1930s Hollywood, 2. LC 99-40065. (Illus.). 256p. 2000. 25.95 (0-8166-3312-6) U of Minn Pr.

Berry, Scott. Monks, Spies & a Soldier of Fortune: The Japanese in Tibet. LC 94-28744. 352p. 1995. text 59.95 (0-312-12398-1) St Martin.

— The Mont Reid Surgical Handbook. 4th ed. LC 97-4039. (Illus.). 920p. (C). (gr. 13). 1997. pap. text 35.95 (0-8151-1007-3, 29155) Mosby Inc.

Berry, Sharon R. 100 Ideas That Work! Discipline in the Classroom. 24p. 1998. reprint ed. pap. text 6.15 (1-58331-006-1) Assn Christ Sch.

***Berry, Sheila M.** Circumstantial Evidence: Anatomy of a Midwestern Murder. 2000. 25.00 (0-9662299-7-5) Archer Books.

Berry, Sheila M. My Name Is Legion. LC 99-31286. 308p. 1999. 25.00 (0-9662299-1-6, Pub. by Archer Books) Midpt Trade.

Berry, Shirley R. Child Abuse & Neglect Prevention Strategies: Milwaukee County. 176p. (Orig.). (C). 1990. pap., teacher ed. 27.50 (0-9627724-0-2) Blckbrry Crtns.

Berry, Skip & Ketzenberger, Jolene. The Insiders' Guide to Greater Indianapolis. 2nd ed. (Insiders' Guide Travel Ser.). 1997. pap. 15.95 (1-57380-015-5, The Insiders Guide) Falcon Pub Inc.

Berry, Stacey, jt. auth. see Eleogram, Tricia.

Berry, Stephen L., et al. Employment Law Handbook: A Complete Reference for Business. 316p. 1993. text 79.00 (0-86587-361-5) Gov Insts.

Berry, Stephen R., ed. see Calhoun, David B.

Berry, Steve. The Boy Who Wouldn't Speak. (Illus.). 32p. (J). (ps-3). 1992. lib. bdg. 14.95 (1-55037-231-9, Pub. by Annick) Firefly Bks Ltd.

Berry, Steve. The Boy Who Wouldn't Speak. (Illus.). 32p. (J). (ps-3). 1992. pap. 5.95 (1-55037-230-0, Pub. by Annick) Firefly Bks Ltd.

Berry, Steven K. The Thunder Dragon Kingdom: A Mountaineering Expedition to Bhutan. (Illus.). 176p. 1988. 29.95 (0-938567-07-1) Mountaineers.

Berry, Susan. Decorating Entrances, Hallways & Stairs. (Illus.). 144p. 1998. pap. 19.95 (0-304-34949-6, Pub. by Cassell) Sterling.

***Berry, Susan.** Garden Plants. (Illustrated Encyclopedias Ser.). (Illus.). 2000. pap. 11.95 (0-7548-0558-1, Lorenz Bks) Anness Pub.

Berry, Susan & Bradley, Steve. Best Plants for Your Garden: A Guide to Choosing the Plants That Will Grow Best in Your Garden. (Illus.). 160p. 1998. 15.98 (0-8317-7491-6) Smithmark.

— Contained Gardens: Creative Designs & Projects. LC 94-45673. (Illus.). 160p. 1995. 25.00 (0-88266-899-4, Garden Way Pub) Storey Bks.

***Berry, Susan & Bradley, Steve.** The Low-Maintenance Garden: A Complete Guide to Designs, Plants & Techniques for Easy-Care Gardens. LC SB473.B47 2000. (Illus.). 144p. 2000. 29.95 (1-55209-514-2); 19.95 (1-55209-531-2) Firefly Bks Ltd.

— The Plant Selector. 160p. 2000. pap. 14.95 (1-84215-080-4) Anness Pub.

— The Practical Guide to Container Gardening. 160p. 2000. pap. 16.95 (1-58017-329-2) Storey Bks.

Berry, Susan & Laura Ashley (Firm) Staff. Laura Ashley Color: Using Color to Decorate Your Home. LC 98-13022. (Illus.). 208p. 1998. pap. 24.95 (0-609-80375-1) C Potter.

Berry, Susan, jt. auth. see Donaldson, Stephanie.

Berry, Susan, jt. auth. see Raworth, Jenny.

Berry, T. Jazz: The Inside Track. 256p. 1985. pap. text 20.95 (0-07-005064-3) McGraw.

Berry, T. E. The Most Common Mistakes in English Usage. 146p. (C). 1971. reprint ed. pap. 7.95 (0-07-005053-8) McGraw.

Berry, T. Sterling. Christianity & Buddhism: A Comparison & a Contrast : Being the Donnellan Lectures for the Year 1889-90. LC 98-904928. 256 p. 1997. write for info. (81-206-1218-3) Asian Educ Servs.

Berry, Terryn L. Essay Writing for Freshman Courses. 80p. (C). 1994. pap. text, spiral bd. 34.95 (0-8403-9594-9, 40959401) Kendall-Hunt.

Berry, Thomas. Creative Energy: Bearing Witness for the Earth. LC 95-44234. (Pathstone Editions Ser.). 96p. (Orig.). 1996. pap. 9.00 (0-87156-854-3, Pub. by Sierra) Random.

— The Dream of Earth. LC 88-42548. (Nature & Natural Philosophy Library). 224p. 1988. 18.95 (0-87156-737-7, Pub. by Sierra) Random.

— The Dream of the Earth. LC 89-42548. (Nature & Natural Philosophy Library). 224p. 1990. pap. 10.00 (0-87156-622-2, Pub. by Sierra) Random.

***Berry, Thomas.** The Great Work. 2000. pap. 12.95 (0-609-80499-5, Pub. by Crown Pub Group) Random House.

Berry, Thomas. The Great Work: Our Way into the Future. LC 99-26350. 1999. 23.00 (0-609-60525-9) Crown.

— Management: The Managerial Ethos & the Future of Planet Earth. (Teilhard Studies: No. 3). 1980. pap. 3.50 (0-89012-016-1) Am Teilhard.

— The New Story: Comments on the Origin, Identification & Transaurian of Values. (Teilhard Studies: No. 1). 1978. 3.50 (0-89012-012-9) Am Teilhard.

— Technology & the Healing of the Earth. (Teilhard Studies: No. 14). 1985. pap. 3.50 (0-89012-043-9) Am Teilhard.

— Teilhard in the Ecological Age. (Teilhard Studies: No. 7). 1982. pap. 3.50 (0-89012-032-3) Am Teilhard.

Berry, Thomas, jt. auth. see Loy, Marc.

Berry, Thomas, jt. auth. see Swimme, Brian.

Berry, Thomas H. Managing the Total Quality Transformation. 223p. 1991. 26.95 (0-07-005071-6) McGraw.

Berry, Thomas M. Buddhism. LC 96-28515. 1996. 14.50 (0-231-10765-X) Col U Pr.

— Religions of India: Hinduism, Yoga, Buddhism. LC 96-28514. 1996. 17.50 (0-231-10781-1) Col U Pr.

Berry, Tim. Cpa's Guide To Developing Effective Business Plans 2000. 1999. pap. text 135.00 (0-15-606881-8) Assessment Sys.

— CPPA'S Guide to Developing Effective Business Plans. 1998. pap. 125.00 (0-15-606295-X) Harcourt Coll Pubs.

***Berry, Tim.** Hurdle the Book on Business Planning: How to Develop & Implement a Successful Business Plan. (Illus.). 1999. pap. 19.95 (0-9664891-2-8) Palo Alto Software.

Berry, Tim. 1999 the Professionals Guide to Purchase & Sale of a Business 2000. 1999. pap. text 135.00 (0-15-606831-1) Harcourt.

***Berry, Tim.** 2001 CPA's Guide to Developing Effective Business Plans. 300p. 2000. pap. 135.00 (0-15-607195-9) Harcourt Legal.

***Berry, Tracy L.** Halloween: Behind the Mask: What Every Christian Parent Should Know. 31p. 1999. pap. 5.95 (1-893555-10-0) Grace Pub TN.

***Berry, Venise T.** All of Me. LC 99-35474. 288p. 2000. 23.95 (0-525-94463-X, Dutt) Dutton Plume.

Berry, Venise T. & Manning-Miller, Carmen L. African-American Media Culture: Contemporary Issues. LC 95-32519. 300p. 1996. 48.00 (0-8039-7277-6); pap. 21.50 (0-8039-7278-4) Sage.

Berry, Vern & Heckert, Connie K. Roots & Recipes: Six Generations of Heartland Cookery. LC 93-44949. (Illus.). 224p. 1995. 16.95 (1-56554-041-7) Pelican.

Berry, W., et al. Sierra Wildlife Coloring Book. 16p. 1971. pap. 1.25 (0-939666-15-4) Yosemite Assn.

Berry, W. B., ed. see Mu, En-Chih, et al.

Berry, W. B. N. Graptolite Faunas of the Marathon Region, West Texas. (Publication Ser.: PUB 6005). (Illus.). 179p. 1960. pap. 3.00 (0-318-03312-7) Bur Econ Geology.

Berry, W. Dennis. A Guide to Training the Swimming Pool Lifeguard. (Illus.). 75p. (C). 1984. pap. text 9.95 (0-89641-140-0) American Pr.

Berry, W. Grinton, ed. see Foxe, John.

Berry, Wallace. Form in Music. 2nd ed. (Illus.). 464p. (C). 1985. text 54.80 (0-13-329285-1) P-H.

— Structural Functions in Music. 480p. 1987. reprint ed. pap. 11.95 (0-486-25384-8) Dover.

Berry, Wayne, jt. auth. see Chen, Weiying.

Berry, Wendell. The Agricultural Crisis: A Crisis of Culture. 41p. (gr. 8-12). 1977. 1.50 (0-913098-28-0) Orion Society.

— Another Turn of the Crank. 128p. 1996. pap. text 13.00 (1-887178-28-7, Pub. by Counterpt DC) HarpC.

— The Collected Poems of Wendell Berry 1957-1982. LC 84-62305. 288p. 1985. 19.95 (0-86547-189-4) N Point Pr.

— A Continuous Harmony: Essays Cultural & Agricultural. LC 74-17016. 192p. 1975. reprint ed. pap. 10.00 (0-15-622575-1, Harvest Bks) Harcourt.

— Entries. LC 97-7191. 88p. 1997. pap. text 12.50 (1-887178-37-6, Pub. by Counterpt DC) HarpC.

— Farming: A Hand Book. LC 71-118828. 132p. 1971. reprint ed. pap. 9.00 (0-15-630171-7, Harvest Bks) Harcourt.

— Fidelity: Five Stories. 1993. pap. 11.00 (0-679-74831-8) Pantheon.

— The Gift of Good Land: Further Essays Cultural & Agricultural. LC 81-81507. 286p. 1982. pap. 13.00 (0-86547-052-9) N Point Pr.

— Harlan Hubbard: Life & Work. rev. ed. (Blazer Lectures). (Illus.). 144p. 1990. pap. 18.00 (0-8131-0942-6) U Pr of Ky.

— The Hidden Wound. LC 88-34555. 150p. 1989. reprint ed. pap. 11.00 (0-86547-358-7) N Point Pr.

— Home Economics. LC 86-62838. 192p. 1987. pap. 11.00 (0-86547-275-0) N Point Pr.

***Berry, Wendell.** Jayber Crow. 384p. 2000. 25.00 (1-58243-029-2, Pub. by Counterpt DC) HarpC.

— Life Is a Miracle: An Essay Against Modern Superstition. 124p. 2000. text 21.00 (1-58243-058-6, Pub. by Counterpt DC) HarpC.

— The Memory of Old Jack. LC PS3552.E75M4 1999. 176p. 1999. pap. text 13.50 (1-58243-043-8, Pub. by Counterpt DC) HarpC.

Berry, Wendell. Nathan Coulter. LC 84-62306. 192p. 1985. 12.00 (0-86547-184-3) N Point Pr.

— A Part: Poems. LC 80-18268. 104p. 1985. pap. 6.95 (0-86547-008-1) N Point Pr.

— A Place on Earth. rev. ed. LC 82-81478. 352p. 1982. reprint ed. pap. 13.00 (0-86547-044-8) N Point Pr.

***Berry, Wendell.** A Place on Earth. rev. ed. 2001. pap. 14.00 (1-58243-124-8) Counterpt DC.

Berry, Wendell. Recollected Essays, Nineteen Sixty-Five to Nineteen Eighty. LC 80-28812. 346p. 1982. pap. 15.00 (0-86547-026-X) N Point Pr.

— Sayings & Doings & an Eastward Look. rev. ed. LC 90-81977. 64p. 1990. reprint ed. pap. 10.00 (0-917788-43-5) Gnomon Pr.

— The Selected Poems of Wendell Berry. LC 98-34793. 160p. 1998. 20.00 (1-887178-84-8, Pub. by Counterpt DC) HarpC.

***Berry, Wendell.** Selected Poems of Wendell Berry. 192p. 1999. pap. text 12.50 (1-58243-037-3, Pub. by Counterpt DC) HarpC.

Berry, Wendell. Sex, Economy, Freedom & Community. 208p. 1994. pap. 11.00 (0-679-75651-5) Pantheon.

— A Timbered Choir: The Sabbath Poems, 1979-1997. LC 98-4925. 240p. 1998. 22.00 (1-887178-68-6, Pub. by Counterpt DC) HarpC.

— A Timbered Choir: The Sabbath Poems, 1979-1997. 240p. 1999. pap. text 12.50 (1-58243-006-3, Pub. by Counterpt DC) HarpC.

***Berry, Wendell.** Two More Stories of the Port William Membership. LC 97-74434. 62p. 1999. reprint ed. pap. 10.50 (0-917788-71-0) Gnomon Pr.

Berry, Wendell. The Unsettling of America: Culture & Agriculture. rev. ed. 236p. 1996. pap. 12.00 (0-87156-877-2, Pub. by Sierra) Random.

— Wendell Berry. Merchant, Paul, ed. LC 91-73134. (American Authors Ser.). 250p. 1991. 25.00 (0-917652-89-4) Confluence Pr.

— What Are People For? LC 89-29848. 224p. 1990. pap. 11.00 (0-86547-437-0) N Point Pr.

— The Wild Birds: Six Stories of the Port William Membership. LC 85-72988. 160p. 1989. pap. 11.00 (0-86547-217-3) N Point Pr.

— A World Lost. 160p. 1997. pap. 12.50 (1-887178-54-6, Pub. by Counterpt DC) HarpC.

Berry, Wendell, et al. From the Heartlands: Photos & Essays from the Midwest. (Midwest Writers Ser.: No. 1). (Illus.). 200p. (Orig.). (C). 1988. pap. 8.95 (0-933087-13-6) Bottom Dog Pr.

— Three on Community. 68p. (Orig.). 1996. pap. 25.00 (0-931659-27-2) Limberlost Pr.

— Three on Community. deluxe limited ed. 68p. (Orig.). 1996. 175.00 (0-931659-28-0) Limberlost Pr.

Berry, William. What Do I Do Next? 101 Steps to Successfully Starting Your Own Business. unabridged ed. 500p. 1989. ring bd. 69.95 (0-9660401-0-4) Success Educ.

Berry, William & Feldman, Stanley. Multiple Regression in Practice. (Quantitative Applications in the Social Sciences Ser.: Vol. 50). 1985. 13.95 (0-8039-2054-7) Sage.

Berry, William & Garber, Judith B. Beery Family History. (Illus.). 783p. 1997. reprint ed. pap. 105.00 (0-8328-7469-8); reprint ed. lib. bdg. 115.00 (0-8328-7468-X) Higginson Bk Co.

Berry, William & Lowery, David. Understanding United States Government Growth: An Empirical Analysis of the Postwar Era. LC 87-11818. 226p. 1987. 62.95 (0-275-92509-9, C2509, Praeger Pubs) Greenwood.

Berry, William, et al. Master Production Scheduling: Principles & Practices. LC 82-236025. 183p. 1983. 25.00 (0-935406-21-2) Am Prod & Inventory.

Berry, William A. Drawing the Human Form: Methods, Sources, Concepts. 2nd ed. LC 93-4354. 306p. 1994. pap. text 40.60 (0-13-219783-9) P-H.

Berry, William A. & Alexander, James E. Justice for Sale: Shocking Scandal of Oklahoma Supreme Court. (Illus.). 224p. 1996. 24.95 (0-939965-12-7) Macedon Prod.

Berry, William A. & Alexander, James Edwin. Prisoner of the Rising Sun. LC 92-50713. 1993. 27.95 (0-8061-2509-8) U of Okla Pr.

Berry, William B. & Wentworth, Chapman. Lost Sierra; Gold, Ghosts & Skis: Legendary Days of Skiing in the California Mining Camps. 256p. 1992. 37.50 (0-9631721-0-7); pap. 25.00 (0-9631721-1-5) W&A Comms.

Berry, William D. Buffalo Land. (Illus.). 48p. (J). (gr. 5-8). 1985. reprint ed. pap. 9.95 (0-938271-01-6) Press N Amer.

— Deneki, An Alaskan Moose. (Illus.). 48p. (J). (gr. 5-8). 1983. reprint ed. pap. 9.95 (0-938271-00-8) Press N Amer.

— Nonrecursive Causal Models. (Quantitative Applications in the Social Science Ser.: Vol. 37). 88p. 1984. pap. 10.95 (0-8039-2265-5) Sage.

— Understanding Regression Assumptions. (Quantitative Applications in the Social Sciences Ser.: Vol. 92). (Illus.). 96p. (C). 1993. pap. text 10.95 (0-8039-4263-X) Sage.

Berry, William D. William D. Berry, 1954-1956, Alaskan Field Sketches. LC 89-4927. xvii, 304p. 1989. 39.95 (0-912006-34-X); pap. 19.95 (0-912006-36-6) U of Alaska Pr.

Berry, William D. & Berry, Elizabeth. Mammals of the San Francisco Bay Region. LC 59-6052. (California Natural History Guides Ser.: No. 2). (Illus.). 80p. reprint ed. pap. 30.00 (0-608-17993-0, 202903900058) Bks Demand.

Berry, William D. & Lewis-Beck, Michael S., eds. New Tools for Social Scientists: Advances & Applications in Research Methods. LC 85-19653. (Illus.). 288p. 1986. reprint ed. pap. 89.30 (0-608-01186-X, 205948400001) Bks Demand.

Berry, William D. & Sanders, Mitchell. Understanding Multivariate Methods. LC 99-57762. (Essentials of Political Science Ser.). 108p. (C). 1999. pap. 16.00 (0-8133-9971-8) Westview.

Berry, William E. Last Rights: Revisiting Four Theories of the Press. Nerone, John C. & McChesney, Robert W., eds. LC 95-3566. (History of Communication Ser.). 200p. (C). 1995. text 29.95 (0-252-02180-0); pap. text 14.95 (0-252-06470-4) U of Ill Pr.

Berry, William L., et al. Integrated Production & Inventory Management: Revitalizing the Manufacturing Enterprise. (APICS Ser.). 270p. 1992. 47.50 (1-55623-604-2, Irwn Prfssnl) McGraw-Hill Prof.

— Manufacturing Planning & Control Systems. 3rd ed. (APICS Series in Production Management). 900p. 1991. 65.00 (1-55623-608-5, Irwn Prfssnl) McGraw-Hill Prof.

— Manufacturing Planning & Control Systems. 3rd ed. 912p. (C). 1991. text 58.00 (0-256-08808-X, Irwn McGrw-H) McGrw-H Hghr Educ.

— Manufacturing Planning & Control Systems. 4th ed. 864p. 1997. text 65.00 (0-7863-1209-2, Irwn McGrw-H) McGrw-H Hghr Educ.

Berryessa, Norman. Global Investing: The Templeton Way. 228p. 1992. text 17.50 (1-55623-873-8, Irwn Prfssnl) McGraw-Hill Prof.

Berryhill, Clint. Rifles & Romance. 200p. 1983. pap. 5.00 (0-942698-09-6) Trends & Events.

— Take a Chance on Me. 268p. 1983. pap. 5.00 (0-685-07464-1) Trends & Events.

Berryhill, Dale A. The Assault: Liberalism's Attack on Religion, Freedom, & Democracy. LC 94-79223. 208p. 1995. pap. 10.99 (1-56384-077-4) Huntington Hse.

— The Media Hates Conservatives: How It Controls the Flow of Information. LC 94-75121. 224p. 1994. pap. 10.99 (1-56384-060-X) Huntington Hse.

Berryhill, Elaine, ed. see Wright, Edward.

Berryhill-Johnson, Jane, jt. auth. see Schafer, Stacey.

B

An Asterisk (*) at the beginning of an entry indicates that the title is appearing for the first time.

Berryhill, Judy. Chuckle & Giggle, Vol. 1. Cornwell, Ilene, ed. (Learning to Obey Ser.: Bk. 8). (Illus.). 30p. (J). (gr. k-4). 1997. 14.00 (*0-9653872-1-6*) Hartford Publns.
— Chuckle & Giggle Vol. 2: Exploring the Natchez Trace. large type ed. (Illus.). 30p. (J). (ps-4). 1998. 14.00 (*0-9653872-4-0*) Hartford Publns.
— Teeny Tiny, the Snowflake: Learns to Obey His Parents. (Illus.). 38p. (Orig.). (J). (ps-6). 1996. pap. 9.99 (*0-9653872-0-8*) Hartford Publns.
Berryhill, Judy & Meeker, Frances. Country Sunshine: The Dottie West Story. 127p. (Orig.). 1995. pap. 12.95 (*0-9653872-3-2*) Hartford Publns.
***Berryhill, Robert.** Bus Across Mexico: A Unique Guide for the Young at Heart. LC 00-133172. (Illus.). 160p. 2000. pap. 19.95 (*0-9700979-5-6*) Bengi Pub.
Berryman. Liberation Theology. 1987. pap. 6.95 (*0-07-545051-8*) McGraw.
Berryman, A. A. Dynamics of Forest Insect Populations: Patterns, Causes & Implications. LC 88-12631. (Population Ecology Ser.). (Illus.). 624p. (C). 1988. text 145.00 (*0-306-42745-1*, Kluwer Plenum) Kluwer Academic.
— Forest Insects: Principles & Practice of Population Management. LC 86-4890. (Population Ecology Ser.). (Illus.). 294p. (C). 1986. text 65.00 (*0-306-42196-8*, Kluwer Plenum) Kluwer Academic.
Berryman, Alan A. Population Systems: A General Introduction. LC 80-26167. 238p. 1981. 29.50 (*0-306-40589-X*, Plenum Trade) Perseus Pubng.
***Berryman, Alan A.** Principles of Population Dynamics & Their Application. (Illus.). 192p. 1999. pap. 47.50 (*0-7487-4015-5*, Pub. by S Thornes Pubs) Trans-Atl Phila.
Berryman, Bryan. Vintage Scarborough. LC 76-378406. (Illus.). 40p. 1976. write for info. (*0-902907-93-X*) Hendon Pubng.
Berryman, Charles. Decade of Novels - Fiction of the 1970s: Form & Challenge. LC 89-51479. vi, 140p. 1990. 39.00 (*0-87875-390-7*) Whitston Pub.
Berryman-Fink, Cynthia. The Manager's Desk Reference. LC 88-48035. 370p. 1991. pap. 19.95 (*0-8144-7759-3*) AMACOM.
Berryman-Fink, Cynthia, et al, eds. Communication & Sex-Role Socialization. LC 92-33993. 592p. 1993. text 25.00 (*0-8153-1256-3*) Garland.
Berryman-Fink, Cynthia & Fink, Charles B. The Manager's Desk Reference. 2nd ed. LC 96-12325. 384p. 1996. 24.95 (*0-8144-0342-5*) AMACOM.
Berryman, Gregg. Designing Creative Portfolios. Gerould, Philip, ed. LC 92-39103. (Illus.). 96p. (Orig.). 1994. pap. 13.95 (*1-56052-113-9*) Crisp Pubns.
— Designing Creative Resumes. rev. ed. Gerould, Philip, ed. LC 91-21443. (Illus.). 175p. 1991. pap. 15.95 (*1-56052-053-1*) Crisp Pubns.
— Notes on Graphic Design & Visual Communications. rev. ed. LC 90-21563. (Illus.). 46p. (C). 1990. pap. 8.95 (*1-56052-044-2*) Crisp Pubns.
Berryman, Jack H. & Markley, Merle, eds. International Association of Fish & Wildlife Agencies, 73rd Convention, 1983: Proceedings. 300p. lib. bdg. 15.00 (*0-932108-10-5*) IAFWA.
Berryman, Jack W. & Park, Roberta J., eds. Sport & Exercise Science: Essays in the History of Sports Medicine. 392p. (C). 1992. text 44.95 (*0-252-01896-6*); pap. text 18.95 (*0-252-06242-6*) U of Ill Pr.
***Berryman, Jeffrey Bruce.** The Law of Equitable Remedies. (Essentials of Canadian Law Ser.). 2000. pap. 35.95 (*1-55221-042-1*, Pub. by Irwin Law) Gaunt.
Berryman, Jerome W. Godly Play: An Imaginative Approach to Religious Education. LC 94-38496. 1994. pap. 14.99 (*0-8066-2785-9*, 9-2785, Augsburg) Augsburg Fortress.
Berryman, Jerome W., jt. auth. see Stewart, Sonja M.
Berryman, Jo B. Circe's Craft: Ezra Pound's Hugh Selwyn Mauberley. LC 83-5936. (Studies in Modern Literature: No. 19). (Illus.). 257p. reprint ed. pap. 79.70 (*0-8357-1431-4*, 207053200001) Bks Demand.
Berryman, John. Berryman's Shakespeare: Essays, Letters & Other Writings. Haffenden, John, ed. LC 98-41000. 416p. 1999. text 30.00 (*0-374-11205-3*) FS&G.
***Berryman, John.** Berryman's Shakespeare: Essays, Letters & Other Writings. Haffenden, John, ed. 416p. 2001. pap. 16.00 (*0-374-52750-4*) FS&G.
Berryman, John. The Dream Songs. LC 74-93811. 427p. 1982. pap. 16.00 (*0-374-51670-7*) FS&G.
Berryman, John, jt. auth. see Reynolds, Barry.
Berryman, Judy C. & Breighner, Kathryn W. Modeling Healthy Behavior: Actions & Attitudes in Schools. LC 93-4787. 1993. 24.95 (*1-56071-357-7*) ETR Assocs.
Berryman, Julia C. Older Mothers: Conception, Pregnancy & Birth After 35. LC 99-215731. 1998. pap. text 17.00 (*0-86358-410-1*) Harper SF.
Berryman, Julia C., ed. Differences Between the Sexes: Their Relevance for Adult Educators. (C). 1989. 40.00 (*1-85041-028-3*, Pub. by Univ Nottingham) St Mut.
Berryman, Julia C., et al. Older Mothers: Conception, Pregnancy & Birth after 35. 276p. 1998. pap. 17.00 (*0-04-440906-0*, Pub. by Rivers Oram) NYU Pr.
Berryman, L. C. Jazz Bass Intonation Plus Double Bass Method. 96p. 1997. pap. 14.95 (*0-7935-7807-8*) H Leonard.
Berryman, L. C. Sex Differences in Behaviour: Their Relevance for Adult Educators. (C). 1988. text 45.00 (*0-7855-3180-7*, Pub. by Univ Nottingham) St Mut.
Berryman-Miller, Sherrill, jt. ed. see Beal, Rayma K.
Berryman, Phillip. Liberation Theology: Essential Facts about the Revolutionary Religious Movement in Latin America & Beyond. 240p. 1987. 37.95 (*0-87722-479-X*) Temple U Pr.
— Religion in the Megacity: Portraits from Two Latin American Cities. LC 96-33367. 200p. (Orig.). 1996. pap. 18.00 (*1-57075-083-1*) Orbis Bks.
— The Religious Roots of Rebellion: Christians in Central American Revolutions. LC 83-19343. 464p. 1984. reprint ed. pap. 143.90 (*0-7837-9801-6*, 206053000005) Bks Demand.
— Stubborn Hope: Religion, Politics, & Revolution in Central America. 288p. 1994. 22.95 (*1-56584-136-0*, Pub. by New Press NY) Norton.
— Stubborn Hope: Religion, Politics, & Revolution in Central America. 288p. 1995. pap. 13.95 (*1-56584-137-9*, Pub. by New Press NY) Norton.
— Stubborn Hope: Religion, Politics, & Revolution in Central America. LC 94-2253. 286p. reprint ed. pap. 88.70 (*0-608-20185-5*, 207144400012) Bks Demand.
Berryman, Phillip, tr. see Boff, Leonardo.
Berryman, Phillip, tr. see Casaldaliga, Pedro.
Berryman, Phillip, tr. see Cleary, Edward L., ed.
Berryman, Phillip, tr. see Comblin, Jose.
Berryman, Phillip, tr. see De Mello, Anthony.
Berryman, Phillip, tr. see Fabella, Virginia & Oduyoye, Mercy Amda, eds.
Berryman, Phillip, tr. see Hoff, Leonardo.
Berryman, Phillip, tr. see Irarrazaval, Diego.
Berryman, Phillip, tr. see Mignone, Emilio F.
Berryman, Phillip, tr. see Richard, Pablo.
Berryman, Phillip, tr. see Sobrino, Jon & Pico, Juan H.
Berryman, Phillip, tr. see Treto, Raul G.
Berryman, Phillip E., tr. from SPA. Report of the Chilean National Commission on Truth & Reconciliation, 2 vols., Set. LC 93-13815.Tr. of Informe de la Comision Nacional de Verdad y Reconciliacion. (C). 1993. text 69.00 (*0-268-01645-3*); pap. text 34.50 (*0-268-01646-1*) U of Notre Dame Pr.
Berryman, Sue & Bailey, Thomas A. The Double Heliz of Education & the Economy. 155p. (C). 1992. pap. 12.00 (*1-882217-00-4*) Inst on Educ.
Berryman, Sue E. Routes into the Mainstream: Career Choices of Women & Minorities. 1988. 2.75 (*0-318-40008-1*, OC 124) Ctr Educ Trng Employ.
Berrywell, Clint. Survivors. 196p. 1983. pap. 5.00 (*0-942698-13-4*) Trends & Events.
Bers, Donald M. Excitation - Contraction Coupling & Cardiac Contractile Force. (Developments in Cardiovascular Medicine Ser.). 258p. (C). 1991. lib. bdg. 118.50 (*0-7923-1186-8*) Kluwer Academic.
— Excitation-Contraction Coupling & Cardiac Contractile Force. (Developments in Cardiovascular Medicine Ser.). 288p. (C). 1993. pap. text 61.00 (*0-7923-2479-X*) Kluwer Academic.
Bers, Eric & Hendrickson, Chris, eds. Managing Urban Transportation As a Business. 382p. 1987. 32.00 (*0-87262-627-X*) Am Soc Civil Eng.
Bers, Lipman. Selected Works of Lipman Bers: Papers on Complex Analysis, 2 vols. Kra, Irwin & Maskit, Bernard, eds. Incl. Vol. 1. LC 98-2927. 1998. 125.00 (*0-8218-0996-2*, CWORKS-BERS-1); Vol. 2. LC 98-2927. 1998. 125.00 (*0-8218-0997-0*, CWORKS-BERS-2); 225.00 (*0-8218-0858-3*) Am Math.
Bers, Lipman, ed. Charles Loewner: Collected Works. (Contemporary Mathematicians Ser.). 272p. 1988. 122.50 (*0-8176-3377-4*) Birkhauser.
Bers, Lipman, et al. Contributions to the Theory of Partial Differential Equations. (Annals of Mathematics Studies: No. 33). 1972. reprint ed. 25.00 (*0-527-02749-9*) Periodicals Srv.
— Partial Differential Equations. LC 63-19664. (Lectures in Applied Mathematics: Vol. 3a). 343p. 1975. reprint ed. pap. 45.00 (*0-8218-0049-3*, LAM/3.1) Am Math.
Bers, Melvin K. Union Policy & the Older Worker. LC 76-14986. 87p. 1976. reprint ed. lib. bdg. 49.50 (*0-8371-8655-2*, BEUP, Greenwood Pr) Greenwood.
Bers, Trudy H. & Mittler, Mary L., eds. Assessment & Testing: Myths & Realities. LC 85-644753. (New Directions for Community Colleges Ser.: No. CC 88). 110p. (Orig.). 1994. pap. 22.00 (*0-7879-9983-0*) Jossey-Bass.
***Bers, Trudy H. & Seybert, Jeffrey A.** Effective Reporting. 99p. (C). 1999. pap. text 15.00 (*1-882393-08-2*) Assn Instl Res.
Bers, Victor. Speech in Speech: Studies in Incorporated Oratio Recta in Attic Drama & Oratory. LC 96-48908. (Greek Studies: Interdisciplinary Approaches). 256p. 1997. 66.00 (*0-8476-8449-0*); pap. 25.95 (*0-8476-8450-4*) Rowman.
Bersani, Ferdinando. Electricity & Magnetism in Biology & Medicine. LC 98-47483. 996p. (C). 1999. text. write for info. (*0-306-46041-6*, Kluwer Plenum) Kluwer Academic.
Bersani, Hank, jt. ed. see Dybwad, Gunnar.
Bersani, Hank A., jt. auth. see Dybwad, Gunnar.
Bersani, Hank A., jt. auth. see Fried-Oken, Melanie.
Bersani, Leo. The Culture of Redemption. (Illus.). 248p. 1990. text 32.00 (*0-674-17977-3*) HUP.
— The Culture of Redemption. (Illus.). 248p. 1999. pap. 16.95 (*0-674-17978-1*) HUP.
— The Freudian Body: Psychoanalysis & Art. LC 85-22334. (Illus.). 126p. 1990. pap. text 18.00 (*0-231-06219-2*, King's Crown Paperbacks) Col U Pr.
Bersani, Leo. A Future for Astyanax: Character & Desire in Literature LC 76-10322. xii, 338 p. 1976. write for info. (*0-316-09213-4*) Little.
Bersani, Leo. A Future for Astynax. 388p. 1984. text 66.50 (*0-231-05938-8*) Col U Pr.
— Homos. LC 94-30987. 218p. 1995. text 22.95 (*0-674-40619-2*, BERHOM) HUP.
— Homos. 224p. 1996. pap. 12.95 (*0-674-40620-6*) HUP.
Bersani, Leo & Dutoit, Ulysse. Arts of Impoverishment: Beckett, Rothko, Resnais. LC 93-16603. (Illus.). 256p. 1994. 42.00 (*0-674-04875-X*); pap. 22.95 (*0-674-04876-8*) HUP.
***Bersani, Leo & Dutoit, Ulysse.** Caravaggio. (BFI Modern Classics). (Illus.). 86p. 1999. pap. 10.95 (*0-85170-724-6*, Pub. by British Film Inst) Ind U Pr.
Bersani, Leo & Dutoit, Ulysse. Caravaggio's Secret. LC 98-17336. (Illus.). 140p. 1998. 25.00 (*0-262-02449-7*) MIT Pr.
Bersaques, J. De, see De Bersaques, J., ed.
Bersaw, Barbara M. The Mystery at Blarney Castle, Vol. 1. (Illus.). viii, 40p. (J). (gr. 4-6). 1997. pap. 3.50 (*0-9660535-0-8*) Castle Pubns MA.
Bersch, Maxine. Storytelling in a Nutshell: A Primer for Storytellers in Christian Education. (Illus.). 244p. 1998. pap. text 12.95 (*0-7673-9104-7*) LifeWay Christian.
Bersche, Paul. Is There a Father in the House? 192p. (Orig.). 1995. pap. 12.99 (*1-56043-834-7*, Treasure Hse) Destiny Image.
Berscheid, Ellen, jt. auth. see Regan, Pamela C.
Berschin, Walter. Bonizo von Sutri: Leben & Werk. (Beitraege zur Geschichte und Quellenkunde des Mittelalters Ser.: Bd 2). 200p. (C). 1972. 102.35 (*3-11-001758-X*) De Gruyter.
— Greek Letters & the Latin Middle Ages: From Jerome to Nicholas of Cusa. expanded rev. ed. Frakes, Jerold C., tr. LC 86-9762.Tr. of Griechisch-lateinisches mittelalter von Hieronymus zu Nikolaus von Kues. (Illus.). 431p. 1988. reprint ed. pap. 133.70 (*0-7837-9198-4*, 204990000004) Bks Demand.
Berschin, Walter, ed. see Hrotsvitha.
Bersee, Harald E. Diaphragm Forming of Continuous Fibre Reinforced Thermoplastics: Process Analysis & Development. (Illus.). 571p. (Orig.). 1996. pap. 47.50 (*90-407-1334-0*, Pub. by Delft U Pr) Coronet Bks.
Bersee, Josefien, compiled by. RARE (Association of European Networking Organizations) "State of the Union" Report. 48p. (Orig.). (C). 1993. pap. text 25.00 (*0-7881-0038-6*) DIANE Pub.
Berselli, Costante. Hymns to Christ. (Illus.). (C). 1988. 60.00 (*0-85439-210-6*, Pub. by St Paul Pubns) St Mut.
— To Him Be Praise. (C). 1988. 39.00 (*0-85439-211-4*, Pub. by St Paul Pubns) St Mut.
Berselli, Costante & Gharib, Georges. Sing the Joys of Mary.Tr. of Lodi alla Madonna. (C). 1988. 45.00 (*0-85439-188-6*, Pub. by St Paul Pubns) St Mut.
Bersen, Dolores. The Adventures of Clyde Cockroach. 26p. (J). (ps-4). 1994. 13.95 (*0-9640986-0-1*); pap. 4.95 (*0-9640986-4-4*); lib. bdg. 14.95 (*0-9640986-1-X*) DUB Pubng.
— Lynda Ladybug. 24p. (J). (ps-2). 1995. 13.95 (*0-9640986-2-8*); pap. 4.95 (*0-9640986-5-2*); lib. bdg. 14.95 (*0-9640986-3-6*) DUB Pubng.
— Rhythmic Phonics. (Illus.). 56p. (J). 1997. pap. 8.95 (*0-933025-65-3*) Blue Bird Pub.
Bersez, J. Practical Explanatory Dictionary of Magical Items & Related Articles.Tr. of Dictionnaire Pratique des Explicatif des Produits Magiques et Articles Usuels. (FRE.). 125p. 1985. pap. 75.00 (*0-7859-4847-3*, M6732) Fr & Eur.
Bershad, Deborah, ed. see Laster, Paul & Riccardo, Renee.
Bershader, Daniel & Hanson, Ronald, eds. Shock Waves & Shock Tubes: Proceedings of the Fifteenth International Symposium on Shock Waves & Shock Tubes. (Illus.). xvi, 922p. 1986. 69.50 (*0-8047-1310-3*) Stanford U Pr.
Bershader, Daniel, ed. see International Symposium on Shock Waves & Shock Tub.
Bershadker, Andrew, jt. auth. see Haveman, Robert.
Bershadsky, A. D. & Vasiliev, J. M. Cytoskeleton. LC 87-38489. (Cellular Organelles Ser.). (Illus.). 310p. (C). 1988. text 69.50 (*0-306-42508-4*, Kluwer Plenum) Kluwer Academic.
Bershady, Harold J. Social Class & Democratic Leadership: Essays in Honor of E. Digby Baltzell. LC 89-4845. 316p. (C). 1989. text 46.50 (*0-8122-8158-6*) U of Pa Pr.
***Bershon, Richard Y.** With the Cross of Jesus: A History of the Church of God Chaplaincy & Ministry to the Military. 2000. pap. 9.99 (*0-87148-955-4*) Pathway Pr.
Bershtel, Sara & Graubard, Allen. Saving Remnants: Feeling Jewish in America. LC 93-1852. 1992. reprint ed. pap. 17.95 (*0-520-08512-4*, Pub. by U CA Pr) Cal Prin Full Svc.
Bersianik, Louky. The Euguelion. Scott, Howard, tr. from FRE. LC 97-121978.Tr. of Euguelionne. 358p. 1997. pap. 17.55 (*1-896743-01-3*, Pub. by Alter Ego Editions) Genl Dist Srvs.
Bersoff, Donald, et al. Law & Mental Health Professionals: Pennsylvania. LC 98-25722. 392p. 1998. 59.95 (*1-55798-555-3*) Am Psychol.
Bersoff, Donald N., ed. Ethical Conflicts in Psychology. 2nd rev. ed. LC 99-14474. 560p. 1999. pap. 39.95 (*1-55798-599-5*, 431-2081); text 59.95 (*1-55798-591-X*, 431-2080) Am Psychol.
Berson. Building Data Mining Applications. 488p. 1999. pap. 49.00 (*0-07-134444-6*) McGraw.
Berson, A. Client - Server Architectures. 2nd ed. (Illus.). 569p. 1996. 55.00 (*0-07-005664-1*) McGraw.
Berson, Alan S., jt. auth. see Association for Advancement of Medical Instrumenta.
Berson, Alex. Data Warehousing. Data Mining, & OLAP. LC 97-27472. (Mcgraw Hill Series on Data Warehousing). (Illus.). 640p. 1997. 54.95 (*0-07-006272-2*) McGraw.
Berson, Alex & Anderson, George. Sybase & Client-Server Computing. LC 94-44228. (Computer Communications Ser.). 1995. write for info. (*0-00-700503-2*) McGraw.
Berson, Alex & Anderson, Geroge. Sybase & Client-Server Computing: Featuring System II. 2nd ed. LC 97-125676. (Illus.). 650p. 1996. pap. 54.95 (*0-07-006080-0*) McGraw.
Berson, Ann, jt. auth. see Walsh, Margaret.
Berson, Dvera & Roy, Sander. Pain-Free Arthritis. (Illus.). 130p. 1982. 23.50 (*0-9609608-0-5*) S & J Books.
Berson, Frank G., ed. Ophthalmology for Medical Students & Primary Care Physicians. 6th ed. LC 93-21474. 1993. write for info. (*1-56055-074-0*) Am Acad Ophthal.
— Ophthalmology Study Guide for Students & Practitioners of Medicine. 5th ed. (Illus.). 166p. 1987. 10.00 (*0-317-94084-8*) Am Acad Ophthal.
Berson, Jon. Foamers. LC 97-2491. 1997. 23.00 (*0-684-83586-X*) S&S Trade.
Berson, Lenora E. Culture Shock: Soviet Jews in Philadelphia. (Illus.). 5.00 (*0-614-32307-X*) Balch IES Pr.
— Culture Shock: Soviet Jews in Philadelphia. (Illus.). 5.00 (*0-614-14844-8*) Balch Inst Ethnic Studies.
Berson, Misha. Performances & Presentations. Link, Terry, ed. 24p. (Orig.). 1994. pap. 5.00 (*0-936434-72-4*, Pub. by Zellerbach Fam Fund) Intl Spec Bk.
— The San Francisco Stage: From Gold Rush to Golden Spike, 1849-1869, Pt. 1. (Journals: No. 2). 100p. 1989. pap. 15.00 (*1-881106-01-2*) SF Perf Arts Lib.
— The San Francisco Stage: From Golden Spike to Great Earthquake, 1869-1906, Pt. 2. Gere, David, ed. (SF Palm Ser.: No. 4). (Illus.). 146p. (Orig.). (C). 1992. pap. 15.00 (*1-881106-03-9*) SF Perf Arts Lib.
Berson, Robin Kadison. Young Heroes in World History. LC 98-46809. (Illus.). 288p. (YA). (gr. 7 up). 1999. 45.00 (*0-313-30257-X*, GR0257, Greenwood Pr) Greenwood.
Berson, Robing K. Marching to a Different Drummer: Unrecognized Heroes of American History. LC 93-49533. 368p. 1994. 49.95 (*0-313-28802-X*, Greenwood Pr) Greenwood.
Berson, Ruth, jt. auth. see Bennett, Anna G.
Berson, T. A. & Beth, T., eds. Local Area Network Security. (Lecture Notes in Computer Science Ser.: Vol. 396). x, 152p. 1989. pap. 31.00 (*0-387-51754-5*) Spr-Verlag.
Berssenbrugge, Mei-Mei. Empathy. 88p. 1988. pap. 14.95 (*0-88268-078-1*) Station Hill Pr.
Berssenbrugge, Mei-mei. Endocrinology. Dienstfrey, Patricia, ed. LC 97-20715. (Illus.). 36p. 1997. pap. 17.00 (*0-932716-41-5*) Kelsey St Pr.
— Endocrinology. deluxe limited ed. LC 97-20715. (Illus.). 36p. 1997. pap. 250.00 (*0-932716-42-3*) Kelsey St Pr.
— Four Year Old Girl. Dienstfrey, Patricia, ed. LC 98-26171. (Illus.). 88p. 1998. pap. 12.00 (*0-932716-44-X*) Kelsey St Pr.
— Four Year Old Girl. LC 98-26171. (Illus.). 80p. 1998. 200.00 (*0-932716-46-6*) Kelsey St Pr.
— The Heat Bird: Poems. (Poetry Ser.). 62p. 1986. reprint ed. pap. 6.00 (*0-930901-03-7*) Burning Deck.
Berssenbrugge, Mei-Mei. Mizu. deluxe limited ed. 1990. pap. 75.00 (*0-685-56973-X*) Chax Pr.
— Rat Pack Steve. (Chapbook Ser.). 24p. (Orig.). (C). 1983. pap. 3.00 (*0-936556-09-9*) Contact Two.
Berssenbrugge, Mei-mei. Summits Move with the Tide. 2nd ed. 70p. (Orig.). 1982. pap. 4.00 (*0-912678-56-9*, Greenfld Rev Pr) Greenfld Rev Lit.
Berssenbrugge, Mei-Mei & Tuttle, Richard. Sphericity. Dienstfrey, Patricia & Rosenwasser, Rena, eds. LC 92-37586. (Illus.). 48p. (C). 1993. pap. 14.00 (*0-932716-30-X*) Kelsey St Pr.
Bersson, Robert. Worlds of Art. 1999. pap. text 31.50 (*0-697-25819-X*) McGraw.
Berst, Barbara J. I Love Softball. LC 84-62470. (Illus.). 72p. (Orig.). (J). (gr. 3-6). 1985. pap. 4.25 (*0-9614126-0-7*) Natl Lilac Pub.
Berst, Charles A. Bernard Shaw & the Art of Drama. LC 73-180884. 363p. reprint ed. pap. 112.60 (*0-8357-6038-3*, 203442600090) Bks Demand.
— Pygmalion. (Twayne's Masterwork Studies). 1995. 29.00 (*0-8057-9447-6*, Twyne); pap. 18.00 (*0-8057-4538-6*, Twyne) Mac Lib Ref.
Berst, Charles A., ed. Shaw & Religion. LC 81-956. (Annual of Bernard Shaw Studies: Vol 1). 264p. 1981. 40.00 (*0-271-00280-8*) Pa St U Pr.
Berst, Jesse. The Magnet Effect. 240p. 2000. 24.95 (*0-07-134803-4*) McGraw.
Berst, Jesse, jt. auth. see Segal, Hillel.
Berstein, Basil. Pedagogy, Symbolic Control & Identity: Theory, Research, Critique. 208p. 1995. 79.95 (*0-7484-0371-X*, Pub. by Tay Francis Ltd); pap. 23.95 (*0-7484-0372-8*, Pub. by Tay Francis Ltd) Taylor & Francis.
Berstein, Charles. Republics of Reality, 1975-1995. (Classics Ser.: No. 120). 361p. 2000. pap. 14.95 (*1-55713-304-2*, Pub. by Sun & Moon CA) Consort Bk Sales.
Berstein, Hank, ed. A Different Latitude: Poems. 120p. 1998. pap. 10.00 (*0-937158-11-9*) Del Valley.
Berstein, Jack. The Life of an American Jew in Racist, Marxist Israel. 48p. 1991. reprint ed. pap. 2.98 (*0-939482-01-0*, 0253, Noontide Pr) Legion Survival.
Berstein, Jane A. Orlando De Lassus, 72-106, Vol. 13. LC 87-750544. (Sixteenth-Century Chanson Ser.). 210p. 1988. text 30.00 (*0-8240-3112-1*) Garland.
Berstein, Jane A., ed. Adrian Willaert: The Complete Five & Six-Voice Chansons. LC 92-750038. (Sixteenth-Century Chanson Ser.: Vol. 23). 224p. 1992. text 83.00 (*0-8240-3122-9*) Garland.
Berstein, Lev M. Macrosomy, Obesity & Cancer. (Illus.). 207p. (C). 1996. lib. bdg. 135.00 (*1-56072-202-9*) Nova Sci Pubs.
Berstein, Malcolm E., et al. Executive Communication Development, 2 vols. (Illus.). 150p. 1983. write for info. (*0-915159-00-7*); write for info. (*0-915159-01-5*); teacher ed. write for info. (*0-915159-02-3*) Human Equat.
Berstein, Michael A. Bitter Carnival: Ressentiment & the Abject Hero. 264p. 1992. text 39.50 (*0-691-06939-5*, Pub. by Princeton U Pr) Cal Prin Full Svc.
Berstein, Nurith, jt. auth. see Wagner, Caroline.

B

Berstein, Samuel. French Political & Intellectual History. LC 83-4731. 224p. 1983. pap. text 29.95 (*0-87855-938-8*) Transaction Pubs.

Berstein, Serge. The Republic of De Gaulle, 1958-1969. Morris, Peter, tr. (History of Modern France Ser.: No. 8). 281p. (C). 1993. text 59.95 (*0-521-25239-3*) Cambridge U Pr.

Berstein, Serge & Milza, Pierre. Dictionnaire Historique des Fascismes et du Nazisme. (FRE.). 1992. 175.00 (*0-7859-8174-8*, 2-87027-463-7) Fr & Eur.

Berstel, J. & Reutenauer, C. Rational Series & Their Languages. (EATCS Monographs on Theoretical Computer Science: Vol. 12). 150p. 1988. 53.95 (*0-387-18626-3*) Spr-Verlag.

Berston & Fisher. Arithmetic Review for Business. rev. ed. 1993. pap. 36.95 (*0-87393-189-0*) Dame Pubns.

Berston, jt. auth. see Fisher.

Berston, Hyman M. California Real Estate Practice. 5th ed. (C). 1988. text 38.95 (*0-256-03477-X*, Irwn McGrw-H) McGrw-H Hghr Educ.

— California Real Estate Principles. 7th ed. LC 94-22609. 544p. (C). 1994. text 46.50 (*0-256-13597-5*, Irwn McGrw-H) McGrw-H Hghr Educ.

Berstrom, Christer, jt. auth. see Sundin, Claes.

Bersuire, Pierre. Dictionarium, Seu Repertorium Morale Petri Berchorii Ordinis Divi Benedicti. (LAT.). civ, 1683p. reprint ed. write for info. (*0-318-72000-0*) G Olms Pubs.

Bersuker, Isaac B. Electronic Structure & Properties of Transition Metal Compounds: Introduction to the Theory. LC 95-461. (Illus.). 696p. 1996. 115.00 (*0-471-13079-6*, Wiley-Interscience) Wiley.

— The Jahn-Teller Effect: A Bibliographic Review. LC 83-17635. 600p. 1984. 130.00 (*0-306-65206-4*, Kluwer Plenum) Kluwer Academic.

— The Jahn-Teller Effect & Vibronic Interactions in Modern Chemistry. LC 88-16070. (Modern Inorganic Chemistry Ser.). 334p. 1984. 79.50 (*0-306-41319-1*, Plenum Trade) Perseus Pubng.

Bersuker, Isaac B. & Polinger, V. Z. Vibronic Interactions in Molecules & Crystals. (Chemical Physics Ser.: Vol. 49). (Illus.). 435p. 1989. 130.95 (*0-387-19259-X*) Spr-Verlag.

Bert, Charles W., ed. see American Society of Mechanical Engineers Staff.

Bert, Charles W., ed. & tr. see Bogdanovich, A.

Bert, Deb, jt. auth. see Bert, Norman A.

Bert, Jacques. Dictionary of Science: English-French. (ENG & FRE.). 400p. 1994. pap. 49.95 (*0-7859-8888-2*) Fr & Eur.

Bert, Joseph C. Colonisation of Indo-China. (C). 1993. 14.00 (*81-85557-21-7*, Pub. by Low Price) S Asia.

Bert, Joseph J. Le, see Le Bert, Joseph J.

Bert, Kendell E., et al. Accommodation of Utility Plant Within the Rights-of-Way of Urban Streets & Highways: Manual of Improved Practice. 102p. (Orig.). 1974. pap. text 25.00 (*0-917084-24-1*) Am Public Works.

Bert, Norman A. Adventure in Discipleship: A Brethren in Christ Heritage Study. rev. ed. LC 92-72132. 153p. 1992. pap., student ed. 5.95 (*0-916035-52-2*) Evangel Indiana.

— One-Act Plays for Acting Students: An Anthology of Short One-Act Plays for One, Two or Three Actors. Zapel, Arthur L., ed. LC 87-42871. 288p. (YA). (gr. 9 up). 1987. pap. 16.95 (*0-916260-47-X*, B159) Meriwether Pub.

— The Scenebook for Actors: Great Monologs & Dialogs from Contemporary & Classical Theatre. Zapel, Arthur L., ed. LC 90-52983. 256p. (YA). (gr. 9-12). 1990. pap. 15.95 (*0-916260-65-8*, B177) Meriwether Pub.

Bert, Norman A., et al, eds. Theatre Alive! An Introductory Anthology of World Drama. rev. ed. LC 94-41533. 848p. (Orig.). 1994. pap. 29.95 (*1-56608-008-8*, B178) Meriwether Pub.

Bert, Norman A. & Bert, Deb. Play It Again! More 1-Act Plays for Acting Students. Zapel, Theodore O., ed. LC 93-312. 288p. (Orig.). (YA). (gr. 9-12). 1993. pap. 14.95 (*0-916260-97-6*, B130) Meriwether Pub.

Berta, Alez G. Understanding Glial Cells. Castellano, Bernardo et al, eds. LC 98-12036. 456p. 1998. 199.00 (*0-7923-8140-8*) Kluwer Academic.

Berta, Annalisa. Enzymology of the Tears. LC 92-9529. 352p. 1992. 190.00 (*0-8493-6050-1*, QP231, CRC Reprint) Franklin.

— Quaternary Evolution & Biogeography of the Large South American Canidae (Mammalia, Carnivora) LC 88-23378. (University of California Publications in Geological Sciences: No. 132). 174p. 1988. pap. 54.00 (*0-7837-7472-9*, 204919400010) Bks Demand.

Berta, Annalisa & Sumich. Marine Mammals: Evolutionary Biology. 460p. 1999. 59.95 (*0-12-093225-3*) Acad Pr.

Berta, Arpad. Lautgeschichte der Tatarischen Dialekte. (Studia Uralo-altaica Ser.: Vol. 31). (GER.). 304p. (Orig.). 1989. pap. 83.00 (*0-685-33594-1*, Pub. by Attila Josef Univ) Advent Bks Div.

Berta, Arpad, ed. Tatarische Etymologische Studien, No. II. (Studia Uralo-altaica Ser.: Vol. 30). (GER.). 283p. (Orig.). 1988. pap. 58.00 (*0-685-33595-X*, Pub. by Attila Josef Univ) Advent Bks Div.

Berta, Arpad, et al. Symbolae Turcologicae: Philological & Languistics Studies in Honor of Lars Hohanson. (Swedish Research Institute in Istanbul: Vol. 6). (ENG & GER.). 246p. (Orig.). 1996. pap. 52.50 (*91-86884-07-7*) Coronet Bks.

Berta of Vilich. Mater Spiritualis: The Life of Adelheid of Vilich. Dyck, Madelyn B., tr. (Translation Ser.). 152p. 1994. pap. 15.00 (*0-920669-48-4*, Pub. by Peregrina Pubng) Cistercian Pubns.

***Berta, R., et al, eds.** Experimental Nuclear Physics in Europe: ENPE 99, Facing the Next Millennium. (AIP Conference Proceeding Ser.: Vol. 495). 547p. 1999. 140.00 (*1-56396-907-6*, Pub. by Am Inst Physics) Spr-Verlag.

Berta, Susan M., et al. Archeology of the Mixed Grass Prairie Phase I: Quartermaster Creek. Baugh, Timothy G., ed. (Archeological Resource Survey Report: No. 20). (Illus.). 313p. (C). 1984. pap. text 8.00 (*1-881346-13-7*) Univ OK Archeol.

***Berta, Victor Thomas.** From the Mind, from the Heart. 2000. 12.95 (*0-533-13440-4*) Vantage.

Bertaccini, G., ed. Mediators & Drugs in Gastrointestinal Motility II: Endogenous & Exogenous Agents. (Handbook of Experimental Pharmacology Ser.: Vol. 59, II). (Illus.). 460p. 1982. 272.00 (*0-387-11333-9*) Spr-Verlag.

— Meditators & Drugs in Gastrointestinal Motility I: Morphological Basis & Neurophysiological Control. (Handbook of Experimental Pharmacology Ser.: Vol. 59, I). (Illus.). 468p. 1982. 312.00 (*0-387-11296-0*) Spr-Verlag.

Bertagna, X., ed. Peptide Hormone Secreting Tumors. (Journal: Hormone Research Ser.: Vol. 32, 1-3, 1989). (Illus.). viii, 166p. 1990. pap. 101.00 (*3-8055-5167-3*) S Karger.

Bertagna, Xavier, ed. Recent Progress on the Molecular Aspects of Endocrine Tumors: Clinical Implications: 39th International Henri-Pierre Kotz Symposium on Hormone Binding Proteins, Paris, May 1996. (Journal: Hormone Research Ser.: Vol. 47, No. 4-6, 1997). (Illus.). 166p. 1997. pap. 120.00 (*3-8055-6504-6*) S Karger.

Bertagnolli, Leslie. Family Photographs. Bensen, Robert, ed. (Chapbook Ser.: No. 1). 24p. 1978. pap. 2.00 (*0-932884-00-8*) Red Herring.

Bertagnolli, Olivia & Rackham, Jeff, eds. Creativity & the Writing Process. (C). 1982. 24.60 (*0-673-15732-6*) Addson-Wesley Educ.

Bertagnolli, Olivia, jt. auth. see Rackham, Jeff.

Bertain, Leonard. New Turnaround. 196p. 1993. 30.00 (*0-88427-096-3*) North River.

Bertain, Leonard & Hales, Lee, eds. A Program Guide for CIM Implementation: A Project of the CASA - SME Technical Council. 2nd ed. LC 87-62381. (Illus.). 216p. reprint ed. pap. 67.00 (*0-7837-6280-1*, 204599500010) Bks Demand.

Bertalan, Dan. Bowhunting Fireside Tales. LC 94-70353. 128p. 1994. pap. 6.95 (*0-9623955-3-6*) Envisage Unlimited.

— Opening Day. LC 94-70352. 256p. 1994. pap. 11.95 (*0-9623955-2-8*) Envisage Unlimited.

Bertalanffy, Ludwig Von, see Von Bertalanffy, Ludwig.

Bertali, Antonio & Dobel, Heinrich. Solo Compositions for Violin & Viola da Gamba with Basso Continue. Brewer, Charles E., ed. (Recent Researches in Music of the Baroque Era Ser.: Vol. RRB82). (Illus.). xviii, 142p. 1997. pap. 55.00 (*0-89579-386-5*) A-R Eds.

Bertalot, John. Five Wheels to Successful Sight-Singing: A Practical Approach to Teach Children & Adults to Read Music. LC 93-2008. 128p. 1993. pap. 8.99 (*0-8066-2692-5*, 11-26925) Augsburg Fortress.

— Five Wheels to Successful Sight-Singing: A Practical Approach to Teach Children & Adults to Read Music. 1994. 38.95 incl. VHS (*0-8066-2694-1*, 11-26941, Augsburg) Augsburg Fortress.

— John Bertalot's Immediately Practical Tips for Choral Directors. LC 94-24996. 1994. pap. 17.95 (*0-8066-2810-3*, 11-28103) Augsburg Fortress.

Bertanzetti, Eileen D. Rich in Love: The Story of Padre Pio of Pietrelcina. LC 99-19027. (Weaver Books). 68p. (YA). (gr. 6-9). 1999. pap. 3.95 (*0-8198-6470-6*) Pauline Bks.

Bertau, Karl, ed. see De Tepla, Johannes & Zacensis, Civis.

Bertaud, Alain & Renaud, Bertrand. Cities Without Land Markets: Lessons of the Failed Socialist Experiment. LC 93-42813. (Discussion Paper Ser.: No. 227). 46p. 1994. pap. 22.00 (*0-8213-2740-2*, 12740) World Bank.

Bertaud du Chazaud, Henri. Robert Dictionnaire des Synonymes. (FRE.). 800p. 1992. 75.00 (*0-8288-9431-0*, 285036035X) Fr & Eur.

Bertaut, E. F., et al. Commensurate - Incommensurate: Crystallography in the Life Sciences: Corrections: Accelerated Convergence Treatment of R-N Lattice Sums: A Special Issue of the Journal Crystallography Reviews. 62p. 1990. pap. text 64.00 (*2-88124-743-1*) Gordon & Breach.

Bertaux, Daniel & Thompson, Paul. Pathways to Social Class: A Qualitative Approach to Social Mobility. (Illus.). 344p. 1997. text 78.00 (*0-19-827931-0*) OUP.

Bertaux, Daniel & Thompson, Paul, eds. International Yearbook of Oral History & Life Stories Vol. 2: Between Generations: Family Models, Myths, & Memories. 240p. (C). 1993. 55.00 (*0-19-820249-0*) OUP.

Bertaux, Pierre. Franzosisch-Deutsches, Deutsch-Franzosisches Woerterbuch, Vol. 1. (FRE & GER.). 1966. 95.00 (*0-8288-6719-4*, M7411, Pub. by O Brandstetter Verlag) Trafalgar.

— Franzosisch-Deutsches, Deutsch-Franzosisches Woerterbuch, Vol. 2. (FRE & GER.). 1967. 95.00 (*0-8288-6720-8*, M7412, Pub. by O Brandstetter Verlag) Trafalgar.

Bertazzoni, Giovanna, jt. auth. see Johnson, Robert F.

Bertch, Barbara A., jt. auth. see Bertch, David P.

Bertch, David P. Biblical Business Ethics: Exploring Secular Ethical Values & Alternative Christian Approaches. Martin, Terry & Martin, Dyna, eds. (Minding Your Own Business Ser.: Bk. 2). (Illus.). 125p. 1994. student ed. 9.95 (*0-9634472-3-8*) Good Works Pr.

— Pursuing God's Purpose: Defining & Determining Direction for Your Life. Martin, Terry & Martin, Dyna, eds. (Minding Your Own Business Ser.). (Illus.). 227p. (Orig.). 1994. pap., student ed. 16.95 (*0-9634472-2-X*) Good Works Pr.

Bertch, David P. & Bertch, Barbara A. The Dynamic Dinosaur of Faith's History Vol. I: From Christ to 1000 AD. Martin, Terry & Martin, Dyna, eds. (Roots of the Past Ser.: Bk. 1). (Illus.). 150p. (J). (gr. 6). student ed. 9.95 (*0-9634472-4-6*) Good Works Pr.

Bertch, Julie. Writing with Insight. 274p. (C). 1996. text 28.40 (*0-536-59365-5*) Pearson Custom.

***Bertcher, Harvey, et al, eds.** Rebuilding Communities: Challenges for Group Work. LC 99-30672. 207p. 1999. pap. 34.95 (*0-7890-0942-0*) Haworth Pr.

Bertcher, Harvey J. Group Participation: Techniques for Leaders & Members. 2nd ed. (Human Services Guides Ser.: Vol. 10). (Illus.). 192p. (C). 1993. text 42.00 (*0-8039-5213-9*); pap. text 18.95 (*0-8039-5214-7*) Sage.

Bertcher, Harvey J. & Maple, Frank F. Creating Groups. 2nd ed. LC 95-50168. (Human Services Guides Ser.: Vol. 2). 96p. (C). 1996. 42.00 (*0-8039-5491-3*); pap. 18.95 (*0-8039-5492-1*) Sage.

***Bertcher, Harvey J., et al.** Rebuilding Communities: Challenges for Group Work. LC 99-30672. 207p. 1999. 59.95 (*0-7890-0722-3*) Haworth Pr.

***Berte, Janell.** The Designer Bride: A Wedding Planner. (Illus.). 200p. 1999. ring bd. 59.95 incl. cd-rom (*0-9674832-0-4*) Berte Ltd.

Berte, Lucia. Developing Performance Standards for Hospital Personnel. LC 89-17872. (Illus.). 92p. 1989. student ed. 25.00 (*0-89189-285-0*, 45-9-027-00) Am Soc Clinical.

Berte, Marjorie. Hit Me - I Need the Money: The Politics of Auto Insurance Reform. 195p. 1991. 18.95 (*1-55815-152-4*) ICS Pr.

Berte, Neal R., ed. Individualizing Education Through Contract Learning. LC 75-9707. 206p. reprint ed. 63.90 (*0-8357-9618-3*, 205129100093) Bks Demand.

Berte, Raymond A. To Speak Again. 196p. 1987. 19.95 (*0-941219-50-X*) Phillips Pub MA.

— To Speak Again: My Victory over Throat Cancer. 192p. 1988. 14.95 (*0-8159-6923-6*) Devin.

Bertea, Cassandra, tr. see Camon, Ferdinando.

Berteau, John T. Estate Planning in Florida. 2nd rev. ed. LC 98-14520. 240p. 1998. 24.95 (*1-56164-151-0*) Pineapple Pr.

Berteau, John T., jt. auth. see McKinney, Anne.

Berteaux, H. O. Buoy Engineering. LC 75-20046. (Ocean Engineering, a Wiley Ser.). 334p. reprint ed. pap. 103.60 (*0-8357-7476-7*, 205560500029) Bks Demand.

Bertech, Wener. Washington D. C. Souvenir Book: English Text - Texte Francais - Deutscher Text - Texto Espanol. rev. ed. (ENG, FRE, GER & SPA.). 96p. 1992. pap. 9.75 (*1-879295-08-3*) L B Prince.

Bertel, E. & Donath, M. Electronic Surface & Interface States on Metallic Systems: Proceedings of the We-Heraeus Seminars. 400p. 1995. text 109.00 (*981-02-2019-7*) World Scientific Pub.

Bertel, Laurent. Introduction to Spacetime. 3000p. 1994. text 518.00 (*981-02-1928-8*) World Scientific Pub.

Bertela, Giovanna G. Donatello. Pearson, Nancy & Brierley, Anthony, trs. from ITA. (Library of Great Masters). (Illus.). 80p. (Orig.). 1991. pap. 12.99 (*1-878351-19-2*) Riverside NY.

Bertele, Hans Von, see Von Bertele, Hans.

Bertele, Otto Von, see Davidson, John & Von Bertele, Otto.

Bertell, Rosalie. No Immediate Danger? Prognosis for a Radioactive Earth. 2nd ed. LC 86-72223. 435p. 1986. pap. 11.95 (*0-913990-25-6*) Book Pub Co.

— No Immediate Danger? Prognosis for a Radioactive Earth. 3rd ed. 400p. pap. write for info. (*0-88961-092-4*, Pub. by Womens Pr) LPC InBook.

Bertelli, A., ed. New Trends in the Therapy of Liver Disease: Proceedings of the International Symposium on Tirrenia, June, 1974. 300p. 1975. 54.50 (*3-8055-2118-9*) S Karger.

Bertels. Book of the World. 2nd ed. 558p. 1998. 465.00 (*0-02-864966-4*) Macmillan.

Bertels, Frank. The First Book on Male Liberation & Sex Equality. LC 81-164329. (Illus.). 415p. 1981. 50.00 (*0-932574-05-X*); pap. 50.00 (*0-932574-06-8*) Brun Pr.

Bertels, Thomas M., Sr. In Pursuit of Agri-Power: The One Thing North American Farmers & Ranchers Can't Produce. (Illus.). 350p. 1988. pap. 12.95 (*0-9625034-0-1*) Silver Lake Col Pr.

Bertelsen, Dale A., jt. auth. see Chesebro, James W.

Bertelsen, Judy S., ed. Non-State Nations in International Politics: Comparative System Analyses. LC 75-36404. 272p. 1976. 59.95 (*0-275-90244-7*, C0244, Praeger Pubs) Greenwood.

Bertelsen, Lance. Henry Fielding at Work. text. write for info. (*0-312-23336-1*) St Martin.

Bertelsen, Lance. The Nonsense Club: Literature & Popular Culture, 1749-1764. (Illus.). 334p. 1986. text 75.00 (*0-19-812859-2*) OUP.

Bertelsen, Lars Kiel, et al, eds. Symbolic Imprints: Essays on Photography & Visual Culture. (Illus.). 200p. 1998. pap. 24.95 (*87-7288-787-7*, Pub. by Aarhus Univ Pr) David Brown.

Bertelsmann. Bertelsmann Universallexikon. (GER.). 1008p. 1997. 95.00 (*0-320-00101-6*) Fr & Eur.

— Macmillan Centennial Atlas of World & Planet Earth World Atlas. 1997. 175.00 (*0-02-864901-X*) Mac Lib Ref.

Bertelsmann, Annekatrin. Bertelsmann Lexikon Astronomie. (GER.). 348p. 1993. 95.00 (*0-7859-8429-1*, 3570016129) Fr & Eur.

— Bertelsmann Lexikon Geschichte. (GER.). 830p. 1991. 95.00 (*0-7859-8433-X*, 3570071901) Fr & Eur.

— Bertelsmann Lexikon Informatik, EDV, Computertechnik. (GER.). 480p. 1993. write for info. (*0-7859-8428-3*, 3570016110) Fr & Eur.

— Bertelsmann Lexikon Wirtschaft. (GER.). 815p. 1992. 95.00 (*0-7859-8686-3*, 357007191x) Fr & Eur.

— English-German/German-English Dictionary of Drug Epidemiology. (ENG & GER.). 182p. 1993. 125.00 (*0-7859-9963-9*) Fr & Eur.

Bertelsmann Cartographic Institute Staff. Planet Earth with Calendar 1998. 432p. 1997. 39.95 (*0-02-862012-7*) Macmillan.

Bertelsmann Cartographic Staff. Macmillan Portable World Atlas. 96p. 1997. pap. 17.95 (*0-02-862105-0*, Pub. by Macmillan) S&S Trade.

***Bertelsmann Foundation Staff.** Future of Foundations in an Open Society. 1999. pap. 16.95 (*3-89204-440-6*) Bertelsmann Stiftung.

Bertelson, David. The Lazy South. LC 80-24033. 284p. 1980. reprint ed. lib. bdg. 65.00 (*0-313-22696-2*, BELS, Greenwood Pr) Greenwood.

— Snowflakes & Snowdrifts: Individualism & Sexuality in America. 294p. (Orig.). (C). 1986. pap. text 25.50 (*0-8191-5579-9*); lib. bdg. 48.00 (*0-8191-5578-0*) U Pr of Amer.

Bertelson, Paul, ed. The Onset of Literacy: Cognitive Processes in Reading Acquisition. (Cognitive Special Issues Ser.). 192p. (Orig.). 1987. pap. text 15.00 (*0-262-52125-3*, Bradford Bks) MIT Pr.

Bertens, Hans. The Idea of Postmodern: A History. LC 94-14352. 192p. (Orig.). (C). 1995. pap. 24.99 (*0-415-06012-5*, B4658) Routledge.

Bertens, Hans & D'Haen, Theo, eds. The Small Town in America: A Multidisciplinary Revisit. (European Contributions to American Studies: Vol. 32). 250p. 1995. pap. 30.00 (*90-5383-385-4*) Paul & Co Pubs.

Bertens, Hans & Fokkema, Douwe W., eds. International Postmodernism: Theory & Literary Practice. LC 96-52208. (Comparative History of Literatures in European Languages Ser.: Vol. 11). xvi, 581p. 1997. lib. bdg. 165.00 (*1-55619-602-4*) J Benjamins Pubng Co.

Bertens, Hans, jt. ed. see D'Haen, Theo.

Bertensson, Sergei, jt. ed. see Leyda, Jay.

Bertera, Martin & Oberholtzer, Ken. The 4th Michigan Volunteer Infantry at Gettysburg: The Battle for the Wheatfield. (Illus.). 187p. 1997. 24.95 (*0-89029-328-7*) Morningside Bkshop.

Bertero, M. & Boccacci, P. Introduction to Inverse Problems in Imaging. LC 98-14461. (Illus.). 392p. 1998. 149.00 (*0-7503-0439-1*); pap. 49.00 (*0-7503-0435-9*) IOP Pub.

Bertero, M. & Pike, E. R., eds. Inverse Problems in Scattering & Imaging. (Malvern Physics Ser.). (Illus.). 550p. 1992. 139.00 (*0-7503-0143-0*) IOP Pub.

Bertero, V., ed. Reducing Earthquake Hazards: Lessons Learned from the Mexico Earthquake. 190p. 1989. pap. 15.00 (*0-943198-29-1*) Earthquake Eng.

Berteville, John. Recit de l'Expedition en Ecosse l'an, 1546. LC 79-39436. (Bannatyne Club, Edinburgh. Publications: No. 10). reprint ed. 37.50 (*0-404-52710-8*) AMS Pr.

Berth, Patte, jt. auth. see Mitchell, Ruth.

***Berthe, Faye.** Raspberry Road. 1999. pap. write for info. (*1-58235-201-1*) Watermrk Pr.

Berthe, Robert. Bridge: Techniques & Tips from the Masters, 4,249 Diagrammed Hands & Plays. (Illus.). 698p. 1997. 29.98 (*1-57912-003-2*) Blck Dog & Leventhal.

Berthelemy, Jean-Claude. Asian Crisis: A New Agenda for Euro-Asian Cooperation Paris, France 11 - 12 May 1998. 260p. 1999. pap. 26.00 (*981-02-3818-5*) World Scientific Pub.

Berthelemy, Jean-Claude, ed. Whither African Economies? LC 96-179008. (Development Centre Seminars Ser.). (ENG & FRE.). 168p. (Orig.). 1995. pap. 27.00 (*92-64-14647-4*, Pub. by Org for Econ) OECD.

Berthelemy, Jean-Claude & Bourguignon, Francois. Growth & Crisis in Cote d'Ivoire. LC 95-14395. (Comparative Macroeconomic Studies). 244p. 1996. pap. 22.00 (*0-8213-2655-4*, 12655) World Bank.

Berthelemy, Jean-Claude & Quenan, Carlos, eds. New Approaches to Financing Development in Africa. 65p. (Orig.). 1996. pap. 8.00 (*92-64-15347-0*, 41-96-12-1) OECD.

Berthelemy, Jean-Claude & Varoudakis, Aristomene. Financial Development Policy & Growth. (Development Center Studies, Long-Term Growth Ser.). 148p. (Orig.). 1996. pap. 25.00 (*92-64-15297-0*, 41-96-09-1) OECD.

Berthelemy, Jean-Claude, et al. Growth in Senegal: A Lost Opportunity? (Development Centre Studies). 180p. 1997. pap. 32.00 (*92-64-15409-4*, 41-97-02-1, Pub. by Org for Econ) OECD.

Berthelet, Arlette & Chavaillon, Jean, eds. The Use of Tools by Human & Non-Human Primates. LC 92-26903. (Fyssen Foundation Symposium Ser.). (Illus.). 448p. 1993. 125.00 (*0-19-852263-0*) OUP.

***Berthelin, J.** Effect of Mineral-Organic-Microorganism Interactions on Soil & Freshwater Environments. LC 99-42966. 1999. write for info. (*0-306-46216-8*, Kluwer Plenum) Kluwer Academic.

Berthelin, J., ed. Diversity of Environmental Biogeochemistry. (Developments in Geochemistry Ser.: No. 6). 538p. 1991. 195.00 (*0-444-88900-0*) Elsevier.

Berthelot, Anne. King Arthur: And the Knights of the Round Table. LC 97-21474. (Discoveries Ser.). (Illus.). 160p. (J). 1997. pap. 12.95 (*0-8109-2887-6*, Pub. by Abrams) Time Warner.

Berthelot, Christine, jt. auth. see Lloyd, Sam.

Berthelot, Dolly A. Perfectly Square: A Fantasy Fable for All Ages. (Illus.). 60p. 1994. pap. 8.99 (*0-9644406-0-1*) Berthelots Consult.

Berthelot, Dolly H. Perfectly Square: A Fantasy Fable for All Ages. 1996. pap. text 8.99 (*0-9644486-0-2*) Lightsmith Prod.

An Asterisk (*) at the beginning of an entry indicates that the title is appearing for the first time.

Berthelot, Helen W. Win Some, Lose Some: G. Mennen Williams & the New Democrats. LC 94-21329. (Illus.). 334p. 1995. 39.95 (*0-8143-2345-6*, Great Lks Bks); pap. 19.95 (*0-8143-2476-2*, Great Lks Bks) Wayne St U Pr.

Berthelot, Jean M. & Cole, J. M. Composite Materials: Mechanical Behavior & Structural Analysis. Ling, F. F., ed. LC 97-48885. (Mechanical Engineering Ser.). (Illus.). 704p. 1998. 99.00 (*0-387-98426-7*) Spr-Verlag.

Berthelot, Joseph A. Michael Drayton. LC 67-19341. (English Authors Ser.). 1967. lib. bdg. 20.95 (*0-8057-1172-4*) Irvington.

Berthelsen, Barbara. Multiple Choice Questions in Preparation for the AP Biology Examination. 3rd ed. 1996. pap. 16.95 (*1-878621-41-6*) D & S Mktg Syst.

— Teacher's Manual to Accompany Multiple Choice Questions in Preparation for the AP Biology Examination. 3rd ed. 1996. pap., teacher ed. write for info. (*1-878621-42-4*) D & S Mktg Syst.

Berthelsen, Bert A. Half Pint Cowpoke: A California Historical Western. (Illus.). 312p. (Orig.). 1993. pap. 6.95 (*1-879700-03-4*) Half Pint Pub.

— How to Survive & Succeed Without a Credit Card: Can't Save Money? This Book Is for You. 192p. (Orig.). 1991. pap. 9.95 (*1-879700-02-6*) Half Pint Pub.

Berthelsen, Walter & Straub, Joseph T. Management & Supervision. 394p. (C). 1992. pap. text 42.69 (*1-56226-102-9*) CAT Pub.

— Management & Supervision Instructor's Manual. 354p. 1992. pap. text. write for info. (*1-56226-124-X*) CAT Pub.

Bertherat, Therese & Bernstein, Carol. The Body Has Its Reasons: Self-Awareness Through Conscious Movement. 176p. 1989. pap. 10.95 (*0-89281-298-2*, Heal Arts VT) Inner Tradit.

Berthiaume, Laurent, jt. ed. see Ackermann, Hans-Wolfgang.

***Berthier, Francois.** Reading Zen in the Rocks: The Japanese Dry Landscape Garden. Parks, Graham, tr. from FRE. LC 99-43678. (Illus.). 136p. 1999. 20.00 (*0-226-04411-4*) U Ch Pr.

Berthier, G., ed. see Julg, A.

Berthier, J. Les Physalacriaceae du Globe: Hymenomacetales, Clavarioides. (Bibliotheca Mycologica Ser.: No. 98). (Illus.). 128p. 1985. pap. text 40.00 (*3-7682-1424-9*) Lubrecht & Cramer.

Berthier, Jacques. Songs & Prayers from Taize. 1991. pap. text 6.00 (*0-941050-30-0*, G-3719) GIA Pubns.

— Taize: Songs for Prayer. 105p. 1998. 9.95 (*1-57999-035-5*, G-4956) GIA Pubns.

— Taize: Songs for Prayer - Instrument Edition. 105p. 1998. spiral bd. 15.95 (*1-57999-036-3*, G-4956A) GIA Pubns.

Berthier, Jacques & Gelineau, Joseph. Taize - Songs for Prayer: Assembly Edition. 65p. 1998. pap. 4.50 (*1-57999-042-8*, G-4956P) GIA Pubns.

***Berthier, Marcelo L.** Transcortical Aphasias. (Brain Damage, Behaviour & Cognition Ser.). 272p. 1999. write for info. (*0-86377-840-2*) L Erlbaum Assocs.

Berthod, Alain. Micellar Liquid Chromatography. (Chromatographic Science Ser.). (Illus.). 418p. Date not set. text. write for info. (*0-8247-9993-3*) Dekker.

Berthod, Rene, jt. auth. see Nau, Paul.

Berthoff, Ann E. The Making of Meaning: Metaphors, Models, & Maxims for Writing Teachers. LC 81-9948. 208p. (Orig.). (C). 1981. pap. text 22.00 (*0-86709-003-0*, 0003, Pub. by Boynton Cook Pubs) Heinemann.

— The Sense of Learning. LC 89-295087. 171p. (Orig.). (C). 1990. pap. text 22.00 (*0-86709-201-7*, 0201, Pub. by Boynton Cook Pubs) Heinemann.

Berthoff, Ann E., ed. Reclaiming the Imagination: Philosophical Perspectives for Writers & Teachers of Writing. LC 83-15537. 286p. (Orig.). (C). 1984. pap. text 23.50 (*0-86709-059-6*, 0059, Pub. by Boynton Cook Pubs) Heinemann.

Berthoff, Ann E. & Stephens, James. Forming - Thinking - Writing. 2nd ed. LC 88-696. 278p. (C). 1988. pap. text 25.00 (*0-86709-238-6*, 0238, Pub. by Boynton Cook Pubs) Heinemann.

Berthoff, Ann E., ed. see Richards, I. A.

Berthoff, Rowland. Republic of the Dispossessed: The Exceptional Old-European Consensus in America. LC 96-36884. 264p. 1997. spiral bd. 39.95 (*0-8262-1101-1*) U of Mo Pr.

Berthoff, Warner. American Trajectories: Authors & Readings, 1790-1970. LC 92-41208. 200p. (C). 1994. 35.00 (*0-271-01051-7*) Pa St U Pr.

— Edmund Wilson. LC 68-64750. (University of Minnesota Pamphlets on American Writers Ser.: No. 67). 47p. (Orig.). reprint ed. pap. 30.00 (*0-7837-2899-9*, 205755600006) Bks Demand.

— The Ferment of Realism: American Literature, 1884-1919. LC 80-42335. 352p. 1981. pap. text 24.95 (*0-521-28435-X*) Cambridge U Pr.

— Literature & the Continuances of Virtue. LC 86-15103. 306p. reprint ed. pap. 94.90 (*0-608-06425-4*, 206663800008) Bks Demand.

Berthold-Bond, Annie. Better Basics for the Home: Simple Solutions for Less Toxic Living. LC 98-48649. 1999. pap. 18.00 (*0-609-80325-5*) Crown Pub Group.

— Clean & Green: The Complete Guide to Non-Toxic & Environmentally Safe Housekeeping. 160p. (Orig.). 1994. pap. text 8.95 (*1-886101-01-9*) Ceres Pr.

— Green Kitchen Handbook, The ST contd: Home Into a Healthy, Livable Place: Practical Advice, References, & Sources for Transforming the Center of Your. LC 96-43028. 304p. 1997. pap. 15.00 (*0-06-095186-9*, Perennial) HarperTrade.

Berthold-Bond, Daniel. Hegel's Grand Synthesis: A Study of Being, Thought, & History. LC 88-15930. (SUNY Series in Hegelian Studies). 233p. (C). 1989. text 65.50 (*0-88706-955-X*); pap. text 21.95 (*0-88706-956-8*) State U NY Pr.

— Hegel's Theory of Madness. LC 94-32809. (SUNY Series in Hegelian Studies). 309p. (C). 1995. text 59.50 (*0-7914-2505-3*); pap. text 19.95 (*0-7914-2506-1*) State U NY Pr.

Berthold, Dennis, ed. see Whitman, Thomas J.

Berthold, George C., ed. Faith Seeking Understanding: Learning & the Catholic Tradition: Selected Papers from the Symposium & Convocation Celebrating the Saint Anselm College Centennial. LC 91-61465. 274p. (C). 1991. pap. 8.95 (*0-9629547-0-5*) St Anselm Coll.

— Maximus the Confessor. (Classics of Western Spirituality Ser.: Vol. 45). 1985. pap. 26.95 (*0-8091-2659-1*) Paulist Pr.

Berthold, John W., jt. ed. see DePaula, Ramon P.

Berthold, M. & Hand, D. J. Intelligent Data Analysis: An Introduction. LC 99-23777. (Illus.). ix, 400p. 1999. 62.00 (*3-540-65808-4*) Spr-Verlag.

Berthold, M., ed. see Cohen, P.

Berthold, Margot. The History of World Theater: From the Beginnings to the Baroque. LC 77-6945. (Illus.). 528p. 1999. pap. 39.95 (*0-8264-1166-5*) Continuum.

Berthold, Mary P. Big Hole Journal: Notes & Excerpts. 1973. 5.25 (*0-8187-0022-X*) Harlo Press.

— Including Two Captains: A Later Look. LC 75-13400. 1975. 6.00 (*0-8187-0023-8*) Harlo Press.

— Turn Here for the Big Hole. 1970. 3.95 (*0-8187-0025-4*) Harlo Press.

Berthold, P., ed. Orientation in Birds. (Experientia Supplementa Ser.: No. 60). 344p. 1991. 174.50 (*0-8176-2618-2*) Birkhauser.

Berthold, Richard M. Rhodes in the Hellenistic Age. LC 83-23127. (Illus.). 243p. 1984. text 42.50 (*0-8014-1640-X*) Cornell U Pr.

Berthold, Robert. The Australian Scuba Divers Illustrated Dictionary. (C). 1993. 85.00 (*0-646-07526-8*, Pub. by R Berthold Photo) St Mut.

Berthold, Robert, Jr. Beeswax Crafting. Connor, Larence J., ed. LC 93-19562. 1993. 17.95 (*1-878075-02-0*) Wicwas Pr.

Berthold, S. Megan, jt. auth. see Maki, Mitchell T.

Berthold, Werner & Loffler, Ullrich. Lexicon of Safety Terminology in Chemistry: Lexikon Sicherheitstechnischer Begriffe in der Chemie. (GER.). 170p. 1981. 75.00 (*0-8288-1311-6*, M15296) Fr & Eur.

Bertholet, Alfred. Dictionary of Religion: Woerterbuch der Religionen. 4th ed. (ENG & GER.). 689p. 1985. 59.95 (*0-8288-2306-5*, M15222) Fr & Eur.

— Woerterbuch der Religionen. (GER.). 379p. 1985. 59.95 (*0-7859-7438-5*, 3520125048) Fr & Eur.

Bertholf, Judy. Tiger Beetles of the Genus Cicindela in Arizona: Coleoptera: Cicindelidae. (Special Publications: No. 19). (Illus.). 44p. 1983. pap. 7.00 (*0-89672-110-8*) Tex Tech Univ Pr.

Bertholf, Kenneth J., Jr. Blairstown. LC 98-88255. (Images of America Ser.). 1998. write for info. (*0-7385-0033-X*) Arcadia Publng.

Bertholf, Robert. Robert Duncan: A Descriptive Bibliography. LC 84-16740. (Illus.). 492p. 1986. 65.00 (*0-87685-620-2*) Black Sparrow.

Bertholf, Robert, ed. see Oppenheimer, Joel.

Bertholf, Robert J., et al, contrib. by. Julian Stanczak: Decades of Light. (Illus.). 180p. 1990. 39.95 (*0-922668-04-3*); 325.00 (*0-922668-06-X*); 750.00 (*0-922668-05-1*) SUNYB Poetry Rare Bks.

Bertholf, Robert J. & Levitt, Annette S., eds. William Blake & the Moderns. LC 82-656. 294p. (C). 1983. pap. text 24.95 (*0-87395-616-8*) State U NY Pr.

Bertholf, Robert J. & Reid, Ian W., eds. Robert Duncan: Scales of the Marvelous. LC 79-19861. (Insights Ser.). 1980. pap. 5.95 (*0-8112-0735-8*, NDP487, Pub. by New Directions) Norton.

Bertholf, Robert J., ed. see Duncan, Robert.

Bertholf, Robert J., ed. see Oppenheimer, Joel.

Bertholf, Stephen D. What Every College Age Woman Should Know about Relationships. LC 98-94808. viii, 120p. 1999. pap. 10.95 (*0-9668691-1-7*, 771) Abbey Hse.

Berthollet, Claude-Louis. Researches into the Laws of Chemical Affinity. 2nd ed. LC 65-23404. 1966. reprint ed. 27.50 (*0-306-70914-7*) Da Capo.

Berthome, Pascal & Ferreira, Afonso, eds. Optical Interconnections & Parallel Processing: Trends at the Interface. LC 97-42015. 410p. 1997. 182.00 (*0-7923-4817-6*) Kluwer Academic.

Berthomieu, Gabrielle & Cribier, Michel, eds. Inside the Sun. (C). 1990. text 206.50 (*0-7923-0662-7*) Kluwer Academic.

Berthon, Guy, ed. Handbook of Metal-Ligand Interactions in Biological Fluid: Bioinorganic Chemistry. LC 95-32797. (Books in Soils, Plants, & the Environment). (Illus.). 746p. 1995. text 545.00 (*0-8247-9296-3*); text 545.00 (*0-8247-9636-5*) Dekker.

— Handbook of Metal-Ligand Interactions in Biological Fluids: Bioinorganic Medicine. LC 95-32798. (Illus.). 1632p. 1995. text 495.00 (*0-8247-9638-1*) Dekker.

— Handbook of Metal-Ligand Interactions in Biological Fluids: Bioinorganic Medicine, Vol. 1. LC 95-32798. (Illus.). 692p. 1995. text 495.00 (*0-8247-9637-3*) Dekker.

Berthon, Simon & Robinson, Andrew. The Shape of the World: The Mapping & Discovery of the Earth. (Illus.). 192p. 1999. reprint ed. text 28.00 (*0-7881-6463-5*) DIANE Pub.

Berthoud, Gerald & Sitter-Liver, Beat, eds. The Responsible Scholar: Ethical Considerations in the Humanities & Social Sciences. LC 95-53708. 303p. 1996. 49.95 (*0-88135-165-2*) Watson Pub Intl.

***Berthoud, Hans-Rudolf & Seeley, Randy J.** Neural Control of Macronutrient Selection: Neural & Metabolic Control of Macronujtrient Intake. LC 99-29233. 528p. 1999. boxed set 89.95 (*0-8493-2752-0*, 2752) CRC Pr.

Berthoud, Jacques. Joseph Conrad: The Major Phase. LC 77-8242. (British Authors Ser.). 264p. 1978. pap. text 18.95 (*0-521-29273-5*) Cambridge U Pr.

Berthoud, Jacques, ed. see Conrad, Joseph.

Berthoud, Jacques, ed. & intro. see Conrad, Joseph.

Berthoud, Jacques, ed. & intro. see Trollope, Anthony.

Berthoud, R., jt. auth. see Rowlingson, K.

Berthoud, Richard. Disadvantages of Inequality: A Study of Social Deprivation. (Illus.). 1976. 25.00 (*0-8464-0338-2*) Beekman Pubs.

Berthouex, P. Mac & Brown, Linfield C. Statistics for Environmental Engineers. LC 94-10699. 352p. 1994. lib. bdg. 85.00 (*1-56670-031-0*, L1031) Lewis Pubs.

***Berthoz, Alain.** Brain's Sense of Movement. 2000. text. write for info. (*0-674-80109-1*) HUP.

Berthoz, Alain, ed. Multisensory Control of Movement. (Illus.). 522p. 1993. 95.00 (*0-19-854785-4*) OUP.

Berthoz, Alain, et al. Head - Neck Sensory Motor System. (Illus.). 784p. 1992. text 150.00 (*0-19-506820-3*) OUP.

Berthrong, Donald J. The Cheyenne & Arapaho Ordeal: Reservation & Agency Life in the Indian Territory, 1875-1907. LC 75-17795. (Civilization of the American Indian Ser.: Vol. 136). (Illus.). 424p. (Orig.). (C). 1992. pap. 17.95 (*0-8061-2416-4*) U of Okla Pr.

— The Southern Cheyennes. LC 63-8990. (Civilization of the American Indian Ser.: No. 66). (Illus.). 456p. 1975. pap. 18.95 (*0-8061-1199-2*) U of Okla Pr.

Berthrong, John. The Divine Deli: Religious Identity in the North American Cultural Mosaic. LC 99-39287. (Faith Meets Faith Ser.). 144p. 1999. pap. 16.00 (*1-57075-268-0*) Orbis Bks.

Berthrong, John, jt. ed. see Tucker, Mary E.

Berthrong, John H. All under Heaven: Transforming Paradigms in Confucian-Christian Dialogue. LC 93-17291. (SUNY Series in Chinese Philosophy & Culture). 273p. (C). 1994. pap. text 21.95 (*0-7914-1858-8*) State U NY Pr.

— All under Heaven: Transforming Paradigms in Confucian-Christian Dialogue. LC 93-17291. (SUNY Series in Chinese Philosophy & Culture). 273p. (C). 1994. text 64.50 (*0-7914-1857-X*) State U NY Pr.

— Concerning Creativity: A Comparison of Chu Hsi, Whitehead & Neville. LC 98-22840. (SUNY Series in Religious Studies). 280p. (C). 1998. text 65.50 (*0-7914-3943-7*); pap. text 21.95 (*0-7914-3944-5*) State U NY Pr.

***Berthrong, John H.** Confucianism: A Short Introduction. 2000. pap. 14.95 (*1-85168-236-8*, Pub. by Onewrld Pubns) Penguin Putnam.

Berthrong, John H. Interfaith Dialogue: An Annotated Bibliography. LC 93-188859. 32p. 1993. pap. 4.25 (*0-9637372-8-7*) Multifaith Res.

— Transformations of the Confucian Way. (Explorations Ser.). 264p. (C). 1998. pap. text 25.00 (*0-8133-2804-7*, Pub. by Westview) HarpC.

Berti, F., et al, eds. Cyclooxygenase & Lipoxygenase Modulators in Lung Reactivity. (Progress in Biochemical Pharmacology Ser.: Vol. 20). (Illus.). x, 146p. 1985. 115.75 (*3-8055-3974-6*) S Karger.

Berti, Gianna Valli. Baby Patchwork: Small Quilts & Other Gifts. LC 99-18124. 1999. 27.95 (*0-8069-9951-9*) Sterling.

***Berti, Gianna Valli.** Baby Patchwork: Small Quilts & Other Gifts. (Illus.). 2000. pap. 14.95 (*0-8069-9933-0*) Sterling.

Berti, Luciano & Tofani, Anna M. The Uffizi. (Illus.). 264p. 1993. 40.00 (*1-870248-81-3*) Scala Books.

Berti, Silvia, et al, eds. Heterodoxy, Spinozism & Free Thought in Early-Eighteenth-Century Europe: Studies on the Trait E des Trois Imposteurs. LC 96-21165. (International Archives of the History of Ideas: Vol. 148). 1996. lib. bdg. 250.00 (*0-7923-4192-9*) Kluwer Academic.

Bertiaux, Michael. A Course in Cosmic Meditation. 49p. (Orig.). 1989. pap. 30.00 (*1-878738-01-1*) Tech Sacred.

Bertiaux, Michael & Jean-Maine, H. F. Hoard of Gold: Voodoo Methods to Obtain Financial & Material Benefits. 51p. (Orig.). 1989. pap. 175.00 (*1-878738-00-3*) Tech Sacred.

Bertie, John E., et al. Tables of Intensities for the Calibration of Infrared Spectroscope Measurements in the Liquid Phase: International Union of Pure & Applied Chemistry, Physical Chemistry Division, Commission on Molecular Structure & Spectroscopy. 272p. 1995. 69.50 (*0-86542-926-X*) Blackwell Sci.

Bertier de Sauvigny, Guillaume De, see De Bertier De Sauvigny, Guillaume.

Bertillon, Alphonse. Alphonse Bertillon's Instructions for Taking Descriptions for the Identification of Criminals, & Others by Means of Anthropometric Indications. LC 72-156004. (Foundations of Criminal Justice Ser.). reprint ed. 41.50 (*0-404-09104-0*) AMS Pr.

Bertilsson, Bo. Classic Hot Rods. LC 99-34068. (Illus.). 128p. 1999. pap. 21.95 (*0-7603-0721-0*, 128960AP, Pub. by MBI Pubg) Motorbooks Intl.

***Bertin, B.J.** Flea Market Makeovers: 25 Projects for Fabulous Home Furnishings. LC 99-86294. (Illus.). 176p. 2000. 30.00 (*0-609-60491-0*) C Potter.

Bertin, Celia. Jean Renoir: A Life in Pictures. Muellner, Mireille & Muellner, Leonard, trs. from FRE. LC 90-23138. 464p. 1991. 42.50 (*0-8018-4184-4*) Johns Hopkins.

— Marie Bonaparte. LC 86-51356. 304p. 1987. pap. 17.00 (*0-300-03901-8*, Y-654) Yale U Pr.

Bertin, Charles. Two Plays: Christopher Columbus & Don Juan. Smith, William J., tr. LC 78-109941. (Minnesota Drama Editions Ser.: No. 6). 148p. reprint ed. pap. 45.90 (*0-608-14094-5*, 205584300039) Bks Demand.

Bertin, E. P. Principles & Practice of X-Ray Spectrometric Analysis. 2nd ed. LC 74-28043. (Illus.). 1080p. (C). 1975. text 175.00 (*0-306-30809-6*, Kluwer Plenum) Kluwer Academic.

Bertin, Emanuel A., jt. auth. see Zanan, Arthur S.

Bertin, Emile M. Unimodality of Probability Measures. LC 96-48825. (Mathematics & Its Applications Ser.). 268p. (C). 1996. text 154.50 (*0-7923-4318-2*) Kluwer Academic.

Bertin, Emile M., ed. Proceedings from the International Conference on Potential Theory, Amersfoort, The Netherlands, August 18-24, 1991. LC 94-6950. 350p. (C). 1994. lib. bdg. 172.50 (*0-7923-2741-1*) Kluwer Academic.

Bertin, Eugene P. Introduction to X-Ray Spectrometric Analysis. LC 77-27244. (Illus.). 500p. 1978. 79.50 (*0-306-31091-0*, Plenum Trade) Perseus Pubng.

***Bertin, G.** The Dynamics of Galaxies. LC 99-14192. (Illus.). 448p. (C). 2000. 80.00 (*0-521-47262-8*); pap. 34.95 (*0-521-47855-3*) Cambridge U Pr.

Bertin, G. & Lin, C. C. Spiral Structure in Galaxies: A Density Wave Theory. LC 95-11635. (Illus.). 280p. (C). 1996. 44.00 (*0-262-02396-2*) MIT Pr.

Bertin, J. The Last Dragonlord. LC 98-21186. 400p. 1998. text 25.95 (*0-312-86429-9*) St Martin.

Bertin, J. & Loeb, J. Experimental & Theoretical Aspects of Induced Polarization. Incl. Experimental & Theoretical Aspects of Induced Polarization Vol. 1: Presentation & Application of the IP Method - Case Histories. (Illus.). xxi, 250p. 1976. 52.00 (*3-443-13009-7*, Pub. by Gebruder Borntraeger); Experimental & Theoretical Aspects of Induced Polarization Vol. 2: Macroscopic & Microscopic Theories. (Illus.). xvi, 85p. 1976. 46.00 (*3-443-13010-0*, Pub. by Gebruder Borntraeger); 1976. write for info. (*0-318-54137-8*) Lubrecht & Cramer.

B

Bertin, J. J., et al, eds. Advances in Hypersonics II, 3 vols., Set. LC 92-26882. 1993. 363.00 (*0-8176-3664-1*) Birkhauser.

— Advances in Hypersonics II, Vol. 1. LC 92-26882. x, 437p. 1992. 157.00 (*0-8176-3639-0*) Birkhauser.

— Advances in Hypersonics II, Vol. 2. LC 92-26882. x, 270p. 1992. 157.00 (*0-8176-3663-3*) Birkhauser.

— Advances in Hypersonics II, Vol. 3. LC 92-26882. x, 427p. 1992. 157.03 (*0-8176-3672-2*) Birkhauser.

Bertin, J. J., et al. Hypersonics: Proceedings of the First Joint Europe-U. S. Short Course, 2 vols. Set. (Progress in Scientific Computing Ser.: Nos. 8 & 9). 1300p. 1989. 194.50 (*0-8176-3420-7*) Birkhauser.

— Hypersonics: Proceedings of the First Joint Europe-U. S. Short Course, 2 vols., Vol. 1. (Progress in Scientific Computing Ser.: Nos. 8 & 9). 547p. 1989. 134.00 (*0-8176-3418-5*) Birkhauser.

— Hypersonics: Proceedings of the First Joint Europe-U. S. Short Course, 2 vols., Vol. 2. (Progress in Scientific Computing Ser.: Nos. 8 & 9). 459p. 1989. 134.00 (*0-8176-3419-3*) Birkhauser.

Bertin, Jacques. Graphics & Graphic Information Processing. Berg, William J. & Scott, Paul, trs. from FRE. (Illus.). 273p. 1981. 46.95 (*3-11-008868-1*); pap. 30.80 (*3-11-006901-6*) De Gruyter.

— Semiology of Graphics: Diagrams, Networks, Maps. Berg, William J., tr. LC 83-47755. (Illus.). 429p. reprint ed. pap. 133.00 (*0-8357-3532-X*, 203427000089) Bks Demand.

Bertin, Jacques, et al. Atlas of Food Crops. (Ecoles Practiques des Hautes Etudes Ser.: Section 6). (Illus.). 41p. 1971. text 78.50 (*90-279-1798-1*) Mouton.

Bertin, Jean C. Lexique de Transport International. (ENG & FRE.). 143p. 1992. 49.95 (*0-8288-7187-6*, 2729892176) Fr & Eur.

***Bertin, Joanne.** Dragon & Phoenix. LC 99-37456. 544p. 1999. 25.95 (*0-312-86430-2*, Pub. by Tor Bks) St Martin.

— Dragon & Phoenix. 2000. mass mkt. 6.99 (*0-8125-4542-7*) Tor Bks.

— The Last Dragonlord. 1999. mass mkt. 5.99 (*0-8125-4541-9*, Pub. by Forge NYC) St Martin.

Bertin, John J. Hypersonic Aerothermodynamics. (Educ Ser.). 600p. 1994. 89.95 (*1-56347-036-5*, 36-5) AIAA.

Bertin, John J. & Smith, Michael L. Aerodynamics for Engineers. 3rd ed. LC 96-29675. 668p. 1997. 105.00 (*0-13-576356-8*) P-H.

Bertin, Marie-Jose, ed. Seminaire de Theorie des Nombres, Paris, 1980-1981, Vol. 22. 360p. 1983. 64.00 (*0-8176-3066-X*) Birkhauser.

Bertin, Marie-Jose & Goldstein, Catherine, eds. Seminaire de Theorie des Nombres, 1982-1983. (Progress in Mathematics Ser.: No. 51). 312p. 1985. 69.00 (*0-8176-3261-1*) Birkhauser.

Bertin, Marie-Jose, et al. Pisot & Salem Numbers. LC 92-32812. xiii, 291p. 1992. 146.50 (*0-8176-2648-4*) Birkhauser.

Bertin, Phyllis & Perlman, Eileen. Preventing Academic Failure: A Multisensory Curriculum for Teaching, Reading, Spelling & Handwriting in the Elementary Classroom. 10th rev. ed. 234p. 1980. spiral bd. 42.00 (*0-9636471-0-5*) Monroe Assocs.

Bertine, Eleanor. Close Relationships: Family, Friendship, Marriage. 160p. 1995. pap. 16.00 (*0-919123-58-9*, Pub. by Inner City Bks) BookWorld.

Bertinetti, Marcello. The Rocky Mountains. (Bertinetti Ser.). (Illus.). 128p. 1989. 14.98 (*0-8317-7428-2*) Smithmark.

Berting, Jan, et al, eds. Human Rights in a Pluralist World: Individuals & Collectivities. LC 89-13170. 280p. 1990. 52.95 (*0-313-28077-0*, BWX/, Greenwood Pr) Greenwood.

Berting, Jan & Blockmans, W. Beyond Progress & Development. 110p. 1987. text 69.95 (*0-566-05397-7*, Pub. by Avebry) Ashgate Pub Co.

Berting, Jan, et al. Problems in International Comparative Research in the Social Sciences. 186p. 1979. 91.00 (*0-08-025247-8*, Pub. by Pergamon Repr) Franklin.

Bertini, Ivano, et al, contrib. by. Bioinorganic Chemistry. LC 95-12983. (Structure & Bonding Ser.: Vol. 83). 1995. write for info. (*0-387-59105-2*) Spr-Verlag.

— Bioinorganic Chemistry. LC 95-12983. (Structure & Bonding Ser.: Vol. 83). (Illus.). 100p. 1995. 85.95 (*3-540-59105-2*) Spr-Verlag.

Bertini, Ivano & Drago, Russell, eds. E S R & N M R of Paramagnetic Species in Biological & Related Systems. (NATO Advanced Study Institute Ser.: No. C-52). 422p. 1979. text 155.50 (*90-277-1063-5*) Kluwer Academic.

Bertini, Ivano & Luchinat, Claudio. Nmr of Paramagnetic Molecules in Biological Systems: Physical Bioinorganic Chemistry Series. (Physical Bioinorganic Ser.). (Illus.). 300p. (C). 1986. text 44.25 (*0-8053-0780-X*) Benjamin-Cummings.

Bertini, Ivano, et al. Bioinorganic Chemistry. LC 91-67870. (Illus.). 611p. (C). 1994. text 72.00 (*0-935702-57-1*) Univ Sci Bks.

— The Coordination Chemistry of Metalloenzymes: The Role of Metals in Reaction Involving Water, Dioxygen & Related Species. 1983. text 184.00 (*90-277-1530-0*) Kluwer Academic.

Bertini, Jo. A Man & His Camel. (Illus.). 32p. (J). 1996. pap. 14.95 (*0-7022-2739-0*, Pub. by Univ Queensland Pr) Intl Spec Bk.

Bertini, Mario, et al, eds. Field Dependence in Psychological Theory Research & Application: Two Symposia in Memory of Herman A. Witkin. 152p. (C). 1985. text 39.95 (*0-89859-668-8*) L Erlbaum Assocs.

Bertini, Mario, jt. ed. see Antrobus, John.

Bertini, Tullio B. Trapped in Tuscany--The True World War II Story of Tullio Bertini. Caso, Adolph, ed. LC 98-2884. (Illus.). 296p. 1998. pap. 19.95 (*0-937832-35-9*) Dante U Am.

Bertino, Elisa. Computer Security, ESORICS 96: 4th European Symposium on Research in Computer Security, Rome, Italy, September 25-27, 1996, Proceedings, Vol. 114. LC 96-43202. (Lecture Notes in Computer Science Ser.). x, 365p. 1996. 62.00 (*3-540-61770-1*) Spr-Verlag.

***Bertino, Elisa.** ECOOP '2000- Object-Oriented Programming: Proceedings of the 14th European Conference, Sophia Antipolis & Cannes, France, June 12-16, 2000. LC 00-41915. (Lecture Notes in Computer Science Ser.). 2000. pap. write for info. (*3-540-67660-0*) Spr-Verlag.

Bertino, Elisa. Indexing Techniques for Advanced Database Systems. LC 97-24536. (International Series on Advances in Database Systems). ix, 250 p. 1997. text 126.50 (*0-7923-9985-4*) Kluwer Academic.

— Intelligent Database Systems. (C). 1997. pap. text. write for info. (*0-201-87736-8*) Addison-Wesley.

Bertino, Elisa, ed. Distributed & Parallel Database Object Management. 132p. (C). 1994. text 113.50 (*0-7923-9440-2*) Kluwer Academic.

Bertino, Elisa & Urban, S., eds. Object-Oriented Methodologies & Systems: Proceedings of the International Symposium ISOOMS '94, Palermo, Italy, September 21-22, 1994. LC 95-236647. (Lecture Notes in Computer Science Ser.: Vol. 858). x, 386p. 1994. 55.95 (*3-540-58451-X*) Spr-Verlag.

Bertino, J. R., ed. Marrow Protection: Transduction of Hematopoietic Cells with Drug Resistance Genes. LC 99-25603. (Progress in Experimental Tumor Research Ser.: Vol. 36). (Illus.). 180p. 1999. 174.00 (*3-8055-6828-2*) S Karger.

Bertino, Joseph R. Encyclopedia of Cancer, 3 vols. LC 96-3046. 1996. text 184.00 (*0-12-093231-8*); text 183.00 (*0-12-093232-6*); text 183.00 (*0-12-093233-4*) Acad Pr.

Bertino, Joseph R., ed. Encyclopedia of Cancer, 3 vols. LC 96-3046. (Illus.). 2133p. 1996. text 578.00 (*0-12-093230-X*) Acad Pr.

Bertling, Claudia. Die Darstellung der Kreuzabnahme und der Beweinung Christi in der Ersten Halfte des 16. Jahrhunderts. (GER.). 264p. 1992. 45.00 incl. 3.5 hd (*0-318-70551-6*) G Olms Pubs.

Bertling, Ed, jt. auth. see Leen, Edie.

Bertling, Tom. A Child Sacrificed to the Deaf Culture. 112p. 1994. pap. 18.95 (*0-9637813-4-0*) Kodiak Media.

— No Dignity for Joshua: More Vital Insight into Deaf Children, Deaf Education & Deaf Culture. LC 96-78647. 112p. (Orig.). 1997. per. 21.95 (*0-9637813-6-7*) Kodiak Media.

Bertling, Tom, ed. see Parsons, Frances M. & Stewart, Larry G.

Bertlmann, R. A. Anomalies in Quantum Field Theory. LC 96-185792. (International Series of Monographs on Physics). (Illus.). 580p. 1996. text 115.00 (*0-19-852047-6*) OUP.

***Bertlung, Tom, ed.** An Intellectual Look at American Sign Langauge. 12p. 2001. pap. 19.95 (*0-9637813-7-5*) Kodiak Media.

Bertman, Martin A. Body & Cause in Hobbes: Natural & Political. LC 91-12806. 235p. 1991. 25.00 (*0-89341-636-3*, Longwood Academic) Hollowbrook.

Bertman, Martin A., jt. auth. see Airaksinen, Timo.

Bertman, Sandra, ed. Grief & the Healing Arts: Creativity As Therapy. LC 97-48681. (Death, Value, & Meaning Ser.). (Illus.). 438p. 1998. 58.95 (*0-89503-189-2*); pap. 29.95 (*0-89503-198-1*) Baywood Pub.

Bertman, Sandra L. Death: A Primer for All Ages. (Illus.). 60p. 1990. pap. 6.95 (*0-930194-21-7*) Ctr Thanatology.

— Facing Death: Images, Insights & Interventions. 232p. 1991. pap. 29.95 (*1-56032-223-5*) Taylor & Francis.

Bertman, Sandra L., et al, eds. Death & Loss: Reflections & Interventions from the Arts. (Current Thanatology Ser.). 120p. 2000. pap. 17.95 (*0-930194-47-0*) Ctr Thanatology.

Bertman, Sandra L., jt. auth. see Halporn, Roberta.

Bertman, Skip. Youth League Baseball. (Illus.). 192p. 1993. reprint ed. pap. 12.95 (*0-940279-68-1*, 79681H, Mstrs Pr) NTC Contemp Pub Co.

Bertman, Stephen. Art & the Romans. (Illus.). 83p. 1975. 15.00 (*0-87291-070-9*) Coronado Pr.

***Bertman, Stephen.** Cultural Amnesia: America's Future & the Crisis of Memory. LC 99-43113. 176p. 2000. 35.00 (*0-275-96230-X*, Praeger Pubs) Greenwood.

Bertman, Stephen. Hyperculture: The Human Cost of Speed. LC 97-32951. 288p. 1998. 24.95 (*0-275-96205-9*, Praeger Pubs) Greenwood.

***Bertness, Mark D.** The Ecology of Atlantic Shorelines. LC 98-39306. (Illus.). 417p. (C). 1998. pap. text 39.95 (*0-87893-056-6*) Sinauer Assocs.

Bertnolli, Edward C. & Tranter, William H., eds. National Electronics Conference: Proceedings, Marriott Oak Brook Hotel, Oak Brook, Illinois, October 24, 25 & 26, 1983, Vol. 37. LC TK0005.N37. 550p. reprint ed. pap. 170.50 (*0-608-13460-0*, 202275800037) Bks Demand.

Berto, Frank J. The Birth of Dirt: The Origins of Mountain Biking. LC 98-61189. (Cycling Resources Ser.). (Illus.). 128p. 1999. pap. 12.95 (*1-892495-10-4*) Van der Plas.

***Berto, Frank J. & Shepherd, Ron.** The Dancing Chain: History & Development of the Derailleur Bicycle. (Cycling Resources Ser.). (Illus.). 356p. 2000. 49.95 (*1-892495-21-X*, 21X, Pub. by Van der Plas) Seven Hills Bk.

Berto, Giuseppe. Sky Is Red. Davidson, Angus, tr. from ITA. LC 76-138575. 397p. 1971. reprint ed. lib. bdg. 79.50 (*0-8371-5774-9*, BESR, Greenwood Pr) Greenwood.

Bertocchi, M., et al, eds. Modelling Techniques for Financial Markets & Bank Management. (Contributions to Management Science Ser.). x, 296p. 1996. pap. 78.00 (*3-7908-0928-4*) Spr-Verlag.

Bertocci, Peter A. The Person & Primary Emotions. (Recent Research in Psychology Ser.). 340p. 1988. 58.95 (*0-387-96812-1*) Spr-Verlag.

— Religion As Creative Insecurity. LC 73-1826. 128p. 1973. reprint ed. lib. bdg. 49.50 (*0-8371-6803-1*, BECI, Greenwood Pr) Greenwood.

Bertocci, U., jt. ed. see Mansfield, F.

Bertoch, Julia B., jt. auth. see Bertoch, Marvin J.

Bertoch, Marvin J. & Bertoch, Julia B. Modern Echoes from Ancient Hills: Our Greek Heritage. Larson, Stan, ed. LC 96-43404. (Illus.). 224p. 1997. text 15.95 (*0-9634732-5-5*, Blue Ribbon Books) Freethinker.

Bertodan, Teresa De, see De Bertodan, Teresa.

Bertoglio, Jan & Hudson, JoLe. A Cooking Affaire I. (Illus.). 413p. 1985. 24.95 (*0-9614367-2-7*) Butchr Blck Pr.

— A Cooking Affaire II. 2nd ed. (Illus.). 429p. 1991. 24.95 (*0-9614367-1-9*) Butchr Blck Pr.

— A Cooking Affaire III. (Illus.). 196p. 1999. spiral bd. 19.95 (*0-9614367-3-5*) Butchr Blck Pr.

Bertoglio, Jan, jt. auth. see Hudson, JoLe.

Bertoia, Jeanne. Doorstops. (Illus.). 176p. 1996. pap. 9.95 (*0-89145-298-2*, 1629) Collector Bks.

Bertoia, Judi. Drawings from a Dying Child: Insights into Death from a Jungian Perspective. LC 92-15267. (Illus.). 176p. (C). 1993. text 49.95 (*0-415-07218-2*, A7169) Routledge.

***Bertoia, Rich.** Antique Motorcycle Toys. LC 99-62042. (Illus.). 160p. 1999. 49.95 (*0-7643-0862-9*) Schiffer.

***Bertoin, J., et al.** Lectures on Probability Theory & Statistics: Ecole d'Ete de Probabilities de Saint-Flour XXVII - 1997. Bernard, P., ed. (Lecture Notes in Mathematics Ser.: Vol. 1717). ix, 289p. 2000. pap. 52.80 (*3-540-66593-5*) Spr-Verlag.

Bertoin, Jean. Levy Processes. (Cambridge Tracts in Mathematics Ser.: No. 121). 275p. (C). 1998. pap. text 27.95 (*0-521-64632-4*) Cambridge U Pr.

Bertol, Daniela. Designing Digital Space: An Architect's Guide to Virtual Reality. LC 96-26224. 368p. 1996. pap. 54.95 (*0-471-14662-5*) Wiley.

— Visualizing with CAD: Why & How to Generate Forms from Geometry to Architecture Using AutoCAD. LC 94-17611. (Illus.). 384p. 1994. pap. 49.95 (*0-387-94275-0*) Spr-Verlag.

***Bertola, Chiara & Falcone, Paolo, texts.** Ilya/Emilia Kabakov. (Illus.). 248p. 1999. pap. 49.95 (*88-8158-222-8*, 920503, Pub. by Charta) Dist Art Pubs.

Bertola, F. & Curi, U., eds. The Anthropic Principle: The Conditions for the Existence of Mankind in the Universe. (Illus.). 191p. (C). 1993. text 74.95 (*0-521-38203-3*) Cambridge U Pr.

***Bertola, Giuseppe, et al, eds.** Welfare & Employment in a United Europe. (Illus.). 320p. (C). 2000. 32.95 (*0-262-02483-7*) MIT Pr.

Bertolacci, Anthony. Agricultural, Commercial & Financial Interests of Ceylon: With an Appendix; Containing Some of the Principal Laws & Usages of the Candians. 1993. reprint ed. 45.00 (*81-7013-102-2*, Pub. by Navarang) S Asia.

Bertolacini, Ralph J., et al, eds. Characterization & Catalyst Development: An Interactive Approach. LC 89-17777. (Symposium Ser.: No. 411). (Illus.). 488p. 1989. text 115.00 (*0-8412-1684-3*, Pub. by Am Chemical) OUP.

Bertolaet, Todd, photos by. Crescent Rivers: Waterways of Florida's Big Bend. LC 98-10218. (Illus.). 80p. 1998. 29.95 (*0-8130-1614-2*) U Press Fla.

Bertolami, O., jt. auth. see Bento, M. C.

***Bertoldi, Paolo, et al.** Energy Efficiency Improvements in Electric Motors & Drives. LC 00-33889. 2000. pap. write for info. (*3-540-67669-6*) Spr-Verlag.

Bertoleio, Noah. I'm with You No Matter How Far Away. LC 97-93544. (Illus.). 52p. (J). (gr. k up). 1997. pap., spiral bd. 15.95 (*0-9658823-1-4*) Love St Publ.

— My Wine. LC 97-72091. 88p. 1997. pap. 20.00 (*0-9658823-0-6*) Love St Publ.

Bertolet, D. H. Bertolet: Genealogical History of the Bertolet Family; the Descendents of Jean Bertolet. (Illus.). 260p. 1991. reprint ed. pap. 41.00 (*0-8328-1872-0*); reprint ed. lib. bdg. 51.00 (*0-8328-1871-2*) Higginson Bk Co.

Bertolet, Mary M. & Goldsmith, Lee S., eds. Hospital Liability: Law & Tactics. 5th ed. 801p. 1987. 10.00 (*0-685-69447-X*) PLI.

Bertolet, Rod. What Is Said: A Theory of Indirect Speech Reports. 266p. (C). 1990. lib. bdg. 144.00 (*0-7923-0792-5*, Pub. by Kluwer Academic) Kluwer Academic.

Bertoletti, T., jt. auth. see Isi.

Bertoli, E., jt. ed. see Chapman, David J.

Bertoline. Fundamentals of Graphics Communications. 3rd ed. 2000. 47.00 (*0-07-232209-8*) McGraw.

— Technical Graphics Communication for Autocad 14. 2nd ed. 1998. text 66.74 (*0-07-561649-1*) McGraw.

— Technical Graphics Communications. 1996. 72.00 (*0-256-25266-1*) McGraw.

Bertoline & Nasman. Fundamental Engineering Graphics. 1996. 51.25 (*0-256-25265-3*) McGraw.

Bertoline, Gary R. CAD Applications: Mechanical. 256p. 1986. teacher ed. 16.00 (*0-8273-2549-5*); pap. 29.95 (*0-8273-2548-7*) Delmar.

— Engineering Graphics Communication. (C). 1997. pap. 28.13 (*0-256-26780-4*) McGraw.

— Engineering Graphics Communication. LC 94-23423. 896p. (C). 1995. text 72.75 (*0-256-11418-8*, Irwn McGrw-H) McGrw-H Hghr Educ.

— Engineering Graphics Communication: Problems for Engineering Graphics Communincation & Technical Graphics Communication, 2. 128p. (C). 1995. text 21.95 (*0-256-11420-X*, Irwn McGrw-H) McGrw-H Hghr Educ.

— Engineering Graphics Communication: Problems for Engineering Graphics Communincation & Technical Graphics Communication, 1. 120p. (C). 1995. text 21.95 (*0-256-11419-6*, Irwn McGrw-H) McGrw-H Hghr Educ.

— Fundamentals of CAD. LC 84-17563. 352p. (C). 1985. pap. 42.95 (*0-8273-2332-8*) Delmar.

— Fundamentals of CAD. 2nd ed. 352p. 1988. mass mkt. 64.95 (*0-8273-3291-2*) Delmar.

— Fundamentals of CAD. 2nd ed. 352p. 1988. pap., teacher ed. 16.00 (*0-8273-3292-0*) Delmar.

***Bertoline, Gary R.** Fundamentals of Graphics Communication. 1998. 65.63 (*0-07-236042-9*) McGraw.

Bertoline, Gary R. Fundamentals of Graphics Communication. 2nd ed. LC 97-38383. (Irwin Graphics Ser.). 1997. write for info. (*0-07-289201-3*) McGraw.

***Bertoline, Gary R.** Graphics Drawing Workbook. 504p. (C). 1999. pap. 27.50 (*0-07-233608-0*) McGrw-H Hghr Educ.

Bertoline, Gary R. Introduction to Graphics Communications for Engineers. LC 98-34941. (McGraw-Hill's Best-Basic Engineering Series & Tools). 224p. 1998. pap. 30.00 (*0-07-229144-3*) McGraw.

— Technical Graphics Communication. 2nd ed. 1997. pap. text. write for info. (*0-256-26668-9*) McGraw.

— Technical Graphics Communication Chapter 16. (C). 1995. pap. text 1.50 (*0-256-20452-7*, Irwn McGrw-H) McGrw-H Hghr Educ.

Bertoline, Gary R., et al. The AutoCAD Solid Modeling Workbook. (Graphics Ser.). 250p. 1995. text, wbk. ed. 19.95 (*0-256-12451-5*, Irwn McGrw-H) McGrw-H Hghr Educ.

— Engineering Graphics Communication. rev. ed. 896p. (C). 1995. text 69.95 (*0-256-21309-7*, Irwn McGrw-H) McGrw-H Hghr Educ.

— Fundamentals of Graphics Communication. (Irwin Graphics Ser.). 1995. write for info. (*0-256-16413-4*, Irwn McGrw-H) McGrw-H Hghr Educ.

— Technical Graphics Communication. LC 95-1599. (Graphics Ser.). 1336p. (C). 1995. text 72.95 (*0-256-11417-X*, Irwn McGrw-H) McGrw-H Hghr Educ.

— Technical Graphics Communication. 2nd ed. LC 96-43009. 1152p. (C). 1996. text 69.95 (*0-256-22981-3*, Irwn McGrw-H) McGrw-H Hghr Educ.

Bertoline, Gary R., jt. auth. see Resetarits, Paul J.

Bertoline, Robert R., et al. Fundamentals of Graphics Communication. 51.95p. (C). 1995. text 51.95 (*0-256-12402-7*, Irwn McGrw-H) McGrw-H Hghr Educ.

Bertolini, Dewey M. Back to the Heart of Youth Work. 228p. 1989. text 16.99 (*0-89693-662-7*, Victor Bks) Chariot Victor.

— Escaping the Subtle Sellout. LC 92-12725. 204p. (Orig.). 1992. pap. 1.80 (*0-89693-065-3*, 6-1065, Victor Bks) Chariot Victor.

— Secret Wounds & Silent Cries. rev. ed. LC 93-18867. Orig. Title: Sometimes I Really Hate You!. 156p. (J). 1993. pap. 9.99 (*1-56476-116-9*, 6-3116, Victor Bks) Chariot Victor.

— Sometimes I Really Hate You. (Straight Talk for Teenagers Ser.). 132p. (YA). 1991. pap. 4.99 (*0-89693-041-6*) Chariot Victor.

Bertolini Guerrieri-Gonzaga, jt. auth. see Rolland, Romain.

Bertolini, John A. The Playwriting Self of Bernard Shaw. LC 89-49568. 208p. (C). 1991. 26.95 (*0-8093-1650-1*) S Ill U Pr.

Bertolini, Joseph C. The Serpent Within: Politics, Literature & American Individualism. LC 96-40871. vii, 116p. (C). 1997. pap. 24.50 (*0-7618-0626-1*) U Pr of Amer.

Bertolini, Rebecca. Growing Seasons for Little Characters. (Illus.). 176p. 1993. pap. 12.99 (*1-56476-114-2*, 6-3114, Victor Bks) Chariot Victor.

— Mom's Big Activity Book for Building Little Characters. 175p. 1992. pap. 12.99 (*0-89693-980-4*, 6-1980, Victor Bks) Chariot Victor.

Bertolini, Vincent J., jt. auth. see Cutrufelli, Maria Rosa.

***Bertolino, Angela & Lewis, Carla.** "Extra" Work for Brain Surgeons. 18th rev. ed. Mancini, Laura Drake, ed. 375p. 2000. pap. 20.00 (*1-893899-05-5*) Holly Op Sys.

Bertolino, Angela, jt. auth. see Lewis, Carla.

Bertolino, Bob. Therapy with Troubled Teenagers: Rewriting Young Lives in Progress. LC 98-9520. 234p. 1998. 47.50 (*0-471-24996-3*) Wiley.

Bertolino, Bob & O'Hanlon, William H. Invitation to Possibility Land: An Intensive Teaching Seminar with Bill O'Hanlon. LC 98-20700. 1998. 39.95 (*0-87630-875-2*) Brunner-Mazel.

Bertolino, Bob & Thompson, Kevin. The Residential Youth Care Worker in Action: A Collaborative, Competency-Based Approach. LC 99-15066. (Illus.). 202p. 1999. lib. bdg. 39.95 (*0-7890-0701-0*) Haworth Pr.

Bertolino, James. First Credo. 2nd ed. (QRL Poetry Bks.: Vol. XXVI). 1986. 20.00 (*0-614-06413-9*) Quarterly Rev.

— New & Selected Poems. LC 77-81274. (Poetry Ser.). 1978. pap. 11.95 (*0-915604-14-0*) Carnegie-Mellon.

— Precinct Kali & the Gertrude Spicer Story: Poems. 116p. 1981. pap. 4.00 (*0-89823-034-9*) New Rivers Pr.

— Snail River. (QRL Poetry Bks.: Vol. XXXIV). 684p. 1995. 20.00 (*0-614-06462-7*) Quarterly Rev.

— What Water Says. (Tanbark Ser.). 32p. (Orig.). 1997. pap. 8.00 (*1-887853-15-4*) Radiolarian.

Bertolino, Jane V. The Many Faces of Pamela. (Literary Criticism Ser.). 138p. (Orig.). (C). 1990. pap. 12.00 (*0-921252-12-9*) LEGAS.

Bertolino, Judie, et al. Fun with Fingerpuppets. (Illus.). 48p. (J). 1996. pap., wbk. ed. 15.95 (*1-56472-103-5*) Edupress Inc.

— Theme Centers for Dramatic Play. (Illus.). 304p. 1996. pap., wbk. ed. 24.95 (*1-56472-106-X*) Edupress Inc.

***Bertolli, Paul & Waters, Alice.** Chez Panisse Cooking. 2000. 31.00 (*0-8446-7110-X*) Peter Smith.

Bertolli, Paul & Waters, Alice L. Chez Panisse Cooking. (Illus.). 448p. 1994. pap. 18.95 (*0-679-75535-7*) Random.

Bertollini, Roberto, et al, eds. Environmental Epidemiology: Exposure & Disease. LC 95-17470. 256p. 1995. lib. bdg. 75.00 (*1-56670-067-1*, L1067) Lewis Pubs.

Bertolotti, Mario. Masers & Lasers: An Historical Approach. (Illus.). 268p. 1988. pap. 65.00 (*0-85274-437-4*) IOP Pub.

Bertolotti, Mario & Andriesh, A. M. Physics & Applications of Non-Crystalline Semiconductors in Optoelectronics. LC 97-20563. (NATO ASI Series: Partnership Sub-Series 3). 1997. text 251.00 (*0-7923-4623-8*) Kluwer Academic.

Bertolotto, Giovanni, jt. ed. see Adjmi, Morris.

Bertolucci, Attilio. Selected Poems. Tomlinson, Charles, tr. from ITA. 160p. 1994. pap. 18.95 (*1-85224-242-6*, Pub. by Bloodaxe Bks) Dufour.

Bertolucci, John, jt. auth. see Scanlan, Michael.

Bertolucci, Miguel, tr. see Kardec, Allan, pseud.

Berton. International Negotiation. LC 98-51658. 1999. text 55.00 (*0-312-21778-1*) St Martin.

Berton, A. Archery Dictionary: French/English/French. (ENG & FRE.). 1998. 35.00 (*0-320-00222-5*) Fr & Eur.

Berton, J. La Toponymie Ecossaise. (ENG & GAE.). 29p. 1990. pap. 11.95 (*0-8288-3377-X*, F119710) Fr & Eur.

Berton, Kathleen. Moscow: An Architectural History. (Illus.). 255p. 1991. 41.00 (*0-685-38703-8*, Pub. by I B T) St Martin.

— Moscow Revealed. (Illus.). 222p. 1991. 29.98 (*1-55859-215-6*) Abbeville Pr.

— Niagara Falls Picture Book. 1994. 19.95 (*0-7710-1214-4*) McCland & Stewart.

Berton, L. Moscow: An Architectural History. (C). 1990. 180.00 (*0-7855-4488-7*, Pub. by Collets) St Mut.

Berton, Laura B. I Married the Klondike. 232p. 1996. pap. text 14.99 (*0-7710-1240-3*) McCland & Stewart.

Berton, Peter. The Russo-Japanese Alliance of 1916. (Pew Caes Studies in International Affairs). 50p. (C). 1988. pap. text 3.50 (*1-56927-326-X*) Geo U Inst Dplmcy.

***Berton, Pierre.** Arctic Grail: The Quest for the Northwest Passage & the North Pole, 1818-1909. 2000. pap. 19.95 (*1-58574-116-7*) Lyons Pr.

Berton, Pierre. Attack on Montreal. LC 96-140218. (Battles of the War of 1812 Ser.). (Illus.). 88p. (J). (gr. 6-9). pap. 4.99 (*0-7710-1419-8*) McCland & Stewart.

— The Battle of Lake Erie. (Battles of the War of 1812 Ser.). (Illus.). 88p. (J). (gr. 6-9). pap. 4.99 (*0-7710-1424-4*) McCland & Stewart.

— Before the Gold Rush. (Great Klondike Gold Rush Ser.). (Illus.). 88p. (J). (gr. 6-9). pap. 4.99 (*0-7710-1449-X*) McCland & Stewart.

— Bonanza Gold. (Great Klondike Gold Rush Ser.). (Illus.). 88p. (J). (gr. 6-9). pap. 4.99 (*0-7710-1432-5*) McCland & Stewart.

— City of Gold. (Great Klondike Gold Rush Ser.). (Illus.). 88p. (J). (gr. 6-9). pap. 4.99 (*0-7710-1445-7*) McCland & Stewart.

— The Death of Tecumseh. (Battles of the War of 1812 Ser.). (Illus.). 88p. (J). (gr. 6-9). pap. 4.99 (*0-7710-1423-6*) McCland & Stewart.

— Directory of Professional Genealogists, 1995. (Illus.). 150p. 1995. pap. text 15.00 (*0-614-05487-7*) Assn Prof Genealogists.

— Dr. Kane of the Arctic Seas: Exploring the Frozen North. (Exploring the Frozen North Ser.). (Illus.). 88p. (J). (gr. 6-9). pap. 4.99 (*0-7710-1446-5*) McCland & Stewart.

— The Great Lakes. (Illus.). 224p. 1996. 40.00 (*0-7737-2971-2*) Stoddart Publ.

— Jane Franklin's Obsession. (Exploring the Frozen North Ser.). (Illus.). 88p. (J). (gr. 6-9). pap. 4.99 (*0-7710-1435-X*) McCland & Stewart.

— Kings of the Klondike. (Great Klondike Gold Rush Ser.). (Illus.). 88p. (J). (gr. 6-9). pap. 4.99 (*0-7710-1448-1*) McCland & Stewart.

— Klondike: The Last Great Gold Rush, 1896-1899. (Illus.). 496p. 1994. pap. 15.95 (*0-7710-1284-5*) McCland & Stewart.

— Klondike Fever. 457p. 1985. pap. 13.95 (*0-88184-139-0*) Carroll & Graf.

— Klondike Quest. 240p. 1997. 32.00 (*1-55046-202-4*, Pub. by Boston Mills) Genl Dist Srvs.

— The Klondike Stampede. (Great Klondike Gold Rush Ser.). (Illus.). 88p. (J). (gr. 6-9). pap. 4.99 (*0-7710-1433-3*) McCland & Stewart.

— The Men in Sheepskin Coats. (Canada Moves West Ser.). (Illus.). 88p. (J). (gr. 6-9). pap. 4.99 (*0-7710-1438-4*) McCland & Stewart.

— My Times: Living. (Illus.). 448p. 1995. 34.95 (*0-385-25528-4*) Doubleday.

— Niagara: A History of the Falls. (Illus.). 480p. 1998. pap. text 7.00 (*0-7881-5350-1*) DIANE Pub.

— Niagara: A History of the Falls. Turner, Philip, ed. (Illus.). 480p. 1997. 27.00 (*1-56836-154-8*) Kodansha.

— Niagara: A History of the Falls. 1993. pap. 8.99 (*0-7710-1217-9*) McCland & Stewart.

— Niagara: A History of the Falls. LC 96-44821. 371p. 1998. pap. 14.95 (*0-14-027016-7*) Viking Penguin.

— Niagara Falls: A Picture Book. (Illus.). 160p. 1993. 29.95 (*0-7710-0218-1*) McCland & Stewart.

— Parry of the Arctic. (Exploring the Frozen North Ser.). (Illus.). 88p. (J). (gr. 6-9). pap. 4.99 (*0-7710-1434-1*) McCland & Stewart.

— A Picture Book of Niagara Falls. (Illus.). 160p. 1998. text 20.00 (*0-7881-5401-X*) DIANE Pub.

— Pierre Berton's Canada: The Land & the People. LC 98-226151. (Illus.). 224p. 1999. 40.00 (*0-7737-3095-8*) Genl Dist Srvs.

— Pierre Berton's Canada: The Land & the People. LC 99-492061. (Illus.). 208p. 1999. 40.00 (*0-7737-3160-1*) Stoddart Publ.

— A Prairie Nightmare. (Canada Moves West Ser.). (Illus.). 88p. (J). (gr. 6-9). pap. 4.99 (*0-7710-1440-6*) McCland & Stewart.

— The Railway Pathfinders. (Canada Moves West Ser.). (Illus.). 88p. (J). (gr. 6-9). pap. 4.99 (*0-7710-1437-6*) McCland & Stewart.

— The Remarkable Past: Tales from My Country & the Wild Frontier. rev. ed. 400p. 1995. pap. 19.99 (*0-7710-1357-4*) McCland & Stewart.

— The Secret World of Og. rev. ed. (Illus.). 60p. (Orig.). (J). (gr. k-4). pap. 12.99 (*0-7710-1399-X*) McCland & Stewart.

— Steel Across the Plains. (Canada Moves West Ser.). (Illus.). 88p. (J). (gr. 6-9). pap. 4.99 (*0-7710-1441-4*) McCland & Stewart.

— Steel Across the Shield. (Canada Moves West Ser.). (Illus.). 88p. (J). (gr. 6-9). pap. 4.99 (*0-7710-1422-8*) McCland & Stewart.

— Trails of '98. (Great Klondike Gold Rush Ser.). (Illus.). 88p. (J). (gr. 6-9). pap. 4.99 (*0-7710-1444-9*) McCland & Stewart.

— Trapped in the Arctic: Exploring the Frozen North. (Adventures in Canadian History Ser.). (Illus.). 88p. (J). (gr. 6-9). pap. 4.99 (*0-7710-1447-3*) McCland & Stewart.

— Welcome To The Twenty-First Century. 256p. 1999. 18.95 (*0-385-25817-8*) Doubleday.

— Winter. (Illus.). 64p. 1994. 50.00 (*0-7737-2505-9*) Genl Dist Srvs.

— Winter. LC 95-128276. (Illus.). 224p. 1996. 40.00 (*0-7737-2805-8*) Stoddart Publ.

— Worth Repeating: A Literary Resurrection. 320p. 1999. pap. 11.95 (*0-385-25737-6*) Bantam.

***Berton, Ralph.** Remembering Bix. 464p. 2000. pap. text 18.00 (*0-306-80937-0*) Da Capo.

Berton, Valerie, ed. Source Book of Sustainable Agriculture for Educators, Producers & Other Agricultural Professionals. (Illus.). 136p. 1998. pap. text 30.00 (*0-7881-4828-1*) DIANE Pub.

Bertoncini, Gene. Approaching the Guitar. 88p. 1991. pap. text 14.95 (*0-8497-6326-6*, GE56) Kjos.

Bertone, Joseph, jt. auth. see Brown, Christopher.

Bertone, Manuela. Carlo Emilio Gadda: Contemporary Perspectives. (Toronto Italian Studies). (Illus.). 352p. 1998. text 60.00 (*0-8020-4171-X*); pap. text 21.95 (*0-8020-8033-2*) U of Toronto Pr.

Bertoneche, Marc, jt. auth. see Knight, Rory.

***Bertoni, Franco.** Claudio Silvestrin. LC 99-89495. 2000. write for info. (*0-8176-6105-0*) Birkhauser.

Bertoni, H. L., et al. Ultra-Wideband, Short-Pulse Electromagnetics, Vol. 1. (Illus.). 554p. (C). 1993. text 125.00 (*0-306-44530-1*, Kluwer Plenum) Kluwer Academic.

Bertoni, H. L., jt. auth. see Das, N. K.

***Bertoni, Henry L.** Radio Propagation for Modern Wireless Systems. 276p. 1999. 79.00 (*0-13-026373-7*) P-H.

Bertoni, Henry L. & Felsen, L. B., eds. Directions in Electromagnetic Wave Modeling. (Illus.). 574p. (C). text 162.00 (*0-306-44023-7*, Kluwer Plenum) Kluwer Academic.

Bertonlini, Luca. Cities on Rails: The Development of Railway Stations & their Surroundings. LC 99-160765. xi, 236p. 1998. pap. 60.00 (*0-419-22760-1*, E & FN Spon) Routledge.

Bertonneau, Thomas F. Declining Standards at Michigan Public Universities. (Illus.). 88p. (Orig.). 1996. pap. 5.00 (*0-9647703-8-5*, S96-04) Mackinac Ctr Public Pol.

— Declining Standards at Michigan Public Universities. 2nd rev. ed. (Illus.). 88p. (Orig.). 1996. pap. 5.00 (*0-9647703-9-3*, S96-04) Mackinac Ctr Public Pol.

Bertorelli, Paul, ed. see Savage, Craig.

Bertorini. Evaluation & Diagnostic Test in Neuromuscular Disorders. 400p. Date not set. 80.00 (*0-7506-7290-0*) Buttrwrth-Heinemann.

Bertot, Francisco L. La Inmovil Carrera. LC 88-80863. (Coleccion Espejo de Paciencia). (SPA.). 112p. (Orig.). 1988. pap. 12.00 (*0-89729-481-5*) Ediciones.

Bertot, John C., jt. auth. see McClure, Charles R.

Bertot, John C., jt. ed. see Fletcher, Patricia D.

***Bertot, John Carlo.** Policy Issues & Strategies Affecting Public Libraries in the National Networked Environment: Moving Beyond Connectivity. 32p. 1998. pap. 2.75 (*0-16-061878-9*) USGPO.

Bertot, Lillian. Separados por la Espuma. LC 80-65223. (Coleccion Espejo de Paciencia). 46p. 1980. pap. 5.95 (*0-89729-250-2*) Ediciones.

Bertot, Lillian D. The Literary Imagination of the Mariel Generation. 105p. (C). 1995. pap. text 14.00 (*1-884619-05-3*) Endowment CAS.

***Bertot, Yves, et al, eds.** Theorem Proving in Higher Order Logics: 12th International Conference, TPHOLS '99, Nice, France, September 14-17, 1999, Proceedings. LC 99-44586. (Lecture Notes in Computer Science Ser.: Vol. 1690). viii, 359p. 1999. pap. 62.00 (*3-540-66463-7*) Spr-Verlag.

Bertotti, Bruno, et al, eds. Modern Cosmology in Retrospect. (Illus.). 446p. (C). 1991. text 95.00 (*0-521-37213-5*) Cambridge U Pr.

Bertotti, Bruno & Farinella, Paolo. Physics of the Earth & the Solar System: Dynamics & Evolution, Space Navigation, Space-Time Structure. (C). 1990. text 236.50 (*0-7923-0535-3*) Kluwer Academic.

Bertotti, Giorgio. Hysteresis in Magnetism: For Physicists, Materials Scientists, & Engineers. LC 98-7054. (Illus.). 558p. 1998. text 99.95 (*0-12-093270-9*) Morgan Kaufmann.

Bertotti-Scamozzi, O. The Buildings & the Designs of Andrea Palladio. LC NA1123.P2B37. 126p. 1976. reprint ed. pap. 39.10 (*0-8357-7474-0*, 202177200023) Bks Demand.

Bertout, C., jt. auth. see Reipurth, Bo.

Bertozzi, Barbara. Jasper Johns Seasons. 1996. pap. 25.00 (*88-8158-079-9*, Pub. by Charta) Dist Art Pubs.

Bertozzi, Elena, tr. see Baldelli, Pia G.

Bertozzi, Stefano, jt. auth. see Babbel, David.

Bertozzi, W., et al, eds. Electron & Pion Interactions with Nuclei at Intermediate Energies. (Studies in High Energy Physics: Vol. 2). xii, 704p. 1980. text 322.00 (*3-7186-0015-3*) Gordon & Breach.

Bertr Computer Society Press Staff, jt. ed. see Mingins, Christine.

Bertram, tr. see Van der Waal, Cornelis.

Bertram, Alexandra, jt. auth. see Trumble, Angus.

Bertram, Anne. In a Pig's Eye! The Dictionary of Country Jawing. LC 97-28167. 400p. 1998. 7.99 (*0-517-18887-2*) Crown Pub Group.

— Life Is Just a Bowl of Cherries: And Other Delicious Sayings. LC 96-51179. (Artful Wordsmith Ser.). (Illus.). 336p. 1997. pap. 12.95 (*0-8442-0900-7*, 09007) NTC Contemp Pub Co.

— NTC Thesaurus of Everyday American English. LC 95-174468. 496p. 1994. 16.95 (*0-8442-5825-3*, 58253) NTC Contemp Pub Co.

— NTC Thesaurus of Everyday American English. 340p. 1994. pap. 12.95 (*0-8442-5826-1*, 58261) NTC Contemp Pub Co.

— NTC's Dictionary of Commonplace Words in Real-Life Contexts: An Essential Guide to the Everyday Objects in American Life. LC 96-26183. (Illus.). 400p. 1998. pap. 14.95 (*0-8442-0846-9*, 08469) NTC Contemp Pub Co.

— NTC's Dictionary of Euphemisms: The Most Practical Guide to Unraveling Euphemisms. LC 97-49341. 320p. 1998. 16.95 (*0-8442-0842-6*, 08426) NTC Contemp Pub Co.

— NTC's Dictionary of Euphemisms: The Most Practical Guide to Unraveling Euphemisms. 320p. 1999. pap. 14.95 (*0-8442-0843-4*, 08434) NTC Contemp Pub Co.

— NTC's Dictionary of Folksy, Regional & Rural Sayings: A Practical Guide to Down-Home Expressions & the Way They Are Used. Spears, Richard A., ed. (Illus.). 400p. 1996. pap. 16.95 (*0-8442-5834-2*, 58342) NTC Contemp Pub Co.

— NTC's Dictionary of Proverbs & Cliches. (Illus.). 320p. 1996. pap. 12.95 (*0-8442-5158-5*, 51585, Natl Textbk Co) NTC Contemp Pub Co.

— NTC's Dictionary of Proverbs & Cliches: Intermediate Through Advanced. Spears, Richard A., ed. (Illus.). 320p. 1994. pap. 16.95 (*0-8442-5159-3*, 51593, Natl Textbk Co) NTC Contemp Pub Co.

Bertram, Anne, ed. In Other Words: Making Better Word Choices in American English. (Artful Wordsmith Ser.). (Illus.). 492p. 1996. pap. 12.95 (*0-8442-0903-1*, 09031) NTC Contemp Pub Co.

Bertram, Anne & Spears, Richard A., eds. Aw Shucks! The Dictionary of Country Jawing. (Artful Wordsmith Ser.). (Illus.). 400p. 1996. pap. 12.95 (*0-8442-0906-6*, 09066) NTC Contemp Pub Co.

***Bertram, Barbara, et al.** Integral Methods in Science & Engineering. LC 99-86281. (Research Notes in Mathematics Ser.). 2000. 94.95 (*1-58488-146-1*, Chap & Hall CRC) CRC Pr.

Bertram, Brian. Lions. LC 98-17626. (Worldlife Library). (Illus.). 72p. (YA). 1998. pap. 16.95 (*0-89658-399-6*) Voyageur Pr.

Bertram, Brian C. The Ostrich Communal Nesting. (Monographs in Behavior & Ecology). (Illus.). 208p. 1992. text 42.50 (*0-691-08785-7*, Pub. by Princeton U Pr) Cal Prin Full Svc.

Bertram, Christoph. Europe in the Balance: Securing the Peace Won in the Cold War. 110p. (C). 1995. pap. 12.95 (*0-87003-068-X*) Carnegie Endow.

Bertram, Christopher. New Conventional Weapons & East-West Security. LC 78-78216. (Praeger Special Studies). 97p. 1979. 55.00 (*0-275-90331-1*, C0331, Praeger Pubs) Greenwood.

Bertram, Christopher & Chitty, Andrew, eds. Has History Ended? Fukuyama, Marx & Modernity. (Avebury Series in Philosophy). 190p. 1994. 72.95 (*1-85628-959-1*, Pub. by Avebury) Ashgate Pub Co.

Bertram, Christopher, jt. auth. see Kincade, William H.

Bertram, David, ed. Butterworths Business Tax Service. ring bd. write for info. (*0-406-99863-9*, BBTSASET, MICHIE) LEXIS Pub.

Bertram, Dora R., Jr. & Martin, Kimberly A. Congressional Hearings Calendar, 10 vols. (AALL Legal Research Ser.). 1987. lib. bdg. 615.00 (*0-89941-558-X*, 305160) W S Hein.

Bertram, Eva, et al. Drug War Politics: The Price of Denial. LC 95-19168. 349p. 1996. pap. 18.95 (*0-520-20598-7*, Pub. by U CA Pr) Cal Prin Full Svc.

Bertram, G. L., tr. see Van der Waal, Cornelis.

Bertram, G. T., jt. ed. see Van Wagoner, J. C.

Bertram, Geoffrey, jt. auth. see Thorp, Rosemary.

Bertram, George T., jt. auth. see Purdy, Edward G.

Bertram, Gordon W. Consolidated Bargaining in California Construction: An Appraisal of Twenty-Five Years' Experience. (Monograph & Research Ser.: No. 12). 259p. 1966, 6.00 (*0-89215-013-0*) U Cal LA Indus Rel.

Bertram, H. Neal. Theory of Magnetic Recording. (Illus.). 372p. (C). 1994. text 95.00 (*0-521-44512-4*); pap. text 42.95 (*0-521-44973-1*) Cambridge U Pr.

Bertram, Hans. The Abbey Cookbook: Inspired Recipes from the Great Atlanta Restaurant. LC 81-20225. (Illus.). 224p. 1982. pap. 10.95 (*0-916782-26-3*) Harvard Common Pr.

Bertram, James. Dan Davin. (New Zealand Writers & Their Work Ser.). 64p. 1983. pap. text 12.95 (*0-19-558095-8*) OUP.

Bertram, James M. First Act in China: The Story of the Sian Mutiny. LC 74-31223. (China in the 20th Century Ser.). Orig. Title: Crisis in China. (Illus.). xxii, 284p. 1975. reprint ed. lib. bdg. 35.00 (*0-306-70687-3*) Da Capo.

— Unconquered: Journal of a Year's Adventure Among the Fighting Peasants of North China. (China in the 20th Century Ser.). (Illus.). ix, 340p. 1975. reprint ed. lib. bdg. 39.50 (*0-306-70688-1*) Da Capo.

Bertram, Jerome, ed. Monumental Brasses As Art & History. LC 96-35981. (Illus.). 256p. 1996. 51.95 (*0-7509-1051-8*, Pub. by Sutton Pub Ltd) Intl Pubs Mktg.

Bertram, Jerome, tr. see Rievaulx, Aelred.

Bertram, Jerome, tr. see St. John Cassiau.

Bertram, John E. Looking Good Is Good Business: A Handbook of Publicity & Promotion Techniques Every Builder Should Use. LC 92-24918. (Illus.). 112p. (Orig.). 1992. pap. 12.00 (*0-86718-379-9*) Home Builder.

Bertram, L. A., et al, eds. Material Parameter Estimation for Modern Constitutive Equations. 289p. 1993. pap. 67.50 (*0-7918-1016-X*) ASME.

***Bertram, Lakshmi.** Choosing Waterbirth: Reclaiming the Sacred Power of Birth. (Illus.). 160p. 2000. pap. 14.95 (*1-57174-152-6*) Hampton Roads Pub Co.

Bertram, M., tr. see Luther, Martin H.

Bertram, Marshall. The Birth of Anglo-American Friendship: The Prime Facet of the Venezuelan Boundary Dispute a Study of the Interreaction of Diplomacy & Public Opinion. 172p. (Orig.). (C). 1992. lib. bdg. 49.50 (*0-8191-8764-X*) U Pr of Amer.

— The Birth of Anglo-American Friendship: The Prime Facet of the Venezuelan Boundary Dispute a Study of the Interreaction of Diplomacy & Public Opinion. 172p. (Orig.). (C). 1992. pap. text 24.50 (*0-8191-8765-8*) U Pr of Amer.

Bertram, Martin, tr. see Luther, Martin H.

Bertram, Martin H., tr. see Luther, Martin.

Bertram, Michael, ed. see Weingarten, John.

Bertram, Paul, ed. see Shakespeare, William.

Bertram, Rainer. Pflanzengesellschaften der Torfstiche Nordniedersaechsischer Moore und die Abhaengigkeit Dieser Vegetationseinheiten Von der Wasserqualitaet. (Dissertationes Botanicae Ser.: Band 126). (GER., Illus.). xii, 192p. 1988. pap. 48.00 (*3-443-64038-9*, Pub. by Gebruder Borntraeger) Balogh.

Bertram, Vicki. Kicking Daffodils: Twentieth-Century Women Poets. 1997. pap. 29.50 (*0-7486-0782-X*, Pub. by Edinburgh U Pr) Col U Pr.

***Bertram, Volker.** Practical Ship Hydrodynamics. 224p. 2000. pap. 54.95 (*0-7506-4851-1*) Buttrwrth-Heinemann.

Bertrams, R. Bank Guarantees in International Trade: The Law & Practice of Independent (First Demand) Guarantees & Standby Letters of Credit in Civil Law & Common Law Jurisdictions. 2nd ed. LC 96-26449. 1996. 147.50 (*90-411-0238-8*) Kluwer Law Intl.

Bertramsen, Rene B., et al. State, Economy & Society. 272p. (C). 1990. text 55.00 (*0-04-445433-3*) Routledge.

Bertran, J., ed. Molecular Aspects of Biotechnology: Computational Models & Theories: Proceedings of the NATO Advanced Research Workshop on the Role of Computational Models & Theories in Biotechnology, Sant Feliu de Guixols, Spain, 13-19 June 1991. LC 92-8531. (NATO Advanced Study Institutes Series C, Mathematical & Physical Sciences: Vol. 368). 352p. 1992. text 185.00 (*0-7923-1728-9*) Kluwer Academic.

Bertran, J. & Csizmadia, Imre G., eds. New Theoretical Concepts for Understanding Organic Reactions. (C). 1989. text 202.50 (*0-7923-0151-X*) Kluwer Academic.

Bertran, Juan, jt. ed. see Tapia, Orlando.

Bertrand. La Information des Cartographes. 1985. pap. 51.00 (*90-70310-09-0*, Pergamon Pr) Elsevier.

— The United Nations Vol. NLSP 25: Past, Present & Future. LC 96-38074. 1997. 88.00 (*90-411-0337-6*) Kluwer Law Intl.

Bertrand, jt. auth. see Hermet, Guy.

***Bertrand, Aloysius.** Flemish School, Old Paris & Night & Its Spells. Lombardo, Glen, tr. 40p. 2000. pap. 5.00 (*0-9656161-7-7*) Quale Pr.

Bertrand, Aloysius. Gaspard de la Nuit. (Poesie Ser.). (FRE.). 338p. 1980. pap. 11.95 (*2-07-032186-X*) Schoenhof.

— Louis "Aloysius" Bertrand's Gaspard de la Nuit: Fantasies in the Manner of Rembrandt & Callot. 2nd ed. Wright, John T., tr. from FRE. & intro. by. 182p. (C). 1994. lib. bdg. 39.00 (*0-8191-9345-3*) U Pr of Amer.

***Bertrand, Anne.** Indoor. 2000. pap. 39.95 (*88-8158-241-4*) Charta.

Bertrand, Anne, tr. see Brachlianoff, Dominique.

Bertrand, Armand L., Jr. How to Start Understanding the Computer. LC 83-90306. (Illus.). 208p. (Orig.). (J). (gr. 7 up). 1986. pap. 12.95 (*0-912447-02-8*) Eclectical.

Bertrand, Carol. Starting an Allen 's Cognitive Level Program in a Geriatric Facility. 38p. 1997. pap. 15.00 (*0-9654111-1-7*) Allen Conf.

Bertrand, Charles A. Expert Witness. LC 98-34026. 204p. 1998. 26.00 (*0-9629017-1-7*) Creat Med Prodns.

***Bertrand, Claude-Jean.** Media Ethics & Accountability Systems. LC 99-56519. 158p. 2000. 29.95 (*1-56000-420-7*) Transaction Pubs.

Bertrand, D. Contribution a l'Etude de l'Environnement et de la Dynamique des Mangroves de Guinee (A Contribution to the Study of the Environment & Dynamics of Mangrove Zones in Guinea)Tr. of A Contribution to the Study of the Environment & Dynamics of Mangrove Zones in Guinea. (FRE.). 202p. 1993. pap. 50.00 (*2-7099-1150-7*, Pub. by LInstitut Francais) Balogh.

Bertrand, David & Bertrand, J. Mark. Making a Difference While You're Making a Living. LC 98-87460. 212p. 1998. pap. 12.95 (*0-9666773-0-7*) New Paradigm TX.

Bertrand, Denis. L' Espace et le sens Germinal d'Emile Zola: Essai de Semiotique Discursive. (Actes Semiotiques Ser.: No. 2). (FRE.). 213p. 1985. pap. 52.00 (*90-272-2262-2*) J Benjamins Pubng Co.

Bertrand, Diane G. Alicia's Treasure. LC 95-37669. 125p. (J). (gr. 3-7). 1996. pap. 7.95 (*1-55885-086-4*, Pinata Bks) Arte Publico.

— Lessons of the Game. LC 98-28340. 192p. (YA). (gr. 6 up). 1998. pap. 9.95 (*1-55885-245-X*, Pinata Bks) Arte Publico.

Bertrand, Diane Gonzales. Trino's Choice. LC 98-56132. 128p. (J). (gr. 4-7). 1999. 16.95 (*1-55885-279-4*, Pinata Bks) Arte Publico.

— Trino's Choice. LC 98-56132. (Illus.). 128p. (YA). (gr. 4-7). 1999. pap. 9.95 (*1-55885-268-9*, Pub. by Arte Publico) SPD-Small Pr Dist.

Bertrand, Didier. Test Yourself French Grammar. LC 96-47422. (Test Yourself Ser.). (ENG & FRE., Illus.). 192p. 1996. pap. 11.95 (*0-8442-2360-3*, 23603, NTC Learningworks) NTC Contemp Pub Co.

Bertrand, Edgard. The Potential for Collaboration in New Sciences & Technology Development Between San Antonio, Texas & Nancy, France. LC 90-63057. 170p. 1990. student ed. 8.50 (*0-945632-04-5*) St Marys Univ Pr.

Bertrand, F. E., ed. Giant Multipole Resonances. Oak Ridge, Tennessee, October 15-17, 1979. (Nuclear Science Research Conference Ser.: Vol. 1). xvi, 482p. 1980. text 267.00 (*3-7186-0029-3*) Gordon & Breach.

Bertrand, Guy. Enough Is Enough: An Attorney's Struggle for Democracy in Quebec. Blanc, Marie T., tr. from FRE. 190p. 1996. pap. 19.95 (*1-55022-302-X*, Pub. by ECW) Genl Dist Srvs.

Bertrand, Ina, ed. Cinema in Australia: A Documentary History. 448p. 1990. 42.95 (*0-86840-075-0*, Pub. by New South Wales Univ Pr) Intl Spec Bk.

Bertrand, J. Dictionnaire Practique des Homonymes.Tr. of Practical Dictionary of Homonyms. (FRE.). 224p. 1980. 29.95 (*0-8288-1929-7*, M12401) Fr & Eur.

Bertrand, J., et al, eds. Modern Group Theoretical Methods in Physics: Proceedings of the Conference in Honour of Guy Rideau. (Mathematical Physics Studies). 300p. (C). 1995. text 169.00 (*0-7923-3645-3*) Kluwer Academic.

Bertrand, J. Mark, jt. auth. see Bertrand, David.

Bertrand, J. W., et al. Production Control: A Structural & Design Oriented Approach. (Manufacturing Research & Technology Ser.: No. 11). 622p. 1990. 177.25 (*0-444-88122-0*) Elsevier.

Bertrand, James O., ed. see Allen, Claudia K.

Bertrand, James O., jt. ed. see Vineyard Publising Staff.

Bertrand, Jean, et al, eds. Pediatric Endocrinology: Physiology, Pathophysiology & Clinical Aspects. 2nd ed. LC 92-49159. (Illus.). 768p. 1993. 129.00 (*0-683-00609-6*) Lppncott W & W.

Bertrand, Jean B., et al. A Historical Relation of the Plague at Marseilles in the Year 1720. LC 76-372873. (Pioneers of Demography Ser.). xxxii, 384p. 1973. write for info. (*0-576-53282-7*) Gregg Intl.

Bertrand, John & Stice, Carole, eds. Empowering Children at Risk of School Failure: A Better Way. 200p. 1995. pap. text 31.95 (*0-926842-45-5*) CG Pubs Inc.

Bertrand, John E., jt. ed. see Stice, Carole F.

Bertrand, Joseph. Calcul des Probabilites. 2nd ed. LC 78-113114. (FRE.). 389p. 1972. text 18.95 (*0-8284-0262-0*) Chelsea Pub.

Bertrand, Luce. Nous Sommes Tous des Apprentis Sages. LC 96-941040. (FRE.). 147p. 1996. 19.95 (*2-89466-003-0*) Edns Roseau.

Bertrand, Lynn W., jt. ed. see Orr, N. Lee.

Bertrand, Lynne. Good Night, Teddy Bear. LC 92-15141. (Illus.). 24p. (J). (ps). 1992. pap. 9.95 (*0-9631591-1-9*, Chapters Bks) HM.

— Let's Go! Teddy Bear. LC 93-71172. (Illus.). 24p. (J). (ps). 1993. pap. 9.95 (*1-881527-15-8*, Chapters Bks) HM.

— Who Sleeps in the City? LC 94-71016. (Illus.). 26p. (J). (ps). 1994. 9.95 (*1-881527-48-4*, Chapters Bks) HM.

Bertrand, M., et al, eds. Handbook of Cardiovascular Interventions. LC 96-16865. 948p. 1996. pap. text 225.00 (*0-443-07970-6*) Church.

B

Bertrand, Marc. L' Oeuvre de Jean Prevost. LC 68-64308. (U. C. Publ. in Modern Philology Ser.: Vol. 90). 133p. reprint ed. 41.30 (0-8357-9634-5, 201380500088) Bks Demand.

Bertrand, Marc, ed. Popular Traditions & Learned Culture in France, 17th-20th Centuries. (Stanford French & Italian Studies: Vol. 35). (Illus.). 350p. 1986. pap. 56.50 (0-915838-02-8) Anma Libri.

Bertrand, Marlene C., jt. auth. see Mihalakis, Diana.

***Bertrand, Marsha.** Fraud!!! How to Protect Yourself from Schemes, Scams & Swindles. LC 99-34601. 265p. 1999. pap. 16.95 (0-8144-7032-7) AMACOM.

Bertrand, Marsha. A Woman's Guide to Savvy Investing: Everything You Need to Know to Protect Your Future. LC 97-21282. 224p. 1997. 24.95 (0-8144-0381-6) AMACOM.

***Bertrand, Marsha.** Woman's Guide to Savvy Investing: Everything You Need to Know to Protect Your Future. 2000. reprint ed. pap. 16.95 (0-8144-7099-8) AMACOM.

Bertrand, Maurice. The Third Generation World Organization. (C). 1989. lib. bdg. 94.50 (0-7923-0382-2) Kluwer Academic.

Bertrand, Maurice & Warner, Daniel M., eds. A New Charter for a Worldwide Organisation? LC 96-36769. 288p. 1996. pap. 125.00 (90-411-0286-8) Kluwer Law Intl.

***Bertrand, Michael T.** Race, Rock & Elvis. LC 99-50895. (Music in American Life Ser.). 320p. 2000. text 32.95 (0-252-02586-5) U of Ill Pr.

Bertrand, P., et al. Organic Matter Accumulation: The Organic Cyclicities of the Kimmeridge Clay Formation (Yorkshire, GB) & the Recent Maar Sediments (Lac du Bouchet, France) (Lecture Notes in Earth Sciences Ser.: Vol. 57). (Illus.). 200p. 1995. 85.95 (3-540-59170-2) Spr-Verlag.

Bertrand, P., jt. auth. see Jourbel, H.

Bertrand, R., jt. auth. see Messerschmid, E.

Bertrand, Roger M. Programmable Controller Circuits. LC 95-17503. 240p. (C). 1995. mass mkt. 39.95 (0-8273-7066-0) Delmar.

— Programmable Controller Circuits. (Electrical Trades Ser.). 104p. 1995. teacher ed. 18.00 (0-8273-7067-9) Delmar.

Bertrand-Sarfati, Janine & Monty, Claude, eds. Phanerozoic Stromatolites II. LC 94-4221. 496p. (C). 1994. text 272.50 (0-7923-2747-0) Kluwer Academic.

***Bertrand, Shirley.** Characters of R. John Wright Identifcation & Price Guide. (Illus.). 128p. 2000. 29.95 (0-87588-592-6) Hobby Hse.

Bertrand, Yann A., photos by. Morocco from the Air. LC 94-16536. (Illus.). 156p. 1994. text 45.00 (0-86565-955-9) Vendome.

Bertrand, Yves. Contemporary Theories & Practice in Education. 279p. 1995. pap. text 24.95 (1-891859-07-2) Atwood Pub LLC.

— Contemporary Theories & Practice in Education. Poisson, Jean-Marc, tr. LC 95-42307. 270p. 1995. 24.95 (0-912150-41-6) Atwood Pub LLC.

— The Ordinary Hero. LC 98-19392.Tr. of Le Heros Ordinaire. 143p. 1998. pap. text 23.95 (1-891859-25-0) Atwood Pub LLC.

Bertsch, Aida C. & Bertsch, Werner J. Florida: America's Tropical Paradise Including the Florida Keys. (Illus.). 32p. (Orig.). 1989. pap. 4.99 (1-877833-00-2) Pro Pub Inc.

— Florida: Educational & Historical Coloring Book. (Illus.). 24p. (Orig.). (J). (gr. 1-6). 1989. pap. 2.99 (1-877833-01-0) Pro Pub Inc.

Bertsch, G., jt. ed. see Brogila, Ricardo A.

Bertsch, Gary K. Crossroads & Conflict: Security & Foreign Policy in the Caucasus & Central Asia. LC 99-20477. 1999. pap. 24.99 (0-415-92274-7) Routledge.

— Dangerous Weapons, Desperate States: Russia, Belarus, Kazakstan & Ukraine. LC 99-11361. 1999. pap. 24.99 (0-415-92237-2) Routledge.

— Engaging India: U.S. Strategic Relations with the World's Largest Democracy. LC 99-20771. 1999. pap. 24.99 (0-415-92283-6) Routledge.

— Values & Community in Multinational Yugoslavia. (East European Monographs: No. 17). 160p. 1970. text 59.00 (0-914710-10-9, Pub. by East Eur Monographs) Col U Pr.

Bertsch, Gary K., ed. Controlling East-West Trade & Technology Transfer: Power, Politics & Policies. LC 88-4101. (Duke Press Policy Studies). xiv, 506p. (C). 1988. text 69.95 (0-8223-0829-0); pap. text 28.95 (0-8223-0843-6) Duke.

***Bertsch, Gary K., ed.** Engaging India: U. S. Strategic Relations with the World's Largest Democracy. LC 99-20771. 288p. 1999. 75.00 (0-415-92282-8) Routledge.

Bertsch, Gary K., et al, eds. International Cooperation on Nonproliferation Export Controls: Prospects for the 1990s & Beyond. 344p. (C). 1994. text 54.50 (0-472-10515-9, 10515) U of Mich Pr.

— U. S. & Japanese Nonproliferation Export Controls: Theory, Description & Analysis. 388p. (Orig.). (C). 1995. pap. text 38.50 (0-7618-0192-8); lib. bdg. 49.00 (0-7618-0191-X) U Pr of Amer.

Bertsch, Gary K. & Elliott-Gower, Steven, eds. Export Controls in Transition: Perspectives, Problems, & Prospects. LC 91-14463. 363p. 1991. pap. text 27.95 (0-8223-1191-7) Duke.

— Export Controls in Transition: Perspectives, Problems, & Prospects. LC 91-14463. 363p. 1992. text 64.95 (0-8223-1186-0) Duke.

Bertsch, Gary K. & Grillot, Suzette. Arms on the Market: Reducing the Risk of Proliferation in the Former Soviet Union. LC 97-47647. 256p. (C). 1998. 75.00 (0-415-92058-2); pap. 22.99 (0-415-92059-0) Routledge.

***Bertsch, Gary K. & Potter, William C.** Dangerous Weapons, Desperate States: Russia, Belarus, Kazakstan & Ukraine. LC 99-11361. 1999. write for info. (0-415-92236-4) Routledge.

Bertsch, Gary K., et al. Comparing Political Systems: Power & Policy in Three Worlds. 4th ed. LC 90-13444. 608p. (C). 1991. 85.00 (0-02-309020-0, Macmillan Coll) P-H.

Bertsch, George F. Nuclear Theory, 1981: Proceedings of the Nuclear Theory Summer Workshop Institute of Theoretical Physics, Santa Barbara, CA, August 1981. 309p. 1982. 52.00 (9971-950-06-5); pap. 30.00 (9971-950-07-3) World Scientific Pub.

Bertsch, George F. & Brogila, Ricardo A. Oscillations in Finite Quantum Systems. LC 92-40596. (Cambridge Monographs on Mathematical Physics). (Illus.). 224p. (C). 1994. text 54.95 (0-521-41148-3) Cambridge U Pr.

Bertsch, Hans, ed. see Gotshall, Daniel W.

Bertsch, Hans, ed. see Michael, Scott W.

Bertsch, Hans, ed. see Wrobel, David & Mills, Claudia E.

Bertsch, Kenneth A. Corporate Giving in the Reagan Years. 97p. (Orig.). 1985. pap. 10.00 (0-931035-04-X) IRRC Inc DC.

— Corporate Philanthropy. 84p. 1982. 10.00 (0-931035-58-9) IRRC Inc DC.

— The MacBride Principles & U. S. Companies in Northern Ireland. 150p. (Orig.). 1991. pap. 25.00 (0-931035-87-2) IRRC Inc DC.

Bertsch, Kenneth A. & Shaw, Linda S. The Nuclear Weapons Industry. 405p. 1984. pap. text 10.00 (0-931035-75-9) IRRC Inc DC.

Bertsch, Steve. Crisis in Our Courts. (Illus.). 320p. 1995. pap., mass mkt. 6.99 (0-914839-35-7) Gollehon Pr.

Bertsch, Werner J., jt. auth. see Bertsch, Aida C.

Bertsche, Karl, ed. see Sancta Clara, Abraham A.

Bertsching. Golden Needle. 1996. text 67.00 (0-443-04390-6, W B Saunders Co) Harcrt Hlth Sci Grp.

Bertschinger, P. P. Know How in Insurance & Reinsurance. 152p. (C). 1977. 90.00 (0-900886-15-3, Pub. by Witherby & Co); 110.00 (0-7855-4109-8, Pub. by Witherby & Co) St Mut.

— Know How in Versicherung und Ruckversicherung. 167p. 1977. 80.00 (0-900886-19-6, Pub. by Witherby & Co) St Mut.

Bertschinger, R. Secret of Everlasting Life. 1994. text 24.95 (1-85230-568-1, Pub. by Element MA) Penguin Putnam.

Bertschmann, Harry, jt. auth. see Sampson, Mary Y.

Bertschmann, Mary, ed. see Sampson, Mary Y.

Bertschmann, Mary, ed. see Sampson, Mary Y. & Bertschmann, Harry.

Bertschmann, Mary, ed. see Sampson, Mary Y. & Hart, Maurice.

Bertschmann, Mary, ed. see Sampson, Mary Y., et al.

Bertsekas, Dimitri P. Constrained Optimization & Lagrange Multiplier Methods. LC 96-79307. 410p. (C). 1996. pap. text 49.50 (1-886529-04-3) Athena Scientific.

— Dynamic Programming & Optimal Control, Vol. I. LC 95-75941. 400p. (C). 1995. text 69.00 (1-886529-12-4) Athena Scientific.

— Dynamic Programming & Optimal Control, Vol. II. LC 95-75941. 304p. (C). 1995. text 55.50 (1-886529-13-2) Athena Scientific.

— Dynamic Programming & Optimal Control, Vols. I-II. LC 95-75941. 704p. (C). 1995. text 99.50 (1-886529-11-6) Athena Scientific.

— Linear Network Optimization: Algorithms & Codes. (Illus.). 275p. 1991. 52.50 (0-262-02334-2) MIT Pr.

— Network Optimization: Continuous & Discrete Models. LC 98-70298. 608p. (C). 1998. text 74.00 (1-886529-02-7) Athena Scientific.

— Nonlinear Programming. 2nd ed. LC 99-73208. 708p. 1999. text 79.00 (1-886529-00-0) Athena Scientific.

Bertsekas, Dimitri P. & Gallager, Robert. Data Networks. 2nd ed. LC 91-35561. 592p. 1991. 105.00 (0-13-200916-1) P-H.

Bertsekas, Dimitri P. & Shreve, Steven E. Stochastic Optimal Control: The Discrete-Time Case. LC 96-80191. 325p. (C). 1996. pap. text 49.50 (1-886529-03-5) Athena Scientific.

Bertsekas, Dimitri P. & Tsitsiklis, John N. Neuro-Dynamic Programming. LC 96-85338. 491p. (C). 1996. text 84.00 (1-886529-10-8) Athena Scientific.

— Parallel & Distributed Computation: Numerical Methods. LC 97-70648. 730p. (C). 1997. pap. text 49.50 (1-886529-01-9) Athena Scientific.

Bertsimas, Dimitris. Quantitative Methods: Data, Models & Decision. (MI - Management Science Ser.). 2000. mass mkt. 85.95 (0-538-85906-7) S-W Pub.

Bertsimas, Dimitris & Tsitsiklis, John N. Introduction to Linear Optimization. LC 96-78786. (Illus.). 608p. (C). 1997. text 74.00 (1-886529-19-1) Athena Scientific.

Bertsky-Zweig, Sarah. Onions & Cucumbers & Plums: 46 Yiddish Poems in English. 259p. 1977. 18.95 (0-8369-6002-5) Ayer.

Bertucci, Bob & Peterson, James. Volleyball Drill Book: Game Action Drills. (Illus.). 224p. 1992. pap. 14.95 (0-940279-42-8, 79428H, Mstrs Pr) NTC Contemp Pub Co.

— Volleyball Drill Book: Individual Skills. (Illus.). 224p. 1992. pap. 14.95 (0-940279-28-2, 79282H, Mstrs Pr) NTC Contemp Pub Co.

Bertucci, Bob, jt. auth. see Crawford, Terry.

Bertucci, Bob, jt. auth. see Fields, Bud.

Bertucci, Lina, jt. auth. see Niemann, Linda.

Bertucci, Paul F. & Ingersoll, Raymond V., eds. Guidebook to the Stony Creek Formation, Great Valley Group, Sacramento Valley, California. (Illus.). 32p. (Orig.). 1983. pap. 2.00 (1-878861-38-7) Pac Section SEPM.

Bertucelli-Papi, Marcella, jt. ed. see Verschueren, Jef.

Bertuglia, C. S., et al, eds. The City & Its Sciences. LC 98-39448. (Illus.). xx, 914p. 1998. 129.00 (3-7908-1075-4) Spr-Verlag.

Bertuglia, Cristoforo S., et al, eds. Technological Change, Economic Development & Space. LC 95-24292. (Advances in Spatial Science Ser.). (Illus.). 354p. 1995. 117.00 (3-540-59288-1) Spr-Verlag.

— Urban Systems: Contemporary Approaches to Modelling. 688p. (C). 1987. text 125.00 (0-7099-3971-X, Pub. by C Helm) Routldge.

Bertuglia, Cristoforo S., et al. Innovative Behaviour in Space & Time. LC 97-15141. (Advances in Spatial Science Ser.). 1997. write for info. (3-540-62542-9) Spr-Verlag.

Bertulani, C. A., et al. Nuclear Physics. LC 98-161797. 350p. 1997. text 74.00 (981-02-3230-6) World Scientific Pub.

Bertuzzi, Frederico. El Despertar de las Misiones.Tr. of Wake up Call to Missions. 5.99 (0-7899-0445-4, 498661) Editorial Unilit.

Bertuzzi, Frederico. Latinos en el Mundo Islamico.Tr. of Latins to the Islamic World. (SPA.). 1990. 4.50 (1-56063-146-5, 498495); pap. write for info. (0-614-27069-3) Editorial Unilit.

— Rios en la Soledad - Streams in the Midst of Loneliness. (SPA.). 226p. write for info. (1-56063-764-1) Editorial Unilit.

***Bertuzzi, Joe.** The Soccer Scouting Guide. (Illus.). 108p. 1999. pap. 12.95 (1-890946-26-5) Reedswain.

***Berty, J. M.** Experiments in Catalytic Reaction Engineering. LC 99-35157. (Studies in Surface Science & Catalysis Ser.). 288p. 1999. 190.50 (0-444-82823-0) Elsevier.

Berty, J. M., ed. Kinetic Model Development: A Special Issue of the Journal Chemical Engineering Communications. 230p. 1989. pap. text 654.00 (2-88124-318-5) Gordon & Breach.

Bertz, William L. & Bowman, Judith. Applications of Research in Music Technology: From Research to the Music Classroom. 96p. 1994. pap. 16.50 (1-56545-026-4, 1625) MENC.

Berube, David G., jt. auth. see Isham, Linda R.

Berube, David M. Non-Policy Debating. 390p. (Orig.). (C). 1994. pap. text 34.50 (0-8191-9348-8) U Pr of Amer.

Berube, John Paul, jt. auth. see Darcy-Berube, Francoise.

Berube, Lawrence. The Brule River: A Guide's Story. (Illus.). 80p. 1998. pap. 9.95 (1-886028-36-2) Savage Pr.

Berube, Maurice R. American Presidents & Education, 46. LC 90-24709. (Contributions to the Study of Education Ser.: No. 46). 184p. 1991. 55.00 (0-313-27848-2, BBQ/, Greenwood Pr) Greenwood.

— American School Reform: Progressive, Equity, & Excellence Movements, 1883-1993. LC 94-25043. 168p. 1994. 59.95 (0-275-95036-0, Praeger Pubs) Greenwood.

— American School Reform: Progressive, Equity & Excellence Movements, 1883-1993. LC 94-25043. 168p. 1994. pap. 18.95 (0-275-95160-X, Praeger Pubs) Greenwood.

— Education & Poverty: Effective Schooling in the United States & Cuba, 13. LC 83-26428. (Contributions to the Study of Education Ser.: No. 13). 163p. 1984. 49.95 (0-313-23468-X, BPV/, Greenwood Pr) Greenwood.

— Eminent Educators: Studies in Intellectual Influence, 76. LC 99-29555. 76. 192p. 2000. 57.95 (0-313-31060-2, Greenwood Pr) Greenwood.

— Teacher Politics: The Influence of Unions, 26. LC 87-29546. (Contributions to the Study of Education Ser.: No. 26). 185p. 1988. 49.95 (0-313-25685-3, BTH/, Greenwood Pr) Greenwood.

— The Urban University in America. LC 77-87917. 149p. 1978. 47.95 (0-313-20031-9, BUU/, Greenwood Pr) Greenwood.

Berube, Michael. The Employment of the English. LC 97-21213. 1997. pap. text 18.00 (0-8147-1301-7) NYU Pr.

— The Employment of the English. LC 97-21213. 1998. text 55.00 (0-8147-1300-9) NYU Pr.

— Life As We Know It. 1998. pap. 14.00 (0-679-75866-6) Random.

— Marginal Forces - Cultural Centers: Tolson, Pynchon, & the Politics of the Canon. LC 91-55555. 368p. 1992. pap. text 17.95 (0-8014-9921-6) Cornell U Pr.

— Public Access: Literary Theory & American Cultural Politics. LC 94-11163. 256p. (C). 1994. pap. 20.00 (0-86091-678-2, Pub. by Verso) Norton.

Berube, Michael & Nelson, Cary, eds. Higher Education under Fire: Politics, Economics & the Crisis of the Humanities. LC 94-17598. 400p. (C). (gr. 13). 1994. 75.00 (0-415-90805-1, B2859); pap. 23.99 (0-415-90806-X, B2863) Routledge.

Berube, Nicole, jt. auth. see Edwards, Viv.

Berube, Paul, ed. see Salazar, Marivel & Cassano, Angelo.

Berube, Paulette. Buddy: A Story about Tolerance & Understanding Differences. LC 94-77204. 24p. (J). (gr. 1-4). 1994. 6.95 (1-884063-24-1) Mar Co Prods.

Berube, Richard H. Computer Simulated Experiments For Digital Electronics Using a Electronics Workbench. annuals 373p. (ps). 1998. pap. text 46.00 (0-13-749475-0) P-H.

***Berube, Richard H.** Computer Simulated Experiments for Electric Circuits Using Electronics Workbench. 2nd ed. 293p. (C). 2000. pap. text 45.00 (0-13-084508-6, Prentice Hall) P-H.

— Computer Simulated Experiments for Electronic Devices Using Electronics Workbench. 2nd ed. (Illus.). 393p. 1999. pap. text 39.00 incl. cd-rom (0-13-084500-0) P-H.

Berube, Richard H. Electric Circuits & Devices Using Micro-Cap III. (Illus.). 288p. (Orig.). (C). 1993. pap. text 24.91 (0-02-309151-7, Macmillan Coll) P-H.

Beruete y Moret, Aureliano De. Velazquez. LC 77-37330. (Select Bibliographies Reprint Ser.). (Illus.). 1977. reprint ed. 41.95 (0-8369-6677-5) Ayer.

Beruff, Jorge R. & Muniz, Humberto G., eds. Security Problems & Policies in the Post-Cold War Caribbean. LC 95-34284. (International Political Economy Ser.). 230p. 1996. text 65.00 (0-312-12828-2) St Martin.

Beruff, Jorge Rodriguez, see Rodriguez Beruff, Jorge.

Berufsgenossenschaft. Toxicological Evaluations, Vol. 10. LC 90-10020. 268p. 1996. 59.95 (3-540-60683-1) Spr-Verlag.

***Berufsgenossenschaft der Chemischen Industrie Heidelberg Staff, ed.** Toxicological Evaluations, Vol. 15. 390p. 1999. 75.00 (3-540-65681-2) Spr-Verlag.

Berufsgenossenschaft der Chemischen Industrie Staf, ed. Toxicological Evaluations Vol. 11: Potential Health Hazards of Existing Chemicals, Vol. 11. (Illus.). vi, 180p. 1997. 52.00 (3-540-61391-9) Spr-Verlag.

Berufsgenossenschaft der Chemischen Industrie Staf & Heidelberg, B. G., eds. Potential Health Hazards of Existing Chemicals. (Toxicological Evaluations Ser.: Vol. 13). 256p. 1997. 52.00 (3-540-62658-1) Spr-Verlag.

Berufsgenossenschaft der Chemischen Industry Staff. Toxicological Evaluations Vol. 11: Potential Health Hazards of Existing Chemicals. LC 90-10020. 200p. 1999. pap. 64.95 (3-540-63084-8) Spr-Verlag.

Berulfsen, B., et al. English-Norwegian Dictionary: Engelsk-Norsk Ordbok. (ENG & NOR.). 475p. 1981. 49.95 (0-8288-0474-5, M9455) Fr & Eur.

Berulfsen, B., jt. auth. see Kirkeby, Willy A.

Berumen, Paula, ed. see Bordelon, Jane A.

Berutti, Alfred, ed. Practical Guide to Ground Fault Protection. (Practical Guide to Ser.). (Illus.). 78p. 1995. pap. 23.95 (0-87288-608-5) Intertec Pub.

— Practical Guide to Motors & Motor Controls. (Practical Guide to Ser.). (Illus.). 88p. 1991. pap. 23.95 (0-87288-457-0) Intertec Pub.

Berutti, Alfred & Hartwell, Frederic P., eds. Understanding NE Code Rules on Hazardous Locations. (Illus.). 160p. 1993. pap. 18.95 (0-87288-513-5) Intertec Pub.

Berutti, Alfred & Lawrie, Robert J., eds. Practical Guide to Electrical Energy Efficiency & Reduced Costs. (Practical Guide to Ser.). (Illus.). 136p. 1994. pap. 23.95 (0-87288-584-4) Intertec Pub.

Berutti, Alfred & Morgan, Robert B., eds. Practical Guide to Applying, Installing, & Maintaining Transformers. rev. ed. (Practical Guide to Ser.). (Illus.). 88p. 1994. pap. 23.95 (0-87288-585-2) Intertec Pub.

Berve, Helmut. Das Alexanderreich: Auf Prosopographischer Grundlage Esterband; Darstellung; Zweiterband; Prosopographie, 2 vols., 1 bk. LC 72-7885. (Greek History Ser.). (GER.). 1973. reprint ed. 57.95 (0-405-04779-7) Ayer.

Berveiller, M., ed. Mechanics of Solids with Phase Changes. (CISM International Center for Mechanical Sciences Ser.: No. 368). (Illus.). vii, 317p. 1997. pap. 80.00 (3-211-82904-0) Spr-Verlag.

Berven, Barry A., jt. ed. see Gammage, Richard B.

Berven, Dikka, ed. Language & Meaning: Word Study in Montaigne's "Essais" LC 94-41683. (Montaigne Ser.: Vol. 4). (Illus.). 344p. 1995. 70.00 (0-8153-1842-1) Garland.

— Montaigne's: Message & Method, 5 vols., Set. LC 94-41683. 433p. 1995. 380.00 (0-8153-1838-3) Garland.

— Montaigne's Message & Method: A Collection of Essays: An Anthology of Scholarly Articles, 5 vols. LC 94-41683. (Montaigne Ser.: Vol. 1). (ENG & FRE.). 456p. 1995. text 85.00 (0-8153-1839-1) Garland.

— Montaigne's Rhetoric: Composing Myself for Others. LC 94-41683. (Montaigne Ser.: Vol. 3). 408p. 1995. reprint ed. text 75.00 (0-8153-1841-3) Garland.

— Reading Montaigne. LC 94-41683. (Montaigne Ser.: Vol. 5). 400p. 1995. text 75.00 (0-8153-1843-X) Garland.

— Sources of Montaigne's Thought. LC 94-41683. (Montaigne Ser.: Vol. 2). 376p. 1995. text 75.00 (0-8153-1840-5) Garland.

Berwald, Rosalind. Remembering Signor Oscar. (Illus.). 44p. 1992. 45.00 (0-930126-39-4) Typographeum.

Berwanger, Eugene H. The British Foreign Service & the American Civil War. LC 94-6468. 216p. 1994. lib. bdg. 29.00 (0-8131-1876-X) U Pr of Ky.

— The Civil War Era. LC 93-78909. 249p. (C). 1994. pap. text 43.00 (0-15-501039-5) Harcourt.

— The Frontier Against Slavery: Western Anti-Negro Prejudice & the Slavery Extension Controversy. LC 67-21850. 186p. reprint ed. pap. 57.70 (0-608-13600-X, 201900600010) Bks Demand.

— The West & Reconstruction. LC 80-26357. (Illus.). 304p. 1981. text 29.95 (0-252-00868-5) U of Ill Pr.

Berwanger, Eugene H. & Russell, William H. My Diary North & South. LC 94-48487. 384p. (C). 1987. pap. 22.19 (0-07-554025-8) McGraw.

Berwanger, Paulo. Family Denial. 14p. (Orig.). 1985. pap. 1.75 (0-89486-319-3, 5280B) Hazelden.

Berwanger, Paulo, tr. see Kamiya, Taeko.

Berwick, Ann. Aromaterapia: Descubra Los Usos Terapeuticos de Los Aceites Esencials. LC 99-32325. (SPA., Illus.). 254p. 1999. pap. text 12.95 (1-56718-066-3) Llewellyn Pubns.

— Aromatherapy - A Holistic Guide: Balance Body & Soul with Essential Oils. LC 93-48571. (Illus.). 240p. 1999. pap. 12.95 (0-87542-033-8) Llewellyn Pubns.

Berwick, D., jt. ed. see Vernon, J.

Berwick, Donald M. Reputation of Jonathan Swift, 1781-1882. LC 65-21096. (Studies in Irish Literature: No. 16). 1969. reprint ed. lib. bdg. 75.00 (0-8383-0508-3) M S G Haskell Hse.

Berwick, Donald M., et al. Curing Health Care: New Strategies for Quality Improvement. LC 90-5229. (Health-Management Ser.). 315p. 1990. text 41.95 (1-55542-294-2) Jossey-Bass.

B

Berwick, Donald M., jt. auth. see Brennan, Troyen A.

Berwick, Lin, ed. Inner Vision. (C). 1990. pap. 24.00 (*0-85305-306-5*, Pub. by Arthur James) St Mut.

Berwick, Richard, jt. ed. see Cumming, Alister.

Berwick, Robert C. The Acquisition of Syntactic Knowledge. LC 85-11460. (Artificial Intelligence Ser.). (Illus.). 350p. 1985. 45.00 (*0-262-02226-5*) MIT Pr.

— Principle-Based Parsing: Computation & Psycholinguistics. (Studies in Linguistics & Philosophy). 418p. (C). 1992. pap. text 61.50 (*0-7923-1637-1*) Kluwer Academic.

Berwick, Robert C., ed. Principle-Based Parsing: Computation & Psycholinguistics. 416p. (C). 1991. lib. bdg. 133.00 (*0-7923-1173-6*) Kluwer Academic.

Berwick, Robert C. & Weinberg, Amy S. The Grammatical Basis of Linguistic Performance: Language Use & Acquisition. 344p. (C). 1986. pap. text 19.50 (*0-262-52110-5*) MIT Pr.

Berwick, Robert C., jt. auth. see Fong, Sandiway.

Berwick, Robert C., jt. ed. see Brady, Michael.

Berwick, Stephen H. & Saharia, V. B., eds. The Development of International Principles & Practices of Wildlife Research & Management: Asian & American Approaches. LC 95-904822. (Illus.). 498p. 1995. text 45.00 (*0-19-563651-1*) OUP.

Berwin, S. J. & Co Staff. U. K. Competition Law, 2 vols. annuals Date not set. ring bd. write for info. (*1-57823-058-6*) Juris Pubng.

Berwitz, Clement J. The Job Analysis Approach to Affirmative Action. LC 75-11660. (Illus.). 341p. reprint ed. pap. 105.80 (*0-608-10869-3*, 201646100002) Bks Demand.

Berxo, Robert L. Consumer's Guide to Home Repair Grants & Subsidized Loans. rev. ed. Spiegel, Monroe, ed. (Illus.). 236p. 1988. pap. 12.00 (*0-934873-07-0*); text 18.00 (*0-934873-08-9*) Consumer Ed Res.

***Bery, Ashok.** Comparing Postcolonial Literatures: Dislocations. 2000. text 55.00 (*0-312-22781-7*) St Martin.

Bery, Odette J. Every Season Cookbook: Elegant Recipes for All Occasions. 1995. 14.98 (*0-88365-913-1*) Galahad Bks.

Bery, Suman K. Preventing Banking Sector Distress & Crises in Latin America: Proceedings of a Conference Held in Washington, D. C., April 15-16, 1996. (Discussion Papers: No. 360). 118p. 1997. pap. 22.00 (*0-8213-3893-5*, 13893) World Bank.

Beryl, Elizabeth, ed. see Thomas, John.

Beryman-Ungar, Robert, ed. Soho Journal. (Illus.). 200p. (Orig.). 1994. pap. 20.00 (*1-885957-00-9*) Map Pubns.

Berz, David R. & Spracker, Stanley M. Environmental Law in Real Estate & Business Transactions, 3 vols., Set. 1992. 445.00 (*0-8205-1792-5*) Bender.

***Berz, Martin, et al, eds.** Advances in Imaging & Electron Physics Vol. 108. 350p. 1999. 130.00 (*0-12-014750-5*) Acad Pr.

Berz, Martin, et al, eds. Computational Differentiation: Techniques, Applications, & Tools. LC 96-71061. (Proceedings in Applied Mathematics Ser.: No. 89). (Illus.). xvi, 421p. 1996. pap. 69.50 (*0-89871-385-4*, PR89) Soc Indus-Appl Math.

— Nonlinear Problems in Accelerator Physics: Proceedings of the International Workshop, Held in Berlin, Germany, 30 March-2 April 1992. (Institute of Physics Conference Ser.: No. 131). (Illus.). 276p. 1993. 161.00 (*0-7503-0238-0*) IOP Pub.

Berzevich, A. Z., tr. see Bokut, L. A. & Kukin, G. P.

Berzin, Alexander. Developing Balanced Sensitivity: Practical Buddhist Exercises for Daily Life. LC 98-22123. 275p. 1998. pap. 14.95 (*1-55939-094-8*) Snow Lion Pubns.

***Berzin, Alexander.** Relating to a Spiritual Teacher. LC 00-8944. 228p. 2000. pap. 15.95 (*1-55939-139-1*) Snow Lion Pubns.

Berzin, Alexander. Taking the Kalachakra Initiation. LC 97-37384. 190p. 1997. pap. 12.95 (*1-55939-084-0*) Snow Lion Pubns.

Berzin, Alexander, tr. from TIB. Kalachakra & Other Six-Session Yoga Texts. LC 98-17366. 52p. 1998. 8.95 (*1-55939-108-1*) Snow Lion Pubns.

Berzin, Alexander & Dalai Lama XIV. The Gelug Kagyu Tradition of Mahamudra. LC 96-48435. 395p. 1997. pap. 22.95 (*1-55939-072-7*) Snow Lion Pubns.

Berzin, Alexander, ed. see Yeshe, Lama Thubten & Rinpoche, Lama Thubten Zopa.

Berzinec, Nancy. Gifts from the Kitchen. 36p. (Orig.). 1986. pap. 3.25 (*0-940844-24-9*) Wellspring.

— Out of the Blue. 36p. (Orig.). 1988. pap. 3.25 (*0-940844-28-1*) Wellspring.

— Pasta Favorites. 36p. (Orig.). 1988. pap. 3.25 (*0-940844-31-1*) Wellspring.

Berzins, Alfreds. Two Faces of Co-Existence. 1967. 15.00 (*0-8315-0018-2*) Speller.

Berzins, Rai. Cerberus. 191p. 1993. pap. 11.95 (*0-86492-166-7*, Pub. by Goose Ln Edits) Genl Dist Srvs.

Berzins, Valdis, ed. Basic Cloning Procedures. LC 97-43014. (Lab Manuals Ser.). (Illus.). 200p. 1998. 64.95 (*3-540-63539-4*) Spr-Verlag.

— Software Merging & Slicing. LC 95-7313. 248p. 1995. pap. 46.00 (*0-8186-6792-3*, PB06792) IEEE Comp Soc.

Berzins, Valdis & Lugi, Lucia. Software Engineering with Abstractions. (Illus.). 640p. (C). 1991. 54.95 (*0-201-08004-4*) Addison-Wesley.

Berzoa, Morton, jt. ed. see Leonhardt, Barbara A.

Berzofsky, J. A. & Sercarz, Eli E. Immunogenicity of Protein Antigens Repertoire & Regulation, Vol. 1. LC 87-5129. 1987. 100.00 (*0-8493-4340-2*, QR186, CRC Reprint) Franklin.

— Immunogenicity of Protein Antigens Repertoire & Regulation, Vol. 2. LC 87-21856. 1987. 92.00 (*0-8493-4341-0*, QR186, CRC Reprint) Franklin.

Berzofsky, Jay A. & Sercarz, Eli E., eds. Immunogenicity of Protein Antigens Repertoire & Regulation: Repertoire & Regulation, 2 vols., Set. (Immunologists & Biochemists Ser.). 1988. 192.00 (*0-8493-4339-9*, QR186, CRC Reprint) Franklin.

Berzon, Betty. The Intimacy Dance: A Guide to Long-Term Success in Gay & Lesbian Relationships. 288p. 1997. pap. 12.95 (*0-452-27747-7*, Plume) Dutton Plume.

— Permanent Partners: Building Gay & Lesbian Relationships That Last. 352p. 1990. pap. 14.95 (*0-452-26308-5*, Plume) Dutton Plume.

— Setting Them Straight. 1999. pap. 21.95 (*0-525-93990-3*) Viking Penguin.

— Setting Them Straight: You Can Do Something about Bigotry & Homophobia in Your Life. 204p. 1996. pap. 12.95 (*0-452-27421-4*, Plume) Dutton Plume.

— Stage 2. 1999. pap. write for info. (*0-525-93991-1*) NAL.

Berzon, Betty, ed. Positively Gay. rev. ed. 288p. 1995. pap. 12.95 (*0-89087-676-2*) Celestial Arts.

Berzon, Betty, jt. ed. see Solomon, Lawrence N.

Berzonsky, Vladimir. The Gift of Love. LC 85-19655. 181p. 1985. pap. 9.95 (*0-88141-041-1*) St Vladimirs.

Berzsenyi, George & Maurer, Stephen B., eds. The Contest Problem Book V: AHSHME & AIME Examinations 1983-1988. LC 96-79944. (New Mathematical Library). 308p. 1997. pap. text 27.95 (*0-88385-640-9*) Math Assn.

Berztiss, Alfs T. Data Structures: Theory & Practice. LC 75-137603. (Computer Science & Applied Mathematics Ser.). xiii, 442 p. 1971. write for info. (*0-12-093550-3*) Acad Pr.

— Software Methods for Business Reengineering. LC 95-19289. (Illus.). 320p. 1995. 60.95 (*0-387-94553-9*) Spr-Verlag.

Bes, D. R. & Kurchan, J., eds. A Treatment of Collective Co-ordinates in Many-Body Systems. (Lecture Notes in Physics Ser.: Vol. 34). 128p. (C). 1990. text 36.00 (*981-02-0306-3*); pap. text 21.00 (*981-02-0307-1*) World Scientific Pub.

Bes, G. C. & Guillotin, T., eds. A Natural Language & Graphics Interface: Results & Perspectives from the ACORD Project. (Research Reports ESPRIT: Vol. 1). vii, 188p. 1992. 39.00 (*0-387-55675-3*) Spr-Verlag.

Besa, E., et al. Hematology. (National Medical Series for Independent Study). (Illus.). 335p. 1993. 26.00 (*0-683-06222-0*) Lppncott W & W.

Besack, Michael. Vocal Arts: The Hermeneutic Dimension. LC 96-52358. (Vocal Arts Ser.: Vol. 1). (Illus.). 287p. (Orig.). 1997. pap. 20.00 (*1-889059-05-6*) Regent Pr.

— Winterreise: Reflections on a Winter Journey/Esoteric Journeys Through Poetry. LC 97-38442. (Esoteric Journeys Through Poetry & Song Ser.: Vol. 2). (Illus.). 370p. 1998. pap. 20.00 (*1-889059-10-2*) Regent Pr.

Besag, Frank P. & Besag, Peter L. Statistics for the Helping Professions. LC 84-13399. 375p. 1985. reprint ed. pap. 116.30 (*0-608-01482-6*, 205952600001) Bks Demand.

Besag, Frank P. & Levine, Leonard P. BASIC for Teachers. LC 84-6953. (Illus.). 208p. reprint ed. pap. 64.50 (*0-8357-8473-8*, 203474100091) Bks Demand.

— Computer Literacy for Teachers. LC 84-6954. (Illus.). 112p. (Orig.). reprint ed. pap. 34.80 (*0-8357-4735-2*, 203765200009) Bks Demand.

Besag, Peter L., jt. auth. see Besag, Frank P.

Besag, Valerie. Bullies & Victims in Schools. 232p. 1989. pap. 33.95 (*0-335-09542-9*) OpUniv Pr.

***Besalel-Azrin, Victoria A. & Azrin, Nathan H.** How to Use Positive Practice, Self-Correction, & Overcorrection. 2nd ed. LC 98-36536. (How to Manage Behavior Ser.). 1999. 8.00 (*0-89079-792-7*) PRO-ED.

Besalel, Victoria A., jt. auth. see Azrin, Nathan H.

Besamusca, B., et al, eds. Cyclification: The Development of the Narrative Cycles in the Chansons de Geste & the Arthurian Romance. LC 94-228178. (Verhandelingen der Koninklijke Nederlandse Akademie van Wetenschappen, Afd. Letterkunde, Nieuwe Reeks Ser.: No. 159). 244p. pap. 48.75 (*0-444-85781-8*) Elsevier.

Besamusca, Bart & Kooper, Erik, eds. Arthurian Literature: Originality & Tradition in the Middle Dutch Roman van Walewein, Vol. 17. (Arthurian Literature Ser.: Vol. 0261-9946). 256p. 1999. 75.00 (*0-85991-546-8*) Boydell & Brewer.

Besanceney, Paul H. Interfaith Marriages: Who & Why. 1970. pap. 14.95 (*0-8084-0165-3*) NCUP.

Besancenot, Jean. The Traditional Costumes of Morocco. Stone, Caroline, tr. 206p. 1990. 87.50 (*0-7103-0359-9*, A3922) Routledge.

Besancon, Alain. The Falsification of the Good. Screech, Matthew, tr. 156p. 1995. pap. 15.95 (*1-870626-53-2*, Pub. by Claridge Pr) Paul & Co Pubs.

Besancon, I. Simha: Visages Limunieux. Dimermanas, Alon, ed. (FRE.). 169p. 1989. pap. 9.00 (*0-930213-25-4*) Breslov Res Inst.

Besanko. Economics of Strategy. 192p. 1996. pap. text, teacher ed. 25.00 (*0-471-12656-X*) Wiley.

***Besanko.** Im Strategy 2nd ed. 1999. pap. text 46.00 (*0-471-36200-X*) Wiley.

Besanko, David & Sappington, David E. Designing Regulatory Policy with Limited Information. LC 87-277. (Fundamentals of Pure & Applied Economics Ser.: Vol. 20). viii, 80p. (C). 1987. pap. text 53.00 (*3-7186-0385-3*) Gordon & Breach.

Besanko, David, et al. Economics of Strategy. 2nd ed. LC 99-20331. 656p. 1999. text 95.95 (*0-471-25454-1*) Wiley.

— The Economics of Strategy A. LC 95-35057. 800p. 1995. text 92.95 (*0-471-59849-6*) Wiley.

Besant, A. Meditations on the Path & Its Qualifications. 1985. 9.50 (*0-8356-7575-0*, Quest) Theos Pub Hse.

Besant, A. & Blavatsky, Helena P. The Nature of Memory. 1935. pap. 4.50 (*81-7059-023-X*, 7647, Quest) Theos Pub Hse.

Besant, A. & Leadbeater, C. W. Thought Forms. 1997. 9.95 (*81-7059-202-X*, 7187, Quest) Theos Pub Hse.

***Besant, Annie W.** The Ancient Wisdom. 364p. 1999. pap. 9.95 (*81-7059-204-6*, Pub. by Theos Pub Hse) Natl Bk Netwk.

Besant, Annie W. Ancient Wisdom: An Outline of Theosophical Teachings. 9th ed. 1998. 14.95 (*81-7059-203-8*, 7038, Quest) Theos Pub Hse.

— The Ancient Wisdom: An Outline of Theosophical Teachings (1939) 390p. 1998. reprint ed. pap. 24.95 (*0-7661-0200-9*) Kessinger Pub.

— Annie Besant: An Autobiography. 1995. 22.95 (*0-8356-7568-8*) Theos Pub Hse.

— Annie Besant, an Autobiography. 1988. reprint ed. lib. bdg. 59.00 (*0-7812-0569-7*) Rprt Serv.

— Annie Besant, an Autobiography. 1976. reprint ed. 29.00 (*0-403-06689-1*, Regency) Scholarly.

— Avataras. 124p. 1983. reprint ed. pap. 5.95 (*0-912181-06-0*) East School Pr.

— Avataras: Four Lectures Delivered at the Twenty-Fourth Anniversary Meeting of the Theosophical Society at Adyar, Madras, December 1899. 124p. 1996. reprint ed. pap. 14.95 (*1-56459-617-6*) Kessinger Pub.

— Beauties of Islam. 1996. pap. 2.50 (*81-7059-143-0*, 7405, Quest) Theos Pub Hse.

— Bhagavad Gita: The Lord's Song. 1987. 7.50 (*81-7059-048-5*, 7027, Quest) Theos Pub Hse.

— Bhagavad Gita: The Lord's Song. 1998. pap. 4.95 (*81-7059-175-9*, 7610, Quest) Theos Pub Hse.

***Besant, Annie W.** Building of the Kosmos (1894) 156p. 1998. reprint ed. pap. 17.95 (*0-7661-0601-2*) Kessinger Pub.

— Changing World (1909) 372p. 1998. reprint ed. pap. 27.95 (*0-7661-0581-4*) Kessinger Pub.

— The Coming of the World Teacher (1926) 50p. 1998. reprint ed. pap. 7.95 (*0-7661-0167-3*) Kessinger Pub.

— Death & After. 100p. 1999. pap. 6.00 (*81-7059-175-1*, Pub. by Theos Pub Hse) Natl Bk Netwk.

Besant, Annie W. Dharma. 1994. pap. 4.50 (*0-8356-7116-X*) Theos Pub Hse.

— Dharma. 70p. 1998. reprint ed. pap. 16.95 (*0-7661-0377-3*) Kessinger Pub.

— Doctrine of the Heart. 1988. 7.50 (*81-7059-109-0*) Theos Pub Hse.

Besant, Annie W. Esoteric Christianity or the Lesser Mysteries. 416p. 1997. reprint ed. pap. 27.95 (*0-7661-0099-5*) Kessinger Pub.

Besant, Annie W. Esoteric Christianity: or The Lesser Mysteries. 8th ed. 285p. 1975. 12.95 (*81-7059-120-1*) Theos Pub Hse.

***Besant, Annie W.** Four Great Religions (1897) 140p. 1998. reprint ed. pap. 16.95 (*0-7661-0602-0*) Kessinger Pub.

Besant, Annie W. The Freethinker's Textbook: Christianity, Its Evidences, Its Origin, Its Morality, Its History. Vol. 2. 3rd ed. LC 77-169205. (Atheist Viewpoint Ser.). 288p. 1978. reprint ed. 23.95 (*0-405-03803-8*) Ayer.

— From the Outer Court to the Inner Sanctum. Nicholson, Shirley, ed. LC 82-42703. 130p. 1983. reprint ed. pap. 5.95 (*0-8356-0574-4*, Quest) Theos Pub Hse.

— Giordano Bruno: Theosophy's Apostle in the Sixteenth Century (1913) 55p. 1996. reprint ed. pap. 14.95 (*1-56459-547-1*) Kessinger Pub.

— Hints on the Study of the Bhagavad Gita. 1984. 7.95 (*0-8356-7079-1*) Theos Pub Hse.

— How India Wrought for Freedom: The Story of the National Congress Told from Official Records. 770p. 1974. reprint ed. 40.00 (*0-88065-057-5*) Scholarly Pubns.

***Besant, Annie W.** How India Wrought for Freedom: The Story of the National Congress Told from Official Records (1915) 784p. 1998. reprint ed. pap. 37.95 (*0-7661-0597-0*) Kessinger Pub.

— Immediate Future (1911) 190p. 1998. reprint ed. pap. 17.95 (*0-7661-0501-6*) Kessinger Pub.

Besant, Annie W. Initiation: The Perfecting of Man. 149p. 1996. reprint ed. pap. 13.95 (*1-56459-618-4*) Kessinger Pub.

— Initiation, the Perfecting of Man. 149p. 1996. reprint ed. spiral bd. 14.00 (*0-7873-0102-7*) Hlth Research.

— The Inner Government of the World. 81p. 1981. pap. 7.00 (*0-89540-092-8*, SB-092) Sun Pub.

— An Introduction to Yoga. 1987. 7.50 (*81-7059-050-7*, 7120) Theos Pub Hse.

— An Introduction to Yoga (1908) 200p. 1998. reprint ed. pap. 17.95 (*0-7661-0277-7*) Kessinger Pub.

— Karma. 10th ed. 1997. 6.50 (*81-7059-300-X*) Theos Pub Hse.

— The Laws of the Higher Life. 1997. pap. 3.25 (*0-8356-7103-8*) Theos Pub Hse.

— Mahabharata: The Story of the Great War. 1992. pap. 12.50 (*81-7059-183-X*, 7605, Quest) Theos Pub Hse.

— Man & His Bodies. 12th ed. 1990. 4.95 (*81-7059-133-8*, 7083, Quest) Theos Pub Hse.

— The Masters. 54p. 1995. pap. 3.95 (*81-7059-159-7*) Theos Pub Hse.

***Besant, Annie W.** The Masters & the Way to Them (1912) 50p. 1998. reprint ed. pap. 9.95 (*0-7661-0166-5*) Kessinger Pub.

— Mysticism. 150p. 1997. reprint ed. pap. 19.95 (*0-7661-0095-2*) Kessinger Pub.

— Pedigree of Man (1908) 208p. 1998. reprint ed. pap. 17.95 (*0-7661-0580-6*) Kessinger Pub.

Besant, Annie W. Popular Lectures on Theosophy, 1919. 121p. 1996. reprint ed. pap. 16.95 (*1-56459-545-5*) Kessinger Pub.

— Reincarnation. 11th ed. 1999. 7.50 (*81-7059-234-8*) Theos Pub Hse.

— Reincarnation, 1919. 73p. 1996. reprint ed. pap. 6.95 (*1-56459-704-0*) Kessinger Pub.

— Reincarnation, Theosophical Manual, No. 2. 73p. 1996. reprint ed. spiral bd. 9.50 (*0-7873-0103-5*) Hlth Research.

***Besant, Annie W.** Religious Problems in India (1902) 134p. 1998. reprint ed. pap. 14.95 (*0-7661-0593-8*) Kessinger Pub.

Besant, Annie W. The Riddle of Life & How Theosophy Answers It. 54p. 1998. reprint ed. pap. 11.00 (*0-7661-0266-1*) Kessinger Pub.

— The Search for Happiness. 1990. pap. 3.50 (*81-7059-158-9*, 7164, Quest) Theos Pub Hse.

— Seven Great Religions. pap. 9.50 (*81-7059-152-X*, 7218, Quest) Theos Pub Hse.

— Seven Principles of Man. 1998. 8.50 (*81-7059-097-3*, 7321, Quest) Theos Pub Hse.

— The Seven Principles of Man. 86p. 1996. reprint ed. pap. 12.95 (*1-56459-628-1*) Kessinger Pub.

***Besant, Annie W.** Shri Rama Chandra the Ideal King: Some Lessons from the Ramayana (1905) 192p. 1998. reprint ed. pap. 17.95 (*0-7661-0589-X*) Kessinger Pub.

— Some Problems of Life (1900) 146p. 1998. reprint ed. pap. 16.95 (*0-7661-0582-2*) Kessinger Pub.

Besant, Annie W. The Spiritual Life. rev. ed. 243p. 1991. pap. 8.95 (*0-8356-0666-X*, Quest) Theos Pub Hse.

***Besant, Annie W.** Study in Consciousness: A Contribution to the Science of Psychology (1915) 472p. 1998. reprint ed. pap. 33.00 (*0-7661-0514-8*) Kessinger Pub.

Besant, Annie W. Super-Human Men in History & Religion. 136p. 1996. reprint ed. pap. 16.95 (*1-56459-621-4*) Kessinger Pub.

***Besant, Annie W.** Theosophy & the New Psychology: A Course of Six Lectures (1904) 136p. 1998. reprint ed. pap. 16.95 (*0-7661-0598-9*) Kessinger Pub.

Besant, Annie W. Thought Power: Its Control & Culture. LC 73-7644. 1988. pap. 9.00 (*0-8356-0312-1*, Quest) Theos Pub Hse.

— Thought Power: Its Control & Culture, 1905. 146p. 1996. reprint ed. pap. 12.95 (*1-56459-713-X*) Kessinger Pub.

— Thought Power, Its Control & Culture. 145p. 1996. reprint ed. spiral bd. 14.00 (*0-7873-0105-1*) Hlth Research.

— Yoga: The Hatha Yoga & the Raja Yoga. 73p. 1996. reprint ed. spiral bd. 12.00 (*0-7873-0104-3*) Hlth Research.

***Besant, Annie W., ed.** Universal Text Book of Religion & Morals (1910), Pts. I & II. 384p. 1998. reprint ed. pap. 27.95 (*0-7661-0603-9*) Kessinger Pub.

***Besant, Annie W., tr.** Bhagavad Gita: The Lord's Song. 260p. 1998. 7.95 (*81-7059-174-0*, Pub. by Theos Pub Hse) Natl Bk Netwk.

Besant, Annie W. & Leadbeater, C. W. The Lives of Alcyone, 2 vols., Set. 737p. 1998. reprint ed. pap. 48.50 (*0-7873-0107-8*) Hlth Research.

— Occult Chemistry. 3rd ed. 397p. 1998. reprint ed. pap. 34.50 (*0-7873-0106-X*) Hlth Research.

— Occult Chemistry: Investigations by Clairvoyant Magnification into the Structure of the Atoms of the Periodic Table & of Some Compounds. 3rd ed. 404p. 1996. reprint ed. pap. 29.95 (*1-56459-678-8*) Kessinger Pub.

Besant, Annie W. & Leadbeater, Charles W. Occult Chemistry: Clairvoyant Observations on the Chemical Elements. rev. ed. 170p. 1996. reprint ed. spiral bd. 16.50 (*0-7873-0108-6*) Hlth Research.

— Talks on the Path of Occultism Vol. 1: At the Feet of the Master. 1998. 17.95 (*81-7059-160-0*, Pub. by Theos Pub Hse) Natl Bk Netwk.

— Talks on the Path of Occultism Vol. 2: Voice of the Silence. 1991. 17.95 (*81-7059-162-7*) Theos Pub Hse.

— Thought Forms. abr. ed. LC 98-32233. (Illus.). 88p. 1999. pap. 13.00 (*0-8356-0008-4*, Quest) Theos Pub Hse.

Besant, Annie W., jt. auth. see Leadbeater, Charles W.

Besant, C. B. & Lui, C. W. Computer-Aided Design & Manufacture. 3rd ed. LC 85-27185. (Engineering Science Ser.). 410p. 1986. text 89.95 (*0-470-20180-0*); pap. text 39.95 (*0-470-20242-4*) P-H.

Besant, C. B., jt. auth. see Bedenick, B.

Besant, Christopher W., jt. ed. see Leonard, E. Bruce.

Besant, D. L., et al. Man, Whence, How & Whither. abr. ed. 540p. 1997. reprint ed. pap. 25.00 (*0-7873-1068-9*) Hlth Research.

Besant, Walter. All Sorts & Conditions of Men. LC 96-52788. (Oxford Popular Fiction Ser.). (Illus.). 464p. 1997. pap. 11.95 (*0-19-283258-1*) OUP.

— Autobiography of Sir Walter Besant. LC 76-144877. 1971. reprint ed. 39.00 (*0-403-00864-6*) Scholarly.

— French Humorists: From the Twelfth to the Nineteenth Century. LC 74-38774. (Essay Index Reprint Ser.). 1977. reprint ed. 25.95 (*0-8369-2635-8*) Ayer.

— In Deacon's Orders, & Other Stories. LC 76-128720. (Short Story Index Reprint Ser.). 1977. 19.95 (*0-8369-3611-6*) Ayer.

— In Deacon's Orders, 1895. Wolff, Robert L., ed. LC 75-1541. (Victorian Fiction Ser.). 1976. lib. bdg. 16.50 (*0-8240-1612-2*) Garland.

— The Rebel Queen. LC 74-27964. (Modern Jewish Experience Ser.). 1975. reprint ed. 40.95 (*0-405-06695-3*) Ayer.

— Studies in Early French Poetry. LC 72-13206. (Essay Index Reprint Ser.). 1977. reprint ed. 23.95 (*0-8369-8147-2*) Ayer.

— Studies in Early French Poetry. LC 72-13206. (Essay Index Reprint Ser.). 319p. reprint ed. lib. bdg. 22.00 (*0-8290-0522-6*) Irvington.

***Besant, Walter & Rice, James.** Twas in Trafalgar Bay. 252p. 2000. pap. 9.95 (*0-594-02941-4*) Eightn Hundrd.

Besant, Walter, jt. auth. see Rice, James.

Besant, Walter, ed. see Conder, Claude R.

B

Besas, Peter. Behind the Spanish Lens: Spanish Cinema under Fascism & Democracy. LC 85-22874. (Illus.). 291p. (Orig.). 1985. 26.00 (*0-912869-06-2*) Arden Pr.

Besch, Werner, et al, contrib. by. Sprachgeschichte: Ein Handbuch zur Geschichte der Deutschen Sprache und Ihrer Erforschung. 850p. 1998. 406.00 (*3-11-011257-4*) De Gruyter.

Besch, Werner, et al, eds. Dialektologie: Ein Handbuch Zur Deutschen Und Allgemeinen Dialektforschung, 2 Pts., Pt. 1. (GER., Illus.). 1344p. 1982. 434.65 (*3-11-005977-0*) De Gruyter.

— Dialektologie: Ein Handbuch Zur Deutschen Und Allgemeinen Dialektforschung, 2 Pts., Pt. 2. (GER., Illus.). 1344p. 1982. 496.15 (*3-11-009571-8*) De Gruyter.

Bescherelle. El Arte de Conjugar en Espanol: Diccionario de 12,000 Verbos. (SPA.). 249p. 1984. 20.95 (*2-218-06140-6*, Pub. by Ed Hatier) Hatier Pub.

— Bescherelle Ecole. (FRE.). 415p. (J). (gr. 2-10). 1997. 16.95 (*2-218-71508-2*, Pub. by Ed Hatier) Hatier Pub.

— Complete Guide to Conjugating 12,000 French Verbs. (ENG & FRE.). 174p. 1995. 22.95 (*0-7859-9229-4*) Fr & Eur.

— La Conjugaison: 12,000 Verbes. (FRE.). 178p. 1990. 22.95 (*0-7859-9230-8*) Fr & Eur.

— La Grammaire Pour Tous. (FRE.). 356p. 1990. 22.95 (*0-7859-9238-3*) Fr & Eur.

— L' Orthographe pour Tous. (FRE.). 256p. 1990. 22.95 (*0-7859-9237-5*) Fr & Eur.

Bescherelle, ed. Bescherelle 1: La Conjugaison pour Tous: Dictionnaire de 12,000 Verbes. (FRE.). 200p. 1997. 13.95 (*2-218-71716-6*) Hatier Pub.

— Bescherelle 2: L'Orthographe pour Tous. (FRE.). 253p. 1997. 17.95 (*2-218-71717-4*) Hatier Pub.

— Bescherelle 3: La Grammaire pour Tous. (FRE.). 351p. 1997. 17.95 (*2-218-71718-2*) Hatier Pub.

— Complete Guide to Conjugating 12,000 French Verbs: English Edition. 174p. 1989. 14.95 (*2-218-06591-6*) Hatier Pub.

Bescherelle, Louis. Le Nouveau Bescherelle: L'Art de Conjuguer. 15.95 (*0-685-11014-1*) Fr & Eur.

Bescherelle, Louis-Nicolas & Devars, G. Grand Dictionnaire de Geographie Universelle Ancienne et Moderne, 4 vols., Set. 3599p. reprint ed. write for info. (*0-318-71320-9*) G Olms Pubs.

Beschi, Joseph. A Grammar of the Common Dialect of the Tamil Language. (ENG & TAM.). 156p. 1992. 39.95 (*0-8288-8420-X*) Fr & Eur.

Beschlebnov. German to Russian Dictionary Veterinary Medicine. (ENG & GER.). 464p. 1996. 105.00 (*0-320-00526-7*) Fr & Eur.

Beschloss, Michael R. The Impeachment & Trial of President Clinton: The Official Transcripts from the House Judiciary Committee Hearings to the Senate Trial. LC 99-25382. 1999. pap. 15.00 (*0-8129-3264-1*, Times Bks) Crown Pub Group.

— Taking Charge: The Johnson White House Tapes, 1963-1964. LC 97-26749. (Illus.). 624p. 1997. 30.00 (*0-684-80407-7*) S&S Trade.

— Taking Charge: The Johnson White House Tapes, 1963-1964. 592p. 1998. pap. 16.00 (*0-684-84792-2*, Touchstone) S&S Trade Pap.

Beschloss, Michael R. & Talbott, Strobe. Bush & Gorbachev. 1989. write for info. (*0-318-65992-1*, E Burlingame Bks) HarpC.

Beschner, George M., jt. auth. see Friedman, Alfred S.

Besdin, Abraham R. Reflections of the Rav: Lessons in Jewish Thought Adapted from the Lectures of Rabbi Joseph B. Soloveitchik, Vol. 1. 1993. 22.95 (*0-88125-330-8*) Ktav.

— Reflections of the Rav: Man of Faith in the Modern World Adapted from the Lectures of Rabbi Joseph B. Soloveitchik, Vol. 2. 1989. 22.95 (*0-88125-312-X*) Ktav.

Besdine, Richard W., et al, eds. Medical Care of the Nursing Home Resident: What Physicians Need to Know. LC 96-12363. 175p. 1996. pap. 29.00 (*0-943126-48-7*) Amer Coll Phys.

Besdine, Richard W., jt. auth. see Rowe, John W.

Besdo, D. & Stein, E., eds. Finite Ineslastic Deformations - Theory & Applications: IUTAM Symposium, Hannover, Germany, 1991. LC 92-28121. (International Union of Theoretical & Applied Mechanics Symposia Ser.). 576p. 1992. 179.00 (*0-387-55849-7*) Spr-Verlag.

Besdo, D., ed. see CISM (International Center for Mechanical Sciences.

Beseacker, Robert. Michigan in the Novel, 1816-1996: An Annotated Bibliography. annot. ed. LC 97-32194. (Great Lakes Books Publication). (Illus.). 448p. 1998. 54.95 (*0-8143-2712-5*) Wayne St U Pr.

Beseler, Dora V. & Jacobs-Wuestefeld, Barbara. Law Dictionary: Technical Dictionary of the Anglo-American Legal Terminology Including Commercial & Political Terms: English-German. 4th ed. LC 86-4496. 1986. 306.15 (*3-11-010429-6*) De Gruyter.

Besemer, Susan P. & Crosman, Christopher, compiled by. From Museums, Galleries, & Studios: A Guide to Artists on Film & Tape, 6. LC 83-22710. (Art Reference Collection Ser.: No. 6). 199p. 1984. lib. bdg. 49.95 (*0-313-23881-2*, BFM/, Greenwood Pr) Greenwood.

Besemeres, John F. Socialist Population Politics: The Political Implications of Demographic Trends in the U. S. S. R. & Eastern Europe. LC 80-65260. 389p. reprint ed. pap. 120.60 (*0-608-18120-X*, 203277200081) Bks Demand.

Besen, Stanley M. & Johnson, Leland L. Regulation of Media Ownership by the Federal Communications Commission: An Assessment. LC 84-26387. 77p. 1984. pap. 7.50 (*0-8330-0627-4*, R-3206-MF) Rand Corp.

Besen, Stanley M., et al. Misregulating Television: Network Dominance & the F. C. C. LC 84-8738. viii, 202p. 1985. 24.00 (*0-226-04415-7*) U Ch Pr.

— Misregulating Television: Network Dominance & the F. C. C. LC 84-8738. viii, 210p. 1986. pap. text 12.00 (*0-226-04416-5*) U Ch Pr.

***Besenfelder, Ann Meade.** Signs of Good Taste: Recollections & Recipes from Richmond's Fan District. (Illus.). 88p. 1999. write for info. (*0-9676204-0-6*) Meade Pr.

Besenhard, J. O. Handbook of Battery Materials. LC 99-186348. 648p. 1999. 450.00 (*3-527-29469-4*) Wiley.

***Besenjak, Carol.** Copyright Plain & Simple. 2nd ed. (Plain & Simple Ser.). 192p. 2000. pap. 12.99 (*1-56414-512-3*) Career Pr Inc.

Besenjak, Cheryl. Copyright Plain & Simple. LC 96-53388. (In Plain English Ser.). 192p. (Orig.). 1997. pap. 11.99 (*1-56414-273-6*) Career Pr Inc.

Beser, Nicholas. Introduction to Data Compression Standards. (Electrical Engineering Ser.). 1996. 49.95 (*0-442-01992-0*, VNR) Wiley.

Beser, Rose. Why Some People Act So Stupid & What You Can Do about It. 180p. 1998. pap. 10.95 (*1-57502-824-7*, PO2270) Morris Pubng.

Besevliev, Veselin. Bulgarisch-Byzantinische Aufsatz. (Collected Studies: No. CS80). (Illus.). 370p. (C). 1978. reprint ed. lib. bdg. 145.95 (*0-86078-024-4*, Pub. by Variorum) Ashgate Pub Co.

Beshara, Raymond & Scott, Leontine D. Time to Think. (Illus.). 1989. pap. text 7.95 (*0-9623161-0-5*) ERN Inc.

Beshara, Raymond, et al. What You Should Know about AIDS. (Illus.). 72p. (YA). (gr. 6-10). 1989. teacher ed. 3.00 (*0-9623161-3-X*); pap. text 9.85 (*0-9623161-2-1*) ERN Inc.

Besharov. Combating Child Abuse: Guidelines for Cooperation Between Law Enforcement & Child Protective Agencies. 50p. (Orig.). 1990. pap. 6.50 (*0-8447-7003-5*) Am Enterprise.

— Recognizing Child Abuse: A Trainer's Manual. LC 97-38384. 256p. 1998. pap. 75.00 (*0-684-83994-6*) S&S Trade.

Besharov, Douglas J. Family Violence: Research & Public Policy Issues. LC 89-18431. 200p. 1990. 33.25 (*0-8447-3707-0*, AEI Pr) Am Enterprise.

— Recognizing Child Abuse: A Guide for the Concerned. 270p. 1990. per. 14.95 (*0-02-903082-X*) Free Pr.

— Understanding Poverty & Dependence. 1994. 26.87 (*0-02-903071-4*) S&S Trade.

— The Vulnerable Social Worker: Liability for Serving Children & Families. LC 85-28437. 275p. 1985. 23.95 (*0-87101-136-0*) Natl Assn Soc Wkrs.

Besharov, Douglas J., ed. Enhancing Early Childhood Programs: Burdens & Opportunities. LC 96-163314. 1996. pap. text 16.95 (*0-87868-605-3*) Child Welfare.

— Legal Services for the Poor: Time for Reform. 283p. 1990. 31.25 (*0-8447-3689-9*, AEI Pr) Am Enterprise.

— When Drug Addicts Have Children: Reorienting Child Welfare's Response. (Orig.). 1994. pap. 26.95 (*0-87868-561-8*) Child Welfare.

Besharov, Douglas J., et al, eds. Why Some Men Don't Use Condoms: Male Attitudes about Condoms & Other Contraceptives. (Sexuality & American Social Policy Ser.). 50p. 1997. pap. text. write for info. (*0-944525-29-6*) H J Kaiser.

Besharov, Douglas J., et al. America's Disconnected Youth: Toward a Preventive Strategy. LC 99-20814. 1999. 28.95 (*0-87868-756-4*, CWLA Pr) Child Welfare.

Besharov, Douglas J., jt. auth. see Fontana, Vincent J.

Beshenkovsky, Eugene, jt. ed. see Kisluk, Eugene J.

Besher, Alexander. Chi. LC 99-21859. 304p. 1999. 23.50 (*0-684-83088-4*) Simon & Schuster.

— Mir: A Novel of Virtual Reality. LC 98-3496. 320p. 1998. 23.00 (*0-684-83087-6*) S&S Trade.

Beshers, James M. Urban Social Structure. LC 80-27972. 207p. 1981. reprint ed. lib. bdg. 59.50 (*0-313-22714-4*, BEUR, Greenwood Pr) Greenwood.

Beshir, Ekram & Beshir, Mohamed R. Meeting the Challenge of Parenting in the West: An Islamic Perspective. LC 98-35846. 160p. 1998. pap. 11.75 (*0-915957-87-6*) amana pubns.

Beshir, Mohamed R., jt. auth. see Beshir, Ekram.

Beshir, Mohammad O. Diversity Regionalism & National Unity. (Research Report Ser.: No. 54). 50p. 1979. write for info. (*91-7106-166-5*, Pub. by Nordic Africa) Transaction Pubs.

Beshoff, Pamela, jt. ed. see Hill, Christopher.

Beshore, George, ed. Sickle Cell Anemia. LC 94-15513. (Venture Bks.). (Illus.). 112p. (YA). (gr. 7-12). 1994. lib. bdg. 24.00 (*0-531-12510-6*) Watts.

***Beshore, George W.** Science in Ancient China. (Science of the Past Ser.). (Illus.). 64p. (J). (gr. 4-6). 1998. pap. 8.95 (*0-531-15914-0*) Watts.

Beshore, George W. Science in Early Islamic Cultures. (Science Of The Past Ser.). (Illus.). 64p. (J). (gr. 4-6). 1998. pap. 8.95 (*0-531-15917-5*) Watts.

***Beshore, Kenton & Young, Woody.** Life at Its Best: Enjoying the Fruits of the Spirit. 2000. write for info. (*0-939513-15-3*) Joy Pub SJC.

Besier, Rudolf. The Barretts of Wimpole Street. 1953. pap. 5.25 (*0-8222-0096-1*) Dramatists Play.

Besilius, Harold A., tr. see Urzidil, Johannes.

Besimo, Christian. Removable Partial Dentures on Osseointegrated Implants: Principles of Treatment Planning & Prosthetic Rehabilitation in Edentulous Mandible. Hassel, Thomas M., tr. from GER. LC 97-3822. 232p. 1997. text 98.00 (*0-86715-329-6*) Quint Pub Co.

Besinger, Curtis. Working with Mr. Wright: What It Was Like. (Illus.). 335p. (C). 1995. text 69.95 (*0-521-48122-8*) Cambridge U Pr.

— Working with Mr. Wright: What It Was Like. (Illus.). 335p. 1997. pap. 19.95 (*0-521-58714-X*) Cambridge U Pr.

Beskeen. CPR: MS Powerpoint 97 Intermed. (Illustrated Ser.). (C). 1997. pap. 20.95 (*0-7600-5826-1*) Course Tech.

Beskeen. Crs Gde-ill Ppt 2000 Basic. (C). 1999. pap. text 21.95 (*0-7600-6395-8*) Course Tech.

Beskeen. Microsoft Powerpoint 97 Basic. (C). 1997. spiral bd. 20.95 (*0-7600-5825-3*) Thomson Learn.

Beskeen, jt. auth. see Reding.

Beskeen, David W. Microsoft Office 2000 Illustrated Introductory. (Illus.). 1999. pap. text 50.95 (*0-7600-6050-9*) Course Tech.

— Microsoft PowerPoint 4.0 for Windows: Illustrated Brief Edition. Johnson, Steven M., ed. (Illustrated Ser.). (Illus.). 104p. (C). 1995. pap. 11.95 (*1-56527-593-4*) Course Tech.

Beskeen, David W. Microsoft Powerpoint 97 - Illustrated Standard Edition. (Illus.). 232p. per. 21.95 (*0-7600-6164-5*, Pub. by Course Tech) Thomson Learn.

Beskeen, David W. Microsoft PowerPoint 97: Illustrated Standard Edition: A First Course. 10th ed. (Illustrated Ser.). (Illus.). 192p. (C). 1997. pap. 16.50 (*0-7600-5160-7*) Course Tech.

— Microsoft PowerPoint 7 for Windows 95 - Illustrated, Incl. instr. resource kit, test mgr., files. (Illustrated Ser.). (Illus.). 200p. 1996. text, mass mkt. 20.95 incl. 3.5 ld (*0-7600-3525-3*) Course Tech.

— Microsoft PowerPoint 7 for Windows 95: Illustrated Brief Edition. (Illustrated Ser.). (Illus.). 96p. 1995. pap. 11.95 (*0-7600-3526-1*) Course Tech.

Beskeen, David W. Microsoft Powerpoint 2000 - Illustrated Brief. (Illus.). 112p. per. 12.95 (*0-7600-6073-8*, Pub. by Course Tech) Thomson Learn.

— Microsoft Powerpoint 2000 Certified: Course CBT. 26.95 (*0-619-00126-7*, Pub. by Course Tech) Thomson Learn.

Beskeen, David W. Microsoft PowerPoint 2000: Illustrated Introductory. 1999. pap. text 21.95 (*0-7600-6074-6*) Course Tech.

***Beskeen, David W.** MOUS PowerPoint 2000 Exam Prep: The Most Comprehensive, Interactive & Visual Microsoft Certification Study Guide on Microsoft PowerPoint 2000. (Exam Prep Ser.). (Illus.). 2000. pap. write for info. incl. cd-rom (*1-57610-579-2*) Coriolis Grp.

Beskeen, David W. PowerPoint 97 Exam Prep. 10th ed. 264p. (C). 1997. pap. 29.99 (*1-57610-233-5*) Coriolis Grp.

Beskeen, David W. & Clemens, Barbara. Course Guide - Microsoft Powerpoint 2000 Illustrated Advanced. 88p. spiral bd. 21.95 (*0-7600-6396-6*, Pub. by Course Tech) Thomson Learn.

Beskeen, David W. & Johnson, Steve M. Microsoft PowerPoint 97: Illustrated Brief Edition. 10th ed. (Illustrated Ser.). (Illus.). 96p. (C). 1997. pap. 12.95 (*0-7600-4704-9*) Course Tech.

Beskeen, David W. & Johnson, Steven M. Microsoft PowerPoint 4 for Windows - Illustrated, Incl. instr. resource kit, test bank, transparency. (Illustrated Ser.). (Illus.). 184p. 1995. pap. 20.95 (*1-56527-523-3*) Course Tech.

Beskeen, David W., et al. Course CBT: Microsoft Office 2000 Certified with Windows 98--Core. 48.95 (*0-619-00106-2*, Pub. by Course Tech) Thomson Learn.

— Microsoft Office 2000 Certified with Windows 98 -- Expert: Course CBT. 56.95 (*0-619-00134-8*, Pub. by Course Tech) Thomson Learn.

— Microsoft Office 2000 with Windows 98 -- Basic: Course CBT. (C). 40.95 (*0-619-00151-8*, Pub. by Course Tech) Thomson Learn.

Beskeen, David W., jt. auth. see Reding, Elizabeth E.

***Besker, Nicholas J.** Beerinsky: Orphan. LC 99-91491. 2000. 25.00 (*0-7388-0834-2*); pap. 18.00 (*0-7388-0835-0*) Xlibris Corp.

Beskin, James E. The Jew Who Chose Jesus: The Life of the Reverend Doctor Nathan Cohen Beskin. 148p. (Orig.). 1995. pap. 12.95 (*0-9633671-5-3*) Greenfield Ctr.

Beskin, V. S., et al. Physics of the Pulsar Magnetosphere. Tsaplina, M. V., tr. from RUS. LC 92-18417. (Illus.). 432p. (C). 1993. text 140.00 (*0-521-41746-5*) Cambridge U Pr.

Beskind, Donald H., jt. auth. see Bocchino, Anthony J.

Beskos, D. E., ed. Boundary Element Methods in Structural Analysis. LC 89-6565. 352p. 1989. 33.00 (*0-87262-694-6*, 694) Am Soc Civil Eng.

Beskos, D. E., et al, eds. Dynamic Soil-Structure Interaction: Proceedings of the International Symposium, Minneapolis, 4-5 Sept. 1984. 184p. (C). 1984. text 123.00 (*90-6191-558-9*, Pub. by A A Balkema) Ashgate Pub Co.

Beskos, D. E. & Anagnostopoulos, S. A., eds. Computer Analysis & Design of Earthquake Resistant Structures: A Handbook. LC 97-68728. (Advances in Earthquake Engineering Ser.: Vol. 3). 936p. 1997. 295.00 (*1-85312-374-9*, 3749, Pub. by WIT Pr) Computational Mech MA.

Beskos, D. E. & Atluri, S. N., eds. Boundary Element Analysis of Plates & Shells. (Computational Mechanics Ser.). (Illus.). viii, 368p. 1991. 129.95 (*0-387-54464-X*) Spr-Verlag.

Beskos, D. E. & Ziegler, F., eds. Advances in Dynamic Systems & Stability: Lectures Given at the Symposium in Atlanta, Georgia, December 1991, on the Occasion of the 65th Birthday of Bruno A. Boley. LC 92-15846. (Acta Mechanical, Supplementum Ser.: No. 3). (Illus.). 210p. 1992. write for info. (*3-211-82368-9*); 188.95 (*0-387-82368-9*) Spr-Verlag.

Beskow, Elsa. Children of the Forest. unabridged ed. (Illus.). 36p. (J). (ps-1). Date not set. 15.95 (*0-86315-049-7*, 20236, Pub. by Floris Bks) Gryphon Hse.

— The Flowers' Festival. (Illus.). 32p. (J). (gr. k-4). 1991. reprint ed. 15.95 (*0-86315-120-5*, Pub. by Floris Bks) Gryphon Hse.

— Ollie's Ski Trip. Ernest Benn Ltd. Staff, tr. (Illus.). (J). (ps-2). 15.95 (*0-86315-091-8*, Pub. by Floris Bks) Gryphon Hse.

— Pelle's New Suit. Woodburn, Marion L., tr. from SWE. (Illus.). 32p. (J). 1989. reprint ed. 15.95 (*0-86315-092-6*, Pub. by Floris Bks) Gryphon Hse.

— Peter in Blueberry Land. (J). (ps-2). 1988. 15.95 (*0-86315-050-0*, 20237, Pub. by Floris Bks) Gryphon Hse.

— Peter's Old House. unabridged ed. Orig. Title: Herr Peter. (Illus.). 26p. (J). (ps-1). 15.95 (*0-86315-102-7*, 25986, Pub. by Floris Bks) Gryphon Hse.

— The Sun Egg. unabridged ed. Orig. Title: Solagget. (Illus.). 32p. (J). (ps-1). 15.95 (*0-86315-163-9*, 28345, Pub. by Floris Bks) Gryphon Hse.

— Tale of the Little, Little Old Woman. (Illus.). 26p. (J). (ps-1). 12.95 (*0-86315-079-9*, 20246, Pub. by Floris Bks) Gryphon Hse.

— Woody, Hazel & Little Pip. Orig. Title: Ocke, Nutta Och Pillerill. 36p. (J). (ps-1). 1939. 15.95 (*0-86315-109-4*, 24578, Pub. by Floris Bks) Anthroposophic.

Beskrovny, L. G. The Russian Army & Fleet in the Nineteenth Century: A Handbook of Armaments, Personnel & Policy. Smith, Gordon E., ed. LC 96-207832. 405p. 1996. lib. bdg. 50.00 (*0-87569-139-0*) Academic Intl.

Besl, H., jt. auth. see Bresinsky, A.

Besley. Essentials of Managerial Finance. 12th ed. (C). 1999. pap. text 44.50 (*0-03-025877-4*) Harcourt Coll Pubs.

— Principles of Finance. (C). 1999. pap. text, student ed. 22.50 (*0-03-025263-6*, Pub. by Harcourt Coll Pubs) Harcourt.

— Principles of Finance. (C). 1999. pap. text 38.00 (*0-03-025258-X*, Pub. by Harcourt Coll Pubs) Harcourt.

Besley, Scott. Principles of Finance. 816p. (C). 1999. text 89.00 (*0-03-025253-9*, Pub. by Harcourt Coll Pubs) Harcourt.

Besmann, T. M., et al, eds. Chemical Vapor Deposition: 13th International Conference. (Proceedings Ser.: Vol. 96-5). (Illus.). 892p. 1996. 86.00 (*1-56677-155-2*) Electrochem Soc.

— Chemical Vapor Deposition of Refractory Metals & Ceramics II. (Symposium Proceedings Ser.: Vol. 250). 393p. 1992. text 17.50 (*1-55899-144-1*) Materials Res.

Besmann, T. M. & Gallois, B. M., eds. Chemical Vapor Deposition of Refractory Metals & Ceramics Vol. 168: Materials Research Society Symposium Proceedings. 402p. 1990. text 17.50 (*1-55899-056-9*) Materials Res.

Besmark, Tracey, ed. see Clark, Billy C.

Besmehn, Bobby. Juggling Step-by-Step. (Illus.). 80p. (Orig.). 1995. pap. 7.95 (*0-8069-0815-7*, Chapelle) Sterling.

Besmer, Fremont E. Horses, Musicians & Gods: The Hausa Cult of Possession-Trance. LC 81-10153. (Illus.). 304p. (C). 1983. 47.95 (*0-89789-020-5*, Bergin & Garvey) Greenwood.

— Kidan Daran Salla: Music for the Eve of the Muslim Festivals of Id Al-Fitr & Id Al-Kabir in Kano, Nigeria. (African Humanities Ser.). (Illus.). 84p. (Orig.). 1974. pap. text 4.00 (*0-941934-10-1*) Indiana Africa.

Besnainou, Denis & Davezies, Laurent. Regional Development & Structural Policy in Mexico. LC 98-133116. 132p. 1997. pap. 26.00 (*92-64-15687-9*, 04-97-05-1, Pub. by Org for Econ) OECD.

Besnard, P. An Introduction to Default Logic. (Symbolic Computation Ser.). xi, 208p. 1989. 63.95 (*0-387-51566-6*) Spr-Verlag.

Besnehard, Daniel. Passengers. Vogel, Stephen J., tr. 89p. (Orig.). 1985. pap. text 8.95 (*0-913745-12-X*) Ubu Repertory.

— The White Bear. Vogel, Stephen J., tr. from FRE.Tr. of L'Ourse Blanche. 78p. (Orig.). 1992. pap. 7.95 (*0-913745-35-9*) Ubu Repertory.

Besner, Derek & Humphreys, Glyn W. Basic Processes in Reading: Visual Word Recognition. 352p. (C). 1990. text 99.95 (*0-8058-0219-3*) L Erlbaum Assocs.

— Basic Processes in Reading: Visual Word Recognition. 352p. (C). 1990. pap. 55.00 (*0-8058-0994-5*) L Erlbaum Assocs.

Besner, Edward, et al. Practical Endodontics: A Clinical Atlas. LC 93-7003. (Illus.). 296p. (C). (gr. 13). 1993. text 77.95 (*0-8016-7798-X*, 07798) Mosby Inc.

Besner, Hilda F. & Spungin, Charlotte I. Gay & Lesbian Students: Understanding Their Needs. LC 95-12727. 174p. 1995. 59.95 (*1-56032-337-X*); pap. 29.95 (*1-56032-338-8*) Taylor & Francis.

— Training for Professionals Who Work with Gay & Lesbian Youth. LC 97-20520. 236p. 1997. pap. 22.95 (*1-56032-566-6*) Hemisp Pub.

Besner, Neil, et al, eds. Uncommon Wealth: An Anthology of Poetry in English. 872p. (C). 1998. pap. text 32.95 (*0-19-541076-9*) OUP.

Besner, Neil K. Introducing Alice Munro's Lives of Girls & Women. (Canadian Fiction Studies: No. 8). 124p. (C). 1990. text 18.95 (*1-55022-122-1*, Pub. by ECW) Genl Dist Srvs.

Besnick, Janet, ed. see Danieri, Cheryl L.

Besnier, Niko. Literacy, Emotion & Authority: Reading & Writing on a Polynesian Atoll. (Studies in the Social & Cultural Foundations of Language: No. 16). (Illus.). 254p. (C). 1995. text 59.95 (*0-521-48087-6*); pap. text 20.95 (*0-521-48539-8*) Cambridge U Pr.

***Besnier, Niko.** Tuvaluan. LC 98-43190. 1999. write for info. (*0-415-02456-0*) Routledge.

Besnier, P. La Reunion des Langues. Cascio, V. L., ed. vi, 92p. 1985. 44.65 (*90-6765-103-6*); pap. 30.80 (*90-6765-095-1*) Mouton.

Besong, Bate. The Grain of Bobe Ngom Jua. 40p. 1997. pap. 15.00 (*0-9655761-3-2*) Kola Tree Pr.

An Asterisk (*) at the beginning of an entry indicates that the title is appearing for the first time.

Besore, Donald H. Success from Failure That Changed History. LC 98-90129. 1999. 16.95 (*0-533-12713-0*) Vantage.

Besov, Oleg V., et al. Nine Papers on Functional Analysis & Numerical Analysis. (Translations Ser.: Series 2, Vol. 40). 290p. 1964. 36.00 (*0-8218-1740-X*, TRANS2/40) Am Math.

Besoyan, Rick. Babes in the Wood. 64p. 1983. pap. 6.95 (*0-88145-011-1*) Broadway Play.

Bespaloff, Alexis. New Schoonmaker Ency Win. exp. rev. ed. LC 88-5270. (Illus.). 544p. 1988. 25.00 (*0-688-05749-7*, Wm Morrow) Morrow Avon.

Bespalov, V. I. & Pasmanik, G. A. Nonlinear Optics & Adaptive Laser Systems. 147p. (C). 1993. lib. bdg. 165.00 (*1-56072-121-9*) Nova Sci Pubs.

Bess, C. W. Children's Object Sermons for the Seasons. (Object Lessons to Spark Imaginations Ser.). 112p. (Orig.). (gr. 11). 1993. pap. 6.99 (*0-8010-1026-8*) Baker Bks.

Bess, Carole, jt. auth. see White, L. M.

Bess, Clayton. Cuento Negro para una Negra Noche (Story for a Black Night) (SPA.). 84p. (YA). 1992. pap. 6.99 (*968-16-3792-5*, Pub. by Fondo) Continental Bk.

— The Mayday Rampage. LC 92-74268. (Illus.). 208p. (YA). (gr. 9-12). 1993. 14.95 (*1-882405-00-5*); pap. 7.95 (*1-882405-01-3*) Lookout Pr.

— The Truth about the Moon. 48p. (J). (ps-3). 1992. pap. 6.95 (*0-395-64371-6*) HM.

Bess, Demaree, jt. auth. see Littlepage, John D.

Bess, Donovan. A Practical Guide to Creative Senility. LC 88-9551. (Illus.). 176p. (Orig.). 1988. pap. 9.95 (*0-931892-16-3*) B Dolphin Pub.

Bess, Fred H., ed. Children with Hearing Impairment: Contemporary Trends. LC 96-61871. (Illus.). 401p. (C). 1998. text 60.00 (*0-9631439-8-0*, B103) Vanderbilt Wilkerson.

Bess, Fred H., et al, eds. Amplification for Children with Auditory Deficits. LC 95-78697. (Illus.). 500p. 1996. 55.00 (*0-9631439-3-X*) Vanderbilt Wilkerson.

Bess, Fred H. & Hall, James W., III, eds. Screening Children for Auditory Function. LC 92-70246. (Illus.). 560p. (C). 1992. text 55.00 (*0-9631439-0-5*) Vanderbilt Wilkerson.

Bess, Fred H. & Humes, Larry E. Audiology: The Fundamentals. 2nd ed. (Illus.). 352p. 1995. 48.00 (*0-683-00620-7*) Lppncott W & W.

Bess, H. David & Farris, Martin T. U. S. Maritime Policy: History & Prospects. LC 81-1503. 218p. 1981. 55.00 (*0-275-90584-5*, C0584, Praeger Pubs) Greenwood.

Bess, Howard H. Pastor, I Am Gay. LC 94-47332. 224p. (Orig.). 1995. pap. 14.95 (*0-9644123-0-6*) Palmer Pubng.

Bess, James L. Collegiality & Bureaucracy in the Modern University: The Influence of Information & Power on Decision-Making Structures. 208p. (C). 1987. text 27.00 (*0-8077-2868-3*) Tchrs Coll.

— Creative R & D Leadership: Insights from Japan. LC 94-46199. 384p. 1995. 75.00 (*0-89930-915-1*, Quorum Bks) Greenwood.

— Teaching Well & Liking It: Motivating Faculty to Teach Effectively. 448p. 1996. text 39.95 (*0-8018-5364-8*) Johns Hopkins.

Bess, James L., ed. Foundations of American Higher Education. (ASHE Reader Ser.). 772p. (C). 1991. pap. text 71.00 (*0-536-58013-8*) Pearson Custom.

***Bess, James L. & Webster, David S., eds.** Foundations of American Higher Education. 2nd rev. ed. (ASHE Reader Ser.). 744p. (C). 1999. pap. text 58.00 (*0-536-01853-7*) Pearson Custom.

***Bess, James L., et al.** Teaching Alone, Teaching Together: Transforming the Structure of Teams for Teaching. LC 99-50828. 288p. 2000. 29.95 (*0-7879-4798-9*, Pfffr & Co) Jossey-Bass.

Bess, Michael. Realism, Utopia, & the Mushroom Cloud: Four Activist Intellectuals & Their Strategies for Peace, 1945-1989. LC 93-9707. (Illus.). 344p. 1993. pap. text 19.95 (*0-226-04421-1*); lib. bdg. 54.95 (*0-226-04420-3*) U Ch Pr.

Bess, Michael D. Changing Face of Progress. 1995. pap. text 16.95 (*0-226-04418-1*); lib. bdg. 40.00 (*0-226-04417-3*) U Ch Pr.

Bess, Patti A. Vegetarian Barbecue. LC 98-10710. 224p. 1999. 26.00 (*1-56565-881-7*, 08817W, Pub. by Lowell Hse) NTC Contemp Pub Co.

— Vegetarian Barbecue. 272p. 1999. reprint ed. pap. 16.95 (*0-7373-0135-X*, 0135XW) NTC Contemp Pub Co.

***Bess, Philip.** City Baseball Magic: Plain Talk & Uncommon Sense about Cities & Baseball Parks. rev. ed. (Illus.). 64p. 1999. reprint ed. pap. 8.95 (*0-9673986-0-6*) Knothole.

— Inland Architecture: Subterranean Essays on Moral Order & Formal Order in Chicago. LC 00-28122. (Illus.). 2000. pap. write for info. (*0-9630969-6-6*) Interalia Des.

Bess, Phyllis & Bess, Tom. Frankoma & Other Oklahoma Potteries. (Illus.). 144p. (Orig.). 1997. pap. 24.95 (*0-7643-0084-9*) Schiffer.

***Bess, Phyllis & Bess, Tom.** Frankoma & other Oklahoma Potteries. LC 99-58372. (Illus.). 144p. 2000. pap. 24.95 (*0-7643-0903-X*) Schiffer.

Bess, Savitri L. Offer Me a Flower. (Illus.). 1999. pap. 13.50 (*0-9668373-8-X*) Bharati Impress.

***Bess, Savitri L.** The Path of the Mother. 432p. 2000. pap. 14.00 (*0-345-42347-X*, Ballantine) Ballantine Pub Grp.

Bess, Tom, jt. auth. see Bess, Phyllis.

Bessa Victor, Geraldo. Poetry by Geraldo Bessa Victor: Debaixo de Ceu, Mucanda, Cubata Abandonada. (B. E. Ser.: No: 33). 1966. 35.00 (*0-8115-2984-3*) Periodicals Srv.

— Poetry from Angola: Ao Som das Marimbas, Poemes Africians. (B. E. Ser.: No. 110). 1967. 25.00 (*0-8115-3041-8*) Periodicals Srv.

Bessac, Jean-Claude. La Pierre en Gaule Narbonnaise et les Carrieres du Bois des Lens (Nimes) Histoire, Archeologie, Ethnographie & Techniques. (JRA Supplementary Ser.: No. 16). (FRE., Illus.). 334p. 1996. lib. bdg. 89.50 (*1-887829-16-4*) Jour Roman Arch.

***Bessamra, Sonia.** Focus on Tunisia: Guide for Doing Business & Investing in Tunisia. (Illus.). 352p. 2000. pap. 35.00 (*9973-31-551-0*) Publi-Performances.

***Bessange, Marc.** Euros 12. (Illus.). 1998. 16.95 (*3-86187-117-3*) B Gmunder.

Bessange, Marc. Marc Bessange. (Illus.). 1998. pap. text 7.95 (*3-86187-125-4*) B Gmunder.

Bessanova, S. Impressionist & Post-Impressionist Paintings in Soviet Museums. (C). 1990. 250.00 (*0-7855-4491-7*, Pub. by Collets) St Mut.

***Bessant, Claire.** The Complete Guide to the Cat. (Complete Animal Guide Ser.). 192p. 1999. 21.95 (*0-7641-5203-3*) Barron.

— Complete Guide to the Cat. (Complete Animal Guides Ser.). (Illus.). 256p. 2000. 14.98 (*1-58663-076-8*) M Friedman Pub Grp Inc.

— The Complete Guide to the Dog. (Complete Animal Guide Ser.). 192p. 1999. 21.95 (*0-7641-5204-1*) Barron.

Bessant, Claire. How to Talk to Your Cat. 120p. 1993. pap. 8.95 (*0-8120-1749-8*) Barron.

Bessant, Claire & Viner, Bradley. The Ultrafit Older Cat. LC 96-43186. 1997. 10.95 (*0-8120-9856-0*) Barron.

Bessant, John. Technology Transfer in Europe. 240p. (C). (gr. 13). 1996. pap. 65.00 (*0-415-08231-5*, B4414) Thomson Learn.

Bessant, John, et al. Technology Centres: Strategies for Best Practice. 1996. pap. 60.00 (*0-415-12503-0*) Thomson Learn.

Bessant, Judith, et al, eds. Cultures of Crime & Violence: The Australian Experience. (Illus.). (C). 1995. pap. 24.95 (*1-86324-417-4*, Pub. by LaTrobe Univ) Intl Spec Bk.

Bessant, Judith & Watts, Rob. Sociology Australia. 288p. 1998. pap. 35.00 (*1-86448-731-3*, Pub. by Allen & Unwin Pty) Paul & Co Pubs.

Bessant, Judith, jt. auth. see Cook, Sandy.

Bessant, P. & Smith, L. Dance. (Dance Guides Ser.). (Illus.). 48p. (J). (gr. 5-9). 1987. pap. 7.95 (*0-7460-0087-1*) EDC.

— Dance. (Dance Guides Ser.). (Illus.). 48p. (J). (gr. 5 up). 1987. lib. bdg. 15.95 (*0-88110-245-8*) EDC.

Bessar, Anthony, jt. auth. see Kraft, Karen.

Bessarion, Agioantonides. The House of Holy Wisdom: A Commentary on Proverbs 9. (Illus.). 60p. (Orig.). 1986. pap. 4.95 (*0-936649-12-7*) St Anthony Orthodox.

Bessason, Haraldur, tr. see Johannesson, Jon.

Bessborough, ed. see Schreiber, Charlotte E.

Besse, A. L. Einstein Manifolds. (Series of Modern Surveys in Mathematics: Vol. 10).Tr. of Ergebnisse der Mathematik und ihrer Grenzgebiete. 3. Folge. (Illus.). 510p. 1986. 98.00 (*0-387-15279-2*) Spr-Verlag.

— Manifolds All of Whose Geodesics Are Closed. (Ergebnisse der Mathematik und Ihrer Grenzgebiete Ser.: Vol. 93). (Illus.). 1978. 93.95 (*0-387-08158-5*) Spr-Verlag.

Besse, Alvin J. & Besse, Kirk J. A China Sailor. LC 93-60730. (Illus.). 128p. (Orig.). 1999. pap. text. write for info. (*1-883141-01-X*) Victoria Pubns.

Besse, B., et al. Lexique Anglais-Francais de L'Aciere Electrique. (ENG & FRE.). 135p. 1975. pap. 8.95 (*0-8288-5927-2*, M9239) Fr & Eur.

Besse, B. De. Termes Techniques Nouveaux: Termes Officielement Recommendes par le Gouvernement Francais: French-English, English-French. (ENG & FRE.). 366p. 1982. pap. 95.00 (*0-7859-7143-2*) Fr & Eur.

Besse, B. De, see De Besse, B.

Besse, Jean M., jt. auth. see Beaunier, Andre.

***Besse, Joseph.** Sufferings of Early Quakers: Yorkshire 1652 to 1690. fac. ed. 1999. pap. 36.00 (*1-85072-212-9*, Pub. by W Sessions) St Mut.

Besse, Kirk J. Grand Times Amid the Sorrows: The Gilmer Family in North America. LC 93-60128. (Illus.). 224p. (Orig.). 1993. pap. 29.95 (*1-883141-00-1*) Victoria Pubns.

— Show Houses: Twin Cities Style. LC 93-60772. (Illus.). 165p. (Orig.). 1997. pap. text 24.95 (*1-883141-02-8*) Victoria Pubns.

Besse, Kirk J., jt. auth. see Besse, Alvin J.

Besse, Susan K. Restructuring Patriarchy: The Modernization of Gender Inequality in Brazil, 1914-1940. LC 95-23353. 1996. lib. bdg. 39.95 (*0-614-07953-5*) U of NC Pr.

— Restructuring Patriarchy: The Modernization of Gender Inequality in Brazil, 1914-1940. LC 95-23353. (Illus.). 300p. (C). 1996. pap. text 19.95 (*0-8078-4559-0*); lib. bdg. 49.95 (*0-8078-2252-3*) U of NC Pr.

Bessel, Richard. Germany after the First World War. (Illus.). 340p. 1995. pap. text 24.95 (*0-19-820586-4*) OUP.

Bessel, Richard, ed. Fascist Italy & Nazi Germany: Comparisons & Contrasts. 256p. (C). 1996. text 59.95 (*0-521-47129-X*) Cambridge U Pr.

— Fascist Italy & Nazi Germany: Comparisons & Contrasts. 256p. (C). 1996. pap. text 18.95 (*0-521-47711-5*) Cambridge U Pr.

— Life in the Third Reich. (Illus.). 144p. 1987. pap. 12.95 (*0-19-285184-5*) OUP.

***Bessel, Richard & Emsley, Clive.** Patterns of Provocation: Police & Public Disorder. LC 99-86560. 208p. 2000. 49.95 (*1-57181-227-X*); pap. 18.50 (*1-57181-228-8*) Berghahn Bks.

Bessel, Richard, jt. ed. see Ehlers, Robert.

Besselaar, A. Van Den, see Van Den Besselaar, A.

Besseling, J. F. & Van Der Giessen, E. Mathematical Modelling of Inelastic Deformation. LC 93-32189. 328p. (gr. 13). 1994. ring bd. 78.95 (*0-412-45280-4*, Chap & Hall CRC) CRC Pr.

Besseling, J. F. & Van Der Heijden, A. M., eds. Trends in Solid Mechanics. 256p. 1980. text 139.00 (*90-286-0699-8*) Kluwer Academic.

Bessell, Harold & Kelly, Thomas. The Parent Book. LC 77-71461. (Creative Parenting Ser.). (Illus.). (C). 1977. pap. 9.95 (*0-915190-15-X*, JP9015-X) Jalmar Pr.

Bessell, Katherine D. & Traina, Cynthia. The New, Revised Restaurateur's Easy Guide to Do-It-Yourself Public Relations. rev. ed. 45p. 1985. pap. 18.50 (*0-9629953-0-4*) Bessell Pub.

Bessemer, Henry. Sir Henry Bessemer, F. R. S. An Autobiography. 496p. 1989. text 33.90 (*0-901462-49-7*, Pub. by Inst Materials) Ashgate Pub Co.

Bessen, A. Howard. Corrugated Boxshop Practices. (Illus.). 256p. 1996. reprint ed. 89.00 (*1-885067-01-1*) Jelmar Pub.

— The Corrugator. LC 99-28536. (Illus.). 202p. 1999. 82.00 (*1-885067-17-8*) Jelmar Pub.

— Design & Production of Corrugated Packaging & Displays. LC 90-5117. (Illus.). 256p. 1991. 89.50 (*0-9616302-4-8*) Jelmar Pub.

***Bessent Bryd, Helen.** Enfranchising Urban Learners for the Twenty-First Century. Freeman, Algeania & Morris, Carole, eds. 196p. 1999. write for info. (*0-7392-0323-1*, PO2260) Morris Pubng.

Besser. Bart's Endocrine Protocols. 1995. pap. text 32.95 (*0-443-04496-1*, W B Saunders Co) Harcrt Hlth Sci Grp.

Besser, G. Michael, ed. Acromegaly. (Journal: Hormone Research Ser.: Vol. 33, Suppl. 1, 1990). (Illus.). vi, 36p. 1990. pap. 19.25 (*3-8055-5207-6*) S Karger.

Besser, Gretchen R. Germaine de Stael, Revisited. LC 93-28437. (Twayne's World Authors Ser.: No. 849). 180p. 1994. 32.00 (*0-8057-8286-9*) Macmillan.

Besser, Howard & Trant, Jennifer. Introduction to Imaging: Issues in Constructing an Image Database. LC 95-20202. (Introduction to Ser.). (Illus.). 48p. (Orig.). 1996. pap. 9.95 (*0-89236-361-4*, Pub. by J P Getty Trust) OUP.

Besser, Jeanne. The First Book of Baking: More Than 200 Delicious Recipes to Get You Started. LC 96-43286. 256p. 1997. per. 16.00 (*0-7615-0727-2*) Prima Pub.

— Working Mom's Fast & Easy One-Pot Cooking: Over 100 Yummy Recipes That Will Have Your Whole Family Begging for More. LC 98-26037. 240p. 1998. pap. 15.00 (*0-7615-1432-5*) Prima Pub.

Besser, Michael, jt. auth. see Hall, Reginald L.

Besser, Pam. A Basic Handbook of Writing Skills: Instructor's Manual. LC 93-30095. 314p. (C). 1994. 28.95 (*1-55934-032-0*, 1032); pap. text, teacher ed. write for info. (*1-55934-321-4*, 1321) Mayfield Pub.

Besser, Terry L. Team Toyota: Transplanting the Toyota Culture to the Camry Plant in Kentucky. LC 96-11692. (Series in the Sociology of Work). 199p. (C). 1996. pap. text 16.95 (*0-7914-3146-0*) State U NY Pr.

Besserman, Lawrence L. Chaucer's Biblical Poetics. LC 98-13350. (Illus.). 352p. 1998. 39.95 (*0-8061-3067-9*); pap. 17.95 (*0-8061-3068-7*) U of Okla Pr.

— The Legend of Job in the Middle Ages. LC 78-14936. 191p. 1979. reprint ed. pap. 59.30 (*0-7837-2224-9*, 205731400004) Bks Demand.

Besserman, Lawrence L., ed. The Challenge of Periodization: Old Paradigms & New Perspectives. LC 96-2710. 272p. 1996. reprint ed. text 60.00 (*0-8153-2103-1*, H1938) Garland.

Besserman, Perle. Owning It: Zen & the Art of Facing Life. LC 97-5153. 192p. 1997. 18.00 (*1-56836-177-7*) Kodansha.

— Shambhala Guide to Kabbalah & Jewish Mysticism. LC 97-19190. 1998. pap. 13.95 (*1-57062-215-9*, Pub. by Shambhala Pubns) Random.

— Teachings of the Jewish Mystics. LC 97-42458. 112p. 1998. pap. 10.00 (*1-57062-351-1*, Pub. by Shambhala Pubns) Random.

Besserwisser, Gertrude. Scheisse! The Real German You Were Never Taught in School. LC 93-48608. (Illus.). 96p. (Orig.). 1994. pap. 10.95 (*0-452-27221-1*, Plume) Dutton Plume.

Besset, Jean-Marie. The Best of Schools. O'Donnell, Mark, tr. from FRE.Tr. of Grande Ecole. 64p. (Orig.). 1992. pap. 7.95 (*0-913745-34-0*) Ubu Repertory.

Bessette, ed. see Storing.

Bessette, Alan E. A Guide to Some Edible & Poisonous Mushrooms of New York. 1985. pap. 6.00 (*0-318-41728-6*) North Country.

— Mushrooms of the Adirondacks: A Field Guide. 148p. 1988. pap. 12.95 (*0-932052-64-9*) North Country.

— Wildflowers of Maine, New Hampshire, & Vermont. LC 99-46641. 2000. pap. text 24.95 (*0-8156-0586-2*) Syracuse U Pr.

Bessette, Alan E., et al. Birds of the Adirondacks: A Field Guide. 240p. 1993. pap. 16.95 (*0-932052-94-0*) North Country.

— Mushrooms of North America in Color: A Field Guide Companion to Seldom-Illustrated Fungi. LC 95-11781. (Illus.). 188p. 1995. 39.95 (*0-8156-2666-5*); pap. 19.95 (*0-8156-0323-1*) Syracuse U Pr.

— Mushrooms of Northeastern North America. (Illus.). xiv, 582p. 1997. 95.00 (*0-8156-2707-6*, BEMU); pap. 45.00 (*0-8156-0388-6*, BEMUP) Syracuse U Pr.

— North American Boletes: A Color Guide to the Fleshy Pored Mushrooms. LC 99-21065. 1999. 95.00 (*0-8156-0588-9*) Syracuse U Pr.

— Wildflowers of Maine, New Hampshire & Vermont. LC 99-46641. (Illus.). 163p. 1999. 59.95 (*0-8156-2803-X*) Syracuse U Pr.

Bessette, Alan E., jt. auth. see Bessette, Arleen R.

Bessette, Alan E., jt. auth. see Fischer, David W.

Bessette, Arleen R. & Bessette, Alan E. Taming the Wild Mushroom: A Culinary Guide to Market Foraging. (Illus.). 125p. (Orig.). 1997. pap. 16.95 (*0-292-70856-4*) U of Tex Pr.

Bessette, Gerard. The Brawl. Lebel, Marc & Sutherland, Ronald, trs. LC 77-473823. (French Writers of Canada Ser.). 230p. reprint ed. pap. 71.30 (*0-8357-7384-1*, 202493100040) Bks Demand.

***Bessette, Gerard.** Not for Every Eye. 2nd ed. Shortliffe, Glen, tr. from FRE. (Picas Ser.: No. 20). Orig. Title: Le Libraire. 92p. 1999. reprint ed. pap. 7.00 (*1-55096-549-2*, Pub. by Exile Edns) Paul & Co Pubs.

Bessette, Guy & Rajasunderam, D. V. La Communication Participative pour le Developpement: Un Agenda Ouest-Africain. LC 97-701328. (FRE.). vi, 162p. 1996. pap. 17.95 (*0-88936-803-1*, Pub. by IDRC Bks) Stylus Pub VA.

Bessette, J. & Yelle, Henri. New Findings on the Loading of Plastic Spur Gear Teeth. (Nineteen Ninety-Two Fall Technical Meeting Ser.: Vol. 92FTM11). (Illus.). 8p. 1993. 30.00 (*1-55589-591-3*) AGMA.

Bessette, Joseph M. The Mild Voice of Reason: Deliberative Democracy & American National Government. LC 93-30669. 256p. (C). 1994. 32.50 (*0-226-04423-8*) U Ch Pr.

— The Mild Voice of Reason: Deliberative Democracy & American National Government. (American Politics & Political Economy Ser.). 1997. pap. text 15.95 (*0-226-04424-6*) U Ch Pr.

— Toward a More Perfect Union: Writings of Herbert J. Storing. LC 94-22771. 180p. 1995. pap. 14.95 (*0-8447-3840-9*) Am Enterprise.

***Bessette, Joseph M., ed.** Encyclopedia of American Government, 4 vols. LC 98-28986. (Illus.). 896p. 1998. lib. bdg. 210.00 (*0-89356-117-7*) Salem Pr.

***Bessette, Joseph M. & Pitney, John J., Jr.** American Government: Democracy & Citizenship. 2002. pap. write for info. (*0-312-24572-6*) St Martin.

Bessette, Joseph M., ed. see Salem Press Editors.

Bessette, Roland L. Mario Lanza: Tenor in Exile. LC 98-24135. (Illus.). 306p. 1999. 24.95 (*1-57467-044-1*, Amadeus Pr) Timber.

Bessey. Management of Trauma. Date not set. text. write for info. (*0-7216-5140-2*, W B Saunders Co) Harcrt Hlth Sci Grp.

***Bessey, Carolyn.** Battle of the WAC. (Illus.). 192p. 1999. per. 11.95 (*0-9670579-0-6*) C H Bessey.

Bessey, Carolyn, ed. see Larsen, Joan S.

Bessey, K. Michal. In Whose Interest? Telecommunications Privatization & Universal Service in Canada, Vol. I-97-2. unabridged ed. LC 98-129043. 29p. 1997. pap. text. write for info. (*1-879716-41-0*) Ctr Info Policy.

Bessey, M. A., ed. see Bradford, Gamaliel.

Bessey, Vance. Only in Maine. Raschack, Jason B., ed. (Illus.). 80p. (Orig.). 1993. pap. 9.95 (*1-885724-00-4*, 01) Edutainment Media.

***Bessho, Koro.** Identities & Security in East Asia. (Illus.). 86p. 1999. pap. text 26.00 (*0-19-922421-8*) OUP.

Bessie, Alvah C. Alvah Bessie's Short Fictions. LC 82-9739. 312p. (Orig.). 1982. pap. 7.95 (*0-88316-546-5*) Chandler & Sharp.

— Bread & a Stone. LC 83-7488. 352p. 1983. pap. 7.95 (*0-88316-553-8*) Chandler & Sharp.

— Spain Again. LC 74-28742. (Illus.). 242p. 1975. pap. 5.95 (*0-88316-516-3*) Chandler & Sharp.

Bessie, Alvah C. & Prago, Albert, eds. Our Fight: Writings by Veterans of the Abraham Lincoln Brigade, Spain 1936-1939. LC 87-5562. 320p. (C). 1987. pap. 12.00 (*0-85345-724-7*, Pub. by Monthly Rev) NYU Pr.

Bessie, Cornelia, ed. see Blumenthal, W. Michael.

Bessie, Cornelia, ed. see Meyer, Karl & Brysac, Shareen Blair.

***Bessie, Dan.** Rare Birds: An American Family. LC 00-28312. (Illus.). 272p. 2000. 25.00 (*0-8131-2179-5*) U Pr of Ky.

Bessie, Joseph & Glennan, Stuart. Elements of Deductive Inference. LC 98-48446. (Philosophy Ser.). 479p. 1999. pap. 55.95 (*0-534-55121-1*) Wadsworth Pub.

Bessie, Michael, ed. see Blumenthal, W. Michael.

Bessie, Michael, ed. see Meyer, Karl & Brysac, Shareen Blair.

Bessieres & Bougouint. Dictionary Hachette Benjamin CP-CE (6-8 Ans) (FRE.). 1998. 14.95 (*0-320-00412-0*) Fr & Eur.

Bessieres, Albert. Wife, Mother & Mystic: Blessed Anna Maria Taigi. Newton, Douglas, ed. Rigby, Stephen, tr. from FRE. 1977. reprint ed. pap. 8.00 (*0-89555-058-X*) TAN Bks Pubs.

***Bessin, Bernice.** Celebration at Sunset: Legacy of Love. 175p. 2000. pap. 14.95 (*0-934953-68-6*) Water Row Pr.

Bessinger, Donivan. Emerging from Chaos: Wholeness, Ethic, & New World Order. 1991. pap. write for info. (*0-9628594-3-5*, Wintergreen-Orchard) Riverside Pub Co.

— Religion Confronting Science: And There Was Light. (Illus.). 176p. 1991. 17.95 (*0-9628594-0-0*); pap. 10.95 (*0-9628594-1-9*) Orchard Pk Pr.

Bessinger, J. D., Jr. Beowulf: In Old English. abr. ed. 1996. audio 12.00 (*0-694-51701-1*, CPN 1161) HarperAudio.

Bessinger, Jess B. A Short Dictionary of Anglo-Saxon Poetry: In a Normalized Early West-Saxon Orthography. LC 61-2144. 105p. reprint ed. pap. 32.60 (*0-608-30146-9*, 202045400018) Bks Demand.

Bessinger, Jess B., Jr. & Yeager, Robert F., eds. Approaches to Teaching Beowulf. LC 83-22124. (Approaches to Teaching World Literature Ser.: No. 4). xvii, 214p. 1984. pap. 18.00 (*0-87352-482-9*, AP04P); lib. bdg. 37.50 (*0-87352-481-0*, AP04C) Modern Lang.

Bessire, Mark. Great Zimbabwe. LC 97-31289. (African Civilizations Ser.). 64p. (J). 1999. 22.50 (*0-531-20285-2*) Watts.

B

Bessire, Mark, et al. Sukuma. LC 96-38236. (Heritage Library of African Peoples: Set 3). (Illus.). 64p. (YA). (gr. 7-12). 1997. lib. bdg. 16.95 (0-8239-1992-7, D1992-7) Rosen Group.

***Bessire, Mark H. C. & Fistenberg, Lauri, eds.** Beyond Decorum: The Photography of Ike Ude. LC TR647.U33 2000. (Illus.). 152p. 2000. pap. 25.00 (0-262-52280-2) MIT Pr.

Bessis, Daniel, ed. see NATO Advanced Study Institute Staff.

Bessis, Joel. Risk Management in Banking. LC 97-25521. 448p. 1998. 120.95 (0-471-97465-X); pap. 54.95 (0-471-97466-8) Wiley.

Bessis, M., et al, eds. Red Cell Shape: Physiology, Pathology, Ultrastructure. LC 73-77351. (Illus.). 180p. 1973. 50.00 (0-387-06257-2) Spr-Verlag.

***Bessler, Ian, ed.** Songwriter's Market: 1,800 Places to Market Your Songs. 528p. 2000. pap. 23.99 (0-89879-980-5) F & W Pubns Inc.

Bessler, Joanne M. Putting "Service" into Library Staff Training: A Patron-Centered Guide. Tramdack, Phil, ed. LC 93-31055. (Occasional Papers - Library Administration & Management Association). 72p. (Orig.). 1994. pap. 20.00 (0-8389-3437-4) ALA.

Bessler, John D. Death in the Dark: Midnight Executions in America. (Illus.). 336p. 1997. pap. text 18.95 (1-55553-357-4) NE U Pr.

Bessman, Jim. Ramones: An American Band. 5th ed. LC 93-16437. (Illus.). 224p. (Orig.). 1993. pap. 16.95 (0-312-09369-1) St Martin.

Bessmer, Sue. The Laws of Rape. LC 84-18202. (Landmark Dissertations in Women's Studies). 400p. 1985. 65.00 (0-275-90061-4, C0061, Praeger Pubs) Greenwood.

Besso, Henry V. Dramatic Literature of the Sephardic Jews of Amsterdam in the XVII & XVIII Centuries. 118p. 1948. 1.00 (0-318-14257-0) Hispanic Inst.

Bessom, Linda. Thumbs Up! Teaching Interdependence to Grades 3 & 4. Keegan, Jane P., ed. (Illus.). 32p. 1989. teacher ed. 5.00 (0-941395-03-0) Maryknoll Wrld Prods.

Besson, Alain, ed. Thornton's Medical Books, Libraries & Collectors. (Illus.). 450p. 1990. text 99.95 (0-566-05481-7, Pub. by Gower) Ashgate Pub Co.

Besson, George. Andre Minaux. (Illus.). 72p. 1967. pap. 175.00 (1-55660-135-2) A Wofsy Fine Arts.

Besson, Gerard, et al. Riemannian Geometry. Lovric, Miroslav et al, eds. LC 95-47659. (Fields Institute Monographs: No. 4). 115p. 1996. text 46.00 (0-8218-0263-1, FIM/4) Am Math.

Besson, Jean-Louis. Livre de l'Histoire de France. (Gallimard - Decouverte Cadet Ser.: No. 25). (FRE.). 124p. (J). (gr. 4-9). 1986. 18.95 (2-07-039525-1) Schoenhof.

Besson, Jean-Marie, jt. ed. see Basbaum, A. I.

Besson, Patrick. Ah! Berlin et Autres Recits. (FRE.). 342p. 1989. pap. 12.95 (0-7859-2237-7, 207038117X) Fr & Eur.

Besson, Paul M. The Goldwater-Nichols Act: A Ten-Year Report Card, Vol. P-98-3. unabridged ed. (Illus.). 69p. 1998. pap. text. write for info. (1-879716-49-6) Ctr Info Policy.

Besson, Tannee S. & Besson, Taunee S. National Business Employment Weekly Guide to Cover Letters. 3rd ed. LC 98-50853. (Illus.). 304p. 1999. pap. 12.95 (0-471-32261-X) Wiley.

Besson, Taunee S., jt. auth. see Besson, Tannee S.

Besson, Taunee S., jt. auth. see National Business Employment Weekly Staff.

Bessonov, M. I. Aromatic Thermotropichi Fluid Crystal Polyesters. 1992. write for info. (0-8493-6703-4, CRC Reprint) Franklin.

— Polyamic Acids & Polyimides Synthesis Transformations Structures. 1993. lib. bdg. 219.00 (0-8493-6704-2, TP1180) CRC Pr.

Bessonov, M. I., et al. Polyimides: Thermally Stable Polymers. Wright, W. W., ed. Backinowsky, L. V. & Chlenov, M. A., trs. from RUS. LC 86-25155. (Macromolecular Compounds Ser.). (Illus.). 332p. (C). 1987. text 132.00 (0-306-10993-X, Kluwer Plenum) Kluwer Academic.

Besst, jt. auth. see Duke.

Best. Cognitive Psychology. 5th ed. LC 98-40566. (Psychology Ser.). (C). 1998. mass mkt. 78.95 (0-534-35417-3) Wadsworth Pub.

— Evidence. LC 93-86409. 1994. 23.95 (0-316-09285-1, Aspen Law & Bus) Aspen Pub.

— Phase-Locked Loops. 4th ed. LC 99-32414. (Professional Engineering Ser.). 408p. 1999. 65.00 (0-07-134903-0); 65.00 (0-07-134904-9) McGraw.

— Quality Supervision: Theory & Practice. (C). 1996. text 51.00 (0-7020-2121-0) Harcourt.

— Understanding Earth. 2nd ed. (C). 1997. pap. text, student ed. 20.95 (0-7167-2804-4) St Martin.

Best & Morey. The Assurance of Quality in Health Care. 1994. write for info. (0-08-042006-0, Pergamon Pr) Elsevier.

Best, jt. auth. see Hein.

Best, A. K. A. K.'s Fly Box. (Illus.). 208p. 1996. 40.00 (1-55821-362-7) Lyons Pr.

— Dyeing & Bleaching Natural Fly-Tying Materials. 144p. 1993. 24.95 (1-55821-214-0) Lyons Pr.

— Production Fly Tying: A Collection of Ideas, Notions, Hints & Variations on the Techniques of Fly Tying. LC 89-37103. (Illus.). 177p. 1989. pap. 29.95 (0-87108-792-8) Pruett.

Best, A. M., Staff. Best's Agents Guide. annuals 550p. 95.00 (0-685-11479-1) A M Best.

— Best's Aggregates & Averages: Life-Health Edition. annuals 75p. pap. 195.00 (0-685-43288-2) A M Best.

— Best's Aggregates & Averages: Property-Casualty Edition. annuals 300p. pap. 325.00 (0-685-11471-6) A M Best.

— Best's Insurance Reports. (Property-Casualty & Life-Health Editions Ser.). 2000p. 695.00 (0-317-53402-5) A M Best.

— Best's Insurance Reports. annuals 2000p. cd-rom 1195.00 (0-318-59845-0) A M Best.

— Best's Key Rating Guide. annuals (Property-Casualty & Life-Health Editions Ser.). 95.00 (0-317-53393-2) A M Best.

— Best's Safety Directory. annuals 1800p. pap. 49.95 (0-685-43285-8) A M Best.

— Best's State/Line Reports & Databases. 1994. ring bd. write for info. (0-318-59847-7); audio, cd-rom, disk. write for info. (0-318-59848-5) A M Best.

Best, Alan D. & Wolfshutz, Hans, eds. Modern Austrian Writing: Literature & Society after 1945. 307p. 1980. 44.00 (0-389-20038-7, 06810) B&N Imports.

Best, Alice, jt. auth. see Jackson, Dennis.

Best, Alyse. Miss Best's Etiquette for Young People. 1990. pap. write for info. (0-945033-02-8) PEP Pr.

***Best, Amy.** Prom Night: Youth & Popular Culture. 2000. pap. 19.99 (0-415-92428-6) Routledge.

— Prom Night: Youth Schools & Popular Culture. 224p. 2000. text 75.00 (0-415-92427-8) Routledge.

Best, Arthur. Evidence: Examples & Explanations. 2nd ed. (Examples & Explanations Ser.). 300p. 1996. pap. write for info. (1-56706-503-1, 65031) Panel Pubs.

— Evidence: Examples & Explanations. 3rd ed. LC 98-41909. 300p. 1998. pap. text 33.95 (0-7355-0240-4) Panel Pubs.

— Torts. LC 97-19844. 1997. pap. text 21.95 (1-56706-487-6) Aspen Law.

***Best, Arthur, et al.** Colorado Evidence Courtroom Manual 2000. rev. ed. 356p. 1999. pap. 42.50 (1-58360-121-X) Anderson Pub Co.

Best, Barbara. A Dream of Her Own. large type ed. (Linford Romance Library). 368p. 1997. pap. 16.99 (0-7089-7981-5, Linford) Ulverscroft.

— The Hound of Truran. large type ed. 1994. pap. 16.99 (0-7089-7601-8, Linford) Ulverscroft.

— Island in the Sun. large type ed. 1995. 27.99 (0-7089-3344-0) Ulverscroft.

— A Most Unusual Marriage. large type ed. (Linford Romance Library). 288p. 1997. pap. 16.99 (0-7089-5076-0, Linford) Ulverscroft.

— Second Spring. large type ed. (Large Print Ser.). 464p. 1996. 27.99 (0-7089-3549-4) Ulverscroft.

***Best, Barbara.** Till You Find Your Love. large type ed. 264p. 1999. 31.99 (0-7089-4141-9) Ulverscroft.

Best, Barbara. Tomorrow Is Ours. large type ed. (Linford Romance Library). 288p. 1997. pap. 16.99 (0-7089-5112-0, Linford) Ulverscroft.

— Wings of Destiny. large type ed. (Linford Romance Library). 272p. 1995. pap. 16.99 (0-7089-7737-5, Linford) Ulverscroft.

***Best, Bill.** From Existence to Essence. deluxe ed. 148p. 1999. pap. 14.95 (0-935680-70-5) Kentucke Imprints.

Best, Bill. The Great Appalachian Sperm Bank & Other Stories. LC 86-82566. (Illus.). 125p. (Orig.). 1986. pap. 6.95 (0-935680-32-2) Kentucke Imprints.

Best, Bill. One Hundred Years of Appalachian Visions. deluxe ed. 216p. 1997. pap. write for info. (0-935680-67-5) Kentucke Imprints.

Best, Bill. The Tragedy of Platitudinous Piety. (Illus.). 14p. (Orig.). 1982. pap. 2.50 (0-685-24883-6) Kentucke Imprints.

Best, Bob, jt. auth. see Pagna, Tom.

Best, Bonnie, jt. auth. see Williams, Patrick.

***Best-Boss, Angie.** Heart of a Shepherd: Meditations for New Pastors. LC 99-40029. 144p. 2000. pap. 13.00 (0-8170-1344-X) Judson.

Best-Boss, Angie. Surviving Your First Year As Pastor: What Seminary Couldn't Teach You. LC 98-49773. 1999. pap. 12.00 (0-8170-1300-8) Judson.

Best, Cari. Getting Used to Harry. LC 95-23176. (Illus.). 32p. (J). (ps-3). 1996. 15.95 (0-531-09494-4); lib. bdg. 16.99 (0-531-08794-8) Orchard Bks Watts.

— Last Licks: A Spaldeen Story. LC 97-43606. (Illus.). 40p. (YA). (gr. 1 up). 1999. text 15.95 (0-7894-2513-0, D K Ink) DK Pub Inc.

— Montezuma's Revenge. LC 99-11716. (Illus.). 32p. (J). (ps-2). 1999. 15.95 (0-531-30198-2); lib. bdg. 16.99 (0-531-33198-9) Orchard Bks Watts.

— Red Light, Green Light, Mama & Me. LC 94-33010. (Illus.). 32p. (J). (ps-2). 1995. lib. bdg. 16.99 (0-531-08752-2) Orchard Bks Watts.

— Red Light, Green Light, Mama & Me. LC 94-33010. (Illus.). 32p. (J). (ps-3). 1995. 15.95 (0-531-09452-9) Orchard Bks Watts.

***Best, Cari.** Shrinking Violet. LC 99-88966. (J). 2000. write for info. (0-7894-6531-0) DK Pub Inc.

Best, Cari. Taxi! Taxi! LC 96-21108. (Illus.). 32p. (J). (ps-3). 1997. pap. 6.95 (0-531-07084-0) Orchard Bks Watts.

— Three Cheers for Catherine the Great. LC 98-41153. (Illus.). 32p. (J). (ps-3). 1999. 16.95 (0-7894-2622-6) DK Pub Inc.

— Top Banana. LC 96-42286. (Illus.). 32p. (J). (ps-3). 1997. 15.95 (0-531-30009-9); lib. bdg. 16.99 (0-531-33009-5) Orchard Bks Watts.

***Best, Carl.** Last Licks: A Spaldeen Story. 40p. (J). 2000. pap. text 5.95 (0-7894-2656-0, D K Ink) DK Pub Inc.

Best, Caroline. Best of All Main Dish Salads. LC 93-80901. 175p. 1993. pap. 16.95 (0-9635257-1-9) Mt Ivy Pr.

Best, Clare & Boisset, Caroline, eds. Leaves from the Garden: Two Centuries of Garden Writing. (Illus.). 412p. 1987. 22.50 (0-393-02451-2) Norton.

Best, Clare, tr. see Morel, Gaud.

Best, D. J., jt. auth. see Rayner, J. C.

Best, David. The Fourth Resource: Information & Its Management. 182p. 1996. 74.95 (0-566-07696-9, Pub. by Gower) Ashgate Pub Co.

Best, David G. Portrait of a Racetrack: A Behind the Scenes Look at a Thoroughbred Horseracing Community. LC 92-97019. (Illus.). 96p. (Orig.). 1992. pap. 24.95 (0-9634241-0-6) Best Edits.

Best, Deborah L., jt. auth. see Williams, John E.

Best, Deborah L., jt. ed. see Intons-Peterson, Magaret J.

***Best, Don.** The Author's Guide to Marketing "Your Book" From Start to Success, for Writers & Publishers. 224p. 2000. pap. 16.95 (1-880656-46-9) Stone Bridge Pr.

— Do-It-Yourself Guide to Home Emergencies: From Breakdowns & Leaks to Cracks & Critters Step by-Step. LC 99-16795. 1999. pap. 15.95 (0-7621-0171-7, Pub. by RD Assn) Penguin Putnam.

Best, Don. Make a Mil-Yen: Teaching English in Japan. LC 93-44380. 176p. (Orig.). 1994. pap. 14.95 (1-880656-11-6) Stone Bridge Pr.

Best, Don & Freeman, Jim. Crystal Clarinets: A Coffee Table Book of Nice. LC 80-83629. (Illus.). 96p. (Orig.). (C). 1980. pap. 6.66 (0-938104-00-4) Cosmotic Concerns.

Best, E. & Fernandez, C. Nonsequential Processes. (EATCS Monographs on Theoretical Computer Science: Vol. 13). vii, 112p. 1988. 43.95 (0-387-19030-9) Spr-Verlag.

Best, E. P. & Baker, J. P., eds. Netherlands-Wetlands. LC 93-20965. (Developments in Hydrobiology Ser.: Vol. 88). 1993. text 267.50 (0-7923-2473-0) Kluwer Academic.

Best, E. P. & Haeck, J., eds. Ecological Indicators for the Assessment of the Quality of Air, Water, Soil, & Ecosystems. 1984. text 145.50 (90-277-1708-7) Kluwer Academic.

Best, Eike. Semenatics of Sequential & Parallel Programs. 352p. 1996. pap. 49.00 (0-13-460643-4) P-H.

Best, Eike, ed. Concurrency Theory--CONCUR '93: Proceedings of the 4th International Conference on Concurrency Theory, Hildesheim, Germany, August 1993. LC 93-30066. (Lecture Notes in Computer Science Ser.: Vol. 715). 1993. 73.95 (0-387-57208-2) Spr-Verlag.

Best, Elizabeth. Mr. McGillicuddy's Clocks. LC 93-26928. (Voyages Ser.). (Illus.). (J). 1994. 4.25 (0-383-03765-4) SRA McGraw.

— What Happened to Aunt Cordelia? LC 93-167. (Voyages Ser.). (Illus.). (J). 1994. write for info. (0-383-03725-5) SRA McGraw.

Best, Elsdon. Astronomical Knowledge of the Maori. LC 75-35226. 1922. reprint ed. 39.50 (0-404-14405-5) AMS Pr.

— Fishing Methods & Devices of the Maori. LC 75-35228. reprint ed. 52.50 (0-404-14406-3) AMS Pr.

— Forest Lore of the Maori. LC 75-35229. reprint ed. 61.50 (0-404-14407-1) AMS Pr.

— The Maori, 2 vols., Set. LC 75-35231. reprint ed. 165.00 (0-404-14310-5) AMS Pr.

— Maori Canoe. LC 75-35234. 1923. reprint ed. 74.50 (0-404-14411-X) AMS Pr.

— Maori Religion & Mythology. LC 75-35236. reprint ed. 62.50 (0-404-14412-8) AMS Pr.

Best, Ernest E. Ephesians. (International Critical Commentary Ser.). 704p. 1998. 69.95 (0-567-08565-1, Pub. by T & T Clark) Bks Intl VA.

— Essays on Ephesians. 224p. 1998. 44.95 (0-567-08566-X, Pub. by T & T Clark) Bks Intl VA.

— The First & Second Epistles to the Thessalonians. (Black's New Testament Commentary Ser.: No. 13). 392p. 1993. 24.95 (1-56563-019-X) Hendrickson MA.

Best, Ernest E. 1 Peter. (New Century Bible Ser.). 188p. 1971. pap. 14.95 (0-551-00989-6, Pub. by Sheffield Acad) CUP Services.

— Following Jesus: Discipleship in Mark's Gospel. (JSNT Supplement Ser.: No. 4). 283p. 1981. 80.00 (0-905774-28-0, Pub. by Sheffield Acad) CUP Services.

Best, Ernest E. Following Jesus: Discipleship in Mark's Gospel. (JSNT Supplement Ser.: No. 4). 283p. 1981. pap. 28.50 (0-905774-29-9, Pub. by Sheffield Acad) CUP Services.

Best, Ernest E. Disciples & Discipleship: Studies in the Gospel According to Mark. 256p. 1986. 39.95 (0-567-09369-7, Pub. by T & T Clark) Bks Intl VA.

— Ephesians. (New Testament Guides Ser.: No. 10). 102p. 1993. pap. 12.50 (1-85075-716-X, Pub. by Sheffield Acad) CUP Services.

— From Text to Sermon. 1996. pap. 19.95 (0-567-29143-X) Bks Intl VA.

— Interpreting Christ. 208p. 1993. pap. text 27.95 (0-567-29215-0, Pub. by T & T Clark) Bks Intl VA.

— Mark: The Gospel As Story. Riches, John E., ed. 164p. 1989. pap. 24.95 (0-567-29153-7, Pub. by T & T Clark) Bks Intl VA.

— Paul & His Converts. 192p. (C). 1988. 39.95 (0-567-09147-3) Bks Intl VA.

— Religion & Society in Transition: The Church & Social Change in England, 1560-1850. LC 82-21699. (Texts & Studies in Religion: Vol. 15). 353p. 1982. lib. bdg. 99.95 (0-88946-804-4) E Mellen.

— Second Corinthians. LC 86-45404. (Interpretation: A Bible Commentary for Teaching & Preaching Ser.). 156p. 1987. 21.00 (0-8042-3135-4) Westminster John Knox.

Best, Ernest E. & Wilson, R. McL., eds. Text & Interpretation: Studies in the New Testament. LC 78-2962. 286p. reprint ed. pap. 81.60 (0-608-12300-5, 2024416) Bks Demand.

Best, Ethel. Nutrient-Drug Interactions. Boykin, Lorraine S., ed. (Illus.). 121p. (Orig.). (C). 1988. pap. text 20.00 (0-317-91261-5); lib. bdg. 10.00 (0-317-91260-7) E Best Pubg.

Best, Felton O. Crossing the Color Line: A Biography of Paul Laurence Dunbar, 1872-1906. LC 96-210203. 200p. (C). 1996. pap. text, per. 32.95 (0-7872-2234-8, 41223401) Kendall-Hunt.

Best, Felton O., ed. Black Religious Leadership from the Slave Community to the Million Man March: Flames of Fire. LC 98-7594. (Black Studies: Vol. 3). 272p. 1998. pap. 89.95 (0-7734-8345-4) E Mellen.

— Black Resistance Movements in the United States & Africa, 1800-1993: Oppression & Retaliation. LC 95-1888. 344p. 1995. text 99.95 (0-7734-9053-1) E Mellen.

Best, Frank E. Amidon: A Record of the Descendants of Roger Amadowne of Rehobeth, MA. 165p. 1994. reprint ed. pap. 26.00 (0-8328-4292-3); reprint ed. lib. bdg. 36.00 (0-8328-4291-5) Higginson Bk Co.

Best, Frank E. & Nye, G. S. Genealogy of the Nye Family. Nye, D. F., ed. (Illus.). 704p. 1989. reprint ed. pap. 99.00 (0-8328-0911-X); reprint ed. lib. bdg. 107.00 (0-8328-0910-1) Higginson Bk Co.

Best, Franklin L., Jr. Pennsylvania Insurance Law. LC 90-84169. 1999. ring bd. 109.50 (1-887024-55-7) Bisel Co.

Best, Fred. Flexible Life Scheduling: Breaking the Education-Work-Retirement Lockstep. LC 80-160. 267p. 1980. 65.00 (0-275-90454-7, C0454, Praeger Pubs) Greenwood.

— Reducing Workweeks to Prevent Layoffs: The Economic & Social Impacts of Unemployment Insurance Supported Work Sharing. LC 87-10097. 228p. (C). 1988. 49.95 (0-87722-506-0) Temple U Pr.

— Work Sharing: Issues, Policy Options & Prospects. LC 81-7567. 204p. 1981. text 14.00 (0-911558-79-9); pap. text 8.00 (0-911558-80-2) W E Upjohn.

Best, G. A., et al, eds. International River Water Quality. (Illus.). 496p. 1997. pap. 175.00 (0-419-21540-9, E & FN Spon) Routledge.

Best, Gary D. The Critical Press & the New Deal: The Press Versus Presidential Power, 1933-38. LC 92-31715. 216p. 1993. 55.00 (0-275-94350-X, C4350, Praeger Pubs) Greenwood.

Best, Gary D. FDR & the Bonus Marchers, 1933-1935. LC 92-1194. 168p. 1992. 55.00 (0-275-93715-1, C3715, Praeger Pubs) Greenwood.

Best, Gary D. Herbert Hoover: The Postpresidential Years, 1933-1964, 2 Vols., Set. (Publication Ser.: No. 276). 538p. 1983. 75.00 (0-8179-7761-9) Hoover Inst Pr.

— The Nickel & Dime Decade: American Popular Culture During the 1930s. LC 93-2855. 184p. 1993. 49.95 (0-275-94395-X, C4395, Praeger Pubs) Greenwood.

— The Politics of American Individualism: Herbert Hoover in Transition, 1918-1921. LC 75-16960. 202p. 1975. 52.95 (0-8371-8160-7, BPA/, Greenwood Pr) Greenwood.

— Pride, Prejudice, & Politics: Roosevelt Versus Recovery, 1933-1938. LC 90-38841. 288p. 1990. 65.00 (0-275-93524-8, C3524, Praeger Pubs) Greenwood.

— To Free a People: American Jewish Leaders & the Jewish Problem in Eastern Europe, 1890 to 1914, 98. LC 81-4265. (Contributions in American History Ser.: No. 98). 240p. 1982. 38.50 (0-313-22532-X, BTO/, Greenwood Pr) Greenwood.

— Witch Hunt in Wise County: The Persecution of Edith Maxwell. LC 94-12351. 192p. 1994. 55.00 (0-275-94892-7, Praeger Pubs) Greenwood.

Best, Geoffrey. The Permanent Revolution: The French Revolution & Its Legacy, 1789-1989. LC 88-26181. 241p. Date not set. reprint ed. pap. 74.80 (0-608-21013-7, 205454100003) Bks Demand.

— War & Law since 1945. 450p. 1997. reprint ed. pap. text 21.00 (0-19-820699-2) OUP.

— War & Society in Revolutionary Europe, 1770-1870. 336p. 1998. pap. 19.95 (0-7735-1761-8, Pub. by McG-Queens Univ Pr) CUP Services.

Best, Geoffrey, ed. The Permanent Revolution: The French Revolution & Its Legacy, 1789-1989. LC 88-26181. 256p. 1994. lib. bdg. 24.95 (0-226-04427-0) U Ch Pr.

— The Permanent Revolution: The French Revolution & Its Legacy, 1789-1989. LC 88-26181. 156p. 1996. pap. text 13.50 (0-226-04428-9) U Ch Pr.

Best, Geoffrey F. Honour among Men & Nations: Transformations of an Idea. LC 83-107843. (Joanne Goodman Lectures: No. 1981). 122p. reprint ed. pap. 37.90 (0-8357-3632-6, 203636000003) Bks Demand.

Best, George W. Problem Solving with Pascal. 209p. 1992. 25.00 (1-886018-01-4) Venture Pubng.

Best, George W. & Fischback, Sally. Using the TI-85 to Explore Precalculus & Calculus. 198p. (C). 1994. 25.00 (1-886018-05-7) Venture Pubng.

Best, George W. & Fischbeck, Sally. AP Calculus with the TI-82 Graphics Calculator. 222p. 1995. 27.00 (1-886018-07-3) Venture Pubng.

Best, George W. & Penner, David A. Calculus. 550p. (YA). (gr. 12). 1992. 48.00 (1-886018-00-6) Venture Pubng.

— Exploring Precalculus & Calculus with the TI-81 Graphics Calculator. 188p. (C). 1993. 25.00 (1-886018-04-9) Venture Pubng.

— Using the TI-82 to Explore Precalculus & Calculus. 204p. 1994. write for info. (1-886018-06-5) Venture Pubng.

Best, Gerald. Nevada County Narrow Gauge. 216p. 1998. 39.95 (0-911581-46-4) Heimburger Hse Pub.

***Best, Gerry.** Environmental Pollution Studies. 156p. 1999. 15.95 (0-85323-923-1, Pub. by Liverpool Univ Pr) Intl Spec Bk.

Best, Gerry, et al, eds. Pesticides - Developments, Impacts, & Controls: Proceedings: Analytical Division's Symposium of the Royal Society of Chemistry Annual Chemical Congress (1995: Edinburgh, UK) 180p. 1995. 78.00 (0-85404-785-9, SB) CRC Pr.

Best Guides Staff. Britain's Top 2000 Days Out: Millennium 99/2000 Ed. 1999. pap. text 12.95 (1-901258-32-7) Best Guides.

— London's Top 500 Days Out: Millennium 99/2000 Ed. 1999. pap. text 7.95 (1-901258-33-5) Best Guides.

Best, Harold. Music Through the Eyes of Faith. LC 92-53911. 240p. 1993. pap. 15.00 (*0-06-060862-5*, Pub. by Harper SF) HarpC.

***Best, Heinrich & Cotta, Maurizio, eds.** Parliamentary Representatives in Europe 1848-2000: Legislative Recruitment & Careers in Eleven European Countries. LC 99-87409. 420p. 2000. text 95.00 (*0-19-829793-9*) OUP.

Best, Henry. The Farming & Memorandum Books of Henry Best of Elmswell, 1642. (British Academy Records of Social & Economic History Ser.). (Illus.). 426p. 1985. 62.00 (*0-19-726029-2*) OUP.

Best, Hugh. Adventures in the Pen Trade. LC 98-75591. (Illus.). 318p. 1999. pap. 15.00 (*0-9668213-0-0*) H Best.

Best, Inc. Staff. Black Males: An African American View on Raising Young Men. 160p. 1994. per. 16.95 (*0-8403-9482-9*) Kendall-Hunt.

Best, Inc. Staff & Alston, Harvey. Book of Wisdom for Speakers. 64p. 1994. pap. text, per. 2.10 (*0-8403-9756-9*) Kendall-Hunt.

— Book Wisdom for Teachers. 64p. 1996. pap. text, per. 2.10 (*0-8403-9755-0*) Kendall-Hunt.

Best, Isaac O. History of the 121st New York State Infantry. 2nd ed. (Army of the Potomac Ser.). (Illus.). 288p. 1996. 35.00 (*0-935523-52-9*) Butternut & Blue.

Best, J. The Digital Organization: Allied Signal's Success with Business Technology. LC 96-34960. 234p. 1997. 29.95 (*0-471-16159-4*) Wiley.

Best, J. L. & Bristow, C. S., eds. Braided Rivers. (Geological Society Special Publications: No. 75). (Illus.). 432p. (C). 1993. 108.00 (*0-903317-93-1*, 289, Pub. by Geol Soc Pub Hse) AAPG.

Best, James. Another Way to Live: Experiencing Intentional Community. LC 78-51384. 32p. (Orig.). 1978. pap. 4.00 (*0-87574-218-1*) Pendle Hill.

Best, James J. American Popular Illustration: A Reference Guide. LC 83-14150. (American Popular Culture Ser.). 171p. 1984. lib. bdg. 55.00 (*0-313-23389-6*, BEI/, Greenwood Pr) Greenwood.

Best, Jan G. & De Vries, Nanny M., eds. Interaction & Acculturation in the Mediterranean, Vol. 1. (Publications of the Henri Frankfort Foundation: Vol. 6). xv, 221p. (Orig.). 1980. pap. 42.00 (*90-6032-194-4*, Pub. by B R Gruner) Humanities.

— Interaction & Acculturation in the Mediterranean, Vol. 2. 238p. (Orig.). 1982. pap. 60.00 (*90-6032-195-2*, Pub. by B R Gruner) Humanities.

Best, Joel. Controlling Vice: Regulating Brothel Prostitution in St. Paul, 1865-1883. LC 98-26486. (History of Crime & Criminal Justice Ser.). xiv, 175p. 1998. pap. text 16.95 (*0-8142-5007-6*, BESCOX) Ohio St U Pr.

— Controlling Vice: Regulating Brothel Prostitution in St. Paul, 1865-1883. LC 98-26486. (History of Crime & Criminal Justice Ser.). 184p. 1999. text 42.50 (*0-8142-0807-X*, BESCON) Ohio St U Pr.

— Random Violence: Worrying about New Crimes & New Victims. LC 98-6234. 1999. 45.00 (*0-520-21571-0*, Pub. by U CA Pr) Cal Prin Full Svc.

— Random Violence: Worrying about New Crimes & New Victims. LC 98-6234. 237p. 1999. 17.95 (*0-520-21572-9*, Pub. by U CA Pr) Cal Prin Full Svc.

— Threatened Children: Rhetoric & Concern about Child-Victims. LC 89-48508. (Illus.). xii, 244p. (C). 1993. pap. text 13.00 (*0-226-04426-2*) U Ch Pr.

— Threatened Children: Rhetoric & Concern about Child-Victims. LC 89-48508. (Illus.). 256p. 1994. 29.95 (*0-226-04425-4*) U Ch Pr.

Best, Joel, ed. Images of Issues: Typifying Contemporary Social Problems. 2nd ed. (Social Problems & Social Issues Ser.). 371p. 1995. pap. text 27.95 (*0-202-30539-2*); lib. bdg. 51.95 (*0-202-30538-4*) Aldine de Gruyter.

— Troubling Children: Children & Social Problems. (Social Problems & Social Issues Ser.). 259p. 1994. pap. text 25.95 (*0-202-30492-2*); lib. bdg. 49.95 (*0-202-30491-4*) Aldine de Gruyter.

Best, Joel & Luckenbill, David F. Organizing Deviance. 2nd ed. LC 93-19690. 292p. (C). 1993. pap. text 25.20 (*0-13-336355-4*) P-H.

Best, Joey. Sedona's Best Guide Book 1999/2000, Vol. 7. 7th ed. (Illus.). 116p. 1999. pap. 9.95 (*1-56457-003-7*) Best Vid AZ.

***Best, Joey.** Sedona;s Best Guidebook Vol. 8: 2000/2001. 116p. 2000. pap. 5.00 (*1-56457-004-5*) Best Vid AZ.

Best, John B. Cognitive Psychology. 3rd ed. Baxter & Crochiere, eds. 550p. (C). 1992. text 48.75 (*0-314-90894-3*) West Pub.

— Cognitive Psychology. 4th ed. LC 94-31727. 508p. (C). 1994. mass mkt. 54.50 (*0-314-04445-0*) West Pub.

Best, John H., ed. Historical Inquiry in Education: A Research Agenda. LC 82-74458. 317p. reprint ed. pap. 98.30 (*0-7837-2988-X*, 205246200006) Bks Demand.

Best, John W. & Kahn, James V. Research in Education. 8th ed. LC 96-53399. 507p. 1997. 77.00 (*0-205-18697-1*) Allyn.

— Research in Education: Instructor's Manual with Test Items. 8th ed. (C). 1997. text, teacher ed. write for info. (*0-205-18698-X*, H8698-6) Allyn.

Best, Jonathan W. Philippines A Journey Through the Archipelago. 1997. 39.95 (*981-3018-99-2*) Tuttle Pubng.

Best, Judah. The Foreign Corrupt Practices Act: A Compliance Approach. LC 99-165625. 36 p. 1997. pap. write for info. (*0-937299-60-X*) Natl Legal Ctr Pub Interest.

Best, Judith A. The Mainstream of Western Political Thought. LC 80-11042. 149p. 1980. pap. text 23.95 (*0-87705-243-3*, Kluwer Acad Hman Sci) Kluwer Academic.

— The Mainstream of Western Political Thought. LC 97-13010. 152p. 1997. pap. 24.50 (*0-7618-0770-5*) U Pr of Amer.

Best, Judith A. & Hatch, Orrin G. National Representation for the District of Columbia. LC 83-21721. 85p. 1984. lib. bdg. 59.95 (*0-313-27083-X*, U7083, Greenwood Pr) Greenwood.

Best, Judith A. & McWilliams, Wilson C., eds. The Choice of the People? Debating the Electoral College. (Enduring Questions in American Political Life Ser.). 192p. (C). 1996. pap. text 17.95 (*0-8476-8217-X*); lib. bdg. 51.00 (*0-8476-8216-1*) Rowman.

Best, Katherine & Brubaker, Louis, eds. Passages of Light: Quotations from "A New Way of Living" the Series. (YA). (gr. 6-12). 1995. pap. 6.95 (*1-56266-109-4*) Anwol.

Best, Katrina, ed. see Franklin, Venus.

Best, L. J. The Belmont Murders. LC 91-33036. 1991. pap. 13.95 (*0-87949-353-4*) Ashley Bks.

Best, Larry & Bacon, Terry R. Writing R&D Proposals. (Illus.). 166p. 1994. write for info. (*1-57740-007-0*, ILW006) Intl LrningWrk.

Best, Leo R., jt. auth. see Johnson.

***Best, Marshall W.** Through the Prophet's Eye. 700p. 2000. pap. 29.99 (*1-57921-246-8*, 924-178, Pub. by WinePress Pub) BookWorld.

Best-Martini, Elizabeth, jt. auth. see Cunninghis, Richelle N.

Best, Mary A. Rebel Saints. LC 68-55839. (Essay Index Reprint Ser.). 1977. 20.95 (*0-8369-0205-X*) Ayer.

Best-Maugard, Adolfo. Method for Creative Design. (Illus.). 192p. 1990. pap. 5.95 (*0-486-26436-X*) Dover.

Best, Melvin L., Jr., et al, eds. Strategic Stability in the Post-Cold War World & the Future of Nuclear Disarmament: Proceedings of the NATO Advanced Research Workshop, Washington, D.C., U. S. A., April 6-10, 1995. (Partnership Sub-Series 1: Disarmament Technologies: Vol. 3, No. 1). 352p. (C). 1995. lib. bdg. 184.00 (*0-7923-3805-7*) Kluwer Academic.

Best, Michael H. The New Competition: Institutions of Industrial Restructuring. LC 90-34371. (Illus.). 304p. 1990. 42.50 (*0-674-60925-5*) HUP.

— The New Competition: Institutions of Industrial Restructuring. (Illus.). 320p. (C). 1993. pap. 21.50 (*0-674-60926-3*) HUP.

Best, Michael R. & Brightman, Frank H., eds. The Book of Secrets of Albertus Magnus: Of the Virtues of Herbs, Stones & Certain Beasts, Also a Book of the Marvels of the World. LC 99-35005. (Illus.). 176p. 1999. pap. 14.95 (*0-87728-925-5*) Weiser.

***Best, Michael R. & Brightman, Frank H., eds.** The Book of Secrets of Albertus Magnus: Of the Virtues of Herbs, Stones & Certain Beasts, Also a Book of the Marvels of the World. 176p. 2000. pap. 14.95 (*0-87728-941-7*) Weiser.

Best, Michael R., ed. see Markham, Gervase.

Best, Myron G. Igneous & Metamorphic Petrology. 630p. 1995. 74.95 (*0-86542-498-5*) Blackwell Sci.

***Best, Myron G. & Christiansen, Eric H.** Igneous Petrology. (Illus.). 450p. 2000. pap. 69.95 (*0-86542-541-8*) Blackwell Sci.

Best, Nicholas. Historic Britain from the Air. (Illus.). 160p. 1995. text 35.00 (*0-86565-965-6*) Vendome.

— The King & Queens of England. LC 95-77250. (Illus.). 96p. 1996. 9.95 (*0-8212-2255-4*, Pub. by Bulfinch Pr) Little.

***Best, Nicholas.** The Kings & Queens of Scotland. 96p. 1999. 9.95 (*0-297-82489-9*) Weidenfeld & Nicolson.

Best, Nicholas. The Presidents of U. S. A. (Illus.). 96p. 1996. 8.95 (*0-8212-2256-2*, Pub. by Bulfinch Pr) Little.

Best, Norman. A Celebration of Work. Robbins, William G., ed. & intro. by. LC 89-30401. (Illus.). xviii, 241p. 1990. text 35.00 (*0-8032-1212-7*) U of Nebr Pr.

— A Celebration of Work. Robbins, William G., ed. & intro. by. LC 89-30401. (Illus.). xviii, 241p. (C). 1996. pap. 12.00 (*0-8032-6127-6*, Bison Books) U of Nebr Pr.

Best, Otto F. Handbuch literarischer Fachbegriffe. (GER.). 624p. 1994. pap. 24.25 (*3-596-11958-8*, Pub. by Fischer Tasch) Intl Bk Import.

Best, P. Implementing Value at Risk. LC 98-4098. 222p. 1998. 85.00 (*0-471-97205-3*) Wiley.

Best, Pat, ed. see Trostel, Scott D.

Best, Patricia, jt. auth. see Sarlos, Andrew.

Best, Pete & Doncaster, Patrick. Beatle! The Pete Best Story. 192p. 1994. per. 14.95 (*0-85965-077-4*, Pub. by Plexus) Publishers Group.

Best Places Editors, ed. Seattle Cheap Eats: 300 Terrific Bargain Eateries. 6th ed. (Best Places Ser.). (Illus.). 224p. 1998. pap. 15.95 (*1-57061-148-3*) Sasquatch Bks.

Best Practices Project Staff. Guidelines for Family Support Practice. LC 96-26929. (Guidelines for Effective Practice Ser.). 128p. (Orig.). 1996. pap. text 35.00 (*1-885429-14-2*) Family Resource.

Best Publishing Co. Staff, ed. Diving Inspection Personnel Log Book. 210p. (C). 1989. text 21.00 (*0-941332-15-2*, D308) Best Pub Co.

— Professional Diver's Log Book. 224p. (C). 1986. text 21.00 (*0-941332-01-2*, D019) Best Pub Co.

— U. S. Navy Diver's Handbook. (Illus.). 212p. (C). 1995. text 27.50 (*0-941332-16-0*, D005) Best Pub Co.

Best Publishing Co. Staff & College of Oceaneering Staff, eds. Commercial Diver Training Manual. (Illus.). 362p. (C). 1996. text 39.75 (*0-941332-10-1*, D263) Best Pub Co.

Best, R. I. Bibliography of Whitley Stokes Works on the Celtic Language & Literature. 1987. pap. text 17.50 (*0-89979-041-0*) British Am Bks.

Best, R. S. The Life of Passmore Edwards. (C). 1989. text 45.00 (*0-907566-18-9*, Pub. by Dyllansow Truran) St Mut.

Best, R. S., ed. Clay Country Remembered: Recollections of a St. Austell Boyhood. (C). 1989. 50.00 (*1-85022-022-0*, Pub. by Dyllansow Truran) St Mut.

Best, Raphaela. We've All Got Scars: What Boys & Girls Learn in Elementary School. LC 82-49198. 192p. 1983. 27.50 (*0-253-36420-5*) Ind U Pr.

Best, Richard A., Jr. Co-Operation with Like-Minded Peoples: British Influences on American Security Policy, 1945-1949, 116. LC 85-27306. (Contributions in American History Ser.: No. 116). 236p. 1986. 55.00 (*0-313-24850-8*, BCT/) Greenwood.

Best, Richard I. Bibliography of the Works of Kuno Meyer on Celtic Language & Literature. 1996. pap. 15.00 (*0-89979-079-8*) British Am Bks.

Best, Robert M. Noah's Ark & the Ziusudra Epic: Sumerian Origins of the Flood Myth. LC 98-93918. 304p. 1999. text 38.00 (*0-9667840-1-4*) Enlil Pr.

***Best, Rod.** Towards Excellence: Understanding the Keyboard - For Beginners to Advanced. 273p. 1998. 27.00 (*0-9577651-0-X*) Heart of God Ministries.

— Towards Excellence - Building a Strong Worship Team. 175p. 1998. 22.00 (*0-9577651-1-8*) Heart of God Ministries.

***Best, Roger J.** Market-Based Management: Strategies for Growing Customer Value & Profitability. 2nd ed. LC 99-37126. (Illus.). 385p. 1999. pap. 51.00 (*0-13-014546-7*) P-H.

Best, Roland E. Phase-Locked Loops: Theory, Design, & Applications. 3rd ed. (Illus.). 365p. 1996. text 60.00 incl. disk (*0-07-006051-7*) McGraw.

***Best, Ron.** Education for Spiritual, Moral, Social & Cultural Development. 2000. pap. 31.95 (*0-304-70696-5*) Continuum.

Best, Ron, ed. Education, Spirituality, & the Whole Child. (Studies in Pastoral Care, Personal & Social Education). 320p. 1996. 90.00 (*0-304-33533-9*); pap. 39.95 (*0-304-33534-7*) Continuum.

Best, Ron, et al, eds. Caring for Children: International Perspectives on Pastoral Care & Personal & Social Education. LC 95-186705. (Studies in Pastoral Care, Personal & Social Education). (Illus.). 224p. 1994. text 100.00 (*0-304-32754-9*); pap. text 35.95 (*0-304-32752-2*) Continuum.

Best, Ron, et al. Pastoral Care & PSE: Entitlement & Provision. (Cassell Studies in Pastoral Care & PSE). (Illus.). 256p. 1995. pap. 39.95 (*0-304-32780-8*) Continuum.

— Pastoral Care & PSE: Entitlement & Provision. Lodge, Caroline, ed. (Cassell Studies in Pastoral Care & PSE). (Illus.). 352p. 1995. 100.00 (*0-304-32781-6*) Continuum.

Best, Ron, ed. see McGuiness, John.

Best, Ron, ed. see Whitaker, Patrick.

Best, Steven. Bestie Things in Life. 1999. 7.00 (*0-7117-1046-5*) Seven Hills Bk.

— The Politics of Historical Vision: Marx, Foucalt, Habermas. LC 94-44894. (Critical Perspectives Ser.). 294p. 1995. lib. bdg. 37.95 (*0-89862-851-2*) Guilford Pubns.

— The Politics of Historical Vision: Marx, Foucault, Habermas. LC 94-44894. (Critical Perspectives Ser.). 294p. 1996. pap. text 17.95 (*1-57230-145-7*, 0145) Guilford Pubns.

Best, Steven & Kellner, Douglas. Postmodern Theory. LC 91-2634. (Critical Perspectives Ser.). 256p. 1991. pap. 18.95 (*0-89862-418-5*); lib. bdg. 42.00 (*0-89862-412-6*) Guilford Pubns.

Best, Steven & Kellner, Douglas. Postmodern Theory: Critical Interrogations LC 92-173607. (Communications & Culture Ser.). xi, 324 p. 1991. write for info. (*0-333-48844-X*) Trans-Atl Phila.

Best, Steven & Kellner, Douglas. The Postmodern Turn. LC 97-15234. (Critical Perspectives Ser.). 306p. 1997. pap. 18.95 (*1-57230-221-6*, 0221); lib. bdg. 40.00 (*1-57230-220-8*, 0220) Guilford Pubns.

Best, Terence, ed. Handel Collections & Their History. (Illus.). 270p. (C). 1993. text 59.00 (*0-19-816299-5*) OUP.

Best, Thomas W. Jacob Bidermann. LC 74-2015. (Twayne's World Authors Ser.). 244p. (C). 1975. 20.95 (*0-8057-2154-1*) Irvington.

— Macropedius. LC 70-185265. (Twayne's World Authors Ser.). 185p. (C). 1972. 20.95 (*0-8290-1755-0*) Irvington.

***Best, Tina McKay.** Fluoroscopy Manual for Pain Management. (Illus.). 178p. 2000. pap. text 80.00 (*0-9678176-0-9*) Pain Mgmt.

Best, Tony. Teaching Children with Visual Impairments. (Children with Special Needs Ser.). 160p. 1991. pap. 34.95 (*0-335-15989-3*) OpUniv Pr.

***Best, Victoria.** Critical Subjectivities: Identity & Narrative in the Work of Colette & Marguerite Duras. (Modern French Identities Ser.: Vol. 5). 243p. 2000. pap. text 40.95 (*0-8204-4631-9*) P Lang Pubng.

***Best, Victoria & Collier, Peter, eds.** Powerful Bodies: Performance in French Cultural Studies. LC 99-40046. (Modern French Identities Ser.: Vol. 1). 220p. (C). 1999. pap. text 32.95 (*0-8204-4239-9*) P Lang Pubng.

Best, Walter, ed. see Pratt, Virginia A.

Best, William. The Churches Plea for Her Right. LC 76-57357. (English Experience Ser.: No. 776). 1977. reprint ed. lib. bdg. 25.00 (*90-221-0776-0*) Walter J Johnson.

Bestard-Camps, Joan. What's in a Relative? Household & Family in Formentera. (Explorations in Anthropology Ser.). 230p. 1991. 25.00 (*0-85496-586-6*) Berg Pubs.

Bestavros, Azer, et al, eds. Real-Time Database Systems: Issues & Applications. LC 97-9510. (International Series in Engineering & Computer Science, Real-Time Systems). 1997. text 152.50 (*0-7923-9897-1*) Kluwer Academic.

Bestavros, Azer & Fay-Wolfe, Victor. Real-Time Database & Information Systems: Research Advances, Vol. 420. LC 97-29142. (Real-Life Systemnational Series in Engineering & Computer Systems). 448p. 1997. text 159.50 (*0-7923-8011-8*) Kluwer Academic.

Bestavros, Azer, jt. auth. see Mueller, Frank.

Beste, J. Richard. Wabash, or Adventures of an English Gentleman's Family in the Interior of America, 2 Vols. LC 75-121498. (Select Bibliographies Reprint Ser.). 1977. 66.95 (*0-8369-5456-4*) Ayer.

Besteman, Catherine. Land Tenure in the Middle Jubba Valley Somalia: Customary Tenure & the Effect of Land Registration. (Research Paper Ser.: Vol. 104). (Illus.). xv, 106p. (C). 1990. pap. 7.00 (*0-934519-14-5*, RP104) U of Wis Land.

— Unraveling Somalia: Race, Violence, & the Legacy of Slavery. LC 98-33372. 1999. 42.50 (*0-8122-3488-X*) U of Pa Pr.

***Besteman, J. C., et al.** The Excavation near Wijnaldum: Reports on Friesland in Roman & Medieval Times. (Illus.). 352p. (C). 2000. text 41.00 (*90-5410-488-0*, Pub. by A A Balkema) Ashgate Pub Co.

***Bester, Alfred.** The Deceivers. (J). 1999. per. 14.00 (*0-671-03889-3*) S&S Trade.

Bester, Alfred. The Demolished Man. 1996. pap. 11.00 (*0-679-76781-9*) Random.

— The Demolished Man. 1993. reprint ed. lib. bdg. 25.95 (*0-89968-329-0*, Lghtyr Pr) Buccaneer Bks.

— Starlight: The Great Short Fiction of Alfred Bester. 1993. reprint ed. lib. bdg. 18.95 (*1-56849-249-9*) Buccaneer Bks.

— The Stars My Destination. 1996. pap. 12.00 (*0-679-76780-0*) Random.

— The Stars My Destination. 1993. reprint ed. lib. bdg. 25.95 (*0-89968-328-2*, Lghtyr Pr) Buccaneer Bks.

— Virtual Unrealities: The Short Fiction of Alfred Bester. LC 97-8738. 384p. 1997. pap. 14.00 (*0-679-76783-5*) Random.

Bester, Alfred & Zelazny, Roger. Psycho Shop. LC 98-6111. 256p. 1998. pap. 12.00 (*0-679-76782-7*) Random.

Bester, Alfred, et al. Hell's Cartographers: Some Personal Histories of Science Fiction Writers. LC 76-353865. 246 p. 1975. 3.50 (*0-297-76882-4*) Weidenfeld & Nicolson.

Bester, Hollis H. Sanitation - Practices & Methods for Health Protection & Disease Prevention: Index of New Information. 160p. 1997. 47.50 (*0-7883-1708-3*); pap. 44.50 (*0-7883-1709-1*) ABBE Pubs Assn.

Bester, John, tr. Traditional Korean Painting: A Lost Art Rediscovered. (Illus.). 176p. 1990. 65.00 (*0-87011-997-4*) Kodansha.

Bester, John, tr. see Agawa, Hiroyuki.

Bester, John, tr. see Doi, Takeo.

Bester, John, tr. see Enchi, Fumiko.

Bester, John, tr. see Hasegawa, Nyozekan.

Bester, John, tr. see Ibuse, Masuji.

Bester, John, tr. see Mishima, Yukio, pseud.

Bester, John, tr. see Miyazawa, Kenji.

Bester, John, tr. see Nippon Bonsai Association Staff.

Bester, John, tr. see Oe, Kenzaburo.

Bester, John, tr. see Ozawa, Hiroyuki.

Bester, John, tr. see Saga, Junichi.

Bester, John, tr. see Senoh, Kappa.

Bester, John, tr. see Ueda, Makoto, et al, eds.

Bester, John, tr. see Yoshiyuki, Junnosuke.

Bester, John, tr. & intro. see Mishima, Yukio, pseud.

***Besterci, Michal.** Dispersion-Strengthened Aluminium Prepared by Mechanical Alloying. 90p. 1998. pap. 50.00 (*1-898326-55-X*, Pub. by CISP) Balogh.

Besterfield. Total Quality Management. 2nd ed. LC 98-24253. 533p. 1998. 94.00 (*0-13-639403-5*) P-H.

Besterfield, Dale H. Quality Control. 5th ed. LC 97-9443. 519p. (C). 1997. pap. 88.00 (*0-13-632571-8*) P-H.

Besterfield, Dale H. & O'Hagan, Robert E. Technical Sketching with Introduction to CAD: For Engineers, Technologists & Technicians. 3rd ed. LC 97-14321. 367p. 1997. pap. text 54.00 (*0-13-472572-7*) P-H.

***Besterman.** Philosophical Dictionary. 2000. pap. write for info. (*0-13-028130-1*) P-H.

Besterman, ed. see Voltaire.

Besterman, Theodore. Art & Architecture: A Bibliography of Bibliographies. LC 74-29568. 216p. 1971. write for info. (*0-87471-045-6*) Rowman.

— The Beginnings of Systematic Bibliography. 1988. lib. bdg. 75.00 (*0-7812-0258-2*) Rprt Serv.

— Bibliography, Library Science, & Reference Books: A Bibliography of Bibliographies. LC 70-29437. 271p. 1971. write for info. (*0-87471-041-3*) Rowman.

— Commerce: Manufactures & Labour: A Bibliography of Bibliographies. LC 72-177932. 1971. write for info. (*0-87471-056-1*) Rowman.

— Crystal Gazing: A Study in the History, Distribution, Theory, & Practice of Scrying. 189p. 1996. reprint ed. pap. 17.95 (*1-56459-542-0*) Kessinger Pub.

— History & Geography: A Bibliography of Bibliographies. LC 72-184975. 1972. write for info. (*0-87471-057-X*) Rowman.

— Law & International Law: A Bibliography of Bibliographies. LC 72-178009. 436p. 1971. write for info. (*0-87471-051-0*) Rowman.

— Literature, English & American: A Bibliography of Bibliographies. LC 74-29403. 457p. 1971. write for info. (*0-87471-052-9*) Rowman.

— Periodical Publications: A Bibliography of Bibliographies. LC 70-29733. 1971. write for info. (*0-87471-043-X*) Rowman.

— Printing, Book Collecting, & Illustrated Books: A Bibiography of Bibliographies. LC 70-29686. 1971. write for info. (*0-87471-042-1*) Rowman.

— Voltaire Essays, & Another. LC 80-17075. (Illus.). 181p. 1980. reprint ed. lib. bdg. 49.75 (*0-313-22527-3*, BEVO, Greenwood Pr) Greenwood.

— A World Bibliography of Bibliographies, 5 Vols. 4th ed. 1963. 417.50 (*0-87471-294-7*) Rowman.

— A World Bibliography of Oriental Bibliographies. 339p. 1975. pap. 23.00 (*0-87471-750-7*) Rowman.

B

Besterman, Theodore & Roman and Little Field Inc. Agriculture: A Bibliography of Bibliographies. LC 71-30167. 302p. 1971. write for info. (*0-87471-049-9*) Rowman.

Besterman, Theodore & Rowman and Little Field Inc. Technology, Including Patents: A Bibliography of Bibliographies. LC 72-30099. 1971. write for info. (*0-87471-053-7*) Rowman.

Besterman, Theodore, ed. see Crawley, Ernest.

Besterman, Theodore, ed. see Voltaire.

Besterman, Theodore, tr. see Driesch, Hans.

Bestle, D., jt. ed. see Schiehlen, W. O.

Bestler, Emily, ed. see Phelan, Laurel.

Bestler, Emily, ed. see Ramer, Andrew.

***Bestman, Monica.** Fantastic Fiber Jewelry. (Illus.). 8p. (J). (gr. 2-9). 1998. pap., boxed set 5.95 (*0-8167-4886-1*) Troll Communs.

Bestmann, jt. auth. see Beyer, H.

Bestmann, Mark. The Only True & Incredible Me. LC 98-225933. 24p. (J). 1998. 12.99 (*0-89900-819-4*) College Pr Pub.

Bestmann, Nancy. Nana, Will You Write Me from Heaven? LC 98-227224. 1998. 12.99 (*0-89900-816-X*) College Pr Pub.

— Plant Your Dreams, My Child. (Illus.). 18p. (J). 1997. 12.99 (*0-89900-665-5*) College Pr Pub.

— Where Does God Sleep, Momma? (Illus.). 18p. (J). 1997. 12.99 (*0-89900-664-7*) College Pr Pub.

***Beston, Henry.** The Best of Beston: The Natural World of Henry Beston, from Cape Cod to the St. Lawrence. Coatsworth, Elizabeth, ed. (Nonpareil Ser.: Vol. 83). 224p. 2000. reprint ed. pap. 16.95 (*1-56792-104-3*) Godine.

Beston, Henry. Herbs & the Earth. LC 89-46185. (Illus.). 168p. 1990. 17.95 (*0-87923-827-5*) Godine.

— Northern Farm. 1995. pap. 9.95 (*0-8050-3092-1*) H Holt & Co.

— Northern Farm A Glorious Year on A Small Maine Farm. LC 99-28762. 1999. 25.95 (*0-7838-8657-8*) Macmillan Gen Ref.

— The Outermost House. 10.00 (*0-614-30536-5*) NAVH.

— The Outermost House: A Year of Life on the Great Beach of Cape Cod. 256p. 1995. pap. 9.95 (*0-8050-1966-9*, Owl) H Holt & Co.

Bestor, Arthur E. Educational Wastelands: The Retreat from Learning in Our Public Schools. 2nd ed. LC 85-1014. 304p. pap. text 14.95 (*0-252-01244-5*) U of Ill Pr.

— Educational Wastelands: The Retreat from Learning in Our Public Schools. 2nd ed. LC 85-1014. 304p. 1985. text 29.95 (*0-252-01226-7*) U of Ill Pr.

Bestor, Arthur E., et al. Three Presidents & Their Books: The Readings of Jefferson, Lincoln, & F. D. Roosevelt. LC 54-12305. (Fifth Annual Windsor Lectures). 141p. reprint ed. pap. 43.80 (*0-608-13777-4*, 202021900016) Bks Demand.

Bestor, Dorothy K. Aside from Teaching, What in the World Can You Do? Career Strategies for Liberal Arts Graduates. LC 82-2009. 352p. 1982. 30.00 (*0-295-95960-6*) U of Wash Pr.

Bestor, George C. & Jones, Holway R., eds. City Planning Bibliography: A Basic Bibliography of Sources & Trends. 3rd ed. 534p. 1972. pap. 5.00 (*0-87262-036-0*) Am Soc Civil Eng.

Bestor, Jane F., jt. auth. see Thornley, Isobel D.

Bestor, Kurt, et al. Fathers. 1998. 24.95 incl. audio compact disk (*1-57008-440-8*) Bookcraft Inc.

Bestor, Robert & Bestor, Tom. The Fifty Best Country Inns & Small, City Hotels of Germany, Austria & Switzerland. (Illus.). 164p. (Orig.). 1989. pap. 10.95 (*0-9625238-0-1*) UpCountry Pub.

Bestor, Sheri Mabry, jt. auth. see Teacher Created Materials, Inc. Staff.

Bestor, Theodore C. Neighborhood Tokyo. LC 88-12383. (Illus.). 368p. 1989. 47.50 (*0-8047-1439-8*); pap. 15.95 (*0-8047-1797-4*) Stanford U Pr.

Bestor, Tom, jt. auth. see Bestor, Robert.

Bestpitch, Barry G. & Parnell, Tere. LAN Times Guide to Wide Area Networks. 528p. 1996. pap. text 34.95 (*0-07-882228-9*) Osborne-McGraw.

Bestsch, Kenneth A., ed. see Gastman, Grant A. & Isaacs, Jack D.

Bestt, Judith. How to Soothe & Amuse Your New Baby: Wonderful, Simple Activities That Will Entertain & Calm Babies While Stimulating Their Growth & Development. LC 94-68361. (From Birth to 3 Months Ser.). (Illus.). 88p. (Orig.). 1995. pap. 7.95 (*1-886147-01-9*) Remedios Pub.

Bestul, Scott, ed. Minnesota Seasons: Classic Tales of Life Outdoors. (Illus.). 240p. 1998. 22.95 (*0-9653381-4-2*) Cabin Bkshelf.

Bestul, Thomas H. Satire & Allegory in "Wynnere & Wastoure" LC 73-77750. 135p. 1974. reprint ed. pap. 41.90 (*0-608-02043-5*, 206269600003) Bks Demand.

— Texts of the Passion: Latin Devotional Literature & Medieval Society. LC 96-26705. (Middle Ages Ser.). 288p. 1996. text 39.95 (*0-8122-3376-X*) U of Pa Pr.

Bestul, Thomas H., ed. A Durham Book of Devotions. (LAT.). viii, 102p. pap. text 7.43 (*0-88844-468-0*) Brill Academic Pubs.

***Bestuzhev-Lada, Igor' Vasil'evich.** Russia in the 20th & 21st Centuries: From Colossus to Collapse & Back. LC 99-44299. 1999. text 34.00 (*1-56072-709-8*) Nova Sci Pubs.

Bestvina, Mladen. Characterizing k-Dimensional Universal Menger Compacta. LC 87-28829. (Memoirs of the American Mathematical Society Ser.: Vol. 380). 110p. 1988. pap. 21.00 (*0-8218-2443-0*, MEMO/71/380C) Am Math.

***Bestwick, Joan.** Life's Little Barry Cookbook: 101 Berry Recipes. 144p. 2000. pap. 11.95 (*1-892384-05-1*) Avery Color.

— Life's Little Rhubarb Cookbook: 101 Rhubarb Recipes. 144p. 1999. pap. 11.95 (*1-892384-00-0*) Avery Color.

Bestwick, Joan. Life's Little Zucchini Cookbook: 101 Zucchini Recipes. LC 97-70281. 144p. (Orig.). 1997. pap. 11.95 (*0-932212-94-8*) Avery Color.

Beswick, A. Synchrotron Radiation & Dynamic Phenomena. (Conference Proceeding Ser.: No. 258). 500p. 1992. 120.00 (*1-56396-008-7*) Am Inst Physics.

Beswick, Barbara A., jt. auth. see Robinson, Ralph E.

***Beswick, Bill.** Focused for Soccer. (Illus.). 208p. 2000. pap. write for info. (*0-7360-3002-6*) Human Kinetics.

Beswick, C. Nice & Easy French Grammar. (FRE., Illus.). 136p. 1995. pap. 4.95 (*0-8442-9497-7*, 94977, Natl Textbk Co) NTC Contemp Pub Co.

Beswick, Dave. Bald Men Always Come Out on Top: 101 Ways to Use Your Head & Win with Skin. LC 95-95139. (Illus.). 104p. (Orig.). 1997. pap. 9.95 (*0-9613176-1-2*) Ama Pub FL.

— Bald Men Never Have a Bad Hair Day: Wit & Wisdom for Men on the Bald Path. (Illus.). 104p. 1998. pap. 9.95 (*0-9613176-2-0*) Ama Pub FL.

Beswick, Raymond & Williams, Alfred, eds. Information Systems & Business Communication. 116p. (Orig.). 1983. pap. text 6.90 (*0-931874-15-7*) Assn Busn Comm.

Beswick, Samuel. Swedenborg Rite & the Great Masonic Leaders of the Eighteenth Century. 210p. 1994. reprint ed. pap. 16.95 (*1-56459-424-6*) Kessinger Pub.

Beswick, Simon & Wine, Humphrey. Beswick & Wine: Buying & Selling Private Companies & Businesses. 5th ed. 1996. pap. write for info. (*0-406-08190-5*, WBBS04, MICHIE) LEXIS Pub.

Beswick, Simon, jt. auth. see Wine, Humphrey.

Besznyak, I., et al. Diagnosis & Surgical Treatment of Mediastinal Tumors & Pseudotumors. (Illus.). 336p. 1984. 112.25 (*3-8055-3582-1*) S Karger.

***Bet-El, Llana.** Conscripts. 1999. 35.95 (*0-7509-2108-0*) Bks Intl VA.

***Bet, Zana Sandra.** No Time to Sew Sewing Pattern. 2001. text. write for info. (*0-87596-786-8*) Rodale Pr Inc.

Beta, Hymenaeons, ed. see Crowley, Aleister.

Beta, Hymenaeus, ed. see Crowley, Aleister.

Beta, Hymenaeus, ed. see Crowley, Aleister & Adams, Evangeline.

Beta, Hymenaeus, ed. see Parsons, Jack W.

Beta Sigma Phi Staff. Food in the Fast Lane. LC 92-23181. 1992. write for info. (*0-87197-346-4*) Favorite Recipes.

Beta, Simone, ed. Lessico Dei Romanzieri Greci, Vol. 4. (Alpha-Omega, Reihe A Ser.: Vol. LXXVIII). (GER.). 378p. 1997. write for info. (*3-487-10556-X*) G Olms Pubs.

Betageri, Guru, et al. Liposome Drug Delivery Systems. LC 93-60519. 140p. 1993. pap. text 84.95 (*1-56676-030-5*) Technomic.

Betances, Emelio. State & Society in the Dominican Republic. (C). 1995. pap. 24.00 (*0-8133-8682-9*, Pub. by Westview) HarpC.

Betances, Emelio & Spalding, Hobart A., Jr., eds. The Dominican Republic Today: Realities & Perspectives. LC 94-33703. (ENG & SPA.). 206p. (C). 1996. 43.95 (*0-929972-18-X*) Bildner Ctr.

Betancourt. Double Helix: Infection, Vol. 1. (Star Trek Ser.: 51). 239p. 1999. mass mkt. 6.50 (*0-671-03255-0*, Star Trek) PB.

Betancourt, Ana. Nearly Complete Works. (SPA.). 100p. (Orig.). 1991. pap. 8.00 (*0-685-26449-1*) Atabex Collection.

Betancourt De Hita, Armando. Emilia Bernal: Su Vida y Su Obra. Labrada, Emilio B., ed. LC 99-62751. (Coleccion Polymita).Tr. of Emilia Bernal: Life & Work. (SPA., Illus.). 186p. Date not set. pap. 15.00 (*0-89729-899-3*) Ediciones.

Betancourt, Donna L. Before College Book for Women: Protecting Yourself from Campus Crime. LC 93-91066. (Illus.). 122p. (Orig.). (YA). 1993. pap. 12.95 (*0-9639693-0-7*) D Betancourt.

Betancourt, Ernesto F. Revolutionary Strategy: A Handbook for Practitioners. 196p. (C). 1991. 34.95 (*0-88738-411-0*) Transaction Pubs.

Betancourt, Ernesto F. & Dizard, Wilson P., III. Castro & the Bankers: The Mortgaging of a Revolution - 1983 Update. 1982. 2.00 (*0-317-90487-6*) Cuban Amer Natl Fndtn.

Betancourt, Ethel Rios De, see De Betancourt, Ethel Rios.

Betancourt, Jeanne. The Baby Pony. (Pony Pals Super Special Ser.: No. 1). (Illus.). (J). (gr. 2-5). 1996. pap. text 5.99 (*0-590-74210-8*) Scholastic Inc.

— The Blind Pony, Vol. 15. (Pony Pals Ser.: No. 15). (Illus.). 96p. (J). (gr. 2-5). 1997. pap. text 3.50 (*0-590-86632-X*) Scholastic Inc.

— Circus Pony. (Pony Pals Ser.: No. 11). (Illus.). (J). (gr. 4-7). 1996. pap. text 2.99 (*0-590-86597-8*) Scholastic Inc.

— Circus Pony. (Pony Pals Ser.: No. 11). (Illus.). (J). (gr. 2-5). 1996. 8.60 (*0-606-09756-2*, Pub. by Turtleback) Demco.

***Betancourt, Jeanne.** Detective Pony. (Pony Pals Ser.: No. 17). (Illus.). (J). (gr. 2-5). 1998. pap. text 3.50 (*0-590-37460-5*, Little Apple) Scholastic Inc.

Betancourt, Jeanne. Don't Hurt My Pony. (Pony Pals Ser.: No. 10). (Illus.). (J). (gr. 4-7). 1996. pap. text 2.99 (*0-590-62975-1*) Scholastic Inc.

— Don't Hurt My Pony. (Pony Pals Ser.: No. 10). (Illus.). (J). 1996. 8.09 (*0-606-09203-X*, Pub. by Turtleback) Demco.

— Eclair Est Malade. Henri, Jocelyne, tr. from ENG. (Pony Pals (Le Cercle des Poneys) Ser.: No. 3).Tr. of Pony in Trouble. (FRE., Illus.). 104p. (J). (gr. 2-5). 1996. mass mkt. 6.99 (*0-590-16039-7*) Scholastic Inc.

***Betancourt, Jeanne.** Fight, Bulldogs, Fight! 128p. (gr. 3-7). 1999. pap. 4.50 (*0-590-97808-X*) Scholastic Inc.

Betancourt, Jeanne. The Ghost Pony With Pony Charm Bracelet, (Pony Pals Super Special Ser.: No. 3). (Illus.). (J). (gr. 2-5). 1997. pap. text 5.99 (*0-590-37461-3*) Scholastic Inc.

— The Girl Who Hated Ponies. (Pony Pals Ser.: No. 13). (Illus.). 96p. (J). (gr. 1-4). 1997. mass mkt. 2.99 (*0-590-86600-1*) Scholastic Inc.

— Give Me Back My Pony. (Pony Pals Ser.: No. 4). (Illus.). 96p. (J). (gr. 4-7). 1995. pap. 2.99 (*0-590-48586-5*) Scholastic Inc.

Betancourt, Jeanne. Give Me Back My Pony. (Pony Pals Ser.: No. 4). (Illus.). (J). (gr. 2-5). 1995. 8.60 (*0-606-07579-8*, Pub. by Turtleback) Demco.

Betancourt, Jeanne. Ce poney est a moi! Henri, Jocelyne, tr. from ENG. (Pony Pals (Le Cercle des Poneys) Ser.: No. 4). Orig. Title: Give Me Back My Pony. (FRE., Illus.). 90p. (J). (gr. 2-5). 1996. mass mkt. 6.99 (*0-590-16040-0*) Scholastic Inc.

***Betancourt, Jeanne.** Go, Girl, Go! 128p. (gr. 3-7). 1999. pap. 4.50 (*0-590-97806-3*) Scholastic Inc.

Betancourt, Jeanne. Good-Bye Pony. (Pony Pals Ser.: No. 8). (Illus.). (J). (gr. 2-4). 1996. pap. text 3.50 (*0-590-54339-3*) Scholastic Inc.

— Good-Bye Pony. (Pony Pals Ser.: No. 8). (Illus.). (J). (gr. 2-5). 1995. 8.60 (*0-606-08529-7*, Pub. by Turtleback) Demco.

— I Want a Pony. (Pony Pals Ser.: No. 1). (Illus.). 103p. (J). (gr. 2-5). 1994. pap. 2.99 (*0-590-48583-0*) Scholastic Inc.

Betancourt, Jeanne. I Want a Pony. (Pony Pals Ser.: No. 1). (Illus.). (J). (gr. 2-5). 1994. 8.60 (*0-606-07688-3*, Pub. by Turtleback) Demco.

Betancourt, Jeanne. Kate's Turn. 144p. (J). 1992. 13.95 (*0-590-43103-X*, Scholastic Hardcover) Scholastic Inc.

— Keep Out Pony. (Pony Pals Ser.: No. 12). (Illus.). (J). (gr. 5-7). 1996. pap. 2.99 (*0-590-86598-6*) Scholastic Inc.

***Betancourt, Jeanne.** Lonely Pony, Vol. 25. (Pony Pals Ser.: No. 25). (Illus.). 144p. (J). (gr. 2-5). 2000. mass mkt. 3.99 (*0-439-06491-0*) Scholastic Inc.

Betancourt, Jeanne. The Missing Pony Pal. (Pony Pals Ser.: No. 16). (Illus.). 96p. (J). (gr. 2-5). 1997. pap. text 3.50 (*0-590-37459-1*) Scholastic Inc.

***Betancourt, Jeanne.** Movie Star Pony. (Pony Pals Ser.: No. 26). (Illus.). 96p. (J). (gr. 2-5). 2000. pap. 3.99 (*0-439-06492-9*) Scholastic Inc.

Betancourt, Jeanne. Moving Pony. (Pony Pals Ser.). 112p. (J). (gr. 2-5). 1999. pap. 3.99 (*0-590-63397-X*) Scholastic Inc.

— My Name Is Brain Brian. LC 92-16513. 144p. (J). (gr. 3-7). 1993. 14.95 (*0-590-44921-4*) Scholastic Inc.

— My Name Is Brain Brian. (J). 1993. 9.09 (*0-606-07907-6*, Pub. by Turtleback) Demco.

***Betancourt, Jeanne.** The Pony & the Bear, (Pony Pals Ser.: No. 23). (Illus.). 85p. (J). (gr. 3-5). 1999. mass mkt. 3.99 (*0-439-06489-9*) Scholastic Inc.

Betancourt, Jeanne. A Pony for Keeps. (Pony Pals Ser.: No. 2). (Illus.). 96p. (J). (gr. 4-7). 1995. pap. 2.99 (*0-590-48584-9*) Scholastic Inc.

— A Pony for Keeps. (Pony Pals Ser.: No. 2). (Illus.). (J). (gr. 2-5). 1995. 8.60 (*0-606-08027-9*, Pub. by Turtleback) Demco.

— A Pony in Trouble. LC 95-209004. (Pony Pals Ser.: No. 3). (Illus.). 96p. (J). (gr. 4-7). 1995. pap. 2.99 (*0-590-48585-7*) Scholastic Inc.

— A Pony in Trouble. (Pony Pals Ser.: No. 3). (Illus.). (J). (gr. 2-5). 1995. 8.60 (*0-606-08028-7*, Pub. by Turtleback) Demco.

— Pony-Sitters, (Pony Pals Ser.: No. 14). (Illus.). 96p. (gr. 2-5). 1997. pap. 3.50 (*0-590-86601-X*, Little Apple) Scholastic Inc.

— Pony to the Rescue. (Pony Pals Ser.: No. 5). (Illus.). 96p. (J). (gr. 2-5). 1995. pap. 2.99 (*0-590-25244-5*) Scholastic Inc.

— Pony to the Rescue. (Pony Pals Ser.: No. 5). (Illus.). (J). (gr. 2-5). 1995. 8.09 (*0-606-08031-7*, Pub. by Turtleback) Demco.

— Perdue Dans les Bois. Henri, Jocelyne, tr. from ENG. (Pony Pals (Le Cercle des Poneys) Ser.: No. 5). Orig. Title: Pony to the Rescue. (FRE., Illus.). 120p. (J). (gr. 2-5). 1996. mass mkt. 6.99 (*0-590-16041-9*) Scholastic Inc.

— Puppy Love. 96p. (J). (gr. 4-8). 1986. pap. 2.50 (*0-380-89958-2*, Avon Bks) Morrow Avon.

— The Rainbow Kid. 112p. (Orig.). (J). (gr. 3-7). 1983. pap. 2.50 (*0-380-84665-9*, Avon Bks) Morrow Avon.

— Ready, Shoot, Score, 1 vol., Vol. 4. (Cheer USA Ser.: Vol. 3). 128p. (gr. 3-7). 1999. pap. text 4.50 (*0-590-97809-8*) Scholastic Inc.

— Runaway Pony. (Pony Pals Ser.: No. 7). (Illus.). (J). (gr. 2-5). 1995. pap. 2.99 (*0-590-54338-5*) Scholastic Inc.

Betancourt, Jeanne. Runaway Pony. (Pony Pals Ser.: No. 7). (Illus.). (J). (gr. 2-5). 1995. 8.60 (*0-606-08593-9*, Pub. by Turtleback) Demco.

Betancourt, Jeanne. The Saddest Pony, (Pony Pals Ser.: No. 18). (Illus.). (J). (gr. 2-5). 1998. pap. 3.99 (*0-590-51295-1*) Scholastic Inc.

— Stolen Ponies, (Illus.). (J). (gr. 2-5). 1999. pap. 3.99 (*0-590-63401-1*) Scholastic Inc.

— The Stories of Our Ponies. (Pony Pals Super Special Ser.: No. 2). (J). (gr. 2-5). 1997. pap. 2.99 (*0-614-29030-9*, Little Apple) Scholastic Inc.

— The Stories of Our Ponies. (Pony Pals Super Special Ser.: No. 2). (J). (gr. 2-5). 1997. mass mkt. 5.99 (*0-590-86631-1*, Little Apple) Scholastic Inc.

— The Stories of Our Ponies. (Pony Pals Super Special Ser.: No. 2). (Illus.). (J). (gr. 2-5). 1997. pap. text 5.99 (*0-590-21240-0*) Scholastic Inc.

— Ten True Animal Rescues. 1998. pap. text 3.99 (*0-590-68117-6*) Scholastic Inc.

— Too Many Ponies. (Pony Pals Ser.: No. 6). (Illus.). 96p. (J). (gr. 2-5). 1995. pap. 2.99 (*0-590-25245-3*) Scholastic Inc.

— Too Many Ponies. (Pony Pals Ser.: No. 6). (Illus.). (J). (gr. 2-5). 1995. 8.60 (*0-606-08312-X*, Pub. by Turtleback) Demco.

— Turtle Time. 112p. 1985. pap. 2.50 (*0-380-89675-3*, Avon Bks) Morrow Avon.

***Betancourt, Jeanne.** Unlucky Pony. (Pony Pals Ser.: No. 24). (Illus.). 96p. (J). (gr. 2-5). 2000. pap. 4.99 (*0-439-06490-2*, Little Apple) Scholastic Inc.

Betancourt, Jeanne. Western Pony, , (Pony Pals Ser.: No. 22). (Illus.). 96p. (gr. 2-5). 1999. pap. text 3.99 (*0-439-06488-0*) Scholastic Inc.

— We've Got Spirit! (Cheer USA Ser.). 1999. pap. text 36.00 (*0-439-11748-8*) Scholastic Inc.

— We've Got Spirit!, 1 vol., Vol. 4. (Cheer USA Ser.). 1999. pap. text 4.50 (*0-590-97876-4*) Scholastic Inc.

— The Wild Pony. (Pony Pals Ser.: No. 9). (Illus.). (J). (gr. 2-5). 1996. pap. 2.99 (*0-590-62974-3*) Scholastic Inc.

— The Wild Pony. (Pony Pals Ser.: No. 10). (Illus.). (J). (gr. 2-5). 1996. 8.09 (*0-606-10071-7*, Pub. by Turtleback) Demco.

***Betancourt, Jeanne.** Winning Pony, (Pony Pals Ser.: No. 21). (Illus.). 89p. (J). (gr. 3-5). 1999. pap. text 3.99 (*0-590-63405-4*) Scholastic Inc.

Betancourt, John, jt. auth. see Fulton, Roger.

Betancourt, John, jt. ed. see McCaffrey, Anne.

Betancourt, John G. The Blind Archer. 240p. 1988. pap. 2.95 (*0-380-75146-1*, Avon Bks) Morrow Avon.

— Cutthroat Island. 1995. mass mkt. 5.99 (*0-8125-4304-1*, Pub. by Tor Bks) St Martin.

— Gates of Hades. (Hercules Ser.). 1997. mass mkt. 7.00 (*0-8125-3912-5*, Pub. by Tor Bks) St Martin.

— Incident at Arbuk. (Star Trek). 1995. mass mkt. 5.99 (*0-671-52048-2*) PB.

— The Sci-Fi Channel Trivia Book. LC 96-232617. 400p. (Orig.). 1996. pap. 15.00 (*1-57297-110-X*) Blvd Books.

— Slab's Tavern & Other Uncanny Tales. LC 90-81728. (Illus.). 96p. 1990. 15.00 (*0-932445-41-1*); 35.00 (*0-932445-42-X*) Wildside.

— The Trojan Spaceship: The/Heart of the Warrior. (Star Trek: Deep Space Nine Ser.). 1996. per. 5.99 (*0-671-00239-2*, Star Trek) PB.

— Vengeance of Hera. (Hercules Ser.). 1997. mass mkt. 4.99 (*0-8125-3911-7*, Pub. by Tor Bks) St Martin.

— The Wrath of Poseidon. (Hercules Ser.). 1997. mass mkt. 4.99 (*0-8125-3910-9*, Pub. by Tor Bks); mass mkt. 4.99 (*0-614-27804-X*) Tor Bks.

Betancourt, John G., jt. auth. see Anderson, Kevin J.

Betancourt, Juan, ed. From the Palm Tree: The Cuban Revolution in Retrospect. 224p. 1983. 12.00 (*0-8184-0344-6*) Carol Pub Group.

Betancourt, Julio L., et al, eds. Packrat Middens: The Last 40,000 Years of Biotic Change. LC 89-38454. 469p. 1990. 67.50 (*0-8165-1115-2*) U of Ariz Pr.

Betancourt, Luiz, jt. auth. see Rivera, Nilda R.

Betancourt, Luz, jt. auth. see Rivera, Nilda R.

Betancourt, Marian. The Best Internet Businesses You Can Start. LC 99-13064. 210p. 1999. pap. 14.95 (*1-58062-157-0*) Adams Media.

— What to Do When Love Turns Violent. 1997. pap. 12.00 (*0-614-27643-8*, Harper Ref) HarpC.

— What To Do When Love Turns Violent: A Practical Resource for Women in Abusive Relationships. LC 97-1710. 288p. 1997. pap. 12.00 (*0-06-273456-3*, Perennial) HarperTrade.

Betancourt, Marian, jt. auth. see Loo, Marcus H.

Betancourt, Marian, jt. auth. see Miskovitz, Paul F.

Betancourt, Marian, jt. auth. see Wallis, Lila A.

Betancourt, Philip P. The Cretan Collection in the University Museum, University of Pennsylvania Vol. 1: Minoan Objects Excavated from Vasilike, Pseira, Sphoungaras, Priniatikos Pyrgos, & Other Sites. (University Museum Monographs: No. 47). (Illus.). 160p. 1983. text 45.00 (*0-934718-46-6*) U Museum Pubns.

— The History of Minoan Pottery. LC 84-22305. (Illus.). 289p. 1985. reprint ed. pap. 89.60 (*0-7837-8161-X*, 204786600008) Bks Demand.

Betancourt, Philip P. & Davaras, Costis, eds. Pseira I: The Minoan Buildings on the West Side of Area A. LC 95-25712. (University Museum Monographs: Vol. 90). (Illus.). 200p. 1995. 40.00 (*0-924171-40-5*) U Museum Pubns.

Betancourt, Philip P. & Silverman, Jean S. The Cretan Collection in the University Museum, University of Pennsylvania Vol. 2: Pottery from Gournia. (University Museum Monographs: No. 72). (Illus.). 111p. 1991. 65.00 (*0-924171-06-5*) U Museum Pubns.

Betancourt, Philip P., et al. East Cretan White-on-Dark Ware. (University Museum Monographs: No. 51). (Illus.). xx, 200p. 1984. 56.00 (*0-934718-57-1*) U Museum Pubns.

***Betancourt, Philip P., et al.** Minoan Buildings in Areas B, C, D & F. LC 99-6974. (PSEIRA Ser.). 1999. write for info. (*0-924171-74-X*) U Museum Pubns.

Betancourt, Philip P., et al. Pseira II: Building AC (the "Shrine") & Other Buildings in Area A. LC 96-25365. (Illus.). xvi, 151p. 1997. 60.00 (*0-924171-44-8*) U Museum Pubns.

— Vasilike Ware: An Early Bronze Age Pottery Style in Crete. (Studies in Mediterranean Archaeology: Vol. LVI). (Illus.). 68p. (Orig.). 1979. pap. 39.50 (*91-85058-88-2*, Pub. by P Astroms) Coronet Bks.

Betancourt, Philip P., jt. auth. see Becker, Marshall J.

Betancourt, Rafael, tr. see Arbdeya, Jesus.

An Asterisk (*) at the beginning of an entry indicates that the title is appearing for the first time.

***Betancur, John & Gills, Douglas, eds.** The Collaborative City: Opportunities & Struggles for Blacks & Latinos in U. S. Cities. LC 99-23665. (Contemporary Urban Affairs Ser.: No. 8). 320p. 1999. 65.00 (*0-8153-3560-1*, SS1461, Pub. by Garland) Taylor & Francis.

Betant, Elie A. Lexicon Thucydideum, 2 vols., Set. 1969. reprint ed. 215.00 (*0-318-72001-9*) G Olms Pubs.

Betanzos-Palacios, Odon. Conciencia y Reforma. (SPA.). 1962. pap. 5.00 (*0-86515-017-6*) Edit Mensaje.

— De Ese Dios de las Totalidades. 1989. pap. 5.00 (*0-86515-004-4*) Edit Mensaje.

— Diosdado de lo Alto: Con la Senal en la Freuto. (SPA., Illus.). 1990. pap. 15.00 (*0-86515-000-1*) Edit Mensaje.

— Hombre de Luz. (SPA., Illus.). 1972. 12.00 (*0-86515-013-3*) Edit Mensaje.

— Poemas del Hombre y las Desolaciones. 1986. pap. 3.00 (*0-86515-014-1*) Edit Mensaje.

Betanzos, Ramon J. Franz Von Baader's: Philosophy of Love. 1999. pap. text 34.95 (*0-8143-2830-X*) Wayne St U Pr.

Betanzos, Ramon J., ed. & tr. see Dilthey, Wilhelm.

Betanzos, Ramon J., tr. & intro. see Heimsoeth, Heinz.

Betcher, R. William & Pollack, William S. In a Time of Fallen Heroes: The Re-Creation of Masculinity. 288p. 1995. pap. text 16.95 (*0-89862-844-X*, C2844) Guilford Pubns.

— In a Time of Fallen Heroes: The Re-Creation of Masculinity. LC 93-12073. 304p. 1993. text 22.50 (*0-689-12177-6*) Macmillan.

Betcher, William. Intimate Play. 384p. 1988. pap. 4.95 (*0-318-32672-8*, Penguin Bks) Viking Penguin.

Betcher, William R. A Student to Student Guide to Medical School. 278p. 1985. pap. 19.95 (*0-316-09246-0*, Little Brwn Med Div) Lppncott W & W.

Beteille, Andre. Backward Classes in Contemporary India. 128p. 1993. pap. text 8.95 (*0-19-563035-1*) OUP.

— Essays in Comparative Sociology. 2nd ed. 182p. 1988. pap. text 9.95 (*0-19-562145-X*) OUP.

— The Idea of Natural Inequality & Other Essays. 2nd ed. 256p. (Orig.). 1988. 22.50 (*0-19-562147-6*) OUP.

— Society & Politics in India: Essays in a Comparative Perspective. LC 91-23882. (London School of Economics Monographs on Social Anthropology: No. 63). 248p. (C). 1991. text 35.00 (*0-485-19563-1*, Pub. by Athlone Pr) Humanities.

— Society & Politics in India: Essays in a Comparative Perspective. (Oxford India Paperbacks Ser.). 328p. 1998. pap. 10.95 (*0-19-564107-8*) OUP.

Beteille, Andre, ed. Equality & Inequality: Theory & Practice. 1989. pap. 14.95 (*0-19-561661-8*) OUP.

Betenbaugh, Michael J. Cell Culture Engineering Vi. LC 99-19003. (Current Applications of Cell Culture Engineering Ser.). 1999. write for info. (*0-7923-5575-X*) Kluwer Academic.

Betensky, Ellis I., et al, eds. Zoom Lenses II. LC 98-122080. 22p. 1997. pap. 59.00 (*0-8194-2551-6*) SPIE.

Betensky, Mala G. What Do You See? Phenomenology of Therapeutic Art Expression. LC 95-5939. 1995. pap. 29.95 (*1-85302-261-6*) Taylor & Francis.

Betenson, Lula P. & Flack, Dora D. Butch Cassidy, My Brother. LC 75-2332. (Illus.). 281p. reprint ed. 87.20 (*0-8357-9044-4*, 201564800095) Bks Demand.

Beterov, I. M. & Chebotaev, V. P. Three-Level Gas Systems & Their Interaction with Radiation. LC 74-159842. (Progress in Quantum Electronics Ser.). 106p. 1974. write for info. (*0-08-017764-6*, Pergamon Pr) Elsevier.

Beteta, Peter, jt. auth. see Fernandez-Carvajal, Francis.

Beteta, Ramon. Jarano. Upton, John, tr. from SPA. LC 75-121124. (Texas Pan-American Ser.). (Illus.). 177p. reprint ed. pap. 54.90 (*0-8357-7769-3*, 203612900002) Bks Demand.

Beth Archer, Brombert, tr. see De Luca, Erri.

Beth, E. W. Aspects of Modern Logic. De Jongh, D. M. & De Jongh-Kearl, Susan, trs. from DUT. LC 79-135102. (Synthese Library: No. 32). 187p. 1970. text 94.00 (*90-277-0173-3*, D Reidel) Kluwer Academic.

— Formal Methods: An Introduction to Symbolic Logic & to the Study of Effective Operations in Arithmetic & Logic. (Synthese Library: No.4). 184p. 1970. text 126.50 (*90-277-0069-9*, D Reidel) Kluwer Academic.

— Mathematical Thought: An Introduction to the Philosophy of Mathematics. xii, 207p. 1965. text 252.00 (*0-677-00600-4*) Gordon & Breach.

— Mathematical Thought: An Introduction to the Philosophy of Mathematics. (Synthese Library: No. 11). 220p. 1965. text 126.50 (*90-277-0070-2*, D Reidel) Kluwer Academic.

— Science, a Road to Wisdom: Collected Philosophical Studies. Wesly, Peter, tr. from DUT. 136p. 1972. text 118.00 (*90-277-0003-6*, D Reidel) Kluwer Academic.

Beth, E. W. & Piaget, J. Mathematical Epistemology & Psychology. Mays, W., tr. from FRE. (Synthese Library: No. 12). 326p. 1974. text 182.50 (*90-277-0071-0*) Kluwer Academic.

Beth, Eliza. Journey Through Life. 23p. 1997. pap. 7.00 (*0-8059-4006-5*) Dorrance.

Beth, Elke, jt. ed. see Giraldo, G.

Beth Jacob Hebrew Teachers College Staff. Deeds of the Righteous. (Illus.). 160p. 6.95 (*0-934390-00-2*) B J Hebrew Tchrs.

— The Rebbe's Treasure. write for info. (*0-934390-01-0*); pap. write for info. (*0-934390-02-9*) B J Hebrew Tchrs.

Beth, Loren P. John Marshall Harlan: The Last Whig Justice. LC 91-36140. (Illus.). 328p. 1992. lib. bdg. 39.95 (*0-8131-1778-X*) U Pr of Ky.

Beth, Mary, jt. auth. see Ancona, George.

Beth Memorial Colloquium Staff. Logic & Foundations of Science: Proceedings of the E. W. Beth Memorial Colloquium, Paris, 1964. Destouches, J. L., ed. 137p. 1967. text 120.00 (*90-277-0076-1*) Kluwer Academic.

Beth, Rae. Lamp of the Goddess: Lives & Teachings of a Priestess. LC 95-16719. (Illus.). 160p. (Orig.). 1995. pap. text 9.95 (*0-87728-848-8*) Weiser.

— The Wiccan Path: A Guide to Solitary Practice. 190p. 1995. pap. 12.95 (*0-89594-744-7*) Crossing Pr.

Beth, T., ed. Cryptography: Burg Feuerstein, FRG 1982. (Lecture Notes in Computer Science Ser.: Vol. 149). 402p. 1986. 37.00 (*0-387-11993-0*) Spr-Verlag.

Beth, T., et al, eds. Public-Key Cryptography: State of the Art & Future Directions. (Lecture Notes in Computer Science Ser.: Vol. 578). xi, 97p. 1992. 31.95 (*0-387-55215-4*) Spr-Verlag.

Beth, T., jt. ed. see Berson, T. A.

Beth, Thomas, et al. Design Theory, Vol. 1. 2nd rev. ed. LC 98-29508. (Encyclopedia of Mathematics & Its Applications Ser.: No. 69). (Illus.). 1120p. (C). 1999. text 95.00 (*0-521-44432-2*) Cambridge U Pr.

Bethall, D., ed. Advances in Physical Organic Chemistry, Vol. 30. (Illus.). 272p. 1995. text 95.00 (*0-12-033530-1*) Acad Pr.

Betham, Matilda. The Lay of Marie, 1816. LC 93-47134. (Revolution & Romanticism Ser.). 1994. 55.00 (*1-85477-164-7*) Continuum.

Betham, R. M. Marathas & Dekhani Musalmans: Handbooks for the Indian Army. (C). 1996. 24.00 (*81-206-1204-3*, Pub. by Asian Educ Servs) S Asia.

Bethancourt, Charles, ed. see Logan, Mike.

Bethancourt, Charles, ed. see Steinman, Philip.

Bethancourt, Chuck. Why I Left the Catholic Church. 70p. 1998. mass mkt. 4.95 (*0-9665868-2-4*) Wisdom Pub Inc.

Bethany Community of the Resurrection of Christ St. Akathist to Saints. Martha & Mary. 1991. pap. 1.00 (*0-89981-112-4*) Eastern Orthodox.

***Bethany House Publishing Staff.** Chang Duvall, M. D., Vols. 5-8. 2000. pap. text 43.99 (*0-7642-8597-1*) Bethany Hse.

Bethany, Michael, jt. ed. see Anderson, Douglas T.

Bethany Productions Staff. Pregnancy Counseling for Success: A Guide to Effective Counseling. 80p. (Orig.). 1990. pap. 16.95 (*1-879058-02-2*) Bethany Prods.

***Bethany World Prayer Center Staff.** Between the Bases Retreats. 64p. 1999. pap. text 5.00 (*1-928772-02-1*) Keepsafe.

— Christianity 101. 48p. 1998. pap. text 3.50 (*1-928772-03-X*) Keepsafe.

— Discipleship 201. 84p. 1998. pap. text 5.00 (*1-928772-04-8*) Keepsafe.

— Leadership 301. 84p. 1999. pap. text 5.00 (*1-928772-05-6*) Keepsafe.

Bethards, Betty. Be Your Own Guru. 123p. 1988. pap. 12.95 (*0-918915-19-8*) Inner Light Found.

— Dream Book: Symbols for Self Understanding. 1985. pap. 9.95 (*0-918915-09-0*) Inner Light Found.

— The Dream Book: Symbols for Self-Understanding. 184p. 1997. pap. 9.95 (*1-86204-098-2*, Pub. by Element MA) Penguin Putnam.

— From My Heart to Yours. (Orig.). 1996. pap. 10.95 (*0-918915-01-5*) Inner Light Found.

— Relationships in the New Age of AIDS: Self Awareness Through Commitment. 55p. (Orig.). 1988. pap. 2.50 (*0-918915-12-0*) Inner Light Found.

— Sex & Psychic Energy. 127p. 1990. pap. 12.95 (*0-918915-25-2*) Inner Light Found.

— Techniques for Health & Wholeness. 108p. 1985. pap. 11.95 (*0-918915-17-1*) Inner Light Found.

— There Is No Death. 94p. 1988. pap. 10.95 (*0-918915-27-9*) Inner Light Found.

Bethards, Betty & Catalfo, Jaclyn. Way of the Mystic: Seven Steps to Developing Your Intuitive Powers. 1995. pap. 12.95 (*1-85230-690-4*, Pub. by Element MA) Penguin Putnam.

Bethards, Betty & Grace, Jaclyn C. Seven Steps to Developing Your Intuitive Powers. LC 97-37751. 200p. 1998. pap. 12.95 (*1-86204-249-7*, Pub. by Element MA) Penguin Putnam.

Bethe, H. A. & Salpeter, E. E. Quantum Mechanics of One- & Two-Electron Atoms. LC 76-30829. (Illus.). 382p. (C). 1977. text 37.50 (*0-306-20022-8*, Kluwer Plenum) Kluwer Academic.

Bethe, Hans A. The Road from Los Alamos: Collected Essays of Hans A. Bethe. (Masters of Modern Physics Ser.). 192p. 1991. 24.95 (*0-88318-707-8*) Am Inst Physics.

— Selected Works of Hans A. Bethe. 500p. 1997. lib. bdg. 49.00 (*981-02-2876-7*) World Scientific Pub.

— Splitting of Terms in Crystals. LC 58-2296. (Translated from Annals of Physics Ser.: Vol. 3). (Illus.). 73p. reprint ed. pap. 30.00 (*0-608-10863-4*, 200337000021) Bks Demand.

Bethe, Hans A., et al, eds. From a Life of Physics. 104p. (C). 1989. pap. text 8.00 (*9971-5-0937-7*) World Scientific Pub.

Bethe, Hans A. & Jackiw, Roman. Intermediate Quantum Mechanics. 3rd ed. LC 97-39327. 1997. pap. 39.00 (*0-201-32831-3*) Addison-Wesley.

Bethe, Hans A. & Jackiw, Roman V. Intermediate Quantum Mechanics: Lecture Notes & Supplements in Physics, Vol. 18. 3rd ed. LC 85-19010. (Illus.). 396p. (C). 1986. pap. 54.00 (*0-8053-0757-5*) Addison-Wesley.

Bethe, Hans A., et al. Basic Bethe: Seminal Articles on Nuclear Physics, 1936-1937. LC 86-10712. (History of Modern Physics & Astronomy Ser.). 488p. 1986. reprint ed. text 37.50 (*0-88318-495-8*) Am Inst Physics.

Bethe, Monica & Brazell, Karen. Dance in the No Theatre, Vol. 1: Dance Analysis. LC 84-151322. (Cornell East Asia Ser.: No. 29). 214p. 1982. pap. 15.30 (*0-939657-09-0*) Cornell East Asia Pgm.

Bethea, David M. Joseph Brodsky & the Creation of Exile. LC 93-31178. 344p. (C). 1994. text 45.00 (*0-691-06773-2*, Pub. by Princeton U Pr) Cal Prin Full Svc.

— Khodasevich: His Life & Art. LC 82-61355. (Illus.). 405p. reprint ed. pap. 125.60 (*0-608-06325-8*, 206668700008) Bks Demand.

— Realizing Metaphors: Alexander Pushkin & the Life of the Poet. LC 98-10320. 1998. 40.00 (*0-299-15970-1*); pap. 17.95 (*0-299-15974-4*) U of Wis Pr.

— The Shape of Apocalypse in Modern Russian Fiction. LC 88-12639. 326p. 1989. reprint ed. pap. 101.10 (*0-608-02530-5*, 206317400004) Bks Demand.

Bethea, David M., ed. Puskin Today. LC 92-7861. 276p. 1993. 31.50 (*0-253-31161-6*) Ind U Pr.

***Bethea-Jones, Karoline.** Someone to Love. 260p. 2000. pap. 12.95 (*0-9679523-0-1*) NovelTwogo Pub.

Bethea, Morrison C., jt. auth. see Steward, H. Leighton.

Bethea, Odessa, ed. see League, V. C.

Bethea, Robert M. Statistical Methods for Engineers & Scientists. 3rd ed. (Statistics - Textbooks & Monographs: Vol. 144). (Illus.). 672p. 1995. text 75.00 (*0-8247-9335-8*) Dekker.

Bethea, Robert M. & Rhinehart, Russell. Applied Engineering Statistics. (Statistics: Textbooks & Monographs: Vol. 121). (Illus.). 416p. 1991. text 85.00 (*0-8247-8503-7*) Dekker.

Bethel, D., ed. Advances in Physical Organic Chemistry, Vol. 24. (Serial Publication Ser.). 225p. 1988. text 142.00 (*0-12-033524-7*) Acad Pr.

Bethel, D., jt. ed. see Gold, V.

Bethel, Dayle M. Makiguchi the Value Creator: Revolutionary Japanese Educator & Founder of Soka Gakkai. (Illus.). 68p. (Orig.). 1994. pap. 14.95 (*0-8348-0318-6*) Weatherhill.

Bethel, Dayle M., ed. Compulsory Schooling & Human Learning: The Moral Failure of Public Education in American & Japan. LC 94-29522. 160p. 1994. pap. 17.95 (*1-880192-13-6*) Caddo Gap Pr.

Bethel, Dayle M., ed. see Tezuka, Ikue.

Bethel, Elizabeth R. AIDS: Readings on a Global Crisis. (Illus.). 448p. 1994. pap. text 34.00 (*0-02-309192-4*, Macmillan Coll) P-H.

— Promiseland: A Century of Life in a Negro Community. LC 97-27292. 346p. 1997. reprint ed. pap. 16.95 (*1-57003-229-7*) U of SC Pr.

Bethel, Elizabeth Rau. Roots of African-American Identity: Memory & History in Antebellum Free Communities. 242p. 1999. pap. 18.95 (*0-312-21836-2*) St Martin.

— Transition from Communism to Capitalism: Ruling Elites from Gorbachev to Yeltsin. LC 98-45020. 331p. 1998. text 55.00 (*0-312-21612-2*) St Martin.

***Bethel, Glynis & Bethel, Orlando.** Be a Model for the Gospel: Sex Talk! Questions & Biblical Answers about Sex. (Illus.). 80p. (YA). (gr. 6-12). 1998. pap. 6.00 (*0-9675738-0-7*) New Life Gospel.

Bethel, James S., ed. World Trade in Forest Products. LC 83-17012. (George S. Long Publications). 551p. (C). 1983. 40.00 (*0-295-96078-7*) U of Wash Pr.

***Bethel, Leonard.** Africana: An Introduction & Study. 682p. (C). 1999. per. 59.00 (*0-7872-6252-8*) Kendall-Hunt.

Bethel, Leonard, jt. auth. see Johnson, Frederick.

Bethel, Leonard L. & Johnson, Frederick A., eds. Plainfield's African-American: From Northern Slavery to Church Freedom. LC 97-25342. (Illus.). 180p. (C). 1997. text 32.50 (*0-7618-0848-5*) U Pr of Amer.

Bethel, May. Healing Power of Herbs. 164p. 1980. pap. 5.00 (*0-87980-047-X*) Wilshire.

— Healing Power of Natural Foods. 1978. pap. 7.00 (*0-87980-363-0*) Wilshire.

Bethel, Orlando, jt. auth. see Bethel, Glynis.

Bethel, Rodman J. First Overseas Highway to Key West Florida. (Illus.). (Orig.). 1989. 11.95 (*0-9614702-4-0*) Rods Bks.

— Flaglers Folly: The Railroad That Went to Sea & Was Blown Away. (Illus.). 111p. (Orig.). 1987. pap. 12.95 (*0-9614702-2-4*) Rods Bks.

— A Halloween Love Story. (Illus.). (Orig.). 1988. pap. 14.95 (*0-9614702-3-2*) Rods Bks.

— Second Overseas Highway to Key West Florida. (Orig.). 1989. write for info. (*0-9614702-5-9*) Rods Bks.

— A Slumbering Giant of the Past. 2nd ed. White, Louise, ed. (Illus.). 91p. (Orig.). 1985. lib. bdg. 19.95 (*0-9614702-1-6*) Rods Bks.

Bethel, Rodman J. & White, Louise. A Slumbering Giant of the Past. (Illus.). 91p. (Orig.). 1984. pap. 11.95 (*0-9614702-0-8*) Rods Bks.

Bethel, Shelia M. Making a Difference: Twelve Qualities That Make You a Leader. 1990. pap. 12.95 (*0-425-12309-X*) Berkley Pub.

Bethel, Terry A., et al. The Common Law of the Workplace: The Views of Arbitrators. St. Antoine, Theodore J., ed. LC 98-36527. 393p. 1998. 85.00 (*1-57018-120-9*, 1120-PR8) BNA Books.

Bethel, William. Questions That Make the Sale. 196p. 1992. pap. 21.95 (*0-85013-196-0*, TE7608) Dartnell Corp.

Bethel, William, et al. Ten Steps to Connecting with Your Customers. LC 94-68812. 278p. 1995. 28.95 (*0-85013-201-0*) Dartnell Corp.

Bethel, William, ed. see Dugan, Eleanor.

Bethel, Youlander. Being & Becoming. 108p. (Orig.). 1996. pap. 6.50 (*1-57502-126-9*) Morris Pubng.

Bethelard, Faith, jt. auth. see Young-Bruehl, Elisabeth.

***Bethell, A. Talbot.** The Early Settlers of the Bahamas & Colonists of North America. 238p. 1999. reprint ed. pap. 20.50 (*0-7884-1249-3*, B173) Heritage Bk.

Bethell, C. B., tr. see Guenon, Rene.

Bethell, Delia R., jt. auth. see Howard, Gary C.

Bethell, Donald, ed. Advances in Physical Organic Chemistry, Vol. 25. (Serial Publication Ser.). 474p. 1989. text 183.00 (*0-12-033525-5*) Acad Pr.

— Advances in Physical Organic Chemistry, Vol. 26. (Illus.). 432p. 1991. text 154.00 (*0-12-033526-3*) Acad Pr.

— Advances in Physical Organic Chemistry, Vol. 27. (Illus.). 320p. 1991. text 123.00 (*0-12-033527-1*) Acad Pr.

— Advances in Physical Organic Chemistry, Vol. 28. (Illus.). 312p. 1993. text 125.00 (*0-12-033528-X*) Acad Pr.

— Advances in Physical Organic Chemistry, Vol. 29. (Illus.). 368p. 1994. text 105.00 (*0-12-033529-8*) Acad Pr.

— Advances in Physical Organic Chemistry, Vol. 31. (Illus.). 336p. 1999. boxed set 140.00 (*0-12-033531-X*) Acad Pr.

— Advances in Physical Organic Chemistry, Vol. 32. (Illus.). 414p. 1999. 140.00 (*0-12-033532-8*) Acad Pr.

Bethell, Donald, jt. ed. see Gold, V.

Bethell, Eloise & Inman, Will, texts. Mexico: A Landscape in People. (C). 1989. text 39.00 (*0-946270-29-5*, Pub. by Pentland Pr) St Mut.

Bethell, Jean. Three Cheers for Mother Jones. LC 79-28655. 48p. (gr. 2-4). 1980. 6.95 (*0-03-054831-4*) Holt R&W.

Bethell, Jean & Axtell, Susan. A Colonial Williamsburg Activities Book: Fun Things to Do for Children 4 & Up. (Illus.). 40p. (J). (ps). 1984. pap. 4.25 (*0-87935-068-7*) Colonial Williamsburg.

Bethell, John & Somerville, Christopher. The English Coast. (Country Ser.). (Illus.). 160p. 1996. pap. 17.95 (*0-297-83215-8*, Pub. by Weidenfeld & Nicolson) Trafalgar.

Bethell, John T. Harvard Observed. LC 98-29816. (Illus.). 320p. 1998. 39.95 (*0-674-37733-8*) HUP.

Bethell, Leslie. A Cultural History of Latin America: Literature, Music & the Visual Arts in the 19th & 20th Century. LC 98-20589. 546p. (C). 1998. text 64.95 (*0-521-62327-8*); pap. text 24.95 (*0-521-62626-9*) Cambridge U Pr.

B

Bethell, Leslie, ed. Argentina since Independence. LC 92-26994. (Illus.). 418p. (C). 1993. text 74.95 (*0-521-43376-2*) Cambridge U Pr.

— Argentina since Independence. LC 92-26994. (Illus.). 418p. (C). 1993. pap. text 22.95 (*0-521-43988-4*) Cambridge U Pr.

— The Cambridge History of Latin America: Bibliographical Essays, Vol. 11. 1070p. (C). 1995. text 105.00 (*0-521-39525-9*) Cambridge U Pr.

— The Cambridge History of Latin America: Colonial Latin America, 5 vols. Incl. Vol. 1. Colonial Latin America. 656p. 1985. text 135.00 (*0-521-23223-6*); Vol. 2. Colonial Latin America. 922p. 1985. text 149.95 (*0-521-24516-8*); Vol. 3. From Independence to 1870. 961p. 1985. text 149.95 (*0-521-23224-4*); Vol. 4. 1870-1930. 684p. 1986. text 139.95 (*0-521-23225-2*); Vol. 5. 1870-1930. 956p. 1986. text 149.95 (*0-521-24517-6*); (Illus.). write for info. (*0-318-57955-3*) Cambridge U Pr.

— The Cambridge History of Latin America Pt. 1: Latin America since 1930, Economy, Society & Politics, Vol. 6. 649p. (C). 1995. text 99.95 (*0-521-23226-0*) Cambridge U Pr.

— The Cambridge History of Latin America Pt. 2: Latin America since 1930, Economy, Society & Politics, Vol. 6. 750p. (C). 1995. text 99.95 (*0-521-46556-7*) Cambridge U Pr.

— The Cambridge History of Latin America Vol. 7: Latin America since 1930. (Illus.). 789p. (C). 1990. text 139.95 (*0-521-24518-4*) Cambridge U Pr.

— The Cambridge History of Latin America Vol. 8: Latin America since 1930. 935p. (C). 1991. text 135.00 (*0-521-26652-1*) Cambridge U Pr.

— The Cambridge History of Latin America Vol. 10: Latin America since 1930, Ideas, Culture, & Society. 659p. (C). 1995. text 110.00 (*0-521-49594-6*) Cambridge U Pr.

— Chile since Independence. LC 92-17160. (Illus.). 250p. (C). 1993. text 74.95 (*0-521-43375-4*); pap. text 24.95 (*0-521-43987-6*) Cambridge U Pr.

— Colonial Brazil. 412p. 1987. pap. text 21.95 (*0-521-34925-7*) Cambridge U Pr.

— Cuba: A Short History. (Illus.). 180p. (C). 1993. text 54.95 (*0-521-43063-1*); pap. text 17.95 (*0-521-43682-6*) Cambridge U Pr.

— Ideas & Ideologies in Latin America since 1870. (Illus.). 350p. (C). 1996. text 64.95 (*0-521-46341-6*); pap. text 19.95 (*0-521-46833-7*) Cambridge U Pr.

— The Independence of Latin America. 272p. 1987. text 89.95 (*0-521-34129-9*); pap. text 19.95 (*0-521-34927-3*) Cambridge U Pr.

— Latin America: Economy & Society since 1930. 532p. (C). 1998. text 59.95 (*0-521-59393-X*); pap. text 19.95 (*0-521-59571-1*) Cambridge U Pr.

— Latin America: Economy & Society, 1870-1930: A Selection of Chapters from Volume V of The Cambridge History of Latin America. 432p. (C). 1989. text 20.95 (*0-521-36376-4*); pap. text 20.95 (*0-521-36898-7*) Cambridge U Pr.

— Latin America: Politics & Society since 1930. LC 97-11735. 500p. (C). 1998. pap. 21.95 (*0-521-59582-7*); text 59.95 (*0-521-59390-5*) Cambridge U Pr.

— Mexico since Independence. (Illus.). 463p. (C). 1991. text 80.00 (*0-521-41306-0*); pap. text 24.95 (*0-521-42372-4*) Cambridge U Pr.

Bethell, Leslie & Roxborough, Ian, eds. Latin America Between the Second World War & the Cold War: Crisis & Containment, 1944-1948. LC 92-15357. (Cambridge Latin American Studies: No. 73). 364p. (C). 1993. text 74.95 (*0-521-43032-1*) Cambridge U Pr.

— Latin America Between the Second World War & the Cold War: Crisis & Containment, 1944-1948. 364p. 1997. pap. text 18.95 (*0-521-57425-0*) Cambridge U Pr.

Bethell, Nicholas, tr. see Solzhenitsyn, Aleksandr.

Bethell, Ruth M., tr. see Zeeden, Ernest W.

***Bethell, Thomas N., et al.** Design Theory, Vol. 2. 2nd ed. (Encyclopedia of Mathematics & Its Applications Ser.: No. 78). 512p. (C). 2000. 95.00 (*0-521-77231-1*) Cambridge U Pr.

Bethell, Thomas N., jt. auth. see Ball, Robert M.

Bethell, Tom. The Noblest Triumph: Property & Prosperity Through the Ages. LC 98-6010. 378p. 1998. 29.95 (*0-312-21083-3*) St Martin.

— The Noblest Triumph: Property & Prosperity Through the Ages. 384p. 1999. pap. 16.95 (0-312-22337-4) St Martin.

Bethell, Tom, ed. see Gilfillan, Corinna.

Bethell, Ursula. Collected Poems. O'Sullivan, Vincent, ed. 128p. 1986. teacher ed. write for info. (0-318-60424-8); pap. text 22.00 (0-19-558139-3) OUP.

Bethell, Ursula & O'Sullivan, Vincent. Collected Poems. LC 98-155702. xxiii, 112 p. 1997. write for info. (0-86473-307-0) Victoria Univ Pr.

Bethemont, Jacques, et al. Italy: A Geographic Introduction. LC 81-15661. 222 p. 1983. 13.50 (0-582-30072-X) Addison-Wesley.

***Bethers, Linda.** Christmas Oranges. LC 99-50326. 1999. pap. 3.95 (1-57734-546-0, 01114387) Covenant Comms.

Bethge, Eberhard. Dietrich Bonhoeffer: A Biography. rev. ed. Barnett, Victoria J., ed. & rev. by. LC 99-39507. 912p. 1999. pap. 39.00 (0-8006-2844-6, 1-2844, Fortress Pr) Augsburg Fortress.

Bethge, Eberhard, ed. see Bonhoeffer, Dietrich.

Bethie. Bethie's "Really Silly Songs about Animals" (J). 1993. 8.95 incl. audio (1-881225-17-8) Discov Music.

Bethin, Christina Y. Polish Syllables: The Role of Prosody in Phonology & Morphology. (Illus.). 278p. (Orig.). 1992. pap. 22.95 (0-89357-234-9) Slavica.

— Slavic Prosody: Language Change & Phonological Theory. LC 97-1215. (Studies in Linguistics: Vol. 86). 360p. (C). 1998. 69.95 (0-521-59148-1) Cambridge U Pr.

B

Bethke, ed. Mineralization in Silicic Calderas: Questa, New Mexico, & San Juan Mountains, Colorado. (IGC Field Trip Guidebooks Ser.). 88p. 1989. 13.00 (0-87590-654-0, T320) Am Geophysical.

Bethke, Bruce. Headcrash. 352p. (Orig.). 1995. mass mkt. 5.50 (0-446-60260-4, Pub. by Warner Bks) Little.

— Headcrash. LC 97-21387. 352p. (Orig.). 1997. mass mkt. 10.99 (0-446-67314-5, Pub. by Warner Bks) Little.

Bethke, Bruce & Day, Vox. Rebel Moon. 1996. per. 5.99 (0-671-00236-8) PB.

Bethke, Graig M. Geochemical Reaction Modeling: Concepts & Applications. LC 95-35674. (Illus.). 416p. (C). 1996. text 65.00 (0-19-509475-1) OUP.

***Bethke, Philip M. & Hay, Richard L.** Ancient Lake Creede: Its Volcano-Tectonic Setting, History of Sedimentation & Relation to Mineralization in the Creede Mining District. LC 00-26436. (Special Paper Ser.). 2000. write for info. (0-8137-2346-9) Geol Soc.

Bethke, Robert D. Americana Crafted: Jehu Camper, Delaware Whittler. LC 95-21142. (Folk Art & Artists Ser.). (Illus.). 72p. 1995. pap. 16.95 (0-87805-763-3); text 32.50 (0-87805-762-5) U Pr of Miss.

Bethlehem, Daniel, et al, eds. The Yugoslav Crisis in International Law. 800p. (C). 1993. pap. text 150.00 (1-85701-016-7, Pub. by Grotius Pubns Ltd) St Mut.

Bethlehem, Daniel L. & Lauterpacht, E., eds. The Kuwait Crisis: Sanctions & Their Economic Consequences. 1045p. (C). 1991. pap. 300.00 (0-949009-88-1, Pub. by Grotius Pubns Ltd) St Mut.

Bethlehem, Daniel L. & Weller, Marc, eds. The Yugoslav Crisis in International Law: General Issues. LC 97-198718. (International Documents Ser.: Vol. 5). 800p. (C). 1997. text 125.00 (0-521-46304-1) Cambridge U Pr.

***Bethlehem, Lael & Goldblatt, Michael, eds.** The Bottom Line: Industry & the Environment in South Africa. LC 98-4432. (Illus.). xiv, 225p. 1998. pap. 17.95 (0-88936-830-9, Pub. by IDRC Bks) Stylus Pub VA.

Bethlehem Public Library Staff. Bethlehem. LC 97-183789. (Images of America Ser.). 1997. pap. 16.99 (0-7524-0805-4) Arcadia Publng.

Bethlem, Jaap & Knobbout, Charlotte E. Neuromuscular Diseases. Krabshuis, J. & Michael, E. J., trs. (Illus.). 166p. 1987. pap. 23.95 (0-19-261586-6) OUP.

Bethlem Royal Hospital & the Maudsley Hospital Sta, jt. ed. see Goldberg, David P.

Bethlen, Julianna. The Ice Witch & the Unicorn. LC 96-54697. (Illus.). 24p. (J). (ps). 1999. 18.99 (0-8037-2085-8, Dial Yng Read) Peng Put Young Read.

Bethlen, Stephen. Treaty of Trianon & European Peace: Four Lectures Delivered in London in November 1933. LC 73-135795. (Eastern Europe Collection). 1971. reprint ed. 16.95 (0-405-02737-0) Ayer.

Bethlenfalvay, G. J. & Linderman, R. G., eds. Mycorrhizae in Sustainable Agriculture. LC 92-32096. (Special Publications: No. 54). 124p. 1992. pap. 12.00 (0-89118-112-1) Am Soc Agron.

Bethmann, L. Making Prints from Nature. LC 97-50633. 1998. pap. 2.95 (1-58017-013-7) Storey Bks.

Bethmann, Laura D. Nature Printing with Herbs, Fruits, & Flowers. Balmuth, Deborah, ed. (Illus.). 96p. 1996. 24.95 (0-88266-929-X, 929-X, Storey Pub) Storey Bks.

***Bethuel, Fabrice, et al.** Calculus of Variations & Geometric Evolution Problems: Lectures Given at the 2nd Session of the Centro Internazionale Estivo (C.I.M.E.) Held in Cetraro, Italy, June 15-22, 1996. Hildebrandt, Stefan & Struwe, Michael, eds. LC 99-51991. (Lecture Notes in Mathematics Ser.: Vol. 1713). (Illus.). vii, 294p. 1999. pap. 59.80 (3-540-65977-3) Spr-Verlag.

Bethuel, Fabrice, et al. Ginzburg-Landau Vortices. (Progress in Nonlinear Differential Equations & Their Applications Ser.: Vol. 13). 158p. 1994. 54.50 (0-8176-3723-0) Birkhauser.

Bethune, Ade. Eye Contact with God Through Pictures: A Clip Book of Pictures from the Ade Bethune Collection. (Illus.). 64p. (Orig.). 1986. pap. 24.95 (0-934134-89-8) Sheed & Ward WI.

— The Way of the Cross: The Pilgrimage at Jerusalem. (Illus.). 32p. (Orig.). 1986. pap. 1.00 (0-934134-94-4) Sheed & Ward WI.

***Bethune-Baker, J. F.** Nestorius & His Teachings: A Fresh Examination of the Evidence. 252p. 1998. pap. 22.00 (1-57910-194-1) Wipf & Stock.

Bethune, George W. British Female Poets: With Biographical & Critical Notices. LC 75-38734. (Essay Index Reprint Ser.). 1977. reprint ed. 30.95 (0-8369-2636-6) Ayer.

***Bethune, Gordon.** From Worst to First: Behind the Scenes of Continental's Remarkable Comeback. 304p. 1999. pap. 16.95 (0-471-35652-2) Wiley.

Bethune-Griffin, Winnifred. Ibo: The Untold Story Behind Mark Clyde Bethune/Ibo Omar. LC 96-75548. (Illus.). viii, 132p. (Orig.). 1995. pap. 9.95 (0-9650550-0-0) Bethune MI.

Bethune, James D. Engineering Graphics with AutoCAD. LC 94-41420. 641p. (C). 1995. 115.00 (0-13-100140-X) P-H.

Bethune, James D. Engineering Graphics with Autocad Release 14. 3rd ed. LC 98-22958. 736p. 1998. 95.00 (0-13-795667-3) P-H.

— Engineering Graphics with AutoCAD 13. 2nd ed. LC 96-22491. 758p. 1996. 99.00 (0-13-567892-7) P-H.

***Bethune, James D.** Engineering Graphics with AutoCAD 2000. LC 99-50068. 2000. write for info. (0-13-022135-X) P-H.

Bethune, James D. Essentials of Drafting. 2nd ed. (Illus.). 416p. 1986. text 57.80 (0-13-284456-7) P-H.

— Modern Drafting: An Introduction to Cad. 480p. (C). 1988. text 53.20 (0-13-591058-7) P-H.

— A Visual Introduction to AutoCAD & 3D Designing with Release 14, Vol. 14. LC 99-14592. (Illus.). 597p. 1999. pap. 53.00 (0-13-020369-6) P-H.

Bethune, James D. & Svatik, Paul T. Introduction to Electrical Mechanical Drafting with Cad. LC 96-22838. 422p. (C). 1996. 84.00 (0-13-213539-6) P-H.

Bethune, John. Bethune on Bass. (Illus.). 88p. 1993. 32.50 (0-86417-511-6, Pub. by Kangaroo Pr) Seven Hills Bk.

Bethune, Jon L. Early Welsh Christianity: A Brief History. LC 97-68392. 49p. 1997. pap. 7.95 (1-889298-23-9) Rhwymbooks.

Bethune, Mary M., et al. Mary Mcleod Bethune Papers: The Bethune Foundation Collection. LC 96-48361. 1996. 2620.00 (1-55655-636-5) U Pubns Amer.

Bethune, Pearl E. Forward to the Past! Hierholzer, Ernest J., tr. from GER. LC 90-93592. (ENG & GER., Illus.). 310p. 1991. text 60.00 (0-9620124-1-6) Bethune Pubns.

— A Texas Child's Harvest: For Anyone Who Has Ever Been a Child. LC 88-70480. (Illus.). 64p. 1988. 29.95 (0-9620124-0-8) Bethune Pubns.

Bethuniensis, Eberhardus. Graecismus. (Corpus Grammaticorum Medii Aevi Ser.: Vol. I). xx, 319p. 1987. reprint ed. write for info. (3-487-07875-9) G Olms Pubs.

Bethwaite, Frank. High Performance Sailing. (Illus.). 416p. 1996. pap. text 32.95 (0-07-005799-0) Intl Marine.

***Bethwann, Laura D. & Fox, Ann R.** Rustic Accents for Your Home: 45 Projects from Vines, Twigs & Branches. LC 99-27368. (Illus.). 128p. 1999. 24.95 (1-58017-135-4) Storey Bks.

Beti, Mongo. Dictionnaire de la Negritude. (FRE.). 246p. 1989. pap. 55.00 (0-7859-8015-6, 2738404944) Fr & Eur.

— Lament for an African Pol. Bjornson, Richard, tr. from FRE. LC 84-51443.Tr. of La/Ruine Preque Cocasse d'un Polichinelle. 370p. 1985. 14.50 (0-89410-304-0, Three Contnts) L Rienner.

— Mission to Kala. (African Writers Ser.). 192p. (C). 1964. pap. 8.95 (0-435-90013-7, 90013) Heinemann.

— Le Pauvre Christ de Bomba. (B. E. Ser.: No. 27). (FRE.). 1956. 25.00 (0-8115-2978-9) Periodicals Srv.

— The Poor Christ of Bomba. (African Writers Ser.). 219p. (C). 1971. pap. 9.95 (0-435-90088-9, 90088) Heinemann.

Betiero, J. T. & Clymer, R. Swinburne. Nedoure: Priestess of the Magi. 248p. 1958. 9.95 (0-932785-34-4) Philos Pub.

— Nedoure: Priestess of the Magi. deluxe ed. 248p. 1958. lthr. 20.00 (0-932785-96-4) Philos Pub.

Betina, Vladimir, ed. Chromatography of Mycotoxins: Techniques & Applications. LC 93-15686. (Journal of Chromatography Library: Vol. 54). 454p. 1993. 214.00 (0-444-81521-X) Elsevier.

Betjeman, John. American's Guide to English Parish Churches. (Illus.). 1959. 20.00 (0-8392-1004-3) Astor-Honor.

— English Cities & Small Towns. (Writers' Britain Ser.). (Illus.). 96p. 1997. 11.95 (1-85375-251-7) Prion.

— Illustrated Poems of John Betjeman. (Illus.). 144p. 1997. pap. 19.95 (0-7195-5532-9, Pub. by John Murray) Trafalgar.

— The Illustrated Summoned by Bells. (Illus.). 144p. 1994. pap. 22.95 (0-7195-5284-2, Pub. by John Murray) Trafalgar.

— In Praise of Churches. (Illus.). 144p. 1998. pap. 19.95 (0-7195-5562-0, Pub. by John Murray) Trafalgar.

— John Betjeman. (Pocket Poet Ser.). 1967. pap. 3.95 (0-8023-9040-4) Dufour.

— John Betjeman: Collected Poems. 351p. 1990. 34.95 (0-7195-3628-6, Pub. by John Murray); pap. 24.95 (0-7195-3632-4, Pub. by John Murray) Trafalgar.

— A Nip in the Air. 1976. pap. 2.50 (0-393-04423-8) Norton.

Betjeman, John, ed. Altar & Pew. (Pocket Poet Ser.). 1960. pap. 3.95 (0-8023-9041-2) Dufour.

Betjeman, John & Hogarth, Paul. In Praise of Churches. (Illus.). 138p. 1996. 24.95 (0-7195-5554-X, Pub. by John Murray) Trafalgar.

Betken, William T., ed. see Shakespeare, William.

Betlem, G., jt. auth. see Backes, C.

Betlem, Gerrit. Civil Liability for Transfrontier Pollution: Dutch Environmental Tort Law in International Cases in the Light of Community Law. (International Environmental Law & Policy Ser.). 640p. (C). 1993. lib. bdg. 127.00 (1-85333-951-2, Pub. by Graham & Trotman) Kluwer Academic.

Betocchi, Silvia, ed. Giuseppe Prezzolini: The American Years, 1929-1962. LC 94-227795. 1994. pap. text 15.00 (0-913298-93-X) S F Vanni.

Betof, Edward & Harwood, Frederic. Just Promoted: How to Survive & Thrive in Your First 12 Months as a Manager. 273p. 1991. pap. 16.95 (0-07-005073-2) McGraw.

— Just Promoted: How to Survive & Thrive in Your First 12 Months as a Manager. 1992. 29.95 (0-07-005072-4) McGraw.

Betounes, D. Partial Differential Equations with Maple & Vector Analysis. LC 97-26381. (Illus.). 592p. 1998. 64.95 (0-387-98300-7) Spr-Verlag.

Betourne, Henriette D., et al. Direct French Conversation, 2 bks., Bk. 2. (FRE.). (Orig.). (gr. 9 up). 1966. pap. text 3.25 (0-88345-041-0, 17471) Prentice ESL.

Betran, J. Antonio, ed. see Hispaliensis, Isidorus.

Betran, J. Antonio, jt. ed. see Magallon, Ana.

Betrancourt, Jeanne. My Name Is Brian. (gr. 4-7). 1995. pap. text 3.99 (0-590-44922-2) Scholastic Inc.

Betro, Maria C. Hieroglyphics: The Writing of Ancient Egypt. LC 96-15588. (Illus.). 252p. 1996. 29.95 (0-7892-0232-8) Abbeville Pr.

Betrock, Alan. The Complete Guide to Cult Magazines Vols. 1 & 2: Scandal Magazines (1952-1962) & Strange & Exotic Hollywood (1945-1967) (Illus.). 96p. 1997. pap. 8.95 (1-893599-00-0) Shake Bks.

***Betrock, Alan.** The Cult Magazine Checklist Guide: Issue by Issue Listings for the Most Collectible Cult Magazines, 1945-1973. (Illus.). 96p. 2000. pap. 11.95 (1-893599-01-9) Shake Bks.

Betrock, Alan. Hitsville: The One Hundred Greatest Rock 'n' Roll Magazines, 1954-1968. LC 91-90477. (Illus.). 112p. (Orig.). 1991. pap. 11.95 (0-9626833-2-9) Shake Bks.

— The Illustrated Price Guide to Cult Magazines 1945-69. LC 94-92046. (Illus.). 160p. (Orig.). 1994. pap. 14.95 (0-9626833-6-1) Shake Bks.

— Sleazy Business: A Pictorial History of Exploitation Tabloids 1959-1974. (Illus.). 128p. (Orig.). 1996. pap. 12.95 (0-9626833-8-8) Shake Bks.

— Unseen America: The Greatest Cult Exploitation Magazines, 1950-1966. LC 90-91696. (Illus.). 112p. (Orig.). 1990. pap. 11.95 (0-9626833-0-2) Shake Bks.

Betrock, Alan, ed. Bikinis & Lingerie: A Pictorial Guide to Pin-Up Magazines, 1945-1960. (Illus.). 96p. 1998. pap. 11.95 (0-9626833-9-6) Shake Bks.

Betrock, Alan & Schneider, Hillard. The Personality Index: To Hollywood Scandal Magazines, 1952-1966. LC 90-92216. (Illus.). 64p. (Orig.). 1990. pap. 6.00 (0-9626833-1-0) Shake Bks.

Betros, Cecil G. Speech-Language Pathology in Home Health Care. LC 98-48636. (Illus.). 225p. 1999. pap. 49.00 (0-8342-0919-5, 20919) Aspen Pub.

Betrus, Michael. The Guide to Executive Recruiters. 2nd rev. ed. 848p. 1997. pap. 24.95 (0-07-006280-3) McGraw.

Betrus, Michael, jt. auth. see Block, Jay A.

Bets, Barnard, ed. see Ericson, Lois.

Betschart, Anne & American Association of Diabetes Educators Staff. Medical Book of Remedies: 50 Ways to Manage Diabetes. LC 96-105879. 80p. 1995. write for info. (0-7853-1233-1) Pubns Intl Ltd.

Betschart, Jean. Diabetes Care for Babies, Toddlers, & Preschoolers: A Reassuring Guide. LC 98-230636. 96p. 1998. pap. 14.95 (1-56561-167-5); pap. 14.95 (0-471-34676-4) Wiley.

Betschart, Jean. In Control: A Guide for Teens with Diabetes. 128p. 1995. pap. 9.95 (0-471-34742-6) Wiley.

— It's Time to Learn about Diabetes. 112p. 1995. pap. 9.95 (0-471-34743-4) Wiley.

— Magic Ride in Foozbah Land: An Inside Look at Diabetes. 48p. 1995. pap. 12.95 (0-471-34755-8) Wiley.

Betschart, Jean, et al. In Control: A Guide for Teens with Diabetes. (Illus.). 125p. 1995. 10.95 (1-56561-061-X) Wiley.

Betschart, Jean, jt. auth. see Siminerio, Linda M.

Betser, Muki. Secret Soldier: The True Life Story of Israel's Greatest Commando. Rosenberg, Robert, ed. (Illus.). 276p. 1998. text 23.00 (0-7881-5639-X) DIANE Pub.

Betsky, Aaron. Architecture & Medicine: I. M. Pei Designs the Kirklin Clinic, University of Alabama at Birmingham Medical Center. LC 92-28149. 144p. (C). 1993. lib. bdg. 34.00 (0-8191-8878-6) U Pr of Amer.

— Drager House: Berkeley, California 1994 Franklin D. Israel. LC 96-172989. (Architecture in Detail Ser.). (Illus.). 60p. 1996. pap. text 29.95 (0-7148-3382-7, Pub. by Phaidon Press) Phaidon Pr.

— James Gamble Rogers & the Architecture of Pragmatism. (American Monographs). (Illus.). 320p. 1994. 50.00 (0-262-02381-4) MIT Pr.

— Paul Tuttle: Three Evolutions Plus. (Illus.). 33p. 1995. pap. text 18.00 (1-880658-09-7) San Barb CAF.

— Queer Space: Architecture & Same-Sex Desire. LC 96-15992. 1997. 27.50 (0-688-14301-6, Wm Morrow) Morrow Avon.

Betsky, Aaron, et al, contrib. by. Sitting on the Edge: Modernist Design from the Collection of Michael & Gabrielle Boyd. LC 98-40463. (Illus.). 164p. 1999. 40.00 (0-8478-2167-6, Pub. by Rizzoli Intl) St Martin.

***Betsky, Aaron & Adigard, Erik.** Architecture Must Burn: Manifestoes for the Future of Architecture. (Illus.). 144p. 2000. pap. 39.95 (1-58423-030-4) Gingko Press.

Betsky, Aaron & Eizenberg, Julie. Koning Eizenberg: Buildings & Projects. LC 96-13261. (Illus.). 224p. 1996. 60.00 (0-8478-1943-4, Pub. by Rizzoli Intl); pap. 40.00 (0-8478-1944-2, Pub. by Rizzoli Intl) St Martin.

Betsky, Aaron & San Francisco Museum of Modern Art Staff. Icons: Magnets of Meaning. LC 96-46759. (Illus.). 272p. 1997. 27.50 (0-8118-1857-8) Chronicle Bks.

***Betsky, Aaron & Sudjic, Deyan.** Vertigo: The City in the Twenty-First Century. Moore, Rowan, ed. (Illus.). 240p. 1999. 55.00 (1-58423-001-0) Gingko Press.

Betsky-Zweig, Sarah. Onions & Cucumbers & Plums: Forty-Six Yiddish Poems. LC 80-20914. (ENG & YID.). 285p. reprint ed. pap. 88.40 (0-608-06270-7, 206659900008) Bks Demand.

Betson, Carol L. Managing the Medical Enterprise: A Study of Physician Managers. Farmer, Richard, ed. LC 85-31834. (Research for Business Decisions Ser.: No. 89). 205p. reprint ed. pap. 63.60 (0-8357-1735-6, 207036300088) Bks Demand.

Betson, Craig E. Signs of Life... Observations of Death. Farese, Susan, ed. LC 94-60686. (Illus.). 92p. 1994. pap. 9.95 (1-880254-18-2) Vista.

Betson, Martin. Here Begynneth a Treatyse to Dyspose Men to Be Vertously Occupyed in Theyr Myndes & Prayers. LC 77-6854. (English Experience Ser.: No. 848). 1977. reprint ed. lib. bdg. 20.00 (90-221-0848-1) Walter J Johnson.

Betsos, P. J. Modern UCC Litigation Forms, 3 vols. 1969. 465.00 (0-8205-2118-3) Bender.

Betsworth, Roger G. The Radical Movement of the 1960s. LC 80-12534. (American Theological Library Association Monograph: No. 14). viii, 363p. 1980. 26.50 (0-8108-1307-6) Scarecrow.

Bett, Brian. Planet Ocean. Balkwill, Fran, ed. (Making Sense of Science Ser.). (Illus.). 32p. (J). 1997. pap. 12.00 (1-85578-094-1, Pub. by Portland Pr Ltd) Ashgate Pub Co.

Bett, Henry. Joachim of Flora. (Great Medieval Churchmen Ser.). vii, 184p. 1976. reprint ed. lib. bdg. 16.50 (0-915172-24-0) Richwood Pub.

***Bett, Richard.** Pyrrho, His Antecedents & His Legacy. 300p. 2000. text 55.00 (0-19-825065-7) OUP.

Bett, Richard, ed. see Sextus Empiricus Staff.

Bett, Richard, tr. & comment see Sextus Empiricus.

Bettagno, Alessandro, et al, texts. The Prado Museum. LC 97-215454. (Illus.). 670p. 1997. 175.00 (0-8109-6346-9, Pub. by Abrams) Time Warner.

Bettane. Classement, 1997: Des Vins et Domaines de France. 527p. 1997. 69.95 (0-7859-9356-8) Fr & Eur.

Bettane & Desseauve. Classement 98 des Vins et Domaines de France. (FRE.). Date not set. 79.95 (0-7859-9584-6) Fr & Eur.

Bettany, George T. The Conquerors of the World: Peoples & Races of Europe. 1977. lib. bdg. 59.95 (0-8490-1664-9) Gordon Pr.

— Dark Peoples of the Land of Sunshine. LC 73-89424. (Black Heritage Library Collection). 1977. 23.95 (0-8369-8510-9) Ayer.

— Eminent Doctors, 2 Vols., Set. LC 76-39663. (Essay Index Reprint Ser.). 1977. 44.95 (0-8369-2747-8) Ayer.

***Bettany, George T.** The Red, Brown, & Black Men of America & Australia, & Their White Supplanters. (LC History-America-E). 289p. 1999. reprint ed. lib. bdg. 79.00 (0-7812-4236-3) Rprt Serv.

Bettany, George T. World's Inhabitants. LC 72-5744. (Black Heritage Library Collection). 1977. reprint ed. 90.95 (0-8369-9134-6) Ayer.

Bettany, W. A., ed. see Byron, George Gordon.

Bettarello, A., ed. Famotidine: A Further Development in the Modern Treatment of Peptic Ulcer Disease. (Journal: Digestion: Vol. 32, Suppl. 1, 1985). (Illus.). 72p. 1985. pap. 19.25 (3-8055-4254-2) S Karger.

Bettas, George A., jt. ed. see Byers, C. Randall.

Bettauer, Evelyn C., jt. auth. see Rohner, Ronald P.

Bettauer, Hugo. The City Without Jews. Brainin, Salomea N., tr. from GER. LC 91-24155. (Stadt Ohne Juden Ser.). 200p. reprint ed. pap. 9.95 (0-8197-0594-2) Bloch.

Bettazzi, Enrico. Tibaldi Fountain Pens. LC 99-232662. 1998. 95.00 (88-422-0788-8) Allemandi.

Bette, Nina K. Heaven Sent. LC 96-36728. (Janet Dailey's Love Scenes Ser.). 1997. pap. 3.50 (1-56853-030-7, Signal Hill) New Readers.

Bettelheim, Bruno. The Empty Fortress: Infantile Autism & the Birth of the Self. LC 67-10886. 484p. 1972. reprint ed. pap. 16.95 (0-02-903140-0) Free Pr.

— Freud & Man's Soul. LC 83-47809. 128p. 1984. pap. 9.00 (0-394-71036-3) Vin Bks.

— A Home for the Heart. 1985. pap. 14.95 (0-226-04439-4) U Ch Pr.

— Individual & Mass Behavior in Extreme Situations. (Reprint Series in Sociology). (C). 1993. reprint ed. pap. text 2.90 (0-8290-2621-5, S-23) Irvington.

— Love Is Not Enough. 1950. 27.95 (0-02-903280-6) Free Pr.

— Obsolete Youth. 1970. pap. 5.00 (0-911302-11-5) San Francisco Pr.

— Truants from Life: The Rehabilitation of Emotionally Disturbed Children. LC 55-7331. 516p. 1964. pap. 16.95 (0-02-903450-7) Free Pr.

— The Uses of Enchantment: The Meaning & Importance of Fairy Tales. 2000. 26.50 (0-8446-7111-8) Peter Smith.

Bettelheim, Bruno. The Uses of Enchantment: The Meaning & Importance of Fairy Tales. 1989. pap. 13.00 (0-679-72393-5) Vin Bks.

Bettelheim, Bruno & Freedgood, Anne. A Good Enough Parent: A Book on Child-Rearing. LC 87-45931. 480p. 1988. reprint ed. pap. 16.00 (0-394-75776-9) Vin Bks.

Bettelheim, Bruno, jt. auth. see Ogburn, William F.

Bettelheim, Charles. Class Struggles in the U. S. S. R. First Period, 1917-1923. Pearce, Brian, tr. LC 76-28986. 567p. 1978. pap. 12.00 (0-85345-434-5, Pub. by Monthly Rev) NYU Pr.

— Class Struggles in the U. S. S. R. Second Period: 1923-1930, Vol. 11. Pearce, Brian, tr. from FRE. LC 76-28976. 640p. 1978. pap. 10.00 (0-85345-514-7, Pub. by Monthly Rev) NYU Pr.

An Asterisk (*) at the beginning of an entry indicates that the title is appearing for the first time.

— Economic Calculation & Forms of Property. Taylor, John, tr. from FRE. LC 74-21473. 168p. 1976. pap. 10.00 (*0-85345-427-2*, Pub. by Monthly Rev) NYU Pr.

— India Independent. LC 67-19254. 428p. reprint ed. pap. 132.70 (*0-608-15885-2*, 203076600070) Bks Demand.

Bettelheim, Charles, jt. auth. see Burton, Neill G.

Bettelheim, Charles, jt. auth. see Sweezy, Paul M.

Bettelheim, D., et al. Fetal Sonographic Biometry: A Guide to Normal & Abnormal Measurements. LC 96-33682. (Illus.). 346p. 1997. 98.00 (*1-85070-725-1*) Prthnon Pub.

Bettelheim, Frederick A. Experiments for Introduction to Organic Chemistry: A Miniscale Approach. (C). 1996. pap. text, teacher ed. 46.50 (*0-03-019238-2*) Harcourt.

— General Organic & Biochemistry. 5th ed. LC 97-13992. (Illus.). 576p. (C). 1997. pap. text, lab manual ed. 54.50 (*0-03-020333-3*, Pub. by SCP) Harcourt.

— General Organic & Biochemistry. 5th ed. (Illus.). 256p. (C). 1997. pap. text, student ed. 33.50 (*0-03-020437-2*, Pub. by SCP) Harcourt.

— Introduction to General Organic & Biochemistry. 3rd ed. (C). 1991. pap. text, teacher ed., lab manual ed. 40.50 (*0-03-054677-X*, Pub. by Harcourt Coll Pubs) Harcourt.

— Introduction to General, Organic & Biochemistry. 4th ed. (C). 1994. pap. text, teacher ed. 33.75 (*0-03-001069-1*) Harcourt Coll Pubs.

— Introduction to General, Organic & Biochemistry. 5th ed. LC 97-66892. (Illus.). 912p. (C). 1997. text 90.00 (*0-03-020217-5*, Pub. by SCP) Harcourt.

— Introduction to General Organic & Biological Chemistry Flashcards. 4th ed. (C). 1995. text 104.50 (*0-03-008437-7*) Harcourt Coll Pubs.

— Introduction to Organic Biochemistry. 3rd ed. LC 97-66891. (Illus.). 640p. (C). 1997. text 96.00 (*0-03-020218-3*, Pub. by SCP) Harcourt.

— Introduction to Organic Biochemistry. 5th ed. (C). 1997. pap. text, teacher ed. 28.00 (*0-03-020433-X*) Harcourt Coll Pubs.

— Introductory Organic Biochemistry. 5th ed. (C). 1997. pap. text, student ed. 26.50 (*0-03-020434-8*, Pub. by Harcourt Coll Pubs) Harcourt.

— Lab Experiments for Organic & Biochemistry. 3rd ed. LC 97-20202. (Golden Sunburst Ser.). 336p. (C). 1997. pap. text, lab manual ed. 45.50 (*0-03-020332-5*) SCP.

Bettelheim, Judith, jt. auth. see Mesa-Bains, Amalia.

Bettelheim, Judith, ed. see Ortiz, Fernando & Brown, David.

Bettell, Charlie. The Art of Lure Fishing. (Illus.). 160p. 1995. 39.95 (*1-85223-797-X*, Pub. by Cro1wood) Trafalgar.

***Bettelyoun, Susan B. & Waggoner, Josephine.** With My Own Eyes: A Lakota Woman Tells Her People's History. LC 97-37884. (Illus.). 199p. 1999. pap. 14.95 (*0-8032-6164-0*, Bison Books) U of Nebr Pr.

Bettelyoun, Susan B., et al. With My Own Eyes: A Lakota Woman Tells Her People's History. LC 97-37884. (Illus.). 199p. 1999. text 45.00 (*0-8032-1280-1*, Bison Books) U of Nebr Pr.

Bettembourg, Georges & Brame, Michael. The White Death. (Illus.). 300p. 1981. 13.95 (*0-685-03582-4*) Reynard Hse.

Betten, Francis S. From Many Centuries: A Collection of Historical Papers. LC 68-16910. (Essay Index Reprint Ser.). 1977. reprint ed. 20.95 (*0-8369-0206-8*) Ayer.

Betten, Lammy, Jr. International Labor Law. 1993. pap. text 66.50 (*90-6544-708-3*) Kluwer Academic.

***Betten, Lammy, ed.** Human Rights Act, 1998: What It Means: The Incorporation Of The European Convention On Human Rights Into the Legal Order of the United Kingdom. LC 98-43912. 336p. 1999. 102.00 (*90-411-1085-2*) Kluwer Academic.

Betten, Lammy, et al, eds. The Employment Contract in Transforming Labour Relations. 1996. pap. 72.00 (*90-411-0149-7*) Kluwer Law Intl.

Betten, Lammy & Grief, Nicholas. European Law & Human Rights. LC 98-11058. (European Law Ser.). 176p. 1998. pap. 28.00 (*0-582-28716-2*) Longman.

Betten, Lammy, jt. auth. see Jaspers, C. M.

Betten, Neil. Catholic Activism & the Industrial Worker. LC 76-17280. 201p. reprint ed. pap. 62.40 (*0-7837-4965-1*, 204463100004) Bks Demand.

Betten, Neil & Austin, Michael J. The Roots of Community Organizing, 1917-1939. 184p. (C). 1990. 27.95 (*0-87722-662-8*) Temple U Pr.

Betten, Neil, jt. auth. see Mohl, Raymond A.

Bettencourt, Carl M., jt. ed. see Jacobs, Karen.

Bettencourt, Christine, ed. see Wright, Peter M.

***Bettencourt, K. C. Theft & Drugs in the Workplace: A Management Guide. rev. ed. LC 90-63054. (Illus.). 138p. (Orig.). 2000. pap. 10.95 (*0-9676979-0-5*) Knighthawk Pub Co.**

"Many employees believe that stealing from their company isn't really stealing. Their philosophy is that 'everyone does it, & no one cares if you take a few things.' Yet this year alone, the United States retail, manufacturing, & banking industries combined will lose nine billion dollars due to employee theft, & that figure increases by 35 percent every five years. Sixty percent of all employees are given the opportunity to steal. If we change employees' perceptions about theft in the workplace, then we go a long way toward solving the problem." So says K. C. Bettencourt, president of The Bettencourt Group, a California-based loss prevention consulting firm. In his book, THEFT & DRUGS IN THE WORKPLACE (Knighthawk Publishing $9.95), Bettencourt explains that devising a company policy to deal with employee theft is the best way to deter a potential criminal. "Many employees steal because of poor communication with the company, bad feelings about the company, & dissatisfaction with their job. Supervisors who can improve their interpersonal & management skills & who can convey the message that loss prevention is everyone's responsibility can help to deter employee theft." Bettencourt says that companies must also take additional measures including "consistently prosecuting, & communicating that fact to other workers." With a consistent policy in place, employee theft is less likely to occur. Also, Bettencourt explains, managers should be taught to recognize warning signs. Internal theft indicators include frequent customer complaints about certain employees, frequent tardiness & absenteeism by an employee, inventory shrinkages or losses, & violations of company policies on a regular basis. According to Bettencourt, employee theft is not a street crime & employees who steal must not be treated the same way as street criminals. "Employees who are otherwise honest people may steal money or merchandise from the company & yet not define their behavior as theft. Exactly what is considered theft needs to be clearly defined. Those firms that establish rules & procedures to detect & to deal with the problem generally have lower levels of theft by employees." He stresses that the company must work as a team to deter internal thievery. "Give employees the message that what hurts the company hurts everybody in the company. Establish rules for acceptable employee behavior, & then provide continuous training to ensure awareness & understanding. Loss prevention should be everyone's responsibility," Bettencourt says. *Publisher Paid Annotation.*

Bettenson, Henry, ed. Documents of the Christian Church. 2nd ed. 362p. 1970. pap. text 15.95 (*0-19-501293-3*) OUP.

Bettenson, Henry, tr. Early Christian Fathers: A Selection from the Writings of the Fathers from St. Clement of Rome to St. Athanasius. 318p. 1969. reprint ed. pap. text 21.95 (*0-19-283009-0*) OUP.

***Bettenson, Henry & Maunder, Chris, eds.** Documents of the Christian Church. 3rd ed. 488p. 1999. pap. 15.95 (*0-19-288071-3*) OUP.

Bettenson, Henry, tr. see Augustine, Saint.

Bettenson, Henry, tr. see Livy.

Better, Cathy D. Don't Hit Your Brother with Your Mouth Full. LC 94-96250. (Illus.). (Orig.). 1995. pap. 10.00 (*0-9629880-7-3*) ACME Pr.

***Better, Cathy Drinkwater.** Excuse Me! 2001. write for info. (*0-8054-2166-1*) Broadman.

— In His Footsteps. 2000. 12.99 (*0-570-07035-X*) Concordia.

— My B-I-B-L-E. (Illus.). 10p. (J). (ps-k). 2000. 8.99 (*0-570-07041-4*) Concordia.

Better Communications Staff, jt. auth. see Dumaine, Deborah.

Better Homes & Gardens. America's Best Loved Community Cookbook Recipes: Casual Suppers. 144p. 1996. 15.95 (*0-696-20547-5*) Meredith Bks.

— America's Best-Loved Community Recipes, Vol. 1. (Better Homes & Gardens Ser.). (Illus.). 464p. 1994. 29.95 (*0-696-20095-3*) Meredith Bks.

— Baths: Your Guide to Planning & Remodeling. LC 96-76679. (Remodeling Ser.: No. 3). (Illus.). 112p. (Orig.). 1996. pap. 12.95 (*0-696-20611-0*) Meredith Bks.

— Best Bread Machine Recipes: For One-&-a-Half & Two Pound Loaf Loaves. LC 96-78799. (Illus.). 128p. 1997. 15.95 (*0-696-20682-X*) Meredith Bks.

— Better Homes & Gardens Baby Book. 1995. mass mkt. 6.99 (*0-553-85061-X*) Bantam.

— Better Homes & Gardens New Baby Book. 416p. 1986. mass mkt. 5.99 (*0-553-26114-2*) Bantam.

— Better Homes & Gardens New Baby Book: The Complete Guide to Pregnancy, Childbirth & Baby Care. rev. ed. 528p. 1999. mass mkt. 6.99 (*0-553-58065-5*) Bantam.

— Better Homes & Gardens New Cook Book. 10th ed. 1995. mass mkt. 8.99 (*0-553-85116-0*) Bantam.

— Better Homes & Gardens New Cook Book. 11th limited ed. (Better Homes & Gardens Ser.). (Illus.). 574p. 1999. 26.95 (*0-696-21002-9*, Better Homes) Meredith Bks.

— Better Homes & Gardens Step-by-Step Cabinets & Shelves. (Illus.). 96p. 1983. pap. 8.95 (*0-696-01065-8*) Meredith Bks.

***Better Homes & Gardens.** Big Book of Healthy Family Dinners. LC 99-75950. (Better Homes & Gardens Ser.). (Illus.). 288p. 2000. 24.95 (*0-696-21088-6*) Meredith Bks.

— Big Book of 30-Minute Dinners. (Illus.). 288p. 2000. 24.95 (*0-696-21027-4*, Better Homes) Meredith Bks.

Better Homes & Gardens. Bread Machine Bounty: More Than 100 Recipes for Your Bread Machine. LC 93-148264. (Better Homes & Gardens Ser.). (Illus.). 144p. 1992. reprint ed. text 14.95 (*0-696-01992-2*) Meredith Bks.

— Chicken. (Cooking for Today Ser). (Illus.). 144p. 1993. 15.95 (*0-696-01843-8*) Meredith Bks.

— Complete Book of Baking. (Better Homes & Gardens Ser.). (Illus.). 336p. 1995. 29.95 (*0-696-20040-6*) Meredith Bks.

— Complete Guide to Flower Gardening. (Illus.). 408p. 1995. 29.95 (*0-696-00057-1*) Meredith Bks.

— Cookies, Cookies, Cookies. 144p. 1992. pap. 12.95 (*0-696-00054-7*) Meredith Bks.

***Better Homes & Gardens.** Crafts to Make & Sell: Over 1,000 Tips & Ideas for Marketing, (Even Giving!) Your Crafts. (Illus.). 216p. 2000. 29.95 (*0-696-21020-7*, Better Homes) Meredith Bks.

Better Homes & Gardens. Crockery Cookbook. (Illus.). 144p. 1994. 14.95 (*0-696-20365-0*) Meredith Bks.

— Decks: Your Guide to Planning & Building. LC 96-75561. (Do-It-Yourself Ser.). 112p. 1996. pap. 12.95 (*0-696-20451-7*) Meredith Bks.

***Better Homes & Gardens.** Easy Cooking with Zing: 90 Recipes Bursting with Fresh Flavor. (Illus.). 96p. 2000. 12.95 (*0-696-21113-0*, ReaLemon) Meredith Bks.

Better Homes & Gardens. Eat & Stay Slim. LC 96-78800. (Illus.). 112p. 1997. 14.95 (*0-696-20649-8*) Meredith Bks.

— Family Favorites Made Lighter. 240p. 1992. pap. 14.95 (*0-696-00079-2*) Meredith Bks.

— 501 Quilt Blocks: A Treasury of Patterns for Patchwork & Applique. LC 94-75959. 320p. 1995. pap. 19.95 (*0-696-20480-0*) Meredith Bks.

***Better Homes & Gardens.** Flea Market Decorating: Creating Style with Vintage Finds. (Illus.). 224p. 2000. 34.95 (*0-696-20882-2*, Better Homes) Meredith Bks.

Better Homes & Gardens. Furniture Projects. LC 96-76680. (Wood Shop Library). (Illus.). 160p. 1996. pap. 14.95 (*0-696-20630-7*, Meredith Pr) Meredith Bks.

***Better Homes & Gardens.** Garden Style Projects: Decorating Ideas for Indoors & Outdoors, 6 vols. LC 98-68018. (Better Homes & Gardens Bks.). (Illus.). 224p. 1999. 34.95 (*0-696-20929-2*, Bttr Homes & Grdns) Meredith Bks.

— Garden Style Projects: Decorating Ideas for Indoors & Outdoors. (Illus.). 168p. 2000. 24.95 (*0-696-21036-3*, Better Homes) Meredith Bks.

Better Homes & Gardens. Gardening Tips: 100's of Tips, Techniques & Ideas for Your Yard. 80p. 1996. pap. 7.95 (*0-696-20119-4*) Meredith Bks.

— Gas Grill Cookbook. LC 93-86596. (Illus.). 144p. 1994. 14.95 (*0-696-00062-8*) Meredith Bks.

— Great Cooking for Two. 240p. 1995. pap. 16.95 (*0-696-20427-4*) Meredith Bks.

***Better Homes & Gardens.** Halloween: 101 Frightfully Fun Ideas. (Illus.). 144p. 2000. pap. 15.95 (*0-696-20975-6*, Better Homes) Meredith Bks.

Better Homes & Gardens. Healthy Family Cookbook. (Better Homes & Gardens Ser.). 360p. 1996. pap. 19.95 (*0-696-20704-4*) Meredith Bks.

— Home Landscaping: Plants, Projects & Ideas for Your Yard. LC 95-81773. 288p. 1996. 29.95 (*0-696-20422-3*) Meredith Bks.

***Better Homes & Gardens.** Home Security: Your Guide to Protecting Your Family. LC 98-68015. (Illus.). 80p. 1999. pap. 12.95 (*0-696-20934-9*) Meredith Bks.

Better Homes & Gardens. Incredibly Awesome Crafts for Kids. (Illus.). 168p. (J). 1992. pap. 16.95 (*0-696-01984-1*) Meredith Bks.

***Better Homes & Gardens.** It's My Party: 12 Great Parties You Can Make Yourself. (Illus.). 96p. (J). 2000. 15.95 (*0-696-20964-0*, Better Homes) Meredith Bks.

Better Homes & Gardens. Kitchens: Your Guide to Planning & Remolding. LC 96-75562. (Do-It-Yourself Ser.). (Illus.). 112p. 1996. pap. 12.95 (*0-696-20452-5*) Meredith Bks.

— Low Fat & Luscious. LC 95-81715. 160p. 1996. 16.95 (*0-696-20373-1*) Meredith Bks.

— Low-Fat & Luscious Italian. LC 96-78798. (Illus.). 160p. 1997. 16.95 (*0-696-00063-6*) Meredith Bks.

— Low-Fat Meals. (Better Homes & Gardens Ser.). 128p. 1990. 12.95 (*0-696-01889-6*) Meredith Bks.

— More Bread Machine Bounty. LC 93-86597. (Better Homes & Gardens Ser.). 144p. 1994. 14.95 (*0-696-00072-5*) Meredith Bks.

— Nestle Make-It-Simple Entertaining: Fabulous Menus for Festive Celebrations. LC 98-164827. (Illus.). 96p. 1996. 12.95 (*0-696-20613-7*, Meredith Pr) Meredith Bks.

— Nestle Toll House Best Loved Cookies. 96p. 1996. 12.95 (*0-696-20554-8*) Meredith Bks.

***Better Homes & Gardens.** New Baking Book. (Better Homes & Gardens Ser.). (Illus.). 416p. 1999. 34.95 (*0-696-20971-3*, Better Homes) Meredith Bks.

Better Homes & Gardens. New Cook Book. 11th ed. Darling, Jennifer, ed. (Illus.). 576p. 1997. boxed set 34.95 (*0-696-20644-7*) Meredith Bks.

— New Crockery Cooker Cook Book. 80p. 1987. 9.95 (*0-696-01740-7*) Meredith Bks.

— New Decorating Book: A Complete Guide. LC 96-78792. 408p. 1997. 34.95 (*0-696-20636-6*) Meredith Bks.

— New Garden Book. (Better Homes & Gardens Ser.). 384p. 1990. 29.95 (*0-696-00042-3*) Meredith Bks.

— New Garden Book. (Better Homes & Gardens Ser.). (Illus.). 384p. 1990. pap. 16.95 (*0-696-02557-4*) Meredith Bks.

***Better Homes & Gardens.** The New Grilling Book: Charcoal, Gas, Smokers, Indoor Grills, Rotisseries. 372p. 2000. ring bd. 29.95 (*0-696-21029-0*, Better Homes) Meredith Bks.

Better Homes & Gardens. New Junior Cookbook: 77 Easy-to-Make Recipes. 6th ed. Darling, Jennifer, ed. LC 97-71329. (Better Homes & Gardens Test Kitchen Ser.). (Illus.). 112p. (J). (gr. 3-7). 1997. 15.95 (*0-696-20708-7*, Better Homes) Meredith Bks.

***Better Homes & Gardens.** New Junior Craft Book: 52 Cool Projects for Kids to Make. (Illus.). 112p. 2000. 15.95 (*0-696-21021-5*, Better Homes) Meredith Bks.

Better Homes & Gardens. 1001 Do-It-Yourself Tips: Hints, Tricks, & Shortcuts for Your Home. (Better Homes & Gardens Ser.). (Illus.). 192p. 1995. pap. 19.95 (*0-696-20478-9*) Meredith Bks.

***Better Homes & Gardens.** Paint Ideas & Decorating Techniques. LC 99-75939. (Better Homes & Gardens Ser.). (Illus.). 160p. 2000. pap. 19.95 (*0-696-21032-0*) Meredith Bks.

Better Homes & Gardens. Pasta. (Cooking for Today Ser.). (Illus.). 144p. 1993. 15.95 (*0-696-01990-6*) Meredith Bks.

***Better Homes & Gardens.** Perennials for Today's Gardens. 288p. 2000. 29.95 (*0-696-20952-7*, Bttr Homes & Grdns) Meredith Bks.

Better Homes & Gardens. Pizzas. (Cooking for Today Ser.). (Illus.). 144p. 1994. 15.95 (*0-696-02569-8*) Meredith Bks.

***Better Homes & Gardens.** Recipes to the Rescue: Thrilling Kitchen Adventures... Just in the Nick of Time! 112p. 2000. 15.95 (*0-696-21052-5*, Better Homes) Meredith Bks.

Better Homes & Gardens. Salads. (Cooking for Today Ser.). (Illus.). 144p. 1994. 15.95 (*0-696-02062-9*) Meredith Bks.

— 75 Years of All-Time Favorites. LC 96-78797. (Illus.). 320p. 1997. 29.95 (*0-696-20633-1*) Meredith Bks.

— Simply Handmade: 365 Easy Gifts & Decorations You Can Make. LC 98-66251. (Illus.). 216p. 1998. 29.95 (*0-696-20782-6*, Meredith Pr) Meredith Bks.

— Soups & Stews. (Cooking for Today Ser.). (Illus.). 144p. 1993. 15.95 (*0-696-01844-6*) Meredith Bks.

— Steaks, Ribs, Chops: And All the Fixin's That Make 'Em Great. 120p. 1998. pap. 19.95 (*0-696-20828-8*) Meredith Bks.

— Step-by-Step Annuals. (Illus.). 132p. 1997. pap. 12.95 (*0-696-20657-9*) Meredith Bks.

***Better Homes & Gardens.** Step-by-Step Cabinets & Shelves. (Better Homes & Gardens Ser.). (Illus.). 112p. 2000. pap. 12.95 (*0-696-20990-X*) Meredith Bks.

Better Homes & Gardens. Step-by-Step Deck Projects. (Step-by-Step Ser.). 112p. 1998. pap. 12.95 (*0-696-20779-6*) Meredith Bks.

***Better Homes & Gardens.** Step-by-Step Garden Basics. LC 99-75942. (Better Homes & Gardens Ser.). (Illus.). 168p. 2000. pap. 16.95 (*0-696-21030-4*) Meredith Bks.

Better Homes & Gardens. Step-by-Step Herbs. (Illus.). 132p. 1997. pap. 12.95 (*0-696-20658-7*) Meredith Bks.

— Step-by-Step Landscaping. (Better Homes & Gardens Ser.). (Illus.). 336p. 1991. pap. 15.95 (*0-696-02558-2*) Meredith Bks.

— Step-by-Step Landscaping: Planning, Planting, Building. LC 90-63292. (Better Homes & Gardens Ser.). (Illus.). 336p. 1991. 29.95 (*0-696-01873-X*) Meredith Bks.

— Step-by-Step Lawns, Ground Covers & Vines. (Illus.). 132p. 1997. pap. 12.95 (*0-696-20654-4*) Meredith Bks.

— Step-by-Step Low-Maintenance Gardens. (Illus.). 132p. 1997. pap. 12.95 (*0-696-20656-0*) Meredith Bks.

— Step-by-Step Ornamental Grasses. (Illus.). 132p. 1997. pap. 12.95 (*0-696-20659-5*) Meredith Bks.

— Step-by-Step Perennials. (Illus.). 132p. 1997. pap. 12.95 (*0-696-20660-9*) Meredith Bks.

— Step-by-Step Shade Gardens. LC 94-74290. (Illus.). 132p. 1997. pap. 12.95 (*0-696-20661-7*) Meredith Bks.

— Step by Step Successful Gardening. (Better Homes & Gardens Ser.). 256p. 1992. pap. 14.95 (*0-696-00736-3*) Meredith Bks.

— Step-by-Step Trees & Shrubs. (Illus.). 132p. 1997. pap. 12.95 (*0-696-20662-5*) Meredith Bks.

— Step-by-Step Vegetables. (Illus.). 132p. 1997. pap. 12.95 (*0-696-20663-3*) Meredith Bks.

— Step-by-Step Wildflowers & Native Plants. (Illus.). 132p. 1997. pap. 12.95 (*0-696-20655-2*) Meredith Bks.

***Better Homes & Gardens.** Step-by-Step Yard Care. Blume, James D., ed. LC 99-15941. (Better Homes & Gardens Ser.). (Illus.). 168p. 2000. pap. 16.95 (*0-696-21031-2*) Meredith Bks.

Better Homes & Gardens. Stir Fries. LC 94-75962. (Cooking for Today Ser.). (Illus.). 144p. 1994. 15.95 (*0-696-02568-X*) Meredith Bks.

— 30 Minute Main Dishes. (Cooking for Today Ser.). 144p. 1996. 15.95 (*0-696-20147-X*) Meredith Bks.

— Vegetarian Recipes. LC 92-82904. (Cooking for Today Ser.). (Illus.). 144p. 1993. 15.95 (*0-696-01989-2*) Meredith Bks.

— Wok Cuisine. (Better Homes & Gardens Ser.). (Illus.). 216p. 1991. 24.95 (*0-696-01950-7*) Meredith Bks.

— Workshop Tools & Techniques. LC 96-76682. (Wood Shop Library). (Illus.). 160p. 1996. pap. 14.95 (*0-696-20631-5*, Meredith Pr) Meredith Bks.

***Better Homes & Gardens, contrib. by.** Better Home & Gardens Homemade Cookies. (Illus.). 96p. 2000. 16.95 (*0-696-21193-9*, Better Homes) Meredith Bks.

— Better Homes & Gardens Bed & Bath: Decorating Ideas & Projects. (Illus.). 112p. 2000. pap. 14.95 (*0-696-21144-0*, Better Homes) Meredith Bks.

— Better Homes & Gardens Christmas All Through the House. (Illus.). 320p. 2000. 34.95 (*0-696-20976-4*, Better Homes) Meredith Bks.

— Better Homes & Gardens Dinnertime Express. (Illus.). 288p. 2000. 24.95 (*0-696-21192-0*, Better Homes) Meredith Bks.

— Better Homes & Gardens Fireplaces: Decorating & Planning Ideas. (Illus.). 160p. 2000. pap. 19.95 (*0-696-21102-5*, Better Homes) Meredith Bks.

— Better Homes & Gardens Indoor Grilling: Recipes for Tabletop Grills & Rangetop Inserts. (Illus.). 96p. 2000. 16.95 (*0-696-21238-2*, Better Homes) Meredith Bks.

— Better Homes & Gardens On-Pack with Book. 2000. ring bd. 29.95 (*0-696-21249-8*) Meredith Bks.

B

— Better Homes & Gardens One Dish Dinners. (Illus.). 240p. 2000. 24.95 (*0-696-20965-9*, Better Homes) Meredith Bks.

— Better Homes & Gardens Porches & Sunrooms: Your Guide to Planning & Remodeling. (Illus.). 112p. 2000. pap. 14.95 (*0-696-21101-7*, Better Homes) Meredith Bks.

— Better Homes & Gardens Real Life Decorating. (Illus.). 168p. 2000. 29.95 (*0-696-21097-5*, Better Homes) Meredith Bks.

— Better Homes & Gardens Second Home: Finding Your Place in the Fun. (Illus.). 216p. 2000. 34.95 (*0-696-21152-1*, Better Homes) Meredith Bks.

— Better Homes & Gardens the New Guide to Step-By-Step Landscaping. (Illus.). 408p. 2001. 34.95 (*0-696-20850-4*, Better Homes) Meredith Bks.

— Better Homes & Gardens Treasured Recipes: 200 Prize Winning Dishes from America's Hometown Cooks. (Illus.). 288p. 2000. 29.95 (*0-696-21159-9*, Better Homes) Meredith Bks.

— A Passion for Chocolate: Seductively Sweet Recipes to Melt Your Heart. (Illus.). 96p. 2000. 16.95 (*0-696-21174-2*, Better Homes) Meredith Bks.

Better Homes & Gardens, ed. Additions: Your Guide to Planning & Design. LC 96-78793. (Better Homes & Gardens Ser.). (Illus.). 112p. 1997. pap. 12.95 (*0-696-20635-8*) Meredith Bks.

***Better Homes & Gardens, ed.** America's All-Time Favorite Canning & Preserving Recipes. LC 95-81717. (Better Homes & Gardens Bks.). (Illus.). 96p. 1999. 12.95 (*0-696-21150-5*) Meredith Bks.

Better Homes & Gardens, ed. At the Circus. (Max the Dragon Project Book Ser.). (Illus.). 32p. (J). (ps-3). 1991. lib. bdg. 12.95 (*1-878363-57-3*) Forest Hse.

***Better Homes & Gardens, ed.** Better Homes & Gardens All-Time Favorites: 70 Years of Best-Loved Recipes. (Illus.). 96p. 1999. 14.95 (*0-696-21128-9*, Better Homes) Meredith Bks.

Better Homes & Gardens, ed. Better Homes & Gardens New Cook Book: New Edition. 1995. mass mkt. 5.95 (*0-553-85078-4*) Bantam.

— Better Homes & Gardens New Cookbook. 11th ed. 540p. 1994. mass mkt. 25.95 (*0-553-85023-7*) Bantam.

— Cooking for Friends. LC 98-66249. (Fresh & Simple Ser.). (Illus.). 96p. 1998. pap. 15.95 (*0-696-20853-9*, Better Homes) Meredith Bks.

— Country America Celebrity Recipes: Great Recipes from Your Favorite Country Music Stars. LC 98-218574. (count). (Illus.). 96p. 1998. 12.95 (*0-696-20885-7*, Country Home) Meredith Bks.

— Food for Health & Healing. (Illus.). 368p. 1999. pap. 24.95 (*0-696-20856-3*, Better Homes) Meredith Bks.

— Let's Go Exploring. (Max the Dragon Project Book Ser.). (Illus.). 32p. (J). (gr. k-3). 1991. lib. bdg. 12.95 (*1-878363-58-1*) Forest Hse.

***Better Homes & Gardens, ed.** New Baking Book. LC 98-66245. (Illus.). 384p. 1998. ring bd. 25.95 (*0-696-20799-0*) Meredith Bks.

Better Homes & Gardens, ed. New Flavors from Your Crockery Cooker. LC 98-66247. (Illus.). 96p. 1998. 15.95 (*0-696-20855-5*, Better Homes) Meredith Bks.

— The New Remodeling Book: Your Complete Guide to Planning Your Dream Project. LC 98-66254. (Illus.). 360p. 1998. 34.95 (*0-696-20740-0*, Better Homes) Meredith Bks.

***Better Homes & Gardens, ed.** Pressure Cooker Cookbook. LC 95-75621. (Better Homes & Gardens Ser.). (Illus.). 96p. 2000. 12.95 (*0-696-21215-3*) Meredith Bks.

Better Homes & Gardens, ed. Quick Simmering Soups. LC 98-66250. (Fresh & Simple Ser.). (Illus.). 96p. 1998. pap. 15.95 (*0-696-20854-7*, Better Homes) Meredith Bks.

— Silly Snacks. LC 98-66248. (Illus.). 112p. (J). (gr. 2-7). 1998. 15.95 (*0-696-20847-4*, Better Homes) Meredith Bks.

— Step-by-Step Outdoor Projects. LC 98-66255. (Illus.). 112p. 1998. pap. 12.95 (*0-696-20817-2*, Better Homes) Meredith Bks.

— Step-by-Step Plumbing. LC 96-78795. (Better Homes & Gardens Ser.). (Illus.). 112p. 1997. pap. 12.95 (*0-696-20634-X*) Meredith Bks.

— Step-by-Step Wiring. LC 96-78794. (Better Homes & Gardens Ser.). (Illus.). 112p. 1997. pap. 12.95 (*0-696-20453-3*) Meredith Bks.

— 301 Stylish Storage Ideas. LC 98-66252. (Illus.). 112p. 1998. pap. 12.95 (*0-696-20857-1*, Better Homes) Meredith Bks.

— 2001 Cross-Stitch Designs: The Essential Reference Book. LC 98-66924. (Illus.). 336p. 1999. 34.95 (*0-696-20780-X*, Better Homes) Meredith Bks.

— Water Wonders. (Max the Dragon Project Book Ser.). (Illus.). 32p. (J). (gr. k-3). 1991. lib. bdg. 12.95 (*1-878363-60-3*) Forest Hse.

— Weekend Decorating Projects. LC 98-66253. (Illus.). 112p. 1998. pap. 12.95 (*0-696-20858-X*, Better Homes) Meredith Bks.

Better Homes & Gardens, ed. At the Zoo. (Max the Dragon Project Book Ser.). 32p. (J). (ps-3). 1991. reprint ed. lib. bdg. 12.95 (*1-878363-30-1*) Forest Hse.

— Bird Buddies. (Max the Dragon Project Book Ser.). 32p. (J). (gr. k-3). 1991. reprint ed. lib. bdg. 12.95 (*1-878363-31-X*) Forest Hse.

— Make Believe. (Max the Dragon Project Book Ser.). 32p. (J). (gr. k-3). 1991. reprint ed. lib. bdg. 12.95 (*1-878363-32-8*) Forest Hse.

— On the Farm. (Max the Dragon Project Book Ser.). 32p. (J). (gr. k-3). 1991. reprint ed. lib. bdg. 12.95 (*1-878363-33-6*) Forest Hse.

Better Homes & Gardens & Mitchell, Carolyn B. Grill It Right. 240p. 1995. pap. 16.95 (*0-696-20472-X*) Meredith Bks.

— Mexican Cooking. LC 96-78801. (Illus.). 96p. 1997. 14.95 (*0-696-20647-1*) Meredith Bks.

Better Homes & Gardens, et al. 30-Minute Vegetarian Recipes. LC 96-76681. (Illus.). 96p. 1996. 12.95 (*0-696-20615-3*) Meredith Bks.

Better Homes & Gardens, jt. auth. see Darling, Jennifer.

Better Homes & Gardens, jt. ed. see Fuller, Kristi.

Better Homes & Gardens Staff. Kraft Springtime Celebrations (MCP) (Illus.). 96p. 1997. 12.95 (*0-696-20719-2*) Meredith Bks.

***Better Homes Fund Staff.** Homeless Children: America's New Outcasts. LC 99-63630. (Illus.). 54p. 1999. pap. text. write for info. (*0-9672165-0-8*) Bettr Homes Fund.

***Better Life Press Staff & Sauvage, Lester R.** Better Life Diet: A Simple Plan for Long & Youthful Life. 74p. 2000. pap. 7.95 (*0-9663788-3-0*, Pub. by Better Life Pr) IPG Chicago.

Better, Maurice B. Contract Bargaining Handbook for Local Union Leaders. LC 93-11496. 308p. 1993. trans. 35.00 (*0-87179-803-4*) BNA Books.

Better, O. S., et al. Diuretics. Gregor, R. F. et al, eds. LC 95-3116. (Handbook of Experimental Pharmacology Ser.: Vol. 117). 1995. write for info. (*0-387-58965-1*) Spr-Verlag.

Better Restaurant Association Staff, ed. Historic Restaurants of America. (Illus.). 1987. pap. 9.95 (*0-913290-72-6*) Camaro Pub.

Betteridge, Barbara, tr. see Steiner, Rudolf.

Betteridge, D. & Morrell, J. M. Clinicians' Guide to Lipids & Coronary Heart Disease. (Illus.). 192p. 1997. pap. 30.00 (*0-412-75720-6*, Pub. by E A) OUP.

***Betteridge, D. John, ed.** Diabetes: Current Perspectives. 359p. 2000. 99.95 (*1-85317-555-2*, Pub. by Martin Dunitz) Blackwell Sci.

Betteridge, D. John, ed. Lipids: Current Perspectives. 312p. (C). 1996. text. write for info. (*1-85317-231-6*) Mosby Inc.

Betteridge, Harold T. Cassell's German Dictionary: German-English, English-German. rev. ed. LC 77-18452. (ENG & GER.). 560p. 1977. 13.95 (*0-02-522650-9*) Macmillan.

— Cassell's German Dictionary: German-English, English-German. rev. ed. LC 77-18452. (ENG & GER.). 1600p. 1978. 25.00 (*0-02-522920-6*); 27.00 (*0-02-522930-3*) Macmillan.

Betteridge, John & Shepherd, James, eds. Lipoproteins in Health & Disease. LC 98-3650. (Arnold Publication Ser.). 1300p. 1998. text 225.00 (*0-340-55269-7*, Pub. by E A) Routldge.

Betteridge, Terry. An Algebraic Analysis of Storage Fragmentation. LC 82-11194. (Computer Science: Systems Programming Ser.: No. 15). (Illus.). 232p. reprint ed. pap. 72.00 (*0-8357-1364-4*, 207035900088) Bks Demand.

Betteridge, Tom. Brief Chronicles & True Accounts: Tudor Histories of the English Reformation, 1530-83. LC 98-54195. (St. Andrews Studies in Reformation History Ser.). 256p. 1999. text 86.95 (*1-84014-281-2*) Ashgate Pub Co.

Betterly, Joan. Good Food Afloat: Tasty & Nutritious Recipes for Healthy Shipboard Meals. LC 95-42381. 204p. 1996. pap. 16.95 (*0-88415-357-6*, 5357) Gulf Pub.

***Betters, Chuck.** Treasures of Faith Leader's Guide: Living Boldly in View of God's Promises. 1999. pap. text 11.99 (*0-87552-094-4*) P & R Pubng.

Betters, Chuck & Betters, Sharon. Treasures of Faith: Living Boldly in View of God's Promises. LC 99-32966. 256p. 1999. pap. 12.99 (*0-87552-096-0*) P & R Pubng.

Betters, Fran. Adirondack Fish & Game Recipes. unabridged ed. Goodman, Jan, ed. (Illus.). 104p. 1993. pap. 9.95 (*0-9616439-8-6*) Adirondack S P.

— Adirondack Tall Tales & Short Stories. unabridged ed. (Illus.). 114p. 1991. pap. 9.95 (*0-9616439-6-X*) Adirondack S P.

— The Collection. unabridged ed. Goodman, Alan, ed. 160p. 1992. pap. 14.95 (*0-9616439-7-8*) Adirondack S P.

— Meet the Animals of the Adirondacks. Balzer, Nadine, ed. (Illus.). 64p. 1993. pap. 9.95 (*0-9616439-9-4*) Adirondack S P.

Betters, Francis E. Something's Fishy in the Adirondacks. 1985. 9.95 (*0-318-20255-7*) Adirondack S P.

Betters, Francis E. & Woods, Craig. Fly Fishing, Fly Tying & Pattern Guide. LC 86-70207. (Illus.). 112p. (Orig.). 1986. pap. 24.95 (*0-9616439-0-0*) Adirondack S P.

Betters, Francis E., et al. Fran Betters' Fly Fishing, Fly Tying & Pattern Guide. (Illus.). 112p. 1986. 12.95 (*0-318-20254-9*) Adirondack S P.

Betters, Paul V. Federal Services to Municipal Governments. LC 77-749330. (American Federalism-the Urban Dimension Ser.). 1978. reprint ed. lib. bdg. 19.95 (*0-405-10479-0*) Ayer.

— The Personnel Classification Board: Its History, Activities & Organization. LC 72-3081. (Brookings Institution. Institute for Government Research. Service Monographs of the U. S. Government: No. 64). reprint ed. 24.00 (*0-404-57164-6*) AMS Pr.

Betters, Paul V., et al. Cities & the 1936 Congress & Recent Federal-City Relations. LC 77-74929. (American Federalism-the Urban Dimension Ser.). 1978. reprint ed. lib. bdg. 19.95 (*0-405-10478-2*) Ayer.

Betters, Paul V., jt. auth. see Smith, Darrell H.

Betters-Reed, Bonita & Crocitto, Madeline, eds. Weaving Partnerships & Communities - Visions, Voices, Ventures: Proceedings of the 34th Annual Meeting - Eastern Academy of Management. 300p. 1997. write for info. (*0-916958-15-9*) Eastrn Acad Mgmt.

Betters, Sharon, jt. auth. see Betters, Chuck.

Betters, Sharon W. Treasures of Encouragement: Women Helping Women in the Church. 208p. (Orig.). 1996. pap. 9.99 (*0-87552-097-9*) P & R Pubng.

Betterton, Alec & Dymond, David. Lavenham Industrial Town. 144p. 1990. 30.00 (*0-86138-069-X*, Pub. by T Dalton) St Mut.

— Lavenham Industrial Town. 1994. pap. 35.00 (*0-86138-070-3*, Pub. by T Dalton) St Mut.

Betterton, Don M. How the Military Will Help You Pay for College. 2nd ed. LC 89-29864. 184p. (Orig.). 1990. pap. 9.95 (*0-87866-996-5*) Petersons.

***Betterton, Don M.** Insider's Guide to Paying for College: The Guide To Understanding College Financing & Getting. LC 99-56877. 160p. 1999. pap. write for info. (*0-7689-0230-4*) Petersons.

Betterton, Rosemary. An Intimate Distance: Women, Artists, & the Body. LC 95-44682. (Illus.). 256p. (C). 1996. pap. 20.99 (*0-415-11085-8*) Routledge.

— An Intimate Distance: Women, Artists, & the Body. LC 95-44682. (Illus.). 256p. (C). 1996. 75.00 (*0-415-11084-X*) Routledge.

— Looking On. 1987. 22.95 (*0-86358-177-3*, Pub. by Pandora) Harper SF.

Bettes, Roger & Watts, Jacqueline, eds. Unsteady Flow & Fluid Transients: Proceedings of the International Conference Durham, U. K. 29 September - 1 October 1992. (Illus.). 380p. (C). 1992. text 138.00 (*90-5410-046-X*, Pub. by A A Balkema) Ashgate Pub Co.

Bettess, R., jt. ed. see Soulsby, R.

Bettetini, Gianfranco. The Language & Technique of the Film. (Approaches to Semiotics Ser.: No. 28). 1973. text 43.10 (*90-279-2412-0*) Mouton.

Bettex, Albert W. German Novel of Today: A Guide to Contemporary Fiction in Germany, to the Novels of the Emigrants & to Those of German-Speaking Swiss Writers. LC 77-99655. (Select Bibliographies Reprint Ser.). 1977. 16.95 (*0-8369-5084-4*) Ayer.

Bettex, M. & Koch, A., eds. Kinderchirurgische Probleme in der paediatrische Praxis. (Paediatrische Fortbildungskurse fuer die Praxis Ser.: Vol. 49). (Illus.). 1980. pap. 35.75 (*3-8055-0232-X*) S Karger.

Bettey, J. H. WESSEX FROM AD 1000 C. (Regional History of England Ser.). 352p. 1986. text 42.95 (*0-582-49207-6*) Longman.

Bettger, Frank. How I Multiplied My Income & Happiness in Selling. 315p. 1982. 12.95 (*0-13-423962-8*); pap. 4.95 (*0-13-423954-7*) P-H.

— How I Raised Myself from Failure to Success in Selling. 192p. 1992. per. 11.00 (*0-671-79437-X*, Fireside) S&S Trade Pap.

Betti, Claudia W. & Sale, Teel. Drawing: A Contemporary Approach. 4th ed. LC 96-76307. 256p. (Orig.). (C). 1996. pap. text 63.50 (*0-15-501580-X*, Pub. by Harcourt Coll Pubs) Harcourt.

Betti, Raimondo, jt. ed. see Meier, Urs.

Betti, Silvello, et al. Coherent Optical Communications Systems. (Series in Microwave & Optical Engineering). 560p. 1995. 110.00 (*0-471-57512-7*) Wiley.

Betti, Ugo. Corruzione Al Palazzo di Giustizia. Luciani, Vincent, ed. (ITA.). (C). 1980. pap. 8.95 (*0-913298-20-4*) S F Vanni.

Bettig, Ronald V. Copyrighting Culture: The Political Economy of Intellectual Property. (Critical Studies in Communication & in the Cultural Industries). 288p. (C). 1996. pap. text 27.00 (*0-8133-3304-0*, Pub. by Westview) HarpC.

Bettignies, Henri-Claude De, see De Bettignies, Henri-Claude.

Bettigole, Neal H. & Robison, Rita. Bridge Decks: Design, Construction, Rehabilitation & Replacement. LC 97-151. 88p. 1997. 24.00 (*0-7844-0223-X*) Am Soc Civil Eng.

Bettigole, Neal H., jt. ed. see Haber, Bernard J.

Bettin, Christopher, ed. see Gale, Jack L.

Bettin, Christopher, ed. see Godi, Art & Reyhons, Kenneth.

Bettin, Christopher, ed. see Jewell, Michael.

Bettin, Christopher, ed. see Kahn, Harold L.

Bettin, Christopher, ed. see Reyhons, Kenneth.

***Bettin, Wayne.** Revelation Revealed: A Verse by Verse Analysis Letting Bible Verses Reveal the Book of Revelation. 360p. 1999. pap. 9.95 (*0-9632172-8-3*) ABS Bks.

Betting. Persuasive Communication. 5th ed. (C). 1994. pap. text 50.00 (*0-03-055352-0*, Pub. by Harcourt Coll Pubs) Harcourt.

Bettinger, Cass. High Performance in the '90s. 312p. 1990. text 55.00 (*1-55623-425-2*, Irwn Prfssnl) McGraw-Hill Prof.

Bettinger, Julie S. & King, Heidi T. Tallahassee: Tradition, Technology, Teamwork. Turner, James E. & Gilreath, Lenita, eds. LC 95-17683. 144p. Date not set. pap. 24.95 (*1-885352-10-7*) Community Comm.

Bettinger, Lillian. Forty-Eight Plus Years in the Same House. 40p. 1994. pap. 5.00 (*1-886303-05-3*) Write to Print.

***Bettinger-Lopez, Caroline.** Cuban-Jewish Journeys: Searching for Identity, Home & History in Miami. LC 00-8613. (Illus.). 352p. (C). 2000. text 40.00 (*1-57233-097-X*, Pub. by U of Tenn Pr); pap. text 15.00 (*1-57233-098-8*, Pub. by U of Tenn Pr) U Ch Pr.

Bettinger, R. L. Hunter-Gatherers: Archaeological & Evolutionary Theory. LC 90-25228. (Interdisciplinary Contributions to Archaeology Ser.). (Illus.). 272p. (C). 1991. 42.50 (*0-306-43650-7*, Plenum Trade) Perseus Pubng.

Bettingham, Erwin P. Persuasive Communication. 5th ed. (C). 1994. pap. text, teacher ed. 4.75 (*0-03-097621-9*) Harcourt Coll Pubs.

Betttinghaus, Erwin P. The Nature of Proof. 2nd ed. LC 76-173979. (Orig.). 1972. pap. 3.50 (*0-672-61295-X*, SC1, Bobbs) Macmillan.

***Bettini, C., et al.** Time Granularities in Databases, Data Mining & Temporal Reasoning. xi, 226p. 2000. 38.00 (*3-540-66997-3*) Spr-Verlag.

Bettini, Maurizio. Anthropology & Roman Culture: Kinship, Time, Images of the Soul. Van Sickle, John, tr. from ITA. LC 90-25887. (Ancient Society & History Ser.). (Illus.). 344p. 1991. text 47.50 (*0-8018-4104-6*) Johns Hopkins.

— Classics in the Age of Indiscretion. 300p. 1999. pap. text 14.95 (*1-56886-064-1*, Pub. by Marsilio Pubs) Consort Bk Sales.

***Bettini, Maurizio.** Portrait of the Lover. LC 99-20905. 353p. 1999. 45.00 (*0-520-20850-1*, Pub. by U CA Pr) Cal Prin Full Svc.

Bettino, M. L. Access to Reading: Electronic Textbook. (Focused Reading Ser.). 155p. (C). 1995. text 14.95 (*1-888971-00-2*) La Vita Nuova.

Bettinson, Craig, jt. auth. see Rogers, Dorothy.

Bettio, Francesca. The Sexual Division of Labour: The Italian Case. (Illus.). 304p. 1988. 64.00 (*0-19-828544-2*) OUP.

Betts, E. Arthur, III, ed. Archaeological Geology of the Archaic Period in North America. LC 94-49522. (Special Papers: Vol. 297). 1995. pap. 45.00 (*0-8137-2297-7*) Geol Soc.

Betts, Richard A. & Thomas, Howard, eds. Risk, Strategy & Management. LC 90-4522. (Strategic Management, Policy & Planning Ser.: Vol. 5). 215p. 1990. 73.25 (*0-89232-801-0*) Jai Pr.

Bettison, Joan. Baba Nangko. LC 93-26225. (Voyages Ser.). (Illus.). (J). 1994. 4.25 (*0-383-03733-6*) SRA McGraw.

Bettison, Sue. Toilet Training to Independence for the Handicapped: A Manual for Trainers. (Illus.). 144p. (C). 1982. pap., spiral bd. 28.95 (*0-398-04678-6*) C C Thomas.

Bettle, Janet. Personal Injury Claims in the County Court. 184p. 1992. 60.00 (*1-85190-166-3*, Pub. by Tolley Pubng) St Mut.

***Bettle, Janet.** Unnatural Causes. 320p. 2000. 23.95 (*0-312-26244-2*, Minotaur) St Martin.

Bettle, Janet & Hamey, John A. Personal Injury Claims in the County Court: Practice & Procedure. 2nd ed. (Lawyers Practice & Procedure Ser.). 289p. (C). 1994. pap. 195.00 (*0-85459-921-5*, Pub. by Tolley Pubng) St Mut.

Bettle, Jonathan, jt. auth. see Finke, Ronald A.

Bettleheim, Bruno & Janowitz, Morris. Ethnic Toleraence: A Function of Social & Personal Control. (Reprint Series in Social Sciences). (C). 1993. reprint ed. pap. text 5.00 (*0-8290-4156-7*, S-24) Irvington.

Bettman, Lynn. Profiles of American Artists. rev. ed. 1984. pap. 25.00 (*0-317-26926-7*) Kennedy Gall.

Bettmann, Michael A., et al. Complications in Diagnostic Interventional Radiology. 3rd rev. ed. (Illus.). 704p. 1996. 265.00 (*0-86542-243-5*) Blackwell Sci.

Bettmann, Otto L. Bettmann: The Picture Man. Sheffield, Norman, Jr., ed. LC 92-10639. (Illus.). 192p. 1992. 37.95 (*0-8130-1153-1*) U Press Fla.

— The Delights of Reading: Quotes, Notes & Anecdotes. 140p. 1992. pap. 12.95 (*0-87923-951-4*) Godine.

— The Good Old Days? They Were Terrible! LC 74-6050. (Illus.). 1974. pap. 15.95 (*0-394-70941-1*) Random.

— Johann Sebastian Bach: As His World Knew Him. (Illus.). 272p. 1995. 22.50 (*1-55972-279-7*, Birch Ln Pr) Carol Pub Group.

— Johann Sebastian Bach: As His World Knew Him. (Illus.). 260p. 1997. pap. 19.95 (*0-8065-1870-7*, Citadel Pr) Carol Pub Group.

— A Pictorial History of Medicine. (Illus.). 336p. 1979. 48.95 (*0-398-00149-9*); pap., spiral bd. 36.95 (*0-398-06019-3*) C C Thomas.

Bettner. Weston Manufacturing. Date not set. pap. text 12.00 (*0-314-03804-3*) West Pub.

Bettner, Betty L. & Lew, Amy. Raising Kids Who Can: Use Good Judgement, Assume Responsibility, Communicate Effectively, Respect Self & Others, Cooperate, Develop Self-Esteem & Enjoy Life. 2nd rev. ed. LC 89-82477. (Illus.). 120p. 1990. pap. 9.50 (*0-9624841-7-2*) Connex Pr.

— Raising Kids Who Can Leader's Guide: Parent Study Group Leader's Guide. 2nd rev. ed. 105p. 1998. pap. 25.00 (*0-9624841-1-3*) Connex Pr.

Bettner, Betty L., jt. auth. see Lew, Amy.

Bettner, Betty Lou, jt. auth. see Lew, Amy.

***Betton, Scott G.** Love Poems of the Sacred Heart. unabridged ed. Thornton, Diana J., ed. 202p. (Orig.). 2000. pap. 15.00 (*1-930507-00-3*) Eternal Pubng.

Bettone, James. Tricks of the Visual Basic 4 Gurus. 744p. 1996. pap. text 49.99 incl. cd-rom (*0-672-30929-7*) Sams.

Bettoney, Fred, ed. see Weissenborn, Julius.

Bettoni, Efrem. Duns Scotus: The Basic Principles of His Philosophy. Bonansea, Berbardine, ed. LC 78-14031. 220p. 1979. reprint ed. lib. bdg. 69.50 (*0-313-21142-6*, BESB, Greenwood Pr) Greenwood.

— St. Bonaventure. Gambatese, Angelus, tr. from ITA. LC 81-13371. (Notre Dame Pocket Library).Tr. of Santa Bonaventura. 127p. 1981. reprint ed. lib. bdg. 55.00 (*0-313-23271-7*, BESB, Greenwood Pr) Greenwood.

Bettotti, B., et al, eds. General Relativity & Gravitation. 1984. text 232.00 (*90-277-1819-9*) Kluwer Academic.

Bettridge, Jack, jt. auth. see Browne, Rick.

Betts. Seizing Control: Live with Epilepsy. Date not set. text. write for info. (*0-7190-3814-6*) Manchester Univ Pr.

— Seizing Control: Live with Epilepsy. 1998. text. write for info. (*0-7190-3813-8*) Manchester Univ Pr.

Betts, A. V., ed. The Harra & the Hamad Vol. 1: Excavations & Explorations in Eastern Jordan. (Sheffield Archaeological Monographs Ser.: Vol. 9). 252p. 1999. 74.00 (*1-85075-614-7*, Pub. by Sheffield Acad) CUP Services.

Betts, Ann. The Journey: Discovering Your Life's Stories. (Illus.). 65p. 1998. 19.95 (*0-9669141-0-4*) Sure Betts Ink.

B

An Asterisk (*) at the beginning of an entry indicates that the title is appearing for the first time.

Betts, Anthony. Green Wood & Chloroform: A Young English Doctor Comes to Rural Maine. LC 97-51605. (Illus.). 208p. 1998. pap. 12.95 (*0-89272-434-X*) Down East.

Betts, Benjamin. Mexican Imperial Coinage: The Medals & Coinage. (Illus.). 1982. reprint ed. pap. 10.00 (*0-915262-75-4*) S J Durst.

Betts, C. J. Early Deism in France. 1984. lib. bdg. 179.50 (*90-247-2923-8*) Kluwer Academic.

Betts, C. J., tr. see De Montesquieu, Charles.

Betts, C. W. & Crane, Stephen W., eds. Manual of Small Animal Surgical Therapeutics. (Illus.). 440p. 1986. text 49.00 (*0-7216-5924-1*, W B Saunders Co) Harcrt Hlth Sci Grp.

Betts, Charles W. & Betts, Frederick. Thomas Betts, (1618-1688) & His Descendants. (Illus.). 136p. 1988. reprint ed. pap. 27.50 (*0-8328-0247-6*); reprint ed. lib. bdg. 35.50 (*0-8328-0246-8*) Higginson Bk Co.

Betts, Chris A. & Penbera, Joseph J. A Guide to One Hundred Publishing Opportunities for Business Faculty. (Illus.). 256p. 1990. 19.95 (*0-912201-22-3*) CSU Pr Fresno.

Betts, Clive. The Political Conundrum. Stephens, Meic, ed. (Changing Wales Ser.). 65p. 1993. pap. 11.95 (*0-8464-4713-4*) Beekman Pubs.

Betts, Clive, ed. Changing Wales Vol. V: The Political Conundrum. 1993. pap. 21.00 (*1-85902-011-9*, Pub. by Gomer Pr) St Mut.

Betts, David S. Introduction to Millikelvin Technology. (Cambridge Studies in Low Temperature Physics: No. 1). (Illus.). 112p. 1989. text 54.95 (*0-521-34456-5*) Cambridge U Pr.

Betts, Diane F. Wool Fibers: Ways to Produce, Select, Process, & Spin Them by Hand. LC 94-94302. (Illus.). 186p. (Orig.). 1995. pap. text 21.95 (*0-9647880-1-2*) D F Betts Enter.

Betts, Dianne C., jt. ed. see Whaples, Robert.

Betts, Donni, jt. auth. see Betts, George.

Betts, Doris. Astronomer & Other Stories. (Voices of the South Ser.). 242p. 1995. pap. 11.95 (*0-8071-2010-3*) La State U Pr.

— Beasts of the Southern Wild & Other Stories. LC 98-16090. 208p. 1998. per. 11.00 (*0-684-83805-2*) Scribner.

— Gentle Insurrection & Other Stories. LC 97-14746. (Voices of the South Ser.). 288p. 1997. pap. 13.95 (*0-8071-2224-6*) La State U Pr.

— The River to Pickle Beach. 1996. per. 12.00 (*0-684-81860-4*, Scribner Pap Fic) S&S Trade Pap.

— The Sharp Teeth of Love. LC 98-10985. 352p. 1998. per. 12.00 (*0-684-84475-3*) S&S Trade.

— Souls Raised from the Dead: A Novel. 352p. 1995. per. 12.00 (*0-684-80104-3*) S&S Trade.

Betts, Edward. Master Class in Watermedia. LC 93-3421. (Illus.). 144p. (Orig.). 1993. 29.95 (*0-8230-3017-2*) Watsn-Guptill.

***Betts, Edward.** Master Class in Watermedia: Techniques in Traditional & Experimental Painting. (Illus.). 144p. 2000. pap. 19.95 (*0-8230-3040-7*) Watsn-Guptill.

Betts, Edwin M. & Bear, James A., Jr., eds. The Family Letters of Thomas Jefferson. LC 85-26599. (Illus.). 506p. 1986. reprint ed. pap. 18.95 (*0-8139-1096-X*) U Pr of Va.

Betts, Edwin M. & Perkins, Hazlehurst B. Thomas Jefferson's Flower Garden at Monticello. 3rd ed. LC 86-5613. (Illus.). xiv, 96p. 1986. pap. 10.95 (*0-8139-1087-0*) U Pr of Va.

Betts, Elaine. Adobe Indesign F/X & Design. LC 99-49156. 1999. pap. text 49.99 (*1-57610-518-0*) Coriolis Grp.

Betts, Frank, ed. Songs & Sayings of Walther Von der Vogelweide. 1973. 250.00 (*0-8490-2631-8*) Gordon Pr.

Betts, Frank, tr. see Walther von der Vogelweide.

Betts, Frederick, jt. auth. see Betts, Charles W.

Betts, Gavin G. Teach Yourself Latin. (Teach Yourself Ser.). 1992. 15.95 (*0-8288-8374-2*) Fr & Eur.

— Teach Yourself Latin: A Complete Course for Beginners. (ENG & LAT., Illus.). 362p. 1995. pap. 12.95 (*0-8442-3811-2*, Teach Yrslf) NTC Contemp Pub Co.

Betts, Gavin G., tr. Three Medieval Greek Romances: Velthandros & Chrysandza, Kallimachos & Chrysorroi, Livistros & Rodamni. LC 94-32655. (Library of Medieval Literature: Vol. 98B). 240p. 1995. text 42.00 (*0-8153-1279-2*) Garland.

Betts, Gavin G. & Blackman, D. R., eds. Mulomedicina Chironis: Concordantia in Mulomedicinam Chironis, 2 vols., Set. write for info. (*0-318-71985-1*) G Olms Pubs.

Betts, Gavin G. & Henry, Alan. Teach Yourself Ancient Greek. (GRE., Illus.). 352p. 1994. pap. 16.95 (*0-8442-3786-8*, Teach Yrslf) NTC Contemp Pub Co.

— Teach Yourself Greek, Ancient: Complete Course. (Teach Yourself Ser.). 1992. 29.95 (*0-8288-8346-7*) Fr & Eur.

Betts, Gavin G., jt. contrib. by see Blackman, Deane R.

Betts, Gavin G., jt. ed. see Blackman, D. R.

Betts, George & Betts, Donni. Seasons of Love. rev. ed. LC 86-11733. (Illus.). 80p. 1986. pap. 5.95 (*0-89087-477-8*) Celestial Arts.

Betts, George H. The Distribution & Functions of Mental Imagery. LC 76-176560. (Columbia University. Teachers College. Contributions to Education Ser.: No. 26). reprint ed. 37.50 (*0-404-55026-6*) AMS Pr.

— Mind & Its Education. LC 77-164694. reprint ed. 29.50 (*0-404-00789-9*) AMS Pr.

***Betts, Heidi.** Cinnamon & Roses. 320p. (Orig.). 2000. pap. 4.99 (*0-8439-4668-7*, Leisure Bks) Dorchester Pub Co.

— A Promise of Roses. 320p. 2000. pap. 4.99 (*0-8439-4738-1*, Leisure Bks) Dorchester Pub Co.

Betts, Ian M., et al. A Corpus of Relief-Patterned Tiles in Roman Britain. (Journal of Roman Pottery Studies: Vol. 7). (Illus.). 100p. 1997. pap. 27.00 (*1-900188-25-2*, Pub. by Oxbow Bks) David Brown.

Betts, J. H., et al, eds. Studies in Honour of T. B. L. Webster, Vol. 1. 264p. 1987. 45.00 (*0-8453-4515-X*) Assoc Univ Prs.

— Studies in Honour of T. B. L. Webster, Vol. 2. (Illus.). 208p. 1988. 48.00 (*0-8453-4523-0*) Assoc Univ Prs.

Betts, James. Bass Scales in Tablature. 56p. 1995. pap. 8.95 (*0-7866-0789-0*, 95604) Mel Bay.

Betts, Janet, et al. The Party's Over: Living Without Leah. 228p. 1999. 25.95 (*1-86105-116-6*, Pub. by Robson Bks) Parkwest Pubns.

Betts, Janice L. & Mathews, Wendell G., eds. Turfgrass: Nature's Constant Benediction: The History of the American Sod Producers Association 1967-1992. 112p. (Orig.). 1992. pap. write for info. (*0-9633510-0-1*) Turfgrass Producers Intl.

Betts, Jeanette G., et al, eds. Santa Barbara & California's Central Coast Region: Images & Encounters. LC 97-149355. (Pathways in Geography Ser.: Vol. 15). (Illus.). 80p. 1996. pap. 8.00 (*1-884136-10-9*) NCFGE.

***Betts, Jim.** Colours in the Storm. 96p. 2000. pap. 14.95 (*0-88754-587-4*) Theatre Comm.

Betts, Joan. Ordinary Stuff: A Simple Guide for Abundant Living. LC 97-66588. 112p. 1997. pap. 12.00 (*1-888604-04-2*) SunShine CO.

***Betts, John.** The Current Status of Prehistoric Resources on Jackson Demonstration State Forest, Mendocino County, California, No. 24. (California Department of Forestry & Fire Protection Ser.). (Illus.). 38p. (C). 1999. pap. text 6.25 (*1-55567-843-2*) Coyote Press.

Betts, John E. Essentials of Applied Physics. 352p. 1988. text 80.00 (*0-13-284407-9*) P-H.

Betts, John H., ed. see Anderson, William S.

Betts, John H., ed. see Clarke, Howard W.

Betts, John H., ed. see Owen, E. T.

Betts, Jonathan D. Keeping Time: The Story of the Marine Chronometer. (Illus.). 224p. 75.00 (*0-917376-49-8*) Mariners Mus.

— Keeping Time: The Story of the Marine Chronometer. deluxe ed. (Illus.). 224p. 150.00 (*0-917376-50-1*) Mariners Mus.

Betts, Judi. Watercolor . . . Let's Think about It! 4th ed. (Illus.). 114p. 1984. pap. 17.00 (*0-9616679-0-7*) Aquarelle Pr.

***Betts, Judi & Huntley, Charlotte.** Painting... A Quest Toward Xtraordinary. LC 99-95214. (Illus.). 1999. write for info. (*0-9616679-3-1*) Aquarelle Pr.

***Betts, Julian R.** The Changing Role of Education in California's Labor Market. LC 00-37278. 2000. pap. write for info. (*1-58213-014-0*) Pub Policy Inst.

***Betts, Julian R., et al.** Equal Resources, Equal Outcomes? The Distribution of School Resources & Student Achievement in California. LC 99-87994. xix, 347p. 2000. pap. 25.00 (*1-58213-015-9*) Pub Policy Inst.

Betts, Katharine. Ideology & Immigration: Australia 1976 to 1987. 244p. 1988. pap. 29.95 (*0-522-84351-4*, Pub. by Melbourne Univ Pr) Paul & Co Pubs.

Betts, Keith & McCollam, Dan. Junior High Game Nights: Wild & Crazy Outreach Events for Junior High Ministry. 96p. (YA). 1991. pap. 12.99 (*0-310-53811-4*) Zondervan.

— More Junior High Game Nights. 96p. 1992. pap. 12.99 (*0-310-54101-8*) Zondervan.

Betts, Louise. Secret Garden. LC 86-46002. (Troll Illustrated Classics). (Illus.). (J). 1988. 9.15 (*0-606-03648-2*, Pub. by Turtleback) Demco.

***Betts, Martin, ed.** Strategic Management of IT in Construction. LC 99-31142. 1999. write for info. (*0-632-04026-2*) Blackwell Sci.

Betts, Martin, jt. auth. see Brandon, Peter.

Betts, Otsie V., jt. ed. see Srygley, Ola P.

Betts, P. W. Supervisory Management. 6th ed. Orig. Title: Supervisory Studies. 560p. 1993. pap. 48.50 (*0-273-60057-5*, Pub. by Pitman Pub) Trans-Atl Phila.

Betts, P. Y. People Who Say Goodbye. large type ed. 303p. 1992. 23.95 (*1-85089-570-8*, Pub. by ISIS Lrg Prnt) Transaction Pubs.

Betts, Raymond F. Decolonization. LC 97-42992. 120p. (C). 1998. 50.00 (*0-415-18682-X*); pap. 14.99 (*0-415-15236-4*) Routledge.

— The False Dawn: European Imperialism in the Nineteenth Century. LC 75-14683. (Europe & the World in the Age of Expansion Ser.: No. 6). 291p. reprint ed. pap. 90.30 (*0-7837-2976-6*, 205747800006) Bks Demand.

Betts, Raymond F., jt. ed. see Munholland, John K.

Betts, Richard K. Cruise Missiles & U. S. Policy. LC 82-72704. 612p. 1982. pap. 8.95 (*0-8157-0933-1*) Brookings.

— Military Readiness: Concepts, Choices, Consequences. LC 94-44266. 280p. (C). 1995. 42.95 (*0-8157-0906-4*); pap. 18.95 (*0-8157-0905-6*) Brookings.

— NATO Deterrence Doctrine: No Way Out. (CISA Working Papers: No. 51). 78p. (Orig.). 1985. pap. 15.00 (*0-86682-064-7*) Ctr Intl Relations.

— Nuclear Blackmail & Nuclear Balance. LC 87-13384. 240p. 1987. 36.95 (*0-8157-0936-6*); pap. 16.95 (*0-8157-0935-8*) Brookings.

— Soldiers, Statesmen & Cold War Crises. 330p. 1991. text 61.50 (*0-231-07468-9*); pap. text 21.00 (*0-231-07469-7*) Col U Pr.

— Surprise Attack: Lessons for Defense Planning. LC 82-70887. 318p. 1982. 36.95 (*0-8157-0930-7*); pap. 16.95 (*0-8157-0929-3*) Brookings.

Betts, Richard K., ed. Conflict After the Cold War: Arguments on Causes of War & Peace. LC 93-10550. 544p. (C). 1993. pap. text 52.00 (*0-02-309191-6*, Macmillan Coll) P-H.

— Cruise Missiles: Technology, Strategy, Politics. LC 81-18149. 612p. 1981. 42.95 (*0-8157-0932-3*); pap. 18.95 (*0-8157-0931-5*) Brookings.

Betts, Richard K., jt. auth. see Gelb, Leslie H.

Betts, Richard M. & Ely, Silas J. Basic Real Estate Appraisal. 4th ed. LC 96-37511. 530p. 1997. 44.00 (*0-13-742891-X*) P-H.

***Betts, Richard M. & Ely, Silas J.** Basic Real Estate Appraisal. 5th ed. LC 00-39182. 2001. pap. write for info. (*0-13-085967-2*, Aspen Law & Bus) Aspen Pub.

Betts, Richard M., jt. auth. see McKenzie, Dennis J.

Betts, Richard T., tr. see Marchenko, Vyacheslav.

Betts, Robert B. Along the Ramparts of the Tetons: The Saga of Jackson Hole, Wyoming. LC 77-94083. 1978. pap. 22.50 (*0-87081-117-7*) Univ Pr Colo.

— Christians of the Arab East: A Political Study. 2nd ed. (Illus.). 318p. 1978. 25.00 (*960-7269-01-2*, Pub. by Lycabettus Pr) Bosphorus Bks.

— The Druze. 192p. (C). 1990. reprint ed. pap. 14.00 (*0-300-04810-6*) Yale U Pr.

Betts, Robert F., jt. auth. see Reese, Richard E.

Betts, Robert F., jt. ed. see Reese, Richard E.

Betts, Robin. Dr. Macnamara, 1861-1930. LC 99-495131. 416p. 1998. 56.95 (*0-85323-863-4*, Pub. by Liverpool Univ Pr) Intl Spec Bk.

Betts, Tim & Kenwood, Claire. Practical Psychiatry. 576p. 1993. 49.95 (*0-19-263027-X*) OUP.

Betts, Timothy. Tarot & the Millennium: The Story of Who's on the Cards & Why. LC 98-91311. (Illus.). 384p. 1998. pap. 24.95 (*0-9641020-5-6*) N Perspective.

— Why Tarot "Seems" to Work: Mathematics Versus Intuition. 64p. 1999. pap. 64.00 (*0-9641020-3-X*) N Perspective.

Betts, V. G., ed. Excavation at Jawa 1972-1986: Excavations & Explorations in the Hashemite Kingdom of Jordan. (Illus.). 408p. 1992. 95.00 (*0-7486-0307-7*, Pub. by Edinburgh U Pr) Col U Pr.

— Excavations at Tell Um Hammad, 1982-1984: The Early Assemblages (EB One-Two) Excavations & Explorations in the Hashemite Kingdom of Jordan. (Illus.). 408p. 1993. 110.00 (*0-7486-0336-0*, Pub. by Edinburgh U Pr) Col U Pr.

Betts, W. B., et al, eds. Protozoan Parasites & Water. No. 168. 260p. 1995. 99.95 (*0-85404-755-7*) CRC Pr.

Betts, W. B. & Robards, Anthony W., eds. Biodegradation: Natural & Synthetic Materials. (Series in Applied Biology). xii, 238p. 1991. 107.95 (*0-387-19705-2*) Spr-Verlag.

Bettschard, Roland & Ernst, E. The Book of Symptoms & Treatments: A Comprehensive Guide to the Safety & Effectiveness of Alternative & Complementary Medical Treatments for Common Ailments. Wood, David, tr. from GER. LC 98-3697. 1999. write for info. (*1-86204-171-7*) Element MA.

Bettschart, Roland. The Complete Book of Symptoms & Treatments. 992p. 1998. pap. 24.95 (*1-86204-424-4*, Pub. by Element MA) Penguin Putnam.

Bettwy. Yo Soy La Guardiana de la Fe. (SPA.). 1994. pap. 5.95 (*0-940535-61-0*, UP161) Franciscan U Pr.

Bettwy, Isabel. I Am the Guardian of the Faith. 124p. 1991. pap. 8.95 (*0-940535-46-7*, UP146) Franciscan U Pr.

Betty & Pansy. Severe Queer Review of New York. (Severe Queer Reviews Ser.). 112p. 1994. pap. 9.95 (*0-9633048-3-6*) Bedpan Prods.

— Severe Queer Review of San Francisco, No. 4. 4th ed. (Severe Queer Review Travel Ser.). (Illus.). 131p. 1995. pap. 10.95 (*0-9633048-4-4*) Bedpan Prods.

— Severe Queer Review of Washington, DC. 2nd ed. 96p. 1993. pap. 8.95 (*0-9633048-2-8*) Bedpan Prods.

***Betty Crocker Editors.** Betty Crocker's Bisquick Cookbook. (Illus.). 2000. pap. 21.99 (*0-7645-6156-1*) IDG Bks.

— Betty Crocker's Cooking for Two: Terrific Tastes Just for Two. (Illus.). 240p. 2000. 21.95 (*0-7645-6108-1*) IDG Bks.

— Betty Crocker's Eat & Lose Weight. 2000. 21.99 (*0-7645-6205-3*, B Crocker) Macmillan Gen Ref.

— Betty Crocker's Flavors of Home. (Illus.). 2000. pap. 27.95 (*0-7645-8143-0*) IDG Bks.

— Betty Crocker's Good & Easy Cookbook: Quick Delicious Dinners. (Illus.). 432p. 2000. 25.00 (*0-7645-6113-8*) IDG Bks.

Betty Crocker Editors, ed. see Crocker, Betty.

Betty, John G. Engineering Contracts: A Practical Guide. LC 92-37010. (International Series in Civil Engineering). 1993. write for info. (*0-07-707779-2*) McGraw.

***Betty, L. Stafford.** Thomas: A Novel. LC 99-934543. 430p. 1998. write for info. (*0-14-027854-0*) Penguin Putnam.

Betty, Patricia. Aromatherapy: A Personal Journey Through Your Senses. Sheldon, Amelia, ed. (Illus.). 100p. (Orig.). 1994. pap. 22.95 (*0-9641205-4-2*) Escent Yours.

***Betty, Patricia & Andrusia, David.** Essential Beauty: Using Natures Essential Oils to Rejuvenate, Replenish & Revitalize. (Illus.). 256p. 2000. pap. 16.95 (*0-658-00280-5*, 002805, Keats Publng) NTC Contemp Pub Co.

Bettye, Collier T. African Americans in the Performing Arts: An Encyclopedia. Date not set. pap. 30.00 (*0-8050-5125-2*) H Holt & Co.

Betulani, Carlos A. Collective Excitations Fermi & Bose Systems: Sao Paulo, Brazil 14-19 September 1998. 1999. 161.00 (*981-02-3735-9*) World Scientific Pub.

Betz. Complete Preparation for the AHPAT, 1999: Allied Health Professions Admission Test. 1998. pap. 27.95 (*0-683-30554-9*) Lppncott W & W.

— Complete Preparation for the DAT, 1999: Dental Admission Test. 1998. pap. 27.95 (*0-683-30550-6*) Lppncott W & W.

— Complete Preparation for the OAT, 1999: Optometry Admission Test. 1998. pap. 27.95 (*0-683-30552-2*) Lppncott W & W.

— Complete Preparation for the PCAT, 1999: Pharmacy College Admission Test. 1998. pap. 27.95 (*0-683-30551-4*) Lppncott W & W.

— Complete Preparation for the VETs, 1999: Vet Entrance Tests. 1998. pap. 27.95 (*0-683-30553-0*) Lppncott W & W.

— High Yield Biology. rev. ed. LC 96-17351. (Illus.). 260p. 1996. pap. 12.95 (*0-683-18069-X*) Lppncott W & W.

***Betz.** Mosby's Pediatric Nursing Reference. 4th ed. 1999. text 34.95 (*0-323-00935-2*) Mosby Inc.

Betz. New Politics of Right. LC 97-50396. 288p. 1998. pap. 18.95 (*0-312-21338-7*); text 55.00 (*0-312-21134-1*) St Martin.

Betz, A. L., jt. auth. see Drewes, L. R.

Betz, Adrienne. Scholastic Treasury of Quotations for Children. LC 97-34153. 256p. (YA). (gr. 4-7). 1998. 16.95 (*0-590-27146-6*, Pub. by Scholastic Inc) Penguin Putnam.

Betz, Albrecht. Hanns Eisler: Political Musician. Hopkins, Bill, tr. from GER. LC 81-12260. (Illus.). 336p. 1982. text 69.95 (*0-521-24022-0*) Cambridge U Pr.

Betz, Ann, ed. see Mott Hospital Staff.

Betz, Cecily L., et al, eds. Family-Centered Nursing Care of Children, Instructor's Manual & Test Questions. 2nd ed. (Illus.). 1994. teacher ed. write for info. (*0-7216-4573-9*, W B Saunders Co) Harcrt Hlth Sci Grp.

Betz, Cecily L. & Sowden, Linda A., eds. Mosby's Pediatric Nursing Reference. 3rd ed. LC 95-26736. (Illus.). 672p. (C). (gr. 13). 1996. pap. text 33.95 (*0-8151-0599-1*, 26571) Mosby Inc.

Betz, Cecily L., et al. Family-Centered Nursing Care of Children. 2nd ed. LC 93-2268. (Illus.). 2272p. 1994. reprint ed. text 68.00 (*0-7216-4489-9*, W B Saunders Co) Harcrt Hlth Sci Grp.

Betz, Charles H. How to Teach the Bible with Power. LC 94-38887. 1994. pap. 7.99 (*0-8280-0787-X*) Review & Herald.

***Betz, Daniel L.** Seven Steps to Riches: How to Program Your Mind to Get Whatever You Want. 256p. 2000. pap. 27.00 (*0-9676270-0-1*, Wenzell Park Pubng) Betz Enter.

Betz Des Chenes, jt. auth. see Nagel, Rob.

Betz, Des Chenes, ed. see Saari, Peggy.

Betz, Eleanor P., et al. Holiday Eating for a Healthy Heart. 1981. pap. write for info. (*0-318-55562-X*) Rush-Presby-St Lukes.

— Summertime Eating for a Healthy Heart: Cook Out-Camp Out-Eat Out the Low Cholesterol Way. (Illus.). 60p. 1981. pap. 3.95 (*0-686-31628-2*) Rush-Presby-St Lukes.

Betz, Frederick. Managing Technological Innovation: Competitive Advantage from Change. LC 97-20307. (Series in Engineering & Technology Management). 384p. 1997. 90.00 (*0-471-17380-0*) Wiley.

Betz, G. & Varga, P. S., eds. Desorption Induced by Electronic Transitions DIET Four: Proceedings of the Fourth International Workshop, Gloggnitz, Austria, October 2-4, 1989. (Surface Sciences Ser.: Vol. 19). (Illus.). xvi, 392p. 1990. 75.00 (*0-387-52386-3*) Spr-Verlag.

Betz, Hans D. Galatians. LC 77-78625. (Hermeneia: A Critical & Historical Commentary on the Bible Ser.). 352p. 1979. 49.00 (*0-8006-6009-9*, 1-6009, Fortress Pr) Augsburg Fortress.

— Second Corinthians Eight & Nine: A Commentary on Two Administrative Letters of the Apostle Paul. LC 84-48904. (Hermeneia: A Critical & Historical Commentary on the Bible Ser.). 184p. (C). 1985. 38.00 (*0-8006-6014-5*, 1-6014, Fortress Pr) Augsburg Fortress.

— The Sermon on the Mount: A Commentary on the Sermon on the Mount, Including the Sermon on the Plain (Matthew 5:3 - 7:27 & Luke 6:20-49) Collins, Adela Y., ed. LC 95-5123. (Hermeneia: A Critical & Historical Commentary on the Bible Ser.). 768p. 1995. 79.00 (*0-8006-6031-5*, 1-6031, Fortress Pr) Augsburg Fortress.

Betz, Hans D., ed. The Bible As a Document of the University. LC 80-23300. (Polebridge Bks.: No. 3). 86p. reprint ed. pap. 30.00 (*0-608-07908-1*, 206788900011) Bks Demand.

— Christology & a Modern Pilgrimage: A Discussion with Norman Perrin. rev. ed. LC 74-31605. 109p. reprint ed. pap. 33.80 (*0-608-13840-1*, 202026800016) Bks Demand.

— The Greek Magical Papyri in Translation, Including the Demonic Spells, Vol. 1: Texts. LC 85-1137. (Illus.). lviii, 340p. 1986. 39.95 (*0-226-04444-0*) U Ch Pr.

Betz, Hans D., ed. The Greek Magical Papyri in Translation, Including the Demotic Spells. 2nd ed. (Illus.). lviii, 348p. 1996. pap. text 24.95 (*0-226-04447-5*) U Ch Pr.

— The Greek Magical Papyri in Translation, Including the Demotic Spells. 2nd ed. LC 92-5617. lviii, 105p. 1997. 49.50 (*0-226-04446-7*) U Ch Pr.

Betz, Hans-Georg. Postmodern Politics in Germany: The Politics of Resentment. LC 90-39843. 224p. 1991. text 45.00 (*0-312-04881-5*) St Martin.

Betz, Hans-Georg, et al. Germany's New Right: Revivial of Nationalism or Call for Normalcy? Dehke, Dieter et al, eds. 70p. 1997. pap. text. write for info. (*0-9647348-2-6*) Friedrich-Ebert Found.

Betz, Ingrid. That Saturday Feeling. LC 97-93724. 192p. 1997. 18.95 (*0-8034-9242-1*, Avalon Bks) Bouregy.

Betz, L., jt. ed. see Hoff, J. T.

Betz, Louis P. Litterature Comparee. LC 77-101092. (BCL Ser. I). (FRE.). 1969. reprint ed. 34.00 (*0-404-00793-7*) AMS Pr.

— Litterature Comparee. LC 68-25307. (Studies in Comparative Literature: No. 35). 1969. reprint ed. lib. bdg. 75.00 (*0-8383-0911-9*) M S G Haskell Hse.

Betz, Margaret B. Centurions: Photorealists. Van Baron, Judith, ed. (Illus.). 27p. 1997. pap. write for info. (*0-9654682-3-2*) Savannah Coll.

***Betz, Michael J.** Writing at Work: A Text for Insurance Personnel. 2nd ed. LC 98-75497. xi, 291 p. 1999. 27.00 (*0-89462-130-0*) IIA.

Betz, Monte L. Kindergartner with AIDS & the Classroom. LC 92-101. 261p. 1992. pap. 24.95 (*0-934753-61-X*) LRP Pubns.

B

Betz, Nancy E. & Fitzgerald, Louise F. The Career Psychology of Women. 283p. 1987. text 74.95 (0-12-094405-7) Acad Pr.

Betz, Nancy E., jt. auth. see Walsh, Bruce.

Betz, Paul, ed. see Wordsworth, William.

Betz, R., ed. Proceedings of the 1984 Dusseldorf Conference on Piezo- & Pyroelectric PVDF Films. iv, 84p. 1987. pap. text 201.00 (2-88124-284-7) Gordon & Breach.

Betz, Randal R., ed. The Child with a Spinal Cord Injury. 888p. 1996. 95.00 (0-89203-155-7) Amer Acad Ortho Surg.

Betz, Randal R. & American Academy of Orthopaedic Surgeons Staff, eds. The Child with a Spinal Cord Injury. 888p. 1996. pap. 95.00 (0-89203-146-8) Amer Acad Ortho Surg.

Betz, Vaughn, et al. Architecture & CAD for Deep-Submicron FPGAS. LC 99-11904. (International Series In Engineering & Computer Science). 23p. 1999. write for info. (0-7923-8460-1) Kluwer Academic.

Betz, Vincent. Florida: Past & Present Visions. 264p. (C). 1996. pap. text, per. 31.95 (0-7872-2391-3, 41239101) Kendall-Hunt.

Betz, W., et al, eds. High Temperature Alloys for Gas Turbines & Other Applications 1986, 2 vols. Incl. Vol. I. 1987. lib. bdg. 286.00 (90-277-2347-8); Vol. II. Pt. II. 1900. lib. bdg. 579.50 (90-277-2348-6); 1986. Set lib. bdg. 479.50 (90-277-2304-4) Kluwer Academic.

Betzel, Christian, jt. ed. see Bott, Richard.

Betzig, Laura, ed. Human Nature: A Critical Reader. (Illus.). 512p. (C). 1996. pap. text 44.95 (0-19-509865-X) OUP.

Betzig, Laura L. Despotism & Differential Reproduction: A Darwinian View of History. LC 85-20010. (Evolutionary Foundations of Human Behavior Ser.). (Illus.). 182p. 1986. lib. bdg. 41.95 (0-202-01171-2) Aldine de Gruyter.

Betzina, Sandra. Fabric Savvy: The Essential Guide for Every Sewer. LC 98-44107. (Illus.). 208p. 1999. spiral bd. 24.95 (1-56158-267-0) Taunton.

— No Time to Sew. (Illus.). 256p. 1996. text 29.95 (0-87596-744-2) St Martin.

*Betzina, Sandra. Power Sewing Step-by-Step. LC 00-23431. (Illus.). 2000. 34.95 (1-56158-363-4) Taunton.

Betzinez, Jason & Nye, Wilbur S. I Fought with Geronimo. LC 87-10839. (Illus.). x, 214p. 1987. reprint ed. pap. 12.95 (0-8032-6086-5, Bison Books) U of Nebr Pr.

Betzold, Michael. Appointment with Doctor Death. LC 93-35550. 360p. 1993. 21.95 (1-879094-37-1); pap. 14.95 (1-879094-42-8) Momentum Bks.

*Betzold, Michael. Casey & the Bat. 182p. 1999. (0-7414-0134-7) Buy Books.

Betzold, Michael, jt. ed. see Feldman, Richard.

Beuchame, L., tr. see Melanchthon, Philip.

Beuchat, Larry R. & Rockland, Louis B. Water Activity: Theory & Applications to Food. (IFT Basic Symposium Ser.: Vol. 2). (Illus.). 424p. 1987. text 145.00 (0-8247-7759-X) Dekker.

Beuchat, Larry R., jt. auth. see Deak, Tibor.

Beuchot, Mauricio. The History of Philosophy in Colonial Mexico. Mill, Elizabeth, tr. LC 98-9210. 204p. (C). 1999. text 64.95 (0-8132-0906-4) Cath U Pr.

Beuckelaer, Gerard M. de, see de Beuckelaer, Gerard M.

Beucken, Jean De, see De Beucken, Jean.

Beucler, Andre. Last of the Bohemians. Sainsbury, Geoffrey, tr. LC 79-108841. 1971. reprint ed. lib. bdg. 65.00 (0-8371-3729-2, BEBO, Greenwood Pr) Greenwood.

Beudert, Monique & Rainbird, Sean. Contemporary Art: The Janet Wolfson de Botton Gift. LC 98-162940. (Illus.). 104p. 1998. pap. 25.00 (1-85437-247-5, Pub. by Tate Gallery) U of Wash Pr.

Beudert, Peter, jt. auth. see Crabtree, Susan.

Beudoin, James J. Handbook of Fiber-Reinforced Concrete: Principles, Properties, Developments & Applications. LC 89-70976. (Illus.). 332p. 1990. 72.00 (0-8155-1236-8) Noyes.

Beueder, R., jt. auth. see Barthel, J.

Beuers, U., jt. ed. see Paumgartner, G.

Beues, R. Resurreccion Realidad o Ilusion? (Resurrection: Fact Or Fiction?) (SPA.). 1.50 (0-685-74980-0, 490257) Editorial Unilit.

Beuf, Ann H. Beauty Is the Beast: Appearance-Impaired Children in America. LC 89-21485. 152p. (C). 1990. text 38.95 (0-8122-8234-5); pap. text 16.95 (0-8122-1310-6) U of Pa Pr.

— Biting off the Bracelet: A Study of Children in Hospitals. 2nd ed. LC 88-15329. 164p. (C). 1988. pap. text 17.95 (0-8122-1278-9) U of Pa Pr.

*Beug, Hans-Jurgen & Miehe, Georg. Vegetation History & Human Impact in the Eastern Central Himalaya (Langtang & Helambu, Nepal) (Dissertationes Botanicae Ser.: Band 318). (Illus.). 98p. 1999. pap. 65.00 (3-443-64230-6, Pub. by Gebruder Borntraeger) Balogh.

*Beug, LaVere Ray. Walking Through Revelation with a Common Man. 336p. 1999. pap. 15.00 (1-892525-06-2) ACW Press.

Beugin, Mary E. Coping: Attention Deficit Disorder: A Guide for Parents & Teachers. 173p. (Orig.). 1990. pap. 15.95 (1-55059-013-8) Temeron Bks.

Beugre, Constant D. Managing Fairness in Organizations. LC 98-6017. 168p. 1998. 49.95 (1-56720-211-X, Quorum Bks) Greenwood.

*Beuke, Arnold. Werbung und Warnung: Australien Als Ziel Deutscher Auswanderer im 19, Jahrhundert. (Deutsch-Australische Studien Ser.). 213p. 1999. 32.95 (3-906763-76-5, Pub. by P Lang) P Lang Pubng.

*Beukel, Dorine Vanden. Architecture Drawings, 1. 1999. pap. text 24.95 (90-5496-041-8) Pepin Pr.

Beukel, Erik. American Perceptions of the Soviet Union As a Nuclear Adversary: From Kennedy to Reagan. 390p. 1990. text 54.00 (0-86187-033-6) St Martin.

Beukelman, David R. & Mirenda, Pat. Augmentative & Alternative Communication: Management of Severe Communication Disorders in Children & Adults. 2nd ed. LC 97-42827. 602p. 1998. 59.95 (1-55766-333-5) P H Brookes.

Beukelman, David R. & Yorkston, Kathryn M., eds. Communication Disorders Following Traumatic Brain Injury: Management of Cognitive, Language, & Motor Impairments. LC 89-14560. (Illus.). 439p. (C). 1991. pap. text 37.00 (0-89079-295-X, 1586) PRO-ED.

*Beukema, Frits & Dikken, Marcel den, eds. Clitic Phenomena in European Languages. LC 99-54884. (Linguistik Aktuell/Linguistics Today Ser.: Vol. 30). x, 324p. 2000. 69.00 (1-55619-914-7, JB2330) J Benjamins Pubng Co.

Beukema, Henry J., jt. auth. see Giachino, Joseph W.

Beukema, J. J., et al, eds. Expected Effects of Climatic Change on Marine Coastal Ecosystems. (C). 1990. text 206.50 (0-7923-0697-X) Kluwer Academic.

*Beukema, John H. Stories from God's Heart: Ten Parables Calling Us to a Life Worth Living. LC 00-25757. 240p. 2000. pap. 9.99 (0-8024-8689-4) Moody.

Beukema, Phyllis, et al. Basic Phonics for Adults. 2nd ed. 156p. 1994. spiral bd. 17.95 (0-8403-5794-X) Kendall-Hunt.

Beuken, W. A. Haggai-Sacharja 1-8: Studien zur Uberlieferungsgeschichte der fruhnachexilischen Prophetie. (Studia Semitica Neerlandica: Vol. 10). xvii, 350p. 1967. text 27.00 (90-232-0368-2, Pub. by Van Gorcum) Eisenbrauns.

*Beuken, W. A. M. Isaiah, Volume II, Chapters 28-39. xxxiv, 420p. 2000. 52.00 (90-429-0813-0, Pub. by Peeters Pub) Bks Intl VA.

Beuken, Wim, et al, eds. The Messiah in History. (Concilium Ser.). 1993. 15.00 (0-88344-869-6) Orbis Bks.

Beukhof, G. & Simons, R. J., eds. German & Dutch Research on Learning & Instruction. (Selecta Reeks Ser.: Vol. 43). 142p. 1986. 17.00 (90-6472-099-1) Taylor & Francis.

Beukhof, G., jt. ed. see Simons, P. R.

Beule, Jurgen. Bildwelten Zu Aids: Die Immunschwache Im Spiegel der Printmedien. (Illus.). 180p. 1998. 37.95 (3-631-33824-4) P Lang Pubng.

Beulens, A. J. & Sebastian, H. J., eds. Optimization-Based Computer-Aided Modelling & Design. (Lecture Notes in Control & Information Sciences: Vol. 174). (Illus.). 268p. 1992. 90.95 (0-387-55135-2) Spr-Verlag.

Beum, Robert L. Modern British Essayists. LC 90-43746. (Dictionary of Literary Biography Ser.). 426p. 1990. text 155.00 (0-8103-4580-3) Gale.

Beuman, Monika E., jt. auth. see Delmar Staff.

Beumer, J. Henri Nouwen: A Restless Seeking for God. 240p. 1998. pap. 16.95 (0-8245-1768-7) Crossroad NY.

Beumer, J., jt. auth. see Lewis, S.

Beumer, John, 3rd, et al. Maxillofacial Rehabilitation: Prosthodontic & Surgical Considerations. (Illus.). xii, 546p. 1996. text 195.00 (1-56386-036-8, Ishiyaku EuroAmerica) Med Dent Media.

Beumer, Jurjen J. Henri Nouwen: A Restless Seeking for God. Schlaver, David E. & Forest-Flier, Nancy, trs. from DUT. LC 97-6808. 240p. 1997. 19.95 (0-8245-1677-X) Crossroad NY.

Beumer, W. G., jt. auth. see De Silva, H. K.

*Beumers, Birgit. Russia on Reels: The Russian Idea in Post-soviet Cinema. 1999. 59.50 (1-86064-389-2, Pub. by I B T) St Martin.

— Russia on Reels: The Russian Idea in Post-Soviet Cinema. 1999. pap. text 24.50 (1-86064-390-6, Pub. by I B T) St Martin.

Beumers, Birgit. Yury Lyubimov: Thirty Years at the Taganka Theatre, 1964-1994. (Contemporary Theatre Studies). 349p. 1997. text 82.00 (3-7186-5875-5, Harwood Acad Pubs); pap. text 27.00 (3-7186-5885-2, Harwood Acad Pubs) Gordon & Breach.

Beumont, Pierre J., jt. auth. see Vandereycken, Walter.

Beun, Robbert-Jan, et al, eds. Dialogue & Instruction: Modelling Interaction in Intelligent Tutoring Systems. LC 95-6511. (NATO ASI Ser.: Series F, Computer & Systems Sciences: Vol. 142). 1995. write for info. (0-387-58834-5) Spr-Verlag.

Beun, Robert-Jan, ed. see Reiner, M.

Beunat, Joseph. Empire Style Designs & Ornaments. LC 73-91877. (Illus.). 95p. 1974. pap. 8.95 (0-486-22984-X) Dover.

Beuque. Dictionnaire des Poincons Officiels Francais et Etrangers, Anciens et Modernes de Leur Creation (14e Siecle) a Nos Jours. (FRE.). 1976. lib. bdg. 250.00 (0-8288-2603-X, F64050) Fr & Eur.

Beurdeley, Jean-Michel. Thai Forms. (Illus.). 128p. 1980. 47.50 (0-8348-0150-7, 28518) Weatherhill.

Beuret, Eric. Contribution a l'etude de la Distribution Geographique et de la Physiologic de Taxons Affines Diet Polyploides. (Bibliotheca Botanica: Vol. 133). (GER., Illus.). x, 80p. 1977. 64.00 (3-510-48004-X, Pub. by E Schweizerbartsche) Balogh.

Beuret, Jean-Eudes, jt. auth. see Saika, Yukiya.

*Beurier, Jean-Pierre, et al, eds. New Technologies & Law of the Marine Environment (Nouvelles Technologies et Droit de l'Environnement Marin) (International Environmental Law & Policy Ser.: Vol. 55). 304p. 2000. text 135.00 (90-411-9756-7) Kluwer Law Intl.

Beurkel-Rothfuss, Nancy, jt. auth. see Yerby, Janet.

Beurlen, Karl. Geologie Von Brasilien. (Beitrage Zur Regionalen Geologie der Erde. Ser.: Vol. 9). (GER., Illus.). viii, 444p. 1970. 92.00 (3-443-11009-6, Pub. by Gebruder Borntraeger) Balogh.

— Die Geologische Entwicklung des Atlantischen Ozeans: Stiefel, Joerg. (Geotektonische Forschungen Ser.: Vol. 46). (GER.). ii, 194p. 1974. 58.00 (3-510-50012-1, Pub. by E Schweizerbartsche) Balogh.

Beurlen, Wolfgang, tr. see Schubring, Walther.

Beurlier, Emile. Le Culte Imperial. vi, 357p. reprint ed. write for info. incl. 3.5 hd (0-318-71321-7) G Olms Pubs.

Beurmann, Maria A. Follow the Mind to Another Place & Time... Poems of the Adirondack Mountains/Poems of Awareness. (Illus.). 75p. (Orig.). 1995. pap. 12.95 (0-9651589-0-X) Hawk Resources.

*Beurmann, Maria A. In Celebration... Adirondack Visions. (Illus.). 64p. 2000. per. 14.95 (0-9651589-1-8) Hawk Resources.

Beurskens, Sarah B. Kayaking: Riding the Rapids. LC 98-207720. (Cover-To-Cover Bks.). 56 p. 1997. write for info. (0-7807-6143-X, Covercraft) Perfection Learn.

*Beurton, Peter, et al, eds. The Concept of the Gene in Development & Evolution: Historical & Epistemological Perspectives. (Cambridge Studies in Philosophy & Biology). (Illus.). 320p. 2000. 59.95 (0-521-77187-0) Cambridge U Pr.

Beus, Alexei A. & Grigorian, S. V. Geochemical Exploration Methods for Mineral Deposits. Levinson, A. A., ed. Teteruk-Schneider, Rita, tr. LC 77-75045. (Illus.). 1977. 32.00 (0-915834-03-0) Applied Pub.

Beus, Carma. One Patch, Two Patch, Three Patch, Four: A Guide to Making Professional-looking Patchwork Quilts. LC 83-81177. 52p. 1983. pap. 9.98 (0-88290-224-5) Horizon Utah.

Beus, H. L., tr. see Rodin, S. N.

Beus, Stanley S., ed. Rocky Mountain Section Field Guide. (DNAG Centennial Field Guides Ser.: No. 2). (Illus.). 489p. 1987. 21.75 (0-8137-5402-X) Geol Soc.

Beus, Stanley S. & Morales, Michael, eds. Grand Canyon Geology. (Illus.). 582p. (C). 1990. pap. text 37.95 (0-19-505015-0) OUP.

Beusch, A., et al. Low Cost Road Construction in Indonesia: Labour-Based Road Projects in Manggarai District, Vol. I, Documentation. 48p. 1998. pap. 19.50 (3-906494-01-2, Pub. by Intermed Tech) Stylus Pub VA.

— Low Cost Road Construction in Indonesia: Labour-Based Road Projects in Manggarai District, Vol. II, Workbook. 110p. 1998. pap., wbk. ed. 17.50 (3-906494-02-0, Pub. by Intermed Tech) Stylus Pub VA.

Beuschel, Richard M. Nakajima KI-44 Shokiin Japanese Army Air Force Service. (Illus.). 64p. (YA). (gr. 10-13). 1996. pap. 14.95 (0-88740-914-8) Schiffer.

Beuscher, Paul, jt. see Dahl, Gary.

*Beuschlein, Marti. Ready, Set, Tell: Active Bible Story-Telling. (Illus.). (J). 1999. pap. 8.99 (0-570-05384-6) Concordia.

Beuschlein, Marti & Hoffman, Patricia A. Early Easter Morning. (Illus.). 32p. (J). (ps-k). 1999. 7.00 (0-570-05473-7, 56-1936GJ) Concordia.

Beusekom, C. F. Van, see Van Beusekom, C. F.

Beushausen, Derwin. Airwalker: A Date with Destiny! Rocket-Belt History & Construction Plans Exhaustive Study Manual. (Illus.). 160p. (Orig.). 1993. pap. 29.95 (0-9637097-0-4) DreamQuest.

Beusichem, M. L. Van, see Van Beusichem, M. L.

Beusman. Drafting & Design for Production. (Drafting Ser.). 1991. text 28.95 (0-8273-3934-8) Delmar.

*Beusse, William E. & Dey, Martha J. DOD Service Academies: More Actions Needed to Eliminate Sexual Harassment. (Illus.). 64p. 2000. pap. text 20.00 (0-7567-0059-0) DIANE Pub.

Beust, Friedrich F. Graf Von, see Graf Von Beust, Friedrich F.

Beust, Friedrich F. Von, see Von Beust, Friedrich F.

Beutel, Frederick K. Democracy or the Scientific Method in Law & Policy Making. 269p. (C). 1965. 5.00 (0-8477-3000-X) U of PR Pr.

— The Operation of the Bad Check Laws of Puerto Rico. 158p. 1967. 3.00 (0-8477-2200-7) U of PR Pr.

Beutel, Frederick K., jt. auth. see Brannan, Joseph D.

Beutel, Helga. Woerterbuch der Chinesischen Wortbildung. (CHI & GER.). 121p. 1993. 150.00 (0-7859-8263-9, 3050023236) Fr & Eur.

Beutel, Jacob, jt. ed. see Van Metter, Richard L.

Beutell, Nicholas J. PC Projects for Human Resource Management. 2nd ed. Fenton, ed. 300p. (C). 1993. pap. text 28.75 incl. audio (0-314-01250-8) West Pub.

— PC Projects for Human Resource Management. 3rd ed. LC 96-128897. 270p. 1996. pap. 41.95 (0-314-07135-0) West Pub.

Beutelspacher, Albrecht. Cryptology. (Spectrum Ser.). 176p. 1994. pap. text 35.95 (0-88385-504-6, CRYPT) Math Assn.

Beutelspacher, Albrecht & Rosenbaum, Ute. Projective Geometry: From Foundations to Applications. LC 97-18012. (Illus.). 268p. (C). 1998. text 64.95 (0-521-48277-1); pap. text 24.95 (0-521-48364-6) Cambridge U Pr.

Beutelspacher, Albrecht, jt. auth. see Batten, Lynn M.

Beutelspacher, Carlos. Las Mariposas Entre los Antiguos Mexicanos (Butterflies among the Ancient Mexicans) (SPA.). 104p. 1989. 23.99 (968-16-3042-4, Pub. by Fondo) Continental Bk.

Beutelspacher, Ludwig. Exploraciones Arqueologicas en Itzantun, Chiapas. 79p. 1993. pap. 8.00 (968-29-4537-2, IN019) UPLAAP.

Beuth, Eugene. We Love Our New Home. LC 93-77946. (Illus.). 34p. (Orig.). (J). (ps). 1993. pap. 12.95 (0-9636417-2-7) Make-Hawk Pub.

*Beuthe, Michel & Nijkamp, Peter, eds. New Contributions to Transportation Analysis in Europe. LC 99-72600. 360p. 1999. 78.95 (0-7546-1082-9, Pub. by Ashgate Pub) Ashgate Pub Co.

Beuthin, R. C. Basic Company Law. 2nd ed. 409p. 1992. pap. 76.00 (0-409-01255-6, SA, MICHIE) LEXIS Pub.

Beuthin, Timothy M., jt. ed. see Moore, Steve.

Beutin, Wolfgang. Anima Teil 2: Untersuchungen Zur Frauenmystik des Mittelalters. Metscher, Thomas, ed. (Bremer Beitrage Zur Literatur und Ideengeschichte Ser.: Bd. 23). (GER.). 235p. 1998. 34.95 (3-631-31489-2) P Lang Pubng.

*Beutin, Wolfgang. Die Revolution Tritt in die Literatur: Beitrage Zur Literatur- und Ideengeschichte von Thomas Muntzer Bis Primo Levi. (Bremer Beitrage Zur Literatur und Ideengeschichte Ser.). 199p. 1999. 31.95 (3-631-34887-8) P Lang Pubng.

Beutin, Wolfgang & Hoppe, Wilfried. Franz Mehring (1846-1919) Beitrage der Tagung Vom 8. Bis 9. November 1996 in Hamburg Anlablich Seines 150. Geburtstags. (GER.). 157p. 1997. 35.95 (3-631-30833-7) P Lang Pubng.

Beutin, Wolfgang, et al. History of German Literature: From the Beginnings to the Present Day. 4th ed. LC 93-3381.Tr. of Deutsche Literaturgeschichte. 800p. (C). (gr. 13). 1994. 125.00 (0-415-06034-6) Routledge.

Beutler, Bruce, ed. Tumor Necrosis Factors: The Molecules & Their Emerging Role in Medicine. 608p. 1991. text 104.00 (0-88167-852-X) Lppncott W & W.

— Tumor Necrosis Factors: The Molecules & Their Emerging Role in Medicine. LC 91-26481. (Illus.). 608p. reprint ed. pap. 188.50 (0-608-09762-4, 206993500007) Bks Demand.

Beutler, Bryce D., jt. auth. see Beutler, Eve R.

Beutler, Cora R. Baptism Journal, Boy. (Illus.). 28p. (J). 1992. pap. 2.95 (1-56684-005-8) Evans Bk Dist.

— Baptism Journal, Girl. (Illus.). 28p. (YA). 1992. pap. 2.95 (1-56684-002-3) Evans Bk Dist.

Beutler, Ernest, et al, eds. Williams Hematology. 5th ed. (Illus.). 1920p. 1994. text 155.00 (0-07-070386-8) McGraw-Hill HPD.

*Beutler, Ernest, et al. Williams Hematology. 6th ed. (Illus.). 1680p. 2000. 169.00 (0-07-070397-3) McGraw-Hill Prof.

Beutler, Eve R. & Beutler, Bryce D. Whinosaurus Rex. (Illus.). 36p. (J). (ps-3). 1993. pap. 6.95 (0-9637262-0-X) Evening Pearl.

Beutler, Gerhard, et al, eds. GPS Trends in Precise Terrestrial, Airborne & Spaceborne Applications: Symposium No. 115 Boulder, Colorado, U. S. A. July 3-4, 1995. LC 96-7080. (International Association of Geodesy Symposia Ser.: Vol. 115). (Illus.). xiv, 355p. 1996. pap. 136.00 (3-540-60872-9) Spr-Verlag.

Beutler, J. Flax for Life. 1997. pap. text 6.95 (1-896817-10-6) ApPubng.

Beutler, Jade. Flax for Life! 101 Deliciuos Recipes & Tips Featuring Fabulous Flax Oil. 1997. pap. text 5.95 (0-9645075-2-8) Prog Hlth Pub.

Beutler, Johann H. & Gutsmuth, Johann C. Allgemeines Sachregister Uber die Wichtigsten Deutschen Zeitund Wochenschriften, 2 vols., Set. 1976. reprint ed. write for info. (3-487-05934-7) G Olms Pubs.

Beutler, Larry E. & Berren, Michael R., eds. Integrative Assessment of Adult Personality. LC 94-19183. 414p. 1994. lib. bdg. 40.00 (0-89862-281-6, 2281) Guilford Pubns.

— Integrative Assessment of Adult Personality. LC 94-19183. 414p. 1996. pap. text 25.00 (1-57230-138-4, 0138) Guilford Pubns.

Beutler, Larry E. & Clarkin, John F. Systemic Treatment Selection: Toward Targeted Therapeutic Interventions. LC 89-71203. (Integrative Psychotherapy Ser.: No. 3). 384p. 1990. text 49.95 (0-87630-576-1) Brunner-Mazel.

Beutler, Larry E. & Crago, Marjorie, eds. Psychotherapy Research: An International Review of Programmatic Studies. 334p. 1991. pap. 19.95 (1-55798-090-X) Am Psychol.

*Beutler, Larry E. & Harwood, T. Mark. Prescriptive Psychotherapy: A Practical Guide to Systematic Treatment Selection. LC 99-42912. 208p. 2000. 29.95 (0-19-513669-1) OUP.

Beutler, Larry E., et al. Am I Crazy, or Is My Shrink? LC 97-43546. 224p. 1998. 24.00 (0-19-510780-2) OUP.

*Beutler, Larry E., et al. A Consumers Guide to Psychotherapy. 256p. 2000. pap. 12.95 (0-19-513920-8) OUP.

— Guidelines for the Systematic Treatment of the Depressed Patient. LC 99-19377. (Guidebooks in Clinical Psychology Ser.). (Illus.). 464p. 2000. text 55.00 (0-19-510530-3) OUP.

Beutler, Larry E., jt. ed. see Bongar, Bruce.

Beutner, Ed. Biblical Ballads. (Illus.). 1985. pap. 4.95 (0-911346-09-0) Christianica.

Beutner, Edward F., ed. see Funk, Robert W.

Beutner, Ernest H., ed. Autoimmunity in Psoriasis. 328p. 1982. 182.00 (0-8493-5473-0, RL321, CRC Reprint) Franklin.

Beutner, Ernest H., et al, eds. Immunopathology of the Skin. 2nd ed. LC 78-24139. (Wiley Medical Publications). (Illus.). 520p. reprint ed. pap. 161.20 (0-608-10335-7, 201783000009) Bks Demand.

Beutter, Manfred H., jt. auth. see Mattenheimer, A.

*Beuttler, Fred W., et al. The University of Illinois at Chicago: A Pictorial History. (College History Ser.). (Illus.). 128p. 2000. pap. 18.99 (0-7385-0706-7) Arcadia Publng.

Beuttler, William. Family, the Future. LC 89-63696. 1990. 15.00 (0-87212-234-4) Libra.

Beuvery, E. C., et al, eds. Animal Cell Technology: Developments Towards the 21st Century. LC 95-38366. 1240p. (C). 1996. text 552.00 (0-7923-3736-0) Kluwer Academic.

Beuys, Joseph. Beuys in America. LC 98-141550. (Illus.). 224p. (C). 1997. 29.95 (3-88243-539-9) Dist Art Pubs.

— Vitrines. 1994. 50.00 (3-88375-168-5, Pub. by Walther Konig) Dist Art Pubs.

Beuys, Joseph, jt. auth. see Bastian, Heiner.

Bev-E Staff. While Passing Through. (Illus.). 103p. 1998. 14.95 (1-881524-41-8) Milligan Bks.

*Bevacqua, Maria.** Rape on the Public Agenda: Feminism & the Politics of Sexual Assault. 256p. 2000. text 50.00 (1-55553-447-3); pap. text 18.95 (1-55553-446-5) NE U Pr.

Bevan. House of Ptolemy. (Illus.). 434p. 1985. pap. 30.00 (0-89005-536-X) Ares.

— House of Seleucus, 2 vols. 1985. 35.00 (0-89005-537-8) Ares.

Bevan, A. Beckford & Wolryche-Whitmore, H. B., eds. A Sailor of King George: The Journals of Captain Frederick Hoffman, RN, 1793-1814. LC 98-35343. (Classics of Naval Literature Ser.). (Illus.). 376p. 1998. 32.95 (1-55750-391-5) Naval Inst Pr.

*Bevan, Amanda.** Tracing Your Ancestors in the Public Record Office. 5th rev. ed. 304p. 1999. pap. 26.00 (1-873162-61-8, Pub. by Statnry Office) Balogh.

*Bevan, Amanda, ed.** Tracing Your Ancestors in the Public Record Office (U. K.) 5th ed. (Illus.). 320p. 1999. pap. text 35.00 (0-7881-8122-X) DIANE Pub.

Bevan, Andy, jt. auth. see Mitchell, Maurice.

Bevan, Antoinina. The Reception of the Church Fathers in the West: From the Carolingians to the Maurists, 2 vols. Backus, Irena D., ed. LC 96-20106. (Illus.). 1996. 318.00 (90-04-09722-8) Brill Academic Pubs.

Bevan, B. King James VI of Scotland & I of England. (Illus.). 1996. 31.95 (0-948695-44-7, Pub. by Rubicon Pr); pap. 20.95 (0-948695-45-5, Pub. by Rubicon Pr) David Brown.

Bevan, B., et al. The Banks & Personal Customers. (C). 1989. 40.00 (0-85297-081-1, Pub. by Chartered Bank) St Mut.

Bevan, Bryan. Edward III: Monarch of Chivalry. (Illus.). 168p. (Orig.). 1992. pap. 17.95 (0-948695-27-7, Pub. by Rubicon Pr) David Brown.

— Henry IV. LC 94-241055. 1994. text 45.00 (0-312-11696-9) St Martin.

— Henry the Fourth. 1994. pap. 19.95 (0-312-11697-7) St Martin.

— Robert Louis Stevenson: Poet & Teller of Tales. (Illus.). 208p. 1993. pap. 17.95 (0-948695-29-3, Pub. by Rubicon Pr) David Brown.

Bevan, Carol S. Foster Care: Too Much Too Little Too Early Too Late; Child Protection: Old Problem, New Paradigm. Bosnick, Anthony J. & Mainwaring, Douglas S., eds. 80p. 1997. pap. write for info. (0-614-31243-4) Natl Adoption.

Bevan, Christopher. Insolvent Trading. 150p. 1994. 54.00 (1-86287-138-8, Pub. by Federation Pr) Gaunt.

Bevan, Clare. Christmas Play, 1 vol. (J). 1999. 12.99 (0-7459-4088-9) Lion USA.

Bevan, David. Andr[00e9] Malraux: Towards the Expression of Transcendence. 144p. 1986. 55.00 (0-7735-0552-0, Pub. by McG-Queens Univ Pr) CUP Services.

— The Art & Poetry of Charles-Ferdinand Ramuz. (Language & Literature Ser.). 1977. 25.00 (0-902675-47-8) Oleander Pr.

— Trade & Fiscal Adjustment in Africa. LC 98-11471. 320p. 1999. text 75.00 (0-312-21464-2) St Martin.

Bevan, David, et al. Controlled Open Economies: A Neoclassical Approach to Structuralism. (Illus.). 380p. (C). 1994. reprint ed. pap. text 26.00 (0-19-828783-6, 14332) OUP.

— Nigeria, Policy Responses to Shocks, 1970-1990. LC 92-22772. 48p. 1992. pap. 9.95 (1-55815-224-5) ICS Pr.

— Peasants & Governments: An Economic Analysis. (Illus.). 362p. 1990. text 95.00 (0-19-828621-X) OUP.

*Bevan, David, et al.** The Political Economy of Poverty, Equity & Growth: Nigeria & Indonesia. (A World Bank Publication). 432p. 1999. 60.00 (0-19-520986-9) OUP.

Bevan, Donald. Stalag 17. 1952. pap. 5.25 (0-8222-1070-3) Dramatists Play.

Bevan, Edwyn R. Christianity, 157. LC 80-24452. (Home University Library of Modern Knowledge: No. 157). 255p. 1981. reprint ed. lib. bdg. 59.50 (0-313-22681-4, BECY, Greenwood Pr) Greenwood.

— Hellenism & Christianity. LC 67-26714. (Essay Index Reprint Ser.). 1980. 20.95 (0-8369-0207-6) Ayer.

— Holy Images: An Inquiry into Idolatry & Image-Worship in Ancient Paganism & in Christianity. LC 77-27191. (Gifford Lectures: 1933). reprint ed. 37.50 (0-404-60489-7) AMS Pr.

— Stoics & Sceptics. 152p. 1980. reprint ed. pap. 15.00 (0-89005-364-2) Ares.

— Stoics & Sceptics. Vlastos, Gregory, ed. LC 78-15852. (Morals & Law in Ancient Greece Ser.). 1979. reprint ed. lib. bdg. 25.95 (0-405-11530-X) Ayer.

Bevan, Edwyn R., ed. Later Greek Religion. LC 76-179282. (Library of Greek Thought: No. 9). reprint ed. 27.50 (0-404-07807-9) AMS Pr.

Bevan, Finn. Beneath the Earth. (Landscapes of Legend Ser.). (Illus.). 32p. (J). (gr. 4-8). 1998. pap. 6.95 (0-516-26298-X) Childrens.

— Beneath the Earth: The Facts & the Fables. LC 97-51338. (Landscapes of Legend Ser.). (Illus.). (J). 1998. 20.00 (0-516-20954-X) Childrens.

— Beneath the Earth: The Facts & the Fables. (Landscapes of Legend Ser.). 1999. pap. text 6.95 (0-516-26302-1) Childrens.

— Cities of Splendor. LC 98-6678. (Landscapes of Legend Ser.). (Illus.). 31p. (J). 1998. student ed. 20.00 (0-516-20955-8) Childrens.

— Cities of Splendor. (Landscapes of Legend Ser.). (Illus.). 32p. (J). (gr. 4-6). 1999. pap. text 6.95 (0-516-26303-X) Childrens.

— Fabulous Beasts. LC 96-45196. (Landscapes of Legend Ser.). (Illus.). (J). 1997. lib. bdg. 20.00 (0-516-20349-5) Childrens.

— Mighty Mountains. (Landscapes of Legend Ser.). (J). 1998. pap. text 6.95 (0-516-26299-8) Childrens.

— Mighty Mountains: The Facts & the Fables. LC 96-48801. (Landscapes of Legend Ser.). (Illus.). (J). 1997. lib. bdg. 20.00 (0-516-20348-7) Childrens.

— Sacred Skies. LC 97-11694. (Landscapes of Legend Ser.). (J). (gr. 4-8). 1997. 20.00 (0-516-20351-7) Childrens.

— Sacred Skies. (Landscapes of Legend Ser.). (J). 1998. pap. text 6.95 (0-516-26300-5) Childrens.

— Waters of Life. LC 97-11697. (Landscapes of Legend Ser.). (Illus.). (J). (gr. 4-8). 1997. 20.00 (0-516-20350-9) Childrens.

— Waters of Life. (Landscapes of Legend Ser.). (J). 1999. pap. 6.95 (0-516-26301-3) Childrens.

Bevan, Gareth A., ed. A Dictionary of the Welsh Language (Geiriadur Prifysgol Cymru) Vol. 1, Pts. I-XXI: A - Ffysur. (ENG & WEL.). xx, 1386p. 1992. 90.00 (0-7083-0504-0, Pub. by Univ Wales Pr) Paul & Co Pubs.

— A Dictionary of the Welsh Language (Geiriadur Prifysgol Cymru) Vols. 2, Pts. XXII-XXXVI: G - Llyys. (ENG & WEL.). xxi, 926p. 1992. 70.00 (0-7083-0981-X, Pub. by Univ Wales Pr) Paul & Co Pubs.

Bevan, J. A., et al, eds. Vascular Neuroeffectors Mechanisms Journal: Blood Vessels, Vol. 28, No. 103, 1991. (Illus.). 268p. 1991. pap. 187.00 (3-8055-5380-3) S Karger.

Bevan, J. A., ed. see Physiology & Pharmacology of Vascular Neuroeffecto.

Bevan, James. A Pictorial Handbook of Anatomy & Physiology. (Illus.). 96p. 1994. pap. text 17.50 (1-85732-392-0) Buttrwrth-Heinemann.

*Bevan, Jan Atchley.** Corky the Bathtub Who Wouldn't Swallow. (Illus.). (J). 2000. write for info. (0-9653895-5-3) Bookmark Pubg.

Bevan, Joan & Pacelli, Maria. The Quintessential Canadian Anaesthetist, Wesley Bourne: A Retrospective on the Foundations of McGill Anesthesia. 10th ed. (Fontanus Monographs). (Illus.). 140p. 1997. 49.95 (0-7735-1455-4, Pub. by McG-Queens Univ Pr) CUP Services.

Bevan, Joan C. & Pacelli, Maria A. The Quinessential Canadian Anaesthetist Wesley Bourne: A Retrospective on the Foundations of McGill Anesthesia. LC 98-121894. 138p. 1996. 45.00 (0-7717-0485-2, Pub. by McGill-Queens Univ Pr) CUP Services.

Bevan, John A., et al, eds. Flow Dependent Regulation of Vascular Function. (Clinical Physiology Series - An American Physiological Society Book). (Illus.). 384p. 1995. text 89.50 (0-19-507842-X) OUP.

— The Resistance Vasculature. LC 91-20884. (Vascular Biomedicine Ser.). (Illus.). 488p. 1991. 120.00 (0-89603-212-4) Humana.

Bevan, John A., jt. ed. see Bevan, Rosemary D.

Bevan, John A., ed. see International Symposium on Vascular Neuroeffector.

Bevan, John A., ed. see International Vascular Neuroeffector Mechanisms Symposium Staff.

Bevan, John A., tr. see Mchedlishvili, George I.

Bevan, John V., jt. auth. see Bevan, Kay.

Bevan, Jonquil, ed. see Walton, Isaak.

Bevan, Kay & Bevan, John V. Learning to Love My Cancer: How a "Silent Killer" Became a Prescription for Living. LC 99-93839. 225p. 1999. pap. 12.95 (0-9671327-0-3) Charhill Voice.

Bevan, P. Gilroy & Donovan, I. A. Handbook of General Surgery. (Illus.). 576p. 1992. pap. 38.95 (0-632-01111-4) Blackwell Sci.

Bevan, Rosemary D. & Bevan, John A., eds. The Human Brain Circulation: Functional Changes in Disease. LC 94-15788. (Vascular Biomedicine Ser.). (Illus.). 470p. 1994. text 125.00 (0-89603-271-X) Humana.

Bevan, Ruth A. Contemporary Political Ideology. 1996. text 50.00 (0-86531-371-7) Westview.

*Bevan, Scott.** Water from the Moon: A Biography of John Fawcett. LC 99-495110. (Illus.). 304p. 1999. pap. 19.95 (1-86368-236-8, Pub. by Fremantle Arts) Intl Spec Bk.

Bevan, Simon & Chidgey, Peter. Accounts & Audit of Property Companies. 1994. pap. write for info. (0-406-01648-8, U.K., MICHIE) LEXIS Pub.

Bevan, Stanley C., et al. A Concise Etymological Dictionary of Chemistry. ix, 140p. 1976. 38.00 (0-85334-653-4) Elsevier.

Bevan, Stanley C., ed. see Conference on Vacuum Microbalance Techniques (9th:.

Bevan, Teleri. Years of My Time. 1997. pap. 29.95 (0-8464-4576-X) Beekman Pubs.

— Years of My Time. 1997. pap. 30.00 (1-85902-464-5, Pub. by Gomer Pr) St Mut.

Bevan, W., jt. ed. see Kennedy, H. E.

*Bevans.** Criminal Law & Procedure. (C). 2002. pap. 44.75 (0-7668-2279-6) Delmar.

Bevans, Charles I. U. S. Treaties . . . Digests . . . Bevans: Bevans: U. S. Treaties & Other International Agreements of the United States of America, General Index. LC 70-600742. 75.00 (1-57588-371-6, 201220) W S Hein.

— U. S. Treaties . . . Digests . . . Bevans: Bevans: U. S. Treaties & Other International Agreements of the United States of America, 1776-1949, 13 vols., Set. LC 70-600742. 1979. 800.00 (1-57588-370-8, 201220) W S Hein.

Bevans, Debbie, jt. auth. see Kdoshim, Jenny.

*Bevans, Neal R.** North Carolina Student Supplement for Litigation. LC 99-88903. 2000. pap. text, student ed. 21.95 (0-7355-1327-9) Panel Pubs.

Bevans, Stephen. John Oman & His Doctrine of God. 185p. (C). 1992. text 65.00 (0-521-41059-2) Cambridge U Pr.

Bevans, Stephen B. Models of Contextual Theology: The Struggle for Cultural Relevance. LC 92-19749. (Faith & Cultures Ser.). 180p. (Orig.). 1992. pap. 20.00 (0-88344-814-9) Orbis Bks.

Bevans, Stephen B., jt. auth. see Scherer, James A.

Bevans, Stephen B., jt. ed. see Scherer, James A.

Bevarly, Elizabeth. Un Acompanante Especial: An Unsuitable Man for the Job. (Deseo Ser.).Tr. of A Special Partner. (SPA.). 1997. per. 3.50 (0-373-35208-5, 1-35208-7) Harlequin Bks.

— Algo para Compartir. (Deseo Ser.: Vol. 128).Tr. of Father on the Brink. (SPA.). 1998. per. 3.50 (0-373-35258-1, 1-35258-2) Harlequin Bks.

— Amor Repentino. (SPA.). 1997. per. 3.50 (0-373-35188-7, 1-35188-1) Harlequin Bks.

— Beauty & the Brain. 1998. per. 3.75 (0-373-76130-9, 1-76130-3) Silhouette.

— Bride of the Bad Boy: Blame It on Bob. (Desire Ser.: No. 1124). 1998. per. 3.75 (0-373-76124-4, 1-76124-6) Silhouette.

*Bevarly, Elizabeth.** Coup de Coeur, Coup de Foudre. (Rouge Passion Ser.: No. 539). (FRE.). 2000. mass mkt. 3.99 (0-373-37539-5, 1-37539-3, Harlequin French) Harlequin Bks.

— Cuestion de Suerte. Vol. 199.Tr. of Matter of Luck. (SPA.). 156p. 2000. per. 3.50 (0-373-35329-4) Harlequin Bks.

Bevarly, Elizabeth. A Dad Like Daniel. (Desire Ser.). 1995. per. 3.25 (0-373-05908-6, 1-05908-8) Silhouette.

— Deseos de Aventura.Tr. of Adventures Desire. (SPA.). 1999. per. 3.50 (0-373-35286-7, 1-35286-3) Harlequin Bks.

— Destinations South. (Men at Work Ser.: Vol. 8). 1995. mass mkt. 4.50 (0-373-81020-2, 1-81020-9) Harlequin Bks.

— Dr. Daddy. (Desire Ser.). 1995. per. 3.25 (0-373-05933-7, 1-05933-6) Silhouette.

— A Doctor in Her Stocking: From Here to Maternity. (Desire Ser.: No. 1252). 1999. mass mkt. 3.75 (0-373-76252-6, 1-76252-5) Silhouette.

*Bevarly, Elizabeth.** Dr. Mommy: (From Here to Maternity) (Desire Ser.: No. 1269). 2000. mass mkt. 3.75 (0-373-76269-0, 1-76269-9) Harlequin Bks.

Bevarly, Elizabeth. Encuentro Con el Ayer (Meeting with Yesterday) (Deseo Ser.). (SPA.). 1998. per. 3.50 (0-373-35233-6, 1-35233-5) Harlequin Bks.

— Father of the Brat (From Here to Paternity) (Desire Ser.). 1996. per. 3.50 (0-373-05993-0, 1-05993-0) Silhouette.

— Father of the Brood: From Here to Paternity. (Desire Ser.). 1996. per. 3.50 (0-373-76005-1, 1-76005-7) Silhouette.

— Father on the Brink. (Desire Ser.). 1996. per. 3.50 (0-373-76016-7, 1-76016-4) Silhouette.

*Bevarly, Elizabeth.** First Comes Love. (Desire Ser.: Bk. 1323). 2000. mass mkt. 3.99 (0-373-76323-9, 1-76323-4) Silhouette.

Bevarly, Elizabeth. Georgia Meets Her Groom. (Desire Ser.: No. 1083). 1997. per. 3.50 (0-373-76083-3, 1-76083-4) Silhouette.

— Her Man Friday. LC 98-94816. 384p. 1999. mass mkt. 5.99 (0-380-80020-9, Avon Bks) Morrow Avon.

*Bevarly, Elizabeth.** How to Trap a Tycoon. 384p. 2000. mass mkt. 5.99 (0-380-81048-4) Morrow Avon.

Bevarly, Elizabeth. Lucy & the Loner. (Man of the Month Ser.). 1997. per. 3.50 (0-373-76063-9, 1-76063-6) Silhouette.

— Mas Que Belleza. 1999. per. 3.50 (0-373-35297-2, 1352970) Harlequin Bks.

*Bevarly, Elizabeth.** Monahan's Gamble. 2001. mass mkt. 3.99 (0-373-76337-9, 1-76337-4) Silhouette.

Bevarly, Elizabeth. My Man Pendleton. 384p. 1998. mass mkt. 5.99 (0-380-80019-5, Avon Bks) Morrow Avon.

— The Perfect Father: (From Here to Maternity) (Desire Ser.). 1995. per. 3.25 (0-373-05920-5, 1-05920-3) Silhouette.

— Promesa Cumplidas: Lucy & the Loner. (Deseo Ser.: Vol. 122).Tr. of Fulfilled Promises. 1998. per. 3.50 (0-373-35252-2, 1-35252-5) Harlequin Bks.

— Proposicion Inocente. (Deseo Ser.). 1996. per. 3.50 (0-373-35145-3, 1-35145-1) Harlequin Bks.

— Return Engagement. (Special Edition Ser.). 1993. per. 3.50 (0-373-09844-8, 5-09844-7) Silhouette.

— Roxy & the Rich Man. (Desire Ser.). 1997. per. 3.50 (0-373-76053-1, 1-76053-7) Silhouette.

— The Sheriff & the Imposter Bride: Follow That Baby. (Desire Ser.: No. 1184). 1998. per. 3.75 (0-373-76184-8, 1-76184-0) Silhouette.

— The Society Bride: The Fortunate Children. 1999. per. 3.75 (0-373-76196-1, Harlequin) Harlequin Bks.

— Un Soltero en Apuros. (Silhouette Deseo Ser.: No. 149). 1996. per. 3.50 (0-373-35149-6, 1-35149-3) Harlequin Bks.

— That Boss of Mine. (Desire Ser.: No. 1231). 1999. per. 3.75 (0-373-76231-3, 1-76231-9) Silhouette.

— Up Close. (Special Edition Ser.: No. 737). 1992. per. 3.39 (0-373-09737-9, 5-09737-3) Harlequin Bks.

*Bevarly, Elizabeth.** Un Viejo Amor. (Deseo Ser.).Tr. of Old Love. (SPA.). 2000. mass mkt. 3.50 (0-373-35347-2, 1-35347-3) Harlequin Bks.

Bevarly, Elizabeth. The Virgin & the Vagabond. 1998. per. 3.75 (0-373-76136-8, 1-76136-0) Silhouette.

Bevege, Margaret. Behind the Barbed Wire: Internment in Australia During World War II. 1993. pap. 19.95 (0-7022-2492-8, Pub. by Univ Queensland Pr) Intl Spec Bk.

Bevel, Virgil T. Bloodstain Pattern Analysis: With an Introduction to Crime Scene Reconstruction. LC 97-57102. (Practical Aspects of Criminal Investigation Ser.). 336p. 1997. boxed set 79.95 (0-8493-8159-2) CRC Pr.

Bevelacqua. Hazardous Materials Chemistry for Emergency Responders: Street Chemistry. (Fire Science Ser.). (C). 2000. pap. 32.95 (0-7668-1434-3) Thomson Learn.

Bevelacqua & Stilp. Emer Med Response/haz Material Study Gde. (FIRE SCIENCE). 1997. student ed. 17.75 (0-8273-7830-0) Delmar.

— Emergency Response to Hazardous Materials Incidents IG. (Career Education Ser.). 112p. 1997. text, teacher ed. 16.50 (0-8273-7831-9) Delmar.

*Bevelacqua, Armando S.** Hazardous Materials Chemistry. LC 00-30679. (Illus.). 2000. write for info. (0-7668-1435-1) Delmar.

Bevelacqua, Armando S. Pocket Guide to EMS Run Reports. 16.00 (0-685-50512-X) P-H.

— Prehospital Documentation: A Systematic Approach. 144p. 1992. pap. text 22.00 (0-89303-948-9) P-H.

Bevelacqua, Armando S. & Stilp, Richard H. Emergency Medical Response to Hazardous Materials Incidents. LC 96-34053. (Career Education Ser.). 448p. 1996. mass mkt. 55.95 (0-8273-7829-7) Delmar.

— Hazardous Materials Field Guide. LC 97-44636. 96p. 1998. pap. 26.95 (0-7668-0155-1) Delmar.

— Terrorism Handbook for Operational Responders. LC 98-7415. 120p. 1998. pap. text 15.95 (0-7668-0475-5) Delmar.

Bevelacqua, Joan. Working with Business. 116p. 29.95 (0-914951-07-6) LERN.

*Bevelacqua, Joseph J.** Basic Health Physics: Problems & Solutions. LC 98-20472. 559p. 1999. 79.95 (0-471-29711-9, Wiley-Interscience) Wiley.

Bevelacqua, Joseph J. Health. 456p. 1995. 92.95 (0-471-01801-5) Wiley.

Bevelander, Gerrit. Abalone, Gross & Fine Structure. (Illus.). 1988. pap. 18.00 (0-940168-05-7) Boxwood.

— Atlas of Oral Histology & Embryology. LC 67-29213. 249p. 1967. reprint ed. pap. 77.20 (0-8357-5843-5, 205632500059) Bks Demand.

Bevell, Ruth Adams. Sheaves of Friendship. xxii, 247p. 1982. text 7.50 (0-88053-325-0, S-100) Macoy Pub.

Beven, K. J., ed. Distributed Hydrological Modelling: Applications of the TOPMODEL Concept. LC 97-19670. (Advances in Hydrological Processes Ser.). 356p. 1998. pap. 80.00 (0-471-97724-1) Wiley.

Beven, Keith J. Channel Network Hydrology. LC 92-5404. 330p. 1993. 265.00 (0-471-93534-4) Wiley.

— Rainfall-Runoff Modelling. text 56.00 (0-471-98553-8) Wiley.

Beven, Keith J., et al, eds. Mixing & Transport in the Environment: A Memorial Volume for Catherine M. Allen (1954-1991) 474p. 1994. 205.00 (0-471-94142-5) Wiley.

Beven, Roy Q. Move with Science: Energy, Force & Motion. LC 98-84914. (Illus.). 160p. 1998. pap. text 21.95 (0-87355-172-9, PB144X) Natl Sci Tchrs.

Beven, Thomas. Negligence in Law, 2 vols. 4th ed. ccxi, 1638p. 1998. reprint ed. 395.00 (1-56169-407-X, 15564) Gaunt.

Bevens, Chris. American Sentences. 14p. (Orig.). 1997. pap. 5.00 (1-891051-02-4) Back Cover Pr.

— Bonjour. 16p. (Orig.). 1997. pap. 5.00 (1-891051-01-6) Back Cover Pr.

— So, What Do We Talk About? 23p. (Orig.). 1997. pap. 5.00 (1-891051-00-8) Back Cover Pr.

Bevens, Darcy, ed. On the Rim of Kilauea: Excerpts from the Volcano House Register, 1865-1955. LC 92-85122. (Illus.). 168p. (Orig.). 1992. pap. text 9.95 (0-940295-11-3) HI Natural Hist.

Bevens, Darcy, et al, eds. Early Serial Publications of the Hawaiian Volcano Observatory, 3 vols., Set. (Illus.). 3062p. (C). 1988. reprint ed. 50.00 (0-940295-03-2) HI Natural Hist.

Bevens, Darcy & Wright, Thomas L. Thomas A. Jaggar Museum Guidebook. (Illus.). 34p. (Orig.). 1992. pap. 6.95 (0-940295-10-5) HI Natural Hist.

Bevens, Darcy, et al. Early Serial Publications of the Hawaiian Volcano Observatory, Vol. 1. (Illus.). 565p. (C). 1988. reprint ed. 20.00 (0-940295-04-0) HI Natural Hist.

— Early Serial Publications of the Hawaiian Volcano Observatory, Vol. 2. 1273p. (C). 1988. reprint ed. 20.00 (0-940295-05-9) HI Natural Hist.

— Early Serial Publications of the Hawaiian Volcano Observatory, Vol. 3. (Illus.). 1224p. (C). 1988. reprint ed. 20.00 (0-940295-06-7) HI Natural Hist.

Bevensee, Robert M. Handbook of Conical Antennas & Scatterers. LC 71-172793. (Illus.). xiv, 173p. 1973. text 323.00 (0-677-00480-X) Gordon & Breach.

Bever. Safety: A Personal Focus. 5th ed. 2000. 65.00 (0-07-289116-5) McGraw.

Bever, Bernie. Hojo Supreme. 1978. 1.00 (0-916866-03-3) Cats Pajamas.

— Hojo Supreme. deluxe ed. 1978. 3.00 (0-916866-04-1) Cats Pajamas.

Bever, Dale N. Northwest Conifers: A Photographic Key. LC 81-65509. (Illus.). 116p. 1981. pap. 18.95 (0-8323-0390-9) Binford Mort.

Bever, Edward. Africa. LC 96-43086. (International Government & Politics Ser.). (Illus.). 304p. 1996. pap. 37.95 (0-89774-954-5) Oryx Pr.

Bever, Michael B., ed. Concise Encyclopedia of Materials Economics, Policy & Management. LC 92-27943. (Advances in Materials Science & Engineering Ser.). (Illus.). 480p. 1992. 215.00 (0-08-037056-X, Pergamon Pr) Elsevier.

Bever, Michael B. & Cahn, Robert W., eds. Encyclopedia of Materials Science & Engineering Supplementary, Vol. 3. 770p. 1993. 453.25 (0-08-040590-8) Elsevier.

Bever, Michael B., jt. auth. see Cahn, Robert W.

Bever, Michael B., jt. ed. see Cahn, Robert W.

Bever, William Van, see Van Bever, William, ed.

Beverage, Gloria, ed. Special Times: 365 Low-Cost Activities for Children. (Illus.). 384p. (J). 1995. pap. 10.00 (0-9635089-0-3) PWC Pub.

Beverage, Richard E. The Hollywood Stars: Baseball in Movieland 1926-57. LC 84-70556. (Illus.). 310p. (Orig.). 1984. pap. 11.95 (0-940684-01-2) Deacon Pr.

B

***Bevere, John.** Asi Dice el Senor? (SPA.). 1999. pap. 9.99 (*0-88419-608-9*) Casa Creacion.

Bevere, John. The Bait of Satan. LC 94-71394. 191p. 1999. pap. 12.99 (*0-88419-374-8*) Dake Pub.

— The Bait of Satan: Study Guide. 1997. pap., student ed. 5.99 (*0-88419-447-7*) Creation House.

***Bevere, John.** Breaking Intimidation: How to Overcome Fear & Release the Gifts of God in Your Life. 206p. 2000. pap. 12.99 (*0-88419-733-6*) Creation House.

Bevere, John. Breaking Intimidation: How to Oversome Fear & Release the Gifts of God in Your Life. 1999. pap. 12.99 (*0-88419-387-X*) Dake Pub.

— The Devil's Door. LC 96-85051. 200p. 1999. pap. 12.99 (*0-88419-442-6*) Dake Pub.

— The Fear of the Lord: Beginning to Know God with Intimacy & Passion. LC 97-35841. 1997. pap. 12.99 (*0-88419-486-8*) Creation House.

— The Fear of the Lord: Discover the Key to Intimately Knowing God. LC 97-35841. 1997. 14.99 (*0-88419-525-2*) Creation House.

***Bevere, John.** A Heart Ablaze. LC 99-39348. 192p. 1999. pap. 12.99 (*0-7852-6990-8*) Nelson.

Bevere, John. Pathway to His Presence: Removing Barriers to Intimacy with God, Vol. 1. LC 99-58695. 1999. 16.99 (*0-88419-654-2*) Creation House.

Bevere, John. Quebrando la Intimidacion. (SPA.). 1995. pap. 9.99 (*0-88419-603-8*) Casa Creacion.

— El Temor de Dios: Descubra la Clave para Conocer Intimamente a Dios. (SPA.). 1997. pap. 9.99 (*0-88419-553-8*) Casa Creacion.

— Thus Saith the Lord: How to Know When God Is Speaking to You Through Another. LC 99-11625. 204p. 1999. pap. 12.99 (*0-88419-575-9*) Creation House.

Bevere, John. Victory in the Wilderness. 1996. pap. 9.99 (*0-9633176-0-1*) J Bevere Minist.

— The Voice of One Crying. 1999. pap. 7.99 (*0-9633176-1-X*) Dake Pub.

***Bevere, Lisa.** Be Angry (But Don't Blow It) A Woman's Guide to Managing Anger. LC 00-35504. 192p. 2000. pap. 12.99 (*0-7852-6988-6*) Nelson.

— Fuera de Control y Disfrutandolo! (SPA.). 1998. pap. 9.99 (*0-88419-555-4*) Casa Creacion.

Bevere, Lisa. Out of Control & Loving It! Giving God Complete Control of Your Life. LC 96-83756. 1996. pap. 12.99 (*0-88419-436-1*) Creation House.

— The True Measure of a Woman: You Are More Than What You See. LC 97-31174. 1997. pap. 11.99 (*0-88419-487-6*) Creation House.

— You Are Not What You Weigh: Discover How God Loves You Just the Way You Are. LC 98-41550. 1998. 14.99 (*0-88419-542-2*) Creation House.

***Bevere, Lisa.** You Are Not What You Weigh: Escaping the Lie & Living the Truth, Vol. 1. 1999. pap. 10.99 (*0-88419-661-5*) Creation House.

***Beveridge, tr.** Maathir - Ul - Umara. 1999. reprint ed. 64.00 (*81-7536-159-X*, Pub. by Low Price) S Asia.

Beveridge & Riley. European Community Taxation. 78.95 (*1-85521-569-1*) Ashgate Pub Co.

Beveridge, jt. auth. see Anderson.

Beveridge, A. D., ed. Forensic Investigations of Explosions. (Series in Forensic Science). 300p. 1996. 89.95 (*0-13-341629-1*, Pub. by Tay Francis Ltd) Taylor & Francis.

Beveridge, Albert J. Abraham Lincoln, 1809-1858, 2 vols., Set. (History - United States Ser.). 1992. reprint ed. lib. bdg. 150.00 (*0-7812-6169-4*) Rprt Serv.

— The Art of Public Speaking. 64p. Date not set. pap. 14.95 (*0-9634672-2-0*) Georgetwn Pub Hse.

— The Life of John Marshall, 4 vols. bound in 2. LC 90-2613. (Illus.). 2496p. 1990. reprint ed. 150.00 (*0-87797-181-1*) Cherokee.

— The Life of John Marshall, 4 vols. 1997. reprint ed. 495.00 (*1-56169-305-7*) Gaunt.

— The Life of John Marshall, 4 vols., Set. (BCL1 - U. S. History Ser.). 1991. reprint ed. lib. bdg. 300.00 (*0-7812-6127-9*) Rprt Serv.

— The Life of John Marshall, Vol. 1 & 2. LC 90-2613. 1998. 85.00 (*0-87797-182-X*) Cherokee.

— The Life of John Marshall, Vol. 3 & 4. 1998. 85.00 (*0-87797-183-8*) Cherokee.

— Meaning of the Times & Other Speeches. LC 68-54327. (Essay Index Reprint Ser.). 1977. 23.95 (*0-8369-0208-4*) Ayer.

Beveridge, Annette S., tr. The History of Humayun. (C). 1989. 16.00 (*81-86142-14-2*, Pub. by BR Pub) S Asia.

Beveridge, Annette S., tr. see Babar Emperor of Hindustan.

Beveridge, Annette S., tr. see Ghazi, Z. M.

Beveridge, Barbara. Honey, My Rabbit. LC 92-34272. (Voyages Ser.). (Illus.). (J). 1993. 2.50 (*0-383-03630-5*) SRA McGraw.

— Hooray for Snow. LC 92-27098. (Voyages Ser.). (Illus.). (J). 1993. 3.75 (*0-383-03573-2*) SRA McGraw.

— Over the Marble Mountain. LC 92-27097. (Illus.). (J). (gr. 4 up). 1993. 2.50 (*0-383-03589-9*) SRA McGraw.

— The Stream. LC 92-33738. (Voyages Ser.). (Illus.). (J). 1993. 3.75 (*0-383-03657-7*) SRA McGraw.

— Waves. LC 92-31948. (Voyages Ser.). (Illus.). (J). 1993. 3.75 (*0-383-03603-8*) SRA McGraw.

Beveridge, Charles & Rocheleau, Paul. Frederick Law Olmsted: Designing the American Landscape. Larkin, David, ed. & des. by. LC 98-26181. (Illus.). 240p. 2000. pap. 25.00 (*0-7893-0228-4*, Pub. by Universe) St Martin.

Beveridge, Charles E. Frederick Law Olmsted: Designing the American Landscape. Larkin, David, ed. & des. by. LC 95-12042. (Illus.). 288p. 1995. 70.00 (*0-8478-1842-X*, Pub. by Rizzoli Intl) St Martin.

Beveridge, Charles E., ed. The Papers of Frederick Law Olmsted Vol. 1: Writings on Public Parks, Parkways, & Park Systems. LC 77-741. (Papers of Frederick Law Olmsted: Vol. 1). (Illus.). 744p. 1997. text 55.00 (*0-8018-5532-2*) Johns Hopkins.

Beveridge, Charles E. & Schuyler, David. The Papers of Frederick Law Olmsted Vol. 3: Creating Central Park, 1857-1861. LC 82-4701. (Olsted Papers). (Illus.). 464p. 1983. text 55.00 (*0-8018-2751-5*) Johns Hopkins.

Beveridge, Charles E., ed. see Olmsted, Frederick L.

Beveridge, Craig & Turnbull, Ronald. The Eclipse of Scottish Culture. 1989. 14.00 (*0-7486-6009-7*, Pub. by Polygon) Subterranean Co.

— Scotland after Enlightenment. 184p. 1997. 20.00 (*0-7486-6223-5*, Pub. by Polygon) Subterranean Co.

Beveridge, David L., et al, eds. Theoretical Biochemistry & Molecular Biophysics Vol. 1: DNA. (Illus.). 431p. 1990. lib. bdg. 95.00 (*0-940030-33-0*) Adenine Pr.

— Theoretical Biochemistry & Molecular Biophysics Vol. 2: Proteins. (Illus.). 335p. 1990. lib. bdg. 95.00 (*0-940030-34-9*) Adenine Pr.

Beveridge, David L. & Lavery, R. V., eds. Theoretical Biochemistry & Molecular Biophysics: DNA; Proteins, 2 vols. (Illus.). 1990. lib. bdg. 190.00 (*0-940030-28-4*) Adenine Pr.

Beveridge, David R., ed. Rethinking Dvorak: Views from Five Countries. (Illus.). 316p. 1996. text 65.00 (*0-19-816411-4*) OUP.

Beveridge, Donna. Henry. (Books for Young Learners).Tr. of Henry. (Illus.). 12p. (J). (gr. k-2). 1999. pap. text 5.00 (*1-57274-263-1*) R Owen Pubs.

***Beveridge, Donna.** Henry. Romo, Alberto, tr. (Books for Young Learners).Tr. of Henry. (SPA., Illus.). 12p. (J). (gr. k-2). 1999. pap. text 5.00 (*1-57274-342-5*, A2866) R Owen Pubs.

Beveridge, Elizabeth. Choosing & Using Home Equipment. 7th ed. LC 76-12577. 118p. 1976. reprint ed. pap. 36.60 (*0-608-00189-9*, 206097100006) Bks Demand.

Beveridge, Henry. Tuzuk-I-Jahangiri: or Memoirs of Jahangir. Rogers, A., tr. 1989. reprint ed. 22.50 (*81-85395-13-6*, Pub. by BR Pub) S Asia.

Beveridge, Henry, tr. The Akbar Nama of Abu-I-Fazal, 3 vols., Set. 1989. reprint ed. 72.50 (*81-85395-03-9*) S Asia.

— The Tarikh-I-Mubarakshahi. 1990. 10.00 (*81-85418-55-1*, Pub. by Low Price) S Asia.

Beveridge, Henry, ed. see Jahangir.

Beveridge, Henry, tr. see Beza, Theodore.

Beveridge, Jim & Wiener, Robert. Multithreading Applications in Win 32: The Complete Guide to Threads in Windows 95 & Windows NT. LC 96-48106. 400p. (C). 1996. pap. 42.95 (*0-201-44234-5*) Addison-Wesley.

Beveridge, John, jt. auth. see Gupta, Jagdish M.

Beveridge, Julian, et al, photos by. Historic Inns of Canada's East Coast: A Select Guide. LC 98-104175. (Illus.). 72p. (Orig.). 1997. pap. 10.95 (*0-88780-400-4*, Pub. by Formac Publ Co) Seven Hills Bk.

Beveridge, Julian, jt. auth. see Elliot, Elaine.

Beveridge, Malcolm C. Cage Aquaculture. 2nd ed. LC 95-48447. 336p. 1996. pap. text 65.00 (*0-85238-235-9*) Blackwell Sci.

***Beveridge, Malcolm C. M. & McAndrew, Brendan J.** Tilapias: Biology & Exploitation. LC 00-33062. (Fish & Fisheries Ser.). 2000. write for info. (*0-412-80090-X*) Plenum.

Beveridge, Martha B. Building Better Boundaries. 2nd rev. ed. Bruce-Phipps, Terrisa, ed. 42p. 1989. pap. 3.50 (*1-889237-03-5*) Options Now.

— Healing & Freeing the Inner Child. 2nd rev. ed. Bruce-Phipps, Terrisa, ed. 30p. 1994. pap. 3.50 (*1-889237-06-X*) Options Now.

— Healthy Sexual Response-Ability. 2nd rev. ed. Bruce-Phipps, Terrisa, ed. 32p. 1994. pap. 3.50 (*1-889237-08-6*) Options Now.

— The Little Book of Love Tips. Bruce-Phipps, Terrisa, ed. 36p. (Orig.). 1996. pap. 5.95 (*1-889237-00-0*) Options Now.

— Loving & Healing Your Inner Adolescent. 2nd rev. ed. Bruce-Phipps, Terrisa, ed. 25p. 1994. pap. 3.50 (*1-889237-05-1*) Options Now.

— Make Friends with Your Feelings. 2nd rev. ed. Bruce-Phipps, Terrisa, ed. 20p. 1994. pap. 3.50 (*1-889237-09-4*) Options Now.

— Making Peace with Your Past. 2nd rev. ed. Bruce-Phipps, Terrisa, ed. 17p. 1994. pap. 3.50 (*1-889237-07-8*) Options Now.

— Meeting & Mastering Your Internal Saboteur. 2nd rev. ed. Bruce-Phipps, Terrisa, ed. 44p. 1989. pap. 3.50 (*1-889237-02-7*) Options Now.

— The Missing Pieces in the Weight Loss Puzzle. Bruce-Phipps, Terrisa, ed. 71p. (Orig.). 1996. pap. 9.95 (*1-889237-01-9*) Options Now.

— Prosperity Consciousness. 2nd rev. ed. Bruce-Phipps, Terrisa, ed. 28p. 1994. pap. 3.50 (*1-889237-04-3*) Options Now.

Beveridge, Mary E., ed. see Brylske, Alex.

Beveridge, Michael & Conti-Ramsden, Gina. Language & Communication in People with Learning Disabilities. 320p. (C). 1997. pap. 24.99 (*0-415-15397-2*) Routledge.

Beveridge, Michael & Reddiford, Gordon, eds. Language, Culture, & Education. 200p. 1993. 59.00 (*1-85359-203-X*, Pub. by Multilingual Matters) Taylor & Francis.

Beveridge, Michael, et al. Language & Communication in Mentally Handicapped People. 200p. 1989. 67.50 (*0-412-32390-7*) Chapman & Hall.

Beveridge, Michael, jt. auth. see Lloyd, P.

Beveridge, Phyllis, jt. auth. see Corbett, Nancy A.

Beveridge, Sally. Special Educational Needs in Schools. LC 92-40455. (Education in Society Ser.). 144p. 1993. pap. write for info. (*0-415-07551-3*) Routledge.

***Beveridge, Sally.** Special Educational Needs in Schools. 2nd ed. LC 99-13192. 184p. (C). 1999. pap. write for info. (*0-415-20294-9*); text. write for info. (*0-415-20293-0*) Routledge.

Beveridge, Terrence J. & Koval, S. F., eds. Advances in Bacterial Paracrystalline Surface Layers. (NATO ASI Ser.: Vol. 252). (Illus.). 354p. (C). 1993. text 115.00 (*0-306-44582-4*, Kluwer Plenum) Kluwer Academic.

Beveridge, Thomas M. FAIRMODEL User's Guide & Introductory Workbook. (Illus.). 219p. (Orig.). (C). 1990. pap. text 18.00 (*0-9627631-1-X*) Macro MA.

Beveridge, Tony & McGlashan, Paul. High Performance ISAPI/NSAPI Web Programming. 10th ed. LC 97-196076. 600p. (C). 1997. pap. text, mass mkt. 39.99 incl. cd-rom (*1-57610-151-7*) Coriolis Grp.

Beveridge, W. I., ed. see International Symposium on Breeding Non-Human Prim.

Beveridge, William. Complete Works, 12 vols. LC 72-39437. (Library of Anglo-Catholic Theology: No. 2). reprint ed. write for info. (*0-404-52040-5*) AMS Pr.

— A Short History of the Westminster Assembly. 160p. (C). 1993. pap. text 9.95 (*1-884416-00-4*) A Press.

Beveridge, William H. Causes & Cures of Unemployment. LC 75-41030. (BCL Ser. II). 1976. reprint ed. 20.00 (*0-404-14798-4*) AMS Pr.

— Unemployment: A Problem of Industry. LC 79-95398. (BCL Ser. II). reprint ed. 25.00 (*0-404-00794-5*) AMS Pr.

Beveridge, William H. & Wells, Alan F., eds. The Evidence for Voluntary Action, Being Memoranda by Organisations & Individuals & Other Materials Relevant to Voluntary Action. LC 78-5650. (Illus.). 343p. 1978. reprint ed. lib. bdg. 55.00 (*0-313-20485-3*, BEEV) Greenwood.

Beveridge, William I. Frontiers in Comparative Medicine. LC 72-79500. (Wesley W. Spink Lectures on Comparative Medicine: No. 1). 104p. reprint ed. pap. 32.30 (*0-8357-8886-5*, 203320600085) Bks Demand.

Beverley, Deena. Flowercrafts: Practical Inspirations for Natural Gifts, Country Crafts & Decorative Displays. (Illus.). 128p. 1997. 19.95 (*1-85967-374-0*, Lorenz Bks) Anness Pub.

— Ribboncraft: More Than 20 Classic Projects. (Illus.). 128p. 1998. 24.95 (*1-85732-789-6*, Pub. by Mitchell Beazley) Trafalgar.

— Stringwork. (New Crafts Ser.). (Illus.). 96p. 1997. 14.95 (*1-85967-377-5*, Lorenz Bks) Anness Pub.

Beverley, Deena, jt. auth. see Newton-Cox, Andrew.

Beverley, George H. Pioneer in the U. S. Air Corps. (Illus.). 70p. (Orig.). 1982. pap. text 12.00 (*0-89745-029-9*) Sunflower U Pr.

Beverley, James A. Christ & Islam: Understanding the Faith of the Muslims. 84p. 1997. pap. 5.99 (*0-89900-715-5*) College Pr Pub.

Beverley, Jo. An Arranged Marriage. 352p. 1999. mass mkt. 6.99 (*0-8217-6401-2*, Zebra Kensgtn) Kensgtn Pub Corp.

— Dangerous Joy. large type ed. (Black Satin Romance Ser.). 505p. 1997. 27.99 (*1-86110-029-9*) Ulverscroft.

— Dark Champion. 400p. (Orig.). 1993. mass mkt. 4.50 (*0-380-76786-4*, Avon Bks) Morrow Avon.

— Deirdre & Don Juan. 224p. 1993. mass mkt. 3.99 (*0-380-77281-7*, Avon Bks) Morrow Avon.

***Beverley, Jo.** Devilish. 352p. 2000. mass mkt. 6.99 (*0-451-19997-9*, Sig) NAL.

— Devilish. large type ed. LC 00-37771. 647p. 2000. pap. 29.95 (*0-7862-2653-6*) Thorndike Pr.

Beverley, Jo. Emily & the Dark Angel. 224p. 1992. mass mkt. 3.99 (*0-380-71555-4*, Avon Bks) Morrow Avon.

— Forbidden. 448p. 1994. mass mkt. 4.99 (*0-8217-4488-7*, Zebra Kensgtn) Kensgtn Pub Corp.

— Forbidden. large type ed. (Black Satin Romance Ser.). 462p. 1997. 27.99 (*1-86110-031-0*, Pub. by Mgna Lrg Print) Ulverscroft.

— Forbidden Magic. 1998. mass mkt. 6.50 (*0-451-40802-0*, Topaz) NAL.

— The Fortune Hunter. 208p. 1992. mass mkt. 3.99 (*0-380-71771-9*, Avon Bks) Morrow Avon.

— Lord of Midnight. (Topaz Historical Romance Ser.). 378p. 1998. mass mkt. 6.50 (*0-451-40801-2*, Onyx) NAL.

— Lord of Midnight. large type ed. LC 98-34893. 1998. 23.95 (*1-56895-662-2*) Wheeler Pub.

— Lord of My Heart. 384p. (Orig.). 1992. mass mkt. 4.50 (*0-380-76784-8*, Avon Bks) Morrow Avon.

— My Lady Notorious. 384p. 1993. mass mkt. 4.50 (*0-380-76785-6*, Avon Bks) Morrow Avon.

— Secrets of the Night. 1999. mass mkt. 6.50 (*0-451-40889-6*, Topaz) NAL.

***Beverley, Jo.** Secrets of the Night. large type ed. LC 99-38386. 1999. 22.95 (*1-56895-770-X*, Wheeler) Wheeler Pub.

Beverley, Jo. The Shattered Rose. 1996. pap. text 5.99 (*0-8217-5310-X*, Zebra Kensgtn) Kensgtn Pub Corp.

— Something Wicked. 352p. 1997. mass mkt. 5.99 (*0-8217-5548-X*, Zebra Kensgtn) Kensgtn Pub Corp.

— Something Wicked. 1997. mass mkt. 5.99 (*0-451-40780-6*, Onyx) NAL.

— Something Wicked. LC 98-27674. (Star Romance Ser.). 1998. 24.95 (*0-7862-1603-4*) Thorndike Pr.

— The Stanforth Secrets. 256p. 1991. mass mkt. 3.99 (*0-380-71438-8*, Avon Bks) Morrow Avon.

— The Stanforth Secrets. large type ed. LC 90-10728. 386p. 1990. lib. bdg. 18.95 (*0-89621-971-2*) Thorndike Pr.

— The Stolen Bride. 224p. 1991. mass mkt. 3.99 (*0-380-71439-6*, Avon Bks) Morrow Avon.

— The Stolen Bride. large type ed. 335p. 1991. reprint ed. lib. bdg. 18.95 (*1-56054-115-6*) Thorndike Pr.

— Tempting Fortune. 448p. 1995. mass mkt. 4.99 (*0-8217-4858-0*, Zebra Kensgtn) Kensgtn Pub Corp.

— An Unwilling Bride. 1994. pap. 3.99 (*0-8217-4475-5*) NAL.

***Beverley, Jo, et al.** The Brides of Christmas: The Wise Virgin; The Vagabond King; The Unexpected Guest. 1999. mass mkt. 5.99 (*0-373-83417-9*, Harlequin) Harlequin Bks.

Beverley, John. Against Literature. LC 92-46356. 192p. 1993. pap. 14.95 (*0-8166-2249-3*); text 37.95 (*0-8166-2248-5*) U of Minn Pr.

— Del Lazarillo al Sandinismo: Estudios Sobre la Funcion Ideologica de la Literatura Espanola e Hispanoamericana. (Towards a Social History of Hispanic & Luso-Brazilian Literature Ser.). (SPA.). 208p. (Orig.). 1987. pap. text 9.95 (*0-910235-18-X*) Prisma Bks.

Beverley, John. Subalternity & Representation: Arguments in Cultural Theory. LC 99-31551. 224p. 1999. pap. text 17.95 (*0-8223-2416-4*) Duke.

***Beverley, John.** Subalternity & Representation: Arguments in Cultural Theory. LC 99-31551. 224p. 1999. 49.95 (*0-8223-2382-6*) Duke.

Beverley, John, et al, eds. The Postmodernism Debate in Latin America. LC 94-23975. (Boundary Two Book Ser.). 336p. 1995. text 49.95 (*0-8223-1586-6*); pap. text 17.95 (*0-8223-1614-5*) Duke.

Beverley, John & Zimmerman, Marc. Literature & Politics in the Central American Revolutions. LC 90-12667. (New Interpretations of Latin America Ser.). 270p. (Orig.). reprint ed. pap. 83.70 (*0-608-20862-0*, 207196100003) Bks Demand.

Beverley, John R. Aspects of Gongora's "Soledades" (Purdue University Monographs in Romance Languages: No. 1). iv, 139p. 1980. 35.00 (*90-272-1711-4*) J Benjamins Pubng Co.

Beverley, M. C., tr. see Aksakov, Sergei.

Beverley, Mary F. Cowbells & Coffins: The Old General Store. Roberts, Melissa, ed. (Illus.). 80p. 1987. 11.95 (*0-89015-593-3*) Sunbelt Media.

Beverley, Peter C., ed. Monoclonal Antibodies. LC 85-19512. (Illus.). 352p. 1986. 132.00 (*0-443-02990-3*) Church.

Beverley, Robert. The East Tennessee Almanac. (Living Almanacs Ser.). (Illus.). xii, 291p. (Orig.). 1992. pap. 12.95 (*0-9629289-1-7*) Sanctuary Pr.

— History & Present State of Virginia. Wright, Louis B., ed. LC 68-58999. (Illus.). 402p. reprint ed. pap. 124.70 (*0-8357-9803-8*, 201574500097) Bks Demand.

— The Western North Carolina Almanac. 2nd ed. (Living Almanacs Ser.). (Illus.). xii, 275p. 1993. pap. 12.95 (*0-9629289-2-5*) Sanctuary Pr.

***Beverly, Deena.** Tiling & Mosaics in a Weekend. 2000. pap. 14.95 (*1-58290-027-2*, Pub. by Jrny Editions) Tuttle Pubng.

Beverly, Don & Dekle, Hal. Florida Trial Evidence. 1995. student ed. 45.00 (*0-07-172774-4*) Shepards.

Beverly, Don, jt. auth. see Morton, Chris.

Beverly, J. Risa Santa y la Bencicion de Toronta.Tr. of Holy Laughter, the Toronto Blessing. (SPA.). 1996. pap. 9.99 (*0-8297-0508-2*) Vida Pubs.

Beverly, Jo. Dangerous Joy. 1995. mass mkt. 5.99 (*0-8217-5129-8*, Zebra Kensgtn) Kensgtn Pub Corp.

— Lord Wraybourne's Betrothed. large type ed. 351p. 1991. reprint ed. lib. bdg. 18.95 (*1-56054-087-7*) Thorndike Pr.

***Beverly, Jo, et al.** Star of Wonder. 368p. 1999. mass mkt. 6.99 (*0-515-12653-5*, Jove) Berkley Pub.

Beverly, John. Del Lazarillo al Sandinisuo. (SPA.). 192p. 1988. pap. 9.95 (*0-318-39831-1*, 3036) Ediciones Norte.

Beverly, Lois R. Prayers & Blessings. 53p. 1998. pap. 5.95 (*1-55630-833-7*) Brentwood Comm.

***Beverly, Sheree L.** 1999 Senate Staff Employment Study. (Illus.). 126p. 1999. pap. text 15.00 (*1-930473-00-1*) Congressional Mgmt Fdnt.

Beverly, Sonnie. Real Saved Folks. 144p. 1999. pap. 8.95 (*1-58169-036-3*, Third Stry Window) Genesis Comm Inc.

Beverly, Suanne. The Kitchenless Cookbook. LC 97-81194. (Illus.). 224p. 1998. 21.95 (*0-9662137-0-X*) InterMedia Pub.

Bevernes, J. & Eberly, D. Mathematical Problems from Combustion Theory. (Applied Mathematical Sciences Ser.: Vol. 83). (Illus.). x, 177p. 1989. 58.95 (*0-387-97104-1*) Spr-Verlag.

Bevers, Holm. Das Rathaus von Antwerpen (1561-65) (Studien zur Kunstgeschichte: Bd. 28). (GER.). 255p. 1985. write for info. (*3-487-07716-7*) G Olms Pubs.

Bevers, Michael, jt. auth. see Hof, John.

***Beversluis, Joel D.** Sourcebook of the World's Religions: An Interfaith Guide to Religion & Spirituality. 3rd rev. ed. 420p. 2000. pap. 24.95 (*1-57731-121-3*, Pub. by New Wrld Lib) Publishers Group.

***Beversluis, John.** Cross-Examining Socrates: A Defense of the Interlocutors in Plato's Early Dialogues. 428p. 2000. 69.95 (*0-521-55058-0*) Cambridge U Pr.

Beverstock, Caroline, jt. auth. see Newman, Anabel P.

Beverton, R. J., et al, eds. Marine Mammals & Fisheries. (Illus.). 350p. (C). 1985. text 100.00 (*0-04-639003-0*) Routledge.

Beverton, R. J. & Holt, S. J. On the Dynamics of Exploited Fish Populations. 533p. (C). 1993. text 97.00 (*0-412-54960-3*, 530.17C) Chapman & Hall.

Bevevino, Mary M., et al. An Educator's Guide to Block Scheduling: Decision Making, Curriculum Design, & Lesson Planning Strategies. LC 98-14869. 175p. (C). 1998. pap. 33.00 (*0-205-27847-7*) Allyn.

Bevevino, Mary M., jt. auth. see Snodgrass, Dawn M.

Bevier, L. Brief Greek Syntax. (College Classical Ser.). (gr. 11-12). 1981. 25.00 (*0-89241-127-9*); pap. 14.00 (*0-89241-343-3*) Caratzas.

BeVier, Lillian R. Is Free TV for Federal Candidates Constitutional? LC 98-208920. (AEI Studies in Telecommunications Deregulation). 59p. 1998. pap. 9.95 (*0-8447-7113-9*, AEI Pr) Am Enterprise.

Bevier, Louis R., ed. Atlas of Breeding Birds of Connecticut. (Illus.). 461p. 1994. 45.00 (*0-942081-05-6*) CT DEP CGNHS.

Bevier, Robert S. The Confederate First & Second Missouri Brigades & from Wakarusa to Appomattox. (Illus.). 500p. 1985. reprint ed. 24.50 (*0-940435-00-4*) Inland Print Ltd.

Bevier, Thomas F. Images of Benzie County. LC 97-46668. 1998. 35.95 (*1-57864-024-5*) Donning Co.

Bevil, Ann. Soaring with Numbers. unabridged ed. (Illus.). 55p. (J). (gr. 3-8). 1997. pap. 15.00 (*1-891022-01-6*) Showboard.

Bevilacqua, Alberto. Eros. McGarrell, Ann, tr. from ITA. 198p. (C). 1998. text 20.00 (*0-7881-5431-1*) DIANE Pub.

— Eros. McGarrell, Ann, tr. from ITA. LC 96-33225. 200p. 1996. 20.00 (*1-883642-35-3*) Steerforth Pr.

***Bevilacqua, Giulio.** Electron-phonon Dynamics & the Jahn-teller Effect: Proceedings for the XIV International Symposium. 1999. 122.00 (*981-02-3900-9*) WSC Inst MA Studies.

Bevilacqua, Jan. Talking Drums. (Illus.). 110p. (Orig.). 1995. pap. 9.95 (*1-886383-13-8*) Pride & Imprints.

Bevilacqua, Louis, jt. auth. see Dattilio, Frank M.

Bevilacqua, Michelle. More Words You Should Know: Fifteen Hundred More Words Every Educated Person Should Be Able to Use & Define. LC 93-47470. 276p. 1994. pap. 8.95 (*1-55850-293-9*) Adams Media.

Bevilacqua, Michelle, jt. auth. see Anastasio, Janet.

Beville, Don, ed. see Rosenbaum, Claire M.

Beville, Hugh M., Jr. Audience Ratings: Radio, Television, & Cable. rev. ed. (Communication Ser.). 424p. 1988. pap., student ed. 39.95 (*0-8058-0174-X*); text 89.95 (*0-8058-0175-8*) L Erlbaum Assocs.

Beville, Hugh M. & Blankenship, A. B. The Market Research Council, 1958-1989. (Illus.). 144p. 1989. 60.00 (*1-877633-02-X*) Luthers.

Beville, Mitchel J. Municipal Structural Reform in Sioux City: The Perennial Question. 1980. 1.00 (*1-55614-067-3*) U of SD Gov Res Bur.

Beville, Mitchel J. & Meyer, Kenneth. The Search for Effectiveness & Efficiency in Government: Policy Analysis, Program Evaluation, Social Indicator, & Quality of Life Research. 1983. 5.00 (*1-55614-112-2*) U of SD Gov Res Bur.

Beville, Mitchel J., et al. Planning Districts in South Dakota: An Assessment of Economic Change & Development. 1984. 1.00 (*1-55614-077-0*) U of SD Gov Res Bur.

Bevin, Keith J. & Moore, I. D., eds. Terrain Analysis & Distributed Modelling in Hydrology. (Advances in Hydrological Processes Ser.). 256p. (Orig.). 1993. pap. 175.00 (*0-471-93886-6*) Wiley.

Bevin, Michael B. & Henstock, M. E., eds. Recycling: Opportunities & Constraints: Proceedings of the Conference Co-Sponsored by the Federation of Materials Science & the U. S. Bureau of Mines, Washington, D. C., U. S. A., 17-19 July 1984. 136p. 1985. pap. 85.00 (*0-08-032635-8*, E135, D145, G13, Pub. by PPL) Elsevier.

Bevin, Michael B., ed. see Henstock, M. E.

Bevin, Teresa. Havana Split. LC 98-10315. 368p. 1998. pap. 12.95 (*1-55885-229-8*) Arte Publico.

Bevin Warehime, Nancy. To Be One of Us: Cultural Conflict, Creative Democracy, & Education. LC 92-3098. (SUNY Series, The Philosophy of Education). 190p. (C). 1993. text 57.50 (*0-7914-1321-7*) State U NY Pr.

Bevingto, Delgadillo. California. (Discover America Ser.). 1985. 6.99 (*0-8442-7472-0*) NTC Contemp Pub Co.

Bevington, Adrian, jt. auth. see Allan, Dave.

Bevington, C. Housing for Children. (Architecture Ser.). 1992. pap. write for info. (*0-442-01119-9*, VNR) Wiley.

Bevington, David. Campaspe & Sappho & Phao: John Lyly. 1999. pap. text 19.95 (*0-7190-3100-1*) St Martin.

Bevington, David & Holbrook, Peter, eds. The Politics of the Stuart Court Masque. LC 97-52957. (Illus.). 368p. (C). 1998. 64.95 (*0-521-59436-7*) Cambridge U Pr.

Bevington, David, et al. Homo, Memento Finis: The Iconography of Just Judgment in Medieval Art & Drama. (Early Drama, Art & Music Monograph: No. 6). 1985. pap. 13.95 (*0-918720-61-3*) Medieval Inst.

Bevington, David, ed. see Marlowe, Christopher.

Bevington, David, ed. see Shakespeare, William.

Bevington, David M. Action Is Eloquence: Shakespeare's Language of Gesture. LC 84-673. 241p. reprint ed. pap. 74.80 (*0-7837-1510-2*, 204178700024) Bks Demand.

Bevington, David M. Medieval Drama, 001. (C). 1975. text 60.36 (*0-395-13915-5*) HM.

Bevington, David M. Shakespeare. LC 76-5220. (Goldentree Bibliographies Series in Language & Literature). (C). 1978. pap. text 14.95 (*0-88295-555-1*) Harlan Davidson.

— Tudor Drama & Politics: A Critical Approach to Topical Meaning. LC 68-17637. 372p. reprint ed. pap. 115.40 (*0-7837-1672-9*, 205720400024) Bks Demand.

Bevington, David M., ed. The Macro Plays. Incl. Castle of Perserverance. Wisdom & Mankind. (Facsimiles Ser.). 42.00 (*0-686-16149-1*) Folger Bks.

Bevington, David M. & Halio, Jay L., eds. Shakespeare, Pattern of Excelling Nature: Shakespearean Criticism in Honor of America's Bicentennial. LC 77-82878. 304p. 38.50 (*0-87413-129-4*) U Delaware Pr.

Bevington, David M. & Rasmussen, Eric, eds. Dr. Faustus A- & B- Texts (1604, 1616) Christopher Marlowe & His Collaborator & Revisers. LC 92-31602. (Revels Plays Ser.). 1993. text 16.95 (*0-7190-1643-6*, Pub. by Manchester Univ Pr) St Martin.

Bevington, David M., et al. Homo, Memento Finis: The Iconography of Just Judgment in Medieval Art & Drama. (Early Drama, Art & Music Monograph: No. 6). 1985. boxed set 22.95 (*0-918720-60-5*) Medieval Inst.

Bevington, David M., ed. see Kyd, Thomas.

Bevington, David M., ed. see Lyly, John.

Bevington, David M., ed. see Shakespeare, William.

Bevington, Fran. Make Way for Triplets. LC 91-66575. 1992. pap. 7.95 (*0-9630697-5-6*) Triple Treat.

Bevington, G. C. Remarkable Miracles: Story of a Godly Man's Walk Producing Miracles. rev. ed. LC 91-78269. 168p. 1992. pap. 9.99 (*0-88270-703-5*) Bridge-Logos.

Bevington, Gary. Maya for Travelers & Students: A Guide to Language & Culture in Yucatan. LC 93-48159. (Illus.). 168p. 1995. text 37.50 (*0-292-70838-6*); pap. text 14.95 (*0-292-70812-2*) U of Tex Pr.

— Where Do Words Come From? 68p. (C). 1995. pap. text, per. 21.95 (*0-7872-1013-7*) Kendall-Hunt.

Bevington, Helen S. The Journey Is Everything: A Journal of the Seventies. LC 83-5582. vii, 208p. 1983. text 39.95 (*0-8223-0553-4*); pap. text 18.95 (*0-8223-0847-9*) Duke.

— The Third & Only Way: Reflections on Staying Alive. LC 96-14208. 224p. 1996. 21.95 (*0-8223-1850-4*) Duke.

— The World & the Bo Tree. LC 91-7608. 224p. 1991. text 49.95 (*0-8223-1153-4*); pap. text 18.95 (*0-8223-1165-8*) Duke.

Bevington, J. C., jt. auth. see Allen, Geoffrey.

Bevington, J. C., jt. ed. see Allen, Geoffrey.

Bevington, Merle M. Saturday Review, 1855-1868: Representative Educated Opinion in Victorian England. LC 41-25970. reprint ed. 20.00 (*0-404-00795-3*) AMS Pr.

Bevington, Philip R. & Robinson, D. Keith. Data Reduction & Error Analysis for the Physical Sciences. 2nd ed. 328p. (C). 1991. pap. 33.13 (*0-07-911243-9*) McGraw.

Bevington, William, jt. auth. see Craig, James.

Bevington, William, jt. auth. see Sanders, Norman.

Bevins, Ann Bolton, et al. Georgetown & Scott County, KY. LC 98-86672. (Images of America Ser.). (Illus.). 128p. 1998. pap. 18.99 (*0-7524-1394-5*) Arcadia Publng.

Bevir, Mark. The Logic of the History of Ideas. LC 98-38079. 360p. (C). 1999. text 59.95 (*0-521-64034-2*) Cambridge U Pr.

Bevirt, W. David, jt. auth. see Gladstone, John.

Bevis. Caring for Women. 4th ed. (C). 1991. pap. text 19.00 (*0-7020-1453-2*) Harcourt.

Bevis, Charlie. Mickey Cochrane: The Life of a Baseball Hall of Fame Catcher. LC 98-13679. (Illus.). 214p. 1998. pap. 26.50 (*0-7864-0516-3*) McFarland & Co.

Bevis, Desmond, jt. ed. see Dickey, Karlene N.

Bevis, Em O. Curriculum Building in Nursing: A Process. 3rd ed. 304p. 1989. 29.95 (*0-88737-439-5*) Natl League Nurse.

Bevis, Em O. & Watson, Jean. Toward a Caring Curriculum: A New Pedagogy for Nursing. 416p. 1989. 28.95 (*0-88737-440-9*) Natl League Nurse.

Bevis, Jean H. & Stratton, Cheryl. Schaum's Electronic Tutor for College Algebra. 2nd ed. (Schaum's Outline Ser.). 384p. (C). 1997. pap. 39.95 (*0-07-913620-6*) McGraw.

Bevis, John. Atlas Celeste. rev. ed. (Mapping of the Stars Ser.). (Illus.). 136p. 1998. reprint ed. pap. 945.00 (*1-85297-023-5*, Pub. by Archival Facs) St Mut.

Bevis, Mary, jt. auth. see Sieck, Jeneanne.

***Bevis, Olivia.** Curriculum Building in Nursing: A Process. 3rd ed. (Illus.). 200p. (C). 1998. pap. text 28.75 (*0-7637-0941-7*) JB Pubns.

Bevis, Richard. The Road to Egdon Heath: The Aesthetics of the Great in Nature. 384p. 75.00 (*0-7735-1800-2*) McG-Queens Univ Pr.

Bevis, William W. Borneo Log: The Struggle for Sarawak's Forests. LC 95-18317. (Illus.). 264p. (C). 1995. 19.95 (*0-295-97416-8*) U of Wash Pr.

— Mind of Winter: Wallace Stevens, Meditation & Literature. LC 88-19814. (Critical Essays in Modern Literature Ser.). 356p. 1988. reprint ed. pap. 110.40 (*0-608-00898-2*, 206169200010) Bks Demand.

— Shorty Harris, or the Price of Gold: A Novel. LC 98-49761. 1999. 29.95 (*0-8061-3124-1*) U of Okla Pr.

— Ten Tough Trips: Montana Writers & the West. LC 89-77570. 248p. 1990. 24.95 (*0-295-96941-5*) U of Wash Pr.

Bevitt, Ann & Stanton, Lisa. Criminal Advocacy: A Practical Guide. xvii, 214p. 1997. pap. 36.00 (*1-85941-356-0*, Pub. by Cavendish Pubng) Gaunt.

Bevitt, Emogene A. Directory of Cultural Resource Education Programs At Colleges, Universities, Craft & Trade Schools in the United States 1994-1995. 105p. 1994. pap. 9.50 (*0-16-045362-3*) USGPO.

— Second Lives: A Survey of Architectural Artifact Collections in the U. S. (Illus.). 100p. (Orig.). (C). 1995. pap. text 30.00 (*0-7881-1829-3*) DIANE Pub.

— Second Lives: A Survey of Architectural Artifact Collections in the United States. 112p. 1994. pap. 5.00 (*0-16-045205-8*) USGPO.

Bevlin, Marjorie E. Design Through Discovery. 6th ed. (C). 1993. pap. text 63.50 (*0-03-076547-1*, Pub. by Harcourt Coll Pubs) Harcourt.

— Design Through Discovery: The Elements & Principles. 2nd ed. LC 93-77624. xv, 205p. (C). 1993. pap. text 49.00 (*0-15-500963-X*) Harcourt.

Bevoise, M. B. De, see De Bevoise, M. B., tr.

Bew, Paul. Charles Stewart Parnell. 2nd ed. (Illus.). 145p. 1998. reprint ed. pap. 13.95 (*0-7171-1886-X*, Pub. by Gill & MacMill) Irish Bks Media.

Bew, Paul. Conflict & Conciliation in Ireland 1890-1910: Parnellites & Radical Agrarians. LC 86-28578. (Illus.). 240p. 1987. 55.00 (*0-19-822758-2*) OUP.

Bew, Paul. Ideology & the Irish Question: Ulster Unionism & Irish Nationalism 1912-1916. (Illus.). 184p. 1998. reprint ed. pap. text 29.95 (*0-19-820708-5*) OUP.

***Bew, Paul & Gillespie, Gordon.** Northern Ireland. 2nd ed. LC 99-48569. 384p. 1999. 45.00 (*0-8108-3735-8*) Scarecrow.

Bew, Paul & Gillespie, Gordon. The Northern Ireland Peace Process, 1993-1996: A Chronology. LC 97-124832. 192p. 1998. pap. 17.95 (*1-897959-28-1*, Pub. by Serif) IPG Chicago.

Bew, Paul, et al. Northern Ireland, 1921-1994. 1995. pap. 23.95 (*1-897959-08-7*) LPC InBook.

— Northern Ireland, 1921-1996: Political Forces & Social Classes. LC 97-115439. 272p. 1998. pap. 24.95 (*1-897959-24-9*, Pub. by Serif) IPG Chicago.

— The Political Future of Northern Ireland. LC 93-150256. 160p. (C). 1997. pap. 18.50 (*0-85315-771-5*, Pub. by Lawrence & Wishart) NYU Pr.

Bewell, Alan J. Romanticism & Colonical Disease. LC 99-33027. (Medicine & Culture Ser.). 356p. 1999. 45.00 (*0-8018-6225-6*) Johns Hopkins.

— Wordsworth & the Enlightenment: Nature, Man, & Society in the Experimental Poetry. LC 88-20644. 352p. (C). 1989. 45.00 (*0-300-04393-7*) Yale U Pr.

Bewer, Julius A. & Kraeling, Emil G. The Literature of the Old Testament. 3rd ed. LC 62-17061. (Records of Civilization: Sources & Studies: No. 5). 512p. reprint ed. pap. 158.80 (*0-608-12520-2*, 202497500040) Bks Demand.

***Bewer, Tim.** Acorn Guide to Northwest Wisconsin. LC 99-23993. (Illus.). 140p. 1999. pap. 9.95 (*1-879483-57-2*) Prairie Oak Pr.

Bewer, Tim. Wisconsin's Outdoor Treasures: A Guide to 150 Natural Destinations. LC 97-12643. (Illus.). 288p. 1997. pap. 17.95 (*1-879483-39-4*) Prairie Oak Pr.

Bewersdorff, A., ed. Materials Science in Space. (Advances in Space Research Ser.: Vol. 1, No. 5). (Illus.). 171p. 1981. pap. 25.00 (*0-08-027161-8*, Pergamon Pr) Elsevier.

— Materials Science in Space: Proceedings of the Topical Meeting of the COSPAR Interdisciplinary Scientific Commission G (Meeting G1) of the COSPAR Twenty-Fifth Plenary Meeting Held in Graz, Austria, 25th June - 7th July 1984. (Illus.). 116p. 1985. pap. 54.00 (*0-08-032733-8*, Pergamon Pr) Elsevier.

Bewersdorff, H. W., jt. auth. see Gyr, Albert.

Bewes, C. To Carol with Love. 11.99 (*1-85792-112-7*, Pub. by Christian Focus) Spring Arbor Dist.

***Bewes, Richard.** Great Quotations of the 20th Century. 2000. pap. 10.99 (*1-85792-536-X*) Christian Focus.

Bewes, Richard, ed. see Wesley, John.

Bewes, Timothy. Cynicism & Postmodernity. LC 97-6372. 1997. pap. 19.00 (*1-85984-196-1*, Pub. by Verso) Norton.

Bewes, Wyndham A. The Romance of the Law Merchant: Being an Introduction to the Study of International & Commercial Law with Some Account of the Commerce & Fairs of the Middle Ages. LC 88-80855. 148p. 1988. reprint ed. 45.00 (*0-912004-65-7*, Pub. by Sweet & Maxwll) Gaunt.

— The Romance of the Law Merchant: Being an Introduction to the Study of International & Commercial Law with Some Account of the Commerce & Fairs of the Middle Ages. (Legal Reprint Ser.). ix, 148p. 1986. reprint ed. lib. bdg. 22.50 (*0-8377-1940-2*, Rothman) W S Hein.

Bewick, Pauline. The Yellow Man. LC 95-237888. (Illus.). 76p. 1997. pap. 19.95 (*0-86327-448-X*, Pub. by Wolfhound Press) Irish Amer Bk.

Bewick, Thomas. Eighteen Hundred Woodcuts by Thomas Bewick & His School. Cirker, Blanche, ed. 247p. 1962. pap. 14.95 (*0-486-20766-8*) Dover.

— Memoir of Thomas Bewick: Written by Himself, 1822-1828. LC NE1212.B5A3. (Centaur Classics Ser.). (Illus.). 294p. reprint ed. pap. 91.20 (*0-8357-6654-3*, 203532300094) Bks Demand.

— Thomas Bewick's Birds: Watercolours & Engravings. (Illus.). 52p. 1982. 10.95 (*0-262-02176-5*) MIT Pr.

Bewick, Thomas, jt. ed. see Ritson, Joseph.

Bewicke, Dhyana & Potter, Beverly A. Chlorella: The Emerald Food. (Illus.). 128p. (Orig.). 1984. pap. 7.95 (*0-914171-02-X*) Ronin Pub.

Bewig, Karen V. Memoirs of a Century in St. Louis. 125p. 1993. pap. 14.95 (*0-9638054-0-1*) K Bewig.

Bewlay, B. P., et al, eds. High-Temperature Silicides & Refractory Alloys Vol. 322: Materials Research Society Symposium Proceedings. LC 94-5806. 567p. 1994. text 30.00 (*1-55899-221-9*) Materials Res.

Bewley. Gentleman Radical: A Life of John Horne Tooke, Vol. 1. 288p. 1998. text 59.50 (*1-86064-344-2*, Pub. by I B T) St Martin.

Bewley, Aisha A., tr. see Anas, Imam Malik Ibn.

Bewley, D. K. The Physics & Radiobiology of Fast Neutron Beams. (Medical Science Ser.). (Illus.). 164p. 1989. 104.00 (*0-85274-093-X*) IOP Pub.

Bewley, J. D. Nitrogen & Carbon Metabolism: Symposium on the Physiology & Bio-Chemistry of Plant Productivity. (Development in Plant & Soil Sciences Ser.: No. 3). 1981. text 112.50 (*90-247-2472-4*) Kluwer Academic.

Bewley, J. D. & Black, M. Seeds: Physiology of Development & Germination. 2nd ed. (Illus.). 462p. (C). 1994. pap. text 45.00 (*0-306-44748-7*, Kluwer Plenum) Kluwer Academic.

— Seeds: Physiology of Development & Germination. 2nd ed. (Illus.). 462p. (C). 1994. 85.00 (*0-306-44747-9*, Plenum Trade) Perseus Pubng.

Bewley, J. D., jt. auth. see Black, M.

Bewley, James G. & McGee, S. W., eds. Progress in Powder Metallurgy, Vol. 38. (Illus.). 634p. 1982. pap. 20.00 (*0-918404-58-4*) Metal Powder.

Bewley, James G., ed. see National Powder Metallurgy Conference Staff.

Bewley, Marius. Complex Fate: Hawthorne, Henry James & Some American Writers. LC 67-28474. 248p. 1967. reprint ed. 35.00 (*0-87752-008-9*) Gordian.

***Bewley, Robert, et al, eds.** Archiving Aerial Photography & Remote Sensing Data. (AHDS Guides to Good Practice Ser.). 45p. 1999. pap. 18.00 (*1-900188-70-8*, Pub. by Oxbow Bks) David Brown.

Bewley, Robert H. Prehistoric & Romano-British Settlement in the Solway Plain, Cumbria. (Oxbow Monographs in Archaeology: No. 36). (Illus.). 110p. 1994. pap. 32.00 (*0-946897-66-2*, Pub. by Oxbow Bks) David Brown.

Bewley, Ronald. Allocation Models: Specification, Estimation, & Applications. LC 85-28777. (Econometrics & Management Sciences Ser.). 368p. 1986. text 34.95 (*0-88730-077-4*, HarpBusn) HarpInfo.

Bewley-Taylor, David R. The United States & International Drug Control, 1909-1997. LC 98-32345. 192p. 1999. 45.00 (*1-85567-610-9*) Continuum.

***Bewley, Truman F.** Why Wages Don't Fall During a Recession. LC 99-16443. 576p. 2000. 55.00 (*0-674-95241-3*) HUP.

Bewley, Truman F., ed. Advances in Econometrics, Fifth World Congress, Vol. 1. (Econometric Society Monographs: No. 13). (Illus.). 321p. (C). 1994. pap. text 19.95 (*0-521-46726-8*) Cambridge U Pr.

— Advances in Econometrics, Fifth World Congress, Vol. 2. (Econometric Society Monographs: No. 14). (Illus.). 267p. (C). 1994. pap. text 18.95 (*0-521-46725-X*) Cambridge U Pr.

Bews, John W. The World Grasses. (C). 1979. text 115.00 (*0-89771-553-5*, Pub. by Intl Bk Distr) St Mut.

— The World Grasses. (Illus.). xii, 408p. 1979. reprint ed. 165.00 (*0-7855-6638-4*, Pub. by Intl Bk Distr) St Mut.

Bewsey, Julia J. Microcomputers & Libraries: An Annotated Bibliography. (CompuBibs Ser.: No. 8). 63p. 1985. pap. 15.00 (*0-914791-07-9*) Vantage Info.

Bewsey, Susan. Home Cleaning Business: Your Step by Step Business Plan. 128p. Date not set. pap. 12.95 (*1-55180-210-4*) Self-Counsel Pr.

Bewsher, Paul. Green Balls: The Adventures of a Night Bomber. 296p. pap. 19.95 (*0-947898-32-8*, 5516) Stackpole.

Bewtra, Chhandra. A Physician's Guide for the Handling of Gynecologic & Obstetric Tissue Specimens. (Illus.). 69p. (Orig.). 1996. pap. 9.95 (*1-880906-15-5*) IDI Pub.

Bex, Tony. Variety in Written English. 240p. (C). 1996. 75.00 (*0-415-10839-X*); pap. 24.99 (*0-415-10840-3*) Routledge.

Bex, Tony & Watts, Richard J. Standard English: The Widening Debate. LC 98-36167. 1999. 85.00 (*0-415-19162-9*); pap. 25.99 (*0-415-19163-7*) Routledge.

***Bexa, Theodore.** The Life of John Calvin. 1999. pap. 10.99 (*0-85234-404-X*) Evangelical Pr.

Bexley, James B. Banking Management: A Guide to More Profitable Banking. LC 78-53195. 208p. reprint ed. pap. 64.50 (*0-8357-5965-2*, 203284200081) Bks Demand.

***Bexleyheath, Kent.** Arts & Crafts Houses I. 1999. 19.95 (*0-7148-3875-6*) Phaidon Pr.

Bexton, Harold W., jt. ed. see Colman, Arthur D.

Bey-Abdul Jami, Amur. Aluta Continua: The Struggle Continues. 76p. 1997. pap. 7.25 (*1-57502-633-3*, PO1794) Morris Pubng.

Bey, Essad. Mohammed. 336p. 1984. 195.00 (*1-85077-019-0*, Pub. by Darf Pubs Ltd) St Mut.

Bey, Faruq Z. Macro-Harmonic Music Manuscript Workbook. (Illus.). 70p. (C). 1992. 15.00 (*1-56439-015-2*) Ridgeway.

Bey, Hakim. Immediatism. (Illus.). 64p. (Orig.). 1995. pap. 7.00 (*1-873176-42-2*) AK Pr Dist.

— Millennium. 1996. pap. 7.00 (*1-57027-045-7*) Autonomedia.

— T. A. Z. The Temporary Autonomous Zone, Ontological Anarchy, Poetic Terrorism. 150p. 1991. pap. 6.00 (*0-936756-76-4*) Autonomedia.

Bey, Hakim, jt. auth. see Grim Reaper Books Staff.

Bey, I., et al, eds. Neutral Interfaces in Design, Simulation, & Programming for Robotics. (Research Reports ESPRIT, Subseries PDT, Project 5109: Vol. 1). xv, 334p. 1994. 50.95 (*0-387-57531-6*) Spr-Verlag.

Bey, Malik R. Adolescent Mothers & Child Abuse & Neglect: The Correlates of Abuse & Mothering. 51p. (Orig.). 1996. pap. 12.95 (*0-9656137-2-0*) M Bey.

***Bey, Malik R.** Benzino: What Goes Around Comes Around! 1999. pap. text 15.95 (*1-890301-13-2*) M Bey.

Bey, Malik R. Citizen's Legal Guide to the Courts. (Illus.). 83p. (Orig.). 1997. pap. text 24.95 (*0-9656137-6-3*) M Bey.

— Languages for the American Traveler: Brief & Basic Expressions Made Easy. 100p. (Orig.). 1996. pap. 12.95 (*0-9656137-1-2*) M Bey.

Bey, Malik R., ed. see Holmes, Nicole C.

Bey, Malik R., ed. see Roland, Christopher P., Jr.

Bey, Malik R., ed. see Roland, Christopher P.

Bey, Malik R., ed. see Sheafe, Valerie.

Bey, Mohammad El-Naggary. Dictionnaire Francais-Arabe, 3 vols., Set. 125.00 (*0-86685-674-9*) Intl Bk Ctr.

Bey, Pilaff, pseud. Venus in the Kitchen: Recipes for Seduction. LC 91-28238. (Illus.). 208p. 1992. pap. 13.95 (*1-879904-01-2*) Halo Bks.

Bey, Rene C., ed. Revue de l'Histoire Juive en Egypte. (Illus.). viii, 178p. 1987. pap. 32.00 (*0-9613805-2-7*) Halgo Inc.

Bey, Salma M. Syria's Quest for Independence, 1939-1945. 1998. pap. text 19.95 (*0-86372-225-3*, Pub. by Garnet-Ithaca) LPC InBook.

Bey, Theresa M. & Holmes, C. Thomas, eds. Mentoring: Contemporary Principles & Issues. 1992. pap. 9.95 (*0-685-74810-3*) Assn Tchr Ed.

— Mentoring: Developing Successful New Teachers. (Orig.). 9.95 (*0-685-57422-9*) Assn Tchr Ed.

— Mentoring: Developing Successful New Teachers. 96p. (Orig.). (C). 1990. pap. text. write for info. (*0-9624818-1-5*) U GA Coll Ed.

B

Bey, Theresa M. & Turner, Gwendolyn Y. Making School a Place of Peace. LC 95-22884. (Illus.). 184p. 1995. 55.95 (*0-8039-6192-8*); pap. 24.95 (*0-8039-6193-6*) Corwin Pr.

Bey, Vahid. English-Turkish Dictionary. (ENG & TUR.). 750p. 1992. 35.00 (*0-86685-578-5*, LDL5785, Pub. by Librairie du Liban) Intl Bk Ctr.

Beyala, Calixthe. Loukoum: The Little Prince of Belleville. LC 96-145955. (African Writers Ser.). 160p. 1995. pap. 10.95 (*0-435-90968-1*) Heinemann.

— The Sun Hath Looked upon Me. (African Writers Ser.). 128p. 1996. pap. 9.95 (*0-435-90951-7*) Heinemann.

— Your Name Shall Be Tanga. (African Writers Ser.). 144p. 1996. pap. 10.95 (*0-435-90950-9*) Heinemann.

— Your Name Shall be Tanga. De Jager, Marjolijn, tr. 1996. pap. 10.95 (*0-614-97781-9*) Heinemann.

Beyand, Islah & Karriem, Jaleelah. Love Period. (Illus.). 48p. (Orig.). 1988. pap. text 5.00 (*0-317-92553-9*) We Did It.

***Beyani, Chaloka.** Human Rights Standards & the Free Movement of People Within States. (Oxford Monographs in International Law). 176p. 2000. text 74.00 (*0-19-826821-1*) OUP.

Beyani, Chaloka, et al. African Exodus: Refugee Crisis, Human Rights, & the 1969 OAU Convention. Black, George, ed. LC 96-131482. 266p. (Orig.). (C). 1995. pap. text 15.00 (*0-934143-73-0*) Lawyers Comm Human.

Beyani, Chaloka, jt. auth. see Leigh, Leonard.

Beyar, R., jt. auth. see Sideman, S.

Beyar, R., jt. auth. see Sideman, Samuel.

***Beyar, Rafael, et al.** Frontiers in Interventional Cardiology. 480p. (C). 1998. text. write for info. (*1-85317-487-4*) Mosby Inc.

Beyar, Rafael, jt. ed. see Sideman, Samuel.

Beyard, Ernest R. Art at Auction in America. Wilson, Laurie, ed. (Premiere Edition). 167p. (Orig.). 1990. pap. 15.00 (*0-9624926-0-4*) Frontier Publng.

— Art at Auction in America: 1991 Edition. 208p. (Orig.). 1991. pap. 15.00 (*0-9624926-1-2*) Frontier Publng.

— Art at Auction in America: 1994 Edition. 1994. pap. 15.00 (*0-9624926-4-7*) Frontier Publng.

Beyard, Michael D. Dollars & Cents of Shopping Centers 1998. 225p. 1998. pap. 239.95 (*0-87420-864-5*, DC8) Urban Land.

Beyard, Michael D. Business & Industrial Park Development Handbook. LC 88-50770. (Community Builders Handbook Ser.). 380p. 1988. 64.95 (*0-87420-678-2*, I11) Urban Land.

Beyard, Michael D. & O'Mara, W. Paul. Shopping Center Development Handbook. 3rd ed. LC 99-61546. (Development Handbook Ser.). 350p. 1998. 89.95 (*0-87420-852-1*, S30) Urban Land.

Beyard, Michael D., et al. Developing Urban Entertainment Centers. 150p. 1998. pap. 59.95 (*0-87420-824-6*, U11) Urban Land.

Beyavsky, A. Uncompromising Chess. 1998. pap. text 18.95 (*1-85744-205-9*) Cadgn Bks.

Beychok, Milton R. Aqueous Wastes: From Petroleum & Petrochemical Plants. LC 67-19834. 380p. reprint ed. 117.80 (*0-8357-9839-9*, 205122900093) Bks Demand.

— Fundamentals of Stack Gas Dispersion. LC 97-204328. 191p. 1994. pap. 75.00 (*0-9644588-0-2*) M R Beychok.

Beyda. Data Communications: From Basics to Broadband. 3rd ed. LC 99-14309. 330p. 1999. pap. 55.00 (*0-13-096139-6*) P-H.

Beyda, Vivian, et al. Combating Iron Deficiency in Chile: A Case Study. Adams, Catherine E. et al, eds. (Illus.). 58p. (Orig.). 1986. pap. text 3.50 (*0-935368-48-5*) ILSI.

— La Lutte Contre la Carence en Fer: Etude de Cas Realisee au Chili. Adams, Catherine E. et al, eds. DeMaeyer, Catherine, tr. (FRE., Illus.). 64p. (Orig.). 1986. pap. text 3.50 (*0-318-35292-3*) ILSI.

— Prevencion de la Deficiencia de Hierro: La Experiencia de Chile. Adams, Catherine E. et al, eds. Hertrampf, Eva, tr. (SPA., Illus.). 64p. (Orig.). 1986. pap. text 3.50 (*0-318-35293-1*) ILSI.

Beydoun, Z. R. Arabian Plate Hydrocarbon Geology & Potential: A Plate Tectonic Approach. LC 91-185003. (AAPG Studies in Geology: No. 33). (Illus.). 96p. 1991. reprint ed. pap. 30.00 (*0-608-04231-5*, 206498800012) Bks Demand.

Beye, Charles R. Ancient Epic Poetry: Homer, Apollonius, Virgil. LC 92-28920. 296p. 1993. 39.95 (*0-8014-2673-1*); pap. text 16.95 (*0-8014-9964-X*) Cornell U Pr.

— Ancient Greek Literature & Society. 2nd rev. ed. LC 86-47979. (Illus.). 376p. 1987. text 47.50 (*0-8014-1874-7*) Cornell U Pr.

— Iliad, the Odyssey & the Epic Tradition. 1990. 20.00 (*0-8446-1674-5*) Peter Smith.

— The Iliad, the Odyssey, & the Epic Tradition. LC 76-10726. 280p. 1976. reprint ed. 50.00 (*0-87752-187-5*) Gordian.

Beye, Eugene. Export Controls: Information on the Decision to Revise High Performance Computer Controls. 83p. (C). 1999. pap. text 25.00 (*0-7881-7828-8*) DIANE Pub.

— Hong Kong's Reversion to China: Effective Monitoring Critical to Assess U. S. Nonproliferation Risks. (Illus.). 49p. (C). 1997. pap. text 25.00 (*0-7881-4739-0*) DIANE Pub.

Beyea, Jan & Rosenthal, Joyce. Long Term Threats to Canada's James Bay from Human Development. (Environmental Policy Analysis Department Reports). (Illus.). 34p. (Orig.). 1989. pap. text. write for info. (*0-930698-31-2*) Natl Audubon.

Beyeler Foundation. Renzo Piano: A Home for Art. 1998. 35.00 (*3-7643-5920-X*) Birkhauser.

Beyeler Foundation Staff. Renzo Piano-Fondation Beyeler: A Home for Art. (Illus.). 120p. 1998. 35.00 (*3-7643-5919-6*) Birkhauser.

— Renzo Piano-Fondation Beyeler: A Home for Art. 1999. write for info. (*0-8176-5919-6*) Birkhauser.

Beyeler Foundation Staff, ed. The Magic of Trees. (Illus.). 148p. 1999. 45.00 (*3-7757-0798-0*, Pub. by Gerd Hatje) Dist Art Pubs.

Beyen, J. W. Money in a Maelstrom. Wilkins, Mira, ed. LC 73-3898. (International Finance Ser.). 1979. reprint ed. lib. bdg. 23.95 (*0-405-11203-3*) Ayer.

Beyenbach, K. W., ed. Cell Volume Regulation. (Comparative Physiology Ser.: Vol. 4). (Illus.). 166p. 1990. text 129.75 (*3-8055-5148-7*) S Karger.

— Structure & Function of Primary Messengers in Invertebrates: Insect Diuretic & Antidiuretic Peptides. (Molecular Comparative Physiology Ser.: Vol. 12). (Illus.). viii, 180p. 1993. 213.25 (*3-8055-5704-3*) S Karger.

Beyene, Asmelash & Mutahabe, Gelase. The Quest for Constitutionalism in Africa: Selected Essays on Constitutionalism, the Nationality Problem, Military Rule, & Party Politics. LC 95-106832. (Illus.). VIII, 253p. 1994. pap. 48.95 (*3-631-47110-6*) P Lang Pubng.

Beyene, Yewoubdar. From Menarche to Menopause: Reproductive Lives of Peasant Women in Two Cultures. LC 88-2244. (SUNY Series in Medical Anthropology). 169p. (C). 1989. pap. text 21.95 (*0-88706-867-7*) State U NY Pr.

Beyenka, Mary B. Sea Scribe & Other Poems. (Illus.). 63p. (C). 1996. spiral bd. 8.00 (*1-57193-201-1*, AP-815) Alliance Pubns.

Beyer. Christmas with Jinny Beyer. (Illus.). 256p. 1999. pap. 19.95 (*1-57954-194-1*) Rodale Pr Inc.

— HB Mathematical Science. 5th ed. 1978. 59.95 (*0-685-48455-6*, 655, CRC Reprint) Franklin.

— Pharmazeutisches Medizinisches Terminologi. 3rd ed. (GER.). 188p. 1990. 39.95 (*0-7859-7439-3*, 3804711197) Fr & Eur.

— Standard Mathamatical Tables. 28th ed. 1986. pap. 34.95 (*0-8493-0625-6*, CRC Reprint) Franklin.

Beyer. What Every Teacher Knows & Thinks. 1995. pap. text 41.50 (*0-205-14250-8*) Allyn.

Beyer, Alfred. Lokale Abbreviationen des Decretum Gratiani. 477p. 1998. 67.95 (*3-631-33430-3*) P Lang Pubng.

Beyer, Andrew. Beyer on Speed. 288p. 1995. pap. 14.00 (*0-395-73523-8*) HM.

— Picking Winners: A Horse Player's Guide. 240p. 1994. pap. 14.00 (*0-395-70132-5*) HM.

Beyer, Andrew. The Winning Horseplayer: A Revolutionary Approach to Thoroughbred Handicapping & Betting, 001. 208p. 1985. pap. 9.95 (*0-395-37761-7*) HM.

Beyer, Andrew. The Winning Horseplayer: An Advances Approach to Thoroughbred Handicapping & Betting. LC 97-133549. 208p. 1994. pap. 14.00 (*0-395-70131-7*) HM.

Beyer, Barnet J., jt. auth. see Fucito, Salvatore.

Beyer, Barry. Improving Student Thinking: A Comprehensive Approach. LC 96-39375. 318p. (C). 1997. 43.00 (*0-205-15062-4*) Allyn.

Beyer, Barry. Teaching Thinking Skills: A Handbook for Secondary Teachers. 320p. (C). 1991. pap. text 41.00 (*0-205-12797-5*, H27972, Longwood Div) Allyn.

Beyer, Barry K. How to Conduct a Formative Evaluation. 1995. pap. 8.95 (*0-87120-244-1*) ASCD.

Beyer, Beverly & Rabey, Ed A. Passport to Europe's Small Hotels & Inns. 9th ed. 272p. 1993. pap. 9.95 (*0-471-58298-0*) Wiley.

Beyer, Bryon E., jt. auth. see Arnold, Bill T.

Beyer, Carl. Max Klinger - The Late Graphic Work: Das Graphische Werk, 1909-1919. (ENG & GER., Illus.). 224p. 1997. 150.00 (*1-55660-170-0*) A Wofsy Fine Arts.

Beyer, Cathy, et al. Surviving Unemployment: A Family Handbook for Weathering Hard Times. LC 92-32402. 320p. 1995. 20.00 (*0-8050-2050-0*, Owl); pap. 10.95 (*0-8050-2051-9*, Owl) H Holt & Co.

Beyer, Charles E., jt. auth. see Iorio, Mary G.

Beyer, Chris, jt. auth. see Petretti, Allan.

***Beyer, Chris H.** Coca-Cola Girls: An Advertising Art History. limited ed. Bennett, Ann Granning, ed. (Illus.). 500p. 2000. 125.00 (*1-888054-45-X*, 54441, Pub. by Collectors Pr) Universe.

— Coca-Cola Girls: An Illustrated History. Bennett, Ann Granning, ed. (Illus.). 500p. 2000. 60.00 (*1-888054-44-1*, 54441, Pub. by Collectors Pr) Universe.

Beyer, D. & Modder, U. Diagnostic Imaging of the Acute Abdomen. (Illus.). 470p. 1988. 169.00 (*0-387-17520-2*) Spr-Verlag.

Beyer, Dave, jt. auth. see Little, Larry.

Beyer, Dick. Dona Maria de Rosa. LC 95-60257. 302p. 1995. pap. 3.95 (*0-9635404-9-1*) TwoForYou Bks.

— Fifty-One. LC 96-60770. 304p. 1994. pap. 5.95 (*0-9635404-1-6*) TwoForYou Bks.

— Golgotha II. LC 93-71005. 260p. 1993. pap. 5.95 (*0-9635404-6-7*) TwoForYou Bks.

— The Lock Box Murders. LC 94-60771. 304p. 1994. pap. 5.95 (*0-9635404-0-8*) TwoForYou Bks.

— The Mousing Owl. LC 96-90439. 278p. 1996. pap. 3.95 (*0-9635404-3-2*) TwoForYou Bks.

— Next Thursday. LC 96-90440. 306p. 1996. pap. 3.95 (*0-9635404-7-5*) TwoForYou Bks.

— The Scorpion Affair. LC 93-71006. 304p. 1993. pap. 5.95 (*0-9635404-8-3*) TwoForYou Bks.

— Treachery in D. C. LC 95-60256. 330p. 1995. pap. 3.95 (*0-9635404-2-4*) TwoForYou Bks.

Beyer, Douglas. La Familia de Dios. Gutierrea, Miriam Z., tr.Tr. of Family of God. (SPA.). 96p. 1992. pap. 6.00 (*0-8170-1179-X*) Judson.

— Family of God: A Handbook for Adult Disciples of Jesus Christ. 1990. pap., student ed. 7.00 (*0-8170-1156-0*) Judson.

— Family of God: A Handbook for Adult Disciples of Jesus Christ. 1990. pap., teacher ed. 6.00 (*0-8170-1166-8*) Judson.

Beyer, E. Dictionary of Sport Science. (ENG, FRE & GER.). 770p. 1987. spiral bd. 75.00 (*0-8288-7615-0*) Fr & Eur.

Beyer, Edward. Album of Virginia: Or Illustrations of the Old Dominion. (Illus.). vii, 40p. 1980. text 39.95 (*0-88490-091-6*) Library of VA.

Beyer, Elmira K. My Lee Comes to America. LC 97-216187. (Illus.). 74p. (Orig.). (J). (gr. 4-5). 1997. pap. 9.99 (*0-88092-044-0*) Royal Fireworks.

Beyer, F. M. Elementary Instruction Book for the Pianoforte: Metodo de Instruccion Elemental. 80p. 1986. pap. 7.95 (*0-7935-5288-5*, 50325580) H Leonard.

Beyer, Francine S. & Houston, Ronald L. Assessment of School Needs for Low-Achieving Students: Staff Survey. 44p. 1989. reprint ed. pap. 16.95 (*1-56602-025-5*) Research Better.

Beyer, Francine S., jt. auth. see Dusewicz, Russell A.

Beyer, Fred. North Carolina, the Years Before Man: A Geologic History. LC 91-70197. (Illus.). 240p. (YA). (gr. 10). 1991. text 34.95 (*0-89089-400-0*) Carolina Acad Pr.

— Science Snapshots: Brief Looks at Common Science Phenomena. (Illus.). 200p. (J). (gr. 6-8). 1998. pap. text. write for info. (*0-89089-680-1*) Carolina Acad Pr.

Beyer, Fred, jt. auth. see Stiffler, Lee A.

Beyer, George R., ed. Guide to the Microfilm of the Simon Cameron Papers. 91p. 1971. pap. 6.00 (*0-911124-64-0*, 1316) Pa Hist & Mus.

Beyer, Gerry W. Teacher's Manual to Accompany Teaching Materials on Estate Planning. (American Casebook Ser.). 254p. (C). 1995. pap. text, teacher ed. write for info. (*0-314-06659-4*) West Pub.

— Teaching Materials on Estate Planning. LC 95-1066. (American Casebook Ser.). 763p. (C). 1995. 57.50 (*0-314-05619-X*) West Pub.

— Wills, Trusts & Estates: Examples & Explanations. LC 98-55960. 640p. 1999. pap. text 33.95 (*0-7355-0061-4*) Panel Pubs.

Beyer, Gerry W. & Redden, Kenneth R. Modern Dictionary for the Legal Profession. 2nd ed. LC 96-26480. xii,818,v, 215p. 1996. 78.00 (*1-57588-114-4*, 310770) W S Hein.

— Modern Dictionary for the Legal Profession: 1997 Supplement. 2nd ed. LC 96-26480. 142p. 1997. 27.50 (*1-57588-406-2*, 310775) W S Hein.

***Beyer, Gerry W. & Redden, Kenneth R.** Modern Dictionary for the Legal Profession: 1999 Supplement. 2nd ed. Beyer, Margaret, ed. LC 96-26480. v, 215p. 1999. pap. 35.00 (*1-57588-600-6*, 310775) W S Hein.

Beyer, Gerry W. & Redden, Kenneth R. Modern Dictionary for the Legal Profession, 1998 Cumulative Supplement: 1998 Cumulative Supplement. 2nd ed. LC 96-26480. 225p. 1998. suppl. ed. 30.00 (*1-57588-454-2*, 310775) W S Hein.

Beyer, Gerry W., jt. auth. see Redden, Kenneth R.

Beyer, Gudrun. Rechtfertigungstheologisch Denken: Rudolf Bultmanns Kerygmatheologie Aus Exegetischen, Genetischen und Systematischen Perspektiven. (Europaische Hochschulschriften Ser.: Reihe 23, Bd. 560). (GER.). 278p. 1996. 54.95 (*3-631-48948-X*) P Lang Pubng.

Beyer, H. & Bestmann. Financial Lexicon: Finanzlexikon. 2nd ed. (GER.). 1988. 49.95 (*0-8288-1410-4*, M8365) Fr & Eur.

Beyer, H. F. & Shevelko, V. P. Atomic Physics with Heavy Ions. LC 99-11675. (Series on Atoms & Plasmas). xi, 407 p. 1999. 100.00 (*3-540-64875-5*) Spr-Verlag.

Beyer, H. F., et al. X-Ray Radiation of Highly Charged Ions. LC 97-25461. (Springer Series on Atoms & Plasmas). 1997. write for info. (*3-540-63185-2*) Spr-Verlag.

***Beyer, H. G.** The Theory of Evolution Strategies. (Natural Computing Ser.). xix, 382p. 2000. 49.00 (*3-540-67297-4*) Spr-Verlag.

Beyer, H. J., et al. Coherence in Atomic Collision Physics. LC 88-9796. (Physics of Atoms & Molecules Ser.). (Illus.). 368p. (C). 1988. text 110.00 (*0-306-42842-3*, Kluwer Plenum) Kluwer Academic.

Beyer, H. K., ed. see ZEOCAT '95 Staff.

Beyer, Hans & Walter, Wolfgang. Organic Chemistry: A Comprehensive Degree Text & Source Book. Lloyd, Douglas, ed. & tr. by. LC 97-178950. 1038p. 1997. pap. 45.00 (*1-898563-37-3*, Pub. by Horwood Pub) Paul & Co Pubs.

Beyer, Hermann W. Der Syrische Kirchenbau. (Studien zur Spaetantiken Kunstgeschichte: Vol. 1). (Illus.). viii, 183p. (C). 1978. reprint ed. 138.50 (*3-11-005705-0*) De Gruyter.

Beyer, Hugh, jt. auth. see Holtzblatt, Karen.

Beyer, Hugh, tr. see Kuietenbrouwer, Maarten.

Beyer, Jan E. Aquatic Ecosystems: An Operational Research Approach. LC 79-57217. (Illus.). 328p. 1981. 25.00 (*0-295-95719-0*) U of Wash Pr.

Beyer, Janet & Deitch, Kenneth M. The Great Depression: A Nation in Distress. Weisman, JoAnne B., ed. LC 95-68771. (Perspectives on History Ser.). (Illus.). 64p. (YA). (gr. 8 up). 1995. pap. 6.95 (*1-878668-46-3*) Disc Enter Ltd.

Beyer, Janice M., jt. auth. see Trice, Harrison M.

Beyer, Jean. Alone with God: Thirty Eucharistic Meditations. 117p. (Orig.). 1990. pap. 8.95 (*1-85390-050-8*, Pub. by Veritas Pubns) St Mut.

— Prayer, Praise, & Glory. 54p. 1991. pap. 6.95 (*1-85390-172-5*, Pub. by Veritas Pubns) St Mut.

Beyer, Jinny. Christmas with Jinny Beyer: Decorate Your Home for the Holidays with Beautiful Quilts, Wreaths, Arrangements, Ornaments & More. LC 96-6166. (Illus.). 256p. 1996. text 29.95 (*0-87596-716-7*) Rodale Pr Inc.

— Designing Tessellations. LC 98-13128. (Illus.). 256p. 1999. 39.95 (*0-8092-2866-1*, 286610, Contemporary Bks) NTC Contemp Pub Co.

— Jinny Beyer's Color Confidence for Quilter's. LC 92-24025. (Illus.). 144p. 1992. pap. 27.95 (*0-8442-2639-4*, Quilt Dgst Pr) NTC Contemp Pub Co.

— Patchwork Patterns. LC 78-32055. (Illus.). 208p. 1979. pap. 21.95 (*0-914440-27-6*, EPM) Howell Pr VA.

— Patchwork Portfolio: A Presentation of 165 Original Quilt Designs with Illustrated Instructions for Easy Drafting, Elegant Fabric Usage, & Dazzling Design Experimentation. LC 88-33446. (Illus.). 248p. 1990. pap. 29.95 (*0-939009-46-3*, EPM) Howell Pr VA.

— The Quilter's Album of Blocks & Borders. LC 86-4262. (Illus.). 208p. 1986. pap. 19.95 (*0-914440-92-6*, EPM) Howell Pr VA.

— Soft-Edge Piecing: Add the Elegance of Applique to Traditional-Style Patchwork Design. LC 94-38483. (Illus.). 144p. 1995. pap. 24.95 (*0-914881-94-9*, 10112) C & T Pub.

Beyer, John L., et al. Electroconvulsive Therapy: A Programmed Text. 2nd ed. LC 97-3184. 211p. 1998. 36.00 (*0-88048-813-1*, 8813) Am Psychiatric.

Beyer, Joy De, see Kronick, Richard & De Beyer, Joy.

***Beyer, Julie.** Jet Fighter. (High Interest Bks.). (Illus.). (J). 2000. 19.00 (*0-516-23340-8*) Childrens.

— Jet Fighter: The Harrier AV-8B. (High Interest Bks.). (Illus.). 48p. (J). (gr. 4-7). 2000. pap. 6.95 (*0-516-23540-0*) Childrens.

— Miniature Cars. (High Interest Bks.). (Illus.). (J). 2000. 19.00 (*0-516-23332-7*) Childrens.

— Miniature Cars. LC 99-40449. (High Interest Bks.). (Illus.). 48p. (J). (gr. 4-7). 2000. pap. 6.95 (*0-516-23532-X*) Childrens.

— Miniature Cars. LC 99-40449. (Cool Collectibles Ser.). (Illus.). 2000. pap. write for info. (*0-531-17620-7*) Watts.

Beyer, Kay. Coping with Teen Parenting. rev. ed. Rosen, Ruth C., ed. (Coping Ser.). (YA). (gr. 7-12). 1995. lib. bdg. 17.95 (*0-8239-2134-4*) Rosen Group.

— The Value of Good Manners. (Ethics Ser.). (Illus.). 160p. (YA). (gr. 7-12). 1991. lib. bdg. 15.95 (*0-8239-1343-0*) Rosen Group.

***Beyer, Keeneth M.** Q-Ship Versus U-Boats: America's Secret Project. LC 98-53195. 1999. 32.95 (*1-55750-044-4*) Naval Inst Pr.

Beyer, Landon E. Critical Reflection & the Culture of Schooling: Empowering Teachers. (C). 1989. 45.00 (*0-7855-6758-5*, Pub. by Deakin Univ) St Mut.

Beyer, Landon E., ed. Creating Democratic Classrooms: The Struggle to Integrate Theory & Practice. (Practitioner Inquiry Ser.: Vol. 1). 192p. (C). 1996. text 44.00 (*0-8077-3519-1*); pap. text 20.95 (*0-8077-3518-3*) Tchrs Coll.

Beyer, Landon E. & Apple, Michael W., eds. The Curriculum: Problems, Politics, & Possibilities. 2nd ed. LC 97-49330. (SUNY Series, Frontiers in Education). 417p. (C). 1998. text 59.50 (*0-7914-3809-0*); pap. text 19.95 (*0-7914-3810-4*) State U NY Pr.

Beyer, Landon E. & Liston, Daniel P. Curriculum in Conflict: Social Visions, Educational Agendas, & Progressive School Reform. LC 95-26770. 264p. (C). 1996. text 44.00 (*0-8077-3529-9*); pap. text 21.95 (*0-8077-3528-0*) Tchrs Coll.

Beyer, Landon E., et al. Preparing Teachers As Professionals: The Role of Educational Studies & Other Liberal Disciplines. 168p. (C). 1989. pap. text 17.95 (*0-8077-2988-4*) Tchrs Coll.

Beyer, Lorraine R. Community Policing: Lessons from Victoria. 222p. 1993. pap. 35.00 (*0-642-19345-2*, Pub. by Aust Inst Criminology) Advent Bks Div.

Beyer, Lynn H. Great German Recipes. 160p. 1988. spiral bd. 6.95 (*0-941016-49-8*) Penfield.

Beyer, Marcel. The Karnau Tapes: A Novel. Brownjohn, John, tr. LC 97-24782. 256p. 1997. 23.00 (*0-15-100255-X*) Harcourt.

Beyer, Margaret, ed. see Beyer, Gerry W. & Redden, Kenneth R.

Beyer, Margaret W. The Art People Love: Stories of Richard S. Beyer's Life & His Sculpture. (Illus.). 136p. 1999. 32.95 (*0-87422-183-8*); pap. 22.95 (*0-87422-184-6*) Wash St U Pr.

***Beyer, Mark.** We're Depressed. (Illus.). 30p. 1999. 45.00 (*0-934953-65-1*) Water Row Pr.

— We're Depressed. limited aut. ed. (Illus.). 30p. 1999. 79.00 (*0-934953-66-X*) Water Row Pr.

Beyer, Marty, jt. auth. see Jaklitsch, Barbara.

Beyer, Peter F. Religion & Globalization. (Theory, Culture & Society Ser.: Vol. 27). (C). 1994. text 69.95 (*0-8039-8916-4*); pap. text 26.95 (*0-8039-8917-2*) Sage.

Beyer, Peter F., tr. see Luhmann, Niklas.

Beyer, R., ed. see Ando, Yoichi.

Beyer, R. T. Sounds of Our Times: Two Hundred Years of Acoustics. LC 98-9607. (Illus.). 400p. 1998. 60.00 (*0-387-98435-6*) Spr-Verlag.

Beyer, Richard J. Medjugorje Day by Day: A Daily Meditation Book Based on the Messages of Our Lady of Medjugorje. LC 92-74779. (Illus.). 544p. (Orig.). 1993. pap. 12.95 (*0-87793-494-0*) Ave Maria.

Beyer, Rick. Decorative Fish Carving. 128p. 1990. pap. 14.95 (*0-07-155819-5*) McGraw.

— Decorative Fish Carving. (Illus.). 128p. 1990. pap. 14.95 (*0-8306-3568-8*) McGraw-Hill Prof.

Beyer, Robert T. Nonlinear Acoustics. LC 97-77103. 452p. 1997. 55.00 (*1-56396-724-3*) Am Inst Physics.

Beyer, Robert T., tr. see Bahkvalov, N. S., et al.

Beyer, Robert T., tr. see Fabelinskii, Immanuil L.

Beyer, Sally, jt. auth. see Ryan, Greg.

Beyer, Stephan V. The Classical Tibetan Language. LC 91-24499. (SUNY Series in Buddhist Studies). 503p. (C). 1992. text 24.50 (*0-7914-1099-4*) State U NY Pr.

Beyer, Stephen. The Cult of Tara: Magic & Ritual in Tibet. LC 74-186109. (Hermeneutics: Studies in the History of Religions: No. 2). (Illus.). 1974. pap. 22.50 (*0-520-03635-2*, Pub. by U CA Pr) Cal Prin Full Svc.

An Asterisk (*) at the beginning of an entry indicates that the title is appearing for the first time.

Beyer, Stephen G. Administrative Law Regulations. 2nd ed. 1208p. 1992. 55.00 (*0-316-10777-8*, Aspen Law & Bus) Aspen Pub.

Beyer, Steve. Upgrading & Trouble Shooting Your PC. Hanson, Kevin C., ed. (Illus.). (Orig.). 1990. pap. text 24.95 (*0-929978-27-7*) M-USA Busn Systs.

— Using dBase IV. Hanson, Kevin C., ed. (Logic Ware Ser.). (Illus.). 1990. 24.95 incl. VHS (*0-929978-22-6*) M-USA Busn Systs.

Beyer, Steve, ed. see Hurtado, Jose.

Beyer, Steven L. The Star Guide: A Unique System for Identifying the Brightest Stars in the Night Sky. LC 85-13039. (Illus.). 404p. 1986. pap. 12.95 (*0-316-09268-1*) Little.

***Beyer, Thomas, Jr.** Learn English the Fast & Fun Way for Russian Speakers. (Illus.). 128p. 2000. pap. 18.95 (*0-7641-1327-5*) Barron.

Beyer, Thomas. Russian at a Glance. (RUS & ENG.). 1991. pap. 6.95 (*0-8120-4299-9*) Barron.

Beyer, Thomas, Jr., tr. see Solovyov, Vladimir.

Beyer, Thomas P. Integrated Life. LC 75-93317. (Essay Index Reprint Ser.). 1977. 21.95 (*0-8369-1393-0*) Ayer.

Beyer, Thomas R., Jr. 501 English Verbs. LC 97-40811. 550p. 1998. pap. 13.95 (*0-7641-0304-0*) Barron.

— 501 Russian Verbs: Fully Conjugated in All the Tenses. (RUS & ENG.). 600p. (C). 1992. pap. text 13.95 (*0-8120-4662-5*) Barron.

Beyer, Thomas R. Getting by in Russian. 2nd ed. LC 96-26364. (Getting by in...Ser.). (ENG & RUS.). 1997. pap. 18.95 incl. audio (*0-8120-8448-9*) Barron.

— Getting by in Russian: A Quick Beginner's Course for Tourists & Business People. 2nd ed. LC 96-26364. 1997. pap. 7.95 (*0-8120-9685-1*) Barron.

— Indians of the Totem Pole. (J). 1991. pap. text 5.95 (*0-516-95607-8*) Childrens.

Beyer, Thomas R., Jr. Learn Russian the Fast & Fun Way, 4 cassettes. (Barron's Fast & Fun Way Ser.). (RUS.). 240p. (J). (gr. 6-9). 1993. 39.95 incl. audio (*0-8120-7857-8*) Barron.

— Learn Russian the Fast & Fun Way: The Activity Kit That Makes Learning a Language Quick & Easy! LC 92-28052. (JPN & ENG.). 240p. 1993. pap. 16.95 (*0-8120-4846-6*) Barron.

— Pronounce It Perfectly in Russian, 2 cass., Set. LC 93-49857. (Pronounce It Perfectly Ser.). (RUS & ENG.). 140p. 1994. pap. 16.95 incl. audio (*0-8120-8016-5*) Barron.

Beyer, Thomas R. Russian on the Go, Level 1. (On the Go Ser.). (RUS.). 1994. pap. 12.95 incl. audio (*0-8120-8128-5*) Barron.

— Russian on the Go, Level 2. (Languages on the Go Ser.). (ENG & RUS.). 1995. pap. 12.95 incl. audio (*0-8120-8211-7*) Barron.

Beyer, Thomas R., tr. see Bely, Andrei.

***Beyer, Tom.** The Miraculous Mystery: Reflections, Devotions & Awakenings. LC 99-96236. (Illus.). vi, 182p. 2000. mass mkt. 14.00 (*0-9672498-0-5*) OneSelf Pubg.

***Beyer, W.** Traceability Strategies for the Calibration of Spline & Serration Gauges. (Technical Papers: Vol. 99FTM2). 5p. 1999. pap. 30.00 (*1-55589-740-1*) AGMA.

***Beyer, W. F. & Keydel, D. F.** Deeds of Valor: How America's Civil War Heroes Won the Congressional Medal of Honor. LC 99-87289. (Illus.). 576p. 2000. 10.98 (*0-7651-1769-X*) Smithmark.

Beyer, W. Nelson, et al, eds. Environmental Contaminants in Wildlife: Interpreting Tissue Concentrations. 512p. 1996. lib. bdg. 95.00 (*1-56670-071-X*, L1071) Lewis Pubs.

Beyer, W. W. Islands Beneath the Moon. LC 95-75369. 236p. 1995. 22.95 (*1-878208-58-6*) Guild Pr IN.

***Beyer, Will & Hunt, Robert D.** Born to Be Wild: Attention Deficit Hyperactivity Disorder, Alcoholism & Addiction. 1999. pap. text 64.50 (*1-886021-12-0*) J W Wood.

Beyer, William H. Handbook of Tables for Probability & Statistics. 2nd ed. (Handbook Ser.). 656p. 1968. lib. bdg. 92.95 (*0-8493-0692-2*, QA) CRC Pr.

— Standard Mathematical Tables & Formulae. 29th ed. 725p. 1991. 39.95 (*0-8493-0629-9*, QA) CRC Pr.

Beyer, William H., ed. Handbook of Mathematical Sciences. 6th ed. (Illus.). 992p. 1987. lib. bdg. 99.95 (*0-8493-0656-6*, QA47) CRC Pr.

— Standard Probability & Statistics Tables & Formulae. 520p. 1990. 41.95 (*0-8493-0680-9*, QA276) CRC Pr.

Beyer, Wolfgang. Traceable Calibration of Master Gears at PTB. (Technical Papers: Vol. 96FTM4). (Illus.). 6p. 1996. pap. text 30.00 (*1-55589-671-5*) AGMA.

Beyerchen, Alan D. Scientists under Hitler: Politics & the Physics Community in the Third Reich. LC 77-2167. (Illus.). 309p. reprint ed. pap. 95.80 (*0-7837-4526-5*, 208018900003) Bks Demand.

Beyerl, Paul. Compendium of Herbal Magick. LC 99-164253. (Illus.). 528p. 1997. pap. 24.50 (*0-919345-45-X*) Phoenix WA.

— The Master Book of Herbalism. (Illus.). 424p. 1984. pap. 14.95 (*0-919345-53-0*) Phoenix WA.

Beyerl, Paul V. The Holy Books of the Devas: The Secret Mythologies of the Herbal World. 4th rev. ed. (Illus.). 216p. 1998. pap. 16.95 (*0-9655687-1-7*) Hermits Grove.

— Painless Astrology: A Simple & Fun Guide to Natal Chart Interpretation. rev. ed. (Illus.). 200p. 1996. pap. write for info. (*0-9655687-0-9*) Hermits Grove.

***Beyerl, Paul V.** A Wiccan Bardo, Revisited: Initiation & Self-Transformation. 2nd rev. ed. 210p. 1999. pap. 16.95 (*0-9655687-2-5*) Hermits Grove.

Beyerle, Shaazka, ed. Completing the Marshall Plan: The Enlargement of Euro-Atlantic Institutions. 36p. 1997. pap. 15.00 (*1-886607-06-0*) European Inst.

Beyerle, Shaazka M., ed. Eu Enlargement: Catalyst for Market Liberalization? A Report of the September 1995 Seminar the Future of Enlarged Translantic Relations: The Impact of Central & Eastern Europe. 30p. (Orig.). 1996. pap. 15.00 (*1-886607-01-X*) European Inst.

— The Transatlantic Technology Agenda: New Policy Dimensions: Report of the European Institute Project on Transatlantic Technology Cooperation (PROTEC) Seminar. LC 95-60868. 46p. (Orig.). 1995. pap. 15.00 (*0-9628287-9-3*) European Inst.

Beyerle, Stefan. Der Mosesegen Im Deuteronomium: Eine Text-, Kompositions- und Formkritische Studie Zu Deuteronomium 33. (Beihefte zur Zeitschrift fuer die Alttestamentliche Wissenschaft Ser.: Vol. 250). (GER.). x, 345p. (C). 1997. lib. bdg. 127.15 (*3-11-015062-X*) De Gruyter.

Beyerlein, Ann, et al. Small Group Leaders Handbook: The Next Generation. 2nd ed. LC 95-43636. 192p. 1995. pap. 10.99 (*0-8308-1139-7*, 1139) InterVarsity.

Beyerlein, Douglas, ed. Beyerlein Beginnings. 117p. (C). 1989. pap. text 18.00 (*0-9623312-0-1*) D Beyerlein.

***Beyerlein, Frederick M.** Drink as Much as You Want & Live Longer: The Intelligent Person's Guide to Healthy Drinking. 213p. 1999. pap. 14.95 (*1-55950-188-X*, 85293) Loompanics.

Beyerlein, Michael M., ed. Advances in Interdisciplinary Studies of Work Teams, Vol. 4. 1997. 78.50 (*0-7623-0173-2*) Jai Pr.

— Advances in Interdisciplinary Studies of Work Teams, Vol. 5. Date not set. 82.50 (*0-7623-0360-3*) Jai Pr.

Beyerlein, Michael M., et al, eds. Advances in Interdisciplinary Studies of Work Teams: Knowledge Work in Teams, Vol. 2. 301p. 1995. 78.50 (*1-55938-926-5*) Jai Pr.

— Advances in Interdisciplinary Studies of Work Teams: Team Leadership, Vol. 3. 320p. 1996. 78.50 (*0-7623-0006-X*) Jai Pr.

— Advances in Interdisciplinary Studies of Work Teams: Theories of Self-Managing Work Teams, Vol. 1. 289p. 1994. 78.50 (*1-55938-858-7*) Jai Pr.

***Beyerlein, Michael Martin, et al.** Team Performance Management. LC 00-32261. (Advances in Interdisciplinary Studies of Work Teams). 2000. write for info. (*0-7623-0655-6*) Jai Pr.

Beyerlein, Steve W., jt. auth. see Carroll, Sarah M.

Beyerlin, Walter. Bleilot, Brecheisen Oder Was Sonst? Revision Einer Amos-Vision. (Orbis Biblicus et Orientalis Ser.: Vol. 81). (GER.). 61p. 1988. pap. text 14.75 (*3-7278-0579-X*, Pub. by Presses Univ Fribourg) Eisenbrauns.

— Im Licht der Traditionen: Psalm 67 und 115, ein Entwicklungszusammenhang. LC 92-13826. (Supplements to Vetus Testamentum Ser.: No. 45). (GER.). x, 154p. 1992. 79.00 (*90-04-09635-3*) Brill Academic Pubs.

— Reflexe der Amosvisionen im Jeremiabuch. (Orbis Biblicus et Orientalis Ser.: Vol. 93). (GER.). 119p. 1989. text 28.00 (*3-7278-0658-3*, Pub. by Presses Univ Fribourg) Eisenbrauns.

— We Are Like Dreamers. Livingstone, Dinah, tr. from GER.Tr. of Wir Sind Wie Traumende. 76p. 1982. 19.95 (*0-567-09315-8*, Pub. by T & T Clark) Bks Intl VA.

— Werden und Wesen des 107 Psalms. (Beiheft zur Zeitschrift fuer die Alttestamentliche Wissenschaft Ser.: No. 153). (C). 1979. 77.70 (*3-11-007755-8*) De Gruyter.

Beyerly, Elizabeth. Eurocentric International Law? Contemporary Doctrinal Perspectives. LC 98-18480. xviii, 160p. 1998. 65.00 (*1-57588-417-8*, 311600) W S Hein.

— The Europe Centric Historiography of Russia: An Analysis of the Contribution by Russian Emigre Historians in the U. S. A., 1925-55, Concerning 19th Century Russian History. LC 72-94444. (Studies in European History: No. 11). 385p. 1973. text 115.40 (*90-279-2515-1*) Mouton.

Beyermann, W. Random Magnetism, High TC Superconductivity. 276p. 1994. text 86.00 (*981-02-1786-2*) World Scientific Pub.

Beyers. Quality in Nursing Services. 1997. text. write for info. (*0-7216-4255-1*, W B Saunders Co) Harcrt Hlth Sci Grp.

Beyers, Robert J. & Odum, Howard T. Ecological Microcosms. LC 93-290. (Advanced Texts in Life Sciences Ser.). 1993. 87.95 (*0-387-97980-8*) Spr-Verlag.

Beyersdorf, Eunice, jt. auth. see Brady, J. D.

***Beyersdorf, Friedhelm.** Ischemia-Reperfusion Injury in Cardiac Surgery. (Medical Intelligence Unit Ser.). 304p. 2000. 99.00 (*1-58706-002-7*, Pub. by Eurekah) Landes Bioscience.

Beyersdorf, Friedhelm. Ischemia-Reperfusion Injury in Cardiac Surgery. LC 99-22059. (Medical Intelligence Unit Ser.). 304p. 2000. 89.00 (*1-57059-588-7*) Landes Bioscience.

Beyerstein, Barry L. & Beyerstein, Dale F., eds. The Write Stuff: Evaluations of Graphology, the Study of Handwriting Analysis. LC 91-21698. 515p. (Orig.). (C). 1992. 55.95 (*0-87975-612-8*); pap. 26.95 (*0-87975-613-6*) Prometheus Bks.

Beyerstein, Dale F., jt. ed. see Beyerstein, Barry L.

Beyette, Beverly, jt. auth. see Schwartz, Jeffrey M.

Beyfus, Drusilla. The You Guide to Modern Dilemmas. (Illus.). 160p. 1998. pap. 19.95 (*1-85626-253-7*, Pub. by Cathie Kyle) Trafalgar.

***Beyfus, Drusilla, et al, contrib. by.** Photographs by Snowdon: A Retrospective. (Illus.). 240p. 2000. 75.00 (*0-8109-4479-0*, Pub. by Abrams) Time Warner.

***Beykont, Zeyhep F., ed.** Lifting Every Voice: Pedagogy & Politics of Bilingualism. 180p. 1999. pap. 18.95 (*1-891792-01-6*) HEPG.

Beyl, Judith. Sunshine, Rainbows & Friends. LC 80-50828. (Illus.). 83p. (Orig.). (J). (ps-k). 1980. pap. 5.95 (*0-933308-01-9*) Harper SF.

Beylard-Ozeroff, Ann, et al, eds. Translator's Strategies & Creativity: Selected Papers from the 9th International Conference on Translation & Interpreting, Prague, September, 1995. In Honor of Jiri Levy & Anton Popovic. LC 98-18682. (Benjamins Translation Library: Vol. 27). xiv, 230p. 1998. 65.00 (*1-55619-711-X*) J Benjamins Pubng Co.

***Beylarian, George & Osborne, Jeffrey J.** Mondo Materials: Materials & Ideas for the Future. 2000. pap. 35.00 (*1-58567-087-1*, Pub. by Overlook Pr) Penguin Putnam.

Beyle, Marie-Henri, see Stendhal, pseud.

Beyle, Noel W. Around on Cape Cod, No. 27. (Illus.) 48p. (Orig.). 1986. pap. 0.95 (*0-912609-10-9*) First Encounter.

— Cape Cod Calamities, No. 20. (Illus.). 48p. (Orig.) 1984. pap. 0.95 (*0-912609-03-6*) First Encounter.

— Cape Cod Jokes (Illustrated), No. 21. (Illus.). 48p. (Orig.). 1984. pap. 0.95 (*0-912609-04-4*) First Encounter.

— The Cape Cod Seafood Cookbook, No. 29. (Illus.) 48p. (Orig.). 1987. pap. 0.95 (*0-912609-12-5*) First Encounter.

— Cape Cod to the Rescue!, No. 22. (Illus.). 48p. (Orig.). 1984. pap. 0.95 (*0-912609-05-2*) First Encounter.

— Curious Cape Cod Oddities, No. 25. (Illus.). 48p. (Orig.). 1985. pap. 0.95 (*0-912609-08-7*) First Encounter.

— Fishy Stories of Cape Cod, No. 28. (Illus.). 48p. (Orig.). 1987. pap. 0.95 (*0-912609-11-7*) First Encounter.

— How to Spot a Cape Cod Native, No. 24. (Illus.). 48p. (Orig.). 1985. pap. 0.95 (*0-912609-07-9*) First Encounter.

— How to Talk Cape Cod Talk, No. 19. (Illus.). 48p. (Orig.). 1983. pap. 0.95 (*0-912609-01-X*) First Encounter.

— Olde Cape Cod, No. 26. (Illus.). 48p. 1986. pap. write for info. (*0-912609-09-5*) First Encounter.

— Part of Cape Cod Is Missing!, No. 17. (Illus.). 48p (Orig.). 1983. pap. 0.95 (*0-912609-00-1*) First Encounter.

— Provincetown! Questions You Don't Dare Ask (& Answers) (No. 18). (Illus.). 48p. (Orig.). 1983. pap. 0.95 (*0-912609-02-8*) First Encounter.

— Salty Stories of Cape Cod, No. 23. (Illus.). 48p. (Orig.). 1984. pap. 0.95 (*0-912609-06-0*) First Encounter.

Beyle, Thad. Governors & Hard Times. 215p. 1992. pap. 22.95 (*0-87187-710-4*) Congr Quarterly.

***Beyle, Thad L.** State & Local Government, 2000-2001. 250p. 2000. 19.95 (*1-56802-558-0*) CQ Pr.

Beyle, Thad L. State Government, 1997-1998: CQ's Guide to Current Issues & Activities. 225p. 1997. pap. 19.95 (*1-56802-097-X*) Congr Quarterly.

— State Government 1996-1997: CQ's Guide to Current Issues & Activities. LC 85-9657. 260p. 1996. pap. 22.95 (*0-87187-891-7*) Congr Quarterly.

Beyle, Thad L., ed. Gubernatorial Transitions: The 1982 Elections. LC 85-6748. (Duke Press Policy Studies). (Illus.). x, 500p. (C). 1985. 58.00 (*0-8223-0642-5*) Duke.

— Gubernatorial Transitions: The 1983 & 1984 Elections. LC 88-14711. x, 384p. (C). 1988. text 58.00 (*0-8223-0858-4*) Duke.

— State & Local Government, 1999-2000. 250p. 1999. pap. 19.95 (*1-56802-099-6*) CQ Pr.

— State Government: CQ's Guide to Current Issues & Activities 1994-1995. LC 85-9657. 250p. 1994. pap. 22.95 (*0-87187-802-X*) Congr Quarterly.

— State Government: CQ's Guide to Current Issues & Activities 1995-96. LC 85-9657. 253p. 1995. pap. 22.95 (*0-87187-824-0*) Congr Quarterly.

— State Government 1998-1999: CQ's Guide to Current Issues & Activities. 240p. 1998. pap. text 19.95 (*1-56802-098-8*) Congr Quarterly.

Beyle, Thad L. & Muchmore, Lynn, eds. Being Governor: The View from the Office. LC 82-24234. (Duke Press Policy Studies). xi, 237p. 1983. text 46.00 (*0-8223-0506-2*) Duke.

Beylerian, George M. Chairmania: Fantastic Miniatures. LC 94-1546. (Illus.). 144p. 1994. 19.95 (*0-8109-3192-1*, Pub. by Abrams) Time Warner.

Beylerian, George M. & Osborne, Jeffrey J. Mondo Materials: Materials & Ideas for the Future. 1990. pap. 24.95 (*0-8109-2468-4*, Pub. by Abrams) Time Warner.

Beyleveld, jt. auth. see Haker.

Beyleveld, Deryck. The Dialectical Necessity of Morality: An Analysis & Defense of Alan Gewirth's Argument to the Principle of Generic Consistency. 562p. 1991 pap. text 26.00 (*0-226-04483-1*); lib. bdg. 63.50 (*0-226-04482-3*) U Ch Pr.

Beylin, Simon. What You Should Know about Jewelry: Buyer's Guide. Hant, Lisa & Carpenter, Jake, eds. (Illus.). 81p. 1995. 12.99 (*0-9648865-0-2*) Romans Pubng.

Beylin, Tanya, tr. see Mesyats, Vadim.

Beylon. Invisible Riddles Magic Picture Book. (Invisible Picture Bks.). 1998. pap. 1.00 (*0-486-40113-8*) Dover.

— Pegatinas de Mis Animales: Favorite Animals (Spanish Edition) (SPA.). 1998. pap. text 1.00 (*0-486-28383-6*) Dover.

Beylon, C. Animals. 1997. pap. text 1.00 (*0-486-29775-4*) Dover.

***Beylon, C.** Freddy, the Fireman: With 28 Sticker Costumes. (J). 1999. pap. 1.00 (*0-486-40754-3*) Dover.

— My Play Kitchen. (Little Activity Bks.). (J). 2000. pap. 1.00 (*0-486-40981-3*) Dover.

Beylon, C. Numbers. 1997. pap. text 1.00 (*0-486-29775-6*) Dover.

— Shapes & Colors. 1997. pap. text 1.00 (*0-486-29774-8*) Dover.

Beylon, C. Wizard of Oz Nested Dolls. (Illus.). 1995. pap. text 4.95 (*0-486-28764-5*) Dover.

***Beylon, Cathy.** Amanda Dresses up Sticker Paper Doll. (Illus.). (J). 1999. pap. 1.00 (*0-486-40753-5*) Dover.

Beylon, Cathy. Animal ABC Stickers. (Illus.). (J). (gr. k-3). 1994. pap. 1.00 (*0-486-27936-7*) Dover.

***Beylon, Cathy.** Aquarium Show. (Little Activity Bks.). (Illus.). (J). 2000. pap. 1.00 (*0-486-40985-6*) Dover.

Beylon, Cathy. Beach Sticker Activity Book. (J). pap. 1.00 (*0-486-29731-4*) Dover.

***Beylon, Cathy.** Birds. (Little Activity Bks.). (Illus.). (J). 1999. pap. 1.00 (*0-486-40744-6*) Dover.

— Circus Sticker Activity Book. (Illus.). (J). 1999. pap. 1.00 (*0-486-40745-4*) Dover.

— Coral Reef. (Little Activity Bks.). (Illus.). (J). 1997. pap. 1.00 (*0-486-29407-2*) Dover.

— Create Your Own Bunnyland Sticker Picture Book. (Illus.). (J). 1996. pap. 3.50 (*0-486-28873-0*) Dover.

— Create Your Own Halloween Sticker Cards. (Little Activity Bks.). (Illus.). (J). 1997. pap. 1.00 (*0-486-29719-5*) Dover.

— Create Your Own St. Patrick's Day Sticker Card Book. (Little Activity Bks.). (Illus.). (J). 1998. pap. text 1.00 (*0-486-40317-3*) Dover.

Beylon, Cathy. Create Your Own Teacher Sticker Cards. 1998. text 1.00 (*0-486-40318-1*) Dover.

— Create Your Own Thank You Sticker Cards. 1998. text 1.00 (*0-486-40097-2*) Dover.

— Decorate a Christmas Tree with 40 Stickers. (Illus.). (J). (gr. k-3). 1994. pap. 1.00 (*0-486-28104-3*) Dover.

Beylon, Cathy. Decorate a Christmas Wreath: With 39 Stickers. (Little Activity Bks.). (Illus.). (J). 1996. pap. 1.00 (*0-486-29180-4*) Dover.

— Decorate a Gingerbread Boy. (Little Activity Bks.). (Illus.). (J). 1999. pap. 1.00 (*0-486-40508-7*) Dover.

Beylon, Cathy. Decorate a Pumpkin with 34 Stickers. (Illus.). 1998. pap. 1.00 (*0-486-29179-0*) Dover.

***Beylon, Cathy.** Decorate a Snowman. (Little Activity Bks.). (Illus.). (J). 1999. pap. 1.00 (*0-486-40507-9*) Dover.

— Doctor's Office. (Little Activity Bks.). (Illus.). (J). 2000. pap. 1.00 (*0-486-40982-1*) Dover.

Beylon, Cathy. Easter Basket Stickers. (Illus.). (J). (gr. k-3). 1993. pap. 1.00 (*0-486-27810-7*) Dover.

Beylon, Cathy. Easter Eggs. (Little Activity Bks.). (Illus.). (J). 1997. pap. 1.00 (*0-486-29408-0*) Dover.

Beylon, Cathy. Fairy Tale Princesses, Vol. 1. 1999. pap. 4.99 (*0-448-42078-3*, G & D) Peng Put Young Read.

— Favorite Animals Coloring Book. (Illus.). (J). (gr. k-3). 1993. pap. 1.00 (*0-486-27727-5*) Dover.

Beylon, Cathy. Gingerbread House. (Little Activity Bks.). (Illus.). (J). 1997. pap. 1.00 (*0-486-29794-2*) Dover.

Beylon, Cathy. Hush Little Baby. (Window Bks.). (J). (ps). 1992. 4.95 (*1-56288-284-8*) Checkerboard.

Beylon, Cathy. Indian Village. (Little Activity Bks.). (Illus.). (J). 1997. pap. 1.00 (*0-486-29644-X*) Dover.

Beylon, Cathy. Invisible Halloween Magic Picture Book. (Illus.). (J). (ps-3). 1998. pap. 1.00 (*0-486-40227-4*, 881889Q) Dover.

***Beylon, Cathy.** Invisible Thanksgiving Magic Picture Book. (Illus.). (J). 1999. pap. 1.00 (*0-486-40527-3*) Dover.

— Jack-O-Lantern Sticker Book. (Little Activity Bks.). (Illus.). (J). 1999. pap. 1.00 (*0-486-40501-X*) Dover.

— Jungle. (Little Activity Bks.). (Illus.). (J). 1997. pap. 1.00 (*0-486-29645-8*) Dover.

Beylon, Cathy. Kitten Stickers. (Illus.). (J). (gr. k-3). 1993. pap. 1.00 (*0-486-27672-4*) Dover.

— Kittens. (Illus.). 32p. (J). pap. 1.00 (*0-486-40020-4*) Dover.

***Beylon, Cathy.** Learning Signs. 2000. pap. 4.50 (*0-486-40816-7*) Dover.

— Lion Sticker Paper Doll. (Illus.) (J). 1995. pap. 1.00 (*0-486-28423-9*) Dover.

— Little Gas Station. (Illus.). (J). 1998. pap. 1.00 (*0-486-40311-4*) Dover.

Beylon, Cathy. Make Your Own Aquarium Sticker Activity Book. (J). pap. text 1.00 (*0-486-28603-7*) Dover.

— Make Your Own Haunted House. (Illus.). 1995. pap. 1.00 (*0-486-28604-5*) Dover.

— Make Your Own Sticker Calendar. 1999. pap. text 4.50 (*0-486-40583-4*) Dover.

— Mr. McGregor's Garden Sticker Activity Book. (J). pap. 1.00 (*0-486-29793-4*) Dover.

— The Mulberry Bush. (Window Bks.). (J). (ps) 1992. 4.95 (*1-56288-282-1*) Checkerboard.

***Beylon, Cathy.** My Clubhouse. (Little Activity Bks.). (Illus.). (J). 1999. pap. 1.00 (*0-486-40746-2*) Dover.

— My Playground Sticker Picture. (Illus.). (J). 1999. pap. 4.50 (*0-486-40584-2*) Dover.

— My Rain Forest Sticker Activity Book. (Illus.). (J). 1999. pap. 1.00 (*0-486-40509-5*) Dover.

— My School. (Little Activity Bks.). (Illus.). (J). 1999. pap. text 1.00 (*0-486-40510-9*) Dover.

Beylon, Cathy. Old Macdonald. (Window Book Ser.). (J). (ps). 1992. 4.95 (*1-56288-281-3*) Checkerboard.

Beylon, Cathy. Old MacDonald's Farm. (Little Activity Bks.). (Illus.). (J). 1997. pap. 1.00 (*0-486-29409-9*) Dover.

— Oz. (Little Activity Bks.). (Illus.). (J). 1998. pap. 1.00 (*0-486-40045-X*) Dover.

— Penguin Stickers. (Illus.). (J). 1995. pap. 1.00 (*0-486-28779-3*) Dover.

Beylon, Cathy. Pet Shop Sticker Activity Book. (J). pap. text 1.00 (*0-486-40312-2*) Dover.

— Petting Zoo Sticker Activity Book. (J). pap. text 1.00 (*0-486-40098-0*) Dover.

Beylon, Cathy. Santa. (Little Activity Bks.). (Illus.). (J). 1995. pap. 1.00 (*0-486-28644-4*) Dover.

— Santas Workshop Sticker Activity Book. (Illus.). (J). 1997. pap. 1.00 (*0-486-29720-9*) Dover.

Beylon, Cathy. Scary Creatures Sticker Storybook. (Illus.). 16p. (Orig.). (J). 1997. pap. text 1.00 (*0-486-29721-7*) Dover.

— Stickers - Create Your Own Valentine. (Illus.). (J). (ps-4). 1998. pap. 1.00 (*0-486-29393-9*, 256769Q) Dover.

B

— There Was a Tree. (Window Bks.). 14p. (J). (ps). 1992. 4.95 (*1-56288-283-X*) Checkerboard.

***Beylon, Cathy.** Tom the Turkey. (Little Activity Bks.). (Illus.). (J). 1999. pap. 1.00 (*0-486-40513-3*) Dover.

— Western Ranch Sticker Activity Book. (Illus.). (J). 1998. pap. 1.00 (*0-486-40099-9*) Dover.

Beylon, Cathy. Berlitz Junior French Dictionary. LC 91-40123. (FRE.). 144p. (J). (ps-2). 1992. pap. 11.95 (*0-689-71539-0*) Aladdin.

— Over in the Meadow. (Baby Shaped Board Bks.). 28p. (J). (ps). 1990. 2.95 (*0-02-689484-X*) Checkerboard.

— We Are Ballerinas: A Sticker Stories Book. (Sticker Stories Ser.). 16p. (J). 1997. pap. text 4.95 (*0-448-41723-5*, G & D) Peng Put Young Read.

Beylon, Cathy, jt. auth. see Bracken, Carolyn.

Beylon, Cathy, jt. auth. see Fremont, Victoria.

Beylsmit, J. J. Linguistic Bibliography for the Year, 1979. 1982. 135.00 (*0-686-37163-1*) Kluwer Academic.

Beylsmit, J. J., ed. Linguistic Bibliography for the Year, 1981. 911p. 1984. lib. bdg. 450.50 (*90-247-2953-X*) Kluwer Academic.

— Linguistic Bibliography for the Year, 1978. 760p. 1981. lib. bdg. 417.00 (*90-247-2509-7*) Kluwer Academic.

Beylsmit, J. J. & Rijlaarsdam, J. C., eds. Linguistic Bibliography for the Year, 1976. xlviii, 736p. 1980. lib. bdg. 306.00 (*90-247-2242-X*) Kluwer Academic.

Beyma, Ron. Conservative Innovation: Kicking the Newness Habit. LC 96-16108. 192p. 1996. 24.95 (*1-56079-596-4*, Petersons Pacesetter) Petersons.

Beyme, Klaus Von, see Von Beyme, Klaus.

Beymer, Lawrence. Meeting the Guidance & Counseling Needs of Boys. LC 94-31000. 108p. 1995. pap. text 23.95 (*1-55620-136-2*, 72562) Am Coun Assn.

Beymer, Robert. Boundary Waters Canoe Area Vol. 1: The Western Region. 5th ed. LC 93-36540. (Illus.). 173p. 1994. pap. 14.95 (*0-89997-165-2*) Wilderness Pr.

***Beymer, Robert.** Boundary Waters Canoe Area Vol. 1: The Western Region, 1. 6th rev. ed. LC 00-25846. (Illus.). 2000. pap. 14.95 (*0-89997-237-3*) Wilderness Pr.

Beymer, Robert. Boundary Waters Canoe Area Vol. 2: The Eastern Region. 3rd ed. LC 85-40197. (Illus.). 160p. 1991. 14.95 (*0-89997-124-5*) Wilderness Pr.

***Beymer, Robert.** Boundary Waters Canoe Area Vol. 2: The Eastern Region, 2. rev. ed. (Illus.). 2000. pap. 14.95 (*0-89997-238-1*) Wilderness Pr.

Beymer, Robert. A Paddler's Guide to Quetico Provincial Park. LC 85-80675. 168p. (Orig.). 1985. pap. 7.95 (*0-933287-00-3*) Fisher Co.

— Ski Country: Nordic Skiers Guide to the Minnesota Arrowhead. LC 86-81167. 224p. (Orig.). 1986. pap. 8.95 (*0-933287-01-1*) Fisher Co.

Beyn, Edgar J. The Twelve Volt Doctor's Alternator Book. rev. ed. (Twelve Volt Doctor's Bks.). (Illus.). 182p. 1989. reprint ed. pap. 21.00 (*1-878797-02-6*) Weems & Plath.

— The Twelve Volt Doctor's Practical Handbook: For the Boat's Electric System. rev. ed. (Twelve Volt Doctor's Bks.). (Illus.). 233p. 1989. reprint ed. pap. 26.50 (*1-878797-00-X*) Weems & Plath.

— 12 Volt Doctor's Practical Handbook: For the Boat's Electric System. 4th rev. ed. (Twelve Volt Doctor's Bks.). (Illus.). 1998. pap. 26.50 (*1-878797-13-1*) Weems & Plath.

— The Twelve Volt Doctor's Project Book. (Twelve Volt Doctor's Bks.). (Illus.). 57p. (Orig.). 1990. pap. 16.00 (*1-878797-01-8*) Weems & Plath.

— The Twelve Volt Doctor's Troubleshooting Book. (Twelve Volt Doctor's Bks.). (Illus.). 58p. (Orig.). 1990. pap. 16.00 (*1-878797-03-4*) Weems & Plath.

Beyne, E. Seminar, et al. Thermal Management of Electronics Systems II: Proceedings of Eurotherm Seminar 45, 20-22 September 1995, Leuven, Belgium. LC 97-19915. 1997. text 191.00 (*0-7923-4612-2*) Kluwer Academic.

Beynen, Anton C. & Solleveid, H. A., eds. New Developments in Biosciences: Their Implication for Laboratory Animal Science. 480p. (C). 1987. text 306.50 (*0-89838-354-4*) Kluwer Academic.

Beynen, Anton C. & West, C. E., eds. Use of Animal Models for Research in Human Nutrition. (Comparative Animal Nutrition Ser.: Vol. 6). (Illus.). v, 190p. 1989. 146.25 (*3-8055-4802-8*) S Karger.

Beynen, Anton C., jt. ed. see Sugano, M.

Beynon. The Complete MRCP3. 2nd ed. (C). 1998. pap. text. write for info. (*0-443-05690-0*) Church.

***Beynon & Geddis.** Learing-to-Teach: Cases & Concepts for Novice Teachers & Teacher Educators. 2000. pap. 34.60 (*0-13-016655-3*) P-H.

Beynon, Barbara. The Complete American Eskimo: A Special Kind of Companion Dog. (Illus.). 224p. 1990. 27.95 (*0-87605-013-5*) Howell Bks.

Beynon-Davies, P. Information Systems Failures & How to Avoid Them. 1996. pap. 129.00 (*1-85953-028-1*, Pub. by Tech Comm) St Mut.

Beynon-Davies, Paul. Information Systems Development. Sumner, F. H., ed. (Computer Science Ser.). 242p. 1989. pap. text 35.00 (*0-333-48035-X*) Scholium Intl.

***Beynon, Donald.** Fantasies in Rhyme & Other Thoughts. LC 99-67770. 100p. 1999. pap. 5.99 (*1-893181-34-0*) Le Gesse Stevens.

Beynon, Granville, ed. Solar-Terrestrial Physics: Proceedings of an International Symposium, Innsbruck, Austria, 1978. (Illus.). 240p. 1979. pap. 52.00 (*0-08-025054-8*, Pergamon Pr) Elsevier.

Beynon, H. Looking at Class. text 65.00 (*1-85489-120-0*) Rivers Oram.

— Looking at Class. (Illus.). 224p. 2000. pap. 24.95 (*1-85489-121-9*) Rivers Oram.

Beynon, H. L., et al, eds. Data Interpretation Questions & Case Histories Pt. 2: MRCP. 2nd ed. (Illus.). 232p. 1998. pap. write for info. (*0-443-05694-3*) Church.

— Multiple Choice Questions Pt. 1: MRCP. 2nd ed. 328p. 1998. pap. write for info. (*0-443-05691-9*) Church.

Beynon, H. L., et al. The Complete Set MRCP, 3 vols. (Complete MRCP Ser.). (Illus.). (Orig.). 1992. pap. text 64.00 (*0-443-04311-6*) Church.

— Multiple Choice Questions. (Complete MRCP Ser.). (Illus.). 265p. (Orig.). 1991. pap. text 26.00 (*0-443-04308-6*) Church.

— Slide Interpretation. (Complete MRCP Ser.). (Illus.). 232p. (Orig.). 1991. pap. text 32.00 (*0-443-04309-4*) Church.

Beynon, Huw. Digging up Trouble: The Environment, Protest & Open-Cost Mining. 1999. pap. text 21.50 (*1-85489-113-8*, Pub. by Rivers Oram) NYU Pr.

Beynon, Huw, et al. Digging up Trouble: The Environment, Protest & Open-Cast Mining. (Illus.). 288p. 1999. 57.50 (*1-85489-112-X*, Pub. by Rivers Oram) NYU Pr.

— A Tale of Two Industries: The Contradiction of Coal & Steel in the North East of England. 128p. 1991. 110.00 (*0-335-09682-4*); pap. 32.95 (*0-335-09681-6*) OpUniv Pr.

Beynon, J. Introductory University Optics. 288p. 1996. pap. 40.00 (*0-13-210824-0*) P-H.

Beynon, J. & Carr, Nicholas D., eds. Recent Advances in Coloproctology. LC 99-24162. 255p. 1999. 149.00 (*1-85233-169-0*, Pub. by Spr-Verlag) Spr-Verlag.

Beynon, J., et al. An Atlas of Rectal Endosonography. (Illus.). 112p. 1991. 130.00 (*0-387-19690-0*) Spr-Verlag.

***Beynon, J. H., et al, eds.** Engineering Against Fatigue: Proceedings of an International Conference, Sheffield, UK, 17-21 March 1997. (Illus.). 15p. 1999. 120.00 (*90-5410-969-6*, Pub. by A A Balkema) Ashgate Pub Co.

Beynon, John, ed. Children, Classrooms & Computers. 250p. 1993. 80.00 (*1-85000-644-X*, Falmer Pr); pap. 29.95 (*1-85000-645-8*, Falmer Pr) Taylor & Francis.

Beynon, John & Mackay, Hughie. Technological Literacy & the Curriculum. 224p. 1992. pap. 32.95 (*1-85000-986-4*, Falmer Pr) Taylor & Francis.

Beynon, John, jt. ed. see Mackay, Hughie.

Beynon, John H. & Gilbert, J. R. Application of Transition State Theory to Unimolecular Reactions: An Introduction. LC 83-17016. (Illus.). 93p. reprint ed. pap. 30.00 (*0-8357-3048-4*, 203930400012) Bks Demand.

Beynon, John H. & McGlashan, M. L., eds. Current Topics in Mass Spectrometry & Chemical Kinetics: Proceedings of the Symposium in Honour of Professor Allan Maccoll, University College, London, 1981. LC QD0096.M3C87. 165p. reprint ed. pap. 51.20 (*0-608-12334-X*, 202519400042) Bks Demand.

***Beynon, Karen & Porter, Andrew.** Valuing Pharmaceutical Companies. 256p. 2000. 170.00 (*1-85573-458-3*, Pub. by Woodhead Pubng) Am Educ Systs.

Beynon, Neville. Pigs: A Guide to Management. (Illus.). 176p. 1994. pap. 29.95 (*1-85223-754-6*, Pub. by Cro1wood) Trafalgar.

Beynon, Par, jt. auth. see Davies, Barry.

Beynon, Peter H., et al, eds. BSAVA Manual of Raptors, Pigeons & Waterfowl. (Illus.). 352p. 1996. pap. 89.95 (*0-8138-2876-7*, Pub. by BSAVA) Iowa St U Pr.

— Manual of Psittacine Birds. LC 96-159979. (Illus.). 240p. 1996. pap. text 72.95 (*0-8138-2349-8*, Pub. by BSAVA) Iowa St U Pr.

— Manual of Reptiles. (Illus.). 228p. 1994. pap. text 72.95 (*0-8138-2296-3*) Iowa St U Pr.

Beynon, Peter H. & Cooper, John E., eds. Manual of Exotic Pets. (Illus.). 312p. 1994. pap. text 72.95 (*0-8138-2294-7*) Iowa St U Pr.

Beynon, R. J. Postgraduate Studies in the Biological Sciences: A Researcher's Companion. 150p. 1993. pap. 20.00 (*1-85578-009-7*, Pub. by Portland Pr Ltd) Ashgate Pub Co.

Beynon, R. J. & Bond, Judith S. Proteolytic Enzymes: A Practical Approach. (Practical Approach Ser.). (Illus.). 278p. 1989. pap. text 50.00 (*0-19-963059-3*) OUP.

Beynon, R. J., ed. see McPherson, M. J. & Moller, S.

Beynon, Rob J., jt. auth. see Munn, R. W.

Beynon, Robert. Routledge Critical Dictionary of Global Economics. LC 98-55077. 416p. 1999. pap. 22.99 (*0-415-92352-2*) Routledge.

***Beyon, Jeffrey Y.** G-programming, Data Acquistion & Analysis With Labview. 300p. 2000. pap. 55.00 (*0-13-030367-4*) P-H.

— Supplementsis with Labview - G-programming, Data Acquistion & Analysis With Labview 1/e: Hands-On Exercise Manual for G-programming, Data Acquision & Analysis With Labview - G-programming, Data Acquistion & Analysis With Labview 1/e. 100p. 2000. cd-rom 29.00 (*0-13-030368-2*) P-H.

Beyond Graphics Staff, ed. see Comstock, Sallyann.

Beyondananda, Swami, pseud. Driving Your Own Karma: Swami Beyondananda's Tour Guide to Enlightenment. LC 89-16769. 128p. 1989. pap. 12.95 (*0-89281-253-2*, Destiny Bks) Inner Tradit.

— Duck Soup for the Soul: The Way of Living Louder & Laughing Longer. 160p. 1999. pap. 9.95 (*1-887166-28-9*, Hysteria Pubns) Sourcebks.

***Beyra M., Angela & Lavin, Matt.** Monograph of Pictetia (Leguminosae-Papilionoideae) & Review of the Aeschynomeneae. Anderson, Christiane, ed. (Systematic Botany Monographs: Vol. 56). (Illus.). 93p. 1999. pap. 13.00 (*0-912861-56-8*) Am Soc Plant.

Beyrer, Mary K. Positive Health: Designs for Action. 2nd ed. LC 76-22769. (Health Education, Physical Education, & Recreation Ser.). 195p. reprint ed. pap. 60.50 (*0-608-13433-3*, 201452500093) Bks Demand.

Beyreuther, Erich & Meyer, Matthias. Georg Heinrich Loskiel. (GER.). 1989. reprint ed. write for info. (*3-487-09243-3*) G Olms Pubs.

Beyreuther, Erich, ed. see Spener, Philipp J.

Beyreuther, K., jt. ed. see Schettler, F. Gotthard.

Beyrle, John R. The Long Good-Bye: The Withdrawal of Russian Military Forces from the Baltic States. (Pew Case Studies in International Affairs). 50p. (C). 1996. text 3.50 (*1-56927-371-5*) Geo U Inst Dplmcy.

Beysade, ed. see Descartes, Rene.

Beysens, D., et al, eds. Dynamical Phenomena at Interfaces: Surfaces & Membranes. 610p. (C). 1993. text 245.00 (*1-56072-089-1*) Nova Sci Pubs.

Beysens, D. & Forgacs, G., eds. Dynamical Networks in Physics & Biology. xxii, 310p. 1999. pap. 89.95 (*3-540-65349-X*) Spr-Verlag.

Beysens, D., et al. Fragmentation Phenomena: Proceedings of the Workshop. 300p. 1995. text 90.00 (*981-02-2259-9*) World Scientific Pub.

— Interplay of Genetic & Physical Processes in the Development of Biological Form. LC 97-106141. (Les Hoches Ser.). 340p. 1995. text 78.00 (*981-02-2374-9*) World Scientific Pub.

Beytagh, Francis X., jt. auth. see Kauper, Paul G.

Beyth-Marom, Ruth, et al. An Elementary Approach to Thinking under Uncertainty. rev. ed. 154p. 1985. text 29.95 (*0-89859-379-4*) L Erlbaum Assocs.

Beytim, Joan F. The First Book of Mezzo-Soprano Solos, Pt. II. 128p. (Orig.). 1993. pap. 10.95 (*0-7935-2495-4*, HL50482065) H Leonard.

Beyton, Cathy. Funny Teddy Bear Stickers. (Illus.). (J). (gr. k-3). 1993. pap. 1.00 (*0-486-27671-6*) Dover.

Beytout, Olivier. Memories of Cuba. (Illus.). 144p. 1998. pap. text 22.95 (*1-56025-182-4*, Thunders Mouth) Avalon NY.

Beyza'i, Bahram, et al. Modern Persian Drama: An Anthology. Yarshater, Ehsan, ed. Kapuscinski, Gisele, tr. (Modern Persian Literature Ser.: No. 8). 248p. (C). 1987. pap. text 24.00 (*0-8191-6579-4*) U Pr of Amer.

Beza, Marcu. Paganism in Roumanian Folklore. LC 74-173102. (Illus.). 172p. 1972. reprint ed. lib. bdg. 17.95 (*0-405-08267-3*, Pub. by Blom Pubns) Ayer.

Beza, Theodore. Bezae Codex Cantabrigiensis: Being an Exact Copy, in Ordinary Type of the Celebrated Uncial Graeco-Latin Manuscript of the Four Gospels & Acts of the Apostles. Scrivener, Frederick H., ed. LC 78-4144. (Pittsburgh Reprint Ser.: No. 5). 1978. pap. 30.00 (*0-915138-39-5*) Pickwick.

— The Life of John Calvin. Sanseri, Gary, ed. Beveridge, Henry, tr. LC 96-84651. (Illus.). 150p. 1996. reprint ed. 19.95 (*1-880045-16-8*) Back Home Indust.

— A Little Book of Christian Questions & Responses in Which the Principal Headings of the Christian Religion Are Briefly Set Forth. Summers, Kirk M., tr. from LAT. LC 86-25583. (Princeton Theological Monographs: No. 9).Tr. of Quaestionum et Responsionum Christianarum Libellus. (Orig.). 1986. pap. 8.00 (*0-915138-91-3*) Pickwick.

***Bezaire, Neil.** First Empty Your Cup: What It Means to Be Human. 147p. 1999. pap. 14.90 (*0-9668453-0-7*) Twin Dolphins Pub.

Bezalel. The Meaning of Biblical Sacrifice. unabridged ed. 280p. 1998. pap. 16.95 (*1-892896-04-4*) Buy Books.

Bezan, Debra, et al. Differential Diagnosis in Primary Eye Care. 496p. 1998. text 85.00 (*0-7506-9462-9*) Buttrwrth-Heinemann.

— Optometric Guide to Surgical Co-Management. LC 92-23818. (Illus.). 118p. 1992. spiral bd. 37.50 (*0-7506-9329-0*) Buttrwrth-Heinemann.

Bezancon, Jean-Noel. A Man Called Jesus. 144p. (C). 1990. 45.00 (*0-85439-334-X*, Pub. by St Paul Pubns) St Mut.

Bezancon, Jean-Noel, et al. How to Understand the Creed. (Adult Christian Formation Program Ser.). (Illus.). 164p. (Orig.). (C). 1988. pap. 14.95 (*0-8245-0868-8*) Crossroad NY.

Bezane, Norm. This Inventive Century. 1994. pap. text 18.95 (*1-55989-580-2*) Underwrtrs Labs.

Bezanson, Mary E., ed. The Right to Communicate Decisions & Dissents: A Supreme Court Reader. LC 93-6015. 486p. (Orig.). (C). 1993. pap. text 39.50 (*0-8191-9301-1*); lib. bdg. 69.50 (*0-8191-9300-3*) U Pr of Amer.

Bezanson, Randall. Speech Stories: How Free Can Speech Be? LC 97-33821. 232p. 1998. pap. text 18.50 (*0-8147-1321-1*) NYU Pr.

Bezanson, Randall P. Speech Stories: How Free Can Speech Be? LC 97-33821. 221p. 1998. text 45.00 (*0-8147-1320-3*) NYU Pr.

— Taxes on Knowledge in America: Exactions on the Press from Colonial Times to the Present. LC 93-44447. 336p. (C). 1994. text 47.50 (*0-8122-3212-7*) U of Pa Pr.

Bezanson, Randall P., et al. Libel Law & the Press: Myth & Reality. LC 86-33579. 1987. 55.00 (*0-02-905870-8*) Free Pr.

Bezanson, Randall P., jt. ed. see Soloski, John.

Bezanson, Walter E., ed. Clarel. annot. ed. (Complete Works of Herman Melville Ser.). 772p. 1959. 29.95 (*0-685-02254-4*) Hendricks House.

Bezar, David D. LAN Times Guide to Telephony. (LAN Times Ser.). 450p. 1995. pap. 34.95 (*0-07-882126-6*) McGraw.

Bezborodova, V. & Ostrikova, O. English-Russian Frequency Dictionary History. 136p. (C). 1984. 35.00 (*0-89771-932-8*, Pub. by Collets) St Mut.

Bezborodova, V. & Ostrikova, O., eds. English-Russian Frequency Dictionary: History. 136p. (C). 1984. 39.00 (*0-7855-5038-0*, Pub. by Collets) St Mut.

***Bezchilbnyk-Butler, Kalyna Z. & Jeffries, J. Joel, eds.** Clinical Handbook of Psychotropic Drugs: Subscription Edition with Quarterly Updates. 9th ed. (Illus.). 240p. 1999. pap. text 89.50 (*0-88937-212-8*) Hogrefe & Huber Pubs.

***Bezchlibnyk-Butler, Kalyna Z. & Jeffries, J. Joel.** Clinical Handbook of Psychotropic Drugs: CD-ROM Version 1.0. 9th ed. 2000. 75.00 (*0-88937-228-4*, 5685448) Hogrefe & Huber Pubs.

***Bezchlibnyk-Butler, Kalyna Z. & Jeffries, J. Joel, eds.** Clinical Handbook of Psychotropic Drugs. 10th rev. ed. 268p. 2000. 49.00 (*0-88937-233-0*); ring bd. 89.50 (*0-88937-234-9*) Hogrefe & Huber Pubs.

Bezdechi, Adrian. Manual & Digital Gymnastics. (Illus.). (Orig.). 1957. pap. 7.95 (*0-9604092-1-1*) Interstate Piano.

— Pianos & Player Pianos: An Informative Guide for Owners & Prospective Buyers. LC 79-318082. (Illus.). 63p. (Orig.). 1979. pap. 10.95 (*0-9604092-0-3*) Interstate Piano.

Bezdek. Czech-English, English-Czech Dictionary of Nuclearing Physics. (CZE & ENG.). 343p. 1985. 29.95 (*0-7859-7462-8*) Fr & Eur.

Bezdek, J. Advances in Artificial Intelligence - Applications & Theory. (Series in Computer Science: Vol. 27). 228p. 1990. text 81.00 (*981-02-0525-2*) World Scientific Pub.

Bezdek, J. C. Pattern Recognition with Fuzzy Objective Function Algorithms. LC 81-4354. (Advanced Applications in Pattern Recognition Ser.). (Illus.). 272p. (C). 1981. text 79.50 (*0-306-40671-3*, Kluwer Plenum) Kluwer Academic.

Bezdek, James C. Analysis of Fuzzy Information: Artificial Intelligence & Decision Systems, Vol. II. 272p. 1987. 149.00 (*0-8493-6297-0*, CRC Reprint) Franklin.

— Analysis of Fuzzy Information Vol. 1: Mathematics & Logic, Vol. I. LC 86-12953. 304p. 1987. 161.00 (*0-8493-6296-2*, QA248, CRC Reprint) Franklin.

— Analysis of Fuzzy Information Vol. 3: Applications in Engineering & Science, Vol. III. LC 86-12953. 304p. 1987. 173.00 (*0-8493-6298-9*, QA248, CRC Reprint) Franklin.

— Fuzzy Models & Algorithms for Pattern Recognition & Image Processing LC 99-27835. (Handbooks of Fuzzy Sets Ser.). 1999. write for info. (*0-7923-8521-7*) Kluwer Academic.

Bezdek, James C., et al, eds. Applications & Science of Neural Networks, Fuzzy Systems & Evolutionary Computation, Vol. 3455. 1998. 80.00 (*0-8194-2910-4*) SPIE.

***Bezdek, James C., et al.** Fuzzy Sets in Approximate Reasoning & Information Systems. LC 99-16664. (Handbooks of Fuzzy Sets). 514p. 1999. write for info. (*0-7923-8584-5*) Kluwer Academic.

Bezdek, Richard H. American Swords & Sword Makers. (Illus.). 648p. 1994. text 79.95 (*0-87364-765-3*) Paladin Pr.

— American Swords & Sword Makers, Vol. II. (Illus.). 376p. 1999. 74.95 (*1-58160-016-X*) Paladin Pr.

***Bezdek, Richard H.** German Swords & Sword Makers: Edged Weapon Makers from the 14th to the 20th Centuries. (Illus.). 248p. 2000. 59.95 (*1-58160-057-7*) Paladin Pr.

Bezdek, Richard H. Swords & Sword Makers of the War of 1812. LC 97-187897. (Illus.). 104p. 1997. text 44.95 (*0-87364-927-3*) Paladin Pr.

Bezdek, Z. English-Czech & Czech-English Dictionary of Nuclear Physics. 344p. (C). 1985. 95.00 (*0-7855-5008-9*, Pub. by Collets) St Mut.

Bezdicek, D. F., et al, eds. Organic Farming: Current Technology & Its Role in a Sustainable Agriculture. (ASA Special Publications: No. 46). 192p. 1984. 8.00 (*0-89118-076-1*) Am Soc Agron.

Bezella, Winfred A. & Ott, Karl O. Introductory Nuclear Reactor Statics. rev. ed. 386p. 1989. 52.00 (*0-89448-033-2*, 350013) Am Nuclear Soc.

Bezem, M. & Groote, J. F., eds. Typed Lambda Calculi & Applications: International Conference on Typed Lambda Calculi & Applications, March 16-18, 1993, Utrecht, The Netherlands, Proceedings. LC 93-21883. (Lecture Notes in Computer Science Ser.: Vol. 664). 1993. 61.95 (*0-387-56517-5*) Spr-Verlag.

Bezemek, Rebecca H., ed. see Eastman, Samuel.

***Bezener, Andy.** Birds of Ontario. (Illus.). 352p. 2000. pap. 19.95 (*1-55105-236-9*) Lone Pine.

Bezener, Andy & Kershaw, Linda J. Rocky Mountain Nature Guide. LC 98-91098. (Illus.). 192p. 1999. pap. 14.95 (*1-55105-178-8*) Lone Pine.

***Bezener, Andy, et al.** Birds of Northern California. (Illus.). 384p. 2000. pap. 19.95 (*1-55105-227-X*) Lone Pine.

Bezener, Andy, jt. auth. see Fisher, Chris.

Bezic, Sandra. Passion to Skate. 176p. 1998. pap. 16.95 (*0-8362-6452-5*) Andrews & McMeel.

***Bezick, Christian J.** Smart Parents, Safe Children - Protect Your Child from the Dangers of Recalled Children's Products & Other Hazards. 169p. 2000. 16.95 (*0-9677001-0-8*) ChildRecall.

Bezier, Pierre. Numerical Control: Mathematics & Applications. LC 70-39230. (Wiley Series in Computing). 256p. reprint ed. 79.40 (*0-8357-9944-1*, 201490000094) Bks Demand.

***Bezigian, Thomas, ed.** The Extrusion Coating Manual. 4th ed. LC 98-53265. 308p. 1999. 110.00 (*0-89852-067-3*) TAPPI.

Bezilla, Michael. The College of Engineering at Penn State: A Century in the Land-Grant Tradition. LC 96-1150. 1996. 25.00 (*0-271-01550-0*) Pa St U Pr.

— Electric Traction on the Pennsylvania Railroad, 1895-1968. LC 79-65858. (Illus.). 1980. 35.00 (*0-271-00241-7*) Pa St U Pr.

Bezilla, Robert. America's Youth: 1977-1988. (Illus.). 320p. 1988. 59.00 (*0-685-24657-4*) GHG Intl Inst.

Bezilla, Robert, jt. auth. see Gallup, George H., Jr.

Bezirgan, Basima Q., jt. ed. see Fernea, Elizabeth W.

Beziven, Jean, jt. auth. see Meyer, Bertrand.

***Bezivin, J. & Muller, P.-A., eds.** The Unified Modeling Language, UML'98: Beyond the Notation: First International Workshop, Mulhouse, France, June 3-4, 1998, Selected Papers. LC 99-38074. (Lecture Notes in Computer Science Ser.: Vol. 1618). ix, 443p. 1999. pap. 73.00 (*3-540-66252-9*) Spr-Verlag.

An Asterisk (*) at the beginning of an entry indicates that the title is appearing for the first time.

Bezkorovainy, Anatoly. Science & Medicine in Imperial Russia. (Illus.). 271p. 1980. pap., spiral bd. 12.00 (*0-9607600-0-8*) Bezkorovainy.

Bezkorovainy, Anatoly, ed. A History of Holy Trinity Russian Orthodox Cathedral of Chicago, 1892-1992. (Illus.). 168p. 1992. 29.95 (*0-9632743-0-9*) H T Russ Ortho Cath.

Bezkorovainy, Anatoly & Miller-Catchpole, Robin. Biochemistry & Physiology of Bifidobacteria. 192p. 1989. lib. bdg. 269.00 (*0-8493-4753-X*, QR82) CRC Pr.

Bezler, P. Piping Benchmark Problems for the Westinghouse AP600 Standardized Plant. 327p. 1997. per. 30.00 (*0-16-062809-1*) USGPO.

Bezmez, Serap. Milet Redhouse Large Portable Dictionary. 1997. pap. text 42.50 (*975-8176-03-X*) MLE Inc.

— Milet Redhouse Smaller Portable Dictionary. 1997. pap. text 17.00 (*975-8176-01-3*) MLE Inc.

Bezner, H. German-English Dictionary of Power Engineering & Automation. 3rd ed. (ENG & GER.). 579p. 1993. 125.00 (*0-7859-8775-4*) Fr & Eur.

Bezner, Heinrich. Dictionary of Power Engineering. 1996. audio compact disk 295.00 (*0-7859-9522-6*) Fr & Eur.

— Dictionary of Power Engineering. 3rd ed. (ENG & GER.). 511p. 1993. 120.00 (*0-7859-8770-3*) Fr & Eur.

— Dictionary of Power Engineering & Automation, Vol. 1. (ENG & GER.). 537p. 1987. 125.00 (*0-8288-0621-7*, M15791) Fr & Eur.

— Dictionary of Power Engineering & Automation, Vol. 2. (ENG & GER.). 545p. 1987. 125.00 (*0-8288-0622-5*, M15792) Fr & Eur.

Bezner, Janet, ed. Physical Therapy Protocols: Guidelines for Rehabilitation. (Illus.). 232p. (C). 1991. pap. text 49.00 (*0-7616-4221-8*) Commun Skill.

Bezner, Kevin. The Tools of Ignorance. 61p. (Orig.). 1997. pap. 10.00 (*0-9633551-3-9*) Cinc Writers Proj.

***Bezner, Kevin.** Wherever. LC 99-90731. 49p. 1999. pap. 12.00 (*0-9633551-7-1*) Cinc Writers Proj.

Bezner, Kevin, jt. auth. see Walzer, Kevin.

***Bezner, Lili Corbus.** Photography & Politics in America: From the New Deal into the Cold War. LC 99-23281. (Illus.). 336p. 1999. 39.95 (*0-8018-6187-X*) Johns Hopkins.

Bezodis, P. A. Spitalfields & Mile End New Town: The Parishes of Christ Church & All Saints & the Liberties of Norton Folgate & the Old Artillery Ground. LC 74-6547. (London County Council. Survey of London Ser.: No. 27). 1957. reprint ed. 84.50 (*0-685-00410-4*) AMS Pr.

Bezold, C. & Knabner, K., eds. Health Care Twenty Ten: Health Care Delivery, Therapies, & Pharmaceutical Industries. LC 93-43683. (Schering Foundation Workshop Ser.: Vol. 8). 1994. 49.00 (*0-387-57373-9*) Spr-Verlag.

Bezold, C., ed. & tr. see Swainson, Charles A.

Bezold, Clement & Olson, Robert L., eds. The Information Millennium: Alternative Futures. 1986. 297.00 (*0-942774-24-8*) Info Indus.

Bezold, Friedrich. Geschichte der Deutschen Reformation. LC 79-149654. (BCL Ser. I). (GER.). reprint ed. 54.50 (*0-404-00797-X*) AMS Pr.

Bezold, G. Protection of Biotechnological Matter: European & German Law. LC 97-213163. 468p. 1997. pap. 125.00 (*3-527-28781-7*, Wiley-VCH) Wiley.

Bezold, Thomas. Zur Messung der Dienstleistungsqualitat: Eine Theoretische und Empirische Studie zur Methodenentwicklung unter Besonderer Berucksichtigung des Ereignisorientierten Ansatzes. (Europaische Hochschulschriften: Reihe 5: Bd. 1932). (GER., Illus.). 288p. 1996. pap. 54.95 (*3-631-30364-5*) P Lang Pubng.

Bezona, jt. auth. see McKeague, Charles P.

Bezooyen, R. Van, see Van Bezooyen, R.

Bezore, Buz, jt. auth. see Waters, Christina.

Bezou, Henry C. Metairie: A Tongue of Land to Pasture. (Illus.). 248p. 1997. pap. 13.95 (*1-56554-279-7*) Pelican.

Bezou, James F., tr. see Goffin, Robert.

Bezruchka, M. D., contrib. by. Nepali for Trekkers: Ninety Minutes of Phrases & Vocabulary. 48p. 1998. pap. 18.95 incl. audio (*0-89886-311-2*) Mountaineers.

Bezruchka, Stephen. Altitude Illness: Prevention & Treatment. (Illus.). 80p. 1994. pap. 6.95 (*0-89886-402-X*) Mountaineers.

— Pocket Doctor: A Passport to Healthy Travel. 3rd ed. LC 98-52801. 96p. 1999. pap. 6.95 (*0-89886-614-6*) Mountaineers.

— The Pocket Doctor: Your Ticket to Good Health While Traveling. 2nd ed. LC 92-19995. (Illus.). 96p. 1992. pap. 4.95 (*0-89886-345-7*) Mountaineers.

— Trekking in Nepal: A Traveler's Guide. 7th ed. LC 97-21915. 384p. 1997. pap. text 16.95 (*0-89886-535-2*) Mountaineers.

Bezrukavnikov, R., et al. Factorizable Sheaves & Quantum Groups. (Lecture Notes in Mathematics Ser.: Vol. 1691). x, 282p. 1998. pap. 49.00 (*3-540-64619-1*) Spr-Verlag.

Bezrukov, Vladislav V. & Frokis, V. V. Aging of the Central Nervous System. (Interdisciplinary Topics in Gerontology Ser.: Vol. 16). (Illus.). 1979. pap. 57.50 (*3-8055-2995-3*) S Karger.

Bezucha, Robert J. The Lyon Uprising of 1834: Social & Political Conflict in the Early July Monarchy. LC 74-75780. (Studies in Urban History). 288p. 1974. 36.50 (*0-674-53965-6*) HUP.

***Bezucha, Robert J.** Nations: Nationality & the European Revolutions of 1848. 2001. pap. 10.95 (*0-312-17217-6*) St Martin.

Bezuidenhout, Jan, jt. auth. see Nel, Francisca.

Bezuidenhout, Jan, jt. ed. see Nel, Francisca.

Bezuidenhout, R. J., jt. auth. see Smuts, Malie M.

Bezuk, Nadine S., jt. auth. see Curcio, Frances R.

Bezuszka, Stanley & Kenney, Margaret J. Wonder-Full World of Numbers. (Contemporary Motivated Mathematics Ser.). 97p. (Orig.). (J). (gr. 3-6). 1971. pap. text 2.50 (*0-917916-05-0*) Boston Coll Math.

Bezuszka, Stanley, et al. Applications of Geometric Series. (Motivated Math Project Activity Booklets). 46p. (Orig.). (YA). (gr. 10-12). 1976. pap. text 2.00 (*0-917916-14-X*) Boston Coll Math.

— Applications of Mathematics Through Models & Formulas. (Motivated Math Project Activity Booklets). 102p. (Orig.). 1987. pap. text 3.50 (*0-317-60037-0*) Boston Coll Math.

— Contemporary Motivated Mathematics, Bk. 1. (Contemporary Motivated Mathematics Ser.). 97p. (Orig.). (J). (gr. 5-8). 1972. pap. text 2.50 (*0-917916-02-6*) Boston Coll Math.

— Contemporary Motivated Mathematics, Bk. 2. 97p. (Orig.). (J). (gr. 6-9). 1973. pap. text 2.50 (*0-917916-03-4*) Boston Coll Math.

— Contemporary Motivated Mathematics, Bk. 3. 97p. (Orig.). (J). (gr. 7-10). 1972. pap. text 2.50 (*0-917916-04-2*) Boston Coll Math.

— Finite Differences. (Motivated Math Project Activity Booklets). 108p. (Orig.). (YA). (gr. 10-12). 1976. pap. text 2.50 (*0-917916-11-5*) Boston Coll Math.

— Fraction Action 1. (Motivated Math Project Activity Booklets). 47p. (Orig.). (J). (gr. 5-8). 1976. pap. text 2.00 (*0-917916-12-3*) Boston Coll Math.

— Fraction Action 2. (Motivated Math Project Activity Booklets). 68p. (Orig.). (YA). (gr. 7-12). 1976. pap. text 2.00 (*0-917916-13-1*) Boston Coll Math.

— Perfect Numbers. (Motivated Math Project Activity Booklets). 169p. (Orig.). (YA). (gr. 7-12). 1980. pap. text 3.50 (*0-917916-19-0*) Boston Coll Math.

— Wonder Square. (Motivated Math Project Activity Booklets). 30p. (Orig.). (YA). (gr. 6-12). 1976. pap. text 1.25 (*0-917916-15-8*) Boston Coll Math.

— Word Problems for Calculator & Computer. (Motivated Math Project Activity Booklets). 250p. (Orig.). 1985. pap. text 4.50 (*0-317-39752-4*) Boston Coll Math.

— Word Problems for Maxima & Minima. (Motivated Math Project Activity Booklets). 96p. (Orig.). 1984. pap. text 4.50 (*0-917916-20-4*) Boston Coll Math.

Bezwinska, J. & Czech, Danuta, eds. Amidst a Nightmare of Crime: Manuscripts of Prisoners in Crematorium Squads Found at Auschwitz. Michalik, K., tr. from POL. LC 91-24978. 207p. 1992. reprint ed. lib. bdg. 35.00 (*0-86527-404-5*) Fertig.

— KL Auschwitz Seen by the SS. FitzGibbon, Constantine & Michalik, K., trs. from GER. LC 83-16512. (Illus.). 331p. 1984. reprint ed. 44.00 (*0-86527-346-4*) Fertig.

Bezy, John. Bryce Canyon: The Story Behind the Scenery. LC 79-93079. (Illus.). 48p. (Orig.). 1980. pap. 7.95 (*0-916122-69-7*) KC Pubns.

Bezy, John V., jt. ed. see Sanchez, Joseph P.

Bezzant, Norman, jt. auth. see Burroughs, David.

Bezzerides, A. I. Thieves' Market. LC 97-18530. 250p. 1998. pap. 13.95 (*0-520-20746-7*, Pub. by U CA Pr) Cal Prin Full Svc.

Bezzola, Tobia. Max Beckmann & Paris: The Exhibition Catalogue. (Jumbo Ser.). 1998. 39.99 (*3-8228-7203-2*) Taschen Amer.

Bezzola, Tobia, et al. Max Beckmann & Paris. (Illus.). 240p. 1998. 39.95 (*0-89178-076-9*) St Louis Art Mus.

BFA Staff, et al. Making the Money Last: Financial Clarity for the Surviving Spouse. limited ed. 288p. 1996. pap. text, per. 29.95 (*0-7872-2172-4*) Kendall-Hunt.

BG Chemie Staff. Toxicological Evaluations Vol. 4: Potential Health Hazards of Existing Chemicals. (Illus.). 336p. 1992. 62.95 (*0-387-54984-6*) Spr-Verlag.

BG Chemie Staff, ed. Toxicological Evaluations Vol. 7: Potential Health Hazards of Existing Chemicals. 205p. 1994. 62.95 (*0-387-57300-3*) Spr-Verlag.

BGA Staff & Doyle, Bryan. Consumers' Guide to Long Term Health Care Facilities, 3 vols., Set. 2nd ed. (Illus.). 200p. 1994. pap. 25.00 (*0-9641280-0-4*) Better Government.

BGU (Jackson) Staff. Hounds of the Road. 224p. 1984. per., boxed set 29.95 (*0-8403-3235-1*) Kendall-Hunt.

Bh/Update. The GP Registrar Handbook. 80p. pap. text 34.00 (*0-7506-4252-1*) Buttrwrth-Heinemann.

Bhabha, Homi. Anish Kapoor. LC 98-204454. (Illus.). 120p. 1998. 35.00 (*0-520-21741-1*, Pub. by U CA Pr) Cal Prin Full Svc.

Bhabha, Homi K. Nation & Narration. 352p. (C). (gr. 13). 1990. pap. 20.99 (*0-415-01483-2*) Routledge.

Bhabuta, Love & Maddison, R. N. Information System Methodologies. LC 83-16684. (Monographs in Informatics). 138p. reprint ed. pap. 42.80 (*0-608-17859-4*, 203267900080) Bks Demand.

Bhacca, Norman S. & William, Dudley H. Applications of NMR Spectroscopy in Organic Chemistry: Illustrations from the Steroid Field. LC 64-25659. (Holden-Day Series in Physical Techniques in Chemistry). 208p. reprint ed. pap. 64.50 (*0-8357-5670-X*, 201628500005) Bks Demand.

Bhachu, Parminder. Twice Migrants: East African Sikh Settlers in Britain. 256p. 1986. text 35.00 (*0-422-78910-0*, 9773, Pub. by Tavistock) Routldge.

Bhadauria, Mridula. Women in India: Some Issues. xii, 160p. 1998. 23.00 (*81-7024-875-2*, Pub. by Ashish Pub Hse) Nataraj Bks.

Bhadeshia, H. K. Bainite in Steels. 400p. 1992. 50.00 (*0-901462-95-0*, Pub. by Inst Materials) Ashgate Pub Co.

Bhadeshia, H. K. Worked Examples in Geometry of Crystals. 1987. 28.00 (*0-904357-94-5*) Institute of Management Consultants.

Bhadeshia, H. K., jt. ed. see Cerjak, H.

Bhadeshia, H. K. D. H., jt. ed. see Pullan, Wendy.

Bhadha, Homi K. The Location of Culture. LC 93-10757. 288p. (C). (gr. 13). 1994. pap. 22.99 (*0-415-05406-0*, A4760) Routledge.

Bhadouria, G. S. Women in Indian Art. (C). 1995. 72.00 (*81-7320-024-6*, Pub. by Agam Kala Prakashan) S Asia.

Bhadra, Bipul K. The Political Sociology of C. Wright Millas. 1989. 23.50 (*81-85195-24-2*, Pub. by Minerva) S Asia.

Bhadra, Gautam, et al, eds. Subaltern Studies: Writings on South Asian History & Society, Vol. X. 264p. 1999. 29.95 (*0-19-564570-7*) OUP.

Bhadra, Madhumit. Sikkim: Democracy & Social Change. (C). 1992. 16.00 (*81-85195-45-5*, Pub. by Abhinav) S Asia.

Bhadra, Mita. Women Workers of Tea Plantations in India. (C). 1992. 20.00 (*81-7026-172-4*, Pub. by Heritage IA) S Asia.

Bhadra, R. K. & Mondal, Sekh R., eds. Stratification, Hierarchy & Ethnicity in Northeast India. (C). 1991. 30.00 (*81-7035-086-7*, Pub. by Daya Pub Hse) S Asia.

Bhadshia, H., jt. auth. see Honeycombe, Robert.

Bhaduri. Mundari-English Dictionary. (ENG.). 228p. 1983. 24.95 (*0-7859-7463-6*) Fr & Eur.

Bhaduri, Amit. Macroeconomics: The Dynamics of Commodity Production. LC 85-18249. (Illus.). 290p. (Orig.). 1986. reprint ed. pap. 89.90 (*0-7837-9930-6*, 206065700006) Bks Demand.

***Bhaduri, Amit.** On the Border of Economic Theory & History. (Illus.). 204p. 2000. text 27.50 (*0-19-564901-X*) OUP.

Bhaduri, Amit. Unconventional Economic Essays: Selected Papers of Amit Bhaduri. 288p. (C). 1993. 29.95 (*0-19-563005-X*, 14452) OUP.

Bhaduri, Amit & Skarstein, Rune, eds. Economic Development & Agricultural Productivity. LC 97-14365. (Centre for Environment & Development, Norwegian University of Science & Technology 1997 Ser.). 304p. (C). 1997. text 90.00 (*1-85898-615-X*) E Elgar.

Bhaduri, Rajat K. Semiclassical Methods in Mean-Field Systems. LC 97-166776. (C). 1997. 61.00 (*0-201-48351-3*) Addison-Wesley.

Bhaduri, Sumit & Mukesh, Doble. Homogeneous Homogeneous Catalysis: Mechanisms & Industrial Applications. LC 99-45532. 224p. 2000. text 79.95 (*0-471-37221-8*) Wiley.

***Bhadury, Bikash.** Managing the Workforce: Challenges in the Manufacturing Industry. LC 00-33274. 2000. pap. write for info. (*0-7619-9414-9*) Pine Forge.

Bhadury, Bikash, jt. ed. see Shenoy, Dinesh.

Bhaerman, Robert, et al. The Role of Service-Learning in Educational Reform. LC 97-67379. 128p. (C). 1998. pap. text 17.95 (*0-536-01028-5*) Pearson Custom.

Bhaerman, Robert D. Integrating Education, Health, & Social Sources in Rural Communities: Service Integration Through the Rural Prism. (Orig.). 1994. pap. text 23.99 (*1-56602-058-1*) Research Better.

— Planning for Adult Career Counseling. 64p. 1985. 6.25 (*0-318-17845-1*, IN 290) Ctr Educ Trng Employ.

Bhaerman, Steve & Denker, Joel. No Particular Place to Go: The Making of a Free High School. LC 81-18248. 263p. (Orig.). 1982. pap. 14.95 (*0-8093-1056-2*) S Ill U Pr.

Bhaerman, Steve, see Beyondananda, Swami, pseud.

Bhaerman, Steve, jt. auth. see Cole, Raymond.

Bhagat, Anjana K. Elections & Electoral Reforms in India. LC 95-911593. (C). 1996. 32.00 (*0-7069-9127-3*, Pub. by Vikas) S Asia.

Bhagat, B. My Kind of Kathmandu. 1994. pap. 310.50 (*0-7855-0461-3*, Pub. by Ratna Pustak Bhandar) St Mut.

Bhagat, Budh D. Mode of Action of Autonomic Drugs. LC 78-58696. (Illus.). 170p. 1979. text 32.95 (*0-932126-00-6*); pap. text 29.50 (*0-932126-01-4*) Graceway.

Bhagat, Ekha. Mass Media & Farm Women. (C). 1989. 12.75 (*81-7076-019-4*, Pub. by Intellectual) S Asia.

Bhagat, R. C., jt. auth. see Fotedar, D. N.

Bhagat, Rabi, jt. ed. see Landis, Dan.

Bhagat, Ram B., ed. Damping of Multiphase Inorganic Materials: Proceedings of the Damping of Multiphase Inorganic Materials Symposium, ASM Materials Week, Held November 2-5, 1992, in Chicago, IL. LC 92-76076. (Illus.). 197p. 1993. reprint ed. pap. 61.10 (*0-608-02621-2*, 206327900004) Bks Demand.

Bhagat, Ram B., et al, eds. Mechanisms & Mechanics of Composites Fracture: Proceedings of ASM 1993 Materials Congress Materials Week '93 Held October 17-21, 1993, Pittsburgh, PA. LC 93-73754. (Illus.). 264p. 1993. reprint ed. pap. 81.90 (*0-608-02642-5*, 206330000004) Bks Demand.

Bhagat, Ram B., ed. see Minerals, Metals & Materials Society Staff.

Bhagat, Shantilal P. Creation in Crisis: Responding to God's Covenant. LC 90-45512. 173p. (Orig.). reprint ed. pap. 53.70 (*0-608-04168-8*, 206490200011) Bks Demand.

— The Family Farm, Can It Be Saved? LC 85-180076. 75p. 1985. reprint ed. pap. 30.00 (*0-608-02152-0*, 206282100004) Bks Demand.

Bhagat, Shantilal P., et al. What Does It Profit...? Christian Dialogue on the U. S. Economy. LC 83-3687. 144p. (Orig.). 1983. reprint ed. pap. 44.70 (*0-608-02153-9*, 206282200004) Bks Demand.

Bhagavad-Gita. The Song of God. Prabhavananda, Swami & Isherwood, Christopher, trs. 1954. mass mkt. 5.99 (*0-451-62757-1*, Ment) NAL.

Bhagavan. Energy Management in Africa, Vol. 1. 1992. pap. text 25.00 (*1-85649-052-1*, Pub. by Zed Books) St Martin.

Bhagavan, M. R. Performing the Power Sector in Africa. 1999. pap. text 29.95 (*1-85649-668-6*) Zed Books.

— Petroleum Marketing in Africa: Issues in Pricing, Taxation & Investment. (Illus.). 192p. 1999. pap. 25.00 (*1-85649-666-X*); text 59.95 (*1-85649-665-1*) St Martin.

— Reforming the Power Sector in Africa. 1999. 69.95 (*1-85649-667-8*, Pub. by Zed Books) St Martin.

— Technological Transformation in the Third World: Strategies & Prospects. LC 88-2682. 128p. (C). 1990. pap. 17.50 (*0-86232-813-6*, Pub. by Zed Books); text 49.95 (*0-86232-812-8*, Pub. by Zed Books) St Martin.

Bhagavan, M. R. & Sweden. New Generic Technologies in Developing Countries. LC 97-11909. 1997. text 79.95 (*0-312-17643-0*) St Martin.

Bhagavan, M. R., ed. see Ali, G. Elfaki, et al.

Bhagavan, M. R., ed. see Baguant, J. & Teferra, M.

Bhagavan, Malur R. Angola: Prospects for Socialist Industrialisation. (Research Report Ser.: No. 57). 48p. 1980. write for info. (*91-7106-175-4*, Pub. by Nordic Africa) Transaction Pubs.

— Angola's Political Economy, 1975-1985. (Research Report Ser.: No. 75). 89p. 1986. write for info. (*91-7106-248-3*, Pub. by Nordic Africa) Transaction Pubs.

— A Critique of "Appropriate" Technology for Underdeveloped Countries. (Research Report Ser.: No. 48). 56p. 1979. write for info. (*91-7106-150-9*, Pub. by Nordic Africa) Transaction Pubs.

— The Energy Sector in the SADCC Countries: Policies, Priorities & Options in the Context of the African Crisis. (Research Report Ser.: No. 74). 42p. 1985. write for info. (*91-7106-240-8*, Pub. by Nordic Africa) Transaction Pubs.

— Inter-Relations Between Technological Choices & Industrial Strategies in Third World Countries. (Research Report Ser.: No. 49). 79p. 1979. write for info. (*91-7106-151-7*, Pub. by Nordic Africa) Transaction Pubs.

— Zambia: Impact of Industrial Strategy on Regional Imbalance & Social Inequality. (Research Report Ser.: No. 44). 76p. 1978. write for info. (*91-7106-119-3*, Pub. by Nordic Africa) Transaction Pubs.

Bhagavan, N. V. Medical Biochemistry. 992p. (C). 1992. 70.00 (*0-86720-030-8*) Jones & Bartlett.

***Bhagavan, Nadhipuram V.** Medical Biochemistry. 2nd ed. 960p. 2000. 79.95 (*0-12-095440-0*) Acad Pr.

Bhagavat Simhaji. A Short History of Aryan Medical Science. LC 75-23683. reprint ed. 45.00 (*0-404-13236-7*) AMS Pr.

Bhagavatam. Bhagavata, Srimad, 4. Tapasyananda, tr. from SAN. 1983. 21.00 (*0-87481-519-3*, Pub. by Ramakrishna Math) Vedanta Pr.

— Bhagavata, Srimad, Vol. 1. Tapasyananda, tr. from SAN. 455p. 1983. 21.00 (*0-87481-516-9*, Pub. by Ramakrishna Math) Vedanta Pr.

— Bhagavata, Srimad, Vol. 2. Tapasyananda, tr. from SAN. 492p. 1983. 21.00 (*0-87481-517-7*, Pub. by Ramakrishna Math) Vedanta Pr.

— Bhagavata, Srimad, Vol. 3. Tapasyananda, tr. from SAN. 447p. 1983. 21.00 (*0-87481-518-5*, Pub. by Ramakrishna Math) Vedanta Pr.

— Srimad Bhagavatam: The Wisdom of God. Prabhavananda, Swami, tr. from SAN. 329p. 1979. pap. 5.95 (*0-87481-490-1*, Pub. by Ramakrishna Math) Vedanta Pr.

Bhagavatam, tr. see Puri, Vishnu.

Bhagowalia, Urmila. Vaisnavism & Society in Northern India. 1980. 22.00 (*0-8364-0664-8*, Pub. by Intellectual) S Asia.

Bhagwandin, Annie. The Chestnut Cookbook: Recipes, Folklore & Practical Information Regarding the Most Diverse of Culinary Nuts. LC 94-65681. (Illus.). 128p. (Orig.). 1996. pap. 9.95 (*0-9648296-0-6*) Shady Grve Pubns.

Bhagwat, Ramachandra K., tr. see Jnanadeva, Sri.

Bhagwat, Ramachandra K., tr. see Juanadeva, Sri.

Bhagwati, Jadish N. A Stream of Windows: Unsettling Reflections on Trade, Immigration, & Democracy. LC 97-35314. (Illus.). 372p. 1998. 32.50 (*0-262-02440-3*) MIT Pr.

Bhagwati, Jagdish. Free Trade, 'Fairness' & the New Protectionism: Reflections on an Agenda for the World Trade Organisation. (IEA Occasional Paper Ser.: No. 96). 43p. 1995. pap. 11.95 (*0-255-36346-X*, Pub. by Inst Economic Affairs) Coronet Bks.

— A Streams of Windows: Unsettling Reflections on Trade, Immigration & Democracy. (Illus.). 592p. 1999. reprint ed. pap. 18.95 (*0-262-52265-9*) MIT Pr.

— Writing on International Economics. Balasubramanyam, V. N., ed. (Illus.). 628p. 1999. pap. text 21.00 (*0-19-564755-6*) OUP.

Bhagwati, Jagdish, et al, eds. Trading Blocs: Alternative Approaches to Analyzing Preferential Trade Agreements. LC 98-30485. (Illus.). 576p. 1999. 55.00 (*0-262-02450-0*) MIT Pr.

Bhagwati, Jagdish N. Anatomy & Consequences of Exchange Control Regimes. LC 78-18799. (National Bureau of Economic Research Ser.). 252p. 1978. reprint ed. pap. 78.20 (*0-8357-5460-X*, 202623700049) Bks Demand.

— Dependence & Independence. Grossmen, Gene M., ed. 1985. 49.50 (*0-262-02230-3*) MIT Pr.

— Essays in Developmental Economics: Wealth & Poverty. Grossmen, Gene M., ed. 1985. 49.50 (*0-262-02229-X*) MIT Pr.

— Essays in International Economic Theory Vol. 2: The International Factor Mobility. Feenstra, Robert, ed. 576p. 1986. reprint ed. pap. text 18.50 (*0-262-52121-0*) MIT Pr.

— Illegal Transactions in International Trade: Theory & Measurement. LC 73-88164. (Studies in International Economics: Vol. 1). 208p. 1975. pap. 20.50 (*0-444-10883-1*, North Holland) Elsevier.

B

— India in Transition: Freeing the Economy. LC 93-16303. (Illus.). 120p. 1993. text 32.00 (*0-19-828816-6*); pap. text 16.95 (*0-19-828847-6*) OUP.

— Political Economy & International Economics. (Illus.). 490p. 1991. 49.95 (*0-262-02322-9*) MIT Pr.

— Political Economy & International Economics. (Illus.). 576p. 1996. pap. text 29.00 (*0-262-52218-7*) MIT Pr.

— Protectionism. (Illus.). 168p. 1988. 30.00 (*0-262-02282-6*) MIT Pr.

— Protectionism. (Ohlin Lectures). 168p. 1989. reprint ed. pap. text 15.00 (*0-262-52150-4*) MIT Pr.

Bhagwati, Jagdish N., ed. The Brain Drain & Income Taxation. 1977. pap. text 16.25 (*0-08-020600-X*, Pergamon Pr) Elsevier.

— Import Competition & Response. LC 81-21831. (National Bureau of Economic Research Conference Report Ser.). (Illus.). 352p. (C). 1982. pap. text 18.00 (*0-226-04539-0*); lib. bdg. 43.50 (*0-226-04538-2*) U Ch Pr.

— International Trade: Selected Readings. 2nd ed. 448p. 1987. 54.00 (*0-262-02264-8*); pap. text 27.00 (*0-262-52119-9*) MIT Pr.

Bhagwati, Jagdish N. & Hirsch, Mathias, eds. Uruguay Round & Beyond: Essays in Honor of Arthur Dunkel. LC 98-23020. (Studies in International Economics & Institutions). (Illus.). xvi, 320p. 1998. 83.50 (*3-540-64461-X*) Spr-Verlag.

— The Uruguay Round & Beyond: Essays in Honor of Arthur Dunkel. LC 98-20651. (Studies in International Economics). 320p. 1998. text 70.00 (*0-472-10980-4*, 10980) U of Mich Pr.

***Bhagwati, Jagdish N. & Hirsch, Mathias, eds.** The Uruguay Round & Beyond: Essays in Honor of Arthur Dunkel. (Studies in International Economics). 320p. (C). 1999. pap. text 29.95 (*0-472-08647-2*, 08647) U of Mich Pr.

Bhagwati, Jagdish N. & Hudec, Robert E., eds. Fair Trade & Harmonization Vol. 1: Prerequisites for Free Trade? Economic Analysis. (Illus.). 608p. 1996. 71.50 (*0-262-02401-2*) MIT Pr.

— Fair Trade & Harmonization Vol. 2: Prerequisites for Free Trade? Economic Analysis. (Illus.). 460p. 1996. 71.50 (*0-262-02402-0*) MIT Pr.

Bhagwati, Jagdish N. & Ruggie, John G., eds. Power, Passions & Purpose: Prospects for North-South Negotiations. (Illus.). 360p. (Orig.). (C). 1984. 37.50 (*0-262-02201-X*); pap. text 18.50 (*0-262-52091-5*) MIT Pr.

Bhagwati, Jagdish N. & Srinivasan, T. N. India. LC 74-82374. (Foreign Trade Regimes & Economic Development Ser.: No. 6). (Illus.). 287p. reprint ed. pap. 89.00 (*0-8357-7578-X*, 205689900096) Bks Demand.

— India. (Special Conference Series on Foreign Trade Regimes & Economic Development: No. 6). 287p. 1975. reprint ed. 74.70 (*0-87014-531-2*) Natl Bur Econ Res.

— Lectures on International Trade. LC 82-18030. (Illus.). 464p. 1983. 49.50 (*0-262-02185-4*) MIT Pr.

Bhagwati, Jagdish N. & Wilson, John D., eds. Income Taxation & International Mobility. 256p. 1989. 35.00 (*0-262-02292-3*) MIT Pr.

Bhagwati, Jagdish N., et al. Lectures on International Trade. 2nd ed. LC 98-10303. (Illus.). 675p. 1998. 55.00 (*0-262-02443-8*) MIT Pr.

Bhagwati, Jagdish N., jt. auth. see Panagariya, Arvind.

Bhagyalakshmi, S., jt. ed. see Krishnananda, Swami.

Bhagyalekshmy, Z. S. Music & Bharathanatyam. (C). 1991. 54.00 (*81-85067-63-5*, Pub. by Sundeep Prak) S Asia.

Bhagyavathi, N. E. Growing from Within: A Study in Self-Actualization. 1991. text 25.00 (*81-85218-30-7*) Advent Bks Div.

Bhai, L. Thara. Changing Patterns of Caste & Class Relations in South India: Social Stratification & Social Mobility. 215p. 1987. 13.00 (*81-212-0087-3*, Pub. by Gian Publng Hse) S Asia.

***Bhairavan, Amarananda.** Kali's Odyya--A Shaman's True Story of Initiation. (Illus.). 288p. 2000. pap. 19.95 (*0-89254-048-6*, Pub. by Nicolas-Hays) Weiser.

Bhaird, Laoiseach Mac An. Cutting down an Ancient Tree: Seventeenth Century. McCormick, Malachi, ed. & tr. by. (Miniatures Ser.). 24p. pap. 7.00 (*0-943984-47-5*) Stone St Pr.

Bhaird, Laoiseach Macan. Cutting Down an Ancient Tree: Seventeenth Century. McCormick, Malachi, ed. & tr. by. 24p. 1989. 7.00 (*0-943984-36-X*) Stone St Pr.

Bhajan, Yogi. The Master's Touch: On Being a Sacred Teacher for the New Age. LC 97-73614. (Illus.). x, 400p. (Orig.). 1997. pap. write for info. (*0-9639991-1-7*) KRI.

— Owner's Manual. Khalsa, Hari J., ed. & illus. by. 50p. 1995. pap. 14.95 (*0-9639847-0-5*) KRI.

— Owner's Manual for the Human Body: Kundalini Yoga As Taught by Yogi Bhajan. (Illus.). iv, 49p. (Orig.). 1997. reprint ed. spiral bd. write for info. (*0-9639991-0-9*) KRI.

— Physical Wisdom. Khalsa, Hari J., ed. & illus. by. 50p. (Orig.). 1995. pap. 14.95 (*0-9639847-1-3*) KRI.

— Physical Wisdom: Kundalini Yoga As Taught by Yogi Bhajan. (Illus.). x, 50p. 1997. reprint ed. spiral bd. write for info. (*0-9639991-2-5*) KRI.

— Self Knowledge: Kundalis Yoga As Taught by Yogi Bhajan. rev. ed. Kaur Klalsa, Harijot, tr. & illus. by. x, 49p. 1998. spiral bd. 16.95 (*0-9639991-3-3*) KRI.

— Seventy-Two Stories of God, Good, & Goods. Khalsa, Tej K., ed. (Illus.). 241p. (Orig.). (YA). (gr. 10). 1989. pap. 9.95 (*0-685-29452-8*) Harimander Pub.

Bhajan, Yogi & Khalsa, Gurucharan S. The Mind: Its Properties & Multiple Facets. Khalsa, Sat K., ed. (Illus.). 224p. 1998. pap. 19.95 (*0-9639991-6-8*) KRI.

Bhajan, Yogi, jt. auth. see Khalsa, Gurucharan Singh.

***Bhakta, Amal.** Mystical Stories from the Bhagavatam: Twenty Timeless Lessons in Self-Discovery. (Illus.). 224p. 2000. 18.95 (*1-887089-27-6*, Pub. by Torchlght Pub) Natl Bk Netwk.

— Mystical Stories from the Mahabharata: Twenty Timeless Lessons in Wisdom & Virtue. LC 99-53807. (Illus.). 264p. 2000. 17.95 (*1-887089-19-5*, Pub. by Torchlght Pub) Natl Bk Netwk.

Bhakta, Ragini J. Ragini's Vegetarian Cuisine Cookbooks. 2nd ed. Collier, Jan & Johnson, Jim, eds. (Illus.). 56p. 1998. reprint ed. pap. 9.99 (*0-9672815-9-8*) Ragini Veg.

Bhakta Vishita, Swami. Genuine Mediumship. reprint ed. 15.00 (*0-911662-34-0*) Yoga.

— Seership. reprint ed. 15.00 (*0-911662-33-2*) Yoga.

Bhakti, Krishna, tr. see Siddheswarananda, Swami.

Bhakti, Sara. The Goldfish Story: And Other Teaching Tales. 60p. (Orig.). 1993. pap. 7.00 (*0-9630514-1-5*) Gaea Pubs.

Bhakti, Sara. Listening with the Heart & Other Communication Skills. 60p. (Orig.). 1997. pap. 7.00 (*0-9630514-2-3*) Gaea Pubs.

***Bhaktisiddhanta.** Art Treasures of the Mahabharata: Illustrated Stories & Relief Sculpture Depicting India's Greatest Spiritual Epic. LC 99-54622. (Illus.). 80p. 2000. 22.95 (*1-887089-21-7*, Pub. by Torchlght Pub) Natl Bk Netwk.

Bhaktivedanta, A. C. In Search of the Ultimate Goal of Life: Sri Ramananda Samvada. (Illus.). 128p. 1999. 12.95 (*1-886069-04-2*, Pub. by Mandala Pub Grp) Bookpeople.

Bhaktivedanta, A. C. The Laws of Nature: An Infallible Justice. 121p. 1991. pap. 7.95 (*0-89213-328-7*) Bhaktivedanta.

Bhaktivedanta, A. C. The Science of Self-Realization. (Illus.). 412p. 1997. 9.95 (*0-89213-286-8*) Bhaktivedanta.

Bhaktivedanta, A. C. & Prabhupada. Dharma: The Way of Transcendence. (Illus.). 145p. 1998. 9.95 (*0-89213-326-0*) Bhaktivedanta.

— Narada Bhakti Sutra: The Secrets of Transcendental Love. 2nd ed. 213p. 1991. reprint ed. pap. 7.95 (*0-89213-273-6*) Bhaktivedanta.

Bhaktivedanta Prabhupada, A. C. Krishna Consciousness: The Matchless Gift. LC 73-76634. (Illus.). 118p. (YA). 1996. pap. 1.95 (*0-912776-61-7*) Bhaktivedanta.

Bhaktivedanta, Swami A. C. Life Comes from Life. 140p. 1979. reprint ed. pap. 2.95 (*0-89213-100-4*) Bhaktivedanta.

***Bhaktivedanta Swami Prabhupada, A. C.** Beyond Illusion & Doubt: A Vedic View of Western Philosophy. (Illus.). 269p. (C). 1999. 9.95 (*0-89213-336-8*) Bhaktivedanta.

Bhala, Rah. International Trade Law. 1450p. 1996. text 62.00 (*1-55834-310-5*, 10617-10, MICHIE) LEXIS Pub.

Bhala, Raj. International Trade Law: Cases & Materials. (Contemporary Legal Education Ser.). 1996. pap. 25.00 (*1-55834-374-1*) LEXIS Pub.

Bhala, Raj. The Law of Foreign Exchange. LC 97-5051. 572p. 1997. 60.00 (*0-89089-682-8*) Carolina Acad Pr.

Bhala, Raj & Frisch, David. Global Business Law: Principles & Practice. LC 99-22352. 1184p. 1999. boxed set 80.00 (*0-89089-683-6*) Carolina Acad Pr.

***Bhala, Raj & Kennedy, Kevin.** World Trade Law: The GATT-WTO System, Regional Arrangements, & U.S. Law. LC 98-65392. 1381p. 1998. write for info. (*1-55834-881-6*) LEXIS Pub.

Bhala, Raj & Kennedy, Kevin. World Trade Law, 1999 Supplement. 395p. 1999. pap., suppl. ed. write for info. (*0-327-01061-4*, 6074410) LEXIS Pub.

Bhala, Raj K. Foreign Bank Regulation after BCCI. LC 94-72117. 346p. (C). 1994. lib. bdg. 49.95 (*0-89089-602-X*) Carolina Acad Pr.

— Towards a Payments System Law for Developing & Transition Economies. LC 95-37718. (Discussion Papers: Vol. 299). 42p. 1995. 7.95 (*0-8213-3438-7*, 13438) Wrld Bank.

Bhalla, A., ed. Ferroelectric Materials & Their Applications to Sensors. x, 390p. 1988. pap. text 1094.00 (*2-88124-337-1*) Gordon & Breach.

Bhalla, A. A., ed. Technology & Employment in Industry: A Case Study Approach. enl. rev. ed. xviii, 436p. 1985. 40.50 (*92-2-103969-2*) Intl Labour Office.

— Technology & Employment in Industry: A Case Study Approach. 3rd enl. rev. ed. xviii, 436p. 1985. pap. 33.75 (*92-2-103970-6*) Intl Labour Office.

Bhalla, A. K. & Williams, P. L. Dictionnaire Illustre de Rhumathologie. (FRE.). 352p. 1990. 150.00 (*0-8288-9535-X*) Fr & Eur.

Bhalla, A. S. Facing the Technological Challenge. 1996. text 69.95 (*0-312-12901-7*) St Martin.

Bhalla, A. S., ed. Environment, Employment & Development: A WEP Study. v, 177p. (Orig.). 1992. pap. 22.50 (*92-2-108250-4*) Intl Labour Office.

— Small & Medium Enterprises: Technology Policies & Options, 124. LC 91-11403. (Contributions in Economics & Economic History Ser.: No. 124). 296p. 1991. 69.50 (*0-313-27594-7*, BHV, Greenwood Pr) Greenwood.

Bhalla, A. S., et al, eds. Ferroic Materials: Design, Preparation & Characteristics. LC 94-27689. (Ceramic Transactions Ser.: Vol. 43). 428p. 1994. 88.00 (*0-944904-77-7*, CT043) Am Ceramic.

Bhalla, A. S., intro. Small-Scale Processing of Beef. (Technical Memorandum, Technology Ser.: No. 10). vi, 121p. (Orig.). 1985. pap. 18.00 (*92-2-105050-5*) Intl Labour Office.

***Bhalla, A. S. & Lapeyre, Frederic.** Poverty & Exclusion in a Global World. LC 98-38452. 256p. 1999. text 65.00 (*0-312-21825-7*) St Martin.

Bhalla, A. S. & Subbarao, E. C., eds. Proceedings of Indo-United States Workshop on Electronic Ceramics & Materials: A Special Issue of the Journal Ferroelectrics. 414p. 1990. pap. text 899.00 (*2-88124-430-0*) Gordon & Breach.

Bhalla, A. S., jt. ed. see Nair, K. M.

Bhalla, Alok. Stories about the Partition of India. (C). 1995. 24.00 (*81-7223-156-3*, Pub. by Indus Pub) S Asia.

— Stories about the Partition of India, Vol. I. (C). 1994. 19.00 (*81-7223-119-9*, Pub. by Indus Pub) S Asia.

— Stories about the Partition of India, Vol. II. (C). 1994. text 9.00 (*81-7223-120-2*, Pub. by Indus Pub) S Asia.

Bhalla, Alok, ed. Life & Works of Saadat Hasan Manto. LC 97-913701. xii, 219p. 1997. 20.00 (*81-85952-48-5*, Pub. by Indian Inst) Nataraj Bks.

— Yatra, No. 5. (C). 1995. pap. 17.50 (*81-7223-188-1*, Pub. by Indus Pub) S Asia.

Bhalla, Alok, et al, eds. Yatra 4. (C). 1994. pap. text 12.50 (*81-7223-160-1*, Pub. by Indus Pub) S Asia.

— Yatra 3. (C). 1994. pap. text 12.50 (*81-7223-148-2*, Pub. by Indus Pub) S Asia.

Bhalla, Alok, tr. see Kumar, Ram.

Bhalla, G. S., et al. Agricultural Growth & Structural Changes in the Punjab. 119p. 1990. 10.00 (*0-89629-085-9*) Intl Food Policy.

Bhalla, Happy. Relaxed Intensity Vol. 1: Transforming the Competitive Experiences. 100p. 1998. pap. 16.00 (*0-939713-08-X*) Carriage House.

Bhalla, J. S., et al, eds. India Nation-State & Communalism. (C). 1989. 20.00 (*81-7050-101-6*, Pub. by Patriot Pubs) S Asia.

Bhalla, R. S. The Institution of Property: Legally, Historically & Philosophically Regarded. (C). 1989. 80.00 (*0-89771-767-8*, Pub. by Eastern Book) St Mut.

— The Institution of Property: Legally, Historically & Philosophically Regarded. 216p. 1984. 240.00 (*0-7855-1410-4*) St Mut.

— The Institution of Property: Legally, Historically & Philosophically Regarded. (C). 1984. 80.00 (*0-7855-5442-4*) St Mut.

Bhalla, R. S., ed. The Institution of Property. (C). 1984. 90.00 (*0-7855-4708-8*) St Mut.

Bhalla, S. I. Fundamentals of International Law. (C). 1990. 115.00 (*0-89771-313-3*) St Mut.

Bhalla, Sarab, jt. auth. see Levine, Jason.

Bhalla, Subhash, ed. Information Systems & Data Management: 6th International Conference, CISMOD 95, Bombay, India, November 1995: Proceedings. LC 95-45833. (Lecture Notes in Computer Science Ser.: No. 1006). 321p. 1995. 56.00 (*3-540-60584-3*) Spr-Verlag.

Bhalla, Sushil K. The Effective Management of Technology: A Challenge for Corporations. LC 86-25847. 220p. (C). 1987. 31.95 (*0-201-10929-8*) Addison-Wesley.

Bhalla, V. K. International Monetary Cooperation. 600p. 1992. 240.00 (*81-7041-563-2*, Pub. by Scientific Pubs) St Mut.

— World Economy in '90s: A Portfolio Approach. 260p. 1990. 100.00 (*81-7041-434-2*, Pub. by Scientific Pubs) St Mut.

Bhalla, V. K., jt. auth. see Sarma, N. A.

Bhambhani, Suresh. Gynecological Cytology Cervix. 1996. 79.95 (*81-85017-78-6*, Pub. by Interprint) St Mut.

Bhambhri, C. P. Elections 1991: An Analysis. (C). 1991. 13.50 (*81-7018-701-X*, Pub. by BR Pub) S Asia.

— Political Process in India, 1947-1990. 1991. text 27.50 (*0-7069-5596-X*, Pub. by Vikas) S Asia.

— Politics in India, 1992-93. xi, 308p. 1993. 25.95 (*1-881338-10-X*) Nataraj Bks.

Bhambri, Arvind & Sinatra, Alessandro. Corporate Transformation. LC 97-12268. 1997. lib. bdg. 154.00 (*0-7923-9767-3*) Kluwer Academic.

Bhambri, Arvind, et al. Strategies & Structure of Real Estate Development Firms. LC 91-66063. 63p. 1991. 30.95 (*0-87420-723-1*, S42) Urban Land.

Bhamidimarri, R., et al, eds. Development & Water Pollution Control in Asia: Selected Proceedings of Asian Waterqual '91, the 3rd IAWPRC Regional Conference on Development & Water Pollution Control, 20-24 November, 1991, Shanghai, China. (Water Science & Technology Ser.: Vol. 28). (Illus.). 266p. 1994. pap. 100.75 (*0-08-042491-0*) Elsevier.

Bhamidimarri, R. & Manderson. Environmental Biotechnology. (Water Science & Technology Ser.: Vol. 36). 1998. write for info. (*0-08-043376-6*, Pergamon Pr) Elsevier.

Bhamidipati, Kishore. SQL Programmer's Reference. (Programmer's Reference Ser.). 337p. 1998. pap. text 16.99 (*0-07-882460-5*) Osborne-McGraw.

Bhamrah, H. S. & Juneja, Kavita. Introduction to Amphibia. 1990. 42.00 (*81-7041-266-8*, Pub. by Anmol) S Asia.

— Introduction to Birds. 1990. 42.00 (*81-7041-268-4*, Pub. by Anmol) S Asia.

— Introduction to Fishes. 1990. 42.00 (*81-7041-265-X*, Pub. by Anmol) S Asia.

— Introduction to Mammals. 1990. 42.00 (*81-7041-269-2*, Pub. by Anmol) S Asia.

— Introduction to Protochordata. 1990. 42.00 (*81-7041-264-1*, Pub. by Anmol) S Asia.

— Introduction to Reptiles. 1990. 42.00 (*81-7041-267-6*, Pub. by Anmol) S Asia.

Bhan, Esme, jt. ed. see Lemert, Charles.

Bhan, Satish. Tissue Culture. (Illus.). viii, 231p. 1998. 26.00 (*81-7099-694-5*, Pub. by Mittal Pubs Dist) Nataraj Bks.

Bhan, Susheela. Child Abuse: An Annotated Bibliography. (C). 1991. 97.50 (*81-7211-002-2*, Pub. by Northern Bk Ctr) S Asia.

— Impact of Ethnic Violence on Youth: A Study of Tribal-Nontribal Violence in Kokrajhar, Assam LC 98-917870. 204 p. 1999. write for info. (*81-7541-015-9*) Nataraj Bks.

— Terrorism: An Annotated Bibliography. (C). 1989. 44.00 (*81-7022-256-7*, Pub. by Concept) S Asia.

Bhan, Susheela, jt. ed. see Shah, A. B.

Bhana, Surendra. Gandhi's Legacy: The Natal Indian Congress 1894-1994. LC 98-106200. (Illus.). 198p. 1997. pap. 27.00 (*0-86980-931-8*, Pub. by Univ Natal Pr) Intl Spec Bk.

— Indentured Indian Emigrants to Natal 1860-1902: A Study Based on Ships' Lists. (Illus.). xi, 157p. 1991. 20.00 (*81-85002-21-5*, Pub. by Promilla) Nataraj Bks.

Bhana, Surendra & Hunt, James D. Gandhi's Editor: The Letters of M. H. Nazar 1902-1903. (C). 1989. 22.00 (*81-85002-08-8*, Pub. by Promilla) S Asia.

Bhandai, Romesh. As I Saw It. LC 98-906931. 326 p. 1998. write for info. (*81-241-0076-4*) Har-Anand Pubns.

Bhandar, Ratna P. Kings, Soldiers & Priests: Nepalese Politics & the Rise of Jung Bahadur Rana 1830-1857. 1990. 125.00 (*0-7855-0256-4*, Pub. by Ratna Pustak Bhandar) St Mut.

Bhandar, Ratna P., ed. Statistical Pocket Book of Nepal, 1992. (C). 1992. 30.00 (*0-7855-0214-9*, Pub. by Ratna Pustak Bhandar) St Mut.

***Bhandar, Ratna Pustak.** Cooking in Nepal. 1999. pap. 59.00 (*0-7855-7532-4*) St Mut.

— Health in Nepal: Realities & Challenges. 1997. pap. 50.00 (*0-7855-7593-6*) St Mut.

Bhandar, Ratna Pustak. Health Statistics of Nepal, 1997. 1997. pap. 22.00 (*0-7855-7412-3*, Pub. by Ratna Pustak Bhandar) St Mut.

Bhandar, Ratna Pustak. The Himalayan Journal, No. 52. 1996. pap. 94.00 (*0-7855-7597-9*) St Mut.

Bhandar, Ratna Pustak. The Himalayan Journal, Vol. 52. 1966. pap. 75.00 (*0-7855-7414-X*, Pub. by Ratna Pustak Bhandar) St Mut.

— Nepal & the World: A Statistical Profile, 1998. 1998. pap. 54.00 (*0-7855-7445-X*, Pub. by Ratna Pustak Bhandar) St Mut.

— Nepalese National Bibliography (NNR), 1987-1989. 1996. pap. 53.00 (*0-7855-7448-4*, Pub. by Ratna Pustak Bhandar) St Mut.

— Occasional Papers in Sociology & Anthropology, Vol. 5. 1996. pap. 27.00 (*0-7855-7468-9*, Pub. by Ratna Pustak Bhandar) St Mut.

— Patan Walk About - Inner City Guide. 1996. pap. 22.00 (*0-7855-7471-9*, Pub. by Ratna Pustak Bhandar) St Mut.

— Plight of the Kamaiyas: A Report of the Kamaiya Conference. 1997. pap. 22.00 (*0-7855-7477-8*, Pub. by Ratna Pustak Bhandar) St Mut.

— Ratna Trekker's Pal Nepali Phrasebook. 1997. pap. 22.00 (*0-7855-7484-0*, Pub. by Ratna Pustak Bhandar) St Mut.

— Studies in Nepali History & Society, December 1996 Vol. L, No. 2: December, 1996. 1997. pap. 34.00 (*0-7855-7496-4*, Pub. by Ratna Pustak Bhandar) St Mut.

***Bhandar, Ratna Pustak.** A Study on Developing Nepal Information System in Science & Technology. 1998. pap. 30.00 (*0-7855-7641-X*) St Mut.

— Sustainability in Mountain Tourism Perspectives for the Himalayan Countries. 1998. pap. 120.00 (*0-7855-7644-4*) St Mut.

— Third General Election: Emerging Scenario 2055. 1999. pap. 22.00 (*0-7855-7647-9*) St Mut.

— Water Nepal, Vol. 5 No. 2. 1997. pap. 22.00 (*0-7855-7658-4*) St Mut.

Bhandar, Ratna Pustak. Water Nepal, January 1997 Vol. 5, No. 1: January, 1997, Vol. 5, No. 1. 1997. pap. 22.00 (*0-7855-7506-5*, Pub. by Ratna Pustak Bhandar) St Mut.

Bhandara, J. S. Kinship, Affinity & Domestic Group: A Study among the Mishing of the Brahmaputra Valley. 1992. 27.50 (*81-212-0388-0*, Pub. by Gian Publng Hse) S Asia.

***Bhandare, Murlidhar C., ed.** World of Gender Justice: Justice Sunanda Bhandare Foundation. 1999. 36.00 (*81-241-0609-6*, Pub. by Har-Anand Pubns) S Asia.

Bhandare, Shaila. Memory in Indian Epistemology: Its Nature & Status. (Sri Garib Dass Oriental Ser.: No. 165). (C). 1993. 17.50 (*81-7030-359-1*) S Asia.

Bhandare, Vasant V. Sanskrit Speech: Habits & Panini. 387p. 1986. 16.00 (*0-8364-1674-0*, Pub. by Ajanta) S Asia.

Bhandari, jt. auth. see Adhikari.

Bhandari, jt. ed. see Smith.

Bhandari, A. India under Janata. 176p. 1980. 12.95 (*0-318-36578-2*) Asia Bk Corp.

***Bhandari, B.** An Inventory of Nepal's Terai Wetlands. 1998. pap. 60.00 (*0-7855-7602-9*) St Mut.

Bhandari, B., jt. auth. see Bhargava, B.

Bhandari, Bishnu. Prospects for Tourism Is Chhekampar. 1998. pap. 27.00 (*0-7855-7481-6*, Pub. by Ratna Pustak Bhandar) St Mut.

Bhandari, Jagdeep S. Exchange Rate Determination & Adjustment. LC 81-11933. 276p. 1982. 65.00 (*0-275-90762-7*, C0762, Praeger Pubs) Greenwood.

— Studies in International Macroeconomics. LC 86-8095. 279p. 1986. 75.00 (*0-275-92087-9*, C2087, Praeger Pubs) Greenwood.

Bhandari, Jagdeep S., ed. Exchange Rate Management under Uncertainty. (Illus.). 296p. 1987. pap. text 16.50 (*0-262-52122-9*) MIT Pr.

Bhandari, Jagdeep S., et al, eds. Corporate Bankruptcy: Economic & Legal Perspectives. (Illus.). 576p. (C). 1996. text 80.00 (*0-521-45107-8*); pap. text 26.95 (*0-521-45717-3*) Cambridge U Pr.

— Economic Interdependence & Flexible Exchange Rates. (Illus.). 560p. 1983. pap. text 21.50 (*0-262-52083-4*) MIT Pr.

Bhandari, Jagdeep S. & Sykes, Alan O., eds. Economic Dimensions in International Law: Comparative & Empirical Perspectives. LC 96-39893. (Illus.). 704p. (C). 1998. text 89.95 (*0-521-57012-3*); pap. text 39.95 (*0-521-57898-1*) Cambridge U Pr.

An Asterisk (*) at the beginning of an entry indicates that the title is appearing for the first time.

Bhandari, M. C. Guide to Company Law Procedures, Vol. 1. (C). 1990. 210.00 (*0-89771-281-1*) St Mut.
— Guide to Company Law Procedures, Vol. 2. (C). 1990. 210.00 (*0-89771-280-3*) St Mut.
Bhandari, M. C. & Makheeja, R. D. Guide to Memorandum, Articles & Incorporation of Companies. 2nd ed. (C). 1989. 225.00 (*0-7855-6126-9*) St Mut.
Bhandari, M. M. Flora of the Indian Desert. 475p. (C). 1978. 100.00 (*81-85046-00-X*, Pub. by Scientific) St Mut.
***Bhandari, Meena.** Global Perspectives: A Media Guide to Progressive Foreign Policy Experts. 94p. 1998. pap. 10.00 (*0-911213-65-1*) Interhemisp Res Ctr.
Bhandari, Ramesh. Survivable Networks: Algorithms for Diverse Routing. LC 98-45585. (International Series in Engineering & Computer Science: Vol. 477). 200p. 1999. 110.00 (*0-7923-8381-8*) Kluwer Academic.
Bhandari, S. Engineering Rock Blasting Operations. (Illus.). 400p. (Orig.). (C). 1997. text 104.00 (*90-5410-658-1*, Pub. by A A Balkema); pap. text 59.00 (*90-5410-663-8*, Pub. by A A Balkema) Ashgate Pub Co.
Bhandari, S., ed. Severe Accidents & Topics in the Nesc Project: Proceedings, ASME/JSMEJoint Pressure Vessels & Piping Conference (1998, San Diego, CA) LC 98-226190. 362. 326p. 1998. pap. 120.00 (*0-7918-1858-6*) ASME.
Bhandari, S. C., jt. auth. see Somani, L. L.
Bhandarkar, Ramkrishna G. Early History of the Dekkan. 160p. 1986. reprint ed. 14.00 (*0-8364-1703-8*, Pub. by Manohar Bk Srv) S Asia.
— Vaisnavism Saivism & Minor Religious Systems. (C). 1995. reprint ed. 16.00 (*81-206-0122-X*, Pub. by Asian Educ Servs) S Asia.
— Vaisnavism Saivism & Minor Religious Systems. 238p. 1986. reprint ed. 14.00 (*0-8364-1704-6*, Pub. by Minerva) S Asia.
Bhandarkar, S. D., jt. auth. see Saroskar, R. S.
Bhandarkar, Suchendra M., jt. auth. see Suk, Minsoo.
Bhandarkar, T. A. Ramakrishna, Sri: Sahasra-Nama-Stotram. (Illus.). 200p. (Orig.). 1988. pap. 6.95 (*0-87481-509-6*, Pub. by Ramakrishna Math) Vedanta Pr.
Bhandarker, A., jt. auth. see Singh, P.
Bhandarker, Dileep. Alpha Implementations & Architecture. 328p. 1995. pap. text 46.95 (*1-55558-130-7*, Digital DEC) Buttrwrth-Heinemann.
Bhanoji Rao, V. V., jt. auth. see Yong Mun Cheong.
Bhanot, G., et al. Some New Directions in Science on Computers. 250p. 1997. text 58.00 (*981-02-3196-2*) World Scientific Pub.
Bhanot, Rashmee P., jt. auth. see Pandya, Meenal A.
Bhansali, K. J., ed. see Metallurgical Society of AIME Staff.
Bhansali, Vineer. Pricing & Managing Exotic & Hybrid Options. LC 97-32770. (Irwin Library of Investment & Finance). 300p. 1998. 70.00 (*0-07-006669-8*) McGraw-Hill Prof.
Bhanu, Bir & Lee, Sungkee. Genetic Learning for Adaptive Image Segmentation, 287. LC 94-22448. (International Series in Engineering & Computer Science). 296p. (C). 1994. text 138.50 (*0-7923-9491-7*) Kluwer Academic.
Bhanu, Bir, jt. auth. see Burger, Wilhelm.
Bhanu, Chitra, jt. auth. see Blackden, C. Mark.
Bhappu, Roshan B., ed. see Mineral Processing Plant Design Symposium Staff.
Bhappu, Roshan B., jt. ed. see Mular, Andrew L.
***Bharadwait, Monisha.** Indian Spice Kitchen. (Illus.). 240p. 2000. reprint ed. pap. 17.50 (*0-7818-0801-4*) Hippocrene Bks.
Bharadwaj, A. N. Problems of Scheduled Caste & Scheduled Tribes in India. 117p. 1979. 14.95 (*0-318-36817-X*) Asia Bk Corp.
Bharadwaj, K. D. The Sanatana Dharma. 80p. (C). 1989. 100.00 (*81-209-0735-3*, Pub. by Pitambar Pub); pap. 25.00 (*81-209-0029-4*, Pub. by Pitambar Pub) St Mut.
— Story of Hanumanji. (C). 1997. 30.00 (*81-209-0081-2*, Pub. by Pitambar Pub) St Mut.
— Valmiki's Ramayana. 152p. (C). 1997. 100.00 (*81-209-0731-0*, Pub. by Pitambar Pub); pap. 25.00 (*81-209-0038-3*, Pub. by Pitambar Pub) St Mut.
— The Wisdom of India. 104p. 1997. pap. 75.00 (*81-209-0999-2*, Pub. by Pitambar Pub) St Mut.
Bharadwaj, Krishna. Accumulation, Exchange & Development: Essays on the Indian Economy. 400p. 1994. 42.00 (*0-8039-9176-2*) Sage.
— Production Conditions in Indian Agriculture: A Study Based on Farm Management Surveys. LC 78-176251. (University of Cambridge, Dept of Applied Economics, Occasional Papers: 33). 138p. reprint ed. pap. 39.40 (*0-608-12291-2*, 2024413) Bks Demand.
Bharadwaj, Krishna & Kaviraj, Sudipta, eds. Perspectives on Capitalism: Marx, Keynes, Schumpeter & Weber. 260p. (C). 1990. text 26.00 (*0-8039-9619-5*) Sage.
Bharadwaj, Krishna & Schefold, Bertram, eds. Essays in Honour of Piero Sraffa. 672p. 1989. text 70.00 (*0-04-445254-3*) Routledge.
***Bharadwaj, Monisha.** India Style. LC 99-14617. (Illus.). 160p. 1999. 30.00 (*1-57959-052-7*, SOMA) BB&T Inc.
— The Indian Kitchen: A Book of Essentail Ingredients with over 200 Easy & Authentic Recipes. 1999. pap. 24.95 (*1-85626-298-7*, Pub. by Cathie Kyle) Trafalgar.
Bharadwaj, O. P. Studies in the Historical Geography of Ancient India. (Illus.). xii, 290p. 1986. 27.00 (*81-85055-89-0*, Pub. by Sundeep Prak) Nataraj Bks.
Bharadwaj, R. & Nadkarni, M. V., eds. Planning for Social & Economic Development: Essays in Honour of Professor D. M. Nanjundappa. LC 92-20729. (Illus.). 276p. (C). 1992. text 36.00 (*0-8039-9444-3*) Sage.
Bharadwaj, Veeravalli, et al. Scheduling Divisible Loads in Parallel & Distributed Systems. LC 96-177. 292p. 1996. 50.00 (*0-8186-7521-7*) IEEE Comp Soc.
Bharadwaja, Koshlesh. A Philosophical Study of the Concept of Vinsu in the Puranas. 416p. (C). 1998. 195.00 (*81-209-0162-2*, Pub. by Pitambar Pub); 250.00 (*81-209-0737-X*, Pub. by Pitambar Pub) St Mut.
Bharadwaja, Vijay. Form & Validity in Indian Logic. 1990. 16.00 (*0-685-37833-0*, Pub. by M Manoharial) S Asia.
Bharait, Agehananda, ed. The Realm of the Extra-Human: Ideas & Actions. (World Anthropology Ser.). (Illus.). xii, 522p. 1976. 51.55 (*90-279-7759-3*) Mouton.
Bharat Heavy Electricals Ltd. Staff. Dictionary of Power Engineering. LC 93-16449. (ENG & GER.). 328p. 1993. 158.50 (*0-444-89984-7*) Elsevier.
Bharat, Shalini, ed. Family Measurement in India. LC 96-17782. 280p. 1996. 35.00 (*0-8039-9329-3*, 93293) Sage.
Bharath, Ramachandran. Neural Network Computing. 1994. pap. 29.95 incl. disk (*0-8306-4523-3*, Windcrest) TAB Bks.
— Prolog: Sophisticated Applications in Artificial Intelligence. (Illus.). 220p. 1989. pap. 17.95 (*0-8306-9392-0*, 3092) McGraw-Hill Prof.
Bharath, Ramachandran & Drosen, James. Neutral Network Computing. LC 94-1199. 1994. pap. 29.95 (*0-07-005145-3*) McGraw-Hill Prof.
Bharatha, S., jt. auth. see Truesdell, Clifford A.
Bharathi, K. S. The Philosophy of Sarvodaya. (C). 1990. 26.00 (*81-85182-36-1*, Pub. by Indus Pub) S Asia.
— The Social Philosophy of Mahatama Gandhi. (C). 1991. 17.50 (*81-7022-362-8*, Pub. by Concept) S Asia.
— Thoughts of Gandhi & Vinoba. (C). 1995. 18.00 (*81-7022-543-4*, Pub. by Concept) S Asia.
Bharathi, Swami P. God Rebirth & the Vedas. (C). 1993. 8.50 (*81-224-0506-1*) S Asia.
Bharati, Agehananda. Hindu Views & Ways & the Hindu-Muslim Interface: An Anthropological Assessment. 1981. 12.50 (*0-8364-5681-5*) S Asia.
— Tantric Traditions. enl. rev. ed. (C). 1993. 38.00 (*81-7075-022-9*, Pub. by Hindustan) S Asia.
Bharati, Agehananda, ed. The Realm of the Extra-Human: Agents & Audiences. (World Anthropology Ser.). (Illus.). xii, 556p. 1976. 58.50 (*90-279-7749-6*) Mouton.
Bharati, Jahadhuru Swami Sri & Maharaja, Krsna Tirthaji. Vedic Mathematics: Sixteen Simple Mathematical Formulae from the Vedas. Agrawala, V. S., ed. 367p. (C). 1994. 21.00 (*81-208-0163-6*, Pub. by Motilal Bnarsidass) S Asia.
Bharati, Saroja & Lev, Maurice. The Cardiac Conduction System in Unexplained Sudden Death. (Illus.). 416p. 1990. 115.00 (*0-87993-362-3*) Futura Pub.
— The Pathology of Congenital Heart Disease: A Personal Experience with More Than 6,300 Congenitally Malformed Hearts, 2 vols. (Illus.). 1608p. 1996. 395.00 (*0-87993-556-1*) Futura Pub.
Bharati, Saroja, et al. Cardiac Surgery & the Conduction System. 2nd rev. ed. (Illus.). 176p. 1991. 75.00 (*0-87993-522-7*) Futura Pub.
Bharati, Shashi. Glossary of Drama, Theatre & Electronic Media. LC 96-900399. (ENG & HIN.). 1996. 21.00 (*81-7018-854-7*, Pub. by BR Pub) S Asia.
Bharati, Veda. The Light of Ten Thousand Suns. (Illus.). 160p. 1998. pap. 15.00 (*0-936663-20-0*) Yes Intl.
Bharatiya, V. P., jt. auth. see Rashid, Syed K.
Bharavi. The Kiratarjuniya by Bharavi, Cantos I-VI. annot. ed. Bahadur, Kaisher, tr. 245p. (C). 1972. 30.00 (*0-7855-6581-7*, Pub. by Ratna Pustak Bhandar) St Mut.
— The Kiratarjuniya by Bharavi, Cantos VII-XII. annot. ed. Bahadur, Kaisher, tr. 223p. (C). 1974. 30.00 (*0-89771-062-2*, Pub. by Ratna Pustak Bhandar) St Mut.
***Bhardwaj.** Hemu-Napoleon of Medieval India. 1999. 26.00 (*81-7099-663-5*, Pub. by Mittal Pubns) S Asia.
Bhardwaj, Arya B. Living Non Violence. xii, 82p. 1986. 9.00 (*1-55528-075-7*, Pub. by Today Tomorrow) Scholarly Pubns.
Bhardwaj, D. S. Domestic Tourism in India LC 98-902046. 310p. 1998. write for info. (*81-7387-078-0*, Pub. by Indus Pub) S Asia.
***Bhardwaj, Gautam.** The Future of India's Debt Market. LC 99-938611. 1998. write for info. (*0-07-463530-1*) McGrw-H Hghr Educ.
Bhardwaj, H. C. Aspects of Ancient Indian Technology. 1979. 18.50 (*0-89684-055-7*, Pub. by Motilal Bnarsidass) S Asia.
Bhardwaj, I. S., ed. Polymer Science: Recent Advances, 2 vols., Set. (Illus.). 1038p. (C). 1994. 560.00 (*2-7108-0670-3*, Pub. by Edits Technip) Enfield Pubs NH.
Bhardwaj, K. K. Combating Communalism in India: Key to National Integration. (C). 1993. 19.50 (*81-7099-478-0*, Pub. by Mittal Pubs Dist) S Asia.
— Pakistan's Democracy at Work. 1998. write for info. (*81-207-2014-8*) Sterling Pubs.
Bhardwaj, Mangat. Colloquial Panjabi: A Complete Language Course. LC 94-33132. (Colloquials Ser.). 304p. (gr. 13). 1995. pap. 22.99 (*0-415-10191-3*, B4031) Routledge.
— Colloquial Panjabi: A Complete Language Course. (Colloquials Ser.). 304p. (C). (gr. 13). 1995. audio 27.99 (*0-415-10192-1*, B4035) Routledge.
— Colloquial Panjabi: A Complete Language Course. (Colloquials Ser.). 304p. (gr. 13). 1995. 49.99 incl. audio (*0-415-10193-X*, B4039) Routledge.
Bhardwaj, R. C. Legislation by Members in the Indian Parliament. LC 95-900347. (C). 1994. 30.00 (*81-7023-409-3*, Pub. by Allied Pubs) S Asia.
Bhardwaj, R. C. & Vijayakrishnan, Shri K. Democracy & Development: Allies or Adversaries. LC 98-18564. (Commonwealth Parliamentary Association Ser.). xi, 222p. 1998. text 68.95 (*1-84014-033-X*, HD82.B469, Pub. by Ashgate Pub) Ashgate Pub Co.
Bhardwaj, R. K. Democracy in India. 346p. 1980. 27.95 (*0-940500-30-2*) Asia Bk Corp.
Bhardwaj, Shyama, jt. ed. see Sapru, R. K.
Bhardwaj, Surinder M. Hindu Places of Pilgrimage in India: A Study in Cultural Geography. LC 73-174454. (Center for South & Southeast Asia Studies, UC Berkeley). (Illus.). 1973. pap. 17.95 (*0-520-04951-9*, Pub. by U CA Pr) Cal Prin Full Svc.
Bhardwaj, V. Bhushan. Medical Examinations: A Preparation Guide. (Illus.). 1979. pap. 9.00 (*0-668-03944-2*, Arco) Macmillan Gen Ref.
Bhardwaj, V. Bhushan, jt. auth. see Yen, Ernest Y.
Bhardwaja, T. N. & Gena, C. B. Perspectives in Pteridology, Present & Future: Prof. S. S. Bir Commemoration Volume, Pt. 1. (Aspects of Plant Sciences Ser.: Vol. 13). (Illus.). 342p. 1991. text 65.00 (*81-7019-385-0*, Pub. by Today Tomorrow) Lubrecht & Cramer.
Bhardwaja, T. N. & Gena, C. B., eds. Perspectives in Pteridology, Present & Future: Prof. S. S. Bir Commemoration Volume, Pt. I. (Aspects of Plant Sciences Ser.: Vol. 13). (Illus.). xxxviii, 342p. 1992. 65.00 (*1-55528-251-2*, Pub. by Today Tomorrow) Scholarly Pubns.
— Perspectives in Pteridology, Present & Future: Prof. S. S. Bir Commemoration Volume, Pt. II. (Aspects of Plant Sciences Ser.: Vol. 14). (Illus.). xxxviii, 342p. 1992. 65.00 (*0-685-66552-6*, Pub. by Today Tomorrow) Scholarly Pubns.
Bhargava, Amit. Integrated Broadband Networks. (Telecommunications Library). 331p. 1990. pap. write for info. (*0-89006-483-0*, C1483) Artech Hse.
Bhargava, B. & Bhandari, B. Direct Taxes Circulars, 1983-1990. (C). 1990. 150.00 (*0-89771-277-3*) St Mut.
— Direct Taxes Digest, 1984-1990. (C). 1990. 275.00 (*0-89771-279-X*) St Mut.
— Direct Taxes Digest, 1988-1990. (C). 1990. 135.00 (*0-89771-278-1*) St Mut.
Bhargava, B. S. & Sivanna, N. The Land Army & Rural Development: A Study of Organisational Innovation in Karnataka. (Illus.). vi, 104p. 1994. 12.00 (*81-7024-630-X*, Pub. by Ashish Pub Hse) Nataraj Bks.
Bhargava, Bharat K. Digital Libraries - Current Issues: Selected Papers of the Digital Libraries Workshop, DL '94, Held in Newark, New Jersey, U. S. A., May 19-20, 1994. Adam, Nabil R. et al, eds. (Lecture Notes in Computer Science Ser.: Vol. 916). (Illus.). 1995. 56.00 (*3-540-59282-2*) Spr-Verlag.
***Bhargava, Bharat K.** Digital Libraries & Multimedia. LC 00-22044. 2000. write for info. (*0-7923-7817-2*) Kluwer Academic.
Bhargava, Bharat K., et al, eds. Digital Libraries: Research & Technology Advances, Vol. 1082. (Lecture Notes in Computer Science Ser.). xiii, 390p. 1996. pap. 56.00 (*3-540-61410-9*) Spr-Verlag.
Bhargava, Bharat K., jt. ed. see Adam, Nabil R.
Bhargava-Fetschrift, K. S. Current Trends in Sugarcane Pathology. Rao, G. P. et al, eds. 400p. 1993. pap. 175.00 (*0-7855-0404-4*, Pub. by Intl Bks & Periodicals) St Mut.
Bhargava, G. S. Bhin Sen Sachar: An Intimate Biography. LC 97-905885. (C). 1997. text 30.00 (*81-241-0526-X*, Pub. by Har-Anand Pubns) S Asia.
— Government Media: Autonomy & After. (C). 1991. 14.00 (*81-7022-366-0*, Pub. by Concept) S Asia.
Bhargava, G. S., jt. auth. see Pal, R. M.
Bhargava, Gopal. Socio-Economic & Legal Implications of Urban Land Ceiling & Regulation. 1983. 12.00 (*0-8364-1053-X*, Pub. by Abhinav) S Asia.
Bhargava, Gopal, ed. Urban Problems & Policy Perspectives. 1981. 38.00 (*0-8364-0720-2*, Pub. by Abhinav) S Asia.
Bhargava, K. S., ed. see Agnihotri, V. P.
Bhargava, Kant K. Shaping South Asia's Future Role of Regional Cooperation. Bongartz, Heinz & Sobhan, Farooq, eds. (C). 1995. 28.00 (*0-7069-9225-3*, Pub. by Vikas) S Asia.
Bhargava, Monohar. The Geography of Rgvedic India: A Physical Geography of Sapta Saindhaval. LC 65-10226. 167p. reprint ed. pap. 51.80 (*0-608-12624-1*, 202542600043) Bks Demand.
Bhargava, Moti L. Hundred Years of Allahabad University. 1987. 42.50 (*81-7024-162-6*, Pub. by Ashish Pub Hse) S Asia.
***Bhargava, P. L.** Retrieval of History from Puranic Myths: Exposure of Late Puranic Myths about Some Great Characters of the Earliest Indian History. rev. ed. LC 98-907196. xiii, 146p. 1998. 18.50 (*81-246-0100-3*, Pub. by D K Printwrld) Nataraj Bks.
Bhargava, P. L. Vedic Religion & Culture: An Exposition of District Facets. LC 93-910171. xiii, 120p. (C). 1998. 13.00 (*81-246-0006-6*, Pub. by D K Printwrld) Nataraj Bks.
Bhargava, Pradeep. Political Economy of the Gulf States. (C). 1988. 17.50 (*81-7003-098-6*, Pub. by S Asia Pubs) S Asia.
Bhargava, Purushottam L. Chandragupta Maurya: A Gem of Indian History. (Illus.). xiii, 160p. (C). 1996. 15.00 (*81-246-0056-2*, Pub. by D K Printwrld) Nataraj Bks.
— Founders of India's Civilization: Lives of Ten Pre-Buddha Great Men of India. LC 92-15606. 135p. 1992. reprint ed. pap. 41.90 (*0-608-01773-6*, 206243100003) Bks Demand.
Bhargava, R., ed. Properties of Wide Bandgap II-VI Semiconductors. (EMIS Datareviews Ser.: No. 17). 320p. 1996. 195.00 (*0-85296-882-5*, EM017) INSPEC Inc.
Bhargava, Raj. Open VMS: Architecture, Use, & Migration. 1995. 50.00 (*0-07-005157-7*) McGraw.
Bhargava, Rajeev. Individualism in Social Science: Forms & Limits of a Methodology. (Oxford Philosophical Monographs). (Illus.). 280p. 1992. text 69.00 (*0-19-824279-4*) OUP.
***Bhargava, Rajeev, et al, eds.** Multiculturalism, Liberalism & Democracy. 444p. 2000. text 29.95 (*0-19-564824-2*) OUP.
Bhargava, Vijay K. & Wicker, Stephen B., eds. Reed-Solomon Codes & Their Applications. LC 94-3160. 336p. 1994. 89.95 (*0-7803-1025-X*, PC03749) Inst Electrical.
Bhargava, Vijay K., et al. Digital Communications by Satellite: Modulaton, Multiple Access & Coding. LC 91-4052. 592p. 1991. reprint ed. text 88.50 (*0-89464-629-X*) Krieger.
Bhargva, Deepali. Manu Smriti: A Sociological Analysis. (C). 1989. 21.50 (*81-7033-078-5*, Pub. by Rawat Pubns) S Asia.
Bharti, C. . . . Out of His Ashes. (C). 1994. text 14.00 (*81-241-0193-0*, Pub. by Har-Anand Pubns) S Asia.
Bharti, Jai P. The Necklace of Diamonds, 2 vols., 1. (C). 1989. 12.00 (*81-209-0507-5*, Pub. by Pitambar Pub) St Mut.
— The Necklace of Diamonds, 2 vols., 2. (C). 1989. 12.00 (*81-209-0508-3*, Pub. by Pitambar Pub) St Mut.
Bharti, Pratap, tr. see Osho.
Bhartia, Prakash & Bahl, Inder J. Microstrip Antennas. LC 80-70174. (Illus.). 364p. 1980. reprint ed. pap. 112.90 (*0-608-16025-3*, 203312400083) Bks Demand.
— Millimeter Wave Engineering & Applications. LC 83-12404. 736p. 1984. 245.00 (*0-471-87083-8*) Wiley.
Bhartia, Prakash, et al. Millimeter-Wave Microstrip & Printed Circuit Antennas. LC 90-1126. (Artech House Antenna Library). 336p. 1991. reprint ed. pap. 104.20 (*0-608-01349-8*, 206208900002) Bks Demand.
Bhartia, Prakash, jt. auth. see Bahl, Inder J.
Bhartiya, V. P. Religion-State Relationship & Constitutional Rights in India. (C). 1987. 54.00 (*81-7100-009-6*, Pub. by Deep & Deep Pubns) S Asia.
Bhartrihari. Vairagya-Satakam: The Hundred Verses on Renunciation. pap. 2.00 (*81-85301-94-8*, Pub. by Advaita Ashrama) Vedanta Pr.
***Bharttrhari & Ghose, Aurobindo.** Bharttrharineitibsatakam = Century of Life: The Nitishataka of Bhartrihari LC 99-931591. 72 p. 1998. write for info. (*81-7060-120-7*) Acrpls Bks CO.
Bharucha, E. S. Zorostrian Religion & Customs. 210p. 1993. 11.95 (*0-318-36786-6*) Asia Bk Corp.
Bharucha, Fershid, ed. see Charyn, Jerome.
Bharucha, Kerman D. dBASE II: A Comprehensive User's Manual. (Illus.). 304p. 1985. 24.95 (*0-8306-0884-2*, 1884); pap. 18.95 (*0-8306-1884-8*, 1884P) McGraw-Hill Prof.
— The dBASE III Plus Users Manual (IBM) 1991. 27.95 (*0-8306-6633-8*) McGraw-Hill Prof.
— The dBASE IV: Complete User's Manual. 1991. 24.95 (*0-8306-5413-5*) McGraw-Hill Prof.
— The dBASE IV for Nonprogrammers. 1990. pap. 22.95 (*0-8306-3570-X*) McGraw-Hill Prof.
Bharucha-Reid, Albert T. Elements in the Theory of Markov Processes & Their Applications. LC 96-44546. 480p. 1997. reprint ed. pap. text 14.95 (*0-486-69539-5*) Dover.
Bharucha, Rustom. Chandralekha. LC 95-904025. (C). 1995. 38.00 (*81-7223-168-7*, Pub. by Indus Pub) S Asia.
— In the Name of the Secular: Cultural Practice & Activism in India Today. LC 97-914017. 210p. (C). 1998. text 22.95 (*0-19-564222-8*) OUP.
***Bharucha, Rustom.** The Politics of Cultural Practice: Thinking Through Theatre in an Age of Globalization. LC 99-85991. 324p. 2000. 19.95 (*0-8195-6439-7*, Wesleyan Univ Pr); 45.00 (*0-8195-6440-0*, Wesleyan Univ Pr) U Pr of New Eng.
Bharucha, Rustom. Theatre & the World: Essays on Performance & Politics of Culture. 1990. 24.00 (*0-945921-13-6*, Pub. by S Asia Pubs) S Asia.
— Theatre & the World: Performance & the Politics of Culture. LC 93-18374. 272p. (C). 1993. pap. 29.99 (*0-415-09216-7*) Routledge.
— Theatre & the World: Performance & the Politics of Culture. LC 93-18374. 272p. (C). (gr. 13). 1993. 90.00 (*0-415-09215-9*) Routledge.
— Theatre of Kanhailal: Pebet & Memoirs of Africa. (C). 1992. pap. text 14.00 (*81-7046-094-8*, Pub. by Seagull Bks) S Asia.
Bhasiin, Kamla. What Is Patriarchy? 41p. 1993. pap. 6.95 (*81-85107-73-4*) Women Ink.
Bhasin, K. B., jt. ed. see Frey, J.
Bhasin, Kamla, et al, eds. Against All Odds: Essays on Women, Religion & Development from India & Pakistan. 2nd ed. 191p. 1995. pap. 12.00 (*81-85107-74-2*, Pub. by Kali for Women) Women Ink.
Bhasin, Kamla, jt. auth. see Menon, Ritu.
Bhasin, M. L. Human Resources Management: The Case Studies. 470p. 1992. 180.00 (*81-7041-506-3*, Pub. by Scientific Pubs) St Mut.
— Indian Management: The Case Studies. 410p. 1992. 200.00 (*81-7041-455-5*, Pub. by Scientific Pubs) St Mut.
— Indian Marketing: The Case Studies. 460p. 1990. 180.00 (*81-7041-456-3*, Pub. by Scientific Pubs) St Mut.
— Inflation Accounting in Public Enterprises. 480p. 1989. 140.00 (*81-7041-081-9*, Pub. by Scientific Pubs) St Mut.
Bhasin, M. M. & Slocum, D. W. Methane & Alkane Conversion Chemistry: Proceedings of the American Chemical Society Symposium in San Diego, California, March 13-18, 1994. (Illus.). 360p. (C). 1996. 125.00 (*0-306-45212-X*, Kluwer Plenum) Kluwer Academic.
Bhasin, Shalender, et al, eds. Biology, Pharmacology, & Clinical Applications of Androgens: Current Status & Future Prospects. LC 95-46146. 529p. 1996. 135.00 (*0-471-13320-5*, Wiley-Interscience) Wiley.
Bhasin, V. K. Super Power Rivalry in the Indian Ocean. 236p. 1981. text 20.00 (*0-685-43584-9*) Coronet Bks.

B

An Asterisk (*) at the beginning of an entry indicates that the title is appearing for the first time.

— Super Power Rivalry in the Indian Ocean. 229p. 1981. 24.95 (*0-940500-16-7*, Pub. by S Chand & Co) Asia Bk Corp.

— Super Power Rivalry in the Indian Ocean. 238p. 1989. 30.00 (*0-7855-1205-5*) St Mut.

Bhasin, Veena. Ecology, Culture & Change: Tribals of Sikkim Himalayas. (C). 1989. 54.00 (*81-210-0217-6*, Pub. by Inter-India Pubns) S Asia.

Bhaskar. Orban's Oral Histology & Embryology. 11th ed. (Illus.). 512p. (C). (gr. 13). 1990. text 61.95 (*0-8016-0239-4*, 00239) Mosby Inc.

Bhaskar, Jayram. A Guide to VHDL Syntax: Based on the New IEEE STD 1076-1993. LC 94-34900. (Innovative Technology Ser.). 280p. 1994. 45.00 (*0-13-324351-6*) P-H.

Bhaskar, K. N. & Housden, R. J. Information Technology Management. 2nd ed. 502p. 1990. pap. 54.95 (*0-434-90077-X*) Buttrwrth-Heinemann.

Bhaskar, Manu. Press & Working Class Consciousness in Developing Societies. 130p. 1988. 10.00 (*81-212-0246-9*, Pub. by Gian Publng Hse) S Asia.

Bhaskar, Roy. Critical Realism: Essential Readings. LC 98-18861. (Critical Realism--Interventions Ser.). 1p. 1998. write for info. (*0-415-19631-0*); pap. 32.99 (*0-415-19632-9*) Routledge.

— Dialectic: The Pulse of Freedom. LC 93-38066. 300p. (C). 1994. pap. 23.00 (*0-86091-583-2*, Pub. by Verso) Norton.

***Bhaskar, Roy.** From East to West: Odyssey of a Soul. LC 99-87584. (Critical Realism--Interventions Ser.). 2000. pap. write for info. (*0-415-23325-9*) Routledge.

Bhaskar, Roy. Plato, Etc. The Problems of Philosophy & Their Resolution. 256p. (C). 1994. pap. 20.00 (*0-86091-649-9*, B4649, Pub. by Verso) Norton.

— The Possibility of Naturalism: A Philosophical Critique of the Contemporary Human Sciences. 3rd ed. LC 98-35442. 1998. 85.00 (*0-415-19873-9*); pap. 24.99 (*0-415-19874-7*) Routledge.

— A Realist Theory of Science. 2nd ed. (Classics Ser.). 284p. (C). 1997. reprint ed. pap. 18.00 (*1-85984-103-1*, Pub. by Verso) Norton.

— Reclaiming Reality: Philosophical Underlabouring. 180p. 1989. 50.00 (*0-86091-237-X*, A3346) Routledge.

Bhaskar, S. Prehistoric & Primitive Hunter-Gatherers of South India. 1990. 38.50 (*81-7141-107-X*) S Asia.

Bhaskar, S., jt. auth. see Gupta, C. Dwarakanath.

Bhaskar, Sepuri & Vijayakumari, A., eds. Social Change among Balijas: Majority Community of Andhra Pradesh. LC 99-931667. 139p. 1998. pap. 87.50 (*81-7533-072-4*, Pub. by Print Hse) St Mut.

Bhaskar, V., jt. auth. see Glyn, Andrew.

Bhaskaran, Vasudev & Konstantinides, Konstantinos. Image & Video Compression Standards: Algorithms & Architectures. LC 95-32739. (International Series in Engineering & Computer Science). 392p. (C). 1995. text 116.00 (*0-7923-9591-3*) Kluwer Academic.

— Image & Video Compression Standards: Algorithms & Architectures. 2nd ed. LC 97-17141. (International Series in Engineering & Computer Science). 454p. 1997. text 107.50 (*0-7923-9952-8*) Kluwer Academic.

Bhaskarananda, Swami. The Essentials of Hinduism: A Comprehensive Overview of the World's Oldest Religion. LC 93-61483. 233p. 1995. pap. 12.95 (*1-884852-02-5*) Viveka Pr.

Bhasker, J. A Verilog HDL Primer. 2nd ed. LC 98-61678. (Illus.). 320p. (C). 1999. text 64.95 (*0-9650391-7-X*) Star Galaxy.

— Verilog HDL Synthesis, a Practical Primer. LC 98-61058. (Illus.). 236p. 1998. 49.95 (*0-9650391-5-3*) Star Galaxy.

— VHDL: Features & Applications, Incl. primer, final exam. Menchini, Paul, ed. 185p. 1995. student ed. 299.00 (*0-7803-2297-5*, HL5712) Inst Electrical.

***Bhasker, J.** VHDL Primer. 3rd ed. 386p. 1998. 73.00 (*0-13-096575-8*) P-H.

Bhasker, J. A VHDL Synthesis Primer. LC 95-73048. 238p. 1996. 49.95 (*0-9650391-0-2*) Star Galaxy.

— A VHOL Synthesis Primer. 2nd rev. ed. LC 97-62293. (Illus.). 312p. 1998. 59.95 (*0-9650391-9-6*) Star Galaxy.

Bhasker, Jayaram. A Verilog HDL Primer. LC 96-93133. 260p. 1997. 59.95 (*0-9656277-4-8*) Star Galaxy Pr.

Bhat, A. Vishnu, jt. auth. see Lockwood, Michael.

Bhat, Barathi, jt. auth. see Koul, Shiban K.

Bhat, D. G., ed. see International Conference on Surface Modification T.

Bhat, D. G., ed. see International Conference on Surface Modifications.

***Bhat, D. N. S.** The Prominence of Tense, Aspect & Mood. LC 99-11172. (Studies in Language Companion Ser.: Vol. 49). xii, 198p. 1999. 65.00 (*1-55619-935-X*) J Benjamins Pubng Co.

Bhat, D. N. S., ed. The Adjectival Category: Criteria for Differentiation & Identification. LC 94-11533. (Studies in Language Companion Ser.: Vol. 24). xii, 295p. 1994. 65.00 (*1-55619-376-9*) J Benjamins Pubng Co.

Bhat, G. K. Sanskrit Drama, Problems & Prospects. 1986. 37.50 (*0-8364-1531-0*, Pub. by Ajanta) S Asia.

— Theatric Aspects of Sanskrit Drama. 1985. 12.50 (*0-8364-1365-2*) S Asia.

Bhat, G. K., ed. Special Melting & Processing Technologies. LC 89-9337. (Illus.). 987p. 1989. 98.00 (*0-8155-1202-3*) Noyes.

Bhat, G. K., jt. ed. see Lherbier, L. W.

Bhat, Krish D. Guide to Indo-American Parenting. deluxe ed. King, Kathy, ed. (Illus.). 418p. 1999. pap. 26.95 (*0-9665082-0-3*) Uma Publ.

Bhat, L. S. Strategy for Integrated Area Development: Case Study of North Kanara District (Karnataka) (C). 1988. 17.00 (*81-7022-198-6*, Pub. by Concept) S Asia.

Bhat, M. Ramakrishna. Fundamentals of Astrology. 1974. lib. bdg. 250.00 (*0-87968-484-4*) Krishna Pr.

— Fundamentals of Astrology. 313p. (C). 1995. reprint ed. 17.50 (*81-208-0275-6*, Pub. by Motilal Bnarsidass); reprint ed. pap. 12.50 (*81-208-0276-4*, Pub. by Motilal Bnarsidass) S Asia.

Bhat, M. S. Vedic Tantrism: A Study of Rgvidhana of Saunaka. 475p. (C). 1987. 31.00 (*81-208-0197-0*, Pub. by Motilal Bnarsidass) S Asia.

Bhat, M. S., jt. auth. see Misri, M. L.

Bhat, Madhuri & Sher, Jonathan P. The 1998 North Carolina Data Guide to Child Well-Being. 156p. 1998. pap. 15.00 (*0-9665180-0-4*) NC Child.

Bhat, N. Shyam. South Kanara, 1799-1860: A Study in Colonial Administration & Regional Response. LC 99-931903. 244 p. 1998. write for info. (*81-7099-586-8*) S Asia.

Bhat, Naras. How to Reverse & Prevent Heart Disease & Cancer. LC 95-69189. (Illus.). 440p. 1995. pap. 19.95 (*0-9624780-8-3*) HealthWorld.

Bhat, Parameshwar R., jt. auth. see Davar, Bhargavi V.

***Bhat, Pushpalatha C. & Prosper, Harrison B.** Multivariate Methods in High Energy Physics: The Neural Network Revolution. 300p. 2000. 58.00 (*981-02-4347-2*) World Scientific Pub.

Bhat, R. V., jt. ed. see Simopoulos, Artemis P.

Bhat, Rajendra R. Managing the Demand for Fashion Items. Farmer, Richard, ed. LC 85-1039. (Research for Business Decisions Ser.: No. 73). 137p. reprint ed. 42.50 (*0-8357-1618-X*, 207036000088) Bks Demand.

Bhat, Ramakrishna M. Essentials of Horary Astrology or Prasnapadavi. (C). 1992. text 21.00 (*81-208-0888-6*, Pub. by Motilal Bnarsidass) S Asia.

Bhat, Ramdas B. & Basawa, Ishwarasa V., eds. Queuing & Related Models. (Oxford Statistical Science Ser.). (Illus.). 366p. 1992. text 95.00 (*0-19-852233-9*) OUP.

Bhat, S. A. Management of Public Enterprises. 132p. 1991. 60.00 (*81-7041-520-9*, Pub. by Scientific Pubs) St Mut.

Bhat, Shama & Gupta, Virendra K. Ichneumonologia Orientalis, Pt. VI The Subfamily Agathidinae (Hym - Braconidae) (Oriental Insects Monographs: No. 6). 1977. 55.00 (*1-877711-05-5*) Assoc Pubs FL.

Bhat, Sudhakar. India & China. 1967. 59.50 (*0-614-01799-8*) Elliots Bks.

Bhat, V. Narayan. Elements of Applied Stochastic Processes. 2nd ed. LC 84-7338. (Probability & Mathematical Statistics Ser.: No. 1-346). 704p. (C). 1984. 199.95 (*0-471-87826-X*) Wiley.

Bhat, Vasanthakumar N. The Green Corporation: The Next Competitive Advantage. LC 95-41389. 280p. 1996. 62.95 (*0-89930-979-8*, Quorum Bks) Greenwood.

— Total Quality Environmental Management: An ISO 14000 Approach. LC 97-19761. 288p. 1998. 59.95 (*1-56720-097-4*, Quorum Bks) Greenwood.

Bhat, Vasanthi. Meditation Throughout the Day. 1999. pap. text 12.95 (*0-9655499-1-7*) Vasantha Yoga.

— The Power of Conscious Breathing in Hatha Yoga: Discover the Tremendous Benefits of Ancient Yoga Techniques to Relieve Stress, Improve Health, Prevent & Heal Ailments, Achieve Inner Peace. Shenoi, Amita & Slogar, Rich, eds. (Illus.). xii, 244p. (Orig.). 1997. pap. 19.95 (*0-9655499-0-9*) Vasantha Yoga.

Bhat, Yashoda, ed. Beyond the Threshold: Indian Women on the Move. 1995. 36.00 (*81-7018-863-6*, Pub. by BR Pub) S Asia.

— Image of Woman in Indian Literature. (C). 1993. text 19.00 (*81-7018-750-8*, Pub. by BR Pub) S Asia.

Bhatacharya, Gargi. Tales of Dark-Skinned Women: Race, Gender & Global Culture. LC 99-161346. (Race & Representation Ser.). 390p. 1998. 85.00 (*1-85728-611-1*) Taylor & Francis.

Bhate, Saroja & Bronkhorst, Johannes, eds. Bhartrhari: Philosopher & Grammarian. LC 97-913613. (C). 1995. reprint ed. 22.00 (*81-208-1198-4*, Pub. by Motilal Bnarsidass) S Asia.

Bhate, Saroja, jt. ed. see Deshpande, Madhav M.

Bhathager, Himanshu. Advanced Asic Chip Synthesis: Using Synopsis Design Compiler & Primetime. LC 99-24720. 1999. write for info. (*0-7923-8537-3*) Kluwer Academic.

Bhathal, Ragbir. Australian Astronomer John Tebbutt: The Life & World of the Man on the 100 Dollar Note. (Illus.). 112p. (Orig.). 1993. pap. 16.95 (*0-86417-522-1*, Pub. by Kangaroo Pr) Seven Hills Bk.

Bhatia, A. B. Ultrasonic Absorption: An Introduction to the Theory of Sound Absorption & Dispersion in Gases, Liquids & Solids. 440p. 1985. reprint ed. pap. 11.95 (*0-486-64917-2*) Dover.

Bhatia, A. B. & Singh, R. N. Mechanics of Deformable Media. (Graduate Student Series in Physics). (Illus.). 204p. (C). 1986. pap. 49.00 (*0-85274-500-1*) IOP Pub.

Bhatia, Ajit S. Rural-Urban Migration: A Study of Socio-Economic Implications. (C). 1992. text 22.00 (*81-7100-443-1*, Pub. by Deep & Deep Pubns) S Asia.

Bhatia, Anita, jt. auth. see White, Oliver C.

Bhatia, B. L. Protozoa: Ciliophora. (Fauna of British India Ser.). (Illus.). xxii, 522p. 1979. reprint ed. 30.00 (*0-88065-058-3*) Scholarly Pubns.

— Protozoa: Sporozoa. (Fauna of British India Ser.). (Illus.). xx, 508p. 1979. reprint ed. 30.00 (*0-88065-103-2*) Scholarly Pubns.

Bhatia, B. M. Indian Agriculture: A Policy Perspective. 190p. (C). 1988. text 22.50 (*0-8039-9550-4*) Sage.

— India's Middle Class: Role in Nation Building. (C). 1994. text 18.00 (*81-220-0341-9*, Pub. by Konark Pubs) S Asia.

— Pakistan's Economic Development: Freedom to Bondage (1948-1988) 332p. 1990. text 35.00 (*81-220-0155-6*, Pub. by Konark Pubs Pvt Ltd) Advent Bks Div.

Bhatia, B. N. Pakistan's Economic Development. 282p. 1979. 24.95 (*0-318-37251-7*) Asia Bk Corp.

Bhatia, Bela, jt. auth. see Vijayaraghavan, M. R.

Bhatia, C. S. & Menon, Aric K., eds. Tribology of Contact-Near Contact Recording for Ultra High Density Magnetic Storage: Proceedings. LC 96-86434. (TRIB Ser.: Vol. 6). 65p. pap. 60.00 (*0-7918-1515-3*) ASME.

Bhatia, H. S. European Women in India - Their Life & Adventures. 224p. 1979. 14.95 (*0-318-37048-4*) Asia Bk Corp.

— Studies in Islamic Law, Religion & Society. (C). 1989. 315.00 (*0-7855-3685-X*) St Mut.

Bhatia, H. S., ed. Studies in Islamic Law, Religion & Society. (C). 1990. 160.00 (*0-89771-146-7*) St Mut.

Bhatia, Hamir, jt. auth. see Bayles, Deborah L.

Bhatia, Harmeet K., ed. see Fosberg, Lorna R.

Bhatia, J. & Tribology Society of India Staff. Advances in Industrial Tribology. LC 98-904602. xvii, 690 p. 1998. write for info. (*0-07-463343-0*) McGraw.

Bhatia, K. L. Judicial Activism & Social Change. (C). 1990. 38.00 (*0-89771-288-9*) St Mut.

Bhatia, K. L., ed. Dr. B. R. Ambedkar: Social Justice & the Indian Constitution. (C). 1994. 34.00 (*81-7100-639-6*, Pub. by Deep & Deep Pubns) S Asia.

Bhatia, K. L., et al. Social Justice of Dr. B. R. Ambedkar. (C). 1995. 28.00 (*81-7100-809-7*, Pub. by Deep & Deep Pubns) S Asia.

Bhatia, Kaushi. Indian Cookbook. (Orig.). (C). 1994. pap. write for info. (*0-614-01847-1*) Sterling Pubs.

Bhatia, Kiran, jt. auth. see Banerjee, B. G.

Bhatia, M. L. Administrative History of Medieval India. (C). 1992. 28.00 (*81-85484-36-8*, Pub. by Manohar) S Asia.

Bhatia, Motir. An Intensive Course in Punjabi. 1985. 11.00 (*0-8364-2078-0*, Pub. by Usha) S Asia.

***Bhatia, Praveen.** Winter's Tale: Special Edition with Introduction, Detailed Notes, Scene-Wise Summary, Annotations & Questions & Answers. 2000. pap. 12.50 (*81-7476-292-2*, Pub. by UBS Pubs) S Asia.

Bhatia, R. R., jt. auth. see Skipper, A. C.

Bhatia, Rajendra. Analysis, Geometry & Probability. 422p. 1997. text 60.00 (*81-85931-12-7*) Am Math.

— Matrix Analysis, Vol. 169. LC 96-32217. (Graduate Texts in Mathematics Ser.). 347p. 1996. 49.95 (*0-387-94846-5*) Spr-Verlag.

Bhatia, Ramesh, et al, eds. Socioeconomic Aspects of Renewable Energy Technologies. LC 87-22890. 226p. 1988. 62.95 (*0-275-92851-9*, C2851, Praeger Pubs) Greenwood.

Bhatia, Rattan J. The West African Monetary Union: An Analytical Review. (Occasional Papers: No. 35). 59p. 1985. pap. 7.50 (*1-55775-083-1*) Intl Monetary.

***Bhatia, S.** Favourite Chinese Dishes. 1998. pap. 45.00 (*81-86982-06-X*, Pub. by Business Pubns) St Mut.

— Favourite Dishes of India. 1998. pap. 63.00 (*81-86982-09-4*, Pub. by Business Pubns) St Mut.

— Favourite Sindi Dishes. 1998. pap. 45.00 (*81-86982-29-9*, Pub. by Business Pubns) St Mut.

Bhatia, S. N. & Leighton, B. C. A Manual of Facial Growth: A Computer Analysis of Longitudinal Cephalometric Growth Data. LC 93-2900. (Illus.). 560p. 1993. text 230.00 (*0-19-261770-2*) OUP.

***Bhatia, Sangeeta.** Microfabrication in Tissue Engineering & Bioartificial Organs. LC 99-35715. (Microsystems Ser.). 145p. 1999. write for info. (*0-7923-8566-7*) Kluwer Academic.

Bhatia, Sanjiv, ed. Industry Analysis: The Consumer Staples Industry. (Orig.). 1996. pap. text 30.00 (*1-879087-59-6*) RFICFA.

— Investing Worldwide, Vol. VI. 78p. (Orig.). 1996. pap. text 30.00 (*1-879087-58-8*) RFICFA.

— Managing Assets for Individual Investors. 94p. (Orig.). 1995. pap. text 30.00 (*1-879087-53-7*) RFICFA.

***Bhatia, Sardar S., et al.** The Sikh Tradition: A Continuing Reality: Essays in History & Religion. LC 99-933517. xxii, 337 p. 1999. write for info. (*81-7380-558-X*, Pub. by Pubn Bureau) S Asia.

Bhatia, Satish C. & Chopra, R. N., eds. Bryophyte Development: Physiology & Biochemistry. (Illus.). 312p. 1990. boxed set 225.00 (*0-8493-5289-4*, QK533) CRC Pr.

Bhatia, Savitri. Delightful Cooking: Best of Indian Cuisine. (C). 1994. 20.00 (*81-7223-095-8*, Pub. by Indus Pub) S Asia.

Bhatia, Shobha & Suits, L. David, eds. Recent Developments in Geotextile Filters & Prefabricated Drainage Geocomposites, No. 1281. LC 96-14901. (STP Ser.: Vol. 1281). (Illus.). 240p. 1996. text 43.00 (*0-8031-2047-8*, STP1281) ASTM.

Bhatia, Shyam. Nuclear Rivals in the Middle East. 160p. 1988. lib. bdg. 57.50 (*0-415-00479-9*) Routledge.

***Bhatia, Shyam & McGrory, Dan.** Brighter Than the Baghdad Sun: Saddam Hussein's Nuclear Threat to the United States. 2000. 27.95 (*0-89526-251-7*) Regnery Pub.

***Bhatia, Singh, ed.** Interface Tribology. 91p. 1999. 70.00 (*0-7918-1969-8*) ASME Pr.

Bhatia, Sitesh. Agricultural Price Policy & Production in India, 1956-1990. viii, 221p. (C). 1991. text 27.50 (*81-220-0210-2*) Advent Bks Div.

Bhatia, Subhash. Zeolite Catalysts: Principles & Applications. 320p. 1989. lib. bdg. 249.00 (*0-8493-5628-8*, TP245, CRC Reprint) Franklin.

Bhatia, Sukhcharan K., ed. Jurisprudence of Amending Process under Indian Constitution. (C). 1990. 113.00 (*0-89771-209-9*) St Mut.

Bhatia, Tej K. Colloquial Hindi: A Complete Language Course. LC 95-14790. 354p. (gr. 13). 1996. pap. 22.99 (*0-415-11087-4*) Routledge.

— Colloquial Hindi: A Complete Language Course. LC 95-14790. (Illus.). (C). (gr. 13). 1996. audio 27.99 (*0-415-11088-2*) Routledge.

— Colloquial Hindi: A Complete Language Course. LC 95-14790. 322p. (gr. 13). 1997. pap. 45.00 incl. audio (*0-415-11089-0*) Routledge.

***Bhatia, Tej K. & Koul, Ashok.** Colloquial Afrikaans: The Complete Course for Beginners. (Colloquials Ser.). 304p. 2000. 55.00 incl. audio (*0-415-20674-X*) Routledge.

Bhatia, Tej K. & Koul, Ashok. Colloquial Urdu: A Complete Language Course. LC 96-3689. (URD., Illus.). 384p. 1998. pap. 24.99 (*0-415-13540-0*); pap. 44.99 incl. audio (*0-415-13542-7*) Routledge.

— Colloquial Urdu: Complete Language Course. (Colloquials Ser.). (Illus.). (C). 1998. audio 27.99 (*0-415-13541-9*) Routledge.

Bhatia, Tej K., jt. ed. see Ritchie, William C.

Bhatia, Vijay K. Analysing Genre: Language Use in Professional Settings. LC 92-30733. (Applied Linguistics & Language Ser.). 1995. pap. text 33.52 (*0-582-08524-1*) Longman.

Bhatkal, G. R. & Bhatkal, Sadanand. Contemporary India: G.r. Bhatkal Memorial Lectures, 1975-1995. LC 98-901679. xiii, 246p. 1998. 24.00 (*81-7154-559-9*, Pub. by Popular Prakashan) S Asia.

Bhatkal, Sadanand, jt. auth. see Bhatkal, G. R.

Bhatkande, V. N. A Comparative Study of Some of the Leading Music Systems of the Fifteenth, Sixteenth, Seventeenth & Eighteenth Centuries. 1990. reprint ed. 9.00 (*81-85395-85-3*, Pub. by Low Price) S Asia.

Bhatkar, Vijay P. & Popovic, Dobrivoje. Distributed Computer Control Systems in Industrial Automation. (Electrical Engineering & Electronics Ser.: Vol. 66). (Illus.). 728p. 1990. text 195.00 (*0-8247-8118-X*) Dekker.

Bhatkar, Vijay P., jt. auth. see Popovic, Dobrivoje.

Bhatla, Ravi. SSRI 6 SIGMA APPRCH PROC. LC 92-25877. (Six Sigma Research Institute Ser.). 1993. pap. text 10.95 (*0-201-63420-1*) Addison-Wesley.

Bhatnagar, jt. ed. see Sinha.

Bhatnagar, A. K., ed. Metallic & Semiconducting Glasses, 3 vols., Set. 960p. (C). 1987. text 316.00 (*0-87849-556-8*, Pub. by Trans T Pub) Enfield Pubs NH.

Bhatnagar, Ajay S., ed. The Anterior Pituitary Gland. LC 81-40373. (Illus.). 471p. 1983. reprint ed. pap. 146.10 (*0-7837-9523-8*, 206027200005) Bks Demand.

Bhatnagar, B. Manual of Railway Laws. (C). 1990. 110.00 (*0-89771-247-1*) St Mut.

Bhatnagar, Bhuvana & Williams, Aubrey C., eds. Participatory Development & the World Bank: Potential Directions for Change. LC 92-34236. (Discussion Papers: Vol. 183). 202p. 1992. pap. 22.00 (*0-8213-2249-4*, 12249) World Bank.

Bhatnagar, G. S. Science & Technology of the Diamond. 220p. 1997. boxed set 108.00 (*1-898326-48-7*, Pub. by CISP) Balogh.

Bhatnagar, J. P. Commentaries on the Muslim Women (Protection of Rights on Divorce) Act, 1986-1987, No. 25. (C). 1987. 50.00 (*0-7855-4756-8*) St Mut.

— Commentaries on the Societies Registration Act, 1860. 314p. 1985. 180.00 (*0-7855-1408-2*) St Mut.

— Commentaries on the Societies Registration Act, 1980. 6th rev. ed. (C). 1991. 95.00 (*0-7855-5418-1*) St Mut.

— Societies Registration Act, 1860. (C). 1993. 110.00 (*81-7012-457-3*, Pub. by Eastern Book) St Mut.

Bhatnagar, K. B., ed. Instability, Chaos & Predictability in Celestial Mechanics & Stellar Dynamics. 402p. (C). 1993. text 225.00 (*1-56072-054-9*) Nova Sci Pubs.

— Space Dynamics & Celestial Mechanics. 1986. text 226.50 (*90-277-2311-7*) Kluwer Academic.

Bhatnagar, K. P. Elsevier's Dictionary of Civil Engineering. 704p. 1988. 246.00 (*0-444-42961-1*) Elsevier.

— Elsevier's Dictionary of Civil Engineering. (ENG & RUS.). 694p. 1988. 350.00 (*0-8288-9264-4*) Fr & Eur.

— Elsevier's Dictionary of Geosciences. (ENG & RUS.). 1036p. 1991. 227.00 (*0-444-88425-4*) Elsevier.

— Elsevier's Dictionary of Geosciences. (ENG & RUS.). 1024p. 1991. 395.00 (*0-8288-9246-6*) Fr & Eur.

Bhatnagar, M. K. Feminist English Literature. LC 99-932722. ix, 318 p. 1999. (*81-7156-824-6*) Atlantic Pubs.

Bhatnagar, P. The Problems of Afforestation in India. (C). 1991. text 150.00 (*0-89771-554-3*, Pub. by Intl Bk Distr) St Mut.

— The Problems of Afforestation in India. 170p. 1991. pap. 250.00 (*81-7089-156-6*, Pub. by Intl Bk Distr) St Mut.

Bhatnagar, P. K. Engineering Networks for Synchronization, CCS 7, & ISDN: Standards, Protocols, Planning, & Testing. LC 96-50010. 528p. 1997. 89.95 (*0-7803-1158-2*) Inst Electrical.

— Medical Physics for Human Health Care. 1997. pap. 300.00 (*81-7233-154-1*, Pub. by Scientific Pubs) St Mut.

Bhatnagar, S. Famous Murder Cases. (C). 1988. 75.00 (*0-7855-3543-8*) St Mut.

— Rural Local Government in India. 278p. 1978. 16.95 (*0-318-36617-7*) Asia Bk Corp.

Bhatnagar, S. K. Network Analysis Techniques. LC 82-23257. 301p. 1987. 28.95 (*0-470-27395-X*) P-H.

Bhatnagar, Subhash C. & Andy, Orlando. Neuroscience for the Study of Communicative Disorders. (Illus.). 369p. 1995. pap. text 37.95 (*0-683-00740-8*) Lppncott W & W.

***Bhatnagar, Subhash C. & Schware, Robert.** Information & Communication Technology in Development: Cases from India. LC 00-28598. 2000. pap. write for info. (*0-7619-9445-9*) Sage.

Bhatnagar, V. P. A Complete Course in Certificate Physics, Vol. 2. 292p. 1996. pap. 70.00 (*81-209-0868-6*, Pub. by Pitambar Pub) St Mut.

Bhatnagar, V. P. A Complete Course in Certificate Physics, VOL.1. 272p. 1997. pap. 80.00 (*81-209-0867-8*) St Mut.

Bhatnagar, V. P. A Complete Course in ISC Physics, Vol. 1. 794p. 1997. pap. 160.00 (*81-209-0385-4*, Pub. by Pitambar Pub) St Mut.

An Asterisk (*) at the beginning of an entry indicates that the title is appearing for the first time.

— A Complete Course in ISC Physics, Vol. 2. 804p. 1997. pap. 150.00 (*81-209-0202-5*, Pub. by Pitambar Pub) St Mut.

Bhatnagar, V. P., et al. The Art of Comprehension, Vol. 1. 272p. 1997. pap. 80.00 (*81-209-0767-1*, Pub. by Pitambar Pub) St Mut.

Bhatnagar, V. S., tr. Padmanabha's Kanhadada: India's Greatest Patriotic Saga of Medieval Times. (C). 1991. 27.50 (*81-85179-54-9*, Pub. by Aditya Prakashan) S Asia.

Bhatnagar, Ved. Challenges to India's Integrity: Terrorism, Casteism, Communalism. LC 98-903023. 243p. 1998. write for info. (*81-7033-442-X*) Rawat Pubns.

Bhatnagar, W. Criminal Minor Acts, 2 vols. (C). 1988. 300.00 (*0-7855-3544-6*) St Mut.

Bhatnagar, Y. C. Foreign Language Teaching in India. (C). 1988. 24.00 (*81-202-0199-X*, Pub. by Ajanta) S Asia.

— Soviet Literature & Glasnost Vol. 1: A Study in Povests. 1990. 16.00 (*81-202-0268-6*, Pub. by Ajanta) S Asia.

Bhatnagar, Y. C., tr. see Belai, Margrita A., et al.

Bhatnager, Damyanti. Bureaucratic Culture in India. (C). 1989. 26.00 (*81-7033-066-1*, Pub. by Rawat Pubns) S Asia.

Bhatt. Liberation & Purity: Race, New Religious Movements & the Ethics of Postmodernity. LC 97-202060. 320p. 1997. 65.00 (*1-85728-423-2*, Pub. by UCL Pr Ltd); pap. 22.95 (*1-85728-424-0*, Pub. by UCL Pr Ltd) Taylor & Francis.

— Programmed Dynamic Analysis Structures. (Civil Engineering Ser.). 1999. pap. 55.00 (*0-419-15610-0*) Thomson Learn.

— Programming the Matrix Analysis of Skeletal Structures. (Civil & Mechanical Engineering Ser.). 1986. text 59.95 (*0-470-20310-2*) P-H.

Bhatt, Anil. Development & Social Justice: Micro-Action by Weaker Sections. 220p. (C). 1989. text 26.00 (*0-8039-9579-2*) Sage.

— Poverty Tribals & Development: A Rehabilitation Approach. 1990. 14.00 (*81-85054-96-7*, Pub. by Manohar) S Asia.

Bhatt, B. D. Women's Education & Social Development. (Modern Education Ser.). (C). 1992. 34.00 (*81-85475-54-7*, Pub. by Kanishka) S Asia.

***Bhatt, B. D. & Praskash, Ravi, eds.** Modern Encyclopaedia of Educational Technology, 4 vols. 1998. pap. 750.00 (*81-7391-026-X*, Pub. by Print Hse) St Mut.

***Bhatt, Chetan.** Hindu Nationalism: Origins, Ideologies & Modern Myths. 192p. 2000. 65.00 (*1-85973-343-3*, Pub. by Berg Pubs); pap. 19.50 (*1-85973-348-4*, Pub. by Berg Pubs) NYU Pr.

Bhatt, Christa, et al, eds. Syntactic Phrase Structure Phenomena in Noun Phrases & Sentences. LC 89-18430. (Linguistik Aktuell/Linguistics Today Ser.: Vol. 6). ix, 187p. 1989. 44.00 (*90-272-2726-8*) J Benjamins Pubng Co.

Bhatt, G. D. Emerging Leadership Pattern in Rural India: An Empirical Study. 221p. 1994. pap. 150.00 (*81-85880-20-4*, Pub. by Print Hse) St Mut.

— Empowerment & Status of Rural Women: A Central Himalayan Perspective. LC 99-931186. 1998. 25.00 (*81-7533-074-0*, Pub. by M D Pubns) S Asia.

Bhatt, G. P. Ancient Indian Tradition & Mythology Vol. 39: Padma-Purana, Pt. 1. (C). 1988. 26.00 (*0-317-93108-3*, Pub. by Motilal Bnarsidass) S Asia.

— The Basic Ways of Knowing: An Indepth Study of Kumarila's Contribution to Indian Epistemology. (C). 1989. 31.00 (*81-208-0580-1*, Pub. by Motilal Bnarsidass) S Asia.

— Vagu Puranas Pt. II: Ancient Indian Tradition & Mythology, Vol. 38. 1988. 26.00 (*81-208-0455-4*, Pub. by Motilal Bnarsidass) S Asia.

Bhatt, G. P., ed. Ancient Indian Tradition & Mythology Vol. 53: The Skanda-Purana V. Tagare, G. V., tr. (C). 1994. text 22.00 (*81-208-1151-8*, Pub. by Motilal Bnarsidass) S Asia.

— Ancient Indian Tradition & Mythology Vol. 55, Pt. VII: The Skanda Purana. Tagare, G. V., tr. (C). 1995. 22.00 (*81-208-1203-4*, Pub. by Motilal Bnarsidass) S Asia.

— Brahma Purana: Gautami Mahatmya, Pt. IV. (Ancient Indian Tradition & Mythology Ser.). 448p. 1987. 28.50 (*0-317-60563-1*, Pub. by Motilal Bnarsidass) S Asia.

— The Skandapurana. 1996. 24.00 (*81-208-1364-2*, Pub. by Motilal Bnarsidass) S Asia.

Bhatt, G. S. Women & Polyandry in Rawain-Jaunpur. (C). 1991. 16.00 (*0-685-59789-X*, Pub. by Rawat Pubns) S Asia.

Bhatt, Harasiddhiprasad G., et al, eds. Management of Toxic & Hazardous Wastes: Development from the Third Ohio Environmental Conference. 418p. 1985. 50.00 (*0-685-18631-8*, 1023) Am Soc Civil Eng.

Bhatt, M. Ramakrishna, ed. & tr. see Varahamihira.

Bhatt, Nikhil J. Endoscopic Sinus Surgery: New Horizons. LC 97-20818. (Illus.). 190p. (Orig.). 1997. pap. 164.95 (*1-56593-897-6*, 1766) Thomson Learn.

Bhatt, P. & Marshall, W. T. Structures. 4th ed. LC 98-36456. 1999. write for info. (*0-582-31222-1*) Longman.

Bhatt, Purnima M. Scholars' Guide to Washington, D. C. for African Studies. LC 79-607774. (Scholar's Guide to Washington D.C. Ser.: No. 4). 348p. (Orig.). 1980. text 29.95 (*0-87474-238-2*); pap. text 12.95 (*0-87474-239-0*) W Wilson Ctr Pr.

Bhatt, R. G., jt. auth. see Oza, S. S.

***Bhatt, Rakesh M.** Verb Movement & the Syntax of Kashmiri. LC 99-55907. (Studies in Natural Language & Linguistic Theory). 308p. 1999. 117.00 (*0-7923-6033-8*) Kluwer Academic.

Bhatt, S. Environment Protection & International Laws. 122p. 1985. text 15.95 (*81-7027-081-2*, Pub. by Radiant Pubs) S Asia.

Bhatt, S. C. Satellite Invasion of India. LC 94-905418. (C). 1996. 30.00 (*81-212-0483-6*, Pub. by Gian Publng Hse) S Asia.

— The Triangle Indian Nepal China: A Study of Treaty Rotations. 1996. pap. 120.00 (*0-7855-7499-9*, Pub. by Ratna Pustak Bhandar) St Mut.

Bhatt, S. C., ed. The Encyclopedia District Gazetteers of India, 10 vols., Set. rev. ed. (C). 1996. 1250.00 (*81-212-0525-5*, Pub. by Gian Publng Hse) S Asia.

Bhatt, S. D. Ecology of the Mountain Waters. (C). 1991. 45.00 (*81-7024-366-1*, Pub. by Ashish Pub Hse) S Asia.

***Bhatt, S. R. & Dignaga.** Buddhist Epistemology, 75. LC 99-44513. (Contributions in Philosophy Ser.). 160p. 2000. 55.00 (*0-313-31087-4*, Greenwood Pr) Greenwood.

Bhatt, S. R., jt. ed. see Pandey, R. C.

Bhatt, Sandeep N., ed. see DIMACS (Group) Staff.

***Bhatt, Sujata.** Augatora. 96p. 1999. pap. (*1-85754-381-5*, Pub. by Carcanet Pr) Paul & Co Pubs.

Bhatt, Sujata. Point No Point: Selected Poems. LC 97-221814. 144p. 1997. pap. 14.95 (*1-85754-306-8*, Pub. by Carcanet Pr) Paul & Co Pubs.

— The Stinking Rose. 128p. 1995. pap. 16.95 (*1-85754-048-4*, Pub. by Carcanet Pr) Paul & Co Pubs.

Bhatt, Vikram. Resorts of the Raj: Hill Stations of India. 1997. 65.00 (*0-944142-98-2*) Grantha.

***Bhatt, Vikram.** Resorts of the Raj: Hill Stations of India. 1998. 140.00 (*81-85822-41-7*) Mapin Pub.

Bhatt, Vinay, ed. GMP Compliance, Productivity & Quality: Achieving Synergy in Healthcare Manufacturing Process Optimization. LC 98-6591. 1998. 229.00 (*1-57491-077-9*) Interpharm.

Bhatt, Vinayak V. Financial Systems, Innovations, & Development. 200p. 1995. 29.95 (*0-8039-9268-8*) Sage.

Bhatta, Anita. The Strategic Role of Indian Ocean in World Politics: A Case Study of Diego Garcita. (C). 1992. 21.00 (*0-8364-2809-9*, Pub. by Ajanta) S Asia.

***Bhatta, Gambhir.** Reforms at the United Nations: Contextualising the Annan Agenda. 366p. 2000. pap. 48.50 (*9971-69-235-X*, Pub. by Sngapore Univ Pr) Coronet Bks.

Bhatta, Gambhir & Gonzalez, Joaquin L., III, eds. Governance Innovations in the Asia-Pacific Region: Trends, Cases & Issues. LC 97-78327. (Illus.). 305p. 1998. text 72.95 (*1-84014-392-4*, Pub. by Ashgate Pub) Ashgate Pub Co.

Bhatta, H. S. Secondary Education. (C). 1990. 56.00 (*81-7024-340-8*, Pub. by Ashish Pub Hse) S Asia.

Bhatta, V. P. Epistemology, Logic & Grammar Vol. 1: In the Analysis of Sentence-Meaning. xxxvii, 313p. (C). 1991. 28.22 (*81-85133-49-2*, Pub. by Eastern Bk Linkers) Nataraj Bks.

— Gadadhara's Saktivada Theory of Expressive Power of Words Vol. 1: With Introduction English Translation, Notes & Sanskrit Text. LC 94-902189. viii, 371p. (C). 1994. 29.00 (*81-85133-70-0*, Pub. by Eastern Bk Linkers) Nataraj Bks.

— Gadadhara's Theory of Expressive Power of Words Saktivada Vol. 2: With English Translation, Notes & Sanskrit Text. LC 94-902189. ix, 424p. 1995. 39.00 (*81-86339-11-6*, Pub. by Eastern Bk Linkers) Nataraj Bks.

Bhatta, V. P., ed. Epistemology, Logic & Grammar Vol. 2: In the Analysis of Sentence-Meaning. ix, 229p. 1992. 18.00 (*0-685-62639-3*, Pub. by Eastern Bk Linkers) Nataraj Bks.

— Epistemology, Logic & Grammar, Vol. 1: In the Analysis of Sentence-Meaning. xxxvii, 313p. 1991. 28.00 (*0-685-62640-7*, Pub. by Eastern Bk Linkers) Nataraj Bks.

— Mandana Misra's Distinction of the Activity Bhavanaviveka: With Introduction, English Translation with Notes, & Sanskrit Text. LC 93-910452. 6, 307p. (C). 1994. 30.00 (*81-85133-81-6*, Pub. by Eastern Bk Linkers) Nataraj Bks.

Bhattachan & Mishra. Developmental Practices in Nepal. 1997. pap. 27.00 (*0-7855-7381-X*, Pub. by Ratna Pustak Bhandar) St Mut.

Bhattacharjea, Ajit. Kashmir: The Wounded Valley. (C). 1994. 18.50 (*81-86112-36-7*, Pub. by UBS Pubs Dist) S Asia.

Bhattacharjea, Ajit, ed. Social Justice & the Constitution. xi, 271p. 1997. 20.00 (*81-85952-44-2*, Pub. by Indian Inst) Nataraj Bks.

Bhattacharjee, Arun. Bharatavarsha: An Account of Early India with Special Emphasis on Social & Economic Aspects. 212p. (C). 1988. 27.00 (*81-7024-169-3*, Pub. by Ashish Pub Hse) S Asia.

— A History of Modern India, Seventeen Seven to Nineteen Forty-Seven. 1988. 28.50 (*81-7024-180-4*, Pub. by Ashish Pub Hse) S Asia.

— History of Political Thought: From Plato to Laski. (C). 1989. 31.00 (*81-7024-246-0*, Pub. by Ashish Pub Hse) S Asia.

— The Prophets of Modern Indian Nationalism: Raja Rammohun Roy, Swami Dayananda Saraswati, Ishwar Chandra Vidyasagar, Bankim Chandra Chatterji, Swami Vivekananda, Dababhai Naoroji, Mahadev Govind-Ranade & Pherozeshah Mehta. viii, 213p. 1993. 25.00 (*81-7024-535-4*, Pub. by Ashish Pub Hse) Nataraj Bks.

— Rajiv Gandhi: Life & Message. xiv, 267p. 1992. 25.00 (*81-7024-484-6*, Pub. by Ashish Pub Hse) Nataraj Bks.

Bhattacharjee, Arun, jt. auth. see Basham, A. L.

Bhattacharjee, Arun, jt. auth. see Muller, Edmund.

Bhattacharjee, I. R. Gravity Dictates Life-Death & Biological Growth (Also Agricultural Productivity) Introductory Concept. 160p. 1988. 5.00 (*1-55528-097-8*) Scholarly Pubns.

Bhattacharjee, J. Convection & Chaos in Fluids. 256p. 1987. text 58.00 (*9971-5-0224-0*) World Scientific Pub.

Bhattacharjee, J. B. Social & Polity Formations in Pre-Colonial North-East India. 1991. text 35.00 (*0-7069-5464-5*, Pub. by Vikas) S Asia.

Bhattacharjee, J. K. Statistical Physics: Equilibrium & Non-Equilibrium Aspects. 1997. 24.00 (*81-7023-631-2*, Pub. by Allied Pubs) S Asia.

Bhattacharjee, J. P., ed. Studies in Indian Agricultural Economics. LC 75-26296. (World Food Supply Ser.). (Illus.). 1976. reprint ed. 30.95 (*0-405-07769-6*) Ayer.

Bhattacharjee, M. Notes of Infinite Permutation Groups. LC 98-39226. (Lecture Notes in Mathematics Ser.: Vol. 169). 1999. pap. write for info. (*3-540-64965-4*) Spr-Verlag.

Bhattacharjee, Nirmal Kanti, jt. auth. see Debi, Mahasveta.

Bhattacharjee, S. B., jt. ed. see Mookherjee, A.

Bhattacharjee, S. M., ed. Polymer Physics: Twenty-Five Years of the Edwards Model: Proceedings of the Workshop - Puri, India, 2-9 January 1991. LC 92-11873. 400p. (C). 1992. text 104.00 (*981-02-0741-7*); pap. text 61.00 (*981-02-1985-7*) World Scientific Pub.

Bhattacharjee, Shivaji. Astrological Healing Gems. 128p. (Orig.). (C). 1990. pap. 7.95 (*1-878423-07-X*) Morson Pub.

Bhattacharji, S., et al, eds. Fluvial Hydraulics of Mountain Regions. (Lecture Notes in Earth Sciences Ser.: Vol. 37). (Illus.). x, 468p. 1991. 86.95 (*0-387-54491-7*) Spr-Verlag.

— GPS for Geodesy, Vol. 60. (Illus.). viii, 416p. 1996. pap. 99.95 (*3-540-60785-4*) Spr-Verlag.

— Thermal Analysis in the Geosciences. (Lecture Notes in Earth Sciences Ser.: Vol. 38). (Illus.). 392p. 1991. 79.95 (*0-387-54520-4*) Spr-Verlag.

Bhattacharji, S., ed. see Allard, B., et al.

Bhattacharji, S., ed. see Koch, K. R.

Bhattacharji, S., ed. see Lehmann, B.

Bhattacharji, S., ed. see Mosbrugger, V.

Bhattacharji, S., ed. see Scherbaum, F.

Bhattacharji, S., ed. see Shangguan, D.

Bhattacharji, S., ed. see Stille, Peter & Shields, Graham.

Bhattacharji, S., ed. see Trappe, J.

Bhattacharji, S., ed. see Westphal, H.

Bhattacharji, Sukumari. Literature in the Vedic Age: Brahmanas, Aranyakas, Upanishads & Sutras, Vol. 2. 400p. 1986. 32.50 (*0-8364-1859-X*, Pub. by KP Bagchi) S Asia.

Bhattacharvya, Amitabha & Ham, Inyong. Design of Cutting Tools: Use of Metal Cutting Theory. LC 68-59237. (American Society of Tool & Manufacturing Engineers Manufacturing Data Ser.). 199p. reprint ed. pap. 61.70 (*0-608-11549-5*, 201600100097) Bks Demand.

Bhattachary, Ed & Gurung. Emerging Ethnicity & Aspects of Community Adoptation. 1996. pap. 27.00 (*0-7855-7392-5*, Pub. by Ratna Pustak Bhandar) St Mut.

Bhattacharya. Dictionary Francais-Bengali. (FRE & BEN.). 273p. 1994. 59.95 (*0-320-00839-8*) Fr & Eur.

Bhattacharya. Metal Filled Polymers. (Plastics Engineering Ser.: Vol. 11). (Illus.). 376p. 1986. text 175.00 (*0-8247-7555-4*) Dekker.

***Bhattacharya, ed.** Globalisation & India: A Multi-Dimensional Perspective. 2000. 29.50 (*81-7095-076-7*, Pub. by Lancer India) S Asia.

Bhattacharya & Thapar, R., eds. Situating Indian History. 463p. 1986. 49.95 (*0-318-36973-7*) Asia Bk Corp.

Bhattacharya, A. A Treatise on Ancient Hindu Music. 176p. 1978. 12.95 (*0-318-36325-9*) Asia Bk Corp.

Bhattacharya, A. K., et al, eds. Proceedings of the IVth Indian Geological Congress Varanasi. (Current Trends in Geology Ser.: Vols. 7-8). 900p. 1985. 95.00 (*1-55528-005-6*) Scholarly Pubns.

Bhattacharya, Anand K. & Fabozzi, Frank J., eds. Asset-Backed Securities. 402p. 1996. 75.00 (*1-883249-10-4*) F J Fabozzi.

Bhattacharya, Anima, et al, eds. Planning in the Perspective of Development. 231p. 1995. pap. 150.00 (*81-85880-62-X*, Pub. by Print Hse) St Mut.

***Bhattacharya, B.** Damage Mechanics Based Approach to Structural Deterioration & Reliability. 201p. 1998. per. 17.00 (*0-16-062892-X*) USGPO.

Bhattacharya, B. Saivism & the Phallic World, 2 vols. (C). 1993. text 110.00 (*81-215-0618-2*, Pub. by M Manoharial) Coronet Bks.

***Bhattacharya, B.** Varanasi Rediscovered. (Illus.). 332p. 1999. 57.50 (*81-215-0860-6*, Pub. by M Manoharial) S Asia.

Bhattacharya, B. The World of Tantra. 1988. 48.50 (*81-215-0080-X*, Pub. by M Manoharial) Coronet Bks.

***Bhattacharya, B.** World of Tantra. 2nd ed. 2000. reprint ed. pap. 26.95 (*81-215-0968-8*, Pub. by M Manoharial) S Asia.

Bhattacharya, B. B. India's Economic Crises, Debt Burden & Stabilization. (C). 1992. 9.00 (*81-7018-714-1*, Pub. by BR Pub) S Asia.

— Public Expenditure, Inflation & Growth: A Macro-Econometric Analysis for India. (Illus.). 250p. (C). 1985. text 21.00 (*0-19-561713-4*) OUP.

Bhattacharya, B. B., ed. Frontiers in Exploration Geophysics. (C). 1988. 36.00 (*81-204-0300-2*, Pub. by Oxford IBH) S Asia.

Bhattacharya, B. B., tr. see Kozlov, E. A.

Bhattacharya, Bhabani, ed. Contemporary Indian Short Stories, Vol. 2. 3rd ed. 1982. pap. 6.50 (*0-8364-1599-X*, Pub. by National Sahitya Akademi) S Asia.

Bhattacharya, Bhabani C., ed. Contemporary Indian Short Stories, Series 1. 132p. 1976. 5.95 (*0-318-36951-6*) Asia Bk Corp.

Bhattacharya, Bhabani C., ed. Contemporary Indian Short Stories, Series 2. 240p. 1977. 6.95 (*0-318-36946-X*) Asia Bk Corp.

Bhattacharya, Bhaswati, jt. auth. see Udayaneacearya Staff.

Bhattacharya, Binay. Kamakhya Hills & Elsewhere: A Novel. 1993. 16.00 (*81-7001-092-6*, Pub. by Chanakya) S Asia.

Bhattacharya, Brojen, jt. auth. see Chakraborty, Phani B.

Bhattacharya, D., ed. Origins of Algae & Their Plastids. (Illus.). 320p. 1998. 179.00 (*3-211-83036-7*) Spr-Verlag.

Bhattacharya, Debashis & Hayes, John P. Hierarchical Modeling for VLSI Circuit Testing. (C). 1989. text 91.50 (*0-7923-9058-X*) Kluwer Academic.

Bhattacharya, Debashish. Origins of Algae & Their Plastids. LC 97-48872. (Plant Systematics & Evolution Ser.). 1997. write for info. (*3-211-83035-9*) Spr-Verlag.

Bhattacharya, Deben. The Mirror of the Sky: Songs of the Bauls of Bengal. 2nd rev. ed. LC 98-45834. (Illus.). 288p. 1999. pap. 24.95 incl. audio compact disk (*0-934252-89-0*, Pub. by Hohm Pr) SCB Distributors.

***Bhattacharya, Dillip.** Musical Instruments of Tribal India. LC 98-915699. 1998. 142.00 (*81-7049-092-8*, Pub. by Manas Pubns) S Asia.

Bhattacharya, Dipak C. Studies in Buddhist Iconography. 1978. 22.50 (*0-8364-0016-X*) S Asia.

Bhattacharya, Hiranmoy. Raj & Literature: Banned Bengali Books. (C). 1989. 21.50 (*0-9514244-0-8*, Pub. by Firma KLM) S Asia.

Bhattacharya, Hrishikes. Banking Strategy, Credit Appraisal & Lending Decisions: A Risk-Return Framework. (Illus.). 744p. 1999. pap. 22.50 (*0-19-564850-1*) OUP.

— Total Management by Ratios: An Integrated Approach for the Control & Monitoring of Business Enterprises. 256p. 1995. 38.00 (*0-8039-9271-8*) Sage.

Bhattacharya, Ishan, jt. auth. see Gress, Frank.

Bhattacharya, J. C. Kabir: In the Light of Kriyayoga. (Illus.). 198p. 1997. reprint ed. pap. 29.95 (*0-937134-21-X*) Amrita Found.

— Yogiraj Shri Shri Lahiri Mahashay. LC 97-196072. (Illus.). 74p. 1997. reprint ed. pap. 21.95 (*0-937134-20-1*) Amrita Found.

Bhattacharya, Jason K. My Trips to India. (Illus.). viii, 24p. (Orig.). (J). 1995. pap. 3.95 (*1-881338-43-6*) Nataraj Bks.

Bhattacharya, Jogendra N. Hindu Castes & Sects. (C). 1995. 34.00 (*81-215-0700-6*, Pub. by M Manoharial) Coronet Bks.

Bhattacharya, Keron. The Pearls of Coromandel. large type ed. (Large Print Ser.). 576p. 1997. 27.99 (*0-7089-3679-2*) Ulverscroft.

Bhattacharya, Krishna. Dialectical Methods of Nagarjuna. vii, 146p. 1986. 15.00 (*81-208-0176-8*, Pub. by Motilal Bnarsidass) S Asia.

Bhattacharya, Krishna, tr. see Saraswati, Madhusudana.

Bhattacharya, N. N. Buddhism in the History of Indian Ideas. (C). 1993. 31.00 (*81-7304-017-6*, Pub. by Manohar) S Asia.

— Glossary of Indian Religious Terms & Concepts. 244p. (C). 1991. 40.00 (*0-685-48705-9*, Pub. by S Asia Pubs) S Asia.

— Medieval Bhakti Movements in India. (C). 1989. 44.00 (*0-685-30850-2*, Pub. by M Manoharial) S Asia.

Bhattacharya, Nalinaksha. A Fistful of Desire. LC 98-900458. 1997. write for info. (*0-14-027050-7*) Penguin Books.

Bhattacharya, Nandini. Reading the Splendid Body: Gender & Consumerism in Eighteenth-Century British Writing on India. LC 97-5222. (Illus.). 232p. 1998. 39.50 (*0-87413-612-1*) U Delaware Pr.

Bhattacharya, Nikhilesh, et al. Poverty, Inequality & Prices in Rural India. 220p. (C). 1991. 28.50 (*0-8039-9685-3*) Sage.

Bhattacharya, P., ed. Properties of Lattice-Matched & Strained Indium Gallium Arsenide. (EMIS Datareviews Ser.: No. 8). 360p. 1993. boxed set 225.00 (*0-85296-865-5*) INSPEC Inc.

Bhattacharya, P. B., et al. Basic Abstract Algebra. 507p. (C). 1994. text 80.00 (*0-521-46081-6*) Cambridge U Pr.

Bhattacharya, P. K., ed. Properties of III-V Quantum Wells & Superlattices. (EMIS Datareviews Ser.: No. 15). 420p. 1996. 195.00 (*0-85296-881-7*, EM015) INSPEC Inc.

Bhattacharya, R. N. & Rao, Ranga R. Normal Approximation & Asymptotic Expansions. LC 83-19559. 306p. (C). 1986. reprint ed. lib. bdg. 49.50 (*0-89874-690-6*) Krieger.

Bhattacharya, R. S., jt. auth. see Larson, G. J.

Bhattacharya, Rabi N. & Denker, Manfred. Asymptotic Systems. (DMV Seminar Ser.: Vol. 14). 122p. 1990. 35.00 (*0-8176-2282-9*); pap. 19.50 (*0-685-45915-2*) Birkhauser.

Bhattacharya, Ram S., jt. ed. see Larson, Gerald J.

Bhattacharya, Ranjit K. Moslems of Rural Bengal. (C). 1991. 20.00 (*0-8364-2761-0*, Pub. by Usha) S Asia.

Bhattacharya, Rinki. Bimal Roy: A Man of Silence. (C). 1994. 28.00 (*81-7223-154-7*, Pub. by Indus Pub) S Asia.

***Bhattacharya, S. K.** Christian Missions, Missionaries & Indian Society: A Socio-Economic Study. LC 99-936611. 1999. 38.00 (*81-7445-084-X*, Pub. by Mehit Pubns) S Asia.

Bhattacharya, S. K. Krishna-Cult in Indian Art. 164p. 1996. pap. 275.00 (*81-7533-001-5*, Pub. by Print Hse) St Mut.

— Trends in Modern Indian Art. 84p. (C). 1994. pap. 200.00 (*81-85880-21-2*, Pub. by Print Hse) St Mut.

Bhattacharya, Sabyasachi, ed. Essays in Modern Indian Economic History. (Indian History Congress Golden Jubilee Year Publication Ser.: Vol. 4). 1988. 32.00 (*81-215-0083-4*, Pub. by M Manoharial) Coronet Bks.

Bhattacharya, Sabyasachi, ed. Mahatma & the Poet: Letters & Debates Between Gandhi & Tagore, 1915-1941. 1997. reprint ed. pap. 5.00 (*81-237-2202-8*, Pub. by Natl Bk Trust) S Asia.

Bhattacharya, Sabyasachi & Thapar, Romila, eds. Situating Indian History: For Savepalli Gopal. 480p. 1987. 24.95 (*0-19-561842-4*) OUP.

Bhattacharya, Sachchidananda. Biotreatment of Hazardous Wastes. (Industrial Health & Safety Ser.). 1992. pap. write for info. (*0-442-00940-2*, VNR) Wiley.

***Bhattacharya, Sachchidananda.** A Dictionary of Indian History, 2 vols. 1998. pap. 375.00 (*81-7020-585-9*, Pub. by Print Hse) St Mut.

Bhattacharya, Sachchidananda. A Dictionary of Indian History. LC 77-1105. 963p. 1977. reprint ed. lib. bdg. 58.50 (*0-8371-9515-2*, BHDI, Greenwood Pr) Greenwood.

Bhattacharya, Sachchidananda, et al, eds. The South Indian Economy: Agrarian Change, Industrial Structure, & State Policy, 1914-1947. 320p. 1992. 27.00 (*0-19-562642-7*) OUP.

Bhattacharya, Sibnath. Rural Poverty in India. (C). 1989. 42.50 (*81-7024-254-1*, Pub. by Ashish Pub Hse) S Asia.

Bhattacharya, Sudipto. Financial Markets & Incomplete Information: Frontiers of Modern Financial Theory. Constantinides, George M., ed. LC 87-32124. (Studies in Financial Economics: Vol. 2). 374p. (C). 1989. lib. bdg. 65.00 (*0-8476-7597-1*) Rowman.

Bhattacharya, Sudipto & Constantinides, George. Theory of Valuation: Frontiers of Modern Financial Theory, Vol. 1. LC 87-32123. (Studies in Financial Economics). 368p. (C). 1988. pap. text 39.50 (*0-8476-7487-8*) Rowman.

Bhattacharya, Sudipto & Constantinides, George M., eds. Financial Markets & Incomplete Information: Frontiers of Modern Financial Theory, Vol. 2. LC 87-32124. (Studies in Financial Economics). 374p. (C). 1989. pap. text 39.50 (*0-8476-7598-X*) Rowman.

Bhattacharya, Suresh C. Vaishnavism in Eastern India. (C). 1995. 12.00 (*81-7102-026-7*, Pub. by Firma KLM) S Asia.

***Bhattacharya, Sutapas.** Oneness/Otherness Mystery: Synthesis of Science & Mysticism. LC 99-932608. 1999. 44.00 (*81-208-1654-4*, Pub. by Motilal Bnarsidass) S Asia.

Bhattacharya, Vidhushekhara, ed. The Agamasastra of Gaudapada. (C). 1989. reprint ed. 32.50 (*81-208-0652-2*, Pub. by Motilal Bnarsidass) S Asia.

Bhattacharya, Vivek. The Spirit of Indian Culture: Saints of India. 622p. 1980. 32.95 (*0-940500-40-X*) Asia Bk Corp.

Bhattacharyas, S. Physical Chemical Treatment of Hazardous Waste. 1992. pap. write for info. (*0-442-00941-0*, VNR) Wiley.

Bhattacharyya. Clinical Medicine. (C). 1989. 500.00 (*0-89771-372-9*, Pub. by Current Dist) St Mut.

***Bhattacharyya.** Indian Mother Goddess. 3rd rev. ed. 1999. 36.00 (*81-7304-324-8*, Pub. by Manohar) S Asia.

Bhattacharyya, et al, eds. The Cultural Heritage of India, Set. Incl. Vol. 1. Early Phases. Radhakrishnan, Sarvepalli, intro. 25.00 (*0-87481-560-6*); Vol. 2. Itihasas, Puranas, Dharma & Other Shastras. 25.00 (*0-87481-561-4*); Vol. 3. Philosophies. 25.00 (*0-87481-562-2*); Vol. 4. Religions. 25.00 (*0-87481-563-0*); Vol. 5. Languages & Literatures. 25.00 (*0-87481-564-9*); (Illus.). 1937. 260.00 (*0-87481-558-4*) Vedanta Pr.

Bhattacharyya, A. K. Pageant of Indian Culture, 2 vols., Set. (C). 1995. 225.00 (*0-317-99886-2*, Pub. by Abhinav) S Asia.

Bhattacharyya, Amitabha. Deformation of Solids - A Treatise on Strength of Materials. (C). 1989. 65.00 (*0-89771-382-6*, Pub. by Current Dist) St Mut.

— Principles of Metal Cutting. (C). 1989. 140.00 (*0-89771-380-X*, Pub. by Current Dist) St Mut.

Bhattacharyya, Amitabha, ed. Robotic Applications in India. (C). 1989. 80.00 (*0-89771-386-9*, Pub. by Current Dist) St Mut.

Bhattacharyya, Anjan. Modern Commercial Concepts in the Mahabharatam. 1987. 15.00 (*0-8364-2317-8*, Pub. by Firma KLM) S Asia.

Bhattacharyya, Arun. Electromagnetic Fields in Multilayered Structures: Theory & Applications. LC 93-38271. 1993. 83.00 (*0-89006-651-5*) Artech Hse.

Bhattacharyya, Asoke K. High-Frequency Electromagnetic Techniques: Recent Advances & Applications. LC 94-23584. (Series in Microwave & Optical Engineering). 512p. 1995. 145.00 incl. disk (*0-471-55903-2*) Wiley.

Bhattacharyya, B. Magnet Dowsing: or The Magnet Study of Life. 150p. 1998. reprint ed. pap. 16.50 (*0-7873-1152-9*) Hlth Research.

— The Science of Tridosha. 57p. 1996. reprint ed. spiral bd. 10.00 (*0-7873-0109-4*) Hlth Research.

Bhattacharyya, B. & Garg, G. Handbook of Direct Taxes. (C). 1990. 230.00 (*0-89771-276-5*) St Mut.

Bhattacharyya, B., jt. auth. see Johri, B. M.

Bhattacharyya, B., jt. auth. see Mullick, M.

Bhattacharyya, B., jt. auth. see Roychowdhury, R.

Bhattacharyya, B., jt. ed. see Sen, S.

Bhattacharyya, B. C., ed. Computer Aided Design (CAD) of Chemical Process Equipment. (C). 1989. 75.00 (*0-89771-384-2*, Pub. by Current Dist) St Mut.

Bhattacharyya, B. K. Humour & Satire in Assamese Literature. 263p. 1982. 45.00 (*0-940500-46-9*, Pub. by Sterling) Asia Bk Corp.

Bhattacharyya, Benoytosh. Indian Buddhist Iconography: Mainly Based on the Sadhanamala & Other Cognate Tantric Texts of Rituals. 1993. reprint ed. 62.00 (*81-206-0842-9*, Pub. by Asian Educ Servs) S Asia.

— An Introduction to Buddhist Esoterism. 1980. reprint ed. 24.00 (*81-208-0625-5*, Pub. by Motilal Bnarsidass) S Asia.

Bhattacharyya, Bhaskar. The Path of the Mystic Lover: Baul Songs of Passion & Ecstasy. Douglas, Nik, ed. LC 86-19780. (Illus.). 192p. 1993. pap. 19.95 (*0-89281-019-X*) Inner Tradit.

Bhattacharyya, Chanchal A. The Concept of Theft in Classical Hindu Law: An Analysis & the Ideas of Punishment. 220p. 1990. reprint ed. 27.50 (*81-215-0475-9*, Pub. by M Manoharial) Coronet Bks.

Bhattacharyya, D., ed. Composite Sheet Forming. LC 97-14822. (Composite Materials Ser.: Vol. 11). 548p. 1997. 273.00 (*0-444-82641-6*) Elsevier.

— Sheet Forming. 1996. write for info. (*0-614-17894-0*) Elsevier.

Bhattacharyya, Deborah P. Pagalami: Ethnopsychiatric Knowledge in Bengal. (Foreign & Comparative Studies Program, South Asian Ser.: No. 11). (Orig.). (C). 1986. pap. 13.00 (*0-915984-89-X*) Syracuse U Foreign Comp.

Bhattacharyya, Gargi. Tales of Dark Skinned Women: Race, Gender & Global Culture. LC 99-161346. (Race & Representation Ser.). 1998. pap. text 25.95 (*1-85728-612-X*) Taylor & Francis.

Bhattacharyya, Gouri K. & Johnson, Richard A. Statistical Concepts & Methods. (Probability & Mathematical Statistics Ser.). 656p. 1977. text 99.95 (*0-471-07204-4*) Wiley.

Bhattacharyya, Gouri K., jt. auth. see Johnson, Richard A.

Bhattacharyya, H. C., jt. auth. see Singh, K. N.

Bhattacharyya, Hiranya K. Economic Development of Assam. LC 97-906925. xiii, 234p. 1998. 26.00 (*81-7024-816-7*, Pub. by APH Pubng) Nataraj Bks.

Bhattacharyya, J. V., tr. Jayantabhatta's Nyaya-Manjari: The Compendium of Indian Speculative Logic, Vol. 1. 1978. 35.00 (*0-89684-000-X*, Pub. by Motilal Bnarsidass) S Asia.

Bhattacharyya, N. N. Ancient Indian History & Civilization Trends & Perspectives. (C). 1988. 27.50 (*0-945921-00-4*, Pub. by S Asia Pubs) S Asia.

— Ancient Indian Rituals & Their Social Contents. (C). 1996. reprint ed. 37.50 (*81-7304-121-0*, Pub. by Manohar) S Asia.

— The Geographical Dictionary: Ancient & Early Medieval India. 1991. 47.50 (*81-215-0078-8*, Pub. by M Manoharial) Coronet Bks.

— History of the Tantric Religion. 1983. 36.00 (*0-8364-0943-4*, Pub. by Manohar) S Asia.

— History of the Tantric Religion: A Historical, Ritualistic & Philosophical Study. (C). 1992. text 34.00 (*81-85054-39-8*) S Asia.

— Indian Religious Historiography, Vol. 1. (C). 1996. 44.00 (*81-215-0637-9*, Pub. by M Manoharial) Coronet Bks.

— Jainism & Prakrit in Ancient & Medieval India. (C). 1994. text 44.00 (*81-7304-051-6*, Pub. by Manohar) S Asia.

— Religious Culture of North-Eastern India. (C). 1995. 22.00 (*81-7304-116-4*, Pub. by Manohar) S Asia.

Bhattacharyya, Narendra N. History of the Sakta Religion. (C). 1996. reprint ed. 30.00 (*81-215-0713-8*, Pub. by M Manoharial) Coronet Bks.

***Bhattacharyya, Narendra N.** History of the Tantric Religion: An Historical, Ritualistic & Philosophical Study. 2nd ed. LC 99-932709. 483p. 1999. write for info. (*81-7304-025-7*) S Asia.

Bhattacharyya, Narendra N. Jain Philosophy: Historical Outline. 1976. 17.00 (*0-685-37837-3*, Pub. by M Manoharial) S Asia.

***Bhattacharyya, Narendra N.** Jain Philosophy: Historical Outline. LC 99-935281. 1999. 35.00 (*81-215-0887-8*, Pub. by M Manoharial) Coronet Bks.

Bhattacharyya, Narendra Nath. Encyclopaedia of Ancient Indian Culture. LC 98-909720. 459 p. 1998. write for info. (*81-7304-077-X*, Pub. by Manohar) S Asia.

Bhattacharyya, Narendra Nath, et al. Tantric Buddhism: Centennial Tribute to Dr. Benoytosh Bhattacharyya. LC 98-909713. 328p. 1999. write for info. (*81-7304-191-1*, Pub. by Manohar) S Asia.

Bhattacharyya, Parnasabari. Conceptualizations in the Manusmrti. (C). 1996. 38.00 (*81-7304-154-7*, Pub. by Manohar) S Asia.

Bhattacharyya, S. Gadadhara's Theory of Objectivity: Visayatavada, Pt. 2. 1990. 17.50 (*81-208-0822-3*, Pub. by Motilal Bnarsidass) S Asia.

Bhattacharyya, S. & Garg, H. R. Valuation under Direct Tax Laws. (C). 1989. 175.00 (*0-7855-4731-2*) St Mut.

Bhattacharyya, S. K. Genocide in East Pakistan-Bangladesh: A Horror Story. Ghosh, A., ed. 323p. (Orig.). 1988. pap. 16.50 (*0-9611614-3-4*) A Ghosh.

Bhattacharyya, S. P. Control of Uncertain Dynamic Systems. 544p. 1991. boxed set 156.95 (*0-8493-0195-5*, TJ210) CRC Pr.

— Robust Stabilization Against Structured Perurbations. (Lecture Notes in Control & Information Sciences: Vol. 99). ix, 172p. 1987. 37.95 (*0-387-18056-7*) Spr-Verlag.

Bhattacharyya, S. P., et al. Robust Control: The Parametric Approach. LC 95-2313. (Information & System Sciences Ser.). 672p. (C). 1995. pap. 75.00 (*0-13-781576-X*) P-H.

Bhattacharyya, Sailendra N. Mahatma Gandhi the Journalist. LC 84-595. (Illus.). 195p. 1984. reprint ed. lib. bdg. 55.00 (*0-313-24461-8*, BHMG, Greenwood Pr) Greenwood.

Bhattacharyya, Shuvra S., et al. Software Synthesis from Dataflow Graphs. (Kluwer International Series in Engineering & Computer Science). 192p. (C). 1996. text 112.00 (*0-7923-9722-3*) Kluwer Academic.

Bhattacharyya, Shuvra S., jt. auth. see Sriram, Sundararajan.

Bhattacharyya, Sibajiban. Gangesa's Theory of Indeterminant Perception, Vol. 1. (C). 1996. 14.00 (*81-85636-22-2*, Pub. by M Manoharial) S Asia.

— Gangesa's Theory of Indeterminant Perception, Vol. 2. (C). 1996. 11.00 (*81-85636-02-8*, Pub. by M Manoharial) S Asia.

Bhattacharyya, Sibajiban, jt. ed. see Potter, Karl H.

Bhattacharyya, Swapan K. Farmers Rituals & Modernization in India: A Sociological Study. 1976. 12.50 (*0-88386-800-8*) S Asia.

Bhattacharyya, Swapan K., jt. auth. see Chakrabortty, Krishna.

Bhattacharyya, Tarapada. The Canons of Indian Art: A Study of Vastuvidya. 3rd rev. ed. 1986. 52.00 (*0-8364-1618-X*) S Asia.

Bhattachavya, N. C., tr. see Annadananda, Swami.

Bhattacherje, S. B. Calcutta: City of Joy. (C). 1997. 8.50 (*81-207-1935-2*, Pub. by Motilal Bnarsidass) S Asia.

Bhattacherjee, Satya B. Encyclopedia of Indian Events & Dates. (C). 1995. write for info. (*81-207-1685-X*); pap. write for info. (*81-207-1343-5*) Sterling Pubs.

Bhattachryya, Sibajiban & Vohra, Ashok, eds. Philosophy of K. Satchidananda Murty. 1995. 31.00 (*81-85636-18-4*, Pub. by M Manoharial) S Asia.

Bhattarai, Dinesh & Khatiwada, Pradip, eds. Nepal India: Democracy in the Making of Mutual Trust. 320p. 1993. 25.00 (*81-85693-36-6*, Pub. by Nirala Pubns) Nataraj Bks.

***Bhatti, Anil & Voigt, Johannes H., eds.** Jewish Exile in India, 1933-1945. 1999. 26.00 (*81-7304-237-3*, Pub. by Manohar) S Asia.

***Bhatti, Ghazala.** Asian Children at Home & at School. LC 98-45315. 1999. write for info. (*0-415-17498-8*); pap. write for info. (*0-415-17499-6*) Routledge.

Bhatti, J. S., tr. see Vogel, Stefan.

Bhatti, M. A. Practical Optimization Methods with Mathematics Applications. (Illus.). 592p. 1999. 64.95 incl. cd-rom (*0-387-98631-6*) Spr-Verlag.

Bhatti, M. Ishaq. Testing Regression Models Based on Sample Survey Data. 216p. (C). 1995. 77.95 (*1-85628-642-8*, Pub. by Avebry) Ashgate Pub Co.

Bhatti, Razzaque H., jt. auth. see Moosa, Imad A.

Bhatty, Margaret R. An Atheist Reports from India. LC 87-19501. 267p. (Orig.). 1987. pap. 9.00 (*0-910309-42-6*, 5026) Am Atheist.

Bhatty, Michael. Geschichte und Vermarktung der Hollywood - Glamour - Photographie. (Europaische Hochschulschriften, Reihe 28: Bd. 297). (GER., Illus.). 199p. 1997. 44.95 (*3-631-31794-8*) P Lang Pubng.

Bhatty, R. S., ed. Barley: Chemistry & Technology. LC 93-72889. (Illus.). 486p. 1993. 159.00 (*0-913250-80-5*) Am Assn Cereal Chem.

Bhattycharya, Panchanan. Ideals of Indian Womanhood. 1989. 50.00 (*81-210-0249-4*, Pub. by Inter-India Pubns) S Asia.

Bhatwadekar, S. M., et al, contrib. by. Trends in Mathematics. 300p. 1999. 99.00 (*3-7643-6058-5*) Princeton Arch.

Bhau, Dhiam S. & Bhau, Singh. Agriculture Productivity in India: Impact of Chemical Fertilizers. 1990. 21.00 (*81-7041-290-0*, Pub. by Anmol) S Asia.

Bhau, Singh, jt. auth. see Bhau, Dhiam S.

***Bhaumik, Dilip K.** Antaral. LC 99-97817. (BEN., Illus.). xii, 324p. 2000. 14.95 (*0-9679229-0-9*) Pratichya Pubns.

Bhaumik, Sankar K. Tenancy Relations & Agrarian Development: A Study of West Bengal. LC 93-7495. (Illus.). 208p. (C). 1993. 32.00 (*0-8039-9118-5*) Sage.

Bhavabhuti. Malatimadhava. Coulson, Michael, ed. 344p. 1990. 29.95 (*0-19-562354-1*) OUP.

Bhave, Vinoba. The Intimate & the Ultimate. Kumar, Satish, ed. 120p. 1992. pap. 14.95 (*0-906540-89-5*, Pub. by Element MA) Penguin Putnam.

— Moved by Love: The Memoirs of Vinoba Bhave. Kalindi, ed. Sykes, Marjorie, tr. from HIN. (Illus.). 271p. 1994. pap. 15.95 (*1-870098-54-4*, Pub. by Resurgence) Chelsea Green Pub.

— Revolutionary Sarvodaya. Nargolkar, Vasant, ed. & tr. by. from HIN. 64p. (Orig.). 1980. pap. 1.50 (*0-934676-23-2*) Greenlf Bks.

— Talks on the Gita. 241p. 1983. pap. 10.00 (*0-934676-37-2*) Greenlf Bks.

— Thoughts on Education. Sykes, Marjorie, ed. 288p. 1983. pap. 16.00 (*0-934676-47-X*) Greenlf Bks.

Bhave, Vinoba, jt. auth. see Mashruwala, K. G.

Bhavikatti, S. S., ed. see Rajashekarappa, K. G.

Bhavnani, Enakshi. The Dance in India. (Illus.). 261p. 1984. 59.95 (*0-318-36311-9*) Asia Bk Corp.

— Decorative Designs & Craftsmanship. (Illus.). 108p. 1978. 39.95 (*0-318-36255-4*) Asia Bk Corp.

***Bhavnani, Kum-Kum, ed.** Feminism & Race. (Oxford Readings in Feminism Ser.). 400p. 2000. pap. 24.95 (*0-19-878236-5*) OUP.

Bhavnani, Kum-Kum & Phoenix, Ann, eds. Shifting Identities, Shifting Racisms: A Feminism & Psychology Reader. 224p. 1994. 69.95 (*0-8039-7786-7*); pap. 26.95 (*0-8039-7787-5*) Sage.

Bhavyananda, Swami, ed. see Monks of the Ramakrishna Order Staff.

***Bhawalkar, Vanamala.** Woman in the Mahabharata. LC 99-931138. 1999. 32.00 (*81-85616-54-X*, Pub. by Sharada Pub Hse) S Asia.

Bhawn, Rabindra. B.K. Thakore. LC 98-915014. 57p. write for info. (*81-260-0373-1*) Rabindra Bhawn.

Bhaya, Amit, jt. auth. see Kaszkurewicz, Eugenius.

BHB International Staff. African Insect Life. 1997. pap. text 59.00 (*0-86977-087-X*, Pub. by New5 Holland) BHB Intl.

***BHB International Staff.** Airplanes. (Our World in Pictures Ser.). (J). 1998. 8.95 (*2-215-06168-5*) CE75.

— All about Animals. (Images Ser.). (J). 1998. pap. text 9.95 (*2-215-06194-4*) CE75.

— Best Guide to Days Out Ever: Around Britain 98/99. 1998. pap. text 17.95 (*1-901258-16-5*, Pub. by Best Guides) BHB Intl.

BHB International Staff. Best of African Folklore. 1997. pap. text 12.95 (*0-86978-476-5*, Pub. by New5 Holland) BHB Intl.

***BHB International Staff.** Birds. (Our Animal World in Pictures Ser.). (J). 1998. 8.95 (*2-215-06158-8*) CE75.

— Christmas. 131p. (J). (gr. 1-4). 1999. pap. text 9.95 (*2-215-06262-2*) Editions Herit.

— Dinosaurs. (Our Animal World in Pictures Ser.). (J). 1998. 8.95 (*2-215-06172-3*) CE75.

— Dogs. (Our Animal World in Pictures Ser.). (J). 1998. 8.95 (*2-215-06166-9*) CE75.

— Earth. (Our World in Pictures Ser.). (J). 1998. 8.95 (*2-215-06162-6*) CE75.

BHB International Staff. Especially for You. 1997. 6.95 (*1-85833-614-7*, Pub. by CLib Bks) Whitecap Bks.

***BHB International Staff.** Farm. (Here We Go Round Ser.). (J). 1998. 5.95 (*2-215-06176-6*) CE75.

BHB International Staff. Field Guide to Insects of Kruger National Park. 1997. pap. text 24.95 (*0-86977-945-1*, Pub. by New5 Holland) BHB Intl.

***BHB International Staff.** Forest. (Here We Go Round Ser.). (J). 1998. 5.95 (*2-215-06182-0*) CE75.

BHB International Staff. Geographical Atlas of the World. 1997. 22.99 (*1-85833-590-6*, Pub. by CLib Bks) Whitecap Bks.

— Herbal Book of Days. (Illus.). 160p. 1997. 9.95 (*1-85833-010-6*, Pub. by CLib Bks) Whitecap Bks.

***BHB International Staff.** Human Body. (Our World in Pictures Ser.). (J). 1998. 8.95 (*2-215-06164-2*) CE75.

BHB International Staff. Irish Woman's Book of Days. 1997. 10.99 (*1-85833-801-8*, Pub. by CLib Bks) Whitecap Bks.

— Jock of the Bushveld. 1997. pap. text 9.95 (*0-86978-477-3*) Struik Timmins.

***BHB International Staff.** Jonah. (Bible Stories For the Very Young Ser.). 1998. 7.95 (*2-7289-0894-X*) CE75.

BHB International Staff. Mexican Cooking. (Illus.). 72p. 1997. 7.95 (*1-85833-676-7*, Pub. by CLib Bks) Whitecap Bks.

— Mother's Album. 1997. 14.95 (*1-85833-599-X*, Pub. by CLib Bks) Whitecap Bks.

***BHB International Staff.** Mountains. (Here We Go Round Ser.). (J). 1998. 5.95 (*2-215-06180-4*) CE75.

BHB International Staff. My Special Friend. 1997. 6.95 (*1-85833-612-0*, Pub. by CLib Bks) Whitecap Bks.

***BHB International Staff.** Nature. (Illus.). 131p. (J). (gr. 1-4). 1999. 9.95 (*2-215-06283-5*, Pub. by CE75) BHB Intl.

BHB International Staff. Nature. 131p. (J). (ps-3). 1999. pap. text 9.95 Editions Herit.

— Rich & Rare Land: Irish Verse & Art. 1998. 12.99 (*1-85833-701-1*, Pub. by CLib Bks) Whitecap Bks.

***BHB International Staff.** Savannah. (Here We Go Round Ser.). (J). 1998. 5.95 (*2-215-06178-2*) CE75.

— Sea Animals. (Our Animal World in Pictures Ser.). (J). 1998. 8.95 (*2-215-06160-X*) CE75.

— Spacecraft. (Our World in Pictures Ser.). (J). 1998. 8.95 (*2-215-06174-X*) CE75.

BHB International Staff. Special Memories. 1997. pap. 6.95 (*1-85833-617-1*, Pub. by CLib Bks) Whitecap Bks.

— Treasured Moments Keepsake. 1997. 6.95 (*1-85833-610-4*, Pub. by CLib Bks) Whitecap Bks.

— Treasury of Irish Verse. 1997. 12.95 (*1-85833-702-X*, Pub. by CLib Bks) Whitecap Bks.

— Victorian Wedding Photograph Album. (Illus.). 12p. 1997. 24.95 (*1-85833-653-8*, Pub. by CLib Bks) Whitecap Bks.

***BHB International Staff.** Witches & Whatnot. 131p. (J). (gr. 1-4). 1999. pap. text 9.95 (*2-215-06260-6*) Editions Herit.

BHB International Staff, ed. Bodypiercing, Vol. 1. 1998. pap. 19.95 (*1-86254-441-7*) Wakefield Pr.

— Namibia: Africa's Harsh Paradise. 1997. pap. text 49.95 (*1-85368-094-X*, Pub. by New5 Holland) Sterling.

BHB International Staff & Teske, Robert T. Aspects of Life. LC 97-139501. 1997. pap. text 49.95 (*1-86825-929-3*, Pub. by New5 Holland) BHB Intl.

— Best Walks in Cape Peninsula. 1997. pap. text 15.95 (*1-86825-861-0*, Pub. by New5 Holland) BHB Intl.

— Complete Guide to Walks & Trails in South Africa. 1997. pap. text 39.95 (*1-86825-448-8*, Pub. by New5 Holland) BHB Intl.

— Drakensburg Walks. 1997. pap. text 14.95 (*1-86825-761-4*) BHB Intl.

— Exploring the Natural Wonders of South Africa. LC 97-134219. 1997. 29.95 (*1-86825-855-6*, Pub. by New5 Holland) BHB Intl.

— Field Guide to Birds of South Africa. 1997. pap. text 24.95 (*1-86825-510-7*, Pub. by New5 Holland) BHB Intl.

— Field Guide to Mammals of Kruger National Park. 1997. pap. text 24.95 (*1-86825-386-4*, Pub. by New5 Holland) BHB Intl.

— Field Guide to Mammals of South Africa. 1997. pap. text 24.95 (*1-86825-519-0*, Pub. by New5 Holland) BHB Intl.

— Field Guide to the Birds of Kruger National Park. 1997. pap. text 24.95 (*1-86825-512-3*, Pub. by New5 Holland) BHB Intl.

— Field Guide to Trees of Kruger National Park. 1997. pap. text 24.95 (*1-86825-508-5*, Pub. by New5 Holland) BHB Intl.

— Field Guide to Trees of Southern Africa. LC 98-135331. 1997. pap. text 24.95 (*1-86825-922-6*, Pub. by New5 Holland) BHB Intl.

— Guide to Caravan Parks in Southern Africa. 1997. pap. text 15.95 (*1-86872-042-X*, Pub. by New5 Holland) BHB Intl.

— Guide to Hotels in Southern Africa. 1997. pap. text 15.95 (*1-86872-044-6*, Pub. by New5 Holland) BHB Intl.

— Guide to the Common Sea Fishes of South Africa. 1997. pap. text 29.95 (*1-86825-394-5*, Pub. by New5 Holland) BHB Intl.

— Handy Guide to Durban. LC 97-131329. 64p. 1997. pap. text 9.95 (*1-86825-894-7*, Pub. by New5 Holland) BHB Intl.

— Handy Guide to Harare. LC 97-131292. 1997. pap. text 9.95 (*1-86825-890-4*, Pub. by New5 Holland) BHB Intl.

B

An Asterisk (*) at the beginning of an entry indicates that the title is appearing for the first time.

— Handy Guide to Johannesburg. LC 97-131284. 64p. 1997. pap. text 9.95 (*1-86825-888-2*, Pub. by New5 Holland) BHB Intl.

— Handy Guide to Victoria Falls. LC 97-131301. 1997. pap. text 9.95 (*1-86825-891-2*, Pub. by New5 Holland) BHB Intl.

— Journey Through South Africa. 1997. pap. text 29.95 (*1-86825-692-8*, Pub. by New5 Holland) BHB Intl.

— Magnificent South Africa. 1997. pap. text 49.95 (*1-86825-976-5*, Pub. by New5 Holland) BHB Intl.

— Namibia: Africa's Harsh Paradise. 1997. pap. text 49.95 (*1-86825-381-3*, Pub. by New5 Holland) BHB Intl.

— Okavango: Sea of Love, Land of Water. 1997. pap. text 39.95 (*1-86825-382-1*, Pub. by New5 Holland) BHB Intl.

— Signs of the Wild. 1997. pap. text 24.95 (*1-86825-896-3*, Pub. by New5 Holland) BHB Intl.

— South Africa: A Visual Celebration. LC 97-192748. 1997. pap. text 49.95 (*1-86825-957-9*, Pub. by New5 Holland) BHB Intl.

— South Africa the Beautiful. 1997. pap. text 49.95 (*1-86825-870-X*, Pub. by New5 Holland) BHB Intl.

— Southern African Birds: A Photographic Guide. LC 95-209304. 1997. pap. text 49.95 (*1-86825-785-1*, Pub. by New5 Holland) BHB Intl.

— Southern African Spiders: An Identification Guide. 1997. pap. text 29.95 (*1-86825-188-8*, Pub. by New5 Holland) BHB Intl.

— This Is Capetown. 1997. pap. text 39.95 (*1-86825-433-X*, Pub. by New5 Holland) BHB Intl.

— This Is South Africa. 1997. pap. text 39.95 (*1-86825-867-X*, Pub. by New5 Holland) BHB Intl.

— Touring Atlas of South Africa. 1997. pap. text 29.95 (*1-86825-928-5*, Pub. by New5 Holland) BHB Intl.

— Touring in South Africa. 1997. 24.95 (*1-86825-328-7*, Pub. by New5 Holland) BHB Intl.

— Trees of Southern Africa. 1997. pap. text 75.00 (*1-86825-171-3*, Pub. by New5 Holland) BHB Intl.

— Visitor's Guide to Kruger National Park. 1997. pap. text 19.95 (*1-86825-926-9*, Pub. by New5 Holland) BHB Intl.

— Wildflowers of South Africa. LC 96-230297. 1997. pap. text 24.95 (*1-86825-897-1*, Pub. by New5 Holland) BHB Intl.

— Zimbabwe the Beautiful. LC 96-232813. 1997. pap. text 49.95 (*1-86825-776-2*, Pub. by New5 Holland) BHB Intl.

Bheavadevaseuri. The Life & Stories of the Jaina Savior Pearpevaneatha. 1979. 25.95 (*0-405-10583-5*) Ayer.

Bhebe & Ranger. Society in Zimbabwe's Liberation War. LC 97-49145. 1996. pap. 27.95 (*0-435-07412-1*) Heinemann.

Bhebe, Ngwabi. Christianity & Traditional Religion in Western Zimbabwe, 1859-1923. LC 79-322844. 206p. reprint ed. pap. 63.90 (*0-8357-2966-4*, 203922800011) Bks Demand.

Bhebe, Ngwabi & Ranger, T. O. Soldiers in Zimbabwe's Liberation War. LC 95-4003. xi, 211p. 1995. write for info. (*0-85255-609-8*) J Currey.

Bhebe, Ngwabi, jt. ed. see Ranger, Terence O.

Bhely-Quenum, Olympe. Snares Without End. Blair, Dorothy S., tr. LC 88-7301. 233p. reprint ed. pap. 72.30 (*0-608-10477-9*, 207109500008) Bks Demand.

Bhengu, Mfuniselwa J. Ubuntu: The Essence of Democracy. 1998. pap. 8.95 (*0-9583885-6-3*, Pub. by Novalis Trust) Anthroposophic.

Bhiday, M. R. From Isolation to Mainstream: Higher Education in India. 314p. 1986. text 32.50 (*81-7027-090-1*, Pub. by Radiant Pubs) S Asia.

Bhide, Amar. The Origins & Evolution of New Businesses. LC 99-38239. (Illus.). 432p. 2000. 35.00 (*0-19-513144-4*) OUP.

Bhide, Shashanka, jt. ed. see Heady, Earl O.

Bhide, Vidhyadhar V. Concise Sanskrit-English Dictionary. (ENG & SAN.). 1986. 195.00 (*0-8288-1155-5*, M9870) Fr & Eur.

Bhikkhu, Ajahn B. Mindfulness with Breathing: A Manual for Serious Beginners. Bhikkhu, Santikaro, tr. 160p. 1996. pap. 14.95 (*0-86171-111-4*) Wisdom MA.

***Bhikkhu, Ajahn Sumano.** Meeting the Monkey Halfway. LC 99-58179. 128p. 2000. pap. 9.95 (*1-57863-146-7*) Weiser.

Bhikkhu, Ajahn Sumano & Phillips, Jeffrey D. Questions from the City, Answers from the Forest: Simple Lessons on Living from a Western Buddhist Monk. LC 99-11828. 224p. 1999. pap. 16.00 (*0-8356-0774-7*, Pub. by Theos Pub Hse) Natl Bk Netwk.

Bhikkhu, Buddhadasa. Heartwood of the Bodhi Tree: The Buddha's Teaching on Voidness. rev. ed. Bhikkhu, Santikaro, tr. from THA. LC 94-9431. 176p. 1994. pap. 15.95 (*0-86171-035-5*, Pub. by Wisdom MA) Natl Bk Netwk.

Bhikkhu, Santikaro, tr. see Bhikkhu, Ajahn B.

Bhikkhu, Santikaro, tr. see Bhikkhu, Buddhadasa.

Bhikshu, Cheng C. Manifestation of the Tathagata: Buddhahood According to the Avatamsaka Sutra. LC 93-24080. 192p. 1993. pap. 12.50 (*0-86171-054-1*) Wisdom MA.

Bhikshu, Guo-gu, tr. see Sheng-Yen, Chang.

Bhikshu Hung Ju & Bhikshu Hung Yo. Three Steps, One Bow. (Illus.). 152p. (Orig.). 1977. pap. 5.00 (*0-917512-18-9*) Buddhist Text.

Bhikshu Hung Yo, jt. auth. see Bhikshu Hung Ju.

Bhikshu, Subhadra. A Buddhist Catechism: An Outline of the Doctrine of the Buddha Gotama. 95p. 1996. pap. 8.00 (*0-89540-293-9*, SB-293) Sun Pub.

Bhikshu, Yogi. Karma Yoga. 1928. reprint ed. 11.00 (*0-911662-20-0*) Yoga.

Bhila, H. H. Trade & Politics in a Shona Kingdom: The Manyika & Their African & Portuguese Neighbors, 1575-1902. LC DT0962.42.B4. (Studies in Zimbabwean History). 307p. reprint ed. pap. 95.20 (*0-608-13145-8*, 202523300043) Bks Demand.

Bhimani, Alnoor, ed. Management Accounting: European Perspectives. LC 97-121421. (Illus.). 274p. (C). 1996. text 69.00 (*0-19-828966-9*) OUP.

Bhimani, Harish. In Search of Lata. LC 95-901485. (C). 1995. 28.00 (*81-7223-170-9*, Pub. by Indus Pub) S Asia.

Bhinda. Stories from Asia, India, Pakistan & Bangladesh. Date not set. pap. text. write for info. (*0-582-03922-3*, Pub. by Addison-Wesley) Longman.

Bhocker, Anita & Havinga, Tetty. Asylum Migration to the European Union: Patterns of Origin & Destination. LC 98-196445. 121p. 1997. 30.00 (*92-828-3306-2*, Pub. by Comm Europ Commun) Bernan Associates.

Bhogilal Leherchand Institute of Indology, jt. auth. see Nyeayavijaya.

Bhohm, G., jt. auth. see Pehnt, Wolfgang.

Bhoite, Anuradha. Women Employees & Rural Development: Problems of Employed Women in Rural Areas. 150p. 1987. write for info. (*81-212-0085-7*, Pub. by Gian Publng Hse) S Asia.

Bhoite, U. B. Sociology of Indian Intellectuals. 342p. (C). 1987. 36.00 (*81-7033-035-1*, Pub. by Rawat Pubns) S Asia.

Bhoite, Uttam, jt. ed. see Hill, John L.

Bhoj, D. S., jt. ed. see Ahsanullah, M.

Bhoja. The Srngara-Prakasa of Bhoja, 2 vols., Set. Raghavan, V., ed. LC 87-33908. (Oriental Ser.). (SAN.). 1888p. 1988. 90.00 (*0-674-83340-6*) HUP.

Bhojwani, S. S., ed. Plant Tissue Culture: Applications & Limitations. (Developments in Crop Science Ser.: No. 19). 462p. 1990. 158.25 (*0-444-88883-7*) Elsevier.

Bhojwani, S. S. & Razdan, M. N. Plant Tissue Culture: Theory & Practice. (Developments in Crop Science Ser.: Vol. 5). vii,502p. 1986. pap. 116.00 (*0-444-42526-8*) Elsevier.

— Plant Tissue Culture: Theory & Practice. rev. ed. LC 96-42141. (Studies in Plant Science). 776p. 1996. 284.50 (*0-444-81623-2*) Elsevier.

Bhojwani, S. S., et al. Plant Tissue Culture: A Classified Bibliography. (Developments in Crop Science Ser.: No. 9). xvi,790p. 1987. 420.00 (*0-444-42663-9*) Elsevier.

Bhojwani, S. S., jt. auth. see Soh, Woong Y.

Bhola, H. S. A Source Book for Literacy Work: Perspective from the Grassroots. 208p. 1994. pap. write for info. (*1-85302-263-2*, Pub. by Jessica Kingsley) Taylor & Francis.

Bhola, H. S., ed. Adult Education Policy & Performance Vol. 13:3/4: An International Perspective. 129p. 1994. pap. 15.00 (*0-944285-42-2*) Pol Studies.

Bhola, Nath T., jt. auth. see Chaturvedi, Mahendra.

Bhola, P. L. Pakistan-China Relations. 304p. 1986. 37.50 (*0-8364-1865-4*, Pub. by Manohar) S Asia.

Bhonsle. Mathematical Modeling for Design. LC 98-13195. 448p. (C). 1998. pap. text 52.00 (*0-13-727231-6*, Prentice Hall) P-H.

Bhonsle, R. K. The Korean War. 220p. (C). 1986. 65.00 (*81-7002-015-8*, Pub. by Himalayan Bks) St Mut.

Bhonsle, R. K., ed. Montgomery & Guderian. 356p. 1986. pap. 35.00 (*81-7002-019-0*, Pub. by Himalayan Bks) St Mut.

— Russo German Campaign, 1941-43. 200p. (C). 1988. 45.00 (*81-7002-037-9*, Pub. by Himalayan Bks) St Mut.

— Wingate & Thimayya: A Biographical Analysis. 150p. (C). 1989. pap. 25.00 (*81-7002-053-0*, Pub. by Himalayan Bks) St Mut.

Bhooshan, B. S., jt. auth. see Misra, R. P.

***Bhoothalingam, Mathuram & Sriraman, T.** Vasaveswaram. LC 99-933850. 1998. pap. 10.00 (*0-333-93189-0*, Pub. by Macmillan) S Asia.

Bhopal, Kalwant. Gender, "Race" & Patriarchy: A Study of South Asian Women. LC 97-73610. (Interdisciplinary Research Series in Ethnic, Gender & Class Relations). (Illus.). 224p. 1997. text 69.95 (*1-84014-139-5*, Pub. by Ashgate Pub) Ashgate Pub Co.

Bhote, Adi K., jt. auth. see Bhote, Keki R.

Bhote, Keki R. Beyond Customer Satisfaction to Customer Loyalty: The Key to Greater Profitability. LC 96-35335. (AMA Management Briefing Ser.). 1996. write for info. (*0-8144-2362-0*) AMACOM.

— Strategic Supply Management: A Blueprint for Revitalizing the Manufacturer-Supplier Partnership. LC 88-48029. 448p. 1989. 65.00 (*0-8144-5925-0*) AMACOM.

— World Class Quality: Using Design of Experiments to Make It Happen. 212p. 1991. 24.95 (*0-8144-5053-9*, 040537) AMACOM.

***Bhote, Keki R. & Bhote, Adi K.** World Class Quality: Using Design of Experiments to Make It Happen. 2nd rev. expanded ed. LC 99-38804. 487p. 1999. 34.95 (*0-8144-0427-8*) AMACOM.

Bhowmick, A. K. & Stephens, Howard L. Handbook of Elastomers: New Developments & Technology. (Plastics Engineering Ser.). (Illus.). 816p. 1988. text 275.00 (*0-8247-7800-6*) Dekker.

Bhowmick, Anil K., et al, eds. Rubber Products Manufacturing Technology. (Illus.). 936p. 1994. text 275.00 (*0-8247-9112-6*) Dekker.

Bhowmick, B. C., jt. ed. see Dhar, Bharat B.

Bhowmick, Pradip K. Dynamics of Tribal Development. (C). 1993. 28.00 (*81-210-0306-7*, Pub. by Inter-India Pubns) S Asia.

— Rural & Tribal Development Practices in India. 212p. 1994. pap. 150.00 (*81-85880-25-5*, Pub. by Print Hse) St Mut.

Bhowmik, jt. auth. see McCutchion.

Bhowmik, Nani G., jt. ed. see Jennings, Marshall E.

Bhown, Ajit S., ed. Protein Peptide Sequence Analysis Current Methodologies: Current Methodologies. LC 87-718. (Biochemists Ser.). 256p. 1988. 144.00 (*0-8493-6583-X*, QP551, CRC Reprint) Franklin.

BHR Group Ltd. Staff, ed. Management & Engineering of Fire Safety & Loss Prevention: Onshore & Offshore - Proceedings of the Third Internat. Conf., 18-20 Feb., 1991, Aberdeen, Scotland, U. K. 358p. 1991. mass mkt. 164.95 (*1-85166-676-1*) Elsevier.

Bhrolchain, Muireann Ni, see Ni Bhrolchain, Muireann, ed.

***Bhuchar, Sudha.** House of the Sun. (Nick Hern Bks.). 2000. pap. 14.95 (*1-85459-447-8*) Theatre Comm.

— Tainted Dawn. 96p. 2000. pap. 14.95 (*1-85459-451-6*) Theatre Comm.

Bhugra, Dinesh, et al. Troublesome Disguises. LC 97-4247. (Illus.). 352p. 1997. 69.95 (*0-86542-674-0*) Blackwell Sci.

Bhugra, Dinesh, jt. auth. see Bhui, Kamaldeep.

Bhugra, Dinesh K. L., ed. Homelessness & Mental Health. (Studies in Social & Community Psychiatry). (Illus.). 343p. (C). 1996. text 90.00 (*0-521-45202-3*) Cambridge U Pr.

— Psychiatry & Religion: Context Consensus & Controversies. 256p. (C). 1997. pap. 25.99 (*0-415-16512-1*) Routledge.

— The Relationship Between Religion & Mental Health. LC 94-47489. 256p. (C). (gr. 13). 1996. 85.00 (*0-415-08955-7*, B4333) Routledge.

Bhugra, Dinesh K. L. & Burns, Alastair. Management Training for Psychiatrists. 264p. 1992. pap. 25.00 (*0-88048-610-4*, 8610, Pub. by Royal Coll Psych) Parkwest Pubns.

Bhugra, Dinesh K. L. & Leff, Julian P. Principles of Social Psychiatry. (Illus.). 600p. 1993. 165.00 (*0-632-03336-3*) Blackwell Sci.

Bhui. Pocket Psychiatry. (C). 1996. pap. text 51.00 (*0-7020-2151-2*) Harcourt.

Bhui, Kam, et al. MRCPsych Tutor Pt. 1: MCQs. 72p. 1992. pap. text 19.95 (*0-7020-1642-X*, Pub. by W B Saunders) Saunders.

***Bhui, Kamaldeep & Bhugra, Dinesh.** Cross Cultural Psychiatry: A Practical Guide. 192p. 2000. pap. text 36.00 (*0-7506-4353-6*) Buttrwrth-Heinemann.

Bhujade, M. R. & Sarda, N. L. Digital Computer Design Principles with Introduction to Microprocessors. 300p. 1996. pap. 125.00 (*81-209-0018-9*, Pub. by Pitambar Pub) St Mut.

Bhukaswan, T., tr. see Boonyubol, M. & Pramokchutima, S.

Bhumichitr, Vatcharin. Thai Vegetarian Cooking. (Illus.). 160p. 1997. pap. 19.95 (*1-85145-891-3*, Pub. by Pavilion Bks Ltd) Trafalgar.

— Vatch's South East Asian Cookbook. LC 97-33264. 1997. text 26.95 (*0-312-18274-0*) St Martin.

***Bhumichitr, Vatcharin.** Vatchs Southeast Asian Cook Book. 192p. 2000. pap. 17.95 (*0-312-25431-8*) St Martin.

Bhumichitr, Vatcharin. Vatch's Thai Cookbook. (Illus.). 192p. 1998. pap. 17.95 (*1-86205-195-X*, Pub. by Pavilion Bks Ltd) Trafalgar.

Bhumralkar, Chandrakant & Teasley, John I., eds. Meteorological Aspects of Acid Rain. (Acid Precipitation Ser.: Vol. 1). 200p. 1984. 79.95 (*0-250-40566-0*) Buttrwrth-Heinemann.

Bhushan, B. Advances in Information Storage Systems, Vol. 6. 400p. 1995. text 109.00 (*981-02-2074-X*) World Scientific Pub.

Bhushan, B., ed. Advances in Information Storage Systems. 400p. 1995. pap. 48.00 (*981-02-2133-9*) World Scientific Pub.

— Advances in Information Storage Systems, Vol. 1. 432p. 1991. 90.00 (*0-7918-0021-0*, 800219) ASME Pr.

— Advances in Information Storage Systems, Vol. 2. 200p. 1991. 72.00 (*0-7918-0022-9*, 800229) ASME Pr.

— Advances in Information Storage Systems, Vol. 3. 200p. 1991. 72.00 (*0-7918-0023-7*, 800237) ASME Pr.

— Advances in Information Storage Systems, Vol. 4. 420p. 1992. 90.00 (*0-7918-0027-X*, 80027-X) ASME Pr.

— Advances in Information Storage Systems, Vol. 5. 540p. 1993. 90.00 (*0-7918-0031-8*, 800318) ASME Pr.

— Advances in Information Storage Systems, Vol. 8. 250p. 1998. 54.00 (*981-02-3347-7*); pap. 27.00 (*981-02-3348-5*) World Scientific Pub.

Bhushan, Bharat. Advances in Information Storage Systems: Selected Papers. (Electrical & Electronic Engineering Ser.). 1999. 84.00 (*981-02-3616-6*); 84.00 (*981-02-3617-4*) World Scientific Pub.

— Handbook of Micro-Nanotribology. 2nd ed. LC 98-24466. (Mechanics & Materials Science Ser.). 880p. 1998. boxed set 149.95 (*0-8493-8402-8*) CRC Pr.

— Mechanics & Reliability of Flexible Magnetic Media. (Illus.). 664p. 1992. 174.95 (*0-387-97708-2*) Spr-Verlag.

***Bhushan, Bharat.** Mechanics & Reliability of Flexible Magnetic Media. 2nd ed. LC 99-45614. (Illus.). 656p. 2000. 179.00 (*0-387-98936-6*) Spr-Verlag.

Bhushan, Bharat. Principles & Applications of Tribology. LC 98-41591. 1020p. 1999. 150.00 (*0-471-59407-5*) Wiley.

— Tribology & Mechanics of Magnetic Storage Devices. (Illus.). xviii, 1019p. 1989. 169.00 (*0-387-96926-8*) Spr-Verlag.

— Tribology & Mechanics of Magnetic Storage Devices. 2nd ed. 1152p. 1996. 149.95 (*0-7803-3406-X*, PC5676) Inst Electrical.

— Tribology & Mechanics of Magnetic Storage Devices. 2nd ed. (Illus.). 1144p. 1996. 149.95 (*0-387-94627-6*) Spr-Verlag.

— Tribology Issues & Opportunities in Mems: Proceedings of the NSF AFSOR ASME Workshop on Tribology Issues & Opportunities in MEMS. LC 98-14438. 655p. 1998. write for info. (*0-7923-5024-3*) Kluwer Academic.

Bhushan, Bharat, ed. Handbook of Micro/Nanotribology. (Mechanical & Materials Science Ser.: Vol. 1). 640p. 1995. boxed set 159.95 (*0-8493-8401-X*, 8401) CRC Pr.

— Micro-Nanotribology & Its Applications: Proceedings of the NATO Advanced Study Institutes, held in Sesimbra, Portugal, June 16-28, 1996. LC 96-40248. (NATO Advanced Science Institutes Series C). 692p. (C). 1997. text 331.50 (*0-7923-4386-7*) Kluwer Academic.

Bhushan, Bharat & Gupta, B. K. Handbook of Tribology: Materials, Coatings, & Surface Treatments. LC 97-8067. (Illus.). 1168p. 1997. reprint ed. 99.50 (*1-57524-050-5*) Krieger.

Bhushan, Bharat, jt. auth. see Kapoor, N. D.

Bhushan, L. S., et al, eds. Soil & Water Conservation: Challenges & Opportunities/Proceedings of the 8th International Conference, New Delhi 1994, 2 vols. 1740p. 1998. text 156.00 (*90-5410-274-8*, Pub. by A A Balkema) Ashgate Pub Co.

***Bhushan, Nalini & Rosenfeld, Stuart.** Of Minds & Molecules: New Philosophical Perspectives on Chemistry. LC 99-40329. (Illus.). 320p. 2000. text. write for info. (*0-19-512834-6*) OUP.

Bhushan, P. The Case That Shook India. 294p. 1978. 14.95 (*0-7069-0594-6*) Asia Bk Corp.

Bhushan, Vikas. First Aid for the USMLE Step 1: 1999 Edition. 9th ed. 351p. 1999. pap. 27.95 (*0-8385-2612-8*, Apple Lange Med) McGraw.

— First Aid for the USMLE Step 2. 2nd ed. 3200p. 1999. pap. 29.95 (*0-8385-2604-7*, Apple Lange Med) McGraw.

Bhushan, Vikas & Amin, Chirag. First Aid for the Match. 162p. (C). 1996. pap. 29.95 (*0-8385-2596-2*, Apple Lange Med) McGraw.

— First Aid for the USMLE Step 1,(1997), Step 1. 7th rev. ed. (C). 1996. pap. text 23.95 (*0-8385-1495-2*, A1495-9) Appleton & Lange.

— First Aid for the Wards. 302p. (C). 1997. pap. 29.95 (*0-8385-2595-4*, A-2595-5, Apple Lange Med) McGraw.

— First Aid USMLE Step 1, 1998 Edition. 8th ed. 432p. (C). 1997. pap. text 24.95 (*0-8385-2603-9*, A-2603-7) Appleton & Lange.

Bhuta, Chandra, jt. intro. see Kumar, Arun.

Bhutani, D. H. The Third Sikh War? Towards or Away from Khalistan? 137p. 1986. 22.95 (*0-318-37216-9*) Asia Bk Corp.

Bhutani, L. K. Color Atlas of Sexually Transmitted Diseases. (Illus.). 208p. 1986. 42.50 (*0-912791-02-0*, Ishiyaku EuroAmerica) Med Dent Media.

— Colour Atlas of Sexually Transmitted Diseases. 208p. (C). 1990. 250.00 (*81-85017-23-9*, Pub. by Interprint) St Mut.

***Bhutani, Manoop S., ed.** Interventional Endoscopic Ultrasonography. 325p. 1999. text 98.00 (*90-5702-601-5*, Harwood Acad Pubs) Gordon & Breach.

Bhuteshananda. Thoughts on Spiritual Life. pap. 4.95 (*0-87481-241-0*) Vedanta Pr.

***Bhutta, Zulfigar Ahmed, ed.** Contemporary Issues in Childhood Diarrhoea & Malnutrition. (Illus.). 450p. 2000. text 34.50 (*0-19-579149-5*) OUP.

Bhutto, Fatima. Whispers of the Desert. Salman & Kureshi, Tarik, eds. LC 98-135948. 78p. 1998. 21.00 (*0-19-577844-8*) OUP.

***Bhutto, Fatima & Kureshi, Salman Tarik.** Whispers of the Desert. LC 98-930015. 1998. write for info. (*0-19-577846-4*) OUP.

Bhuvan, Unhelkar. After the Fireworks: Business & Technology Strategies for Surviving Y2K Hits. LC 98-55541. (Advanced & Emerging Communications Technologies Ser.). 464p. 1999. boxed set 59.95 (*0-8493-9599-2*, 9599) CRC Pr.

Bhuvanbhanusuri, Acarya G. Ganadharavada: A Treatise on the Question & Answers between Eleven Brahmin Scholars & Mahavir Bhagavan. (C). 1989. 21.50 (*81-208-0677-8*, Pub. by Motilal Bnarsidass) S Asia.

Bhuvanendran, N. Interpretation of Indian Art. (C). 1991. 42.00 (*0-8364-2593-6*, Pub. by Heritage IA) S Asia.

Bhuyan, Laxmi N. & Zhang, Xiaodong, eds. Multiprocessor Performance Measurement & Evaluation. LC 94-21718. 488p. 1994. 50.00 (*0-8186-6522-X*, BP06522) IEEE Comp Soc.

Bhuyan, Suryya K. Anglo-Assamese Relations: Seventeen Seventy-One to Eighteen Twenty-Six. LC 77-87072. reprint ed. 46.00 (*0-404-16795-0*) AMS Pr.

Bhyrappan, S. L. Parva: A Tale of War, Peace, Love, Death, God & Man. Rao, K. Raghavendra, tr. (C). 1994. 20.00 (*81-7201-659-X*, Pub. by Indian Pubs) S Asia.

— The Uprooted: Translation of the Original Novel Vamshavriksha in Kannada. Rao, K. Raghavendra, tr. (C). 1992. 17.50 (*81-7018-734-6*, Pub. by BR Pub) S Asia.

Bi-Nabi, Malik. Bayn al-Rashad wa-al-Tih. (Mushkilat al-Hadarah Ser.). 216p. 1988. pap. 6.95 (*1-57547-024-1*) Dar Al-Fikr.

Bia, Fred & McCarthy, T. L. Of Mother Earth & Father Sky. (Illus.). 69p. 1983. pap. 8.00 (*0-685-42612-2*) Rough Rock Pr.

Biacindo. Educational Psychology. (C). 1998. pap. text 16.36 (*0-395-90256-8*) HM.

Biacs, P. A., ed. Biological Role of Plant Lipids. LC 88-43522. (Illus.). 644p. 1990. 145.00 (*0-306-43181-5*, Plenum Trade) Perseus Pubng.

Biadene, Susanna, ed. Titian: Prince of Painters. (Illus.). 452p. 1990. 95.00 (*3-7913-1102-6*, Pub. by Prestel) te Neues.

Biafra, Jello. Burning Down the Magic Kingdom. 1999. pap. text 17.95 (*1-902593-01-4*) AK Pr Dist.

Biaggi, Cristina. Habitations of the Great Goddess. LC 93-30386. (Illus.). 200p. 1994. text 50.00 (*1-879198-18-5*) Knwldg Ideas & Trnds.

B

***Biaggi, Cristina.** In the Footsteps of the Goddess: Paths to Self-Discovery. 176p. 2000. 20.00 (*1-879198-30-4*) Knwldg Ideas & Trnds.

Biaggi, Mildred, ed. see Hamlin, Janet L. & Smith, Sandra J.

Biaggi, Virgilio. Las Aves de Puerto Rico. 4th rev. ed. LC 96-36080. (Illus.). 389p. 1997. 34.95 (*0-8477-0242-1*) U of PR Pr.

— Manual Ilustrado de Laboratorio Para Zoologia. 129p. (C). 1975. pap. text, student ed. 24.95 (*1-881375-11-0*) Libreria Univ.

Biaggi, Virgilio, jt. auth. see Aguayo, Carlos A.

***Biaggio, Maryka & Hersen, Michel.** Issues in the Psychology of Women. LC 00-21555. 2000. write for info. (*0-306-46321-0*, Kluwer Plenum) Kluwer Academic.

Biagi. Media Impact. 2nd ed. (Mass Communication Ser.). 1992. text, teacher ed. write for info. (*0-534-16244-4*) Wadsworth Pub.

***Biagi.** Media Impact: An Introduction to Mass Medial. 5th ed. (Mass Communication Ser.). 2000. 43.75 (*0-534-57510-2*) Wadsworth Pub.

Biagi. Media Impact: Intro to Mass Media. 3rd ed. (Mass Communication Ser.). 1995. teacher ed. 48.00 (*0-534-21745-1*) Wadsworth Pub.

Biagi, Adele, jt. auth. see Ragazzini, Giuseppe.

Biagi, Dan. Advanced Computer Applications in Business. (Management Information Systems Ser.). 1996. pap. 30.95 (*0-534-24858-6*) S-W Pub.

Biagi, M., jt. ed. see Blanpain, Roger.

Biagi, Robert C. Working Together: A Manual to Help Groups Work More Effectively. LC 79-624736. (Illus.). (Orig.). (C). 1978. pap. 7.00 (*0-934210-05-5*) Devlp Commy.

Biagi, Ron, jt. auth. see Eyres, Tresa.

Biagi, Shirley. Interviews That Work: A Practical Guide for Journalists. 184p. (C). 1985. pap. write for info. (*0-534-05664-4*) Wadsworth Pub.

— Media-Impact: An Introduction to Mass Media. 411p. (C). 1988. pap. write for info. (*0-534-08946-1*) Wadsworth Pub.

— Media-Impact: An Introduction to Mass Media. 411p. (C). 1989. pap. write for info. (*0-534-12660-X*) Wadsworth Pub.

— Media-Impact: An Introduction to Mass Media. 2nd ed. 564p. (C). 1992. pap. 35.95 (*0-534-16242-8*) Wadsworth Pub.

— Media-Impact: An Introduction to Mass Media. 2nd ed. 564p. 1993. mass mkt. 33.75 (*0-534-20184-9*) Wadsworth Pub.

— Media-Impact: An Introduction to Mass Media. 3rd ed. LC 95-2932. 1996. pap. 46.95 (*0-534-21744-3*) Wadsworth Pub.

— Media Impact: An Introduction to Mass Media. 4th ed. LC 98-22567. 1998. pap. 60.95 (*0-534-54810-5*) Wadsworth Pub.

***Biagi, Shirley.** Media Impact: An Introduction to Mass Media. 5th ed. LC 00-27152. 2000. pap. write for info. (*0-534-57511-0*) Wadsworth Pub.

Biagi, Shirley. Media-Reader: Perspectives on Mass Media Industries, Effects, & Issues. 366p. (C). 1989. pap. write for info. (*0-534-08955-0*) Wadsworth Pub.

— Media-Reader: Perspectives on Mass Media Industries, Effects, & Issues. 2nd ed. 340p. (C). 1993. mass mkt. 25.75 (*0-534-19086-3*) Wadsworth Pub.

— Media/Impact: An Introduction to Mass Media. 3rd rev. ed. LC 97-14636. (Mass Communication Ser.). (C). 1997. pap. 40.50 (*0-534-50482-5*) Wadsworth Pub.

Biagi, Susan. Louisbourg: Un Guide en Couleurs a Histoire Vivante. Rioux, Marie-Claude, tr. LC 97-950059.Tr. of Louisbourg - A Living History Colourguide. (ENG & FRE., Illus.). 72p. 1997. pap. 16.95 (*0-88780-363-6*, Pub. by Formac Publ Co) Formac Dist Ltd.

Biagi, Susan. Louisbourg - A Living History Colour Guide. LC 96-950145. (Illus.). 72p. (Orig.). 1997. pap. 10.95 (*0-88780-362-8*, Pub. by Formac Publ Co) Seven Hills Bk.

***Biagi, Susan & Vaughan, Keith.** Touring the Cabot Trail. (Living History Colourguides Ser.). (Illus.). 72p. 1999. pap. 12.95 (*0-88780-476-4*, Pub. by Formac Publ Co) Formac Dist Ltd.

Biagini, Emilio. Northern Ireland & Beyond. (GeoJournal Library: Vol. 33). 1996. lib. bdg. 129.00 (*0-7923-4046-9*) Kluwer Academic.

Biagini, Emilio & Hoyle, Brian S., eds. Insularity & Development: International Perspectives on Islands. LC 97-50239. (Island Studies). xxi, 378p. 1999. 90.00 (*1-85567-460-2*) Bks Intl VA.

***Biagini, Eugenio F.** Gladstone. LC 99-22262. (British History in Perspective Ser.). 2000. text 49.95 (*0-312-22738-8*) St Martin.

Biagini, Eugenio F., ed. Citizenship & Community: Liberals, Radicals & Collective Identities in the British Isles, 1865-1931. 380p. (C). 1996. text 69.95 (*0-521-48035-3*) Cambridge U Pr.

Biagini, Mary K. A Handbook of Contemporary Fiction for Public Libraries & School Libraries. LC 89-27859. 257p. 1989. 31.00 (*0-8108-2275-X*) Scarecrow.

Biagioli, Mario. Galileo, Courtier: The Practice of Science in the Culture of Absolutism. LC 92-33736. (Science & Its Conceptual Foundations Ser.). (Illus.). 416p. (C). 1993. 32.95 (*0-226-04559-5*) U Ch Pr.

— Galileo, Courtier: The Practice of Science in the Culture of Absolutism. (Illus.). 416p. 1994. pap. 19.00 (*0-226-04560-9*) U Ch Pr.

Biagioli, Mario, ed. The Science Studies Reader. LC 98-36335. 500p. (C). (gr. 13). 1998. 85.00 (*0-415-91867-7*, D3232) Routledge.

— The Science Studies Reader. LC 98-36335. 592p. (C). 1999. pap. 35.00 (*0-415-91868-5*) Routledge.

Biagioni, H. A. A Nonlinear Theory of Generalized Functions. Dold, A. et al, eds. (Lecture Notes in Mathematics Ser.: Vol. 1421). xii, 214p. 1990. 34.80 (*0-387-52408-8*) Spr-Verlag.

Biagioni, Louis F. Managerial Accounting: Computer Assisted Practice Set 1, 5 Disk, Ibm. 2nd ed. (C). 1994. pap. text 22.00 (*0-07-839911-4*) McGraw.

Biagiotti, Aldo P. Impact: The Historical Account of the Italian Immigrants of Ridgefield, Connecticut. LC 90-61386. (Illus.). 345p. 1990. mass mkt. 14.95 (*0-9627278-0-6*) Romald Pr.

Biais, B., et al. Financial Mathematics Vol. 165: Lectures Given at the 3rd Session of the Centro Internazionale Matematico Estivo (C.I.M.E.) Held in Bressanone, Italy, July 8-13, 1996. LC 97-7799. (Lecture Notes in Mathematics Ser.). 1997. write for info. (*3-540-62642-5*) Spr-Verlag.

***Biaising, Craig.** Progressive Dispensationalism. 2000. pap. 19.99 (*0-8010-2243-6*) Baker Bks.

Bial, Daniel. Arnold Schwarzenegger: Man of Action. LC 97-29323. (Book Report Biography Ser.). (Illus.). 112p. (YA). (gr. 6-8). 1998. 22.00 (*0-531-11485-6*) Watts.

***Bial, Daniel.** Arnold Schwarzenegger: Man of Action. LC 97-29323. (Book Report Biographies). (Illus.). 112p. (YA). (gr. 6-8). 1999. pap. text 6.95 (*0-531-15933-7*) Watts.

Bial, Henry, jt. auth. see Martin, Carol.

Bial, Linda L., ed. see Bial, Raymond.

Bial, Morrison D., jt. auth. see Simon, Solomon.

Bial, Morrison D., ed. see Stadtler, Bea.

Bial, Morrison David. Liberal Judaism at Home. rev. ed. 1971. reprint ed. pap. 6.95 (*0-8074-0075-0*, 383110) UAHC.

— Liberal Judaism at Home: The Practices of Modern Reform Judaism. rev. ed. 1971. reprint ed. pap., teacher ed. 5.00 (*0-8074-0245-1*, 203110) UAHC.

— Your Jewish Child. 1978. 5.00 (*0-8074-0012-2*, 101200) UAHC.

Bial, Raymond. Amish Home. (Illus.). 40p. (J). (gr. 4-7). 1993. 17.00 (*0-395-59504-5*) HM.

— Amish Home. LC 92-4406. (Illus.). 40p. (J). (gr. 3-7). 1995. pap. 5.95 (*0-395-72021-4*, Sandpiper) HM.

— Amish Home. 1993. 11.15 (*0-606-07186-5*, Pub. by Turtleback) Demco.

***Bial, Raymond.** The Apache. LC 99-44717. (Lifeways Ser.). (J). 2001. 32.79 (*0-7614-0939-4*, Benchmark NY) Marshall Cavendish.

Bial, Raymond. Cajun Home. LC 97-20646. 48p. 1998. 16.00 (*0-395-86095-4*) HM.

— The Cherokee. LC 97-26574. (Lifeways Ser.). (J). 1998. lib. bdg. 32.79 (*0-7614-0801-0*, Benchmark NY) Marshall Cavendish.

***Bial, Raymond.** The Cheyenne. LC 00-23075. (Lifeways Ser.). 2001. 32.79 (*0-7614-0938-6*, Benchmark NY) Marshall Cavendish.

Bial, Raymond. The Comanche. LC 99-24133. (Lifeways Ser.). (Illus.). 128p. (YA). (gr. 4-7). 1999. lib. bdg. 32.79 (*0-7614-0864-9*) Marshall Cavendish.

— Common Ground: Photographs of Rural & Small Town Life. Bial, Linda L., ed. LC 85-63625. (Illus.). 110p. (Orig.). 1986. pap. 10.00 (*0-935153-01-2*) Stormline Pr.

— Corn Belt Harvest. (Illus.). 48p. (J). (gr. 3-6). 1991. 17.00 (*0-395-56234-1*, Sandpiper) HM.

— The Fresh Grave: And Other Ghostly Stories. LC 97-29651. 192p. (YA). (gr. 3 up). 1997. 18.95 (*1-883953-23-5*, Face to Face) Midwest Trad.

— The Fresh Grave: And Other Ghostly Stories. LC 97-29651. (Illus.). 192p. (YA). (gr. 3 up). 1997. pap. 13.95 (*1-883953-22-7*, Face to Face) Midwest Trad.

— Frontier Home. LC 92-36449. 40p. (J). (gr. 4-7). 1993. 18.00 (*0-395-64046-6*) HM.

— The Ghost of Honeymoon Creek. LC 99-40590. 128p. (J). (gr. 3-7). 1999. pap. 13.95 (*1-883953-27-8*, Pub. by Midwest Trad) Partners Pubs Grp.

***Bial, Raymond.** The Ghost of Honeymoon Creek. LC 99-40590. 128p. (J). (gr. 4-7). 2000. 18.95 (*1-883953-28-6*, Pub. by Midwest Trad) Partners Pubs Grp.

— The Haida. LC 00-22225. (Lifeways Ser.). 2001. 32.79 (*0-7614-0937-8*, Benchmark NY) Marshall Cavendish.

— A Handful of Dirt. LC 99-53632. (Illus.). 32p. (J). (gr. 3-7). 2000. 16.95 (*0-8027-8698-7*) Walker & Co.

— A Handful of Dirt. LC 99-53632. (Illus.). 32p. (J). (gr. 2-6). 2000. lib. bdg. 17.85 (*0-8027-8699-5*) Walker & Co.

— The Huron. LC 99-49261. (Lifeways Ser.). 2001. 32.79 (*0-7614-0940-8*, Benchmark NY) Marshall Cavendish.

Bial, Raymond. The Iroquois. LC 97-26573. (Lifeways Ser.). (J). 1998. lib. bdg. 32.79 (*0-7614-0802-9*, Benchmark NY) Marshall Cavendish.

— Ivesdale: A Photographic Essay. LC 82-73325. (Champaign County Historical Archives Historical Publications Ser.: No. 5). (Illus.). 126p. 1982. 12.00 (*0-9609646-0-6*) Urbana Free Lib.

***Bial, Raymond.** Lifeways, 4 vols. 2000. boxed set 131.14 (*0-7614-0860-6*) M Cavendish.

— Lifeways, No. 3. (Illus.). (J). 2000. 131.14 (*0-7614-0936-X*, Benchmark NY) Marshall Cavendish.

Bial, Raymond. Mist over the Mountains: Appalachia & Its People. (Illus.). 48p. (J). 1997. 14.95 (*0-395-73569-6*) HM.

— The Navajo. LC 97-53248. (Lifeways Ser.). (Illus.). (YA). (gr. 6 up). 1998. lib. bdg. 32.79 (*0-7614-0803-7*, Benchmark NY) Marshall Cavendish.

— The Ojibwe. LC 99-12202. (Lifeways Ser.). (Illus.). 128p. (YA). (gr. 4-7). 1999. lib. bdg. 32.79 (*0-7614-0863-0*) Marshall Cavendish.

***Bial, Raymond.** One-Room School. LC 98-43241. (Illus.). 48p. (J). (gr. 3-7). 1999. 15.00 (*0-395-90514-1*) HM.

Bial, Raymond. Portrait of a Farm Family. (Illus.). 48p. (J). (gr. 3-7). 1995. 15.95 (*0-395-69936-3*) HM.

— The Pueblo. LC 98-48299. (Lifeways Ser.). (Illus.). 128p. (YA). (gr. 4-7). 1999. lib. bdg. 32.79 (*0-7614-0861-4*) Marshall Cavendish.

— The Seminole. LC 98-50427. (Lifeways Ser.). (Illus.). 128p. (YA). (gr. 4-7). 1999. lib. bdg. 32.79 (*0-7614-0862-2*) Marshall Cavendish.

— Shaker Home. LC 93-17917. 40p. (J). 1994. 15.95 (*0-395-64047-4*) HM.

— The Sioux. LC 98-2915. (Lifeways Ser.). (Illus.). (YA). (gr. 6 up). 1998. lib. bdg. 32.79 (*0-7614-0804-5*, Benchmark NY) Marshall Cavendish.

— The Strength of These Arms: Life in the Slave Quarters. LC 96-39860. (Illus.). 48p. (J). (gr. 3-7). 1997. 16.00 (*0-395-77394-6*) HM.

— The Underground Railroad. LC 94-19614. (Illus.). 48p. (J). (gr. 3-7). 1995. 16.00 (*0-395-69937-1*) HM.

***Bial, Raymond.** The Underground Railroad. (Illus.). 48p. (J). (gr. 3-7). 1999. pap. 5.95 (*0-395-97915-3*) HM.

Bial, Raymond. Visit to Amish Country. (Illus.). 112p. 1995. 23.95 (*1-886154-02-3*) U of Ill Pr.

— Where Lincoln Walked. LC 97-9922. (Illus.). 48p. (J). (gr. 3-7). 1998. 16.95 (*0-8027-8630-8*); lib. bdg. 17.85 (*0-8027-8631-6*) Walker & Co.

— With Needle & Thread: A Book about Quilts. LC 95-16416. (Illus.). 48p. (J). (gr. 3-7). 1996. 14.95 (*0-395-73568-8*) HM.

— Zoom Lens Photography. (Illus.). 112p. 1996. pap. 15.95 (*0-936262-45-1*) Amherst Media.

Bial, Raymond, photos by. Stopping By: Portraits from Small Towns. LC 88-17407. (Visions of Illinois Ser.). (Illus.). 200p. 1988. 24.95 (*0-252-01587-8*) U of Ill Pr.

Bial, Raymond & Schlipf, Frederick A., eds. Upon a Quiet Landscape: The Photographs of Frank Sadorus. LC 83-72993. (Champaign County Historical Archives Historical Publications Ser.: No. 6). (Illus.). 155p. 1983. 18.00 (*0-9609646-1-4*) Urbana Free Lib.

Bial, Raymond, jt. auth. see Kerr, Kathryn.

Bial, Raymond S. Looking Good: Photographing Your Library. 1991. 15.00 (*0-8389-0575-7*) ALA.

Biala, Arlene. Continental Drift. 36p. 1999. pap. 7.95 (*0-931122-95-3*) West End.

Bialas, A., et al. Soft Physics & Fluctuations: Cracow Workshop on Multiparticle Production. 344p. 1994. text 116.00 (*981-02-1588-6*) World Scientific Pub.

Bialas, Wolfgang & Iggers, Georg G., eds. Intellektuelle in der Weimarer Republik. 2nd ed. (GER.). 465p. 1997. pap. 67.95 (*3-631-32195-3*) P Lang Pubng.

Bialas, Wolfgang & Raulet, Gerard. Die Historismusdebatte in der Weimarer Republik. (Schriften Zur Politischen Kultur der Weimarer Republik Ser.: Bd. 2). (GER.). 276p. 1996. 49.95 (*3-631-30801-9*) P Lang Pubng.

***Bialas, Zbigniew.** East-Central European Traumas & a Millennial Condition. 2000. 34.50 (*0-88033-441-X*, 543, Pub. by East Eur Monographs) Col U Pr.

***Bialaski, Tom.** High Availability: Directory Services & Authentication. 250p. 2001. pap. 32.00 (*0-13-030678-9*) Prntice Hall Bks.

Bialaski, Tom. Solaris Guide for Windows NT Administrators. LC 99-41137. 147p. (C). 1999. pap. text 29.00 (*0-13-025854-7*) P-H.

Biale, David. Childhood, Marriage & the Family in the Eastern European Jewish Enlightement. 24p. 1983. pap. 1.50 (*0-87495-049-X*) Am Jewish Comm.

— Eros & the Jews: From Biblical Israel to Contemporary America. LC 97-13465. 334p. 1997. pap. 17.95 (*0-520-21134-0*, Pub. by U CA Pr) Cal Prin Full Svc.

— From Intercourse to Discourse: Control of Sexuality in Rabbinic Literature. LC 92-28287. (Protocol of the Sixty Second Colloquy Ser.: No. 0098-0900). 1992. write for info. (*0-89242-063-4*) Ctr Hermeneutical.

— Gershom Scholem: Kabbalah & Counter-History. 2nd ed. 216p. 1982. pap. 15.00 (*0-674-36332-9*) HUP.

— Insider Outsider: American Jews & Multiculturalism. LC 97-2508. 288p. 1998. pap. 16.95 (*0-520-21122-7*, Pub. by U CA Pr) Cal Prin Full Svc.

— The Invention of Judaism. 1997. write for info. (*0-8052-4126-4*); pap. write for info. (*0-8052-1027-X*) Schocken.

— Schocken History of the Jews, 5. 1999. write for info. (*0-8052-4132-9*) Schocken.

— Schocken History of the Jews, Vol. 3. 1999. write for info. (*0-8052-4133-7*) Knopf.

— Schocken History of the Jews #5, 5. 1999. write for info. (*0-8052-4131-0*) Schocken.

Biale, David, et al, eds. Insider Outsider: American Jews & Multiculturalism. LC 97-2508. 288p. 1998. 45.00 (*0-520-21108-1*, Pub. by U CA Pr) Cal Prin Full Svc.

Biale, David, jt. auth. see Bayme, Steven.

Biale, Rachel. My Pet Died: A Let's Make a Book About It Book. (Let's Make a Book about It Ser.). (Illus.). 48p. (J). (ps-3). 1997. pap. 7.95 (*1-883672-51-1*) Tricycle Pr.

— We Are Moving: A Let's Make a Book about It Book. LC 96-157866. (Illus.). 48p. (J). (ps-3). 1996. pap. 7.95 (*1-883672-32-5*) Tricycle Pr.

— Women & Jewish Law: The Essential Texts, Their History, & Their Relevance for Today. LC 95-234656. 312p. 1995. pap. 15.00 (*0-8052-1049-0*) Schocken.

Bialecki, Ireneusz, et al, eds. Crisis & Transition: Polish Society in the 1980s. 184p. 1987. 19.50 (*0-85496-525-4*) Berg Pubs.

Bialecki, R., et al, eds. Advanced Computational Methods in Heat Transfer V. LC 98-84576. (Computational Studies: Vol. 1). 600p. 1998. 295.00 (*1-85312-591-1*, 5911, Pub. by WIT Pr) Computational Mech MA.

Bialek, Jacques. Productivity Improvement Management. LC 87-6557. (Illus.). 339p. (Orig.). 1987. pap. 18.00 (*0-941883-01-9*, HD56.B49) CA Mgmt Pr.

Bialek, Jacques, et al. Power System Dynamics & Stability. LC 96-39033. 484p. 1997. 149.95 (*0-471-97174-X*) Wiley.

Bialek, Janusz, jt. auth. see Machowski, Jan.

Bialek, Joseph. Half-Cocked. 26p. 1998. pap. 3.00 (*0-9664124-3-5*) Sweet Lady Moon.

Bialek, Kathy, et al. Historic Courthouses of Florida. 2nd ed. Cole, Vicki, ed. (Lesson Plans Series 2: No. 21). (Illus.). 16p. (YA). (gr. k up). 1997. 1.00 (*1-889030-12-0*) FL Div Hist Res.

Bialek, William. Princeton Lectures on Biophysics. 424p. 1993. text 109.00 (*981-02-1325-5*); pap. text 48.00 (*981-02-1326-3*) World Scientific Pub.

Bialer, Seweryn. Stalin's Successors: Leadership, Stability & Change in the Soviet Union. LC 80-12037. 416p. 1982. pap. text 22.95 (*0-521-28906-8*) Cambridge U Pr.

— The U. S. S. R. after Brezhnev. LC 83-83061. (Headline Ser.: No. 265). (Illus.). 64p. (Orig.). (YA). (gr. 11-12). 1983. pap. 5.95 (*0-87124-086-6*) Foreign Policy.

Bialer, Seweryn, ed. The Domestic Context of Soviet Foreign Policy. LC 80-11877. 442p. 1981. text 50.50 (*0-89158-783-7*) Westview.

— The Domestic Context of Soviet Foreign Policy. LC 80-11877. 442p. 1981. pap. text 24.90 (*0-89158-891-4*) Westview.

— Stalin & His Generals: Soviet Military Memoirs of World War II. (Encore Edition Ser.). 650p. 1984. pap. text 75.50 (*0-86531-610-4*) Westview.

Bialer, Seweryn & Gustafson, Thane, eds. Russia at the Crossroads: The Twenty-Sixth Congress of the CPSU. 256p. 1982. text 55.00 (*0-04-329039-6*) Routledge.

Bialer, Seweryn, jt. ed. see Jervis, Robert.

Bialer, Uri. Between East & West: Israel's Foreign Policy Orientation, 1948-1956. (London School of Economics Monographs in International Studies). 302p. (C). 1990. text 64.95 (*0-521-36249-0*) Cambridge U Pr.

Bialeschki, M. Deborah, jt. auth. see Henderson, Karla A.

Bialestowski, Alice & Sainderichin, Ginette. Paris. 80p. 1999. text 18.95 (*0-7893-0379-5*) Universe.

Bialestowski, Alice, jt. auth. see Sainderichin, Ginette.

Bialick, Craig, ed. see Rinpoche, Khenpo P.

Bialik, Hayim N. & Ravnitzky, Yehoshua H., eds. The Book of Legends (Sefer Ha-aggadah) Legends from the Talmud & Midrash. Braude, William G., tr. from HEB. LC 91-52700. 896p. 1992. 75.00 (*0-8052-4113-2*) Schocken.

Bialik, Hayyim Nahman. Knight of Onions & Knight of Garlic. 55p. 1934. 6.95 (*0-88482-734-8*) Hebrew Pub.

— Selected Poems of Hayyim Nahman Bialik. Efros, I., ed. 1999. pap. 15.95 (*0-8197-0666-3*) Bloch.

Bialik, Loren J. Unclaimed Fortunes: How to Get Your Share. 176p. 1994. pap. 150.00 (*0-9639772-0-2*) Mazel Pubng.

Bialkin, Kenneth J., Jr., et al. New Techniques in Acquisitions & Takeovers. vi, 528p. write for info. (*0-318-58372-0*) Harcourt.

Bialko, Michal & Crampagne, R. Basic Methods for Microcomputer-Aided Analysis of Electronic Circuits. 472p. 1995. pap. 53.00 (*0-13-061284-7*) P-H.

Bialkowski, Carol, jt. auth. see Opler, Lewis A.

Bialkowski, Stephen E. Photothermal Spectroscopy Methods for Chemical Analysis. LC 95-34049. (Chemical Analysis Ser.). 584p. 1995. 110.00 (*0-471-57467-8*, Wiley-Interscience) Wiley.

Biallas, Leonard J. Myths: Gods, Heroes & Saviors. LC 85-52140. 312p. (Orig.). 1986. pap. 12.95 (*0-89622-290-X*) Twenty-Third.

— World Religions: A Story Approach. LC 91-65738. (Illus.). 336p. (C). 1991. pap. 14.95 (*0-89622-493-7*) Twenty-Third.

Bialosiewicz, Frank & Burns, Julie. Game of Childhood Diseases. (Technical Notes Ser.: No. 23). (Illus.). 30p. (Orig.). 1983. pap. text 2.00 (*0-932288-70-7*) Ctr Intl Ed U of MA.

Bialosiewicz, Frank, jt. auth. see Burns, Julie.

Bialosky, Jill. The End of Desire: Poems. LC 96-43695. 80p. 1997. 21.00 (*0-679-45455-1*) Knopf.

— The End of Desire: Poems. 88p. 1999. pap. 13.00 (*0-679-76606-5*) Knopf.

Bialosky, Jill, et al, eds. Wanting a Child. LC 97-32348. 272p. 1998. 25.00 (*0-374-28634-5*) FS&G.

Bialosky, Jill & Schulman, Helen, eds. Wanting a Child. 288p. 1999. pap. text 13.00 (*0-374-52594-3*) FS&G.

Bialostok, Steve. But Will He Read? A Teacher's Guide to Helping Parents Understand Whole Language. LC 96-920098. 128p. 1996. pap., teacher ed. 12.00 (*1-895411-83-1*) Peguis Pubs Ltd.

— Raising Readers: Helping Your Child to Literacy. Norget, Judy, ed. 176p. 1992. pap. 14.00 (*1-895411-37-8*) Peguis Pubs Ltd.

Bialostosky, Don H. Making Tales: The Poetics of Wordsworth's Narrative Experiments. LC 83-5069. 208p. 1984. pap. text 12.50 (*0-226-04576-5*) U Ch Pr.

— Making Tales: The Poetics of Wordsworth's Narrative Experiments. LC 83-5069. 208p. 1984. lib. bdg. 25.00 (*0-226-04575-7*) U Ch Pr.

— Making Tales: The Poetics of Wordsworth's Narrative Experiments. LC 83-5069. 220p. Date not set. reprint ed. pap. 68.20 (*0-608-20666-0*, 207210300003) Bks Demand.

— Wordsworth, Dialogics & the Practice of Criticism. (Literature, Culture, Theory Ser.: No. 2). 316p. (C). 1992. text 69.95 (*0-521-41249-8*) Cambridge U Pr.

Bialostosky, Don H. & Needham, Lawrence D., eds. Rhetorical Traditions & British Romantic Literature. LC 94-19475. 320p. 1995. 39.95 (*0-253-31180-2*) Ind U Pr.

Bialoszewski, Miron. A Memoir of the Warsaw Uprising. Levine, Madeline, tr. from POL. & intro. by. 234p. 1991. reprint ed. pap. 12.95 (*0-8101-1026-1*) Northwestern U Pr.

— The Revolution of Things. Czaykowski, Bogdan & Busza, Andrzej, trs. LC 74-81212. 1974. 7.50 (*0-910350-01-9*) Charioteer.

Bialy, Harvey, ed. Biopoesis. 350p. 1974. pap. 5.00 (*0-913028-25-8*) North Atlantic.

Bialy, Harvey, ed. see Ritundo, R. L.

Bialyncki-Birula, Iwo, et al. Theory of Quanta. Furdyna, Anna M., tr. (Illus.). 512p. (C). 1992. text 68.00 (*0-19-507157-3*) OUP.

Bialynicki-Birula, A., et al, eds. Group Actions & Invariant Theory: Proceedings of the 1988 Montreal Conference. LC 89-17605. (Canadian Math Society Conference Proceedings Ser.: Vol. 10). 228p. 1989. pap. 46.00 (*0-8218-6015-1*, CMSAMS/10) Am Math.

Bialystok, Ellen, ed. Language Processing in Bilingual Children. 251p. (C). 1991. pap. text 21.95 (*0-521-37918-0*) Cambridge U Pr.

Bialystok, Ellen & Hakuta, Kenji. In Other Words: The Science & Psychology of Second-Language Acquisition. 256p. 1995. pap. 15.00 (*0-465-03281-8*, Pub. by Basic) HarpC.

Bialystok, Ellen, jt. auth. see Olson, David R.

Biammatteo, Tom, ed. see Kain, Jay & Weiselfish-Giammatteo, Sharon.

Biamonte, Edgar. Window of Eternity. LC 83-9944. 145p. 1984. 21.95 (*0-87949-230-9*) Ashley Bks.

Bian, Tonda R. The Drug Lords... America's Pharmaceutical Cartel. LC 96-92687. (Illus.). 192p. (Orig.). 1998. per. 12.95 (*0-9654568-0-3*) No Barriers.

Bian, Yanjie. Work & Inequaltiy in Urban China. LC 93-14708. (SUNY Series in the Sociology of Work). 286p. (C). 1994. text 64.50 (*0-7914-1801-4*); pap. text 21.95 (*0-7914-1802-2*) State U NY Pr.

Bian, Ying, jt. auth. see Chen, Lydia.

Bian, Ying, ed. see Ah Cheng, et al.

Bianca, C. M., et al, eds. Commentary on the International Sales Law: The Vienna Sales Convention, 1988. 903p. 125.00 (*88-14-01276-8*) Juris Pubng.

***Biancalana, Stefano, et al.** Vespa: From Italy with Love. (Illus.). 128p. 2000. 24.95 (*88-7911-162-0*, 130752AE, Pub. by Giorgio Nada Editore) Motorbooks Intl.

Bianchi. In the Studio. 96p. 1999. pap. 25.00 (*0-312-24304-9*) St Martin.

Bianchi, et al. The Fetal Patient: Multi Approach to Management. (Illus.). 528p. (C). 2000. pap. 145.00 (*0-8385-2570-9*, Apple Lange Med) McGraw.

Bianchi, A. & Richeri, G., eds. Telecommunications: New Dynamics & Driving Forces. LC 96-7508. (European Communication Policy Research Ser.). 135p. (YA). (gr. 12). 1996. pap. 72.00 (*90-5199-256-4*, 256-4) IOS Press.

Bianchi, A. L. & Denavit-Saubie, M., eds. Neurogenesis of Central Respiratory Rhythm: Electrophysiological, Pharmacological & Pathological Aspects. 1985. text 322.00 (*0-85200-903-8*) Kluwer Academic.

Bianchi, Andres. Politica Cambiaria, Desarrollo Exportador y Estabilizacion en Chile, 1990-92, Vol. 12. (SPA.). 54p. 1994. pap. text 8.00 (*0-940602-87-3*) IADB.

Bianchi, Anne. C. Everett Koop: The Health of a Nation. LC 92-1230. (New Directions Ser.). (Illus.). 104p. (YA). (gr. 7 up). 1992. lib. bdg. 21.90 (*1-56294-103-8*) Millbrook Pr.

— From Tables Tuscan Women. LC 95-10075. (Illus.). 326p. 1995. 26.00 (*0-88001-425-3*) HarpC.

— Music Lover's Guide to Great Britain. Spinella, Dan, ed. (Illus.). 350p. (Orig.). 1995. pap. 14.95 (*0-8442-9006-8*, Passprt Bks) NTC Contemp Pub Co.

— 101 Great Choices: San Francisco. LC 97-18693. (101 Great Choices Ser.). (Illus.). 128p. 1997. pap. text 8.95 (*0-8442-8989-2*, 89892) NTC Contemp Pub Co.

— Solo Verdura: The Complete Cookbook of Tuscan Vegetables. LC 97-9344. (Illus.). 352p. 1997. 28.95 (*0-88001-543-8*) HarpC.

— Zuppa: Soups From The Italian Countryside. LC 96-19067. (Cooking with Ser.). (Illus.). 2524p. 1996. 25.00 (*0-88001-513-6*) HarpC.

Bianchi, Anne & Lotti, Sandra. Dolci Toscani: The Book Of Tuscan Desserts. LC 98-8312. 224p. 1998. 28.95 (*0-88001-587-X*) HarpC.

Bianchi, Antonio, et al, eds. The Supramolecular Chemistry of Anions. 250p. 1996. 69.95 (*1-56081-906-5*, Wiley-VCH) Wiley.

Bianchi, Antonio, et al. The Supramolecular Chemistry of Anions. LC 97-7640. 480p. 1997. 98.95 (*0-471-18622-8*) Wiley.

Bianchi, C. P., ed. Kidney, Small Proteins & Drugs. (Contributions to Nephrology Ser.: Vol. 42). (Illus.). x, 262p. 1985. 29.75 (*3-8055-3913-4*) S Karger.

Bianchi, C. P., et al, eds. Kidney & Proteins in Health & Disease. (Contributions to Nephrology Ser.: Vol. 68). (Illus.). xi, 274p. 1988. 29.75 (*3-8055-4821-4*) S Karger.

— Kidney, Proteins & Drugs. (Contributions to Nephrology Ser.: Vol. 83). (Illus.). xii, 276p. 1991. 29.75 (*3-8055-5190-8*) S Karger.

— Kidney, Proteins & Drugs: An Update. (Contributions to Nephrology Ser.: Vol. 101). (Illus.). x, 270p. 1993. 49.75 (*3-8055-5668-3*) S Karger.

— Skeletal Muscle Toxicity of 6-Mercaptopurine, Vol. 11, 14. LC 86-61951. (Toxicology & Industrial Health Ser.: Vol. 2, No. 2). (Illus.). 144p. 1986. 24.00 (*0-911131-95-7*) Specialist Journals.

Bianchi, C. P., ed. see International Symposium on Unilateral Renal Functions Studies Staff.

Bianchi, Chuck. Code Talkers. 1990. mass mkt. 3.95 (*1-55817-448-6*, Pinncle Kensgtn) Kensgtn Pub Corp.

Bianchi, Emanuela, ed. Is Feminist Philosophy Philosophy? LC 99-46794. 312p. 1999. 69.95 (*0-8101-1594-8*); pap. 26.95 (*0-8101-1595-6*) Northwestern U Pr.

Bianchi, Enzo. Praying the Word: An Introduction to Lectio Divina. Elder, E. Rozanne, ed. Zona, James W., tr. from ITA. LC 98-55938. (Cistercian Studies: Vol. CS182). 119p. 1999. pap. 11.95 (*0-87907-682-8*) Cistercian Pubns.

Bianchi, Eugene C. Aging As a Spiritual Journey. 304p. 1984. pap. 19.95 (*0-8245-0622-7*) Crossroad NY.

Bianchi, Ferrari P., et al. Collins Gem Dictionary: Francais-Italien-Francais. (FRE & ITA.). 738p. 1981. 12.95 (*0-8288-1506-2*) Fr & Eur.

***Bianchi, G., ed.** Environmental Applications of Mechanics & Computer Science: Proceedings of the CISM 30th Anniversary Conference, Udine, May 29, 1999. (CISM International Centre for Mechanical Sciences Ser.: No. 409). (Illus.). vi, 135p. 1999. pap. 32.00 (*3-211-83152-5*) Spr-Verlag.

Bianchi, G. & Schiehlen, W. O., eds. Dynamics of Multibody Systems. 310p. 1986. 94.95 (*0-387-16347-6*) Spr-Verlag.

Bianchi, Herman. Justice As Sanctuary: Toward a New System of Crime Control. LC 93-8386. 215p. reprint ed. pap. 66.70 (*0-608-09328-9*, 205407400002) Bks Demand.

Bianchi, John. The Artist. (Illus.). 32p. (YA). (gr. 2 up). 1993. pap. 4.95 (*0-921285-28-0*, Pub. by Bungalo Books); lib. bdg. 14.95 (*0-921285-29-9*, Pub. by Bungalo Books) Firefly Bks Ltd.

— The Bungalo Boys: Flight of the Space Quester. (Illus.). 24p. (J). (gr. k-3). 1993. pap. 4.95 (*0-921285-30-2*, Pub. by Bungalo Books); lib. bdg. 14.95 (*0-921285-31-0*, Pub. by Bungalo Books) Firefly Bks Ltd.

— The Bungalo Boys: The Last of the Tree Ranchers. (Illus.). 24p. (J). (gr. k-3). 1986. lib. bdg. 16.95 (*0-921285-02-7*, Pub. by Bungalo Books) Firefly Bks Ltd.

— The Bungalo Boys: The Last of the Tree Ranchers. (Illus.). 24p. (J). (ps-8). 1986. pap. 5.95 (*0-921285-00-0*, Pub. by Bungalo Books) Firefly Bks Ltd.

— The Bungalo Boys III: Champions of Hockey. (Illus.). 24p. (J). (ps-8). 1989. pap. 5.95 (*0-921285-16-7*, Pub. by Bungalo Books); lib. bdg. 16.95 (*0-921285-18-3*, Pub. by Bungalo Books) Firefly Bks Ltd.

— The Bungalo Boys II: Bushmen Brouhaha. (Illus.). 24p. (J). (ps-8). 1987. pap. 5.95 (*0-921285-08-6*, Pub. by Bungalo Books); lib. bdg. 16.95 (*0-921285-10-8*, Pub. by Bungalo Books) Firefly Bks Ltd.

— The First Big Bungalo Boys Book: Three Stories High. (Illus.). 72p. (J). (ps-2). 1995. pap. 8.95 (*0-921285-42-6*, Pub. by Bungalo Books); lib. bdg. 18.95 (*0-921285-43-4*, Pub. by Bungalo Books) Firefly Bks Ltd.

— The Lab Rats of Doctor Eclair. (Illus.). 32p. (J). (gr. k-3). 1997. pap. 6.95 (*0-921285-48-5*) Bungalo Books.

— Penelope Penguin: The Incredibly Good Baby. (Illus.). 24p. (J). (ps-3). 1992. pap. 4.95 (*0-921285-11-6*, Pub. by Bungalo Books); lib. bdg. 14.95 (*0-921285-13-2*, Pub. by Bungalo Books) Firefly Bks Ltd.

— Princess Frownsalot. (Illus.). 24p. (J). (ps-8). 1987. pap. 4.95 (*0-921285-04-3*, Pub. by Bungalo Books); lib. bdg. 16.95 (*0-921285-06-X*, Pub. by Bungalo Books) Firefly Bks Ltd.

— Sapo Duerme Fuera de Casa.Tr. of Toad Sleeps Over. (SPA., Illus.). 24p. (Orig.). (J). (ps-3). 1997. pap. 5.95 (*0-921285-56-6*, Pub. by Bungalo Books) Firefly Bks Ltd.

— Snowed in at Pokeweed Public School. (Illus.). 24p. (J). (gr. 6-9). 1991. lib. bdg. 16.95 (*0-921285-07-8*) Bungalo Books.

— Snowed In At Public School. (Illus.). 24p. (J). (gr. 1-5). 1999. pap. 4.95 (*1-894323-12-2*, Pub. by Genl Dist Srvs) Genl Dist Srvs.

— Spring Break at Pokeweed Public School. (Illus.). 24p. (J). (ps-2). 1994. lib. bdg. 16.95 (*0-921285-33-7*, Pub. by Bungalo Books) Firefly Bks Ltd.

— Spring Break at Pokeweed Public School. (Illus.). 24p. (J). (ps-3). 1994. pap. 4.95 (*0-921285-32-9*, Pub. by Bungalo Books) Firefly Bks Ltd.

Bianchi, John. Spring Break at Pokeweed Public School. (YA). 1994. 10.15 (*0-606-06764-7*, Pub. by Turtleback) Demco.

Bianchi, John. The Toad Sleeps Over. (Illus.). 24p. (J). (ps-2). 1995. pap. 4.95 (*0-921285-40-X*, Pub. by Bungalo Books); lib. bdg. 16.95 (*0-921285-41-8*, Pub. by Bungalo Books) Firefly Bks Ltd.

— Welcome Back to Pokeweed Public School. (Illus.). 24p. (J). (gr. 1-5). 1996. 15.95 (*0-921285-45-0*, Pub. by Bungalo Books); pap. 4.95 (*0-921285-44-2*, Pub. by Bungalo Books) Firefly Bks Ltd.

***Bianchi, John.** Young Author's Day at Pokeweed Public School. (Illus.). 24p. (YA). (gr. 6-9). 1999. text 14.95 (*1-894323-14-9*, Pub. by Genl Dist Srvs) Genl Dist Srvs.

— Young Author's Day at Pokeweed Public School. large type ed. (Public School Ser.). (Illus.). 24p. (J). (gr. 1-5). 1999. pap. 15.95 (*1-894323-13-0*, Pub. by Genl Dist Srvs) Genl Dist Srvs.

Bianchi, L., et al, eds. Aging in Liver & Gastrointestinal Tract. (Falk Ser.). (C). 1988. text 209.50 (*0-7462-0066-8*) Kluwer Academic.

Bianchi, L., et al. Infectious Diseases of the Liver. (C). 1990. text 192.00 (*0-7923-8902-6*) Kluwer Academic.

Bianchi, L., jt. ed. see Boyer, J. L.

Bianchi, Luciana & Gilmozzi, Roberto. Mass Outflows from Stars & Galactic Nuclei. (C). 1988. text 237.50 (*90-277-2698-1*) Kluwer Academic.

Bianchi, M., et al. String Theory & Grand Unification: Proceedings of the Conference. 450p. 1993. text 109.00 (*981-02-1161-9*) World Scientific Pub.

Bianchi, M. V., et al, eds. Proceedings of the 32nd National Heat Transfer Conference, Baltimore, Maryland, August 8-12, 1997, Vol. 6. (HTD Ser.: Vol. 344). 148p. 1997. 70.00 (*0-7918-1811-X*, H01092) ASME Pr.

Bianchi, Marina. The Active Consumer: Novelty & Surprise in Consumer Choice. LC 97-32108. 288p. (C). 1998. 90.00 (*0-415-17190-3*) Routledge.

Bianchi, Martha D. The Life & Letters of Emily Dickinson. LC 70-162296. 386p. 1972. reprint ed. 32.00 (*0-8196-0276-0*) Biblo.

***Bianchi, P. & Doswald, C.** Die Nonchalance der Zeichen: Kleines ABC der Gegenwartskunst. (GER.). 160p. 1998. pap. text 16.00 (*90-5705-101-X*, Verlag Kunst) Gordon & Breach.

Bianchi, Paolo. Wherever We Are Is Museum. 1999. 19.95 (*3-89322-979-5*) Dr Cantz sche Druckerei GmbH.

Bianchi, Patrizio. Industrial Policies & Economic Integration: Learning from European Experiences. LC 97-21642. 224p. (C). 1998. write for info. (*0-415-14910-X*) Routledge.

Bianchi-Porro, G., et al, eds. Clinical Challenges in Inflammatory Bowel Diseases: Diagnosis, Prognosis & Treatment. (Falk Symposium Ser.). 288p. 1998. 125.00 (*0-7923-8733-3*) Kluwer Academic.

Bianchi, Porro G. & Scarpignato, C., eds. Clinical Investigation of Gastric Function. (Frontiers of Gastrointestinal Research Ser.: Vol. 17). (Illus.). viii, 300p. 1990. 233.25 (*3-8055-5100-2*) S Karger.

Bianchi, Robert. Interest Groups & Political Development in Turkey. LC 83-10999. 443p. 1984. reprint ed. pap. 137.40 (*0-608-03335-9*, 206404700008) Bks Demand.

Bianchi, Robert, tr. see Donadoni, Sergio.

Bianchi, Robert S. Splendors of Ancient Egypt: From the Egyptian Museum, Cairo. (Illus.). 224p. 1998. text 30.00 (*0-7881-5901-1*) DIANE Pub.

Bianchi, Robert S., jt. auth. see Rubin, Arnold.

Bianchi, Robert S., ed. see Mercatante, Anthony S.

Bianchi, Roland R. The Migration of Moro: My Other Grandfather's Story. LC 97-535. (Illus.). 112p. (Orig.). 1997. pap. 9.95 (*1-56474-209-1*) Fithian Pr.

Bianchi, Susan & Butler, Jan. Warm Ups for Meeting Leaders. Parcher, Jean & Lewis, Cathy, eds. LC 84-61535. (Illus.). 138p. (Orig.). 1984. 29.95 (*0-930733-00-2*) Quality Groups Pub.

Bianchi, Susan, et al. Warmups for Meeting Leaders. LC 84-61535. (Illus.). 138p. 1990. ring bd. 59.95 (*0-88390-249-4*, Pfffr & Co) Jossey-Bass.

Bianchi, Susan, ed. see Forrest, Judith M. & Richey, David L.

Bianchi, Susan, ed. see Richey, David & Richey, Fred.

Bianchi, Susanne M. & Spain, Daphne. American Women in Transition. LC 85-62809. (Population of the United States in the 1980s: A Census Monograph Ser.). 312p. (C). 1986. pap. text 14.95 (*0-87154-112-2*) Russell Sage.

Bianchi, Suzanne M., jt. auth. see Spain, Daphne.

Bianchi, Thomas S., et al, eds. Biogeochemistry of Gulf of Mexico Estuaries. LC 98-15977. 448p. 1998. 89.95 (*0-471-16174-8*) Wiley.

Bianchi, Tom. In Defense of Beauty. LC 95-664. 1995. 12.00 (*0-517-70223-1*) Crown Pub Group.

— In the Studio. LC 96-37058. (Illus.). 96p. 1998. text 50.00 (*0-312-15150-0*) St Martin.

— Men I've Loved. 1998. 49.95 (*3-925443-81-9*) Janvid Pubs.

***Bianchi, Valentina.** Consequences of Antisymmetry. LC 99-34346. (Studies in Generative Grammar: No. 46). 357p. 1999. 110.00 (*3-11-016250-4*) De Gruyter.

***Bianchin, Helen.** Boda de Sociedad (Wedding in Society) A Convenient Bridegroom. (Bianca Ser.: No. 193). (SPA.). 2000. per. 3.50 (*0-373-33543-1*, 1-33543-9) Silhouette.

Bianchin, Helen. Bridal Bed. 1999. 21.95 (*0-263-15952-3*, G K Hall & Co) Mac Lib Ref.

— The Bridal Bed: (Top Author - Do Not Disturb) (Presents Ser.: No. 1996). 1998. per. 3.75 (*0-373-11996-8*, 0-11996-6) Harlequin Bks.

***Bianchin, Helen.** Convenient Bridegroom. large type ed. (Thorndike Harlequin Romance Ser.). 2000. 22.95 (*0-263-16282-6*) Mills & Boon.

— A Convenient Bridegroom: Society Weddings. (Harlequin Presents Ser.). 1999. mass mkt. 3.75 (*0-373-12067-2*, Harlequin) Harlequin Bks.

Bianchin, Helen. Dangerous Alliance. LC 95-7047. (Presents Ser.). 188p. 1995. per. 3.25 (*0-373-11741-8*, 1-11741-5) Harlequin Bks.

— Dangerous Alliance. large type ed. (Harlequin Romance Ser.). 284p. 1995. lib. bdg. 19.95 (*0-263-14100-4*) Mac Lib Ref.

— Desert Mistress. (Presents Ser.). 1997. per. 3.50 (*0-373-11872-4*, 1-11872-8) Harlequin Bks.

— Desert Mistress. large type ed. 283p. 1997. 20.95 (*0-263-14795-9*) Thorndike Pr.

— Forgotten Husband. (Top Author Ser.). 1996. per. 3.50 (*0-373-11809-0*, 1-11809-0) Harlequin Bks.

***Bianchin, Helen.** The Husband Assignment. (Harlequin Presents Ser.). 2000. mass mkt. 3.99 (*0-373-12115-6*, 1121151) Harlequin Bks.

Bianchin, Helen. An Ideal Marriage? 1997. per. 3.50 (*0-373-11905-4*, 1-11905-6) Harlequin Bks.

— An Ideal Marriage. large type ed. (Harlequin Ser.). 287p. 1998. 20.95 (*0-263-15371-1*) Thorndike Pr.

— The Marriage Campaign. (Presents Ser.). 1998. per. 3.75 (*0-373-11960-7*, 1-11960-1) Harlequin Bks.

— The Marriage Campaign. large type ed. 1998. 21.95 (*0-263-15747-4*, Pub. by Mills & Boon) Chivers N Amer.

— Master of Uluru. large type ed. (Linford Romance Library). 326p. 1984. pap. 16.99 (*0-7089-6038-3*, Linford) Ulverscroft.

— Mistress by Arrangement. (Romance Ser.). 1999. per. 3.75 (*0-373-12049-4*, 1-12049-2) Harlequin Bks.

***Bianchin, Helen.** Mistress by Arrangement. large type ed. (Thorndike Harlequin Romance Ser.). 2000. 22.95 (*0-263-16367-9*) Mills & Boon.

Bianchin, Helen. No Gentle Seduction. (Presents Ser.). 1993. pap. 2.89 (*0-373-11527-X*, 1-11527-8) Harlequin Bks.

— No Gentle Seduction. large type ed. 1992. reprint ed. lib. bdg. 18.95 (*0-263-12898-9*) Mac Lib Ref.

***Bianchin, Helen.** Noces de Feu. (Azur Ser.: No. 789). (FRE.). 1999. mass mkt. 3.99 (*0-373-34789-8*, 1-34789-7) Harlequin Bks.

Bianchin, Helen. Passion's Mistress. large type ed. 1994. 19.95 (*0-263-13902-6*) Thorndike Pr.

— Passion's Mistress: (Presents Plus) (Presents Ser.). 1994. per. 2.99 (*0-373-11704-3*, 1-11704-3) Harlequin Bks.

— The Reluctant Captive. large type ed. (Harlequin Ser.). 1993. 19.95 (*0-263-13403-2*) Thorndike Pr.

— The Reluctant Captive: Year down Under. (Presents Ser.). 1993. per. 2.99 (*0-373-11601-2*, 1-11601-1) Harlequin Bks.

— Stormfire. (Presents Ser.). 1993. per. 2.99 (*0-373-11561-X*, 1-11561-7) Harlequin Bks.

— Union Peligrosa. (Bianca Ser.). 1996. per. 3.50 (*0-373-33371-4*, 1-33371-5) Harlequin Bks.

***Bianchin, Helen, et al.** Christmas Affairs: The Seduction Season; A Miracle on Christmas Eve; Yuletide Reunion. 1999. mass mkt. 5.99 (*0-373-83416-0*, Harlequin) Harlequin Bks.

Bianchina, Paul. Attic, Basement & Garage Conversion: A Do-It-Yourselfer's Guide. (Illus.). 208p. 1989. 24.95 (*0-8306-9271-1*); pap. 16.95 (*0-8306-3271-9*) McGraw-Hill Prof.

— Bathroom Remodeling: A Do-It-Yourselfer's Guide. (Illus.). 208p. 1988. 23.95 (*0-8306-9001-8*, 3001) McGraw-Hill Prof.

— Builder's Guide to New Materials & Techniques. LC 96-49070. (Builder's Guide Ser.). (Illus.). 337p. 1997. pap. 24.95 incl. disk (*0-07-006052-5*) McGraw.

— Illustrated Dictionary of Building Materials & Techniques: An Invaluable Sourcebook to the Tools, Terms, Materials, & Techniques Used by Building Professionals. LC 92-15437. (Illus.). 256p. 1993. 49.95 (*0-471-57656-5*); pap. 16.95 (*0-471-57657-3*) Wiley.

— Kitchen Remodeling. 1991. 23.95 (*0-8306-5313-9*) McGraw-Hill Prof.

Bianchina, Paul, jt. auth. see Ruegg, Frank.

Bianchini, A., et al, eds. Cataclysmic Variables: Proceedings of the Conference Held in Abvano Terme, Italy, on 20-24 June, 1994, Vol. 205. LC 95-34348. (Astrophysics & Space Science Library). 536p. (C). 1995. text 202.50 (*0-7923-3676-3*) Kluwer Academic.

***Bianchini, Angela.** The Edge of Europe. Jeannet, Angela M. & Castronuovo, David, trs. LC 00-24176. (European Women Writers Ser.). 128p. 2000. pap. 15.00 (*0-8032-6171-3*, Bison Books); text 45.00 (*0-8032-1308-5*) U of Nebr Pr.

Bianchini, Ellen, tr. see Burke, Peter, ed.

Bianchini, Ellen, jt. tr. see Dorey, Claire.

Bianchini, Ellen, tr. see Settis, Salvatore.

Bianchini, Thomas. The Overlord. 92p. (Orig.). 1983. pap. 5.00 (*0-9612286-0-1*) Whitewater.

Bianciotti, Hector. Sans le Misericorde du Christ. (FRE.). 352p. 1987. pap. 11.95 (*0-7859-2066-8*, 2070378470) Fr & Eur.

— Seules les Larmes Seront Comptees. (FRE.). 441p. 1991. pap. 14.95 (*0-7859-2178-8*, 2070384276) Fr & Eur.

— Le Traite de Saisons. (FRE.). 256p. 1984. pap. 11.95 (*0-7859-1998-8*, 2070375730) Fr & Eur.

— What the Night Tells the Day. Coverdale, Linda, tr. from FRE. LC 94-43354.Tr. of Ce Que la Nuit Raconte au Jour. 272p. 1995. 22.00 (*1-56584-240-5*, Pub. by New Press NY) Norton.

— What the Night Tells the Day: A Novel. Coverdale, Linda, tr. from FRE. (International Fiction Ser.). 272p. 1996. pap. 11.00 (*1-56584-241-3*, Pub. by New Press NY) Norton.

Bianco. Little Wooden Doll. (Illus.). 32p. (J). Date not set. 15.95 (*0-06-028277-0*); pap. 4.95 (*0-06-443548-2*) HarpC.

— Oregon Rediscovered. 1994. 16.95 (*0-9643408-0-1*) Bianco Pub.

Bianco, Anthony. Rainmaker: The Saga of Jeff Beck, Wall Street's Mad Dog. 1993. mass mkt. write for info. (*0-449-22135-0*) Fawcett.

— Rainmaker: The Saga of Jeff Beck, Wall Street's Mad Dog. (Illus.). 486p. 1999. reprint ed. text 25.00 (*0-7881-6198-9*) DIANE Pub.

— The Reichmanns. (Illus.). 848p. 1998. pap. 20.00 (*0-8129-3063-0*, Times Bks) Crown Pub Group.

Bianco, Bob. The Guitar in Fourths. 64p. (Orig.). pap. 7.95 (*0-9605912-2-2*) Calliope Music.

Bianco, Carla. The Two Rosetos. LC 73-16523. (Illus.). 254p. reprint ed. 78.80 (*0-8357-9249-8*, 205523400011) Bks Demand.

Bianco, David. Gay Essentials: Facts for Your Queer Brain. LC 99-36465. 288p. 1999. pap. 12.95 (*1-55583-508-2*, Pub. by Alyson Pubns) Consort Bk Sales.

Bianco, David. Heat Wave: The Motown Fact Book. LC 86-60558. (Rock & Roll Reference Ser.). write for info. (*0-87650-204-4*) Popular Culture.

Bianco, David. Heat Wave: The Motown Fact Book. (Rock & Roll Reference Ser.: No. 25). (Illus.). 560p. 1989. reprint ed. 55.00 (*1-56075-011-1*) Popular Culture.

— Modern Jewish History for Everyone. (Illus.). 216p. 1997. pap. text 24.95 (*0-9657981-0-0*) History Everyone.

— Who's New Wave in Music: An Illustrated Encyclopedia, 1976-1982. (Rock & Roll Reference Ser.: No. 14). (Illus.). 430p. 1989. reprint ed. 55.00 (*1-56075-008-1*) Popular Culture.

Bianco, David, ed. see Griswold, Denny.

Bianco, David J. Professional & Occupational Licensing Directory: A Descriptive Guide to State & Federal Licensing Registration, & Certification Requirements. 2nd ed. Moran, Amanda, ed. 439p. 1995. 105.00 (*0-8103-9050-7*, 030306) Gale.

Bianco, David P. Parents Aren't Supposed to Like It: People & Trends in Popular Music. LC 97-34040. (J). 1997. write for info. (*0-7876-1732-6*, UXL) Gale.

Bianco, David P. Parents Aren't Supposed to Like It: People & Trends in Popular Music, 3 vols., Set. LC 97-34040. 672p. (YA). (gr. 7 up). 1997. text 69.00 (*0-7876-1731-8*, UXL) Gale.

B

***Bianco, Diana.** Tales from a Walking Shadow. 1999. pap. write for info. (*1-58235-167-8*) Watermrk Pr.

Bianco, Frank. Voices of Silence: Lives of the Trappists Today. 256p. 1992. pap. 11.95 (*0-385-42430-2*, Anchor NY) Doubleday.

— Voices of Silence: Lives of the Trappists Today. (Illus.). 220p. 1991. 18.95 (*1-55778-305-5*) Paragon Hse.

Bianco, Joe. Cooking Italian: From My Dear Italian Mother's Peasant Recipes. rev. ed. (Illus.). 84p. 1977. reprint ed. pap. text 9.95 (*0-9643408-4-4*) Bianco Pub.

— Portland Step-by-Step: A Walking Guide to Scenic & Historic Points of Interest. (Illus.). 88p. (Orig.). 1988. pap. 9.95 (*0-911518-79-7*) F Amato Pubns.

Bianco, Jose. La Perdida del Reino (The Loss of the Kingdom) 2nd ed. (SPA.). 382p. 1990. 24.99 (*968-16-3396-2*, Pub. by Fondo) Continental Bk.

— Shadow Play, The Rats: Two Novellas. Miller, Yvette E., ed. Balderston, Daniel, tr. from SPA. LC 83-775. (Discoveries Ser.). 88p. 1983. pap. 9.50 (*0-935480-11-0*) Lat Am Lit Rev Pr.

Bianco, Juliette M., jt. auth. see Rand, Richard.

***Bianco, Katalina M., et al.** Financial Services Modernization: Gramm-Leach-Bliley Act of 1999 Law & Explanation. 256p. 1999. pap. text 45.00 (*0-8080-0449-2*) CCH INC.

Bianco, L. & Toth, Paolo. Advanced Methods in Transportation Analysis. LC 96-20125. (Transportation Analysis Ser.). 619p. 1996. 157.00 (*3-540-61118-5*) Spr-Verlag.

Bianco, L., et al. Modelling & Simulation in Air Traffic Management. LC 97-22629. (Transportation Analysis Ser.). xii, 202p. 1997. text. write for info. (*3-540-63093-7*) Spr-Verlag.

Bianco, Lucien. Origins of the Chinese Revolution, 1915-1949. Bell, Muriel, tr. from FRE. LC 75-150321. xvii, 220p. 1971. reprint ed. pap. 12.95 (*0-8047-0827-4*) Stanford U Pr.

— Peasant Movements in Twentieth Century China. 300p. 2000. 64.95 (*1-56324-839-5*) M E Sharpe.

Bianco, Lucio. Large Scale Computation & Information Processing in Air Traffic Control. Odoni, Amedeo R., ed. (Transportation Analysis Ser.). (Illus.). xiv, 240p. 1993. write for info. (*3-540-56950-2*) Spr-Verlag.

Bianco, Lucio & La Bella, A., eds. Freight Transport Planning & Logistics. (Lecture Notes in Economics & Mathematical Systems Ser.: Vol. 317). (Illus.). x, 568p. 1988. 69.95 (*0-387-50232-7*) Spr-Verlag.

Bianco, Lucio & Odoni, Amedeo R., eds. Large Scale Computation & Information Processing in Air Traffic Control. LC 93-11819. (Transportation Analysis Ser.). 1993. 95.95 (*0-387-56950-2*) Spr-Verlag.

Bianco, Margery, tr. see Cendrars, Blaise.

Bianco, Margery W. The Velveteen Rabbit: or How Toys Become Real. LC 99-217055. (Illus.). 48p. (J). 1995. 13.95 (*1-883746-16-7*) Vermilion.

— The Velveteen Rabbit: or How Toys Become Real. (Illus.). 48p. (J). (ps). 1995. 19.95 (*1-883746-06-X*) Vermilion.

— The Velveteen Rabbit: or How Toys Become Real. unabridged ed. (Illus.). 48p. (J). (ps up). 1995. 14.95 (*1-883746-07-8*) Vermilion.

Bianco, Margery W., jt. auth. see Noble, Marty.

Bianco, Marie, jt. auth. see Hirsch, George.

Bianco-Mathis, Virginia & Chalofsky, Neal. The Full-Time Faculty Handbook. LC 98-40062. 1998. 69.95 (*0-7619-1222-3*) Sage.

Bianco-Mathis, Virginia & Chalofsky, Neal, eds. The Adjunct Faculty Handbook. LC 96-4516. 266p. 1996. 52.00 (*0-7619-0277-5*); pap. 24.00 (*0-7619-0278-3*) Sage.

Bianco-Mathis, Virginia, jt. auth. see Chalofsky, Neal.

Bianco, Roberta Del, see Del Bianco, Roberta.

Bianco, S., et al, eds. Reversible Airway Obstruction: Neurohumoral Mechanisms & Treatment. (Journal: Respiration: Vol. 50, Suppl. 2, 1986). (Illus.). vi, 326p. 1987. pap. 102.75 (*3-8055-4524-X*) S Karger.

Bianco, S., jt. ed. see Olivieri, D.

***Bianco, Stefano.** Urban Form in the Arab World. LC 99-67630. (Illus.). 400p. 2000. pap. 39.95 (*0-500-28205-6*, Pub. by Thames Hudson) Norton.

***Bianco, Terri & Haggart, Bill.** The Kaleidoscope Profile: Guide for Educators. 2nd rev. ed. (The Kaleidoscope Profile Ser.: Vol. 2). Orig. Title: PLS Educator Learning Styles Inventory: Directions & Applications. 2000. pap. 19.95 (*1-892334-10-0*) Perf Lrn Systs.

— The Kaleidoscope Profile: Guide for Students. 2nd rev. ed. (The Kaleidoscope Profile Ser.: Vol. 1). Orig. Title: PLS Student Learning Styles Inventory: Directions & Applications. 2000. pap. 19.95 (*1-892334-09-7*) Perf Lrn Systs.

— The Kaleidoscope Profile: Guide for the Workplace. (The Kaleidoscope Profile Ser.: Vol. 3). 2000. pap. 19.95 (*1-892334-11-9*) Perf Lrn Systs.

Bianco, William. American Politics. (C). pap. text. write for info. (*0-393-97610-6*) Norton.

Bianco, William T. Trust: Representatives & Constitutents. 232p. 1994. text 47.50 (*0-472-10510-8*, 10510); pap. text 19.95 (*0-472-08267-1*, 08267) U of Mich Pr.

***Bianco, William T., ed.** Congress on Display, Congress at Work. (Illus.). 198p. (C). 2000. text 69.50 (*0-472-11118-3*, 11118); pap. text 25.95 (*0-472-08711-8*, 08711) U of Mich Pr.

Biancolli, Amy. Fritz Kreisler: Love's Sorrow, Love's Joy. LC 98-12200. (Illus.). 350p. 1998. 34.95 (*1-57467-037-9*, Amadeus Pr) Timber.

Biancolli, Louis L. The Mozart Handbook: A Guide to the Man & His Music. LC 75-32504. (Illus.). 629p. 1975. reprint ed. lib. bdg. 45.00 (*0-8371-8496-7*, BIMH, Greenwood Pr) Greenwood.

Biancolli, Louis L. & Farkas, Andrew. The Flagstad Manuscript. LC 76-29935. (Opera Biographies Ser.). (Illus.). 1977. reprint ed. lib. bdg. 29.95 (*0-405-09677-1*) Ayer.

Biancolli, Louis L. & Peyser, Herbert F. Masters of the Orchestra from Bach to Prokofieff. LC 70-94578. 481p. 1969. reprint ed. lib. bdg. 75.00 (*0-8371-2545-6*, BIMO, Greenwood Pr) Greenwood.

Biancolli, Louis L., jt. auth. see Garden, Mary.

Bianconi, A., et al, eds. EXAFS & Near Edge Structures: Proceedings, Frascati, Italy, 1982. (Chemical Physics Ser.: Vol. 27). (Illus.). 420p. 1983. 85.95 (*0-387-12411-X*) Spr-Verlag.

Bianconi, A. & Marcelli, A., eds. High Tc Superconductors: Electronic Structure. (Proceedings of the International Symposium on Transport Phenomena, Dynamics & Design of Rotating Machinery Ser.). (Illus.). 349p. 1989. pap. 43.00 (*0-08-037543-X*, Pergamon Pr) Elsevier.

Bianconi, Betty, ed. see Shimer, Porter.

Bianconi, Lorenzo. History of Italian Opera, Vol. 5. 1993. 60.00 (*0-226-04591-9*) U Ch Pr.

— History of Italian Opera, Vol. 6. 1993. 60.00 (*0-226-04592-7*) U Ch Pr.

Bianconi, Lorenzo & Pestelli, Giorgio, eds. History of Italian Opera, 4. Cochrane, Lydia G., tr. LC 97-25421. (Illus.). 440p. 1998. 50.00 (*0-226-04590-0*) U Ch Pr.

Bianculli, David. Dictionary of Teleliteracy: Television's 500 Biggest Hits, Misses, & Events. LC 97-17305. (The Television Ser.). 420p. 1997. pap. 22.95 (*0-8156-0505-6*) Syracuse U Pr.

***Bianculli, David.** Teleliteracy: Taking Television Seriously. LC 00-35759. 320p. 2000. pap. 19.95 (*0-8156-0653-2*) Syracuse U Pr.

Biancuzzo. Promoting Successful Breastfeeding. LC 98-42525. (Illus.). 480p. (C). (gr. 13). 1998. pap. text 26.95 (*0-8151-2453-8*, 31178) Mosby Inc.

Biancuzzo, Marie & Freda, Margaret Comberford. Breastfeeding the Healthy Newborn: A Nursing Perspective. Damus, Karla, ed. 1994. write for info. (*0-86525-064-2*) March of Dimes.

Biane, P., et al. Lectures on Probability Theory: Ecole d'Ete de Probabilities de Saint-Flour XXIII - 1993. Dold, A. et al, eds. (Lecture Notes in Mathematics Ser.: Vol. 1608). 210p. 1995. pap. 44.95 (*3-540-60015-9*) Spr-Verlag.

Bianki, V. L. The Mechanisms of Brain Laterilization. (Monographs in Neuroscience: Vol. 4). 296p. 1993. text 94.00 (*2-88124-460-2*) Gordon & Breach.

— The Right & Left Hemispheres of the Animal Brain: Cerebral Lateralization of Function. (Monographs in Neuroscience: Vol. 3). xvi, 423p. 1987. text 189.00 (*2-88124-197-2*) Gordon & Breach.

Bianming, Zhou, tr. see Kong, Judy W., ed.

Bianquis, T. H., ed. see Bosworth, C. E.

Biard, Phillip & Delafosse, Claude. Pyramids. LC 94-49424. (First Discovery Book).Tr. of Pyramide. (ENG & FRE., Illus.). 24p. (J). (ps-3). 1995. 11.95 (*0-590-42786-5*, Cartwheel) Scholastic Inc.

Biard, Roland. Dictionnaire de l'Extreme-Gauche: De 1945 a Nos Jours: Dictionary of the Extreme Left from 1945 to Present. (FRE.). 384p. 1978. pap. 39.95 (*0-8288-5176-X*, M6033) Fr & Eur.

Biardeau, Madeleine. Hinduism: The Anthropology of a Civilization. Nice, Richard, tr. from FRE. (French Studies on South Asian Culture & Society; Oxford India Paperbacks). 196p. 1994. pap. text 8.95 (*0-19-563389-X*) OUP.

Biardi, G., jt. ed. see Gioda, M.

Biardo, John C. Anyone Can Write a "Best-Seller"...& Get It Published. LC 90-85647. (Illus.). 176p. (Orig.). (C). 1991. pap. 9.95 (*0-933181-07-8*) Elmwood Park Pub.

— Five Hundred & One Patio Party Cocktails. LC 85-81526. 136p. 1986. spiral bd. 4.95 (*0-933181-02-7*) Elmwood Park Pub.

— Help Your Child Discover the Joys of Learning. LC 89-82639. (Illus.). 120p. (Orig.). 1990. pap. 5.95 (*0-933181-06-X*) Elmwood Park Pub.

— The Safe Driving Handbook: A Guide to Driving Defensively. 2nd ed. LC 95-90695. (Illus.). 128p. (Orig.). (YA). (gr. 10-12). 1996. pap. 9.95 (*0-933181-08-6*) Elmwood Park Pub.

— Sing a New Song unto the Lord: Poems of Joyful Praise. LC 86-83240. 80p. (Orig.). 1987. pap. 3.95 (*0-933181-03-5*) Elmwood Park Pub.

***Biardo, John C.** Your Pet Parakeet: A Complete Care Guide. 2nd rev. ed. (Illus.). 120p. (Orig.). 2000. pap. 9.95 (*0-933181-09-4*) Elmwood Park Pub.

Biarez, Jean & Gourves, R., eds. Powders & Grains: Proceedings of an International Congress on Micromechanics of Granular Media, Clermont-Ferrand, 4 - 8 September 1989. (Illus.). 528p. (C). 1989. text 220.00 (*90-6191-984-3*, Pub. by A A Balkema) Ashgate Pub Co.

Biarez, Jean & Hicher, Pierre-Yves. Elementary Mechanics of Soil Behaviour: Saturated Remoulded Soils. (Illus.). 184p. (C). 1994. pap. text 45.00 (*90-5410-157-1*, Pub. by A A Balkema) Ashgate Pub Co.

Biart, Lucien. The Aztecs: Their History, Manners & Customs. 1976. reprint ed. 59.00 (*0-685-71094-7*, Regency) Scholarly.

Bias, Clifford. Qabalah, Tarot & the Western Mystery Tradition: The 22 Connecting Paths on the Tree of Life. rev. ed. LC 97-29495. Orig. Title: The Way Back. (Illus.). 160p. 1997. pap. 12.95 (*1-57863-031-2*) Weiser.

Bias, Clifford, ed. Qabalah, Tarot & the Western Mystery Tradition: The 22 Connecting Paths on the Tree of Life. Orig. Title: The Way Back. (Illus.). 158p. 1998. pap. 12.95 (*1-57281-106-4*, BK177) US Games Syst.

Bias, Doug De, see De Bias, Doug.

Bias, Randolph G. & Mayhew, Deborah J., eds. Cost-Justifying Usability. LC 93-38583. (Illus.). 334p. 1994. text 53.00 (*0-12-095810-4*) Acad Pr.

***Bias, Tim.** Emmanuel! Celebrating God's Presence with Us. LC 97-69411. 64p. 1998. pap. 12.95 (*0-88177-236-4*, DR236) Discipleship Res.

Bias, Tim. The Key Event Celebration: A Guidebook for Leaders. LC 97-69410. 80p. 1998. pap. 14.95 (*0-88177-235-6*, DR235) Discipleship Res.

***Biasca, Cynthia Brott.** Supplement to Descendants of Albert & Arent Andriessen Bradt. fac. ed. 190p. 1999. reprint ed. 37.00 (*0-7404-0000-2*); reprint ed. pap. 27.00 (*0-7404-0001-0*) Higginson Bk Co.

Biasca, Cynthis B. Bradt: Descendants of Albert & Arent Andriessen Bradt. (Illus.). 776p. 1994. reprint ed. pap. 89.50 (*0-8328-4302-4*); reprint ed. lib. bdg. 99.50 (*0-8328-4301-6*) Higginson Bk Co.

Biase, Fausto Di, see Di Biase, Fausto.

Biasetto, Wendy. The Ultimate Guide: To Forms for Early Childhood Programs. LC 95-78356. 238p. 1995. 29.95 (*0-9625907-1-1*) Learning Expo.

Biasin, Gain-Paolo. The Flavors of Modernity: Food & the Novel. 192p. 1993. text 22.50 (*0-691-03275-0*, Pub. by Princeton U Pr) Cal Prin Full Svc.

Biasin, Gian-Paolo. Italian Literary Icons. LC 84-42876. (Princeton Essays in Literature Ser.). 210p. 1985. reprint ed. pap. 65.10 (*0-7837-9298-0*, 206003700004) Bks Demand.

— Literary Diseases: Theme & Metaphor in the Italian Novel. LC 74-30345. 188p. reprint ed. pap. 58.30 (*0-8357-7718-9*, 203607500002) Bks Demand.

— Montale, Debussy & Modernism. LC 89-10516. (Princeton Essays on the Arts Ser.). (Illus.). 171p. 1989. reprint ed. pap. 53.10 (*0-608-02560-7*, 206320500004) Bks Demand.

Biasin, Gian-Paolo & Gieri, Manuela, eds. Pirandello: Contemporary Perspectives. (Toronto Italian Studies). 256p. 1998. text 45.00 (*0-8020-4387-9*) U of Toronto Pr.

***Biasing Rivera, Charles & Wilde, Betty, eds.** NUEVA LUZ. (SPA.). (YA). (gr. 9 up). 2000. 5.00 En Foco.

Biasini, Emile & Lebrat, Jean. The Grand Louvre: A Museum Transfigured, 1981-1993. (Illus.). 166p. 1989. 59.50 (*0-89397-340-8*) Nichols Pub.

Biasini, Gian-Paolo. The Smile of the Gods: A Thematic Study of Cesare Pavese's Works. LC 68-9748. 337p. 1968. 20.00 (*0-915042-19-3*) Lib Soc Sci.

Biasiotto, Judd. Hypnotize Me & Make Me Great. Trunzo, Jim & McClellan, Tim, eds. 100p. (Orig.). 1985. pap. 7.00 (*0-933079-00-1*) World Class Enterprises.

— The Odyssey Continues. Foote, Tom, ed. & illus. by. 250p. (Orig.). 1987. pap. 10.00 (*0-933079-06-0*) World Class Enterprises.

— Power. 80p. (Orig.). 1988. pap. 6.00 (*0-933079-07-9*) World Class Enterprises.

— Psyching. 80p. (Orig.). 1988. pap. 6.00 (*0-933079-08-7*) World Class Enterprises.

— Sports, Sex, Drugs . . . & Other American Pastimes. (Illus.). 175p. (Orig.). 1988. pap. 10.00 (*0-933079-09-5*) World Class Enterprises.

— Take Control: Weight Reduction. (Illus.). 134p. (Orig.). 1986. pap. 8.00 (*0-933079-05-2*) World Class Enterprises.

— 2001: A Sports Odyssey Hypnosis Cybernetics Conditioning Biofeedback. 160p. (Orig.). 1984. pap. 8.00 (*0-933079-04-4*) World Class Enterprises.

Biasiotto, Judd & Ritter, Ed. Fundamentals of Fitness. 100p. (Orig.). 1983. pap. 7.00 (*0-933079-02-8*) World Class Enterprises.

Biasiotto, Judd, jt. auth. see Foote, Tom.

Biasiotto, Judson & Campbell, Wilbur. Progressive Resistance: Building Muscular Strength & Endurance. Kirchdorfer, Uef, ed. (Illus.). 124p. (Orig.). (C). 1996. pap. 19.95 (*0-9648775-1-1*) Solaris GA.

Biasiotto, Peter R. History of the Development of the Devotion to the Holy Name. xiv, 189p. 1943. pap. 3.00 (*1-57659-110-7*) Franciscan Inst.

Biaut, Alan, jt. auth. see Liang, Yun.

Biava, A. Dizionario Portoghese-Italiano-Portoghese: Portuguese-Italian, Italian-Portuguese Dictionary. (ITA & POR.). 318p. 1980. 14.95 (*0-8288-1635-2*, M9172) Fr & Eur.

— Italian-Portuguese - Portuguese-Italian Dictionary: Dizionario Italiano-Portoghese-Italiano. (ITA & POR.). 370p. 1982. 12.95 (*0-8288-1634-4*, F45870) Fr & Eur.

Biavdi, G., et al. Chaos & Fractals in Chemical Engineering: Proceedings of the 1st Italian Conference. 328p. 1995. text 86.00 (*981-02-1904-0*) World Scientific Pub.

Biays. Responding to Literature. 1988. teacher ed. 21.56 (*0-07-005161-5*) McGraw.

Biays, John S. & Wershoven, Carol. Along These Lines: A Course for Developing Writers. LC 97-26234. 441p. 1997. pap. text 39.80 (*0-13-398447-8*) P-H.

— Along These Lines: Writing Paragraphs & Essays. 2nd ed. LC 00-26135. 532p. 2000. pap. 37.33 (*0-13-086817-5*) P-H.

Biays, John S. & Wershoven, Carol. Responding to Literature: A Step-by-Step Guide for Student Writers. 474p. (C). 1988. pap. 35.00 (*0-07-005160-7*) McGraw.

Bib. Catalogue d'Articles de Periodiques Arts Decoratifs et Beau Arts. (FRE.). 1980. 420.00 (*0-8161-1277-0*, G K Hall & Co) Mac Lib Ref.

Biba, Otto & Jones, David W., eds. Studies in Music History: Presented to H. C. Robbins Landon. LC 95-62054. (Illus.). 272p. 1996. 34.95 (*0-500-01696-8*, Pub. by Thames Hudson) Norton.

Bibace, Roger, et al. Partnerships in Research, Clinical & Educational Settings LC 99-26833. (Advances in Applied Developmental Psychology Ser.). 1999. write for info. (*1-56750-455-8*) Ablx Pub.

Bibas, David. Immigrants & the Formation of Community: A Case Study. LC 91-9084. (Immigrant Communities & Ethnic Minorities in the U. S. & Canada Ser.: No. 77). 298 p. 1998. 62.50 (*0-404-19487-7*) AMS Pr.

Bibaud, Michel. Histoire du Canada et Des Canadiens Sous la Domination Anglaise. (Canadiana Avant 1867 Ser.: No. 2). 1968. 50.00 (*90-279-6323-1*) Mouton.

Bibb & Associates, Inc., jt. ed. see Francovigli, N. C.

Bibb, C. W. Bibb Family in America, 1640-1940. 149p. 1993. reprint ed. pap. 24.00 (*0-8328-3265-0*); reprint ed. lib. bdg. 34.00 (*0-8328-3264-2*) Higginson Bk Co.

Bibb, Elizabeth. In the Japanese Garden. (Illus.). 108p. 1995. pap. 24.95 (*1-55591-308-3*) Fulcrum Pub.

Bibb, Eloise. Poems. LC 71-173601. (Black Heritage Library Collection). 1977. reprint ed. 20.95 (*0-8369-8897-3*) Ayer.

***Bibb, Henry.** The Life & Adventures of Henry Bibb: An American Slave. 2000. 40.00 (*0-299-16890-5*); pap. 16.95 (*0-299-16894-8*) U of Wis Pr.

Bibb, Henry. Narrative & Adventures of Henry Bibb. (C). 1992. reprint ed. pap. text 21.95 (*0-88143-143-5*) Ayer.

— Narrative of the Life & Adventures of Henry Bibb, an American Slave. LC 70-89423. (Black Heritage Library Collection). 1977. 19.98 (*0-8369-8511-7*) Ayer.

Bibb, Kaye, et al, eds. The Heritage of Morgan County, Alabama. (Heritage of Alabama Ser.: No. 52). (Illus.). 540p. 1998. 70.00 (*1-891647-19-9*) Herit Pub Consult.

Bibb, Kenneth D. & Wake, Larry. Practical XView Programming. LC 92-30943. 480p. 1993. pap. 34.95 (*0-471-57460-0*) Wiley.

Bibb, Porter. Ted Turner: It Ain't As Easy As It Looks. rev. ed. LC 97-23805. (Illus.). 496p. 1997. pap. 20.00 (*1-55566-203-X*) Johnson Bks.

Bibb, Stephanie. Women's Liberation, Jesus Style: Messages of Spirituality & Wisdom for Today's Woman. 1999. 19.95 (*0-9663124-0-6*) Ruach Communs.

Bibber, Joyce K. Bath & West Bath. (Images of America Ser.). 1995. pap. 16.99 (*0-7524-0245-5*) Arcadia Publng.

— Bruswick & Topsham. LC 95-163237. (Images of America Ser.). 1994. pap. 16.99 (*0-7524-0081-9*) Arcadia Publng.

— Harpswell. (Images of America Ser.). 128p. 1996. pap. 16.99 (*0-7524-0297-8*) Arcadia Publng.

— A Home for Every Man: The Greek Revival & Maine Domestic Architecture. (Illus.). 250p. 1988. 22.50 (*0-318-41168-7*) Greater Portland.

***Bibber, Joyce K.** Maine Coast Postcards. (Postcard History Ser.). 128p. 1999. pap. 18.99 (*0-7524-1338-4*) Arcadia Publng.

Bibbero, Robert J. & Young, Irving G. Systems Approach to Air Pollution Control. LC 74-8905. 542p. reprint ed. pap. 168.10 (*0-608-11770-6*, 205515700008) Bks Demand.

Bibbero, Robert J., ed. see Instrument Society of America Staff.

Bibbo, Marluse. Comprehensive Cytopathology. 2nd ed. Day, Lesley, ed. LC 95-48273. (Illus.). 1216p. 1996. text 205.00 (*0-7216-5752-4*, W B Saunders Co) Harcrt Hlth Sci Grp.

Bibbs, C. Susheel. Heritage of Power: Marie LaVeau - Mary Ellen Pleasant. rev. ed. LC 98-96443. (Illus.). 92p. 1998. per. 24.95 (*1-892516-03-9*) MEP Publications.

— Mary Ellen Pleasant, 1817-1904: Mother of Human Rights in California. 2nd rev. ed. (Illus.). 20p. (J). (gr. 5-12). 1996. reprint ed. mass mkt. 7.95 (*1-892516-00-4*) MEP Publications.

Bibbs, Susheel. The Legacies of Mary Ellen Pleasant: Mother of Civil Rights in California. unabridged ed. (Illus.). 28p. (YA). (gr. 9 up). 1998. mass mkt. 9.95 (*1-892516-01-2*) MEP Publications.

Bibby. Personal Safety for Health Care Workers. 248p. 1995. pap. 33.95 (*1-85742-196-5*) Ashgate Pub Co.

Bibby, Bob & Wade, Barrie. English & the Ofsted Experience. 128p. 1995. pap. text 24.95 (*1-85346-357-4*, Pub. by David Fulton) Taylor & Francis.

Bibby, Brian. Deeper Than Gold: Indian Life along California's Highway 49. (Illus.). 192p. 2000. pap. 18.00 (*0-930588-96-7*) Heyday Bks.

Bibby, Brian, ed. The Fine Art of California Indian Basketry. (Illus.). 128p. (Orig.). 1996. pap. 20.00 (*0-930588-87-8*) Heyday Bks.

***Bibby, Colin J., et al.** Bird Census Techniques. 2nd ed. 350p. 2000. 55.00 (*0-12-095831-7*) Acad Pr.

Bibby, Colin J., et al. Birs Census Techniques Apl. (Illus.). 257p. 1992. text 55.00 (*0-12-095830-9*) Acad Pr.

Bibby, Geoffrey. Four Thousand Years Ago: A World Panorama of Life in the Second Millennium B. C. LC 83-12743. (Illus.). 398p. 1983. reprint ed. lib. bdg. 89.50 (*0-313-23411-6*, BIFT, Greenwood Pr) Greenwood.

Bibby, Geoffrey. Looking for Dilmun. (Illus.). 286p. 1997. 39.95 (*0-905743-90-3*, Pub. by Stacey Intl) Intl Bk Ctr.

Bibby, John & Toutenburg, Helge. Prediction & Improved Estimation in Linear Models. LC 76-7533. 202p. reprint ed. pap. 62.70 (*0-8357-3394-7*, 203965100013) Bks Demand.

Bibby, John, tr. see Bunke, Helga & Bunke, Olaf, eds.

Bibby, John F. Governing by Consent: An Introduction to American Politics. 2nd ed. LC 94-32850. 664p. (YA). (gr. 11). 1995. pap. text 39.95 (*0-87187-827-5*) Congr Quarterly.

— Politics, Parties & Elections in America. 4th ed. LC 99-12827. 1999. 35.95 (*0-8304-1547-5*) Thomson Learn.

Bibby, John F., jt. auth. see Maisel, L. Sandy.

Bibby, M. C., jt. ed. see Double, John.

Bibby, Michael. Hearts & Minds: Bodies, Poetry, & Resistance in the Vietnam Era. LC 95-52261. (Perspectives on the Sixties Ser.). 300p. (C). 1996. text 50.00 (*0-8135-2297-8*); pap. text 17.95 (*0-8135-2298-6*) Rutgers U Pr.

Bibby, Michael, ed. The Vietnam War & Postmodernity. LC 99-36757. 248p. 2000. 50.00 (*1-55849-237-2*); pap. 16.95 (*1-55849-238-0*) U of Mass Pr.

Bibby, Pauline, ed. Personal Safety for Social Workers. 224p. 1994. pap. 33.95 (*1-85742-195-7*, Pub. by Arena) Ashgate Pub Co.

An Asterisk (*) at the beginning of an entry indicates that the title is appearing for the first time.

Bibby, Peter, ed. Organised Abuse. LC 96-83248. 304p. 1996. 64.95 (*1-85742-284-8*, Pub. by Arena) Ashgate Pub Co.

Bibby, Peter & Payne, Sebastian. Effective Use of Judicial Review. 264p. 1995. pap. 195.00 (*0-85459-761-1*, Pub. by Tolley Pubng) St Mut.

Bibby, Reginald W. Fragmented Gods: The Poverty & Potential of Religion in Canada. 319p. 1987. pap. 12.95 (*0-7725-1666-9*) Genl Dist Srvs.

— Fragmented Gods: The Poverty & Potential of Religion in Canada. 319p. 1990. pap. 15.95 (*0-7737-5422-9*) Genl Dist Srvs.

— Mosaic Madness: Pluralism Without a Cause. 224p. 1990. pap. 15.95 (*0-7737-5399-0*) Genl Dist Srvs.

Bibby, T. G. Preliminary Survey in East Arabia. (Jutland Archaeological Society Publications: No. 12). (Illus.). 67p. (C). 1967. pap. 9.95 (*87-00-91091-0*, Pub. by Aarhus Univ Pr) David Brown.

Bibeau, Anita, jt. auth. see Muther, Connie.

Bibeau, Gilles & Corin, Ellen, eds. Beyond Textuality: Asceticism & Violence in Anthropological Interpretation. (Approaches to Semiotics Ser.: No. 120). xiv, 364p. (C). 1994. lib. bdg. 136.95 (*3-11-013889-1*) Mouton.

Bibeau, Simone. Cash in on Today's Educational Market: Teachers-Make Real Money Outside the Classroom! (Illus.). 256p. (Orig.). (C). pap. 14.95 (*0-940406-11-X*) Perception Pubns.

— Developing the Early Learner: Level 1. rev. ed. (Pre-Reading Experience Ser.). (Illus.). 64p. (J). (ps-2). 1983. pap. text 8.75 (*0-940406-01-2*) Perception Pubns.

— Developing the Early Learner: Level 2. rev. ed. (Pre-Reading Experience Ser.). (Illus.). 64p. (J). (ps-2). 1983. pap. text 8.75 (*0-940406-02-0*) Perception Pubns.

— Developing the Early Learner: Level 3. rev. ed. (Pre-Reading Experience Ser.). (Illus.). 64p. (J). (ps-2). 1983. pap. text 8.75 (*0-940406-03-9*) Perception Pubns.

— Developing the Early Learner: Level 4. (Pre-Reading Experience Ser.). (Illus.). 64p. 1983. pap. text 8.75 (*0-940406-04-7*) Perception Pubns.

— One Hundred Fifty-One Fun Activities to Increase Your Child's IQ: Will Your Children Be Successful? This Program Is for People Who Care! unabridged ed. 16p. (J). (ps-6). 1986. pap. text 25.00 incl. audio (*0-940406-15-2*, 015) Perception Pubns.

— Raise Your Child's Creative IQ: All Children Are Born Gifted. unabridged ed. (Illus.). 128p. (J). (gr. 1-6). 1986. pap. text 99.00 incl. audio (*0-940406-14-4*, 014) Perception Pubns.

— Writing the Advanced Short Story. (Illus.). 32p. (J). (gr. 1-12). 1983. pap. text 8.75 (*0-940406-07-1*) Perception Pubns.

— Writing the Beginning Short Story. (Illus.). 32p. (J). (gr. 1-9). 1983. pap. text 8.75 (*0-940406-06-3*) Perception Pubns.

— Writing the Fantasy Story. (Illus.). 32p. (J). (gr. 1-9). 1983. pap. text 8.75 (*0-940406-08-X*) Perception Pubns.

Bibee, John. Bicycle Hills: How One Halloween Almost Got out of Hand. LC 89-15316. (Spirit Flyer Ser.: Vol. 4). (Illus.). 204p. (Orig.). (J). (gr. 7-8). 1989. pap. 6.99 (*0-8308-1203-2*, 1203) InterVarsity.

— The Home School Detectives, 4 vols., Set, Nos. 1-4. (Orig.). (J). (gr. 3-7). 1996. mass mkt., boxed set 18.99 (*0-8308-1919-3*, 1919) InterVarsity.

— The Home School Detectives Series, 8 vols., Set. Incl. Bk. 1. Mystery of the Homeless Treasure. LC 94-18832. 120p. (Orig.). (J). 1994. pap. 4.99 (*0-8308-1911-8*, 1911); Bk. 2. Mystery of the Missing Microchips. 128p. (Orig.). (J). (gr. 3-7). 1995. pap. 4.99 (*0-8308-1912-6*, 1912); Bk. 3. Mystery of the Mexican Graveyard. LC 95-33595. 128p. (Orig.). (J). 1995. pap. 4.99 (*0-8308-1913-4*, 1913); Bk. 4. Mystery of the Campus Crook. LC 96-71. 122p. (Orig.). (J). (gr. 3-7). 1996. pap. 4.99 (*0-8308-1914-2*, 1914); Bk. 5. Mystery of the Vanishing Cave. LC 96-16142. (Illus.). 128p. (J). (gr. 3-7). 1996. pap. 4.99 (*0-8308-1915-0*, 1915); Bk. 6. Mystery at the Broken Bridge. LC 96-37894. 128p. (Orig.). (J). (gr. 3-7). 1997. mass mkt. 4.99 (*0-8308-1916-9*, 1916); (J). (gr. 3-7). 1998. Set mass mkt. 39.92 (*0-8308-1910-X*, 1910) InterVarsity.

— The Journey of Wishes. LC 93-8173. (Spirit Flyer Ser.: Bk. 8). (Illus.). 192p. (Orig.). (J). (gr. 4-8). 1993. pap. 6.99 (*0-8308-1207-5*, 1207) InterVarsity.

— The Last Christmas. LC 90-4870. (Spirit Flyer Ser.: Vol. 5). (Illus.). 204p. (Orig.). (J). (gr. 3-8). 1990. pap. 6.99 (*0-8308-1204-0*, 1204) InterVarsity.

— The Magic Bicycle. LC 83-240. (Spirit Flyer Ser.: Vol. 1). (Illus.). 215p. (Orig.). (J). (gr. 4-9). 1983. pap. 6.99 (*0-87784-348-1*, 348) InterVarsity.

— The Mystery in Lost Canyon. LC 97-15600. (Home School Detectives Ser.: Vol. 7). 128p. (J). (gr. 3-7). 1997. mass mkt. 4.99 (*0-8308-1917-7*, 1917) InterVarsity.

— The Mystery of the Widow's Watch. LC 98-21210. (Home School Detectives Ser.: Vol. 8). 128p. (J). 1998. mass mkt. 4.99 (*0-8308-1918-5*, 1918) InterVarsity.

***Bibee, John.** The Mystery of the Widow's Watch Bk. 8. (Home School Detectives Ser.). (Illus.). (J). 1999. 18.99 (*0-8308-8661-3*) InterVarsity.

Bibee, John. The Only Game in Town. LC 88-9369. (Spirit Flyer Ser.: Vol. 3). (Illus.). 209p. (Orig.). (J). (gr. 5-8). 1988. pap. 6.99 (*0-8308-1202-4*, 1202) InterVarsity.

— The Perfect Star. LC 92-5686. (Spirit Flyer Ser.: Bk. 7). (Illus.). 192p. (Orig.). (J). (gr. 5-8). 1992. pap. 6.99 (*0-8308-1206-7*, 1206) InterVarsity.

— The Runaway Parents: A Parable of Problem Parents. LC 91-22762. (Spirit Flyer Ser.: Bk. 6). (Illus.). 204p. (Orig.). (J). (gr. 3-8). 1991. pap. 6.99 (*0-8308-1205-9*, 1205) InterVarsity.

— The Spirit Flyer Series, 8 bks., Set. (Illus.). 1993. pap. 53.13 (*0-8308-1200-8*, 1200) InterVarsity.

— The Spirit Flyer Series, Set, Bks. 1-4. (Illus.). (J). 1992. boxed set 24.99 (*0-8308-1208-3*, 1208) InterVarsity.

— The Spirit Flyer Series, Set, Bks. 5-8. (Illus.). (J). 1993. boxed set 24.99 (*0-8308-1289-X*, 1289) InterVarsity.

— The Toy Campaign. LC 87-3261. (Spirit Flyer Ser.: Vol. 2). (Illus.). 225p. (Orig.). (J). (gr. 4-8). 1987. pap. 6.99 (*0-8308-1201-6*, 1201) InterVarsity.

Bibel-Archiv, Deutches, jt. ed. see Reinitzer, Heimo.

Bibel-Archiv, Deutsches, jt. ed. see Reinitzer, Heimo.

Bibel, Debra J. A Collection of Clouds: Zen Haiku & Other Poetry. LC 96-61629. (Orig.). 1997. pap. 11.95 (*0-614-26962-8*) E Metchnikoff Mem Lib.

— Freeing the Goose in the Bottle: Discovering Zen Through Science, Understanding Science Through Zen. LC 92-97036. (Illus.). xvi, 325p. (Orig.). 1992. pap. 16.95 (*0-9634067-0-1*) E Metchnikoff Mem Lib.

Bibel, Wolfgang. Automated Deduction A Basis for Applications, 003. LC 99-164724. 1248p. 1998. 480.00 (*0-7923-5132-0*) Kluwer Academic.

— Automated Deduction: A Basis For Applications: Applications. Iii. 346p. 1998. 159.00 (*0-7923-5131-2*) Kluwer Academic.

— Automated Deduction: A Basis For Applications: Foundations - Calculi & Methods. I. 500p. 1998. 227.00 (*0-7923-5129-0*) Kluwer Academic.

— Automated Deduction: A Basis For Applications: Systems & Implementation Techniques. Ii. 448p. 1998. 205.00 (*0-7923-5130-4*) Kluwer Academic.

— Deduction: Automated Logic. (Illus.). 253p. 1993. text 54.00 (*0-12-095835-X*) Acad Pr.

— Fifth Conference on Automated Deduction: Les Arcs Proceedings. Kowalski, R. A., ed. (Lecture Notes in Computer Science Ser.: Vol. 87). (Illus.). 385p. 1980. 34.00 (*0-387-10009-1*) Spr-Verlag.

Bibel, Wolfgang & Jantke, K. P., eds. Mathematical Methods of Specification & Synthesis of Software Systems '85. (Lecture Notes in Computer Science Ser.: Vol. 215). 245p. 1986. 33.00 (*0-387-16444-8*) Spr-Verlag.

Bibel, Wolfgang & Jorrand, P., eds. Fundamentals of Artificial Intelligence. vii, 313p. 1990. 38.00 (*0-387-18265-9*) Spr-Verlag.

Biber, Douglas. Dimensions of Register Variation: A Cross-Linguistic Comparison. 446p. (C). 1995. text 69.95 (*0-521-47331-4*) Cambridge U Pr.

— Longman Grammar of Spoken & Written English. LC 99-29033. 1999. pap. text 119.00 (*0-582-23725-4*) Addison-Wesley.

— Variation Across Speech & Writing. (Illus.). 315p. (C). 1992. pap. text 28.95 (*0-521-42556-5*) Cambridge U Pr.

Biber, Douglas & Finegan, Edward, eds. Sociolinguistic Perspectives on Register. LC 92-44536. (Illus.). 400p. 1994. text 75.00 (*0-19-508364-4*) OUP.

Biber, Douglas, et al. Corpus Linguistics: Investigating Language Structure & Use. LC 97-16560. (Approaches to Linguistics Ser.). (Illus.). 310p. (C). 1998. text 59.95 (*0-521-49622-5*); pap. text 19.95 (*0-521-49957-7*) Cambridge U Pr.

Biber, Marjorie, jt. auth. see Biber, Rene.

Biber, Rene & Biber, Marjorie. Heurs et Malheurs d'Une Famille Angevine et Vendeene, 1754-1794: Rene et Genevieve: Cours de Civilisation Francaise. (FRE., Illus.). 432p. 1993. pap. 39.95 (*0-7734-1970-5*) E Mellen.

Biberaj, Elez. Albania in Transition: The Rocky Road to Democracy. LC 97-52976. (Nations of the Modern World Ser.). 400p. (C). 1998. text 79.00 (*0-8133-3502-7*, Pub. by Westview) HarpC.

— Albania in Transition: The Rocky Road to Democracy. (Nations of the Modern World Ser.). 400p. 1999. pap. 30.00 (*0-8133-3688-0*, Pub. by Westview) HarpC.

Biberdorf, Daryl & Glidden, Keith. PowerBuilder 5 How-To: The Definitive PowerBuilder 5 Problem-Solver. 800p. (Orig.). 1996. pap. 49.99 incl. cd-rom (*1-57169-055-7*) Sams.

Biberman, Herbert. The Salt of the Earth: The Story of a Film. Cortes, Carlos E., ed. LC 76-1248. (Chicano Heritage Ser.). (Illus.). 1977. reprint ed. 17.95 (*0-405-09486-8*) Ayer.

***Biberman, Jerry & Alkhafaji, Abbass, eds.** Business Research Yearbook Vol. VI: Global Business Perspectives, 1999. (Illus.). 850p. 1999. write for info. (*1-889754-03-X*) McNaughton & Gunn Inc.

Biberman, Jerry, jt. ed. see Alkhafaji, Abbass F.

Biberman, Jerry, jt. ed. see Alkhafaji, Abbass.

Biberman, L. M. Thermal Physics Reviews Vol. 2, Pt. 5: Condensation of Supersaturated Vapor in a Field of Electromagnetic Radiation, Vol. 2. (Soviet Technology Reviews Ser.: Section B). iv, 48p. 1989. pap. text 52.00 (*3-7186-5002-9*, Harwood Acad Pubs) Gordon & Breach.

Biberman, L. M., ed. Perception of Displayed Information. LC 72-97695. (Optical Physics & Engineering Ser.). (Illus.). 346p. 1973. 79.50 (*0-306-30724-3*, Plenum Trade) Perseus Pubng.

Biberman, L. M. & Legault, R. Reticles in Electro Optical Devices. LC 65-28562. (International Series of Monographs in Interdisciplinary & Advanced Topics: Vol. 1). 1966. 84.00 (*0-08-011683-3*, Pub. by Pergamon Repr) Franklin.

Biberman, L. M., et al. Kinetics of Nonequilibrium Low-Temperature Plasmas. LC 87-12018. (Illus.). 498p. (C). 1987. text 145.00 (*0-306-10998-0*, Kluwer Plenum) Kluwer Academic.

Bibesco, Elizabeth. Whole Story. LC 75-403493. (Short Story Index Reprint Ser.). 1977. 21.95 (*0-8369-3235-8*) Ayer.

Bibesco, Marthe. The Green Parrot. Cowley, Malcolm, tr. LC 94-60638. 250p. (Orig.). 1995. pap. 12.95 (*0-9627987-9-7*) Turtle Point Pr.

Bibhutibhushan Bandyopadhyay. A Strange Attachment & Other Stories. Granoff, Phyllis, tr. 277p. 1995. pap. 12.95 (*0-88962-222-1*) Mosaic.

Bibib, T., jt. auth. see Fries, Y.

Bibiena, Ferdinando G. Da. Architettura Civile. LC 68-57184. (ITA., Illus.). 1972. 55.95 (*0-405-08268-1*, Pub. by Blom Pubns) Ayer.

Bibik, Janice, et al. Aerobic Dance: Fitness for College & Beyond. 192p. 1994. per. 19.95 (*0-8403-8229-4*) Kendall-Hunt.

Bibik, Janusz, jt. auth. see Galazka, Jacek.

Bibikov. Russian-Hungarian Dictionary. (HUN & RUS.). 223p. 1982. 14.95 (*0-8288-1065-6*, F47675) Fr & Eur.

Bibin, T., jt. auth. see Fries, Yvonne.

Biblarz. Social Statistics. (C). 1996. text 51.00 (*0-02-309417-6*, Macmillan Coll) P-H.

Bible. Ratio & Invention: A Study of Medieval Lyric & Narrative. 1989. 22.95 (*0-310-91481-7*) Zondervan.

— Respiratory Distress Syndromes: Molecules to Man. 1990. 49.50 (*0-310-91516-3*) Zondervan.

Bible, ed. Bible: Pocket Ed. 1472p. 1999. 49.99 (*0-19-528220-5*) OUP.

Bible, Carolyn. Texas A & M: Traditions & Spirit. (Illus.). 80p. (Orig.). 1990. pap. 5.95 (*0-9627306-0-2*) C Bible.

Bible, Debbie. Adventure Gear for God's Kids: How Jesus Can Help When You're All Mixed Up. Dall, Jeanette & Oliver, Marian, eds. (Nineteen Ninety-Six 50-Day Spiritual Adventure Ser.). (Illus.). 64p. (Orig.). (J). (gr. 3-6). 1995. pap., wbk. ed. 6.00 (*1-879050-73-0*) Chapel of Air.

Bible, G. T., jt. auth. see Halperin, Don A.

Bible, Jon D. & McWhirter, Darien A. Privacy in the Workplace: A Guide for Human Resource Managers. LC 90-9075. 320p. 1990. 65.00 (*0-89930-473-7*, BPJ/, Quorum Bks) Greenwood.

Bible, Jon D., jt. auth. see McWhirter, Darien A.

Bible, Ken. Beacon Small-Group Bible Studies, Genesis Pt. II, Chapters 26-50: Faithful to His Promises. Wolf, Earl C., ed. 72p. (Orig.). 1986. pap. 4.99 (*0-8341-1108-X*) Beacon Hill.

— For Servants of God. 64p. 1999. pap. write for info. (*1-892078-06-6*) Liv the Natural.

— His Personal Presence: Trusting the One Who Is Always with Us. 152p. 1993. per. 4.99 (*1-882854-00-4*); audio 4.99 (*0-685-74727-1*, TA-4007C); audio compact disk 7.99 (*0-685-74728-X*, DC-4007) Allegis.

— Knowing God. 64p. 1998. pap. 19.99 (*1-892078-00-7*) Liv the Natural.

— Master Chorus Book II: 100 Contemporary, Traditional & New Choruses, Words Only. 1994. 2.25 (*0-8341-9182-2*, BCMB-698A) Lillenas.

***Bible, Ken.** The Most Beautiful Way to Live. 64p. 1999. pap. write for info. (*1-892078-08-2*) Liv the Natural.

Bible, Ken. Praying in His Presence: Enjoying Constant Communication with God. 160p. (Orig.). 1993. pap. 4.99 (*1-882854-02-0*) Allegis.

— The Satisfied Life. 64p. 1998. pap. write for info. (*1-892078-04-X*) Liv the Natural.

— Simple Prayers to Draw Your Heart to God. 64p. 1998. pap. 19.99 (*1-892078-02-3*) Liv the Natural.

***Bible, Ken.** Step by Step: With Jesus. 64p. 1999. pap. write for info. (*1-892078-10-4*) Liv the Natural.

Bible, Ken, compiled by. Dare to Run. 1989. audio 19.99 (*0-685-68413-X*, TA-9108S) Lillenas.

— Dare to Run. 12p. 1989. 1.99 (*0-8341-9239-X*, MB-602A); 7.99 (*0-8341-9072-9*, BCMB-602) Lillenas.

— Dare to Run. 1989. audio 12.99 (*0-685-68412-1*, TA-9108C) Lillenas.

— Magnify the Lord. 125p. 1986. ring bd. 7.99 (*0-8341-9254-3*, MB-559) Lillenas.

— Magnify the Lord, Vols. 1 & 2. 1986. audio 19.99 (*0-685-68425-3*, TA-9077B) Lillenas.

— Moving up to Gloryland. 171p. 1987. 7.99 (*0-8341-9334-5*, MB-579) Lillenas.

— A Pocketful of Praise. 62p. (J). (gr. 3-7). 1987. 4.99 (*0-8341-9283-7*, MB-574) Lillenas.

— Primary Praise. 60p. 1990. 7.99 (*0-8341-9306-X*, MB-620) Lillenas.

— Sing a Song of Scripture. 144p. (J). (gr. 3-7). 1985. 7.99 (*0-8341-9050-8*, MB-558) Lillenas.

— Wesley Hymns. 1982. 5.99 (*0-685-69276-0*, MB-510) Lillenas.

Bible, Ken, compiled by. Wesley Hymns. 1982. pap. 5.99 (*0-8341-9737-5*) Lillenas.

***Bible, Leon.** The Finis J. Drake Annotated Biography. annot. ed. 1999. pap. 4.99 (*1-55829-119-9*) Dake Pub.

Bible, Leon. Tithe & Offering Scriptures: Scriptures for Receiving Titles & Offerings God's Way. LC 99-90367. 128p. 1999. ring bd. 19.95 (*0-9671995-0-6*) Ministry Helps.

Bible, Like Moms. Bible Like Mom's. 1999. 19.99 (*0-7852-0085-1*) Nelson.

Bible Pew Staff. New Living Translation Pew Bible, Blue. 1997. 10.99 (*0-8423-3346-0*) Tyndale Hse.

Bible, Roy H. Interpretation of NMR Spectra: An Empirical Approach. LC 64-20741. (Illus.). 160p. reprint ed. pap. 49.60 (*0-608-05415-1*, 206588400006) Bks Demand.

Bible Science Association Editors, jt. auth. see Bartz, Paul A.

Bible Staff. Philippians, Colossians, & Philemon. LC 97-25920. (Shepherd's Notes). 1997. pap. text 5.95 (*1-55819-689-7*) Broadman.

Bible Training Institute Staff. Los Diez Mandimientos. (Serie Conozca Su Biblia - Know Your Bible Ser.).Tr. of Ten Commandments. (SPA., Illus.). 140p. (Orig.). 1996. pap. text 5.95 (*1-889505-04-8*) White Wing Pub.

***Bibleman ICB Staff.** Bibleman ICB Bible: The Official Bible of Bibleman: Holy Bible. (Illus.). 1500p. (gr. k-5). 2000. pap. text 17.99 (*0-8499-7615-4*) Tommy Nelson.

Biblia Sacra Staff, ed. Concordantiae Bibliorum Sacrorum Vulgatae Editionis. xxiii, 1484p. 1986. reprint ed. 400.00 (*3-487-05839-1*) G Olms Pubs.

Biblical Passages Staff. Sacred Solos by Adrienne Tindall Vol. I: 12 Scriptural Solos: 4 Songs from the Psalms, Song of the Law (7 Songs from Ps. 119); I Cor. 13. Tindall, Adrienne, ed. 46p. 1987. pap., student ed. 25.00 (*1-889079-03-0*) Darcey Pr.

— Sacred Solos by Robert J. Powell: 12 Solos from the Scriptures. 46p. 1997. pap. 25.00 (*1-889079-19-7*) Darcey Pr.

Bibliena, Giuseppe. Architectural & Perspective Designs. (Illus.). 103p. 1964. pap. 10.95 (*0-486-21263-7*) Dover.

Biblio Institute Staff. Kleine Duden Deutsches Woerterbuch. 3rd ed. (GER.). 442p. 1992. 29.95 (*0-7859-7440-7*, 3411046635) Fr & Eur.

Biblio Press Staff. Telegram & Other Gram Rhymes for All Occasions: Any Occasion, That Occasion & Most Occasions. 15p. pap. text 27.95 (*0-939476-12-6*) Prosperity & Profits.

Bibliograf Staff. Diccionario de Botanica y Zoologia Gran Vox. (SPA.). 412p. 1990. 150.00 (*0-7859-3360-3*, 8471533413) Fr & Eur.

— Diccionario de Matematicas Gran Vox. (SPA.). 400p. 1984. 195.00 (*0-7859-9793-8*) Fr & Eur.

Bibliografia Historica Mexicana Staff. Bibliografia Historica Mexicana, Vol. 28: 1986-87. LC 68-101966. (SPA.). 415p. 1987. reprint ed. pap. 128.70 (*0-7837-6834-6*, 204666300003) Bks Demand.

Bibliographic Instruction Section, Editorial Board. Sourcebook for Bibliographic Instruction. 96p. 1993. pap. 19.00 (*0-8389-7673-5*) Assn Coll & Res Libs.

Bibliographic Standards Committee of the Rare Book. Genre Terms: A Thesaurus for Use in Rare Book & Special Collections Cataloguing. 2nd ed. 90p. 1991. pap. 22.00 (*0-8389-7516-X*) Assn Coll & Res Libs.

Bibliotecas Para La Gente Periodical Committee. Revistas: An Annotated Bibliography of Spanish Language Periodicals for Public Libraries. (Ethnic Studies Library Publications: No. 9). 31p. (Orig.). 1983. pap. 10.00 (*0-918520-07-X*) Ethnic Stud Lib.

Bibliotech Anutech Pty., Ltd. Staff, ed. New Technologies for Rainfed Rice-Based Farming Systems in the Philippines & Sri Lanka. 1988. pap. 36.00 (*0-949511-63-3*, Pub. by ACIAR) St Mut.

Bibliotheca Press Staff. Black English, Chocolate Grammar: or English Too??? 15p. (YA). (gr. 9-12). 1989. pap. text 6.50 (*0-318-42724-9*) Prosperity & Profits.

— Boom Cities & Towns U. S. A. A Report. rev. ed. 50p. 1998. ring bd. 29.95 (*0-939476-51-7*) Prosperity & Profits.

— Bread Pudding Recipe Greetings. (Illus.). 56p. (Orig.). 1992. ring bd. 25.95 (*0-939476-81-9*) Prosperity & Profits.

— The Creator or Almighty Always Has an Answer. 7.95 (*0-317-00012-8*); pap. text 2.95 (*0-939476-23-1*) Prosperity & Profits.

— Fragrant Choices: A Word Mapping Guide to Fragrant Leaves, Seeds, Roots, Flowers & More. 60p. (C). 1991. ring bd. 36.95 (*0-317-04652-7*) Prosperity & Profits.

— I Can, I Shall, I Will: A Story Rhyme. 50p. Date not set. pap. text 6.95 (*0-939476-54-1*) Prosperity & Profits.

— Obey Your Signal Only: A Poetry Book. 7.95 (*0-939476-20-7*) Prosperity & Profits.

— One Woman's Feelings: A Poetry Book. 1981. pap. text 8.95 (*0-939476-13-4*) Prosperity & Profits.

— Posie the Positive Train: Story Edition. (J). (gr. 4-9). 1990. pap. 12.95 (*0-939476-28-2*) Prosperity & Profits.

— Posie the Positive Train: Story Edition. (J). (gr. 4-9). 1996. 17.95 (*0-939476-27-4*) Prosperity & Profits.

— Potpourri Recipe Encyclopedia. 100p. 1991. ring bd. 115.00 (*0-317-04653-5*) Prosperity & Profits.

— Recipe Greetings - A Poetry Reference for Greeting Cards to Duplicate & Use. rev. ed. 50p. (Orig.). 1993. ring bd. 25.95 (*0-317-01784-5*, Bibliotheca Pr) Prosperity & Profits.

— Scenterpieces of Fragrance: Creative Recipe Pages. rev. ed. (Illus.). 60p. 1991. student ed., ring bd. 25.95 (*0-939476-88-6*) Prosperity & Profits.

— Small Business Entrepreneural Services - Suggestions for a Small Business Entrepreneural Service Center: A Business Workbook. rev. ed. 70p. 1992. ring bd. 26.95 (*0-939476-95-9*) Prosperity & Profits.

— Story Rhyme Greetings for the Fax Machine: Correspondence, Etc. (Illus.). 50p. 1991. ring bd. 26.95 (*0-939476-46-0*) Prosperity & Profits.

— Survival Suggestions for Libraries: A Report. rev. ed. 1995. reprint ed. ring bd. 25.95 (*0-939476-48-7*) Prosperity & Profits.

— Temporary Help Services: Possibilities for Home Businesses, School & College Placements, Community Job Services, Seminar Workshop Workbook. 125p. 1993. ring bd. 495.00 (*0-939476-97-5*) Prosperity & Profits.

— The Thrift Book Index. LC 82-70344. 100p. (C). 1982. ring bd. 28.95 (*0-939476-45-2*) Prosperity & Profits.

— Thrift Book-Possibilities for Saving & Budgeting Plus Work Pages. 70p. 1991. ring bd. 24.95 (*0-939476-09-6*) Prosperity & Profits.

Bibliotheca Press Staff, compiled by. The Baby Shower Ideas Index. 200p. 1992. ring bd. 25.95 (*0-939476-66-5*) Prosperity & Profits.

— Registering Agent Services for Delaware Incorporators & Other States: A How to Find or Locate Reference. 150p. 1992. ring bd. 39.95 (*0-939476-87-8*) Prosperity & Profits.

Bibliotheca Press Staff, ed. Business Possibilities: A Report. 300p. 1983. ring bd. 75.00 (*0-939476-92-4*) Prosperity & Profits.

— Cookbooks & Recipes for Almost Nothing & More: A How to Find or Locate Workbook. 75p. 1983. ring bd. 25.95 (*0-939476-67-3*) Prosperity & Profits.

B

— Farmer's Markets in the U. S. & Some Other Countries: A How to Locate Workbook. rev. ed. 60p. 1991. ring bd. 25.95 (*0-939476-78-9*) Prosperity & Profits.

— Fundraiser's Workbook: Based on Guide for Fundraisers. 1992. ring bd. 25.95 (*0-939476-76-2*) Prosperity & Profits.

— Guide for Fundraisers. rev. ed. 106p. 1995. ring bd. 25.95 (*0-939476-30-4*) Prosperity & Profits.

— How to Be Your Own Publisher, Advertiser, Promoter, Etc. A Report. ring bd. 39.95 (*0-939476-18-5*) Prosperity & Profits.

— Meat Substitution Cookbook: Nutritional Foods that Can Be Prepared to Taste Like Meat. rev. ed. 50p. 1998. ring bd. 25.95 (*0-939476-60-6*) Prosperity & Profits.

— Prescriptions for Survival Index. LC 82-70345. 102p. 1982. ring bd. 25.95 (*0-939476-43-6*) Prosperity & Profits.

— Recycling Workbook: Based on Recycling for Living, Fun & Profit. 50p. 1983. ring bd. 24.95 (*0-939476-50-9*) Prosperity & Profits.

— Single Source: A Workbook Reference for Singles. 75p. 1982. student ed., ring bd. 35.95 (*0-939476-71-1*, Bibliotheca Pr) Prosperity & Profits.

— Small Press Publishing: A Report. 70p. 1991. reprint ed. student ed., ring bd. 34.95 (*0-939476-77-0*) Prosperity & Profits.

— Story Tide Collectus. 68p. (Orig.). 1982. pap. text 17.95 (*0-939476-44-4*) Prosperity & Profits.

— Unescorted Women. Date not set. pap. 12.95 (*0-939476-26-6*) Prosperity & Profits.

— Vegetarian Cookbooks Etc. A How to Find or Locate Workbook. 70p. 1983. ring bd. 24.95 (*0-939476-68-1*) Prosperity & Profits.

Bibliotheek der Rijksuniversiteit Utrecht, Departm, ed. Bibliografie van Nederlandse Proefschriften/Dutch Theses Vol. 8: 1989. x, 174p. 1989. pap. 62.75 (*90-265-1023-3*) Swets.

— Bibliografie van Nederlandse Proefschriften/Dutch Theses Vol. 9: 1985. x, 182p. 1990. pap. 60.75 (*90-265-1095-0*) Swets.

— Bibliografie van Nederlandse Proefschriften/Dutch Theses Vol. 10: 1986. xii, 180p. 1990. pap. 60.75 (*90-265-1137-X*) Swets.

Bibliothek, Deutsche. Richard A. Berman-Osterreicher, Demokrat, Weltburger: Ein Kapitel Deutsh-Osterreichischer Kuturgeschichte. 1995. 60.00 (*3-598-11297-1*) K G Saur Verlag.

Bibliothek, Herzog A., ed. see Mortzfeld, Peter.

Bibliotheque du Musee de l'Homme, Paris Staff. Catalogue Systematique de la Section Afrique (Classified Catalog of the Africa Section), 2 Vols, Set. 1970. 175.00 (*0-8161-0827-7*, G K Hall & Co) Mac Lib Ref.

Bibliotheque Nationale Staff. Catalogue Generale des Livres Imprimes: Auteurs, Collectivites-Auteurs, Anonymes, 1960-1969, 15 vols. (Serie I). 2995.00 (*0-685-11067-2*) Fr & Eur.

Biblis, Margaret, ed. see Andress, Alice A.

Biblis, Margaret, ed. see Bates, Andrea & Hanson, Norm.

Biblis, Margaret, ed. see Baxter, Richard.

Biblis, Margaret, ed. see Buck, Carol J.

Biblis, Margaret, ed. see Chabner, Davi-Ellen.

Biblis, Margaret, ed. see De Domenico, Giovanni & Wood, Elizabeth C.

Biblis, Margaret, ed. see Diehl, Marcy O. & Fordney, Marilyn T.

Biblis, Margaret, ed. see Frazier, Margaret S., et al.

Biblis, Margaret, ed. see Goodman, Catherine C. & Bossonnault, William G.

Biblis, Margaret, ed. see Jenkins, David B. & Hollinshead, W. Henry.

Biblis, Margaret, ed. see Magee, David J., et al.

Biblis, Margaret, ed. see Montone, Deborah.

Biblis, Margaret, ed. see Porterfield, James A. & DeRosa, Carl.

Biblis, Margaret, ed. see Purtilo, Ruth B. & Haddad, Amy.

Biblis, Margaret, ed. see Salvo & Breaux.

Biblis, Margaret, ed. see Sloane, Sheila B.

Biblis, Margaret, ed. see Stepp, Craig A. & Woods, MaryAnn.

Biblis, Margaret, ed. see Walker, Joan M. & Helewa, Antoine.

Biblograf Editorial Staff, compiled by. Vox Traveler's Spanish & English Dictionary. LC 99-23187. (SPA & ENG., Illus.). 510p. 1994. vinyl bd. 7.95 (*0-8442-7987-0*, 79870, Natl Textbk Co) NTC Contemp Pub Co.

Bibo, Bai, jt. compiled by see Lewis, Paul W.

Bibo, Istvan. Democracy, Revolution, Self-Determination. Nagy, Karoly, ed. 520p. 1991. text 107.50 (*0-88033-214-X*, Pub. by East Eur Monographs) Col U Pr.

Bibo, James. Zen, Eastern Wisdom. LC 92-42257. (Eastern Wisdom Ser.). 192p. 1993. boxed set 29.95 (*0-8118-0438-0*) Chronicle Bks.

Bibring, Grete L., ed. The Teaching of Dynamic Psychiatry: A Reappraisal of the Goals & Techniques in the Teaching of Psychoanalytic Psychiatry. LC 67-27426. 277p. 1968. 40.00 (*0-8236-6380-9*) Intl Univs Pr.

Bibring, Grete L. & Kahana, Ralph J. Lectures in Medical Psychology: An Introduction to the Care of Patients. LC 68-57279. 289p. 1969. 42.50 (*0-8236-2970-8*) Intl Univs Pr.

Bibring, J. P., jt. auth. see Encrenaz, T.

Bibus, Ethel & Marshall, Louise. Carroll County, Mississippi Cemetery Records. 310p. (Orig.). 1995. pap. 34.00 (*1-885480-04-0*) Pioneer Pubng.

Bic, Frances, jt. auth. see Bic, Zuzana.

Bic, J. C., et al. Elements of Digital Communication. LC 91-9086. (Series in Communication & Distributed Systems). 636p. 1991. 345.00 (*0-471-91571-8*) Wiley.

Bic, Lubomir, ed. Parallel Language & Compiler Research in Japan. 536p. (C). 1995. text 193.50 (*0-7923-9506-9*) Kluwer Academic.

Bic, Lubomir, et al, eds. Advanced Topics in Dataflow Computing & Multithreading. LC 94-25601. 412p. 1995. 55.00 (*0-8186-6542-4*, BP06542) IEEE Comp Soc.

Bic, Zuzana & Bic, Frances. No More Headaches, No More Migraines: A Proven Approach to Preventing Headaches & Migraines. 134p. 1999. pap. 10.95 (*0-89529-924-0*, Avery) Penguin Putnam.

Bica, L. Diane. Dreamwish. 1991. 8.95 (*0-924663-05-7*) Alaskan Viewpoint.

Bicak, Charles J. & Bicak, Laddie J. Discovering Connections Within the History, Methods & Applications of Science. (Illus.). 204p. 1993. teacher ed. 20.00 (*1-878276-31-X*) Educ Systs Assocs Inc.

Bicak, Laddie J., jt. auth. see Bicak, Charles J.

***Bicalho, Alexander.** MAXScript for Advanced Users. 2000. pap. 49.99 (*0-7821-2794-0*) Sybex.

Bican, Ladislav, et al. Rings, Modules, & Preradicals. LC 81-22209. (Lecture Notes in Pure & Applied Mathematics Ser.: No. 75). 255p. reprint ed. pap. 79.10 (*0-7837-0800-9*, 204111400019) Bks Demand.

Bicanic, D. D., ed. Photoacoustic & Photothermal Phenomena III: Proceedings of the International Topical Meeting, 7th, Doorwerth, the Netherlands, August 26-30, 1991. LC 92-21891. (Optical Sciences Ser.: Vol. 69). xxviii, 731p. 1992. 132.00 (*3-540-55669-9*); 132.00 (*0-387-55669-9*) Spr-Verlag.

Bicanic, Rudolf. Problems of Planning, East & West. (Publications of the Institute of Social Studies: No. 15). 1967. text 22.35 (*90-279-0112-0*) Mouton.

Bicarregui, J. C., ed. Proof in VDM: Case Studies. LC 97-29213. (Formal Approaches to Computing & Information Technology Ser.). (Illus.). xvi, 228p. 1998. pap. 69.95 (*3-540-76186-1*) Spr-Verlag.

Bicarregui, Juan C. Proof in the VDM: A Practitioner's Guide. LC 93-23655. (Formal Approaches to Computing & Information Technology Ser.). 1993. 50.95 (*0-387-19813-X*) Spr-Verlag.

***Bicay, Michael, et al, eds.** Astrophysics with Infrared Surveys: A Prelude to SIRTF. (Conference Series Proceedings: Vol. 177). 483p. 1999. text 52.00 (*1-58381-001-3*) Astron Soc Pacific.

BICC Cables Ltd. Staff, jt. auth. see Moore, G. F.

Bicchieri, Cristina. Rationality & Coordination. (Studies in Probability, Induction & Decision Theory). (Illus.). 286p. (C). 1994. text 69.95 (*0-521-38123-1*) Cambridge U Pr.

— Rationality & Coordination. (Cambridge Studies in Probability, Induction & Decision Theory). 288p. 1997. pap. text 20.95 (*0-521-57444-7*) Cambridge U Pr.

Bicchieri, Cristina, et al, eds. The Dynamics of Norms. (Studies in Probability, Induction & Decision Theory). (Illus.). 231p. (C). 1996. text 69.95 (*0-521-56062-4*) Cambridge U Pr.

— The Logic of Strategy. LC 98-50190. (Illus.). 208p. 1999. text 45.00 (*0-19-511715-8*) OUP.

Bicchieri, Cristina & Chiara, Maria L., eds. Knowledge, Belief & Strategic Interaction. (Studies in Probability, Induction & Decision Theory). 429p. (C). 1992. text 89.95 (*0-521-41674-4*) Cambridge U Pr.

Bicchieri, M. G., ed. Hunters & Gatherers Today. (Illus.). 494p. (C). 1988. reprint ed. pap. text 22.95 (*0-88133-351-4*) Waveland Pr.

Biccum, Gerald. Handology: How to Unlock the Hidden Secrets of Your Life. LC 88-70817. 342p. 1989. pap. 12.95 (*0-941831-39-6*) Beyond Words Pub.

***Biccum, Gerald E.** Gerald E. Picard's Handology: The Power to Master Destiny with Character. 2nd ed. Simms, Maurice, ed. Orig. Title: Handology - How to Unlock the Hidden Secrets of Your Life. 558p. 1999. pap. text. write for info. (*1-929961-00-6*) Gordon.

— Your Affection. Simms, Maurice, ed. (Gerald E. Picard's Handology Collection Ser.: No. 6). (Illus.). 36p. 1999. pap. text. write for info. (*1-929961-06-5*) Gordon.

— Your Character. Simms, Maurice, ed. (Gerald E. Picard's Handology Collection Ser.: No. 1). (Illus.). 168p. 1999. pap. text. write for info. (*1-929961-01-4*) Gordon.

— Your Fate. Simms, Maurice, ed. (Gerald E. Picard's Handology Collection Ser.: No. 8). (Illus.). 57p. 1999. pap. text. write for info. (*1-929961-08-1*) Gordon.

— Your Health. Simms, Maurice, ed. (Gerald E. Picard's Handology Collection Ser.: No. 9). (Illus.). 46p. 1999. pap. text. write for info. (*1-929961-09-X*) Gordon.

— Your Heart. Simms, Maurice, ed. (Gerald E. Picard's Handology Collection Ser.: No. 2). 60p. 1999. pap. text. write for info. (*1-929961-02-2*) Gordon.

— Your Influence. Simms, Maurice, ed. (Gerald E. Picard's Handology Collection Ser.: No. 5). (Illus.). 36p. 1999. pap. text. write for info. (*1-929961-05-7*) Gordon.

— Your Minor Lines. Simms, Maurice, ed. (Gerald E. Picard's Handology Collection Ser.: No. 10). (Illus.). 50p. 1999. pap. text. write for info. (*1-929961-10-3*) Gordon.

***Biccum, Gerald E. & Simms, Maurice.** Your Career. (Gerald E. Picard's Handology Collection Ser.: No. 7). (Illus.). 66p. 1999. pap. text. write for info. (*1-929961-07-3*) Gordon.

— Your Head. (Gerald E. Picard's Handology Collection Ser.: No. 3). (Illus.). 96p. 1999. pap. text. write for info. (*1-929961-03-0*) Gordon.

— Your Life. (Gerald E. Picard's Handology Collection Ser.: No. 4). (Illus.). 70p. 1999. pap. text. write for info. (*1-929961-04-9*) Gordon.

Bice, Christopher. Cornish Phrase Book: Lyver Lavarow Kernewek. pap. 9.95 (*0-89979-012-7*) British Am Bks.

Bice, David A. People Make the Difference. Kurten, Mary J., ed. 134p. 1987. 25.00 (*0-940213-15-X*) Walsworth Pub.

Bice, Joe, jt. auth. see Kline, Troy.

Bice, John. Tap into the Great Lakes. (Illus.). 200p. 1999. pap. 12.95 (*1-882376-67-6*) Thunder Bay Pr.

Bice-Stephens, Wynona. The Art of Nursing. 2nd ed. 64p. 1992. 9.95 (*0-8059-3254-2*) Dorrance.

Bicentennial Book Committee. Bicentennial History of Union Presbyterian Church: Robinson Township, Pennsylvania, Pittsburgh Presbytery, 1794-1994. (Illus.). 128p. 1993. 19.95 (*1-881576-15-9*) Providence Hse.

Bicentennial Committee Staff. History of Sidney, Maine. LC 91-68229. (Illus.). 288p. 1992. 25.00 (*0-929539-88-5*, 1323) Picton Pr.

Bicentennial Genealogy Committee. History & Genealogy of the Families of Chesterfield, Mass., 1762-1962. 427p. 1989. reprint ed. lib. bdg. 48.50 (*0-8328-0818-0*, MA0109) Higginson Bk Co.

Bicentennial History Committee. Historical Notes & Pictures of Milan, 1771-1971. (Illus.). 352p. 1998. reprint ed. lib. bdg. 42.00 (*0-8328-9724-8*) Higginson Bk Co.

Bicentennial History Committee Staff. The History of the Town of Cortlandt Westchester County, New York. Keefe, Regina et al, eds. (Illus.). 176p. 1988. pap. 10.00 (*0-9621119-0-2*) Town Cortlandt Bicent.

Bicentennial Symposium Staff. Eighteenth-Century Florida & the Caribbean. Proctor, Samuel, ed. LC 76-2673. 117p. reprint ed. pap. 36.30 (*0-7837-4937-6*, 204460300004) Bks Demand.

Bicerano, Jozef. Prediction of Polymer Properties. LC 92-44567. (Plastics Engineering Ser.: Vol. 27). (Illus.). 427p. reprint ed. pap. 132.40 (*0-608-08914-1*, 206954900005) Bks Demand.

— Prediction of Polymer Properties. 2nd ed. LC 96-25977. (Plastics Engineering Ser.: Vol. 38). (Illus.). 552p. 1996. text 180.00 (*0-8247-9781-7*) Dekker.

Bicerano, Jozef, ed. Computational Modeling of Polymers. (Plastics Engineering Ser.: Vol. 25). (Illus.). 648p. 1992. text 255.00 (*0-8247-8438-3*) Dekker.

Bich Thuan, Nguyen. Contemporary Vietnamese Readings. (Southeast Asian Language Ser.). 218p. 1997. pap. 27.95 (*1-891134-00-0*) SE Asia.

Bicha, Karel D. C. C. Washburn & the Upper Mississippi Valley. LC 94-45653. (Studies in Entrepreneurship). (Illus.). 232p. 1995. text 15.00 (*0-8153-2013-2*) Garland.

— The Czechs in Oklahoma. LC 79-19734. (Newcomers to a New Land Ser.: Vol. 2). (Illus.). 81p. (Orig.). 1980. pap. 6.95 (*0-8061-1618-8*) U of Okla Pr.

— Western Populism: Studies in an Ambivalent Conservatism. (Illus.). 1976. 10.50 (*0-87291-085-7*) Coronado Pr.

Bichakjian, Bernard H., ed. From Linguistics to Literature: Romance Studies Offered to Francis M. Rogers. x, 292p. 1981. 65.00 (*90-272-2007-7*) J Benjamins Pubng Co.

Bichakjian, Bernard H., et al, eds. Language Origin: A Multidisciplinary Approach. 544p. (C). 1992. lib. bdg. 247.50 (*0-7923-1369-0*, Pub. by Kluwer Academic) Kluwer Academic.

Bichart, K. J. & Chandler, R. M. Recent Advances in the Study of Neogene Fossil Birds: I-The Birds of the Late Miocene - Early Pliocene Big Sandy Formation, Mohave County; II-Fossil Birds of the San Diego Formation, Late Pliocene, Blancan, San Diego County, California. (Ornithological Monographs: Vol. 44). (Illus.). 161p. 1990. 19.75 (*0-943610-57-5*) Am Ornithologists.

Bichat, Marie F. Physiological Researches on Life & Death. Kastenbaum, Robert J., ed. Gold, F. et al, trs. LC 76-19561. (Death & Dying Ser.). 1977. reprint ed. lib. bdg. 33.95 (*0-405-09557-0*) Ayer.

Bichat, Xavier. Physiological Researches on Life & Death. 2. Gold, F., tr. from FRE. LC 77-72191. (Contributions to the History of Psychology Ser.: Vol. II, Pt. E, Physiological Psychology). 302p. 1978. reprint ed. lib. bdg. 89.50 (*0-313-26950-5*, U6950, Greenwood Pr) Greenwood.

***Bicheldei, Kaadyr-ool A., et al.** Let's Speak Tuvan. Slone, J. Eric, ed. LC 99-69185. 110p. 2000. pap. 40.00 (*1-58490-029-6*) Scientific Consulting.

Bicheno, John. Time, Quality & Production: Measurement, Planning Improvement. (C). 1995. text. write for info. (*0-201-56517-X*) Addison-Wesley.

Bicheno, John & Elliott, Brian B. Operations Management: An Active Learning Approach. LC 97-44918. 656p. 1997. pap. 68.95 (*0-631-20180-7*) Blackwell Pubs.

Bicher, Haim I., et al, eds. Consensus on Hyperthermia for the 1990's: Clinical Practice in Cancer Treatment. LC 90-7312. (Advances in Experimental Medicine & Biology Ser.: Vol. 267). (Illus.). 572p. (C). 1990. text 174.00 (*0-306-43533-0*, Kluwer Plenum) Kluwer Academic.

Bichler, Joyce, jt. auth. see Harris, Phyllis B.

Bichon, Pierre, jt. auth. see Gomez, Philippe.

Bichowsky, F. Russell. Industrial Research. LC 72-5033. (Technology & Society Ser.). (Illus.). 132p. 1972. reprint ed. 17.95 (*0-405-04686-3*) Ayer.

Bichsel, Peter. Hug Schapler - Uberlieferung und Stilwandel: Ein Beitrag Zum Fruhneuhochdeutschen Prosaroman und Zur Lexikalischen Paarform. 384p. 1999. 54.95 (*3-906761-79-7*) P Lang.

Bichteler, Julie, ed. see Geoscience Information Society Staff.

Bichteler, K. Stochastic Integration & Stochastic Differential Equations. 1984. write for info. (*0-318-57812-3*, North Holland) Elsevier.

Bichteler, Klaus., et al. Malliavin Calculus for Processes with Jumps. (Stochastics Monographs: Theory & Applications of Stochastic Processes: Vol. 2). x, 158p. 1987. text 101.00 (*2-88124-185-9*) Gordon & Breach.

Bichteler, Klaus. Integration: A Functional Approach. LC 98-18100. 1998. 49.50 (*0-8176-5936-6*) Birkhauser.

— Integration - A Functional Approach. LC 98-18100. (Advanced Texts Ser.). 204p. 1998. 49.50 (*3-7643-5936-6*) Birkhauser.

Bick, Barbara, ed. Culture & Politics. 55p. 1976. pap. 19.95 (*0-87855-659-1*) Transaction Pubs.

Bick, David. Gloucester & Cheltenham Tramroad & the Leckhampton Quarry Lines. 96p. (C). 1985. 50.00 (*0-85361-336-2*) St Mut.

Bick, David G. Proud Words on a Dusty Shelf. 107p. (Orig.). 1990. pap. text 7.95 (*0-9625775-0-2*) Modern Printing.

Bick, Etta, jt. auth. see Steinberg, Gerald.

Bick, Hans. Die Moorvegetation der Zentralen Hochvogesen. (Dissertationes Botanicae Ser.: Band 91). (GER., Illus.). 288p. 1985. pap. 53.00 (*3-443-64001-X*, Pub. by Gebruder Borntraeger) Balogh.

Bick, J. Up-to-Date Technical Dictionary of Computer, Electricity, Electronic, Communication, Internet. (ENG & HEB.). 1998. 69.95 (*0-320-00695-6*) Fr & Eur.

***Bick, Jonathan.** 101 Things You Need to Know about Internet Law. LC 00-37726. (Illus.). 224p. 2000. pap. 12.95 (*0-609-80633-5*, Three Riv Pr) Crown Pub Group.

Bick, Joram. Dictionary of Electronic & Computer Terms: Hebrew-English, English-Herbrew. (ENG & HEB.). 466p. 1991. 125.00 (*0-7859-9403-3*) Fr & Eur.

Bick, Julie. All I Really Need to Know I Learned at Microsoft: Insider Strategies to Help You Succeed. 1997. 15.00 (*0-684-82124-9*) S&S Trade.

— All I Really Need to Know in Business, I Learned at Microsoft. 1984. pap. 1.50 (*0-671-00914-1*, PB Trade Paper) PB.

— All I Really Need to Know in Business I Learned at Microsoft: Insider Strategies to Help You Succeed. LC 97-219048. 1984. 1.50 (*0-671-00913-3*) PB.

— All i Really Need to Know in Business I Learned at Microsoft: Insider Strategies to Help You Succeed. 160p. 1999. reprint ed. pap. text 16.00 (*0-7881-6230-6*) DIANE Pub.

***Bick, Julie.** Microsoft Edge: Insider Strategies for Building Sucess. 176p. 1999. 20.00 (*0-671-03413-8*, PB Hardcover) PB.

Bick, Lois. Messy Moose: Big Book. large type ed. (Little Books & Big Bks.). (Illus.). 8p. (J). (ps-1). 1998. pap. text 19.89 (*0-8215-0842-3*) Sadlier.

— The Trash Can Band: Big Book. large type ed. (Little Books & Big Bks.). (Illus.). 16p. (J). (gr. 1-3). 1997. pap. text 29.85 (*0-8215-0975-6*) Sadlier.

Bick, Margaret. Preparing to Celebrate in Schools. LC 96-52681. (Preparing for Liturgy Ser.). 48p. (Orig.). 1997. pap. 3.95 (*0-8146-2481-2*) Liturgical Pr.

Bick, Paul. Construction Contract Law: Text Cases & Materials. 700p. 1996. pap. write for info. (*1-85941-038-3*, Pub. by Cavendish Pubng) Gaunt.

Bick, Roger L. Basic Concepts of Hemostasis & Thrombosis. Murano, Genesio, ed. 304p. 1980. 118.00 (*0-8493-5393-9*, RC633, CRC Reprint) Franklin.

— Disorders of Thrombosis & Hemostasis: Clinical & Laboratory Practice. 2nd ed. (Illus.). 323p. 1998. text 105.00 (*0-397-51690-8*) Lppncott W & W.

Bick, Roger L., ed. Disseminated Intravascular Coagulation & Related Syndromes. 144p. 1983. 88.00 (*0-8493-6636-4*, RC647, CRC Reprint) Franklin.

Bick, T.A. Elementary Boundary Value Problems. (Pure & Applied Mathematics Ser.: Vol. 173). (Illus.). 264p. 1993. text 65.00 (*0-8247-8899-0*) Dekker.

Bickart, Theodore A. & Balabanian, Norman. Linear Network Theory: Analysis, Properties, Design & Synthesis. (Illus.). 648p. 1985. 64.95 (*0-916460-10-X*, Matrix Pubs Inc) Weber Systems.

***Bickart, Toni S. & Dodge, Diane Trister.** Reading Right from the Start: What Parents Can Do in the First Five Years. 62p. (C). 2000. pap. 2.95 (*1-879537-55-9*) Tchng Strtgs.

Bickart, Toni S., et al. Building the Primary Classroom: A Complete Guide to Teaching & Learning. 2nd ed. Orig. Title: Constructing Curriculum for the Primary Grades. (Illus.). 462p. (C). 1999. pap. text 32.50 (*1-879537-38-9*) Tchng Strtgs.

— What Every Parent Needs to Know about 1st, 2nd & 3rd Grades: An Essential Guide to Your Child's Education. LC 97-1802. (Illus.). 184p. 1997. pap. 12.95 (*1-57071-156-9*) Sourcebks.

Bickart, Toni S., jt. auth. see Dodge, Diane T.

***Bickel.** Small War Lessons. 214p. 2000. 65.00 (*0-8133-9775-8*, Pub. by Westview) HarpC.

Bickel & Jantz, Stan. Bruce & Stan's Guide to the Bible: Understanding God's All-Time Bestseller. LC 98-4072. (Illus.). 304p. 1998. pap. 11.99 (*1-56507-795-4*) Harvest Hse.

Bickel, jt. auth. see Hering.

Bickel, Alexander M. The Least Dangerous Branch: The Supreme Court at the Bar of Politics. 2nd ed. LC 85-52084. 328p. (C). 1986. pap. 20.00 (*0-300-03299-4*, Y-585) Yale U Pr.

Bickel, Alexander M. The Morality of Consent. LC 75-10988. 176p. 1977. pap. 14.00 (*0-300-02119-4*) Yale U Pr.

— Politics & the Warren Court. LC 73-398. (American Constitutional & Legal History Ser). 314p. 1973. reprint ed. lib. bdg. 35.00 (*0-306-70573-7*) Da Capo.

Bickel, Alexander M. & Schmidt, Benno C., Jr. History of the Supreme Court of the United States: The Judiciary & Responsible Government 1910-1921, Vol. 9. (Illus.). 1985. 75.00 (*0-02-541420-8*) Macmillan.

***Bickel, Annette & Whittaker, Hilary.** Guinea Pre-Election Technical Assessment: December 7-21, 1997. ii, 40p. 1998. pap. text 6.00 (*1-879720-55-8*) Intl Fndt Elect.

Bickel, Branden E. The Condominium Bluebook: California Edition. 10th ed. 320p. 1998. pap. 14.95 (*1-882889-15-0*) Piedmont CA.

— The Condominium Bluebook: 1999 Edition. 340p. 1999. pap. 14.95 (*1-882889-16-9*) Piedmont CA.

***Bickel, Bruce.** God Is in the Small Stuff & It All Matters. large type ed. (Inspirational Ser.). 187p. 2000. 27.95 (*0-7838-9115-6*, G K Hall Lrg Type) Mac Lib Ref.

Bickel, Bruce. Life's Little Handbook of Wisdom. deluxe ed. 1995. boxed set 9.97 (*1-55748-681-6*) Barbour Pub.

B

B

An Asterisk (*) at the beginning of an entry indicates that the title is appearing for the first time.

Vol. 5: Legislative Histories - Funding Act (HR-63) Through Militia Bill (HR-112) LC 84-15465. 864p. 1986. text 75.00 (*0-8018-3167-9*) Johns Hopkins.

— Documentary History of the First Federal Congress of the United States of America, March 4, 1789-March 3, 1791 Vol. 6: Legislative Histories - Mitigation of Fines Bill (HR-38) Through Resolution on Unclaimed Western Lands. LC 84-15465. 720p. 1986. text 75.00 (*0-8018-3169-5*) Johns Hopkins.

Bickford, Christopher P. Farmington in Connecticut. LC 82-18575. (Illus.). 496p. 1982. 19.95 (*0-914016-92-X*) Phoenix Pub.

Bickford, Christopher P. & McNulty, J. Bard, eds. John Warner Barber's View of Connecticut Towns, 1834-36. 123p. 1990. 22.00 (*0-940748-98-3*) Conn Hist Soc.

Bickford, Dennis F., et al, eds. Environmental & Waste Management Issues in the Ceramic Industry II. (Ceramic Transactions Ser.: Vol. 45). 1994. 88.00 (*0-944904-79-3*, CT045) Am Ceramic.

Bickford, Gail H., ed. see Hall, Lawrence P.

Bickford, Gail H., ed. see Morse, Gladys K.

Bickford, Gail H., ed. see Nowell, John.

Bickford, Gail H., ed. see Roberts-Herrick, Lyn.

Bickford, Gail H., ed. see Senter, Don.

***Bickford, J. Albert, contrib. by.** Tools for Analyzing the World's Languages: Morphology & Syntax. 410p. 1998. pap. 39.00 (*1-55671-057-7*) S I L Intl.

Bickford, James R. The American Dreams Collection, Vol. 1. Jacobs, Don, ed. (Illus.). 180p. 1998. pap. 19.95 (*0-9661558-0-7*) Amer Dreams.

Bickford, Jayne E. Watkins: A Beginning Genealogy. (Illus.). 704p. 1994. reprint ed. pap. text 72.50 (*1-55613-903-9*) Heritage Bk.

Bickford, Jayne E., jt. auth. see Bartlett, Charlene.

Bickford, John H., ed. Gaskets & Gasketed Joints. LC 97-38711. (Illus.). 616p. 1997. text 165.00 (*0-8247-9877-5*) Dekker.

Bickford, John H. & Nassar, Sayed, eds. The Handbook of Bolts & Bolted Joints. LC 98-14949. (Illus.). 906p. 1998. text 195.00 (*0-8247-9977-1*) Dekker.

Bickford, Kathleen. Everyday Patterns: Factory Printed Cloth of Africa. (Illus.). 32p. (Orig.). 1997. 10.00 (*0-914489-17-8*) Univ Miss-KC Art.

Bickford, Kathleen E., et al. The Art Institute of Chicago Museum Studies: African Art at the Art Institute of Chicago. (Museum Studies: Vol. 23, No. 2). (Illus.). 104p. 1997. pap. 14.95 (*0-86559-149-0*) Art Inst Chi.

***Bickford, Lawrence.** A Mac School Primer: A User's Guide to the Mac School Student Information System. 206p. 1998. spiral bd. 32.00 (*0-9637294-9-7*) Sugar Hill Pr.

Bickford, Lawrence. A Scheduler's Notebook: A Guide to School Scheduling Using the Mac School Student Information System. 3rd rev. ed. (Illus.). 254p. 1998. pap. 44.00 (*0-9637294-6-2*) Sugar Hill Pr.

— Sumo & the Woodblock Print Masters. LC 94-15433. 152p. 1994. 45.00 (*4-7700-1752-9*) Kodansha.

Bickford, Maggie. Bones of Jade, Soul of Ice: The Flowering Plum in Chinese Art. LC 84-52148. (Illus.). 318p. (Orig.). reprint ed. pap. 98.60 (*0-8357-6406-0*, 203576700096) Bks Demand.

Bickford, Maggie, et al. The Crawford Bequest: Chinese Objects in the Collection of the Museum of Art, Rhode Island School of Design. (Illus.). 120p. (Orig.). 1993. pap. 20.00 (*0-933519-24-9*) D W Bell Gallery.

Bickford, Marion, jt. auth. see Strode, William.

Bickford, Marion E. & Mose, D. G. Geochronology of Precambrian Rocks in the St. Francois Mountains, Southeastern Missouri. LC 75-25345. (Geological Society of America, Special Paper: No. 165). 54p. reprint ed. pap. 30.00 (*0-608-14464-9*, 202503300041) Bks Demand.

Bickford, Peter. Interface Design: The Art of Developing Easy-to-Use Software. LC 97-22135. (Illus.). 306p. 1997. pap. text 34.95 (*0-12-095860-0*) Morgan Kaufmann.

Bickford, Russell S., ed. Publishments, Marriages, Births & Deaths from the Earlier Records of Gorham, Maine. LC 91-60228. 192p. 1991. 29.50 (*0-929539-83-4*, 1183) Picton Pr.

Bickford, Russell S., ed. see King, Marquis F.

Bickford, Sam. Pilipino-English - English-Pilipino Concise Dictionary. 389p. 1989. pap. 8.95 (*0-87052-491-7*) Hippocrene Bks.

Bickford-Smith, S., et al, eds. Emden: Building Contracts & Practice, 5 vols. 8th ed. 1990. student ed., ring bd. write for info. (*0-318-67321-5*, MICHIE) LEXIS Pub.

Bickford-Smith, S. & Sydenham, Colin. Party Walls: The New Law. LC 98-165409. xxiv, 190p. 1997. write for info. (*0-85308-401-7*) Jordan Pubng.

Bickford-Smith, Vivian. Ethnic Pride & Racial Prejudice in Victorian Cape Town: Group Identity & Social Practice, 1875-1902. (African Studies: No. 81). (Illus.). 310p. (C). 1995. text 80.00 (*0-521-47203-2*) Cambridge U Pr.

Bickford, Susan. The Dissonance of Democracy: Listening, Conflict, & Citizenship. LC 96-26038. 224p. 1996. text 42.50 (*0-8014-3219-7*); pap. text 15.95 (*0-8014-8377-8*) Cornell U Pr.

Bickford-Swarthout, Doris. The Best of Times, 1870-1915: Heritage Gardening at Cradle Knoll Farm. LC 98-74387. (Illus.). 145p. 1999. 25.00 (*0-9646900-3-9*, Berry Hill) Berry Hill NY.

— Mary Hallock Foote: Pioneer Woman Illustrator. LC 96-95072. (Illus.). 130p. 1996. 35.00 (*0-9646900-2-0*) Berry Hill NY.

Bickford, Thomas. Care & Feeding of the Long White Cane: Instructions in Cane Travel for Blind People. large type ed. (Illus.). 110p. (Orig.). 1993. pap. 2.00 (*0-9624122-7-9*) Natl Fed Blind.

Bickford, William B. A First Course in the Finite Element Method. 2nd ed. LC 93-20874. 672p. (C). 1993. text 76.25 (*0-256-14472-9*, Irwn McGrw-H) McGrw-H Hghr Educ.

— Mechanics of Solids: Concepts & Applications. 2nd ed. LC 96-2837. 864p. (C). 1997. 72.75 (*0-256-19271-5*, Irwn McGrw-H) McGrw-H Hghr Educ.

Bickham, David P. Blackberry Juice from Blues Bones. (Orig.). 1988. pap. 4.00 (*0-938535-80-3*) Salt-Works Pr.

Bickham, George. The Beauties of Stow: or A Description of the Pleasant Seat, & Noble Gardens, of the Right Honourable Lord Viscount Cobham. LC 92-25465. (Augustan Reprints Ser.: Nos. 185-186). 1992. reprint ed. 18.50 (*0-404-70185-X*, NA7625) AMS Pr.

— George Bickham's Penmanship Made Easy (Young Clerks Assistant) LC 97-16502. (Illus.). 64p. 1997. pap. 5.95 (*0-486-29779-9*) Dover.

Bickham, George. Musical Entertainer, Bickham's Musical Entertainer. fac. ed. (Monuments of Music & Music Literature in Facsimile Ser., Series I: Vol. 6). (Illus.). 1965. lib. bdg. 125.00 (*0-8450-2006-4*) Broude.

Bickham, George. The Universal Penman. (Illus.). 212p. 1954. pap. 17.95 (*0-486-20616-5*) Dover.

Bickham, Jack M. Breakfast at Wimbledon. 1991. 19.95 (*0-312-51195-7*) St Martin.

— Breakfast at Wimbledon. (Brad Smith Ser.: No. 4). 384p. 1992. mass mkt. 3.99 (*0-8125-1195-6*) Tor Bks.

— The Davis Cup Conspiracy. 384p. 1995. pap. 5.99 (*0-8125-5055-2*, Pub. by Forge NYC) St Martin.

— Double Fault. 352p. 1994. mass mkt. 4.50 (*0-8125-2161-7*) Tor Bks.

— Dropshot. 1991. mass mkt. 4.50 (*0-8125-0052-0*) Tor Bks.

— Murder at Oklahoma. 1998. mass mkt. 5.99 (*0-425-16381-4*, Prime Crime) Berkley Pub.

— Overhead. (Brad Smith Ser.: No. 3). 352p. 1993. mass mkt. 4.50 (*0-8125-1194-8*) Tor Bks.

— Scene & Structure. (Elements of Fiction Writing Ser.). 168p. 1999. pap. 12.00 (*0-89879-906-6*, Wrtrs Digest Bks) F & W Pubns Inc.

— Setting. (Elements of Fiction Writing Ser.). 176p. 1994. 14.99 (*0-89879-635-0*, 10646, Wrtrs Digest Bks) F & W Pubns Inc.

***Bickham, Jack M.** Setting. (Elements of Fiction Writing Ser.). 176p. 1999. pap. 12.00 (*0-89879-948-1*, Wrtrs Digest Bks) F & W Pubns Inc.

Bickham, Jack M. The 38 Most Common Fiction Writing Mistakes. 128p. 1997. pap. 12.99 (*0-89879-821-3*, Wrtrs Digest Bks) F & W Pubns Inc.

— Writing & Selling Your Novel. 208p. 1996. 17.99 (*0-89879-788-8*, Wrtrs Digest Bks) F & W Pubns Inc.

— Writing the Short Story. 224p. 1998. pap. 14.99 (*0-89879-880-9*, Wrtrs Digest Bks) F & W Pubns Inc.

Bickham, William. Liberating the Human Spirit in the Workplace. 2192p. 1995. 25.00 (*0-7863-0454-5*, Irwn Prfssnl) McGraw-Hill Prof.

Bickham, William D. & Ham, Randall E. A Buckeye in the Land of Gold: The Letters & Journal of William Dennison Bickham. LC 96-33028. (American Trail Ser.). 290p. 1996. 37.50 (*0-87062-263-3*) A H Clark.

Bickhard, Mark H. Cognition, Convention, & Communication. LC 80-20799. 270p. 1980. 69.50 (*0-275-90455-5*, C0455, Praeger Pubs) Greenwood.

Bickhard, Mark H. & Campbell, R. L. Knowing Levels & Developmental Stages. (Contributions to Human Development Ser.: Vol. 16). 148p. 1986. 38.50 (*3-8055-4262-3*) S Karger.

Bickhard, Mark H. & Terveen, Loren. Foundational Issues in Artificial Intelligence & Cognitive Science: Impasse & Solution. LC 95-2373. (Advances in Psychology Ser.: Vol. 109). 396p. 1995. 152.50 (*0-444-82048-5*, North Holland) Elsevier.

— Foundational Issues in Artificial Intelligence & Cognitive Science: Impasse & Solutions. LC 96-36526. 396p. 1996. pap. 92.00 (*0-444-82520-7*) Elsevier.

Bickimer, David A. Christ the Placenta. LC 82-24097. 239p. (Orig.). 1983. pap. 16.95 (*0-89135-034-9*) Religious Educ.

Bickish, David. Backwoods Bucks. LC 98-132251. (Bush Pilot Bowman Ser.: Vol. 2). (Illus.). 192p. 1997. pap. 18.95 (*0-9658673-1-5*) D Bickish.

— Bush Pilot Bowman. LC 98-162201. (Illus.). 192p. 1997. pap. 18.95 (*0-9658673-0-7*) D Bickish.

Bickle, Ian. Turmoil & Triumph: The Controversial Railway to Hudson Bay. LC 96-118978. (Illus.). 224p. 1995. write for info. (*1-55059-107-X*) Detselig Ents.

***Bickle, John.** Psychoneural Reduction: The New Wave. LC 97-28252. (Illus.). 372p. 1998. 35.00 (*0-262-02432-2*, Bradford Bks) MIT Pr.

Bickle, M. J., ed. see Nisbet, Evan G.

Bickle, Mike. Creciendo en el Ministerio Profetico. (SPA.). 1996. pap. 10.99 (*0-88419-550-3*) Casa Creacion.

Bickle, Mike. Growing in the Prophetic. LC 95-83824. 220p. 1996. pap. 12.99 (*0-88419-426-4*) Creation House.

— Passion for Jesus. 204p. 1993. pap. 12.99 (*0-88419-258-X*) Creation House.

— Pleasures of Loving God, Vol. 1. 2000. pap. 12.99 (*0-88419-662-3*) Creation House.

Bickleman, Eric J. The Story of the Stewartstown Railroad. (Illus.). 80p. (Orig.). 1995. pap. 19.95 (*0-9651235-0-2*) Baltimore Chap.

Bickler, Graham, jt. auth. see Solity, Jonathan.

Bickley, Dan. No Bull: The Unauthorized Biography of Dennis Rodman. LC 97-17046. (Illus.). 288p. 1997. text 23.95 (*0-312-17119-6*) St Martin.

Bickley, Francis L. Manuscripts of Allan George Finch, 1692 & Addenda, 1690-1691. (Reports & Calendars, Series 58: Vol. 4). 626p. 1965. 16.00 (*0-11-440140-3*, HM01403, Pub. by Statnry Office) Bernan Associates.

— Matthew Arnold & His Poetry. LC 77-120977. (Poetry & Life Ser.). reprint ed. 16.00 (*0-404-52501-6*) AMS Pr.

Bickley, George, jt. ed. see Culp, Robert D.

Bickley, Gillian. The Golden Needle: The Biography of Frederick Stewart (1836-1889) LC 97-49596. 1998. write for info. (*962-8027-08-5*) David Co.

Bickley, John A. Field Manual for Maturity & Pullout Testing on Highway Surfaces. 84p. (C). 1993. pap. text 15.00 (*0-309-05754-X*, SHRP-C-376) SHRP.

Bickley, Lynn S. & Hoekelman, Robert A. Bates' Guide to Physical Examination & History Taking. 7th ed. LC 98-21795. 789p. 1998. text 59.95 (*0-7817-1655-1*) Lppncott W & W.

— Bates' Pocket Guide to Physical Examination & History Taking. 3rd ed. LC 99-38243. 256p. 2000. pap. text 24.95 (*0-7817-1869-4*) Lppncott W & W.

***Bickley, Mary C., et al.** Marketing, Distribution & Users of Annuities. LC 00-30200. 2000. write for info. (*1-57974-077-4*) Life Office.

Bickley, R. Bruce, Jr. & Keenan, Hugh T. Joel Chandler Harris: An Annotated Bibliography of Criticism, 1977-1996 with Supplement, 1892-1976, 27. LC 97-39754. (Bibliographies & Indexes in American Literature Ser.: Vol. 27). 208p. 1997. lib. bdg. 72.95 (*0-313-29263-9*, Greenwood Pr) Greenwood.

Bickley, Verner C. & Puthenparampil, J. Philip, eds. Cultural Relations in the Global Community: Problems & Prospects. 1981. 17.50 (*0-8364-0728-8*, Pub. by Abhinav) S Asia.

Bickman, Connie. Children of Australia. LC 94-13308. (Through the Eyes of Children Ser.). (J). (gr. 3 up). 1994. lib. bdg. 15.98 (*1-56239-326-X*) ABDO Pub Co.

— Children of Ecuador. LC 95-39542. (Through the Eyes of Children Ser.). (J). 1996. lib. bdg. 15.98 (*1-56239-546-7*) ABDO Pub Co.

— Children of Israel. LC 94-29483. (Through the Eyes of Children). (J). (gr. 1-8). 1994. lib. bdg. 15.98 (*1-56239-330-8*) ABDO Pub Co.

— Children of Mexico. LC 94-12497. (Through the Eyes of Children Ser.). (J). 1994. lib. bdg. 15.98 (*1-56239-328-6*) ABDO Pub Co.

— Children of Peru. LC 94-9905. (Through the Eyes of Children Ser.). (J). 1994. lib. bdg. 15.98 (*1-56239-325-1*) ABDO Pub Co.

— Children of Russia. LC 94-19299. (Through the Eyes of Children Ser.). (J). (gr. 4 up). 1994. lib. bdg. 15.98 (*1-56239-329-4*) ABDO Pub Co.

— Children of Tanzania. LC 95-39543. (Through the Eyes of Children Ser.). (Illus.). (J). 1996. lib. bdg. 15.98 (*1-56239-547-5*) ABDO Pub Co.

— Children of Turkey. LC 94-14801. (Through the Eyes of Children Ser.). (J). 1994. lib. bdg. 15.98 (*1-56239-327-8*) ABDO Pub Co.

— Egypt. LC 95-38549. (Through the Eyes of Children Ser.). (J). 1996. lib. bdg. 15.98 (*1-56239-548-3*) ABDO Pub Co.

— Nepal. Berg, Julie, ed. (Through the Eyes of Children Ser.). (J). 1996. lib. bdg. 15.98 (*1-56239-549-1*) ABDO Pub Co.

— Roots & Wings . . . A Scrapbook of Time: Cannon Falls, Minnesota. (Illus.). 448p. (Orig.). 1996. pap. 50.00 (*1-889644-13-7*) Yatra Publns.

Bickman, Connie, tr. see Bickman, Kelli & Gaiman, Neil.

Bickman, Jack M. Tiebreaker. 320p. 1990. pap. 4.99 (*0-8125-0050-4*) Tor Bks.

Bickman, Kelli & Gaiman, Neil. What I Thought I Saw: New York - London. Bickman, Connie, tr. LC 96-90532. (Illus.). 96p. (Orig.). 1996. pap. 23.95 (*1-889644-03-X*) Yatra Publns.

Bickman, Leonard, ed. Advances in Program Theory. LC 85-644749. (New Directions for Program Evaluation Ser.: No. PE 47). 1990. pap. 22.00 (*1-55542-813-4*) Jossey-Bass.

***Bickman, Leonard, ed.** Research Design Vol. 2: Donald Campbell's Legacy. LC 99-50461. 247p. 2000. 64.95 (*0-7619-1085-9*) Sage.

Bickman, Leonard & Ellis, Henry, eds. Preparing Psychologists for the Twenty-First Century: Proceedings of the National Conference on Graduate Education in Psychology. 256p. 1990. text 69.95 (*0-8058-0574-5*) L Erlbaum Assocs.

Bickman, Leonard & Rog, Debra A., eds. Handbook of Applied Social Research Methods. LC 97-4858. 604p. 1997. 85.00 (*0-7619-0672-X*) Sage.

Bickman, Leonard & Rog, Debra J. Handbook of Applied Social Research Methods. LC 97-4858. 1997. pap. write for info. (*0-7619-0673-8*) Sage.

Bickman, Leonard & Rog, Debra J., eds. Children's Mental Health Services. 256p. 1995. 45.00 (*0-8039-7348-9*) Sage.

— Children's Mental Health Services, Vol. 1. 256p. 1995. pap. 19.95 (*0-8039-7349-7*) Sage.

— Evaluating Mental Health Services for Children. LC 85-644749. (New Directions for Evaluation Ser.: No. PE 54). 105p. 1992. pap. 22.00 (*1-55542-760-X*) Jossey-Bass.

Bickman, Leonard, et al. Evaluating Managed Mental Health Services: The Fort Bragg Experiment. (Illus.). 219p. 1995. 42.50 (*0-306-45044-5*, Plenum Trade) Perseus Pubng.

Bickman, Martin. Approaches to Teaching Melville's Moby Dick. LC 85-4892. (Approaches to Teaching World Literature Ser.: No. 8). x, 157p. 1985. pap. 18.00 (*0-87352-490-X*, AP08P); lib. bdg. 37.50 (*0-87352-489-6*, AP08C) Modern Lang.

— The Unsounded Centre: Jungian Studies in American Romanticism. LC 79-26042. 192p. reprint ed. pap. 59.60 (*0-8357-3895-7*, 203662700004) Bks Demand.

— Walden: Volatile Truths. (Twayne's Masterworks Ser.). 130p. (Orig.). 1992. 29.00 (*0-8057-7958-2*) Macmillan.

— Walden: Volatile Truths. LC 92-1187. (Twayne's Masterworks Ser.: Vol. 91). 130p. (Orig.). 1992. pap. 18.00 (*0-8057-8012-2*) Macmillan.

Bickman, Martin, ed. see Thoreau, Henry David.

***Bickmann, Isa.** Leonardismus und Symbolistische Asthetik: Ein Beitrag Zur Wirkungsgeschichte Leonardo Da Vincis In Paris und Brussel. (GER., Illus.). 295p. 1999. 57.00 (*3-631-34146-6*) P Lang Pubng.

Bickmore. Further Examples of Environmental Maps. (Illus.). 1985. pap. 51.00 (*90-70310-06-6*, Pergamon Pr) Elsevier.

Bickmore, Barbara. The Back of Beyond. 576p. 1995. mass mkt. 5.99 (*0-8217-4893-9*, Zebra Kensgtn) Kensgtn Pub Corp.

***Bickmore, Barbara.** The Back of Beyond. large type ed. LC 99-23577. 1999. write for info. (*1-57490-194-X*, Beeler LP Bks) T T Beeler.

Bickmore, Barbara. Beyond the Promise. LC 97-71646. 384p. 1997. 23.00 (*1-57566-220-5*, Knsington) Kensgtn Pub Corp.

— Beyond the Promise. 480p. 1998. pap. 5.99 (*1-57566-329-5*) Kensgtn Pub Corp.

— Beyond the Promise. large type ed. LC 97-39081. 1997. 25.95 (*1-57490-129-X*, Beeler LP Bks) T T Beeler.

— Deep in the Heart. 448p. 1997. mass mkt. 5.99 (*1-57566-225-6*, Knsington) Kensgtn Pub Corp.

— Deep in the Heart. large type ed. LC 96-41030. 1996. lib. bdg. 24.95 (*1-57490-067-6*, Beeler LP Bks) T T Beeler.

— Distant Star. (Illus.). 544p. (Orig.). 1993. pap. 10.00 (*0-345-36109-1*) Ballantine Pub Grp.

— East of the Sun. 608p. 1990. mass mkt. 5.99 (*0-8041-0730-0*) Ivy Books.

— Homecoming. 1995. text 18.95 (*0-8217-4923-4*, Pinncle Kensgtn) Kensgtn Pub Corp.

— Homecoming. 1996. mass mkt. 6.99 (*1-57566-005-9*) Kensgtn Pub Corp.

— The Moon Below. 624p. 1994. mass mkt. 5.99 (*0-8217-4454-2*, Zebra Kensgtn) Kensgtn Pub Corp.

Bickmore-Brand, Jennie, ed. Language in Mathematics. LC 92-46790. 128p. (C). 1993. pap. text 17.00 (*0-435-08340-6*, 08340) Heinemann.

Bickmore, Kathy, et al. Alternatives to Violence: A Manual for Teaching Peacemaking to Youth & Adults. 2nd ed. Soltis, Kathy, ed. (Illus.). 126p. 1994. reprint ed. pap. text 9.95 (*0-9619819-2-X*) Peace Grows.

***Bickmore, Wendy A., ed.** Chromosome Structural Analysis: A Practical Approach. LC 98-46718. (Practical Approach Ser.: 200). (Illus.). 234p. 1999. pap. text 55.00 (*0-19-963698-2*) OUP.

— Chromosome Structural Analysis: A Practical Approach. LC 98-46718. (Practical Approach Ser.: No. 200). (Illus.). 234p. 1999. text 115.00 (*0-19-963699-0*) OUP.

Bicknell, A. J. Wooden & Brick Buildings with Details. LC 77-363. (Architecture & Decorative Art Ser.). 1977. reprint ed. 95.00 (*0-306-70832-9*) Da Capo.

Bicknell, A. J., & Co. Staff. Bicknell's Victorian Buildings. LC 79-52830. (Illus.). 192p. 1980. pap. 9.95 (*0-486-23904-7*) Dover.

***Bicknell, Alf & Ferguson, Alasdair.** Ticket to Ride: The Ultimate Beatles Tour Diary! 9.95p. 1999. pap. 9.95 (*1-902588-01-0*, Pub. by Glitter Bks) Subterranean Co.

Bicknell, Arthur. Masterpieces. 1979. pap. 5.25 (*0-8222-0739-7*) Dramatists Play.

Bicknell, Barbara A. & Bicknell, Kris D. The Road Map to Repeatable Success: Using QFD to Implement Change. LC 94-17627. (Systems Engineering Ser.). 368p. 1994. lib. bdg. 74.95 (*0-8493-8019-7*) CRC Pr.

***Bicknell Crane, Ellery.** The Treatment of the Indians by the Colonists. (LC History-America-E). 248p. 1999. reprint ed. lib. bdg. 79.00 (*0-7812-4250-9*) Rprt Serv.

Bicknell, David L. & Brengle, Richard L., eds. Image & Event: America Now. LC 75-146363. (Illus.). (Orig.). (C). 1971. pap. text 16.95 (*0-89197-225-0*) Irvington.

Bicknell, David L., jt. auth. see Collins, Tony.

Bicknell, John W., ed. Selected Letters of Leslie Stephen, 1864-1882, Vol. 1. LC 96-1738. 309p. 1996. text 67.50 (*0-8142-0690-5*) Ohio St U Pr.

— Selected Letters of Leslie Stephen, 1882-1904, Vol. 2. LC 96-1738. 301p. 1996. text 67.50 (*0-8142-0691-3*) Ohio St U Pr.

Bicknell, Kris D., jt. auth. see Bicknell, Barbara A.

Bicknell, P. The Picturesque Scenery of the Lake District, 1752-1855: A Bibliographical Study. 1990. 40.00 (*0-906795-60-5*) Oak Knoll.

Bicknell, Robert, ed. see Maher, Larry.

Bicknell, Roy, ed. Endothelial Cell Culture. (Handbooks in Practical Animal Cell Biology Ser.). (Illus.). 148p. (C). 1996. text 64.95 (*0-521-55024-6*); pap. text 23.95 (*0-521-55990-1*) Cambridge U Pr.

Bicknell, Roy, et al, eds. Tumour Angiogenesis. LC 96-52106. (Illus.). 396p. 1997. text 195.00 (*0-19-854937-7*) OUP.

Bicknell, Stephen. The History of the English Organ. (Illus.). 428p. (C). 1996. text 69.95 (*0-521-55026-2*) Cambridge U Pr.

— The History of the English Organ. (Illus.). 433p. (C). 1999. pap. text 27.95 (*0-521-65409-2*) Cambridge U Pr.

Bicknell, Susan J., ed. see LeGwin, J. Hardy.

Bicknell, Thomas W. Barrington: With Ancient Records of Sowams & Parts Adjacent. (Illus.). 204p. 1997. reprint ed. lib. bdg. 29.00 (*0-8328-6474-9*) Higginson Bk Co.

— History & Genealogy of the Bicknell Family & Some Collateral Lines. (Illus.). 620p. 1988. reprint ed. pap. 93.00 (*0-8328-0249-2*); reprint ed. lib. bdg. 101.00 (*0-8328-0248-4*) Higginson Bk Co.

— History of Barrington, R. I. (Illus.). 620p. 1993. reprint ed. lib. bdg. 65.00 (*0-8328-3506-4*) Higginson Bk Co.

***Bicknell, Thomas Williams.** A History of Barrington, Rhode Island, 2 vols. (Illus.). 730p. 1999. pap. 48.50 (*0-7884-1302-3*, B143) Heritage Bk.

— Sowams: With Ancient Records of Sowams & Parts Adjacent. (Illus.). 261p. 1999. pap. 19.50 (*0-7884-1247-7*) Heritage Bk.

Bicknell, Treld P. Seven Is Heaven. LC 86-45415. (Illus.). 64p. (J). (gr. 2). 1986. 8.95 (*0-15-200580-3*, Gulliver Bks) Harcourt.

Bicknell, Treld P. & Trotman, Felicity, eds. How to Write & Illustrate Children's Books. (Illus.). 144p. 1988. 24.99 (*0-89134-264-8*, North Lght Bks) F & W Pubns Inc.

***Bicknell, Treld Pelkey & Trotman, Felicity, eds.** How to Write & Illustrate Children's Books & Get Them Published. (Illus.). 144p. 2000. pap. 19.99 (*1-58297-013-0*, Wrtrs Digest Bks) F & W Pubns Inc.

Bickner, Robert. An Introduction to the Thai Poem Lilit Phra Law: The Story of King Law. (Special Reports: No. 25). 254p. 1991. pap. 16.95 (*1-877979-75-9*) SE Asia.

Bickner, Robert J., et al, eds. Papers from a Conference on Thai Studies in Honor of William J. Gedney. LC 84-45446. (Michigan Papers on South & Southeast Asia: No. 25). (Illus.). 265p. 1986. 31.95 (*0-89148-030-7*) Ctr S&SE Asian.

Bickner, Robert J., ed. see Gedney, William J.

Bicks, Jane R. Dr. Jane's Natural Care for a Healthy, Happy Dog: The Complete Guide to Nutrition & Health. LC 98-46936. 176p. 1999. pap. 11.95 (*0-399-52482-7*, Perigee Bks) Berkley Pub.

— Dr. Jane's 30 Days to a Healthier, Happier Cat: The Complete Guide to Nutrition & Health. 1997. pap. 21.95 (*0-614-27823-6*, Perigee Bks) Berkley Pub.

Bicksler, Harriet. Perspectives on Social Issues. LC 92-72846. 192p. 1992. pap., student ed. 5.95 (*0-916035-54-9*) Evangel Indiana.

— Perspectives on Social Issues. LC 92-73335. 96p. 1992. pap., teacher ed. 4.95 (*0-916035-55-7*) Evangel Indiana.

Bicksler, Harriet, jt. auth. see Gephart, Lynda W.

Bickston, Diana. Street Birth. (Prison Writing Ser.). 36p. 1982. pap. 2.00 (*0-912678-52-6*, Greenfld Rev Pr) Greenfld Rev Lit.

Bicos, Olga. More Than Magic. 544p. 1994. mass mkt. 4.99 (*0-7860-0049-X*, Pinncle Kensgtn) Kensgtn Pub Corp.

— Perfect Timing. 416p. 1998. pap. 5.99 (*0-8217-5947-7*, Zebra Kensgtn) Kensgtn Pub Corp.

— Risky Games. 416p. 1997. pap. 5.99 (*0-8217-5679-6*, Zebra Kensgtn) Kensgtn Pub Corp.

— Sweeter Than Dreams. 512p. 1995. mass mkt. 4.99 (*0-8217-0142-8*, Zebra Kensgtn) Kensgtn Pub Corp.

— Wrapped in Wishes. 432p. 1996. mass mkt. 5.50 (*0-8217-5370-3*, Zebra Kensgtn) Kensgtn Pub Corp.

***Bicos, Olga.** Wrapped in Wishes. large type ed. LC 99-31992. 1999. write for info. (*1-56895-759-9*) Wheeler Pub.

Bicout, D., et al, eds. Quantum Mechanical Simulation Methods for Studying Biological Systems: Les Houches Workshops, 2-7 May, 1995. xvii, 314p. 1996. pap. 98.50 (*3-540-60869-9*) Spr-Verlag.

Bicrford. Strength of Materials: Solutions Manual. (C). 1997. pap. text, teacher ed. write for info. (*0-673-97505-3*) Addison-Wesley.

BICSI Staff. LAN & Internetworking Applications Guide: How Network Software Impacts Network Design. (Illus.). 250p. 1999. pap. 29.99 (*1-928886-00-0*) B I C S I.

— LAN & Internetworking Design Manual. 3rd rev. ed. Orig. Title: LAN Design Manual. (Illus.). 1200p. 1999. ring bd. 329.00 (*1-928886-01-9*) B I C S I.

Bicudo, Carlos E., et al, eds. Phycologia Latino-Americana, Vol. 2. 213p. 1984. text 60.00 (*3-7682-1410-9*) Lubrecht & Cramer.

Bicudo, Carlos E. & Azevedo, M. T. Desmidioflorula Paulista I: Genero Arthordesmus Ehr. ex Ralfs Emend. Arch. (Bibliotheca Phycologica Ser.: No. 36). (POR., Illus.). 1978. text 32.00 (*3-7682-1156-8*) Lubrecht & Cramer.

Bicudo, Carlos E. & Samanez, I. M. Desmidioflorula Paulista III: Generos Bambu ina, Desmidium, Groenbladia, Nyalotheca, Onychonema, Phymatodos, Spondylosium, Teilingia. (Bibliotheca Phycologica Ser.: No. 68). (POR., Illus.). 138p. 1984. pap. text 40.00 (*3-7682-1388-9*) Lubrecht & Cramer.

Bicudo, Carlos E. & Sormus, L. Desmidioflorula Paulista II: Genero Micrasterias C. Agardh ex Ralfs. (Bibliotheca Phycologica Ser.: No. 57). (SPA., Illus.). 230p. 1982. pap. text 65.00 (*3-7682-1225-4*) Lubrecht & Cramer.

Bicudo, Carlos E. de Mattos, see De Mattos Bicudo, Carlos E.

Bicudo, P. W., jt. ed. see Eduardo, J.

Bicycle Federation of America Staff & Federal Highway Administration Staff. Implementing Bicycle Improvements at the Local Level. (Illus.). 100p. 1999. pap. text 35.00 (*0-935403-31-0*, LP-471) Inst Trans Eng.

Bicycling Magazine Editors. Bicycling Magazine's Basic Maintenance & Repair. LC 89-70255. 1990. pap. 8.95 (*0-87857-902-8*, 12-008-1) Rodale Pr Inc.

— Bicycling Magazine's Bicycle Commuting Made Easy. LC 91-45292. (Illus.). 128p. (Orig.). 1992. pap. 8.95 (*0-87596-101-0*, 12-147-1) Rodale Pr Inc.

— Bicycling Magazine's Bike Touring in the 90's. LC 92-34608. 120p. 1993. pap. 6.95 (*0-87596-154-1*) Rodale Pr Inc.

— Bicycling Magazine's Cycling for Women. (Illus.). 96p. 1989. pap. 8.95 (*0-87857-811-0*) Rodale Pr Inc.

— Bicycling Magazine's Long-Distance Cycling. LC 92-33508. 128p. 1993. pap. 8.95 (*0-87596-155-X*) Rodale Pr Inc.

— Bicycling Magazine's Mountain Biking Skills. LC 89-77243. 128p. 1990. pap. 8.95 (*0-87857-900-1*, 12-012-1) Rodale Pr Inc.

— Bicycling Magazine's New Bike Owners Guide. LC 89-70310. 128p. 1990. pap. 8.95 (*0-87857-872-2*, 12-651-1) Rodale Pr Inc.

— Bicycling Magazine's Nutrition for Cyclists. LC 90-25277. 128p. 1991. pap. 8.95 (*0-87857-935-4*, 12-326-1) Rodale Pr Inc.

— Bicycling Magazine's Ride Like a Pro. LC 91-4529. (Illus.). 128p. (Orig.). 1992. pap. 6.95 (*0-87596-102-9*, 12-028-1) Rodale Pr Inc.

— Bicycling Magazine's Six Hundred Tips for Better Bicycling. LC 90-25330. 128p. 1991. pap. 8.95 (*0-87857-936-2*, 12-327-1) Rodale Pr Inc.

— Bicycling Magazine's Training for Fitness & Endurance. LC 89-77188. 128p. 1990. pap. 8.95 (*0-87857-899-4*, 12-010-1) Rodale Pr Inc.

Bicycling Magazine Editors & Mountain Bike Magazine Editors. Bicycling Magazine's Complete Guide to Bicycle Maintenance & Repair. rev. ed. LC 90-8057. (Illus.). 352p. 1994. pap. 16.95 (*0-87596-207-6*, 12-762-1) Rodale Pr Inc.

Bicycling Magazine Editors, jt. auth. see Mountain Bike Magazine Editors.

BID (Banco Interamericano De Desarrollo) Staff, jt. ed. see CEPAL Staff.

Bidal, Lillian. The Run of the Elk. LC 98-68155. (Illus.). 180p. 1999. 27.50 (*0-9646793-3-7*) R E McKee Fnd.

Bidal, Lillian, ed. see Von Bosse, Hennig.

Bidal, Lillian H. Pisacah: A Place of Plenty. (Illus.). 352p. 1996. 32.50 (*0-9646793-0-2*) R E McKee Fnd.

Bidan, P. & Boverie, S., eds. Intelligent Components for Autonomous & Semi-Autonomous Vehicles. LC 96-41665. (IFAC Postprint Ser.). 142p. 1996. pap. text 65.50 (*0-08-042603-4*, Pergamon Pr) Elsevier.

Bidani, Jayne Hinds. Jayne Hinds Bidaut: Tintypes. 192p. 1999. text 50.00 (*1-888001-79-8*) Graphis US.

Bidart Campos, German J. The Argentine Supreme Court: The Court of Constitutional Guarantees. Brisk, William J., tr. from SPA. viii, 143p. 1982. reprint ed. pap. 15.00 (*950-06-2114-2*) W S Hein.

Bidart, Frank. Desire. LC 97-9098. 64p. 1997. 20.00 (*0-374-13824-9*) FS&G.

***Bidart, Frank.** Desire. 64p. 1999. pap. text 11.00 (*0-374-52599-4*) FS&G.

Bidart, Frank. In the Western Night: Collected Poems, 1965-90. 280p. 1991. pap. 14.00 (*0-374-52271-5*) FS&G.

Bidart, Frank, ed. see Lowell, Robert.

Bidasio, John. E Ninth Pedal Steel. 112p. (C). 1988. student ed. 19.95 incl. audio (*0-931759-19-6*) Centerstream Pub.

Bidault, Francis. Leveraged Innovation: Unlocking the Innovation Potential of Strategic Supply. LC 98-50469. 200p. 1999. text 40.00 (*0-312-22154-1*) St Martin.

Bidaux, Maurice. Glossaire Patois-Francais. (FRE.). 360p. 1983. pap. 75.00 (*0-8288-1714-6*, F1942) Fr & Eur.

Bidder, Alex Von, see Mariani, John F. & Von Bidder, Alex.

Bidder, Hans. Carpets from Eastern Turkestan: Known As Khotan, Samarkand & Kansu Carpets. Allen, Grace M., tr. from GER. LC 79-66596. (Illus.). 96p. 1979. reprint ed. 36.00 (*0-317-01331-9*); reprint ed. 36.00 (*0-318-21254-4*) Wash Intl Assocs.

— Carpets from Eastern Turkestan: Known As Khotan, Samarkand & Kansu Carpets. Allen, Grace M. & Wasmuth, Gunther, trs. from GER. LC 79-66596. (Illus.). 96p. 1979. reprint ed. 36.00 (*0-915036-02-9*) Wash Intl Assocs.

***Bidder, Sean.** The Rough Guide to House. 288p. 1999. pap. 9.95 (*1-85828-432-5*) Penguin Putnam.

Biddick, Kathleen. The Other Economy: Pastoral Husbandry on a Medieval Estate. 274p. (C). 1989. 50.00 (*0-520-06388-0*, Pub. by U CA Pr) Cal Prin Full Svc.

— The Shock of Medievalism. LC 97-32456. 1998. write for info. (*0-8223-2182-3*); pap. write for info. (*0-8223-2199-8*) Duke.

Biddick, Kathleen, ed. Archaeological Approaches to Medieval Europe. LC 84-14759. (Studies in Medieval Culture: No. 18). 1984. pap. 16.95 (*0-918720-52-4*); boxed set 27.95 (*0-918720-53-2*) Medieval Inst.

Biddis, K. J. Homeopathy in Veterinary Practice. 86p. (Orig.). pap. 11.95 (*0-8464-4236-1*) Beekman Pubs.

— Homoeopathy in Veterinary Practice. 86p. 1996. pap. 9.95 (*0-85207-196-5*, Pub. by C W Daniel) Natl Bk Netwk.

Biddiscombe, Perry. Werewolf! The History of the National Socialist Guerrilla Movement, 1944-1946. LC 98-129905. (Illus.). 464p. 1998. text 39.95 (*0-8020-0862-3*) U of Toronto Pr.

— Werwolf! The History of the National Socialist Guerrilla Movement 1944-1946. 462p. 1998. write for info. (*0-7083-1446-5*, Pub. by Univ Wales Pr) Paul & Co Pubs.

Biddiss, Michael & Wyke, Maria, eds. The Uses & Abuses of Antiquity. LC 99-32206. (Illus.). 281p. 1999. pap. 41.95 (*0-8204-4217-8*) P Lang Pubng.

Biddiss, Michael, jt. auth. see Cartwright, Frederick F.

Biddle. Angles of Vision. 1992. teacher ed. 9.68 (*0-07-005216-6*) McGraw.

— Dark Side of the Moon. 1995. 29.95 (*0-8050-2235-X*) H Holt & Co.

Biddle, Arthur. A Treatise on the Law of Warranties in the Sale of Chattels. xx, 308p. 1981. reprint ed. 45.00 (*0-8377-0316-6*, Rothman) W S Hein.

Biddle & Associates. Career Passport: OPAC System Test Preparation Manual. LC 98-50570. (Illus.). 192p. 1999. pap. text 49.00 incl. disk (*0-13-084114-5*) P-H.

Biddle, Arthur W. & Bien, Gloria, eds. Global Voices: Contemporary Literature from the Non-Western World. LC 94-24288. 1056p. 1994. pap. text 51.00 (*0-13-299793-2*) P-H.

Biddle, Arthur W. & Fulwiler, Toby. Angles of Vision: An Introduction to Literature. 1802p. (C). 1991. pap. 42.81 (*0-07-005214-X*) McGraw.

Biddle, Arthur W. & Fulwiler, Toby, eds. Reading, Writing, & the Study of Literature. 192p. (C). 1988. pap. 29.38 (*0-07-553538-6*) McGraw.

Biddle, Arthur W., jt. auth. see Fulwiler, Toby.

Biddle, Arthur W., ed. see Bien, Gloria & Dharwadker, Vinay.

Biddle, Arthur W., ed. see Bond, Lynne A., et al.

Biddle, Arthur W., ed. see Holland, Kenneth & Fulwiler, Toby.

Biddle, Arthur W., ed. see Merton, Thomas & Lax, Robert.

Biddle, Arthur W., ed. see Steffens, Henry J., et al.

Biddle, Bruce J. Role Theory: Expectations, Identities & Behaviors. 1979. text 70.00 (*0-12-095950-X*) Acad Pr.

Biddle, Bruce J., jt. auth. see Berliner, David C.

Biddle, Bruce J., jt. ed. see Rossi, Peter H.

Biddle-Bruckman, Laura, ed. HomeOwners '91 Policy. 254p. 1998. teacher ed. 35.00 (*1-56461-250-3*) Rough Notes.

— 1991 Businessowners Policy. 76p. 1996. 19.95 (*1-56461-170-1*) Rough Notes.

— 1996 Business Owner's Policy. 72p. 1996. 19.95 (*1-56461-174-4*) Rough Notes.

Biddle, Charles J. The Way of the Eagle. 7th ed. (Great War Ser.: No. 7). (Illus.). 297p. 1990. reprint ed. 34.95 (*0-89839-152-0*) Battery Pr.

Biddle, Chuck, jt. auth. see Aker, John.

Biddle-Cope, J. C. Cope. Memoirs of the Copes of Wiltshire. (Illus.). 100p. 1997. reprint ed. pap. 19.00 (*0-8328-8046-9*); reprint ed. lib. bdg. 29.00 (*0-8328-8045-0*) Higginson Bk Co.

Biddle, Cordelia F., jt. auth. see Hearst, Particia.

Biddle, Derek & Evenden, Robin. Human Aspects of Management. 200p. (C). 1989. 72.00 (*0-85292-395-3*) St Mut.

Biddle, Edward & Fielding, Mantle. Life & Works of Thomas Sully. LC 74-77716. (Library of American Art). 1970. reprint ed. lib. bdg. 52.50 (*0-306-71354-3*) Da Capo.

Biddle, Flora Miller. The Whitney Women & the Museum They Made: A Family Memoir. LC 99-35730. (Illus.). 432p. 1999. 28.95 (*1-55970-509-4*, Pub. by Arcade Pub Inc) Time Warner.

Biddle, Francis. Fear of Freedom. LC 76-138496. (Civil Liberties in American History Ser.). 1971. reprint ed. lib. bdg. 39.50 (*0-306-70073-5*) Da Capo.

— In Brief Authority. LC 76-5432. (Illus.). 494p. 1976. reprint ed. lib. bdg. 75.00 (*0-8371-8807-5*, BIIB, Greenwood Pr) Greenwood.

— Llanfear Pattern. 1993. reprint ed. lib. bdg. 89.00 (*0-7812-5426-4*) Rprt Serv.

***Biddle, Francis.** Mr. Justice Holmes. 216p. 1999. reprint ed. 68.00 (*1-56169-484-3*) Gaunt.

Biddle, Francis. Mr. Justice Holmes. LC 86-15042. (Illus.). 215p. 1986. reprint ed. lib. bdg. 75.00 (*0-313-25215-7*, BIJH, Greenwood Pr) Greenwood.

— The World's Best Hope: A Discussion of the Role of the United States in the Modern World. LC E 0744.B48. (Midway Reprint Ser.). 189p. Date not set. reprint ed. pap. 58.60 (*0-608-21014-5*, 205454200003) Bks Demand.

Biddle, Francis B. The World's Best Hope. (History - United States Ser.). 175p. 1993. reprint ed. lib. bdg. 69.00 (*0-7812-4815-9*) Rprt Serv.

— The World's Best Hope. (Midway Reprint Ser.). xiv, 176p. 1974. reprint ed. pap. text 8.50 (*0-226-04621-4*) U Ch Pr.

Biddle, Geoffrey. Alphabet City. 1992. pap. 24.95 (*0-520-07949-3*, Pub. by U CA Pr) Cal Prin Full Svc.

— Alphabet City. 1992. 55.00 (*0-520-07360-6*, Pub. by U CA Pr) Cal Prin Full Svc.

Biddle, H. D. A Sketch of Owen Biddle. (Illus.). 87p. 1988. reprint ed. pap. 17.50 (*0-8328-0251-4*); reprint ed. lib. bdg. 25.50 (*0-8328-0250-6*) Higginson Bk Co.

***Biddle, Jeff E. & Backhouse, Roger E., eds.** Toward a History of Applied Economics. 330p. 2000. lib. bdg. 59.95 (*0-8223-6485-9*) Duke.

Biddle, Jeff E., jt. ed. see Samuels, Warren J.

Biddle, Julian. 214 Ways to Say I Love You. 96p. 1996. mass mkt. 4.99 (*0-7860-0234-4*, Pinncle Kensgtn) Kensgtn Pub Corp.

— What Was Hot. 192p. 1994. mass mkt. 4.50 (*1-55817-894-5*, Pinncle Kensgtn) Kensgtn Pub Corp.

Biddle, Kevin T., ed. Active Margin Basins. (AAPG Memoir Ser.: No. 52). (Illus.). 324p. 1991. 29.00 (*0-89181-330-6*, 561) AAPG.

Biddle, Kevin T. & Christie-Blick, Nicholas, eds. Strike-Slip Deformation, Basin Formation, & Sedimentation Based on a Symposium Sponsored by the Society of Economic Paleontologists & Mineralogists. LC 87-160028. (Society of Economic Paleontologists & Mineralogists Ser.: No. 37). (Illus.). 395p. 1985. pap. 122.50 (*0-608-05189-6*, 206572600001) Bks Demand.

Biddle, Livingston L. Our Government & the Arts: A Perspective from the Inside. LC 88-6168. 554p. 1988. 19.95 (*0-915400-67-7*, ACA Bks) Am for the Arts.

Biddle, Mark. Fishlake National Forest: Backcountry Guide for Hikers & Horsemen. (Illus.). 128p. (Orig.). 1993. pap. 8.00 (*0-915272-38-5*) Wasatch Pubs.

***Biddle, Mark.** Fishlake National Forest: Backcountry Guide for Hiking & Horseback Riding. 1999. pap. 7.95 (*0-87480-625-9*) U of Utah Pr.

Biddle, Mark E. Polyphony & Symphony in Prophetic Literature: Rereading Jeremiah 7-20. (Studies in Old Testament Interpretation: Vol. 2). 160p. 1996. text 30.00 (*0-86554-503-0*, MUP/H394) Mercer Univ Pr.

Biddle, Mark E., tr. see Gunkel, Hermann.

Biddle, Mark E., tr. see Jenni, Ernst & Westermann, Claus, eds.

Biddle, Martin. Object & Economy in Medieval Winchester, 2 vols. (Winchester Studies: Vol. 7, Pt. 2). (Illus.). 1990. text 295.00 (*0-19-813175-5*) OUP.

— The Tomb Of Christ. 2000. reprint ed. pap. 21.95 (*0-7509-2525-6*, Pub. by Sutton Publng) Intl Pubs Mktg.

Biddle, Martin. What Future for British Archaeology? (Oxbow Lectures: No. 1, 1994). (Illus.). 20p. 1994. 5.30 (*0-946897-80-8*, Pub. by Oxbow Bks) David Brown.

***Biddle, Martin, et al.** Church of the Holy Sepulchre. (Illus.). 240p. 2000. text 85.00 (*0-8478-2282-6*, Pub. by Rizzoli Intl) St Martin.

Biddle, Mason & Dewitt, Martin. Deep Woods: Concerning Nature in Contemporary Painting, Sculpture, & Drawing. (Illus.). 16p. (Orig.). 1989. pap. 5.00 (*1-889523-06-2*) Tweed Mus.

Biddle, Megumi, jt. auth. see Biddle, Steve.

Biddle, Pamela C. & Fishman, Joel E. All I Need to Know I Learned from My Horse. (Illus.). 128p. 1996. pap. 8.95 (*0-385-48267-1*) Doubleday.

Biddle, Pamela C., jt. auth. see Fishman, Joel E.

Biddle, Perry H., Jr. A Funeral Manual. rev. ed. 192p. 1994. pap. 16.00 (*0-8028-0697-X*) Eerdmans.

— A Funeral Manual: A Hospital Visitation Manual; A Marriage Manual, 3 vols. 1994. pap. 48.00 (*0-8028-0775-5*) Eerdmans.

Biddle, Perry H. Goodness of Marriage. 1984. 9.95 (*0-687-60426-5*) Abingdon.

Biddle, Perry H., Jr. A Hospital Visitation Manual. rev. ed. 208p. 1994. pap. 16.00 (*0-8028-0698-8*) Eerdmans.

— Humor & Healing. 2nd ed. 52p. 1994. pap. 4.95 (*0-914733-19-2*) Desert Min.

— Lectionary Preaching Workbook, II, C, Vol. II, Pt. C. (Orig.). 1988. pap., wbk. ed. 39.50 (*1-55673-064-0*, 8861) CSS OH.

— A Marriage Manual. rev. ed. 192p. 1994. pap. 16.00 (*0-8028-0699-6*) Eerdmans.

— Reflections on Suicide. 2nd ed. 36p. 1996. pap. 2.95 (*0-914733-22-2*) Desert Min.

Biddle, Richard. Memoir of Sebastian Cabot, with a Review of the History of Maritime Discovery, Illustrated by Documents from the Rolls. LC 73-107793. (Select Bibliographies Reprint Ser.). 1977. 26.95 (*0-8369-5211-1*) Ayer.

Biddle, Stanton F. Planning in the University Library, 28. LC 92-8678. (New Directions in Information Management Ser.: No. 28). 238p. 1992. 55.00 (*0-313-27788-5*, BLO/, Greenwood Pr) Greenwood.

Biddle, Stanton F., ed. The African-American Yellow Pages: A Comprehensive Resource Guide & Directory. LC 96-15092. 384p. 1995. pap. 19.95 (*0-8050-4070-6*, Owl) H Holt & Co.

— Culture Keepers: Enlightening & Empowering Our Communities: Proceedings of the First National Conference of African American Librarians. 364p. (Orig.). 1993. pap. 19.95 (*0-9640292-0-0*) Black Caucus Am Lib.

Biddle, Stanton F. & Conference Proceedings Committee, eds. Culture Keepers Vol. II: Unity Through Diversity: Proceedings of the Second National Conference of African American Librarians, Milwaukee, Wisconsin, August 5-7, 1994. (Illus.). 526p. (Orig.). 1995. pap. 19.95 (*0-9640292-1-9*) Black Caucus Am Lib.

Biddle, Stephen D. & Feaver, Peter D., eds. Battlefield Nuclear Weapons: Issues & Options. LC 89-22275. (Occasional Papers: No. 5). 170p. (Orig.). (C). 1990. pap. text 21.00 (*0-8191-7605-2*); lib. bdg. 43.50 (*0-8191-7604-4*) U Pr of Amer.

Biddle, Steve. Essential Origami. 1991. pap. 15.95 (*0-312-05716-4*) St Martin.

— Horrorgami. (Illus.). 32p. (J). (gr. 4 up). 1996. pap. 8.95 (*0-8120-9771-8*) Barron.

— Origami: Inspired by Japanese Prints. 48p. 1998. 22.00 (*0-670-88206-2*) Viking Penguin.

***Biddle, Steve.** Underwater Origami. (Illus.). 32p. (J). (gr. 4). 2000. pap. 9.95 (*0-7641-1446-8*) Barron.

***Biddle, Steve & Biddle, Megumi.** Handmade Flowers from Paper & Fabric. (Illus.). 160p. 2000. pap. 19.95 (*0-7153-0985-4*, Pub. by D & C Pub) Sterling.

Biddle, Steve & Biddle, Megumi. Horrorgami: Spooky Paper Folding for Children. (Drawing, Paper Folding & Craft Books for Kids). (Illus.). 32p. (J). (gr. 3 up). 1996. lib. bdg. 17.95 (*1-56674-173-4*, HTS Bks) Forest Hse.

— New Directions in Origami. LC 92-2209. 1993. pap. 15.95 (*0-312-08037-9*) St Martin.

— Origami Safari. (Illus.). 80p. (YA). (gr. 4 up). 1994. pap. 8.95 (*0-688-13570-6*, Wm Morrow) Morrow Avon.

— Planet Origami. (Illus.). 32p. (J). (gr. 4 up). 1998. pap. 8.95 (*0-7641-0694-5*) Barron.

***Biddle, Stuart, et al.** Physical Activity & Psychological Well-Being. LC 00-28617. 2000. pap. write for info. (*0-415-23439-5*) Routledge.

Biddle, Stuart J., ed. European Perspectives on Exercise & Sport Psychology. LC 94-32258. 360p. 1995. text 42.00 (*0-87322-826-X*, BBID0826) Human Kinetics.

Biddle, Wayne. A Field Guide to Germs. (Illus.). 224p. 1996. pap. 13.95 (*0-385-48426-7*, Anchor NY) Doubleday.

— A Field Guide to Germs. LC 94-48204. (Illus.). 88p. (YA). 1995. 22.50 (*0-8050-3531-1*) H Holt & Co.

— A Field Guide to the Invisible. LC 97-39178. 224p. 1998. 23.00 (*0-8050-5069-8*) H Holt & Co.

Biddlecombe, George. The Art of Rigging. LC 76-57844. 1977. lib. bdg. 250.00 (*0-8490-1453-0*) Gordon Pr.

— Art of Rigging. (Illus.). 192p. 1990. pap. 7.95 (*0-486-26343-6*) Dover.

— English Opera from 1834 to 1864 with Particular Reference to the Works of Michael Balfe. rev. ed. LC 94-26321. (Outstanding Dissertations in Music from British Universities Ser.). 368p. 1994. text 25.00 (*0-8153-1436-1*) Garland.

Biddlecombe, Peter. Faster, They're Gaining. 464p. 1999. pap. 16.00 (*0-316-07890-5*) Little.

Biddulph, Fiona. Metropolitan: A Portrait of Paris. (Illus.). 240p. 1994. text 55.00 (*0-7148-3156-5*, Pub. by Phaidon Press) Phaidon Pr.

Biddulph, Howard L. The Morning Breaks: Stories of Conversion & Faith in the Former Soviet Union. LC 96-13912. 188p. 1996. 15.95 (*1-57345-152-5*) Deseret Bk.

Biddulph, John. Pirates of Malabar & an Englishwoman in India Two Hundred Years Ago. (C). 1995. reprint ed. 34.00 (*81-206-0919-0*, Pub. by Asian Educ Servs) S Asia.

B

Biddulph, Lewis. The Rosicrucian "Three Treasures" The Curious Prophecies of Paracelsus. 1994. pap. 6.95 (*1-55818-309-4*, Sure Fire) Holmes Pub.

Biddulph, Michael. The Golf Shot. 74p. 1999. 40.00 (*1-897676-60-3*, Pub. by Nottingham Univ Pr) St Mut.

Biddulph, Michael & Murray, Deryck. The Natural Sportsman. 87p. 1999. 60.00 (*1-897676-63-8*, Pub. by Nottingham Univ Pr) St Mut.

Biddulph, Peter, jt. auth. see Biddulph, William.

Biddulph, Stephan, jt. auth. see Terry, Keith.

Biddulph, Steve. Manhood: An Action Plan for Changing Men's Lives. LC 98-42354. 272p. 1999. pap. 12.95 (*0-89087-852-8*) Celestial Arts.

— More Secrets of Happy Children. 1999. pap. 11.95 (*0-207-18941-2*) HarpC.

— Raising Boys: Why Boys Are Different & How to Help Them Become Happy & Well-Balanced Men. LC 98-72441. 192p. 1998. pap. 12.95 (*0-89087-853-6*) Celestial Arts.

— The Secret of Happy Children: Parent's Guide. 1998. pap. text 11.95 (*0-207-18945-5*) HarpC.

Biddulph, William & Biddulph, Peter. Travels of Certaine Englishmen into Africa, Asia & to the Blacke Sea, Finished 1608. LC 72-6344. (English Experience Ser.: No. 22). 144p. 1968. reprint ed. 25.00 (*90-221-0022-7*) Walter J Johnson.

B

Bideau, Alain, et al, eds. Infant & Child Mortatlity in the Past. LC 97-3696. (International Studies in Demography). (Illus.). 330p. 1998. text 80.00 (*0-19-828995-2*) OUP.

Bideau, D. & Dodds, J. A., eds. Physics of Granular Media. 435p. 1992. text 175.00 (*1-56072-034-4*) Nova Sci Pubs.

Bideau, D. & Hansen, A., eds. Disorder & Granular Media. LC 92-46778. (Random Materials & Processes Ser.). 348p. 1993. pap. 89.00 (*0-444-88925-6*, North Holland) Elsevier.

Bideaud, Jacqueline, et al, eds. Pathways to Number: Children's Developing Numerical Abilities. rev. ed. 408p. 1992. text 89.95 (*0-8058-0866-3*) L Erlbaum Assocs.

Bideleux, Robert. Communism & Development. 320p. 1987. pap. 17.95 (*0-416-73420-0*) Routledge.

Bideleux, Robert, ed. European Integration & Disintegration. 312p. (C). 1996. pap. 27.99 (*0-415-13741-1*) Routledge.

Bideleux, Robert & Jeffries, Ian. A History of Eastern Europe: Crisis & Change. LC 97-12358. 552p. (C). 1998. 100.00 (*0-415-16111-8*); pap. 32.99 (*0-415-16112-6*) Routledge.

Bidelman, Patrick K. Pariahs Stand Up! The Founding of the Liberal Feminist Movement in France, 1858-1889, 31. LC 81-4222. (Contributions in Women's Studies: No. 31). 285p. 1982. 49.95 (*0-313-23006-4*, BPU/, Greenwood Pr) Greenwood.

Biden, Joe, jt. ed. see McConnell, Mitch.

Biden, Joseph R. & United States. Meeting the Challenges of a Post-cold War World: Nato Enlargement & U.s.-Russia Relations : A Report to the Committee on Foreign Relations, United States Senate. LC 98-110367. vii, 59 p. 1997. write for info. (*0-16-055004-1*) USGPO.

Biden, Joseph R. & USGPO Staff. To Stand Against Aggression: Milosevic, the Bosnian Republic & the Conscience of the West: A Report to the Committee on Foreign Relations, United States Senate LC 93-233887. vi, 98 p. 1993. pap. write for info. (*0-16-040868-7*) USGPO.

Biderberg Conference Staff. The Structure of the Quiet Photosphere & the Low Chromosphere: Proceedings of the Biderberg Conference, Arnhem, Holland, April 17-21, 1967. De Jager, C., ed. 240p. 1968. text 152.50 (*90-277-0120-2*) Kluwer Academic.

Biderman, A. D., et al. Understanding Crime Incidence Statistics. (Research in Criminology Ser.). (Illus.). 112p. 1991. 79.95 (*0-387-97045-2*) Spr-Verlag.

Biderman, Albert D. March to Calumny. Kohn, Richard H., ed. LC 78-22376. (American Military Experience Ser.). 1980. reprint ed. lib. bdg. 23.95 (*0-405-11853-8*) Ayer.

Biderman, Beverly. Wired for Sound: A Journey into Hearing. Thomas, Wendy, ed. (Illus.). 256p. 1998. pap. 21.95 (*1-895579-32-5*) Trifolium Inc.

Biderman, Bob. The Genesis Files. Hutchings, Janet, ed. 248p. 1991. 17.95 (*0-8027-5797-9*) Walker & Co.

Biderman, Bob. Judgement of Death. 224p. 1992. 19.95 (*0-8027-3217-8*) Walker & Co.

Biderman, Shlomo. Scriptures & Knowledge. (Numen Bookseries: No. 69). 250p. 1995. 94.50 (*90-04-10154-3*) Brill Academic Pubs.

***Biderman, Shlomo & Rotem, Ornan.** Relativism & Beyond. Yoav, Ariel, ed. (Philosophy & Religion: Vol. 4). (Illus.). X, 427p. 1998. text 114.50 (*90-04-10930-7*) Brill Academic Pubs.

Biderman, Shlomo & Scharfstein, Ben-Ami, eds. Interpretation in Religion. LC 92-6242. (Philosophy & Religion Ser.: Vol. 2). (Illus.). xi, 290p. 1992. 93.00 (*90-04-09519-5*) Brill Academic Pubs.

— Myths & Fictions. LC 93-29158. (Philosophy & Religion Ser.: Vol. 3). 1993. 137.50 (*90-04-09838-0*) Brill Academic Pubs.

— Rationality in Question: On Eastern & Western Views of Rationality. (Studies in the History of Religions: Vol. LII). xix, 256p. 1989. 87.00 (*90-04-09212-9*) Brill Academic Pubs.

Biderman, Stan. Everything Changes: A Spiritual Journey. 120p. pap. 14.95 (*0-911051-87-2*) Plain View.

***Bidermann, Gottlob Herbert.** In Deadly Combat: A German Soldier's Memoir of the Eastern Front. Zumbro, Derek S., tr. from GER. LC 99-55738. 336p. 2000. 34.95 (*0-7006-1016-2*) U Pr of KS.

Bidey, Stephen, ed. Endocrine Cell Culture. LC 98-14244. (Handbooks in Practical Animal Cell Biology). (Illus.). 166p. (C). 1998. text 69.95 (*0-521-59399-9*); pap. text 26.95 (*0-521-59563-0*) Cambridge U Pr.

Bidez, J. & Parmentier, L., eds. The Ecclesiastical History of Evagrius. LC 76-24994. (Byzantine Texts: No. 4). reprint ed. 46.00 (*0-404-60004-2*) AMS Pr.

Bidez, Joseph. La Biographie d'Empedocle. (Recueil de Travaux Publies par la Faculte de Philosophie et Lettres de l'Universite de Gande Ser.: No. 12). xii, 176p. 1973. reprint ed. lib. bdg. 35.00 (*3-487-04664-4*) G Olms Pubs.

— EOS: Ou, Platon et l'Orient. LC 77-27185. (Gifford Lectures: 1939). reprint ed. 45.00 (*0-404-60496-X*) AMS Pr.

— Vie de Porphyre: Le Philosophe Neo-Platonicien. vii, 166p. 1980. reprint ed. lib. bdg. 50.00 (*3-487-07018-9*) G Olms Pubs.

Bidez, Joseph & Cumont, Franz. Les Mages Hellenises: Zoroastre, Ostanes & Hystaspe d'Apres la Tradition Grecque, 2 vols. LC 75-10629. (Ancient Religion & Mythology Ser.). (FRE & GRE.). 1976. reprint ed. 58.95 (*0-405-07005-5*) Ayer.

Bidgen, Richard & Carteret, Carriede. Data Modelling for Information Systems. 416p. (Orig.). 1994. pap. 67.50 (*0-273-60262-4*, Pub. by Pitman Pub) Trans-Atl Phila.

Bidgoli, Hossein. Advanced Lotus 1-2-3 with Applications. (DF - Computer Applications Ser.). (C). 1988. mass mkt. 35.75 (*0-314-47211-8*) West Pub.

***Bidgoli, Hossein.** Handbook of Business Data Communications: A Managerial Perpective. 512p. 2000. 115.00 (*0-12-095976-3*) Acad Pr.

Bidgoli, Hossein. Handbook of Management Information Systems. LC 98-87237. (Illus.). 680p. (C). 1999. boxed set 99.95 (*0-12-095975-5*) Acad Pr.

— Information Systems Literacy. (Illus.). 320p. (C). 1994. teacher ed. write for info. (*0-318-72451-0*) Macmillan.

— Information Systems Literacy. (Illus.). 290p. (C). 1994. teacher ed. write for info. (*0-318-72452-9*) Macmillan.

— Intelligent Management Support Systems. LC 97-13411. 248p. 1998. 65.00 (*1-56720-176-8*, Quorum Bks) Greenwood.

— Modern Information Systems for Managers. LC 97-9582. (Illus.). 438p. 1997. text 54.95 (*0-12-095970-4*) Morgan Kaufmann.

— Windows 95 Explorer. (DF - Computer Applications Ser.). 1996. pap. 40.95 (*0-7895-0659-9*) Course Tech.

Bidgood, Lee, jt. auth. see Alvord, Clarence W.

Bidgood, Ruth. The Fluent Moment. LC 97-101630. 66p. 1997. pap. 14.95 (*1-85411-170-1*, Pub. by Seren Bks) Dufour.

— Lighting Candles: New & Selected Poems. 75p. 1982. pap. 9.95 (*0-907476-13-9*) Dufour.

— Selected Poems. 138p. 1993. pap. 17.95 (*1-85411-069-1*, Pub. by Seren Bks) Dufour.

Bidgood, Tony, jt. auth. see Holloway, Simon.

Bidingmeyer, B. A. Preparative Liquid Chromatography. (Journal of Chromatography Library: Vol. 38). xiv,342p. 1987. 201.50 (*0-444-42832-1*) Elsevier.

Bidini, G., jt. ed. see Sucharov, L. J.

Bidinotto, Robert J., ed. Criminal Justice? The Legal System Versus Individual Responsibility. 2nd ed. LC 95-61017. 324p. 1995. 14.95 (*1-57246-016-4*) Foun Econ Ed.

Bidlack, Gerald H. Unlikely Beginnings. LC 82-90984. 1984. 10.95 (*0-87212-164-X*) Libra.

Bidlack, Mary K., ed. American Cooperation. LC 26-276. 1991. write for info. (*0-938868-13-6*); pap. write for info. (*0-938868-12-8*) Nat Coun of Farmer.

— American Cooperation. LC 26-276. 1992. write for info. (*0-938868-15-2*); pap. write for info. (*0-938868-14-4*) Nat Coun of Farmer.

— American Cooperation, Set, 1987-1990. LC 26-276. write for info. (*0-614-17580-1*); pap. write for info. (*0-614-17579-8*) Nat Coun of Farmer.

— American Cooperation, 1985. (Illus.). 504p. 1985. 12.00 (*0-938868-09-8*); pap. write for info. (*0-938868-08-X*) Nat Coun of Farmer.

— American Cooperation, 1986: Including Journal of Agricultural Cooperation. (Illus.). 400p. 1986. 14.50 (*0-938868-11-X*); pap. 14.50 (*0-938868-10-1*) Nat Coun of Farmer.

Bidlack, Wayne R., et al, eds. Phytochemicals: A New Paradigm. LC 98-86874. 200p. 1998. 104.95 (*1-56676-684-2*) Technomic.

***Bidlack, Wayne R., et al, eds.** Phytochemicals As Bioactive Agents. LC 99-69881. 296p. 2000. text 99.95 (*1-56676-788-1*) Technomic.

Bidlak, Wayne R. & Omaye, Stanley T., eds. Natural Protectants & Natural Toxicants in Food, Vol. 1. LC 94-61655. 137p. 1994. pap. text 39.95 (*1-56676-206-5*) Technomic.

Bidlingmaier, F. & Knorr, D. Oestrogens: Physiological & Clinical Aspects. (Pediatric & Adolescent Endocrinology Ser.: Vol. 4). (Illus.). 1978. 59.25 (*3-8055-2845-0*) S Karger.

Bidlingmeyer, Brian A. Practical HPLC Methodology & Applications. LC 92-4680. 464p. 1993. 89.95 (*0-471-57246-2*) Wiley.

— Preparative Liquid Chromatography. (Journal of Chromatography Library: Vol. 38). 1988. 193.75 (*0-318-32589-6*) Elsevier.

Bidlo, Mike. Fountain Drawings. 1999. pap. text 50.00 (*1-891475-15-0*) T Shafrazi.

Bidner, Jenni. Great Photos with the Advanced Photo System. LC 96-69484. (Illus.). 80p. (Orig.). (YA). (gr. 7-12). 1998. pap. 9.95 (*0-87985-773-0*, AC-300, Kodak) Saunders Photo.

— The Lighting Cookbook: Foolproof Recipes for Perfect Glamour, Portrait, Still Life & Corporate Photographs. LC 96-51982. (Illus.). 44p. 1997. pap. 24.95 (*0-8174-4196-4*, Amphoto) Watsn-Guptill.

Bidney, David. Theoretical Anthropology. 2nd ed. LC 95-12862. 550p. (C). 1995. pap. text 24.95 (*1-56000-832-6*) Transaction Pubs.

Bidney, David, ed. Concept of Freedom in Anthropology. (Studies in General Anthropology). 1963. text 45.40 (*90-279-0316-6*) Mouton.

Bidney, Martin. Blake & Goethe: Psychology, Ontology, Imagination. LC 87-19157. 190p. 1988. text 27.50 (*0-8262-0651-4*) U of Mo Pr.

— Patterns of Epiphany: From Wordsworth to Tolstoy, Pater & Barrett Browning. LC 96-38623. 1997. 34.95 (*0-8093-2116-5*) S Ill U Pr.

Bidoglio, Giovanni & Stumm, Werner, eds. Chemistry of Aquatic Systems: Local & Global Perspectives - Based on the Lectures Given During the Eurocourse Held at the Joint Research Centre, Ispra, Italy, September 27-October 1, 1993. LC 94-15441. (Eurocourses: Chemical & Environmental Science Ser.: Vol. 5). 544p. (C). 1994. text 272.50 (*0-7923-2867-1*) Kluwer Academic.

Bidois, Le, see Le Bidois.

Bidoit, M. & Choppy, C., eds. Recent Trends in Data Type Specification: Eighth Workshop on Specification of Abstract Data Types, Joint with the 3rd COMPASS Workshop, Dourdan, France, August 26-30, 1991: Selected Papers. LC 92-42107. (Lecture Notes in Computer Science Ser.: Vol. 655). 1993. 55.95 (*0-387-56379-2*) Spr-Verlag.

Bidol, Patricia. Improving Local Union Women's Committees. Kleiner, Lydia et al, eds. (Program on Women & Work Ser.). 38p. 1981. pap. 3.50 (*0-87736-345-5*) U of Mich Inst Labor.

Bidwai, Praful & Vanaik, Achin. New Nukes: India, Pakistan & Global Nuclear Disarmament. LC 99-23965. 2000. 40.00 (*1-56656-318-6*); pap. 17.95 (*1-56656-317-8*) Interlink Pub.

Bidwai, Praful, et al. India under Siege: Challenges Within & Without. LC 94-907160. (C). 1995. pap. 10.00 (*81-224-0692-0*) S Asia.

— Religion, Religiosity & Communialism. 1996. 34.00 (*81-7304-132-6*, Pub. by Manohar) S Asia.

Bidwell. Investigating Family Issues. 304p. 2000. pap. text, teacher ed. write for info. (*0-02-309673-X*, Macmillan Coll) P-H.

Bidwell, jt. auth. see Holbrook.

Bidwell, Bruce W. History of the Military Intelligence Division, Department of the Army General Staff: 1775-1941. LC 85-32286. 625p. 1986. lib. bdg. 75.00 (*0-313-27038-4*, U7038, Greenwood Pr) Greenwood.

Bidwell, Charles E. & Kasarda, John D. The Organization & Its Ecosystem Vol. 2: A Theory of Structuring in Organizations. LC 85-7992. (Monographs in Organizational Behavior & Industrial Relations: Vol. 2). 364p. 1985. 78.50 (*0-89232-500-3*) Jai Pr.

Bidwell, Charles E. & Wise, Sheldon. English for Jugo-Slavs. (Spoken English As a Second Language Ser.).Tr. of Kurs Govornog Engleskog Jezika. (CRO, ENG & SER.). 374p. 1980. pap. 110.00 incl. audio (*0-87950-609-1*); pap., student ed. 20.00 (*0-87950-305-X*) Spoken Lang Serv.

Bidwell, Charles E. & Wise, Sheldon. English for Jugo-Slavs. (Spoken English As a Second Language Ser.).Tr. of Kurs Govornog Engleskog Jezika. (CRO, ENG & SER.). 1980. audio 90.00 (*0-87950-608-3*) Spoken Lang Serv.

Bidwell, Charles E., et al. Structuring in Organizations Vol. 7: Ecosystem Theory Evaluated. Bacharach, Samuel B., ed. LC 87-2749. (Monographs in Organizational Behavior & Industrial Relations: Vol. 7). 397p. 1987. 78.50 (*0-89232-732-4*) Jai Pr.

Bidwell, Edwin M. Genealogy of the Seventh Generation of the Bidwell Family in America. 123p. 1988. reprint ed. pap. 25.00 (*0-8328-0253-0*); reprint ed. lib. bdg. 33.00 (*0-8328-0252-2*) Higginson Bk Co.

Bidwell, Glen I. How to Use the Repertory. 128p. (Orig.). pap. 8.95 (*0-8464-4237-X*) Beekman Pubs.

— How to Use the Repertory. 162p. (Orig.). 1983. pap. 5.95 (*0-85032-150-6*, Pub. by C W Daniel) Natl Bk Netwk.

***Bidwell, Jeffrey L.** Histocompatibility Testing. LC 99-87762. (Illus.). 400p. 2000. 84.00 (*1-86094-156-7*) World Scientific Pub.

Bidwell, Jeffrey L., jt. auth. see Hui, Kam M.

***Bidwell, John.** A Boy at Seven: Fear & Loathing in Aspen. 2000. pap. 3.95 (*1-86092-022-5*, Pub. by Travelman Pub) IPG Chicago.

Bidwell, John. Echoes of the Past: An Account of the First Emigrant Train to California, Fremont in the Conquest of California, the Discovery of Gold & Early Reminiscences. LC 72-9428. (Far Western Frontier Ser.). (Illus.). 824p. 1973. reprint ed. 13.95 (*0-405-04959-5*) Ayer.

Bidwell, John, et al. First Three Wagon Trains. (Illus.). 120p. (YA). (gr. 7-9). 1993. reprint ed. pap. 11.95 (*0-8323-0504-9*) Binford Mort.

Bidwell, John, ed. see Thompson, John S.

Bidwell, Joseph P. & Spotte, Stephen H. Artificial Seawaters: Formulas & Methods. LC 85-12556. (Life Science Ser.). 327p. 1985. 100.00 (*0-86720-057-X*) Jones & Bartlett.

Bidwell, Lee D. Miller. Sociology of the Family: Investigating Family Issues. LC 99-51525. 540p. (C). 1999. 61.00 (*0-02-309672-1*, Pub. by Allyn) P-H.

Bidwell, Percy W. History of Agriculture in the Northern United States: 1620-1860. 1990. 19.50 (*0-8446-1075-5*) Peter Smith.

— Rural Economy in New England at the Beginning of the 19th Century. LC 68-55480. (Reprints of Economic Classics Ser.). (Illus.). 159p. 1972. reprint ed. 35.00 (*0-678-00815-9*) Kelley.

Bidwell, Percy W. & Falconer, John I. History of Agriculture in the Northern United States 1620-1860. LC 72-11914. (Library of Early American Business & Industry: No. 59). xii, 512p. 1973. reprint ed. 65.00 (*0-678-00956-2*) Kelley.

Bidwell, Percy W., jt. auth. see Spiess, Mathias.

***Bidwell, Percy Wells.** Rural Economy in New England at the Beginning of the Nineteenth Century. (Facsimile Edition Series of Historic Papers Published by the Academy: Vol. 1). Orig. Title: Transactions of the Connecticut Academy of Arts & Sciences, Vol. 20. 400p. 1999. pap. 15.00 (*1-878508-14-8*) CT Acad Arts & Sciences.

Bidwell, R. L., ed. The Arab Bulletin 1916-1919: Bulletin of the Arab League in Cairo, 4 vols., Set. 1900p. (C). 1986. reprint ed. lib. bdg. 595.00 (*1-85207-025-0*, Pub. by Archive Editions) N Ross.

Bidwell, R. L., et al, eds. New Arabian Studies, Vol. 1. 224p. 1994. text 39.95 (*0-85989-408-8*, Pub. by Univ Exeter Pr) Northwestern U Pr.

— New Arabian Studies, Vol. 2. 245p. 1995. text 39.95 (*0-85989-452-5*, Pub. by Univ Exeter Pr) Northwestern U Pr.

Bidwell, R. L. & Smith, Rex, eds. Arabian & Islamic Studies: Articles Presented to R.B. Serjeant on the Occasion of His Retirement from the Sir Thomas Adams. LC 83-12027. (Illus.). 320p. (C). 1984. text 45.95 (*0-582-78308-9*) Longman.

Bidwell, R. L., jt. ed. see Serjeant, R. B.

***Bidwell, Ralph.** You Be the Judge: Is Justice for Sale? 1998. pap. 15.00 (*1-58339-161-4*) Triangle Press.

Bidwell, Robert E. Skills for Managerial Excellence. 250p. (C). 1995. pap. 43.00 (*0-536-58877-5*) Pearson Custom.

Bidwell, Robin L. The Dictionary of Modern Arab History: An A to Z of over 2000 Entries from 1798 to the Present Day. 2,400p. 1996. 255.00 (*0-7103-0505-2*, Pub. by Kegan Paul Intl) Col U Pr.

— Morocco under Colonial Rule: French Administration of Tribal Areas, 1912-1956. 349p. 1973. 52.50 (*0-7146-2877-8*, Pub. by F Cass Pubs) Intl Spec Bk.

Bidwell, Robin L., ed. Affairs of Arabia: 1905-1906, 2 vols., Set. 1971. 195.00 (*0-7146-2694-5*, Pub. by F Cass Pubs) Intl Spec Bk.

Bidwell, Robin L., intro. Arabian Personalities of the Early 20th Century. (Arabia Past & Present Ser.: Vol. 19). (Illus.). 380p. 1986. 60.00 (*0-906672-39-2*) Oleander Pr.

Bidwell, Shelford. Brassey's Artillery of the World. 2nd rev. ed. 270p. 1981. 67.50 (*0-08-027035-2*, Pergamon Pr) Elsevier.

— The Women's Royal Army Corps. LC 78-317843. (Famous Regiments Ser.). (Illus.). 156p. 1977. 8.95 (*0-85052-099-1*, Pub. by Leo Cooper) Trans-Atl Phila.

Bidwell, Shelford & Graham, Dominick. Fire Power: British Army Weapons & Theories (1904-1945) (Illus.). 366p. 1985. reprint ed. pap. text 24.95 (*0-04-942190-5*) Routledge.

Bidwell, Shelford, jt. auth. see Graham, Dominick.

Bidwell, William B., jt. ed. see Cole, Maija J.

Bidyadhar, Misra. Village Life in India: Past & Present. (C). 1988. 22.50 (*81-202-0194-9*, Pub. by Ajanta) S Asia.

Bidzinski, Martin. The Soccer Coaching Handbook. (Illus.). 224p. 1996. pap. 29.95 (*1-85223-973-5*, Pub. by Cro1wood) Trafalgar.

Bie, Catherine F. De, see De Bie, Catherine F.

Bie, Oskar. A History of the Pianoforte & Pianoforte Players. rev. ed. Naylor, Edward W. & Kellett, E. E., trs. 336p. 1990. reprint ed. lib. bdg. 79.00 (*0-7812-9110-0*) Rprt Serv.

— History of the Pianoforte & Pianoforte Players. 2nd ed. LC 66-28445. 1966. reprint ed. lib. bdg. 37.50 (*0-306-70938-4*) Da Capo.

— Schubert, the Man. LC 77-107794. (Select Bibliographies Reprint Ser.). 1977. 26.95 (*0-8369-5177-8*) Ayer.

— Schubert, the Man. 215p. 1990. reprint ed. lib. bdg. 69.00 (*0-7812-9086-4*) Rprt Serv.

Biebel, Andrew R., et al. PPC's 1120S Deskbook, 2 vols. Incl. Vol. 1. 1997. ring bd. 150.00 (*0-7646-0345-0*); Vol. 2. 1997. ring bd. 150.00 (*0-7646-0346-9*); Set ring bd. 150.00 (*0-7646-0344-2*) Prctnrs Pub Co.

Biebel, Belle M. The Small Business Reference Guide For: Home-Based Business, Small Manufacturers, Self-Publishers, Entrepreneurs, Craftsmen, Retailers, Writers, Artists. 63p. pap. 12.95 (*0-941825-02-7*) Bluechip Bks.

Biebel, David B. If God Is So Good, Why Do I Hurt So Bad? 176p. (gr. 10). 1995. reprint ed. mass mkt. 4.99 (*0-8007-8628-9*, Spire) Revell.

Biebel, Elizabeth M., jt. ed. see Beidler, Peter G.

Biebel, Kenneth, ed. see Miller, Floyd C.

Biebel, Paul, et al, eds. Symposium on Desmids & Other Zygnematales: Proceedings of the Second International Desmid Symposium, Lake Itasca, Minnesota, 21-25 Sept. 1976. (Nova Hedwigia Beihefte Ser.: Vol. 56). (Illus.). 203p. 1986. pap. 53.00 (*3-443-51004-3*, Pub. by Gebruder Borntraeger) Balogh.

Bieber, Doris M., ed. Energy & Congress, (1974-1978) LC 80-82112. 801p. 1982. lib. bdg. 50.00 (*0-89941-060-X*, 300750) W S Hein.

Bieber, Doris M., jt. auth. see Prince, Mary M.

Bieber, Eric & Loffer, F. The Gynecologic Resectoscope. (Minimally Invasive Gynecology Ser.). (Illus.). 256p. 1995. 75.00 (*0-86542-349-0*) Blackwell Sci.

***Bieber, Eric J. & Maclin, Victoria M.** Myomectomy. LC 98-21524. (Illus.). 310p. 1998. 105.00 (*0-86542-381-4*) Blackwell Sci.

Bieber, Hugo, ed. see Heine, Heinrich.

Bieber, Irving. Cognitive Psychoanalysis: Cognitive Processes in Psychopathology. 1996. pap. 50.00 (*1-56821-760-9*) Aronson.

Bieber, Irving, et al. Homosexuality. LC 88-14560. 358p. 1988. 50.00 (*0-87668-989-6*) Aronson.

Bieber, Janet. Highland Bride. 1999. mass mkt. 5.50 (*0-449-00284-5*, GM) Fawcett.

Bieber, Judy. Plantation Societies in the Era of European Expansion. LC 96-40468. (Expanding World Ser.: No. 18). 372p. 1997. text 124.95 (*0-86078-506-8*, Pub. by Variorum) Ashgate Pub Co.

An Asterisk (*) at the beginning of an entry indicates that the title is appearing for the first time.

Bieber, Judy. Power, Patronage & Political Violence: State Building on a Brazilian Frontier, 1822-1889. LC 99-22581. (Illus.). 304p. 1999. text 45.00 (*0-8032-1297-6*) U of Nebr Pr.

Bieber, Konrad, tr. see Aubrac, Lucie.

Bieber, Margarete. Alexander the Great in Greek & Roman Art. (Illus.). 98p. 1979. 30.00 (*0-916710-69-6*) Obol Intl.

— Laocoon: The Influence of the Group since Its Rediscovery. LC 67-16850. (Illus.). 78p. reprint ed. pap. 30.00 (*0-7837-3826-9*, 204364700010) Bks Demand.

Bieber, Margarete, ed. see Caviness, Madeline, et al.

Bieber, Nancy. Communion for a Quaker. LC 97-69932. 1997. write for info. (*0-87574-331-5*) Pendle Hill.

Bieber, Ralph P., ed. see Webb, James J.

***Bieberbach, Ludwig.** Conformal Mapping. LC 00-21321. (Illus.). 2000. write for info. (*0-8218-2105-9*) Am Math.

Bieberbach, Ludwig. Conformal Mapping. LC 53-7209. 1986. 12.00 (*0-8284-0090-3*) Chelsea Pub.

Bieberich, G. Sampson. Illustration File Environments: Complete Pond Environment. (Series One). (Illus.). 48p. 1994. 31.95 (*1-57289-006-1*) Meanderings.

— Illustration File Environments: Complete Prehistoric Cretaceous Period. (Series Two). (Illus.). 48p. 1994. 31.95 (*1-57289-013-4*) Meanderings.

— Illustration Files: Bullfrog. (Series Outlines). (Illus.). 8p. 1994. 5.95 (*1-57289-000-2*) Meanderings.

— Illustration Files: Dragonfly. (Series One). (Illus.). 1994. 5.95 (*1-57289-001-0*) Meanderings.

— Illustration Files: Euoplocephalus. (Series V). (Illus.). 8p. 1994. 5.95 (*1-57289-007-X*) Meanderings.

— Illustration Files: Large-Mouth Bass. (Series One). (Illus.). 8p. 1994. 5.95 (*1-57289-002-9*) Meanderings.

— Illustration Files: Mallard Duck. (Series One). (Illus.). 8p. 1994. 5.95 (*1-57289-003-7*) Meanderings.

— Illustration Files: Painted Turtle. (Series One). (Illus.). 8p. 1994. 5.95 (*1-57289-004-5*) Meanderings.

— Illustration Files: Pond Environment. (Series One). (Illus.). 8p. 1994. 5.95 (*1-57289-005-3*) Meanderings.

— Illustration Files: Prehistoric Environment - Cretaceous Period. (Series Two). (Illus.). 8p. 1994. 5.95 (*1-57289-012-6*) Meanderings.

— Illustration Files: Pteranodon. (Series Two). (Illus.). 8p. 1994. 5.95 (*1-57289-008-8*) Meanderings.

— Illustration Files: Spinosaurus. (Series Two). (Illus.). 8p. 1994. 5.95 (*1-57289-009-6*) Meanderings.

— Illustration Files: Triceratops. (Series Two). (Illus.). 8p. 1994. 5.95 (*1-57289-010-X*) Meanderings.

— Illustration Files: Tyrannosaurus Rex. (Series Two). (Illus.). 8p. 1994. 5.95 (*1-57289-011-8*) Meanderings.

Bieberstein, F. A. Marschall Von, see Marschall von Bieberstein, F. A.

Bieberstein, Klaus. Josua - Jordan - Jericho: Archaologie, Geschichte und Theologie der Landnahmeerzahlungen Josua 1-6. (Orbis Biblicus et Orientalis Ser.: Vol. 143). (GER.). 492p. 1995. text 98.00 (*3-7278-1016-5*, Pub. by Presses Univ Fribourg) Eisenbrauns.

***Bieberstein, Sabine.** Verschwiegene Jungerinnen - Vergessene Zeuginnen: Gebrochene Konzepte im Lukasevangelium. (Novum Testamentum et Orbis Antiquus Ser.: Vol. 38). (GER.). xii, 314p. 1998. text 66.00 (*3-7278-1180-3*, Pub. by Ed Univ Fri) Eisenbrauns.

***Biebesheimer, Christina.** Justice Beyond Our Borders. 216p. 2000. pap. 21.95 (*1-886938-80-6*) IADB.

***Biebesheimer, Christina & Cordovez, Carlos, eds.** La Justicia Mas Alla de Nuestras Fronteras: Experiencias de Reforma Utiles Para America Latina y el Caribe. (SPA.). 237p. 2000. 21.95 (*1-886938-67-9*) IADB.

***Biebl, Andrew R. & Ranweiler, Robert J.** A CPA's Guide to Saving Tax Dollars for Farm Clients. 2nd rev. ed. 252p. 1999. pap. 45.00 (*0-87051-248-X*, 090460) Am Inst CPA.

***Biebl, Andrew R., et al.** Guide to Choice of Business Entity, Vol. 1. 1999. ring bd. 79.00 (*0-7646-0759-6*) Prctnrs Pub Co.

Biebl, Andrew R., et al. PPC Tax Planning Guide - S Corporations, 3 vols. Incl. Vol. 1. PPC Tax Planning Guide - S Corporations. Carefoot, George M. & Esch, John B. 1998. ring bd. (*0-7646-0470-8*); Vol. 2. PPC Tax Planning Guide - S Corporations. Carefoot, George M. & Esch, John B. 1998. ring bd. 180.00 (*0-7646-0471-6*); Vol. 3. PPC Tax Planning Guide - S Corporations. Carefoot, George M. & Esch, John B. 1998. ring bd. 180.00 (*0-7646-0472-4*); Vol. 1. Carefoot, George M. & Burris, Richard L. 1997. ring bd. (*0-7646-0176-8*); Vol. 2. Carefoot, Gerorge M. & Burris, Richard L. 1997. ring bd. (*0-7646-0177-6*); Vol. 3. Carefoot, George M. & Burris, Richard L. 1997. ring bd. (*0-7646-0178-4*); 170.00 (*0-7646-0175-X*); 180.00 (*0-7646-0469-4*) Prctnrs Pub Co.

***Biebl, Andrew R., et al.** PPC's 1120S Deskbook, 2 vols. Incl. Vol. 1. PPC's 1120S Deskbook. 1999. ring bd. (*0-7646-0908-4*); Vol. 2. PPC's 1120S Deskbook. 1999. ring bd. (*0-7646-0909-2*); 1999. Set ring bd. 150.00 (*0-7646-0907-6*) Prctnrs Pub Co.

Biebl, Andrew R., et al. PPC's 1120S Deskbook, Vol. 1. 1998. ring bd. write for info. (*0-7646-0561-5*) Prctnrs Pub Co.

— PPC's 1120S Deskbook, Vol. 2. 1998. ring bd. write for info. (*0-7646-0562-3*) Prctnrs Pub Co.

— PPC's 1120S Deskbook, Vols. 1 & 2. 1998. ring bd. 150.00 (*0-7646-0560-7*) Prctnrs Pub Co.

— PPC's 1040 Deskbook, 2 vols. Incl. Vol. 1. 1997. ring bd. 150.00 (*0-7646-0263-2*); Vol. 2. 1997. ring bd. 150.00 (*0-7646-0264-0*); 150.00 (*0-7646-0052-4*); 150.00 (*0-7646-0262-4*) Prctnrs Pub Co.

***Biebl, Andrew R., et al.** PPC's 1040 Deskbook, 2 vols. 1999. ring bd. 150.00 (*0-7646-0850-9*) Prctnrs Pub Co.

— PPC's 1040 Deskbook, Vol. 1. 1999. ring bd. write for info. (*0-7646-0851-7*) Prctnrs Pub Co.

— PPC's 1040 Deskbook, Vol. 2. 1999. ring bd. write for info. (*0-7646-0852-5*) Prctnrs Pub Co.

Biebl, Andrew R., jt. auth. see Behrenfeld, William H.

Biebuych, Tony, jt. auth. see Drake, Madeline.

Biebuyck, Benjamin, et al, eds. Faith & Fiction: Interdisciplinary Studies on the Interplay Between Metaphor & Religion: A Selection of Papers from the 25th LAUD-Symposium of the Gerhard Mercator University of Duisburg on "Metaphor & Religion" (Duisburg Papers on Research in Language & Culture: Vol. 37). 253p. (C). 1998. pap. text 45.95 (*0-8204-3624-0*) P Lang Pubng.

— Faith & Fiction: Interdisciplinary Studies on the Interplay Between Metaphor & Religion a Selection of Papers from the 25th Laud-symposium of the Gerhard Mercator University of Duisburg on 'Metaphor & Religion' (Duisburg Papers on Research in Language & Culture: Vol. 37). 253p. 1998. pap. 45.95 (*3-631-33760-4*) P Lang Pubng.

Biebuyck, Brunhilde, tr. see Rouget, Gilbert.

Biebuyck, Daniel P. & Biech, E. The ASTD Trainer's Sourcebook Series, Creativity. Roe, Richard L., ed. LC 96-75330. 302p. 1996. pap. 39.95 (*0-07-053445-4*) McGraw.

Biebuyck, Daniel P. & Mateene, Kahombo C., eds. The Mwindo Epic from the Banyanga (Congo Republic) 1969. pap. 12.95 (*0-520-02049-9*, Pub. by U CA Pr) Cal Prin Full Svc.

Biebuyck, Julian F., jt. ed. see Lydic, Ralph.

Biebuyck, Julien. Anesthesia: Biologic Foundations. LC 97-23913. 1585p. 1997. text 229.00 (*0-397-58742-2*) Lppncott W & W.

Biech, E., jt. auth. see Biebuyck, Daniel P.

Biech, Elaine. The Business of Consulting: The Basics & Beyond. LC 98-7265. (Business & Management Ser.). 240p. 1998. 39.95 (*0-7879-4021-6*) Jossey-Bass.

— Consultant's Legal Guide. LC 99-6480. 300p. 1999. 49.95 (*0-7879-4763-6*) New Lexington.

***Biech, Elaine.** Consulting 2001. 2000. 94.95 (*0-7879-5335-0*); pap. 44.95 (*0-7879-5336-9*) Jossey-Bass.

Biech, Elaine. TQM for Training. (Illus.). 221p. 1992. 29.95 (*0-07-005210-7*) McGraw.

***Biech, Elaine.** Training 2001. 2000. 94.95 (*0-7879-5334-2*) Jossey-Bass.

— Training 2001, Vol. 1. 2000. pap. 44.95 (*0-7879-5333-4*) Jossey-Bass.

Biech, Elaine, ed. The 1999 Annual, 2 vols. 320p. 1998. pap. 79.95 (*0-7879-4452-1*) Jossey-Bass.

— The 1999 Annual Vol. 1: Training. 320p. 1998. pap. 44.95 (*0-7879-4541-2*) Jossey-Bass.

— The 1999 Annual Vol. 2: Consulting. 320p. 1998. pap. 44.95 (*0-7879-4542-0*) Jossey-Bass.

— The 2000 Annual Vol. 1: Training. 320p. 1999. pap. 44.95 (*0-7879-4712-1*) Jossey-Bass.

— The 2000 Annual Vol. 2: Consulting. 320p. 1999. pap. 44.95 (*0-7879-4713-X*) Jossey-Bass.

***Biech, Elaine & Vander Linde, Karen.** Building High Performance: Tools & Techniques for Training & Learning. LC 98-67403. 360p. 1998. pap. 49.95 (*0-944533-25-6*) Am Soc Train & Devel.

Biechler, James E. The Religious Language of Nicholas of Cusa. LC 75-23096. (American Academy of Religion, Dissertation Ser.: Vol. 8). 248p. reprint ed. pap. 76.90 (*0-608-08842-0*, 206948100004) Bks Demand.

Biechler, James E. & Bond, H. Lawrence, eds. Nicholas of Cusa on Interreligious Harmony: Text, Concordance & Translation of De Pace Fidei. LC 90-25778. (Texts & Studies in Religion: Vol. 55). 254p. 1991. lib. bdg. 89.95 (*0-88946-736-6*) E Mellen.

Bieck, Peter R., ed. Colonic Drug Absorption & Metabolism. LC 93-17265. (Drugs & the Pharmaceutical Sciences Ser.: Vol. 60). (Illus.). 240p. 1993. text 155.00 (*0-8247-9013-8*) Dekker.

Bieda, John. Practical Product Assurance Management. LC 97-27776. 350p. 1997. 41.00 (*0-87389-375-1*, H0966) ASQ Qual Pr.

Biedak, Aleksander. Zeby Polska . . . (Let Poland Be . . .) (POL., Illus.). 60p. (Orig.). 1986. 6.00 (*0-930401-06-9*) Artex Pub.

Biedenbender, Richard E. Logistics Support Analysis Management. 574p. 1992. 60.00 (*0-07-005220-4*) McGraw.

Biedenbender, Richard E., et al. The ILS Manager's LSA Toolkit: Availability Engineering. 1993. 60.00 (*0-318-69748-3*) McGraw.

Biedenharn, L. C. Quantum Group Symetry & Q-Tensor Algebras. 270p. 1995. text 64.00 (*981-02-2331-5*) World Scientific Pub.

***Biedenweg, Kaarl.** Personal Finance. (Illus.). 80p. (YA). (gr. 5). 1999. pap. text 9.95 (*1-58037-091-8*, Pub. by M Twain Media) Carson-Dellos.

***Biedenweg, Karl.** Basic Economics. (Illus.). 80p. 1999. pap. text 9.95 (*1-58037-090-X*, Pub. by M Twain Media) Carson-Dellos.

Bieder, Robert E. Native American Communities in Wisconsin, 1600-1960. LC 94-24314. (Illus.). 272p. (C). 1995. pap. text 18.95 (*0-299-14524-7*); lib. bdg. 39.95 (*0-299-14520-4*) U of Wis Pr.

— Science Encounters the Indian, 1820-1880: The Early Years of American Ethnology. LC 86-40068. (Illus.). 304p. 1989. pap. 15.95 (*0-8061-2176-9*) U of Okla Pr.

Biederbick, Karl-Heinrich. Untersuchungen Zur Reliefbedingten Variation Von Vegetation und Standort. (Dissertationes Botanicae Ser.: Band 176). (GER., Illus.). viii, 189p. 1991. pap. 48.00 (*3-443-64088-5*, Pub. by Gebruder Borntraeger) Balogh.

Biederman, Charles. Art Mirrors Psychological Humanizing Experience of Reality. 158p. (Orig.). 1996. pap. 15.50 (*0-614-29906-3*) Art History.

— Art, Science, Realty. 77p. 1988. 15.50 (*0-9600002-5-9*) Art History.

— The Dehumanization & Denaturalization of Modern Art. 131p. 1992. 15.50 (*0-9600002-6-7*) Art History.

— The End of Modernism; Figurative or Abstract. 136p. (Orig.). 1994. pap. 15.50 (*0-614-29905-5*) Art History.

— Nature Art Anew. 218p. 1993. 15.50 (*0-9600002-7-5*) Art History.

— The New Cezanne. LC 58-10644. 1958. boxed set, bds. 25.00 incl. audio, Apple II (*0-9600002-2-4*) Art History.

— Search for New Arts. LC 79-90835. 1979. 25.00 (*0-9605614-0-4*); pap. 25.00 (*0-9605614-1-2*) Art History.

Biederman, Charles, jt. auth. see Bohm, David.

Biederman, David, jt. auth. see Zuckerman, Amy.

Biederman, H. & Osada, Y. Plasma Polymerization Processes. (Plasma Technology Ser.: Vol. 3). x, 210p. 1992. 140.00 (*0-444-88724-5*) Elsevier.

Biederman, Jerry. Earth Angels: True Stories about Real People Who Bring Heaven to Earth. 272p. 1998. reprint ed. pap. 10.00 (*0-7679-0005-7*) Broadway BDD.

Biederman, Jerry & Biederman, Lorin M. Earth Angels: True Stories about Real People Who Bring Heaven to Earth. LC 97-15365. 256p. 1997. 18.00 (*0-7679-0004-9*) Broadway BDD.

Biederman, Jerry & Michelle, Lorin. 101 Ways to See the Light: How You Can Have a Near-Death Experience. 1996. mass mkt. 6.99 (*0-312-95665-7*, Pub. by Tor Bks) St Martin.

Biederman, Lorin M., jt. auth. see Biederman, Jerry.

Biederman, Marcia. The Makeover. (Academy First Mystery Ser.). 240p. 1984. pap. 5.95 (*0-89733-226-1*) Academy Chi Pubs.

Biederman, Marcia. Sismo. LC 93-1866. 210p. 1993. 21.95 (*0-8027-3243-7*) Walker & Co.

Biederman, Patricia W., jt. auth. see Bennis, Warren.

Biederman, Paul. The U. S. Airline Industry: End of an Era. LC 81-17845. 198p. 1982. 38.50 (*0-275-90763-5*, C0763, Praeger Pubs) Greenwood.

Biederman, Robert, ed. see Schmitt.

Biederman-Thorson, M. A., tr. Physiological Plant Ecology. rev. ed. LC 79-26396. (Illus.). 304p. 1980. 34.00 (*3-540-09795-3*) Spr-Verlag.

Biederman-Thorson, M. A., tr. see Barth, F. G.

Biederman-Thorson, M. A., tr. see Schmidt, Richard F., ed.

Biederman-Thorson, M. A., tr. see Schmidt, Richard F. & Thews, G. E., eds.

Biederman-Thorson, M. A., tr. see Thews, G. E. & Vaupel, P.

Biederman-Thorson, M. Ann, tr. see Kummer, Hans.

Biedermann, Gertrude & Anderson, Martha. Traditional Bobbin Lace: Patterns in Torchin, Guipure & India. Kliot, Jules & Kliot, Kaethe, eds. 1975. reprint ed. pap. 21.00 (*0-916896-07-2*) Lacis Pubns.

Biedermann, Hans. Dictionary of Symbolism: Cultural Icons & the Meanings Behind Them. Hulbert, James, tr. from GER. (Illus.). 480p. 1992. lib. bdg. 45.00 (*0-8160-2593-2*) Facts on File.

— Dictionary of Symbolism: Cultural Icons & the Meanings Behind Them. Hulbert, James, tr. LC 93-30616. (Illus.). 480p. 1994. reprint ed. pap. 21.95 (*0-452-01118-3*, Mer) NAL.

— Dictionary of Symbols. (SPA.). 1993. 69.95 (*0-7859-9726-1*) Fr & Eur.

Biedermann-Thorson, M. A., tr. see Schmidt, Richard F., ed.

Biedermen, Edwin W., ed. Atlas of Selected Oil & Gas Reservoir Rocks from North America: A Color Guidebook to the Petrology of Selected Oil & Gas Reservoir Rocks from the United States & Canada. LC 85-29467. (Wiley-Interscience Publications). 419p. reprint ed. pap. 129.90 (*0-7837-2385-7*, 204007100006) Bks Demand.

Biederwolf, William E. Prophecy Handbook. 728p. 1991. pap. 14.99 (*0-529-06991-1*, PHB) World Pubng.

***Biederwolf, William Edward.** The Millennium Bible: Complete Commentary on All Scripture Passages Related to the Second Coming. 728p. 1999. pap. 6.99 (*1-58558-002-3*) Global Pubs.

***Biedrzycki, Anita.** The Radiography Procedure & Competency Manual. (Illus.). 472p. (C). 2000. pap. text 29.00 (*0-8036-0672-9*) Davis Co.

***Biefang, Sibylle, ed.** Strategies for Communication on Food Biotechnology. (Illus.). 80p. (C). 2000. reprint ed. pap. text 20.00 (*0-7881-8991-3*) DIANE Pub.

Biefeld, R. M., ed. Compound Semiconductor Strained-Layer Superlattices. 320p. 1989. text 81.00 (*0-87849-587-8*, Pub. by Trans T Pub) Enfield Pubs NH.

Bieg. Payroll Accounting Test Key. 93rd ed. (Swc-Accounting). 1992. mass mkt. 7.00 (*0-538-81209-5*) S-W Pub.

— Payroll Accounting Tests. 93rd ed. (Swc-Accounting). 1992. mass mkt. 14.75 (*0-538-81208-7*) S-W Pub.

— 2000 Payroll Accounting. 10th ed. (SWC-Accounting Ser.). 1999. pap. 54.95 (*0-324-01458-9*) Sth-Wstrn College.

Bieg, Bernard. Payroll Accounting. 7th ed. (Payroll Accounting Ser.). 1996. pap. 46.95 (*0-538-86702-7*) S-W Pub.

Bieg, Bernard J. Managing Payroll Systems: Payroll Accounting. 6th ed. (AH - Payroll Accounting Ser.). 1996. 4.95 (*0-538-86457-5*) S-W Pub.

— Payroll Accounting LC 99-158517. 1999. write for info. (*0-324-00389-7*) Sth-Wstrn College.

— Payroll Accounting, 1998 Edition. 8th ed. (Miscellaneous/Catalogs Ser.). 416p. 1999. pap. 40.95 (*0-538-86742-6*) Thomson Learn.

— Payroll Accounting, 1997. 7th ed. (Miscellaneous/Catalogs Ser.). 1999. mass mkt. 39.95 (*0-538-86694-2*) S-W Pub.

— Payroll Accounting 1996 Edition. 6th ed. (SWC-Accounting). 416p. 1995. mass mkt. 35.75 (*0-538-85723-4*) S-W Pub.

— Payroll Accounting, 8th ed. 8th ed. 1999. pap. text 53.95 (*0-538-86743-4*) S-W Pub.

Bieg, Bernard J., jt. auth. see Keeling, B. Lewis.

Biega, B. C. Thirteen Is My Lucky Number: The Dramatic True Story of a Polish Resistance Fighter. (Illus.). 328p. 1996. 21.95 (*1-57087-204-X*) Prof Pr NC.

Biegel, David E. Social Networks & Mental Health: An Annotated Bibliography. LC 84-23585. 391p. 1985. reprint ed. pap. 121.30 (*0-608-01475-3*, 205951900001) Bks Demand.

Biegel, David E. & Blum, Arthur. Innovations in Practice & Service Delivery Across the Lifespan. LC 98-9710. (Innovations in Practice & Service Delivery with Vulnerable Populations Ser.). (Illus.). 368p. (C). 1998. text 47.95 (*0-19-511155-9*) OUP.

Biegel, David E. & Blum, Arthur, eds. Aging & Caregiving: Theory, Research & Policy. (Focus Editions Ser.: Vol. 110). (Illus.). 296p. (C). 1990. text 59.95 (*0-8039-3566-8*); pap. text 24.95 (*0-8039-3567-6*) Sage.

— Aging & Caregiving: Theory, Research, & Policy. LC 89-27848. (Sage Focus Editions Ser.: Vol. 110). 294p. 1990. reprint ed. pap. 91.20 (*0-608-02982-3*, 205962200006) Bks Demand.

Biegel, David E., et al. Building Support Networks for the Elderly: Theory & Applications. LC 84-8337. (Sage Human Services Guides Ser.: Vol. 36). 160p. 1984. reprint ed. pap. 49.60 (*0-608-02227-6*, 204409100003) Bks Demand.

— Family Caregiving in Chronic Illness: Alzheimer's Disease, Cancer, Heart Disease, Mental Illness, & Stroke. (Family Caregiver Applications Ser.: Vol. 1). (Illus.). 368p. (C). 1990. text 45.00 (*0-8039-3213-8*); pap. text 22.50 (*0-8039-3214-6*) Sage.

— Family Caregiving in Chronic Illness: Alzheimer's Disease, Cancer, Heart Disease, Mental Illness, & Stroke. LC 90-43952. (Family Caregiver Applications Ser.: No. 1). 332p. 1991. reprint ed. pap. 103.00 (*0-608-01267-X*, 206201600001) Bks Demand.

— Social Support Networks: A Bibliography, 15. LC 88-32824. 347p. 1989. lib. bdg. 79.50 (*0-313-26604-2*, BSX, Greenwood Pr) Greenwood.

Biegel, David E., jt. auth. see Wells, Kathleen.

Biegel, David E., jt. ed. see Wells, Kathleen.

Biegel, Harvey M. Battleship Country: The Battle Fleet at Long Beach-San Pedro, California, 1919-1940. LC 82-63060. (Illus.). 76p. 1983. 7.95 (*0-933126-30-1*) Pictorial Hist.

Biegel, Richard A. Easy Object Programming with DBase for Windows. 1994. pap. 34.95 incl. disk (*0-13-185540-9*) P-H.

Biegel, Richard A. & Pendharkar, Sumant S. Visual dBASE 5.5 for Windows. LC 95-48342. 1996. text. write for info. (*0-02-802618-7*) Glencoe.

Biegel, Richard A., jt. auth. see Pendharkar, Sumant S.

Biegel, Richard A., jt. auth. see Pendharker, Sumant S.

Biegel, Thomas. Sprachwahlverhalten Bei Deutschfranzosischer Mehrsprachigkeit. (Studien zur Allgemeinen und Romanischen Sprachwissenschaft Ser.: Bd. 4). (GER., Illus.). XII, 252p. 1996. 51.95 (*3-631-31074-9*) P Lang Pubng.

***Biegelbauer, Peter S.** 130 Years of Catching up with the West: A Comparative Perspective of Hungarian Science & Technology Policy-Making since Industrialization. LC 99-75542. 250p. 2000. text 74.95 (*1-84014-930-2*, Pub. by Ashgate Pub) Ashgate Pub Co.

Biegeleisen, J. I. Classic Type Faces & How to Use Them: Including 91 Complete Fonts. LC 95-15727. Orig. Title: Art Directors' Workbook of Type Faces. 256p. 1995. pap. 12.95 (*0-486-28727-0*) Dover.

Biegeleisen, J. I. & Ubinas, Dave. 1001 Cartoon-Style Illustrations. LC 95-39683. (Pictorial Archive Ser.). (Illus.). 144p. 1996. pap. 8.95 (*0-486-29047-6*) Dover.

Biegeleisen, Jacob I. Complete Book of Silk Screen Printing Production. (Illus.). 253p. (Orig.). (C). 1963. pap. 6.95 (*0-486-21100-2*) Dover.

— Job Resumes. rev. ed. 112p. 1991. reprint ed. pap. 8.95 (*0-399-51692-1*, Perigee Bks) Berkley Pub.

— Make Your Job Interview a Success. 4th ed. 240p. 1994. per. 12.95 (*0-671-87070-X*, Arc) IDG Bks.

Biegeleisen, Jacob I. & Cohn, J. A. Silk Screen Techniques. (Illus.). 185p. 1958. pap. 6.95 (*0-486-20433-2*) Dover.

Biegeleisen, Jacob I. & Cohn, M. A. Silk Screen Techniques. (Illus.). 1990. 22.50 (*0-8446-0491-7*) Peter Smith.

Biegelsen, D. K., et al, eds. Energy Beam - Solid Interactions & Transient Thermal Processing, 1984, Vol. 35. LC 85-5113. 1985. text 17.50 (*0-931837-00-6*) Materials Res.

Bieger, George R., jt. auth. see Gerlach, Gail J.

Biegert, E., ed. A Topical Guide to "Folia Primatologica", (1963-1978), Vols. 1-30. 160p. 1980. pap. 34.00 (*3-8055-0781-X*) S Karger.

Biegert, John E. Listening to the Spirit: Prayers for All Occasions. LC 95-51674. 104p. (Orig.). 1996. pap. 11.95 (*0-8298-1075-7*) Pilgrim OH.

— Looking up . . . While Lying Down: Thoughts, Poems, & Prayers for Those in the Hospital. (Looking up Ser.). 24p. 1979. pap. 1.95 (*0-8298-0364-5*) Pilgrim OH.

— Mirando Hacia Arriba en Medio de la Enfermedad (Looking up . . . While Lying Down) (Looking up Ser.).Tr. of Looking Up While Lying Down (Thoughts, Poems & Prayers for Those in the Hospital). (SPA.). 24p. (Orig.). 1983. pap. 1.95 (*0-8298-0663-6*) Pilgrim OH.

— My Loved One Is Dying. (Looking up Ser.). 24p. (Orig.). 1990. pap. 1.95 (*0-8298-0846-9*) Pilgrim OH.

— So We're Growing Older. (Looking up Ser.). 1982. pap. 1.95 (*0-8298-0436-6*) Pilgrim OH.

B

— Staying In . . . (Looking up Ser.). 24p. 1985. pap. 1.95 (*0-8298-0567-2*) Pilgrim OH.
— When Death Has Touched Your Life: Thoughts, Poems, & Prayers at a Time of Loss. (Looking up Ser.). 24p. 1981. pap. 1.95 (*0-8298-0455-2*) Pilgrim OH.
Biegler, Lorenz T., et al, eds. Large-Scale Optimization with Applications Pt. 1: Optimization in Inverse Problems & Design. LC 97-22879. (IMA Volumes in Mathematics & Its Applications Ser.: No. 93). (Illus.). 352p. 1997. text 59.95 (*0-387-98287-6*) Spr-Verlag.
— Large-Scale Optimization with Applications Pt. 1: Optimization in Inverse Problems & Design, Pt. I. LC 97-22879. (IMA Volumes in Mathematics & Its Applications Ser.: No. 92). (Illus.). 230p. 1997. 59.95 (*0-387-98286-8*) Spr-Verlag.
— Large-Scale Optimization with Applications Pt. 1: Optimization in Inverse Problems & Design, Pt. III. LC 97-22879. (IMA Volumes in Mathematics & Its Applications Ser.: No. 94). (Illus.). 224p. 1997. text 59.95 (*0-387-98288-4*) Spr-Verlag.
Biegler, Lorenz T., et al. Systematic Methods for Chemical Process Design. LC 96-52100. 700p. (C). 1997. 99.00 (*0-13-492422-3*) P-H.
Biegler, Lorenz T., ed. see Fourth International Conference on Foundations of.
Biegman, Nicolaas H. Egypt: Moulids, Saints & Sufis. (Illus.). 176p. 1991. 49.95 (*0-7103-0415-3*, A5534) Routledge.
Biegon, Anat & Volkow, Nora D., eds. Sites of Drug Action in the Human Brain. LC 94-25232. 192p. 1995. boxed set 199.95 (*0-8493-7653-X*, 7653) CRC Pr.
Biegun, Virginia, ed. see Joachim, Kitty.
Biehak, N., et al. Moving on - Young People & Leaving Care Schemes. LC 96-183828. 320p. 1995. pap. 45.00 (*0-11-321891-5*, HM18915, Pub. by Statnry Office) Bernan Associates.
Biehal. Buyer Analysis. 2000. pap. 47.74 (*0-07-005221-2*) McGraw.
Biehal, Nina, jt. auth. see Wade, Jim.
Biehl, ed. Euripidis: Cyclops. (GRE.). 1983. 18.95 (*3-322-00833-9*, T1324, Pub. by B G Teubner) U of Mich Pr.
— Euripidis: Ion. (GRE.). 1979. 34.50 (*3-322-00834-7*, T1331, Pub. by B G Teubner) U of Mich Pr.
— Euripidis: Orestes. (GRE.). 1975. 31.50 (*3-322-00835-5*, T1335, Pub. by B G Teubner) U of Mich Pr.
— Euripidis: Troades. (GRE.). 1970. 19.95 (*3-322-00136-9*, T1339, Pub. by B G Teubner) U of Mich Pr.
Biehl, Allen, jt. auth. see Hadfield, Jeff.
Biehl, B. Heirloom Memories. 1994. 29.95 (*0-00-504371-9*) Collins SF.
Biehl, Bobb. Dreaming. 1996. 19.99 (*0-345-39565-4*) Ballantine Pub Grp.
— The Effective Board Member: Secrets of Making a Significant Contribution to Any Organization You Serve. LC 97-38552. 1998. pap. write for info. (*0-08-546174-1*, Pergamon Pr) Elsevier.
— Masterplanning: A Complete Guide for Building a Strategic Plan for Your Business, Church, or Organization. LC 97-958. 288p. (Orig.). 1997. pap. 16.99 (*0-8054-6096-9*) Broadman.
Biehl, Bobb. Memories: A Priceless Heirloom. 266p. 1997. 40.00 (*0-9664049-1-2*) Premiere Publng.
Biehl, Bobb. Mentoring: Confidence in Finding a Mentor & Becoming One. 1997. pap. 11.99 (*0-8054-6347-X*) Broadman.
— On My Own Handbook: 100 Secrets of Success. 320p. (Orig.). 1991. pap. 10.99 (*1-55513-338-X*) Chariot Victor.
— Stop Setting Goals If You Would Rather. 1996. pap. 9.99 (*0-345-40778-4*, Moorings) Ballantine Pub Grp.
— 30 Days to Confident Leadership. LC 97-35170. Orig. Title: Increasing Your Leadership Confidence. 240p. 1998. pap. 11.99 (*0-8054-0173-3*) Broadman.
— Weathering the Midlife Storm. LC 96-23081. 224p. 1996. 17.99 (*1-56476-583-0*, Victor Bks) Chariot Victor.
— Wisdom for Men. Davis, Cathy, ed. 144p. (Orig.). 1994. pap. 6.99 (*0-7814-0183-6*) Chariot Victor.
Biehl, Bobb & Engstrom, Ted W. The Effective Board Member: Secrets of Making a Significant Contribution to Any Organization. 240p. 1998. pap. 11.99 (*0-8054-0174-1*) Broadman.
Biehl, Cathleen S., jt. ed. see Biehl, Michael M.
Biehl, Dieter, ed. see International Institute of Public Finance Congress.
Biehl, Janet. Finding Our Way: Rethinking Eco-Feminist Politics. LC 90-83625. 159p. 48.99 (*0-921689-79-9*, Pub. by Black Rose); pap. 19.99 (*0-921689-78-0*, Pub. by Black Rose) Consort Bk Sales.
— Murray Bookchin Reader. 288p. 1999. 53.99 (*1-55164-119-4*); pap. 24.99 (*1-55164-118-6*) Black Rose CA.
— The Politics of Social Ecology: Libertarian Municipalism. 204p. 1997. pap. 19.99 (*1-55164-100-3*, Pub. by Black Rose) Consort Bk Sales.
— The Politics of Social Ecology: Libertarian Municipalism. 204p. 1997. 48.99 (*1-55164-101-1*, Pub. by Black Rose) Consort Bk Sales.
— Rethinking Eco-Feminist Politics. 188p. (C). 1991. 25.00 (*0-89608-392-6*); pap. 12.00 (*0-89608-391-8*) South End Pr.
Biehl, Janet & Staudenmaier, Peter. Ecofascism: Lessons from the German Experience. LC 95-40752. 73p. (Orig.). 1996. pap. 7.00 (*1-873176-73-2*, AK Pr San Fran) AK Pr Dist.
Biehl, Janet, jt. auth. see Bookchin, Murray.
***Biehl, Kathy & Calishain, Tara.** The Lawyer's Guide to Internet Legal Research. LC 00-41336. 2000. pap. write for info. (*0-8108-3885-0*) Scarecrow.
Biehl, Maria Loreto, jt. auth. see Morrison, Andrew.
Biehl, Maria Loreto, jt. ed. see Morrison, Andrew R.
Biehl, Michael M. & Biehl, Cathleen S., eds. The Medical Staff: Legal Issues. 136p. 1990. 30.00 (*0-918945-07-0*) Am Hlth Lawyers.
Biehle, Garrett. The MCAT Physics Book. 444p. 2000. pap. 29.95 (*1-889057-00-2*) Nova Pr.
Biehler. Psychology: Applied Teaching, 7 vols. (C). 1992. pap., teacher ed. 3.96 (*0-395-63771-6*) HM.
— Psychology Applied Teaching, 8 vols. (C). 1996. pap., teacher ed. 11.96 (*0-395-82880-5*) HM.
— Psychology Applied Teaching: Testbank, 8 vols. (C). 1996. pap., suppl. ed. 11.96 (*0-395-82881-3*) HM.
Biehler, Robert F. Psychology: Applied Teaching, 7 vols. (C). 1992. pap. 61.56 (*0-395-61598-4*) HM.
Biehler, Robert F., et al, eds. Applications & Modelling in Learning & Teaching Mathematics. 1989. text 97.00 (*0-470-21315-9*) P-H.
Biehler, Robert F. & Snowman, Jack. Psychology Applied to Teaching. 5th ed. LC 85-60849. 752p. (C). 1985. 47.96 (*0-395-40820-2*); 47.96 (*0-395-40822-9*); 47.96 (*0-395-40821-0*); audio 5.00 (*0-395-40823-7*) HM.
— Psychology Applied to Teaching, 6 vols. 6th ed. (C). 1989. pap. text 2.76 (*0-395-52634-5*); pap. text 3.16 (*0-395-52636-1*) HM.
— Psychology Applied to Teaching, 6 vols. 6th ed. (C). 1990. 80.36 (*0-395-52906-9*) HM.
— Psychology Applied to Teaching, 7 vols. 6th ed. (C). 1990. pap. text 9.96 (*0-395-53286-8*) HM.
— Psychology Applied to Teaching, 8 vols. 8th ed. LC 96-76870. 672p. (C). 1996. pap. text 63.16 (*0-395-77685-6*) HM.
— Psychology Applied to Teaching, 8 vols. 8th ed. (C). 1996. pap. text, student ed. 21.56 (*0-395-83817-7*) HM.
Biehler, Rolf, et al, eds. Didactics of Mathematics as a Scientific Discipline. LC 93-39782. (Mathematics Education Library: Vol. 13). 1993. lib. bdg. 223.00 (*0-7923-2613-X*) Kluwer Academic.
Biehler, Scott, jt. auth. see Burdenko, Igor.
***Biehn, Janice, et al.** The Complete Idiot's Guide to Beating Debt for Canadians. 400p. 2000. pap. 25.95 (*0-13-086726-8*, Prentice Hall) P-H.
Biehn, Michel. Colors of Provence. LC 97-11487. (Illus.). 176p. 1997. 50.00 (*1-55670-619-7*) Stewart Tabori & Chang.
Biehn, Michel. Recipes from a Provencal Kitchen. (Illus.). 200p. 1995. 35.00 (*2-08-013586-4*, Pub. by Flammarion) Abbeville Pr.
— Recipes from a Provencal Kitchen. (Illus.). 200p. 2000. text 19.95 (*2-08-013679-8*, Pub. by Flammarion) Abbeville Pr.
Biehn, Miriam. Mother to Mother on Breastfeeding. LC 99-185764. 1998. pap. 6.50 (*1-884377-06-8*) Green Psturs Pr.
Biek, David. Flora of Mount Rainier National Park. LC 99-57564. (Illus.). 488p. 1999. pap. 29.95 (*0-87071-470-8*) Oreg St U Pr.
***Biek, Robert F.** The Geology of Quail Creek State Park. (Public Information Ser.: Vol. 63). (Illus.). 21p. 1999. mass mkt. 3.50 (*1-55791-630-6*, PI-63) Utah Geological Survey.
Biek, Robert F. A Visitor's Guide to the North Dakota Capitol Grounds: Buildings, Monuments, & Stones. (Illus.). vi, 55p. 1995. pap. 3.00 (*1-891419-13-7*) State Hist ND.
***Biekart, Kees.** The Politics of Civil Society Building: European Private Aid Agencies & Democratic Transitions in Central America. LC 99-514789. 400p. 1999. pap. 29.95 (*90-5727-025-0*, Pub. by Intl Bks) Paul & Co Pubs.
Biekert, Russell & Berling, David. CIM Technology: Fundamentals & Applications. LC 97-34787. 1997. 37.28 (*1-56637-426-X*) Goodheart.
Biel. Political Economics. (C). 1998. pap. 30.00 (*0-06-500864-2*) HarpC.
Biel, Alexander, jt. ed. see Aaker, David A.
Biel, Andrew R. Trail Guide to the Body: How to Locate Muscles, Bones & More! LC 97-93767. (Illus.). 302p. 1997. reprint ed. pap. text 42.95 (*0-9658534-0-3*) Bks of Discov.
Biel, Gabriel. Collectorium in IV Libros Sententiarum Guillelmi Occam, No. 2. (GER.). 1266p. 1977. reprint ed. write for info. (*3-487-06146-5*) G Olms Pubs.
Biel, Jane, ed. see Guilds of the Orange County Performing Arts Center.
Biel, John H. & Abood, Leo G., eds. Biogenic Amines & Physiological Membranes in Drug Therapy, 2 pts., Pt. A. LC 77-180643. (Medicinal Research Ser.: No. 5). 174p. reprint ed. pap. 54.00 (*0-7837-0738-X*, 204106100001) Bks Demand.
— Biogenic Amines & Physiological Membranes in Drug Therapy, 2 pts., Pt. B. LC 77-180643. (Medicinal Research Ser.: No. 5). 376p. reprint ed. pap. 116.60 (*0-7837-0739-8*, 204106100002) Bks Demand.
Biel, Pamela. Doorkeepers at the House of Righteousness: Heinrich Bullinger & the Zurich Clergy 1535-1575. Busser, Fritz, ed. (Zurcher Beitrage Zur Reformationsgeschichte Ser.: Vol. 15). 250p. 1991. pap. 45.00 (*3-261-04317-2*) P Lang Pubng.
Biel, Steven. Down with the Old Canoe: A Cultural History of the Titanic Disaster. 320p. 1996. 25.00 (*0-393-03965-X*) Norton.
— Down with the Old Canoe: A Cultural History of the Titanic Disaster. (Illus.). 320p. 1997. pap. 13.00 (*0-393-31676-9*) Norton.
— Independent Intellectuals in the United States, 1910-1945. LC 92-14935. (American Social Experience Ser.: No. 25). 296p. (C). 1995. pap. text 18.50 (*0-8147-1232-0*) NYU Pr.
Biel, Steven, ed. Titanica: The Disaster of the Century in Poetry, Song, & Prose. LC 98-7986. 128p. 1998. pap. 11.00 (*0-393-31873-7*) Norton.
Biel, Timothy. Tigers. (Zoobooks Ser.). (Illus.). 24p. (J). (gr. 1-6). 1997. 13.95 (*1-888153-43-1*) Wildlife Educ.
Biel, Timothy & Quality Productions Staff. Owls. (Zoobooks Ser.). (Illus.). 24p. (J). (gr. 1-6). 1997. 13.95 (*1-888153-44-X*) Wildlife Educ.
Biel, Timothy L. The Age of Feudalism. LC 93-19290. (World History Ser.). (J). (gr. 6-9). 1994. lib. bdg. 22.45 (*1-56006-232-0*) Lucent Bks.
— Charlemagne. LC 96-45625. (Importance of Ser.). (Illus.). (YA). (gr. 4-12). 1997. lib. bdg. 22.45 (*1-56006-074-3*) Lucent Bks.
Biel, Timothy L. The Crusades. (World History Ser.). (Illus.). 128p. (J). (gr. 5-9). 1995. lib. bdg. 22.45 (*1-56006-245-2*) Lucent Bks.
Biel, Timothy L. Life in the North During the Civil War. LC 96-34422. (Way People Live Ser.). (Illus.). 112p. (YA). 1996. lib. bdg. 22.45 (*1-56006-334-3*) Lucent Bks.
— Skunks & Their Relatives. (Zoobooks Ser.). 24p. (J). (gr. 1-7). 1993. 13.95 (*1-888153-03-2*) Wildlife Educ.
— Wild Dogs. (Zoobooks Ser.). 24p. (J). (gr. 1-7). 1993. 13.95 (*1-888153-04-0*) Wildlife Educ.
***Bielak, Robert.** Global Capitalism: Its Dynamics & the Impact on the Prospects of Poor Countries. LC 99-55043. 2000. pap. 27.50 (*1-85649-747-X*) Zed Books.
— The New Imperialism: Crisis & Contradiction in North & South. 2000. text 69.50 (*1-85649-746-1*, Pub. by Zed Books) St Martin.
Bielanski, Adam & Haber, Jerzy, eds. Oxygen in Catalysis. (Chemical Industries Ser.: Vol. 43). (Illus.). 488p. 1990. text 195.00 (*0-8247-8320-4*) Dekker.
Bielasiak, Jack. Poland: The Politics of Crisis. (WVSS on the Soviet Union & Eastern Europe Ser.). 1996. text 26.50 (*0-86531-441-1*) Westview.
Bielasiak, Jack, ed. Polish Politics: Edge of the Abyss. LC 83-24759. 366p. 1984. 65.00 (*0-275-91128-4*, C1128, Praeger Pubs) Greenwood.
Bielawa, R. L. Rotary Wing Structural Dynamics & Aeroelasticity. (Educ Ser.). 584p. (C). 1992. text 75.95 (*1-56347-031-4*, 31-4) AIAA.
***Bielawski, Jill.** Stretching for Health: Your Handbook for Ultimate Wellness, Longevity & Productivity. (Illus.). 128p. 2000. pap. 14.95 (*0-8092-2436-4*, Contemporary Bks) NTC Contemp Pub Co.
Bielawski, Jill & Weinert, Jerry. Head to Toe: A Manual of Wellness & Flexibility. McDaniel, Judith, ed. LC 97-92362. (Illus.). 96p. 1997. spiral bd. 16.95 (*0-9659331-0-5*) Southwest Well.
Bielawski, Larry. Intelligent Systems Design: Integrating Expert Systems, Hypermedia & Database Technologies. 302p. 1991. pap. 29.95 (*0-471-52535-9*) Wiley.
Bielawski, Maxwell M. How to Heal & Cure Anything: My Favorite Remedies. 300p. (Orig.). 1984. 125.00 (*0-317-14873-7*) Bielawski.
Bielawski, Shraga F. & Liebovich, Louis W., eds. The Last Jew from Wengrow: The Memoirs of a Survivor of the Step-by-Step Genocide in Poland. LC 90-24127. 184p. 1991. 52.95 (*0-275-93896-4*, C3896, Praeger Pubs) Greenwood.
Bielby, Denise D., jt. auth. see Harrington, C. Lee.
Bielby, Diane D., jt. auth. see Harirngton, C. Lee.
Bielby, Nicholas. Teaching Reading: Key Stage 2. (Stanley Thornes Teaching Primary English Ser.). (Illus.), 224p. 1999. pap. 37.50 (*0-7487-4040-6*, Pub. by S Thornes Pubs) Trans-Atl Phila.
Biele, Albert M., jt. auth. see Piotrowski, Zygmunt a.
Biele, Pam, jt. auth. see Walter, Susan.
Bielec, Dana. Polish: An Essential Grammar. LC 97-44254. (POL & ENG.). 296p. (C). 1998. 75.00 (*0-415-16405-2*); pap. 22.99 (*0-415-16406-0*) Routledge.
Bielecki, Mother T. Teresa of Avila: Ecstasy & Common Sense. LC 96-13513. 168p. (Orig.). 1996. pap. 12.95 (*1-57062-167-5*, Pub. by Shambhala Pubns) Random.
Bielecki, Tessa. Holy Daring: An Outrageous Gift to Modern Spirituality from Saint Teresa, the Grand Wild. 1994. pap. 9.95 (*1-85230-483-9*, Pub. by Element MA) Penguin Putnam.
— Teresa of Avila: An Introduction to Her Life & Writings. 208p. 1994. pap. 40.00 (*0-86012-233-6*, Pub. by Srch Pr) St Mut.
— Teresa of Avila: Mystical Writings. (Spiritual Legacy Ser.). 176p. (Orig.). 1994. pap. 12.95 (*0-8245-2504-3*) Crossroad NY.
Bielefeld, Wolfgang, jt. auth. see Galaskiewicz, Joseph.
Bielefeldt, Carl. Dogen's Manuals of Zen Meditation. 267p. 1988. pap. 17.95 (*0-520-06835-1*, Pub. by U CA Pr) Cal Prin Full Svc.
Bielefeldt, Gerald, jt. auth. see Burt, Richard.
Bielefield, Arlene & Cheeseman, Lawrence. Interpreting & Negotiating Licensing Agreements: A Guidebook for the Library, Research & Teaching Professions. 4th ed. LC 98-55929. 162p. 1999. pap. 59.95 (*1-55570-324-0*) Neal-Schuman.
Bielefield, Arlene C. Libraries & the Law Series, 6 vols. Incl. Libraries & Copyright Law. Cheeseman, Lawrence. 148p. 1993. 45.00 (*1-55570-130-2*); Library Contracts & the Law. Cheeseman, Lawrence. 150p. 1998. pap. 45.00 (*1-55570-134-5*); Library Employment Within the Law. Cheeseman, Lawrence G. LC 93-31839. 150p. 1993. pap. 45.00 (*1-55570-131-0*); Library Facilities & the Law. Cheeseman, Lawrence. 150p. 1999. pap. 45.00 (*1-55570-133-7*); Library Patrons & the Law. Cheeseman, Lawrence. 142p. (Orig.). 1995. pap. 45.00 (*1-55570-132-9*); Trustees, Friends, & the Law. Cheeseman, Lawrence. 150p. 1998. pap. 45.00 (*1-55570-135-3*); Set pap. 220.00 (*1-55570-136-1*) Neal-Schuman.
Bielefield, Arlene C. & Cheeseman, Lawrence. Maintaining the Privacy of Library Records: A Handbook & Guide. LC 94-7153. 203p. 1994. 49.95 (*1-55570-066-7*) Neal-Schuman.
— Technology & Copyright Law: A Guidebook for the Library, Research, & Teaching Professions. LC 96-48255. 213p. 1997. pap. 55.00 (*1-55570-267-8*) Neal-Schuman.
Bieleman, B., et al. Lines Across Europe: Nature & Extent of Cocaine Use in Barcelona, Rotterdam & Turin. x, 222p. 1993. pap. 44.00 (*90-265-1347-X*) Swets.
***Bieleman, Johan.** Additives for Coatings. 392p. 2000. 185.00 (*3-527-29785-5*) Wiley.
Bielen, E. The Inheritance of Cardiac Structure & Function at Rest & During Dynamic Exercise: An Echocardiographic Study in Twins. No. 32. 149p. (Orig.). 1990. pap. 39.50 (*90-6186-419-4*, Pub. by Leuven Univ) Coronet Bks.
Bielen, F. Sodium-Proton Exchange in Cardiac Cells: Role in Mulations of Intracellular Sodium & Sodium-Dependent Processes. No. 42. 169p. (Orig.). 1991. pap. 37.50 (*90-6186-450-X*, Pub. by Leuven Univ) Coronet Bks.
***Bielen, Kenneth G.** The Lyrics of Civility: Biblical Images & Popular Music Lyrics in American Culture. LC 99-33782. 1999. write for info. (*0-8153-3193-2*) Garland.
Bielen, Peggy, jt. auth. see McDaniel, Sandy.
Bielenberg, Andy. Cork's Industrial Revolution, 1780-1880: Development Or Decline? LC 92-118675. 1991. pap. text 16.95 (*0-902561-59-6*) Intl Spec Bk.
— Cork's Industrial Revolution 1780-1880: Development or Decline? 1991. 34.95 (*0-902561-58-8*) Cork Univ.
— The Irish Diaspora. LC 99-53717. 376p. 2000. 69.95 (*0-582-36998-3*) Longman.
— The Irish Diaspora. LC 99-53717. 376p. 2000. pap. 18.00 (*0-582-36997-5*) Longman.
Bielenberg, Carl & Allen, Hugh. How to Make & Use the Treadle Irrigation Pump. 77p. 1995. pap. 17.50 (*1-85339-312-6*, Pub. by Intermed Tech) Stylus Pub VA.
***Bielenberg, Christabel.** The Road Ahead. 2000. pap. 12.95 (*0-552-99469-3*, Pub. by Transworld Publishers Ltd) Trafalgar.
Bielenberg, Christabel. When I Was a German, 1934-1945: An Englishwoman in Nazi Germany. LC 98-33491. 1998. pap. 15.00 (*0-8032-6151-9*, Bison Books) U of Nebr Pr.
Bielenda, S., intro. Oregon, Greyhound of the Atlantic: A Diver's Scrapbook. (Illus.). 185p. (Orig.). 1993. pap. 20.00 (*0-9635879-0-0*) H F Kaasmann.
Bieler, E. F. Three Great Gothic Novels. 25.95 (*0-8488-0060-5*) Amereon Ltd.
Bieler, Henry G. & Block, Maxine. Food Is Your Best Medicine. 236p. 1987. mass mkt. 5.99 (*0-345-35183-5*) Ballantine Pub Grp.
Bieler, Henry G. & Nichols, Sarah. Natural Way to Sexual Health. Fried, Jerome, ed. LC 72-83312. 231p. 1972. text 12.95 (*0-912880-03-1*) Charles Pub.
Bieler, Ludwig. Studies on the Life & Legend of St. Patrick. Sharpe, Richard, ed. (Collected Studies: No. CS244). (ENG & GER.). 342p. (C). 1986. reprint ed. lib. bdg. 113.95 (*0-86078-192-5*, Pub. by Variorum) Ashgate Pub Co.
Bieler, Ludwig, ed. see Lowe, E. A.
Bieler, Peter & Costas, Suzanne. This Business Has Legs: The Inside Story of the Infomercial Entrpreneur Who Turned the Thigh-Master into a Household Name. LC 96-18232. 206p. 1996. 24.95 (*0-471-14749-4*) Wiley.
Bieler, Rudiger & Mikkelsen, Paula M., eds. Abstracts of the World Congress of Malacology: Washington, D. C., 25-30 July 1998. 400p. 1998. pap. write for info. (*0-914868-22-5*) Field Mus.
Bieler, T. K., jt. ed. see Ghosh, A. K.
Bieler, Thomas R., et al. Hot Deformation of Aluminum Alloys Ii: Proceedings of the Second Symposium Held At the 1998 Tms Fall Meeting, in Rosemont, Illinois, on October 11-15, 1998. LC 98-67357. 20p. 1998. 94.00 (*0-87339-412-7*) Minerals Metals.
Bieler, Thomas R., jt. ed. see Ghosh, Amit K.
Bieleski, R. L., jt. ed. see Lauchli, Andre.
Bielfeld, Horst. Mice. (Pet Care Ser.). 1985. pap. 6.95 (*0-8120-2921-6*) Barron.
Bielfeldt, Dennis D. & Schwarzwaller, Klaus, eds. Freiheit Als Liebe Bei Martin Luther (Freedom As Love in Martin Luther) 8th International Congress for Luther Research in St. Paul, Minnesota, 1993: Seminar I Referate - Papers. (ENG & GER.). 181p. 1995. 37.95 (*3-631-47787-2*) P Lang Pubng.
Bielfeldt, Hans H. Deutsch-Russiches Woerterbuch, 2 vols. 3rd ed. (GER & RUS.). 2253p. 1991. 295.00 (*0-7859-7441-5*, 3050017767) Fr & Eur.
— Russian-German Dictionary: Russisch-Deutsches Woerterbuch. 14th ed. (GER & RUS.). 1119p. 1982. 55.00 (*0-8288-0793-0*, F60180) Fr & Eur.
Bielier, E. F. The Big Bow Mystery. 19.95 (*0-8488-0063-X*) Amereon Ltd.
— My Lady's Money. 17.95 (*0-8488-0062-1*) Amereon Ltd.
— Three Supernatural Novels of the Victorian Period. 25.95 (*0-89190-697-5*) Amereon Ltd.
Bielier, E. F., ed. Five Victorian Ghost Novels. 29.95 (*0-89190-683-5*) Amereon Ltd.
Bieling, David. Archaeological Investigations at CA-MRN-254, the Dominican College Site, San Rafael, Marin County, California. fac. ed. (Illus.). 353p. (C). 1998. reprint ed. pap. text 36.88 (*1-55567-716-9*) Coyote Press.
Bieling, David G. Perspective on Behavior Gained from Lithic Analysis & Archaeological Investigations near Bridgeport, Mono County, California. 188p. (C). 1992. pap. text 20.00 (*1-55567-100-4*) Coyote Press.
Bielinski, Leo S. The Back Road to Thurber. (Illus.). 282p. 1993. 24.00 (*0-9638476-0-0*) Joy Presswrk.
Bielinski, Michael S. Holusion Art, How & Why It Works. LC 94-220611. (Illus.). 36p. 1994. 15.99 (*0-9640923-0-1*) NVision Grafix.
Bielinski, Sue, jt. auth. see Vandenberg, Dawn.

An Asterisk (*) at the beginning of an entry indicates that the title is appearing for the first time.

B

An Asterisk (*) at the beginning of an entry indicates that the title is appearing for the first time.

B

***Bierbrier, Morris L.** Ancient Faces: Mummy Portraits in Roman Egypt. Walker, Susan, ed. LC 99-58352. (Illus.). 168p. 2000. 55.00 (0-415-92744-7); pap. 35.00 (0-415-92745-5) Routledge.

Bierbrier, Morris L. Historical Dictionary of Ancient Egypt. Woronoff, Jon, ed. LC 98-50361. (Historical Dictionaries of Ancient Civilizations & Historical Eras Ser.). 320p. 1999. 49.50 (0-8108-3614-9) Scarecrow.

— The Tomb-Builders of the Pharaohs. (Illus.). 160p. 1975. pap. 15.00 (977-424-210-6, Pub. by Am Univ Cairo Pr) Col U Pr.

Bierce, Ambrose. Ambrose Bierce's Civil War. McCann, William, ed. & intro. by. 258p. 1996. pap. 12.95 (0-89526-716-0, Gateway Editions) Regnery Pub.

— Ambrose Bierce's Civil War. McCann, William, ed. & intro. by. 272p. 1996. 9.99 (0-517-15013-1) Wings Bks.

— Black Beetles in Amber. (Principle Works of Ambrose Gwinett Bierce). 1989. reprint ed. lib. bdg. 79.00 (0-7812-1961-2) Rprt Serv.

— Can Such Things Be? 24.95 (0-89190-185-X, Rivercity Pr) Amereon Ltd.

— Can Such Things Be? 427p. 1977. 23.95 (0-8369-3767-8) Ayer.

— Can Such Things Be? 1977. pap. 6.95 (0-8065-0550-8, Citadel Pr) Carol Pub Group.

— Can Such Things Be? (Principle Works of Ambrose Gwinett Bierce). 1989. reprint ed. lib. bdg. 79.00 (0-7812-1963-9) Rprt Serv.

— Chickamauga. (Classic Short Stories on Tape Ser.). (YA). (gr. 9-12). 1988. ring bd. 38.00 (1-878298-23-2) Balance Pub.

— The Civil War Short Stories of Ambrose Bierce. Hopkins, Ernest J., ed. LC 87-27970. vi, 139p. 1988. pap. 9.95 (0-8032-6087-3, Bison Books) U of Nebr Pr.

— Civil War Short Stories of Ambrose Bierce. Date not set. lib. bdg. 18.95 (0-8488-1900-4) Amereon Ltd.

— Civil War Stories. LC 93-46121. (Illus.). 128p. (Orig.). 1994. pap. 1.00 (0-486-28038-1) Dover.

— Cobwebs from an Empty Skull. (Principle Works of Ambrose Gwinett Bierce). 1989. reprint ed. lib. bdg. 79.00 (0-7812-1956-6) Rprt Serv.

— Collected Works of Ambrose Bierce, 1909-1912, 12 Vols, Set. LC 66-14638. 1966. 800.00 (0-87752-010-0) Gordian.

— The Collected Writings of Ambrose Bierce. 41.95 (0-88411-859-2) Amereon Ltd.

— Collected Writings of Ambrose Bierce. Fadiman, Clifton, ed. 832p. 1983. pap. 16.95 (0-8065-0180-4, 70, Citadel Pr) Carol Pub Group.

— Collected Writings of Ambrose Bierce. LC 72-13283. (Biography Index Reprint Ser.). 1977. reprint ed. 45.95 (0-8369-8141-3) Ayer.

— The Complete Short Stories of Ambrose Bierce. Hopkins, Ernest J., ed. LC 84-8575. iv, 496p. 1984. pap. 16.00 (0-8032-6071-7, Bison Books) U of Nebr Pr.

— The Dance of Death. (Principle Works of Ambrose Gwinett Bierce). 1989. reprint ed. lib. bdg. 79.00 (0-7812-1957-4) Rprt Serv.

— The Dance of Life. (Principle Works of Ambrose Gwinett Bierce). 1989. reprint ed. lib. bdg. 79.00 (0-7812-1958-2) Rprt Serv.

— The Devil's Dictionary. LC 98-22576. (Illus.). 256p. 1999. pap. 12.95 (0-19-512627-0) OUP.

— Devil's Dictionary. (Reference Library). 219p. 1998. pap. 6.95 (1-85326-364-8, 3648WW, Pub. by Wrdsworth Edits) NTC Contemp Pub Co.

— Devils Dictionary. (Illus.). 256p. 1999. 25.00 (0-19-512626-2) OUP.

— The Devil's Dictionary. 376p. reprint ed. lib. bdg. 23.95 (0-89190-186-8) Amereon Ltd.

— The Devil's Dictionary. 1990. reprint ed. lib. bdg. 22.95 (0-89968-478-5) Buccaneer Bks.

— The Devil's Dictionary. LC 92-46179. (Thrift Editions Ser.). 144p. 1993. reprint ed. pap. 1.00 (0-486-27542-6) Dover.

— The Devil's Dictionary. (Principle Works of Ambrose Gwinett Bierce). 1989. reprint ed. lib. bdg. 79.00 (0-7812-1966-3) Rprt Serv.

— 10 Relatos de Terror. 1996. pap. text 14.95 (84-01-54003-8) Plaza.

— Eyes of the Panther: Tales of Soldiers & Civilians. LC 76-169541. (Short Story Index Reprint Ser.). 1977. reprint ed. 24.95 (0-8369-4002-4) Ayer.

***Bierce, Ambrose.** The Fall of the Republic & Other Political Satires. Joshi, S. T. & Schultz, David E., eds. LC 00-8439. 288p. 2000. pap. text 18.95 (1-57233-096-1, Pub. by U of Tenn Pr) U Ch Pr.

— The Fall of the Republic & Other Political Satires. Joshi, S. T. & Schultz, David E., eds. LC 00-8439. 288p. (C). 2000. text 40.00 (1-57233-095-3, Pub. by U of Tenn Pr) U Ch Pr.

Bierce, Ambrose. Fantastic Fables. 160p. 1976. reprint ed. lib. bdg. 20.95 (0-89190-184-1, Rivercity Pr) Amereon Ltd.

— Fantastic Fables. 1990. reprint ed. lib. bdg. 16.95 (0-89968-479-3) Buccaneer Bks.

— Fantastic Fables. LC 73-92026. 116p. 1970. reprint ed. pap. 3.95 (0-486-22225-X) Dover.

— Fantastic Fables. (Principle Works of Ambrose Gwinett Bierce). 1989. reprint ed. lib. bdg. 79.00 (0-7812-1964-7) Rprt Serv.

— The Fiend's Delight. (Principle Works of Ambrose Gwinett Bierce). 1989. reprint ed. lib. bdg. 79.00 (0-7812-1954-X) Rprt Serv.

— Ghost & Horror Stories of Ambrose Bierce. Bleiler, Everett F., ed. 199p. 1964. pap. 6.95 (0-486-20767-6) Dover.

— A Horseman in the Sky. rev. ed. (Read-along Radio Dramas Ser.). (YA). (gr. 7-12). 1985. ring bd. 38.00 (1-878298-17-8) Balance Pub.

— In the Midst of Life, 2 vols. Incl. Pt. 1. Tales of Soldiers. 215p. 1976. lib. bdg. 21.95 (0-89190-182-5); Pt. 2. Tales of Civilians. 1976. lib. bdg. 19.95 1976. reprint ed. write for info. (0-318-50515-0, Rivercity Pr) Amereon Ltd.

— In the Midst of Life, Part I: Tales of Soldiers. 1990. reprint ed. lib. bdg. write for info. (0-89968-480-7) Buccaneer Bks.

— In the Midst of Life, Part II: Tales of Civilians. 1990. reprint ed. lib. bdg. 15.95 (0-89968-481-5) Buccaneer Bks.

— Letters. Pope, B. C., ed. LC 67-30702. 252p. 1967. reprint ed. 50.00 (0-87752-009-7) Gordian.

— Letters. (BCL1-PS American Literature Ser.). 204p. 1992. reprint ed. lib. bdg. 79.00 (0-7812-6675-0) Rprt Serv.

— The Monk & the Hangman's Daughter. 143p. 1976. reprint ed. lib. bdg. 19.95 (0-89190-183-3, Rivercity Pr) Amereon Ltd.

— The Monk & the Hangman's Daughter. 1990. reprint ed. lib. bdg. 15.95 (0-89968-482-3) Buccaneer Bks.

— The Monk & the Hangman's Daughter. (Principle Works of Ambrose Gwinett Bierce). 1989. reprint ed. lib. bdg. 79.00 (0-7812-1962-0) Rprt Serv.

***Bierce, Ambrose.** The Moonlit Road & Other Ghost & Horror Stories. Grafton, John, ed. LC 98-2677. (Dover Thrift Editions Ser.). 96p. 1998. pap. 1.00 (0-486-40056-5) Dover.

Bierce, Ambrose. Nuggets & Dust Panned Out in California. (Principle Works of Ambrose Gwinett Bierce). 1989. reprint ed. lib. bdg. 79.00 (0-7812-1955-8) Rprt Serv.

Bierce, Ambrose. Occurence at Owl Creek. abr. ed. LC 73-750986. 1973. audio 14.00 (0-694-50220-0, SWC 1345, Caedmon) HarperAudio.

— An Occurrence at Owl Creek Bridge. 2000. pap. 3.95 (1-86092-006-3, Pub. by Travelman Pub) IPG Chicago.

Bierce, Ambrose. Poems of Ambrose Bierce. Grenander, M. E., ed. & intro. by. LC 94-13761. xliv, 202p. 1995. pap. 12.00 (0-8032-6133-0, Bison Books) U of Nebr Pr.

— Sardonic Humor of Ambrose Bierce. Barkin, George, ed. 232p. (Orig.). 1963. pap. 6.95 (0-486-20768-4) Dover.

— The Shadow on the Dial & Other Essays. (Principle Works of Ambrose Gwinett Bierce). 1989. reprint ed. lib. bdg. 79.00 (0-7812-1967-1) Rprt Serv.

— Shapes of Clay. (Principle Works of Ambrose Gwinett Bierce). 1989. reprint ed. lib. bdg. 79.00 (0-7812-1965-5) Rprt Serv.

— The Shorter Devil's Dictionary. (Illus.). 80p. 1998. 13.95 (0-86281-632-7, Pub. by Appletree Pr) Irish Bks Media.

— Skepticism & Dissent: Selected Journalism, 1898-1901. Berkove, Lawrence I., ed. LC 85-24588. (Nineteenth-Century Studies). 337p. reprint ed. 104.50 (0-8357-1727-5, 207046500095) Bks Demand.

— A Sole Survivor: Bits of Autobiography. Joshi, S. T. & Schultz, David E., eds. LC 98-8981. 384p. 1998. text 38.00 (1-57233-018-X) U of Tenn Pr.

— Tales of Horror & Fantasy. 228p. reprint ed. lib. bdg. 21.95 (0-89190-187-6, Rivercity Pr) Amereon Ltd.

— Tales of Soldiers & Civilians. LC 70-121522. (Short Story Index Reprint Ser.). 1980. 23.95 (0-8369-3478-4) Ayer.

— Tales of Soldiers & Civilians. (Principle Works of Ambrose Gwinett Bierce). 1989. reprint ed. lib. bdg. 79.00 (0-7812-1959-0) Rprt Serv.

***Bierce, Ambrose.** Tales of Soldiers & Civilians: And Other Stories. LC 99-16212. (Penguin Classics Ser.). 256p. 2000. pap. 12.95 (0-14-043756-8, Penguin Classics) Viking Penguin.

Bierce, Ambrose. Twenty-One Letters of Ambrose Bierce. (American Biography Ser.). 1p. 1991. reprint ed. lib. bdg. 59.00 (0-7812-8019-2) Rprt Serv.

***Bierce, Ambrose.** The Unabridged Devil's Dictionary. Schultz, David E. & Joshi, S. T., eds. LC 99-87396. 400p. 1999. 34.95 (0-8203-2196-6) U of Ga Pr.

Bierce, Ambrose. The Works of Ambrose Gwinett Bierce, Set. 1989. reprint ed. lib. bdg. 79.00 (0-7812-1969-8) Rprt Serv.

— Write It Right. Gannon, Edward B. & Gannon, Richard S., eds. LC 86-71638. 73p. 1987. 12.95 (0-9617270-0-4) Terripam Pubs.

— Write It Right. (Principle Works of Ambrose Gwinett Bierce). 1989. reprint ed. lib. bdg. 79.00 (0-7812-1968-X) Rprt Serv.

Bierce, Ambrose & Bufe, Charles Q. The Devil's Dictionaries: The Best of "The Devil's Dictionary" & "The American Heretic's Dictionary. expanded ed. (Illus.). 144p. 1995. pap. 9.95 (1-884365-06-X) See Sharp Pr.

Bierce, Ambrose & Fadiman, Clifton. The Collected Writings of Ambrose Bierce. 830p. 1999. reprint ed. 48.95 (0-7351-0081-0) Replica Bks.

***Bierce, Ambrose & Joshi, S. T.** The Collected Fables of Ambrose Bierce. LC 99-52375. 413p. 2000. 65.00 (0-8142-0842-8) Ohio St U Pr.

Bierce, Ambrose & Wilson, Gahan. The Devil's Dictionary & Other Works. (Classics Illustrated Ser.). (Illus.). 52p. (YA). pap. 4.95 (1-57209-018-9) Classics Int Ent.

Bierce, L. V. Historical Reminiscences of Summit County. 157p. 1997. reprint ed. lib. bdg. 25.00 (0-8328-6366-1) Higginson Bk Co.

Bierce, Rose, ed. see Center for Environmental Education Staff.

Bierce, T. H. & Cottrell, L. Bierce: Ancestors in the U. S. of Byron Bierce & His Wife Mary Ida Cottrell, of Cortland Co., N.Y. 289p. 1992. reprint ed. pap. 44.00 (0-8328-2634-0); reprint ed. lib. bdg. 54.00 (0-8328-2633-2) Higginson Bk Co.

Bierds, Linda. Flights of the Harvest-Mare. 2nd ed. Boyer, Dale K., ed. LC 84-73272. (Ahsahta Press Modern & Contemporary Poets of the West Ser.). 50p. 1984. pap. 6.95 (0-916272-27-3) Ahsahta Pr.

— The Ghost Trio: Poems. LC 94-26063. 1995. 20.00 (0-8050-3485-4); pap. 12.95 (0-8050-3486-2) H Holt & Co.

— Heart & Perimeter. 64p. 1995. pap. 12.95 (0-8050-1765-8, Owl) H Holt & Co.

— The Profile Makers. 1997. 25.00 (0-614-29408-8); 23.00 (0-8050-5535-5); pap. 12.00 (0-614-29409-6); pap. 12.95 (0-8050-5536-3) H Holt & Co.

— The Stillness, the Dancing. 1995. pap. 10.95 (0-8050-0766-0, Owl) H Holt & Co.

Bierens, Herman J. Robust Methods & Asymptotic Theory in Nonlinear Econometrics. (Lecture Notes in Economics & Mathematical Systems Ser.: Vol. 192). (Illus.). 198p. 1981. 35.00 (0-387-10838-6) Spr-Verlag.

— Topics in Advanced Econometrics: Estimation, Testing & Specification of Cross-Section & Time Series Models. LC 92-47068. 270p. (C). 1994. text 64.95 (0-521-41900-X) Cambridge U Pr.

— Topics in Advanced Econometrics: Estimation, Testing & Specification of Cross-Section & Time Series Models. 270p. 1996. pap. text 23.95 (0-521-56511-1) Cambridge U Pr.

Bierens, Herman J. & Gallant, A. Ronald, eds. Nonlinear Models, 2 vols. (International Library of Critical Writings in Econometrics: Vol. 8). 1016p. 1997. 360.00 (1-85898-382-7) E Elgar.

Bierer, Doug. Inside Intranet Ware. LC 96-46750. 1408p. 1997. 59.99 (1-56205-707-3) New Riders Pub.

— Inside NetWare 4.1. 1200p. 1995. 39.99 (1-56205-291-8) New Riders Pub.

— Inside NetWare 4.1. 2nd ed. LC 96-110421. (Illus.). 1344p. 1995. pap. 45.00 (1-56205-534-8) New Riders Pub.

***Bierer, Doug.** Novell's Guide to Integrating Linux & NetWare. (Illus.). 700p. 2000. pap. text 49.99 (0-7645-4725-9) IDG Bks.

***Bieresborn, Dirk.** Klage und Klageerwiderung im Deutschen und Englischen Zivilprozess: Eine Rechtshistorische und Rechtsvergleichende Untersuchung Unter Besonderer Berucksichtigung der Beeinflussung Durch das Romisch-kanonische Verfahren. XXXI, 669p. 1999. 73.95 (3-631-34712-X) P Lang Pubng.

Bierfelder, W. Handwoerterbuch des Oeffentlichen Dienster: Das Personalwesen. (GER.). 1800p. 1976. 275.00 (0-8288-5702-4, M7440) Fr & Eur.

Bierhaus, Jere, jt. auth. see Fisher, Bruce.

Bierhoff, H. W., et al. Justice in Social Relations. LC 86-15089. (Critical Issues in Social Justice Ser.). (Illus.). 380p. (C). 1986. 70.00 (0-306-42181-X, Plenum Trade) Perseus Pubng.

Bierhoff, Hans-Werner. Person Perception & Attribution. (Social Psychology Ser.). (Illus.). 370p. 1989. 86.95 (0-387-50356-0) Spr-Verlag.

Bierhoff, Hans-Werner & Montada, Leo, eds. Altruism in Social Systems. (Illus.). 268p. 1991. text 43.00 (0-88937-045-1) Hogrefe & Huber Pubs.

Bierhorst. Four Masterworks. LC 84-8462. 371p. 1984. reprint ed. pap. 19.95 (0-8165-0886-0) U of Ariz Pr.

— History & Mythology of Aztecs: The Codex Chimalpopoca. LC 91-42267. 248p. 1998. pap. 17.95 (0-8165-1886-6) U of Ariz Pr.

***Bierhorst.** Is My Friend at Home. LC 99-29214. 2000. text. write for info. (0-374-33550-8) FS&G.

Bierhorst, John. Codex Chimalpopoca: The Text in Nahuatl with a Glossary & Grammatical Notes. LC 91-46411. 210p. 1992. 58.50 (0-8165-1306-6) U of Ariz Pr.

— A Cry from the Earth: Music of the North American Indians. LC 91-59002. (Illus.). 113p. (J). 1992. reprint ed. pap. 15.95 (0-941270-53-X) Ancient City Pr.

— Doctor Coyote. (J). 1998. pap. 5.99 (0-87628-341-5) Ctr Appl Res.

— Doctor Coyote: A Native American Aesop's Fables. (J). (gr. 2-5). 1996. mass mkt. 5.99 (0-689-80739-2) S&S Childrens.

Bierhorst, John. Doctor Coyote: A Native American Aesop's Fables. 1996. 11.19 (0-606-10788-6, Pub. by Turtleback) Demco.

Bierhorst, John. Is My Friend at Home? Pueblo Fireside Tales. LC 93-14249. (Illus.). 32p. (J). 1996. 14.95 (0-02-709733-1, Mac Bks Young Read) S&S Childrens.

***Bierhorst, John.** Lightning Inside You: And Other Native American Riddles. (Illus.). 112p. (gr. 4-7). 1999. mass mkt. 5.95 (0-688-17298-9, Grenwillow Bks) HarpC Child Bks.

Bierhorst, John. The Mythology of Mexico & Central America. LC 90-5879. (Illus.). 256p. (YA). (gr. 7 up). 1990. 17.00 (0-688-06721-2, Wm Morrow) Morrow Avon.

— The Mythology of North America: Introduction to Classic Native American Gods, Heroes & Tricksters. LC 85-281. (Illus.). 272p. (YA). (gr. 7 up). 1986. pap. 13.00 (0-688-06666-6, Wm Morrow) Morrow Avon.

— Mythology of the Lenape: Guide & Texts. LC 95-11567. 147p. 1995. 36.00 (0-8165-1523-9); pap. 19.95 (0-8165-1573-5) U of Ariz Pr.

— A Nahuatl-English Dictionary & Concordance to the "Cantares Mexicanos" With an Analytic Transcription & Grammatical Notes. LC 82-61070. 760p. 1985. 95.00 (0-8047-1183-6) Stanford U Pr.

— Native American Stories. LC 97-29253. (Illus.). 160p. (J). (gr. 5-9). 1998. 16.00 (0-688-14837-9, Wm Morrow) Morrow Avon.

— The Way of the Earth: Native America & the Environment. LC 93-28971. (Illus.). 336p. (YA). (gr. 7 up). 1994. 15.00 (0-688-11560-8, Wm Morrow) Morrow Avon.

Bierhorst, John, ed. The Dancing Fox: Arctic Folktales. LC 96-17146. (Illus.). 142p. (YA). (gr. 5 up). 1997. 15.00 (0-688-14406-3, Wm Morrow) Morrow Avon.

— In the Trail of the Wind: American Indian Poems & Ritual Orations. 1993. 22.50 (0-8446-6694-7) Peter Smith.

— In the Trail of the Wind: American Indian Poems & Ritual Orations. rev. ed. LC 97-77213. (Illus.). 224p. (YA). (gr. 7 up). 1998. pap. 6.95 (0-374-43609-6) FS&G.

— The Monkey's Haircut: And Other Stories Told by the Maya. LC 85-28471. (Illus.). 160p. (J). (gr. 5 up). 1986. 16.00 (0-688-04269-4, Wm Morrow) Morrow Avon.

— The White Deer: And Other Stories Told by the Lenape. LC 94-30962. (Illus.). 160p. (YA). (gr. 7 up). 1995. 15.00 (0-688-12900-5, Wm Morrow) Morrow Avon.

Bierhorst, John, ed. Lightning Inside You: And Other Native American Riddles. LC 91-21744. (Illus.). 112p. (J). (ps-3). 1992. 14.00 (0-688-09582-8, Wm Morrow) Morrow Avon.

Bierhorst, John, intro. Cantares Mexicanos: Songs of the Aztecs. LC 82-61071. (Illus.). xiv, 559p. 1985. 69.50 (0-8047-1182-8) Stanford U Pr.

Bierhorst, John, tr. History & Mythology of the Aztecs: The Codex Chimalpopoca. LC 91-42267. 238p. 1992. 38.95 (0-8165-1126-8) U of Ariz Pr.

Bierhorst, John, tr. Doctor Coyote: A Native American Aesop's Fables. LC 86-8669. (Illus.). 48p. (J). (gr. 2-5). 1987. lib. bdg. 15.95 (0-02-709780-3, Mac Bks Young Read) S&S Childrens.

Bierhorst, John & Olive Natural Heritage Society Staff. The Ashokan Catskills: A Natural History. 2nd ed. Crawford, Ann et al, eds. LC 95-4639. (Illus.). 128p. 1995. pap. 18.00 (0-935796-61-4) Purple Mnt Pr.

Bierhorst, John, tr. see Vicuna, Cecilia, ed.

Bieri, H. & Noltemeier, H., eds. Computational Geometry - Methods, Algorithms & Applications: International Workshop on Computational Geometry CG '91 Bern, Switzerland, March 1991 Proceedings. (Lecture Notes in Computer Science Ser.: Vol. 553). viii, 320p. 1991. 43.00 (0-387-54891-2) Spr-Verlag.

***Bieri, Peter.** Action Games. rev. ed. (Illus.). 56p. (J). (gr. k-6). 1999. pap. 7.95 (1-58107-021-7, Pub. by New Forums) Booksource.

Bierkoff, Nicholas, tr. see Panova, Vera.

Bierl, Maja M. Canaries As a New Pet. (Illus.). 64p. 1991. pap. 6.95 (0-86622-529-3, TU-018) TFH Pubns.

Bierlaagh, Jos J., jt. auth. see Govin, Marc H.

***Bierle, Donald A.** Faith Search. 1999. pap. text 12.99 (1-883002-68-0) YWAM Pub.

Bierle, Donald A. Surprised by Faith. rev. ed. 120p. 1993. pap. write for info. (0-9647488-0-0) Emerald WA.

— Surprised by Faith: A Scientist Shares His Personal, Life-Changing Discoveries about God, the Bible & Personal Fulfillment. 120p. (Orig.). 1996. pap. 8.99 (1-883002-33-8) Emerald WA.

Bierlein, J. F. Living Myths: How Myth Gives Meaning to Human Experience. LC 98-38533. 1999. pap. 14.95 (0-345-42207-4) Ball Well.

— Parallel Myths. 368p. 1994. pap. 14.00 (0-345-38146-7) Ballantine Pub Grp.

***Bierlein, J. F.** Parallel Myths. 1999. pap. 14.00 (0-345-91529-1) Ballantine Pub Grp.

Bierlein, Lawrence W. Update to Redbook on Transport, No. 1. 2nd ed. (Industrial Health & Safety Ser.). 1990. text. write for info. (0-442-20576-7, VNR) Wiley.

— Update to Redbook on Transport, No. 2. 2nd ed. (Industrial Health & Safety Ser.). 1990. text. write for info. (0-442-20577-5, VNR) Wiley.

— What to Do When the Dot Hazardous Materials Inspector Calls. 1986. 24.95 (0-940394-20-0) Labelmaster.

Bierlein, Louann A. Controversial Issues in Educational Policy. (Controversial Issues In Public Policy Ser.: Vol. 5). (Illus.). 200p. (C). 1992. 42.00 (0-8039-4832-8); pap. 18.95 (0-8039-4833-6) Sage.

Bierley, Paul E. Hallelujah Trombone! The Story of Henry Fillmore. LC 82-90686. (Illus.). 172p. 1982. 19.95 (0-918048-05-2) Integrity.

— John Philip Sousa, American Phenomenon. rev. ed. LC 86-80682. (Illus.). 293p. 1986. 17.95 (0-918048-07-9) Integrity.

— The Music of Henry Fillmore & Will Huff. LC 82-81491. (Music Catalog Ser.). 71p. 1982. pap. 5.95 (0-918048-02-8) Integrity.

— Sousa Band Fraternal Society News Index. LC 97-76978. 176p. 1998. spiral bd. 33.00 (0-918048-38-9) Integrity.

— The Works of John Philip Sousa. LC 84-80665. (Illus.). 245p. 1984. 19.95 (0-918048-04-4) Integrity.

Bierley, Paul E., ed. Later Operetta Pt. I: El Capitan (1896), Music by John Philip Sousa, Libretto by Charles Klein. fac. ed. LC 94-2238. (Nineteenth-Century American Musical Theater Ser.: Vol. 14). (Illus.). 336p. 1994. text 110.00 (0-8153-1378-0) Garland.

Bierley, Paul E., ed. see Rehrig, William H.

Bierley, Paul E., ed. see Sousa, John P.

Bierly, Steve R. Help for the Small-Church Pastor: Unlocking the Potential of Your Congregation. 160p. 1995. pap. 12.99 (0-310-49951-8) Zondervan.

— How to Thrive As a Small-Church Pastor: A Guide to Spiritual & Emotional Well-Being. LC 97-32368. 160p. 1998. pap. 12.99 (0-310-21655-9) Zondervan.

Bierma, Lyle D. German Calvinism in the Confessional Age: The Covenant Theology of Caspar Olevianus. LC 97-7373. 208p. (Orig.). (gr. 12). 1997. pap. text 14.99 (0-8010-2111-1, Labyrinth) Baker Bks.

Bierma, Lyle D., ed. & tr. see Olevianus, Caspar.

Bierma, Lyle D., tr. see Selderhuis, Herman J.

Bierma, Lyle D., tr. see Van't Spijker, Willem.

Bierma, Thomas J. & Waterstraat, Frank. Waste Minimization through Shared Savings: Chemical Supply Strategies. LC 99-16024. 344p. (C). 1999. 80.00 (0-471-33284-4) Wiley.

Biermaier, Ann M., jt. contrib. by see Raiche, Annabelle.

Bierman. Financial Accounting. (C). 1987. student ed. write for info. (0-15-527488-0) Harcourt Coll Pubs.

Bierman, A., jt. auth. see Treganza, A. E.

Bierman, Arthur K. Logic: A Dialogue. LC 64-16572. (Illus.). 433p. reprint ed. pap. 134.30 (0-608-30657-6, 201628600005) Bks Demand.

An Asterisk (*) at the beginning of an entry indicates that the title is appearing for the first time.

Bierman, Arthur K. & Gould, James A. Philosophy for a New Generation. 4th ed. 576p. (C). 1980. pap. text 39.73 (*0-02-309640-3*, Macmillan Coll) P-H.

Bierman, Arthur K., et al. The Critical Thinking Handbook. LC 95-1330. 560p. 1995. pap. text 63.00 (*0-02-309660-8*, Macmillan Coll) P-H.

Bierman, Bernard. A Translator-Warrior Speaks: A Personal History of the American Translators Association, 1959-1970. Rothstein, Evelyn, ed. (Illus.). 220p. (Orig.). 1987. pap. text 19.95 (*0-913935-43-3*) ERA-CCR.

***Bierman, Carol.** Journey to Ellis Island: How My Father Came to America. LC 98-10987. 48p. (J). 1998. 17.45 (*0-7868-0377-0*, Pub. by Hyperion) Time Warner.

Bierman, D., et al, eds. Artificial Intelligence & Education: Proceedings of the 4th International Conference on AI & Education, Amsterdam, Netherlands, 1989. (Frontiers in Artificial Intelligence & Applications Ser.). 339p. (gr. 12). 1989. pap. 70.00 (*90-5199-014-6*, Pub. by IOS Pr) IOS Press.

Bierman, Harold. Analisis Cuantitativo para Decisiones Empresariales. 8th ed. (SPA.). 784p. (C). 1994. pap. text. write for info. (*0-201-60127-3*) Addison-Wesley.

Bierman, Harold, Jr. The Causes of the 1929 Stock Market Crash: A Speculative Orgy or a New Era?, 195. LC 97-32007. (Contributions in Economics & Economic History Ser.: Vol. 195). 184p. 1998. 55.00 (*0-313-30629-X*, Greenwood Pr) Greenwood.

— Corporate Financial Strategy & Decision Making to Increase Shareholder Value. (Illus.). 200p. 1999. pap. 45.00 (*1-883249-67-8*) F J Fabozzi.

— The Great Myths of 1929 the Lessons to Be Learned, 118. LC 90-19917. (Contributions in Economics & Economic History Ser.: No. 118). 208p. 1991. 55.00 (*0-313-27365-0*, BGF/, Greenwood Pr) Greenwood.

— Implementation of Capital Budgeting Techniques: Survey & Synthesis. (Financial Management Survey & Synthesis Ser.). (Illus.). 69p. (Orig.). (C). 1986. 10.00 (*0-936795-01-8*) Finan Mgmt Assn.

— Implementing Capital Budgeting Techniques. rev. ed. (Financial Management Association Survey & Synthesis Series, the International Investor Series in Finance). 128p. 1988. text 39.95 (*0-88730-359-5*, HarpBusn) HarpInfo.

Bierman, Harold, Jr. & Smidt, Seymour. The Capital Budgeting Decision: Economic Analysis of Investment Projects. 8th ed. (Illus.). 608p. (C). 1992. teacher ed. write for info. (*0-318-69338-0*) Macmillan.

— The Capital Budgeting Decision: Economic Analysis of Investment Projects. 8th ed. (Illus.). 591p. (C). 1992. 63.80 (*0-02-309943-7*, Macmillan Coll) P-H.

Bierman, Harold, et al. Analisis Cuantitativo para la Toma de Decisiones. 8th ed. (SPA.). (C). 1996. text 32.00 (*0-8151-0802-8*, Irwn McGrw-H) McGrw-H Hghr Educ.

Bierman, Harold, Jr., et al. Hedge Accounting: An Exploratory Study of the Underlying Issues. LC 91-70656. (Financial Accounting Standards Board Research Report Ser.). 240p. (Orig.). 1991. pap. 17.50 (*0-910065-41-1*) Finan Acct Found.

Bierman, Harold, et al. Quantitative Methods for Management. 9th ed. 768p. (C). 1997. text 71.95 (*0-256-14021-9*, Irwn McGrw-H) McGrw-H Hghr Educ.

Bierman, Irene A. Writing Signs: The Fatimid Public Text. LC 97-50204. 247p. 1998. 50.00 (*0-520-20801-3*, Pub. by U CA Pr); pap. 20.00 (*0-520-20802-1*, Pub. by U CA Pr) Cal Prin Full Svc.

Bierman, Irene A., et al, eds. The Ottoman City & Its Parts: Urban Structure & Social Order. (Subsidia Balcanica, Islamica et Turcica Ser.: No. 3). (Illus.). x, 256p. 1991. text 60.00 (*0-89241-473-1*) Caratzas.

Bierman, John & Smith, Colin. Fire in the Night: Wingate of Burma, Ethiopia & Zion. LC D767.6.B54 1999. 352p. 1999. 29.95 (*0-375-50061-8*) Random.

Bierman, Judah, jt. ed. see Laszlo, Ervin.

Bierman, Kenneth J. & Mason, Florence M. New Jersey Library Network: Interlibrary Loan Study. (Illus.). 92p. (Orig.). (C). 1996. pap. text 30.00 (*0-7881-3717-4*) DIANE Pub.

***Bierman, Leonard, et al.** The Legal Environment of Business. 2nd ed. 2000. 74.95 (*1-57879-012-3*) E Bowers Pub.

Bierman, Masten. Guerilla GT Bankruptcy 2000. pap. write for info. (*0-312-20411-6*) St Martin.

Bierman, Pieke. Violetta. Reider, Ines, tr. from GER. (Mask Noir Ser.). 256p. 1996. pap. 13.99 (*1-85242-289-0*) Serpents Tail.

Bierman, Stanley M. More of the World's Greatest Stamp Collectors. (Illus.). 224p. 1990. 30.00 (*0-940403-28-5*); pap. 14.95 (*0-940403-27-7*) Linns Stamp News.

— World's Greatest Stamp Collectors. (Illus.). 288p. 1990. 30.00 (*0-940403-26-9*); pap. 14.95 (*0-940403-25-0*) Linns Stamp News.

— World's Greatest Stamp Collectors & More of the World's Greatest Stamp Collectors, 2 vols. (Illus.). 512p. 1990. boxed set 60.00 (*0-940403-35-8*); boxed set 29.95 (*0-940403-34-X*) Linns Stamp News.

Bierman, Todd & Masten, David. Fix Your Credit Workbook. LC 97-12114. (Illus.). 160p. 1997. pap., wbk. ed. 11.95 (*0-312-15530-1*) St Martin.

Bierman, Todd & Wice, Nathaniel. The Guerrilla Guide to Credit Repair: How to Find out What's Wrong with Your Credit Rating--& How to Fix It. 176p. (Orig.). 1994. pap. 10.95 (*0-312-10734-X*) St Martin.

Biermann, Alan W. Great Ideas in Computer Science: A Gentle Introduction. 2nd ed. LC 96-41198. (Illus.). 568p. 1997. pap. text 40.00 (*0-262-52223-3*) MIT Pr.

Biermann, Alan W. & Guiho, Gerard. Computer Program Synthesis Methodologies. 1982. text 192.50 (*90-277-1504-1*) Kluwer Academic.

Biermann, Berthold, ed. see Goethe, Johann Wolfgang Von.

***Biermann, Carol A.** Journey to Ellis Island: Book Club Edition. 48p. (J). 1999. pap. 8.95 (*0-7868-1411-X*, Pub. by Disney Pr) Little.

Biermann, Carol A., ed. see Rose, Rose K.

Biermann, Christopher J. Handbook of Pulping & Papermaking. 2nd ed. (Illus.). 754p. 1996. text 82.00 (*0-12-097362-6*) Acad Pr.

Biermann, Christopher J. & McGinnis, Gary D., eds. Analysis of Carbohydrates by GLC & MS. 288p. 1988. lib. bdg. 239.00 (*0-8493-6851-0*, QP701) CRC Pr.

***Biermann, Derek.** Samadhi: Personal Journeys to Spiritual Truth. LC 99-88975. (Illus.). 2000. 29.95 (*1-57062-579-4*, Pub. by Shambhala Pubns) Random.

Biermann, June & Toohey, Barbara. The Diabetic's Book: All Your Questions Answerable. 4th rev. ed. LC 98-4630. 272p. 1998. pap. 13.95 (*0-87477-924-3*) Putnam Pub Group.

— The Diabetic's Total Health Book. 3rd rev. ed. 272p. 1992. pap. 13.95 (*0-87477-689-9*, Tarcher Putnam) Putnam Pub Group.

Biermann, Veronica & Alberti, Leon Battista. Ornamentum. (Studien Zur Kunstgeschichte Ser.: Band 111). (GER.). 232p. 1997. 60.00 (*3-487-10260-9*) G Olms Pubs.

***Biermann, Werner, ed.** African Crisis Response Initiative. (Social Research on Africa Ser.: Vol. 6). 184p. 1999. pap. 24.95 (*3-8258-4155-3*, Pub. by CE24) Transaction Pubs.

— The Tanzanian Economy, 1920-1985: Colonial Valorisation, Reconstruction & Crisis. (Social Research on Africa Ser.). 220p. 1998. pap. text 27.95 (*3-8258-2525-6*, Pub. by CE24) Transaction Pubs.

Biermann, Werner & Moshi, Humphrey, eds. Tanganyika Railways, Carrier of Colonialism: An Account of Economic Indicators & Social Fragments. 150p. 1995. pap. text 24.95 (*3-8258-2524-8*) Transaction Pubs.

Biermann, Werner, jt. ed. see Moshi, Humphrey.

Biermann, Wolfgang & Vadset, Martin, eds. U. N. Peacekeeping in Trouble. LC 98-70987. (Illus.). 400p. 1998. text 86.95 (*1-84014-176-X*, Pub. by Ashgate Pub) Ashgate Pub Co.

***Biermann, Wolfgang & Vadset, Martin, eds.** U. N. Peacekeeping in Trouble: Lessons Learned from the Former Yugoslavia: Peacekeepers' Views on the Limits & Possibilities of the United Nations in a Civil War-Like Conflict. 408p. 1999. pap. 34.95 (*0-7546-1026-8*) Ashgate Pub Co.

Biermans, John T. The Odyssey of New Religions Today. rev. ed. LC 88-1631. (Illus.). 388p. 1988. lib. bdg. 109.95 (*0-88946-035-3*) E Mellen.

— The Odyssey of New Religious Movements: Persecution, Struggle, Legitimation - a Case Study of the Unification Church. LC 87-5476. (Symposium Ser.: Vol. 19). 240p. 1986. lib. bdg. 99.95 (*0-88946-710-2*) E Mellen.

Biermant, H. Scott. Game Theory with Economic Applications. 2nd ed. LC 97-37181. (Illus.). 452p. (C). 1997. pap. text 70.00 (*0-201-84758-2*) Addison-Wesley.

Biernacki, Daniel G. Erie USRA Heavy Pacifics No. 1: Locomotive Study. LC 92-71544. (Illus.). 80p. (Orig.). 1992. pap. 18.00 (*0-9632787-0-3*) E L Hist Soc.

Biernacki, Richard. The Fabrication of Labor: Germany & Britain, 1640-1914. LC 93-39487. 1995. 58.00 (*0-520-08491-8*, Pub. by U CA Pr) Cal Prin Full Svc.

— The Fabrication of Labor: Germany & Britain, 1640-1914. LC 93-39487. (Studies on the History of Society & Culture: Vol. 22). (Illus.). 1997. pap. 22.50 (*0-520-20878-1*, Pub. by U CA Pr) Cal Prin Full Svc.

Biernacki, Wladyslaw. Prophecies. 2nd ed. Dzierzynski, Nellie & Szewczyk, Henryk, trs. from POL. (Illus.). 84p. 1992. pap. text 8.50 (*0-933731-07-8*) Children of Mary.

Biernat & Manson. Legal Ethics Management & Their Counsel: 1997 Edition. LC 97-73751. 416p. 1997. pap. text 90.00 (*1-55834-591-4*, 60561-12, MICHIE) LEXIS Pub.

***Biernat, Len & Manson, R. Hunter.** Legal Ethics for Management & Their Counsel: 1999 Edition. 420p. 1999. 100.00 (*0-327-10014-1*, 6056114) LEXIS Pub.

Biernat, Len & Mason, R. Hunter. Legal Ethics for Management & Their Counsel, 1998 Edition. LC 99-461912. 410p. 1998. write for info. (*0-327-00715-X*, 6056113) LEXIS Pub.

Bierne-Smith, Mary, et al. Mental Retardation. 5th ed. LC 97-30617. 647p. (C). 1997. 73.00 (*0-13-894908-5*, Merrill Coll) P-H.

Biernson, George A. Principles of Feedback Control Vol. 1: Feedback System Design. LC 87-30539. 497p. 1988. 172.00 (*0-471-82167-5*) Wiley.

— Principles of Feedback Control Vol. 2: Advanced Control Topics, Vol. 2, Advanced Control Topics. 637p. 1988. 192.00 (*0-471-50120-4*) Wiley.

Bierny, Jean-Paul, tr. see Van Hamme, Jean.

Bierovic. Synergetic Technical Analysis. 288p. 1999. 76.50 (*0-471-14547-5*) Wiley.

Bierregaard, Richard O., jt. auth. see Laurance, Willaim F.

Bierregaard, Richard O., jt. auth. see Laurance, William F.

Biers, jt. auth. see Rhodes.

Biers, Ariel, et al. Spirit in Nature: Teaching Judaism & Ecology on the Trail. 96p. pap. 9.95 (*0-87441-686-8*) Behrman.

Biers, Jane C. The Great Bath on the Lechaion Road. LC 85-2746. (Corinth Ser.: Vol. 17). (Illus.). 128p. 1985. 35.00 (*0-87661-171-4*) Am Sch Athens.

Biers, William R. The Archaeology of Greece: An Introduction. rev. ed. LC 87-5447. (Illus.). 344p. (C). 1987. 55.00 (*0-8014-2082-2*); pap. 19.95 (*0-8014-9406-0*) Cornell U Pr.

— The Archaeology of Greece: An Introduction. 2nd ed. (Illus.). 364p. 1996. pap. text 22.50 (*0-8014-8280-1*) Cornell U Pr.

— The Archaeology of Greece: An Introduction. 2nd ed. LC 95-48905. (Illus.). 364p. (C). 1996. text 57.50 (*0-8014-3173-5*) Cornell U Pr.

— Art, Artefacts & Chronology in Classical Archaeology. LC 92-45632. (Approaching the Ancient World Ser.). (Illus.). 120p. (C). 1992. pap. 17.99 (*0-415-06319-1*, A7626) Routledge.

Biersach, Jeffrey W. Voting by Institutional Investors on Corporate Governance Issues in the 1990 Proxy Season. 6th ed. (Annual Ser.). 118p. 1990. pap. 25.00 (*0-931035-74-0*) IRRC Inc DC.

Biersach, William L. Of Mary, There Is Never Enough. 110p. (Orig.). (YA). (gr. 8 up). 1995. pap. 3.95 (*1-885692-01-3*) Cath Treas.

Biersack, Aletta, ed. Papuan Borderlands: Huli, Duna, & Ipili Perspectives on the Papua New Guinea Highlands. LC 95-30130. 456p. 1995. text 65.00 (*0-472-10601-5*, 10601) U of Mich Pr.

Biersack, H. J. & Winkler, C., eds. Amphetamines & PH-Shift Agents for Brain Imaging: Basic Research & Clinical Results. (Illus.). 208p. 1986. 119.25 (*3-11-010772-4*) De Gruyter.

Biersack, Hans J. & Cox, Peter H., eds. Nuclear Medicine in Gastroenterology. (Developments in Nuclear Medicine Ser.). 264p. 1991. text 180.50 (*0-7923-1074-8*) Kluwer Academic.

— Radioisotope Studies in Cardiology. (Developments in Nuclear Medicine Ser.). 1985. text 233.50 (*0-89838-733-7*) Kluwer Academic.

Biersack, J. P., jt. auth. see Ziegler, J. F.

Biersack, Robert, et al, eds. Risky Business? PAC Decisionmaking & Congressional Elections. LC 94-18902. (American Political Institutions & Public Policy Ser.). (Illus.). 328p. (C). (gr. 13). 1994. text 74.95 (*1-56324-294-X*); pap. text 35.95 (*1-56324-295-8*) M E Sharpe.

***Biersack, Robert, et al.** After the Revolution: PACs, Lobbies & the Republican Congress. LC 98-39203. 216p. 1999. pap. text 33.53 (*0-205-26913-3*) Allyn.

***Bierschenk, Thomas & Le Meur, Pierre-Yves, eds.** Negotiated Development: Brokers, Knowledge, Technologies. 174p. 1998. pap. 24.95 (*3-8258-3234-1*, Pub. by CE24) Transaction Pubs.

Bierschwale, Margaret. Fort McKavett, Texas. (Illus.). 1966. 35.00 (*0-685-05001-7*) A Jones.

Bierstadt, Edward Hale, ed. & intro. see Walker, Stuart.

Bierstadt, O. A., tr. see Blok, Petrus J.

Bierstedt, Klaus D., et al, eds. Functional Analysis. LC 93-28421. (Lecture Notes in Pure & Applied Mathematics Ser.: Vol. 150). (Illus.). 552p. 1993. pap. text 195.00 (*0-8247-9066-9*) Dekker.

Bierstedt, Robert, ed. see Znaniecki, Florian.

Bierstedt, Robin, jt. auth. see Metcalf, Slade R.

Biersteker, Ann. Kujibizana: Questions of Language & Power in 19th- & 20th- Century Poetry in Kiswahili. (MSU Press African Ser.: No. 4). 1996. 35.00 (*0-87013-390-X*) Mich St U Pr.

— Masomo Ya Kisasa: Contemporary Readings in Swahili. 480p. (C). 1990. 29.95 (*0-300-04811-4*) Yale U Pr.

Biersteker, Ann & Shariff, Ibrahim N. Mashairi Ya Vita Vya Kuduhu: War Poetry in Kiswahili Exchanged at the Time of Kuduhu. LC 92-35316. (African Historical Sources Ser.: Vol. 7). (ENG & SWA.). 1995. 26.95 (*0-87013-323-3*) Mich St U Pr.

Biersteker, Thomas J. Multinationals, the State, & Control of the Nigerian Economy. LC 86-25214. (Illus.). 365p. reprint ed. pap. 113.20 (*0-608-06385-1*, 206674600008) Bks Demand.

— Reaching Agreement with the IMF: The Nigerian Negotiations, 1983-1986. (Pew Case Studies in International Affairs). 54p. (C). 1989. pap. text 3.50 (*1-56927-205-0*) Geo U Inst Dplmcy.

Biersteker, Thomas J. & Weber, Cynthia, eds. State Sovereignty As Social Construct. (Studies in International Relations: No. 46). 311p. (C). 1996. text 59.95 (*0-521-56252-X*) Cambridge U Pr.

Bierstone, Edward, ed. see Arnold, V. I.

Bierut, Michael, et al, eds. Looking Closer: Critical Writings on Graphic Design. LC 93-71922. 256p. (Orig.). 1994. pap. 18.95 (*1-880559-15-3*) Allworth Pr.

— Looking Closer No. 2: Critical Writings on Graphic Design. 2nd ed. LC 93-83003. 256p. (Orig.). 1997. pap. 18.95 (*1-880559-56-0*) Allworth Pr.

— Looking Closer Vol. 3: Classic Writings on Graphic Design. LC 98-74536. 304p. 1999. pap. 18.95 (*1-58115-022-9*) Allworth Pr.

Bierut, Michael, jt. ed. see Hall, Peter.

Bierwag, G. O. The Primary Market for Municipal Debt: Bidding Rules & Cost of Long Term Borrowing. Altman, Edward I. & Walter, Ingo I., eds. LC 80-82480. (Contemporary Studies in Economic & Financial Analysis: Vol. 29). 272p. 1981. 78.50 (*0-89232-167-9*) Jai Pr.

Bierwagen, Gordon P., ed. Organic Coatings for Corrosion Control. (ACS Symposium Ser.: No. 689). (Illus.). 468p. 1998. text 145.00 (*0-8412-3549-X*) OUP.

Bierwagen, R. M. GATT Article VI & the Protectionist Bias in Anti-Dumping Laws. (Studies in Transnational Economic Law: Vol. 7). 240p. 1990. 117.00 (*90-6544-497-1*) Kluwer Law Intl.

Bierwert, Crisca. Brushed by Cedar, Living by the River: Coast Salish Figures of Power. LC 98-40108. 320p. 1999. 35.00 (*0-8165-1919-6*) U of Ariz Pr.

Bierwert, Crisca, ed. Lushootseed Texts: An Introduction to Puget Salish Narrative Aesthetics. Hilbert, Vi & Hess, Thomas M., trs. LC 95-37060. (Studies in the Anthropology of North American Indians). (Illus.). xii, 325p. 1996. text 55.00 (*0-8032-1262-3*) U of Nebr Pr.

Bierwirth, Johanna, jt. auth. see Raab, Susan S.

Bierwisch, Manfred. Modern Linguistics, Its Development Methods & Problems. (Janua Linguarum, Ser. Minor: No. 110). 103p. 1971. pap. text 24.65 (*90-279-1657-8*) Mouton.

Bierwisch, Manfred & Heidolph, Karl E., eds. Progress in Linguistics: A Collection of Papers. LC 78-123127. (Janua Linguarum, Ser.: No. 43). 1970. text 63.10 (*90-279-0723-4*) Mouton.

Bierwisch, Manfred & Lang, E. K., eds. Dimensional Adjectives. (Language & Communication Ser.: Vol. 26). (Illus.). x, 523p. 1989. 128.00 (*0-387-50633-0*, 3157) Spr-Verlag.

Bierwolf, D., et al. Geschwuelste - Tumors Two. LC 56-2297. (Handbuch der Allgemeinen Pathologie Ser.: Vol. 6, Pt. 6). (Illus.). 908p. 1975. 368.00 (*0-387-06820-1*) Spr-Verlag.

Biery, Darryl N., jt. auth. see Owens, Jerry M.

Biery, Ken D., Jr. & Schaub, James L. Women & Children First: How to Avoid Crime. 164p. 1998. pap. text 8.00 (*0-7881-5758-2*) DIANE Pub.

Biery, Ken D., jt. auth. see Schaub, James L.

Biery, Thomas A. Alco's to Allentown. (Illus.). 112p. 1998. pap. 29.95 (*0-9657709-1-5*) Railroad Pr.

Bies, David A. & Hansen, Colin H. Engineering Noise Control: Theory & Practice. (Illus.). 448p. 1988. 85.00 (*0-04-620021-5*); pap. 39.95 (*0-04-620022-3*) Routledge.

— Engineering Noise Control: Theory & Practice. 2nd ed. (Illus.). 640p. (C). 1995. pap. 75.00 (*0-419-20430-X*, E & FN Spon) Routledge.

***Bies, Fred.** Common Basketball Rules & Violations Made Simple. (Illus.). 66p. 1999. pap. 10.95 (*0-9677152-0-2*) Basketball Res.

Bies, John D. The Maintenance Mechanic's-Machinist's Toolbox Manual. 380p. 1992. pap. text 9.95 (*0-13-545666-5*) P-H.

— Mapping & Topographic Drafting. (Drafting Ser.). 1983. teacher ed. 17.50 (*0-538-33331-6*); text 42.95 (*0-538-33330-8*) S-W Pub.

— Sheet Metal Work. 472p. 1985. 19.95 (*0-8161-1706-3*) Macmillan.

Bies, Robert J., jt. ed. see Sitkin, Sim B.

Biesanz, John B., jt. auth. see Biesanz, Mavis H.

Biesanz, Mavis H. Helmi Mavis: A Finnish-American Girlhood. LC 89-15948. 1989. pap. 12.95 (*0-87839-052-9*) North Star.

Biesanz, Mavis H. & Biesanz, John B. Costa Rican Life. LC 78-12865. (Illus.). 272p. 1979. lib. bdg. 35.00 (*0-313-21125-6*, BICR, Greenwood Pr) Greenwood.

Biesanz, Mavis H., et al. The Ticos: Culture & Social Change in Costa Rica. LC 98-7422. 307p. 1998. pap. 19.95 (*1-55587-737-0*); lib. bdg. 55.00 (*1-55587-724-9*) L Rienner.

Biesanz, Richard, et al. The Costa Ricans. (Illus.). 250p. (C). 1988. reprint ed. pap. text 12.50 (*0-88133-340-9*) Waveland Pr.

***Biesboer, P. & Togneri, Carol.** Collections of Paintings in Harlem, 1572-1745. LC 00-28420. (Illus.). 2000. write for info. (*0-89236-573-0*) J P Getty Trust.

Biesboer, Pieter, jt. ed. see Welu, James A.

Biesbrouck, Wouter, jt. ed. see Jackson, Marvin.

Biesch, June. Take Notes. (Paper Moon Bks.). 30p. (Orig.). pap. text 5.00 (*1-884438-02-4*) Epiphany AR.

Bieschke, Ken. Whispers of the Heart: A Collection of Poems. 1998. pap. write for info. (*1-57553-857-1*) Watermrk Pr.

Biesecker, Courtney. Infinity Plus One. 1998. 10.00 (*0-533-12317-8*) Vantage.

Biesecker-Mast, Gerald, jt. ed. see Biesecker-Mast, Susan.

***Biesecker-Mast, Susan & Biesecker-Mast, Gerald, eds.** Anabaptists & Postmodernity. (C. Henry Smith Ser.: 1). 440p. 2000. pap. 26.95 (*0-9665021-2-4*) Pandora PA.

Biesel, David B. Can You Name That Team? A Guide to Professional Baseball, Football, Soccer, Hockey, & Basketball Teams & Leagues. LC 91-26356. 240p. 1991. 39.50 (*0-8108-2458-2*) Scarecrow.

Biesel, Diane, jt. ed. see Okiko, Miyake.

Biesel, Diane, ed. see Wright, Kieth C. & Davie, Judith F.

Biesel, Diane de Cordova, ed. see Hachten Wee, Patricia.

Biesele, Megan. Women Like Meat: The Folklore & Foraging Ideology of the Kalahari Ju - 'hoan. LC 93-12414. 247p. 1993. 31.50 (*0-253-31565-4*); pap. 15.95 (*0-253-31566-2*) Ind U Pr.

Biesele, Megan & Loloo, Kxao. San. LC 96-38235. (Heritage Library of African Peoples: Set 4). (Illus.). 64p. (YA). (gr. 7-12). 1996. lib. bdg. 16.95 (*0-8239-1997-8*, D1997-8) Rosen Group.

***Biesele, Megan, et al.** Hunters & Gatherers in Modern Context: Conflict, Resistance & Self-Determination. LC 98-44905. 512p. 2000. 69.95 (*1-57181-101-X*) Berghahn Bks.

Biesele, Rudolf. The History of German Settlements in Texas. (Illus.). 280p. 21.95 (*1-57168-236-8*) Sunbelt Media.

Biesele, Rudolph L. The History of the German Settlements in Texas 1831-1861. (Illus.). x, 266p. 1987. reprint ed. 20.00 (*0-944779-02-6*) German-TX Herit Soc.

— History of the German Settlements in Texas, 1831-1861. 1993. reprint ed. lib. bdg. 75.00 (*0-7812-5916-9*) Rprt Serv.

Biesemans, S., jt. ed. see De Meyer, K.

***Biesemeier, Chris, et al.** Connective Leadership. LC 00-36350. 2000. write for info. (*0-88091-178-6*) Am Dietetic Assn.

Biesenberger, Joseph A. & Sebastican, Donald H. Principles of Polymerization Engineering. 768p. 1993. reprint ed. 92.00 (*0-89464-603-6*) Krieger.

Bieshman, Margot S., jt. auth. see Biestman, Margot S.

Biesiot, Elizabeth. Natural Treasures Field Guide for Kids. (Illus.). 64p. (Orig.). (J). (gr. 3-6). 1996. pap. 12.95 (*1-57098-082-9*) Roberts Rinehart.

Biesiot, Wouter, jt. auth. see Mulder, Henk A.

B

Biesman, Brian S. Lasers in Facial Aesthetic & Reconstructive Surgery. LC 98-21399. 182p. 1998. 99.00 (*0-683-30414-3*) Lppncott W & W.

Biesold, D., jt. ed. see Steriade, Mircea.

Biesold, Horst. Crying Hands: Eugenics & Deaf People in Nazi Germany. LC 99-27291. 208p. 1999. 39.95 (*1-56368-077-7*) Gallaudet Univ Pr.

Biespiel, David. Shattering Air. (New Poets of America Ser.: Vol. 17). 65p. 1996. 20.00 (*1-880238-34-9*); pap. 12.50 (*1-880238-35-7*) BOA Edns.

Biesseling, J. F. & Eckhaus, Wiktor, eds. Trends in Applications of Mathematics to Mechanics. (Illus.). ix, 361p. 1988. 71.95 (*0-387-50075-8*) Spr-Verlag.

Biestek, T. & Weber, J. Electrolytic & Chemical Conversion Coatings. 434p. 1989. 300.00 (*0-901994-78-2*, Pub. by Fuel Metallurgical Jrnl) St Mut.

Biester, James. Lyric Wonder: Rhetoric & Wit in Renaissance English Poetry. LC 96-35473. (Rhetoric & Society Ser.). 232p. 1996. text 39.95 (*0-8014-3313-4*) Cornell U Pr.

Biestman, Margot S. Travel for Two: The Art of Compromise. (Illus.). 192p. (Orig.). 1986. pap. 10.95 (*0-936865-07-5*) Pergot Pr.

Biestman, Margot S. & Bieshman, Margot S. Grammie Stories - When Grammie Was Little, Vol. 1: Grammie Finds a Way Out of Camp; Grammie As a Bully. unabridged ed. Boatwright, Alice, ed. (Grammie Stories Ser.: Vol. 2). (Illus.). 26p. (J). (gr. k-6). 1993. pap. 7.95 incl. audio (*0-936865-09-1*) Pergot Pr.

— Grammie Stories - When Grammie Was Little, Vol. 2: Grammie & the Rosebud Fairy; Grammie & Good Times with Her Mother. unabridged ed. Boatwright, Alice, ed. (Grammie Stories Ser.: Vol. 1). (Illus.). 24p. (J). (gr. k-6). 1992. pap. 7.95 incl. audio (*0-936865-10-5*) Pergot Pr.

Biesty, Stephen. Barco de Guerra del Siglo XVII: Cross Sections, Man of War. 1995. 25.99 (*84-372-4536-2*) Santillana.

— Look Inside Cross-Sections: Planes. (Illus.). 32p. (J). pap. 8.99 (*0-590-24341-1*) Scholastic Inc.

— Look Inside Cross-Sections: Ships. (Illus.). 32p. (J). pap. 8.99 (*0-590-24342-X*) Scholastic Inc.

— Stephen Biesty's Incredible Pop-Up Cross-Sections. LC 97-214690. (Illus.). (J). 1995. 16.95 (*0-7894-0199-1*, 5-70612) DK Pub Inc.

Biesty, Stephen & Platt, Richard. Stephen Biesty's Incredible Explosions: Exploded Views of Astonishing Things. (Illus.). 32p. (J). 22.99 (*0-590-24893-6*) Scholastic Inc.

Biesty, Stephen & Platt, Roger. Cross-Sections: Castle. LC 93-30158. (Illus.). 32p. (J). 1994. 16.95 (*1-56458-467-4*) DK Pub Inc.

Biesty, Stephen, jt. auth. see Platt, Richard.

Bietenholz, Peter G. Historia & Fabula: Myths & Legends in Historical Thought from Antiquity to the Modern Age. LC 94-33178. (Studies in Intellectual History). 464p. 1994. 114.50 (*90-04-10063-6*) Brill Academic Pubs.

Bietenholz, Peter G., ed. The Correspondence of Erasmus Vol. 8: Letters 1122-1251 (1520-1521) Mynors, Roger A., tr. 1988. text 85.00 (*0-8020-2607-9*) U of Toronto Pr.

Bietenholz, Peter G. & Deutscher, Thomas B., eds. Contemporaries of Erasmus: A Biographical Register of the Renaissance, Vol. 3 (N-Z) 1987. text 100.00 (*0-8020-2575-7*) U of Toronto Pr.

— Contemporaries of Erasmus: A Biographical Register of the Renaissance & Reformation, Vol. 2. 504p. 1986. text 95.00 (*0-8020-2571-4*) U of Toronto Pr.

Bietenholz, Peter G., et al. The Correspondence of Erasmus: Letters 842-992 (May 1518 - June 1519) Mynors, Roger A., tr. (Collected Works of Erasmus: Vol. 6). 1981. text 85.00 (*0-8020-5500-1*) U of Toronto Pr.

Bietenholz, Peter G., ed. see Erasmus, Desiderius.

***Bieter, John & Bieter, Mark.** An Enduring Legacy: A Story of Basques in Idaho. LC 00-8233. (Basque Ser.). 2000. write for info. (*0-87417-333-7*) U of Nev Pr.

Bieter, Mark, jt. auth. see Bieter, John.

Bieth, J. G., et al. Practical Dictionary of English for Biologists, Chemists & Doctors: Dictionnaire Pratique de l'Anglais pour les Biologistes, Chimistes, Medecins. (ENG & FRE.). 272p. 1983. 89.95 (*0-8288-0560-1*, M14532) Fr & Eur.

Biethahn, Jorg & Nissen, Volker. Evolutionary Algorithms in Management Applications. LC 95-45889. 378p. 1995. 115.00 (*3-540-60382-4*) Spr-Verlag.

Bieto, Gretchen U. Coya Come Home: A Congresswoman's Journey. (Illus.). 336p. 1998. pap. 17.95 (*0-938817-45-0*) Pomegranate Pr.

Bietz, J. A. HPLC High Performance Liquid Chromatography of Cereal & Legume Proteins. Kruger, James E., ed. LC 94-76856. (Illus.). 426p. 1994. 129.00 (*0-913250-82-1*) Am Assn Cereal Chem.

Bietz, R. R. Happy Home Farm. LC 94-60336. 128p. 1994. per. 6.95 (*0-945383-87-8*) Teach Servs.

Bietze, Andreas, tr. see Froese, Arno.

Bievenue, Lisa A., jt. auth. see Nagel, Stuart S.

Biever, Bruce F. Religion, Culture & Values: A Cross-Cultural Analysis of Motivational Factors in Native Irish & American Irish Catholicism. LC 76-6322. (Irish Americans Ser.). 1976. 68.95 (*0-405-09319-5*) Ayer.

Biever, Dale, et al. Four Pennsylvania German Studies. (Pennsylvania German Folklore Ser.: Vol. 3). 1970. 20.00 (*0-911122-26-5*) Penn German Soc.

Biever, Vernon J. The Glory of Titletown: The Classic Green Bay Packers Photography of Vernon Biever. LC 97-20810. (Illus.). 256p. 1997. 36.95 (*0-87833-990-6*) Taylor Pub.

Biey, Mario & Premoli, Amedeo. Tables for Active Filter Design: Based on Cauer MCPER Functions. LC 84-73279. (Illus.). 576p. 1985. reprint ed. pap. 178.60 (*0-7837-9770-2*, 206049800005) Bks Demand.

Biezad, Daniel J. Integrated Navigation & Guidance Systems. LC 98-54413. (AIAA Education Ser.). 1999. write for info. (*1-56347-291-0*) AIAA.

Bifano, Thomas G., ed. Proceedings from ASPE, 1994 Annual Meeting. 473p. 1994. pap. write for info. (*1-887706-12-7*) Am Soc Prec Engr.

Bifano, Thomas G., et al, eds. Proceedings from ASPE Spring Topical Meeting on Precision Grinding of Brittle Materials. (Illus.). 128p. 1996. pap. write for info. (*1-887706-15-1*) Am Soc Prec Engr.

***Biffar, Donna.** Events Preceding Death: Poems. LC 99-55331. 92p. 2000. pap. text 19.95 (*0-7734-2794-5*) E Mellen.

Biffar, Donna. Water Witching in the Garden: Poems. LC 95-39508. 64p. 1995. pap. 14.95 (*0-7734-2670-1*, Mellen Poetry Pr) E Mellen.

Biffen, John. Inside Westminster. (Illus.). 288p. 1996. 22.95 (*0-233-98979-X*, Pub. by Andre Deutsch) Trafalgar.

Biffi, Inos. An Introduction to the Liturgical Year. LC 94-40623.Tr. of Piccola Guida al Messale. (ENG & ITA., Illus.). 100p. (YA). (gr. 5 up). 1995. 17.00 (*0-8028-5103-7*) Eerdmans.

— The Sacraments. LC 93-39150. (My First Catechism Ser.). (Illus.). 29p. (J). 1994. 12.00 (*0-8028-3757-3*, Eerdmans Bks) Eerdmans.

— The Way of the Cross. LC 96-45055. (Illus.). 48p. (YA). (gr. 5 up). 1997. 12.00 (*0-8028-5135-5*, Eerdmans Bks) Eerdmans.

— The Way to Bethlehem. LC 97-21274. (Illus.). 47p. (YA). (gr. 5 up). 1997. 14.00 (*0-8028-5159-2*, Eerdmans Bks) Eerdmans.

Biffignandi, Silvia, ed. Micro- & Macrodata of Firms: Statistical Analysis & International Comparison. LC 98-55551. (Contibutions to Statistics Ser.). (Illus.). xii, 751p. 1999. pap. 119.00 (*3-7908-1143-2*) Spr-Verlag.

Biffle, Christopher. A Guided Tour of Five Works by Plato: With Complete Translations of Euthyphro, Apology, Crito, Phaedo Death Scene & Allegory of the Cave. 2nd ed. LC 94-29164. viii, 125p. (C). 1994. pap. text 10.95 (*1-55934-356-7*, 1356) Mayfield Pub.

***Biffle, Christopher.** A Guided Tour of Renbe Descartes' Meditations on First Philosophy. 3rd ed. LC 00-37225. 2000. write for info. (*0-7674-0975-2*) Mayfield Pub.

Biffle, Christopher. A Guided Tour of Rene Descartes' Meditations on First Philosophy. 2nd ed. Rubin, Ronald, tr. LC 95-25339. 130p. 1995. pap. text 10.95 (*1-55934-512-8*, 1512) Mayfield Pub.

— Landscape of Wisdom: A Guided Tour of Western Philosophy. LC 98-39193. 792p. 1998. pap. text 49.95 (*1-55934-724-4*, 724-4) Mayfield Pub.

***Biffle, Christopher & Plato.** A Guided Tour of Five Works by Plato: With Complete Translations of Euthyphro, Apology, Crito, Phaedo (Death Scene) & "Allegory of the Cave" 3rd ed. LC 00-21557. 2000. write for info. (*0-7674-1033-5*) Mayfield Pub.

Biffle, Christopher, ed. see Aristotle.

Biffle, Kent. A Month of Sundays. LC 93-7882. 261p. 1993. pap. 12.95 (*0-929398-56-4*) UNTX Pr.

Bifsso, John, ed. see Dorian, Michael.

Bifulco, Antonia & Moran, Patricia. Wednesday's Child Is Full of Woe: Research into Women's Experience of Neglect & Abuse in Childhood & Adult Depression. LC 97-26564. 224p. (C). 1998. 80.00 (*0-415-16526-1*); pap. 24.99 (*0-415-16527-X*) Routledge.

BiFulco, Michael. Superman on Television: Tenth Anniversary Edition. 10th anniversary rev. ed. (Illus.). 240p. 1998. pap. 24.95 (*0-9619596-3-0*) M Bifulco.

Big Bend National Park Staff & Big Bend Natural History Association Staff. Hiking Big Bend National Park. LC 96-12282. (Travel Guide Ser.). (Illus.). 176p. (Orig.). 1993. pap. 12.95 (*1-56044-286-7*) Falcon Pub Inc.

Big Bend Natural History Association Staff, jt. auth. see Big Bend National Park Staff.

Big D Unlimited Staff. A Guidebook to the Psilocybin Mushrooms of Mexico. (Illus.). (Orig.). 1976. pap. 3.00 (*0-934600-01-5*) Mother Duck Pr.

Big Entertainment Staff. Beach High, Vol. 1. (Illus.). 24p. (Orig.). 1996. pap. text 3.25 (*1-57780-000-1*) Big Enter Inc.

***Big Fish Staff.** Sensuality: Great Minds Explore the Senses. 144p. 2000. 16.00 (*0-688-17275-X*, Wm Morrow) Morrow Avon.

***Big Guy Books Staff.** American Trucks. (Illus.). (J). 2000. 11.95 (*1-929945-04-3*) Big Guy Books.

— Arthur. (Illus.). (J). 2000. 16.95 (*1-929945-05-1*) Big Guy Books.

— Dinosaurs & Machines. (Illus.). (J). 2000. 11.95 (*1-929945-09-4*) Big Guy Books.

— Heavy Equipment. (Illus.). (J). 2000. 11.95 (*1-929945-08-6*) Big Guy Books.

— Man on the Cross. (Illus.). (J). 2001. 16.95 (*1-929945-06-X*) Big Guy Books.

— Patch. (Illus.). (J). 2000. 16.95 (*1-929945-02-7*) Big Guy Books.

— Rex. (Illus.). (J). 2000. 16.95 (*1-929945-00-0*) Big Guy Books.

— Rex II. (Illus.). (J). 2000. 16.95 (*1-929945-01-9*) Big Guy Books.

— Robin Hood. (Illus.). (J). 2001. 16.95 (*1-929945-07-8*) Big Guy Books.

— Tanks & Army Stuff. (Illus.). (J). 2000. 11.95 (*1-929945-10-8*) Big Guy Books.

Big Ten Conference Staff. Official Big Ten Football Fan's Guide, 1997-1998. rev. ed. (Illus.). 128p. 1997. pap. 9.95 (*1-57243-203-9*) Triumph Bks.

Big Ten Conference Staff & Triumph Books Staff. Official Big Ten Football Fan's Guide, 1998-1999. (Illus.). 132p. 1998. pap. 9.95 (*1-57243-268-3*) Triumph Bks.

Big Twelve Conference Staff & Triumph Books Staff. Official Big 12 Football Guide, 1998-1999. (Illus.). 192p. 1998. pap. 9.95 (*1-57243-271-3*) Triumph Bks.

Big 12 Conference Staff. Official Big 12 Football Guide, 1997-1998. (Illus.). 128p. (Orig.). 1997. pap. 9.95 (*1-57243-206-3*) Triumph Bks.

Bigaham, Chris. Promise of God's Presence. 1999. pap. text 9.99 (*0-8474-1713-1*) Back to Bible.

***Bigaj, Agnieszka Joanna.** Structural Dependence of Rotation Capacity of Plactic Hinges in RC Beams & Slabs. (Illus.). 236p. 1999. pap. 57.50 (*90-407-1926-8*, Pub. by Delft U Pr) Coronet Bks.

Bigalk. Craft of Composition: The Activities & Advice for College Writers. LC 99-52342. 110p. 1999. pap. text 16.80 (*0-13-080603-X*) P-H.

Bigan, Tammy. Nail Art & Design. LC 93-28383. (NAILS). 90p. 1993. pap. 41.95 (*1-56253-118-2*) Thomson Learn.

— Tech Nails. (NAILS). (Illus.). 160p. (C). 1991. pap. 31.95 (*0-87350-382-1*) Thomson Learn.

Bigandet, Paul A. The Life, or Legend of Gaudama: The Buddha of the Burmese, 2 vols., Set. 4th ed. LC 77-8749. reprint ed. 75.00 (*0-404-16800-0*) AMS Pr.

Bigar, F., ed. Microsurgery Update, 1982-1984. (Developments in Ophthalmology Ser.: Vol. 11). (Illus.). x, 206p. 1985. 110.50 (*3-8055-4004-3*) S Karger.

Bigar, Jacqueline. Women & Their Moon Signs: Discover the Power of the Moon in Your Life. LC 98-23587. 368p. 1998. pap. 14.00 (*0-380-79779-8*, Avon Bks) Morrow Avon.

Bigarelli, Alessandro. Ethik Und Diskurs Im Weiblichen Schreiben Am Beispiel Von Helga Schuberts Geschichten: Eine Interdisziplinare Untersuchung: Literatur, Philosophie, Psychologie. 281p. 1998. 48.95 (*3-631-33846-5*) P Lang Pubng.

Bigart, Robert. Name of Salish & Kootenai Nation: The 1855 Hell Gate Treaty & the Origin of the Flathead Indian Reservation. LC 96-4730. (Illus.). 180p. 1996. pap. 14.95 (*0-295-97545-8*) U of Wash Pr.

Bigart, Robert, ed. see Arlee, Johnny.

Bigas, Sylvia. La Narrativa Indigenista Mexicana del Siglo, No. XX. 488p. 1990. pap. 25.00 (*0-8477-3647-4*) U of PR Pr.

Bigazzi, Pierluigi E. & Reichlin, Seymour, eds. Systemic Autoimmunity. (Immunology Ser.: Vol. 54). (Illus.). 320p. 1991. text 195.00 (*0-8247-8550-9*) Dekker.

Bigbee, Ivy. Optical Allusions: An Art Photographer's Poems. unabridged ed. (Illus.). 119p. 1998. 47.50 (*0-9663161-0-X*) Reddi-Arts.

— Successful Slides: Photographing Your Artwork. Stevens, Marilyn, ed. (Art Calendar Guide Ser.). (Illus.). 35p. 1999. pap. 9.95 (*0-945388-12-8*) Art Calendar.

***Bigby, Christine.** Moving on Without Parents: Planning, Transitions & Sources of Support for Middle-Aged & Older Adults with Intellectual Disability. LC 00-33668. 2000. write for info. (*1-55766-478-1*) P H Brookes.

Bigel, Alan I. Justices William J. Brennan, Jr. & Thurgood Marshall on Capital Punishment: Its Constitutionality, Morality, Deterrent Effect, & Interpretation by the Court. 164p. 1997. 37.50 (*0-7618-0614-8*) U Pr of Amer.

Bigel-Casher, Rita. Bride's Guide to Emotional Survival. LC 95-20683. (Illus.). 256p. 1995. pap. 14.00 (*0-7615-0296-3*) Prima Pub.

— Bride's Guide to Emotional Survival. 256p. 1997. per. 14.00 (*0-7615-1156-3*) Prima Pub.

Bigel Institute for Health Policy Staff & United Hospital Fund Staff. New York City's Hospital Occupancy Crisis: Caring for a Changing Patient Population. 36p. 1988. 25.00 (*0-934459-50-9*) United Hosp Fund.

Bigell, Donovan. Digital Electronics. 4th ed. (C). 1999. pap. text, lab manual ed. 22.00 (*0-7668-0330-9*) Thomson Learn.

Bigelow. Plug & Play Book. 1999. 29.99 (*0-07-134775-5*) McGraw.

— Type Design in the Digital Realm. (Design & Graphic Design Ser.). 1995. text 49.95 (*0-442-02218-2*, VNR) Wiley.

***Bigelow, Alister, ed.** Encyclopaedia of Sex Education, 3 vols. 1999. 185.00 (*81-7020-860-2*, Pub. by Cosmo Pubn) S Asia.

Bigelow, Ann C., ed. Current Soviet Policies Vol. II: Documents from the 28th Congress of the Communist Party. Current Digest of the Soviet Press Staff, tr. from RUS. 128p. (Orig.). (C). 1991. pap. 27.00 (*0-913601-11-X*) Current Digest.

Bigelow, Ann C., jt. ed. see Schulze, Fred.

Bigelow, Ann C., tr. see Cosic, Bora.

Bigelow, B. William. Woodworking Techniques, Tips & Projects from a Master Craftsman. (Illus.). 224p. 1989. 24.95 (*0-8306-9255-X*) McGraw-Hill Prof.

Bigelow, Bill & Peterson, Bob, eds. Global Sweatshops: The Lives Behind the Labels. (Illus.). 160p. 1998. pap. 8.00 (*0-942961-22-6*) Rethinking Schls.

— Rethinking Columbus: The Next 500 Years. 2nd ed. (Illus.). 192p. 1998. pap. 6.00 (*0-942961-20-X*) Rethinking Schls.

Bigelow, Bill, et al. Rethinking Our Classrooms: Teaching for Equity & Justice. Miner, Barbara, ed. (Illus.). 216p. 1994. pap. 6.00 (*0-942961-18-8*) Rethinking Schls.

Bigelow, Brian J., et al. Learning the Rules: The Anatomy of Children's Relationships. LC 96-15609. (Series on Personal Relationships). 255p. 1996. lib. bdg. 36.00 (*1-57230-084-1*) Guilford Pubns.

Bigelow, Charles, et al, eds. Fine Print on Type: The Best of Fine Print Magazine on Type & Typography, 1977-1988. LC 88-17729. (Illus.). 1988. pap. 25.00 (0-9607290-2-X) Pro Arte Libri.

This collection of essays on type design & typography, written by some of the most foremost designers & scholars in the field, will appeal to those who use, study, & love type - from advertising designers to desktop publishers, from research bibliographers to just plain discerning readers, all of whom have observed & been fascinated by the way TYPE, apparently a neutral conveyor, can radically affect the meaning & impact of the message. FINE PRINT magazine has regularly published a series of articles under the title "On Type," exploring the history & development of type design from its scribal roots to the best in digital type for the new electronic media. This anthology makes for a stimulating & instructive mix of the aesthetic & the technical, the traditional & the avant-garde. Types covered include the up-to-date & quotidian like ITC Zapf Chancery, Galliard, & Iridium, as well as little-known but interesting historical faces like Fleischmann Antiqua, Hiero-Rhode Italic, & Hammer Uncial. Here sixteenth- & seventeenth-century type designers like Claude Garamond & Miklos Kis share the stage with "bit wizards" of our own time like Kris Holmes, Sumner Stone & Adrian Frutiger. Pro Arte Libri, P.O. Box 193397, San Francisco, CA 94119-3397. e-mail: wordpusher@aol.com. $25.00 plus $3.50 shipping. 30 discount on 3 or more copies. ***Publisher Paid Annotation.***

Bigelow, Charles R. Hazardous Materials Management in Physical Distribution. 234p. 1994. 90.00 (*0-471-29067-X*, VNR) Wiley.

Bigelow, David. Thinking Pro/Engineer: Mastering Design Methodology. (Illus.). 368p. (C). 1995. pap. 76.50 (*1-56690-065-4*, 1910) Thomson Learn.

Bigelow, Deborah, ed. Gilded Wood, History & Conservation. (Illus.). 432p. 1992. boxed set 89.00 (*0-932087-21-3*) Sound View Pr.

Bigelow, Donald N. William Conant Church & the Army & Navy Journal. LC 68-59264. (Columbia University. Studies in the Social Sciences: No. 576). reprint ed. 27.50 (*0-404-51576-2*) AMS Pr.

Bigelow, Ernest N. Mommy Isn't Sick; She's Just Dying. 157p. (Orig.). 1993. pap. 9.50 (*0-9632030-0-2*) Bigelow Pub.

Bigelow, Gary. Sisters of Interment. LC 98-36273. (Literature Ser.). (Illus.). 264p. 1998. pap. 16.95 (*1-878610-67-8*) Red Crane Bks.

Bigelow, Gladys M. & Knowles, Ruth M. History of St. Albans, ME. (Illus.). 418p. 1995. reprint ed. pap. text 30.00 (*0-7884-0213-7*) Heritage Bk.

Bigelow, Gordon E. Frontier Eden: The Literary Career of Marjorie Kinnan Rawlings. LC 66-26808. (Illus.). xviii, 162p. 1966. pap. 17.95 (*0-8130-0672-4*) U Press Fla.

— Rhetoric & American Poetry of the Early National Period. LC 60-63133. (University of Florida Humanities Monographs: No. 4). 86p. reprint ed. pap. 30.00 (*0-7837-5027-7*, 204469500004) Bks Demand.

Bigelow, Gordon E. & Monti, Laura V., eds. Selected Letters of Marjorie Kinnan Rawlings. LC 82-2674. (Illus.). vi, 414p. 1983. pap. 19.95 (*0-8130-0899-9*) U Press Fla.

Bigelow, Jacob. The History of Mount Aubum Cemetery. 288p. 1989. 14.95 (*1-55709-121-8*) Applewood.

— The Useful Arts. LC 72-5034. (Technology & Society Ser.). (Illus.). 762p. 1972. reprint ed. 46.95 (*0-405-04687-1*) Ayer.

Bigelow, James H., et al. Using the Force & Support Costing System: An Introduction Guide & Tutorial. LC 98-29721. 72p. 1999. pap. 15.00 (*0-8330-2641-0*, MR-991-OSD) Rand Corp.

Bigelow, James H., jt. auth. see Davis, Paul K.

Bigelow, Jim. The Joy of Uncircumcising! 2nd ed. (Illus.). 240p. (Orig.). 1998. pap. 19.95 (*0-934061-22-X*) Marketscope Bks.

Bigelow, Jo, ed. see Rea, Sara W.

Bigelow, John. The Campaign of Chancellorsville. (Illus.). 528p. 1983. reprint ed. 200.00 (*0-89029-075-X*) Morningside Bkshop.

— The Campaign of Chancellorsville: A Strategic & Tactical Study. (Illus.). 528p. 1991. reprint ed. lthr. 250.00 (*0-89029-097-0*) Morningside Bkshop.

— Earth Energy: The Entrancing Force with a Thousand Names. 54p. 1996. spiral bd. 14.00 (*0-7873-0111-6*) Hlth Research.

— Frogstein's Saucer Technology. 18p. 1996. reprint ed. spiral bd. 8.00 (*0-7873-0110-8*) Hlth Research.

— Jamaica in Eighteen-Hundred Fifty: The Effects on Sixteen Years of Freedom on a Slave Colony. LC 72-106880. 214p. 1970. reprint ed. lib. bdg. 45.00 (*0-8371-3276-2*, BIJ&) Greenwood.

— Mystery of Sleep (1905) 224p. 1998. reprint ed. pap. 17.95 (*0-7661-0579-2*) Kessinger Pub.

— The Peach Orchard: Gettysburg, July 2, 1863. 57p. 1987. reprint ed. pap. 10.00 (*0-942211-25-1*) Olde Soldier Bks.

— The Reality of Numbers: A Physicalist's Philosophy of Mathematics. (Illus.). 208p. 1988. text 55.00 (*0-19-824957-8*) OUP.

— Toleration, & Other Essays & Studies. LC 78-84298. (Essay Index Reprint Ser.). 1977. 17.95 (*0-8369-1075-3*) Ayer.

— William Cullen Bryant. LC 70-125678. (American Journalists Ser.). 1978. reprint ed. 25.95 (*0-405-01653-0*) Ayer.

Bigelow, John & Pargetter, Robert. Science & Necessity. (Cambridge Studies in Philosophy). 422p. (C). 1991. text 85.00 (*0-521-39027-3*) Cambridge U Pr.

Bigelow, John, ed. see Tilden, Samuel J.

An Asterisk (*) at the beginning of an entry indicates that the title is appearing for the first time.

Bigelow, John D. Managerial Skills: Explorations in Applied Knowledge. (Illus.). 320p. 1991. text 55.00 (*0-8039-4095-5*); pap. text 25.00 (*0-8039-4096-3*) Sage.

Bigelow, Josette, ed. see Berlandier, Jean L., et al.

Bigelow, M. M., ed. Commentaries on the Constitution of the United States, 2 vols., Set. 5th ed. LC 94-76119. 1610p. 1994. reprint ed. 150.00 (*0-89941-883-X*, 308260) W S Hein.

Bigelow, Melville M. Elements of the Law of Torts for the Use of Students: For the Use of Students. 5th ed. LC 98-10849. xxviii, 386p. 1998. reprint ed. 47.50 (*0-8377-1988-7*, Rothman) W S Hein.

— History of Procedure in England from the Norman Conquest. LC 87-81278. viii, 411p. 1987. reprint ed. lib. bdg. 48.50 (*0-89941-561-X*, 305190) W S Hein.

— History of Procedure in England from the Norman Conquest: The Norman Period (1066-1204) LC 80-2235. reprint ed. 49.50 (*0-404-18752-8*) AMS Pr.

— Law of Bills, Notes, & Checks: Illustrated by Leading Cases. 2nd ed. LC 96-42490. xliii, 692p. 1996. reprint ed. 75.00 (*0-8377-1983-6*, Rothman) W S Hein.

— Law of Fraud & the Procedure Pertaining to the Redress Thereof. lix, 696p. 1981. reprint ed. 85.00 (*0-8377-0317-4*, Rothman) W S Hein.

*__Bigelow, Melville M.__ Law of Torts. 7th ed. 1999. reprint ed. 145.00 (*1-56169-454-1*) Gaunt.

Bigelow, Melville M. Law of Wills for Students. xxxii, 398p. 1996. reprint ed. 52.50 (*0-8377-1984-4*, Rothman) W S Hein.

— Papers on the Legal History of Government: Difficulties Fundamental & Artificial. 256p. 1982. reprint ed. 35.00 (*0-8377-0326-3*, Rothman) W S Hein.

— Placita Anglo-Normannica. lxiv, 328p. 1974. reprint ed. 90.00 (*3-487-05293-8*) G Olms Pubs.

— Placita Anglo-Normannica: Law Cases from William I to Richard I. lxiv, 328p. 1970. reprint ed. 35.00 (*0-8377-1928-3*, Rothman) W S Hein.

— Treatise on the Law of Estoppel & Its Application in Practice. lxiv, 656p. 1991. reprint ed. 75.00 (*0-8377-1923-2*, Rothman) W S Hein.

Bigelow, Melville M., intro. Centralization & the Law, Scientific Legal Education: An Illustration. LC 72-181856. xx, 296p. 1972. reprint ed. 35.00 (*0-8377-2004-4*, Rothman) W S Hein.

Bigelow, Melville M., jt. auth. see Story, Joseph.

Bigelow, Otis. The Giants' Dance. 1965. pap. 5.25 (*0-8222-0441-X*) Dramatists Play.

— The Peacock Season. 1971. pap. 13.00 (*0-8222-0882-2*) Dramatists Play.

Bigelow, Pat. The Conning, the Cunning of Being: Being a Kierkegaardian Demonstration of the Postmodern Implosion of Metaphysical Sense in Aristotle & the Early Heidegger. 264p. 1990. 49.95 (*0-8130-0952-9*) U Press Fla.

— Kierkegaard & the Problem of Writing. LC 87-6182. (Kierkegaard & Postmodernism Ser.). 192p. 1988. pap. 24.95 (*0-8130-0856-5*) U Press Fla.

Bigelow, Patricia, ed. see Bigelow Society, Inc. Staff.

Bigelow, Roberta, et al. Nuclear & Particle Physics Simulations: The Consortium of Upper-Level Physics Software. LC 95-35662. 240p. 1995. pap., pap. text 46.95 incl. disk (*0-471-54883-9*) Wiley.

Bigelow, S. Tupper. The Baker Street Briefs. (Illus.). 178p. 1993. pap. 16.00 (*0-88773-409-X*, Pub. by MTLB) Battered Silicon.

Bigelow, S. Tupper. The Baker Street Briefs. Hollyer, Cameron, ed. LC 93-95451. (Illus.). 178p. 1993. pap., spiral bd. 16.00 (*0-88773-040-X*) Battered Silicon.

Bigelow, S. Tupper. An Irregular Anglo-American Glossary of More or Less Unfamiliar Words, Terms & Phrases in the Sherlock Holmes Saga. 1995. pap. 16.00 (*1-896032-31-1*, Pub. by Grg A Vanderburgh) Battered Silicon.

— An Irregular Anglo-American Glossary of More or Less Unfamiliar Words, Terms & Phrases in the Sherlock Holmes Saga. 1998. 24.00 (*1-896032-30-3*, Pub. by Grg A Vanderburgh) Battered Silicon.

Bigelow Society, Inc. Staff. Bigelow Families in 1850, Extracted from the 1850 U. S. Census. Bigelow, Patricia, ed. 165p. (Orig.). 1986. pap. 18.95 (*0-9616682-0-2*) Bigelow Soc.

— The Bigelow Family Genealogy: The First Six Generations in America, Vol. 1. Bigelow, Patricia, ed. LC 86-72956. (Family Genealogy Ser.). 385p. (Orig.). 1987. 55.00 (*0-9616682-1-0*) Bigelow Soc.

*__Bigelow, Stacie.__ Fibromyalgia: Simple Relief Through Movement. 144p. 2000. pap. 14.95 (*0-471-34802-3*) Wiley.

Bigelow, Stephen J. Bigelow's Build Your Own PC Pocket Reference. LC 97-48321. (Bigelow's Pocket Reference Ser.). 256p. 1998. pap. 19.95 (*0-07-037139-3*) McGraw.

— Bigelow's Computer Repair Toolkit. LC 96-29780. (Illus.). 464p. 1997. pap., pap. text 39.95 incl. cd-rom (*0-07-912979-X*) McGraw.

— Bigelow's PC Technician's Troubleshooting Pocket Reference. LC 97-17119. (Illus.). 421p. 1997. pap. 19.95 (*0-07-006988-3*) McGraw.

— Bigelow's Printer Troubleshooting Pocket Reference. LC 99-27803. 1999. pap. text 19.99 (*0-07-135420-4*) Osborne-McGraw.

*__Bigelow, Stephen J.__ Drive & Memory Troubleshooting Pocket Reference. LC 99-59391. (Hardware Ser.). 2000. pap. 19.99 (*0-07-135453-0*) McGrw-H Intl.

Bigelow, Stephen J. FAT FAQs PC Hardware: Troubleshooting, Upgrading, Maintaining, & Repairing. LC 98-108279. (Illus.). 704p. 1997. pap. 29.95 (*0-07-036939-9*) McGraw.

— Maintain & Repair Your Computer Printer & Save a Bundle. 240p. 1991. 26.95 (*0-8306-2563-1*) McGraw-Hill Prof.

— Maintain & Repair Your Notebook, Palmtop, & Pen Computers: A Technician's Guide. 1994. 27.00 (*0-07-005275-1*) McGraw-Hill Prof.

— Maintain & Repair Your Notebook, Palmtop, or Pen Computer. LC 93-28420. 300p. 1993. 27.00 (*0-8306-4454-7*, Windcrest) TAB Bks.

— The TAB Electronics Technician's Online Resource Reference. LC 96-42140. (Illus.). 384p. 1997. 44.95 (*0-07-036219-X*); pap. 24.95 (*0-07-036220-3*) McGraw.

— Telephone Repair Illustrated. LC 92-32381. 1993. write for info. (*0-8306-4033-9*); pap. 17.95 (*0-8306-4034-7*) McGraw-Hill Prof.

— Telephone Repair Illustrated. 1993. 28.95 (*0-07-005238-7*); 18.95 (*0-07-005239-5*) McGraw-Hill Prof.

— Troubleshooting & Repairing Computer Monitors. 2nd ed. LC 96-34038. (Illus.). 304p. 1996. 44.95 (*0-07-005733-8*); pap. 24.95 (*0-07-005734-6*) McGraw.

— Troubleshooting & Repairing Computer Printers. 2nd ed. (Illus.). 496p. 1996. 44.95 (*0-07-005731-1*); pap. 29.95 (*0-07-005732-X*) McGraw.

— Troubleshooting & Repairing PC Drives & Memory Systems. 2nd ed. LC 97-26273. 368p. 1997. 44.95 (*0-07-006384-2*); pap. 29.95 (*0-07-006385-0*) McGraw.

— Troubleshooting, Maintaining, & Repairing PCs. 2nd ed. LC 98-20453. 1520p. 1998. 59.99 incl. cd-rom (*0-07-913732-6*) McGraw.

— Troubleshooting, Maintaining & Repairing PC's: A Technician's Guide. 2nd ed. 1692p. 1998. 79.95 (*0-07-913733-4*) McGraw.

*__Bigelow, Stephen J.__ Troubleshooting, Maintaining & Repairing PCs, Millennium Ed. (Illus.). 1616p. 1999. 59.99 (*0-07-212223-4*) McGraw.

Bigelow, Stephen J. Troubleshooting, Maintaining, & Repairing Personal Computers: A Technician's Guide. LC 95-22071. (Illus.). 896p. 1995. pap. 44.95 (*0-07-912099-7*) McGraw.

— Understanding Telephone Electronics. 3rd ed. LC 97-142162. (Illus.). 367p. 1997. pap. text 24.95 (*0-7506-9944-2*) Buttrwrth-Heinemann.

Bigelow, Stephen J. & Allen, George. Understanding Telephone Electronics. 4th ed. 384p. 2000. pap. 29.95 (*0-7506-7175-0*) Buttrwrth-Heinemann.

Bigelow, Steve. Easy Laser Printer Maintenance & Repair. 205p. 1994. pap. 19.95 (*0-07-035976-8*) McGraw.

*__Bigelow, Steven J.__ Plug & Play Book. LC 99-14542. (Illus.). 243p. 1999. pap. 29.99 incl. cd-rom (*0-07-134774-7*) McGraw.

Bigelow, Suzzanne F., jt. auth. see Knudson, R. R.

Bigelow, W. C. Vacuum Methods in Electron Microscopy. Glauert, A. M., ed. (Practical Methods in Electron Microscopy Ser.: Vol. 15). (Illus.). 512p. (Orig.). (C). 1994. text 187.00 (*1-85578-053-4*, Pub. by Portland Pr Ltd); pap. text 85.00 (*1-85578-052-6*, Pub. by Portland Pr Ltd) Ashgate Pub Co.

Bigelow, William. Strangers in Their Own Country: A Curriculum Guide on South Africa. LC 85-71369. (Illus.). 104p. (Orig.). (YA). (gr. 8 up). 1987. pap. 12.95 (*0-86543-010-1*) Africa World.

Bigelow, William, jt. auth. see Diamond, Norman.

Bigelow, William S. Buddhism & Immortality. LC 78-72379. reprint ed. 32.50 (*0-404-17228-8*) AMS Pr.

Bigelsen, Sylvia. The Ties That Bind . . . And Bind . . . And Bind: A Survival Guide to In-Law Relationships. LC 99-19528. 256p. 1999. pap. 13.95 (*1-86204-487-2*, Pub. by Element MA) Penguin Putnam.

Biger, Gideon. An Empire in the Holy Land: Historical Geography of the British Administration in Palestine, 1917-1929. LC 94-16866. 289p. 1995. text 55.00 (*0-312-12269-1*) St Martin.

Biger, Gideon, jt. ed. see Baker, Alan R.

Biger, Godeon, ed. Encyclopedia of International Boundaries. (Illus.). 496p. 1995. 125.00 (*0-8160-3233-5*) Facts on File.

Bigg, Charles. The Christian Platonists of Alexandria. xvii, 304p. 1981. reprint ed. 65.00 incl. 3.5 hd (*3-487-07044-8*) G Olms Pubs.

*__Bigg, Charles.__ Christian Platonists of Alexandria: Eight Lectures. 332p. 1999. pap. 28.00 (*1-57910-303-0*) Wipf & Stock.

Bigg, Charles. Christian Platonists of Alexandria: Eight Lectures. LC 75-123764. reprint ed. 39.50 (*0-404-00799-6*) AMS Pr.

— The Epistles of St. Peter & St. Jude: Critical & Exegetical Commentary. Driver, Samuel R. et al, eds. (International Critical Commentary Ser.). 376p. 1978. reprint ed. 39.95 (*0-567-05036-X*, Pub. by T & T Clark) Bks Intl VA.

Bigg, Grant R. The Oceans & Climate. 256p. 1996. pap. text 27.95 (*0-521-58268-7*) Cambridge U Pr.

Bigg, Sandy. Pets. 1995. 3.95 (*1-55708-484-X*, MCT1015) McDonald Pub Co.

Biggar, Charles R. Sir Oliver Mowat: A Biographical Sketch, 2 vols., Set. LC 71-136404. (BCL Ser. I). reprint ed. 105.00 (*0-404-00858-5*) AMS Pr.

— Sir Oliver Mowat: A Biographical Sketch, 2 vols., Set. (BCL1 - History - Canada Ser.). 1991. reprint ed. lib. bdg. 150.00 (*0-7812-6360-3*) Rprt Serv.

Biggar, H. P. The Early Trading Companies of New France: A Contribution to the History of Commerce & Discovery in North America. LC 70-136303. (Reprints of Economic Classics Ser.). (Illus.). xii, 308p. 1972. reprint ed. lib. bdg. 45.00 (*0-678-00822-1*) Kelley.

Biggar, Henry P. The Early Trading Companies of New France. (BCL1 - History - Canada Ser.). 308p. 1991. reprint ed. lib. bdg. 89.00 (*0-7812-6350-6*) Rprt Serv.

Biggar, James W. & Seiber, James H. Fate of Pesticides in the Environment. LC 86-73098. (Illus.). 168p. (Orig.). 1987. pap. 12.00 (*0-931876-77-X*, 3320) ANR Pubns CA.

Biggar, Joan R. Missing on Castaway Island. LC 97-12850. (Megan Parnell Mysteries Ser.). (J). (gr. 5-9). 1997. pap. text 5.99 (*0-570-05015-4*, 56-1842) Concordia.

— Mystery at Camp Galena. LC 97-12849. (Megan Parnell Mysteries Ser.). (J). (gr. 5-9). 1997. pap. text 5.99 (*0-570-05016-2*, 56-1843) Concordia.

*__Biggar, Joan R.__ Trapped at Haunted Canyon. LC 98-2617. (Megan Parnell Mysteries Ser.). 160p. (J). (gr. 4-7). 1998. 5.99 (*0-570-05069-3*, 56-1893) Concordia.

Biggar, Joan R. Treasure at Morning Gulch. (Adventure Quest Ser.). (Illus.). 152p. (Orig.). (J). (gr. 5-8). 1991. pap. 4.99 (*0-570-04193-7*, 56-1652) Concordia.

— Trouble in Yakima Valley. LC 97-18134. (Megan Parnell Mysteries Ser.). (J). (gr. 5-9). 1998. 5.99 (*0-570-05031-6*, 56-1855) Concordia.

Biggar, Joanna. Travels: Poems by Joanna Biggar. Baker, R. D., ed. (Poetry Chapbook Ser.). (Illus.). 28p. (Orig.). 1996. pap. 4.00 (*1-887641-12-2*) Argonne Hotel Pr.

Biggar, Myron J., Group Inc. Staff. O Gauge Railroading the Primer. 96p. 1997. per. 9.95 (*0-9650291-0-7*) O Gauge Railrd.

Biggar, Nigel. The Hastening That Waits: Karl Barth's Ethics. (Oxford Studies in Theological Ethics). 204p. 1996. reprint ed. pap. text 17.95 (*0-19-826390-2*) OUP.

Biggar, Nigel, et al. Cities of Gods: Faith, Politics & Pluralism in Judaism, Christianity & Islam, 16. LC 85-9879. (Contributions to the Study of Religion Ser.: No. 16). 253p. 1986. 49.95 (*0-313-24944-X*, BCG/, Greenwood Pr) Greenwood.

Biggar, Patricia, jt. auth. see James, Jeanne.

Biggar, Robert J., jt. auth. see Laurent, Simon.

Biggar, W. D., et al. Thymus Involvement in Immunity & Disease. LC 72-13558. (Illus.). 220p. (C). 1973. text 32.50 (*0-8422-7068-X*) Irvington.

Biggart, John, et al, eds. Alexander Bogdanov & the Origins of Systems Thinking in Russia. LC 97-76943. 370p. 1998. 72.95 (*1-85972-678-X*, Pub. by Ashgate Pub) Ashgate Pub Co.

Biggart, John, et al. Bogdanov & His Work: A Guide to the Published & Unpublished Works of Alexander A. Bogdanov (Malinovsky), 1873-1928. LC 97-77890. 510p. 1998. text 85.95 (*1-85972-623-2*, Pub. by Ashgate Pub) Ashgate Pub Co.

Biggart, Nicole W. Charismatic Capitalism: Direct Selling Organizations in America. LC 88-19833. 232p. 1989. 24.95 (*0-226-04785-7*) U Ch Pr.

— Charismatic Capitalism: Direct Selling Organizations in America. LC 88-19833. 236p. 1990. pap. text 15.00 (*0-226-04786-5*) U Ch Pr.

Bigge, June L. Adapting Curriculum & Instruction for Special Needs Students. LC 98-34355. (Special Education Ser.). 512p. 1999. pap. 57.95 (*0-534-16770-5*) Brooks-Cole.

Bigge, June L. Teaching Individuals with Physical & Multiple Disabilities. 3rd ed. 640p. (C). 1990. 92.00 (*0-675-21017-8*, Merrill Coll) P-H.

Bigge, Morris L. & Shermis, S. Samuel. Learning Theories for Teachers. 6th ed. LC 98-19891. 384p. (C). 1998. pap. 53.00 (*0-321-02343-9*) Addson-Wesley Educ.

Bigge, Tanya. Gardening Projects for Children. (J). 1992. pap. 10.95 (*1-878767-31-3*) Murdoch Bks.

Bigger, Charles P. Kant's Methodology: An Essay in Philosophical Archeology. LC 95-9639. (Series in Continental Thought : No. 23). 464p. (C). 1995. text 55.00 (*0-8214-1124-1*) Ohio U Pr.

— Participation: A Platonic Inquiry. fac. ed. LC 68-21802. 239p. 1968. reprint ed. pap. 74.10 (*0-7837-7935-6*, 204769100008) Bks Demand.

Bigger, Elise D., jt. auth. see Taylor, John R.

Bigger, Margaret. MotherHoot. LC 98-71924. (Illus.). 128p. 1999. pap. 9.95 (*0-9640606-8-X*) A Borough Bks.

— There's No Such Thing As a Perfect Wedding. LC 91-71001. (Illus.). 90p. 1991. pap. 7.95 (*1-878086-04-9*, Pub. by Down Home NC) Blair.

Bigger, Margaret & Webb, Betsy. You Can Tell You're a Charlottean If . . . large type ed. LC 98-71923. (Illus.). 96p. 1998. pap. 7.95 (*0-9640606-6-3*) A Borough Bks.

*__Bigger, Margaret G.__ Churchgoers' Chuckles: True Tales - You Can't Make This Stuff Up! large type ed. LC 00-131766. (Illus.). 96p. 2000. pap. 7.50 (*1-893597-02-4*) A Borough Bks.

Bigger, Margaret G. Recalling Your Memories on Paper, Tape or Videotape: How to Preserve Valuable Memoirs for Your Family or the Public. LC 96-84100. (Illus.). 160p. (Orig.). 1996. pap. 13.95 (*0-9640606-4-7*) A Borough Bks.

— You've GOT to Have a Sense of Humor to Have a Wedding. LC 96-86617. (Illus.). 128p. (Orig.). 1997. pap. 9.95 (*0-9640606-5-5*) A Borough Bks.

*__Bigger, Margaret G., ed.__ Kitties & All That Litter. large type ed. LC 99-73609. (Illus.). 96p. 1999. pap. 7.50 (*1-893597-00-8*) A Borough Bks.

— MEN! Cry Flustered, Frustrated Females Everywhere. large type ed. LC 00-90090. (Illus.). 96p. 2000. pap. 7.50 (*1-893597-01-6*) A Borough Bks.

Bigger, Margaret G. & Dunlap, Katherine M. Small Church with a Big Mission: The History of the First 50 Years of Seigle Avenue Presbyterian Church. LC 95-79297. (Illus.). 128p. (Orig.). 1995. pap. 12.95 (*0-9640606-2-0*) A Borough Bks.

Bigger, Margaret G., ed. see Abrams, Susie, et al.

Bigger, Margaret G., ed. see Barnes, Bob, et al.

Biggers. Charge Nurse Survival Skills, No. 2. 1997. text 24.95 (*0-8151-2459-7*) Mosby Inc.

Biggers & Vivian. Taking Charge: Survival Skills for the Take Charge Nurse. 32p. (gr. 13). 1997. pap. text 129.95 (*0-8151-1297-1*) Mosby Inc.

Biggers, Don H. Buffalo Guns & Barbed Wire: Two Frontier Accounts. (Illus.). 280p. 1991. 39.95 (*0-89672-242-2*) Tex Tech Univ Pr.

Biggers, Earl D. The Agony Column. 1976. reprint ed. lib. bdg. 25.95 (*0-89966-074-6*) Buccaneer Bks.

— The Black Camel. 224p. Date not set. 21.95 (*0-8488-2211-0*) Amereon Ltd.

— The Black Camel. 1978. reprint ed. lib. bdg. 27.95 (*0-89966-077-0*) Buccaneer Bks.

— Charlie Chan: House Without a Key. 21.95 (*0-8488-0917-3*) Amereon Ltd.

— Fifty Candles. 1979. reprint ed. lib. bdg. 25.95 (*0-89966-079-7*) Buccaneer Bks.

— The House Without a Key. Date not set. lib. bdg. 24.95 (*0-8488-1956-X*) Amereon Ltd.

— The House Without a Key. 316p. 1994. 35.00 (*1-883402-23-9*) S&S Trade.

— The House Without a Key. 1979. reprint ed. lib. bdg. 35.95 (*0-89966-081-9*) Buccaneer Bks.

— Seven Keys to Baldpate. 1976. reprint ed. lib. bdg. 28.95 (*0-89966-076-2*) Buccaneer Bks.

— Seven Keys to Balpate. 414p. Date not set. 27.95 (*0-8488-2210-2*) Amereon Ltd.

Biggers, Jeff. Transgenerational Addiction. (Drug Abuse Prevention Library). 64p. (J). (gr. 7-12). 1998. pap. 6.95 (*1-56838-247-2*) Hazelden.

— Transgenerational Addiction. LC 97-43052. (Drug Abuse Prevention Library). (Illus.). 64p. (YA). (gr. 7-12). 1998. lib. bdg. 17.95 (*0-8239-2757-1*) Rosen Group.

Biggers, John & Alexander, Margaret W. Ananse: The Web of Life in Africa. (Illus.). 131p. 1996. reprint ed. pap. 24.95 (*0-292-70345-7*) U of Tex Pr.

*__Biggers, Shirley Hoover.__ American Author Houses, Museums, Memorials & Libraries: A State-by-State Guide. LC 99-59558. (Illus.). 215p. 2000. 39.95 (*0-7864-0777-8*) McFarland & Co.

*__Biggers, W. Watts.__ The Man Inside. 150p. 1999. 14.00 (*0-917453-37-9*, Pub. by Bamberger) SPD-Small Pr Dist.

Biggers, W. Watts, jt. auth. see Goodman, Joseph I.

Biggerstaff. Modern China & Japan. 1988. 34.75 (*0-07-557264-8*) McGraw.

Biggerstaff, Knight. Nanking Letters, 1949. (Cornell East Asia Ser.: No. 23). 114p. 1999. reprint ed. pap. 11.90 (*0-939657-23-6*) Cornell East Asia Pgm.

Biggerstaff, Knight, jt. ed. see Teng Ssu-Yu.

Biggerstaff, Ted J. Systems Software Tools. (Illus.). 320p. 1986. text 32.00 (*0-13-821869-2*) P-H.

— Systems Software Tools, Software Builder's Kit Version 1.0. rev. ed. 48p. 1987. write for info. (*0-318-61641-6*) P-H.

Biggins, Alan. Argentina. LC 92-146745. (World Bibliographical Ser.). 488p. 1991. lib. bdg. 112.50 (*1-85109-109-2*) ABC-CLIO.

*__Biggins, Alan.__ Buenos Aires. 2000. lib. bdg. 64.00 (*1-85109-284-6*) ABC-CLIO.

Biggins, J., ed. Progress in Photosynthesis Research, 4 vols., Set. 1986. text 1668.50 (*90-247-3449-5*) Kluwer Academic.

Biggins, John. Two-Headed Eagle. LC 96-8482. 368p. 1996. 24.95 (*0-312-14751-1*) St Martin.

Biggins, Michael, tr. see Debelijak, Ales.

Biggins, Michael, tr. see Jackson, Richard, ed.

Biggins, Michael, tr. see Jancar, Drago.

Biggins, Michael, tr. see Pahor, Boris.

Biggins, Michael, tr. see Potokar, Jure.

Biggins, Michael, tr. see Vishevsky, Anatoly.

Biggio, Giovanni, et al, eds. Central & Peripheral Dopamine Receptors: Biochemistry & Pharmacology. (FIDIA Research Ser.: Vol. 5). ix, 283p. 1988. 130.00 (*0-387-96736-2*) Spr-Verlag.

— GABAergic Synaptic Transmission: Molecular, Pharmacological & Clinical Aspects. LC 92-11898. (Advances in Biochemical Psychopharmacology Ser.: No. 47). (Illus.). 493p. 1992. reprint ed. pap. 152.90 (*0-608-05836-X*, 205980200007) Bks Demand.

— GABA(in)a Receptors & Anxiety: From Neurobiology to Treatment. LC 95-164375. (Advances in Biochemical Psychopharmacology Ser.: Vol. 48). (Illus.). 157p. 1995. text 79.00 (*0-7817-0308-5*) Lppncott W & W.

— Neuronal Plasticity & Trophic Factors. (FIDIA Research Ser. - Symposia on Neuroscience: Vol. 7). 1988. 75.00 (*0-387-96796-6*) Spr-Verlag.

— Receptors As Surramolecular Entities: Proceedings of the Biannual Capo Bio Conference, Cagliari, Italy, 7-10 June, 1981. (Advances in the Biosciences Ser.: Vol. 44). (Illus.). 476p. 1983. 101.50 (*0-08-029804-4*, Pergamon Pr) Elsevier.

— Voltage-Sensitive Ion Channels: Modulation by Neurotransmitters & Drugs. (FIDIA Research Ser.: Vol. 6). viii, 189p. 1988. 88.00 (*0-387-96737-0*) Spr-Verlag.

Biggio, Giovanni & Costa, E., eds. Benzodiazepine Recognition Site Ligands: Biochemistry & Pharmacology. LC 83-23069. (Advances in Biochemical Psychopharmacology Ser.: No. 38). (Illus.). 272p. reprint ed. pap. 84.40 (*0-7837-7100-2*, 204692900004) Bks Demand.

— Chloride Channels & Their Modulation by Neurotransmitters & Drugs. LC 88-42745. (Advances in Biochemical Psychopharmacology Ser.: Vol. 45). 400p. 1988. reprint ed. pap. 124.00 (*0-608-04716-3*, 206543700004) Bks Demand.

— GABAergic Transmission & Anxiety. LC 86-6553. (Advances in Biochemical Psychopharmacology Ser.: Vol. 41). (Illus.). 272p. reprint ed. pap. 84.40 (*0-608-09730-6*, 206990700007) Bks Demand.

Biggio, Giovanni & Costa, Erminio, eds. GABA & Benzodiazepine Receptor Subtypes: Molecular Biology, Pharmacology & Clinical Aspects. LC 90-8829. (Advances in Biochemical Psychopharmacology Ser.: Vol. 46). 256p. 1990. reprint ed. pap. 79.40 (*0-608-04728-7*, 206544900004) Bks Demand.

Biggio, Giovanni, et al. Excitatory Amino Acids & Brain Ischemia: Pharmacological & Clinical Aspects, Proceedings of the Biannual Capo Boi Conference on Neuroscience, June 1989, Villasimius, Italy. (Advances in the Biosciences Ser.: No. 78). 156p. 1990. 109.00 (*0-08-040783-8*, Pergamon Pr) Elsevier.

B

— Neuromodules & Brain Function. (Advances in the Biosciences Ser.). 460p. 1984. 80.50 (*0-08-030782-5*, Pergamon Pr) Elsevier.

Bigglestone, William E. Tucson's Korean War Dead. (Illus.). v, 42p. 1997. pap. 10.00 (*0-9653649-8-4*) Thirteenth Bomb Sqndrn.

***Biggot.** From Cottage to Bungalow. 1998. 40.00 (*0-226-04875-6*) U Ch Pr.

***Biggs, et al.** Biology: The Dynamics of Life, Teacher Wraparound Edition. 1998. teacher ed. 65.18 (*0-02-825432-5*) Glencoe.

Biggs, A. K. Matrimonial Proceedings. 1980. 100.00 (*0-7855-7332-1*, Pub. by Fourmat Pub) St Mut.

— Matrimonial Proceedings. 174p. 1984. 90.00 (*0-906840-78-3*, Pub. by Fourmat Pub) St Mut.

— Matrimonial Proceedings. 240p. (C). 1989. 110.00 (*1-85190-064-0*, Pub. by Fourmat Pub) St Mut.

Biggs, A. K., ed. Butterworths Rules of Court: Family Court Practice 1996. 1996. pap. write for info. (*0-406-99893-0*, BRCF1996, MICHIE) LEXIS Pub.

Biggs, A. K. & Rogers, A. P. Probate Practice & Procedure. 1981. 40.00 (*0-7855-7334-8*, Pub. by Fourmat Pub) St Mut.

— Probate Practice & Procedure. 1988. 112.00 (*1-85190-040-3*, Pub. by Fourmat Pub) St Mut.

— Probate Practice & Procedure. 4th ed. 348p. 1992. 105.00 (*1-85190-154-X*, Pub. by Tolley Pubng) St Mut.

— Probate Practice & Procedure. 5th ed. (Lawyers Practice & Procedure Ser.). 365p. (C). 1994. 175.00 (*0-85459-891-X*, Pub. by Tolley Pubng) St Mut.

— Probate Practice & Procedure. 6th ed. 1998. pap. write for info. (*1-86012-935-8*, Pub. by Tolley Pubng) St Mut.

Biggs, A. K. & Strong, J. Matrimonial Causes & Proceedings. 4th ed. 265p. (C). 1992. 150.00 (*1-85190-164-7*, Pub. by Tolley Pubng) St Mut.

Biggs, A. R., jt. ed. see Blanchette, R. A.

Biggs, Alan R., ed. Handbook of Cytology, Histology, & Histochemistry of Fruit Tree Diseases. 352p. 1992. lib. bdg. 199.00 (*0-8493-2939-6*, SB608) CRC Pr.

Biggs, Andy, et al. Design & Make It! Systems & Control Technology. 144p. 1998. pap. 30.00 (*0-7487-3664-6*, Pub. by S Thornes Pubs) Trans-Atl Phila.

***Biggs, Andy, et al.** Product Design for Key Stage 3 Course Guide: Pupil's Book. (Design & Make It Ser.). (Illus.). 144p. (YA). (gr. 6-9). 2000. pap. 22.50 (*0-7487-4429-0*, Pub. by S Thornes Pubs) Trans-Atl Phila.

— Product Design for Key Stage 3 Course Guide: Teacher Support Pack. (Design & Make It Ser.). (Illus.). 223p. (YA). (gr. 6-9). 2000. pap. 99.50 (*0-7487-4430-4*, Pub. by S Thornes Pubs) Trans-Atl Phila.

— Product Design for Key Stage 3 Course Guide: Teacher Support Pack CD-Rom. (Design & Make It Ser.). (Illus.). 144p. (YA). (gr. 6-9). 2000. audio compact disk 187.50 (*0-7487-5455-5*, Pub. by S Thornes Pubs) Trans-Atl Phila.

Biggs, Anne. Through Their Eyes: A Story of Doylestown Hospital. LC 98-71524. (Illus.). 224p. 1998. 24.95 (*0-941668-08-8*) Tower Hill Pr.

Biggs, B. J., ed. see Thomas, a Kempis.

Biggs, Bradley. The Triple Nickles: America's First All-Black Paratroop Unit. LC 85-28732. (Illus.). x, 92p. (C). 1986. pap. 17.50 (*0-208-02402-6*, Archon Bks) Shoe String.

***Biggs, Brian.** Dear Julia. (Illus.). 108p. 2000. pap. 12.95 (*1-891830-12-0*, Pub. by Top Shelf Prodns) LPC InBook.

Biggs, Brian. Frederick & Eloise. 32p. 1993. pap. 4.95 (*1-56097-096-0*) Fantagraph Bks.

Biggs, Bruce. Let's Learn Maori. rev. ed. LC 98-215797. 208p. 1998. pap. 18.95 (*1-86940-186-7*, Pub. by Auckland Univ) Paul & Co Pubs.

Biggs, Bruce, ed. He Whiriwhiringa: Selected Readings in Maori. LC 97-189633. 250p. 1997. pap. 24.95 (*1-86940-168-9*, Pub. by Auckland Univ) Paul & Co Pubs.

Biggs, Bruce, jt. auth. see Jones, Pe Te H.

Biggs, Bud & Marshall, Lois. Watercolor Workbook. (Illus.). 160p. 1987. pap. 22.99 (*0-89134-203-6*, 8841, North Lght Bks) F & W Pubns Inc.

Biggs, Carol R. Wild Edible & Medicinal Plants Alaska, Canada & Pacific Northwest Rainforest Vol. 1: An Introductory Pocket Trail Guide. (Illus.). 88p. 1999. pap. 11.95 (*0-9669192-0-3*) Alaska Nature Conn.

— Wild Edible & Medicinal Plants Alaska, Canada & Pacific Northwest Rainforest Vol. 2: An Introductory Pocket Trail Guide. (Illus.). 1999. pap. 11.95 (*0-9669192-1-1*) Alaska Nature Conn.

Biggs, Charles R. Book of Ezekiel. (Commentary Ser.). 1996. pap. text 17.00 (*0-7162-0505-X*) Epworth Pr.

Biggs, Cherlyn. The Cowboy She Never Forgot: Way Out West. 1999. per. 4.25 (*0-373-07911-7*, Harlequin) Harlequin Bks.

Biggs, Cheryl. Across a Rebel Sea. 416p. 1993. mass mkt. 4.50 (*0-8217-4385-6*, Zebra Kensgtn) Kensgtn Pub Corp.

— Blackjack's Lady. 320p. 1999. mass mkt. 4.99 (*0-8217-6180-3*, Zebra Kensgtn) Kensgtn Pub Corp.

— Denim & Lace. (Lucky in Love Ser.: No. 11). 304p. 1992. mass mkt. 3.99 (*0-8217-3977-8*, Zebra Kensgtn) Kensgtn Pub Corp.

— Family Tradition. 320p. 1993. mass mkt. 3.99 (*0-8217-4054-7*, Zebra Kensgtn) Kensgtn Pub Corp.

— Hearts Denied. 400p. 1994. mass mkt. 4.50 (*0-8217-4776-2*, Zebra Kensgtn) Kensgtn Pub Corp.

— Hearts Divided. 352p. 1996. mass mkt. 4.99 (*0-8217-5461-0*, Zebra Kensgtn) Kensgtn Pub Corp.

— Remembering Jake. (Intimate Moments Ser.: No. 953). 1999. mass mkt. 4.25 (*0-373-07953-2*, 1-07953-2) Silhouette.

— The Return of the Cowboy. 1997. per. 3.99 (*0-373-07762-9*, 1-07762-7) Silhouette.

— Silver Linings. 304p. 1998. pap. 4.99 (*0-8217-5910-8*) Kensgtn Pub Corp.

Biggs, Chester M., Jr. Behind the Barbed Wire: Memoir of a World War II U. S. Marine Captured in North China in 1941 & Imprisoned by the Japanese until 1945. LC 94-32415. (Illus.). 232p. 1994. lib. bdg. 29.95 (*0-89950-972-X*) McFarland & Co.

Biggs, Cliff, ed. see Biggs, Marjorie I.

Biggs, D. L., ed. North-Central Section Field Guide. (DNAG Centennial Field Guides Ser.: No.3). (Illus.). 490p. 1988. 21.75 (*0-8137-5403-8*) Geol Soc.

***Biggs, David.** The Cocktail Handbook. 2000. 24.95 (*1-85974-098-7*, Pub. by New5 Holland) Sterling.

Biggs, Deb R., ed. ProCite in Libraries: Applications in Bibliographic Database Management. 221p. 1995. 39.50 (*0-938734-90-3*) Info Today Inc.

Biggs, Dick. If Life Is a Balancing Act, Why Am I So Darn Clumsy? Progressing Beyond Professional Success to Personal Happiness. 3rd ed. LC 93-70774. 221p. 1993. 22.95 (*0-9635977-6-0*) Chattahoo Pubs.

***Biggs, Dick.** Maximize Your Moments with the Masters. 48p. 2000. mass mkt. 8.00 (*0-9635977-0-1*) Chattahoo Pubs.

Biggs, Donald A. Dictionary of Counseling. LC 93-39352. 256p. 1994. lib. bdg. 65.00 (*0-313-28367-2*, Greenwood Pr) Greenwood.

Biggs, Donald A., jt. auth. see Williamson, Edmund G.

Biggs, Donna L. Getting Real with Geometry: A Resorve of Real-Life Activites. 80p. (YA). (gr. 9 up). 1996. pap. text, teacher ed. 12.95 (*1-881641-47-3*) Pencil Point.

Biggs, Earlene. How to Plan & Conduct a Customer Satisfaction Survey. (Illus.). 52p. 1998. wbk. ed. 49.95 (*0-9667059-0-4*) MERIT.

Biggs, Edith & Shaw, Kathleen. Maths Alive! Inset Mathematics for the National Curriculum (Key States 1, 2, & 3) (Cassell Education Ser.). (Illus.). 144p. 1995. 110.00 (*0-304-32994-0*); pap. 33.95 (*0-304-32990-8*) Continuum.

Biggs, Emma. The Encyclopedia of Mosaic Techniques: A Step-by-Step Visual Directory with an Inspirational Gallery of Finished Works. (Encyclopedia of Arts Ser.). (Illus.). 160p. 1999. 24.95 (*0-7624-0444-2*) Running Pr.

Biggs, Emma & Hunkin, Tessa. Mosaic Workshop: A Guide to Designing & Creating Mosaics. 1999. 24.95 (*1-57076-149-3*, Trafalgar Sq Pub) Trafalgar.

— Stylish & Simple Mosaic. LC 98-5061. (Illus.). 96p. 1998. 17.95 (*1-57145-627-9*, Laurel Glen Pub) Advantage Pubs.

***Biggs, Frank.** Easy Beats & Breaks. 64p. 1998. pap. 17.95 incl. audio compact disk (*0-7866-3271-2*, 97060BCD) Mel Bay.

— Essential Reading. 40p. 1999. pap. 14.95 incl. audio compact disk (*0-7866-3273-9*, 97062BCD) Mel Bay.

— Funky Beats & Breaks. 56p. 1998. pap. write for info. incl. audio compact disk (*0-7866-3272-0*, 97061BCD) Mel Bay.

— Jazz Time Part One: The Basics Book/CD. 40p. 2000. pap. 14.95 (*0-7866-3506-1*, 97215BCD) Mel Bay.

Biggs, Hayes & Orzel, Susan. Musically Incorrect: Conversations about Music at the End of the 20th Century. LC 98-28553. 1998. pap. 12.95 (*0-938856-07-3*) C F Peters Corp.

Biggs, Howard. The River Medway. 160p. 1990. pap. 24.00 (*0-86138-005-3*, Pub. by T Dalton) St Mut.

— The Sound of Maroons: The Story of Life-Saving Services on the Kent & Sussex Coasts. 176p. 1994. 40.00 (*0-900963-83-2*, Pub. by T Dalton) St Mut.

Biggs, J. M., et al. Topics in Engineering Meteorology. (Meteorological Monograph: Vol. 4, No. 22). (Illus.). 98p. 1960. pap. 17.00 (*0-933876-10-6*) Am Meteorological.

Biggs, Jeffrey & Foley, Thomas S. Honor in the House: Speaker Tom Foley. LC 99-12845. (Illus.). 384p. 1999. 35.00 (*0-87422-172-2*); pap. 25.00 (*0-87422-173-0*) Wash St U Pr.

Biggs, John. The Guilty Mind: Psychiatry & the Law of Homicide. LC 55-10812. (Isaac Ray Award Ser.). 250p. 1967. reprint ed. pap. 77.50 (*0-608-04077-0*, 206480900011) Bks Demand.

Biggs, John, ed. Teaching for Learning. (C). 1992. 70.00 (*0-86431-080-3*, Pub. by Aust Council Educ Res) St Mut.

Biggs, John & Watkins, David, eds. Classroom Learning: Educational Psychology of the Asian Teacher. LC 95-30415. 1995. 34.95 (*0-13-504093-0*) P-H.

Biggs, John, jt. auth. see Telfer, Ross.

Biggs, John, tr. see Firishtah, Muhammad K.

Biggs, John, tr. see Firishtah, Muhammed K.

***Biggs, John B.** Teaching for Quality Learning at University. LC 98-44938. 208p. 1999. pap. 29.95 (*0-335-20171-7*) OpUniv Pr.

Biggs, John B. Teaching for Quality Learning at University: What the Student Does. LC 98-44938. 1999. 99.00 (*0-335-20172-5*) Taylor & Francis.

Biggs, John B., jt. ed. see Watkins, John.

Biggs, John M. Introduction to Structural Dynamics. 341p. (C). 1964. 99.38 (*0-07-005255-7*) McGraw.

Biggs, John S. & Rubin, Stephen. Teachers That Sexually Abuse Students: An Administrative & Legal Guide. LC 98-85050. 232p. 1998. pap. 34.95 (*1-56676-627-3*) Scarecrow.

Biggs, Jonathan. Riding in Motion: A Three-Dimensional Guide to Horses for Young People. LC 87-45765. (Illus.). 14p. (J). (gr. 3-6). 1988. 15.95 (*0-397-32258-5*) HarpC Child Bks.

***Biggs, Kathy R.** Common Dragonflies of California: A Beginner's Pocket Guide. LC 00-100376. (Illus.). 96p. 2000. pap. 10.95 (*0-9677934-0-8*) Azalea Creek Pub.

Biggs, Keith & Donnelly, Kevin. A Step by Step Guide to Wills & Probate. 164p. 1991. 33.00 (*1-85190-119-1*, Pub. by Tolley Pubng) St Mut.

***Biggs, Lewis.** New Thing Breathing: Recent Work by Tony Cragg. (Illus.). 156p. 2000. pap. 40.00 (*1-85437-324-2*) U of Wash Pr.

Biggs, Lindy. The Rational Factory: Architecture, Technology, & Work in America's Age of Mass Production. LC 96-10947. (Johns Hopkins Studies in Industry & Society: No. 11). (Illus.). 224p. 1996. text 39.95 (*0-8018-5261-7*) Johns Hopkins.

Biggs, Margaret K. Magnolias & Such. (Illus.). 1982. 2.50 (*0-943696-00-3*) Red Key Pr.

— Nocturnal Woman LC 98-67339. 95 p. 1998. write for info. (*0-9636529-5-8*) Mulberry Riv.

— The Plumage of the Sun. LC 85-62534. (Illus.). 92p. 1986. 12.00 (*0-942544-10-2*) Negative Capability Pr.

Biggs, Marjorie I. Madame Alexander "Little People" Biggs, Cliff, ed. LC 79-66461. (Ser. I). (Illus.). 1979. 35.00 (*0-9603218-0-2*) M Biggs.

Biggs, Mark. Complete Dulcimer Handbook. 196p. 1985. pap. 17.95 (*0-87166-892-0*, 94047); pap. 26.95 incl. audio (*0-7866-0965-6*, 94047P); audio 9.98 (*1-56222-338-0*, 94047C) Mel Bay.

***Biggs, Mark.** Mountain Dulcimer. 80p. 1998. pap. 17.95 (*0-7866-3444-8*, 93859BCD) Mel Bay.

Biggs, Mary. A Gift That Cannot Be Refused: The Writing & Publishing of Contemporary American Poetry, 34. LC 89-11939. (Contributions to the Study of World Literature Ser.: No. 34). 282p. 1990. 59.95 (*0-313-26673-5*, BER/, Greenwood Pr) Greenwood.

Biggs, Mary, ed. Publishers & Librarians: A Foundation for Dialogue Proceedings of the 42nd Conference of the Graduate Library School, May 13-15, 1983. LC 83-18124. (University of Chicago Studies in Library Science Ser.). 106p. Date not set. reprint ed. pap. 32.90 (*0-608-21016-1*, 205454400003) Bks Demand.

— Publishers & Librarians: A Foundation for Dialogue: Proceedings of the 42nd Annual Conference of the Graduate Library School. LC 83-18124. (Studies in Library Science). 112p. 1984. pap. text 7.50 (*0-226-04847-0*) U Ch Pr.

— Women's Words: The Columbia Book of Quotations by Women. 384p. 1996. 26.50 (*0-231-07986-9*) Col U Pr.

Biggs, Mary, jt. ed. see Sklar, Morty.

Biggs, Matthew. Practical Guide to Growing Healthy Houseplants. 1997. 16.95 (*1-85833-525-6*, Pub. by CLib Bks) Whitecap Bks.

Biggs, Matthew, jt. auth. see Lancaster, Roy.

Biggs, Melissa E. French Films, 1945-1993: A Critical Filmography of the 400 Most Important Releases. LC 95-10539. (Illus.). 365p. 1996. lib. bdg. 52.50 (*0-7864-0024-2*) McFarland & Co.

Biggs, Michael. Amazing Whitetails. LC 94-61042. (Illus.). 192p. 1994. 39.95 (*0-9642915-0-9*) T P W.

***Biggs, Michael.** Just the Facts: Investigative Report Writing. LC 99-88616. (Illus.). 142p. (C). 2000. pap. 34.80 (*0-13-014301-4*) P-H.

Biggs, Michael. Whitetails in Action, 2 vols. unabridged ed. LC 96-90530. (Illus.). 192p. 1996. 39.95 (*0-9642915-2-5*) T P W.

Biggs, Michael & Monty, Lise. Images of Delaware. LC 98-30751. 1998. 45.00 (*0-9663337-0-5*) Miller Pub.

Biggs, Michael & Quillman, Catherine. Chester County: A Photographic Journey. LC 97-26070. 1997. write for info. (*0-89802-692-X*) Miller Pub.

Biggs, Michael, jt. auth. see Abedian, Iraj.

Biggs, Mike. Amazing Whitetails. limited ed. LC 94-61042. (Illus.). 192p. 1994. lthr. 95.00 (*0-9642915-1-7*) T P W.

— The Whitetail Chronicles: Real Deer & the Times of Their Lives. unabridged ed. LC 98-90565. (Illus.). 192p. 1998. 39.95 (*0-9642915-4-1*) T P W.

Biggs, Mouzon, jt. auth. see Allen, Charles L.

Biggs, Murray, et al, eds. The Arts of Performance in Elizabethan & Early Stuart Drama. 248p. 1991. text 76.50 (*0-7486-0266-6*, Pub. by Edinburgh U Pr) Col U Pr.

***Biggs, Nancy & Britt, Peggy.** Exploring Science Writing: An Environmental Focus. 73p. 1998. spiral bd. 10.00 (*1-883097-23-1*) U Ill Ofc Agricult.

Biggs, Neva, et al. Make Time for This. 70p. 1985. 10.00 (*0-911051-23-6*) Plain View.

Biggs, Norman L. Algebraic Graph Theory. 2nd ed. LC 73-86042. (Cambridge Mathematical Library). (Illus.). 213p. (C). 1994. pap. text 27.95 (*0-521-45897-8*) Cambridge U Pr.

— Discrete Mathematics. 2nd rev. ed. (Illus.). 494p. (C). 1993. reprint ed. pap. text 49.95 (*0-19-853427-2*) OUP.

— Introduction to Computing with Pascal. (Illus.). 230p. (C). 1989. pap. text 24.95 (*0-19-853756-5*) OUP.

Biggs, Norman L. & Anthony, M. H. Computational Learning Theory. (Cambridge Tracts in Theoretical Computer Science Ser.: No. 30). (Illus.). 157p. 1997. pap. text 22.95 (*0-521-59922-9*) Cambridge U Pr.

— Mathematics for Economics & Finance: Methods & Modelling. (Illus.). 394p. (C). 1996. text 74.95 (*0-521-55113-7*); pap. text 27.95 (*0-521-55913-8*) Cambridge U Pr.

***Biggs, Norman L., et al.** Graph Theory, 1736-1936: Seventeen Thirty-Six to Nineteen Thirty-Six. (Illus.). 240p. 1999. pap. text 45.00 (*0-19-853916-9*) OUP.

Biggs, P. & Dalwood, C. Les Orleanais ont la Parole. (Illus.). 1977. teacher ed. 7.95 (*0-582-33122-6*); pap. text 8.95 (*0-582-33121-8*); audio 14.00 (*0-582-37885-0*) Longman.

Biggs, P. M., et al, eds. Oncogenesis & Herpesviruses I. (IARC Scientific Publications: No. 2). (Illus.). 515p. 1986. 65.00 (*0-19-723001-6*) OUP.

Biggs, R. D., jt. ed. see Gibson, Mcguire.

Biggs, R. D., jt. ed. see Gibson, M.

Biggs, R. Hilton & Joyner, Margaret E., eds. Stratospheric Ozone Depletion - UV-B Radiation in the Biosphere. LC 94-5044. (NATO ASI Series I: Global Environmental Change). xv, 358p. 1994. 202.95 (*0-387-57810-2*) Spr-Verlag.

Biggs, Rick W., ed. see Hammer, William H. & Gadotti, George A.

Biggs, Robert D. Inscriptions from Al-Hiba-Lagash: The First & Second Seasons. LC 76-47770. (Bibliotheca Mesopotamica Ser.: Vol.3). (Illus.). vi, 47p. 1992. reprint ed. pap. 11.00 (*0-89003-017-0*) Undena Pubns.

— Inscriptions from Tell Abu Salabikh. LC 73-91231. (Oriental Institute Publications: Vol. 99). (Illus.). xiii, 114p. 1974. lib. bdg. 60.00 (*0-226-62202-9*) U Ch Pr.

Biggs, Robert D., ed. Discoveries from Kurdish Looms. LC 83-19535. (Illus.). 116p. (Orig.). 1983. pap. 22.50 (*0-941680-02-9*) M&L Block.

Biggs, Robert D. & Jackson, Danny P. The Epic of Gilgamesh. 2nd rev. ed. Shore, Paul, tr. from AKK. LC 97-25048. (Illus.). 1997. pap. 6.95 (*0-86516-352-9*) Bolchazy-Carducci.

***Biggs, Simon.** The Mature Imagination: Dynamics of Identity in Midlife & Beyond. LC 98-33196. 224p. 1999. pap. 26.95 (*0-335-20102-4*) OpUniv Pr.

— Mature Imagination: Dynamics of Identity in Midlife & Beyond: Dynamics of Identity in Midlife & Beyond. LC 98-33196. 1999. 85.00 (*0-335-20103-2*) Taylor & Francis.

Biggs, Simon, et al. Elder Abuse in Perspective. LC 95-15366. (Rethinking Aging Ser.). 160p. 1995. 104.95 (*0-335-19147-9*); pap. 28.95 (*0-335-19146-0*) OpUniv Pr.

Biggs, Simon J. Understanding Aging: Images, Attitudes & Professional Practice. LC 92-46227. 1993. pap. 35.95 (*0-335-15724-6*) OpUniv Pr.

Biggs, Simon J., jt. ed. see Dowrick, Peter W.

Biggs, Stephen & Grosvenor-Alsop, Ruth. Developing Technologies for the Rural Poor. (ITDG Occasional Papers). 122p. (Orig.). 1984. pap. 11.50 (*0-614-09535-2*) Women Ink.

Biggs, Tyler, et al. Africa Can Compete! Export Opportunities & Challenges for Garments & Home Products in the U. S. Market. LC 94-16198. (Discussion Papers; Africa Technical Department Ser.: Vol. 242). 84p. 1994. pap. 22.00 (*0-8213-2838-7*, 12838) World Bank.

— Africa Can Compete! Export Opportunities & Challenges in Garments & Home Products in the European Market. LC 95-36039. (Discussion Paper Ser.: No. 300). 154p. 1996. pap. 22.00 (*0-8213-3439-5*, 13439) World Bank.

***Biggs, Undra E.** When You Look at Me. LC 00-35214. 2000. pap. write for info. (*0-9647635-6-7*) La Caille-Nous.

Biggs, Walter C., Jr. & Parnell, James F. State Parks of North Carolina. LC 89-6976. (Illus.). 339p. (Orig.). 1989. pap. 14.95 (*0-89587-071-1*) Blair.

Biggs, William. Narrative of William Biggs. 34p. 1988. pap. 6.95 (*0-87770-425-2*) Ye Galleon.

Bigham, Annette. Computerized Accounting with Peachtree. LC 98-30274. 635p. (C). 1999. pap. text 70.00 (*0-13-751421-2*) P-H.

Bigham, Darrel. Evansville. LC 98-87450. (Images of America Ser.). 1998. 18.99 (*0-7524-0811-9*) Arcadia Publng.

Bigham, Darrel E. Towns & Villages of the Lower Ohio. LC 97-30247. (Ohio River Valley Ser.). (Illus.). 400p. (C). 1998. text 39.95 (*0-8131-2042-X*) U Pr of Ky.

— We Ask Only a Fair Trial: A History of the Black Community of Evansville, Indiana. LC 86-45892. (Midwestern History & Culture Ser.; Blacks in the Diaspora Ser.). (Illus.). 302p. 1987. 39.95 (*0-253-36326-8*) Ind U Pr.

Bigham, Elizabeth, jt. auth. see Coles, Janet.

Bigham, George D., jt. auth. see Bigham, Vicki S.

Bigham, J., jt. ed. see Hayzelden, A.

Bigham, J. M., et al, eds. Soil Color. LC 93-16678. (Special Publications: No. 31). 172p. 1993. 25.00 (*0-89118-802-9*) Soil Sci Soc Am.

Bigham, Stephen, tr. see Behr-Sigel, Elisabeth.

Bigham, Stephen, tr. see Ignatius, IV.

Bigham, Steven. The Image of God the Father in Orthodox Theology & Iconography & Other Studies. 200p. 1995. per. 9.95 (*1-879038-15-3*) Oakwood Pubns.

Bigham, Steven, ed. Heroes of the Icon: People, Places Events. (Illus.). 208p. 1998. pap. 9.95 (*1-879038-91-9*) Oakwood Pubns.

— Icons in Early Christianity: The Genesis of Images. 225p. 1999. pap. 9.95 (*1-879038-92-7*) Oakwood Pubns.

Bigham, Steven, tr. see Evdokimov, Paul.

Bigham, Steven, tr. see Montand, Y.

Bigham, Steven, tr. see Sendler, Egon.

Bigham, Vicki S. & Bigham, George D. Prentice Hall Directory of Online Education Resources. LC 98-15621. (Illus.). 450p. (C). 1998. pap. text 34.95 incl. cd-rom (*0-13-618588-6*) P-H.

Bighami, Muhammad Ibn A. Love & War: Adventures from the Firuz Shah Namah of Sheikh Bighami. LC 74-6039. (Unesco Collection of Representative Works). 224p. 1974. 50.00 (*0-8201-1126-0*) Schol Facsimiles.

Bighorse, Tiana. Bighorse the Warrior. Bennett, Noel, ed. LC 90-10874. 113p. 1990. 24.95 (*0-8165-1189-6*) U of Ariz Pr.

— Bighorse the Warrior. Bennett, Noel, ed. LC 90-10874. (Illus.). 113p. 1994. reprint ed. pap. 13.95 (*0-8165-1444-5*) U of Ariz Pr.

Bigi, I.I. & Sanda, A. I. CP Violation. LC 98-38616. (Cambridge Monographs on Particle Physics, Nuclear Physics & Cosmology: No. 9). 350p. (C). 1999. text 95.00 (*0-521-44349-0*) Cambridge U Pr.

An Asterisk (*) at the beginning of an entry indicates that the title is appearing for the first time.

B

Bihari, O. The Constitutional Models of Socialist State Organization. 372p. (C). 1979. 90.00 (*963-05-2077-X*, Pub. by Akade Kiado) St Mut.

Bihari Vajpayee, Atal. Four Decades in Parliament, 3 vols. 1725p. 1996. pap. 1125.00 (*81-85402-69-8*, Pub. by Print Hse) St Mut.

Bihl, H. & Wannenmacher, M., eds. Systemic Radiotherapy with Monoclonal Antibodies: Options & Problems. (Recent Results in Cancer Research Ser.: Vol. 141). 192p. 1996. 135.00 (*3-540-60209-7*) Spr-Verlag.

Bihn, M., ed. see Behar, J.

Bihn, M., ed. see Malakellis, Michael.

Bihr, E., et al. Renal Sonography. 2nd rev. ed. (Illus.). 225p. 1986. 171.00 (*0-387-15343-8*) Spr-Verlag.

***BIischops, Klaus.** Soccer: One-On-One, Vol. 1. 2000. pap. 14.95 (*1-84126-013-4*) Meyer & Meyer.

Bijan, Nancy N. Alphabet. 2nd ed. (First Ser.). (PER., Illus.). 19p. (J). (ps-6). 1998. pap. 5.95 (*1-880710-15-3*) Monterey Pacific.

— Animals & Plants. 2nd large type ed. (First Ser.). (Illus.). 27p. (J). (ps-6). 1998. pap. 5.95 (*1-880710-14-5*) Monterey Pacific.

— Aunt Cockroach. 2nd large type ed. (First Ser.). (Illus.). 17p. (J). (ps-6). 1998. pap. 5.95 (*1-880710-09-9*) Monterey Pacific.

— Colors & Transportation. 2nd large type ed. (First Ser.). (Illus.). 25p. (J). (ps-6). 1998. pap. 5.95 (*1-880710-12-9*) Monterey Pacific.

— Fruits & Vegetables. 2nd large type ed. (First Ser.). (Illus.). 23p. (J). (ps-6). 1998. pap. 5.95 (*1-880710-13-7*) Monterey Pacific.

— Hunch above Hunch. 2nd ed. (First Ser.). (PER., Illus.). 17p. (J). (ps-6). 1998. pap. 5.95 (*1-880710-07-2*) Monterey Pacific.

— Let's Celebrate! large type ed. (Second Ser.). (Illus.). 22p. (J). (ps-6). 1998. pap. 6.95 (*1-880710-19-6*) Monterey Pacific.

— Numbers, Seasons, Months & Days. 2nd ed. (First Ser.). (PER., Illus.). 21p. (J). (ps-6). 1998. pap. 5.95 (*1-880710-11-0*) Monterey Pacific.

— Picky Ali. 2nd ed. (First Ser.). (PER., Illus.). 15p. (J). (ps-6). 1998. pap. 5.95 (*1-880710-08-0*) Monterey Pacific.

— Rhymes 1. 2nd large type ed. (First Ser.). (Illus.). 23p. (J). (ps-6). 1998. pap. 5.95 (*1-880710-16-1*) Monterey Pacific.

— Rhymes 2. 2nd large type ed. (First Ser.). (Illus.). 21p. (J). (ps-6). 1998. pap. 5.95 (*1-880710-17-X*) Monterey Pacific.

— Rolling Pumpkin. 2nd ed. (First Ser.). (PER., Illus.). 17p. (J). (ps-6). 1998. pap. 5.95 (*1-880710-10-2*) Monterey Pacific.

***Bijaoui, Pierre.** Scaling Microsoft Exchange 2000: Create & Optimize High-Performance Exchange Messaging Systems. (Illus.). 2000. pap. 34.95 (*1-55558-239-7*, Digital DEC) Buttrwrth-Heinemann.

Bijker, Wiebe E. Of Bicycles, Bakelites, & Bulbs: Toward a Theory of Sociotechnical Change. (Inside Technology Ser.). 1995. 45.00 (*0-262-02376-8*) MIT Pr.

— Of Bicycles, Bakelites, & Bulbs: Toward a Theory of Sociotechnical Change. (Inside Technology Ser.). (Illus.). 392p. 1997. reprint ed. pap. text 22.50 (*0-262-52227-6*) MIT Pr.

Bijker, Wiebe E., et al, eds. The Social Construction of Technological Systems: New Directions in the Sociology & History of Technology. LC 86-27600. (Illus.). 424p. 1989. pap. text 22.50 (*0-262-52137-7*) MIT Pr.

Bijker, Wiebe E. & Law, John, eds. Shaping Technology - Building Society: Studies in Sociotechnical Change. (Illus.). 352p. 1994. pap. text 19.50 (*0-262-52194-6*) MIT Pr.

Bijker, Wiebe E., ed. see Mack, Pamela E.

Bijl, Aart. Computer Discipline & Design Practice. (Illus.). 186p. 1990. 68.00 (*0-85224-644-7*, Pub. by Edinburgh U Pr) Col U Pr.

Bijl, Nicholas Van Der, see Van Der Bijl, Nicholas.

Bijl, Simon W. Erasmus in the Netherlands to 1617: Extensive English Summaries. (DUT.). 441p. 1978. text 77.50 (*90-6004-356-1*, Pub. by B De Graaf) Coronet Bks.

Bijlani, H. U. & Roy, Prodipto. Slum Habitat. 1990. text 30.00 (*0-7069-5324-X*, Pub. by Vikas) S Asia.

Bijlefeld, Marjolijn. The Gun Control Debate: A Documentary History. LC 96-53518. (Primary Documents in American History & Contemporary Issues Ser.). 336p. 1997. 49.95 (*0-313-29903-X*, Greenwood Pr) Greenwood.

***Bijlefeld, Marjolijn.** People for & Against Gun Control: A Biographical Reference. LC 98-53383. (Making a Difference Ser.). 336p. 1999. 49.95 (*0-313-30690-7*) Greenwood.

***Bijlefeld, Marjolijn K. & Zoumbaris, Sharon.** Teen Guide to Personal Financial Management. LC 00-20464. 2000. write for info. (*0-313-31107-2*) Greenwood.

Bijleveld, Catrien C. J. H., ed. see Mooijaart, Ab, et al.

Bijlmakers, Leon A. & Basset, Mary T. Socioeconomic Stress, Health, & Child Nutritional Status In Zimbabwe at A Time of Economic Structural Adjustment: A Three-year Longitudinal Study. LC 99-165862. (Research Report Ser.). 123 p. 1999. write for info. (*91-7106-434-6*) Nordisk Afrikainstitutet.

Bijlmer, Hendricus J. Outlines of the Anthropology of the Timor Archipelago. LC 77-87480. (Illus.). reprint ed. 48.00 (*0-404-16697-0*) AMS Pr.

Bijlsma, R. & Loeschcke, V. Environmental Stress, Adaptation, & Evolution. LC 97-22248. (EXS Ser.). 1997. write for info. (*0-8176-5695-2*) Birkhauser.

— Environmental Stress, Adaptation, & Evolution. LC 97-22248. (EXS Ser.). 1997. 99.50 (*3-7643-5695-2*) Birkhauser.

Bijmakers, Leon A., et al. Health & Structural Adjustment in Rural & Urban Zimbabwe. (Scandinavian Institute of African Studies: No. 101). 78p. (Orig.). 1996. pap. 20.00 (*91-7106-393-5*) Coronet Bks.

Bijou, Sidney W. Behavior Analysis of Child Development. 3rd ed. (C). 1993. text 39.95 (*1-878978-09-8*); pap. text 19.95 (*1-878978-03-9*) Context Pr.

Bijou, Sidney W. & Ghezzi, Patrick M. Outline of J. R. Kantor's Psychological Linguistics. 79p. (C). 1994. student ed. 12.95 (*1-878978-11-X*) Context Pr.

Bijou, Sidney W. & Ribes, Emilio, eds. New Directions in Behavioral Development. (Illus.). 189p. (C). 1996. text 29.95 (*1-878978-24-1*) Context Pr.

Bijou, Sidney W. & Ruiz, Roberto, eds. Behavior Modification: Contributions to Education. LC 80-278780. 352p. 1981. text 69.95 (*0-89859-051-5*) L Erlbaum Assocs.

Bijster, Fred. Dancing Is Pleasure for Two: The Story of Ballroom & Social Dance. 1985. lib. bdg. 78.95 (*0-8490-3249-0*) Gordon Pr.

Bijsterveld, O. P. Van, see Van Bijsterveld, O. P.

Bijutsu Shuppan-Sha Editorial Staff. Architectural Illustrations: Bird's-Eye View. (BIS Ser.: No. 3). (Illus.). 104p. 1992. pap. 29.95 (*4-568-50151-2*, Pub. by Bijutsu Shuppan-Sha) Bks Nippan.

Bijvoet, Marga. Art as Inquiry: Toward New Collaborations Between Art, Science, & Technology. LC 96-33375. (American University Studies XX: Vol. 32). X, 283p. (C). 1997. text 46.95 (*0-8204-3382-9*) P Lang Pubng.

Bijvoet, Olav L., et al, eds. Biophosphonate on Bones. 474p. 1995. 268.50 (*0-444-89132-3*) Elsevier.

Bik, Jerzy. English Grammar for Polish Speaking People. (ENG & POL.). 112p. 1995. 19.95 (*0-7859-9756-3*) Fr & Eur.

Bikaki, Aliki H. Ayia Irini: The Potters' Marks. (Illus.). xv, 64p. 1984. write for info. (*3-8053-0791-8*, DM65, Pub. by P Zabern) Eisenbrauns.

Bike, William S. Winning Political Campaigns: A Comprehensive Guide to Electoral Success. LC 97-52338. 240p. 1998. pap. 27.00 (*0-938737-35-X*) Denali Press.

Bike World Editors. Traveling by Bike. 96p. 1977. pap. 3.95 (*0-89037-065-6*) Anderson World.

Bike World Staff, ed. Traveling by Bike. 1982. pap. 3.95 (*0-02-499830-3*, Macmillan Coll) P-H.

Bikhovets, N. M., et al, eds. English-Ukrainian Ukrainian-English Dictionary. 696p. 1995. 25.00 (*0-8285-5133-2*) Firebird NY.

Bikhovsky, Anatoly. Closed Spanish Karpov-Zaitsev Systems. 136p. 1995. pap. 14.95 (*0-8050-2938-9*) H Holt & Co.

Bikkhu Silacara Staff. Four Noble Truths (1922) 64p. 1998. reprint ed. pap. 7.95 (*0-7661-0670-5*) Kessinger Pub.

Bikkie, James A. Careers in Marketing. 2nd ed. Dorr, Eugene L., ed. LC 77-3865. (Occupational Manuals & Projects in Marketing Ser.). 1978. text 12.28 (*0-07-005236-0*) McGraw.

Bikle, D. D., ed. Assay of Calcium Regulating Hormones. (Illus.). 290p. 1983. 135.00 (*0-387-90841-2*) Spr-Verlag.

Bikle, Daniel E. & Negro-Vilar, Andres, eds. Hormonal Regulation of Bone Mineral Metabolism. (Endocrine Reviews Monographs: Vol. 4). 400p. 1995. pap. 15.00 (*1-879225-19-0*) Endocrine Soc.

Bikle, George B., Jr. The New Jerusalem: Aspects of Utopianism in the Thought of Kagawa Toyohiko. LC 75-36125. (Monographs: No. 30). v, 343p. 1976. 15.00 (*0-8165-0550-0*) Assn Asian Studies.

Bikle, George B. The New Jerusalem: Aspects of Utopianism in the Thought of Kagawa Toyohiko. fac. ed. LC 75-36125. (Association for Asian Studies, Monographs & Papers: No. 30). 351p. 1976. pap. 108.90 (*0-7837-7672-1*, 204742500007) Bks Demand.

Bikle, Lucy L. George W. Cable: His Life & Letter, by His Daughter. (BCL1-PS American Literature Ser.). 306p. 1992. reprint ed. lib. bdg. 89.00 (*0-7812-6683-1*) Rprt Serv.

Bikle, Nancy. Museum of Westward Expansion: A Photographic Collection. 126p. 1997. pap. 5.95 (*0-931056-11-X*) Jefferson Natl.

Biklen, Douglas P. Communication Unbound: How Facilitated Communication Is Challenging Traditional Views of Autism & Ability-Disability. LC 92-34555. (Special Education Ser.: No. 13). 240p. (C). 1993. text 39.00 (*0-8077-3222-2*); pap. text 17.95 (*0-8077-3221-4*) Tchrs Coll.

— Schooling Without Labels: Parents, Educators & Inclusive Education. (Health, Society, & Policy Ser.). (C). 1992. 69.95 (*0-87722-875-2*); pap. 22.95 (*0-87722-876-0*) Temple U Pr.

Biklen, Douglas P., et al, eds. Schooling & Disability. (National Society for the Study of Education Publication Ser.: No. 88, Pt. 2). 302p. 1989. 27.00 (*0-226-60150-1*) U Ch Pr.

Biklen, Douglas P., et al. Achieving the Complete School: Strategies for Effective Mainstreaming. (Special Education Ser.). 224p. (C). 1985. pap. text 19.95 (*0-8077-2772-5*) Tchrs Coll.

Biklen, Sari K. School Work: Gender & the Cultural Construction of Teaching. (Series on School Reform). 216p. (C). 1994. text 44.00 (*0-8077-3408-X*); pap. text 19.95 (*0-8077-3407-1*) Tchrs Coll.

Biklen, Sari K. & Pollard, Diane S., eds. Gender & Education. (National Society for the Study of Education Publication Ser.: No. 92, Pt. 1). 288p. (C). 1993. 27.50 (*0-226-60159-5*) U Ch Pr.

Biklen, Sari K., jt. auth. see Bogdan, Robert C.

Biklen, Sari K., jt. ed. see Antler, Joyce.

Biklin, D., et al. The Least Restrictive Alternative: Principles & Practices. Turnbull, H. Rutherford, III, ed. 80p. (Orig.). 1981. pap. 6.00 (*0-940898-06-3*) Am Assn Mental.

Biklin, Doug. Contested Words, Contested Science: Unraveling the Facilitated Communication Controversy. Cardinal, Don, ed. LC 96-52240. (Special Education Ser.: Vol. 18). 256p. (C). 1997. text 54.00 (*0-8077-3602-3*); pap. text 24.95 (*0-8077-3601-5*) Tchrs Coll.

Biko, Steve. Escribo lo Que Me Da la Gana: " I Write What I Like" LC 89-11105. (SPA.). 160p. 1989. pap. 9.95 (*0-932727-07-7*) Hope Pub Hse.

— Escribo lo Que Me da la Gana: "I Write What I Like" LC 89-11105. (SPA.). 160p. 1989. lib. bdg. 16.95 (*0-932727-25-5*) Hope Pub Hse.

— I Write What I Like. 196p. 1996. pap. text 14.95 (*0-906097-49-5*, Pub. by Bowerdean Pub) Capital VA.

Bikowski, J. New Perspectives on Dermatological Infections (Handbook) 1995. 9.95 (*1-873413-16-5*) Merit Pub Intl.

Bikowski, Joseph, jt. auth. see Connolly, Coyle.

Bikram-Kisor, Maharaj-Kumar Sahadev & Gan-Chaudhuri, Jagadis. Tripura: Historical Documents. (C). 1994. 24.00 (*0-8364-2894-3*, Pub. by Firma KLM) S Asia.

Bikson, Tora K. New Technology in the Office: Planning for People. (Studies in Productivity: Highlights of the Literature Ser.: Vol. 40). 1985. 55.00 (*0-08-029514-2*) Work in Amer.

***Bikson, Tora K. & Panis, Constantijn W. A.** Citizens, Computers & Connectivity: A Review of Trends. (Illus.). xiv, 50p. (C). 1999. pap. 7.50 (*0-8330-2778-6*, MR-1109-MF) Rand Corp.

Biktashev, Val, jt. auth. see Moran, Elizabeth.

Bil, Albert. The Shieling, 1600-1840: The Case of the Central Scottish Highlands. 400p. (C). 1997. text 60.00 (*0-85976-158-4*, Pub. by J Donald) St Mut.

Bil, Cornelis. Development & Application of a Computer-Based System for Conceptual Aircraft Design. (Illus.). 258p. (Orig.). 1988. pap. 43.50 (*90-6275-484-8*, Pub. by Delft U Pr) Coronet Bks.

Bila, Dennis & Ross, Donald. Precalculus. 480p. (gr. 12). 1986. 18.36 (*0-935115-00-5*) Instruct Tech.

Bila, Dennis, et al. Mathematics for Business Occupations. 567p. (gr. 10-12). 1986. reprint ed. 18.36 (*0-935115-01-3*) Instruct Tech.

— Mathematics for Health Occupations. 526p. 1986. reprint ed. student ed. write for info. (*0-935115-04-8*); reprint ed. pap. text 18.36 (*0-87626-570-0*) Instruct Tech.

— Mathematics for Technical Occupations. 606p. (gr. 10-12). 1985. reprint ed. 18.36 (*0-935115-02-1*) Instruct Tech.

Bilagody, Harry, Jr., tr. see Luckert, Karl W.

***Bilal, Enki.** The Nikopol Trilogy. deluxe ed. (Illus.). 176p. 1999. 39.95 (*0-9672401-2-3*) Humanoids.

Bilancia, Philip R. Chinese-English Dictionary of Chinese Law & Government. (CHI & ENG.). 822p. 1981. 125.00 (*0-8288-0972-0*, M3879) Fr & Eur.

— Dictionary of Chinese Law & Government: Chinese-English. LC 73-80618. (CHI & ENG.). 832p. 1981. 89.50 (*0-8047-0864-9*) Stanford U Pr.

Bilanich, Bud. Supervisory Leadership & the New Factory: Getting Extraordinary Things Done on the Shop Floor. 120p. 1993. pap. 19.95 (*0-9638280-0-2*) Front Row Pr.

— Using Values to Turn Vision into Reality. large type ed. 1998. pap. text 15.95 (*0-9638280-1-0*) Front Row Pr.

Bilaniuk, Larissa T., jt. auth. see Newton, Thomas H.

Bilardi, G. Solving Irregularly Structured Problems in Parallel: 4th International Symposium, Irregular '97, Paderborn, Germany, June 12-13, 1997, Proceedings, Vol. 125. LC 97-17625. (Lecture Notes in Computer Science). 1997. write for info. (*3-540-63138-0*) Spr-Verlag.

Bilardi, G., et al, eds. Algorithms - ESA, '98: 6th Annual European Symposium, Venice, Italy, August 24-26, 1998, Proceedings. LC 98-36219. (Lecture Notes in Computer Science Ser.: Vol. 1461). xii, 516p. 1998. pap. 75.00 (*3-540-64848-8*) Spr-Verlag.

***Bilas, Charles.** French Riviera 20's /30's. (Illus.). 160p. 1999. 24.95 (*2-7450-0051-9*) Telleri Edit.

Bilas, Ram. Rural Water Resource Utilization & Planning: A Geographical Approach in Varanasi District. (C). 1988. 24.00 (*81-7022-027-0*, Pub. by Concept) S Asia.

Bilash, Borislaw, II. A Demo a Day: A Year of Physical Science Demonstrations. (Illus.). 333p. (Orig.). 1997. pap. text 35.95 (*0-614-29832-6*) Flinn Scientific.

Bilash, Borislaw, 2nd, et al. A Demo a Day: A Year of Chemical Demonstrations. Meszaros, Mark W., ed. (Illus.). 295p. (Orig.). 1995. pap. text 33.95 (*1-877991-36-8*) Flinn Scientific.

Bilash, Radomir & Wilberg, Barbara, eds. Tkanyna: An Exhibit of Ukrainian Weaving. (Illus.). 63p. pap. 9.95 (*0-920862-58-6*) Ukrainian Acad.

Bilateral Commission on the Future of United State. The Challenge of Interdependence: Mexico & the United States. 260p. (Orig.). (C). 1988. pap. text 25.00 (*0-8191-7274-X*); lib. bdg. 48.00 (*0-8191-7273-1*) U Pr of Amer.

Bilbao, Andres. Lexico de Economia: Talasa Ediciones, 1993. (Illus.). 140p. 1993. 39.95 (*84-88119-16-X*) Fr & Eur.

***Bilbao, J. Mario.** Cooperative Games on Combinatorial Structures. 344p. 2000. 139.95 (*0-7923-7782-6*) Kluwer Academic.

Bilbao, Juan, jt. auth. see Midroni, Gyl.

Bilbrey, Burt, illus. see Fries, Derrick.

Bilbrey, Darrell. PeopleSoft Administrator's Guide. LC 99-60011. 560p. 1999. pap. 59.99 (*0-7821-2396-1*) Sybex.

Bilbrey, David. Born to Sell: What It Really Takes to Succeed in Sales. 1995. pap. 9.95 (*0-614-07781-8*) D Bilbrey & Co.

***Bilbrough, Norman.** Desert Shorts: And Other Stories. 160p. (Orig.). 1999. pap. 24.95 (*0-908812-81-7*, Pub. by Canterbury Univ) Accents Pubns.

***Bilbrough, Paola.** Bell Tongue. 80p. 2000. pap. 14.95 (*0-86473-363-1*, Pub. by Victoria Univ Pr) Paul & Co Pubs.

Bilby, Joseph. Irish Brigade in the Civil War. 1998. pap. 19.95 (*0-938289-97-7*, 289997) Combined Pub.

Bilby, Joseph G. Civil War Firearms: Their Historical Background & Tactical Use. LC 96-33314. 1996. 34.95 (*0-938289-79-9*, 289799) Combined Pub.

— Forgotten Warriors: New Jersey's African American Soldiers in the Civil War. (Illus.). 72p. 1994. pap. text 7.95 (*0-944413-28-5*) Longstreet Hse.

— Remember Fontenoy! The 69th New York & the Irish Brigade in the Civil War. (Illus.). 269p. 1995. 28.00 (*0-944413-37-4*) Longstreet Hse.

Bilby, Joseph G. & Goble, William C. Remember You Are Jerseymen! A Military History of New Jersey's Troops in the Civil War. (Illus.). 734p. 1998. 48.00 (*0-944413-54-4*, 141) Longstreet Hse.

Bilby, Joseph G. & O'Neill, Stephan D., eds. My Sons Were Faithful & They Fought the Irish Brigade at Antietam: An Anthology. LC 98-220798. (Illus.). 131p. 1997. pap. 18.00 (*0-944413-42-0*, 132) Longstreet Hse.

Bilby, R. E., jt. ed. see Naiman, R. J.

Bilby, Robert E., jt. ed. see Naiman, Robert J.

Bilchik, Shay. Guide for Implementing the Balanced & Restorative Justice Model. 90p. (C). 1999. pap. text 25.00 (*0-7881-7686-2*) DIANE Pub.

— Juvenile Court Statistics, 1994. Butts, Jeffrey A. et al, eds. (Illus.). xvi, 96p. 1996. pap. text 30.00 (*1-57979-259-6*) DIANE Pub.

***Bilchik, Shay.** Juvenile Mentoring Program: 1998 Report to Congress. (Illus.). 65p. 1999. pap. text 20.00 (*0-7881-8083-5*) DIANE Pub.

Bilchik, Shay. Reducing Your Gun Violence: An Overview of Programs & Initiatives: Program Report. 73p. (C). 1998. reprint ed. pap. text 30.00 (*0-7881-3926-6*) DIANE Pub.

***Bilchik, Shay.** Title V Incentive Grants for Local Delinquency Preventive Programs: 1996 Report. (Illus.). 65p. 1999. reprint ed. pap. text 15.00 (*0-7881-8080-0*) DIANE Pub.

Bilchik, Shay. When Your Child Is Missing: A Family Survival Guide. (Illus.). 93p. 1999. pap. text 20.00 (*0-7881-7690-0*) DIANE Pub.

Bilchik, Shay, ed. Child Abuse: Guide to Investigating Child Abuse. 227p. (C). 1999. pap. text 35.00 (*0-7881-7633-1*) DIANE Pub.

— Matrix of Community Based Initiatives: Violence & Delinquency Prevention. (Illus.). 49p. (C). 1997. reprint ed. pap. text 30.00 (*0-7881-4037-X*) DIANE Pub.

***Bilchik, Shay, ed.** National Gang Survey (1996) Summary. (Illus.). 75p. 1999. pap. text 20.00 (*0-7881-8453-9*) DIANE Pub.

— National Youth Gang Survey, 1996: Summary. (Illus.). 75p. (C). 2000. pap. text 20.00 (*0-7881-8795-3*) DIANE Pub.

— Promising Strategies to Reduce Gun Violence. (Illus.). 253p. (C). 1999. pap. text 40.00 (*0-7881-8203-X*) DIANE Pub.

Bild, Linda, jt. auth. see Franco, Betsy.

Bild, Sharon, ed. see Nelson, Doris.

Bildarchiv Foto Marburg Staff & Deutches Dokumentationszentrum fur Kuntsgeschichte, eds. Marburger Informations, Dokumentations und Administrations-System (MIDAS) Handbuch: Lutz Heusinger. (Literatur und Archiv Ser.). (GER.). xxvi, 577p. 1992. lib. bdg. 54.00 (*3-598-22086-3*) K G Saur Verlag.

Bilde, Per, et al, eds. Apocryphon Severin: Studies in Ancient Manichaeism & Gnosticism Presented to Soren Giversen. 258p. (C). 1993. 27.00 (*87-7288-101-1*, Pub. by Aarhus Univ Pr) David Brown.

— Aspects of Hellenistic Kingship. (Studies in Hellenistic Civilization: No. 7). (Illus.). 160p. (C). 1996. 30.00 (*87-7288-474-6*, Pub. by Aarhus Univ Pr) David Brown.

— Centre & Periphery in the Hellenistic World. (Studies in Hellenistic Civilization: No. 4). (Illus.). 360p. (C). 1994. 40.00 (*87-7288-317-0*, Pub. by Aarhus Univ Pr) David Brown.

— Conventional Values of the Hellenistic Greeks. (Studies in Hellenistic Civilization: Vol. VIII). (Illus.). 320p. 1997. 39.95 (*87-7288-555-6*, Pub. by Aarhus Univ Pr) David Brown.

— Ethnicity in Hellenistic Egypt. (Studies in Hellenistic Civilization: No. 3). 210p. (C). 1992. text 27.00 (*87-7288-359-6*, Pub. by Aarhus Univ Pr) David Brown.

— Religion & Religious Practice in the Seleucid Kingdom. (Studies in Hellenistic Civilization: No. 1). (Illus.). 269p. (C). 1990. text 35.00 (*87-7288-322-7*, Pub. by Aarhus Univ Pr) David Brown.

Bilde, Per, ed. see Engberg-Pedersen, Troels.

Bilde, Per, ed. see Nielsen, Inge.

Bilde, Pia G., et al, eds. Aspects of Hellenism in Italy: Acta Hyperborea, Vol. 5. (Illus.). 400p. 1994. pap. 40.00 (*87-7289-208-0*, Pub. by Mus Tusculanum) Paul & Co Pubs.

Bilder, Erica, ed. Theandric: Julian Beck's Last Notebooks, 2, Vol. 2. (Contemporary Theatre Studies). xii, 195p. 1992. text 30.00 (*3-7186-5192-0*, Harwood Acad Pubs); pap. text 15.00 (*3-7186-5193-9*, Harwood Acad Pubs) Gordon & Breach.

Bilder, Richard B. Managing the Risks of International Agreement. LC 80-52288. 315p. 1981. reprint ed. pap. 97.70 (*0-7837-9777-X*, 206050600005) Bks Demand.

Bilder, Robert M. & LeFever, F. Frank, eds. Neuroscience of the Mind on the Centennial of Freud's "Project for a Scientific Psychology" On the Centennial of Freud's Project for a Scientific Psychology. LC 98-13652. (Annals of the New York Academy of Sciences Ser.: Vol. 843). 1998. 80.00 (*1-57331-063-8*); 80.00 (*1-57331-062-X*) NY Acad Sci.

An Asterisk (*) at the beginning of an entry indicates that the title is appearing for the first time.

Bilderback, Allen H. Revelation & Apocalyptic Symbols: Bible Stories of the Planets & Stars. (Revelations of God's Glory & Hidden Identities Ser.). (Illus.). 180p. (YA). (gr. 8 up). 1992. 24.95 (*0-9630710-1-7*); pap. 10.00 (*0-9630710-0-9*) ABCO Pub.

— The Revelation of Christ's Glory: A Scientific Exposition of John's Apocalypse. 93p. 1995. pap. text 10.00 (*0-9630710-3-3*) ABCO Pub.

Bilderback, Allen H. & Bilderback, Lillian A. Our African Journal, 1945-1950. 156p. (Orig.). (YA). (gr. 8 up). 1993. pap. text 10.00 (*0-9630710-2-5*) ABCO Pub.

Bilderback, Carolyn. Gatherings from a Dancer's Journal. (Orig.). 1992. pap. 12.00 (*0-913660-25-6*) Magic Cir Pr CT.

Bilderback, Lillian A., jt. auth. see Bilderback, Allen H.

Bilderbeck, James B. Chaucer's Legend of Good Women. LC 78-39441. reprint ed. 34.50 (*0-404-00859-3*) AMS Pr.

Bilderbeek, A. S. & Van Buitenen, A., eds. Biodiversity & International Law: Effectiveness of International Environmental Law. LC 91-7765. 200p. (gr. 12). 1992. 55.00 (*90-5199-067-7*, Pub. by IOS Pr) IOS Press.

Bilderdijk, Willem. Remarkable Aerial Voyage. Vincent, Paul, tr. from DUT. & intro. by. LC 87-70814. 88p. 1987. pap. 13.95 (*0-905075-24-2*, Pub. by Wilfion Bks) Dufour.

Bildersee, A. State Scholarship Students at Hunter College of the City of New York. LC 77-176563. (Columbia University. Teachers College. Contributions to Education Ser.: No. 540). reprint ed. 37.50 (*0-404-55540-3*) AMS Pr.

Bildner, Jim & Dodson, James. J Bildner & Sons Cookbook: Casual Feasts, Food on the Run, & Special Celebrations. Doubleday Staff, ed. LC 93-30686. (Illus.). 256p. 1993. reprint ed. pap. 12.95 (*1-55832-064-4*) Harvard Common Pr.

Bildner, Phil. Shoeless Joe & Black Betsy. LC 99-40563. (J). 2002. pap. text 16.00 (*0-689-82913-2*) S&S Childrens.

Bildstein, Jay. The King of Clubs: The Story of Scores - The Famed Topless Club & the Lurid Life Behind the Glitter. Schmetterer, Jerry, tr. LC 95-51181. 288p. 1996. 24.00 (*1-56980-073-1*) Barricade Bks.

Bildstein, Keith L. Behavioral Ecology of Red-Tailed Hawks (Buteo Jamaicensis), Rough-Legged Hawks (Buteo Lagopus), Northern Harriers (Circus Cyaneus) & American Kestrels (Falco Sparvarius) in South Central Ohio. LC 85-62834. (Biological Notes Ser.: No. 18). (Illus.). 50p. (C). 1986. pap. text 5.00 (*0-86727-102-7*) Ohio Bio Survey.

— White Ibis: Wetland Wanderer. LC 92-38961. (Illus.). 272p. 1993. 24.95 (*1-56098-223-3*) Smithsonian.

***Bildt, Carl.** Peace Journey. LC 99-220726. 1998. 50.00 (*0-297-84131-9*, Pub. by Weidenfeld & Nicolson) Trafalgar.

Bildungswerk des Verbands Deutscher Tonmeister, ed. Tagungsbericht der 20, Tonmeistertagung Karlsuiile 1998: International Convention on Social Design vom. 20, G. S. 23, November 1998. 1276p. 1999. lib. bdg. write for info. (*3-598-20361-6*) K G Saur Verlag.

Bilej, Martin. Immunology of Annelids. 320p. 1993. lib. bdg. 210.00 (*0-8493-4909-5*) CRC Pr.

Bilello, Jack. Bonds of War. ii, 350p. (Orig.). 1998. pap. 16.95 (*1-892509-50-4*) Chambers Pubg Grp.

— Bonds of War. 352p. (Orig.). 1998. pap. 16.95 (*1-58446-010-5*, Eva Bks) Temple Pubg.

Bilello, Suzanne, et al. Attacks on the Press in 1996. Chasan, Alice, ed. 376p. 1997. pap. 30.00 (*0-944823-16-5*) Comm to Protect Jrnlists.

***Bilenko, M. V.** Free-Radical Mechanisms of Ischemic & Reperfusion Injuries of Various Organs. LC 00-25271. (Illus.). 347p. 2000. lib. bdg. 79.00 (*1-56072-800-0*) Nova Sci Pubs.

Bilenky, S. M. Introduction to the Physics of Electroweak Interactions. LC 81-15839. (Illus.). 250p. 1982. 125.00 (*0-08-026502-2*, Pub. by Pergamon Repr) Franklin.

Biler, I. & Sternlicht, Manny. The Psychology of Mental Retardation. LC 77-4137. 800p. 1977. 39.95 (*0-88437-013-5*) Psych Dimensions.

Biler, Piotr & Nadzieja, Tadeusz, eds. Problems & Examples in Differential Equations. (Pure & Applied Mathematics Ser.: Vol. 164). (Illus.). 264p. 1992. text 65.00 (*0-8247-8637-8*) Dekker.

Biler, Piotr & Witkowski, Alfred. Problems in Mathematical Analysis. (Pure & Applied Mathematics Ser.: Vol. 132). (Illus.). 240p. 1990. text 65.00 (*0-8247-8312-3*) Dekker.

Biles. Statistics: A Health Sciences Introduction Minitab. 160p. 1993. pap. 16.95 (*0-8016-6534-5*) Mosby Inc.

Biles, D. & McDonald, D., eds. Deaths in Custody in Australia, 1980-1989. 605p. 1992. pap. 50.00 (*0-642-18077-6*, Pub. by Aust Inst Criminology) Advent Bks Div.

Biles, D. & Vernon, J., eds. Private Sector & Community Involvement in the Criminal Justice System. LC 95-173937. (Australian Institute Conference Proceedings Ser.: Vol. 23). 478p. 1994. pap. 45.00 (*0-642-20156-0*, Pub. by Aust Inst Criminology) Advent Bks Div.

Biles, D., jt. ed. see McKillop, Sandra.

Biles, Daniel V., jt. auth. see Cumberworth, Sheila M.

Biles, David. Current Australian Trends in Corrections. 1988. pap. 30.00 (*1-86287-003-9*, Pub. by Federation Pr) Gaunt.

— Current International Trends in Corrections. 222p. (C). 1988. text 30.00 (*1-86287-002-0*, Pub. by Federation Pr) Gaunt.

Biles, Fay, et al, eds. Play for Power: Creating Leaders Through Sport. 265p. (Orig.). 1996. pap. text 26.00 (*0-88314-801-3*, A801-3) AAHPERD.

Biles, Frances H. Biles-Herzog Genealogy. LC 84-81998. 88p. 1984. 22.50 (*0-943480-58-2*) Friis-Pioneer Pr.

Biles, George E. & Tuckman, Howard P. Part-Time Faculty Personnel Management Policies. (ACE-Oryx Series on Higher Education). 188p. 1986. 27.95 (*0-02-903500-7*) Free Pr.

— Part-Time Faculty Personnel Management Policies. 224p. 1986. text. write for info. (*0-318-62004-9*, 2009) Macmillan.

Biles, Jack I., ed. British Novelists since Nineteen Hundred. LC 85-48000. (Georgia State Literary Studies: No. 1). 1987. 55.00 (*0-404-63201-7*) AMS Pr.

Biles, Jack I. & Evans, Robert O., eds. William Golding: Some Critical Considerations. LC 77-73705. 295p. reprint ed. pap. 91.50 (*0-608-12694-2*, 202435700037) Bks Demand.

Biles, Roger. Big City Boss in Depression & War: Mayor Edward J. Kelly of Chicago. LC 83-19391. 219p. 1984. 25.00 (*0-87580-098-X*) N Ill U Pr.

— Memphis in the Great Depression. LC 85-22575. (Illus.). 185p. 1986. reprint ed. pap. 57.40 (*0-608-07780-1*, 206786800010) Bks Demand.

— A New Deal for the American People. LC 90-27715. 274p. 1991. pap. 15.00 (*0-87580-554-X*); lib. bdg. 32.00 (*0-87580-161-7*) N Ill U Pr.

— Richard J. Daley: Politics, Race & the Governing of Chicago. LC 94-48268. (Illus.). 305p. 1995. 32.00 (*0-87580-199-4*); pap. 18.00 (*0-87580-566-3*) N Ill U Pr.

— The South & the New Deal. LC 93-20816. (New Perspectives on the South Ser.). 216p. (C). 1994. 24.95 (*0-8131-1836-0*) U Pr of Ky.

Biletzki, Anat. Biletzki Talking Wolves. LC 96-54216. 1997. text 113.50 (*0-7923-4425-1*) Kluwer Academic.

Biletzki, Anat & Matar. The Story of Analytic Philosophy: Plot & Heroes. LC 97-23396. 276p. (C). 1998. 70.00 (*0-415-16251-3*) Routledge.

Biletzky, I. Ch. God, Jew, Satan in the Works of Isaac Bashevis-Singer. 154p. (Orig.). (C). 1995. pap. text 24.50 (*0-8191-9829-3*); lib. bdg. 47.00 (*0-8191-9828-5*) U Pr of Amer.

Biley. Contemporary Issues in Nursing. 1996. pap. text 17.95 (*0-443-05351-0*, W B Saunders Co) Harcrt Hlth Sci Grp.

Bilezikian, Gilbert. Beyond Sex Roles: What the Bible Says about a Woman's Place in Church & Family. 2nd ed. LC 84-73199. 352p. 1985. pap. 14.99 (*0-8010-0885-9*) Baker Bks.

— Christianity One Hundred One: Your Guide to Eight Basic Christian Beliefs. 288p. 1993. pap. 16.99 (*0-310-57701-2*) Zondervan.

Bilezikian, Gilbert G. Community 101: Reclaiming the Local Church As a Community of Oneness. LC 97-14458. 208p. 1997. pap. 14.99 (*0-310-21741-5*) Zondervan.

Bilezikian, John P., et al, eds. The Parathyroids: Basic & Clinical Concepts. LC 93-4126. (Illus.). 889p. 1994. reprint ed. pap. 200.00 (*0-608-07316-4*, 206754400009) Bks Demand.

— Principles of Bone Biology. LC 96-32323. (Illus.). 1398p. 1996. text 165.00 (*0-12-098650-7*) Acad Pr.

Bilezikian, John P., jt. ed. see Becker, Kenneth L.

Bilezikian, Monique A., jt. ed. see Romanowski, Sylvie.

Bilezkian, Gilbert & Willow Creek Resources Staff. The Church as a Community. (Defining Moments Ser.: Vol. 2). 1994. audio 12.99 (*0-310-20979-X*) Zondervan.

Bilfinger, Georg B. Gesammelte Werke: Abteilung: Ergaenzungsreihe, Vol. 18. (GER.). 618p. 1982. write for info. (*3-487-07234-3*) G Olms Pubs.

— Gesammelte Werke: Abteilung: Ergaenzungsreihe, Vol. 21. (GER.). 24p. 1984. write for info. (*3-487-07379-X*) G Olms Pubs.

Bilfinger, Georg B. & Wolff, Christian. Gesammelte Werke: Abteilung: Ergaenzungsreihe, Bd. 22. (Gesammelte Werke Abteilung: Erganzungsreihe: Materialien und Dokumente Ser. Three: Pt. 22). (GER.). 110p. 1985. reprint ed. write for info. (*3-487-07641-1*) G Olms Pubs.

Bilge, Barbara, jt. ed. see Aswad, Barbara C.

Bilger, Andrea, jt. auth. see Liebermann, Loni.

Bilger, Audrey. Laughing Feminism: Subversive Comedy in Frances Burney, Maria Edgeworth, & Jane Austen. LC 98-10828. (Humor in Life & Letters Ser.). 1998. text 39.95 (*0-8143-2722-2*) Wayne St U Pr.

Bilger, Burkhard. Global Warming. (Earth at Risk Ser.). (Illus.). 128p. (YA). (gr. 5 up). 1992. lib. bdg. 19.95 (*0-7910-1575-0*) Chelsea Hse.

***Bilger, Burkhard.** Noodling for Flatheads: Moonshine, Monster Catfish & Other Southern Comforts. (Illus.). 256p. 2000. write for info. (*0-684-85010-9*) Scribner.

Bilger, Burkhard, et al. Environmental Awareness Case Studies. 94p. 1994. pap. text 81.32 (*0-669-30820-X*) HM Trade Div.

Bilger, Burkhard, jt. ed. see Quammen, David.

Bilgere, Dmitiri. Beyond the Blame Game: Creating Compassion & Ending the Sex War in Your Life. LC 97-147784. 172p. 1997. pap., per. 10.95 (*0-9613177-3-6*) MPC Pr.

Bilgere, George. Big Bang: Poems. LC 98-45303. 64p. 1999. pap. 11.00 (*0-914278-76-2*) Copper Beech.

— The Going. 64p. 1994. pap. 12.95 (*0-8262-0966-1*) U of Mo Pr.

Bilginer, Sadettin. Deutsch-Turkisches Worterbuch Fur Technische Berufe. 2nd deluxe ed. (GER & TUR.). 448p. 1966. 75.00 (*0-8288-6701-1*, M7348) Fr & Eur.

Bilgram, Hugo. The Remedy for Overproduction & Unemployment. 1979. lib. bdg. 250.00 (*0-87700-287-8*) Revisionist Pr.

— A Study of the Money Question. 1973. 59.95 (*0-8490-1157-4*) Gordon Pr.

Bilgram, Hugo & Levy, L. The Cause of Business Depressions. 1973. 250.00 (*0-87968-095-4*) Gordon Pr.

Bilgrami, K. S., et al. Changes in Nutritional Components of Stored Seeds Due to Fungal Association. (International Bioscience Monographs: No. 9). 90p. 1979. 8.00 (*0-88065-061-3*) Scholarly Pubns.

— Fungi of India - List & References. 2nd enl. rev. ed. (Illus.). 800p. 1992. 95.00 (*1-55528-259-8*, Pub. by Today Tomorrow) Scholarly Pubns.

Bilgrami, K. S., ed. see All India Symposium Staff.

Bilgrami, Syed A. Landmarks of the Deccan: A Comprehensive Guide to the Archaeological Remains of the City & Suburbs of Hyderabad. (C). 1992. 20.30 (*81-206-0543-8*, Pub. by Asian Educ Servs) S Asia.

Bilgrien, Marie V. Solidarity: A Principle, an Attitude, a Duty?: or The Virtue for an Interdependent World? LC 97-52194. (American University Studies VII: Vol. 204). XI, 278p. (C). 1999. text 48.95 (*0-8204-3985-1*, 39851) P Lang Pubng.

Bilhart. Effective Group Discussion. 10th ed. 448p. 2000. pap. 39.38 (*0-07-231568-7*) McGraw.

***Bilhartz, Lyman E. & Croft, Carol Lynn.** Gastrointestinal Disease in Primary Care. LC 99-55265. 224p. 2000. pap. text 39.95 (*0-683-30444-5*) Lppncott W & W.

Bilhartz, Lyman E., jt. auth. see Weisiger, Richard A.

Bilhartz, Terry D. Francis Asbury's America. 1984. pap. 7.99 (*0-685-70967-1*) Schmul Pub Co.

— Urban Religion & the Second Great Awakening. LC 83-49455. 240p. 1986. 36.50 (*0-8386-3227-0*) Fairleigh Dickinson.

Bilhartz, Terry O., ed. Francis Asbury's America: An Album of Early American Methodism. LC 83-18275. 128p. 1984. pap. 4.70 (*0-310-44791-7*, 18275P) Zondervan.

Bilharz, Joy A. The Allegany Senecas & Kinzua Dam: Forced Relocation Through Two Generations. LC 97-35056. (Illus.). xxvii, 204p. 1998. text 45.00 (*0-8032-1282-8*) U of Nebr Pr.

Bilheimer, Linda T. Designing Program Evaluations. Glass, Karen, ed. (Strategies for Improving State Perinatal Programs Ser.). 70p. (Orig.). 1989. pap. text 15.00 (*1-55877-060-7*) Natl Governor.

Bilheimer, Robert S. Breakthrough: The Emergence of the Ecumenical Tradition. LC 89-7705. 245p. (Orig.). reprint ed. pap. 76.00 (*0-7837-3179-5*, 204278300006) Bks Demand.

— What Must the Church Do? LC 70-134053. (Essay Index Reprints - Interseminary Ser.: Vol. 5). 1977. reprint ed. 19.95 (*0-8369-2384-7*) Ayer.

Bilheux, Roland. Basic Bread Making Techniques. (Special & Decorative Breads Ser.). 304p. 1997. text 69.95 (*0-470-25005-4*) Halsted Pr.

— Creams, Confections, Finished Desserts. (French Professional Pastry Ser.). 224p. 1997. 80.00 (*0-470-24409-7*) Wiley.

— Doughs, Batters, Merigues. (French Professional Pastry Ser.). 200p. 1997. 80.00 (*0-470-24408-9*) Wiley.

— Petits Fours, Chocolate, Frozen Desserts, Sugar Work. LC 98-158019. (French Professional Pastry Ser.). 240p. 1998. text 69.95 (*0-470-25000-3*) Halsted Pr.

Bilheux, Roland. Petits Fours, Chocolate, Frozen Desserts, Sugar Work. (French Professional Pastry Ser.). 22-p. 1998. 80.00 (*0-470-24410-0*) Wiley.

***Bilibin, A. Yu., et al.** Macromolecular Symposia 128. Jung, B. et al, eds. 264p. 1998. pap. 75.00 (*3-527-29886-X*) Wiley.

Bilibin, Ivan I. Russian Fairy Tales. LC 95-15334. (Everyman's Library of Children's Classics). 1995. write for info. (*0-614-07798-2*, Evrymans Lib Childs) Knopf.

Bilic, N., et al, eds. Frontiers in Particle Physics, 1983: Adriatic Meeting on Particle Physics, IV, Dubrovnik, Yugoslavia, 6-15 June, 1983. 550p. (C). 1984. 98.00 (*9971-950-57-X*) World Scientific Pub.

Bilich, Marion. Weight Loss from the Inside Out: Help for the Compulsive Eater. LC 83-633. 192p. 1984. 9.95 (*0-8164-2485-3*) Harper SF.

***Bilich, Marion, et al, eds.** Shared Grace: Therapists & Clergy Working Together. LC 99-462143. 237p. 2000. 49.95 (*0-7890-0878-5*, Haworth Pastrl); pap. text 24.95 (*0-7890-1110-7*, Haworth Pastrl) Haworth Pr.

Bilicki, Bettie Y. & Goetz, Masa. Getting Back Together: How to Create a New, Loving Relationship with Your Old Partner & Make It Last. 1990. pap. 9.95 (*1-55850-862-7*) Adams Media.

Bilides, David G., et al. Macedonian Folk Songs for Voice & Tambura, Vol. 1. (Illus.). 113p. (Orig.). 1997. pap. 42.00 (*0-9658579-0-5*) Izvor Music.

— Macedonian Folk Songs for Voice & Tambura, Vol. 2. 110p. (Orig.). 1999. pap. 42.00 (*0-9658579-1-3*) Izvor Music.

Bilik, Dorothy. Immigrant-Survivors: Post-Holocaust Consciousness in Recent Jewish American Fiction. 10.95 (*0-931848-87-3*) Dryad Pr.

— Immigrant-Survivors: Post-Holocaust Consciousness in Recent Jewish American Fiction. LC 80-15326. 225p. 1981. reprint ed. pap. 69.80 (*0-608-02300-0*, 206294100004) Bks Demand.

Bilik, Jen. Women of Taste: A Collaboration Celebrating Quilt Artists & Chefs. LC 99-6295. 1999. pap. text 24.95 (*1-57120-078-9*) C & T Pub.

Bilimoria, Purusottama. Hinduism in Australia: Mandala for the Gods Yoga, Meditation & the Guru. 178p. (C). 1989. 65.00 (*0-86786-201-7*, Pub. by Deakin Univ) St Mut.

— Sabdapramana: Word & Knowledge. 400p. (C). 1988. lib. bdg. 245.00 (*90-277-2675-2*, Pub. by Kluwer Academic) Kluwer Academic.

— Yoga, Meditation & the Guru: Critical Reflections on the Australian Scenario. 79p. (C). 1989. 45.00 (*0-7855-6753-4*, Pub. by Deakin Univ) St Mut.

— Yoga, Meditation & the Guru: Critical Reflections on the Australian Scenario. (Illus.). 64p. 1997. pap. 14.95 (*0-9587718-2-0*, Pub. by Indra Pub) Intl Spec Bk.

Bilimoria, Purusottama & Mohanty, J. N., eds. Relativism, Suffering & Beyond: Essays in Memory of Bimal K. Matilal. LC 97-900347. (Illus.). 392p. 1997. text 38.00 (*0-19-563858-1*) OUP.

Bilimoria, Purusottama, jt. auth. see Sharma, Renuka M.

Bilimoria, Purusottama, ed. see Mohanty, J. N.

Bilingual Haitian Students of Solomon Lewenberg Mi. A New Beginning: The World of Poetry. Jerome, Lunine P., ed. (CRP & ENG.). 181p. (J). (gr. 7-10). 1997. 10.00 (*1-885566-15-8*) Oresjozef.

Bilingual Staff. New American Standard Update (La Biblia de las Americas) Bilingual Bible - Indexed. (SPA & ENG.). 1998. bond lthr. 47.99 (*1-58135-037-6*) Foun Pubns.

Bilinkoff, Jodi. The Avila of Saint Teresa: Religious Reform in a Sixteenth-Century City. LC 89-42886. (Illus.). 240p. 1989. text 37.50 (*0-8014-2203-5*) Cornell U Pr.

— The Avila of Saint Teresa: Religious Reform in a Sixteenth-Century City. LC 89-42886. (Illus.). 240p. 1992. pap. text 14.95 (*0-8014-8052-3*) Cornell U Pr.

***Bilinsky, David J.** Amicus Attorney in One Hour for Lawyers. (Illus.). 100p. 2000. pap. 34.95 (*1-57073-681-2*, Pub. by Amer Bar Assn) IPG Chicago.

Bilinsky, Yaroslav. Endgame in NATO's Enlargement. LC 98-33573. 168p. 1999. 55.00 (*0-275-96363-2*, Praeger Pubs) Greenwood.

Bilio, Beth De, see De Bilio, Beth.

Bilirakis, Michael, ed. Assisted Suicide - Legal, Medical, Ethical & Social Issues: Hearing Before the Committee on Commerce, U. S. House of Representatives. 143p. (C). 1998. pap. text 30.00 (*0-7881-4971-7*) DIANE Pub.

— Medicaid Reform: The Governors' View: Hearing Before the Committee on Commerce, U. S. House of Representatives. 89p. (C). 1998. pap. text 20.00 (*0-7881-4970-9*) DIANE Pub.

— Medical Devices: Technological Innovation & Patient-Provider Perspectives. (Illus.). 86p. (C). 1999. reprint ed. pap. text 20.00 (*0-7881-8099-1*) DIANE Pub.

***Bilirakis, Michael, ed.** Medical Records Confidentiality in the Modern Delivery of Health Care: Congressional Hearing. 121p. 2000. pap. text 30.00 (*0-7567-0138-4*) DIANE Pub.

— The Medicare & Choice Program after One Year: Congressional Hearing. (Illus.). 128p. (C). 2000. reprint ed. pap. text 25.00 (*0-7881-8957-3*) DIANE Pub.

— Medicare Provider Service Networks: Congressional Hearing. 112p. 1999. reprint ed. pap. text 25.00 (*0-7881-8553-5*) DIANE Pub.

— Overview on NIH Programs: Congressional Hearing. 56p. (C). 1999. reprint ed. pap. text 20.00 (*0-7881-8301-X*) DIANE Pub.

— Putting Patients First: Resolving Allocations of Transplant Organs: Congressional Hearings. 240p. (C). 1999. reprint ed. pap. text 40.00 (*0-7881-8452-0*) DIANE Pub.

— The State Children's Health Insurance Program: A Progress Report: Congressional Hearing. (Illus.). 94p. (C). 2000. reprint ed. pap. text 20.00 (*0-7881-8958-1*) DIANE Pub.

Bilitewski, Bernd, et al. Waste Management. LC 96-35760. 650p. 1996. 69.00 (*3-540-59210-5*) Spr-Verlag.

***Bilitewski, Ursula & Turner, Anthony, eds.** Biosensors in Environmental Monitoring. 505p. 1999. text 120.00 (*90-5702-449-7*, Harwood Acad Pubs) Gordon & Breach.

Bilitski, Joan & Taylor, Margaret C., eds. Nursing in the Year 2000. 70p. (Orig.). 1984. pap. 7.95 (*0-937058-20-3*) West Va U Pr.

Bilitza, D., et al. Ionospheric Models. (Advances in Spatial & Network Economics Ser.: No. 14). 216p. 1994. pap. 176.00 (*0-08-042489-9*, Pergamon Pr) Elsevier.

Bilitza, D., jt. ed. see Rawer, K.

Bilke, Ernst. Pferdepassion: Von Pferdezucht und Pferdeschonheit. (Documenta Hippologica Ser.). (Illus.). 321p. 1976. 105.00 (*3-487-08111-3*) G Olms Pubs.

Bilker, Melissa, ed. see Wainwright, Barry W.

Bilker, Scott. Credit Card & Debt Management: A Step-by-Step How-To Guide for Organizing Debts & Saving Money on Interest Payments. LC 95-71626. 144p. 1996. pap. 19.95 (*0-9648401-9-7*) Pr One Pubng.

Bill. Daddy I'm Pregnant. LC 97-50108. 1998. pap. text 7.99 (*0-89900-800-3*) College Pr Pub.

Bill. Holiday Game Book, 1992. (Illus.). pap. 12.95 (*0-8069-5627-5*) Sterling.

— Politics in the Middle East. 5th ed. LC 99-29689. 350p. (C). 1999. pap. text 48.00 (*0-321-00537-6*) Addison-Wesley.

Bill, Albert D. Carey: The Careys of Kansas & Some of Their Ancestors. (Illus.). 81p. 1997. reprint ed. pap. 15.00 (*0-8328-7849-9*); reprint ed. lib. bdg. 25.00 (*0-8328-7848-0*) Higginson Bk Co.

Bill, Alfred H. Alas, Poor Yorick. LC 71-110180. (Short Story Index Reprint Ser.). 1977. 20.95 (*0-8369-3331-1*) Ayer.

— The Beleaguered City: Richmond, 1861-1865. LC 80-16702. (Illus.). 313p. 1980. reprint ed. lib. bdg. 52.50 (*0-313-22568-0*, BIBE, Greenwood Pr) Greenwood.

— The Campaign of Princeton, 1776-1777. LC 75-7660. 154p. 1975. reprint ed. pap. 47.80 (*0-608-07810-7*, 205987700010) Bks Demand.

— New Jersey & the Revolutionary War. (New Jersey Historical Ser.). (Illus.). 117p. 1970. reprint ed. pap. 12.95 (*0-8135-0642-5*) Rutgers U Pr.

Bill, Buffalo, Jr. Buffalo Bill Museum. (Illus.). 64p. (C). 1995. pap. 20.00 (*0-295-97489-3*) U of Wash Pr.

— Treasures from Our West. (Illus.). 60p. (C). 1995. pap. 15.00 (*0-295-97488-5*) U of Wash Pr.

Bill, E. G., ed. A Catalogue of Manuscripts in Lambeth Palace Library: MSS 2431-3119. 1983. 67.00 (*0-19-920135-8*) OUP.

Bill, Erastus D. Citizen: An American Boy's Early Manhood Aboard a Sag Harbor Whale-Ship Chasing Delirium & Death Around the World, 1843-1849. LC 78-50525. (World Discovery Bks.). (Illus.). 1978. 10.00 (*0-930766-01-6*); pap. 4.95 (*0-930766-02-4*) O W Frost.

Bill Harris Studios, tr. see Stephens, Richard E.

B

B

Bill, James A. The Eagle & the Lion: The Tragedy of American-Iranian Relations. 520p. (C). 1989. reprint ed. pap. 20.00 (*0-300-04412-7*) Yale U Pr.
— George Ball: Behind the Scenes in U. S. Foreign Policy. LC 96-33991. (Illus.). 320p. 1997. 35.00 (*0-300-06969-3*) Yale U Pr.
— George Ball: Behind the Scenes in U. S. Foreign Policy. (Illus.). 320p. 1998. pap. 16.00 (*0-300-07646-0*) Yale U Pr.
— The Shah, the Ayatollah & the U. S. LC 88-70867. (Headline Ser.: No. 285). (Illus.). 72p. 1988. pap. 5.95 (*0-87124-120-X*) Foreign Policy.
Bill, Ledyard. History of Paxton. 121p. 1995. reprint ed. pap. 19.50 (*0-8328-4697-X*) Higginson Bk Co.
— History of the Bill Family. 368p. 1988. reprint ed. pap. 55.50 (*0-8328-0255-7*); reprint ed. lib. bdg. 63.50 (*0-8328-0254-9*) Higginson Bk Co.
Bill, M. Le Corbusier Vol. 3: Complete Works, 1934-1938. (Le Corbusier Ser.). 1996. 75.00 (*3-7643-5505-0*) Birkhauser.
Bill Ong Hing. Making & Remaking Asian America Through Immigration Policy, 1850-1990. LC 92-25507. (Asian America Ser.). 354p. 1994. 55.00 (*0-8047-2118-1*) Stanford U Pr.
Bill, Patricia, ed. see Minnesota Council on Foundations Staff.
***Bill, Robert.** Medical Mathematics & Dosage Calculations for Veterinary Professionals. LC 00-33438. (Illus.). 2000. write for info. (*0-8138-2099-5*) Iowa St U Pr.
Bill, Robert. Pharmacology for Veterinary Technicians. 2nd ed. LC 97-11. (Illus.). 352p. (C). (gr. 13). 1997. pap. text 29.00 (*0-8151-0902-4*, 28335) Mosby Inc.
Bill, Stephen. Curtains. LC 98-113145. 1997. pap. 5.25 (*0-8222-1564-0*) Dramatists Play.
Bill, V. Tschebotarioff, ed. The Russian People: A Reader on their History & their Culture. 3rd ed. LC 74-17005. 191p. reprint ed. pap. 59.30 (*0-608-15104-1*, 202578400046) Bks Demand.
Bill W, pseud. The Language of the Heart: Bill W.'s Grapevine Writings. LC 88-71930. 432p. 1988. 10.00 (*0-933685-16-5*) A A Grapevine.
Billa, Madam. Tales You Do Tell. LC 97-67291. 27p. (Orig.). 1997. pap. 8.95 (*1-57197-069-X*) Pentland Pr.
Billac, Pete. The Annihilator: All Must Die. Davis, Sharon K., ed. LC 80-85318. 176p. (Orig.). (YA). (gr. 12 up). 1987. mass mkt. 1.95 (*0-943629-02-0*) Swan Pub.
***Billac, Pete.** Become an Internet Millionaire: How to Succeed in a Home-Based Business. Zaruca, Dale & Purcell, Stuart, eds. LC 00-101730. 96p. 2000. pap. 9.95 (*0-943629-45-4*, Pub. by Swan Pub) Herveys Bklink.
Billac, Pete. How Not to Be Lonely. Davis, Sharon K. & Horton, Jo A., eds. LC 87-60965. 224p. 1987. pap. 9.95 (*0-943629-00-4*) Swan Pub.
— How Not to Be Lonely. rev. ed. 224p. 1989. per. 9.95 (*0-943629-03-9*) Swan Pub.
— Lose Fat While You Sleep: No Dieting, No Drugs, No Exercise. 7th ed. Evans, Cliff, ed. Patrick, Myra, tr. from ENG.Tr. of Pierda Grasa Mientras Usted Duerme. (SPA., Illus.). 96p. 1998. reprint ed. pap. 9.95 (*0-943629-38-1*) Swan Pub.
— Lose Fat While You Sleep No Dieting No Drugs No Exercise. large type ed. Evans, Cliff, ed. LC 98-84047. 96p. 1998. pap. 9.95 (*0-943629-33-0*) Swan Pub.
***Billac, Pete.** Managing Stress Through the Magic of Adaptogens. 2nd ed. Kroll, Ken et al, eds. LC 99-65296. 93p. 1999. pap. 9.95 (*0-943629-42-X*) Swan Pub.
Billac, Pete. The Millionaires Are Coming! Davis, Sharon, ed. LC 98-86954. (Illus.). 120p. 1998. pap. 9.95 (*0-943629-36-5*) Swan Pub.
— New Father's Baby Guide. (Illus.). 128p. 1994. per. 9.95 (*0-943629-10-1*) Swan Pub.
***Billac, Pete.** The New Millionaires How to Succeed in Network Marketing. Harris, Ken & Jones, Bill, eds. LC 99-65295. 93p. 1999. pap. 9.95 (*0-943629-41-1*) Swan Pub.
— The Silent Killer: Indoor Air Pollution. Newell, Kimberly, ed. LC 99-68643. 96p. 1999. pap. 9.95 (*0-943629-44-6*, Pub. by Swan Pub) Herveys Bklink.
Billac, Pete. Willie the Wisp. large type ed. Evans, Cliff, ed. LC 97-69463. (Illus.). 192p. 1998. pap. 14.95 (*1-888224-02-9*) Prestige LA.
Billac, Pete & Ragusa, Shirley. All about Cruises. large type ed. Davis, Sharon, ed. LC 96-68889. (Illus.). 144p. (Orig.). 1996. pap. 9.95 (*0-943629-23-3*) Swan Pub.
Billac, Pete, ed. see Burrow, John.
Billac, Pete, ed. see Dade, Tom.
Billac, Pete, ed. see Durrani, A. M.
Billac, Pete, ed. see Evans, Cliff.
Billac, Pete, ed. see Gehrlein, Steve & Evans, Cliff.
Billac, Pete, ed. see Hill, Barbara.
Billac, Pete, ed. see Killebrew, Charley.
Billac, Pete, ed. see Lemmon, Randy.
Billac, Pete, ed. see Orr, James R., et al.
Billac, Pete, ed. see Shaughnessy, Joyce.
Billac, Pete, ed. see Tynan, Tom.
Billac, Pete, ed. see Weber, Lynda.
Billac, Pete, ed. see Wilson, Steven K. & Mobley, David F.
Billacois, Francois. The Duel: Its Rise & Fall in Early Modern France. 288p. (C). 1990. 40.00 (*0-300-04028-8*) Yale U Pr.
***Billard, E.** Spanish for Dummies. (For Dummies Ser.). 384p. 1999. pap. 24.99 (*0-7645-5194-9*) IDG Bks.
***Billard, Jean-Antonin, et al.** French for Dummies: Le Moyen le Plus Facile et le Plus Amusant D'Apprendre. (For Dummies Ser.). 384p. 1999. pap. 24.99 (*0-7645-5193-0*) IDG Bks.
Billard, John, jt. auth. see Vockell, Edward L.
Billard, Lynne, jt. auth. see LePage, Raoul.
Billard, R. The Carp: Biology & Culture. LC 98-50710. 385p. 1999. 119.00 (*1-85233-118-6*) Spr-Verlag.
Billard, Ruth S. Ralph Morrill's Museum Quality Fish Taxidermy: A Guide to Molding with Plaster, Casting with Resin, Painting with an Airbrush. LC 84-70664. (Illus.). 275p. 1984. lib. bdg. 32.50 (*0-9611112-0-8*) BillArt.
Billard, Wayne, jt. ed. see Tucker, Dennis.
Billatos, Samir B. Green Technology & Design for the Environment. 304p. 1996. text 47.95 (*1-56032-460-0*) Taylor & Francis.
Billatos, Samir B. & Basaly, Nadia A., eds. Design for Manufacturing & Assembly: Proceedings, ASME International Mechanical Engineering Congress & Exposition, 1996, Atlanta, Georgia. LC 96-78660. (DE Ser.: Vol. 89). 91p. 1996. pap. text 56.00 (*0-7918-1517-X*) ASME Pr.
***Billatos, Samir B. & Sung Kim, Byoung, eds.** Conceptual & Innovative Design for Manufacturing: Proceedings International Mechanical Engineering Congress & Exposition, Nashville, Tennessee, 1999. LC 99-75417. (DE Ser.: Vol. 103). 117p. 1999. 70.00 (*0-7918-1648-6*) ASME Pr.
Billatos, Samir B. & Zhang, Hong C., eds. Concurrent Product Design & Environmentally Conscious Manufacturing: Proceedings, ASME International Mechanical Engineering Congress & Exposition, Dallas, TX, 1997. LC 97-76703. (DE - MED Ser.: Vols. 94 & 5). 295p. 1997. pap. 120.00 (*0-7918-1819-5*, TD170) ASME Pr.
***Billatos, Samir B., et al.** Applications of Design for Manufacturing: Presented at the 1998 ASME International Mechanical Engineering Congress & Exposition, November 15-20, 1998, Anaheim, California. LC 98-74428. (MED Ser.). v, 93 p. 1998. write for info. (*0-7918-1601-X*) ASME.
Billawaria, Anita, jt. auth. see Charak, S. D.
Billberg, Rudy. In the Shadow of Eagles: From Barnstormer to Alaska Bush Pilot: A Flyer's Story. 2nd ed. LC 98-22727. (Caribou Classic Ser.). 1998. 8.95 (*0-88240-507-1*, Alaska NW Bks) Gr Arts Ctr Pub.
***Billboard Books Publishing Staff.** Backstreet Boys: Larger Than Life; the Unofficial Poster Book. (Illus.). 48p. 1999. pap. 12.95 (*0-8230-7859-0*) Watsn-Guptill.
— Bewitched: Destination Everywhere. (Illus.). 1999. pap. 16.95 (*0-8230-7855-8*) Watsn-Guptill.
— Boy Power. 1999. pap. 12.95 (*0-8230-8306-3*, Billboard Bks) Watsn-Guptill.
— Girl Power. 1999. pap. 12.95 (*0-8230-8320-9*, Billboard Bks) Watsn-Guptill.
Billboard Staff. All Saints: The Unofficial Book. LC 98-85530. 63p. 1998. pap. 12.95 (*0-8230-8255-5*, Billboard Bks) Watsn-Guptill.
— Backstreet Boys: The Unofficial Book. (Illus.). 64p. (J). (gr. 4-7). 1998. pap. 10.95 (*0-8230-7861-2*, Billboard Bks) Watsn-Guptill.
Billboard Staff & Whitburn, Joel. Pop Annual, 1955-1994. 850p. pap. 39.95 (*0-7935-5016-5*, 00330153) H Leonard.
Billboard Staff, jt. auth. see Whitburn, Joel.
Billboard Staff, jt. ed. see Whitburn, Joel.
Billcliffe, R. Mackintosh Watercolours. pap. text 34.95 (*0-7195-3678-2*, Pub. by John Murray) Trafalgar.
Billcliffe, Roger. Charles Rennie Mackintosh: Textile Designs. rev. ed. LC 93-20632. (Illus.). 112p. 1993. 39.95 (*1-56640-314-6*) Pomegranate Calif.
— The Scottish Colourists: Cadell, Fergusson, Hunter & Peploe. (Illus.). 176p. 1997. pap. 40.00 (*0-7195-5437-3*, Pub. by John Murray) Trafalgar.
Bille, Albertus. The Joy of the Simple Life. 88p. (Orig.). 1993. pap. 5.95 (*0-938711-16-4*) Tecolote Pubns.
— The Time Killers. LC 96-60702. 260p. (Orig.). 1996. pap. 10.00 (*0-938711-38-5*) Tecolote Pubns.
Bille-de Mot, Eleonore. La Grece Antique. Rollin, A., ed. (FRE., Illus.). 200p. 1958. lib. bdg. 35.00 (*0-8288-3933-6*) Fr & Eur.
Bille, Matthew A. Rumors of Existence: Newly Discovered, Supposedly Extinct, & Unconfirmed Inhabitants of the Animal Kingdom. LC 96-146109. (Illus.). 192p. 1995. pap. 12.95 (*0-88839-335-0*) Hancock House.
Bille, Patricia A. & McQuaig, Douglas J. Camp Kits: Practice Set, 6 vols. 6th ed. (C). 1997. pap. text, teacher ed. 21.56 (*0-395-82916-X*) HM.
— Contemporary College Accounting. annot. ed. (C). 1995. text, teacher ed. 35.56 (*0-395-59289-5*) HM.
Bille, Patricia A. & Williamson, Suzanne M. The Book Loft, 001. (C). 1986. pap. 25.96 (*0-395-39046-X*) HM.
— Sailsports: Complete Practice Set, 001. (C). 1986. pap. text 21.16 (*0-395-39042-7*) HM.
Bille, Patricia A., jt. auth. see McQuaig, Douglas J.
Billeaud, Frances P. Communication Disorders in Infants & Toddlers: Assessment & Intervention. 2nd ed. LC 97-43983. 304p. 1998. text 47.50 (*0-7506-9952-3*) Buttrwrth-Heinemann.
Billeb, Emil. Mining Camp Days. (Illus.). 229p. 1968. pap. 12.95 (*0-913814-05-9*) Nevada Pubns.
Billen, J., ed. Biology & Evolution of Social Insects. 398p. (Orig.). 1992. pap. 77.50 (*90-6186-487-9*, Pub. by Leuven Univ) Coronet Bks.
Biller, Geraldine P., et al. Latin American Women Artists, 1915-1995 (Artistas Latinoamericanas, 1915-1995) Rosenthal, Liliana H. et al, trs. (SPA., Illus.). 204p. 1995. pap. 34.95 (*0-944110-50-9*) Milwauk Art Mus.
Biller, Henry B. Fathers & Families: Paternal Factors in Child Development. LC 92-18361. 328p. 1993. 65.00 (*0-86569-208-4*, T208, Auburn Hse); pap. 27.95 (*0-86569-227-0*, R227, Auburn Hse) Greenwood.
Biller, Hugh F., jt. auth. see Bailey, Byron J.
Biller, Jose. Iatrogenic Neurology. 530p. 1998. 110.00 (*0-7506-9840-3*) Buttrwrth-Heinemann.
— Practical Neurology. LC 97-4327. 752p. 1997. pap. text 59.95 (*0-316-09483-8*) Lppncott W & W.
Biller, Jose, et al, eds. Cerebral Ischemia: From Pathophysiology to Treatment - Journal: Cerebrovascular Diseases, Vol. 1, Suppl. 1, 1991. (Illus.). iv, 140p. 1991. pap. 62.75 (*3-8055-5448-6*) S Karger.
— Stroke in Children & Young Adults. LC 93-49468. 280p. 1994. text 87.50 (*0-7506-9203-0*) Buttrwrth-Heinemann.
***Biller, Jose & Bogousslavsky, Julien.** Clinical Trials in Neurologic Practice. (Illus.). 380p. 2000. 95.00 (*0-7506-7140-8*) Buttrwrth-Heinemann.
Biller, Peter & Dobson, Barrie, eds. The Medieval Church: Universities, Heresy & the Religious Life. LC 99-18328. (Ecclesiastical History Society Ser.). 352p. 1999. 75.00 (*0-9529733-3-2*) Boydell & Brewer.
Biller, Peter & Hudson, Anne. Heresy & Literacy, 1000-1530. (Cambridge Studies in Medieval Literature: No. 23). 344p. 1996. pap. text 20.95 (*0-521-57576-1*) Cambridge U Pr.
Biller, Peter & Minnis, A. J. Handling Sin: Confession in the Middle Ages. LC 98-17971. (York Studies in Medieval Theology). x, 219p. 1998. 60.00 (*0-9529734-1-3*) Boydell & Brewer.
Biller, Peter, jt. ed. see Minnis, Alastair J.
Biller, Rudolf. Garnishing & Decoration. 160p. 1988. 44.95 (*0-471-28988-4*, VNR) Wiley.
Biller, Rudolph. Garnishing & Decorating. 160p. 1987. text 42.95 (*0-900778-31-8*, VNR) Wiley.
Biller, Walter, ed. The San Francisco Almanac. (Illus.). 224p. (Orig.). 1992. pap. 6.95 (*0-9628427-1-0*) S F Almanac.
Biller, Walter, ed. see Hunter, Samuel F.
Billera, Louis J., et al, eds. Formal Power & Algebraic Combinatorics, 1994: Proceedings. LC 95-38140. (DIMACS Series in Discrete Mathematics & Theoretical Computer Science: Vol. 24). 198p. 1995. text 45.00 (*0-8218-0324-7*, DIMACS/24) Am Math.
— New Perspectives in Algebraic Combinatorics. LC 99-34738. (Mathematical Sciences Research Institute Publications: Vol. 38). 320p. (C). 1999. 49.95 (*0-521-77087-4*) Cambridge U Pr.
Billerbeck, Franklin, ed. Anglican - Orthodox Pilgrimage. LC 93-23496. 1993. pap. 4.50 (*0-9622713-5-7*) Conciliar Pr.
Billerbeck-Gentz, F., tr. see May, Karl.
***Billerbeck, Kristin, et al.** Lessons of the Heart. 352p. 2000. 4.97 (*1-57748-792-3*) Barbour Pub.
Billerbeck, Margarethe. Seneca: Hercules Furens: Einleitung, Text, Ubersetzung Und Kommentar. (Mnemosyne, Supplements Ser.: No. 187). 752p. 1999. 194.00 (*90-04-11245-6*) Brill Academic Pubs.
— Seneca Tragodien: Sprachliche Und Stilistische Untersuchungen. LC 88-4114. (Supplements to Mnemosyne Biblioteca Classica Batava Ser.: Vol. 105). (GER.). vi, 219p. (Orig.). 1988. pap. 56.50 (*90-04-08631-5*) Brill Academic Pubs.
Billerbeck, Margarethe, ed. Die Kyniker in der Modernen Forschung: Aufsatze mit Einfuhrung und Bibliographie. (Bochumer Studien zur Philosophie Ser.: Vol. 15). (ENG, GER & ITA.). 326p. 1991. 47.00 (*90-6032-316-5*, Pub. by B R Gruner) Humanities.
***Billet, Bret L.** Cultural Relativism in the Face of the West: The Plight of Women. 1999. pap. write for info. (*0-312-22132-0*); text. write for info. (*0-312-22131-2*) St Martin.
Billet, Bret L. Investment Behavior of Multinational Corporations in Developing Areas: Comparing the Development Assistance Committee, Japanese, & American Corporations. 128p. (C). 1990. 39.95 (*0-88738-379-3*) Transaction Pubs.
— Modernization Theory & Economic Development: Discontent in the Developing World. LC 93-19115. 160p. 1993. 49.95 (*0-275-94446-8*, C4446, Praeger Pubs) Greenwood.
Billet, Bret L. & Formwalt, Lance J. America's National Pastime: A Study of Race & Merit in Professional Baseball. LC 95-3331. 200p. 1995. 55.00 (*0-275-95193-6*, Praeger Pubs) Greenwood.
Billet, Donald F. & Dellinger, Edward A. The Chronicles & Genealogy of the Jacob Dellinger Family of York County, Pennsylvania. LC 93-73800. 420p. 1993. 40.00 (*0-9638721-0-9*) D Billet.
Billet, Donald F & Ellis, Marie B. Billet Families of York, Lancaster & Dauphin Counties, Pennsylvania: 1751-1997. LC 97-78210. 402p. 1998. 34.00 (*0-9638721-1-7*) D Billet.
Billet, M. L. & Morgan, W. B., eds. Cavitation Inception 1993. LC 79-54430. 159p. pap. 50.00 (*0-7918-1048-8*) ASME.
Billet, Reinhard. Packed Towers: In Processing & Environmental Technology. LC 94-45292. 383p. 1995. 250.00 (*3-527-28616-0*, Wiley-VCH) Wiley.
Billet, Sanford L. Partnership Games: The Musings of a Recently Retired Psychiatrist. LC 97-94034. 298p. 1997. 28.00 (*0-9659365-0-3*) Auth Village Pubns.
Billetdoux, Francois. La Nostalgie Camarade. 49.95 incl. audio (*0-685-21219-X*) Fr & Eur.
***Billeter.** Problem Solving in Biology. 152p. 1999. pap. text 13.00 (*0-536-02762-5*) Pearson Custom.
Billeter, Erika. Lucio Fontana, 1899-1968: A Retrospective. LC 77-88448. (Illus.). 1977. pap. 6.98 (*0-89207-010-2*) S R Guggenheim.
Billeter, M. A., jt. ed. see Meulen, V. Ter.
Billett, Michael. Highwaymen & Outlaws. LC 97-178288. (Illus.). 160p. 1997. pap. 27.95 (*1-85409-318-5*, Pub. by Arms & Armour) Sterling.
Billett, Roy O. Preparing Theses & Other Typed Manuscripts. (Quality Paperback Ser.: No. 63). (Orig.). 1968. reprint ed. pap. 11.00 (*0-8226-0063-3*) Littlefield.
***Billey, S. & Lakshmibai, V.** Singular Loci of Schubert Varieties. (Progress in Mathematics Ser.: Vol. 182). 240p. 1999. 49.95 (*0-8176-4092-4*, Pub. by Birkhauser) Spr-Verlag.
Billheimer, John. The Contrary Blues: An Owen Allison Mystery. 1999. mass mkt. 5.99 (*0-440-23504-9*) Dell.
— The Contrary Blues: An Owen Allison Mystery. LC 98-2628. 256p. 1998. text 21.95 (*0-312-18565-0*) St Martin.
***Billheimer, John.** Highway Robbery: An Owen Allison Mystery. LC 99-54823. 304p. 2000. text 24.95 (*0-312-25247-1*) St Martin.
Billheimer, Paul E. Destinados a Vencer.Tr. of Destined to Overcome. 96p. 1984. pap. 5.99 (*0-88113-048-6*) Caribe Betania.
— Destined for the Throne: A Remarkable New Perspective on the Eternal Destiny of the Bride of Christ. 2nd rev. ed. Messerschmidt, Edwin, ed. 144p. 1996. pap. 8.99 (*1-55661-739-9*, Hampshire MN) Bethany Hse.
— Destined to Overcome. LC 82-4537. 128p. 1982. pap. 7.99 (*0-87123-287-1*) Bethany Hse.
— Destined to Overcome. 123p. 1993. pap. 8.99 (*0-87508-044-8*) Chr Lit.
— Don't Waste Your Sorrows. LC 83-15821. 128p. 1983. pap. 7.99 (*0-87123-310-X*) Bethany Hse.
— Don't Waste Your Sorrows. 1992. pap. 8.99 (*0-87508-007-3*) Chr Lit.
— Love Covers. 1980. pap. 8.99 (*0-87508-006-5*) Chr Lit.
— O Amor Cobre Todo.Tr. of Love Covers. (POR.). 192p. 1990. pap. 8.95 (*0-8297-1633-5*) Vida Pubs.
Billiar, Timothy R. Hepatocyte: Kupfer Cell Interactions. 320p. 1992. lib. bdg. 225.00 (*0-8493-6109-5*, RC846) CRC Pr.
Billiard, Barbara R. Van, see Van Billiard, Barbara R.
Billiard Congress of America Staff. Billiards: Official Rules. 160p. 1992. pap. 10.95 (*1-55821-189-6*) Lyons Pr.
Billias, George A. The Massachusetts Land Bankers of 1740. LC 59-63155. 1959. pap. 8.95 (*0-89101-005-X*) U Maine Pr.
Billias, George A., ed. American Constitutionalism Abroad: Selected Essays in Comparative Constitutional History, 16. LC 89-27277. (Contributions to the Study of World History Ser.: No. 16). 176p. 1990. 52.95 (*0-313-26757-X*, BAO/, Greenwood Pr) Greenwood.
— George Washington's Generals. LC 79-28195. (Illus.). 327p. 1980. reprint ed. lib. bdg. 35.00 (*0-313-22280-0*, BIGW, Greenwood Pr) Greenwood.
— George Washington's Generals & Opponents: Their Exploits & Leadership. LC 93-33603. (Illus.). 7166p. 1994. reprint ed. pap. 19.95 (*0-306-80560-X*) Da Capo.
Billias, George A., ed. see Great Britain Historical Manuscripts Commission.
Billias, George A., jt. ed. see Grob, Gerald N.
Billias, George A., ed. see Mackesy, Piers.
Billias, George A., ed. see New York Historical Society Staff.
Billias, George A., ed. see Raynal, Guillaume T.
Billias, George A., ed. see Society of Gentlemen Staff.
Billias, George A., ed. see United Empire Loyalists Centennial Committee.
Billias, George A., ed. see Vinovskis, Maris A.
Billias, Stephen. The American Book of the Dead. 224p. 1987. mass mkt. 2.95 (*0-445-20335-8*, Pub. by Warner Bks) Little.
— The Quest for the Thirty-Six. 208p. 1988. mass mkt. 3.95 (*0-445-20670-5*, Pub. by Warner Bks) Little.
Billick, Brian. Developing an Offensive Game Plan. LC 96-69211. (Art & Science of Coaching Ser.). (Illus.). 102p. 1996. pap. 16.95 (*1-57167-046-7*) Coaches Choice.
Billick, David, intro. Indexing Tradition & Innovations: Proceedings of the 22nd Annual Conference of the American Society of Indexers. 118p. (Orig.). pap. 30.00 (*0-936547-13-8*) Am Soc Index.
Billick, David J., jt. auth. see Dworkin, Steven N.
Billie. Contemporary College Accounting. (C). 1995. pap., teacher ed. 11.96 (*0-395-72394-9*); pap., teacher ed., suppl. ed. 11.96 (*0-395-71906-2*) HM.
— Contemporary College Accounting. (C). 1995. pap., teacher ed. 19.96 (*0-395-63777-5*) HM.
Billie, Patricia A. Contemporary College Accounting. (C). 1995. pap. text 40.36 (*0-395-59288-7*) HM.
Billiet, Jaak, jt. ed. see Voye, Liliane.
Billiet, Walter E. Automotive Engines: Maintenance & Repair. 4th ed. LC 72-88611. 526p. reprint ed. pap. 163.10 (*0-8357-5922-9*, 202682500052) Bks Demand.
— Do-It-Yourself Automotive Maintenance & Repair. LC 78-15055. (Illus.). 1979. 17.95 (*0-13-217190-2*, Spectrum IN) Macmillan Gen Ref.
— Do-It-Yourself Automotive Maintenance & Repair. LC 78-15055. (Illus.). 1979. pap. 7.95 (*0-13-217182-1*) P-H.
Billiet, Walter E. & Alley, Walter. Automotive Suspensions, Steering, Alignment, & Brakes. 5th ed. LC 73-80444. (Illus.). 364p. reprint ed. pap. 112.90 (*0-8357-8811-3*, 203329000085) Bks Demand.
Billiet, Walter E., jt. auth. see Frazee, Irving A.
Billiet, Walter E., jt. auth. see Venk, Ernest A.
Billig, Florence G. A Technique for Developing Content for a Professional Course in Science for Teachers in Elementary Schools. (Columbia University. Teachers College. Contributions to Education Ser.: No. 397). reprint ed. 37.50 (*0-404-55397-4*) AMS Pr.
Billig, Harvey E. The Ambulatory Care & Outpatient Services Manual: Includes Facility Design, Operations, Case Costing, Contracting, Integrated Delivery Systems, Reimbursement. LC 96-40918. 340p. (C). 1997. text 250.00 (*1-55738-641-2*, Irwn Prfssnl) McGraw-Hill Prof.
Billig, Leslie. Crypto-Quotes. (Mighty Mini Ser.). 1999. pap. text 4.95 (*0-8069-9672-2*) Sterling.
Billig, Michael. Banal Nationalism. 208p. 1995. 42.50 (*0-8039-7524-4*); pap. 14.99 (*0-8039-7525-2*) Sage.
***Billig, Michael.** Freudian Repression: Conversation Creating the Unconscious. LC 99-12788. 275p. (C). 1999. 59.95 (*0-521-65052-6*); pap. 22.95 (*0-521-65956-6*) Cambridge U Pr.

Billig, Michael. Ideology & Opinions: Studies in Rhetorical Psychology. 224p. (C). 1991. 55.00 (*0-8039-8331-X*); pap. 14.99 (*0-8039-8332-8*) Sage.

— Talking of the Royal Family. 272p. (Orig.). (C). 1991. pap. 25.99 (*0-415-06746-4*, A6504) Routledge.

— Talking of the Royal Family. 272p. (Orig.). (C). (gr. 13). 1991. text 85.00 (*0-415-06745-6*, A6500) Routledge.

Billig, Michael, et al. Ideological Dilemmas: A Social Psychology of Everyday Thinking. 224p. (C). 1988. text 45.00 (*0-8039-8095-7*); pap. text 16.95 (*0-8039-8096-5*) Sage.

Billig, Michael, ed. see Simons, Herbert W.

Billig, Nathan. Growing Older & Wiser. 230p. 1995. pap. 12.00 (*0-669-27679-0*) Lxngtn Bks.

— Growing Older & Wiser: Coping with Expectations, Challenges, & Change in the Later Years. LC 92-24310. 230p. 1992. 20.95 (*0-669-27678-2*) Lxngtn Bks.

Billig, Nathan & Rabins, Peter V., eds. Issues in Geriatric Psychiatry. (Advances in Psychosomatic Medicine Ser.: Vol. 19). (Illus.). vii, 184p. 1989. 90.50 (*3-8055-4972-5*) S Karger.

Billig, Otto. Flying Saucers: Magic in the Skies. 265p. 1982. pap. 18.95 (*0-87073-940-9*) Schenkman Bks Inc.

Billig, Shelley H. & Kraft, Nancy P. Linking Federal Programs & Service Learning: A Planning, Implementation & Evaluation Guide. LC 98-89827. 376p. 1999. pap. text 59.95 (*1-56676-745-8*) Scarecrow.

Billigheimer, C. E., tr. see Polya, George & Szego, Gabor.

Billigmeier, Robert H. A Crisis in Swiss Pluralism: The Romanisch & Their Relations with the German & the Italian-Swiss in the Perpective of a Millenium. (Contributions to the Sociology of Language Ser.: No. 26). 1979. 96.15 (*90-279-7577-9*) Mouton.

Billigmeier, Robert H. & Picard, Fred A., eds. The Old Land & the New: Journals of Two Swiss Families in America in the 1820s. LC 65-15544. (Illus.). 291p. reprint ed. pap. 90.30 (*0-608-14093-7*, 205584400039) Bks Demand.

Billimoria, H. M. Attitude of Parsi Women to Marriage. (C). 1991. 24.00 (*81-7040-430-4*, Pub. by Manohar) S Asia.

***Billin-Frye, Paige.** Cowboys, 1 vol. (Sticker Stories Ser.). (ps-1). 1999. pap. text 4.99 (*0-448-41982-3*) Putnam Pub Group.

Billin-Frye, Paige. Meet the Sweet-Hearts: A Sticker Stories Book. (Sticker Stories Ser.). (Illus.). 16p. (J). 1997. pap. text 4.95 (*0-448-41715-4*, G & D) Peng Put Young Read.

Billin-Frye, Paige, jt. illus. see Herman, Gail.

Billin-Frye, Paige, jt. illus. see Penner, Lucille R.

Billing, Billie & Ratner, Megan. Pool Pointers. 96p. 1992. pap. 10.00 (*0-380-76136-X*, Avon Bks) Morrow Avon.

Billing, D. E., ed. see Aylett, B. J.

***Billing, Gert D.** Dynamics of Molecule Surface Interactions. LC 99-38866. 235p. 1999. 99.95 (*0-471-33108-2*) Wiley.

Billing, Gert D. & Mikkelsen, Kurt V. Advanced Molecular Dynamics & Chemical Kinetics. LC 96-43762. 288p. 1997. 79.95 (*0-471-12740-X*) Wiley.

— Introduction to Molecular Dynamics & Chemical Kinetics. LC 95-23950. 200p. 1996. 59.95 (*0-471-12739-6*, Wiley-Interscience) Wiley.

Billing, Graham. Forbush & the Penguins. LC 95-222196. 168p. (Orig.). 1995. pap. 24.95 (*0-908812-40-X*, Pub. by Canterbury Univ) Accents Pubns.

Billing, Yvonne D. & Alvesson, Mats. Gender, Managers & Organizations, Vol. IX. LC 93-26380. (Studies in Organization: Vol. 50). 260p. (C). 1994. 49.95 (*3-11-012984-1*) De Gruyter.

***Billinge, S. J. & Thorpe, M. F., eds.** Local Structure from Diffraction: Proceedings of a Conference Held in Traverse City, Michigan, August 10-13, 1997. LC 98-4348. (Fundamental Materials Research Ser.). (Illus.). 412p. (C). 1998. 120.00 (*0-306-45827-6*, Plenum Trade) Perseus Pubng.

***Billinger, Robert D., Jr.** Hitler's Soldiers in the Sunshine State: German POWs in Florida. LC 99-31274. (History & Culture Ser.). (Illus.). 288p. 2000. 24.95 (*0-8130-1740-8*) U Press Fla.

Billinger, Robert D. Metternich & the German Question: States' Rights & Federal Duties, 1820-1834. LC 90-50002. 1991. 40.00 (*0-87413-407-2*) U Delaware Pr.

Billingham, Brenda. Lilly to the Rescue. LC 96-950186. (First Novels). (Illus.). 64p. (J). (gr. 1-4). 1998. mass mkt. 3.99 (*0-88780-386-5*, Pub. by Formac Publ Co) Formac Dist Ltd.

Billingham, E. J. Spectrophotometric Determination of Copper in Brass. Neidig, H. Anthony, ed. (Modular Laboratory Program in Chemistry Ser.). 8p. (C). 1989. pap. text 1.50 (*0-87540-357-3*, ANAL 357-3) Chem Educ Res.

***Billingham, John & King, Andrew.** Wave Motion. (Texts in Applied Mathematics Ser.: Vol. 24). (Illus.). 475p. (C). 2000. write for info. (*0-521-63257-9*); pap. write for info. (*0-521-63450-4*) Cambridge U Pr.

***Billingham, John, et al.** Social Implications of the Detection of Extraterrestrial Civilization: Report on Workshops as the Cultural Aspects of SETI. Shostak, Seth, ed. (Illus.). 150p. 1999. pap. 15.00 (*0-9666335-0-4*) SETI Pr.

Billingham, John, ed. see Cyclops Design Team Staff.

Billingham, Richard. Ray's a Laugh. 112p. 1996. pap. 39.95 (*3-931141-18-7*, Pub. by Scalo Pubs) Dist Art Pubs.

Billinghurst, Carmen A. De, see De Billinghurst, Carmen A.

Billinghurst, Jane. Grey Owl: The Many Faces of Archie Belaney. LC 99-20137. (Illus.). 160p. 1999. 22.00 (*1-56836-293-5*) Kodansha.

***Billinghurst, Jane.** The Spirit of the Whale: Legend, History, Conservation. LC 99-40265. (Illus.). 144p. 2000. 29.95 (*0-89658-409-7*) Voyageur Pr.

Billinghurst, Mervyn W., ed. Studies of Cellular Function Using Radiotracers. 272p. 1982. 149.00 (*0-8493-6025-0*, QP519, CRC Reprint) Franklin.

Billinghurst, Mervyn W. & Fritzberg, Alan R. Chemistry for Nuclear Medicine. LC 81-2957. (Illus.). 339p. reprint ed. pap. 105.10 (*0-8357-7588-7*, 205690900096) Bks Demand.

Billingiere, Joseph & Reynosa, Larry. A Beginner's Guide to Aikido. (Illus.). 180p. (Orig.). (C). 1989. pap. 12.95 (*0-9625269-0-8*) R & B Pub.

Billingley, jt. auth. see Watson.

Billings. Bizarre Endings. (Wild Side Ser.). (Illus.). (YA). (gr. 6-12). 1998. 13.00 (*0-89061-803-8*, R0803-8E, Jamestwn Pub) NTC Contemp Pub Co.

— The Clinical Encounter: A Guide to the Medical Interview & Case Presentation. 2nd ed. LC 98-21886. (Illus.). 368p. (C). (gr. 13). 1998. pap. text 29.95 (*0-8151-1374-9*, 29932) Mosby Inc.

— Crime & Punishment. (Wild Side Ser.). (Illus.). (YA). (gr. 6-12). 1998. 13.00 (*0-89061-799-6*, R0799-6E, Jamestwn Pub) NTC Contemp Pub Co.

— Extreme Sports. (Wild Side Ser.). (Illus.). (YA). (gr. 6-12). 1998. 13.00 (*0-89061-800-3*, R0800-3E, Jamestwn Pub) NTC Contemp Pub Co.

— Plants Man & Ecosystem. 2nd ed. (Biology Ser.). 1970. pap. 5.50 (*0-534-02027-5*) Wadsworth Pub.

— Total Panic. (Wild Side Ser.). (Illus.). (YA). (gr. 6-12). 1998. 13.00 (*0-89061-804-6*, R0804-6E, Jamestwn Pub) NTC Contemp Pub Co.

— Weird Science. (Wild Side Ser.). (Illus.). (YA). (gr. 6-12). 1998. 13.00 (*0-89061-798-8*, R0798-8E, Jamestwn Pub) NTC Contemp Pub Co.

— World History. 90th ed. 1990. pap. text, teacher ed., wbk. ed. 18.00 (*0-03-028903-3*); pap. text, wbk. ed. 15.50 (*0-03-028902-5*) Holt R&W.

— World History: Skills Activity Book. 90th ed. 1990. pap. text, wbk. ed. 9.50 (*0-03-028909-2*) Holt R&W.

Billings, Andrew. Carnage. 1999. mass mkt. 6.50 (*0-515-12564-4*, Jove) Berkley Pub.

— Tainted Blood. 544p. 1997. mass mkt. 6.99 (*0-515-12046-4*, Jove) Berkley Pub.

Billings, Anna H. A Guide to Middle English Metrical Romances: Dealing with English & Germanic Legends, & with the Cycles of Charlemagne & of Arthur. 232p. (C). 1965. lib. bdg. 75.00 (*0-8383-0522-9*) M S G Haskell Hse.

Billings, B. H., ed. Selected Papers on Polarization. 736p. 1990. pap. 35.00 (*0-8194-0495-0*, VOL. MS23) SPIE.

Billings, Bart. An Anthology of Machine Postal Markings. 2nd ed. 110p. 1992. pap. 10.00 (*1-880065-03-7*) Machine Cancel Soc.

— Flag Cancellation Dies: Same Year Use of Different Dies. (Illus.). 134p. 1991. pap. 10.00 (*0-9621481-7-2*) Machine Cancel Soc.

— Flag Cancellation Dies: Transfers Between Towns. (Illus.). 279p. 1991. pap. 20.00 (*0-9621481-8-0*) Machine Cancel Soc.

— A Handbook of U. S. Postal Markings Impressed by Machines. Morris, Reg et al, eds. (Illus.). 145p. 1991. 17.50 (*0-9621481-3-X*) Machine Cancel Soc.

— Handbook of U. S. Postal Markings Impressed by Machines: Revision 1. Payne, Robert J., ed. (Illus.). 160p. 1992. pap. 17.50 (*1-880065-04-5*) Machine Cancel Soc.

— International Postal Supply Co. Hey-Dolphin Cancelling Machine Model HD-2. (Illus.). 250p. 1995. pap. 20.00 (*1-880065-12-6*) Machine Cancel Soc.

— Ohio Doane Cancels. (Illus.). 125p. (Orig.). (C). 1987. pap. 7.00 (*0-685-24135-1*) Machine Cancel Soc.

— Universal Stamping Machine Company. (Illus.). 250p. 1994. pap. 20.00 (*1-880065-10-X*) Machine Cancel Soc.

— Universal Stamping Machine Company: Machines & Postal Markings, 1909-1920. Morris, Reg & Payne, Robert J., eds. (Illus.). 121p. (Orig.). (C). 1988. pap. text 7.00 (*0-9621481-0-5*) Machine Cancel Soc.

— Universal Stamping Machine Company Machines & Postal Markings, Catalog Revision No. 1. (Illus.). 120p. (Orig.). 1990. pap. text 7.00 (*0-9621481-2-1*) Machine Cancel Soc.

Billings, Bart, ed. see Morris, R. & Payne, R.

Billings, Beverley & Merkley, Steve R., eds. Student Energy Awareness Journal: Project Energy, '93. LC 93-78830. (Illus.). 450p. 1993. 20.00 (*0-9631634-3-4*) Intl Acad Science.

Billings, Bradley B. U. S.-E.E.C. Trade Negotiations on the Acession of Spain & Portugal. (Pew Case Studies in Internatioanl Affairs). 50p. (C). 1993. pap. text 3.50 (*1-56927-147-X*) Geo U Inst Dplmcy.

Billings, Bruce, jt. auth. see Erichsen, Kurt.

Billings, Bruce H., ed. Selected Papers on Applications of Polarized Light. LC 92-19413. (Milestone Ser.: Vol. 57). 1992. pap. 35.00 (*0-8194-0990-1*) SPIE.

— Selected Papers on Applications of Polarized Light. LC 92-19413. (Milestone Ser.: Vol. MS 57/HC). 1992. 45.00 (*0-8194-0989-8*) SPIE.

Billings, Charlene W. Lasers: The New Technology of Light. LC 92-7324. (Science Sourcebooks Ser.). (Illus.). 128p. (YA). (gr. 7-12). 1992. lib. bdg. 19.95 (*0-8160-2630-0*) Facts on File.

— Supercomputers: Shaping the Future. LC 94-44111. (Science Sourcebooks Ser.). 144p. 1995. 19.95 (*0-8160-3096-0*) Facts on File.

Billings, Charles E. Principles of Human-Centered Aviation Automation. (Human Factors in Transportation Ser.). 376p. (C). 1996. 69.95 (*0-8058-2126-0*); pap. 45.00 (*0-8058-2127-9*) L Erlbaum Assocs.

Billings, Chris & Billings, Maria. Rapid Development with Oracle CASE: A Workshop Approach. LC 93-8205. 144p. (C). 1993. pap. 36.95 (*0-201-63344-2*) Addison-Wesley.

Billings, Chris, et al. Rapid Application Development with Oracle Designer/2000. LC 96-32379. 480p. (C). 1996. pap. 41.95 (*0-201-63444-9*) Addison-Wesley.

Billings, Clayton H., ed. Manual of Wastewater Collection. (Illus.). 232p. 1981. text 16.19 (*0-933317-03-4*) Texas Water.

— Manual of Wastewater Treatment. 5th ed. (Illus.). 572p. 1983. text 19.19 (*0-933317-02-6*) Texas Water.

Billings, D. McGovern. Lippincott's Review for NCLEX-RN. 6th ed. LC 97-3490. 720p. 1997. pap. text 29.95 (*0-397-55452-4*) Lppncott W & W.

Billings, Deborah A. An Analysis of Lithic Workshop Debris from Iron Mountain, Union County, Illinois. LC 87-71130. (Center for Archaeological Investigations Research Paper Ser.: No. 47). (Illus.). ix, 63p. (Orig.). 1984. pap. 7.50 (*0-88104-023-1*) Center Archaeol.

Billings, Diane M. NurseNotes: Psychiatric-Mental Health Nursing. LC 96-9116. 272p. 1997. pap. text 29.95 (*0-7817-1127-4*) Lppncott W & W.

Billings, Diane M. & Halstead, Judith. Teaching in Nursing: A Guide to Curriculum, Teaching & Evaluation. Eoyang, Thomas, ed. LC 97-44011. (Illus.). 640p. 1998. text 49.00 (*0-7216-3037-5*, W B Saunders Co) Harcrt Hlth Sci Grp.

Billings, Diane M., jt. auth. see Colombrari, Geraldine C.

Billings, Don, jt. auth. see Asmus, Barry.

Billings, Donald B. & Asmus, E. Barry. Crossroads - The Great American Experiment: The Rise, Decline, & Restoration of Freedom & the Market Economy. LC 84-20962. 420p. (Orig.). 1985. lib. bdg. 56.00 (*0-8191-4362-6*) U Pr of Amer.

Billings, Dwight B. Planters & the Making of a New South: Class, Politics & Development in North Carolina, 1865-1900. LC 78-25952. 298p. reprint ed. pap. 92.40 (*0-7837-0299-X*, 204062000018) Bks Demand.

***Billings, Dwight B., et al, eds.** Back Talk from Appalachia: Confronting Stereotypes. 368p. (C). 2001. reprint ed. pap. 19.00 (*0-8131-9001-0*) U Pr of Ky.

Billings, Dwight B., et al, eds. Confronting Appalachian Stereotypes: Back-Talk from an American Region. LC 98-43591. 344p. 1999. 29.95 (*0-8131-2099-3*) U Pr of Ky.

***Billings, Dwight B. & Blee, Kathleen M.** The Road to Poverty: The Making of Wealth & Hardship in Appalachia. LC 98-51561. (Illus.). 520p. (C). 2000. 59.95 (*0-521-65229-4*); pap. 24.95 (*0-521-65546-3*) Cambridge U Pr.

Billings, Edward C. The Struggle Between the Civilization of Slavery & That of Freedom. LC 76-164379. (Black Heritage Library Collection). 1977. reprint ed. 13.95 (*0-8369-8838-8*) Ayer.

Billings, Gene, jt. auth. see Rosgen, Dave.

Billings, Harold, ed. Edward Dahlberg, American Ishmael of Letters: Selected Critical Essays. 1968. 35.50 (*0-911796-01-0*) Beacham.

Billings, Harold, ed. & intro. see Dahlberg, Edward.

Billings, Harold C., Jr. Watergrate: How to Train Taxed Prisoners. LC 84-90959. 276p. 1985. pap. 14.95 (*0-9613642-0-3*) H C Billings.

Billings-Harris, Lenora. The Diversity Advantage: A Guide to Making Diversity Work. LC 98-9576. 144p. 1998. 19.95 (*1-886939-25-X*, Pub. by OakHill Pr VA) ACCESS Pubs Network.

Billings, Henry. Economics, It's Your Business. LC 98-178666. 142 p. 1993. 19.59 (*1-56256-047-6*) Peoples Pub Grp.

Billings, Henry. Economics: Principles & Applications: Workbook. 2nd ed. 7.95 (*0-8219-1090-6*) EMC-Paradigm.

— Economics:Principles & Applications: Teacher's annotated edition. 2nd ed. 39.00 (*0-8219-1088-4*) EMC-Paradigm.

— Economics:Principles & Applications: Workbook teacher's edition. 2nd ed. 8.95 (*0-8219-1091-4*) EMC-Paradigm.

Billings, Henry. The Joys of Cheap Wine: A Spirited Guide to Buying, Serving, & Enjoying the World's Greatest Inexpensive (Cheap) Wines. LC 84-61651. (Illus.). 112p. (Orig.). 1984. pap. 4.95 (*0-933050-26-7*) New Eng Pr VT.

— States & Regions. (Maps Globes Graphs for Adults Ser.: Bk. 1). (Illus.). 1997. pap., student ed. 9.16 (*0-8114-6212-9*) Raintree Steck-V.

— The United States. (Maps Globes Graphs for Adults Ser.: Bk. 2). (Illus.). 1997. pap., student ed. 9.16 (*0-8114-6213-7*) Raintree Steck-V.

— The World. (Maps Globes Graphs for Adults Ser.: Bk. 3). (Illus.). 1997. pap., student ed. 9.16 (*0-8114-6214-5*) Raintree Steck-V.

Billings, Henry & Billings, Melissa. Angry Animals. (Wild Side Ser.). (Illus.). 114p. (YA). (gr. 6-12). 1998. 13.00 (*0-89061-801-1*, R0801-1E, Jamestwn Pub) NTC Contemp Pub Co.

— Eccentrics. (Illus.). 160p. (YA). (gr. 6 up). 1987. pap. text 12.64 (*0-89061-464-4*, Jamestwn Pub) NTC Contemp Pub Co.

— Heroes. (Illus.). 160p. (YA). (gr. 6 up). 1985. pap. text 12.64 (*0-89061-450-4*, Jamestwn Pub) NTC Contemp Pub Co.

— Phenomena. (Illus.). 160p. (J). (gr. 6-8). 1984. pap. text 12.64 (*0-89061-363-X*, 762, Jamestwn Pub) NTC Contemp Pub Co.

Billings, Henry, jt. auth. see EMC-Paradigm Publishing Staff.

Billings, Johanna S. & Billings, Sean. Collectible Glass Rose Bowls: A History & Identification Guide. (Illus.). 208p. 1999. pap. 26.95 (*1-58221-009-8*, Antique Trader) Krause Pubns.

Billings, John. Everybody's Friend: Or, Josh Billing's Encyclopedia & Proverbial Philosophy of Wit & Humor. LC 71-39442. (Classics of Modern American Humor Ser.). reprint ed. 49.50 (*0-404-00864-X*) AMS Pr.

— My Pet Crocodile: And Other Slightly Outrageous Verse. LC 93-72718. (Illus.). 128p. (J). (gr. k-12). 1994. 16.95 (*1-884035-55-8*) Chokecherry.

Billings, John. Ovulation Method: Natural Family Planning. 40p. 1973. pap. 9.95 (*0-8146-1011-0*) Liturgical Pr.

Billings, John D. Hardtack & Coffee: The Unwritten Story of Army Life, 1861-1865. 3rd unabridged ed. Eames, Stephen C., ed. (Illus.). 428p. 1996. reprint ed. pap. 18.95 (*0-87928-113-8*) Corner Hse.

— Hardtack & Coffee or, The Unwritten Story of Army Life. LC 93-19440. (Illus.). xx, 413p. 1996. pap. 15.95 (*0-8032-6111-X*, Bison Books) U of Nebr Pr.

Billings, John S. Census of the United States: Tenth Decennial Census, 1880: Report on the Mortality & Vital Statistics of the United States . . . Part I: Statistics of Deaths by States, Principal Cities, Etc., 22 vols., Vol. 11, Series 34. LC 07-18862. (Illus.). lxiii, 767p. 1991. reprint ed. lib. bdg. 575.00 incl. fiche (*0-88354-434-2*) N Ross.

— Census of the United States: Tenth Decennial Census, 1880: Report on the Mortality & Vital Statistics of the United States . . . Part II: Statistics of Deaths by Locality, Cause, Etc., 22 vols., Vol. 12, Series 35. LC 07-18862. (Illus.). clviii, 803p. 1991. reprint ed. lib. bdg. 400.00 incl. fiche (*0-88354-435-0*) N Ross.

— History & Literature of Surgery. 1970. reprint ed. 20.00 (*0-87266-038-9*) Argosy.

— Report on the Barracks & Hospitals of the United States Army, No. 4. 1870. 102.00 (*0-914074-08-3*, J M C & Co) Amereon Ltd.

— Report on the Hygiene of the United States Army, No. 8. 1875. 102.00 (*0-914074-09-1*, J M C & Co) Amereon Ltd.

Billings, John S. & Atwater, Wilbur O. Physiological Aspects of the Liquor Problem, 2 Vols. 1977. 40.95 (*0-8369-6965-0*, 7846) Ayer.

Billings, Josh, pseud. Josh Billings, Hiz Sayings. LC 75-39443. (Illus.). reprint ed. 25.00 (*0-404-00865-8*) AMS Pr.

— Josh Billings on Ice & Other Things. (Illus.). reprint ed. 26.50 (*0-404-00866-6*) AMS Pr.

Billings, Keith. Master Planning for Architecture: Theory & Practice of Designing Building Complexes as Development Frameworks. 184p. 1993. 69.95 (*0-471-29086-6*) Wiley.

— Switchmode Power Supply Handbook. 2nd ed. LC 98-53827. 1999. 89.95 (*0-07-006719-8*) McGraw.

Billings, Laura, jt. auth. see Roberts, Terry.

Billings, Malcolm. The Crusades: Five Centuries of Holy Wars. (Illus.). 240p. 1996. pap. 14.95 (*0-8069-9410-X*) Sterling.

— The English: The Making of a Nation from 430-1700. (Illus.). 144p. 1992. 27.95 (*0-563-36114-X*, BBC-Parkwest) Parkwest Pubns.

Billings, Maria, jt. auth. see Billings, Chris.

Billings, Melissa, jt. auth. see Billings, Henry.

Billings, Patricia C., jt. auth. see Delmar Staff.

Billings, Patrick. The Quiet. 256p. (Orig.). 1994. mass mkt. 4.50 (*0-8125-2131-5*, Pub. by Tor Bks) St Martin.

Billings, Paul R., ed. DNA on Trial: Genetic Identification & Criminal Justice. LC 92-19236. (Illus.). 164p. 1992. reprint ed. pap. 50.90 (*0-608-05398-8*, 206586700006) Bks Demand.

Billings, Peggy. Paradox & Promise in Human Rights. fac. ed. LC 79-10325. (Illus.). 142p. (Orig.). 1979. pap. 44.10 (*0-7837-7706-X*, 204746500007) Bks Demand.

Billings, Peggy, et al. Fire Beneath the Frost. LC 83-16525. (Illus.). 106p. (Orig.). 1984. reprint ed. pap. 32.90 (*0-608-00236-4*, 206073800006) Bks Demand.

Billings, R. Bruce & Jones, C. Vaughan. Forecasting Urban Water Demand. LC 95-44740. 179p. 1996. 100.00 (*0-89867-827-7*, 20410) Am Water Wks Assn.

Billings, R. E., jt. ed. see Veziroglu, T. Nejat.

Billings, Richard. The Forty-Year War. 1992. write for info. (*0-201-08014-1*) Addison-Wesley.

Billings, Richard N. & Schirra, Walter M. Schirra's Space. LC 95-24817. (Bluejacket Bks.). (Illus.). 240p. 1995. pap. 15.95 (*1-55750-792-9*) Naval Inst Pr.

Billings, Richard W. The Village & the Hill Vol. 1: Growing up in Seal Harbor, Maine, in the 1930's. (Illus.). 126p. (Orig.). 1996. pap. 10.00 (*0-9654287-0-2*) Day Mtn Pubns.

Billings, Robert. The Elizabeth Trinities. 78p. 1980. 5.95 (*0-920806-18-X*, Pub. by Penumbra Pr) U of Toronto Pr.

— Northern Poems. 1986. 5.00 (*0-920806-84-8*, Pub. by Penumbra Pr) U of Toronto Pr.

Billings, Robert S. Adam & Mackie the Monster. (Illus.). 16p. (J). (gr. k-7). 1997. pap., per. 6.95 (*0-938911-12-0*) Indiv Ed - Poppy Ln.

Billings, Roger D. Handling Auto Warranty & Repossession Cases. 2nd ed. LC 91-78047. 1992. ring bd. 135.00 (*0-685-59827-6*) West Group.

Billings, Roger D., Jr. Handling Business Opportunities in the European Community. LC 93-13814. (International Business & Law Ser.: Vol.5). 1993. ring bd. 135.00 (*0-87632-916-4*) West Group.

Billings, Roger E. The Hydrogen World View. LC 91-77512. 192p. 1991. 44.95 (*0-9631634-0-X*) Intl Acad Science.

— WideBand Networking. LC 96-76053. (Illus.). 144p. (C). 1996. pap. 19.95 (*0-9631634-5-0*) Intl Acad Science.

— WideBand Networking. 2nd rev. ed. LC 96-61770. (Illus.). 128p. (C). 1996. pap. text 19.95 (*0-9631634-6-9*) Intl Acad Science.

Billings, Roger E., ed. Project Energy, '93: Conference Proceedings. LC 93-61304. (Illus.). 528p. 1993. 40.00 (*0-9631634-4-2*) Intl Acad Science.

Billings, Rolland G. & Goldman, Errol. Professional Negotiations for Media-Library Professionals: District & School. LC 80-67724. 70p. 1980. pap. 8.50 (*0-89240-037-4*) Assn Ed Comm Tech.

Billings, Ronald F., jt. ed. see Appel, David N.

B

An Asterisk (*) at the beginning of an entry indicates that the title is appearing for the first time.

Billings, S. A., jt. ed. see Harris, C. J.
Billings, Scott, et al. Access 97 Programming Unleased. LC 96-72075. 912p. 1997. 49.99 (*0-672-31049-X*) Sams.
Billings, Sean, jt. auth. see Billings, Johanna S.
Billings, Susan V. Sarah's Awakening. (Orig.). 1979. mass mkt. 2.50 (*0-89083-536-5*, Zebra Kensgtn) Kensgtn Pub Corp.
Billings, Vicky. Bethany Learns about Giving. 1989. pap. 3.85 (*0-89137-057-9*) Quality Pubns.
— Bethany Learns about Prayer. 1990. pap. 3.85 (*0-89137-063-3*) Quality Pubns.
— Bethany Learns about the Lord's Supper. 1988. pap. 3.85 (*0-89137-053-6*) Quality Pubns.
— Bethany Learns about the Preaching of the Gospel. 1997. pap. text 3.85 (*0-89137-067-6*) Quality Pubns.
Billings, Warren M. The Historic Rules of the Supreme Court of Louisiana, 1813-1879. (U. S. L. History Ser.). 90p. 1985. 10.00 (*0-940984-26-1*) Univ LA Lafayette.
— Jamestown & the Founding of a Nation. (Illus.). 144p. (C). 1991. pap. text 6.95 (*0-939631-27-X*) Thomas Publications.
Billings, Warren M., ed. The Old Dominion in the Seventeenth Century: A Documentary History of Virginia, 1606-1689. LC 74-8302. (Institute of Early American History & Culture Ser.). xxiv, 324p. 1975. pap. 22.95 (*0-8078-1237-4*) U of NC Pr.
Billings, Warren M., et al, eds. An Uncommon Experience: Law & Judicial Institutions in Louisiana, 1803-2003. LC 96-84494. (Louisiana Purchase Bicentennial Series in Louisiana History: Vol. 13). 885p. 1997. 40.00 (*1-887366-11-3*) Univ LA Lafayette.
Billings, Warren M., pref. The Papers of Francis Howard, Baron Howard of Effingham, 1643-1695. xxxvii, 473p. 1989. text 35.00 (*0-88490-165-3*) Library of VA.
***Billings, Warren M. & Fernandez, Mark F., eds.** A Law unto Itself? Essays in the New Louisiana Legal History. 208p. 2000. 34.95 (*0-8071-2583-0*) La State U Pr.
Billings, William. The Complete Works of William Billings, Vol. I. Kroeger, Karl, ed. (Illus.). 388p. 1981. 50.00 (*1-878528-11-4*) Am Musicological.
— The Complete Works of William Billings, Vol. II. Nathan, Hans, ed. (Illus.). 366p. 1977. 50.00 (*1-878528-12-2*) Am Musicological.
— The Complete Works of William Billings, Vol. III. Kroeger, Karl, ed. (Illus.). 402p. 1986. 50.00 (*1-878528-13-0*) Am Musicological.
— The Complete Works of William Billings: Volume 2: The Singing Master's Assistant(1778), Music in Miniature (1779) Nathan, Hans et al, eds. LC 76-28587. 362p. 1977. text 50.00 (*0-8139-0839-6*) U Pr of Va.
— The Complete Works of William Billings Vol. 1: The New England Psalm-Singer (1770) Kroeger, Karl & Crawford, Richard, eds. LC 80-69464. (Illus.). 383p. 1981. text 50.00 (*0-8139-0917-1*) U Pr of Va.
— The Complete Works of William Billings Vol. 3: The Psalm-Singer's Amusement (1781), The Suffolk Harm (1786) & Independent Publications. Kroeger, Karl & Crawford, Richard, eds. (Illus.). 399p. 1986. text 50.00 (*0-8139-1130-3*) U Pr of Va.
— The Complete Works of William Billings Vol. 4: The Continental Harmony, 1794. Kroeger, Karl, ed. (Illus.). 332p. 1990. text 50.00 (*1-878528-01-7*) U Pr of Va.
— The Psalm Singer's Amusement. LC 73-5100. (Earlier American Music Ser.: No. 20). 104p. 1974. reprint ed. lib. bdg. 25.00 (*0-306-70587-7*) Da Capo.
Billings, William, et al. The Core Repertory of Early American Psalmody. Crawford, Richard, ed. (Recent Researches in American Music Ser.: No. RRAM11-12). (Illus.). 165, lxxxivp. 1984. pap. 75.00 (*0-89579-198-6*) A-R Eds.
Billings, William Dwight, jt. ed. see Barbour, Michael G.
Billings-Yun, Melanie. Decision Against War: Eisenhower & Dien Bien Phu, 1954. Leuchtenburg, William E., ed. 200p. 1988. text 44.00 (*0-231-06622-8*) Col U Pr.
Billingslea-Brown, Alma J. Crossing Borders Through Folklore: African American Women's Fiction & Art. LC 98-31339. (Illus.). 160p. 1999. 27.50 (*0-8262-1199-2*) U of Mo Pr.
Billingsley, jt. auth. see Watson.
Billingsley, Andrew. Climbing Jacob's Ladder: The Enduring Legacy of African-American Families. 528p. 1994. pap. 15.00 (*0-671-67709-8*, Touchstone) S&S Trade Pap.
— Mighty Like a River: The Black Church & Social Reform. LC 98-13875. (Illus.). 288p. 1999. 26.00 (*0-19-510617-2*) OUP.
Billingsley, Ann V. Getting the Time of Day from Your Kids. 38p. 1989. pap. 3.95 (*0-923672-02-8*) Hearth Pubns.
— Getting the Twenty-Fifth Hour. 60p. (Orig.). 1988. pap. 6.95 (*0-923672-00-1*) Hearth Pubns.
Billingsley, Berry-Anne. Space. (Fact Finders Ser.). (Illus.). 48p. (Orig.). (J). (gr. 4 up). 1993. pap. 8.95 (*0-563-34789-9*, BBC-Parkwest) Parkwest Pubns.
Billingsley, Carolyn E. Eighteen Forty Saline County, Arkansas, Census. 24p. 1987. pap. 7.25 (*0-9618123-1-1*) C E Billingsley.
— Eighteen Ninety Saline County, Arkansas, Taxpayers. (Illus.). 103p. (Orig.). 1987. pap. 12.50 (*0-9618123-0-3*) C E Billingsley.
— The Family History of Eula Mae Miller Fisher. (Illus.). 41p. 1987. pap. 11.00 (*0-9618123-2-X*) C E Billingsley.
— Pleasant Grove Families: Saline County, Arkansas, Recollections of a Church, a Cemetery, a Community of the Past. 2nd ed. (Illus.). 216p. 1997. pap. 28.00 (*1-56546-108-8*) Arkansas Res.
— Pleasant Grove Families (Saline County, Arkansas) Recollections of a Church, a Cemetery, a Community of the Past. (Illus.). 202p. 1988. pap. 23.50 (*0-9618123-5-4*) C E Billingsley.
Billingsley, Carolyn E. Saline County, Arkansas Census, 1850. 260p. 1987. pap. 23.00 (*0-9618123-3-8*) C E Billingsley.
Billingsley, Carolyn E. The Saline, 1987. (Illus.). 201p. 1988. ring bd. 13.75 (*0-945183-09-7*) Saline Cnty Hist Heritage Soc.
Billingsley, Carolyn E., ed. The Saline, 1986. (Illus.). 132p. 1986. ring bd. 13.75 (*0-945183-00-3*) Saline Cnty Hist Heritage Soc.
Billingsley, Carolyn E. & Allen, Desmond W. How to Become a Professional Genealogist. 3rd ed. 50p. (Orig.). 1997. pap. 5.95 (*1-56546-103-7*) Arkansas Res.
Billingsley, Carolyn E., jt. auth. see Allen, Desmond W.
***Billingsley, Carolyn Earle.** Early Saline County, Arkansas, Records: Transcriptions of the 1840 Federal Census & 1846 Tax Book. (Illus.). 50p. 2000. pap. 12.00 (*1-56546-168-1*) Arkansas Res.
— 1890 Saline County, Arkansas, Taxpayers. (Illus.). 53p. 2000. pap. 12.00 (*1-56546-169-X*) Arkansas Res.
Billingsley, David S. Descendants of Richard Billingsley & Elizabeth Pearson of New Carlisle, P.Q., Canada; Second Son, Richard. (Illus.). 298p. 1992. 65.00 (*0-317-04959-3*) D S Billingsley.
Billingsley, Franny. The Folk Keeper. LC 98-48778. (Illus.). 176p. (J). (gr. 4-6). 1999. 16.00 (*0-689-82876-4*) Atheneum Yung Read.
***Billingsley, Franny.** The Folk Keeper. large type ed. (Thorndike Young Adult Ser.). (YA). 2000. 20.95 (*0-7862-2461-4*) Thorndike Pr.
Billingsley, Franny. Well Wished. 176p. (J). 2000. pap. 4.99 (*0-689-83255-9*) Aladdin.
— Well Wished. LC 96-24511. 176p. (J). (gr. 3-7). 1997. 16.00 (*0-689-81210-8*) S&S Childrens.
Billingsley, George H., et al. Quest for the Pillar of Gold: The Mines & Miners of the Grand Canyon. LC 96-80426. (Monograph Ser.: Vol. 10). (Illus.). 112p. 1997. pap. 15.00 (*0-938216-56-2*) GCA.
Billingsley, Hobie. Hobie Billingsley's Diving Illustrated. LC 90-70956. (Illus.). 301p. 1994. pap. 18.95 (*1-878958-04-6*) Taylor FL.
***Billingsley, J.** Mechatronics & Machine Vision. LC 00-32338. (Robotics & Mechatronics Ser.). 2000. write for info. (*0-86380-261-3*, Pub. by Research Studies Pr Ltd) Taylor & Francis.
Billingsley, J., ed. Robots & Automated Manufacture. (Control Engineering Ser.: No. 28). 248p. 1985. boxed set 75.00 (*0-86341-053-7*, CE028) INSPEC Inc.
Billingsley, John. A Stoney Gaze: Investigating Celtic & Other Stone Heads. (Illus.). (Orig.). 1998. pap. 19.95 (*1-898307-71-7*, Pub. by Capall Bann Pubng) Holmes Pub.
Billingsley, K. L. From Mainline to Sideline: The Social Witness of the National Council of Churches. 220p. (C). 1990. pap. text 14.95 (*0-89633-142-3*); lib. bdg. 29.95 (*0-89633-141-5*) Ethics & Public Policy.
***Billingsley, K. L.** The Seductive Image: Cinema & the Christian Faith. 236p. 1999. pap. 22.00 (*1-57910-263-8*) Wipf & Stock.
Billingsley, K. L., ed. Voices of Choice: The Education Reform Debate. LC 93-36884. 1993. write for info. (*0-936488-75-1*) PRIPP.
Billingsley, Lloyd. Hollywood Party: The Untold Story of How Communism Seduced the American Film Industry in the '30s & '40s. LC 98-27188. 272p. 1998. boxed set 25.00 (*0-7615-1376-0*) Prima Pub.
Billingsley, Martin. The Pens Excellencie or the Secretaries Delight. LC 77-6852. (English Experience Ser.: No. 849). 1977. reprint ed. lib. bdg. 20.00 (*90-221-0849-X*) Walter J Johnson.
Billingsley, Melvin L. Pharmacology: Review for New National Boards. LC 95-75271. (Illus.). 186p. 1995. pap. 25.00 (*0-9632873-7-0*) J & S Pub VA.
Billingsley, Patrick. Weak Convergence of Measures: Applications in Probability. (CBMS-NSF Regional Conference Ser.: No. 5). v, 31p. 1972. pap. text 14.50 (*0-89871-176-2*) Soc Indus-Appl Math.
***Billingsley, Patrick.** Convergence of Probability Measures. 2nd ed. LC 99-30372. 296p. 1999. 79.95 (*0-471-19745-9*) Wiley.
Billingsley, Patrick. Probability & Measure. 3rd ed. LC 94-28500. (Series in Probability & Mathematical Statistics). 608p. 1995. 84.95 (*0-471-00710-2*) Wiley.
— Statistical Inference for Markov Processes. LC 61-8646. (Statistical Research Monographs: No. 2). 83p. reprint ed. pap. 30.00 (*0-608-09388-2*, 205413300004) Bks Demand.
Billingsley, Patrick, jt. auth. see Huntsberger, David V.
Billingsley, Peter B., jt. ed. see Lehane, Michael J.
Billingsley, Phil. Bandits in Republican China. LC 87-30518. (Illus.). 400p. 1988. 47.50 (*0-8047-1406-1*) Stanford U Pr.
Billingsley, Randall S., ed. Corporate Financial Decision Making & Equity Analysis. 67p. (Orig.). 1995. pap. text 30.00 (*1-879087-52-9*) RFICFA.
Billingsley, Ronald G., jt. auth. see Lewan, Lloyd S.
Billingsley, Rosario B. He's Not the Right One (Divorce & Dating Thereafter) LC 96-85644. 200p. (Orig.). 1996. pap. 16.95 (*0-9653361-0-7*) Fell St Pr.
Billingsley, Stanley & Zevely, Wilbur M. Kentucky Driving under the Influence Law. 471p. (Orig.). 1996. pap. 67.50 (*0-8322-0663-6*) Banks-Baldwin.
Billingsley, William J. Communists on Campus: Race, Politics, & the Public University in Sixties North Carolina. LC 99-11408. (Illus.). 336p. 1999. 29.95 (*0-8203-2109-5*) U of Ga Pr.
***Billingsly, Kenneth Lloy.** Hollywood Party. 2000. pap. 16.00 (*0-7615-2166-6*) Prima Pub.
Billington, Ann, jt. auth. see Evans, Jimmy.
Billington, Anthony, et al, eds. Mission & Meaning: Essays Presented to Peter Cotterell. xvi, 375p. 1995. reprint ed. pap. 25.00 (*0-85364-676-7*, Pub. by Paternoster Pub) OM Literature.
Billington, Cecil. Shrubs of Michigan. 2nd ed. LC 44-1024. (Bulletin Ser.: No. 20). (Illus.). 339p. 1949. text 12.00 (*0-87737-005-2*) Cranbrook.
Billington, D., et al. Radioisotopes. (Introduction to Biotechniques Ser.). 168p. (Orig.). 1992. pap. 47.50 (*1-872748-85-6*, Pub. by Bios Sci) Coronet Bks.
Billington, David & Goldsmith, Myron, eds. Technique & Aesthetics in the Design of Tall Buildings. (Illus.). 100p. (C). 1986. text 24.00 (*0-939493-01-2*) Coun Tall Bldg.
Billington, David P. The Innovators: The Engineering Pioneers Who Transformed America. LC 95-43653. 256p. 1996. 24.95 (*0-471-14026-0*) Wiley.
— The Innovators: The Engineering Pioneers Who Transformed America. 258p. (C). 1996. pap. 28.95 (*0-471-14096-1*) Wiley.
— Robert Maillart: Builder, Designer, & Artist. LC 96-23133. (Illus.). 364p. 1997. text 70.00 (*0-521-57132-4*) Cambridge U Pr.
— Robert Maillart & the Art of Reinforced Concrete. (Illus.). 151p. 1990. 70.00 (*0-262-02310-5*) MIT Pr.
— Robert Maillart's Bridges: The Art of Engineering. LC 78-70279. (Illus.). 168p. 1979. pap. text 27.50 (*0-691-02421-9*, Pub. by Princeton U Pr) Cal Prin Full Svc.
— Robert Maillart's Bridges: The Art of Engineering. LC 78-70279. (Illus.). 162p. reprint ed. pap. 50.30 (*0-608-09113-8*, 206974500005) Bks Demand.
— The Tower & the Bridge: The New Art of Structural Engineering. LC 85-42667. (Illus.). 328p. 1985. pap. text 22.50 (*0-691-02393-X*, Pub. by Princeton U Pr) Cal Prin Full Svc.
Billington, Dottie. Life Is an Attitude: How to Grow Forever Better. rev. ed. 276p. 2000. pap. text 12.95 (*0-9671837-5-8*) Lowell Leigh.
Billington, E. W. An Introduction to the Mechanics & Physics of Solids. (Illus.). 356p. 1986. 40.00 (*0-85274-491-9*) IOP Pub.
Billington, Elisabeth. Czech in Three Months. LC 98-31745. (Hugo's Simplified Language Course Ser.). 1999. write for info. (*0-7894-4433-X*); pap. 14.95 (*0-7894-4399-6*) DK Pub Inc.
Billington, J., et al, eds. Application & Theory of Petri Nets 1996: 17 International Conference, Osaka, Japan, June 24-28, 1996 Proceedings, Vol. 1091. (Lecture Notes in Computer Science Ser.). viii, 549p. 1996. pap. 87.00 (*3-540-61363-9*) Spr-Verlag.
***Billington, J., et al, eds.** Application of Petri Nets to Communication Networks: Advances in Petri Nets. LC 99-26574. (Lecture Notes in Computer Science Ser.: Vol. 1605). ix, 303p. 1999. pap. 43.00 (*3-540-65870-X*) Spr-Verlag.
Billington, James, jt. auth. see Sandler, Martin W.
Billington, James H. The Face of Russia. (Illus.). 296p. 1998. 29.95 (*1-57500-104-7*, Pub. by TV Bks) HarpC.
***Billington, James H.** Face of Russia. 272p. 1999. pap. 16.00 (*1-57500-089-X*) HarpC.
Billington, James H. Fire in the Minds of Men. LC 98-24144. 695p. 1998. pap. 29.95 (*0-7658-0471-9*) Transaction Pubs.
— Icon & the Axe: An Interpretive History of Russian Culture. LC 66-18687. (Illus.). 1970. pap. 22.00 (*0-394-70846-6*, V620) Knopf.
— The Icon & the Axe: An Interpretive History of Russian Culture. 1994. 29.25 (*0-8446-6754-4*) Peter Smith.
— Russia Transformed: Breakthrough to Hope, August, 1991. 202p. 1992. 22.95 (*0-02-903515-5*) Free Pr.
Billington, Jill. Planting Companions. LC 96-49089. (Illus.). 160p. 1997. 32.50 (*1-55670-543-3*) Stewart Tabori & Chang.
— Really Small Gardens: A Practical Guide to Gardening in a Truly Small Space. 192p. 1999. pap. 29.95 (*1-57076-128-0*) Trafalgar.
— Small Gardens with Style. (Illus.). 144p. (Orig.). 1996. pap. 16.95 (*0-7063-7475-4*, Pub. by WrLock) Sterling.
— The Summer Garden: Planning - Preparing - Enjoying. (Illus.). 144p. pap. 17.95 (*0-7063-7568-8*, Pub. by WrLock) Sterling.
— Summer Garden: Planning, Preparing, Enjoying. LC 97-175365. (Illus.). 144p. 1997. 24.95 (*0-7063-7455-X*) Ward Lock Ltd UK.
Billington, Joy, ed. see deTagle, Lillian Lorca.
Billington, Ken. People, Politics & Public Power. LC 87-51001. (Illus.). 480p. 1988. 24.95 (*0-9619682-0-6*); pap. 19.95 (*0-9619682-1-4*) WA Public Util Dist Assn.
Billington, M. J., jt. auth. see Powell-Smith, Vincent.
Billington, Michael. The Life & Work of Harold Pinter. (Illus.). 384p. 1997. 24.95 (*0-571-17103-6*) Faber & Faber.
— One Night Stands: A Critic's View of British Theatre from 1971-1991. 382p. 1994. pap. 15.95 (*0-435-08644-8*, 08644) Heinemann.
— Stoppard the Playwright. 192p. 1988. write for info. (*0-413-45850-4*, A0272, Methuen Drama) Methn.
Billington, Mike. Cowboys of the Heart. 2nd ed. 104p. 1996. pap. 12.95 (*0-9660486-1-X*) White Rose Bks.
Billington, Mike & DeSantis, Cari. Faith in Action: Medical Missionaries in Central America. LC 97-91255. (Illus.). 104p. pap. 25.00 (*0-9660486-0-1*) White Rose Bks.
Billington, Monroe L. New Mexico's Buffalo Soldiers, 1866-1900. (Illus.). 278p. 1993. pap. 22.50 (*0-87081-346-3*) Univ Pr Colo.
— Southern Politics since the Civil War. LC 83-23885. 208p. 1984. pap. 11.50 (*0-89874-673-6*) Krieger.
Billington, Monroe L. & Hardaway, Roger D., eds. African Americans on the Western Frontier. (Illus.). 336p. 1998. 27.50 (*0-87081-491-5*) Univ Pr Colo.
Billington, N. S., jt. auth. see Baturin, V.
Billington, Neil, jt. auth. see Kaye, Connie.
Billington, R. Life of Jesus. mass mkt. 11.95 (*0-340-69357-6*, Pub. by Hodder & Stought Ltd) Trafalgar.
— Perfect Happiness. mass mkt. 15.95 (*0-340-67513-6*, Pub. by Hodder & Stought Ltd) Trafalgar.
Billington, R. A. & Ridge, Martin, eds. America's Frontier Story: A Documentary History of Westward Expansion. LC 79-28118. 680p. 1980. reprint ed. pap. text 30.00 (*0-89874-090-8*) Krieger.
Billington, Rachel. The First Christmas. LC 87-20383. (Illus.). 32p. (J). (ps-5). 1987. pap. 7.95 (*0-8192-1410-8*) Morehouse Pub.
— The Garish Day. large type ed. 560p. 1986. 11.50 (*0-7089-8361-8*) Ulverscroft.
Billington, Rachel. The Life of Jesus. (Illus.). 144p. 1997. pap. 19.95 (*0-340-69356-8*, Pub. by Hodder & Stought Ltd) Trafalgar.
Billington, Rachel. Occasion of Sin. large type ed. 512p. 1984. 11.50 (*0-7089-1123-4*) Ulverscroft.
— Perfect Happiness. large type ed. (Charnwood Large Print Ser.). 448p. 1997. 27.99 (*0-7089-8969-1*) Ulverscroft.
Billington, Rachel & Austen, Jane. Perfect Happiness: The Sequel to Jane Austen's Emma. 240p. 1996. text 29.95 (*0-340-67512-8*, Pub. by Hodder & Stought Ltd) Trafalgar.
Billington, Ray. East of Existentialism: The Tao of the West. 320p. (C). 1990. text 55.00 (*0-04-445542-9*) Routledge.
— Living Philosophy: An Introduction to Applied Ethics. 288p. 1988. text 15.50 (*0-7102-1303-4*, Routledge Thoemms) Routledge.
— Living Philosophy: An Introduction to Moral Thought. 2nd rev. ed. LC 93-19012. 352p. (C). 1993. pap. 22.99 (*0-415-10028-3*, B2595) Routledge.
— Understanding Eastern Philosophy. LC 97-224463. 208p. (C). 1997. pap. 19.99 (*0-415-12965-6*) Routledge.
— Understanding Eastern Philosophy. LC 97-224463. 208p. (C). 1997. 65.00 (*0-415-12964-8*) Routledge.
Billington, Ray A. American History Before 1877: With Questions & Answers. (Quality Paperback Ser.: No. 26). 288p. (Orig.). 1981. reprint ed. pap. 17.95 (*0-8226-0026-9*) Littlefield.
— America's Frontier Culture: Three Essays. LC 77-89510. (Elma Dill Russell Spences Series in the West & Southwest: No. 3). 100p. 1977. 11.95 (*0-89096-036-4*) Tex A&M Univ Pr.
— The Genesis of the Frontier Thesis: A Study in Historical Creativity. LC 74-171108. 329p. reprint ed. pap. 102.00 (*0-7837-6680-7*, 204629600011) Bks Demand.
— The Origins of Nativism in the United States, 1800-1844. LC 73-19129. (Politics & People Ser.). (Illus.). 716p. 1979. reprint ed. 57.95 (*0-405-05854-3*) Ayer.
— People of the Plains & Mountains: Essays in the History of the West Dedicated to Everett Dick, 25. LC 72-784. (Contributions in American History Ser.: No. 25). (Illus.). 227p. 1973. 55.00 (*0-8371-6358-7*, BID/, Greenwood Pr) Greenwood.
Billington, Ray A., ed. The Far Western Frontier, 47 bks., Set. 1269.00 (*0-405-04955-2*) Ayer.
— The Frontier Thesis: Valid Interpretation of American History? LC 77-9103. (American Problem Studies). 128p. 1977. reprint ed. pap. 11.50 (*0-88275-586-2*) Krieger.
Billington, Ray A. & Ridge, Martin. American History after Eighteen Sixty-Five. 9th ed. (Quality Paperback Ser.: No. 27). 382p. (C). 1981. pap. text 17.95 (*0-8226-0027-7*) Littlefield.
Billington, Ray A. & Whitehill, Walter M., eds. Dear Lady: The Letters of Frederick Jackson Turner & Alice Forbes Perkins Hooper, 1910-1932. LC 76-134261. (Illus.). 487p. 1970. 9.00 (*0-87328-046-6*) Huntington Lib.
Billington, Ray Allen. America's Frontier Heritage. LC 66-13289. (Histories of the American Frontier Ser.). 310p. 1994. 14.95 (*0-8263-1463-5*) U of NM Pr.
— America's Frontier Heritage. LC 66-13289. (Histories of the American Frontier Ser.). 328p. 1994. reprint ed. pap. 14.95 (*0-8263-0310-2*) U of NM Pr.
Billington, Sandra. Mock Kings in Medieval Society & Renaissance Drama. (Illus.). 300p. 1991. text 90.00 (*0-19-811967-4*, 1894) OUP.
Billington, Sandra & Green, Miranda, eds. The Concept of Goddess. LC 95-53942. (Illus.). 208p. (C). 1996. 65.00 (*0-415-14421-3*) Routledge.
— The Concept of the Goddess. (Illus.). 208p. 1998. reprint ed. pap. 22.99 (*0-415-19789-9*) Routledge.
Billington, Shirley, jt. auth. see Clegg, David.
Billington, Shirley, jt. auth. see Clegg, David W.
Billington, Shirly, jt. auth. see Clegg, David.
***Billington, Tom.** Separating, Losing & Excluding Children: Narratives of Difference. LC 00-32832. (Master Classes in Education Ser.). 2000. pap. write for info. (*0-415-23089-6*) Routledge.
Billinton, R. & Allan, R. Reliability Evaluation of Engineering Systems: Concepts & Techniques. 2nd ed. LC 92-10368. (Illus.). 472p. (C). 1992. 75.00 (*0-306-44063-6*, Plenum Trade) Perseus Pubng.
Billinton, Roy. Power System Reliability Evaluation. x, 300p. 1970. text 220.00 (*0-677-02870-9*) Gordon & Breach.
Billinton, Roy & Allan, Ronald N. Reliability Assessment of Large Electric Power Systems. (C). 1988. text 104.50 (*0-89838-266-1*) Kluwer Academic.
— Reliability Evaluation of Power Systems. 2nd ed. (Illus.). 508p. (C). 1996. 107.00 (*0-306-45259-6*, Plenum Trade) Perseus Pubng.
Billinton, Roy & Li, W., eds. Reliability Assessment of Electrical Power Systems Using Monte Carlo Methods. LC 96-21880. (Illus.). 368p. (C). 1994. 95.00 (*0-306-44781-9*, Plenum Trade) Perseus Pubng.
Billion, Anna. Kundalini: Secret of the Ancient Yogis. 1982. pap. 4.95 (*0-686-97516-2*, Reward) P-H.
Billion, Frederic L. Annals of St. Louis in Its Early Days under the French & Spanish Dominations. (Illus.). x, 507p. 1997. pap. 35.00 (*0-7884-0690-6*, B344) Heritage Bk.

An Asterisk (*) at the beginning of an entry indicates that the title is appearing for the first time.

— Annals of St. Louis in Its Territorial Days from 1804 to 1821. (Illus.). vi, 463p. 1997. reprint ed. pap. 32.50 (0-7884-0691-4, 13345) Heritage Bk.

Billips, Annie. That Man: Reading Level 3. (Sundown Fiction Collection). 1993. 3.95 (0-88336-766-1) New Readers.

Billips, Connie J. Janet Gaynor: A Bio-Bibliography, 23. LC 91-36239. (Bio-Bibliographies in the Performing Arts Ser.: No. 23). 184p. 1992. lib. bdg. 49.95 (0-313-27574-2, BJG/, Greenwood Pr) Greenwood.

— Maureen O'Sullivan: A Bio-Bibliography, 13. LC 90-31763. (Bio-Bibliographies in the Performing Arts Ser.: No. 13). 224p. 1990. lib. bdg. 45.00 (0-313-26470-8, BMF, Greenwood Pr) Greenwood.

Billips, Connie J. & Pierce, Arthur. Lux Presents Hollywood: A Show-by-Show History of the Lux Radio Theater & the Lux Video Theater, 1934-1957. LC 94-11517. (Illus.). 739p. 1995. lib. bdg. 95.00 (0-89950-938-X) McFarland & Co.

Billis, jt. auth. see Taylor, D. A.

Billis, David. Welfare Bureaucracies: Their Design & Changes in Response to Social Problems. 252p. 1985. 41.95 (0-435-82059-1, Pub. by Avebry) Ashgate Pub Co.

Billis, David, jt. auth. see Rowbottom, Ralph.

Billitt, Arthur. Vegetable Growing. 96p. 1988. 55.00 (1-85283-226-6, Pub. by Boxtree) St Mut.

***Billitteri, Thomas J.** The Gault Case: Legal Rights for Young People. (Landmark Supreme Court Cases Ser.). (Illus.). 112p. (YA). (gr. 6 up). 2000. lib. bdg. 20.95 (0-7660-1340-5) Enslow Pubs.

Billman, Brian R. & Feinman, Gary M., eds. Settlement Pattern Studies in the Americas: Fifth Years since Viru. LC 98-39513. (Series in Archaeological Inquiry). (Illus.). 328p. 1999. 65.00 (1-56098-826-6) Smithsonian.

Billman, Jean. Starting & Operating a Child Care Center. 272p. (C). 1992. text. write for info. (0-697-14550-6) Brown & Benchmark.

Billman, Jean B. & Sherman, Janice. Observation & Participation in Early Childhood Birth Through Age Five. LC 98-121623. 186p. 1996. pap. text 31.00 (0-205-26474-3) Allyn.

— Observation & Participation in Early Childhood Settings: A Practicum Guide. 256p. 1995. pap. text 38.00 (0-205-15993-1) Allyn.

Billman, Jon. When We Were Wolves. LC 99-14952. 256p. 1999. 21.95 (0-375-50258-0) Random.

***Billman, Kathleen D. & Migliore, Daniel L.** Rachel's Cry: Prayer of Lament & Rebirth of Hope. LC 99-30816. 192p. 1999. pap. 18.95 (0-8298-1353-5) Pilgrim OH.

Billman, Larry. Betty Grable: A Bio-Bibliography, 40. LC 93-17579. 328p. 1993. text 55.00 (0-313-28156-4, Greenwood Pr) Greenwood.

Billman, Larry. Film Choreographers & Dance Directors: An Illustrated Biographical Encyclopedia, with a History & Filmographies, 1893 Through 1995. LC 96-31756. (Illus.). 664p. 1997. boxed set 125.00 (0-89950-868-5) McFarland & Co.

— Fred Astaire: A Bio-Bibliography, 76. LC 97-12281. (Bio-Bibliographies in the Performing Arts: Vol. 76). 424p. 1997. lib. bdg. 69.50 (0-313-29010-5, Greenwood Pr) Greenwood.

Billman, Ruth. Destined to Share the Throne. 1990. pap. 4.95 (0-87508-032-4) Chr Lit.

Billmeyer, Fred W. Synthetic Polymers-Building the Giant Molecule. LC 77-171279. (Science Study Ser.). 204p. reprint ed. pap. 63.30 (0-608-16223-X, 202650800050) Bks Demand.

Billmeyer, Fred W., Jr. Textbook of Polymer Science. 3rd ed. LC 83-19870. 608p. 1984. 89.95 (0-471-03196-8) Wiley.

Billmeyer, Fred W. & Kelley, Richard N. Entering Industry: A Guide for Young Professionals. LC 75-22283. 295p. reprint ed. pap. 91.50 (0-608-11411-1, 202224300025) Bks Demand.

Billmeyer, Patricia. The Complete Encyclopedia of Wild Game & Fish Cleaning & Cooking, 3 Vols., 1. LC 83-50091. (Illus.). 96p. 1983. pap. 4.95 (0-9606262-4-7) Yesnaby Inc.

— The Complete Encyclopedia of Wild Game & Fish Cleaning & Cooking, 3 Vols., 2. LC 83-50091. (Illus.). 96p. 1983. pap. 4.95 (0-9606262-5-5) Yesnaby Inc.

— The Complete Encyclopedia of Wild Game & Fish Cleaning & Cooking, 3 Vols., 3. LC 83-50091. (Illus.). 96p. 1983. pap. 4.95 (0-9606262-6-3) Yesnaby Inc.

— The Complete Encyclopedia of Wild Game & Fish Cleaning & Cooking, 3 Vols., Set. LC 83-50091. (Illus.). 96p. 1983. pap. 13.00 (0-9606262-3-9) Yesnaby Inc.

— The Encyclopedia of Wild Game & Fish Cleaning & Cooking. LC 79-54388. 116p. 1979. reprint ed. pap. 4.95 (0-9606262-0-4) Yesnaby Inc.

Billo, E. J. Microsoft Excel for Chemists: A Comprehensive Guide. 400p. 1997. pap. 49.95 incl. disk (1-56081-959-6) Wiley.

Billo, E. Joseph. Excel for Chemists: A Comprehensive Guide. LC 97-1274. 480p. 1997. pap. 54.95 (0-471-18896-4) Wiley.

Billon. Clinical Case Studies. 3rd ed. (Health Sciences Ser.). 1999. pap. 39.95 (0-534-54657-9) Wadsworth Pub.

Billon & Catalod. Clinical Nutrition. (Health Sciences Ser.). 1991. pap., student ed. 20.26 (0-314-88786-5) Wadsworth Pub.

Billon, B. M. Death's an End & a Beginning Without. 1981. 45.00 (0-7223-1388-8, Pub. by A H S Ltd) St Mut.

Billon, Frederic L. Annals of St. Louis in Its Early Days under the French & Spanish Dominations. LC 72-146373. (First American Frontier Ser.). (Illus.). 1971. reprint ed. 41.95 (0-405-02824-5) Ayer.

— Annals of St. Louis in Its Territorial Days from 1804 to 1821: Being a Continuation of the Author's Previous Work, the Annals of the French & Spanish Period. LC 76-146374. (First American Frontier Ser.). (Illus.). 1971. reprint ed. 41.95 (0-405-02825-3) Ayer.

Billon, Frederoc L. Annals of Saint Louis in Its Early Days: Under the French & Spanish Dominations. (Illus.). 499p. 1997. reprint ed. lib. bdg. 52.00 (0-8328-6857-4) Higginson Bk Co.

Billon, Wayne E. Clinical Nutrition Case Studies. 2nd ed. 293p. 1996. 25.25 (0-314-07169-5) West Pub.

***Billoni, Michael J. & Rich, Robert E.** Robert E. Rich: Memoirs of an Innovator. (Illus.). 320p. 2000. 29.95 (0-9671480-1-4); pap. 19.95 (0-9671480-2-2) Canisius Coll Pr.

Billot, Antoine. Economic Theory of Fuzzy Equilibria: An Axiomatic Analysis, Vol. XVIII. 2nd enl. rev. ed. (Illus.). 180p. 1995. 99.00 (3-540-60200-3) Spr-Verlag.

Billot, Diane. Free Money for Writers. LC 97-11091. 224p. 1997. 14.95 (0-8050-5312-3) H Holt & Co.

Billot, Michel, tr. see Olsen, Maryann, et al.

Billout, Guy. Journey. (Illus.). 32p. (YA). (gr. 3 up). 1993. 22.60 (1-56846-081-3, Creative Eds) Creative Co.

Billows, Dick. Project & Program Management: People, Budgets & Software. (Illus.). 250p. (Orig.). 1996. pap. text 49.95 (0-9642865-2-1) Hampton Grp.

Billows, Dick, et al. At-Home Workers: Converting In-Office Departments to At-Home Jobs. (Illus.). 160p. (Orig.). 1995. pap. 19.95 (0-9642865-1-3) Hampton Grp.

***Billows, Richard.** Essentials of Project Management. (Illus.). 78p. 1999. pap. 29.95 (0-9642865-7-2) Hampton Grp.

— Project & Program Management: Managing Complex Projects. 7th ed. (Illus.). 322p. 2000. pap. 65.00 (0-9642865-9-9) Hampton Grp.

— Project & Program Management: People, Budgets & Software. (Illus.). 153p. 1999. pap. 39.95 incl. cd-rom (0-9642865-8-0) Hampton Grp.

Billows, Richard A. Antigonos the One-Eyed & the Creation of the Hellenistic State. LC 89-4677. (Hellenistic Culture & Society Ser.: Vol. 4). 1997. pap. 24.95 (0-520-20880-3, Pub. by U CA Pr) Cal Prin Full Svc.

— Kings & Colonists: Aspects of Macedonian Imperialism. LC 94-33774. (Columbia Studies in the Classical Tradition: 22). xv, 240p. 1994. 97.00 (90-04-10177-2) Brill Academic Pubs.

— Project & Program Management: Managing Complex Projects with PC Software. LC 94-96302. (Illus.). 178p. (Orig.). 1994. pap. text 30.00 (0-9642865-0-5) Hampton Grp.

Billroth-Gottlieb, Hans, jt. auth. see Absolon, Karel B.

Billroth, Theodor. Mechanism - Prevention - Treatment of Aspiration Pneumonia: Theodor Billroth's M.D. Thesis in 1852 on Cervical Vagotomy. fac. ed. (LAT.). 50p. (C). 1994. pap. text 19.50 (0-930329-67-8) Kabel Pubs.

Bills. Principles of Pharmacology. 96p. 1997. text, teacher ed. 19.95 (0-8273-8300-2) Delmar.

— Principles of Pharmacy for Respiratory Care. (Respiratory Care Ser.). 1994. 15.00 (0-8273-6360-5) Delmar.

Bills, D. D. & Kung, Shain-Dow. Biotechnology & Plant Protection. 352p. 1994. text 99.00 (981-02-1833-8) World Scientific Pub.

— Biotechnology & Plant Protection - Viral Pathogenesis & Disease Resistance. 350p. 1995. text 99.00 (981-02-2274-2) World Scientific Pub.

Bills, David B., ed. The New Modern Times: Factors Reshaping the World of Work. LC 94-1044. (SUNY Series in the Sociology of Work). 319p. (C). 1995. pap. text 21.95 (0-7914-2228-3) State U NY Pr.

Bills, Diane. Trust in the Lord: Letting the Spirit Be Your Guide. LC 96-30355. 1996. 13.95 (1-55503-983-9, 01112341) Covenant Comms.

Bills, Donald D. & Mussinan, Cynthia J., eds. Characterization & Measurement of Flavor Compounds. LC 85-22913. (ACS Symposium Ser.: Vol. 289). 192p. 1985. reprint ed. pap. 59.60 (0-608-03917-9, 206436400009) Bks Demand.

Bills, Donald D., jt. auth. see Kung, Shain-dow.

Bills, Garland D., jt. ed. see Bergen, John J.

Bills, Georgine W. & Soderberg, Robert C. Principles of Pharmacology. 2nd ed. LC 97-22776. 400p. 1997. mass mkt. 50.95 (0-8273-8299-5) Delmar.

— Principles of Pharmacology for Respiratory Care. LC 93-48582. 333p. 1994. pap. 34.95 (0-8273-5274-3) Delmar.

— Principles of Pharmacology for Respiratory Care Workbook. 111p. 1994. 17.95 (0-8273-5275-1) Delmar.

Bills, Greg. Consider This Home. 1994. 21.00 (0-671-79873-1) S&S Trade.

Bills, Jay & Bills, Shirley. Home Food Dehydrating: Economical "Do-It Yourself" Methods for Preserving, Storing, & Cooking. 151p. 1974. pap. 10.98 (0-88290-035-8) Horizon Utah.

Bills, Jay, et al. Food Storage Basics: Just Add Water, Beginners Guide to Family Preparedness, Home Food Dehydrating, 3 bks., Set. 1994. pap. 27.98 (0-88290-464-7) Horizon Utah.

Bills, Jerold, et al. Fireproof Children Handbook. (Illus.). 150p. 1990. ring bd. 49.95 (0-9626076-0-6) Natl Fire Serv Support Systs.

Bills, Joe, jt. auth. see Loehr, David.

Bills, Leslie W. A Medal for Life: A Biography of Capt. Leefe Robinson VC (WWI) 144p. (C). 1991. 110.00 (0-946771-56-1, Pub. by Spellmnt Pubs) St Mut.

Bills, Mark. Edwin Longsden Long RA. LC 98-25759. (Illus.). 256p. 1998. 65.00 (0-8386-3821-X) Fairleigh Dickinson.

— Victorian Salon Paintings from the Russell-Cotes Art Gallery, 1. 1999. pap. text 29.95 (0-85331-748-8) Lund Humphries.

Bills, Martha, et al. Options for U. S. Military Support to the United Nations. fac. ed. LC JX1981.P7O6. (Illus.). 47p. 1992. reprint ed. pap. 30.00 (0-608-00957-1, 206180400011) Bks Demand.

Bills, Peter. Carling. 224p. 1996. pap. 15.95 (0-575-06260-6, Pub. by V Gollancz) Trafalgar.

Bills, Peter, jt. auth. see Richards, Dean.

Bills, Rex H. The Rulership Book. 1994. 21.95 (0-86690-431-X, B1022-034) Am Fed Astrologers.

Bills, Scott L. The Libyan Arena: The U. S., Britain & the Council of Foreign Ministers, 1945-1948. LC 94-33134. (American Diplomatic History Ser.: No. 8). (Illus.). 232p. 1995. 30.00 (0-87338-511-X) Kent St U Pr.

Bills, Scott L., ed. Kent State - May 4th: Echoes Through a Decade. LC 87-31685. (Illus.). 344p. 1988. pap. 14.00 (0-87338-360-5) Kent St U Pr.

Bills, Scott L. & Smith, E. Timothy, eds. The Romance of History: Essays in Honor of Lawrence S. Kaplan. LC 96-27660. 1997. 35.00 (0-87338-563-2) Kent St U Pr.

Bills, Shirley, jt. auth. see Bills, Jay.

Billsberry, Jon. Finding & Keeping the Right People: How to Select Motivated Employees. (Institute of Management Ser.). 250p. 1996. pap. 47.50 (0-273-61698-6, Pub. by Pitman Pub) Trans-Atl Phila.

Billsberry, Jon, ed. The Effective Manager: Perspectives & Illustrations. (Illus.). 320p. (C). 1996. 79.95 (0-7619-5110-5); pap. 29.95 (0-7619-5111-3) Sage.

Billsberry, Jon & Thomson. Competent Manager. 1999. pap. text 32.95 (0-7506-2401-9) Buttrwrth-Heinemann.

Billson, A., et al. Key Questions in Paediatrics. (Key Topics - Questions Ser.). (Illus.). 128p. (Orig.). 1997. pap. 27.95 (1-85996-116-9, Pub. by Bios Sci) Bks Intl VA.

Billson, A. L., jt. auth. see Davies, A. E.

Billson, Anne. The Thing. (Modern Classics Ser.). (Illus.). 96p. 1998. pap. 10.95 (0-85170-566-9, Pub. by British Film Inst) Ind U Pr.

Billson, Charles J. Popular Poetry of the Finns. (Popular Studies in Mythology, Romance & Folklore: No. 5). reprint ed. 27.50 (0-404-53505-4) AMS Pr.

Billson, Janet M. Pathways to Manhood: Young Black Males Struggle for Identity. 2nd exp. ed. 382p. 1996. pap. text 24.95 (1-56000-871-7) Transaction Pubs.

Billson, Janet M., jt. auth. see Majors, Richard G.

Billson, Janet Mancine, ed. Clinical Sociology Review, Vol. II. 160p. 1984. 34.95 (0-930390-56-3); pap. text 12.50 (0-942756-01-0) Clin Soc Assn.

Billstein. Math for Elementary School Teachers. 5th ed. (C). 1996. text 45.00 (0-201-40241-6) Addison-Wesley.

Billstein. Mathematics for Elementary School Teachers: A Problem Solving Approach. 5th ed. 1995. pap. text 165.00 (0-201-52718-9) Addison-Wesley.

Billstein. A Problem Solving Approach to Mathematics for Elementary School Teachers. 6th ed. (C). 1996. write for info. (0-201-59130-8) Addison-Wesley.

— A Problem Solving Approach to Mathematics with Student Solutions Manual Bundle. 1995. write for info. (0-201-85718-9) Addison-Wesley.

***Billstein & Libeskind.** Problem Solving Appraoch Math Bridgewater State. 1998. pap. text 73.00 (0-201-63627-1) Addison-Wesley.

— Problem Solving Approach: Mathematics for Elementary School Teachers. 1998. pap. text 69.00 (0-201-47228-7) Addison-Wesley.

***Billstein, Reinhold, et al.** Working for the Enemy: Ford, General Motors & Forced Labor in Germany during the Second World War. Levis, Nicholas, ed. & tr. by. (Illus.). 350p. 2000. 39.95 (1-57181-224-5) Berghahn Bks.

Billstein, Richard. Mathematics for Elementary School Teachers: A Problem Solving Approach. 5th ed. 176p. (C). 1992. pap. text, student ed. 23.00 (0-201-52778-2) Addison-Wesley.

— A Problem Solving Approach to Mathematics. 6th ed. Guardino, Karen, ed. LC 96-12195. 928p. (C). 1996. 81.00 (0-201-84664-0) Addison-Wesley.

Billstein, Richard & Lott, Johnny W. Math Liberal Arts. (Illus.). 646p. (C). 1986. text 52.75 (0-8053-0863-6) Addison-Wesley.

Billstein, Richard, et al. Apple LOGO: Programming & Problem Solving. 416p. (C). 1986. pap. text 32.25 (0-8053-0866-0) Addison-Wesley.

— IBM Tst Sftw Math Elem. 4th ed. Moller, Lisa, ed. 360p. (C). 1990. disk 129.25 (0-8053-0393-6) Benjamin-Cummings.

— Logo: Mit Logo for the Apple. LC 84-24229. 415p. (C). 1985. pap. text, teacher ed. 41.00 (0-8053-0860-1) Addison-Wesley.

— Mathematics for Elementary School Teachers: A Problem Solving Approach. 5th ed. (Illus.). 976p. (C). 1992. text 63.00 (0-201-52565-8) Addison-Wesley.

— A Problem Solving Approach to Mathematics for Elementary School Teachers. 5th ed. LC 92-32185. 1992. text 40.75 (0-201-60250-4) Addison-Wesley.

Billstrom, Beth, ed. see Elliott, Ryan.

Billups, Annie, ed. see Bosley, Judith A.

***Billups, Don.** Taking a Christian Break: Bible Verses, Spiritual Poems, Biblical Puzzles. Taylor, Kendrick, ed. Searle, Helen W., tr. (Illus.). 64p. (YA). 2000. pap. 10.00 (0-9664709-3-1) Mountain Empire.

Billups, Hvacinth, ed. see Innerarity, Al.

***Billups, Norman.** American Drug Index 2000. 44th ed. 1999. 54.95 (1-57439-051-1) Facts & Comparisons.

Billups, Norman & Billups, Shirley M. American Drug Index 2000. 1056p. 85.00 (1-57439-053-8) Lppncott W & W.

Billups, Norman, ed. see Facts & Comparisons Staff.

Billups, Shirley M., jt. auth. see Billups, Norman.

Billups, W. E. & Ciufolini, Marco A., eds. Buckminsterfullerenes. 339p. 1993. 89.95 (0-471-18845-X) Wiley.

Billups, W. Edward & Ciufolini, Marco A., eds. Buckminsterfullerenes. LC 93-3028. 339p. 1993. 59.00 (1-56081-608-2, Wiley-VCH) Wiley.

Billy, Andre, ed. see Diderot, Denis.

Billy, Dennis. Soliloquy Prayer Series 1: Unfolding Our Hearts to God. LC 98-20160. 144p. 1998. pap. 12.00 (0-7648-0222-4) Liguori Pubns.

Billy, Dennis J. Evangelical Kernels: Towards a Theological Spirituality of the Religious Life. LC 92-45146. 316p. 1993. pap. 15.95 (0-8189-0669-3) Alba.

— Holy Spirit. 1981. mass mkt. 3.50 (0-446-36176-3, Pub. by Warner Bks) Little.

— Into the Heart of Faith: Ten Steps on the Journey. LC 98-35068. 144p. 1999. pap. 11.95 (0-7648-0336-0, Liguori Triumph) Liguori Pubns.

***Billy, Dennis J.** The Way of a Pilgrim: Complete Text & Reader's Guide. LC 99-54857. 192p. 2000. pap. 15.95 (0-7648-0568-1) Liguori Pubns.

Billy, Dennis J., ed. Even Today: Theology & the Inner Child. LC 94-45232. 124p. (Orig.). 1995. pap. 6.95 (0-8189-0708-8) Alba.

Billy, Dennis J. & Orsuto, Donna L., eds. Spirituality & Morality: Integrating Prayer & Action. LC 95-37835. 192p. (Orig.). 1996. pap. 14.95 (0-8091-3611-2) Paulist Pr.

***Billy, Dennis Joseph.** Experiencing God: Fostering a Contemplative Life. LC 00-29604. 2000. pap. 12.95 (0-7648-0658-0) Liguori Pubns.

Billy, George J. Palmerston's Foreign Policy, 1848. LC 91-30737. (American University Studies: History: Ser. IX, Vols. 120). XV, 256p. (C). 1993. text 53.95 (0-8204-1730-0) P Lang Pubng.

***Billy, Molly L., et al.** Inuqguaq. large type ed.Tr. of A Small Doll. (ESK., Illus.). 8p. 2000. pap. text 6.00 (1-58084-210-0) Lower Kuskokwim.

— A Small Doll. large type ed. (Illus.). 8p. (J). (gr. k-3). 2000. pap. text 6.00 (1-58084-209-7) Lower Kuskokwim.

— A Small Doll (Cup'ik) large type ed. (ESK., Illus.). 8p. (J). (gr. k-3). 2000. pap. text 6.00 (1-58084-211-9) Lower Kuskokwim.

Billy, Pierre-Henri. Atlas Linguae Gallicae. (GER.). x, 254p. 1995. write for info. (3-487-10038-X) G Olms Pubs.

— Thesaurus Linguae Gallicae. (GER.). 260p. 1993. write for info. (3-487-09746-X) G Olms Pubs.

Billy, Ted. A Wilderness of Words: Closure & Disclosure in Conrad's Short Fiction. LC 97-24388. 320p. 1997. 37.50 (0-89672-389-5) Tex Tech Univ Pr.

Billy, Ted, jt. ed. see Orr, Leonard.

Bilmanis, Alfred. History of Latvia. LC 69-13827. 441p. 1970. reprint ed. lib. bdg. 45.00 (0-8371-1446-2, BIHL, Greenwood Pr) Greenwood.

Bilmes, J. Discourse & Behavior. (Illus.). 236p. (C). 1986. 54.50 (0-306-42307-3, Plenum Trade) Perseus Pubng.

Bilodeau, Gerald G. & Thie, Paul R. An Introduction to Analysis. LC 96-33319. (International Series in Pure & Applied Mathematics). 336p. (C). 1996. 74.06 (0-07-005662-5) McGraw.

Bilodeau, Lorrainne. Anger Workbook. 128p. 1997. 5.98 (1-56731-202-0, MJF Bks) Fine Comms.

— Anger Workbook. 128p. pap. 10.95 (1-56838-054-2) Hazelden.

Bilodeau, Louis, ed. see Verne, Jules & D'Ennery, Adolphe.

***Bilodeau, M. & Brenner, D.** Theory of Multivariate Statistics. Casella, G. et al, eds. LC 99-26378. (Texts in Statistics Ser.). 312p. 1999. 74.95 (0-387-98739-8) Spr-Verlag.

Bilokur, Borys. A Concordance to the Russian Poetry of Fedor I. Tiutchev. LC 75-9419. 357p. reprint ed. pap. 110.70 (0-608-16791-6, 200897800055) Bks Demand.

Bilon, Linda, jt. auth. see Haverluck, Bob.

Bilotta. Connections in Electronic Assemblies. (Manufacturing Engineering & Materials Processing Ser.: Vol. 17). (Illus.). 288p. 1985. text 125.00 (0-8247-7319-5) Dekker.

Bilotta, Peter A. Advanced Fuel Injection Systems. Gorham, Kelly, ed. 17p. 1994. student ed. 7.00 (0-8064-0272-5, A44) Bergwall.

Bilotti-Alia. Interactive Statistics. LC 98-47370. 676p. 1999. spiral bd. 77.00 (0-13-231036-8) P-H.

Bilotto, Gerardo & Washam, Veronica. Work Independence & the Severely Disabled: A Bibliography. LC 79-91351. 108p. 1980. 7.50 (0-686-38821-6) Human Res Ctr.

Bilovsky, Frank. Lion Country: Inside Penn State Football: The Triumphs & Glories of Penn State Football As Told by Lettermen from Different Eras, 1948-1981. fac. ed. LC 82-81802. (Illus.). 176p. 1982. reprint ed. pap. 54.60 (0-608-00948-2, 206176200011) Bks Demand.

Bilsborough, A. Human Evolution. (Tertiary Level Biology Ser.). (Illus.). 200p. 1990. 69.95 (0-412-02111-0, A3609, Chap & Hall NY); pap. 32.00 (0-412-02121-8, A3613, Chap & Hall NY) Chapman & Hall.

Bilsborrow, Richard E. Population in Development Planning: Background & Bibliography. 1976. pap. 5.00 (0-89055-048-4) Carolina Pop Ctr.

Bilsborrow, Richard E., ed. Migration, Urbanization & Development: New Directions & Issues. LC 97-31606. 544p. 1997. 137.50 (0-7923-8032-0) Kluwer Academic.

Bilsborrow, Richard E., et al. International Migration Statistics: Guidelines for Improvement of Data Collection Systems. LC 98-131022. 426p. 1997. 67.50 (92-2-109517-7) Intl Labour Office.

— Migration Surveys in Low-Income Countries: Guidelines for Survey & Questionnaire Design. LC 84-11354. 560p. 1984. 45.00 (0-7099-3266-9, Pub. by C Helm) Routldge.

Bilsen, F. A., ed. see International Symposium on Hearing Staff.

Bilsen, J. Children of the Sultan, 1. 1999. pap. text 9.99 (0-9680432-3-2) IDG Bks.

Bilsen, Jonathan Van, see Van Bilsen, Jonathan.

Bilsen, Valentijn, jt. ed. see Jackson, Marvin.

***Bilski, Emily, ed.** The Berlin Metropolis: Jews & the New Culture, 1890-1918. LC 99-32029. (Illus.). 256p. 1999. 60.00 (0-520-22241-5, Pub. by U CA Pr) Cal Prin Full Svc.

B

— The Berlin Metropolis: Jews & the New Culture, 1890-1918. LC 99-32029. (Illus.). 265p. 2000. pap. 29.95 (0-520-22242-3, Pub. by U CA Pr) Cal Prin Full Svc.

Bilski, R., et al, eds. Can Planning Replace Politics? (Van Leer Jerusalem Foundation Ser.: No. 11). 338p. 1980. text 126.50 (90-247-2324-8) Kluwer Academic.

Bilsky, Terry L. Expectations: Best Kept Secrets Every New Mother Should Know. LC 96-164656. (Illus.). 46p. 1996. 9.95 (0-8362-1089-1) Andrews & McMeel.

— Expectations: Best Kept Secrets Every New Mother Should Know. LC 98-84237. (Little Bks.). (Illus.). 80p. 1998. 4.95 (0-8362-6918-7) Andrews & McMeel.

***Bilsky, Terry Lee.** Newborn Expectations: My First Journal. (Illus.). 128p. 2000. pap. 10.95 (0-7407-0988-7) Andrews & McMeel.

Bilsky, Terry Lee, jt. auth. see Engelbreit, Mary.

Bilson. The Canadian Law of Nuisance. 232p. 1991. 59.00 (0-409-80573-4, MICHIE) LEXIS Pub.

Bilson, Elizabeth, jt. ed. see Terzian, Yervant.

Bilson, Geoffrey. A Darkened House: Cholera in Nineteenth-Century Canada. LC 80-154432. (Social History of Canada Ser.: No. 31). 236p. reprint ed. pap. 73.20 (0-608-16997-8, 202642300049) Bks Demand.

Bilson, Geoffrey. Death Over Montreal. 112p. (J). 1982. pap. 4.95 (0-919964-45-1) Kids Can Pr.

— Goodbye Sarah. 64p. (J). 1981. pap. 4.95 (0-919964-38-9) Kids Can Pr.

— Hockeybat Harris. 160p. (J). 1984. pap. 4.95 (0-919964-57-5) Kids Can Pr.

Bilson, John F. & Marston, Richard C., eds. Exchange Rate Theory & Practice. LC 84-2441. (National Bureau of Economic Research Conference Report Ser.). 464p. (C). 1985. lib. bdg. 62.00 (0-226-05096-3) U Ch Pr.

— Exchange Rate Theory & Practice. LC 84-2441. (National Bureau of Economic Research Conference Report Ser.). 538p. (C). 1988. pap. text 20.50 (0-226-05097-1) U Ch Pr.

Bilstein, Roger E. American Aerospace Industry. 1996. per. 28.95 (0-8057-9838-2, Twyne) Mac Lib Ref.

— Flight in America. rev. ed. LC 93-36027. 386p. (C). 1994. 50.00 (0-8018-4827-X); pap. 18.95 (0-8018-4828-8) Johns Hopkins.

***Bilstein, Roger E.** Stages to Saturn: A Technological History of the Apollo/Saturn Launch Vehicle. (Illus.). 511p. (C). 1999. reprint ed. pap. text 60.00 (0-7881-8186-6) DIANE Pub.

— Stages to Saturn: A Technological History of the Apollo/Saturn Launch Vehicles. 536p. 1997. per. 39.00 (0-16-048909-1) USGPO.

Bilton, Helen. Outdoor Play in the Early Years: Management & Innovation. 1998. 24.95 (1-85346-519-4) Taylor & Francis.

Bilton, Michael & Sim, Kevin. Four Hours in My Lai. 448p. 1993. pap. 15.99 (0-14-017709-4, Penguin Bks) Viking Penguin.

***Bilton, Paul.** The Xenophobe's Guide to the Swiss. (Xenophobe's Guides Ser.). 64p. 1999. pap. 5.95 (1-902825-45-4) Oval Bks.

Bilton, Ray & Tibbs, Mike. Orchids. LC 99-170945. (Growing Classic Ser.). (Illus.). 96p. 1998. pap. 12.95 (0-8069-6285-2) Sterling.

Biltz, Karl. Neuer Deutscher Bucherschatz. viii, 264p. 1967. reprint ed. 75.00 (0-318-71740-9) G Olms Pubs.

Bilu, Dalya, jt. auth. see Horn, Shifra.

Bilu, Dalya, tr. see Almog, Ruth.

Bilu, Dalya, tr. see Appelfeld, Aharon.

Bilu, Dalya, tr. see Goor, Batya.

Bilu, Dalya, tr. see Kenaz, Yehoshua.

Bilu, Dalya, tr. see Koren, Yeshayahu.

Bilu, Dalya, tr. see Shaked, Gershon, ed.

Bilu, Dalya, tr. see Shalev, Zeruya.

Bilu, Dalya, tr. see Yehoshua, Abraham B.

***Bilu, Yoram.** Without Bounds: The Life & Death of Rabbi Ya'aqov Wazana. LC 99-54753. (Illus.). 192p. 2000. 39.95 (0-8143-2902-0); pap. 17.95 (0-8143-2903-9) Wayne St U Pr.

Bilu, Yoram, jt. ed. see Ben-Ari, Eyal.

Bily, Matej, ed. Cyclic Deformation & Fatigue of Metals. LC 92-31855. (Materials Science Monographs: No. 78). xiv,372p. 1993. 189.50 (0-444-98790-8) Elsevier.

Bily, S. The Buprestidae (Coleoptera) of Fennoscandia & Denmark. (Fauna Entomologica Scandinavica Ser.: No. 10). (Illus.). 1982. pap. 30.00 (87-87491-42-7) Lubrecht & Cramer.

— World Catalogue of the Genus Anthaxia Eschscholtz. 190p. 1998. pap. 79.95 (1-57309-287-8) Intl Scholars.

Bilz. Legal Document Preparation. 1988. teacher ed. write for info. (0-8273-3617-9) Thomson Learn.

Bilz, H. & Kress, W. Phonon Dispersion Relations in Insulators. (Solid-State Sciences Ser.: Vol. 10). (Illus.). 1979. 62.95 (0-387-09399-0) Spr-Verlag.

Bilz, Reed K. & McGlew, Polly A. Legal Document Preparation: The Guide for Preparing & Handling Legal Documents. 172p. (C). 1990. pap. text 19.95 (1-885477-05-8) Fut Horizons.

Bilzer, B. Begriffslexikon der Bildenden Kuenste, 2 vols., Set. (GER.). 320p. 1971. pap. 49.95 (0-8288-6435-7, M7305) Fr & Eur.

Bilzer, Richard. Louisiane. 2nd ed. LC 99-23998. (FRE., Illus.). 416p. 1999. pap. text 23.95 (1-56554-678-4) Pelican.

Bilzing-Ernst, Deborah. The Wisconsin Developmental Guidance Model: A Resource & Planning Guide for School-Community Teams. rev. ed. LC 98-163974. 110p. (C). 1999. pap. text 24.00 (1-57337-047-9) WI Dept Pub Instruct.

Bimba, Anthony. History of the American Working Class. 3rd ed. LC 68-30818. (Illus.). 385p. 1968. reprint ed. lib. bdg. 75.00 (0-8371-0020-8, BIWC, Greenwood Pr) Greenwood.

— The Molly Maguires. LC 75-15046. 144p. 1970. reprint ed. pap. 4.50 (0-7178-0273-6) Intl Pubs Co.

Bimbenet, J. J., et al. Automatic Control of Food & Biological Processes: Proceedings of the ACoFoP III Symposium, Paris, France, 25-26 October, 1994. LC 94-36658. (Developments in Food Science Ser.: Vol. 36). 472p. 1994. 250.50 (0-444-81959-2) Elsevier.

Bimbenet-Privat, Michele, jt. auth. see Cloulas, Ivan.

Bimbenet-Privat, Michele, jt. auth. see Gruber, Alain.

Bimber, Bruce. The Decentralization Mirage: Comparing Decisionmaking Arrangements in Four High Schools. LC 94-26055. 1994. pap. text 7.50 (0-8330-1561-3, MR-459-GGF/LE) Rand Corp.

— The Politics of Expertise in Congress: The Rise & Fall of the Office of Technology Assessment. LC 96-7386. 127p. (C). 1996. text 48.50 (0-7914-3059-6); pap. text 15.95 (0-7914-3060-X) State U NY Pr.

Bimber, Bruce A. School Decentralization: Lessons from the Study of Bureaucracy. LC 93-11802. 1993. pap. 15.00 (0-8330-1354-8, MR-157-GGS/LE) Rand Corp.

***Bimberg, Dieter, et al.** Quantum Dot Heterostructures. LC 98-7734. 338p. 1999. 205.00 (0-471-97388-2) Wiley.

Bimberg, L. The Moroccan Goums: Tribal Warriors in a Modern War, 177. LC 98-52989. (Contributions in Military Studies Ser.: Vol. 177). 176p. 1999. 55.00 (0-313-30913-2) Greenwood.

Bimbo, Alberto Del, see Del Bimbo, Alberto.

***Bimes-Michalak, Beverly.** Teaching for Achievement in Urban Middle Schools. LC 98-206643. xi, 319 p. 1998. 24.00 (0-931054-49-4) Clark Pub.

Bimler, Richard. Angels Can Fly Because They Take Themselves Lightly. LC 92-8586. 96p. 1992. pap. 9.99 (0-570-04577-0, 12-3177) Concordia.

— Word to My Sponsor. 48p. 1998. pap. 4.00 (0-570-03561-9) Concordia.

Bimler, Richard & Schroeder, Theodore W. Miracles in the Middle: Men Who Live the Promise in Midlife. LC 96-44487. 288p. 1997. pap. 10.99 (0-570-04890-7, 12-3307) Concordia.

***Bimler, Richard W. & Bimler, Robert D.** Let There Be Laughter. LC 99-20570. 128p. 1999. pap. 9.99 (0-570-05356-0, 12-3407) Concordia.

Bimler, Robert D., jt. auth. see Bimler, Richard W.

Bimson, John J., ed. see Edersheim, Alfred.

Bin Abd al-Salam, Al-Izz. Maqasid al-Ri'ayah li-Huquq Allah 'Azza wa-Jall, aw Mukhtasar Ri'ayat al-Muhasabi. 192p. 1995. pap. 5.95 (1-57547-210-4) Dar Al-Fikr.

Bin, Alberto & Hill, Richard. Desert Storm: A Forgotten War. LC 98-24040. 304p. 1998. 59.95 (0-275-96319-5, Praeger Pubs); pap. 22.95 (0-275-96320-9, Praeger Pubs) Greenwood.

bin Ali al Mazru'i, Shaykh Al-Amin, see Al-Amin bin Ali al Mazru'i, Shaykh.

Bin, Andrzej K., tr. & contrib. by see Wronski, Stanislaw, et al.

***Bin Idris, Nazmul.** Enterprise Development with JFC Swing: A4, Version 3.07. Oberman, David, ed. (CIW Enterprise Developer Track A4 Ser.). (Illus.). 1999. pap. write for info. (1-58143-081-7) Prosoft I-net.

Bin, Li, tr. see Rusong, Wu, et al.

Bin Mukhtar Tulaymat, Ghazi, jt. auth. see Al-Ilah al-Nabhan, Abd.

Bin-Nabi, Malik. Al-Muslim fi'Alam al-Iqtisad. (Mushkilat al-Hadarah Ser.). 112p. 1987. pap. 3.95 (1-57547-035-7) Dar Al-Fikr.

— Al-Qadaya al-Kubra. (Mushkilat al-Hadarah Ser.). 224p. 1991. pap. 6.95 (1-57547-033-0) Dar Al-Fikr.

— Al-Sira'al-Fikri fi al-bilad al-Musta' Marah. (Mushkilat al-Hadarah Ser.). 144p. 1988. pap. 3.95 (1-57547-028-4) Dar Al-Fikr.

— Al-Zahirah al-Qur'aniyah. (Mushkilat al-Hadarah Ser.). 328p. 1987. pap. 7.95 (1-57547-029-2) Dar Al-Fikr.

— Dawr al-Muslim wa-Risalatuhu fi al-Thuluth al-Akhir min al-Qarn al-'Ishrin. (Mushkilat al-Hadarah Ser.). 64p. 1978. pap. 1.95 (1-57547-026-8) Dar Al-Fikr.

— Fi Mahabb al-Ma 'rakah. (Mushkilat al-Hadarah Ser.). 176p. 1981. pap. 4.95 (1-57547-032-2) Dar Al-Fikr.

— Fikrat al-Afriqiyah al-Asyawiyah. (Mushkilat al-Hadarah Ser.). 268p. 1981. pap. 6.95 (1-57547-030-6) Dar Al-Fikr.

— Fikrat Kumunwilth Islami. (Mushkilat al-Hadarah Ser.). 96p. 1990. pap. 3.95 (1-57547-031-4) Dar Al-Fikr.

— Milad Mujtama': Shabakat Al-Alaqat Al-Ijtima Iyah. (Mushkilat al-Hadarah Ser.). 128p. 1986. pap. 3.95 (1-57547-038-1) Dar Al-Fikr.

— Min Ajl Al-Taghyir. (Mushkilat al-Hadarah Ser.). 144p. 1995. pap. 4.95 (1-57547-211-2) Dar Al-Fikr.

— Mudhakkarat Shahid lil-Qarn. (Mushkilat al-Hadarah Ser.). 456p. 1984. pap. 9.95 (1-57547-034-9) Dar Al-Fikr.

— Mushkilat al-Afkar fi al-'lam al-Islami. (Mushkilat al-Hadarah Ser.). 184p. 1988. pap. 4.95 (1-57547-036-5) Dar Al-Fikr.

— Mushkilat al-Thaqafah. (Mushkilat al-Hadarah Ser.). 152p. 1984. pap. 3.95 (1-57547-037-3) Dar Al-Fikr.

— Shurut al-Nahdah. (Mushkilat al-Hadarah Ser.). 176p. 1987. pap. 4.95 (1-57547-027-6) Dar Al-Fikr.

— Ta'ammulat. (Mushkilat al-Hadarah Ser.). 220p. 1979. pap. 6.95 (1-57547-025-X) Dar Al-Fikr.

— Wijhat al-'lam al-Islami. (Mushkilat al-Hadarah Ser.). 200p. 1986. pap. 4.95 (1-57547-039-X) Dar Al-Fikr.

Bin-Nun, Ariel. The Law of the State of Israel - An Introduction. 2nd ed. 216p. 1992. 34.00 (965-09-0112-4, 73816, Pub. by R Mass Ltd) Lambda Pubs.

Bin-Nun, Judy & Einhorn, Franne. Rosh Hashanah: A Holiday Funtext. (Illus.). (J). (gr. 1-3). 1978. pap. 5.00 (0-8074-0230-3, 101300) UAHC.

Bin-Nun, Judy, et al. Pesach: A Holiday Funtext. (Illus.). 32p. (Orig.). (J). (gr. 1-3). 1983. pap. text 5.00 (0-8074-0161-7, 101310) UAHC.

***Bin-Sallik, Mary Ann.** Aboriginal Women by Degrees: Their Stories of the Journey Towards Academic Achievement. (Illus.). 2000. pap. 19.95 (0-7022-3147-9, Pub. by Univ Queensland Pr) Intl Spec Bk.

***Bin Sayeed, Omer.** Organizational Commitment & Conflict: Studies in Healthy Organizational Processes. LC 99-89252. 2000. pap. write for info. (81-7036-866-9) Sage.

Bin Talal, El H. Christianity in the Arab World. LC 98-10273. 128p. 1998. 12.95 (0-8264-1094-4) Continuum.

Bin Ulwan, Ahmad. Al-Futuh (Diwan wa-Kitab) 576p. 1995. 15.95 (1-57547-209-0) Dar Al-Fikr.

— Al-Mihrajan. 120p. 1995. pap. 3.95 (1-57547-208-2) Dar Al-Fikr.

Bin Wahad, Dhoruba, et al. Still Black, Still Strong: Survivors of the War Against Black Revolutionaries. 270p. Date not set. 7.00 (0-936756-74-8) Autonomedia.

Bin, Yu, ed. The North Pacific Quadrangle Fifty Years After: Balance of Power & Back to the Future. LC 97-11124. 157p. (C). 1997. lib. bdg. 39.00 (1-56072-428-5) Nova Sci Pubs.

Bin, Yu & Tsungting, Chung, eds. Dynamics & Dilemma: Mainland, Taiwan & Hong Kong in a Changing World. LC 96-28731. 237p. (C). 1996. lib. bdg. 95.00 (1-56072-303-3) Nova Sci Pubs.

Bina, Cyrus, et al, eds. Beyond Survival: Wage Labor in the Late Twentieth Century. LC 95-42401. (Labor & Human Resources Ser.). 272p. (C). (gr. 13). 1996. text 74.95 (1-56324-515-9) M E Sharpe.

Bina, Cyrus, et al, eds. Beyond Survival: Wage Labor in the Late Twentieth Century. LC 95-42401. (Labor & Human Resources Ser.). 272p. (C). (gr. 13). 1996. pap. text 34.95 (1-56324-516-7) M E Sharpe.

Bina, Cyrus & Zangeneh, Hamid, eds. Modern Capitalism & Islamic Ideology in Iran. LC 91-12418. 256p. 1992. text 45.00 (0-312-04780-0) St Martin.

Binaghi, Elisabetta, et al. Soft Computing in Remote Sensing Data Analysis: Proceedings of the International Workshop, Milan Italy, Dec. 4-5, 1995. LC 96-8559. (Series in Remote Sensing). 276p. 1996. write for info. (981-02-2757-4) World Scientific Pub.

Binam, Sharyn. By the Sea. (Illus.). 62p. 1999. pap. 10.95 (1-57377-077-9, 0 19884-02300) Easl Pubns.

— Desert Holiday, Vol. 1. (Illus.). 54p. 1997. pap. 10.95 (1-57377-026-4) Easl Pubns.

— Down in the Meadow. 1997. pap. text 9.95 (1-57377-004-3) Easl Pubns.

***Binam, Sharyn.** The Sideload Book, Vol. 2. (Illus.). 56p. 2000. pap. 10.95 (1-57377-093-0, 0-19884-2324) Easl Pubns.

Binam, Sharyn. Sideload Rose Garden. (Illus.). 58p. 1999. pap. 10.95 (1-57377-063-9, O19884-2272) Easl Pubns.

— The Sideload Sea Shells, Vol. 1. (Illus.). 52p. 1998. pap. 10.95 (1-57377-034-5) Easl Pubns.

***Binam, Sharyn, et al.** Etching to Paint. (Illus.). 2000. 10.95 (1-57377-105-8, 0-1988-4-02348-7) Easl Pubns.

Binard, Arthur, tr. see Kijima, Hajime.

Binari, S., et al, eds. Wide-Bandgap Semiconductors for High-Power, High-Frequency & High-Temperature Applications, 1999 Vol. 572: Materials Research Society Symposium Proceedings. LC 99-40454. 559p. 1999. text 74.00 (1-55899-479-3) Materials Res.

Bincer, Adam, tr. see Glasko, V. B.

Binch, Caroline. Since Dad Left. LC 96-37644. (Illus.). 32p. (J). (gr. k-5). 1998. 15.95 (0-7613-0290-5); lib. bdg. 21.40 (0-7613-0357-X) Millbrook Pr.

Binch, Caroline. Down by the River: Afro-Caribbean Rhymes, Games, & Songs for Children. LC 96-2043. 40p. (J). (ps-3). 1996. 16.95 (0-590-69320-4, Cartwheel) Scholastic Inc.

Binchy, D. A. Church & State in Fascist Italy, (Royal Institute of International Affairs Ser.). 1971. 54.00 (0-19-821486-3) OUP.

***Binchy, Maeve.** Aches & Pains. LC 99-87352. (Illus.). 96p. 2000. 10.00 (0-385-33510-5) Delacorte.

Binchy, Maeve. Circle of Friends. 608p. 1991. mass mkt. 7.50 (0-440-21126-3) Dell.

***Binchy, Maeve.** Circle of Friends. LC 99-16780. 1999. write for info. (0-7621-0252-7) RD Assn.

Binchy, Maeve. The Copper Beech. 400p. 1993. mass mkt. 7.50 (0-440-21329-0) Dell.

— Echoes. 494p. 1989. mass mkt. 7.50 (0-440-12209-0) Dell.

— Evening Class. 1997. pap. 6.99 (0-440-29550-5) Dell.

— Evening Class. 544p. 1998. mass mkt. 7.50 (0-440-22320-2, Dell Trade Pbks) Dell.

— Evening Class. large type ed. LC 97-1694. (Core Ser.). 661p. 1997. 28.95 (0-7838-8112-6, G K Hall Lrg Type) Mac Lib Ref.

— Evening Class. large type ed. LC 97-1694. 1999. pap. 26.95 (0-7838-8113-4, G K Hall Lrg Type) Mac Lib Ref.

— Firefly Summer. 672p. 1989. mass mkt. 7.50 (0-440-20419-4) Dell.

— The Glass Lake. LC 94-36104. 592p. 1995. 23.95 (0-385-31354-3) Delacorte.

— The Glass Lake. 768p. 1996. mass mkt. 7.50 (0-440-22159-5) Dell.

— The Glass Lake. large type ed. 911p. 1995. lib. bdg. 26.95 (0-7838-1118-7, G K Hall Lrg Type) Mac Lib Ref.

— The Glass Lake. large type ed. LC 94-38990. 911p. 1996. 23.95 (0-7838-1119-5, G K Hall Lrg Type) Mac Lib Ref.

— Light a Penny Candle. 592p. 1997. mass mkt. 7.50 (0-451-19202-8, Sig) NAL.

— The Lilac Bus. 400p. 1992. mass mkt. 7.50 (0-440-21302-9) Dell.

— The Lilac Bus. large type ed. LC 92-17122. (General Ser.). 480p. 1992. 18.95 (0-8161-5384-1, G K Hall Lrg Type) Mac Lib Ref.

— London Transports. 376p. 1995. mass mkt. 7.50 (0-440-21235-9) Dell.

— London Transports. large type ed. LC 95-16438. (Large Print Bks.). 1995. pap. 22.95 (1-56895-226-0) Wheeler Pub.

— The Return Journey. 240p. 1999. mass mkt. 6.99 (0-440-22459-4) Broadway BDD.

— The Return Journey. LC 97-52624. 224p. 1998. 16.95 (0-385-31506-6) Delacorte.

— Silver Wedding. 432p. 1990. reprint ed. mass mkt. 7.50 (0-440-20777-0) Dell.

— The Storyteller. 1997. pap. text. write for info. (0-582-05063-4) Addison-Wesley.

Binchy, Maeve. Tara Road. Date not set. 24.95 (0-385-31581-3) Delacorte.

Binchy, Maeve. Tara Road. LC 98-33768. 512p. 1999. 24.95 (0-385-33395-1) Delacorte.

***Binchy, Maeve.** Tara Road. 512p. 1999. 1.11 (0-385-33512-1) Dell.

— Tara Road. 656p. 2000. mass mkt. 7.99 (0-440-23559-6) Dell.

— Tara Road. large type ed. LC 98-56658. 743p. 1999. write for info. (0-7540-2212-9) Chivers N Amer.

Binchy, Maeve. Tara Road. large type ed. LC 98-56658. (Paperback Bestsellers Ser.). 1950. pap. 28.95 (0-7862-1837-1) Thorndike Pr.

— Tara Road. large type ed. LC 98-56658. 1999. 30.95 (0-7862-1836-3) Thorndike Pr.

— This Year It Will Be Different: And Other Stories. 272p. 1997. mass mkt. 6.99 (0-440-22357-1, Dell Trade Pbks) Dell.

— Three Complete Novels: The Lilac Bus; Firefly Summer; Silver Wedding. LC 95-10831. 704p. 1995. 13.99 (0-517-14864-1) Random.

***Binchy, Maeve, et al.** Ladies' Night at Finbar's Hotel. Bolger, Dermot, ed. LC 99-56093. 288p. 2000. pap. 14.00 (0-15-600866-1) Harcourt.

Binchy, William. Irish Conflict of Laws. 765p. 1988. boxed set 173.00 (0-86205-220-3, U.K., MICHIE) LEXIS Pub.

Binchy, William, jt. auth. see Burne, R.

Binchy, William, jt. auth. see McMahon, Bryan M.

Bindari-Hammad, A. El & Smith, D. L. Primary Health Care Reviews: Guidelines & Methods. (ENG & FRE.). xiv, 226p. 1992. pap. text 40.00 (92-4-154437-6, 1150374) World Health.

Bindas, Kenneth J. All of This Music Belongs to the Nation: The WPA's Federal Music Project & American Society. LC 95-4375. (Illus.). 184p. 1996. text 26.50 (0-87049-909-2) U of Tenn Pr.

Bindas, Kenneth J., ed. America's Musical Pulse: Popular Music in Twentieth-Century Society. LC 92-893. (Contributions to the Study of Popular Culture Ser.: No. 33). 320p. 1992. pap. 24.95 (0-275-94306-2, B4306, Praeger Pubs) Greenwood.

— America's Musical Pulse: Popular Music in Twentieth-Century Society. 33. LC 92-1122. (Contributions to the Study of Popular Culture Ser.: No. 33). 328p. 1992. 59.95 (0-313-27465-7, BIZ/, Greenwood Pr) Greenwood.

Bindels, J. G., ed. Recent Developments in Infant Nutrition. 416p. (C). 1996. text 147.00 (0-7923-8707-4) Kluwer Academic.

Bindels, J. G., jt. ed. see Viser, H. K.

***Bindemann, Kirsten.** The Future of European Financial Centres. LC 99-20645. 1999. 85.00 (0-415-20403-8) Routledge.

— The Future of European Financial Centres. 4th ed. LC 99-20645. 1999. write for info. (0-415-20520-4) Routledge.

Binder. Fact Investigation. Date not set. text. write for info. (0-314-06534-2); pap. text, teacher ed. write for info. (0-314-86352-4) West Pub.

***Binder, Alan, ed.** Ward's GM Report: GM in the Twentieth Century. (Illus.). 400p. (C). 2000. 100.00 (0-910589-52-6) Wards Comm.

Binder-Arain, Laurel, jt. auth. see Douglas, James A.

Binder, Arnold & Geis, Gilbert. Methods of Research in Criminology & Criminal Justice. 288p. (C). 1983. 35.00 (0-07-005286-7) McGraw.

Binder, Arnold, et al. Juvenile Delinquency: Historical, Cultural, & Legal Perspectives. 2nd ed. LC 97-70226. (C). 1997. pap. 46.95 (0-87084-106-8) Anderson Pub Co.

***Binder, Arnold, et al.** Juvenile Delinquency: Historical, Cultural & Legal Perspectives. 3rd ed. LC 00-38040. 2000. pap. write for info. (1-58360-503-7) Anderson Pub Co.

Binder, Arnold, jt. auth. see Scharf, Peter L.

Binder, Bettye B. Discovering Your Past Lives & Other Dimensions. LC 94-66821. 144p. 1994. pap. 10.00 (1-879005-12-3) Reincarnation Bks.

— Past Life Regression Guidebook: How Our Past Lives Influence Us Now. 2nd rev. ed. 128p. (Orig.). 1993. pap. 13.00 (1-879005-11-5) Reincarnation Bks.

— Past Lives, Present Karma Workbook. 160p. 1986. pap., wbk. ed. 15.00 (1-879005-01-8) Reincarnation Bks.

Binder, Bettye B. & Vito, Mark. Finding Your Life's Purpose Through Astrology Workbook. 60p. (Orig.). 1986. pap. 12.00 (1-879005-03-4) Reincarnation Bks.

Binder, Cynthia, ed. see Kaufman, Julie.

Binder, Daniel. Music for the Listener. 304p. (C). 1995. ring bd. 66.95 (0-7872-1087-0) Kendall-Hunt.

Binder, Daniel J. Civil War Collector's Guide to Albert's Button Book. (Illus.). 84p. 1993. pap. 14.95 (0-942365-05-4) North South Trader.

Binder, David A. & Bergman, Paul. Fact Investigation: From Hypothesis to Proof. LC 84-3676. (American Casebook Ser.). 354p. (C). 1984. reprint ed. 31.50 (0-314-81258-X) West Pub.

An Asterisk (*) at the beginning of an entry indicates that the title is appearing for the first time.

Binder, David A. & Price, Susan C. Legal Interviewing & Counseling: A Client-Centered Approach. (Miscellaneous Ser.). 217p. (C). 1979. pap. text. write for info. (*0-314-51174-1*) West Pub.

— Legal Interviewing & Counselling: A Client-Centered Approach. LC 77-84550. (Hornbook Ser.). 232p. (C). 1977. reprint ed. pap. 21.25 (*0-314-33557-9*) West Pub.

Binder, David A., et al. Lawyers As Counsellors: A Client-Centred Approach. (American Casebook Ser.). 427p. (C). 1990. pap. 28.00 (*0-314-77002-X*) West Pub.

Binder, David F. Hearsay Handbook. LC 83-17600. (Trial Practice Ser.). 521p. 1983. text 95.00 (*0-07-005287-5*) Shepards.

— Hearsay Handbook. 2nd ed. (Trial Practice Ser.). 600p. 1991. text 95.00 (*0-07-172780-9*) Shepards.

Binder, Deanna, jt. auth. see Dheensaw, Cleve.

***Binder, Donald D.** Into the Temple Courts: The Place of the Synagogues in the Second Temple Period. LC 99-44123. (Dissertation Ser.). 566p. 1999. 60.00 (*0-88414-008-3*, 062169, Pub. by Soc Biblical Lit) Scholars Pr GA.

Binder, Eric. Villains Pop-Up: A Pop-Up Book. LC 94-68708. 12p. (J). 1995. 12.95 (*0-7868-3056-5*, Pub. by Disney Pr) Little.

Binder, Frederick M. James Buchanan & the American Empire. LC 94-8922. 1994. 45.00 (*0-945636-64-4*) Susquehanna U Pr.

Binder, Frederick M. & Reimers, David M. All the Nations under Heaven: An Ethnic & Racial History of New York City. LC 94-45085. 368p. 1995. 43.50 (*0-231-07878-1*) Col U Pr.

— The Way We Lived: Essays & Sources in American Social History, 2 vols., Vol. II. LC 87-81182. 328p. (C). 1988. pap. text 29.96 (*0-669-09031-X*) HM Trade Div.

Binder, Frederick M. & Reimers, David M., eds. The Way We Lived: Essays & Documents in American Social History, Vol. 1. 3rd ed. 322p. (C). 2000. pap. text 29.96 (*0-669-39714-8*) HM Trade Div.

— The Way We Lived: Essays & Documents in American Social History, Vol. 2. 3rd ed. 323p. (C). 1996. pap. text 29.96 (*0-669-39715-6*) HM Trade Div.

Binder, Frederick M., jt. auth. see Reimers, David M.

Binder, Guyora. Treaty Conflict & Political Consideration: The Dialectic of Duplicity. LC 88-11756. 234p. 1988. 59.95 (*0-275-93046-7*, C3046, Praeger Pubs) Greenwood.

***Binder, Guyora & Weisberg, Robert.** Literary Criticisms of Law. LC 99-37484. 2000. write for info. (*0-691-00723-3*); pap. text. write for info. (*0-691-00724-1*) Princeton U Pr.

Binder, Henry, ed. see Crane, Stephen.

Binder, Jeffrey L., jt. auth. see Strupp, Hans H.

Binder, Jenni. Digital Photography. LC 98-38214. (Kodak Workshop Ser.). 1999. pap. 24.95 (*0-87985-797-8*, Pub. by Saunders Photo) Sterling.

Binder, K., et al, eds. Cohesion & Structure of Surfaces. (Cohesion & Structure Ser.: Vol. 4). 398p. 1995. 172.00 (*0-444-89829-8*) Elsevier.

Binder, K. & Heermann, Dieter W. Monte Carlo Simulation in Statistical Physics: An Introduction. 3rd ed. LC 97-28559. (Series in Solid-State Sciences: Vol. 80). (Illus.). x, 130p. 1997. pap. 24.95 (*3-540-63265-4*) Spr-Verlag.

Binder, Kate. Easy Edobe Photoshop 5. LC 98-86039. (Easy Ser.). 1998. pap. 19.99 (*0-7897-1770-0*) Que.

Binder, Kate, jt. auth. see Gibbs, Al.

Binder, Kathryn. QuarkXpress Studio Skills. 350p. 1997. 35.00 (*1-56830-391-2*) Hayden.

Binder, Kurt, ed. Applications of the Monte Carlo Method in Statistical Physics. 2nd ed. (Topics in Current Physics Ser.: Vol. 36). (Illus.). 360p. 1987. 57.95 (*0-387-17650-0*) Spr-Verlag.

— Monte Carlo & Molecular Dynamics Simulations in Polymer Science. (Topics in Polymer Science Ser.). (Illus.). 608p. 1995. text 110.00 (*0-19-509438-7*) OUP.

— The Monte-Carlo Method in Condensed Matter Physics. (Topics in Applied Physics Ser.: Vol. 71). (Illus.). 392p. 1992. 67.00 (*0-387-54369-4*) Spr-Verlag.

— The Monte Carlo Method in Condensed Matter Physics, Vol. 71. LC 95-33224. (Topics in Applied Physics Ser.). 430p. 1995. 59.95 (*3-540-60174-0*) Spr-Verlag.

Binder, Kurt & Heermann, D. W. Monte Carlo Simulation in Statistical Physics: An Introduction. (Solid-State Sciences Ser.: Vol. 80). (Illus.). 135p. 1988. 37.00 (*0-387-19107-0*) Spr-Verlag.

— Monte Carlo Simulation in Statistical Physics: An Introduction. 2nd ed. (Illus.). 135p. 1992. 31.95 (*0-387-55729-6*) Spr-Verlag.

Binder, Kurt, jt. auth. see Landau, David.

Binder, L. James. Front & Center: Heroes, War Stories & Army Life. (Association of the U. S. Army Book Ser.). (Illus.). 265p. 1991. 32.00 (*0-08-040586-X*, 3993M); pap. 12.00 (*0-08-041063-4*, 3993M) Brasseys.

Binder, L. James, II. Lemnitzer: A Soldier for His Time. LC 97-19134. (Association of the U. S. Army Book Ser.). 400p. 1997. 32.95 (*1-57488-107-8*) Brasseys.

***Binder, L. James.** Lemnitzer: A Soldier for His Time. (Illus.). 386p. 2000. text 33.00 (*0-7881-9028-8*) DIANE Pub.

Binder, Leonard. In a Moment of Enthusiasm: Political Power & the Second Stratum in Egypt. LC 77-15480. (Illus.). 460p. 1978. lib. bdg. 45.00 (*0-226-05144-7*) U Ch Pr.

— In a Moment of Enthusiasm: Political Power & the Second Stratum in Egypt. LC 77-15480. 459p. Date not set. reprint ed. pap. 142.30 (*0-608-20667-9*, 207210400003) Bks Demand.

— Islamic Liberalism: A Critique of Development Ideologies. LC 88-5455. 416p. 1988. pap. text 24.00 (*0-226-05147-1*) U Ch Pr.

— Islamic Liberalism: A Critique of Development Ideologies. 416p. 1999. lib. bdg. 72.00 (*0-226-05146-3*) U Ch Pr.

Binder, Leonard, ed. The Study of the Middle East: Research & Scholarship in the Humanities & the Social Sciences. LC 76-7408. 655p. reprint ed. pap. 200.00 (*0-608-11654-8*, 205541200021) Bks Demand.

Binder, Leonard, et al. Crises & Sequences in Political Development. LC 79-141952. (Studies in Political Development: No. 7). 337p. reprint ed. pap. 104.50 (*0-8357-6081-2*, 203429400089) Bks Demand.

Binder, Louis R. Modern Religious Cults & Society. LC 77-113556. reprint ed. 34.50 (*0-404-00867-4*) AMS Pr.

***Binder, M. D., ed.** Peripheral & Spinal Mechanisms in the Neural Control of Movement. (Progress in Brain Research Ser.). 498p. 1999. 228.50 (*0-444-50288-2*, Excerpta Medica) Elsevier.

Binder, Marc D. & Mendell, Lorne M., eds. The Segmental Motor System. (Illus.). 416p. 1989. text 68.00 (*0-19-505484-9*) OUP.

Binder, Marilyn R., jt. ed. see Fang, Madeleine W.

Binder, Mark. Crumbs Don't Count: The Rationalization Diet. LC 98-92810. 176p. 1998. pap. 6.50 (*0-380-80015-2*, Avon Bks) Morrow Avon.

— The Everything Bedtime Story Book. LC 98-47668. 1999. pap. 12.95 (*1-58062-147-3*) Adams Media.

***Binder, Mark & Helman, Beth.** Everything Build Your Own Home Page Book. (Illus.). 304p. 2000. pap. 12.95 (*1-58062-339-5*) Adams Media.

Binder, Martin, et al. Choosing Lovers: Patterns of Romance: How You Select Partners in Intimacy, The Ways You Connect & Why You Break Apart. LC 88-83381. 222p. 1989. 21.95 (*0-944435-04-1*) Glenbridge Pub.

Binder, Michael B. Videotex & Teletext: New Online Resources for Libraries. LC 85-5246. (Foundations in Library & Information Science: Vol. 21). 160p. 1985. 78.50 (*0-89232-612-3*) Jai Pr.

Binder, Otto, ed. see Shelley, Mary Wollstonecraft.

Binder, Otto, ed. see Verne, Jules.

Binder, Otto, ed. see Wells, H. G.

Binder, Otto O., jt. auth. see Flind, Max H.

Binder, Pam. The Inscription. Goodfellow, Pamela R., ed. 384p. 1997. pap. 12.99 (*0-9639882-7-1*) Goodfellow Pr.

***Binder, Pam.** The Inscription. 384p. 2000. per. 6.50 (*0-671-04765-5*, Sonnet Bks) PB.

— The Quest. 2000. 19.99 (*1-891761-10-2*) Goodfellow Pr.

— The Quest. 336p. 2000. reprint ed. mass mkt. 6.50 (*0-671-77451-4*) PB.

Binder, Perry S. Cornea, Refractive Surgery, & Contact Lens. LC 87-9633. (Transactions of the New Orleans Academy of Ophthalmology Ser.). 336p. 1987. reprint ed. pap. 104.20 (*0-608-04700-7*, 206542100004) Bks Demand.

Binder, Raymond C. Fluid Mechanics. 5th ed. (Illus.). 448p. 1973. text 67.00 (*0-13-322594-1*) P-H.

Binder, Robert. Testing Object-Oriented Systems: Models Patterns. LC 99-45602. 1152p. (C). 1999. 69.95 (*0-201-80938-9*) Addison-Wesley.

Binder, Rudi. The Meaning: An Odyssey in Medicine. 291p. (YA). 1998. per. 11.95 (*1-893309-01-0*, 2) Red Maple Pubg.

— More Than Meets the Eye: A Candid Journal of Two Eye Surgeons. 2nd rev. ed. 210p. (YA). 1999. reprint ed. per. 11.95 (*1-893309-00-2*, 1) Red Maple Pubg.

Binder, Rudolph M., jt. ed. see Bliss, William D.

Binder, Sarah A. Minority Rights, Majority Rule. 250p. 1997. text 59.95 (*0-521-58239-3*); pap. text 18.95 (*0-521-58792-1*) Cambridge U Pr.

Binder, Sarah A. & Smith, Steven S. Politics or Principle? Filibustering in the United States Senate. 247p. 1997. 38.95 (*0-8157-0952-8*); pap. 16.95 (*0-8157-0951-X*) Brookings.

***Binder, Sibylle L. & Wolf, Gefion.** Horseback Riding for Beginners. (Illus.). 144p. 1998. 19.95 (*0-8069-6205-4*) Sterling.

Binder, Steffen. Die Idee der Konsumentensouveranitat in der Wettbewerbstheorie: Teleokratische vs. Nomokratische Auffassung. (GER.). (Orig.). 1996. 63.95 (*3-631-30688-1*) P Lang Pubng.

Binder, Timothy, jt. auth. see Russell, Walter.

Binder, Tonia, ed. Mystic Aquarium Cookbook. (Illus.). 160p. (Orig.). 1995. write for info. (*0-915897-06-7*) Mystic Marinelife Aquarium.

Binder, Wolfgang, ed. Creoles & Cajuns: French Louisiana - La Louisiane Francaise. LC 98-205648. (Illus.). XIII, 344p. 1998. per. text 51.95 (*0-8204-3244-X*) P Lang Pubng.

Binder, Wolfgang & Breinig, Helmbrecht, eds. American Contradictions: Interviews with Nine American Writers. LC 94-39055. (Illus.). 205p. 1995. text 19.95 (*0-8195-5282-8*, Wesleyan Univ Pr) U Pr of New Eng.

***Binder, Z., et al.** Management & Control of Production & Logistics (MCPL '97) A Proceedings Volume from the IFAC IFIP Conference, Campinas, SP, Brazil, 31 August-3 September, 1997. LC 98-24451. 1998. 166.50 (*0-08-043036-8*, Pergamon Pr) Elsevier.

Binder, Zane. Go for Broke! Wealth & Happiness after Bankruptcy. LC 97-226706. 104p. 1997. pap. 14.00 (*0-87364-942-7*) Paladin Pr.

Binderman, Murray B., et al. The Life: The Love & Poetry of the Black Hustler. 224p. 1986. mass mkt. 3.50 (*0-87067-367-X*, BH367) Holloway.

***Bindert, Patricia M.** Bide-a-While Mobile Home Park. 28p. 1999. pap. 6.00 (*0-9648232-7-6*) Frith Pr.

Bindewald, Helene. Die Sprache der Reichskanzlei Zur Zeit Konig Wenzels. (GER.). lxix, 270p. 1985. reprint ed. write for info. (*3-487-07527-X*) G Olms Pubs.

Bindiganavale, Sunil & Volakis, John L. Scattering by a Groove in an Impedance Plane. LC QC0676.7. (University of Michigan Reports: No. 030601-2-T). 21p. reprint ed. pap. 30.00 (*0-7837-6784-6*, 204661600003) Bks Demand.

***Binding, Guenther.** High Gothic: The Age of the Great Cathedrals. (World Architecture Ser.: No. 12). (Illus.). 240p. 1999. 29.99 (*3-8228-7055-2*) Taschen Amer.

Binding, H., jt. ed. see Reinert, J.

***Binding, Paul.** Babel Guide to Scandinavian Fiction. 224p. 2000. pap. 19.95 (*1-899460-30-6*, Pub. by Boulevard-Babel) Paul & Co Pubs.

Binding, Rudolf G. Das Heiligtum der Pferde. (GER., Illus.). 108p. 1982. write for info. (*3-487-08242-X*) G Olms Pubs.

— Reitvorschrift fur eine Geliebte. (GER., Illus.). 80p. 1995. write for info. (*3-487-08369-8*) G Olms Pubs.

Binding, Tim. Lying with the Enemy. 368p. 1999. 24.00 (*0-7867-0657-0*) Carroll & Graf.

***Binding, Tim.** Lying with the Enemy. 368p. 2000. reprint ed. pap. 12.95 (*0-7867-0809-3*, Pub. by Carroll & Graf) Publishers Group.

Binding, Tim. A Perfect Execution. 320p. 1996. write for info. (*0-385-25587-X*) Doubleday.

Bindler. Developing Child. 1999. pap. text 35.95 (*0-8385-1586-X*, Medical Exam) Appleton & Lange.

Bindler, Paul R., ed. Proceedings of the Association of Orthodox Jewish Scientists: Behavioral & Social Sciences, Vol. 10. 160p. (Orig.). 1989. pap. 12.50 (*0-87203-131-4*) Hermon.

Bindler, Ruth M. & Howry, Linda Berner. Pediatric Drugs & Nursing Implications. 2nd rev. ed. LC 96-18530. 640p. (C). 1996. pap. text 39.95 (*0-8385-8085-8*, A8085-1) Appleton & Lange.

Bindler, Ruth M., jt. auth. see Ball, Jane.

Bindley, T. Herbert. Letter of the Churches of Vienne & Lyons to the Churches of Asia & Phrygia in 177 A. D. 1991. reprint ed. pap. 2.95 (*0-89981-220-1*) Eastern Orthodox.

Bindley, T. Herbert, ed. The Ecumenical Documents of the Faith: The Creed of Nicea; Three Epistles of Cyril; The Tome of Leo; The Chalcedonian Definition. 4th ed. LC 79-8708. 246p. 1980. reprint ed. lib. bdg. 59.50 (*0-313-22197-9*, BIOD) Greenwood.

Bindloss, H. & Pinnock, J. In the Niger Country, Benin: The Surrounding Country, Inhabitants, Customs, & Trade. 398p. 1968. reprint ed. 47.50 (*0-7146-1791-1*, Pub. by F Cass Pubs) Intl Spec Bk.

Bindman, Catherine, ed. see Dubansky, Mindell.

Bindman, David. Hogarth. LC 86-51572. (World of Art Ser.). (Illus.). 216p. 1985. pap. 14.95 (*0-500-20182-X*, Pub. by Thames Hudson) Norton.

— Hogarth. LC 86-51572. (World of Art Ser.). (Illus.). 216p. 1985. 19.95 (*0-500-18182-9*, Pub. by Thames Hudson) Norton.

— Hogarth & His Times. LC 97-20496. 192p. 1998. pap. 29.95 (*0-520-21300-9*, Pub. by U CA Pr) Cal Prin Full Svc.

— Roubiliac & the Eighteenth Century Monument. 1995. 65.00 (*0-300-06333-4*) Yale U Pr.

Bindman, David, ed. The Illuminated Books of William Blake. Date not set. pap. 165.00 (*0-691-00179-0*, Pub. by Princeton U Pr) Cal Prin Full Svc.

Bindman, David, ed. The Thames & Hudson Encyclopaedia of British Art. LC 84-51499. (World of Art Ser.). (Illus.). 320p. 1988. pap. 14.95 (*0-500-20229-X*, Pub. by Thames Hudson) Norton.

Bindman, David, et al, eds. The Illuminated Books of William Blake: Jerusalem: the Emanation of the Giant Albion. (Illus.). 292p. 1991. 85.00 (*0-691-06935-2*, Pub. by Princeton U Pr) Cal Prin Full Svc.

***Bindman, David, intro.** William Blake: The Complete Illuminated Books. LC 00-101383. (Illus.). 464p. 2000. 60.00 (*0-500-51014-8*, Pub. by Thames Hudson) Norton.

Bindman, David & Wilcox, Scott, eds. Among the Whores & Thieves: William Hogarth & the Beggar's Opera. LC 96-61829. (Illus.). 112p. 1997. pap. 12.95 (*0-930606-80-9*) Yale Ctr Brit Art.

Bindman, David, ed. see Schinkel, Karl F.

Bindman, Geoffrey, ed. see International Commission of Jurists.

Bindman, L., et al, eds. Women Physiologists: An Anniversary Celebration of Their Contribution to British Physiology. (Illus.). 164p. (Orig.). (C). 1993. pap. text 20.00 (*1-85578-049-6*, Pub. by Portland Pr Ltd) Ashgate Pub Co.

Bindman, Lynn, et al. Multiple Choice Questions in Physiology: With Answers & Explanatory Comments. 3rd ed. LC 96-46366. (An Arnold Publication). (Illus.). 144p. 1997. pap. text 17.50 (*0-340-67677-9*, Pub. by E A) OUP.

Bindman, Yirmeyahu. Rabbi Moshe Chaim Luzzatto: His Life & Works. LC 94-12660. 200p. 1995. 30.00 (*1-56821-293-3*) Aronson.

— The Seven Colors of the Rainbow: Torah Ethics for Non-Jews. LC 95-19163. (Or L'amim Ser.). 173p. 1995. pap. 14.95 (*0-89390-332-9*, Pub. by Resource Pubns) Feldheim.

Bindman, Yirmeyanu. Lord George Gordon. 250p. 1991. 15.95 (*1-56062-056-0*); pap. 12.95 (*1-56062-057-9*) CIS Comm.

Bindman, Yirmiyahu. On Two Fronts. LC 90-82062. (C). 1990. 14.95 (*1-56062-028-5*) CIS Comm.

Bindmann, W. Dictionary of Solid State Physics & Electronics Technology: English-German, German-English. (Technical Dictionary Ser.). (ENG & GER.). 1973. 31.50 (*0-685-27547-7*) Adlers Foreign Bks.

Bindmann, Werner. Dictionary of Optics & Optical Engineering: German-English, English-German. 2nd ed. (ENG & GER.). 688p. 1992. 195.00 (*0-8288-7380-1*, M7402) Fr & Eur.

— English - German, German - English Dictionary of Microelectronics. 4th ed. (ENG & GER.). 688p. 1992. 125.00 (*0-8288-0286-6*, M15114) Fr & Eur.

— Festkoerperphysik und Elektronische Technik. (ENG & GER.). 1104p. 1972. 125.00 (*0-8288-6392-X*, M7410, Pub. by O Brandstetter Verlag) Trafalgar.

Bindmann, Werner, ed. German Dictionary of Microelectronics: Worterbuch Mikroelektronik Englisch. (GER.). 800p. (C). 1999. 110.00 (*0-415-17340-X*) Routledge.

— Optics & Optical Instrumentation: Dictionary, Vol. 1: E to G. (ENG & GER.). 450p. 1974. 59.50 (*3-7684-6411-3*) Adlers Foreign Bks.

— Optics & Optical Instrumentation: Dictionary, Vol. 2: G to E. (ENG & GER.). 450p. 1974. 59.50 (*3-7684-6512-8*) Adlers Foreign Bks.

Bindocci, Cynthia G. Women & Technology: An Annotated Bibliography. LC 92-34400. (Women's History & Culture Ser.: Vol. 7). 248p. 1993. text 20.00 (*0-8240-5789-9*, SS517) Garland.

Bindon, Kathleen R. Inventories & Foreign Currency Translation Requirements. LC 82-21729. (Research for Business Decisions Ser.: No. 56). 157p. reprint ed. pap. 48.70 (*0-8357-1391-1*, 207036100088) Bks Demand.

Bindra, Dalbir. Motivation: A Systematic Reinterpretation. LC 59-6101. (Illus.). 371p. reprint ed. pap. 115.10 (*0-608-11275-5*, 201255900081) Bks Demand.

Bindra, Dalbir, ed. The Brain's Mind: A Neuroscience Perspective on the Mind-Body Problem. LC 80-13998. (Illus.). 128p. 1980. text 23.95 (*0-89876-003-8*) Gardner Pr.

Bindslev, Anne M. Mrs. Humphrey Ward: A Study in Late-Victorian Feminine Consciousness & Creative Expression. 172p. (Orig.). 1985. pap. text 35.00 (*91-22-00731-8*) Coronet Bks.

Bine, Linda, jt. auth. see Levine, Judith.

Bines, Hazel, jt. ed. see Roaf, Caroline.

***Bines, Jonathan & Greenberg, Gary.** Self-Helpless: The Greatest Self-Help Books You'll Never Read. LC 99-11636. (Illus.). 160p. (Orig.). 1999. pap. 12.99 (*1-56414-411-9*) Career Pr Inc.

Binet, Alfred. Alterations of Personality, 5. Baldwin, Helen G., tr. from FRE. LC 77-72191. (Contributions to the History of Psychology Ser.). 346p. 1977. reprint ed. lib. bdg. 79.50 (*0-313-26944-0*, U6944, Greenwood Pr) Greenwood.

— Las Ideas Modernas Sobre los Ninos. (SPA.). pap. 9.99 (*968-16-2111-5*, Pub. by Fondo) Continental Bk.

— Modern Ideas about Children. Heisler, Suzanne, tr. from FRE. LC 86-162049. 235p. (Orig.). 1984. pap. 20.00 (*0-9617054-1-8*) S Heisler.

Binet, Alfred. The Psychology of Reasoning. 201p. 55.00 (*1-85506-674-2*) Thoemmes Pr.

Binet, Alfred & Simon, Thomas. The Development of Intelligence in Children. LC 73-2962. (Classics in Psychology Ser.). 1975. reprint ed. 25.95 (*0-405-05135-2*) Ayer.

Binet, Calla M. Tears Flow, Ice Melts, Spring Comes! A Soul Blossoms. LC 97-177579. 200p. (Orig.). 1997. pap. 14.00 (*1-889245-03-8*) Glden Reed.

Binet, Helene, photos by. House of the Book - Beth Sepher: Zvi Hecker's Jewish Community School in Berlin. (Illus.). 112p. 1999. pap. 29.95 (*1-901033-15-5*, Pub. by Black Dog Pubg) RAM Publications.

***Binet, Helene & Muller, Lars, eds.** The Architecture of Zaha Hadid in Photographs by Helene Binet. (Illus.). 176p. 2000. 65.00 (*3-907078-12-8*, Pub. by Lars Muller) Princeton Arch.

Binet, Helene, jt. auth. see Zumthor, Peter.

Binet, Pere. Divine Favors Granted to Saint Joseph. LC 82-50590. 177p. 1992. reprint ed. pap. 5.00 (*0-89555-187-X*) TAN Bks Pubs.

Binette, Andre, jt. auth. see Boucher, Francine.

Binette, Dennis A., jt. auth. see Martins, Michael.

Binette, Reynald. French - English Vocabulary of Panels Derived from Wood. (ENG & FRE.). 83p. 1985. pap. 29.95 (*0-8288-9383-7*) Fr & Eur.

— French - English Vocabulary of Upholstery. (ENG & FRE.). 91p. 1985. pap. 29.95 (*0-8288-9384-5*) Fr & Eur.

— French - English Vocabulary of Wood Turning. (ENG & FRE.). 39p. 1985. pap. 19.95 (*0-8288-9407-8*) Fr & Eur.

***Binetti, Marianne.** Annuals for Washington & Oregon. (Illus.). 256p. 2000. pap. 18.95 (*1-55105-160-5*) Lone Pine.

— Carefree Landscapes: 500 Simple Ideas. 1999. 14.95 (*1-58017-211-3*) Storey Bks.

— Easy Answers for Great Gardens: 500 Tips, Techniques & Outlandish Ideas. LC 99-47199. (Illus.). 272p. 2000. pap. 14.95 (*1-57061-213-7*) Sasquatch Bks.

Binetti, Marianne. Shortcuts for Accenting Your Garden: Over Five Hundred Easy & Inexpensive Tips. Webb, Sandra, ed. LC 92-54654. (Illus.). 144p. (Orig.). 1993. pap. 9.95 (*0-88266-829-3*, Garden Way Pub) Storey Bks.

— Tips for Carefree Landscapes: Over Five Hundred Sure-Fire Ways to Beautify Your Yard & Garden. Watson, Ben, ed. LC 89-45739. (Illus.). 168p. (Orig.). 1990. 16.95 (*0-88266-604-5*, Garden Way Pub); pap. 9.95 (*0-88266-572-3*, Garden Way Pub) Storey Bks.

***Binetti, Marianne & Beck, Alison.** Perennials for Washington & Oregon. (Illus.). 352p. 2000. pap. 18.95 (*1-55105-162-1*) Lone Pine.

Binetti, Marianne, jt. auth. see Beck, Alison.

Binfield, Clyde. Sainthood Revisioned: Studies in Hagiography & Biography. (Individual Titles in Religion Ser.). 143p. 1995. 47.50 (*1-85075-289-3*, Pub. by Sheffield Acad) CUP Services.

Binfield, Clyde, jt. ed. see Hey, David.

Binford. El Mozote Massacre: Anthropology & Human Rights. LC 96-10097. (Hegemony & Experience Ser.). (Illus.). 263p. 1996. pap. 19.95 (*0-8165-1662-6*) U of Ariz Pr.

Binford, Carol. Natures Palette. 100p. 1992. pap. text 10.50 (*1-56770-248-1*) S Scheewe Pubns.

Binford, Henry C. The First Suburbs: Residential Communities on the Boston Periphery, 1815-1860. LC 84-16127. (Illus.). 273p. 1985. 25.00 (*0-226-05158-7*) U Ch Pr.

— The First Suburbs: Residential Communities on the Boston Periphery, 1815-1860. LC 84-16127. (Illus.). 320p. 1996. pap. text 16.95 (*0-226-05159-5*) U Ch Pr.

— The First Suburbs: Residential Communities on the Boston Periphery, 1815-1860. LC 84-16127. (Illus.). 318p. Date not set. reprint ed. pap. 98.60 (*0-608-21017-X*, 205454500003) Bks Demand.

Binford, J. C. History of Hancock County, Indiana. (Illus.). 536p. 1992. reprint ed. lib. bdg. 54.00 (*0-8328-2538-7*) Higginson Bk Co.

Binford, L. C. A Distributional Survey of the Birds of the Mexican State of Oaxaca. (Ornithological Monographs: Vol. 43). (Illus.). 418p. 1989. 20.00 (*0-943610-54-0*) Am Ornithologists.

Binford, Leigh. The El Mozote Massacre: Anthropology & Human Rights. LC 96-10097. (Hegemony & Experience Ser.). (Illus.). 263p. 1996. 45.00 (*0-8165-1661-8*) U of Ariz Pr.

Binford, Leigh, jt. auth. see Cook, Scott.

Binford, Lewis R. Working at Archaeology. (Studies in Archaeology). 1983. text 60.00 (*0-12-100060-5*) Acad Pr.

Binford, Lewis R., ed. Debating Archaeology. 534p. 1989. text 45.00 (*0-12-100045-1*) Acad Pr.

***Binford, Lewis Roberts.** Constructing Frames of Reference: An Analytical Method for Archaeological Theory Building Using Hunter-Gatherer & Enviromental Data Sets. LC 00-28714. 2001. write for info. (*0-520-22393-4*) U CA Pr.

Binford, Tom & Kichler, Florrie B. A Checkered Past: My Twenty Years As Indy 500 Chief Steward. LC 93-90170. (Illus.). 144p. (Orig.). 1993. pap. 14.95 (*1-882859-01-4*) Patria Pr.

***Binford, Virgie M. & Cowling, Dorothy N.** Self-Esteem Enhancers: Inner-Directed Guidelines for Successful Living. LC 99-66910. 128p. 1999. 18.95 (*1-57736-166-0*) Providence Hse.

Bing, Alexander M. War-Time Strikes & Their Adjustment. LC 79-156405. (American Labor Ser., No. 2). 1977. reprint ed. 25.95 (*0-405-02915-2*) Ayer.

***Bing, Benny.** High-Speed Wireless ATM & LANs. LC 99-52311. 268p. 2000. 75.00 (*1-58053-092-3*) Artech Hse.

Bing, Caryn, ed. see Chamallas, Stan, et al.

Bing, Charles C. Lordship Salvation Grace Life Edition: A Biblical Evaluation & Response. 205p. 1997. pap. 10.00 (*0-9701365-0-1*) Grace Life.

***Bing, Charlie.** Dear John. 16p. 1998. pap. 0.50 (*0-9701365-1-X*) Grace Life.

Bing, Christopher H., jt. auth. see Thayer, Ernest Lawrence.

Bing, Claudine. Painting Out of Sorrow. LC 98-43468. (Illus.). 88p. 1999. 19.95 (*1-883280-12-5*) Font & Ctr Pr.

Bing, Elisabeth D. Elisabeth Bing's Guide to Moving Through Pregnancy: Advice from America's Foremost Childbirth Educator on Making Pregnancy as Physically Comfortable as Possible, at Home & at Work. (Illus.). 166p. 1992. pap. 12.00 (*0-374-52297-9*) FS&G.

— Moving Through Pregnancy. LC 74-17673. 144p. 1975. pap. write for info. (*0-672-52095-8*) Macmillan.

— Six Practical Lessons for an Easier Childbirth. 3rd rev. ed. LC 93-26507. (Illus.). 176p. 1994. pap. 11.95 (*0-553-37369-2*) Bantam.

Bing, Elizabeth. Laughter & Tears: The Emotional Life of New Mothers. LC 96-46089. (Illus.). 272p. (Orig.). 1995. pap. 16.95 (*0-8050-4157-5*, Owl) H Holt & Co.

Bing, Gordon. Corporate Acquisitions. fac. ed. LC 80-22386. 260p. pap. 80.60 (*0-7837-7422-2*, 204721700006) Bks Demand.

— Corporate Divestment. LC 77-86528. 180p. reprint ed. pap. 55.80 (*0-608-18153-6*, 203284300081) Bks Demand.

— Due Diligence Techniques & Analysis: Critical Questions for Business Decisions. LC 95-51411. 288p. 1996. 69.50 (*1-56720-029-X*, Quorum Bks) Greenwood.

Bing, John. Handbook of Legal Information Retrieval. LC 84-1177. 1984. 136.00 (*0-444-87576-X*) Elsevier.

Bing, John W., jt. ed. see Kinsey, David C.

Bing, Jonathan, ed. Writing for Your Life, Vol. 4. 295p. 2000. 28.00 (*1-888889-12-8*, Pub. by Pushcart Pr) Norton.

Bing, Jonathan, jt. ed. see Steinberg, Sybil S.

Bing, Leon. Do or Die: For the First Time, Members of L.A.'s Most Notorious Teenage Gangs - The Crips & the Bloods Speak for Themselves. LC 90-55922. 304p. 1992. reprint ed. pap. 13.00 (*0-06-092291-5*, Perennial) HarperTrade.

Bing, Peter. Games of Venus: An Anthology of Greek & Roman Erotic Verse from Sappho to Ovid. 224p. (C). (gr. 13). 1993. pap. 20.99 (*0-415-90261-4*, Pub. by Tavistock) Routldge.

Bing, Peter, tr. see Burkert, Walter.

Bing, R. H. The Geometric Topology of 3-Manifolds. LC 83-14962. (Colloquium Publications: Vol. 40). 238p. 1983. text 74.00 (*0-8218-1040-5*, COLL/40) Am Math.

Bing, R. H., ed. see Topology Seminar (1965: University of Wisconsin) S.

Bing, Richard J. Cardiology: Evolution of Ideas. LC 92-1542. 319p. 1992. text 74.00 (*3-7186-0549-X*) Gordon & Breach.

Bing, Richard J., ed. Cardiology: The Evolution of the Science & the Art. LC 92-1542. 319p. 1992. pap. text 29.00 (*3-7186-0554-6*) Gordon & Breach.

— Cardiology: The Evolution of the Science & the Art. 2nd ed. LC 98-44410. (Illus.). 368p. (C). 1999. text 55.00 (*0-8135-2627-2*); pap. text 24.00 (*0-8135-2628-0*) Rutgers U Pr.

Bing, Richard J., jt. ed. see Morin, Robert J.

Bing, Rudolf. Five Thousand Nights at the Opera. 27.95 (*0-8488-0430-9*) Amereon Ltd.

— Five Thousand Nights at the Opera. 360p. reprint ed. lib. bdg. 49.00 (*0-685-14894-7*) Rprt Serv.

Bing, Stanley. Lloyd: What Happened. 432p. 1999. pap. 15.00 (*0-375-70564-3*) Vin Bks.

***Bing, Stanley.** What Would Machiavelli Do: The Ends Justify the Meanness. LC 99-52084. 176p. 2000. 21.00 (*0-06-662011-2*) HarpC.

Bingam, Stephen & Brinkmeier, Hermina. Genealogy of Bingham Family. 1208p. 1999. boxed set 75.00 (*1-886855-29-3*) Tavenner Pub.

Bingaman, Ron, jt. auth. see Doody, Alan F.

Bingay, Malcolm. Of Me I Sing. (American Autobiography Ser.). 300p. 1995. reprint ed. lib. bdg. 79.00 (*0-7812-8459-7*) Rprt Serv.

Bingea, Marian L., jt. auth. see Brammer, Lawrence M.

Bingel, Christina, jt. auth. see Bartelme, Nicole.

Bingelis, Tony. Firewall Forward: Airplane Engine Installation Methods. Rivers, David A., ed. (Illus.). 303p. reprint ed. pap. 19.95 (*0-940000-93-8*, 21-13950) EAA Aviation.

— Firewall Forward: Engine Installation Methods. Rivers, David A., ed. (Tony Bingelis Ser.). (Illus.). 295p. 1992. reprint ed. pap. 19.95 (*0-940000-29-6*) EAA Aviation.

— The Shortplane Builder: Aircraft Construction Methods. Rivers, David A., ed. (Tony Bingelis Ser.). (Illus.). 319p. 1992. reprint ed. pap. 17.95 (*0-940000-57-1*) EAA Aviation.

— The Sportplane Builder. rev. ed. Rivers, David A., ed. (Illus.). 320p. 1992. pap. 19.95 (*0-940000-30-X*) EAA Aviation.

— Sportplane Construction: A Builder's Handbook. Hawkins, Teresa, ed. (Illus.). 366p. 1986. reprint ed. pap. 20.95 (*0-940000-92-X*, 21-01395) EAA Aviation.

— Sportplane Construction Techniques: A Builder's Handbook. Hawkins, Tressa, ed. (Tony Bingelis Ser.). (Illus.). 368p. 1992. reprint ed. pap. 20.95 (*0-940000-31-8*) EAA Aviation.

— Tony Bingelis on Engines, Vol. 4. 240p. 1995. pap. 21.95 (*0-940000-54-7*) EAA Aviation.

Bingemer, Maria C., jt. auth. see Gebara, Ivone.

Bingen, Hildegard Von, see Von Bingen, Hildegard.

***Bingen, R. James, et al, eds.** Democracy & Development in Mali. 352p. 2000. pap. 29.95 (*0-87013-560-0*) Mich St U Pr.

Binger, Brian, ed. Microeconomics with Calculus. 2nd ed. LC 97-25855. (Illus.). 633p. (C). 1997. 98.00 (*0-321-01225-9*) Addson-Wesley Educ.

Binger, Cathy, jt. auth. see Light, Janice B.

Binger, Tilde. Asherah: Goddesses in Ugarit, Israel & the Old Testament. LC 97-205267. (JSOTS Ser.: No. 232). 190p. 1997. 57.50 (*1-85075-637-6*, Pub. by Sheffield Acad) CUP Services.

Bingham. Blitzed: The Battle of France, May-June, 1940. write for info. (*1-871187-07-9*) Air Res Pubns.

— Buying Jewelry. pap. 5.99 (*0-685-69319-8*, Harp PBks) HarpC.

***Bingham.** Economics of Central City Neighborhoods. 2000. 69.00 (*0-8133-9771-5*, Pub. by Westview) HarpC.

Bingham. Edge of Despair. 1997. pap. 6.99 (*0-907927-72-6*) Emerald House Group Inc.

— Freedom Fighter. 1997. pap. 5.99 (*1-85792-371-5*, Pub. by Christian Focus) Spring Arbor Dist.

— The Nightingale Sings. LC 96-209224. 1997. mass mkt. 8.99 (*0-553-40895-X*) Bantam.

***Bingham.** The Nightingale Sings. 2000. 29.95 (*0-385-40610-X*, Pub. by Transworld Publishers Ltd) Trafalgar.

Bingham. Paws Presents: ClarisWorks 4.0 Mac Tutorial. (DA - K-8 Computer Education Ser.). (YA). 1997. text 22.95 (*0-538-66075-9*) S-W Pub.

— Paws Presents: Using ClarisWorks for MAC. (DA - Computer Education Ser.). (J). (gr. k-8). 1997. text 22.95 (*0-538-65118-0*); text 22.95 (*0-538-65126-1*) S-W Pub.

— Paws Presents: Using ClarisWorks for MAC. (DA - Computer Education Ser.). (J). (gr. k-8). 1997. text 22.95 (*0-538-65122-9*) S-W Pub.

— Paws Presents: Using ClarisWorks for MAC. (DA - Computer Education Ser.). (J). (gr. k-8). 1997. text 22.95 (*0-538-65114-8*) S-W Pub.

***Bingham.** To Hear A Nightingale. 2000. pap. 10.95 (*0-553-17635-8*, Pub. by Transworld Publishers Ltd) Trafalgar.

Bingham. Trailblazer. 1998. pap. 5.99 (*1-85792-370-7*, Pub. by Christian Focus) Spring Arbor Dist.

Bingham & Stryker, Sandy. Mother Nature Nursery Rhymes. Paine, ed. (Illus.). 32p. (J). (ps up). 1990. 14.95 (*0-911655-01-8*) Advocacy Pr.

Bingham, Kevin. Black in Business. (Illus.). 31p. 1999. pap. 10.00 (*0-9670906-0-1*, KDB0001) FourUTwoC Prods.

Bingham, A. Walker. The Snake-Oil Syndrome: Patent Medicine Advertising. LC 93-72216. (Illus.). 1994. 40.00 (*0-8158-0484-9*) Chris Mass.

Bingham, Al, jt. auth. see Finger, Alan.

Bingham, Alfred M. The Tiffany Fortune: And Other Chronicles of a Connecticut Family. LC 96-1360. (Illus.). 448p. 1996. 35.00 (*0-9650357-1-9*) Abeel Pubs.

Bingham, Alfred M. & Rodman, Selden, eds. Challenge to the New Deal. LC 79-156614. (Essay Index Reprint Ser.). 1977. reprint ed. 26.95 (*0-8369-2269-7*) Ayer.

***Bingham, Alfred M. & Shapere, Alfreda.** Explorer of Machu Picchu: Portrait of Hiram Bingham. 2nd unabridged ed. LC 99-10336. (Illus.). 408p. 2000. reprint ed. pap. 15.95 (*0-9613602-2-4*) Triune Bks.

Bingham, Allen H., et al, eds. Acoustic Emission Testing of Aerial Devices & Associated Equipment Used in the Utility Industries. LC 92-19624. (Special Technical Publication Ser.: No. 1139). (Illus.). 90p. 1992. text 21.00 (*0-8031-1433-8*, STP1139) ASTM.

Bingham, Anne, et al. Exploring the Multiage Classroom. LC 95-12556. (Illus.). 264p. (C). 1995. pap. text 21.00 (*1-57110-013-X*) Stenhse Pubs.

Bingham, Anne, jt. auth. see MacDonald, Jeffrey A.

Bingham, Anson. Law of Executory Contracts for the Sale of Real Property. xlviii, 862p. 1997. reprint ed. 110.00 (*0-8377-1986-0*, Rothman) W S Hein.

***Bingham, Areta.** Tole-Painted Outdoor Projects: Decorative Designs for Gardens, Patios, Decks & More. LC 99-87166. (Illus.). 2000. write for info. (*0-8069-4486-2*) Sterling.

Bingham, B. Negligence, All Modern Cases On. 3rd rev. ed. (C). 1978. 800.00 (*0-7855-4073-3*, Pub. by Witherby & Co) St Mut.

Bingham, Berek. C.S. the Storyteller. 1999. pap. text 5.99 (*1-85792-487-8*) Christian Focus.

Bingham, Bruce. The Sailor's Sketchbook. (Illus.). 144p. 1987. pap. text 15.95 (*0-07-155096-8*) Intl Marine.

Bingham, C. T. Hymenoptera: Ants & Cuckoowasps, Vol. 2. (Fauna of British India Ser.). xx, 508p. 1975. reprint ed. 25.00 (*0-88065-063-X*) Scholarly Pubns.

— Hymenoptera: Wasps & Bees, Vol. 1. (Fauna of British India Ser.). xxx, 590p. 1975. reprint ed. 30.00 (*0-88065-062-1*) Scholarly Pubns.

Bingham, Caleb. The American Preceptor, 1818: Lessons in Reading & Speaking. 226p. 1998. reprint ed. pap. 35.00 (*0-87556-867-X*) Saifer.

— Columbian Orator: Containing a Variety of Original & Selected Pieces Together with Rules Calculated to Improve Youth & Others in the Ornamental & Useful Art of Eloquence (1811) 302p. 1999. reprint ed. pap. 19.95 (*0-7661-0821-X*) Kessinger Pub.

— Young Lady's Accidence. LC 81-5663. (American Linguistics Ser.). 168p. 1981. reprint ed. 50.00 (*0-8201-1360-3*) Schol Facsimiles.

Bingham, Caleb & Blight, David W. The Columbian Orator: Containing a Variety of Original & Selected Pieces Together with Rules, Which Are Calculated to Improve Youth & Others, in the Ornamental & Useful Art of Eloquence. LC 97-35955. 296p. 1997. text 50.00 (*0-8147-1322-X*); pap. text 16.00 (*0-8147-1323-8*) NYU Pr.

Bingham, Caroline. Big Book of Trucks. LC 99-20409. 32p. (J). (gr. k-4). 1999. 14.95 (*0-7894-4739-8*) DK Pub Inc.

***Bingham, Caroline.** DK Big Book of Rescue Vehicles. LC 99-42517. (Illus.). 31p. (J). (ps-3). 2000. 14.95 (*0-7894-5454-8*) DK Pub Inc.

Bingham, Caroline & Foster, Karen, eds. Crafts for Decoration. (Millbrook Arts Library). (Illus.). 48p. (J). (gr. 3-6). 1993. lib. bdg. 22.90 (*1-56294-098-8*) Millbrook Pr.

***Bingham, Charlotte.** At Home. 2000. pap. 6.95 (*0-553-40429-6*, Pub. by Transworld Publishers Ltd) Trafalgar.

— Belgravia. 2000. pap. 6.95 (*0-553-40427-X*, Pub. by Transworld Publishers Ltd) Trafalgar.

Bingham, Charlotte. By Invitation. large type ed. 22.95 (*1-85695-363-7*, Pub. by ISIS Lrg Prnt) Transaction Pubs.

***Bingham, Charlotte.** Change of Heart. 2000. 27.95 (*0-385-40999-0*, Pub. by Transworld Publishers Ltd) Trafalgar.

Bingham, Charlotte. The Debutantes. 1997. mass mkt. 8.99 (*0-553-40890-9*) Bantam.

***Bingham, Charlotte.** The Debutantes. 2000. 27.95 (*0-385-40605-3*, Pub. by Transworld Publishers Ltd) Trafalgar.

— Grand Affair. 2000. 29.95 (*0-385-40843-9*, Pub. by Transworld Publishers Ltd) Trafalgar.

— Grand Affair. large type ed. 496p. 1999. 31.99 (*0-7089-9082-7*, Linford) Ulverscroft.

— Love Song. large type ed. 472p. 1999. 31.99 (*0-7089-9107-6*) Ulverscroft.

Bingham, D. Jeffrey. Irenaeus' Use of Matthews Gospel. 1998. 75.00 (*90-6831-964-7*, Pub. by Peeters Pub) Bks Intl VA.

Bingham, Dan, ed. see Gallagher, Jane.

***Bingham, Deann Lee.** Andrew--Catch That Cat! (First Flight Ser.). (Illus.). (J). 1999. 9.95 (*1-55041-411-9*) Fitzhenry & W Ltd.

Bingham, Deanna L. It's a Jungle in Here. (Illus.). 24p. 1995. pap. 5.95 (*0-929005-75-9*, Pub. by Sec Story Pr) LPC InBook.

***Bingham, Deanne L.** Andrew's Magnificent Mountain of Mittens. (First Flight Ser.). (Illus.). 48p. (J). (gr. 2-4). 1999. 9.95 (*1-55041-397-X*); pap. 3.95 (*1-55041-389-9*) Fitzhenry & W Ltd.

Bingham, Deanne L. It's a Jungle in Here. (Illus.). 24p. 1995. 12.95 (*0-929005-77-5*, Pub. by Sec Story Pr) LPC InBook.

— Just Imagine. (Illus.). 24p. (J). 1998. 11.95 (*1-55041-381-3*) Fitzhenry & W Ltd.

***Bingham, Deanne Lee.** Andrew--Catch That Cat! (First Flight Ser.). (J). 1999. pap. 3.95 (*1-55041-413-5*) Fitzhenry & W Ltd.

— Just Imagine. (Illus.). 24p. 2000. pap. text 5.95 (*1-55041-544-1*) Fitzhenry & W Ltd.

Bingham, Denis A. Marriages of the Bourbons, 2 vols. LC 70-113557. (Illus.). reprint ed. 95.00 (*0-404-00890-9*) AMS Pr.

Bingham, Dennis. Acting Male: Masculinities in the Films of James Stewart, Jack Nicholson, & Clint Eastwood. LC 93-37678. (Illus.). 280p. (C). 1994. pap. 15.95 (*0-8135-2074-6*); text 45.00 (*0-8135-2073-8*) Rutgers U Pr.

***Bingham, Derick.** Joseph & Ruth. (Illus.). 154p. 1999. pap. 9.99 (*1-84030-055-8*) Emerald House Group Inc.

— On Highest Ground: Surveying Your Resources in Christ. 360p. 1999. 9.99 (*1-84030-068-X*) Emerald House Group Inc.

Bingham, Derick. Worry. 1997. pap. 3.99 (*0-907927-92-0*) Emerald House Group Inc.

Bingham, Derrick. Backsliding. 1997. pap. 3.99 (*1-898787-02-6*) Emerald House Group Inc.

— Diary of a Longing Heart. 287p. 1992. pap. 9.99 (*0-907927-82-3*) Emerald House Group Inc.

Bingham, Derrick. For All Seasons. 291p. 1997. pap. 11.99 (*1-84030-000-0*) Emerald House Group Inc.

Bingham, Derrick. Guidance. 1997. pap. 3.99 (*1-898787-01-8*) Emerald House Group Inc.

— Invitation. 1997. pap. text 12.99 (*1-898787-81-6*) Emerald House Group Inc.

— Ruth. 1997. pap. 7.99 (*0-907927-76-9*) Emerald House Group Inc.

— Suffering. 1997. pap. 3.99 (*0-907927-93-9*) Emerald House Group Inc.

Bingham, Don & Bingham, Joan. Recycled Elegance: Decorating with Second-Hand Treasures. LC 97-27546. (Illus.). 300p. 1998. 16.95 (*0-8038-9408-2*) Hastings.

— Tuttle Dictionary of Antiques & Collectibles Terms. LC 91-67337. 272p. (Orig.). 1992. pap. 19.95 (*0-8048-1756-1*) Tuttle Pubng.

Bingham, Don, jt. auth. see Bingham, Joan.

Bingham, E. R., jt. auth. see Walker, G.

Bingham, Edwin, ed. see Wood, Charles E., et al.

Bingham, Edwin R. Charles F. Lummis: Editor of the Southwest. LC 73-15058. (Illus.). 218p. 1973. reprint ed. lib. bdg. 69.50 (*0-8371-7149-0*, BICL, Greenwood Pr) Greenwood.

Bingham, Edwin R., ed. California Gold: Selected Source Materials for College Research Papers. LC 81-2001. 117p. 1981. reprint ed. lib. bdg. 35.00 (*0-313-22776-4*, BICAG, Greenwood Pr) Greenwood.

Bingham, Edwin R. & Love, Glen A., eds. Northwest Perspectives: Essays on the Culture of the Pacific Northwest. LC 77-15189. 264p. 1979. 22.00 (*0-295-95594-5*); pap. 10.95 (*0-295-95805-7*) U of Wash Pr.

Bingham, Eileen, ed. & compiled by see Bingham, Richard.

Bingham, Eula, et al, eds. Public Health Aspects of Criminal Prosecution of Workplace-Related Deaths, Injury, & Disease. (International Journal of Occupational Medicine, Immunology, & Toxicology Ser.: Vol. 3, No. 4). (Illus.). 1994. pap. text 50.00 (*0-911131-79-5*) Specialist Journals.

Bingham, Eula & Rall, David, eds. Preventive Strategies for Living in a Chemical World: A Symposium in Honor of Irving J. Selikoff. LC 97-39041. (Annals of the New York Academy of Sciences Ser.: No. 837). 588p. 1998. 110.00 (*1-57331-074-3*); pap. 110.00 (*1-57331-075-1*) NY Acad Sci.

***Bingham, Eula, et al.** Patty's Toxicology, Vol. 1. 5th ed. 1056p. 2000. 295.00 (*0-471-31932-5*) Wiley.

Bingham, Eula, jt. auth. see Ashford, Nicholas A.

Bingham, F. F. Log of the Peep O'Day: Summer Cruises in West Florida Waters, 1912-1915. Rucker, Brian R. & Woolsey, Nathan F., eds. (Illus.). 203p. (Orig.). 1991. pap. 9.95 (*1-882695-03-8*) Patagonia Pr.

Bingham, F. F. & Rucker, Brian R. From Pensacola to Belize: An American's Odyssey Through Mexico in 1903. LC 98-100815. (Illus.). 122p. 1997. pap. 8.95 (*1-882695-09-7*) Patagonia Pr.

Bingham, Frank G. Business Marketing Management. LC 97-13370. 1997. 71.95 (*0-8442-2964-4*) NTC Contemp Pub Co.

Bingham, Fred P. Boat Joinery & Cabinetmaking Simplified. 1993. pap. 24.95 (*0-07-005307-3*) Intl Marine.

— Boat Joinery & Cabinetmaking Simplified. 1993. pap. text 21.95 (*0-87742-354-7*) McGraw.

***Bingham-Hall, Patrick.** Olympic Architecture 2000: Building Sydney. (Illus.). 280p. 2000. 60.00 (*0-949284-39-4*, Pub. by Watermark) Antique Collect.

Bingham, Helen M. History of Green County. (Illus.). 310p. 1997. reprint ed. lib. bdg. 37.50 (*0-8328-6967-8*) Higginson Bk Co.

Bingham, Hiram. The Dawnwatchers. 344p. 1999. reprint ed. pap. 12.95 (*0-9613602-0-8*, Pub. by Triune Bks) Anthroposophic.

— Elementary Lessons in Hawaiian. (Works of Hiram Bingham). 1989. reprint ed. lib. bdg. 79.00 (*0-685-27342-3*) Rprt Serv.

— First Book for Children. (Works of Hiram Bingham). 1989. reprint ed. lib. bdg. 79.00 (*0-685-27264-8*) Rprt Serv.

— Lost City of the Incas. LC 81-7196. (Illus.). 263p. 1981. reprint ed. lib. bdg. 69.75 (*0-313-22950-3*, BILC, Greenwood Pr) Greenwood.

***Bingham, Hiram.** Lost City of the Incas. 2nd unabridged ed. LC 99-26171. (Illus.). 288p. 2000. reprint ed. pap. 15.95 (*0-9613602-1-6*) Triune Bks.

Bingham, Hiram. A Residence of Twenty-One Years in the Sandwich Islands. (Works of Hiram Bingham). 1989. reprint ed. lib. bdg. 79.00 (*0-7812-0305-8*) Rprt Serv.

— Scripture Catechism. (Works of Hiram Bingham). 1989. reprint ed. lib. bdg. 79.00 (*0-685-27263-X*) Rprt Serv.

— The Works of Hiram Bingham. 1989. reprint ed. lib. bdg. 63.00 (*0-685-27261-3*) Rprt Serv.

Bingham, Howard & Wallace, Max. Muhammad Ali's Greatest Fight: Cassius Clay vs. the United States of America. LC 99-50269. (Illus.). 272p. 2000. 21.95 (*0-87131-900-4*) M Evans.

Bingham, Isabel. Profile of a Manic Depressive. 1997. pap. write for info. (*1-57553-637-4*) Watermrk Pr.

Bingham, J. Science Experiments. (Illus.). 64p. (J). (gr. 4 up). 1992. pap. 8.95 (*0-7460-0806-6*, Usborne) EDC.

An Asterisk (*) at the beginning of an entry indicates that the title is appearing for the first time.

Bingham, J. Science Experiments. (Illus.). 64p. (J). (gr. 5 up). 1992. lib. bdg. 16.95 (*0-88110-515-5*, Usborne) EDC.

Bingham, J., tr. see Xenophon.

***Bingham, Jane.** Medieval World. (World History Ser.). (Illus.). 96p. 1999. 29.95 (*0-7460-2762-1*, Usborne) EDC.

Bingham, Jane. Medieval World. (World History Ser.). (Illus.). 96p. (gr. 3-7). 1999. 29.95 (*1-58086-200-4*) EDC.

— The Usborne Book of Science Experiments. (Usborne Kid Kits Ser.). (Illus.). (J). (gr. 4 up). 1996. 19.95 (*0-88110-871-5*, Usborne) EDC.

Bingham, Jane & Scholt, Grayce, eds. Fifteen Centuries of Children's Literature: An Annotated Chronology of British & American Works in Historical Context. LC 79-8584. (Illus.). 1540p. 1980. lib. bdg. 59.95 (*0-313-22164-2*, BCL/, Greenwood Pr) Greenwood.

Bingham, Jane, jt. ed. see Wardley, Rachel.

Bingham, Joan. A Year of Delicious Low-Fat Diet Desserts: 365 Quick & Easy Low-Calorie Recipes. LC 96-1567. (Illus.). 272p. (Orig.). 1997. pap. 14.95 (*0-940159-35-X*) Camino Bks.

Bingham, Joan & Bingham, Don. Buying & Selling Antiques & Collectibles: For Fun & Profit. LC 94-7707. 224p. 1994. pap. 16.95 (*0-8048-1986-6*) Tuttle Pubng.

Bingham, Joan, jt. auth. see Bingham, Don.

Bingham, Joan, jt. auth. see Riccero, Delores.

Bingham, Joan, jt. ed. see Owen, David.

Bingham, John. Brock. large type ed. 352p. 1982. 27.99 (*0-7089-0884-5*) Ulverscroft.

— Brock & the Defector. large type ed. 416p. 1984. 27.99 (*0-7089-1082-3*) Ulverscroft.

— The Courage to Start: A Guide to Running for Your Life. LC 99-17797. (Illus.). 208p. 1999. per. 13.00 (*0-684-85455-4*) S&S Trade Pap.

— The Penguin Brigade Training Log. (Illus.). 160p. 1998. spiral bd. 12.95 (*1-55821-672-3*, Pub. by Breakaway Bks) Consort Bk Sales.

***Bingham, John A.** ADSL, VDSL & Multicarrier Modulation. LC 99-15963. 289p. 1999. 84.95 (*0-471-29099-8*) Wiley.

Bingham, John A. The Theory & Practice of Modem Design. LC 87-37262. 480p. 1988. 148.00 (*0-471-85108-6*) Wiley.

Bingham, Jonathan B. Shirt-Sleeve Diplomacy. LC 77-133512. (Select Bibliographies Reprint Ser.). 1977. 21.95 (*0-8369-5544-7*) Ayer.

Bingham, Julie E. Hal Plain & Simple: Learning Hal with Lotus 1-2-3 Release 2. 1987. pap. 17.95 (*0-201-08002-8*) Addison-Wesley.

Bingham, June. Courage to Change: An Introduction to the Life & Thought of Reinhold Nieburh. LC 92-484. 1992. pap. 36.50 (*0-8191-8731-3*) U Pr of Amer.

Bingham, Kate. Cohabitation. LC 99-168018. 64p. 1998. pap. 17.95 (*1-85411-215-5*, Pub. by Seren Bks) Dufour.

***Bingham, Kate.** Mummy's Legs. LC 99-36028. 224p. 2000. 20.00 (*0-684-86470-3*) S&S Trade.

Bingham, Kathleen, see Jwala, pseud.

Bingham, Linda S. FlashPoint. write for info. (*0-945199-16-3*) Double SS Pr.

Bingham, Linda S. Up in Flames. (John & Mary Bolt Mystery Ser.: Vol. 1). 256p. 1998. pap. 9.95 (*0-945199-10-4*) Double SS Pr.

Bingham, Lisa. And Babies Make Ten: New Arrivals. (Presents Ser.: Bk. 784). 1999. per. 3.99 (*0-373-16784-9*, 1-16784-0) Harlequin Bks.

— The Bengal Rubies. Tolley, Carolyn, ed. 288p. (Orig.). 1993. mass mkt. 5.50 (*0-671-77095-0*) PB.

— The Butler & the Bachelorette. (American Romance Ser.). 1996. per. 3.75 (*0-373-16635-4*, 1-16635-4) Harlequin Bks.

— The Daddy Hunt. (American Romance Ser.). 1996. per. 3.75 (*0-373-16651-6*, 1-16651-1) Harlequin Bks.

— Dana & the Calendar Man. 1997. per. 3.75 (*0-373-16662-1*, 1-16662-8) Silhouette.

***Bingham, Lisa.** Man Behind the Voice, Vol. 835. (American Romance Ser.). 2000. mass mkt. 4.25 (*0-373-16835-7*, 1-16835-0) Harlequin Bks.

Bingham, Lisa. Nanny Jake. LC 96-569. 249p. 1995. per. 3.50 (*0-373-16602-8*, 1-16602-4) Harlequin Bks.

— The Princess & the Frog. (Fairy Tale Ser.). 1997. per. 3.75 (*0-373-16692-3*, 1-16692-5) Harlequin Bks.

— Runner-Up Bride. (Love & Laughter Ser.: No. 22). 1997. per. 3.50 (*0-373-44022-7*, 1-44022-1) Harlequin Bks.

— Sweet Dalliance. Tolley, Carolyn, ed. 256p. (Orig.). 1994. mass mkt. 5.50 (*0-671-88711-4*) PB.

— Sweet Decadence. 1996. pap., mass mkt. 5.99 (*0-671-88713-0*, PB Trade Paper) PB.

— Sweet Defiance. 1995. mass mkt. 5.99 (*0-671-88712-2*) PB.

— Temptation's Kiss. Tolley, Carolyn, ed. 336p. (Orig.). 1992. mass mkt. 4.99 (*0-671-74564-6*) PB.

— Tender Conquest. 352p. (Orig.). 1989. pap. 3.95 (*0-380-75734-6*, Avon Bks) Morrow Avon.

— When Night Draws Near. (Intrigue Ser.: No. 540). 1999. per. 3.99 (*0-373-22540-7*, 1-22540-8) Harlequin Bks.

— Wild Escapade. 1996. mass mkt. 5.99 (*0-671-52804-1*) PB.

— Wild Masquerade. 1997. per. 5.99 (*0-671-52811-4*) PB.

— Wild Serenade. 320p. 1997. per. 5.99 (*0-671-52810-6*, Pocket Books) PB.

Bingham, Marjorie W. Women & the Constitution. Donaldson, Janet, ed. 228p. (C). 1990. pap. text, student ed. 14.95 (*1-879413-00-0*) Emory U Carter Ctr.

Bingham, Marjorie W. & Gross, Susan H. Women in Africa of the Sub-Sahara: Ancient Times to the 20th Century, Vol. I. (Illus.). 143p. 1982. pap. 15.00 (*0-86596-006-2*) UM Womens Hist.

— Women in Ancient Greece & Rome. LC 83-14016. (Women in World Area Studies). (Illus.). 125p. (Orig.). 1983. pap. 15.00 (*0-914227-00-9*) UM Womens Hist.

— Women in Islam. (Illus.). 130p. 1980. pap. 15.00 (*0-86596-000-3*) UM Womens Hist.

— Women in Japan: From Ancient Times to the Present. Donaldson, Janet M., ed. (Women in World Area Studies). (Illus.). 317p. (Orig.). 1987. pap. 18.00 (*0-914227-08-4*) UM Womens Hist.

— Women in Latin America: From Pre-Columbian Times to the 20th Century, Vol. I. Donaldson, Janet M., ed. LC 84-73429. (Women in World Area Studies). (Illus.). 210p. (Orig.). 1985. pap. 15.00 (*0-914227-04-1*) UM Womens Hist.

— Women in Modern China. (Women in World Area Studies). (Illus.). 107p. 1980. pap. 15.00 (*0-86596-003-8*) UM Womens Hist.

— Women in the U. S. S. R. (Woman in World Area Studies). (Illus.). 151p. 1980. pap. 15.00 (*0-86596-005-4*) UM Womens Hist.

Bingham, Marjorie W., jt. auth. see Gross, Susan H.

Bingham, Mark E., ed. see Dobbins, Durell C.

Bingham, Mary. God Never Changes: A Woman's Bible Study on the Unchanging Nature of God. Hansen, Susan, ed. 65p. 1995. pap. text 4.95 (*1-56309-110-0*, W954101) Womans Mission Union.

Bingham, Mike & Shemish, Joe. Tasmania. (Illus.). 112p. 1999. 39.95 (*1-86436-338-X*, Pub. by New Holland) BHB Intl.

Bingham, Mindy. Berta Benz & the Motorwagen. (Illus.). 48p. (J). (gr. 1 up). 1992. 14.95 (*0-911655-38-7*) Advocacy Pr.

— Minou. LC 86-26539. (Illus.). 64p. (J). (ps up). 1987. 14.95 (*0-911655-36-0*) Advocacy Pr.

Bingham, Mindy & Stryker, Sandy. Career Choices: A Guide for Teens & Young Adults: Who Am I? What Do I Want? How Do I Get It? Shafer, Robert, ed. LC 90-81785. (Illus.). 288p. (Orig.). (YA). (gr. 9 up). 1990. pap. 22.95 (*1-878787-02-0*) Acad Innovat.

— Career Choices & Changes: A Guide for Discovering Who You Are, What You Want, & How to Get It. Shafer, Robert, ed. LC 94-135960. (Illus.). 304p. (Orig.). (C). 1994. pap. 22.95 (*1-878787-06-3*) Acad Innovat.

— More Choices: A Strategic Planning Guide for Mixing Career & Family. Paine, Penelope C. & Greene, Barbara, eds. LC 87-11494. (Illus.). 240p. (Orig.). 1993. pap. 19.95 (*0-911655-28-X*) Advocacy Pr.

— More Choices Workbook: A Strategic Planning Guide for Mixing Career & Family. rev. ed. Greene, Barbara et al, eds. LC 87-11494. (Illus.). 104p. (Orig.). 1992. pap. 6.95 (*0-911655-29-8*) Advocacy Pr.

— Women Helping Girls with Choices: A Handbook. (Illus.). 132p. 1989. pap. 14.95 (*0-911655-00-X*) Advocacy Pr.

— Workbook for Career Choices: A Guide for Teens & Young Adults, Who Am I? What Do I Want? How Do I Get It? Shafer, Robert, ed. (Illus.). 128p. 1990. pap. text 6.95 (*1-878787-03-9*) Acad Innovat.

Bingham, Mindy, et al. Challenges: A Young Man's Journal for Self-Awareness & Personal Planning. rev. ed. Greene, Barbara et al, eds. LC 84-70108. (Illus.). 240p. (YA). (gr. 7 up). 1993. pap. 19.95 (*0-911655-24-7*) Advocacy Pr.

— Choices: A Teen Woman's Journal for Self-Awareness & Personal Planning. Green, Barbara & Peters, Kathleen, eds. (Illus.). 240p. (YA), (gr. 7 up). 1993. pap. 19.95 (*0-911655-22-0*) Advocacy Pr.

— Choices & Challenges Workbook. Greene, Barbara et al, eds. LC 84-70108. (Illus.). 240p. (YA). (gr. 7 up). 1993. student ed. 6.95 (*0-911655-25-5*) Advocacy Pr.

— Instructor's & Counselor's Guide for Career Choices: An Interdisciplinary Curriculum for High Schools & College. Light, Laura & Hoyt, Kenneth B., eds. (Illus.). 288p. (Orig.). 1994. pap. text 20.95 (*1-878787-04-7*) Acad Innovat.

— Lifestyle Math Your Financial Planning Portfolio: A Supplemental Mathematics Unit for Career Choices. (Illus.). 112p. 1994. pap. 6.95 (*1-878787-07-1*) Acad Innovat.

— Mother-Daughter Choices: A Handbook for the Coordinator. Greene, Barbara & Stryker, Sandy, eds. (Illus.). 150p. 1988. pap. 14.95 (*0-911655-44-1*) Advocacy Pr.

— Things Will Be Different for My Daughter: A Practical Guide to Building Her Self-Esteem. LC 94-18517. 494p. 1995. pap. 15.95 (*0-14-024125-6*, Penguin Bks) Viking Penguin.

Bingham, Mindy, jt. auth. see Paine, Penelope C.

Bingham, Mindy, jt. auth. see Poynter, Dan.

Bingham, Mindy, jt. ed. see Goode, Janet.

Bingham, N. H. Risk Neutral Valuation: Pricing & Hedging of Financial Derivatives. LC 98-4663. (Springer Finance). 1998. 79.95 (*1-85233-001-5*) Spr-Verlag.

Bingham, N. H., et al. Regular Variation. (Encyclopedia of Mathematics & Its Applications Ser.: No. 27). (Illus.). 512p. 1987. text 155.00 (*0-521-30787-2*) Cambridge U Pr.

— Regular Variation. (Encyclopedia of Mathematics & Its Applications Ser.: No. 27). (Illus.). 516p. (C). 1989. pap. text 54.95 (*0-521-37943-1*) Cambridge U Pr.

Bingham, Neil. Christopher Nicholson. (RIBA Drawings Monographs: No. 4). (Illus.). 113p. (Orig.). 1996. pap. 38.00 (*1-85490-445-0*, Pub. by Wiley) Wiley.

Bingham, Peregrine. Law of Infancy & Coverture. 2nd ed. viii, 396p. 1980. reprint ed. 45.00 (*0-8377-0311-5*, Rothman) W S Hein.

Bingham, Pete. The Picture Framing Course. 1997. 24.95 (*0-8117-1246-X*) Stackpole.

Bingham, Rebecca. Opals. deluxe ed. (Illus.). 48p. 1982. lthr. 30.00 (*0-88014-042-9*) Mosaic Pr OH.

Bingham, Richard. Richard Bingham's Poems & Short Stories. Bingham, Eileen, ed. & compiled by by. LC 96-90959. 103p. 1997. 13.95 (*0-533-12232-5*) Vantage.

***Bingham, Richard & Felbinger, Clare.** Evaluation in Practice. 2nd ed. 445p. (C). 2000. pap. text 55.00 (*1-889119-57-1*, Chatham House Pub) Seven Bridges.

Bingham, Richard D. Industrial Policy American Style: From Hamilton to HDTV. LC 97-20514. 236p. 1997. pap. 27.95 (*1-56324-597-3*, East Gate Bk) M E Sharpe.

— Industrial Policy American Style: From Hamilton to HDTV. LC 97-20514. 236p. (C). 1997. 61.95 (*1-56324-596-5*) M E Sharpe.

— Managing Local Government: Public Administration in Practice. (Illus.). 368p. 1991. text 65.00 (*0-8039-3938-8*); pap. text 27.95 (*0-8039-3939-6*) Sage.

Bingham, Richard D., ed. Economic Restructuring of the American Midwest: Proceedings of the Midwest Economic Restructuring Conference of the Federal Reserve Bank of Cleveland. (C). 1990. lib. bdg. 113.50 (*0-7923-9066-0*) Kluwer Academic.

Bingham, Richard D., et al, eds. Financing Economic Development: An Institutional Response. (Illus.). 318p. (C). 1990. text 58.00 (*0-8039-3571-4*); pap. text 26.50 (*0-8039-3572-2*) Sage.

— The Homeless in Contemporary Society. LC 86-27922. (Sage Focus Editions Ser.: No. 87). 276p. reprint ed. pap. 85.60 (*0-7837-6578-9*, 204614300011) Bks Demand.

Bingham, Richard D. & Blair, John P., eds. Urban Economic Development. LC 84-11456. (Urban Affairs Annual Reviews Ser.: No. 27). 287p. 1984. reprint ed. pap. 89.00 (*0-608-01514-8*, 205955800002) Bks Demand.

Bingham, Richard D. & Felbinger, Claire L. Evaluation in Practice: A Methodological Approach. 324p. (C). 1989. pap. text 26.95 (*0-8013-0216-1*, 75874) Longman.

Bingham, Richard D. & Hedge, David M. State & Local Government in a Changing Society. 2nd ed. 576p. (C). 1990. 72.50 (*0-07-005303-0*) McGraw.

Bingham, Richard D. & Hill, Edward W., eds. Global Perspectives on Economic Development: Government & Business Finance. LC 96-34691. 549p. 1997. pap. 21.95 (*0-88285-157-8*) Ctr Urban Pol Res.

Bingham, Richard D. & Mier, Robert. Theories of Local Economic Development: Perspectives from Across the Disciplines. (Illus.). 360p. (C). 1993. text 62.00 (*0-8039-4867-0*); pap. text 28.50 (*0-8039-4868-9*) Sage.

Bingham, Richard D. & Mier, Robert, eds. Dilemmas of Urban Economic Development: Issues in Theory & Practice. (Urban Affairs Annual Review Ser.: Vol. 47). 352p. (C). 1997. 62.00 (*0-8039-5919-2*, 59192); pap. 26.00 (*0-8039-5920-6*, 59206) Sage.

Bingham, Richard D., et al. Beyond Edge Cities. Urban Center Staff et al, eds. LC 97-27959. (Contemporary Urban Affairs Ser.: Vol. 2). (Illus.). 272p. 1997. text 60.00 (*0-8153-3046-4*, SS1180) Garland.

— Professional Associations & Municipal Innovation. LC 80-5119. 197p. 1981. reprint ed. pap. 61.10 (*0-608-01918-6*, 206257000003) Bks Demand.

Bingham, Richard D., jt. auth. see Gibson, James L.

Bingham, Richard D., ed. see Alex-Assensoh, Yvette M.

Bingham, Richard D., ed. see Reese, Laura A. & Urban Center Staff.

Bingham, Rita. Country Beans. (Natural Meals in Minutes Ser.: Bk. 4). (Illus.). 192p. (Orig.). 1994. 14.95 (*1-882314-11-5*) Nat Meals Pub.

— Food Combing: Better Health - The Natural Way. (Illus.). 80p. 1998. pap. 6.95 (*1-882314-15-8*) Nat Meals Pub.

— Natural Meals in Minutes: Whole Grains, Beans, Seeds, Sprouting, Powdered Milk Cheeses. Orig. Title: Introduction to Natural Foods, Sprouting, Powdered Milk Cheeses. (Illus.). 200p. 1997. reprint ed. student ed. 14.95 (*1-882314-09-3*) Nat Meals Pub.

— 1-2-3 Smoothies: 123 Quick Frosty Drinks - Delicious & Nutritious. (Illus.). 200p. 1998. pap. 14.95 (*1-882314-14-X*) Nat Meals Pub.

— Sauces, Seasonings & Natural Foods: Low Fat, No Fat Sauces, Seasonings & Fast Easy Meals. 40p. Date not set. 3.95 (*1-882314-08-5*) Nat Meals Pub.

Bingham, Rita & Dickey, Esther. The New Passport to Survival: 12 Steps to Self-Sufficient Living. (Illus.). 240p. 1999. pap. 15.95 (*1-882314-27-7*) Nat Meals Pub.

Bingham, Rita, jt. auth. see Moulton, LeArta.

Bingham, Robert. Pure Slaughter Value. 208p. 1998. pap. 11.00 (*0-385-48867-X*) Doubleday.

***Bingham, Robert & D'Erasmo, Stacey.** Lightning on the Sun: A Novel. LC 99-47900. 288p. 2000. 23.95 (*0-385-48856-4*) Doubleday.

Bingham, Robert, jt. auth. see Oberman, Joseph.

Bingham, Robert C. Economic Concepts: A Programmed Approach. 10th ed. LC 92-27518. (C). 1992. pap. text 32.50 (*0-07-045591-0*) McGraw.

Bingham, Robert J. Photogenic Manipulation. LC 72-9182. (Literature of Photography Ser.). (Illus.). 1973. reprint ed. 15.95 (*0-405-04893-9*) Ayer.

Bingham, Rosie & Daniels, Jacquie. Developing Student Support Groups. LC 99-191753. 100p. 1999. pap. 42.95 (*0-566-08117-2*) Ashgate Pub Co.

Bingham, Rosie & Drew, Sue. Key WorkSkills. LC 98-53695. 255p. 1999. pap. 25.95 (*0-566-08183-0*, Pub. by Ashgate Pub) Ashgate Pub Co.

***Bingham, Rosie & Drew, Sue.** Key WorkSkills. LC 98-53695. 200p. 1999. ring bd. 262.95 (*0-566-08208-X*, Pub. by Ashgate Pub) Ashgate Pub Co.

Bingham, Rosie, jt. auth. see Drew, Sue.

Bingham, Sallie. Matron of Honor. LC 93-33845. 192p. 1996. reprint ed. pap. 10.95 (*0-944072-63-1*) Zoland Bks.

— Passion & Prejudice: A Family Memoir. 1993. pap. 12.95 (*1-55783-077-0*) Applause Theatre Bk Pubs.

— Small Victories. LC 91-66474. 312p. 1993. pap. 9.95 (*0-944072-25-9*) Zoland Bks.

— Straight Man. LC 96-16398. 244p. 1996. 22.95 (*0-944072-65-8*) Zoland Bks.

— Upstate. 2nd ed. LC 92-34345. 128p. 1993. pap. 16.00 (*1-877946-50-8*) Permanent Pr.

Bingham, Sam. The Last Ranch: A Colorado Community & the Coming Desert. LC 97-20012. 1997. pap. 14.00 (*0-15-600539-5*, Harvest Bks) Harcourt.

Bingham, Shereen G., ed. Conceptualizing Sexual Harrassment as Discursive Practice. LC 93-37025. 224p. 1994. 59.95 (*0-275-94593-6*, Praeger Pubs) Greenwood.

Bingham Summers Welsh & Spilman. Environmental Compliance Handbook: An Overview of Indiana & Federal Environmental Laws for Indiana Business. 2nd ed. 376p. 1996. pap., per. 84.00 (*1-883698-12-X*) IN Chamber Comm.

Bingham Summers Welsh & Spilman Attorneys at Law S. Environmental Compliance Handbook: An Overview of Indiana & Federal Environmental Laws for Indiana Business. 380p. (Orig.). 1994. pap., per. 84.00 (*1-883698-00-6*) IN Chamber Comm.

Bingham, Theodore A. Genealogy of the Bingham Family in the United States. (Illus.). 288p. 1988. reprint ed. pap. 43.00 (*0-8328-0257-3*); reprint ed. lib. bdg. 51.00 (*0-8328-0256-5*) Higginson Bk Co.

Bingham, Thomas, frwd. Guidelines for the Assessment of General Damages in Personal Injury Cases. 2nd ed. LC 95-144590. 72p. 1994. pap. 36.00 (*1-85431-378-9*, Pub. by Blackstone Pr) Gaunt.

***Bingham, Tom.** The Business of Judging: Selected Essays & Speeches. (Illus.). 480p. 2000. text 60.00 (*0-19-829912-5*) OUP.

Bingham, W. G., ed. Recent Advances in Brain Tumor Research. (Progress in Experimental Tumor Research Ser.: Vol. 17). 1972. 121.75 (*3-8055-1402-6*) S Karger.

Bingham, William H., jt. ed. see Holcombe, R. I.

Bingham, Woodbridge. Hiram Bingham: A Personal History. 1989. 45.00 (*0-685-29186-3*) Dsktp Pub Servs.

Binghamton Symposium in Geomorphology Staff. Geomorphology & Natural Hazards: Proceedings of the 25th Binghamton Symposium on Geomorphology, Held September 24-25, 1994 at SUNY, Binghamton, U. S. A. Morisawa, Marie E., ed. LC 94-41213. 366p. 1994. 244.50 (*0-444-82012-4*) Elsevier.

Bingle, Robert J. How to Try a Personal Injury Case: Strategies & Techniques from the Experts : A Satellite Program. LC 98-223139. (Litigation & Administration Practice Ser.). 176 p. 1998. 55.00 (*0-87224-517-9*) PLI.

Bingley, A. H. Handbook on Rajputs. (Illus.). 204p. 1986. reprint ed. 20.00 (*0-8364-1756-9*, Pub. by Usha) S Asia.

Bingley, David. Long Range Deserter. large type ed. (Linford Mystery Library). 400p. 1997. pap. 16.99 (*0-7089-5100-7*, Linford) Ulverscroft.

Bingley, Margaret. After Alice. 1989. mass mkt. 3.95 (*0-445-20528-8*, Mysterious Paperbk) Warner Bks.

— Deadtime Story. 1990. mass mkt. 4.95 (*0-445-20722-1*, Mysterious Paperbk) Warner Bks.

— Dramatic Death. 208p. (YA). (gr. 7-9). 1995. pap. 3.50 (*0-590-20371-1*) Scholastic Inc.

— Dramatic Death. (Point Crime Ser.). 1994. 8.60 (*0-606-07447-3*, Pub. by Turtleback) Demco.

***Bingley, Margaret.** A Dramatic Death. large type ed. (J). 1998. pap. 16.95 (*0-7540-6019-5*, Galaxy Child Lrg Print) Chivers N Amer.

— Point Crime: Bored to Death. 1999. 16.95 (*0-7540-6071-3*) Chivers N Amer.

Bingley, Margaret. Time to Kill. (Crime & Passion Ser.). (Orig.). 1997. mass mkt. 5.95 (*0-7535-0164-3*, Pub. by Virgin Bks) London Brdge.

Bingman, Charles F. Japanese Government Leadership & Management. LC 88-3162. 144p. 1989. text 55.00 (*0-312-01181-4*) St Martin.

Bingren, Li. Introduction to Operator Algebras. 750p. 1992. text 78.00 (*981-02-0941-X*) World Scientific Pub.

Bingulac, Stanoje & Van Landingham, Hugh F. Algorithms for Computer-Aided Design of Multivariable Control Systems. LC 93-10191. (Electrical Engineering & Electronics Ser.: Vol. 84). (Illus.). 424p. 1993. text 175.00 (*0-8247-8913-X*) Dekker.

Binh, Duong T. Tagmemic Comparison of the Structure of English & Vietnamese Sentences. LC 74-123126. (Janua Linguarum, Ser. Practica: No. 110). (Orig.). 1971. pap. text 110.80 (*90-279-1598-9*) Mouton.

Binh Nhu Ngo. Elementary Vietnamese. LC 99-30228. (VIE & ENG., Illus.), 256p. 1999. text 34.95 (*0-8048-3207-2*) Tuttle Pubng.

Binham, Philip, jt. ed. see Dauenhauer, Richard.

Binham, Philip, tr. see Friis, Erik J., ed.

Bini, Daniela. Carlo Michelstaedter & the Failure of Language. (Illus.). 314p. (C). 1992. 49.95 (*0-8130-1111-6*) U Press Fla.

— A Fragrance from the Desert: Poetry & Philosophy in Giacomo Leopardi. (Stanford French & Italian Studies: Vol. 27). 200p. 1983. pap. 56.50 (*0-915838-10-9*) Anma Libri.

— Pirandello & His Muse: The Plays for Marta Abba. LC 97-33089. (Crosscurrents Ser.). 248p. 1998. 49.95 (*0-8130-1548-0*) U Press Fla.

Bini, Daniela, jt. auth. see Pease, Antonella.

Bini, Daniela, intro. see Leopardi, Giacomo.

Bini, Dario & Pan, Victor. Polynomial & Matrix Computations Vol. 1: Fundamental Algorithms. LC 94-27577. (Progress in Theoretical Computer Science Ser.). xvi, 415p. 1994. 71.00 (*0-8176-3786-9*) Birkhauser.

***Bini-Smaghi, Lorenzo & Gros, Daniel.** Open Issues in European Central Banking LC 99-40985. 1999. text 69.95 (*0-312-22845-7*) St Martin.

B

An Asterisk (*) at the beginning of an entry indicates that the title is appearing for the first time.

Bini-Smaghi, Lorenzo, et al. The Transition to EMU in the Maastricht Treaty. LC 94-23847. (Essays in International Finance Ser.: No. 194). 74p. 1994. pap. 10.00 (*0-88165-101-X*) Princeton U Int Finan Econ.

Bining, Arthur C. British Regulation of the Colonial Iron Industry. LC 68-55481. (Library of Early American Business & Industry: No. 60). xii, 163p. 1973. reprint ed. 35.00 (*0-678-00924-4*) Kelley.

— Pennsylvania Iron Manufacture in the Eighteenth Century. LC 72-120547. (Library of Early American Business & Industry: No. 39). 227p. 1970. reprint ed. lib. bdg. 35.00 (*0-678-00678-4*) Kelley.

Binion, jt. auth. see Butler.

Binion, Rudolph. Hitler among the Germans. LC 76-26937. 207p. 1981. lib. bdg. 39.95 (*0-444-99033-X*, BHA/) Greenwood.

— Hitler among the Germans. LC 84-1198. 207p. 1984. reprint ed. pap. 15.00 (*0-87580-531-0*) N Ill U Pr.

— Love Beyond Death: The Anatomy of a Myth in the Arts. LC 92-35152. (C). 1993. text 45.00 (*0-8147-1189-8*) NYU Pr.

— Sounding the Classics: From Sophocles to Thomas Mann. LC 97-1693. 176p. 1997. pap. 18.95 (*0-275-95965-1*, Praeger Pubs) Greenwood.

— Sounding the Classics: From Sophocles to Thomas Mann, 83. LC 97-1693. (Contributions to the Study of World Literature Ser.: Vol. 83). 176p. 1997. 55.00 (*0-313-30458-0*, Greenwood Pr) Greenwood.

Binker, A. J., ed. see Paul, Richard W.

Binker, A. J., ed. see Paul, Richard W., et al.

Binkert, Peter J. Generative Grammar Without Transformations. LC 83-27034. viii, 240p. 1984. 72.35 (*3-11-009720-6*) Mouton.

Binkhorst, J., et al, eds. Education-Training & Labour Market Policy: Bibliography & Summaries. (Selecta Reeks Ser.: Vol. 48). viii, 90p. 1986. 17.00 (*90-6472-083-5*) Taylor & Francis.

Binkhorst, Rob A., ed. see International Congress on Pediatric Work Physiolog.

Binkhorst, Rob A., ed. see International Congress on Pediatric Work Physiology (11th, 1983, Papendal, Netherlands) Staff.

Binkin, Martin. America's Volunteer Military: Progress & Prospects. LC 84-14943. (Studies in Defence Policy). 63p. 1984. pap. 8.95 (*0-8157-0975-7*) Brookings.

— The Military Pay Muddle. LC 75-4422. (Studies in Defense Policy). 66p. 1975. pap. 8.95 (*0-8157-0961-7*) Brookings.

— Military Technology & Defense Manpower. LC 85-48204. (Studies in Defense Policy). 143p. 1986. 28.95 (*0-8157-0978-1*); pap. 10.95 (*0-8157-0977-3*) Brookings.

— Support Costs in the Defense Budget: The Submerged One-Third: A Staff Paper. LC 72-646. (Studies in Defense Policy). 59p. reprint ed. pap. 30.00 (*0-608-17110-7*, 202773900056) Bks Demand.

— U. S. Reserve Forces: The Problem of the Weekend Warrior. LC 73-23109. (Studies in Defense Policy). 63p. 1974. pap. 8.95 (*0-8157-0959-5*) Brookings.

— Who Will Fight the Next War? The Changing Face of the American Military. 224p. (C). 1993. 31.95 (*0-8157-0956-0*); pap. 14.95 (*0-8157-0955-2*) Brookings.

Binkin, Martin & Bach, Shirley J. Women & the Military. LC 77-24040. (Studies in Defense Policy). 134p. 1977. 26.95 (*0-8157-0966-8*); pap. 9.95 (*0-8157-0965-X*) Brookings.

Binkin, Martin & Clark, Rolf H. Shaping the Defense Civilian Work Force: Economics, Politics, & National Security. LC 78-14897. (Studies in Defense Policy). 113p. 1978. pap. 7.95 (*0-8157-0967-6*) Brookings.

Binkin, Martin & Kaufmann, William W. U. S. Army Guard & Reserve: Rhetoric, Realities, Risks. (Studies in Defense Policy). 160p. 1989. pap. 12.95 (*0-8157-0979-X*) Brookings.

Binkin, Martin & Kyriakopoulos, Irene. Youth or Experience? Manning the Modern Military. LC 79-12633. (Studies in Defense Policy). 84p. 1979. pap. 8.95 (*0-8157-0969-2*) Brookings.

Binkin, Martin & Record, Jeffrey. Where Does the Marine Corps Go from Here? LC 75-45068. (Studies in Defense Policy). 105p. reprint ed. pap. 32.60 (*0-608-14560-2*, 202496200040) Bks Demand.

Binkin, Martin, et al. Blacks & the Military. LC 82-70886. (Studies in Defense Policy). 190p. 1982. 26.95 (*0-8157-0974-9*) Brookings.

Binkley. Notable Black American Scientists. LC 98-36338. (Illus.). 500p. 1998. 80.00 (*0-7876-2789-5*, GML00298-112329) Gale.

Binkley, Barbara, jt. auth. see Piaget, Gerald W.

Binkley, Barbara M., jt. auth. see Piaget, Gerald W.

***Binkley, Clark S. & Forgacs, Otto L.** Status of Forest Sector Research & Development in Canada. 28p. 1998. 10.20 (*1-896742-23-8*) Pulp & Paper.

Binkley, D., et al, eds. The Response of Western Forests to Air Pollution. LC 92-21992. (Ecological Studies: Vol. 97). (Illus.). xii, 532p. 1992. 120.00 (*0-387-97895-X*) Spr-Verlag.

Binkley, D., et al. Acidic Depostion & Forest Soils. (Ecological Studies: Vol. 72). (Illus.). 150p. 1990. 89.95 (*0-387-96889-X*) Spr-Verlag.

Binkley, Dan. Forest Nutrition Management. LC 86-7779. 304p. 1986. 140.00 (*0-471-81883-6*) Wiley.

Binkley, Dan & Brown, Thomas C. Management Impacts on Water Quality of Forests & Rangelands. (Illus.). 120p. 1997. reprint ed. 19.00 (*0-89904-595-2*, Bear Meadows Resrch Grp); reprint ed. pap. 13.00 (*0-89904-596-0*, Bear Meadows Resrch Grp) Crumb Elbow Pub.

Binkley, David A. A Taste for the Beautiful: Zairian Art from the Hampton University Museum. (Illus.). 116p. 1993. pap. 24.95 (*0-9616982-6-8*); text 40.00 (*0-9616982-7-6*) Hampton Univ Muse.

Binkley, Edith R. & Binkley, Roger W. Carbohydrate Photochemistry, Vol. 191. LC 98-8007. (ACS Monographs ; An American Chemical Society Publication: No. 191). (Illus.). 448p. 1998. text 169.95 (*0-8412-3539-2*, Pub. by Am Chemical) OUP.

Binkley, Frederick. Mark It Like It Is. LC 87-90901. 1988. 15.00 (*0-87212-205-0*) Libra.

Binkley, Jim, jt. auth. see Eisenhammer, Fred.

Binkley, Margaret, ed. see Forte, Imogene & Schurr, Sandra.

Binkley, Margaret, ed. see Philpot, Jan G.

Binkley, Marian. Risks, Dangers & Rewards in the Nova Scotia Offshore Fishery. LC 96-154377. (Illus.). 208p. 1995. 55.00 (*0-7735-1313-2*, Pub. by McG-Queens Univ Pr) CUP Services.

Binkley, Marilyn. Reading Literacy in the United States: Findings from the LEA Reading Literacy Study. 79p. 1996. pap. 9.50 (*0-16-048670-X*) USGPO.

Binkley, Marilyn & Williams, Trevor. Reading Literacy in the U. S. Findings from the IEA Reading Literacy Study. (Illus.). 67p. 1997. reprint ed. pap. text 30.00 (*0-7881-4512-6*) DIANE Pub.

Binkley, Peter, ed. Pre-Modern Encyclopedia Texts: Proceedings of the Second COMERS Congress, Groningen, 1-4 July 1996. LC 97-18515. (Studies in Intellectual History: Vol. 79). (Illus.). 400p. 1997. 131.00 (*90-04-10830-0*) Brill Academic Pubs.

Binkley, Roger W. Modern Carbohydrate Chemistry. (Food Science & Technology Ser.: Vol. 27). (Illus.). 344p. 1987. text 175.00 (*0-8247-7789-1*) Dekker.

Binkley, Roger W., jt. auth. see Binkley, Edith R.

Binkley, Sue. Biological Clocks: Your Owner's Manual. (Illus.). 234p. 1998. text 40.00 (*90-5702-533-7*, Harwood Acad Pubs); pap. text 19.00 (*90-5702-534-5*, Harwood Acad Pubs) Gordon & Breach.

Binkley, Sue A. Clockwork Sparrow. 1989. 24.95 (*0-13-073701-1*) P-H.

— The Endocrine Role of the Pineal Gland. (Illus.). 288p. (C). 1988. pap. text 48.00 (*0-13-277146-2*) P-H.

Binkley, T. Wittgenstein's Language. 236p. 1973. pap. text 78.50 (*90-247-1541-5*, Pub. by M Nijhoff) Kluwer Academic.

Binkley, Thomas & Frenk, Margit. Spanish Romances of the Sixteenth Century. LC 94-44095. 192p. 1995. pap. text 20.00 (*0-253-20964-1*) Ind U Pr.

Binkley, Thomas, ed. see Apel, Willi.

Binkley, Thomas, tr. see Winckel, Fritz.

Binkley, Timothy, jt. auth. see Gartel, Laurence.

Binkley, Wilfred E. The Man in the White House: His Powers & Duties. LC JK0516.B49. (Johns Hopkins Paperbacks Ser.). 320p. reprint ed. pap. 99.20 (*0-608-10154-0*, 202075900018) Bks Demand.

Binkley, William C. The Expansionist Movement in Texas, 1836-1850. 1993. reprint ed. lib. bdg. 75.00 (*0-7812-5866-9*) Rprt Serv.

— The Texas Revolution. LC 79-63065. x, 132p. 1979. reprint ed. 12.95 (*0-87611-041-3*) Tex St Hist Assn.

Binko, James B. & Neubert, Gloria A. Teaching Geography in the Disciplines. LC 96-67180. (Fastback Ser.: No. 400). 64p. (Orig.). 1996. pap. 3.00 (*0-87367-600-9*) Phi Delta Kappa.

Binko, James B., jt. auth. see Neubert, Gloria A.

Binko, Patricia G. The Resistant Reader. (Illus.). 180p. (Orig.). 1997. spiral bd. 14.95 (*0-9662300-0-0*) Binko Info.

Binkowski, Carol J. Musical New York: An Informal Guide to Its History & Legends & a Walking Tour of Its Sites & Landmarks. LC 98-11733. (Illus.). 304p. 1999. pap. 12.95 (*0-940159-47-3*) Camino Bks.

Binkowski, Don. Colonel P. W. Norris: Yellowstone's Greatest Superintendent. (Illus.). 362p. (Orig.). 1995. pap. 14.95 (*0-9646527-0-6*) C & D of Warren.

Binkowski, Edward, ed. Oxymoron Vol. 2: The Fringe. 2nd ed. (Illus.). 200p. 1998. pap. 49.95 (*0-9653852-1-3*) Oxymoron Media.

Binkowski, Edward, jt. ed. see Hagood, Patricia.

Binkowski, Edward S. Satellite Information Systems. (Professional Librarian Ser.). 237p. (C). 1988. 45.00 (*0-8161-1856-6*, Hall Reference); 30.00 (*0-8161-1880-9*, Hall Reference) Macmillan.

Binkowski, F. P. & Doroshov, S. I., eds. North American Sturgeons: Biology & Aquaculture Potential. 1986. text 192.00 (*90-6193-539-3*) Kluwer Academic.

Binks, B. P., ed. Modern Aspects of Emulsion Science. 450p. 1999. 165.00 (*0-85404-439-6*) Royal Soc Chem.

***Binks, Bernard P.** Modern Characterization Methods of Surfactant Systems. LC 99-22026. (Surfactant Science Ser.). (Illus.). 624p. 1999. text 195.00 (*0-8247-1978-6*) Dekker.

Binks, Robert, et al. Tables for Use in High Resolution Mass Spectrometry. LC 75-130645. 208p. 1970. reprint ed. pap. 64.50 (*0-608-10347-0*, 202403100035) Bks Demand.

Binmore, Ken G. Mathematical Analysis: A Straightforward Approach. 2nd ed. LC 81-21728. 376p. 1983. pap. text 32.95 (*0-521-28882-7*) Cambridge U Pr.

Binmore, Ken G. Fun & Games: A Text on Game Theory. 602p. (C). 1992. text 73.56 (*0-669-24603-4*); pap. text 8.36 (*0-669-28502-1*) HM Trade Div.

— Game Theory & the Social Contract: Just Playing, 2. LC 93-29610. (Economic Learning & Social Evolution Ser.). (Illus.). 600p. 1998. 50.00 (*0-262-02444-6*) MIT Pr.

— Game Theory & the Social Contract Vol. 1: Playing Fair. LC 93-29610. 365p. 1994. 50.00 (*0-262-02363-6*) MIT Pr.

Binmore, Ken G., et al. Frontiers of Game Theory. (Illus.). 368p. 1993. 50.00 (*0-262-02356-3*) MIT Pr.

Binnamin, Vivian. The Case of the Anteater's Missing Lunch. Brook, Bonnie, ed. (Field Trip Mysteries Ser.). (Illus.). 32p. (J). (gr. k-3). 1990. pap. 2.95 (*0-671-68820-0*, Silver Pr NJ); lib. bdg. 4.95 (*0-671-68816-2*, Silver Pr NJ) Silver Burdett Pr.

— The Case of the Mysterious Mermaid. Brook, Bonnie, ed. (Field Trip Mysteries Ser.). (Illus.). 32p. (J). (gr. k-3). 1990. pap. 2.95 (*0-671-68821-9*, Silver Pr NJ); lib. bdg. 4.95 (*0-671-68817-0*, Silver Pr NJ) Silver Burdett Pr.

— The Case of the Planetarium Puzzle. Brook, Bonnie, ed. (Field Trip Mysteries Ser.). (Illus.). 32p. (J). (gr. k-3). 1990. pap. 2.95 (*0-671-68823-5*, Silver Pr NJ); lib. bdg. 4.95 (*0-671-68819-7*, Silver Pr NJ) Silver Burdett Pr.

— The Case of the Snoring Stegosaurus. Brook, Bonnie, ed. (Field Trip Mysteries Ser.). (Illus.). 32p. (J). (gr. k-3). 1990. pap. 2.95 (*0-671-68822-7*, Silver Pr NJ); lib. bdg. 4.95 (*0-671-68818-9*, Silver Pr NJ) Silver Burdett Pr.

— Field Trip Mysteries Series, 4 vols., Set. (Illus.). 128p. (J). (gr. k-3). 1990. pap. 11.80 (*0-671-94437-1*); lib. bdg. 19.80 (*0-671-94436-3*) Silver Burdett Pr.

Binneberg, Karl. Padagogische Fallstudien. (GER., Illus.). 272p. 1997. 45.95 (*3-631-32368-9*) P Lang Pubng.

Binneddijk, Hans & Clawson, Patrick L., eds. Strategic Assessment, 1995: U. S. Security Challenges in Transition. (Illus.). 206p. (C). 1997. reprint ed. pap. text 35.00 (*0-7881-4586-X*) DIANE Pub.

***Binnendijk, Hans.** Strategic Assessment 1999: Priorities for a Turbulent World. 334p. 1999. per. 38.00 (*0-16-059032-9*) USGPO.

— Strategic Trends in China. 140p. 1998. per. 6.50 (*0-16-061220-9*) USGPO.

— Transforming Nuclear Deterrence. 81p. 1997. per. 4.50 (*0-16-061202-0*) USGPO.

Binnendijk, Hans & Clawson, Patrick L., eds. Strategic Assessment (1997) Flashpoints & Force Structure. (Illus.). 300p. (C). 1997. pap. text 50.00 (*0-7881-4648-3*) DIANE Pub.

Binnendijk, Hans, et al. Strategic Trends in China. LC 98-173507. (Illus.). 140p. 1998. pap., per. 6.50 (*1-57906-011-0*) Natl Defense.

Binnendijk, Hans A., ed. National Negotiating Styles. 147p. (Orig.). (C). 1995. pap. text 30.00 (*0-7881-1570-7*) DIANE Pub.

Binnendijk, Hans A., et al. Strategic Assessment, 1997: Flashpoints & Force Structure. LC 96-52237. 1997. write for info. (*1-57906-029-3*) Natl Defense.

Binnendijk, Leendert. Properties of Double Stars: A Survey of Parallaxes & Orbits. LC 58-8011. 357p. reprint ed. pap. 110.70 (*0-608-30344-5*, 205527900012) Bks Demand.

Binner, J. G. & Yeomans, J. M., eds. Better Ceramics Through Processing. (British Ceramics Proceedings Ser.: Vol. 58). (Illus.). 220p. 1998. 150.00 (*1-86125-033-9*, Pub. by Inst Materials) Ashgate Pub Co.

Binner, Jon G., ed. Advanced Ceramic Processing & Technology, Vol. 1. 415p. 1990. 129.00 (*0-8155-1256-2*) Noyes.

Binneveld, Hans. From Shell Shock to Combat Stress: A Comparative History of Military Psychiatry. 224p. 1998. pap. text 34.50 (*90-5356-270-2*, Pub. by Amsterdam U Pr) U of Mich Pr.

Binneweis, Rudi. The Options Course: A Winning Program for Investors & Traders. LC 96-109673. 300p. 1995. 50.00 incl. disk (*1-55738-871-7*, Irwn Prfssnl) McGraw-Hill Prof.

Binney, Charles J. Genealogy of the Binney Family in the United States. 278p. 1988. reprint ed. pap. 41.00 (*0-8328-0259-X*); reprint ed. lib. bdg. 49.00 (*0-8328-0258-1*) Higginson Bk Co.

— The History & Genealogy of the Prentice or Prentiss Family in New England from 1631 to 1833. 2nd ed. (Illus.). 453p. 1989. reprint ed. pap. 68.00 (*0-8328-0989-6*); reprint ed. lib. bdg. 76.00 (*0-8328-0988-8*) Higginson Bk Co.

— Life of Horace Binney. LC 72-2577. (Select Bibliographies Reprint Ser.). 1977. reprint ed. 29.95 (*0-8369-6849-2*) Ayer.

Binney, George & Williams, Colin. Leaning into the Future: Changing the Way People Change Organizations. LC 95-210676. (Illus.). 192p. 1997. pap. 15.95 (*1-85788-083-8*) Nicholas Brealey.

Binney, J. J., et al. The Theory of Critical Phenomena: An Introduction to the Renormalization Group. LC 92-8130. (Illus.). 476p. 1992. pap. text 55.00 (*0-19-851393-3*, Clarendon Pr) OUP.

Binney, James. Galactic Astronomy. LC 98-24385. (Princeton Series in Astrophysics). 850p. 1998. pap. text 35.00 (*0-691-02565-7*, Pub. by Princeton U Pr) Cal Prin Full Svc.

Binney, James & Merrifield, Michael. Galactic Astronomy. LC 98-24385. (Series in Astrophysics). 850p. 1998. text 99.50 (*0-691-00402-1*, Pub. by Princeton U Pr) Cal Prin Full Svc.

Binney, James J. & Tremaine, Scot. Galactic Dynamics. (Illus.). 640p. 1988. text 135.00 (*0-691-08444-0*, Pub. by Princeton U Pr); pap. text 39.50 (*0-691-08445-9*, Pub. by Princeton U Pr) Cal Prin Full Svc.

Binney, James J., jt. auth. see Mihalas, Dimitri M.

Binney, Judith. Mihaia: The Prophet Rua Kenana & His Community at Maungapohatu. 208p. 1996. pap. 39.95 (*1-86940-148-4*, Pub. by Auckland Univ) Paul & Co Pubs.

— Nga Morehu/The Survivors: The Life Story of Eight Maori Women. 228p. 1996. pap. 39.95 (*1-86940-147-6*, Pub. by Auckland Univ) Paul & Co Pubs.

— Redemption Songs: A Life of Nineteenth-Century Maori Leader Te Kooti Arikirangi Te Turuki. LC 97-7318. 1997. pap. text 34.00 (*0-8248-1975-6*) UH Pr.

— Redemption Songs: A Life of Te Kooti Arikirangi Te Turuki. (Illus.). 676p. 1996. 55.00 (*1-86940-131-X*, Pub. by Auckland Univ) Paul & Co Pubs.

Binney, Judith & Chaplin, Gillian. Nga Morehu: The Survivors. 144p. 1987. pap. 34.50 (*0-19-558135-0*) OUP.

***Binney, Marcus.** Airport Builders. (Illus.). 224p. 1999. 85.00 (*0-471-98445-0*) Wiley.

Binney, Marcus. The Chateaux of France: From the Archives of Country Life. (Illus.). 192p. 1994. 60.00 (*1-85732-531-1*, Pub. by Reed Illust Books) Antique Collect.

— Country Manors of Portugal. (Illus.). 229p. 1993. 55.00 (*0-935748-74-1*) M T Train.

— The Ritz Hotel: London. LC 99-70942. (Illus.). 128p. 1999. 50.00 (*0-500-01934-7*, Pub. by Thames Hudson) Norton.

— Town Houses: Urban Houses from 1200 to the Present Day. LC 98-4148. 176p. 1998. 45.00 (*0-8230-6962-1*) Watsn-Guptill.

Binney, Marcus, ed. Great Railway Stations of Europe. (Illus.). 144p. 1985. 29.95 (*0-317-65910-3*, TH02) Am Soc Civil Eng.

Binney, Marcus & Burman, Peter. Change & Decay: The Future of Our Churches LC 77-370575. 192p. 1977. write for info. (*0-289-70774-9*, Pub. by SVista Bks) Sterling.

Binney, Marcus, et al. The Save Britain's Heritage Action Guide. LC 91-218910. 160p. 1991. write for info. (*1-85585-056-7*, Pub. by Collins & Br) Trafalgar.

Binney, Newman. Pick for Humans. 1991. 29.95 (*0-8306-1800-7*) McGraw-Hill Prof.

Binney, Ruth, jt. ed. see Reader's Digest Editors.

Binnick, Robert I. Modern Mongolian: A Transformational Syntax. LC 79-311196. (Illus.). 167p. reprint ed. pap. 51.80 (*0-8357-8227-1*, 203402400088) Bks Demand.

Binnie & Parners Staff & EEC Commission. Islands for Offshore Nuclear Power Stations. 167p. 1982. pap. text 118.00 (*0-86010-373-0*) G & T Inc.

***Binnie, Alison & Tichen, Angie.** Freedom to Practise: The Development of Patient-Centred Nursing. LC 99-32977. 251p. 2000. pap. text 32.00 (*0-7506-4075-8*) Buttrwrth-Heinemann.

Binnie-Clark, Georgina. Wheat & Women. LC 80-463250. (Social History of Canada Ser.: No. 30). 364p. reprint ed. pap. 112.90 (*0-608-17002-X*, 202642400049) Bks Demand.

Binnie, Colin D., et al. Clinical Neurophysiology: Electromyography, Nerve Conduction & Evoked Potentials, Vol. 1. Osselton, John W., ed. (Illus.). 544p. 1995. text 175.00 (*0-7506-1183-9*) Buttrwrth-Heinemann.

Binnie, Eric. The Theatrical Designs of Charles Ricketts. Beckerman, Bernard, ed. LC 84-23921. (Theater & Dramatic Studies: No. 23). 199p. reprint ed. pap. 61.70 (*0-8357-1584-1*, 207043000089) Bks Demand.

Binnie, Jean. Bring Phonics to Life: Individual Book. text, student ed. write for info. (*0-943343-72-0*) Lrn Wrap-Ups.

Binnie, Jon, jt. auth. see Bell, David.

Binnie, Patricia, ed. see Peele, George.

Binnie, Susan W., jt. ed. see Knafla, Louis A.

Binning, William C., et al. Encyclopedia of American Parties, Campaigns & Elections. LC 98-46810. 480p. 1999. lib. bdg. 99.50 (*0-313-30312-6*) Greenwood.

Binns, Alison. Dedications of Monastic Houses in England & Wales, 1066-1216. (Studies in the History of Medieval Religion: No. 1). 238p. 1989. 75.00 (*0-85115-521-9*) Boydell & Brewer.

Binns, Archie. The Land Is Bright. LC 91-694. (Northwest Reprints Ser.). 376p. 1992. reprint ed. text 24.95 (*0-87071-508-9*) Oreg St U Pr.

— Lightship. 345p. 1962. 19.95 (*0-8323-0109-4*) Binford Mort.

— Mighty Mountain. 440p. 1951. 14.95 (*0-8323-0110-8*); pap. 9.95 (*0-8323-0259-7*) Binford Mort.

— Northwest Gateway: The Story of the Port of Seattle. (Illus.). 325p. 1958. 14.95 (*0-8323-0004-7*) Binford Mort.

— Peter Skene Ogden, Fur Trader. LC 67-23627. (Illus.). 376p. 1967. 16.95 (*0-8323-0054-3*) Binford Mort.

Binns, Bernard & Dale, Peter. Cadastral Surveys & Records of Rights in Land. LC 96-146487. (Land Tenure Studies: Vol. 1). 102p. 1995. pap. 9.00 (*92-5-103627-6*) Food & Agri Org UN.

Binns, Betty. Better Type: Learn to See Subtle Distinctions in the Faces & the Spaces of Text Type: Achieve Legible, Beautiful, & Expressive Type Every Time. (Illus.). 191p. 1998. reprint ed. text 30.00 (*0-7881-5886-4*) DIANE Pub.

Binns, Bright L. Jody Maroni's Sausage Kingdom Cookbook. (Illus.). 96p. 1997. pap. 16.95 (*0-7893-0109-1*, Pub. by Universe) St Martin.

Binns, Brigit. Low-Fat Cooking. (Complete Idiot's Guides Ser.). 320p. 1999. pap. text 16.95 (*0-02-862888-8*) Macmillan Gen Ref.

Binns, Brigit L. Polenta. (Illus.). 120p. 1996. pap. 14.95 (*0-8118-1185-9*) Chronicle Bks.

Binns, Brigit L., jt. auth. see Spears, Grady.

Binns, Donald & Koch, Gunther. Meyer & Meyer Form Articulated Locomotives. LC 94-26002. 1994. write for info. (*0-87315-005-8*) Golden Bell.

Binns, Donald & Koch, Gunther, eds. Meyer & Meyer Form Articulated Locomotives, Vol. 1. 104p. 1994. pap. 25.90 (*1-873150-05-9*) Taylor & Francis.

Binns, H. B., jt. auth. see Rowntree, J. W.

Binns, Henry B. Life of Walt Whitman. LC 78-92937. (Studies in Whitman). 1969. reprint ed. lib. bdg. 75.00 (*0-8383-1001-X*) M S G Haskell Hse.

— Walt Whitman & His Poetry. LC 75-120971. (Poetry & Life Ser.). reprint ed. 16.00 (*0-404-52502-4*) AMS Pr.

***Binns, J. W., et al.** Latin Treatises on Poetry from Renaissance England. LC 99-44198. (Library of Renaissance Humanism: Vol. 6). 1999. lib. bdg. 45.00 (*1-893009-03-3*) Summertown.

An Asterisk (*) at the beginning of an entry indicates that the title is appearing for the first time.

***Binns, Jack, ed.** The Memoirs & Memorials of Sir Hugh Cholmley of Whitby, 1600-1657. (Illus.). 352p. 2000. 60.00 (*0-902122-83-5*, Pub. by Yorkshire) Boydell & Brewer.

***Binns, Jack R.** The United States in Honduras, 1980-1981: An Ambassador's Memoir. (Illus.). 407p. 2000. per. 39.95 (*0-7864-0734-4*) McFarland & Co.

Binns, John. Ascetics & Ambassadors of Christ: The Monasteries of Palestine 314-631. (Oxford Early Christian Studies). 288p. 1996. pap. text 26.00 (*0-19-826934-X*) OUP.

Binns, John & Jones, Mark. The ER Files: The Unauthorized Companion. (Illus.). 256p. 1998. pap. 13.95 (*0-233-99280-4*, Pub. by Chameleon) Trafalgar.

***Binns, John & Jones, Mark.** The New ER Files: The Unauthorized Companion. (Illus.). 338p. 2000. pap. 13.95 (*0-233-99612-5*, Pub. by Andre Deutsch) Trafalgar.

Binns, K. J., et al. The Analytical & Numerical Solution of Electric & Magnetic Fields. 486p. 1992. 320.00 (*0-471-92460-1*) Wiley.

Binns, Katherine, ed. The American Teacher, 1993: Violence in America's Public Schools. (Illus.). 126p. 1998. pap. text 25.00 (*0-7881-7291-3*) DIANE Pub.

Binns, M. Sierra Leone. LC 93-202732. (World Bibliographical Ser.). 282p. 1992. lib. bdg. 81.50 (*1-85109-101-7*) ABC-CLIO.

***Binns, M. R., et al.** Sampling & Monitoring in Crop Protection: The Theoretical Basis for Designing Practical Decision Guides. (CABI Publishing Ser.). 280p. 2000. text 85.00 (*0-85199-347-8*, Pub. by C A B Intl) OUP.

Binns, Margaret. Guinea. LC 97-180603. (World Bibliographical Ser.: Vol. 191). 122p. 1996. lib. bdg. 64.75 (*1-85109-148-3*, DT620) ABC-CLIO.

Binns, Mathew M. Recombinant Poxviruses. 368p. 1992. lib. bdg. 229.00 (*0-8493-6179-6*, QR412) CRC Pr.

***Binns, Michael Elliot.** Finding Through War: Poems of Fifty Years Ago. 1999. pap. 21.00 (*1-85072-165-3*, Pub. by W Sessions) St Mut.

***Binns, Niall.** Un Vals en un Monton de Escombros: Poesia Hispanoamericana Entre la Modernidad Y la Postmodernidad (Nicanor Parra, Enrique Lihn) 175p. 1999. 30.95 (*3-906762-07-6*, Pub. by P Lang) P Lang Pubng.

Binns, Nijel L., jt. auth. see Watt, Robert L.

Binns, Richard. French Leave Finesse. 1997. 16.95 (*0-9516930-8-5*) Seven Hills Bk.

Binns, Ronald. The Loch Ness Mystery Solved. LC 84-43103. (Science & the Paranormal Ser.). (Illus.). 240p. 1984. 19.95 (*0-87975-278-5*); pap. 19.95 (*0-87975-291-2*) Prometheus Bks.

***Binns, Stewart & Wood, Adrian.** The Second World War in Color. LC 00-31404. (Illus.). 208p. 2000. 29.95 (*0-8092-9967-4*, Contemporary Bks) NTC Contemp Pub Co.

Binns, Tony. Tropical Africa. LC 93-35489. (Introductions to Development Ser.). (Illus.). 208p. (C). 1993. pap. 18.99 (*0-415-04801-X*, B2449) Routledge.

Binns, Tony & Bowden, Rob. East Africa. LC 97-40221. (Country Fact Files Ser.). 1998. 24.26 (*0-8172-5401-3*) Raintree Steck-V.

— West Africa. LC 97-40252. (Country Fact Files Ser.). 1998. 24.26 (*0-8172-5400-5*) Raintree Steck-V.

Binns, Tony, jt. auth. see Fisher, Chris.

Bins, Susan K., jt. auth. see Kraus, Anne Marie.

Binsacca, Rich. The Home Building Process: Everything You Need to Know to Work with Contractors & Subcontractors. LC 99-72938. (Illus.). 224p. 1999. pap. 14.95 (*1-881955-63-X*) Home Planners.

Binsacca, Richard, jt. auth. see Yapp, Bob.

Binsack, Rudolf, jt. ed. see Soeder, Carl J.

Binsbergen, Wim M., jt. ed. see Geschiere, Peter.

Binsbergen, Wim M. Van, see Van Binsbergen, Wim M.

Binski, Paul. Medieval Death: Ritual & Representation. LC 96-6007. (Illus.). 232p. (C). 1996. text 39.95 (*0-8014-3315-0*) Cornell U Pr.

— The Painted Chamber at Westminster. (Illus.). 256p. 1986. pap. 32.50 (*0-500-99044-1*, Pub. by Soc Antiquaries) David Brown.

— Painters. (Medieval Craftsmen Ser.). (Illus.). 72p. 1991. pap. text 19.95 (*0-8020-6918-5*) U of Toronto Pr.

— Westminster Abbey & the Plantagenets: Kingship & the Representation of Power, 1200-1400. LC 94-24291. 241p. 1995. 65.00 (*0-300-05980-9*) Yale U Pr.

Binski, Paul, jt. auth. see Pointon, Marcia.

Binsse, Harry, tr. see Roy, Gabrielle.

Binsse, Harry L., tr. see Maritain, Jacques.

Binst, G. V., ed. Design & Synthesis of Organic Molecules Based on Molecular Recognition. (Illus.). 410p. 1986. 172.95 (*0-387-16123-6*) Spr-Verlag.

***Binstadt, Chari Yost.** Up North in Michigan. (Illus.). 32p. (J). (ps-7). 2000. 19.95 (*0-9662399-7-0*) Petunia Pr Inc.

Binstock, Andrew, et al, eds. Technology Forecast, 1998. 72p. 1998. pap. 450.00 (*1-891865-00-5*) PrcewtrhseCprs.

— Technology Forecast, 1999. 824p. 1998. pap. 450.00 (*1-891865-01-3*) PrcewtrhseCprs.

Binstock, Andrew & Rex, John. Practical Algorithms for Programmers. 592p. (C). 1995. pap. text 34.95 (*0-201-63208-X*) Addison-Wesley.

Binstock, Cathy L. After Your Child's Diagnosis: A Practical Guide for Families Raising Children with Disabilities. LC 97-16991. 158p. (Orig.). 1997. pap. 21.95 (*1-880664-21-6*) E M Pr.

Binstock, Dayan, et al, eds. The Chief Rabbi's Children Siddur. (Illus.). 256p. (J). 1996. 14.95 (*1-888162-01-5*) Kuperand USA.

Binstock, R. C. The Light of Home. 176p. 1992. text 19.00 (*0-689-12156-3*) Atheneum Yung Read.

— The Soldier. LC 95-26356. 288p. 1996. 24.00 (*1-56947-059-6*) Soho Press.

— Tree of Heaven. LC 94-41552. 212p. 1995. 22.00 (*1-56947-038-3*) Soho Press.

— Tree of Heaven. LC 94-41552. 220p. 1996. pap. 12.00 (*1-56947-069-3*) Soho Press.

Binstock, Robert H. Agenda for an Aging Society. Date not set. 19.95 (*0-465-00087-8*, Pub. by Basic) HarpC.

— Aging Society. Date not set. pap. 15.00 (*0-465-00066-5*, Pub. by Basic) HarpC.

Binstock, Robert H., et al, eds. Dementia & Aging: Ethics, Values, & Policy Choices. 224p. 1992. pap. text 19.95 (*0-8018-4545-9*) Johns Hopkins.

— Dementia & Aging: Ethics, Values & Policy Choices. 224p. 1992. text 50.00 (*0-8018-4424-X*) Johns Hopkins.

— The Future of Long-Term Care: Social & Policy Issues. LC 96-2146. 288p. 1996. text 38.50 (*0-8018-5320-6*) Johns Hopkins.

— Too Old for Health Care? Controversies in Medicine, Law, Economics, & Ethics. LC 90-23237. (Johns Hopkins Series in Contemporary Medicine & Public Health). 229p. reprint ed. pap. 71.00 (*0-608-06040-2*, 206637200008) Bks Demand.

***Binstock, Robert H. & Cluff, Leighton E., eds.** Home Care Advances: Essential Research & Policy Issues. LC 99-54282. (Illus.). 256p. 2000. text 42.95 (*0-8261-1304-4*) Springer Pub.

Binstock, Robert H. & George, Linda K., eds. The Handbook of Aging & the Social Sciences. 4th ed. (Handbooks of Aging Ser.). (Illus.). 531p. 1995. pap. text 54.95 (*0-12-099193-4*) Acad Pr.

Binstock, Robert H., jt. auth. see Woll, Peter.

Binswanger, Barbara & Charlton, Jim. On the Night the Hogs Ate Willie: And Other Quotations on All Things Southern. 1996. pap. 9.95 (*0-614-97891-2*, Plume) Dutton Plume.

Binswanger, Barbara & Mark, Lisbeth. The Best Name for Your Baby: A Creative Guide to Proper Nomenclature. 256p. (Orig.). 1995. pap. 9.95 (*0-8050-0877-2*, Owl) H Holt & Co.

Binswanger, Hans P. Money & Magic: A Critique of the Modern Economy in the Light of Goethe's Faust. Harrison, John E., tr. from GER. LC 93-38470.Tr. of Geld und Magie. 144p. 1994. 21.50 (*0-226-05185-4*) U Ch Pr.

Binswanger, Hans P. & Landell-Mills, Pierre. The World Bank's Strategy for Reducing Poverty & Hunger. LC 95-1366. (Environmentally Sustainable Development Studies & Monographs: No. 4). 68p. 1995. pap. 22.00 (*0-8213-3174-4*, 13174) World Bank.

Binswanger, Hans P. & Rosenzweig, Mark R., eds. Contractual Arrangements, Employment, & Wages in Rural Labor Markets in Asia. LC 83-5944. (Publication of the Economic Growth Center, Yale University Ser.). 350p. reprint ed. pap. 108.50 (*0-7837-3282-1*, 205768400006) Bks Demand.

Binswanger, Hans P., et al. Induced Innovation: Technology, Institutions, & Development. LC 77-23387. 440p. 1978. reprint ed. pap. 136.40 (*0-608-06700-8*, 206689700009) Bks Demand.

Binswanger, Harry, ed. see Rand, Ayn.

Binswanger, Ludwig, jt. auth. see Foucault, Michel.

Binswanger, Mathias. Stock Markets, Speculative Bubbles & Economic Growth: New Dimensions in the Co-evolution of Real & Financial Markets. LC 99-19286. 384p. 1999. 110.00 (*1-84064-071-5*) E Elgar.

Binswanger, U. & Kretschmer, G., eds. Schweizerisches Erythropoietin Symposium: Beatenberg-CH, Maerz, 1988. (Journal: Nephron: Vol. 51, Suppl. 1, 1989). (Illus.). vi, 46p. 1988. pap. 76.75 (*3-8055-4941-5*) S Karger.

Bint. MCQS in Clinical Pathology. 1995. pap. text 21.00 (*0-7020-1782-5*, W B Saunders Co) Harcrt Hlth Sci Grp.

Binta, Ashaki, et al, eds. The Chords That Bind: Traditions in Southern Music. (Southern Exposure Ser.). (Illus.). 64p. (Orig.). (C). 1996. pap. 5.00 (*0-943810-25-6*) Inst Southern Studies.

Bintliff, John, ed. The Annales School & Archaeology. 132p. (C). 1991. text 42.50 (*0-8147-1168-5*) NYU Pr.

— Structure & Contingency: Evolutionary Processes in Life & Human Society. LC 97-22671. (Illus.). 128p. 1998. 75.00 (*0-7185-0025-3*); pap. 24.95 (*0-7185-0026-1*) Bks Intl VA.

Bintliff, Russell. Police Procedural: A Writer's Guide to the Police & How They Work. (Howdunit Ser.). 272p. 1993. pap. 16.99 (*0-89879-596-6*, Wrtrs Digest Bks) F & W Pubns Inc.

Bintliff, Russell L. The Complete Manual of Corporate & Industrial Security. LC 92-19744. 640p. (C). 1992. text 79.95 (*0-13-159641-1*) P-H.

Bintulisham, Saumiyah, ed. see Hussaini, Mohammad M.

Binuia, Von G. American Jones Building & Maintenance: Fall 1998. 140p. 1998. pap. 6.00 (*1-892034-04-2*) Missing Spoke.

— American Jones Building & Maintenance: Summer 1999. 1999. pap. 6.00 (*1-892034-08-5*, Pub. by Missing Spoke) Partners Pubs Grp.

Binuia, Von G., ed. American Jones Building & Maintenance: Spring, 1999. 1999. pap. 6.00 (*1-892034-07-7*, AJBM5) Missing Spoke.

— American Jones Building & Maintenance: Summer 1998 Issue. 150p. 1998. pap. 6.00 (*1-892034-00-X*) Missing Spoke.

— American Jones Building & Maintenance: Winter 1998-99. 144p. 1998. pap. 6.00 (*1-892034-06-9*, AJBM4) Missing Spoke.

— American Jones Building & Maintenance Issue 1: February, 1998. (Illus.). 120p. 1998. pap. 6.00 (*1-57502-707-0*, PO1992) Morris Pubng.

Binyan, Liu. China's Crisis, China's Hope. (Interpretations of Asia Ser.). 192p. 1990. text 25.00 (*0-674-11882-0*) HUP.

— People or Monsters? And Other Stories & Reportage from China after Mao. Link, Perry, ed. LC 82-48594. (Chinese Literature in Translation Ser.). 160p. 1983. pap. 4.95 (*0-253-20313-9*, MB-313) Ind U Pr.

Binyon, C. M., tr. see Blochet, Edgar.

Binyon, Helen. Eric Ravilious: Memoir of an Artist. LC 83-71366. (Illus.). 144p. 1986. 30.00 (*0-913720-42-9*) Beil.

— Eric Ravilious: Memoir of an Artist. LC 95-82206. (Illus.). 144p. 1996. 34.95 (*0-7188-2920-4*, Lutterworth-Parkwest) Parkwest Pubns.

Binyon, Laurence. Followers of William Blake. LC 68-56526. (Illus.). 39p. 1972. reprint ed. 30.95 (*0-405-08270-3*, Pub. by Blom Pubns) Ayer.

Binyon, Pamela M. The Concepts of Spirit & Demon: A Study in the Use of Different Languages Describing the Same Phenomena. (IC-Studies in the International History of Christianity: Vol. 8). 132p. 1977. pap. 30.00 (*3-261-01787-2*) P Lang Pubng.

Binyon, T. J. Greek Gifts. large type ed. 323p. 1990. reprint ed. 19.95 (*1-85089-324-1*, Pub. by ISIS Lrg Prnt) Transaction Pubs.

— Pushkin. 1999. pap. 11.95 (*0-14-011152-2*, Viking); pap. 23.00 (*0-670-82278-7*) Viking Penguin.

Binyong, Yin & Rohsenow, John. Modern Chinese Characters. (Illus.). 397p. 1994. 16.95 (*0-8351-2474-6*) China Bks.

Binz, Carl. Doctor Johann Weyer: Ein Rheinischer Arzt der Erste Bekampfer Des Hexenwahns Beitrag Zur Geschicte der Aufklarung und der Heilkunde. 2nd rev. ed. LC 75-16683. (Classics in Psychiatry Ser.). (GER.). 1976. reprint ed. 18.95 (*0-405-07415-8*) Ayer.

Binz, Stephen J. Advent of the Savior: A Commentary on the Infancy Narratives of Jesus. 72p. 1996. pap. 4.95 (*0-8146-2410-3*) Liturgical Pr.

— El Dios de la Libertad y de la Vida: El Comentario para le Libro D'Exodo. (SPA.). 152p. 1995. pap. 6.95 (*0-8146-2357-3*) Liturgical Pr.

— The God of Freedom & Life: A Commentary on the Book of Exodus. LC 93-2104. 148p. (Orig.). 1994. pap. 5.95 (*0-8146-2260-7*) Liturgical Pr.

— The Passion & Resurrection Narratives of Jesus: A Commentary. 120p. 1989. pap. 5.95 (*0-8146-1771-9*) Liturgical Pr.

Binzel, Philip E., Jr. Alive & Well: One Doctor's Experience with Nutrition in the Treatment of Cancer Patients. (Illus.). 144p. (Orig.). (C). 1994. pap. 9.95 (*0-912986-17-4*) Am Media.

Binzen, Bill. The Berkshires. rev. ed. LC 94-24549. (Illus.). 96p. 1995. 24.95 (*0-936399-67-8*) Berkshire Hse.

Binzen, Peter. Nearly Everybody Read It: Snapshots of the Philadelphia Bulletin. LC 97-16200. (Illus.). 192p. 1998. 22.00 (*0-940159-40-6*) Camino Bks.

Binzen, Peter, ed. see Gold, Aaron A.

Binzen, Susanna C., ed. see Wolff, James A., et al.

Bioacoustics Research Program Staff. Whales '93: Finback. 1995. pap. 19.95 incl. audio compact disk (*0-938027-26-3*) Crows Nest Bird.

— Whales '93: Greatest Hits. 1995. pap. 14.95 incl. audio compact disk (*0-938027-25-5*) Crows Nest Bird.

— Whales '93: Minke. 1995. pap. 19.95 incl. audio compact disk (*0-938027-28-X*) Crows Nest Bird.

Bioacoutics Research Program Staff. Whales '93: Blue. 1995. pap. 19.95 incl. audio compact disk (*0-938027-27-1*) Crows Nest Bird.

Biocca, Dario, tr. see Calvi, Giulia.

Biocca, Ettore. Yanoama: The Narrative of a Young Girl Kidnapped by Amazonian Indians. Turner, Philip, ed. LC 96-42704. (Illus.). 368p. 1996. pap. 16.00 (*1-56836-108-4*, Kodansha Globe) Kodansha.

Biocca, Frank. Television & Political Advertising, 2 vols. (Communication Ser.). (C). 1991. text 90.00 (*0-8058-1101-X*) L Erlbaum Assocs.

— Television & Political Advertising, Vol. I. (Communication Ser.). 376p. (C). 1991. text 79.95 (*0-8058-0655-5*) L Erlbaum Assocs.

— Television & Political Advertising, Vol. II. (Communication Ser.). 280p. (C). 1991. text 59.95 (*0-8058-0662-8*) L Erlbaum Assocs.

Biocca, Frank & Levy, Mark R., eds. Communication in the Age of Virtual Reality. (Communication Ser.). 408p. 1995. pap. 39.95 (*0-8058-1550-3*); text 99.95 (*0-8058-1549-X*) L Erlbaum Assocs.

Biocca, Silvia, jt. auth. see Cattaneo, Antonio.

Biocca, Silvia, jt. ed. see Cattaneo, Antonio.

BioCycle Staff, ed. Composting for Manure Management. LC 98-231091. 77 p. 1998. write for info. (*0-932424-19-8*) JG P.

***Biodiversity Support Program Staff.** Priority-Setting in Conservation. LC 99-42659. (ENG, TAR, UKR, RUS & CRE.). 1999. pap. write for info. (*1-887531-31-9*) Biodivers Supp Prog.

Biodiversity Support Program Staff, jt. auth. see Meine, Curt.

Biody, Evelyn, et al. Partnership Tax Practice Manual: 1992 Edition. 550p. 1991. ring bd. 99.00 (*1-878375-70-9*) Panel Pubs.

Bioedon, Patricia, tr. see Tomberg, Valentin.

Bioedon, Richard, tr. see Tomberg, Valentin.

Biogeomon, the Symposium on Ecosystem Behaviour: E. Biogeochemical Monitoring in Small Catchments: Refereed Papers for BIOGEOMON, the Symposium of Ecosystem Behaviour: Evaluation of Integrated Monitoring in Small Catchments Held in Prague, Czech Republic, September 18-20, 1993. Cerny, Jiri et al, eds. LC 95-14. 432p. (C). 1995. text 291.00 (*0-7923-3383-7*) Kluwer Academic.

Biographical Review Staff. Biographical Review Containing Life Sketches of Leading Citizens of Essex County, Massachusetts. (Illus.). 619p. 1997. reprint ed. pap. 40.00 (*0-7884-0750-3*, B356) Heritage Bk.

— Biographical Sketches of the Leading Citizens of Otsego County, New York. (Illus.). 874p. 1995. pap. 56.50 (*0-7884-0258-7*) Heritage Bk.

Biographical Review Staff, ed. Biographical Sketches of the Leading Citizens of Otsego County, New York. (Illus.). 857p. 1997. reprint ed. lib. bdg. 87.50 (*0-8328-6198-7*) Higginson Bk Co.

Biography Master Hsuan Hua Publication Committee Staff. Records of the Life of the Venerable Master Hsuan Hua, Vol. 1. (Illus.). 90p. 1981. pap. 5.00 (*0-917512-07-3*) Buddhist Text.

Biography Master Hsuan Hua Publication Committee Staff. Records of the Life of the Venerable Master Hsuan Hua, Vol. 2. (Illus.). 182p. 1976. pap. 8.00 (*0-917512-10-3*) Buddhist Text.

Biological Council, Animal Research & Welfare Pane & U F A W Staff. Guidelines on Handling & Training of Laboratory Animals. 1992. pap. 25.00 (*0-900767-77-4*, Pub. by Univs Fed Animal Welfare) St Mut.

Biological Sciences Curriculum Study Staff. Biological Science: Interaction of Experiments & Ideas (BSCS Second Course) 3rd ed. (gr. 10-12). 1977. teacher ed. 15.96 (*0-13-076919-3*); text 30.64 (*0-13-076562-7*) P-H.

***Biological Sciences Curriculum Study Staff.** Making Sense of Integrated Science: A Guide for High Schools. (Illus.). xii, 243p. 2000. pap. text 24.00 (*1-929614-03-9*) Biological Sciences.

B

Biolsi. Organizing the Lakota: The Political Economy of the New Deal on the Pine Ridge & Rosebud Reservations. LC 92-182. 280p. 1998. pap. 17.95 (*0-8165-1885-8*) U of Ariz Pr.

Biolsi, Thomas. Organizing the Lakota: The Political Economy of the New Deal on the Pine Ridge & Rosebud Reservations. LC 92-182. (Illus.). 240p. 1992. 38.50 (*0-8165-1127-6*) U of Ariz Pr.

Biolsi, Thomas & Zimmerman, Larry J., eds. Indians & Anthropologists: Vine Deloria, Jr., & the Critique of Anthropology. LC 96-45804. 240p. 1997. 45.00 (*0-8165-1606-5*); pap. 19.95 (*0-8165-1607-3*) U of Ariz Pr.

Biomechanical & Human Factors Conference Staff. Biomechanical & Human Factors Symposium: Proceedings of the Biomechanical & Human Factors Conference, 2nd, Washington, D. C., 1967. Gage, Howard, ed. LC 67-21480. (Illus.). 184p. reprint ed. pap. 57.10 (*0-8357-7248-9*, 201681400005) Bks Demand.

Biomechanics Symposium (1977, Yale University). Biomechanics Symposium, 1977: Presented at the 1977 Joint Applied Mechanics, Fluids Engineering , & Bioengineering Conference, Yale University , New Haven, CT, June 15-17, 1977, (Sponsored by the Applied Mechanics Division, ASME, the Bioengineering Division, ASME, the Fluids Engineering Division, ASME. Skalak, Richard & Schultz, Albert B., eds. LC 77-151677. (AMD Ser.: Vol. 23). 244p. reprint ed. pap. 75.70 (*0-8357-7250-0*, 205616200052) Bks Demand.

Biomedical Engineering Society Staff. Bioengineering Approaches to Pulmonary Physiology & Medicine. Khoo, Michael C., ed. LC 96-28918. (Illus.). 253p. (C). 1996. text 107.00 (*0-306-45370-3*, Kluwer Plenum) Kluwer Academic.

Biomedical Sciences Instrumentation Staff. Biomedical Sciences Instrumentation: Technical Papers Composing the Proceedings of the 33rd Annual Rocky Mountain Symposium & 33rd International ISA Symposium, Presented at United States Air Force Academy, Colorado Springs, CO, April 12-13, 1996. Valenta, Harry L., Jr., ed. LC 63-25575. (Illus.). 346p. 1996. reprint ed. pap. 107.30 (*0-608-04250-1*, 206500600032) Bks Demand.

Bion. Current Topics in Intensive Care, Vol. 2. 2nd ed. 1995. text 61.00 (*0-7020-1871-6*, W B Saunders Co) Harcrt Hlth Sci Grp.

Bion, Francesca, ed. see Bion, Wilfred R.

Bion, M. The Construction & Principal Uses of Mathematical Instruments. Stone, Edmund, tr. from FRE. (Illus.). 400p. 1995. reprint ed. 59.50 (*1-879335-60-3*) Astragal Pr.

Bion, Wilfred R. All My Sins Remembered: Another Part of a Life - The Other Side of Genius: Family Letters. 243p. 1991. pap. 41.50 (*1-85575-003-1*, Pub. by H Karnac Bks Ltd) Other Pr LLC.

Bion, Wilfred R. All My Sins Remembered: Another Part of Life - The Other Side of Genius: Family Letters. 246p. 1990. reprint ed. text 41.95 (*0-9507895-1-8*, Pub. by H Karnac Bks Ltd) Brunner-Mazel.

— Brazilian Lectures: 1973 Sao Paolo, 1974 Rio de Janeiro/Sao Paolo. 224p. 1990. reprint ed. pap. 31.00 (*0-946439-78-8*, Pub. by H Karnac Bks Ltd) Brunner-Mazel.

Bion, Wilfred R. Clinical Seminars & Other Works. expanded ed. 352p. 1994. pap. 42.00 (*1-85575-061-9*, Pub. by H Karnac Bks Ltd) Other Pr LLC.

— Cogitations. expanded ed. 416p. 1994. pap. 50.00 (*0-946439-98-2*, Pub. by H Karnac Bks Ltd) Brunner-Mazel.

Bion, Wilfred R. Experiences in Groups: And Other Papers. 148p. (C). 1991. pap. 22.99 (*0-415-04020-5*, A5774) Routledge.

— Ginduri Secunde: Lucrari Selectate de Psihanaliza. Vladescu, Florin V., ed. & tr. by. Bujdei, Carmen et al, trs. (Illus.). 240p. (Orig.). 1993. pap. text 19.95 (*1-883881-00-5*) S Freud RT&PF.

— The Long Week-End, 1897-1919: Part of a Life. 299p. 1990. reprint ed. pap. text 41.95 (*0-9507895-0-X*, Pub. by H Karnac Bks Ltd) Brunner-Mazel.

Bion, Wilfred R. The Long Weekend 1897-1919: Part of a Life. 287p. 1991. pap. 41.50 (*1-85575-000-7*, Pub. by H Karnac Bks Ltd) Other Pr LLC.

Bion, Wilfred R. A Memoir of the Future. 678p. 1991. pap. 50.00 (*0-946439-79-6*, Pub. by H Karnac Bks Ltd) Other Pr LLC.

An Asterisk (*) at the beginning of an entry indicates that the title is appearing for the first time.

Bion, Wilfred R. Taming Wild Thoughts. 72p. 1997. pap. 15.00 (1-85575-168-2, Pub. by H Karnac Bks Ltd) Other Pr LLC.

Bion, Wilfred R. Transformations. LC 84-45130. 192p. 1983. 40.00 (0-87668-723-0) Aronson.

Bion, Wilfred R. Two Papers: The Grid & Caesura. 72p. 1989. reprint ed. pap. 15.00 (0-946439-77-X, Pub. by H Karnac Bks Ltd) Other Pr LLC.

— War Memoirs, 1917-1919. Bion, Francesca, ed. LC 98-150438. 320p. 1997. 42.00 (1-85575-179-8, Pub. by H Karnac Bks Ltd); pap. 55.00 (1-85575-153-4, Pub. by H Karnac Bks Ltd) Other Pr LLC.

Bionda, Richard & Blotkamp, Carel, eds. The Age of Van Gogh: Dutch Painting, 1880-1895. (Illus.). 262p. 1997. pap. 40.00 (90-6630-128-7, Pub. by Waanders) U of Wash Pr.

***Biondi, Al.** Swing Jazz Duets - Clarinet Edition. 32p. 1999. pap. 8.95 (0-7866-4827-9, 98127) Mel Bay.

— Swing Jazz Duets - E-Flat Alto Sax Edition. 32p. 1999. pap. 8.95 (0-7866-4826-0, 98126) Mel Bay.

— Swing Jazz Duets - Guitar Edition. 32p. 1999. pap. 8.95 (0-7866-4823-6, 98123) Mel Bay.

— Swing Jazz Duets - Tenor Sax Edition. 32p. 1999. pap. 8.95 (0-7866-4828-7, 98128) Mel Bay.

— Swing Jazz Duets - Trumpet Edition. 32p. 1999. pap. 8.95 (0-7866-4825-2, 98125) Mel Bay.

— Swing Jazz Duets - Violin Edition. 32p. 1999. pap. 8.95 (0-7866-4824-4, 98124) Mel Bay.

B

Biondi, Albano, et al, eds. Eresia e Riforma Nell'italia del Cinquecento: Miscellanea I. LC 74-30505. (Corpus Reformatorum Italicorum & Biblioteca Ser.). (ITA.). 357p. 1974. pap. 40.00 (0-87580-520-5) N Ill U Pr.

Biondi, Andrea, jt. auth. see Lonbay, Julian.

Biondi, Bob, jt. auth. see Congdon-Martin, Douglas.

***Biondi, Joann.** Miami. LC 00-26018. (Citylife Pictorial Guides Ser.). (Illus.). 96p. 2000. 24.95 (0-89658-445-3) Voyageur Pr.

Biondi, Joann & Haskins, James. Black New York. (U. S. A. Guides Ser.). 141p. (Orig.). 1994. pap. 14.95 (0-7818-0172-9) Hippocrene Bks.

Biondi, Joann, jt. auth. see Haskins, James.

Biondi, Joann, jt. auth. see Haskins, Jim.

Biondi-Morra, Brizio N. Hungry Dreams: The Failure of Food Policy in Revolutionary Nicaragua, 1979-1990. LC 92-56782. (Food Systems & Agrarian Change Ser.). 256p. 1993. text 39.95 (0-8014-2663-4) Cornell U Pr.

***BIONDI, PAOLA.** Design in Italian Furnishing. 1999. 70.00 (88-422-0839-6) Dist Art Pubs.

Biondi, Ray & Hecox, Walter. All His Father's Sins: Inside the Gerald Gallego Sex-Slave Murders. rev. ed. (Illus.). 208p. 1991. 15.95 (0-914629-34-4) Prima Pub.

— All His Father's Sins: The Shocking Truth about California's Most Gruesome Serial Killer. 224p. 1990. mass mkt. 4.99 (0-671-67265-7) PB.

— The Dracula Killer. Tobias, Eric, ed. 232p. (Orig.). 1992. mass mkt. 4.99 (0-671-74003-2) PB.

Biondo, Lisa A., ed. Father William Boyle: A Teacher Remembered. LC 98-41910. 150p. 1999. 22.00 (0-8232-1896-1) Fordham.

Biondo, Ronald J. Introduction to Plant & Soil Science & Technology. LC 96-75865. (Agriscience & Technology Ser.). 544p. 1997. 58.75 (0-8134-3079-8) Interstate.

Biondo, Ronald J. & Lee, Jasper S. Introduction to Plant & Soil Science & Technology. 1998. teacher ed. 9.95 (0-8134-3080-1, 3080) Interstate.

— Introduction to Plant & Soil Science & Technology Activity Manual. 1998. teacher ed. 14.95 (0-8134-3132-8, 3132); student ed. 19.95 (0-8134-3131-X, 3131) Interstate.

Biondo, Ronald J. & Schroeder, Charles B. Introduction to Landscaping: Design, Construction, & Maintenance. 2nd ed. (Illus.). 1998. teacher ed. 12.95 (0-8134-3122-0, 3122) Interstate.

— Introduction to Landscaping: Design, Construction, & Maintenance. 2nd ed. LC 99-71469. (Agriscience & Technology Ser.). (Illus.). viii, 440 p. 2000. 74.95 (0-8134-3171-9) Interstate.

— Introduction to Landscaping: Design, Construction, & Maintenance: Activity Manual. 2nd ed. 1998. 19.95 (0-8134-3133-6, 3133) Interstate.

— Introduction to Landscaping: Design, Construction, & Maintenance: Instructor's Guide for Activity Manual. 2nd ed. 1998. teacher ed. 14.95 (0-8134-3134-4, 3134) Interstate.

Biorklund, Elis. International Atomic Policy During a Decade: An Historical-Political Investigation into the Problems of Atomic Weapons During the Period 1945-55. Reed, Albert, tr. LC 78-13715. 148p. 1979. reprint ed. lib. bdg. 55.00 (0-313-20633-3, BIIA) Greenwood.

Biorklund, George & Barnard, Osbert H. Rembrandt's Etchings True & False. LC 87-80027. (Illus.). 200p. 1988. reprint ed. lib. bdg. 50.00 (0-87817-319-6) Hacker.

BIOS Agency Staff, jt. auth. see Tracqui, Valerie.

Biot, M. A. Acoustics, Elasticity & Thermodynamics of Porous Media: Twenty-One Papers by M. A. Biot. Tolstoy, Ivan, ed. LC 91-41032. 272p. 1991. 33.00 (1-56396-014-1) Acoustical Soc Am.

Biot, Yvan, et al. Rethinking Research on Land Degradation in Developing Countries. LC 95-22327. (Discussion Paper Ser.: Vol. 289). 152p. 1995. pap. 22.00 (0-8213-3329-1, 13329) World Bank.

Biotelemetry International Symposium Staff. Biotelemetry International Symposium, 2nd, Davos, May 1974. Neukomm, P. A. et al, eds. 1974. 55.75 (3-8055-2103-0) S Karger.

Biotol. Principles of Enzymology for Technological Applications. (BIOTOL Ser.). 300p. 1993. pap. text 66.95 (0-7506-0689-4) Buttrwrth-Heinemann.

— Techniques Used in Bioproduct Analysis. 302p. 1992. pap. text 47.95 (0-7506-1501-X) Buttrwrth-Heinemann.

Biotol Board Staff. Bioreactor Design & Product Yield. 275p. 2000. pap. text 36.95 (0-7506-1509-5) Buttrwrth-Heinemann.

BIOTOL Partners Staff. A Compendium of Good Practices in Biotechnology. (BIOTOL Ser.). (Illus.). 318p. 1994. pap. text 75.00 (0-7506-1600-8) Buttrwrth-Heinemann.

BIOTOL Partners Staff, et al. Biotechnological Innovations in Chemical Synthesis. (BIOTOL Ser.). (Illus.). 400p. 1997. pap. text 74.95 (0-7506-0561-8) Buttrwrth-Heinemann.

— In Vitro Cultivation of Animal Cells. (Biotechnology by Open Learning Ser.). (Illus.). 264p. 1994. pap. text 66.95 (0-7506-0555-3) Buttrwrth-Heinemann.

BIOTOL Project Members. Analysis of Amino Acids, Proteins & Nucleic Acids. (Illus.). 255p. 1992. pap. text 54.95 (0-7506-1502-8) Buttrwrth-Heinemann.

BIOTOL Project Staff, jt. auth. see Green.

BIOTOL Staff. Technological Application of Immunochemicals. (BIOTOL Ser.). 1994. pap. text 66.95 (0-7506-0508-1) Buttrwrth-Heinemann.

Biott, Colin. Semi-Detached Teachers: Building Advisory & Support Relationships in Classrooms. 1990. pap. 34.95 (1-85000-443-9, Falmer Pr) Taylor & Francis.

Biott, Colin & Easen, Patrick. Collaborative Learning in Staffrooms & Classrooms. LC 94-224867. (Primary Curriculum Ser.). 176p. 1994. pap. 29.00 (1-85346-201-2, Pub. by David Fulton) Taylor & Francis.

Biott, Colin & Nias, Jennifer, eds. Working & Learning Together for Change. (Developing Teachers & Teaching Ser.). 160p. 1992. pap. 36.95 (0-335-09716-2) OpUniv Pr.

Biow, Douglas. Mirabile Dictu: Representations of the Marvelous in Medieval & Renaissance Epic. LC 96-3475. (Stylus Ser.). (Illus.). 216p. (C). 1996. text 42.50 (0-472-10691-0, 10691) U of Mich Pr.

Biow, Lisa. HELP! Paradox for Windows. (HELP! Ser.). (Illus.). 1042p. (Orig.). 1993. pap. 27.95 (1-56276-039-4, Ziff-Davis Pr) Que.

— How to Use Computers Visually. LC 98-84267. 1998. pap. text 24.99 (0-7897-1645-3) Que.

Bioy Casares, Adolfo. Asleep in the Sun. Levine, Suzanne J., tr. from SPA. LC 77-91846. 1978. 8.95 (0-89255-030-9) Persea Bks.

— Breve Diccionario del Argentino Exquisito. (SPA.). 162p. 1978. 19.95 (0-8288-4865-3, S33074) Fr & Eur.

— A Russian Doll & Other Stories. Levine, Suzanne J., tr. from SPA. LC 92-10432. 128p. 1992. 22.95 (0-8112-1211-4, Pub. by New Directions); pap. 10.95 (0-8112-1212-2, NDP745, Pub. by New Directions) Norton.

— Selected Stories. LC 96-6744. (SPA., Illus.). 176p. 1994. 21.95 (0-8112-1275-0, Pub. by New Directions) Norton.

Bippen, Linda, jt. auth. see Pullis, Joe M.

Bippes, Thomas. Die Europaische Nahostpolitik. (Illus.). 230p. 1997. 42.95 (3-631-31705-0) P Lang Pubng.

BipQuiz Staff & Mitchell, Carolyn B. American History. LC 97-181089. (BipQuiz Ser.). (Illus.). 64p. (J). 1996. pap. 2.95 (0-8069-4855-8) Sterling.

— Revolutionary War. LC 97-181097. (BipQuiz Ser.). (Illus.). 64p. (J). 1996. pap. 2.95 (0-8069-4853-1) Sterling.

Biqin, Zhong & Xianshen, Zhou, annos. Ten Vernacular Tales from Ancient China. 536p. 1992. 19.95 (0-8351-2471-1) China Bks.

Bir Krishna Goswami, pseud. Encounters: A Higher Dimension in Consciousness. 64p. (Orig.). pap. 0.50 (0-944969-00-3) ISKCON NC.

Bir, Richard E. Growing & Propagating Showy Native Woody Plants. LC 91-35993. (Illus.). x, 192p. (C). 1992. 39.95 (0-8078-2027-X); pap. 24.95 (0-8078-4366-0) U of NC Pr.

Bir, S. S. Aspects of Plant Sciences, Vol. III: Pteridophytes: Some Aspects - Their Structure & Morphology, Vol. III. 170p. 1980. 15.00 (0-88065-172-5) Scholarly Pubns.

— Pteridophytes: Some Aspects of Their Structure & Morphology. (Aspects of Plant Sciences Ser.: Vol. III). 170p. 1980. 15.00 (0-88065-064-8) Scholarly Pubns.

— Pteridophytes: Some Aspects of Their Structure Morphology. (C). 1988. 40.00 (0-7855-3259-5, Pub. by Scientific) St Mut.

— Pteridophytes: Their Morphology, Cytology, Taxonomy & Phylogeny. (C). 1988. 60.00 (0-7855-3260-9, Pub. by Scientific) St Mut.

— Pteridophytes: Their Morphology, Cytology, Taxonomy & Phytogeny. (Aspects of Plant Sciences Ser.: Vol. 6). vii, 253p. 1983. 19.00 (1-55528-012-9, Pub. by Today Tomorrow) Scholarly Pubns.

Bir, S. S., ed. Aspects of Plant Sciences, Vol. VI. (Illus.). 261p. (C). 1983. 19.00 (0-88065-235-7, Pub. by Today Tomorrow) Scholarly Pubns.

Bir, S. S., ed. Essays on Plant Cytogenetics in India. (Aspects of Plant Sciences Ser.: Vol. IX). (Illus.). 360p. 1987. 45.00 (1-55528-087-0) Scholarly Pubns.

Bir, S. S. & Chatha, G. S. Forest Vegetation Characteristics of Indian Hills (Palni Hills S. India) (International Bioscience Monographs: Vol. XIX). (Illus.). 130p. 1988. 45.00 (1-55528-095-1) Scholarly Pubns.

Bir, S. S. & Saggoo, M. I., eds. Perspectives in Plant Sciences in India: Proceedings of the Section of Botany of Indian Science Congress Platinum Jubilee Session, June 1988. (Aspects of Plant Sciences Ser.: Vol. X). xvi, 279p. 1989. 45.00 (1-55528-163-X) Scholarly Pubns.

Bir, S. S., jt. auth. see Satija, C. K.

Bir, S. S., jt. auth. see Vasudeva, S. M.

Biracree, Tom. Althea Gibson: Tennis Champion. (Black American Ser.). (Illus.). (YA). 1990. mass mkt. 3.95 (0-87067-563-X, Melrose Sq) Holloway.

Biracree, Tom. Don't Know Much about Geography. 1993. mass mkt. 7.99 (0-8125-2224-9) Tor Bks.

Biracree, Tom. Wilma Rudolph: Champion Athlete. (Black American Ser.). (Illus.). 192p. (YA). 1991. mass mkt. 3.95 (0-87067-565-6, Melrose Sq) Holloway.

Biracree, Tom, jt. auth. see Christian, Spencer.

Biracree, Tom, jt. auth. see Pargh, Andy.

Biracree, Tom, jt. auth. see Taylor, Stu.

Biraimah, Karen. Unequal Knowledge Distribution: The Schooling Experience in a Togolese Secondary School. (Special Studies in Comparative Education: No. 9). 56p. (Orig.). 1983. pap. text 10.00 (0-937033-00-6) Grad Schl of Educ.

Biram, John, tr. see Wegener, Alfred.

***Biran.** Ship Hydrostatics & Stability. 320p. 2001. 75.95 (0-7506-4988-7) Buttrwrth-Heinemann.

***Biran, Adrian.** Matlab 5.0 for Engineers. 2nd ed. LC 98-44898. 672p. (C). 1999. pap. 56.00 (0-201-36043-8) Addison-Wesley.

Biran, Michal. Qaidu & the Rise of the Independent Mongol State in Central Asia. LC 98-170584. 288p. 1997. 75.00 (0-7007-0631-3, Pub. by Curzon Pr Ltd) Paul & Co Pubs.

Biran, Pierre Maine De, see Maine De Biran, Pierre.

Birand, Mehmet A. Shirts of Steel: An Anatomy of the Turkish Officer Corps. 1991. text 59.95 (1-85043-326-7, Pub. by I B T) St Martin.

Birau, N. & Schlott, W., eds. Melatonin - Current Status & Perspectives: Proceedings of an International Symposium on Melatonin, Held in Bremen, F. R. Germany, September 18-30, 1980. (Advances in the Biosciences Ser.: Vol. 29). 420p. 1981. 72.50 (0-08-026400-X, Pergamon Pr) Elsevier.

Birbalsingh, Frank, ed. Frontiers of Caribbean Literature in English. LC 95-19517. 264p. 1996. pap. 19.95 (0-312-12638-7); text 49.95 (0-312-12637-9) St Martin.

Birbaum, Alfred & Kammei, Riku. Zen for Cats: Postcard Book. (Illus.). 48p. (Orig.). 1993. pap. 8.95 (0-8348-0294-5) Weatherhill.

Birbaumer, Niels & Kimmel, H. D., eds. Biofeedback & Self-Regulation. LC 79-19203. 480p. reprint ed. pap. 148.80 (0-8357-2583-9, 204028800015) Bks Demand.

***Birbeck, Mark, et al.** Professional XML. 2000. pap. 49.99 (1-86100-311-0) Wrox Pr Inc.

Birberick, Anne L. Reading Undercover: Audience & Authority in Jean de la Fontaine. LC 98-12829. 160 p. 1999. 33.50 (0-8387-5388-4) Bucknell U Pr.

Birberick, Anne L., ed. Refiguring La Fontaine: Tercentenary Studies. LC 95-33255. 242p. 1996. lib. bdg. 45.00 (1-886365-00-8) Rookwood Pr.

Birbo, Yvette. Profane Mythology: The Savage Mind of the Cinema. LC 81-48384. 158p. reprint ed. pap. 49.00 (0-7837-6096-5, 205914200008) Bks Demand.

***Bircee, Loverne.** True Tales from the Top of Mt. Alyeska: A Story of Glacier Valley. (Illus.). 117p. 1998. pap. text 12.00 (1-57833-098-X) Todd Commns.

Birch. Automotive Braking Systems. 3rd ed. LC 98-34476. (Automotive Technology Ser.). 544p. (C). 1999. pap. 62.95 (0-8273-9097-1) Delmar.

***Birch.** Automotive Braking Systems: Instructor's Manual. 128p. 1999. teacher ed. 15.95 (0-8273-9098-X) Delmar.

Birch. Automotive Chassis Systems. LC 99-26156. (Automotive Technology Ser.). (C). 1999. pap. text 66.95 (0-7668-0001-6) Delmar.

— Automotive Suspension & Steering Systems. 3rd ed. LC 98-22157. (Automotive Technology Ser.). 640p. (C). 1998. text 62.95 (0-8273-9099-8) Delmar.

Birch, jt. auth. see Mauch.

Birch, Alan. The Economic History of the British Iron & Steel Industry, 1784-1879: Essays in Industrial & Economic History with Special Reference to the Development of Technology. LC 67-29908. xv, 397p. 1967. 49.50 (0-678-05026-0) Kelley.

***Birch, Alexander.** Age of E-Tail: Conquering the New World of Electronic Shopping. 2000. 24.95 (1-84112-092-8) Capstone Pub NH.

Birch, Anthony H. The British System of Government. 10th ed. LC 97-33484. 288p. (C). 1998. pap. 24.99 (0-415-18389-8) Routledge.

— The Concepts & Theories of Modern Democracy. LC 92-33977. 272p. (C). 1993. pap. 24.99 (0-415-09108-X, B0408) Routledge.

— The Concepts & Theories of Modern Democracy. LC 92-33977. 272p. (C). (gr. 13). 1993. text 85.00 (0-415-09107-1, B0404) Routledge.

— Nationalism & National Integration. LC 88-31365. 272p. (C). (gr. 13). 1989. text 76.00 (0-04-320180-6) Routledge.

Birch, Anthony H. Representative & Responsible Government: An Essay on the British Constitution. LC 71-465276. 252p. reprint ed. pap. 78.20 (0-608-16226-4, 202650900050) Bks Demand.

***Birch, Anthony Harold.** Concepts & Theories of Modern Democracy. 2nd ed. LC 00-42219. 2000. pap. write for info. (0-415-22605-8) Routledge.

Birch, Arthur J. Arthur J. Birch: To See the Obvious. LC 95-18601. (Profiles, Pathways, & Dreams Ser.). (Illus.). 304p. 1995. text 38.00 (0-8412-1840-4, Pub. by Am Chemical) OUP.

Birch, B. Science Museum Book of Discoveries. (Illus.). (J). 1997. mass mkt. 8.95 (0-340-68999-4, Pub. by Hodder & Stought Ltd) Trafalgar.

Birch, Beryl B. Power Yoga: The Total Strength & Flexibility Workout. 286p. 1995. per. 15.00 (0-02-058351-6) Macmillan.

***Birch, Beryl Bender.** Beyond Power Yoga: 8 Levels of Practice for Body & Soul. LC 99-55145. 272p. 2000. per. 16.00 (0-684-85526-7) S&S Trade.

Birch, Beverley. Benjamin Franklin: Adventures with Electricity. (Science Stories Ser.). (Illus.). 48p. (J). (gr. 2-4). 1996. lib. bdg. 14.95 (1-56674-190-4) Forest Hse.

— Benjamin Franklin's Adventures with Electricity. (Science Stories Ser.). (Illus.). 48p. (J). (gr. 4-7). 1996. 10.95 (0-8120-6622-7); pap. text 5.95 (0-8120-9790-4) Barron.

— Benjamin Franklin's Adventures with Electricity. (Science Stories). (J). 1996. 11.15 (0-606-11106-9, Pub. by Turtleback) Demco.

— Marconi's Battle for Radio. (Science Stories Ser.). (Illus.). 48p. (J). (gr. 4-7). 1996. 10.95 (0-8120-6620-0); pap. text 5.95 (0-8120-9792-0) Barron.

— Marconi's Battle for Radio. (Science Stories Ser.). (Illus.). 48p. (J). (gr. 2-4). 1996. lib. bdg. 14.95 (1-56674-191-2) Forest Hse.

***Birch, Beverley.** Marie Curie. LC 00-8806. (Illus.). 64p. (gr. 4-7). 2000. write for info. (1-56711-333-8) Blackbirch.

Birch, Beverley. Marie Curie's Search for Radium. (Science Stories Ser.). (Illus.). 48p. (J). (gr. 4-7). 1996. 10.95 (0-8120-6621-9); pap. text 5.95 (0-8120-9791-2) Barron.

— Marie Curie's Search for Radium. (Science Stories Ser.). (Illus.). 48p. (J). (gr. 2-4). 1996. lib. bdg. 14.95 (1-56674-192-0) Forest Hse.

— Pasteur's Fight Against Microbes. LC 96-83307. (Science Stories Ser.). (Illus.). 48p. (J). (gr. 4-7). 1996. pap. text 5.95 (0-8120-9793-9) Barron.

— Pasteur's Fight Against Microbes. (Science Stories Ser.). (Illus.). 48p. (J). (gr. 2-4). 1996. lib. bdg. 14.95 (1-56674-193-9) Forest Hse.

— Pastuer's Fight Against Microbes. LC 96-83307. (Science Stories Ser.). (Illus.). 48p. (J). (gr. 4-7). 1996. 10.95 (0-8120-6623-5) Barron.

Birch, Beverley & Gardner, Sally. Suzi, Sam, George & Alice. (Illus.). 32p. (J). (ps-1). 1994. 17.95 (0-370-31771-8, Pub. by Bodley Head) Trafalgar.

Birch, Beverly. Marconi's Battle for Radio. (Science Stories). 1996. 11.15 (0-606-11597-8, Pub. by Turtleback) Demco.

— Marie Curie's Search for Radium. (Science Stories). 1996. 11.15 (0-606-11598-6, Pub. by Turtleback) Demco.

— Pasteur's Fight Against Microbes. (Science Stories). 1996. 11.15 (0-606-11723-7, Pub. by Turtleback) Demco.

— Science Stories: The History of Famous Discoveries, 4 vols., Set. 192p. (J). (gr. 2-4). 1997. lib. bdg. 59.80 (1-56674-934-4) Forest Hse.

Birch, Bruce C. Hosea, Joel, & Amos. LC 97-616. (Bible Companion Ser.). 280p. 1997. pap. 19.00 (0-664-25271-0) Westminster John Knox.

— Let Justice Roll Down: The Old Testament, Ethics, & Christian Life. 320p. (Orig.). 1991. pap. 32.95 (0-664-24026-7) Westminster John Knox.

— To Love As We Are Loved: The Bible & Relationships. 128p. (Orig.). 1992. pap. 8.95 (0-687-42188-8) Abingdon.

Birch, Bruce C. & Rasmussen, Larry L. Bible & Ethics in the Christian Life. enl. rev. ed. LC 88-39769. 224p. 1989. pap. 16.99 (0-8066-2397-7, 10-0706, Augsburg) Augsburg Fortress.

***Birch, Carol.** The Whole Story Handbook: Using Imagery to Complete the Story Experience. 2000. pap. 12.95 (0-87483-566-6) August Hse.

Birch, Carol, jt. auth. see Rouse, Geraldine.

Birch, Carol L. & Heckler, Melissa A. Who Says: Essays on Pivotal Issues in Contemporary Storytelling. 1996. pap. text 16.95 (0-87483-454-6) August Hse.

***Birch, Cathy.** Asserting Your Self: How to Feel Confident about Getting More from Life. 144p. 2000. pap. 14.95 (1-85703-433-3, Pub. by How To Bks) Midpt Trade.

Birch, Cathy. Awakening the Writer Within: How to Discover & Release Your True Writer's Voice. 144p. 2000. pap. 14.95 (1-85703-281-0, Pub. by How To Bks) Midpt Trade.

***Birch, Charles.** Biology & the Riddle of Life. 224p. 1999. pap. 19.95 (0-86840-785-2, Pub. by New South Wales Univ Pr) Intl Spec Bk.

Birch, Charles. Feelings. 132p. 1995. pap. 25.95 (0-86840-151-X, Pub. by New South Wales Univ Pr) Intl Spec Bk.

— Regaining Compassion: For Humanity & Nature. 250p. (Orig.). 1993. pap. 17.99 (0-8272-3214-4) Chalice Pr.

— Regaining Compassion for Humanity & Nature. 251p. 1993. pap. 19.95 (0-86840-213-3, Pub. by New South Wales Univ Pr) Intl Spec Bk.

Birch, Charles & Cobb, John B., Jr. The Liberation of Life: From the Cell to the Community. 2nd ed. Hargrove, Eugene C., ed. 353p. (C). 1990. reprint ed. pap. 14.95 (0-9626807-0-2) Environ Ethics Bks.

Birch, Cordelia M., ed. Caesar - Concordantia et Index Caesaris, 2 vols., Set. (Alpha Omega, Reihe A Ser.: Bd. C). (GER.). 1550p. 1989. 465.00 (3-487-07991-7) G Olms Pubs.

Birch, Cyril. Scenes for Mandarins: The Elite Theater of the Ming. 1999. pap. text 17.50 (0-231-10263-1) Col U Pr.

Birch, Cyril, ed. Chinese Myths & Fantasies. (Oxford Myths & Legends Ser.). (Illus.). 205p. (YA). (gr. 5-12). 1993. pap. 12.95 (0-19-274152-7) OUP.

— Studies in Chinese Literary Genres. LC 77-157825. 408p. reprint ed. pap. 126.50 (0-608-18431-4, 203228200080) Bks Demand.

Birch, Cyril, ed. from CHI. Anthology of Chinese Literature: From the Fourteenth Century to the Present Day, Vol. 2. LC 65-14202. Vol. 2.. (Illus.). 512p. 1988. pap. 14.95 (0-8021-5090-X, Grove) Grove-Atltic.

— Stories from a Ming Collection. LC 68-44187. 208p. 1968. pap. 12.00 (0-8021-5031-4, Grove) Grove-Atltic.

Birch, Cyril, tr. Scenes for Mandarins: The Elite Theater of the Ming. LC 95-3382. (Translations from the Asian Classics Ser.). (Illus.). (CHI & ENG.). 1995. 39.00 (0-231-10262-3) Col U Pr.

Birch, Cyril & Keene, Donald, eds. Anthology of Chinese Literature Vol. 1: From the Earliest Times to the Fourteenth Century. LC 65-14202. Vol. 1. (Illus.). 528p. 1988. pap. 15.95 (*0-8021-5038-1*, E417, Grove) Grove-Atltic.

Birch, Cyril, jt. auth. see Meng, Cheng-Shun.

Birch, Cyril, tr. see Tang, Xian Zu.

Birch, David. The King's Chessboard. (Illus.). 32p. (J). (gr. k up). 1993. pap. 5.99 (*0-14-054880-7*, PuffinBks) Peng Put Young Read.

Birch, David. King's Chessboard. (Picture Puffin Ser.). (Illus.). (J). 1988. 11.19 (*0-606-05394-8*, Pub. by Turtleback) Demco.

— Language, Literature & Critical Practice: Ways of Analysing Text. 256p. (C). 1989. pap. 24.99 (*0-415-02941-4*) Routledge.

— Language, Literature & Critical Practice: Ways of Analysing Text. 256p. 1989. 39.95 (*0-415-03121-4*) Routledge.

— The Language of Drama. LC 90-9082. (Language of Literature Ser.). 184p. 1991. text 39.95 (*0-312-05269-3*) St Martin.

***Birch, David & Cleary, Michael.** Valdosta Customized Edition Insert. 5th ed. (Illus.). (C). 1998. pap. text. write for info. (*0-7637-0895-X*) JB Pubns.

Birch, David & Marte, Rebecca. HIV/AIDS Education for Students with Special Needs: A Guide for Teachers. 43p. 1995. pap. 8.00 (*0-88314-601-0*, 301-10030) AAHPERD.

Birch, David & O'Toole, Michael, eds. The Function of Style. (Open Linguistics Ser.). 260p. 1988. text 49.00 (*0-86187-918-X*) St Martin.

Birch, David, ed. see Lackie-Tarry, Helen.

Birch, David, ed. see Leckie-Tarry, Helen.

Birch, David A. Step by Step to Involving Parents in Health Education. LC 95-24324. 1995. write for info. (*1-56071-474-3*) ETR Assocs.

Birch, David A. & Cleary, Michael J. Managing Your Health: Assessment & Action. LC 96-1779. (Health Science Ser.). 304p. 1996. pap. 29.50 (*0-7637-0139-4*) Jones & Bartlett.

***Birch, Debra J.** Pilgrimage to Rome in the Middle Ages. (Studies in the History of Medieval Religion: Vol. 0955-2480). 256p. 2000. pap. 24.95 (*0-85115-771-8*, Pub. by Camden Hse) Boydell & Brewer.

Birch, Derek W. & Latcham, Jack. Managing Open Learning. 1985. 70.00 (*0-907659-39-X*) St Mut.

Birch, Desmond A. Trial, Tribulation & Triumph: Before, During, & after Antichrist. LC 96-68461. 635p. (Orig.). 1996. pap. text 19.50 (*1-882972-73-2*, 3411) Queenship Pub.

Birch, Dinah. Ruskin's Myths. (Oxford English Monographs). 224p. 1988. text 70.00 (*0-19-812872-X*) OUP.

Birch, Dinah, ed. Ruskin & the Dawn of the Modern. LC 98-47181. (Illus.). 204p. 1999. text 62.00 (*0-19-818454-9*) OUP.

Birch, Gordon G., et al, eds. Glucose Syrups & Related Carbohydrates. (Illus.). 118p. 1971. 38.00 (*0-444-20103-3*) Elsevier.

Birch, Helen, ed. Moving Targets: Women, Murder, & Representation. LC 93-25139. 1994. 48.00 (*0-520-08573-6*, Pub. by U CA Pr); pap. 18.95 (*0-520-08574-4*, Pub. by U CA Pr) Cal Prin Full Svc.

Birch, Ian & Richter, Ingo, eds. Comparative School Law. LC 90-43333. 377p. reprint ed. pap. 116.90 (*0-608-06258-8*, 206658700008) Bks Demand.

Birch, Isobel, jt. auth. see Palmer, Robin.

Birch, J. R., ed. Fourier Transform Spectroscopy: Proceedings of the International Conference, Durham, U. K., 19-22 September, 1983. 290p. 1984. pap. 70.00 (*0-08-030265-3*, Pergamon Pr) Elsevier.

Birch, J. R. & Lennox, E. S., eds. Monoclonal Antibodies: Principles & Applications. 344p. 1995. 110.00 (*0-471-05147-0*) Wiley.

Birch, Jack W., jt. auth. see Mauch, James E.

Birch, Jennie. Diagnosis of Defective Colour Vision. 204p. 1993. pap. text 50.00 (*0-7506-4047-2*) Buttrwrth-Heinemann.

***Birch, Jennie.** Diagnosis of Defective Colourvision. (Illus.). 224p. 2000. pap. 55.00 (*0-7506-4174-6*) Buttrwrth-Heinemann.

Birch, Jennie, jt. auth. see Rudnicka, Alicja.

Birch, Jennifer. Diagnosis of Defective Colour Vision. LC 92-48986. (Oxford Medical Publications). (Illus.). 204p. 1993. write for info. (*0-19-261870-9*) OUP.

Birch, Jeremy. Loving Change: The Secrets of Lifelong, Joy, Fulfillment & Opportunity. (Illus.). 267p. (Orig.). 1994. pap. 19.95 (*0-9613102-5-1*) StressPress.

Birch, Jeremy, jt. auth. see Loring, Honey.

Birch, Jesse S. History of Benton County, Indiana, & Historic Oxford. (Illus.). 386p. 1993. reprint ed. lib. bdg. 41.50 (*0-8328-2901-3*) Higginson Bk Co.

Birch, John E. So, You Want to Be a Slave? Miley, David A., ed. (Illus.). 48p. 1997. pap. 12.95 (*0-9631226-1-4*) Selective Pub.

Birch, John G., ed. see Shriners Hospitals for Crippled Children Staff, et al.

Birch-Jones, Sonia. A First Class Funeral. 1983. text 16.95 (*0-88982-062-7*, Pub. by Oolichan Bks); pap. text 8.95 (*0-88982-058-9*, Pub. by Oolichan Bks) Genl Dist Srvs.

Birch, Judith L. Profiles in Poverty. Goodman, Jack, ed. LC 90-24740. (Orig.). 1992. pap. 13.95 (*0-87949-308-9*) Ashley Bks.

Birch, L. C., jt. auth. see Andrewartha, Herbert G.

Birch Lane Press Staff. Cinderella. (Upside Down Tales Ser.). (Illus.). (J). (ps-3). 1990. 12.95 (*1-55972-054-9*, Birch Ln Pr) Carol Pub Group.

Birch, Linda. How to Draw & Paint Animals in Pencil, Charcoal, Line & Watercolor. (Illus.). 128p. 1999. pap. 17.95 (*0-7153-0930-7*, Pub. by D & C Pub) Sterling.

— How to Draw & Paint Animals in Pencil, Charcoal, Line & Watercolor. LC 97-192027. (Illus.). 128p. 1997. 24.95 (*0-7153-0499-2*) Sterling.

***Birch, Melissa H. & Haar, Terry, eds.** The Impact of Privatization in the Americas. 256p. 2000. pap. 26.95 (*1-57454-054-8*, Pub. by U Miami N-S Ctr) L Rienner.

Birch, Melissa H., jt. ed. see Baer, Werner.

Birch, Neville H. Passenger Protection Technology in Aircraft Accident Fires. 200p. 1987. text 86.95 (*0-291-39734-4*, Pub. by Avebury Technical) Ashgate Pub Co.

Birch, Neville H. & Bramson, A. E. Flight Briefing for Ultralight Pilots. Christy, Joe, ed. (Illus.). 288p. 1986. pap. 14.95 (*0-8306-2417-1*, 2417P) McGraw-Hill Prof.

Birch, Nicholas J., ed. Lithium & the Cell: Pharmacology & Biochemistry. (Illus.). 351p. 1991. text 104.00 (*0-12-099300-7*) Acad Pr.

— Magnesium & the Cell. (Illus.). 289p. 1993. text 104.00 (*0-12-099620-0*) Acad Pr.

***Birch, Paul.** Instant Leadership: Reach Your Full Potential Now! 128p. 1999. pap. 12.95 (*0-7494-3026-5*, Kogan Pg Educ) Stylus Pub VA.

***Birch, Paul & Clegg, Brian.** Imagination Engineering: A Toolkit for Business Creativity. 2nd ed. (Illus.). 224p. 2000. pap. 34.00 (*0-273-64929-9*, Pub. by F T P H) Trans-Atl Phila.

Birch, Paul & Clegg, Brian. Imagination Engineering: How to Generate & Implement Great Ideas. (Illus.). 225p. (Orig.). 1996. pap. 17.95 (*0-273-62064-9*) F T P-H.

Birch, Paul, jt. auth. see Clegg, Brian.

Birch, Paul, jt. auth. see DeVillers, Victor.

Birch, Penny. In for a Penny. 1999. mass mkt. 6.95 (*0-352-33449-5*) London Brdge.

***Birch, Penny.** Plaything. 2000. mass mkt. 6.95 (*0-352-33493-2*) Nexus.

Birch, Peter. To Die For. (Crime & Passion Ser.). (Orig.). 1997. mass mkt. 5.95 (*0-7535-0034-5*, Pub. by Virgin Bks) London Brdge.

Birch, R., et al. Surgical Disorders of the Peripheral Nerves. (Illus.). 450p. 1998. write for info. (*0-443-04443-0*) Church.

Birch, R., jt. auth. see Harris, N. H.

Birch, R. C. The Shaping of the Welfare State. (Seminar Studies in History). 126p. (C). 1974. pap. text 6.95 (*0-582-35200-2*) Longman.

Birch, Richard. Worry-Free RRSPs. 144p. 1989. pap. 12.95 (*0-7737-5252-8*) Genl Dist Srvs.

Birch, Robert L., jt. auth. see Fauver, William.

Birch, Robert W. Male Sexual Endurance: A Man's Book about Ejaculatory Control. 190p. 1997. 19.95 (*1-57074-349-5*) PEC.

Birch, Robert William. Improper Limericks: An Original Bawdy Collection. 190p. 1997. pap. 7.95 (*1-57074-357-6*) PEC.

***Birch, Robert William.** Limericks for Lechers: Lacivious Lyrics, Rambling Ruminations & Titillating Trivia. (Illus.). 249p. 1999. pap. 17.95 (*1-57074-391-6*, Pub. by PEC) ACCESS Pubs Network.

— More Improper Limericks: Thirty Dirty Ditties. 57p. 1998. spiral bd. 3.00 (*1-57074-414-9*) PEC.

Birch, Robert William. Oral Caress: The Loving Guide to Exciting a Woman. 150p. 1996. 19.95 (*1-57074-307-X*) Greyden Pr.

Birch, Robert William. A Sex Therapist's Manual: Assessment Questionnaires, Therapeutic Stories & Other Practical Clinical Materials. 152p. 1996. spiral bd. 24.95 (*1-57074-320-7*) PEC.

— Still More Improper Limericks: Writings of a Limericks Addict. 72p. 1998. spiral bd. 3.25 (*1-57074-425-4*) PEC.

***Birch, Robert William & Ruberg, Cynthia Lief.** Pathways to Pleasure: A Woman's Guide to Orgasm. 210p. 2000. pap. 14.95 (*1-57074-479-3*, Pub. by PEC) ACCESS Pubs Network.

Birch, Sally, jt. auth. see Hill, Michael.

Birch, Sarah. Christine Brooke-Rose & Contemporary Fiction. LC 93-24543. 262p. (C). 1994. text 55.00 (*0-19-812375-2*) OUP.

***Birch, Sarah.** Elections & Democratization in the Ukraine. LC 00-24439. 2000. write for info. (*0-312-23457-0*) St Martin.

Birch, Silas B., Jr. Public Works Inspector's Manual. 5th ed. 1996. pap. 49.95 (*1-55701-169-9*) BNI Pubns.

Birch, Stephen & Ida, Junko. Japanese Acupuncture: A Clinical Guide. Felt, Robert L. & Lincoln, Jack, eds. LC 94-18574. (Illus.). 350p. (Orig.). (C). 1998. pap. 40.00 (*0-912111-42-9*) Paradigm Publns.

Birch, Stephen, jt. auth. see Felt, Robert L.

Birch, Stephen, jt. auth. see Matsumoto, Kiiko.

Birch, Stewart, jt. auth. see Carss, Bob.

Birch, Thomas W. Automotive Cooling Systems: Operation & Service. (Illus.). 224p. 1986. text 27.95 (*0-8359-9359-0*) P-H.

— Court & Times of James the First, 2 vols. LC 74-113558. reprint ed. 115.00 (*0-404-00906-9*) AMS Pr.

— The History of the Royal Society of London for Improving of Natural Knowledge, 4 vols., Set. (Anglistica & Americana Ser.: No. 7). 1968. reprint ed. 640.00 (*0-685-66432-5*, 05101966) G Olms Pubs.

— The Life of the Honourable Robert Boyle. 476p. reprint ed. write for info. (*0-318-71887-1*) G Olms Pubs.

— Manual Drive Trains & Axles. 2nd ed. LC 98-6983. 422p. (C). 1998. pap. text 65.00 (*0-13-924069-1*) P-H.

— Memoirs of the Reign of Queen Elizabeth, 2 vols. LC 79-131513. reprint ed. lib. bdg. 135.00 (*0-404-00909-3*) AMS Pr.

— Private Forest-Land Owners of the United States, 1994. (Illus.). 183p. 1998. pap. text 25.00 (*0-7881-7373-1*) DIANE Pub.

Birch, Thomas W., ed. see Boyle, Robert.

Birch, Tom. Automotive Heating & Air Conditioning. 2nd ed. LC 99-19588. (Illus.). 403p. 1999. pap. 64.00 (*0-13-013575-5*) P-H.

Birch, Una. Secret Societies & the French Revolution. 1976. lib. bdg. 59.95 (*0-8490-2585-0*) Gordon Pr.

Birch, W. J. An Inquiry into the Philosophy & Religion of Shakespeare. LC 72-3660. (Studies in Shakespeare: No. 24). 1972. reprint ed. lib. bdg. 75.00 (*0-8383-1569-0*) M S G Haskell Hse.

Birch, Walter D., ed. see Kemble, John.

Birch, William. Inquiry into the Philosophy & Religion of Shakespeare. LC 76-39446. reprint ed. 37.50 (*0-404-00868-2*) AMS Pr.

Birch, William D., tr. see Birch, Williiam D., ed.

Birch, William G. Guide to Pregnancy & Childbirth. 1993. pap. 6.00 (*0-318-37514-1*) Budlong.

Birch, William G. & Meilach, Dona Z. Doctor Discusses Pregnancy. (Illus.). 1994. pap. 6.00 (*0-318-37507-9*) Budlong.

Birch, Williiam D., ed. Vita Haroldi: The Romance of the Life of Harold, King of England. Birch, William D., tr. LC 80-2232. reprint ed. 36.00 (*0-404-18753-6*) AMS Pr.

Birchak, Barb, et al. Teacher Study Groups: Building a Professional Community. LC 98-38170. 148p. 1998. pap. 22.95 (*0-8141-4846-8*) NCTE.

Birchall. International Co-Operative Movement. LC 97-18479. 1997. pap. 24.95 (*0-7190-4824-9*, Pub. by Manchester Univ Pr) St Martin.

Birchall, jt. auth. see Colwill.

Birchall, Brian. The Magic Wheel. LC 93-18048. (Illus.). (J). 1994. pap. write for info. (*0-383-03701-8*) SRA McGraw.

Birchall, Christopher, tr. see Holy Transfiguration Monastery Staff, ed.

Birchall, Christopher, tr. see Khrapovitsky, Antony.

Birchall, David & Lyons, Laurence. Creating Tomorrows Organization Today: Unlock the Benefits of Future Work. 256p. (C). 1995. 30.00 (*0-273-61094-5*) F T P-H.

Birchall, David W. The New Flexi-Manager. LC 96-38885. 152p. 1996. pap., wbk. ed. 12.99 (*0-415-12502-2*) Thomson Learn.

Birchall, Ian H. Spectre of Babeuf. LC 96-52824. 276p. 1997. text 65.00 (*0-312-17365-2*) St Martin.

Birchall, John. Dictionary of Economics. (Professional Ser.). 2000. pap. text 17.95 (*0-948549-91-2*, Pub. by P Collin) IPG Chicago.

Birchall, Johnston. The International Co-Operative Movement. LC 97-18479. 1997. text 69.95 (*0-7190-4823-0*, Pub. by Manchester Univ Pr) St Martin.

Birchall, Lorrie. Cauldron of Halloween Ideas: Literature-Based & Cross Curricular. 1993. pap. 7.95 (*0-590-49342-6*) Scholastic Inc.

***Birchall, Mark.** Rabbit's Wooly Sweater. LC 00-9035. (Illus.). (J). 2001. pap. write for info. (*1-57505-465-5*) Carolina Acad Pr.

Birchall, Martin A. & Murphy, Siobhan M. HIV Infection & AIDS. LC 92-12583. (Colour Guide Ser.). 121p. 1992. pap. text 17.95 (*0-443-04578-X*) Harcrt Hlth Sci Grp.

Birchall, Peter. Longest Walk: The World of Bomb Disposal. LC 98-140295. (Illus.). 240p. 1998. 27.95 (*1-85409-398-3*, Pub. by Arms & Armour) Sterling.

Birchall, Simon, jt. auth. see Ramus, Jack.

Birchard, Bill, jt. auth. see Epstein, Marc J.

Birchard, Bruce. The Burning Oneness Blinding Everything. LC 97-69933. 1997. write for info. (*0-87574-332-3*) Pendle Hill.

Birchard, Bruce, ed. see American Friends Service Committee Staff.

Birchard, Carl R. & Birchard, Delores S. The Christian Home. 40p. 1988. pap. 3.50 (*0-8341-1259-0*) Beacon Hill.

Birchard, Delores S., jt. auth. see Birchard, Carl R.

***Birchard, Harry.** Brandywine County: A Novel of World War II. LC 00-190965. 2000. 25.00 (*0-7388-2025-3*); pap. 18.00 (*0-7388-2026-1*) Xlibris Corp.

— Hoover Dam: An Historical Novel. LC 00-190344. 308p. 2000. 18.00 (*0-7388-1732-5*); pap. 18.00 (*0-7388-1733-3*) Xlibris Corp.

— Massachusetts Bay: An Historical Novel. LC 00-190966. 463p. 2000. 25.00 (*0-7388-2027-X*); pap. 18.00 (*0-7388-2028-8*) Xlibris Corp.

Birchard, John. Doormaking: A Do-It-Yourself Guide. rev. ed. LC 99-14530. (Illus.). 1999. pap. 19.95 (*0-8069-4840-X*) Sterling.

— Make Your Own Handcrafted Doors & Windows. LC 87-33701. (Illus.). 296p. (Orig.). 1988. pap. 19.95 (*0-8069-6544-4*) Sterling.

— Projects for Woodworkers. Beckstrom, Robert J., ed. LC 94-69603. (Illus.). 96p. (Orig.). 1995. pap. 9.95 (*0-87921-258-6*, 05994, Ortho Bks) Meredith Bks.

Birchard, Robert S. Cecil B. DeMille: In Pursuit of the Grand Award. (Illus.). 288p. 1999. write for info. (*1-887322-07-8*) Emprise NY.

— King Cowboy: Tom Mix & the Movies. (Illus.). 160p. 1993. pap. 24.95 (*1-880756-05-6*) Riverwood Pr.

Birchard, Stephen J. & Sherding, Robert G. Saunders Manual of Small Animal Practice. (Illus.). 1424p. 1993. text 130.00 (*0-7216-3219-X*, W B Saunders Co) Harcrt Hlth Sci Grp.

— Saunders' Manual of Small Animal Practice. 2nd ed. LC 98-26528. (C). 1999. text 110.00 (*0-7216-7078-4*, W B Saunders Co) Harcrt Hlth Sci Grp.

***Birchard, William, Jr. & Proudman, Robert D.** Appalachian Trail Design, Construction & Maintenance. 2nd ed. 240p. 1999. 14.95 (*0-917953-72-X*) Appalachian Trail.

Birchard, William, Jr. & Proudman, Robert D. Appalachian Trail Fieldbook: A Self-Help Guide for Trail Maintainers. (Illus.). 52p. 1982. pap. 3.95 (*0-917953-08-8*) Appalachian Trail.

Birchenall. Sociology Applied to Nursing. (C). 1998. pap. text 25.00 (*0-7020-1932-1*, W B Saunders Co) Harcrt Hlth Sci Grp.

Birchenall, Joan. Mosby's Textbook for the Home Care Aide: Instructor's Resource Kit. (Illus.). 1997. teacher ed. write for info. (*0-8151-0730-7*) Mosby Inc.

Birchenall, Joan M. & Steight, Eileen. The Home Care Aide. LC 97-118486. (Illus.). 496p. (C). (gr. 13). 1996. pap. text 31.00 (*0-8151-0726-9*, 24172) Mosby Inc.

Birchenall, Joan M. & Streight, Mary E. Health Occupations: Explorations & Career Planning. 1990. teacher ed. write for info. (*0-8151-2689-1*) Mosby Inc.

Birchenall, Joan M. & Streight, Mary E. Mosby's Textbook for the Home Care Aide. teacher ed. write for info. (*0-8151-0728-5*) Mosby Inc.

— Mosby's Textbook for the Home Care Aide. 1997. pap. text, wbk. ed. 16.00 (*0-8151-0727-7*) Mosby Inc.

Birchenall, Joan M. & Streight, Mary Eileen. Geriatric Nursing: Care of the Older Adult. 3rd ed. (Illus.). 352p. 1993. pap. text 24.95 (*0-397-54840-0*) Lppncott W & W.

— Health Occupations: Explorations & Career Planning. (Illus.). 400p. (C). (gr. 13). 1989. text 22.95 (*0-8016-0477-X*, 00477) Mosby Inc.

Bircher, ed. see Spangenberg, Wolfhart.

Bircher, A. J., et al, eds. Exogenous Dermatology: Advances in Skin-Related Allergology, Bioengineering, Pharmacology, & Toxicology. (Current Problems in Dermatology Ser.: Vol. 22). (Illus.). xviii, 242p. 1995. 224.50 (*3-8055-6062-1*) S Karger.

Bircher-Benner, M., tr. see Eiloart, Arnold, ed.

Bircher-Glueckswechsel, M., ed. see Spangenberg, Wolfhart.

***Bircher, J.** Oxford Textbook of Clinical Hepatology. 2nd ed. LC 98-30555. (Illus.). 1999. write for info. (*0-19-263039-3*); write for info. (*0-19-263040-7*) OUP.

Bircher, Johannes, et al, eds. Oxford Textbook Of Clinical Hepatology, 2 vols. 2nd ed. LC 98-30555. (Illus.). 2392p. 1999. text 350.00 (*0-19-262515-2*) OUP.

Bircher, Johannes, jt. ed. see Conn, Harold O.

Bircher, Katy. I Want to Get Fit. 1999. pap. 6.95 (*1-84024-063-6*) Seven Hills Bk.

Bircher, Martin, ed. Deutsche Drucke des Barock, 1600-1720 in der Herzog August Bibliothek Wolfenbuttel Abeteilung B Vol. 3: Mittlere Aufstellung: Theologica 1. (Illus.). ix, 445p. 1986. lib. bdg. 160.00 (*3-598-32133-3*) K G Saur Verlag.

— Deutsche Drucke des Barock, 1600-1720 in der Herzog August Bibliothek Wolfenbuttel Abteilung B Vol. 5: Mittlere Aufstellung: Theologica 3. (Illus.). ix, 491p. 1986. lib. bdg. 160.00 (*3-598-32135-X*) K G Saur Verlag.

— Deutsche Drucke des Barock, 1600-1720 in der Herzog August Bibliothek Wolfenbuttel Abteilung B Vol. 4: Mittlere Aufstellung: Theologica 2. (Illus.). ix, 572p. 1986. lib. bdg. 160.00 (*3-598-32134-1*) K G Saur Verlag.

— Deutsche Drucke des Barock, 1600-1720 in der Herzog August Bibliothek Wolfenbuttel Abtwilung B Vol. 6: Mittlere Aufstellung: Theologica 4. (Illus.). 303p. 1986. lib. bdg. 160.00 (*3-598-32136-8*) K G Saur Verlag.

— Deutsche Drucke des Barock, 1600-1720 in der Herzog August Bibliothek Wolfenmittel, Abteilung A: Bibliotheca Augusta, 13 vols., Set. write for info. (*3-598-32100-7*) K G Saur Verlag.

— Deutsche Drucke des Barock, 1600-1720 in der Herzog August Bibliothek Wolfenmittel, Abteilung A: Bibliotheca Augusta: Abstract A, 7 vols., Vol. 1. 346p. 1977. 160.00 (*3-598-32101-5*) K G Saur Verlag.

— Deutsche Drucke des Barock, 1600-1720 in der Herzog August Bibliothek Wolfenmittel, Abteilung A: Bibliotheca Augusta: Abstract A, 7 vols., Vol. 2. 1979. 160.00 (*3-598-32102-3*) K G Saur Verlag.

— Deutsche Drucke des Barock, 1600-1720 in der Herzog August Bibliothek Wolfenmittel, Abteilung A: Bibliotheca Augusta: Abstract A, 7 vols., Vol. 3. 311p. 1980. 160.00 (*3-598-32103-1*) K G Saur Verlag.

— Deutsche Drucke des Barock, 1600-1720 in der Herzog August Bibliothek Wolfenmittel, Abteilung A: Bibliotheca Augusta: Abstract A, 7 vols., Vol. 4. 348p. 1987. 160.00 (*3-598-32104-X*) K G Saur Verlag.

— Deutsche Drucke des Barock, 1600-1720 in der Herzog August Bibliothek Wolfenmittel, Abteilung A: Bibliotheca Augusta: Abstract A, 7 vols., Vol. 5. 271p. 160.00 (*3-598-32105-8*) K G Saur Verlag.

— Deutsche Drucke des Barock, 1600-1720 in der Herzog August Bibliothek Wolfenmittel, Abteilung A: Bibliotheca Augusta: Abstract A, 7 vols., Vol. 6. 271p. 1987. 160.00 (*3-598-32106-6*) K G Saur Verlag.

— Deutsche Drucke des Barock, 1600-1720 in der Herzog August Bibliothek Wolfenmittel, Abteilung A: Bibliotheca Augusta: Abstract A, 7 vols., Vol. 7. 270p. 1987. 160.00 (*3-598-32107-4*) K G Saur Verlag.

— Deutsche Drucke des Barock, 1600-1720 in der Herzog August Bibliothek, Wolfenmittel, Abteilung B: Mittlere Aufstellung, 20 vols. write for info. (*3-598-32130-9*) K G Saur Verlag.

— Deutsche Drucke des Barock, 1600-1720 in der Herzog August Bibliothek, Wolfenmittel, Abteilung B: Mittlere Aufstellung: Abstract B, 2 vols., Vol. 1. 332p. 1987. 160.00 (*3-598-32131-7*) K G Saur Verlag.

— Deutsche Drucke des Barock, 1600-1720 in der Herzog August Bibliothek, Wolfenmittel, Abteilung B: Mittlere Aufstellung: Abstract B, 2 vols., Vol. 2. 339p. 1982. 160.00 (*3-598-32132-5*) K G Saur Verlag.

— Deutsche Drucke des Barock, 1600-1720 in der Herzog August Bibliothek, Wolfenmittel, Abteilung C: Helmstedter Bestande, 6 vols. write for info. (*3-598-32160-0*) K G Saur Verlag.

— Deutsche Drucke des Barock, 1600-1720 in der Herzog August Bibliothek, Wolfenmittel, Abteilung C: Helmstedter Bestande: Abstract C, 3 vols., Vol. 1. 1983. 160.00 (*3-598-32161-9*) K G Saur Verlag.

B

An Asterisk (*) at the beginning of an entry indicates that the title is appearing for the first time.

— Deutsche Drucke des Barock, 1600-1720 in der Herzog August Bibliothek, Wolfenmittel, Abteilung C: Helmstedter Bestande: Abstract C, 3 vols., Vol. 3. vi, 365p. 1988. 160.00 (*3-598-32163-5*) K G Saur Verlag.

Bircher, Martin, ed. see Greiffenberg, Catharina Regina von.

Bircher, Paul. From the Companies Act of 1929 to the Companies Act of 1948: A Study of Change in the Law & Practice of Accounting. LC 90-21475. (New Works in Accounting History). 348p. 1991. reprint ed. text 15.00 (*0-8153-0002-6*) Garland.

Bircher, Robert. A-Z of Conspiracy Theory, 1. 1998. pap. text 16.95 (*1-84024-069-5*) Summers.

— 101 Reasons Not to Do Anything: A Collection of Cynical & Defeatist Quotations, 1. 1998. pap. text 6.95 (*1-84024-043-1*, Pub. by Summers) Seven Hills Bk.

— The Unofficial Book of Star Wars Trivia. 1998. pap. 15.95 (*1-84024-024-5*, Pub. by Summers) Howell Pr VA.

Bircher, William. A Drummer Boy's Diary. Chester, Newell L., ed. (Illus.). 160p. 1995. reprint ed. 24.95 (*0-87839-094-4*) North Star.

Birchett, Colleen. How to Help Hurting People. 200p. (Orig.). 1989. pap., teacher ed. 6.95 (*0-940955-09-1*); pap. text 7.95 (*0-940955-08-3*) Urban Ministries.

Birchett, Colleen, ed. Biblical Strategies for a Community in Crisis: What African Americans Can Do. 207p. (Orig.). 1992. pap., teacher ed. 6.95 (*0-940955-20-2*); pap. text 7.95 (*0-940955-19-9*) Urban Ministries.

Birchett, Colleen, intro. How I Got Over. 183p. (Orig.). 1994. pap., teacher ed. 6.95 (*0-940955-27-X*); pap. text 7.95 (*0-940955-26-1*) Urban Ministries.

Birchett, Colleen, ed. see Abatso, George & Abatso, Yvonne.

Birchett, Colleen, ed. see Banks, Walter L., Sr.

Birchett, Colleen, jt. ed. see Goodwin, Bennie E.

Birchett, Colleen, ed. & intro. see Wright, Jeremiah A., Jr.

Birchett, Collen, ed. see Abatso, George & Abatso, Yvonne.

Birchfield, D. L. Jim Thorpe, World's Greatest Athlete. (Illus.). (J). (gr. 1-4). 1995. pap. 4.95 (*0-8136-5766-0*); lib. bdg. 10.60 (*0-8136-5760-1*) Modern Curr.

— The Oklahoma Basic Intelligence Test. (Greenfield Review Writers Memorial Ser.). 182p. 1999. pap. 14.95 (*0-912678-97-6*) Greenfld Rev Lit.

— Tecumseh, Leader. (Illus.). (J). (gr. 1-4). 1995. pap. 4.95 (*0-8136-5768-7*); lib. bdg. 10.60 (*0-8136-5762-8*) Modern Curr.

Birchfield, D. L. & Smelcer, John E., eds. Durable Breath: Contemporary Native American Poetry. (Illus.). 169p. (C). 1994. pap. 14.00 (*0-9634000-7-X*, Pub. by Salmon Run) SPD-Small Pr Dist.

Birchfield, H. W. Insuring Home-Based Businesses: A Key to Unlocking Personal & Commerical Opportunities. LC 99-218144. 69p. 1998. pap. 30.00 (*1-878204-59-9*) APIS Inc.

Birchfield, James. Kentucky Countess: Mona Bismarck in Art & Fashion. LC 97-60334. (Illus.). 88p. 1997. pap. 15.00 (*1-882007-14-X*) Univ KY Art Mus.

Birchfield, James D., et al. Thomas Satterwhite Noble, 1835-1907. LC 88-50136. (Illus.). 144p. 1989. pap. text 18.00 (*0-929007-00-X*) Univ KY Art Mus.

Birchfield, Jane. Words from an Old Wife: Tips & Tales from Great Aunt Jane. 192p. (Orig.). 1992. pap. 10.00 (*0-9631760-0-5*) Possumwood Pr.

Birchfield, John C. Design & Layout Foodservice Facilities. 2nd ed. (Hospitality, Travel & Tourism Ser.). 1998. text 44.95 (*0-442-02373-1*, VNR) Wiley.

— Design & Layout of Foodservice Facilities. 264p. 1988. 54.95 (*0-471-28865-9*, VNR) Wiley.

Birchfield, Mary E., ed. The Complete Reference Guide to United Nations Sales Publications, 1946-1978 Vols. I & II: The Catalogue & Indexes, 2 vols. 1982. write for info. (*3-11-008719-7*) De Gruyter.

Birchfield, Maureen. Connie: Life Story of a Political Activist. (Illus.). 1998. pap. 29.95 (*1-877133-53-1*, Pub. by Univ Otago Pr) Intl Spec Bk.

***Birchler, James A. & Newton, Kathleen J.** Plant Genetics. (Illus.). 2000. pap. 50.00 (*0-86542-244-3*) Blackwell Sci.

Birchman, David F. A Green Horn Blowing. LC 93-34054. (Illus.). 32p. (J). 1997. lib. bdg. 14.93 (*0-688-12389-9*) Lothrop.

— A Green Horn Blowing. LC 93-34054. (Illus.). 32p. (J). (ps up). 1997. 15.00 (*0-688-12388-0*) Lothrop.

— Jigsaw Jackson. LC 94-48815. (Illus.). 32p. (J). (ps-3). 1996. 16.00 (*0-688-11632-9*) Lothrop.

— The Raggly, Scraggly, No-Soap, No-Scrub Girl. LC 92-40339. (Illus.). 32p. (J). (gr. k up). 1995. 16.00 (*0-688-11060-6*) Lothrop.

Birchman, Willis. Faces & Facts, by & About Twenty-Six Contemporary Artists. LC 68-25600. (Essay Index Reprint Ser.). 1977. 18.95 (*0-8369-0211-4*) Ayer.

Birchmeier, Carmen, jt. ed. see Birchmeier, Walter.

Birchmeier, W., jt. auth. see Gunthert, U.

***Birchmeier, Walter & Birchmeier, Carmen, eds.** Epithelial Morphogenesis in Development & Disease. (Cell Adhesion & Communication Ser.). 496p. 1999. text 150.00 (*90-5702-419-5*, Harwood Acad Pubs) Gordon & Breach.

Birchmire, Tom. From the Hoard: Because We Can. iii, 64p. 1998. pap. 12.50 (*0-9664993-0-1*) T Birchmire.

Birchmore, Daniel A. Harry, the Happy Snake of Happy Hollow. LC 96-4227. (Harry, the Happy Snake of Happy Hollow Ser.: No. 1). (Illus.). 40p. (J). (ps-3). 1997. 15.95 (*1-887813-06-3*) Cucumber Island.

— The Reluctant Santa: Christmas Has Been Cancelled. LC 95-20584. (Illus.). 32p. (J). (ps-3). 1997. 15.95 (*1-887813-00-4*) Cucumber Island.

— The Rock. LC 95-20585. (Illus.). 32p. (J). (ps-3). 1997. 14.95 (*1-887813-03-9*) Cucumber Island.

— The White Curtain. Musick, Melinda B., ed. LC 96-7762. (Illus.). 32p. (J). (ps-3). 1997. 15.95 (*1-887813-09-8*) Cucumber Island.

Birchmore, Fred A. Around the World on a Bicycle. 2nd ed. Musick, Melinda B., ed. (Illus.). 406p. (YA). (gr. 5 up). 1997. reprint ed. 24.95 (*1-887813-12-8*) Cucumber Island.

— Miracles in My Life: Tales of a Happy Wanderer. LC 96-14854. (Illus.). 136p. 1997. 19.95 (*1-887813-30-6*) Cucumber Island.

Birchwater, Sage, told to. Chiwid. (Transmontanus Ser.: Vol. 2). (Illus.). 128p. 1995. pap. 12.00 (*0-921586-39-6*, Pub. by New Star Bks) Genl Dist Srvs.

***Birchwood, M. J., et al.** Early Intervention in Psychosis: A Guide to Concepts, Evidence & Interventions. LC 00-33039. (Series in Clinical Psychology). 2000. pap. write for info. (*0-471-97866-3*) Wiley.

***Birchwood, Max J.** Early Intervention in Psychosis: A Guide to Concepts, Evidence & Interventions. 300p. 2000. text 59.95 (*0-471-97865-5*) Wiley.

***Birchwood, Max J. & Jackson, Chris.** Schizophrenia. 196p. 1999. 49.95 (*0-86377-552-7*, Pub. by Psychol Pr); pap. 24.95 (*0-86377-553-5*, Pub. by Psychol Pr) Taylor & Francis.

Birchwood, Max J. & Tarrier, Nicholas, eds. Psychological Management of Schizophrenia. LC 94-6698. 176p. 1994. pap. 65.95 (*0-471-95056-4*) Wiley.

Birck, Sixt. Saemtliche Dramen, Vol. 2. Brauneck, M., ed. (Ausgaben Deutscher Literatur des XV bis XVIII Jahrhunderts Ser.). (C). 1976. 361.55 (*3-11-006758-7*) De Gruyter.

Birckbichler, Diane W., ed. see Anouilh, Jean, et al.

Birckmayer, Jennifer. Discipline Is Not a Dirty Word: A Workshop Outline for Parents, Teachers & Caregivers of Young Children. 3rd rev. ed. (Illus.). 56p. 1995. pap. 6.25 (*1-57753-018-7*, 321HDFS51) Corn Coop Ext.

Birckmayer, Jennifer & Westendorf, Bonnie J. Bookstart: Selected Activities for Babies, Toddlers, & Young Children. Calvert, Trudie, ed. (Illus.). 104p. 1996. ring bd. 14.75 (*1-57753-102-7*, 3211B 239) Corn Coop Ext.

Birckmayer, Jennifer, et al. Teens As Parents of Babies & Toddlers. 2nd rev. ed. 222p. 1997. ring bd. 26.25 (*1-57753-095-0*, 321TP) Corn Coop Ext.

Bird. Calculus for Techncian. 2nd ed. 1985. pap. text. write for info. (*0-582-41370-2*, Pub. by Addison-Wesley) Longman.

— Coasts. (Australian National University Press Ser.). 1996. text. write for info. (*0-08-033024-X*, Pergamon Pr); pap. text. write for info. (*0-08-033021-5*, Pergamon Pr) Elsevier.

***Bird.** Cox-Inhibitors: Pocketbook Edition. 2000. 14.95 (*1-85317-795-4*, Pub. by Martin Dunitz) Blackwell Sci.

Bird. Exercise Physiology for Health Professionals. 322p. 1992. pap. 42.50 (*1-56593-006-1*, 0247) Thomson Learn.

***Bird.** Newnes Engineering Mathematics Pocket Book. 384p. 2001. 32.95 (*0-7506-4992-5*, Newnes) Buttrwrth-Heinemann.

— Newnes Engineering Science Pocket Book. 512p. 2001. 32.95 (*0-7506-4991-7*, Newnes) Buttrwrth-Heinemann.

— PowerPoint 97 Essentials. LC 97-67229. (Illus.). 240p. 1997. 22.99 (*1-57576-824-0*) Sams.

— Sonnet. pap. write for info. (*0-86547-528-8*) N Point Pr.

Bird. Technician Maths 1. 1996. pap. write for info. (*0-582-23426-3*, Pub. by Addison-Wesley) Longman.

Bird & Falk. Cold at Five. (New Trend Fiction B Ser.). (J). 1993. pap. text. write for info. (*0-582-80034-X*, Pub. by Addison-Wesley) Longman.

— A Face in the Water. (New Trend Fiction B Ser.). (J). 1993. pap. text. write for info. (*0-582-91198-2*, Pub. by Addison-Wesley) Longman.

— Funny Kid, Monkey. (New Trend Fiction C Ser.). (J). 1993. pap. text. write for info. (*0-582-91199-0*, Pub. by Addison-Wesley) Longman.

— Go Home, Kid! (New Trend Fiction B Ser.). (J). 1993. pap. text. write for info. (*0-582-80030-7*, Pub. by Addison-Wesley) Longman.

— Hey, That's My Bike! (New Trend Fiction B Ser.). (J). 1993. pap. text. write for info. (*0-582-80031-5*, Pub. by Addison-Wesley) Longman.

— I Bet You. (New Trend Fiction B Ser.). (J). 1993. pap. text. write for info. (*0-582-91196-6*, Pub. by Addison-Wesley) Longman.

— If He Fell. (New Trend Fiction C Ser.). (J). 1993. pap. text. write for info. (*0-582-91197-4*, Pub. by Addison-Wesley) Longman.

— Last Train. (New Trend Fiction A Ser.). (J). 1993. pap. text. write for info. (*0-582-80032-3*, Pub. by Addison-Wesley) Longman.

— Night Cats. (New Trend Fiction A Ser.). (J). 1993. pap. text. write for info. (*0-582-80033-1*, Pub. by Addison-Wesley) Longman.

— A Real City Kid. (New Trend Fiction C Ser.). (J). 1993. pap. text. write for info. (*0-582-80036-6*, Pub. by Addison-Wesley) Longman.

— A Real Hero. (New Trend Fiction C Ser.). (J). 1993. pap. text. write for info. (*0-582-80038-2*, Pub. by Addison-Wesley) Longman.

— Red Hot Mountain. (nc). (J). 1993. pap. text. write for info. (*0-582-80037-4*, Pub. by Addison-Wesley) Longman.

— Red Surf. (New Trend Fiction A Ser.). (J). 1993. pap. text. write for info. (*0-582-80042-0*, Pub. by Addison-Wesley) Longman.

— Sudden Death. (New Trend Fiction B Ser.). (J). 1993. pap. text. write for info. (*0-582-80043-9*, Pub. by Addison-Wesley) Longman.

— That Old Tin Can. (New Trend Fiction A Ser.). (J). 1993. pap. text. write for info. (*0-582-91192-3*, Pub. by Addison-Wesley) Longman.

— Vroom! Vroom! (New Trend Fiction A Ser.). (J). 1993. pap. text. write for info. (*0-582-80044-7*, Pub. by Addison-Wesley) Longman.

— Watcher on the Wharf. (New Trend Fiction C Ser.). (J). 1993. pap. text. write for info. (*0-582-80041-2*, Pub. by Addison-Wesley) Longman.

— White Lie. (New Trend Fiction B Ser.). (J). 1993. pap. text. write for info. (*0-582-80039-0*, Pub. by Addison-Wesley) Longman.

— Wild Dog. (New Trend Fiction B Ser.). (J). 1993. pap. text. write for info. (*0-582-80040-4*, Pub. by Addison-Wesley) Longman.

Bird & Sporakowski. Taking Sides: Family & Persona. 4th ed. 1998. pap., student ed. 18.44 (*0-07-292716-X*) McGraw.

Bird, et al. A World View of Art History Vol. I: Selected Readings. 188p. (C). 1998. 44.95 (*0-7872-3706-X*) Kendall-Hunt.

Bird, A., et al. Combined Care of the Rheumatic Patient. (Illus.). 320p. 1985. 73.95 (*0-387-13557-X*) Spr-Verlag.

Bird, A. Graham, ed. Immunology of HIV Infection. (Immunology & Medicine Ser.). 192p. (C). 1991. text 126.50 (*0-7923-8962-X*) Kluwer Academic.

Bird, Adren & Bird, Josephine P. Hawaiian Flower Lei Making. LC 87-24347. (Illus.). 152p. 1987. pap. 18.95 (*0-8248-1137-2*, Kolowalu Bk) UH Pr.

Bird, Adren J., et al. The Craft of Hawaiian Lauhala Weaving. LC 82-4818. (Illus.). 163p. 1982. pap. 16.95 (*0-8248-0779-0*, Kolowalu Bk) UH Pr.

Bird, Alan. A History of Russian Painting. LC 86-22145. (Illus.). 304p. 1987. 65.00 (*0-8161-8911-0*, Hall Reference) Macmillan.

Bird, Alan F. & Bird, Jean. The Structure of Nematodes. 2nd ed. (Illus.). 316p. (C). 1991. text 90.00 (*0-12-099651-0*) Acad Pr.

Bird, Alexander. Philosophy of Science. 224p. 1998. text 55.00 (*0-7735-1772-3*, Pub. by McG-Queens Univ Pr); pap. text 19.95 (*0-7735-1773-1*, Pub. by McG-Queens Univ Pr) CUP Services.

Bird, Allan, jt. ed. see Beechler, Schon L.

Bird, Allan G. Bordellos of Blair Street: The Story of Silverton, Colorado's Notorious Red Light District. rev. ed. (Illus.). (Orig.). 1993. pap. 11.95 (*0-9619382-1-8*) A G Bird.

— Silverton - Then & Now. 2nd rev. ed. (Illus.). 176p. 1999. pap. 11.95 (*0-9619382-4-2*) A G Bird.

— Silverton Gold: The Story of Colorado's Largest Underground Gold Mine. 1999. 11.95 (*0-9619382-5-0*) A G Bird.

Bird, Allison. Heart of the Dragonfly: Historical Development of the Cross Necklaces of the Pueblo & Navajo Peoples. (Illus.). 224p. (Orig.). 1992. pap. 39.95 (*0-936755-20-2*) Avanyu Pub.

Bird, Anat. Can S&Ls Survive? The Emerging Recovery, Restructuring & Repositioning of America's Savings & Loans. 250p. 1992. text 35.00 (*1-55738-329-4*, Irwn Prfssnl) McGraw-Hill Prof.

— The Community Banker. 2nd ed. 1996. per. 225.00 (*0-7602-0043-2*, Irwn Prfssnl) McGraw-Hill Prof.

— SuperCommunity Banking: A Super Strategy for Surviving & Thriving in the Year 2000. LC 94-128791. 1993. text 42.50 (*1-55738-388-X*, Irwn Prfssnl) McGraw-Hill Prof.

— Supercommunity Banking: Superstrategy For Success. 1996. 6995.00 (*0-7863-1179-7*) McGraw.

Bird, Arthur. Looking Forward: A Dream of the United States of the Americas in 1999. LC 76-154429. (Utopian Literature Ser.). 1974. reprint ed. 18.95 (*0-405-03512-8*) Ayer.

Bird, Augusto. Bibliografia Puertorriquena Nineteen Thirty to Nineteen Forty-Five, 4 vols., Set. (Puerto Rico Ser.). 1979. lib. bdg. 800.00 (*0-8490-2872-8*) Gordon Pr.

Bird, B. M., et al. An Introduction to Power Electronics. 2nd ed. 392p. 1992. 240.00 (*0-471-92616-7*); pap. 84.95 (*0-471-92617-5*) Wiley.

Bird, Bettina & Short, Joan. Insects. LC 96-23059. (Mondo Animals Ser.). (Illus.). (J). (gr. 2-7). 1997. pap. 5.95 (*1-57255-216-6*) Mondo Pubng.

Bird, Bettina, jt. auth. see Short, Joan.

Bird, Beverly. Comes the Rain. 512p. (Orig.). 1990. mass mkt. 4.95 (*0-380-75525-4*, Avon Bks) Morrow Avon.

— Compromising Positions. 1997. mass mkt., per. 3.99 (*0-373-07777-7*, 1-07777-5) Silhouette.

***Bird, Beverly.** I'll Be Seeing You. (Intimate Moments Ser.: Vol. 1030). 2000. mass mkt. 4.50 (*0-373-27100-X*, 1-27100-6) Harlequin Bks.

— It Had to Be You. (Intimate Moments Ser.). 1999. mass mkt. 4.25 (*0-373-07970-2*) Silhouette.

Bird, Beverly. Loving Mariah. (Intimate Moments Ser.: No. 790). 1997. per. 3.99 (*0-373-07790-4*, 1-07790-8) Silhouette.

— A Man Without a Haven. (Intimate Moments Ser.). 1995. mass mkt. 3.75 (*0-373-07641-X*, 1-07641-3) Silhouette.

— A Man Without a Wife. (Intimate Moments Ser.). 1995. per. 3.75 (*0-373-07652-5*, 1-07652-0) Silhouette.

— A Man Without Love. (Wounded Warriors) (Wounded Warriors Ser.). 1995. per. 3.75 (*0-373-07630-4*, 1-07630-6) Silhouette.

— Marrying Jake. 1997. per. 3.99 (*0-373-07802-1*, 1-07802-1) Silhouette.

— The Marrying Kind. (Intimate Moments Ser.). 1996. per. 3.99 (*0-373-07732-7*, 1-07732-0) Silhouette.

— The Pony Wife. 464p. (Orig.). 1995. mass mkt. 5.99 (*0-515-11629-7*, Jove) Berkley Pub.

— Saving Susannah. 1997. per. 3.99 (*0-373-07814-5*, 1-07814-6) Silhouette.

— Undercover Cowboy. (Intimate Moments Ser.). 1996. per. 3.99 (*0-373-07711-4*, 1-07711-4) Silhouette.

— Walk into the Night. 480p. 1996. mass mkt. 5.99 (*0-7860-0220-4*, Pinncle Kensgtn) Kensgtn Pub Corp.

***Bird, Beverly.** When Winter Comes. rev. ed. 376p. 1999. pap. 19.95 (*1-58444-067-8*) DiscUs Bks.

Bird, Bob. Fourteen Short Pieces. 184p. 1991. pap. 7.95 (*0-934804-11-7*) Happiness.

— Happiness. 220p. (Orig.). 1983. pap. 8.95 (*0-934804-10-9*) Happiness.

— Help Yourself to Happiness. 20p. (Orig.). 1979. pap. 2.00 (*0-934804-07-9*) Happiness.

— You Are a Special Person. 16p. (Orig.). 1974. pap. 2.00 (*0-934804-06-0*) Happiness.

Bird, C. J. & McLachlan, J. L. Seaweed Flora of the Maritimes: One: Rhodophyta - the Red Algae. (Illus.). 177p. 1992. 90.00 (*0-948737-18-2*, Pub. by Biopress) Balogh.

Bird, Carmel. The Bluebird Cafe. LC 90-13243. 192p. 1991. 19.95 (*0-8112-1156-8*, Pub. by New Directions); pap. 10.95 (*0-8112-1155-X*, NDP707, Pub. by New Directions) Norton.

— The White Garden. 232p. 1995. pap. 16.95 (*0-7022-2821-4*, Pub. by Univ Queensland Pr) Intl Spec Bk.

— Woodpecker Point & Other Stories. LC 88-1819. 160p. 1988. 19.95 (*0-8112-1072-3*, Pub. by New Directions); pap. 9.95 (*0-8112-1073-1*, NDP662, Pub. by New Directions) Norton.

Bird, Carolyn J. & Ragan, Mark A., eds. Proceedings of the 11th International Seaweed Symposium. (Developments in Hydrobiology Ser.). 1984. text 450.50 (*90-6193-773-6*) Kluwer Academic.

Bird, Charles. The Dialects of Mandekan. LC 81-70547. 423p. (Orig.). 1982. pap. text 20.00 (*0-941934-09-8*) Indiana Africa.

Bird, Charles, et al. The Songs of Seydou Camara Vol. 1: Kambili. (Occasional Papers in Mande). 120p. (Orig.). 1974. pap. text 7.00 (*0-941934-12-8*) Indiana Africa.

Bird, Charles E. Organizing Your Practices: A New Swimming Manual. 3rd rev. ed. (Illus.). 416p. (C). 1988. pap. 19.95 (*0-317-93356-6*) Bird Pub Co.

Bird, Charles S., jt. ed. see Karp, Ivan.

***Bird, Chloe, et al.** Handbook of Medical Sociology. 5th ed. 438p. (C). 2000. 58.00 (*0-13-014456-8*) P-H.

***Bird, Chris.** Concealed Handgun Manual. 2nd ed. 2000. pap. text 17.95 (*0-9656784-6-6*) Privateer Pubns.

Bird, Christiane. The Jazz & Blues Lover's Guide to the U. S. With More than 900 Hot Clubs, Cool Joints, Landmarks & Legends from Boogie-Woogie to Bop & Beyond. 2nd ed. 1994. pap. 15.00 (*0-201-62648-9*) Addison-Wesley.

***Bird, Christiane.** Moon Handbooks: New York City. 2nd rev. ed. (Illus.). 300p. 2000. pap. 13.95 (*1-56691-202-4*, Moon Handbks) Avalon Travel.

— Moon Handbooks: New York State. 2nd rev. ed. (Illus.). 780p. 2000. pap. 19.95 (*1-56691-201-6*, Moon Handbks) Avalon Travel.

Bird, Christina. Implementing Virtual Private Networks: A Practitioner's Guide. 1999. pap. text 32.99 (*0-7357-0047-8*) New Riders Pub.

Bird, Christine. Jazz & Blues Lover's Guide to the U. S. 1991. pap. 14.95 (*0-201-52332-9*) Addison-Wesley.

Bird, Christine M. All I Need to Know about Money, I Learned in Arithmetic Class. (Illus.). 138p. (Orig.). 1995. pap. 9.95 (*0-9649019-0-0*, Arithmetic Pr) C Bird.

Bird, Christopher, jt. auth. see Tompkins, Peter.

Bird, Christopher O. The Divining Hand: The 500 Year-Old Mystery of Dowsing. (Illus.). 372p. 1996. pap. 29.95 (*0-924608-16-1*, Whitford) Schiffer.

— Modern Vegetable Gardening. 192p. 1993. pap. 13.95 (*1-55821-256-6*) Lyons Pr.

Bird, Christopher O., jt. auth. see Tompkins, Peter.

Bird, Chuch, jt. auth. see Peters, Susan.

Bird, Chuck & Peters, Susan. Christmas Songs for Folk Harp. 128p. 1994. pap. 14.95 (*0-7866-0151-5*, 95307) Mel Bay.

Bird, Chuck & Peters, Susan. Classics for Pedal-Free Harp. 120p. 1996. pap. 24.95 incl. audio compact disk (*0-7866-0569-3*, 95500BCD) Mel Bay.

Bird, Colin. The Myth of Liberal Individualism. LC 98-38601. (Social Philosophy & Policy Ser.). (Illus.). 280p. (C). 1999. text 54.95 (*0-521-64128-4*) Cambridge U Pr.

Bird, D. Dickie Bird. (Illus.). mass mkt. 15.95 (*0-340-68458-5*, Pub. by Hodder & Stought Ltd) Trafalgar.

— Dickie Bird: My Autobiography. (Illus.). (J). text 35.00 (*0-340-68457-7*) Hodder & Stought Ltd.

Bird, Dave. Preparing Public Writing. 4th ed. 160p. (C). 1998. pap. text 29.95 (*1-56226-411-7*) CAT Pub.

— Yap Regains Its Sovereignty: The Story of the First Yap State Constitutional Convention, Vol. I, Background & Preparations. 275p. 1994. pap. 17.00 (*0-9642897-0-9*) Koolau Writ.

***Bird, David.** The Abbot & the Sensational Squeeze. 128p. 1999. pap. 15.95 (*0-575-06741-1*, Pub. by V Gollancz) Trafalgar.

— Famous Bridge Disasters. (Illus.). 128p. 2000. pap. 14.95 (*0-575-06745-4*, Pub. by V Gollancz) Trafalgar.

Bird, David. Famous Leads & Defences. 128p. 1998. pap. 15.95 (*0-575-06597-4*, Pub. by V Gollancz) Trafalgar.

— Token Ring Network Design. 232p. (C). 1994. 39.95 (*0-201-62760-4*) Addison-Wesley.

Bird, David, et al, eds. Raptors in Human Landscapes: Adaptations to Built & Cultivated Environments. (Illus.). 416p. 1996. text 72.00 (*0-12-100130-X*) Acad Pr.

Bird, David & Bourke, Tim. Tournament Acol: A System for Winners. 160p. 1996. pap. 17.95 (*0-575-06113-8*, Pub. by V Gollancz) Trafalgar.

Bird, David & Cocheme, Simon. Bachelor Bridge: The Amorous Adventures of Jack O'Hearts. 144p. 1995. pap. 13.95 (*0-575-05814-5*, Pub. by V Gollancz) Trafalgar.

— Bridge with a Feminine Touch. 128p. 1996. pap. 13.95 (*0-575-06361-0*, Pub. by V Gollancz) Trafalgar.

An Asterisk (*) at the beginning of an entry indicates that the title is appearing for the first time.

Bird, David & Klinger, Ron. Kosher Bridge. 128p. 1998. pap. 15.95 (*0-575-06632-6*, Pub. by V Gollancz) Trafalgar.
— Kosher Bridge, No. 2. 128p. 1994. pap. 14.95 (*0-575-05727-0*, Pub. by V Gollancz) Trafalgar.
— The Rabbi's Magic Trick: More Kosher Bridge. 128p. 1998. pap. 15.95 (*0-575-06595-8*, Pub. by V Gollancz) Trafalgar.

Bird, David, et al. Receiving the Vision: The Anglican-Roman Catholic Reality Today. 184p. (Orig.). 1995. pap. 14.95 (*0-8146-2173-2*, Liturg Pr Bks) Liturgical Pr.

Bird, David, jt. auth. see Reece, Terence.

Bird, David, jt. auth. see Reese, Terence.

Bird, David D., jt. auth. see Maloy, Richard H.

Bird, David M. The Bird Almanac: The Ultimate Guide to Essential Facts & Figures of the World's Birds. (Illus.). 462p. 1999. pap. 19.95 (*1-55209-323-9*) Firefly Bks Ltd.

***Bird, Delys, ed.** Katharine Susannah Prichard: Stories, Journalism & Essays. 224p. 2000. pap. 29.95 (*0-7022-3089-8*, Pub. by Univ Queensland Pr) Intl Spec Bk.

Bird, Dennis K., jt. auth. see Krauskopf, Konrad B.

Bird, Dick. The Art of Freehand Pinstriping. rev. ed. (Illus.). 64p. 1994. pap. 14.95 (*0-9641470-0-9*) Eastwood PA.
— Freehand Lettering. rev. ed. (Illus.). 78p. 1994. pap. 14.95 (*0-9641470-1-7*) Eastwood PA.

***Bird, Doni & Robinson, Debbie.** Examaster to Accompany Torres & Ehrlich Modern Dental Assisting. 6th ed. 1999. 165.00 (*0-7216-7631-6*, W B Saunders Co) Harcrt Hlth Sci Grp.
— Instructor's Manual to Accompany Torres & Ehrlich Modern Dental Assisting. 6th ed. Kuhn, Shirley, ed. 135p. 1999. pap. text, teacher ed. write for info. (*0-7216-7638-3*, W B Saunders Co) Harcrt Hlth Sci Grp.
— Student Workbook to Accompany Torres & Ehrlich Modern Dental Assisting. 6th ed. Kuhn, Shirley, ed. (Illus.). 240p. 1999. pap. text, student ed., wbk. ed. write for info. (*0-7216-7629-4*, W B Saunders Co) Harcrt Hlth Sci Grp.

Bird, Doni & Robinson, Debbie S. Torres & Ehrlich Modern Dental Assisting. 6th ed. Kuhn, Shirley, ed. LC 98-40582. (Illus.). 765p. (C). 1999. text 47.00 (*0-7216-7627-8*, W B Saunders Co) Harcrt Hlth Sci Grp.

Bird, Dorothy & Greenberg, Joyce. Bird's Eye View: Dancing with Martha Graham & on Broadway. LC 97-4730. (Illus.). 261p. 1997. text 29.95 (*0-8229-3980-0*) U of Pittsburgh Pr.

Bird, Drayton. Commonsense Direct Marketing. 2nd ed. 352p. 1994. 29.95 (*0-8442-3182-7*, NTC Business Bks) NTC Contemp Pub Co.
— Commonsense Direct Marketing. 3rd ed. (Illus.). 372p. 1999. pap. 35.00 (*0-7494-2584-9*) Kogan Page Ltd.
— Commonsense Direct Marketing. 3rd ed. Knudsen, Anne, ed. LC 94-16183. (Illus.). 376p. 1994. 37.95 (*0-8442-3543-1*, NTC Business Bks) NTC Contemp Pub Co.

***Bird, Drayton.** Marketing Insights & Outrages. 2000. pap. 17.95 (*0-7494-3215-2*) Kogan Page Ltd.

Bird, Dutch D. The Sword's Revenge. 247p. 1998. per. 6.50 (*0-9664699-0-9*) Presage Publishing.

Bird, E. J. How Do Bears Sleep? (Picture Bks.). (Illus.). 32p. (J). (ps-3). 1989. lib. bdg. 19.95 (*0-87614-384-2*, Carolrhoda) Lerner Pub.
— How Do Bears Sleep? (Picture Bks.). (Illus.). 32p. (J). (ps-3). reprint ed. pap. 5.95 (*0-87614-522-5*, Carolrhoda) Lerner Pub.
— The Rainmakers. LC 92-29789. (Illus.). (J). (gr. 4-7). 1993. lib. bdg. 15.95 (*0-87614-748-1*, Carolrhoda) Lerner Pub.

Bird, Elizabeth A., et al, eds. Planting the Future: Developing an Agriculture That Sustains Land & Community. LC 94-41959. (Illus.). 300p. 1995. pap. text 17.95 (*0-8138-2072-3*) Iowa St U Pr.

Bird, Elizabeth S., ed. Dressing in Feathers: The Construction of the Indian in American Popular Culture. (C). 1996. pap. 30.00 (*0-8133-2667-2*, Pub. by Westview) HarpC.

Bird, Eric C. Beach Management. LC 96-11165. (Coastal Morphology & Research Ser.). 292p. 1996. 100.00 (*0-471-96337-2*) Wiley.
— The Coast of Victoria: Shaping of Scenery. (Illus.). 416p. 1993. 49.95 (*0-522-84544-4*, Pub. by Melbourne Univ Pr) Paul & Co Pubs.
— Submerging Coasts: The Effects of a Rising Sea Level on Coastal Environments. LC 92-30175. (Coastal Morphology & Research Ser.). 192p. 1993. pap. 145.00 (*0-471-93807-6*) Wiley.

Bird, Eric C., ed. Geomorphology of Changing Coastlines. (Annals of Gemorphology Supplement Ser.: Bd. 57). (Illus.). 202p. (Orig.). 1986. pap. text 80.00 (*0-317-63559-X*) Lubrecht & Cramer.

Bird, Eric C., et al. The Impact of Opencast Mining on the Rivers & Coasts of New Caledonia. 53p. 1985. pap. 9.00 (*92-808-0505-3*, 85.III.A.6) UN.

Bird, F. E., Jr. & Germain, George L. Practical Loss Control Leadership. (Illus.). ix, 446p. 1986. pap. text 65.00 (*0-88061-054-9*) Intl Loss Cntrl.

Bird, Floyd. Bird CCP Review Course. 280p. 1989. 265.00 incl. audio (*0-9616174-1-1*) Bird Prof Pubns.
— Bird CDP Review Course. 300p. 1989. 250.00 incl. audio (*0-9616174-0-3*) Bird Prof Pubns.

Bird, Frances. Laws of the Kingdom: As Presented by the Spirit World Through the Automatic Writings of Frances Bird. LC 87-22714. (Laws of the Kingdom Ser.: Vol. II). 382p. (Orig.). 1988. pap. 16.95 (*1-55768-702-1*) LC Pub.
— Laws of the Kingdom Volume I: As Presented by the Spirit World, Through the Automatic Writings of Frances Bird. unabridged ed. LC 87-22714. (Automatic Writings Ser.: Vol. I). 249p. 1988. pap. 44.95 incl. audio (*1-55768-701-3*) LC Pub.
— The New Dispensation: As Presented by the Spirit World, Through the Automatic-Writings of Frances Bird. LC 87-22789. (Automatic Writings Ser.). 400p. 1988. pap. 53.95 incl. audio (*1-55768-703-X*) LC Pub.
— The Transition, Explained Earth Questions-Spirit Answers: As Presented by the Spirit World, Through the Automatic-Writings of Frances Bird. unabridged ed. LC 87-22788. (Automatic Writings Ser.). 172p. 1990. pap. 26.95 incl. audio (*1-55768-700-5*) LC Pub.

Bird, Frank E., Jr. Profits Are in Order. 90p. 1992. pap. text 35.00 (*0-88061-128-6*) Intl Loss Cntrl.

Bird, Frank E., Jr. & Davies, Ray J. Safety & the Bottom Line. (Illus.). 345p. 1996. 55.00 (*0-9656516-1-4*) FEBCO.

Bird, Frank E., Jr. & Germain, George L. Commitment. 1988. pap. text 30.00 (*0-88061-073-5*) Intl Loss Cntrl.
— Practical Loss Control Leadership: French Home Study. (FRE.). Date not set. student ed. 35.00 (*0-88061-152-9*) Intl Loss Cntrl.
— Practical Loss Control Leadership: French Version. (FRE.). Date not set. 65.00 (*0-88061-151-0*) Intl Loss Cntrl.
— Practical Loss Control Leadership: German Version. (GER.). Date not set. 65.00 (*0-88061-150-2*) Intl Loss Cntrl.
— Practical Loss Control Leadership: Spanish Home Study. (SPA.). Date not set. student ed. 35.00 (*0-88061-154-5*) Intl Loss Cntrl.
— Practical Loss Control Leadership: Spanish Version. (SPA.). (C). Date not set. 65.00 (*0-88061-153-7*) Intl Loss Cntrl.
— The Property Damage Accident: The Neglected Part of Safety. (Illus.). 325p. 1997. 70.00 (*0-9656516-3-0*) FEBCO.

Bird, Frederick B. The Muted Conscience: Moral Silence & the Practice of Ethics in Business. LC 96-591. 280p. 1996. 59.95 (*0-89930-652-7*, Quorum Bks) Greenwood.

***Bird, G.** Russian Punchneedle Embroidery. 1998. pap. text 4.95 (*0-486-40262-2*) Dover.

Bird, G. A. Molecular Gas Dynamics & the Direct Simulation of Gas Flows. 2nd ed. (Engineering Science Ser.: Vol. 42). (Illus.). 476p. 1994. text 135.00 (*0-19-856195-4*) OUP.

Bird, Gail B. Cases & Materials on California Community Property. 6th ed. LC 94-6691. (American Casebook Ser.). 603p. (C). 1994. 57.50 (*0-314-03491-9*) West Pub.

Bird, Gary, compiled by. Program Notes for the Solo Tuba. LC 93-34073. (Illus.). 160p. (C). 1994. 19.95 (*0-253-31189-6*) Ind U Pr.

***Bird, Gary E.** The Wrap-Up Guide. 3rd rev. ed. 196p. 2000. pap. 53.00 (*1-886813-51-5*) Intl Risk Mgt.

Bird, George & Stokes, Richard, trs. The Fischer-Dieskau Book of Lieder. LC 84-743. 448p. 1984. reprint ed. pap. 18.95 (*0-87910-004-4*) Limelight Edns.

Bird, Glenn, jt. auth. see Kavanagh, Barry F.

Bird, Gloria. Full Moon on the Reservation. 1994. pap. 9.95 (*0-912678-86-0*) Greenfld Rev Lit.
— The River of History. LC 97-26529. 32p. (Orig.). 1996. pap. 7.00 (*0-932264-13-1*) Trask Hse Bks.

Bird, Gloria & Melville, Keith. Families & Intimate Relationships. LC 93-43169. (C). 1993. text 51.74 (*0-07-041701-6*) McGraw.
— Families & Intimate Relationships. (C). 1994. text, student ed. 52.74 (*0-07-911721-X*) McGraw.
— Families & Intimate Relationships. (C). 1994. pap. text, student ed. 10.62 (*0-07-041704-0*) McGraw.
— Families & Intimate Relationships. LC 93-43169. (C). 1994. text, student ed. write for info. (*0-07-041703-2*) McGraw.

Bird, Gloria, jt. ed. see Harjo, Joy.

Bird, Gloria W. & Sporakowski, Michael J. Taking Sides: Clashing Views on Controversial Issues in Family & Personal Relationships. 3rd ed. LC 96-85806. (Orig.). (C). 1996. text 19.50 (*0-697-35715-5*, WCB McGr Hill) McGrw-H Hghr Educ.
— Taking Sides: Clashing Views on Controversial Issues in Family Personal Relationships. 3rd ed. (C). 1997. text. write for info. (*0-697-39268-6*, WCB McGr Hill) McGrw-H Hghr Educ.

Bird, Gloria W. & Sporakowski, Michael J., eds. Taking Sides: Clashing Views on Controversial Issues in Family & Personal Relationships. 2nd rev. ed. LC 94-2256. (Illus.). 384p. (Orig.). (C). 1994. text 13.95 (*1-56134-250-5*, Dshkn McG-Hill) McGrw-H Hghr Educ.

Bird, Graham. Economic Reform in Eastern Europe. 208p. 1992. 90.00 (*1-85278-594-2*) E Elgar.
— IMF Lending to Developing Countries: Issues & Evidence. LC 94-47967. (Development Policy Studies). 208p. (C). 1995. pap. 25.99 (*0-415-11700-3*, C0363) Routledge.
— Loan-Loss Provisions & Third-World Debt. LC 89-28013. (Essays in International Finance Ser.: No. 176). 34p. 1989. pap. text 10.00 (*0-88165-083-8*) Princeton U Int Finan Econ.
— William James. LC 86-6569. 221p. 1987. 39.95 (*0-7100-9602-X*, Routledge Thoemms) Routledge.

Bird, Graham, ed. International Aspects of Economic Development. (Surrey Seminars in Applied Economics Ser.). 256p. 1992. text 100.00 (*0-12-099742-8*) Acad Pr.
— International Financial Regimes. (Surrey Seminars in Applied Economics Ser.). 343p. 1990. text 99.95 (*0-12-099745-2*) Acad Pr.
— Third World Debt: The Search for a Solution. (Illus.). 256p. 1989. text 90.00 (*1-85278-162-9*) E Elgar.

Bird, Graham & Bird, Heather, eds. Contemporary Issues in Applied Economics. 304p. 1991. text 90.00 (*1-85278-404-0*) E Elgar.

Bird, Graham & Bird, Heather, eds. Contemporary Issues in Applied Economics. 304p. 1991. pap. text 30.00 (*1-85278-405-9*) E Elgar.

Bird, Graham & Helwege, Ann, eds. Latin America's Economic Future. (Surrey Seminars in Applied Economics Ser.). (Illus.). 339p. 1994. text 79.95 (*0-12-099645-6*) Acad Pr.

Bird, Graham & Snowden, P. Nicholas, eds. International Debt, 2 vols. LC 95-13457. (International Library of Critical Writings in Economics: No. 56). 968p. 1995. 370.00 (*1-85278-789-9*) E Elgar.

Bird, Graham, ed. see James, William.

Bird, Graham R. Economic Assistance to Low-Income Countries: Should the Link Be Resurrected? LC 94-29473. (Essays in International Finance Ser.: 193). 34p. 1994. pap. 10.00 (*0-88165-100-1*) Princeton U Int Finan Econ.

Bird, Greta, et al, eds. Majah: Indigenous Peoples & the Law. 298p. 1996. pap. 39.00 (*1-86287-197-3*, Pub. by Federation Pr) Gaunt.

Bird, H. A., jt. ed. see Scott, J. S.

Bird, H. W., tr. from LAT. Aurelius Victor: De Caesaribus. (Translated Texts for Historians Ser.). 256p. (Orig.). 1994. pap. text 18.50 (*0-85323-218-0*, Pub. by Liverpool Univ Pr) U of Pa Pr.
— Eutropius: Breviarium. (Translated Texts for Historians Ser.). 194p. (Orig.). 1993. pap. text 17.50 (*0-85323-208-3*, Pub. by Liverpool Univ Pr) U of Pa Pr.

Bird, Heather, jt. ed. see Bird, Graham.

Bird, Henry. The Narrative of Henry Bird. 15p. 1973. pap. 6.95 (*0-87770-115-6*) Ye Galleon.

Bird, Howard A. & Snaith, Michael L. Challenges in Rheumatoid Arthritis. LC 98-42399. (Illus.). 1999. 95.00 (*0-632-04939-1*) Blackwell Sci.

Bird, Ian, ed. Phospholipid Signaling Protocols. LC 98-3874. (Methods in Molecular Biology Ser.). (Illus.). 400p. 1998. 89.50 (*0-89603-491-7*) Humana.

***Bird, Isabella.** Unbeaten Tracks in Japan. 408p. 2000. pap. 14.95 (*1-885211-57-0*) Trvlers Tale.

Bird, Isabella Lucy. The Englishwoman in America. LC 65-16359. 525p. 1966. reprint ed. pap. 162.80 (*0-7837-9778-8*, 206050700005) Bks Demand.
— Korea & Her Neighbours. (Pacific Basin Bks.). 400p. (Orig.). 1985. pap. 19.95 (*0-7103-0135-9*) Routledge.
— A Lady's Life in the Rocky Mountains. (Cloth Bound Pocket Ser.). 354p. 1999. 7.95 (*3-8290-0881-3*, 520653) Konemann.
— Lady's Life in the Rocky Mountains. LC 60-8748. (Western Frontier Library: No. 14). (Illus.). 1960. reprint ed. pap. 7.95 (*0-8061-1328-6*) U of Okla Pr.
— Six Months in Hawaii. pap. 19.95 (*0-7103-0232-0*, 02320) Routledge.
— Six Months in the Sandwich Islands. 318p. 1998. reprint ed. mass mkt. 7.95 (*1-56647-050-1*) Mutual Pub HI.

Bird, Isabella Lucy & Bernard, Ernest S. Isabella Lucy Bird's "A Lady's Life in the Rocky Mountains" An Annotated Text. LC 98-41396. 1999. 24.95 (*0-8061-3112-8*) U of Okla Pr.

Bird, Isabella Lucy & Havely, Cicely Palser. This Grand Beyond: The Travels of Isabella Bird Bishop. LC 84-201847. 190 p. 1984. write for info. (*0-7126-0392-1*) CEN3.

Bird, Izola. Ethos of the Unfolding. unabridged ed. 180p. (Orig.). 1997. pap. 8.95 (*1-56411-130-X*, 4BBG0134) Untd Bros & Sis.

Bird, J. M., jt. auth. see Harrison, Glynn.

***Bird, J. O.** Basic Engineering Mathematics. (Illus.). 218p. 1999. pap. 39.95 (*0-7506-4109-6*, Newnes) Buttrwrth-Heinemann.

Bird, J. O. Bird's Pocket Reference Guide for Electrical Engineers. 2nd ed. (Illus.). 160p. (C). 1994. pap. text 29.95 (*0-582-23795-5*, Pub. by Addison-Wesley) Trans-Atl Phila.
— Early Engineering Mathematics: "Learn by Example" with 600 Worked Problems. LC 94-22234. 288p. 1995. pap. text 32.95 (*0-7506-2133-8*) Buttrwrth-Heinemann.
— Electrical Circuit Theory & Technology. 128p. 1999. pap. text 39.95 (*0-7506-3552-5*) Buttrwrth-Heinemann.

***Bird, J. O.** Electrical Circuit Theory & Technology. 2001. 39.95 (*0-7506-4989-5*, Newnes) Buttrwrth-Heinemann.

Bird, J. O. Electrical Principles & Technology for Engineering. LC 94-46419. (Illus.). 352p. 1999. pap. text 29.95 (*0-7506-2196-6*) Buttrwrth-Heinemann.

***Bird, J. O.** Engineering Mathematics. 480p. 2001. pap. 32.95 (*0-7506-4990-9*, Newnes) Buttrwrth-Heinemann.

Bird, J. O. Higher Electrical Technology. 2nd ed. (Illus.). 496p. 1996. pap. text 32.95 (*0-7506-2599-6*) Buttrwrth-Heinemann.
— Higher Engineering Mathematics. 2nd ed. 1996. pap. text 36.95 (*0-7506-2627-5*) Buttrwrth-Heinemann.
— Mathematical Formula. 2nd ed. 1994. pap. 7.95 (*0-582-22910-3*, Pub. by Addison-Wesley) Longman.
— Mathematics for Electrical Technicians. 2nd ed. 1996. pap. (*0-582-23421-2*) Addison-Wesley.
— MCQs in Science & Mathematics for Engineering: Intermediate GNVQ. LC 95-45355. 64p. 1995. spiral bd. write for info. (*0-7506-2664-X*) Buttrwrth-Heinemann.
— Multiple Choice Questions in Electrical Principles & Technology: Advanced GNVQ. LC 95-45356. 64p. 1995. spiral bd. write for info. (*0-7506-2667-4*) Buttrwrth-Heinemann.
— Multiple Choice Questions in Mathematics for Engineering Advanced GNVQ. LC 95-45357. 64p. 1995. spiral bd. write for info. (*0-7506-2666-6*) Buttrwrth-Heinemann.
— Newnes Engineering & Physical Science Pocket Book. 2nd ed. LC 96-17119. (Illus.). 624p. 1996. 32.95 (*0-7506-2897-9*, Pub. by Newtech) Buttrwrth-Heinemann.
— Newnes Mathematics Pocket Book for Engineers. (Illus.). 352p. 1988. 26.95 (*0-7506-0264-3*) Buttrwrth-Heinemann.
— Newnes Mathematics Pocket Book for Engineers. 1988. 21.00 (*0-434-90129-6*) CRC Pr.
— Newnes Mathematics Pocket Book for Engineers. 2nd ed. LC 97-27319. (Pocket Book Ser.). 384p. 1999. text 28.95 (*0-7506-3004-3*, Newnes) Buttrwrth-Heinemann.
— Science for Engineering. 2nd ed. LC 94-31866. 380p. 2000. pap. text 36.95 (*0-7506-2150-8*) Buttrwrth-Heinemann.
— Technician Mathematics. 2nd ed. 1994. pap. 20.95 (*0-582-23424-7*, Pub. by Addison-Wesley); pap. 25.95 (*0-582-23425-5*, Pub. by Addison-Wesley) Longman.

Bird, J. O. & Chivers, P. Newnes Physical Science Pocket Book for Engineers. 4201st ed. 1988. 22.00 (*0-408-01343-5*) CRC Pr.

Bird, J. O. & May, A. J. Algebra & Calculus for Technicians: Level 3. LC 85-38627. (Longman Technician Ser.). 367p. 1991. reprint ed. pap. 113.80 (*0-608-03620-X*, 206444700009) Bks Demand.
— Mathematics for Electrical & Telecommunications Technicians: Level 2. LC TA0330.. (Longman Technician Series, Mathematics & Sciences). (Illus.). 383p. reprint ed. pap. 118.80 (*0-608-18736-4*, 203033300068) Bks Demand.
— Mathematics for Science Technicians, Level 2. LC TA0330.. (Longman Technician Series, Mathematics & Sciences). (Illus.). 330p. reprint ed. pap. 102.30 (*0-8357-2979-6*, 203924100011) Bks Demand.
— Statistics for Technicians. LC 79-41681. (Longman Technician Series, Mathematics & Sciences). 133p. reprint ed. pap. 41.30 (*0-8357-3551-6*, 203446900090) Bks Demand.

Bird, J. Roger & Williams, James S., eds. Ion Beams for Materials Analysis. 719p. 1989. text 136.00 (*0-12-099740-1*) Acad Pr.

Bird, J. Roger, et al. Ion Beam Techniques in Archaeology & the Arts, Vol. 1. 172p. 1983. pap. text 112.00 (*3-7186-0188-5*) Gordon & Breach.

Bird, James H. The Changing World of Geography: A Critical Guide to Concepts & Methods. 2nd ed. LC 92-29463. (Illus.). 328p. 1993. pap. text 35.00 (*0-19-874182-0*, Clarendon Pr) OUP.

Bird, Jean. In-Service Training in Public Library Authorities: British Library R & D Report 5898. LC 86-19330. (Library Association Research Publication: Vol. 23). 165p. 1986. reprint ed. pap. 51.20 (*0-7837-9413-4*, 206000500004) Bks Demand.

Bird, Jean, jt. auth. see Bird, Alan F.

Bird, Joanna, et al, eds. Interpreting Roman London: Papers in Memory of Hugh Chapman. (Monographs in World Archaeology: Vol. 58). (Illus.). 270p. 1996. pap. 63.00 (*1-900188-02-3*, Pub. by Oxbow Bks) David Brown.

Bird, Joanna, jt. ed. see O'Connell, M. G.

***Bird, John.** Basic Engineering Mathematics. 2nd ed. 256p. 2000. 39.95 (*0-7506-4750-7*, Newnes) Buttrwrth-Heinemann.

Bird, John. Beyond the Millenium. 50p. 1997. pap. 5.95 (*1-57918-052-3*, 3741) Queenship Pub.
— Black Students & Higher Education: Rhetorics & Realities. LC 96-12068. (Illus.). 132p. 1996. 122.95 (*0-335-19627-6*); pap. 37.00 (*0-335-19626-8*) OpUniv Pr.

***Bird, John.** Electrical & Electronic Principles & Technology. 2nd ed. 352p. 2000. pap. 29.95 (*0-7506-4748-5*, Newnes) Buttrwrth-Heinemann.

Bird, John. Higher Engineering Mathematics. 512p. 1999. pap. text 32.95 (*0-7506-4110-X*) Buttrwrth-Heinemann.
— Percy Grainger. 2nd ed. (Illus.). 424p. 1999. text 45.00 (*0-19-816652-4*) OUP.

Bird, John. Percy Granger. (Illus.). (Orig.). pap. 29.95 (*0-86819-570-7*, Pub. by Currency Pr) Accents Pubns.

Bird, John. Queen of Ukraine. 65p. 1992. pap. 4.00 (*1-890137-28-6*) One Hund-One Fnd.

***Bird, John.** Science for Engineering. 352p. 2000. pap. 34.95 (*0-7506-4747-7*, Newnes) Buttrwrth-Heinemann.

Bird, John, jt. ed. see Englestad, Diane.

Bird, John B. The Physiography of Arctic Canada, with Special Reference to the Area South of Perry Channel. LC 67-16232. 427p. reprint ed. pap. 132.40 (*0-608-11893-1*, 202308300032) Bks Demand.

Bird, John T. Twin Killing: The Bill Mazeroski Story. 316p. 1995. 24.95 (*0-9649011-0-2*) Esmerelda AL.

Bird, Jon, et al, eds. Mapping the Futures: Local Cultures, Global Change. LC 92-8718. (Futures Ser.). (Illus.). 256p. (C). 1993. pap. 23.99 (*0-415-07018-X*, A7914) Routledge.

Bird, Jon, et al. Nancy Spero. (Contemporary Artists Ser.). (Illus.). 160p. (Orig.). 1996. pap. 29.95 (*0-7148-3340-1*, Pub. by Phaidon Press) Phaidon Pr.
— Rachel Whiteread: House. Lingwood, James, ed. LC 96-147143. (Illus.). 144p. (Orig.). 1995. pap. 24.95 (*0-7148-3459-9*, Pub. by Phaidon Press) Phaidon Pr.

Bird, Jonathan. Beneath the North Atlantic. LC 96-60420. (Illus.). 160p. 1997. 39.95 (*1-55949-314-3*, 314-3) Tide-Mark.

Bird, Josephine P., jt. auth. see Bird, Adren.

Bird, Junius B. Travels & Archaeology in South Chile. LC 87-30245. (Illus.). 278p. 1988. text 34.95 (*0-87745-202-4*) U of Iowa Pr.

Bird, Kai. The Chairman: John J. McCloy - The Making of the American Establishment. 608p. 1992. 30.00 (*0-671-45415-3*) S&S Trade.
— The Color of Truth: McGeorge & William Bundy - Brothers in Arms - A Biography. LC 98-24676. (Illus.). 480p. 1998. 27.50 (*0-684-80970-2*) Simon & Schuster.

B

***Bird, Kai.** The Color of Truth: Mcgeorge Bundy & William Bundy Brothers in Arms. (Illus.). 496p. 2000. per. 15.00 (*0-684-85644-1*) S&S Trade.

Bird, Kai & Lifschultz, Lawrence. Hiroshima's Shadow: Writings on the Denial of History & the Smithsonian Controversy. 584p. 1997. 35.95 (*0-9630587-3-8*); pap. 25.00 (*0-9630587-4-6*) Pamphleteers.

Bird, Kermit M., ed. Quill of the Wild Goose: Civil War Letters & Diaries of Private Joel Molyneux, 141st Pennsylvania Volunteers. LC 96-17600. 326p. 1996. 30.00 (*1-57249-038-1*, Burd St Pr) White Mane Pub.

Bird, Larry. Drive: The Story of My Life. (J). 1989. 12.09 (*0-606-04657-7*, Pub. by Turtleback) Demco.

Bird, Larry & Bischoff, John. Bird on Basketball: How-to Strategies from the Great Celtics Champion. 3rd rev. ed. (Illus.). 128p. 1988. pap. 15.00 (*0-201-14209-0*) Addison-Wesley.

***Bird, Larry & MacMullan, Jackie.** Bird Watching: On Playing & Coaching the Game I Love. LC 99-18906. 320p. 1999. 24.95 (*0-446-52464-6*, Pub. by Warner Bks) Little.

— Bird Watching: On Playing & Coaching the Game I Love. 2000. mass mkt. 7.99 (*0-446-60888-2*) Warner Bks.

Bird, Larry & Ryan, Bob. Drive: The Story of My Life. 304p. 1990. reprint ed. mass mkt. 7.50 (*0-553-28758-3*) Bantam.

Bird, Leah H. Two Communities in Stitches: A History of Dale & McLoud, OK. 323p. 1977. 20.00 (*0-9601364-0-1*); text 20.00 (*0-685-60798-4*); pap. text 15.00 (*0-9601364-1-X*) Henrys Postscript.

Bird, Leslie, jt. auth. see Buckingham, Linda.

***Bird, Linda.** Mous Essentials Powerpoint 2000. 2nd ed. 350p. 2000. pap. 42.67 (*0-13-019105-1*) P-H.

— Powerpoint for Windows 95 Essentials. 2nd ed. 181p. (C). 1997. pap. text 18.67 (*1-58076-029-5*) Que Educ & Trng.

Bird, Linda. PowerPoint 97 Essentials, Level 1. LC 97-65586. 192p. 1997. 22.99 (*1-57576-785-6*) Sams.

***Bird, Linda.** PowerPoint 2000 Essentials Advanced. 2000. pap. text 14.00 (*1-58076-286-7*) Que Educ & Trng.

— Powerpoint 2000 Essentials Basic with CD-ROM. 300p. (C). 1999. spiral bd. 21.33 (*1-58076-095-3*) Que Educ & Trng.

Bird, Linda. PowerPoint 95 Essentials. 1996. 22.99 (*1-57576-257-9*) Que Educ & Trng.

— PowerPoint 97 Essentials: Level II. 1997. teacher ed. 49.99 (*1-57576-810-0*) Que Educ & Trng.

— PowerPoint 97 Essentials Level II. LC 97-65621. 192p. 1997. 22.99 (*1-57576-802-X*) Sams.

***Bird, Linda.** Transition from Powerpoint 4.0 to Powerpoint for Windows 95. 120p. 1998. pap. text 17.33 (*1-58076-067-8*) Que Educ & Trng.

— Transition From Word 6 To Word For Windows 95 Essentials. 101p. (C). 1998. pap. text 17.33 (*1-58706-063-9*) P-H.

Bird, Linda A., ed. see Logan, John W.

Bird, Lizzie. Wreck Diving Manual. (Illus.). 160p. 1997. pap. 29.95 (*1-86126-023-7*, Pub. by Crolwood) Trafalgar.

Bird, Lois B., ed. Becoming a Whole Language School: The Fair Oaks Story. LC 89-3094. 151p. (Orig.). (C). 1989. pap. text 16.95 (*0-913461-15-6*, 24) R Owen Pubs.

Bird, Lois B., jt. auth. see Gust, John.

***Bird, Lonnie.** Bandsaw Book. LC 99-29603. 208p. 1999. 19.95 (*1-56158-289-1*) Taunton.

Bird, Lonnie. The Shaper Book. LC 96-35740. 144p. 1997. pap. 19.95 (*1-56158-120-8*, 70251) Taunton.

Bird, Lori b., jt. auth. see Franklin, Carolyn.

Bird, Lydia. Sonnet: One Woman's Voyage from Maryland to Greece. LC 96-50352. 256p. 1997. pap. 23.00 (*0-86547-507-5*) N Point Pr.

Bird, M. B. The Black Man. LC 70-164380. (Black Heritage Library Collection). 1977. reprint ed. 37.95 (*0-8369-8839-6*) Ayer.

***Bird, M. Catherine, et al, eds.** The Keeshin Farm Site & Rock River Langford Tradition in Northern Illinois. LC 99-28570. (Transportation Archaeological Research Reports). (Illus.). 284p. 1999. pap. 15.00 (*0-9644881-8-3*) ITARP.

Bird, Madeline & Prestedge, Margie. Smocking. (C). 1989. 30.00 (*1-85368-077-X*, Pub. by New5 Holland) St Mut.

Bird, Malcolm. Complete Guide to Business & Sales Presentation. (C). (gr. 13). 1990. mass mkt. 18.95 (*0-442-30288-6*) Chapman & Hall.

— Effective Leadership: A Practical Guide to Leading Your Team to Success. (Illus.). 1996. pap. 9.95 (*0-563-36416-5*, BBC-Parkwest) Parkwest Pubns.

Bird, Marion H. Mathematics for Young Children: An Active Thinking Approach. (Illus.). 176p. (C). (gr. 13). 1991. text 79.95 (*0-415-06479-1*, A6270) Routledge.

Bird, Martyn & Lewis, H. Hotel Europa - France: Business French for Beginners. (Illus.). 184p. 1991. pap. 27.00 (*0-340-54697-2*, Pub. by Hodder & Stought Ltd) Lubrecht & Cramer.

Bird, Mary. Playing Tree & Other Stories. 1995. pap. text 12.95 (*1-887650-00-8*) Factor Pr.

Bird, Michael, jt. ed. see May, John R.

Bird, Michael S. Art & Interreligious Dialogue: Six Perspectives. (Illus.). 160p. (C). 1995. reprint ed. pap. text 22.50 (*0-8191-9555-3*) U Pr of Amer.

— Art & Interreligious Dialogue: Six Perspectives. (Illus.). 160p. (C). 1995. reprint ed. lib. bdg. 49.50 (*0-8191-9554-5*) U Pr of Amer.

— Canadian Country Furniture: 1675-1950. (Illus.). 400p. 60.00 (*1-55046-087-0*, Pub. by Boston Mills) Genl Dist Srvs.

Bird, Mike. The Economic Development of Colorado in Historical Perspective. 23p. 1993. pap. text 8.00 (*1-57655-104-0*) Independ Inst.

Bird Observer Staff & Van Dusen, Barry W. A Birder's Guide to Eastern Massachusetts. Baicich, Paul J., ed. LC 94-71892. (ABA Birdfinding Guides). (Illus.). 292p. (Orig.). 1994. pap., pap. text, spiral bd. 18.95 (*1-878788-08-6*, 266) Amer Birding Assn.

Bird, Otto, ed. see Maritain, Jacques.

Bird, Otto, tr. see Bochenski, J. M.

Bird, Otto A. Seeking a Center: My Life As a "Great Bookie" LC 91-71555. 145p. (Orig.). 1991. pap. 9.95 (*0-89870-370-0*) Ignatius Pr.

Bird, P. E., ed. Elements of Sport Airplane Design for the Homebuilder. 3rd ed. (Illus.). 105p. 1986. pap. 19.95 (*0-911720-25-1*) Aviation.

Bird, P. M. The Solicitor's Duty in Law & Conduct. (Practitioner's Library). 224p. 1989. 99.00 (*0-08-033073-8*) Macmillan.

Bird, P. M. & Weir, J. B. The Concise Law on Solicitors. (Waterlow Practitioner's Library). (Illus.). 352p. 1989. 63.00 (*0-685-24819-4*) Macmillan.

Bird, Peter L., jt. ed. see Lilja, David J.

Bird, Phyllis A. Missing Persons & Mistaken Identities: Women & Gender in Ancient Israel. LC 97-27404. (Overtures to Biblical Theology Ser.). 320p. 1997. pap. 20.00 (*0-8006-3128-5*, Fortress Pr) Augsburg Fortress.

***Bird, Polly.** Helping Your Child to Learn at Primary School: How to Support & Improve Your Child's Learning Potential. (Illus.). 144p. (Orig.). 1999. pap. 19.95 (*1-85703-383-3*, Pub. by How To Bks) Trans-Atl Phila.

Bird, Polly. Time Management. (Illus.). 192p. 1998. pap. 11.95 (*0-8442-0016-6*, 00166, Teach Yrslf) NTC Contemp Pub Co.

Bird, R. The Computer in Experimental Psychology. LC 80-41610. (Computers & People Ser.). 256p. 1981. text 147.00 (*0-12-099760-6*) Acad Pr.

— A History of Russian Painting. (C). 1990. 350.00 (*0-7855-4493-3*, Pub. by Collets) St Mut.

Bird, R. Byron & Floyd, Sigmund. Polymer Science & Engineering. LC 94-42316. (Technical Japanese Supplements Ser.). 96p. 1995. pap. 22.95 (*0-299-14694-4*) U of Wis Pr.

Bird, R. Byron, et al. Dynamics of Polymer Liquids, 2 vols. 2nd ed. 1086p. 1989. 265.00 (*0-471-51844-1*) Wiley.

— Dynamics of Polymeric Liquids: Fluid Mechanics, Vol. 1, 2 vols., Vol. 1, Fluid Mechanics. 2nd ed. LC 86-13230. 672p. 1987. 156.00 (*0-471-80245-X*) Wiley.

— Dynamics of Polymeric Liquids: Kinetic Theory, Vol. 2, 2 vols., Vol. 2, Kinetic Theory. 2nd ed. LC 86-13230. 464p. 1987. 156.00 (*0-471-80244-1*) Wiley.

— Transport Phenomena. 808p. 1960. text 99.95 (*0-471-07392-X*) Wiley.

Bird, R. S., et al, eds. Mathematics of Program Construction: Proceedings of the 2nd International Conference, Oxford, U. K., June-July 1992. LC 93-16952. (Lecture Notes in Computer Science Ser.: Vol. 669). 1993. 55.95 (*0-387-56625-2*) Spr-Verlag.

***Bird, Richard.** Annuals & Perennials. 192p. 2000. 19.95 (*1-84215-103-7*) Anness Pub.

Bird, Richard. Beds & Borders. LC 97-35548. (Garden Project Workbooks Ser.). 1998. write for info. (*1-55670-613-8*) Stewart Tabori & Chang.

— Border Pinks. (Illus.). 174p. 1994. 29.95 (*0-88192-304-4*) Timber.

***Bird, Richard.** The Border Planner. LC 00-32760. 2000. 19.95 (*1-57145-675-9*, Laurel Glen Pub) Advantage Pubs.

Bird, Richard. Climbers: The Complete Guide to Successful Climbing Plants. 1998. pap. text 12.95 (*1-85967-663-4*, Lorenz Bks) Anness Pub.

— Companion Planting. (Illus.). 144p. 1998. pap. 14.95 (*0-8069-3785-8*) Sterling.

— The Eunuch: A Dark Tale. LC 95-69970. 200p. (Orig.). 1995. pap. 14.95 (*0-9646471-0-9*) Cerberus Bks.

— Fences & Hedges & Other Garden Dividers: A Garden Project Workbook. LC 98-17156. (Garden Project Workbooks Ser.: Vol. 7). (Illus.). 122p. 1998. 22.50 (*1-55670-836-X*) Stewart Tabori & Chang.

— 50 Recipes for Colourful Containers. (Illus.). 128p. 1996. 22.95 (*0-7063-7493-2*, Pub. by WrLock) Sterling.

— 50 Recipes for Colorful Hanging Baskets. LC 97-175775. 1997. 22.95 (*0-7063-7557-2*, Pub. by WrLock) Sterling.

— 50 Recipes for Colorful Window Boxes. LC 97-175406. (Illus.). 128p. 1997. 22.95 (*0-7063-7492-4*) Ward Lock Ltd UK.

— Garden Year: Practical Gardening Month by Month. 1998. 29.95 (*0-7063-7633-1*, Pub. by WrLock) Sterling.

— The Garden Year: Practical Gardening Month by Month. (Illus.). 192p. 1999. pap. 19.95 (*0-7063-7809-1*, Pub. by WrLock) Sterling.

***Bird, Richard.** Glorious Climbers. (Illus.). 2000. 14.95 (*0-7548-0550-6*, Lorenz Bks) Anness Pub.

Bird, Richard. Hardy Perennials: A Complete Guide to Care & Cultivation. (Illus.). 256p. 1998. pap. text 19.95 (*0-7063-7764-8*, Pub. by WrLock) Sterling.

— Identifying Guide to Ornamental Conifers. 80p. 1995. 6.98 (*0-7858-0324-6*) Bk Sales Inc.

— Introduction to Functional Programming, Haskell 1.3. LC 98-5681. 200p. (Series in Computer Science). 1998. write for info. (*0-13-484338-X*) P-H.

***Bird, Richard.** The Kitchen Garden. LC 99-58856. (Garden Project Workbook Ser.: Vol. 9). (Illus.). 112p. 2000. 22.50 (*1-55670-960-9*) Stewart Tabori & Chang.

Bird, Richard. Kitchen Garden Book: Vegetables from Seed to Table. 1999. 35.00 (*0-7548-0198-5*, Lorenz Bks) Anness Pub.

— Lagonda Heritage. (Color Library). (Illus.). 128p. 1994. pap. 15.95 (*1-85532-363-X*, Pub. by Osprey) Motorbooks Intl.

— Lilies. 1991. 12.98 (*1-55521-706-0*) Bk Sales Inc.

***Bird, Richard.** Perennials: A Complete Guide to Successful Growing. (Illus.). 2000. 16.95 (*0-7548-0562-X*, Lorenz Bks) Anness Pub.

Bird, Richard. Planning a Small Garden: Big Inspirations for Compact Plots. LC 98-36923. (Illus.). 128p. 1998. pap. 25.00 (*1-57959-035-7*, SOMA) BB&T Inc.

— Programs & Machines: An Introduction to the Theory of Computation. LC 75-38893. (Wiley Series in Computing). 224p. reprint ed. pap. 69.50 (*0-7837-3213-9*, 204323100007) Bks Demand.

— Rolls-Royce Heritage. (Osprey Colour Library). (Illus.). 128p. 1994. pap. 15.95 (*1-85532-410-5*, Pub. by Ospry) Motorbooks Intl.

***Bird, Richard.** The Scented Garden. LC 99-58855. (Garden Project Workbook Ser.: Vol. 10). (Illus.). 112p. 2000. 22.50 (*1-55670-961-7*) Stewart Tabori & Chang.

— Sensational Shrubs. (Illus.). 2000. 14.95 (*0-7548-0555-7*, Lorenz Bks) Anness Pub.

Bird, Richard. Shrubs. 1998. pap. text 12.95 (*1-85967-677-4*, Lorenz Bks) Anness Pub.

Bird, Richard, compiled by. General Index. LC 79-21840. (Heibonsha Survey of Japanese Art Ser.: Vol. 31). 104p. 1980. 20.00 (*0-8348-1031-X*) Weatherhill.

Bird, Richard, et al, eds. Decentralization of the Socialist State: Intergovernmental Finance in Transition Economics. (World Bank Ser.). 464p. 1996. 97.95 (*1-85972-308-X*, Pub. by Avebry) Ashgate Pub Co.

Bird, Richard & De Moor, Oege. The Algebra of Programming. 352p. 1996. pap. 48.00 (*0-13-507245-X*) P-H.

Bird, Richard & Tarrant, David. New Perennials: The Latest & Best Perennials. (Illus.). 144p. pap. 14.95 (*1-55110-821-6*) Whitecap Bks.

Bird, Richard & Vaillancourt, Francois, eds. Fiscal Decentralisation in Developing Countries. LC 98-20491. (Trade & Development Ser.). (Illus.). 320p. (C). 1999. text 59.95 (*0-521-64143-8*) Cambridge U Pr.

Bird, Richard, et al. Beds & Borders: A Garden Project Workbook, Vol. 4. LC 97-35548. 112p. 1998. 22.50 (*1-55670-689-8*) Stewart Tabori & Chang.

— Introduction to Functional Programming. 2nd ed. 460p. 1998. pap. 74.00 (*0-13-484346-0*) P-H.

Bird, Richard, jt. auth. see Lloyd, Christopher.

Bird, Richard M. Bibliography on Taxation in Developing Countries. LC 68-20366. 198p. (Orig.). 1968. pap. 5.00 (*0-915506-08-4*) Harvard Law Intl Tax.

— Intergovernmental Finance in Colombia: Final Report of the Mission on Intergovernmental Finance. LC 83-22752. 434p. 1984. pap. 20.00 (*0-915506-28-9*) Harvard Law Intl Tax.

— Tax Policy & Economic Development. LC 91-16243. (Studies in Development). 264p. 1991. pap. text 19.95 (*0-8018-4265-4*) Johns Hopkins.

— Taxation & Development: Lessons from Colombian Experience. LC 77-89965. 294p. reprint ed. pap. 91.20 (*0-7837-4447-1*, 205797700012) Bks Demand.

— Taxing Agricultural Land in Developing Countries. LC 73-77991. (Harvard Law School International Tax Program Ser.). 384p. 1974. 43.00 (*0-674-86855-2*) HUP.

Bird, Richard M., et al, eds. Decentralization of the Socialist State: Intergovernmental Finance in Transition Economies. LC 95-2528. (Regional & Sectoral Studies). 464p. 1995. pap. 28.00 (*0-8213-3186-8*, 13186) World Bank.

Bird, Richard M. & Casanegra De Jantscher, Milka, eds. Improving Tax Administration in Developing Countries. LC 92-34718. 403p. 1992. pap. 23.50 (*1-55775-317-2*) Intl Monetary.

Bird, Richard M. & Oldman, Oliver, eds. Taxation in Developing Countries. 4th ed. LC 89-28367. 544p. 1990. reprint ed. pap. 168.70 (*0-608-07331-8*, 206755900009) Bks Demand.

Bird, Richard M. & Slack, N. E. Residential Property Tax Relief in Ontario. LC 79-322196. (Ontario Economic Council Research Studies: No. 15). 198p. reprint ed. pap. 61.40 (*0-8357-4030-7*, 203672200005) Bks Demand.

***Bird, Robert, ed.** A Bibliography of Russian Idealist Philosophy in English. (Readings in Russian Philosophy Ser.: Vol. 7). 61p. 1999. pap. 5.00 (*1-929829-07-8*) Variable Pr.

Bird, Robert, ed. see Khomiakov, Aleksey & Kieerevsky, Ivan.

Bird, Robert, ed. & tr. see Bulgakov, Sergius.

Bird, Robert, ed. & tr. see Florenskij, Pavel & Lopatin, Lev.

Bird, Robert, tr. see Florenskij, Pavel.

Bird, Robert J., tr. see Poznansky, Alexander.

Bird, Robert M. The Adventures of Robin Day. (Works of Robert Montgomery Bird). 1989. reprint ed. lib. bdg. 90.00 (*0-7812-1993-0*) Rprt Serv.

— A Belated Revenge. (Works of Robert Montgomery Bird). 1989. reprint ed. lib. bdg. 79.00 (*0-7812-1994-9*) Rprt Serv.

— Calavar. (Works of Robert Montgomery Bird). 1989. reprint ed. lib. bdg. 79.00 (*0-7812-1988-4*) Rprt Serv.

— City Looking Glass: A Philadelphia Comedy. LC 74-177511. 1972. reprint ed. 23.95 (*0-405-08271-1*, Pub. by Blom Pubns) Ayer.

— Hawks of Hawk Hollow. 1993. reprint ed. lib. bdg. 89.00 (*0-7812-5427-2*) Rprt Serv.

— The Hawks of Hawks Hollow. (Works of Robert Montgomery Bird). 1989. reprint ed. lib. bdg. 79.00 (*0-7812-1990-6*) Rprt Serv.

— The Infidel. (Works of Robert Montgomery Bird). 1989. reprint ed. lib. bdg. 79.00 (*0-7812-1989-2*) Rprt Serv.

— Miscellaneous - Peter Pilgrim. (Works of Robert Montgomery Bird). 1989. reprint ed. lib. bdg. 79.00 (*0-7812-1995-7*) Rprt Serv.

— Nick of the Woods. Dahl, Curtis, ed. (Masterworks of Literature Ser.). 1967. pap. 15.95 (*0-8084-0235-8*) NCUP.

— Nick of the Woods. (Works of Robert Montgomery Bird). 1989. reprint ed. lib. bdg. 79.00 (*0-7812-1992-2*) Rprt Serv.

— Sheppard Lee. (Works of Robert Montgomery Bird). 1989. reprint ed. lib. bdg. 79.00 (*0-7812-1991-4*) Rprt Serv.

— The Works of Robert Montgomery Bird. 1989. reprint ed. lib. bdg. 63.00 (*0-685-27343-1*) Rprt Serv.

Bird, Roger. Practice & Procedure in District Registries. 165p. 1991. 65.00 (*1-85190-143-4*, Pub. by Tolley Pubng) St Mut.

Bird, Roger C., ed. The Frank M. Engle Lectures, 1978-1997. LC 98-73516. 1000p. (C). 1998. text 15.00 (*1-57996-008-1*) Amer College.

***Bird, Roger C. & Graber, Robert S.** Fundamentals of Investments for Financial Planning. 1000p. (C). 2000. text 78.00 (*1-57996-022-7*, Pub. by Amer College) Maple-Vail Bk.

Bird, Roland T. Bones for Barnum Brown: Adventures of a Dinosaur Hunter. Schreiber, V. Theodore, ed. LC 84-24047. (Illus.). 226p. 1985. 29.95 (*0-87565-007-4*); pap. 14.95 (*0-87565-011-2*) Tex Christian.

Bird-Romero, Allison, jt. auth. see Baxter, Paula A.

Bird-Romero, Allison, jt. auth. see Krena, John.

Bird, Rose Elizabeth & Galloway, Russell W. A Student's Guide to Basic Constitutional Analysis 1996. annuals 1996. text 24.00 (*0-8205-3081-6*) Bender.

Bird, Roy. Kansas Day by Day. (Illus.). 280p. (Orig.). 1996. pap. 12.95 (*1-880397-13-7*) Patrice Pr.

— Topeka: An Illustrated History of the Kansas Capital. 152p. 1985. 19.95 (*0-941974-06-5*) Baranski Pub Co.

Bird, Roy K. Wright Morris: Memory & Imagination. (American University Studies: English Language & Literature: Ser. IV, Vol. 20). 155p. (C). 1985. text 23.30 (*0-8204-0181-1*) P Lang Pubng.

Bird, S., et al. Exercise Benefits & Prescription. 2nd ed. (Illus.). 1998. pap. 52.50 (*0-7487-3362-0*, Pub. by S Thornes Pubs) Trans-Atl Phila.

***Bird, S., et al.** Sports Injuries: Causes, Diagnosis, Treatment & Prevention. 320p. (Orig.). 1999. pap. 57.50 (*0-7487-3181-4*, Pub. by S Thornes Pubs) Trans-Atl Phila.

Bird, S., et al. Sports Injuries: Causes, Diagnosis, Treatment & Prevention. (Illus.). 320p. (Orig.). 1997. pap. 55.00 (*1-56593-196-3*, 0511) Singular Publishing.

Bird, S. Elizabeth. For Enquiring Minds: A Cultural Study of Supermarket Tabloids. LC 91-13989. (Illus.). 248p. (C). 1992. pap. 16.95 (*0-87049-729-4*); text 34.00 (*0-87049-728-6*) U of Tenn Pr.

Bird, S. J., jt. auth. see Kavanagh, Barry F.

Bird, Sarah. Virgin of the Rodeo. LC 99-36651. 352p. 1999. pap. 15.00 (*0-8032-6169-1*) U of Nebr Pr.

Bird, Sophie G. Maneater. (Orig.). 1993. mass mkt. 6.95 (*1-56333-103-9*, Rhinoceros) Masquerade.

Bird-Sporakowsk. Taking Sides: Family Edition. 2nd ed. 1994. teacher ed. 13.53 (*0-697-32899-6*, WCB McGr Hill) McGrw-H Hghr Educ.

— Taking Sides: Family Edition. 3rd ed. 1996. 13.53 (*0-697-35737-6*, WCB McGr Hill) McGrw-H Hghr Educ.

Bird, Stacey, ed. Impact: Working with Sexual Abusers. LC 98-194776. 96p. (Orig.). 1997. pap. 20.00 (*1-884444-42-3*) Safer Soc.

Bird, Stephanie. Recasting Historical Women: Female Identity in German Biographical Fiction. 224p. 1998. 55.00 (*1-85973-962-8*, Pub. by Berg Pubs) NYU Pr.

Bird, Stephen, jt. auth. see Fawcett, Trevor.

Bird, Stephen M. Prayers That Bring Miracles. rev. ed. LC 97-44694. 176p. 1997. reprint ed. 15.95 (*1-56236-238-0*, Pub. by Aspen Bks) Origin Bk Sales.

Bird, Steven. Computational Phonology: A Constraint-Based Approach. (Studies in Natural Language Processing). 219p. (C). 1995. text 49.95 (*0-521-47496-5*) Cambridge U Pr.

— Mikhail Bakhtin: Between Phenomenology & Marxism. (Studies in Natural Language Processing: No. 11). 205p. (C). 1995. pap. text 19.95 (*0-521-46647-4*) Cambridge U Pr.

Bird, Steven, et al. Exercise Benefits & Prescription. 2nd ed. 344p. 1999. pap. 42.50 (*0-7487-3315-9*, Pub. by S Thornes Pubs) Trans-Atl Phila.

Bird, Stewart & Robilotta, Peter. The Wobblies. (Orig.). 1980. pap. 1.00 (*0-918266-13-0*) Smyrna.

Bird, Stewart & Robilotta, Peter T. The Wobblies: The U. S. vs. Wm. D. Haywood, et al. LC 88-107256. (Illus.). 79p. 1980. reprint ed. pap. 30.00 (*0-7837-9093-7*, 204984300003) Bks Demand.

Bird, Stewart, et al. Solidarity Forever: An Oral History of the I. W. W. LC 84-82491. (Illus.). 256p. 1985. 29.95 (*0-941702-11-1*); pap. 12.95 (*0-941702-12-X*) Lake View Pr.

Bird, Tate, ed. see McClure, Patricia.

Bird, Thomas E., ed. Foreign Language Learning: Research & Development. 118p. 1968. pap. 10.95 (*0-915432-68-4*) NE Conf Teach Foreign.

— Foreign Languages: Reading, Literature, Requirements. 124p. 1967. pap. 10.95 (*0-915432-67-6*) NE Conf Teach Foreign.

Bird, Thomas E., jt. ed. see Marshall, Richard H., Jr.

Bird, Tia. Dream Like Ezra: A Story of Pioneer Ezra Meeker. Lent, Penny, ed. LC 94-76616. (Illus.). 24p. (Orig.). (J). (gr. k-6). 1994. pap. 2.95 (*1-885371-04-7*) Kldoscope Pr.

Bird, Tom. American POWs of World War II: Forgotten Men Tell Their Stories. LC 91-46991. 184p. 1992. 49.95 (*0-275-93707-0*, C3707, Praeger Pubs) Greenwood.

Bird, Tom, jt. auth. see Dawson, Andre.

Bird, Tom, jt. auth. see Niekro, Phil.

An Asterisk (*) at the beginning of an entry indicates that the title is appearing for the first time.

Bird, Twila. Build unto My Holy Name: The Story of the Denver Temple. England, Breck, ed. LC 87-51134. (Illus.). 208p. 1987. 15.00 (*0-9619296-0-X*) DCAPCC.

— A Century of Saints: The Church of Jesus Christ of Latter-Day Saints along the Front Range of the Rocky Mountains. unabridged ed. (Illus.). 130p. 1997. 15.00 (*0-9619296-1-8*) DCAPCC.

Bird, Virgil H. A World View of Art History: Selected Readings, Vol. II. 200p. (C). 1994. ring bd. 41.95 (*0-8403-9286-9*) Kendall-Hunt.

Bird, Vivian. By Lock & Pound. 208p. (C). 1989. 75.00 (*0-947712-06-2*, Pub. by S A Baldwin) St Mut.

Bird, Vivian, tr. see Grimm, Jacob W.

Bird, Warren, jt. auth. see George, Carl F.

Bird Watcher's Digest Editors & Thompson, Bill, III. Bird Watching for Dummies. LC 97-80179. (For Dummies Ser.). (Illus.). 448p. 1997. pap. 19.99 (*0-7645-5040-3*) IDG Bks.

Bird, William L., Jr. Better Living: Advertising, Media, & the New Vocabulary of Business Leadership. LC 98-45398. (Media Topographies Ser.). (Illus.). 192p. 1999. 30.00 (*0-8101-1585-9*) Northwestern U Pr.

Bird, William L. "Better Living" Advertising, Media & the New Vocabulary of Business Leadership, 1935-1955 LC 98-45398. (Media Topographies Ser.). 1999. 30.00 (*0-8101-1586-7*) Northwestern U Pr.

Bird, William L. & Rubenstein, Harry R. Design for Victory: World War II Posters on the American Home Front. LC 97-48361. (Illus.). 120p. 1998. pap. 17.95 (*1-56898-140-6*) Princeton Arch.

Bird Wright, Sarah, jt. auth. see Caws, Mary Ann.

Birdi, K. S. Fractals in Chemistry, Geochemistry & Biophysics: An Introduction. (Illus.). 278p. (C). 1993. text 55.00 (*0-306-44140-3*, Kluwer Plenum) Kluwer Academic.

— Handbook of Surface & Colloid Chemistry. LC 97-3758. 784p. 1997. boxed set 149.95 (*0-8493-9459-7*) CRC Pr.

— Lipid & Biopolymer Monolayers at Liquid Interfaces. LC 88-23172. (Illus.). 336p. (C). 1989. text 110.00 (*0-306-42870-9*, Kluwer Plenum) Kluwer Academic.

***Birdi, K. S.** Self-Assembly Monolayer Structures of Lipids & Macromolecules at Interfaces LC 99-37361. 1999. write for info. (*0-306-46099-8*, Kluwer Plenum) Kluwer Academic.

— Surface & Colloid Chemistry Handbook: CRC Net BASE, 1999. (Illus.). 1999. pap. text (*0-8493-2148-4*, Chap & Hall CRC) CRC Pr.

Birdine, Steven T. A Common Sense Approach to Retaining Students of Color. 50p. (Orig.). (C). 1994. 25.00 (*0-9644477-0-3*) Creat Diversity.

Birds Australia, WA Group Staff. Birding Sites Around Perth. LC 99-204444. (Illus.). 160p. 1997. pap. 19.95 (*1-876268-03-4*, Pub. by Univ of West Aust Pr) Intl Spec Bk.

Birds, John. Modern Insurance Law. 2nd ed. (C). 1988. 250.00 (*0-7855-4076-8*, Pub. by Witherby & Co); pap. 170.00 (*0-7855-4077-6*, Pub. by Witherby & Co) St Mut.

— Reminders for Company Secretaries. 25th ed. 136p. 1986. 60.00 (*0-85308-077-1*) St Mut.

Birdsad, Virginia Freld, tr. see Grobmann, Gerbert.

Birdsall, B. P. History of Wright County, Iowa. (Illus.). 1061p. 1994. reprint ed. lib. bdg. 107.00 (*0-8328-3829-2*) Higginson Bk Co.

Birdsall, Ben. Blue Charm. 200p. 1996. pap. 16.95 (*0-85640-544-2*, Pub. by Blackstaff Pr) Dufour.

Birdsall, C. K. & Langdon, A. B. Plasma Physics Via Computer Simulation. (Plasma Physics Ser.). (Illus.). 504p. 1991. 90.00 incl. disk (*0-7503-0117-1*) IOP Pub.

Birdsall, Carole & Sperry, Sandra. Clinical Paths in Medical-Surgical Nursing. (Illus.). 448p. (C). (gr. 13). 1996. text 59.95 (*0-8151-0484-7*, 27084) Mosby Inc.

Birdsall, David L., jt. auth. see Mair, W. Austyn.

Birdsall, Doug, intro. Enter...Save...Delete... Libraries Pioneering into the Next Century - Mountain Plains Library Association Academic Section Research Forum. 86p. 1989. pap. 7.50 (*0-934068-06-2*) Memorial Union.

Birdsall, Eric, ed. see Wordsworth, William.

Birdsall, George. The Feng Shui Companion: A User-Friendly Guide to the Ancient Art of Placement. LC 97-640. (Illus.). 208p. 1997. pap. 12.95 (*0-89281-616-3*) Inner Tradit.

Birdsall, John, jt. auth. see Mayhew, Bob.

Birdsall, Kathryn. In Poetry We Bond. 64p. (Orig.). 1995. pap. write for info. (*1-884257-10-0*) AGEE Keyboard.

***Birdsall, Nancy.** New Markets, New Opportunities? Economic & Social Mobility in a Changing World. LC 99-50451. 1999. pap. 24.95 (*0-8157-0917-X*) Brookings.

Birdsall, Nancy, et al, eds. Beyond Tradeoffs: Market Reforms & Equitable Growth in Latin America. 330p. 1998. pap. 22.95 (*0-8157-0921-8*) Brookings.

Birdsall, Nancy & Jaspersen, Frederick, eds. Pathways to Growth: Comparing East Asia & Latin America. LC 97-71220. (Inter-American Development Bank Ser.). 330p. 1997. pap. text 21.95 (*1-886938-13-X*) IADB.

Birdsall, Nancy & Sabot, Richard, eds. Opportunity Foregone: Education in Brazil. LC 96-77344. (Inter-American Development Bank Ser.). 566p. (C). 1996. pap. 14.50 (*1-886938-03-2*) IADB.

Birdsall, Stephen S., et al. North America. 5th ed. LC 98-51000. (Illus.). 464p. 1999. text 87.95 (*0-471-00998-9*) Wiley.

Birdsall, Steve. Pride of Seattle: The First 300 Boeing B-17FS. LC 98-201480. (Illus.). 64p. 1998. pap. 9.95 (*0-89747-389-2*, 6074) Squad Sig Pubns.

Birdsall, Virginia O. Defoe's Perpetual Seekers: A Study of the Major Fiction. LC 83-46154. 208p. 1985. 32.50 (*0-8387-5076-1*) Bucknell U Pr.

Birdsall, William F. The Myth of the Electronic Library: Librarianship & Social Change in America, 82. LC 93-49534. (Contributions in Librarianship & Information Science Ser.: No. 82). 224p. 1994. 59.95 (*0-313-29210-8*, Greenwood Pr) Greenwood.

Birdsell, David S., jt. auth. see Jamieson, Kathleen H.

Birdsell, Polly G. How Magicians Relate the Occult to Modern Magic: An Investigation & Study. 75p. (Orig.). 1989. pap. 6.95 (*0-9623139-0-4*) Silver Dawn.

Birdsell, Sandra. Agassiz: A Novel in Stories. LC 90-22663. (Illus.). 352p. 1991. 18.95 (*0-915943-61-1*) Milkweed Ed.

— Agassiz: A Novel in Stories. 1997. pap. 14.95 (*0-88801-123-7*, Pub. by Turnstone Pr) Genl Dist Srvs.

— Chrome Suite. 1995. pap. 14.95 (*0-7710-1452-X*) McCland & Stewart.

— Chrome Suite. 384p. 1995. reprint ed. pap. 10.95 (*0-7710-1453-8*) McCland & Stewart.

— The Two-Headed Calf. LC 97-930052. 267p. 1997. pap. 19.99 (*0-7710-1454-6*) McCland & Stewart.

Birdsey, Richard A., ed. see Hom, John L.

Birdseye, Clarence & Birdseye, Eleanor G. Growing Woodland Plants. (Illus.). 1972. reprint ed. pap. 5.95 (*0-486-20661-0*) Dover.

Birdseye, Debbie H. & Birdseye, Tom. Under Our Skin: Kids Talk about Race. LC 97-9395. (Illus.). 32p. (J). (gr. 4-6). 1997. lib. bdg. 15.95 (*0-8234-1325-X*) Holiday.

— What I Believe: Kids Talk about Faith. LC 96-11240. (Illus.). 32p. (J). (gr. 4-6). 1996. 15.95 (*0-8234-1268-7*) Holiday.

Birdseye, Debbie H., jt. auth. see Birdseye, Tom.

Birdseye, Eleanor G., jt. auth. see Birdseye, Clarence.

Birdseye, Harvey E. ABC's of Microchips: An Introduction to Silicon Process & Microelectronics. LC 97-61368. (Illus.). 102p. (Orig.). 1997. pap. text 11.00 (*0-9659207-0-4*) Tech Ed.

— The ABC's of Microchips Vol. 1: An Introduction to Microelectronics Manufacturing. 2nd ed. Breymer, Sylvia, ed. (Illus.). 110p. 1998. pap. text 10.95 (*0-9659207-1-2*) Tech Ed.

Birdseye, Tom. Airmail to the Moon. LC 87-21199. (Illus.). 32p. (J). (ps-3). 1988. lib. bdg. 15.95 (*0-8234-0683-0*) Holiday.

— Airmail to the Moon. LC 87-21199. (Illus.). 32p. (J). (ps-3). 1989. pap. 6.95 (*0-8234-0754-3*) Holiday.

***Birdseye, Tom.** The Eye of the Stone. LC 00-24322. 144p. (J). (gr. 3-7). 2000. 15.95 (*0-8234-1564-3*) Holiday.

Birdseye, Tom. I'm Going to Be Famous. LC 86-45401. 144p. (J). (gr. 4-6). 1986. 15.95 (*0-8234-0630-X*) Holiday.

— Just Call Me Stupid. 192p. (J). (gr. 4-5). 1993. 15.95 (*0-8234-1045-5*) Holiday.

— Just Call Me Stupid. 192p. (J). (gr. 3-7). 1996. pap. 4.99 (*0-14-037954-1*) Viking Penguin.

— A Kids' Guide to Building Forts. LC 92-45908. (Illus.). 64p. (Orig.). (J). (gr. 3-9). 1993. pap. 10.95 (*0-943173-69-8*) Roberts Rinehart.

— A Regular Flood of Mishap. LC 93-9888. (Illus.). 32p. (J). (ps-3). 1994. lib. bdg. 16.95 (*0-8234-1070-6*) Holiday.

— A Regular Flood of Mishap. (Illus.). 32p. (J). (gr. k-3). 1994. reprint ed. pap. 6.95 (*0-8234-1338-1*) Holiday.

— Tarantula Shoes. LC 94-38424. 144p. (J). (gr. 4-7). 1995. 15.95 (*0-8234-1179-6*) Holiday.

— Tarantula Shoes. LC 94-38424. 144p. (J). (gr. 4-7). 1996. pap. 4.99 (*0-14-037955-X*, PuffinBks) Peng Put Young Read.

— Tarantula Shoes. 1996. 9.60 (*0-606-09951-4*, Pub. by Turtleback) Demco.

— Tucker. LC 89-46243. 120p. (J). (gr. 4-6). 1990. 15.95 (*0-8234-0813-2*) Holiday.

— Waiting for Baby. LC 90-29076. (Illus.). 32p. (J). (gr. k-3). 1991. lib. bdg. 14.95 (*0-8234-0892-2*) Holiday.

Birdseye, Tom & Birdseye, Debbie H. She'll Be Comin' Round the Mountain. LC 92-37641. (Illus.). 32p. (J). (gr. k-3). 1994. lib. bdg. 15.95 (*0-8234-1032-3*) Holiday.

Birdseye, Tom, jt. auth. see Birdseye, Debbie H.

Birdsong, D. Metalinguistic Performance & Interlinguistic Competence. (Language & Communication Ser.: Vol. 25). ix, 246p. 1989. 86.95 (*0-387-50351-X*) Spr-Verlag.

Birdsong, David, ed. Second Language Acquisition & the Critical Period Hypothesis. (Second Language Acquisition Research Series: Theoretical & Methodical Issues). 208p. 1998. 45.00 (*0-8058-3084-7*) L Erlbaum Assocs.

Birdsong, Mirian S., jt. auth. see Harrell, Robert W., Jr.

Birdsong, Robert E. Mission to Mankind: A Cosmic Autobiography. LC 74-18195. 1975. 6.35 (*0-917108-12-4*); pap. 3.50 (*0-917108-08-6*) Sirius Bks.

— Sensory Awareness & Psychic Manifestation LC 78-65000. ii, 114p. 1978. write for info. (*0-917108-24-8*) Sirius Bks.

***Birdwell, Dwight W. & Nolan, Keith William.** Hundred Miles of Bad Road: An Armored Cavalryman in Vietnam, 1967-1968. (Illus.). 256p. 2000. pap. 17.95 (*0-89141-712-5*) Presidio Pr.

***Birdwell, Michael E.** Celluloid Soldiers: Warner Bro.'s Campaign Against Nazism. 2001. pap. 19.50 (*0-8147-9871-3*) NYU Pr.

Birdwell, Michael E. Celluloid Soldiers: Warner Bros. Campaign Against Nazism, 1934-1941. LC 98-58058. 1999. text 35.00 (*0-8147-1338-6*) NYU Pr.

Birdwell-Pheasant, Donna & Lawrence-Zuniga, Denise, eds. House Life: Space, Place & Family in Europe. LC 99-220597. (Illus.). 224p. 1998. 55.00 (*1-85973-230-5*, Pub. by Berg Pubs); pap. 19.50 (*1-85973-235-6*, Pub. by Berg Pubs) NYU Pr.

Birdwell, Russell. Mount Horeb. LC 77-187991. (Illus.). 104p. 1972. 12.00 (*0-8315-0122-7*) Speller.

Birdwhistell, Anne D. Li Yong (1627-1705) & Epistemological Dimensions of Confucian Philosophy. LC 95-31977. 300p. 1996. 45.00 (*0-8047-2605-1*) Stanford U Pr.

— Transition to Neo-Confucianism: Shao Yung on Knowledge & Symbols of Reality. 336p. 1989. 42.50 (*0-8047-1550-5*) Stanford U Pr.

Birdwhistell, Ira V. A Heart for Missions: A History of First Baptist Church, Murray, Kentucky, 1846-1996. LC 96-70297. 256p. 1996. 24.95 (*1-57736-015-X*) Providence Hse.

Birdwhistell, Ray L. Kinesics & Context: Essays on Body Motion Communication. LC 77-122379. (Conduct & Communication Ser.). 352p. 1970. pap. 20.95 (*0-8122-1012-3*) U of Pa Pr.

— Kinesics & Context: Essays on Body Motion Communication. LC 77-122379. (University of Pennsylvania Publications in Conduct & Communication). 352p. reprint ed. pap. 109.20 (*0-608-07407-1*, 206763400009) Bks Demand.

Birdwhistell, Terry L., jt. ed. see Allen, Susan E.

Birdwood, G. Understanding Osteoporosis & It's Treatment. (Illus.). 192p. 1995. 55.00 (*1-85070-409-0*) Prthnon Pub.

Birdwood, G. T. Practical Bazar Medicines with over 200 Useful Prescriptions. 220p. 1986. reprint ed. 15.00 (*0-8364-1768-2*, Pub. by Manohar) S Asia.

Birdwood, L., ed. see Lorimer, John G.

Birdwood, Vere, ed. see Pitt, Hester.

Birdzell, L. E., Jr. Ethical Problems of Inside Counsel. Vol. C2. text 82.00 (*0-8205-2393-3*) Bender.

Birdzell, L. E., Jr., jt. auth. see Rosenberg, Nathan.

Birecki, Henryk & Kwiecien, James Z., eds. Optical Data Storage 1997 Topical Meeting, Vol. 3109. LC 98-122078. 262p. 1997. 69.00 (*0-8194-2530-3*) SPIE.

Bireda, Martha R. & Link, Mike. Love Addiction: A Guide to Emotional Independence. (Illus.). 224p. 1990. pap. 14.95 (*0-934986-91-6*) New Harbinger.

Bireley, Marlene. Crossover Children: A Sourcebook for Helping Children Who Are Gifted & Learning Disabled. 2nd ed. LC 95-23133. 94p. 1995. pap. text 28.00 (*0-86586-264-8*, P5121) Coun Exc Child.

Bireley, Marlene & Genshaft, Judy L., eds. Understanding the Gifted Adolescent. (Education & Psychology of the Gifted Ser.: No. 5). 296p. (C). 1991. pap. text 22.95 (*0-8077-3072-6*) Tchrs Coll.

***Bireley, Robert.** The Refashioning of Catholicism, 1450-1700: A Reassessment of the Counter Reformation. LC 99-19230. 1999. 39.95 (*0-8132-0950-1*) Cath U Pr.

— The Refashioning of Catholicism, 1450-1700: A Reassessment of the Counter Reformation. LC 99-19230. 1999. pap. 19.95 (*0-8132-0951-X*) Cath U Pr.

Bireline, George. George Bireline. LC 94-68630. (Illus.). 20p. (Orig.). 1994. pap. 46.00 (*1-885449-01-1*) City Gallery Cntmprry Art.

Biren, James E., et al, eds. Handbook of the Psychology of Aging, 3 vols. 4th ed. 1996. pap. 112.00 (*0-12-044520-4*) Acad Pr.

***Biren, Richard L.** Don't Worry...Take Action! A Worry-Education Manual for Grades 3-5. (Illus.). 80p. (J). (gr. 3). 2000. pap. 13.95 (*1-57543-085-1*) Mar Co Prods.

Biren, Richard L. I Wonder Who: A Self Study Manual for Inv. or Group on Friendship. (Illus.). 94p. (Orig.). (J). (gr. 4-8). 1990. pap. 10.95 (*1-57543-011-8*) Mar Co Prods.

***Biren, Richard L.** I'm Telling on You: A Tattling Educational Manual for Use with Students Grade 2-5. (Illus.). 56p. (J). (gr. 2-5). 1999. pap. 13.95 (*1-57543-075-4*) Mar Co Prods.

Biren, Richard L. Managing School Conflict: Procedures, Conflict Lessons, Skills Lessons, Problem-Solving Lessons, Signed Agreements, & Mediating Conflicts. LC 95-78485. 64p. 1995. 11.95 (*1-884063-69-1*) Mar Co Prods.

— Nah Nah Nah! Teasing. LC 96-79863. (Illus.). 72p. (Orig.). (J). (gr. 3-5). 1997. pap. 13.95 (*1-57543-020-7*) Mar Co Prods.

Birenbaum, Arnold. Disability & Managed Care: Problems & Opportunities at the End of the Century. LC 99-23415. 200p. 1999. 55.00 (*0-275-96552-X*) Greenwood.

— In the Shadow of Medicine: Remaking the Division of Labor in Health Care. LC 90-80203. (Illus.). 184p. (Orig.). 1990. text 35.95 (*0-930390-28-8*) Gen Hall.

— Managed Care: Made in America. LC 97-5578. 208p. 1997. 39.95 (*0-275-95916-3*, Praeger Pubs) Greenwood.

— Putting Health Care on the National Agenda. LC 95-3861. 256p. 1995. 65.00 (*0-275-95163-4*, Praeger Pubs) Greenwood.

— Putting Health Care on the National Agenda. rev. ed. LC 95-3861. 256p. 1995. pap. 20.95 (*0-275-95164-2*, Praeger Pubs) Greenwood.

Birenbaum, Arnold & Cohen, Herbert J. Community Services for the Mentally Retarded. LC 84-15905. (Illus.). 208p. (C). 1985. 48.00 (*0-86598-151-5*) Rowman.

Birenbaum, Barbara. Amazing Bald Eaglet. LC 93-17659. (Illus.). 32p. (J). 1999. 19.95 (*0-935343-50-4*) Peartree.

— Candle Talk. LC 90-33299. (Kindl Adventure Ser.: No. 7). (Illus.). 54p. (J). (gr. 2-5). 1991. pap. 5.95 (*0-935343-15-6*); lib. bdg. 12.95 (*0-935343-10-5*) Peartree.

— The Gooblins Night. LC 85-62585. (Historical Adventure Ser.: No. 1). (Illus.). 44p. (J). (gr. 2-5). 1985. 12.95 (*0-935343-32-6*); pap. 5.95 (*0-935343-31-8*) Peartree.

— Lady Liberty's Light. LC 85-32061. (Historical Adventure Ser.: No. 3). (Illus.). 50p. (J). (gr. 3-5). 1986. 12.95 (*0-935343-12-1*); pap. 5.95 (*0-935343-11-3*) Peartree.

— The Lighthouse Christmas. LC 90-7284. (Kindl Adventure Ser.). (Illus.). 48p. (Orig.). (J). (gr. k-5). 1991. pap. 5.95 (*0-935343-25-3*) Peartree.

— The Lighthouse Christmas. LC 90-7284. (Historical Adventure Ser.: No. 8). (Illus.). 48p. (Orig.). (J). (gr. k-5). 1991. 12.95 (*0-935343-26-1*) Peartree.

— The Olympic Glow. LC 93-34122. (Historical Adventure Ser.: No. 9). (Illus.). 56p. (YA). 1994. pap. 5.95 (*0-935343-46-6*) Peartree.

— The Olympic Glow. LC 93-34122. (Historical Adventure Ser.: No. 9). (Illus.). 56p. (J). (gr. 3-6). 1994. lib. bdg. 12.95 (*0-935343-45-8*) Peartree.

***Birenbaum, Barbara.** Up till Now, Yet-- Yardage of Thought Imprinted in a Prism of Words. LC 99-22595. 1999. write for info. (*0-935343-49-0*) Peartree.

Birenbaum, David E. Business Ventures in Eastern Europe & Russia, 2 vols. 2nd ed. 1526p. 1993. ring bd. 185.00 (*0-13-291394-1*) Aspen Law.

Birenbaum, Eric, jt. ed. see Perry, William E.

Birenbaum, Halina. Hope Is the Last to Die: A Coming of Age under Nazi Terror. LC 95-49342. 240p. (YA). (gr. 13). 1996. 55.95 (*1-56324-746-1*) M E Sharpe.

— Hope Is the Last to Die: A Coming of Age under Nazi Terror. Dyrcz-Freeman, Dosia, tr. LC 95-49342. 240p. (C). (gr. 13). 1996. pap. 20.95 (*1-56324-747-X*) M E Sharpe.

Birenbaum, Harvey. The Art of Our Necessities: Form & Consciousness in Shakespeare. (American University Studies: English Language & Literature: Ser. IV, Vol. 84). XXII, 320p. (C). 1988. text 43.80 (*0-8204-0799-2*) P Lang Pubng.

— Between Blake & Nietzsche: The Reality of Culture. LC 91-58182. 184p. 1992. 32.50 (*0-8387-5222-5*) Bucknell U Pr.

— The Happy Critic: A Serious but Not Solemn Guide to Thinking & Writing about Literature. LC 96-23360. 263p. (Orig.). (C). 1996. pap. text 22.95 (*1-55934-706-6*, 706-6) Mayfield Pub.

Birenbaum, Menucha & Dochy, Filip J., eds. Alternatives in Assessment of Achievements, Learning Processes & Prior Knowledge. (Evaluation in Education & Human Services Ser.). 416p. (C). 1995. lib. bdg. 139.00 (*0-7923-9615-4*) Kluwer Academic.

Birenheide, R. Chaetetida und Tabulate Korallen des Devon. (Leitfossilien Ser.: Nr. 3). vi, 249p. 1985. 47.00 (*3-443-27003-4*, Pub. by Gebruder Borntraeger) Balogh.

— Rugose Korallen des Devon. (Leitfossilien Ser.: Nr. 2). vi, 265p. 1978. 45.00 (*3-443-27002-6*, Pub. by Gebruder Borntraeger) Balogh.

Biresaw, Girma, ed. Tribology & the Liquid-Crystalline State. LC 90-14427. (ACS Symposium Ser.: No. 441). (Illus.). 144p. 1990. text 45.00 (*0-8412-1874-9*, Pub. by Am Chemical) OUP.

Birge, Darice E., et al. Excavations at Nemea Vol. 1: Topographical & Architectural Studies, the Sacred Square, the Xenon & the Bath. LC 90-41003. (C). 1992. 85.00 (*0-520-07027-5*, Pub. by U CA Pr) Cal Prin Full Svc.

***Birge, Debra L.** The World of My Little Pony, An Unauthorized Guide for Collectors. (Illus.). 128p. 1999. pap. 24.95 (*0-7643-1013-5*) Schiffer.

Birge, E. A. Bacterial & Bacteriophage Genetics. 2nd ed. (Microbiology Ser.: Vol. 3). (Illus.). 470p. 1988. 49.95 (*0-387-96696-X*) Spr-Verlag.

Birge, Edward A. Bacterial & Bacteriophage Genetics. 3rd ed. LC 94-245. (Illus.). 440p. 1994. 58.95 (*0-387-94270-X*) Spr-Verlag.

***Birge, Edward A.** Bacterial & Bacteriophage Genetics. 4th ed. LC 99-31015. (Illus.). 544p. 1999. 69.95 (*0-387-98730-4*) Spr-Verlag.

Birge, Edward A. Modern Microbiology: Principles & Applications. 496p. (C). 1991. text. write for info. (*0-697-07628-8*, WCB McGr Hill) McGrw-H Hghr Educ.

Birge, Edward B. History of Public School Music in the United States. 330p. 1988. reprint ed. 11.00 (*0-940796-40-6*, 1020) MENC.

— History of Public School Music in the United States. (Music Book Index Ser.). 323p. 1992. reprint ed. lib. bdg. 89.00 (*0-7812-9495-9*) Rprt Serv.

Birge, John K. The Bektashi Order of Dervishes. 320p. 1996. 40.00 (*1-898942-00-5*, Pub. by Luzac Oriental) Weatherhill.

— The Bektashi Order of Dervishes. LC 77-87662. reprint ed. 45.00 (*0-404-16400-5*) AMS Pr.

Birge, John R. & Louveaux, Francois. Introduction to Stochastic Programming. LC 97-6931. 448p. 1997. 49.95 (*0-387-98217-5*) Spr-Verlag.

Birge, Robert R., ed. see Chemical Congress of North America Staff.

Birgegard, Ulla. Johan Gabriel Sparwengeld & the Lexicon Slavonicom: His Contribution to 17th Century Slavonic Lexicography. x, 160p. 1985. lib. bdg. 61.50 (*0-317-68022-6*) Coronet Bks.

Birgegard, Ulla, ed. see Sparwenfeld, Johan G.

***Birger, Zev.** No Time for Patience: My Road from Kaunas to Jerusalem; a Memoir of a Holocaust Survivor. LC 99-30229. 150p. 1999. 18.95 (*1-55704-386-8*, Pub. by Newmarket) Norton.

***Birget, J. C.** Algorithmic Problems in Groups & Semigroups. LC 99-52747. 2000. write for info. (*3-7643-4130-0*) Birkhauser.

***Birget, J.-C., et al, eds.** Algorithmic Problems in Groups & Semigroups. LC QA174.2.A44 2000. (Trends in Mathematics Ser.). (Illus.). 352p. 1999. 69.95 (*0-8176-4130-0*, Pub. by Birkhauser) Spr-Verlag.

Birggs, John. Fractals: The Patterns of Chaos. LC 92-16886. 1992. 20.00 (*0-671-74218-3*, Touchstone) S&S Trade Pap.

Birglen, J. H. Van, see Van Birglen, J. H., ed.

***Birgus, Vladimir.** Czech Photographic Avant-Garde 1918-1948. (Illus.). 2000. 65.00 (*80-86217-09-4*) Kant.

B

Birgus, Vladimir. Frantisek Drtikol: Modernist Nudes. Koch, Robert & Takahashi, Ada, eds. LC 97-72933. (Illus.). 88p. (Orig.). 1997. pap. 45.00 (*0-929196-02-3*) R Koch Gallery.

Birgus, Vladimir, et al. Certainty & Searching in Czech Photography of the 1990s. (Illus.). 200p. 1997. 65.00 (*80-901903-5-9*) Dist Art Pubs.

***Birin, Eileen, ed.** Go Ahead Self-Publish! Fifteen Authors Share Experiences & Tips for Turning Your Book into a Reality. LC 99-90781. 154p. 2000. pap. 11.95 (*0-9655339-1-3*) Neelie Pub.

Birindelli, Ben. The 200 Year Legacy of Stephen Decatur, 1798-1998. LC 98-7647. 1998. 39.95 (*0-9653759-4-3*) Hallmark Publng.

***Biringen, Sedat, et al, eds.** Industrial & Environmental Applications of Direct & Large Eddy Simulation: Proceedings of a Workshop Held in Istanbul, Turkey, August 5-7, 1998. LC 99-39808. (Lecture Notes in Physics Ser.: Vol. 529). xvi, 301p. 1999. 74.00 (*3-540-66171-9*) Spr-Verlag.

Biringuccio, Vannoccio. Pirotechnia. 507p. 1990. pap. 14.95 (*0-486-26134-4*) Dover.

Biriotti, Sophie, ed. Gardens of the Imagination: A Literary Anthology. LC 98-42838. (Illus.). 144p. 1999. 24.95 (*0-8118-1884-5*) Chronicle Bks.

Biriotti, Sophie & Malone, Peter. The Possibility of Angels: A Literary Anthology. LC 96-53498. (Illus.). 144p. 1997. 24.95 (*0-8118-1530-7*) Chronicle Bks.

Biriouk, Leonid, ed. see Stamps, Donald C.

Birjukov, A. P., et al. Sixteen Papers on Number Theory & Algebra. LC 51-5559. (Translations Ser.: Series 2, Vol. 82). 264p. 1969. 49.00 (*0-8218-1782-5*, TRANS2/82) Am Math.

Birjukov, B. V. Two Soviet Studies on Frege. Angelelli, Ignacio, tr. from RUS. (Sovietica Ser.: No. 15). 101p. 1964. lib. bdg. 113.00 (*90-277-0072-9*) Kluwer Academic.

Birk, Andreas, et al, eds. Learning Robots: 6th European Workshop, EWLR '96, Brighton, U. K., Proceedings. LC 98-55093. (Lecture Notes in Computer Science Ser.: Vol. 1545). ix, 188p. 1999. pap. 37.00 (*3-540-65480-1*) Spr-Verlag.

Birk, Andreas, jt. ed. see Demiris, John.

Birk, Ann W., jt. ed. see Bassuk, Ellen L.

Birk, David M. & Lathrop, James K. 1997 Life Safety Code Field Guide for Health Care Facilities. (Illus.). 176p. 1998. pap. text 145.00 (*1-57839-045-1*) Opus Communs.

— 1997 Life Safety Code Workbook & Study Guide. (Illus.). 416p. 1998. pap. text 495.00 (*1-57839-046-X*) Opus Communs.

— The Statement of Conditions Manual: A Comprehensive Guide to JCAHO Compliance. LC 99-212068. (Illus.). 850p. 1998. pap. text 247.00 (*1-57839-048-6*) Opus Communs.

Birk, David M., jt. auth. see Koffel, William E.

Birk, Dorothy D. The World Came to St. Louis: A Visit to the 1904 World's Fair. LC 79-10396. (Illus.). 1979. 9.99 (*0-8272-4213-1*) Chalice Pr.

Birk, James P. Chemistry. (C). 1994. pap. text, student ed. 20.36 (*0-395-69057-9*) HM.

— Chemistry. annot. ed. (C). 1993. text, teacher ed. 90.76 (*0-395-69231-8*) HM.

— General Chemistry. (C). 1993. pap., teacher ed. 6.76 (*0-395-69052-8*); pap., teacher ed., suppl. ed. 7.96 (*0-395-68362-9*); text 89.16 (*0-395-51535-1*) HM.

— General Chemistry. (C). 1994. pap., student ed. 22.76 (*0-395-69056-0*); pap. text, student ed. 28.36 (*0-395-51536-X*); pap. text, lab manual ed. 46.36 (*0-395-51537-8*) HM.

— General Chemistry Videodisc Guide. (C). 1994. pap. text 7.96 (*0-395-69641-0*) HM.

Birk, James P., jt. auth. see Gunter, S. Kay.

***Birk, Jim.** Electronic Companion to General Chemistry. (Electronic Companion Ser.). 2000. text 34.95 (*1-58032-050-3*) Cogito Lrning.

Birk, John F. Herman Melville's Billy Budd & the Cybernetic Imagination. LC 95-723. (Studies in American Literature: Vol. 20). 1995. write for info. (*0-7734-9025-6*) E Mellen.

***Birk, John F.** Tracing the Round - The Astrological Framework of Moby-Dick. (Illus.). 348p. 2000. 29.95 (*0-7541-0994-1*, Pub. by Minerva Pr) Unity Dist.

Birk, Lance A. The Paphiopedilum Grower's Manual. (Illus.). 208p. 1984. 75.00 (*0-9612826-0-6*) Pisang Pr.

Birk, Ron. St. Murphy's Commandments. LC 97-35613. (Illus.). 104p. (Orig.). 1998. pap. 8.95 (*1-880292-57-2*) LangMarc.

— What's a Nice God Like You Doing in a Place Like This? 110p. 1991. pap. 10.00 (*0-9629331-0-4*) Golden Goat.

— You Can't Walk on Water If You Stay in the Boat: And More "Rondom Thoughts" LC 93-91678. 112p. (Orig.). 1993. pap. 10.00 (*0-9629331-1-2*) Golden Goat.

— You Might Be in a Country Church If . . . LC 98-28123. (Illus.). 104p. 1998. pap. 8.95 (*1-880292-23-8*) LangMarc.

Birkbeck, John. Longitudes. 64p. 1999. pap. 12.00 (*0-9671757-1-2*) Carmine Creek.

Birkbeck, Lyn. Do It Yourself Astrology: A User-Friendly Guide to Your Personality. (Illus.). 312p. 1997. pap. 19.95 (*1-85230-892-3*, Pub. by Element MA) Penguin Putnam.

***Birkbeck, Lyn.** Do It Yourself Life Plan Astrology: How Planetary Cycles Affect Your Whole Life. (Illus.). 2000. pap. 19.95 (*1-86204-733-2*, Pub. by Element MA) Penguin Putnam.

Birkbeck, Morris. Notes of a Journey in America & Letters from Illinois. 3rd ed. LC 71-119545. 1971. reprint ed. 45.00 (*0-678-00686-5*) Kelley.

— Notes on a Journey in America: From the Coast of Virginia to the Territory of Illinois. (American Biography Ser.). 156p. 1991. reprint ed. lib. bdg. 59.00 (*0-7812-8020-6*) Rprt Serv.

Birkbeck, Paul H. From Statism to Pluralism: Democracy, Civil Society & Global Politics. LC 98-101794. 192p. 1997. 69.95 (*1-85728-749-5*, Pub. by UCL Pr Ltd); pap. 19.95 (*1-85728-750-9*) UCL Pr Ltd.

Birkbeck, Sandra C., ed. Of Amorous Love: Elizabethan Erotic Verse. 300p. 1994. 8.50 (*0-460-87530-2*, Everyman's Classic Lib) Tuttle Pubng.

Birkby, Evelyn. Neighboring on the Air: Cooking with the KMA Radio Homemakers. rev. ed. LC 91-6304. (Bur Oak Original Ser.). (Illus.). 349p. (Orig.). 1991. pap. 16.95 (*0-87745-340-0*) U of Iowa Pr.

— Up a Country Lane Cookbook. LC 93-20659. (Bur Oak Original Ser.). (Illus.). 276p. 1993. 22.95 (*0-87745-420-5*) U of Iowa Pr.

***Birkby, Evelyn.** Up a Country Lane Cookbook. LC 93-20659. (Illus.). 276p. 2000. reprint ed. pap. 14.95 (*0-87745-743-3*) U of Iowa Pr.

Birkby, Evelyn M. Come again Cookie Book. (Illus.). 144p. (Orig.). 1987. pap. 6.00 (*0-9615083-2-9*) KMA Broadcast.

Birkby, Jeff. Touring Montana & Wyoming Hot Springs. LC 99-17813. (Illus.). 241p. 1999. pap. 14.95 (*1-56044-679-X*) Falcon Pub Inc.

Birkby, Phyllis, et al, eds. Amazon Expedition: A Lesbian-Feminist Anthology. LC 73-79902. (Illus.). 96p. (Orig.). 1973. pap. 4.95 (*0-87810-026-1*) Times Change.

Birkby, Robert C. KMA Radio: The First 60 Years. (Illus.). 248p. (Orig.). (C). 1985. pap. 5.00 (*0-9615083-0-2*) KMA Broadcast.

— Learn How to Canoe in One Day: Quickest Way to Start Paddling, Turning, Portaging, & Maintaining. LC 89-34189. (Illus.). 112p. (Orig.). 1990. pap. 10.95 (*0-8117-2249-X*) Stackpole.

Birkby, Robert C. & Student Conservation Association Staff. Lightly on the Land: The SCA Trail Building & Maintenance Manual. LC 96-17213. (Illus.). 272p. 1996. pap. 19.95 (*0-89886-491-7*) Mountaineers.

Birkby, Robert C., jt. auth. see Boy Scouts of America.

***Birke, Lynda.** Feminism & the Biological Body. LC 99-55850. 224p. 2000. text 49.00 (*0-8135-2822-4*); pap. text 19.00 (*0-8135-2823-2*) Rutgers U Pr.

Birke, Lynda. Feminism, Animals & Science: The Naming of the Shrew. LC 94-19790. 160p. 1994. 114.95 (*0-335-19198-3*); pap. 31.95 (*0-335-19197-5*) OpUniv Pr.

— Women, Feminism & Biology. 232p. 1986. text 27.50 (*0-416-01221-3*, 9810); pap. text 12.95 (*0-416-01231-0*, 9828) Routledge.

Birke, Lynda & Hubbard, Ruth, eds. Reinventing Biology: Respect for Life & the Creation of Knowledge. LC 95-1443. (Race, Gender, & Science Ser.). 312p. 1995. pap. 15.95 (*0-253-20981-1*) Ind U Pr.

Birke, Lynda, jt. auth. see Barr, Jean.

Birke, Veronika. Masterworks from the Albertina: Italian Drawings, 1350-1800. 1992. pap. 45.00 (*0-89835-276-2*) Abaris Bks.

Birke, Veronika, ed. The Illustrated Bartsch Vol. 40: Italian Masters of the Sixteenth Century. 1983. lib. bdg. 149.00 (*0-89835-040-9*) Abaris Bks.

— The Illustrated Bartsch Vol. 40-1, Commentary: Italian Masters of the Sixteenth & Seventeenth Centuries. (Illus.). 1983. lib. bdg. 149.00 (*0-89835-139-1*) Abaris Bks.

Birkedahl, Nonie. The Habit Control Workbook. 224p. (Orig.). 1993. pap. 12.95 (*0-934986-98-3*) New Harbinger.

Birkedal-Hansen, Hennig, et al, eds. Matrix Metalloproteinases & Inhibitors: Proceedings of the Matrix Metalloproteinase Conference, Held Sept. 11-15, 1989, Sandestin Beach, Florida. (Illus.). 650p. 1992. 275.00 (*1-56081-309-1*, Pub. by Gustav Fischer) Balogh.

***Birkel, Dee A.** Hatha Yoga: Developing the Body, Mind & Inner Self. 3rd ed. 134p. 2000. pap. text 34.95 (*1-57879-013-1*) E Bowers Pub.

Birkel, J. Damian & Miller, Stacey J. Career Bounce-Back! The Professionals in Transition Guide to Recovery & Reemployment. LC 97-23243. 224p. 1997. pap. 14.95 (*0-8144-7954-5*) AMACOM.

Birkel, Michael L. & Newman, John W., eds. The Lamb's War: Quaker Essays to Honor Hugh Barbour. 305p. (Orig.). 1992. pap. 19.95 (*1-879117-00-2*) Earlham Pr.

Birkel, Michael L., jt. ed. see Newman, John W.

Birkeland, Brian, jt. ed. see Campbell, Dennis.

Birkeland, Charles, ed. Acanthaster Planci: Major Management Problem of Coral Reefs. 272p. 1990. lib. bdg. 229.00 (*0-8493-6599-6*, QL384) CRC Pr.

Birkeland, John H., jt. auth. see Postlewaite, Philip F.

Birkeland, Jorgen, jt. ed. see Bowman, Craig T.

Birkeland, Peter. Soils & Geomorphology. 3rd ed. LC 98-3589. (Illus.). 448p. (C). 1999. pap. text 45.00 (*0-19-507886-1*) OUP.

Birkeland, Peter W. & Larson, Edwin E. Putnam's Geology. 5th rev. ed. (Illus.). 656p. (C). 1989. pap. text 49.95 (*0-19-505517-9*) OUP.

Birkeland, Peter W., et al. Soils As a Tool for Applied Quaternary Geology. (Miscellaneous Publication Ser.: Vol. 91-3). (Illus.). 63p. 1991. pap. 6.50 (*1-55791-312-9*, MP-91-3) Utah Geological Survey.

Birkelbach, Alan. Bone Song. LC 96-84211. (Illus.). 52p. (Orig.). 1996. pap. 7.50 (*1-878149-36-9*) Counterpoint Pub.

Birkelbach, Mary R. On the Bright Winter Hills. LC 90-86059. (Illus.). 53p. (Orig.). 1991. pap. 10.95 (*0-9628619-0-1*) Bun Pubns.

Birken, Lawrence. Consuming Desire: Sexual Science & the Emergence of a Culture of Abundance, 1871-1914. LC 88-47719. 168p. 1988. 29.95 (*0-8014-2058-X*) Cornell U Pr.

— Consuming Desire: Sexual Science & the Emergence of a Culture of Abundance, 1871-1914. LC 88-47719. 181p. reprint ed. pap. 56.20 (*0-608-20874-4*, 207197300003) Bks Demand.

— Cv:und Western Civiliz: A Chaos Approach. 2nd ed. (C). 1996. pap. text 31.00 (*0-15-505396-5*) Harcourt Coll Pubs.

— Hitler as Philosopher: Remnants of the Enlightenment in National Socialism. LC 94-37200. 128p. 1995. 47.95 (*0-275-95065-4*, Praeger Pubs) Greenwood.

Birken-Silverman, Gabriele. Sprachkontakt Italienisch - Albanisch In Kalabrien Teil 1-3: Die Italienischen Lehnworter in Den Kalabroalbanischen Mundarten des Cratitals: Handwerks-, Land- und Hauswirtschaftsterminologie, 2 vols. (Illus.). XXX, 765p. 1997. 95.95 (*3-631-31540-6*) P Lang Pubng.

Birkenhager, W. H., jt. ed. see Hansson, L.

Birkenhager, Willem H., ed. Practical Management of Hypertension. 2nd ed. LC 96-115. (Developments in Cardiovascular Medicine Ser.: Vol. 184). 224p. 1996. text 100.50 (*0-7923-3952-5*) Kluwer Academic.

Birkenhager, William H., ed. Practical Management of Hypertension. (Developments in Cardiovascular Medicine Ser.). (C). 1991. lib. bdg. 124.50 (*0-7923-0918-9*) Kluwer Academic.

Birkenhake, C., jt. auth. see Lange, H.

Birkenhake, Christina & Lange, H. Complex Tori LC 99-32326. (Progress In Mathematics Ser.). 1999. write for info. (*3-7643-4103-3*) Birkhauser.

Birkenhake, Christina, jt. auth. see Lange, Herbert.

Birkenhead, Frederick E. America Revisited. LC 68-16911. (Essay Index Reprint Ser.). 1977. reprint ed. 19.95 (*0-8369-0212-2*) Ayer.

— Contemporary Personalities. LC 69-17562. (Essay Index Reprint Ser.). 1977. 21.95 (*0-8369-0061-8*) Ayer.

— Contemporary Personalities. LC 69-17562. (Essay Index Reprint Ser.). 326p. reprint ed. lib. bdg. 16.00 (*0-8290-0480-7*) Irvington.

— Last Essays. LC 78-104996. (Essay Index Reprint Ser.). 1977. 28.95 (*0-8369-1546-1*) Ayer.

— Law, Life & Letters, 2 Vols. LC 71-10997. (Essay Index Reprint Ser.). 1977. reprint ed. 42.95 (*0-8369-1450-3*) Ayer.

— Points of View, 2 Vols. LC 77-111815. (Essay Index Reprint Ser.). 1977. 40.95 (*0-8369-1594-1*) Ayer.

— Turning Points in History. LC 78-86730. (Essay Index Reprint Ser.). 1977. 26.95 (*0-8369-1246-2*) Ayer.

Birkenhead, Frederick W. Rudyard Kipling. LC 79-303455. xi, 423 p. 1978. write for info. (*0-297-77535-9*) Weidenfeld & Nicolson.

Birkenhead, R., jt. ed. see John, R.

Birkenmaier, Julie, jt. auth. see Berg-Weger, Marla.

Birkens. Apprenons par la Musique. (FRE.). (C). 1981. pap. write for info. (*0-03-929569-9*) Harcourt Coll Pubs.

Birkenstock, James M. The ISO 9000 Quality System Checklist. LC 96-20986. 286p. 1997. text 150.00 (*0-7863-1089-8*, Irwn Prfssnl) McGraw-Hill Prof.

Birkerts, Gunnar. Gunnar Birkerts Buildings, Projects & Thoughts, 1960 to 1985. LC 85-50641. (Illus.). 96p. (Orig.). 1985. pap. 23.50 (*0-9614792-0-5*) U Mich Arch.

— Process & Expression in Architectural Form. LC 93-40030. (Bruce Alonzo Goff Series in Creative Architecture: Vol. 1). (Illus.). 192p. 1994. 39.95 (*0-8061-2642-6*); pap. 17.95 (*0-8061-2645-0*) U of Okla Pr.

Birkerts, Sven. Readings. LC 98-84453. 274p. 1999. pap. 16.00 (*1-55597-283-7*) Graywolf.

Birkerts, Sven P. The Gutenberg Elegies: The Fate of Reading in an Electronic Age. 256p. 1995. pap. 12.50 (*0-449-91009-1*) Fawcett.

Birkerts, Sven P. Literature: The Evolving Canon. 2nd ed. LC 95-19938. 1698p. 1995. 54.00 (*0-205-17515-5*) Allyn.

Birkerts, Sven P. Literature: The Evolving Canon: Examination Copy. 2nd ed. 1728p. (C). 1995. text. write for info. (*0-205-19390-0*, H9390-9) Allyn.

Birkerts, Sven P., ed. Tolstoy's Dictaphone: Technology & the Muse. LC 96-75790. (Forum Ser.: Vol. 1). 256p. (Orig.). 1996. pap. 16.00 (*1-55597-248-9*) Graywolf.

Birkerts, Sven P., jt. auth. see Hall, Donald.

Birkes, David & Dodge, Yadolah. Alternative Methods of Regression. LC 92-31165. (Probability & Mathematical Statistics Ser.). 240p. 1993. 99.95 (*0-471-56881-3*) Wiley.

Birket, James. Some Cursory Remarks. LC 77-150169. (Select Bibliographies Reprint Ser.). 1977. 15.95 (*0-8369-5682-6*) Ayer.

Birket, Sallie C., jt. auth. see Josephson-Millman, Linda.

Birket-Smith, Kaj. Anthropological Observations on the Central Eskimos. Calvert, W. E., tr. LC 76-22525. (Thule Expedition, 1921-24 Ser.: Vol. 3, No. 2). (Illus.). reprint ed. 42.50 (*0-404-58312-1*) AMS Pr.

— The Caribou Eskimos. LC 76-21702. (Thule Expedition Ser.: Vol. 5). reprint ed. 137.50 (*0-404-58316-4*) AMS Pr.

— Contributions to Chipewyan Ethnology. LC 76-21701. (Thule Expedition Ser.: Vol. 6, No. 3). reprint ed. 38.50 (*0-404-58319-9*) AMS Pr.

— Ethnographical Collections from the Northwest Passage. Calvert, W. E., tr. LC 76-21697. (Thule Expedition Ser.: Vol. 6 No. 2). (Illus.). reprint ed. 89.50 (*0-404-58318-0*) AMS Pr.

Birket-Smith, Kaj. Ethnography of the Egedesminde District, with Aspects of the General Culture of West Greenland. LC 74-5827. (Illus.). reprint ed. 73.00 (*0-404-11630-2*) AMS Pr.

Birket-Smith, Kaj. Five Hundred Eskimo Words. LC 76-21770. (Thule Expedition, 5th, 1921-1924 Ser.: Vol. 3, No. 3). reprint ed. 32.50 (*0-404-58313-X*) AMS Pr.

— Geographical Notes on the Barren Grounds. LC 76-21642. (Thule Expedition, 5th, 1921-1924 Ser.: Vol. 1, No. 4). (Illus.). reprint ed. 49.50 (*0-404-58304-0*) AMS Pr.

Birket-Smith, Kaj & De Laguna, Frederica. The Eyak Indians of the Copper River Delta, Alaska. LC 74-7932. (Illus.). reprint ed. 42.50 (*0-404-11817-8*) AMS Pr.

Birkets, Sven. An Artificial Wilderness: Essays on Twentieth-Century Literature. LC 89-45387. 1989. pap. 14.95 (*0-87923-807-0*) Godine.

***Birkett.** Samuel Beckett. LC 99-12251. 304p. 1999. pap. 30.73 (*0-582-29807-5*) Addison-Wesley.

Birkett, Alaric. Vikings. LC 85-72965. 72p. (J). (gr. 5-8). 1985. pap. 12.95 (*0-7175-1321-1*) Dufour.

***Birkett, Bill.** Classic Treks: The 30 Most Spectacular Hikes in the World. (Illus.). 144p. 2000. 40.00 (*0-8212-2655-X*, Pub. by Bulfinch Pr) Little.

Birkett, D. Peter. Psychiatry in the Nursing Home: Assessment, Evaluation, & Intervention. 192p. 1991. pap. text 19.95 (*1-56024-069-5*) Haworth Pr.

— Psychiatry in the Nursing Home: Assessment, Evaluation, & Intervention. 192p. 1991. text 49.95 (*1-56024-068-7*) Haworth Pr.

Birkett, D. Peter, ed. The Psychiatry of Stroke. LC 95-17692. 416p. 1996. 56.00 (*0-88048-540-X*, 8540) Am Psychiatric.

Birkett, Dea. Jella: A Woman of the Sea. large type ed. (Non-Fiction Ser.). 432p. 1993. 27.99 (*0-7089-2964-8*) Ulverscroft.

— Serpent in Paradise. 320p. 1998. pap. 12.95 (*0-385-48871-8*) Doubleday.

Birkett, Donald J. Pharmacokinetics Made Easy. 119p. 1998. pap. write for info. (*0-07-470609-8*) McGraw-Hill HPD.

***Birkett, Frederick A.** Parent's Complete Guide to Charter Schools: Is it Right for My Child? (Illus.). 304p. 2000. pap. 16.00 (*0-7615-2516-5*) Prima Pub.

Birkett, G., jt. ed. see Struve, Gleb.

Birkett, G. A., ed. see Boronina, E.

Birkett, G. A., ed. see Fedin, Konstantin.

Birkett, G. A., ed. see Gorky, Maxim.

Birkett, Jennifer & Harvey, Elizabeth D., eds. Determined Women: Studies in the Construction of the Female Subject, 1900-1990. 224p. (C). 1991. text 69.00 (*0-389-20950-3*) B&N Imports.

Birkett, Jennifer & Kearns, James. A Guide to French Literature: Early Modern to Postmodernism. LC 97-1766. 373p. 1997. pap. 18.95 (*0-312-17476-4*) St Martin.

Birkett, John. The Last Private Eye. 192p. 1988. pap. 2.95 (*0-380-75488-6*, Avon Bks) Morrow Avon.

— The Queen's Mare. 240p. 1990. pap. 3.50 (*0-380-75683-8*, Avon Bks) Morrow Avon.

Birkett, Joseph. Birkett Diary: Voyage & Visit to America, 1784-1785. Tazewell, Calvert W., ed. LC 90-84741. 86p. (Orig.). 1990. pap. 12.00 (*1-878515-53-5*) W S Dawson.

Birkett, Julian. Word Power: A Guide to Creative Writing. 3rd ed. 1998. pap. 19.95 (*0-7136-4850-3*, Pub. by A & C Blk) Midpt Trade.

Birkett, K. R., jt. auth. see Jensen, Phillip D.

Birkett, Ken & Worman, Dianah, eds. Getting on with Disabilities: An Employer's Guide. 300p. (C). 1988. 72.00 (*0-85292-407-0*) St Mut.

Birkett, Ken, jt. ed. see Palmer, Steve.

Birkett, Mary E. Lamartine & the Poetics of Landscape. LC 82-82427. (French Forum Monographs: No. 38). 105p. (Orig.). 1982. pap. 10.95 (*0-917058-37-2*) French Forum.

Birkett, N., tr. see Babitsky, V. I.

Birkett, Norman. Six Great Advocates. 109p. 1977. 11.95 (*0-8369-8132-4*) Ayer.

***Birkett, Stephen.** Ulster Alien. 240p. 1999. pap. 14.95 (*1-902852-01-X*, Pub. by Prowler GMP) LPC InBook.

Birkey, Del. The House Church: A Model for Renewing the Church. LC 87-31055. 182p. (Orig.). 1988. pap. 18.99 (*0-8361-3467-2*) Herald Pr.

Birkey, Verna. Women Connecting with Women. LC 97-62495. 272p. 1998. pap. 14.99 (*1-57921-087-2*, Pub. by WinePress Pub) BookWorld.

— Women Connecting with Women Study Guide. LC 98-60297. 80p. 1998. pap. 5.99 (*1-57921-106-2*, Pub. by WinePress Pub) BookWorld.

— You Are Very Special: A Biblical Guide to Self-Worth. LC 77-23805. 168p. (gr. 10). 1987. pap. 7.99 (*0-8007-5032-2*) Revell.

Birkhaeuser, H., et al, eds. Advances in Tuberculosis Research, Vol. 18. 1972. 85.25 (*3-8055-1301-1*) S Karger.

Birkhaeuser, H. & Fox, W., eds. Advances in Tuberculosis Research, Vol. 20. (Illus.). 1980. 61.00 (*3-8055-2954-6*) S Karger.

Birkhahu-Rommelfanger, Daniel, ed. see Erickson, Karen L.

***Birkhan, Helmut.** Celts: Images of Their Culture. (Illus.). 454p. 2000. 125.00 (*3-7001-2814-2*) U of Wash Pr.

Birkhauser. Dominique Perrault - Des Natures: Beyond Architecture. (Illus.). 80p. 1996. pap. 35.00 (*3-7643-5434-8*, Pub. by Birkhauser) Princeton Arch.

— Place des Nations, Geneve: International Competition. (Illus.). 124p. 1996. pap. 34.50 (*3-7643-5358-9*, Pub. by Birkhauser) Princeton Arch.

Birkhauser, Kaspar. Light from the Darkness: Paintings by Peter Birkhauser. Wertenschlag, Eva, ed. (ENG & GER., Illus.). 80p. 1991. 34.50 (*0-8176-1190-8*) Birkhauser.

Birkhauser, M., jt. ed. see Neves-e-Castro, M.

Birkhauser-Oeri, Sibylle. The Mother. 176p. 1995. pap. 18.00 (*0-919123-33-3*, Pub. by Inner City Bks) BookWorld.

Birkhauser Staff. Architecture for the Retail Trade. (GER., Illus.). 336p. 1996. 89.00 (*3-7643-5268-X*, Pub. by Birkhauser) Princeton Arch.

— Berlinmodel Industriekultur: Redesigning the Urban

An Asterisk (*) at the beginning of an entry indicates that the title is appearing for the first time.

Factory. Orig. Title: Berlinmodel Industriekultur. (ENG & GER.). 176p. 1996. pap. 34.50 (*3-7643-2340-X*, Pub. by Birkhauser) Princeton Arch.
— Calatrava - Berlin: Five Projects. (Illus.). 212p. 1996. 65.00 (*3-7643-2985-8*, Pub. by Birkhauser) Princeton Arch.
— Capital Berlin: Central District Soreeinsel International Competition for Urban Design Ideas, 1. (GER., Illus.). 212p. 1996. pap. 65.00 (*3-7643-5040-7*, Pub. by Birkhauser) Princeton Arch.
— Capital Berlin: Parliament District at the Spreebogen. (GER., Illus.). 256p. 1996. pap. 65.00 (*3-7643-2893-2*, Pub. by Birkhauser) Princeton Arch.
— City Invasions: 14 International Projects for Vienna. 1996. 80.00 (*3-7643-5110-1*, Pub. by Birkhauser) Princeton Arch.
***Birkhauser Staff.** Extra-Ordinary. IN-EX Project Staff, ed. (Illus.). 304p. 1999. pap. 29.95 (*3-7643-6128-X*) Birkhauser.
— Frank O. Gehry & Associates: Architecture Postcards. (Illus.). 18p. 2000. pap. 9.95 (*3-7643-6240-5*) Birkhauser.
— Herzog & De Meuron. (Illus.). 18p. 2000. pap. 9.95 (*3-7643-6242-1*) Birkhauser.
— Jean Nouvel: Architecture Postcards. (Illus.). 18p. 2000. pap. 9.95 (*3-7643-6241-3*) Birkhauser.
Birkhauser Staff. Santiago Calatrava - Dynamic Equilibrium: Recent Projects. (Illus.). 80p. 1991. pap. 35.00 (*3-7643-5525-5*, Pub. by Birkhauser) Princeton Arch.
Birkhauser Staff, ed. Le Corbusier: Complete Works. 1996. boxed set 500.00 (*3-7643-5515-8*) Birkhauser.
Birkhead, Alice. Heroes of Modern Europe. LC 67-22073. (Essay Index Reprint Ser.). 1977. 18.95 (*0-8369-0213-0*) Ayer.
— Heroes of Modern Europe. (Essay Index Reprint Ser.). (Illus.). 239p. reprint ed. text 17.00 (*0-8290-0525-0*) Irvington.
Birkhead, Edith. Christina Rossetti & Her Poetry. LC 75-148751. reprint ed. 16.00 (*0-404-52503-2*) AMS Pr.
Birkhead, Guthrie S., ed. Administrative Problems in Pakistan. LC 66-25174. 239p. reprint ed. pap. 74.10 (*0-8357-5110-4*, 202739800055) Bks Demand.
Birkhead, Mike & Birkhead, Tim R. The Survival Factor. 208p. (C). 1990. 60.00 (*1-85283-245-2*, Pub. by Boxtree) St Mut.
Birkhead, Pat. We've a Story to Tell: A History of First Baptist Church, Orlando, Florida, 1871-1996. LC 96-70690. 320p. 1996. 26.95 (*1-57736-020-6*) Providence Hse.
Birkhead, Tim R. Great Auk Islands: A Field Biologist in the Arctic. (Poyser Popular Bird Bks.). (Illus.). 275p. 1993. text 39.00 (*0-85661-077-1*) Acad Pr.
— The Magpies: The Ecology & Behavior of Black-Billed & Yellow-Billed Magpies. (Poyser Popular Bird Bks.). (Illus.). 270p. 1991. text 39.00 (*0-85661-067-4*, 784667) Acad Pr.
***Birkhead, Tim R.** Promiscuity: An Evolutionary History of Sperm Competition & Sexual Conflict. (Illus.). 280p. 2000. 24.95 (*0-674-00445-0*) HUP.
Birkhead, Tim R. & Moller, A. P. Sperm Competition in Birds: Evolutionary Causes & Consequences. (Illus.). 282p. 1991. text 99.00 (*0-12-100540-2*); pap. text 53.00 (*0-12-100541-0*) Acad Pr.
Birkhead, Tim R. & Moller, Anders P., eds. Sperm Competition & Sexual Selection. (Illus.). 650p. (C). 1998. pap. text 59.95 (*0-12-100543-7*) Morgan Kaufmann.
Birkhead, Tim R., jt. auth. see Birkhead, Mike.
Birkhead, Tim R., jt. ed. see Nettleship, David N.
Birkhoff, Garrett & Hall, Marshall, Jr., eds. Computers in Algebra & Number Theory. LC 76-167685. (SIAM-AMS Proceedings Ser.: No. 4). (Illus.). 208p. 1971. pap. 64.50 (*0-608-05173-X*, 205259400001) Bks Demand.
Birkhoff, Garrett D. Dynamical Systems. LC 28-28411. (Colloquium Publications: Vol. 9). 305p. 1927. pap. 29.00 (*0-8218-1009-X*, COLL/9) Am Math.
— Garrett Birkhoff: Collected Papers. (Contemporary Mathematicians Ser.). 1987. 149.50 (*0-8176-3114-3*) Birkhauser.
— Hydrodynamics: A Study in Logic, Fact, & Similitude. LC 77-18143. (Illus.). 184p. 1978. reprint ed. lib. bdg. 35.00 (*0-313-20118-8*, BIHY, Greenwood Pr) Greenwood.
— Lattice Theory. LC 66-23707. (Colloquium Publications: Vol. 25). 418p. 1940. reprint ed. pap. 34.00 (*0-8218-1025-1*, COLL/25) Am Math.
— The Numerical Solution of Elliptic Equations. (CBMS-NSF Regional Conference Series in Applied Mathematics: No. 1). xi, 82p. 1971. pap. text 21.00 (*0-89871-001-4*) Soc Indus-Appl Math.
Birkhoff, Garrett D., et al, eds. Hydrodynamic Instability: Proceedings. LC 50-1183. (Proceedings of the Symposium in Applied Mathematics Ser.: Vol. 13). 319p. 1969. reprint ed. pap. 36.00 (*0-8218-1313-7*, PSAPM/13) Am Math.
Birkhoff, Garrett D. & Lynch, Robert E. Numerical Solution of Elliptic Problems. LC 84-51823. (Studies in Applied Mathematics: No. 6). (Illus.). ix, 319p. 1984. text 52.00 (*0-89871-197-5*) Soc Indus-Appl Math.
Birkhoff, Garrett D. & Mac Lane, Saunders. A Survey of Modern Algebra. 5th rev. ed. LC 97-372. (Illus.). 512p. (C). 1996. text 59.00 (*1-56881-068-7*) AK Peters.
Birkhoff, Garrett D. & Merzbach, Uta C., eds. A Source Book in Classical Analysis. LC 72-85144. (Source Books in the History of the Sciences). 484p. reprint ed. pap. 150.10 (*0-7837-4448-X*, 205797800012) Bks Demand.
Birkhoff, Garrett D. & Rota, Gian-Carlo. Ordinary Differential Equations. 4th ed. LC 88-14231. 416p. 1989. text 117.95 (*0-471-86003-4*) Wiley.
Birkhoff, Garrett D. & Varga, R. S., eds. Numerical Solution of Field Problems in Continuum Physics: Proceedings of the SIAM-AMS Symposia, North Carolina, April, 1968. LC 75-92659. (SIAM-AMS Proceedings Ser.: Vol. 2). 280p. 1970. text 38.00 (*0-8218-1321-8*, SIAMS/2) Am Math.
Birkhoff, Garrett D. & Wigner, E. P., eds. Nuclear Reactor Theory: Proceedings. LC 50-1183. (Proceedings of Symposia in Applied Mathematics Ser.: Vol.11). 339p. 1961. reprint ed. pap. 51.00 (*0-8218-1311-0*, PSAPM/11) Am Math.
Birkhoff, Garrett D. & Wigner, Eugene P., eds. Nuclear Reactor Theory: Proceedings of the Eleventh Symposium in Applied Mathematics of the American Mathematical Society, Held at the Hotel New Yorker, April 23-25, 1959. fac. ed. LC 50-1183. (Proceedings of Symposia in Applied Mathematics Ser.: No. 11). 345p. 1961. reprint ed. pap. 107.00 (*0-608-01007-3*, 206186500012) Bks Demand.
Birkhoff, Garrett D., jt. auth. see Mac Lane, Saunders.
Birkhoff, Garrett D., ed. see Applied Mathematics Symposium Staff.
Birkhoff, Garrett D., ed. see Society for Industrial & Applied Mathematics Staff & American Mathematical Society Staff.
***Birkhoff, George D. & Beatley, Ralph.** Basic Geometry. 3rd ed. LC 99-50340. 1999. write for info. (*0-8218-2101-6*) Am Math.
Birkhoff, George D. & Beatley, Ralph. Basic Geometry. 3rd ed. (Illus.). 294p. 1992. text 19.95 (*0-8284-0120-9*, 120) Chelsea Pub.
— Basic Geometry: Answer Book. (AMS/Chelsea Ser.). 76p. 1997. pap. 8.00 (*0-8284-0162-4*) Am Math.
— Basic Geometry: Manual for Teachers. LC 49-2197. (AMA/Chelsea Ser.). 160p. 1997. text 8.00 (*0-8284-0034-2*) Am Math.
Birkholz, Heinz. Flugzeug Archiv. Chapman, A. R., tr. (Foto-Archiv Ser.: Vol. 1). (GER., Illus.). 96p. 1999. pap. 15.95 (*1-57427-095-8*) Howell Pr VA.
— Flugzeug Archiv. Chapman, A. R., tr. (Foto-Archiv Ser.: Vol. 2). (GER., Illus.). 96p. 1999. pap. 15.95 (*1-57427-096-6*) Howell Pr VA.
— Flugzeug Archiv. Chapman, A. R., tr. (Foto-Archiv Ser.: Vol. 3). (GER., Illus.). 96p. 1999. pap. 15.95 (*1-57427-097-4*) Howell Pr VA.
Birkin, jt. see Price.
***Birkin, Malcolm A.** Building the Integrated Company. LC 99-49654. 232p. 2000. 84.95 (*0-566-07950-X*, Pub. by Ashgate Pub) Ashgate Pub Co.
Birkin, Mark, et al. Intelligent GIS: Location Decisions & Strategic Planning. 292p. 1996. pap. text 44.95 (*0-470-23614-0*) Halsted Pr.
Birkin, Stanley J., ed. Business Communications: An Annotated Bibliography. LC 79-8296. 686p. 1980. lib. bdg. 65.00 (*0-313-20923-5*, WBW/, Greenwood Pr) Greenwood.
Birkin, Stanley J., jt. compiled by see Walsh, Ruth M.
Birkinshaw, Elsye. Think Slim - Be Slim: A New 21-Day Plan for "Mental Dieting" That Can Give You Perfect Weight Control. rev. ed. LC 80-7115. 144p. (Orig.). 1981. pap. 8.95 (*0-912800-91-7*) Woodbridge Pr.
— Think Young - Be Young! You Can Look & Feel Years Younger. rev. ed. LC 86-28240. Orig. Title: Turn Off Your Age. 160p. (Orig.). 1988. pap. 7.95 (*0-88007-157-5*) Woodbridge Pr.
***Birkinshaw, Julian & Hagstrom, Peter, eds.** The Flexible Firm: Capability Management in Network Organizations. (Illus.). 250p. 2000. text 65.00 (*0-19-829651-7*) OUP.
***Birkinshaw, Marie.** Race for Survival. (Dorling Kindersley Readers). 48p. (J). (gr. 2-4). 2000. 12.95 (*0-7894-6096-3*, D K Ink) DK Pub Inc.
— Race for Survival. LC 99-55202. (Dorling Kindersley Readers). (Illus.). 48p. (J). (gr. 2-4). 2000. pap. text 3.95 (*0-7894-5458-0*, D K Ink) DK Pub Inc.
— Trouble at the Bridge. (Dorling Kindersley Readers). 32p. (J). (ps-1). 2000. 12.95 (*0-7894-6093-9*, D K Ink) DK Pub Inc.
— Trouble at the Bridge. LC 99-53094. (Dorling Kindersley Readers). (Illus.). 32p. (J). (ps-1). 2000. pap. text 3.95 (*0-7894-5457-2*, D K Ink) DK Pub Inc.
Birkinshaw, Patrick. Birkinshaw: Freedom of Information - the Law, the Practice & the Ideal. 2nd ed. LC 97-102515. 280p. 1996. 46.95 (*0-406-04972-6*, MICHIE) LEXIS Pub.
— Freedom of Information: The Law, the Practice & the Ideal. (Law in Context Ser.). xxii, 291p. 1988. 37.50 (*0-297-79344-6*) W S Hein.
— Government & Information - The Law Relating to Access, Disclosure & Regulation. 1990. pap. 67.00 (*0-406-10411-5*, U.K., MICHIE) LEXIS Pub.
— Grievances, Remedies & the State. 2nd ed. LC 95-139182. (Modern Legal Studies). 1994. pap. 31.00 (*0-421-48510-8*, Pub. by Sweet & Maxwll) Gaunt.
Birkinshaw, Patrick, jt. auth. see Lewis, Norman.
Birkitt, James, ed. see Howerton, Liz.
Birkitt, Malcolm. Harley-Davidson Electraglide. (Color Library). (Illus.). 128p. 1994. pap. 15.95 (*1-85532-402-4*, Pub. by Ospry) Motorbooks Intl.
— Honda Gold Wing & Valkyrie. (Illus.). 144p. 1999. 17.95 (*1-85532-879-8*, 128408AE) Motorbooks Intl.
— Honda Goldwing. (Osprey Colour Library). (Illus.). 128p. 1995. pap. 15.95 (*1-85532-443-1*, Pub. by Ospry) Motorbooks Intl.
Birkj, Edward L., et al. Florida Evidence. Stein, Linda S., ed. LC 96-77661. (American Inns of Court Ser.). 450p. 1996. text. write for info. (*0-7620-0095-3*) West Group.
Birkland, Barbara J. & Kernes, Steven T. Military Police Guide to the Federal Criminal Code, 1999-2000. 247p. 1996. pap. 15.20 (*0-937935-43-3*) Justice Syst Pr.
— Peace Officer's Guide to the Georgia Criminal Code, 1999-2000. 164p. 1999. 8.95 (*0-937935-44-1*) Justice Syst Pr.
Birkland, Barbara J. & Kernes, Steven T. Peace Officer's Guide to the Hawaii Criminal Code. 100p. 1994. pap. 8.95 (*0-937935-29-8*) Justice Syst Pr.
— Peace Officer's Guide to the Idaho Criminal Code, 1998-1999. 164p. 1998. pap. 9.95 (*0-937935-35-2*) Justice Syst Pr.
***Birkland, Barbara J. & Kernes, Steven T.** Peace Officer's Guide to the Washington Criminal Code, 2000-2001. 178p. 2000. pap. 9.95 (*0-937935-47-6*) Justice Syst Pr.
— Peace Officer's Guide to the Washington Traffic Code, 2000-2001. 143p. 2000. reprint ed. pap. 9.95 (*0-937935-48-4*) Justice Syst Pr.
Birkland, Barbara J., et al. Guide to Police Supervision. (Police Supervision Ser.). (Illus.). 48p. 1997. pap. 8.95 (*0-937935-08-5*) Justice Syst Pr.
— Law Enforcement Administrative File System. (Illus.). 90p. 1987. pap. 19.95 (*0-937935-04-2*) Justice Syst Pr.
— Police Supervisor's Guide to Discipline & Commendation. Mund, Ed, ed. (Police Supervision Ser.). (Illus.). 48p. 1997. pap. 7.95 (*0-937935-09-3*) Justice Syst Pr.
Birkland, Barbara J., jt. auth. see Kernes, Steven T.
Birkland, Carol J. Unified in Hope: Arabs & Jews Talk about Peace. 160p. 1987. reprint ed. pap. 8.95 (*0-377-00177-5*) Friendship Pr.
Birkland, Thomas A. After Disaster: Agenda Setting, Public Policy, & Focusing Events. LC 97-7908. (American Governance & Public Policy Ser.). 256p. 1997. 53.00 (*0-87840-652-2*); pap. 20.95 (*0-87840-653-0*) Georgetown U Pr.
***Birkler, John, et al.** An Acquisition Strategy, Process & Organization for Innovative Systems. LC 99-87113. xvi, 69p. (C). 2000. pap. 10.00 (*0-8330-2802-2*, MR-1098-OSD) Rand Corp.
Birkler, John, et al. Gaining New Military Capability: An Experiment in Concept Development. LC 98-5157. 69p. 1998. pap. 15.00 (*0-8330-2586-4*, MR-912) Rand Corp.
Birkler, John L. A Framework for Precision Conventional Strike in Post-Cold War Military Strategy. LC 96-1953. 1996. pap. 15.00 (*0-8330-2386-1*, MR-743-CRMAF) Rand Corp.
Birkler, John L. & Schank, J. The U. S. Submarine Production Base: An Analysis of Cost, Schedule & Risk for Selected Force Structures. LC 94-28415. 230p. 1994. pap. 15.00 (*0-8330-1548-6*, MR-456-OSD) Rand Corp.
Birkler, John L., et al. Reconstituting a Production Capability: Past Experience, Restart Criteria & Suggested Policies. LC 93-29793. 127p. 1993. pap. 15.00 (*0-8330-1445-5*, MR-273-ACQ) Rand Corp.
— The U. S. Aircraft-Carrier Industrial Base: Force Structure, Cost, Schedule & Technology Issues for CVN-77. LC 98-6126. (Illus.). 196p. 1998. pap. text 15.00 (*0-8330-2597-X*, MR-948-OSD) Rand Corp.
— The U. S. Submarine Production Base: An Analysis of Cost, Schedule & Risk for Selected Force Structures, Executive Summary. LC 94-32570. 1994. pap. 7.50 (*0-8330-1587-7*, MR-456/1-OSD) Rand Corp.
Birkman, Roger. Los Colores de la Personalidad.Tr. of True Colors. 1997. pap. text 10.99 (*0-88113-423-6*) Caribe Betania.
Birkmann, Thomas. Von Agedal Bis Malt: Die Skandinavischen Runeninschriften Vom Ende Des 5. Bis Ende Des 9. Jahrhunderts, Bd. 11. (Ergaenzungsbaende zum Reallexikon der Germanischen Alterumskunde: Vol. 12). (GER.). xi, 418p. 1995. lib. bdg. 176.95 (*3-11-014510-3*) De Gruyter.
Birkmayer, Georg. NADH: The Energizing Coenzyme. LC 99-163562. (Good Health Guides Ser.). 1998. pap. 3.95 (*0-87983-862-0*, 38620K, Keats Publng) NTC Contemp Pub Co.
Birkmayer, J. G. Tumorbiologie. (Illus.). viii, 230p. 1984. 49.75 (*3-8055-3892-8*) S Karger.
Birkmayer, W. & Duvoisin, R. C., eds. Extrapyramidal Disorders. (Illus.). 340p. 1984. 130.00 (*0-387-81756-5*) Spr-Verlag.
Birkmayer, W. & Riederer, P. Parkinson's Disease: Biochemistry, Clinical Pathology, & Treatment. Reynolds, G., tr. from GER. (Illus.). 194p. 1983. 82.95 (*0-387-81722-0*) Spr-Verlag.
— Understanding the Neurotransmitters: Key to the Workings of the Brain. (Illus.). 160p. 1989. 35.95 (*0-387-82100-7*) Spr-Verlag.
Birkmeier, Rana. The Astrological Cookbook: Your Culinary Guide to Celestial Harmony. Dejauregui, Ruth & Yenne, Bill, eds. (Illus.). 128p. 1994. text 12.95 (*0-912517-11-5*) Bluewood Bks.
Birkmire, William H. Skeleton Construction in Buildings. LC 72-5035. (Technology & Society Ser.). (Illus.). 200p. 1978. reprint ed. 21.95 (*0-405-04688-X*) Ayer.
Birkner, Hans-Joachim. Schleiermacher-Studien. Fischer, Hermann, ed. (Schleiermacher-Archiv Ser.: Vol. 16). (GER., Illus.). xvi, 421p. (C). 1996. lib. bdg. 145.70 (*3-11-014253-8*, 125/96) De Gruyter.
Birkner, Hans-Joachim, ed. Friedrich Daniel Ernst Schleiermacher - Kritische Gesamtausgabe Vol. 10: Theologisch-Dogmatische Abhandlungen un Gelegenheitsschriften. (GER.). cxvi, 616p. (C). 1990. lib. bdg. 267.70 (*3-11-011594-8*) De Gruyter.
Birkner, Katherine M. Breaking the Sugar Habit Cookbook. 2nd ed. LC 90-81658. 100p. (Orig.). 1995. pap. text 8.95 (*0-9625914-1-6*) Pain & Stress.
Birkner, Katherine M., jt. auth. see Sahley, Billie J.
Birkner, Michael J. A Country Place No More: The Transformation of Bergenfield, New Jersey, 1894-1994. LC 94-11783. 1994. 45.00 (*0-8386-3574-1*) Fairleigh Dickinson.
***Birkner, Michael J.** McCormick of Rutgers: Scholar, Teacher, Public Historian, 6. Vol. 6. 2000. write for info. (*0-313-30356-8*, Greenwood Pr) Greenwood.
Birkner, Michael J. Samuel L. Southard: Jeffersonian Whig. LC 82-48517. 1984. 37.50 (*0-8386-3160-6*) Fairleigh Dickinson.
Birkner, Michael J., ed. James Buchanan & the Political Crisis of the 1850s. LC 95-45041. (Illus.). 215p. (C). 1996. 29.50 (*0-945636-89-X*) Susquehanna U Pr.
Birks, Albert S., et al, eds. ASNT Nondestructive Testing Handbook, Vol. 7: Ultrasonic Testing. 2nd ed. (Illus.). 915p. (C). 1991. text 140.00 (*0-931403-04-9*, 132) Am Soc Nondestructive.
Birks, Beverly. Sophisticated Silhouettes: The Shape of Fashion, 1910-1960. (Illus.). 24p. 1986. 8.00 (*0-915171-06-6*) Katonah Gal.
Birks, Ee-Kheng. Coping with 'Morning' Sickness. 95p. 1993. pap. 24.95 (*0-908569-76-9*, Pub. by Univ Otago Pr) Intl Spec Bk.
Birks, H. J. & Gordon, A. D. Numerical Methods in Quarternary Pollen Analysis. 1985. text 142.00 (*0-12-101250-6*) Acad Pr.
Birks, Hilary H. Plant Macrofossils in Quaternary Lake Sediments. (Advances in Limnology Ser.: Vol. 15). (GER., Illus.). 60p. 1980. 20.00 (*3-510-47013-3*, Pub. by E Schweizerbartsche) Balogh.
Birks, J. & Fry, D. Theory & Practice of Scintillation Counting. LC 63-19244. (International Series of Monographs in Electronics Instrumentation: Vol. 27). 1964. 303.00 (*0-08-010472-X*, Pub. by Pergamon Repr) Franklin.
Birks, J. S. Across the Savannas to Mecca: The Overland Pilgrimage Route from West Africa. (Illus.). 161p. 1978. 35.00 (*0-7146-6005-1*, Pub. by F Cass Pubs) Intl Spec Bk.
Birks, J. W., ed. Chemiluminescence & Photochemical Reaction Detection in Chromatography. 291p. 1989. 110.00 (*0-471-18698-8*) Wiley.
Birks, John B., ed. Excited States of Biological Molecules: Based on the Proceedings of the International Conference at the Calouste Gulbenkian Foundation Centre, Lisbon, Portugal, on April 18-24, 1974. LC 75-6985. (Wiley Monographs in Chemical Physics). 670p. reprint ed. pap. 200.00 (*0-608-14066-X*, 202400500035) Bks Demand.
— Organic Molecular Photophysics, Vol. 1. LC 72-8594. 618p. reprint ed. pap. 191.60 (*0-608-09944-9*, 203048100001) Bks Demand.
— Organic Molecular Photophysics, Vol. 2. LC 72-8594. (Wiley Monographs in Chemical Physics). 670p. 1975. reprint ed. pap. 200.00 (*0-608-09945-7*, 203048100002) Bks Demand.
Birks, John W., ed. Chemiluminescence & Photochemical Reaction Detection in Chromatography. LC 89-5734. 291p. 1989. 75.00 (*0-89573-281-5*, Wiley-VCH) Wiley.
Birks, John W., et al, eds. The Chemistry of the Atmosphere: Its Impact on Global Change, Perspectives & Recommendations. LC 92-41499. (An American Chemical Society Publication). (Illus.). 170p. 1993. text 38.00 (*0-8412-2532-X*, Pub. by Am Chemical); pap. text 29.95 (*0-8412-2533-8*, Pub. by Am Chemical) OUP.
Birks, Peter, ed. The Classification of Obligation. (SPTL Seminar Ser.). 336p. 1998. text 96.50 (*0-19-826598-0*) OUP.
***Birks, Peter, ed.** English Private Law, 2 vols. (Oxford English Law Ser.). 1800p. 2000. text 250.00 (*0-19-876500-2*) OUP.
Birks, Peter, ed. Lessons from the Swaps Litigation. 188p. 1999. 74.00 (*0-9526499-3-4*, Pub. by Hart Pub) Northwestern U Pr.
— Privacy & Loyalty: In the Law of Obligations. LC 97-23790. (SPTL Seminar Ser.). 342p. (C). 1997. text 92.00 (*0-19-876488-X*) OUP.
Birks, Peter B. H. An Introduction to the Law of Restitution. (Clarendon Law Ser.). 488p. 1985. text 85.00 (*0-19-876074-4*) OUP.
— An Introduction to the Law of Restitution. 2nd rev. ed. (Illus.). 522p. 1989. pap. text 42.00 (*0-19-825645-0*) OUP.
— Restitution: The Future. 1992. 25.00 (*1-86287-088-8*, Pub. by Blackstone Pr) Gaunt.
Birks, Peter B. H., ed. Examining the Law Syllabus: Beyond the Core. LC 93-16304. 118p. 1993. pap. text 19.95 (*0-19-876319-0*, Clarendon Pr) OUP.
— Laundering & Tracing. 388p. 1996. text 80.00 (*0-19-826101-2*) OUP.
— The Life of the Law: Proceedings of the Tenth British Legal History Conference, Oxford, 1991. LC 93-4567. 256p. 1993. 60.00 (*1-85285-102-3*) Hambledon Press.
— New Perspectives in the Roman Law of Property: Essays for Barry Nicholas. (Illus.). 244p. 1989. text 59.00 (*0-19-825614-0*) OUP.
— Pressing Problems in Law: Criminal Justice & Human Rights. 176p. 1995. pap. text 42.00 (*0-19-826042-3*) OUP.
— Pressing Problems in Law Vol. 2: What are Law Schools for? LC 97-111444. 138p. 1996. pap. text 55.00 (*0-19-826293-0*) OUP.
— Wrongs & Remedies in the Twenty-First Century. LC 96-229826. 348p. 1996. text 80.00 (*0-19-826292-2*) OUP.
Birks, Peter B. H., jt. ed. see MacCormick, D. Neil.
Birks, Peter B.H., ed. Examining the Law Syllabus: The Core. 90p. 1992. pap. text 21.00 (*0-19-876269-0*) OUP.
— Frontiers of Liability, Vol. 2. 240p. 1994. pap. text 55.00 (*0-19-825951-4*) OUP.
— Frontiers of Liability Vol. I. 214p. 1994. pap. text 39.95 (*0-19-825902-6*) OUP.
Birks, Peter B.H., tr. see Justinian.
***Birks, Tony.** Complete Potter's Companion. (Illus.). 208p. 1998. pap. 26.95 (*0-8212-2495-6*, Pub. by Bulfinch Pr) Little.
Birks, Tony. Tony Birks Pottery: A Complete Guide to Pottery-Making Techniques. 2nd ed. (Illus.). 136p. 1998. reprint ed. pap. 27.95 (*1-889250-14-7*) Gentle Br.

Birks, Walter. The Treasure of Montsegur: A Study of the Cathar Heresy & the Nature of the Cathar Secret. 1990. pap. 12.95 (*0-85030-424-5*) Aqm Pr.

Birksett, Bill. The Lakeland Fells Almanac. 160p. 1997. 15.00 (*1-897784-59-7*, Pub. by N Wilson Pubng) Interlink Pub.

Birksted-Breen, Dana, ed. The Gender Conundrum: Psychoanalytic Perspectives on Masculinity & Femininity. LC 92-37650. (New Library of Psychoanalysis Ser.: No. 18). 664p. (C). 1993. pap. 29.99 (*0-415-09164-0*, B0875) Routledge.

Birksted, Jan. Relating Architecture to Landscape. LC 98-18215. 320p. (C). 1999. pap. 49.99 (*0-419-23150-1*, E & FN Spon) Routledge.

***Birkwood, Ilene.** Stress for Success: How to Cope with Stress & Enjoy Life. rev. ed. LC 99-24440. 128p. 1999. reprint ed. pap. 14.95 (*0-8397-7930-5*, Pub. by Eriksson) IPG Chicago.

Birla, G. D. Bapu, A Unique Association: Correspondence with Mahatma Gandhi, 4 vols., Set. 1838p. 1983. 60.00 (*0-934676-33-X*) Greenlf Bks.

Birla, Ghanshyam S. Love in the Palm of Your Hand: How to Use Palmistry for Successful Relationships. LC 98-38310. (Illus.). 208p. 1998. pap. 19.95 (*0-89281-718-6*) Inner Tradit.

***Birla, Ghanshyam Singh.** Destiny in the Palm of Your Hand: Creating Your Future Through Vedic Palmistry. (Illus.). 160p. 2000. 19.95 (*0-89281-770-4*, Destiny Bks) Inner Tradit.

Birla, Ghanshyamdas. Alive in Krishna. LC 86-4936. (Patterns of World Spirituality Ser.). (Illus.). 219p. 1986. pap. 8.95 (*0-913757-65-9*) Paragon Hse.

Birla Institute of Scientific Research, Staff. Capital & Technological Progress in the Indian Economy, 1950-51-1980-81. xvi, 198p. 1986. text 25.00 (*81-7027-080-4*, Pub. by Radiant Pubs) S Asia.

Birla, Madan. Balanced Life & Leadership Excellence: A Nurturing Relationship. Kerr, Robert, ed. LC 97-71401. (Illus.). 200p. (Orig.). 1997. pap. 11.95 (*0-9657644-0-0*) Balance Group.

***Birlew, Dan.** Nemesis, Vol. 3. (Resident Evil Ser.). 1999. pap. 12.99 (*1-56686-955-2*) Brady Pub.

***Birley, Anthony.** Hadrian: The Restless Emperor. (Roman Imperial Biographies Ser.). 2000. pap. 24.95 (*0-415-22812-3*) Routledge.

Birley, Anthony. Septimus Severus: The African Emperor. (Illus.). 320p. 1999. reprint ed. pap. 24.99 (*0-415-16591-1*) Routledge.

Birley, Anthony, ed. see Stemmler, Michael.

Birley, Anthony, ed. see Syme, Ronald.

Birley, Anthony, tr. see Tacitus.

Birley, Anthony R. Hadrian: The Restless Emperor. LC 96-49232. (Roman Imperial Biographies Ser.). (Illus.). 424p. 1997. 50.00 (*0-415-16544-X*) Routledge.

— Marcus Aurelius: A Biography. rev. ed. LC 86-51355. 334p. reprint ed. pap. 103.60 (*0-7837-2349-0*, 208024400004) Bks Demand.

Birley, Anthony R., tr. Lives of the Later Caesars. (Classics Ser.). 336p. (C). 1976. pap. 12.95 (*0-14-044308-8*, Penguin Classics) Viking Penguin.

Birley, Anthony R., ed. see Syme, Ronald.

Birley, Arthur W., et al. Physics of Plastics: Processing, Properties & Materials Engineering. 549p. 1992. 95.00 (*1-56990-003-5*); pap. 59.95 (*1-56990-004-3*) Hanser-Gardner.

— Plastics Materials: Properties & Applications. 2nd ed. 208p. (C). (gr. 13). 1988. mass mkt. 47.50 (*0-412-01781-4*, Chap & Hall NY) Chapman & Hall.

Birley, Derek. Land of Sport & Glory: Sport & British Society, 1887-1910. LC 94-26464. 1995. text 79.95 (*0-7190-4494-4*) Manchester Univ Pr.

— Playing the Game: Sport & British Society, 1914-1945. (International Studies in the History of Sport). 256p. 1996. text 29.95 (*0-7190-4497-9*, Pub. by Manchester Univ Pr) St Martin.

— Sport & the Making of Britain. LC 93-81. (International Studies in the History of Sport). 1993. text 29.95 (*0-7190-3759-X*, Pub. by Manchester Univ Pr) St Martin.

Birley, Eric. The Roman Army: Papers, Nineteen Twenty-Nine to Nineteen Eighty-Six. (Mavors Roman Army Researches Ser.: Vol. IV). 460p. (C). 1988. 134.00 (*90-5063-002-2*, Pub. by Gieben) J Benjamins Pubng Co.

Birley, Graham & Moreland, Neil. A Practical Guide to Academic Research. 192p. 1998. pap. 25.00 (*0-7494-2277-7*, Kogan Pg Educ) Stylus Pub VA.

Birley, M. H. Guidelines for Forecasting the Vector-Borne Disease Implications of Water Resources Development. (PEEM Guidelines Ser.: No. 2). (ENG & SPA.). xi, 128p. 1991. pap. text 29.70 (*0-614-08056-8*, 1930026) World Health.

Birley, Sue, ed. Entrepreneurship. LC 97-45887. (History of Management Thought Ser.). 580p. 1998. text 162.95 (*1-85521-966-2*, Pub. by Ashgate Pub) Ashgate Pub Co.

Birley, Sue, et al, eds. Frontiers of Entrepreneurship Research, 1993: Proceedings of 13th Annual Conference. (Illus.). 698p. (Orig.). 1994. pap. text 65.00 (*0-910897-14-X*) Babson College.

— Frontiers of Entrepreneurship Research, 1994: Proceedings of the 14th Annual Entrepreneurship Research Conference. (Frontiers on Entrepreneurship Research Ser.: No. 14). 711p. 1995. pap. text 65.00 (*0-910897-15-8*) Babson College.

Birley, Sue & Muzycka, Daniel F., eds. Financial Times Mastering Enterprise. (Financial Times Mastering Ser.). 350p. (Orig.). 1997. pap. text 29.95 (*0-273-63031-8*) F T P-H.

***Birley, Sue & Muzyka, Daniel F.** Mastering Entrepreneurship. 448p. 2000. pap. 34.00 (*0-273-64928-0*) S&S Trade.

Birley, Susan & MacMillan, I. C. International Perspectives on Entrepreneurship Research. (Advanced Series in Management: Vol. 18). 404p. 1992. 111.00 (*0-444-89526-4*, Pergamon Pr) Elsevier.

Birley, Susan & MacMillan, Ian C. Entrepreneurship in a Global Context. LC 96-18550. (International Business & the World Economy Ser.). 208p. (C). 1997. 85.00 (*0-415-13132-4*) Routledge.

Birley, Susan & MacMillan, Ian C., eds. Entrepreneurship Research: Global Perspectives: Proceedings of the Second Annual Global Conference on Entrepreneurship Research, London, U. K., March 1992. LC 93-15465. (Advanced Series in Management: Vol. 19). 534p. 1993. 111.00 (*0-444-89988-X*, North Holland) Elsevier.

Birman, Carl D. Little Brother Goes Down: An Erotic Exorcism. LC 95-67314. (Illus.). 80p. (Orig.). 1995. pap. 9.95 (*0-9635181-1-9*) Plutonia Pr.

Birman, David. The Book of Billy. 2nd ed. LC 92-97191. 209p. 1993. pap. 11.95 (*0-9635181-0-0*) Plutonia Pr.

Birman, Igor. Secret Incomes of the Soviet State Budget. 330p. 1981. lib. bdg. 181.50 (*90-247-2550-X*) Kluwer Academic.

Birman, J. & Libgober, A. Braids. LC 88-26283. (Contemporary Mathematics Ser.: Vol. 78). 730p. 1983. pap. 72.00 (*0-8218-5088-1*, CONM/78) Am Math.

Birman, J. L. Theory of Crystal Space Groups & Lattice Dynamics: Infra-Red & Raman Optical Processes of Insulating Crystals. (Illus.). 570p. 1984. pap. 69.00 (*0-387-13395-X*) Spr-Verlag.

Birman, J. L., et al, eds. Laser Optics of Condensed Matter. LC 88-2513. (Illus.). 578p. 1988. 135.00 (*0-306-42816-4*, Plenum Trade) Perseus Pubng.

Birman, J. L., ed. see Hecht, K. T.

Birman, J. L., ed. see Hladik, J.

Birman, J. L., ed. see Kaku, M.

Birman, J. L., ed. see Metcalf, Harold J. & Van der Straten, P.

Birman, J. L., ed. see Oberhummer, H.

Birman, J. L., ed. see Phillies, George D.

Birman, Joan S. Braids, Links & Mapping Class Groups. LC 74-2961. (Annals of Mathematics Studies: No. 82). 300p. 1974. pap. text 49.50 (*0-691-08149-2*, Pub. by Princeton U Pr) Cal Prin Full Svc.

Birman, Kenneth P. & Renesse, Robert V. Reliable Distributed Computing with the Isis Toolkit. LC 93-39785. 416p. 1994. 57.00 (*0-8186-5342-6*, 5342) IEEE Comp Soc.

Birman, Linda. Stewart: Seattle's Skyscraper Falcon. LC 96-910393. 32p. (J). (gr. k-5). 1997. 14.95 (*0-88839-389-X*) Hancock House.

Birman, Lisa. Some Things: Poems & Translations. 33p. 1998. pap. write for info. (*0-9665341-1-5*) Dristil Pr.

Birman, M., ed. Spectral Theory. LC 78-93768. (Topics in Mathematical Physics Ser.: Vol. 3). 99p. reprint ed. pap. 30.70 (*0-608-11841-9*, 202069300018); reprint ed. pap. 28.30 (*0-608-30437-9*, 2020693) Bks Demand.

Birman, M. S. Estimates & Asymptotics for Discrete Spectra of Integral & Differential Equations. LC 91-640741. (Advances in Soviet Mathematics Ser.: Vol. 7). 204p. 1991. text 118.00 (*0-8218-4106-8*, ADVSOV/7) Am Math.

Birman, M. S., ed. Wave Propagation, Scattering Theory. LC 93-31285. (Translations Ser.: Series 2, Vol. 157). 256p. 1993. text 105.00 (*0-8218-7507-8*, TRANS2/157) Am Math.

Birman, M. S. & Solomjak, M. Z. Quantitative Analysis in Sobolev Imbedding Theorems & Applications to Spectral Theory. LC 79-27339. (Translations Ser. 2: Vol. 114). 132p. 1980. text 47.00 (*0-8218-3064-3*, TRANS2/114) Am Math.

— Spectral Theory of Self-Adjoint Operators in Hilbert Space. 1987. text 211.50 (*90-277-2179-3*) Kluwer Academic.

Birman, M. S., et al. Fifteen Papers on Analysis. LC 51-5559. (Translations Ser.: Series 2, Vol. 54). 281p. 1966. 50.00 (*0-8218-1754-X*, TRANS2/54) Am Math.

***Birmbach, Hodgman.** 1,003 Great Things about Friends. 416p. 2000. 7.98 (*1-56731-394-9*, MJF Bks) Fine Comms.

Birmele, Ricardo. Access for Windows Quickstart Corporate Version. 1994. 29.99 (*1-56529-729-6*) Que.

— The Complete Idiot's Guide to Excel for Windows 95. (Illus.). 351p. (Orig.). 1995. 19.99 (*0-7897-0375-0*) Que.

— Complete Idiot's Guide to Excel 5. 286p. 1993. 19.99 (*1-56761-318-7*, Alpha Ref) Macmillan Gen Ref.

***Birmelin, I. & Wolter, Annette.** The Parakeet Handbook: Everything about the Purchase, Diet, Diseases & Behavior of Parakeets with a Special Chapter on Raising Parakeets. 2nd ed. LC 99-41233. (Pet Handbks.). 144p. 2000. 9.95 (*0-7641-1018-7*) Barron.

Birmelin, Immanuel. Budgerigars. LC 98-20371. (Barron's Complete Pet Owner's Manuals). (Illus.). 64p. 1998. pap. 6.95 (*0-7641-0662-7*) Barron.

Birmingham. History of Central Africa: The Contemporary Years Since 1960. (C). 1998. pap. text. write for info. (*0-582-27907-0*) Addison-Wesley.

— Portugal & Africa, 1815-1910: A Study in Uneconomic Imperialism. LC 99-11300. 1999. text 59.95 (*0-312-22319-6*) St Martin.

Birmingham, Peggy, ed. see Wyatt, R. G.

Birmingham Children's Theatre Staff. Once upon a Stove. LC 86-47955. (Cookbook Ser.). 400p. (Orig.). 1986. pap. 12.95 (*0-9617659-0-9*) Birmingham Child.

Birmingham, Christian, jt. illus. see Morpurgo, Michael.

***Birmingham Colloquium on the Textual Criticism of the New Testament Staff.** Studies in the Early Text of the Gospels & Acts: The Papers of the First Birmingham Colloquium on the Textual Criticism of the New Testament. Taylor, David G. K., ed. LC 99-49530. (Text-Critical Studies). 283p. 1999. 55.00 (*0-88414-007-5*, 067001, Pub. by Soc Biblical Lit) Scholars Pr GA.

Birmingham, D. HIST CNTRL AFRICA V1. (C). 1983. pap. text 37.50 (*0-582-64674-X*) Addison-Wesley.

Birmingham, David. Central Africa to 1870: Zambezia, Zaire & the South Atlantic. LC 81-9947. (Illus.). 176p. 1982. pap. text 16.95 (*0-521-28444-9*) Cambridge U Pr.

— A Concise History of Portugal. LC 92-33824. (Cambridge Concise Histories Ser.). (Illus.). 223p. (C). 1993. pap. 17.95 (*0-521-43880-2*); text 54.95 (*0-521-43308-8*) Cambridge U Pr.

— The Decolonization of Africa. LC 95-41640. (Illus.). 117p. (Orig.). (C). 1995. pap. text 12.95 (*0-8214-1153-5*) Ohio U Pr.

— Frontline Nationalism in Angola & Mozambique. LC 92-32977. 1992. 39.95 (*0-86543-367-4*); pap. 12.95 (*0-86543-368-2*) Africa World.

— History De Portugal - A Concise History of Portugal. Garcia, M. Angeles, tr. (SPA., Illus.). 308p. (C). 1995. pap. 16.95 (*0-521-47830-8*) Cambridge U Pr.

— Kwame Nkrumah: The Father of African Nationalism. rev. ed. LC 98-7888. xi, 142p. (C). 1998. pap. text 14.95 (*0-8214-1242-6*) Ohio U Pr.

***Birmingham, David.** Switzerland: A Village History. LC 99-51698. (Illus.). 2000. text 65.00 (*0-312-23076-1*) St Martin.

Birmingham, David & Martin, Phyllis. History Central Africa. LC 97-25419. (C). 1998. 73.13 (*0-582-27608-X*, Pub. by Addison-Wesley) Longman.

Birmingham, David & Martin, Phyllis M., eds. HIST CNTRL AFRICA V2, Vol. 2. (Illus.). 432p. (C). 1983. pap. text 33.50 (*0-582-64676-6*) Longman.

— History Central Africa, Vol. 2. (Illus.). 432p. (C). 1983. pap. text 63.50 (*0-582-64675-8*) Longman.

Birmingham, Duncan. Fantasy Mobiles. (Illus.). 32p. (Orig.). (J). (gr. 3-5). 1990. pap. 6.50 (*0-906212-52-9*, Pub. by Tarquin Pubns) Parkwest Pubns.

— Look Twice: Mirror Reflections, Logical Thinking. (J). (gr. 3 up). 1991. pap. 7.50 (*0-906212-86-3*, Pub. by Tarquin Pubns) Parkwest Pubns.

— The Maya, Aztecs & Incas Pop-Up. (Tarquin Pop-up Ser.). (Illus.). 32p. (J). (gr. 3 up). 1985. pap. 8.95 (*0-906212-37-5*, Pub. by Tarquin Pubns) Parkwest Pubns.

— Pop-Up! A Manual of Paper Mechanisms. 1997. pap. 12.95 (*1-899618-09-0*, Pub. by Tarquin Pubns) Parkwest Pubns.

Birmingham, Edgar. Biochemistry & Food Science. 162p. 1998. pap. 34.50 (*0-7487-1806-0*) St Mut.

Birmingham, Elizabeth, tr. see Janicaud, Dominique.

Birmingham Historical Society Staff, ed. Go to Town, Birmingham: Update on a Vital City Center. (Illus.). 32p. (Orig.). 1985. pap. 4.00 (*0-943994-12-8*) Birmingham Hist Soc.

Birmingham Historical Society Staff & Auburn University, Department of Architecture Staf, eds. Old Birmingham, New Architecture: Student Projects for an Historic Downtown Context. (Illus.). 48p. (Orig.). 1984. pap. 4.00 (*0-943994-10-1*) Birmingham Hist Soc.

Birmingham, Jacqueline J. Discharge Planning: A Practitioner's Guide to Policies, Procedures & Protocols, Guideline Manual. 1992. 90.00 (*1-879575-25-6*) Acad Med Sys.

***Birmingham, Jacqueline J.** Medical Terminology: A Self-Learning Text. 3rd ed. 1999. teacher ed. write for info. (*0-323-00456-3*) Mosby Inc.

Birmingham, Jacqueline J. Medical Terminology: A Self-Learning Text. 3rd ed. LC 98-42213. 1999. pap. text 31.95 (*0-323-00406-7*) Mosby Inc.

Birmingham Jewish History Research Group Staff & Josephs, Zoe. Survivors: Jewish Refugees in Birmingham, 1933-1945. (Illus.). 217p. 1988. pap. 25.00 (*1-869922-02-6*) Denali Press.

Birmingham, Kelly J. Junior High: Good Grief!!! Lalonde, Beverly, ed. LC 91-92234. (Illus.). 160p. (Orig.). 1992. pap. text 10.95 (*0-9621042-3-X*) IMPEL.

Birmingham, Madeline & Connolly, William J. Witnessing to the Fire: Spiritual Direction & the Development of Directors. LC 93-27071. 256p. (Orig.). 1994. pap. 16.95 (*1-55612-666-2*) Sheed & Ward WI.

Birmingham, Maisie. The Heat of the Sun. large type ed. (Linford Mystery Library). 300p. 1987. pap. 16.99 (*0-7089-6362-5*, Linford) Ulverscroft.

— Sleep in a Ditch. large type ed. (Linford Mystery Library). 320p. 1987. pap. 16.99 (*0-7089-6452-4*, Linford) Ulverscroft.

— You Can Help Me. large type ed. (Linford Mystery Library). 320p. 1987. pap. 16.99 (*0-7089-6358-7*, Linford) Ulverscroft.

Birmingham, Mary. Word & Worship Workbook for Year A: Religious Education & Formation. 688p. 1998. wbk. ed. 44.95 (*0-8091-3826-3*) Paulist Pr.

— Word & Worship Workbook for Year B: For Ministry in Initiation, Preaching, Religious Education. 736p. 1999. pap., wbk. ed. 44.95 (*0-8091-3898-0*) Paulist Pr.

— Word & Worship Workbook for Year C: For Ministry in Initiation Preaching, Religious Education & Formation. LC 97-22382. 688p. (Orig.). 1997. pap. 39.95 (*0-8091-3747-X*, 3747-X) Paulist Pr.

Birmingham, Maureen & Quesenberry, Peter, eds. Where There Is No Animal Doctor. (Illus.). Date not set. pap. write for info. (*1-886532-11-7*) Christian Vet.

Birmingham News Staff. Champions on the Field: Undefeated Season Lauches Bowden Era. 1993. pap. 10.00 (*0-9635413-2-3*) Birm News.

Birmingham, Peg, tr. see Janicaud, Dominique.

Birmingham-Pokorny, Elba D. An English Anthology of Afro-Hispanic Writers of the Twentieth Century. LC 94-61078. (Coleccion Ebano y Canela). 126p. (Orig.). 1995. pap. 19.00 (*0-89729-758-X*) Ediciones.

Birmingham-Pokorny, Elba D., ed. The Demythologization of Language, Gender & Culture & the Re-Mapping of Latin American Identity in Luis Rafael Sanche's Works. LC 98-86579. (Coleccion Ebano y Canela Ser.). (SPA.). 144p. 1999. pap. 16.00 (*0-89729-877-2*) Ediciones.

— Denouncement & Reaffirmation of the Afro-Hispanic Identity in Carlos Guillermo Wilson's Works. LC 91-78227. (Coleccion Ebano y Canela). (SPA.). 150p. (Orig.). 1993. pap. 19.95 (*0-89729-635-4*) Ediciones.

Birmingham Pokorny, Elba D., ed. Critical Perspectives in Enrique Jaramillo-Levi's Work: A Collection of Critical Essays. LC 95-83321. (Coleccion Ebano y Canela). 123p. (Orig.). 1996. pap. 16.00 (*0-89729-788-1*) Ediciones.

Birmingham-Pokorny, Elba D., tr. see Wilson, Carlos G.

***Birmingham, Robert A. & Eisenberg, Leslie E.** Indian Mounds of Wisconsin. 2000. 45.00 (*0-299-16870-0*) U of Wis Pr.

— Indian Mounds of Wisconsin. LC 00-8925. (Illus.). 2000. pap. 18.95 (*0-299-16874-3*) U of Wis Pr.

Birmingham, Ruth. Atlanta Graves. 1998. mass mkt. 5.99 (*0-425-16267-2*) Berkley Pub.

— Fulton County Blues, Vol. 2. Vol. 2. 288p. 1999. pap. 5.99 (*0-425-16697-X*, Prime Crime) Berkley Pub.

***Birmingham, Ruth.** Sweet Georgia. (Sunny Childs Mysteries Ser.). 2000. mass mkt. 5.99 (*0-425-17671-1*) Berkley Pub.

Birmingham, Sonya. Almost a Lady. 400p. (Orig.). 1993. mass mkt. 4.50 (*0-380-76766-X*, Avon Bks) Morrow Avon.

***Birmingham, Sonya.** The Brightest Flame, 1. 400p. 1999. mass mkt. 5.99 (*0-8439-4564-8*, Pub. by Dorchester Pub Co) CMG.

Birmingham, Sonya. Renegade Lady. 384p. (Orig.). 1992. mass mkt. 4.50 (*0-380-76765-1*, Avon Bks) Morrow Avon.

— Scarlet Leaves. 368p. (Orig.). 1996. mass mkt. 5.50 (*0-8439-4081-6*, Leisure Bks) Dorchester Pub Co.

— Song of the Lark. 368p. 1998. mass mkt. 5.50 (*0-8439-4393-9*, Leisure Bks) Dorchester Pub Co.

— Spitfire. 368p. (Orig.). 1991. pap. 3.95 (*0-380-76294-3*, Avon Bks) Morrow Avon.

Birmingham, Stephen. Carriage Trade. large type ed. 1994. 110.95 (*1-56054-868-1*) Thorndike Pr.

— Carriage Trade. large type ed. 1993. 25.95 (*1-56895-027-6*) Wheeler Pub.

— The Grandees: The Story of America's Sephardic Elite. 386p. 1997. pap. 17.95 (*0-8156-0459-9*) Syracuse U Pr.

— Life at the Dakota: New York's Most Unusual Address. 263p. (C). 1996. pap. 18.95 (*0-8156-0338-X*, BILDP) Syracuse U Pr.

— Our Crowd: The Great Jewish Families of New York. LC 96-32954. 404p. 1996. reprint ed. pap. 17.95 (*0-8156-0411-4*, BIOCP) Syracuse U Pr.

— Real Lace. LC 97-21262. xi, 322p. 1997. pap. 17.95 (*0-8156-0509-9*) Syracuse U Pr.

— The Rest of Us: The Rise of America's Eastern European Jews. 384p. 1984. 19.95 (*0-316-09647-4*) Little.

***Birmingham, Stephen.** Rest of Us: The Rise of America's Eastern European Jews. LC 99-36991. 428p. 1999. pap. text 22.95 (*0-8156-0614-1*) Syracuse U Pr.

Birmingham, Stephen. Shades of Fortune: A Novel. 400p. 1989. 18.95 (*0-316-09655-5*) Little.

— The Wrong Kind of Money. 1997. 23.95 (*0-614-27942-9*) NAL.

— The Wrong Kind of Money. 480p. 1998. mass mkt. 6.99 (*0-451-19304-0*, Onyx) NAL.

Birmingham, T. J. & Dessler, A. J., eds. Comet Encounters. 352p. 1988. pap. 35.00 (*0-87590-239-1*, CR0232391) Am Geophysical.

***Birmingham, Walter.** Eightieth Birthday Verses. 1999. pap. 21.00 (*1-85072-158-0*, Pub. by W Sessions) St Mut.

Birminham, Duncan. M Is for Mirror. (Illus.). 33p. (J). (ps-3). 1989. pap. 7.50 (*0-906212-66-9*, Pub. by Tarquin Pubns) Parkwest Pubns.

Birn, Randi. Aksel Sandemose: Exile in Search of a Home, 2. LC 83-13034. (Contributions to the Study of World Literature Ser.: No. 2). 150p. 1984. 45.00 (*0-313-24163-5*, BAS/, Greenwood Pr) Greenwood.

Birn, Randi & Gould, Karen, eds. Orion Blinded: Essays on Claude Simon. LC 79-17687. 320p. 1981. 38.50 (*0-8387-2420-5*) Bucknell U Pr.

Birn, Raymond. Crisis, Absolutism, Revolution: Europe, 1648-1789. 2nd ed. 432p. (C). 1992. pap. text 37.50 (*0-03-053328-7*, Pub. by Harcourt Coll Pubs) Harcourt.

Birn, Robin. Effective Use Of Market Research: A Guide For Management To Grow The Business, 2nd Ed. 2nd ed. 1999. pap. text 29.95 (*0-7494-2772-8*, Kogan Pg Educ) Stylus Pub VA.

Birn, Robin, jt. auth. see Forsyth, Patrick.

Birn, Ruth Bettina, jt. auth. see Finkelstein, Norman G.

***Birnam, Stewart.** Distributed Enterprise Development with Java Technology. 2000. pap. 44.99 (*0-13-026861-5*, Prentice Hall) P-H.

Birnaum, Mayer. Tefillah Workbooks Series Pt. II: Shema II & Shemoneh Esray. (ENG & HEB.). 1997. pap. 8.00 (*1-878895-19-2*, A086) Torah Umesorah.

Birnbach, Allen. Colorado: Photographs by Allen Birnbach. (Illus.). 28p. (Orig.). 1992. pap. 9.95 (*0-9633763-0-6*) Antero Pub.

— Colorado, Aspen. 1994. pap. text 9.95 (*0-9633763-1-4*) Antero Pub.

Birnbach, David J. Ostheimer's Manual of Obstetric Anesthesia. 3rd ed. LC 99-35204. (Illus.). 315p. 2000. pap. text. write for info. (*0-443-06554-3*, W B Saunders Co) Harcrt Hlth Sci Grp.

***Birnbach, David J., et al.** Obstetrics Anesthesia. LC 99-462024. (Illus.). 795p. Date not set. text. write for info. (*0-443-06560-8*, W B Saunders Co) Harcrt Hlth Sci Grp.

Birnbach, Lisa. 1,003 Great Things about Kids. 320p. 1999. 6.98 (*1-56731-357-4*, MJF Bks) Fine Comms.
— Welcome to the Real World. 1987. write for info. (*0-318-61412-X*) Villard Books.
***Birnbach, Lisa, et al.** 1,003 Great Things about Teachers. 2000. pap. 8.95 (*0-7407-0989-5*) Andrews & McMeel.
Birnbach, Lisa, et al. 1,003 Great Things about Kids. LC 98-7624. (Illus.). 320p. 1998. pap. 8.95 (*0-8362-6964-0*) Andrews & McMeel.
— 1,003 Great Things about Getting Older. LC 97-3825. 315p. (Orig.). 1997. pap. 8.95 (*0-8362-2699-2*) Andrews & McMeel.
Birnbach, Lisa, jt. auth. see Hodgman.
Birnbach, Martin. Neo-Freudian Social Philosophy. vi, 283p. 1961. 39.50 (*0-8047-0076-1*) Stanford U Pr.
— Neo-Freudian Social Philosophy. fac. ed. LC 61-12389. 291p. 1961. reprint ed. pap. 30.00 (*0-7837-7910-0*, 204766600008) Bks Demand.
Birnbach, Nettie & Lewenson, Sandra B., eds. First Words: Selected Addresses from NLN 1894-1933. 408p. 1991. 28.95 (*0-88737-526-X*) Natl League Nurse.
— Legacy of Leadership: Presidential Addresses from the Superintendents' Society & the National League for Nursing 1894-1952. 416p. (C). 1993. pap. text 29.95 (*0-88737-575-8*, 14-2514) Natl League Nurse.
Birnback, George, jt. auth. see Gibson.
Birnbaum. Birnbaum's Disneyland, 1999: Expert Advice from the Inside Source. (Illus.). 160p. (J). 1998. pap. 11.45 (*0-7868-8369-3*, Pub. by Hyperion) Time Warner.
— Cultural Landscapes: Expanding the Realm of Historic Preservation. 300p. 49.95 (*0-471-13783-9*) Wiley.
Birnbaum & Free, eds. Eddy-Current Characterization of Materials & Structures - STP 722. 505p. 1981. 44.50 (*0-8031-0752-8*, STP722) ASTM.
Birnbaum, jt. auth. see Murray.
Birnbaum, Alfred, tr. see Miyabe, Miyuki.
Birnbaum, Alfred T. & Kanmei, Riku. Zen for Cats. (Illus.). 96p. 1993. 12.95 (*0-8348-0292-9*); pap. 9.95 (*0-8348-0275-9*) Weatherhill.
Birnbaum, Alfred T., tr. see Koizumi, Kazuko.
Birnbaum, Alfred T., tr. see Murakami, Haruki.
Birnbaum, Asher, jt. auth. see Tilden, William T.
***Birnbaum, Barry W.** Connecting Special Education & Technology for the 21st Century. LC 99-33111. (Studies in Education: Vol. 45). 117p. 1999. text 59.95 (*0-7734-7991-0*) E Mellen.
Birnbaum, Bette. Jane Goodall & the Wild Chimpanzees. (Real Readers Ser.: Level Red). (Illus.). 32p. (J). (gr. 1-4). 1989. pap. 4.95 (*0-8114-6709-0*) Raintree Steck-V.
— Jane Goodall & the Wild Chimpanzees. (Real Readers Ser.: Level Red). (Illus.). 32p. (J). (ps-3). 1989. lib. bdg. 21.40 (*0-8172-3509-4*) Raintree Steck-V.
— My School, Your School. (Ready-Set-Read Ser.). (Illus.). 32p. (J). (ps-3). 1990. lib. bdg. 21.40 (*0-8172-3583-3*) Raintree Steck-V.
— My School, Your School. 28p. (J). (ps-3). 1990. pap. text 4.95 (*0-8114-6743-0*) Raintree Steck-V.
Birnbaum, Burton H., jt. auth. see Kirkpatrick, Beth.
Birnbaum, Charles A. Pioneers of American Landscape Design: An Annotated Bibliography. 148p. 1994. per. 15.00 (*0-16-041974-3*) USGPO.
Birnbaum, Charles A. Pioneers of American Landscape Design 2: An Annotated Bibliography. 186p. 1995. per. 13.00 (*0-16-048060-4*) USGPO.
— Protecting Cultural Landscapes: Planning, Treatment & Management of Historic Landscapes. 20p. 1994. pap. 1.75 (*0-16-061666-2*) USGPO.
Birnbaum, Charles A., et al, eds. Making Educated Decisions: A Landscape Preservation Bibliography. LC 94-41041. (NPS Reading List Ser.). 1994. per. 5.50 (*0-16-045145-0*, 024-005-01142-1) USGPO.
Birnbaum, Charles A. & Wagner, Cheryl, eds. Making Educated Decisions: A Landscape Preservation Bibliography. (Illus.). 160p. 1998. pap. text 30.00 (*0-7881-7158-5*) DIANE Pub.
Birnbaum, Charles A., et al. Secretary of the Interior's Standards for the Treatment of Historic Properties: With Guidelines for the Treatment of Cultural Landscapes. LC 96-37575. 1997. per. 16.00 (*0-16-048700-5*, 024-005-01171-4) USGPO.
Birnbaum, Daniel. The Hospitality of Presence: Problems of Otherness in Husserl's Phenomenology. LC 98-167551. (Stockholm Studies in Philosophy: Vol. 20). 200p. 1998. pap. 37.50 (*91-22-01803-4*) Coronet Bks.
Birnbaum, David. God & Evil. 1989. 25.00 (*0-88125-307-3*) Ktav.
Birnbaum, David A., jt. auth. see Lane, Fred.
Birnbaum, David J., jt. ed. see Ostrowski, Donald.
Birnbaum, Debra, jt. auth. see Freed, Jennifer.
Birnbaum, Eduard. Jewish Musicians at the Court of the Mantuan Dukes, 1542-1628. (Documentations & Studies, Dept. of Musicology, Tel-Aviv University: No. 1). (Illus.). 52p. 1978. pap. 6.00 (*0-685-45773-7*) Theodore Front.
Birnbaum, Eleazar. Books on Asia from the Near East to the Far East: A Guide for the General Reader. LC 75-151361. 357p. reprint ed. pap. 110.70 (*0-8357-7348-5*, 201413300090) Bks Demand.
Birnbaum, Ervin. In the Shadow of the Struggle. 344p. 1992. 19.95 (*965-229-037-8*, Pub. by Gefen Pub Hse) Gefen Bks.
— Politics of Compromise: State & Religion in Israel. LC 70-92557. 348p. 1975. 39.50 (*0-8386-7567-0*) Fairleigh Dickinson.
Birnbaum, H., et al, eds. Studia Linguistica Alexandro Vasilii Filio Issatschenko: A Collegis Amicusque Oblata. (ENG, FRE, GER & RUS.). xxvi, 517p. (Orig.). 1978. pap. 85.00 (*0-686-32343-2*) J Benjamins Pubg Co.
Birnbaum, Harold F., jt. auth. see Birnbaum, Ruth F.
Birnbaum, Henrik. Aspects of the Slavic Middle Ages & Slavic Renaissance Culture. (American University Studies: Slavic Languages & Literature: Ser. XII, Vol. 4). (Illus.). 838p. (C). 1992. text 110.95 (*0-8204-1057-8*) P Lang Pubng.
— Linguistic Reconstruction: Its Potentials & Limitations in New Perspective. (Journal of Indo-European Studies: No.2). 1976. pap. text 20.00 (*0-941694-26-7*) Inst Study Man.
— Novgorod in Focus: Selected Essays. 192p. 1996. 24.95 (*0-89357-261-6*) Slavica.
— On Medieval & Renaissance Slavic Writings. LC 73-85243. (Slavistic Printings & Reprintings Ser.: No. 266). 381p. 1974. text 100.00 (*90-279-2680-8*) Mouton.
— Problems of Typological & Genetic Linguistics Viewed in a Generative Framework. LC 70-123298. (Janua Linguarum, Ser. Minor: No. 106). (Orig.). (C). 1970. pap. text 29.25 (*90-279-1541-5*) Mouton.
Birnbaum, Henrik, et al, eds. California Slavic Studies, Vol. 14. LC 90-37039. (C). 1993. 50.00 (*0-520-07025-9*, Pub. by U CA Pr) Cal Prin Full Svc.
Birnbaum, Henrik & Eekman, Thomas. Fiction & Drama in Eastern & Southeastern Europe: Evolution & Experiment in the Postwar Period. (UCLA Slavic Studies: Vol. 1). ix, 463p. 1980. 34.95 (*0-89357-064-8*) Slavica.
Birnbaum, Henrik & Merrill, Peter T. Recent Advances in the Reconstruction of Common Slavic (1971 to 1982) vi, 141p. (Orig.). 1985. pap. 17.95 (*0-89357-116-4*) Slavica.
Birnbaum, Henrik & Speros, V. Aspects of the Balkans: Continuity & Change. (Slavistic Printings & Reprintings Ser.: No. 27). 1972. text 126.95 (*90-279-2172-5*) Mouton.
Birnbaum, Herbert C. KODAK Pocket Guide to Great Picture Taking. LC 84-10683. (Pocket Guide Ser.). (Illus.). 112p. (YA). (gr. 7-12). 1998. pap. 6.95 (*0-87985-770-6*, AR-24a, Kodak) Saunders Photo.
Birnbaum, Howard, et al. Public Pricing of Nursing Home Care. (Illus.). 222p. 1984. reprint ed. lib. bdg. 52.00 (*0-8191-4065-1*) U Pr of Amer.
Birnbaum, Hubert C. Black & White Darkroom Techniques. 3rd ed. LC 96-71713. (Kodak Workshop Ser.). (Illus.). 96p. (Orig.). (C). 1998. pap. 17.95 (*0-87985-274-7*, KW-15, Kodak) Saunders Photo.
— Existing-Light Photography. 3rd ed. LC 96-69137. (Kodak Workshop Ser.). (Illus.). 88p. (C). 1998. pap. 17.95 (*0-87985-744-7*, KW-17, Kodak) Saunders Photo.
Birnbaum, Irina, tr. see Davis, George D., et al.
Birnbaum, Irwin, et al. Health Care M & A: How to Structure the Transaction. LC 97-153504. (Corporate Law & Practice Course Handbook Ser.). 384p. 1997. 129.00 (*0-87224-323-0*) PLI.
Birnbaum, Irwin M. Health Care Law Treatise (Treatise on Health Care Law), Vol. 4. Capron, Alexander M. et al, eds. 1991. 650.00 (*0-8205-1407-1*) Bender.
Birnbaum, Jacob, jt. auth. see Taylor, Jason R.
Birnbaum, Jacob S. The Musculoskeletal Manual. 2nd ed. LC 79-594. 384p. 1985. text 55.00 (*0-8089-1796-X*, 790594, Grune & Strat) Harcrt Hlth Sci Grp.
Birnbaum, Jeff, et al, eds. Passing the Obesity & Nutrition Exams in Primary Care. 208p. 1997. pap. text 49.95 (*1-888628-22-7*) Southlnd Tutor.
***Birnbaum, Jeffrey.** The Money Men: The Real Story of Political Power in the U. S. A. LC 00-23463. 320p. 2000. 25.95 (*0-8129-3119-X*, Times Bks) Crown Pub Group.
Birnbaum, Jeffrey H. The Lobbyists: How Influence Peddlers Work Their Way in Washington. 1993. pap. 15.00 (*0-8129-2314-6*, Times Bks) Crown Pub Group.
Birnbaum, Jeffrey H. & Murray, Alan S. Showdown at Gucci Gulch: Lawmakers, Lobbyists, & the Unlikely Triumph of Tax Reform. Osnos, Peter, ed. LC 87-45971. 336p. 1988. reprint ed. pap. 16.00 (*0-394-75811-0*) Knopf.
Birnbaum, Jonathan. Civil Rights since 1787: A Reader. LC 00-8112. 704p. 2000. pap. 29.95 (*0-8147-8249-3*); text 85.00 (*0-8147-8215-9*) NYU Pr.
Birnbaum, Jonathan, jt. ed. see Ollman, Bertell.
Birnbaum, Karl E. The Politics of East-West Communication in Europe. 182p. 1979. text 82.95 (*0-566-00254-X*, Pub. by Dartmth Pub) Ashgate Pub Co.
Birnbaum, Karl E., jt. auth. see Andren, Nils.
Birnbaum, Lawrence A. & Collins, Gregg C., eds. Machine Learning: Proceedings of the Eighth International Workshop. 1998. pap. text 39.95 (*1-55860-200-3*) Morgan Kaufmann.
Birnbaum, M. & Rosenblum, Yonoson. Lieutenant Birnbaum: A Soldier's Story. 1993. 19.99 (*0-89906-822-7*); 16.99 (*0-89906-823-5*) Mesorah Pubns.
Birnbaum, M. D. & Matejka, Ladislav, eds. History - Another Text: Essays on the Fiction of Kazimierz Brandys, Dauilo Kis, Gyorgy Konrad, & Christa Wolf. (Michigan Studies in the Humanities: No. 7). (C). 1988. pap. 15.00 (*0-936534-06-0*) Mich Studies Human.
Birnbaum, Marianna D. Humanists in a Shattered World: Croatian & Hungarian Latinity in the Sixteenth Century. (UCLA Slavic Studies: Vol. 15). (Illus.). 433p. 1986. 34.95 (*0-89357-155-5*) Slavica.
Birnbaum, Martha R., tr. from HEB. Timeless Jewish Songs. 31p. (Orig.). (C). pap. 10.00 (*1-878617-14-1*) Leyerle Pubns.
Birnbaum, Martin H. Optometric Management of Nearpoint Vision Disorders. 416p. 1992. text 92.50 (*0-7506-9193-X*) Buttrwrth-Heinemann.
Birnbaum, Mayer. Tefillah Workbooks Series Pt. 1: Brachos & Shema. (ENG & HEB., Illus.). 1997. pap., wbk. ed. 8.00 (*1-878895-16-8*, A085) Torah Umesorah.
Birnbaum, Meyer. Pathway to Prayer. 1997. 9.95 (*1-58330-109-7*) Feldheim.
Birnbaum, Michael, et al, eds. Measurement Judgment & Decision Making. 2nd ed. (Handbook of Perception & Cognition Ser.). (Illus.). 367p. 1997. text 85.00 (*0-12-099975-7*) Morgan Kaufmann.
***Birnbaum, Michael H.** Introduction to Behavioral Experimentation on the Internet. LC 00-29673. (Illus.). 2000. write for info. (*0-13-085362-3*) Aspen Law.
— Psychological Experiments on the Internet. LC 99-68195. (Illus.). 352p. 1999. 59.95 (*0-12-099980-3*) Acad Pr.
Birnbaum, Milton. Aldous Huxley's Quest for Values. LC 71-142146. 230p. 1971. 20.00 (*0-87049-127-X*) Lib Soc Sci.
Birnbaum-More, Philip H., et al. International Research Management: Studies in Interdisciplinary Methods from Business, Government & Academia. (Illus.). 232p. 1990. text 80.00 (*0-19-506252-3*) OUP.
Birnbaum, N. Conflicting Interpretations of the Rise of Capitalism: Marx & Weber. (Reprint Series in Social Sciences). (C). 1993. reprint ed. pap. text 5.00 (*0-8290-3702-0*, S-26) Irvington.
***Birnbaum, Norman.** After Progress: American Social Reform & European Socialism In The 20th Century. 432p. 2001. 35.00 (*0-19-512005-1*) OUP.
Birnbaum, Norman. Social Structure & the German Reformation. Zuckerman, Harriet & Merton, Robert K., eds. LC 79-8976. (Dissertation on Sociology Ser.). 1980. lib. bdg. 44.95 (*0-405-12952-1*) Ayer.
Birnbaum, Philip. Encyclopedia of Jewish Concepts. rev. ed. 1979. 29.50 (*0-88482-876-X*); pap. 24.50 (*0-88482-930-8*) Hebrew Pub.
— Five Megilloth. 124p. 1973. pap. 11.50 (*0-88482-380-9*) Hebrew Pub.
— Hasiddur Hashalem (Daily Prayer Book) 790p. 1977. 15.95 (*0-88482-054-8*) Hebrew Pub.
— Hasiddur Hashalem (Daily Prayer Book) Ashkenaz. 790p. 1977. 25.00 (*0-88482-045-9*) Hebrew Pub.
— Hasiddur Hashalem Daily Prayer Book: Sephardic. 860p. 1977. 29.50 (*0-88482-053-X*) Hebrew Pub.
— Mahzor Hashalem: High Holiday Prayer Book, Vol. 1, Rosh Hashahah. 646p. 1988. 24.00 (*0-88482-245-X*) Hebrew Pub.
— Mahzor Hashalem: High Holyday Prayer Book, 5 vols. 1971. 98.00 (*0-88482-169-2*) Hebrew Pub.
— Mahzor Hashalem: High Holyday Prayer Book. 1042p. 1979. 27.00 (*0-88482-240-0*) Hebrew Pub.
— Mahzor Hashalem: High Holyday Prayer Book, 2 vols. 1988. 44.00 (*0-88482-170-6*) Hebrew Pub.
— Mahzor Hashalem: Prayer Book for Pesah, Vol. 4. 459p. 1971. 20.00 (*0-88482-172-2*) Hebrew Pub.
— Mahzor Hashalem: Prayer Book for Shavuot, Vol. 5. 358p. 1971. 20.00 (*0-88482-173-0*) Hebrew Pub.
— Mahzor Hashalem: Prayer Book for Sukkot, Vol. 3. 478p. 1971. 20.00 (*0-88482-174-9*) Hebrew Pub.
— Mahzor Hashalem High Holiday Prayer Book Vol. 2: Yom Kippur. 770p. 1988. 24.00 (*0-88482-247-8*) Hebrew Pub.
— Mahzor Leshalosh Regalim: Prayer Book for Three Festivals. 641p. 1971. 24.50 (*0-88482-149-8*) Hebrew Pub.
— Passover Haggadah - Mini Haggadah. 77p. pap. 2.95 (*0-88482-367-9*) Hebrew Pub.
— Selihot. 63p. pap. 3.50 (*0-88482-344-X*) Hebrew Pub.
— Siddur Leshabbat Veyom Tov: Prayer Book for Sabbath & Festivals. large type ed. 384p. 1978. 29.00 (*0-88482-126-9*) Hebrew Pub.
— Siddur Leshabbat Veyom Tov: Prayer Book for Sabbath & Festivals with Torah Readings. 724p. 1978. 24.50 (*0-88482-062-9*) Hebrew Pub.
Birnbaum, Philip, tr. The Concise Jewish Bible. large type ed. (Large Print Jewish Classics Ser.). 373p. 1991. reprint ed. pap. 16.95 (*0-8027-2644-5*) Walker & Co.
***Birnbaum, Phillip, ed.** Karaite Studies. xii, 318p. 2000. pap. 20.00 (*0-9700775-2-1*, Gan Elden Pr) Karaism.com.
Birnbaum, Phyllis. Modern Girls, Shining Stars, the Skies of Tokyo: Five Japanese Women. LC 98-15268. (Illus.). 240p. 1999. 26.50 (*0-231-11356-0*) Col U Pr.
***Birnbaum, Phyllis.** Modern Girls, Shining Stars, the Skies of Tokyo: Five Japanese Women. 2000. pap. text 14.95 (*0-231-11357-9*) Col U Pr.
Birnbaum, Phyllis, tr. Rabbits, Crabs, Etc. Stories by Japanese Women. LC 82-8365. 160p. 1984. pap. 9.95 (*0-8248-0817-7*) UH Pr.
Birnbaum, Phyllis, tr. see Uno Chiyo.
Birnbaum, Pierre. The Heights of Power: An Essay on the Power Elite in France. Goldhammer, Arthur, tr. from FRE. LC 81-16101. (Illus.). 176p. (C). 1982. pap. text 20.50 (*0-226-05202-8*) U Ch Pr.
— The Heights of Power: An Essay on the Power Elite in France. Goldhammer, Arthur, tr. from FRE. LC 81-16101. (Chicago Original Ser.). 184p. reprint ed. pap. 57.10 (*0-608-09389-0*, 205413400004) Bks Demand.
***Birnbaum, Pierre.** The Idea of France. DeBevoise, M. B., tr. from FRE.Tr. of France Imaginie. 352p. 2001. 30.00 (*0-8090-4650-4*) Hill & Wang.
— Jewish Destinies: Citizenship, State & Community in Modern France. Goldhammer, Arthur, tr. from FRE. LC 99-16275. 288p. 2000. 30.00 (*0-8090-6101-5*) Hill & Wang.
Birnbaum, Pierre. The Jews of the Republic: A Political History of State Jews of France from Gambetta to Vichy. Todd, Jane M., tr. LC 96-10603. (Jewish History & Culture Ser.). 1996. write for info. (*0-8047-2633-7*) Stanford U Pr.
— States & Collective Action: The European Experience. (Illus.). 240p. 1988. text 54.95 (*0-521-32548-X*) Cambridge U Pr.
Birnbaum, Pierre & Katznelson, Ira, eds. Paths of Emancipation: Jews, States, & Citizenship. 320p. 1995. text 59.50 (*0-691-03460-5*, Pub. by Princeton U Pr); pap. text 17.95 (*0-691-03461-3*, Pub. by Princeton U Pr) Cal Prin Full Svc.
Birnbaum, Pierre & Leca, Jean, eds. Individualism: Theories & Methods. Gaffney, John, tr. (Illus.). 348p. 1990. text 95.00 (*0-19-827324-X*) OUP.
Birnbaum, Pierre, jt. auth. see Badie, Bertrand.
Birnbaum, Robert. How Academic Leadership Works: Understanding Success & Failure in the College Presidency. LC 92-8766. (Higher & Adult Education Ser.). 280p. 1992. text 34.45 (*1-55542-466-X*) Jossey-Bass.
— How Colleges Work: The Cybernetics of Academic Organization & Leadership. fac. ed. LC 88-42777. (Jossey-Bass Higher Education Ser.). (Illus.). 275p. 1988. reprint ed. pap. 85.30 (*0-7837-8045-1*, 204779800008) Bks Demand.
— How Colleges Work: The Cybernetics of Academic Organization & Leadership. LC 88-4277. (Higher & Adult Education Ser.). 275p. 1991. reprint ed. pap. text 25.00 (*1-55542-354-X*) Jossey-Bass.
— Maintaining Diversity in Higher Education. LC 83-48156. (Jossey-Bass Higher Education Ser.). 227p. reprint ed. pap. 70.40 (*0-7837-0162-4*, 204045900017) Bks Demand.
***Birnbaum, Robert.** Management Fads in Higher Education: Where They Come From, What They Do, Why They Fail. 320p. 2000. 32.95 (*0-7879-4456-4*) Jossey-Bass.
Birnbaum, Robert, ed. Faculty in Governance: The Role of Senates & Joint Committees in Academic Decision Making. LC 84-644752. (New Directions for Higher Education Ser.: No. HE 75). 1991. pap. 22.00 (*1-55542-771-5*) Jossey-Bass.
Birnbaum, Robert, et al. Cooperation in Academic Negotiations: A Guide to Mutual Gains Bargaining. 70p. 1985. pap. 7.00 (*0-88111-006-X*) Inst Mgmt & Labor.
Birnbaum, Ruth F. & Birnbaum, Harold F. The Prometheus Trilogy. 1978. 10.00 (*0-87291-125-X*) Coronado Pr.
Birnbaum, S. L. & Crawford, G. E. How to Protect Your Company from Product Liability Exposure. 16p. 1984. 2.50 (*0-317-07504-7*) P-H.
Birnbaum, Salomo A. Yiddish: A Survey & a Grammar. LC 80-480492. (Illus.). 415p. reprint ed. pap. 128.70 (*0-8357-6357-9*, 203571100096) Bks Demand.
Birnbaum, Solomon A. The Bar Menasheh Marriage Deed: Its Relation with Other Jewish Marriage Deeds. (Illus.). vi, 26p. 1962. pap. text 17.50 (*0-614-03988-6*, Pub. by Netherlands Inst) Eisenbrauns.
Birnbaum, Stephen. Birnbaum's U. S. A. for Business Travelers, 1986. 1985. pap. 7.95 (*0-685-11176-8*) HM.
— Birnbaum's Walt Disney World for Kids, by Kids, 1999. Safro, Jill & Goytizolo, Suzy, eds. (Birnbaum's Walt Disney World for Kids, by Kids). (Illus.). 160p. (J). (gr. 3-7). 1998. pap. 10.45 (*0-7868-8368-5*, Pub. by Hyperion) Time Warner.
— Birnbaum's Walt Disney World, 1999: Expert Advice from the Inside Source. Safro, Jill & Garrard, Alice, eds. (Illus.). 256p. (J). 1998. pap. 13.95 (*0-7868-8367-7*, Pub. by Hyperion) Time Warner.
— Birnbaum's Walt Disney World without Kids, 1999: Official Guide for Fun-Loving Adults. (Illus.). 224p. (J). 1998. pap. 11.45 (*0-7868-8370-7*, Pub. by Hyperion) Time Warner.
— Canada, 1989. (Birnbaum's Travel Guides Ser.). 624p. 1988. pap. 12.95 (*0-318-35548-5*) HM.
— Caribbean, 1985. (Birnbaum's Travel Guides Ser.). pap. 11.95 (*0-685-42766-8*) HM.
— Disneyland - 1990: The Official Guide. 160p. 1989. pap. 8.95 (*0-380-71003-X*, Avon Bks) Morrow Avon.
— Disneyland, 1991: The Official Guide. 160p. (Orig.). 1990. pap. 8.95 (*0-380-71215-6*, Avon Bks) Morrow Avon.
— United States, 1985. (Birnbaum's Travel Guides Ser.). pap. 11.95 (*0-685-09374-3*) HM.
— United States, 1989. (Birnbaum's Travel Guides Ser.). 1008p. 1988. pap. 12.95 (*0-318-35549-3*) HM.
— Walt Disney World, 1989. 1989. pap. write for info. (*0-318-64763-X*) HM.
— Walt Disney World, 1991: The Official Guide. 240p. (Orig.). 1991. pap. 10.95 (*0-380-71216-4*, Avon Bks) Morrow Avon.
***Birnbaum, Steven M., et al, eds.** The Longshore Textbook. 4th rev. ed. LC 99-33489. 464p. 1999. 85.00 (*0-913875-88-0*, 0861-N) Lawyers & Judges.
Birnbaum Travel Guides Staff. Birnbaum's Disneyland 2000: Expert Advice from the Inside Source. (Illus.). 160p. 1999. pap. 11.95 (*0-7868-8480-0*, Pub. by Hyperion) Time Warner.
— Birnbaum's Walt Disney World: The Official Guide, 1997. (Illus.). 256p. (J). 1996. pap. 12.95 (*0-7868-8192-5*) Hyperion.
— Birnbaum's Walt Disney World For Kids, By Kids 2000: Real Kids Give Honest Advice for the Most Awesome Vacation in the World. 160p. 1999. pap. text 10.95 (*0-7868-8481-9*, Pub. by Hyperion) Time Warner.
— Birnbaum's Walt Disney World 2000: Expert Advice from the Inside Source. LC 93-644493. (Illus.). 256p. 1999. pap. text 13.95 (*0-7868-8483-5*, Pub. by Hyperion) Time Warner.
— Birnbaum's Walt Disney World Without Kids 2000: The Official Guide for Fun-Loving Adults. (Illus.). 224p. 1999. pap. 11.95 (*0-7868-8482-7*, Pub. by Hyperion) Time Warner.
— Birnbaum's Walt Disney World Without Kids: The Official Guide to Fun-Loving Adults, 1997. (Illus.). 224p. (J). 1996. pap. 10.95 (*0-7868-8194-1*) Hyperion.
Birnbaum, William S. If Your Strategy Is So Terrific, How Come It Doesn't Work? LC 90-55199. 250p. reprint ed. pap. 77.50 (*0-7837-7060-X*, 204687200004) Bks Demand.
***Birnbaum, William S. & Dunne, Stephen M.** Oral Diagnosis: The Clinician's Guide. (Illus.). 314p. 2000. pap. 35.00 (*0-7236-1040-1*) Buttrwrth-Heinemann.
Birnbaum, Yochai, jt. auth. see Kloner, Robert A.

B

Birnbaum, Yochai, jt. ed. see Kloner, Robert.

Birnbaumer. Emergency Medicine. 2000. pap. text. write for info. (*0-7216-6452-0*, W B Saunders Co) Harcrt Hlth Sci Grp.

Birnbaumer, Lutz, ed. see Aktories, K., et al.

Birnberg, Howard G. Project Management for Building Designers & Owners. 2nd ed. LC 98-17157. 256p. 1998. boxed set 54.95 (*0-8493-1265-5*) CRC Pr.

Birner, Betty J. & Ward, Gregory L. Information Status & Noncanonical Word Order in English. LC 98-6210. (Studies in Language Companion Ser.: Vol. 40). xiv, 314p. (C). 1998. 69.00 (*1-55619-926-0*) J Benjamins Pubng Co.

Birner, Louis. Get Creative No Depressed. LC 98-89505. 375p. 1998. text 25.00 (*0-7388-0229-8*); pap. text 15.00 (*0-7388-0230-1*) Xlibris Corp.

Birner, Regina. The Role of Livestock in Agricultural Development: Theoretical Approaches & Their Applications in the Case of Sri Lanka. LC 98-74760. 336p. 1999. text 74.95 (*1-84014-871-3*) Ashgate Pub Co.

Birnes, William J. The Apple Megabook. 1985. pap. 12.95 (*0-671-54386-5*) S&S Trade.

***Birnes, William J. & Burtt, Harold E.** Unsolved UFO Mysteries: Twenty Compelling Cases of Alien Encounter. 2000. mass mkt. 6.50 (*0-446-60901-3*, Aspect) Warner Bks.

Birnes, William J., jt. auth. see Corso, Philip J.

Birnes, William J., jt. auth. see Keppel, Robert D.

Birnes, William J., jt. auth. see Mastrich, James L.

Birnes, William J., jt. auth. see Phillips, Ethan.

Birney, Alice. The Literary Lives of Jesus: An International Bibliography. LC 88-24727. 224p. 1989. text 15.00 (*0-8240-8475-6*) Garland.

Birney, Betty. Let's Play Hide & Seek! (Lift-the-Flap Bk.). (Illus.). 24p. (J). (ps). 1997. bds. 9.95 (*0-590-92960-7*) Scholastic Inc.

— Oh, Bother! Someone Won't Share. (Look-Look Bks.). (Illus.). 24p. (J). (ps-3). 1993. pap. 3.29 (*0-307-12766-4*, 12766) Gldn Bks Pub Co.

— Oh, Bother! Someone's Afraid of the Dark! LC 97-225449. (Look-Look Bks.). (Illus.). 24p. (J). (ps-3). 1994. 3.29 (*0-307-12843-1*, 12843) Gldn Bks Pub Co.

— Oh, Bother! Someone's Grumpy. LC 98-102593. (Look-Look Bks.). (Illus.). 24p. (J). (ps-3). 1997. 3.29 (*0-307-12667-6*, 12667, Goldn Books) Gldn Bks Pub Co.

— Oh, Bother! Someone's Jealous. LC PZ7.B52285Sog 1997. (Look-Look Bks.). (Illus.). 24p. (J). (ps-3). 1997. 3.29 (*0-307-12820-2*, 12820, Goldn Books) Gldn Bks Pub Co.

— Oh, Bother! Someone's Messy. LC 98-102581. (Look-Look Bks.). (Illus.). 24p. (J). (ps-3). 1997. 3.29 (*0-307-12690-0*, 12690, Goldn Books) Gldn Bks Pub Co.

— Snowy Day. (Golden Look-Look Ser.). 24p. (J). 1998. pap. 3.29 (*0-307-13156-4*, 13156, Goldn Books) Gldn Bks Pub Co.

— Who Am I? (Riddle Flap Bks.). (Illus.). 16p. (J). (ps). 1992. pap. 5.95 (*0-671-76914-6*) Litle Simon.

— Winnie the Pooh: The Merry Christmas Mystery. (Look-Look Bks.). (J). (ps-3). 1993. pap. 3.29 (*0-307-12774-5*, 12774) Gldn Bks Pub Co.

Birney, Betty, retold by. Toy Story. (Look-Look Bks.). (Illus.). 24p. (J). (ps-3). 1995. pap. 3.29 (*0-307-12908-X*, 12908, Goldn Books) Gldn Bks Pub Co.

Birney, Betty & Fulton, Mary J. Oh, Bother! Someone's Baby-Sitting. LC 98-102599. (Look-Look Bks.). (Illus.). (J). (ps-3). 1997. 3.29 (*0-307-12634-X*, 12634, Goldn Books) Gldn Bks Pub Co.

— Oh Bother! Someone's Fibbing. LC 98-102595. (Look-Look Bks.). (Illus.). 24p. (J). (ps-3). 1997. 3.29 (*0-307-12636-6*, 12636, Goldn Books) Gldn Bks Pub Co.

— Oh, Bother! Someone's Fighting. LC 98-102548. (Look-Look Bks.). (Illus.). (J). (ps-3). 1997. 3.29 (*0-307-12635-8*, 12635, Goldn Books) Gldn Bks Pub Co.

Birney, Betty G. Tyrannosaurus Rex. LC 93-30727. (Illus.). 32p. (J). (ps-3). 1996. pap. 7.95 (*0-395-81654-8*) HM.

— Tyrannosaurus Tex. LC 93-30727. (Illus.). 32p. (J). 1994. 14.95 (*0-395-67648-7*) HM.

— Tyrannosaurus Tex. LC 93-30727. 1994. 11.15 (*0-606-10960-9*, Pub. by Turtleback) Demco.

***Birney, Bill & Michalakias, John.** Microsoft Windows Movie Maker Handbook. 336p. 2000. 29.99 (*0-7356-1180-7*) Microsoft.

Birney, Catherine H. The Grimke Sisters. (History - United States Ser.). 319p. 1992. reprint ed. lib. bdg. 89.00 (*0-7812-6159-7*) Rprt Serv.

— Grimke Sisters: Sarah & Angelina Grimke, the First American Women Advocates of Abolition & Women's Rights. LC 69-13828. 319p. 1970. reprint ed. lib. bdg. 38.50 (*0-8371-1303-2*, BIGS, Greenwood Pr) Greenwood.

— Grimke Sisters, Sarah & Angelina Grimke: The First America Women Advocates of Abolition & Women's Rights. LC 70-108461. 1970. reprint ed. 13.00 (*0-403-00230-3*) Scholarly.

— Grimke Sisters, Sarah & Angelina Grimke: The First American Women Advocates of Abolition & Women's Rights. LC 68-24971. (American Biography Ser.: No. 32). 1969. reprint ed. lib. bdg. 75.00 (*0-8383-0912-7*) M S G Haskell Hse.

Birney, Earle. Big Bird in the Bush: Stories & Sketches. (Illus.). (J). 1990. pap. 9.95 (*0-88962-068-7*) Mosaic.

— Essays on Chaucerian Irony. Rowland, Beryl, ed. LC 86-182313. 192p. reprint ed. pap. 59.60 (*0-8357-3633-4*, 203636100003) Bks Demand.

— Last Makings. LC 91-167607. 1991. pap. 14.95 (*0-7710-1471-6*) McCland & Stewart.

— Turvey. 360p. 1996. pap. text 8.95 (*0-7710-9953-3*) McCland & Stewart.

Birney, Elmer C. Systematics of Three Species of Woodrats (Genus Neotom) in Central North America. (Miscellaneous Publications: No. 58). 173p. 1973. 9.00 (*0-317-04956-9*) U KS Nat Hist Mus.

Birney, Elmer C., jt. auth. see Jones, J. Knox, Jr.

Birney, James G. American Churches: The Bulwarks of American Slavery. LC 79-82174. (Anti-Slavery Crusade in America Ser.). 1975. reprint ed. 16.95 (*0-405-00611-X*) Ayer.

— Collection of Valuable Documents, Being Birney's Vindication of Abolitionists. reprint ed. 27.50 (*0-404-00247-1*) AMS Pr.

— Letter on the Political Obligations of Abolitionists, by James G. Birney: With a Reply by William Lloyd Garrison. LC 71-82172. (Anti-Slavery Crusade in America Ser.). 1969. reprint ed. 7.50 (*0-405-00613-6*) Ayer.

— Letters, 1831-1857, Vols. 1 & 2. Dumond, Dwight L., ed. 1990. 29.00 (*0-8446-1078-X*) Peter Smith.

Birney, James G., ed. Correspondence Between the Honorable F. H. Elmore & James G. Birney. LC 75-82173. (Anti-Slavery Crusade in America Ser.). 1970. reprint ed. 17.95 (*0-405-00612-8*) Ayer.

Birney, William. James G. Birney & His Times: The Genesis of the Republican Party with Some Account of Abolition Movements in the South Before 1828. LC 71-77190. 443p. 1969. reprint ed. lib. bdg. 59.50 (*0-8371-1313-X*, BIB&) Greenwood.

Birngruber, R. & Gabel, V. P., eds. Laser Treatment & Photocoagulation of the Eye. (Documenta Ophthalmologica Proceedings Ser.). 1984. text 225.00 (*90-6193-732-9*) Kluwer Academic.

Birngruber, Reginald, et al, eds. Lasers in Ophthalmology IV, Vol. 2930. (Europto Ser.). 238p. 1996. 66.00 (*0-8194-2332-7*) SPIE.

Birnhack, Sarah. One Day & Forever: A Novel. 1993. 16.99 (*0-89906-133-8*); 13.99 (*0-89906-143-5*) Mesorah Pubns.

— Search My Heart: A Novel. 308p. 1986. 14.00 (*0-940118-66-1*) Moznaim.

Birnhack, Sarah, ed. see Malach, Atara.

Birnham, Robert. Creative Academic Bargaining: Managing Conflict in the Unionized College & University. LC 80-18806. 288p. reprint ed. pap. 89.30 (*0-8357-2763-7*, 203988800014) Bks Demand.

Birnholz, Mary B., et al. Fast Fat Facts: The Percentage of Calories from Fat Guide. Meitam, Carol & Mansell, Mary, eds. LC 94-94280. (Illus.). 75p. (Orig.). 1994. pap. 10.00 (*0-9641232-0-7*) Athene Bks.

Birnie, Dianna. North American Trade Guide 1999. 2072p. 1998. pap. 475.00 (*1-891131-02-8*) Primedia Directories.

Birnie, Dianna & Moran-Lever, Tery, eds. North American Trade Guide: 1998 Edition. (ISSN Ser.: No. 1071-958X). (Illus.). 2056p. 1997. pap. text 419.00 (*0-9649630-7-8*) Primedia Directories.

Birnie, Esmond & Hitchens, David M. The Northern Ireland Economy: Performance, Prospects & Policy. LC HC257.N58B57 1999. 210p. 1999. text 65.95 (*1-84014-848-9*) Ashgate Pub Co.

Birnie, J. E., jt. auth. see Hitchins, D. M.

Birnie, J. E., ed. see Hitchens, D. M. & Wagner, K.

Birnie, Jane, ed. Three Rivers Cookbook, Vol. Three. (Illus.). 254p. 1990. vinyl bd. 14.95 (*0-9607634-2-2*) T Rivers Cookbook.

Birnie, Patricia & Boyle, Alan. International Environmental Law. 590p. 1993. pap. text 48.00 (*0-19-876283-6*) OUP.

— International Law & the Environment. 576p. 2000. text 98.00 (*0-19-876552-5*); pap. text 49.95 (*0-19-876553-3*) OUP.

Birnie, Patricia, jt. auth. see Boyle, Alan.

Birnie, Shelley, jt. auth. see Coward, Sylvia.

***Birnios, Baltazar & Birnios, Mariano.** MS Visual Basic 6.0 - Manual de Referencia en Espanol - Spanish con CD-ROM: Manual de Referencia del Lenguaje mas Utilizado al Alcance. (SPA., Illus.). 617p. 1999. pap. 29.90 incl. cd-rom (*987-526-018-5*, Pub. by MP Ediciones) Am Wholesale.

***Birnios, Baltazer & Birnios, Mariano.** Creacion de Aplicaciones Multimedia con Visual Basic con CD-ROM en Espanol: Desarrollo Desde Cero de un Proyecto Completo Multimedial. (Manuales PC Users Ser.). (SPA., Illus.). 308p. 1999. pap. 19.90 incl. cd-rom (*987-9131-85-1*, Pub. by MP Ediciones) Am Wholesale.

Birnios, Mariano, jt. auth. see Birnios, Baltazar.

Birnios, Mariano, jt. auth. see Birnios, Baltazer.

Birnkrant, Sam. Mama, Say I Do: (A Whisper in God's Ear), a 3-Act Comedy. (Illus.). 58p. 1970. pap. 4.00 (*0-88680-126-5*) I E Clark.

Birns, B. & Hay, D. The Different Faces of Motherhood. LC 88-16878. (Perspectives in Developmental Psychology Ser.). (Illus.). 312p. (C). 1988. 54.50 (*0-306-42887-3*, Plenum Trade) Perseus Pubng.

Biro, Adam & Passeron, Rene. Dictionnaire General de Surrealisme et de ses Environs. (FRE.). 468p. 1982. 150.00 (*0-8288-9530-9*) Fr & Eur.

— General Dictionary of Surrealism: Dictionnaire General du Surrealisme et de Ses Environs. (FRE.). 468p. 1982. 135.00 (*0-8288-1416-3*, F30200) Fr & Eur.

Biro, Brian D. Beyond Success: The 15 Secrets of a Winning Life! (Illus.). 368p. 1995. 24.00 (*0-9647453-0-5*) Pygmalion MT.

— Beyond Success: The 15 Secrets of a Winning Life! 2nd ed. LC 96-53664. (Illus.). 384p. 1997. pap. 14.95 (*0-9647453-2-1*); pap. 14.95 (*0-9647453-1-3*) Pygmalion MT.

— The Joyful Spirit! How to Become the Happiest Person You Know. LC 97-36377. 200p. 1998. pap. 14.00 (*0-9647453-3-X*) Pygmalion MT.

Biro, Charles, jt. auth. see Harvey, R. C.

Biro, Charlotte S. Flavors of Hungary. 3rd ed. (One Hundred One Productions Ser.). 192p. (Orig.). 1992. pap. 11.95 (*1-56426-502-1*, One Hund One Prods) Cole Group.

***Biro, David.** One Hundred Days: My Unexpected Journey from Doctor to Patient. LC 99-34956. 304p. 2000. 23.00 (*0-375-40715-4*) Pantheon.

Biro, J. I. & Shahan, Robert W. Mind, Brain & Function: Essays in the Philosophy of Mind. LC 81-40296. 208p. 1982. 29.95 (*0-8061-1783-4*) U of Okla Pr.

Biro, John, et al, eds. Frege: Sense & Reference Once Hundred Years Later. (Philosophical Studies: Vol. 65). 224p. (C). 1995. text 132.50 (*0-7923-3795-6*) Kluwer Academic.

Biro, Lajos & Cohen, Marc J., eds. The United States in Crisis: Marxist Analysis. LC 78-61686. (Studies in Marxism: Vol. 4). 245p. 1979. 8.95 (*0-930656-08-3*); pap. 3.00 (*0-930656-07-5*) MEP Pubns.

Biro, Matthew. Anselm Kiefer & the Philosophy of Martin Heidegger. LC 98-20892. (Contemporary Artists & Their Critics Ser.). (Illus.). 336p. (C). 1998. text 75.00 (*0-521-59170-8*) Cambridge U Pr.

***Biro, Matthew.** Anselm Kiefer & the Philosophy of Martin Heidegger. (Contemporary Artists & Their Critics Ser.). (Illus.). 336p. (C). 2000. pap. 27.95 (*0-521-59834-6*) Cambridge U Pr.

Biro, Maureen, ed. see Griggs, Rick.

Biro, P. & Talling, J. F., eds. Trophic Relationships in Inland Waters. (Developments in Hydrobiology Ser.). (C). 1990. lib. bdg. 236.00 (*0-7923-0414-4*) Kluwer Academic.

Biro, P., jt. auth. see Salanki, J.

Biro-Ripeau. To Dress a Nude: Exercises In Imagination. LC 99-177614. 192p. (C). 1998. per. 31.95 (*0-7872-4219-5*, 41421901) Kendall-Hunt.

Biro, T. S., et al. Chaos & Gauge Field Theory. (Lecture Notes in Physics Ser.: Vol. 56). 300p. 1995. text 61.00 (*981-02-2079-0*) World Scientific Pub.

Biro, V. Nonlinear Oscillation in Feedback Systems. 208p. (C). 1985. 140.00 (*963-05-3425-8*, Pub. by Akade Kiado) St Mut.

— Nonlinear Oscillations in Feedback Systems. 208p. (C). 1985. 160.00 (*0-7855-4971-4*, Pub. by Collets) St Mut.

Biro, Val. The Donkey That Sneezed. (J). write for info. (*0-19-272275-1*) OUP.

— The Donkey That Sneezed. LC 98-60510. (Illus.). 32p. (J). (gr. 1-3). 1998. pap. 4.99 (*1-887734-47-3*) Star Brght Bks.

Biro, Val. Gumdrop & the Bulldozer. (Illus.). (J). text 22.95 (*0-340-71444-1*, Pub. by Hodder & Stought Ltd); mass mkt. 11.95 (*0-340-71445-X*, Pub. by Hodder & Stought Ltd) Trafalgar.

— Gumdrop & the Martians. (Illus.). (J). text 22.95 (*0-340-71485-9*, Pub. by Hodder & Stought Ltd) Trafalgar.

— Gumdrop & the Monster. (Illus.). (J). text 22.95 (*0-340-71446-8*, Pub. by Hodder & Stought Ltd); mass mkt. 11.95 (*0-340-71447-6*, Pub. by Hodder & Stought Ltd) Trafalgar.

— Gumdrop Forever. (Illus.). (J). text 22.95 (*0-340-71448-4*, Pub. by Hodder & Stought Ltd); pap. text 11.95 (*0-340-71449-2*, Pub. by Hodder & Stought Ltd) Trafalgar.

— Gumdrops & the Elephant. (Illus.). (J). text 22.95 (*0-340-71442-5*, Pub. by Hodder & Stought Ltd); pap. text 11.95 (*0-340-71443-3*, Pub. by Hodder & Stought Ltd) Trafalgar.

— Gumdrop's Magic Journey. (Illus.). (J). text 22.95 (*0-340-71455-7*, Pub. by Hodder & Stought Ltd); pap. text 11.95 (*0-340-71441-7*, Pub. by Hodder & Stought Ltd) Trafalgar.

Biro, Val. The Hobyahs. (J). write for info. (*0-19-272278-6*) OUP.

— The Hobyahs. LC 98-60914. (Val Biro Bks.). (Illus.). 32p. (J). (gr. 1-3). 1998. pap. 4.99 (*1-887734-44-9*) Star Brght Bks.

— Hungarian Folk-Tales. (Oxford Myths & Legends Ser.). (J). 1992. 18.05 (*0-606-05365-4*, Pub. by Turtleback) Demco.

— Jack & the Robbers. (J). write for info. (*0-19-272274-3*) OUP.

— Lazy Jack. (Illus.). 32p. (J). 1995. (*0-19-279956-8*) OUP.

— The Three Billy Goats Gruff. (J). write for info. (*0-19-272280-8*) OUP.

— The Three Billy Goats Gruff. LC 98-60512. (Illus.). 32p. (J). (gr. 1-3). 1998. pap. 4.99 (*1-887734-46-5*) Star Brght Bks.

Biro, Val. Hungarian Folk-Tales. (Oxford Myths & Legends Ser.). 192p. (YA). (gr. 4 up). 1992. pap. 12.95 (*0-19-274148-9*) OUP.

Biroli, Marco, ed. Potential Theory & Degenerate Partial Differential Operators. LC 95-37538. 1995. text 99.50 (*0-7923-3596-1*) Kluwer Academic.

Birolini, A. On the Use of Stochastic Processes in Modeling Reliability Problems. (Lecture Notes in Economics & Mathematical Systems Ser.: Vol. 252). (Illus.). vi, 105p. 1985. 29.50 (*0-387-15699-2*) Spr-Verlag.

— Quality & Reliability of Technical Systems: Theory, Practice & Management. Podaras, C., tr. from GER. xiii, 524p. 1994. 135.95 (*0-387-50603-9*) Spr-Verlag.

— Quality & Reliability of Technical Systems: Theory, Practice & Management. LC 94-7744. 1994. write for info. (*0-387-57569-3*) Spr-Verlag.

Birolini, Alessandro. Quality & Reliability of Technical Systems: Theory, Practice & Management. 2nd ed. LC 97-27839. (Illus.). xiii, 502p. 1997. 129.00 (*3-540-63310-3*) Spr-Verlag.

***Birolini, Alessandro.** Reliability Engineering: Theory & Practice. 3rd ed. LC 99-44341. Orig. Title: Quality & Reliability of Technical Systems. (Illus.). 500p. 1999. 119.00 (*3-540-66385-1*) Spr-Verlag.

Biron, jt. auth. see Koike.

Biron, Armand D. The Letters & Documents of Armand De Gontaut, Baron De Biron, Marshal of France, 1524-1592, 2 vols., Set. Ehrman, Sidney H., ed. LC 76-29405. reprint ed. 82.50 (*0-404-15351-8*) AMS Pr.

Biron, Armand L. Memoirs of the Duc de Lauzun. 1969. 18.95 (*0-405-01158-X*, 13254) Ayer.

Biron, Cemal. Design of Supports in Mines. 270p. 1987. text 45.95 (*0-471-86726-8*) Krieger.

Biron, Henry C. & Chalmers, Kenneth E. The Law & Practice of Extradition. xv, 432p. 1981. reprint ed. lib. bdg. 58.00 (*0-8377-0315-8*, Rothman) W S Hein.

Biron, Joce-Lyne. Vocabulary of Education. 2nd ed. (ENG & FRE.). 229p. 1988. pap. 39.95 (*0-8288-9390-X*) Fr & Eur.

Biron, Paul J. Terminology of Water Supply & Environmental Sanitation: A World Bank-UNICEF Glossary. 176p. 1987. pap. 24.00 (*0-8213-0585-9*, 10585) World Bank.

***Biron, Rebecca E.** Murder & Masculinity: Violent Fictions of Twentieth-Century Latin America. LC 99-6496. 192p. 1999. 45.00 (*0-8265-1342-5*) Vanderbilt U Pr.

Biron, Rebecca E. Murder & Masculinity: Violent Fictions of Twentieth Century Latin America. LC 99-6497. 192p. 1999. pap. 21.95 (*0-8265-1347-6*) Vanderbilt U Pr.

Biros, Florence K. Dog Jack. 2nd ed. (Illus.). (Orig.). (YA). (gr. 5 up). 1990. pap. 9.95 (*0-936369-47-7*) Son-Rise Pubns.

Biros, Florence K., jt. auth. see Lacho, Lubomir.

Biros, Florence K., ed. see Carr, Marc.

Biros, Florence K., ed. see Conningham, Jewell.

Biros, Florence K., ed. see Whitten, Beryle E.

Biros, Florence W., et al. Crossing Paths Treasury, Vol. 1. McKenna, Judy, ed. (Illus.). 240p. 1998. pap. 12.95 (*0-936369-99-X*) Son-Rise Pubns.

Birosik, P. J. The Burrito Book. 160p. (Orig.). 1991. pap. 8.95 (*0-380-76428-8*, Avon Bks) Morrow Avon.

— Salsa. LC 92-35699. 134p. 1993. pap. 10.00 (*0-02-041641-5*, Pub. by Macmillan) S&S Trade.

Birou, Alain. Lexico de Sociologia. 5th ed. (SPA.). 114p. 1975. pap. 14.95 (*0-8288-5914-0*, S50041) Fr & Eur.

— Vocabulaire Pratique des Sciences Sociales. (FRE.). 384p. 49.95 (*0-686-57277-7*, F136960); 49.95 (*0-8288-7617-7*, F136960) Fr & Eur.

Birou, Laura M. & Ellram, Lisa M. Purchasing for Bottom Line Impact: Improving the Organization Through Strategic Procurement. 240p. 1995. pap. 45.00 (*0-7863-0217-8*, Irwn Prfssnl) McGraw-Hill Prof.

Birr, Kendall, jt. auth. see Curti, Merle E.

Birr, Kendall A. A Tradition of Excellence: The Sesquicentennial History of the University at Albany, 1884 to 1994. LC 94-2894. 1994. write for info. (*0-89865-889-6*) Donning Co.

***Birr, Tim.** Public & Media Relations for the Fire Service. LC 98-48123. 156p. 1998. pap. 32.50 (*0-912212-79-9*) Fire Eng.

Birr, Ursula, et al. Dog's Best Friend: Journey to the Roots of an Ancient Partnership. LC 99-14170. (Illus.). 144p. 1999. 19.95 (*0-89281-829-8*, Park St Pr) Inner Tradit.

Birr, Uschi. Beautiful Cats: The Most Popular Breeds. LC 97-50631. (Illus.). 96p. 1998. 12.95 (*0-8069-9993-4*) Sterling.

— A Cat in the Family. (Illus.). 64p. 1997. 12.95 (*0-7938-0206-7*, WW-040) TFH Pubns.

— The Shoshone. LC 96-49702. (Junior Library of the Indians of North America). 76p. (J). (gr. 3 up). 1997. pap. 19.95 (*0-7910-4601-X*, Chelsea Juniors) Chelsea Hse.

***Birrell, Anne.** Chinese Myths. LC 00-39296. (Legendary Past Ser.). (Illus.). 80p. 2000. pap. 14.95 (*0-292-70879-3*) U of Tex Pr.

— Classic of Mountains & Seas. (Classics Ser.). 336p. 2000. pap. 13.95 (*0-14-044719-9*, Penguin Classics) Viking Penguin.

Birrell, Anne. Popular Songs & Ballads of Han China. 370p. 1988. 39.95 (*0-04-895028-9*) Routledge.

— Popular Songs & Ballads of Han China. LC 93-18715. 240p. (C). 1993. reprint ed. pap. text 15.00 (*0-8248-1548-3*) UH Pr.

Birrell, Anne M. Chinese Mythology: An Introduction. 1999. pap. text 18.95 (*0-8018-6183-7*) Johns Hopkins.

Birrell, Augustine. Andrew Marvell. LC 77-39666. (Select Bibliographies Reprint Ser.). 1977. reprint ed. 17.95 (*0-8369-9929-0*) Ayer.

— Collected Essays & Addresses, Eighteen Eighty to Nineteen Twenty, 3 Vols., Set. LC 68-24844. (Essay Index Reprint Ser.). 1977. 66.95 (*0-8369-0214-9*) Ayer.

— Essays about Men, Women & Books. (BCL1-PR English Literature Ser.). 24p. 1992. reprint ed. lib. bdg. 79.00 (*0-7812-7437-0*) Rprt Serv.

— Essays & Addresses. LC 75-104998. (Essay Index Reprint Ser.). 1977. 21.95 (*0-8369-1451-1*) Ayer.

— Et Cetera: A Collection. LC 72-167310. (Essay Index Reprint Ser.). 1977. reprint ed. 20.95 (*0-8369-2453-3*) Ayer.

— Et Cetera: A Collection. (BCL1-PR English Literature Ser.). 277p. 1992. reprint ed. lib. bdg. 79.00 (*0-7812-7438-9*) Rprt Serv.

— In the Name of the Bodleian: And Other Essays. LC 70-177952. (Essay Index Reprint Ser.). 1977. reprint ed. 19.95 (*0-8369-2893-8*) Ayer.

— Life of Charlotte Bronte. Robertson, E. S., ed. LC 78-148752. reprint ed. 32.50 (*0-404-08726-4*) AMS Pr.

— More Obiter Dicta. LC 68-57304. (Essay Index Reprint Ser.). 1977. 19.95 (*0-8369-0062-6*) Ayer.

— More Obiter Dicta. (BCL1-PR English Literature Ser.). 212p. 1992. reprint ed. lib. bdg. 79.00 (*0-7812-7439-7*) Rprt Serv.

— Obiter Dicta. LC 17-21084. (First & Second Ser.). 1969. reprint ed. 9.00 (*0-403-00131-5*) Scholarly.

An Asterisk (*) at the beginning of an entry indicates that the title is appearing for the first time.

— Seven Lectures on the Law & History of Copyright in Books. 228p. 1971. reprint ed. 35.00 (*0-8377-1929-1*, Rothman) W S Hein.

— William Hazlitt. (BCL1-PR English Literature Ser.). 244p. 1992. reprint ed. lib. bdg. 79.00 (*0-7812-7557-1*) Rprt Serv.

Birrell, Derek & Murie, Alan. Policy & Government in Northern Ireland: Lessons of Devolution. LC 79-53790. 353p. 1980. 50.00 (*0-389-20019-0*, 06348) B&N Imports.

Birrell, Francis, tr. see Diderot, Denis.

Birrell, Jean, tr. see Bois, Guy.

Birrell, Jean, tr. see Corbin, Alain.

Birrell, Jean, tr. see Duby.

Birrell, Jean, tr. see Duby, Georges.

Birrell, Jean, tr. see Richard, Jean.

Birrell, Jean, tr. see Roche, Daniel.

Birrell, Jean, tr. see Vauchez, Andre.

Birrell, N. D. & Ould, Martyn A. A Practical Handbook for Software Development. (Illus.). 272p. 1988. pap. text 37.95 (*0-521-34792-0*) Cambridge U Pr.

Birrell, Susan & Cole, Cheryl L., eds. Women, Sport, & Culture. LC 93-38013. 416p. 1994. text 42.00 (*0-87322-650-X*, BBIR0650) Human Kinetics.

***Birrell, Susan & McDonald, Mary G., eds.** Reading Sport: Critical Essays on Power & Representation. LC 99-88217. 304p. 2000. text 50.00 (*1-55553-430-9*); pap. text 20.00 (*1-55553-429-5*) NE U Pr.

Birrell, T. A. The Library of John Morris: The Reconstruction of a Seventeenth-Century Collection LC 77-362673. xxiv, 83 p. 1976. write for info. (*0-7141-0365-9*) BRI5.

Birren, Bruce, et al, eds. Analyzing DNA. (Genome Analysis Ser.: Vol. 1). (Illus.). 675p. (C). 1997. text, lab manual ed. 230.00 (*0-87969-495-5*); pap. text, lab manual ed. 140.00 (*0-87969-496-3*) Cold Spring Harbor.

— Cloning Systems: A Laboratory Manual. (Genome Analysis Ser.: No. 3). (Illus.). 650p. (C). 1998. text 230.00 (*0-87969-512-9*); pap. text 140.00 (*0-87969-513-7*) Cold Spring Harbor.

— Detecting Genes: A Laboratory Manual. LC 97-17117. (Genome Analysis Ser.: No. 2). (Illus.). 463p. (C). 1998. text, lab manual ed. 230.00 (*0-87969-510-2*); pap. text, lab manual ed. 140.00 (*0-87969-511-0*) Cold Spring Harbor.

— Mapping Genomes: A Laboratory Manual. (Genome Analysis Ser.: No. 4). (Illus.). 650p. (C). 1998. text 230.00 (*0-87969-514-5*); pap. text 140.00 (*0-87969-515-3*) Cold Spring Harbor.

Birren, Bruce W. & Lai, Eric. Pulsed Field Gel Electrophoresis: A Practical Guide. (Illus.). 272p. 1993. pap. 34.00 (*0-12-101290-5*) Acad Pr.

Birren, Bruce W. & Lai, Eric, eds. Nonmammalian Genomes Analysis: A Practical Guide. (Illus.). 353p. 1996. pap. text 39.95 (*0-12-101285-9*, QH445) Acad Pr.

Birren, Bruce W., jt. ed. see Lai, Eric.

Birren, Faber. Color: A Survey in Words & Pictures. (Illus.). 256p. 1984. reprint ed. pap. 14.95 (*0-8065-0849-3*, Citadel Pr) Carol Pub Group.

— Color & Human Response. LC 77-12505. (Illus.). 120p. 1978. pap. 29.95 (*0-442-20961-4*, VNR) Wiley.

Birren, Faber. Color & Human Response: Aspects of Light & Color Bearing on the Reactions of Living Things & the Welfare of Human Beings. 168p. 1984. pap. 34.95 (*0-471-28864-0*, VNR) Wiley.

Birren, Faber. Color Perception in Art. LC 86-61199. (Illus.). 88p. 1986. pap. 14.95 (*0-88740-064-7*) Schiffer.

— Color Psychology & Color Therapy. (Illus.). 302p. 1984. pap. 12.95 (*0-8065-0653-9*, Citadel Pr) Carol Pub Group.

— Creative Color. LC 87-60000. (Illus.). 128p. 1987. pap. 19.95 (*0-88740-096-5*) Schiffer.

— Light, Color & Environment. rev. ed. LC 88-61470. (Illus.). 128p. 1988. pap. 24.95 (*0-88740-131-7*) Schiffer.

— The Power of Color: How It Can Reduce Fatigue, Relieve Monotony, Enhance Sexuality, & More. LC 96-49751. 320p. 1997. pap. 14.95 (*0-8065-1857-X*, Citadel Pr) Carol Pub Group.

— Principles of Color. rev. ed. LC 88-61471. (Illus.). 96p. 1987. pap. 14.95 (*0-88740-103-1*) Schiffer.

— The Symbolism of Color: The Beauty & Magic of Color Has Been a Vital Part of Living, Religion & Mysticism. (Illus.). 196p. (gr. 9-12). 1988. 15.95 (*0-8065-1099-4*, Citadel Pr); pap. 7.95 (*0-8065-1109-5*, Citadel Pr) Carol Pub Group.

Birren, Faber, ed. see Itten, Johannes.

Birren, James E. Where to Go from Here: Discovering Your Own Life's Wisdom in the Second Half of Your Life. LC 97-22499. 160p. 1997. 21.50 (*0-684-83057-4*) S&S Trade.

Birren, James E., ed. Encyclopedia of Gerontology, Vol. 1. LC 95-47195. (Illus.). 1996. text 175.00 (*0-12-226861-X*) Acad Pr.

— Encyclopedia of Gerontology, Vol. 2. LC 95-47195. (Illus.). 1996. text 175.00 (*0-12-226862-8*) Acad Pr.

— Encyclopedia of Gerontology: Age, Aging & the Aged, 2 vols. LC 95-47195. (Illus.). 1474p. 1996. text 350.00 (*0-12-226860-1*) Acad Pr.

Birren, James E., et al, eds. Aging & Biography: Explorations in Adult Development. (Illus.). 368p. 1995. 52.95 (*0-8261-8980-6*) Springer Pub.

— The Concept & Measurement of Quality of Life in the Frail Elderly. (Illus.). 385p. (C). 1991. text 64.95 (*0-12-101275-1*) Acad Pr.

— Handbook of Mental Health & Aging. 2nd ed. (Illus.). 996p. 1992. text 69.95 (*0-12-101277-8*) Acad Pr.

— Handbook of the Psychology of Aging. 4th ed. LC 95-19905. (Handbooks of Aging Ser.). (Illus.). 416p. 1996. text 69.95 (*0-12-101260-3*); pap. text 49.95 (*0-12-101261-1*) Acad Pr.

— Human Aging. LC 79-8658. (Growing Old Ser.). (Illus.). 1980. reprint ed. lib. bdg. 33.95 (*0-405-12776-6*) Ayer.

— Metaphors of Aging in Science & the Humanities. LC 91-12798. 272p. (C). 1991. text 33.95 (*0-8261-7440-X*) Springer Pub.

Birren, James E. & Deutchman, Donna E. Guiding Autobiography Groups for Older Adults: Exploring the Fabric of Life. LC 90-15625. (Series in Contemporary Medicine & Public Health). 176p. 1991. pap. text 18.95 (*0-8018-4213-1*) Johns Hopkins.

***Birren, James E. & Schroots, Johannes J. F., eds.** A History of Geropsychology in Autobiography. LC 99-51564. 400p. 1999. pap. 29.95 (*1-55798-631-2*, 431740A) Am Psychol.

Birren, James E. & Stein, Leon, eds. Relations of Development & Aging. LC 79-8659. (Growing Old Ser.). (Illus.). 1980. reprint ed. lib. bdg. 30.95 (*0-405-12775-8*) Ayer.

Birren, James E., et al. Age, Health & Employment. 192p. (C). 1986. text 49.00 (*0-13-018524-8*) P-H.

Birren, James E., jt. auth. see Welford, A. T.

Birrer, Christina D., jt. auth. see Birrer, Richard B.

Birrer, G. Eddy & Carrica, Jean L. Present Value Applications for Accountants & Financial Planners. LC 89-10218. 148p. 1990. 55.00 (*0-89930-307-2*, BPI/, Greenwood Pr) Greenwood.

Birrer, R., ed. Urban Family Medicine. (Illus.). 350p. 1986. 150.00 (*0-387-96301-4*) Spr-Verlag.

Birrer, Richard B. Office Urgencies & Emergencies: Quick Reference Guides for Family Physicians. (The Academy Collection Ser.). 208p. pap. text 29.95 (*0-7817-2055-9*) Lppncott W & W.

Birrer, Richard B., ed. Sports Medicine for the Primary Care Physician. 2nd ed. LC 93-45708. 656p. 1994. per. 83.95 (*0-8493-2741-5*) CRC Pr.

Birrer, Richard B. & Birrer, Christina D. Medical Injuries in the Martial Arts. (Illus.). 240p. 1981. pap. 29.95 (*0-398-04134-2*) C C Thomas.

Birrer, Richard B., et al. Common Foot Problems in Primary Care. 2nd ed. LC 97-41961. 1998. 54.00 (*1-56053-222-X*) Hanley & Belfus.

Birringer, Johannes. Theatre, Theory, Postmodernism. LC 90-24442. (Drama & Performance Studies). (Illus.). 256p. 1991. 39.95 (*0-253-31195-0*) Ind U Pr.

***Birringer, Johannes H.** Media & Performance: Along the Border. LC 98-12702. (Paj Bks.). (Illus.). 288p. 1998. pap. 19.95 (*0-8018-5852-6*) Johns Hopkins.

Birringer, Johannes H. Media & Performance: Along the Border. LC 98-12702. (Paj Bks.). 1998. 48.00 (*0-8018-5851-8*) Johns Hopkins.

***Birringer, Johannes H.** Performance on the Edge: Transformations of Culture. LC 99-86429. 2000. write for info. (*0-485-00418-6*) Athlone Pr.

Birsan, Edi, jt. ed. see Hartley, Nina.

Birsch, Douglas. Ethical Insights: A Brief Introduction. LC 98-27070. 144p. 1998. pap. text 13.95 (*0-7674-0712-1*) Mayfield Pub.

Birsch, Douglas & Fielder, John, eds. The Ford Pinto Case: A Study in Applied Ethics, Business, & Technology. LC 94-838. (SUNY Series, Case Studies in Applied Ethics, Technology, & Society). 312p. (C). 1994. text 59.50 (*0-7914-2233-X*); pap. text 21.95 (*0-7914-2234-8*) State U NY Pr.

Birse, M. C., et al, eds. Hadron 95: Proceedings of the 6th International Conference on Hadron Spectroscopy, University of Manchester 10 - 14 July 1995. 500p. 1996. text 112.00 (*981-02-2468-0*, Ph-P2939) World Scientific Pub.

Birsh, Judith R., ed. Multisensory Teaching of Basic Language Skills: Theory & Practice. LC 99-21233. 624p. 1999. 59.00 (*1-55766-349-1*, 3491) P H Brookes.

Birsner, E. Patricia. Job Hunting for the 40+ Executive. 3rd ed. 1996. pap. 14.00 (*0-671-51728-7*) S&S Trade.

Birsner, E. Patricia & Balsley, Ronald D. Practical Guide to Customer Service Management & Operations. LC 81-69366. 224p. reprint ed. pap. 69.50 (*0-608-12403-6*, 205214000040) Bks Demand.

Birsner, E. Patricia, ed. see Davis, Dorinne S.

Birsner, Patricia E. Mid-Career Job Hunting. 2nd ed. 272p. 1991. pap. 14.00 (*0-13-508532-2*, Arco) Macmillan Gen Ref.

Birss, Helen. Making Wood Work: Value Added Policies & Programs. 92p. (Orig.). (YA). (gr. 12 up). 1994. pap. text 30.00 (*0-7881-0843-3*) DIANE Pub.

Birss, Robert R., jt. auth. see Gerber, Richard.

Birss, V., jt. ed. see Oyama, N.

Birstein, Vadim J., et al. Sturgeon Biodiversity & Conservation. LC 97-8149. (Developments in Environmental Biology of Fishes Ser.). 1997. text 267.50 (*0-7923-4517-7*) Kluwer Academic.

Birt, jt. auth. see Fletcher.

Birt, Anita. The House at Bridal Veil. LC 92-70383. (Illus.). 288p. (Orig.). 1992. pap. 19.95 (*0-8323-0495-6*) Binford Mort.

Birt, David. The Black Prince. (Resouces Units: Middle Ages, 1066-1484 Ser.). (Illus.). 24p. 1974. reprint ed. pap. text 12.95 (*0-582-39382-5*) Longman.

— Knights & Tournaments. (Resource Units: Middle Ages, 1066-1485 Ser.). (Illus.). 24p. 1974. pap. text, teacher ed. 12.95 (*0-582-39374-4*) Longman.

— The Medieval Town. (Resource Units: Middle Ages, 1066-1485 Ser.). (Illus.). 24p. (Orig.). 1974. pap. text, teacher ed. 12.95 (*0-582-39389-2*) Longman.

— The Monastery. (Resource Units: Middle Ages, 1066-1485 Ser.). (Illus.). 1974. pap. text, teacher ed. 12.95 (*0-582-39380-9*) Longman.

— The Murder of Becket. (Resource Units: Middle Ages, 1066-1485 Ser.). (Illus.). 24p. 1974. pap. text, teacher ed. 12.95 (*0-582-39376-0*) Longman.

— The Norman Conquest, 10 bks., Set. (Resource Units: Middle Ages, 1066-1485 Ser.). (Illus.). 24p. 1974. pap. text, teacher ed. 12.95 (*0-582-39372-8*) Longman.

— Stephen & Matilda. (Resource Units: Middle Ages, 1066-1485 Ser.). (Illus.). 24p. 1974. pap. text, teacher ed. 12.95 (*0-582-39375-2*) Longman.

Birt, David & Carstairs, Ian. The Tudors Briefings Unit. (History Units Ser.). (Illus.). 1975. pap. text 18.95 (*0-582-39616-6*) Longman.

Birt, Michael P., jt. auth. see Colby, Mark A.

Birt, Robert F., jt. auth. see Morrison, Leger R.

Birt, Theodor. Die Buchrolle in der Kunst. ix, 352p. 1976. reprint ed. 115.00 (*3-487-05950-9*) G Olms Pubs.

Birtchnell, J., et al. Effects of Early Parent Death. (Attitudes Toward Death Ser.: Vol. 1). 177p. (C). 1973. text 37.00 (*0-8422-7145-7*) Irvington.

Birtchnell, John. How Humans Relate: A New Interpersonal Theory. LC 93-20296. 320p. 1993. 67.95 (*0-275-94405-0*, C4405, Praeger Pubs) Greenwood.

— Relating in Psychotherapy: The Application of a New Theory. LC 98-38281. (Human Evolution, Behavior & Intelligence Ser.). 288p. 1999. 65.00 (*0-275-96376-4*, Praeger Pubs) Greenwood.

Birth Defects Annual Conference Staff. Annual Review of Birth Defects, 1977: Proceedings of the Birth Defects Annual Conference, 10th, Memphis, Tenn., June, 1977, 3 vols. Summitt, Robert L. & Bergsma, Daniel, eds. Incl. Vol. XIV, No. 6A. Cell Surface Factors,Immune Deficiencies, Twin Studies. 240p. 1978. 41.00 (*0-8451-1020-9*); Vol. XIV, No. 6B. Recent Advances & New Syndromes. 400p. 1978. 68.00 (*0-8451-1021-7*); Vol. XIV, No. 6C. Sex Differentiation & Chromosomal Abnormalities. 440p. 1978. 74.00 (*0-8451-1022-5*); Vol. 14, No. 6. (Illus.). 1978. write for info. (*0-318-50125-2*) A R Liss.

Birth, Kevin K. Any Time Is Trinidad Time: Social Meanings & Temporal Consciousness. LC 99-20574. 1999. 49.95 (*0-8130-1713-0*) U Press Fla.

Birtha, Becky. For Nights Like This One: Stories of Loving Women. LC 82-21087. 128p. (Orig.). 1983. pap. 4.95 (*0-9603628-4-3*) Frog in Well.

— Lovers' Choice. LC 87-17281. 152p. (Orig.). 1994. pap. 10.95 (*1-878067-41-9*) Seal Pr WA.

Birtle, A. J., ed. Rearming the Phoenix: U. S. Military Assistance to the Federal Republic of Germany, 1950-1960. LC 91-19695. (Modern American History Ser.). 464p. 1991. text 25.00 (*0-8240-1899-0*) Garland.

Birtle, Andrew J. Sicily: The United States Army Campaigns of World War 2. 28p. 1994. pap. 1.75 (*0-16-042081-4*) USGPO.

— U. S. Army Counterinsurgency & Contingency Operations Doctrine, 1860-1941. (Illus.). 319p. (C). 1998. pap. text 35.00 (*0-7881-7327-8*) DIANE Pub.

***Birtle, Andrew J.** United States Army Counterinsurgency & Contingency Operations Doctrine, 1860-1941. 331p. 1998. per. 19.00 (*0-16-061324-8*) USGPO.

Birtle, Jan, jt. auth. see Wheeler, Sue.

Birtles, Bill & Hewitt, Patricia. Your Rights at Work. 1983. 35.00 (*0-946088-06-3*, Pub. by NCCL) St Mut.

Birtles, Ellinor F., jt. ed. see Scharff, David E.

Birtles, Jasmine. A Father's Little Instruction Book. 128p. (Orig.). 1997. pap. 10.95 (*0-7522-1107-2*, Pub. by Boxtree) Trans-Atl Phila.

— A Mother's Little Instruction Book. 128p. (Orig.). 1997. pap. 10.95 (*0-7522-1104-8*, Pub. by Boxtree) Trans-Atl Phila.

Birtles, Jasmine. Women on Men. pap. 8.95 (*1-85479-963-0*, Pub. by M OMara) Trafalgar.

Birtles, Jasmine, compiled by. Bumper Joke Book for Kids. 168p. (J). 1996. write for info. (*1-85479-622-4*, Pub. by M OMara) Assoc Pubs Grp.

Birtles, Philip. Boeing 777: Jetliner for a New Century. LC 98-41747. (Airline Markings Ser.). 128p. 1998. pap. 24.95 (*0-7603-0581-1*) MBI Pubg.

— Lockheed L-1011: Tristar. LC 98-42469. (Airliners In Color Ser.). 128p. 1998. pap. 24.95 (*0-7603-0582-X*) MBI Pubg.

***Birtles, Philip J.** Boeing 767 Vol. 7: Airline Color History. LC 99-58615. (Airliner Color History Ser.). (Illus.). 128p. 1999. pap. 24.95 (*0-7603-0826-8*, 129399AP, Pub. by MBI Pubg) Motorbooks Intl.

— Mosquito: The Illustrated History. LC 99-187988. (Illus.). 192p. 1998. 39.95 (*0-7509-1495-5*, Pub. by Sutton Pub Ltd) Intl Pubs Mktg.

***Birtles, Philip J.** Mosquito: The Illustrated History. (Illus.). 256p. 1999. pap. 22.95 (*0-7509-2327-X*) Sutton Pub Ltd.

Birts, Anthony N. Balance Sheet Structures. (Association of Corporate Treasurers Ser.). 250p. 2000. 270.00 (*1-85573-247-5*, Pub. by Woodhead Pubng) Am Educ Systs.

Birts, Donald & Fisher, Joseph. Risk Taker: The Autobiography of Donald "Ducky" Birts. Woolfolk, Thomas, Jr. & Bell-Hughes, Janice, eds. LC 99-1287. 350p. 1999. 39.95 (*1-886098-05-0*, 1553) Woolfolk Pubns.

Birts, Peter & Willis, Alan. Trespass - Summary Procedure for Possession of Land. 155p. 1987. pap. 50.00 (*0-406-10481-6*, U.K., MICHIE) LEXIS Pub.

Birttan, Leon, ed. Competition Policy & Merger Control in the Single European Market. 68p. (C). 1991. 60.00 (*0-949009-92-X*, Pub. by Grotius Pubns Ltd) St Mut.

Birtton, David. Motherfuckers: The Auschwitz of Oz. Butterworth, Michael, ed. 250p. 1996. 30.95 (*0-86130-098-X*, Pub. by Savoy Bks) AK Pr Dist.

Birtwell, Charles W., jt. ed. see Spencer, Anna G.

Birtwhistle, John. The Conversion to Oil. Date not set. pap. 7.95 (*0-900977-36-1*, Pub. by Anvil Press) Dufour.

— Our Worst Suspicions. 64p. 1985. pap. 13.95 (*0-85646-131-8*, Pub. by Anvil Press) Dufour.

— A Selection of Poems. 40p. 1989. pap. 9.95 (*0-85646-215-2*, Pub. by Anvil Press) Dufour.

— Tidal Models. Date not set. pap. 14.95 (*0-85646-052-4*, Pub. by Anvil Press) Dufour.

Birtwistle. Making of Pride & Predjudice. 1995. pap. 20.95 (*0-14-025157-X*, Pub. by Pnguin Bks Ltd) Trafalgar.

Birtwistle, G. M. Discrete Event Modelling on Simula. 176p. 1987. 39.95 (*0-387-91301-7*) Spr-Verlag.

Birtwistle, G. M., et al, eds. Asynchronous Digital Circuit Design. LC 95-20349. (Workshops in Computing Ser.). (Illus.). vii, 263p. 1995. 59.00 (*0-387-19901-2*) Spr-Verlag.

Birtwistle, G. M. & Davis, A., eds. Asynchronous Digital Circuit Design. LC 95-1009. (Workshops in Computing Ser.). 1995. write for info. (*3-540-19901-2*) Spr-Verlag.

Birtwistle, G. M. & Subrahmanyam, P. A., eds. Current Trends in Hardware Verification & Automated Theorem Proving. (Illus.). x, 489p. 1989. 79.95 (*0-387-96988-8*) Spr-Verlag.

Birtwistle, G. M. & Van Rijsbergen, C. J., eds. Fourth Higher Order Workshop Banff 1990: Proceedings, September 10-14, 1990, Alberta, Canada. (Workshops in Computing Ser.). x, 283p. 1991. 59.00 (*0-387-19660-9*) Spr-Verlag.

Birtwistle, Graham, jt. auth. see Moller, Faron.

Birtwistle, Graham, jt. ed. see Suaya, Robert.

Birutta, Gale. A Guide to Raising Llamas: Care, Showing, Breeding, Packing, Profiting. LC 96-54288. (Storey Animal Handbook Ser.). (Illus.). 304p. (Orig.). 1997. pap. 18.95 (*0-88266-954-0*) Storey Bks.

***Birutta, Gale.** Storey's Guide to Raising Llamas. LC 00-30803. (Illus.). 2000. pap. write for info. (*1-58017-328-4*) Storey Bks.

Birx, H. James. Human Evolution. (Illus.). 378p. (C). 1988. text 59.95 (*0-398-05417-7*) C C Thomas.

— Interpreting Evolution: Darwin & Teilhard de Chardin. LC 90-44530. 326p. (C). 1991. 33.95 (*0-87975-636-5*) Prometheus Bks.

Birx, H. James, tr. see Huxley, Julian S.

Biryukov, Nikolai & Sergeyev, Victor. Russian Politics in Transition. LC 97-30129. (Centre for Democratization Ser.). 342p. 1997. text 78.95 (*1-85521-975-1*, Pub. by Ashgate Pub) Ashgate Pub Co.

Biryukov, Nikolai, jt. auth. see Sergeyev, Victor.

Biryukov, S. V. Surface Acoustic Wave in Inhomogenous Media. (Series on Wave Phenomena: Vol. 20). 1995. write for info. (*0-387-58460-9*) Spr-Verlag.

— Surface Acoustic Wave in Inhomogenous Media. (Series on Wave Phenomena: Vol. 20). 1995. 99.95 (*3-540-58460-9*) Spr-Verlag.

Biryukov, Valery M., et al. Crystal Channeling & Its Application at High-Energy Accelerators. LC 96-28616. 1996. write for info. (*3-540-60769-2*) Spr-Verlag.

Birznieks, Gunther. Building an Online Store. LC 97-5728. 432p. 1997. pap. text 39.95 (*1-55851-559-3*, M&T Bks) IDG Bks.

Birzvalka, I. & Sosare, M. English - Latvian, Latvian - English Dictionary. (ENG & LAV.). 1989. 49.95 (*0-8288-2487-8*) Fr & Eur.

— English-Latvian Latvian-English Dictionary. 360p. 1993. 25.00 (*0-8285-5139-1*) Firebird NY.

Birzvalka, I., jt. auth. see Sosare, M.

Bisaccia, Andy. Hannibal by the Sea: Boyhood Recollections of Growing up in Santa Barbara from 1923 to 1945. LC 97-48358. (Illus.). 416p. 1998. pap. 16.95 (*1-56474-252-0*) Fithian Pr.

Bisagno, John R. Positive Obedience: The Christian's Response to the Ten Commandments. 80p. (Orig.). 1987. pap. 4.95 (*0-310-38141-X*, 9249P) Zondervan.

— Power of Positive Praying. 91p. 1965. mass mkt. 6.99 (*0-310-21212-X*, 9238P) Zondervan.

— Power of Positive Praying. large type ed. (Large Print Inspirational Ser.). 256p. 1987. pap. 8.95 (*0-8027-2580-5*) Walker & Co.

— The Secret of Positive Praying. Ruark, Jim, ed. 128p. 1986. pap. 4.95 (*0-310-21152-2*, 09239P) Zondervan.

Bisaillon, Teresa. TCP/IP with Windows NTIllustrated. LC 97-41022. (McGraw Hill NT Professional Reference Ser.). (Illus.). 736p. 1998. pap., pap. text 44.95 incl. cd-rom (*0-07-913648-6*) McGraw.

***Bisang, Bruno.** Bruno Bisang Photographs. 2000. 35.00 (*3-8238-5451-8*) te Neues.

Bisang, Irene. Biosystematische Studien an Lophozia Subgen: Schistochilopsis (Hepaticae) Gradstein, S. R., ed. (Bryophytorum Bibliotheca: Vol. 43). (GER., Illus.). 225p. 1991. 65.00 (*3-443-62015-9*, Pub. by Gebruder Borntraeger) Balogh.

Bisanz, J., et al, eds. Learning in Children: Progress in Cognitive Development Research. (Cognitive Development Ser.). (Illus.). 201p. 1983. 84.95 (*0-387-90802-1*) Spr-Verlag.

Bisanz, J., et al. Formal Methods in Developmental Psychology. LC 96-35385. (Cognitive Development Ser.). (Illus.). 370p. 1987. 171.95 (*0-387-96441-X*) Spr-Verlag.

Bisanz, Rudolf M. German Romanticism & Philipp Otto Runge: A Study in Nineteenth-Century Art Theory & Iconography. LC 74-98388. (Illus.). 144p. 1970. 35.00 (*0-87580-013-0*) N Ill U Pr.

Bisarsh, A., ed. Superconductivity: An Annotated Bibliography with Abstracts. 148p. 1998. lib. bdg. 115.00 (*1-56072-106-5*) Nova Sci Pubs.

Bisbas, Dorthea, et al. Finding What Is Lost: An Anthology. 58p. 1999. pap. write for info. (*0-7392-0096-8*, PO2983) Morris Pub.

Bisbee, A. The History & Practice of Daguerreotyping. LC 72-9183. (Literature of Photography Ser.). 1978. reprint ed. 12.95 (*0-405-04894-7*) Ayer.

Bisbee, Chester A. Bioinformatics: Biotechnology Enters the Information Age, 7 vols. DiClemente, Susan C., ed. LC 98-227800. 218p. 1997. spiral bd. 4950.00 (*1-57936-096-3*, 964, Drug & Market Dev) IBC USA.

Bisbee, M. Lauren. Of Land & Labor: Gunston Hall Plantation Life in the 18th Century. (Illus.). 32p. 1994. pap. 4.95 (*1-884085-06-7*) Bd Regents.

Bisberg-Youkelson, Feigl & Youkelson, Rubin, eds. The Life & Death of a Polish Shtetl. Bluestein, Gene, tr. from YID. LC 99-30394. 128p. 2000. pap. text 12.95 (*0-8032-6167-5*) U of Nebr Pr.

Bisbey, Lori B., jt. auth. see Bisbey, Stephen.

Bisbey, Stephen & Bisbey, Lori B. Brief Therapy for PTSD: Traumatic Incident Reduction & Related Techniques. LC 97-45185. 192p. 1998. pap. 48.95 (*0-471-97567-2*) Wiley.

Bisbing, Steven B. & Jorgenson, Linda M. Sexual Abuse by Professionals: A Legal Guide, 1999 Cumulative Supplement. 200p. 1999. suppl. ed. write for info. (*0-327-01057-6*, 6055612) LEXIS Pub.

Bisbing, Steven B., et al. Sexual Abuse by Professionals: A Legal Guide, 1999 Cumulative Supplement. 950p. 105.00 (*0-327-01941-7*) LEXIS Pub.

Bisbort, Alan. Charles Bragg: The Works! A Retrospective. LC 99-29080. 223p. 1999. 60.00 (*0-7649-1028-0*) Pomegranate Calif.

— Sunday Afternoon, Looking for the Car: The Aberrant Art of Barry Kite. LC 97-14852. (Illus.). 96p. (Orig.). 1997. pap. 25.00 (*0-7649-0362-4*, A903) Pomegranate Calif.

— The White Rabbit & Other Delights: East Totem West, a Hippie Company, 1967-1969. LC 96-26464. (Illus.). 88p. (Orig.). 1996. pap. 26.95 (*0-7649-0011-0*) Pomegranate Calif.

***Bisbort, Alan & Bragg, Charles.** Charles Bragg: The Works! LC 99-29080. 1999. boxed set 250.00 (*0-7649-1053-1*) Pomegranate Calif.

***Bisbort, Alan & Osborne, Linda Barrett.** The Nation's Library: The Library of Congress. (Illus.). 144p. 2000. pap. 16.95 (*1-85759-235-2*, Pub. by Scala Books) Antique Collect.

***Bisbort, Alan & Puterbaugh, Parke.** Rhino's Psychedelic Trip. (Illus.). 192p. 2000. pap. 19.95 (*0-87930-626-2*, M Freeman Bks) Miller Freeman.

Bisbort, Alan, jt. auth. see Puterbaugh, Parke.

Bisbrouck, Marie-Francoise, jt. ed. see Chauveinc, Marc.

Bisbrown, A. J. Fumigable Warehouses: Design & Construction. 1992. pap. 25.00 (*0-85954-309-9*, Pub. by Nat Res Inst) St Mut.

Bisby, Frank A. Plant Taxonomic Database Standards: Plant Names in Botanical Databases, No. 3. 30p. 1994. pap. 8.00 (*0-913196-62-2*) Hunt Inst Botanical.

Bisby, Frank A., jt. auth. see Ainsworth.

Bisby, Mark A., ed. see International Union of Physiological Sciences Cong.

***Bisceglia, Michael F., Jr.** Border Storm. LC 99-64383. 253p. 1999. 25.00 (*0-7388-0448-7*); pap. 18.00 (*0-7388-0449-5*) Xlibris Corp.

Bisceglie, A. M. Di, see Bacon, B. R. & Di Bisceglie, A. M., eds.

***Bisch, Philippe, et al, eds.** Earthquake Engineering / Invited Papers: Proceedings of the 11th European Conference, Paris, France, 6-11 September 1998. 361p. 1998. 85.00 (*90-5809-027-2*) Ashgate Pub Co.

Bischak, Gregory A., jt. ed. see Cassidy, Kevin J.

Bischel, John D., jt. auth. see Sikking, C. Thomas.

Bischel, Margaret D. The Credentialing & Privileges Manual. (Illus.). 275p. 1997. ring bd. 199.00 (*1-893826-03-1*) Apollo Managed.

— Disease State Management Vol. I: Clinical Guidelines for the Primary Physician. (Illus.). 163p. 1997. ring bd. 195.00 (*1-893826-05-8*) Apollo Managed.

— Disease State Management, Clinical Behavioral Vol. II: Health Guidelines. 195p. 1997. ring bd. 195.00 (*1-893826-06-6*) Apollo Managed.

— Glossary of Managed Care Medical Terms, Abbreviations & Acronyms. 97p. 1997. ring bd. 25.00 (*1-893826-08-2*) Apollo Managed.

— Managed Behavioral Healthcare Manual. 275p. 1997. ring bd. 225.00 (*1-893826-02-3*) Apollo Managed.

— The Managed Care Provider's Toolbox. (Illus.). 415p. 1998. ring bd. write for info. (*1-893826-04-X*) Apollo Managed.

— The Managed Physical/Occupational Therapy & Rehabilitation Care Manual. (Illus.). 275p. 1996. ring bd. 225.00 (*1-893826-01-5*) Apollo Managed.

— Managing Post-Acute Care & Other Extented Care Services. 405p. 1998. ring bd. 225.00 (*1-893826-09-0*) Apollo Managed.

— Medical Review Criteria Guidelines for Managed Care. (Illus.). 605p. 1997. ring bd. 495.00 (*1-893826-00-7*) Apollo Managed.

— Utilization Management & Capitation Strategies. (Illus.). 413p. 1998. ring bd. 225.00 (*1-893826-07-4*) Apollo Managed.

Bischiniotis, George, ed. CD-ROM Directory 1996: With Multimedia CDs. 15th ed. 1197p. 1996. pap. 159.00 (*1-870889-46-0*) TFPL.

Bischke, Richard E., jt. auth. see Tearpock, Daniel.

Bischke, Scott. Two Wheels Around New Zealand: A Bicycle Journey on Friendly Roads. LC 89-35041. (Illus.). 286p. 1996. reprint ed. pap. 12.95 (*0-9639705-1-8*) Ecopress.

Bischko, Johannes. An Introduction to Acupuncture, Vol. 1. 2nd rev. ed. (Illus.). 135p. 1985. 19.95 (*3-7760-0842-3*, Pub. by K F Haug Pubs) Medicina Bio.

Bischler-Causse, Helene. Marchantia L. The Asiatic & Oceanic Taxa. Gradstein, S. R., ed. (Bryophytorum Bibliotheca: Vol. 38). (GER., Illus.). 317p. 1989. pap. text 77.00 (*3-443-62010-8*, Pub. by Gebruder Borntraeger) Balogh.

— Marchantia L. The European & African Taxa. Gradstein, S. R., ed. (Bryophytorum Bibliotheca: Vol. 45). (GER., Illus.). 129p. 1993. pap. 42.00 (*3-443-62017-5*, Pub. by Gebruder Borntraeger) Balogh.

Bischler, H. Marchantia I: The New World Species. (Bryophytorum Bibliotheca Ser.: Vol. 26). (Illus.). 228p. 1984. text 48.00 (*3-7682-1401-X*) Lubrecht & Cramer.

Bischler, H., ed. see Bonner, C. E. B.

Bischler, Helene. Systematics & Evolution of the Genera of the Marchantiales. Gradstein, S. R., ed. (Bryophytorum Bibliotheca: Vol. 51). (GER., Illus.). 1998. 71.00 (*3-443-62023-X*, Pub. by Gebruder Borntraeger) Balogh.

Bischler, Helene, jt. ed. see Geissler, Patricia.

Bischof. College Accounting Practice, Set B. (C). 1988. student ed. write for info. (*0-03-017118-0*) Harcourt Coll Pubs.

— Comp Connection (3.5"DISK) 2nd ed. (C). 1992. 45.00 incl. 3.5 ld (*0-15-512628-8*) Harcourt Coll Pubs.

— Introduction to College Accounting, Chapters 1-28. 2nd ed. 1992. 10.00 (*0-15-541713-4*) Harcourt Coll Pubs.

— OHT-Intro to College Acct:1-14 2E. 2nd ed. 1992. 125.00 (*0-15-541715-0*, Pub. by Harcourt Coll Pubs) Harcourt.

Bischof-Delaloye, A. & Blaufox, M. Donald, eds. Radionuclides in Nephrology. (Contributions to Nephrology Ser.: Vol. 56). (Illus.). x, 278p. 1987. 29.75 (*3-8055-4445-6*) S Karger.

Bischof, Gunter, et al, eds. Austria in the Nineteen Fifties. (Contemporary Austrian Studies: Vol. 3). 311p. (C). 1994. pap. 35.00 (*1-56000-763-X*) Transaction Pubs.

— The Kreisky Era in Austria. LC 93-22851. (Contemporary Austrian Studies: Vol. 2). 276p. (C). 1993. pap. text 35.00 (*1-56000-705-2*) Transaction Pubs.

— The Vranitzky Era in Austria. LC 98-33871. (Contemporary Austrian Studies: Vol. 7). 300p. 1999. pap. 35.00 (*0-7658-0490-5*) Transaction Pubs.

— Women in Austria. LC 97-24055. (Contemporary Austrian Studies: Vol. 6). 340p. 1997. pap. 35.00 (*0-7658-0404-2*) Transaction Pubs.

Bischof, Gunter & Ambrose, Stephen E., eds. Eisenhower: Centenary Assessment. LC 94-27045. (Eisenhower Center Studies on War & Peace). 312p. (C). 1995. text 42.50 (*0-8071-1942-3*) La State U Pr.

— Eisenhower & the German POWs: Facts Against Falsehood. LC 92-3908. (Eisenhower Center Studies on War & Peace). (Illus.). 296p. (C). 1992. 24.95 (*0-8071-1758-7*) La State U Pr.

Bischof, Gunter & Dockrill, Saki, eds. Cold War Respite: The Geneva Summit of 1955. (Eisenhower Center Studies on War & Peace). (Illus.). 312p. 1999. text 60.00 (*0-8071-2370-6*) La State U Pr.

Bischof, Gunter & Dupont, Robert L., eds. Pacific War Revisited. LC 97-5178. (Eisenhower Center Studies on War & Peace). (Illus.). 200p. 1997. text 25.00 (*0-8071-2156-8*) La State U Pr.

Bischof, Gunter & Pelinka, Anton, eds. Austrian Historical Memory & National Identity. (Contemporary Austrian Studies: Vol. 5). 399p. (Orig.). 1996. pap. text 35.00 (*1-56000-902-0*) Transaction Pubs.

— Austro-Corporatism: Past, Present, Future. (Contemporary Austrian Studies: Vol. 4). 314p. (Orig.). (C). 1995. pap. text 35.00 (*1-56000-833-4*) Transaction Pubs.

Bischof, Gunter, jt. ed. see Pelinka, Anton.

Bischof, Hans-Joachim, jt. ed. see Zeigler, H. Philip.

Bischof, Horst. Pyramidal Neural Networks. 216p. 1995. text 39.95 (*0-8058-1913-4*); pap. text 24.50 (*0-8058-1914-2*) L Erlbaum Assocs.

***Bischof, Jens.** Ice Drift, Ocean Circulation & Climate Change. LC 00-44030. (Books in Environmental Sciences). (Illus.). 2000. write for info. (*1-85233-648-X*) Spr-Verlag.

Bischof, Joy. Capture the Wind. 112p. 1991. write for info. (*0-8187-0146-3*) Harlo Press.

Bischof, Larry & Lowry, William B. Amazon Adventure. LC 92-12844. (Widgets Ser.). (J). (gr. 2). 1992. lib. bdg. 13.99 (*1-56239-150-X*) ABDO Pub Co.

Bischof, M. & Kessling, V. Landeskunde und Literaturdidaktik. Neuner, Gerd, ed. (Fernstudienangebot Ser.). (GER.). 184p. 1996. 11.25 (*3-468-49677-X*) Langenscheidt.

Bischof, P. Placental Proteins. (Contributions to Gynecology & Obstetrics Ser.: Vol. 12). (Illus.). viii, 96p. 1984. 57.50 (*3-8055-3853-7*) S Karger.

Bischof, P. & Klopper, A., eds. Proteins of the Placenta. (Illus.). viii, 208p. 1985. 155.75 (*3-8055-4034-5*) S Karger.

Bischof, Phyllis, jt. ed. see Scheven, Yvette.

Bischof, W. F., jt. auth. see Caelli, T.

Bischof, Werner A. After the War: Photographs by Werner Bischof. LC 97-1269. (Motta Photography Ser.: Vol. 1). (Illus.). 64p. 1997. 24.95 (*1-56098-721-9*) Smithsonian.

Bischofberger, W., jt. auth. see Pomberger, Gustav.

Bischoff. P/S A-Intro to College: 1-14 2E, Chapters 1-14. 2nd ed. (C). 1992. pap. text, student ed. 20.50 (*0-15-541701-0*) Harcourt Coll Pubs.

— World Civilizations: The Global Experience. (C). Date not set. write for info. (*0-673-97073-6*) Addson-Wesley Educ.

***Bischoff.** World Civilizations: The Global Experience. 3rd ed. (C). 1999. pap. text, student ed. Price not set. (*0-321-00522-8*) Addison-Wesley.

Bischoff. World History Atlas. (C). 1996. text 16.88 (*0-673-98177-0*) Addson-Wesley Educ.

Bischoff, Armin. Vegetations- und Populationsdynamik in N-Belasteten Agraroekosystemen Nach Dem Ubergang Zu Einer Extensivierten Nutzung. (Dissertationes Botanicae Ser.: Band 268). (Illus.). vii, 184p. 1996. pap. 53.00 (*3-443-64180-6*, Pub. by Gebruder Borntraeger) Balogh.

Bischoff, Bernhard. Latin Palaeography: Antiquity & the Middle Ages. 303p. (C). 1990. text 80.00 (*0-521-36473-6*) Cambridge U Pr.

— Latin Palaeography: Antiquity & the Middle Ages. 303p. (C). 1990. pap. text 27.95 (*0-521-36726-3*) Cambridge U Pr.

— Manuscripts & Libraries in the Age of Charlemagne. Gorman, Michael M., tr. & compiled by by. LC 92-44509. (Studies in Palaeography & Codicology: No. 1). (ENG & GER.). 211p. (C). 1994. text 69.95 (*0-521-38346-3*) Cambridge U Pr.

Bischoff, Bernhard & Lapidge, Michael. Biblical Commentaries from the Canterbury School of Theodore & Hadrian. LC 93-42766. (Cambridge Studies in Anglo-Saxon England: Vol. 10). 626p. (C). 1995. text 115.00 (*0-521-33089-0*) Cambridge U Pr.

Bischoff, Cynthia L. Business Writing That Works. unabridged ed. 150p. (Orig.). 1997. pap. 16.95 (*1-890842-00-1*) White Raven Pr.

Bischoff, David. Abduction: The UFO Conspiracy. 1990. mass mkt. 4.95 (*0-446-35489-9*) Warner Bks.

— Aliens: Genocide, No. 4. LC 94-125059. 288p. 1993. mass mkt. 5.50 (*0-553-56371-8*) Bantam.

— Aliens Vs. Predator: Hunter's Planet. 272p. 1994. mass mkt. 5.50 (*0-553-56556-7*, Spectra) Bantam.

***Bischoff, David.** The Crow: Quoth the Crow. LC 98-146176. 288p. 1998. mass mkt. 13.00 (*0-06-105825-4*, HarperPrism) HarpC.

Bischoff, David. Deception: The UFO Conspiracy. 1991. mass mkt. 4.95 (*0-446-35491-0*) Warner Bks.

— Gremlins 2: The New Batch. 1990. pap. 3.95 (*0-380-76061-4*, Avon Bks) Morrow Avon.

— Hackers. 208p. 1995. mass mkt. 4.99 (*0-06-106375-4*, Harp PBks) HarpC.

— Quest. LC 76-44815. 64 p. (J). 1977. 3.95 (*0-8172-0528-4*) Raintree Steck-V.

— Revelation: The UFO Conspiracy. 368p. (Orig.). 1991. mass mkt. 5.99 (*0-446-35493-7*) Warner Bks.

Bischoff, David, jt. auth. see Harrison, Harry.

Bischoff, David, jt. auth. see Sheffield, Charles.

Bischoff, Donald C., ed. The Effect of Increased Speed Limits in the Post-NMSL Era. (Illus.). 80p. (C). 1999. pap. text 20.00 (*0-7881-7621-8*) DIANE Pub.

Bischoff, Erich. The Kabbala: An Introduction to Jewish Mysticism & Its Secret Doctrine. LC 84-52262. (Illus.). 96p. 1985. pap. 7.95 (*0-87728-564-0*) Weiser.

Bischoff, Ernst. Microscopic Analysis of the Anastomoses Between the Cranial Nerves. Sachs, Ernst, Jr. & Valtin, Eva W., eds. LC 77-72520. 148p. reprint ed. pap. 45.90 (*0-608-11919-9*, 202323100032) Bks Demand.

Bischoff, Gregory W. Introduction to College Accounting. 2nd ed. (C). 1992. pap. text, teacher ed. 23.75 (*0-15-541697-9*) Harcourt Coll Pubs.

— Introduction to College Accounting, Chapters 1-28. 1033p. (C). 1988. teacher ed. 18.50 (*0-15-541587-5*) Harcourt Coll Pubs.

— Introduction to College Accounting, Chapters 1-14. 551p. (C). 1988. teacher ed. 6.15 (*0-15-541617-0*) Harcourt Coll Pubs.

— Introduction to College Accounting, Chapters 1-14. 2nd ed. (C). 1992. pap. text, teacher ed., suppl. ed. 10.50 (*0-15-541699-5*, Pub. by Harcourt Coll Pubs) Harcourt.

— Introduction to College Accounting, Chapters 1-28. 1004p. (C). 1988. teacher ed. 5.00 (*0-685-22031-1*); teacher ed. 4.00 (*0-685-44224-1*) Harcourt Coll Pubs.

— Introduction to College Accounting, Chapters 1-28. 3rd ed. 1040p. (C). 1994. pap. text 32.00 (*0-03-007423-1*) Dryden Pr.

— Introduction to College Accounting, Chapters 15-28. 2nd ed. (C). 1992. pap. text, teacher ed. 8.75 (*0-15-541709-6*) Harcourt Coll Pubs.

— Introduction to College Accounting, Chapts. 1/14. 2nd ed. (C). 1992. pap. text 12.50 (*0-15-541703-7*, Pub. by Harcourt Coll Pubs) Harcourt.

— Introduction to College Accounting: Test Bank, Chapters 15-28. 2nd ed. (C). 1992. pap. text, teacher ed., suppl. ed. 10.50 (*0-15-541710-X*, Pub. by Harcourt Coll Pubs) Harcourt.

***Bischoff, Gunter, et al, eds.** The Marshall Plan in Austria. LC 99-87781. (Contemporary Austrian Studies: Vol. 8). 475p. 2000. pap. 40.00 (*0-7658-0679-7*) Transaction Pubs.

Bischoff, Harry W. & Bold, Harold C., eds. Phycological Studies: Some Soil Algae from Enchanted Rock & Related Algae Species. (Phycological Studies Ser.: Vol. 4). 195p. 1975. pap. 38.00 (*3-87429-099-9*, Pub. by Koeltz Sci Bks) Lubrecht & Cramer.

Bischoff, Henry. Ramapo College of New Jersey: The First Quarter Century, 1971-1996. unabridged ed. (Illus.). 150p. (Orig.). 1997. pap. write for info. (*0-927351-02-1*) Ramapo College.

Bischoff, J. Comprehensive History of the Woollen & the Worsted Manufacturers, 2 vols. (Illus.). 1968. reprint ed. 75.00 (*0-7146-1387-8*, Pub. by F Cass Pubs) Intl Spec Bk.

Bischoff, J. L. & Piper, D. Z., eds. Marine Geology & Oceanography of the Pacific Manganese Nodule Province. LC 79-12475. (Marine Science Ser.: Vol. 9). 856p. 1979. 145.00 (*0-306-40187-8*, Plenum Trade) Perseus Pubng.

Bischoff, J. L., jt. ed. see Smith, G. I.

Bischoff, John, jt. auth. see Bird, Larry.

Bischoff, John Paul. Mr. Iba: Basketball's Aggie Iron Duke. (Oklahoma Trackmaker Ser.). (Illus.). 276p. 1980. 12.95 (*0-86546-001-9*) OK Heritage.

Bischoff, Karen, jt. auth. see PURSLEY, JOAN MUYSKENS.

Bischoff, Kenneth B., jt. auth. see Froment, G. F.

Bischoff, Martin B. Successful Pharmaceutical Selling: Frank Advice from the Frontlines. LC 97-15126. 1997. 21.95 (*0-7863-1211-4*, Irwn Prfssnl) McGraw-Hill Prof.

***Bischoff, Matt C.** The Desert Training Center, California - Arizona Maneuver Area, 1942-1944: Historical & Archaeological Contexts. (Technical Ser.: Vol. 75). (Illus.). 156p. 2000. pap. 25.00 (*1-879442-75-2*) Stats Res.

Bischoff, Matt C. Touring Arizona Hot Springs. LC 99-11764. (Illus.). 125p. 1999. pap. 12.95 (*1-56044-737-0*) Falcon Pub Inc.

— Touring California & Nevada Hot Springs. LC 97-14037. (Illus.). 168p. (Orig.). 1997. pap. 16.95 (*1-56044-578-5*) Falcon Pub Inc.

Bischoff, Paul-Henri. Swaziland's International Relations & Foreign Policy: A Study of a Small African State in International Relations. (European University Studies: Political Science: Ser. 31, Vol. 158). 555p. 1990. pap. 79.00 (*3-261-04226-5*) P Lang Pubng.

Bischoff, Ralph F. Nazi Conquest Through German Culture. LC 78-63651. (Studies in Fascism: Ideology & Practice). reprint ed. 37.50 (*0-404-16906-6*) AMS Pr.

Bischoff, Robin N., jt. auth. see Reynolds, John D.

Bischoff, Ulrich. Ernst. 1994. pap. 9.99 (*3-8228-0073-2*) Taschen Amer.

Bischoff, Ulrich. Ernst. 1996. 12.99 (*3-8228-0235-2*) Taschen Amer.

— Munch. (SPA.). 1996. pap. 12.99 (*3-8228-0224-7*) Benedikt Taschen.

Bischoff, Ulrich. Munch. 1996. pap. 9.99 (*3-8228-0569-6*) Taschen Amer.

Bischoff, Volker, ed. Ezra Pound Criticism, 1905-1985. 264p. 1991. reprint ed. pap. 19.95 (*3-8185-0092-4*) Natl Poet Foun.

Bischoff, William. Choosing Right Business Entity. 1997. pap. 197.00 (*0-15-606072-8*, Pub. by Harcourt Coll Pubs) Harcourt.

***Bischoff, William.** Choosing the Right Business Entity. 1999th ed. 400p. 1999. pap. text 197.00 (*0-15-606771-4*) Harcourt Coll Pubs.

— 2000 Choosing the Right Business Entity. 400p. 2000. pap. 197.00 (*0-15-607112-6*) Harcourt.

Bischoff, William L., ed. The Coinage of El Peru. (Coinage of the Americas Conference Ser.: No. 5). (Illus.). 250p. 1989. 15.00 (*0-89722-234-2*) Am Numismatic.

Bischoff, William N. We Were Not Summer Soldiers: The Indian War Diary of Plympton J. Kelly, 1855-1856. LC 76-11999. (Illus.). 191p. 1976. 8.75 (*0-917048-00-8*) Wash St Hist Soc.

***Bischoff, William R., et al.** Guide to Buying & Selling a Business, 2 vols. 1999. ring bd. 180.00 (*0-7646-0807-X*) Prctnrs Pub Co.

Bischoff, William R., et al. Guide to Buying & Selling a Business, 2 vols. Incl. Vol. 2. 1997. ring bd. 170.00 (*0-7646-0245-4*); Vol. 1. 1997. ring bd. (*0-7646-0246-2*); 168.00 (*1-56433-964-5*) Prctnrs Pub Co.

Bischoff, William R., et al. Guide to Buying & Selling a Business, 2 vols. Incl. Vol. 2. 1997. ring bd. 170.00 (*0-7646-0245-4*); Vol. 1. 1997. ring bd. (*0-7646-0246-2*); 170.00 (*0-7646-0244-6*) Prctnrs Pub Co.

— Guide to Buying & Selling a Business, Vol. 1. 1999. ring bd. write for info. (*0-7646-0808-8*) Prctnrs Pub Co.

— Guide to Buying & Selling a Business, Vol. 2. 1999. ring bd. write for info. (*0-7646-0809-6*) Prctnrs Pub Co.

— PPC's 1065 Deskbook, 2 vols. 1999. ring bd. 150.00 (*0-7646-0871-1*) Prctnrs Pub Co.

— PPC's 1065 Deskbook, Vol. 1. 1999. ring bd. write for info. (*0-7646-0872-X*) Prctnrs Pub Co.

— PPC's 1065 Deskbook, Vol. 2. 1999. ring bd. write for info. (*0-7646-0873-8*) Prctnrs Pub Co.

Bischoff, William R., et al. PPC's 1065 Deskbook, 2 vols. Incl. Vol. 1. 1997. 150.00 (*0-7646-0226-8*); Vol. 2. 1997. ring bd. 150.00 (*0-7646-0227-6*); 150.00 (*0-7646-0026-5*); 150.00 (*0-7646-0225-X*) Prctnrs Pub Co.

Bischoff, Wolfgang. Marketing-Forschung fur Agrarfakultaten: Analyse der Berufsfelder & Evaluierung des Studiums der Studiengange Allgemeine Agrarwissenschaften & Agrarbiologie. (GER., Illus.). XVI, 304p. 1996. 57.95 (*3-631-30529-X*) P Lang Pubng.

Bischofsberger, W. Lexikon der Abwassertechnik. (ENG & GER.). 717p. 1990. lib. bdg. 115.00 (*0-8288-3595-0*, F99120) Fr & Eur.

Bischofsberger, W. & Hegemann, W. Lexicon of Sewage Processing: Lexikon der Abwassertechnik. 4th ed. (ENG & GER.). 671p. 1990. 125.00 (*0-685-53795-1*, F38010) Fr & Eur.

***Bischops, Klaus.** Soccer: Warming-Up & Cooling Down. 1999. pap. 14.95 (*1-84126-014-2*) Meyer & Meyer.

Biscoe, C. E. Kashmir in Sunlight & Shade. (C). 1995. reprint ed. 34.00 (*0-8364-2905-2*, Pub. by Motilal Bnarsidass) S Asia.

Biscoe, Joseph D. You Can Be an Effective Board Member. (Christian Living Ser.). 40p. 1988. pap. 3.50 (*0-8341-1233-7*) Beacon Hill.

Biscoff, Joyce & Alexander, Ted. Data Warehouse. LC 97-8262. 428p. (C). 1997. 49.99 (*0-13-577370-9*) P-H.

Biscoglio, Frances M. The Wives of the "Canterbury Tales" & the Tradition of the Valiant Woman of Proverbs 31: 10-31. LC 92-23974. (Illus.). 272p. 1992. text 89.95 (*0-7734-9803-6*) E Mellen.

Biscombe, Tony & Drewett, Peter. Rugby: Steps to Success. LC 97-29732. (Steps to Success Activity Ser.). (Illus.). 168p. (Orig.). 1997. pap. 16.95 (*0-88011-509-2*, PBIS0509) Human Kinetics.

Biscotti, M. L. & Hill, Gene. A Bibliography of American Sporting Books: 1926-1985. LC 97-72599. (Illus.). 573p. 1997. 75.00 (*1-886967-06-7*) Meadow Run Pr.

Biscotti, Matthew L. American Sporting Book Series. LC 94-66135. 328p. 1994. 150.00 (*1-881755-03-7*); pap. 45.00 (*1-881755-05-3*) Sunrise OH.

— American Sporting Book Series. deluxe ed. LC 94-66135. 328p. 1994. boxed set 750.00 (*1-881755-04-5*) Sunrise OH.

— The Borzoi Books for Sportsmen. 300p. 1992. 80.00 (*1-881755-00-2*) Sunrise OH.

— The Borzoi Books for Sportsmen. deluxe ed. 300p. 1992. 225.00 (*1-881755-01-0*) Sunrise OH.

Bisdorf, Rita, jt. ed. see Bolander, Donald O.

An Asterisk (*) at the beginning of an entry indicates that the title is appearing for the first time.

Bise, Christopher J. Mining Engineering Analysis. LC 85-62660. (Illus.). 160p. (C). 1986. text 61.00 (*0-87335-057-X*, 057-X) SMM&E Inc.

Biseartei, Murhammad & Johnson-Davies, Denys. A Last Glass of Tea & Other Stories LC 95-960303. 139 p. 1994. write for info. (*977-424-349-8*) Col U Pr.

Bisel, Steve. AS/400 Power Tips & Techniques. (Illus.). 387p. (Orig.). 1995. pap. 99.00 (*1-883884-13-6*, 524) Midrange Comput.

Bisen, Malini, tr. see Osho.

Biser, David. Kokanee: A Complete Fishing Guide. LC 99-179483. (Illus.). 168p. 1998. pap. 14.95 (*1-57188-120-4*) F Amato Pubns.

Biser, Len. The Ignorant Majority: Our Reason for National Gridlock. LC 92-85271. 192p. (Orig.). 1993. pap. 9.95 (*1-880015-13-7*) Petra Pub.

— Jumpstart to Reemployment: A Nation-Wide Guide to Beat Unemployment. LC 91-90314. (Illus.). 124p. (Orig.). 1991. pap. 6.95 (*1-880015-12-9*) Petra Pub.

Bisese, John H. Spinal MRI: A Teaching File Approach. (Illus.). 305p. 1991. text 45.00 (*0-07-005406-1*) McGraw-Hill HPD.

Bisese, John H. & Ay-Ming Wang. Pediatric Cranial MRI: An Atlas of Normal Development. LC 93-47186. (Illus.). 208p. 1994. 165.00 (*0-387-94218-1*) Spr-Verlag.

Bisesi, Michael S. & Kohn, James P. Industrial Hygiene Evaluation Methods. 304p. (C). 1995. boxed set 84.95 (*1-56670-024-8*, L1024) Lewis Pubs.

Bisesi, Michael S., jt. auth. see Koren, Herman.

Bisexual Anthology Collective Staff. Plural Desires: Writing Bisexual Women's Realities. LC 95-231609. 320p. Date not set. pap. 19.95 (*0-920813-19-4*) Sister Vis Pr.

Bisgaard, Daniel J. Social Conscience in Sanskrit Literature. (C). 1994. 14.00 (*81-208-1116-X*, Pub. by Motilal Bnarsidass) S Asia.

Bisgaard, Erling & Aaron, Tossi. In Canon: Explorations of Familiar Canons for Voices, Recorders & Orff Instruments. 32p. 1978. pap. 6.00 (*0-918812-03-8*, SE 0103) MMB Music.

Bisgaard, Erling & Stehouwer, Gulle. Musicbook: O Songs, Games, Movement Activities for Teaching Music to Young Children. Aaron, Tossi, ed. 80p. 1976. pap. 8.95 (*0-918812-04-6*, SE 0016) MMB Music.

Bisgaard, Torkild, jt. auth. see Clasen, Gry.

Bisgrove, Margaret O. Where Two Are Gathered: Stories of 12 Small Christian Communities. LC 97-214412. 160p. 1997. pap. 14.95 (*0-88489-499-1*) St Marys.

Bisgrove, Richard. Gardens of Gertrude Jekyll. 1998. 100.00 (*0-7112-0746-1*, Pub. by F Lincoln) St Mut.

***Bisgrove, Richard.** The Gardens of Gertrude Jekyll. (Illus.). 192p. 2000. pap. 29.95 (*0-520-22620-8*, Pub. by U CA Pr) Cal Prin Full Svc.

Bisguier, Arthur & Maddox, Don. Bisguier! The Career of IGM Arthur Bisguier. (ChessBase University American Grandmaster Ser.). (Illus.). 64p. (Orig.). pap. 10.95 (*1-883358-03-5*) R&D Pub NJ.

***Bish, Barry.** Body Art. (Illus.). 64p. 1999. 6.95 (*1-85626-310-X*, Pub. by Cathie Kyle) Trafalgar.

— Body Art Chic: The First Step-By-Step Guide to Body Painting, Temporary Tattoos, Piercing, Hair Designs, Nail Art. 1999. pap. 13.00 (*1-57076-156-6*) Trafalgar.

Bish, D. L. & Post, J. E. Modern Powder Diffraction. (Reviews in Mineralogy Ser.: Vol. 20). 384p. 1989. per. 28.00 (*0-939950-24-3*) Mineralogical Soc.

Bish, Diane. Classical Organ Collection Organ. 1997. pap. 12.95 (*0-634-00350-X*) H Leonard.

— The Diane Bish Organ Book, Vol. 1. 1997. pap. 10.95 (*0-634-00352-6*); pap. 9.95 (*0-634-00353-4*); pap. 10.95 (*0-634-00355-0*) H Leonard.

— The Diane Bish Organ Book: Christmas, Vol. 3. 1997. pap. 9.95 (*0-634-00354-2*) H Leonard.

— Favorite Organ Selections. 1998. pap. 18.95 (*0-634-00351-8*) H Leonard.

— The Joy of Music: Organ, Vol. 2. 1997. pap. 10.95 (*0-634-00359-3*) H Leonard.

Bish, Douglas & Agnew, John. The Fundamental Band Director: A Guide to Teaching the Modern Concert Band. 144p. (C). 1993. per. 20.95 (*0-8403-8595-1*) Kendall-Hunt.

Bish, Robert. Governing Puget Sound. LC 82-2743. (Illus.). 136p. 1986. pap. 8.95 (*0-295-95886-3*) U of Wash Pr.

Bishai, William R., et al. How to Prepare for the Medical College Admission Test (MCAT) rev. ed. LC 86-3162. 484p. 1987. pap. 12.95 (*0-15-600933-1*) Harcourt.

Bishan, Swarup. Theory of Indian Music. 233p. (C). 1987. 21.00 (*0-8364-2081-0*, Pub. by Mittal Pubs Dist) S Asia.

Bishara. Textbook of Orthodontics. (C). 2001. text. write for info. (*0-7216-8289-8*, W B Saunders Co) Harcrt Hlth Sci Grp.

Bisharat, Fred. Format for Building Detailing. LC 89-51917. (Illus.). 496p. (Orig.). 1989. pap. 37.50 (*0-936029-21-8*) Western Bk Journ.

Bisharat, George E. Palestinian Lawyers & Israeli Rule: Law & Disorder in the West Bank. 263p. 1990. text 30.00 (*0-292-76513-4*) U of Tex Pr.

Bishay, Adli. Desert Development Pt. 1: Desert Agriculture, Ecology & Biology, Vol.5. (Advances in Desert & Arid Land Technology & Development Ser.). xiv, 654p. 1991. text 223.00 (*3-7186-0396-9*, Harwood Acad Pubs) Gordon & Breach.

Bishay, Adli, ed. Desert Development Pt. 2: Socio-Economic Aspects & Renewable Energy Applications, Vol. 5. (Advances in Desert & Arid Land Technology & Development Ser.). xiii, 655p. 1991. text 223.00 (*3-7186-0522-8*, Harwood Acad Pubs) Gordon & Breach.

Bishay, Adli & McGinnies, William G., eds. Advances in Desert & Arid Land Technology & Development. (Advances in Desert & Arid Land Technology & Development Ser.: Vol. 1). xii, 618p. 1979. text 431.00 (*3-7186-0002-1*) Gordon & Breach.

Bishay, F. K., et al. Agricultural Policy Analysis in Egypt: Selected Papers. (Economic & Social Development Papers: No. 129). 186p. 1995. pap. 17.00 (*92-5-103594-6*, F35946, Pub. by FAO) Bernan Associates.

Bishay, Milad. Bishay' New Illustrated Medical Dictionary: English-Arabic. (ARA & ENG.). 800p. 1991. 125.00 (*0-7859-7464-4*) Fr & Eur.

Bisher, Furman. Thankful. LC 96-79793. 96p. 1997. 9.95 (*1-56352-384-1*) Longstreet.

Bisher, Furman & Sibley, Celestine. Atlanta's Half-Century: As Seen Through the Eyes of Columnists Furman Bisher & Celestine Sibley. (Illus.). 192p. 1997. 20.00 (*1-56352-460-0*) Longstreet.

Bishin, William & Stone. Law, Language & Ethics. 1972. text 38.00 (*0-88277-379-8*) Foundation Pr.

Biship, Neal. Everywhere the Light. Young, Billie, ed. LC 78-14861. 1979. 22.95 (*0-87949-137-X*) Ashley Bks.

Bishir, Catherine. Unpainted Aristocracy: The Beach Cottages of Old Nags Head. (Illus.). 28p. 1992. pap. 4.00 (*0-86526-105-9*) NC Archives.

Bishir, Catherine W. North Carolina Architecture: Published for the Historic Preservation Foundation of North Carolina Inc. LC 90-30662. (Illus.). xvi, 516p. (C). 1990. 85.00 (*0-8078-1923-9*) U of NC Pr.

Bishir, Catherine W. & Southern, Michael T. A Guide to the Historic Architecture of Eastern North Carolina. LC 95-50149. (Illus.). 504p. (C). 1996. pap. 19.95 (*0-8078-4594-9*) U of NC Pr.

— A Guide to the Historic Architecture of Eastern North Carolina. LC 95-50149. (Illus.). 504p. (C). (gr. 13). 1996. 39.95 (*0-8078-2285-X*) U of NC Pr.

Bishir, Catherine W., et al. Architects & Builders in North Carolina: A History of the Practice of Building. LC 89-22521. (Illus.). xvi, 540p. (C). 1990. 27.50 (*0-8078-1898-4*) U of NC Pr.

— A Guide to the Historic Architecture of Western North Carolina. LC 98-29626. (Richard Hampton Jenrette Series in Architecture & the Decorative Arts). (Illus.). 496p. 1999. 34.95 (*0-8078-2465-8*); pap. 19.95 (*0-8078-4767-4*) U of NC Pr.

Bishirjian, Richard. The Nature of Public Philosophy. LC 82-20170. 62p. 1983. reprint ed. pap. text 11.50 (*0-8191-2861-9*) U Pr of Amer.

Bishnoi, P. R., jt. auth. see Holder, Gerald D.

Bishoff, David. Grounded, No. 25. Stern, David, ed. (Star Trek: The Next Generation Ser.: Vol. 25). 288p. 1993. mass mkt. 5.50 (*0-671-79747-6*) PB.

— Seaquest DSV: The Ancient. 240p. (Orig.). 1994. mass mkt. 4.99 (*0-441-00042-8*) Ace Bks.

Bishoff, Jay T., jt. auth. see Kavoussi, Louis R.

Bishoff, Tonya & Rankin, Jo, eds. Seeds from a Silent Tree: An Anthology by Korean Adoptees. LC 97-69561. 180p. 1997. pap. 15.00 (*0-9659360-0-7*) Pandal Pr.

Bishofs, Maris. The Alien Diaries. LC 86-1080. (Illus.). 116p. 1986. pap. text 9.95 (*0-915361-44-2*) Lambda Pubs.

— Feisty Virginia Woolf. LC 85-1306. (Illus.). 96p. (Orig.). 1985. pap. 9.95 (*0-915361-17-5*) Lambda Pubs.

— Soho: Drawings on Drawings. (Illus.). (Orig.). 1988. pap. 9.95 (*1-55774-040-2*) Lambda Pubs.

— Soho: Drawings on Drawings. limited ed. (Illus.). (Orig.). 1988. 32.00 (*0-318-33428-3*) Lambda Pubs.

Bishop. Adventure Human Spirit. 2nd ed. 88p. 1998. pap. text, student ed. 17.80 (*0-13-759804-1*) P-H.

— Adventures of the Human Spirit. 2nd ed. 464p. 1998. pap. text 62.00 (*0-13-727306-1*) P-H.

— Dictionary Catalog of the Library of the Bernice P. Bishop Museum. 1970. 160.00 (*0-8161-1448-X*, G K Hall & Co); 160.00 (*0-8161-1449-8*, G K Hall & Co) Mac Lib Ref.

— Experiments in General Chemistry. 3rd ed. (C). 1995. pap. text, teacher ed. 28.00 (*0-03-015633-5*) Harcourt Coll Pubs.

— Fitness Thru Aerobics. 4th ed. LC 98-23793. 205p. 1998. pap. text 25.00 (*0-205-28584-8*, Longwood Div) Allyn.

— Gateway to America. (C). 1995. 24.95 (*0-13-343021-9*, Macmillan Coll) P-H.

— Himalayan Herders. LC 97-74701. (C). 1997. pap. text 23.50 (*0-15-505172-5*) Harcourt.

***Bishop.** Instructor's Manual t/a Standard & Microscale Experiments in General Chemistry. 4th ed. 80p. 1999. write for info. (*0-03-021018-6*, Pub. by SCP) Harcourt.

Bishop. Nursing Ethics. (Philosophy Ser.). (C). 1996. 35.95 (*0-534-54245-X*) Wadsworth Pub.

— The Process Reader. 2000. text 26.00 (*0-07-237939-1*) McGraw.

— Psychology. 9th ed. 1996. pap. text, student ed. 21.00 (*0-13-443243-6*) P-H.

— Standard & Microscale Experiments in General Chemistry. 3rd ed. (C). 1996. pap. text 57.50 (*0-03-007429-0*, Pub. by Harcourt Coll Pubs) Harcourt.

***Bishop.** Standard & Microscale Experiments in General Chemistry. 4th ed. 672p. 1999. text 38.00 (*0-03-021017-8*, Pub. by SCP) Harcourt.

— Twenty-Five Roleplays for Assertiveness Training. 328p. 1995. pap. 131.95 (*0-566-07681-0*) Ashgate Pub Co.

— Understanding Electronic Control Systems. 2000. pap. 39.95 (*0-7506-4601-2*) Buttrwrth-Heinemann.

Bishop. Understanding Psychic. 4th ed. 1998. pap. text, student ed. 20.00 (*0-13-081058-4*) P-H.

— Understanding Psychology. 3rd ed. 1996. pap. text, student ed. 20.00 (*0-13-443508-7*) P-H.

Bishop, ed. Thirteen Ways of Looking for a Poem: A Guide to Writing Poetry. LC 99-45079. 437p. (C). 1999. pap. text 35.33 (*0-321-01130-9*) Addson-Wesley Educ.

Bishop & Aldana. Step up to Wellness. LC 98-33568. 412p. 1998. pap. text 36.00 (*0-205-27970-8*) Allyn.

Bishop & Dowley, Tim. La Oveja Perdida. (Libros de Carton).Tr. of Lost Sheep. (SPA.). (J). 1991. bds. 2.99 (*1-56063-224-0*, 490390) Editorial Unilit.

Bishop, et al. Keys to Success Reader. LC 98-45121. 382p. 1998. pap. text 24.00 (*0-13-010799-9*) P-H.

— Keys to Workplace Skills. LC 98-47210. 186p. 1998. pap. text 31.60 (*0-13-914086-7*) P-H.

Bishop, jt. auth. see Carter.

Bishop, jt. auth. see Carter, Carol.

Bishop, jt. auth. see Dowley.

Bishop, jt. auth. see Venit.

***Bishop, Brett.** Clayton's Path. (Illus.). 40p. (J). (gr. k-4). 2000. 12.95 (*0-9700035-3-6*) Apogee Publng.

Bishop, A., et al. Nonlinear Evolution Equations & Dynamical Systems, '94. 404p. 1995. text 113.00 (*981-02-2219-X*) World Scientific Pub.

Bishop, A. A. & Kulacki, Frank A., eds. Nuclear Reactor Safety Heat Transfer: Presented at the Winter Meeting of the ASME. LC 77-87329. 68p. reprint ed. pap. 30.00 (*0-608-10290-3*, 201690400005) Bks Demand.

Bishop, A. A., ed. see American Society of Mechanical Engineers Staff.

Bishop, A. A., jt. ed. see Chen, John C.

***Bishop, A. Kingsley.** Six Vital Patient Contacts. (Illus.). iii, 71p. 1999. ring bd. 259.00 (*1-929798-00-8*) Greystone Intl Inc.

Bishop, A. R., et al, eds. Disorder & Nonlinearity. (Proceedings in Physics Ser.: Vol. 39). (Illus.). 150p. 1989. 63.95 (*0-387-51374-4*, 3263) Spr-Verlag.

— Nonlinearity in Condensed Matter: Proceedings of the Sixth International Conference, Los Alamos, New Mexico, 5-9 May, 1986. (Solid-State Sciences Ser.: Vol. 69). (Illus.). 410p. 1987. 74.95 (*0-387-17561-X*) Spr-Verlag.

— Special Issue on Incommensurate Phase Transitions. (Journal Ferroelectrics). 412p. 1986. text 604.00 (*2-88124-121-2*) Gordon & Breach.

Bishop, A. R. & Schneider, T., eds. Solitons & Condensed Matter Physics: Proceedings. rev. ed. (Solid-State Sciences Ser.: Vol. 8). (Illus.). 342p. 1981. 57.95 (*0-387-09138-6*) Spr-Verlag.

Bishop, A. R., et al. Microscopic Aspects of Nonlinearity in Condensed Matter. (NATO ASI Ser.: Vol. 264). (Illus.). 374p. (C). 1991. text 115.00 (*0-306-44001-6*, Kluwer Plenum) Kluwer Academic.

Bishop, A. R., jt. auth. see Baeriswyl, D.

Bishop, A. R., ed. see Abdullaev, Fatkhulla K., et al.

Bishop, A. W. Loyalty on the Frontier. Sperry, Phillip A., ed. (Illus.). 244p. 1993. reprint ed. 34.95 (*1-56869-046-0*); reprint ed. pap. 22.95 (*1-56869-047-9*) Oldbuck Pr.

Bishop, Adela. The Christmas Polar Bear. (Illus.). 32p. (J). (gr. k-3). 1991. 12.95 (*0-9625620-2-5*) DOT Garnet.

— The Easter Wolf: An Easter Fable. (Illus.). 32p. (J). (ps-5). 1991. 12.95 (*0-9625620-1-7*) DOT Garnet.

Bishop, Alan J. Mathematical Enculturation: A Cultural Perspective on Mathematics Education. (C). 1991. pap. text 49.00 (*0-7923-1270-8*) Kluwer Academic.

Bishop, Alan J., ed. Mathematical Knowledge: Its Growth Through Teaching. 200p. (C). 1991. lib. bdg. 126.50 (*0-7923-1344-5*) Kluwer Academic.

— Mathematics Education & Culture. (C). 1988. lib. bdg. 98.50 (*90-277-2802-X*) Kluwer Academic.

Bishop, Alan J., et al, eds. International Handbook of Mathematics Education. LC 96-53300. (International Handbooks of Education KHE Ser.: Vol. 4). 1364p. (C). 1997. lib. bdg. 395.00 (*0-7923-3533-3*) Kluwer Academic.

Bishop, Amelia. Lengthening Legacy: Eula Mae Henderson. LC 98-28405. 1998. 15.95 (*1-57168-261-9*, Eakin Pr) Sunbelt Media.

Bishop, Andrea. Mother Wit: 365 Meditations for African American Women. 336p. 1996. pap. 12.95 (*0-687-04794-3*) Abingdon.

Bishop, Ann. Slides: Planning & Producing Slide Programs. LC 81-67828. (Illus.). 160p. (Orig.). (C). 1998. pap. 19.95 (*0-87985-238-0*, S-30, Kodak) Saunders Photo.

Bishop, Ann P., ed. Emerging Communities: Integrating Networked Information into Library Services: Proceedings of the Clinic on Library Applications of Data Processing, 1993. 1994. 30.00 (*0-87845-094-7*) U of Ill Grad Sch.

Bishop, Anne. Daughter of Blood. 1998. mass mkt. 5.99 (*0-451-45671-8*, ROC) NAL.

— Heir to the Shadows, Bk. 2. (Black Jewels Trilogy Ser.). 464p. 1999. mass mkt. 5.99 (*0-451-45672-6*) NAL.

***Bishop, Anne.** Invisible Ring. 2000. mass mkt. 6.99 (*0-451-45802-8*, ROC) NAL.

— Queen of the Darkness. (Black Jewels Trilogy Ser.: Vol. 3). (J). 2000. mass mkt. 5.99 (*0-451-45673-4*, ROC) NAL.

Bishop, Anne H. & Scudder, John R., Jr. The Practical, Moral, & Personal Sense of Nursing: A Phenomenological Philosophy of Practice. LC 89-11480. 185p. (C). 1990. pap. text 21.95 (*0-7914-0252-5*) State U NY Pr.

Bishop, Anne H. & Scudder, John R., Jr., eds. Caring, Curing, Coping: Nurse, Physician, Patient Relationships. LC 84-8836. 142p. 1985. pap. 44.10 (*0-608-05146-2*, 206570700005) Bks Demand.

Bishop, Ashley. Teaching Phonics, Phonemic Awareness & Word Recognition. LC 97-146488. 1997. pap. text 9.95 (*1-57690-126-2*) Tchr Create Mat.

***Bishop, Barbara J.** God's Gifted Helpers. ii, 90p. 1999. pap. 9.95 (*0-9673337-1-7*) Bar-Lor Pubng.

Bishop, Barbara J. Numerology: The Universal Vibrations of Numbers. LC 89-77886. (Self-Help Ser.). (Illus.). 224p. (Orig.). 1999. pap., wbk. ed. 12.95 (*0-87542-056-7*) Llewellyn Pubns.

***Bishop, Barbara J.** Plane Facts, Here & Now. iv, 100p. 1999. pap. 10.95 (*0-9673337-0-9*) Bar-Lor Pubng.

Bishop, Barry C. Karnali under Stress: Livelihood Strategies & Seasonal Rhythms in a Changing Nepal Himalaya. LC 89-20206. (Geography Ser.: Vol. 228-). (Illus.). 300p. 1990. pap. text 29.00 (*0-89065-135-3*) U Ch Pr.

Bishop, Beata. Time to Heal. 320p. 1996. pap. 17.95 (*0-14-019517-3*, Pub. by Pnguin Bks Ltd) Trafalgar.

Bishop, Beata, jt. auth. see Gerson, Charlotte.

Bishop, Bernice P., Museum Editors. Dictionary Catalog of the Library of the Bernice P. Bishop Museum, 9 vols., Set. 1970. 1020.00 (*0-8161-0679-7*, G K Hall & Co) Mac Lib Ref.

Bishop, Bernie. Foreign Direct Investment in Korea: The Role of the State. LC 97-74451. 174p. 1997. 64.95 (*1-84014-196-4*, HG5782, Pub. by Ashgate Pub) Ashgate Pub Co.

Bishop, Betty. Flaubert's Introduction to Art: A Tale for Childish Adults. (Illus.). 40p. (Orig.). 1993. pap. 2.50 (*1-883456-02-9*) Malthus Pr.

Bishop, Betty Webster. The Life & Times of Ralf: Only a Dog. unabridged ed. (Illus.). 20p. 1997. spiral bd. 4.00 (*1-929326-36-X*) Hal Bar Pubg.

— Welcome to Dollyland: A Picturesque Look at Puns. unabridged ed. (Illus.). 72p. 1998. spiral bd 29.95 (*1-929326-27-0*) Hal Bar Pubg.

Bishop, Beverly C. Cowboys, Lumberjacks, & Frontier Justice: A Pictorial History of Flagstaff, AZ. 32p. 1993. pap. 2.95 (*0-9638484-0-2*) Mtn Media.

***Bishop, Bill.** Global Marketing for the Digital Age: Globalize Your Business with Digital & Online Technology. 2000. pap. 20.00 (*0-00-638632-6*) HarpC.

Bishop, Bill. Global Marketing for the Digital Age: Globalize Your Business with Digital & Online Technology. LC 98-36504. xvi, 270p. 1999. 34.95 (*0-8442-2254-2*, NTC Business Bks) NTC Contemp Pub Co.

***Bishop, Bill.** Global Marketing for the Digital Age: Globalize Your Business with Digital & Online Technology. 272p. 2000. pap. 16.95 (*0-658-00058-6*, 000586) NTC Contemp Pub Co.

— The Strategic Enterprise: Growing a Business for the 21st Century. (Illus.). 192p. 2000. 20.95 (*0-7737-3223-3*) Stoddart Publ.

— Strategic Marketing in the Digital Age: Grow Your Company with Online & Digital Technology. 300p. 1999. pap. 80.00 (*0-85297-496-5*, Pub. by Chartered Bank) St Mut.

Bishop, Bob. Shades of Reality: How the New Fuzzy Philosophy Will Change Your World View. LC 97-74302. (Illus.). 217p. 1998. 21.95 (*0-944435-44-0*) Glenbridge Pub.

Bishop, Bob & Thomas, Matt. Protecting Children from Danger: Learning Self-Reliance & Emergency Skills. LC 93-5977. (Illus.). 192p. (Orig.). 1993. pap. 12.95 (*1-55643-159-7*) North Atlantic.

Bishop, Bob, jt. auth. see Whitlock, Flint.

***Bishop, Bonnie K.** California Probate Workflow Manual - 6/98 Update, 2 vols. rev. ed. Tom, Janette, ed. LC 79-53359. 318p. 1998. ring bd. 56.00 (*0-7626-0241-4*, ES-31568) Cont Ed Bar-CA.

Bishop, Budd H., jt. intro. see Columbus Museum of Art Staff.

Bishop, C. James, jt. auth. see Kopf, David S.

***Bishop, C. M., ed.** Generalization in Neural Networks & Machine Learning. LC 98-40870. (Illus.). 353p. 1999. 79.00 (*3-540-64928-X*) Spr-Verlag.

Bishop, Carl. Out of the Ashes: An Abuser's Story of Hope & Restoration. LC 96-68496. 231p. 1996. pap. 10.95 (*1-880451-18-2*) Rainbows End.

Bishop, Carly. Angel with an Attitude. 1997. per. 3.75 (*0-373-22440-0*, 1-22440-1) Harlequin Bks.

— Breathless: (Pulse) LC 95-8357. (Intrigue Ser.). 248p. 1995. per. 3.50 (*0-373-22319-6*, 1-22319-7) Harlequin Bks.

— Falling Stars. (Intrigue Ser.). 1993. per. 2.99 (*0-373-22232-7*, 1-22232-2) Harlequin Bks.

— Harlequin Dreamscape, No. 4. 1990. per. 3.25 (*0-373-79004-X*) Harlequin Bks.

— Heart Throb: (Pulse) LC 95-13558. (Intrigue Ser.). 248p. 1995. per. 3.50 (*0-373-22323-4*, 1-22323-9) Harlequin Bks.

— Hot Blooded. LC 95-7079. (Intrigue Ser.). 248p. 1995. per. 3.50 (*0-373-22314-5*, 1-22314-8) Harlequin Bks.

— McQuaid's Justice: The/Cowboy Code. 1998. per. 3.99 (*0-373-22497-4*, 1-22497-1, Mira Bks) Harlequin Bks.

— No Baby but Mine: Lovers under Cover. (Intrigue Ser.: No. 538). 1999. per. 3.99 (*0-373-22538-5*, 1-22538-2) Harlequin Bks.

***Bishop, Carly.** No Bride but His: Lovers Under Cover. 2000. per. 4.25 (*0-373-22564-4*) Harlequin Bks.

Bishop, Carly. Reckless Lover. LC 96-2466. (Intrigue Ser.). 248p. 1996. per. 3.75 (*0-373-22357-9*, 1-22357-7) Harlequin Bks.

— Shadow Lover. 1996. per. 3.75 (*0-373-22394-3*, 1-22394-0) Harlequin Bks.

— The Soulmate. (Intrigue Ser.). 1996. per. 3.75 (*0-373-22370-6*, 1-22370-0) Harlequin Bks.

— Watch over Me. (Intrigue Ser.: No. 454). 1998. per. 3.99 (*0-373-22454-0*, 1-22454-2) Harlequin Bks.

Bishop, Carol K. Under the Lens: A Look at the American Media. LC 96-61724. 192p. (Orig.). 1997. pap., teacher ed. 15.95 (*0-472-08429-1*, 08429); pap. text 16.95 (*0-472-08403-8*, 08403) U of Mich Pr.

Bishop, Carolyn, jt. ed. see Richards, Delphene.

Bishop, Carter G. & Brooks, Jennifer J. Federal Partnership Taxation: A Guide to the Leading Cases, Statutes, & Regulations. 545p. (C). 1990. pap. 27.50 (*0-314-79329-1*) West Pub.

Bishop, Carter G. & Kleinberger, Daniel S. Limited Liability Companies: Tax & Business Law. 1994. ring bd. 185.00 (*0-685-69541-7*, LIM) Warren Gorham & Lamont.

— Limited Liability Companies: Tax & Business Law. LC 93-61890. 1072p. 1994. 175.00 (*0-7913-1879-6*) Warren Gorham & Lamont.

Bishop, Carter G., jt. auth. see Hogg, James F.

Bishop, Catherine M., jt. auth. see Moskovitz, Myron.

B

B

***Bishop, Charles E.** Radon-Hazard Potential of Beaver Basin Area, Beaver County, Utah. (Special Study Ser.: Vol. 94). (Illus.). 39p. 1998. pap. 7.45 (*1-55791-616-0*, SS-94) Utah Geological Survey.

***Bishop, Charles H., Jr.** Making Change Happen One Person at a Time: Assessing Change Capacity Within Your Organization. LC 00-29965. 2000. 27.95 (*0-8144-0528-2*) AMACOM.

Bishop, Charlie, Jr. & Pittman, Bill. To Be Continued: The Alcoholics Anonymous World Bibliography 1935-1994. 2nd ed. LC 95-107772. 528p. (Orig.). 1994. pap., mass mkt. 25.00 (*1-877686-07-7*) Bishop Bks.

Bishop, Chris. Air Warfare. (Firepower Ser.). 1999. 19.99 (*0-7858-1088-9*) Bk Sales Inc.

— Encyclopedia of Air Warfare, Vol. 2. (Illus.). 1998. 34.95 (*1-880588-26-9*) AIRtime Pub.

***Bishop, Chris.** 1400 Days. 256p. 1998. write for info. (*1-57215-260-5*) World Pubns.

Bishop, Chris. Guns in Combat. 1998. 19.99 (*0-7858-0844-2*) Bk Sales Inc.

— Mechanized Combat. 1998. 19.99 (*0-7858-0842-6*) Bk Sales Inc.

— Neural Networks for Pattern Recognition. (Illus.). 500p. 1996. pap. text 49.95 (*0-19-853864-2*) OUP.

— Sea Warefare. (Firepower Ser.). 1999. 19.99 (*0-7858-1087-0*) Bk Sales Inc.

Bishop, Chris, ed. The Encyclopedia of Civil Aircraft. LC 99-46376. (Illus.). 816p. 1999. 39.98 (*1-57145-183-8*, Thunder Bay) Advantage Pubs.

— The Vital Guide to Combat Guns & Infantry Weapons. (Illus.). 128p. 1996. 14.95 (*1-85310-539-2*) Specialty Pr.

Bishop, Chris, jt. auth. see Dorr, Robert F.

***Bishop, Christina.** Miller's Collecting Kitchenware. (Illus.). 144p. 1999. 25.00 (*1-85732-565-6*, Pub. by Millers Pubns) Antique Collect.

Bishop, Christina. Miller's Collecting Kitchenware. LC 96-141831. (Illus.). 144p. 1996. 25.00 (*1-85732-767-5*, Pub. by Reed Illust Books) Antique Collect.

***Bishop, Christine.** Schwalm Embroidery. 112p. 1999. pap. text 14.95 (*1-86351-220-9*) Sally Milner.

Bishop, Christopher M. Snowmobile Handbook. (Chilton's Total Car Care). (C). 1999. pap. text 29.00 (*0-8019-9124-2*) Thomson Learn.

Bishop, Christopher M., jt. ed. see Maass, Wolfgang.

Bishop, Claire H. The Five Chinese Brothers. LC 38-27908. (Illus.). 64p. (J). (ps-3). 1996. pap. 5.99 (*0-698-11357-8*, PapStar) Peng Put Young Read.

— The Five Chinese Brothers. (J). 1988. 13.99 (*0-399-23319-9*) Putnam Pub Group.

— The Five Chinese Brothers. (J). 1989. 11.15 (*0-606-04223-7*, Pub. by Turtleback) Demco.

— Twenty & Ten. (Illus.). (J). (gr. 3-7). 1978. pap. 4.99 (*0-14-031076-2*, PuffinBks) Peng Put Young Read.

— Twenty & Ten. (Illus.). (J). (gr. 5-9). 1984. 18.75 (*0-8446-6168-6*) Peter Smith.

— Twenty & Ten. 1991. 9.19 (*0-606-02303-8*, Pub. by Turtleback) Demco.

Bishop, Claire Huchet. Twenty & Ten. 76p. (J). (gr. 3-5). pap. 4.99 (*0-8072-1418-3*) Listening Lib.

Bishop, Claudia. Death Dines Out. (Hemlock Falls Mystery Ser.). 256p. 1997. mass mkt. 5.99 (*0-425-16111-0*, Prime Crime) Berkley Pub.

***Bishop, Claudia.** Marinade for Murder. 2000. mass mkt. 5.99 (*0-425-17611-8*, Prime Crime) Berkley Pub.

Bishop, Claudia. Murder Well-Done. 1996. mass mkt. 5.99 (*0-425-15336-3*) Berkley Pub.

— A Pinch of Poison. (Hemlock Falls Mystery Ser.). 1995. mass mkt. 5.99 (*0-425-15104-2*) Berkley Pub.

— A Steak in Murder. 1999. mass mkt. 5.99 (*0-425-16966-9*, Prime Crime) Berkley Pub.

— A Taste for Murder. 240p. (Orig.). 1994. mass mkt. 5.99 (*0-425-14350-3*, Prime Crime) Berkley Pub.

— A Touch of the Grape. (Hemlock Falls Mystery Ser.). 256p. 1998. mass mkt. 5.99 (*0-425-16397-0*, Prime Crime) Berkley Pub.

***Bishop, Clifford.** Sex & Spirit: An Illustrated Guide to Sacred Sexuality. (Illus.). 192p. 2000. pap. 16.95 (*1-56975-212-5*, Pub. by Ulysses Pr) Publishers Group.

Bishop, Conrad & Fuller, Elizabeth. Full Hookup. 1986. pap. 5.25 (*0-8222-0427-4*) Dramatists Play.

— Get Happy: Acting Edition. 36p. (Orig.). (YA). (gr. 9-12). 1990. pap. 4.00 (*0-9624511-0-X*) WordWorkers.

— Loveplay. 90p. (Orig.). 1993. pap. 5.00 (*0-9624511-1-8*) WordWorkers.

— Marie Antoinette. 62p. (C). 1994. pap. 5.00 (*0-9624511-2-6*) WordWorkers.

— Mating Cries. 70p. 1998. pap. 5.00 (*0-9624511-6-9*) WordWorkers.

— Rash Acts: 18 Snapshots for the Stage. LC 89-51731. 208p. (Orig.). (C). 1989. pap. 14.95 (*0-9624511-3-4*) WordWorkers.

***Bishop, Conrad & Fuller, Elizabeth.** Seismic Stages: Five Plays for Teens. LC 99-91942. 256p. (YA). 2000. pap. 18.95 (*0-9624511-7-7*) WordWorkers.

Bishop, Cortlandt F. History of Elections in the American Colonies. LC 78-137277. (Columbia University. Studies in the Social Sciences: No. 8). reprint ed. 29.50 (*0-404-51008-6*) AMS Pr.

Bishop, Cynthia, ed. see Akron-Summit County Public Library Staff.

Bishop, D. F. & Desnick, R. J., eds. Assays of the Heme Biosynthetic Enzymes. (Journal: Enzyme: Vol. 28, No. 2-3). (Illus.). vi, 144p. 1982. pap. 84.50 (*3-8055-3573-2*) S Karger.

Bishop, D. H., ed. Thinkers of Indian Renaissance. 420p. 1986. 36.95 (*0-318-37041-7*) Asia Bk Corp.

Bishop, D. V. Handedness & Developmental Disorder. (Clinics in Developmental Medicine Ser.: No. 110). (Illus.). 208p. (C). 1991. text 54.95 (*0-521-41195-5*, Pub. by Mc Keith Pr) Cambridge U Pr.

— Uncommon Understanding: Development & Disorders of Language Comprehension in Children. LC 97-212683. (Illus.). viii, 277p. 1997. write for info. (*0-86377-260-9*, Pub. by Psychol Pr) Taylor & Francis.

Bishop, Daniel A., et al, eds. Remote Sensing for Geography, Geology, Land Planning & Cultural Heritage. (Europto Ser.: Vol. 2960). 280p. 1996. 66.00 (*0-8194-2364-5*) SPIE.

Bishop, Daniel B. & Weber, Jack A. Impacts of Demand Reduction on Water Utilities. LC 96-137169. (Illus.). 133p. 1996. pap. 90.00 (*0-89867-838-2*, 90690) Am Water Wks Assn.

Bishop, David. Cursed Earth Asylum. (Judge Dredd Ser.). 1995. mass mkt. 5.95 (*0-352-32893-2*, Pub. by Virgin Bks) London Brdge.

— The Savage Amusement. (Judge Dredd Ser.). 256p. (Orig.). 1996. mass mkt. 5.95 (*0-352-32874-6*, Pub. by Virgin Bks) London Brdge.

Bishop, David & Holloway, R. Ross. Wheaton College Collection of Greek & Roman Coins. (Ancient Coins in North American Collections 4). (Illus.). 64p. 1981. 30.00 (*0-89722-190-7*) Am Numismatic.

Bishop, David H. Rhabdoviruses, Vol. I. 208p. 1979. 92.95 (*0-8493-5913-9*, QR415) CRC Pr.

— Rhabdoviruses, 3 vols., Vol. II. 256p. 1980. 141.00 (*0-8493-5914-7*, QR415, CRC Reprint) Franklin.

— Rhabdoviruses, 3 vols., Vol. III. 272p. 1980. 148.00 (*0-8493-5915-5*, CRC Reprint) Franklin.

Bishop, David M. Group Theory & Chemistry. rev. ed. LC 92-39688. (Illus.). 294p. 1993. reprint ed. pap. text 10.95 (*0-486-67355-3*) Dover.

Bishop, David N. Electrical Systems for Oil & Gas Production Facilities. LC 89-1726. 86p. reprint ed. pap. 30.00 (*0-7837-5147-8*, 204487500004) Bks Demand.

Bishop, David S. Effective Communication. LC 76-58043. 1996. reprint ed. pap. 9.99 (*0-87148-286-X*) Pathway Pr.

— Into His Presence. LC 89-60456. 1989. pap. 11.99 (*0-87148-439-0*) Pathway Pr.

Bishop, Debbie & Berg, Cori. Martha's Got Nothin' on Me: The Pre-Fab Cookbook. (Illus.). 174p. 1998. pap. 14.95 (*0-9664737-0-1*, PF2001) Lft Field Prods.

***Bishop, Deborah & Levy, David.** Hello Midnight: The Insomniac's Literary Bedside Companion. 2000. pap. 13.00 (*0-684-84834-1*, Touchstone) S&S Trade Pap.

Bishop, Denis & Ellis, Christopher. Vehicles at War. 25.00 (*0-8453-1699-0*, Cornwall Bks) Assoc Univ Prs.

Bishop, Dennis. Cellular Telephone Product Operation Handbook. (Illus.). 1000p. 2000. ring bd. 159.00 (*0-945592-04-3*) Telecom Pubng.

— Cellular Telephone Program Handbook. 400p. 2000. ring bd. 149.00 (*0-945592-05-1*) Telecom Pubng.

— Simplified Cellular. 160p. 1991. pap. 29.00 (*1-880008-00-9*) Bishop & Assoc.

Bishop, Donald G. The Administration of British Foreign Relations. LC 74-3761. 410p. 1974. reprint ed. lib. bdg. 79.50 (*0-8371-7461-9*, BIBF, Greenwood Pr) Greenwood.

— The Roosevelt - Litvinov Agreements: The American View. LC 65-15852. 305p. reprint ed. pap. 94.60 (*0-608-07592-2*, 205990700010) Bks Demand.

Bishop, Donald H., ed. Chinese Thought: Introduction. (C). 1994. reprint ed. 24.00 (*81-208-1139-9*, Pub. by Motilal Bnarsidass) S Asia.

— Mysticism & the Mystical Experience: East & West. LC 94-35278. 1995. 49.50 (*0-945636-73-3*) Susquehanna U Pr.

Bishop, Doris T., ed. see Blake, Marion E.

Bishop, Dorothy. The Musician as Athlete: Alternative Approaches to Healthy Performance. Carlson, Jude, ed. (Illus.). 395p. (Orig.). (C). 1992. pap. 18.95 (*0-9695590-0-3*, Pub. by Kava Pubns) Rosenthals.

Bishop, Dorothy & Mogford-Bevan, Kay, eds. Language Development in Exceptional Circumstances. (Illus.). 324p. 1988. text 56.00 (*0-443-03800-7*) Church.

Bishop, Dorothy S. Chiquita y Pepita (Chiquita & Pepita) Dos Ratoncitas (The City Mouse & the Country Mouse) (Bilingual Ser.). (ENG & SPA.). (J). 1978. 10.15 (*0-606-01255-9*, Pub. by Turtleback) Demco.

— The City Mouse & the Country Mouse. (French/English Bilingual Fables Ser.). (ENG & FRE., Illus.). 72p. (J). 1989. pap. 4.95 (*0-8442-1086-2*, 10862, Natl Textbk Co) NTC Contemp Pub Co.

— Habia Una Vez. (Once upon a Time Ser.). (SPA., Illus.). 96p. (J). 1991. pap. 15.95 incl. audio (*0-8442-7349-X*, 7349X, Natl Textbk Co) NTC Contemp Pub Co.

— Habia Una Vez. (SPA., Illus.). 96p. (J). 1994. pap. 7.95 (*0-8442-7333-3*, 73333) NTC Contemp Pub Co.

— Habia Una Vez. (SPA.). (J). 1985. 12.05 (*0-606-01283-4*, Pub. by Turtleback) Demco.

— Leonardo el Leon y Ramon el Raton (Leonard the Lion & Raymond the Mouse) (Bilingual Ser.). (ENG & SPA.). (J). 1986. 10.15 (*0-606-01306-7*, Pub. by Turtleback) Demco.

— Le Lion et la Souris - The Lion & the Mouse. (French/English Bilingual Fables Ser.). (ENG & FRE., Illus.). 72p. (J). 1992. pap. 4.95 (*0-8442-1084-6*, 10846, Natl Textbk Co) NTC Contemp Pub Co.

— Tina la Tortuga y Carlos el Conejo (Tina the Turtle & Carlos the Rabbit) (Bilingual Ser.). (ENG & SPA.). (J). 1992. 10.15 (*0-606-01454-3*, Pub. by Turtleback) Demco.

— The Tortoise & the Hare (La Tortue et le Lievre) (French-English Bilingual Fables Ser.). (ENG & FRE., Illus.). 72p. (J). (gr. 4 up). 1992. pap. 4.95 (*0-8442-1085-4*, 10854, Natl Textbk Co) NTC Contemp Pub Co.

Bishop, Dorothy S., et al. Chiquita y Pepita: The City Mouse & the Country Mouse. (SPA., Illus.). 64p. 6.95 (*0-8442-7446-1*, 74461) NTC Contemp Pub Co.

— La Lechera y Su Cubeta.Tr. of Milkmaid & Her Pail. (SPA., Illus.). 64p. 6.95 (*0-8442-7250-7*, 72507) NTC Contemp Pub Co.

— Leonardo el Leon y Ramon el Raton.Tr. of Lion & The Mouse. (Illus.). 64p. 6.95 (*0-8442-7445-3*, 74453) NTC Contemp Pub Co.

Bishop, Dorothy S., et al. Las Manchos del Sapo.Tr. of How the Toad Got Its Spots. (ENG & SPA., Illus.). 64p. (J). 1994. pap. 4.95 (*0-8442-7171-3*, Natl Textbk Co) NTC Contemp Pub Co.

Bishop, Dorothy S., et al. El Muchacho Que Grito el Lobo! (Spanish/English Bilingual Ser.).Tr. of Boy Who Cried Wolf. (ENG & SPA., Illus.). 64p. (J). 1994. pap. 6.95 (*0-8442-7295-7*, 72957, Natl Textbk Co) NTC Contemp Pub Co.

— El Pajaro Cu.Tr. of Cu Bird. (ENG & SPA., Illus.). 64p. (J). 1995. pap. 6.95 (*0-8442-7163-2*, 71632, Natl Textbk Co) NTC Contemp Pub Co.

— Perez y Martina. (SPA., Illus.). 64p. 6.95 (*0-8442-7167-5*, 71675) NTC Contemp Pub Co.

— Poniendo el Cascabel el Gato.Tr. of Belling the Cat. (SPA., Illus.). 64p. 6.95 (*0-8442-7282-5*, 72825) NTC Contemp Pub Co.

— Tina la Tortuga y Carlos el Conejo. (Spanish/English Bilingual Ser.).Tr. of Tortoise & the Hare. (SPA & ENG., Illus.). 64p. 6.95 (*0-8442-7444-5*, 74445, Natl Textbk Co) NTC Contemp Pub Co.

Bishop, Dorothy Sword. Christmas in Russia. (Christmas in...Ser.). (Illus.). 80p. 1995. 12.95 (*0-8442-4291-8*, 42918, Passprt Bks) NTC Contemp Pub Co.

***Bishop, Dorothy V.** Uncommon Understanding: Development & Disorders of Language Comprehension in Children. 288p. 1998. pap. 27.95 (*0-86377-501-2*, Pub. by Psychol Pr) Taylor & Francis.

Bishop, Douglas D. Working in Plant Science. Amberson, Max L. et al, eds. (Illus.). (gr. 9-10). 1978. text 19.96 (*0-07-000835-3*) McGraw.

Bishop, Douglas D., et al. Crop Science & Food Production. 416p. 1983. text 25.96 (*0-07-005431-2*) McGraw.

Bishop, E. Indicators. 756p. (C). 1972. 334.00 (*0-08-016617-2*, Pub. by Pergamon Repr) Franklin.

Bishop, E. & Bridges, Douglas. Constructive Analysis. (Grundlehren der Mathematischen Wissenschaften Ser.: Vol. 279). 500p. 1985. 135.95 (*0-387-15066-8*) Spr-Verlag.

Bishop, Edward. Hurricane. LC 89-69825. (Illus.). 150p. 1990. text 29.95 (*0-87474-221-8*) Smithsonian.

Bishop, Edward L. A Virginia Woolf Chronology. 192p. 1988. 40.00 (*0-8161-8982-X*, Hall Reference) Macmillan.

Bishop, Edward L., ed. see Woolf, Virginia.

Bishop, Eleanor. Prints in the Sand: The U. S. Coast Guard Beach Patrol During WWII. LC 89-62184. (Illus.). 92p. 1989. pap. 9.95 (*0-929521-22-6*) Pictorial Hist.

Bishop, Eleanor C. Ponies, Patriots & Powder Monkeys: A History of Children in America's Armed Forces, 1776-1916. (Illus.). 180p. 1983. 14.95 (*0-911329-00-5*) Bishop Pr.

Bishop, Elizabeth. The Collected Prose. Giroux, Robert, ed. LC 83-16418. 278p. 1984. pap. 14.00 (*0-374-51855-6*) FS&G.

— The Complete Poems, 1927-1979. LC 69-15407. 287p. 1984. pap. 13.00 (*0-374-51817-3*) FS&G.

Bishop, Elizabeth. Edgar Allen Poe & the Jukebox: Uncollected Poems. Date not set. text. write for info. (*0-374-14645-4*) FS&G.

Bishop, Elizabeth. Exchanging Hats: Paintings. Benton, William, ed. & intro. by. LC 96-7963. 128p. 1996. text 40.00 (*0-374-15090-7*) FS&G.

— Geography III. 50p. 1978. pap. 9.00 (*0-374-51440-2*) FS&G.

— One Art: Letters. Giroux, Robert, ed. & selected by by. 725p. 1994. 35.00 (*0-374-22640-7*) FS&G.

— One Art: Letters. Giroux, Robert, ed. & selected by by. 668p. 1995. pap. 16.00 (*0-374-52445-9*) FS&G.

Bishop, Elizabeth & Brasil, Emanuel, eds. An Anthology of Twentieth-Century Brazilian Poetry. LC 75-184359. (Wesleyan Poetry Classics Ser.). (ENG & POR.). 203p. 1997. reprint ed. pap. 19.95 (*0-8195-6023-5*, Wesleyan Univ Pr) U Pr of New Eng.

Bishop, Elizabeth, jt. auth. see Swenson, May.

Bishop, Elizabeth, tr. see Cabral de Melo Neto, Joao.

Bishop, Elizabeth, tr. see Cabral De Melo Neto, Joao.

Bishop, Elizabeth, tr. see Morley, Helena.

***Bishop, Ellen, ed.** Cinema(-to-)graphy: Using Film to Teach Composition. LC 98-54808. 183p. 1999. pap. text 21.00 (*0-86709-458-3*, Pub. by Boynton Cook Pubs) Heinemann.

Bishop, Ellen G. Managing in Black & White. 48p. 1989. 11.95 (*0-87920-105-3*) WNY Wares.

Bishop, Ellen M. & Allen, John E. Hiking Oregon's Geology. (Illus.). 256p. (Orig.). 1996. pap. 16.95 (*0-89886-485-2*) Mountaineers.

Bishop, Emie. Joyous Occasions: A Collection of Heirloom Hardanger Designs. Jolly, Michael, ed. LC 95-71956. (Illus.). 144p. 1996. 29.95 (*0-932437-06-0*) Symbol Exc Pubs.

Bishop, Erin, ed. My Darling Danny: Letters from Mary O'Connell to Her Son Daniel, 1830-1832. LC 99-175819. (Irish Narrative Ser.). 96p. 1998. pap. 12.95 (*1-85918-173-2*, Pub. by Cork Univ) Intl Spec Bk.

***Bishop, Erin I.** The World of Mary O'Connell, 1778-1836. LC 99-198036. 216p. 1999. pap. 29.95 (*1-901866-19-X*, Pub. by Lilliput Pr) Irish Bks Media.

Bishop, Ernest S. The Narcotic Drug Problem. LC 75-17204. (Social Problems & Social Policy Ser.). 1976. reprint ed. 17.95 (*0-405-07476-X*) Ayer.

Bishop, Errett. Selected Papers of Errett Bishop. 440p. 1986. text 79.00 (*9971-5-0127-9*) World Scientific Pub.

Bishop, Errett & Cheng, Henry. Constructive Measure Theory. LC 52-42839. (Memoirs Ser.: No. 1/116). 85p. 1972. pap. 16.00 (*0-8218-1816-3*, MEMO 1/116) Am Math.

— Constructive Measure Theory. LC 72-181247. (American Mathematical Society Ser.: Vol. 116). 92p. reprint ed. pap. 30.00 (*0-608-10510-4*, 205279300009) Bks Demand.

Bishop, Eugene A. The Development of a State School System: New Hampshire. LC 78-176566. (Columbia University. Teachers College. Contributions to Education Ser.: No. 391). reprint ed. 37.50 (*0-404-55391-5*) AMS Pr.

Bishop, Evelyn M. Blake's Hayley: The Life, Works, & Friendships of William Hayley. LC 72-5490. (Biography Index Reprint Ser.). 1977. reprint ed. 30.95 (*0-8369-8133-2*) Ayer.

Bishop, F. Michler. Relapse Prevention with REBT. wbk. ed. 22.95 incl. audio (*0-917476-26-3*, C050) Inst Rational-Emotive.

***Bishop, F. Michler.** Techniques of Treating Addiction: Cognitive, Emotive & Treating Addiction. 2000. 50.00 (*0-7657-0267-3*) Aronson.

***Bishop-Firth, Rachel.** The Ultimate CV for Managers & Professionals: Win Senior Managerial Positions with an Outstanding CV. (Jobs & Careers Ser.). (Illus.). 144p. 2000. pap. 19.95 (*1-85703-584-4*, Pub. by How To Bks) Midpt Trade.

Bishop, G. Reginald, Jr., ed. Culture in Language & Learning. 1960. pap. 10.95 (*0-915432-60-9*) NE Conf Teach Foreign.

— Foreign Language Teaching: Challenges to the Profession. 158p. 1965. pap. 10.95 (*0-915432-65-X*) NE Conf Teach Foreign.

Bishop, Garth, ed. Master Chefs of the World Vol. 1: U. S. A. (Illus.). 1985. pap. 5.95 (*0-913290-57-2*) Camaro Pub.

Bishop, Garth W., ed. Restaurant Redbook: San Francisco, Vol. 2. (Illus.). 1987. pap. 4.95 (*0-913290-91-2*) Camaro Pub.

— Restaurant Redbook Vol. 1: Los Angeles. (Illus.). 1988. pap. 4.95 (*0-913290-89-0*) Camaro Pub.

Bishop, Gary. Shifting Gears. McClain, Cindy, ed. 190p. (Orig.). 1992. pap. text 7.95 (*1-56309-017-1*, N924102, New Hope) Womans Mission Union.

***Bishop, Gavin.** Conejito y el Mar. Acevedo, Pilar, tr.Tr. of Little Rabbit & the Sea. (SPA., Illus.). 32p. (J). (ps). 2000. 15.95 (*0-7358-1313-2*, Pub. by North-South Bks NYC) Chronicle Bks.

— Conejito y el Mar. Acevedo, Pilar, tr.Tr. of Little Rabbit & the Sea. (SPA., Illus.). 32p. (J). (ps-1). 2000. pap. 6.95 (*0-7358-1314-0*, Pub. by North-South Bks NYC) Chronicle Bks.

— Conejito y el Mar.Tr. of Little Rabbit & the Sea. (SPA., Illus.). (J). 2000. 12.40 (*0-606-18317-5*) Turtleback.

Bishop, Gavin. Little Rabbit & the Sea. LC 97-16444. (Illus.). 32p. (J). (ps-1). 1997. 15.95 (*1-55858-809-4*, Pub. by North-South Bks NYC); lib. bdg. 15.88 (*1-55858-810-8*, Pub. by North-South Bks NYC) Chronicle Bks.

***Bishop, Gavin.** Little Rabbit & the Sea. LC 97-16444. (Illus.). 32p. (J). (ps-1). 2000. pap. 6.95 (*0-7358-1312-4*, Pub. by North-South Bks NYC) Chronicle Bks.

— Little Rabbit & the Sea. (Illus.). (J). 2000. 12.40 (*0-606-18322-1*) Turtleback.

— Stay Awake, Bear! LC 99-29514. (Illus.). 32p. (J). (ps-1). 2000. 15.95 (*0-531-30249-0*); lib. bdg. 16.99 (*0-531-33249-7*) Orchard Bks Watts.

***Bishop, Gay.** Miss Hallberg's Butterfly Garden. LC 99-97783. (Illus.). 32p. (J). (ps-6). 2000. pap. 10.95 (*0-9676839-0-4*) Pinevine Pr.

Bishop, George. Every Women Her Own Lawyer: A Private Guide in All Matters of Law, of Essential Interest to Women & by the Aid of Which Every Female May, in Whatever Situation, Understand Her Legal Course & Redress & Be Her Own Legal Advisor. (Women & the Law Reprint Ser.). 1992. reprint ed. 47.50 (*0-8377-1921-6*, Rothman) W S Hein.

— Travels in Imperial China: The Intrepid Explorations & Discoveries of Pere Armand David. (Illus.). 192p. 1996. pap. 19.95 (*0-304-34802-3*, Pub. by Cassell) Sterling.

— When the Master Relents: The Neglected Short Fictions of Henry James. Litz, A. Walton, ed. LC 87-25543. (Studies in Modern Literature: No. 80). 128p. reprint ed. 39.70 (*0-8357-1826-3*, 207069300004) Bks Demand.

Bishop, George F., ed. see Meadow, Robert G. & Jackson-Beeck, Marilyn.

Bishop, George W. Barry Jackson & the London Theatre. LC 76-81972. 230p. 1972. 24.95 (*0-405-08272-X*, Pub. by Blom Pubns) Ayer.

Bishop, Gillian, jt. auth. see Hillman, Ken.

Bishop, Gordon. Gateway to America. LC 98-36231. (Illus.). 200p. 1998. pap. 14.95 (*1-887714-27-8*, 887714) Summerhse Pr.

***Bishop, Greg.** Wake up down There! The Excluded Middle Anthology. 420p. 2000. pap. 25.00 (*0-932813-82-8*, Pub. by Adventures Unltd) SCB Distributors.

Bishop, Greta, ed. see Fournier, Larry.

Bishop, H. L., jt. ed. see Uys, J. M.

Bishop, Haskell H. The Fake Book. 250p. 1996. pap. 5.00 (*1-887146-21-0*) Ark Works.

Bishop, Henry F. Historical Sketch of Lisbon, from 1786 to 1900. 83p. 1997. reprint ed. pap. 16.00 (*0-8328-5658-4*) Higginson Bk Co.

Bishop Herman, ed. The Living Word: A Collection of Sermons for the Liturgical Year, Vols. 1 & 2. 1988. 29.90 (*1-878997-05-X*); 14.95 (*1-878997-03-3*); 14.95 (*1-878997-04-1*) St Tikhons Pr.

Bishop Hipps, Carol. In a Southern Garden. 256p. 1994. 25.00 (*0-671-87151-X*) P-H.

***Bishop, Hugh E.** The Night the Fitz Went Down. LC 00-30459. 2000. pap. write for info. (*0-942235-37-1*) LSPC Inc.

Bishop, Hugh E., jt. ed. see Hayden, Paul L.

Bishop, Hugh E., ed. see Stonehouse, Frederick.

An Asterisk (*) at the beginning of an entry indicates that the title is appearing for the first time.

Bishop, Hunter, ed. see MacDonald, J. E.

Bishop, I. E. Bishop Families in America, Bk. III Bk. III: Richard of Salem. 80p. 1991. reprint ed. pap. 16.00 (*0-8328-2096-2*) Higginson Bk Co.

Bishop, Ian C. The Gibson Guitar since 1950, Vol. 1. 2nd ed. (Illus.). 96p. 1977. reprint ed. pap. 17.95 (*0-933224-46-X*, T14) Bold Strummer Ltd.

Bishop, Ila A. You Can't Spoil a Child with Love! 52p. 1994. pap. 6.95 (*0-9639089-0-1*) Hali Prods.

Bishop Innocent of Kamchatka. Indication of the Way into the Kingdom of Heaven. 48p. (Orig.). 1993. pap. 4.95 (*1-880364-10-7*) New Sarov.

***Bishop, Isabella L.** Among the Tibetans. 160p. 2001. text 110.00 (*0-7103-0695-4*) Col U Pr.

Bishop, Isabella L. Among the Tibetans. 1996. reprint ed. 24.00 (*81-206-1147-0*, Pub. by Asian Educ Servs) S Asia.

— The Aspects of Religion in the United States of America. LC 75-38438. (Religion in America, Ser. 2). 200p. 1979. reprint ed. 23.95 (*0-405-04059-8*) Ayer.

— A Lady's Life in the Rocky Mountains. (American Biography Ser.). 252p. 1991. reprint ed. lib. bdg. 69.00 (*0-7812-8021-4*) Rprt Serv.

Bishop, J. A., et al, eds. Skin Cancer. LC 96-190934. (Cancer Surveys Ser.: Vol. 26). (Illus.). 300p. (C). 1996. text 56.00 (*0-87969-483-1*) Cold Spring Harbor.

Bishop, J. B. Criminal Procedure. 1983. 50.00 (*0-409-49460-7*, AT, MICHIE); pap. 33.00 (*0-409-49201-9*, AT, MICHIE) LEXIS Pub.

— Prosecution Without Trial. 1989. 59.00 (*0-409-49478-X*, AT, MICHIE) LEXIS Pub.

Bishop, J. E., et al, eds. Pulmonary Vascular Remodelling. (Portland Press Research Monographs: Vol. 7). 288p. (C). 1995. 136.00 (*1-85578-041-0*, Pub. by Portland Pr Ltd) Ashgate Pub Co.

Bishop, J. L. History of American Manufacturers, 1608-1860, 2 vols., Set. 1993. reprint ed. lib. bdg. 180.00 (*0-7812-5209-1*) Rprt Serv.

Bishop, J. M. Data Abstraction in Programming Languages. 192p. (C). 1987. pap. text 23.75 (*0-201-14222-8*) Addison-Wesley.

Bishop, J. M., jt. auth. see Barron, D. W.

Bishop, Jack. The Complete Italian Vegetarian Cookbook: 350 Essential Recipes for Inspired Everyday Eating. Martin, Rux, ed. LC 97-16879. (Illus.). 688p. 1997. 35.00 (*1-57630-044-7*, Chapters Bks) HM.

— Lasagna. 144p. 1994. pap. 9.95 (*0-8092-3699-0*, 369900, Contemporary Bks) NTC Contemp Pub Co.

— Pasta e Verdura: 140 Vegetable Sauces for Spaghetti, Fusilli, Rigatoni, & All Other Noodles. 336p. 1996. 27.00 (*0-06-017402-1*) HarpC.

***Bishop, Jack.** Pasta e Verdura: 140 Vegetable Sauces for Spaghetti, Fusilli, Rigatoni, & All Other Noodles. 336p. 2000. pap. 15.00 (*0-06-093245-7*, Quil) HarperTrade.

Bishop, Jack. Ralph Ellison: Author. Huggins, Nathan I., ed. (Black Americans of Achievement Ser.). (Illus.). 124p. (YA). (gr. 5 up). 1987. lib. bdg. 19.95 (*1-55546-585-4*) Chelsea Hse.

— Ralph Ellison: Author. Huggins, Nathan I., ed. (Black Americans of Achievement Ser.). (Illus.). 124p. (YA). (gr. 5 up). 1989. pap. 8.95 (*0-7910-0202-0*) Chelsea Hse.

— Something Sweet. 1995. 15.00 (*0-684-80187-6*) S&S Trade.

***Bishop, Jack.** Vegetables Every Day: The Definitive Guide to Buying & Cooking Today's Fresh Produce. LC 00-40823. (Illus.). 2001. write for info. (*0-06-019221-6*) HarpC.

Bishop, Jack, jt. auth. see Casella, Cesare.

***Bishop, Jacqueline.** The Colors of Rhythm: New Orleans Artists Reflect on Music & the Musician. (Illus.). 27p. (Orig.). 1998. pap. 15.00 (*0-9663846-0-1*) Lavender Ink.

— Em Memoria Chico Mendes: A Tribute on the Ten Year Anniversary of His Death. Otto, Sylvia et al, trs. (POR, SPA & ENG.). 64p. (Orig.). 1998. pap. 25.00 (*0-9663846-1-X*) Lavender Ink.

Bishop, Jacqui & Grate, Mary. How to Love Yourself When You Don't Know How: Healing All Your Inner Children. 165p. 1991. pap. 12.95 (*0-88268-131-1*) Station Hill Pr.

Bishop, James, Jr. Epitaph for a Desert Anarchist: The Life & Legacy of Edward Abbey. 1996. pap. 12.00 (*0-614-14726-3*, Riverhd Trade) Berkley Pub.

— Epitaph for a Desert Anarchist: The Life & Legacy of Edward Abbey. 320p. 1994. pap. 22.00 (*0-689-12195-4*, Pub. by Ctrl Bur voor Schimmel) Macmillan.

Bishop, James. Remembering Bruce: The Enduring Legend of the Martial Arts Superstar. (Illus.). 176p. 1999. pap. 19.95 (*1-890723-21-5*, Pub. by Cyclone Bks) SCB Distributors.

***Bishop, James F.** Cancer Facts: A Concise Oncology Text. 432p. 1999. pap. text 38.00 (*90-5702-470-5*, Harwood Acad Pubs) Gordon & Breach.

— Cancer Facts: A Concise Oncology Text. 432p. 1999. text 75.00 (*90-5702-365-2*, Harwood Acad Pubs) Gordon & Breach.

Bishop, Jane, tr. Hildegard of Bingen: Scivias. (Classics of Western Spirituality Ser.). 1990. pap. 24.95 (*0-8091-3130-7*) Paulist Pr.

Bishop, Jane, tr. see Furlog, Nicola.

Bishop, Jane, tr. see Walsh, Kathleen A.

Bishop, Janice, ed. see Mathie, Mellissa.

***Bishop, Jennie.** Crayon Kingdom: Lion Cub Storybooks, Teaches Children about Unity. (Illus.). (J). 1999. 12.95 (*0-87162-853-8*) Warner Pr.

Bishop, Jennifer A., jt. auth. see Bishop, Patrick.

Bishop, Jim. The Day Christ Died. 288p. 1991. pap. 12.00 (*0-06-060816-1*, Pub. by Harper SF) HarpC.

Bishop, Jim. Day Christ Was Born. large type ed. (Large Print Inspirational Ser.). 128p. 1986. pap. 8.95 (*0-8027-2548-1*) Walker & Co.

Bishop, Jim. The Day Christ Was Born. large type ed. reprint ed. 10.00 (*0-318-65646-9*) NAVH.

— The Day Christ Was Born & the Day Christ Died, 2 vols. in 1. 544p. 1993. 11.98 (*0-88365-830-5*) Galahad Bks.

— The Day Kennedy Was Shot. 736p. 1984. 11.99 (*0-517-43100-9*) Random Hse Value.

Bishop, Jim. The Day Lincoln Was Shot. 320p. 1942. mass mkt. 19.00 (*0-06-080005-4*, P5, Perennial) HarperTrade.

Bishop, Jim. The Day Lincoln Was Shot. 320p. 1984. 9.99 (*0-517-44649-9*) Random Hse Value.

Bishop, Jodi, jt. auth. see Hale, Sarah L.

***Bishop, Jodie.** Customer-Effective Web Sites. LC 00-29128. 274p. 2000. pap. 39.99 (*0-13-087827-8*) P-H.

Bishop, Joel P. Commentaries on the Criminal Law, 2 vols. 7th enl. rev. ed. LC 87-80149. No. 4. 1630p. 1987. reprint ed. lib. bdg. 110.00 (*0-89941-547-4*, 305120) W S Hein.

— Commentaries on the Criminal Law, 2 vols., Set. LC 76-156005. (Foundations of Criminal Justice Ser.). reprint ed. 155.00 (*0-404-09105-9*) AMS Pr.

— Commentaries on the Law of Married Women under the Statutes of the Several States, & at Common Law & in Equity, 2 vols. LC 87-80147. (Historical Writings in Law & Jurisprudence Ser.: No. 14). 1475p. 1987. reprint ed. lib. bdg. 105.00 (*0-89941-548-2*, 305130) W S Hein.

— First Book of the Law. LC 89-80599. xi, 466p. 1989. reprint ed. 50.00 (*0-89941-678-0*, 305900) W S Hein.

***Bishop, Joel Prentiss.** The Doctrines of the Law of Contracts, in Their Principal Outlines, Stated, Illustrated & Condensed. LC 99-73244. 1999. 120.00 (*1-56169-539-4*) Gaunt.

Bishop, John. Bishop's: The Cookbook. (Illus.). 164p. 1997. 29.95 (*1-55054-437-3*, Pub. by DGL); pap. 22.95 (*1-55054-633-3*, Pub. by DGL) Orca Bk Pubs.

— Borderlines. 1989. pap. 5.25 (*0-8222-0135-6*) Dramatists Play.

— Cabin Twelve: A One Act Play. 1978. pap. 3.25 (*0-8222-0171-2*) Dramatists Play.

— Confluence & The Skirmishers: Two Short Plays. 1982. pap. 5.25 (*0-8222-0236-0*) Dramatists Play.

***Bishop, John.** Cooking at My House. (Illus.). 168p. 2000. 40.00 (*1-55054-727-5*, Pub. by DGL) Orca Bk Pubs.

Bishop, John. The Harvesting. 1984. pap. 5.25 (*0-8222-0499-1*) Dramatists Play.

— Joyce's Book of the Dark: Finnegan's Wake. LC 86-40045. 288p. (C). 1993. reprint ed. pap. text 27.95 (*0-299-10824-4*) U of Wis Pr.

— The Musical Comedy Murders of 1940. 1987. pap. 5.25 (*0-8222-0792-3*) Dramatists Play.

— Natural Agency: An Essay on the Causal Theory of Action. (Cambridge Studies in Philosophy). 223p. (C). 1990. text 80.00 (*0-521-37430-8*) Cambridge U Pr.

Bishop, John A. & Howitt, Idelle A. Federal Tax Valuation Digest Annual. per. 175.00 (*0-7913-0157-5*) Warren Gorham & Lamont.

Bishop, John L., ed. Studies in Chinese Literature. LC 65-13836. (Harvard-Yenching Institute Studies: No. 21). 253p. (Orig.). 1965. pap. 8.50 (*0-674-84705-9*) HUP.

— Studies of Governmental Institutions in Chinese History. LC 68-17622. (Harvard-Yenching Institute Studies: No. 23). 280p. 1968. pap. 8.50 (*0-674-85110-2*) HUP.

Bishop, John M. An Ever-Changing Place: A Year among Snow Monkeys & Shepas in the Himalayas. 1975. 45.00 (*0-7855-0226-2*, Pub. by Ratna Pustak Bhandar) St Mut.

— An Ever-Changing Place: A Year among Snow Monkeys & Sherpas in the Himalayas. 192p. (C). 1975. 285.00 (*0-89771-040-1*, Pub. by Ratna Pustak Bhandar) St Mut.

Bishop, John Michael. Molecular Oncology. 1996. 71.95 (*0-89454-023-8*) Mosby Inc.

Bishop, John P. The Republic of Letters in America: The Correspondence of John Peale Bishop & Allen Tate. Young, Thomas D. & Hindle, John J., eds. LC 80-5186. 240p. reprint ed. pap. 74.40 (*0-7837-5779-4*, 204544500006) Bks Demand.

Bishop, John P. & Wilson, Edmund. The Undertaker's Garland. LC 74-4263. (American Literature Ser.: No. 49). 1974. lib. bdg. 75.00 (*0-8383-2041-4*) M S G Haskell Hse.

Bishop, John S., Jr., jt. auth. see Thayer, Ralph E.

Bishop, John W., et al. The Jewish-Christian Connection: An Interfaith Experience. LC 86-24051. (Illus.). 64p. 1987. 10.00 (*0-8159-5903-6*) Devin.

Bishop, Jonathan. The Covenant: A Reading. 458p. (Orig.). 1983. pap. 9.95 (*0-87243-113-4*) Templegate.

— Emerson on the Soul. LC 80-2527. reprint ed. 29.50 (*0-404-19251-3*) AMS Pr.

Bishop, Joseph B. Notes & Anecdotes of Many Years. LC 78-128210. (Essay Index Reprint Ser.). 1977. 20.95 (*0-8369-1904-1*) Ayer.

Bishop, Joseph M. A Mariner's Guide to Radiofacsimile Weather Charts. (Illus.). 115p. (Orig.). 1981. pap. 14.95 (*0-9607004-1-2*) Alden Electronics.

Bishop, Joseph W. Law of Corporate Officers & Directors: Indemnification & Insurance. LC 82-4383. 1990. 130.00 (*0-685-10649-7*) West Group.

Bishop, Joyce, jt. auth. see Carter, Carol.

Bishop, Judith. The Burning Place: Poems. LC 94-12622. 80p. (Orig.). 1994. pap. 8.50 (*1-56474-110-9*) Fithian Pr.

— Java Gently for Engineers & Scientists: Programming. LC 99-55691. 436p. (C). 2000. pap. 51.00 (*0-201-34304-5*) Addison-Wesley.

Bishop, Judson W. The Story of a Regiment: Being a Narrative of the Service of the Second Regiment, Minnesota Veteran Volunteer Infantry in the Civil War of 1861-1865. Chester, Newell, ed. 256p. 1999. pap. 14.95 (*0-87839-114-2*) North Star.

Bishop, Judy. Bishop Java Gently. 2nd rev. ed. LC 98-142940. 420p. (C). 1998. pap. 51.00 (*0-201-34297-9*) Addison-Wesley.

— Pascal Precisely. 256p. (C). 1987. pap. text 19.95 (*0-201-17525-8*) Addison-Wesley.

***Bishop, Julia C. & Curtis, Mavis.** Play Today in the Primary School Playground: Life, Learning & Creativity. LC 00-44120. 2001. pap. write for info. (*0-335-20715-4*, Pub. by OpUniv Pr) Taylor & Francis.

Bishop, June, jt. ed. see Norman, Anthony W.

Bishop, Kate, ed. see Ardagh, Arjuna Nick.

Bishop, Kathleen, et al. Working with Kids Who Hurt: A Program for Working with Students from Dysfunctional Families. (Illus.). 44p. (Orig.). (J). (gr. 3-8). 1992. pap. 9.95 (*1-884063-99-3*) Mar Co Prods.

Bishop, Keith. Factfinders: Environment. (Fact Finders Ser.). (J). pap. 8.95 (*0-563-37352-0*, BBC-Parkwest) Parkwest Pubns.

Bishop, Keith P. Nevada Corporation Law & Practice. LC 93-39070. (National Corporation Law Ser.). 1993. 110.00 (*0-13-108499-2*) Aspen Law.

— Nevada Law of Corporations & Business Organizations. LC 97-2473. 1000p. 1997. 155.00 (*1-56706-329-2*) Aspen Law.

Bishop, Kevin. China's Imperial Way. (Illus.). 240p. 1997. pap. 19.95 (*0-8351-2599-8*) China Bks.

***Bishop, Kevin.** Xi'an. 2000. pap. 19.95 (*962-217-621-6*) Norton.

Bishop, L. J., et al. After the Smoke Clears: A Fire & Smoke Damage Restoration Technical Reference Guide. (Illus.). 230p. 1993. pap. 169.00 (*0-944352-34-0*) Cleaning Cons.

— Fire's Out... Now What? Disaster Restoration: Marketing & Sales. (Illus.). 200p. 1993. pap. 249.00 (*0-944352-33-2*) Cleaning Cons.

Bishop, Lea, jt. auth. see Bailey, Covert.

Bishop, Lee. Gunblaze. large type ed. 1990. pap. 5.00 (*0-7451-1288-9*, Pub. by Chivers N Amer) Chivers N Amer.

Bishop, Lee E., Jr. & Elliott, J. Robert, II. American Society Medals: An Identification Guide. unabridged ed. LC 96-96836. (Illus.). 320p. 1998. 69.95 (*0-9653338-0-9*) Bishop & Elliott.

Bishop, Leonard. Dare to Be a Great Writer. 320p. 1992. pap. 15.99 (*0-89879-464-1*, Wrtrs Digest Bks) F & W Pubns Inc.

Bishop, Lilli & Dawson, Janet. Comprehensive Articulation Resource Directory. (Illus.). 152p. (Orig.). 1997. pap. 24.95 (*1-890265-00-4*, 1000) Janelle Pubns.

Bishop, Lloyd. Romantic Irony in French Literature: From Diderot to Beckett. LC 89-35563. 256p. 1989. 29.95 (*0-8265-1233-X*) Vanderbilt U Pr.

Bishop, Lloyd & Lester, Paula. Instrumentation in Education: An Anthology. LC 92-40361. (Source Books on Education: Vol. 39). 368p. 1993. text 66.00 (*0-8153-0638-5*) Garland.

Bishop, Lloyd, jt. auth. see Lester, Paula.

Bishop, Lloyd K., jt. auth. see Lester, Paula E.

Bishop, M. C. Finds from Roman Aldborough. (Monographs in Archaeology: Vol. 65). (Illus.). 116p. 1996. pap. 20.00 (*1-900188-09-0*, Pub. by Oxbow Bks) David Brown.

Bishop, M. C., ed. Journal of Roman Military Equipment Studies, Vol. 1. annuals (Illus.). 166p. 1990. pap. 32.50 (*0-614-21876-4*, Pub. by Oxbow Bks) David Brown.

— Journal of Roman Military Equipment Studies, Vol. 2. annuals (Illus.). 126p. 1991. pap. 32.50 (*0-614-21875-6*, Pub. by Oxbow Bks) David Brown.

— Journal of Roman Military Equipment Studies, Vol. 3. annuals (Illus.). 128p. 1994. pap. 45.00 (*0-946897-74-3*, Pub. by Oxbow Bks) David Brown.

— Journal of Roman Military Equipment Studies, Vol. 4. annuals (Illus.). 103p. 1995. 45.00 (*0-946897-95-6*, Pub. by Oxbow Bks) David Brown.

— Journal of Roman Military Equipment Studies, Vol. 5. annuals 200p. 1996. pap. 60.00 (*0-614-21874-8*, Pub. by Oxbow Bks) David Brown.

Bishop, M. C. & Dore, J. N. Corbridge: Excavations of the Roman Fort & Town, 1947-80. (Historic Buildings & Monuments Commission for England Archaeological Report Ser.: No. 8). 323p. 1989. 72.00 (*1-85074-209-X*) Balogh.

Bishop, M. Guy. Henry William Bigler: Soldier, Gold Miner, Missionary, Chronicler, 1815-1900. LC 98-25354. xiv, 200 p. 1998. pap. 19.95 (*0-87421-254-5*) Utah St U Pr.

— Henry William Bigler: Soldier, Gold Miner, Missionary, Chronicler, 1815-1900. (Illus.). 200p. 1998. 36.95 (*0-87421-253-7*) Utah St U Pr.

Bishop, M. J. & Rawlings, C. J., eds. Nucleic Acid & Protein Sequence Analysis. (Practical Approach Ser.). 436p. 1987. 75.00 (*1-85221-007-9*); pap. 49.95 (*1-85221-006-0*) OUP.

Bishop, Margaret M. The ABCs & All Their Tricks: The Complete Reference Book of Phonics & Spelling. (J). 1986. 22.99 (*0-88062-149-4*) Mott Media.

Bishop, Marilyn E. Religion & Disability: Perspectives in Scripture, Theology & Ethics. LC 94-44885. 80p. (Orig.). 1995. pap. 6.95 (*1-55612-713-8*) Sheed & Ward WI.

Bishop, Mark. Okinawan Karate. pap. write for info. (*0-7136-5666-2*, Pub. by A & C Blk) Midpt Trade.

— Okinawan Karate. rev. ed. 1999. pap. 16.95 (*0-8048-3205-6*) Tuttle Pubng.

— Seeing Is Believing: A Christmas Gift. 24.95 (*1-883755-10-7*) Lost Riv Pr.

— Spiritual Jurisdiction. LC 93-195360. 1996. pap. text 6.99 (*0-9628301-0-0*) M Bishop Minis.

— Zen Kobudo: Mysteries of Okinawan Weaponry & Te. 96p. 1995. pap. 12.95 (*0-8048-2027-9*) Tuttle Pubng.

Bishop, Markus. Our Covenant of Prosperity: Crossing the Threshold to Supernatural Abundance. LC 97-213780. 112p. 1997. pap. 6.99 (*0-89274-959-8*) Harrison Hse.

Bishop, Marsha B. & Polk, David P., eds. And the Angels Wept: From the Pulpits of Oklahoma after the Bombing. 136p. (Orig.). 1995. pap. 15.00 (*0-8272-0021-8*) Chalice Pr.

Bishop, Martha. Browning, for Five Viols: Two Trebles, Tenor, Two Basses. (Charney Manor Ser.: No. 5). i, 19p. 1992. pap. text 10.00 (*1-56571-048-7*, CM5) PRB Prods.

— Eight Canonic Duets for Bass Viols. (Contemporary Consort Ser.: No. 15). i, 14p. 1991. pap. text 8.00 (*1-56571-001-0*) PRB Prods.

— Eight Duets for Two Cellos. i, 14p. 1992. pap. text 8.00 (*1-56571-050-9*, CC19) PRB Prods.

— Elegy & Passacaglia for Tenor Viol & Two Bass Viols. (Contemporary Consort Ser.: No. 9). i, 11p. 1990. pap. text 10.00 (*1-56571-012-6*) PRB Prods.

— Mosaics for Four Viols & Optional Recorder Quartet. (Contemporary Consort Ser.: No. 12). i, 22p. 1990. 12.00 (*1-56571-014-2*) PRB Prods.

***Bishop, Martha.** Prellidio & Passacaglia: For Seven-String Bass Viol. (Contemporary Instrumental Ser.: Vol. 10). 6p. 1999. pap. 5.00 (*1-56571-173-4*, CI010) PRB Prods.

Bishop, Martha. Recorders on Parade, for Recorder Quintet. (Contemporary Consort Ser.: No. 26). i, 16p. 1993. pap. text 12.00 (*1-56571-076-2*, CC026) PRB Prods.

— Suite for Two Bass Viols. (Contemporary Consort Ser.: No. 5). i, 18p. 1990. pap. text 10.00 (*1-56571-003-7*) PRB Prods.

— Two Fantasias for Three Viols. (Contemporary Consort Ser.: No. 6). i, 21p. 1990. pap. text 10.00 (*1-56571-010-X*) PRB Prods.

Bishop, Martin. The Fourth Horseman. large type ed. (Linford Western Library). 1991. pap. 16.99 (*0-7089-7037-0*) Ulverscroft.

— Genetic Databases. 272p. 1999. pap. 49.95 (*0-12-101625-0*) Acad Pr.

Bishop, Martin, ed. Guide to Human Genome Computing. 2nd ed. LC 98-14458. (Illus.). 320p. 1998. boxed set 69.95 (*0-12-102051-7*) Morgan Kaufmann.

Bishop, Martin & Rawlings, Chris, eds. DNA & Protein Sequence Analysis: A Practical Approach. (The Practical Approach Ser.: No. 171). (Illus.). 374p. 1997. text 110.00 (*0-19-963464-5*); pap. text 55.00 (*0-19-963463-7*) OUP.

***Bishop, Mary.** Financial Reporting Analysis & Planning. 444p. 1999. pap. 120.00 (*0-85297-532-5*, Pub. by Chartered Bank) St Mut.

Bishop, Matthew, et al, eds. Privatization & Economic Performance. LC 94-10326. (Illus.). 392p. 1994. text 65.00 (*0-19-877343-9*); pap. text 26.00 (*0-19-877344-7*) OUP.

— The Regulatory Challenge. (Illus.). 468p. 1995. pap. text 35.00 (*0-19-877342-0*) OUP.

Bishop, Matthew & Kay, John A., eds. European Mergers & Merger Policy. (Illus.). 376p. 1993. pap. text 26.00 (*0-19-877346-3*) OUP.

Bishop, Matthew A. The Art & Science of Computer Security. (C). 2000. 54.95 (*0-201-44099-7*) Addison-Wesley.

Bishop, Maurice. Maurice Bishop Speaks: The Grenada Revolution & Its Overthrow, 1979-83. LC 83-63309. 352p. 1983. reprint ed. pap. 20.95 (*0-87348-612-9*); reprint ed. lib. bdg. 55.00 (*0-87348-611-0*) Pathfinder NY.

Bishop, Maurice & Castro, Fidel. La Revolucion Granadina, 1979-83. (SPA.). 86p. 1984. pap. 6.95 (*0-87348-483-5*) Pathfinder NY.

Bishop, Meg, jt. ed. see Gibson, Graeme.

***Bishop, Melanie.** Blue Parabolas. 14p. 1999. pap. write for info. (*1-929896-01-8*) Jump & Shout.

Bishop, Michael. Ancient of Days. LC 84-28324. 384p. 1995. 13.95 (*0-312-89027-3*) Orb NYC.

— At the City Limits of Fate. LC 97-111100. 328p. (Orig.). 1996. pap. 14.00 (*0-9629066-6-2*) Edgewood Pr.

— Blooded on Arachne. LC 81-10830. (Illus.). 352p. 1982. 15.95 (*0-87054-093-9*) Arkham.

***Bishop, Michael.** Blue Kansas Sky. 270p. 2000. 23.95 (*0-9655901-0-0*, Pub. by Golden Gryphon) IPG Chicago.

Bishop, Michael. Brittle Innings. LC 93-31150. 528p. 1995. mass mkt. 5.99 (*0-553-56943-0*) Bantam.

— Count Geiger's Blues. 384p. 1994. pap. 12.95 (*0-312-89008-7*) Orb NYC.

— Critical History of French Poetry. (Twayne's Critical History of Poetry Ser.). 384p. 1993. pap. 33.00 (*0-8057-8453-5*, Twyne) Mac Lib Ref.

— Nebula Awards No. 4: SFWA's Choices for the Best Science Fiction & Fantasy, 1988. 1990. pap. 13.95 (*0-15-665474-1*) Harcourt.

— Nebula Awards No. 25: SFWA's Choices for the Best Science Fiction & Fantasy of the Year. 1991. 24.95 (*0-15-164933-2*) Harcourt.

— Nebula Awards No. 25: SFWA's Choices for the Best Science Fiction & Fantasy (1989) 346p. 1991. pap. 14.95 (*0-15-665473-3*, Harvest Bks) Harcourt.

— Philip K. Dick Is Dead, Alas. 352p. 1993. pap. 12.95 (*0-312-89002-8*) Orb NYC.

— The Secret Ascension. 1989. mass mkt. 4.50 (*0-8125-3157-4*) Tor Bks.

— Seven Deadly Sins. 304p. 1999. 22.00 (*0-9669888-0-9*); pap. 14.95 (*0-9669888-1-7*) Checkmate.

— Stolen Faces. LC 76-26262. 176p. 1977. 25.00 (*0-06-010362-0*) Ultramarine Pub.

— Who Made Stevie Cry? LC 84-9251. (Illus.). 325p. 1984. 18.95 (*0-87054-099-8*) Arkham.

Bishop, Michael, ed. Nebula Awards No. 4: SFWA's Choices for the Best Science Fiction & Fantasy, 1988. 1990. 22.95 (*0-15-164932-4*) Harcourt.

— Nebula Awards No. 23: SFWA's choices for the Best Science Fiction & Fantasy 1987. 352p. 1989. 21.95 (*0-15-164930-8*); pap. 12.95 (*0-15-665475-X*) Harcourt.

Bishop, Michael, tr. Women's Poetry in France, 1965-1995: A Bilingual Anthology. (French Poetry in Translation Ser.). (FRE.). 175p. (Orig.). 1997. pap. 17.95 (*0-916390-79-9*) Wake Forest.

B

Bishop, Michael, et al. Clinical Chemistry: Principles, Procedures, Correlations. 4th ed. LC 99-36820. 682p. 2000. text. write for info. (*0-7817-1776-0*) Lppncott W & W.

— The New Color Portfolio. (Illus.). 10p. 1989. 3000.00 (*0-89659-243-X*) Abbeville Pr.

Bishop, Michael G., et al. A History of Sevier County. LC 96-60163. (Centennial County History Ser.). 321p. 1997. write for info. (*0-913738-07-7*) Utah St Hist Soc.

Bishop, Mike. Fiat Service-Repair Handbook, 128 & X1/9, 1971-1975 LC 76-364914. 213p. 1976. write for info. (*0-89287-089-3*) Clymer Pub.

***Bishop, Mike & Tardel, Vern.** How to Build a Traditional Ford Hot Rod. LC 00-20537. (Illus.). 160p. 2000. pap. 24.95 (*0-7603-0900-0*, 130550AP, Pub. by MBI Pubg) Motorbooks Intl.

Bishop, Mike, et al. Fiat Service, Repair Handbook, 128 & XI/9, 1971-1977 LC 77-374506. x, 195 p. 1977. write for info. (*0-89287-165-2*) Clymer Pub.

Bishop, Morris. A History of Cornell. LC 62-17815. (Illus.). 663p. 1962. text 52.50 (*0-8014-0036-8*) Cornell U Pr.

— Middle Ages. (American Heritage Library). 352p. 1986. pap. 15.00 (*0-8281-0487-5*) HM.

***Bishop, Morris.** Middle Ages. (Illus.). 368p. 2001. reprint ed. pap. 16.00 (*0-618-05703-X*, Mariner Bks) HM.

Bishop, Morris. A Survey of French Literature, 2 vols. rev. ed. Incl. Vol. 1. Survey of French Literature. rev. ed. 462p. (C). 1965. text 64.50 (*0-15-584963-8*, Pub. by Harcourt Coll Pubs); Vol. 2. Survey of French Literature. rev. ed. 462p. (C). 1965. text 64.50 (*0-15-584964-6*); 462p. (C). 1965. text. write for info. (*0-685-02107-6*) Harcourt Coll Pubs.

— A Survey of French Literature, 2 vols., Vol. 1. 1955. 6.75 (*0-15-584961-1*) Harcourt.

— A Survey of French Literature, 2 vols., Vol. 2. 1955. 6.75 (*0-15-584962-X*) Harcourt.

Bishop, Morris, ed. Treasury of British Humor. (Granger Index Reprint Ser.). 1977. 38.95 (*0-8369-6194-3*) Ayer.

Bishop, Morris, tr. see Petrarca, Francesco.

Bishop, Nancy, jt. auth. see Holloway, Diane.

Bishop, Nancy, ed. see Womack, Pam.

Bishop, Natalie. A Love Like Romeo & Juliet. 1993. per. 3.50 (*0-373-09840-5*, 5-09840-5) Silhouette.

— The Princess of Coldwater Flat. (Special Edition Ser.). 1994. per. 3.50 (*0-373-09882-0*, 5-09882-7) Silhouette.

— Valentine's Child. 1997. per. 3.99 (*0-373-24086-4*, 1-24086-0) Silhouette.

***Bishop, Nathaniel H.** Voyage of the Paper Canoe. 2nd ed. LC 00-34068. (North Carolina Maritime Museum's Seascape Ser.). (Illus.). 2000. pap. write for info. (*1-928556-13-2*) Coastal NC.

***Bishop, Nic.** Digging for Bird-Dinosaurs: An Expedition to Madagascar. LC 99-36145. (Illus.). 48p. (J). (gr. 4-7). 2000. 16.00 (*0-395-96056-8*) HM.

Bishop, Nic. Katydids. (Books for Young Learners). (Illus.). 8p. (J). (gr. k-2). 1998. pap. text 5.00 (*1-57274-135-X*, A2170) R Owen Pubs.

— Strange Plants. (Books for Young Learners). (Illus.). 12p. (J). (gr. k-2). 1997. pap. text 5.00 (*1-57274-112-0*, A2198) R Owen Pubs.

Bishop, Nick. The Secrets of Animal Flight. LC 96-23131. (Illus.). 32p. (J). (ps-3). 1997. 16.00 (*0-395-77848-4*) HM.

Bishop Nikodim. Maria of Olonets. (Illus.). 111p. 1996. pap. 8.95 (*0-938635-74-3*) St Herman Pr.

Bishop, O. N. Essential Analog Electronics. LC 96-42137. 304p. 1999. pap. text 37.95 (*0-7506-2898-7*) Buttrwrth-Heinemann.

Bishop of Amiens, Guy. The Carmen De Hastingae Proelio of Guy, Bishop of Amiens. 2nd ed. Barlow, Frank, ed. LC PA8445.W48C3 1999. (Oxford Medieval Texts Ser.). (Illus.). 160p. 1999. text 73.00 (*0-19-820758-1*) OUP.

Bishop Otto of Freising. The Deeds of Frederick Barbarossa. (MART Thirty-One Medieval Academy Reprints for Teaching Ser.: No. 31). 368p. 1994. reprint ed. pap. text 16.95 (*0-8020-7574-6*) U of Toronto Pr.

***Bishop, Owen.** Electronics: Circuits & Systems. 512p. 1999. pap. 34.95 (*0-7506-4195-9*) Buttrwrth-Heinemann.

— Microelectronics: Systems & Devices. 288p. 2000. pap. 29.95 (*0-7506-4723-X*, Newnes) Buttrwrth-Heinemann.

Bishop, Owen. Understand Electronic Filters. LC 96-8190. (Illus.). 180p. 1996. pap. text 29.95 (*0-7506-2628-3*) Buttrwrth-Heinemann.

— Understanding Amplifiers. LC 98-218077. (Illus.). 180p. 1998. pap. text 32.95 (*0-7506-3743-9*, Newnes) Buttrwrth-Heinemann.

— Understanding Electronics. LC 95-15088. (Illus.). 256p. 1999. pap. text 34.95 (*0-7506-2100-1*) Buttrwrth-Heinemann.

Bishop, P., jt. ed. see Khanpara, J. C.

***Bishop, Patrick.** The Irish Empire. (Illus.). 192p. 2000. 24.95 (*0-312-26527-1*, Thomas Dunne) St Martin.

***Bishop, Patrick & Bishop, Jennifer A.** Money-Tree Marketing: Innovative Secrets That Will Double Your Small-Business Profits. 256p. 2000. pap. 18.95 (*0-8144-7055-6*) AMACOM.

***Bishop, Paul.** Chalk Whispers. 368p. 2000. 24.50 (*0-684-87157-2*) S&S Trade.

— Chalk Whispers: A Fey Croaker LAPD Crime Novel. LC 99-49408. 368p. 2000. 24.50 (*0-684-83010-8*) S&S Trade.

Bishop, Paul. Chapel of the Ravens. 352p. 1992. mass mkt. 4.99 (*0-8125-0583-2*) Tor Bks.

— The Dionysian Self: C. G. Jung's Reception of Friedrich Nietzsche. LC 95-32811. (Monographien und Texte Zur Nietzsche-Forschung Ser.: Vol. 30). xvi, 411p. (C). 1995. lib. bdg. 166.15 (*3-11-014709-2*) De Gruyter.

— Five Grails. 1996. write for info. (*0-312-85371-8*) Tor Bks.

— Jung in Contexts: A Reader. LC 98-45954. 1999. pap. 32.99 (*0-415-20558-1*) Routledge.

— Jung in Contexts: A Reader. LC 98-45954. 1999. 100.00 (*0-415-20557-3*) Routledge.

— Kill Me Again. 288p. 1994. mass mkt. 4.99 (*0-380-76890-9*, Avon Bks) Morrow Avon.

***Bishop, Paul.** Pattern of Behavior: A Short Story Collection. LC 00-30841. (Standard Print Mystery Ser.). 2000. write for info. (*0-7862-2670-6*) Five Star.

Bishop, Paul. Sand Against the Tide. 1992. mass mkt. 4.99 (*0-8125-0918-8*) Tor Bks.

— Tequila Mockingbird: A Fey Croaker Novel. LC 97-24569. 395p. 1997. 22.50 (*0-684-83009-4*) S&S Trade.

— Tequila Mockingbird: A Fey Croaker Novel. 448p. 1998. mass mkt. 6.50 (*0-671-02531-7*) S&S Trade.

— Twice Dead. 336p. 1996. mass mkt. 5.50 (*0-380-77862-9*, Avon Bks) Morrow Avon.

— The World of Stoical Discourse in Goeth's Novel "Die Wahlverwandtschaften" LC 99-23076. (Studies in German Language & Literature: Vol. 25). 132p. 1999. text 69.95 (*0-7734-7992-9*) E Mellen.

Bishop, Paul & Dixon, Don. Foreign Exchange Handbook: Managing Risk & Opportunity in Global Currency Markets. 432p. 1992. 69.95 (*0-07-005474-6*) McGraw.

Bishop, Paul, et al. Adapted Physical Education: A Comprehensive Resource Manual of Definition, Assessment, Programming & Future Prediction. (Illus.). 184p. 1994. teacher ed. 45.00 (*1-878276-01-8*) Educ Systs Assocs Inc.

***Bishop, Paul L.** Pollution Prevention: Fundamentals & Practice LC 99-16020. 768p. 1999. 81.88 (*0-07-366147-3*) McGraw.

Bishop Percy, et al. Bishop Percy's Folio Manuscript Ballards & Romances, 3 vols. Hales, John W., ed. 1968. reprint ed. 210.00 (*1-55888-936-1*) Omnigraphics Inc.

Bishop, Peter. An Archetypal Constable: National Identity & the Geography of Nostalgia. LC 95-210. 1995. 45.00 (*0-8386-3645-4*) Fairleigh Dickinson.

— Dreams of Power: Tibetan Buddhism, Western Imagination. LC 92-53943. (Illus.). 168p. (C). 1993. 29.50 (*0-8386-3510-5*) Fairleigh Dickinson.

— Fifth Generation Computers: Concepts, Implementations & Uses. LC 85-27337. (Computers & Their Applications Ser.). 128p. 1986. text 39.95 (*0-470-20269-6*) P-H.

— The Greening of Psychology: The Vegetable World in Myth, Dream & Healing. LC 90-27418. (Illus.). 238p. (Orig.). 1991. pap. 14.00 (*0-88214-345-X*) Spring Pubns.

— The Myth of Shangri-la: Tibet, Travel Writing & the Western Creation of Sacred Landscape. 400p. 1989. 48.00 (*0-520-06686-3*, Pub. by U CA Pr) Cal Prin Full Svc.

***Bishop, Peter.** 100 Woods: A Guide to the Popular Timbers of the World. (Illus.). 224p. 1999. 40.00 (*1-86126-167-5*, Pub. by Cro1wood) Trafalgar.

Bishop, Peter, jt. auth. see Duck, Michael.

Bishop, Peter, jt. auth. see Naish, Paul.

***Bishop, Peter D.** Written on the Flyleaf: A Christian Faith in the Light of Other Faiths. 176p. 1998. pap. 15.00 (*0-7162-0519-X*) Epworth Pr.

Bishop, Philip E. Literature for Adventures in the Human Spirit, Vol. 1. LC 94-28737. 320p. (C). 1994. pap. text 28.00 (*0-13-141251-5*) P-H.

— Literature for Adventures in the Human Spirit: Literature, Vol. 2. LC 94-28737. Vol. 2. 320p. (C). 1995. pap. text 28.00 (*0-13-141269-8*) P-H.

Bishop, Philip R. Thomas Bird Mosher, the Pirate Prince of Publishers. LC 97-47040. (Illus.). 552p. 1998. 125.00 (*1-884718-49-3*, 50308) Oak Knoll.

Bishop, Phyllis, et al. I Am Somebody God Loves. LC 93-74551. (Living Stones Ser.). (Illus.). 170p. (J). (ps-8). 1994. pap. 32.95 (*0-87303-204-7*) Faith & Life.

Bishop, R. The Borden Limner & His Contemporaries. (Illus.). 90p. 1976. pap. 3.95 (*0-912303-10-7*) Michigan Mus.

— Christopher Sphere, Vol. 1. LC 98-120287. (Illus.). 128p. (YA). (gr. 3-12). 1997. pap. 4.95 (*0-87505-409-9*) Borden.

Bishop, R. E. & Price, W. G. Hydroelasticity of Ships. LC 78-67297. 434p. 1980. text 135.00 (*0-521-22328-8*) Cambridge U Pr.

Bishop, R. F., jt. ed. see Nielson, D.

Bishop, R. J., jt. auth. see Smallman, R. E.

Bishop, R. S., ed. see Newsome, Effie Lee.

Bishop, Rand. African Literature, African Critics: The Forming of Critical Standards, 1947-1966, 115. LC 87-36091. (Contributions in Afro-American & African Studies: No. 115). 225p. 1988. 55.00 (*0-313-25918-6*, BHR/, Greenwood Pr) Greenwood.

Bishop, Raymond F. Microscopic Approaches to the Structure of Light Nuclei. (Series on Advances in Quantum Many-Body Theory - Vol. 2: Vol. 2). 400p. 1999. 85.00 (*981-02-3875-4*) World Scientific Pub.

***Bishop, Raymond F., et al, eds.** Recent Progress in Many-Body Theories. 480p. 2000. 98.00 (*981-02-4318-9*) World Scientific Pub.

Bishop, Richard & Goldberg, Samuel. Tensor Analysis on Manifolds. (Illus.). 288p. 1980. reprint ed. pap. 8.95 (*0-486-64039-6*) Dover.

Bishop, Richard C. & Romano, Donato. Environmental Resource Valuation: Applications of the Contingent Valuation Method in Italy. LC 98-13256. (Studies in Risk & Uncertainty). 1998. 100.00 (*0-7923-8143-2*) Kluwer Academic.

Bishop, Robert. Control Systems Analysis & Design Using Matlab. (C). 1996. pap. text. write for info. (*0-201-56866-7*) Addison-Wesley.

— The Investor's Guide to Penny Mining Stocks. 200p. (Orig.). 1986. pap. 24.95 (*0-938691-21-X*) Justim Pub.

— Learning with Labview. LC 98-27202. 450p. (C). 1999. pap. 54.00 (*0-201-36166-3*, Prentice Hall) P-H.

***Bishop, Robert & Atkins, Jacqueline M.** Folk Art in American Life. (Illus.). 228p. 2000. reprint ed. text 30.00 (*0-7881-9094-6*) DIANE Pub.

Bishop, Robert & Coblentz, Patricia. Furniture One: Prehistoric Through Rococo. Gilchrist, Brenda, ed. LC 78-62733. (Smithsonian Illustrated Library of Antiques). (Illus.). 128p. (Orig.). 1979. 9.95 (*0-910503-23-0*) Cooper-Hewitt Museum.

Bishop, Robert H. Matlab & Simulink for Control Systems. LC 96-46978. 250p. (C). 1996. pap. text 19.80 (*0-201-49846-4*) Addison-Wesley.

***Bishop, Robert H., et al, eds.** Spaceflight Mechanics 1999, 2 vols. (Advances in the Astronautical Sciences Ser.: Vol. 102, Nos. I & II). (Illus.). 1600p. 1999. lib. bdg. 280.00 (*0-87703-458-3*, Am Astronaut Soc) Univelt Inc.

Bishop, Robert H., jt. auth. see Dorf, Richard C.

Bishop, Robert L. Qi Lai: Mobilizing One Billion Chinese: The Chinese Communication System. LC 87-36153. (Illus.). 208p. 1989. reprint ed. pap. 64.50 (*0-608-00153-8*, 206093400006) Bks Demand.

Bishop, Roma. Animals. (Nursery Board Mini Pop Bks.). (Illus.). 14p. (J). (ps). 1991. ring bd., boxed set 2.95 (*0-671-74833-5*) Litle Simon.

— Christmas Nativity. (Little Christmas Pop-Ups Ser.). (Illus.). 10p. (J). (ps up). 1994. 3.95 (*0-671-89517-6*) Litle Simon.

— Christmas Songs. LC 95-150076. (Little Christmas Pop-Ups Ser.). (Illus.). 10p. (J). (ps-k). 1994. 3.95 (*0-671-89516-8*) Litle Simon.

— Easter Babies. (Little Easter Pop-Up Bks.). (Illus.). 12p. (J). (ps-1). 1996. 4.50 (*0-689-80611-6*) S&S Childrens.

— Easter Counting. LC 96-144899. (Little Easter Pop-Up Bks.). (Illus.). 12p. (J). (ps-3). 1996. 4.50 (*0-689-80612-4*) S&S Childrens.

— Easter Egg Hunt. LC 96-144898. (Little Easter Pop-Up Bks.). (Illus.). 12p. (J). (ps-3). 1996. 4.50 (*0-689-80613-2*) S&S Childrens.

— Easter Sunday. LC 96-133067. (Little Easter Pop-Up Bks.). (Illus.). 12p. (J). (ps-3). 1996. 4.50 (*0-689-80614-0*) S&S Childrens.

— Fairy Tale Tower. (Illus.). (J). 1996. bds. write for info. (*1-85479-743-3*, Pub. by M OMara) Assoc Pubs Grp.

— Festive Fun. (Little Christmas Pop-Ups Ser.). (Illus.). 10p. (J). (ps up). 1994. 3.95 (*0-671-89518-4*) Litle Simon.

— In the Forest. 1994. pap. 3.95 (*0-671-88307-0*) Litle Simon.

— Look at Insects. 1994. pap. 3.95 (*0-671-88310-0*) Litle Simon.

— My First Pop-Up Book of Prehistoric Animals. (Illus.). (J). (ps-3). 1994. 12.95 (*0-671-89556-7*) S&S Bks Yung.

— On a Safari. 1994. pap. 3.95 (*0-671-88309-7*) Litle Simon.

— Pop up My First Book of Dinosaurs. (J). 1993. pap. 13.00 (*0-671-86723-7*) S&S Bks Yung.

— Santa Pays a Visit. (Little Christmas Pop-Ups Ser.). (Illus.). 10p. (J). (ps up). 1994. 3.95 (*0-671-89519-2*) Litle Simon.

— See the Dinosaurs. 1994. pap. 3.95 (*0-671-88308-9*) Litle Simon.

— Toys. (Nursery Board Mini Pop Bks.). (Illus.). 14p. (J). (ps). 1991. 2.95 (*0-671-74831-9*) Litle Simon.

Bishop, Ron. Getting to Know You. (Illus.). 344p. (Orig.). 1996. pap. 6.95 (*0-9652496-0-3*) Juggernaut Co.

— Rebuilding the Famous Ford Flathead. 140p. 1981. pap. 10.95 (*0-07-156316-4*) McGraw.

— Rebuilding the Famous Ford Flathead. (Illus.). 140p. 1981. 9.95 (*0-8306-9965-1*, 2066H); pap. 9.95 (*0-8306-2066-4*, 2066P) McGraw-Hill Prof.

Bishop, Ronald L. & Lange, Frederick W., eds. The Ceramic Legacy of Anna O. Shepard. (Illus.). 480p. 1991. text 49.95 (*0-87081-195-9*) Univ Pr Colo.

***Bishop, Rosemarie E.** A Matter of Conscience. LC 99-64381. (Moral Vampire Ser.: Bk. 2). 1999. 25.00 (*0-7388-0452-5*); pap. 18.00 (*0-7388-0453-3*) Xlibris Corp.

— Noah's Garden. LC 00-190569. 229p. 2000. 25.00 (*0-7388-1838-0*); pap. 18.00 (*0-7388-1839-9*) Xlibris Corp.

Bishop, Rosemarie E. Search for a Soul. 325p. 1998. 25.00 (*0-7388-0197-6*); pap. 15.00 (*0-7388-0198-4*) Xlibris Corp.

Bishop, Ross & Ursky, Allison. Healing the Shadow. (Illus.). 325p. 1998. pap. 19.95 (*0-9669822-0-7*) Blue Lotus Pr.

Bishop, Rudine S. Presenting Walter Dean Myers. (Twayne's United States Young Adult Authors Ser.: No. 565). 136p. (C). 1990. 28.00 (*0-8057-8214-1*, Twyne) Mac Lib Ref.

Bishop, Rudine S., ed. Kaleidoscope: A Multicultural Booklist for Grades K-8. (Bibliography Ser.). 170p. 1994. pap. 14.95 (*0-8141-2543-3*) NCTE.

***Bishop, Rudine Sims.** Free Within Ourselves: The Development of African American Children's Literature. 2000. pap. text. write for info. (*0-325-00269-X*) Heinemann.

Bishop, Russell, jt. auth. see Watson-Jarvis, Karen.

Bishop, Ryan & Robinson, Lillian S. Night Market: Sexual Cultures & the Thai Economic Miracle. LC 97-29451. 288p. 1997. pap. 20.99 (*0-415-91429-9*) Routledge.

— Night Market: Sexual Cultures & the Thai Economic Miracle. LC 97-29451. 288p. (C). 1997. 75.00 (*0-415-91428-0*) Routledge.

Bishop, S. G., jt. ed. see Taylor, P. C.

Bishop, S. L., jt. auth. see Topping, S. L.

***Bishop, S. P. & Kerns, W. D.** Cardiovascular Toxicology, 13 vols. (Comprehensive Toxicology Ser.: Vol. 6). 523p. 1999. 165.00 (*0-08-042971-8*) Elsevier.

Bishop, Schuyler. A Passion for Golf: The Best of Golf Writing. 1999. pap. 15.95 (*0-312-20668-2*) St Martin.

Bishop, Schuyler, ed. A Passion for Golf. LC 98-10263. 384p. 1998. 24.95 (*0-312-19027-1*, Thomas Dunne) St Martin.

Bishop, Selma L. Isaac Watts's Hymns & Spiritual Songs (1707) A Publishing History & a Bibliography. LC 73-78316. 1974. 35.00 (*0-87650-033-5*) Pierian.

Bishop, Sheila. Consequences. large type ed. 1995. 27.99 (*0-7089-3325-4*) Ulverscroft.

— The Favourite Sister. large type ed. 1991. 27.99 (*0-7089-2493-X*) Ulverscroft.

— Goldsmiths' Row. large type ed. 368p. 1994. 27.99 (*0-7089-3089-1*) Ulverscroft.

— No Hint of Scandal. large type ed. (Large Print Ser.). 320p. 1997. 27.99 (*0-7089-3680-6*) Ulverscroft.

— The Parson's Daughter. large type ed. 1991. 27.99 (*0-7089-2383-6*) Ulverscroft.

— The Phantom Garden. large type ed. (Historical Romance Ser.). 320p. 1992. 27.99 (*0-7089-2619-3*) Ulverscroft.

— Rosalba. large type ed. 416p. (Orig.). 1994. 27.99 (*0-7089-3128-6*) Ulverscroft.

— The School in Belmont. large type ed. 1995. 27.99 (*0-7089-3305-X*) Ulverscroft.

— The Second Husband. large type ed. 1991. 27.99 (*0-7089-2424-7*) Ulverscroft.

— A Speaking Likeness. large type ed. 1990. 27.99 (*0-7089-2197-3*) Ulverscroft.

— Sweet Nightingale. large type ed. (Large Print Ser.). 384p. 1996. 27.99 (*0-7089-3642-3*) Ulverscroft.

— The Wilderness Walk. large type ed. 1990. 27.99 (*0-7089-2275-9*) Ulverscroft.

Bishop, Sherman C. Handbook of Salamanders: The Salamanders of the United States, of Bishop, Sherman C. LC 94-14253. (Comstock Classic Handbooks Ser.: Vol. 3). (Illus.). 555p. 1994. pap. text 39.95 (*0-8014-8213-5*) Cornell U Pr.

Bishop, Sherry. Immaculate Misconceptions: A Self-Help Book for Former Catholics. 208p. (Orig.). 1996. pap. 14.95 (*0-9648756-0-8*) Veranda Pr.

Bishop Shigley, Sally. Dazzling Dialectics: Elizabeth Bishop's Resonating Feminist Reality. LC 96-8413. (Studies in Modern Poetry: Vol. 7). IX, 181p. (C). 1997. text 42.95 (*0-8204-3353-5*) P Lang Pubng.

***Bishop, Shigley Sally.** Fun Sex: Exciting Ideals for Better Love Making. 2000. pap. 16.95 (*1-85868-780-2*, Pub. by Carlton Bks Ltd) Natl Bk Netwk.

Bishop, Stephen. IPC Author Guide. 1990. ring bd. write for info. (*0-201-54437-7*) Addison-Wesley.

— Songs in the Rough: Rock's Greatest Songs in Rough-Draft Form. LC 95-45128. 160p. 1996. text 27.95 (*0-312-14048-7*) St Martin.

— Songs in the Rough: Rock's Greatest Songs in Rough-Draft Form. (Illus.). 160p. 2000. pap. 19.95 (*0-312-17029-7*) St Martin.

Bishop, Steven R., jt. auth. see Kapitaniak, Tomasz.

***Bishop, Sue.** The Complete Feedback Skills Training Book. LC 99-46136. 180p. 2000. 113.95 (*0-566-08218-7*, Pub. by Gower) Ashgate Pub Co.

Bishop, Sue. The Complete Guide to People Skills. LC 96-37782. 192p. 1997. text 69.95 (*0-566-07777-9*, Pub. by Gower) Ashgate Pub Co.

— Training Games for Assertiveness & Conflict Resolution: 50 Ready to Use Activities. 256p. 1996. 99.95 (*0-07-913052-6*) McGraw.

Bishop, Sue & Taylor, David Conrad. Fifty Activities for Interpersonal Skills Training. 275p. 1992. ring bd. 139.95 (*0-87425-182-6*) HRD Press.

Bishop, Susan, jt. auth. see Taylor, David Conrad.

Bishop, Susy. Black-Eyed Susan. 208p. 1995. pap. text, per. 19.95 (*0-7872-1907-X*) Kendall-Hunt.

Bishop, Suzette. Cold Knife Surgery. 36p. 1998. pap. 5.00 (*1-891387-00-6*) Red Dragon VA.

Bishop, T. G. Shakespeare & the Theatre of Wonder. (Cambridge Studies in Renaissance Literature & Culture: No. 9). 236p. (C). 1996. text 54.95 (*0-521-55086-6*) Cambridge U Pr.

Bishop, Tanya. Silent Seduction. (Black Lace Ser.). (Orig.). 1997. mass mkt. 5.95 (*0-352-33193-3*, Pub. by BLA4) London Brdge.

Bishop, Thomas, jt. auth. see Lentner, Marvin.

***Bishop, Tim & Sham, Pak.** Analysis of Multifactorial Diseases. (Human Molecular Genetics Ser.). 320p. 2000. 115.00 (*0-12-101610-2*) Acad Pr.

Bishop, Tom. From the Left Bank: Reflections on the Modern French Theater & Novel. LC 96-45819. Date not set. pap. write for info. (*0-8147-1261-4*) NYU Pr.

— From the Left Bank: Reflections on the Modern French Theater & Novel. LC 96-45819. (Illus.). 288p. (C). 1997. text 35.00 (*0-8147-1260-6*) NYU Pr.

— Gold! The Way to Roadside Riches. (Illus.). 52p. 1971. pap. 4.95 (*0-933472-31-5*) Johnson Bks.

Bishop, Tony. Field Guide to the Orchids of New South Wales & Victoria. (Illus.). 250p. 1996. pap. 24.95 (*0-86840-375-X*, Pub. by New South Wales Univ Pr) Intl Spec Bk.

***Bishop, Tony.** Field Guide to the Orchids of New South Wales & Victoria. 2nd ed. (Illus.). 250p. 2000. pap. 29.95 (*0-86840-706-2*, Pub. by NSW U Pr) Intl Spec Bk.

Bishop, Twyla D. Secrets Within. Koger, Dorothy P. & Battle, Jackie, eds. (Illus.). 1999. pap. write for info. (*1-882821-16-5*) DPK Pubns.

Bishop, Verna Hall. On Wings of Faith. LC 98-93794. (Illus.). 112p. 1998. pap. 12.95 (*1-57579-092-0*) Pine Hill Pr.

Bishop, Virginia E. Teaching Visually Impaired Children. 2nd ed. LC 96-1751. Orig. Title: Teaching the Visually Limited Child. (Illus.). 274p. 1996. 51.95 (*0-398-06595-0*); pap. 35.95 (*0-398-06596-9*) C C Thomas.

Bishop, Virginia E., et al, eds. Low Vision: Reflections of the Past, Issues for the Future. 181p. 1993. pap. 29.95 (*0-89128-218-1*) Am Foun Blind.

An Asterisk (*) at the beginning of an entry indicates that the title is appearing for the first time.

Bishop, W. E., et al, eds. Aquatic Toxicology & Hazard Assessment - STP 802: Sixth Symposium. LC 82-73772. 560p. 1983. text 59.00 (*0-8031-0255-0*, STP802) ASTM.

Bishop, Walter W., ed. Geological Background to Fossil Man: Recent Research in the Gregory Rift Valley, East Africa. LC 78-323378. 640p. reprint ed. pap. 198.40 (*0-608-15664-7*, 203193400077) Bks Demand.

Bishop, Walter W. & Clark, J. Desmond, eds. Background to Evolution in Africa. LC 66-30212. (Illus.). 1967. lib. bdg. 70.00 (*0-226-05393-8*) U Ch Pr.

Bishop, Wayne, jt. auth. see Venit, Stewart M.

Bishop, Wayne S., jt. auth. see McFarland, Alan R.

Bishop, Wendy. Ethnographic Writing Research: Writing It Down, Writing It up & Reading It. LC 98-55915. 1999. 28.00 (*0-86709-486-9*, Pub. by Boynton Cook Pubs) Heinemann.

— Mid-Passage. (Poetry Chapbook Ser.). (Illus.). 36p. 1998. pap. 7.95 (*1-879205-77-7*) Nightshade Pr.

— Released into Language: Options for Teaching Creative Writing. 2nd rev. ed. LC 98-15992. 264p. 1998. pap. text 22.50 (*0-9663233-1-9*, 323319) Calendar Islands.

— Something Old, Something New: College Writing Teachers & Classroom Change. LC 89-27529. (Studies in Writing & Rhetoric). 192p. (C). 1990. pap. text 14.95 (*0-8093-1601-3*) S Ill U Pr.

— The Subject Is Writing: Essays by Teachers & Students. 2nd ed. LC 98-56012. 1999. 25.00 (*0-86709-457-5*, Pub. by Boynton Cook Pubs) Heinemann.

— Teaching Lives: Essays & Stories. LC 97-21168. (Illus.). 352p. 1997. pap. 19.95 (*0-87421-224-3*) Utah St U Pr.

— Working Words: The Process of Creative Writing. (C). 1992. pap., teacher ed. write for info. (*1-55934-166-1*, 1166); pap. text 31.95 (*1-55934-076-2*, 1076) Mayfield Pub.

Bishop, Wendy, ed. Elements of Alternate Style: Essays on Writing & Revision. LC 97-3435. 185p. 1997. pap. text 22.50 (*0-86709-423-0*, 0423, Pub. by Boynton Cook Pubs) Heinemann.

***Bishop, Wendy, ed.** The Subject is Reading. LC 99-58141. 310p. 2000. pap. text 23.00 (*0-86709-472-9*, Pub. by Boynton Cook Pubs) Heinemann.

Bishop, Wendy, ed. The Subject Is Writing: Essays by Teachers & Students. LC 92-39430. 278p. (C). 1993. pap. text 24.00 (*0-86709-314-5*, 0314, Pub. by Boynton Cook Pubs) Heinemann.

Bishop, Wendy & Ostrum, Hans, eds. Genre & Writing: Issues, Arguments, Alternatives. LC 97-18461. (Orig.). (C). 1997. pap. text 29.50 (*0-86709-421-4*, 0421, Pub. by Boynton Cook Pubs) Heinemann.

***Bishop, Wendy & Starkey, David, eds.** In Praise of Pedagogy: Poetry, Flash Fiction & Essays on Composing. LC 00-25410. 230p. 2000. pap. text 25.00 (*1-893056-08-2*, 056082) Calendar Islands.

***Bishop, Wendy & Zemliansky, Pavel.** The Subject is Research. 2001. pap. write for info. (*0-86709-572-5*, Pub. by Boynton Cook Pubs) Heinemann.

Bishop, Wiley L., jt. auth. see Weaver, Barbara N.

***Bishop, William.** The Blue Idol. 211p. 1999. pap. 14.95 (*0-7414-0175-4*) Buy Books.

Bishop, William. Strategic Marketing for the Digital Age. LC 97-49938. 272p. 1998. 34.95 (*0-8442-3441-9*, NTC Business Bks) NTC Contemp Pub Co.

Bishop, William H. History of Roane County, West Virginia. (Illus.). 711p. 1993. reprint ed. lib. bdg. 72.00 (*0-8328-2961-7*) Higginson Bk Co.

— St. Louis in 1884. Jones, William R., ed. (Illus.). 24p. 1977. reprint ed. pap. 2.00 (*0-89646-024-X*) Vistabooks.

Bishop, William H. & Newcomb. Southern California One Hundred Years Ago, Vol. 1. (Historical Ser.). (Illus.). 1976. pap. 3.50 (*0-89540-033-2*, SB-033) Sun Pub.

Bishop, William H. & Roberts, Edward. Southern California One Hundred Years Ago, Vol. 2. (Historical Ser.). (Illus.). 1976. pap. 3.50 (*0-89540-034-0*, SB-034) Sun Pub.

Bishop, William H., et al. Northern California One Hundred Years Ago. (Historical Ser.). (Illus.). (Orig.). 1976. pap. 3.50 (*0-89540-032-4*, SB-032) Sun Pub.

Bishop, William W. Backs of Books, & Other Essays in Librarianship. LC 68-54328. (Essay Index Reprint Ser.). 1977. reprint ed. 20.95 (*0-8369-0215-7*) Ayer.

Bishop, William W., Jr. International Law: Cases & Materials. 3rd ed. 1168p. 1971. 57.00 (*0-316-09664-4*, Aspen Law & Bus) Aspen Pub.

Bishop, William W. & Keogh, Andrew. Essays Offered to Herbert Putnam by His Colleagues & Friends on His 30th Anniversary As Librarian of Congress, 5 April Nineteen Twenty-Nine. 1929. 89.50 (*0-686-51379-7*) Elliots Bks.

Bishop, Yvonne, et al. Discrete Multivariate Analysis: Theory & Practice. 1977. pap. text 37.50 (*0-262-52040-0*) MIT Pr.

Bishops' Committee for Pastoral Research Staff & Practices National Conference of Catholic Bishops. Growing Together in Spirit. (Marriage Is a Sacrament Ser.). 48p. (Orig.). (C). 1990. pap. 2.95 (*1-55586-353-1*) US Catholic.

Bishops' Committee for Pastoral Research Staff & Practices National Conference of Catholic Bishops. Making Marriage Work. (Marriage Is a Sacrament Ser.). 48p. (Orig.). (C). 1990. pap. 2.95 (*1-55586-355-8*) US Catholic.

— Our Future Together. (Marriage Is a Sacrament Ser.). 72p. (C). 1990. pap. 3.95 (*1-55586-351-5*) US Catholic.

— Parenthood. (Marriage Is a Sacrament Ser.). 48p. (Orig.). (C). 1990. pap. 2.95 (*1-55586-352-3*) US Catholic.

— Planning Your Wedding Ceremony. (Marriage Is a Sacrament Ser.). 48p. (Orig.). (C). 1990. pap. 2.95 (*1-55586-354-X*) US Catholic.

Bishop's Committee on Marriage & Family Staff & National Conference of Catholic Bishops Staff. Always Our Children: A Pastoral Message to Parents of Homosexual Children & Suggestions to Pastoral Ministers. (Illus.). 16p. 1997. pap. 1.25 (*1-57455-131-0*) US Catholic.

Bishops' Committee on Priestly Formation, jt. auth. see Bishops' Committee on Vocations.

Bishops' Committee on Priestly Life & Ministry Sta & National Conference of Catholic Bishops Staff. Retreats for Diocesan Priests. 5p. (Orig.). 1990. pap. 1.25 (*1-55586-344-2*) US Catholic.

Bishops' Committee on the Laity Staff. Gifts Unfolding: The Lay Vocation Today with Questions for Tomorrow. National Conference of Catholic Bishops Staff, ed. 60p. (Orig.). 1990. pap. 3.95 (*1-55586-348-5*) US Catholic.

Bishops, Committee On The Litur. Order of Christian Funerals Appendix 2: Cremation. 16p. 1997. pap. 2.95 (*0-89942-352-3*, 352/04) Catholic Bk Pub.

Bishops' Committee on the Liturgy, National Confer, ed. see Vatican Congregation for Divine Worship Staff.

Bishops' Committee on the Liturgy Staff & United States Catholic Conference of Bishops Staff, eds. Rito De la Iniciacion Cristiana De Adultos. 364p. 1991. 34.95 (*0-929650-54-9*, S/RCIA) Liturgy Tr Pubns.

— Rito De la Iniciacion Cristiana De Adultos. 364p. 1993. pap. 12.95 (*0-929650-75-1*, SSRCIA) Liturgy Tr Pubns.

Bishops' Committee on Vocations & Bishops' Committee on Priestly Formation. Handbook for Vocation & Seminary Personnel. 290p. (Orig.). 1987. pap. 29.95 (*1-55586-184-9*) US Catholic.

Bishops' Committee on Vocations Staff & National Conference of Catholic Bishops Staff. A Reflection on the Relationship Between Seminary & Vocation Personnel. 78p. (Orig.). 1988. pap. 8.95 (*1-55586-248-9*) US Catholic.

***Bishops, Kevin.** Countryside Protection. 320p. 2000. pap. 24.99 (*0-415-12880-3*) Routledge.

Bishops of the United States & Canada Staff. The Gospel of Life & the Vision of Health Care: Proceedings of the Fifteenth Bishops' Workshop, Dallas, Texas. Smith, Russell E., ed. LC 96-46483. 212p. (Orig.). 1996. pap. 19.95 (*0-935372-40-7*) NCBC.

Bishops of the United States Staff, jt. auth. see John Paul, II, pseud.

Bishopsgate Press Ltd. Staff, ed. Tombleson's Thames & the Medway. 254p. 1985. 45.00 (*0-900873-30-2*, Pub. by Bishopsgate Pr Ltd) St Mut.

Bishri, Tariq A. & Alwani, Taha J. Mushkilatan wa Qira'ah Fihima: Two Issues & a Critical Study on Them. 2nd ed. (Silsilat Qadaya al Fikr al Islami Ser.: No. 8). (ARA.). 86p. 1992. pap. 4.00 (*1-56564-113-2*) IIIT VA.

Bisht, B. S. Tribes of India, Nepal, Tibet Borderland: A Study of Cultural Transformation. (C). 1994. 24.00 (*81-212-0454-2*, Pub. by Gian Publng Hse) S Asia.

Bisht, B. S., jt. ed. see Pant, V. K.

Bisht, D. S. Agricultural Development in India. 332p. 1989. 140.00 (*81-7041-161-0*, Pub. by Scientific Pubs) St Mut.

Bisht, Harshwanti. Tourism in Garhwal Himalaya: With Special Reference to Mountaineering & Trekking in Uttarkashi & Chamoli Districts. (C). 1995. 32.00 (*81-7387-006-3*, Pub. by Indus Pub) S Asia.

Bisht, Narendra S., et al, eds. Entrepreneurship Reflections & Investigations. (C). 1989. 44.00 (*81-85076-62-6*, Pub. by Chugh Pubns) S Asia.

Bisht, R. S. Tribes of India, Nepal, Tibet Borderland: A Study of Cultural Transformation. 1994. pap. 72.00 (*0-7855-0489-3*, Pub. by Ratna Pustak Bhandar) St Mut.

Bisiach, E., jt. ed. see Marcel, A. J.

***Bisignani, Joe D.** Moon Handbooks: Hawaii: The All-Island Guide. 5th rev. ed. (Illus.). 1030p. 1999. pap. 19.95 (*1-56691-160-5*, Moon Handbks) Avalon Travel.

— Moon Handbooks: Honolulu-Waikiki: The Island of Oahu. 3rd rev. ed. Vol. 3. (Illus.). 360p. 1999. pap. 14.95 (*1-56691-128-1*, Moon Handbks) Avalon Travel.

Bisignani, Joe D. Moon Handbooks: Kauai: Including the Island of Niihau. 3rd ed. (Illus.). 320p. 1997. pap. text 15.95 (*1-56691-091-9*, Moon Handbks) Avalon Travel.

***Bisignani, Joe D.** Moon Handbooks: Maui: Including Molokai & Lanai. 5th rev. ed. (Illus.). 450p. 1999. pap. 15.95 (*1-56691-138-9*, Moon Handbks) Avalon Travel.

Bisignani, Joe D. & Nilsen, Robert. Moon Handbooks: Big Island of Hawaii: Including Hawaii Volcanoes National Park, the Kona Coast & Waipio Valley. 3rd rev. ed. Vol. 3. (Illus.). 390p. 1998. pap. 15.95 (*1-56691-100-1*, Moon Handbks) Avalon Travel.

Bisignano, Alphonse. Cooking the Italian Way. LC 82-12641. (Easy Menu Ethnic Cookbooks Ser.). (Illus.). 48p. (J). (gr. 5 up). 1982. lib. bdg. 19.93 (*0-8225-0906-7*, Lerner Publctns) Lerner Pub.

***Bisignano, Alphonse.** Cooking the Italian Way. LC 00-9537. (Easy Menu Ethnic Cookbks.). (Illus.). 2002. lib. bdg. write for info. (*0-8225-4113-0*) Lerner Pub.

Bisignano, Joseph. Life's Financial Instruction Book. 1996. pap. 7.95 (*0-614-12593-6*) Pelican Books.

— Life's Little Financial Instruction Book. LC 95-48161. 96p. 1996. pap. 7.95 (*1-56554-153-7*) Pelican.

Bisignano, Joseph & Bisignano, Judith. Creating Your Future: Level 4. (Illus.). 64p. 1983. student ed. 6.95 (*0-910141-01-0*, KP115) Kino Pubns.

Bisignano, Joseph, et al. Creating Your Future: Level 3. (Illus.). 72p. 1982. student ed. 6.95 (*0-9607366-9-7*, KP109) Kino Pubns.

***Bisignano, Joseph, et al.** Global Financial Crisis: Lessons from Recent Events. LC 00-25874. 2000. pap. write for info. (*0-7923-7865-2*, Kluwer Plenum) Kluwer Academic.

Bisignano, Judith. Advent Activities for Home & Classroom. (Illus.). 64p. 1986. pap. 6.95 (*0-934134-97-9*) Sheed & Ward WI.

Bisignano, Judith & Gellman, Rayna. Pathways to a Grand Canyon Adventure. (Illus.). 28p. (Orig.). (J). (gr. 3-9). 1996. pap. 9.95 (*0-9642469-1-0*) Lrning to Lrn.

Bisignano, Judith, jt. auth. see Bisignano, Joseph.

Bisignano, Judith, jt. auth. see Cera, Mary J.

Bisignano, Judith, jt. auth. see Kino Learning Center Staff.

Bisignano, Judith, jt. auth. see Robinson, Marilyn.

Bisignano, Judith, jt. auth. see Sanders, Corinne.

Bisignano, Judy. Relating. (Illus.). 64p. (J). (gr. 3-8). 1985. student ed. 8.99 (*0-86653-331-1*, GA 678) Good Apple.

Bisignano, Judy, jt. auth. see Carswell, Evelyn.

Bisilliat, Jeanne, et al. Women of the Third World. Amann, Enne & Amann, Peter, trs. LC 86-46328. 104p. 1987. 26.50 (*0-8386-3311-0*) Fairleigh Dickinson.

Bisio, Attilio. Synthetic Rubber: The Story of an Industry. (Illus.). 58p. 1993. 40.00 (*0-9638167-1-3*) IIOSRP.

Bisio, Attilio & Boots, Sharon. Wiley Encyclopedia of Energy & the Environment, 2 vols. abr. ed. LC 96-2734. 1562p. 1996. 225.00 (*0-471-14827-X*) Wiley.

Bisio, Attilio & Boots, Sharon, eds. Encyclopedia of Energy Technology & the Environment, 4 vols. LC 94-44119. (Wiley Encyclopedia Series in Environmental Sciences). 3024p. 1995. 900.00 (*0-471-54458-2*) Wiley.

Bisio, Attilio & Gastwirt, Lawrence. Turning Research & Development into Profits: A Systematic Approach. LC 78-10239. 287p. reprint ed. pap. 89.00 (*0-608-12906-2*, 202354100033) Bks Demand.

Bisio, Attilio & Kabel, Robert L. Scaleup in the Chemical Process Industries: Conversion from Laboratory Scale Tests to Successful Commercial Size Design. LC 84-25767. 712p. 1985. 175.00 (*0-471-05747-9*) Wiley.

Bisio, Attilio & Xanthos, Marino, eds. How to Manage Plastics Waste: Technology & Market Opportunities. LC 94-28957. (Polymer Processing Institute Ser.). 253p. 1994. 75.00 (*1-56990-136-8*) Hanser-Gardner.

Bisio, Attilio, jt. auth. see Herbert, Vernon.

Bisistha, Chitta R. Dravidian India & Aponymous Bharata: An Indo-Sociological Dimension. (C). 1992. 24.00 (*0-8364-2790-4*, Pub. by Firma KLM) S Asia.

Bisk, John, tr. see Shur, Leonid, ed.

Bisk, Leonard. Entrepreneur Magazine: Guide to Professional Services. LC 96-46319. (Entrepreneur Magazine Small Business Ser.). 294p. 1997. pap. 19.95 (*0-471-15517-9*) Wiley.

Bisk, Nathan M. Accounting & Reporting. (CPA Comprehensive Exam Review Ser.). 1994. pap. 31.95 (*0-88128-639-7*) Bisk-Totaltape.

— Accounting & Reporting. 28th ed. (CPA Comprehensive Exam Review Ser.: No. 2). 1997. pap. text 34.95 (*1-57961-015-3*) Bisk-Totaltape.

***Bisk, Nathan M.** Accounting & Reporting, 4 vols., Vol. 2. 30th ed. (CPA Comprehensive Examination Review Ser.). 2000. pap. 37.95 (*1-57961-097-8*) Bisk-Totaltape.

Bisk, Nathan M. Auditing. (CPA Comprehensive Exam Review Ser.). 1994. pap. 31.95 (*0-88128-640-0*) Bisk-Totaltape.

— Auditing. 28th ed. (CPA Comprehensive Exam Review Ser.: No. 3). 1997. pap. text 34.95 (*1-57961-016-1*) Bisk-Totaltape.

— Business Law & Professional Responsibilities. (CPA Comprehensive Exam Review Ser.). 1994. pap. 31.95 (*0-88128-641-9*) Bisk-Totaltape.

— Business Law & Professional Responsibilities. 28th ed. (CPA Comprehensive Exam Review Ser.: No. 4). 1997. pap. text 34.95 (*1-57961-017-X*) Bisk-Totaltape.

***Bisk, Nathan M.** Business Law & Professional Responsibilities. 30th ed. (CPA Comprehensive Examination Review Ser.). 2000. pap. 37.95 (*1-57961-099-4*) Bisk-Totaltape.

Bisk, Nathan M. CPA Accounting & Reporting. 27th ed. 1996. pap. text 39.95 (*0-88128-942-6*); pap. text 34.95 (*0-88128-943-4*) Bisk-Totaltape.

— CPA Accounting & Reporting: Taxation, Managerial, Governmental & Not-for-Profit. 1994. pap. 29.95 (*0-88128-765-2*) Bisk-Totaltape.

— CPA Accounting & Reporting: Taxation, Managerial, Governmental & Not-For-Profit Organization. 1995. pap. text 32.95 (*0-88128-883-7*) Bisk-Totaltape.

— CPA Auditing. 1994. pap. 29.95 (*0-88128-766-0*) Bisk-Totaltape.

— CPA Auditing. 1995. pap. text 32.95 (*0-88128-884-5*) Bisk-Totaltape.

— CPA Auditing. 27th ed. 1996. pap. text 34.95 (*0-88128-944-2*) Bisk-Totaltape.

— CPA Business Law & Professional Responsibilites. 1994. pap. 29.95 (*0-88128-767-9*) Bisk-Totaltape.

— CPA Business Law & Professional Responsibilities. 1995. pap. text 32.95 (*0-88128-885-3*) Bisk-Totaltape.

— CPA Business Law & Professional Responsibilities. 27th ed. 1996. pap. text 34.95 (*0-88128-945-0*) Bisk-Totaltape.

— CPA Comprehensive Exam Review Vol. 1: Topic Summaries & Exam Preparation Guides. 1994. pap. 41.95 (*0-88128-632-X*) Bisk-Totaltape.

— CPA Comprehensive Exam Review Vol. 2: Questions, Problems & Essays with Solutions. 1994. pap. 41.95 (*0-88128-633-8*) Bisk-Totaltape.

— CPA Comprehensive Examination Review: Questions, Problems & Essays with Solutions, Vol. 2. 1994. pap. 41.95 (*0-88128-704-0*) Bisk-Totaltape.

— CPA Comprehensive Examination Review: Topic Summaries & Exam Preparation Guides, Vol. 1. 1994. pap. 41.95 (*0-88128-703-2*) Bisk-Totaltape.

— CPA Comprehensive Examination Review Vol. 1: Topic Summaries & Exam Preparation Guides. 1995. pap. text 44.95 (*0-88128-834-9*) Bisk-Totaltape.

— CPA Comprehensive Examination Review Vol. 2: Questions, Problems & Essays with Solutions. 1995. pap. text 44.95 (*0-88128-835-7*) Bisk-Totaltape.

— CPA Financial Accounting & Reporting: Business Enterprise. 1995. pap. text 39.95 (*0-88128-882-9*) Bisk-Totaltape.

— CPA Financial Accounting & Reporting: Business Enterprises. 1994. pap. 32.95 (*0-88128-764-4*) Bisk-Totaltape.

— Financial Accounting & Reporting. (CPA Comprehensive Exam Review Ser.). 1994. pap. 38.95 (*0-88128-638-9*) Bisk-Totaltape.

— Financial Accounting & Reporting. 28th ed. (CPA Comprehensive Exam Review Ser.: No. 1). 1997. pap. text 34.95 (*1-57961-014-5*) Bisk-Totaltape.

***Bisk, Nathan M.** Financial Accounting & Reporting, 4 vols., Vol. 1. 30th ed. (CPA Comprehensive Examination Review Ser.). 2000. pap. 39.95 (*1-57961-096-X*) Bisk-Totaltape.

Bisk, Nathan M. & Bisk Publishing Staff. Accounting & Reporting. 29th ed. (CPA Comprehensive Exam Review Ser.: Vol. 2). 1998. pap. text 34.95 (*1-57961-067-6*) Bisk-Totaltape.

— Business Law & Professional Responsibilities. 29th ed. (CPA Comprehensive Exam Review Ser.: Vol. 4). 1998. pap. text 34.95 (*1-57961-069-2*) Bisk-Totaltape.

— Financial Accounting & Reporting. 29th ed. (CPA Comprehensive Exam Review Ser.: Vol. 1). 1998. pap. text 34.95 (*1-57961-066-8*) Bisk-Totaltape.

Bisk, Nathan M. & Brisk Publishing Staff. Auditing. 29th ed. (CPA Comprehensive Exam Review Ser.: Vol. 3). 1998. pap. text 34.95 (*1-57961-068-4*) Bisk-Totaltape.

***Bisk Publishing Staff.** Auditing, 4 vols., Vol. 3. 30th ed. (CPA Comprehensive Examination Review Ser.). 2000. pap. 37.95 (*1-57961-098-6*) Bisk-Totaltape.

Bisk Publishing Staff, jt. auth. see Bisk, Nathan M.

***Biskamp, Dieter.** Magnetic Reconnection in Plasmas. LC 99-87680. (Cambridge Monographs on Plasma Physics: Vol. 3). (Illus.). 496p. 2000. write for info. (*0-521-58288-1*) Cambridge U Pr.

Biskamp, Dieter. Nonlinear Magnetohydrodynamics. (Cambridge Monographs on Plasma Physics: No. 1). (Illus.). 392p. 1997. pap. text 44.95 (*0-521-59918-0*) Cambridge U Pr.

Biskeborn, Susan. Artists at Work: Twenty-Five Northwest Glassmakers, Ceramists, & Jewelers. LC 90-1089. (Illus.). 172p. 1990. pap. 24.95 (*0-88240-405-9*, Alaska NW Bks) Gr Arts Ctr Pub.

Bisker, Jeffrey. Clinical Applications of Medical Imaging. LC 86-15093. (Illus.). 242p. (C). 1986. text 78.00 (*0-306-42199-2*, Kluwer Plenum) Kluwer Academic.

Biskin, Miriam. Three Spinning Fairies. 24p. 1973. pap. 3.50 (*0-87129-180-0*, T26) Dramatic Pub.

Biskind, Peter. Easy Riders, Raging Bulls: How the Sex - Drugs - & - Rock 'n Roll Generation Saved Hollywood. (Illus.). 512p. 1999. per. 15.00 (*0-684-85708-1*, Touchstone) S&S Trade Pap.

— Easy Riders, Raging Bulls: The Generation That Transformed Hollywood. LC 98-2919. 416p. 1998. 24.50 (*0-684-80996-6*) S&S Trade.

***Biskind, Peter.** Seeing Is Believing: How Hollywood Taught Us to Stop Worrying & Love the Fifties. LC 00-36971. (Illus.). 384p. 2000. pap. text 16.00 (*0-8050-6563-6*, Owl) H Holt & Co.

Bisko, Waclaw, et al. A Beginner's Course of Polish. (ENG & POL.). 329p. 1979. pap. 14.95 (*0-8288-4722-3*, M9130) Fr & Eur.

Biskup, J., et al, eds. MFDBS 87. (Lecture Notes in Computer Science Ser.: Vol. 305). v, 249p. 1988. 36.00 (*0-387-19121-6*) Spr-Verlag.

Biskup, J. & Hull, R., eds. Database Theory - ICDT '92: Fourth International Conference, Berlin, Germany, October 1992, Proceedings. LC 92-32100. (Lecture Notes in Computer Science Ser.: Vol. 646). 1992. 69.95 (*0-387-56039-4*) Spr-Verlag.

Biskup, Joachim, et al, eds. Database Security VIII: Status & Prospects: Results of the IFIP WG 11.3 Workshop on Databas Security, Bad Salzdetfurth, Germany, 23-26 August 1994. LC 94-45583. (IFIP Transactions: Computer Science & Technology Ser.: Vol. 60A). 412p. 1994. 139.50 (*0-444-81976-2*, North Holland) Elsevier.

Biskup, Manfred, et al, eds. The Family & Its Culture: An Investigation in Seven East & West European Countries. 2nd ed. 496p. (C). 1987. 171.00 (*963-05-4646-9*, Pub. by Akade Kiado) St Mut.

Biskup, Manfred, et al. The Family & Its Culture: An Investigation in Seven East & West European Countries. 496p. 1987. 171.00 (*963-05-6446-7*, Pub. by Akade Kiado) St Mut.

Biskup, Michael D., ed. Criminal Justice: Opposing Viewpoints. (Opposing Viewpoints Ser.). (Illus.). 216p. (YA). (gr. 10 up). 1993. pap. text 16.20 (*0-89908-623-3*); lib. bdg. 26.20 (*0-89908-624-1*) Greenhaven.

Biskup, Michael D. & Cozic, Charles P., eds. Youth Violence. LC 92-23592. (Current Controversies Ser.). 272p. (YA). (gr. 10 up). 1992. pap. text 16.20 (*1-56510-016-6*); lib. bdg. 26.20 (*1-56510-017-4*) Greenhaven.

Biskup, Michael D. & Swisher, Karin L., eds. AIDS: Opposing Viewpoints. LC 92-19874. (Opposing Viewpoints Ser.). (Illus.). 216p. (YA). (gr. 10 up). 1992. pap. text 16.20 (*0-89908-165-7*) Greenhaven.

Biskup, Michael D., jt. ed. see Wekesser, Carol.

Biskupic, Joan. Supreme Court Yearbook, 1989-1990. 1991. 33.95 (*0-87187-590-X*) Congr Quarterly.

— Supreme Court Yearbook 1990-1991. 250p. 1991. 33.95 (*0-87187-637-X*); pap. 23.95 (*0-87187-638-8*) Congr Quarterly.

— Supreme Court Yearbook, 1991-1992. 250p. 1992. 33.95 (*0-87187-716-3*) Congr Quarterly.

Biskupic, Joan & Witt, Elder. Congressional Quarterly's Guide to the U. S. Supreme Court, 2 vols., Set. 3rd ed. LC 96-8222. Vol. 3. 1172p. (YA). (gr. 11). 1996. text 315.00 (*1-56802-130-5*) Congr Quarterly.

— Congressional Quarterly's Guide to the U. S. Supreme Court, Vol. 1. 3rd ed. LC 96-8222. 1996. write for info. (*1-56802-236-0*) Congr Quarterly.

B

— Congressional Quarterly's Guide to the U. S. Supreme Court, Vol. 2. 3rd ed. LC 96-8222. 1996. write for info. (*1-56802-237-9*) Congr Quarterly.
— The Supreme Court & Individual Rights. 3rd ed. LC 96-8220. 360p. (YA). (gr. 11). 1997. pap. text 23.97 (*1-56802-239-5*) Congr Quarterly.
— The Supreme Court & the Powers of the American Government. LC 96-9856. 434p. (YA). (gr. 11). 1997. pap. text 23.97 (*1-56802-324-3*) Congr Quarterly.
— The Supreme Court at Work. 2nd ed. LC 96-29102. 402p. (YA). (gr. 11). 1997. pap. text 23.97 (*1-56802-323-5*) Congr Quarterly.
Biskupski, M. B., jt. ed. see Pula, James S.
Bisler, Ludwig, tr. see Eugippius.
Bislev, Sven, jt. auth. see De Appendini, Kirsten A.
Bisley, Geoffrey G. A Handbook of Ophthalmology for Developing Countries. 2nd ed. (Illus.). 1981. pap. text 14.95 (*0-19-261244-1*) OUP.
Bislo, Robin, jt. auth. see Anderson, Cynthia.
Bisman, Cynthia. Social Work Practice: Cases & Principles. LC 93-23213. 314p. 1993. mass mkt. 37.00 (*0-534-22230-7*) Brooks-Cole.
Bisman, Cynthia & Hardcastle, David A. Integrating Research into Practice: A Model for Effective Social Work. LC 98-35449. 1998. mass mkt. 42.95 (*0-534-36215-X*) Brooks-Cole.
Bismarck, Beatrice Von, see Von Bismarck, Beatrice.
Bismarck-Nas, Maher N. Structural Dynamics in Aeronautical Engineering. LC 99-12326. (AIAA Education Ser.). 297p. 1999. write for info. (*1-56347-323-2*) AIAA.
Bismut, Jean-Michel. Large Deviations & the Malliavin Calculus. (Progress in Mathematics Ser.: Vol. 45). 216p. 1984. 45.00 (*0-8176-3220-4*) Birkhauser.
— Theorie Probabiliste du Controle des Diffusions. LC 75-41602. (Memoirs Ser.: No. 4/167). 130p. 1976. pap. 22.00 (*0-8218-1867-8*, MEMO/4/167) Am Math.
Bismut, Roger, jt. auth. see Maupassant, Guy de.
Bismuth, Chantal & Hall, Alan H., eds. Paraquat Poisoning: Mechanisms, Prevention, Treatment. LC 94-39917. (Drug & Chemical Toxicology Ser.: Vol. 10). (Illus.). 382p. 1995. reprint ed. pap. 118.50 (*0-608-05322-8*, 206586000010) Bks Demand.
***Bismuth, Gil & Neumann, Shosh.** Cleaning Validation: A Practical Approach. LC 99-47401. 1999. 179.00 (*1-57491-108-2*) Interpharm.
Bismuth, Gil, jt. auth. see Ginsbury, Karen.
Bisnauth, Dale. History of Religions in the Caribbean. 236p. 1995. pap. 16.95 (*0-86543-342-9*) Africa World.
— History of Religions in the Caribbean. 236p. 1996. 49.95 (*0-86543-341-0*) Africa World.
***Bisnauth, Dale.** The Settlement of Indians in Guyana, 1890-1930. 260p. 1999. pap. (*1-900715-16-3*, Pub. by Peepal Tree Pr) Paul & Co Pubs.
Bisnignano, Judith. Living with Death - Middle School. 64p. (J). (gr. 5-9). 1991. 8.99 (*0-86653-584-5*, GA1317) Good Apple.
Bisno, Abraham. Abraham Bisno, Union Pioneer: An Autobiographical Account of Bisno's Early Life & the Beginnings of Unionism in the Women's Garment Industry. LC 67-20752. 262p. reprint ed. pap. 81.30 (*0-8357-5018-3*, 202371900033) Bks Demand.
Bisno, Alan L. & Waldvogel, Francis A., eds. Infections Associated with Indwelling Medical Devices. 2nd ed. LC 94-12592. (Illus.). 390p. 1994. 72.00 (*1-55581-077-2*) ASM Pr.
Bisno, Alan L., jt. ed. see Waldvogel, Francis.
Bisno, Herb. Managing Conflict. (Human Services Guides Ser.: Vol. 52). 160p. (C). 1988. pap. text 18.95 (*0-8039-2585-9*) Sage.
***Bisnovatyi-Kogan, G. S.** Stellar Physics Vol. I: Fundamental Concepts & Stellar Equilibrium. Blinov, A. Y. & Romanova, M., trs. from RUS. LC 00-38607. (Astronomy & Astrophysics Library). (Illus.). xvi, 328p. 2000. 84.95 (*3-540-63262-X*) Spr-Verlag.
Bisnt, G. S. Impact of Land Use on Nutrition & Health: A Study of Kosi Basin, U. P. (C). 1988. 44.00 (*81-202-0210-4*, Pub. by Ajanta) S Asia.
Bisognano, Joseph J. & Mondelli, Alfred A., eds. Computational Accelerator Physics. (AIP Conference Proceedings Ser.: No. 391). 425p. 1997. 120.00 (*1-56396-671-9*, CP# 391, AIP Pr) Spr-Verlag.
Bison, John C. Genesis, Vol. 1. 224p. 1993. pap. 22.00 (*0-7152-0465-3*, Pub. by St Andrew) St Mut.
— Genesis, Vol. 2. 336p. 1993. pap. 22.00 (*0-7152-0539-0*, Pub. by St Andrew) St Mut.
Bison, Jutta. Die Regulierung des Mietwohnungsmarktes in der Bundesrepublik Deutschland: Eine Positive Okonomische Analyse. (GER., Illus.). 299p. 1996. 57.95 (*3-631-30997-X*) P Lang Pubng.
Bispels, William C. Stephen Girard: A Great American. 1998. 6.95 (*0-533-12723-8*) Vantage.
Bispham, David. A Quaker Singer's Recollections. Farkas, Andrew, ed. LC 76-29927. (Opera Biographies Ser.). (Illus.). 1977. reprint ed. lib. bdg. 30.95 (*0-405-09669-0*) Ayer.
Bispham, W. Bispham: Memoranda Concerning the Family of Bispham in Great Britain & the U. S. 348p. 1992. reprint ed. pap. 57.00 (*0-8328-2636-7*); reprint ed. lib. bdg. 67.00 (*0-8328-2635-9*) Higginson Bk Co.
Bisplinghoff, A. Engaging Teachers. LC 98-172810. 1998. pap. 19.00 (*0-325-00037-9*) Heinemann.
Bisplinghoff, R., jt. auth. see Cox, H.
Bisplinghoff, Raymond L. & Ashley, Holt. Principles of Aeroelasticity. 2nd ed. LC 74-20442. (Illus.). 527p. (C). 1975. reprint ed. 12.95 (*0-486-61349-6*) Dover.
Bisplinghoff, Raymond L., et al. Aeroelasticity. unabridged ed. LC 96-5412. (Illus.). 880p. 1996. reprint ed. pap. 24.95 (*0-486-69189-6*) Dover.
— Statics of Deformable Solids. (Illus.). xii, 322p. 1990. pap. 10.95 (*0-486-66360-4*) Dover.
Bissantz, ed. see Instructors of Introduction to Language, the Ohio.
Bisschop, W. R. Rise of the London Money Market, 1640-1826. 256p. 1968. reprint ed. 37.50 (*0-7146-1206-5*, Pub. by F Cass Pubs) Intl Spec Bk.
***Bisschops, Ralph & Francis, James, eds.** Metaphor, Canon & Community: Jewish, Christian & Islamic Approaches. (Religions & Discourse Ser.). 307p. 1999. 45.95 (*3-906762-40-8*, Pub. by P Lang) P Lang Pubng.
— Metaphor, Canon & Community: Jewish, Christian & Islamic Approaches. LC 99-15409. (Religions & Discourse Ser.: Vol. 1). 307p. (C). 1999. pap. text 45.95 (*0-8204-4234-8*) P Lang Pubng.
Bisseland, James, III, jt. auth. see Tolve, Arthur P.
Bissell. Sensory Motor Handbook. 2nd ed. (C). 1998. pap. text 42.00 (*0-12-785072-4*) Acad Pr.
Bissell, Beryl S., ed. see Bennett, Sandy & Sullivan, Tom J.
Bissell, C. C. Control Engineering. (Illus.). 192p. 1988. 30.95 (*0-278-00060-6*) Chapman & Hall.
— Control Engineering. 2nd ed. 266p. 1994. pap. 34.95 (*0-412-57710-0*, Chap & Hall NY) Chapman & Hall.
Bissell, Chris & Chapman, David. Digital Signal Transmission. (Illus.). 331p. (C). 1992. text 125.00 (*0-521-41537-3*); pap. text 44.95 (*0-521-42557-3*) Cambridge U Pr.
Bissell, Claude. Ernest Buckler Remembered. 208p. 1989. 25.95 (*0-8020-5814-0*) U of Toronto Pr.
Bissell, Claude T. Halfway up Parnassus: A Personal Account of the University of Toronto, 1932-1971. LC 74-82289. (Illus.). 207p. reprint ed. pap. 64.20 (*0-8357-3634-2*, 203636200003) Bks Demand.
— The Imperial Canadian: Vincent Massey in Office. (Illus.). 1986. 32.50 (*0-8020-5656-3*) U of Toronto Pr.
Bissell, Claude T., ed. Our Living Tradition: Seven Canadians. LC 58-526. (Canadian University Paperbooks Ser.: No. 5). 159p. reprint ed. pap. 49.30 (*0-8357-4151-6*, 203692500007) Bks Demand.
Bissell, D. C. The First Conglomerate: 145 Years of the Singer Sewing Machine Company. LC 98-73207. (Illus.). 239p. 1999. 14.95 (*1-879418-72-X*) Audenreed Pr.
Bissell, Dee & Creurer, Michael. Good Grief, No. 2. 16p. (Orig.). 1997. pap. 4.50 (*0-915708-47-7*) Cheever Pub.
Bissell, Elaine. Empire. 384p. 1988. pap. 4.50 (*0-373-97066-8*) Harlequin Bks.
Bissell, Frances. The Book of Food: A Cook's Guide to Over 1,000 Exotic & Everyday Ingredients. 276p. 1995. write for info. (*0-8050-3006-9*) H Holt & Co.
— Ten Dinner Parties for Two. LC 89-32090. (Ten Menus Ser.). (Illus.). 128p. 1989. 19.95 (*0-940793-30-X*) Interlink Pub.
— The Times Cookbook. (Illus.). 654p. 1996. pap. 24.95 (*0-7011-6366-6*, Pub. by Chatto & Windus) Trafalgar.
Bissell, Frances, intro. Food Lover's Introduction to Britain. (Illus.). 96p. (Orig.). 1991. pap. 12.95 (*0-948817-52-6*, Pub. by Grub St) Seven Hills Bk.
***Bissell, Joan S., et al.** Cybereducator: The Internet & World Wide Web for K-12 Education. 80p. (C). 1998. pap., student ed. 9.38 (*0-07-366308-5*) McGrw-H Hghr Educ.
Bissell, Joan S. Guide to the Internet for Educational Psychology. 80p. (C). 1996. text. write for info. (*0-697-35413-X*, WCB McGr Hill) McGrw-H Hghr Educ.
— Guide to the Internet for Educational Psychology. 2nd ed. 96p. (C). 1996. text 8.50 (*0-697-37158-1*, WCB McGr Hill) McGrw-H Hghr Educ.
Bissell, Julie. Sensory Motor Handbook: A Guide for Implementing & Modifying Activities in the Classroom. 2nd ed. LC 98-16011. 1998. 44.00 (*0-7616-4386-9*, Thrpy Skill Bldrs) Commun Skill.
Bissell, Julie, et al. Sensory Motor Handbook: A Guide for Implementing & Modifying Activities in the Classroom. LC 88-60760. (Illus.). 150p. 1988. pap. 18.00 (*1-882068-02-5*) Sensory Integration.
Bissell, Kathlene. Fred Couples. LC 99-17944. (Illus.). 320p. 1999. 23.95 (*0-8092-2778-9*, 277890, Contemporary Bks) NTC Contemp Pub Co.
***Bissell, Kathlene.** Fred Couples: Golf's Reluctant Superstar. 288p. 2000. pap. 14.95 (*0-8092-2485-2*, 248520, Contemporary Bks) NTC Contemp Pub Co.
Bissell, LeClair & Royce, James. Ethics for Addiction Professionals. LC 94-32433. 60p. (Orig.). 1987. pap. 10.00 (*0-89486-454-8*) Hazelden.
Bissell, LeClair & Watherwax, Richard. The Cat Who Drank Too Much. (Illus.). 48p. (J). (gr. 4 up). 1982. pap. 8.00 (*0-911153-00-4*) Bibulophile Pr.
— El Gato Que Bebia Demasiado. (SPA., Illus.). 48p. (J). (gr. 4 up). 1982. pap. 6.00 (*0-911153-01-2*) Bibulophile Pr.
Bissell, LeClair, jt. auth. see Crosby, Linda.
Bissell, LeClair, jt. auth. see Crosby, Linda R.
Bissell, Michael E., jt. ed. see McCormick, Gordon H.
***Bissell, Michael G., ed.** Laboratory Related Measures of Patient Outcomes: An Introduction. 2000. pap. text 49.00 (*1-890883-26-3*) Am Assn Clinical Chem.
Bissell, Michael G. & Petersen, John R., eds. Automated Integration of Clinical Laboratories: A Reference. 153p. 1998. pap. 49.00 (*1-890883-03-4*, 202028) Am Assn Clinical Chem.
Bissell, R. Ward. Artemisia Gentileschi & the Authority of Art: Critical Reading & Catalogue Raisonne E. LC 97-48437. 1999. 85.00 (*0-271-01787-2*) Pa St U Pr.
— Orazio Gentileschi & the Poetic Tradition in Caravaggesque Painting. LC 80-11452. (Illus.). 404p. 1982. 75.00 (*0-271-00263-8*) Pa St U Pr.
Bissell, Richard. High Water. LC 87-20317. 290p. 1987. reprint ed. pap. 8.95 (*0-87351-221-9*, Borealis Book) Minn Hist.
— A Stretch on the River. LC 87-20390. 252p. 1987. reprint ed. pap. 8.95 (*0-87351-220-0*, Borealis Book) Minn Hist.
Bissell, Richard E. South Africa & the United States: The Erosion of an Influence Relationship. LC 81-22663. (Studies of Influence in International Relations). 147p. 1982. 57.95 (*0-275-90764-3*, C0764, Praeger Pubs) Greenwood.
— Southern Africa in the World: Autonomy or Interdependence? LC 78-102899. (Foreign Policy Research Institute. Monograph: No. 23). 74p. reprint ed. pap. 30.00 (*0-7837-1776-8*, 204197400001) Bks Demand.
Bissell, Richard E. & Gasteyger, Curt, eds. The Missing Link: West European Neutrals & Regional Security. LC 89-17010. (Duke Press Policy Studies). (Illus.). 270p. 1990. text 42.95 (*0-8223-0953-X*) Duke.
Bissell, Richard E. & Radu, Michael, eds. Africa in the Post-Decolonization Era. 278p. 1984. text 39.95 (*0-87855-496-3*) Transaction Pubs.
Bissell, Richard M., Jr., et al. Reflections of a Cold Warrior: From Yalta to the Bay of Pigs. LC 95-43084. 261p. (C). 1996. 37.00 (*0-300-06430-6*) Yale U Pr.
Bissell, Robert. Dream Road: And Other Tales from Hidden Hills (Some Involving Rabbits) 1997. 14.95 (*0-9656082-1-2*) Dreamroads Pr.
Bissell, Ronald. Reflections: Mirrors of Light. 1997. pap. 12.95 (*0-9639446-4-9*) Inn Voice Prods.
Bissell, Ronald D. Eban's World: The Colors of Change. Concepts, Triamond, ed. 136p. (Orig.). 1995. pap. 10.00 (*0-9639446-2-2*) Inn Voice Prods.
— Souls of Light: A Beginners Guide to Spiritual Transformation. (Orig.). pap. 10.95 (*0-9639446-0-6*) Inn Voice Prods.
— Unity: Life's Essence. 168p. 1998. pap. 12.95 (*0-9639446-3-0*) Inn Voice Prods.
***Bissell, Trim, ed.** Globalization in Our Own Front Yard. (Illus.). 24p. 2000. pap. write for info. (*0-9679024-1-X*) Allil Global Justice.
Bissell, William G. A Little Off the Top at the Barber Shop. x, 300p. (Orig.). 1999. pap. 12.00 (*0-9673223-0-8*) William Bissell.
Bissen, Joan, et al. Cholesterol Connections. 56p. 1990. student ed. write for info. (*1-884153-02-X*) Prk Nicollet.
— Weight Control Ways. 56p. 1990. student ed. write for info. (*1-884153-01-1*) Prk Nicollet.
Bissert, Ellen M. The Immaculate Conception of the Blessed Virgin Dyke. LC 75-27883. (Illus.). 1977. pap. 3.00 (*0-9601224-1-9*) Thirteenth Moon.
Bisset, James. Walk to Glory: A Daily Journey with James Bisset. 394p. 1998. pap. write for info. (*0-7392-0017-8*, PO2766) Morris Pubng.
Bisset, James & Stephensen, P. R. Tramps & Ladies. LC 59-12193. (Illus.). 1959. 44.95 (*0-87599-014-2*) S G Phillips.
Bisset, John T. Why Christian Kids Leave the Faith. LC 97-20794. 224p. 1997. pap. 11.99 (*1-57293-026-8*) Discovery Hse Pubs.
Bisset, Norman G., jt. ed. see Wichtl, Max.
Bisset, R. A. & Khan, A. N. Differential Diagnosis in Abdominal Ultrasound. (Illus.). 374p. 1990. pap. text 29.50 (*0-7020-1483-4*, Pub. by W B Saunders) Saunders.
Bisset, R. A., et al. Differential Diagnosis in Obstetric & Gynecologic Ultrasound. (Illus.). 350p. 1996. text 30.00 (*0-7020-2171-7*, Pub. by W B Saunders) Saunders.
Bisset, Tom. Good News about Prodigals: Why Prodigals Return & How We Can Help Them. LC 97-14646. 192p. 1997. pap. 11.99 (*1-57293-025-X*) Discovery Hse Pubs.
Bisset, Virgil, jt. ed. see Hunting, Constance.
Bisset, William P. & Matla, Ihor. Educational Crossword Puzzles in Mathematics. 64p. (YA). (gr. 9-12). 1995. pap. text 4.90 (*0-921369-07-7*) J C George Ent.
Bissett. Inkorrect Thots. LC 92-204021. 136p. 1992. pap. 12.95 (*0-88922-303-3*, Pub. by Talonbks) Genl Dist Srvs.
— Selected Poems: Beyond Even Faithful Legends. LC 81-91051. 160p. 1980. pap. 12.95 (*0-88922-172-3*, Pub. by Talonbks) Genl Dist Srvs.
Bissett, Bill. The Last Photo of the Human Soul. LC 94-150289. (Illus.). 144p. 1993. pap. 12.95 (*0-88922-322-X*, Pub. by Talonbks) Genl Dist Srvs.
— Loving Without Being Vulnerable. LC 98-135811. 144p. 1997. pap. 12.95 (*0-88922-372-6*, Pub. by Talonbks) Genl Dist Srvs.
***Bissett, Bill.** Scars on the Seehors. 144p. 1999. pap. 12.95 (*0-88922-387-4*, Pub. by Talonbks) Genl Dist Srvs.
Bissett, Bill. TH Influenza UV Logik. LC 96-106232. 144p. 1995. pap. 12.95 (*0-88922-357-2*, Pub. by Talonbks) Genl Dist Srvs.
Bissett, D., jt. auth. see Cassidy, James.
Bissett, Isabel. Here Comes Annette! LC 92-27267. (Voyages Ser.). (Illus.). (J). 1993. 3.75 (*0-383-03628-3*) SRA McGraw.
— How to Make Cheese Muffins. LC 93-21247. (Illus.). (J). 1994. 4.25 (*0-383-03748-4*) SRA McGraw.
— Molly's Bracelet. LC 92-34337. (Voyages Ser.). (Illus.). (J). 1993. 3.75 (*0-383-03641-0*) SRA McGraw.
— That's Dangerous. LC 92-31947. (Voyages Ser.). (Illus.). (J). 1993. 3.75 (*0-383-03596-1*) SRA McGraw.
— Wheels. LC 92-21399. (Voyages Ser.). (Illus.). (J). 1993. 3.75 (*0-383-03605-4*) SRA McGraw.
Bissett, Jim. Agrarian Socialism in America: Marx, Jefferson, & Jesus in the Oklahoma Countryside, 1904-1920. LC 99-12917. 272p. 1999. 33.95 (*0-8061-3148-9*) U of Okla Pr.
Bissett, Lesley. Going for the Gold: Winning the Gold Medal for Financial Independence. Scanlon, Kelly & Guthrie, Jane D., eds. LC 95-72994. 130p. (Orig.). 1996. pap. 15.95 (*1-57294-001-8*, 13-0014) SkillPath Pubns.
Bissett, Roni. Don't Trip over the Pebbles in Your Path. Griffith, Joyce, ed. (Illus.). 194p. 1998. pap. 14.98 (*0-9661622-0-X*) Veronika Pr.
Bissette, Stephen R. & O'Connor, Nancy J., eds. Taboo, Vol. 3. (Illus.). 144p. (Orig.). 1989. pap. 9.95 (*0-922003-02-5*) Spiderbaby Grafix Pubns.
— Taboo, Vol. 4. Lofficier, Randy & Lofficier, Jean-Marc, trs. (FRE., Illus.). 144p. (Orig.). 1990. pap. write for info. (*0-922003-03-3*) Spiderbaby Grafix Pubns.
Bissette, Stephen R. & Totleben, John, eds. Taboo, No. 1. (Illus.). 112p. (Orig.). 1988. pap. 9.95 (*0-922003-00-9*) Spiderbaby Grafix Pubns.
— Taboo, No. 2. (Illus.). 112p. (Orig.). 1989. pap. 9.95 (*0-922003-01-7*) Spiderbaby Grafix Pubns.
Bissette, Stephen R., ed. see Grimes, Rick.
Bissette, Steve. Age of Monsters. (Godzilla Ser.). (Illus.). 1998. pap. text 17.95 (*1-56971-277-8*) Dark Horse Comics.
Bissette, Steve & Dorman, Dave. Aliens: Tribes. limited ed. (Illus.). 80p. 1993. 75.00 (*1-56971-014-7*) Dark Horse Comics.
Bissex, Glenda L. Gnys at Work: A Child Learns to Write & Read. 235p. 1985. pap. 15.50 (*0-674-35490-7*) HUP.
— Partial Truths: A Memoir & Essays on Reading, Writing & Researching. LC 96-26639. 1996. pap. text 25.00 (*0-435-07224-2*) Heinemann.
Bissex, Glenda L. & Bullock, Richard, eds. Seeing for Ourselves: Case-Study Research by Teachers of Writing. LC 86-27153. 228p. (C). 1987. pap. text 25.00 (*0-435-08436-4*, 08436) Heinemann.
Bissex, Sandra, ed. see Lupton, James F.
***Bissinger.** Friday Night Lights: A Town, a Team, & a Dream. anniversary ed. (Illus.). 400p. 2000. reprint ed. pap. 14.00 (*0-306-80990-7*, Pub. by Da Capo) HarpC.
Bissinger, Buzz. A Prayer for the City: The True Story of a Mayor & Five Heroes in a Race Against Time. (Illus.). 448p. 1999. pap. 15.00 (*0-679-74494-0*) Vin Bks.
Bissinger, H. G. Friday Night Lights: A Town, a Team & a Dream. 1991. 19.10 (*0-606-12297-4*, Pub. by Turtleback) Demco.
— Friday Night Lights: A Town, a Team, & a Dream. large type ed. (General Ser.). 491p. 1991. lib. bdg. 20.95 (*0-8161-5237-3*, G K Hall Lrg Type) Mac Lib Ref.
— Friday Night Lights: A Town, a Team, & a Dream. LC 90-56421. (Illus.). 416p. 1991. reprint ed. pap. 14.00 (*0-06-097406-0*, Perennial) HarperTrade.
Bissinger, Margie. Osteoporosis: An Exercise Guide. (Illus.). 27p. 1998. pap., wbk. ed. 9.95 (*0-9668792-0-1*) Workfit Consult.
Bissland, Ted. Modern Canoe. 160p. 1994. pap. 18.95 (*0-385-25463-6*) Doubleday.
Bisso, Ray. Buddy Bolden of New Orleans: A Jazz Poem. LC 98-13969. 80p. 1998. pap. 10.00 (*1-56474-268-7*) Fithian Pr.
Bisson. Chaucer & Late Medieval World. 2000. pap. 18.95 (*0-312-22466-4*) St Martin.
Bisson & de Schonen. L'Enfant Derriere la Porte: Level B. text 8.95 (*0-8219-1459-6*) EMC-Paradigm.
Bisson, David. The Boy Behind the Door. Date not set. pap. 4.99 (*0-7493-2123-7*) Heinemann.
Bisson, Douglas R. The Merchant Adventurers of England: The Company & the Crown, 1474-1564. LC 92-50759. 1993. 29.50 (*0-87413-465-X*) U Delaware Pr.
Bisson, I. J., ed. see Shakespeare, William.
Bisson, Julie. Celebrate! An Anti-Bias Guide to Enjoying Holidays in Early Childhood Programs. LC 97-23504. (Orig.). 1997. pap. 16.95 (*1-884834-32-9*, 1724) Redleaf Pr.
***Bisson, Michael S., et al.** Ancient African Metallurgy: The Socio-Cultural Context. (Illus.). 344p. 2000. 65.00 (*0-7425-0260-0*); 26.95 (*0-7425-0261-9*) AltaMira Pr.
Bisson, Terry. Bears Discover Fire & Other Stories. 256p. 1994. pap. 12.00 (*0-312-89035-4*) Orb NYC.
— Fire on the Mountain. 176p. 1990. pap. 3.50 (*0-380-75369-3*, Avon Bks) Morrow Avon.
— Hardwire. Todd, Rebecca, ed. (Orig.). 1995. mass mkt. 5.50 (*0-671-52300-7*) PB.
— Harriet Tubman: Antislavery Activist. Huggins, Nathan I., ed. (Black Americans of Achievement Ser.). (Illus.). 124p. (YA). (gr. 5 up). 1991. pap. 8.95 (*0-7910-0249-7*); lib. bdg. 19.95 (*1-55546-612-5*) Chelsea Hse.
***Bisson, Terry.** In the Upper Room & Other Likely Stories: And Other Likely Stories. LC 00-25138. 304p. 2000. 23.95 (*0-312-87404-9*, Pub. by Tor Bks) St Martin.
Bisson, Terry. Miracle Man. (X-Files Ser.). 144p. (J). 1998. pap. 4.50 (*0-06-447192-6*) HarpC Child Bks.
***Bisson, Terry.** Mumia: His Story. 2001. write for info. (*0-87486-901-3*) Plough.
— Nat Turner: Prophet & Slave Revolt Leader. (Black American Ser.). (Illus.). 192p. 1989. reprint ed. mass mkt. 4.95 (*0-87067-895-7*, Melrose Sq) Holloway.
Bisson, Terry. Nat Turner: Slave Revolt Leader. Huggins, Nathan I., ed. (Black Americans of Achievement Ser.). (Illus.). 124p. (YA). (gr. 5 up). 1988. lib. bdg. 19.95 (*1-55546-613-3*) Chelsea Hse.
— Nat Turner: Slave Revolt Leader. Huggins, Nathan I., ed. (Black Americans of Achievement Ser.). (Illus.). 124p. (YA). (gr. 5 up). 1989. pap. 8.95 (*0-7910-0214-4*) Chelsea Hse.
— Pirates of the Universe. 1997. pap. 12.95 (*0-312-86295-4*) St Martin.
— Pirates of the Universe. 1997. pap. 12.95 (*0-614-27318-8*) Tor Bks.
***Bisson, Terry.** The Sixth Day. 2000. mass mkt. write for info. (*0-8125-7947-X*) Tor Bks.
Bisson, Terry. Talking Man. 192p. 1987. pap. 2.95 (*0-380-75141-0*, Avon Bks) Morrow Avon.
— Virtuosity. 1995. mass mkt. 5.99 (*0-671-53752-0*) PB.
— Voyage to the Red Planet. 240p. 1991. mass mkt. 3.50 (*0-380-75574-2*, Avon Bks) Morrow Avon.
— Wyrldmaker. 176p. 1988. mass mkt. 2.95 (*0-380-75359-6*, Avon Bks) Morrow Avon.

An Asterisk (*) at the beginning of an entry indicates that the title is appearing for the first time.

***Bisson, Terry.** X Files: Miracle Man, Vol. 16. 128p. (YA). 2000. mass mkt. 4.50 (*0-06-106617-6*) HarpC Child Bks.

Bisson, Terry, jt. auth. see Spinner, Stephanie.

Bisson, Thomas A. American Policy in the Far East, 1931-1941. LC 75-30096. (Institute of Pacific Relations Ser.). reprint ed. 39.50 (*0-404-59505-7*) AMS Pr.

— America's Far Eastern Policy. LC 75-30095. (Institute of Pacific Relations Ser.). reprint ed. 39.50 (*0-404-59506-5*) AMS Pr.

Bisson, Thomas N. Assemblies & Representation in Languedoc in the Thirteenth Century. LC 63-23400. 379p. reprint ed. pap. 117.50 (*0-7837-0044-X*, 204029100016) Bks Demand.

— Conservation of Coinage: Monetary Exploitation & Its Restraint in France, Catalonia, & Aragon C.1000-1225 A.D. (Illus.). 1979. 65.00 (*0-19-828275-3*) OUP.

— The Medieval Crown of Aragon: A Short History. (Illus.). 250p. 1991. reprint ed. pap. text 26.00 (*0-19-820236-9*, 11916) OUP.

— Medieval France & Her Pyrenean Neighbours. (Studies in Early Institutional History). 464p. 1989. 65.00 (*0-907628-69-9*) Hambledon Press.

— Tormented Voices: Power, Crisis, & Humanity in Rural Catalonia, 1140-1200. LC 97-46083. 224p. 1998. pap. 18.95 (*0-674-89528-2*) HUP.

— Tormented Voices: Power, Crisis, & Humanity in Rural Catalonia, 1140-1200. LC 97-46083. 224p. 1999. text 35.00 (*0-674-89527-4*) HUP.

Bisson, Thomas N., ed. Cultures of Power: Lordship, Status, & Process in Twelfth-Century Europe. (Middle Ages Ser.). (Illus.). 400p. 1995. pap. text 19.95 (*0-8122-1555-9*) U of Pa Pr.

— Cultures of Power: Lordship, Status, & Process in Twelfth-Century Europe. LC 95-12349. (Middle Ages Ser.). (Illus.). 400p. 1995. text 47.50 (*0-8122-3290-9*) U of Pa Pr.

Bisson, Thomas N., jt. auth. see Brussel, Nicolas.

Bisson, Thomas N., ed. see Benton, John F.

Bisson, Wilfred J. Countdown to Violence: The Charlestown Convent Riot of 1834. (Nineteenth Century American Political & Social History Ser.). 154p. 1989. reprint ed. 54.00 (*0-8240-4064-3*) Garland.

Bisson, Wilfred J., compiled by. Franklin Pierce: A Bibliography, 14. LC 93-4195. 192p. 1993. lib. bdg. 65.00 (*0-313-28172-6*, Greenwood Pr) Greenwood.

Bissonette, Bruce. Travel Air: A Photo History: A Timeless Collection of Photos from the Beginnings of the Travel Air Company. LC 96-84927. (Aviation Heritage Library Ser.). 101p. 1996. write for info. (*0-9652727-0-2*) Aviation Publng.

Bissonette, John A. & Krausman, Paul R., eds. Integrating People & Wildlife for a Sustainable Future. LC 95-60231. (Illus.). 715p. (C). 1995. pap. 30.00 (*0-933564-12-0*) Wildlife Soc.

Bissonette, John A. & Wildlife Society Staff. Wildlife & Landscape Ecology: Effects of Pattern & Scale. LC 97-7739. 223p. 1997. 29.95 (*0-387-94789-2*) Spr-Verlag.

***Bissonnette, Bruno & Dalens, Bernard J.** Companion Handbook of Pediatric Symptoms. (Illus.). 500p. 2000. Price not set. (*0-07-135455-7*) McGraw.

— Textbook of Pediatric Anesthesia. (Illus.). 928p. 2000. Price not set. (*0-07-135454-9*) McGraw.

Bissonnette, Denise. Beyond Traditional Job Development: The Art of Creating Opportunity. LC 94-21858. 256p. (Orig.). (C). 1995. pap., pap. text 74.95 incl. audio (*0-942071-29-8*, 250BC) M Wright & Assocs.

Bissonnette, Denise. Contacting Employers - Takin' It to the Streets. Lamendella, John & Wright, Anita Lee, eds. (Cultivating True Livelihood Ser.: Course 7). (Illus.). 127p. 1997. teacher ed., student ed., ring bd. 200.00 (*0-942071-47-6*, 277M) M Wright & Assocs.

Bissonnette, Denise. Crossroads: Motivation & Self-Esteem for Employment Preparation & Job Retention. 269p. 1991. reprint ed. teacher ed. 115.00 (*0-942071-12-3*) M Wright & Assocs.

Bissonnette, Denise. Cultivating True Livelihood: Work in the 21st Century: Curriculum Guide. Wright, Anita Lee, ed. (Cultivating True Livelihood Ser.). (Illus.). 189p. 1997. teacher ed., ring bd. 90.00 (*0-942071-41-7*, 280M) M Wright & Assocs.

— Interviewing with Ease - Mastering the Art of Self Presentation. Lamendella, John & Wright, Anita Lee, eds. (Cultivating True Livelihood Ser.: Course 8). (Illus.). 179p. 1997. teacher ed., student ed., ring bd. 200.00 (*0-942071-48-4*, 278M) M Wright & Assocs.

— Knowing Thyself - Assets, Strengths, & Choices. Lamendella, John & Wright, Anita Lee, eds. (Cultivating True Livelihood Ser.: Course 2). (Illus.). 169p. 1997. teacher ed., student ed., ring bd. 200.00 (*0-942071-42-5*, 272M) M Wright & Assocs.

— Personal Power - Responding to Challenges. Lamendella, John & Wright, Anita Lee, eds. (Cultivating True Livelihood Ser.: Course 3). (Illus.). 145p. 1997. teacher ed., student ed., ring bd. 200.00 (*0-942071-43-3*, 273M) M Wright & Assocs.

— Researching Options & Opportunities. Lamendella, John & Wright, Anita Lee, eds. (Cultivating True Livelihood Ser.: Course 6). (Illus.). 171p. 1997. teacher ed., student ed., ring bd. 200.00 (*0-942071-46-8*, 276M) M Wright & Assocs.

— The Spirit to Work - Fostering Hope & Shifting Perspective. Lamendella, John & Wright, Anita Lee, eds. (Cultivating True Livelihood Ser.: Course 1). (Illus.). 155p. 1997. teacher ed., student ed., ring bd. 200.00 (*0-942071-40-9*, 271M) M Wright & Assocs.

— 30 Ways to Shine As a New Employee: A Guide to Success in the Workplace. Wright, Anita Lee, ed. (Illus.). 130p. 1999. pap. text 18.00 (*0-942071-36-0*, 253B) M Wright & Assocs.

— Tools for the Journey - Proposals, Resumes & Letters. Lamendella, John & Wright, Anita Lee, eds. (Cultivating True Livelihood Ser.: Course 5). (Illus.). 167p. 1997. teacher ed., student ed., ring bd. 200.00 (*0-942071-45-X*, 275M) M Wright & Assocs.

— Work Search Planning - Laying the Groundwork in the New Millennium. Lamendella, John & Wright, Anita Lee, eds. (Cultivating True Livelihood Ser.: Course 4). (Illus.). 191p. 1997. teacher ed., student ed., ring bd. 200.00 (*0-942071-44-1*, 274M) M Wright & Assocs.

Bissonnette, Denise & Pimentel, Richard. Interactions: Customer Service for Persons with Disabilities. 92p. 1992. teacher ed. 695.00 (*0-942071-22-0*) M Wright & Assocs.

Bissonnette, Donald R., ed. see Ang, Eng T.

Bissonnette, Georges. Moscow Was My Parish. LC 78-16489. 272p. 1978. reprint ed. lib. bdg. 65.00 (*0-313-20594-9*, BIMM, Greenwood Pr) Greenwood.

Bissonnette-Lamendella, Denise. Pathways: A Job Search Curriculum. 275p. (Orig.). (YA). 1987. student ed. 7.95 (*0-942071-05-0*) M Wright & Assocs.

— Pathways: A Job Search Curriculum. rev. ed. 265p. (Orig.). (J). 1987. reprint ed. teacher ed. 87.95 (*0-942071-02-6*) M Wright & Assocs.

Bissonnette, Lise. Affairs of Art. Fischman, Sheila, tr. LC 97-113171. (ENG & FRE.). 128p. 1996. pap. text 13.95 (*0-88784-583-5*, Pub. by Hse of Anansi Pr) Genl Dist Srvs.

— Following the Summer. Fischman, Sheila, tr. from FRE. 112p. (Orig.). 1993. pap. 12.95 (*0-88784-543-6*, Pub. by Hse of Anansi Pr) Genl Dist Srvs.

Bissonnette, Luc R., ed. Propagation & Imaging Through the Atmosphere II, Vol. 3433. LC 99-200354. 1998. 99.00 (*0-8194-2888-4*) SPIE.

Bissonnette, Luc R. & Dainty, Christopher, eds. Propagation & Imaging Through the Atmosphere. x, 458 p. 1997. pap. 99.00 (*0-8194-2547-8*) SPIE.

Bissonnette, Luc R., jt. ed. see Dainty, Christopher.

Bissonnette, Luc R., jt. ed. see Roggemann, Michael C.

Bissonnette, William E. The Jazz Crusade: The Inside Story of the Great New Orleans Jazz Revival of the 1960s. (Illus.). 432p. (Orig.). 1992. pap. 29.95 incl. cd-rom (*0-9632297-0-2*) Spec Req Bks Rec.

Bissoondath, Neil. Digging up the Mountains: Selected Stories. 247p. 1986. pap. 4.95 (*0-7715-9246-9*) Genl Dist Srvs.

Bissort, Alan, jt. auth. see Puterbaugh, Parke.

Bista, Dor B. People of Nepal. 1987. 125.00 (*0-7855-0233-5*, Pub. by Ratna Pustak Bhandar) St Mut.

— People of Nepal. 210p. (C). 1987. 285.00 (*0-89771-044-4*, Pub. by Ratna Pustak Bhandar) St Mut.

Bister-Broosen, Helga. Sprachwandel im Dialekt von Krefeld. (Berkeley Insights in Linguistics & Semiotics Ser.: Vol. 3). (GER.). IX, 139p. (C). 1989. text 31.95 (*0-8204-1006-3*) P Lang Pubng.

Bister-Broosen, Helga, et al, eds. Niederlandisch Am Niederrhein. (Duisburger Arbeiten zur Sprach- und Kulturwissenschaft Ser.: Band 35). (GER., Illus.). 171p. 1998. pap. 37.95 (*3-631-32578-9*) P Lang Pubng.

Bister, Donna, jt. auth. see Cleveland, Richard.

Bister, Helga, et al. Spektrum: Grammatik im Kontext. 416p. (C). 1992. text 38.20 (*0-13-517293-4*) P-H.

Bistline, John L., jt. auth. see Winegar, Norman.

Bistner, Stephen I., et al, eds. Handbook of Veterinary Procedures & Emergency Treatment. 7th ed. LC 99-41999. (Illus.). 1020p. 2000. text. write for info. (*0-7216-7166-7*, W B Saunders Co) Harcrt Hlth Sci Grp.

Bistner, Stephen I. & Ford, Richard B. Kirk & Bistner's Handbook of Veterinary Procedures & Emergency Treatment. 6th ed. (Illus.). 912p. 1994. pap. text 63.00 (*0-7216-4972-6*, W B Saunders Co) Harcrt Hlth Sci Grp.

***Bistrian, B. R. & Walker-Smith, J. A., eds.** Inflammatory Bowel Diseases: 2nd Nestle Nutrition Workshop Clinical & Performance Programme, "Inflammatory Bowel Diseases", Pasadena, California, November 1998. LC 99-27294. (Nestle Nutrition Workshop Series : Clinical & Performance Programme). (Illus.). xiv, 268p. 1999. 172.25 (*3-8055-6885-1*) S Karger.

Bistry, David, et al. Complete Guide to MMX Technology. LC 97-7978. (Illus.). 313p. 1997. pap., pap. text 59.95 incl. cd-rom (*0-07-006192-0*) McGraw.

Biswa, K. & Chopra, R. N. Common Medicinal Plants of Darjeeling & the Sikkim Himalayas. 158p. (C). 1982. 50.00 (*0-7855-3302-8*, Pub. by Scientific) St Mut.

Biswag, A. Climate & Development. 154p. 1983. pap. text 50.00 (*0-907567-37-1*, Tycooly Pub) Weidner & Sons.

Biswag, A., jt. auth. see Golubev, G. N.

Biswas. Samsad Bengali-English Dictionary. (BEN & ENG.). 932p. 1992. 29.95 (*0-7859-7465-2*) Fr & Eur.

Biswas & Ramadurai, S. Galactic Cosmic Ray Heavy Ions. (Advances in Space Research Ser.: Vol. 15, No. 1). 76p. 1994. pap. 176.00 (*0-08-042535-6*, Pergamon Pr) Elsevier.

Biswas, A.K. & Davenport, W. G., eds. Extractive Metallurgy of Copper. 3rd ed. LC 94-12685. 518p. 1994. 100.75 (*0-08-042124-5*, Pergamon Pr) Elsevier.

Biswas, Arun K. Swami Vivekananda & the Indian Quest for Socialism. 300p. 35.00 (*0-8364-1949-9*) S Asia.

Biswas, Arun K. & Biswas, Sulekha. Minerals & Metals in Ancient India, 2 vols., Set. (C). 1996. 210.00 (*81-246-0048-1*, Pub. by DK Pubs Ind) S Asia.

***Biswas, Asit K.** Management of Latin American River Basins: Amazon, Plata & San Francisco. LC 98-58084. 1999. pap. 29.95 (*92-808-1012-X*) UN Univ Pr.

Biswas, Asit K., ed. International Waters of the Middle East: From Euphrates-Tigris to Nile. (Water Resources Management Ser.: No. 2). (Illus.). 238p. 1994. text 35.00 (*0-19-563467-5*) OUP.

— Water Resources: Environmental Planning, Management, & Development. LC 96-38133. (Illus.). 737p. 1997. 69.95 (*0-07-005483-5*) McGraw.

Biswas, Asit K., et al, eds. National Water Master Plans for Developing Countries. (Water Resources Management Ser.: No. 6). (Illus.). 288p. 1998. text 27.50 (*0-19-564061-6*) OUP.

Biswas, Asit K. & Agarwal, B. C., eds. Environmental Impact Assessment for Developing Countries. LC 92-3236. (Illus.). 259p. 1992. reprint ed. pap. 80.30 (*0-608-07927-8*, 206790100012) Bks Demand.

Biswas, Asit K. & Agarwal, S. B., eds. Environmental Impact Assessment for Developing Countries. 256p. 1994. reprint ed. pap. text 44.95 (*0-7506-2139-7*) Buttrwrth-Heinemann.

Biswas, Asit K. & Davenport, W. G. Extractive Metallurgy of Copper. 2nd ed. LC 96-20338. (Illus.). 328p. 1980. pap. 170.00 (*0-08-024735-0*, Pub. by Pergamon Repr) Franklin.

Biswas, Asit K. & Geping, Qu. Environmental Impact Assessment for Developing Countries, Vol. E19. 240p. 1987. pap. 60.00 (*1-85148-008-0*) Weidner & Sons.

Biswas, Asit K. & Hashimoto, Tsuyoshi, eds. Asian International Waters: From Ganges-Brahmaputra to Mekong. LC 96-912034. (Water Resources Management Ser.: Vol. 4). (Illus.). 304p. (C). 1997. text 28.00 (*0-19-563860-3*) OUP.

Biswas, Asit K. & International Workshop on the Intercomparison of National Water Master Plans. National Water Master Plans for Developing Countries. LC 97-906437. (Illus.). 1997. write for info. (*0-19-564366-6*) OUP.

Biswas, Asit K., et al. Core & Periphery: A Comprehensive Approach to Middle Eastern Water. (Water Resources Management Ser.: No. 5). (Illus.). 180p. 1997. text 24.95 (*0-19-564062-4*) OUP.

Biswas, Asit K., jt. auth. see Abu-Zeid, Mahmoud A.

Biswas, Asit K., jt. auth. see Ausebel, J.

Biswas, Asit K., jt. auth. see Modak, Prasad.

Biswas, Asit K., jt. ed. see El-Hinnawi, Essam E.

Biswas, Asit K., jt. ed. see Thanh, N. C.

Biswas, B. Handbook of Pathology, 2 vols. (C). 1984. 210.00 (*0-7855-6119-6*, Pub. by Current Dist) St Mut.

Biswas, B. B. & Biswas, S., eds. Subcellular Biochemistry Vol. 26: Myoinositol Phosphates, Phosphoinositides & Signal Transduction, Vol. 26. (Illus.). 413p. (C). 1996. text 125.00 (*0-306-45221-9*, Kluwer Plenum) Kluwer Academic.

Biswas, B. B. & Das, H. K. Subcellular Biochemistry Vol. 29: Plant-Microbe Interactions. (Illus.). 396p. (C). 1998. text 129.50 (*0-306-45678-8*, Kluwer Plenum) Kluwer Academic.

Biswas, B. C. Agroclimatology of the Sugar-Cane Crop. (WMO, No. 703 & Technical Note Ser.: No. 193). xvi, 90p. 1988. pap. 23.00 (*92-63-10703-3*, Pub. by Wrld Meteorological) St Mut.

Biswas, C. & Johri, B. M. The Gymnosperms. 300p. 1997. 159.00 (*3-540-61283-1*) Spr-Verlag.

***Biswas, Gautam & McIlraith, Sheila, eds.** Hybrid Systems & AI - Modeling Analysis & Control of Discrete Plus Continuous Systems: Papers from the AAAI Spring Symposium. (Technical Reports: Vol. SS-99-05). (Illus.). 265p. 1999. spiral bd. 30.00 (*1-57735-101-0*) AAAI Pr.

Biswas, Goutam. Art As Dialogue: Essays in Phenomonology of Aesthetic Experience. LC 97-900807. (C). 1995. 18.00 (*81-246-0043-0*, Pub. by Abhinav) S Asia.

Biswas, J., ed. see Pung, H. K.

Biswas, Jayasee. U. S. - Bangladesh Relations: A Study of the Political & Economic Developments During 1971-1981. 1985. 12.50 (*0-8364-1309-1*) S Asia.

Biswas, K. Common Fresh & Brackish Water Algal Flora: India & Burma. 105p. (C). 1980. text 100.00 (*0-89771-555-1*, Pub. by Intl Bk Distr) St Mut.

Biswas, K. & Calder, C. Hand-Book of Common Water & Marsh Plants of India & Burma. 2nd ed. (Illus.). 177p. 1984. text 30.00 (*0-614-03285-7*, Pub. by B Singh) Lubrecht & Cramer.

Biswas, M., et al, eds. The Web of Life. (Perspectives in Science & Engineering Ser.: Vol. 1). 224p. 1997. text 35.00 (*3-7186-5927-1*, Harwood Acad Pubs) Gordon & Breach.

Biswas, Manju. Mentally Retarded & Normal Children: A Comparative Study of Their Family Conditions. 157p. 1980. 19.95 (*0-940500-50-7*, Pub. by Sterling) Asia Bk Corp.

Biswas, Margaret R., et al, eds. Food, Climate & Man. LC 78-15154. (Environmental Science & Technology Ser.). (Illus.). 311p. 1979. reprint ed. pap. 96.50 (*0-7837-3428-X*, 205774900008) Bks Demand.

Biswas, Margaret R. & Gabr, Madouh, eds. Nutrition in the 90s: Policy Issues. (Illus.). 220p. (C). 1994. 18.95 (*0-19-563393-8*) OUP.

Biswas, O'Neil. From Justice to Welfare. 1985. 30.00 (*0-8364-1513-2*, Pub. by Intellect Pub Hse) S Asia.

Biswas, R. K., ed. Innovative Austrian Architecture. (Illus.). 223p. 1996. pap. 51.00 (*3-211-82728-5*) Spr-Verlag.

Biswas, S. Applied Stochastic Processes: Biostatistical & Population Oriented Approach. 1995. write for info. (*81-224-0691-2*, Pub. by Wiley Estrn) Franklin.

***Biswas, S.** Cosmic Perspectives in Space Physics LC 99-15697. (Astrophysics & Space Science Library). 1999. write for info. (*0-7923-5813-9*) Kluwer Academic.

Biswas, S., jt. ed. see Biswas, B. B.

Biswas, S. C., ed. Gandhi: Theory & Practice, Social Impact & Contemporary Relevance. 1990. 32.00 (*81-7074-058-4*, Pub. by KP Bagchi) S Asia.

— Union Catalogue of Philosophical Periodicals. (C). 1989. 11.00 (*0-685-30704-2*, Pub. by M Manoharial) S Asia.

Biswas, S. K. Samsad English-Bengali Dictionary. (BEN & ENG.). 932p. 1992. 59.95 (*0-8288-1119-9*, M14243) Fr & Eur.

Biswas, S. K., et al, eds. Cosmic Perspectives. (Illus.). 272p. (C). 1989. text 74.95 (*0-521-34354-2*) Cambridge U Pr.

— Energetic Charged Particles in Space: Proceedings of Symposium 11 & of the Topical Meeting of the COSPAR Interdisciplinary Scientific Commission D of the COSPAR 27th Plenary Meeting Held in Espoo, Finland, 18-29 July, 1988. (Advances in Space Research Ser.: Vol. 9). 210p. 1989. pap. 99.00 (*0-08-040155-4*, 1702; 2308, Pergamon Pr) Elsevier.

— Foundations of Software Technology & Theoretical Computer Science: 11th Conference, New Delhi, India December 17-19, 1991 Proceedings. (Lecture Notes in Computer Science Ser.: Vol. 560). x, 420p. 1992. 57.00 (*0-387-54967-6*) Spr-Verlag.

***Biswas, S. S.** Protecting the Cultural Heritage: National Legislations & International Conventions LC 99-931901. 263p. 1999. write for info. (*81-7305-150-X*, Pub. by Aryan Bks Intl) S Asia.

Biswas, Saroj K., ed. see Jameson, William J.

***Biswas, Subhas C. & Prajapati, M. K., eds.** Bibliographic Survey of Indian Manuscript Catalogues: Being a Union List of Manuscript Catalogues. 1998. 65.00 (*81-86339-75-2*) Eastern Bk Linkers.

Biswas, Suddhendu. Applied Stochastic Processes: A Biostatistical & Population Oriented Approach. 427p. 1995. text 49.95 (*0-470-22159-3*) Halsted Pr.

***Biswas, Sugata & Twitchell, Daryl.** Management Consulting: A Complete Guide to the Industry. LC 98-30144. 304p. 1998. 34.95 (*0-471-29352-0*) Wiley.

Biswas, Sulekha, jt. auth. see Biswas, Arun K.

Biswas, T. K. Horse in Early Indian Art. (C). 1987. 34.00 (*81-215-0046-X*, Pub. by M Manoharial) Coronet Bks.

Biswass, Jayshree. Children of Prejudiced Parents. 1990. text 27.50 (*0-7069-5323-1*, Pub. by Vikas) S Asia.

Biswell, Harold. Prescribed Burning In California Wildlands Vegetation Management. 295p. 1999. pap. 18.95 (*0-520-21945-7*, Pub. by U CA Pr) Cal Prin Full Svc.

Bisyak, Steven & McDermott, Michael. Mastering Fear: The Ultimate Challenge. LC 94-234825. 195p. (Orig.). (C). 1994. 9.95 (*0-9640871-1-1*) Frog & Latte.

Bisztray, George. Hungarian-Canadian Literature. 128p. 1987. text 30.00 (*0-8020-5715-2*) U of Toronto Pr.

Bisztriczky, T., ed. Polytopes - Abstract, Convex & Computational: Proceedings of the NATO Advanced Study Institute, Scarborough, Ontario, Canada, August 20-September 3, 1993. (NATO ASI Series C). 528p. (C). 1994. text 309.50 (*0-7923-3016-1*) Kluwer Academic.

Bit, Seanglim. The Warrior Heritage: A Psychological Perspective of Cambodian Trauma. 250p. 1991. 19.95 (*0-9628625-0-9*) Seanglim Bit.

Bita, Lili. The Scorpion & Other Stories. Zaller, Robert, tr. from GRE. LC 98-65050. 224p. 1998. pap. 15.00 (*0-918618-69-X*) Pella Pub.

Bita, Lili, tr. see Stocke, Joy E.

Bitar, Farid, ed. Treasury of Arabic Love Poems, Quotations & Proverbs. (Hippocrene Treasury of Love Ser.). 128p. 1995. 11.95 (*0-7818-0395-0*) Hippocrene Bks.

Bitar, Walid. Maps with Moving Parts. 60p. 1988. pap. 9.95 (*0-919626-37-8*, Pub. by Brick Bks) Genl Dist Srvs.

— Two Guys on Holy Land. LC 92-25033. (Wesleyan Poetry Ser.). 68p. 1993. pap. 12.95 (*0-8195-1209-5*, Wesleyan Univ Pr); text 25.00 (*0-8195-2206-6*, Wesleyan Univ Pr) U Pr of New Eng.

Bitbol, Michel. Schrodinger's Philosophy of Quantum Mechanics. LC 96-42123. (Boston Studies in the Philosophy of Science: Vol. 188). 300p. (C). 1996. lib. bdg. 120.50 (*0-7923-4266-6*) Kluwer Academic.

Bitchaeva, O., jt. auth. see Ronneau, C.

***Bitchin, Bob.** Letters from the Lost Soul: A Five Year Voyage of Discovery & Adventure. LC 00-36555. (Illus.). 272p. 2000. 29.95 (*1-57409-112-3*) Sheridan.

Bitcon, Carol H. Risk It-Express! Expression in Creative Practice. (Horizon Ser.: No. 8). 56p. (Orig.). (C). 1989. pap. text 12.00 (*0-918812-63-1*, ST 200) MMB Music.

***Bitcon, Carol Hampton.** Alike & Different: The Clinical & Educational Uses of Orff-Schulwerk. 2nd rev. ed. (Illus.). 375p. (C). 2000. pap. text. write for info. (*1-891278-09-6*) Barcelona Pubs.

Bitel, Lisa M. Isle of the Saints: Monastic Settlement & Christian Community in Early Ireland. LC 90-55118. (Illus.). 288p. 1994. text 39.95 (*0-8014-2471-2*); pap. text 17.95 (*0-8014-8157-0*) Cornell U Pr.

— Land of Women: Tales of Sex & Gender from Early Ireland. LC 95-39296. (Illus.). 296p. 1996. 42.50 (*0-8014-3095-X*) Cornell U Pr.

— Land of Women: Tales of Sex & Gender from Early Ireland. (Illus.). 336p. 1998. pap. text 16.95 (*0-8014-8544-4*) Cornell U Pr.

Bitensky, Lucille, jt. auth. see Chayen, Joseph.

Bitensky, Lucille, jt. ed. see Chayen, Joseph.

***Bitetti, Marge.** Millennium: Twenty First Century Orange County LC 98-67812. 170p. 1998. write for info. (*1-881547-27-2*) Pioneer Pubns.

***Bitetto, Marco A. V.** Ada & You. braille ed. 2000. write for info. (*1-58578-022-7*) Inst of Cybernetics.

— Biological Foundations of the Nervotron. braille ed. (Illus.). 100p. 1999. 570.00 (*1-58578-002-2*) Inst of Cybernetics.

— Biological Foundations of the Nervotron. 5th unabridged ed. (Illus.). 100p. 1999. pap. 23.50 (*1-58578-000-6*) Inst of Cybernetics.

— Confessions of a Nerd. 4p. 1999. pap. 1.50 (*1-58578-004-9*) Inst of Cybernetics.

— Confessions of a Nerd. braille ed. 1999. 224.50 (*1-58578-006-5*) Inst of Cybernetics.

— Cybernetics Laboratory. braille ed. (Illus.). (YA). 2000. write for info. (*1-58578-025-1*) Inst of Cybernetics.

— Futurist. braille ed. (Looking into the Future Ser.). 2000. write for info. (*1-58578-019-7*) Inst of Cybernetics.

— Science Fact of Space Warfare. 225p. (YA). 2000. pap. 49.95 (*1-58578-351-X*) Inst of Cybernetics.

Bitetto, Marco A. V. Scientific Foundation Behind the Nervotron. 2nd braille rev. ed. 400p. 1989. pap. 570.00 (*1-893375-98-6*) Inst of Cybernetics.

B

B

***Bitetto, Marco A. V.** SCIFI Zone: A How to Guide for Science Fiction Writers. large type ed. (Illus.). 1200p. 2000. pap. write for info. (*1-58578-015-4*) Inst of Cybernetics.

***Bitetto, Marco A. V., ed.** Aircraft Flight Simulators. braille ed. (C). 2000. write for info. (*1-58578-079-0*) Inst of Cybernetics.

— Black Watch. braille ed. (J). 2000. write for info. (*1-58578-070-7*) Inst of Cybernetics.

— A Joystick Nation. braille ed. (J). 2000. write for info. (*1-58578-085-5*) Inst of Cybernetics.

— NASA Case Studies. braille ed. (YA). 2000. write for info. (*1-58578-082-0*) Inst of Cybernetics.

— Space Enterprise. braille ed. (YA). 2000. write for info. (*1-58578-076-6*) Inst of Cybernetics.

— Test Pilot Stories. braille ed. (J). 2000. write for info. (*1-58578-073-1*) Inst of Cybernetics.

Bithell, Jethro, tr. see Zweig, Stefan.

Bithell, Sherry B. Educator Sexual Abuse: A Guide for Prevention in the Schools. LC 91-75096. 115p. (Orig.). 1992. pap. 19.95 (*0-9630575-0-2*) Tudor Hse.

Bither, Eve. Blue Ribbon Schools: Outstanding Practices in the Arts. 60p. (Orig.). (C). 1995. pap. text 25.00 (*0-7881-1546-4*) DIANE Pub.

Bititci, Umit S. & Carrie, Allan. Strategic Management of the Manufacturing Value Chain: Proceedings of the International Conference of the Manufacturing Value-Chain, August, 1998, Troon, Scotland, Uk LC 98-29390. x, 652 p. 1998. write for info. (*0-412-82710-7*) Chapman & Hall.

— Strategic Management of the Manufacturing Value Chain: Proceedings of the International Conference of the Manufacturing Value-Chain, August '98, Troon, Scotland, U. K. LC 98-29390. 1998. write for info. (*0-7923-8240-4*) Kluwer Academic.

Bitker, Marian. Thanks for Giving & Other Poems. LC 90-93454. 63p. (Orig.). (YA). 1991. 15.00 (*0-9628150-0-4*); pap. 10.00 (*0-9628150-1-2*) M Bitker.

Bitker, Steve. The Original San Francisco Giants: The Giants of '58. LC 98-84764. (Illus.). 295p. 1998. 29.95 (*1-57167-182-X*) Sports Pub.

Bitler, Dougless S. Ask Dougless: More Questions & Answers on Period Authenticity & Miniaturia. (Ask Dougless Ser.: Vol. II). (Illus.). 113p. 1987. 9.95 (*0-938685-01-5*) Dees Delights.

— Ask Dougless: More Questions & Answers on Period Authenticity & Miniaturia. Hacker, Deanna, ed. (Ask Dougless Ser.: Vol. III). (Illus.). 100p. 1990. pap. text 9.95 (*0-938685-06-6*) Dees Delights.

— Ask Dougless: One Hundred One Questions & Answers on Period Authenticity & Miniaturia. rev. ed. LC 86-71018. (Ask Dougless Ser.: Vol. II). (Illus.). 64p. 1986. pap. 9.95 (*0-938685-00-7*) Dees Delights.

Bitling, Athene, ed. & illus. see Newhouse, Flower A.

***Bitmead, Robert R., et al.** Adaptive Systems in Control & Signal Processing, 1998: A Proceedings Volume from the IFAC Workshop, Glasgow, Scotland, U. K., 26-28 August 1998. IFAC Workshop on Adaptive Systems in Control & Signal Processing Staff & International Federation of Automatic Control Staff, eds. LC 00-24954. 2000. pap. write for info. (*0-08-043238-7*, Pergamon Pr) Elsevier.

Bitner, Alvah C. Advances in Industrial Ergonomics & Safety, Vol. 7. 800p. 1995. 195.00 (*0-7484-0325-6*, Pub. by Tay Francis Ltd) Taylor & Francis.

Bitner, John W., et al. Successful Bank Asset-Liability Management: A Guide to the Future Beyond GAP. LC 91-41363. 288p. 1992. 99.95 (*0-471-52731-9*) Wiley.

Bitney, Greg. Bohemian Mobility Tales. 69p. (Orig.). (YA). (gr. 3-12). 1994. pap. 9.95 (*0-9638668-0-X*) AV Mobility.

Bitney, James. Bright Intervals: Prayers for Paschal People. 96p. (gr. 9-12). 1982. 5.95 (*0-86683-669-1*) Harper SF.

— First Communion: A Parish Celebration Family Book. 48p. (J). 1993. reprint ed. pap. text 6.30 (*1-55944-038-4*) Franciscan Comns.

Bitney, James, ed. All Things New: A Celebration of Forgiveness Family Book. (Illus.). 48p. 1992. reprint ed. pap. text 6.30 (*1-55944-016-3*, 2536316) Franciscan Comns.

— Johnson Institute No-Bullying Program Vol. 5: Preventing Bully/Victim Violence at School: Director's Manual. 80p. (Orig.). 1996. pap., teacher ed. 65.95 (*1-56246-114-1*, 3076, HazeldenJohnson Inst) Hazelden.

— No-Bullying Program Grades 4-5: Preventing Bully/Victim Violence at School. 75p. 1996. pap., teacher ed. 54.95 (*1-56246-121-4*, 3079, HazeldenJohnson Inst) Hazelden.

— No-Bullying Program Grades K-1: Preventing Bully/Victim Violence at School. (Illus.). 75p. (Orig.). 1996. pap., teacher ed. 54.95 (*1-56246-119-2*, 3077, HazeldenJohnson Inst) Hazelden.

— No-Bullying Program Grades 2-3: Preventing Bully/Victim Violence at School. (Illus.). 75p. (Orig.). 1996. pap., teacher ed. 54.95 (*1-56246-120-6*, 3078, HazeldenJohnson Inst) Hazelden.

— No-Bullying Program Grades 6-8: Preventing Bully/Victim Violence at School. (Illus.). 125p. (Orig.). 1996. pap., teacher ed. 54.95 (*1-56246-122-2*, 3081, HazeldenJohnson Inst) Hazelden.

Bitney, James L. & Schaffhausen, Suzanne. Sunday's Children: Prayers in the Language of Children. LC 86-60172. (Illus.). 80p. 1986. 5.95 (*0-89390-076-1*); 5.95 (*0-89390-110-5*) Resource Pubns.

Bitney, Jim, jt. auth. see Bell, Peter.

Bitov, Andrei. A Captive of the Caucasus. Brownsberger, Susan, tr. 352p. 1992. text 23.00 (*0-374-11883-3*) FS&G.

— A Captive of the Caucasus. 323p. 1994. pap. 15.00 (*0-00-271668-2*, Pub. by HarpC) HarpC.

— The Monkey Link. Brownsberger, Susan, tr. LC 94-18864. 400p. 1994. text 30.00 (*0-374-10578-2*) FS&G.

— Novyi Gulliver (New Gulliver) LC 97-6900. (RUS.). 220p. 1997. 15.00 (*1-55779-089-2*) Hermitage Pubs.

— Pushkin House. Brownsberger, Susan, tr. from RUS. (Contemporary Russian Prose Ser.). 414p. 1990. pap. 13.95 (*0-679-73009-5*) Vin Bks.

— Pushkin House. Brownsberger, Susan, tr. from RUS. LC 98-23360. 371p. 1998. reprint ed. pap. 13.95 (*1-56478-200-X*) Dalkey Arch.

Bitov, Andrei, et al, contrib. by. Childhood. (Glas Ser.: No. 16). 224p. 1998. pap. 14.95 (*1-56663-198-X*) I R Dee.

Bitov, Andrei & Guidieri, Remo. Monumental Propaganda. Ashton, Dore, ed. 96p. 1995. pap. 20.00 (*0-916365-42-5*) Ind Curators.

Bitoy, Earl, jt. auth. see Hauswald, Carol.

Bitran & Golomb. Lung Cancer: A Comprehensive Treatise. 1987. 94.00 (*0-685-18913-9*, Grune & Strat) Harcrt Hlth Sci Grp.

***Bitran, Jacob D.** Expert Guide to Oncology. LC 99-44526. (Illus.). 232p. 1999. pap. text 35.00 (*0-943126-88-6*) Amer Coll Phys.

Bitran, Ricardo A. A Supply-Demand Model of Health Care Financing with an Application to Zaire. LC 93-20079. (EDI Technical Materials Ser.). 92p. 1994. pap. 24.00 (*0-8213-2342-3*, 12342) World Bank.

Bitran, Ricardo A. & McInnes, D. Keith. The Demand for Health Care in Latin America: Lessons from the Dominican Republic & El Salvador. LC 93-18214. (EDI Seminar Ser.: No. 46). 66p. 1993. pap. 22.00 (*0-8213-2341-5*, 12341) World Bank.

Bitsadze, A., ed. Partial Differential Equations. 300p. (C). 1993. text 55.00 (*981-02-0593-7*) World Scientific Pub.

Bitsadze, A. V. Integral Equations of the First Kind. (Series on Soviet & East European Mathematics: Vol. 7). 260p. 1995. text 55.00 (*981-02-2263-7*) World Scientific Pub.

— Some Classes of Partial Differential Equations, Vol. 4. xii, 504p. 1988. text 176.00 (*2-88124-662-1*) Gordon & Breach.

Bitsakis, Eftichios & Nicolaides, Cleanthes A., eds. The Concept of Probability. 464p. (C). 1989. lib. bdg. 255.50 (*90-277-2679-5*, Pub. by Kluwer Academic) Kluwer Academic.

Bitsch, Marie-Therese, ed. Jalons pour Une Histoire du Conseil de l'Europe: Actes du Colloque de Strasbourg (8-10 Juin, 1995) (Euroclio Ser.). (FRE.). xiv, 376p. 1997. 53.95 (*3-906758-06-0*, Pub. by P Lang) P Lang Pubng.

***Bitskey, Istvan.** Konfessionen Und Literarische Gattungen Der Fruhen Neuzeit in Ungarn. (Illus.). 209p. 1999. 37.95 (*3-631-34543-7*) P Lang Pubng.

Bitstrisky, Levi & Zalman, Schneur. Sha'Alois Ve'Tshuvois Admur Hazoken.Tr. of Questions & Answers of Rabbi Schneur Zalman of Liadi. (HEB.). 512p. 1988. 17.00 (*0-8266-5511-4*) Kehot Pubn Soc.

Bittan, Bradley M. The Public Defender Experience: A Student Career Guide into the Heads & Hearts of America's "Real Lawyers" 1997. 30.00 (*0-938609-11-4*) Graduate Group.

Bittanti, S., ed. Software Reliability Modelling & Identification. (Lecture Notes in Computer Science Ser.: Vol. 341). vii, 209p. 1989. 34.00 (*0-387-50695-0*) Spr-Verlag.

— Time Series & Linear Systems. (Lecture Notes in Control & Information Sciences: Vol. 86). xvii, 243p. 1986. 40.95 (*0-387-16903-2*) Spr-Verlag.

Bittanti, S., et al, eds. The Riccati Equation. (Communications & Control Engineering Ser.). x, 338p. 1991. 149.95 (*0-387-53099-1*) Spr-Verlag.

Bittanti, Sergio & Picci, Giorgio, eds. Identification, Adaptation, Learning: The Science of Learning Models from Data. LC 96-14783. (NATO ASI Ser.: Vol. 153). 549p. 1996. 149.50 (*3-540-61080-4*) Spr-Verlag.

Bittar, E. Edward. Advances in Molecular & Cell Biology, Vol. 1. Miller, Kenneth R. et al, eds. 200p. 1987. 128.50 (*0-89232-792-8*) Jai Pr.

— Fundamentals of Medical Cell Biology Vol. 1: Evolutionary Biology. 352p. 1991. 128.50 (*1-55938-303-8*) Jai Pr.

Bittar, E. Edward, ed. Advances in Medical Biology, Vol. 1. Date not set. 128.50 (*0-7623-0386-7*) Jai Pr.

— Cell Biology in Medicine. LC 75-19060. 733p. reprint ed. 200.00 (*0-8357-9853-4*, 201259500083) Bks Demand.

— Fundamentals of Medical Cell Biology: A Multi-Volume Work, 8 vols. (Illus.). 3100p. 1285.00 (*1-55938-302-X*) Jai Pr.

— Fundamentals of Medical Cell Biology: Structural Biology, Vol. 2. 208p. 1991. 128.50 (*1-55938-304-6*) Jai Pr.

— Fundamentals of Medical Cell Biology Vol. 3A: Chemistry of the Living Cell, Vol. 3A. 352p. 1992. 128.50 (*1-55938-305-4*) Jai Pr.

— Fundamentals of Medical Cell Biology Vol. 3B: Chemistry of the Living Cell, Vol. 3B. 368p. 1992. 128.50 (*1-55938-306-2*) Jai Pr.

— Fundamentals of Medical Cell Biology Vol. 4: Membranology & Subcellular Organelles, Vol. 4. 560p. 1992. 128.50 (*1-55938-307-0*) Jai Pr.

— Fundamentals of Medical Cell Biology Vol. 5A: Membrane Dynamics & Signaling, Vol. 5A. 344p. 1992. 128.50 (*1-55938-309-7*) Jai Pr.

— Fundamentals of Medical Cell Biology Vol. 5B: Pumps & Intracellular Homeostasis, Hormones & Cell Function, Intercellular Communication, Cell Motility & Contractility, Vol. 5B. 272p. 1992. 128.50 (*1-55938-310-0*) Jai Pr.

— Fundamentals of Medical Cell Biology Vol. 6: Neurobiology, Thermobiology, Cytobiology, Vol. 6. 400p. 1992. 128.50 (*1-55938-311-9*) Jai Pr.

— Fundamentals of Medical Cell Biology Vol. 7: Developmental Biology, Vol. 7. 248p. 1992. 128.50 (*1-55938-312-7*) Jai Pr.

— Ionic Pumps, 2 pts. (Advances in Molecular & Cell Biology Ser.: Vol. 23). 1998. 257.00 (*0-7623-0287-9*) Jai Pr.

— Membranes & Ion Transport, Vol. 1. LC QH0601.M45. 494p. reprint ed. pap. 153.20 (*0-608-14367-7*, 201617600001) Bks Demand.

— Protein Structural Biology in Biomedical Research, 2 pts., Set. (Advances in Molecular & Cell Biology Ser.: Vol. 22). 627p. 1997. 257.00 (*0-7623-0283-6*) Jai Pr.

Bittar, E. Edward, ed. Fundamentals of Medical Cell Biology Vol. 8: Cumulative Index, Vols. 1-7, 1991-1992, Vol. 8. 224p. 1993. 128.50 (*1-55938-308-9*) Jai Pr.

Bittar, E. Edward, et al, eds. Advances in Molecular & Cell Biology, Vol. 2. 320p. 1989. 128.50 (*0-89232-886-X*) Jai Pr.

— Advances in Molecular & Cell Biology, Vol. 3. 286p. 1990. 128.50 (*1-55938-013-6*) Jai Pr.

— Advances in Molecular & Cell Biology, Vol. 4. 280p. 1992. 128.50 (*1-55938-209-0*) Jai Pr.

— Improving Educational Performance: Local & Systemic Reforms. (Advances in Educational Administration Ser.: Vol. 5). 246p. 1997. 78.50 (*0-7623-0081-7*) Jai Pr.

— The Synapse: In Development, Health, & Disease. (Advances in Organ Biology Ser.: Vol. 2). 416p. 1997. 128.50 (*0-7623-0222-4*) Jai Pr.

Bittar, E. Edward & Bartles, James. Advances in Molecular & Cell Biology Vol. 26: Cell Polarity, Vol. 26. 1998. 128.35 (*0-7623-0381-6*) Jai Pr.

Bittar, E. Edward & Bittar, Neville. Principals of Medical Biology Vol. 12: Reproductive Endocrinology & Biology. LC 98-18709. 1998. 128.50 (*1-55938-817-X*) Jai Pr.

— Principles of Medical Biology Vol. 11: Developmental Biology. LC 98-18490. 1998. 128.50 (*1-55938-816-1*) Jai Pr.

— Principles of Medical Biology Vol. 13: Cell Injury, Vol. 13. LC 98-16467. 1998. 128.50 (*1-55938-818-8*) Jai Pr.

Bittar, E. Edward & Bittar, Neville, eds. Principles of Medical Biology, 2 vols., Vol. 1. 616p. 1994. 257.00 (*1-55938-779-3*) Jai Pr.

— Principles of Medical Biology: Membranes & Cell Signaling, 7 part 2. 1997. 257.00 (*0-614-16885-6*) Jai Pr.

— Principles of Medical Biology Vol. 1A: Bioethics. LC 94-15763. 208p. 1994. 128.50 (*1-55938-801-3*) Jai Pr.

— Principles of Medical Biology Vol. 1B: Evolutionary Biology. LC 94-11633. 392p. 1994. 128.50 (*1-55938-802-1*) Jai Pr.

— Principles of Medical Biology Vol. 2: Cellular Organelles. LC 95-16568. 304p. 1995. 128.50 (*1-55938-803-X*) Jai Pr.

— Principles of Medical Biology Vol. 3: Cellular Organelles & the Extracellular Matrix. LC 95-24345. (Principles of Medical Biology Ser.). 304p. 1995. 128.50 (*1-55938-804-8*) Jai Pr.

— Principles of Medical Biology Vol. 4, Pt. I: Cell Chemistry & Physiology. 400p. 1995. 128.50 (*1-55938-805-6*) Jai Pr.

— Principles of Medical Biology Vol. 4, Pt. II: Cell Chemistry & Physiology. 416p. 1996. 128.50 (*1-55938-806-4*) Jai Pr.

— Principles of Medical Biology Vol. 4, Pt. III: Cell Chemistry & Physiology. 360p. 1996. 128.50 (*1-55938-807-2*) Jai Pr.

— Principles of Medical Biology Vol. 4, Pt. IV: Cell Chemistry & Physiology. 572p. 1996. 128.50 (*1-55938-808-0*) Jai Pr.

— Principles of Medical Biology Vol. 5: Molecular & Cellular Genetics. LC 96-20598. 432p. 1996. 128.50 (*1-55938-809-9*) Jai Pr.

— Principles of Medical Biology Vol. 6: Immunobiology. LC 96-35160. 352p. 1996. 128.50 (*1-55938-811-0*) Jai Pr.

— Principles of Medical Biology Vol. 7, Pts. I & II: Membranes & Cell Signalling. LC 97-5100. 680p. 1997. 257.00 (*1-55938-812-9*) Jai Pr.

— Principles of Medical Biology Vol. 8A, B & C: Molecular & Cellular Pharmacology. LC 97-15195. 1208p. 1997. 375.00 (*1-55938-813-7*) Jai Pr.

— Principles of Medical Biology Vol. 9A & B: Microbiology. LC 97-36100. 743p. 1998. 257.00 (*1-55938-814-5*) Jai Pr.

— Principles of Medical Biology Vol. 10A & B: Molecular & Cellular Endocrinology. LC 97-41660. 684p. 1998. 257.00 (*1-55938-815-3*) Jai Pr.

— Principles of Medical Biology Vol. 14: Psychiatry. Date not set. 128.50 (*1-55938-819-6*) Jai Pr.

Bittar, E. Edward & Das, Dipak K. Advances in Organ Biology Vol. 6: Myocardial Prevention & Cellular Adaption. 1998. 128.50 (*0-7623-0391-3*) Jai Pr.

Bittar, E. Edward & Hesketh, John, eds. Cytoskeleton. (Advances in Molecular & Cell Biology Ser.: Vol. 12). 256p. 1995. 128.50 (*1-55938-845-5*) Jai Pr.

Bittar, E. Edward & Rivett, A. J. Advances in Molecular & Cell Biology Vol. 27: Intracellular Protein Degradation, Vol. 27. 1998. 128.50 (*0-7623-0387-5*) Jai Pr.

Bittar, E. Edward & Sherbet, G. V., eds. Retinoids, Their Physiological Function & Therapeutic Potential. (Advances in Organ Biology Ser.: Vol. 3). 312p. 1997. 128.50 (*0-7623-0285-2*) Jai Pr.

Bittar, E. Edward & Zaidi, Mone. Advances in Organ Biology Vol. 5: Molecular & Cellular Biology of Bone, 3 pts. 1998. 375.00 (*0-7623-0390-5*) Jai Pr.

Bittar, E. Edward & Zakar, Tamas, eds. Advances in Organ Biology Vol. 1: Pregnancy & Parturition. xii, 230 p. 1996. 128.50 (*1-55938-639-8*) Jai Pr.

Bittar, E. Edward, jt. auth. see Edwards, Rem B.

Bittar, E. Edward, jt. auth. see Heppner, Gloria.

Bittar, E. Edward, jt. ed. see Heppner, Gloria.

Bittar, E. Edward, jt. ed. see Rosenberg, William.

Bittar, E. Edward, jt. ed. see Rothman, Stephen.

Bittar, E. Edward, jt. ed. see Timiras, Paola S.

Bittar, Edward & Garrod, D. R. Advances in Molecular & Cell Biology Vol. 28: The Adhesive Interaction of Cells. 1999. 128.50 (*0-7623-0495-2*) Jai Pr.

Bittar, Neville, jt. auth. see Bittar, E. Edward.

Bittar, Neville, jt. ed. see Bittar, E. Edward.

Bittel. Business Accounting. 3rd ed. 1987. student ed. 19.44 (*0-07-005566-1*) McGraw.

Bittel. Practice Management/Communication Skills. (SPA.). 395.00 incl. VHS (*0-8068-8289-1*, 8289) AIMS Multimedia.

— Practice Management/Difficult Situations. 395.00 incl. VHS (*0-8068-8187-9*, 8187) AIMS Multimedia.

— Practice Management/Leadership Skills. (SPA.). 395.00 incl. VHS (*0-8068-8290-5*, 8290) AIMS Multimedia.

Bittel. What Every Super Cour Guide. 6th ed. 1989. 20.94 (*0-07-005582-3*) McGraw.

Bittel, Ella, ed. see Zidonis, Nancy A., et al.

Bittel, K., et al, eds. Anatolian Studies Presented to Hans Gustav Guterbock on the Occasion of His 65th Birthday. xii, 278p. 1974. pap. text 87.50 (*0-614-03989-4*, Pub. by Netherlands Inst) Eisenbrauns.

Bittel, Lester R. The Complete Guide to Supervisory Training & Development. LC 86-22267. 1987. 41.00 (*0-201-12220-0*) Addison-Wesley.

Bittel, Lester R. Practical Management for Supervisors. 1993. teacher ed. 16.12 (*0-02-802485-0*) Glencoe.

Bittel, Lester R. Practical Management for Supervisors. 2nd ed. LC 92-36417. 1992. 20.00 (*0-02-802484-2*) Glencoe.

Bittel, Lester R. Right on Time: The Complete Guide for Time-Pressured Managers. 1991. 9.95 incl. audio (*0-07-005586-6*) McGraw.

Bittel, Lester R. & Newstrom, John W. What Every Supervisor Should Know: Supervision-in-Action: An In-Basket Simulation by Reese & Manning. 1990. 14.82 (*0-07-051488-7*) McGraw.

— What Every Supervisor Should Know: The Basics of Supervisory Management. 1990. teacher ed. 19.28 (*0-07-051489-5*) McGraw.

Bittel, Lester R., et al. Business in Action. 3rd ed. 608p. 1987. text 64.50 (*0-07-005565-3*) McGraw.

Bittel, Lester R., jt. auth. see Burke, Ronald S.

Bittel, Lester R., jt. auth. see Newstrom, John W.

Bittel, Patricia Thomas, et al, eds. Discipline & Discharge in Arbitration. LC 98-42447. 527p. 95.00 (*1-57018-060-1*, 1060-PR8) BNA Books.

Bittel, William H. Adult Learners Survival Skills. LC 89-33605. (Illus.). 74p. (Orig.). 1990. pap. 8.50 (*0-89464-403-3*) Krieger.

***Bittenbinder, J. J. & Neal, William.** Tough Target: The Street-Smart Guide to Staying Safe. 191p. 2000. reprint ed. text 19.00 (*0-7881-6909-2*) DIANE Pub.

Bittencourt, J. A., et al, eds. Ionospheric & Thermospheric Studies: Proceedings of the Topical Meetings of the COSPAR Interdisciplinary Scientific Commission P (Meeting P2) & C (Meetings C4 & C8) of the COSPAR 28th Plenary Meeting Held in The Hague, The Netherlands, June-July, 1990. (Advances in Space Research Ser.: Vol. 12). (Illus.). 342p. 1992. pap. 176.00 (*0-08-041851-1*, Pergamon Pr) Elsevier.

Bittencourt, Luciana A. Spinning Lives. (Illus.). 242p. 1995. lib. bdg. 45.00 (*0-7618-0121-9*) U Pr of Amer.

Bittenger, Marvin L. Elementary Algebra: Concepts & Applications. 4th ed. 304p. (C). 1994. pap. text, student ed. 25.00 (*0-201-53784-2*) Addison-Wesley.

Bitter. Clarisworks: Testbank. Date not set. pap. text, teacher ed. write for info. (*0-314-02221-X*) West Pub.

Bitter, ed. Macmillan Encyclopedia of Computers, Vol. 1. 1992. 110.00 (*0-02-897046-2*) Mac Lib Ref.

Bitter & Pierson. Using Technology Classroom. 4th ed. 316p. 1998. pap. text 59.00 (*0-205-28769-7*) Allyn.

Bitter, Cynthia N. Good Enough: When Losing Is Winning, Perfection Becomes Obsession, & Thin Enough Can Never Be Achieved. LC 97-93354. 285p. 1998. pap. 14.95 (*0-9657755-6-9*) HopeLines.

Bitter, Francis & Medicus, Heinrich A. Fields & Particles: An Introduction to Electromagnetic Wave Phenomena & Quantum Physics. LC 72-87209. 704p. reprint ed. pap. 200.00 (*0-608-30922-2*, 200776300064) Bks Demand.

Bitter, Gary. Understanding & Using Microsoft Works 3.0 on the Macintosh. Leyh, ed. LC 94-2549. (Microcomputing Ser.). 400p. (C). 1994. mass mkt. 28.25 (*0-314-02856-0*) West Pub.

Bitter, Gary G. Claris Works Smartstart for Macintosh. LC 96-67324. 348p. 1996. 29.99 (*1-57576-258-7*) Que Educ & Trng.

Bitter, Gary G. Understanding & Using ClarisWorks. Leyh, ed. LC 92-31308. (Microcomputing Ser.). 450p. (C). 1993. mass mkt. 26.75 (*0-314-01249-4*) West Pub.

— Understanding & Using Microsoft Works for Windows 3.0. LC 94-19253. 450p. (C). 1994. mass mkt. 28.25 (*0-314-03973-2*) West Pub.

— Understanding & Using Microsoft Works 2.0, PC. Leyh, ed. 394p. (C). 1991. pap. text 37.00 (*0-314-77286-3*) West Pub.

— Understanding & Using Microsoft Works 2.0, Macintosh. Leyh, ed. 378p. (C). 1991. pap. text 37.00 (*0-314-76542-5*) West Pub.

— Using the Explorer Plus Calculator. 352p. 1997. pap. 15.95 (*1-57232-853-3*) Seymour Pubns.

Bitter, Gary G., ed. Macmillan Encyclopedia of Computers, Vol. 2. 1992. 110.00 (*0-02-897047-0*) Mac Lib Ref.

Bitter, Gary G. & Camuse, Ruth A. Using a Microcomputer in the Classroom. 2nd ed. (Illus.). 384p. 1988. pap. text 38.67 (*0-13-938978-4*) P-H.

***Bitter, Gary G. & Skintik, Catherine.** Working with Computers. (Illus.). 348p. 1998. spiral bd. 46.60 (*1-57426-020-0*) Computer Lit Pr.

Bitter, Gary G., et al. Mathematics Classroom Management Guide, Grade 1-8. (Mathematics Ser.). (J). (gr. 2). 1981. pap. text 2.80 (*0-07-006092-4*) McGraw.

An Asterisk (*) at the beginning of an entry indicates that the title is appearing for the first time.

— Mathematics Classroom Management Guide, Grade 1-8. (Mathematics Ser.). (J). (gr. 3). 1981. pap. text 2.80 (*0-07-006093-2*) McGraw.
— Mathematics Classroom Management Guide, Grade 1-8. (Mathematics Ser.). (J). (gr. 4). 1981. pap. text 2.80 (*0-07-006094-0*) McGraw.
— Mathematics Classroom Management Guide, Grade 1-8. (Mathematics Ser.). (J). (gr. 5). 1981. pap. text 2.80 (*0-07-006095-9*) McGraw.
— Mathematics Classroom Management Guide, Grade 1-8. (Mathematics Ser.). (J). (gr. 6). 1981. pap. text 2.80 (*0-07-006096-7*) McGraw.
— Mathematics Classroom Management Guide, Grade 1-8. (Mathematics Ser.). (J). (gr. 7). 1981. pap. text 2.80 (*0-07-006097-5*) McGraw.
— Mathematics Classroom Management Guide, Grade 1-8. (Mathematics Ser.). (J). (gr. 8). 1981. pap. text 2.80 (*0-07-006098-3*) McGraw.

Bitter, J. G. Transport Mechanisms in Membrane Separation Processes. (Chemical Engineering Ser.). (Illus.). 212p. (C). 1991. 85.00 (*0-306-43849-6*, Plenum Trade) Perseus Pubng.

***Bitter, James.** Adlerian Therapy. 2000. 95.00 (*0-205-33203-X*) Allyn.

Bitter, James A. & Goodyear, Don L., eds. Rehabilitation Evaluation: Some Application Guidelines. LC 75-9719. 1975. text 32.50 (*0-8422-5223-1*); pap. text 12.95 (*0-8422-0502-0*) Irvington.

***Bitter, Richard.** LabVIEW Advanced Programming Techniques. (Illus.). 2000. 84.95 (*0-8493-2049-6*) CRC Pr.

***Bitter Root Valley Historical Society Staff.** Bitter Root Trails III. LC 98-61500. (Illus.). 455p. 1998. 29.95 (*0-912299-80-0*); pap. 19.95 (*0-912299-79-7*) Stoneydale Pr Pub.

Bitterauf, Theodor. Geschichte des Rheinbundes. (GER.). xiii, 459p. 1983. reprint ed. write for info. (*3-487-07310-2*) G Olms Pubs.

Bitterli, Konrad. Jonathan Lasker, 1977-1997. 1998. 42.95 (*3-89322-943-4*) Edition Cantz.
— McCaslin Works-Sites. 1998. 45.00 (*3-89322-416-5*, Pub. by Edition Cantz) Dist Art Pubs.

***Bitterli, Konrad.** Roman Signer: Biennale di Venezia 1999. (Illus.). 96p. 2000. 35.00 (*3-908617-01-4*, Pub. by Unikate) Dist Art Pubs.

***Bitterli, Robert.** The Hoover Print. LC 99-90133. 336p. 1999. 24.95 (*1-893980-00-6*) Devin Lane Publishing.

Bitterli, Urs. Cultures in Conflict: Encounters Between European & Non-European Cultures, 1492-1800. Robertson, Ritchie, tr. LC 88-64050. 215p. 1989. 39.50 (*0-8047-1737-0*) Stanford U Pr.

Bitterlich, W. Relascope Idea: Relative Measurements in Forestry. 242p. 1996. text 65.00 (*0-85198-539-4*) OUP.

Bitterman, M. E., et al, eds. Animal Learning: Survey & Analysis. LC 78-9894. (NATO ASI Series A, Life Sciences: Vol. 19). 522p. 1979. 115.00 (*0-306-40061-8*, Plenum Trade) Perseus Pubng.

Bitters, Barbara A. & Foxwell, Susan. Wisconsin Model for Sex Equity in Career & Vocational Education. 296p. (C). 1993. pap. text 33.00 (*1-57337-025-8*) WI Dept Pub Instruct.

Bitters, Warren E. The New Science of Asset Allocation. (Glenlake Business Monographs). 320p. 1998. 55.00 (*1-884964-70-2*) Fitzroy Dearborn.
— The New Science of Asset Allocation. 320p. 1998. 55.00 (*1-888998-02-4*) Glenlake Pub.

Bittiger, H. & Schnebli, H. P., eds. Concanavalin A as a Tool. LC 75-37841. (Wiley-Interscience Publications). 659p. reprint ed. pap. 200.00 (*0-608-12375-7*, 205206600033) Bks Demand.

Bitting, Christina, ed. see Looff, Carolyn.

Bitting, Katherine. Gastronomic Bibliography. 718p. 1994. reprint ed. 75.00 (*1-888262-38-9*) Martino Pubng.

Bitting, Terry H., jt. auth. see Frey, Martin A.

Bittinger. Alg & Trig Grpg & Mod Ti Pk. (C). 1998. 84.00 (*0-201-39332-8*) Addison-Wesley.

***Bittinger.** Algebra. 1999. pap. text 75.00 (*0-201-66995-1*) Addison-Wesley.
— Algebra Class Test. 3rd ed. 2001. 82.00 (*0-201-66381-3*) Addison-Wesley.
— Algebra & Trigonometry: Graphs & Models. 2001. 72.00 (*0-201-66346-5*) Addison-Wesley.

Bittinger. Algebra for College Students. 2nd ed. (C). 1998. text. write for info. (*0-201-82491-4*) Addison-Wesley.
— Basic Math Custom. 8th ed. 704p. (C). 1998. text 75.00 (*0-201-43532-2*) Addison-Wesley.
— Basic Mathematics Interact Math 5.25 Preview. 7th ed. (C). 1995. text 61.66 incl. 5.25 hd (*0-201-80888-9*) Addison-Wesley.
— Basic Mathematics Interact Plus Win. 7th ed. (C). 1996. 26.00 (*0-201-42191-7*) Addison-Wesley.
— Bitt Interm Alg C&A/ACS Bndl. 4th ed. 1995. pap. text 70.00 (*0-201-83243-7*) Addison-Wesley.

***Bittinger.** Calculus & Its Applications. 7th ed. 1999. pap. 6.00 (*0-201-65864-X*) Addison-Wesley.

Bittinger. College Alg Graphs & ModelsTI Rebate Coupon. (C). 1998. 79.00 (*0-201-39331-X*) Addison-Wesley.
— Elementary Algebra. 5th ed. (C). 1998. text. write for info. (*0-201-32274-9*) Addison-Wesley.

***Bittinger.** Elementary Algebra: Concepts & Applications. 5th ed. 1998. student ed. 82.00 (*0-201-61942-3*) Addison-Wesley.

Bittinger. Elementary Algebra: Concepts & Applications Interact Math Macintosh. 4th ed. 1995. 26.00 (*0-201-88052-0*) Addison-Wesley.
— Elementary Algebra: Concepts & Applications with Student Solutions Manual Bundle. 4th ed. (C). 1995. 85.00 (*0-201-58959-1*) Addison-Wesley.

***Bittinger.** Fundamental Mathematics. 2nd ed. 1999. 47.81 (*0-201-66355-4*) Addison-Wesley.

Bittinger. Inro Alg Intro Alg SSM. 7th ed. (C). 1996. 93.00 (*0-201-30128-8*) Addison-Wesley.
— Interact Math Version 1.1 to Accompany Basic Mathematics. 7th ed. 1996. 23.44 incl. 3.5 hd (*0-201-89998-1*) Addison-Wesley.
— Interact Math Windows for Elementary Algebra: Concepts & Applications. 4th ed. (C). 1996. 27.40 (*0-201-43020-7*) Addison-Wesley.
— Interact Math Windows for Intermediate Algebra: Concepts & Applications. 4th ed. (C). 1996. 26.00 (*0-201-43021-5*) Addison-Wesley.
— Interact Plus. (C). 1996. write for info. (*0-201-51000-6*) Addison-Wesley.
— Interact Plus Combined Macintosh Demonstration. 7th ed. (C). 1996. write for info. (*0-201-42193-3*) Addison-Wesley.
— Intermediate Algebra. 1995. write for info. (*0-201-89851-9*) Addison-Wesley.
— Intermediate Algebra. 7th ed. (C). 1995. pap. text 23.66 (*0-201-59129-4*) Addison-Wesley.
— Intermediate Algebra: Annotated Instructor's Edition. 8th ed. (Mathmax Ser.). 848p. 1999. 71.00 (*0-201-33876-9*) Addison-Wesley.
— Intermediate Algebra: Answer Book. 8th ed. (Mathmax Ser.). 80p. 1999. 18.00 (*0-201-43847-X*) Addison-Wesley.
— Intermediate Algebra: Concepts & Applications Interact Math Macintosh. 4th ed. 1995. 23.44 (*0-201-88055-5*) Addison-Wesley.
— Intermediate Algebra: Concepts & Applications Interact Math 3.5. 4th ed. 1995. 23.44 (*0-201-88054-7*) Addison-Wesley.

***Bittinger.** Intermediate Algebra: Graphs & Models. (C). 2000. text 82.00 (*0-201-66319-8*) Addison-Wesley.

Bittinger. Intermediate Algebra: Instructor's Solutions Manual. 8th ed. (Mathmax Ser.). 176p. 1999. 24.00 (*0-201-43845-3*) Addison-Wesley.
— Intermediate Algebra Interact Math Windows Version. 7th ed. (C). 1996. 26.00 (*0-201-42197-6*) Addison-Wesley.
— Introductory Algebra. 8th ed. 752p. (C). 1998. text 71.00 (*0-201-43533-0*) Addison-Wesley.
— Introductory Algebra. 8th ed. 240p. (C). 1998. pap. text, student ed. 21.00 (*0-201-34023-2*) Addison-Wesley.
— Introductory Algebra: Instructor's Solutions Manual. 8th ed. (Mathmax Ser.). 144p. 1998. 24.00 (*0-201-43411-3*) Addison-Wesley.

Bittinger. Introductory Algebra Interact Math Windows. 7th ed. 1996. pap. text 27.40 (*0-201-42194-1*) Addison-Wesley.
— Supplement. 4th ed. 1994. suppl. ed. 19.00 (*0-201-53785-0*) Addison-Wesley.
— Supplement. 6th ed. 1995. suppl. ed. 67.00 (*0-201-59342-4*) Addison-Wesley.
— Supplement: Ia Math Developmental Mathematics. 4th ed. 1996. suppl. ed. 26.00 (*0-201-88933-1*) Addison-Wesley.
— Supplement Prealgebra. 2nd ed. 1995. suppl. ed. 67.00 (*0-201-88075-X*) Addison-Wesley.

***Bittinger & Beecher.** Algebra & Trigonometry: Graphs & Models. 2nd ed. 2000. pap., teacher ed. 24.00 (*0-201-70874-4*) Addison-Wesley.
— Fundamentals of College Algebra: Graphs & Models 1/e: Graphing Calculator Manual. 2000. pap., suppl. ed. 24.00 (*0-201-70878-7*) Addison-Wesley.

Bittinger & Ellenbogen. Intermediate Algebra: Concepts & Applications Instructor's Resource Manual. 5th ed. (Bittinger/Ellenbogen Ser.). 592p. 1997. 24.00 (*0-201-30504-6*) Addison-Wesley.

Bittinger & Ellenbogen. Intermediate Algebra: Concepts & Applications Instructor's Solutions Manual/printed Test Bank. 5th ed. (Bittinger/Ellenbogen Ser.). 512p. 1997. 24.00 (*0-201-30503-8*) Addison-Wesley.

***Bittinger, et al.** Elementary & Intermediate Algebra: Graphs & Models. 2000. pap. text 108.60 (*0-201-70250-9*) Addison-Wesley.

Bittinger, et al. Trigonometry: Graphs & Models Student Edition. 1998. 76.00 (*0-201-42849-0*) Addison-Wesley.

Bittinger, Emmet F. Heritage & Promise: Perspectives on the Church of the Brethren. rev. ed. 1983. pap. 6.95 (*0-87178-357-6*, 8576) Brethren.

Bittinger, Gayle. All about Weather. (Rhyme & Reason Workbook Ser.). (Illus.). 32p. (J). (ps-k). 1999. pap. 3.95 (*1-57029-255-8*, 01107) Totline Pubns.
— At the Zoo. (Rhyme & Reason Workbook Ser.). (Illus.). 32p. (J). (ps-k). 1999. pap. 3.95 (*1-57029-256-6*, 01108) Totline Pubns.
— Beginning Fun with Bugs & Butterflies. (Beginning Fun with Science Ser.). (Illus.). 16p. (Orig.). (J). (ps). 1997. pap. 1.95 (*1-57029-146-2*, 3013) Totline Pubns.
— Beginning Fun with Magnets. (Beginning Fun with Science Ser.). (Illus.). 16p. (Orig.). (J). (ps). 1997. pap. 1.95 (*1-57029-148-9*, 3015) Totline Pubns.
— Beginning Fun with Plants & Flowers. (Beginning Fun with Science Ser.). (Illus.). 16p. (Orig.). (J). (ps). 1997. pap. 1.95 (*1-57029-147-0*, 3014) Totline Pubns.
— Beginning Fun with Rainbows & Colors. (Beginning Fun with Science Ser.). (Illus.). 16p. (Orig.). (J). (ps). 1997. pap. 1.95 (*1-57029-149-7*, 3016) Totline Pubns.
— Beginning Fun with Sand & Shells. (Beginning Fun with Science Ser.). (Illus.). 16p. (Orig.). (J). (ps). 1997. pap. 1.95 (*1-57029-150-0*, 3017) Totline Pubns.
— Beginning Fun with Water & Bubbles. (Beginning Fun with Science Ser.). (Illus.). 16p. (Orig.). (J). (ps). 1997. pap. 1.95 (*1-57029-151-9*, 3018) Totline Pubns.
— Best of Totline Newsletter: For New Teachers. Warren, Jean, ed. LC 94-61017. (Illus.). 400p. (Orig.). 1995. pap. text 27.95 (*1-57029-045-8*) Totline Pubns.
— Dramatic Play. (101 Tips for Toddler Teachers Ser.). (Illus.). 24p. (Orig.). 1997. pap. 3.95 (*1-57029-154-3*, 4015) Totline Pubns.
— Exploring Sand: And the Desert. Cubley, Kathleen, ed. LC 92-62463. (Exploring Ser.). (Illus.). 96p. (Orig.). (J). (ps-1). 1993. pap. 8.95 (*0-911019-58-8*, WPH 1801) Totline Pubns.
— Exploring Water & the Ocean. Cubley, Kathleen, ed. LC 92-62462. (Exploring Ser.). (Illus.). 96p. (Orig.). (J). (ps-1). 1993. pap. 8.95 (*0-911019-59-6*, WPH 1802) Totline Pubns.
— Investigation Station. LC 97-62535. (Kinderstation Ser.). (Illus.). 160p. (J). (gr. k). 1998. pap. 14.95 (*1-57029-190-X*, W04504) Totline Pubns.
— Kindergarten Theme Calendar. LC 98-61489. (Theme Calendar Ser.). (Illus.). 48p. 1999. pap. 6.95 (*1-57029-244-2*, 00192) Totline Pubns.
— 1-2-3 Science: Pre-Science Activities for Young Children. LC 93-60024. (Totline 1-2-3 Ser.). (Illus.). 160p. (Orig.). (J). (ps-k). 1993. pap. 14.95 (*0-911019-62-6*, 0410) Totline Pubns.
— 1-2-3 Shapes: Beginning Shape Activities for Young Children. Cubley, Kathleen, ed. LC 94-60690. (1-2-3 Ser.). (Illus.). 160p. (J). (ps). 1995. 14.95 (*1-57029-006-7*, WPH 0411) Totline Pubns.
— Our World: Environmental Awareness. McKinnon, Elizabeth, ed. LC 89-52145. (Learning & Caring About Ser.). (Illus.). 80p. (J). (ps-1). 1990. pap. 8.95 (*0-911019-30-8*, WPH 1201) Totline Pubns.
— Ready to Listen & Explore the Senses: Help Your Child Develop the Skills Necessary for School Success. LC 96-60426. (Getting Ready for School Ser.). (Illus.). 96p. (Orig.). (J). (ps-k). 1997. pap. 6.95 (*1-57029-115-2*, 3205) Totline Pubns.
— Teaching Snacks: Teaching Concepts at Snack Time. Cubley, Kathleen, ed. (Illus.). 48p. (Orig.). (J). (ps-1). 1994. pap. 6.95 (*0-911019-82-0*, WPH 1603) Totline Pubns.
— Under the Sea. (Rhyme & Reason Workbook Ser.). (Illus.). 32p. (J). (ps-k). 1999. pap. 3.95 (*1-57029-259-0*, 01111) Totline Pubns.

Bittinger, Gayle, ed. Animal Piggyback Songs. LC 89-51957. (Piggyback Songs Ser.). (Illus.). 96p. (Orig.). (J). (ps-k). 1990. pap. 8.95 (*0-911019-29-4*, WPH 0207) Totline Pubns.
— Best of Totline Parent Flyers. LC 95-61611. (Best of Totline Ser.). (Illus.). 160p. (Orig.). 1996. pap. text 14.95 (*1-57029-095-4*) Totline Pubns.
— Holiday Patterns: Multi-Sized Patterns for Making Cut-Outs, Puppets & Learning Games. (Mix & Match Pattern Ser.). (Illus.). 128p. (Orig.). (J). (ps). 1991. pap. text 9.95 (*0-911019-45-6*, WPH 1304) Totline Pubns.
— Holiday Piggyback Songs. LC 88-50593. (Piggyback Songs Ser.). (Illus.). 96p. (Orig.). (J). (ps-1). 1988. pap. 8.95 (*0-911019-18-9*, WPH 0206) Totline Pubns.
— Multisensory Theme-a-Saurus. LC 96-60384. (Illus.). 160p. (Orig.). (J). (ps). 1997. pap. 14.95 (*1-57029-131-4*, 1008) Totline Pubns.
— Piggyback Songs for School. LC 85-50433. (Piggyback Songs Ser.). (Illus.). 96p. (Orig.). (J). (ps-1). 1991. pap. 8.95 (*0-911019-44-8*, WPH 0208) Totline Pubns.
— Songs & Games for Fours. LC 96-61895. (Learn with Piggyback Songs Ser.). (Illus.). 48p. (Orig.). (J). (ps). 1997. pap. 3.95 (*1-57029-166-7*, 3304) Totline Pubns.

Bittinger, Gayle & Cubley, Kathleen, eds. One Thousand One Teaching Props: Simple Props to Make for Working with Young Children. LC 91-65931. (1001 Ser.). (Illus.). 248p. (Orig.). (J). (ps). 1992. pap. text 19.95 (*0-911019-46-4*, WPH 1501) Totline Pubns.

Bittinger, Gayle & McKinnon, Elizabeth. Busy Bees - Fall: Fun for Two's & Three's. LC 93-61897. (Busy Bees Ser.). (Illus.). 136p. (J). (ps). 1994. pap. 14.95 (*1-57029-008-3*, WPH 2405) Totline Pubns.

Bittinger, Gayle & Warren, Jean. Creation Station. LC 97-62225. (Kinderstation Ser.). (Illus.). 160p. (J). (ps). 1998. pap. 14.95 (*1-57029-161-6*, 4503) Totline Pubns.

Bittinger, Gayle, et al. Busy Bees - Winter: Fun for Two's & Three's. LC 94-60564. (Busy Bees Ser.). (Illus.). 136p. (J). (ps-k). 1994. pap. 14.95 (*1-57029-023-7*, 2406) Totline Pubns.
— Busy Bees Spring: Fun for Two's & Three's. LC 94-61016. (Busy Bee Ser.). (Illus.). 136p. (Orig.). (J). (ps). 1995. pap. text 14.95 (*1-57029-026-1*, 2407) Totline Pubns.
— Busy Bees Summer: Fun for Two's & Three's. LC 94-61734. (Busy Bees Ser.). (Illus.). 136p. (J). (ps). 1995. pap. text 14.95 (*1-57029-066-0*, WPH 2408) Totline Pubns.

Bittinger, Gayle, jt. auth. see Claycomb, Patty.
Bittinger, Gayle, ed. see Babler, Susan.
Bittinger, Gayle, ed. see Backer, Barbara F.
Bittinger, Gayle, ed. see Clark, Silvana.
Bittinger, Gayle, ed. see Douglas, Kathy.
Bittinger, Gayle, ed. see Hodge, Mary A.
Bittinger, Gayle, ed. see Hodges, Susan.
Bittinger, Gayle, ed. see McKinnon, Elizabeth.
Bittinger, Gayle, ed. see McKinnon, Elizabeth S.
Bittinger, Gayle, jt. ed. see McKinnon, Elizabeth.
Bittinger, Gayle, ed. see Miller, Susan A.
Bittinger, Gayle, ed. see Petersen, Evelyn.
Bittinger, Gayle, ed. see Rose, Jenny C.
Bittinger, Gayle, ed. see Totline Staff.
Bittinger, Gayle, ed. see Warren, Jean.

Bittinger, J. Q. History of Haverhill, N.H. 443p. 1988. reprint ed. lib. bdg. 47.00 (*0-8328-0053-8*, NH0050) Higginson Bk Co.

Bittinger, Judith, ed. see Grigsby, Carolyn.

Bittinger, Judith, ed. see Skidmore, Charles, et al.

Bittinger, Lucy F. Bittinger & Bedinger Families: Descendants of Adam Budinger. 63p. 1996. reprint ed. pap. 13.00 (*0-8328-5336-4*); reprint ed. lib. bdg. 23.00 (*0-8328-5335-6*) Higginson Bk Co.
— The Germans in Colonial Times. 314p. 1998. reprint ed. pap. 25.00 (*0-917890-90-6*, B300) Heritage Bk.

Bittinger, Martin L. Students Solutions Manual to Accompany Intermediate Algebra Concepts & Applications. 5th ed. 384p. (C). 1997. pap. text 21.00 (*0-201-30502-X*) Addison-Wesley.

Bittinger, Marv. Elementary Algebra: Concepts & Applications Interact Math 3.5. 4th ed. 1995. 23.44 (*0-201-88051-2*) Addison-Wesley.

Bittinger, Marvin. Algebra & Trigonometry: Graphs & Models Interact. 1997. text 25.00 (*0-201-87358-3*) Addison-Wesley.
— Algebra & Trigonometry: Graphs & Models Interact. 1997. text 25.00 (*0-201-87359-1*) Addison-Wesley.
— Basic Mathematics. 8th ed. 704p. (C). 1998. pap. text 75.00 (*0-201-43530-6*) Addison-Wesley.
— Collaborative Learning Manual to Accompany Intemediate Algebra. 8th ed. 64p. (C). 1999. pap. text 24.00 (*0-201-66040-7*) Addison-Wesley.
— College Algebra: Graphs & Models Interact. 1997. text 23.44 (*0-201-87357-5*) Addison-Wesley.
— Developmental Mathematics. 5th ed. LC 99-40860. 1120p. (C). 1999. pap. text 80.00 (*0-201-34027-5*) Addison-Wesley.
— Developmental Mathematics: Tasp Version. 5th ed. 1120p. (C). 1999. pap. text 72.00 (*0-201-34028-3*) Addison-Wesley.
— Elementary Algebra: Concepts & Applications & Mac Mathlab Plus Bundle. 1995. 76.00 (*0-201-59554-0*) Addison-Wesley.
— Elementary & Intermediate Algebra: Concepts & Applications a Combined Approach. 384p. (C). 1996. pap. text, student ed. 22.00 (*0-201-41726-X*) Addison-Wesley.

***Bittinger, Marvin.** Elementary & Intermediate Algebra Combined: A Graphing Approach. LC 99-55014. 832p. (C). 2000. 84.00 (*0-201-63676-X*) Addison-Wesley.

Bittinger, Marvin. Elementary & Intermediate Algebra, Concepts & Applications: A Combined Approach with Answer Books. 2nd ed. 1p. (C). 1998. text 84.00 (*0-201-34034-8*) Addison-Wesley.
— Fundamental Mathematics. 2nd ed. LC 98-34319. 400p. (C). 1998. pap. text 44.00 (*0-201-33877-7*) Addison-Wesley.
— General Medical Knowledge for Eyecare Paraprofessionals. LC 98-21940. (Basic Bookshelf for Eyecare Professionals Ser.). (Illus.). 112p. 1998. pap. text 30.00 (*1-55642-334-9*, 63349) SLACK Inc.
— Intermediate Algebra. 8th ed. LC 98-49224. 746p. (C). 1999. pap. text 78.00 (*0-201-95960-7*) Addison-Wesley.
— Intermediate Algebra. 8th ed. LC 99-26865. 830p. (C). 1999. pap. text 78.00 (*0-201-63672-7*) Addison-Wesley.
— Intermediate Algebra: Concept & Applications with Student Solutions Manual Bundle. 4th ed. 1995. 75.00 (*0-201-54239-0*) Addison-Wesley.
— INTRO ALG 99MATHPASS PK. 8th ed. (C). 1998. pap. text 90.20 (*0-201-43401-6*) Addison-Wesley.
— Introduction to Algebra. 8th ed. 752p. (C). 1998. pap. text 75.00 (*0-201-43531-4*) Addison-Wesley.
— Introductory Algebra. 8th ed. LC 98-34318. 704p. (C). 1998. pap. text 78.00 (*0-201-95959-3*) Addison-Wesley.
— Introductory & Intermediate Algebra. LC 99-14098. 928p. (C). 1999. pap. text 91.00 (*0-201-34020-8*) Addison-Wesley.
— Introductory & Intermediate Algebra. 304p. (C). 1999. pap. text, student ed. 21.00 (*0-201-34021-6*) Addison-Wesley.

***Bittinger, Marvin.** Mathpass for Intermediate Algebra. 8th ed. (C). 1999. pap. text 82.00 (*0-201-43402-4*) Addison-Wesley.

Bittinger, Marvin. Prealgebra. 3rd ed. LC 99-26893. 693p. (C). 1999. pap. text 75.00 (*0-201-34024-0*) Addison-Wesley.
— Toliver's Secret. 2nd ed. (C). 1999. pap. text 44.00 (*0-201-66064-4*) Addison-Wesley.
— Windows Version Interact Math Tutorial Software to Accompany Prealgebra. 2nd ed. 1996. 26.00 (*0-201-49914-2*) Addison-Wesley.

Bittinger, Marvin, et al. Elementary & Intermediate Algebra: Concepts & Applications a Combined Approach. 2nd ed. LC 97-44959. (Illus.). 816p. (C). 1997. 89.00 (*0-201-76804-6*) Addison-Wesley.

Bittinger, Marvin L. Algebra & Trigonometry. 2nd ed. 480p. (C). 1994. pap. text, student ed., suppl. ed. 26.00 (*0-201-52512-7*) Addison-Wesley.
— Algebra & Trigonometry: Graphs & Models. (C). 1996. pap. text 79.00 (*0-201-30371-X*) Addison-Wesley.
— Algebra & Trigonometry: Student's Solutions Manual. 288p. (C). 1996. pap. text, student ed. 25.00 (*0-201-49809-X*) Addison-Wesley.
— Algebra for College Students. (C). 1992. pap. text 57.66 (*0-201-65026-6*) Addison-Wesley.
— Algebra for College Students. 288p. (C). 1995. pap. text 25.00 (*0-201-56683-4*) Addison-Wesley.
— Answer Book to Accompany Intermediate Algebra. 7th ed. (C). 1995. pap. text 19.00 (*0-201-82483-3*) Addison-Wesley.
— Applied Calculus. 3rd ed. (C). 1993. pap. text, student ed. 25.00 (*0-201-52988-2*) Addison-Wesley.
— Applied Calculus. 4th ed. (C). 1996. text. write for info. (*0-201-59337-8*) Addison-Wesley.
— Basic Mathematics. 7th ed. (C). 1995. pap. text 72.00 (*0-201-87874-7*) Addison-Wesley.
— Basic Mathematics. 8th ed. LC 98-4836. 720p. (C). 1998. pap. text 78.00 (*0-201-95958-5*) Addison-Wesley.

***Bittinger, Marvin L.** Basic Mathematics: Collaborative Learning Manual. 8th ed. 128p. (C). 1998. pap. text 21.00 (*0-201-34574-9*) Addison-Wesley.

Bittinger, Marvin L. Basic Mathematics Answer Book. 7th ed. 32p. (C). 1994. pap. text 20.00 (*0-201-82481-7*) Addison-Wesley.
— Basic Mathematics Interact Plus Macintosh. 7th ed. 1996. write for info. (*0-201-42192-5*) Addison-Wesley.

B

An Asterisk (*) at the beginning of an entry indicates that the title is appearing for the first time.

— Cactuplot. 2nd ed. (C). 1988. pap. text, student ed. 17.66 (*0-201-12239-1*) Addison-Wesley.
— Calculus. 5th ed. (C). 1994. pap. text, student ed. 28.00 (*0-201-53259-X*) Addison-Wesley.
— Calculus: A Modeling Approach. 3rd ed. LC 83-6334. (Illus.). 544p. 1984. write for info. (*0-201-11217-5*); student ed. write for info. (*0-201-11218-3*) Addison-Wesley.
— Calculus & Its Applications. 6th ed. LC 95-12150. 656p. (C). 1995. pap. text 93.00 (*0-201-59338-6*) Addison-Wesley.
Bittinger, Marvin L. Calculus & Its Applications. 6th ed. 1997. student ed. 89.60 (*0-201-30271-3*) Addison-Wesley.
Bittinger, Marvin L. Calculus & Its Applications. 7th ed. LC 99-47368. 569p. (C). 1999. 96.00 (*0-201-33864-5*) Addison-Wesley.
— Calculus & Its Applications: Instructor's Solutions Manual. 6th ed. 1996. 24.00 (*0-201-59340-8*) Addison-Wesley.
— Calculus & Its Applications: Professional Copy. 4th ed. (C). 1996. text. write for info. (*0-201-42994-2*) Addison-Wesley.
— Collaborative Learning Manual to Accompany Prealgebra. 3rd ed. 128p. (C). 2000. pap. text 24.00 (*0-201-66198-5*) Addison-Wesley.
— Collaborative Learning Manual to Accompany Prealgebra. 8th ed. 64p. (C). 1999. pap. text 24.00 (*0-201-35993-6*) Addison-Wesley.
— College Algebra. 2nd ed. 368p. (C). 1993. pap. text 25.00 (*0-201-52585-2*) Addison-Wesley.
— College Algebra. 2nd ed. (C). 1995. text 72.00 (*0-201-85909-2*) Addison-Wesley.
— College Algebra & Trigonometry: Graphs & Modules. LC 96-21889. 723p. (C). 1996. 91.00 (*0-201-84888-0*) Addison-Wesley.
— College Algebra Graphs & Models. LC 96-21890. 608p. (C). 1996. 88.00 (*0-201-84890-2*) Addison-Wesley.
— Developmental Mathematics: TASP Version. 4th ed. (C). 1996. pap. text. write for info. (*0-201-41765-0*) Addison-Wesley.
— Elementary Algebra & Intermediate Algebra Math Lab Demo Macintosh. 4th ed. (C). 1995. text 13.33 (*0-201-54242-0*) Addison-Wesley.
— Elementary Algebra Concepts & Applications. 5th ed. LC 97-8476. 624p. (C). 1997. 83.00 (*0-201-84749-3*) Addison-Wesley.
— Elementary & Intermediate Algebra. (C). 1996. pap. text 22.50 (*0-201-85205-5*) Addison-Wesley.
— Essential Mathematics. 7th ed. (C). 1996. pap. text. write for info. (*0-201-84502-4*) Addison-Wesley.
— Fundamentals of College Algebra. 3rd ed. (C). 1991. pap. text 52.33 (*0-201-56696-6*) Addison-Wesley.
— Graphing Calculator Manual to Accompany Trigonometry, Graphs & Models. 192p. (C). 1997. pap. text 11.60 (*0-201-34568-4*) Addison-Wesley.
— Graphing Calculator Resource Guide to Accompany College Algebra & Trigonometry. 240p. (C). 1996. pap. text 21.00 (*0-201-87360-5*) Addison-Wesley.
— Hewlett Packard 48G Graphing Calculator. 80p. (C). 1997. ring bd., lab manual ed. 8.00 (*0-201-31231-X*) Addison-Wesley.
— Intermediate Algebra. 288p. (C). 1995. pap. text 25.00 (*0-201-55558-1*) Addison-Wesley.
— Intermediate Algebra. 7th ed. 784p. (C). 1996. text 72.00 (*0-201-88996-X*) Addison-Wesley.
— Intermediate Algebra. 7th ed. (C). 1997. pap. text 64.69 (*0-201-91448-4*) Addison-Wesley.
***Bittinger, Marvin L.** Intermediate Algebra. 8th ed. (C). 1999. pap. text. write for info. (*0-201-65882-8*) Addison-Wesley.
Bittinger, Marvin L. Intermediate Algebra: Concepts & Applications. 4th ed. 1996. text. write for info. (*0-201-46153-6*) Addison-Wesley.
— Intermediate Algebra: Concepts & Applications. 4th alternate ed. 736p. (C). 1995. text 85.00 (*0-201-88929-3*) Addison-Wesley.
— Intermediate Algebra: Concepts & Applications, a Graphing Approach Updated Printing Graphing Appendix As a Supplement. 4th ed. 64p. (C). 1997. ring bd. write for info. (*0-201-34567-6*) Addison-Wesley.
— Intermediate Algebra: Concepts & Applications with ACS Sticker Bundle with Student Solutions Manual. 4th ed. (C). 1995. 75.00 (*0-201-40019-7*) Addison-Wesley.
***Bittinger, Marvin L.** Intermediate Algebra: Graphs & Models. LC 99-15726. 752p. (C). 1999. 75.00 (*0-201-35994-4*) Addison-Wesley.
Bittinger, Marvin L. Intermediate Algebra: Graphs & Models. 192p. (C). 2000. pap. text 22.20 (*0-201-64808-3*) Addison-Wesley.
— Intermediate Algebra Interact Plus Macintosh. 1995. write for info. (*0-201-42198-4*) Addison-Wesley.
— Intermediate Algebra with Answer Book Glued In. 2nd ed. (C). 1996. text. write for info. (*0-201-87369-9*) Addison-Wesley.
— Introduction to Algebra. 7th ed. 704p. (C). 1995. pap. text 72.00 (*0-201-87875-5*) Addison-Wesley.
— Introductory Algebra. 7th ed. 224p. (C). 1994. pap. text, student ed. 21.00 (*0-201-58962-1*) Addison-Wesley.
— Introductory Algebra. 7th ed. (C). 1995. 64.69 (*0-201-91447-6*) Addison-Wesley.
— Introductory Algebra. 7th ed. 688p. (C). 1997. text. write for info. (*0-201-88995-1*) Addison-Wesley.
***Bittinger, Marvin L.** Introductory Algebra: Collaborative Learning Manual. 8th ed. 80p. (C). 1998. pap. text 21.00 (*0-201-34575-7*) Addison-Wesley.
Bittinger, Marvin L. Introductory Algebra Interact Plus Macintosh. 7th ed. 1996. write for info. (*0-201-42195-X*) Addison-Wesley.
— Logic, Proof, & Sets. 2nd ed. LC 81-14913. 144p. 1982. pap. text. write for info. (*0-201-10384-2*) Addison-Wesley.
— Prealgebra Custom Version. 3rd ed. 752p. (C). 1999. pap. 69.00 (*0-201-66059-8*) Addison-Wesley.
— Prealgebra: Student Solutions Manual. 2nd ed. 192p. (C). 1995. pap. text, student ed. 21.00 (*0-201-85525-9*) Addison-Wesley.
— Prealgebra Student Solutions Manual. (C). 1994. pap. text 24.00 (*0-201-50845-1*) Addison-Wesley.
— Precalculus: Graphs & Models. Guardino, Karen, ed. LC 96-8880. 832p. (C). 1996. 95.00 (*0-201-69442-5*) Addison-Wesley.
— Professional Copy to Developmental Mathematics. 4th ed. (C). 1995. pap. text. write for info. (*0-201-88078-4*) Addison-Wesley.
— Professional Copy to Elementary & Intermediate Algebra: Combined. (C). 1995. pap. text. write for info. (*0-201-88080-6*) Addison-Wesley.
— Professional Copy to Prealgebra. 2nd ed. (C). 1996. pap. text. write for info. (*0-201-88079-2*) Addison-Wesley.
— Student's Solutions Manual to Accompany Elementary &d Intermediate Algebra, Concepts & Applications: A Combined Approach. 2nd ed. 496p. (C). 1998. pap. text 21.00 (*0-201-31225-5*) Addison-Wesley.
— Trigonometry Update. 224p. (C). 1994. pap. text 5.00 (*0-201-60010-2*) Addison-Wesley.
Bittinger, Marvin L. & Beecher. Foundations of Algebra. (C). 1998. pap. text. write for info. (*0-201-76690-6*) Addison-Wesley.
Bittinger, Marvin L. & Beecher, Judith A. College Algebra. (Illus.). (C). 1989. text 50.50 (*0-201-09164-X*) Addison-Wesley.
***Bittinger, Marvin L. & Beecher, Judith A.** Fundamentals of College Algebra: Graphs & Models. 640p. 2000. 78.00 (*0-201-70733-0*) Addison-Wesley.
Bittinger, Marvin L. & Crown, J. Conrad. Finite Mathematics. 3rd ed. (Illus.). 768p. (C). 1989. 100.00 (*0-201-10814-3*) Addison-Wesley.
— Mathematics & Calculus with Applications. 2nd ed. (Illus.). 928p. (C). 1989. text 61.25 (*0-201-05941-X*) Addison-Wesley.
— Mathematics for Business, Economics & Management. 1982. write for info. (*0-201-10104-1*) Addison-Wesley.
Bittinger, Marvin L. & Ellenbogen, David. Prealgebra. 2nd ed. 672p. (C). 1995. pap. text 72.00 (*0-201-55753-3*) Addison-Wesley.
Bittinger, Marvin L. & Ellenbogen, David J. Algebra for College Students. (Illus.). 650p. (C). 1991. 83.00 (*0-201-19657-3*) Addison-Wesley.
— Intermediate Algebra: Concepts & Applications. 5th ed. Guardino, Karen, ed. LC 96-36430. 655p. (C). 1997. 83.00 (*0-201-84750-7*) Addison-Wesley.
— Prealgebra. (Illus.). 640p. (C). 1991. pap. text 63.00 (*0-201-50843-5*) Addison-Wesley.
Bittinger, Marvin L. & Keedy, Mervin L. Basic Mathematics. 7th ed. (Illus.). 704p. (C). 1994. pap. text 72.00 (*0-201-59560-5*) Addison-Wesley.
— Essential Algebra with Problem Solving. 624p. (C). 1987. pap. 28.66 (*0-201-14293-7*) Addison-Wesley.
— Essential Math. 4th ed. 736p. 1984. teacher ed. 3.25 (*0-201-14834-X*) Addison-Wesley.
— Essential Mathematics. 4th ed. 736p. 1984. pap. write for info. (*0-201-14806-4*) Addison-Wesley.
— Introductory Algebra. 7th ed. LC 94-17324. 688p. (C). 1994. pap. text 72.00 (*0-201-59561-3*) Addison-Wesley.
Bittinger, Marvin L. & Morell, Bernard B. Applied Calculus. 2nd ed. (Illus.). 768p. (C). 1988. text 40.76 (*0-201-12211-1*) Addison-Wesley.
Bittinger, Marvin L. & Morrell, Bernard B. Applied Calculus. 3rd ed. LC 92-1729. (Illus.). 736p. (C). 1993. text 81.00 (*0-201-52984-X*) Addison-Wesley.
Bittinger, Marvin L. & Penna, Judith A. Fundamental Mathematics. 8th ed. 192p. (C). 1998. pap. text 21.00 (*0-201-34022-4*) S&S Trade.
Bittinger, Marvin L. & Rudolph, William B. Business Mathematics for College Students. 3rd ed. 528p. (C). 1987. pap. text 43.25 (*0-201-11212-4*); pap. text, teacher ed. 40.00 (*0-201-11213-2*) Addison-Wesley.
Bittinger, Marvin L., et al. Algebra & Trigonometry: Right Triangle. 2nd ed. LC 92-44347. (Illus.). 832p. (C). 1993. pap. text 91.00 (*0-201-52510-0*) Addison-Wesley.
— College Algebra. 2nd ed. LC 92-44344. (Illus.). 536p. (C). 1993. pap. text 86.00 (*0-201-52526-7*) Addison-Wesley.
— Developmental Mathematics. 4th ed. LC 95-36700. 1024p. (C). 1995. pap. text 76.00 (*0-201-62978-X*) Addison-Wesley.
— Elementary & Intermediate Algebra: A Combined Approach, Preliminary Version. (Illus.). 768p. (C). 1994. pap. text 66.00 (*0-201-76558-6*) Addison-Wesley.
Bittinger, Marvin L., jt. auth. see Crown, J. Conrad.
Bittinger, Marvin L., jt. auth. see Keedy, Mervin L.
Bittker, et al. Federal Income Taxation of Corporations & Shareholders Forms. 2368p. 1989. ring bd. 195.00 (*0-7913-0259-8*) Warren Gorham & Lamont.
— Federal Income Taxation of Corporations & Shareholders Forms, 2 vol. set, No. 270. 2368p. 1991. suppl. ed. 69.50 (*0-7913-0328-4*) Warren Gorham & Lamont.
— Federal Income Taxation of Corporations & Shareholders Forms, 2 vols., Vol. 2. 2368p. 1991. suppl. ed. 66.25 (*0-7913-0329-2*) Warren Gorham & Lamont.
Bittker, Boris I. Collected Legal Essays. xii, 717p. 1989. reprint ed. 52.50 (*0-8377-0358-1*, Rothman) W S Hein.
— Federal Taxation of Income Estates & Gifts, 5 vols., index, No. 1. LC 80-50773. 1991. suppl. ed. 83.75 (*0-685-42406-5*) Warren Gorham & Lamont.
— Federal Taxation of Income Estates & Gifts, 5 vols., index, No. 2. rev. ed. LC 80-50773. 1991. suppl. ed. 85.75 (*0-685-05297-4*) Warren Gorham & Lamont.
— Federal Taxation of Income Estates & Gifts, 5 vols., index, No. 3. rev. ed. LC 80-50773. 1991. suppl. ed. 86.25 (*0-685-05298-2*) Warren Gorham & Lamont.
— Federal Taxation of Income Estates & Gifts, 5 vols., index, No. 4. rev. ed. LC 80-50773. 1991. suppl. ed. 85.00 (*0-685-42407-3*) Warren Gorham & Lamont.
— Federal Taxation of Income Estates & Gifts, 5 vols., index, Set. rev. ed. LC 80-50773. 1981. suppl. ed. 465.00 (*0-88262-460-1*, BTT) Warren Gorham & Lamont.
— Income Tax: Adaptable to Courses Utilizing Materials by Bittker. 9th ed. 210p. write for info. (*0-318-62085-5*) Harcourt.
Bittker, Boris I. & Benning, Brannon P. Bittker on the Regulation of Interstate & Foreign Commerce. LC 99-19483. 1999. boxed set 195.00 (*0-7355-0364-8*) Panel Pubs.
Bittker, Boris I. & Clark, Elias. Federal Estate & Gift Taxation. 5th ed. LC 83-82904. 608p. (C). 1984. 35.00 (*0-316-09687-3*, Aspen Law & Bus) Aspen Pub.
Bittker, Boris I. & Euistice, James S. Federal Income Taxation of Corporations & Shareholders. 5th rev. ed. 1376p. 1987. 165.00 (*0-88712-811-4*) Warren Gorham & Lamont.
Bittker, Boris I. & Eustice, James S. Federal Income Taxation of Corporations & Shareholders. 6th ed. LC 93-60349. 1996. text 355.00 (*0-7913-1616-5*, BE) Warren Gorham & Lamont.
— Federal Income Taxation of Corporations & Shareholders, No. 2664. 1264p. 1987. student ed., per. 52.00 (*0-88712-991-9*) Warren Gorham & Lamont.
Bittker, Boris I. & Lokken, Lawrence. Federal Taxation of Income, Estates, & Gifts, Vols. I-IV. 2nd ed. 1993. text 770.00 (*0-7913-0741-7*, BTT) Warren Gorham & Lamont.
— Fundamentals of International Taxation: U. S. Taxation of Foreign Income & Foreign Taxpayers. 2nd ed. LC 96-61224. 1997. 65.00 (*0-7913-2844-9*) Warren Gorham & Lamont.
Bittker, Boris I. & McMahon, Martin H. Federal Income Taxation of Individuals. 1300p. 1988. 135.00 (*0-7913-0009-9*) Warren Gorham & Lamont.
— Federal Income Taxation of Individuals. LC 95-61349. 1300p. 1995. student ed. 165.00 (*0-7913-2403-6*, IIT) Warren Gorham & Lamont.
— Federal Income Taxation of Individuals, No. 1. 1300p. 1991. suppl. ed. 50.25 (*0-7913-0560-0*) Warren Gorham & Lamont.
— Federal Income Taxation of Individuals, No. 2. 1300p. 1991. suppl. ed. 53.25 (*0-7913-0944-4*) Warren Gorham & Lamont.
Bittker, Boris I., et al. Federal Estate & Gift Taxation. 7th ed. LC 95-82171. 667p. 1996. teacher ed. 65.00 (*0-316-09700-4*, 97004) Aspen Law.
***Bittker, Boris I., et al.** Federal Estate & Gift Taxation. 8th ed. LC 00-40597. 2000. pap. write for info. (*0-7355-1683-9*) Panel Pubs.
Bittker, Boris I., et al. Federal Income Taxation of Corporations & Shareholders: Forms. 4th ed. LC 95-116696. 1995. ring bd. 235.00 (*0-7913-2193-2*, BEF) Warren Gorham & Lamont.
— Federal Taxation of Income, Estates, & Gifts. 3rd ed. LC 98-87333. 1999. write for info. (*0-7913-3590-9*) Warren Gorham & Lamont.
— Index to Federal Tax Articles, 7 vols. 1976. pap. 425.00 (*0-685-69580-8*, IFTA) Warren Gorham & Lamont.
Bittker, Boris J., et al. Fundamentals of International Taxation: U. S. Taxation of Foreign Income & Foreign Taxpayers. LC 98-86200. 1998. write for info. (*0-7913-3512-7*) Warren Gorham & Lamont.
Bittle, Berchmans, tr. see Felder, Hilarin.
Bittle, Camilla R. Friends of the Family. large type ed. LC 94-13821. 376p. 1994. lib. bdg. 19.95 (*0-7862-0260-2*) Thorndike Pr.
Bittle, Chris & Smith, Harry. Experiences in Microbiology. 112p. (C). 1994. pap. text, per. 13.95 (*0-8403-8231-6*) Kendall-Hunt.
Bittle, Edgar H., ed. Planning & Financing School Improvement & Construction Projects. (Monograph Ser.: Vol. 57). 160p. 1996. text 32.00 (*1-56534-093-0*) Ed Law Assn.
Bittle, Jerry. Geech: The Moosical. 52p. 1989. pap. text 5.95 (*0-685-28072-1*) New Mus Theater Lib.
Bittle, Lester R. & Newstrom, John W. What Every Supervisor Should Know: Trade Edition. 6th ed. 614p. 1993. pap. 27.95 (*0-07-005589-0*) McGraw.
Bittle, Polly, jt. auth. see Sanders, Helen.
Bittle, Robert R., et al, eds. ASME Advanced Energy Systems Division: Proceedings, ASME International Mechanical Engineering Congress & Exposition, 1996, Atlanta, Georgia. LC 96-78670. (Advanced Energy Systems Ser.: Vol. 36). 542p. 1996. 160.00 (*0-7918-1527-7*) ASME Pr.
Bittle, William G. James Nayler (1618-1660) 1999. pap. 30.00 (*1-85072-015-0*, Pub. by W Sessions) St Mut.
Bittler, Merrily. II Joshua: The Battle for Life. (Orig.). 1996. pap. text 12.95 (*1-884687-05-9*) N Horzns Pub.
— III Joshua: The Journey Continues. 160p. 1997. pap. 13.95 (*1-884687-09-1*) N Horzns Pub.
Bittleston, Adam. Counselling & Spiritual Development & Other Essays from the "Golden Blade" 270p. 1990. 29.50 (*0-86315-074-8*, 1316, Pub. by Floris Bks) Anthroposophic.
— Human Needs & Cosmic Answers. pap. 15.95 (*0-86315-170-1*, 1752, Pub. by Floris Bks) Anthroposophic.
— Loneliness. 94p. 1990. 17.50 (*0-86315-056-X*, 1244, Pub. by Floris Bks) Anthroposophic.
— Meditative Prayers for Today. 56p. 1990. 8.95 (*0-903540-54-1*, 631, Pub. by Floris Bks) Anthroposophic.
Bittleston, Adam, ed. see Steiner, Rudolf.
Bittleston, John & Shorter, Barbara. The Book of Business Communications Checklists. 180p. 1982. 50.00 (*0-85227-263-4*) St Mut.
Bittleston, Kalmia. The Gospel of John. 192p. 1990. pap. 9.95 (*0-86315-012-8*, 884, Pub. by Floris Bks) Anthroposophic.
— Gospel of Luke. pap. 9.95 (*0-86315-097-7*, 1416, Pub. by Floris Bks) Anthroposophic.
Bittleston, Kalmia, tr. The Gospel of Mark. 160p. 1990. pap. 9.95 (*0-86315-038-1*, 1115, Pub. by Floris Bks) Anthroposophic.
— The Gospel of Matthew. 240p. 1990. pap. 9.95 (*0-86315-070-5*, 1303, Pub. by Floris Bks) Anthroposophic.
Bittlingmayer, George, jt. auth. see Gould, John P.
Bittman. Flavors. 1996. pap. 30.00 (*0-02-511051-9*) Macmillan.
Bittman, Barry B. Reprogramming Pain: Transform Pain & Suffering into Health & Success. LC 95-42990. (Developments in Clinical Psychology Ser.). 220p. 1996. pap. 39.50 (*1-56750-208-3*); text 73.25 (*1-56750-207-5*) Ablx Pub.
Bittman, Barry B. & DeFail, Anthony J. Healing Imagery for People Facing Cancer. 104p. 1999. write for info. incl. audio (*0-9650240-6-7*, TSA-1007) TouchStar.
Bittman, James. Options for the Stock Investor: How Any Investor Can Use Options to Enhance & Protect Their Return. LC 95-21707. 225p. 1995. 29.95 incl. disk (*1-55738-872-5*, Irwn Prfssnl) McGraw-Hill Prof.
Bittman, James B. Trading Index Options. LC 97-39222. (Illus.). 250p. 1998. 34.95 incl. disk (*0-7863-1230-0*, Irwn McGrw-H) McGrw-H Hghr Educ.
Bittman, Mark. Fish. 544p. 1994. 27.50 (*0-02-510775-5*) Macmillan.
— Fish: The Complete Guide to Buying & Cooking. (Illus.). 367p. 1999. pap. 16.95 (*0-02-863152-8*) Macmillan.
***Bittman, Mark.** How to Cook Everything. (Illus.). 2000. 39.99 (*0-7645-6258-4*) IDG Bks.
Bittman, Mark. How to Cook Everything: Simple Recipes for Great Food. LC 98-22959. (Illus.). 832p. 1998. 25.00 (*0-02-861010-5*, Pub. by Macmillan) S&S Trade.
— Leafy Greens. LC 95-11777. 288p. 1995. 15.00 (*0-02-860355-9*) Macmillan.
***Bittman, Mark.** The Minimalist Cooks at Home: Recipes That Give You More Flavor from Fewer Ingredients in Less Time. LC 99-36291. (Illus.). 288p. 2000. 25.00 (*0-7679-0361-7*) Broadway BDD.
Bittman, Mark, jt. auth. see Vongerichten, Jean-Georges.
Bittman, Michael & Pixley, Jocelyn. The Double Life of the Family: Myth, Hope & Experience. LC 98-220243. 328p. 1998. pap. 32.95 (*1-86373-629-8*, Pub. by Allen & Unwin Pty) Paul & Co Pubs.
Bittman, Robert, ed. Cholesterol Vol. 28: Its Functions & Metabolism in Biology & Med. (Illus.). 576p. (C). 1997. text 167.00 (*0-306-45478-5*, Kluwer Plenum) Kluwer Academic.
Bittman, Robert, jt. auth. see Paquette, Leo.
Bittman, Sam & Zalk, Sue R. Expectant Fathers. 1983. pap. 7.95 (*0-345-31763-7*, Ballantine) Ballantine Pub Grp.
Bittnar, Zdenek & Sejnoha, Jiri. Numerical Methods in Structural Mechanics. LC 96-14306. 480p. 1996. 72.00 (*0-7844-0170-5*) Am Soc Civil Eng.
Bittner. Mass Communication. 6th ed. 1995. pap. text, teacher ed. write for info. (*0-205-17844-8*) Allyn.
Bittner & Swokowski, Earl W. Calculation of a Single Variable. 2nd ed. (Mathematics Ser.). 1995. mass mkt., student ed. 26.75 (*0-534-93927-9*) PWS Pubs.
Bittner, Bob. The Thank-You Book. LC 96-30242. 1996. 5.99 (*0-87788-804-3*, H Shaw Pubs) Waterbrook Pr.
***Bittner, Drew.** GURPS Magic Items II: More Sorcerous Shops & Mysterious Magics. Koke, Jeff, ed. (Illus.). 128p. 1999. pap. 19.95 (*1-55634-207-1*, Pub. by S Jackson Games) BookWorld.
Bittner, Drew. The Jedi Academy Entrance Exam: Tantilizing Trivia from the Star Wars Trilogy. LC 97-19910. 192p. 1997. pap. write for info. (*0-8065-1907-X*) Carol Pub Group.
Bittner, Egon. The Police on Skid-Row: A Study of Peace Keeping. (Reprint Series in Social Sciences). (C). 1993. reprint ed. pap. text 5.00 (*0-8290-3743-8*, S-551) Irvington.
— Popular Interset in Psychiatric Remedies: A Study in Social Control. Zuckerman, Harriet & Merton, Robert K., eds. LC 79-8977. (Dissertations on Sociology Ser.). 1980. lib. bdg. 26.95 (*0-405-12953-X*) Ayer.
Bittner, Egon, ed. see Criminology Review Yearbook Staff.
Bittner, Gina & Gladstone, Neil, eds. Caffe Philadelphia: Coffee Coupon & Guide Book 1995-1996. (Illus.). 144p. 1995. spiral bd. 9.95 (*0-9649295-0-3*) Caffe Philadelphia.
Bittner, J. W. Bittner, Genealogical Record & History of the Bittner-Werley Families: Descendants of Michael Bittner & Sebastian Werley, 1753-1930. (Illus.). 239p. 1992. reprint ed. pap. 28.00 (*0-8328-2638-3*); reprint ed. lib. bdg. 38.00 (*0-8328-2637-5*) Higginson Bk Co.
Bittner, James W. Approaches to the Fiction of Ursula K. Le Guin. Scholes, Robert, ed. LC 84-8507. (Studies in Speculative Fiction: No. 4). 179p. reprint ed. pap. 55.50 (*0-8357-1573-6*, 207069400004) Bks Demand.
Bittner, John R. Mass Communication. 6th ed. LC 95-10813. 514p. 1995. pap. text 61.00 (*0-13-560798-1*) Allyn.
— Mass Communication. 6th annot. ed. 1995. text, teacher ed. write for info. (*0-205-17842-1*) Allyn.
Bittner, L. & Kl Otzler, R. Variational Calculus, Optimal Control, & Applications: International Conference in Honour of L. Bittner & R. Kl Otzler, Trassenheide, Germany, September 23-27, 1996. LC 98-14510. (International Series Of Numerical Mathematics ;). 1998. write for info. (*0-8176-5906-4*); write for info. (*3-7643-5906-4*, Pub. by Birkhauser) Princeton Arch.

An Asterisk (*) at the beginning of an entry indicates that the title is appearing for the first time.

Bittner, Maria. Case, Scope, & Binding. LC 93-42241. (Studies in Natural Language & Linguistic Theory: Vol. 30). 216p. (C). 1994. lib. bdg. 119.00 (*0-7923-2649-0*, Pub. by Kluwer Academic) Kluwer Academic.

Bittner, Reinhard, jt. auth. see Jatzko, Gerhard.

Bittner, Robert. Teacher Is a Class Act. LC 99-164160. (Shaw Greetings Ser.). 1998. pap. text 5.99 (*0-87788-562-1*, H Shaw Pubs) Waterbrook Pr.

— Under His Wings: Meeting the Spiritual Needs of the Mentally Disabled. LC 94-31611. 192p. 1994. pap. 12.99 (*0-89107-805-3*) Crossway Bks.

Bittner, Rosanne. Arizona Bride. 1985. mass mkt. 3.75 (*0-8217-1597-6*, Zebra Kensgtn) Kensgtn Pub Corp.

— Arizona Bride. 496p. 1996. pap. 2.99 (*0-8217-5483-1*) Kensgtn Pub Corp.

— Caress. 480p. 1992. mass mkt. 5.99 (*0-8217-3791-0*, Zebra Kensgtn) Kensgtn Pub Corp.

— Climb the Highest Mountain. 448p. 1996. mass mkt. 5.99 (*0-8217-5431-9*, Zebra Kensgtn) Kensgtn Pub Corp.

— Destiny's Dawn. 384p. 1987. mass mkt. 3.95 (*0-445-20468-0*) Warner Bks.

— The Eagle's Song (Savage Destiny) 7th ed. Vol. 7. 448p. 1996. mass mkt. 5.99 (*0-8217-5326-6*) Kensgtn Pub Corp.

— Embrace the Wild Land. 448p. 1996. mass mkt. 5.99 (*0-8217-5413-0*, Zebra Kensgtn) Kensgtn Pub Corp.

— Full Circle. 480p. 1994. mass mkt. 5.99 (*0-8217-4711-8*, Zebra Kensgtn) Kensgtn Pub Corp.

— Love Me Tomorrow. 320p. 1998. mass mkt. 5.99 (*0-8217-5818-7*, Zebra Kensgtn) Kensgtn Pub Corp.

— Meet the New Dawn. 480p. 1996. mass mkt. 5.99 (*0-8217-5471-8*, Zebra Kensgtn) Kensgtn Pub Corp.

— Mystic Dreamers. LC 98-50567. 1999. 22.95 (*0-312-86511-2*, Pub. by Forge NYC) St Martin.

***Bittner, Rosanne.** Mystic Dreamers. 384p. 2000. mass mkt. 6.99 (*0-8125-6540-1*, Pub. by Tor Bks) St Martin.

— Mystic Visions. 320p. 2000. 22.95 (*0-312-86512-0*) Forge NYC.

— Mystic Warriors. 2001. text. write for info. (*0-312-86513-9*) St Martin.

Bittner, Rosanne. Rapture's Gold. 496p. 1986. mass mkt. 3.95 (*0-8217-1889-4*, Zebra Kensgtn) Kensgtn Pub Corp.

— Ride the Free Wind. (Savage Destiny Ser.: No. 2). 1989. mass mkt. 3.95 (*0-8217-2636-6*, Zebra Kensgtn) Kensgtn Pub Corp.

— Ride the Free Wind. (Savage Destiny Ser.: No. 2). 448p. 1996. mass mkt. 5.99 (*0-8217-5343-6*, Zebra Kensgtn) Kensgtn Pub Corp.

— River of Love. (Savage Destiny Ser.: No. 3). 1990. mass mkt. 4.50 (*0-8217-3005-3*, Zebra Kensgtn) Kensgtn Pub Corp.

— River of Love. 1996. pap. 5.99 (*0-8217-5396-7*); mass mkt. 5.99 (*0-8217-5344-4*, Zebra Kensgtn) Kensgtn Pub Corp.

— Savage Destiny, No. 5. 1985. mass mkt. 4.50 (*0-8217-3171-8*, Zebra Kensgtn) Kensgtn Pub Corp.

— Savage Destiny, No. 6. 1986. mass mkt. 4.50 (*0-8217-3172-6*, Zebra Kensgtn) Kensgtn Pub Corp.

— Savage Horizons. 448p. 1987. mass mkt. 3.95 (*0-445-20372-2*, Pub. by Warner Bks) Little.

— Shameless. 512p. 1993. mass mkt. 5.99 (*0-8217-4056-3*, Zebra Kensgtn) Kensgtn Pub Corp.

— Sioux Splendor. 448p. 1995. mass mkt. 4.99 (*0-8217-5157-3*, Zebra Kensgtn) Kensgtn Pub Corp.

— Sweet Prairie Passion. (Savage Destiny Ser.: No. 1). 1996. mass mkt. 5.99 (*0-8217-5342-8*, Zebra Kensgtn) Kensgtn Pub Corp.

— Tame the Wild Wind. 1996. mass mkt. 5.99 (*0-614-20500-X*) Bantam.

— Tender Betrayal. large type ed. LC 93-33651. 730p. 1994. lib. bdg. 22.95 (*0-7862-0069-3*) Thorndike Pr.

— Texas Bride. 352p. 1988. mass mkt. 4.50 (*0-445-20636-5*, Pub. by Warner Bks) Little.

— Texas Embrace. 320p. 1997. mass mkt. 5.99 (*0-8217-5625-7*, Zebra Kensgtn) Kensgtn Pub Corp.

— Texas Passions. 320p. 1999. mass mkt. 5.99 (*0-8217-6166-8*) Kensgtn Pub Corp.

— Until Tomorrow. 400p. 1995. mass mkt. 5.99 (*0-8217-5064-X*, Zebra Kensgtn) Kensgtn Pub Corp.

Bittner, Rosanne, et al. Love by Chocolate. 320p. 1997. mass mkt. 5.99 (*0-515-12014-6*, Jove) Berkley Pub.

Bittner, Rudiger. What Reason Demands: On Justifications of Morality & Autonomy. Talbot, Theodore, tr. 208p. (C). 1989. text 64.95 (*0-521-35215-0*); pap. text 22.95 (*0-521-37710-2*) Cambridge U Pr.

Bittner, Vernon J. Twelve Steps for Christian Living: Growth in a New Way of Living. 4th rev. ed. Froyland, Eric, tr. 138p. 1994. pap., student ed. 10.00 (*0-9643105-0-3*) ICL Renewed.

— You Can Help with Your Healing: A Guide for Recovering Wholeness in Body, Mind, & Spirit. rev. ed. LC 92-34279. 160p. 1992. pap. 14.99 (*0-8066-2656-9*, 9-2656) Augsburg Fortress.

Bittner, William C. Frank J. Lausche: A Political Biography. LC 76-361526. (Studia Slovenica, Special Ser.). 78p. 1975. 7.00 (*0-686-28389-9*) Studia Slovenica.

Bittner, Wolfgang. Despierta, Osogris! LC 98-37187. (SPA., Illus.). (J). (ps-1). 1999. 15.95 (*0-7358-1125-3*, Pub. by North-South Bks NYC) Chronicle Bks.

— Despierta, Osogris! Antreasyan, Agustin, tr. LC 95-37187. (Illus.). 32p. (J). (gr. k-3). 1999. pap. 6.95 (*0-7358-1126-1*, Pub. by North-South Bks NYC) Chronicle Bks.

— Wake up, Grizzly! James, J. Alison, tr. LC 95-36758. (Illus.). 32p. (J). (gr. k-3). 1996. 15.95 (*1-55858-518-4*, Pub. by North-South Bks NYC); lib. bdg. 15.88 (*1-55858-519-2*, Pub. by North-South Bks NYC) Chronicle Bks.

— Wake up, Grizzly! James, J. Alison, tr. LC 95-36758. (Illus.). 32p. (J). (gr. k-3). 1999. pap. 6.95 (*1-55858-955-4*, Pub. by North-South Bks NYC) Chronicle Bks.

Bitto, Ronald J. Blind Sidetrack. unabridged ed. 455p. 1998. pap. 21.95 (*1-892896-11-7*) Buy Books.

Bitton. Wastewater Microbiology. 478p. 1995. pap. text 99.95 (*0-471-12729-9*) Wiley.

Bitton, Dave. Historical Dictionary of Mormonism. LC 93-35972. (School Library Media Ser.: No. 2). 339p. 1993. 46.00 (*0-8108-2779-4*) Scarecrow.

Bitton, Davis. French Nobility in Crisis, 1560-1640. LC 69-13177. xii, 180p. 1969. 32.50 (*0-8047-0684-0*) Stanford U Pr.

— George Q. Cannon: A Biography. LC 98-50054. 400p. 1999. 19.95 (*1-57345-490-7*) Deseret Bk.

— Images of the Prophet Joseph Smith. LC 96-6416. 208p. 1996. pap. 11.95 (*1-56236-223-2*, Pub. by Aspen Bks) Origin Bk Sales.

— The Ritualization of Mormon History & Other Essays. LC 93-28931. 208p. (C). 1994. text 25.95 (*0-252-02079-0*) U of Ill Pr.

Bitton, Davis & Beecher, Maureen U., eds. New Views of Mormon History: A Collection of Essays in Honor of Leonard J. Arrington. LC 87-18787. 500p. reprint ed. pap. 155.00 (*0-7837-6871-0*, 204670100003) Bks Demand.

Bitton, Davis, jt. auth. see Arrington, Leonard J.

Bitton, Davis, jt. auth. see Bunker, Gary L.

Bitton, Davis, jt. auth. see Sorenson, John L.

Bitton, Gabriel. Formula Handbook for Environmental Engineers & Scientists. LC 97-12769. (Environmental Science & Technology Ser.). 290p. 1997. pap. 54.95 (*0-471-13905-X*) Wiley.

— Wastewater Microbiology. (Ecological & Applied Microbiology Ser.). 488p. 1994. 189.95 (*0-471-30985-0*, Wiley-Interscience); pap. 125.00 (*0-471-30986-9*) Wiley.

— Wastewater Microbiology. 2nd ed. LC 98-25192. (Series in Ecological & Applied Microbiology). 592p. 1999. 99.95 (*0-471-32047-1*) Wiley.

Bitton, Gabriel & Gerba, Charles P., eds. Groundwater Pollution Microbiology. LC 92-17213. 388p. (C). 1994. reprint ed. lib. bdg. 69.50 (*0-89464-745-8*) Krieger.

Bitton, Gabriel, jt. auth. see Dutka, Bernard J.

Bitton-Jackson, Livia. I Have Lived a Thousand Years: Growing up in the Holocaust. LC 96-19971. 224p. (YA). (gr. 7 up). 1997. 17.00 (*0-689-81022-9*) S&S Childrens.

— I Have Lived a Thousand Years: Growing up in the Holocaust. 224p. (YA). (gr. 7). 1999. per. 4.99 (*0-689-82395-9*) S&S Childrens.

***Bitton-Jackson, Livia.** My Bridges of Hope: Searching for Life & Love after Auschwitz. LC 98-8046. 272p. (YA). (gr. 7 up). 1999. per. 17.00 (*0-689-82026-7*) S&S Childrens.

***Bittrick, Cathy Sherman.** Something Beautiful Remains. (Illus.). 167p. 1998. 19.95 (*0-9663399-0-8*) Morgan Reid.

Bitz, Gregory W. War Hangover. LC 87-71864. (Illus.). 272p. (Orig.). 1988. pap. 11.95 (*0-944357-67-9*) Angel Wing Pr.

***Bitz, Steve.** Microsoft Excel Simple Projects: Challenging. Teacher Created Materials Staff, ed. (Illus.). 96p. 2000. pap., teacher ed. 18.95 (*1-57690-734-1*, TCM 2734) Tchr Create Mat.

Bitzel, Diane. Bernardo Zamagna: Navis Aeria: Eine Metamorphose des Lehrgedichts Im Zeichen des Technischen Fortschritts. Von Albrecht, Michael, ed. (Studien Zur Klassischen Philologie Ser.: Bd. 109). (GER.). 241p. 1997. 44.95 (*3-631-31733-6*) P Lang Pubng.

Bitzer, Juergen, jt. auth. see von Hirschhausen, Christian.

Bitzer, Lloyd F. & Rueter, Theodore. Carter vs. Ford: The Counterfeit Debates of 1976. LC 80-5110. 441p. 1980. reprint ed. pap. 136.80 (*0-608-01902-X*, 206255400003) Bks Demand.

Bitzer, Lloyd F., ed. & intro. see Campbell, George.

Bitzer, Robert. Collected Essays of Robert Bitzer. LC 89-51300. (Mentors of New Thought Ser.). 192p. (Orig.). 1990. pap. 9.95 (*0-87516-620-2*) DeVorss.

Bitzer, T. Honeycomb Technology. (gr. 13). 1993. text 55.95 (*0-442-23831-2*) Chapman & Hall.

Bitzes, John G. Greece in World War II: To April 1941. (Illus.). 216p. (Orig.). 1989. pap. 21.95 (*0-89745-093-0*) Sunflower U Pr.

Biuso, Joseph & Newman, Brian. Receiving Love. 240p. 1996. 16.99 (*1-56476-539-3*, 6-3539, Victor Bks) Chariot Victor.

Biuso, Julie. Julie Biusi Cooks Vegetables. (Illus.). 312p. 1992. pap. 29.95 (*0-340-54902-5*, Pub. by Hodder & Stought Ltd) Trafalgar.

Biv, Roy G. LMB Author's Guide. (Illus.). 57p. 1998. 5.95 (*1-57914-028-9*) Campbell-Smith.

Bivans, Ann-Marie. Miss America: In Pursuit of the Crown. (Illus.). 232p. 1998. reprint ed. text 27.00 (*0-7881-5572-5*) DIANE Pub.

***Bivans, Ann-Marie.** The Miss America Cookbook: Favorite Recipes from All 50 States. (Illus.). 256p. 1999. reprint ed. text 20.00 (*0-7881-6710-3*) DIANE Pub.

Bivans, Ann-Marie. 101 Secrets to Winning Beauty Pageants. (Illus.). 240p. 1995. pap. 12.95 (*0-8065-1643-7*, Citadel Pr) Carol Pub Group.

Bivar, A. D. The Personalities of Mithra in Archaeology & Literature. LC 98-43663. (Biennial Yarshater Lecture Ser.: Vol. 1). xii, 164p. 1998. text 28.00 (*0-933273-28-2*) Bibliotheca Persica.

Bivens, Allison, ed. The High Museum of Art Recipe Collection. exp. ed. (Illus.). 209p. (Orig.). 1992. reprint ed. pap. 14.95 (*0-939802-14-7*) High Mus Art.

Bivens, Arthur C. Of Nukes & Nose Cones: A Submarine Story. LC 96-76395. (Illus.). iv, 125p. 1996. 12.00 (*0-9655171-0-1*) A C Bivens.

Bivens, Forrest L. & Vallesky, David. New Life in Christ: Study Guide. Fischer, William E., ed. (Bible Class Course for Young Adults Ser.). 120p. (Orig.). 1986. pap. text 8.00 (*0-938272-07-1*, 07N2161) WELS Board.

— New Life in Christ: Teacher's Guide. (Bible Class Course for Young Adults Ser.). 40p. (Orig.). 1986. pap. text 8.00 (*0-938272-03-9*, 07-2162) WELS Board.

Bivens, Kay S. Home Accent: The Complete Home Organizer. 63p. 1989. ring bd. 19.95 (*0-9624968-1-2*) HKS Co.

Bivens, Ruth. Aunt Ruth's Puppet Scripts, Bk. I. (J). (gr. 1-8). 1986. pap. 19.95 incl. audio (*0-89265-096-6*) Randall Hse.

— Aunt Ruth's Puppet Scripts, Bk. II. (J). 1986. 19.95 incl. audio (*0-89265-114-8*) Randall Hse.

— Aunt Ruth's Puppet Scripts, Bk. III. 55p. (J). (gr. 1-6). 1987. 19.95 incl. audio (*0-89265-119-9*) Randall Hse.

— Aunt Ruth's Puppet Scripts, Bk. IV. (J). 1987. ring bd. 19.95 incl. audio (*0-89265-122-9*) Randall Hse.

Bivens, Sheldon. Raising Healthy Rabbits under Primitive Conditions. 108p. 1994. pap. text 7.50 (*1-886532-01-X*) Christian Vet.

Bivens, William E., jt. auth. see Ankner, William.

Biver, Paul. Pere Lamy. O'Connor, John, tr. from FRE. 1992. reprint ed. pap. 12.00 (*0-89555-055-5*) TAN Bks Pubs.

Bivin, David & Blizzard, Roy B. Understanding the Difficult Words of Jesus. LC 94-79108. 160p. (Orig.). 1994. pap. 10.99 (*1-56043-550-X*, Treasure Hse) Destiny Image.

Bivins, Betty. Operating a Really Small Business: An Owner's Guide. Manber, Beverly, ed. LC 92-54350. (Small Business & Entrepreneurship Ser.). 150p. (Orig.). 1993. pap. 15.95 (*1-56052-169-4*) Crisp Pubns.

Bivins, Billie F. Florida Critters. (Illus.). 1999. pap. write for info. (*0-9665550-2-3*, Faxsimile) Faxon-Gordon.

— The Talisman. (Illus.). 189p. 1999. pap. write for info. (*0-9665550-1-5*) Faxon-Gordon.

Bivins, Charles. Music in Silence. Peditto, C. Natale, ed. LC 94-12722. (Open Mouth Poetry Ser.). 129p. (Orig.). 1994. pap. 9.95 (*1-884773-00-1*) Heat Press.

Bivins, Frank J. The Farmer's Political Economy. McCurry, Dan C. & Rubenstein, Richard E., eds. LC 74-30619. (American Farmers & the Rise of Agribusiness Ser.). (Illus.). 1975. reprint ed. 16.95 (*0-405-06766-6*) Ayer.

Bivins, John. The Art of the Fire-Lock, Twentieth Century: Being a Discourse upon the Present & Past Practices of Stocking & Mounting the Sporting Fire-Lock Rifle-Gun, 2 vols. (Longrifle Ser.). Date not set. write for info. (*0-87387-091-3*) Shumway.

Bivins, John, Jr. Furniture of Coastal North Carolina, 1700-1820. LC 88-5328. (Frank L. Horton Ser.). (Illus.). 562p. 1988. 125.00 (*0-945578-00-8*) Mus South Deco.

— Longrifles of North Carolina. 2nd ed. LC 87-63592. (Illus.). 240p. 1988. boxed set 50.00 (*0-87387-097-2*) Shumway.

Bivins, John. The Moravian Potters in North Carolina. LC 70-172396. (Illus.). 315p. reprint ed. pap. 97.70 (*0-7837-5234-2*, 204496800005) Bks Demand.

Bivins, John, Jr. & Alexander, Forsyth. The Regional Arts of the Early South: A Sampling from the Collection of the Museum of Early Southern Decorative Arts. LC 91-60524. (Illus.). 176p. (C). 1991. pap. text 29.95 (*0-945578-02-4*) Mus South Deco.

Bivins, Marianne. The Peacekeeper Series, Level 2. (Illus.). 9p. (J). (ps-k). 1997. pap. 22.00 (*1-890697-09-5*) Bivins Pubs.

— The Peacekeeper Series Level III. (Illus.). 9p. (J). (ps-1). 1997. pap. 22.00 (*1-890697-26-5*) Bivins Pubs.

***Bivins, Roberta E.** Acupuncture, Expertise & Cross-Cultural Medicine. LC 00-33326. (Science, Technology & Medicine in Modern History Ser.). (Illus.). 2000. write for info. (*0-312-23761-8*) St Martin.

Bivins, Thomas. Fundamentals of Successful Newsletters: Everything You Need to Write, Design, & Publish More Effective Newsletters. (Illus.). 256p. 1993. 39.95 (*0-8442-3483-4*, NTC Business Bks) NTC Contemp Pub Co.

Bivins, Thomas H. Fundamentals of Successful Newsletters: Everything You Need to Write, Design, & Publish More Effective Newsletters. (Illus.). 256p. 1994. pap. 24.95 (*0-8442-3484-2*, NTC Business Bks) NTC Contemp Pub Co.

— Handbook for Public Relations Writing. 2nd ed. LC 91-23548. 352p. (C). 1992. text 29.95 (*0-8442-3263-7*, NTC Business Bks) NTC Contemp Pub Co.

— Handbook for Public Relations Writing. 2nd ed. LC 91-23548. 352p. (C). 1994. pap. 17.95 (*0-8442-3264-5*, NTC Business Bks) NTC Contemp Pub Co.

— Handbook for Public Relations Writing. 3rd ed. (Illus.). 352p. 1995. 39.95 (*0-8442-3435-4*, NTC Business Bks) NTC Contemp Pub Co.

— Handbook for Public Relations Writing. 3rd ed. (Illus.). 352p. 1996. pap. 24.95 (*0-8442-3436-2*, NTC Business Bks) NTC Contemp Pub Co.

— Handbook for Public Relations Writings. LC 98-47955. 1999. 24.95 (*0-8442-0350-5*) NTC Contemp Pub Co.

***Bivins, Thomas H.** Public Relations Writing: The Essentials of Style & Format. 4th ed. LC 98-45630. 1998. pap. write for info. (*0-8442-0352-1*) NTC Contemp Pub Co.

— Public Relations Writing: The Essentials of Style & Format. 4th ed. LC 98-45630. 1999. pap. text 29.95 (*0-8442-0351-3*) NTC Contemp Pub Co.

Bivins, Thomas H. & Keding, Ann. How to Produce Creative Advertising: Traditional Techniques & Computer Applications. 200p. 1993. 37.95 (*0-8442-3481-8*, NTC Business Bks) NTC Contemp Pub Co.

Bivins, Thomas H. & Ryan, William E. How to Produce Creative Publications: Traditional Techniques & Computer Applications. (Illus.). 480p. 1994. pap. 32.95 (*0-8442-3495-8*, NTC Business Bks) NTC Contemp Pub Co.

Bivins, Thomas H., jt. auth. see Keding, Ann.

Bivon, R. Advanced Russian Grammar. 99p. (C). 1979. 50.00 (*0-7855-2311-1*, Pub. by Collets) St Mut.

— The Russian Verb: A Guide to Its Forms & Usage for Advanced Learners. 202p. (C). 1992. 60.00 (*0-569-09311-2*, Pub. by Collets) St Mut.

Bivon, R., jt. auth. see Culhane, P. T.

Bivon, Roy, jt. auth. see Culhane, Terry.

Bivona, Daniel. British Imperial Literature, 1870-1940: Writing & the Administration of Empire. LC 97-27249. 300p. (C). 1998. 59.95 (*0-521-59100-7*) Cambridge U Pr.

Bivona, Francesco. A Handful of Plays. 96p. (Orig.). 1989. pap. 12.00 (*0-88734-802-5*) Players Pr.

— Strange Plays. 80p. (Orig.). 1993. pap. 10.00 (*0-88734-808-4*) Players Pr.

Bivona, Ginnie S. Dirty Dining: A Cookbook, & More, for Lovers. (Illus.). 144p. (Orig.). 1992. pap. 12.95 (*1-55622-258-0*) Wordware Pub.

— Top Texas Chefs Cook at Home. LC 99-36974. 1998. pap. text 18.95 (*1-55622-651-9*, Rep of TX Pr) Wordware Pub.

***Bix, Amy S.** Inventing Ourselves Out of Jobs? America's Debate over Technological Unemployment, 1929-1981. LC 99-32829. (Studies in Industry & Society). 2000. 45.00 (*0-8018-6244-2*) Johns Hopkins.

***Bix, Brian.** Jurisprudence: Theory & Context. 2nd ed. LC 99-68765. 288p. 2000. pap. 25.00 (*0-89089-676-3*) Carolina Acad Pr.

Bix, Brian. Law, Language, & Legal Determinancy. 232p. (C). 1993. text 49.95 (*0-19-825790-2*, 8942) OUP.

— Law, Language, & Legal Determinancy. 232p. 1996. pap. text 32.00 (*0-19-826050-4*) OUP.

Bix, Brian, ed. Analyzing Law: New Essays in Legal Theory. 340p. 1999. text 55.00 (*0-19-826583-2*) OUP.

***Bix, Brian, ed.** Contract Law, Vols. I & II. LC 99-16848. (International Library of Essays in Law & Legal Theory). 970p. 2000. text 175.95 (*1-84014-767-9*, Pub. by Ashgate Pub) Ashgate Pub Co.

Bix, Cynthia O. Arizona: The Spirit of America, State by State. Landau, Diana, ed. LC 98-3990. (Art of the State Ser.). (Illus.). 96p. 1998. 12.95 (*0-8109-5555-5*, Pub. by Abrams) Time Warner.

— New Mexico: The Spirit of America State by State. Landau, Diana, ed. LC 97-12019. (Art of the State Ser.). (Illus.). 86p. 1998. 12.95 (*0-8109-5553-9*, Pub. by Abrams) Time Warner.

Bix, Cynthia O., jt. auth. see Rauzon, Mark J.

Bix, Herbert. Hirohito & the Making of Modern Japan. Date not set. pap. 15.00 (*0-06-093130-2*) HarpC.

Bix, Herbert P. Hirohito And The Making Of Modern Japan. LC 99-89427. (Illus.). 784p. 2000. 35.00 (*0-06-019314-X*, HarpCollins) HarperTrade.

Bix, Herbert P., tr. see Masanori, Nakamura.

Bix, Robert. Conics & Cubics: A Concrete Introduction to Algebraic Curves. LC 97-46950. (Undergraduate Texts in Mathematics Ser.). 1998. 48.95 (*0-387-98401-1*) Spr-Verlag.

Bix, Robert. Topics in Geometry. (Illus.). 538p. 1993. text 71.00 (*0-12-102740-6*) Acad Pr.

Bixby, Donald E., et al. Taking Stock: The North American Livestock Census. LC 93-47249. (Illus.). vii, 182p. (Orig.). 1994. pap. 16.95 (*0-939923-35-1*) M & W Pub Co.

Bixby, Kathleen, ed. see Beal, John R.

Bixby, Louis W. The Excitement of Learning: The Boredom of Education. LC 76-24282. 1977. 12.95 (*0-87212-056-2*) Libra.

Bixby, Mae S., ed. see Smith, Warren S.

Bixby, Mary K. Learning in College: I Can Relate. LC 99-15638. (Illus.). 216p. 1999. pap. text 30.00 (*0-13-011465-0*) P-H.

***Bixby, Michael B., et al.** The Legal Environment of Business. 832p. 2000. pap. 94.00 (*0-13-019492-1*, Prentice Hall) P-H.

Bixby, Michael B., et al. The Legal Environment of Business. LC 96-9283. (C). 1995. mass mkt. 102.95 (*0-538-84484-1*) S-W Pub.

Bixby, Robert, et al. WordPerfect Macros: The Windows Version. 576p. 1992. pap. 29.95 (*0-07-157888-9*) McGraw.

Bixby, Robert, jt. auth. see Benedict, Elinor.

Bixby, Robert, jt. auth. see Bolocan, David.

Bixby, Robert, jt. auth. see Hadella, Paul.

Bixby, Robert, jt. auth. see Hettich, Michael.

Bixby, Robert, jt. auth. see Kessler, Sydney.

Bixby, Robert, jt. auth. see Rosenzweig, Geri.

Bixby, Robert, ed. see Alejandro, Ann.

Bixby, Robert, ed. see Bayer, Deborah.

Bixby, Robert, ed. see Beal, John R.

Bixby, Robert, ed. see Benedict, Elinor.

Bixby, Robert, ed. see Breeden, David.

Bixby, Robert, ed. see Brown, Andrew.

Bixby, Robert, ed. see Cherry, Kelly.

Bixby, Robert, ed. see Chorlton, David.

Bixby, Robert, ed. see Dunning, Stephen.

Bixby, Robert, ed. see Forhan, Chris.

Bixby, Robert, ed. see Gill, Michael J.

Bixby, Robert, ed. see Haymon, Ava L.

Bixby, Robert, ed. see Hettich, Michael.

Bixby, Robert, ed. see Hopper, William F.

Bixby, Robert, ed. see James, David.

Bixby, Robert, ed. see Kearns, Josie.

Bixby, Robert, ed. see Kerlikowske, Elizabeth.

Bixby, Robert, ed. see Kincaid, Joan P.

Bixby, Robert, ed. see Markus, Peter.

Bixby, Robert, ed. see Matherne, Beverly.

Bixby, Robert, ed. see Miller, Errol.

Bixby, Robert, ed. see Miller, Ray.

B

An Asterisk (*) at the beginning of an entry indicates that the title is appearing for the first time.

Bixby, Robert, ed. see Minty, Judith.
Bixby, Robert, ed. see Persun, Terry L.
Bixby, Robert, ed. see Pestana, Emily.
Bixby, Robert, ed. see Petrouske, Rosalie S.
Bixby, Robert, ed. see Powell, Joseph.
Bixby, Robert, ed. see Riley, Joanne M.
Bixby, Robert, ed. see Rutkowski, Thaddeus.
Bixby, Robert, ed. see Schofield, Don.
Bixby, Robert, ed. see Spring, Justin.
Bixby, Robert, ed. see Stringer, David.
Bixby, Robert, ed. see Taylor, Keith.
Bixby, Robert, ed. see Thorburn, Russell.
Bixby, Robert, ed. see Torgersen, Eric.
Bixby, Robert, ed. see Trudell, Dennis.
Bixby, Robert, ed. see Washburn, Laura L.
Bixby, Robert, ed. see Whitney, J. D.
Bixby, Robert, ed. & illus. see Kerlikowske, Elizabeth.
Bixby, Robert, ed. & illus. see Thorburn, Russell.

Bixby, Robert E., et al, eds. Integer Programming & Combinatorial Optimization: 6th International IPCO '98 Conference, Houston, Texas, June 22-24, 1998. Proceedings, Vol. 141. LC 98-26206. (Lecture Notes in Computer Science Ser.: Vol. 1412). ix, 437p. 1998. pap. 67.00 (*3-540-64590-X*) Spr-Verlag.

Bixby, W. G. Bixby: A Genealogy of the Descendants of Joseph Bixby, 1621-1701, of Ipswich & Boxford, Mass. (Illus.). 707p. 1990. reprint ed. pap. 99.00 (*0-8328-1441-5*); reprint ed. lib. bdg. 109.00 (*0-8328-1440-7*) Higginson Bk Co.

***Bixel, Patricia Bellis & Turner, Elizabeth Hayes.** Galveston & the 1900 Storm: Castastrophe & Catalyst. LC 99-87876. (Illus.). 192p. 2000. 60.00 (*0-292-70883-1*); pap. 27.95 (*0-292-70884-X*) U of Tex Pr.

Bixel, Patricia Bellis, see Bellis Bixel, Patricia.

Bixler & Durbin. Oklahoma Real Estate Forms, 3 vols., Issue 11. 151p. 1998. ring bd. write for info. (*0-327-00588-2*, 8225214) LEXIS Pub.

Bixler, Barron J. Ascension. (Illus.). 23p. 1996. ring bd. 9.95 (*0-9651808-0-8*) Ascension CA.

Bixler, C. Temple & Durbin, Alan C. Oklahoma Real Estate Forms, 3 vols. 1994. ring bd., suppl. ed. 89.00 (*0-685-74602-X*, MICHIE) LEXIS Pub.

— Oklahoma Real Estate Forms, 3 vols., Set. 1390p. 1994. spiral bd. 309.00 (*0-87189-978-7*, 82247-10, MICHIE) LEXIS Pub.

Bixler-Clark, Alice. Briards. (Illus.). 1996. pap. 9.95 (*0-7938-2396-X*, KW-231S) TFH Pubns.

Bixler, Dave. MCSE Silmulation Guide: Windows NT Server 4 & Enterprise. LC 98-87236. 1998. pap. 29.99 (*1-56205-914-9*) New Riders Pub.

Bixler, David. Internet Information Server 4. 4th ed. LC 99-62817. 1999. 49.99 (*0-7357-0865-7*) New Riders Pub.

Bixler, David P. Welfare Reform: States' Early Experiences with Benefit Termination. (Illus.). 112p. 1998. pap. text 25.00 (*0-7881-4759-5*) DIANE Pub.

— Welfare Reform: Three States' Spproaches Show Promise of Increasing Work Participation. (Illus.). 60p. 1997. pap. text 20.00 (*0-7881-4758-7*) DIANE Pub.

Bixler, David P. & Mascia, Janet L. Welfare Reform: Implications of Increased Work Participation for Child Care. (Illus.). 48p. (C). 1998. pap. text 20.00 (*0-7881-4775-7*) DIANE Pub.

Bixler, Floyd J. The History with Reminiscences of the Early Taverns & Inns of Easton. 29p. (Orig.). 1931. pap. text 3.00 (*1-877701-09-2*) NCH&GS.

Bixler, Frances. Richard Wilbur: A Reference Guide. (Reference Guides to Literature Ser.). 459p. 1991. 50.00 (*0-8161-7262-5*, Hall Reference) Macmillan.

Bixler, Garvin S., Jr., jt. ed. see Atassi, M. Zouhair.

Bixler, Glenn C., jt. auth. see Jones, L. R.

Bixler, Jacqueling E. Convention & Transgression: The Theatre of Emilio Carballido. LC 97-18859. 256p. 1997. 39.50 (*0-8387-5354-X*) Bucknell U Pr.

Bixler, James P. & Margolis, Bernard P. The Miracle of Print: An Exhibition on the Art of the Printed Word. 84p. 1993. pap. 6.00 (*1-884003-02-8*) Frnds Pikes Peak.

Bixler, Julius S. Immortality & the Present Mood. LC 75-3047. reprint ed. 34.50 (*0-404-59044-6*) AMS Pr.

— Religion for Free Minds. LC 75-3048. (Philosophy in America Ser.). 1976. reprint ed. 18.00 (*0-404-59045-4*) AMS Pr.

— Religion in the Philosophy of William James. LC 75-3049. reprint ed. 42.50 (*0-404-59046-2*) AMS Pr.

Bixler, Kim & Gordon, Jon. 365 Great Things about Atlanta. (Illus.). 96p. (Orig.). 1996. pap. 5.95 (*0-9652426-0-9*) Clue Guides.

Bixler, Margaret T. Winds of Freedom: The Story of the Navajo Code Talkers of World War II. 202p. 1966. pap. text 16.95 (*1-881907-01-5*) Two Bytes Pub.

— Winds of Freedom: The Story of the Navajo Code Talkers of World War II. 189p. 1994. text 23.95 (*1-881907-00-7*) Two Bytes Pub.

Bixler-Marquez, et al. Chicano Studies. 380p. (C). 1999. per. 55.95 (*0-7872-5690-0*, 41569002) Kendall-Hunt.

***Bixler, N. E.** Victoria 2.0: Mechanistic Model for Radionuclide Behavior in a Nuclear Reactor Coolant System under Severe Accident Conditions. 301p. 1999. per. 24.00 (*0-16-062989-6*) USGPO.

Bixler, Norma. Burmese Journey. LC 67-11440. 246p. reprint ed. pap. 76.30 (*0-8357-7480-5*, 201611100098) Bks Demand.

Bixler, Paul, ed. The Antioch Review Anthology. (Essay Index Reprint Ser.). 480p. reprint ed. lib. bdg. 27.00 (*0-8290-0793-8*) Irvington.

Bixler, Paul, ed. see American Library Association Committee, on Intelle.

Bixler, Paul, ed. see Antioch Staff.

Bixler, Phyllis. Secret Garden. LC 96-20031. 1996. 29.00 (*0-8057-8814-X*, Twyne) Mac Lib Ref.

— Secret Garden. (Illus.). 144p. 1996. pap. 18.00 (*0-8057-8815-8*, Twyne) Mac Lib Ref.

Bixler, R. Russell. Earth, Fire & Sea: The Untold Drama of Creation. (Illus.). 214p. 1986. text 16.95 (*0-9617094-0-5*) Baldwin Manor Pr.

***Bixler, R. Russell.** Earth, Fire & Sea: The Untold Drama of Creation. 224p. 1999. pap. 12.99 (*1-56043-342-6*) Destiny Image.

Bixler, R. Russell. Unbreakable Promises: How to Know & Receive all that God Has Given You. 192p. (Orig.). 1987. pap. 5.95 (*0-9617094-1-3*) Baldwin Manor Pr.

***Bixler, Russel.** Faith Works. 1999. pap. text 14.99 (*1-56043-338-8*, Treasure Hse) Destiny Image.

Bixler, Susan. New Professional Image: From Corporate Casual to the Ultimate Power Look, How to Tailor Your Appearance. LC 97-6553. 1997. pap. text 12.95 (*1-55850-729-9*) Adams Media.

***Bixler, Susan & Dugan, Lisa Scherver.** 5 Steps to Professional Presence: How to Project Confidence, Competence & Credibility at Work. 272p. 2000. pap. 12.95 (*1-58062-442-1*) Adams Media.

Bixler, Susan & Scherrer, Lisa. Take Action: 18 Proven Strategies for Advancing in Today's Business World. LC 96-43909. 1997. pap. 12.95 (*0-449-91061-X*) Fawcett.

Bixon, M., jt. auth. see Jortner, Joshua.

Biza, Ted, jt. auth. see Passi, Delia.

Bizais, Yves, et al, eds. Information Processing in Medical Imaging: Proceedings: International Conference on Information Processing in Medical Imaging (14th: 1995: Ile de Berder, France) (Computational Imaging & Vision Ser.: Vol. 3). 408p. (C). 1995. text 197.00 (*0-7923-3593-7*) Kluwer Academic.

Bizar, Jodi. Tripping Out in the Land of the Sun: A User Friendly Outdoor Guide to the El Paso - Juarez - Las Cruces Southwest. Moses, Michael, ed. & photos by by. Peebles, Kelly, photos by. (Illus.). 120p. 1994. pap. 9.95 (*0-944551-07-6*) Sundance Pr TX.

***Bizar, Marilyn & Barr, Rebecca, eds.** School Leadership in Times of Urban Reform. (Topics in Educational Leadership Ser.). 256p. 2000. pap. write for info. (*0-8058-2451-0*) L Erlbaum Assocs.

Bizar, Marilyn, jt. auth. see Daniels, Harvey.

Bizdikian, Jerair. Introduction to the New Testament. LC 98-70223. (ARM.). 340p. 1998. pap. 10.00 (*1-883131-01-4*) Armenian Mission.

Bizek, Hana M. Mathematics of the Rubik's Cube Design. LC 98-137444. (Illus.). 332p. 1996. pap. 20.00 (*0-8059-3919-9*) Dorrance.

Bizet, Georges. L' Arlesienne Suites Nos. 1 & 2 in Full Score. 1998. pap. 10.95 (*0-486-29815-9*) Dover.

— Bizet's Carmen. (Music Ser.). 96p. (Orig.). 1984. pap. 2.95 (*0-486-24556-X*) Dover.

— Carmen. 1998. pap. 7.95 (*963-8303-19-0*) Konemann.

— Carmen. John, Nicholas, ed. Moody, Nell & Moody, John, trs. from FRE. (English National Opera Guide Series: Bilingual Libretto, Articles: No. 13). (Illus.). 128p. 1982. pap. 9.95 (*0-7145-3937-6*) Riverrun NY.

— Carmen: Vocal Score. (ENG & FRE.). 400p. 1986. pap. 22.95 (*0-7935-5360-1*, 50337190) H Leonard.

— Carmen in Full Score. 574p. 1988. pap. 21.95 (*0-486-25820-3*) Dover.

— Carmen Libretto. (ENG & FRE.). 56p. 1986. pap. 4.95 (*0-7935-2620-5*, 50340070) H Leonard.

— Carmen Libretto: Dialogue Version. 64p. 1986. pap. 4.95 (*0-7935-5631-7*, 50340600) H Leonard.

— Carmen Suites Nos. 1 & 2 in Full Score. 144p. Date not set. 11.95 (*0-486-40067-0*) Dover.

— Doctor Miracle. Harris, David, tr. 1968. 2.00 (*0-19-335300-8*) OUP.

— Georges Bizet's Carmen. Friedman, Sonya, tr. 1996. pap. 15.00 (*0-614-20799-1*) Park Lane Pr.

Bizet, Georges & Foil, David. Carmen. (Black Dog Opera Library). (Illus.). 160p. 1996. 19.98 (*1-884822-81-9*) Blck Dog & Leventhal.

***Bizette, Donnice.** Hidden Gold in the Lords Prayer. 84p. 2000. pap. 6.95 (*1-928772-06-4*) Keepsafe.

***Bizier, Richard.** Loisiane. 2nd ed. (Travel Guide (French Guides) Ser.). 1998. pap. text 29.95 (*2-89464-069-2*) Ulysses Travel.

Bizier, Richard. Louisiana. (Illus.). 416p. 1999. pap. text 23.95 (*1-56554-350-5*) Pelican.

— New Orleans. (Illus.). 240p. 1998. pap. text 13.95 (*1-56554-352-1*) Pelican.

Bizier, Richard. La Nouvelle-Orleans. (Illus.). 264p. 1997. pap. text 14.95 (*1-56554-351-3*) Pelican.

***Bizier, Richard.** La Nouvelle-Orleans. (Travel Guide (French Guides) Ser.). 1998. pap. text 17.95 (*2-89464-065-X*) Ulysses Travel.

***Bizier, Richard & Nadeau, Roch.** Ulysses Due South Puerto Vallarta. 2nd ed. (Due South Guide Ser.). (Illus.). 192p. 1999. pap. 10.95 (*2-89464-150-8*, Pub. by Ulysses Travel) Globe Pequot.

Biziere, Jean-Maurice. Dictionnaire des Biographies Vol. 1: L'Antiquite. (FRE.). 272p. 1992. pap. 34.95 (*0-7859-7753-8*, 2200211074) Fr & Eur.

— Dictionnaire des Biographies Vol. 2: Le Moyen Age. (FRE.). 309p. 1993. pap. 39.95 (*0-7859-7757-0*, 2200213719) Fr & Eur.

— Dictionnaire des Biographies Vol. 3: La France Moderne. (FRE.). 272p. 1993. pap. 36.95 (*0-7859-7754-6*, 2200211082) Fr & Eur.

— Dictionnaire des Biographies Vol. 5: XIXe Siecle. (FRE.). 256p. 1994. pap. 36.95 (*0-7859-7755-4*, 2200211090) Fr & Eur.

— Dictionnaire des Biographies Vol. 6: Twentieth Century. (FRE.). 272p. 1992. pap. 39.95 (*0-7859-7756-2*, 2200212313) Fr & Eur.

Biziere, Kathleen E. & Kurth, Matthias C. Living with Parkinson's Disease. LC 96-46633. 160p. 1996. pap. 24.95 (*1-888799-10-2*) Demos Medical.

***Biziou, Barbara.** Joy of Family Rituals: Recipes for Everyday Living. LC 99-87434. (Illus.). 176p. 2000. text 19.95 (*0-312-25328-1*) St Martin.

Bizjack, Carmen, tr. see Phelps De Cordova, Loretta.

Bizjak, jt. auth. see Bergeron.

Bizjak, Gloria & IFSTA Instructor Staff. Fire & Emergency Services Instructor. 6th ed. Adams, Barbara, ed. LC 99-62199. (Illus.). 416p. 1999. pap. 30.00 (*0-87939-167-7*) IFSTA.

Bizjak, Gloria J., jt. auth. see Bergeron.

Bizjak, Gloria J., jt. auth. see Bergeron, J. David.

Bizjak, Marybeth. Coffee Crazy: A Guide to the 100 Best Coffeehouses in America. LC 95-11122. 176p. (Orig.). 1996. pap. 12.95 (*0-944031-64-1*) Aslan Pub.

***Bizley, Kirk.** Gymnastics. LC 99-22662. (You Can Do It! Ser.). 1999. lib. bdg. write for info. (*1-57572-961-X*) Heinemann Lib.

— Mountain Biking. LC 99-24038. (Radical Sports Ser.). 1999. lib. bdg. write for info. (*1-57572-944-X*) Heinemann Lib.

— Soccer. LC 99-22661. (You Can Do It! Ser.). (Illus.). 24p. (J). (gr. k-2). 1999. lib. bdg. 13.95 (*1-57572-962-8*) Heinemann Lib.

— Surfing. LC 99-24039. (Radical Sports Ser.). 1999. write for info. (*1-57572-947-4*) Heinemann Lib.

— Swimming. LC 99-22663. (You Can Do It! Ser.). (Illus.). 24p. (J). (gr. k-2). 1999. lib. bdg. 13.95 (*1-57572-963-6*) Heinemann Lib.

Bizollon, C. A., ed. Physiological Peptides & New Trends in Radioimmunology. 370p. 1984. 136.25 (*0-444-80358-0*) Elsevier.

Bizony, Piers. The Exploration of Mars: Searching for the Cosmic Origins of Life. 1998. pap. 19.95 (*1-85410-584-1*, Pub. by Aurum Pr) London Brdge.

***Bizony, Piers.** Island in the Sky: Building the International Space Station. (Illus.). 142p. 1999. reprint ed. pap. 19.00 (*0-7881-6579-8*) DIANE Pub.

Bizony, Piers. Island in the Sky: The International Space Station. LC 97-173471. (Illus.). 160p. (Orig.). 1996. pap. 19.95 (*1-85410-436-5*, Pub. by Aurum Pr) London Brdge.

— The Rivers of Mars: Searching for Cosmic Origins of Life. (Illus.). 192p. (Orig.). 1997. pap. 14.95 (*1-85410-495-0*, Pub. by Aurum Pr) London Brdge.

— 2001: Filming the Future. (Illus.). 168p. 1995. pap. 19.95 (*1-85410-365-2*, Pub. by Aurum Pr) London Brdge.

Bizub, Paul. Body Diction: A Compilation of Words, Phrases, & Sayings Using Body Parts. 112p. 1999. 14.00 (*0-8059-4671-3*) Dorrance.

Bizuheh, Moques & Keck, Robert. A&P Lecture Notes I. 128p. (C). 1995. spiral bd. 17.95 (*0-8403-9421-7*) Kendall-Hunt.

Bizuneh, Moques & Elias, Katie. A&P Lecture Notes II. 112p. (C). 1996. spiral bd. 17.95 (*0-8403-9517-5*) Kendall-Hunt.

Bizzack, John W. Authentic Leadership: Lifetime Tools That Make a Difference. pap. 20.00 (*0-9630878-6-X*) Autumn Hse KY.

— No Nonsense Leadership. 122p. 1993. 28.95 (*0-8062-3956-5*) Autumn Hse KY.

— Police Management for the 1990's: A Practitioner's Road Map. 170p. 1989. 41.95 (*0-398-05583-1*); pap. 29.95 (*0-398-06020-7*) C C Thomas.

— Professionalism & Law Enforcement Accreditation: The First Ten Years. 1993. pap. 32.95 (*0-9630878-7-8*) Autumn Hse KY.

Bizzaro, Patrick, ed. Dream Garden: The Poetic Vision of Fred Chappell. LC 97-14265. (Southern Literary Studies). 256p. 1997. text 30.00 (*0-8071-2202-5*) La State U Pr.

Bizzarro, Salvatore. Historical Dictionary of Chile. 2nd ed. LC 87-4681. (Latin American Historical Dictionaries Ser.: No. 7). (Illus.). 601p. 1987. 65.00 (*0-8108-1964-3*) Scarecrow.

— Pablo Neruda: All Poets the Poet. LC 78-24437. 204p. 1979. lib. bdg. 21.00 (*0-8108-1189-8*) Scarecrow.

Bizzarro, Tina W. Romanesque Architectural Criticism: A Pre-History. (Illus.). 263p. (C). 1992. text 85.00 (*0-521-41017-7*) Cambridge U Pr.

***Bizzell.** Bedford Bibliography. 5th ed. 2000. pap. text 9.95 (*0-312-24073-2*) St Martin.

Bizzell. Negotiating Differences. 1995. pap. text 5.00 (*0-312-11706-X*) St Martin.

— Negotiating Different Rules. 3rd ed. 1996. pap. text 31.50 (*0-312-14963-8*) St Martin.

Bizzell, et al. Bedford Bibliography. 3rd ed. 1991. pap. text. write for info. (*0-312-05319-3*) St Martin.

Bizzell, Patricia. Academic Discourse & Critical Consciousness. LC 92-11967. (Series in Composition, Literacy, & Culture). 304p. (C). 1993. pap. 19.95 (*0-8229-5485-0*); text 49.95 (*0-8229-3730-1*) U of Pittsburgh Pr.

— The Rhetorical Tradition: Readings from Classical Times to the Present. 2nd ed. 2000. pap. text 69.95 (*0-312-14839-9*) St Martin.

Bizzell, Patricia & Herzberg, Bruce. Negotiating Difference. 963p. 1995. pap. text 38.95 (*0-312-06846-8*) St Martin.

Bizzell, Patricia & Herzberg, Bruce, eds. The Rhetorical Tradition: Readings from Classical Times to the Present. LC 88-63071. 1282p. (C). 1990. pap. text 69.95 (*0-312-00348-X*) St Martin.

Bizzell, William. Rural Texas. 1993. reprint ed. lib. bdg. 75.00 (*0-7812-5917-7*) Rprt Serv.

Bizzell, William B. The Green Rising: An Historical Survey of Agrarianism with Special Reference to the Organized Efforts of the Farmers of the United States to Improve Their Economic & Social Status. LC 72-89078. (Rural America Ser.). 1973. reprint ed. 29.00 (*0-8420-1475-6*) Scholarly Res Inc.

Bizzio, Sergio. El Son de Africa (The African Sound) (SPA.). 152p. (YA). 1993. pap. 6.99 (*968-16-4043-8*, Pub. by Fondo) Continental Bk.

Bizzoco, Dennis, ed. The Exhaustive Concordance to the United States Constitution. 1994. 45.00 (*1-884858-00-7*) Firm Fnd Pr.

Bizzoco, Rick. 1969 Stingray Guidebook. LC 93-74519. 220p. 1995. pap. text 69.95 (*1-884562-01-9*) CA Trader.

Bizzoco, Rick W. Tropical Rainforest Letters. LC 93-74549. 104p. (Orig.). 1994. pap. text 6.95 (*1-884562-00-0*) CA Trader.

BJA (Bureau of Justice Assistance) Staff, jt. auth. see PERF (Police Executive Research Forum) Staff.

Bjarkman, Peter. Duke Snider. (Baseball Legends Ser.). (Illus.). 64p. (J). (gr. 3 up). 1994. lib. bdg. 15.95 (*0-7910-1190-9*) Chelsea Hse.

Bjarkman, Peter C. Baseball with a Latin Beat: A History of the Latin American Game. LC 94-3526. (Illus.). 486p. 1994. pap. 32.50 (*0-89950-973-8*) McFarland & Co.

— The Biographical History of Basketball. LC 97-49369. (Illus.). 608p. 1999. pap. 24.95 (*1-57028-134-3*, 81343H, Mstrs Pr) NTC Contemp Pub Co.

***Bjarkman, Peter C.** The Boston Celtics Encyclopedia. (Illus.). 400p. 1999. 34.95 (*1-58261-062-2*, Pub. by Sprts Pubng) Partners-West.

Bjarkman, Peter C. Brooklyn Dodgers. 1992. 10.98 (*1-55521-761-3*) Bk Sales Inc.

— Ernie Banks. (Baseball Legends Ser.). (Illus.). 64p. (J). (gr. 3 up). 1994. lib. bdg. 15.95 (*0-7910-1167-4*) Chelsea Hse.

Bjarkman, Peter C. Hoopla: A Century of College Basketball. 384p. pap. 15.00 (*1-57028-216-1*, 82616H, Mstrs Pr) NTC Contemp Pub Co.

Bjarkman, Peter C. Hoopla: One Hundred Years of College Basketball. (Illus.). 320p. 1996. 22.95 (*1-57028-039-8*, Mstrs Pr) NTC Contemp Pub Co.

***Bjarkman, Peter C.** The New York Mets Encyclopedia. (Illus.). 250p. 2001. 34.95 (*1-58261-055-5*) Sports Pub.

Bjarkman, Peter C. Reggie Miller: Star Guard. LC 98-33312. (Sports Reports Ser.). (Illus.). 104p. (YA). (gr. 4-10). 1999. lib. bdg. 20.95 (*0-7660-1082-1*) Enslow Pubs.

— Roberto Clemente. (Baseball Legends Ser.). (Illus.). 64p. (J). (gr. 3 up). 1991. lib. bdg. 14.95 (*0-7910-1171-2*) Chelsea Hse.

— Sports Great Dominique Wilkins. (Sports Great Bks.). (Illus.). 64p. (J). (gr. 4-10). 1996. lib. bdg. 17.95 (*0-89490-754-9*) Enslow Pubs.

— Sports Great Scottie Pippen. LC 95-51440. (Sports Great Bks.). (Illus.). 64p. (J). (gr. 4-10). 1996. lib. bdg. 17.95 (*0-89490-755-7*) Enslow Pubs.

— Top 10 Basketball Slam Dunkers. LC 94-45889. (Sports Top 10 Ser.). (Illus.). 48p. (J). (gr. 4-10). 1995. lib. bdg. 18.95 (*0-89490-608-9*) Enslow Pubs.

— Top 10 Baseball Base Stealers. LC 94-45890. (Sports Top 10 Ser.). (Illus.). 48p. (J). (gr. 4-10). 1995. lib. bdg. 18.95 (*0-89490-609-7*) Enslow Pubs.

— Warren Spahn. (Baseball Legends Ser.). (Illus.). 64p. (J). (gr. 3 up). 1994. lib. bdg. 15.95 (*0-7910-1191-7*) Chelsea Hse.

Bjarkman, Peter C., ed. Encyclopedia of Major League Baseball Team Histories Vol. 1: The American League. (Baseball & American Society Ser.: No. 7). (Illus.). 575p. 1991. 65.00 (*0-88736-373-3*) Mecklermedia.

— Encyclopedia of Major League Baseball Team Histories Vol. 2: National League. (Baseball & American Society Ser.: No. 8). 600p. 1991. 65.00 (*0-88736-374-1*) Mecklermedia.

— The National Pastime. (Illus.). 96p. 1993. pap. 7.95 (*0-910137-48-X*) Soc Am Baseball Res.

Bjarkman, Peter C., ed. Baseball & the Game of Ideas: Essays for the Serious Fan. (Sporting Life Ser.). 212p. 1993. 30.00 (*0-913559-19-9*) Birch Brook Pr.

Bjarkman, Peter C. & Hammond, Robert M., eds. American Spanish Pronunciation. LC 89-17189. 283p. (Orig.). 1989. pap. 19.95 (*0-87840-099-0*) Georgetown U Pr.

Bjarkman, Peter C. & Raskin, Victor, eds. Real-World Linguist: Linguistic Applications in the 1980's. LC 85-46067. 384p. 1986. text 73.25 (*0-89391-357-X*) Ablx Pub.

Bjarkman, Peter C. & Rucker, Mark. Smoke: The Romance of Cuban Baseball. (Illus.). 256p. 1999. pap. 29.95 (*1-892129-32-9*) Total Sprts.

Bjarkman, Peter C., ed. see Coover, Robert & Kinsella, W. P.

Bjarnar, Ove, jt. auth. see Kipping, Matthias.

***Bjarnason, Martin.** Getting into Canada: A Guide for Prospective Migrants to Gaining Permanent Residence. 2nd ed. (Living & Working Abroad Ser.). (Illus.). 229p. 1999. pap. 22.50 (*1-85703-537-2*, Pub. by How To Bks) Trans-Atl Phila.

Bjarnson, B. A. & Carlesi, M. Handlining & Squid Jigging. (Fishing Ser.: No. 23). 66p. 1993. pap. 20.00 (*92-5-103100-2*, F31002, Pub. by FAO) Bernan Associates.

Bjedov, G., jt. auth. see Andersen, P. K.

***Bjelajac, David.** American Art: A Cultural History. (Illus.). 416p. 2000. 75.00 (*0-8109-4214-3*, Pub. by Abrams) Time Warner.

— American Art: A Cultural History. 400p. 2000. pap. 49.00 (*0-13-083816-0*) P-H.

Bjelajac, David. Washington Allston, Secret Societies & the Alchemy of Anglo-American Painting. (Cambridge Studies in American Visual Culture). (Illus.). 249p. (C). 1997. text 69.95 (*0-521-43153-0*) Cambridge U Pr.

Bjeldanes, Leonard F., jt. auth. see Shibamoto, Takayuki.

Bjelfvenstam, Bo. Eritrea - Tre Resor. 136p. 1978. write for info. (*91-7106-146-0*, Pub. by Nordic Africa) Transaction Pubs.

— Hur Ska Det Ga For Botswana? 133p. 1981. write for info. (*91-7106-183-5*, Pub. by Nordic Africa) Transaction Pubs.

— I Somalia. 144p. 1982. write for info. (*91-7106-200-9*, Pub. by Nordic Africa) Transaction Pubs.

Bjelke, Rolf, jt. auth. see Shapiro, Deborah.

Bjelkhagen, H. I. Silver-Halide Recording Materials: For Holography & Their Processing. 2nd ed. Schawlow, Arthur L. et al, eds. (Springer Series in Optical Sciences: Vol. 66). (Illus.). 440p. 1995. 74.95 (*3-540-58619-9*) Spr-Verlag.

Bjelkhagen, Hans I. Selected Papers on Holographic Recording Materials. LC 96-35808. (SPIE Milestone Ser.). 1996. write for info. (*0-8194-2371-8*) SPIE.

— Silver Halide Recording Materials for Holography & Their Processing. LC 93-3705. (Optical Sciences Ser.: Vol. 66). (Illus.). 450p. 1993. 89.00 (*0-387-56576-0*); write for info. (*3-540-56576-0*) Spr-Verlag.

Bjelkhagen, Hans I., ed. see Second International Conference on Optics in Life.

Bjelland, Harley. Business Writing the Modular Way: How to Research, Organize & Compose Effective Memos, Letters, Articles, Reports, Proposals, Manuals, Specifications & Books. fac. ed. LC 91-53049. (Illus.). 283p. 1992. pap. 87.80 (*0-7837-8358-2*, 204914800010) Bks Demand.

— Free & Low-Cost Software for Scientists & Engineers. LC 94-5085. 1994. 26.95 (*0-07-005856-3*) McGraw.

— Online Systems for Medical Professionals: How to Use & Access Computer Data Base. Brittenham, Jill, ed. 200p. 1992. 39.95 (*1-878487-44-2*, ME045) Practice Mgmt Info.

— Using Online Scientific & Engineering Databases. 1992. pap. 26.95 (*0-07-005854-7*) McGraw-Hill Prof.

— Using Online Scientific & Engineering Databases. 232p. 1992. pap. 26.95 (*0-8306-3056-2*, 3967, Windcrest) TAB Bks.

Bjelos, Henad, jt. auth. see Forlan, Marian.

***Bjercke, Alf R.** Norwegische Katnersohne Als Konigliche Dragoner: Eine Abhandlung Uber Den Dragonerdienst In Norwegen und die Grenzwache In Schleswig-Holstein, 1758-1762. (GER., Illus.). 247p. 1999. 46.00 (*3-631-34727-8*) P Lang Pubng.

Bjeren, Gunilla. Migration to Shashemene: Ethnicity, Gender & Occupation in Urban Ethiopia. (Illus.). xiv, 292p. (Orig.). 1985. pap. text 41.00 (*91-7106-245-9*, Pub. by Nordisk Afrikainstitutet) Coronet Bks.

Bjeren, Gunilla & Elgqvist-Saltzman, Inga, eds. Gender & Education in a Life Perspective: Lessons from Scandinavia. LC 94-6463. 1994. 78.95 (*1-85628-846-3*, Pub. by Avebry) Ashgate Pub Co.

Bjerhagen, Torbjorn & Savfors, Ingemar. L' Habitat Traditionnel dans la Republique Populaire du Congo. 120p. 1972. write for info. (*91-7106-055-3*, Pub. by Nordic Africa) Transaction Pubs.

***Bjerke, Bjhorn.** Business Leadership & Culture: National Management Styles in the Global Economy. LC 99-28282. 304p. 2000. 95.00 (*1-84064-171-1*) E Elgar.

Bjerke, Bjorn, jt. auth. see Arbnor, Ingeman.

Bjerke, Gene. Writing for Video. LC 96-92002. (Illus.). 176p. (Orig.). 1997. pap. 15.95 (*0-9631505-3-7*) Petrel Pub.

— Writing Video Scripts with WordPerfect. 1992. 3.5 hd 5.00 (*0-9631505-2-9*); 5.25 hd 5.00 (*0-9631505-1-0*) Petrel Pub.

— Writing Video Scripts with WordPerfect. large type ed. LC Z52.5.W65.B4 1991. (Illus.). 96p. 1992. pap. 12.00 (*0-9631505-0-2*, Z52.5.W65.B4 19) Petrel Pub.

Bjerke, Luther. From a Stinker to a Thinker. Rosevold, Doreen, ed. 120p. (Orig.). 1993. write for info. (*0-9619152-1-8*) Beaver Crk Pub.

Bjerken, R. S. The Archaic Smile: A Post-Modern Cosmology: A Post-Religion Spirituality. LC 98-91288. (Illus.). 156p. 1998. pap. 18.95 (*0-9662918-1-6*) ORON Bks.

Bjerkholt, Olav, ed. Foundations of Modern Econometrics: The Selected Essays of Ragnar Frisch, 2 vols. LC 95-16389. (Economists of the Twentieth Century Ser.). 1072p. 1995. 275.00 (*1-85278-840-2*) E Elgar.

Bjerkholt, Olav & Offederal, E., eds. Macroeconomic Prospects for a Small Oil Exporting Country. 1985. lib. bdg. 160.00 (*90-247-3183-6*) Kluwer Academic.

Bjerknes, R., jt. ed. see Laerum, Ole D.

Bjerkoe, Ethel H. Cabinetmakers of America. 2nd ed. LC 57-7278. (Illus.). 272p. 1978. 22.50 (*0-685-04519-6*) Schiffer.

Bjerre, Andreas. The Psychology of Murder: A Study in Criminal Psychology. Classen, E., tr. from SWE. (Historical Foundations of Forensic Psychiatry & Psychology Ser.). 164p. 1980. reprint ed. lib. bdg. 22.50 (*0-306-76067-3*) Da Capo.

Bjerregaard, Carl H. Lectures on Mysticism & Nature Worship. (Second Ser.). 132p. 1996. reprint ed. spiral bd. 14.00 (*0-7873-0112-4*) Hlth Research.

— Lectures on Mysticism & Nature Worship, 1897. 132p. 1996. reprint ed. pap. 12.95 (*1-56459-753-9*) Kessinger Pub.

***Bjerregaard, Marcia.** First Heroes for Freedom. (Adventures in America Ser.). (Illus.). 96p. (J). (gr. 3-7). 2000. lib. bdg. 14.95 (*1-893110-17-6*) Silver Moon.

— Seasons of the Trail. (Adventures in America Ser.). (Illus.). 96p. (J). (gr. 4-6). 2000. lib. bdg. 14.95 (*1-893110-20-6*) Silver Moon.

Bjerring, N., tr. see Basaroff, F.

Bjerring, Nicholas, tr. see Anatolius of Mohilew & Mstislaw.

Bjerring, Peter, et al, eds. Medical Applications of Lasers in Dermatology, Cardiology, Gynecology, Ophthalmology & Dentistry II. (Europto Ser.: Vol. 3564). 1998. 89.00 (*0-8194-3026-9*) SPIE.

Bjerrum, Ole J. & Heegaard, Niels H., eds. Handbook of Immunoblotting of Proteins, 2 vols., Vol. I. 280p. 1988. boxed set 260.00 (*0-8493-0549-7*, QP519) CRC Pr.

— Handbook of Immunoblotting of Proteins, 2 vols., Vol. II. 224p. 1988. boxed set 273.95 (*0-8493-0550-0*, QP519) CRC Pr.

Bjerstedt, Ake, ed. Peace Education: Global Perspectives. (Studia Psychologica et Paedagogica.: Vol. CVII). 214p. 1993. 45.00 (*91-22-01564-7*) Coronet Bks.

***Bjhorntorp, P., et al.** Obesity: Pathology & Therapy. LC 00-44025. (Handbook of Experimental Pharmacology Ser.). 2000. write for info. (*3-540-66133-6*) Spr-Verlag.

Bjoccara, Nino, et al, eds. Cellular Automata & Cooperative Systems. LC 93-3697. (NATO Advanced Study Institutes Series C, Mathematical & Physical Sciences: Vol. 396). 1993. text 285.50 (*0-7923-2272-X*) Kluwer Academic.

Bjomson, Richard. The African Quest for Freedom & Identity: Cameroonian Writing & the National Experience. LC 90-39423. (Illus.). 528p. 1994. reprint ed. pap. 19.95 (*0-253-20908-0*) Ind U Pr.

Bjorck, Ake. Numerical Methods for Least Squares Problems. LC 96-3908. (Miscellaneous Bks.: No. 51). xvii, 408p. 1996. pap. 51.00 (*0-89871-360-9*, OT51) Soc Indus-Appl Math.

Bjorck, Ake, et al, eds. Large Scale Matrix Problems. LC 80-22058. 412p. reprint ed. pap. 127.80 (*0-608-16381-3*, 202627500049) Bks Demand.

***Bjorck, Jeffrey P., et al.** Casebook for Managing Managed Care: A Self-Study Guide. LC 99-40833. 2000. 30.00 (*0-88048-783-6*) Am Psychiatric.

***Bjordahl, Rod G.** Double Feature. LC 99-96695. 2000. 17.95 (*0-533-13301-7*) Vantage.

Bjordal, Asmund & Lolkkeborg, Svein. Longlining. 156p. (Orig.). 1996. text 75.00 (*0-85238-200-6*) Blackwell Sci.

Bjorge, Gary, ed. & tr. see Ling, Ding.

Bjorgo, Tore, ed. Terror from the Extreme Right. LC 95-21435. (Cass Series on Political Violence: Vol. 1). 200p. 1995. 49.50 (*0-7146-4663-6*, Pub. by F Cass Pubs); pap. 24.50 (*0-7146-4196-0*, Pub. by F Cass Pubs) Intl Spec Bk.

Bjorgo, Tore, jt. ed. see Kaplan, Jeffrey.

Bjorhovde, Reidar, et al, eds. Connections in Steel Structures: Behaviour, Strength, & Design. 398p. 1988. mass mkt. 116.95 (*1-85166-177-8*) Elsevier.

— Connections in Steel Structures III: Behavior, Strength & Design: Proceedings of the Third International Workshop Held at Hotel Villa Madruzzo, Trento, Italy, 29-31 May 1995. LC 96-4290. 560p. 1996. text. write for info. (*0-08-042821-5*, Pergamon Pr) Elsevier.

Bjork, Christina. Big Bear's Book. Sandin, Joan, tr. LC 94-66897. (Illus.). 80p. (J). 1994. 17.95 (*91-29-62912-8*) FS&G.

— Elliot's Extraordinary Cookbook. Sandin, Joan, tr. (Illus.). 60p. (J). 1991. 11.95 (*91-29-59658-0*, Pub. by R & S Bks) FS&G.

Bjork, Christina. Linna en el Jardin de Monet. 1996. 15.95 (*968-6582-15-0*) Samara Ediciones.

Bjork, Christina. Linnea in Monet's Garden. Sandin, Joan, tr. from SWE. LC 87-45163. (Illus.). 52p. (J). (gr. 4-7). 1987. 13.00 (*91-29-58314-4*, Pub. by R & S Bks) FS&G.

— Linnea's Alamanac. Sandin, Joan, tr. LC 89-83540. (Illus.). 60p. (J). (gr. 2-5). 13.00 (*91-29-59176-7*, Pub. by R & S Bks) FS&G.

— Linnea's Windowsill Garden. LC 87-15016. (Illus.). 60p. (J). 13.00 (*91-29-59064-7*, Pub. by R & S Bks) FS&G.

— The Other Alice: The Story of Alice Liddell & Alice in Wonderland. Sandlin, Joan, tr. from SWE. LC 93-662. (Illus.). 100p. (J). 1993. 18.00 (*91-29-62242-5*, Pub. by R & S Bks) FS&G.

***Bjork, Christina.** Vendela in Venice. Crampton, Patricia, tr. from SWE. LC 98-49243. (Illus.). 96p. (YA). (gr. 4-7). 1999. 18.00 (*91-29-64559-X*, Pub. by R&S Bks SW) FS&G.

***Bjork, Christina & Erikkson, Inga-Karin.** The Other Alice: The Story of Alice Liddell & Alice in Wonderland. (Illus.). 93p. 1999. reprint ed. text 18.00 (*0-7881-6848-7*) DIANE Pub.

Bjork, Christopher, jt. auth. see Rohlen, Thomas P.

Bjork, Claude. Early Pottery in Greece: A Technological & Functional Analysis of the Evidence from the Neolithic Achilleion Thessaly. (Studies in Mediterranean Archaeology: Vol. CXV). (Illus.). 176p. 1995. 78.00 (*91-7081-091-5*, Pub. by P Astroms) Coronet Bks.

Bjork, Daniel W. B. F. Skinner: A Life. 2nd ed. LC 96-40385. (Illus.). 298p. 1997. reprint ed. pap. 19.95 (*1-55798-416-6*, 4316850) Am Psychol.

— The Compromised Scientist: William James in the Development of American Psychology. LC 82-14690. (Illus.). 221p. 1983. text 61.50 (*0-231-05500-5*) Col U Pr.

— William James: The Center of His Vision. LC 97-25815. 338p. 1997. 19.95 (*1-55798-454-9*) Am Psychol.

Bjork, David E. Unfamiliar Paths: The Challenge of Recognizing the Work of Christ in Strange Clothing. (Illus.). 192p. 1997. pap. 12.95 (*0-87808-278-6*, WCL278-6) William Carey Lib.

Bjork, Eva L. Campus Clowns & the Canon: David Lodge's Campus Fiction. (Umea Studies in the Humanities: No. 15). 139p. (Orig.). 1993. pap. 40.00 (*91-7174-831-8*) Coronet Bks.

Bjork, Gordon C. The Way It Worked & Why It Won't: Structural Change & the Slowdown of U. S. Economic Growth. LC 98-53395. 320p. 1999. pap. 27.95 (*0-275-96532-5*, C6531, Praeger Pubs) Greenwood.

— The Way It Worked & Why It Won't: Structural Change & the Slowdown of U. S. Economic Growth. LC 98-53395. 320p. 1999. 69.50 (*0-275-96531-7*, C6531, Praeger Pubs) Greenwood.

Bjork, James E. & Goodman, Allan E. Yugoslavia, 1991-1992: Could Diplomacy Have Prevented a Tragedy? (Pew Case Studies in International Affairs). 50p. (C). 1992. pap. text 3.50 (*1-56927-453-3*) Geo U Inst Dplmcy.

Bjork, Jan-Erik. Analytic D-Modules & Applications. LC 92-44826. (Mathematics & Its Applications Ser.: Vol. 239). 1993. text 353.00 (*0-7923-2114-6*) Kluwer Academic.

Bjork, Kenneth O. Saga in Steel & Concrete: Norwegian Engineers in America. 504p. 1947. 20.00 (*0-87732-028-4*) Norwegian-Am Hist Assn.

— West of the Great Divide: Norwegian Migration to the Pacific Coast, 1847-1893. LC 58-4511. (Publications of the Norwegian-American Historical Association). 678p. reprint ed. pap. 200.00 (*0-608-13280-2*, 205602100044) Bks Demand.

Bjork, Kenneth O., ed. Norwegian-American Studies, Vol. 21. 311p. 1962. 15.00 (*0-87732-043-8*) Norwegian-Am Hist Assn.

— Norwegian-American Studies, Vol. 22. 264p. 1965. 15.00 (*0-87732-045-4*) Norwegian-Am Hist Assn.

— Norwegian-American Studies, Vol. 23. 256p. 1967. 15.00 (*0-87732-048-9*) Norwegian-Am Hist Assn.

— Norwegian-American Studies, Vol. 25. 293p. 1972. 15.00 (*0-87732-052-7*) Norwegian-Am Hist Assn.

— Norwegian-American Studies, Vol. 26. 271p. 1974. 15.00 (*0-87732-054-3*) Norwegian-Am Hist Assn.

— Norwegian-American Studies, Vol. 27. 323p. 1977. 15.00 (*0-87732-058-6*) Norwegian-Am Hist Assn.

— Norwegian-American Studies, Vol. 28. 367p. 1979. 15.00 (*0-87732-063-2*) Norwegian-Am Hist Assn.

Bjork, Kenneth O., jt. auth. see Lovoll, Odd Sverre.

Bjork, L. E., et al. Technical Dictionary: Tietotekniikan Sanasto. (FIN.). 59p. 1984. 29.95 (*0-8288-1367-1*, F24070) Fr & Eur.

Bjork, Lars-Eric & Brolin, Hans. Calculus Explorations with the TI-82 Graphing Calculator. (Illus.). 80p. 1995. pap. text 12.95 (*0-9623629-5-6*) MathWare.

Bjork, Lars G. & Justiz, Manuel J. Higher Education Research & Public Policy. LC 88-1504. (Ace/Oryx Series on Higher Education). 336p. (C). 1988. text 27.95 (*0-02-916300-5*) Oryx Pr.

— Minorities in Higher Education. LC 91-11397. 415p. 1994. reprint ed. pap. text 34.95 (*1-57356-211-4*) Oryx Pr.

Bjork, Lennart & Zadworna-Fjellestad, Danuta, eds. Criticism in the Twilight Zone: Postmodern Perspectives on Literature & Politics. (Stockholm Studies in English: No. LXXVII). 153p. (Orig.). 1990. pap. 42.50 (*91-22-01314-8*) Coronet Bks.

Bjork, Lennart A. Psychological Vision & Social Criticism in the Novels of Thomas Hardy. 178p. (Orig.). 1987. pap. 40.00 (*91-22-00868-3*) Coronet Bks.

Bjork, Lewis. Piloting at Night. LC 98-4236. (Practical Flying Ser.). (Illus.). 250p. 1998. 39.95 (*0-07-006698-1*); pap. 29.95 (*0-07-006697-3*) McGraw.

***Bjork, Lewis.** Piloting Basics Handbook. (Illus.). 650p. 2000. 49.95 (*0-07-136104-9*) McGraw.

Bjork, Lewis. Piloting For Maximum Performance. LC 96-13568. (Illus.). 295p. 1996. pap. 29.95 (*0-07-005699-4*) McGraw.

Bjork, Patrick B. The Novels of Toni Morrison: The Search for Self & Place Within the Community. LC 91-24571. (American Univ. Studies, XXIV, Am. Lit.: Vol. 31). 172p. (C). 1994. pap. text 29.95 (*0-8204-2569-9*) P Lang Pubng.

***Bjork, Patrick B. & Cummins, Richard.** Reading, Writing & the World Wide Web. LC 97-8498. 200p. (C). 1999. pap. text 29.95 (*0-8204-3799-9*) P Lang Pubng.

Bjork, Ragnar, ed. Contemplating Evolution & Doing Politics: Historical Scholars & Students in Sweden & Hungary Facing Historical Change, 1840-1920. (Royal Academy of Letters, Konferenser Ser.: No. 27). 133p. (Orig.). 1993. pap. 45.00 (*91-7402-233-4*) Coronet Bks.

Bjork, Rebecca S. The Strategic Defense Initiative: Symbolic Containment of the Nuclear Threat. LC 91-34487. (SUNY Series in the Making of Foreign Policy). 182p. (C). 1992. pap. text 21.95 (*0-7914-1162-1*) State U NY Pr.

Bjork, Robert A., jt. auth. see Druckman, Daniel.

Bjork, Robert A., ed. see Druckman, Daniel.

Bjork, Robert A., ed. see National Research Council Staff.

Bjork, Robert E. The Old English Verse Saints Lives: A Study in Direct Discourse & the Iconography of Style. 192p. 1985. text 32.50 (*0-8020-2569-2*) U of Toronto Pr.

Bjork, Robert E. & Niles, John D., eds. A Beowulf Handbook. LC 96-41312. (Illus.). xi, 466p. 1997. text 65.00 (*0-8032-1237-2*) U of Nebr Pr.

— A Beowulf Handbook. LC 96-41312. (Illus.). xi, 466p. 1997. pap. text 27.50 (*0-8032-6150-0*) U of Nebr Pr.

Bjork, Robert E., ed. see Berkhout, Carl.

Bjork, Robert E., tr. & afterword by see Fridegard, Jan.

Bjork, Robert E., tr. & afterword by see Lo-Johansson, Ivar.

Bjork, Robert E., tr. & frwd. see Fridegard, Jan.

Bjork, Robert E., tr. & intro. see Fridegard, Jan.

Bjork, Russell, jt. auth. see Townsley, David.

Bjork, Sven, jt. ed. see Scharf, Burkhard W.

Bjork, Tomas. Arbitrage Theory in Continuous Time. LC 99-185339. (Illus.). 328p. 1999. text 45.00 (*0-19-877518-0*) OUP.

Bjorke, Oyvind, ed. Computer-Aided Tolerancing. 2nd ed. 220p. 1989. 44.00 (*0-7918-0010-5*, 800105) ASME Pr.

Bjorkegren, Dag. The Culture Business: Management Strategies for the Arts-Related Business. LC 95-32342. 216p. 1996. pap. 64.95 (*0-415-12234-1*) Thomson Learn.

— The Culture Business: Management Strategies for the Arts-Related Business. LC 95-32342. 216p. 1996. pap. 16.99 (*0-415-12235-X*) Thomson Learn.

Bjorkegren, Hans. Aleksandr Solzhenitsyn: A Biography. Eneberg, Kaa, tr. from SWE. 200p. 1972. 15.95 (*0-89388-050-7*) Okpaku Communications.

Bjorkelo, Anders, jt. auth. see Shouk, Ahmad I.

Bjorken, James D. In Conclusion: A Collection of Summary Talks in High Energy Physics. 1999. 84.00 (*981-02-3869-X*) World Scientific Pub.

Bjorken, James D. & Drell, S. D. Relativistic Quantum Fields. (International Series in Pure & Applied Physics). 396p. (C). 1965. 96.88 (*0-07-005494-0*) McGraw.

— Relativistic Quantum Mechanics. (International Series in Pure & Applied Physics). (C). 1964. text 69.50 (*0-07-005493-2*) McGraw.

Bjorkholm, Magnus, jt. ed. see Holm, Goran.

Bjorkholm, Peter B., ed. Measurement of the Nucleon Structure Functions F2 & R in Deep Inelastic Muon Scattering. (Uppsala Dissertations from the Faculty of Science Ser.: No. 7). (Illus.). 124p. 1995. pap. 37.50 (*91-554-3570-X*) Coronet Bks.

Bjorklund. Children's Thinking. 2nd ed. (Psychology Ser.). 1994. pap. write for info. (*0-534-21001-5*) Brooks-Cole.

— Custer Leaves on 1876. pap. 10.95 (*0-19-875323-3*, J M C & Co) Amereon Ltd.

— Looking at Children. (Psychology Ser.). 1992. pap., student ed. 20.95 (*0-534-13705-9*) Brooks-Cole.

Bjorklund, A., jt. ed. see Dunnett, S. B.

Bjorklund, Anders T., et al, eds. Analysis of Neuronal Microcircuits & Synaptic Interactions, No. 8: Handbook of Chemical Neuroanatomy. 548p. 1990. 308.00 (*0-444-81231-8*) Elsevier.

— Classical Transmitters in the CNS, Pt. I. (Handbook of Chemical Neuroanatomy Ser.: Vol. 2, pt. I). 464p. 1985. 273.00 (*0-444-90330-5*, Excerpta Medica) Elsevier.

Bjorklund, Anders T. & Hokfelt, Tomas B., eds. GABA & Neuropeptides in the CNS: Handbook of Chemical Neuroanatomy, Vol. 4, Pt. 1. 652p. 1985. 364.50 (*0-444-90353-4*) Elsevier.

— Methods in Chemical Neuroanatomy. (Handbook of Chemical Neuroanatomy Ser.: No. 1). xxvi,548p. 1983. 320.00 (*0-444-90281-3*, Excerpta Medica) Elsevier.

Bjorklund, Anders T. & Swanson, Larry W. Integrated Systems of the CNS, Pt.II. Hokfelt, Tomas B., ed. (Handbook of Chemical Neuroanatomy Ser.: Vol. 7). 436p. 1990. 304.50 (*0-444-81232-6*) Elsevier.

Bjorklund, Anders T. & Swanson, Larry W., eds. Integrated Systems of the CNS. (Handbook of Chemical Neuroanatomy Ser.: No. 4). 1986. 342.50 (*0-318-12535-8*, Excerpta Medica) Elsevier.

Bjorklund, Anders T., et al. Classical Transmitters in the CNS, Pt. II. (Handbook of Chemical Transmitters in the CNS, Pt. II. (Handbook of Chemical Neuroanatomy Ser.: Vol. 3, pt. II). xvi,436p. 1984. 254.50 (*0-444-90352-6*) Elsevier.

— Labour Market Policy & Unemployment Insurance. (FIEF Studies in Labor Markets & Economic Policy: No. 2). (Illus.). 216p. 1991. 55.00 (*0-19-828323-7*) OUP.

— Neuropeptide Receptors in the CNS. (Handbook of Chemical Neuroanatomy Ser.: Vol. 11). xviii,406p. 1992. 293.00 (*0-444-89486-1*) Elsevier.

— Ontogeny of Transmitters & Peptides in the CNS. (Handbook of Chemical Neuroanatomy Ser.: Vol. 10). xxii,664p. 1992. 346.00 (*0-444-89283-4*) Elsevier.

Bjorklund, Anders T., jt. ed. see Dunnett, Stephen B.

Bjorklund, Barbara & Bjorklund, David. Parents Book of Discipline. 1999. mass mkt. 5.98 (*0-345-43640-7*) Ballantine Pub Grp.

Bjorklund, Beth, ed. Contemporary Austrian Poetry. LC 84-46116. Orig. Title: Ger.. 328p. 1986. 48.50 (*0-8386-3178-9*) Fairleigh Dickinson.

Bjorklund, Beth & Cory, Mark, eds. Politics in German Literature: Essays in Memory of Frank G. Ryder. LC 97-31383. (Studies in German Literature & Culture). 230p. 1998. 60.00 (*1-57113-082-9*) Camden Hse.

Bjorklund, Beth, tr. & afterword by see Mayrocker, Friederike.

Bjorklund, Beth, tr. & afterword by see Welsh, Renate.

Bjorklund, David, jt. auth. see Bjorklund, Barbara.

Bjorklund, David, jt. auth. see Pellegrini, Anthony D.

Bjorklund, David F. Children's Thinking: Development Function & Individual Differences. 3rd ed. LC 99-34362. (Psychology Ser.). 587p. 1999. pap. text 55.95 (*0-534-35660-5*) Brooks-Cole.

— Children's Thinking: Developmental Function & Individual Differences. LC 88-22241. 357p. (C). 1988. text 44.95 (*0-534-09384-1*) Brooks-Cole.

— Children's Thinking: Developmental Function & Individual Differences. 2nd ed. LC 94-34020. 384p. 1994. pap. 34.25 (*0-534-21000-7*) Brooks-Cole.

***Bjorklund, David F.** False-Memory Creation in Children & Adults: Theory, Research & Implications. LC 99-55909. (C). 1999. write for info. (*0-8058-3169-X*) L Erlbaum Assocs.

Bjorklund, David F., ed. Children's Strategies: Contemporary Views of Child Development. 348p. 1990. text 69.95 (*0-8058-0315-7*) L Erlbaum Assocs.

Bjorklund, Dennis. Drunk Driving Laws: Rules of the Road When Crossing State Lines. LC 98-68103. 96p. (Orig.). 1998. pap. 19.95 (*1-57502-987-1*, PO2692) Morris Pubng.

Bjorklund, Dennis J. Toasting Cheers: An Episode Guide to the 1982-1993 Comedy Series, with Cast Biographies & Character Profiles. LC 96-31359. (Illus.). 419p. 1997. lib. bdg. 60.00 (*0-89950-962-2*) McFarland & Co.

B

***Bjorklund, Diane.** Interpreting the Self: Two Hundred Years of American Autobiography. 264p. 2000. pap. text 14.00 (*0-226-05448-9*) U Ch Pr.
— Vocabularies of Self. LC 98-23914. (Illus.). 258p. 1999. 25.00 (*0-226-05447-0*) U Ch Pr.
Bjorklund, Lorence, jt. auth. see Carroll, John M.
Bjorklund, Paul. What Is Spirituality? 15p. (Orig.). 1983. pap. 1.75 (*0-89486-182-4*, 1451B) Hazelden.
Bjorklund, Paul E. Step Four for Young Adults. 44p. 1981. pap. 3.25 (*0-89486-118-2*, 1129B) Hazelden.
Bjorklund, Raymond C. Dollars & Sense of Command & Control. (Illus.). 289p. (Orig.). (C). 1995. pap. text 45.00 (*0-7881-2062-X*) DIANE Pub.
***Bjorklund, Ruth.** Kansas. 5 vols. , Set. LC 99-16627. (Celebrate the States Ser.). 144p. (J). 2000. 35.64 (*0-7614-0646-8*) Marshall Cavendish.
Bjorklund, Victoria B., et al. New York Nonprofit Law & Practice: With a Tax Analysis. LC 97-71606. 795p. 1997. text 100.00 (*1-55834-494-2*, 62546-10, MICHIE) LEXIS Pub.
Bjorkman, Adaline. While It Was Still Dark: One Person's Pilgrimage Through Grief. rev. ed. 1993. pap. 7.95 (*0-910452-77-6*) Covenant.
***Bjorkman, Bart.** Recreational Nitrox Gas Blending Manual. LC 99-69201. (Illus.). 62p. 2000. pap. 9.95 (*0-941332-85-3*, B1009) Best Pub Co.
Bjorkman, Bruce. Great Barbecue Companion: Mops, Sops, Sauces & Rubs. (Illus.). 112p. (Orig.). 1996. pap. text 12.95 (*0-89594-800-0*) Crossing Pr.
Bjorkman, David A., jt. auth. see Thomas, Victoria.
Bjorkman, E. Scandinavian Loan-Words in Middle English. LC 68-24897. (Studies in Language: No. 41). 1969. reprint ed. lib. bdg. 75.00 (*0-8383-0913-5*) M S G Haskell Hse.
Bjorkman, Edwin. Gates of Life. LC 75-144882. (Literature Ser.). 384p. 1972. reprint ed. 39.00 (*0-403-00868-9*) Scholarly.
— The Soul of a Child. LC 79-144883. (Literature Ser.). 322p. 1972. reprint ed. 39.00 (*0-403-00869-7*) Scholarly.
Bjorkman, Edwin, tr. see Bjornson, Bjornstjerne.
Bjorkman, Edwin A. Voices of Tomorrow: Critical Studies of the New Spirit in Literature. LC 74-98818. 328p. 1970. reprint ed. lib. bdg. 65.00 (*0-8371-2962-1*, BJVT, Greenwood Pr) Greenwood.
Bjorkman, Edwin A., tr. see Christiansen, Sigurd.
Bjorkman, Erik. Scandinavian Loan-Words in Middle English. LC 75-107161. 360p. 1972. reprint ed. 14.00 (*0-403-00450-0*) Scholarly.
Bjorkman, Gwen B. The Descendants of John Meridy Turner (1747-1815) of Fauquier Co. VA. (Illus.). 163p. 1995. pap. text 15.50 (*0-7884-0145-9*) Heritage Bk.
— Pasquotank County, North Carolina: Record of Deed, 1700-1751. 502p. (Orig.). 1990. pap. 35.00 (*1-55613-308-1*) Heritage Bk.
***Bjorkman, Ingmar.** Nature of the International Firm: Nordic Contributions to International Business Research. LC 98-106378. 1999. 48.00 (*87-16-13359-5*) Mksgaard.
Bjorkman, James W. & Altenstetter, Christa, eds. Health Policy. LC 97-44515. (International Library of Comparative Public Policy: No. 7). 800p. 1998. 290.00 (*1-85898-587-0*) E Elgar.
Bjorkman, James W., jt. ed. see Altenstetter, Christa.
Bjorkman, James W., jt. ed. see Freddi, Giorgio.
***Bjorkman, Steve.** The Flyaway Kite. (Illus.). 40p. (J). (ps-2). 2000. 9.95 (*1-57856-264-3*) Waterbrook Pr.
— Good Night, Little One. (Illus.). 40p. (J). 1999. 9.95 (*1-57856-275-9*) Waterbrook Pr.
Bjorkman, Steve. One Minute Bible Devotions for Kids. (J). 1998. 16.99 (*0-8054-9297-6*) Broadman.
Bjorkman, Steve, jt. auth. see Gross, Ruth Belov.
Bjorkman, Steven, jt. auth. see Levine, Ellen.
Bjorkman, Steven, jt. auth. see Marzollo, Jean.
Bjorkman, Stig, et al. Bergman on Bergman: Interviews with Ingmar Bergman. Austin, Paul B., tr. from SWE. (Illus.). 288p. 1993. reprint ed. pap. 13.95 (*0-306-80520-0*) Da Capo.
Bjorkman, Stig, ed. see Allen, Woody.
Bjorkquist Ng, Anne, jt. compiled by see Renkiewicz, Frank.
Bjorkqvist, Kaj & Niemela, Pirkko, eds. Of Mice & Women: Aspects of Female Aggression. (Illus.). 414p. 1992. text 55.00 (*0-12-102590-X*) Acad Pr.
Bjorkqvist, Kaj, jt. ed. see Fry, Douglas P.
Bjorksten, Bengt, jt. auth. see Blumenthal, Malcolm N.
Bjorksten, Johan A. Learn to Write Chinese Characters. LC 93-41542. 123p. 1994. pap. 16.95 (*0-300-05771-7*) Yale U Pr.
Bjorksten, Oliver J. W., ed. New Clinical Concepts in Marital Therapy. LC 85-11201. (Clinical Insights Ser.). 177p. reprint ed. pap. 54.90 (*0-8357-7828-2*, 203620100002) Bks Demand.
Bjorland, Dennis. Drunk Driving Defense: How to Beat the Rap. LC 98-68104. 106p. 1998. pap. 19.95 (*1-57502-986-3*, PO2690) Morris Pubng.
Bjorling, Anna L. & Farkas, Andrew. Jussi. (Opera Biography Ser.: No. 7). (Illus.). 520p. 1996. 39.95 (*1-57467-010-7*, Amadeus Pr) Timber.
Bjorling, Joel. Channeling: A Bibliographic Exploration. LC 91-13554. (Sects & Cults in America Ser.: Vol. 15). 380p. 1992. text 25.00 (*0-8240-5691-4*, 589) Garland.
— Consulting Spirits: A Bibliography, 46. LC 97-53107. (Bibliographies & Indexes in Religious Studies: Vol. 46). 224p. 1998. lib. bdg. 65.00 (*0-313-30284-7*, Greenwood Pr) Greenwood.
— Reincarnation: An Annotated Bibliography. LC 95-19357. (Sects & Cults in America Ser.: Vol. 18). 194p. 1995. text 39.00 (*0-8153-1129-X*, SS874) Garland.
Bjorling, Stefan, jt. auth. see Whitaker, Lawrence.
Bjorlykke, K. O. Sedimentology & Petroleum Geology. (Illus.). 310p. 1989. 70.95 (*0-387-17691-8*) Spr-Verlag.
Bjorn, A., jt. auth. see Ashworth, P.
Bjorn Magnusson Staaf. An Essay on Copper Flat Axes. (Acta Archaeologica Lundensia, Series Prima in 4). (Illus.). 211p. (Orig.). 1996. pap. 44.50 (*91-22-01731-3*) Coronet Bks.
Bjorn, Thyra F. Mama's Way. 220p. 1986. reprint ed. lib. bdg. 35.95 (*0-89966-569-1*) Buccaneer Bks.
— Papa's Daughter. 180p. 1992. reprint ed. 29.95 (*0-89966-882-8*) Buccaneer Bks.
— Papa's Wife. 180p. 1992. reprint ed. lib. bdg. 33.95 (*0-89966-883-6*) Buccaneer Bks.
Bjornager, Kjeld, et al, eds. The Slavic World & Scandinavia: Cultural Relations. 191p. (C). 1987. pap. 23.00 (*87-7288-173-9*, Pub. by Aarhus Univ Pr) David Brown.
Bjornberg, S. O. Inspection Methods That Give a New Conception of Gear Accuracy. (Technical Papers: Vol. P115). (Illus.). 18p. 1935. pap. text 30.00 (*1-55589-327-9*) AGMA.
Bjornberg, Ulla, ed. European Parents in the Nineteen Nineties: Contradictions & Comparisons. 325p. (C). 1991. 39.95 (*0-88738-426-9*) Transaction Pubs.
Bjornberg, Ulla, et al, eds. Families with Small Children in Eastern & Western Europe. LC 97-73379. 192p. 1997. text 64.95 (*1-85972-481-7*, Pub. by Ashgate Pub) Ashgate Pub Co.
Bjornberg, Ulla & Kollind, Anna-Karin, eds. Men's Family Relations: Report from an International Seminar. (Goteborg University Department of Sociology Research Reports: Vol. 60). 192p. (Orig.). 1996. pap. 47.50 (*91-972940-0-4*) Coronet Bks.
Bjorndal, Jane A. & Ison, Linda K. Mastering Market Data: An Approach to Analyzing & Applying Salary Survey Information. (Building Blocks Ser.: Vol. 2). (Illus.). 24p. (Orig.). 1991. pap. 24.95 (*1-57963-005-7*, A0002) Am Compensation.
Bjorndal, Karen A., ed. Biology & Conservation of Sea Turtles. rev. ed. LC 95-18872. 616p. 1995. pap. text 34.95 (*1-56098-619-0*) Smithsonian.
Bjorneberg, Paul. Music U. S. A., 1989. rev. ed. 28p. 1989. pap. 40.00 (*0-918196-15-9*) American Music.
— Music U. S. A., 1991. rev. ed. 32p. 1991. pap. write for info. (*0-918196-18-3*) American Music.
Bjorneberg, Paul, ed. Music U. S. A., 1988. rev. ed. 28p. 1988. pap. 40.00 (*0-918196-13-2*) American Music.
Bjorneberg, Paul & Stearns, Betty. Music U. S. A., 1987. rev. ed. (Illus.). 24p. 1987. pap. text 35.00 (*0-918196-12-4*) American Music.
— Music U. S. A., 1986. rev. ed. (Illus.). 20p. 1986. pap. text 35.00 (*0-918196-11-6*) American Music.
Bjorneberg, Paul & Stearns, Betty, eds. Music U. S. A., 1985. (Illus.). 1985. pap. text 35.00 (*0-918196-10-8*) American Music.
Bjorneboe, Jens. The Bird Lovers. Wasser, Frederick, tr. from NOR. (Sun & Moon Classics Ser.: No. 43). 160p. (Orig.). 1994. pap. 9.95 (*1-55713-146-5*) Sun & Moon CA.
— Moment of Freedom: The Heiligenberg Manuscript. LC 98-32050. 220p. 2000. pap. 15.95 (*0-8023-1328-0*) Dufour.
***Bjorneboe, Jens.** Powderhouse: Scientific Postscript & Last Protocol. Murer, Esther G., tr. from NOR. LC 99-39925. (History of Bestiality Ser.: No. 2). 180p. 2000. pap. 15.95 (*0-8023-1331-0*) Dufour.
Bjorneboe, Jens. Semmelweis. Martin, Joe, tr. from NOR. & intro. by. (Classics Ser.: No. 129). 120p. (Orig.). 1998. pap. 10.95 (*1-55713-350-6*) Sun & Moon CA.
— The Sharks: The History of a Crew & a Shipwreck. Murer, Esther G., tr. from NOR. 241p. 1993. pap. 24.00 (*1-870041-20-8*, Pub. by Norvik Pr) Dufour.
***Bjorneboe, Jens.** The Silence. Murer, Esther Greenleaf, tr. from NOR. (History of Bestiality Ser.: No. 3). 200p. 2000. pap. 15.95 (*0-8023-1333-7*) Dufour.
***Bjorner, Anders, et al.** Oriented Matroids. (Encyclopedia of Mathematics & Its Applications Ser.: No. 46). (Illus.). 550p. (C). 2000. pap. 49.95 (*0-521-77750-X*) Cambridge U Pr.
Bjorner, B. & Oest, O. N., eds. Towards a Formal Description of Ada. (Lecture Notes in Computer Science Ser.: Vol. 98). 630p. 1980. 39.00 (*0-387-10283-3*) Spr-Verlag.
Bjorner, D., et al, eds. Partial Evaluation & Mixed Computation: Proceedings of the IFIP TC2 Workshop, Gammel Avernaes, Denmark, 18-24 Oct., 1987. 1988. 207.50 (*0-444-70491-4*, North Holland) Elsevier.
— Perspectives of System Informatics Vol. XVII: Proceedings, 2nd International Andrei Ershov Memorial Conference, Akademgorodok, Novosibirsk, Russia, June 25-28, 1966, Vol. 1181. LC 96-50358. (Lecture Notes in Computer Science Ser.). 447p. 1996. pap. 75.00 (*3-540-62064-8*) Spr-Verlag.
— VDM, '87: VDM - A Formal Method at Work. (Lecture Notes in Computer Science Ser.: Vol. 252). x, 422p. 1987. 45.00 (*0-387-17654-3*) Spr-Verlag.
— VDM '90 VDM & Z - Formal Methods in Software Development: Third International Symposium of VDM Europe Kiel, FRG, April 17-21, 1990 Proceedings. (Lecture Notes in Computer Science Ser.: Vol. 428). xviii, 580p. 1990. 57.90 (*0-387-52513-0*) Spr-Verlag.
Bjorner, D., jt. ed. see Barzdins, J.
Bjorner, Susanne, ed. see Berinstein, Paula.
Bjorngard, Bengt E., jt. ed. see Kase, Kenneth R.
Bjornlund, Eric, jt. ed. see Garber, Larry.
***Bjornlund, Lydia.** The Constitution & Founding of the United States. LC 99-39423. (World History Ser.). (Illus.). 128p. (YA). (gr. 6-9). 2000. lib. bdg. 23.70 (*1-56006-586-9*) Lucent Bks.
— The Iroquois. LC 99-50908. (Indigenous Peoples of North America Ser.). 2000. write for info. (*1-56006-618-0*) Lucent Bks.
Bjornlund, Lydia. Media Relations for Local Governments: Communicating for Results. LC 97-138025. 106p. (Orig.). 1996. pap. text 60.00 (*0-87326-117-8*, 42093) Intl City-Cnty Mgt.
Bjornlund, Lydia D. The U. S. Constitution: Blueprint for Democracy. LC 98-29605. (Words That Changed History Ser.). (Illus.). 128p. (YA). (gr. 4-12). 1998. lib. bdg. 23.70 (*1-56006-486-2*) Lucent Bks.
Bjornlund, Lydia D. & International City/County Management Association Staff. Selling Recyclables: Local Governments as Entrepreneurs. LC 98-144546. (Special Data Issue Ser.). 97 p. 1997. write for info. (*0-87326-876-8*) Intl City-Cnty Mgt.
Bjorno, L., ed. Underwater Acoustics & Signal Processing. 1981. text 234.00 (*90-277-1255-7*) Kluwer Academic.
Bjornsen, Peter K. & Rie-mann, Bo, eds. Microbial Ecology of Pelagic Environments: Proceedings of the Fifth International Workshop on the Measurement of Microbial Activities in the Carbon Cycle in Aquatic Environments. (Advances in Limnology Ser.: Vol. 37). (GER., Illus.). vi, 278p. 1992. pap. text 99.00 (*3-510-47038-9*, Pub. by E Schweizerbartsche) Balogh.
Bjornson, Bjornstjerne. Bridal March & Other Stories. Anderson, Rasmos B., tr. LC 74-98562. (Short Story Index Reprint Ser.). 1977. 19.95 (*0-8369-3136-X*) Ayer.
— Captain Mansana & Other Stories. Anderson, Rasmos B., tr. LC 79-103494. (Short Story Index Reprint Ser.). 1977. 20.95 (*0-8369-3236-6*) Ayer.
— Synnove Solbakken. Sutter, Julie, tr. LC 79-38341. (Select Bibliographies Reprint Ser.). 1977. 18.95 (*0-8369-6758-5*) Ayer.
— Three Plays: The Gauntlet, Beyond Our Power, The New System. Bjorkman, Edwin, tr. from NOR. LC 87-38139. vi, 280p. 1989. reprint ed. lib. bdg. 35.00 (*0-86527-383-9*) Fertig.
Bjornson, Helen, jt. auth. see Kavanaugh, Donna.
***Bjornson, Howard.** Weeds. LC 99-40234. (Illus.). 72p. 2000. pap. 19.95 (*0-8118-2721-6*) Chronicle Bks.
Bjornson, Karin S., jt. auth. see Jonassohn, Kurt.
Bjornson, Richard. The Picaresque Hero in European Fiction. LC 76-11312. (Illus.). 319p. 1977. reprint ed. pap. 98.90 (*0-608-07465-9*, 206769200009) Bks Demand.
Bjornson, Richard, ed. Approaches to Teaching Cervantes' Don Quixote. LC 83-23797. (Approaches to Teaching World Literature Ser.: No. 3). x, 188p. 1984. pap. 18.00 (*0-87352-480-2*, AP03P); lib. bdg. 37.50 (*0-87352-479-9*, AP03C) Modern Lang.
Bjornson, Richard, jt. ed. see Mowoe, Isaac J.
Bjornson, Richard, tr. see Beti, Mongo.
Bjornson, Richard, tr. see Hazoume, Paul.
Bjornson, Richard, tr. see Oyono, Ferdinand.
Bjornson, Richard, tr. see Philombe, Rene.
Bjornsson, Johannes, ed. Slow Infections of the Central Nervous System: The Legacy of Dr. Bjorn Sigurdsson. LC 94-12040. (Annals Ser.: Vol. 724). 1994. write for info. (*0-89766-843-X*); pap. 135.00 (*0-89766-844-8*) NY Acad Sci.
Bjornstad, A. M. Morgan. 320p. mass mkt. 5.99 (*1-896329-10-1*) Picasso Publ.
Bjornstad, David J. & Kahn, James R., eds. The Contingent Valuation of Environmental Resources: Methodological Issues & Research Needs. LC 95-39639. (New Horizons in Environmental Economics Ser.). 320p. 1996. 100.00 (*1-85898-321-5*) E Elgar.
Bjornstad, Eric. Desert Rock Vol. 1: Rock Climbs in the National Parks. LC 96-165053. (Desert Rock Ser.: Vol. 1). (Illus.). 256p. (Orig.). 1996. pap. 20.00 (*0-934641-92-7*) Falcon Pub Inc.
Bjornstad, Eric. Desert Rock: Wall Street & the San Rafael Swell Vol. 3: Rock Climbs West of the Colorado River. (Illus.). 180p. (Orig.). 1997. pap. 25.00 (*1-57540-004-9*) Falcon Pub Inc.
— Rock Climbing Desert Rock III: Moab. LC 99-13538. (Illus.). 369p. 1998. pap. 25.00 (*1-56044-754-0*) Falcon Pub Inc.
Bjornstad, Harvey. Mandatory Motorcycle Helmets? 112p. (Orig.). 1996. pap. 7.95 (*1-888824-03-4*) Bridgeport Bks.
Bjornstad, James. Hare Krishna & TM. LC 97-50218. (Zondervan Guide to Cults & Religious Movements Ser.). 64p. 1998. pap. 5.99 (*0-310-70391-3*) Zondervan.
***Bjornstad, Ketil.** Story of Edvard Munch. 2001. pap. 17.95 (*1-900850-44-3*) Arcadia Bks.
Bjornsti, Mary-Ann & Osheroff, Neil. DNA Topoisomerase Protocols Vol. 1: DNA Topology & Enzymes. LC 99-13390. (Methods in Molecular Biology Ser.: Vol. 94). (Illus.). 344p. 1999. 79.50 (*0-89603-444-5*) Humana.
— DNA Topoisomerase Protocols Vol. II: Enzymology & Drugs. (Methods in Molecular Biology Ser.: Vol. 95). 328p. 2000. 79.50 (*0-89603-512-3*) Humana.
Bjornvig, Thorkild. The Pact: My Friendship with Isak Dinesen. Schousboe, Ingvar & Smith, William J., trs. from DAN. LC 83-9335. 183p. 1983. pap. 56.80 (*0-7837-8513-5*, 204932200011) Bks Demand.
— The World Tree: Selected Poems. Rossel, Sven Hakon, ed. Hostrup-Jessen, Paula, tr. from DAN. 66p. (Orig.). (C). 1993. pap. 6.95 (*1-880755-07-6*) Mermaid Pr.
Bjoroy, Malvin, ed. see International Meeting on Organic Geochemistry Staf.
Bjorseth, A. Handbook of Polycyclic Aromatic Hydrocarbons: Emission Sources & Recent Progress in Analytical Chemistry, Vol. 1. 744p. 1983. 275.00 (*0-8247-1845-3*) Dekker.
Bjorseth, Alf & Angeletti, G., eds. Analysis of Organic Micropollutants in Water. 1982. text 171.00 (*90-277-1398-7*) Kluwer Academic.
Bjorseth, Alf & Becher, G. PAH in Work Atmospheres: Occurrence & Determination. LC 85-30731. 184p. 1986. 106.00 (*0-8493-6064-1*, CRC Reprint) Franklin.
Bjorseth, Alf & Dennis, Anthony J., eds. Polynuclear Aromatic Hydrocarbons: Chemistry & Biological Effects. LC 80-17877. (Fourth International Symposium on Polynuclear Aromatic Hydrocarbons Ser.). (Illus.). 1097p. 1980. 65.00 (*0-935470-05-0*) Battelle.
Bjorseth, Alf & Ramdahl. Handbook of Polycyclic Aromatic Hydrocarbons: Emission Sources & Recent Progress in Analytical Chemistry, Vol. 2. (Illus.). 432p. 1985. text 235.00 (*0-8247-7442-6*) Dekker.
Bjorseth, Alf, jt. ed. see Angeletti, G.
Bjorseth, Lillian D. Breakthrough Networking: Building Relationships that Last. LC 95-92656. (Illus.). 256p. (Orig.). 1996. pap. 19.95 (*0-9648839-0-2*) Duoforce Ent.
***Bjorstad, P. & Luskin, M., eds.** Prallel Solution of Partial Differential Equation. (IMA Volumes in Mathematics & Its Applications Ser.: Vol. 120). (Illus.). 316p. 2000. 79.95 (*0-387-95008-7*) Spr-Verlag.
Bjouchon-Meunier, B., et al, eds. IPMU, Advanced Methods in Artificial Intelligence, 1992: Proceedings, Fourth International Conference on Information Processing & Management of Uncertainty in Knowledge-Based Systems, Palma de Mallorca, Spain, July 6-10, 1992. LC 93-29038. (Lecture Notes in Computer Science Ser.: Vol. 682). ix, 367p. 1993. 55.95 (*0-387-56735-6*) Spr-Verlag.
Bjrner, Dines, et al, eds. Formal Methods in Programming & Their Applications: International Conference, Academgorodok, Russia, June - July 1993 Proceedings. LC 93-21317. (Lecture Notes in Computer Science Ser.: Vol. 735). 1993. 61.95 (*0-387-57316-X*) Spr-Verlag.
Bjrseth, A. & Angeletti, G., eds. Organic Micropollutants in the Aquatic Environment. 1986. text 237.50 (*90-277-2242-0*) Kluwer Academic.
Bjurstrom, Per. Nicola Pio As a Collector of Drawings. (Illus.). 291p. 1995. 67.50 (*91-7042-151-X*, Pub. by P Astroms) Coronet Bks.
Bjurstrom, Per, ed. The Art of Drawing in France. (Illus.). 224p. 1987. 50.00 (*0-85667-328-5*, Pub. by P Wilson) Scala Books.
— The Genesis of the Art Museum in the 18th Century. (Illus.). 130p. 1993. 52.50 (*91-7100-447-5*) Coronet Bks.
Bjurstrom, Per, et al. Durer to Delacroix: Great Master Drawings from Stockholm. LC 85-80676. (Illus.). 197p. (Orig.). 1985. pap. 24.95 (*0-912804-21-1*) Kimbell Art.
Bkaily, G. Ion Channels in Vascular Smooth Muscle. LC 94-43011. (Molecular Biology Intelligence Unit Ser.). 119p. 1994. 99.00 (*1-57059-137-7*, LN9137) Landes Bioscience.
Bkaily, Ghassan, ed. Membrane Physiopathology. (Developments in Cardiovascular Medicine Ser.). 432p. (C). 1994. text 198.00 (*0-7923-3062-5*) Kluwer Academic.
BKSTS Staff. BKSTS Dictionary of Image Technology. 3rd rev. ed. LC 94-2192. 168p. 1994. pap. 39.95 (*0-240-51364-9*, Focal) Buttrwrth-Heinemann.
***Blaas-Pratscher, Katharina.** Public Art in Lower Austria, Vol. 5 5. (Illus.). 240p. 2000. 45.00 (*3-211-83416-8*) Spr-Verlag.
Blaas, Wolfgang. A New Perspective for European Spatial Development Policies. LC 97-76941. (Illus.). 172p. 1998. text 59.95 (*1-84014-342-8*, Pub. by Ashgate Pub) Ashgate Pub Co.
Blaas, Wolfgang & Foster, John, eds. Mixed Economies in Europe: An Evolutionary Perspective on Their Emergence, Transition & Regulation. (European Association for Evolutionary Political Economy Ser.). 320p. 1993. 95.00 (*1-85278-728-7*) E Elgar.
Blaauw, Adriaan. History of the IAU: The Birth & First Half-Century of the International Astronomical Union. 300p. 1994. pap. text 63.50 (*0-7923-2980-5*); lib. bdg. 106.00 (*0-7923-2979-1*) Kluwer Academic.
Blaauw, Gerrit A. & Brooks, Frederick P., Jr. Computer Architecture: A Computer Zoo, Vol. II. (Computer Science Ser.). (Illus.). 512p. (C). 1996. text. write for info. (*0-201-10558-6*) Addison-Wesley.
— Computer Architecture Vol. 1: Design Decisions. LC 89-6697. (Computer Science Ser.). (Illus.). 1264p. (C). 1997. 69.95 (*0-201-10557-8*) Addison-Wesley.
Blaazer, David. The Popular Front & the Progressive Tradition: Socialists, Liberals & the Quest for Unity, 1884-1939. 263p. (C). 1992. text 59.95 (*0-521-41383-4*) Cambridge U Pr.
Blaber, Gina, ed. see Bracewell, Mark & Karp, David.
Blaber, S. J. & Copland, J. W. Tuna Baitfish in the Indo-Pacific Region. 211p. 1990. pap. 156.00 (*1-86320-011-8*, Pub. by ACIAR) St Mut.
Blaber, S. J. M., et al. Tuna Baitfish in Fiji & Solomon Islands. 136p. 1994. pap. 93.00 (*1-86320-110-6*, Pub. by ACIAR) St Mut.
Blach, Reg. Celebrations of Nature: Photographs. 108p. 1991. 24.95 (*0-86492-107-1*, Pub. by Goose Ln Edits) Genl Dist Srvs.
Blache, J., et al. Cles de Determination des Poissons de Mer Signales dans l'Atlantique Oriental Entre le 20eme Parallele Nord et le 15eme Parallele Sud (Keys for the Determination of Sea Fish Reported in the Eastern Atlantic Between 20 Degrees North & 15 Degrees South) (Faune Tropicale Ser.: Vol. XVIII).Tr. of Keys for the Determination of Sea Fish Reported in the Eastern Atlantic Between 20 Degrees North & 15 Degrees South. (FRE., Illus.). 480p. 1970. pap. 24.00 (*2-7099-0139-0*, Pub. by LInstitut Francais) Balogh.
Blache, J., jt. auth. see Cadenat, J.
Blache, K. Success Factors for Implementing Change. 393p. 1988. 9.95 (*0-87263-318-7*) SME.
Blache, Monica & Goodridge, Walt F., eds. Come into Our Whirl: The Unique Story of the Creation of the Poets Niche & a Collection of Member's Poetry. (Illus.). 200p. 1999. pap. 14.95 (*0-9629202-6-6*) Co Called W.
Blache, Roberta, tr. see Slide, Anthony, ed.
Blache, Simone, tr. see Slide, Anthony, ed.

An Asterisk (*) at the beginning of an entry indicates that the title is appearing for the first time.

Blacher, Jan B., ed. When There's No Place Like Home: Options for Children Living Apart from Their Natural Families. LC 93-49692. 384p. 1994. 29.95 (*1-55766-145-6*) P H Brookes.

***Blacher, Richard M., et al.** A Primer on Death & Dying for Medical Students. rev. ed. 60p. 2000. reprint ed. 8.95 (*0-930194-91-8*) Ctr Thanatology.

Blachere, J. R. & Pettit, F. S. High Temperature Corrosion of Ceramics. LC 88-38242. (Illus.). 188p. 1989. 58.00 (*0-8155-1188-4*) Noyes.

Blachere, Regis & Chouemi, Moustafa. Dictionnaire Arabe-Francais-Anglais, 1, 4 vols., Set.Tr. of Arabic - French - Arabic Dictionary. (ARA, ENG & FRE.). 1967. 750.00 (*0-8288-6674-0*, M6034) Fr & Eur.

Blachford, G., jt. auth. see Divine, J. A.

***Blachley, Annie.** Good Medicine: Four Las Vegas Doctors & the Golden Age of Medicine. Sohn, Anton P., ed. LC 99-88657. (Illus.). 224p. 1999. 35.00 (*0-9649759-7-1*, Pub. by Greasewood) U of Nev Pr.

Blachly, Frederick F. & Oatman, Miriam E. Government & Administration of Germany. (Brookings Institution Reprint Ser.). reprint ed. lib. bdg. 39.50 (*0-697-00152-0*) Irvington.

Blachman, Benita, ed. Foundations of Reading Acquisition & Dyslexia: Implications for Early Intervention. LC 96-53068. 480p. 1997. 99.95 (*0-8058-2362-X*); pap. 49.95 (*0-8058-2363-8*) L Erlbaum Assocs.

***Blachman, Benita A.** Road to the Code: A Phonological Awareness Program for Young Children. 2000. pap. text 49.95 (*1-55766-438-2*) P H Brookes.

Blachman, Morris J. & Hellman, Ronald G., eds. Terms of Conflict: Ideology in Latin American Politics. LC 76-54814. (Inter-American Politics Ser.: Vol. 1). 288p. reprint ed. pap. 89.30 (*0-608-15017-7*, 202570900046) Bks Demand.

Blachman, Morris M., ed. see Reyna, Jose L., et al.

Blachman, Nancy. Mathematica: A Practical Approach. 384p. 1992. pap. text 38.20 (*0-13-563826-7*) P-H.

Blachman, Nancy & Williams, Colin. Mathematica: A Practical Approach. 2nd ed. LC 98-44766. 640p. (C). 1998. pap. 58.00 (*0-13-259201-0*) P-H.

Blachman, Nancy, et al. CalcLabs with Mathematica. LC 95-34374. (Brooks - Cole Symbolic Computation Ser.). 1995. mass mkt. 30.95 (*0-534-34086-5*) Brooks-Cole.

Blachman, Nancy, jt. auth. see Capulet, Nancy.

Blachman, Nancy R. & Mossinghoff, Michael J. Maple V Quick Reference. LC 94-10459. 1994. mass mkt. 26.50 (*0-534-20478-3*) Brooks-Cole.

Blachman, Nelson M. Noise & Its Effect on Communication. 2nd ed. LC 81-8140. 274p. (C). 1982. lib. bdg. 31.50 (*0-89874-256-0*) Krieger.

Blachowicz, Camille & Fisher, Peter. Teaching Vocabulary. 229p. 1995. pap. text 34.00 (*0-02-310172-5*, Macmillan Coll) P-H.

Blachowicz, James. Of Two Minds: The Nature of Inquiry. LC 97-13473. (SUNY Series in Philosophy). 448p. (C). 1998. text 73.50 (*0-7914-3641-1*); pap. text 24.95 (*0-7914-3642-X*) State U NY Pr.

Black. Biological Performance of Materials. 3rd ed. LC 99-35165. (Illus.). 480p. 1999. text 150.00 (*0-8247-7106-0*) Dekker.

— Blacks Medical Dictionary. 38th ed. 1996. 130.75 (*0-389-21014-5*) B&N Imports.

Black. British Foreign Policy in the Age of Walpole. 216p. 1993. 61.95 (*0-7512-0193-6*) Ashgate Pub Co.

Black. Business Statistics: Contemporary Decision Making. 2nd ed. 1996. pap. text 43.50 (*0-314-20644-2*) West Pub.

— Business Statistics: Contemporary Decision Making. 2nd ed. 1997. text 18.25 (*0-314-20999-9*) West Pub.

— Business Statistics: Contemporary Decision Making. 3rd ed. 2000. pap. 91.95 (*0-324-00920-8*) Sth-Wstrn College.

— Business Statistics: Contempory Decision. (ME - Statistics Ser.). 1994. pap. write for info. (*0-314-03318-1*) West Pub.

— Cost Engineering Management Techniques. (Cost Engineering Ser.: Vol. 4). (Illus.). 272p. 1984. text 125.00 (*0-8247-7088-9*) Dekker.

— Culture & Society In Britain, 1660-1800. LC 96-26248. (Illus.). 224p. 1997. text 69.95 (*0-7190-4947-4*, Pub. by Manchester Univ Pr) St Martin.

Black. Economic Thought & the Irish Question. 1993. 76.95 (*0-7512-0124-3*) Ashgate Pub Co.

— Excel Manual-Business Statistics: Contemporary Decision. 2nd ed. 1997. pap. 12.00 (*0-314-22351-7*) Thomson Learn.

Black. Good Neighbor. 1988. 11.95 (*0-07-541782-0*) McGraw.

— Heat Transfer. (C). 2001. text. write for info. (*0-06-040733-6*) Addson-Wesley Educ.

— Heat Transfer: With Solutions Manual. (C). 1994. pap. text. write for info. (*0-06-500758-1*) Addison-Wesley.

Black. History of Jamaica. 1989. pap. text. write for info. (*0-582-03898-7*, Pub. by Addison-Wesley) Longman.

Black. Introduction to Media Communication. 6th ed. 2000. 37.00 (*0-07-231467-2*) McGraw.

— Mathematics. 2nd ed. 1980. pap. text 38.95 (*0-471-27660-X*) Wiley.

— Medical-Surgical Nursing, 2 vols. 5th ed. 1997. text 82.00 (*0-7216-7484-4*) Harcourt.

— A Military Revolution? Military Change & European Society, 1550-1800. Overy, Richard et al, eds. (Studies in European History Ser.). 1996. text 11.95 (*0-333-51906-X*, Pub. by Macmillan) St Martin.

— New Vegetables on Your Barbecue. 1995. pap. 6.95 (*0-572-01623-9*, Pub. by Foulsham UK) Assoc Pubs Grp.

— Rugby & South African Nation: Sport, Culture, Politics & Power in the Old & New Africa. LC 98-20906. 200p. 1998. text 79.95 (*0-7190-4931-8*, Pub. by Manchester Univ Pr) St Martin.

— Rugby & South African Nation: Sport, Culture, Politics & Power in the Old & New South Africa. LC 98-20906. 200p. 1998. pap. text 29.95 (*0-7190-4932-6*, Pub. by Manchester Univ Pr) St Martin.

***Black.** Supplement: Video Tapes - Internet Architecture & Protocols - The Complete Video Course 1/e: VIDEO TAPES. 2000. VHS 81.99 (*0-13-030410-7*) Pearson Custom.

Black. A System of Ambition? 1991. pap. text. write for info. (*0-582-00475-6*, Pub. by Addison-Wesley) Longman.

— Verbal & Analytical Review for the GRE, Workbook. 203p. 1982. pap. 8.95 (*0-15-600025-3*) Harcourt.

Black, ed. Management: Meeting New Challenges. LC 99-26073. 648p. (C). 1999. 96.00 (*0-321-01407-3*, Prentice Hall) P-H.

***Black & Dinger.** Life Insurance. 13th ed. LC 99-22004. (Illus.). 1072p. 1999. 84.00 (*0-13-891250-5*) P-H.

Black & Hartley, James G. Thermodynamics: English SI Version. 3rd ed. LC 95-24455. (C). 1997. pap. text, teacher ed. 10.67 (*0-673-97060-4*) Addson-Wesley Educ.

Black, jt. auth. see Campbell, Henry.

Black, jt. auth. see Gilmore.

Black, jt. auth. see Gilson.

Black, jt. auth. see Schweitzer.

Black & Decker Incorporated Staff. The Complete Guide to Painting & Decorating. LC 99-23622. 288p. 1999. pap. 19.95 (*0-86573-632-4*) Creat Pub Intl.

Black & Decker Incorporated Staff, jt. auth. see Cy DeCosse Incorporated Staff.

Black & Decker Manufacturing Company Staff, jt. auth. see Creative Publishing International, Inc. Staff.

Black & Decker Staff. Kitchen & Bathroom Ideas. LC 94-7891. (Black & Decker Home Improvement Library). 192p. 1994. 16.95 (*0-86573-738-X*) Creat Pub Intl.

— Popular Mechanics: Houseworks :Guide to Understanding Your Home. LC 98-36739. (Illus.). 160p. 1998. pap. text 19.95 (*0-86573-772-X*) Creat Pub Intl.

Black & Decker Staff, jt. auth. see Cowles Creative Publishing, Inc. Staff.

Black & Decker Staff, jt. auth. see Creative Publishing International, Inc. Staff.

Black, A. N., jt. auth. see Coles, K. Adlard.

Black, Al. Coaching Run-&-Shoot Football. LC 90-24857. (Illus.). 112p. 1991. pap. text 14.00 (*0-9624779-2-3*) Harding Pr.

***Black, Al.** Pro-Style Multiple Defense for High School Football. LC 99-53443. (Illus.). 128p. 2000. pap. 15.00 (*1-890450-05-7*) Harding Pr.

Black, Alan. Urban Mass Transportation Planning. LC 94-33904. 448p. (C). 1995. 95.94 (*0-07-005557-2*) McGraw.

Black, Alexander. American Husbands & Other Alternatives. LC 68-57305. (Essay Index Reprint Ser.). 1977. 18.95 (*0-8369-1021-4*) Ayer.

***Black, Alexander & Murata, Noboru.** The Japanese House. (Illus.). 224p. 2000. 39.95 (*962-593-848-6*) Tuttle Pubng.

Black, Alexander J., ed. Complications of Coronary Angioplasty. (Fundamental & Clinical Cardiology Ser.: Vol. 3). (Illus.). 280p. 1991. text 135.00 (*0-8247-8440-5*) Dekker.

***Black, Alexandra & Murata, Noboru.** The Japanese House: Architecture & Interiors. (Illus.). 2000. 39.95 (*0-8048-3262-5*, Periplus Eds) Tuttle Pubng.

Black, Alfred B. & Smith, Robert M. Shakespeare Allusions & Parallels. LC 78-113559. reprint ed. 32.50 (*0-404-00893-3*) AMS Pr.

Black, Algernon D. The People & the Police. LC 75-40991. 246p. 1976. reprint ed. lib. bdg. 59.50 (*0-8371-8699-4*, BLPP, Greenwood Pr) Greenwood.

Black, Alice. The Joy of Collecting: Butter Pats & Miniature Plates. LC 92-90130. (Illus.). 100p. (gr. 8 up). 1991. 59.95 (*0-9632075-0-4*) A Black.

Black, Alida M. Casting Her Own Shadow: Eleanor Roosevelt & the Shaping of Postwar Liberalism. LC 95-23500. (Illus.). 300p. (C). 1996. boxed set 42.00 (*0-231-10404-9*) Col U Pr.

Black, Alison H. Man & Nature in the Philosophical Thought of Wang Fu-Chih. 346p. 1987. 30.00 (*0-295-96338-7*) U of Wash Pr.

Black, Alistair & Muddiman, David, eds. Understanding Community Librarianship. LC 97-70015. (Studies in Librarianship). (Illus.). 184p. 1997. text 69.95 (*1-85972-243-1*, Pub. by Avebry) Ashgate Pub Co.

Black, Allen, jt. auth. see Black, Mark.

Black, Allida M. Casting Her Own Shadow: Eleanor Roosevelt & the Shaping of Postwar Liberalism. 1997. pap. 18.00 (*0-231-10405-7*) Col U Pr.

Black, Allida M., ed. What I Hope to Leave Behind: The Essential Essays of Eleanor Roosevelt. LC 95-38101. 683p. 1995. 75.00 (*0-926019-88-0*) Carlson Pub.

Black, Allida M., jt. auth. see Roosevelt, Eleanor.

Black, Allida M., ed. see Roosevelt, Eleanor.

Black, Andrea, ed. see Black, Chuck.

Black, Andrew, et al. In Search of Shareholder Value: Managing the Drivers of Performance. (Illus.). 280p. 1997. 25.00 (*0-273-63027-X*) F T P-H.

Black, Andy. A Can of Tuna: The Complete Guide to Cooking with Tuna. (Illus.). 115p. (Orig.). 1995. pap. 7.95 (*1-85327-091-1*, Pub. by Prism Pr) Assoc Pubs Grp.

***Black, Andy.** Leonardo DiCaprio: The Top Ten Movies. 96p. 1999. pap. 14.95 (*1-902588-05-3*, Pub. by Glitter Bks) Subterranean Co.

— Oliver Reed: Ten Top Movies. (Illus.). 2000. pap. 14.95 (*1-902588-06-1*) Glitter Bks.

Black, Andy, ed. Necronomicon No. 2: The Journal of Horror & Erotic Cinema. (Illus.). 192p. 1998. pap. 17.95 (*1-871592-38-0*) Creation Books.

— Necronomicon Vol. 1: The Journal of Horror & Erotic Cinema. (Illus.). 192p. (Orig.). 1996. pap. 16.95 (*1-871592-37-2*) Creation Books.

Black, Angela K. Bitterbrush. LC 94-72417. 274p. (Orig.). 1994. pap. 9.95 (*0-9642571-0-6*) ABCDE Pubng.

Black, Ann. New Era of Benefits Communication. Brzezinski, Mary Jo, ed. LC 96-77776. 1996. pap. 29.00 (*0-89154-505-0*) Intl Found Employ.

Black, Ann N., et al. Ten Tools of Language-Written. 2nd ed. (Illus.). 166p. (J). (gr. 11-12). 1982. pap. text 12.60 (*0-910513-00-7*) Mayfield Printing.

Black, Anthony. Council & Commune: The Conciliar Movement & the Fifteenth-Century Heritage. LC 79-89220. x, 253p. 1979. 25.95 (*0-915762-08-0*) Patmos Pr.

— An Edition of the Cavendish Irish Parliamentary Diary, 1776-1778, 3 vols., Set. LC 84-81378. 750p. 1985. text 49.95 (*0-87319-031-9*) Hallberg Pub Corp.

— Monarchy & Community: Politial Ideas in the Later Conciliar. 3rd ed. LC 72-108101. (Cambridge Studies in Medieval Life & Thought: Vol. 2, 3rd). 201p. reprint ed. pap. 57.30 (*0-608-30062-4*, 2022436) Bks Demand.

Black, Antony. Council & Commune: The Conciliar Movement & the Council of Basle. 264p. 1990. 60.00 (*0-86012-077-5*, Pub. by Srch Pr) St Mut.

— El Pensamiento Politico en Europa, 1250-1450.Tr. of Political Thought in Europe, 1250-1450. (SPA.). 337p. (C). 1996. pap. 17.95 (*0-521-47831-6*) Cambridge U Pr.

— Political Thought in Europe, 1250-1450. (Cambridge Medieval Textbooks Ser.). 223p. (C). 1992. text 54.95 (*0-521-38451-6*); pap. text 18.95 (*0-521-38609-8*) Cambridge U Pr.

Black, Arthur. Arthur! Arthur! More Comic Sketches from the Master's Pen. 233p. 1991. 24.95 (*0-7737-2513-X*) Genl Dist Srvs.

— Arthur! Arthur! More Comic Sketches from the Master's Pen. 1995. pap. 16.95 (*0-7737-5536-5*) Genl Dist Srvs.

— Back to Black: Comic Sketches. (Illus.). 229p. 1987. 19.95 (*0-458-81210-2*) Genl Dist Srvs.

— Black in the Saddle Again. LC 99-203448. 208p. 1998. pap. 16.95 (*0-7737-5914-X*) Stoddart Publ.

***Black, Arthur.** Black Tie & Tales. large type ed. 224p. 1999. 16.95 (*0-7737-3193-8*, Pub. by Stoddart Publ) Genl Dist Srvs.

Black, Auguste R. Miracles at the Inn. (Illus.). 24p. (Orig.). (J). (gr. 1-12). 1990. pap. 4.95 (*0-9628010-1-1*) A R Black.

— The Shelby Avenue Gang. (Illus.). 66p. (Orig.). (J). (gr. 2-5). 1990. pap. 3.95 (*0-9628010-0-3*) A R Black.

— The Year That Santa Goofed & Other Short Stories. (Illus.). 22p. (Orig.). (J). (gr. 1-5). 1990. pap. 2.95 (*0-9628010-2-X*) A R Black.

***Black, Ayanna.** Fiery Spirits & Voices: Canadian Writers of African Descent. rev. ed. 320p. 2000. pap. 15.00 (*0-00-648521-9*) HarpCollins.

Black, Ayanna, et al. Daughters of the Sun, Women of the Moon: An Anthology of Canadian Black Women Poets. Wallace, Ann, ed. 107p. (Orig.). 1991. pap. text 11.95 (*0-88795-091-4*, Pub. by Willms Wallce) Distributors.

Black, Barbara. Corporate Dividends & Stock Repurchases. 1990. ring bd. 130.00 (*0-685-44912-2*) West Group.

***Black, Barbara J.** On Exhibit: Victorians & Their Museums. LC 99-16415. (Victorian Literature & Culture Ser.). 256p. 2000. 37.50 (*0-8139-1897-9*) U Pr of Va.

Black, Baxter. Cactus Tracks & Cowboy Philosophy. LC 96-54507. (Illus.). 288p. 1997. 23.00 (*0-609-60122-9*) Crown Pub Group.

— Cactus Tracks & Cowboy Philosophy. LC 96-54507. 1997. 23.00 (*0-517-70677-6*) Crown Pub Group.

— Cactus Tracks & Cowboy Philosophy. (Illus.). 275p. 1998. pap. 12.95 (*0-14-027683-1*) Viking Penguin.

— Cow Attack. (Illus.). 64p. 1996. pap. 13.95 (*0-939343-23-1*) Coyote Cowboy.

***Black, Baxter.** A Cowfull of Cowboy Poetry. (Illus.). 224p. 2000. 24.95 (*0-939343-30-4*) Coyote Cowboy.

Black, Baxter. Coyote Cowboy Poetry. (Illus.). 208p. 1986. 24.95 (*0-939343-00-2*) Coyote Cowboy.

— Croutons on a Cow Pie, Vol. II. LC 88-71575. Vol. 2. (Illus.). 208p. 1992. 24.95 (*0-939343-12-6*) Coyote Cowboy.

— Dunny & the Duck. LC 94-70585. (Illus.). 64p. 1994. pap. 13.95 (*0-939343-14-2*) Coyote Cowboy.

— Hey, Cowboy, Wanna Get Lucky. 240p. 1995. pap. 11.95 (*0-14-025093-X*, Penguin Bks) Viking Penguin.

— Loose Cow Party. (Illus.). 1998. pap. 13.95 (*0-939343-29-0*) Coyote Cowboy.

Black, Becky, jt. auth. see Virtue, Doreen.

Black Belt Magazine Editors. The Legendary Bruce Lee. Lee, Mike & Vaughn, Jack, eds. LC 86-42770. (Specialties Ser.). 160p. (Orig.). 1986. pap. 10.95 (*0-89750-106-3*, 446) Ohara Pubns.

***Black Belt Publishing Staff.** Backroads of Alabama. 1999. pap. 9.95 (*1-57966-007-X*) Black Belt Communs.

Black, Benjamin, jt. auth. see Black, Gordon S.

Black, Bernadette, jt. auth. see Hecklinger, Fred J.

Black, Bernard. Vasse's Bambinelli: The Child Portraits of an Eighteenth-Century French Sculptor Bernard Black. (Illus.). 100p. (C). 1994. text 49.95 (*0-485-11444-5*, Pub. by Athlone Pr) Humanities.

Black, Bernard & Nadeau, Hugues W. Michel Anguier's Pluto: The Marble of 1669: New Light on the French Sculptor's Career. LC 90-37517. (Illus.). 104p. (C). 1990. text 42.00 (*0-485-11400-3*, Pub. by Athlone Pr) Humanities.

Black, Bernard S., et al. Guide to the Russian Law on Joint Stock Companies. LC 98-19899. 1998. 195.00 (*90-411-0606-5*) Kluwer Law Intl.

Black, Bernard S., jt. auth. see Gilson, Ronald J.

Black, Bert. Minnesota Corporations Practice Manual, 1986-1993. 400p. 1993. ring bd. 78.00 (*0-86678-501-9*, MICHIE); suppl. ed. 37.50 (*1-56257-818-9*, MICHIE) LEXIS Pub.

Black, Bert & Lee, Patrick W. Expert Evidence: A Practitioner's Guide to Law, Science & the FJC Manual. LC 97-223458. xii, 637p. 1997. write for info. (*0-314-22846-2*) West Pub.

Black, Bertram J. The Mentally Ill Child Grows Up: Transitions to the World of Work. LC 93-31218. 222p. 1993. text 31.95 (*0-87630-711-X*) Brunner-Mazel.

— Work & Mental Illness: Transitions to Employment. LC 87-26084. (Johns Hopkins Series in Contemporary Medicine & Public Health). 280p. 1988. reprint ed. pap. 86.80 (*0-608-07379-2*, 206760600009) Bks Demand.

Black, Beryl. Coping with Sexual Harassment. Rosen, Ruth C., ed. (Coping Ser.). 149p. (YA). (gr. 7 up). 1987. lib. bdg. 17.95 (*0-8239-0732-5*) Rosen Group.

Black, Bill. Golden Age Greats Vol. 2: Lady Phantom. (Illus.). 84p. 1995. pap. 9.95 (*1-56225-006-X*) A C Comics.

— Golden Age Greats Vol. 3: The Black Terror. (Illus.). 84p. 1995. pap. 9.95 (*1-56225-007-8*) A C Comics.

— Golden Age Greats Vol. 4: Fawcett Heroes. (Illus.). 100p. 1995. pap. 9.95 (*1-56225-009-4*) A C Comics.

— Golden Age Greats Vol. 6: Fighting Females. (Illus.). 84p. 1995. reprint ed. pap. 9.95 (*1-56225-010-8*) A C Comics.

— Golden Age Greats Vol. 8: Fighting Females Strike Back! (Illus.). 84p. 1996. reprint ed. pap. 9.95 (*1-56225-012-4*) A C Comics.

— King of the Rocketmen: Republic Picture's Original Flying Hero. (Illus.). 1991. pap. 12.95 (*1-56225-003-5*) A C Comics.

— Music's the Very Best Thing Vol. 1: Bill Black Irish Tune Collection. 1996. spiral bd. 28.00 (*0-9652458-0-2*) Sunphone.

Black, Bill, ed. Thrilling Planet Tales. (Illus.). 68p. (Orig.). 1991. pap. 9.95 (*1-56225-001-9*) A C Comics.

Black, Bill, intro. Best of the West. (Illus.). 68p. (Orig.). 1992. pap. 9.95 (*1-56225-004-3*) A C Comics.

Black, Bill & Feret, Bill. TV's Sheena Irish McCalla. 100p. 1992. pap. 19.95 (*0-685-60576-0*) A C Comics.

Black, Bill, ed. see Harvey, R. C. & Biro, Charles.

Black, Bill, ed. see Lewis, Rik.

Black, Bill D. Radon-Hazard Potential of Western Salt Lake Valley, Salt Lake County, Utah. LC 97-111671. (Special Study of the Utah Geological Survey Ser.: Vol. 91). (Illus.). 27p. 1996. pap. 6.00 (*1-55791-398-6*, SS-91) Utah Geological Survey.

Black, Bill D. & Solomon, Barry J. Radon-Hazard Potential of the Lower Weber River Area, Tooele Valley & Southeastern Cache Valley, Cache, Davis, Tooele & Weber Counties, Utah. (Special Study of the Utah Geological Survey Ser.: Vol. 90). (Illus.). 56p. 1996. pap. 6.00 (*1-55791-379-X*, SS90) Utah Geological Survey.

Black, Bill D., et al. Paleoseismic Investigation on the Salt Lake City Segment of the Wasatch Fault Zone at the South Fork Dry Creek & Dry Gulch Sites, Salt Lake County, Utah. LC 97-103871. (Special Study of the Utah Geological Survey Ser.: Vol. 92). (Illus.). 22p. 1996. pap. 5.25 (*1-55791-399-4*, SS-92) Utah Geological Survey.

Black, Bill D., jt. auth. see Lund, William R.

Black, Bob. Anarchy after Leftism. 176p. (Orig.). 1997. pap. 7.95 (*1-890532-00-2*) Columbia Alternat.

— Friendly Fire. (Illus.). 1992. pap. 6.00 (*0-936756-89-6*) Autonomedia.

Black-Branch, Jonathan L. Rights & Realities: The Judicial Impact of the "Canadian Charter of Rights & Freedoms" on Education, Case Law & Political Jurisprudence. LC 97-7850. 256p. 1997. text 82.95 (*1-85521-936-0*, Pub. by Ashgate Pub) Ashgate Pub Co.

Black, Breanda, ed. see Leak, Alexander.

***Black, Brian.** Petrolia: The Landscape of America's First Oil Boom. LC 99-42473. (Creating the North American Landscape Ser.). 248p. 2000. 42.50 (*0-8018-6317-1*) Johns Hopkins.

Black, Bruce. An Introduction to Ear Disease. LC 98-36570. (Illus.). 90p. 1998. reprint ed. pap. 63.95 (*0-7693-0012-X*, 2002) Thomson Learn.

Black, Bruce, jt. auth. see Marks, Susan.

Black, Bruce J. Workshop Processes, Practices & Material. 2nd ed. (Mechanical Engineering Ser.). 336p. 1997. pap. text 27.95 (*0-340-69252-9*, VNR) Wiley.

Black, Bruce L., jt. ed. see Scott, W. Richard.

Black, Bruce W. The Spiritual Gifts Handbook: A Complete Guide to Discovering & Using Your Spiritual Gift. LC 94-43446. 142p. 1995. pap. 9.99 (*0-87213-058-4*) Loizeaux.

Black, C. A., ed. Methods of Soil Analysis, 2 pts. rev. ed. Incl. Pt. 1. (Illus.). 1965. 17.50 (*0-89118-010-9*); Pt. 2. (Illus.). 1982. 36.00 (*0-89118-072-9*); write for info. (*0-318-59617-2*) Am Soc Agron.

Black, C. Clifton. The Disciples According to Mark: Markan Redaction in Current Debate. (JSNT Supplement Ser.: No. 27). 392p. 1989. 85.00 (*1-85075-157-9*, Pub. by Sheffield Acad) CUP Services.

Black, C. Clifton. Mark. (Abingdon New Testament Commentaries Ser.). pap. 23.95 (*0-687-05841-4*) Abingdon.

— Mark: Images of an Apostolic Interpreter. LC 93-37578. (Studies on Personalities of the New Testament). 347p. (C). 1994. text 34.95 (*0-87249-973-1*) U of SC Pr.

Black, C. Clifton, jt. ed. see Culpepper, R. Alan.

Black, C. E. & Falk, Richard A., eds. The Future of the International Legal Order, 4 vols. Incl. Vol. 3. DP-Report. 416p. 1971. 35.00 (*0-691-09220-6*); write for info. (*0-318-55357-0*) Princeton U Pr.

Black, C. F. Cultural Atlas of the Renaissance. 1993. 45.00 (*0-671-86523-4*) Prntice Hall Bks.

B

An Asterisk (*) at the beginning of an entry indicates that the title is appearing for the first time.

Black, C. Stewart. Jennifer. LC 98-55443. 1999. pap. 5.00 (*0-88734-830-0*) Players Pr.

Black, C. T. & Smith, C. R., compiled by. Bird Finding Guide to Michigan. (Illus.). 57p. (Orig.). 1994. pap. 12.95 (*0-9642477-0-4*) MI Audubon Soc.

***Black, Cara.** Murder in Belleville. 368p. 2000. 23.00 (*1-56947-211-4*) Soho Press.

— Murder in the Marais. LC 98-52070. 368p. 1999. 22.00 (*1-56947-159-2*) Soho Press.

***Black, Cara.** Murder in the Marais. 360p. 2000. pap. 13.00 (*1-56947-212-2*) Soho Press.

Black, Caren. Getting Out of Line: A Guide for Teachers Redefining Themselves & Their Profession. LC 97-4859. (Illus.). 112p. 1997. 43.95 (*0-8039-6502-8*); pap. 18.95 (*0-8039-6503-6*) Corwin Pr.

***Black, Caren.** What You Don't Know: The Information Crisis in Public Education. 2001. pap. text. write for info. (*0-325-00281-9*) Heinemann.

Black, Carla, jt. auth. see Rodriguez, Angel.

Black, Carol Gault. Seasonal Artic Word Searches: 256 Word Searches for S, R, L, Blends, SH, CH TH. (Illus.). 280p. (J). (gr. 1-6). 1996. spiral bd., wbk. ed. 31.95 (*1-58650-049-X*, BK-246) Super Duper.

Black, Carol M., jt. ed. see Jayson, Malcolm I.

Black, Catharine F., jt. ed. see Dilts, James D.

Black, Celeste. The Pearl of Cripple Creek: The Story of Cripple Creek's Most Famous Madam, Pearl DeVere. (Illus.). 32p. 1997. pap. 4.95 (*0-9658535-0-0*) Blck Bear Pubns.

— Queen of Glen Eyrie: Story of Mary Lincoln Mellen Palmer, Wife of General William Palmer, Founder of Colorado Springs, CO. (Illus.). 128p. 1999. pap. 9.95 (*0-9658535-1-9*) Blck Bear Pubns.

Black, Charlene & Seerley, Norma, eds. Introductory Sociology: A Set of Syllabi. 233p. 1978. 13.50 (*0-317-33279-1*) Am Sociological.

Black, Charles. Owls Bay in Babylon. (American Dust Ser.: No. 13). 90p. 1980. 7.95 (*0-913218-92-8*); pap. 2.95 (*0-913218-91-X*) Dustbooks.

— The Waking Passenger. Cassin, Maxine, ed. (Journal Press Bks.: Louisiana Legacy). 80p. 1983. pap. 12.00 (*0-938498-03-7*) New Orleans Poetry.

Black, Charles A. & DeWall, Skip. Soil Fertility Evaluation & Control. 768p. 1993. lib. bdg. 104.95 (*0-87371-834-8*, 2596) Lewis Pubs.

Black, Charles L., Jr. The Humane Imagination. LC 86-8797. 201p. 1987. 22.50 (*0-918024-43-9*) Ox Bow.

Black, Charles L. Impeachment: A Handbook. LC 98-88356. 80 p. 1998. write for info. (*0-300-07954-0*) Yale U Pr.

— Impeachment: A Handbook. LC 98-88356. 80p. 1998. pap. 6.95 (*0-300-07950-8*) Yale U Pr.

Black, Charles L., Jr. A New Birth of Freedom. LC 98-88790. 175p. 1998. pap. 14.00 (*0-300-07734-3*) Yale U Pr.

— A New Birth of Freedom: Human Rights, Named & Unnamed. LC 96-52967. 192p. 1997. 22.95 (*0-399-14230-4*, Grosset-Putnam) Putnam Pub Group.

Black, Charles L. Structure & Relationship in Constitutional Law. LC 69-17621. (Edward Douglass White Lectures: 1968). 107p. 1969. reprint ed. pap. 33.20 (*0-608-08388-7*, 205530000013) Bks Demand.

Black, Charles L., Jr. Structure & Relationship in Constitutional Law. LC 85-13904. 98p. (C). 1986. reprint ed. 24.00 (*0-918024-42-0*); reprint ed. pap. 14.00 (*0-918024-44-7*) Ox Bow.

Black, Charles T. & Worden, Diane D., compiled by. Michigan Nature Centers & Other Environmental Education Facilities. 64p. 1982. pap. 6.50 (*0-939294-06-0*, LB 1047-M5) Beech Leaf.

Black, Chauncey F. & Smith, Samuel B., eds. Some Account of the Work of Stephen J. Field As a Legislator, State Judge & Judge of the Supreme Court of the United States. (Illus.). 63, 464p. 1986. reprint ed. 47.50 (*0-8377-1139-8*, Rothman) W S Hein.

Black, Cheryl, ed. see James, Breggie.

Black, Christina W. & Pybus, Beverly E. A Guide to Centralized Credentialing: Evaluating Current Issues & Trends. (Illus.). 180p. 1997. ring bd. 157.00 (*1-57839-005-2*) Opus Communs.

Black, Christine M. The Pursuit of the Presidency: 'Ninety-Two & Beyond. LC 93-37593. (Illus.). 216p. 1993. pap. 24.50 (*0-89774-845-X*) Oryx Pr.

***Black, Chuck.** Kingdom's Edge. Black, Andrea, ed. (Kingdom Ser.). 128p. 2000. pap. 7.95 (*0-9679240-0-6*) Perfect Praise.

Black, Cilla. Through the Years: My Life in Pictures. 160p. 1994. pap. text 34.95 (*0-7472-0918-9*, Pub. by Headline Bk Pub) Trafalgar.

Black, Claudia. Anger Guide. 86p. 1997. spiral bd. 39.95 (*0-910223-24-6*) MAC Pub.

***Black, Claudia.** Changing Course. 2nd ed. 210p. 1999. pap. 14.95 (*0-910223-25-4*) MAC Pub.

Black, Claudia. Double Duty: Chemically Dependent. 74p. (Orig.). 1990. pap. 7.95 (*0-910223-17-3*) MAC Pub.

— Double Duty: Food Addiction. 84p. (Orig.). 1990. pap. 7.95 (*0-910223-16-5*) MAC Pub.

— Double Duty: Gay-Lesbian. 75p. (Orig.). 1990. pap. 7.95 (*0-910223-14-9*) MAC Pub.

— Double Duty: Sexual Abuse. 81p. (Orig.). 1990. pap. 7.95 (*0-910223-15-7*) MAC Pub.

— It Will Never Happen to Me. LC 59-776. (Illus.). 183p. 1982. pap. 9.95 (*0-910223-00-9*) MAC Pub.

— It Will Never Happen to Me! 224p. 1987. mass mkt. 5.99 (*0-345-34594-0*) Ballantine Pub Grp.

— It's Never Too Late to Have a Happy Childhood: Inspirations for Adult Children. 80p. 1989. pap. 15.00 (*0-345-36279-9*) Ballantine Pub Grp.

— My Dad Loves Me, My Dad Has a Disease: A Child's View: Living with Addiction. 3rd rev. ed. (Illus.). 84p. (J). (gr. k-6). 1997. pap. 12.95 (*0-910223-23-8*) MAC Pub.

***Black, Claudia.** Relapse Toolkit. 206p. 2000. spiral bd. 59.00 (*0-910223-26-2*) MAC Pub.

Black, Claudia. Repeat after Me II. 190p. (Orig.). 1995. pap. 15.95 (*0-910223-22-X*) MAC Pub.

Black, Clinton. Pirates of the West Indies. (Illus.). 144p. (C). 1989. pap. text 17.95 (*0-521-35818-3*) Cambridge U Pr.

Black, Clinton L. We as a Black People: "Our Time Has Come" LC 90-93252. (Illus.). 140p. (YA). 1999. pap. 20.00 (*0-9620180-1-5*) C L Black.

Black, Colin R., jt. ed. see Jackson, Michael B.

Black Community Crusade for Children Staff. A Black Community Crusade & Covenant for Protecting Children. 1995. pap. 5.95 (*1-881985-09-1*) Childrens Defense.

— Progress & Peril: Black Children in America. 156p. (Orig.). 1993. pap. 6.00 (*0-938008-99-4*) Childrens Defense.

— Prophetic Voices: Black Preachers Speak on Behalf of Children. 76p. (Orig.). 1993. pap. 10.95 (*1-881985-00-8*) Childrens Defense.

Black, Cynthia. Natural & Herbal Family Remedies. LC 96-53552. (Storey Publishing Bulletin Ser.: Vol. A-168). 1997. pap. 2.95 (*0-88266-716-5*) Storey Bks.

***Black, Cynthia, ed.** Our Turn, Our Time: Women Truly Coming of Age. LC 00-28920. 272p. 2000. pap. 14.95 (*1-58270-029-X*) Beyond Words Pub.

Black, Cynthia, ed. see Joyer, Mike & Robert, Zack.

Black, Cynthia, ed. see Leeson, Tom & Leeson, Pat.

Black, Cyril E. & Thompson, John M., eds. American Teaching about Russia. LC 59-15377. 189p. reprint ed. pap. 58.60 (*0-8357-5402-2*, 200573400059) Bks Demand.

Black, Cyril E., et al. The Modernization of Inner Asia. LC 90-23385. 424p. (C). (gr. 13). 1994. pap. text 38.95 (*0-87332-779-9*, East Gate Bk) M E Sharpe.

— Neutralization & World Politics. LC 68-29388. 216p. reprint ed. pap. 67.00 (*0-8357-8967-5*, 203340000085) Bks Demand.

— Rebirth: A Political History of Europe since World War II. LC 99-34967. 720p. 1999. pap. text 29.00 (*0-8133-3664-3*) Westview.

Black, Cyril E., ed. see Barbir, Karl K., et al.

Black, Cyrus. Black. Historical Record of the Posterity of William Black, Who Settled in This Country in the Year 1775: Also, a Sketch of 23 English Families & Some Early Settlers from New England Who Settled at the Head of the Bay of Fundy about the Same Time. 209p. 1998. reprint ed. pap. 32.00 (*0-8328-9635-7*); reprint ed. lib. bdg. 42.00 (*0-8328-9634-9*) Higginson Bk Co.

Black, D. A., jt. auth. see Baye, Michael R.

Black, D. S. The Music of the Zeros. 52p. (Orig.). 1996. pap. 4.95 (*0-9626708-9-8*) Talisman IN.

***Black, Dan.** Cast a Dark Shadow. large type ed. 240p. 1999. pap. 18.99 (*0-7089-5562-2*, Linford) Ulverscroft.

Black, Dana. Kau Kau Kitchen. LC 86-18700. (Illus.). 108p. 1987. pap. 4.95 (*0-916630-50-1*) Pr Pacifica.

Black, Daniel L. A Layman's Guide to the Holy Spirit. LC 88-60360. 1988. pap. 6.99 (*0-87148-529-X*) Pathway Pr.

Black, Daniel P. Dismantling Black Manhood: An Historical & Literary Analysis of the Legacy of Slavery. LC 96-53852. (Studies in African American History & Culture). 200p. 1997. text 45.00 (*0-8153-2857-5*) Garland.

Black, Darryl. Managing Switched Local Area Networks: A Practical Guide. LC 97-36656. (Illus.). 384p. (C). 1997. pap. text 44.95 (*0-201-18554-7*) Addison-Wesley.

***Black, Daryl Paul.** Building Switched Networks. LC 98-43438. 320p. (C). 1999. 44.95 (*0-201-37953-8*) Addison-Wesley.

Black, Dave, jt. auth. see Feldstein, Sandy.

Black, David. Acid: The Secret History of LSD. (Illus.). 202p. 1999. pap. 15.95 (*1-883319-79-X*) Frog Ltd CA.

— Actor's Audition. LC 90-50153. 112p. (Orig.). 1990. pap. 11.00 (*0-679-73228-4*) Vin Bks.

***Black, David.** Atlanta: The Making of a World Class City. LC 99-44236. (Millennium Ser.). (Illus.). 448p. 1999. 45.00 (*1-58192-002-4*) Community Comm.

Black, David. Design & Implementation of the Machine Operating System. (C). 1995. text. write for info. (*0-201-52898-3*) Addison-Wesley.

— Drumset Independence & Syncopation. 1998. pap. 10.95 (*0-88284-899-2*, 17317) Alfred Pub.

— Ekstagy: Out-of-the-Body Experiences. LC 74-17679. 224p. 1975. 7.95 (*0-672-51972-0*, Bobbs) Macmillan.

— An Impossible Life. LC 97-44877. 200p. 1998. pap. 18.95 (*1-55921-222-5*) Moyer Bell.

— Impossible Life: A False Family History. 224p. 1996. 22.95 (*1-882206-13-4*) Argonaut Pr.

Black, David & Gerou, Tom. Essential Dictionary of Orchestration. LC 98-45507. 1998. pap. 5.95 (*0-7390-0021-7*, 17894) Alfred Pub.

Black, David & Huxley, Anthony. Plants. (World of Science Ser.). (Illus.). 64p. 1985. 15.95 (*0-8160-1065-X*) Facts on File.

Black, David, jt. auth. see De Moubray, Amicia.

Black, David A. Law in Film: Resonance & Representation. LC 98-25506. 208p. 1999. 39.95 (*0-252-02459-1*); pap. 17.95 (*0-252-06765-7*) U of Ill Pr.

Black, David A. Learn to Read New Testament Greek. exp. ed. LC 94-25747. (ENG & GRE.). 224p. 1994. 29.99 (*0-8054-1612-9*) Broadman.

Black, David A. Linguistics & New Testament Interpretation. (Orig.). 1993. pap. 15.99 (*0-8054-1509-2*, 4215-09) Broadman.

— Linguistics for Students of New Testament Greek: A Survey of Basic Concepts & Applications. 2nd ed. LC 95-15091. 222p. 1995. pap. 14.99 (*0-8010-2016-6*) Baker Bks.

— The Myth of Adolescence: Raising Responsible Children in an Irresponsible Society. LC 98-89234. 166p. 1999. 17.00 (*1-891833-51-0*) Davidson Pr.

— New Testament Textual Criticism: A Concise Guide. (Illus.). 80p. (C). 1994. pap. 9.99 (*0-8010-1074-8*) Baker Bks.

Black, David A., ed. Scribes & Scripture: New Testament Essays in Honor of J. Harold Greenlee. LC 92-2921. (American Schools of Oriental Research Dissertation Ser.). xvi, 128p. 1992. text 32.50 (*0-931464-70-6*) Eisenbrauns.

Black, David Alan. It's Still Greek To Me: An Easy-To-Understand Guide to Intermediate Greek. LC 98-7826. 192p. (C). 1998. pap. 14.99 (*0-8010-2181-2*) Baker Bks.

— Using New Testament Greek in Ministry: The Practical Guide for Students & Pastors. LC 92-42175. 128p. (Orig.). (C). 1993. pap. 8.99 (*0-8010-1043-8*) Baker Bks.

Black, David B. Document Capture for Document Imaging Systems. (Illus.). 99p. 1992. per. 59.00 (*0-89258-239-1*, R055) Assn Inform & Image Mgmt.

Black, David L., ed. Drug Testing in Sports. 238p. (Orig.). 1995. pap. 60.00 (*0-912474-20-3*) Preston Pubns.

Black, David R. Bridging the Rift: The New South Africa in Africa. Swatuk, Larry A., ed. LC 96-49701. 260p. (C). 1997. text 75.00 (*0-8133-2752-0*, Pub. by Westview) HarpC.

Black, David R., ed. Eating Disorder among Athletes: Theory, Issues & Research. 92p. 1991. pap. 5.00 (*0-88314-497-2*) AAHPERD.

Black, David W. Vico & Moral Perception. LC 95-35041. (Emory Vico Studies: Vol. 5). XIII, 280p. (C). 1997. 49.95 (*0-8204-2898-1*) P Lang Pubng.

Black, David W., et al, eds. Commonplaces: Essays on the Nature of Place. LC 89-30263. 148p. (C). 1989. lib. bdg. 32.00 (*0-8191-7387-8*) U Pr of Amer.

Black, Davidson, ed. Fossil Man in China. LC 73-38049. reprint ed. 76.50 (*0-404-56903-X*) AMS Pr.

Black, Dean. Health at the Crossroads: Exploring the Conflict Between Natural Healing & Conventional Medicine. 168p. 1988. pap. 8.95 (*0-929283-07-4*) Tapestry Pr.

Black, Deborah, tr. see Gyaltsab, Zhechen.

Black, Deborah, tr. see Padma-Chos-Phel & Semendra, K.

Black, Denise. Around Atlanta with Children. 5th ed. 1997. pap. text 14.95 (*1-56352-455-4*) Longstreet.

Black, Denise, jt. auth. see Schwartz, Janet.

Black, Dennis. Maintaining Perspective. LC 96-32404. (Orig.). 1996. pap. 37.95 (*0-912150-39-4*) Atwood Pub LLC.

— Maintaining Perspective: A Decade of Collegiate Legal Challenges. 294p. 1997. pap. text 37.95 (*1-891859-11-0*) Atwood Pub LLC.

Black, Dianna M., jt. auth. see Paxman, David B.

Black Dog & Leventhal Publis. Staff. New York Bartender's Guide. (Illus.). 256p. 9.98 (*1-884822-13-4*) Blck Dog & Leventhal.

Black, Don. Pocket Full of Miracles. 1991. pap. 8.95 (*1-57734-649-1*) Covenant Comms.

Black, Don & Hampton, Christopher. Sunset Boulevard. 128p. (Orig.). 1993. pap. 8.95 (*0-571-17214-8*) Faber & Faber.

Black, Don E. Black on White: Listening to the Corn Grow Beyond the 'Burbs. 154p. (Orig.). 1995. pap. 11.95 (*0-9648306-0-4*) Vger Pubng.

Black, Don J. The Little Shepherd. 1991. pap. 3.95 (*1-55503-191-9*, 0111783) Covenant Comms.

— Mary's Story of Christmas. 1996. pap. 3.95 (*1-55503-343-1*, 29004764) Covenant Comms.

Black, Donald. The Behavior of Law. 1980. reprint ed. pap. text 29.95 (*0-12-102652-3*) Acad Pr.

— Smart Dating: A Guide to Starting & Keeping a Healthy Relationship. rev. ed. 240p. 1998. pap. 14.95 (*1-879706-76-8*) Paper Chase.

— The Social Structure of Right & Wrong. 2nd rev. ed. LC 97-80734. (Illus.). 224p. 1997. pap. text 48.00 (*0-12-102803-8*) Morgan Kaufmann.

— Sociological Justice. (Illus.). 192p. (C). 1993. reprint ed. pap. text 20.95 (*0-19-508558-2*, 11141) OUP.

Black, Donald, ed. Virginia Review of Sociology, Vol. 2. 1996. 73.25 (*1-55938-903-6*) Jai Pr.

Black, Donald D., jt. compiled by see Karnes, Elizabeth L.

Black, Donald E. Louie Llama, the Beanstalk, & the Magic Ring: The Llama Family in America. 2nd rev. ed. Georgetown University Professor & Professional Sta & Organization of American States Staff, trs. (ENG & SPA., Illus.). 32p. (J). (gr. 3 up). 1997. pap. 9.95 (*0-9625753-4-8*) SuperAmerican Bks.

***Black, Donald F.** Do Something Different This Sunday. 120p. 1999. pap. 14.95 (*1-885631-44-8*, 44-8, Family Of Man Pr) G F Hutchison.

Black, Donald F. Do Something Different This Sunday: Biblical Comedies & Drama for Youth & Adults. (Orig.). 1993. pap. 10.95 (*1-55673-538-3*) CSS OH.

— Lord, I Want to Be A Christian Inna My Church. 1993. pap. 9.95 (*1-55673-576-6*, 7975, Fairway Pr) CSS OH.

***Black, Donald F.** Lord, I Want to Be a Christian Inna My Church. 125p. 1999. reprint ed. pap. 13.95 (*1-885631-38-3*, 38-3, Family Of Man Pr) G F Hutchison.

— Pulpit Psycho. 220p. 1999. pap. 14.95 (*1-885631-43-X*, 43-X, Family Of Man Pr) G F Hutchison.

— The Woman in Your Wife's Body. 60p. 1999. pap. 12.50 (*1-885631-37-5*, 37-5, Family Of Man Pr) G F Hutchison.

Black, Donald J. The Jamaica Triangle: A Novel. LC 98-194458. 177 p. 1991. write for info. (*976-625-033-2*) Kingston Pub.

Black, Donald O. Lama's SuperAmerican Coloring Book. (Illus.). 7p. (J). (gr. 3). 1991. pap. write for info. (*0-9625753-1-3*) SuperAmerican Bks.

— Something Beautiful Came to Earth: The Angel Bird Story. limited ed. LC 90-70072. (Illus.). 64p. 1990. pap. 17.95 (*0-9625753-0-5*) SuperAmerican Bks.

Black, Donald V., jt. auth. see Peterkin, Karen.

Black, Donald W. Bad Boys, Bad Men: Confronting Antisocial Personality Disorder. LC 98-23579. 256p. 1999. 25.00 (*0-19-512113-9*) OUP.

***Black, Donald W. & Larson, C. Lindon, contrib. by.** Bad Boys, Bad Men: Confronting Antisocial Personality Disorder. 256p. 2000. pap. 14.95 (*0-19-513783-3*) OUP.

Black, Donald W., jt. auth. see Andreasen, Nancy C.

Black, Dora, et al, eds. Child Psychiatry & the Law. 2nd ed. 200p. 1991. text 32.00 (*0-88048-608-2*, 8608, Pub. by Royal Coll Psych) Parkwest Pubns.

Black, Dora, et al. When Father Kills Mother: Helping Children Move from Trauma to Grief. LC 92-48528. 240p. (C). 1993. text 69.95 (*0-415-07662-5*, B0869) Routledge.

Black, Doris. Reach for Your Spiritual Potential. 1986. pap. 7.15 (*0-89137-438-8*) Quality Pubns.

***Black-Downes, Jim.** Word 2000 - Module 4: Working with Long Documents. Yackell, Nicole & Amstutz, Irina, eds. (Illus.). (J). 2000. pap. write for info. (*0-7423-0472-8*, WORD2K004LG) ComputerPREP.

Black, Duncan. Incidence of Income Taxes. 136p. 1965. reprint ed. 32.50 (*0-7146-1207-3*, Pub. by F Cass Pubs) Intl Spec Bk.

— The Theory of Committees & Elections. (C). 1986. lib. bdg. 119.00 (*0-89838-189-4*) Kluwer Academic.

Black, E. R., et al. Ten Tools of Language-Written: Revised Edition II, Form B. rev. ed. (Illus.). 166p. (C). 1983. pap. text 12.60 (*0-910513-01-5*) Mayfield Printing.

Black, Earl. Southern Governors & Civil Rights: Racial Segregation As a Campaign Issue in the Second Reconstruction. 446p. 1976. 49.95 (*0-674-82510-1*) HUP.

Black, Earl & Black, Merle. Politics & Society in the South. LC 86-18421. (Illus.). 384p. 1987. 41.50 (*0-674-68958-5*) HUP.

— Politics & Society in the South. 384p. 1989. reprint ed. pap. 20.50 (*0-674-68959-3*) HUP.

— The Vital South: How Presidents Are Elected. (Illus.). 416p. (C). 1993. pap. 19.50 (*0-674-94131-4*) HUP.

Black, Eddie L. Daily Bible Reading Record Book. (Orig.). (YA). 1994. pap. 2.99 (*0-9636455-0-1*) Daily Bible.

***Black, Edwin.** Format C: 414p. 1999. pap. 15.00 (*0-914153-02-1*) Dialog.

Black, Edwin. Format C. unabridged ed. LC 99-19611. 385p. 1999. 24.95 (*1-57129-078-8*) Brookline Bks.

— Rhetorical Criticism: A Study in Method. LC 77-91050. 197p. reprint ed. pap. 61.10 (*0-608-07455-1*, 206768200009) Bks Demand.

— Rhetorical Criticism: A Study in Method. LC 77-91050. 1978. reprint ed. pap. text 19.95 (*0-299-07554-0*) U of Wis Pr.

— Rhetorical Questions: Studies of Public Discourse. LC 91-28534. 220p. 1992. 28.95 (*0-226-05501-9*) U Ch Pr.

***Black, Edwin.** The Transfer Agreement: The Dramatic Story of the Pact Between the Third Reich & Jewish Palestine. rev. ed. (Illus.). 454p. 1999. reprint ed. pap. 15.00 (*0-914153-01-3*) Dialog.

Black, Edwin. The Transfer Agreement: The Untold Story of the Secret Pact Between the Third Reich & Jewish Palestine. rev. ed. LC 99-33552. 450p. 1999. 24.95 (*1-57129-077-X*, Pub. by Brookline Bks) Natl Bk Netwk.

Black, Edwin R. Divided Loyalties: Canadian Concepts of Federalism. LC 75-319658. 286p. reprint ed. pap. 88.70 (*0-7837-6896-6*, 204672600003) Bks Demand.

Black, Eldon. Direct Intervention: Canada-France Relations, 1967-1974. 203p. pap. 27.95 (*0-88629-289-1*, Pub. by McG-Queens Univ Pr) CUP Services.

Black, Eleanor & Robertson, Sidney, eds. The Gold Rush Song Book. (Illus.). 72p. 1998. reprint ed. pap. 9.95 (*1-55709-445-4*) Applewood.

Black, Elizabeth. McCandlish - Black Family History. 201p. 1995. reprint ed. pap. 30.00 (*0-8328-4926-X*); reprint ed. lib. bdg. 40.00 (*0-8328-4925-1*) Higginson Bk Co.

Black, Elizabeth M., jt. auth. see Scheer, Julian.

Black Elk, Wallace. Black Elk Speaks. (American Biography Ser.). 238p. 1991. reprint ed. lib. bdg. 69.00 (*0-7812-8022-2*) Rprt Serv.

***Black Elk, Wallace & Neihardt, John Gneisenau.** Black Elk Speaks: Being the Life Story of a Holy Man of the Oglala Sioux. 21st ed. LC 00-36382. (Illus.). 288p. 2000. pap. 12.95 (*0-8032-6170-5*) U of Nebr Pr.

Black, Ellen, jt. auth. see Schmidt, Robert.

Black, Ellen, jt. tr. see Schmidt, Robert.

Black, Eric. Bosnia: Splintered Region. LC 96-24951. (World in Conflict Ser.). 96p. (YA). (gr. 7-10). 1997. lib. bdg. 25.26 (*0-8225-3553-X*, Lerner Publctns) Lerner Pub.

Black, Eric. Northern Ireland: Troubled Land. LC 96-43639. (World in Conflict Ser.). 1997. lib. bdg. 25.26 (*0-8225-3552-1*, Lerner Publctns) Lerner Pub.

Black, Eric. Our Constitution: The Myth That Binds Us. 192p. (C). 1988. pap. 25.00 (*0-8133-0695-7*, Pub. by Westview) HarpC.

Black, Esther B. Stories of Old Upland: Early Years Picture Album, Pt. 5. 3rd ed. Orig. Title: Stories of Old Upland for Young Listeners. (Illus.). 124p. 1979. pap. text 12.95 (*0-9603586-0-9*) Chaffey Commun Cult Ctr.

Black, Ethan. The Broken Hearts Club. LC 98-24619. 336p. 1999. 24.00 (*0-345-42602-9*) Ballantine Pub Grp.

— The Broken Hearts Club. 2000. mass mkt. 6.99 (*0-345-42603-7*) Ballantine Pub Grp.

***Black, Ethan.** Irresistible. LC 99-34691. 400p. 2000. 24.00 (*0-345-43347-5*, Ballantine) Ballantine Pub Grp.

Black, Eugene C. The Association: British Extraparliamentary Political Organization, 1769-1793. LC 63-17195. (Historical Monographs: No. 54). (Illus.). 358p. 1963. 30.00 (*0-674-05000-2*) HUP.

Black, Eugene R. The Madagascar Corundum. Baber, Lawrence, ed. 256p. 1979. pap. 6.95 (*0-9666256-0-9*, B10011) Hardwick Pubns.

Black, Evelyn S. Cloudcroft - What Have They Done with My Meadow? (Illus.). 64p. (Orig.). 1995. pap. 7.00 (*0-9636577-2-0*) Trego-Hill.

***Black Excel Staff, Black.** The African American Student's College Guide. LC 99-88892. 400p. 2000. pap. 19.95 (*0-471-29552-3*) Wiley.

Black, F. William, jt. auth. see Strub, Richard L.

***Black, Fiona C., et al, eds.** The Labour of Reading: Desire, Alienation & Biblical Interpretation. LC 99-44174. (Semeia Studies). 317p. 1999. pap. 30.00 (*0-88414-011-3*) Soc Biblical Lit.

Black, Fischer. Exploring General Equilibrium. 280p. 1995. 40.50 (*0-262-02382-2*) MIT Pr.

Black Forest Group Staff. Immunodiagnostic Markets. (Modern Greek Writers Ser.: No. 502). (Illus.). 115p. 1995. 995.00 (*0-614-09907-2*) Theta Corp.

— U. S. & World Blood Pressure Equipment Markets. (Illus.). 142p. 1995. 995.00 (*0-614-09908-0*) Theta Corp.

— U. S. Vaccines Markets. (Market Research Reports: No. 501). (Illus.). 91p. 1995. 995.00 (*0-614-09906-4*) Theta Corp.

Black Forest Press Staff. What Parents Must Know & Can Do about Teenage Alcohol & Drug Abuse. 1998. pap. text 14.95 (*1-881116-70-0*, Pub. by Black Forest Pr) Epic Bk Promo.

***Black, Frank M.** Grandma Always Knows What to Do for Me. (Illus.). (J). 1999. pap. write for info. (*1-929157-06-1*) Inside-OUT.

— Grandpa Knows Everyone. (J). 1999. pap. write for info. (*1-929157-07-X*) Inside-OUT.

— It's Not Your Fault Sweetheart. (Illus.). 24p. 1999. pap. write for info. (*1-929157-05-3*) Inside-OUT.

— There Are Some Real Special Kids in Our Class. (Illus.). 24p. (J). 1999. pap. 6.95 (*1-929157-04-5*) Inside-OUT.

— A Visit with Daddy. (Illus.). 20p. (J). 1999. pap. 6.95 (*1-929157-00-2*) Inside-OUT.

— A Visit with Mommy. (Illus.). 20p. (J). 1999. pap. 6.95 (*1-929157-01-0*) Inside-OUT.

— Una Visita a Mami. (SPA., Illus.). 20p. (J). 1999. pap. 6.95 (*1-929157-03-7*) Inside-OUT.

— Una Visita a Papi. (SPA., Illus.). 20p. (J). 1999. pap. write for info. (*1-929157-02-9*) Inside-OUT.

Black, Franklin O., et al. Congenital Deafness: A New Approach to Early Detection of Deafness Through a High Risk Register. LC 76-135285. (Illus.). 84p. reprint ed. pap. 30.00 (*0-8357-5513-4*, 203512900093) Bks Demand.

Black, G. F. County Folklore Vol. III: Printed Extracts No. 5, Examples of Printed Folklore Concerning the Orkeny & Shetland Islands. Thomas, Northcote W., ed. (Folk-Lore Society, London Monographs). 1972. reprint ed. pap. 30.00 (*0-8115-0522-7*) Periodicals Srv.

Black, G. Monroe. Murray (S. Carolina) Echoes in Time: The Murray, Connor & Moorer Families of South Carolina. 399p. 1997. pap. 59.00 (*0-8328-7004-8*); lib. bdg. 69.00 (*0-8328-7003-X*) Higginson Bk Co.

Black, Gale. The Sun Sign Diet. 1997. pap. 18.95 (*0-614-27339-0*) Alive & Well.

Black, Gavin. A Dragon for Christmas. 1996. 19.50 (*0-7451-8681-5*, Black Dagger) Chivers N Amer.

Black, Gayle. The Sun Sign Diet: 12 Exclusive Astrological Diets Personally Designed Just for You. rev. ed. (Illus.). 430p. 1997. pap. 18.95 (*0-9651511-2-3*) Alive & Well.

Black, Geoff. Students Guide to Accounting & Financial Reporting Standards, 1995-96. 270p. 1995. pap. 59.95 (*1-85805-125-8*, Pub. by DP Publns) St Mut.

Black, Geoff & Colson, Brett. Dreams to Reality: A Profile of Modern Day Anaheim. Malone, Myrtle D., ed. (Illus.). 87p. 1993. 20.00 (*1-881547-16-7*) Pioneer Pubns.

Black, George. Contemporary Stage Directing. LC 90-5138. (Illus.). 432p. (C). 1991. text 32.75 (*0-03-016633-0*, PN2053.B525) Harcourt Coll Pubs.

Black, George, ed. At the Crossroads: Human Rights & the Northern Ireland Peace Process. LC 97-131668. 143p. (Orig.). 1996. pap. 12.00 (*0-934143-83-8*) Lawyers Comm Human.

— Critique: Review of the Department of State's Country. (Reports on Human Rights Conditions for 1993 Ser.). 426p. (Orig.). 1994. pap. text 19.95 (*0-934143-68-4*) Lawyers Comm Human.

— Halfway to Reform: The World Bank & the Venezuelan Justice System. 149p. (Orig.). 1996. pap. 15.00 (*0-934143-86-2*) Lawyers Comm Human.

— Improvising History: A Critical Evaluation of the United Nations Observer Mission in El Salvador. LC 96-136909. 175p. (Orig.). 1995. pap. 15.00 (*0-934143-79-X*) Lawyers Comm Human.

— In the National Interest: 1996 Quadrennial Report on Human Rights & U. S. Foreign Policy. (Human Rights & U. S. Foreign Policy Ser.: Vol. 3). 82p. (Orig.). 1996. pap. 15.00 (*0-934143-81-1*) Lawyers Comm Human.

— Islam & Justice: Debating the Future of Human Rights in the Middle East & North Africa. LC 97-154494. 178p. (Orig.). 1997. pap. 15.00 (*0-934143-87-0*) Lawyers Comm Human.

***Black, George, ed.** Obstacles to Reform: Exceptional Courts, Police Impunity & Persecution of Human Rights Defenders in Turkey. 129p. 1999. pap. 15.00 (*0-934143-92-7*) Lawyers Comm Human.

Black, George, ed. Shackling the Defenders: Legal Restrictions on Independent Human Rights Advocacy Worldwide. 2nd ed. 135p. 1995. pap. 12.00 (*0-934143-76-5*) Lawyers Comm Human.

— Wrongs & Rights: A Human Rights Analysis of China's Revised Criminal Law. LC 99-188765. 71p. 1998. pap. 12.00 (*0-934143-90-0*) Lawyers Comm Human.

Black, George, et al, eds. Representing Asylum Applicants: An Attorney's Guide to Law & Procedure. 217p. 1995. pap. text 50.00 (*0-934143-71-4*) Lawyers Comm Human.

Black, George & Armstrong, Patricia, eds. World Bank Governance & Human Rights. 2nd rev. ed. LC 96-126772. 126p. 1995. pap. 12.00 (*0-934143-78-1*) Lawyers Comm Human.

Black, George & Munro, Robin. Black Hands of Beijing: Lives of Defiance in China's Democracy Movement. (Robert L. Bernstein Bk.). (Illus.). 400p. 1993. 24.95 (*0-471-57977-7*) Wiley.

***Black, George & Munro, Robin.** Black Hands of Beijing (to 1992) Lives of Defiance in China's Democracy Movement. (Illus.). 390p. 2000. reprint ed. 25.00 (*0-7881-9438-0*) DIANE Pub.

Black, George, et al. Garrison Guatemala. 208p. 1984. 25.00 (*0-85345-665-8*, Pub. by Monthly Rev) NYU Pr.

Black, George, ed. see Beyani, Chaloka, et al.

Black, George, ed. see Hecht, Jonathan.

Black, George, ed. see Hicks, Neil.

Black, George, ed. see Lawyers Committee for Human Rights.

Black, George, ed. see Lawyers Committee for Human Rights Staff.

Black, George, ed. see Lewis, Ann E.

Black, George, ed. see Naughton, Emma & Smith, Turner.

Black, George A. History of Municipal Ownership of Land on Manhattan Island to the Beginning of Sales by the Commissioner of the Sinking Fund in 1844. LC 12-28238. (Columbia University. Studies in the Social Sciences: No. 3). reprint ed. 31.50 (*0-404-51003-5*) AMS Pr.

Black, George F. Grammar of the Coptic Language with Easy Reading Lessons. 1996. pap. 12.50 (*0-89979-089-5*) British Am Bks.

— Surnames of Scotland: Their Origin, Meaning & History. LC 47-1716. 838p. 1946. reprint ed. 50.00 (*0-87104-172-3*) NY Pub Lib.

Black, George F., ed. Calendar of Cases of Witchcraft in Scotland, 1510-1727. LC 78-137707. (New York Public Library Publications in Reprint). (Illus.). 1971. reprint ed. 8.00 (*0-405-01751-0*) Ayer.

Black, Gerry. Lender to the Lords, Given to the Poor. 389p. 1992. text 30.00 (*0-85303-249-1*, Pub. by M Vallentine & Co) Intl Spec Bk.

Black, Ginger E. Making the Grade: How to Help Your Elementary School Child Have a Happy & Successful School Experience. 1989. pap. 8.95 (*0-8184-0501-5*) Carol Pub Group.

Black Girl Talk Collective Staff. Black Girl Talk. 220p. 1996. per. 12.95 (*0-920813-03-8*) Sister Vis Pr.

Black, Gladys. Iowa Birdlife. enl. ed. LC 92-11196. (Bur Oak Original Ser.). (Illus.). 220p. 1992. pap. 19.95 (*0-87745-393-4*) U of Iowa Pr.

Black, Glenn A. Angel Site: An Archaeological, Historical, & Ethnological Study, Vols. I & II. LC 79-19508. (Illus.). x, 616p. 1967. 20.00 (*0-253-30700-7*) Ind Hist Soc.

Black, Glenn D., ed. An Empowered Witness: Sermons & Writings of Paul S. Rees. LC 97-8967. 120p. (Orig.). 1997. pap. 10.99 (*0-8341-1660-X*) Beacon Hill.

Black, Glenn D., jt. auth. see Chambers, Oswald.

Black, Gloria J. The Unspoken Bond. 2nd ed. (Illus.). 80p. (Orig.). (ps-12). 1986. pap. 6.00 (*0-9616466-1-6*) G Black.

Black, Gordon. Mountain Biking Washington. LC 99-25894. (Illus.). 256p. 1999. pap. 14.95 (*1-56044-806-7*) Falcon Pub Inc.

Black, Gordon S. & Black, Benjamin. The Politics of American Discontent: How a New Party Can Make Democracy Work Again. 262p. 1994. 22.95 (*0-471-59853-4*) Wiley.

Black, Gregory D. The Catholic Crusade Against the Movies, 1940-1975. LC 97-10932. (Illus.). 320p. (C). 1998. pap. text 18.95 (*0-521-62905-5*) Cambridge U Pr.

— Hollywood Censored: Morality Codes, Catholics & the Movies. 348p. 1996. pap. 19.95 (*0-521-56592-8*) Cambridge U Pr.

Black, Gregory D., jt. auth. see Koppes, Clayton R.

Black, H. Delano, et al. Exercises in Plant Biology. 214p. 1991. pap. text 21.95 (*0-88725-153-6*) Hunter Textbks.

Black, Harold A. & Zambito, Raymond F. Hospital Dentistry. (Illus.). 448p. (C). (gr. 13). 1996. pap. text 42.00 (*0-8151-9855-8*, 25547) Mosby Inc.

Black, Harry. Achieving Economic Development Success: Tools That Work. (Special Reports). 156p. 1991. pap. 32.00 (*0-87326-062-7*) Intl City-Cnty Mgt.

***Black, Harvey W.** My Tenant, "Bobo" LC 99-94958. 1999. 21.95 (*0-533-13234-7*) Vantage.

***Black Hawk.** Black Hawk's Autobiography. Nichols, Roger L., ed. LC 99-35792. (Illus.). 106p. 1999. 21.95 (*0-8138-2637-3*) Iowa St U Pr.

Black Hawk. Life of Black Hawk. LC 93-47326. (Illus.). 128p. 1994. reprint ed. pap. 6.95 (*0-486-28105-1*) Dover.

— Life of Black Hawk. Patterson, J. B., ed. LC 93-7289. (Native American Voices Ser.). 1993. reprint ed. 21.99 (*0-7835-1770-X*) Time-Life.

— Life of Ma-Ka-Tai-Me-She-Kia-Kiak, or Black Hawk. (American Biography Ser.). 206p. 1991. reprint ed. lib. bdg. 69.00 (*0-7812-8023-0*) Rprt Serv.

Black, Helen C. Notable Women Authors of the Day. 342p. 1977. 26.95 (*0-8369-2637-4*) Ayer.

— Notable Women Authors of the Day. 342p. reprint ed. lib. bdg. 49.00 (*0-685-10416-8*) Rprt Serv.

***Black, Helen K. & Rubinstein, Robert L.** Old Souls: Aged Women, Poverty & the Experience of God. LC 99-54971. 216p. 2000. lib. bdg. 47.95 (*0-202-30633-X*) Aldine de Gruyter.

— Old Souls: Aged Women, Poverty & the Experience of God. LC 99-54971. 216p. 2000. reprint ed. pap. text 23.95 (*0-202-30634-8*) Aldine de Gruyter.

Black, Henry C. Dictionary of Law, Containing Definitions of Terms & Phrases of American & English Jurisprudence, Ancient & Modern: Including the Principal Terms of International, Constitutional & Commercial Law; with a Collection of Legal Maxims & Numerous Select Titles from the Civil Law & Other Foreign Systems, 1891, First Edition. LC 91-62383. x, 1253p. 1991. reprint ed. lib. bdg. 125.00 (*0-9630106-0-3*, 307290) Lawbk Exchange.

— Essay on the Constitutional Prohibitions Against Legislation Impairing the Obligation of Contracts & Against Retroactive & Ex Post Facto Laws. xxvi, 355p. 1980. reprint ed. 32.50 (*0-8377-0312-3*, Rothman) W S Hein.

— A Law Dictionary Containing Definitions of the Terms & Phrases of American & English Jurisprudence, Ancient & Modern, 1910 Second Edition. 2nd ed. LC 9?-10320. 1314p. 1995. reprint ed. 125.00 (*1-886363-10-2*) Lawbk Exchange.

— The Relation of the Executive Power to Legislation. LC 73-19130. (Politics & People Ser.). 192p. 1974. reprint ed. 15.95 (*0-405-05855-1*) Ayer.

— A Treatise on the Law of Judgments, 2 vols. LC 97-70483. 1997. reprint ed. 165.00 (*1-57588-210-8*, 311130) W S Hein.

Black, Henry C., et al. Black's Law Dictionary: Definitions of the Terms & Phrases of American & English Jurisprudence, Ancient & Modern. 6th abr. ed. Connolly, M. J. et al, eds. 1136p. (C). 1991. reprint ed. pap. 29.00 (*0-314-88536-6*) West Pub.

***Black, Henry Campbell.** Black's Law Dictionary 1999. 7th ed. 1999. 39.00 (*0-314-22864-0*) West Pub.

Black, Herbert L., ed. see American Society for Metals Staff.

Black, Hermina. Who Is Lucinda? 1982. mass mkt. 2.95 (*0-451-11934-7*, AE1934, Sig) NAL.

Black, Hillel. The Watchdogs of Wall Street. LC 75-2621. (Wall Street & the Security Market Ser.). 1975. reprint ed. 23.95 (*0-405-06948-0*) Ayer.

Black, Hillel, ed. see Ganey, Terry.

Black, Hillel, ed. see Guisso, Richard W., et al.

Black, Hillel, ed. see Johnson, Fenton.

Black, Hillel, ed. see Norris, Helen.

Black, Hillel, ed. see Rose, Tom.

Black, Hillel, ed. see Schiller, Ronald.

Black, Hillel, ed. see Spalding, Linda.

Black, Hillel, ed. see Taraborrelli, J. Randy.

Black, Howard, jt. auth. see Parks, Sandra.

Black, Hubert P. The Beatitudes: Eight-Step Path to Happiness. LC 96-96097. 73p. (Orig.). 1996. pap. 5.00 (*0-9651127-0-5*) H P Black.

***Black, Hugh.** The Art of Being a Good Friend: How to Bring Out the Best in Your Friends & in Yourself. LC 99-38478. 160p. 1999. reprint ed. pap. 13.95 (*0-918477-62-X*) Sophia Inst Pr.

Black, Hugh C. Silvicultural Approaches to Animal Damage Management in Pacific Northwest Forests. (Illus.). 460p. 1998. reprint ed. 52.00 (*0-89904-924-9*); reprint ed. pap. 50.00 (*0-89904-923-0*) Crumb Elbow Pub.

Black, Hugo L. The Bill of Rights. (Reprint Series in Political Science). (C). 1993. reprint ed. pap. text 1.90 (*0-8290-2615-0*, P-26) Irvington.

Black, Ian. Israel's Secret Wars: A History of Israel's Intelligence Services. LC 90-49373. 656p. 1992. pap. 18.00 (*0-8021-3286-3*, Grove) Grove-Atltic.

— Last of the Lightnings: Nostalgic Farewell RAF. (Illus.). 160p. 1996. 52.95 (*1-85260-541-3*, Pub. by J H Haynes & Co) Motorbooks Intl.

— Tales of the Tartan Army. 192p. 1997. pap. 19.95 (*1-85158-899-X*, Pub. by Mainstream Pubng) Trafalgar.

— Tornado Pilot. (Osprey Colour Library). (Illus.). 128p. 1994. pap. 15.95 (*1-85532-429-6*, Pub. by Osprey) Motorbooks Intl.

Black, Ian D. A Gambling Style of Government: The Establishment of Chartered Company Rule in Sabah, 1878-1915. (Illus.). 1983. 29.95 (*0-19-582535-7*) OUP.

Black, Indigo. How to Keep Yo' Man in Check: (You Go Girl) (Illus.). 28p. (Orig.). pap. 3.50 (*0-9647036-7-X*) You Go Girl.

***Black, Ira B.** Dying of Enoch Wallace: Life, Death & the Changing Brain. 256p. 2000. 24.95 (*0-07-136208-8*) McGraw.

Black, Ira B. Information in the Brain: A Molecular Perspective. (Illus.). 240p. 1994. pap. text 18.00 (*0-262-52188-1*, Bradford Bks) MIT Pr.

Black, Ira R. Information in the Brain: A Molecular Perspective. (Illus.). 261p. 1991. 32.50 (*0-262-02321-0*, Bradford Bks) MIT Pr.

Black, Irene L. A Determinded Lady. 320p. 1996. mass mkt. 4.50 (*0-8217-5467-X*, Zebra Kensgtn) Kensgtn Pub Corp.

— The Duke's Easter Lady. 320p. 1993. mass mkt. 3.99 (*0-8217-4103-9*, Zebra Kensgtn) Kensgtn Pub Corp.

— Husband for the Countess. 1990. mass mkt. 3.95 (*0-8217-3081-9*, Zebra Kensgtn) Kensgtn Pub Corp.

— Mischievous Miss. 1991. mass mkt. 3.95 (*0-8217-3519-5*, Zebra Kensgtn) Kensgtn Pub Corp.

Black, J. Liquid Fuels in Australia: A Social Science Research Perspective. 280p. 1983. 42.00 (*0-08-024834-9*, Pergamon Pr); pap. 23.00 (*0-08-024833-0*, Pergamon Pr) Elsevier.

Black, J. A., jt. auth. see Blunden, W. R.

Black, J. B. The Reign of Elizabeth, 1558-1603. 2nd ed. (Oxford History of England Ser.). (Illus.). 568p. 1959. text 65.00 (*0-19-821701-3*) OUP.

Black, J. D., jt. auth. see Mighell, Ronald L.

Black, J. E. & Thompson, K. W., eds. Foreign Policies in a World of Change. (New Reprints in Essay & General Literature Index Ser.). 1977. reprint ed. 64.95 (*0-518-10196-7*, 10196) Ayer.

Black, J. Jay & Bryant, Jennings. Introduction to Media Communication. 4th ed. LC 94-72066. 624p. (C). 1995. text. write for info. (*0-697-20124-4*) Brown & Benchmark.

Black, J. L. Citizens of the Fatherland: Education, Educators, & Pedagogical Ideals in Eighteenth Century Russia. (East European Monographs: No. 53). 273p. 1979. text 72.50 (*0-914710-46-X*, Pub. by East Eur Monographs) Col U Pr.

— G.-F. Muller & the Imperial Russian Academy. 300p. 1986. 60.00 (*0-7735-0553-9*, Pub. by McG-Queens Univ Pr) CUP Services.

***Black, J. L.** Russia Faces NATO Expansion: Bearing Gifts or Bearing Arms? LC 99-41681. 288p. 1999. text 29.95 (*0-8476-9866-1*) Rowman.

Black, J. L., ed. Essays on Karamzin: Russian Man of Letters, Political Thinker, Historian, 1766-1826. (Slavistic Printings & Reprintings Ser.: No.309). 232p. 1975. pap. text 69.25 (*90-279-3251-4*) Mouton.

— U. S. S. R. Documents Annual, 1987-1991. 97.00 (*0-87569-110-2*) Academic Intl.

Black, J. L. & Buse, D. K. G.F. Muller & Siberia, Seventeen Thirty-Three to Seventeen Forty-Three. Moessner, Victoria J., tr. from GER. (Russia & Asia Ser.: No. 1). (Illus.). 1990. 28.00 (*0-919642-23-3*) Limestone Pr.

***Black, J. M.** Divorce: The Things You Thought You'd Never Need to Know. 192p. 2000. pap. 8.95 (*0-7160-2119-6*, Pub. by Elliot RW Bks) Midpt Trade.

Black, J. R. One Slimy Summer. (Shadow Zone Ser.). 132p. (Orig.). (J). (gr. 3-7). 1994. pap. 3.50 (*0-685-71035-1*) Random Bks Yng Read.

— Skeleton in My Closet. (Shadow Zone Ser.). (J). 1995. 9.09 (*0-606-08170-4*, Pub. by Turtleback) Demco.

Black, J. S. Human Resource Management: A Strategic & Global Perspective. (C). 1997. text. write for info. (*0-201-54718-X*) Addison-Wesley.

Black, J. S., jt. ed. see Cheyne, T. K.

Black, J. Stewart. Organizational Behavior. 6th ed. Steers, Richard M., ed. (C). 1998. text. write for info. (*0-321-01404-9*) Addison-Wesley Educ.

Black, J. Stewart, et al. Global Assignments: Successfully Expatriating & Repatriating International Managers. LC 92-13928. (Management Ser.). 347p. 1992. text 34.95 (*1-55542-473-2*) Jossey-Bass.

Black, J. Stewart, jt. auth. see Sundaram, Anant K.

Black, J. T. The Design of the Factory with a Future. 256p. (C). 1991. text 58.75 (*0-07-005551-3*); pap. text 45.94 (*0-07-005550-5*) McGraw.

Black, J. Temple, jt. auth. see Degarmo, E. Paul.

Black, Jack. The Card-Counting Guide to Winning Blackjack. Valente, John, ed. (Illus.). 80p. (Orig.). 1983. 14.95 (*0-914087-00-2*) Consumer Pubn.

— Gold Prospector's Handbook. (Illus.). 176p. 1987. pap. 10.95 (*0-935182-32-2*) Gem Guides Bk.

***Black, Jack.** Thrasher Skate & Destroy. LC 99-67473. (Prima's Official Strategy Guides). (Illus.). 79p. 1999. pap. 12.99 (*0-7615-2683-8*) Prima Pub.

Black, Jack. You Can't Win. LC 92-17682. 1992. reprint ed. 18.95 (*0-944204-15-5*) Omniun.

— You Can't Win: An Autobiography. 340p. 1999. pap. text 16.00 (*1-902593-02-2*, Pub. by AK Pr) SPD-Small Pr Dist.

Black, Jacquelyn G. Microbiology: Principles & Applications. 3rd ed. (Illus.). 880p. (C). 1995. text 90.00 (*0-13-190745-X*) P-H.

***Black, Jacquelyn G.** Microbiology: Principles & Applications. 4th ed. 376p. 1999. pap., student ed. 37.95 (*0-471-36835-0*) Wiley.

— Microbiology: Principles & Explorations. 4th ed. 912p. 1999. pap. 84.95 (*0-471-38322-8*) Wiley.

— Microbiology; Principles & Applications. 4th ed. 912p. 1999. text 102.95 (*0-471-36819-9*) Wiley.

— Microbiology Study Guide Set: Principles & Applications. 3rd ed. (Illus.). 1996. student ed. 137.90 (*0-471-37533-0*) Wiley.

— Microbiology Study Guide Set Principles & Applications. 4th ed. 1999. text 137.90 (*0-471-37532-2*) Wiley.

Black, James. Church of Scotland Yearbook, 1993. 392p. 1993. pap. 50.00 (*0-86153-166-3*) St Mut.

— The Word Organizer, 2 vols. 1998. ring bd. 29.99 (*0-9671222-2-8*) Enhance Creatv.

— The Word Organizer: Companion Notebook. 38p. 1998. ring bd. 19.99 (*0-9671222-1-X*) Enhance Creatv.

— The Word Organizer: New Testament. 27p. 1998. ring bd. 12.99 (*0-9671222-4-4*) Enhance Creatv.

— The Word Organizer: Old Testament. 39p. 1998. ring bd. 12.99 (*0-9671222-3-6*) Enhance Creatv.

— The Word Organizer: WO Companion Notebook - WO Old Testament - WO New Testament, 3 vols. 104p. 1998. ring bd. 49.99 (*0-9671222-0-1*) Enhance Creatv.

Black, James, ed. see Shakespeare, William.

Black, James A. & Champion, Dean J. Methods & Issues in Social Research. LC 75-26659. 457p. reprint ed. pap. 141.70 (*0-608-13446-5*, 202018700016) Bks Demand.

Black, James C. & Cantor, Donald. Child Custody. 250p. 1989. text 52.50 (*0-231-06248-6*) Col U Pr.

Black, James M. How to Get Results from Interviewing: A Practical Guide for Operating Management. LC 81-20952. 222p. 1982. reprint ed. 22.00 (*0-89874-417-2*) Krieger.

B

Black, James R. & Motapanyane, Virginia, eds. Clitics, Pronouns & Movement. LC 97-8792. (Current Issues in Linguistic Theory Ser.: Vol. 140). 375p. 1997. lib. bdg. 85.00 (*1-55619-595-8*) J Benjamins Pubng Co.

— Microparametric Syntax & Dialect Variation. LC 96-38230. (Current Issues in Linguistic Theory Ser.: No. 139). xviii, 269p. 1996. lib. bdg. 69.00 (*1-55619-594-X*) J Benjamins Pubng Co.

Black, James T., et al. Private-Market Housing Renovation in Older Urban Areas. LC 77-80214. (ULI Research Reports: No. 26). (Illus.). 47p. reprint ed. pap. 30.00 (*0-8357-8284-0*, 203394800087) Bks Demand.

Black, James Thomas, et al. Downtown Office Growth & the Role of Public Transit. LC 82-50921. (Illus.). 128p. (Orig.). reprint ed. pap. 39.70 (*0-8357-8102-X*, 203394600087) Bks Demand.

— Downtown Retail Development: Conditions for Success & Project Profiles. LC 83-81784. 90p. (Orig.). 1983. pap. 32.95 (*0-87420-650-2*, D35) Urban Land.

— Mixed-Use Development Projects in North America: Project Profiles. LC 82-84338. 96p. (Orig.). reprint ed. pap. 30.00 (*0-8357-8598-X*, 203497400091) Bks Demand.

Black, James Thomas, ed. see Goldberg, Michael A., et al.

Black, Jan & Enns, Greg. Better Boundaries: Owning & Treasuring Your Life. LC 97-75478. 240p. 1998. pap. 14.95 (*1-57224-107-1*) New Harbinger.

Black, Jan, jt. auth. see Enns, Greg.

Black, Jan, jt. auth. see Enns, Gregory.

Black, Jan K. Development in Theory & Practice: Paradigms & Paradoxes. 2nd ed. 320p. 1999. pap. text 25.00 (*0-8133-3446-2*, Pub. by Westview) HarpC.

— Development on a Human Scale. (C). 1929. text 48.00 (*0-8133-0705-8*); pap. text 18.95 (*0-8133-0706-6*) Westview.

— The Dominican Republic: Politics & Development in an Unsovereign State. (Illus.). 160p. (C). 1986. text 39.95 (*0-04-497000-5*); pap. text 13.95 (*0-04-497001-3*) Routledge.

— Inequity in the Global Village: Recycled Rhetoric & Disposable People. LC 99-29730. 288p. 1999. 60.00 (*1-56549-100-9*); pap. 24.95 (*1-56549-099-1*) Kumarian Pr.

— Sentinels of Empire: The United States & Latin American Militarism, 144. LC 85-21850. (Contributions in Political Science Ser.: No. 144). 249p. 1986. 57.95 (*0-313-25155-X*, BKS/, Greenwood Pr) Greenwood.

Black, Jan K., ed. Latin America, Its Problems & Its Promise: A Multidisciplinary Introduction. 3rd ed. LC 97-40415. 672p. (C). 1998. pap. text 37.00 (*0-8133-2757-1*, Pub. by Westview) HarpC.

Black, Janet K. & Puckett, Margaret B. The Young Child: Development from Prebirth Through Age 8. 2nd rev. ed. LC 95-8646. 539p. 1995. pap. text 53.00 (*0-02-310241-1*) P-H.

Black, Janet K., jt. auth. see Puckett, Margaret B.

Black, Jay, ed. Mixed News: The Public/Civic/Communitarian Journalism Debate. LC 96-48127. (LEA's Communication Ser.). 225p. 1996. 59.95 (*0-8058-2542-8*); pap. 27.50 (*0-8058-2543-6*) L Erlbaum Assocs.

Black, Jay & Barney, Ralph, eds. Privacy I: Exploring Questions of Media Morality: A Special Issue of the "Journal of Mass Media Ethics", Vol. 9, No. 3. 64p. 1995. pap. 20.00 (*0-8058-9951-0*) L Erlbaum Assocs.

— Privacy II: Exploring Questions of Media Morality: A Special Issue of the "Journal of Mass Media Ethics", Vol. 9, No. 4, 1994. 71p. 1995. pap. 20.00 (*0-8058-9950-2*) L Erlbaum Assocs.

Black, Jay, et al. Doing Ethics in Journalism: A Handbook with Case Studies. 3rd ed. LC 98-231022. 310p. 1998. pap. text 34.00 (*0-205-28535-X*, T8535-1) Allyn.

Black, Jay, jt. auth. see Barney, Ralph D.

Black, Jay, jt. ed. see Barney, Ralph.

Black, Jay J. Introduction to Media Communication. 5th ed. LC 97-27676. 512p. (C). 1997. text. write for info. (*0-697-32715-9*, WCB McGr Hill) McGrw-H Hghr Educ.

*__Black, Jean Blashfield.__ Toni Morrison. (Women of Achievement Ser.). 2000. 19.95 (*0-7910-5885-9*) Chelsea Hse.

— Toni Morrison. (Women of Achievement Ser.). (Illus.). 2001. pap. 9.95 (*0-7910-5886-7*) Chelsea Hse.

Black, Jean F. Penny Wise. 1945. pap. 5.25 (*0-8222-0883-0*) Dramatists Play.

Black, Jeanne. Keyboarding: Course Code S04-3. Schroeder, Bonnie, ed. (Illus.). 60p. (Orig.). 1988. pap. text 3.95 (*0-917531-51-5*) CES Compu-Tech.

Black, Jeanne & Forker, Vickie. BASIC Programming 2: Lab Pack, Pt. 1. Schroeder, Bonnie & Dohney, Catherine, eds. (Illus.). 179.95 (*1-56177-080-9*, L393-1); teacher ed. 19.95 (*1-56177-082-5*, T393-1); disk 6.95 (*1-56177-078-7*, D393-1); disk 6.95 (*1-56177-079-5*, D393-2) CES Compu-Tech.

— BASIC Programming 2: Lab Pack, Pt. 2. Schroedder, Bonnie. & Doheny, Catherine, eds. (Illus.). 179.95 (*1-56177-081-7*, L393-2); teacher ed. 19.95 (*1-56177-083-3*, TE393-2) CES Compu-Tech.

Black, Jeanne, et al. Introduction to Computing: Lab Pack 1. Schroeder, Bonnie & Doheny, Cathy, eds. (Illus.). teacher ed. 19.95 (*1-56177-058-2*, TE391-1); teacher ed., student ed. 229.95 incl. disk (*1-56177-056-6*, L391-1); disk 15.95 (*1-56177-054-X*, D391-1) CES Compu-Tech.

— Introduction to Computing: Lab Pack 2. Schroeder, Bonnie & Doheny, Cathy, eds. (Illus.). 100p. teacher ed. 19.95 (*1-56177-059-0*, TE391-2); teacher ed., student ed. 229.95 incl. disk (*1-56177-057-4*, L391-2); disk 15.95 (*1-56177-055-8*, D391-2) CES Compu-Tech.

— Primary Program 2: Course Code 391-1. Doheny, Catherine & Schroeder, Bonnie, eds. (Illus.). 85p. 1989. pap., student ed. 5.95 (*0-917531-83-3*) CES Compu-Tech.

— Primary Program 2: Course Code 391-2. Doheny, Cathy & Schroeder, Bonnie, eds. (Illus.). 95p. (gr. 2). 1989. pap., student ed. 5.95 (*0-917531-84-1*) CES Compu-Tech.

Black, Jeffrey M., ed. Partnerships in Birds: The Study of Monogamy. (Oxford Ornithology Ser.). (Illus.). 432p. (C). 1996. text 125.00 (*0-19-854861-3*); pap. text 55.00 (*0-19-854860-5*) OUP.

Black, Jeffrey M., jt. auth. see Owen, Myrfyn.

Black, Jennifer A., jt. auth. see Walker, Moira.

Black, Jeremy. America or Europe? British Foreign Policy, 1739-63. LC 98-150896. 1998. 69.95 (*1-85728-185-3*, Pub. by UCL Pr Ltd) Taylor & Francis.

— Britain as a Military Power. 25p. 1998. 49.95 (*1-85728-772-X*) UCL Pr Ltd.

— British Abroad: The Grand Tour in the Eighteenth Century. 1997. pap. text 19.95 (*0-7509-1414-9*, Pub. by Sutton Pub Ltd) Intl Pubs Mktg.

— British Foreign Policy in an Age of Revolution, 1783-1793. (Illus.). 573p. (C). 1994. pap. text 37.95 (*0-521-46684-9*) Cambridge U Pr.

— The Cambridge Illustrated Atlas of Warfare: Renaissance to Revolution, 1492-1792. LC 95-36852. (Illustrated Atlases Ser.). (Illus.). 192p. (C). 1996. 39.95 (*0-521-47033-1*) Cambridge U Pr.

*__Black, Jeremy.__ Culloden & the '45. 320p. 2000. pap. 16.95 (*0-7509-2462-4*) Sutton Publng.

Black, Jeremy. Dictionary of 18th Century History. 928p. 1997. pap. 17.95 (*0-14-051258-6*) Viking Penguin.

— Eighteenth-Century Europe, 1700-1789. LC 89-10915. 480p. 1990. text 45.00 (*0-312-04009-1*) St Martin.

— Eighteenth Century Europe 1700-1789. (History of Europe Ser.). 1990. pap. text 18.00 (*0-333-37943-8*, Pub. by Macmillan) Humanities.

*__Black, Jeremy.__ Eighteenth-century Europe, 2nd Ed. 2nd ed. LC 99-15610. 1999. pap. 22.95 (*0-312-22539-3*) St Martin.

Black, Jeremy. The English Press in Eighteenth Century. (Modern Revivals in History Ser.). 338p. 1992. 61.95 (*0-7512-0007-7*, Pub. by Gregg Revivals) Ashgate Pub Co.

— European Warfare 1453-1815. LC 98-46680. 304p. 1999. pap. 21.95 (*0-312-22118-5*) St Martin.

Black, Jeremy. European Warfare, 1660-1815. LC 94-60602. 288p. 1994. 35.00 (*0-300-06170-6*) Yale U Pr.

— From Louis XIV to Napoleon: The Fate of a Great Power. (Illus.). 304p. 1999. 74.00 (*1-85728-933-1*, Pub. by UCL Pr Ltd); pap. 25.95 (*1-85728-934-X*, Pub. by UCL Pr Ltd) Taylor & Francis.

— The Historical Atlas of Great Britain: The End of the Middle Ages to the Georgian Era. (Illus.). 2000. 39.95 (*0-7509-2128-5*, Pub. by Sutton Publng) Intl Pubs Mktg.

Black, Jeremy. A History of the British Isles. 365p. 1996. text 39.95 (*0-312-16063-1*) St Martin.

— History of the British Isles. 1996. 29.95 (*0-333-66281-4*) St Martin.

— An Illustrated History of Eighteenth-Century Britain, 1688-1793. LC 96-15120. (Illus.). 304p. 1997. text 45.00 (*0-7190-4267-4*, Pub. by Manchester Univ Pr) St Martin.

— Maps & History: Constructing Images of the Past. LC 96-41293. (Illus.). 278p. 1997. 40.00 (*0-300-06976-6*) Yale U Pr.

*__Black, Jeremy.__ Maps & History: Constructing Images of the Past. (Illus.). 278p. 2000. pap. 18.95 (*0-300-08693-8*) Yale U Pr.

Black, Jeremy. Maps & Politics. LC 97-28355. 192p. 1998. 35.00 (*0-226-05493-4*) U Ch Pr.

*__Black, Jeremy.__ New History of England. 288p. 2000. pap. 15.95 (*0-7509-2319-9*) Sutton Publng.

— A New History of Wales. 256p. 2000. pap. 15.95 (*0-7509-2320-2*) Sutton Publng.

Black, Jeremy. Pitt The Great Commoner. 2000. pap. text 22.95 (*0-7509-2276-1*) Sutton Pub Ltd.

— The Politics of Britain, 1688-1800. LC 93-10228. (New Frontiers in History Ser.). 1993. text 29.95 (*0-7190-3761-1*, Pub. by Manchester Univ Pr) St Martin.

*__Black, Jeremy.__ The Politics of James Bond: From Fleming's Novels to the Big Screen. LC 00-25127. 264p. 2000. 25.00 (*0-275-96859-6*, Praeger Trade) Greenwood.

Black, Jeremy. Reading Sumerian Poetry. LC 98-40316. 288p. 1998. 65.00 (*0-8014-3598-6*) Cornell U Pr.

— The Rise of the European Powers, Sixteen Seventy-Nine to Seventeen Ninety-Three. (Illus.). 224p. 1995. pap. text 19.95 (*0-7131-6537-5*, A4340, Pub. by E A) St Martin.

*__Black, Jeremy.__ A System of Ambition: British Foreign Policy, 1660-1793. 336p. 2000. pap. 24.95 (*0-7509-2278-8*) Sutton Publng.

— War: Past, Present & Future. LC 00-41499. (Illus.). 2000. write for info. (*0-312-23823-1*) St Martin.

Black, Jeremy. War & the World: Military Power & the Fate of the Continents, 1450-2000. LC 97-28169. (Illus.). 344p. 1998. 40.00 (*0-300-07202-3*) Yale U Pr.

*__Black, Jeremy.__ War & the World: Military Power & the Fate of the Continents, 1450-2000. (Illus.). 344p. 2000. pap. 17.95 (*0-300-08285-1*) Yale U Pr.

Black, Jeremy. War in the Early Modern World, 1450-1815. 1998. pap. text 23.95 (*1-85728-688-X*) Taylor & Francis.

— Warfare in the 18th Century. (Illus.). 224p. 1999. 29.95 (*0-304-35245-4*, Pub. by Cassell) Sterling.

— Why Wars Happen. LC 98-5805. 271p. 1998. text 30.00 (*0-8147-1333-5*) NYU Pr.

*__Black, Jeremy, ed.__ European Warfare 1453-1815. LC 98-46680. 304p. 1999. text 59.95 (*0-312-22117-7*) St Martin.

Black, Jeremy, ed. Knights Errant & True Englishmen: British Foreign Policy, 1660-1800. 280p. (C). 1989. 75.00 (*0-85976-226-2*, Pub. by J Donald) St Mut.

— War in the Early Modern World, 1450-1815. LC 98-39245. 280p. 1998. pap. text 23.00 (*0-8133-3611-2*, Pub. by Westview) HarpC.

— War in the Early Modern World, 1450-1815. LC 98-39245. 280p. 1998. text 55.00 (*0-8133-3612-0*, Pub. by Westview) HarpC.

Black, Jeremy, et al, eds. The Oxford Illustrated History of Modern War. (Illus.). 366p. 1997. 49.95 (*0-19-820427-2*) OUP.

Black, Jeremy & Green, Anthony. Gods, Demons & Symbols of Ancient Mesopotamia: An Illustrated Dictionary. LC 92-80151. (Illus.). 192p. (Orig.). 1992. pap. 19.95 (*0-292-70794-0*) U of Tex Pr.

Black, Jeremy, ed. see Dorling Kindersley Publishing Co. Staff.

Black, Jeremy, ed. see Prestwich, Michael.

Black, Jill, et al. A Practical Approach to Family Law. 4th ed. LC 95-157702. 560p. 1994. pap. 46.00 (*1-85431-326-6*, Pub. by Blackstone Pr) Gaunt.

— A Practical Approach to Family Law. 5th ed. 357p. 1998. pap. 48.00 (*1-85431-653-2*, Pub. by Blackstone Pr) Gaunt.

Black, Jim. Black's 1998 Fly Fishing. (Illus.). 224p. 1998. pap. 14.95 (*1-57028-192-0*, Mstrs Pr) NTC Contemp Pub Co.

— Black's 1999 Fly Fishing: The Complete Angler's Guide to Equipment, Instruction & Destinations. (Illus.). 224p. 1999. pap. 14.95 (*0-8092-2653-7*) NTC Contemp Pub Co.

*__Black, Jim.__ Blacks 2000 Fly Fishing: Complete Anglers Guide to Equipment Instruction & Destinations. 2000. pap. text 14.95 (*0-8092-9823-6*) NTC Contemp Pub Co.

Black, Jim. Black's 2000 Wing & Clay: The Complete Shotgunner's Guide to Equipment, Instruction & Destinations. 336p. 1999. pap. 14.95 (*0-8092-2102-0*, 210200, Mstrs Pr) NTC Contemp Pub Co.

*__Black, Jim.__ Black's Wing & Clay: The Complete Shotgunner's Guide to Equipment, Instruction & Destinations. (Illus.). 2000. pap. 14.95 (*0-8092-9980-1*, Contemporary Bks) NTC Contemp Pub Co.

Black, Jim. Black's Wing & Clay-Shotgunner's Handbook: 1998 Edition. rev. ed. (Illus.). 544p. 1997. pap. 14.95 (*1-57028-156-4*, Mstrs Pr) NTC Contemp Pub Co.

Black, Jim, ed. Black's Fly Fishing. (Illus.). 224p. (Orig.). 1997. pap. 12.95 (*1-57028-119-X*, Mstrs Pr) NTC Contemp Pub Co.

Black, Jim N. When Nations Die. 1995. pap. 10.99 (*0-8423-8007-8*) Tyndale Hse.

Black, Jim Nelson, jt. auth. see Franklin, Kirk.

Black, Jim Nelson, jt. auth. see Sanders, Deion.

Black, Jimmy. The Glasgow Graveyard Guide. 160p. (C). 1992. pap. 35.00 (*0-7855-6841-7*, Pub. by St Andrew) St Mut.

— The Glasgow Graveyard Guide. 160p. 1993. pap. 30.00 (*0-7152-0670-2*, Pub. by St Andrew) St Mut.

— History's Mysteries. 160p. 1993. pap. 22.00 (*0-7152-0677-X*, Pub. by St Andrew) St Mut.

Black, Joanne C. The Spirits Are Willing. Lewis, Lynne E., ed. LC 95-79251. 230p. (Orig.). 1995. pap. 12.95 (*1-885487-09-6*) Brownell & Carroll.

Black, Joe. Passing Through: Reflections on Life. LC 96-94968. 112p. 1997. 14.95 (*0-9628474-4-5*) Life Vision Bks.

Black, John. A Dictionary of Economics. LC 96-52401. (Oxford Paperback Reference Ser.). (Illus.). 518p. 1997. pap. 12.95 (*0-19-280018-3*) OUP.

— Mutiny in the Indies. 26p. 1993. pap. 2.50 (*0-89567-114-X*) World View Forum.

— Shore Dream. Hampton, William, ed. LC 98-87466. (Illus.). 96p. 1998. 10.95 (*0-9667077-0-2*) Hampton Publ.

— Urban Transport Planning: Theory & Practice. LC 80-8860. 248p. reprint ed. pap. 76.90 (*0-608-14662-5*, 202583100045) Bks Demand.

Black, John, ed. The Systems Engineer's Handbook: A Guide to Building VME & VXI Systems. (Illus.). 1112p. 1992. text 94.00 (*0-12-102820-8*) Acad Pr.

Black, John & Black, Marguerite. Ruch & the Upper Applegate Valley: An Oregon Documentary. enl. ed. Webber, Bert, ed. LC 89-19917. (Illus.). 240p. 1994. pap. 12.95 (*0-936738-39-1*) Webb Research.

Black, John & Evans, Patrick. John Black Presents Power Build. (Illus.). 92p. (YA). 1990. pap. 16.00 (*0-929994-05-1*) Crains Muscle.

Black, John & Stafford, David. Housing Policy & Finance. 176p. 1988. text 49.95 (*0-415-00419-5*) Routledge.

Black, John & Stafford, David C. Housing Policy & Finance. LC 89-113539. (Illus.). 152p. reprint ed. pap. 47.20 (*0-608-20388-2*, 207164100002) Bks Demand.

Black, John, tr. see Von Humboldt, Alexander.

Black, John, tr. see Von Schlegel, Augustus W.

*__Black, John A.__ The Four Elements in Plato's Timaeus. LC 00-36436. (Studies In The History Of Philosophy Ser.: Vol. 54). 112p. 2000. 59.95 (*0-7734-7771-3*) E Mellen.

Black, John A. & English, Fenwick W. What They Don't Tell You in Schools of Education about School Administration. LC 86-50183. 339p. 1997. 44.95 (*0-87762-461-5*) Scarecrow.

Black, John B., jt. ed. see Britton, Bruce K.

Black, John B., jt. ed. see Graesser, Arthur C.

Black, John D. Parity, Parity, Parity. LC 72-2364. (FDR & the Era of the New Deal Ser.). 367p. 1972. reprint ed. 45.00 (*0-306-70482-X*) Da Capo.

Black, John R. A World Class Production System: Lessons of 20 Years in Pursuit of World Class. Christopher, Bill, ed. LC 98-73101. (Management Library: Vol. 20). 120p. 1998. pap. 12.95 (*1-56052-487-1*) Crisp Pubns.

Black, John W. & Moore, Wilbur E. Speech: Code, Meaning, & Communication. LC 72-6686. (Illus.). 430p. 1973. reprint ed. lib. bdg. 69.50 (*0-8371-6493-1*, BLSC, Greenwood Pr) Greenwood.

Black, John W., et al. The Use of Words in Context: The Vocabulary of College Students. (Cognition & Language). (Illus.). 276p. (C). 1985. 96.00 (*0-306-42206-9*, Plenum Trade) Perseus Pubng.

Black, Jonathan. Biological Performance of Materials: Fundamentals of Biocompatibility. LC 80-26153. (Biomedical Engineering & Instrumentation Ser.: No. 8). (Illus.). 266p. reprint ed. pap. 82.50 (*0-8357-7233-0*, 203224200078) Bks Demand.

— Electrical Stimulation: Its Role in Growth, Repair & Remodeling of the Musculoskeletal System. LC 86-9413. 237p. 1986. 75.00 (*0-275-92170-0*, C2170, Praeger Pubs) Greenwood.

— Idols. 1998. 29.95 (*3-86187-127-0*) B Gmunder.

— Oil. large type ed. 608p. 1983. 27.99 (*0-7089-8102-X*, Charnwood) Ulverscroft.

Black, Jonathan, ed. Biological Performance of Materials: Fundamentals of Biocompatibility. 2nd ed. (Illus.). 400p. 1992. text 145.00 (*0-8247-8439-1*) Dekker.

Black, Jonathan & Amos, Thomas, eds. Descriptive Inventories of Manuscripts Microfilmed for the Hill Monastic Manuscript Library, No. 1: Biblioteca Nacional de Lisboa, Fundo Alcobaca, Pt. 3. 1990. 50.00 (*0-940250-20-9*) Hill Monastic.

Black, Jonathan & Dumbleton, John H., eds. Clinical Biomechanics: A Case History Approach. LC 80-23094. 432p. reprint ed. pap. 134.00 (*0-7837-2554-X*, 204271300006) Bks Demand.

Black, Joseph, jt. auth. see Watt, James.

Black, Joseph T. The Attitude Connection: Focus on Quality. Witt, Stacey, ed. LC 90-92235. (Illus.). 144p. 1991. 14.95 (*0-9628474-2-9*) Life Vision Bks.

— Looking Back on the Future: Building a Quality Foundation. 192p. 1993. 16.95 (*0-9628474-3-7*) Life Vision Bks.

Black, Joyce M. & Matassarin-Jacobs, Esther. Medical-Surgical Nursing: Clinical Management for Continuity of Care. 5th ed. (Illus.). 1997. teacher ed. write for info. (*0-7216-6400-8*, W B Saunders Co) Harcrt Hlth Sci Grp.

— Medical-Surgical Nursing: Clinical Management for Continuity of Care. 5th ed. Eoyang, Thomas, ed. LC 96-7419. (Illus.). 2395p. 1997. text 75.00 (*0-7216-6399-0*, W B Saunders Co) Harcrt Hlth Sci Grp.

— Medical-Surgical Nursing: Clinical Management for Continuity of Care. 5th ed. (Illus.). 1997. pap. text, student ed. 18.95 (*0-7216-6950-6*, W B Saunders Co) Harcrt Hlth Sci Grp.

— Medical-Surgical Nursing: Clinical Management for Continuity of Care, Pocket Companion by Sorrentino & Chunka. 5th ed. (Illus.). 800p. 1997. pap. text 23.00 (*0-7216-7287-6*, W B Saunders Co) Harcrt Hlth Sci Grp.

— Medical-Surgical Nursing: Clinical Management for Continuity of Care, Test Manual. 5th ed. (Illus.). 2399p. 1997. write for info. (*0-7216-7086-5*, W B Saunders Co) Harcrt Hlth Sci Grp.

Black, Joyce M. & Matassarin-Jacobs, Esther, eds. Luckmann & Sorensen's Medical-Surgical Nursing: A Psychophysiologic Approach. 4th ed. (Illus.). 1993. teacher ed. write for info. (*0-7216-3786-8*, W B Saunders Co) Harcrt Hlth Sci Grp.

— Luckmann & Sorensen's Medical-Surgical Nursing: A Psychophysiologic Approach, Manual of Test Questions. 4th ed. (Illus.). 1993. write for info. (*0-7216-3891-0*, W B Saunders Co) Harcrt Hlth Sci Grp.

Black, Judi. North American Official Cellular Users Guide. (Illus.). iv, 200p. 1988. pap. 15.95 (*0-929051-00-9*) Cellmark Pub.

Black, Judith, jt. ed. see Page, Clive.

Black, Judith, tr. see Pedretti, Erica.

Black, Judy. Fashion. LC 93-4639. (YA). (gr. 9 up). 1994. pap. 5.95 (*0-382-24747-7*, Crstwood Hse) Silver Burdett Pr.

Black, Judy, jt. auth. see Black, Kenny.

Black, Julia. Rules & regulators. LC 97-185398. (Oxford Socio-Legal Studies). 298p. 1997. text 65.00 (*0-19-826294-9*) OUP.

Black, Julia, et al, eds. Commercial Regulation & Judicial Review. LC 98-198315. 224p. 1998. 60.00 (*1-901362-65-5*, Pub. by Hart Pub) Northwestern U Pr.

Black, Julie. Dream Catchers: Myths & History. (Illus.). 128p. 1999. pap. 19.95 (*1-55209-439-1*) Firefly Bks Ltd.

Black, K. D., jt. auth. see Joffe, M. S.

Black, K. S., et al, eds. Sedimentary Processes in the Inter-Tidal Zone. (Geological Society Special Publication Ser.: No. 139). 400p. 1998. 132.00 (*1-86239-013-4*, Pub. by Geol Soc Pub Hse) AAPG.

Black, Katherine. Women May Be from Venus, but Men Are Really from Uranus. LC 98-47785. (Illus.). 200p. 1999. pap. 12.95 (*1-892343-04-5*) Oak Tree Pr.

Black, Katherine D. A House of Order: A Family Organizer. 306p. 1996. pap. 19.95 (*0-9656153-5-9*) Advocate Pub.

Black, Katherine D. & Black, Stephen T. Family Law in Utah. 661p. 1997. pap. 39.95 (*0-9656153-6-7*) Advocate Pub.

Black, Kathleen. Short-Term Counseling: Theory & Practice. 1982. pap. write for info. (*0-201-00073-3*, 00073, Health Sci) Addison-Wesley.

— Spirited Miss Caroline. (Zebra Regency Romance Ser.). 224p. 1998. mass mkt. 4.99 (*0-8217-6049-1*, Zebra Kensgtn) Kensgtn Pub Corp.

Black, Kathryn. In the Shadow of Polio. 1997. pap. 12.00 (*0-201-15490-0*) Addison-Wesley.

Black, Kathryn G. The Sun in the North. 215p. 1990. 12.85 (*0-9626891-0-6*) Dika.

Black, Kathy. Accessible Preaching: Healing, Disability, & the Word of God. Franklin, Paul, ed. 144p. 1996. pap. 14.95 (*0-687-00291-5*) Abingdon.

*__Black, Kathy.__ Culturally-Conscious Worship. 2000. pap. 19.99 (*0-8272-0481-7*) Chalice Pr.

B

An Asterisk (*) at the beginning of an entry indicates that the title is appearing for the first time.

— Worship Across Cultures: A Handbook. LC 98-38022. 248p. 1998. pap. 17.00 (*0-687-05652-7*) Abingdon.

Black, Kay E., jt. auth. see Kim, Kumja P.

Black, Kaye. KidVid: Fun-Damentals of Video Instruction. (Illus.). 96p. 1989. pap., teacher ed. 27.00 (*0-913705-44-6*) Zephyr Pr AZ.

Black, Kelly, jt. auth. see Bradley, Julia C.

Black, Ken. Business Statistics: Contemporary Decision Making. 2nd ed. LC 96-38396. 950p. 1996. pap. 95.95 (*0-314-20128-9*) West Pub.

— Business Statistics: Contemporary Decision Making. 2nd ed. LC 96-38396. 1997. pap., teacher ed. write for info. (*0-314-20643-4*) West Pub.

***Black, Ken.** Business Statistics: Contemporary Decision Making. 3rd ed. LC 00-36997. 2000. write for info. (*0-324-00922-4*) Sth-Wstrn College.

Black, Ken. Business Statistics: Contemporary Decision Making. Leyh, ed. LC 93-34134. (SWC-Business Statistics). 1000p. (C). 1994. text 67.00 (*0-314-02474-3*) West Pub.

Black, Kenneth, jt. auth. see Heubner, Solomon S.

Black, Kenneth, Jr., jt. auth. see Russell, G. Hugh.

***Black, Kenneth D.** Environmental Impacts of Aquaculture. LC 00-29762. 2000. write for info. (*0-8493-0501-2*) CRC Pr.

Black, Kenneth D. & Pickering, Alan D., eds. Biology of Farmed Fish: Sheffield Life Science. 400p. 1998. write for info. (*1-85075-877-8*, Pub. by Sheffield Acad) CUP Services.

Black, Kenny & Black, Judy. Rodeo Stars. LC 98-125121. (Illus.). 116p. 1997. pap. 19.95 (*0-9665185-0-0*) Rodeo Stars.

Black, Kirby S., jt. auth. see Hewitt, Charles W.

Black, Kitty. Upper Circle: A Theatrical Chronicle. large type ed. 416p. 1993. 23.95 (*1-85695-020-4*, Pub. by ISIS Lrg Prnt) Transaction Pubs.

Black Koltuv, Barbara. Weaving Woman: Musings & Meditations on the Feminine Mythos. rev. ed. LC 90-6736. (Illus.). 143p. 1995. pap. 9.95 (*0-89254-019-2*) Nicolas-Hays.

Black, Kristen V., ed. see Athay, Sherri L. & Athay, Lawrence D.

Black, Larry. It Couldn't Happen Here. LC 84-90462. 1985. 10.95 (*0-87212-187-9*) Libra.

Black, Laura. Strathgallant. 1983. mass mkt. 3.50 (*0-446-30318-6*, Pub. by Warner Bks) Little.

Black, Laura K. "Give Them Hope" Winning the Battle for Our Heavenly Hope. (Illus.). 130p. 1999. pap. 10.00 (*0-7392-0176-X*, PO3137) Morris Pubng.

Black, Laurel J. Between Talk & Teaching: Reconsidering the Writing Conference. LC 97-45436. 190p. 1998. pap. 19.95 (*0-87421-241-3*) Utah St U Pr.

***Black, Lawrence.** Microtrading CDROM Course. 2000. 125.00 (*1-883272-37-8*) Traders Lib.

Black, Lendley C. Mikhail Chekhov As Actor, Director, & Teacher. LC 87-5995. (Theater & Dramatic Studies: No. 43). 130p. 1987. reprint ed. pap. 40.30 (*0-8357-1800-X*, 207059200004) Bks Demand.

Black, Leo, tr. see Eimert, Herbert & Stockhausen, Karlheinz, eds.

Black, Leo, tr. see Schoenberg, Arnold.

Black, Leo, tr. see Webern, Anton.

Black, Leyardia, jt. auth. see Wescott, Patsy.

***Black, Linda & Denny, Cathy.** Handouts, Etc. 192p. (C). 1999. pap. text 33.95 (*0-7872-6550-0*, 41655001) Kendall-Hunt.

Black, Linda, tr. see Khadra, Yasmina.

Black, Linda J. My Nine Month Diary. (Illus.). 42p. (Orig.). 1993. pap. 7.50 (*1-881459-05-5*) Eagle Pr SC.

Black Liturgy Subcommittee of the Bishop's Committ. In Spirit & Truth: Black Catholic Reflections on the Order of Mass. 36p. (Orig.). 1988. pap. 3.95 (*1-55586-198-9*) US Catholic.

Black, Lowell D. & Black, Sara H. An Officer & a Gentleman: The Military Career of Lieutenant Henry O. Flipper. LC 89-183245. (Illus.). 202p. (Orig.). (C). 1985. 19.95 (*0-9624659-0-9*); pap. 12.95 (*0-685-29035-2*) Lora Co Ltd.

Black, Lowell-Dwight. The Negro Volunteer Militia Units of the Ohio National Guard, 1870-1954: The Struggle for Military Recognition & Equality in the State of Ohio. 422p. 1976. pap. text 51.95 (*0-89126-031-5*) MA-AH Pub.

Black, Loyd. Touch of Merry. 1995. pap. text 4.50 (*0-8217-5175-1*) NAL.

Black, Lydi. Glory Remembered: Wooden Headgear of Alaska Sea Hunters. (Illus.). 176p. (C). 1992. reprint ed. pap. 26.95 (*0-295-97151-7*) U of Wash Pr.

Black, Lydia T. History & Ethnohostory of the Aleutians East. 37.50 (*1-895901-26-X*) Todd Commns.

Black, Lydia T., et al. Faces, Voices & Dreams: A Celebration of the Centennial of the Sheldon Jackson Museum. Corey, Peter, ed. (Illus.). 202p. (Orig.). 1987. pap. text 24.95 (*0-295-96619-X*) AK State Musms.

Black, Lydia T., tr. see Pierce, Richard A., ed.

Black, Lydia T., tr. see Veniaminov, Ivan.

Black, Lynette R., ed. see Cherry, Winky.

Black, Lynnette R. Dream Sewing Spaces: Design & Organization for Spaces Large & Small. Palmer, Pati & Gosche, Ann, eds. (Illus.). 128p. (Orig.). 1996. pap. 19.95 (*0-935278-41-9*, DRM) Palmer-Pletsch.

Black, M. First Reading First Night: A Candid Look at Stage Directing. LC 75-20336. (Illus.). 102p. 1975. 20.00 (*0-295-95432-9*) U of Wash Pr.

Black, M., ed. Christian Palestinian Syriac Horologion (Berlin MS. OR. Oct. 1019) (Texts & Studies Ser.). 1972. reprint ed. 90.00 (*0-8115-1714-4*) Periodicals Srv.

Black, M. & Bewley, J. D. Physiology & Biochemistry of Seeds in Relation to Germination: Viability, Dormancy, & Environmental Control, Vol. 2. (Illus.). 380p. 1983. 163.95 (*0-387-11656-7*) Spr-Verlag.

Black, M. & Reed, J., eds. Perspectives on the American South: An Annual Review, Vol. 1. xii, 410p. 1981. text 125.00 (*0-677-16260-X*) Gordon & Breach.

Black, M., jt. auth. see Bewley, J. D.

Black, M., tr. & intro. see Carnap, Rudolf.

Black, Maggie. Barbecue with an International Flavor. (Illus.). 80p. (Orig.). 1995. pap. 9.95 (*0-572-01215-2*, Pub. by Foulsham UK) Assoc Pubs Grp.

— A Cause for Our Times: Oxfam: The First Fifty Years. (Illus.). 336p. (C). 1992. 42.50 (*0-85598-172-5*, Pub. by Oxfam Pub) Stylus Pub VA.

— Children First: The Story of UNICEF, Past & Present. (Illus.). 378p. 1996. pap. 15.95 (*0-19-828088-2*); text 72.00 (*0-19-828094-7*) OUP.

— In the Twilight Zone: Child Workers in the Hotel, Tourism & Catering Industry. LC 96-113422. xii, 92p. 1995. pap. 13.50 (*92-2-109194-5*) Intl Labour Office.

— The Medieval Cookbook. LC 92-81536. (Illus.). 144p. 1992. 24.95 (*0-500-01548-1*, Pub. by Thames Hudson) Norton.

Black, Malacai. Scout's Honor. 432p. 1988. mass mkt. 3.95 (*0-8217-2508-4*, Zebra Kensgtn) Kensgtn Pub Corp.

Black, Margaret L. Sacramental Ministry to a Diverse Generation. LC 97-20331. 136p. 1997. pap. 12.95 (*1-55612-976-9*, LL1976) Sheed & Ward WI.

Black, Marge, ed. see Anderson, Jacqueline M.

Black, Marguerite, ed. The Oregon & Overland Trail Diary of Mary Louisa Black in 1865: The Unabridged Diary with Introduction & Contemporary Comments by Bert Webber, Includes Genealogy. LC 87-8170. (Illus.). 86p. 1989. pap. 7.50 (*0-936738-36-7*) Webb Research.

Black, Marguerite, jt. auth. see Black, John.

Black, Marguerite, jt. auth. see Halvorsen, Henry H.

Black, Mark & Black, Allen. First & Second Peter. LC 98-43494. (NIV Commentary Ser.). 210p. 1998. 21.99 (*0-89900-648-5*) College Pr Pub.

Black, Marsha W., jt. auth. see McAuliffe, Michelle M.

Black, Martha. Bella Bella: A Season of Heiltsuk Art. LC 96-52048. (Illus.). 224p. 1997. pap. 40.00 (*0-295-97608-X*) U of Wash Pr.

***Black, Martha.** Out of the Mist: Treasures of the Nuu-Chah-Nulth Chiefs. (Illus.). 112p. 2000. pap. 35.00 (*0-7718-9547-X*) BC Archives.

Black, Martha F. Shaw & Joyce: The Last Word in Stolentelling. LC 94-27516. (Florida James Joyce Ser.). 456p. (C). 1995. 49.95 (*0-8130-1328-3*) U Press Fla.

Black, Martha L. & Whyard, Florence. Martha Black: Her Story from the Dawson Gold Fields to the Halls of Parliament. 3rd ed. LC 98-18361. (Caribou Classics Ser.). (Illus.). ix, 190 p. 1998. pap. 8.95 (*0-88240-508-X*, Alaska NW Bks) Gr Arts Ctr Pub.

Black, Martin M., et al. Color Atlas & Text of Obstetric & Gynecologic Dermatology. (Illus.). 192p. 1996. text 95.00 (*0-7234-2009-2*, Pub. by Martin Dunitz) Mosby Inc.

Black, Mary. American Advertising Posters of the Nineteenth Century. (Illus.). (Orig.). 1976. pap. 16.95 (*0-486-23356-1*) Dover.

— Old New York in Early Photographs, 1853-1901. (Illus.). 288p. (Orig.). 1973. pap. 13.95 (*0-486-22907-6*) Dover.

Black, Mary, et al. American Paintings in the Detroit Institute of Arts Vol. 1: Works by Artists Born Before 1816. LC 90-85027. (Collections of the Detroit Institute of Arts). (Illus.). 303p. 1991. 75.00 (*1-55595-044-2*, Pub. by Hudson Hills) Natl Bk Netwk.

Black, Mary H. E-Z Find Puzzles: African Americans. x, 70p. (Orig.). (YA). (gr. 5-12). 1997. pap. 10.00 (*0-9657775-0-2*) EZ Print.

— Mary Herd Black, Her Story: Autobiography: Letterography: Pictography. (Illus.). 600p. (Orig.). (YA). (gr. 6-12). 1998. pap. 35.00 (*0-9657775-1-0*) EZ Print.

Black, Mary L., tr. see Mitchell, Patricia B.

Black, Matthew. An Aramaic Approach to the Gospels & Acts. 400p. 1998. pap. 24.95 (*1-56563-086-6*) Hendrickson MA.

Black, Matthew & Rowley, H H, eds. Peake's Commentary on the Bible. (Illus.). 1142p. (C). 1997. 160.00 (*0-415-05147-9*) Routledge.

Black, Matthew W. A Midsummer Night's Dream Notes. (Cliffs Notes Ser.). 64p. 1961. pap. 4.95 (*0-8220-0057-1*, Cliff) IDG Bks.

— Romans. (New Century Bible Ser.). 191p. 1973. 7.50 (*0-551-00447-9*) Attic Pr.

Black, Matthew W., jt. ed. see Schelling, Felix E.

Black, Matthew W., ed. see Schurer, Emil.

Black, Matthew W., ed. see Shakespeare, William.

***Black, Maurine M.** Essentials of Byley Scales of Infant Development II Assessment. LC 99-34622. (Essentials of Psychological Assessment Ser.). 162p. 1999. pap. 29.95 (*0-471-32651-8*) Wiley.

Black, Max. A Companion to Wittgenstein's Tractatus. 466p. 1964. text 57.50 (*0-8014-0039-2*) Cornell U Pr.

— Language & Philosophy: Studies in Method. LC 81-6206. (Illus.). 264p. 1981. reprint ed. lib. bdg. 45.00 (*0-313-23082-X*, BLLP, Greenwood Pr) Greenwood.

— Perplexities: Rational Choice, the Prisoner's Dilemma, Metaphor, Poetic Ambiguity, & Other Puzzles. LC 89-34777. 224p. 1990. text 37.50 (*0-8014-2230-2*) Cornell U Pr.

— The Prevalence of Humbug & Other Essays. LC 82-22211. 188p. (Orig.). (C). 1983. pap. text 15.95 (*0-8014-9321-8*) Cornell U Pr.

— Problems of Analysis: Philosophical Essays. LC 74-139124. 304p. (C). 1971. reprint ed. lib. bdg. 59.75 (*0-8371-5740-4*, BLPA, Greenwood Pr) Greenwood.

Black, Max, ed. The Importance of Language. fac. ed. LC 62-13720. (Cornell Paperbacks Ser.). 187p. 1969. reprint ed. pap. 58.00 (*0-608-01009-X*, 206186700012) Bks Demand.

— Philosophical Analysis: A Collection of Essays. LC 78-152158. (Essay Index Reprint Ser.). 1980. reprint ed. 30.95 (*0-8369-2214-X*) Ayer.

— Philosophical Analysis: A Collection of Essays. LC 78-152158. (Essay Index Reprint Ser.). 405p. reprint ed. lib. bdg. 52.00 (*0-8290-0796-2*) Irvington.

Black, Merle & Reed, John S. Perspectives on the American South, Vol. 2. xii, 272p. 1984. text 90.00 (*0-677-16450-5*) Gordon & Breach.

Black, Merle, jt. auth. see Black, Earl.

***Black, Michael.** Cambridge University Press, 1584-1984. (Illus.). 349p. (C). 2000. pap. 19.95 (*0-521-66497-7*) Cambridge U Pr.

— Seed Technology. LC 99-27805. 1999. write for info. (*0-8493-9749-9*) CRC Pr.

***Black, Michael A.** Tanks: The M1A1 Abrams. LC 00-27944. (High Interest Bks.). (Illus.). 48p. (J). (gr. 4-7). 2000. pap. write for info. (*0-516-23542-7*) Childrens.

— Volunteering to Help Kids. (Service-Learning Ser.). (Illus.). (YA). 2000. 19.00 (*0-516-23372-6*) Childrens.

— Volunteering to Help Kids. LC 00-26677. (High Interest Bks.). (Illus.). 48p. (J). (gr. 4-7). 2000. pap. write for info. (*0-516-23572-9*) Childrens.

Black, Michael H. Cambridge University Press, 1584-1984. (Illus.). 349p. 1984. text 69.95 (*0-521-26473-1*) Cambridge U Pr.

— D. H. Lawrence: The Early Fiction. 320p. 1986. text 69.95 (*0-521-32293-6*) Cambridge U Pr.

— D. H. Lawrence: The Early Philosophical Works. 488p. (C). 1992. text 64.95 (*0-521-41584-5*) Cambridge U Pr.

— Lawrence: "Sons & Lovers" (Landmarks of World Literature Ser.). (Illus.). 123p. (C). 1992. pap. text 11.95 (*0-521-36924-X*) Cambridge U Pr.

Black, Michael H., jt. auth. see Pierce, Richard A.

Black, Michael H., ed. see Fischer, Frank.

Black, Michael J., jt. ed. see Meyer, Viktor E.

***Black, Michaela.** Tanks: The M1A1 Abrams. (High Interest Bks.). (Illus.). (J). 2000. 19.00 (*0-516-23342-4*) Childrens.

Black, Michelle. Lightning in a Drought Year: A Novel of the Heartland. LC 99-63575. 260p. 1999. 22.95 (*0-9658014-2-X*) WinterSun Pr.

***Black, Michelle.** Lightning in a Drought Year: A Novel of the Heartland. LC 99-63575. 260p. 2000. pap. 13.95 (*1-929705-00-X*) WinterSun Pr.

Black, Michelle. Never Come Down. 270p. 1996. pap. 9.95 (*1-57502-210-9*, P0849) Morris Pubng.

— Never Come Down. rev. ed. LC 96-60498. 300p. 1997. pap. 12.00 (*0-9658014-0-3*) WinterSun Pr.

***Black, Mike.** Stereophonics: High Times & Head Lines. 2000. pap. text 15.95 (*1-897783-18-3*) Indep Music Pr.

Black, Mike & Lovisi, Gary. Doc Atlas: Artic Terror & The Nemesis: Claws of the Falcon. LC 96-133945. (Gryphon Double Novel Ser.: No. 9). 100p. 1994. per. 12.00 (*0-936071-42-7*) Gryphon Pubns.

Black, Mitchell. Taxi That Hurried, 10. 24p. (ps-2). 1999. pap. text 9.95 (*0-307-10222-X*) Gldn Bks Pub Co.

Black, Moishe, ed. & tr. see Jacob, Max.

Black, Moishe, tr. see Jacob, Max.

Black, Moishe, tr. see Otte, Jean-Pierre.

Black, N., jt. auth. see Handrek, K.

Black, Nancy A. Gert Fram: A Kid's Book for Grownups. 112p. (Orig.). 1991. pap. 5.95 (*0-9624049-4-2*) Hatrack River.

Black, Nancy B., ed. The Perilous Cemetery (L'Atre Perilleux) LC 94-18392. (Garland Library of Medieval Literature: Vol. 104A). (Illus.). 480p. 1994. text 20.00 (*0-8153-1897-9*) Garland.

Black, Nancy J. The Frontier Mission & Social Transformation in Western Honduras: The Order of Our Lady of Mercy, 1525-1773. LC 95-2093. (Studies in Christian Mission: Vol. 14). xiii, 194p. 1995. 75.00 (*90-04-10219-1*) Brill Academic Pubs.

Black, Nancy J. & Turck, Mary. Guatemala: Land of the Maya. LC 97-37458. (Discovering Our Heritage Ser.). (J). 1998. 23.00 (*0-382-39718-5*); pap. write for info. (*0-382-39719-3*) Silver Burdett Pr.

Black, Nancy J., jt. auth. see Turck, Mary.

Black, Nancy Johnson, jt. auth. see Mascia-Lees, Frances E.

Black, Nancy K., et al. PPC's 5500 DeskBook, 2 vols. Incl. Vol. 1. 1998. ring bd. 150.00 (*0-7646-0394-9*); Vol. 2. 1998. ring bd. 150.00 (*0-7646-0395-7*); 150.00 (*0-7646-0393-0*) Prctnrs Pub Co.

Black, Naomi. Social Feminism. LC 88-47937. 416p. 1988. pap. text 19.95 (*0-8014-9573-3*) Cornell U Pr.

Black, Naomi, ed. Celebration: The Book of Jewish Festivals. 160p. 1989. 26.95 (*0-8246-0340-0*) Jonathan David.

Black, Naomi & Cuthbert Brandt, Gail. Feminist Politics on the Farm: Rural Catholic Women in Southern Quebec & Southwestern France. 65.00 (*0-7735-1828-2*) McG-Queens Univ Pr.

Black, Nick, et al, eds. Health Services Research Methods: A Guide to Best Practice. 268p. 1998. 30.00 (*0-7279-1275-5*) BMJ Pub.

Black, O. F., jt. auth. see Igarashi, M.

Black, Patricia S. Favorite Montana Recipes: With Bits of History Stirred in. (Illus.). 225p. 1994. pap. 14.95 (*0-9642310-0-X*) Heart West Pr.

Black, Patti C. Art in Mississippi, 1720-1980. LC 98-25119. (Heritage of Mississippi Ser.). (Illus.). 320p. 1998. text 60.00 (*1-57806-084-2*) U Pr of Miss.

— The Southern Writers Quiz Book. LC 98-48346. (Illus.). 80p. 1999. pap. 10.00 (*1-57806-149-0*) U Pr of Miss.

— Welty. LC 77-82045. (Old Capitol Museum Ser.). (Illus.). 28p. 1977. pap. text 6.95 (*0-87805-337-9*) U Pr of Miss.

Black, Patti C., ed. Mississippi Patent Models. (Illus.). 24p. 1981. pap. 3.50 (*0-938896-32-6*) Mississippi Archives.

— Persistence in Pattern in Mississippi Choctaw Culture. (Old Capitol Museum Ser.). (Illus.). 44p. 1987. pap. 9.95 (*0-938896-51-2*) Mississippi Archives.

***Black, Patti C., et al.** Of Home & Family: Art in Nineteenth Century Mississippi. Greenberg, Kathy L., ed. LC 99-39646. (Illus.). 48p. 1999. pap. 20.00 (*1-887422-04-8*) Miss Mus Art.

Black, Patti C., ed. see Anderson, Agnes G.

Black, Patti C., ed. see Welty, Eudora.

Black, Patti C., ed. & intro. see Anderson, Walter.

Black, Paul & Lucas, Arthur, eds. Children's Informal Ideas about Science. LC 92-41878. 240p. (C). 1993. 80.00 (*0-415-00539-6*, A1783) Routledge.

Black, Paul, ed. see Atkin, J. Myron, et al.

Black, Penny. The Book of Pressed Flowers: A Complete Guide to Pressing, Drying, & Arranging. (Illus.). 120p. 1988. 22.00 (*0-671-66071-3*) S&S Trade.

— A Passion for Flowers. (Illus.). 144p. 1992. 30.00 (*0-671-75106-9*) S&S Trade.

Black, Perry, ed. Brain Dysfunction in Children: Etiology, Diagnosis & Management. LC 74-21975. (Illus.). 320p. 1981. reprint ed. pap. 99.20 (*0-608-00616-5*, 206120300007) Bks Demand.

— Drugs & the Brain: Papers on the Action, Use, & Abuse of Psychotropic Agents. LC 68-31642. 416p. reprint ed. pap. 129.00 (*0-608-30503-0*, 200119100068) Bks Demand.

Black, Perry O. & Scahill. Diesel Engine Manual. 4th ed. LC 82-20635. (Audel Ser.). 1983. text 22.50 (*0-672-23371-1*) Macmillan.

Black, Peter. Geoffrey Clarke Symbols for Man: Sculpture & Graphic Work, 1949-94. LC 95-212265. (Illus.). 88p. 1995. pap. 30.00 (*0-85331-665-1*, Pub. by Lund Humphries) Antique Collect.

***Black, Peter.** Orchid Growing. LC 98-212488. 160p. 1998. pap. 17.95 (*0-7063-7743-5*, Pub. by WrLock) Sterling.

Black, Peter, et al, eds. Astrocytomas: Diagnosis, Treatment, & Biology. LC 92-10543. (Contemporary Issues in Neurological Surgery Ser.). (Illus.). 320p. 1993. 95.00 (*0-86542-217-6*) Blackwell Sci.

***Black, Peter, photos by.** Bush: 8 Frames per Sec. 104p. (YA). 1999. pap. 19.95 (*0-8256-1781-2*, BU10000) Omnibus NY.

Black, Peter, photos by. Bush Sixteen Stone Tour. LC 97-177201. (Illus.). 96p. (Orig.). 1996. pap. 14.95 (*0-8256-1601-8*, OP 47889) Omnibus NY.

Black, Peter & Moorhead, Desiree. The Prints of Stanley William Hayter: A Complete Catalogue. (Illus.). 416p. 1992. 250.00 (*1-55921-049-4*) Moyer Bell.

Black, Peter A. & Scimecca, Joseph. Conflict Resolution: Cross-Cultural Perspectives. Avruch, Kevin W., ed. LC 91-15991. 256p. 1998. pap. 22.95 (*0-275-96442-6*, Praeger Pubs) Greenwood.

Black, Peter E. Conservation of Water & Related Land Resources. 2nd ed. 352p. (C). 1988. 62.50 (*0-8476-7567-X*) Rowman.

— Watershed Hydrology. 2nd ed. 512p. 1990. text 70.00 (*0-13-946591-X*, 320102) CRC Pr.

— Watershed Hydrology. 2nd ed. 460p. (C). 1996. boxed set 64.95 (*1-57504-027-1*) CRC Pr.

Black, Peter E., ed. Clinical Neurosurgery, Vol. 35. (Proceedings of the Congress of Neurological Surgeons Ser.). (Illus.). 576p. 1988. 65.00 (*0-683-02032-3*) Lppncott W & W.

— Readings in Environmental Impact. LC 74-13079. 345p. 1974. text 39.50 (*0-8422-5201-0*) Irvington.

Black, Peter E., jt. ed. see Eschner, Arthur R.

Black, Peter E., ed. see Symposium on Monitoring, Modeling, & Mediating Wat.

Black, Peter M. Clinical Neurosurgery: Proceedings of the Congress of Neurological Surgeons, Vol. 36. (Illus.). 512p. 1989. 65.00 (*0-683-02033-1*) Lppncott W & W.

— Clinical Neurosurgery Vol. 37: Proceedings of the Congress of Neurological Surgeons. (Illus.). 844p. 1990. 66.00 (*0-683-02034-X*) Lppncott W & W.

— Informatica: The Best Tools for Accessing & Managing Information. LC 99-29069. 1999. pap. 22.95 (*0-375-70628-3*) Random.

— Informatica: The Best Tools for Accessing & Managing Information. 400p. 1999. pap. 34.95 incl. cd-rom (*0-375-70637-2*) Random.

Black, Peter M., et al, eds. Secretory Tumors of the Pituitary Gland. LC 84-15991. (Progress in Endocrine Research & Therapy Ser.: No. 1). (Illus.). 416p. 1984. reprint ed. pap. 129.00 (*0-7837-9565-3*, 206031400005) Bks Demand.

Black, Peter M. & Loeffler, Jay S. Cancer of the Nervous System. (Illus.). 935p. 1997. text 150.00 (*0-86542-384-9*) Blackwell Sci.

Black, Peter M. & Rossitch, Eugene. Neurosurgery: An Introductory Text. (Illus.). 248p. 1995. text 49.95 (*0-19-504448-7*); pap. text 24.95 (*0-19-504449-5*) OUP.

Black, Peter R. Ernst Kaltenbrunner, Ideological Soldier of the Third Reich. LC 83-42550. 367p. reprint ed. pap. 113.80 (*0-8357-3423-4*, 203968000013) Bks Demand.

Black-Plomeau, Leslie. Homeownership: Potential Effects of Reducing FHA's Insurance Coverage for Home Mortgages. (Illus.). 80p. (C). 1998. pap. text 20.00 (*0-7881-4744-7*) DIANE Pub.

Black Public Sphere Collective Staff, ed. The Black Public Sphere. LC 95-21303. (Black Literature & Culture Ser.). 355p. 1995. pap. 17.95 (*0-226-07192-8*); lib. bdg. 35.00 (*0-226-07190-1*) U Ch Pr.

Black, R. Angola. LC 93-205389. (World Bibliographical Ser.). 206p. 1993. lib. bdg. 69.00 (*1-85109-143-2*) ABC-CLIO.

Black, R. Collison. A Catalogue of Pamphlets on Economic Subjects 1750-1900 & Now Housed in Irish Libraries. LC 79-81989. ix, 632p. 1969. 75.00 (*0-678-08002-X*) Kelley.

B

— Economic Theory & Policy in Context: Selected Essays of R. D. Collison Black. LC 95-7196. (Economists of the Twentieth Century Ser.). 304p. 1995. 95.00 (*1-85898-123-9*) E Elgar.

Black, R. D., ed. Ideas In Economics. LC 86-10853. 256p. 1986. 66.00 (*0-389-20644-X*, N8201) B&N Imports.

Black, R. D., ed. see Longfield, Mountiford.

Black, R. H. Manual of Epidemiology & Epidemiological Services in Malaria Programmes. (Illus.). 223p. 1968. pap. text 8.00 (*92-4-154015-X*, 1150098) World Health.

Black, R. L. The Church of God of Prophecy: Pastor. 1977. 4.25 (*0-934942-29-3*) White Wing Pub.

— Discerning the Body. 98p. (Orig.). 1984. pap. 3.95 (*0-934942-42-0*, 1264) White Wing Pub.

— Is Marriage Till Death? Orig. Title: Pastor, Why Can't I Remarry?. 91p. (Orig.). 1988. pap. 3.50 (*0-934942-68-4*) White Wing Pub.

Black, R. M. A History of Electric Wires & Cables. (History of Technology Ser.: No. 4). 304p. 1983. boxed set 99.00 (*0-86341-001-4*, HT004) INSPEC Inc.

Black, R. M., ed. A History of Dickey County, North Dakota. (Illus.). 333p. 1993. reprint ed. lib. bdg. 39.50 (*0-8328-3478-5*) Higginson Bk Co.

***Black, Ralph.** Turning over the Earth. LC 99-88540. 95p. 2000. pap. 13.95 (*1-57131-411-3*) Milkweed Ed.

***Black, Rebecca.** Lactation Specialist: Marketing Your Lactation Practice, Vol. 5. (Illus.). 228p. (C). 1999. pap. text 40.00 (*0-7637-1037-7*) JB Pubns.

Black, Rebecca F., et al. Lactation Specialist Self-Study Series. 900p. 1998. pap. 125.00 (*0-7637-0664-7*) Jones & Bartlett.

— Management of Breastfeeding, Module 4. LC 97-25569. (Nursing Ser.). 280p. 1998. spiral bd. 39.95 (*0-7637-0193-9*) Jones & Bartlett.

— Process of Breastfeeding, Module 2. LC 97-25569. (Nursing Ser.). 264p. 1997. spiral bd. 39.95 (*0-7637-0195-5*) Jones & Bartlett.

— Science of Breastfeeding, Module 3. LC 97-25569. (Nursing Ser.). 304p. 1998. spiral bd. 39.95 (*0-7637-0194-7*) Jones & Bartlett.

— Support of Breastfeeding, Module 1. LC 97-25569. (Nursing Ser.). 208p. 1997. spiral bd. 39.95 (*0-7637-0208-0*) Jones & Bartlett.

Black Relocation Assn., Inc. Staff. New Connections: African American Newcomers & Visitors to the Twin Cities Guide. (Illus.). 108p. (Orig.). 1997. pap. 6.95 (*0-9652905-1-4*) Blck Relocat.

Black Relocation Association, Inc., Staff. New Connections: African American Newcomers & Visitors to the Twin Cities Guide. (Illus.). 108p. (Orig.). 1996. pap. 6.95 (*0-9652905-0-6*) Blck Relocat.

Black, Rex E. Managing the Testing Process. LC 99-27358. 350p. 1999. pap. 39.99 (*0-7356-0584-X*) Microsoft.

Black, Rex E., jt. auth. see Richmond, Michael D.

Black, Rhona M. The Elements of Palaeontology. 2nd ed. (Illus.). 416p. 1989. pap. text 34.95 (*0-521-34836-6*) Cambridge U Pr.

Black, Rhonda M. & Sweetmore, A. Plant Quarantine: A Primer to Development Workers. 1995. pap. 45.00 (*0-85954-397-8*, Pub. by Nat Res Inst) St Mut.

Black, Rhonda M., et al. Plant Clinic: A Training System for Decision-Making & Resource Management in Plant Disease Diagnostics. 1995. pap. 39.00 (*0-85954-396-X*, Pub. by Nat Res Inst) St Mut.

Black, Ricardo A., ed. & illus. see Ingram, Wesley T.

Black, Richard. Crisis & Change in Rural Europe: Agricultural Development in the Portuguese Mountains. 208p. 1992. 82.95 (*1-85628-272-4*, Pub. by Avebry) Ashgate Pub Co.

— Ferrari Guides' Gay Mexico. (Orig.). 1997. pap. 17.95 (*0-942586-62-X*) Ferrari Intl Pub.

— Refugees, Environment & Development. 1p. (C). 1998. pap. 33.53 (*0-582-31564-6*) Addison-Wesley.

— Rural Europe. 256p. pap. text. write for info. (*0-340-59699-6*, Pub. by E A) Routldge.

Black, Richard & Koser, Khalid, eds. The End of the Refugee Cycle? Refugee Repatriation & Reconstruction. LC 98-50558. (Refugees & Forced Migration Studies: No. 4). 256p. 1998. 69.95 (*1-57181-987-8*) Berghahn Bks.

— The End of the Refugee Cycle? Vol. 4: Refugee Repatriation & Reconstruction. LC 98-50558. (Illus.). 256p. 1998. pap. 22.50 (*1-57181-715-8*) Berghahn Bks.

Black, Richard & Robinson, Vaughan, eds. Geography & Refugees: Patterns & Processes of Change. LC 93-15085. 256p. 1993. pap. 150.00 (*0-471-94481-5*) Wiley.

Black, Richard, jt. ed. see King, Russell.

Black, Richard W. The Complete Family Guide to College Financial Aid. LC 95-8201. 1995. pap. 12.00 (*0-399-52158-5*, Perigee Bks) Berkley Pub.

Black, Rita B., jt. ed. see Schild, Sylvia.

Black River Group Staff & Dallmann-Jones, Anthony S. The Expert Educator: A Reference Manual of Teaching Strategies for Quality Education. LC 93-61442. 328p. (C). 1994. text 29.95 (*1-881952-23-1*) Three Blue Herons.

Black River Group Staff, jt. auth. see Dallman-Jones, Anthony S.

***Black River Historical Society Staff.** Lorain. (Images of America Ser.). 128p. 1999. pap. 18.99 (*0-7385-0178-6*) Arcadia Publng.

Black, Rob. Military Transition Series. Dean, Becky et al, eds. 60p. 1998. reprint ed. pap. 14.95 (*1-891726-13-7*) Aviation Info.

Black, Robert. Commentaries on the Law of Scotland (1870) 1580p. 1990. text 210.00 (*0-406-17899-2*, UK, MICHIE) LEXIS Pub.

***Black, Robert.** Dr. Reynard's Experiment. (Idol Ser.). 256p. 1998. mass mkt. 9.95 (*0-352-33252-2*, Pub. by BLA4) London Brdge.

Black, Robert. Hard Time. 1999. mass mkt. 9.95 (*0-352-33304-9*) Nexus Contemp.

— Hell of Mirrors. 224p. (Orig.). 1997. pap. text 9.95 (*0-352-33209-3*, Pub. by Virgin Bks) London Brdge.

Black, Robert, et al, eds. Laws of Scotland: Stair Memorial Encyclopaedia. write for info. (*0-406-04849-5*, LS1SET, MICHIE) LEXIS Pub.

Black, Robert, jt. auth. see Rose, Burton D.

Black, Robert, tr. see Guizot, Francois P., ed.

Black, Robert C., III. The Railroads of the Confederacy. LC 97-44268. (Illus.). 400p. 1998. pap. 19.95 (*0-8078-4729-1*) U of NC Pr.

Black, Robert F., et al, eds. The Wisconsinan Stage. LC 72-89466. (Geological Society of America, Memoir Ser.: No. 136). 344p. reprint ed. pap. 106.70 (*0-608-14461-4*, 202503000041) Bks Demand.

Black, Robert G. Cockatiels: Overcoming Problems in Their Care, Feeding & Breeding. LC F473.C6B57 1985 8. write for info. (*0-668-06316-5*) Prntice Hall Bks.

Black, Robert G., ed. Texts & Concordances of Manuscript Esp. 226 of the Bibliotheque Nationale, Paris: Cancionero Castellano Y Catalan de Paris. (Spanish Ser.: No. 23). 16p. 1985. text 10.00 incl. fiche (*0-942260-65-1*) Hispanic Seminary.

Black, Robert J. Florida Lawn Handbook. 1997. pap. text 19.95 (*0-916287-22-X*) Univ Fla Food.

Black, Robert J. & Gilman, Edward F. Your Florida Guide to Bedding Plants: Selection, Establishment, & Maintenance. LC 98-25884. (Illus.). 1997. pap. 14.95 (*0-8130-1642-8*) U Press Fla.

— Your Guide to Florida Bedding Plants: Selection, Establishment & Maintenance. LC 96-46935. (Illus.). 71p. (Orig.). 1996. pap. 14.95 (*0-916287-17-3*, SP 185) Univ Fla Food.

Black, Robert J. & Ruppert, Kathleen C., eds. Your Florida Landscape. (Illus.). 234p. 1995. pap. 9.00 (*0-916287-08-4*, SP135) Univ Fla Food.

— Your Florida Landscape: A Complete Guide to Planting & Maintenance. (Illus.). 1998. pap. 19.95 (*0-8130-1641-X*) U Press Fla.

Black, Robert J., jt. auth. see Gilman, Edward F.

Black, Robert J., jt. ed. see Dunn, R. A., et al.

Black, Robert J., jt. ed. see Ruppert, Kathleen C.

Black, Robert M. Rose & Black's Clinical Patterns in Nephrology. 597p. 1995. text 109.00 (*0-316-75652-0*, Little Brwn Med Div) Lppncott W & W.

Black, Robert N. Edith Stein: A Ceremony of Remembrance. 88p. 1998. pap. 5.00 (*0-87440-062-7*) Bakers Plays.

Black, Robert U. 1999 Pilot's Guide to Flying in the Guard & Reserve. Waymire, Montina L. & Mattice, Dave, eds. 368p. 1999. pap. 40.95 (*1-891726-22-6*, AIR Inc) Aviation Info.

Black, Rod. Design & Manufacture: An Integrated Approach. (Illus.). 328p. (C). 1996. pap. text 39.95 (*0-333-60915-8*) Scholium Intl.

Black, Ronald, ed. An Anthology of Twentieth Century Scottish Gaelic Verse. 344p. Date not set. pap. 28.00 (*0-7486-6219-7*, Pub. by Polygon) Subterranean Co.

Black, Roy. Black's Law: A Criminal Lawyer Reveals His Defence Strategies in Four Cliffhanger Cases. 320p. 2000. per. 13.00 (*0-684-86306-5*) S&S Trade.

— Black's Law: A Famous Criminal Lawyer Reveals His Defense Strategies in Four Cliffhanger Cases. LC 98-31544. 320p. 1999. 24.50 (*0-684-81022-0*) S&S Trade.

Black, S. Fabulous Facts about the Fifty States. LC 98-110559. 224p. (J). (gr. 4-7). 1991. pap. 2.75 (*0-590-44886-2*) Scholastic Inc.

Black, S. & Newberger, D. Coast to Coast: Facts & Fun about the Fifty States. 64p. (J). (gr. 3-7). 1991. 1.95 (*0-590-43970-7*) Scholastic Inc.

Black, S. F. Double Trouble. 1997. pap. 3.95 (*0-8167-4427-0*) Troll Communs.

— Invasion of the Body Thieves. (Cyber Zone Ser.: No. 4). 1997. pap. 3.95 (*0-8167-4344-4*) Troll Communs.

— Lost in Dino World. (J). 1997. pap. 3.95 (*0-8167-4280-4*) Troll Communs.

— Meltdown Man, Vol. 1. (Cyber Zone Ser.). (J). 1997. pap. 3.95 (*0-8167-4279-0*) Troll Communs.

— Virtual Nightmare. (Cyber Zone Ser.: Vol. 3). (J). (gr. 3-7). 1997. pap. 3.95 (*0-8167-4343-6*) Troll Communs.

— Visitor from the Beyond. 1997. pap. 3.95 (*0-8167-4428-9*) Troll Communs.

Black, S. Jason & Hyatt, Christopher S. Pacts with the Devil: A Chronicle of Sex, Blasphemy & Liberation. 2nd ed. (Illus.). 256p. (Orig.). 1993. pap. 14.95 (*1-56184-058-0*) New Falcon Pubns.

— Urban Voodoo: A Beginner's Guide to Afro-Caribbean Magic. LC 94-66064. (Illus.). 192p. (Orig.). 1995. pap. 14.95 (*1-56184-059-9*) New Falcon Pubns.

Black, S. Jason, jt. auth. see Hyatt, Christopher S.

Black Sabbath. We Sold Our Soul for Rock 'n Roll. 80p. 1990. per. 14.95 (*0-7935-6205-8*) H Leonard.

Black, Sam. Exhibiting Overseas. 1971. pap. 25.00 (*0-8464-0393-5*) Beekman Pubs.

Black, Sam, ed. The Practice of Public Relations. 4th ed. (Marketing Ser.). 186p. 2000. pap. text 49.95 (*0-7506-2318-7*) Buttrwrth-Heinemann.

Black, Samuel P., Jr. Entrepreneurship & Innovation in Automobile Insurance. 250p. 1998. 50.00 (*0-8153-2915-6*) Garland.

Black, Samuel W., et al. Yet Still We Rise: African American Art in Cleveland 1920-1970. Korneitchouk, Ursula, ed. (Illus.). 90p. (Orig.). (C). 1996. pap. text 20.00 (*0-9639562-4-8*) Clevelnd Art.

Black, Sandra Baton. Color-Coding Your Scriptures. LC 98-116795. 1997. pap. 4.95 (*1-57734-191-0*, 01113232) Covenant Comms.

Black, Sara, jt. auth. see Djurovic, Liliana.

Black, Sara H., jt. auth. see Black, Lowell D.

***Black, Sharon.** The Gigs Handbook: A Beginner's Guide to Playing Professionally. LC 99-75432. (Illus.). 200p. 2000. pap. 18.95 (*0-9674813-0-9*) Benny Pubg.

Black, Sharon. Telecommunications Law. 400p. 1999. 49.95 (*1-55860-546-0*, Pub. by Morgan Kaufmann) Harcourt.

Black, Sheila. Sitting Bull. Furstinger, Nancy, ed. (Alvin Josephy's Biography of the American Indians Ser.). (Illus.). 144p. (J). (gr. 5-7). 1989. pap. 7.95 (*0-382-09761-0*, Silver Pr NJ); lib. bdg. 12.95 (*0-382-09572-3*, Silver Pr NJ) Silver Burdett Pr.

— Will the Real Ms. X Please Report to the Principal! 144p. (J). (gr. 3-7). 1998. pap. 3.95 (*0-8167-4813-6*) Troll Communs.

Black, Shelia. Hansel & Gretel & the Witch's Story. (J). (ps-3). 1991. 13.95 (*1-55972-080-8*, Birch Ln Pr) Carol Pub Group.

Black, Shelley, ed. see Stephens, Herb.

Black, Shirley B. Local Government, Law & Order in a Pre-Reform English Parish, 1790-1834. LC 92-45202. (Illus.). 448p. 1993. text 109.95 (*0-7734-9239-9*) E Mellen.

***Black, Shirley J.** Napoleon III & Mexican Silver. rev. ed. (Illus.). vii, 220p. 2000. write for info. (*0-9676777-0-X*) Ferrell Pubns.

Black, Simon. The Book of Frank. Putnam, Jeff, ed. 228p. 1994. pap. 11.00 (*1-880909-28-6*) Baskerville.

— The Book of Frank. 2nd ed. 228p. 1994. 19.00 (*1-880909-25-1*) Baskerville.

— Me & Kev. LC 93-70995. 263p. 1993. 20.00 (*1-880909-08-1*) Baskerville.

***Black, Simon.** A Scientist's Story. LC 99-93930. 83p. 2000. pap. 10.00 (*0-533-13190-1*) Vantage.

Black, Sonia W. All about Baby Animals Activity Book. 32p. (J). (ps-3). 1993. pap. 1.95 (*0-590-46286-5*) Scholastic Inc.

— All about My Skeleton. 32p. (J). (ps-3). 1995. pap. 1.95 (*0-590-48721-3*) Scholastic Inc.

— Full House Trivia & Puzzle Fun Book. 64p. (J). (gr. 4-7). 1993. pap. 2.95 (*0-590-47145-7*) Scholastic Inc.

— Hanging Out with Mom. LC 96-21308. (Hello Reader! Ser.). (Illus.). 32p. (J). (ps-3). 2000. 3.99 (*0-590-86636-2*) Scholastic Inc.

***Black, Sonia W.** Hanging Out with Mom. (Hello, Reader! Ser.). (Illus.). (J). 2000. 9.44 (*0-606-18554-2*) Turtleback.

— Mae Jemison. 64p. (J). (gr. 3-7). 2000. pap. 3.95 (*1-57255-801-6*) Mondo Pubng.

Black, Sonia W. Plenty of Penguins. LC 99-26237. (Hello Reader! Science Ser.). (Illus.). 32p. (J). (ps-k). 1999. 3.99 (*0-439-09832-7*) Scholastic Inc.

Black, Sonia W. & Brigandi, Pat. The Baby-Sitters Club Notebook. (Baby-Sitters Club Ser.). (Illus.). 64p. (J). (gr. 4-6). 1991. pap. 2.50 (*0-590-45074-3*) Scholastic Inc.

***Black, Sonia W. & MacCombie, Turi.** Follow the Polar Bears. LC 00-38795. (Hello Science Reader! Ser.). 2000. write for info. (*0-439-20641-3*) Scholastic Inc.

Black, Sophie C. The Misunderstanding of Nature: Poetry. LC 93-23114. 96p. 1994. 22.50 (*1-55597-190-3*); pap. 12.00 (*1-55597-201-2*) Graywolf.

Black, Stanley. Globalization, Technological Change, & Labor Markets. LC 98-31087. 1998. 129.95 (*0-7923-8318-4*) Kluwer Academic.

Black, Stanley W. Learning from Adversity: Policy Responses to 2 Oil Shocks. LC 85-23726. (Essays in International Finance Ser.: No. 160). 24p. 1985. pap. text 10.00 (*0-88165-067-6*) Princeton U Int Finan Econ.

Black, Stanley W., ed. Europe's Economy Looks East: Implications for Germany & the European Union. (Illus.). 379p. (C). 1997. text 69.95 (*0-521-57242-8*) Cambridge U Pr.

— Productivity Growth & the Competitiveness of the American Economy. (C). 1989. lib. bdg. 80.00 (*0-7923-9001-6*) Kluwer Academic.

Black, Stanley W., et al. Competition & Convergence in Financial Markets: The German & Anglo-American Models. LC 97-50532. (Advances in Finance, Investment, & Banking Ser.: 5). 426p. 1998. 129.50 (*0-444-82776-5*) Elsevier.

Black, Star. Balefire. LC 99-13052. 1999. 12.00 (*1-891305-16-6*) Painted Leaf.

— October for Idas. LC 96-45638. 1997. pap. 12.00 (*0-9651558-1-1*) Painted Leaf.

— Waterworn. (Gathering of the Tribes Ser.: No. 9). 112p. (Orig.). 1995. pap. 10.00 (*0-9639585-4-2*) Fly by Nght.

Black, Star, jt. auth. see Lehman, David.

***Black, Stella.** Shameless. 2000. mass mkt. 6.95 (*0-352-33485-1*) BLA4.

Black, Stephanie J., jt. auth. see Plonien, Michael J.

Black, Stephen. Internal Corporate Investigations. Vol. C5. text 82.00 (*0-8205-2406-9*) Bender.

Black, Stephen. The Pokey & Horse Latitudes: Manuscript Edition. 1976. pap. 13.00 (*0-8222-0903-9*) Dramatists Play.

Black, Stephen, jt. auth. see Witten, Roger M.

***Black, Stephen A.** Eugene O'Neill: Beyond Mourning & Tragedy. LC 99-33897. (Illus.). 480p. 1999. 29.95 (*0-300-07676-2*) Yale U Pr.

Black, Stephen A. Whitman's Journeys into Chaos: A Psychoanalytic Study of the Poetic Process. LC 75-2979. 272p. 1975. pap. 84.40 (*0-7837-7446-X*, 201054700068) Bks Demand.

Black, Stephen F. & Witten, Roger M. Business Law Monographs, 36 vols. LC 86-125012. 1999. ring bd. 1450.00 (*0-8205-1080-7*) Bender.

Black, Stephen T., jt. auth. see Black, Katherine D.

Black, Stewart. Management: Meeting New Challenges. 656p. (C). 1999. pap. write for info. (*0-321-04655-2*) Addson-Wesley Educ.

Black, Stewart, et al. Global Explorers: The Next Generation of Leaders. 288p. 1999. 29.99 (*0-415-92148-1*) Routledge.

— Globalizing People through International Assignments. LC 98-45109. 720p. (C). 1998. pap. 47.00 (*0-201-43389-3*, Prentice Hall) P-H.

Black, Stewart, jt. ed. see Connor, Anne.

Black, Sue M. Essential Anatomy for Anesthesia. 1998. 70.95 (*0-443-05054-6*) Church.

Black, Susan. Asphyxiation. LC 96-60922. 116p. 1996. 14.95 (*1-881636-08-9*) Windsor Hse Pub Grp.

— Bono: In His Own Words. rev. ed. (In Their Own Words Ser.). (Illus.). 96p. pap. 15.95 (*0-7119-5299-X*, OP 47797) Omnibus NY.

Black, Susan E. The Mormon Temple Square: The Story Behind the Scenery. Petzinger, Saori, tr. (JPN., Illus.). 48p. (Orig.). 1993. pap. 8.95 (*0-88714-760-7*) KC Pubns.

— The Mormon Temple Square: The Story Behind the Scenery. LC 93-77026. (Illus.). 48p. (Orig.). 1993. pap. 7.95 (*0-88714-076-9*) KC Pubns.

— The Mormon Temple Square: The Story Behind the Scenery. Morales, Brigitte, tr. (GER., Illus.). 48p. (Orig.). 1993. pap. 8.95 (*0-88714-758-5*) KC Pubns.

— The Mormon Temple Square: The Story Behind the Scenery. Le Bras, Yvon, tr. (FRE., Illus.). 48p. (Orig.). 1993. pap. 8.95 (*0-88714-759-3*) KC Pubns.

— The Mormon Temple Square: The Story Behind the Scenery. Marapodi, Carlos, tr. (SPA., Illus.). 48p. (Orig.). 1993. pap. 8.95 (*0-88714-761-5*) KC Pubns.

— Who's Who in the Doctrine & Covenants. 1997. 21.95 (*1-57008-292-8*) Bookcraft Inc.

Black, Susan E., ed. Expressions of Faith: Testimonies of Latter-Day Saint Scholars. LC 95-51330. xiv, 252p. 1996. 15.95 (*1-57345-091-X*) Deseret Bk.

Black, Susan E. & Porter, Larry C., eds. Lion of the Lord: Essays on the Life & Service of Brigham Young. LC 95-42591. xii, 462p. 1996. 19.95 (*1-57345-112-6*) Deseret Bk.

Black, Susan E., jt. ed. see Porter, Larry C.

***Black, Susan Eastman & Telford, John.** In the Footsteps of Jesus: Images of the Holy Land. LC 99-36557. 1999. 29.95 (*1-57734-510-X*, 01114107) Covenant Comms.

Black, Susan Easton & Hartley, William G., eds. The Iowa Mormon Trail: Legacy of Faith & Courage. LC 96-80167. (Illus.). 304p. 1997. pap. 14.95 (*0-9655572-0-0*, Pub. by Helix Pub) Origin Bk Sales.

***Black, Susan Eston & Telford, John.** Salt Lake 2002: An Official Book of the Olympic Winter Games. LC 00-38747. (Illus.). 2000. pap. 39.95 (*1-57345-795-7*, Shadow Mount) Deseret Bk.

Black, Susan H., et al. Federal Appellate Procedure - 11th Circuit: Federal Practice Guide. LC 96-77083. (American Inns of Court Ser.). 1500p. 1996. text. write for info. (*0-7620-0078-3*) West Group.

Black, Suzi. Nirvana Tribute: The Life & Death of Kurt Cobain - The Full Story. LC 95-188018. (Illus.). 48p. 1994. pap. 11.95 (*0-7119-4244-7*, OP 47696) Omnibus NY.

— The Story of Nirvana: Omnibus Press Presents the Story Of. (Illus.). 48p. (Orig.). pap. 11.95 (*0-8256-1539-9*, OP 47808) Omnibus NY.

Black, T. C. The Trader's Wife. 288p. 1998. mass mkt. 5.99 (*0-380-79444-6*, Avon Bks) Morrow Avon.

Black, T. D., et al, eds. Foundations of Quantum Mechanics: Santa Fe, New Mexico, 27-31 May 1991. 400p. 1992. text 95.00 (*981-02-0980-0*) World Scientific Pub.

Black, Terry. Terry Black: Fiery Vision Bright. Gasque, Laurel & Schindell, Dal, eds. 36p. (Orig.). (C). 1995. reprint ed. pap. write for info. (*1-57383-044-5*) Regent College.

Black, Thom. 55 Waverly Street. LC 97-34061. (Illus.). 48p. (J). 1998. 14.99 (*0-310-20792-4*) Zondervan.

Black, Thomas. Black's Texas Evidence Manual, 2 vols., Set. LC 85-393. 1990. 165.00 (*0-8321-0024-2*) West Group.

— Evaluating Social Science Research: An Introduction. (Illus.). 224p. (C). 1993. text 55.00 (*0-8039-8852-4*); pap. text 22.95 (*0-8039-8853-2*) Sage.

Black, Tom & Stephenson, Lynda R. Born to Fly: How to Discover & Encourage Your Child's Natural Gifts. 224p. 1994. 14.99 (*0-310-40281-6*) Zondervan.

— Born to Fly: How to Discover & Encourage Your Child's Natural Gifts. 96p. 1994. pap., wbk. ed. 7.99 (*0-310-40283-2*) Zondervan.

Black, Trevor. Intellectual Property in Industry. 310p. 1989. pap. 64.00 (*0-406-10140-X*, UK, MICHIE) LEXIS Pub.

Black, Tricis M., ed. Issues in Midwifery. LC 94-29342. 1995. pap. text 32.95 (*0-443-04864-9*) Church.

Black, Ulyesses. Architecture for Carrier Transport Systems. LC 97-6009. 352p. (C). 1997. 69.99 (*0-13-259193-6*) P-H.

Black, Ulysses D. Computer Networks. 2nd ed. 432p. 1993. 60.00 (*0-13-175605-2*) P-H.

Black, Ulysses D. Data Link Protocols. LC 92-21202. 320p. 1993. 84.00 (*0-13-204918-X*) P-H.

— Emerging Communications Technologies. 2nd ed. LC 97-866. 480p. (C). 1997. 51.99 (*0-13-742834-0*) P-H.

— Frame Relay Networks: Specifications & Implementations. 2nd ed. (McGraw-Hill Computer Communications Series). (Illus.). 256p. 1996. 45.00 (*0-07-005590-4*) McGraw.

— Mobile & Wireless Networks. LC 96-11741. 384p. 1996. 60.00 (*0-13-440546-3*) P-H.

— Network Management Standards: SNMP, CMIP, TMN, MIBs & Object Libraries. 2nd ed. LC 94-22288. 351p. 1994. 50.00 (*0-07-005570-X*) McGraw.

— OSI: A Model for Computer Communications Standards. 336p. (C). 1990. text 54.75 (*0-13-637133-7*) P-H.

— Physical Level Interfaces & Protocols. 2nd ed. LC 94-47597. 232p. 1995. 58.00 (*0-8186-5697-2*, BP05697) IEEE Comp Soc.

Black, Ulysses D. & Waters, Sharlean. SONET & T1: Architecture for Carrier Transport Systems. LC 96-38443. 352p. (C). 1996. 73.00 (*0-13-447590-9*) P-H.

Black, Uyless. The Advanced Intelligent Network. LC 97-47329. 224p. (C). 1998. 72.00 (*0-13-793019-4*, Prentice Hall) P-H.

— ATM Resource Library Vol. 1: ATM Foundation for Broadband Networks; ATM Signaling, Vol. 2. 1p. (C). 1997. pap. text 149.99 (*0-13-793779-2*) P-H.

***Black, Uyless.** Internet Architecture & Protocols. 2000. pap. 129.99 (*0-13-030329-1*) P-H.

— Internet Architectures. 400p. 2000. 49.99 (*0-13-019906-0*, Prentice Hall) P-H.

Black, Uyless. Internetworking, Vol. 3. (ATM Ser.: Vol. 3). 256p. (C). 1997. 64.00 (*0-13-784182-5*) P-H.

***Black, Uyless.** IP Telephony - The Complete Video Course. 2000. VHS 129.99 (*0-13-030549-9*) Pearson Custom.

— PPP & L2TP: Remote Access Communications. LC 99-47025. 240p. 1999. 39.99 (*0-13-022462-6*) P-H.

Black, Uyless. Residential Broadband Networks. LC 97-47106. (Prentice Hall Series in Advanced Communications). 400p. (C). 1997. 64.00 (*0-13-956442-X*) P-H.

— Second Generation Mobile & Wireless Technologies. LC 98-29585. 400p. (C). 1998. 70.00 (*0-13-621277-8*) P-H.

— TCP/IP & Related Protocols: Includes IPv6, Frame Relay & ATM. 3rd ed. LC 97-33278. (Illus.). 416p. 1997. pap. 44.95 (*0-07-913282-0*) McGraw.

Black, Uyless D. Advanced Internet Technologies. LC 98-36914. 380p. (C). 1998. 49.99 (*0-13-759515-8*) P-H.

— The ATM Resource Library, 3 vols. 2nd ed. 1999. pap. 149.00 (*0-13-083786-5*) P-H.

— Foundation for Broadband Networks, Vol. 1. 2nd ed. LC 99-462443. (ATM Ser.: Vol. 1). (Illus.). 450p. 1998. 63.00 (*0-13-083218-9*) P-H.

— Frame Relay Networks Signature Edition: Specifications & Implementations. LC 98-33582. 1998. pap. 59.99 (*0-07-006890-9*) McGraw.

***Black, Uyless D.** IP Routing Protocols: OSPF, RIP, BGP, & Cisco Protocols. 300p. 2000. 48.99 (*0-13-014248-4*) P-H.

Black, Uyless D. Signaling in Broadband Networks, Vol. 2. LC 95-5961. (ATM Ser.: Vol. 2). (Illus.). 224p. (C). 1997. 77.00 (*0-13-571837-6*) P-H.

— Voice Over IP Networks. LC 99-31326. 328p. 1999. 50.00 (*0-13-022463-4*) P-H.

***Black, Veronica.** Dangerous Inheritance. large type ed. 352p. 2000. 20.99 (*1-84137-002-9*, Pub. by Mgna Lrg Print) Ulverscroft.

Black, Veronica. Flame in the Snow. large type ed. (Dales Large Print Ser.). 235p. 1997. pap. 18.99 (*1-85389-669-1*) Ulverscroft.

— A Footfall in the Mist. large type ed. (Large Print Ser.). 352p. 1996. 27.99 (*0-7089-3566-4*) Ulverscroft.

— Greengirl. large type ed. 224p. 1995. pap. 17.99 (*0-7089-5341-7*) Ulverscroft.

— Hoodman Blind LC 98-36969. 200 p. 1999. write for info. (*0-7540-3550-6*) Chivers N Amer.

— Hoodman Blind. large type ed. LC 98-36969. (Large Print Bks.). 1999. 19.95 (*0-7838-0371-0*, G K Hall Lrg Type) Mac Lib Ref.

— Last Seen Wearing. large type ed. (Dales Ser.). 278p. 1994. pap. 18.99 (*1-85389-422-2*, Dales) Ulverscroft.

— Master of Malcarew. large type ed. 272p. 1995. 27.99 (*0-7089-3233-9*) Ulverscroft.

— My Name Is Polly Winter. large type ed. (Ulverscroft). 352p. 1994. 27.99 (*0-7089-3036-0*) Ulverscroft.

— A Vow of Adoration: A Sister Joan Mystery. LC 99-168436. 190p. 1997. text 20.95 (*0-312-18205-8*) St Martin.

— A Vow of Chastity: A Sister Joan Mystery. large type ed. (Linford Mystery Library). 400p. 1992. pap. 15.99 (*0-7089-7262-4*, Linford) Ulverscroft.

— A Vow of Compassion: A Sister Joan Mystery. LC 98-41424. (Sister Joan Mystery Ser.). 208p. 1998. text 20.95 (*0-312-19354-8*) St Martin.

— A Vow of Devotion: A Sister Joan Mystery. (Dead Letter Mysteries Ser.). 1997. mass mkt. 5.50 (*0-312-96005-0*) St Martin.

— A Vow of Devotion: A Sister Joan Mystery. large type ed. LC 97-32591. (Sister Joan Mystery Ser.). 276p. 1998. pap. 18.95 (*0-7838-8388-9*, G K Hall & Co) Mac Lib Ref.

— A Vow of Fidelity: A Sister Joan Mystery. large type ed. (Large Print Ser.). 352p. 1997. 27.50 (*0-7089-3697-0*) Ulverscroft.

— A Vow of Obedience: A Sister Joan Mystery. 1996. pap. 143.76 (*0-312-95718-1*) St Martin.

— A Vow of Obedience: A Sister Joan Mystery. large type ed. LC 94-28137. 298p. 1994. pap. 19.95 (*0-8161-7472-5*, G K Hall Lrg Type) Mac Lib Ref.

— A Vow of Penance: A Sister Joan Mystery. large type ed. 352p. 1995. 25.99 (*0-7089-3326-2*) Ulverscroft.

— A Vow of Poverty: A Sister Joan Mystery. LC 96-25531. 208p. 1996. 20.95 (*0-312-14756-2*) St Martin.

— A Vow of Poverty: A Sister Joan Mystery. large type ed. (Ulverscroft Large Print Ser.). 388p. 1997. 27.50 (*0-7089-3733-0*) Ulverscroft.

— A Vow of Sanctity: A Sister Joan Mystery. large type ed. 1994. 25.99 (*0-7089-3197-9*) Ulverscroft.

— A Vow of Silence: A Sister Joan Mystery. 1992. mass mkt. 4.99 (*0-8041-0814-5*) Ivy Books.

— A Vow of Silence: A Sister Joan Mystery. large type ed. 1991. 25.99 (*0-7089-2529-4*) Ulverscroft.

Black, W. Bruce & Preston, J., eds. High-Modulus Wholly Aromatic Fibers: Papers. LC 73-78499. (Fiber Science Ser.: No. 5). (Illus.). 388p. reprint ed. pap. 120.30 (*0-7837-0774-6*, 204108800019) Bks Demand.

Black, W. Wayne. An Introduction to On-Line Computers. LC 70-141580. (Illus.). xii, 450p. (C). 1972. text 421.00 (*0-677-02930-6*) Gordon & Breach.

Black, Wallace B. Slaves to Soldiers: African-American Fighting Men in the Civil War. LC 96-31630. (First Bks.). 64p. (J). (gr. 4-6). 1997. lib. bdg. 22.00 (*0-531-20252-6*) Watts.

Black, Wallace B. & Blashfield, Jean F. America Prepares for War. LC 90-46581. (World War II 50th Anniversary Ser.). (Illus.). 48p. (J). (gr. 5-6). 1991. lib. bdg. 12.95 (*0-89686-554-1*, Crstwood Hse) Silver Burdett Pr.

— Bataan & Corregidor. (World War II 50th Anniversary Ser.). (Illus.). 48p. (J). (gr. 5-6). 1991. lib. bdg. 12.95 (*0-89686-557-6*, Crstwood Hse) Silver Burdett Pr.

— Battle of Britain. LC 90-46579. (World War II 50th Anniversary Ser.). (Illus.). 48p. (J). (gr. 5-6). 1991. lib. bdg. 12.95 (*0-89686-553-3*, Crstwood Hse) Silver Burdett Pr.

— Battle of the Atlantic. LC 91-7989. (World War II 50th Anniversary Ser.). (Illus.). 48p. (J). (gr. 5-6). 1991. lib. bdg. 12.95 (*0-89686-558-4*, Crstwood Hse) Silver Burdett Pr.

— Battle of the Bulge. LC 92-1722. (World War II 50th Anniversary Ser.). (Illus.). 48p. (J). (gr. 5-6). 1993. lib. bdg. 12.95 (*0-89686-568-1*, Crstwood Hse) Silver Burdett Pr.

— Blitzkrieg. LC 90-46580. (World War II 50th Anniversary Ser.). (Illus.). 48p. (J). (gr. 5-6). 1991. lib. bdg. 12.75 (*0-89686-552-5*, Crstwood Hse) Silver Burdett Pr.

— Blockade-Runners & Ironclads: Naval Action in the Civil War. LC 96-31643. (First Bk.). (J). (gr. 4-6). 1997. 22.00 (*0-531-20272-0*) Watts.

— Bombing Fortress Europe. LC 91-31452. (World War II 50th Anniversary Ser.). (Illus.). 48p. (J). (gr. 5-6). 1992. lib. bdg. 12.95 (*0-89686-562-2*, Crstwood Hse) Silver Burdett Pr.

— D-Day. LC 91-45951. (World War II 50th Anniversary Ser.). (Illus.). 48p. (J). (gr. 5-6). 1992. lib. bdg. 12.95 (*0-89686-566-5*, Crstwood Hse) Silver Burdett Pr.

— Desert Warfare. LC 91-27186. (World War II 50th Anniversary Ser.). (Illus.). 48p. (J). (gr. 5-6). 1992. lib. bdg. 12.95 (*0-89686-561-4*, Crstwood Hse) Silver Burdett Pr.

— Flattops at War. LC 91-7916. (World War II 50th Anniversary Ser.). (Illus.). 48p. (J). (gr. 5-6). 1991. lib. bdg. 12.95 (*0-89686-559-2*, Crstwood Hse) Silver Burdett Pr.

— Guadalcanal. LC 91-19902. (World War II 50th Anniversary Ser.). (Illus.). 48p. (J). (gr. 5-6). 1992. lib. bdg. 12.95 (*0-89686-560-6*, Crstwood Hse) Silver Burdett Pr.

— Hiroshima & the Atomic Bomb. LC 92-33974. (World War II 50th Anniversary Ser.). (Illus.). 48p. (J). (gr. 5-6). 1993. lib. bdg. 12.95 (*0-89686-571-1*, Crstwood Hse) Silver Burdett Pr.

— Invasion of Italy. LC 91-41484. (World War II 50th Anniversary Ser.). (Illus.). 48p. (J). (gr. 5-6). 1992. lib. bdg. 12.95 (*0-89686-565-7*, Crstwood Hse) Silver Burdett Pr.

— Island Hopping in the Pacific. LC 92-2505. (World War II 50th Anniversary Ser.). (Illus.). 48p. (J). (gr. 5-6). 1992. lib. bdg. 12.95 (*0-89686-567-3*, Crstwood Hse) Silver Burdett Pr.

— Iwo Jima & Okinawa. LC 92-25868. (World War II 50th Anniversary Ser.). (Illus.). 48p. (J). (gr. 5-6). 1993. lib. bdg. 12.95 (*0-89686-569-X*, Crstwood Hse) Silver Burdett Pr.

— Jungle Warfare. LC 91-31533. (World War II 50th Anniversary Ser.). (Illus.). 48p. (J). (gr. 5-6). 1992. lib. bdg. 12.95 (*0-89686-563-0*, Crstwood Hse) Silver Burdett Pr.

— Pearl Harbor! LC 90-45621. (World War II 50th Anniversary Ser.). (Illus.). 48p. (J). (gr. 5-6). 1991. lib. bdg. 4.95 (*0-89686-555-X*, Crstwood Hse) Silver Burdett Pr.

— Russia at War. (World War II 50th Anniversary Ser.). (Illus.). 48p. (J). (gr. 5-6). 1991. lib. bdg. 12.95 (*0-89686-556-8*, Crstwood Hse) Silver Burdett Pr.

— Victory in Europe. LC 92-23234. (World War II 50th Anniversary Ser.). (Illus.). 48p. (J). (gr. 5-6). 1993. lib. bdg. 12.95 (*0-89686-570-3*, Crstwood Hse) Silver Burdett Pr.

— War Behind the Lines. LC 91-40866. (World War II 50th Anniversary Ser.). (Illus.). 48p. (J). (gr. 5-6). 1992. lib. bdg. 12.95 (*0-89686-564-9*, Crstwood Hse) Silver Burdett Pr.

Black, Wendy. Deception of Color: The New Generation. 64p. 1999. pap. 8.00 (*0-8059-4560-1*) Dorrance.

Black, Wendy, jt. auth. see Hotels Magazine Staff.

Black, Wesley. An Introduction to Youth Ministry. 1998. pap. 19.99 (*0-8054-1869-5*) Broadman.

Black, Will. Avenger from Hell. large type ed. (Linford Western Library Ser.). 224p. 1997. pap. 16.99 (*0-7089-5142-2*) Ulverscroft.

— The Legend of Broken Saddle. large type ed. (Linford Western Large Print Ser.). 224p. 1998. pap. 17.99 (*0-7089-5281-X*, Linford) Ulverscroft.

Black, William. A Daughter of Heth, 3 vols., 1 bk. LC 79-8237. reprint ed. 44.50 (*0-404-61781-6*) AMS Pr.

— Goldsmith. Morley, John, ed. LC 68-58370. (English Men of Letters Ser.). reprint ed. lib. bdg. 27.50 (*0-404-51702-1*) AMS Pr.

***Black, William.** The International Platinum Group Metals Trade. LC 99-27807. 1999. write for info. (*0-8493-2384-3*) CRC Pr.

Black, William. Magic Ink & Other Stories. LC 79-37537. (Short Story Index Reprint Ser.). 1977. reprint ed. 21.95 (*0-8369-4096-2*) Ayer.

— Maid of Killeena & Other Stories. LC 71-152936. (Short Story Index Reprint Ser.). 1977. reprint ed. 20.95 (*0-8369-3794-5*) Ayer.

— Penance of John Logan & Two Other Tales. LC 73-106248. (Short Story Index Reprint Ser.). 1977. 20.95 (*0-8369-3284-6*) Ayer.

— The Platinum Group Metals Industry. 192p. 2000. ring bd. 710.00 (*1-85573-346-3*, Pub. by Woodhead Pubng) Am Educ Systs.

Black, William, jt. auth. see Grigson, Sophie.

Black, William C. Blue Chip Flies: A Guide to Choosing & Fishing the Most Productive Trout Patterns. 96p. 1995. pap. 10.95 (*1-882418-18-2*) Centenn Pubns.

Black, William C., ed. see Academy of Marketing Science Staff.

***Black, William Electric, et al.** The Nightingale (Musical) 44p. 1999. pap. 5.50 (*0-87129-880-5*, N04) Dramatic Pub.

Black, William G. Folk-Medicine: A Chapter in the History of Culture. (Folk-Lore Society, London Monographs: Vol. 12). 1972. reprint ed. pap. 30.00 (*0-8115-0504-9*) Periodicals Srv.

Black, William H. Illustrations of Ancient State & Chivalry. LC 78-63488. reprint ed. 38.50 (*0-404-17136-2*) AMS Pr.

Black, William K., ed. Libraries & Student Assistants: Critical Links. 176p. 1995. 39.95 (*1-56024-755-X*) Haworth Pr.

Black, William O. History of Slavery & the Slave Trade, Ancient & Modern. LC 78-83956. (Black Heritage Library Collection). 1977. 58.95 (*0-8369-8512-5*) Ayer.

Black, William R. Railroads for Rent: The Local Rail Service Assistance Program. LC 84-48546. 351p. reprint ed. pap. 108.90 (*0-7837-3692-4*, 205787000009) Bks Demand.

Black, William Z. & Hartley, James G. Thermodynamics: English SI Version. 3rd ed. LC 95-24455. (Illus.). 896p. (C). 1997. 105.00 (*0-673-99648-4*) Addson-Wesley Educ.

Blackaby, Anita, et al. An Image of Peace: The Penn Treaty Collection of Mr. & Mrs. Meyer P. Potamkin. (Illus.). 44p. 1996. pap. 11.95 (*0-89271-069-1*, 0201) Pa Hist & Mus.

Blackaby, Anita D. Washington & the American Revolution: A Guide to the Campaigns in Pennsylvania & New Jersey. LC 86-70173. 112p. (Orig.). 1986. pap. 8.50 (*0-9616323-0-5*) CARS.

Blackaby, Frank T., et al, eds. No-First-Use. LC 84-2467. (Peace Studies). (Illus.). 156p. 1984. 45.00 (*0-85066-274-5*); pap. 21.00 (*0-85066-260-5*) Taylor & Francis.

Blackaby, Henry & Blackaby, Richard. When God Speaks: How to Recognize God's Voice & Respond in Obedience. 96p. 1995. pap. text 7.95 (*0-8054-9822-2*) Broadman.

***Blackaby, Henry & Blackaby, Tom.** The Man God Uses. LC 99-37776. 224p. 1999. 15.99 (*0-8054-2145-9*) Broadman.

Blackaby, Henry & King, Claude. Fresh Encounter: Experiencing God Through Prayer, Humility & a Heartfelt Desire to Know Him. 1997. pap. text 12.99 (*0-8054-6368-2*) Broadman.

***Blackaby, Henry T.** Created to Be God's Friend. 2000. pap., student ed. 15.99 (*0-7852-9719-7*) Nelson.

— Created to Be God's Friend: How God Shapes Those He Loves. LC 99-39349. 224p. 1999. 19.99 (*0-7852-6982-7*) Nelson.

Blackaby, Henry T. Experience: Day by Day with God; A Devotional & Journal, Vol. 1. 1999. 19.99 (*0-8054-1846-6*) Broadman.

— Experiencing God: How to Live the Full Adventure of Knowing & Doing the Will of God. LC 98-109874. 1998. 16.99 (*0-8054-0196-2*) Broadman.

— Experiencing God: How to Live the Full Adventure of Knowing & Doing the Will of God. rev. ed. 1998. pap. 12.99 (*0-8054-0197-0*) Broadman.

Blackaby, Henry T. Waiting on God: A Guide for Helping People in Time of Decision. Skinner, Kerry L., ed. 32p. Date not set. pap. 5.95 (*0-9648743-3-4*) H Blackaby.

***Blackaby, Henry T. & Blackaby, Richard.** Experiencing God Day-by-Day. large type ed. 480p. 2000. reprint ed. pap. 17.95 (*0-8027-2761-1*) Walker & Co.

Blackaby, Henry T. & Blackaby, Richard. Experiencing God Day-by-Day: A Devotional. LC 98-24530. 392p. 1998. 14.99 (*0-8054-1776-1*) Broadman.

— Experiencing God Day by Day: A Devotional & Journal. 384p. 1997. 19.99 (*0-8054-6298-8*) Broadman.

***Blackaby, Henry T. & Edgemon, Roy.** The Ways of God: Working Through Us to Reveal Himself to a Watching World. 192p. 2000. 17.99 (*0-8054-2373-7*) Broadman.

Blackaby, Henry T. & King, Claude V. Experiencing God: How to Live the Full Adventure of Knowing & Doing the Will of God. (Illus.). 224p. 1990. pap. 11.95 (*0-8054-9954-7*, LifeWy Press) LifeWay Christian.

— Experiencing God: How to Live the Full Adventure of Knowing & Doing the Will of God. 40p. 1995. pap. text 4.95 (*0-8054-9859-1*, LifeWy Press) LifeWay Christian.

— Experiencing God: How to Live the Full Adventure of Knowing & Doing the Will of God. 160p. 1995. pap., wbk. ed. 9.95 (*0-8054-9925-3*, LifeWy Press) LifeWay Christian.

***Blackaby, Henry T. & King, Claude V.** Experiencing God: How to Live the Full Adventure of Knowing & Doing the Will of God. large type ed. LC 99-23013. 416p. 2000. reprint ed. pap. 16.95 (*0-8027-2749-2*) Walker & Co.

— Mi Experiencia con Dios.Tr. of Experiencing God. (SPA.). 288p. 1996. pap. text 12.99 (*0-311-11053-3*, Edit Mundo) Casa Bautista.

— Refrescante Experiencia con Dios. Ericson, Raimundo, tr.Tr. of Fresh Encounter with God. (SPA.). 272p. 1999. pap. text 13.50 (*0-311-46154-9*) Casa Bautista.

***Blackaby, Henry T. & Skinner, Kerry L.** Created to Be God's Friend Workbook: How God Shapes Those He Loves. 224p. 2000. pap., wbk. ed. 15.99 (*0-7852-6758-1*) Nelson.

Blackaby, Henry T., et al. The Power of the Call. LC 97-11964. 256p. 1997. 19.99 (*0-8054-6297-X*) Broadman.

Blackaby, James R., et al. The Revised Nomenclature for Museum Cataloging: A Revised & Expanded Version of Robert G. Chenhall's System for Classifying Man-Made Objects. 2nd expanded rev. ed. LC 95-50544. (American Association for State & Local History Book Ser.). 513p. 1988. 69.95 (*0-7619-9147-6*) AltaMira Pr.

Blackaby, M. Look What They Have Done to the Blu. LC 97-179828. 1997. text 17.95 (*0-575-06393-9*, Pub. by V Gollancz) Trafalgar.

Blackaby, Mark. You'll Never Be Here Again. 320p. 1995. pap. 10.95 (*0-575-05897-8*, Pub. by V Gollancz) Trafalgar.

***Blackaby, Richard.** Cross Seekers: Discipleship Covenant for a New Generation. LC 99-178931. (Cross Seekers Ser.). 126p. 1998. write for info. (*0-7673-9084-9*) LifeWay Christian.

Blackaby, Richard, jt. auth. see Blackaby, Henry.

Blackaby, Richard, jt. auth. see Blackaby, Henry T.

Blackaby, Tom, jt. auth. see Blackaby, Henry.

Blackadar, Alfred K. Turbulence & Diffusion in the Atmosphere. LC 96-35289. (Illus.). 200p. 1997. 59.95 (*3-540-61406-0*) Spr-Verlag.

Blackadar, Alfred K., ed. Meteorological Research Reviews: Summaries of Progress from 1951 to 1955. (Meteorological Monograph: Vol. 3, No. 12-20). (Illus.). 283p. 1957. pap. 29.00 (*0-933876-07-6*) Am Meteorological.

Blackadar, Alfred K. & Droessler, Earl G., eds. Report on Workshop on the Future of National Atmospheric Research. 143p. (Orig.). 1977. pap. 11.00 (*0-933876-45-9*) Am Meteorological.

Blackadar, Bruce. K-Theory for Operator Algebras. 2nd rev. ed. LC 98-34543. (Mathematical Sciences Research Institute Publications: No. 5). 320p. (C). 1998. pap. text 29.95 (*0-521-63532-2*) Cambridge U Pr.

Blackadder, D. A. Some Aspects of Basic Polymer Science. 1988. 9.00 (*0-85186-939-4*) CRC Pr.

Blackadder, Elizabeth. Favourite Flowers. 112p. 1999. pap. 16.95 (*1-85793-865-8*, Pub. by Pavilion Bks Ltd) Trafalgar.

Blackall, Bernie. Baseball. LC 98-43109. 1999. write for info. (*1-57572-839-7*) Heinemann.

— Basketball. LC 97-37724. (Top Sport Ser.). (Illus.). 32p. (J). 1998. write for info. (*1-57572-632-7*) Heinemann Lib.

— Golf. LC 97-37723. (Top Sport Ser.). 1998. lib. bdg. write for info. (*1-86391-823-X*) Heinemann.

— Golf. (Top Sport Ser.). (Illus.). 32p. (YA). 1998. lib. bdg. 14.95 (*1-57572-633-5*) Heinemann Lib.

— Gymnastics. LC 98-19585. (Top Sport Ser.). (Illus.). 32p. 1998. write for info. (*1-57572-704-8*) Heinemann Lib.

***Blackall, Bernie.** In-Line Skating. LC 99-27916. (Radical Sports Ser.). 1999. lib. bdg. write for info. (*1-57572-942-3*) Heinemann Lib.

Blackall, Bernie. Martial Arts. LC 98-19590. (Top Sport Ser.). 1998. write for info. (*1-57572-705-6*) Heinemann Lib.

— Rock Climbing. LC 99-27917. (Radical Sports Ser.). 1999. lib. bdg. write for info. (*1-57572-945-8*) Heinemann Lib.

— Soccer. LC 98-45917. 32p. (J). (gr. 4-8). 1999. 21.36 (*1-57572-840-0*) Heinemann Lib.

— Softball. LC 97-31493. (Top Sport Ser.). (Illus.). 32p. (J). 1998. write for info. (*1-57572-634-3*) Heinemann Lib.

— Swimming. LC 98-45919. (Top Sport Ser.). 1999. 21.36 (*1-57572-841-9*) Heinemann Lib.

— Tennis. LC 98-45918. (Top Sport Ser.). 32p. (J). (gr. 4-8). 1999. 21.36 (*1-57572-842-7*) Heinemann Lib.

— Track & Field. LC 98-45916. (Top Sport Ser.). 1999. 21.36 (*1-57572-843-5*) Heinemann Lib.

— Volleyball. LC 98-19591. (Top Sport Ser.). (Illus.). 32p. 1998. write for info. (*1-57572-706-4*) Heinemann Lib.

Blackall, Eric A., ed. & tr. see Goethe, Johann Wolfgang Von.

Blackall, Sophie & Hillard, Leith. 20 Party Tricks to Amuse & Amaze Your Friends. LC 96-33497. 1997. 8.95 (*0-8118-1659-1*) Chronicle Bks.

Blackall, W. E. & Grieve, B. J. How to Know Western Australian Wildflowers Pt. I: Dicotyledons (Casuinaceae to Chenopodiaceae) 49.95 (*0-85564-252-1*, Pub. by Univ of West Aust Pr) Intl Spec Bk.

— How to Know Western Australian Wildflowers Pt. IIIB: Epacridaceae to Lamiaceae. (Illus.). 45p. 34.95 (*0-85564-161-4*, Pub. by Univ of West Aust Pr) Intl Spec Bk.

— How to Know Western Australian Wildflowers Vol. IV: Second Edition with Supplement. 2nd ed. suppl. ed. 39.95 (*0-85564-197-5*, Pub. by Univ of West Aust Pr) Intl Spec Bk.

***Blackard, Kirk.** Managing Change in a Unionized Workplace: Countervailing Collaboration. LC 99-40352. 272p. 2000. write for info. (*1-56720-348-5*) Greenwood.

Blackbeard, Bill. Bizarre Detective. Schreiner, Dave, ed. (Illus.). 36p. 1993. ring bd. 10.95 (*0-87816-183-X*) Kitchen Sink.

Blackbeard, Bill, ed. see Foster, Harold.

Blackbeard, Bill, ed. see Outcault, Richard F.

Blackberry Castle Productions Staff, et al. KC Kidz Recipeez, Vol. 1. Blessman, T. Denise, ed. (Illus.). 108p. 1996. pap., mass mkt. 12.75 (*0-9655439-0-0*) R B S R Ent.

Blackbirch. Antietam. 1998. 16.98 (*0-8050-5228-3*) H Holt & Co.

— Children's Causes. LC 97-38924. 1998. 16.98 (*0-8050-5235-6*) H Holt & Co.

— Economic Causes. 1998. 16.98 (*0-8050-5234-8*) H Holt & Co.

— Gettysburg. 1998. 16.98 (*0-8050-5227-5*) St Martin.

B

Blackbirch Graphics Staff. Alternate Energy Sources. LC 96-23065. (J). 1996. lib. bdg. 16.98 (*0-8050-4621-6*) H Holt & Co.

— Beating Pollution. LC 96-23067. (J). 1996. lib. bdg. 16.98 (*0-8050-4625-9*) H Holt & Co.

— Guardians of Wildlife. LC 96-2912. (J). 1996. lib. bdg. 16.98 (*0-8050-4626-7*) H Holt & Co.

— Natural Harvest. LC 96-15565. (J). 1996. lib. bdg. 16.98 (*0-8050-4623-2*) H Holt & Co.

— New Food Sources. LC 96-22659. (J). 1996. lib. bdg. 16.98 (*0-8050-4624-0*) H Holt & Co.

— Recycling. LC 96-23068. (J). 1996. lib. bdg. 16.98 (*0-8050-4622-4*) H Holt & Co.

Blackbirch Press Editors, ed. see Tesar, Jenny.

***Blackbirch Press Staff, ed.** Creating by Recycling. LC 99-38943. (Crafts for All Seasons Ser.). (Illus.). 32p. (J). (gr. 3-7). 2000. lib. bdg. 18.95 (*1-56711-436-9*) Blackbirch.

— Creating with Paper. LC 99-38941. (Crafts for All Seasons Ser.). (Illus.). 32p. (J). (gr. 3-7). 2000. lib. bdg. 18.95 (*1-56711-434-2*) Blackbirch.

— Creating with Salt Dough. LC 99-38942. (Crafts for All Seasons Ser.). (Illus.). 32p. (J). (gr. 3-7). 2000. lib. bdg. 18.95 (*1-56711-435-0*) Blackbirch.

— Materials from Nature. LC 99-38940. (Crafts for All Seasons Ser.). (Illus.). 32p. (J). (gr. 3-7). 2000. lib. bdg. 18.95 (*1-56711-433-4*) Blackbirch.

Blackbirch Staff, ed. America's Top 100: Our Nation's Most Awe-Inspiring Natural Features & Landmarks. LC 99-35827. (Illus.). 240p. (J). (gr. 3-6). 1999. 39.95 (*1-56711-151-3*) Blackbirch.

Blackbird, Kat S. White Sustenance. LC 93-35959. (Wick Poetry Chapbook Ser.: No. 1). 38p. (Orig.). 1994. pap. 4.75 (*0-87338-503-9*) Kent St U Pr.

Blackbourn. Interfaces le Commerce la Technologie et la Vie de Tous les Jours. (FRE.). 336p. 1997. pap., wbk. ed. 27.95 (*0-471-13894-0*) Wiley.

Blackbourn, Barbara & Marin, Catherine. Interfaces: Les Affaires et la Technologie a Travers la Vie de tous les Jours. LC 97-1443. (FRE.). 480p. 1997. pap. 53.95 (*0-471-13893-2*) Wiley.

Blackbourn, Barbara & Marin, Catherine. Interfaces Texts/Home SG/CS: Les Affaires et la Technologie a Travers la Vie de tous les Jours. 480p. 1997. pap. text 49.95 (*0-471-17827-6*) Wiley.

Blackbourn, David. The Long Nineteenth Century: A History of Germany, 1780-1918. LC 97-29535. (Illus.). 624p. 1998. pap. 24.95 (*0-19-507672-9*); text 60.00 (*0-19-507671-0*) OUP.

— Marpingen: Apparitions of the Virgin Mary in Bismarckian Germany. LC 92-46119. (Illus.). 480p. 1993. text (*0-19-821783-8*) OUP.

— Populists & Patricians: Essays in Modern German History. 304p. (C). 1987. text 55.00 (*0-04-943047-5*) Routledge.

Blackbourn, David, ed. German Bourgeoisie: Essays on the Social History of the German Middle Class. (Illus.). 368p. (C). 1993. pap. 24.99 (*0-415-09358-9*) Routledge.

Blackbourn, David & Eley, Geoffrey. The Peculiarities of German History: Bourgeois Society & Politics in 19th Century Germany. 308p. 1984. pap. text 23.00 (*0-19-873057-8*) OUP.

Blackbourne, Lorne. Anatomy Recall. 500p. 26.00 (*0-683-30436-4*) Lppncott W & W.

— Surgical Recall. (Illus.). 352p. 1994. pap. 26.00 (*0-683-00835-8*) Lppncott W & W.

Blackbourne, Lorne H. Surgical Recall. 2nd ed. LC 97-25166. (Recall Ser.). 608p. 1997. pap. 28.00 (*0-683-30102-0*) Lppncott W & W.

Blackbourne, Lorne H. & Fleischer, Kirk J. Advanced Surgical Recall. LC 96-35097. (Illus.). 600p. 1997. pap. 34.95 (*0-683-00834-X*) Lppncott W & W.

***Blackbridge, Persimmon.** Prozac Highway. 373p. 2000. pap. 14.95 (*0-7145-3059-X*) M Boyars Pubs.

Blackbridge, Persimmon. Prozac Highway: A Novel. LC PR9199.3.B466P7 1997. 256p. 1997. pap. 14.95 (*0-88974-078-X*, Pub. by Press Gang Pubs) LPC InBook.

— Sunnybrook: A True Story with Lies. LC 97-121759. (Illus.). 320p. 1996. 21.95 (*0-88974-068-2*) LPC InBook.

— Sunnybrook: A True Story with Lies. LC PR9199.3.B466S86 199. (Illus.). 108p. 1996. pap. 15.95 (*0-88974-060-7*, Pub. by Press Gang Pubs) LPC InBook.

Blackbridge, Persimmon & Gilhooly, Sheila. Still Sane. (Illus.). 104p. 1985. pap. 12.95 (*0-88974-028-3*, Pub. by Press Gang Pubs) LPC InBook.

Blackburn. Catalysis of Organic Reactions. (Chemical Industries Ser.: Vol. 40). (Illus.). 376p. 1989. text 185.00 (*0-8247-8286-0*) Dekker.

***Blackburn.** Legal Environment of Business. 5th ed. 708p. 1998. pap. text 45.00 (*0-536-01714-X*) Pearson Custom.

Blackburn. Maternal, Fetal & Neonatal Physiology: A Clinical Perspective. (Illus.). 735p. 1991. text 95.00 (*0-7216-2936-9*, W B Saunders Co) Harcrt Hlth Sci Grp.

— The Psychology of Criminal Conduct: Theory, Research & Practice. 506p. 1998. pap. 79.95 (*0-471-96175-2*) Wiley.

— The West & the World since 1945. 4th ed. 176p. 1995. pap. 23.95 (*0-312-11193-2*) St Martin.

— Whole Music: A Whole Language Approach to Teaching Music. LC 97-41403. 1997. pap. text 28.50 (*0-435-07043-6*) Heinemann.

Blackburn, Kelly. Exercises for Elite Golf Performance. LC 99-25148. (Illus.). 168p. 1999. pap. 17.95 (*0-7360-0235-9*, PBLA0235) Human Kinetics.

Blackburn, Al. Aces Wild: The Race for Mach 1. LC 98-22438. (Illus.). 240p. 1998. 24.95 (*0-8420-2732-7*, SR Bks) Scholarly Res Inc.

Blackburn, Albert. Now-Consciousness: Exploring the World Beyond Thought. LC 83-82540. 154p. 1983. reprint ed. pap. 8.95 (*0-9613054-0-1*) Idylwild Bks.

— Worlds Beyond Thought: Conversations on Now-Consciousness. LC 87-82604. 218p. (Orig.). 1988. pap. 12.00 (*0-9613054-3-6*) Idylwild Bks.

Blackburn, Alex, ed. Writers Forum, No. 7. LC 78-649046. 1981. pap. 8.95 (*0-9602992-1-1*) Writers Forum.

— Writers Forum, No. 8. LC 78-649046. 1982. pap. 8.95 (*0-9602992-2-X*) Writers Forum.

— Writers Forum, No. 10. LC 78-649046. 1984. pap. 8.95 (*0-9602992-4-6*) Writers Forum.

— Writers' Forum, No. 13. LC 78-649046. 245p. (Orig.). 1987. pap. 8.95 (*0-9602992-7-0*) Writers Forum.

— Writers' Forum, No. 14. LC 78-649046. (Orig.). 1988. pap. 8.95 (*0-9602992-8-9*) Writers Forum.

— Writers Forum, No. 16. LC 78-649046. 200p. (C). 1990. pap. 8.95 (*1-878359-00-2*) Writers Forum.

— Writers' Forum, No. 17. LC 78-649046. (Illus.). 220p. (Orig.). 1991. pap. text 8.95 (*1-878359-01-0*) Writers Forum.

— Writers' Forum, No. 18. LC 78-649046. (Illus.). 200p. (Orig.). 1992. pap. text 10.00 (*1-878359-02-9*) Writers Forum.

— Writers' Forum, No. 19. LC 78-649046. 228p. (Orig.). 1993. pap. text 10.00 (*1-878359-03-7*) Writers Forum.

— Writers' Forum, Vol. 12. LC 78-649046. 240p. (Orig.). (C). 1986. pap. text 8.95 (*0-9602992-6-2*) Writers Forum.

— Writers Forum 9, 1983. LC 78-649046. 1983. pap. 8.95 (*0-9602992-3-8*) Writers Forum.

— Writers' Forum, 1989, No. 15. LC 78-649046. 1989. pap. 8.95 (*0-9602992-9-7*) Writers Forum.

— Writers' Forum, September 1994, No. 20. LC 78-649046. 245p. 1994. pap. 10.00 (*1-878359-04-5*) Writers Forum.

***Blackburn, Alexander.** Creative Spirit. LC 99-66710. 288p. 2000. pap. 15.95 (*0-88739-315-2*) Creat Arts Bk.

Blackburn, Alexander. The Myth of the Picaro: Continuity & Transformation of the Picaresque Novel, 1554-1954. LC 78-23605. 279p. reprint ed. pap. 86.50 (*0-7837-2070-X*, 204234400004) Bks Demand.

— Suddenly, a Mortal Splendor. 309p. 1995. 20.00 (*1-880909-23-5*) Baskerville.

— A Sunrise Brighter Still: The Visionary Novels of Frank Waters. LC 91-18370. 192p. (C). 1991. text 37.95 (*0-8040-0947-3*) Ohio U Pr.

Blackburn, Alexander, ed. The Interior Country: Stories of the Modern West. LC 87-1968. 352p. 1987. pap. 16.95 (*0-8040-0888-4*) Swallow.

Blackburn, Alexander & Pellow, C. Kenneth, eds. Higher Elevations: Stories from the West: A Writers Forum Anthology. LC 93-10346. 288p. 1993. 29.95 (*0-8040-0971-6*) Swallow.

Blackburn, Barbara. The Life Project: Forming Christian Attitudes Toward Death & Dying. 32p. (J). (gr. k-2). 1995. pap. 2.95 (*0-89243-761-8*) Liguori Pubns.

— The Life Project: Forming Christian Attitudes Toward Death & Dying. 64p. (gr. 3-5). 1995. pap. 3.95 (*0-89243-762-6*) Liguori Pubns.

— The Life Project: Forming Christian Attitudes Toward Death & Dying. 64p. (gr. 6-8). 1995. pap. 3.95 (*0-89243-763-4*) Liguori Pubns.

— Old West Cookbook. LC 86-81884. (Illus.). 150p. 1987. pap. 14.95 (*0-934188-23-8*) Evans Pubns.

Blackburn, Barry. Theios Aner & the Markan Miracle Traditions: A Critique of the Theios Aner Concept As an Interpretative Background of the Miracle Traditions Used by Mark. (WissUNT Neuen Testament Ser.: No. 2-40). 308p. (Orig.). 1990. pap. 61.00 (*3-16-145503-7*, Pub. by JCB Mohr) Coronet Bks.

Blackburn, Benjamin. Blackburn's Introduction to Clinical Radiation Therapy Physics. LC 88-13905. (Illus.). 220p. (Orig.). (C). 1989. text 31.95 (*0-944838-06-5*) Med Physics Pub.

Blackburn, Bill. Old Guitar Mania: A Guide to Guitar Collecting, Vol. 1. (Illus.). 108p. 1992. pap. 10.95 (*0-931759-60-9*, 00000141) Centerstream Pub.

Blackburn, Bob & Strasbaugh, Paul. A History of the State Fair of Oklahoma. (Oklahoma Horizons Ser.). (Illus.). 233p. 1994. 24.95 (*0-86546-089-2*) OK Heritage.

Blackburn, Bonnie J. Music for the Cathedral of Treviso in the Late Sixteenth Century: A Reconstruction of the Lost Manuscripts 29 & 30. (Royal Musical Association Monographs: No. 3). 168p. 1993. 29.95 (*0-947854-02-9*) U Ch Pr.

Blackburn, Bonnie J., et al, eds. A Correspondence of Renaissance Musicians. (Illus.). 1,112p. 1991. text 189.00 (*0-19-315153-7*) OUP.

Blackburn, Bonnie J. & Blackburn, Leofranc. The Oxford Companion to the Year: An Exploration of Calendar Customs & Time Reckoning. (Illus.). 957p. 2000. 49.95 (*0-19-214231-3*) OUP.

***Blackburn, Bonnie J. & Holford-Strevens, Leofranc.** Oxford Book of Days. 640p. 2000. 18.95 (*0-19-866260-2*) OUP.

Blackburn, Bonnie J., ed. see Fubini, Enrico.

***Blackburn, Carole.** Harvest of Souls: The Jesuit Missions in North America, 1632-1650. (Native & Northern Ser.). 184p. 2000. 60.00 (*0-7735-2047-3*, Pub. by McG-Queens Univ Pr) CUP Services.

Blackburn, Charles, jt. ed. see Blair, Peter D.

Blackburn, Charles, jt. ed. see Blondin, Pam.

Blackburn, Charles F., ed. New Perspectives on Environmental Education & Research: A Report on the University Colloquium on Environmental Research & Education. 58p. (Orig.). 1993. pap. 4.00 (*0-914446-05-3*) Sigma Xi.

— Summary, Conclusions, & Recommendations from Global Change & the Human Prospect: Issues in Population, Science, Technology & Equity. 36p. (Orig.). 1992. pap. text 2.50 (*0-914446-02-9*) Sigma Xi.

Blackburn, Charles F., jt. ed. see Ahearne, John F.

Blackburn, Christopher. Napoleon & the Szlachta. 260p. 1998. 36.00 (*0-88033-394-4*, 497, Pub. by East Eur Monographs) Col U Pr.

Blackburn, Clare. Improving Health & Welfare Work with Families in Poverty, a Handbook. LC 91-46006. 119p. 1992. pap. 41.95 (*0-335-09732-4*, RA418) OpUniv Pr.

— Poverty & Health: Working with Families. 160p. 1991. pap. 37.95 (*0-335-09734-0*) OpUniv Pr.

***Blackburn, Claude.** Restorative Drying: Complete Guide to Water Damage Restoration. (Illus.). 300p. 1999. pap. 145.00 (*0-944352-39-1*) Cleaning Cons.

Blackburn, David & Holister, Geoffrey, eds. The G. K. Hall Encyclopedia of Modern Technology. (Illus.). 256p. 1987. 45.00 (*0-8161-9056-9*, Hall Reference) Macmillan.

Blackburn, David L. Deadly Games. 400p. (Orig.). (C). 1995. pap. write for info. (*1-883793-12-2*) Wolfe Pubng.

Blackburn, Dean W. Memoirs with Emphasis on the Immediate Family of Mansul W. & Ida King Blackburn of Johnson County, Arkansas, & upon Arkansas Land: Memoirs with Emphasis upon Family & Arkansas. LC 86-90708. vi, 286p. 1990. 24.00 (*0-9618865-0-1*) D W Blackburn.

Blackburn, Denise A. & Murphy, Nora. Art, Crafts, & Origami from Paper Bags. LC 98-6371. 1998. 14.95 (*1-884830-04-8*) Columbia San Fran.

***Blackburn, Dilys.** Creative Embroidery. (Illus.). 96p. 2000. spiral bd. 29.95 (*1-86126-252-3*, Pub. by Cro1wood) Trafalgar.

Blackburn, Douglas. Leaven: A Black & White Story. (Illus.). 224p. 1991. pap. 24.95 (*0-86980-803-6*, Pub. by Univ Natal Pr) Intl Spec Bk.

Blackburn, E. Howard & Welfley, W. H. History of Bedford & Somerset Counties, with Genealogical & Personal History, 3 vols. Koontz, W. H., ed. (Illus.). 1802p. 1997. reprint ed. lib. bdg. 184.50 (*0-8328-6388-2*) Higginson Bk Co.

Blackburn, E. T., jt. auth. see Caskey, John L.

Blackburn, Earl. Una Presentacion del Evangelio del Senor Jesucristo. 2nd ed.Tr. of Presentation of the Gospel of Our Lord Jesus Christ. (SPA., Illus.). 32p. 1983. reprint ed. pap. 0.99 (*1-56632-093-3*) Revival Lit.

Blackburn, Earl. A Presentation of the Gospel of the Lord Jesus Christ. pap. 0.99 (*1-56632-005-4*) Revival Lit.

Blackburn, Elizabeth. Think Health. 46p. 1991. spiral bd. 7.95 (*0-87516-633-4*) DeVorss.

— Think Love. 30p. 1991. spiral bd. 7.95 (*0-87516-634-2*) DeVorss.

— Think Success. 30p. 1991. spiral bd. 7.95 (*0-87516-635-0*) DeVorss.

Blackburn, Elizabeth H. & Greider, Carol W., eds. Telomeres. LC 95-69539. (Monographs: Vol. 29). (Illus.). 396p. 1995. 80.00 (*0-87969-457-2*) Cold Spring Harbor.

Blackburn, Frances. Computer Yellow Pages: For Students & Teachers. Janke, Jennifer E., ed. LC 99-71592. (Illus.). 64p. (J). 1999. pap. text 8.95 (*0-86530-439-4*) Incentive Pubns.

Blackburn, Francis, ed. see White, Terence.

Blackburn, Francis A., ed. Exodus & Daniel. LC 76-144440. (Belles Lettres Ser., Section I: No. 6). reprint ed. 35.00 (*0-404-53607-7*) AMS Pr.

Blackburn, Fred M. & Williamson, Ray A. Cowboys & Cave Dwellers: Basketmaker Archaeology in Utah's Grand Gulch. LC 96-29572. (Illus.). 196p. 1997. pap. 27.95 (*0-933452-47-0*) Schol Am Res.

Blackburn, G. A. John L. Girardeau's Life's Work & Sermons. 1995. 41.99 (*0-87377-164-8*) GAM Pubns.

Blackburn, G. Meredith, III, compiled by. Index to Poetry for Children & Young People, 1988-1992: A Title, Subject, Author & First Line Index to Poetry in Collections for Children & Young People. LC 94-13171. 400p. 1994. 58.00 (*0-8242-0861-7*) Wilson.

Blackburn, G. Meredith, III & Blackburn, Lorraine A. Index to Poetry for Children & Young People: 1970-1975. Brewton, John E., ed. 471p. 1978. 53.00 (*0-8242-0621-5*) Wilson.

Blackburn, G. Meredith, III & Blackburn, Lorraine A., compiled by. Index to Poetry for Children & Young People: 1982-1987. 392p. 1989. 58.00 (*0-8242-0773-4*) Wilson.

Blackburn, G. Meredith & Blackburn, Lorraine A., eds. Index to Poetry for Children & Young People, 1976-1981. 320p. 1983. 53.00 (*0-8242-0681-9*) Wilson.

Blackburn, G. Meredith, III, jt. auth. see Brewton, Sara W.

Blackburn, G. Michael & Gait, Michael J., eds. Nucleic Acids in Chemistry & Biology. 2nd ed. (Illus.). 538p. (C). 1996. pap. text 59.95 (*0-19-963533-1*) OUP.

Blackburn, Gabriele. The Light of Krishnamurti. LC 96-94645. (Illus.). 256p. 1996. pap. 14.00 (*0-9613054-4-4*) Idylwild Bks.

— The Science & Art of the Pendulum: A Complete Course in Radiesthesia. LC 83-83220. (Illus.). 96p. (Orig.). (C). 1984. pap. 10.00 (*0-9613054-1-X*) Idylwild Bks.

Blackburn, George G. The Guns of Normandy: A Soldier's Eye View, France 1944. LC 96-156242. (Illus.). 536p. 1996. text 34.99 (*0-7710-1500-3*) McCland & Stewart.

— The Guns of Normandy: A Soldier's Eye View, France 1944. LC 97-10228. (Illus.). 536p. 1997. pap. 19.95 (*0-7710-1503-8*) McCland & Stewart.

— The Guns of Victory: A Soldier's Eye View, Belgium, Holland & Germany, 1944-45. (Illus.). 520p. 1997. text 34.99 (*0-7710-1501-1*) McCland & Stewart.

— The Guns of Victory: A Soldier's Eye View, Belgium, Holland & Germany, 1944-45, Vol. 2. (Illus.). 520p. 1998. pap. 24.99 (*0-7710-1505-4*) McCland & Stewart.

— Where the Hell Are the Guns? A Soldier's Eye View of the Anxious Years, 1939-44. LC 98-139337. (Illus.). 439p. 1998. 34.99 (*0-7710-1504-6*) McCland & Stewart.

— Where the Hell Are the Guns? A Soldier's Eye View of the Anxious Years, 1939-44. 384p. 1999. pap. 21.95 (*0-7710-1506-2*) McCland & Stewart.

Blackburn, George L., jt. auth. see Shikora, Scott A.

Blackburn, George M. French Newspaper Opinion on the American Civil War, 171. LC 96-30583. (Contributions in American History Ser.). 176p. 1997. 57.95 (*0-313-30261-8*, Greenwood Pr) Greenwood.

Blackburn, George M., III. Index to Poetry for Children & Young People, 1993-1997. LC 98-39545. 461p. 1998. 70.00 (*0-8242-0939-7*) Wilson.

Blackburn, George M., ed. Dear Carrie... The Civil War Letters of Thomas N. Stevens. LC 84-222354. (Illus.). 1984. 17.50 (*0-916699-10-2*) CMU Clarke Hist Lib.

Blackburn, Gilmer W. Education in the Third Reich: Race & History in Nazi Textbooks. LC 83-17866. 288p. (C). 1985. text 19.50 (*0-87395-822-5*) State U NY Pr.

Blackburn, Glen A. Apache Half-Breed. large type ed. (Linford Western Library). 288p. 1992. pap. 16.99 (*0-7089-7170-9*, Linford) Ulverscroft.

Blackburn, Glenn. Western Civilization: A Concise History: From Early Societies to the Present. 640p. (Orig.). (C). 1990. teacher ed. write for info. (*0-318-68117-X*) St Martin.

— Western Civilization: A Concise History, Vol. I: From Early Societies to the Reformation. 267p. (Orig.). (C). 1990. teacher ed. write for info. (*0-318-68115-3*) St Martin.

— Western Civilization: A Concise History, Vol. II: From the Birth of Modern Science to the Present. 554p. (Orig.). (C). 1990. teacher ed. write for info. (*0-318-68116-1*) St Martin.

Blackburn, Graham. Furniture by Design: Lessons in Craftsmanship from a Master Woodworker. LC 96-48141. (Illus.). 144p. 1997. 30.00 (*1-55821-512-3*) Lyons Pr.

— The Illustrated Book of Housebuilding & Carpentry. (Illus.). 336p. Date not set. pap. 18.95 (*0-87951-651-8*, Pub. by Overlook Pr) Penguin Putnam.

— Illustrated Encyclopedia of Ships & Boats. 448p. 1999. pap. 26.95 (*0-87951-932-0*, Pub. by Overlook Pr) Penguin Putnam.

— The Illustrated Encyclopedia of Ships, Boats & Vessels. LC 78-16565. (Illus.). 448p. 1978. 37.95 (*0-87951-082-X*, Pub. by Overlook Pr) Penguin Putnam.

— The Illustrated Encyclopedia of Ships, Boats & Vessels. LC 78-16565. (Illus.). 448p. 1982. pap. 24.95 (*0-87951-141-9*, Pub. by Overlook Pr) Penguin Putnam.

— The Illustrated Encyclopedia of Woodworking Handtools, Instruments & Devices. 3rd rev. ed. (Illus.). 160p. 1999. 30.00 (*1-892585-01-4*) Blkburn Bks.

— The Overlook Illustrated Dictionary of Nautical Terms. LC 80-39640. (Illus.). 368p. 1981. 35.00 (*0-87951-124-9*, Pub. by Overlook Pr) Penguin Putnam.

— The Overlook Illustrated Dictionary of Nautical Terms. LC 80-39640. (Illus.). 368p. 1984. pap. 15.95 (*0-87951-950-9*, Pub. by Overlook Pr) Penguin Putnam.

Blackburn, Graham. Traditional Woodworking Handtools: A Manual for the Woodworker. LC 98-71242. (Illus.). 384p. 1998. 50.00 (*1-892585-00-6*) Blkburn Bks.

— Traditional Woodworking Handtools: A Manual for the Woodworker. (Illus.). 384p. 1999. pap. 29.95 (*1-55821-874-2*) Lyons Pr.

***Blackburn, Graham.** Traditional Woodworking Handtools: A Manual for the Woodworker. (Illus.). 368p. 2000. 14.99 (*0-517-16202-4*) Random Hse Value.

Blackburn, H., et al. Lessons for Science from the Seven Countries Study: A 35-Year Collaborative Experience. 240p. 1994. write for info. (*4-431-70140-0*) H Blackburn.

Blackburn, H., jt. auth. see Rose, G. A.

Blackburn, Harvey, jt. auth. see Cartwright, Thomas.

Blackburn, Henry. On the Trail of Heart Attacks in Seven Countries. 180p. 1995. write for info. (*1-887268-00-6*) H Blackburn.

***Blackburn, Ian, et al.** Professional Visual Interdev 6 Programming. (Professional Ser.). 700p. 1999. pap. 49.99 (*1-86100-264-5*) Wrox Pr Inc.

Blackburn, Ivy-Marie & Davidson, Kate M. Cognitive Therapy for Anxiety & Depression: A Practitioner's Guide. 2nd ed. LC 95-22027. 1995. pap. 39.95 (*0-632-03986-8*) Blackwell Sci.

Blackburn, Ivy-Marie & Twaddle, Vivien. Cognitive Therapy in Action: A Practitioner's Casebook. 320p. 1996. pap. text 16.95 (*0-285-63282-5*, Pub. by Souvenir Pr Ltd) IPG Chicago.

Blackburn, J. A., ed. The Economic Outlook for Textiles & Clothing in the 1990s - Journal of the Textile Institute: Special Edition. 1991. pap. 54.00 (*0-614-20908-0*, Pub. by Textile Inst) St Mut.

Blackburn, J. K., et al. Terry Texas Ranger Trilogy: Reminiscences of the Terry Rangers, Terry's Texas Rangers, & the Diary of Ephraim Shelby Dodd. LC 96-22469. (Illus.). 256p. 1996. 24.95 (*1-880510-45-6*); pap. 17.95 (*1-880510-46-4*) State House Pr.

— Terry Texas Ranger Trilogy: Reminiscences of the Terry Rangers, Terry's Texas Rangers, & the Diary of Ephraim Shelby Dodd. limited ed. LC 96-22469. (Illus.). 256p. 1996. 60.00 (*1-880510-47-2*) State House Pr.

Blackburn, J. Lewis. Protective Relaying: Principles & Applications. 2nd ed. LC 97-33110. (Power Engineering Ser.: Vol. 2). (Illus.). 560p. 1997. text 99.75 (*0-8247-9918-6*) Dekker.

— Symmetrical Components for Power Systems Engineering. (Electrical Engineering & Electronics Ser.: Vol. 85). (Illus.). 448p. 1993. text 125.00 (*0-8247-8767-6*) Dekker.

Blackburn, J. Vernon, jt. auth. see Nowlin, James E.

Blackburn, J. Vernon, jt. auth. see Seymour, John C.

An Asterisk (*) at the beginning of an entry indicates that the title is appearing for the first time.

Blackburn, J. Walton & Bruce, Willa M. Mediating Environmental Conflicts: Theory & Practice. LC 94-34271. 320p. 1995. 69.50 (*0-89930-846-5*, Quorum Bks) Greenwood.

Blackburn, J. Walton, jt. auth. see Bruce, Willa M.

Blackburn, James & Holland, Jeremy. Who Changes? Institutionalizing Participation in Development. 192p. 1998. pap. 10.00 (*1-85339-420-3*, Pub. by Intermed Tech) Stylus Pub VA.

Blackburn, James, jt. auth. see Holland, Jeremy.

***Blackburn, James A.** Instrumentation for Scientists. LC 00-40040. 2000. write for info. (*0-387-95056-7*) Spr-Verlag.

Blackburn, James A., ed. Spectral Analysis: Methods & Techniques. LC 70-107752. (Illus.). 303p. reprint ed. pap. 94.00 (*0-7837-0955-2*, 204126000019) Bks Demand.

Blackburn, James W., jt. auth. see Stephenson, Ralph.

Blackburn, Jeanne M. & Seniz, Refah. Say It in Turkish. (Orig.). 1958. pap. 3.95 (*0-486-20821-4*) Dover.

***Blackburn, Jennifer & Aguirre-Happordt, Ingrid.** Medi-Cal Outstationing in California: Findings from a Statewide Survey. unabridged ed. (Illus.). 38p. 1999. pap. write for info. (*1-929008-15-5*) CA HlthCare Fnd.

***Blackburn, Joe.** Coley Running Wild Bk. 2: Caged Heat. (Eros Graphic Novels Ser.: Vol. 33). (Illus.). 144p. 1998. pap. 16.95 (*1-56097-245-9*, Eros Comics) Fantagraph Bks.

Blackburn, John. Coley Running Wild: The Blade & the Whip, Bk. 1. (Eros Graphic Novel Ser.: No. 16). 144p. 1995. pap. 16.95 (*1-56097-214-9*) Fantagraph Bks.

***Blackburn, John.** Coley Running Wild: The Destiny Coast. (Eros Graphic Novels Ser.: Vol. 41). (Illus.). 160p. 1999. mac hd 19.95 (*1-56097-360-9*, Eros Comics) Fantagraph Bks.

Blackburn, John D. Legal Environment of Business & Study Guide Package. (C). 1992. text 59.95 (*0-256-13149-X*, Irwn McGrw-H) McGrw-H Hghr Educ.

Blackburn, John D., et al. Legal Environment of Business Environmental Issues in Marketing. 5th ed. (C). 1994. text 32.95 (*0-256-17397-4*, Irwn McGrw-H) McGrw-H Hghr Educ.

Blackburn, John D., jt. auth. see Getman, Julius G.

Blackburn, John H. Elsie's Story. 392p. 1998. pap. 21.00 (*0-8059-4341-2*) Dorrance.

Blackburn, John O. The Renewable Energy Alternative: How the United States & the World Can Prosper Without Nuclear Energy or Coal. LC 86-29273. xi, 201p. 1987. text 49.95 (*0-8223-0687-5*); pap. text 21.95 (*0-8223-0744-8*) Duke.

— Solar Florida: A Sustainable Energy Future. LC 93-71423. 237p. (Orig.). 1993. pap. 24.95 (*0-913207-07-1*) FL Conser Fnd.

Blackburn, Joseph. Time-Based Competition: The Next Battle Ground in American Manufacturing. (APICS Ser.). 240p. 1990. 50.00 (*1-55623-321-3*, Irwn Prfssnl) McGraw-Hill Prof.

Blackburn, Joseph & Green, Simon. Peter Womersley. 88p. (C). 1994. pap. 35.00 (*1-873190-19-0*, Pub. by Rutland Pr) St Mut.

Blackburn, Joyce. James Edward Oglethorpe. 148p. 1993. 9.95 (*0-89176-044-X*, Mckingbird) R Bemis Pub.

— James Edward Oglethorpe. 184p. 1994. pap. 8.95 (*0-89176-995-1*) R Bemis Pub.

— Martha Berry: A Woman of Courageous Spirit & Bold Dreams. (J). (gr. 7-12). 1992. pap. 8.95 (*1-56145-071-5*) Peachtree Pubs.

— Suki & the Old Umbrella. rev. ed. LC 96-14846. (Illus.). 64p. (J). (gr. 3-5). 1996. 14.95 (*1-881576-71-X*) Providence Hse.

Blackburn, Joyce K. The Bloody Summer of Seventeen Forty-Two: A Colonial Boy's Journal. (Illus.). 64p. (J). (gr. 5-8). 1985. pap. 7.95 (*0-930803-00-0*) Fort Frederica.

— Phoebe's Secret Diary: Daily Life & First Romance of a Colonial Girl, 1742. (Illus.). 56p. (Orig.). (J). (gr. 5-8). 1993. pap. 7.95 (*0-930803-01-9*) Fort Frederica.

— Suki & the Invisible Peacock. rev. ed. LC 96-14852. (Illus.). 64p. (J). (gr. 3-5). 1996. 14.95 (*1-881576-69-8*) Providence Hse.

— Suki & the Magic Sand Dollar. rev. ed. LC 96-14851. (Illus.). 64p. (J). (gr. 3-5). 1996. 14.95 (*1-881576-70-1*) Providence Hse.

— Suki & the Wonder Star. rev. ed. LC 96-14845. (Illus.). 64p. (J). (gr. 3-5). 1996. 14.95 (*1-881576-72-8*) Providence Hse.

Blackburn, Julia. The Book of Color. 192p. 1996. pap. 11.00 (*0-679-75837-2*) Random.

— Daisy Bates in the Desert. 240p. 1995. pap. 12.00 (*0-679-74446-0*) Random.

— Daisy Bates in the Desert. large type ed. 400p. 1996. 27.99 (*0-7089-3442-0*) Ulverscroft.

— Emperors Last Island. 1999. pap. 7.95 (*0-14-014861-2*, Viking); pap. 18.95 (*0-670-83814-4*) Viking Penguin.

— The Emperor's Last Island: A Journey to St. Helena. LC 92-50597. 1993. pap. 13.00 (*0-679-73937-8*) Vin Bks.

***Blackburn, Julia.** Leper's Companion. (International Ser.). 208p. 2000. pap. 12.00 (*0-679-75838-0*) Vin Bks.

Blackburn, Julia. The Leper's Companion. LC 98-27026. 208p. 1999. 22.00 (*0-679-43984-6*) Pantheon.

Blackburn, Kate. Woman Maps. 68p. Date not set. pap. 8.95 (*0-932622-70-4*) St Andrews NC.

Blackburn, Ken. The World Record Paper Airplane Book. LC 94-7800. (Illus.). 224p. 1994. pap. 14.95 (*1-56305-631-3*, 3631) Workman Pub.

Blackburn, Ken & Lammers, Jeff. Kids' Paper Airplane Book. (Illus.). 160p. (J). (gr. 1-4). 1996. pap. 12.95 (*0-7611-0478-X*, 10478) Workman Pub.

— Pocket Flyers Paper Airplane Book. LC 98-36689. (Illus.). 160p. 1998. pap. 7.95 (*0-7611-1362-2*) Workman Pub.

Blackburn, Ken, jt. auth. see Lammers, Jeff.

Blackburn, Leofranc, jt. auth. see Blackburn, Bonnie J.

Blackburn, Lorraine A., jt. auth. see Blackburn, G. Meredith, III.

Blackburn, Lorraine A., jt. compiled by see Blackburn, G. Meredith, III.

Blackburn, Lorraine A., jt. ed. see Blackburn, G. Meredith.

Blackburn, Lynn B. The Class in Room Forty-Four: When a Classmate Dies. rev. ed. Johnson, Joy, ed. (Illus.). 24p. (J). (gr. 1-6). 1999. pap. 6.95 (*1-56123-025-1*) Centering Corp.

— I Know I Made It Happen: A Book about Children & Guilt. Johnson, Joy, ed. (Illus.). 24p. (J). (ps-1). 1990. pap. 3.95 (*1-56123-016-2*) Centering Corp.

— Timothy Duck: The Story of the Death of a Friend. rev. ed. Johnson, Joy, ed. (Illus.). 24p. (Orig.). (J). (gr. 1-6). 1989. pap. 4.95 (*1-56123-013-8*) Centering Corp.

Blackburn, Marc K. The United States Army & the Motor Truck: A Case Study in Standardization, 163. LC 95-24770. (Contributions in Military Studies Ser.: No. 163). 136p. 1996. 55.00 (*0-313-29808-4*, Greenwood Pr) Greenwood.

Blackburn, Mark. Hawaiiana: The Best of Hawaiian Design. 256p. 1996. 59.95 (*0-7643-0109-8*) Schiffer.

***Blackburn, Mark.** Hula Girls & Surfer Boys. (Illus.). 112p. 1999. pap. 19.95 (*0-7643-1042-9*) Schiffer.

Blackburn, Mark. Tattoos from Paradise: Traditional Polynesian Patterns. LC 99-37553. (Illus.). 224p. 1999. 69.95 (*0-7643-0941-2*) Schiffer.

Blackburn, Mark, jt. auth. see Grierson, Philip.

Blackburn, Mark A. & Dumville, David N., eds. Kings, Currency & Alliances: History & Coinage of Southern England in the 9th Century. (Studies in Anglo-Saxon History: Vol. 9). 284p. 1998. 99.00 (*0-85115-598-7*, Boydell Pr) Boydell & Brewer.

***Blackburn, Mattie & Davies, Liz.** Child Protection Clinical Practice & the Law. 256p. 2000. pap. 32.00 (*0-7506-4319-6*) Buttrwrth-Heinemann.

Blackburn, McKinley L. Comparing Poverty: The United States & Other Industrial Nations. LC 98-109782. 50p. 1997. pap. 9.95 (*0-8447-7099-X*) Am Enterprise.

Blackburn, MSc, RGN, Maddie. Sexuality & Disability. 192p. 2000. pap. text 27.50 (*0-7506-2252-0*) Buttrwrth-Heinemann.

Blackburn, N. & Huppert, B. Finite Groups. (Grundlehren der Mathematischen Wissenschaften Ser.: Vol. 242). 550p. 1982. 150.95 (*0-387-10632-4*) Spr-Verlag.

Blackburn, N., jt. auth. see Huppert, B.

Blackburn, Patrick & De Rijke, Maarten, eds. Specifying Syntactic Structures. LC 96-52733. (Studies in Logic, Language & Information). 312p. (C). 1997. 64.95 (*1-57586-085-6*) CSLI.

— Specifying Syntactic Structures. LC 96-52733. (Studies in Logic, Language & Information). 303p. (C). 1997. pap. 23.95 (*1-57586-084-8*) Cambridge U Pr.

***Blackburn, Patrick, et al.** Logic, Language & Computation. (Lecture Notes Ser.: No. 111). 350p. (C). 2000. pap. text. write for info. (*1-57586-268-9*, Pub. by CSLI) Cambridge U Pr.

— Logic, Language & Computation, Vol. 3. (Lecture Notes Ser.: No. 111). 350p. (C). 2000. text. write for info. (*1-57586-267-0*, Pub. by CSLI) Cambridge U Pr.

Blackburn, Paul. The Collected Poems of Paul Blackburn. Jarolim, Edith, ed. LC 85-9309. (Lamplighter Ser.). 728p. 1985. 37.50 (*0-89255-086-4*) Persea Bks.

— Halfway down the Coast. LC 75-20727. (Illus.). 64p. 1975. 6.00 (*0-913142-10-7*); pap. 3.50 (*0-913142-09-3*) Mulch Pr.

— The Parallel Voyages. (Illus.). 136p. (Orig.). 1987. 50.00 (*0-933313-02-0*); 75.00 (*0-933313-08-X*); pap. 8.95 (*0-933313-03-9*) SUN Gemini Pr.

— The Selected Poems of Paul Blackburn. Jarolim, Edith, ed. & intro. by. (Lamplighter Ser.). 286p. (Orig.). 1989. pap. 14.95 (*0-89255-123-2*) Persea Bks.

Blackburn, Paul, tr. Peire Vidal. LC 72-83856. (Illus.). 6.00 (*0-913142-02-6*) Mulch Pr.

Blackburn, Paul, jt. ed. see Unger, Daniel.

Blackburn, Paul, tr. see Cortazar, Julio.

Blackburn, Paul, tr. see Economou, George, ed.

Blackburn, Philip & Partch, Harry. Enclosure Three: Harry Partch. LC 97-14032. (Enclosures Ser.). (Illus.). 528p. 1997. 75.00 (*0-9656569-0-X*, IN402) Am Composers Forum.

Blackburn, R. M., ed. see Stewart, Alexander, et al.

Blackburn, Randy. Your Guided Hunt: And What You Should Know. (Illus.). 126p. (Orig.). 1996. pap. 14.95 (*0-9654123-0-X*) R Blackburn.

Blackburn, Richard J. The Vampire of Reason: An Essay in the Philosophy of History. 272p. (C). 1990. pap. 19.00 (*0-86091-972-2*, A4511, Pub. by Verso) Norton.

Blackburn, Richard M. Mercenaries & Lyndon Johnson's "More Flags" The Hiring of Korean, Filipino & Thai Soldiers in the Vietnam War. LC 93-42174. 220p. 1994. lib. bdg. 28.50 (*0-89950-931-2*) McFarland & Co.

Blackburn, Robert. The Meeting of Parliament: A Study of the Law & Practice Relating to the Frequency & Duration of the United Kingdom Parliament. 128p. 1990. text 72.95 (*1-85521-080-0*, Pub. by Dartmth Pub) Ashgate Pub Co.

— Towards a Constitutional Bill of Rights for the United Kingdom: Commentary & Documents. LC 97-44743. (Constitutional Reform Ser.). 704p. 1999. 165.00 (*1-85567-529-3*, Pub. by P P Pubs) Cassell & Continuum.

Blackburn, Robert, ed. Constitutional Studies: Contemporary Issues & Controversies. 224p. 1994. 110.00 (*0-7201-2125-6*); pap. 37.95 (*0-7201-2204-X*) Continuum.

— The European Convention on Human Rights: The Impact of the European Convention on Human Rights in the Legal & Political Systems of Member States. 256p. 1999. 99.50 (*0-7201-2229-5*) Continuum.

— Rights of Citizenship. (Citizenship & the Law Ser.). 348p. 1993. pap. 35.95 (*0-7201-2213-9*) Continuum.

— Rights of Citizenship. LC 92-43396. (Citizenship & the Law Ser.). 348p. 1993. 89.50 (*0-7201-2124-8*) Continuum.

Blackburn, Robert & Busuttil, James. Human Rights for the 21st Century. LC 97-202763. 160p. 1996. 79.50 (*1-85567-440-8*) Bks Intl VA.

Blackburn, Robert & Jennings, Peter, eds. Small Firms: Contributions to Economic Regeneration. 208p. 1996. pap. 74.00 (*1-85396-339-9*, Pub. by P Chapman) Taylor & Francis.

***Blackburn, Robert & Plant, Raymond, eds.** Constitutional Reform: The Labour Government's Constitutional Reform Agenda. LC 99-492154. 517p. 1999. pap. text. write for info. (*0-582-36999-1*, Pub. by Addison-Wesley) Gaunt.

Blackburn, Robert, ed. see Juss, Satvinder S.

Blackburn, Robert, jt. ed. see North, Julian.

Blackburn, Robert T. & Lawrence, Janet H. Faculty at Work: Motivation, Expectation, Satisfaction. 432p. 1995. text 39.95 (*0-8018-4942-X*) Johns Hopkins.

Blackburn, Robert T., jt. auth. see Risenhoover, Morris.

Blackburn, Robin. The Making of New World Slavery: From the Baroque to the Modern, 1492-1800. LC 96-45603. 496p. 1997. 65.00 (*1-85984-890-7*, Pub. by Verso) Norton.

— Making of New World Slavery: From the Baroque to the Modern, 1492-1800. 608p. 1998. pap. 25.00 (*1-85984-195-3*, Pub. by Verso) Norton.

— The Overthrow of Colonial Slavery, 1776-1848. 576p. (C). 1989. pap. 25.00 (*0-86091-901-3*, Pub. by Verso) Norton.

***Blackburn, Robin.** Pension Power: How Progressive Social Funds Can Transform Capitalism. 160p. 2001. 22.00 (*1-85984-795-1*, Pub. by Verso) Norton.

Blackburn, Roderic H. Cherry Hill: The History & Collections of a Van Rensselaer Family. LC 75-44844. (Illus.). 176p. 1976. pap. 15.00 (*0-943366-01-1*) Hist Cherry Hill.

— Okiek. (Kenya People Ser.). (Illus.). 42p. (YA). (gr. 6-9). 1991. pap. write for info. (*0-237-50631-9*) EVN1 UK.

— Remembrance of Patria: Dutch Arts & Culture in Colonial America, 1609-1776. LC 88-14645. (Illus.). 318p. 1988. 65.00 (*0-939072-06-8*) Albany Hist & Art.

Blackburn, Roderic H. & Kelley, Nancy A., eds. New World Dutch Studies: Dutch Arts & Culture in Colonial America, 1609-1776. (Illus.). 219p. (Orig.). 1987. pap. 21.95 (*0-939072-10-6*) Albany Hist & Art.

Blackburn, Roderic H., jt. auth. see Piwonka, Ruth.

Blackburn, Ronald. Jesus the Proclaimer Proclaimed. (C). 1989. pap. 30.00 (*1-85072-105-X*, Pub. by W Sessions) St Mut.

Blackburn, Ruth H. Old Testament As Living Literature. 1976. 4.95 (*0-671-00964-8*, Arco) Macmillan Gen Ref.

Blackburn, S. M., jt. ed. see Walton, D. G.

Blackburn, Sara, ed. see De Salvo, Donna, et al.

Blackburn, Simon. Essays in Quasi-Realism. LC 92-37005. 272p. 1993. text 75.00 (*0-19-508041-6*); pap. text 24.95 (*0-19-508224-9*) OUP.

— The Oxford Dictionary of Philosophy. (Illus.). 416p. 1994. 49.95 (*0-19-211694-0*) OUP.

— The Oxford Dictionary of Philosophy. (Oxford Paperback Reference Ser.). (Illus.). 428p. 1996. pap. 14.95 (*0-19-283134-8*) OUP.

— Ruling Passions: A Theory of Practical Reason. 344p. 1999. text 29.95 (*0-19-824785-0*) OUP.

***Blackburn, Simon.** Ruling Passions: A Theory of Practical Reasoning. 344p. 2000. pap. 18.95 (*0-19-924139-2*) OUP.

Blackburn, Simon. Spreading the Word: Groundings in the Philosophy of Language. (Illus.). 378p. (C). 1984. pap. text 24.00 (*0-19-824651-X*) OUP.

— Think: A Compelling Introduction to Philosophy. 320p. 1999. 22.00 (*0-19-210024-6*) OUP.

Blackburn, Simon, ed. Meaning, Reference, & Necessity: New Studies in Semantics. LC 74-31785. 220p. reprint ed. pap. 62.70 (*0-608-12281-5*, 2024425) Bks Demand.

***Blackburn, Simon & Simmons, Keith, eds.** Truth. LC 99-19787. 412p. 1999. text 65.00 (*0-19-875251-2*); pap. text 19.95 (*0-19-875250-4*) OUP.

Blackburn, Stanley. Enzyme Structure & Function. LC 75-11420. (Enzymology Ser.: No. 3). (Illus.). 540p. reprint ed. pap. 167.40 (*0-7837-0698-7*, 204103100019) Bks Demand.

— Handbook of Chromatography: Amino Acids & Amines, Vol. II. 480p. 1989. lib. bdg. 259.00 (*0-8493-3066-1*, QD79) CRC Pr.

— Handbook of Chromatography: Peptides. LC 86-6133. (Series in Chromatography). 320p. 1986. 222.00 (*0-8493-3065-3*, QP552, CRC Reprint) Franklin.

— Protein Sequence Determination: Methods & Techniques. LC 77-130746. 301p. reprint ed. pap. 93.40 (*0-608-30332-1*, 205541000021) Bks Demand.

Blackburn, Stanley, ed. Handbook of Chromatography: Amino Acids & Amines, Vol. I. LC 82-9561. (Series in Chromatography). 312p. 1983. lib. bdg. 151.00 (*0-8493-3064-5*, QD79, CRC Reprint) Franklin.

Blackburn, Stuart, tr. see Aiyar, B. R.

Blackburn, Stuart H. Inside the Drama-House: Rama Stories & Shadow Puppets in South India. LC 95-10678. (Illus.). 310p. 1996. pap. 22.50 (*0-520-20206-6*, Pub. by U CA Pr) Cal Prin Full Svc.

— Inside the Drama-House: Rama Stories & Shadow Puppets in South India. LC 95-10678. (Illus.). 310p. (C). 1996. 60.00 (*0-520-20205-8*, Pub. by U CA Pr) Cal Prin Full Svc.

— Singing of Birth & Death: Texts in Performance. LC 87-30137. 299p. 1988. reprint ed. pap. 92.70 (*0-608-03631-5*, 206445800009) Bks Demand.

Blackburn, Stuart H., ed. see Ramanujan, A. K.

Blackburn, Stuart H., ed. & pref. see Ramanujan, A. K.

Blackburn, Susan. Practical Visionaries: A Study of Community Aid Abroad. 272p. (Orig.). 1993. pap. 29.95 (*0-522-84562-2*, Pub. by Melbourne Univ Pr) Paul & Co Pubs.

Blackburn, T. Henry & Sorensen, Jan, eds. Nitrogen Cycling in Coastal Marine Environments: Scope 33. LC 86-26803. (Scientific Committee on Problems of the Environment Ser.). 478p. 1988. 460.00 (*0-471-91404-5*) Wiley.

Blackburn, T. Henry, jt. ed. see Knowles, Roger.

***Blackburn, Tammie.** It Takes Two. (Illus.). 16p. (J). 2000. pap. 5.95 (*1-891846-16-7*) Busn Word.

***Blackburn, Terri W. & Russell, Garfield B.** Near Misses in Neuro Anesthesia. (Illus.). 176p. 2000. pap. 35.00 (*0-7506-7065-7*) Buttrwrth-Heinemann.

Blackburn, Thomas. Adjacent Kingdom: Last Poems. MacVean, Jean, ed. LC 88-61443. 94p. (Orig.). 1988. pap. 15.95 (*0-7206-0707-8*, Pub. by P Owen Ltd) Dufour.

Blackburn, Thomas C., ed. December's Child: A Book of Chumash Oral Narratives. LC 74-27284. 360p. 1976. pap. 17.95 (*0-520-04088-0*, Pub. by U CA Pr) Cal Prin Full Svc.

Blackburn, Thomas C., ed. Before the Wilderness: Environmental Management by Native Californians. LC 93-6936. (Anthropological Papers: No. 40). 476p. 1993. 42.50 (*0-87919-127-9*) Ballena Pr.

Blackburn, Thomas C. & Anderson, Kat, compiled by. Before the Wilderness: Environmental Management by Native Californians. LC 93-6936. (Anthropological Papers: No. 40). (Illus.). 476p. 1993. pap. 32.50 (*0-87919-126-0*) Ballena Pr.

Blackburn, Thomas C., jt. auth. see Hudson, Travis.

Blackburn, Thomas C., jt. auth. see Milliken, Randall.

Blackburn, Thomas C., ed. see Hohenthal, William D., Jr.

Blackburn, Thomas C., jt. ed. see Stickel, E. Gary.

Blackburn, Thomas G., ed. see Shoup, Laurence H. & Milliken, Randall T.

Blackburn, Thomas W. Yanqui. large type ed. LC 97-35651. 304p. 1998. 18.95 (*0-7838-8292-0*, G K Hall Lrg Type) Mac Lib Ref.

Blackburn, Thomas Wakefield. Buckskin Man. LC 98-50924. 1999. write for info. (*1-57490-180-X*) T T Beeler.

***Blackburn, Thomas Wakefield.** Patron. LC 00-31960. 2000. write for info. (*0-7838-9112-1*, G K Hall & Co) Mac Lib Ref.

— Ranchero. large type ed. LC 00-21093. 287p. 2000. pap. 23.95 (*0-7838-9045-1*) Mac Lib Ref.

— El Segundo. large type ed. LC 00-21092. 244p. 2000. 23.95 (*0-7838-9041-9*, G K Hall & Co) Mac Lib Ref.

Blackburn, Tim M., jt. auth. see Gaston, Kevin J.

Blackburn, Tom. Jolly Rogers. McCarthy, Paul, ed. 352p. 1990. reprint ed. mass mkt. 5.99 (*0-671-69493-6*) PB.

Blackburn, Tom & Hammel, Eric. The Jolly Rogers: The Story of Tom Blackburn & Navy Fighting Squadron VF-17. LC 96-42244. (Illus.). 288p. 1997. reprint ed. 29.95 (*0-935553-19-3*) Pacifica Military.

Blackburn, Tom W. A Good Day to Die. 288p. 1996. reprint ed. mass mkt. 4.99 (*0-8439-4110-3*) Dorchester Pub Co.

Blackburn, Tom W. Patron. 1998. 17.50 (*0-7540-8018-8*, Gunsmoke) Chivers N Amer.

— Sierra Baron. 304p. 1997. reprint ed. mass mkt. 4.99 (*0-8439-4304-1*, Leisure Bks) Dorchester Pub Co.

Blackburn-Tyson, Jackie, ed. The Silver Season: Twenty-Five Years of Braves Baseball in Atlanta. LC 90-70280. (Illus.). 64p. (Orig.). 1990. pap. 6.95 (*0-9626248-0-2*) SportsPrint.

Blackburn, W. H., ed. Variability in Rangeland Water Erosion Process. LC 94-26299. (Special Publications: No. 38). 106p. 1994. 24.00 (*0-89118-812-6*) Soil Sci Soc Am.

***Blackburn, Warren D., Jr.** Approach to the Patient with a Musculoskeletal Disorder. 304p. 1999. pap. text 19.95 (*1-884735-38-X*) Prof Comms.

Blackburn, William H. & Dennen, William H. Principles of Mineralogy. 2nd ed. 432p. (C). 1993. text 53.65 (*0-697-15078-X*, WCB McGr Hill) McGrw-H Hghr Educ.

Blackburn, William M. Under Twenty-Five: Duke Narrative & Verse, 1945-1962. LC 63-9005. 250p. reprint ed. pap. 77.50 (*0-608-15101-7*, 202618700048) Bks Demand.

— William Farel & the Story of the Swiss Reform. reprint ed. 44.50 (*0-404-19870-8*) AMS Pr.

Blackburn, William M., ed. Under Twenty-Five: Duke Narrative & Verse, 1945-1962: A Collection of Short Stories & Verse by Sixteen Duke Authors. LC 63-9005. xi, 240p. 1963. pap. text 19.95 (*0-8223-0349-3*) Duke.

Blackburn, William R., ed. see Baxter Healthcare Corporation Staff.

Blackburn, William R., ed. see Baxter Healthcare Corporation Staff, et al.

Blackburn, William W. Young Calvin in Paris: or The Scholar & the Cripple. LC 83-45602. reprint ed. 40.00 (*0-404-19869-4*) AMS Pr.

Blackcurn, Robert R., et al. Development of Anti-Icing Technology. 479p. (Orig.). (C). 1993. pap. text 20.00 (*0-309-95761-3*, SHRP-H-385) SHRP.

Blackdeer, Muriel J. An Eagle Blessed Our Home. (Illus.). 160p. (YA). (gr. 8 up). 1994. pap. 12.95 (*0-9615394-5-3*) Skandisk.

Blackden, C. Mark & Bhanu, Chitra. Gender, Growth, & Poverty Reduction: Special Program of Assistance for Africa, 1998 Status Report on Poverty. LC 99-12536. (Technical Paper Ser.: No. 428). 135p. 1999. pap. 22.00 (*0-8213-4468-4*, 14468) World Bank.

B

An Asterisk (*) at the beginning of an entry indicates that the title is appearing for the first time.

B

*__Blackden, C. Mark & Bhanu, Chitra.__ Gender, Growth & Poverty Reduction: Special Program of Assistance for Africa, 1998 Status Report on Poverty in Sub-Saharan Africa. (Technical Paper Ser.: No. 428). (FRE.). 148p. 1999. pap. 22.00 (*0-8213-4529-X*, 14529) World Bank.

Blackden, M. W., ed. Ritual of the Mystery of the Judgement of the Soul: From an Ancient Egyptian Papyrus. 1986. pap. 6.95 (*0-916411-58-3*) Holmes Pub.

Blacke, John D. Herman the Hamster: Beware of Ignoring Me. LC 95-67894. (Illus.). 32p. (Orig.). (J). (gr. 1-5). 1995. 10.98 (*1-882786-19-X*) New Dawn NY.

— The Witch of Burchard Street: Biography of a Witch. Groff, Richard L., Jr., ed. 193p. 1991. 22.95 (*0-9630718-0-7*) New Dawn NY.

Blacke, Terry L. & Rider, Debra. Pabulum Pig: The Yule Swine. LC 91-68193. (Illus.). 41p. (J). (gr. 4). 1992. pap. 7.98 (*0-9630718-2-3*) New Dawn NY.

Blacker. By My Laugh It's Jewish. 1982. pap. 5.50 (*0-85303-198-3*, Pub. by M Vallentine & Co) Intl Spec Bk.

Blacker, Carmen. The Catalpa Bow: A Study of Shamanistic Practices in Japan. (Japan Library Classics). 382p. (C). 1999. pap. text 28.00 (*1-873410-85-9*, Pub. by Japan Library) UH Pr.

*__Blacker, Carmen.__ Collected Writings of Carmen Blacker. (Collected Writings of Modern Western Scholars on Japan: Vol. 1). 480p. 2000. text 140.00 (*1-873410-92-1*, Pub. by Japan Library) UH Pr.

Blacker, Carmen, jt. ed. see Davidson, Hilda Ellis.

Blacker, Carmen, jt. ed. see Shils, Edward.

Blacker, Coit D. Hostage to Revolution: Gorbachev & Soviet Security Policy, 1985-1991. LC 93-9800. 267p. 1993. reprint ed. pap. 82.80 (*0-608-02000-1*, 206265600003) Bks Demand.

— Reluctant Warrior: The Soviet Union & Arms Control. LC 86-32011. (Political Science Ser.). (Illus.). 850p. (C). 1989. pap. text 15.95 (*0-7167-1862-6*) W H Freeman.

Blacker, Coit D. & Davenport, Brian A. The Beijing Summit to Normalize Sino-Soviet Relations. (Pew Case Studies in International Affairs). 50p. (C). 1993. pap. text 3.50 (*1-56927-357-X*) Geo U Inst Dplmcy.

Blacker, Coit D., jt. ed. see Bellany, Ian.

Blacker, Coit D., jt. ed. see Lewis, John W.

Blacker, Coit D., ed. see Stanford Arms Control Group Staff.

Blacker, David J. Dying to Teach: The Educator's Search for Immortality. LC 96-40843. (Advances in Contemporary Educational Thought Ser.). 160p. 1997. 44.00 (*0-8077-3592-2*) Tchrs Coll.

Blacker, Irwin R. The Elements of Screenwriting. LC 96-18961. 144p. 1996. pap. 9.95 (*0-02-861450-X*) Macmillan Gen Ref.

Blacker, Irwin R., ed. Old West in Fact. 1962. 27.95 (*0-8392-1081-7*) Astor-Honor.

— Old West in Fiction. 1961. 27.95 (*0-8392-1082-5*) Astor-Honor.

Blacker, Jean. The Faces of Time: Portrayal of the Past in Old French & Latin Historical Narrative of the Anglo-Norman Regnum. LC 93-46605. 304p. (C). 1994. text 40.00 (*0-292-70808-4*) U of Tex Pr.

*__Blacker, John.__ Have You Forgotten Yet? The First World War Memoirs of C. P. Blacker. 2000. 36.95 (*0-85052-729-5*, Pub. by Pen & Sword Bks Ltd) Combined Pub.

Blacker, Keith. The Basics of Business Process Re-Engineering. (Illus.). 64p. 1995. 12.95 (*1-897815-05-0*, Pub. by Edistone Bks) D R Lambert.

— The Basics of Electronic Data Interchange. 2nd rev. ed. (Illus.). 49p. 1994. 12.95 (*1-897815-04-2*, Pub. by Edistone Bks) D R Lambert.

— The Basics of Electronic Data Interchange. 2nd rev. ed. Lambert, David R., ed. (Illus.). 49p. 1994. 16.95 incl. disk (*1-897815-07-7*, Pub. by Edistone Bks) D R Lambert.

— The Basics of Electronic Data Interchange in Manufacturing. (Illus.). 53p. 1993. 12.95 (*1-897815-01-8*, Pub. by Edistone Bks) D R Lambert.

— The Basics of Electronic Data Interchange in Smaller Companies. (Illus.). 49p. 1994. 12.95 (*1-897815-02-6*, Pub. by Edistone Bks) D R Lambert.

Blacker, Keith & Cronbach, Steve. The Basics of Electronic Data Interchange in Supermarkets & Stores. (Illus.). 47p. 1994. 12.95 (*1-897815-03-4*, Pub. by Edistone Bks) D R Lambert.

*__Blacker, Mary Rose.__ Flora Domestica: A History of British Flower Arranging, 1500-1930. (Illus.). 256p. 2000. 49.50 (*0-8109-6703-0*, Pub. by Abrams) Time Warner.

Blacker, Terence. If I Could Work. LC 87-3972. (Illus.). 32p. (J). (ps-2). 1988. 12.95 (*0-397-32245-3*); lib. bdg. 12.89 (*0-397-32255-0*) HarpC Child Bks.

Blackerby. Geology Workbook for the Web. (Earth Science Ser.). 1997. 17.95 (*0-314-21072-5*) Wadsworth Pub.

Blackerby, Don A. Rediscover the Joy of Learning. 196p. (Orig.). 1996. pap. 24.95 (*1-889997-00-5*) Success Skills.

Blackerby, Peter. Not Now! Maybe Later. Hardly, Roman, ed. LC 97-66998. (Illus.). 48p. (J). (gr. 1-3). 1997. lib. bdg. 19.95 (*0-912495-33-2*) San Diego Pub Co.

Blackerby, Phillip, jt. auth. see Blackerby, Rae F.

Blackerby, Rae F. Application of Chaos Theory to Psychological Models. LC 98-93259. 174p. (C). 1998. pap. text 22.00 (*0-9632885-3-9*) Perf Strategies.

Blackerby, Rae F. & Blackerby, Phillip. Strategic Planning for the Public Sector Video Seminar: Instructor's Guide. LC 92-80908. (Illus.). 94p. 1992. pap. text, teacher ed. 995.00 (*0-9632885-0-4*) Perf Strategies.

— Workbook for Public Sector Strategic Planning. (Illus.). 93p. 1992. pap. text 15.00 (*0-9632885-1-2*) Perf Strategies.

*__Blacket, William S.__ Researches into the Lost Histories of America: or The Zodiac Shown to Be an Old Terrestrial Map in Which the Atlantic Isle Is Dejineated: So That Light Can Be Thrown upon the Obscure Histories of the Earthworks & Ruined Cities of America. (LC History-America-E). 336p. 1999. reprint ed. lib. bdg. 99.00 (*0-7812-4309-2*) Rprt Serv.

Blacketer, Raymond & Blacketer, Sandy. Dare to Care: Leader Guide. (Prime-Time Ser.). 56p. 1999. pap. 8.95 (*1-56212-382-3*, 1210-3077) CRC Pubns.

Blacketer, Raymond & Blacketer, Sandyb. Dare to Care: Student. (Prime-Time Ser.). 42p. 1999. mass mkt. 4.35 (*1-56212-383-1*, 1210-3076) CRC Pubns.

Blacketer, Sandy, jt. auth. see Blacketer, Raymond.

Blacketer, Sandyb, jt. auth. see Blacketer, Raymond.

Blackett, Monica. The Mark of the Maker: A Portrait of Helen Waddell. LC 73-161815. 258p. reprint ed. pap. 80.00 (*0-608-15681-7*, 203199700077) Bks Demand.

Blackett, Patrick M. Studies of War: Nuclear & Conventional. LC 78-16364. (Illus.). 242p. 1978. reprint ed. lib. bdg. 35.00 (*0-313-20575-2*, BLSW, Greenwood Pr) Greenwood.

Blackett, R. J. Beating Against the Barriers: The Lives of Six Nineteenth-Century Afro-Americans. LC 89-42927. (Illus.). 418p. 1989. pap. text 18.95 (*0-8014-9675-6*) Cornell U Pr.

— Building an Antislavery Wall: Black Americans in the Atlantic Abolitionist Movement, 1830-1860. LC 89-42928. 238p. 1989. pap. text 16.95 (*0-8014-9624-1*) Cornell U Pr.

— Building an Antislavery Wall: Black Americans in the Atlantic Abolitionist Movement, 1830-1860. LC 82-21724. 264p. 1983. text 37.50 (*0-8071-1082-5*) La State U Pr.

— Thomas Morris Chester, Black Civil War Correspondent: His Dispatches from the Virginia Front. LC 89-30169. (Illus.). 376p. 1989. text 50.00 (*0-8071-1516-9*) La State U Pr.

*__Blackett, R. J. M.__ Divided Hearts: Britain & the American Civil War. (Illus.). 312p. 2000. 49.95 (*0-8071-2595-4*); pap. 24.95 (*0-8071-2645-4*) La State U Pr.

Blackett, Robert E. & Shubat, Michael A. A Case Study of the Newcastle Geothermal System, Iron County, Utah. LC TN24.U8 A322. (Special Study Ser.: Vol. 81). (Illus.). 30p. 1992. pap. 5.50 (*1-55791-200-9*, SS-81) Utah Geological Survey.

Blackett, Robert E., et al. Effect of Geothermal Drawdown on Sustainable Development, Newcastle Area, Iron County, Utah. LC 97-199810. (Circular of the Utah Geological Survey Ser.: Vol. 97). (Illus.). 31p. 1997. pap. 5.00 (*1-55791-609-8*, C-97) Utah Geological Survey.

Blackett, Ruth & Millhollin, Bonnie. Apple Cellar. Shreves, Kathey, ed. (Illus.). 102p. (C). 1981. 5.95 (*0-940158-05-1*) Zucchini Patch.

— Country Cellar. Shreves, Kathey, ed. (Illus.). 114p. (C). 1981. spiral bd. 5.95 (*0-940158-01-9*) Zucchini Patch.

Blackett, Ruth, ed. see Sherves, Kathey L. & Millhollin, Bonnie.

*__Blackett, Tom & Boad, Bob.__ Co-Branding: The Science of Alliance. LC 99-44845. 2000. text 49.95 (*0-312-22897-X*) St Martin.

Blackey, Eileen. Eileen Blackey: Pathfinder for the Profession, Commentary & Analysis by Werner W. Boehm. Kendall, Katherine A., ed. LC 86-5405. (Leaders in Social Work Ser.). 159p. reprint ed. pap. 49.30 (*0-7837-5361-6*, 204512400005) Bks Demand.

Blackey, Robert, ed. History Anew: Innovations in the Teaching of History Today. LC 92-34909. 336p. (C). 1992. pap. text 22.50 (*1-878981-04-8*); lib. bdg. 65.00 (*1-878981-03-X*) CSULB Univ Pr.

Blackey, Robert & Paynton, Clifford T. Revolution & the Revolutionary Ideal. 256p. 1976. 22.95 (*0-87073-986-7*) Schenkman Bks Inc.

Blackey, Robert, jt. auth. see Paynton, Clifford T.

Blackfield, Neil. Starting Gate Series, 5 vols., Set. Kratoville, Betty L., ed. 48p. (YA). (gr. 6-12). 1999. pap. 17.00 (*1-57128-107-X*) High Noon Bks.

Blackford. Business Enterprise in American History, 3 vols. 3rd ed. LC 93-78665. (C). 1993. pap. text 39.56 (*0-395-66849-2*) HM.

Blackford, Barbara J. & Cramer, Betty. Success in Reading & Writing. 2nd ed. (Illus.). 288p. (J). (gr. k). 1991. 27.95 (*0-673-36000-8*, GoodYrBooks) Addson-Wesley Educ.

Blackford, Bland, et al. Bassett Hall: The Williamsburg Home of Mr. & Mrs. John D. Rockefeller, Jr. LC 84-17600. (Illus.). 43p. (Orig.). 1984. pap. 3.95 (*0-87935-107-1*) Colonial Williamsburg.

Blackford, Charles M. The Campaign & Battle of Lynchburg, Virginia. rev. ed. Houck, Peter W., ed. & illus. by. LC 94-60398. 127p. 1994. 14.95 (*0-9638455-1-9*) Warwick Hse.

Blackford, Charles M. & Blackford, Susan L. Memoirs of Life in & Out of the Army in Virginia During the War Between the States, 2 vols. 2nd rev. ed. Houck, Peter W., ed. Incl. Vol. 1. 2nd rev. ed. LC 96-61733. 288p. 1996. reprint ed. bond lthr. (*0-9638455-7-8*); Vol. 2. 2nd rev. ed. LC 96-61733. 264p. 1996. reprint ed. bond lthr. (*0-9638455-8-6*); LC 96-61733. 1996. reprint ed. 95.00 (*0-9638455-9-4*) Warwick Hse.

Blackford, Charles M., jt. anno. see Blackford, Susan L.

Blackford, George H. ASP Student Guide - Version 3. (Illus.). 127p. (C). 1999. pap. text 16.95 (*1-881564-28-2*) DMC Sftware.

*__Blackford, George H.__ ASP Student Guide - Version 3 with Software: Student Version of ASP. (Illus.). 127p. 1999. pap. text 4.95 (*1-881564-29-0*) DMC Sftware.

Blackford, George H. ASP Tutorial & Student Guide. 96p. (C). 1992. 29.95 incl. 3.5 hd (*1-881564-27-4*); 24.95 incl. 5.25 hd (*1-881564-26-6*); 14.95 (*1-881564-25-8*) DMC Sftware.

— ASP User's Manual (Version 2.00) 224p. (C). 1992. student ed. 29.95 (*1-881564-00-2*) DMC Sftware.

— ASPG Graphics Supplement & Installation Guide. (Illus.). 24p. 1994. 3.00 (*1-881564-01-0*) DMC Sftware.

Blackford, Jason C. Baldwin's Ohio Practice, Business Organizations. LC 96-184243. 588p. 1996. 195.00 (*0-8322-0632-6*) Banks-Baldwin.

Blackford, Mansel G. A History of Small Business in America. (Twayne's Evolution of American Business Ser.: No. 10). 250p. (C). 1992. pap. 13.95 (*0-685-52969-X*, Twayne) Mac Lib Ref.

— A History of Small Business in America. (Twayne's Evolution of American Business Ser.: No. 10). 250p. (C). 1992. 24.95 (*0-8057-9824-2*) Macmillan.

— Pioneering a Modern Small Business: Wakefield Seafoods & the Alaskan Frontier. Porter, Glenn, ed. LC 77-7794. (Industrial Development & the Social Fabric Ser.: Vol. 6). 222p. 1979. 73.25 (*0-89232-088-5*) Jai Pr.

— A Portrait Cast in Steel: Buckeye International & Columbus, Ohio, 1881-1980, 49. LC 82-6114. (Contributions in Economics & Economic History Ser.: No. 49). (Illus.). 225p. 1982. 45.00 (*0-313-23393-4*, BPC/) Greenwood.

— The Rise of Modern Business in Great Britain, the United States, & Japan. 2nd rev. ed. LC 97-32867. (Illus.). 264p. 1998. pap. 17.95 (*0-8078-4732-1*); lib. bdg. 39.95 (*0-8078-2426-7*) U of NC Pr.

Blackford, Mansel G., ed. On Board the U. S. S. Mason: The World War II Diary of James A. Dunn. LC 95-48969. (Illus.). 130p. (C). 1996. text 18.95 (*0-8142-0698-0*) Ohio St U Pr.

Blackford, Mansel G. & Kerr, K. Austin. BFGoodrich: Tradition & Transformation, 1870-1995. (Historical Perspectives on Business Enterprise Ser.). (Illus.). 507p. 1996. text 40.00 (*0-8142-0696-4*) Ohio St U Pr.

Blackford, Russell, et al, eds. Strange Constellations: A History of Australian Science Fiction, 80. LC 98-37716. (Contributions to the Study of Science Fiction & Fantasy Ser.: Vol. 80). 264p. 1999. 65.00 (*0-313-25112-6*, Greenwood Pr) Greenwood.

Blackford, S., et al, eds. Scalapack Users' Guide. LC 97-68164. (Software, Environments & Tools Ser.: Vol. 4). (Illus.). xxvi, 325p. 1997. pap. 53.00 (*0-89871-397-8*, SE04) Soc Indus-Appl Math.

Blackford, Simon. Rights of Way. 112p. 1995. pap. 33.00 (*1-85811-055-6*, Pub. by CLT Prof) Gaunt.

*__Blackford, Simon.__ Rights of Way. 2nd ed. 112p. 1999. pap. 40.00 (*1-85811-166-8*, Pub. by CLT Prof) Gaunt.

Blackford, Susan L. & Blackford, Charles M., annos. Letters from Lee's Army. LC 98-29020. xx, 312p. 1998. pap. 15.00 (*0-8032-6149-7*) U of Nebr Pr.

Blackford, Susan L., jt. auth. see Blackford, Charles M.

Blackford, William W. War Years with Jeb Stuart. LC 93-8969. (Illus.). 322p. 1993. pap. 14.95 (*0-8071-1880-X*) La State U Pr.

— War Years with Jeb Stuart. (History - United States Ser.). 322p. 1993. reprint ed. lib. bdg. 89.00 (*0-7812-4819-1*) Rprt Serv.

Blackhall, David S. This House Had Windows. 1962. 12.95 (*0-8392-1115-5*) Astor-Honor.

Blackhall, James C. Planning Law & Practice. xlv, 418p. 1998. pap. 45.00 (*1-85941-391-9*, Pub. by Cavendish Pubng) Gaunt.

Blackham, Garth J. Modification in Child Behavior. (Education Ser.). 1970. pap. 5.00 (*0-534-00005-3*) Wadsworth Pub.

Blackham, H. J. The Fable As Literature. LC 84-21674. 280p. (C). 1985. text 15.00 (*0-485-11278-7*, Pub. by Athlone Pr) Humanities.

— The Future of Our Past: From Ancient Greece to Global Village. Smoker, Barbara, ed. LC 95-26135. 411p. 1996. 33.95 (*1-57392-042-8*) Prometheus Bks.

— Six Existentialist Thinkers. 179p. 1983. pap. 13.95 (*0-7100-4611-1*, Routledge Thoemms) Routledge.

— Six Existentialist Thinkers. 190p. (C). 1983. pap. 19.99 (*0-415-05098-7*) Routledge.

Blackham, H. J., et al. Objections to Humanism. LC 73-16796. 128p. 1974. reprint ed. lib. bdg. 49.50 (*0-8371-7235-7*, BLOH, Greenwood Pr) Greenwood.

Blackhawk, Ned. The Shoshone. LC 99-23347. (Indian Nations Ser.). (Illus.). 48p. (ps-3). 1999. 25.69 (*0-8172-5468-4*) Raintree Steck-V.

Blackhawk, Terry. Body & Field. LC 99-6069. xi, 107 p. 1999. pap. 15.95 (*0-87013-518-X*) Mich St U Pr.

— Trio: Woman & Myth. (Writer's Voice Series of YMCA). (Illus.). 28p. 1998. pap. text 10.00 (*1-56439-074-8*, Pub. by Ridgeway) Partners Pubs Grp.

*__Blackhorse, Buck.__ Empty Bedrooms: The International Adoption of a Deaf Filipino Boy. LC 99-93733. 2000. 15.95 (*0-533-13135-9*) Vantage.

Blackhurst, A. Edward & Berdine, William H. Intro Special Education. 3rd ed. (C). 1993. pap. text, student ed. 21.56 (*0-673-52315-2*) Addson-Wesley Educ.

Blackhurst, Hector. East & Northeast Africa Bibliography. (Scarecrow Area Bibliographies Ser.: Vol. 7). 360p. 1996. 62.50 (*0-8108-3090-6*) Scarecrow.

Blackie. Community Healthcare Nursing. LC 98-10211. (C). 1998. pap. text 29.95 (*0-443-05291-3*, W B Saunders Co) Harcrt Hlth Sci Grp.

Blackie & Son Staff. Victorian Cabinet-Maker's Assistant. (Illus.). 217p. 1970. reprint ed. pap. 16.95 (*0-486-22353-1*) Dover.

Blackie, John & Patrick, Hilary. Blackie & Patrick: Mental Health: the Law in Scotland. 2nd ed. 1997. pap. write for info. (*0-406-07756-8*, BPMH2, MICHIE) LEXIS Pub.

Blackie, John S. Life of Burns. LC 75-30844. (English Literature Ser.: No. 33). 1975. lib. bdg. 75.00 (*0-8383-2102-X*) M S G Haskell Hse.

— Scottish Song. LC 70-144563. reprint ed. 52.50 (*0-404-08579-2*) AMS Pr.

Blackie, Lorna. Clans & Tartans: The Fabric of Scotland. (Illus.). 72p. 1997. 12.98 (*0-7858-0274-6*) Bk Sales Inc.

Blackie, Malcolm J. & Dent, J. B., eds. Information Systems for Agriculture. (Illus.). 176p. 1979. 47.00 (*0-85334-829-4*) Elsevier.

Blacking, John. How Musical Is Man? LC 72-6710. (Jessie & John Danz Lecture Ser.). (Illus.). 132p. 1990. audio 20.00 (*0-295-75517-2*) U of Wash Pr.

— How Musical Is Man? LC 72-6710. (Jessie & John Danz Lectures). (Illus.). 132p. (C). 1973. reprint ed. pap. 14.95 (*0-295-95338-1*) U of Wash Pr.

— Music, Culture, & Experience: Selected Papers of John Blacking. Byron, Reginald, ed. 282p. 1995. pap. text 17.95 (*0-226-08830-8*) U Ch Pr.

— Venda Children's Songs: A Study in Ethnomusicological Analysis. 210p. 1995. pap. text 15.95 (*0-226-05511-6*); lib. bdg. 35.00 (*0-226-05510-8*) U Ch Pr.

Blacking, John & Kealiinohomoku, Joann W., eds. The Performing Arts: Music & Dance. (World Anthropology Ser.). (Illus.). xii, 346p. 1979. text 57.70 (*90-279-7870-0*) Mouton.

Blacking, John & Nettl, Bruno. Music, Culture, & Experience: Selected Papers of John Blacking. LC 94-25598. 282p. 1995. lib. bdg. 45.95 (*0-226-08829-4*) U Ch Pr.

Blackistone, Mick. Broken Wings Will Fly. (Illus.). 32p. (J). (gr. 4-6). 1992. 10.95 (*0-87033-439-5*, Tidewtr Pubs) Cornell Maritime.

— The Buffalo & the River. LC 90-84005. (Illus.). 44p. (J). (gr. 4-6). 1990. reprint ed. text 14.95 (*0-9627726-0-7*) Blue Crab MD.

— The Day They Left the Bay. 3rd ed. LC 91-76591. (Illus.). 36p. (J). (gr. 2-5). 1988. reprint ed. text 14.95 (*0-9627726-3-1*) Blue Crab MD.

Blacklaw, Jerry. Plain Talk about Women in the Church. (Illus.). 64p. (Orig.). 1992. pap. 8.95 (*1-881576-04-3*) Providence Hse.

Blackle, Lorna. Clans & Tartans. 1998. 12.99 (*0-7858-0882-5*) Bk Sales Inc.

Blackledge. The Job You Want--How to Get It. 3rd ed. (CA - Career Development Ser.). 1983. pap. 11.95 (*0-538-11260-3*) S-W Pub.

*__Blackledge, Adrian.__ Literacy, Power & Social Justice. 204p. 2000. pap. 24.94 (*1-85856-158-2*, Trentham Bks) Stylus Pub VA.

Blackledge, David & Hunt, Barry. Sociological Interpretation of Education. LC 85-4145. (Social Analysis Ser.). 353p. 1985. pap. 18.95 (*0-7099-0676-5*, Pub. by C Helm) Routldge.

*__Blackledge, Dennis A.__ We Gotta Go Now. Blackledge, Holly Adair, ed. 270p. 2000. pap. 19.95 (*0-9677566-0-X*) Windholme Pubng.

Blackledge, G. R., et al, eds. Textbook of Gynecologic Oncology. (Illus.). 512p. 1991. text 160.00 (*0-7020-1410-9*, Pub. by W B Saunders) Saunders.

Blackledge, Holly Adair, ed. see Blackledge, Dennis A.

*__Blackledge, J. M.__ Imaging & Digital Image Processing. 350p. 2000. 95.00 incl. cd-rom (*1-898563-49-7*, Pub. by Horwood Pub) Paul & Co Pubs.

Blackledge, Jonathan, ed. Image Processing: Mathematical Methods & Applications. LC 97-1172. (Institute of Mathematics & Its Applications Conference Ser.: No. 61). (Illus.). 536p. 1997. text 165.00 (*0-19-851197-3*) OUP.

*__Blackledge, Jonathan M., ed.__ Image Processing Research: Mathematical Methods, Algorithms & Applications. 300p. 1999. 95.00 (*1-898563-61-6*, Pub. by Horwood Pub) Paul & Co Pubs.

Blackledge, Jonathan M. & Turner, Martin. Digital Signal Processing: Software Solutions & Applications. 200p. 1998. 39.95 incl. cd-rom (*1-898563-48-9*, Pub. by Horwood Pub) Paul & Co Pubs.

Blackledge, Patricia. Face to Face with Christ. 96p. 1996. pap. 39.95 (*0-85439-517-2*, Pub. by St Paul Pubns) St Mut.

Blackledge, Robert C., et al, eds. Space - A Call for Action: Proceedings of the 10th Annual International Space Development Conference. 404p. 1991. pap. 27.50 (*0-912183-05-5*) Univelt Inc.

Blackleeds, Alistair. A New History of the English Public Library: Social & Intellectual Contexts, 1850-1914. LC 95-41411. 352p. 1996. 95.00 (*0-7185-0015-6*) Bks Intl VA.

Blackler, Frank, ed. Social Psychology & Developing Countries. fac. ed. LC 83-6560. 311p. 1983. reprint ed. pap. 96.50 (*0-7837-8283-7*, 204906500009) Bks Demand.

Blackley, Becky. The Autoharp Book. LC 83-81145. (Illus.). 256p. (Orig.). 1983. pap. 19.95 (*0-912827-01-7*) I A D Pubns.

— The Becky Blackley Songbook. (Illus.). 36p. 1986. pap. 6.95 (*0-912827-10-6*) I A D Pubns.

— Classical Autoharp: Music of the Masters. 42p. (Orig.). 1995. pap. 12.00 (*0-912827-21-1*) I A D Pubns.

— Goodtime Autoharp! Rags, Waltzes, Polkas & the Can-Can Arranged for the Autoharp. (Illus.). 52p. 1993. pap. 10.00 (*0-912827-20-3*) I A D Pubns.

Blackley, Becky, ed. The Care & Feeding of the Autoharp, Vol. 1. 2nd ed. LC 82-108061. 100p. (Orig.). 1991. pap. 10.00 (*0-912827-15-7*) I A D Pubns.

— The Care & Feeding of the Autoharp, Vol. 2. 2nd ed. LC 82-108061. (Illus.). 88p. (Orig.). 1991. pap. 10.00 (*0-912827-16-5*) I A D Pubns.

— The Care & Feeding of the Autoharp, Vol. 3. LC 82-108061. (Illus.). 93p. (Orig.). 1984. pap. 10.00 (*0-912827-03-3*) I A D Pubns.

— The Care & Feeding of the Autoharp, Vol. 4. LC 82-108061. (Illus.). 89p. (Orig.). 1986. pap. 10.00 (*0-912827-07-6*) I A D Pubns.

An Asterisk (*) at the beginning of an entry indicates that the title is appearing for the first time.

— The Care & Feeding of the Autoharp, Vol. 5. LC 82-108061. (Care & Feeding of the Autoharp Ser.). (Illus.). 89p. (Orig.). 1986. pap. 10.00 (*0-912827-08-4*) I A D Pubns.
— The Care & Feeding of the Autoharp, Vol. 6. LC 82-108061. (Illus.). 82p. (Orig.). 1989. pap. 10.00 (*0-912827-12-2*) I A D Pubns.
— The Care & Feeding of the Autoharp, Vol. 7. LC 82-108061. (Illus.). 68p. (Orig.). 1991. pap. 10.00 (*0-912827-13-0*) I A D Pubns.
— The Care & Feeding of the Autoharp, Vol. 8. LC 82-108061. (Illus.). 82p. (Orig.). 1991. pap. 10.00 (*0-912827-14-9*) I A D Pubns.
— The Care & Feeding of the Autoharp, Vol. 9. LC 82-108061. (Illus.). 94p. (Orig.). 1991. pap. 10.00 (*0-912827-17-3*) I A D Pubns.
— The Care & Feeding of the Autoharp, Vol. 10. LC 82-108061. (Illus.). (Orig.). 1991. pap. 12.00 (*0-912827-18-1*) I A D Pubns.
— The Care & Feeding of the Autoharp, Vol. 11. LC 82-108061. (Illus.). 112p. (Orig.). 1993. pap. 12.00 (*0-912827-19-X*) I A D Pubns.
— The Care & Feeding of the Autoharp, Vol. 12. LC 82-108061. (Illus.). 142p. (Orig.). 1993. pap. 15.00 (*0-912827-22-X*) I A D Pubns.

Blackley, Becky, ed. see Beck, Stevie, et al.

Blackley, Becky, ed. see Schroeder, Tom.

Blackley, Meera. Indian Home Cooking. 1994. 12.98 (*0-7858-0196-0*) Bk Sales Inc.

Blackley, Stuart, jt. auth. see Fuller, Janine.

Blackley, Stuart, jt. auth. see Fuller, Janine.

***Blacklock, Craig.** Border Country: Photographs from the Quetico-Superior Wilderness. 1999. 45.00 (*1-892472-03-1*); pap. 27.00 (*1-892472-04-X*) Blacklock Nature.

Blacklock, Craig. The Lake Superior Images. 2nd rev. ed. (Illus.). 192p. 1998. 49.95 (*1-892472-00-7*) Blacklock Nature.

Blacklock, Craig & Adventure Publishing Staff. The Lake Superior Images. 2nd rev. ed. (Illus.). 192p. 1998. pap. 29.95 (*0-9634991-8-1*) Blacklock Nature.

Blacklock, Craig & Blacklock, Nadine. Photographing Wildflowers: Techniques for the Advanced Amateur & Professional. (Illus.). 64p. 1990. reprint ed. pap. 12.95 (*0-89658-069-5*) Voyageur Pr.

Blacklock, Craig, et al. Border Country: The Quetico-Superior Wilderness. LC 88-61091. 180p. 1988. 35.00 (*0-942802-82-9*) Blacklock Nature.

Blacklock, Craig, jt. auth. see Blacklock, Nadine.

Blacklock, Dyan. Nudes & Nikes: Champions & Legends of the First Olympics. (True Stories Ser.). (Illus.). 100p. (Orig.). (J). (gr. 3-8). 1997. pap. 6.95 (*1-86448-455-1*, Pub. by Allen & Unwin Pty) IPG Chicago.
— Pankration: The Ultimate Game. LC 98-38559. 192p. (J). (gr. 5-9). 1999. lib. bdg. 15.95 (*0-8075-6323-4*) A Whitman.

Blacklock, Fran. Our Minnesota. enl. rev. ed. (Illus.). 144p. 2000. 24.95 (*0-89658-221-3*) Voyageur Pr.

Blacklock, Gene W., jt. auth. see Rappole, John H.

Blacklock, Judith. Flower Arranging Style: An International Collection of Ideas & Inspirations for All Seasons. LC 96-79047. 320p. 1997. 35.00 (*0-8212-2386-0*, Pub. by Bulfinch Pr) Little.
— Teach Yourself Flower Arranging. (Illus.). 176p. 1995. pap. 10.95 (*0-8442-3919-4*, Teach Yrslf) NTC Contemp Pub Co.

Blacklock, Les, et al, photos by. Our Minnesota. 3rd rev. ed. LC 92-28228. (Illus.). 144p. 1992. pap. 16.95 (*0-89658-258-2*) Voyageur Pr.

Blacklock, Nadine. 15 Years in a Photographer's Life. (Illus.). 112p. 1997. pap. text 17.50 (*0-9634991-7-3*) Blacklock Nature.

Blacklock, Nadine & Blacklock, Craig. The Duluth Portfolio. limited ed. Gustafson, Susan, ed. LC 95-67900. (Illus.). 108p. 1995. 35.00 (*1-57025-073-1*) Pfeifer-Hamilton.
— Gooseberry. LC 94-29105. (Illus.). 80p. 1994. text 22.95 (*1-57025-024-3*) Pfeifer-Hamilton.

Blacklock, Nadine, jt. auth. see Blacklock, Craig.

Blacklock, Ryan. Comet Vomit. 112p. (Orig.). (J). (gr. 5-9). 1996. pap. 6.95 (*1-86373-810-X*, Pub. by Allen & Unwin Pty) IPG Chicago.

***Blacklow.** New Dimensions in Photo Imaging. 3rd ed. (Illus.). 160p. 2000. pap. 36.95 (*0-240-80431-7*, Focal) Buttrwrth-Heinemann.

Blacklow, Laura. New Dimensions in Photo Imaging: A Step-by-Step Manual. 2nd ed. LC 94-48311. (Illus.). 112p. 1995. pap. text 37.95 (*0-240-80209-8*, Focal) Buttrwrth-Heinemann.

***Blackman.** A.N.T.I.D.O.T.E. 2000. 17.95 (*0-385-40679-7*, Pub. by Transworld Publishers Ltd) Trafalgar.
— Aphids on the World's Crops. 2nd ed. LC 99-40230. 476p. 2000. 169.95 (*0-471-85191-4*) Wiley.
— Aphids on the World's Plants. text. write for info. (*0-471-48973-5*) Wiley.
— Blood Sugar. 150p. 1999. pap. 13.00 (*1-888277-17-3*, Pub. by Incommcdo San Diego) Consort Bk Sales.
— Hacker. 2000. pap. 6.95 (*0-552-52751-3*, Pub. by Transworld Publishers Ltd) Trafalgar.

Blackman. Medical Aspects of Developmental Disabilities in Children Birth to Three. 3rd ed. LC 96-44579. 320p. 1997. 40.00 (*0-8342-0759-1*) Aspen Pub.

***Blackman.** Operation Gadgetman. (J). 2000. pap. 5.95 (*0-440-86307-4*, Pub. by Transworld Publishers Ltd) Trafalgar.
— Pig-Heart Boy. (J). 2000. pap. 6.95 (*0-552-52841-2*, Pub. by Transworld Publishers Ltd) Trafalgar.
— Space Race. 2000. pap. 6.95 (*0-552-54542-2*, Pub. by Transworld Publishers Ltd) Trafalgar.
— Thief. 2000. 16.95 (*0-385-40504-9*, Pub. by Transworld Publishers Ltd); pap. 6.95 (*0-552-52808-0*, Pub. by Transworld Publishers Ltd) Trafalgar.

Blackman, Alyward M. Gods, Priests & Men: Studies in the Religion of Pharaonic Egypt. Lloyd, Alan B., ed. (Studies in Egyptology). (Illus.). 452p. 1998. 212.50 (*0-7103-0412-9*, A6984, Pub. by Kegan Paul Intl) Col U Pr.

Blackman, Ann. Seasons of Her Life: A Biography of Madeleine Korbel Albright. LC 98-28124. (Illus.). 400p. 1998. 27.00 (*0-684-84564-4*) Scribner.

Blackman, Aylward M., tr. see Erman, Adolf.

Blackman, Aylward M., tr. see Erman, Johann P.

Blackman, Barry. Creating Digital Illusions: The Blackman Portfolio. (Design & Graphic Design Ser.). (Illus.). 208p. 1996. text 49.95 (*0-442-02141-0*, VNR) Wiley.

Blackman, Barry. Creating Digital Illusions: The Blackman Portfolio. (Illus.). 195p. 1996. 49.95 (*0-471-28731-8*, VNR) Wiley.

***Blackman, Bill.** Acrylic Painting the Easy Way. (Illus.). 32p. 1999. pap. 10.50 (*1-56770-460-3*) S Scheewe Pubns.

Blackman, Bill. Lighted Windows & Gardens. 48p. 1996. pap. 10.50 (*1-56770-355-0*) S Scheewe Pubns.
— Oil Painting the Easy Way, Vol. 2. 71p. 1995. pap. 10.50 (*1-56770-337-2*) S Scheewe Pubns.

Blackman, Carol & Browning Miller, Elise. Life Is a Stretch: Easy Yoga Anytime, Anywhere. LC 98-27724. (Illus.). 224p. 1999. 17.95 (*1-56718-067-1*, K067) Llewellyn Pubns.

Blackman, Carolyn. Negotiating China: Case Studies & Strategies. LC 97-199211. 224p. 1997. pap. 24.95 (*1-86448-070-X*, Pub. by Allen & Unwin Pty) Paul & Co Pubs.

Blackman, Claudia, ed. see Paup, Donald C. & Fernhall, Bo.

Blackman, Claudia, ed. see Pellett, Tracy L. & Lox, Curt.

Blackman, Claudia, ed. see Rutherford, Jack.

Blackman, Courtney. Managing Foreign Exchange Reserves in Small Developing Countries. (Occasional Paper Ser.: No. 11). 19p. 1982. pap. 7.00 (*1-56708-010-3*) Grp of Thirty.

Blackman, D. R. & Betts, Gavin G., eds. Itinerarium Egeriae - Concordantia in Itinerarium Egeriae. (Alpha-Omega, Reihe A Ser.: Bd. XCVI). (GER.). v, 204p. 1989. 80.00 (*3-487-09075-9*) G Olms Pubs.
— Mulomedicina Chironis - Concordantia in Mulomedicinam Chironis. 1000p. write for info. (*0-318-70669-5*) G Olms Pubs.
— Tacitus - Concordantia Tacitea, 2 vols., Set. (Alpha-Omega, Reihe A Ser.: Bd. LXXIV). (GER.). 1932p. 1986. 480.00 (*3-487-07748-5*) G Olms Pubs.
— Vegetius - Concordantia in Vegetii Opera. (Alpha-Omega, Reihe A Ser.: Bd. LXXXV). (GER.). vi, 830p. 1988. 280.00 (*3-487-09059-7*) G Olms Pubs.

Blackman, D. R., jt. ed. see Betts, Gavin G.

Blackman, David. The Logic of Biochemical Sequencing. LC 93-12778. 192p. 1993. lib. bdg. 54.95 (*0-8493-4497-2*, QP551) CRC Pr.

Blackman, Deane R. & Betts, Gavin G., contrib. by. Concordantia in Mulomedicinam Chironis. (Alpha-Omega, Reihe A Ser.: Vol. LXXXVI). (GER.). vi, 974p. 1998. write for info. (*3-487-10641-8*) G Olms Pubs.

Blackman, Dee. Yesterday & Today, Luther Burbank Home & Gardens. (Illus.). 36p. 1998. pap. 8.25 (*0-9637883-2-9*) L Burbank Home.

Blackman, Derek E., jt. auth. see Leslie, Julian C.

Blackman, Edward B, jt. auth. see Abrams, Edwin D.

Blackman, Edwin C. Marcion & His Influence. LC 77-84695. reprint ed. 39.50 (*0-404-16103-0*) AMS Pr.

Blackman, Ellen. Harvest in the Snow: My Crusade to Rescue the Lost Children of Bosnia. LC 96-49218. 320p. 1997. 24.95 (*1-57488-085-3*) Brasseys.

Blackman, Emily C. History of Susquehanna County, Pennsylvania: From a Period Preceding Settlement to Recent Times. (Illus.). 640p. 1992. reprint ed. lib. bdg. 69.00 (*0-8328-1414-8*) Higginson Bk Co.

Blackman, Eric. Airman at the Helm. 116p. 1987. 40.00 (*0-85937-167-0*, Pub. by K Mason Pubns Ltd) St Mut.

Blackman, Everett. Astrology: Worlds Visible & Invisible. 100p. 1974. 10.50 (*0-86690-059-4*, B1104-034) Am Fed Astrologers.
— So You Want to Be President. 88p. 1972. 6.00 (*0-86690-060-8*, B1024-014) Am Fed Astrologers.

Blackman, Everett A. From the Tales of Burdock Mountain. 55p. (C). 1991. lib. bdg. 10.95 (*0-9622469-8-0*) Norcor Enterprises.
— The General's Pants. 100p. (C). 2000. lib. bdg. 10.95 (*0-9622469-7-2*) Norcor Enterprises.
— Old-Fashioned Girl. 96p. (C). 1999. lib. bdg. 10.95 (*0-9622469-5-6*) Norcor Enterprises.
— Pyramids & Puns Vol. 1: The First Book of Egyptian Humor. (Illus.). 112p. (Orig.). (C). 1988. pap. 2.95 (*0-9622469-9-9*) Norcor Enterprises.
— Saleable Livestock Receipts. 88p. 1999. lib. bdg. 10.95 (*0-9622469-6-4*) Norcor Enterprises.

Blackman, Evertt A. Crisis Studies in Human Affairs: Historic Patterns & New Age Formats. (Illus.). 106p. 1999. spiral bd. 16.95 (*0-86690-489-1*, B3751-014) Am Fed Astrologers.

Blackman, George C., jt. auth. see Tripler, Charles S.

Blackman, Haden. North American Monster. LC 97-43243. 272p. 1998. pap. 15.00 (*0-609-80017-5*) Crown Pub Group.

Blackman, Harold S., jt. auth. see Gertman, David I.

Blackman, Irving & Dorman, Michael. How to Value Your Marine Dealership. 140p. 1996. ring bd. 70.00 (*0-912474-23-8*) Preston Pubns.

Blackman, Irving L. The Complete Guide to Building Your Automobile Deductions - Legally. LC 84-102939. (Special Report Ser.: No. 6). 78p. 1988. pap. 2 .00 (*0-916181-05-7*) Blackman Kallick Bartelstein.
— The Complete Guide to Building Your Entertainment Deductions - Legally. LC 84-102962. (Special Report Ser.: No. 7). 44p. 1987. pap. 21.00 (*0-916181-06-5*) Blackman Kallick Bartelstein.
— The Complete Guide to Building Your Travel Deductions - Legally. (Special Report Ser.: No. 8). 50p. 1987. pap. 21.00 (*0-916181-07-3*) Blackman Kallick Bartelstein.
— Divorce, Taxes & You. (Special Report Ser.: No. 5). 64p. 1987. pap. 29.00 (*0-685-42678-5*) Blackman Kallick Bartelstein.
— How to Cash Out Tax Free, Yet Keep Your Business ... Go ESOP. (Special Report Ser.). 1992. pap. 27.00 (*0-916181-31-6*) Blackman Kallick Bartelstein.
— How to Take Money Out of Your Closely Held Corporation. (Special Report Ser.: No. 10). 57p. 1991. pap. 29.00 (*0-916181-09-X*) Blackman Kallick Bartelstein.
— How to Triple Your Pension, Profit Sharing or IRA Value. (Special Report Ser.: No. 28). 1993. pap. 39.00 (*0-916181-34-0*) Blackman Kallick Bartelstein.
— How to Value an Oil Jobbership. 91p. 1981. 65.00 (*0-318-16169-9*, F-4); 50.00 (*0-318-16170-2*) Mkters Assn of Am.
— How to Value Your Business for Tax Purposes & Win the Tax Game. LC 84-102879. (Special Report Ser.: No. 2). 55p. 1992. pap. 29.00 (*0-916181-01-4*) Blackman Kallick Bartelstein.
— How to Value Your Restaurant. 76p. 1989. pap. 45.00 (*0-929663-01-2*) Natl Restaurant Assn.
— Passing Your Family Business on to Your Family: Creating a Lifetime Succession Plan to Meet Your Changing Tax, Estate & Business Needs. 440p. 1995. per. 32.50 (*1-55738-898-9*, Irwn Prfssnl) McGraw-Hill Prof.
— The Secret of How the Rich Create Wealth & Income Without Risk: The Junk Money Concept. 1995. pap. 39.00 (*0-916181-33-2*) Blackman Kallick Bartelstein.
— Transferring the Privately-Held Business: Creating a Succession Plan to Meet Your Changing Tax, Estate & Business Needs. 400p. 1993. text 75.00 (*1-55738-433-9*, Irwn Prfssnl) McGraw-Hill Prof.
— The Twenty-Five Best Tax-Saving Ideas of the '90s. (Special Report Ser.). 1992. pap. 27.00 (*0-91618.-30-8*) Blackman Kallick Bartelstein.
— Valuing the Privately-Held Business: The Art & Science of Establishing a Company's Worth. rev. ed. 500p. 1992. text 70.00 (*1-55738-287-5*, Irwn Prfssnl) McGraw-Hill Prof.
— Valuing Your Privately-Held Business: The Art & Science of Establishing Your Company's Worth, Revised Edition. 1995. per. 32.50 (*1-55738-897-0*, Irwn Prfssnl) McGraw-Hill Prof.
— Valuing Your Privately-Held Business: The Art & Science of Establishing Your Own Company's Worth. 500p. 1995. 29.95 (*1-55738-879-2*, Irwn Prfssnl) McGraw-Hill Prof.
— Your Business-America's Best Tax Shelter. LC 84-102848. (Special Report Ser.: No. 1). 51p. 1987. pap. 27.00 (*0-916181-00-6*) Blackman Kallick Bartelstein.

Blackman, Irving L. & Andresen, Gregory G. A New Tax Superstar: S Corporation. (Special Report Ser.: No. 17). 61p. 1991. pap. 29.00 (*0-916181-16-2*) Blackman Kallick Bartelstein.

Blackman, Irving L. & Dorman, Michael A. The Right Way to Value Your Company Stock When Owned By An ESOP. (Special Report Ser.: No.29). 25p. 1995. pap. 29.00 (*0-916181-36-7*) Blackman Kallick Bartelstein.

Blackman, Irving L. & Fensin, Daniel J. How to Value an Oil Jobbership. 238p. 1982. 42.00 (*0-318-16168-0*) Mkters Assn of Am.

Blackman, Irving L. & Russ, Donald J. Pay Zero Estate Tax: The Super Trust Way. (Special Report Ser.: No.21). 52p. (Orig.). 1998. pap. 25.00 (*0-916181-29-4*) Blackman Kallick Bartelstein.

Blackman, Irving L. & Whitlock, Brian T. How to Transfer Your Corporation to the Next Generation Tax Free (Special Report Ser.: No. 11). 54p. 1991. pap. 27.00 (*0-916181-10-3*) Blackman Kallick Bartelstein.
— Tax Secrets of the Wealthy: A New System to Pass All Your Wealth - Intact & Tax-Free - To Your Family. 2nd ed. (Special Report Ser.). 400p. 1998. ring bd. 367.00 (*0-916181-38-3*) Blackman Kallick Bartelstein.
— Transferring Your Business When You Have Two or More Children. (Special Report Ser.: No. 12). 57p. 1991. pap. 27.00 (*0-916181-26-X*) Blackman Kallick Bartelstein.
— Unlocking the Secret to Tax Free Wealth Transfer: Family Limited Partnerships. (BK Special Reports). 1995. pap. 29.00 (*0-916181-37-5*) Blackman Kallick Bartelstein.

Blackman, Irving L., ed. see Wilson, Robert A.

Blackman, James. Warning Signals: Basic Criteria for Tracking at-Risk Infants & Toddlers. 10p. 1986. pap. 3.50 (*0-943657-08-3*, 67) ZERO TO THREE.

Blackman, James A. The Infants & Young Children Series. 1995. 198.00 (*0-8342-0652-8*) Aspen Pub.
— Medical Aspects of Early Intervention. 240p. 1995. 33.00 (*0-8342-0648-X*) Aspen Pub.

Blackman, James A., ed. Identification & Assessment in Early Intervention. LC 94-24184. (Infants & Young Children Ser.). 298p. 1995. 33.00 (*0-8342-0644-7*) Aspen Pub.
— Infant Development & Mental Health in Early Intervention. LC 94-24186. (Infants & Young Children Ser.). 258p. 1995. 33.00 (*0-8342-0647-1*) Aspen Pub.
— Innovations in Practice in Early Intervention. LC 94-38451. (Infants & Young Children Ser.). 240p. 1995. 33.00 (*0-8342-0651-X*) Aspen Pub.
— Technology in Early Intervention. LC 94-39482. (Infants & Young Children Ser.). 240p. 1995. pap. 33.00 (*0-8342-0649-8*) Aspen Pub.
— Training & Continuing Education in Early Intervention. LC 94-24185. (Infants & Young Children Ser.). 240p. 1995. pap. 33.00 (*0-8342-0650-1*) Aspen Pub.
— Treatment Options in Early Intervention. LC 94-38449. (Infants & Young Children Ser.). 260p. 1995. pap. 35.00 (*0-8342-0645-5*) Aspen Pub.
— Working with Families in Early Intervention. LC 94-38450. (Infants & Young Children Ser.). 240p. 1995. 33.00 (*0-8342-0646-3*) Aspen Pub.

Blackman, John. Heavy Metal: Classic Armoured Fighting Vehicles in Color. LC 98-228801. (Illus.). 128p. 1998. pap. 24.95 (*1-85409-441-6*) Sterling.

Blackman, John L. Presidential Seizure in Labor Disputes. LC 67-20871. (Wertheim Publications in Industrial Relations). 367p. reprint ed. pap. 113.80 (*0-7837-4449-8*, 205797900012) Bks Demand.

Blackman, Joshua. How to Use the Internet for Legal Research. LC 96-86120. 221p. 1996. write for info. (*1-56241-390-2*) FIND-SVP.

Blackman, Joshua. Internet Fact Finder for Lawyers: How to Find Anything on the Net. LC 98-70386. 1998. pap. 39.95 (*1-57073-535-2*) Amer Bar Assn.

Blackman, Julie. Intimate Violence: A Study of Injustice. 205p. 1989. text 40.50 (*0-231-05094-1*) Col U Pr.

Blackman, Linda S. Sales Coach: Selling Tips from the Pros. 1997. pap. text 19.95 (*1-889944-02-5*) Imago Pr.

Blackman, Lorraine C., ed. What Works? Synthesizing Effective Bio-Medical & Psychosocial Strategies for Healthy Families in the 21st Century. (Illus.). 172p. (Orig.). (C). 1994. pap. text 29.95 (*0-9643817-0-2*) IN U Schl Soc Wrk.

Blackman, Lynne, ed. see Severens, Martha R.

Blackman, Malorie. Not So Stupid: Incredible Short Stories. (Livewire Ser.). (YA). (gr. 6-9). pap. 6.95 (*0-7043-4924-8*, Pub. by Womens Press) Trafalgar.
— Trust Me. (Livewire Ser.). (YA). (gr. 6-9). pap. 7.95 (*0-7043-4931-0*, Pub. by Womens Press) Trafalgar.
— Whizziwig. large type ed. (Illus.). (J). 1998. pap. 16.95 (*0-7540-6026-8*, Galaxy Child Lrg Print) Chivers N Amer.

***Blackman, Malorie, abr.** A.N.T.I.D.O.T.E. 2000. pap. 6.95 (*0-552-52839-0*, Pub. by Transworld Publishers Ltd) Trafalgar.

Blackman, Marc R., ed. GHRH, GH, & IGF-1: Basic & Clincial Advances. 1995. 138.00 (*0-387-94404-4*) Spr-Verlag.

Blackman, Marci. Flying in Nowhere Land. 12p. 1993. pap. 1.50 (*1-884047-52-1*) Mass Extinct.
— Po Man's Child: A Novel. LC 99-6198. 240p. 1999. pap. 12.95 (*0-916397-59-9*, Pub. by Manic D Pr) SPD-Small Pr Dist.

Blackman, Marci & Healey, Trebor, eds. Beyond Definition: New Writing from Gay & Lesbian San Francisco. LC 94-12818. 168p. (Orig.). 1994. pap. 10.95 (*0-916397-30-0*) Manic D Pr.

Blackman, Margaret B. & Davidson, Florence E. During My Time: Florence Edenshaw Davidson, a Haida Woman. enl. rev. ed. LC 91-45973. (Illus.). 228p. 1992. pap. 15.95 (*0-295-97179-7*) U of Wash Pr.

Blackman, Martha Ann, ed. Watching from the Sky. (Illus.). 32p. (Orig.). 1989. pap. 6.00 (*0-914485-12-1*) Trill Pr.

Blackman, Maurice. The Design of Real Time Applications. LC 74-26960. (Illus.). 283p. reprint ed. pap. 87.80 (*0-8357-6302-1*, 203557500096) Bks Demand.

Blackman, Maurice, tr. see Wenz, Paul.

Blackman, Michelle & Chall, Miriam. LLBA Linguistics & Language Behavior Abstracts: User's Reference Manual. 3rd ed. 82p. 1987. ring bd. 47.50 (*0-930710-05-3*) Soc Abstracts.

Blackman, N. S. & Bailey, C. P. Liability in Medical Practice: A Reference for Physicians. x, 476p. 1990. text 77.00 (*3-7186-0506-6*); pap. text 38.00 (*3-7186-0512-0*) Gordon & Breach.

Blackman, Nancy. Mathemtca Quik Ref&Begnn. (C). 1995. pap. text 39.95 (*0-201-82085-4*) Addison-Wesley.

Blackman, Paddy & Figge, Jennifer. Running Home: An Across-Iowa Journal. (Illus.). 126p. (Orig.). 1989. pap. text 8.95 (*0-9625942-0-2*) Bawden Printing.

Blackman, Paul. The Kansas City Trivia Quiz, Vol. 1. Zoglin, Richard, ed. (American Metropolitan Area Trivia Quizzes Ser.). (Illus.). 1983. pap. 4.95 (*0-916399-00-1*) Normandy Pubns.
— The Kansas City Trivia Quiz, Vol. 2. Zoglin, Richard, ed. (American Metropolitan Area Trivia Quizzes Ser.). (Illus.). 1985. pap. 4.95 (*0-916399-02-8*) Normandy Pubns.

Blackman, Philip. Learn Hebrew for English Speakers, Romanized. (ENG & HEB.). pap. 20.95 (*0-87557-032-1*) Saphrograph.

Blackman, Philip, tr. Ethics of the Fathers: Hebrew Text, English Translation & Commentary Digest. 166p. 1980. reprint ed. pap. 7.95 (*0-910818-15-0*) Judaica Pr.
— The Mishnah, 7 vols. (ENG & HEB.). 4050p. 1962. 125.00 (*0-910818-00-2*) Judaica Pr.

Blackman, R. L. & Eastop, V. F. Aphids on the World's Trees: An Identification & Information Guide. (Illus.). 1012p. 1994. text 225.00 (*0-85198-877-6*) OUP.

***Blackman, Rodney J.** Procedural Natural Law. LC 99-48920. 206p. 1999. pap. text 20.00 (*0-89089-688-7*) Carolina Acad Pr.

Blackman, Samuel S. Multiple-Target Tracking with Radar Applications. LC 85-73389. (Artech House Radar Library). (Illus.). 464p. 1986. reprint ed. pap. 143.90 (*0-608-00563-0*, 206144600009) Bks Demand.

Blackman, Samuel S. & Popoli, Richard. Design & Analysis of Modern Tracking Systems. LC 99-27662. (Radar Library). 1200p. 1999. 159.00 (*1-58053-006-0*) Artech Hse.

B

An Asterisk (*) at the beginning of an entry indicates that the title is appearing for the first time.

Blackman, Shane. Youth: Position & Oppositions. LC 96-140378. 288p. 1995. 72.95 (*1-85628-637-1*, Pub. by Avebry) Ashgate Pub Co.

Blackman, Steven. Space Travel. LC 93-13310. (Technology Craft Topics Ser.). (Illus.). 32p. (J). (gr. 5-7). 1993. lib. bdg. 20.00 (*0-531-14275-2*) Watts.

Blackman, Susan, ed. Mattress Factory: Installation & Performance, 1982-1989. (Illus.). 223p. (Orig.). 1991. pap. 35.00 (*0-9623290-0-2*) Mattress Factory.

Blackman, Sushila, ed. Graceful Exits: How Great Beings Die. LC 97-2451. (Illus.). 160p. 1997. pap. 12.95 (*0-8348-0391-7*) Weatherhill.

Blackman, Tannis. Delilah Power. LC 97-69650. (Illus.). 240p. 1999. pap. 11.95 (*0-9652540-1-1*) Swing St Pub.

***Blackman, Tannis.** Delilah Power. LC 99-76930. (Illus.). 264p. 2000. pap. 11.95 (*0-9652540-4-6*) Swing St Pub.

— The Mystical Seductress Handbook. Clark, Gina, ed. (Illus.). 96p. 2000. 4.95 (*0-9652540-5-4*) Swing St Pub.

Blackman, Thomas. Art 1998 Chicago: At Navy Pier. 1998. pap. text 35.00 (*0-89733-468-X*) Academy Chi Pubs.

Blackman, Trevlin. In Pursuit of Truth: Mysteries of Life Unveiled. 56p. 1997. pap. 9.00 (*0-8059-4196-7*) Dorrance.

Blackman, W. Haden. The Field Guide to North American Hauntings. LC 98-4086. (Illus.). 272p. 1998. pap. 15.00 (*0-609-80021-3*) Crown Pub Group.

Blackman, William C., Jr. Basic Hazardous Waste Management. 2nd ed. 416p. (C). 1995. boxed set 84.95 (*1-56670-168-6*, L1168) Lewis Pubs.

— Solutions Manual for Basic Hazardous Waste Management. 2nd ed. LC 95-48341. 98p. 1995. lib. bdg. write for info. (*1-56670-221-6*) CRC Pr.

Blackman, William F. The Making of Hawaii: A Study in Social Evolution. 2nd ed. LC 75-35175. 37.50 (*0-404-14204-4*) AMS Pr.

Blackman, William J. Building Sad & Happy Faces. LC 94-66998. (Illus.). 9p. (J). (gr. k). 1994. 6.95 (*0-9641791-0-5*) Stimey Toys.

Blackmar, Elizabeth. Manhattan for Rent, 1785-1850. LC 88-47926. (Illus.). 336p. 1991. pap. text 17.95 (*0-8014-9973-9*) Cornell U Pr.

Blackmar, Elizabeth, jt. auth. see Rosenzweig, Roy.

Blackmar, Frank W. The Life of Charles Robinson: The First State Governor of Kansas. LC 70-169751. (Select Bibliographies Reprint Ser.). 1977. reprint ed. 30.95 (*0-8369-5971-X*) Ayer.

— Spanish Colonization in the Southwest. LC 78-63794. (Johns Hopkins University. Studies in the Social Sciences. Thirtieth Ser. 1912: 4). reprint ed. 27.50 (*0-404-61059-5*) AMS Pr.

— Spanish Institutions of the Southwest. LC 78-64254. (Johns Hopkins University. Studies in the Social Sciences. Thirtieth Ser. 1912: 10). reprint ed. 47.50 (*0-404-61358-6*) AMS Pr.

Blackmarr, Amy. Going to Ground: Simple Life on a Georgia Pond. LC 97-9471. 192p. 1998. pap. 11.95 (*0-14-026692-5*) Viking Penguin.

***Blackmarr, Amy.** House of Steps: Adventures of a Southerner Removed in Kansas. LC 98-53767. 154p. 1999. 22.95 (*0-670-88237-2*, Viking) Viking Penguin.

Blackmer, Carolyn. Essays on Spiritual Psychology. Larsen, Stephen, ed. & intro. by. LC 87-60495. (Illus.). 68p. 1991. pap. 10.95 (*0-87785-135-2*) Swedenborg.

Blackmer, Corinne E. & Smith, Patricia J., eds. En Travesti: Women, Gender Subversion, Opera. (Between Men - Between Women Ser.). (Illus.). 381p. 1995. pap. 19.50 (*0-231-10269-0*) Col U Pr.

Blackmer, Donald L. Unity in Diversity: Italian Communism & the Communist World. (Studies in Communism, Revisionism & Revolution). 1968. 40.00 (*0-262-02030-0*) MIT Pr.

Blackmer, Donald L. & Tarrow, Sidney, eds. Communism in Italy & France. LC 74-25612. 670p. reprint ed. pap. 200.00 (*0-7837-9299-9*, 206003800004) Bks Demand.

Blackmer, Joan D. Acrobats of the Gods. (Illus.). 128p. 1995. pap. 16.00 (*0-919123-38-4*, Pub. by Inner City Bks) BookWorld.

Blackmer, Joan D., ed. see Edinger, Edward F.

Blackmer, Rollin C. The Lodge & the Craft. viii, 295p. 1994. reprint ed. pap. 12.95 (*0-88053-043-X*, M 092) Macoy Pub.

Blackmon, Carolyn P., et al. Open Conversations: Strategies for Professional Development in Museums. (Illus.). 125p. (Orig.). 1988. pap. 6.00 (*0-914868-10-1*) Field Mus.

Blackmon, Glenn. Incentive Regulation & the Regulation of Incentives. LC 94-18160. (Topics in Regulatory Economics & Policy Ser.: Vol. 17). 160p. (C). 1994. lib. bdg. 98.50 (*0-7923-9470-4*) Kluwer Academic.

***Blackmon, Mandral.** Shadows of a Vision: Selected Poems for Those Who Dream. 88p. 1999. pap. 10.00 (*1-929016-01-8*) My World Pubg.

Blackmon, Marilyn & S. D. Evelyn, David. Charter Schools, Colorado's Mandate for Change: A Primer on the Educational Idea That Almost Everyone & David s. D'Evelyn. 14p. 1993. pap. text 8.00 (*1-57655-103-2*) Independ Inst.

Blackmon, Richard, Jr. Pass Those Cabrini Greens, Please!! 168p. 1994. pap. 10.00 (*0-9642826-1-5*) Seven Hund Fourteen Prods.

— Pass Those Cabrini Greens, Please!! (with Hot Sauce) 170p. (Orig.). 1994. pap. 10.00 (*0-9642826-0-7*) Seven Hund Fourteen Prods.

Blackmoor, Brandon & Blackmoor, Susan. Dwellers in Darkness. 150p. (YA). (gr. 10 up). 2000. pap. 15.00 (*0-9641722-5-9*) Black Gate.

— Legacy: War of Ages. 252p. (YA). (gr. 10 up). 1994. pap. 25.00 (*0-9641722-0-8*) Black Gate.

— Warlock: Black Spiral. 250p. (YA). (gr. 10 up). 1999. pap. 25.00 (*0-9641722-4-0*) Black Gate.

Blackmoor, Susan, jt. auth. see Blackmoor, Brandon.

Blackmore. Science & Technology: Science & Technology. Date not set. pap. 8.95 (*0-7453-0927-5*, Pub. by Pluto GBR) Stylus Pub VA.

***Blackmore, A. M. & Blackmore, E. H., eds.** Six Nineteenth Century French Poets: With Parallel French Text. (Oxford World's Classics Ser.). 400p. 2000. pap. 12.95 (*0-19-283973-X*) OUP.

Blackmore, Anauta, jt. auth. see Washburne, Heluiz.

Blackmore, Charles. The Worst Desert on Earth: Crossing the Taklamakan. LC 96-148140. (Illus.). 224p. 1996. 35.00 (*0-7195-5436-5*, Pub. by John Murray) Trafalgar.

Blackmore, D. J., et al, eds. Animal Clinical Biochemistry: The Future. 398p. (C). 1988. text 110.00 (*0-521-35518-4*) Cambridge U Pr.

Blackmore, D. K., et al. Some Observations on the Diseases of Brunus Edwardii. (Illus.). 1983. pap. 5.00 (*0-912184-04-3*) Synergistic Pr.

Blackmore, E. H., jt. ed. see Blackmore, A. M.

***Blackmore, Hilary.** Inside New York: The Ultimate Guide to Style & Substance. (Illus.). 2000. 18.00 (*1-929439-03-2*) City & Co.

Blackmore, Howard L. British Military Firearms, 1650-1850. (Illus.). 144p. 1994. 50.00 (*1-85367-172-X*, 5406) Stackpole.

— Gunmakers of London: 1350-1850. (Illus.). 224p. 1986. boxed set 50.00 (*0-87387-094-8*) Shumway.

***Blackmore, Howard L.** Hunting Weapons: From the Middle Ages to the Twentieth Century. LC 00-20296. (Illus.). 2000. pap. 18.95 (*0-486-40961-9*) Dover.

Blackmore, Jill. Assessment & Accountability. 170p. (C). 1988. 54.00 (*0-7300-0591-7*, Pub. by Deakin Univ) St Mut.

— Making Educational History: A Feminist Perspective. 117p. 1992. pap. 60.00 (*0-7300-1361-8*, ESA846, Pub. by Deakin Univ) St Mut.

— Troubling Women: Feminism, Leadership, & Educational Change. LC 98-25024. (Feminist Educational Thinking Ser.). 1998. 95.00 (*0-335-19480-X*); pap. 28.95 (*0-335-19479-6*) OpUniv Pr.

Blackmore, Jill & Kenway, Jane, eds. Gender Matters in Educational Administration & Policy: A Feminist Introduction. LC 92-39888. 204p. 1993. 89.95 (*0-7507-0147-1*, Falmer Pr) Taylor & Francis.

Blackmore, Joan. A Dog Owner's Guide to the Rottweiler. (Illus.). 118p. 1995. 10.95 (*1-56465-122-3*, 16028) Tetra Pr.

Blackmore, John T. Ludwig Boltzmann Bk. 2: His Later Life & Philosophy, 1900-1906. (Boston Studies in the Philosophy of Science: Vol. 174). 332p. 1995. lib. bdg. 132.50 (*0-7923-3464-7*, Pub. by Kluwer Academic) Kluwer Academic.

Blackmore, John T., ed. Ernst Mach-a Deeper Look: Documents & New Perspectives. LC 92-20024. (Boston Studies in the Philosophy of Science: Vol. 143). 484p. 1992. lib. bdg. 203.00 (*0-7923-1853-6*, Pub. by Kluwer Academic) Kluwer Academic.

— Ludwig Boltzmann Bk. 1: His Later Life & Philosophy, 1900-1906: A Documentary History. LC 94-39753. (Boston Studies of Philosophy & History: Vol. 168). 280p. (C). 1995. lib. bdg. 102.50 (*0-7923-3231-8*, Pub. by Kluwer Academic) Kluwer Academic.

***Blackmore, Josiah H.** Queer Iberia: Crossing Cultures, Crossing Sexualities. LC 98-32016. (Queer Ser.). 424p. 1999. 59.95 (*0-8223-2326-5*) Duke.

Blackmore, Josiah H. & Hutcheson, Gregory S. Queer Iberia: Crossing Cultures, Crossing Sexualities. LC 98-32016. (Series Q). 424p. 1999. pap. 19.95 (*0-8223-2349-4*) Duke.

Blackmore, Kate, jt. auth. see Ashton, Paul.

Blackmore, Mae M., ed. see Gjovig, Bruce.

Blackmore, Michael. Your Book of Watching Wildlife. (YA). (gr. 7 up). 1972. 7.95 (*0-571-08347-1*) Transatl Arts.

***Blackmore, Nancy J.** The Story of Big Bone Lick. (Illus.). 72p. (J). 1998. 24.95 (*0-9666172-0-7*); per. 14.95 (*0-9666172-1-5*) Thoroughbred Publ KY.

Blackmore, R. D. Lorna Doone. (Andre Deutsch Classics). 319p. (J). (gr. 5-8). 1996. 9.95 (*0-233-99076-3*, Pub. by Andre Deutsch) Trafalgar.

***Blackmore, R. D.** Lorna Doone. 1999. lib. bdg. 21.95 (*1-56723-172-1*) Yestermorrow.

Blackmore, R. D., jt. auth. see Hyem, Jill.

Blackmore, R. W., tr. Duties of Parish Priests in the Russian Orthodox Church. 1972. reprint ed. 15.00 (*0-89981-017-9*) Eastern Orthodox.

Blackmore, R. W., tr. see Mouravieff, A. N.

Blackmore, Rachel. Creative Chicken. 1993. 12.98 (*1-55521-849-0*) Bk Sales Inc.

Blackmore, Richard. Essays upon Several Subjects. (Anglistica & Americana Ser.: No. 164). viii, 439p. 1976. reprint ed. 130.00 (*3-487-05931-2*) G Olms Pubs.

Blackmore, Richard D. Christowell: A Dartmoor Tale, 3 vols., 2 bks., Set. LC 79-3327. reprint ed. 84.50 (*0-404-61783-2*) AMS Pr.

— Lorna Doone. (Classics Library). Date not set. pap. 3.95 (*1-85326-076-2*, 0762WW, Pub. by Wrdsworth Edits) NTC Contemp Pub Co.

— Lorna Doone. 345p. (J). 1976. reprint ed. lib. bdg. 27.95 (*0-89966-350-8*) Buccaneer Bks.

— Lorna Doone. 378p. (J). 1981. reprint ed. lib. bdg. 24.95 (*0-89967-024-5*, Harmony Rain) Buccaneer Bks.

— Lorna Doone: A Romance of Exmoor. Shuttleworth, Sally, ed. (Oxford World's Classics Ser.). 710p. 1999. pap. 11.95 (*0-19-283627-7*) OUP.

— Slain by the Doones, & Other Stories. LC 74-86137. (Short Story Index Reprint Ser.). 1977. 19.95 (*0-8369-3041-X*) Ayer.

Blackmore, Stephen. Bee Orchids. (Natural History Ser.: Nol. 3). (Illus.). 24p. 1989. pap. 5.25 (*0-85263-745-4*, Pub. by Shire Pubns) Parkwest Pubns.

— Buttercups. (Natural History Ser.: No. 6). (Illus.). 24p. 1989. pap. 5.25 (*0-85263-763-2*, Pub. by Shire Pubns) Parkwest Pubns.

Blackmore, Stephen & Barnes, S. H., eds. Pollen & Spores: Patterns of Diversification. (Systematics Association Special Volume Ser.: Vol. 44). 408p. 1992. 125.00 (*0-19-857746-X*) OUP.

Blackmore, Stephen & Knox, R. B., eds. Microspores: Evolution & Ontogeny. 347p. 1990. text 104.00 (*0-12-103458-5*) Acad Pr.

Blackmore, Stephen, jt. auth. see Punt, W.

Blackmore, Stephen, jt. ed. see Crane, Peter R.

***Blackmore, Susan.** The Meme Machine. LC 98-49180. 288p. 1999. 25.00 (*0-19-850365-2*) OUP.

— The Meme Machine. 288p. 2000. pap. 14.95 (*0-19-286212-X*) OUP.

Blackmore, Susan J. Beyond the Body: An Investigation of Out-of-the-Body Experiences. (Illus.). 256p. 1992. pap. 13.00 (*0-89733-344-6*) Academy Chi Pubs.

— Dying to Live: Near-Death Experiences. LC 93-24749. (Illus.). 291p. 1993. reprint ed. 25.95 (*0-87975-870-8*) Prometheus Bks.

— In Search of the Light: The Adventures of a Parapsychologist. LC 96-16260. 286p. 1996. pap. text 17.95 (*1-57392-061-4*) Prometheus Bks.

Blackmore, Susan J. & Hart-Davis, Adam. Test Your Psychic Powers. LC 96-52315. 168p. 1997. pap. 9.95 (*0-8069-9669-2*) Sterling.

***Blackmore, Vernon.** God on the Net: A Guide to the Best Sites for Study, Inspiration & Resources 2000. 160p. 1999. pap. (*0-551-03214-6*) HarperCllins Intl.

Blackmun, Ora. Western North Carolina: Its Mountains & Its People to 1880. 2nd ed. LC 76-53030. (Illus.). (Orig.). 1977. 15.95 (*0-913239-31-3*) Appalach Consortium.

Blackmun, Susie, ed. see Pfeifer, Diane.

Blackmur, Douglas. Strikes: Causes, Conduct & Consequences. 216p. 1993. pap. 39.00 (*1-86287-114-0*, Pub. by Federation Pr) Gaunt.

Blackmur, L. L. Love Lies Slain. large type ed. LC 90-10849. 397p. 1990. 17.95 (*0-89621-995-X*) Thorndike Pr.

Blackmur, R. P. Studies in Henry James. Makowsky, Veronica A., ed. LC 82-18911. 256p. 1983. 19.50 (*0-8112-0863-X*, Pub. by New Directions); pap. 9.25 (*0-8112-0864-8*, NDP552, Pub. by New Directions) Norton.

Blackmur, Richard P. The Double Agent: Essays in Craft & Elucidation. (BCL1-PS American Literature Ser.). 302p. 1993. reprint ed. lib. bdg. 89.00 (*0-7812-6583-5*) Rprt Serv.

— The Expense of Greatness. 1988. reprint ed. lib. bdg. 59.00 (*0-7812-0271-X*) Rprt Serv.

— The Expense of Greatness. reprint ed. 9.00 (*0-403-04062-0*) Somerset Pub.

— Henry Adams. Makowsky, Veronica A., ed. LC 84-11419. (Quality Paperbacks Ser.). 381p. (C). 1984. pap. 10.95 (*0-306-80219-8*) Da Capo.

— Language As Gesture: Essays in Poetry. LC 77-10141. 440p. 1977. reprint ed. lib. bdg. 52.50 (*0-8371-9782-1*, BLLG, Greenwood Pr) Greenwood.

— Selected Essays of R. P. Blackmur. Donoghue, Denis, ed. 350p. (C). 1988. pap. 10.50 (*0-88001-103-3*) HarpC.

Blackmur, Richard P., ed. Henry Adams. LC 79-1812. 384p. 1980. 19.95 (*0-15-139997-2*) Harcourt.

Blackorby, C., ed. see Gorman, W. M.

Blacks. Law Dictionary: Pocket Edition. LC 96-231638. 1996. pap. text 26.00 (*0-314-06690-X*) West Pub.

***Blacksburg's AAS Council Members.** Arts Alive 2000! Anthology of the New River Valley Writers & Poets. Goehe, Ann & Spencer, Elizabeth, eds. 76p. 2000. pap. write for info. (*0-936015-88-8*) Pocahontas Pr.

Blacksell, Mark. Justice Outside the City Access to Legal Services in Rural Britain. 1991. write for info. (*0-470-21739-1*) Halsted Pr.

Blacksell, Mark & Williams, Allan M., eds. The European Challenge: Geography & Development in the EC. (Illus.). 444p. 1994. pap. text 29.95 (*0-19-874177-4*) OUP.

Blackshaw, D. M., et al, eds. Laser Metrology & Machine Performance. 1993. 146.00 (*1-85312-241-6*) Computational Mech MA.

Blackshaw, Ian S. & Hogg, Gillian, eds. Sports Marketing Europe: The Legal & Tax Aspects. LC 93-5893. 1993. 158.00 (*90-6544-678-8*) Kluwer Law Intl.

Blackshaw, Ric & Farrely, Liz. Scrawl: Dirty Graphics & Strange Characters. Booth-Clibborn, Edward, ed. (Illus.). 176p. 1999. pap. 39.95 (*1-58423-003-7*) Gingko Press.

Blackshear, Helen F. Alabama Album: Collected Poems. LC 96-21177. 1996. 20.00 (*1-881320-85-5*, Black Belt) Black Belt Communs.

— The Creek Captives: And Other Alabama Stories. (Illus.). 112p. (Orig.). (J). (gr. 4-9). 1990. pap. 9.95 (*0-9622815-2-2*, Black Belt) Black Belt Communs.

Blackshear, Marlton. Sea of Words: Modern & Romantic Poetry. 1998. pap. write for info. (*1-57553-833-4*) Watermrk Pr.

Blackshear, Perry J. Key References in Endocrinology: An Annotated Guide. LC 82-14662. (Key References in Internal Medicine Ser.). 144p. reprint ed. pap. 44.70 (*0-7837-2591-4*, 204275300006) Bks Demand.

Blackshield, A. R. Legal Change: Essays in Honour of Julius Stone. (Essay in Honour of Julius Stone Ser.). 391p. 1983. boxed set 82.00 (*0-409-49130-6*, Austral, MICHIE) LEXIS Pub.

Blackshield, Tony, et al, comments. Australian Constitutional Law & Theory: Commentary & Materials. 1033p. 1996. pap. 89.00 (*1-86287-191-4*, Pub. by Federation Pr) Gaunt.

Blackshield, Tony & Williams, George. Australian Constitutional Law & Theory: Commentary & Materials. 2nd ed. 1256p. 1998. pap. 90.00 (*1-86287-284-8*, Pub. by Federation Pr) Gaunt.

Blackshire-Belay, Carol Aisha. Current Issues in Second Language Acquisition & Development. 210p. (Orig.). (C). 1993. lib. bdg. 54.50 (*0-8191-9181-7*) U Pr of Amer.

— Foreign Workers' German: A Concise Glossary of Verbal Phrases. 152p. (Orig.). (C). 1991. pap. text 26.00 (*0-8191-8218-4*); lib. bdg. 46.00 (*0-8191-8217-6*) U Pr of Amer.

— The Germanic Mosaic: Cultural & Linguistic Diversity in Society, 33. LC 93-1664. (Contributions in Ethnic Studies: Vol. 33). 336p. 1993. 75.00 (*0-313-28629-9*, Greenwood Pr) Greenwood.

Blackshire-Belay, Carol Aisha, ed. The African-German Experience: Critical Essays. LC 96-6355. 152p. 1996. 55.00 (*0-275-95079-4*, Praeger Pubs) Greenwood.

— The Germanic Mosaic. LC 93-1664. (Contributions in Ethnic Studies: No. 33). 1994. write for info. (*0-313-28269-2*, Greenwood Pr) Greenwood.

— Language & Literature in the African American Imagination, 154. LC 92-12509. (Contributions in Afro-American & African Studies: No. 154). 224p. 1992. 55.00 (*0-313-27826-1*, BGG/, Greenwood Pr) Greenwood.

Blackside, Inc. Staff & Lavelle, Robert, eds. America's New War on Poverty: A Reader for Action. LC 94-40666. (Illus.). 288p. (Orig.). 1994. pap. 12.95 (*0-912333-37-5*, KQED Bks) BB&T Inc.

Blacksin, Andrea. Revelations of the Dark Mother. (Vampire Ser.). (Illus.). 1998. pap. 10.95 (*1-56504-237-9*, 2024) White Wolf.

Blacksmith, E. A., ed. Women in the Military. LC 92-34712. (Reference Shelf Ser.: Vol. 64, No. 5). 1992. pap. 25.00 (*0-8242-0829-3*) Wilson.

Blacksnake, Governor. Chainbreaker: The Revolutionary War Memoirs of Governor Blacksnake As Told to Benjamin Williams. Abler, Thomas S., ed. & intro. by. LC 88-28085. (American Indian Lives Ser.). 325p. 1989. reprint ed. pap. 100.80 (*0-608-03490-8*, 206420500008) Bks Demand.

Blackson, Lorenzo D. The Rise & Progress of the Kingdoms of Light & Darkness. LC 72-78568. (Illus.). 288p. reprint ed. lib. bdg. 32.50 (*0-8398-0166-1*) Irvington.

Blackson, Thomas A. Inquiry, Forms, & Substances: A Study in Plato's Metaphysics & Epistemology. LC 94-41768. (Philosophical Studies: Vol. 62). 1995. lib. bdg. 121.50 (*0-7923-3275-X*, Pub. by Kluwer Academic) Kluwer Academic.

Blackstaff, Michael. Finance for It Decision Makers. LC 98-38348. 1998. pap. text 49.95 (*3-540-76232-9*) Spr-Verlag.

Blackstead, Katharina J., jt. ed. see Gleason, Maureen.

Blackstock, Allan. An Ascendancy Army: The Irish Yeomanry, 1796-1834. LC 98-206063. 320p. 1998. boxed set 49.50 (*1-85182-329-8*, Pub. by Four Cts Pr) Intl Spec Bk.

Blackstock, C. M. All the Journey Through. (Illus.). 291p. 1997. text 29.95 (*0-8020-0966-2*) U of Toronto Pr.

Blackstock, Charity. The Bitter Conquest. 21.95 (*0-685-10844-9*) Amereon Ltd.

— A House Possessed. 1990. reprint ed. lib. bdg. 17.95 (*0-89968-483-1*) Buccaneer Bks.

***Blackstock, David T.** Fundamentals of Physical Acoustics. LC 99-42186. 576p. 2000. 90.00 (*0-471-31979-1*, Wiley-Interscience) Wiley.

Blackstock, David T., jt. ed. see Hamilton, Mark F.

Blackstock, James C. Biochemistry. LC 98-27208. (Biomedical Sciences Explained Ser.). 320p. 1998. pap. text 40.00 (*0-7506-3256-9*) Buttrwrth-Heinemann.

Blackstock, Laurie & Zubot, Carla. Discovering Canadian Pioneers. (Illus.). 1999. pap., student ed. 12.95 (*0-19-541325-3*) OUP.

— Discovering Today's Japan. (Illus.). 64p. 1998. pap. 12.95 (*0-19-541329-6*) OUP.

***Blackstock, Nelson.** Cointelpro: The FBI's Secret War on Political Freedom. 2000. pap. 15.95 (*0-87348-877-6*) Pathfinder NY.

Blackstock, Nelson. Cointelpro: The FBI's Secret War on Political Freedom. LC 88-62040. 190p. 1988. reprint ed. pap. 15.95 (*0-937091-04-9*); reprint ed. lib. bdg. 45.00 (*0-937091-05-7*) Pathfinder NY.

Blackstock, Peter, jt. ed. see Alden, Grant.

Blackstock, Terri. Blind Trust. LC 97-2726. (Second Chances Ser.: Vol. 3). 208p. 1997. pap. 8.99 (*0-310-20710-X*) Zondervan.

— Blind Trust. large type ed. LC 97-32568. (Second Chances Ser.). 1998. 21.95 (*0-7862-1305-1*) Thorndike Pr.

— Broken Wings. LC 97-36086. (Second Chances Ser.). 224p. 1998. pap. 8.99 (*0-310-20708-8*) Zondervan.

— Broken Wings. large type ed. LC 98-4364. 413p. 1998. 22.95 (*0-7862-1468-6*) Thorndike Pr.

— Emerald Windows. 2000. pap. 10.99 (*0-310-22807-7*) Zondervan.

— Evidence of Mercy. large type ed. LC 98-9953. (Sun-Coast Chronicles Ser.). 1998. 22.95 (*0-7862-1402-3*) Thorndike Pr.

Blackstock, Terri. Justifiable Means. (Sun Coast Chronicles Ser.: Bk. 2). 288p. 1996. pap. 9.99 (*0-310-20016-4*) Zondervan.

Blackstock, Terri. Justifiable Means. large type ed. LC 98-4393. 1998. 22.95 (*0-7862-1471-6*) Thorndike Pr.

— Never Again Good-Bye. LC 96-17275. (Second Chances Ser.: No. 1). 208p. 1996. pap. 8.99 (*0-310-20707-X*) Zondervan.

— Never Again Goodbye. large type ed. LC 98-42040. (Christian Fiction Ser.). 1999. 23.95 (*0-7862-1675-1*) Thorndike Pr.

An Asterisk (*) at the beginning of an entry indicates that the title is appearing for the first time.

— Presumption of Guilt. LC 97-254. (Sun Coast Chronicles Ser.: Vol. 4). 352p. 1997. pap. 9.99 (*0-310-20018-0*) Zondervan.
— Presumption of Guilt, Vol. 4. LC 99-21873. (Sun Coast Chronicles Ser.). 1999. 24.95 (*0-7862-1959-9*, G K Hall & Co) Mac Lib Ref.
— Private Justice. LC 98-56119. 1999. pap. text 22.95 (*0-7862-1823-1*) Mac Lib Ref.
— Private Justice. LC 97-36571. (Newpointe 911 Ser.: Bk. 1). 304p. 1998. pap. 10.99 (*0-310-21757-1*) Zondervan.
— Shadow of Doubt. LC 98-19195. 304p. 1998. pap. 10.99 (*0-310-21758-X*) Zondervan.
— The Sun Coast Chronicles. 1999. pap. 12.99 (*0-88486-237-2*, Inspirational Pr) Arrowood Pr.
— Ulterior Motives. abr. ed. (Sun Coast Chronicles Ser.). 1996. audio 14.99 (*0-310-21055-0*) Zondervan.
— Ulterior Motives. large type ed. LC 98-27480. (Sun-Coast Chronicles Ser.). 1998. 22.95 (*0-7862-1556-9*) Thorndike Pr.
— Ulterior Motives, No. 3. (Sun Coast Chronicles Ser.: Bk. 3). 304p. 1996. pap. 9.99 (*0-310-20017-2*) Zondervan.
— When Dreams Cross. LC 96-35255. (Second Chances Ser.: Vol. 2). 256p. (Orig.). 1997. pap. 8.99 (*0-310-20709-6*) Zondervan.
***Blackstock, Terri.** Word of Honor. LC 00-28804. 2000. write for info. (*0-7862-2572-6*) Five Star.
Blackstock, Terri. Word of Honor, Vol. 3. LC 99-30016. 352p. 1999. pap. 10.99 (*0-310-21759-8*) Zondervan.
***Blackstock, Terri, et al.** Sweet Delights. 2001. pap. 9.99 (*0-8423-3573-0*) Tyndale Hse.
Blackstock, Terri, jt. auth. see LaHaye, Beverly.
Blackstock, Terry. Love's Second Chances. 1999. 24.99 (*0-310-23045-4*) HarpC.
Blackstock, Tom, Jr., ed. see Vaughn, Kirby L.
Blackstone. Production & Inventory Management. 3rd ed. (GC - Principles of Management Ser.). (C). 2001. mass mkt. 42.00 (*0-538-83909-0*) S-W Pub.
— This Is Basketball, Vol. 1. (J). 1995. text 14.95 (*0-8050-3387-4*) St Martin.
Blackstone, A. Lee. Manage Globally, Sell Locally: The Art of Strategic Account Management. LC 94-11218. 216p. 1994. text 27.50 (*0-7863-0330-1*, Irwn Prfssnl) McGraw-Hill Prof.
Blackstone, Alexandra. Texas Kiss. (Wildflower Ser.). 320p. (Orig.). 1995. mass mkt. 5.50 (*0-515-11638-6*, Jove) Berkley Pub.
Blackstone, Bellamie. Everyday Magic. LC 98-130890. (Blackstone Family Magic Shoppe Ser.). (Illus.). 48p. (J). (gr. 1 up). 1997. pap. 6.95 (*1-57102-301-1*, Ideals Child) Hambleton-Hill.
Blackstone, Bernard. The Lost Travellers: A Romantic Theme with Variations. LC 83-1546. 292p. 1983. reprint ed. lib. bdg. 65.00 (*0-313-23882-0*, BLLT, Greenwood Pr) Greenwood.
Blackstone, D. Laurence. Credit Department Management. 2nd ed. Smith, Daphne & Geehr, Shelley W., eds. (Illus.). 258p. 1992. pap. text 65.00 (*0-936742-94-1*, 32061) Robt Morris Assocs.
Blackstone, Elizabeth. Virtual Strangers: A Woman's Guide to Love & Sex on the Internet. Moore, Denton, ed. LC 98-67504. 208p. 1998. pap. 14.50 (*1-888756-14-4*) Prospector Pr.
Blackstone, Erwin A. & Hakim, Simon. Police Services: The Private Challenge. (Independent Policy Reports). 44p. (Orig.). 1996. pap. 6.95 (*0-945999-49-6*) Independent Inst.
Blackstone, Erwin A., jt. auth. see Hakim, Simon.
Blackstone-Ford, Jan. Custody Solutions Sourcebook. LC 98-56041. 272p. 1999. pap. 16.95 (*0-7373-0075-2*, 00752w) NTC Contemp Pub Co.
Blackstone, Gay. Around the House Magic. LC 98-130891. (Blackstone Family Magic Shoppe Ser.). (Illus.). 48p. (J). (gr. 1 up). 1997. pap. 6.95 (*1-57102-302-X*, Ideals Child) Hambleton-Hill.
Blackstone, Harry. Blackstone's Modern Card Tricks. 1974. pap. 7.00 (*0-87980-282-0*) Wilshire.
— Blackstone's Secrets of Magic. 1980. pap. 7.00 (*0-87980-260-X*) Wilshire.
Blackstone, Harry, Jr., et al. The Blackstone Book of Magic & Illusion. rev. ed. LC 84-29486. (Illus.). 248p. 1995. pap. 19.95 (*1-55704-177-6*, Pub. by Newmarket) Norton.
Blackstone, John H., Jr. & Winter, Peter J. Operations Management Using Lotus 1-2-3. LC 89-84346. 45p. (Orig.). 1990. 105.00 (*1-55822-020-8*) Am Prod & Inventory.
Blackstone, Judith. Enlightenment Process: How It Deepens Your Experience of Self, Body & Community. LC 97-1882. 128p. 1997. pap. 12.95 (*1-86204-059-1*, Pub. by Element MA) Penguin Putnam.
— The Subtle Self: Personal Growth & Spiritual Practice. LC 91-35756. 122p. (Orig.). 1991. pap. 9.95 (*1-55643-066-3*) North Atlantic.
Blackstone, Judith & Josipovic, Zoran. Zen for Beginners. (Writers & Readers Documentary Comic Bks.). (Illus.). 176p. (Orig.). 1986. pap. 11.95 (*0-86316-116-2*) Writers & Readers.
Blackstone, Kathryn R. Women in the Footsteps of the Buddha: Struggle for Liberation in the Therigatha. (Critical Studies in Buddhism: Vol. 4). 260p. 1998. text 45.00 (*0-7007-0962-2*, Pub. by Curzon Pr Ltd) UH Pr.
Blackstone, Margaret. Beat Diabetes! LC 99-15823. 304p. 1999. pap. 12.95 (*1-58062-183-X*) Adams Media.
— This Is Baseball. 1997. pap. text 5.95 (*0-8050-5169-4*) H Holt & Co.
— This Is Baseball. 1997. 11.15 (*0-606-11980-9*, Pub. by Turtleback) Demco.
— This Is Figure Skating. LC 94-45695. (Illus.). (J). (gr. 1-3). 1998. 15.95 (*0-8050-3706-3*, Bks Young Read) H Holt & Co.
— This Is Soccer, Vol. 1. LC 98-23474. (J). (ps-2). 1999. text 15.95 (*0-8050-2801-3*) St Martin.
***Blackstone, Margaret & Guest, Elissa Haden.** Girl Stuff: A Survival Guide to Growing Up. LC RJ144.B53 2000. (Illus.). 144p. (J). (gr. 3-7). 2000. 14.95 (*0-15-201830-1*, Gulliver Bks) Harcourt.
Blackstone, Margaret & Segal, John. This is Maine. 89p. (J). 1995. 15.95 (*0-8050-2800-5*, Bks Young Read) H Holt & Co.
***Blackstone, Margaret, et al.** Girl Stuff: A Survival Guide to Growing Up. LC 99-48021. (Illus.). 144p. (J). (gr. 3-7). 2000. pap. 8.95 (*0-15-202644-4*, Gulliver Bks) Harcourt.
Blackstone, Meg. The Drug-Free Diabetic: New Hope for Healing. 256p. 1998. mass mkt. 14.00 (*0-446-67344-7*) Warner Bks.
Blackstone, Mick. Just Passing Through. LC 90-84171. (Illus.). 116p. (Orig.). 1990. pap. 13.95 (*0-9627726-1-5*) Blue Crab MD.
Blackstone, Orin. Index to Jazz: Jazz Recordings, 1917-1944. LC 77-27076. 118p. 1978. reprint ed. lib. bdg. 55.00 (*0-313-20178-1*, BLIJ, Greenwood Pr) Greenwood.
Blackstone, Peg. Things They Never Told Me in Therapy School: Serious Problems - Surprising Solutions. 256p. 1991. text 19.95 (*0-9630291-0-X*) Port Gamble.
Blackstone Press Ltd. Staff. Civil Litigation & Remedies. (C). 1991. text 150.00 (*1-85431-159-X*, Pub. by Blackstone Pr) Gaunt.
— Criminal Litigation & Sentencing. (C). 1991. text 150.00 (*1-85431-158-1*, Pub. by Blackstone Pr) Gaunt.
— Evidence & Casework Skills. 363p. (C). 1992. pap. 48.00 (*1-85431-157-3*, Pub. by Blackstone Pr) Gaunt.
Blackstone Press Ltd. Staff, ed. Professional Conduct & Practical Background. (C). 1991. text 65.00 (*1-85431-160-3*, Pub. by Blackstone Pr) Gaunt.
Blackstone Press Pty. Ltd. Staff. Debt Collection Manuals for NSW. 100p. (C). 1989. 130.00 (*1-875114-06-8*, Pub. by Blackstone Pr) Gaunt.
Blackstone Research Assoc. Staff. Defining the Document Industry: Economic Impact & Future Growth Trends. EDSF Staff, ed. (Illus.). 46p. Date not set. pap., spiral bd. 200.00 (*0-9658790-0-3*) EDSF.
Blackstone, Sandra L. Mineral Severance Taxes in Western States: Economic, Legal, & Policy Considerations, Vol. 75, No. 3. Raese, Jon W., ed. LC 80-29698. (Colorado School of Mines Quarterly Ser.). (Illus.). 39p. 1981. pap. text 8.00 (*0-317-06078-3*) Colo Sch Mines.
Blackstone, Sarah J. Buckskins, Bullets, & Business: A History of Buffalo Bill's Wild West, 14. LC 85-17760. (Contributions to the Study of Popular Culture Ser.: No. 14). (Illus.). 168p. 1986. lib. bdg. 47.95 (*0-313-24596-7*, BBU/, Greenwood Pr) Greenwood.
Blackstone, Sarah J., ed. The Business of Buffalo Bill: Selected Letters of William F. Cody, Eighteen Seventy-Nine to Nineteen Seventeen. LC 87-32694. 143p. 1988. 45.00 (*0-275-92889-6*, C2889, Praeger Pubs) Greenwood.
Blackstone, Sarah W., et al, eds. Augmentative Communication: Implementation Strategies. (Illus.). 914p. (C). 1989. student ed. 22.50 (*0-910329-47-8*, 0110727) Am Speech Lang Hearing.
Blackstone, Sarah W. & Bruskin, Deborah M., eds. Augmentative Communication: An Introduction. LC 86-72931. 505p. 1986. pap. 15.00 (*0-910329-36-2*) Am Speech Lang Hearing.
***Blackstone, Stella.** Animal Boogie. (Illus.). 24p. (J). (ps-1). 2000. 14.99 (*1-84148-094-0*) Barefoot Bks NY.
Blackstone, Stella. Baby High, Baby Low. LC 97-21371. (Illus.). (J). (ps-k). 1998. lib. bdg. 14.95 (*0-8234-1345-4*) Holiday.
— Baby Rock, Baby Roll. LC 96-48779. (Illus.). 24p. (J). 1997. lib. bdg. 13.95 (*0-8234-1311-X*) Holiday.
***Blackstone, Stella.** Bear about Town. (Illus.). 24p. (J). (ps-1). 2000. 13.95 (*1-902283-57-0*) Barefoot Bks NY.
— Bear about Town. (Illus.). 24p. (ps-1). 2001. pap. 5.99 (*1-84148-152-1*) Barefoot Pub.
— Bear about Town. (Illus.). 24p. (J). (ps-1). 2000. reprint ed. pap. 5.99 (*1-902283-69-4*) Barefoot Bks NY.
Blackstone, Stella. Bear in a Square. (Illus.). 24p. (J). (ps-1). 1998. 13.95 (*1-901223-58-2*) Barefoot Bks NY.
***Blackstone, Stella.** Bear in a Square. (Illus.). 24p. (J). (ps-1). 2000. pap. 5.99 (*1-84148-120-3*) Barefoot Bks NY.
— Bear in a Square. (Illus.). 24p. (J). (ps). 2000. reprint ed. bds. 6.99 (*1-84148-287-0*) Barefoot Bks NY.
Blackstone, Stella. Bear on a Bike. (Illus.). 32p. (J). (ps-10). 1999. 13.95 (*1-901223-49-3*) Barefoot Bks NY.
***Blackstone, Stella.** Bear on a Bike. (Illus.). 32p. (J). (ps-1). 2000. pap. 5.99 (*1-84148-121-1*) Barefoot Bks NY.
Blackstone, Stella. Bear's Busy Family. (Illus.). 24p. (J). (gr. k-3). 2000. 13.95 (*1-902283-90-2*) Barefoot Bks NY.
***Blackstone, Stella.** Bears Busy Family. (Illus.). (J). 1999. 13.95 (*1-902283-89-9*) Barefoot Bks NY.
— Bear's Busy Family. (Illus.). 24p. (J). (ps). 2000. reprint ed. pap. 5.99 (*1-84148-153-X*); reprint ed. bds. 6.99 (*1-84148-391-5*) Barefoot Bks NY.
Blackstone, Stella. Can You See the Red Balloon? LC 97-26673. (Illus.). 32p. (J). (ps-k). 1998. 14.95 (*0-531-30077-3*) Orchard Bks Watts.
***Blackstone, Stella.** Cleo the Cat. (Illus.). 24p. (J). (ps). 2000. 14.99 (*1-84148-259-5*) Barefoot Bks NY.
Blackstone, Stella. Grandma Went to Market: A Round-the-World Counting Rhyme. LC 94-47079. (Illus.). 32p. (J). (ps-1). 1996. 13.95 (*0-395-74045-2*) HM.
***Blackstone, Stella.** How Big Is a Pig? (Illus.). 24p. (J). (ps-1). 2000. 14.99 (*1-84148-077-0*) Barefoot Bks NY.
— Making Minestrone. (Illus.). 32p. (J). (ps-3). 2000. 15.99 (*1-84148-211-0*) Barefoot Bks NY.
Blackstone, Stella. Where Is the Cat? LC 97-146160. (Illus.). 24p. (J). (ps-1). 1996. 8.95 (*0-7892-0290-5*, Abbeville Kids) Abbeville Pr.
— Who Are You? LC 97-146161. (Illus.). 24p. (J). (ps-1). 1996. 8.95 (*0-7892-0291-3*, Abbeville Kids) Abbeville Pr.
***Blackstone, Stella.** You & Me. (Illus.). 32p. (J). (ps-1). 2000. 15.99 (*1-84148-263-3*) Barefoot Bks NY.
Blackstone, Terri. Shadow of Doubt Bk. 2: New Pointe 911. LC 99-22271. (Christian Fiction Ser.). 1999. 22.95 (*0-7862-2097-X*, Five Star MI) Mac Lib Ref.
Blackstone, Tessa & Plowden, William. The Think Tank: Advising the Cabinet, 1971-1983. LC 89-124896. 258p. 1990. pap. write for info. (*0-7493-0302-6*, Mandarin) Random.
Blackstone, Tessa & Vines, Peter. Social Policy & Administration in Britain: A Bibliography. 130p. 1975. 27.00 (*0-87471-811-2*) Rowman.
Blackstone, Tessa, et al. Race Relations in Britain. LC 97-27327. 272p. (C). 1998. 85.00 (*0-415-15009-4*); pap. 25.99 (*0-415-15010-8*) Routledge.
Blackstone, William. An Analysis of the Laws of England. 3rd ed. LC 97-80478. lxxviii, 204p. 1997. reprint ed. 70.00 (*1-57588-413-5*, 311570) W S Hein.
Blackstone, William. Blackstone's Commentaries, 4 vols. 1915. 50.00 (*0-87511-493-8*) Claitors.
— Blackstone's Commentaries on the Laws of England, 4 vols., Set. LC 91-73627. 1993. reprint ed. 310.00 (*0-89941-775-2*, 307250) W S Hein.
— Commentaries on the Laws of England: A Facsimile of the First Edition of 1765-1769, 4 vols. LC 79-11753. 496p. 1979. pap. 24.00 (*0-226-05538-8*) U Ch Pr.
— Commentaries on the Laws of England: A Facsimile of the First Edition of 1765-1769, 4 vols., III. LC 79-11753. 504p. 1979. pap. 23.95 (*0-226-05543-4*) U Ch Pr.
— Commentaries on the Laws of England: A Facsimile of the First Edition of 1765-1769, Vol. 2. LC 79-11753. 564p. 1979. pap. 24.00 (*0-226-05541-8*) U Ch Pr.
— Commentaries on the Laws of England: A Facsimile of the First Edition of 1765-1769, Vol. 4. LC 79-11753. 512p. 1979. pap. 25.00 (*0-226-05545-0*) U Ch Pr.
— The Sovereignty of the Law: Selections from Blackstone's Commentaries on the Laws of England. LC 72-94916. 312p. reprint ed. pap. 96.80 (*0-8357-4720-4*, 203763600009) Bks Demand.
Blackstone, William & Tucker, St. George. Blackstone's Commentaries - With Notes of Reference to the Constitution & Laws, of the Federal Government of the United States, & of the Commonwealth of Virginia: In Five Volumes, with an Appendix to Each Volume, Containing Short Tracts upon Such Subjects As Appeared Necessary to Form a Connected View of the Laws of Virginia As a Member of the Federal Union, 1803, 5 vols., Set. LC 96-12566. 1996. reprint ed. 450.00 (*1-886363-15-3*) Lawbk Exchange.
Blackstone, William E. Jesus Is Coming: God's Hope for a Restless World. LC 89-2581. 256p. 1989. reprint ed. pap. 11.99 (*0-8254-2275-2*, Kregel Class) Kregel.
Blacksun. The Spell of Making. 208p. (C). 1995. pap. 12.50 (*1-57353-109-X*, Eschaton Bks) Eschaton Prods.
Blackthorn, John, pseud. I, Che Guevara: A Novel. LC 99-39243. 352p. 2000. 24.00 (*0-688-16760-8*, Wm Morrow) Morrow Avon.
— Sins of the Fathers: A Novel. LC 98-24575. 384p. 1999. 25.00 (*0-688-16191-X*, Wm Morrow) Morrow Avon.
Blackwater, Norman, jt. auth. see Teller, Joanne.
Blackwelder, Edward F. For the First Time. LC 98-89483. 375p. 1998. text 25.00 (*0-7388-0263-8*); pap. text 15.00 (*0-7388-0264-6*) Xlibris Corp.
Blackwelder, Julia K. Women of the Depression: Caste of Culture in San Antonio, 1929-1939. (Southwestern Studies: Vol. 2). (Illus.). 304p. 1999. reprint ed. pap. 17.95 (*0-89096-864-0*) Tex A&M Univ Pr.
Blackwelder, Julia Kirk. Now Hiring: The Feminization of Work in the United States, 1900-1995. LC 97-15922. (Illus.). 320p. 1997. 39.95 (*0-89096-776-8*); pap. 17.95 (*0-89096-798-9*) Tex A&M Univ Pr.
Blackwelder, Kathy, ed. see Anderson, Jill.
***Blackwelder, Kraig.** Aberrant Storytellers Screen. (Aberrant Ser.). (Illus.). 72p. 1999. pap. 14.95 (*1-56504-627-7*, 8501) White Wolf.
— Dharma Book: Bone Flowers. 2000. pap. text 14.95 (*1-56504-240-9*) White Wolf.
— Hunter Storytellers Screen. (Hunter Ser.). (Illus.). 72p. 1999. pap. 14.95 (*1-56504-736-2*, 8101) White Wolf.
Blackwelder, Richard E. A Tolkien Thesaurus. LC 89-25949. 286p. 1990. text 15.00 (*0-8240-5296-X*, H1326) Garland.
Blackwelder, Richard E. & Garoian, George S. Handbook of Animal Diversity. 568p. 1986. 311.00 (*0-8493-2992-2*, QH408, CRC Reprint) Franklin.
Blackwelder, Richard E. & Shepherd, Benjamin A., eds. Diversity of Animal Reproduction. 152p. 1981. 91.00 (*0-8493-6355-1*, QP251, CRC Reprint) Franklin.
Blackwell. Consumer Behavior. 9th ed. (C). 1999. text 92.00 (*0-03-021108-5*, Pub. by Harcourt Coll Pubs) Harcourt.
Blackwell, jt. auth. see Carr.
Blackwell, Albert, tr. & intro. see Schleiermacher, Friedrich Daniel Ernst.
***Blackwell, Albert L.** The Sacred in Music. (Illus.). 288p. 2000. 29.95 (*0-664-22171-8*, Pub. by Westminster John Knox) Presbyterian Pub.
Blackwell, Albert L., et al. Friedrich Schleiermacher & the Founding of the University of Berlin: The Study of Religion As a Scientific Discipline. LC 88-12763. (Shorter Studies in German Thought: Vol. 1). 300p. 1988. lib. bdg. 89.95 (*0-88946-358-1*) E Mellen.
Blackwell, Albert L., tr. see Schleiermacher, Friedrich Daniel Ernst.
Blackwell, Alice S., ed. Armenian Poems. LC 78-14975. 308p. 1978. reprint ed. 25.00 (*0-88206-022-8*) Caravan Bks.
Blackwell, Alice S., tr. Some Spanish-American Poets. LC 68-22694. (ENG & SPA.). 1968. reprint ed. 30.00 (*0-8196-0217-5*) Biblo.
***Blackwell, Alice Stone.** Lucy Stone: Pioneer of Woman's Rights. 324p. 2000. pap. 17.50 (*0-8139-1990-8*) U Pr of Va.
Blackwell, Anna, tr. see Kardec, Allan, pseud.
***Blackwell, Antigone D.** Kami's Korner: The Move: The Kids on the Corner Learn about African-American Scientists & Inventors. LC 99-90001. (Illus.). 32p. (J). (gr. k-4). 1999. pap. 9.95 (*1-893802-00-0*) Leedan.
Blackwell, B. Believe It or Not Stories. 15p. (J). (gr. 7-10). 1986. 40.00 (*0-7223-2003-5*, Pub. by A H S Ltd) St Mut.
Blackwell, B. & Pepper, D. W., eds. Benchmark Problems for Heat Transfer Codes. (HTD Ser.: Vol. 222). 96p. 1992. 30.00 (*0-7918-1065-8*, G00709) ASME.
Blackwell, B. F. & Armaly, B. F., eds. Computational Aspects of Heat Transfer Benchmark Problems. LC 93-73716. 115p. 1993. pap. 40.00 (*0-7918-1003-8*) ASME.
Blackwell, Barbara J. Faces & Figures: Prints from the Herbert F. Johnson Museum of Art, Cornell University. (Illus.). 8p. 1986. 10.00 (*0-685-70715-6*) Gal Assn NY.
Blackwell, Barbara L. & Cartwright, Lillian K. Program Consultation with Human Service Programs: A Clinical Perspective. LC 88-50021. 238p. 1988. pap. 15.95 (*0-89914-026-2*) Third Party Pub.
Blackwell, Barry, ed. Treatment Compliance & the Therapeutic Alliance. (Chronic Mental Illness Ser.). 368p. 1997. text 39.00 (*90-5702-546-9*, Harwood Acad Pubs) Gordon & Breach.
— Treatment Compliance & the Therapeutic Alliance. (Chronic Mental Illness Ser.: Vol. 5). 368p. 1997. text 58.00 (*90-5699-525-1*, Harwood Acad Pubs) Gordon & Breach.
Blackwell, Barry, jt. ed. see Ayd, Frank.
Blackwell, Basil H., jt. ed. see Makower, Stanley V.
***Blackwell, Charles.** The Fiery Responses to Love's Calling. 1999. pap. write for info. (*0-7392-0475-0*, PO3579) Morris Pubng.
***Blackwell, Christine, et al, eds.** The Orlando Group & Friends: A Collection of Writings & Art. (Illus.). 2000. write for info. (*0-9621385-2-5*) Arbiter Pr.
Blackwell, Christopher W. In the Absence of Alexander: Harpalus & the Failure of Macedonian Authority. LC 97-52032. (Classical Studies: Vol. 12). 185p. (C). 1998. text 44.95 (*0-8204-3987-8*) P Lang Pubng.
***Blackwell, Constance & Kusukawa, Sachiko.** Philosophy in the Sixteenth & Seventeenth Centuries: Conversations with Aristotle. LC 99-15647. 1999. 110.95 (*0-86078-668-4*, Pub. by Ashgate Pub) Ashgate Pub Co.
Blackwell, Cynthia, jt. ed. see Harris, Gill.
Blackwell, D. Eric, jt. ed. see Fruhwald, Franz X.
Blackwell, Dana J. Naugatuck. LC 97-133975. (Images of America Ser.). 1996. pap. 16.99 (*0-7524-0415-6*) Arcadia Publng.
Blackwell, David & Carter, Andrew, eds. In the Mood: 17 Choral Arrangements of Classic Popular Songs. 184p. 1995. pap. 18.95 (*0-19-330201-2*) OUP.
Blackwell, David & Henkin, Leon. Mathematics: Report of the Project 2061 Phase I Mathematics Panel. LC 89-103. 48p. 1989. pap. 8.00 (*0-87168-344-X*, 89-03S) AAAS.
Blackwell, David A. & Girshick, M. A. Theory of Games & Statistical Decisions. 368p. (C). 1980. reprint ed. pap. 9.95 (*0-486-63831-6*) Dover.
Blackwell, David S. & Rajhans, Gyan S. Practical Guide to Respirator Usage in Industry. (Illus.). 144p. 1985. 42.95 (*0-7506-9232-4*) Buttrwrth-Heinemann.
Blackwell, Donald A. Rounding Third. Rodriguez, Pamela S. & Rothkopf, Michelle, eds. LC 95-96120. (Illus.). 32p. (Orig.). 1997. pap. write for info. (*0-9650332-1-0*) D A Blackwell.
Blackwell, E. M. Blackwell Genealogy, Bk. 1 Genealogy Only: Ancestors, Descendants & Connections of Moore Carter & Sarah Alexander (Foote) Blackwell. (Illus.). 126p. 1993. reprint ed. pap. 23.00 (*0-8328-3269-3*); reprint ed. lib. bdg. 33.00 (*0-8328-3268-5*) Higginson Bk Co.
Blackwell, Elizabeth. Essays in Medical Sociology, 2 vols. LC 73-180555. (Medicine & Society in America Ser.). 580p. 1974. reprint ed. 36.95 (*0-405-03935-2*) Ayer.
— The Laws of Life: With Special Reference to the Physical Education of Girls. rev. ed. Whatley, Elizabeth M., ed. (Illus.). 133p. reprint ed. pap. text 8.95 (*0-940151-10-3*) Statesman-Exam.
— Pioneer Work in Opening the Medical Profession to Women: Autobiographical Sketches. (American Biography Ser.). 264p. 1991. reprint ed. lib. bdg. 69.00 (*0-7812-8025-7*) Rprt Serv.
Blackwell, F. F. & Hohmann, C. K-3 Science. LC 90-22885. (K-Three Curriculum Ser.). 216p. 1991. pap. 22.95 (*0-929816-25-0*, E3003) High-Scope.
Blackwell, Frank. Elementary Science Activity Series: Life & Environment. LC 96-6806. (Illus.). 216p. 1996. 22.95 (*1-57379-009-5*, E3008) High-Scope.
Blackwell, Frank F. Elementary Science Activity Series: Energy & Change. (Illus.). 176p. 1996. pap. 22.95 (*1-57379-011-7*, D3010) High-Scope.
— Elementary Science Activity Series: Structure & Form. (Illus.). 184p. 1996. pap. 22.95 (*1-57379-010-9*, E3009) High-Scope.
Blackwell, Glenn R. The Electronic Packaging Handbook. LC 99-41244. (Electrical Engineering Handbook Ser.). 616p. 1999. 89.95 (*0-8493-8591-1*) CRC Pr.
Blackwell, Harold E., jt. auth. see Carlson, Gerald P.

B

An Asterisk (*) at the beginning of an entry indicates that the title is appearing for the first time.

Blackwell, Henry C. From a Dark Stream: The Story of Cornwall's Amazing People & Their Impact on the World. (C). 1989. 150.00 (*1-85022-019-0*, Pub. by Dyllansow Truran) St Mut.

Blackwell, Ian, jt. auth. see Fowler, Peter.

Blackwell, James E. The Black Community: Diversity & Unity. 3rd ed. 416p. (C). 1997. pap. text 49.00 (*0-06-040737-9*) Addson-Wesley Educ.

— Mainstreaming Outsiders: The Production of Black Professionals. LC 81-82121. (Illus.). 345p. (C). 1981. 39.95 (*0-930390-39-3*) Gen Hall.

— Mainstreaming Outsiders: The Production of Black Professionals. 2nd ed. LC 87-80426. (Illus.). 400p. (C). 1987. text 44.95 (*0-930390-76-8*) Gen Hall.

Blackwell, James E. & Hart, Philip S. Cities, Suburbs & Blacks: A Study of Concerns, Distrust & Alienation. LC 82-80239. 228p. (Orig.). 1982. lib. bdg. 38.95 (*0-930390-45-8*) Gen Hall.

Blackwell, James E. & Janowitz, Morris, eds. Black Sociologists: Historical & Contemporary Perspectives. LC 73-84187. (Heritage of Sociology Ser.). 437p. Date not set. reprint ed. pap. 135.50 (*0-608-20581-8*, 205454600003) Bks Demand.

— Black Sociologists: Historical & Contemporary Perspectives. LC 73-84187. (Heritage of Sociology Ser.). xxii, 416p. 1975. reprint ed. pap. text 11.00 (*0-226-05566-3*) U Ch Pr.

Blackwell, Jeannine & Zantop, Susanne, eds. Bitter Healing: German Women Writers, 1700-1830. An Anthology. LC 89-24953. (European Women Writers Ser.). (Illus.). viii, 539p. 1990. text 50.00 (*0-8032-1207-0*) U of Nebr Pr.

— Bitter Healing: German Women Writers, 1700-1830. An Anthology. LC 89-24953. (European Women Writers Ser.). (Illus.). viii, 539p. 1990. pap. text 25.00 (*0-8032-9909-5*) U of Nebr Pr.

Blackwell, Jeannine, jt. ed. see Jarvis, Shawn C.

Blackwell, Jennifer, jt. ed. see Rollison, David.

Blackwell, Joel. Personal Political Power: How Ordinary People Can Get What They Want from Government. 160p. 1998. pap. 19.95 (*0-9669236-0-X*, 1487) Issue Mgmt.

Blackwell, John. American Bulldog. (Illus.). 1997. pap. 9.95 (*0-7938-2369-2*, KW221S) TFH Pubns.

Blackwell, John & Thornton, Shane. Mastering Optics: Applications Guide to Optical Engineering. LC 95-47412. 1996. pap. write for info. (*0-07-707875-6*) McGrw-H Intl.

Blackwell, John A., jt. auth. see Pentiuc, Eugen.

***Blackwell, Johnny.** Jimi Hendrix: The Ultimate Experience. LC 99-29460. (Illus.). 256p. 1999. pap. 21.95 (*1-56025-240-5*, Thunders Mouth) Avalon NY.

Blackwell, Johnny S. Poor Man's U-Build Handbook: Lawn & Garden Tools. (U-Build Ser.: No. 7). (Illus.). 64p. 1993. 32.95 (*1-883964-07-5*) Poor Mans Pubns.

— Poor Man's U-Build Handbook: Metal Turning Lathes & Accessories. (U-Build Ser.: No. 1). 70p. 1993. 37.95 (*1-883964-01-6*) Poor Mans Pubns.

— Poor Man's U-Build Handbook: Metal Working Tools. (U-Build Ser.: No. 3). (Illus.). 64p. 1993. 34.95 (*1-883964-03-2*) Poor Mans Pubns.

— Poor Man's U-Build Handbook: Photographic Equipment. (U-Build Ser.: No. 8). (Illus.). 64p. 1993. 34.95 (*1-883964-08-3*) Poor Mans Pubns.

— Poor Man's U-Build Handbook: Power Sanders & Accessories. (U-Build Ser.: No. 6). (Illus.). 64p. 1993. 30.95 (*1-883964-06-7*) Poor Mans Pubns.

— Poor Man's U-Build Handbook: Power Saws & Accessories. (U-Build Ser.: No. 5). (Illus.). 64p. 1993. 30.95 (*1-883964-05-9*) Poor Mans Pubns.

— Poor Man's U-Build Handbook: Wood Turning Lathes & Accessories. (U-Build Ser.: No. 2). (Illus.). 64p. 1993. 36.95 (*1-883964-02-4*) Poor Mans Pubns.

— Poor Man's U-Build Handbook: Wood Working Tools & Accessories. (U-Build Ser.: No. 4). (Illus.). 64p. 1993. 32.95 (*1-883964-04-0*) Poor Mans Pubns.

Blackwell, Jonathan M., et al. Environment & Development in Africa: Selected Case Studies. (EDI Development Policy Case Series: Analytical Case Studies: No. 6). 144p. 1991. 22.00 (*0-8213-1608-7*, 11608) World Bank.

Blackwell, Kate & Ferguson, Karen. The Pension Book: What You Need to Know to Prepare for Retirement. LC 96-84308. (Illus.). 288p. 1996. pap. 12.45 (*1-55970-331-8*, Pub. by Arcade Pub Inc) Time Warner.

Blackwell, Kate, jt. auth. see Ferguson, Karen.

Blackwell, Ken, jt. auth. see Cullens, Chane.

Blackwell, Kenneth, ed. A Bibliography of Bertrand Russell, 3 vols., Set. (Collected Papers of Bertrand Russell). (Illus.). 1504p. (C). (gr. 13). 1994. 450.00 (*0-415-11644-9*, B4525) Routledge.

Blackwell, Kenneth & Roja, Harry. A Bibliography of Bertrand Russell, 2 vols., 1. LC 94-5168. (Illus.). 1994. write for info. (*0-415-10487-4*) Routledge.

— A Bibliography of Bertrand Russell, 2 vols., 2. LC 94-5168. (Illus.). 1994. write for info. (*0-415-11086-6*) Routledge.

Blackwell, Kenneth & Spadoni, Carl. A Detailed Catalogue of the Second Archives of Bertrand Russell. 464p. 1992. 95.00 (*1-85506-162-7*) Bks Intl VA.

Blackwell, Kenneth, jt. auth. see Eames, Elizabeth R.

Blackwell, Kenneth, ed. see Russell, Bertrand.

Blackwell, Laird. Western Apache Language/Culture: Essays in Linguistic Anthropology. LC 89-20242. (Illus.). 195p. 1992. reprint ed. pap. 14.95 (*0-8165-1323-6*) U of Ariz Pr.

— Who's to Blame? Child Sexual Abuse & Non-Offending Mothers. (Illus.). 256p. 1999. text 40.00 (*0-8020-2847-0*); pap. text 17.95 (*0-8020-7727-7*) U of Toronto Pr.

— Wildflowers of the Sierra Nevada & the Central Valley. (Illus.). 1999. pap. 15.95 (*1-55105-226-1*) Lone Pine.

Blackwell, Laird & Tharlet, Eve. What's the Matter, Davy? LC 97-34509. (Illus.). 32p. (J). (gr. k-3). 1998. 15.95 (*1-55858-899-X*, Pub. by North-South Bks NYC); lib. bdg. 15.88 (*1-55858-900-7*, Pub. by North-South Bks NYC) Chronicle Bks.

Blackwell, Laird, et al. West Coast Fly Fisher: A Photographic Celebration. (Illus.). 152p. 1998. pap. 19.95 (*0-88839-440-3*) Hancock House.

***Blackwell, Laird R.** Wildflowers of Mount Rainer. (Illus.). 192p. 2000. pap. text 11.95 (*1-55105-230-X*) Lone Pine.

Blackwell, Laird R. Wildflowers of the Tahoe Sierra. LC 96-910853. (Illus.). 144p. (Orig.). 1997. pap. 9.95 (*1-55105-085-4*) Lone Pine.

Blackwell, Lawana. The Courtship of the Vicar's Daughter. (Gresham Chronicles Ser.: Bk. 2). 416p. 1998. pap. 11.99 (*1-55661-948-0*) Bethany Hse.

— Dowry of Miss Lydia Clark, Vol. 3. LC 99-6390. (Gresham Chronicles Ser.). 400p. 1999. pap. text 11.99 (*0-7642-2149-3*) Bethany Hse.

— Gresham Chronicles Mix. 1999. boxed set 35.99 (*0-7642-8462-2*) Bethany Hse.

— Jewels for a Crown. LC 96-18986. (Victorian Serenade Ser.: No. 3). 398p. 1996. pap. 10.99 (*0-8423-7960-6*) Tyndale Hse.

— Like a River Glorious. LC 95-14548. (Victorian Serenade: No. 1). 1995. pap. 10.99 (*0-8423-7954-1*) Tyndale Hse.

— Measures of Grace. LC 95-36082. (Victorian Serenade Ser.: No. 2). (Illus.). 368p. 1996. pap. 10.99 (*0-8423-7956-8*) Tyndale Hse.

— Song of a Soul. LC 96-47577. (Victorian Serenade Ser.: No. 4). 340p. 1997. pap. 10.99 (*0-8423-7965-7*) Tyndale Hse.

— The Widow of Larkspur Inn. LC 97-33858. (Gresham Chronicles Ser.: Vol. 1). 432p. 1998. pap. 11.99 (*1-55661-947-2*) Bethany Hse.

Blackwell, Lee, jt. auth. see Wilson, Mary.

Blackwell, Lewis. David Carson: 2nd Sight: Graphic Design After the End of Print. 1997. pap. 35.00 (*0-7893-0128-8*, Pub. by Universe) St Martin.

***Blackwell, Lewis.** Edward Fella: Letters on America. (Illus.). 176p. 2000. 50.00 (*1-56898-217-8*) Princeton Arch.

Blackwell, Lewis. International Contract Design, Vol. 2. (Illus.). 256p. 1990. 59.95 (*1-55859-013-7*) Abbeville Pr.

— Twentieth-Century Type: Remix. rev. ed. (Illus.). 192p. 1998. pap. 39.95 (*3-927258-89-X*) Gingko Press.

Blackwell, Lewis, jt. auth. see Carson, David.

Blackwell, Lewis, jt. auth. see Leslie, Jeremy.

Blackwell, Lewis, ed. see Burgoyne, Patrick & Faber, Liz.

Blackwell, Lewis, ed. see Makela, Scott & Makela, Laurie.

Blackwell, Luther. Power to Get Wealth. 160p. 1995. pap. 11.99 (*0-927936-35-6*) Vincom Pubng Co.

— Power to Get Wealth: Enjoying Prosperity. 160p. 1996. pap. 8.99 (*1-880089-89-0*, AP-989, Pub. by Albury Pub) Appalach Bk Dist.

Blackwell, Marian. Care of the Mentally Retarded. 1979. 19.50 (*0-316-09890-6*, Little Brwn Med Div) Lppncott W & W.

Blackwell, Marian W. Glassworks. Inman, Sue L. & Freeman, K. Cushing, eds. (Poetry Ser.). 60p. (Orig.). 1996. pap. 10.00 (*0-9645778-1-X*) Emrys Pr.

Blackwell, Marilyn J. Gender & Representation in the Films of Ingmar Bergman. LC 96-36937. (SCAN Ser.). viii, 232p. 1997. 60.00 (*1-57113-094-2*) Camden Hse.

Blackwell, Marilyn J., ed. Structures of Influence: A Comparative Approach to August Strindberg. LC 80-29545. (University of North Carolina Studies in Comparative Literature: No. 98). 323p. reprint ed. pap. 100.20 (*0-7837-3771-8*, 204358800010) Bks Demand.

Blackwell, Marilyn S., jt. auth. see Hill, Ellen C.

***Blackwell, Mary Alice & Chaff, Lin.** The Insiders' Guide to Virginia's Blue Ridge. 7th ed. (Insiders' Guide Travel Ser.). (Illus.). 480p. 1999. pap. 15.95 (*1-57380-127-5*, The Insiders Guide) Falcon Pub Inc.

Blackwell, Meredith, jt. auth. see Wheeler, Quentin.

Blackwell, Michael. Clinging to Grandeur: British Attitudes & Foreign Policy in the Aftermath of the Second World War, 36. LC 92-30012. (Contributions to the Study of World History Ser.: No. 36). 208p. 1993. 55.00 (*0-313-28616-7*, BGZ/, Greenwood Pr) Greenwood.

***Blackwell, Michael C.** New Millennium Families: How You Can Soar above the Coming Flood of Change. LC 99-48420. 160p. 2000. pap. 17.95 (*1-887905-21-9*) Pkway Pubs.

Blackwell, Michael D. Pacifism in the Social Ethics of Walter George Muelder: With His Social Ethics. LC 94-37006. 472p. 1995. text 109.95 (*0-7734-2283-8*) E Mellen.

***Blackwell, Mike D.** The Bloodstained Wall: A Modern Day Adaptation of the Book of Nehemiah. LC 99-63603. 208p. 1999. pap. 12.99 (*1-57921-182-8*) WinePress Pub.

***Blackwell, Muriel F.** How Do I Become a Christian? (Illus.). 48p. (J). (gr. 3 up). 2000. pap. 6.99 (*0-8054-2378-8*) Broadman.

Blackwell North America Staff. Living in the Light. 15.95 (*1-882591-01-1*) Nataraj Pub.

— Matilda. (Illus.). (J). pap. text 6.95 (*2-07-033555-0*) Gallimard Edns.

— Les Souris de Leglise. (FRE.). 15.95 (*2-07-056096-1*) Gallimard Edns.

Blackwell, Pam. Ephraim's Seed. LC 96-68894. (Millennial Ser.: Bk. 1). 408p. 1996. pap. 15.95 (*1-57636-018-0*) SunRise Pbl.

— Ephraim's Seed. 2nd rev. ed. LC 96-68894. (Millennial Ser.: Vol. 1). 430p. 1998. pap. 15.95 (*0-9653327-6-4*) BF Publng.

— Jacob's Cauldron. (Millennial Ser.: Vol. 2). 325p. 1998. pap. 15.95 (*0-9653327-8-0*) BF Publng.

— Michael's Fire. 350p. 1999. pap. 15.95 (*0-9653327-5-6*) BF Publng.

Blackwell, Peter M. Teaching Hearing-Impaired Children in Regular Classrooms. LC LC4401.. (Language in Education: Theory & Practice Ser.: No. 54). 55p. reprint ed. pap. 30.00 (*0-8357-3353-X*, 203958800013) Bks Demand.

Blackwell, Peter M., et al. Sentences & Other Systems: A Language & Learning Curriculum for Hearing-Impaired Children. LC 78-51922. 200p. reprint ed. pap. 62.00 (*0-7837-1254-5*, 204139100020) Bks Demand.

Blackwell, Rebecca L. Descendents of John Michael Kreider of Montgomery County, Pennsylvania: Crider Families of Virginia, Kentucky & Tennessee. LC 99-199274. 192p. 1999. pap. 20.00 (*0-7884-1091-1*, B399) Heritage.

Blackwell, Richard E. Women's Medicine. 644p. 1995. 99.95 (*0-86542-373-3*) Blackwell Sci.

Blackwell, Richard E. & Grotting, James C., eds. Diagnosis & Management of Breast Disease. 664p. 1996. 54.95 (*0-86542-405-5*) Blackwell Sci.

Blackwell, Richard E. & Olive, David L., eds. Chronic Pelvic Pain: Evaluation & Management. LC 97-9562. (Illus.). 296p. 1997. 59.00 (*0-387-98207-8*) Spr-Verlag.

Blackwell, Richard E., jt. auth. see Carr, Bruce R.

Blackwell, Richard E., jt. ed. see Seibel, Machelle M.

Blackwell, Richard J. Galileo, Bellarmine & the Bible. LC 90-70858. (C). 1992. pap. text 17.50 (*0-268-01027-7*) U of Notre Dame Pr.

— Science, Religion & Authority: Lessons from the Galileo Affair, Vol. 199. LC 97-45287. (Aquinas Lecture Ser.). 1998. 15.00 (*0-87462-165-8*) Marquette.

Blackwell, Richard J., compiled by. A Bibliography of the Philosophy of Science: Nineteen Forty-Five to Nineteen Eighty-One. LC 83-5671. 585p. 1983. lib. bdg. 105.00 (*0-313-23124-9*, BLB/, Greenwood Pr) Greenwood.

Blackwell, Richard J., ed. see Bruno, Giordano.

Blackwell, Richard J., tr. see Aquinas, Thomas, Saint.

Blackwell, Richard J., tr. & intro. see Campanella, Tommaso.

Blackwell, Robert, jt. ed. see Pancsofar, Ernest.

Blackwell, Robert S. Rigid Fire Codes Fail to Protect Public Safety. (Issue Papers: No. 15-93). 27p. 1993. pap. text 8.00 (*1-57655-043-5*) Independ Inst.

Blackwell, Roger D. From Mind to Market: Reinventing the Retail Supply Chain. LC HF5415.55.B58. Date not set. pap. 15.00 (*0-88730-927-5*, HarpBusn) HarpInfo.

— From Mind to Market: Reinventing the Retail Supply Chain. LC 97-25822. (Illus.). 239p. 1997. 25.00 (*0-88730-833-3*, HarpBusn) HarpInfo.

Blackwell, Roger D., et al. Consumer Behavior. 8th ed. 1024p. (C). 1994. text 102.50 (*0-03-098464-5*) Dryden Pr.

— Contemporary Cases in Consumer Behavior. 4th ed. LC 93-6545. (C). 1993. pap. text 53.00 (*0-03-097038-5*) Dryden Pr.

— Contemporary Cases in Consumer Behavior: Instructor's Manual. 4th ed. 140p. (C). 1993. pap. text 5.75 (*0-03-097596-4*) Dryden Pr.

Blackwell, Ruby Chapin. A Girl in Washington Territory. LC 72-619693. (Illus.). 31p. 1973. pap. 3.50 (*0-917048-13-X*) Wash St Hist Soc.

Blackwell, Russell T., jt. auth. see Todd, Charles L.

***Blackwell Science Inc., Publishing Staff & Decker, Jane.** Immunology. (11th Hour Ser.). (Illus.). 1999. pap. text 18.95 (*0-632-04415-2*) Blackwell Sci.

***Blackwell Science Inc., Publishing Staff & Inczedy, J.** Compendium of Analytical Nomenclature: The Orange Book. 3rd ed. LC 98-131046. (IUPAC Chemical Data Ser.). (Illus.). 1998. 200.00 (*0-86542-615-5*) Blackwell Sci.

***Blackwell Science Inc., Publishing Staff & Raineri, Deanna.** 11th Hour Molecular Biology. (Eleventh Hour Ser.). (Illus.). 225p. 2000. pap. 18.95 (*0-632-04379-2*) Blackwell Sci.

***Blackwell Science Inc., Publishing Staff & Smiley, Jeffrey.** Biochemistry. (11th Hour Ser.). (Illus.). 2000. pap. text 18.95 (*0-632-04446-2*) Blackwell Sci.

***Blackwell Science Inc., Publishing Staff, et al.** Cell Biology. (11th Hour Ser.). (Illus.). 225p. 2000. pap. text 18.95 (*0-632-04476-4*) Blackwell Sci.

— 11th Hour Introduction to Microbiology. (Eleventh Hour Ser.). (Illus.). 225p. 2000. pap. 18.95 (*0-632-04418-7*) Blackwell Sci.

Blackwell Science Incorporated, ed. see Alexander, William.

***Blackwell, Stephen H.** Zina's Paradox: The Figured Reader in Nabokov's "Gift" LC 99-52904. (Middlebury Studies in Russian Language & Literature: Vol. 23). 232p. (C). 2000. text 55.95 (*0-8204-4883-4*) P Lang Pubng.

Blackwell, Thomas. An Enquiry into the Life & Writings of Homer. 2nd ed. (Anglistica & Americana Ser.: No. 173). iv, 438p. 1976. reprint ed. lib. bdg. 105.00 (*3-487-06001-9*) G Olms Pubs.

Blackwell, Thomas & Schumer, Stan. Restructuring: Methods & Models. (Illus.). 160p. (C). 1997. pap. text 12.95 (*0-9621042-6-4*) IMPEL.

Blackwell, Thomas E., ed. College Law Digest, 1935-1970. xi, 256p. 1974. pap. 12.00 (*0-8377-9115-4*, Rothman) W S Hein.

— College Law Digest, 1935-1970. xi, 256p. 1974. pap. 12.00 (*0-8377-0307-7*, Rothman) W S Hein.

Blackwell, Thomas T. The Hierarchy of Achievement. LaLonde, Beverly, ed. (Illus.). 150p. (Orig.). 1989. pap. 9.95 (*0-9621042-1-3*) IMPEL.

— How to Become Successful at Personal Leadership: Five Steps to Success & Happiness. LaLonde, Beverly, ed. (Illus.). 160p. (Orig.). 1988. pap. 9.95 (*0-9621042-0-5*) IMPEL.

Blackwell, William E. Observations on Life. 132p. 1991. 17.95 (*0-9630477-0-1*) W E Blackwell.

Blackwell, William L. The Industrialization of Russia: A Historical Perspective. 3rd ed. Eubank, Keith, ed. (European History Ser.). 240p. (C). 1994. pap. text 12.95 (*0-88295-905-0*) Harlan Davidson.

Blackwell, Winfield. Sky-High Love. Kelly, Jane, ed. x, 86p. (Orig.). 1996. reprint ed. write for info. (*0-9621194-1-5*) Stratford NC.

***Blackwill, Robert D. & Dibb, Paul, eds.** America's Asian Alliances. (BCSIA Studies in International Security). 160p. 2000. 45.00 (*0-262-02489-6*) MIT Pr.

— America's Asian Alliances. (BCSIA Studies in International Security). 160p. (C). 2000. pap. 17.95 (*0-262-52285-3*) MIT Pr.

Blackwill, Robert D. & Karaganov, Sergei A. Damage Limitation or Crisis? Russia & the Outside World. (CSIA Studies in International Security: Vol. 5). 352p. 1994. pap. 18.50 (*0-02-881119-4*) Brasseys.

Blackwill, Robert D. & Sturmer, Michael, eds. Transatlantic Policies for the Greater Middle East: Transatlantic Policies for the Greater Middle East. LC 97-21781. (CSIA Studies in International Security). (Illus.). 350p. 1997. pap. text 22.50 (*0-262-52244-6*) MIT Pr.

Blackwill, Robert D., et al. Engaging Russia: A Report to the Trilateral Commision. LC 95-12234. (Triangle Papers: Vol. 46). 127p. (C). 1995. pap. 12.00 (*0-930503-72-4*) Trilateral Comm.

Blackwood, Adam. History of Mary Queen of Scots. MacDonald, Alexander, ed. LC 73-39448. (Maitland Club, Glasgow. Publications: No. 31). reprint ed. 47.50 (*0-404-52991-7*) AMS Pr.

Blackwood, Alan. Hungarian Uprising. LC 86-20341. (Flashpoints Ser.: Set I). (Illus.). 80p. (YA). (gr. 7 up). 1988. lib. bdg. 25.27 (*0-86592-032-X*) Rourke Enter.

— Hungarian Uprising, Reading Level 8. LC 86-20341. (Flashpoints Ser.: Set I). (Illus.). 80p. (J). (gr. 7 up). 1988. lib. bdg. 18.60 (*0-685-58793-2*) Rourke Corp.

— Kingdom of the Blind. 544p. 1999. 26.00 (*0-7278-5425-9*, Pub. by Severn Hse) Chivers N Amer.

***Blackwood, Alan.** Kingdom of the Blind. 2000. pap. 8.95 (*0-552-14645-5*) Transworld Publishers Ltd.

Blackwood, Alan. Tales Mysterious & Macabre, Set. 32.95 (*0-8488-0195-4*) Amereon Ltd.

— Tales Mysterious & Macabre, Vol. 2. 20.95 (*0-8488-0194-6*) Amereon Ltd.

Blackwood, Algernon. Best Ghost Stories of Algernon Blackwood. (Orig.). Date not set. lib. bdg. 25.95 (*0-8488-2134-3*) Amereon Ltd.

— Best Ghost Stories of Algernon Blackwood. Bleiler, Everett F., ed. (Illus.). 366p. (Orig.). 1973. pap. 8.95 (*0-486-22977-7*) Dover.

— The Centaur. Reginald, R. & Menville, Douglas A., eds. LC 75-46254. (Supernatural & Occult Fiction Ser.). 1976. reprint ed. lib. bdg. 29.95 (*0-405-08113-8*) Ayer.

— Complete John Silence Stories. Joshi, S. T., ed. & intro. by. LC 97-29663. (Illus.). 380p. 1998. reprint ed. pap. 9.95 (*0-486-29942-2*) Dover.

— The Empty House & Other Ghost Stories. 1993. reprint ed. lib. bdg. 18.95 (*0-89968-418-1*, Lghtyr Pr) Buccaneer Bks.

— The Fruit Stoners: Being the Adventures of Maria among the Fruit Stoners. Reginald, R. & Melville, Douglas, eds. LC 77-84200. (Lost Race & Adult Fantasy Ser.). 1978. reprint ed. lib. bdg. 26.95 (*0-405-10958-X*) Ayer.

— The Listener, & Other Stories. LC 70-150537. (Short Story Index Reprint Ser.). 1977. reprint ed. 19.95 (*0-8369-3834-8*) Ayer.

— Lost Valley, & Other Stories. LC 70-167442. (Short Story Index Reprint Ser.). (Illus.). 1977. reprint ed. 23.95 (*0-8369-3968-9*) Ayer.

— Pan's Garden: A Volume of Nature Stories. LC 74-157772. (Short Story Index Reprint Ser.). (Illus.). 1977. reprint ed. 30.95 (*0-8369-3884-4*) Ayer.

— Strange Stories. Reginald, R. & Menville, Douglas A., eds. LC 75-46255. (Supernatural & Occult Fiction Ser.). 1976. reprint ed. lib. bdg. 60.95 (*0-405-08114-6*) Ayer.

— Tales of Mysterious & Macabre, Vol. 1. 20.95 (*0-8488-0193-8*) Amereon Ltd.

— Tales of the Uncanny & Supernatural, Set. 432p. reprint ed. lib. bdg. 32.95 (*0-88411-145-8*) Amereon Ltd.

— Tales of the Uncanny & Supernatural, Vol. 1. 20.95 (*0-8488-0196-2*) Amereon Ltd.

— Tales of the Uncanny & Supernatural, Vol. 2. 20.95 (*0-8488-0197-0*) Amereon Ltd.

— Ten Minute Stories. LC 72-103495. (Short Story Index Reprint Ser.). 1977. 20.95 (*0-8369-3237-4*) Ayer.

Blackwood, Andres W. Tu Puedes Recobrar el Gozo. (Serie Tu Puedes - You Can Ser.).Tr. of You Can Recover Joy. (SPA.). 24p. 1982. pap. 1.79 (*1-56063-153-8*, 490487) Editorial Unilit.

Blackwood, Beatrice. Both Sides of Buka Passage. LC 76-44691. reprint ed. 64.50 (*0-404-15907-9*) AMS Pr.

Blackwood, Easley. Complete Book of Opening Leads. 475p. 1991. pap. 14.95 (*0-910791-05-8*) Devyn Pr.

— The Structure of Recognizable Diatonic Tunings. LC 85-42972. (Illus.). 329p. reprint ed. pap. 102.00 (*0-608-06379-7*, 206674000008) Bks Demand.

***Blackwood, Evelyn.** Female Desires: Same-Sex Relations & Transgender Practices Across Cultures. LC 98-37847. (Between Men - Between Women Ser.). 352p. 1998. pap. 18.50 (*0-231-11261-0*); lib. bdg. 49.50 (*0-231-11260-2*) Col U Pr.

— Webs of Power. LC 99-45666. 224p. 1999. text 65.00 (*0-8476-9910-2*) Rowman.

— Webs of Power: Women, Kin, & Community in a Sumatran Village. LC 99-45666. 224p. 1999. pap. 21.95 (*0-8476-9911-0*) Rowman.

Blackwood, Evelyn, ed. The Many Faces of Homosexuality: Anthropological Approaches to Homosexual Behavior. LC 85-17757. (Journal of Homosexuality Ser.: Vol. 11, Nos. 3 & 4). 217p. 1986. pap. 19.95 (*0-918393-20-5*, Harrington Park) Haworth Pr.

Blackwood, Evelyn, et al. Anthropology & Homosexual Behavior. LC 85-17758. (Journal of Homosexuality: Vol. 11, No. 3-4). 217p. 1986. 6.95 (*0-86656-328-8*); text 19.95 (*0-86656-420-9*) Haworth Pr.

Blackwood, Gary L. Al Otro Lado de la Puerta (Beyond the Door) Dominguez, Catalina, tr. (Illus.). (YA). 1993. pap. 5.99 (*968-16-4233-3*, Pub. by Fondo) Continental Bk.

— Alien Astronauts. LC 97-13. (Illus.). 80p. (YA). (gr. 4-12). 1998. lib. bdg. 28.50 (*0-7614-0469-4*, Benchmark NY) Marshall Cavendish.

— Attack of the Mushroom People. LC 90-52521. (Orig.). 1984. pap. 6.00 (*0-88734-308-2*) Players Pr.

— Extraordinary Events & Oddball Occurrences. LC 98-30261. (Secrets of the Unexplained Ser.). (J). (gr. 5-9). 1999. lib. bdg. 28.50 (*0-7614-0748-0*, Benchmark NY) Marshall Cavendish.

— Fateful Forebodings. LC 97-11078. (Secrets of the Unexplained Ser.). (YA). (gr. 4-12). 1998. lib. bdg. 28.50 (*0-7614-0467-8*, Benchmark NY) Marshall Cavendish.

— Futures. LC 96-45245. 55p. (Orig.). 1996. pap. 6.00 (*0-88734-715-0*) Players Pr.

***Blackwood, Gary L.** Highwaymen. LC 99-86663. (Bad Guys Ser.). 2001. lib. bdg. write for info. (*0-7614-1017-1*, Benchmark NY) Marshall Cavendish.

— Life in a Medieval Castle. LC 99-26848. (Way People Live Ser.). (Illus.). 112p. (YA). (gr. 6-9). 2000. lib. bdg. 23.70 (*1-56006-582-6*) Lucent Bks.

— Life on the Oregon Trail. (Way People Live Ser.). (Illus.). 112p. (YA). (gr. 4-12). 1999. lib. bdg. 23.70 (*1-56006-540-0*) Lucent Bks.

Blackwood, Gary L. The Lion & the Unicorn. LC 82-90758. 291p. (Orig.). 1983. pap. 6.95 (*0-910971-00-5*) Eagle Bks.

— Moonshine. LC 99-10756. 144p. (J). (gr. 3-7). 1999. 14.95 (*0-7614-5056-4*, Cav Child Bks) Marshall Cavendish.

— Paranormal Powers. Stanton, Joyce, ed. LC 97-48478. (Secrets of the Unexplained Ser.). (Illus.). 80p. (YA). (gr. 4-12). 1998. lib. bdg. 28.50 (*0-7614-0468-6*, Benchmark NY) Marshall Cavendish.

***Blackwood, Gary L.** Pirates. LC 99-86674. (Bad Guys Ser.). 2001. lib. bdg. write for info. (*0-7614-1019-8*, Benchmark NY) Marshall Cavendish.

— Shakespeare Stealer. (Illus.). 208p. (J). (gr. 4-8). 2000. pap. 5.99 (*0-14-130595-9*, PuffinBks) Peng Put Young Read.

— Shakespeare's Scribe. (Illus.). 224p. (J). (gr. 4-6). 2000. 15.99 (*0-525-46444-1*, Dutton Child) Peng Put Young Read.

Blackwood, Gary L. Spooky Spectres. large type ed. LC 98-28281. (Secrets of the Unexplained Ser.). (J). (gr. 5-9). 1999. lib. bdg. 28.50 (*0-7614-0746-4*, Benchmark NY) Marshall Cavendish.

Blackwood, George, jt. auth. see Levin, Murray B.

***Blackwood, James R.** Essential James Blackwood & the Light Crust Doughboys. (Illus.). 1999. 19.99 (*1-888092-14-9*) Lght Crust Dghboys.

Blackwood, John, jt. auth. see Fulder, Stephen.

Blackwood, Karen S. Espresso! Seattle '96. (Illus.). 240p. (Orig.). Date not set. pap. 14.95 (*0-9652852-0-0*) K B Co.

Blackwood, Mary. Derek the Knitting Dinosaur. (Illus.). 32p. (J). (ps-3). 1990. lib. bdg. 19.93 (*0-87614-400-8*, Carolrhoda) Lerner Pub.

— Derek the Knitting Dinosaur. (Illus.). 32p. (J). (ps-3). 1991. pap. 5.95 (*0-87614-540-3*, First Ave Edns) Lerner Pub.

— Derek the Knitting Dinosaur, 4 bks. (J). (gr. k-3). 1997. pap., teacher ed. 33.95 incl. audio (*0-87499-392-X*) Live Oak Media.

— Derek the Knitting Dinosaur. unabridged ed. (J). (gr. k-3). 1997. 24.95 incl. audio (*0-87499-391-1*); pap. 15.95 incl. audio (*0-87499-390-3*) Live Oak Media.

***Blackwood, Mary Jo.** Old Love: Lessons Learned along the Way. 72p. 1999. pap. 7.95 (*0-9671840-0-2*, Hepp U Pr) Healthsite Assocs.

Blackwood, P. L., jt. illus. see Ziegler, J. F.

Blackwood, R., jt. auth. see Turner, Robert C.

Blackwood, Ray. The Whitsunday Islands: An Historical Dictionary. (Illus.). 283p. 1997. pap. 49.95 (*1-875998-27-6*, Pub. by Central Queensland) Accents Pubns.

Blackwood, Roger, jt. auth. see Falk, Bernard.

Blackwood, Roger A., jt. auth. see Turner, Robert C.

Blackwood, Susan & Dilworth, Anne. Temptations. 396p. 1986. 14.95 (*0-9617154-0-5*, Pub. by Presby Day Schl) Wimmer Bks.

Blacque-Belair, Alain. Dictionnaire des Constantes Biologiques et Physiques. 5th ed.Tr. of Dictionary of Biological & Physical Constants. (FRE.). 2200p. 1980. 175.00 (*0-8288-1219-5*, M15349) Fr & Eur.

— Medical, Clinical, Pharmacological & Therapeutic Dictionary: Dictionnaire Medical, Clinique, Pharmacologique et Therapeutique. 3rd ed. 1938p. 1981. 150.00 (*0-8288-1789-8*, M6036) Fr & Eur.

Blacque-Belair, Alain & Fossey, Bernard M. de. Dictionnaire de Diagnostic Clinique et Topographique. (FRE.). 1250p. 1969. 75.00 (*0-8288-6586-8*, M6037) Fr & Eur.

Blacque, I. M. White Women Got Flat Butts. C & C Publishing, Inc. Staff, ed. 182p. (Orig.). 1993. pap. 12.95 (*0-9639017-0-2*) C & C Pubng.

Blacs, Pater A. Biological Role of Plant Lipids: Proceedings of the 8th International Symposium on the Biological Role of Plant Lipids Held at Budapest, Hungary, July 25-28, 1988. Gruiz, Katalin & Kremmer, Tibor, eds. 625p. (C). 1989. 150.00 (*963-05-5375-9*, Pub. by Akade Kiado) St Mut.

Blad, M. C. & Keiding, H. Microeconomics: Institutions, Equilibrium & Optimality. (Advanced Textbooks in Economics Ser.: No. 30). 424p. 1990. 88.00 (*0-444-88644-3*, North Holland) Elsevier.

Blade, Richard A. The Del Operator in Theoretical Physics. (Textbooks in Science & Mathematics Ser.). (Illus.). 161p. (Orig.). (C). 1991. pap. text 16.00 (*1-880930-00-5*) IPI Pr.

Blade, Richard A., ed. see Maccone, Claudio.

Bladel, J. Van, see Van Bladel, J.

Bladen, Vincent W. From Adam Smith to Maynard Keynes: The Heritage of Political Economy. LC 73-91568. 548p. reprint ed. pap. 169.90 (*0-608-16230-2*, 202651000050) Bks Demand.

Bladen, Wilford A., jt. auth. see Karan, P. P.

Blader, Susan. Tales of Magistrate Bao & His Valiant Lieutenants: Selections from Sanxia Wuyi. LC 98-165563. 426p. 1998. pap. 26.50 (*962-201-775-4*, Pub. by Chinese Univ) U of Mich Pr.

Blader, Susan, jt. ed. see Le Blanc, Charles.

Blades, Ann. Back to the Cabin. (Illus.). 32p. (J). (ps-2). 1997. pap. 6.95 (*1-55143-051-7*) Orca Bk Pubs.

— A Boy of Tache. LC 94-62178. (Illus.). 32p. (J). (gr. 3-6). 1995. pap. 5.95 (*0-88776-350-2*) Tundra Bks.

— Boy of Tache. 1995. 13.15 (*0-606-08703-6*, Pub. by Turtleback) Demco.

— Mary of Mile 18. LC 74-179430. (Illus.). 40p. (J). (gr. 1-4). 1996. reprint ed. pap. 8.95 (*0-88776-059-7*) Tundra Bks.

***Blades, Ann.** Too Small. (Illus.). (J). 2000. 15.95 (*0-88899-400-1*) Grndwd Bks.

Blades, Ann. Wolf & the Seven Little Kids. 32p. (J). 1999. text 15.95 (*0-88899-364-1*) Gro1undwood-Douglas.

Blades, Ann. The Singing Basket. 32p. (J). (ps-3). 1991. 13.95 (*0-88899-104-5*) Publishers Group.

Blades, C., et al, eds. Quasar Absorption Lines: Probing The Universe. (Space Telescope Science Institute Symposium Ser.). 360p. 1988. text 69.95 (*0-521-34561-8*) Cambridge U Pr.

Blades, David. Procedures of Power & Curriculum Change: Focault & the Quest for Possibilities in Science Education. (Counterpoints: Studies in the Postmodern Theory of Education: Vol. 35). XIII, 290p. (C). 1997. pap. text 29.95 (*0-8204-3325-X*) P Lang Pubng.

Blades, J. Future Now Past. 1990. pap. text 3.00 (*0-919957-61-7*) Genl Dist Srvs.

Blades, James. Percussion Instruments & Their History. (Illus.). 512p. 1992. reprint ed. pap. 50.00 (*0-933224-61-3*, ST114) Bold Strummer Ltd.

Blades, James & Dean, Johnny. How to Play Drums. (How-to-Play Ser.). (Illus.). 112p. (Orig.). 1992. pap. 9.95 (*0-312-08212-6*) St Martin.

Blades, Joe. Cover Makes a Set. 1990. pap. 6.75 (*0-919957-60-9*) Genl Dist Srvs.

— Open Road West. 2000. pap. 10.50 (*1-896647-30-8*) Genl Dist Srvs.

— Paper Bags. 1989. pap. text 3.00 (*0-921411-14-6*) Genl Dist Srvs.

Blades, Joe. River Suite: Poems. LC 98-231923. 112p. 1999. pap. 9.99 (*1-895837-46-4*) Insomniac.

Blades, Joe. Synopsis. 1994. pap. text 3.00 (*0-921411-27-8*) Genl Dist Srvs.

***Blades, Joe, ed.** Fredericton Bast: A Photo Album. (Illus.). 112p. 1999. pap. 14.00 (*0-921411-73-1*) Genl Dist Srvs.

— In the Dark: Poets & Publishing. 56p. 1997. pap. text 7.50 (*0-921411-62-6*) Genl Dist Srvs.

— May Contain and/Or: A BS Poetry Drop-in Centre Anthology. 1995. pap. text 3.00 (*0-921411-39-1*) Genl Dist Srvs.

Blades, Joe & Stranach, Matt, eds. Burnt Poems Served Hot. 1995. pap. 3.00 (*0-9694127-1-1*) Genl Dist Srvs.

Blades, Joe, et al. Danger Falling Ice: The League of Canadian Poets' Writes of Spring Reading in Fredericton, 1997. 1997. 3.75 (*0-9694127-2-X*) Genl Dist Srvs.

Blades, Joe, ed. see Grace, M. E., et al.

Blades, John, ed. see Barghini, Sandra.

Blades, Joseph D., Jr. A Comparative Study of Selected American Film Critics, 1958-1974. Jowett, Garth S., ed. LC 75-21429. (Dissertations on Film Ser.). 1976. lib. bdg. 20.95 (*0-405-07532-4*) Ayer.

Blades, Margaret B. Two Hundred Years of Chairs & Chairmaking: An Exhibition of Chairs from the Chester County Historical Society. LC 87-11676. (Illus.). 32p. (Orig.). 1987. pap. 6.50 (*0-685-21897-X*) Chester Co Hist Soc.

Blades, William. Shakespeare & Typography. LC 72-113560. reprint ed. 29.50 (*0-404-00894-1*) AMS Pr.

Blades, William H. Selling, the Mother of All Enterprise. 152p. 1994. pap. 12.95 (*0-9624798-7-X*) Mktg Methods Pr.

***Bladey, Conrad Jay.** Brigid of the Gael: A Complete Collection of Primary Resources, Relating to Saint. (Illus.). 154p. 2000. pap. 19.00 (*0-9702386-0-6*) Hutman Prodns.

— Conrad Bladey's Irish Teatime Companion: Being a Collection of the Famous & Essential Teatime Recip. 2nd ed. (Illus.). 92p. (YA). 2000. pap. 14.00 (*0-9702386-2-2*) Hutman Prodns.

— The Good Saint Brigid of Kildare: A Guide to the Primary Stories & Instructions for Celebrat. (Illus.). 20p. 2000. pap. 3.75 (*0-9702386-1-4*) Hutman Prodns.

— The Irish Customs, Crafts & Recipes of November Night, or, Samhain, or Halloween. (Illus.). 31p. (J). 1999. pap. write for info. (*0-9702386-5-7*) Hutman Prodns.

— Possadh & Bainis: A Guide to the Traditional Irish Wedding. (Illus.). 96p. (J). 2000. pap. 15.00 (*0-9702386-3-0*) Hutman Prodns.

— The Wake Which Knows No Sleeping: A Guide to Traditional Irish Funerary Customs & Folklore. 2nd ed. (Illus.). 92p. (J). 2000. pap. 14.00 (*0-9702386-4-9*) Hutman Prodns.

Bladgen, Tom, et al. Lowcountry: The Natural Landscape. (Illus.). 106p. 1988. 49.95 (*0-933101-12-0*) Legacy Pubns.

Bladholm, Cheri. Love Stories: Reading Level 2-3. LC 93-12038. (Timeless Tales Ser.). 1993. 4.95 (*0-88336-462-X*); audio 9.95 (*0-88336-539-1*) New Readers.

***Bladholm, Linda.** Indian Grocery Store Demystified. 256p. 2000. pap. 14.95 (*1-58063-143-6*) Renaissance.

Bladholm, Linda & Eismann, Jonathan. The Asian Grocery Store Demystified: A Food Lover's Guide to All the Best Ingredients. LC 98-55397. (Illus.). 256p. 1999. pap. 14.95 (*1-58063-045-6*, Pub. by Renaissance) St Martin.

Bladin, P. F., jt. auth. see Eadie, M. J.

Bladon Lawrence, Patricia, ed. see Roberts, Perry L., et al.

Bladon, Rachel. French for Beginners Workbook. (Illus.). 32p. (J). (gr. 4-7). 1994. pap. 8.13 (*0-8442-1415-9*, 14159, Passprt Bks) NTC Contemp Pub Co.

— German for Beginners Workbook. (Illus.). 32p. (J) (gr. 4-7). 1994. pap. 6.95 (*0-8442-2181-3*, 21813, Passprt Bks) NTC Contemp Pub Co.

— Insect Sticker Book. (Spotter's Guide Sticker Bks.). (Illus.). 32p. (J). (gr. 2 up). 1997. pap. 7.95 (*0-7460-3003-7*, Usborne) EDC.

— Test Your Grammar. (Test Yourself Ser.). (Illus.). 32p. (J). (gr. 5-9). 1995. pap. 5.95 (*0-7460-1723-5*, Usborne) EDC.

— Test Your Grammar. (Test Yourself Ser.). (Illus.). 32p. (J). (gr. 5 up). 1999. lib. bdg. 13.95 (*0-88110-740-9*, Usborne) EDC.

Bladon, Rachel, et al. Improve Your English. (Test Yourself Ser.). 96p. (J). (gr. 5 up). 1998. pap. 14.95 (*0-7460-3049-5*, Usborne); lib. bdg. 22.95 (*1-58086-000-1*, Usborne) EDC.

Bladt, Sabine, jt. auth. see Wagner, Hildebert H.

Bladwin, William P., Jr. & Baldwin, Agnes. Plantations of the Low Country: South Carolina, 1697-1865. LC 84-82499. (Illus.). 144p. 1986. 29.95 (*0-933101-08-2*) Legacy Pubns.

***Blady, Ken.** Jewish Communities in Exotic Places. LC 99-34824. 280p. 2000. 30.00 (*0-7657-6112-2*) Aronson.

Blaeser, H. Dictionary Personality: German/English/German. (GER.). 442p. 1997. 150.00 (*0-320-00122-9*) Fr & Eur.

— Taschworterbuch der Personalarbeit. (ENG & GER.). 120p. 1989. pap. 95.00 (*0-8288-3881-X*, F93160) Fr & Eur.

Blaeser, Kimberly. Trailing You. 1994. pap. 9.95 (*0-912678-88-7*) Greenfld Rev Lit.

Blaeser, Kimberly, ed. Stories Migrating Home. 304p. 1999. pap. 16.95 (*0-926147-08-0*) Loonfeather.

Blaeser, Kimberly M. Gerald Vizenor: Writing in the Oral Tradition. LC 96-18188. 246p. 1996. 29.95 (*0-8061-2874-7*, 2874) U of Okla Pr.

Blaesser, Brian. Discretionary Land Use Controls. (Real Property - Zoning Ser.). 1996. pap. write for info. (*0-614-06264-0*) West Group.

Blaesser, Brian & Weinstein, Alan, eds. Land Use & the Constitution. LC 88-72355. 291p. (Orig.). 1989. pap. 38.95 (*0-918286-58-1*, Planners Press) Am Plan Assn.

***Blaesser, Brian W.** Discretionary Land Use Controls Avoiding Invitations to Abuse of Discretion LC 98-208673. 1998. write for info. (*0-87632-424-3*) West Group.

Blaesser, Christine, ed. see Graham, Terry L. & Camp, Linda.

Blaeuer, Mark. Hot Springs National Park in Pictures. 2nd ed. (Illus.). 32p. 1996. pap. 4.75 (*0-915992-96-5*) Eastern National.

Blaga, Jeffrey. Wisconsin State Studies: Activity Manual. rev. ed. (Graphic Learning Integrated Social Studies Ser.). (Illus.). 94p. (J). (gr. 4). 1998. 125.00 (*0-87746-159-7*) Graphic Learning.

— Wisconsin State Studies: Teacher's Guide. rev. ed. (Graphic Learning Integrated Social Studies Ser.). (Illus.). 22p. (J). (gr. 4). 1998. teacher ed. 11.00 (*0-87746-160-0*) Graphic Learning.

Blaga, Lucian. At the Court of Yearning: Poems. LC 89-30175. (Romanian Literature & Thought in Translation Ser.). (Illus.). 231p. reprint ed. pap. 71.70 (*0-608-09654-7*, 206976900006) Bks Demand.

***Blagburn, Byron L. & Dryden, Michael W., eds.** Pfizer Atlas of Veterinary Clinical Parasitology. (Illus.). 48p. 2000. write for info. (*0-9678005-3-6*) Gloyd Grp Inc.

Blagdan, Donna, ed. see Albee, Edward, et al.

Blagden, Charles O., jt. auth. see Skeat, Walter W.

Blagden, Cyprian. The Stationers' Company: A History, 1403-1959. LC 76-48000. 320p. 1960. 39.50 (*0-8047-0935-1*) Stanford U Pr.

***Blagden, Julia W., et al.** Sapphire Blue Birthday Album. (J). 2000. 14.00 incl. audio compact disk (*0-9659511-3-8*, Pub. by Multifaceted) Sparkling Recs.

— Sapphire Blue Birthday Album. (J). (ps-4). 2000. audio 12.00 (*0-9659511-2-X*, Pub. by Multifaceted) Sparkling Recs.

Blagden, Tom, Jr., photos by. South Carolina Reflections. LC 98-2847. (Littlebook Ser.). (Illus.). 64p. 1998. 14.95 (*1-56579-299-8*) Westcliffe Pubs.

— South Carolina's Wetland Wilderness: The ACE Basin. (Illus.). 112p. 1992. 29.95 (*0-929969-71-5*) Westcliffe Pubs.

Blagdon, F. W. The European in India: From a Collection of Drawings from Charles Doyley. (C). 1995. 64.00 (*81-206-0882-8*, Pub. by Asian Educ Servs) S Asia.

Blagg, Max. Pink Instrument: Poems by Max Blagg; Photographs by Ralph Gibson. (Illus.). 168p. 1998. pap. 21.95 (*1-57129-054-0*) Brookline Bks.

Blagg, Nigel. School Phobia & Its Treatment. 240p. 1987. pap. 22.95 (*0-7099-5050-0*, Pub. by C Helm); lib. bdg. 49.95 (*0-7099-3938-8*, Pub. by C Helm) Routldge.

Blagg, Thomas M. & Wadsworth, Arthur, eds. Abstracts of Nottinghamshire Marriage Licences Vol. 1: Archdeaconry Court, 1577-1700; Peculiar of Southwell, 1588-1754. (British Record Society Index Library: Vol. 58). 1972. reprint ed. pap. 60.00 (*0-8115-1503-6*) Periodicals Srv.

Blagodat, V. I., jt. ed. see Karatsuba, A. A.

Blagonidow, Beorge. The Last Train from Berlin. 206p. 1995. pap. 9.95 (*0-7818-0368-3*) Hippocrene Bks.

Blagowidow, George. American Phrasebook for Russians. (ENG & RUS.). 144p. 1992. pap. 8.95 (*0-7818-0054-4*) Hippocrene Bks.

— In Search of the Lady Lion Tamer. 249p. (J). 1987. 15.95 (*0-15-144500-1*) Harcourt.

— Operation Parterre. 286p. 1982. 10.95 (*0-88254-712-7*) Hippocrene Bks.

— Traveler's I. Q. Test: Rate Your Globetrotting Knowledge. 194p. 1987. pap. 6.95 (*0-87052-307-4*) Hippocrene Bks.

— Traveler's Trivia Test: 1101 Questions & Answers for the Sophisticated Globetrotter. rev. ed. 224p. 1991. pap. text 6.95 (*0-87052-915-3*) Hippocrene Bks.

Blagrave, John. Astrolabium Vranicum Generale: Nova Orbis Terrarum Descripto (A Map to Accompany the Astrolabium) LC 78-38156. (English Experience Ser.: No. 435). (Illus.). 69p. 1972. reprint ed. 20.00 (*90-221-0435-4*) Walter J Johnson.

— Baculum Familliare, a Booke of the Making & Use of a Staffe. LC 71-26001. (English Experience Ser.: No. 225). 1970. reprint ed. 20.00 (*90-221-0225-4*) Walter J Johnson.

— The Mathematicall Iewell. LC 74-171735. (English Experience Ser.: No. 294). 1971. reprint ed. 45.00 (*90-221-0294-7*) Walter J Johnson.

Blagrave, Joseph. Astrological Practice of Physick: Discovering the True Way to Cure All Kinds of Diseases & Infirmities Which Are Naturally Incident to the Holy Man (1617) 166p. 1998. reprint ed. pap. 18.95 (*0-7661-0583-0*) Kessinger Pub.

— Astrological Practice of Physick: True Way to Cure All Diseases. rev. ed. Wiggers, Carol A., ed. Cochran, Kathleen R., tr. (Illus.). 173p. 1996. pap. 20.00 (*1-878935-37-2*) JustUs & Assocs.

Blagrove, Luanna C. AMERCE Business. abr. ed. (AMERCE Business Ser.). 250p. 1987. text 24.95 (*0-939776-36-7*) Blagrove Pubns.

— Amerce Malpractice. abr. ed. 235p. 1988. 24.95 (*0-939776-40-5*) Blagrove Pubns.

— AMERCE Tribute Account. abr. ed. (Illus.). 250p. 1988. 24.95 (*0-939776-28-6*); write for info. (*0-939776-29-4*); write for info. (*0-939776-30-8*) Blagrove Pubns.

— AMERCE Tribute Account: Accounting. abr. ed. (AMERCE Tribute Account Ser.). (Illus.). 250p. 1987. text 24.95 (*0-939776-31-6*) Blagrove Pubns.

— Amerce Tribute Account: Accounting. abr. ed. (AMERCE Tribute Account Ser.). (Illus.). 235p. 1988. 24.95 (*0-939776-27-8*) Blagrove Pubns.

— American Business. abr. ed. (AMERCE Business Ser.). 250p. 1987. text 24.95 (*0-939776-32-4*) Blagrove Pubns.

— The American Language: AMERCE Language. abr. ed. 250p. 1987. 24.95 (*0-939776-20-0*) Blagrove Pubns.

— Anabasis of American Dialect. abr. ed. (Illus.). 235p. 1988. 24.95 (*0-317-67239-8*) Blagrove Pubns.

— Anabasis of Insurance. abr. ed. (Illus.). 235p. 1988. 24.95 (*0-939776-41-3*) Blagrove Pubns.

— Business Problems & Solutions for Proprietors & Partnerships. LC 81-65224. 160p. (C). 1981. 24.95 (*0-9604466-8-0*); pap. 19.95 (*0-9604466-9-9*) Blagrove Pubns.

— Polity Law Lost Art: Law Arithmetic. abr. ed. (Illus.). 237p. 1988. 29.95 (*0-939776-46-4*) Blagrove Pubns.

— The Professional's Business Guide for Proprietor & Partnerships. rev. ed. LC 81-65223. (Illus.). 185p. (C). 1981. 29.95 (*0-9604466-5-6*) Blagrove Pubns.

— Teach, Teacher. abr. ed. (Illus.). 1988. 24.95 (*0-939776-42-1*) Blagrove Pubns.

Blagrove, Luanna C., intro. AMERCE Diatribe Covenant Government. abr. ed. (Illus.). 250p. 1988. 24.95 (*0-939776-25-1*); text 24.95 (*0-317-55116-7*) Blagrove Pubns.

— AMERCE Management. abr. ed. (AMERCE Management Ser.). (Illus.). 250p. 1988. 24.95 (*0-939776-06-5*) Blagrove Pubns.

— AMERCE Read, Write, or Arithmetic. abr. ed. (Illus.). 250p. 1988. 24.95 (*0-939776-33-2*) Blagrove Pubns.

— AMERCE Subcontractor. abr. ed. (Illus.). 275p. 1988. 24.95 (*0-939776-24-3*) Blagrove Pubns.

— Astrology Lost Magic. (Illus.). 250p. 1988. 24.95 (*0-939776-38-3*) Blagrove Pubns.

— Corporate, Corporation. abr. ed. (Illus.). 250p. 1988. 24.95 (*0-939776-21-9*) Blagrove Pubns.

— Economy, Economics. abr. ed. (Illus.). 235p. 1988. 24.95 (*0-939776-23-5*) Blagrove Pubns.

— Educate, Education. abr. ed. (Illus.). 250p. 1988. 24.95 (*0-939776-26-X*) Blagrove Pubns.

— Hidden Lawyer's Judicial Court Tactics. (Illus.). 235p. 1988. 24.95 (*0-939776-45-6*) Blagrove Pubns.

— Hidden Lawyer's Tactics. (Illus.). 235p. 1988. 24.95 (*0-939776-44-8*) Blagrove Pubns.

— How to Have an Ideal Business Client. abr. rev. ed. (Illus.). 150p. 1988. pap. 10.95 (*0-939776-16-2*) Blagrove Pubns.

— How to Start & Operate a Business Manual: How to Stay

B

An Asterisk (*) at the beginning of an entry indicates that the title is appearing for the first time.

Competent in Business. abr. rev. ed. (AMERCE Business Ser.). (Illus.). 250p. 1988. 24.95 (*0-939776-13-8*) Blagrove Pubns.
— Introduction to Proprietors & Partnerships Businesses. abr. rev. ed. (AMERCE Business Ser.). (Illus.). 1988. 24.95 (*0-939776-11-1*) Blagrove Pubns.
— Law: Allegory Roman Civil & Merchant Laws. abr. ed. (AMERCE Law Ser.). (Illus.). 250p. 1988. 24.95 (*0-939776-09-X*) Blagrove Pubns.
— Law: AMERCE. abr. ed. (AMERCE Law Ser.). (Illus.). 250p. 1988. 24.95 (*0-939776-35-9*) Blagrove Pubns.
— Law: American AMERCE Emporium. abr. ed. (AMERCE Law Ser.). (Illus.). 250p. 1988. 24.95 (*0-939776-37-5*) Blagrove Pubns.
— Law: Lay Urania Deuteronomy Digamma. abr. ed. (AMERCE Law Ser.). (Illus.). 250p. 1988. 24.95 (*0-939776-08-1*) Blagrove Pubns.
— Management: Account (Accounting) abr. ed. (AMERCE Management Ser.). (Illus.). 250p. 1988. 24.95 (*0-939776-04-9*) Blagrove Pubns.
— Management: Covenants, Contracts. abr. ed. (AMERCE Management Ser.). (Illus.). 250p. 1988. 24.95 (*0-939776-02-2*) Blagrove Pubns.
— Management: Manage Mensurate. (AMERCE Management Ser.). (Illus.). 250p. 1988. 24.95 (*0-939776-05-7*) Blagrove Pubns.
— Management for Proprietors & Partnerships. abr. rev. ed. (AMERCE Management Ser.). (Illus.). 250p. 1988. 24.95 (*0-939776-03-0*) Blagrove Pubns.
— Problems & Solutions for Proprietors & Partnerships Business. abr. rev. ed. (AMERCE Business Ser.). (Illus.). 250p. 1988. 24.95 (*0-939776-12-X*) Blagrove Pubns.
— Proprietor, Proprietary. abr. ed. (Illus.). 250p. 1988. 24.95 (*0-939776-19-7*) Blagrove Pubns.
— Stratagem, Strategy. abr. ed. (Illus.). 275p. 1988. 24.95 (*0-685-17760-2*) Blagrove Pubns.
— Strategy for Minority Businesses. abr. rev. ed. (Illus.). 235p. 1988. pap. 10.95 (*0-685-17761-0*) Blagrove Pubns.
— Untapped Profits by Profession. abr. rev. ed. (Illus.). 250p. 1988. 29.95 (*0-939776-15-4*) Blagrove Pubns.
— Untold Facts about the Small Business Game: How to Be Competent in Business. abr. rev. ed. (Illus.). 250p. 1988. 24.95 (*0-939776-14-6*) Blagrove Pubns.
— Voodoo Lost Arts & Sciences. abr. ed. (Illus.). 250p. 1988. 24.95 (*0-939776-22-7*) Blagrove Pubns.
— Your Horoscope Hidden Magic. abr. ed. (Illus.). 225p. 1987. 24.95 (*0-939776-39-1*) Blagrove Pubns.
***Blagrove, Pauline E.** Ahem, a Medley of Poems. 40p. 1998. pap. 8.00 (*0-8059-4359-5*) Dorrance.
Blaha, Franz G. One Day in the Life of Ivan Denisovich Notes. (Cliffs Notes Ser.). 64p. (Orig.). (C). 1986. pap. text 4.95 (*0-8220-0960-9*, Cliff) IDG Bks.
Blaha, K & Malon, P., eds. Peptides, 1982: Proceedings of the 17th European Peptide Symposium, Prague, Czechoslovakia, August 29-September 3, 1982. (Illus.). 846p. 1982. 253.85 (*3-11-009574-2*) De Gruyter.
Blaha, Michael & Premerlain, William. Object-Oriented Modeling & Design for Database Applications. LC 97-27029. 484p. (C). 1997. 60.00 (*0-13-123829-9*) P-H.
Blaha, Robert B. Beyond Survival: Creating Prosperity Through People. 184p. 1995. 19.95 (*1-880156-04-0*) Air Acad Pr.
Blaha, Stephen. Java Jiving on the Net. (C). 2001. pap. 39.99 incl. cd-rom (*0-13-262197-5*) P-H.
Blaha, Stephen, jt. auth. see Rumbaugh, James.
Blaha, T., ed. Applied Veterinary Epidemiology. (Developments in Animal & Veterinary Science Ser.). 344p. 1989. 162.00 (*0-444-98854-8*) Elsevier.
Blahnik, G. Michael. Experience: An Exploration into the Structure & Dynamics of Human Consciousness. 428p. (C). 1997. 60.00 (*0-7618-0914-7*); pap. 32.50 (*0-7618-0915-5*) U Pr of Amer.
— Sense, Sex & Sin: Foundations for an Experientialist Ethics. LC 98-36801. 232p. 1998. 52.00 (*0-7618-1240-7*); pap. 34.50 (*0-7618-1241-5*) U Pr of Amer.
Blahnik, Jim, jt. auth. see Chiras, Daniel D.
Blahnik, Judith. Checklist for a Perfect Christmas. LC 96-12956. 128p. 1996. pap. 6.99 (*0-385-48221-3*) Doubleday.
Blahnik, Judith, jt. auth. see Leader, Daniel.
Blahnik, Roger J. A Revision of the Neotropical Species of the Genus Chimarra, Subgenus Chimarra (Trichoptera - Philopotamidae) (Memoirs of the American Entomological Institute Ser.: Vol. 59). (Illus.). 328p. 1998. 65.00 (*1-887988-03-3*) Am Entomol Inst.
***Blaho, Kari & Winbery, Stephen, eds.** Handbook of Chemical & Pharmacological Restraint. 450p. 2000. 125.00 (*0-89603-600-6*) Humana.
***Blahous, Charles P., III.** Reforming Social Security: For Ourselves & Our Posterity. LC 00-35968. 288p. 2000. 49.00 (*0-275-97044-2*, C7044) Greenwood.
***Blahut, Richard E.** Algebraic Codes for Data Transmission. (Illus.). 425p. (C). 2000. Price not set. (*0-521-55374-1*) Cambridge U Pr.
Blahut, Richard E., et al, eds. Communications & Cryptography: Two Sides of One Tapestry. LC 94-20006. (International Series in Engineering & Computer Science, VLSI, Computer Architecture, & Digital Screen Processing). 504p. (C). 1994. text 127.00 (*0-7923-9469-0*) Kluwer Academic.
Blahut, Richard E., et al. Radar & Sonar, Pt. 1. (IMA Volumes in Mathematics & Its Applications Ser.: Vol. 32). (Illus.). xi, 260p. 1991. 54.95 (*0-387-97516-0*) Spr-Verlag.
Blaich, Robert. New & Notable Product Design 2. 2nd ed. (Illus.). 192p. 1994. 39.99 (*1-56496-120-6*) Rockport Pubs.
Blaicher, Guenther. Freie Zeit-Langeweile-Literatur. Studien Zur Therapeutischen Funktion der Englischen Prosaliteratur im 18 Jahrhundert. (C). 1977. 102.35 (*3-11-006951-2*) De Gruyter.
Blaidsell, F. William & Trunkey, Donald D., eds. Abdominal Trauma: With Additional Chapters from Urogenital Trauma, 2 vols. in 1, Vol. II. 2nd ed. LC 92-49807. (Trauma Management Ser.: Vol. 1-2). 1992. 92.00 (*0-86577-453-6*) Thieme Med Pubs.
Blaikie, Andrew. Ageing & Popular Culture. LC 98-36035. (Illus.). 275p. (C). 1999. 59.95 (*0-521-55150-1*); pap. 24.95 (*0-521-64547-6*) Cambridge U Pr.
Blaikie, Andrew. Illegitimacy, Sex & Society: Mores in Northeast Scotland, 1750-1900. (Illus.). 286p. (C). 1994. text 59.00 (*0-19-828680-5*) OUP.
Blaikie, Norman W. Approaches to Social Enquiry. LC 93-19942. 280p. (C). 1993. 61.95 (*0-7456-1172-9*); pap. 26.95 (*0-7456-1173-7*) Blackwell Pubs.
— Designing Social Research: The Logic of Anticipation. LC 99-31730. 350p. (C). 2000. text 59.95 (*0-7456-1766-2*, Pub. by Polity Pr) Blackwell Pubs.
— Designing Social Research: The Magic of Anticipation. LC 99-31730. 350p. 2000. pap. text 29.95 (*0-7456-1767-0*, Pub. by Polity Pr) Blackwell Pubs.
Blaikie, Piers & Brookfield, Harold. Environment Land Management & Society. (C). 1999. write for info. (*0-415-08827-5*); pap. write for info. (*0-415-08828-3*) Routledge.
Blaikie, Piers, et al. At Risk: Natural Hazards, People's Vulnerability, & Disasters. LC 93-41114. (Illus.). 320p. (C). 1994. pap. 29.99 (*0-415-08477-6*, B3822) Routledge.
Blaikie, Piers, et al. Biodiversity, Human Welfare & Development. 1998. pap. text 29.95 (*0-471-96986-9*) Wiley.
***Blaikie, Piers, et al.** Biodiversity, Human Welfare & Development. 350p. 2000. 80.00 (*0-471-96985-0*) Wiley.
Blaikie, Piers, jt. auth. see Barnett, Tony.
Blaikie, William. How to Get Strong & How to Stay So. (Physical Education Reprint Ser.). (Illus.). reprint ed. lib. bdg. 32.50 (*0-697-00100-8*) Irvington.
Blaikie, William G. Personal Life of David Livingstone. LC 69-19353. (Illus.). 508p. 1969. lib. bdg. 35.00 (*0-8371-0518-8*, BLL&, Greenwood Pr) Greenwood.
Blaiklock, Edward M. The Pastoral Epistles. 128p. 1972. pap. 7.99 (*0-310-21233-2*, 9232P) Zondervan.
— The Zondervan Pictorial Bible Atlas. (Illus.). 1963. 27.95 (*0-310-21240-5*, 6763) Zondervan.
Blaiklock, Edward M. & Harrison, R. K., eds. The New International Dictionary of Biblical Archaeology. 1983. 34.99 (*0-310-21250-2*, 9277) Zondervan.
Blaiklock, M., tr. see Rolland, Romain.
Blail, N., et al. Physician's Guide to the Laboratory Diagnosis of Inherited Metabolic Diseases. (Arnold Publication Ser.). (Illus.). 544p. 1996. text 69.00 (*0-412-57560-4*) OUP.
Blain, Alexander. Clackshant. Leo, Kathleen R., ed. LC 82-80034. (Illus.). (Orig.). 1982. pap. 5.00 (*0-9606678-1-4*) Sylvan Pubns.
Blain, Angeline Kearns. Tactical Textiles: A Genealogy of the Boise Peace Quilt Project. 112p. (C). 1996. pap. text, per. 18.95 (*0-8403-9683-X*) Kendall-Hunt.
***BLAIN, C. R.** Bonus Study of Incentive Scheme's Operating in the Construction Industry. 70p. (C). (gr. 13). 1998. pap. text 32.99 (*1-85032-026-8*) ITCP.
Blain, Christophe, et al. Travel Tales: Ten Fun-Filled Adventures. LC 98-21103. (Illus.). 80p. (J). 1998. 14.95 (*0-8109-3895-2*, Pub. by Abrams) Time Warner.
Blain, Diane. The Boxcar Children Cookbook. Tucker, Kathy, ed. LC 91-15080. (Illus.). 96p. (J). (gr. 2-8). 1991. pap. 9.95 (*0-8075-0856-X*) A Whitman.
Blain, Hugh M. Favorite Huey Long Stories. 1996. pap. text 5.95 (*0-87511-713-9*) Claitors.
— Favorite Huey P. Long Stories. 1977. pap. 5.95 (*0-87511-712-0*) Claitors.
***Blain, Jean-Baptiste.** The Life of John Baptist de La Salle, Founder of the Brothers of the Christian Schools: A Biography in Three Books. Salm, Luke, ed. Arnandez, Richard, tr. from FRE. (Lasallian Resources Ser.: Vol. 2, Bk. 1). Orig. Title: La Vie de Jean-Baptiste de La Salle, Instituteur des Freres des Ecoles Chretiennes. (Illus.). xiv, 158p. 2000. 25.00 (*0-944808-33-6*); pap. 20.00 (*0-944808-34-4*) Lasallian Pubns.
Blain, Jennifer & Burton, Lesley. A Book of Beasts & Monsters. (Illus.). 48p. 1992. 3.98 (*1-55859-444-2*) Abbeville Pr.
— A Book of Birds. (Illus.). 48p. 1992. 6.95 (*1-55859-442-6*) Abbeville Pr.
— A Book of Sea Creatures. (Illus.). 48p. 1992. 3.98 (*1-55859-443-4*) Abbeville Pr.
Blain, Jonathan, jt. auth. see Elkington, Gray.
Blain, Michael J. Introduction to Sociology: A Lecture & Study Guide. 112p. (C). 1995. spiral bd. 11.95 (*0-8403-7914-5*) Kendall-Hunt.
***Blain, Michael J.** Introduction to Sociology: A Lecture & Study Guide. 2nd ed. 100p. (C). 1998. spiral bd. 12.95 (*0-7872-4717-0*) Kendall-Hunt.
Blain, Michael J., jt. auth. see Roche, Edward M.
Blain, Neil, et al. Sport & the Mass Media: National & European Identities. 256p. 1993. pap. text 29.00 (*0-7185-1451-3*, Pub. by Leicester U Pr) Cassell & Continuum.
Blain, Peter G. & Harris, John B., eds. Medical Neurotoxicology: Occupational & Environmental Causes of Neurological Dysfunction. LC 99-16934. (An Arnold Publication). (Illus.). 388p. 1999. text 150.00 (*0-340-59665-1*, Pub. by E A) OUP.
Blain, R., ed. Marina Developments. 301p. 1993. 81.00 (*0-614-16833-3*, CM149) Am Soc Civil Eng.
***Blain, Rony.** Miroir du Soleil. 98p. 2000. pap. 15.00 (*1-886699-31-3*) Five Corners.
Blain, Rony. Reflexions. (ENG & FRE.). 64p. 1999. pap. 9.95 (*1-886699-16-X*) Five Corners.
Blain, Susan A., ed. Imaging the Word: An Arts & Lectionary Resource, Vol. 3. (Illus.). 280p. 1996. pap. 34.95 (*0-8298-1086-2*) Pilgrim OH.
— Imaging the Word Vol. 3: An Arts & Lectionary Resource, Vol. 3. (Illus.). 280p. 1996. 44.95 (*0-8298-1085-4*) Pilgrim OH.
Blain, Virginia. Caroline Bowles Southey, 1786-1854: The Making of a Woman Writer. LC 97-39920. (Nineteenth Century Ser.). 250p. 1997. text 86.95 (*1-85928-197-4*, Pub. by Ashgate Pub) Ashgate Pub Co.
Blain, Virginia, et al. The Feminist Companion to Literature in English: Women Writers from the Middle Ages to the Present. LC 90-70515. 1200p. (C). 1990. 60.00 (*0-300-04854-8*) Yale U Pr.
Blain, Virginia, ed. & intro. see Collins, Wilkie.
Blain, W. Edward. Passion Play. 320p. 1991. pap. 3.95 (*0-380-71450-7*, Avon Bks) Morrow Avon.
Blain, W. R., ed. Hydraulic Engineering Software VII. LC 99-220815. (Water Studies: Vol. 4). 624p. 1998. 295.00 (*1-85312-599-7*, 5997) Computational Mech MA.
— Hydraulic Engineering Software VI. LC 96-83662. (HYDROSOFT Ser.: Vol. 6). 650p. 1996. text 243.00 (*1-85312-405-2*, 4052) Computational Mech MA.
Blain, W. R., ed. Marina Technology. 644p. 1992. 198.00 (*1-85312-161-4*) Computational Mech MA.
Blain, W. R., ed. Marina Technology. 632p. 1992. text 156.00 (*0-7277-1689-1*, Pub. by T Telford) RCH.
— Marina Technology II. LC 91-77630. (Marinas Ser.: Vol. 2). 644p. 1992. 198.00 (*1-56252-089-X*, 1614) Computational Mech MA.
Blain, W. R., ed. Marina III: Planning, Design & Operation. 338p. 1995. 147.00 (*1-85312-312-9*) Computational Mech MA.
Blain, W. R. & Brebbia, Carlos A., eds. Hydraulic Engineering Software VIII. (Water Studies : Vol. 7). 480p. 2000. 222.00 (*1-85312-814-7*, 8147, Pub. by WIT Pr) Computational Mech MA.
Blain, W. R. & Cabrera, E., eds. Hydraulic Engineering Software Copublished With Computational Mechanics Publications UK, 2 vols., Set, Vol. IV. (Illus.). 1200p. (C). (gr. 13). 1992. text 460.00 (*1-85166-852-7*) Elsevier Applied Sci.
Blain, W. R. & Cabrera, E., eds. Hydraulic Engineering Software IV: Computer Techniques & Applications, Vol. 2. 628p. 1992. 199.00 (*1-85312-202-5*) Computational Mech MA.
— Hydraulic Engineering Software IV: Fluid Flow Modeling, Vol. 1. 654p. 1992. 206.00 (*1-85312-201-7*) Computational Mech MA.
Blain, W. R. & De Wilde, W. P., eds. Computer Aided Design in Composite Material Technology. LC 96-83658. (CADCOMP Ser.: Vol. 5). 376p. 1996. 169.00 (*1-85312-401-X*, 401X) Computational Mech MA.
Blain, W. R. & DeWilde, W. P., eds. Computer Aided Design in Composite Material Technology IV. LC 94-70405. (CADCOMP Ser.: Vol. 4). 440p. 1994. 167.00 (*1-56252-187-X*, 2637) Computational Mech MA.
Blain, W. R. & Katsafarakis, K. L., eds. Hydraulic Engineering Software V, 2 vols., Set. LC 94-72457. (HYDROSOFT Ser.: Vol. 5). 760p. 1994. text 321.00 (*1-56252-194-2*, 270X) Computational Mech MA.
Blain, W. R. & Katsifarakis, K. L., eds. Hydraulic Engineering Software V: Free Surface Flow & Hydraulic Software, Vol. 2. 344p. 1994. 158.00 (*1-85312-366-8*) Computational Mech MA.
Blain, W. R. & Katsifarakis, L. Hydraulic Engineering Software V: Free Surface Flow & Hydraulic Software, Vol. 2. LC 94-72457. (HYDROSOFT Ser.: Vol. 5). 344p. 1994. 158.00 (*1-56252-290-6*, 3660) Computational Mech MA.
— Hydraulic Engineering Software V: Water Resources & Distribution, Vol. 1. LC 94-72457. (Hydrosoft Ser.: Vol. 5). 416p. 1994. 189.00 (*1-56252-289-2*, 365X) Computational Mech MA.
Blain, W. R. & Ouazar, D., eds. Hydraulic Engineering: Software Applications. LC 89-82715. (HYDROSOFT Ser.: Vol. 3). 500p. 1990. 150.00 (*0-945824-43-2*) Computational Mech MA.
Blain, W. R., jt. ed. see De Wilde, W. P.
Blaine. Diagnosis & Severity of Drug Abuse & Drug Dependence. 1996. lib. bdg. 252.75 (*0-8490-6893-2*) Gordon Pr.
Blaine, et al. Abstracts of Lucas County Wills: Volumes 1 to 6, to the Year 1874. (Illus.). 125p. 1997. reprint ed. pap. 17.50 (*0-8328-6339-4*) Higginson Bk Co.
Blaine, jt. auth. see Tepperman.
Blaine, B. Michael. Joseph Is Alive: A Scriptural Study of the Restoration of Israel in God's Covenant Promises. 112p. 1995. pap. 6.95 (*0-945460-18-X*) Upward Way.
***Blaine, Bruce E.** The Psychology of Diversity: Perceiving & Experiencing Social America. LC 99-44172. 1999. pap. text 29.95 (*1-55934-938-7*) Mayfield Pub.
Blaine, Carolyn, ed. see Blaine, Chris.
Blaine, Charles G. Federal Regulation of Bank Holding Companies: An Analysis of the Bank Holding Company Act of 1956, as Amended. LC 73-75982. 499p. reprint ed. pap. 154.70 (*0-608-12742-6*, 202434300037) Bks Demand.
Blaine, Chris. Beyond Hocus - Pocus, Vol. 1. Blaine, Sally, ed. (Illus.). 76p. (YA). (gr. 6 up). 1997. 6.95 (*1-892250-00-4*) Barnett Educ.
— Beyond Hocus - Pocus, Vol. 2. Blaine, Sally, ed. (Illus.). 81p. (YA). (gr. 6 up). 1998. 6.95 (*1-892250-01-2*) Barnett Educ.
— Beyond Hocus - Pocus, Vol. 3. Blaine, Sally, ed. (Illus.). 84p. (YA). (gr. 6 up). 1998. 6.95 (*1-892250-02-0*) Barnett Educ.
— Beyond Hocus-Pocus, Vol. IV. Blaine, Sally & Blaine, Carolyn, eds. (Illus.). 68p. 1999. per. 6.95 (*1-892250-03-9*) Barnett Educ.
***Blaine, G. James & Horii, Steven C., eds.** PACS Design & Evaluation. 460p. 1999. pap. text 111.00 (*0-8194-3134-6*) SPIE.
Blaine, G. James, jt. ed. see Horii, Steven C.
Blaine, Hal & Goggin, David. Hal Blaine & the Wrecking Crew. LC 89-18364. 192p. 1990. pap. 19.95 (*0-918371-01-5*, 00330037, MixBooks) Intertec Pub.
Blaine, J. C. End of an Era in Space Exploration. Jacobs, H., ed. (Science & Technology Ser.: Vol. 42). 216p. 1976. 25.00 (*0-87703-084-7*) Univelt Inc.
— The End of an Era in Space Exploration, from International Rivalry to International Cooperation. (Science & Technology Ser.: Vol. 42). (Illus.). 216p. 1976. 25.00 (*0-87703-080-4*, Am Astronaut Soc) Univelt Inc.
Blaine, Jack D., et al, eds. Diagnosis & Severity of Drug Abuse & Drug Dependence. (Illus.). 84p. (C). 1997. reprint ed. pap. text 25.00 (*0-7881-4602-5*) DIANE Pub.
Blaine, Jack D. & Julius, Demetrios A., eds. Psychodynamics of Drug Dependence. LC 93-35969. 196p. 1994. pap. 40.00 (*1-56821-157-0*) Aronson.
Blaine, Jeff. Black Jo of the Pecos. large type ed. (Linford Western Library). 256p. 1997. pap. 16.99 (*0-7089-5000-0*, Linford) Ulverscroft.
Blaine, Martha R. Pawnee Passage, 1870-1875. LC 90-50228. (Civilization of the American Indian Ser.: Vol. 202). (Illus.). 352p. 1990. 31.95 (*0-8061-2300-1*) U of Okla Pr.
— Some Things Are Not Forgotten: A Pawnee Family Remembers. LC 97-2187. (Illus.). xxii, 286p. 1997. text 55.00 (*0-8032-1275-5*) U of Nebr Pr.
Blaine, Marty, jt. auth. see Cobb, Suzanne.
Blaine, Mary R. The Ioway Indians. LC 94-41426. (Civilization of the American Indian Ser.: Vol. 151). (Illus.). 384p. 1995. pap. 19.95 (*0-8061-2728-7*) U of Okla Pr.
Blaine, Micahel. The Desperate Season. LC 99-14262. 304p. 1999. 24.00 (*0-688-16441-2*, Wm Morrow) Morrow Avon.
Blaine, Michael J. Co-Operation in International Business: The Use of Limited Equity Arrangements. 240p. 1994. 77.95 (*1-85628-683-5*, Pub. by Avebry) Ashgate Pub Co.
Blaine, Michael J. & Roche, Edward Mosley, eds. Information Technology In Multinational Enterprises. (New Horizons in International Business Ser.). 336p. 2000. text 95.00 (*1-85898-979-5*) E Elgar.
Blaine, R. L. & Schoff, C. K., eds. Purity Determinations by Thermal Methods - STP 838. LC 83-72815. 150p. 1984. text 24.00 (*0-8031-0222-4*, STP838) ASTM.
Blaine, Sally, ed. see Blaine, Chris.
Blaine, Tom R. Goodbye Allergies. 1988. pap. 6.95 (*0-8065-1088-9*, Citadel Pr) Carol Pub Group.
Blaine, William L., ed. see California Continuing Education of the Bar Staff.
Blainey, Geoffrey. The Causes of War. 3rd ed. 344p. 1988. pap. 14.95 (*0-02-903591-0*) Free Pr.
— The Causes of War. 3rd ed. 312p. 1988. 29.95 (*0-02-903592-9*) Free Pr.
— Essington Lewis: The Steel Master. 1996. pap. 19.95 (*0-522-84709-9*, Pub. by Melbourne Univ Pr) Paul & Co Pubs.
— The Rush That Never Ended: A History of Australian Mining. 4th ed. 404p. 1993. pap. 29.95 (*0-522-84557-6*, Pub. by Melbourne Univ Pr) Paul & Co Pubs.
— Triumph of the Nomads: A History of Aboriginal Australia. LC 75-37122. 304p. 1982. 22.95 (*0-87951-043-9*, Pub. by Overlook Pr); pap. 13.95 (*0-87951-084-6*, Pub. by Overlook Pr) Penguin Putnam.
Blainey, P. D. Parents: The Astonishing Secret Benefits for Kids to Play Sports. 220p. 1994. 27.00 (*0-9642277-0-3*) Cicero Better.
Blair. Measuring Learning in Organizations. 300p. 1998. 39.95 (*0-88415-476-9*, 5476) Gulf Pub.
***Blair.** Sweetest Thing. 2000. pap. 8.95 (*0-553-40373-7*, Pub. by Transworld Publishers Ltd) Trafalgar.
Blair. William & Caroline Herschel. (J). 1995. pap. text. write for info. (*0-7167-6596-9*); pap. text. write for info. (*0-7167-6597-7*) W H Freeman.
Blair & Tobey. Prealgebra. (C). 1998. pap. text, student ed. write for info. (*0-13-020669-5*) P-H.
— Prealgebra. LC 99-10558. 704p. 1999. pap. text 78.00 (*0-13-260936-3*, Pub. by P-H) S&S Trade.
***Blair, A. M. & Hitchcock, David.** Environment & Business. LC 00-38256. (Introductions to Environment Ser.). 2000. pap. write for info. (*0-415-20831-9*) Routledge.
Blair, Adam. Adam Blair. 208p. 1989. pap. 36.00 (*1-873644-37-X*, Pub. by Mercat Pr Bks) St Mut.
Blair, Al. Adam & Eve Bad Advice Rag. 4p. 1990. pap. 3.95 (*0-930366-24-7*) Northcountry Pub.
— Ain't No Cure for Rock & Roll. 6p. 1988. pap. 3.95 (*0-930366-21-2*) Northcountry Pub.
— Cockroach Crawl. 4p. 1990. pap. 3.95 (*0-930366-25-5*) Northcountry Pub.
— The Data Processing Salvation Jump. 6p. 1988. pap. 3.95 (*0-930366-33-6*) Northcountry Pub.
— Dayton's Shopping Glide, a Pocketbook Flattener. 4p. 1990. pap. 3.95 (*0-930366-18-2*) Northcountry Pub.
— Doin' the Minneapolis Mammy Jammy Sleaze. 4p. 1988. pap. 3.95 (*0-930366-16-6*) Northcountry Pub.
— Fool Is My Middle Name. 6p. 1990. pap. 3.95 (*0-930366-42-5*) Northcountry Pub.
— Fruit Soup & Lefse Waddle. 4p. 1990. pap. 3.95 (*0-930366-26-3*) Northcountry Pub.
— Iggy's Gone to Snowmobile Heaven. 6p. 1988. pap. 3.95 (*0-930366-32-8*) Northcountry Pub.
— Janitor Holler. 4p. 1990. pap. 3.95 (*0-930366-45-X*) Northcountry Pub.
— Jesus Is a Nice Jewish Boy. 4p. 1990. pap. 3.95 (*0-930366-17-4*) Northcountry Pub.

An Asterisk (*) at the beginning of an entry indicates that the title is appearing for the first time.

— Little Garage of Love. 4p. 1990. pap. 3.95 (*0-930366-34-4*) Northcountry Pub.
— Minnesota Mummy, Don't You Try to Tut Tut Me. 8p. 1990. pap. 3.95 (*0-930366-44-1*) Northcountry Pub.
— Minnesota Shouts, Stomps, & Syncopated Hollers. 54p. 1988. pap. 9.75 (*0-930366-50-6*) Northcountry Pub.
— Moosewhopper: A Juicy, Moosey Min-Min-Minnesota Burger Tale. 3rd ed. LC 83-61092. (Illus.). 32p. (J). (gr. 3). 1983. pap. 3.95 (*0-930366-04-2*) Northcountry Pub.
— Never Too Old to Rock & Roll. 4p. 1988. pap. 3.95 (*0-930366-20-4*) Northcountry Pub.
— Painless Ingebretsen, The Rock & Roll Dentist. 4p. 1988. pap. 3.95 (*0-930366-28-X*) Northcountry Pub.
— Pig's Eye Sewage Treatment Plant Rock. 6p. 1988. pap. 3.95 (*0-930366-49-2*) Northcountry Pub.
— Pork Chop Santa. 6p. 1990. pap. 3.95 (*0-930366-41-7*) Northcountry Pub.
— Snotball Rock. 6p. 1990. pap. 3.95 (*0-930366-53-0*) Northcountry Pub.
— Syncopated Minnesota Novelties for Young People in Schools & Other Bad Places. 22p. 1988. pap. 12.75 (*0-930366-54-9*) Northcountry Pub.
— Syncopated Songs That Are Banned in Forade, Starbuck & Thief River Falls. 14p. 1988. pap. 7.25 (*0-930366-35-2*) Northcountry Pub.
— Teenage Shitkicker Shout. 4p. 1990. pap. 3.95 (*0-930366-31-X*) Northcountry Pub.
— Teenage Spaceblob Love. 6p. 1990. pap. 3.95 (*0-930366-43-3*) Northcountry Pub.
— They're Yodeling Rock & Roll Songs. 6p. 1988. pap. 3.95 (*0-930366-51-4*) Northcountry Pub.
— Vasectomy Blues. 6p. 1990. pap. 3.95 (*0-930366-22-0*) Northcountry Pub.

Blair, Alan, tr. see Lagerkvist, Par.

Blair, Alan, tr. see Sjowall, Maj & Wahloo, Per.

***Blair, Alaric Wendell.** The End of Innocence: A Journey into the Life. LC 98-67788. 249 p. 1998. write for info. (*0-9667183-0-5*) Mirage Pubg Co.

Blair, Alasdair. Dealing with Europe: Britain & the Negotiation of the Maastricht Treaty. LC 99-72241. 276p. 1999. 69.95 (*1-84014-762-8*, Pub. by Ashgate Pub) Ashgate Pub Co.
— The Longman Companion to the European Union since 1945. LC 98-51662. (Companions to History Ser.). 400p. 1999. pap. text 27.95 (*0-582-36884-7*) Longman.

***Blair, Alasdair.** Longman Companion to the European Union, 1945-1999. LC 98-51662. 400p. 1999. 76.50 (*0-582-36885-5*) Addison-Wesley.

Blair, Alice C. No-Nonsense Principal Handbook for Educators. LC 82-50907. (Illus.). 112p. 1982. 14.50 (*0-941484-02-5*) Urban Res Pr.

Blair, Allen M. Concise Economic Overview of Japanese Money. 12p. 1996. pap. 6.95 (*0-930366-91-3*) Northcountry Pub.
— Concise Economic Overview of Southeast Asia Money. 12p. 1996. pap. 6.95 (*0-930366-90-5*) Northcountry Pub.
— A Concise Historical Economic Overview of Chinese Money. LC 97-221365. 12p. 1997. pap. 6.95 (*0-930366-92-1*) Northcountry Pub.
— Minnesota Rock & Roll Novelties for People Who Aren't Deaf Yet. 13p. 1987. pap. 7.25 (*0-930366-11-5*) Northcountry Pub.
— Syncopated Gospel & Bible-Related Songs for Minnesotans Who Don't Go to Church Much. 13p. 1987. pap. 6.25 (*0-930366-38-7*) Northcountry Pub.
— A World of Money from the Earliest Times: A Concise Non-Eurocentric History of the World's Native Currencies. 2nd ed. LC 97-183110. (Illus.). 166p. (Orig.). 1997. pap., spiral bd. 37.50 (*0-930366-93-X*); per. 29.95 (*0-930366-94-8*) Northcountry Pub.

Blair, Alma. The Dark Side of Paradise. large type ed. 238p. 1992. reprint ed. lib. bdg. 13.95 (*1-56054-537-2*) Thorndike Pr.

Blair, Andrea L. Not My Way. 128p. 1996. 9.95 (*1-883520-23-1*) Jeremiah Pr.

Blair, Ann, jt. ed. see Grafton, Anthony.

Blair, Anna. Croft & Creel: A Hundred Years of Coastal Memories. LC 87-60970. (Illus.). 240p. 1992. pap. 7.95 (*0-85683-096-8*, Pub. by Shepheard-Walwyn Pubs) Paul & Co Pubs.
— More Tea at Miss Cranston's. (Illus.). 240p. 1985. pap. 8.95 (*0-85683-127-1*, Pub. by Shepheard-Walwyn Pubs) Paul & Co Pubs.
— Seed Corn & Other Short Stories. 192p. 1981. pap. 7.95 (*0-85683-118-2*, Pub. by Shepheard-Walwyn Pubs) Paul & Co Pubs.
— Tea at Miss Cranston's: A Century of Glasgow Memories. (Illus.). 224p. (Orig.). 1984. pap. 7.95 (*0-85683-081-X*, Pub. by Shepheard-Walwyn Pubs) Paul & Co Pubs.
— Tea at Miss Cranston's: A Century of Glasgow Memories. 2nd large type ed. 288p. (Orig.). 1993. 23.95 (*1-85695-326-2*, Pub. by ISIS Lrg Prnt) Transaction Pubs.

***Blair, Anne.** Ratter Chatter: An Anthology of Rat Terrier Conversations. deluxe ed. (Illus.). 120p. 1999. 18.95 (*0-9675670-0-9*) A J Enter.

Blair, Anne E. Lodge in Vietnam: A Patriot Abroad. LC 94-38192. 200p. 1995. 32.00 (*0-300-06226-5*) Yale U Pr.

***Blair, Annette J.** Thee, I Love! (Zebra Splendor Historical Romances Ser.). 1999. mass mkt. 4.99 (*0-8217-6355-5*, Zebra Kensgtn) Kensgtn Pub Corp.

Blair, Anthony, jt. auth. see Johnson, Ralph.

Blair, Arthur H. At War in the Gulf: A Chronology. LC 91-33371. (Illus.). 144p. (Orig.). 1992. pap. 10.95 (*0-89096-507-2*) Tex A&M Univ Pr.

Blair, B. M. & Hitchens, D. M. Campus Companies - U. K. & Ireland. LC 97-78427. (Illus.). 346p. 1998. text 72.95 (*1-84014-198-0*, Pub. by Ashgate Pub) Ashgate Pub Co.

Blair, Barry, jt. auth. see Pini, Richard.

Blair, Beryl. Road Charging in the 90s: An Overview & Guide to the Literature. LC 95-132780. (Keynote Ser.). 112p. 1994. pap. 39.95 (*0-7123-0814-8*, Pub. by SRIS) L Erlbaum Assocs.

Blair, Beryl, jt. auth. see Worsford, Frank.

Blair, Beth L., jt. auth. see Ericsson, Jennifer A.

Blair, Betty, ed. Azerbaijan: Land of Fire. LC 97-127167. (Illus.). 1996. pap. 25.00 (*0-9654388-0-5*) Azerbaijan Intl.

Blair, Betty, jt. auth. see Aliev, Gefidar H.

***Blair, Bevelyn W.** Bevelyn Blair's Everyday Cakes: The Ultimate Workday, Weekend, & Special Occasion Cake Book! LC 99-88834. (Illus.). 282p. 2000. 22.50 (*1-892514-61-3*) Hill St Pr.
— Bevelyn Blair's Everyday Pies. (Illus.). 2000. 22.50 (*1-892514-90-7*) Hill St Pr.

Blair, Bevelyn W. Country Cakes. LC 84-72948. (Illus.). 240p. 1984. 18.95 (*0-9613709-0-4*) Blair Columbus.
— Meet Me in the Kitchen: A Timeless Collection of Kitchen Tested Recipes! (Illus.). 320p. (Orig.). 1990. pap. 15.95 (*0-9613709-1-2*) Blair Columbus.

Blair, Billie & Fischer, Cheryl. Curriculum: Key to Schooling. 2nd ed. LC 95-236467. 288p. (C). 1995. per. 39.95 (*0-7872-1595-3*, 41159501) Kendall-Hunt.

Blair, Billie G. & Caine, Renate N., eds. Integrative Learning As the Pathway to Teaching for Holism, Complexity & Interconnectedness. LC 94-40518. 128p. 1995. pap. 14.95 (*0-7734-9153-8*) E Mellen.

Blair, Bonnie & Brown, Greg. A Winning Edge. LC 96-456. (Illus.). 40p. (J). (gr. 3-7). 1996. 14.95 (*0-87833-931-0*) Taylor Pub.

Blair, Brenda R. Supervisors & Managers As Enablers. 16p. 1983. pap. 2.75 (*0-935908-13-7*, 3281, HazeldenJohnson Inst) Hazelden.
— The Supervisor's Role in Early Recovery. 24p. 1991. pap. 3.25 (*1-56246-014-5*, 3285, HazeldenJohnson Inst) Hazelden.

Blair, Bruce. Rail Trail Handbook. 1996. pap. 13.95 (*0-931714-71-0*, Pub. by Nodin Pr) Bookmen Inc.

Blair, Bruce, et al. The Nuclear Turning Point: A Blueprint for Deep Cuts & De-Alerting of Nuclear Weapons. LC 98-58149. 420p. 1999. 52.95 (*0-8157-0954-4*); pap. 22.95 (*0-8157-0953-6*) Brookings.

Blair, Bruce G. De-Alerting Strategic Forces. 90p. 1998. pap. 14.95 (*0-8157-1007-0*) Brookings.
— Global Zero Alert for Nuclear Forces. 108p. (C). 1995. pap. 10.95 (*0-8157-0941-2*) Brookings.
— The Logic of Accidental Nuclear War. 364p. 1993. 49.95 (*0-8157-0984-6*); pap. 22.95 (*0-8157-0983-8*) Brookings.
— Strategic Command & Control: Redefining the Nuclear Threat. LC 84-73164. 341p. 1985. 42.95 (*0-8157-0982-X*); pap. 18.95 (*0-8157-0981-1*) Brookings.

Blair, Bruce G. & Brewer, Garry D. Verifying SALT Agreements. (CISA Working Papers: No. 19). 61p. (Orig.). 1980. pap. 15.00 (*0-86682-018-3*) Ctr Intl Relations.

Blair, Bruce Van, see Van Blair, Bruce.

Blair, Burton F. Amid His Pain...He Said: Sermons on the Seven Words from the Cross. LC 95-39882. (Orig.). 1996. pap. 6.95 (*0-7880-0730-0*) CSS OH.
— The Christ Who Is Hidden. 1991. pap. 6.95 (*1-55673-295-3*, 9128) CSS OH.

Blair, C., jt. ed. see Tarassuk, L.

Blair, Carroll. Facing the Circle. LC 98-42606. 88p. 1998. pap. 14.95 (*0-7734-3094-6*) E Mellen.
— Reel to Real. LC 99-25554. 104p. 1999. pap. 19.95 (*0-7734-3111-X*) E Mellen.

Blair, Carvel H. & Ansel, Willits D. Chesapeake Bay: Notes & Sketches. fac. ed. LC 76-124311. (Illus.). 184p. pap. 57.10 (*0-7837-7301-3*, AU0045000007) Bks Demand.
— A Guide to Fishing Boats & Their Gear. LC 68-19048. (Illus.). 154p. reprint ed. pap. 47.80 (*0-7837-4378-5*, 204411800012) Bks Demand.

***Blair, Catherine.** Hero Returns. 1999. mass mkt. 4.99 (*0-8217-6448-9*) Kensgtn Pub Corp.
— His Bride to Be. (Zebra Regency Romance Ser.). 2000. mass mkt. 4.99 (*0-8217-6610-4*, Zebra Kensgtn) Kensgtn Pub Corp.

Blair, Chad. Money, Color & Sex in Hawai'i's Politics. 208p. 1998. pap. 12.95 (*1-56647-218-0*) Mutual Pub HI.

Blair, Charesa M. & Patrick, Randy R. Hiking Indiana No. 2: Turkey Run State Park. (Illus.). 96p. 1998. pap. 8.95 (*0-9659927-1-3*, HI2) Memories Forever.

Blair, Charesa M., jt. auth. see Patrick, Randy R.

Blair, Charles. Lose the Weight of the World: The Five Days Spiritual Fitness Plan for Your Soul. LC 97-65168. 284p. 1997. pap. 11.95 (*0-89221-346-9*) New Leaf.

Blair, Chauncey J. Heat in the Rig Veda & Atharva Veda. (American Oriental Ser.: Vol. 45). xvi, 190p. 1961. 8.00 (*0-940490-45-5*) Am Orient Soc.

Blair, Christopher, jt. auth. see Quest-Ritson, Charles.

Blair, Claude, et al. The Crown Jewels: The History of the Coronation Regalia in the Jewel House of the Tower of London, 2 vols. limited ed. (Illus.). 1492p. 1998. boxed set 2190.00 (*0-11-701359-5*, Pub. by Statnry Office) Balogh.
— Studies in European Arms & Armor: The C. Otto von Kienbusch Collection in the Philadelphia Museum of Art. LC 91-47037. (Illus.). 208p. 1992. pap. 30.00 (*0-87633-088-X*) Phila Mus Art.

Blair, Clay. Hitler's U-Boat War: The German Navy in World War II: The Hunters, 1939-1942. LC 96-2275. 864p. 1996. 45.00 (*0-394-58839-8*) Random.

***Blair, Clay.** Hitler's U-Boat War: The Hunted, 1942-1944. Vol. 1. 944p. 2000. pap. 18.95 (*0-679-64033-9*) Modern Lib NY.
— Hitler's U-Boat War: The Hunters, 1939-1942, Vol. 2. Vol. 2. 848p. 2000. pap. 18.95 (*0-679-64032-0*) Modern Lib NY.

Blair, Clay. Hitler's U-Boat War Vol. 2: The Hunted, 1942-1944. LC 96-2275. (Illus.). 864p. 1998. 45.00 (*0-679-45742-9*) Random.
— Hitler's U-Boat War, the German Navy in World War II Vol. 1: The Hunters, 1939-1942. LC 96-2275. 1996. write for info. (*0-614-98005-4*) Random.

Blair, Clay, jt. auth. see Bradley, Omar N., Jr.

Blair, Clay, jt. auth. see Bradley, Omar N.

Blair, Clay, Jr., jt. auth. see Crossfield, A. Scott.

Blair, Clay, jt. auth. see Shepley, James R., Jr.

Blair, Clifford. Devil's Canyon Double Cross. large type ed. 251p. 1992. reprint ed. lib. bdg. 14.95 (*1-56054-572-0*) Thorndike Pr.
— Ghost-Town Gold. large type ed. (Popular Ser.). 239p. 1993. reprint ed. lib. bdg. 14.95 (*1-56054-633-6*) Thorndike Pr.
— The Guns of Sacred Heart. 192p. 1991. 18.95 (*0-8027-4123-1*) Walker & Co.
— The Guns of Sacred Heart. large type ed. 301p. 1992. reprint ed. lib. bdg. 15.95 (*1-56054-404-X*) Thorndike Pr.
— Peacemaker for Hire. (Peacemaker Western Ser.: Bk. 1). 1995. 18.95 (*0-8034-9110-7*, 095141, Avalon Bks) Bouregy.
— Peacemaker Law. LC 96-95285. (Peacemaker Western Ser.: Bk. 2). 192p. 1997. 18.95 (*0-8034-9195-6*, Avalon Bks) Bouregy.

***Blair, Clifford.** Peacemaker Prey. LC 00-190023. 192p. 2000. 18.95 (*0-8034-9420-3*, Avalon Bks) Bouregy.

Blair, Clifford. Peacemaker Rawhide. LC 97-94277. (Peacemaker Western Ser.: Bk. 3). 192p. 1997. 17.95 (*0-8034-9271-5*, Avalon Bks) Bouregy.
— Showdown at Viking Cave. LC 93-37908. 198p. 1994. 19.95 (*0-8027-4136-3*) Walker & Co.
— Showdown at Viking Cave. large type ed. LC 94-27154. 255p. 1994. pap. 18.95 (*0-8161-7473-3*, G K Hall Lrg Type) Mac Lib Ref.
— Storm over the Lightning L. 192p. 1993. 19.95 (*0-8027-1236-3*) Walker & Co.
— Storm over the Lightning L. large type ed. LC 93-1387. 316p. 1993. lib. bdg. 17.95 (*1-56054-719-7*) Thorndike Pr.

***Blair, Cornelia, ed.** Homeless in America: How Could It Happen Here? rev. ed. (Information Plus Reference Ser.). (Illus.). 108p. 1999. pap. text 25.95 (*1-57302-098-2*) Info Plus TX.
— Water: No Longer Taken for Granted. rev. ed. (Information Plus Reference Ser.). (Illus.). 156p. 1999. pap. text 25.95 (*1-57302-099-0*) Info Plus TX.

Blair, Cornelia, et al, eds. Endangered Species: Must They Disappear? 4th rev. ed. (Information Plus Reference Ser.). (Illus.). 172p. 1998. pap. text 25.95 (*1-57302-075-3*) Info Plus TX.
— The Environment: A Revolution in Attitudes. 4th rev. ed. (Information Plus Reference Ser.). (Illus.). 192p. 1998. pap. text 26.95 (*1-57302-076-1*) Info Plus TX.
— Garbage & Other Pollution. 3rd rev. ed. (Information Plus Reference Ser.). (Illus.). 160p. 1998. pap. text 25.95 (*1-57302-064-8*) Info Plus TX.
— Growing Old in America. 10th rev. ed. (Information Plus Reference Ser.). (Illus.). 168p. 1998. pap. text 26.95 (*1-57302-065-6*) Info Plus TX.

***Blair, Cornelia, et al, eds.** Recreation: Having a Good Time in America. (Reference Ser.). (Illus.). 100p. 1999. pap. text 25.95 (*1-57302-084-2*) Info Plus TX.

***Blair, Cynthia.** Curse. 2000. mass mkt. 1.99 (*0-06-106261-8*) HarpC.

Blair, Cynthia & Bell, Mike. The Skier's Book of Trail Maps. (Illus.). 88p. 1997. pap. 19.95 (*0-9660031-2-8*) Dandelion NY.

Blair, D. C. Language & Representation in Information Retrieval. xiv,336p. 1990. 135.00 (*0-444-88437-8*) Elsevier.

Blair, D. G. & Buckingham, M. J. Marcel Grossmann Meeting: Fifth (in 2 Vols.) (Proceedings of the Fifth Meeting Ser.). 1989. pap. 94.00 (*9971-5-0785-4*); text 282.00 (*9971-5-0784-6*) World Scientific Pub.

Blair, Dan. Credit Reform: Key Credit Agencies Had Difficulty Making Reasonable Loan Program Cost Estimates. 68p. (C). 1999. pap. text 20.00 (*0-7881-8149-1*) DIANE Pub.

***Blair, David.** Ripples on a Cosmic Sea: The Search for Gravitational Waves. 224p. 1999. pap. text 12.00 (*0-7382-0137-5*, Pub. by Perseus Pubng) HarpC.

Blair, David, jt. ed. see Collins, Peter.

***Blair, David E.** Inversion Theory & Conformal Mapping. (STML Ser.). 128p. 2000. 19.00 (*0-8218-2636-0*) Am Math.

Blair, David G., ed. The Detection of Gravitational Radiation. (Illus.). 505p. (C). 1991. text 160.00 (*0-521-35278-9*) Cambridge U Pr.

Blair, David J. Trade Negotiations in the OECD: Structures, Institutions & States. 280p. 1992. 93.50 (*0-7103-0432-3*, A7586) Routledge.

Blair, Diane D. Arkansas Politics & Government: Do the People Rule? LC 87-31423. (Politics & Governments of the American States Ser.). (Illus.). xxvi, 362p. 1988. pap. text 27.50 (*0-8032-6073-3*) U of Nebr Pr.
— Arkansas Politics & Government: Do the People Rule? LC 87-31423. (Politics & Governments of the American States Ser.). (Illus.). xxvi, 362p. 1988. text 55.00 (*0-8032-1188-0*) U of Nebr Pr.

Blair, Don & Cohen, Skip. Body Parts: Don Blair's Guide to Lighting & Posing. LC 99-17293. 1999. write for info. (*0-9658571-7-4*) Marathon NE.

Blair, Donald F. Arborist Equipment: A Guide to the Tools & Equipment of Tree Maintenance & Removal. 2nd ed. (Illus.). 291p. (C). 1995. text 95.00 (*1-881956-12-1*); pap. text 80.00 (*1-881956-13-X*) Int Soc Arboricult.

Blair, Donald S. Great Opera Singers of the Twentieth Century, 1927-1990. LC 90-29109. (Illus.). 156p. 1991. lib. bdg. 69.95 (*0-7734-9850-8*) E Mellen.

Blair, Dorothy, tr. see Amrouche, Fadhma.

Blair, Dorothy, tr. see Lemsine, Aicha.

Blair, Dorothy, tr. see Maalouf, Amin.

Blair, Dorothy, tr. see Oyono-Mbia, Guillaume, et al.

Blair, Dorothy S., tr. see Bhely-Quenum, Olympe.

Blair, Dorothy S., tr. see Djebar, Assia.

Blair, Dorothy S., tr. see Fantoure, Alioum.

Blair, Dorothy S., tr. see Huet, Michel.

Blair, Dorothy S., tr. see Lemsine, Aicha.

Blair, Dorothy S., tr. see Maalouf, Amin.

Blair, Dorothy S., tr. see Sebbar, Leila.

Blair, E. D., et al. Antiviral Therapy. LC 97-41321. (Medical Perspectives Ser.). (Illus.). 176p. 1997. pap. 38.95 (*0-387-91510-9*) Spr-Verlag.

Blair, Ectyl H., ed. Chlorodioxins: Origin & Fate. LC 73-84139. (Advances in Chemistry Ser.: No. 120). 1973. 27.95 (*0-8412-0181-1*) Am Chemical.

Blair, Edward. Leadville: Colorado's Magic City. LC 95-13481. (Illus.). 247p. 1996. pap. 25.00 (*0-9623868-9-8*) F Pruett.

Blair, Edward E. & Kamakura, Wagner A., eds. AMA Winter Educators' Conference, 1996 Vol. 7: Marketing Theory & Applications. 440p. 1996. pap. 50.00 (*0-87757-258-5*) Am Mktg.

Blair, Edward P. Basic Bible Commentary Vol. 25: Philippians, Colossians, & First & Second Thessalonians. Deming, Lynne M., ed. LC 94-10965. 160p. (Orig.). 1994. pap. 5.95 (*0-687-02645-8*) Abingdon.

***Blair, Emily N.** Bridging Two Eras: The Autobiography of Emily Newell Blair, 1877-1951. Laas, Virginia J., ed. & intro. by. LC 99-42668. (Illus.). 408p. 1999. 29.95 (*0-8262-1254-9*) U of Mo Pr.

Blair, Emma. An Apple from Eden. large type ed. 560p. 1998. 29.99 (*0-7089-9044-4*) Ulverscroft.

***Blair, Emma.** The Daffodil Sea. 2000. 26.95 (*0-593-02828-7*, Pub. by Transworld Publishers Ltd); pap. 8.95 (*0-553-40614-0*, Pub. by Transworld Publishers Ltd) Trafalgar.
— Goodnight, Sweet Prince. large type ed. 496p. 2000. write for info. (*0-7089-9127-0*) Ulverscroft.

Blair, Emma. Half Hidden. large type ed. (Charnwood Large Print Ser.). 528p. 1997. 27.99 (*0-7089-8926-8*, Charnwood) Ulverscroft.
— Maggie Jordan. large type ed. (Charnwood Ser.). 720p. 1994. 27.99 (*0-7089-8757-5*, Charnwood) Ulverscroft.

***Blair, Emma.** Passionate Times. 2000. pap. 10.95 (*0-553-40615-9*, Pub. by Transworld Publishers Ltd) Trafalgar.

Blair, Emma. Passionate Times. large type ed. (Charnwood Large Print Ser.). 560p. 1997. 27.99 (*0-7089-8952-7*, Charnwood) Ulverscroft.
— The Sweetest Thing. large type ed. (Charnwood Large Print Ser.). 1995. 27.99 (*0-7089-8832-6*, Charnwood) Ulverscroft.
— The Water Meadows. large type ed. 752p. 1994. 27.99 (*0-7089-8777-X*) Ulverscroft.

Blair, Emma H., ed. Indian Tribes of the Upper Mississippi Valley & Region of the Great Lakes, 2 vols. in 1. LC 96-5129. (Illus.). ix, 414p. 1996. pap. 25.00 (*0-8032-6099-7*, Bison Books) U of Nebr Pr.

Blair, Esmond. The Environment of Thebes. 1994. pap. 9.99 (*0-913412-71-6*) Brandon Hse.
— Imagery Experience of Classical Literature. (Orig.). 1990. pap. 9.00 (*0-913412-27-9*) Brandon Hse.
— Pliny's Images Through Prose. (C). 1991. pap. 8.98 (*0-913412-53-8*) Brandon Hse.

Blair, Etcyl H., ed. Chlorodioxins - Origin & Fate. LC 73-84139. (Advances in Chemistry Ser.: Vol. 120). 151p. 1973. reprint ed. pap. 46.90 (*0-608-03898-9*, 206434500008) Bks Demand.

Blair-Ewart, Alexander, ed. Mindfire: Dialogues in the Other Future. 360p. pap. (*1-895897-43-2*) Somerville Hse.

Blair, Farnham. The Movie Queen. Hunting, Constance, ed. 60p. 1996. pap. 8.95 (*0-913006-62-9*) Puckerbrush.

Blair, Farnham & Hunting, Constance. The Blue Line. 33p. 1989. pap. 6.95 (*0-685-45308-1*) Puckerbrush.

Blair, Floy, ed. see Blair, W. Charles & McGill, John K.

Blair, Frank. Survey on a Shoestring: A Manual for Small-Scale Language Survey. LC 90-71834. (Publications in Linguistics Ser.: Vol. 96). xii, 141p. 1991. pap. 11.00 (*0-88312-644-3*) S I L Intl.

Blair, Frank, ed. International Marketing Handbook. 3rd ed. 4036p. 1988. 235.00 (*0-8103-2580-2*) Gale.

Blair, G. Eric, et al, eds. Modulation of MHC Antigen Expression & Disease. (Illus.). 480p. (C). 1995. pap. write for info. (*0-521-49921-6*) Cambridge U Pr.
— Modulation of MHC Antigen Expression & Disease. (Illus.). 458p. (C). 1995. text 95.00 (*0-521-49578-4*) Cambridge U Pr.

Blair, G. J., et al, eds. Forages in Southeast Asian & South Pacific Agriculture. 202p. (Orig.). 1985. pap. 105.00 (*0-949511-19-6*) St Mut.

Blair, Gary R. Balance & Fulfillment: Ten Goals You Must Pursue to Land a Balanced Life! 48p. 1998. pap. 6.95 (*1-889770-05-1*, BNF) GoalsGuy.
— Building Your Bridge: Ten Rules for Success in the New Millennium. 48p. 1998. pap. 6.95 (*1-889770-04-3*, BYB) GoalsGuy.
— The Collegiate Guide to Goal-Setting. 48p. (C). 1998. pap. 6.95 (*1-889770-18-3*, GSC) GoalsGuy.
— The Couples Guide for Goal-Setting. 48p. 1998. pap. 6.95 (*1-889770-19-1*, CGG) GoalsGuy.
— Everything Counts! A High Velocity Formula for Maximum Achievement. 48p. 1998. pap. 6.95 (*1-889770-03-5*, ETC) GoalsGuy.

B

— Failure & Progress: A Powerful Performance Acceleration Strategy. 48p. 1998. pap. 6.95 (*1-889770-07-8*, FNP) GoalsGuy.
— The Family Guide to Goal-Setting: Building a Healthy, Happy & Successful Family. 48p. 1998. pap. 6.95 (*1-889770-17-5*, GSF) GoalsGuy.
— Goal-Setting for Knuckleheads: An Easy, Step-by-Step Guide for Setting & Achieving Goals. 48p. 1998. pap. 6.95 (*1-889770-14-0*, GSK) GoalsGuy.
***Blair, Gary R.** Goal Setting 101: How to Set & Achieve a Goal. 80p. 2000. pap. 6.95 (*1-889770-64-7*) GoalsGuy.
Blair, Gary R. Goals Guy Success Pack: 24 Inspirational Messages. 48p. 1998. pap. 6.95 (*1-889770-08-6*, GSP) GoalsGuy.
— Jesus on Goal Setting: Powerful Lessons from the Bible. 48p. 1998. pap. 6.95 (*1-889770-21-3*, JGS) GoalsGuy.
— The Kid's Guide to Goal-Setting. 48p. (J). (gr. 2 up). 1998. pap. 6.95 (*1-889770-15-9*, GSK) GoalsGuy.
— Mentors & Proteges: How to Select, Manage & Lead Dynamic Relationships. 48p. 1998. pap. 6.95 (*1-889770-12-4*, MNP) GoalsGuy.
— Millennium Resolutions: 100 Things to Do Before, During & after the Millennium! 48p. 1998. pap. 6.95 (*1-889770-06-X*, MLR) GoalsGuy.
***Blair, Gary R.** Mind Munchies: An Assortment of Delicious Brain Snacks! 80p. 2000. pap. 6.95 (*1-889770-63-9*) GoalsGuy.
Blair, Gary R. The Myths & Realities: Guidelines for Designing an Extraordinary Life! 48p. 1998. pap. 6.95 (*1-889770-02-7*, MRG) GoalsGuy.
— Personal Action Plan: Building Your Blueprint for Business & Personal Excellence. 40p. 1998. pap. 19.95 (*1-889770-55-8*, PAP) GoalsGuy.
— Personal Balance Profile: Charting Your Life's Current Reality. 40p. 1998. pap. 19.95 (*1-889770-23-X*, PBP) GoalsGuy.
— Personal Board of Directors: Building Your Team of Trusted Advisors. 40p. 1998. pap. 19.95 (*1-889770-61-2*, PBD) GoalsGuy.
— Personal Brand Identity: Creating Brand You! 40p. 1998. pap. 19.95 (*1-889770-53-1*, PBI) GoalsGuy.
— Personal Excellence Award: The "Oscar" of Personal Mastery. 40p. 1998. pap. 19.95 (*1-889770-59-0*, PEA) GoalsGuy.
— Personal Goal Plan: Designing an Extraordinary Life. 40p. 1998. pap. 19.95 (*1-889770-54-X*, PGP) GoalsGuy.
— Personal Goal Planner: Your Monthly Companion. 52p. 1998. pap. 2.95 (*1-889770-62-0*, PGP2) GoalsGuy.
— Personal Goal Planner No. 12: Your Monthly Companion. 52p. 1997. pap. 19.95 (*1-889770-01-9*, PGP1) GoalsGuy.
— Personal Goal-Setting Forms: An Assortment of Planning Sheets & Other Helpful Resources. 40p. 1998. pap. 19.95 (*1-889770-58-2*, PGF) GoalsGuy.
— Personal Goal Setting 101: Mastering the Fundamentals of Goal-Setting & Personal Strategic Planning. 40p. 1998. pap. 19.95 (*1-889770-22-1*, PGS) GoalsGuy.
— Personal Goals Journal: A Record of Your Life's Accomplishments. 48p. 1998. pap. 6.95 (*1-889770-13-2*, PGJ) GoalsGuy.
— Personal Legacy Statement: Determining How You Will Be Remembered. 40p. 1998. pap. 19.95 (*1-889770-51-5*, PLS) GoalsGuy.
— Personal Maintenance Plan: Your 3000-Mile Performance Checkup. 40p. 1998. pap. 19.95 (*1-889770-60-4*, PMP) GoalsGuy.
— Personal Mission Statement: Defining Your Life's Purpose. 40p. 1998. pap. 19.95 (*1-889770-52-3*, PMS) GoalsGuy.
— Personal Reading Journal: Your Record of Quotations, Reflections & Impressions. 48p. 1998. pap. 6.95 (*1-889770-09-4*, PRJ) GoalsGuy.
— Personal Reality Assessment: Preparing Your Future by Understanding Your Past. 40p. 1998. pap. 19.95 (*1-889770-24-8*, PRA) GoalsGuy.
— Personal Reference Guide: Resources to Assist You on Life's Journey. 40p. 1998. pap. 19.95 (*1-889770-57-4*, PRG) GoalsGuy.
— Personal Strategic Plan: Putting It All Together. 40p. 1998. pap. 19.95 (*1-889770-56-6*, PSP) GoalsGuy.
— Personal Value Statements: Writing Your Personal Operating System. 40p. 1998. pap. 19.95 (*1-889770-50-7*, PVS) GoalsGuy.
— The Power of Focus: Your Future Depends upon It! 48p. 1998. pap. 6.95 (*1-889770-10-8*) GoalsGuy.
— The Purpose of Life: Experience Your True Calling. 48p. 1998. pap. 6.95 (*1-889770-20-5*, POL) GoalsGuy.
— The Teenager's Guide to Goal-Setting. 48p. (YA). 1998. pap. 6.95 (*1-889770-16-7*, GST) GoalsGuy.
— The Ten Commandments: Violate Them at Your Own Risk! 48p. 1998. pap. 6.95 (*1-889770-11-6*, TCG) GoalsGuy.
— What Are Your Goals? Powerful Questions to Discover What You Want Out of Life! (Orig.). 1997. pap. text 14.95 (*1-889770-00-0*) GoalsGuy.
— What Are Your Goals? Powerful Questions to Discover What You Want Out of Life! LC 93-61575. (Illus.). 189p. (Orig.). 1994. pap. 14.95 (*1-56912-096-X*) Wharton Pub.
***Blair, Gary Ryan.** Goal Setting Forms: Tools to Help You Set, Focus, & Celebrate. 2nd ed. (Illus.). 85p. 2000. pap. text 14.95 (*1-889770-67-1*) GoalsGuy.
— Personal Goal Planner: Your Monthly Goal Setting Companion. (GoalsGuy Library). (Illus.). 72p. 2000. pap. 19.95 (*1-889770-65-5*) GoalsGuy.
Blair, Gene. Knowing Jesus. (YouthSearch: Small-Group Resources Ser.: Vol. 9). 64p. 1996. pap. 5.95 (*0-687-05574-1*) Abingdon.
Blair, George & Meadows, Sandy. A Real-Life Guide to Organizational Change. LC 96-8723. 200p. 1996. text 69.95 (*0-566-07711-6*, Pub. by Gower) Ashgate Pub Co.
Blair, George A., tr. see Plato.
Blair, Gerald H., et al. 1997 ITS Technology Review: 4th World Congress on ITS, Berlin, Germany. LC 99-173357. (Illus.). 47p. 1998. pap. text. write for info. (*0-935403-20-5*, PP-066) Inst Trans Eng.
Blair, Gerard. Starting to Manage: The Essential Skills. (IEEE Engineers Guide to Business Ser.: Vol. 8). 180p. 1995. pap. 19.95 (*0-7803-2295-9*, EG108) Inst Electrical.
Blair, Gerry. Predator Calling with Gerry Blair. LC 95-77319. (Illus.). 208p. 1995. pap. 14.95 (*0-87341-359-8*, PCG01) Krause Pubns.
— Rockhounding Arizona: 75 Rock-Hunting Sites Throughout Arizona. (Illus.). 176p. 1995. pap. text 12.95 (*1-56044-389-8*) Falcon Pub Inc.
Blair, Gertrude, jt. auth. see Engle, Fannie.
Blair, Glenn M. Mentally Superior & Inferior Children of Junior & Senior High School Age: A Comparative Study of Their Backgrounds, Interests & Ambitions. LC 71-176567. (Columbia University. Teachers College. Contributions to Education Ser.: No. 766). reprint ed. 37.50 (*0-404-55766-X*) AMS Pr.
Blair, Gorden. Open Distributed Processing & Multimedia. LC 97-17905. 480p. (C). 1998. 44.95 (*0-201-17794-3*) Addison-Wesley.
Blair, Gordon, et al. Formal Specifications of Distributed Multimedia Systems. LC 98-117234. 256p. 1997. pap. 55.00 (*1-85728-677-4*, Pub. by UCL Pr Ltd) Taylor & Francis.
***Blair, Gordon P.** Design & Simulation of Four-Stroke Engines LC 99-27316. 1999. 89.00 (*0-7680-0440-3*) Soc Auto Engineers.
— Design & Simulation of Four-Stroke Engines, Computer Software. 1999. 200.00 incl. disk (*0-7680-0507-8*, R-186SW) Soc Auto Engineers.
Blair, Gordon P. Design & Simulation of Two-Stroke Engines. LC 95-25748. 647p. 1996. 99.00 (*1-56091-685-0*, R-161) Soc Auto Engineers.
***Blair, Gordon P.** Virtual 4-Stroke: Design & Simulation of Four-Stroke Engines. 1999. 800.00 incl. cd-rom (*0-7680-0506-X*, R-186M) Soc Auto Engineers.
Blair, Graeme. Sulfur in the Tropics. (Technical Bulletin Ser.: No. T-12). (Illus.). 71p. (Orig.). 1979. pap. 4.00 (*0-88090-011-3*) Intl Fertilizer.
Blair, Graeme & LeFroy, Rod, eds. Sulfur Fertilizer Policy for Lowland & Upland Cropping Systems in Indonesia. 142p. (Orig.). 1989. pap. 108.00 (*1-86320-009-6*) St Mut.
— Technologies for Sustainable Agriculture on Marginal Uplands in Southeast Asia. 128p. (Orig.). 1991. pap. 78.00 (*1-86320-033-9*) St Mut.
Blair, Grandpa. The Gospel Rag: Adam & Eve Straight Up. 2nd ed. 16p. (YA). (gr. 11 up). 1992. pap. 5.95 (*0-930366-71-9*) Northcountry Pub.
— The Gospel Rag: Noah Straight Up. 16p. (YA). (gr. 11 up). 1992. pap. 5.95 (*0-930366-69-7*) Northcountry Pub.
— Vexillophily: A Capsule History of the Stars & Stripes. 2nd rev. ed. (Illus.). 46p. (YA). (gr. 11 up). 1992. pap. 9.95 (*0-930366-74-3*) Northcountry Pub.
— Victor the Vulture. 7p. (YA). (gr. 9 up). 1991. pap. 4.75 (*0-930366-64-6*) Northcountry Pub.
— Willie the Groundhog. 6p. (YA). (gr. 10 up). 1991. pap. 4.75 (*0-930366-63-8*) Northcountry Pub.
— Ziggy the Zombie from Zumbrota. 14p. (YA). (gr. 10 up). 1991. pap. 5.75 (*0-930366-62-X*) Northcountry Pub.
Blair, Gwenda. Almost Golden: Jessica Savitch & the Selling of Television News. 368p. 1989. mass mkt. 4.50 (*0-380-70752-7*, Avon Bks) Morrow Avon.
***Blair, Gwenda.** The Trumps: Three Generations That Built an Empire. 592p. 2000. 30.00 (*0-684-80849-8*) Simon & Schuster.
Blair, H., jt. ed. see Greene, M.
Blair, Harry W. The Political Economy of Participation in Local Development Programs: Short-Term Impasse & Long-Term Change in South Asia & the United States from the 1950s to the 1970s. (Monograph). 180p. (Orig.). 1981. pap. text 10.65 (*0-86731-055-3*) Cornell CIS RDC.
Blair, Hugh. Lectures on Rhetoric & Belles Lettres. LC 93-22920. 528p. 1993. 75.00 (*0-8201-1467-7*) Schol Facsimiles.
Blair, Ian M. Taming the Atom: Facing the Future with Nuclear Power. fac. ed. LC 83-124844. (Illus.). 257p. 1983. reprint ed. pap. 79.70 (*0-7837-7993-3*, 204774900008) Bks Demand.
Blair, J. A., ed. Chemistry & Biology of Pteridines: Pteridines & Folic Acid Derivatives. LC 83-7666. xxxvi, 1070p. 1983. 265.40 (*3-11-008560-7*) De Gruyter.
Blair, J. Allen. Living Consistently: When Life Goes up & Down. LC 94-38138. 112p. 1995. pap. 7.99 (*0-8254-2187-X*) Kregel.
— Living Patiently: When God Seems Far Away. LC 93-41450. 384p. 1994. pap. 13.99 (*0-8254-2185-3*) Kregel.
— Living Peacefully: When the World Won't Leave You Alone. LC 93-41447. 256p. 1994. pap. 11.99 (*0-8254-2183-7*) Kregel.
— Living Victoriously: When Winning It All Isn't Enough. LC 93-41448. 128p. 1994. pap. 7.99 (*0-8254-2184-5*) Kregel.
Blair, J. Anthony, jt. auth. see Johnson, Ralph H.
Blair, J. Anthony, jt. ed. see Johnson, Ralph H.
Blair, J. Antony & Johnson, Ralph H., eds. Informal Logic: The First International Symposium. LC 80-67674. 175p. (Orig.). 1980. pap. 9.95 (*0-918528-09-7*) Edgepress.
***Blair, J. H., ed.** The Good Parts: The Best Erotic Writing in Modern Fiction. 256p. 2000. pap. 12.95 (*0-425-17225-2*) Berkley Pub.
Blair, James, jt. auth. see Holland, Alex.
Blair, James, jt. auth. see Toulmin, Harry.
Blair, Jane & Oleksowicz, Ruth J. Silent Tears, Joyous Joys. 18p. (Orig.). 1986. 15.00 (*0-910147-29-9*); pap. 12.00 (*0-317-60033-8*) World Poetry Pr.
***Blair, Jason, et al.** Illegible Stone. 184p. 1999. pap. 6.00 (*0-7392-0342-8*, PO3515) Morris Pubng.
Blair, Jayne. Justice. Carlton Press Staff, ed. 95p. 1998. 19.95 (*0-9668498-0-9*) J L Blair.
Blair, Jessica. Dangerous Dreams. large type ed. (Magna Large Print Ser.). 597p. 1997. 27.99 (*0-7505-0974-0*) Ulverscroft.
— The Other Side of the River. large type ed. (Magna Large Print Ser.). 496p. 1998. 29.99 (*0-7505-1181-8*, Pub. by Mgna Lrg Print) Ulverscroft.
— The Restless Spirit. large type ed. (Magna Large Print Ser.). 592p. 1997. 27.99 (*0-7505-1018-8*) Ulverscroft.
***Blair, Jessica.** The Seaweed Gatherers. large type ed. 432p. 1999. 31.99 (*0-7505-1360-8*, Pub. by Mgna Lrg Print) Ulverscroft.
Blair, Jim. The Blue Flame Lingers. 40p. (Orig.). 1994. pap. 7.00 (*0-9645871-1-4*) Jim Blair.
— Conversations with My Daughter Sigmund. 42p. (Orig.). 1981. pap. 3.00 (*0-9645871-0-6*) Jim Blair.
Blair, Joane E. Fashion Terminology. 192p. (C). 1991. pap. 11.96 (*0-13-299355-4*) P-H.
Blair, Joe. Introducing the New Testament. LC 93-33581. 1994. 21.99 (*0-8054-2123-8*, 4221-23) Broadman.
Blair, John. Anglo-Saxon Oxfordshire. (Illus.). 230p. 1998. pap. 27.95 (*0-7509-1750-4*, Pub. by Sutton Pub Ltd) Intl Pubs Mktg.
— Industrial Polarization & the Location of New Manufacturing Firms: An Empirical Application. (Discussion Papers: No. 89). 1976. pap. 10.00 (*1-55869-058-1*) Regional Sci Res Inst.
— Tracing Subversive Currents in Goethe's Wilhelm Meister's Apprenticeship. LC 96-46641. (GERM Ser.). x, 200p. 1997. 55.00 (*1-57113-092-6*) Camden Hse.
Blair, John, compiled by. The Illustrated Discography of Surf Music 1961-1965. 3rd ed. LC 95-69560. 264p. 1995. 45.00 (*1-56075-040-5*) Popular Culture.
Blair, John & Golding, Brian. The Cloister & the World: Essays in Medieval History in Honour of Barbara Harvey. (Illus.). 354p. (C). 1996. text 75.00 (*0-19-820440-X*) OUP.
Blair, John & McParland, Stephen. The Illustrated Discography of Hot Rod Music, 1961-1965. LC 89-92312. (Rock & Roll Reference Ser.: No. 32). (Illus.). 180p. 1990. 34.50 (*1-56075-002-2*) Popular Culture.
Blair, John & Ramsay, Nigel, eds. English Medieval Industries: Craftsmen, Techniques, Products. 480p. 1991. 80.00 (*0-907628-87-7*) Hambledon Press.
Blair, John & Sharp, Richard, eds. Pastoral Care Before the Parish. 256p. 1992. text 59.00 (*0-7185-1372-X*, Pub. by Leicester U Pr) Cassell & Continuum.
Blair, John, jt. auth. see Salway, Peter.
***Blair, John D.** Samba: Integrating Linux & Windows. 2nd ed. LC 00-21581. (Illus.). 2000. 34.95 (*1-886411-38-7*) No Starch Pr.
Blair, John D. Samba: Integrating UNIX & Windows. 300p. 1998. pap. 29.95 incl. cd-rom (*1-57831-006-7*) Specialized Sys.
Blair, John D. & Fottler, Myron D. Strategic Leadership for Medical Groups: Navigating Your Strategic Web. LC 97-50436. 1998. 44.95 (*0-7879-0853-3*) Jossey-Bass.
Blair, John D., et al. Medical Group Practices Face the Uncertain Future: Challenges, Opportunities & Strategies. 63p. (Orig.). 1995. pap. text 27.00 (*1-56829-009-8*) Med Group Mgmt.
Blair, John D., jt. auth. see Stanley, Jay.
Blair, John G. Modular America: Cross-Cultural Perspectives on the Emergence of an American Way, 92. LC 88-3111. (Contributions in American Studies: No. 92). 196p. 1988. 49.95 (*0-313-26317-5*, BMW/, Greenwood Pr) Greenwood.
***Blair, John N.** ADD Children: A Handbook for Parents. (Illus.). xii, 154p. 1999. pap. 12.95 (*0-9674306-0-7*) JB Enterp.
Blair, John P. Local Economic Development: Analysis & Practice. LC 95-3023. 330p. 1995. 45.00 (*0-8039-5376-3*) Sage.
Blair, John P. & Reese, Laura A. Approaches to Economic Development: Readings from EDQ LC 98-40126. 1998. 37.44 (*0-7619-1884-1*) Sage.
— Approaches to Economic Development: Readings from EDQ. LC 98-40126. 328p. 1998. 58.00 (*0-7619-1883-3*) Sage.
Blair, John P., jt. auth. see Barrett, G. Vincent.
Blair, John P., jt. ed. see Bingham, Richard D.
Blair, John S. & Tindall, Barry S. Effective Utilization of Abandoned Railroad Rights-of-Way for Park - Recreation Purposes: Potential Problems & Solutions. Briner, Patricia J., ed. LC HD0205.B49. (Illus.). 92p. reprint ed. pap. 30.00 (*0-7837-1536-6*, 204181700024) Bks Demand.
Blair, Johnny, jt. auth. see Czaja, Ronald.
Blair, Joseph M., jt. ed. see Schein, Jeffrey L.
Blair, K. Forestry in Development Planning: Lessons from the Rural Experience. 217p. 1988. reprint ed. pap. 275.00 (*81-7089-096-9*, Pub. by Intl Bk Distr) St Mut.
Blair, Karen. The Clubwoman As Feminist: True Womanhood Redefined, 1868 to 1914. LC 79-26390. 199p. 1980. 37.50 (*0-8419-0538-X*) Holmes & Meier.
— The Clubwoman As Feminist: True Womanhood Redefined, 1868 to 1914. LC 79-26390. 199p. 1988. pap. 17.50 (*0-8419-1261-0*) Holmes & Meier.
Blair, Karen J. History of American Women's Organizations, 1810-1960: A Guide to Sources. 1988. 50.00 (*0-8161-8648-0*, Hall Reference) Macmillan.
— The Torchbearers: Women & Their Amateur Arts Associations in America, 1890-1930. LC 93-485. (Philanthropic Studies). 276p. 1994. 31.50 (*0-253-31192-6*) Ind U Pr.
Blair, Karen J., ed. Northwest Women: An Annotated Bibliography of Sources on the History of Oregon & Washington Women 1787-1970. (Illus.). 150p. (Orig.). 1997. pap. 32.95 (*0-87422-145-5*) Wash St U Pr.
Blair, Katherine D. Scandalous Miss Delaney. 256p. 1999. mass mkt. 4.99 (*0-8217-6292-3*) Kensgtn Pub Corp.
Blair, Kathryn, ed. see Milani, Michael.
***Blair, Kay R.** Ladies of the Lamplight. 2nd ed. LC 00-102174. (Illus.). 112p. 2000. pap. 11.95 (*1-890437-41-7*) Western Reflections.
Blair, Kerry. The Heart Has Its Reasons. LC 99-15658. 1999. pap. 13.95 (*1-57734-479-0*, 01114034) Covenant Comms.
Blair, Kevin, ed. see Shea, Carol Stratman.
Blair, Kristine & Takayoshi, Pamela, eds. Feminist Cyberscapes: Mapping Gendered Academic Spaces. LC 98-43687. (New Directions in Computers & Composition Studies Ser.). 1999. 73.25 (*1-56750-438-8*); pap. 24.95 (*1-56750-439-6*) Ablx Pub.
Blair, Larry, et al, contrib. by. Fifty Famous Butter Pats. (Illus.). 52p. 1995. 49.95 (*0-9632075-1-2*) A Black.
***Blair-Larsen, Susan M., et al.** The Balanced Reading Program: Helping All Students Achieve Success. LC 99-37781. 1999. 22.95 (*0-87207-252-5*) Intl Reading.
Blair-Larson, Susan. Reading in the Middle School: An Integrated Approach. 108p. (C). 1997. per. 33.95 (*0-7872-3783-3*, 41378301) Kendall-Hunt.
Blair-Larson, Susan M., jt. auth. see Bercik, Janet.
Blair, Laurence, jt. auth. see Blair, Mary Ellen.
Blair, Laurence R. & Blair, Mary E. Margaret Tafoya: A Tewa Potter's Heritage & Legacy. McDonald, Susan, ed. LC 86-62249. 200p. 1986. 45.00 (*0-88740-080-9*) Schiffer.
Blair, Lawrence. Rhythms of Vision: Changing Patterns of Myth & Consciousness. (Illus.). 256p. 1991. reprint ed. pap. 12.95 (*0-89281-320-2*, Destiny Bks) Inner Tradit.
Blair, Lawrence & Blair, Lorne. Ring of Fire: An Indonesian Odyssey. (Illus.). 272p. 1991. reprint ed. pap. 24.95 (*0-89281-430-6*, Park St Pr) Inner Tradit.
Blair, Leigh, jt. auth. see Bernstein, Bonnie.
Blair, Leon B. Western Window in the Arab World. LC 78-131423. 350p. reprint ed. pap. 108.50 (*0-608-15865-8*, 203073600070) Bks Demand.
Blair, Leona. Fascination. 544p. 1998. reprint ed. mass mkt. 6.99 (*0-553-57229-6*) Bantam.
***Blair, Les.** Ha Ha Tonka: Land of the Laughing Water. (Illus.). 2000. write for info. (*0-9700473-0-4*) Main St Pubng MO.
Blair, Linda. Design Sense: A Guide to Getting the Most from Your Interior Design Investment. LC 96-12445. (Illus.). 208p. 1996. 29.95 (*0-471-14104-6*) Wiley.
— Design Sense: A Guide to Getting the Most from Your Interior Design Investment. LC 96-12445. 208p. 1998. pap. 14.95 (*0-471-31880-9*) Wiley.
***Blair, Linda.** Passport to Practical & Vocational Nursing. (Illus.). 288p. 1998. teacher ed. write for info. (*1-55664-438-8*) Mosby Inc.
Blair, Linda L. Becoming a Practical & Vocational Nurse: A Complete Planning Guide. LC 97-49685. (Illus.). 288p. (C). (gr. 13). 1998. pap. text 23.00 (*0-8151-2620-4*, 31636) Mosby Inc.
Blair, Lindsay. Joseph Cornell's Vision of Spiritual Order. (Essays in Art & Culture Ser.). (Illus.). 224p. 1998. pap. 24.95 (*0-948462-49-3*, Pub. by Reaktion Bks) Consort Bk Sales.
***Blair, Lisa M.** George Sand's "Nouvelles" Reflections, Perceptions & the Self. LC 98-20811. (Currents in Comparative Romance Languages & Literatures Ser.: Vol. 79). ix, 126p. (C). 1999. text 43.00 (*0-8204-4095-7*) P Lang Pubng.
Blair, Lorne, jt. auth. see Blair, Lawrence.
Blair, Louis H., et al. Guidelines for School-Business Partnerships in Science & Mathematics. LC 90-32170. (Illus.). 222p. (Orig.). 1990. pap. text 24.00 (*0-87766-476-5*) Urban Inst.
Blair, Lowell, tr. see Rostand, Edmond.
Blair, Malcolm, et al, eds. Steel Castings Handbook. 6th ed. 500p. 1995. 198.00 (*0-87170-556-7*, 6820) ASM.
Blair, Marcia. The Final Guest. (Mystery Puzzler Ser.: No. 16). (Illus.). (Orig.). 1979. mass mkt. 1.95 (*0-89083-436-9*, Zebra Kensgtn) Kensgtn Pub Corp.
— The Final Lie. (Mystery Puzzler Ser.: No. 6). (Illus.). (Orig.). 1978. mass mkt. 1.95 (*0-89083-409-1*, Zebra Kensgtn) Kensgtn Pub Corp.
Blair, Margaret. House of Spies: Danger in the Civil War. LC 99-21659. (White Mane Kids Ser.: Vol. 7). (Illus.). 177p. (J). (gr. 4-12). 1999. pap. 8.95 (*1-57249-161-2*, WM Kids) White Mane Pub.
***Blair, Margaret M.** New Relationship: Human Capital in the American Corporation. LC 99-50476. 2000. pap. 22.95 (*0-8157-0901-3*) Brookings.
Blair, Margaret M. Ownership & Control: What's at Stake in the Corporate Governance Debates? 384p. 1995. 44.95 (*0-8157-0948-X*); pap. 19.95 (*0-8157-0947-1*) Brookings.
Blair, Margaret M., ed. The Deal Decade: What Takeovers & Leveraged Buyouts Mean for Corporate Governance. 390p. (C). 1993. 49.95 (*0-8157-0946-3*); pap. 22.95 (*0-8157-0945-5*) Brookings.
— Wealth Creation & Wealth Sharing: A Colloquium on Corporate Governance & Investment in Human Capital. 100p. 1996. pap. 12.95 (*0-8157-0949-8*) Brookings.
***Blair, Margaret M. & Kochan, Thomas A., eds.** New Relationship: Human Capital in the American Corporation. LC 99-50476. 395p. 1999. 49.95 (*0-8157-0902-1*) Brookings.

B

An Asterisk (*) at the beginning of an entry indicates that the title is appearing for the first time.

*Blair, Margaret M. & Roe, Mark J., eds. Employees & Corporate Governance. 1999. 39.95 (0-8157-0944-7) Brookings.

Blair, Margaret M. & Uppal, Girish. The Deal Decade Handbook. LC 93-18026. 72p. 1993. pap. 9.95 (0-8157-0943-9) Brookings.

Blair, Margaret W. Brothers at War. LC 96-45384. (WM Kids Ser.: No. 4). 144p. (YA). (gr. 5 up). 1996. pap. 7.95 (1-57249-049-7, WM Kids) White Mane Pub.

Blair, Margot. The Red String. LC 95-39555. (Illus.). 40p. (J). (ps up). 1996. 16.95 (0-89236-340-1, Pub. by J P Getty Trust) OUP.

Blair, Martha. Johnny Texas Teacher Resource Guide: Including Texas Cultures. (Illus.). 54p. (Orig.). 1994. pap., student ed. 12.95 (0-937460-98-2) Hendrick-Long.

Blair, Martha, et al. When the Ground Fails: Planning & Engineering Response to Debris Flows. (Program on Environment & Behavior Monograph Ser.: No. 40). 110p. (Orig.). (C). 1985. pap. 20.00 (0-685-28114-0) Natural Hazards.

Blair, Martha, jt. ed. see Kasberger, Peggy.

Blair, Mary. Mary Blair's Hors D'Oeuvres Cookbook. LC 84-25850. 433p. 1985. 25.00 (0-88191-004-X) Freundlich.

Blair, Mary E., jt. auth. see Blair, Laurence R.

Blair, Mary Ellen & Blair, Laurence. Legacy of a Master Potter: Nampeyo & Her Descendants. (Illus.). 1999. pap. 29.95 (1-887896-06-6, Rio Nuevo) Treas Chest Bks.

Blair, Matt & Blumberg, Mike. Homeless Dreams: Dream Portraits of Minnesota Celebrities to Aid the Homeless. 104p. 1991. text 35.00 (0-9630190-1-5); pap. text 14.95 (0-9630190-0-7) M Blairs Celeb.

Blair, Maud, et al, eds. Identity & Diversity: Gender & the Experience of Education. (Equality & Difference: Gender Issues in Education Ser.). 250p. 1994. 74.95 (1-85359-248-X); pap. 29.95 (1-85359-247-1) Taylor & Francis.

Blair, Maxine, jt. auth. see Baker, James.

Blair, May. Once upon the Lagan: The Story of the Lagan Canal. LC 95-101891. (Illus.). 139p. 1995. reprint ed. pap. 19.95 (0-85640-245-1, Pub. by Blackstaff Pr) Dufour.

Blair, Michael. Financial Services: The New Core Rules. 212p. 1991. pap. 42.00 (1-85431-072-0, Pub. by Blackstone Pr) Gaunt.

Blair, Michael, et al. Blackstone's Guide to the Bank of England Act, 1998. LC 99-166103. 252p. 1998. pap. 54.00 (1-85431-847-0, Pub. by Blackstone Pr) Gaunt.

Blair, Mike. Prairie Chronicles. (Illus.). 176p. (Orig.). 1993. pap. 12.95 (0-9637862-3-7) Creator Pub.

Blair, Mirpah & Kraps, Sylvia, eds. Marion County History, Vol. 2. (Illus.). 62p. 1956. pap. 5.00 (0-943297-15-X) Marion Coun Hist Soc.

Blair, Mirpah, jt. ed. see Kaiser, Chester C.

Blair, Nancy. Amulets of the Goddess: Oracle of Ancient Wisdom. LC 92-35945. (Illus.). 190p. 1993. pap. 39.95 (0-914728-80-6) Wingbow Pr.

— Goddesses for Every Season. 1995. text 64.75 (1-85230-689-0, Pub. by Element Bks) Penguin Putnam.

Blair, Nancy. Goddesses for Every Season. 128p. 1995. pap. 13.95 (1-85230-686-6, Pub. by Element MA) Penguin Putnam.

Blair, Nancy L., ed. Crossing the Bridge to the Future: Managing Geoscience Information in the Next Decade. (Proceedings Ser.: Vol. 26). (Illus.). 65p. 1996. pap. 45.00 (0-934485-26-7) Geosci Info.

Blair, Pamela D., jt. auth. see Noel, Brook.

Blair, Pat. Know Your Medicines. 144p. (C). 1991. 55.00 (0-86242-100-4, Pub. by Age Concern Eng) St Mut.

Blair, Pat, jt. auth. see Gray, J. A.

Blair, Penny, ed. see Dixon, Steve.

*Blair, Peter. Last Heat. LC 99-72869. 72p. 2000. pap. 10.00 (0-915380-44-7) Word Works.

Blair, Peter D. Multi-Objective Regional Energy Planning. (Studies in Applied Regional Science: Vol. 14). 1979. lib. bdg. 61.00 (0-89838-008-1) Kluwer Academic.

Blair, Peter D. & Blackburn, Charles, eds. Trends in Industrial Innovation: Industry Perspectives & Policy Implications. 1998. pap. text. write for info. (0-914446-12-6) Sigma Xi.

Blair, Peter Hunter. The World of Bede. (Studies in Anglo-Saxon England). 354p. (C). 1990. text 69.95 (0-521-39138-5); pap. text 25.95 (0-521-39819-3) Cambridge U Pr.

Blair, Peter J. An Introduction to Anglo-Saxon England. 2nd ed. LC 77-71404. (Illus.). 395p. 1977. pap. text 26.95 (0-521-29219-0) Cambridge U Pr.

Blair, Philip M. Federalism & Judicial Review in West Germany. 1981. 72.00 (0-19-827427-0) OUP.

Blair, Phillip M. Job Discrimination & Education: An Investment Analysis, a Case Study of Mexican-Americans in Santa Clara County, California. LC 70-180842. (Special Studies in U. S. Economic, Social & Political Issues). 1972. 42.50 (0-89197-807-0) Irvington.

Blair, Preston. Cartoon Animation. (How to Draw & Paint Ser.). (Illus.). 40p. (Orig.). 1989. pap. 6.95 (0-929261-51-8, HT26) W Foster Pub.

— Cartoon Animation. (Collector's Ser.). (Illus.). 224p. (Orig.). 1994. pap. 24.95 (1-56010-084-2, CS03) W Foster Pub.

— How to Animate Film Cartoons. (How to Draw & Paint Ser.). (Illus.). 40p. (Orig.). 1989. pap. 6.95 (1-56010-069-9, HT190) W Foster Pub.

Blair, Raymond N. God's Managers. 32p. 1986. pap., suppl. ed. 3.99 (0-8361-3387-0) Herald Pr.

Blair, Rhonda L., ed. see Crabbe, George.

Blair, Richardson. Inspector Collier & the Bird of Prey. LC 90-27553. 1991. 12.95 (0-87949-349-6) Ashley Bks.

Blair, Rob, ed. The Western San Juan Mountains: Their Geology, Ecology, & Human History. (Illus.). 1996. pap. text 27.50 (0-87081-378-1) Univ Pr Colo.

Blair, Robert. The Funeral & Wedding Handbook. LC 98-20968. 1998. pap. 12.99 (0-89900-809-7) College Pr Pub.

— The Grave: A Poem. LC 92-23645. (Augustan Reprints Ser.: No. 161). 1973. reprint ed. 14.50 (0-404-70161-2, PR3318) AMS Pr.

— Tales of the Superstitions: Origins of the Lost Dutchman Legend. LC 35-35054. 1975. 100.00 (0-910152-07-1) AZ Hist Foun.

Blair, Robert, et al. Greater Lynchburg: The Real Virginia. (Illus.). 208p. 1995. 35.00 (1-885352-16-6) Community Comm.

— Northern Ireland. LC 86-8296. (Illus.). 116p. 1986. 25.00 (0-85640-365-2, Pub. by Blackstaff Pr) Dufour.

Blair, Robert W. In Every Tongue: French for Latter-Day Saints. 1993. pap., student ed. 39.95 (0-87579-758-X) Deseret Bk.

— In Every Tongue: Japanese for Latter-Day Saints. (Orig.). 1994. pap., student ed. 39.95 (0-87579-763-6) Deseret Bk.

— In Every Tongue: Russian for Latter-Day Saints. viii, 232p. (Orig.). 1994. pap., student ed. 39.95 (0-87579-760-1) Deseret Bk.

Blair, Robin. Digital Techniques in Broadcasting Transmission. LC 99-18132. 192p. 1999. pap. text 34.95 (0-240-80366-3, Focal) Buttrwth-Heinemann.

Blair, Roger D. & Harrison, Jeffrey L. Monopsony: Antitrust Law & Economics. (Illus.). 193p. 1993. text 45.00 (0-691-04309-4, Pub. by Princeton U Pr) Cal Prin Full Svc.

Blair, Ruth, ed. see Melville, Herman.

Blair, Ruth M., jt. ed. see Cousens, Michael.

Blair, S. S. The Monumental Inscriptions from Early Islamic Iran & Transoxiana. LC 90-29890. (Muqarnas Supplements Ser.: No. 5). (Illus.). xvi, 307p. 1991. 129.50 (90-04-09367-2) Brill Academic Pubs.

Blair, Sam, jt. auth. see Harmon, Merle.

Blair, Sam, jt. auth. see Lilly, Bob.

Blair, Sam, jt. auth. see Trevino, Lee.

Blair, Sandra, et al. California Marital Settlement & Other Family Law Agreements. 2nd ed. Pickus, Bob, ed. LC 97-68155. 620p. 1997. ring bd. 129.00 (0-7626-0068-3, FA-32960) Cont Ed Bar-CA.

Blair, Sara. Henry James & the Writing of Race & Nation. (Studies in American Literature & Culture: No. 99). (Illus.). 271p. (C). 1996. text 54.95 (0-521-49750-7) Cambridge U Pr.

Blair, Seabury, Jr. Backcountry Ski! Washington: The Best Trails & Descents for Free-Heelers & Snowboarders. LC 98-28096. (Illus.). 224p. 1998. pap. 15.95 (1-57061-151-3) Sasquatch Bks.

— Op-Olympic Peninsula. Baumann, J. Bruce, ed. (Illus.). 112p. 1994. 19.95 (1-884850-03-0) Scripps Howard.

Blair, Sheila. Islamic Inscriptions. LC 97-42757. 224p. 1998. 59.95 (0-8147-1328-9) NYU Pr.

Blair, Sheila, jt. auth. see Grabar, Oleg.

Blair, Sheila S. The Art & Architecture of Islam, 1250-1800. (Illus.). 336p. 1996. pap. 30.00 (0-300-06465-9) Yale U Pr.

Blair, Sheila S. A Compendium of Chronicles: Rashid al Din's Illustrated History of the World - The Earliest Arabic Manuscript. (Nasser D. Khalili Collection of Islamic Art: Vol. XXVII). (Illus.). 126p. 1995. text 255.00 (0-19-727627-X) OUP.

Blair, Sheila S., ed. Images of Paradise in Islamic Art. 140p. 1996. pap. 29.95 (0-614-21578-1, 489) Kazi Pubns.

Blair, Sheila S. & Bloom, Jonathan M. The Art & Architecture of Islam, 1250-1800. LC 93-49561. (Pelican History of Art Ser.). (Illus.). 336p. 1994. 70.00 (0-300-05888-8) Yale U Pr.

Blair, Sheila S., jt. auth. see Bloom, Jonathan.

Blair, Sheila S., jt. auth. see Grabar, Oleg.

Blair, Skippy. Dance Power: Own the Experience. Orig. Title: Dance! Dance! Dance!. (Illus.). 190p. (J). 1997. spiral bd. 39.95 (0-932980-21-X) Golden St Dance Teach Assn.

*Blair, Skippy. Dance Power: Own the Experience. 2nd rev. ed. Orig. Title: Dance! Dance! Dance!. (Illus.). 134p. (J). 1999. pap. 39.95 (0-932980-24-4) Golden St Dance Teach Assn.

Blair, Skippy. Dance Terminology Notebook: Advancing Communication in the 90's. (Illus.). 113p. (Orig.). 1994. ring bd. 39.95 (0-932980-11-2) Golden St Dance Teach Assn.

— Disco to Tango & Back: Skippy Blair on Contemporary Social Dance. 1978. pap. 22.50 incl. audio (0-932980-01-5) Golden St Dance Teach Assn.

— Disco to Tango & Back: Skippy Blair on Contemporary Social Dance. rev. ed. (Illus.). 196p. 1992. pap., ring bd. 39.95 incl. audio (0-932980-06-6) Golden St Dance Teach Assn.

Blair, Susan K., ed. & intro. see Davis, Leslie A.

Blair, Susan M. Unexpected Company. (Little Girl Ser.). (Illus.). 56p. (J). (ps-7). 1992. 19.95 (0-9631956-0-3) Pendant Pr.

Blair, Suzanne, jt. auth. see Collins, Victoria F.

Blair, Thomas. Oqua. LC 79-15861. 1990. pap. 13.95 (0-87949-163-9) Ashley Bks.

Blair, Thomas L., ed. Strengthening Urban Management: International Perspectives. (Urban Innovation Abroad Ser.). 368p. 1985. 75.00 (0-306-42081-3, Plenum Trade) Perseus Pubng.

— Urban Innovation Abroad: Problem Cities in Search of Solutions. 424p. 1984. 95.00 (0-306-41492-9, Plenum Trade) Perseus Pubng.

Blair, Timothy R. & Jones, Deneese L. Student Teaching Handbook. LC 97-28839. 256p. 1997. pap. text 36.00 (0-205-26761-0) P-H.

Blair, Timothy R., jt. auth. see Rupley, William H.

*Blair, Toni. Hotbed Honey. (Temptation Ser.: Vol. 800). 2000. mass mkt. 3.99 (0-373-25900-X, 1-25900-) Harlequin Bks.

Blair, Tony. New Britain: My Vision of a Young Country. LC 96-40377. 352p. 1997. 28.00 (0-8133-3338-5, Pub. by Westview) HarpC.

Blair, Tracy, ed. see Fiese, Bryan R.

Blair, W. Charles & McGill, John K. Employing Family Members in Your Business: A Tax Bonanza. Blair, Floy & McGill, Meredith, eds. 258p. 1983. pap. 24.95 (0-915771-00-4) Blair McGill Co.

Blair, W. Frank. The Rusty Lizard: A Population Study. LC 59-8122. 205p. reprint ed. pap. 63.60 (0-608-14614-7, 205552100024) Bks Demand.

Blair, W. G., ed. see Schultz, E. B., et al.

Blair, Walter. Davy Crockett, Frontier Hero. rev. ed. (Illus.). 225p. 1985. reprint ed. pap. 7.95 (0-942936-08-6) Lincoln-Herndon Pr.

— Essays on American Humor: Blair Through the Ages. LC 92-35534. (Illus.). 306p. (Orig.). (C). 1993. pap. 14.95 (0-299-13624-8) U of Wis Pr.

— Mike Fink: King of Mississippi Keelboatmen. LC 74-138143. (Illus.). 283p. 1971. reprint ed. lib. bdg. 35.00 (0-8371-5600-9, BLMF, Greenwood Pr) Greenwood.

— Tall Tale America: A Legendary History of Our Humorous Heroes. (J). 1987. 23.05 (0-606-04341-1, Pub. by Turtleback) Demco.

— Tall Tale America: A Legendary History of Our Humorous Heroes. (Illus.). 284p. (C). 1987. pap. 17.95 (0-226-05596-5) U Ch Pr.

Blair, Walter & Franklin, Meine J., eds. Half Horse Half Alligator: The Growth of the Mike Fink Legend. LC 77-70578. (International Folklore Ser.). 1977. reprint ed. lib. bdg. 26.95 (0-405-10079-5) Ayer.

Blair, Walter & McDavid, Raven I., Jr., eds. The Mirth of a Nation: America's Great Dialect Humor. LC 81-16403. 331p. 1983. reprint ed. pap. 102.70 (0-7837-2975-8, 205747900006) Bks Demand.

Blair, Walter, ed. see Twain, Mark, pseud.

Blair, William. An Inquiry into the State of Slavery Amongst the Romans. LC 72-92417. 1833. 39.00 (0-403-00152-8) Scholarly.

*Blair, William. Virginia's Private War. (Illus.). 208p. 2000. pap. 13.95 (0-19-514047-8) OUP.

Blair, William. Virginia's Private War: Feeding Body & Soul in the Confederacy, 1861-1865. (Illus.). 216p. 1998. 32.50 (0-19-511864-2) OUP.

Blair, William A., ed. A Politician Goes to War: The Civil War Letters of John White Geary. LC 94-6497. (Illus.). 286p. 1995. 29.50 (0-271-01338-9) Pa St U Pr.

— A Politician Goes to War: The Civil War Letters of John White Geary. 259p. 1997. reprint ed. pap. text 27.00 (0-7881-5057-X) DIANE Pub.

Blair, William A. & Clark, W. A. The Historical Sketch of Banking in North Carolina & the History of the Banking Institutions Organized in South Carolina Prior to 1860, 2 vols. Bruchey, Stuart, ed. LC 80-1134. (Rise of Commercial Banking Ser.). (Illus.). 1981. reprint ed. lib. bdg. 52.95 (0-405-13634-X) Ayer.

*Blair, William Alan & Pencak, William. Making & Remaking Pennsylvania's Civil War. LC 00-37330. (Illus.). 2000. write for info. (0-271-02079-2) Pa St U Pr.

Blair, William D., Jr. Katharine Ordway: The Lady Who Saved the Prairies. (Illus.). 115p. 1989. text 20.00 (0-9624590-0-3) Nature VA.

Blair, William D., jt. auth. see Beachy, John A.

Blair, William F. & Steyers, Curtis M., eds. Techniques in Hand Surgery. LC 95-7309. (Illus.). 1216p. 1996. 225.00 (0-683-00842-0) Lppncott W & W.

Blair, Yogi. Minnesota Fortune Cookies. 5th ed. 26p. (YA). (gr. 11 up). 1993. pap. 8.95 (0-930366-73-5) Northcountry Pub.

Blais. Exam Study Guide for Vet Techs. 1998. pap. text. write for info. (0-7216-4971-8) Harcourt.

Blais, jt. auth. see Carmony.

*Blais, Andre. To Vote or Not to Vote? The Merits & Limits of Rational Choice Theory. 242p. 2000. 45.00 (0-8229-4129-5); pap. 19.95 (0-8229-5734-5) U of Pittsburgh Pr.

Blais, Andre & Dion, Stephane, eds. The Budget-Maximizing Bureaucrat: Appraisals & Evidence. LC 90-29888. (Policy & Institutional Studies). 384p. 1991. text 49.95 (0-8229-3679-8) U of Pittsburgh Pr.

Blais, Andre, et al. Governments, Parties & Public Sector Employees: Canada, United States, Britain & France. 220p. 1997. text 49.95 (0-7735-1702-2, Pub. by McG-Queens Univ Pr); pap. text 22.95 (0-7735-1703-0, Pub. by McG-Queens Univ Pr) CUP Services.

— Governments, Parties & Public Sector Employees: Canada, United States, Britain & France. (Policy & Institutional Studies). 208p. 1997. pap. 17.95 (0-8229-5639-X); text 35.00 (0-8229-3971-1) U of Pittsburgh Pr.

Blais, Andrew L. On the Plurality of Actual Worlds. LC 96-51454. 240p. (C). 1997. text 35.00 (1-55849-072-8) U of Mass Pr.

*Blais, Genevieve. Dalai Lama. (Guides for Beginners - Great Lives Ser.). 2000. pap. 11.95 (0-340-78017-8, Pub. by Headway) Trafalgar.

Blais, Gil, jt. auth. see Keil, Wayne.

Blais, J. F., jt. auth. see Tyagi, R. D.

Blais, Jacqueline, ed. see Curtis, Richard A.

Blais, Jean-Jacques, jt. auth. see Canada.

Blais, Jean-Marc. Les Langages de l'Interpretation Personnalisi (The Languages of Live Interpretation) L'Animation dans les Musies (Animation in Museums) (Illus.). 199p. 1998. pap. 19.95 (0-660-50757-9, Pub. by CN Mus Civilization) U of Wash Pr.

Blais, Madeleine. The Heart Is an Instrument: Portraits in Journalism. LC 91-48358. (Illus.). 360p. (C). 1992. 37.50 (0-87023-772-1) U of Mass Pr.

— The Heart Is an Instrument: Portraits in Journalism. LC 91-48358. (Illus.). 360p. 1994. pap. 18.95 (0-87023-942-2) U of Mass Pr.

— In These Girls, Hope Is a Muscle. 272p. (J). 1996. mass mkt. 12.95 (0-446-67210-6, Pub. by Warner Bks) Little.

Blais, Marie-Claire. American Notebooks: A Writer's Journey. 208p. 1996. pap. text 14.95 (0-88922-358-0) Genl Dist Srvs.

— The Angel of Solitude. Hodes, Laura, tr. LC 93-91901. 168p. 1993. pap. 12.95 (0-88922-337-8, Pub. by Talonbks) Genl Dist Srvs.

— Deaf to the City. Dunlop-Hebert, Carol, tr. LC 86-43063. 224p. 1987. 18.95 (0-87951-276-8, Pub. by Overlook Pr) Penguin Putnam.

— The Execution. Lobdell, David, tr. 104p. 1973. pap. 11.95 (0-88922-103-0, Pub. by Talonbks) Genl Dist Srvs.

— Mad Shadows. 134p. 1996. pap. text 7.95 (0-7710-9867-7) McCland & Stewart.

— A Season in the Life of Emmanuel. 144p. 1996. pap. text 6.95 (0-7710-9880-4) McCland & Stewart.

Blais, Marie-Claire, et al, trs. Durer's Angel. LC 77-357898. 112p. 1993. pap. 11.95 (0-88922-111-1, Pub. by Talonbks) Genl Dist Srvs.

*Blais, Philippe. Leonardo's Flight: A Fantastic Novel. 340p. 2000. 21.00 (1-929953-00-3) Gates & Bridges.

Blais, Steven M., Sr. Adam's Lost Lives: Night Scenes - Theory of Regression. unabridged ed. (Illus.). 90p. 1998. pap. 9.95 (0-9666550-0-1) Steven M Blais.

Blaisde. Study Guide T/A Statistics In. (C). 1993. pap. text, student ed. 27.00 (0-03-032227-8) Harcourt Coll Pubs.

Blaisdell. Formula & Table Cards-stats In Practice. (C). 1993. pap. text 6.00 (0-03-098334-7) Harcourt.

— Statistics in Practice. 2nd ed. (C). 1996. pap. text, teacher ed. 28.00 (0-03-019849-6) Harcourt Coll Pubs.

— Statistics in Practice. 2nd ed. (C). 1997. pap. text 29.50 (0-03-019843-7, Pub. by Harcourt Coll Pubs) Harcourt.

— Statistics in Practice. 2nd ed. 1997. 83.50 (0-03-027114-2) Harcourt Coll Pubs.

— Statistics in Practice. 2nd ed. 304p. (C). 1998. pap. text, student ed. 29.50 (0-03-019844-5) SCP.

— Statistics in Practice, Chapts. 13-16. 2nd ed. (Illus.). 368p. (C). 1997. pap. text, suppl. ed. 3.00 (0-03-023499-9) SCP.

— STATISTICS IN PRACTICE 2E. 2nd ed. LC 97-80332. (Illus.). 720p. (C). 1997. text 83.50 (0-03-019374-5) SCP.

Blaisdell, Anne. Greenmask! (Black Dagger Crime Ser.). 224p. 1997. 19.50 (0-7451-8939-3, Black Dagger) Chivers N Amer.

*Blaisdell, B. Great Speeches by Native Americans. 2000. pap. 2.00 (0-486-41122-2) Dover.

Blaisdell, Bob. Favorite Greek Myths. (Illus.). 96p. (Orig.). (J). 1995. pap. text 1.00 (0-486-28859-5) Dover.

Blaisdell, Bob, jt. auth. see Collodi, Carlo.

Blaisdell, Bob, ed. see Lawrence, D. H.

Blaisdell, Bob, ed. see Tolstoy, Leo.

Blaisdell, Bob, ed. & intro. see Hardy, Thomas.

Blaisdell, David, jt. auth. see Stewart, Meiji.

Blaisdell, Donald C. European Financial Control in the Ottoman Empire. LC 29-15742. reprint ed. 32.50 (0-404-00895-X) AMS Pr.

— Government & Agriculture: Growth of Federal Farm Aid. LC 72-2365. (FDR & the Era of the New Federal Ser.). 217p. 1974. reprint ed. lib. bdg. 32.50 (0-306-70488-9) Da Capo.

— International Organization. LC 66-16837. 539p. reprint ed. pap. 167.10 (0-608-30686-X, 201246800081) Bks Demand.

*Blaisdell, F. William & Holcroft, James W. Scientific American Surgery Handbook of Trauma. LC 99-38987. (Illus.). 1999. write for info. (0-89454-033-5) Scientific Am Inc.

Blaisdell, F. William & Trunkey, Donald D. Cervicothoracic Trauma. 2nd ed. LC 93-4002. (Trauma Management Ser.). (Illus.). 424p. 1993. text 105.00 (0-86577-492-7) Thieme Med Pubs.

Blaisdell, F. William, jt. auth. see Kennedy, J.

Blaisdell, Foster W. Erex Saga & Ivens Saga: The Old Norse Versions of Chretien de Troyes's, Erec & Yvain. Kalinke, Marianne E., tr. & intro. by. LC 77-5395. (Illus.). 112p. reprint ed. pap. 34.80 (0-7837-5312-8, 204438700002) Bks Demand.

Blaisdell, G. L., jt. ed. see Elliot, D. H.

Blaisdell, James P. & Holmgren, Ralph C. Managing Intermountain Rangelands - Salt Desert Shrub Ranges. (Illus.). 56p. 1997. reprint ed. 13.40 (0-89904-653-3, Bear Meadows Resrch Grp); reprint ed. pap. 7.40 (0-89904-654-1, Bear Meadows Resrch Grp) Crumb Elbow Pub.

Blaisdell, Lowell L. The Desert Revolution, Baja California, 1911. LC 85-30528. 281p. 1986. reprint ed. lib. bdg. 65.00 (0-313-25043-X, BLDR, Greenwood Pr) Greenwood.

Blaisdell, Mary J., jt. auth. see Berda, Marty.

Blaisdell, Muriel L. Darwinism & Its Data: The Adaptive Coloration of Animals. rev. ed. LC 91-47029. (Harvard Dissertations in the History of Science Ser.). (Illus.). 418p. 1992. reprint ed. text 35.00 (0-8240-7253-7) Garland.

Blaisdell, Richard E. Dragon Slayer. 110p. 1992. write for info. (1-882359-04-6); pap. write for info. (1-882359-03-8) At Ease Pubns.

Blaisdell, Robert. Imagist Poetry: An Anthology. LC 99-25589. (Dover Thrift Editions Ser.). 176p. 1999. pap. 2.00 (0-486-40875-2) Dover.

— The Story of Hercules. LC 97-11715. (Dover Children's Thrift Classics Ser.). (Illus.). (J). 1997. pap. 1.00 (0-486-29768-3) Dover.

B

Blaisdell, Robert & Scott, Sir Walter. Ivanhoe. LC 97-44614. (Children's Thrift Classics). (Illus.). (J). 1998. pap. 1.00 (*0-486-40143-X*) Dover.

Blaisdell, Robert, jt. auth. see Alcott, Louisa May.

Blaisdell, Robert, jt. auth. see Spyri, Johanna.

***Blaisdell, Thomas.** The Saintly Face of Evil. 1999. pap. 8.00 (*1-888716-12-6*) Xandex Pr.

Blaisdell, Thomas C., Jr. Federal Trade Commission. LC 32-26900. reprint ed. 29.50 (*0-404-00896-8*) AMS Pr.

Blaisdell, Tim & Urmston, Ed, Sr. Standard Guide to Athearn Model Trains. LC 98-84619. (Illus.). 288p. 1998. pap. 24.95 (*0-87341-631-7*, ACBI) Krause Pubns.

Blaisdell, Tom. Eat Sane, Be Sane: Foods That Nourish the Brain. 1999. pap. 8.00 (*1-888716-13-4*) Xandex Pr.

***Blaisdell, Tom.** Good Ole Boys & Girls. 2000. pap. 8.00 (*1-888716-14-2*) Xandex Pr.

Blaise, Clark. The Border As Fiction. (Borderlands Monographs: No. 4). 12p. (C). 1990. pap. text 5.00 (*0-9625055-1-X*) Canadian-Amer Ctr.

— If I Had a Father: A Post-Modern Autobiography. 1994. pap. 12.00 (*0-201-62694-2*) Addison-Wesley.

— If I Were Me. LC 97-157791. 120p. 1997. pap. write for info. (*0-88984-185-3*) Porcup Quill.

— Lunar Attractions. 300p. 1990. pap. write for info. (*0-88984-105-5*) Porcup Quill.

— Man & His World. 144p. 1993. per. write for info. (*0-88984-148-9*) Porcup Quill.

Blaise, Clark & Mukherjee, Bharati. Days & Nights in Calcutta. LC 95-79537. 303p. 1995. reprint ed. pap. 14.00 (*1-886913-01-3*) Ruminator Bks.

***Blaise, Denis & Plisnier, Andre.** Belgo Cookbook. (Illus.). 160p. 2000. pap. 25.00 (*0-609-80636-X*, Three Riv Pr) Crown Pub Group.

Blaise, Denis, et al. Belgo Cookbook. 160p. 1997. 35.00 (*0-297-83603-X*, Pub. by Weidenfeld & Nicolson) Trafalgar.

Blaise, Donald, jt. ed. see Strausbaugh, John.

Blaising, Craig A. & Bock, Darrell L. Progressive Dispensationalism. LC 93-23467. 336p. (gr. 12). 1993. 20.99 (*0-8010-2117-0*, Bridgept Bks) Baker Bks.

Blaivas, Gerry, jt. ed. see Chancellor, Michael B.

***Blaivas, Jerry G.** Conquering Bladder & Prostate Problems: The Authoritative Guide for Men & Women. LC 98-12045. (Illus.). 340p. (C). 1998. 26.95 (*0-306-45864-0*, Plenum Trade) Perseus Pubng.

Blaivas, Jerry G., ed. Evaluation & Treatment of Urinary Incontinence. (Topics in Clinical Urology Ser.). (Illus.). 208p. 1996. 67.50 (*0-89640-306-8*) Igaku-Shoin.

Blaivas, Jerry G., jt. auth. see Chancellor, Michael B.

Blaizot, Jean-Paul & Ripka, Georges. Quantum Theory of Finite Systems. (Illus.). 680p. (C). 1985. 70.00 (*0-262-02214-1*) MIT Pr.

Blajan, Daniel E. Foxgloves & Hedgehog Days: Secrets in a Country Garden. LC 96-43524. 170p. 1997. 19.00 (*0-395-85729-5*) HM.

Blake. Clown. (J). 1996. 15.95 (*0-8050-4583-X*) H Holt & Co.

— Comprehensive Electronic Communication. 1997. pap. text, lab manual ed. 26.25 (*0-314-20746-5*) West Pub.

Blake. Financial Market Analysis. pap. text 39.95 (*0-471-87728-X*) Wiley.

Blake. Handbook of Classical Architecture. 200p. 1997. text 66.00 (*0-419-15700-X*, E & FN Spon) Routledge.

— Medical Transciptionist's Handbook - IML. 2nd ed. 96p. 1998. teacher ed. 12.95 (*0-8273-8324-X*) Delmar.

— Medical Transcriptionist's Handbook. 2nd ed. 112p. (C). 1997. mass mkt., wbk. ed. 9.25 (*0-8273-8323-1*) Delmar.

— Practical Stress Analysis in Engineering Design. 2nd rev. ed. (Mechanical Engineering Ser.: Vol. 69). (Illus.). 712p. 1989. text 85.00 (*0-8247-8152-X*) Dekker.

***Blake.** Readings in the Humanities. 590p. 1999. pap. text 44.00 (*0-536-02812-5*) Pearson Custom.

Blake. 10 Frogs. (J). write for info. (*0-06-205935-1*) HarpC.

***Blake.** Wireless Communication. (Electronics Technology Ser.). 2000. pap. 70.95 (*0-7668-1266-9*) Delmar.

Blake, ed. Tectonic Evolution of Northern California. (IGC Field Trip Guidebooks Ser.). 80p. 1989. 21.00 (*0-87590-614-1*, T108) Am Geophysical.

Blake & DeVries, Mary A. Elements of Correspondence. (Illus.). 288p. 1995. 19.95 (*0-02-531305-3*) Macmillan.

Blake & Falco. Thought of Writing. 126p. 1998. pap. text 12.00 (*0-536-01183-4*) Pearson Custom.

Blake, jt. auth. see Dixon.

Blake, A. Design of Mechanical Joints. (Mechanical Engineering Ser.: Vol. 42). (Illus.). 576p. 1985. text 175.00 (*0-8247-7351-9*) Dekker.

Blake, A. These Sporting Times Soundings13. pap. text 19.50 (*0-85315-920-3*) Lawrence & Wishart.

Blake, A. G. The Intelligent Enneagram. 400p. (Orig.). 1996. pap. 19.00 (*1-57062-213-2*, Pub. by Shambhala Pubns) Random.

— A Seminar on Time. LC 79-52756. 1980. 5.95 (*0-934254-00-1*) Claymont Comm.

Blake, A. G., ed. & frwd. see Bennett, J. G.

Blake, Adriana. Women Can Win the Marriage Lottery: Share Your Man with Another Wife (The Case for Plural Marriage) LC 95-73073. 232p. 1996. pap. 19.95 (*1-887922-03-2*) Orange Cty Univ Pr.

Blake, Alexander. Design of Curved Members for Machines. LC 79-12202. 288p. 1979. reprint ed. lib. bdg. 34.50 (*0-88275-970-1*) Krieger.

— Handbook of Mechanics, Materials & Structures. LC 85-5373. (Mechanical Engineering Practice Ser.). 736p. 1985. 230.00 (*0-471-86239-8*) Wiley.

— Practical Fracture Mechanics. (Mechanical Engineering Ser.: Vol. 102). (Illus.). 456p. 1996. text 140.00 (*0-8247-9678-0*) Dekker.

— WEESKA Threaded Fasteners: Materials & Design. (What Every Engineer Should Know Ser.: Vol. 18). (Illus.). 308p. 1986. text 59.75 (*0-8247-7554-6*) Dekker.

Blake, Alice A. Presbyterian Mission Work in New Mexico: Memoirs of Alice Blake. Roper, Beryl C., ed. Ning, Jimmy, tr. (Illus.). 1997. pap. 24.95 (*1-885812-03-5*) Aquamarine.

Blake, Alison. Gray-eyed Glory. LC 98-96999. 192p. 1999. lib. bdg. 18.95 (*0-8034-9342-8*, Avalon Bks) Bouregy.

Blake, Allan & Bond, Helen J. SWOT Company Law. 240p. (C). 1990. 80.00 (*1-85431-055-0*) St Mut.

— SWOT Company Law. 5th ed. 275p. 1996. pap. 22.00 (*1-85431-478-5*, Pub. by Blackstone Pr) Gaunt.

Blake, Allison. The Chesapeake Bay Book: A Complete Guide. 4th ed. LC 98-46737. (Great Destinations Ser.). (Illus.). 320p. 1999. pap. 17.95 (*1-58157-005-8*) Berkshire Hse.

Blake, Andrew. The Body Language: The Meaning of Modern Sport. 224p. 1996. pap. 25.00 (*0-85315-834-7*, Pub. by Lawrence & Wishart) NYU Pr.

***Blake, Andrew.** Living Through Pop. LC 99-34829. 192p. 1999. pap. write for info. (*0-415-16199-1*) Routledge.

***Blake, Andrew, ed.** Living Through Pop. LC 99-34829. 192p. (C). 1999. text 75.00 (*0-415-16198-3*) Routledge.

***Blake, Andrew & Austin, John.** The Employer's Survival Guide: How to Find & Keep Those Good Employees. 115p. 2000. pap. 16.95 (*0-9662015-3-1*) Marvin Bks.

Blake, Andrew & Isard, M. Active Contours: The Application of Techniques from Graphics, Control Theory & Statistics to Visual Tracking of Shapes in Motion. LC 98-13199. (Illus.). xii, 356p. 1998. pap. 74.95 (*3-540-76217-5*) Spr-Verlag.

Blake, Andrew & Troscianko, Tom, eds. AI & the Eye. LC 90-11926. (Illus.). 308p. 1990. reprint ed. pap. 95.50 (*0-608-05309-0*, 206584700001) Bks Demand.

Blake, Andrew & Yuille, Alan. Active Vision. LC 92-22427. (Artificial Intelligence Ser.). (Illus.). 171p. 1992. 55.00 (*0-262-02351-2*) MIT Pr.

***Blake, Ann.** Christina Stead's Politics of Place. 200p. 1999. pap. 34.95 (*1-876268-35-2*, Pub. by Univ of West Aust Pr) Intl Spec Bk.

Blake, Anne Catharine. Sheep Care. (Illus.). 24p. (J). 1998. 4.99 (*0-570-05090-1*) Concordia.

— Sheep Lost. (Illus.). 24p. (J). 1998. 4.99 (*0-570-05091-X*) Concordia.

Blake, Anthony, jt. auth. see Collister, Linda.

***Blake, Anthony George.** Intelligence. rev. ed. 65p. 1999. (*1-891802-01-1*) By The Way Bks.

Blake, Arthur. The Scopes Trial: Defending the Right to Teach. LC 93-37018. (Spotlight on American History Ser.). (Illus.). 64p. (J). (gr. 4-6). 1994. lib. bdg. 21.90 (*1-56294-407-X*) Millbrook Pr.

Blake, Avril. Milner Gray. 100p. 1987. 60.00 (*0-85072-158-X*) St Mut.

— Misha Black. 108p. (Orig.). 1987. 65.00 (*0-85072-152-0*) St Mut.

Blake, Barbara. A Guide to Children's Books about Asian Americans. 215p. 1995. 78.95 (*1-85928-014-5*, Pub. by Scolar Pr) Ashgate Pub Co.

Blake, Barbara & Kruger, Tom. Bridging Cultures: A Program Kit for Schools & Public Libraries. LC 94-28100. 186p. 1994. 29.95 (*1-55570-166-3*) Neal-Schuman.

Blake, Barry J. Australian Aboriginal Grammar. 240p. 1986. 62.00 (*0-7099-3989-2*, Pub. by C Helm) Routldge.

— Case. (Textbooks in Linguistics Ser.). (Illus.). 247p. (C). 1994. text 64.95 (*0-521-44114-5*); pap. text 20.95 (*0-521-44661-9*) Cambridge U Pr.

Blake, Barry J., et al. Case, Typology & Grammar: In Honor of Barry J. Blake. Siewierska, Anna & Jae Jung Song, eds. LC 98-17515. (Typological Studies in Language: Vol. 38). 395p. (C). 1998. 85.00 (*1-55619-651-2*) J Benjamins Pubng Co.

Blake, Barry J., jt. auth. see Dixon, R. M. W.

Blake, Barry J., jt. ed. see Dixon, R. M. W.

Blake, Barry J., jt. ed. see Dixon, R. M.

***Blake, Beatrice.** New Key to Costa Rica. 15th ed. (Illus.). 2000. pap. 17.95 (*1-56975-219-2*) Ulysses Pr.

Blake, Beatrice & Beecher, Anne. The New Key to Costa Rica. 14th ed. (New Key Travel Ser.). (Illus.). 512p. 1998. reprint ed. pap. 17.95 (*1-56975-146-3*) Ulysses Pr.

Blake, Ben, ed. Four Soviet Plays. LC 77-174873. 1972. reprint ed. 34.95 (*0-405-08273-8*, Pub. by Blom Pubns) Ayer.

Blake, Benjamin, et al. The Kingston Trio on Record. LC 85-50660. (Illus.). 260p. (Orig.). 1986. pap. 17.95 (*0-9614594-0-9*) Kingston Korner.

Blake, Benjamin, jt. auth. see Erickson, Hannah.

Blake, Bennie, ed. see Ruland-Thorne, Kate.

Blake, Bernard. Australian Aboriginal Languages. (C). 1991. pap. 29.95 (*0-7022-2353-0*, Pub. by Univ Queensland Pr) Intl Spec Bk.

— International Electronic Countermeasures Handbook (INTECH) 2nd expanded ed. 266p. 1999. 99.00 (*0-89006-929-8*) Artech Hse.

Blake, Bernard, ed. Jane's Radar & Electronic Warfare Systems, 98-99. (Illus.). 800p. 1998. 350.00 (*0-7106-1807-7*) Janes Info Group.

Blake, Brenda C. Egg Cups: An Illustrated History & Price Guide. (Illus.). 192p. (Orig.). 1995. 44.95 (*1-57080-014-6*); pap. 34.95 (*1-57080-013-8*) Antique Pubns.

Blake, Brett E. She Say, He Say: Urban Girls Write Their Lives. LC 96-45352. 176p. (C). 1997. pap. text 14.95 (*0-7914-3480-X*) State U NY Pr.

— She Say, He Say: Urban Girls Write Their Lives. LC 96-45352. 176p. (C). 1997. text 44.50 (*0-7914-3479-6*) State U NY Pr.

Blake, Bruce. What's Different about the United Methodist Church. 60p. 1997. pap. text 4.95 (*0-9632495-4-1*) Koinonia Pr.

***Blake, Bruce P.** Intimacy, Family & Marriage: A Biblical Perspective. 48p. 1999. pap. 5.00 (*0-9632495-5-X*) Koinonia Pr.

Blake, Carlton E. Blake: Descendants of Jasper Blake, Emigrant from England to Hampton, NH, 1643, 1649-1979. (Illus.). 553p. 1994. reprint ed. pap. 79.50 (*0-8328-3972-8*); reprint ed. lib. bdg. 89.50 (*0-8328-3971-X*) Higginson Bk Co.

***Blake, Casey N.** Beloved Community. 2000. pap. 15.00 (*0-465-04416-6*) HarpC.

Blake, Casey N. Beloved Community: The Cultural Criticism of Randolph Bourne, Van Wyck Brooks, Waldo Frank, & Lewis Mumford. Date not set. 25.00 (*0-465-04415-8*, Pub. by Basic) HarpC.

— Beloved Community: The Cultural Criticism of Randolph Bourne, Van Wyck Brooks, Waldo Frank, & Lewis Mumford. LC 90-50013. (Cultural Studies of the United States). (Illus.). xvi, 365p. (C). 1990. pap. 18.95 (*0-8078-4296-6*) U of NC Pr.

Blake, Catherine, tr. see d'Esprit, Jurella.

***Blake, Charles.** Free to Dream: Discovering Your Divine Destiny. 208p. 2000. 19.99 (*1-57778-183-X*) Albury Pub.

Blake, Charles, jt. ed. see Drewry, Gavin.

***Blake, Chris.** Searching for a God to Love: The One You Always Wanted Is Really There. Thomas, Jerry D., ed. LC 99-26630. 256p. 1999. pap. 11.99 (*0-8163-1719-4*) Pacific Pr Pub Assn.

— Searching for a God to Love: The One You Always Wanted is Really There. 220p. 2000. pap. 12.99 (*0-8499-4226-8*) Word Pub.

Blake, Christopher. Cooking with & for Alcoholics: Amazingly Delicious Alcohol-Free Recipes. 1997. pap. text 5.95 (*0-9645356-5-3*) Morris-Lee Pub.

— Fair, Fair Ladies of Chartres Street. 1965. pap. 5.95 (*0-87651-203-1*) Southern U Pr.

***Blake, Cindy.** Foreign Correspondents. 352p. 2000. 24.95 (*0-312-24193-3*, Thomas Dunne) St Martin.

— Second Wives. LC 99-21985. 336p. 1999. 23.95 (*0-312-19328-9*, Thomas Dunne) St Martin.

***Blake, Cindy.** Second Wives. 1999. mass mkt. 6.99 (*0-312-97121-4*) St Martin.

— Second Wives. 2000. mass mkt. write for info. (*0-312-97568-6*) St Martin.

Blake, Claire, et al. The Paper Chain. LC 97-35088. (Illus.). 32p. (J). (gr. k-6). 1999. pap. 8.95 (*0-929173-28-7*) Health Press.

Blake-Coleman, B. C. Copper Wire & Electrical Conductors: The Shaping of a Technology. LC 91-40910. 320p. 1992. text 104.00 (*3-7186-5200-5*) Gordon & Breach.

Blake, D. Steven, jt. auth. see Curtis, Jerome J., Jr.

Blake, Dan. Killing Frost. (Illus.). 270p. (Orig.). 1997. mass mkt. 6.99 (*1-57532-115-7*) Press-Tige Pub.

***Blake, David.** Finance: A Characteristics Approach. LC 99-45910. 168p. 2000. 85.00 (*0-415-21290-1*) Routledge.

Blake, David. Financial Market Analysis. (C). 1990. text 36.87 (*0-07-707228-6*) McGraw.

— Pension Schemes & Pension Funds in the United Kingdom. LC 93-33140. (Illus.). 630p. 1995. text 110.00 (*0-19-828623-6*) OUP.

Blake, David, ed. Hanns Eisler. (Contemporary Music Studies: Vol. 9). 500p. 1995. text 58.00 (*3-7186-5573-X*, ECU63, Harwood Acad Pubs); pap. text 19.00 (*3-7186-5575-6*, ECU32, Harwood Acad Pubs) Gordon & Breach.

Blake, David, et al, eds. Researching School-Based Teacher Education. 320p. 1995. 77.95 (*1-85972-000-5*) Ashgate Pub Co.

Blake, David & Ormerod, Paul. The Economics of Prosperity: Social Priorities in the Eighties. LC 80-489087. 230 p. 1980. 3.95 (*0-86216-013-8*, Galaxy Child Lrg Print) Chivers N Amer.

Blake, David & Winyard, Paul G., eds. Immunopharmacology of Free Radical Species. (Handbook of Immunopharmacology Ser.). (Illus.). 322p. 1995. text 63.00 (*0-12-103520-4*) Acad Pr.

Blake, David, ed. see Varma, Ved P.

Blake, David H. A Short Course of Economics. LC 93-12209. 1993. 15.95 (*0-07-707726-1*) McGraw.

Blake, David H. & Lambert, Richard D., eds. The Multinational Corporation. LC 72-85688. (Annals of the American Academy of Political & Social Science Ser.: No. 403). 300p. (C). 1972. 28.00 (*0-685-00182-2*); pap. 18.00 (*0-87761-153-X*) Am Acad Pol Soc Sci.

Blake, David H. & Walters, Robert H. The Politics of Global Economic Relations. 4th ed. 208p. (C). 1991. pap. text 45.00 (*0-13-682394-7*) P-H.

Blake, Dixon. Handbook of Australian Languages, Vol. 3. (Australian National University Press Ser.). 1995. pap. text. write for info. (*0-08-032841-5*, Pergamon Pr) Elsevier.

Blake, Don. Alberta Trivia Book. 1990. pap. 7.95 (*1-55105-024-2*) Lone Pine.

— B. C. Trivia. pap. 7.95 (*1-55105-025-0*) Lone Pine.

Blake, Donna J., jt. auth. see Glerum, Richard Z.

Blake, Doreen G. Mom . . . I Will Remember. (Illus.). 128p. 1998. mass mkt. 9.95 (*0-9666137-0-8*) R W Blake.

Blake, Doron W. The Adventure of George the Dinosaur (La Adventura de Jorge il Dinosaurio) Lucas, Winafred B., ed. Gremard, Anna, tr. LC 93-73875. (Illus.). 32p. (J). (gr. k-3). 1994. 14.95 (*1-882530-04-7*); 14.95 (*1-882530-05-5*) Deep Forest Pr.

Blake, Duane L. Dynamics of Human Relations in Vocational Education: The Development of Self-Confidence & a Sense of Mastery. LC 77-91416. 152p. 1979. pap. 11.00 (*0-910328-26-9*) Sulzburger & Graham Pub.

Blake, Dudley D., jt. auth. see Young, Bruce H.

Blake, E. & Wisskirchen, P., eds. Advances in Object-Oriented Graphics I. (Eurographic Seminars Ser.). (Illus.). viii, 218p. 1991. 100.95 (*0-387-53480-6*) Spr-Verlag.

Blake, E. H., jt. ed. see Veltkamp, Remco C.

Blake, Elizabeth, ed. see Harth, Willow.

Blake, Elizabeth J. Up & Down. LC 78-144726. (Yale Series of Younger Poets: No. 19). reprint ed. 18.00 (*0-404-53819-3*) AMS Pr.

Blake, Ellen S. Know Yourself: Achieve Your Goals Through Better Self-knowledge. 1999. pap. 17.95 (*0-7494-2900-3*) Kogan Page Ltd.

— To The Waters & the Wild: Petroleum Geology, 1918 to 1941. (Illus.). 207p. 1991. 15.00 (*0-89181-804-9*, 713) AAPG.

Blake, Emmet R. Manual of Neotropical Birds: Spheniscidae (Penguins) to Laridae (Gulls & Allies), Vol. 1. LC 75-43229. (Illus.). 714p. 1977. lib. bdg. 120.00 (*0-226-05641-4*) U Ch Pr.

Blake, Eve. Old Age Is Contagious but You Don't Have to Catch It. 119p. (Orig.). 1986. pap. 8.95 (*0-939171-00-7*) Lee Pub NV.

Blake, Fanny, jt. auth. see McCloud, Kevin.

Blake, Fay M. & Newman, H. Morton. Verbis non Factis: Words Meant to Influence Political Choices in the United States, 1800-1980. LC 84-1325. 143p. 1984. 25.00 (*0-8108-1688-1*) Scarecrow.

Blake, Francis. Increase Blake of Boston, His Ancestors & Descendants. (Illus.). 147p. 1988. reprint ed. pap. 24.00 (*0-8328-0265-4*); reprint ed. lib. bdg. 32.00 (*0-8328-0264-6*) Higginson Bk Co.

Blake, Francis E., ed. Worcester County, Mass. Warnings, 1737-1788. LC 91-68586. 128p. 1992. reprint ed. 24.50 (*0-929539-99-0*, 1368) Picton Pr.

Blake, G. H. & Lawless, R. I., eds. The Changing Middle Eastern City. LC 80-479247. (Illus.). 273p. 1980. 44.00 (*0-06-490451-2*, 06353) B&N Imports.

Blake, Gary. Elements of Copywriting: The Essential Guide to Creating Copy That Gets the Results You Want. LC 97-2717. 176p. 1997. 22.95 (*0-02-861338-4*) Macmillan.

— Elements of Copywriting: The Essential Guide to Creating Copy That Gets the Results You Want. 192p. 1998. pap. text 10.95 (*0-02-862630-3*) Macmillan Gen Ref.

— Quick Tips for Better Business Writing. LC 95-3942. 186p. 1995. pap. 12.95 (*0-07-005691-9*) McGraw.

Blake, Gary & Bly, Robert W. The Elements of Business Writing. 160p. 1992. reprint ed. pap. 9.95 (*0-02-008095-6*) Macmillan Gen Ref.

— Elements of Technical Writing. 192p. 1995. per. 9.95 (*0-02-013085-6*) Macmillan Gen Ref.

— I Hate Kathy Lee Gifford. LC 97-126824. 112p. 1997. pap. 11.00 (*1-57566-144-6*, Knsington) Kensgtn Pub Corp.

***Blake, George.** Single Again. 176p. 2000. pap. 9.95 (*1-58062-280-1*) Adams Media.

Blake, George. The Woman Who Loved to Shop & Other Stories. LC 98-71313. 140p. 1998. pap. 14.00 (*1-888105-27-5*) Avisson Pr.

Blake, George, ed. The Trials of Patrick Carraher. (Notable British Trials Ser.). xii, 278p. 1995. reprint ed. 88.00 (*1-56169-183-6*) Gaunt.

Blake, George C. History of Radio Telegraphy & Telephony. LC 74-4667. (Telecommunications Ser.). (Illus.). 425p. 1980. reprint ed. 39.95 (*0-405-06034-3*) Ayer.

***Blake, George S.** Death of the Dow LC 98-88558. vi, 77 p. 1998. write for info. (*1-882194-44-6*) TN Valley Pub.

Blake, Gerald, et al, eds. International Boundaries & Environmental Security: Frameworks for Regional Cooperation, Vol. IBOS 1. LC 97-203421. 400p. 1997. 140.00 (*90-411-0669-3*) Kluwer Academic.

Blake, Gerald H. The Peaceful Management of Transboundary Resources. LC 95-3397. (International Environmental Law & Policy Ser.). 1995. lib. bdg. 155.00 (*1-85966-173-4*, Pub. by Graham & Trotman) Kluwer Academic.

Blake, Gerald H., ed. Maritime Boundaries. LC 93-35761. (World Boundaries Ser.: Vol. 5). (Illus.). 192p. (C). 1994. 85.00 (*0-415-08835-6*) Routledge.

— Maritime Boundaries & Ocean Resources. LC 87-907. 304p. 1987. 65.50 (*0-389-20726-8*, N8284) B&N Imports.

Blake, Gerald H., et al, eds. International Environmental Law & Policy Series, Set. LC 95-3397. 1995. write for info. (*1-85333-275-5*, Pub. by Graham & Trotman) Kluwer Academic.

Blake, Gerald H., jt. auth. see Drysdale, Alasdair.

Blake, Gerald H., ed. see Kelly, Harry.

Blake, Gerald Henry. Boundaries & Energy: Problems & Prospects. LC 98-40320. (International Boundary Studies Ser.). 566 p. 1998. write for info. (*90-411-0656-1*) Kluwer Law Intl.

— Boundaries & Energy: Problems & Prospects. LC 98-40320. (International Boundary Studies Ser.). 1999. 149.00 (*90-411-0690-1*) Kluwer Law Intl.

***Blake, Glenn.** Drowned Moon. LC 00-30210. (Poetry & Fiction Ser.). 112p. 2000. 22.50 (*0-8018-6549-2*) Johns Hopkins.

Blake, Haynesly R. Visions of Reality. 53p. (Orig.). 1996. mass mkt. 9.95 (*0-9655656-0-2*) Rhythmic Images.

Blake, Henry. Horse Sense: How to Develop Your Horse's Intelligence. (Illus.). 206p. 1994. pap. 11.95 (*0-943955-89-0*, Trafalgar Sq Pub) Trafalgar.

— Talking with Horses. (Illus.). 172p. 1991. pap. 11.95 (*0-943955-37-8*, Trafalgar Sq Pub) Trafalgar.

Blake, Holly J., jt. auth. see Langley, Donald J.

***Blake, I., et al.** Elliptic Curves in Cryptography. LC 99-19696. (London Mathematical Society Lecture Note Ser.: No. 265). 220p. (C). 1999. pap. 39.95 (*0-521-65374-6*) Cambridge U Pr.

Blake, Ian F. An Introduction to Applied Probability. LC 87-3784. 544p. (C). 1987. reprint ed. lib. bdg. 64.50 (*0-89464-211-1*) Krieger.

Blake, Ian F. & Poor, H. Vincent, eds. Communications & Networks: A Survey of Recent Advances. (Illus.). x, 433p. 1985. 159.95 (*0-387-96253-0*) Spr-Verlag.

B

An Asterisk (*) at the beginning of an entry indicates that the title is appearing for the first time.

Blake, J. Accounting Standards. 6th ed. 1997. pap. 57.50 (*0-273-62697-3*, Pub. by Pitman Pub) Trans-Atl Phila.

Blake, J. B. & Slavin, J. A., eds. Particle Acceleration in Space Plasmas. 128p. 1998. pap. 123.50 (*0-08-043312-X*, Pergamon Pr) Elsevier.

Blake, J. D. The Concise Guide to Interpreting Accounts. 176p. 1990. pap. 22.95 (*0-412-02631-7*, A4432, Chap & Hall NY) Chapman & Hall.

— The Concise Guide to Interpreting Accounts. 2nd ed. (Concise Guide Ser.). (Illus.). 158p. Date not set. pap. text 26.00 (*0-412-38280-6*, Chap & Hall NY) Chapman & Hall.

Blake, J. R., ed. Bubble Dynamics & Interface Phenomena: Proceedings IUTAM Symposium, Held in Birmingham, U. K., 6-9 September 1992. (Fluid Mechanics & Its Applications Ser.). 512p. (C). 1994. text 306.50 (*0-7923-3008-0*) Kluwer Academic.

***Blake, Jack.** Comes the Millennium. 183p. 1999. reprint ed. text 22.00 (*0-7881-6340-X*) DIANE Pub.

Blake, James. Introduction to Landscape Design & Construction. LC 98-9674. 250p. 1999. 74.95 (*0-566-07769-8*, Pub. by Ashgate Pub); pap. 43.95 (*0-566-07775-2*, Pub. by Ashgate Pub) Ashgate Pub Co.

***Blake, James.** Twentieth Century Irish Language Literature: A Survey of Fiction & Poetry. 264p. 1999. 74.95 (*1-57309-393-9*) Intl Schol Pr.

Blake, James A., et al, eds. Taxonomic Atlas of the Benthic Fauna of the Santa Maria Basin & Western Santa Barbara Channel Vol. 5, Pt. 2: The Annelida: Polychaeta: Phyllodocida (Syllidae & Scale-Bearing Families), Amphinomida, & Eunicida. LC 94-68651. (Illus.). viii, 378p. (Orig.). 1995. pap. 34.00 (*0-936494-10-7*) Santa B Museum.

— Taxonomic Atlas of the Benthic Fauna of the Santa Maria Basin & Western Santa Barbara Channel Vol. 6, Pt. 3: The Annelida: Polychaeta: Orbiniidae to Cossuridae. LC 94-68651. (Illus.). vii, 418p. (Orig.). 1996. pap. 39.00 (*0-936494-11-5*) Santa B Museum.

— Taxonomic Atlas of the Benthic Fauna of the Santa Maria Basin & Western Santa Barbara Channel Vol. 12, Pt. 3: The Crustacea: The Amphipoda. LC 94-68651. (Illus.). xiv, 251p. (Orig.). 1995. pap. 28.00 (*0-936494-17-4*) Santa B Museum.

— Taxonomic Atlas of the Benthil Fauna of the Santa Maria Basin & Western Santa Barbara Channel Vol. 14: Miscellaneous Taxa. (Illus.). 305p. (Orig.). 1996. pap. 36.00 (*0-936494-19-0*) Santa B Museum.

Blake, James A. & Hilbig, Brigitte, eds. Taxonomic Atlas of the Benthic Fauna of the Santa Maria Basin & Western Santa Barbara Channel Vol. 4, Pt. 1: The Annelida: Oligochaeta & Polychaeta: Phyllodocida (Phyllodocidae to Paralacydoniidae) LC 94-68651. (Illus.). xviii, 377p. (Orig.). 1994. pap. 36.00 (*0-936494-09-3*) Santa B Museum.

Blake, James A. & Lissner, Andrew, eds. Taxonomic Atlas of the Benthic Fauna of the Santa Maria Basin & Western Santa Barbara Channel Vol. 1: Introduction, Benthic Ecology, Platyhelminthes, & Nemertea. LC 94-68651. (Illus.). viii, 132p. (Orig.). 1993. pap. 34.00 (*0-936494-06-9*) Santa B Museum.

Blake, James A. & Scott, Paul H., eds. Taxonomic Atlas of the Benthic Fauna of the Santa Maria Basin & Western Santa Barbara Channel Vol. 10, Pt. 1: The Arthropoda - the Pychnogonida - the Crustacea - the Pecapoda. (Illus.). 151p. (Orig.). 1997. pap. write for info. (*0-936494-15-8*) Santa B Museum.

— Taxonomic Atlas of the Benthic Fauna of the Santa Maria Basin & Western Santa Barbara Channel Vol. 11, Pt. 2: The Crustacea - the Isopoda, Lumacea & Tanaidacea. LC 94-68651. (Illus.). 278p. (Orig.). 1997. pap. 34.00 (*0-936494-16-6*) Santa B Museum.

Blake, James A., ed. see Green, Karen D. & Bakus, Gerald J.

Blake, James A., jt. ed. see Scott, Paul V.

Blake, James A., ed. see Soule, Dorothy F., et al.

Blake, James C. Borderlands. 256p. 1999. pap. 12.50 (*0-380-79485-3*, Avon Bks) Morrow Avon.

— Borderlands. aut. ed. LC 99-207597. 256p. 1999. 24.00 (*0-380-97807-5*, Avon Bks) Morrow Avon.

— The Friends of Pancho Villa. 272p. 1996. pap. text 13.00 (*0-425-15304-5*) Berkley Pub.

— Friends of Pancho Villa: A Novel. 1998. mass mkt. 5.99 (*0-425-16235-4*) Berkley Pub.

— In the Rogue Blood. LC 97-11647. 352p. 1997. 23.00 (*0-380-97492-4*, Avon Bks) Morrow Avon.

— In the Rogue Blood. LC 97-11647. 352p. 1998. pap. 12.50 (*0-380-79241-9*, Avon Bks) Morrow Avon.

— The Pistoleer. 368p. (Orig.). 1995. pap. 12.00 (*0-425-14782-7*) Berkley Pub.

— The Pistoleer. (Orig.). 1996. mass mkt. 6.99 (*0-425-15412-2*) Berkley Pub.

— The Pistoleer. large type ed. (Niagara Large Print Ser.). 512p. (Orig.). 1996. pap. 29.50 (*0-7089-5823-0*) Ulverscroft.

***Blake, James C.** Red Grass River: A Legend. 384p. 2000. pap. 14.00 (*0-380-79242-7*, Perennial) HarperTrade.

Blake, James C. Red Grass River: A Legend. LC 98-18692. 384p. 1998. 23.00 (*0-380-97493-2*, Avon Bks) Morrow Avon.

***Blake, James C.** Wildwood Boys: A Novel. 384p. 2000. 24.00 (*0-380-97749-4*, Wm Morrow) Morrow Avon.

Blake, James N. Run Your Car on Sunshine: Using Solar Energy for a Solar Powered Car. LC 80-82734. (Illus.). 64p. 1981. pap. 2.95 (*0-915216-65-5*) Marathon Intl Bk.

Blake, Jan. Give Me My Yam: Level Two, Yellow. LC 98-88068. (Reading Together Ser.). (Illus.). 32p. (J). 1999. pap. write for info. (*0-7636-0873-4*) Candlewick Pr.

Blake, Janet & Halligan, Katherine. Arthur Dominique Rozaire: Poet with a Brush. (Illus.). 64p. 1998. pap. write for info. (*0-9666692-0-7*) G Stern Fine Arts.

Blake, Jeanne. Risky Times: How to Be AIDS-Smart & Stay Healthy. LC 89-40728. (Illus.). 196p. (YA). (gr. 8 up). 1999. pap. 5.95 (*0-89480-656-4*, 1656) Workman Pub.

— Risky Times - How to Be AIDS-Smart & Stay Healthy: A Guide for Teenagers. (YA). 1990. 11.05 (*0-606-05567-3*, Pub. by Turtleback) Demco.

— Tiempos de Riesgo. LC 89-40728. (SPA., Illus.). 196p. 1993. pap. 5.95 (*1-56305-436-1*, 3436) Workman Pub.

Blake, Jennifer. Arrow to the Heart. 1995. mass mkt. 5.99 (*0-449-14734-7*) Fawcett.

— Arrow to the Heart. large type ed. LC 96-50221. (Large Print Bks.). 1997. pap. 23.95 (*1-56895-404-2*) Wheeler Pub.

— Embrace & Conquer. 352p. 1987. mass mkt. 4.99 (*0-449-13323-0*) Fawcett.

— Garden of Scandal. 1999. mass mkt. write for info. (*1-55166-281-7*, 0-66281-7, Mira Bks) Harlequin Bks.

***Blake, Jennifer.** Garden of Scandal. LC 00-37743. 2001. write for info. (*0-7862-2618-8*) Thorndike Pr.

Blake, Jennifer. Golden Fancy. 416p. 1987. mass mkt. 5.99 (*0-449-13261-7*, GM) Fawcett.

— Kane. (Mira Bks.). 384p. 1998. per. 5.99 (*1-55166-429-1*, 1-66429-1, Mira Bks) Harlequin Bks.

— Louisiana Dawn. (Orig.). 1993. mass mkt. 5.99 (*0-449-14820-3*, GM) Fawcett.

— Love's Wild Desire. LC 96-96440. 1996. mass mkt. 4.99 (*0-449-14878-5*) Fawcett.

— Love's Wild Desire. large type ed. LC 97-3568. (Large Print Book Ser.). 1997. 25.95 (*1-56895-419-0*) Wheeler Pub.

— Luke. 1999. mass mkt. 5.99 (*1-55166-490-9*, 1-66490-3, Mira Bks) Harlequin Bks.

— Midnight Waltz. 352p. 1995. reprint ed. 20.00 (*0-7278-4719-8*) Severn Hse.

— Notorious Angel. 384p. 1996. 24.00 (*0-7278-4992-1*) Severn Hse.

— Perfume of Paradise. large type ed. LC 98-22080. (Large Print Book Ser.). 511 p. 1998. 24.95 (*1-56895-604-5*) Wheeler Pub.

— Prisoner of Desire: Historical Romance. 1994. 22.00 (*0-7278-4588-8*) Severn Hse.

— The Quilting Circle. (Orig.). 1996. mass mkt. 5.99 (*0-425-14980-3*) Berkley Pub.

***Blake, Jennifer.** Roan. 384p. 2000. mass mkt. 6.50 (*1-55166-630-8*, 1-66630-4, Mira Bks) Harlequin Bks.

Blake, Jennifer. Royal Passion. 384p. 1986. pap. 8.95 (*0-449-90101-7*, Columbine) Fawcett.

— Royal Passion. 384p. 1991. mass mkt. 5.99 (*0-449-14790-8*, GM) Fawcett.

— Royal Seduction. 416p. 1985. mass mkt. 5.95 (*0-449-12979-9*, GM) Fawcett.

— Shameless. 1997. mass mkt. 5.99 (*0-449-15002-X*, GM) Fawcett.

— Shameless. large type ed. LC 94-27172. 511p. 1994. lib. bdg. 22.95 (*0-7862-0269-6*) Thorndike Pr.

— Silver-Tongued Devil. 384p. 1996. 24.00 (*0-7278-5114-4*) Severn Hse.

— Silver-Tongued Devil. large type ed. 541p. 1996. 23.95 (*0-7862-0669-1*) Thorndike Pr.

— Southern Rapture. 1987. pap. 8.95 (*0-449-90177-7*) Fawcett.

— Southern Rapture. 1991. mass mkt. 5.95 (*0-449-14729-0*, GM) Fawcett.

— Spanish Serenade. 1994. mass mkt. 5.99 (*0-449-14603-0*) Fawcett.

— Spanish Serenade. large type ed. (Niagara Large Print Ser.). 525p. 1996. pap. 29.50 (*0-7089-5831-1*) Ulverscroft.

— The Storm & the Splendor. 1987. reprint ed. mass mkt. 4.95 (*0-449-13196-3*, GM) Fawcett.

— The Storm & the Splendor. 1994. reprint ed. lib. bdg. 22.00 (*0-7278-4652-3*) Severn Hse.

— Surrender in Moonlight. LC 97-38423. 1997. 24.95 (*0-7862-1264-0*) Thorndike Pr.

— Tender Betrayal. 1993. mass mkt. 5.99 (*0-449-14877-7*, GM) Fawcett.

— Tender Betrayal. 416p. 1984. mass mkt. 3.50 (*0-446-31314-9*, Pub. by Warner Bks) Little.

— Tigress. 1996. mass mkt. 4.99 (*0-449-14954-4*) Fawcett.

— Tigress. large type ed. LC 96-32353. 1996. 25.95 (*1-56895-361-5*, Compass) Wheeler Pub.

— Wildest Dreams. large type ed. 652p. 1992. reprint ed. lib. bdg. 17.95 (*1-56054-578-X*) Thorndike Pr.

Blake, Jennifer & Richards, Emilie. Southern Gentlemen: John "Rip" Peterson; Billie Ray Wainwright. (Mira Bks.). 384p. 1998. mass mkt. 5.99 (*1-55166-419-4*, 1-66419-2, Mira Bks) Harlequin Bks.

Blake, Jennifer, et al. A Purrfect Romance. large type ed. LC 95-46652. (Large Print Bks.). 1996. pap. 22.95 (*1-56895-284-8*) Wheeler Pub.

Blake, Jennifer, jt. auth. see Postman, Sheryl Lynn.

Blake, Jill. Cushions & Covers. (Quick & Easy Ser.). (Illus.). 96p. 1997. pap. text 14.95 (*0-7063-7676-5*, Pub. by WrLock) Sterling.

— Healthy Home: An Eco-Friendly Guide for Making Your Home Fit for Body, Mind, & Spirit. LC 98-86307. 192p. 1998. 29.95 (*0-8230-2235-8*) Watsn-Guptill.

— Tile Style Pattern Guide. 160p. 1996. 24.95 (*1-57715-006-6*) Knckerbocker.

Blake, Jill, jt. auth. see Taylor, Lesley.

***Blake, Jim.** Station Point. (Illus.). 65p. 1999. pap. 14.12 (*0-9640223-1-1*) Two Steps.

***Blake, Joanna.** Routes to Child Language: Evolutionary & Developmental Precursors. LC 99-52883. (Illus.). 288p. 2000. write for info. (*0-521-59299-2*) Cambridge U Pr.

Blake, Jody. Le Tumulte Noir: Modernist Art & Popular Entertainment in Jazz-Age Paris, 1900-1930. LC 97-29714. 224p. 1999. 65.00 (*0-271-01753-8*) Pa St U Pr.

Blake, Jody & Lasansky, Jeannette. Rural Delivery: Real Photo Postcards from Central Pennsylvania 1905-1935. Ruhl, Jean M., ed. LC 96-4372. 136p. (Orig.). 1996. 40.00 (*0-917127-09-9*); pap. 25.00 (*0-917127-10-2*) Oral Traditions.

— Rural Delivery: Real Photo Postcards from Central Pennsylvania, 1905-1935. (Illus.). 136p. 1996. 40.00 (*0-271-01625-6*); pap. 25.00 (*0-271-01626-4*) Pa St U Pr.

Blake, John. Creative Bread Baking: How to Bake Bread Without Recipes. LC 91-91847. 55p. 1990. pap. 7.95 (*0-9628966-0-8*) J & D Blake Assocs.

— Creative Bread Baking Two: Specialty Breads & the Rule of Two. 1991. pap. 7.95 (*0-9628966-1-6*) J & D Blake Assocs.

— Short Title Catalogue of Eighteenth Century Printed Books in the National Library of Medicine. 501p. 1998. reprint ed. 75.00 (*1-57898-086-0*) Martino Pubng.

Blake, John & Amat, Oriol. Interpreting Company Accounts. 3rd rev. ed. LC 96-38891. 208p. 1996. pap. 17.99 (*1-86152-022-0*) Thomson Learn.

Blake, John & Gao, Simon, eds. Perspectives on Accounting & Finance in China. LC 94-39780. 320p. (C). (gr. 13). 1995. pap. 60.00 (*0-415-11812-3*, C0476) Thomson Learn.

Blake, John & Hooks, Mike. Forty Years at Farnborough. (Illus.). 192p. 1991. 29.95 (*0-85429-741-3*, Pub. by GT Foulis) Haynes Manuals.

Blake, John & Hossein, Mahmud, eds. Readings in International Accounting. 304p. 1996. mass mkt. 94.95 (*0-415-13685-7*); mass mkt. 19.99 (*0-415-13686-5*) Chapman & Hall.

***Blake, John & Lunt, Henry J.** Accounting Standards. 7th ed. LC 00-34087. 2001. pap. write for info. (*0-273-64673-7*) Pearson Educ.

Blake, John, et al. Ethical Issues in Accounting. LC 98-13837. (Professional Ethics Ser.). 280p. (C). 1998. 75.00 (*0-415-17172-5*); pap. 24.99 (*0-415-17173-3*) Routledge.

Blake, John A., ed. see Blake, Susanne S.

Blake, John B. Public Health in the Town of Boston, 1630-1822. LC 59-10314. (Historical Studies: No. 72). (Illus.). 288p. 1959. 20.00 (*0-674-72250-7*) HUP.

Blake, John B., ed. see Conference on the History of Medicinal Drug Contro.

Blake, John F. The Role of the Attorney in Financial Planning. LC 90-11209. 1990. 35.00 (*1-55871-201-1*, TMFP-01) BNA.

Blake, John F., ed. Financial Planning after the Tax Reform Act of 1986. LC 87-30931. 751p. reprint ed. pap. 200.00 (*0-7837-4606-7*, 204432500002) Bks Demand.

Blake, Jon. You're a Hero, Daley B.! LC 91-58725. Orig. Title: Daley B.!. (Illus.). 32p. (J). (ps up). 1994. reprint ed. 13.95 (*1-56402-078-9*) Candlewick Pr.

Blake, Jonathan. History of the Town of Warwick, MA. 240p. 1993. reprint ed. lib. bdg. write for info. (*0-8328-2871-8*) Higginson Bk Co.

Blake, Judith. Family Size & Achievement. (Studies in Demography: Vol. 3). 384p. (C). 1989. pap. 22.50 (*0-520-08041-6*, Pub. by U CA Pr) Cal Prin Full Svc.

Blake, Judith, et al, eds. Annual Review of Sociology, Vol. 18. 1992. text 49.00 (*0-8243-2218-5*) Annual Reviews.

— Annual Review of Sociology, Vol. 19. (Illus.). 1993. text 49.00 (*0-8243-2219-3*) Annual Reviews.

Blake, Judith & Donovan, Jerry J. Western European Censuses, 1960, Vol. 7. LC 76-4558. (Population Monograph: No. 8). 421p. 1976. reprint ed. lib. bdg. 48.50 (*0-8371-8831-8*, BLWE, Greenwood Pr) Greenwood.

Blake, Judith, et al. Family Structure in Jamaica: The Social Context of Reproduction. LC 80-12362. (Illus.). 262p. 1980. reprint ed. lib. bdg. 59.75 (*0-313-22448-X*, BLFS, Greenwood Pr) Greenwood.

Blake, Kathleen, ed. Approaches to Teaching Eliot's Middlemarch. LC 90-39518. (Approaches to Teaching World Literature Ser.: No. 30). ix, 187p. 1990. pap. text 18.00 (*0-87352-534-5*, AP30P); lib. bdg. 37.50 (*0-87352-533-7*, AP30C) Modern Lang.

Blake, Kathryn A. Educating Exceptional Pupils: An Introduction to Contemporary Practices. LC 80-15222. (Illus.). 528p. (C). 1981. teacher ed. write for info. (*0-201-00084-9*); text. write for info. (*0-201-00083-0*) Addison-Wesley.

Blake, Kathryn A., jt. auth. see Johnson, G. Orville.

Blake, Kathy. America's Bounty Down-To-Earth Foods from the Garden, Orchard, Field, River & Ocean, 1. 1998. 12.98 (*1-880908-34-4*) Todtri Prods.

***Blake, Kathy.** Farmhouse Cooking: Traditional & Contemporary Meals from Our Country Kitchens, 1. 1998. 12.98 (*1-880908-41-7*) Todtri Prods.

Blake, Kathy. Handmade Books: A Step-By-Step Guide to Crafting Your Own Books. LC 96-51438. 128p. 1997. 24.95 (*0-8212-2220-1*, Pub. by Bulfinch Pr) Little.

Blake, Kathy & Milne, Bill. Making & Decorating Your Own Paper: Innovative Techniques & Original Projects. LC 93-45440. (Illus.). 144p. 1994. 27.95 (*0-8069-0544-1*) Sterling.

— Making & Decorating Your Own Paper: Innovative Techniques & Original Projects. (Illus.). 144p. 1995. pap. 14.95 (*0-8069-0545-X*) Sterling.

Blake, L. L. The Prince & the Professor: A Dialogue on the Place of the Monarchy in the 21st Century LC 96-162612. 126p. 1995. pap. write for info. (*0-85683-165-4*, Pub. by Shepheard-Walwyn Pubs) Paul & Co Pubs.

Blake, L. S., ed. Civil Engineer's Reference Book. 4th rev. ed. (Illus.). 1246p. 1994. pap. text 115.00 (*0-7506-1964-3*) Buttrwrth-Heinemann.

Blake, Lamont V. Antennas. 2nd ed. LC 91-66381. (Illus.). 461p. (C). 1991. reprint ed. text 45.00 (*0-9629720-1-0*) Munro Pub Co.

— Radar Range: Performance Analysis. LC 91-90362. (Illus.). 443p. 1991. reprint ed. 45.00 (*0-9629720-0-2*) Munro Pub Co.

Blake, Lillie D. Fettered for Life. LC 96-34923. 432p. 1997. pap. 18.95 (*1-55861-155-X*); lib. bdg. 45.00 (*1-55861-159-2*) Feminist Pr.

Blake, Lisabeth. Brewsie & Willie. 1960. pap. 3.25 (*0-8222-0149-6*) Dramatists Play.

Blake, Lord, ed. Oxford Illustrated Encyclopedia Vol. 4: World History from 1800 to the Present Day. (Illus.). 400p. 1988. 49.95 (*0-19-869136-X*) OUP.

Blake, Lord, jt. ed. see Nicholls, Christine S.

Blake, Lord, ed. see Smith, George.

Blake, Lynn M., ed. see Mallory, F. R.

Blake, M. B., et al. Education of the Modern Girl. LC 67-30208. (Essay Index Reprint Ser.). 1977. 19.95 (*0-8369-0406-0*) Ayer.

Blake, M. C., Jr., ed. Franciscan Geology of Northern California. (Illus.). 254p. (Orig.). 1984. pap. text 9.00 (*1-878861-29-8*) Pac Section SEPM.

Blake, Marcia & Liverside, Peggy, eds. College Admissions Data Handbook, 1991-1992: Midwest Regional Vol. 32nd ed. 3175p. (Orig.). 1991. pap. 45.00 (*1-878172-10-7*, Wintergreen-Orchard) Riverside Pub Co.

— College Admissions Data Handbook, 1991-1992: Northeast Regional Vol. 32nd ed. 3175p. (Orig.). 1991. pap. 45.00 (*1-878172-08-5*, Wintergreen-Orchard) Riverside Pub Co.

— College Admissions Data Handbook, 1991-1992: Southeast Regional Vol. 32nd ed. 3175p. (Orig.). 1991. pap. 45.00 (*1-878172-09-3*, Wintergreen-Orchard) Riverside Pub Co.

— College Admissions Data Handbook, 1991-1992: West Regional Vol. 32nd ed. 3175p. 1991. 45.00 (*1-878172-11-5*, Wintergreen-Orchard) Riverside Pub Co.

***Blake, Marie.** You Can Paint Pastels. (Illus.). 96p. 2000. pap. 9.95 (*0-8230-5990-1*) Watsn-Guptill.

Blake, Marion E. Roman Construction in Italy from Nerva Through the Antonines. Bishop, Doris T., ed. LC 72-83463. (American Philosophical Society, Memoirs Ser.: No. 96). 454p. reprint ed. pap. 140.80 (*0-7837-1112-3*, 204164200021) Bks Demand.

Blake, Michael. Airman Mortensen. 1991. 20.00 (*0-9627387-7-8*) Seven Wolves.

— Dances with Wolves. 320p. 1988. mass mkt. 5.95 (*0-449-13448-2*, GM) Fawcett.

Blake, Michael. Dances with Wolves. 1988. 11.05 (*0-606-04898-7*, Pub. by Turtleback) Demco.

Blake, Michael. Marching to Valhalla: A Novel of Custer's Last Days. 304p. 1997. pap. 12.95 (*0-449-00044-3*) Fawcett.

— Marching to Valhalla: A Novel of Custer's Last Days. large type ed. LC 97-4448. 412p. 1997. 23.95 (*0-7838-8091-X*, G K Hall Lrg Type) Mac Lib Ref.

Blake, Michael, ed. Pacific Latin America in Prehistory: The Evolution of Archaic & Formative Cultures. LC 98-43834. (Illus.). 234p. 1999. pap. text 50.00 (*0-87422-166-8*) Wash St U Pr.

Blake, Michael, et al. Teaching the New Library: A How-to-Do-It Manual for Planning & Designing Instructional Programs. LC 96-43647. (How-to-Do-It Manuals Ser.). 171p. 1996. pap. 49.95 (*1-55570-214-7*) Neal-Schuman.

Blake, Michael, ed. see Dickson, Murray.

Blake, Michael F. The Films of Lon Chaney. LC 97-34935. (Illus.). 220p. 1998. 35.00 (*1-879511-26-6*, Vestal Pr) Madison Bks UPA.

— Lon Chaney: The Man Behind the Thousand Faces. LC 93-20212. (Illus.). 408p. 1994. pap. 19.95 (*1-879511-09-6*, Vestal Pr) Madison Bks UPA.

— A Thousand Faces: Lon Chaney's Unique Artistry in Motion Pictures. 398p. 1995. pap. 19.95 (*1-879511-21-5*, Vestal Pr) Madison Bks UPA.

Blake, Michael J., jt. ed. see Kavass, Igor I.

***Blake, Michelle.** Tentmaker. (Lily Connor Mysteries Ser.). 2000. mass mkt. 5.99 (*0-425-17668-1*) Berkley Pub.

Blake, Michelle. The Tentmaker: A Lily Connor Mystery. LC 99-27380. 304p. 1999. 23.95 (*0-399-14577-X*, G P Putnam) Peng Put Young Read.

Blake, N. 10 Relatos de Detectives. 1996. pap. text 14.95 (*84-01-54008-9*) Plaza.

Blake, N. F. The English Language in Medieval Literature. 1979. pap. 10.95 (*0-416-72470-1*, NO.2024) Routledge.

— A History of the English Language. LC 96-12951. (Illus.). 372p. (C). 1996. text 75.00 (*0-8147-1292-4*) NYU Pr.

— A History of the English Language. (Illus.). 382p. 1998. pap. text 25.00 (*0-8147-1313-0*) NYU Pr.

— Language of Shakespeare. 2nd ed. LC 95-106830. 154p. 1994. text 17.95 (*0-333-49778-3*, Pub. by Macmillan) St Martin.

— William Caxton & English Literary Culture. 320p. 1991. 55.00 (*1-85285-051-5*) Hambledon Press.

Blake, N. F., ed. The Cambridge History of the English Language Vol. 2: 1066-1476. (Illus.). 732p. (C). 1992. text 135.00 (*0-521-26475-8*) Cambridge U Pr.

— History of Reynard the Fox Translated from the Dutch Original by William Caxton. (OS 263 Ser.). (Illus.). 1970. 24.95 (*0-19-722267-6*) OUP.

— Phoenix. 136p. 1990. pap. text 15.00 (*0-85989-342-1*, Pub. by Univ Exeter Pr) Northwestern U Pr.

Blake, Nayland, et al, eds. In a Different Light: Visual Culture, Sexual Identity, Queer Practice. LC 94-49371. (Illus.). 368p. 1995. pap. 16.95 (*0-87286-300-X*) City Lights.

Blake, Nayland, et al. David Cannon Dashiell: "Queer Mysteries" LC 93-84527. (Illus.). 32p. (Orig.). 1993. pap. 8.00 (*0-930495-20-9*) San Fran Art Inst.

Blake, Neil Ffrench. The World of Show Jumping. 1973. reprint ed. 15.95 (*0-912830-29-8*) Printed Horse.

B

An Asterisk (*) at the beginning of an entry indicates that the title is appearing for the first time.

Blake, Nelson M. Land into Water - Water into Land: A History of Water Management in Florida. LC 79-21836. (Florida State University Bks.). 352p. reprint ed. pap. 109.20 (*0-8357-6924-0*, 203798300009) Bks Demand.
— The Road to Reno: A History of Divorce in the United States. LC 77-11070. 269p. 1977. reprint ed. lib. bdg. 66.50 (*0-8371-9797-X*, BLRR, Greenwood Pr) Greenwood.
— Water for the Cities: A History of the Urban Water Supply Problem in the United States. LC 56-13576. (Maxwell School Ser.: No. 3). 357p. 1995. reprint ed. pap. 110.70 (*0-608-17478-5*, 202997100067) Bks Demand.

Blake, Nelson M., ed. see Kinsley, Jessie C.

Blake, Nicholas. Murder with Malice. large type ed. (Linford Mystery Library). 528p. 1997. pap. 16.99 (*0-7089-5094-9*, Linford) Ulverscroft.
— A Penknife in My Heart. large type ed. (Linford Mystery Library). 400p. 1997. pap. 16.99 (*0-7089-5106-6*, Linford) Ulverscroft.
— A Tangled Web. 224p. 1987. mass mkt. 3.50 (*0-88184-292-3*) Carroll & Graf.

***Blake, Nicholas & Lawrence, Richard.** Illustrated Companion to Nelson's Navy. (Illus.). 208p. 2000. 29.95 (*0-8117-0864-0*) Stackpole.

Blake, Nicholas J., jt. auth. see MacDonald, Ian A.

Blake, Nigel, et al. Thinking Again: Education after Postmodernism. LC 97-27886. (Critical Studies in Education & Culture). 224p. 1998. 55.00 (*0-89789-511-8*, Bergin & Garvey); pap. 19.95 (*0-89789-512-6*, Bergin & Garvey) Greenwood.

***Blake, Norman.** The Norman Blake Anthology. 200p. 1998. pap. 24.95 (*0-7866-4088-X*, 96641) Mel Bay.

Blake, Osbourne C. Belly of Reason. 1998. pap. write for info. (*1-57553-912-8*) Watermrk Pr.

Blake, P. Gynaecological Oncology: A Guide to Clinical Management. Lambert, H. & Crawford, R., eds. (Illus.). 284p. 1998. text 79.50 (*0-19-262798-8*) OUP.

Blake, Patricia, ed. see Mayakovsky, Vladimir.

Blake, Peter. The Architecture of Ulrich Franzen. 198p. 1999. 45.00 (*3-7643-5905-6*, Pub. by Birkhauser) Princeton Arch.
— How to Design the Perfect Building. 300p. 1997. text 35.00 (*0-393-73019-0*) Norton.
— An Introduction to Sailing. (Illus.). 128p. (Orig.). 1993. pap. 17.50 (*0-924486-54-6*) Sheridan.
— The Master Builders. LC 96-229682. (Illus.). 448p. 1996. reprint ed. pap. 16.95 (*0-393-31504-5*) Norton.
— No Place Like Utopia: Modern Architecture & the Company We Kept. 352p. 1996. pap. 18.95 (*0-393-31503-7*) Norton.
— Philip Johnson. LC 96-195790. (Studio Paperback Ser.). (Illus.). 256p. 1996. pap. 29.95 (*3-7643-5393-7*, Pub. by Birkhauser) Princeton Arch.

Blake, Peter, et al. Ethics of Change: Man & Nature: Conflict or Cooperation. Fetscher, Elmar, ed. (Proceedings of the February ForumSer.: Vol. 5). 150p. (Orig.). 1991. pap. text. write for info. (*1-882070-06-2*) Atlantic Ctr Arts.

Blake, Peter R., jt. ed. see Lambert, Hannah E.

Blake, Philip. Information Technology & Financial Services. Gandy, A. & Chapman, C. S., eds. (Glenlake Business Monographs). 225p. 1998. 67.50 (*1-884964-86-9*) Fitzroy Dearborn.

***Blake, Philippa.** Heat of the Moment. large type ed. 288p. 1999. 31.99 (*0-7089-4094-3*, Linford) Ulverscroft.

Blake, Philippa. Waiting for the Sea to Be Blue. 234p. 1997. 26.00 (*0-7528-0157-0*, Pub. by Orion Pubng Grp) Trafalgar.

Blake, Quentin. All Join In. (J). (ps-3). 1991. 14.95 (*0-316-09934-1*) Little.
— Clown. LC 95-12811. (Illus.). 32p. (J). (ps-3). 1995. 15.95 (*0-8050-4399-3*) H Holt & Co.
— Clown. 32p. (J). (ps-3). 1998. pap. 6.95 (*0-8050-5933-4*) H Holt & Co.
— Nonsense Verse. 288p. 1999. pap. 4.99 (*0-14-036660-1*) Viking Penguin.
— Quentin Blake's Nursery Rhyme Book. LC 83-48171. (Illus.). 32p. (J). (gr. k-3). 1984. 7.95 (*0-06-020533-4*) HarpC Child Bks.
— Simpkin. 1999. pap. write for info. (*0-14-050608-X*) Viking Penguin.

***Blake, Quentin.** 10 Frogs. LC 99-65115. (Michael di Capua Bks.). (Illus.). 24p. (J). 2000. 12.95 (*0-06-205200-4*) HarpC Child Bks.
— Ten Frogs. LC 99-65115. 24p. (J). 2000. lib. bdg. 12.89 (*0-06-205201-2*) HarpC Child Bks.

Blake, Quentin. Zagazoo. LC 98-42420. (Illus.). 32p. (J). 1999. 15.95 (*0-531-30178-8*) Orchard Bks Watts.

Blake, Quentin, ed. Nonsense Verse. LC 97-112693. 1997. pap. 12.95 (*0-14-058757-8*) Viking Penguin.

Blake, Quentin. Mrs. Armitage & the Big Wave. LC 97-15420. 32p. (J). (gr. k-3). 1998. 15.00 (*0-15-201642-2*) Harcourt.

***Blake, Quentin, selected by.** Puffin Book of Nonsense Stories. (Illus.). 288p. (YA). (gr. 2 up). 2000. pap. 10.95 (*0-14-038213-5*, Pub. by Pnguin Bks Ltd) Trafalgar.

Blake, Quentin & Cassidy, John. Drawing for the Artistically Undiscovered. (Illus.). 106p. (YA). (gr. 5 up). 1999. spiral bd. 19.95 (*1-57054-320-8*) Klutz.

Blake, Quentin, jt. auth. see Dahl, Roald.

Blake, R., jt. auth. see Ruttkowski, W.

Blake, R. A. The Lutheran Milieu of the Films of Ingmar Bergman. LC 77-22905. (Dissertation on Film Ser.). 1978. lib. bdg. 29.95 (*0-405-10751-X*) Ayer.

Blake, R. L. The Crimean War. (Illus.). 192p. 1994. reprint ed. 24.95 (*0-85052-404-0*, Pub. by Leo Cooper) Trans-Atl Phila.

Blake, R. M., et al. Theories of Scientific Method: The Renaissance Through the Nineteenth Century. (Classics in the History & Philosophy of Science Ser.: Vol. 2). viii, 364p. 1960. pap. text 75.00 (*2-88124-351-7*) Gordon & Breach.

Blake, Rachelle S. Delmar's Medical Transcriptionist Handbook. 2nd ed. LC 97-18408. 272p. (C). 1997. pap. 32.95 (*0-8273-8325-8*) Thomson Learn.
— The Medical Transcriptionist's Handbook. 352p. 1993. pap., teacher ed. write for info. (*0-538-70678-3*) S-W Pub.

Blake, Ralph E. Basic Electrical Math. 1987. ring bd. 59.95 (*0-945035-00-4*) Ctrl UT Pub.
— Mathematics for Principles of Technology. 1988. ring bd. 39.95 (*0-945035-01-2*) Ctrl UT Pub.

Blake, Randolph, jt. auth. see Sekuler, Robert.

Blake, Raymond B. Canadians at Last: The Integration of Newfoundland As a Province. (Illus.). 272p. (C). 1994. text 55.00 (*0-8020-0554-3*); pap. text 19.95 (*0-8020-6978-9*) U of Toronto Pr.

Blake, Raymond B. & Kesheny, Jeff, eds. Social Welfare Policy in Canada: Historical Readings. LC 94-932821. viii, 397p. 1995. write for info. (*0-7730-5448-0*) Addison-Wesley.

Blake, Reed H., jt. auth. see Harris, John S.

***Blake, Richard A.** Afterimage: The Indelible Catholic Imagination of Six American Filmmakers. LC 99-42549. 268p. 2000. 22.00 (*0-8294-1550-5*) Loyola Pr.
— Afterimage: The Indelible Catholic Imagination of Six American Filmmakers. LC 99-42549. (Illus.). 2000. pap. write for info. (*0-8294-1378-2*) Loyola Pr.

Blake, Richard A. Screening American Reflections: Critical Contexts of Five Classic Films. 1991. pap. 14.95 (*0-8091-3193-5*) Paulist Pr.
— Woody Allen: Profane & Sacred. LC 95-3312. 250p. (YA). 1995. 47.50 (*0-8108-2993-2*) Scarecrow.

Blake, Robert. Disraeli. (Lost Treasure Ser.). 850p. 1998. pap. 29.95 (*1-85375-275-4*) Prion.
— Gladstone, Disraeli & Queen Victoria: The Centenary Romanes Lecture Delivered Before the University of Oxford on 10 November 1992. LC 93-16307. (Romanes Lectures). 26p. 1993. pap. text 4.50 (*0-19-951361-9*, Clarendon Pr) OUP.
— Winston Churchill. LC 99-170156. (New Pocket Biographies Ser.). (Illus.). 128p. 1998. pap. 9.95 (*0-7509-1507-2*, Pub. by Sutton Pub Ltd) Intl Pubs Mktg.

Blake, Robert & Louis, William R., eds. Churchill. 480p. 1993. 35.00 (*0-393-03409-7*) Norton.
— Churchill. LC 92-21814. 1993. 20.00 (*0-19-820317-9*) OUP.

Blake, Robert, jt. auth. see Marks, Martha A.

Blake, Robert, jt. auth. see Mazel, David.

Blake, Robert, jt. ed. see Judge, Harry.

Blake, Robert A., jt. auth. see Orbaker, Douglas.

Blake, Robert A., Jr., jt. auth. see Pipes, R. Byron.

Blake, Robert J. Akiak: A Tale from the Iditarod. LC 97-2251. (Illus.). 32p. (J). (gr. k-3). 1997. 15.95 (*0-399-22798-9*, Philomel) Peng Put Young Read.
— Dog. LC 92-39313. (Illus.). 32p. (J). (ps-3). 1994. 14.95 (*0-399-22019-4*, Philomel) Peng Put Young Read.

***Blake, Robert J.** Dog. 32p. (ps-3). 1999. pap. 5.99 (*0-698-11758-1*, PapStar) Peng Put Young Read.
— Fledgling. LC 99-54838. (Illus.). 32p. (J). (ps-3). 2000. 15.99 (*0-399-23321-0*, Philomel) Peng Put Young Read.

Blake, Robert J. The Perfect Spot. LC 91-16006. (Illus.). 32p. (J). (ps-3). 1992. 15.95 (*0-399-22132-8*, Philomel) Peng Put Young Read.
— The Perfect Spot. (Illus.). 32p. (J). (ps-3). 1997. pap. 5.95 (*0-698-11431-0*, PapStar) Peng Put Young Read.

Blake, Robert J. The Perfect Spot. LC 91-16006. (J). 1997. 11.15 (*0-606-11738-5*, Pub. by Turtleback) Demco.

Blake, Robert J. Spray. LC 94-32514. (Illus.). 32p. (J). (ps-3). 1996. 15.95 (*0-399-22770-9*, Philomel) Peng Put Young Read.
— Yudonsi: A Tale from the Canyons. LC 98-33755. 32p. (J). (gr. 1-3). 1999. 15.99 (*0-399-23320-2*, Philomel) Peng Put Young Read.

***Blake, Robert J., et al, eds.** Essays in Hispanic Linguistics Dedicated to Paul M. Lloyd. (Homenajes Ser.: Vol. 15). (SPA.). 258p. 1999. pap. 22.00 (*0-936388-81-1*) Juan de la Cuesta.

Blake, Robert R. & McCanse, Anne E. Leadership Dilemmas - Grid Solutions: An All-New Presentation of the Managerial Grid. 4th ed. 376p. 1991. 26.95 (*0-87201-488-6*, 1488) Gulf Pub.

Blake, Robert R. & Mouton, Jane S. Consultation: A Comprehensive Approach to Individual & Organization Development. 2nd ed. LC 82-6746. (Illus.). 528p. 1983. 30.95 (*0-201-10165-3*) Addison-Wesley.
— Corporate Excellence Through Grid Organization Development. LC 68-21510. 394p. reprint ed. pap. 122.20 (*0-8357-2575-8*, 204026600015) Bks Demand.
— Productivity: The Human Side: A Social Dynamics Approach. LC 80-69695. 143p. reprint ed. pap. 44.40 (*0-608-30692-4*, 202261900028) Bks Demand.

Blake, Robert R., et al. The Academic Administrator Grid. LC 80-8908. (Jossey-Bass Series in Higher Education). (Illus.). 443p. reprint ed. pap. 137.40 (*0-8357-4806-5*, 203774300009) Bks Demand.
— Change by Design. (Organization Development Ser.). (Illus.). 221p. (C). 1989. pap. text 27.80 (*0-201-50748-X*) Addison-Wesley.
— Managing Intergroup Conflict in Industry. LC 64-8696. 224p. reprint ed. pap. 69.50 (*0-608-18158-7*, 203287400081) Bks Demand.

Blake, Robert R., jt. auth. see Mouton, Jane S.

Blake, Robert W., ed. Efficiency & Economy in Animal Physiology. 199p. (C). 1992. text 64.95 (*0-521-40066-X*) Cambridge U Pr.

Blake, Robert W., intro. Reading, Writing & Interpreting Literature: Pedagogy, Positions & Research. 273p. (C). 1989. pap. text 10.00 (*0-930348-15-X*) NY St Eng Coun.

***Blake, Robin.** Anthony Van Dyck: A Life, 1599-1641. LC 99-58351. (Illus.). 435p. 2000. text 30.00 (*1-56663-282-X*, Pub. by I R Dee) Natl Bk Netwk.

Blake, Robin & Stephens, Eleanors. Compulsion. 160p. 1988. 40.00 (*1-85283-208-8*, Pub. by Boxtree) St Mut.

Blake, Roger. Adriatic Pilot Supplement, 1996. 60p. 1996. pap. 125.00 (*0-85288-371-4*, Pub. by Laurie Norie & Wilson Ltd) St Mut.

Blake, Rory. Market Democracy: The Decline of American Ideals & Rise of a Two Class Society. LC 96-85861. 288p. 1997. pap. text 15.00 (*0-9653521-0-2*) BC Bks.

Blake, Rose & Yeats, Cameron. The Camrose Vision. LC 99-62033. 365p. 1999. 25.00 (*0-7388-0398-7*); pap. 15.00 (*0-7388-0399-5*) Xlibris Corp.

Blake, Roy. Comprehensive Electronic Communication. LC 96-41373. (C). 1996. mass mkt. 104.95 (*0-314-20140-8*) West Pub.

***Blake, Roy M. & McDonald, Archie P.** Uncommon Valor... Common Virtue: A Tribute to Bennett P. Blake, U. S. Marine on Iwo Jima. 160p. 1999. 19.95 (*1-878096-53-2*, Epigram Pr) Best E TX Pubs.

Blake, S. F. & Atwood, Alice C. Geographical Guide to Floras of the World Vol. 1: Africa, Australia, North America, South America & Islands of the Atlantic, Pacific & Indian Oceans. (Illus.). 336p. 1941. reprint ed. 50.00 (*3-87429-068-9*, 001271, Pub. by Koeltz Sci Bks) Lubrecht & Cramer.
— Geographical Guide to Floras of the World Vol. 2: Western Europe: Finland, Sweden, Norway, Denmark, Iceland, Great Britain with Ireland, Netherlands, Belgium, Luxembourg, France, Spain, Portugal, Andorra, Monaco, Italy, San Marino, & Switzerland. 742p. 1974. reprint ed. 130.90 (*3-87429-060-3*, 001275, Pub. by Koeltz Sci Bks) Lubrecht & Cramer.

Blake, Sally. The Devil's Kiss. large type ed. (Magna Historical Fiction Ser.). 372p. 1992. 27.99 (*0-7505-0396-3*) Ulverscroft.
— Far Distant Shores. large type ed. 357p. 1994. 27.99 (*0-7505-0645-8*, Pub. by Mgna Lrg Print) Ulverscroft.

***Blake, Sally.** A Gentleman's Masquerade. large type ed. 320p. 1999. 25.99 (*0-263-16020-3*, Pub. by Mills & Boon) Ulverscroft.

Blake, Sally. Lady of Spain. large type ed. 1995. 27.99 (*0-7505-0646-6*, Pub. by Mgna Lrg Print) Ulverscroft.
— Marrying for Love. large type ed. (Mills & Boon Large Print Ser.). 350p. 1998. 24.99 (*0-263-15528-5*, Pub. by Mills & Boon) Ulverscroft.
— Outback Woman. large type ed. (Magna Large Print Ser.). 1994. 27.99 (*0-7505-0647-4*, Pub. by Mgna Lrg Print) Ulverscroft.

Blake, Sally S., jt. auth. see Shaw, Jean M.

Blake, Samuel. A Genealogical History of William Blake of Dorchester & His Descendants. (Illus.). 140p. 1988. reprint ed. pap. 21.00 (*0-8328-0263-8*); reprint ed. lib. bdg. 29.00 (*0-8328-0262-X*) Higginson Bk Co.

Blake, Sara M. & Madden, Janet. Facets: Writing Skills in Context. (Illus.). 400p. (Orig.). (C). 1994. teacher ed. write for info. (*0-318-72453-7*) Macmillan.
— Facets: Writing Skills in Context. LC 93-43228. (Illus.). 464p. (Orig.). (C). 1994. pap. 50.00 (*0-02-310841-X*, Macmillan Coll) P-H.
— Facets: Writing Skills in Context. annot. ed. LC 93-43228. 400p. (Orig.). 1993. pap., teacher ed. write for info. (*0-02-310842-8*, U0920-1) Allyn.

Blake, Sara M., jt. auth. see Madden, Janet.

Blake, Sarah. Full Turn. (Blue Ser.). (Illus.). 32p. (Orig.). 1989. pap. 5.00 (*0-938631-08-X*) Pennywhistle Pr.

***Blake, Sarah.** Grange House. LC 00-25912. 320p. 2000. text 24.00 (*0-312-24544-0*, Picador USA) St Martin.

Blake, Sarah, jt. auth. see Kahn, Robin.

***Blake, Scott & Lloyd, Scott.** The Keys to Avalon: The True Location of Arthur's Kingdom Revealed. 2000. 29.95 (*1-86204-735-9*, Pub. by Element MA) Penguin Putnam.

Blake Staff. Blake's United Kingdom Book of Parliament. 19th ed. (Illus.). 250p. 1998. 50.00 (*1-85782-189-0*, Pub. by Blake Publng) Seven Hills Bk.

Blake, Stephen. Loving Your Long-Distance Relationship. 96p. 1996. pap. 6.99 (*0-9680971-0-3*) Anton.
— Loving Your Long-Distance Relationship, Vol. 1. 1998. text 13.95 incl. audio (*0-9680971-1-1*) Anton.

***Blake, Stephen.** Loving Your Long Distance Relationship for Women. 1998. text 6.99 (*0-9680971-6-2*) Anton.

Blake, Stephen & Bryan, Kimberli. Still Loving Your Long-Distance Relationship. 96p. 1998. pap. 6.99 (*0-9680971-3-8*) Anton.

***Blake, Stephen P.** Half the World: The Social Architecture of Safavid Isfahan, 1590-1722. LC 99-30291. (Islamic Art & Architecture Ser.: Vol. 9). (Illus.). 216p. 1999. lib. bdg. 65.00 (*1-56859-087-3*) Mazda Pubs.

Blake, Steve, jt. auth. see Tierra, Michael.

Blake, Susan. Letters from Togo. LC 91-20943. (Singular Lives: The Iowa Series in North American Autobiography). (Illus.). 203p. 1991. pap. 13.95 (*0-87745-340-3*) U of Iowa Pr.
— A Practical Approach to Legal Advice & Drafting. 4th ed. 472p. 1993. 44.00 (*1-85431-253-7*, Pub. by Blackstone Pr) Gaunt.
— A Practical Approach to Legal Advice & Drafting. 5th ed. 412p. 1997. pap. 46.00 (*1-85431-541-2*, Pub. by Blackstone Pr) Gaunt.

Blake, Susan & Mayson, Stephen W. Mayson on Revenue Law. 728p. (C). 1991. 90.00 (*1-85431-146-8*, Pub. by Blackstone Pr) Gaunt.
— Revenue Law. 710p. (C). 1990. 225.00 (*1-85431-052-6*, Pub. by Blackstone Pr) St Mut.
— Revenue Law. 13th ed. 1993. 64.00 (*1-85431-269-3*, Pub. by Blackstone Pr) Gaunt.

Blake, Susan, et al. Family Law in Practice. 2nd ed. (Inns of Court School of Law Ser.). 243p. 1998. pap. 48.00 (*1-85431-714-8*, 15581, Pub. by Blackstone Pr) Gaunt.
— Family Law in Practice. 3rd ed. 253p. 1999. pap. 50.00 (*1-85431-898-5*, Pub. by Blackstone Pr) Gaunt.

***Blake, Susan, et al.** Family Law in Practice. 4th ed. (Inns of Court School of Law Ser.). 278p. 2000. pap. 46.00 (*1-84174-001-2*, Pub. by Blackstone Pr) Gaunt.

Blake, Susan, et al. Negotiation, 1998-99. 3rd ed. (Inns of Court School of Law Ser.). 198p. 1998. pap. 42.00 (*1-85431-769-5*) Gaunt.
— Negotiation, 1997-98. 2nd ed. (Inns of Court School of Law Ser.). 198p. 1997. pap. 40.00 (*1-85431-671-0*, Pub. by Blackstone Pr) Gaunt.
— Property Disputes in Practice. 151p. 1998. pap. 48.00 (*1-85431-719-9*, Pub. by Blackstone Pr) Gaunt.
— Property Disputes in Practice. 2nd ed. 151p. 1999. pap. 50.00 (*1-85431-903-5*, Pub. by Blackstone Pr) Gaunt.

***Blake, Susan, et al.** Property Disputes in Practice. 3rd ed. 149p. 2000. pap. 46.00 (*1-84174-006-3*, Pub. by Blackstone Pr) Gaunt.

Blake, Susan, et al. Remedies, 1998-99. 3rd ed. (Inns of Court School of Law Ser.). 357p. 1998. pap. 42.00 (*1-85431-777-6*) Gaunt.
— Remedies, 1997-98. 2nd ed. (Inns of Court School of Law Ser.). 355p. 1997. pap. 40.00 (*1-85431-679-6*, Pub. by Blackstone Pr) Gaunt.

Blake, Susan, jt. auth. see Mayson, Stephen W.

Blake, Susanne S. When Spirit Speaks: A Woman's Mystical Journey & Her Transformation Through the Power of Prayer. Blake, John A., ed. LC 97-182755. (Illus.). 330p. 1998. reprint ed. pap. 18.95 (*1-890247-00-6*) Yellow Bird Commun.

Blake, Sylvia & Kaufman, Sy. Keys to Comprehension: Reading Through Cloze. 1984. student ed. 2.95 (*0-910307-00-8*) Comp Pr.
— Practice Book for the Degrees of Reading Power Test. 1981. 4.95 (*0-9602800-6-5*) Comp Pr.
— Practice Book for the Regents Competency Test in Reading. 103p. 1981. 4.50 (*0-9602800-0-6*) Comp Pr.
— Turn on to Reading (All Night Long) 1984. student ed. 1.00 (*0-910307-04-0*) Comp Pr.

Blake, Sylvia, jt. auth. see Kaufman, Seymour.

Blake, Sylvia, jt. auth. see Tominberg, Larry.

Blake, Thomas M. Annotated Atlas of Electrocardiography: A Guide to Confident Interpretation. LC 98-36685. (Contemporary Cardiology Ser.: Vol. 3). 248p. 1998. 89.50 (*0-89603-762-2*); pap. 49.50 (*0-89603-768-1*) Humana.
— The Practice of Electrocardiography: A Problem-Solving Guide to Confident Interpretation. 5th ed. LC 93-39587. (Illus.). 336p. 1994. 59.50 (*0-89603-292-2*); pap. 39.00 (*0-89603-261-2*) Humana.

Blake, Tom. Hawaiian Surfriders. 21.95 (*0-681-02752-5*) Booklines Hawaii.
— Middle Aged & Dating Again. LC 97-92964. 188p. (Orig.). 1997. pap. 12.95 (*1-57502-423-3*, PO1300) Tooters Pub.

Blake, Toni, ed. Enduring Issues in Psychology. (Enduring Issues Ser.). 336p. (C). 1995. pap. text 17.45 (*1-56510-253-3*, 2533); lib. bdg. 27.45 (*1-56510-254-1*, 2541) Greenhaven.

Blake, Toni, jt. auth. see Karns, Michelle.

Blake, Tonya M., jt. auth. see Quince, Pamela-Denise.

Blake, Tupper A., photos by. Two Eagles - Dos Aguilas: The Natural World of the United States-Mexico Borderlands. LC 93-32431. (Illus.). 1994. 55.00 (*0-520-08482-9*, Pub. by U CA Pr) Cal Prin Full Svc.

***Blake, Tupper Ansel, et al.** Balancing Water: Restoring the Klamath Basin. LC 99-44878. (Illus.). 172p. 2000. 45.00 (*0-520-21314-9*, Pub. by U CA Pr) Cal Prin Full Svc.

Blake, Vanessa. Bride of Chance. large type ed. 304p. 1988. 27.99 (*0-7089-1892-1*) Ulverscroft.

Blake, Vernon. The Art & Craft of Drawing. LC 95-5436. (Illus.). 608p. 1995. pap. text 14.95 (*0-486-28594-4*) Dover.

Blake, Veronica. Sioux Sunrise. 448p. 1994. pap. 4.50 (*0-8217-4718-5*) NAL.

Blake, Virgil & Tjoumas, Renee, eds. Information Literacies for the Twenty-first Century. (Professional Librarian Ser.). 350p. 1990. 30.00 (*0-8161-1921-X*, Hall Reference) Macmillan.

Blake, Virgil L., ed. Mapping Curricular Reform in Library & Information Studies: The American Mosaic. LC 95-37925. (Public & Access Services Quarterly Ser.: Vol. 1, No. 3). 130p. 1995. 39.95 (*1-56024-740-1*) Haworth Pr.

Blake, W. O. History of Slavery & the Slave Trade, 2 vols., Set. LC 73-100496. (Studies in Black History & Culture: No. 54). 1970. lib. bdg. 150.95 (*0-8383-1105-9*) M S G Haskell Hse.

Blake, W. P. Lykanthropus. LC 98-90442. 1998. pap. 11.95 (*0-533-12809-9*) Vantage.

Blake, Wendon. Acrylic Painting. (Artist's Painting Library). (Illus.). 80p. 1979. pap. 9.95 (*0-8230-0068-0*) Watsn-Guptill.
— Acrylic Painting: A Complete Course. LC 97-23763. 1997. pap. 14.95 (*0-486-29912-0*) Dover.
— Acrylic Painting: A Complete Guide. LC 97-23763. (Illus.). 200p. 1997. reprint ed. pap. text 16.95 (*0-486-29589-3*) Dover.
— Creative Color for the Oil Painter. LC 98-48445. 160p. 1999. pap. text 19.95 (*0-486-40472-2*) Dover.
— Figure Drawing Step by Step. LC 98-21530. (Illus.). 80p. 1998. pap. 6.95 (*0-486-40200-2*) Dover.
— Landscape Drawing Step by Step. unabridged ed. LC 98-21529. (Illus.). 80p. 1998. pap. 6.95 (*0-486-40201-0*) Dover.
— Oil Portraits Step by Step. rev. ed. LC 98-28210. (Illus.). 64p. 1998. pap. 8.95 (*0-486-40279-7*) Dover.

An Asterisk (*) at the beginning of an entry indicates that the title is appearing for the first time.

— Portrait Drawing. (Artist's Painting Library). (Illus.). 80p. (Orig.). 1981. pap. 8.95 (*0-8230-4094-1*) Watsn-Guptill.
— Starting to Draw. (Artist's Painting Library). (Illus.). 80p. 1981. pap. 9.95 (*0-8230-4916-7*) Watsn-Guptill.
— Watercolor Landscapes Step by Step. rev. ed. LC 98-36278. (Illus.). 64p. 1998. pap. 8.95 (*0-486-40280-0*) Dover.
— Watercolor Painting. (Artist's Painting Library). (Illus.). 80p. 1979. pap. 12.95 (*0-8230-5673-2*) Watsn-Guptill.
***Blake, Wendon.** Watercolor Painting Step-by-Step. LC 99-45605. 2000. pap. 8.95 (*0-486-40948-1*) Dover.
Blake, William. Blake's America, a Prophecy, & Europe, a Prophecy: Facsimile Reproductions of Two Illuminated Books, with 35 Plates in Color. (Fine Art Ser.). (Illus.). 48p. 1984. reprint ed. pap. 8.95 (*0-486-24548-9*) Dover.
— Blake's Illustrations for the Book of Job. (Illus.). 64p. 1995. reprint ed. pap. text 9.95 (*0-486-28765-3*) Dover.
— Blake's Job: William Blake's Illustrations of the Book of Job. Damon, S. Foster, ed. LC 82-13585. (Illus.). 76p. 1966. reprint ed. pap. 11.95 (*0-87451-241-7*) U Pr of New Eng.
— Blake's Poetry & Designs. Johnson, Mary L. & Grant, John F., eds. (Critical Editions Ser.). (Illus.). 661p. (C). 1979. pap. text 20.25 (*0-393-09083-3*) Norton.
— Blake's Selected Poems. unabridged ed. Erdman, David V. & Erdman, Virginia, eds. (Thrift Editions Ser.). 96p. (Orig.). 1995. pap. text 1.00 (*0-486-28517-0*) Dover.
— Bloomsbury Classic Poetry Series. 2nd ed. 1995. text 9.95 (*0-312-11937-2*) St Martin.
— The Book of Thel: A Facsimile & a Critical Text. Bogen, Nancy, ed. LC 74-155857. 98p. reprint ed. pap. 30.40 (*0-8357-7343-4*, 202301100031) Bks Demand.
— The Book of Urizen. (BCL1-PR English Literature Ser.). 25p. 1992. reprint ed. lib. bdg. 59.00 (*0-7812-7443-5*) Rprt Serv.
Blake, William. The Book of Urizen: A Facsimile in Full Color. LC 97-27426. (Illus.). 48p. 1997. pap. 4.95 (*0-486-29801-9*) Dover.
Blake, William. The Complete Poems: Complete Poems. Ostriker, Alicia S., ed. 1,072p. 1978. pap. 16.95 (*0-14-042215-3*, Penguin Classics) Viking Penguin.
— The Complete Poetry & Prose of William Blake. rev. ed. Erdman, David V., ed. LC 81-40323. 1000p. 1981. 58.00 (*0-520-04473-8*, Pub. by U CA Pr) Cal Prin Full Svc.
— Complete Writings of William Blake, with Variant Readings. 2nd ed. Keynes, Geoffrey L., ed. (Oxford Standard Authors Ser.). (Illus.). 960p. 1966. pap. 22.00 (*0-19-281050-2*) OUP.
— Continental Prophecies. Worrall, David & Dorrbecker, Detlef W., eds. LC 93-43943. (Illuminated Manuscripts of William Blake Ser.: Vol. 4). 372p. 1995. 90.00 (*0-691-03674-8*, Pub. by Princeton U Pr) Cal Prin Full Svc.
— Continental Prophecies, Vol. 4. (Blake's Illuminated Bks.). 1998. pap. text 35.00 (*0-691-00145-6*, Pub. by Princeton U Pr) Cal Prin Full Svc.
— Drawings of William Blake: Ninety-Two Pencil Studies. Keynes, Geoffrey L., ed. LC 74-100545. (Illus.). 178p. (Orig.). 1970. pap. 10.95 (*0-486-22303-5*) Dover.
— Early Illuminated Books, Vol. 3. (Blake's Illuminated Bks.). 1998. pap. 35.00 (*0-691-00147-2*, Pub. by Princeton U Pr) Cal Prin Full Svc.
— The Essential Blake. Kunitz, Stanley, ed. LC 96-76473. 92p. 1996. reprint ed. 8.98 (*1-56731-159-8*, MJF Bks) Fine Comms.
— Favorite Works of William Blake, 3 vols., Set. 160p. 1996. pap. 14.85 (*0-486-29086-7*) Dover.
— The Grave: An Illustrated Poem. (Illus.). 38p. 1984. reprint ed. pap. 25.00 (*0-87556-386-4*) Saifer.
— Illuminated Manuscripts of William Blake Vol. 6: Urizen Books. Worrall, David, ed. 228p. 1995. 70.00 (*0-691-04416-3*, Pub. by Princeton U Pr) Cal Prin Full Svc.
— Infant Joy & Other Poems: Mini Edition. 1996. pap. 1.99 (*0-679-77518-8*) Modern Lib NY.
— An Island in the Moon. O'Keefe, Gavin, ed. (Illus.). 32p. 1998. pap. 6.00 (*0-9603300-5-4*) Purple Mouth.
— Jerusalem: The Emanation of the Giant Albion, Vol. 1. (The Illuminated Books of William Blake). 302p. 1991. pap. 29.95 (*0-691-02907-5*, Pub. by Princeton U Pr) Cal Prin Full Svc.
— The Marriage of Heaven & Hell. LC 94-13248. (Illus.). 82p. 1975. pap. text 13.95 (*0-19-281167-3*) OUP.
— The Marriage of Heaven & Hell. limited ed. (Illus.). 50p. 1993. 3000.00 (*1-887123-03-2*) Granary Bks.
— The Marriage of Heaven & Hell: A Facsimile in Full Color. LC 94-471. (Illus.). 48p. 1994. reprint ed. pap. 4.95 (*0-486-28122-1*) Dover.
— Milton, A Poem, Vol. 5. (Blake's Illuminated Bks.). 1998. pap. 29.95 (*0-691-00148-0*, Pub. by Princeton U Pr) Cal Prin Full Svc.
— Night Thoughts: or The Complaint & the Consolation. Essick, Robert & LaBelle, Jenijoy, eds. LC 96-12356. Orig. Title: The Complaint, & The Consolation. (Illus.). 128p. 1996. reprint ed. pap. text 8.95 (*0-486-29214-2*) Dover.
— Poems. LC 91-52990. Vol. 34. 496p. 1991. 20.00 (*0-679-40552-6*) Everymns Lib.
— Poems: William Blake. LC 95-105107. 256p. 1994. 12.50 (*0-679-43633-2*) Random.
— Poetical Works. Rosetti, William M., ed. LC 79-13496. reprint ed. 47.50 (*0-404-07259-3*) AMS Pr.
— Poetical Works. (BCL1-PR English Literature Ser.). 453p. 1992. reprint ed. lib. bdg. 99.00 (*0-7812-7441-9*) Rprt Serv.
— The Portable Blake. Kazin, Alfred, ed. (Portable Library: No. 26). 728p. 1977. pap. 15.95 (*0-14-015026-9*, P26, Penguin Bks) Viking Penguin.
— The Prophetic Writings of William Blake, 2 vols., Set. (BCL1-PR English Literature Ser.). 1992. reprint ed. lib. bdg. 150.00 (*0-7812-7442-7*) Rprt Serv.
— Selected Poems. Stevens, David, ed. (Literature Ser.). (Illus.). 144p. (C). 1995. pap. 8.50 (*0-521-48546-0*) Cambridge U Pr.
— Selected Poems. Butter, P. H., ed. 256p. 1993. pap. 7.95 (*0-460-87309-1*, Everyman's Classic Lib) Tuttle Pubng.
— Selected Poetry. LC 93-40488. 320p. 1989. pap. 8.95 (*0-14-058596-6*) OUP.
— Selected Poetry. Mason, Michael, ed. (Oxford World's Classics Ser.). 328p. 1998. pap. 9.95 (*0-19-283489-4*) OUP.
— The Selected Poetry & Prose. Frye, Northrop, ed. (Modern Library College Editions). 475p. (C). 1966. pap. 8.44 (*0-07-553661-7*, T86) McGraw.
— Selections from the Symbolical Poems of William Blake. Pierce, F. E., ed. 1915. 49.50 (*0-686-51308-8*) Elliots Bks.
— Songs of Experience. (Fine Art Ser.). (Illus.). 48p. 1984. reprint ed. pap. 4.95 (*0-486-24636-1*) Dover.
— Songs of Innocence. LC 70-165396. (Illus.). 64p. 1971. reprint ed. pap. 4.95 (*0-486-22764-2*) Dover.
— Songs of Innocence & Experience. (Illus.). 64p. (J). 1997. 6.95 incl. audio (*0-486-29828-0*) Dover.
— Songs of Innocence & of Experience. (Illus.). 226p. 1977. pap. text 14.95 (*0-19-281089-8*) OUP.
— Songs of Innocence & Songs of Experience. (Thrift Editions Ser.). 64p. 1992. reprint ed. pap. 1.00 (*0-486-27051-3*) Dover.
— Songs of Innocence & Songs of Experience, 2 bks., Set. 112p. 1986. pap. 9.90 (*0-486-25264-7*) Dover.
— Urizen Books, Vol. 6. (Blake's Illuminated Bks.). 1998. pap. text 29.95 (*0-691-00146-4*, Pub. by Princeton U Pr) Cal Prin Full Svc.
— William Blake's Design for Edward Young's Night Thoughts: Complete, Vols. 1 & 2. Grant, John E. et al, eds. (Illus.). 1980. 450.00 (*0-19-817312-1*) OUP.
— William Blake's Works in Conventional Typography. LC 82-10815. 232p. 1984. 75.00 (*0-8201-1388-3*) Schol Facsimiles.
— William Maitland of Lethington, 1528-1573: A Study of the Policy of Moderation in the Sixteenth-Century Scottish Reformation. (Studies in British History: Vol. 17). 368p. 1990. write for info. (*0-88946-468-5*) E Mellen.
— Works of William Blake, Poetic, Symbolic & Critical, 3 vols. LC 79-13496. (Illus.). reprint ed. 145.50 (*0-404-08990-9*) AMS Pr.
Blake, William, et al. English Romantic Poetry, Set. abr. ed. 1996. audio 18.00 (*0-694-51682-1*, CPN 3005) HarperAudio.
Blake, William, et al. The Illuminated Books of William Blake: Songs of Innocence & of Experience. Lincoln, Andrew & Paley, Morton D., eds. (Blake's Illuminated Bks.: Vol. 2). (Illus.). 212p. 1991. pap. 24.95 (*0-691-03790-6*, Pub. by Princeton U Pr) Cal Prin Full Svc.
— Songs of Innocence & of Experience. Paley, Morton D. & Lincoln, Andrew, eds. (Blake's Illuminated Bks.: Vol. 2). (Illus.). 212p. 1991. 80.00 (*0-691-06936-0*, Pub. by Princeton U Pr) Cal Prin Full Svc.
Blake, William F. Premises Security: A Guide for Attorneys & Security Professionals. LC 98-34862. 128p. 1998. pap. 34.95 (*0-7506-7030-4*) Buttrwrth-Heinemann.
Blake, William P. History of the Town of Hamden, Ct. 350p. 1993. reprint ed. lib. bdg. 39.00 (*0-8328-2886-6*) Higginson Bk Co.
Blake, Winafred. Through My Looking Glass: A Personal Journey into Vaster States of Awareness. 290p. 1998. write for info. (*1-882530-03-9*) Deep Forest Pr.
Blakeley, Ann & Moore, Julia. The Other Rules: Never Wear Panties on a First Date & Other Tips. 1998. mass mkt. 6.95 (*1-56333-658-8*) Masquerade.
Blakeley, Barbara, et al. Activities for School-Age Child Care. rev. ed. LC 89-60449. (Illus.). 92p. 1989. pap. text 6.00 (*0-935989-26-9*, NAEYC#214) Natl Assn Child Ed.
***Blakeley, Barry B.** Defining Chu: Image & Reality in Ancient China. Major, John S. & Cook, Constance A., eds. LC 99-27952. (Illus.). 312p. 1999. text 59.00 (*0-8248-1885-7*) UH Pr.
Blakeley, Brian L. The Colonial Office, 1868-1892. LC 71-161357. 211p. reprint ed. pap. 65.50 (*0-608-15099-1*, 202618800048) Bks Demand.
Blakeley, Brian W. & Siegel, Mary E. Feeling Dizzy: Understanding & Treating Vertigo, Dizziness, & Other Balance Disorders. (Illus.). 256p. 1995. 21.95 (*0-02-860009-6*) Macmillan.
Blakeley, Burnie. Messaging & Queuing Using the MQI: Concepts, Analysis, Design & Implementation. 1995. 55.00 (*0-07-005730-3*) McGraw.
Blakeley, D. R. & Hrusa, C. T. Inland Aquaculture Development Handbook. (Illus.). 192p. 1990. pap. 29.95 (*0-85238-162-X*) Blackwell Sci.
***Blakeley, Elizabeth.** The San Antonio TEX-MEX Cookbook. (Illus.). 160p. 2000. pap. 10.95 (*0-9644411-0-1*) Caxton Hse Pub.
Blakeley, Gwendolynne A., ed. see Clovis, Donna L.
Blakeley, Gwendolynne A., ed. see Davis-Adeshote, Jeanette.
Blakeley, Janet. Welcome to Sharmunding. 64p. (Orig.). 1991. pap. 12.00 (*0-910973-08-3*) Arrowhead AZ.
Blakeley, Jeffrey A. & Toombs, Lawrence E. The Tell El-Hesi Field Manual. LC 80-21724. (Joint Archaeological Expedition to Tell El-Hesi Ser.: Vol. 1). xix, 134p. (C). 1980. pap. 17.95 (*0-89757-203-3*, Pub. by Sheffield Acad) CUP Services.
Blakeley, Thomas J. Bibliographie der sowjetischen Philosophie, 7 vols. Incl. Buecher und Aufsaetze, 1959-1960. 73p. 1962. lib. bdg. 67.50 (*90-277-0046-X*); Buecher und Aufsaetze 1961-1963. 195p. 1968. lib. bdg. 107.00 (*90-277-0049-4*); Buecher und Aufsaetze 1964-1966. 311p. 1968. lib. bdg. 126.50 (*90-277-0050-8*); Buecher, 1947-1956, Buecher und Aufsaetze, 1957-1958, Namenverzeichnis 1947-1958. 109p. 1960. lib. bdg. 73.50 (*90-277-0045-1*); Ergaenzungen, Supplement, 1947-1960. (GER.). 158p. 1963. lib. bdg. 81.00 (*90-277-0047-8*); Register, Indices, 1947-1960. 144p. 1964. lib. bdg. 73.50 (*90-277-0048-6*); Voprosy Filosophie, 1947-1956. 75p. 1960. lib. bdg. 67.50 (*90-277-0044-3*); (Sovietica Ser.). (GER.). write for info. (*0-318-53997-7*) Kluwer Academic.
— Philosophical Sovietology. 282p. (C). 1987. text 155.50 (*90-277-2637-X*, D Reidel) Kluwer Academic.
— Soviet Philosophy: A General Introduction to Contemporary Soviet Thought. (Sovietica Ser.: No. 18). 81p. 1964. lib. bdg. 104.50 (*90-277-0038-9*) Kluwer Academic.
— Soviet Scholasticism. (Sovietica Ser.: No. 6). 176p. 1961. lib. bdg. 130.50 (*90-277-0039-7*) Kluwer Academic.
— Soviet Theory of Knowledge. (Sovietica Ser.). 203p. 1964. lib. bdg. 73.50 (*90-277-0040-0*) Kluwer Academic.
Blakeley, Thomas J., ed. Themes in Soviet Marxist Philosophy: Selected Articles from the Sovetskaja Enciklopedija. (Sovietica Ser.: No. 37). 235p. 1975. text 126.50 (*90-277-0637-9*, D Reidel) Kluwer Academic.
Blakeley, Thomas J. & O'Rourke, James J. The Varieties of Contemporary Marxism. 379p. 1984. text 179.50 (*90-277-1636-6*, D Reidel) Kluwer Academic.
Blakeley, Thomas J., jt. auth. see Gavin, William J.
Blakeley, Thomas J., jt. ed. see Bochenski, J. M.
Blakeley, Thomas J., tr. see Fleischer, H.
Blakeley, Thomas J., tr. see Thiel, C.
Blakeley, Thomas J., tr. see Von Boeselager, Wolfhard.
Blakeley, Thomas J., tr. see Zinov'ev, A. A.
Blakelock, John H. Automatic Control of Aircraft & Missiles. 2nd ed. LC 90-12393. 672p. 1991. 150.00 (*0-471-50651-6*) Wiley.
Blakely, Allison. Blacks in the Dutch World: The Evolution of Racial Imagery in a Modern Society. LC 92-43743. (Blacks in the Diaspora Ser.). (Illus.). 356p. 1993. 35.00 (*0-253-31191-8*) Ind U Pr.
— Russia & the Negro: Blacks in Russian History & Thought. LC 85-5251. (Illus.). 224p. 1987. pap. 14.95 (*0-88258-175-9*) Howard U Pr.
Blakely, April. Math Brainteasers. (Illus.). 96p. (YA). (gr. 6 up). 1996. pap. 9.95 (*0-673-36318-X*, GoodYrBooks) Addson-Wesley Educ.
Blakely, Brian & Collins, Jacquelin. Documents in British History, 2. 2nd ed. 256p. (C). 1993. 32.81 (*0-07-005701-X*) McGraw.
Blakely, Darlene & Evans, Christopher. The Complete Guide to Yearbook Journalism. 263p. (C). 1991. ring bd. 49.95 (*0-9629406-0-7*) Advise Pubns.
Blakely, Diann. Farewell, My Lovelies. LC 99-55821. 80p. 2000. pap. 12.95 (*1-885266-83-9*, Pub. by Story Line) Consort Bk Sales.
Blakely, Edward J., ed. Community Development Research: Concepts, Issues & Strategies. LC 78-11568. 224p. 1979. 36.95 (*0-87705-334-0*, Kluwer Acad Hman Sci); pap. 20.95 (*0-87705-348-0*, Kluwer Acad Hman Sci) Kluwer Academic.
— Planning Local Economic Development: Theory & Practice. 2nd ed. (C). 1994. text 58.00 (*0-8039-5209-0*); pap. text 26.50 (*0-8039-5210-4*) Sage.
Blakely, Edward J. & Snyder, Mary G. Fortress America: Gated Communities in the United States. LC 97-21231. (Illus.). 208p. 1997. 24.95 (*0-8157-1002-X*) Brookings.
— Fortress America: Gated Communities in the United States. 1999. pap. 16.95 (*0-8157-1003-8*) Brookings.
Blakely, Edward J., jt. auth. see Bradshaw, Ted K.
Blakely, Edward J., jt. auth. see Goldsmith, William W.
Blakely, Eleanor H., jt. auth. see Gibbs, Patty.
Blakely, George. Bang: The Gun As Image. LC 97-166500. (Illus.). 48p. (Orig.). 1997. pap. 18.95 (*1-889282-02-2*) FSU Mus Fine Arts.
Blakely, Hunter B. Religion in Shoes. 199p. (Orig.). 1989. reprint ed. pap. text 5.00 (*0-87651-992-3*) Southern U Pr.
Blakely, Jack. Introduction to the Properties of Crystal Surfaces. 1973. 118.00 (*0-08-017641-0*, Pub. by Pergamon Repr) Franklin.
Blakely, James. Horses & Horse Sense: The Practical Science of Horse Husbandry. 450p. 1996. pap. 24.95 (*1-55622-483-4*, Rep of TX Pr) Wordware Pub.
Blakely, James & Bade, David H. The Science of Animal Husbandry. 5th ed. 736p. 1989. boxed set 43.00 (*0-685-44714-6*) P-H.
— The Science of Animal Husbandry. 6th ed. LC 93-7574. 656p. (C). 1993. 73.60 (*0-13-793365-7*) P-H.
Blakely, James, et al. How the Platform Professionals "Keep 'Em Laughin'" Rich Publishing Company Staff, ed. (Illus.). 310p. 1987. text 20.00 (*0-9607256-4-4*) Rich Pub Co.
Blakely, James D. Doc Blakeley's Handbook of Wit & Pungent Humor. rev. ed. LC 83-61029. 228p. 1993. 20.00 (*0-9607256-2-8*) Rich Pub Co.
— Doc Blakely's "Push Button Wit" LC 85-61515. (Illus.). 272p. 1986. text 20.00 (*0-9607256-3-6*) Rich Pub Co.
— Shoot, Luke! The Air Is Full of Pigeons. (Illus.). 249p. 1989. 20.00 (*0-9607256-7-9*) Rich Pub Co.
Blakely, James M. Exchange Administration Guide. 512p. 1996. pap. text 39.99 incl. cd-rom (*0-7821-2004-0*) Sybex.
Blakely, Jeffrey A., et al, eds. The Joint Expedition to Casearea Maritima: Excavation Reports, American School of Oriental Research Excavation Reports. 179.95 (*0-88946-376-X*) E Mellen.
Blakely, Jeffrey A. & Bennett, W. J., Jr. The Pottery of Palestine: Neolithic to Modern. (Illus.). Date not set. text 24.95 (*0-931464-98-6*) Eisenbrauns.
Blakely, Jeffrey A. & Toombs, Lawrence E. The Tell El-Hesi Field Manual. LC 80-21724. (Joint Archaeological Expedition to Tell El-Hesi Ser.: Vol. 1). xix, 134p. (C). 1980. text 20.00 (*0-89757-205-X*) Am Sch Orient Res.
Blakely, Jeffrey A., et al. Caesarea Maritima: The Pottery & Dating of Vault 1: Horreum, Mithraeum & Later Uses. LC 86-23906. (Joint Expedition to Caesarea Maritima Excavation Reports: Vol. 4). (Illus.). 288p. 1987. lib. bdg. 179.95 (*0-88946-377-8*) E Mellen.
Blakely, Jeffrey A., jt. auth. see Bennett, W. J., Jr.
Blakely, John M., ed. see ASM Seminar on Interfacial Segregation.
Blakely, Julia, jt. auth. see Tomasi, Lucia T.
Blakely, Kandis. Your Body Remembers: A Conscious Choice to Live. 96p. (Orig.). (C). 1994. pap. text 12.95 (*1-886531-49-8*) K Blakely.
Blakely, Kim S. & Lang, Mary A. AIDS, Blindness, & Low Vision: A Training Manual for Health Organizations. (Illus.). 193p. 1993. 50.00 (*1-888504-05-6*, P280) Lighthouse NYC.
Blakely, Kristine, ed. see Meisterfeld, C. W. & Pecci, Ernest F.
Blakely, Mary Kay. American Mom: Motherhood, Politics, & Humble Pie. Ng, Donna, ed. 304p. 1995. reprint ed. pap. 14.00 (*0-671-53520-X*, PB Trade Paper) PB.
— Red, White & Oh So Blue. 1996. 20.00 (*0-614-19886-0*, Scribners Ref) Mac Lib Ref.
***Blakely, Mary Kay.** Red, White & Oh So Blue: A Memoir of a Political Depression. 192p. 1999. reprint ed. text 20.00 (*0-7881-6619-0*) DIANE Pub.
Blakely, Mary Kay, ed. see Kaufman, Gloria J.
Blakely, Mary Kay, jt. ed. see Kaufman, Gloria.
Blakely, Michael. Caleb's Hill. (Orig.). mass mkt. 4.50 (*0-8125-3028-4*) Tor Bks.
Blakely, Mike. Comanche Dawn. LC 98-23738. 416p. 1998. 25.95 (*0-312-86575-9*, Pub. by Forge NYC) St Martin.
— Comanche Dawn. 576p. 1999. mass mkt. 6.50 (*0-8125-4833-7*, Pub. by Forge NYC) St Martin.
— Dead Reckoning. 1997. mass mkt. 4.99 (*0-8125-4830-2*, Pub. by Forge NYC) St Martin.
— The Last Chance. 320p. (Orig.). 1995. 4.99 (*0-8125-3027-6*, Pub. by Forge NYC) St Martin.
— More Wild Camp Tales. 208p. 1995. pap. 12.95 (*1-55622-392-7*, Rep of TX Pr) Wordware Pub.
— Shortgrass Song. 608p. 1995. 4.99 (*0-8125-3029-2*, Pub. by Forge NYC) St Martin.
— Snowy Range Gang. 1996. mass mkt. 4.99 (*0-8125-6357-3*, Pub. by Forge NYC) St Martin.
— Snowy Range Gang. LC 91-43639. 192p. 1992. 16.95 (*0-87131-670-6*) M Evans.
— Spanish Blood, Vol. 1. 1996. mass mkt. 4.99 (*0-8125-4831-0*, Pub. by Forge NYC) St Martin.
***Blakely, Mike.** Summer of Pearls. 224p. 2000. text 22.95 (*0-312-87516-9*) St Martin.
Blakely, Mike. Too Long at the Dance. LC 95-33673. 352p. 1996. 23.95 (*0-312-86093-5*) Forge NYC.
— Too Long at the Dance. 1998. mass mkt. 6.50 (*0-8125-4832-9*, Pub. by Forge NYC) St Martin.
— Vendetta Gold. 1998. mass mkt. 4.99 (*0-8125-8915-7*, Pub. by Forge NYC) St Martin.
— Wild Camp Tales. LC 95-32. 208p. 1995. pap. 12.95 (*1-55622-383-8*, Rep of TX Pr) Wordware Pub.
***Blakely, Mike & Goldman, Mary Elizabeth.** Forever Texas. 208p. 2000. text 22.95 (*0-312-86776-X*) St Martin.
Blakely, Newell H., et al. Texas Rules of Evidence Handbook & Supplement. 878p. 1987. 61.40 (*0-317-61183-6*) Houston Law Review.
Blakely, Richard. Potential Theory in Gravity & Magnetic Applications. 461p. 1996. pap. text 37.95 (*0-521-57547-8*) Cambridge U Pr.
Blakely, Robert. Object Security. LC 99-40091. 128p. (C). 1999. pap. 29.95 (*0-201-32565-9*) Addison-Wesley.
Blakely, Robert J. The New Environment: Questions for Adult Educators. (Occasional Papers: No. 23). 1971. pap. text 2.00 (*0-87060-004-4*, OCP 23) Syracuse U Cont Ed.
— To Serve the Public Interest: Educational Broadcasting in the United States. (C). 1979. pap. 16.95 (*0-8156-0153-0*) Syracuse U Pr.
— Toward a Homeodynamic Society. 1965. 2.50 (*0-8156-7028-1*, NES 49) Syracuse U Cont Ed.
— Use of Instructional Television in Adult Education. LC 73-13295. (Occasional Papers: No. 40). 1974. pap. text 2.00 (*0-87060-064-8*, OCP 40) Syracuse U Cont Ed.
Blakely, Robert J. & Lappin, Ivan M. Knowledge Is Power to Control Power: New Institutional Arrangement & Organizational Patterns for Continuing Education. LC 71-106557. (Notes & Essays Ser.: No. 63). 1969. pap. 2.50 (*0-87060-027-3*, NES 63) Syracuse U Cont Ed.
Blakely, Robert L. & Harrington, Judith M., eds. Bones in the Basement: Postmortem Racism in Nineteenth-Century Medical Training. LC 96-53982. (Illus.). 464p. 1997. text 45.00 (*1-56098-750-2*) Smithsonian.
Blakely, Robert W. The Mayor Is Black. 156p. (Orig.). (C). 1996. pap. 19.95 (*1-877858-42-0*, TMIB) Amer Focus Pub.
Blakely, Romaine, ed. see Mitchell, Edith A.
Blakely, T. J., tr. see Kirschenmann, P. K.
Blakely, Thomas D., et al, eds. Religion in Africa: Experience & Expression. LC 92-30302. (Monograph Series of the David M. Kennedy Center for International Studies at Brigham Young University: Vol. 4). 512p. (C). 1994. pap. 24.95 (*0-435-08083-0*, 08083) Heinemann.
Blakely, W. A., ed. American State Papers Bearing on Sunday Legislation. LC 79-122165. (Civil Liberties in American History Ser.). 1970. reprint ed. lib. bdg. 95.00 (*0-306-71973-8*) Da Capo.
***Blakely, William Addison & Colcord, Willard Allen.** American State Papers Bearing on Sunday Legislation. rev. enl. ed. LC 00-21682. 800p. 2000. 85.00 (*1-57588-627-8*, 324360) W S Hein.
Blakeman, J. P. & Williamson, B., eds. Ecology of Plant Pathogens. (Illus.). 384p. 1994. text 130.00 (*0-85198-876-8*) OUP.

Blakeman, Sarah. Elephant. LC 91-44728. (Life Story Ser.). (Illus.). 32p. (J). (gr. 4-6). 1997. lib. bdg. 17.25 (*0-8167-2769-4*) Troll Communs.

Blakeman, Stanley L. Ikons. LC 90-42902. 1992. pap. 14.95 (*0-87949-345-3*) Ashley Bks.

Blakemore. Introduction to Social Policy: An Introduction. LC 97-45910. 227p. 1998. 95.00 (*0-335-19494-X*); pap. 26.95 (*0-335-19493-1*) OpUniv Pr.

Blakemore-Brown, Lisa. Reweaving the Autistic Tapestry: Autism, Asperger's Syndrome & ADHD. LC 98-42737. 1999. 22.95 (*1-85302-748-0*) Taylor & Francis.

Blakemore, Catherine. A Public School of Your Own: Your Guide to Creating & Running a Charter School. LC 97-77067. xiii, 256p. 1998. pap. 22.95 (*0-9661009-1-3*) Adams-Pomeroy.

Blakemore, Colin. Development of the Cerebral Cortex, No. 193. LC 95-21512. (CIBA Foundation Symposium Ser.: Vol. 193). 246p. 1996. 128.00 (*0-471-95705-4*) Wiley.

Blakemore, Colin, ed. Vision: Coding & Efficiency. (Illus.). 464p. (C). 1993. pap. text 44.95 (*0-521-44769-0*) Cambridge U Pr.

*__Blakemore, Colin & Iversen, Susan D.__ Gender & Society: The Herbert Spencer Lectures. LC 99-57194. 180p. 2000. 29.95 (*0-19-829792-0*) OUP.

Blakemore, Connie L., jt. auth. see Harrison, Joyce M.

Blakemore, Derek, jt. auth. see Anderson, Charles.

Blakemore, Diane. Understanding Utterances: An Introduction to Pragmatics. (Blackwell Textbooks in Linguistics Ser.). (C). 1992. pap. text 28.95 (*0-631-15867-7*) Blackwell Pubs.

Blakemore, Harold. Chile. LC 89-103741. (World Bibliographical Ser.: No. 97). 214p. 1988. lib. bdg. 50.00 (*1-85109-026-6*) ABC-CLIO.

Blakemore, Harold & Smith, Clifford, eds. Latin America: Geographical Perspectives. 2nd ed. LC 82-20877. 600p. (C). 1983. pap. 25.99 (*0-416-32830-X*, NO.3814) Routledge.

Blakemore, J. S. Semiconductor Statistics. 416p. 1987. reprint ed. pap. text 12.95 (*0-486-65362-5*) Dover.

— Solid State Physics. 2nd ed. (Illus.). 506p. 1985. pap. text 49.95 (*0-521-31391-0*) Cambridge U Pr.

Blakemore, James C., et al. The Veterinary Dermatology International Slide Bank Collection: Collection Content Reference & Laser Videodisc Index. LC 97-36208. 1997. write for info. (*0-931682-65-7*) Veterinary Med.

Blakemore, John S., ed. Gallium Arsenide. LC 87-932. (Key Papers in Physics: No. 1). 424p. 1987. text 75.00 (*0-88318-525-3*); text 99.95 (*0-88318-758-2*) Spr-Verlag.

Blakemore, Ken & Boneham, Margaret. Age, Race & Ethnicity: A Comparative Approach. (Rethinking Aging Ser.). 160p. 1993. pap. 33.95 (*0-335-19086-3*) OpUniv Pr.

Blakemore, Kenneth. The Retail Jeweller's Guide. 5th ed. 416p. 1988. 64.95 (*0-408-02913-7*) Buttrwrth-Heinemann.

— The Retail Jeweller's Guide. 5th rev. ed. (Illus.). 424p. 1994. pap. 39.95 (*0-7506-2042-0*) Buttrwrth-Heinemann.

*__Blakemore, Kenneth & Stanley, Eddie.__ Retail Jeweler's Guide. 6th ed. 320p. 2000. pap. 39.95 (*0-7506-4650-0*) Buttrwrth-Heinemann.

Blakemore, Michael. Next Season: A Novel. 364p. 1995. pap. 12.95 (*1-55783-223-4*) Applause Theatre Bk Pubs.

Blakemore, Michael & Georgiou, George A., eds. Mathematical Modelling in Non-Destructive Testing. (Institute of Mathematics & Its Applications Conference Series, New Ser.: New Series 16). (Illus.). 378p. 1988. 79.00 (*0-19-853622-4*) OUP.

Blakemore, Neville, et al, eds. The Serious Sides of Sex: Sex Medicine, Law, Ethics & Psychology Related to Sexual Behavior. LC 91-72213. (Illus.). 254p. (Orig.). 1991. pap. 14.95 (*0-9627611-1-7*) Nevbet.

Blakemore, Phyllis, jt. auth. see Sidoli, Mara.

Blakemore, R., jt. auth. see Frankel, R.

Blakemore, Robbie G. History of Interior Design & Furniture: From Ancient Egypt to Nineteenth-Century Europe. 400p. 1996. 59.95 (*0-471-28676-1*, VNR) Wiley.

Blakemore, Robbie G. History of Interior Design & Furniture: From Ancient Egypt to Nineteenth-Century Europe. LC 96-36414. (Illus.). 392p. 1996. text 52.95 (*0-442-01956-4*, VNR) Wiley.

Blakemore, Steven. Crisis in Representation: Thomas Paine, Mary Wollstonecraft, Helen Maria Williams, & the Rewriting of the French Revolution. LC 96-38535. (Illus.). 272p. 1997. 39.50 (*0-8386-3714-0*) Fairleigh Dickinson.

— Intertextual War: Edmund Burke & the French Revolution in the Writings of Mary Wollstonecraft, Thomas Paine, & James Mackintosh. LC 96-52533. 256p. 1997. 39.50 (*0-8386-3751-5*) Fairleigh Dickinson.

Blakemore, Timothy & Greene, Brendan. Law for Legal Executives, Pt. 1 Year 1. xxi, 350p. (C). 1991. pap. 60.00 (*1-85431-179-4*, Pub. by Blackstone Pr) Gaunt.

— Law for Legal Executives Pt. 1: Year One. 3rd ed. 1996. write for info. (*1-85431-583-8*, Pub. by Blackstone Pr) Gaunt.

— Q & A a Level Law. 240p. 1998. pap. 22.00 (*1-85431-534-X*, Pub. by Blackstone Pr) Gaunt.

Blakemore, Timothy, et al. Law for Legal Executives, Pt. 1, Year 2. (C). 1992. 95.00 (*1-85431-194-8*, Pub. by Blackstone Pr) Gaunt.

*__Blakeney, A. B. & O'Brian, L., eds.__ Pacific People & Their Food. (Illus.). 225p. 1998. 79.00 (*1-891127-03-9*) Am Assn Cereal Chem.

Blakeney, Allan & Borins, Sanford. Political Management in Canada: Conversations on Statecraft. 2nd ed. LC 99-167884. 320p. 1998. text 60.00 (*0-8020-4290-2*); pap. text 21.95 (*0-8020-8123-1*) U of Toronto Pr.

Blakeney, Edward, ed. Horace on the Art of Poetry. LC 73-119934. (Select Bibliographies Reprint Ser.). (ENG & LAT.). 1977. reprint ed. 19.95 (*0-8369-5377-0*) Ayer.

Blakeney, Erica T. Moms & Their Young Spirited Boys: An Inspirational & Lighthearted Expose of Moms' Experiences with Their Young Male Charges. (Illus.). 96p. 1998. pap. 8.95 (*0-9662451-0-5*) Publish It Write.

— Moms & Their Young Spirited Boys Gift Set. 96p. 1999. pap. 14.95 (*0-9662451-1-3*) Publish It Write.

Blakeney, Laurie, ed. see Lamothe, Denise C.

Blakeney, M. L. & McKeough, J. Intellectual Property: Commentary & Materials. xlviii, 741p. 1987. pap. 82.00 (*0-455-20695-3*, Pub. by LawBk Co) Gaunt.

Blakeney, Robert. A Boy in the Peninsular War. 400p. 40.00 (*1-85367-029-4*, 5450) Stackpole.

Blakenship, Frank J. Prentice Hall Real Estate Investors Encyclopedia. 1990. pap. 24.95 (*0-685-32931-3*) P-H.

Blaker, Alfred A. Applied Depth of Field. LC 84-28771. (Illus.). 313p. 1985. pap. text 60.00 (*0-240-51730-X*, Focal) Buttrwrth-Heinemann.

Blaker, Charles W. College Application: The Decision-Making Process. 61p. (Orig.). (YA). (gr. 9-12). 1997. pap. write for info. (*0-9604614-3-4*) Rekalb Pr.

— The College Matchmaker. LC 80-67604. (Illus.). 56p. (Orig.). (YA). (gr. 11-12). 1980. pap. text 5.50 (*0-9604614-0-X*) Rekalb Pr.

Blaker, Charles W. & Blaker, Elizabeth D. Chanticleer: A Collection from the Muses. (Illus.). 92p. (Orig.). 1997. pap. 5.25 (*0-9604614-1-8*) Rekalb Pr.

Blaker, Elizabeth D., jt. auth. see Blaker, Charles W.

Blaker, Frances. The Recorder Player's Companion: A Compendium of Technical Exercises for Recorder Players. (Educational Ser.: No. 3). (Illus.). i, 41p. 1993. pap. text 19.00 (*1-56571-059-2*, ED003) PRB Prods.

— The Recorder Player's Companion: A Compendium of Technical Exercises for Recorder Players. 2nd rev. ed. (Educational Ser.: No. 3). (Illus.). i, 42p. 1994. pap. text 19.00 (*1-56571-120-3*) PRB Prods.

Blaker, Gordon A. Iron Knights: The United States 66th Armored Regiment. LC 99-10002. 360p. 1999. 39.95 (*1-57249-122-1*, Burd St Pr) White Mane Pub.

Blaker, J. Warren. Geometric Optics: The Matrix Theory. LC 73-157832. (Illus.). 141p. reprint ed. pap. 43.80 (*0-8357-6128-2*, 203451600090) Bks Demand.

Blaker, James R. United States Overseas Basing: An Anatomy of the Dilemma. LC 90-35145. 206p. 1990. 49.95 (*0-275-93665-1*, C3665, Praeger Pubs) Greenwood.

Blaker, Michael K. Beginner's Guide to Oil Painting. 1994. 12.98 (*0-7858-0017-4*) Bk Sales Inc.

Blaker, Peter, et al. Europe Right Ahead. LC 81-459611. 35p. 1978. write for info. (*0-85070-625-4*) Conserv Poli Ctr.

Blaker, Peter, jt. auth. see Rose, Clive.

Blaker, Richard. The Needle-Watcher: The Will Adams Story, British Samurai. LC 72-89743. 512p. 1973. pap. 16.95 (*0-8048-1094-X*) Tuttle Pubng.

Blakers, Anderson, jt. auth. see Anderson.

Blakers, Catherine. Is Anyone Listening? (C). 1992. pap. 70.00 (*0-86431-090-0*, Pub. by Aust Council Educ Res) St Mut.

Blakes, Gerald, jt. auth. see Schofield, Richard.

Blakeslee, A. F. Sexual Reproduction in the Mucorinaeae. (Bibliotheca Mycologica Ser.: No. 48). 1976. reprint ed. text 32.00 (*3-7682-1064-2*) Lubrecht & Cramer.

Blakeslee, Ann R. Different Kind of Hero. LC 96-32786. (J). (gr. 5-9). 1997. lib. bdg. 14.95 (*0-7614-5000-9*) Marshall Cavendish.

*__Blakeslee, Ann R.__ Interacting with Audiences: Social Influences on the Production of Scientific Writing. (A Volume in the Rhetoric, Knowledge & Society Series). 300p. 2000. write for info. (*0-8058-2299-2*) L Erlbaum Assocs.

— Summer Battles. (Illus.). 128p. (YA). (gr. 5-9). 2000. 14.95 (*0-7614-5064-5*, Cav Child Bks) Marshall Cavendish.

Blakeslee, Carolyn, et al. Washington Art: A Guide to Galleries, Art Consultants & Museums. (Illus.). 1988. pap. 13.95 (*0-945388-00-4*) Art Calendar.

Blakeslee, Carolyn, ed. see Carter, Michelle & Dougherty, Barbara.

Blakeslee, Carolyn, ed. see Steis, Drew, et al.

Blakeslee, Carolyn, ed. & frwd. see Holly, Bruce.

Blakeslee, Donald J. Along Ancient Trails: The Mallet Expedition of 1739. (Illus.). 432p. 1995. 39.95 (*0-87081-410-9*) Univ Pr Colo.

Blakeslee, Mary. Hal. unabridged ed. 160p. (YA). (gr. 7-11). 1991. pap. 4.95 (*0-7736-7432-2*) STDK.

Blakeslee, Mary E. Death Drop. 128p. (J). (gr. 3-6). 1991. pap. 4.95 (*0-7736-7321-0*) Stoddart Publ.

— Four Eyes & French Fries. 128p. (J). (gr. 3-6). 1991. pap. 5.95 (*0-7736-7296-6*) Stoddart Publ.

— Holy Joe. 160p. (J). (gr. 7-9). 1996. pap. write for info. (*0-614-17730-8*) Stoddart Publ.

— Holy Joe. 160p. (gr. 7-11). 1996. pap. 7.95 (*0-7737-5343-5*) Stoddart Publ.

— Stop the Presses, Ida Mae! 116p. (J). (gr. 4-7). 1994. pap. 9.99 (*0-7710-1537-2*) McCland & Stewart.

Blakeslee, Mermer. In Dark Water. LC 97-45815. 304p. 1998. 22.50 (*0-345-41777-1*) Ballantine Pub Grp.

— In Dark Water. 1999. pap. 12.00 (*0-345-41778-X*) Ballantine Pub Grp.

Blakeslee, Merritt R. Love's Masks: Identity, Intertextuality & Meaning in the Old French Tristan Poems. LC 88-22225. (Arthurian Studies: No. XV). 175p. 1989. 70.00 (*0-85991-264-7*) Boydell & Brewer.

Blakeslee, S. The Death of American Antisemitism. LC 99-29576. 304p. 2000. 69.95 (*0-275-96508-2*) Greenwood.

Blakeslee, Sandra & Shaps, Dale E., eds. Human Heart Replacement: A New Challenge for Physicians & Reporters. LC 86-82064. 99p. (Orig.). 1986. pap. 5.00 (*0-910755-04-3*) Foun Am Comm.

Blakeslee, Sandra, jt. auth. see Ramachandran, V. S.

Blakeslee, Sandra, jt. auth. see Wallerstein, Judith S.

Blakeslee, Scott. The Wizard, the Warrior & Me. LC 97-91186. 246p. 1997. pap. 12.95 (*0-9665985-0-4*) B W G Clark.

*__Blakeslee, Thomas R.__ Attitude Factor: Extend Your Life by Changing the Way You Think. 2000. pap. 15.95 (*0-7225-3546-5*) Thorsons PA.

Blakesley, Christopher L. Louisiana Family Law. 450p. 1993. spiral bd. 110.00 (*0-250-42752-4*, MICHIE) LEXIS Pub.

— Louisiana Family Law. 1995. ring bd. 110.00 (*0-327-03964-7*, 81341-10, MICHIE) LEXIS Pub.

— Terrorism, Drugs, International Law & the Protection of Human Liberty. 349p. (C). 1992. lib. bdg. 75.00 (*0-941320-62-6*) Transnatl Pubs.

*__Blakesley, John.__ Garland of Faith: Sequences, Prayers & Poems of the Medieval Church Arranged for the Three Year Lectionary. 1999. pap. 20.95 (*0-85244-462-1*) Gra1cewing.

Blakesley, John. Paths of the Heart: Prayers of Medieval Christians. 1994. pap. text 8.95 (*0-687-85983-2*) Abingdon.

Blakesley, Lance. Presidential Leadership: From Eisenhower to Clinton. LC 94-45059. 1995. pap. text 31.95 (*0-8304-1308-1*) Thomson Learn.

Blakeslsee, Leroy L., et al. World Food Production, Demand, & Trade. LC 72-2785. (Illus.). 423p. 1973. reprint ed. pap. 131.20 (*0-608-00017-5*, 206078300006) Bks Demand.

Blakeson, Ken, et al. Best Radio Plays of 1988: The BBC Giles Cooper Award Winners. (Methuen Drama Ser.). 209p. (C). 1989. write for info. (*0-413-61780-7*, A0390, Methuen Drama) Methn.

Blakeway, Claire. Jacques Prevert: Popular French Theatre & Cinema. LC 87-46426. (Illus.). 224p. 1990. 39.50 (*0-8386-3309-9*) Fairleigh Dickinson.

Blakey, Arch F. General John H. Winder, C. S. A. 304p. 1990. 39.95 (*0-8130-0977-9*) U Press Fla.

Blakey, Arch F., et al, eds. Rose Cottage Chronicles: Civil War Letters of the Bryant-Stephens Families of North Florida. LC 97-44236. (Illus.). 416p. 1998. 34.95 (*0-8130-1550-2*) U Press Fla.

*__Blakey, Brenda Totten.__ Salt Mountain Girl. 2000. pap. 8.95 (*0-533-13479-X*) Vantage.

Blakey, Durocher L. Sharing Divine Life: The Story of My Life & My Teaching Ministry. LC 97-68791. (Illus.). 134p. (Orig.). 1997. pap. write for info. (*1-57502-551-5*, P01607) Morris Pubng.

Blakey, Ellen S. Oil on Their Shoes: Petroleum Geology to 1918. LC 85-20021. (Illus.). 204p. reprint ed. pap. 63.30 (*0-608-20301-7*, 207155600001) Bks Demand.

Blakey, Ellen S., ed. see Sewell, John W.

Blakey, George T. Hard Times & New Deal in Kentucky, 1929-1939. LC 86-1513. (Illus.). 268p. 1986. reprint ed. pap. 83.10 (*0-7837-9580-7*, 206032900005) Bks Demand.

Blakey, Nancy. Lotions, Potions, & Slime: Mudpies & More! LC 95-41082. (Illus.). 120p. (J). (ps-7). 1996. pap. 8.95 (*1-883672-21-X*) Tricycle Pr.

— More Mudpies: 101 Alternatives to Television. LC 94-11709. (Illus.). 144p. (J). (ps-7). 1994. pap. 8.95 (*1-883672-11-2*) Tricycle Pr.

— The Mudpies Activity Book: Recipes for Invention. LC 93-26779. (Illus.). 144p. (J). (ps-7). 1994. pap. 8.95 (*1-883672-19-8*) Tricycle Pr.

— The Mudpies Book of Boredom Busters. LC 99-17791. (Illus.). 120p. (J). (ps-7). 1999. pap. 8.95 (*1-883672-86-4*) Tricycle Pr.

*__Blakey, Paul.__ The Muscle Book. 56p. 2000. pap. 12.95 (*0-89389-182-7*) Himalayan Inst.

Blakey, Robert. The History of Political Literature from the Earliest Times, 2 vols., 1. (Reprints in History Ser.). reprint ed. lib. bdg. 52.00 (*0-697-00029-X*) Irvington.

— The History of Political Literature from the Earliest Times, 2 vols., 2. (Reprints in History Ser.). reprint ed. lib. bdg. 52.00 (*0-697-00030-3*) Irvington.

— The History of Political Literature from the Earliest Times, 2 vols., Set. (Reprints in History Ser.). reprint ed. lib. bdg. 98.00 (*0-89197-790-2*) Irvington.

Blakey, Roy G. United States Beet Sugar Industry & the Tariff. LC 77-76717. (Columbia University. Studies in the Social Sciences: No. 119). reprint ed. 37.50 (*0-404-51119-8*) AMS Pr.

Blakey, Walker J., jt. auth. see Broun, Kenneth S.

Blakey, Walker J., jt. auth. see Howe, Joseph.

Blakiston. Blakiston's Gould Pocket Medical Dictionary. 4th ed. Stander, Richard et al, eds. 992p. 1979. text 29.95 (*0-07-005715-X*) McGraw-Hill HPD.

— Blakiston's Gould Pocket Medical Dictionary. 4th ed. Weiss, Leon et al, eds. 992p. 1979. pap. text 27.50 (*0-07-005714-1*) McGraw-Hill HPD.

Blakiston, Georgiana. Lord William Russell & His Wife, 1815-1846. LC 73-75710. 1974. 30.00 (*0-8420-1681-3*) Scholarly Res Inc.

Blakiston, Noel. The Roman Question. LC 79-91770. 474p. 1980. 65.00 (*0-89453-150-6*) Scholarly Res Inc.

Blakley, Brian W. Feeling Dizzy: Understanding & Treating Dizziness, Vertigo & Other Balance Disorders. 244p. 1997. 14.95 (*0-02-861680-4*, Pub. by Macmillan) S&S Trade.

Blakley, Lonnett D., jt. auth. see Lewis, Sondra K.

Blakley, Mike. Forver Texas. pap. write for info. (*0-312-87685-8*) St Martin.

Blakley, Raymond L. & Benkovic, Stephen J., eds. Folates & Pterins Vol. 1: Chemistry & Biochemistry of Folates. LC 84-3592. 648p. reprint ed. pap. 200.00 (*0-7837-2837-9*, 205763500001) Bks Demand.

— Folates & Pterins Vol. 2: Chemistry & Biochemistry of Pterins. LC 84-3592. 430p. reprint ed. pap. 133.30 (*0-7837-2386-5*, 204007200002) Bks Demand.

— Folates & Pterins Vol. 3: Nutritional, Pharmacological, & Physiological Aspects. LC 84-3592. 496p. reprint ed. pap. 153.80 (*0-7837-2387-3*, 204007200003) Bks Demand.

Blakley, Tim, jt. auth. see Sturdivant, Lee.

Blakney-Barton, Marilyn. Be Happier. 48p. 1995. pap. 8.00 (*0-8059-3799-4*) Dorrance.

*__Blakstad & Cooper.__ Communicating Organisation. 208p. 2000. pap. 56.95 (*0-8464-5012-7*) Beekman Pubs.

Blakstad-Cooke, Katie. Hypermedia Publishing: How to Build a Web Site. LC 96-9387. 352p. (C). 1996. pap. text 29.95 (*0-13-237694-6*) P-H.

Blakstad, Michael. The Risk Business. 144p. (C). 1979. pap. text 50.00 (*0-85072-098-2*) St Mut.

Blakstad, Michael & Cooper, Aldwyn. The Communicating Organisation. 192p. 1995. 125.00 (*0-85292-575-1*, Pub. by IPM Hse) St Mut.

Blalock. The Bedford Handbook for Writers: Background Reading. 4th ed. 1994. pap. text, teacher ed. 10.00 (*0-312-09728-X*) St Martin.

— Social Statistics. 2nd ed. 1979. 21.56 (*0-07-005753-2*) McGraw.

Blalock, Ann B., ed. Evaluating Social Programs at the State & Local Level: The JTPA Evaluation Design Project. LC 89-21488. 410p. 1990. text 39.00 (*0-88099-089-9*); pap. text 21.00 (*0-88099-090-2*) W E Upjohn.

Blalock, Ednah B. Growing. (Scots Plaid Press Fine Poetry Ser.). (Illus.). 40p. 1998. pap. text 12.00 (*1-879009-35-8*) Old Barn Entrprs.

*__Blalock, Gaffney.__ The Clarion Grill: A New Look at Christianity. LC 99-93869. 1999. pap. 7.95 (*0-533-13171-5*) Vantage.

Blalock, Ginger & Benz, Michael R. Using Community Transition Teams to Improve Transition Services. LC 98-33327. (Series on Transition). 1999. 8.00 (*0-89079-811-7*) PRO-ED.

Blalock, Ginger, jt. ed. see Patton, James R.

Blalock, Glenn B. The Bedford Handbook: Background Readings for Instructors. 5th ed. 480p. 1997. pap. text 13.95 (*0-312-16622-2*) St Martin.

Blalock, H. M., Jr., ed. Causal Models in Panel & Experimental Designs. LC 84-24276. (Illus.). 297p. (C). 1985. pap. text 34.95 (*0-202-30316-0*) Aldine de Gruyter.

— Causal Models in the Social Sciences. 2nd ed. LC 84-24258. (Illus.). 458p. (C). 1985. pap. text 37.95 (*0-202-30314-4*); lib. bdg. 56.95 (*0-202-30313-6*) Aldine de Gruyter.

Blalock, Hubert M. Basic Dilemmas in the Social Sciences. LC 83-24590. 184p. reprint ed. pap. 57.10 (*0-7837-6588-6*, 204615300011) Bks Demand.

Blalock, Hubert M., Jr. Black-White Relations in the Nineteen Eighties: Towards a Long-Term Policy. LC 79-10224. 208p. 1979. 55.00 (*0-275-90332-X*, C0332, Praeger Pubs) Greenwood.

Blalock, Hubert M. Conceptualization & Measurement in the Social Sciences. LC 81-23269. (Illus.). 285p. reprint ed. pap. 88.40 (*0-608-01116-9*, 205942000001) Bks Demand.

— Power & Conflict: Toward a General Theory. LC 89-10215. (Violence, Cooperation, Peace Ser.). (Illus.). 280p. 1989. pap. 86.80 (*0-608-05069-5*, 206562400005) Bks Demand.

Blalock, Hubert M., Jr. Power & Conflict: Toward a General Theory. (Violence, Cooperation, & Peace Ser.: Vol. 4). 280p. (C). 1989. text 55.00 (*0-8039-3594-3*); pap. text 24.95 (*0-8039-3595-1*) Sage.

— Race & Ethnic Relations. (Foundations of Modern Sociology Ser.). (Illus.). 160p. (C). 1982. pap. text 19.40 (*0-13-750174-9*) P-H.

— Social Statistics. 2nd rev. ed. 592p. (C). 1979. 93.75 (*0-07-005752-4*) McGraw.

Blalock, Hubert M. Understanding Social Inequality: Modeling Allocation Processes. (Library of Social Research: Vol. 188). 256p. (C). 1991. text 59.95 (*0-8039-4339-3*); pap. text 26.00 (*0-8039-4340-7*) Sage.

— Understanding Social Inequality: Modeling Allocation Processes. LC 91-22015. (Sage Library of Social Research Ser.: Vol. 188). (Illus.). 272p. 1991. reprint ed. pap. 84.40 (*0-608-07688-0*, 206777800010) Bks Demand.

Blalock, J. Edwin, ed. Neuroimmunoendocrinology. 3rd enl. rev. ed. (Chemical Immunology Ser.: Vol. 69, 1997). (Illus.). xiv, 228p. 1997. 194.00 (*3-8055-6524-0*) S Karger.

Blalock, Joan. Quilted Landscapes: Machine-Embellished Fabric Images. LC 95-48414. (Illus.). 88p. (Orig.). 1996. pap. 21.95 (*1-56477-144-X*, B261) Martingale & Co.

Blalock, Rick & Oglesby, K. Thomas, eds. Remembering Diana: The People's Tribute to Their Princess. 250p. 1998. pap. 15.95 (*1-881524-23-X*) Milligan Bks.

Blalock, Roy, Jr., jt. auth. see Huneycutt, C. D.

Blalock, Steven F., jt. auth. see North Carolina Bar Association Foundation Staff.

Blalock, Susan E. Guide to the Secular Poetry of T. S. Eliot. LC 96-17059. (Reference Publication in Literature Ser.). 1996. 50.00 (*0-8161-7341-9*, G K Hall & Co) Mac Lib Ref.

Blamey. Atlas of Breast Disease: 50 Illustrations. (Illus.). 1997. text 98.00 (*0-7020-2252-7*) Bailliere Tindall.

Blamey, Kathleen, tr. see Ricoeur, Paul.

Blamey, Kathleen, tr. see Ricur, Paul, et al.

Blamey, M., jt. auth. see Grey-Wilson, C.

Blamey, Marjorie. Flowers in Watercolour. (Learn to Paint Ser.). (Illus.). 1999. pap. 15.95 (*0-00-413339-0*, Pub. by HarpC) Trafalgar.

An Asterisk (*) at the beginning of an entry indicates that the title is appearing for the first time.

Blamey, Marjorie & Wilson, Christopher G. The Illustrated Flora of Britain & Northern Europe: Over 2400 Plants, Native & Introduced, Described & Illustrated in Colour. (Illus.). 544p. 1989. lib. bdg. 75.00 (*0-340-40170-2*, Pub. by Hodder & Stought Ltd) Lubrecht & Cramer.

Blamey, R., et al. Atlas of Breast Cancer. (Illus.). 100p. 1994. 29.95 (*1-873413-70-X*) Merit Pub Intl.

Blamire. Exploring Life: Principles of Biology. 1993. 124.37 (*0-697-14541-7*, WCB McGr Hill) McGrw-H Hghr Educ.

— Life Explored. 1994. teacher ed. 14.06 (*0-697-24020-7*, WCB McGr Hill) McGrw-H Hghr Educ.

— Life Explored. 1994. pap. text 325.31 (*0-697-24024-X*, WCB McGr Hill) McGrw-H Hghr Educ.

— Trans Masters Exploring Lif. 1994. 16.87 (*0-697-21981-X*) McGraw.

Blamire, John. Exploring Life. (C). 1994. text, student ed. write for info. (*0-697-24622-1*, WCB McGr Hill) McGrw-H Hghr Educ.

Blamire, John. Exploring Life: The Principles of Biology. 528p. (C). 1993. text. write for info. (*0-697-14537-9*, WCB McGr Hill) McGrw-H Hghr Educ.

Blamire, John. Exploring Life: The Principles of Biology. 528p. (C). 1993. text, student ed. 16.25 (*0-697-14539-5*, WCB McGr Hill) McGrw-H Hghr Educ.

— Exploring Life: The Principles of Biology. 528p. (C). 1994. text. write for info. (*0-697-22359-0*, WCB McGr Hill) McGrw-H Hghr Educ.

— Life Explored. 192p. (C). 1994. text, student ed. 16.25 (*0-697-24021-5*, WCB McGr Hill) McGrw-H Hghr Educ.

— Life Explored: The Principles of Biology. (C). 1994. text, student ed. 16.50 (*0-697-24022-3*) McGraw.

— Life Explored: The Principles of Biology. 528p. (C). 1994. text. write for info. (*0-697-23370-7*, WCB McGr Hill) McGrw-H Hghr Educ.

Blamire, Susanna. The Poetical Works, 1842. LC 93-47133. (Revolution & Romanticism, 1789-1834 Ser.). 1994. 55.00 (*1-85477-165-5*) Continuum.

Blamires, Alcuin. The Case for Women in Medieval Culture. LC 97-193252. 288p. 1997. text 75.00 (*0-19-818256-2*) OUP.

— The Case of Women in Medieval Culture. 288p. 1998. reprint ed. pap. text 24.95 (*0-19-818630-4*) OUP.

Blamires, Alcuin, ed. Woman Defamed & Woman Defended: An Anthology of Medieval Texts. (Illus.). 342p. 1992. pap. text 19.95 (*0-19-871039-9*) OUP.

Blamires, Cyprian P., tr. see Fanno, Marco.

Blamires, Cyprian P., tr. see Vattimo, Gianni.

Blamires, David. Fortunatus in His Many English Guises. LC 95-49931. (Illus.). 172p. 1996. text 79.95 (*0-7734-1350-2*) E Mellen.

Blamires, Harry. The Cassell Guide to Common Errors in English. (Illus.). 336p. 1999. pap. 16.95 (*0-304-35028-1*) Continuum.

— The Christian Mind: How Should a Christian Think? LC 97-22820. 230p. 1997. pap., student ed. 10.99 (*1-56955-044-1*, Vine Bks) Servant.

— The New Bloomsday Book: A Guide Through Joyce's Ulysses: The New Text. 2nd rev. ed. 288p. 1988. pap. text 14.95 (*0-415-00704-6*) Routledge.

— The New Bloomsday Book: A Guide Through Ulysses. 3rd ed. LC 95-44440. 272p. 1996. pap. 20.99 (*0-415-13858-2*) Routledge.

— The New Bloomsday Book: A Guide Through Ulysses. 3rd ed. LC 95-44440. 272p. (C). 1996. 85.00 (*0-415-13857-4*) Routledge.

— The Post-Christian Mind. LC 99-14076. 218p. 1999. pap. 10.99 (*1-56955-142-1*) Servant.

***Blamires, Mike, ed.** Enabling Technology for Inclusion. 208p. 2000. pap. 31.00 (*1-85396-394-1*, Pub. by P Chapman); lib. bdg. 82.00 (*1-85396-436-0*, Pub. by P Chapman) Sage.

Blamires, Mike, et al. Parent-Teacher Partnership: Practical Approaches to Meet Special Educational Needs. LC 97-202739. (Resource Materials for Teachers Ser.). 112p. 1997. pap. 24.95 (*1-85346-470-8*, Pub. by David Fulton) Taylor & Francis.

Blamires, Steve. Celtic Tree Mysteries: Secrets of the Ogham. LC 96-36866. (World Religion & Magic Ser.). (Illus.). 312p. (Orig.). 1997. pap. 14.95 (*1-56718-070-1*) Llewellyn Pubns.

— Glamoury: Magic of the Celtic Green World. LC 95-39750. (Llewellyn's Celtic Wisdom Ser.). (Illus.). 352p. 1999. pap. 16.95 (*1-56718-069-8*) Llewellyn Pubns.

Blampain, Daniel. Nouveau Dictionnaire des Difficultes du Francais Moderne. 3rd ed. 983p. 1994. 95.00 (*0-7859-8750-9*) Fr & Eur.

Blamton, Claire & Hawcock, David. Egyptian Mummies. (Zoomers Ser.). 4p. (J). (gr. 4-6). 1999. 2.99 (*1-57584-285-8*, RD Childrens) Rdrs Digest.

Blan, Evelyn. Krishnamurti: 100 Years. (Illus.). 284p. 1997. pap. 17.95 (*1-55670-678-2*) Stewart Tabori & Chang.

Blan, Julie, jt. auth. see Drysdale, Bryan.

Blan, L. B. Special Study of the Incidence of Retardation. LC 79-176569. (Columbia University. Teachers College. Contributions to Education Ser.: No. 40). reprint ed. 37.50 (*0-404-55040-1*) AMS Pr.

Blana, Hubert. Die Herstellung: Ein Handbuch fur die Gestaltung Technik und Kalkuation von Buch, Zeitschrift und Zeitung, Mit 250 Abbidungen. 4th ed. (Grundwissen Buchhandel-Verlage Ser.: Vol. 5). (GER., Illus.). 380p. 1998. pap. write for info. (*3-598-20067-6*) K G Saur Verlag.

Blanas, Kate, tr. see Knuth, Bruce G.

***Blanc.** Computer Applications: Text. (Computer Applications Ser.). (C). 2000. text 41.95 (*0-538-72330-0*) Sth-Wstrn College.

Blanc, Alan. Desktop Publishing Projects. 1997. mass mkt. 29.95 (*0-538-67790-2*) S-W Pub.

— Internal Components. (Mitchell's Building Ser.). 216p. (C). 1996. pap. text 45.95 (*0-582-21257-X*) Addison-Wesley.

— Landscape Construction & Detailing. LC 96-4922. (Illus.). 210p. 1996. 74.95 (*0-07-005957-8*) McGraw.

— Potter's Perinatal Pathology. 1991. write for info. (*0-8151-0868-0*) Mosby Inc.

— Stairs, Steps & Ramps. (Illus.). 192p. 1996. text 95.00 (*0-7506-1526-5*) Buttrwrth-Heinemann.

— Word Processing to Desktop Publishing: Exercises & Applications. (DF - Computer Applications Ser.). 1994. mass mkt. 27.95 (*0-538-62352-7*) S-W Pub.

Blanc, Alan, et al, eds. Architecture & Construction in Steel. (Illus.). 640p. (C). 1993. 165.00 (*0-419-17660-8*, E & FN Spon) Routledge.

***Blanc, B., et al.** Office Hysteroscopy & Operative Hysteroscopy on One Day Basis. (Illus.). 260p. 1999. 124.00 (*2-287-59652-6*, Pub. by Spl France Editions) Spr-Verlag.

Blanc, C., ed. Leonhardi Euleri Opera Omnia. (Series Secunda: Vol. 24). 356p. 1990. 202.00 (*0-8176-1454-0*) Birkhauser.

Blanc, Cristina S., et al. Urban Children in Distress: Global Predicaments & Innovative Strategies. LC 94-401. 481p. 1994. text 61.00 (*2-88124-622-2*); pap. text 31.00 (*2-88124-623-0*) Gordon & Breach.

Blanc, Elaine Le, see Fredericks, Anthony & Le Blanc, Elaine.

Blanc, Esther S. Berchick. LC 87-37172. (Illus.). 32p. (J). (gr. k-5). 1989. 14.95 (*0-912078-81-2*) Volcano Pr.

— Wars I Have Seen. LC 93-60727. (Illus.). 126p. (Orig.). 1996. pap. 12.95 (*0-912078-80-4*) Volcano Pr.

Blanc, Felice. I am a Quaker. LC 98-11796. (Religions of the World Ser.). 24p. (J). (gr. k-4). 1999. 17.26 (*0-8239-5264-9*, PowerKids) Rosen Group.

Blanc, Georges. The French Vineyard Table. LC 97-12569. 1997. 55.00 (*0-609-60000-1*) C Potter.

Blanc, H. Le, see Wyatt, J. & Le Blanc, H.

Blanc, Henry. Narrative of Captivity in Abyssinia with Some Account of the Late Emperor Theodore, His Country & People. (Illus.). 410p. 1970. reprint ed. 55.00 (*0-7146-1792-X*, Pub. by F Cass Pubs) Intl Spec Bk.

Blanc, Iris. Advanced Word 7. (Short Course Texts Ser.). (Illus.). (Orig.). 1996. pap. 25.00 (*1-56243-339-3*, AB-19) DDC Pub.

— Aprendido Microsoft Office 97. 1999. pap. 27.00 (*1-56243-614-7*) DDC Pub.

— Computer Applications for Business. 318p. 1990. 25.00 (*0-936862-91-2*, 55/TX); teacher ed. 10.00 (*0-936862-93-9*, 5-TM); teacher ed. 325.00 incl. trans. (*0-936862-79-3*, T-55); spiral bd. 19.50 (*0-936862-77-7*, 55); disk 65.00 (*1-56243-003-3*); disk 65.00 (*1-56243-002-5*); disk 65.00 (*0-936862-99-8*); disk 65.00 (*0-936862-97-1*) DDC Pub.

— Computer Applications for Business (Generic) 2nd rev. ed. (Illus.). 1996. text 22.00 (*1-56243-321-0*, 552) DDC Pub.

— Corel Wordperfect Suite 7 for Windows 95, Quick Reference. (Quick Reference Guides Ser.). (Orig.). 1996. pap. 12.00 (*1-56243-333-4*, G-11) DDC Pub.

— DisplayWrite 4 Quick Reference Guide. (DDC Quick Reference Guides Ser.). 82p. (Orig.). 1989. spiral bd. 12.00 (*0-936862-70-X*, D-4) DDC Pub.

— Intermediate Word 7. (Short Course Texts Ser.). (Illus.). (Orig.). 1996. pap. 25.00 (*1-56243-338-5*, AB-18) DDC Pub.

— Introduction to Microsoft Office for Windows 95. (Short Course Texts Ser.). (Illus.). (Orig.). 1996. pap. 25.00 (*1-56243-325-3*, AB-15) DDC Pub.

— Introduction to Microsoft Office 4.3. LC 96-192661. (Short Course Texts Ser.). (Illus.). (Orig.). 1996. pap. 25.00 (*1-56243-324-5*, AB-14) DDC Pub.

— Introduction to Word 7. LC 97-140645. (Short Course Texts Ser.). (Illus.). 242p. (Orig.). 1996. pap. 25.00 (*1-56243-337-7*, AB-17) DDC Pub.

— Learning Desktop Publishing for Wordperfect 6 for Windows. LC 95-127568. 1994. pap. 27.00 (*1-56243-191-9*, F9) DDC Pub.

— Learning Desktop Publishing with WordPerfect 6.1 for Windows. LC 95-202883. 1995. pap. 25.00 (*1-56243-260-5*, Z5) DDC Pub.

— Learning Keyboarding & Word Processing with Word 97. 1997. 29.00 (*1-56243-358-X*, Z-24HC) DDC Pub.

— Learning Lotus 1-2-3 (DOS) 1992. teacher ed. 10.00 (*1-56243-078-5*, L6-TM); pap. 27.00 (*1-56243-077-7*, L-9); trans. 250.00 (*1-56243-079-3*, L-68) DDC Pub.

— Learning Microsoft Office for Windows 95. 1996. pap. text 27.00 (*1-56243-294-X*, Z-6) DDC Pub.

— Learning Microsoft Office' Professional Version. 1996. 31.00 (*1-56243-300-8*, M-9HC); pap. text 27.00 (*1-56243-261-3*, M-9) DDC Pub.

— Learning Microsoft Word 97. (Fast-Teach Learning Ser.). spiral bd. 29.00 incl. cd-rom (*1-56243-462-4*, Z-20HC) DDC Pub.

***Blanc, Iris.** Learning Microsoft Word 97. LC 98-151845. (Fast-Teach Learning Ser.). 1998. pap., spiral bd. 27.00 (*1-56243-440-3*, Z-20) DDC Pub.

Blanc, Iris. Learning Word 7 for Windows 95. 1996. 31.00 (*1-56243-317-2*, Z-10HC) DDC Pub.

— Learning Word 7 for Windows 95. 1996. pap. text 27.00 (*1-56243-316-4*, Z-10) DDC Pub.

— Learning WordPerfect 5.0 & 5.1: Through Step-by-Step Exercises & Applications. (YA). (gr. 9-12). 1991. teacher ed. 10.00 (*1-56243-047-5*, W-106); teacher ed. 7.50 incl. disk (*1-56243-048-3*, SW-25); trans. 250.00 (*1-56243-049-1*, PW-1) DDC Pub.

— Learning WordPerfect 5.0 & 5.1: Through Step-by-Step Exercises & Applications. (Fast-Teach Learning Ser.). 1991. spiral bd. 27.00 (*1-56243-046-7*, W-9) DDC Pub.

— Learning WordPerfect 5.0 & 5.1: Through Step-by-Step Exercises & Applications. large type ed. 1992. 86.50 (*0-614-09875-0*, L-18281-00) Am Printing Hse.

— Learning WordPerfect 6 (DOS) 1993. pap. 27.00 (*1-56243-097-1*, P-9) DDC Pub.

— Learning WordPerfect 6.1 for Windows. 1995. pap. 27.00 (*1-56243-256-7*, H9) DDC Pub.

— Learning WordPerfect 6.1 for Windows. 1996. 29.00 (*1-56243-302-4*, H-9HC) DDC Pub.

— Learning Works 3.0 for Windows. (Fast-Teach Learning Ser.). 1995. spiral bd. 27.00 (*1-56243-180-3*, 1-VKW3) DDC Pub.

— Lotus for Windows. 1993. pap. 12.00 (*1-56243-111-0*, LW-17) DDC Pub.

— Lotus 1-2-3 (Ver. 3.1) Quick Reference Guide. (Illus.). 1992. spiral bd. 12.00 (*1-56243-031-9*, J-18) DDC Pub.

— Lotus 1-2-3 (Ver. 2.2) Quick Reference Guide. (DDC Quick Reference Guides Ser.). (YA). (gr. 9-12). 1990. spiral bd. 12.00 (*1-56243-000-9*, L2-17) DDC Pub.

— Lotus 1-2-3, Version 3.4, IBM PC: Quick Reference Guide. 1993. spiral bd. 12.00 (*1-56243-090-4*, L317) DDC Pub.

— Quick Reference Guide for Lotus 123 Release 4 DOS. 1995. spiral bd. 12.00 (*1-56243-229-X*, G4) DDC Pub.

— Quick Reference Guide for Lotus 123 Release 5 for Windows. 1994. spiral bd. 12.00 (*1-56243-247-8*, L-19) DDC Pub.

— Step-by-Step Skill Building Exercises for the Word Processor. 2nd ed. Dembo, Shirley & Lorton, Elizabeth, eds. 224p. 1989. 20.00 (*0-936862-54-8*, RWP-9-0); teacher ed. 10.00 (*0-936862-65-3*, RP-TM); teacher ed. 10.00 (*1-56243-409-8*, RP-TM); student ed. 175.00 incl. trans. (*0-936862-58-0*, T-100E); disk 20.00 (*0-936862-67-X*, 10-TEWP) DDC Pub.

Blanc, Iris & Hildebrandt, Elinore J. Database Applications & Exercises. Montero, Julio, ed. 106p. 1990. 20.00 (*0-936862-50-5*, DB-1); 20.00 (*1-56243-058-0*, 10-TEDB); teacher ed. 10.00 (*0-936862-52-1*, DB-TM); trans. 100.00 (*1-56243-054-8*, DT-200); disk 65.00 (*0-936862-30-0*, SD1) DDC Pub.

— Lotus 1-2-3 (Intro.) Quick Reference Guide. (DDC Quick Reference Guides Ser.). 40p. 1986. 12.00 (*0-936862-31-9*, L-17) DDC Pub.

Blanc, Iris & Vento, Cathy. Learning Microsoft Excel 97. (Fast-Teach Learning Ser.). pap., spiral bd. 25.00 (*1-56243-441-1*, Z-21) DDC Pub.

— Learning Microsoft Office 97. (Fast-Teach Learning Ser.). 29.00 incl. cd-rom (*1-56243-461-6*, Z-19HC) DDC Pub.

— Learning Microsoft Office 97. LC 97-222711. (Fast-Teach Learning Ser.). (Illus.). 494p. 1997. pap. 27.00 (*1-56243-439-X*, Z-19) DDC Pub.

— Spreadsheets Skill Building Exercises & Applications. 124p. 1986. 20.00 (*0-936862-22-X*, 369); teacher ed. 10.00 (*0-936862-45-9*, SAE/TM); teacher ed. 10.00 (*1-56243-410-1*, SAE/TM); student ed. 20.00 incl. disk (*1-56243-056-4*, 10-TESP); trans. 250.00 (*0-936862-19-X*, 1359); trans. 250.00 (*1-56243-055-6*, S-124); disk 65.00 (*0-936862-43-2*, T-L34/LW4EX40); disk 65.00 (*0-936862-48-3*, SS10SL) DDC Pub.

Blanc, Iris, jt. auth. see Hildebrandt, Elinore J.

Blanc, Jean-Jacques, et al. Neurally Mediated Syncope: Pathophysiology, Investigations & Treatment. (Bakken Research Center Ser.: No. 10). (Illus.). 188p. 1996. 55.00 (*0-87993-644-4*) Futura Pub.

Blanc, Karen. Dear Hilda. (Illus.). 400p. 1983. reprint ed. pap. 9.95 (*0-937776-01-7*, Fowler) Good Commun Inc.

Blanc, Karen, jt. auth. see Woolf, Marsha.

Blanc, L. Le, see Le Blanc, L.

Blanc, La, see La Blanc.

Blanc, Louis. Decorative French Ironwork Designs. LC 99-19600. (Illus.). 96p. 1999. pap. text 9.95 (*0-486-40487-0*) Dover.

— Histoire de la Revolution Francaise, 12 vols. LC 79-39452. (FRE.). reprint ed. 270.00 (*0-404-07150-3*) AMS Pr.

Blanc, Madame, see De Solms, Marie T., pseud.

Blanc, Marcel Le, see Le Blanc, Marcel.

Blanc, Marie T., tr. see Bertrand, Guy.

Blanc, Michel, et al. Numerical Simulation of Magnetospheric Electron Transport Phenomena. (Applied Mathematics Ser.: Vol. 1). xvii, 62p. 1987. pap. text 82.00 (*2-88124-165-4*) Gordon & Breach.

Blanc, Michel, jt. auth. see Hamers, Josiane.

Blanc, Nero. The Crossword Murder. LC 00-265195 320p. (Orig.). 1999. pap. 13.00 (*0-425-16977-4*, Prime Crime) Berkley Pub.

***Blanc, Nero.** Crossword Murder. 2000. mass mkt. 5.99 (*0-425-17701-7*) Berkley Pub.

— Two Down. 2000. pap. 13.00 (*0-425-17510-3*, Prime Crime) Berkley Pub.

Blanc, Oliver. Mansions of Paris. (Illus.). 208p. 1998. pap. text 27.50 (*2-87939-180-6*, Pub. by Pierre Terrail) Rizzoli Intl.

Blanc, Paul Le, see McLemee, Scott & Le Blanc, Paul, eds.

Blanc, Paul Le, see Le Blanc, Paul.

Blanc, Raymond. Blanc Mange: The Mysteries of the Kitchen Revealed. LC 97-77083. 1996. pap. text 21.95 (*0-563-38724-6*) BBC.

— Blanc Mange: The Mysteries of the Kitchen Revealed. (Illus.). 320p. 1996. pap. 21.95 (*0-563-37016-5*) BBC.

***Blanc, Raymond.** Blanc Vite: Fast Fresh Food from Raymond Blanc. (Illus.). 320p. 2000. 55.00 (*0-7472-1708-4*, Pub. by Headline Bk Pub) Trafalgar.

***Blanc-Rerat, Martine.** All about Jesus: The Life & Teachings of Jesus in the Bible's Own Words. 2000. 15.95 (*0-8294-1506-8*) Loyola Pr.

Blanc, Roger D., et al. Nuts & Bolts of Financial Products: The Evolving World of Capital Market & Investment Management Products. LC 98-112539. (Corporate Law & Practice Course Handbook Ser.). 640 p. 1997. 129.00 (*0-87224-357-5*) PLI.

Blanc, Sydney Le, see Le Blanc, Sydney.

***Blanc, Sylvia.** Stairs, Steps & Ramps. 240p. 2000. pap. 47.95 (*0-7506-4846-5*, Architectural Pr) Buttrwrth-Heinemann.

Blanc, Tara. The First Seventy-Five Years of Los Altos Golf & Country Club. Nelson, Rodney, ed. 110p. 1999. 100.00 (*0-929690-41-9*) Herit Pubs AZ.

— Sifting Through the Years: A History of Bay State Milling Company. 110p. 1999. 18.99 (*0-929690-31-1*) Herit Pubs AZ.

Blanc, Tara, jt. auth. see Finnerty, Margaret.

Blanc, Tara, jt. auth. see Heritage Publishers Staff.

Blanc, Tara, jt. auth. see Myers, John L.

***Blanc, Tara A.** Oasis in the City: The History of the Desert Botanical Garden. Zeloznicki, Susan, ed. 88p. 2000. 22.00 (*0-929690-51-6*) Herit Pubs AZ.

Blanc, Tara A., jt. auth. see Myers, John L.

Blanc, Warren, jt. auth. see Howell, Carol L.

Blanca, Bahia, jt. ed. see Barrantes, Francisco J.

Blanca, Cano Puertos. Cocina Economica. (SPA.). 1997. pap. text 7.98 (*968-403-951-4*) Selector.

Blanca, N. P. De La, see De La Blanca, N. P.

Blanca, Nieto. Cocina Tradicional Mexicana. (SPA.). 1997. pap. text 7.98 (*968-403-710-4*) Selector.

Blanca, Nieto. Postres Mexicanos. 1997. pap. text 7.98 (*968-403-960-3*) Selector.

Blanca, Oscar T., ed. The International Design Yearbook 5, Vol. 5. (International Design Yearbooks Ser.). (Illus.). 240p. 1989. 90.00 (*1-55859-005-6*) Abbeville Pr.

Blancard, D. A Colour Atlas of Tomato Diseases: Observation, Identification & Control. 212p. 1994. text 119.95 (*0-470-23417-2*) Halsted Pr.

Blancard, D., et al. A Colour Atlas of Cucurbit Diseases: Observation, Identification & Control. LC 94-20419.Tr. of Maladies des Cucurbitacees. (Illus.). 299p. 1995. text 129.00 (*0-470-23416-4*) Halsted Pr.

Blancart, jt. auth. see Bernot, Denise.

Blancarte, Roberto. Cultura E Identidad Nacional (Culture & National Identity) (SPA.). 424p. 1994. pap. 15.99 (*968-16-4237-6*, Pub. by Fondo) Continental Bk.

Blancato, Jerry N., et al, eds. Biomarkers for Agrochemicals & Toxic Substances: Applications & Risk Assessment, Vol. 643. LC 96-28772. (ACS Symposium Ser.: No. 643). (Illus.). 296p. 1996. text 105.00 (*0-8412-3449-3*, Pub. by Am Chemical) OUP.

Blance & Cook. Lady Monster Has a Plan. Date not set. pap. text. write for info. (*0-582-19312-5*, Pub. by Addison-Wesley) Longman.

— Monster & Magic Umbrella. Date not set. pap. text. write for info. (*0-582-18593-9*, Pub. by Addison-Wesley) Longman.

— Monster & Surprise Cookie. Date not set. pap. text. write for info. (*0-582-19308-7*, Pub. by Addison-Wesley) Longman.

— Monster & the Mural. Date not set. pap. text. write for info. (*0-582-19301-X*, Pub. by Addison-Wesley) Longman.

— Monster at School. Date not set. pap. text. write for info. (*0-582-18597-1*, Pub. by Addison-Wesley) Longman.

— Monster Buys a Pet. Date not set. pap. text. write for info. (*0-582-19311-7*, Pub. by Addison-Wesley) Longman.

— Monster Cleans His House. Date not set. pap. text. write for info. (*0-582-18590-4*, Pub. by Addison-Wesley) Longman.

— Monster Comes to the City. Date not set. pap. text. write for info. (*0-582-18588-2*, Pub. by Addison-Wesley) Longman.

— Monster Gets a Job. Date not set. pap. text. write for info. (*0-582-19307-9*, Pub. by Addison-Wesley) Longman.

— Monster Goes Around Town. Date not set. pap. text. write for info. (*0-582-19309-5*, Pub. by Addison-Wesley) Longman.

— Monster Goes to Circus. Date not set. pap. text. write for info. (*0-582-19304-4*, Pub. by Addison-Wesley) Longman.

— Monster Goes to School. Date not set. pap. text. write for info. (*0-582-18596-3*, Pub. by Addison-Wesley) Longman.

— Monster Goes to the Beach. Date not set. pap. text. write for info. (*0-582-19306-0*, Pub. by Addison-Wesley) Longman.

— Monster Goes to the Hospital. Date not set. pap. text. write for info. (*0-582-19305-2*, Pub. by Addison-Wesley) Longman.

— Monster Goes to the Zoo. Date not set. pap. text. write for info. (*0-582-18599-8*, Pub. by Addison-Wesley) Longman.

— Monster Looks for a House. Date not set. pap. text. write for info. (*0-582-18589-0*, Pub. by Addison-Wesley) Longman.

— Monster Looks for Friend. Date not set. pap. text. write for info. (*0-582-18591-2*, Pub. by Addison-Wesley) Longman.

— Monster Meets Lady Monster. Date not set. pap. text. write for info. (*0-582-18592-0*, Pub. by Addison-Wesley) Longman.

— Monster on the Bus. Date not set. pap. text. write for info. (*0-582-18595-5*, Pub. by Addison-Wesley) Longman.

— Monstruo, 12 bks., Set. Incl. Monstruo Compre un Animalito. 1.98 (*0-8372-3482-4*); Monstruo Encuentra Trabajo. 1.98 (*0-8372-3485-9*); Monstruo, la Senorita Monstruo y el Paseo en Bicicleta. 1.98 (*0-8372-3488-3*); Monstruo Recorre la Ciudad. 1.98 (*0-8372-3490-5*); Monstruo Va a la Playa. 1.98 (*0-8372-3479-4*); Monstruo Va Al Circo. 1.98 (*0-8372-3483-2*); Monstruo Va Al Hospital. 1.98 (*0-8372-3489-1*); Monstruo y el

B

Muro. 1.98 (0-8372-3487-5); Monstruo y la Galleta de Sorpresa. 1.98 (0-8372-3486-7); Monstruo y la Liquidacion de Juguetes. 1.98 (0-8372-3480-8); Plan de la Senorita Monstruo. 1.98 (0-8372-3481-6); Senorita Monstruo Ayuda. 1.98 (0-8372-3484-0); (gr. k-4). Set pap. 215.00 (0-8372-3493-X) Bowmar-Noble.

Blance & Cooke. Lady Monster Helps Out. Date not set. pap. text. write for info. (0-582-19302-8, Pub. by Addison-Wesley) Longman.

Blance, A. Norie's Nautical Tables. 636p. (C). 1991. 29.95 (0-85288-160-6, Pub. by Laurie Norie & Wilson Ltd) Bluewater Bks.

Blance, A. G., ed. Norie's Nautical Tables. rev. ed. (Illus.). 600p. (C). 1983. 100.00 (0-85288-091-X, Pub. by Laurie Norie & Wilson Ltd) St Mut.

Blancero & Marron. Pak: Women, Culture & Society. 2nd ed. 544p. (C). 1998. pap. text 42.95 (0-7872-5385-5, 41538501) Kendall-Hunt.

Blancett, Suzanne S. & Flarey, Dominick L. Outcomes in Path-Based Collaborative Practice. 400p. 1998. pap. 99.00 (0-8342-1048-7, 10487) Aspen Pub.

— Reengineering Nursing & Health Care Delivery: The Handbook for Organizational Transformation. 416p. 1995. 65.00 (0-8342-0660-9, 20660) Aspen Pub.

Blancett, Suzanne S. & Flarey, Dominick L., eds. Case Studies in Nursing Case Management: Health Care Delivery in a World of Managed Care. 470p. 1996. 69.00 (0-8342-0789-3) Aspen Pub.

Blancett, Suzanne S., ed. see Flarey, Dominick L.

Blanch. Italian Men: Love & Sex. 2000. 20.00 (0-7893-0126-1, Pub. by Universe) St Martin.

Blanch, Harvey W., et al, eds. Foundations of Biochemical Engineering: Kinetics & Thermodynamics in Biological Systems. LC 82-20694. (ACS Symposium Ser.: No. 207). 522p. 1983. lib. bdg. 60.95 (0-8412-0752-6) Am Chemical.

— Foundations of Biochemical Engineering: Kinetics & Thermodynamics in Biological Systems. LC 82-20694. (ACS Symposium Ser.: No. 207). (Illus.). 537p. 1983. reprint ed. pap. 166.50 (0-608-03223-9, 206374200007) Bks Demand.

Blanch, Harvey W. & Clark, D. S., eds. Biochemical Engineering. (Illus.). 720p. 1997. pap. text 39.75 (0-8247-0099-6) Dekker.

Blanch, Harvey W. & Clark, Douglas S. Biochemical Engineering. LC 95-37549. (Illus.). 720p. 1995. text 125.00 (0-8247-8949-0) Dekker.

Blanch, Harvey W. & Clark, Douglas S., eds. Applied Biocatalysis, Vol. 1. (Illus.). 248p. 1991. text 160.00 (0-8247-8533-9) Dekker.

Blanch, John, et al. Mercantilist Views of Trade & Monopoly: Four Essays, 1645-1720. LC 77-38468. (Evolution of Capitalism Ser.). 140p. 1978. reprint ed. 37.95 (0-405-04127-6) Ayer.

Blanch, Jose M., tr. see Pink, Arthur W.

Blanch, Jose Maria, tr. see Douma, J.

Blanch, Juan M., tr. see Spurgeon, Charles H.

Blanch, Lesley. The Sabres of Paradise. 495p. 1984. pap. 12.95 (0-88184-042-4) Carroll & Graf.

— The Wilder Shores of Love. 336p. 1996. pap. 12.95 (0-7867-0260-5) Carroll & Graf.

Blanch, Montserrat. Manolo: Escultura, Pintura y Dibujo. (Grandes Monografias). (SPA., Illus.). 338p. 1993. 200.00 (84-343-0087-7) Elliots Bks.

Blanch, Robert J., ed. "Sir Gawain & the Green Knight" A Reference Guide. LC 82-50412. vi, 298p. 1984. 45.00 (0-87875-244-7) Whitston Pub.

Blanch, Robert J., ed. Style & Symbolism in Piers Plowman: A Modern Critical Anthology. LC 69-20115. 290p. (Orig.). reprint ed. pap. 89.90 (0-608-15456-3, 202937200060) Bks Demand.

Blanch, Robert J., et al, eds. Text & Matter: New Critical Perspectives of the "Pearl"-Poet. xx, 254p. 1990. 49.50 (0-87875-402-4) Whitston Pub.

Blanch, Robert J. & Wasserman, Julian N. From Pearl to Gawain: Forme to Fynisment. LC 94-40999. (Illus.). 224p. (C). 1995. 49.95 (0-8130-1348-8) U Press Fla.

Blanch, Santiago A. The Prado. LC 96-3896. (Illus.). 474p. 1996. pap. 39.98 (0-8109-8147-5, Pub. by Abrams) Time Warner.

Blanch, Stuart Y. Living by Faith. LC 84-10182. 156p. reprint ed. 48.40 (0-608-16652-9, 202753600055) Bks Demand.

Blanchaert, Remy H., jt. auth. see Ord, Robert A.

***Blanchan, Neltje.** Birds Every Child Should Know. (Illus.). 296p. 2000. reprint ed. 34.95 (0-87745-716-6); reprint ed. pap. 15.95 (0-87745-705-0) U of Iowa Pr.

Blanchard. Instrumento Para Diagnosticar Lecturas: Instrument for the Diagnosis of Reading. 144p. (C). 1989. spiral bd. 20.95 (0-8403-5199-2) Kendall-Hunt.

— Litig/trial Prac F/legal Asst Stdy Gde 4e. 4th ed. (Paralegal). (C). 1995. student ed. 16.25 (0-314-04936-3) Delmar.

— Manual of Equine Reproduction. (Illus.). 224p. (gr. 13). 1997. pap. text 39.95 (0-8151-4378-8, 31124) Mosby Inc.

— Mission Possible. 1999. pap. 14.95 (0-07-134827-1) McGraw.

— Trial Practice. 3rd ed. Date not set. pap. text, teacher ed. write for info. (0-314-68774-2) West Pub.

Blanchard & Devaney. Differential Equations. (Mathematics Ser.). Date not set. 58.00 (0-534-95268-2) Brooks-Cole.

— Differential Equations. 1998. mass mkt., student ed. 24.95 (0-534-35253-7) Brooks-Cole.

— Differential Equations. LC 97-34431. (Miscellaneous/Catalogs Ser.). 1998. 97.95 (0-534-34550-6) Course Tech.

— Differential Equations. (Mathematics Ser.). 1996. pap. 65.95 (0-534-95008-6) PWS Pubs.

Blanchard, et al. Dynamics of Complex & Irregular Systems - Biefefeld Encounters in Mathematics & Physics VIII. 372p. 1993. text 106.00 (981-02-1570-3) World Scientific Pub.

Blanchard, A., jt. auth. see Lago, M. T.

Blanchard, Alice. Darkness Peering. LC 99-24823. 352p. 1999. 23.95 (0-553-11153-1) Bantam.

***Blanchard, Alice.** Darkness Peering: A Novel. large type ed. LC 99-88115. 2000. 25.95 (1-56895-829-3) Wheeler Pub.

— Darkness Piercing. 464p. 2000. mass mkt. 6.99 (0-553-58129-5) Bantam.

Blanchard, Alice. The Stuntman's Daughter. LC 95-26177. 155p. (Orig.). 1996. pap. 14.95 (1-57441-009-1) UNTX Pr.

Blanchard, Arlene. The Dump Truck. LC 94-25704. (Illus.). (J). (ps up). 1995. pap. 3.99 (1-56402-506-3) Candlewick Pr.

— The Naughty Lamb. LC 88-4098. (Illus.). 32p. (J). (ps-1). 1989. 9.95 (0-8037-0577-8, Dial Yng Read) Peng Put Young Read.

— The Tugboat. LC 94-25705. (Illus.). (J). (ps-3). 1995. pap. 3.99 (1-56402-524-1) Candlewick Pr.

Blanchard, B. Everard. A New System of Education. LC 74-23970. 1975. 19.95 (0-88280-012-4) ETC Pubns.

Blanchard, Barbara. From Pawns to Kings Vol. I: In the Game of Cancer. 200p. 1999. pap. 9.98 (0-9670630-0-0, 1516) Legacy NY.

Blanchard, Benjamin S. Logistic Engineering & Management. 5th ed. LC 98-9446. 526p. (C). 1998. 99.00 (0-13-905316-6, Prentice Hall) P-H.

— System Engineering Management. 2nd ed. LC 97-3546. 504p. 1997. 79.00 (0-471-19086-1) Wiley.

Blanchard, Benjamin S. & Fabrycky, W. J. Systems Engineering & Analysis. 3rd ed. LC 97-44423. 704p. 1998. 99.00 (0-13-135047-1) P-H.

Blanchard, Benjamin S. & Fabrycky, Walter J. Systems Engineering & Analysis. 2nd ed. 720p. 1990. text 92.00 (0-13-880758-2) P-H.

Blanchard, Benjamin S., et al. Maintainability: A Key to Effective Serviceability & Maintenance Management. LC 94-13474. 560p. 1995. 120.00 (0-471-59132-7) Wiley.

Blanchard, C., jt. ed. see Goodspeed, Weston A.

Blanchard, Calvin. Art of Real Pleasure: That New Pleasure, for Which an Imperial Reward Was Offered. LC 70-154430. (Utopian Literature Ser.). (Illus.). 1976. reprint ed. 20.95 (0-405-03513-6) Ayer.

Blanchard, Charles. Counties of Clay & Owen, Indiana. (Illus.). 966p. 1992. reprint ed. lib. bdg. 95.00 (0-8328-2535-2) Higginson Bk Co.

— Why Is the Past Important? 2nd ed. (Series of Lesson Plans: Ser. 1, No. 2). (Illus.). 8p. 1996. write for info. (0-9642289-2-0) FL Div Hist Res.

Blanchard, Charles, ed. Counties of Howard & Tipton: Historical & Biographical. (Illus.). 1997. reprint ed. lib. bdg. 92.50 (0-8328-6653-9) Higginson Bk Co.

— Counties of Morgan, Monroe, & Brown, Indiana. (Illus.). 800p. 1992. reprint ed. lib. bdg. 79.50 (0-8328-2550-6) Higginson Bk Co.

Blanchard, Charles, jt. auth. see Payne, Claudine.

Blanchard, Charles, jt. ed. see Goodspeed, Weston A.

Blanchard, Charles A. Revised Knight Templarism Illustrated (1880) Complete Rituals of the Knight Templars. (Illus.). 346p. 1998. reprint ed. pap. 24.95 (0-7661-0476-1) Kessinger Pub.

Blanchard, Charles E. New Words, Old Songs: Understanding the Lives of Ancient Peoples in Southwest Florida Through Archaeology. LC 94-46955. (Illus.). 136p. (Orig.). 1995. 24.95 (1-881448-02-9) IAPS Bks.

— New Words, Old Songs: Understanding the Lives of Ancient Peoples in Southwest Florida Through Archaeology. LC 94-46955. (Illus.). 136p. (Orig.). 1995. pap. 14.95 (1-881448-03-7) IAPS Bks.

— The Romance of Proctology. LC 75-23684. reprint ed. 49.50 (0-404-13237-5) AMS Pr.

Blanchard, Cherie. Greek 2 Latin Root Words Flipper. 49p. (YA). (gr. 7-12). 1998. 6.95 (1-878383-39-6) C Lee Pubns.

Blanchard, Cherie A. Word-Wiz Get to the Roots of a Word! No. 1: A Study of Latin & Greek Roots Workbook & Dictionary. unabridged ed. (Illus.). 104p. (YA). (gr. 7-12). 1996. spiral bd. 19.95 (0-9663148-0-8) C B Educ.

Blanchard, Clarise. I'm a Precious Creation. (Illus.). 168p. (Orig.). (J). (gr. 1-4). 1996. pap. text 19.95 (1-56550-036-9) Vis Bks Intl.

Blanchard, Claude. Journal of Claude Blanchard, Commissary of the French Auxiliary Army Sent to the U. S. During the American Revolution, 1780-1783. Balch, Thomas W., ed. Duane, William, tr. LC 76-76241. (Eyewitness Accounts of the American Revolution Ser.). 1969. reprint ed. 16.95 (0-405-01143-1) Ayer.

Blanchard, Clay, ed. see Caputo, Larry.

Blanchard, Dallas A. Anti-Abortion Movement. (Social Movements Past & Present Ser.). 200p. 1994. pap. 20.00 (0-8057-3871-1, Twyne) Mac Lib Ref.

— Anti Abortion Movement. 1996. 40.00 (0-8161-7258-7, G K Hall & Co) Mac Lib Ref.

— The Anti-Abortion Movement & the Rise of the Religious Right. (Social Movements Past & Present Ser.). 200p. 1994. 33.00 (0-8057-3872-X, Twyne) Mac Lib Ref.

***Blanchard, Dallas A.** The Anti-Abortion Movement & the Rise of the Religious Right: From Polite to Fiery Protest. 177p. 1999. reprint ed. text 25.00 (0-7881-6496-1) DIANE Pub.

Blanchard, Dallas A. & Prewitt, Terry J. Religious Violence & Abortion: The Gideon Project. LC 92-39693. (Illus.). 368p. 1993. 49.95 (0-8130-1193-0); pap. 18.95 (0-8130-1194-9) U Press Fla.

Blanchard, David. Intelligent Systems: Applications & Analysis. 1994. 129.00 (0-9629217-6-9) Lionheart Pub.

Blanchard, David & Beard, Paul. Intelligent Applications. (Illus.). (Orig.). 1991. 39.95 (0-9629217-0-X) Lionheart Pub.

Blanchard, David S. A Temporary State of Grace: Meditations. LC 97-190468. 64p. 1997. pap. 7.00 (1-55896-354-5, Skinner Hse Bks) Unitarian Univ.

Blanchard, Donald, tr. see Bartisch, George.

Blanchard, Donald, tr. see Batisch, George.

Blanchard, Donald, tr. & intro. see Jaeger, E.

Blanchard, Donald, tr. & intro. see Stromayr, Caspar.

Blanchard, Dorothy A. Along the Damariscotta. (Images of America Ser.). 1995. pap. 16.99 (0-7524-0083-5) Arcadia Publng.

— Old Sebec Lake. LC 97-183784. (Images of America Ser.). 128p. 1999. pap. 16.99 (0-7524-0273-0) Arcadia Publng.

Blanchard, Duncan C. From Raindrops to Volcanoes: Adventures with Sea Surface Meteorology. LC 80-19134. (Science Study Ser.: Selected Topics in Atmospheric Sciences). (Illus.). 180p. 1980. reprint ed. lib. bdg. 49.75 (0-313-22638-5, BLFR) Greenwood.

— The Snowflake Man: A Biography of Wilson A. Bentley. LC 98-6561. (Illus.). 180p. 1998. pap. 17.95 (0-939923-71-8) M & W Pub Co.

Blanchard, E. P. Boring Mills in a Gear Shop. (Technical Papers: Vol. P210). (Illus.). 11p. 1940. pap. text 30.00 (1-55589-213-2) AGMA.

Blanchard, Edward & Andraisk, F. Management of Chronic Headaches. 216p. (C). 1992. pap. text 60.95 (0-205-14285-0, H4285) Allyn.

***Blanchard, Edward B.** Irritable Bowel Syndrome: Psychosocial Assessment & Treatment. LC 00-40583. 2000. write for info. (1-55798-730-0) Am Psychol.

Blanchard, Edward B., ed. Journal of Consulting & Clinical Psychology. Special Issue: Behavioral Medicine. 156p. 1992. pap. 16.00 (1-55798-179-5) Am Psychol.

Blanchard, Edward B. & Hickling, Edward J. After the Crash: Assessment & Treatment of Motor Vehicle Accident Survivors. LC 97-5336. (Illus.). 353p. 1997. boxed set 39.95 (1-55798-424-7) Am Psychol.

Blanchard, Edward B., jt. auth. see Hickling, Edward J.

Blanchard, Edward B., jt. ed. see Gatchel, Robert J.

Blanchard, F. A. & Crosby, F. J., eds. Affirmative Action in Perspective. (Recent Research in Psychology Ser.). (Illus.). 240p. 1989. 70.95 (0-387-96971-3) Spr-Verlag.

Blanchard-Fields, Fredda & Hess, Thomas. Perspectives on Cognitive Change in Adulthood & Aging. LC 95-81973. 528p. (C). 1996. pap. 45.31 (0-07-028450-4) McGraw.

Blanchard-Fields, Fredda, ed. see Hess, Thomas M.

Blanchard, Francis, intro. Employment & Poverty in a Troubled World: Report of a Meeting of High-Level Experts on Employment. 55p. (Orig.). 1985. pap. 11.25 (92-2-100528-3) Intl Labour Office.

Blanchard, Frederick L. Engineering Project Management. (Cost Engineering Ser.: Vol. 16). (Illus.). 264p. 1990. text 165.00 (0-8247-8119-8) Dekker.

Blanchard, G. L., jt. auth. see Turner, Herschell.

Blanchard, Geral. Sex Offender Treatment: A Psychoeducational Model. 154p. (Orig.). 1989. student ed. 15.00 (0-685-30795-6) Golden Val Inst Behav Med.

Blanchard, Geral T. The Difficult Connection: The Therapeutic Relationship in Sex Offender Treatment. Bear, Euan, ed. 76p. (Orig.). (C). 1998. pap. text 12.00 (1-884444-15-6) Safer Soc.

Blanchard, Gerald. The Black West Print Set. (J). (gr. 4-6). 1992. 99.00 incl. VHS (1-882205-04-9) All Media Prods.

— Lender Liability Law, Practice & Prevention, 3 vols. 1992. 350.00 (0-685-30640-2) West Group.

Blanchard, Gerald, jt. auth. see Turner, Herschell.

Blanchard, Gerry, et al. Problem Loan Workouts, 2 vols. 230.00 (0-685-63103-6) West Group.

Blanchard Gross, Diana L. It's All Relative: Family Relationships in Art. (Illus.). 9p. 1999. pap. 3.50 (1-886845-06-9) Penin Fine Arts.

Blanchard Gross, Diana L. & Wessells, D. Thomas. Made in Virginia: Furniture from the 1830's to the Present. (Illus.). 24p. 1998. pap. 3.00 (1-886845-04-2) Penin Fine Arts.

Blanchard, Hal, ed. see Adler, Cyrus.

Blanchard, Homer D. The Bach Organ Book. LC 84-62572. (Illus.). 250p. 1985. 45.00 (0-930112-07-5) Organ Lit.

Blanchard, Homer D., ed. Organs of Our Time II. LC 81-185580. (Illus.). 176p. (Orig.). 1981. pap. 20.00 (0-930112-05-9) Organ Lit.

Blanchard, Homer D., jt. auth. see Lindow, C. W.

Blanchard, Ian. Russia's Age of Silver: Precious Metal Production & Economic Production & Economic Growth in the Eighteenth Century. 384p. 1989. 79.95 (0-415-00831-X, A3631) Routledge.

Blanchard, Ira. I Marched with Sherman: Civil War Memoirs of the 20th Illinois Volunteer Infantry. 176p. 1992. 18.95 (0-9630274-2-5); pap. 10.95 (0-9630274-5-X) J D Huff.

Blanchard, J. Knight Templarism. rev. ed. 17.95 (0-685-22013-3) Wehman.

— Standard Freemasonry. 15.95 (0-685-22116-4) Wehman.

— Ultimate Questions. 1994. pap. 1.95 (2-906287-01-6, Pub. by Evangelical Pr) P & R Pubng.

— What in the World Is a Christian? 1996. pap. 11.99 (0-85234-342-6, Pub. by Evangelical Pr) P & R Pubng.

Blanchard, J., et al. Principles & Perspective in Drug Bioavailability. 1978. 85.25 (3-8055-2440-4) S Karger.

Blanchard, James. Behind the Embassy Door: Canada, Clinton & Quebec. LC 99-159270. (Illus.). 288p. 1998. text 21.95 (0-7710-1478-3) McCland & Stewart.

— Silver Bonanza: How to Profit from the Coming Bull Market in Silver. 272p. 1995. 25.00 (0-671-50297-2) S&S Trade.

Blanchard, James, jt. auth. see Ford, Phyllis M.

Blanchard, James J. Behind the Embassy Door: Canada, Clinton, & Quebec. 300p. 1998. 24.95 (1-886947-59-7) Sleepng Bear.

Blanchard, James U., III, ed. see Veneroso, Frank.

***Blanchard, Jay S.** Educational Computing in the Schools: Technology, Communication & Literacy. LC 99-39844. (Computers in the Schools Monograph Ser.: Vol. 15, No. 1). 116p. 1999. pap. text 19.95 (0-7890-0814-9) Haworth Pr.

***Blanchard, Jay S., ed.** Educational Computing in the Schools: Technology, Communication & Literacy. LC 99-39844. (Computers in the Schools Monograph Ser.: Vol. 15, No. 1). 116p. 1999. 39.95 (0-7890-0779-7) Haworth Pr.

Blanchard, Jay S., et al, eds. The Computer in Reading & Language Arts. LC 87-8704. (Computers in the Schools Ser.: Vol. 4, No. 1). 132p. 1987. text 39.95 (0-86656-667-8) Haworth Pr.

***Blanchard, Jean-Marc F., et al, eds.** The Power & the Purse: Economic Statecraft, Interdependence & National Security. 354p. 2000. 59.50 (0-7146-5067-6, Pub. by F Cass Pubs); pap. 24.50 (0-7146-8116-4, Pub. by F Cass Pubs) Intl Spec Bk.

Blanchard, Jean O., et al, eds. The Transition in Eastern Europe: Restructuring, Vol. 2. 384p. (C). 1994. 48.00 (0-226-05662-7) U Ch Pr.

Blanchard, John. Aceptado por Dios.Tr. of Right with God. 128p. 1989. reprint ed. pap. 4.99 (0-85151-406-5) Banner of Truth.

***Blanchard, John.** Does God Believe in Atheists? 2000. 24.99 (0-85234-460-0) Evangelical Pr.

Blanchard, John. How to Enjoy Your Bible. 1978. pap. 4.99 (0-85234-182-2, Pub. by Evangelical Pr) P & R Pubng.

— Invitation to Live. 1991. pap. 7.99 (0-85234-285-3, Pub. by Evangelical Pr) P & R Pubng.

— Luke Comes Alive. 1986. pap. 4.99 (0-85234-223-3, Pub. by Evangelical Pr) P & R Pubng.

— The Mystic Shrine Illustrated: The Fully Illustrated Ritual of the Nobles of the Mystic Shrine. (Illus.). 50p. 1994. reprint ed. pap. 8.95 (1-56459-444-0) Kessinger Pub.

— Pop Goes the Gospel. rev. ed. 1983. pap. 6.99 (0-85234-263-2, Pub. by Evangelical Pr) P & R Pubng.

— Read Mark Learn. 1987. pap. 2.99 (0-85234-234-9, Pub. by Evangelical Pr) P & R Pubng.

— Right with God. rev. ed. 126p. 1985. pap. 4.99 (0-85151-045-0) Banner of Truth.

— Truth for Life. 1986. pap. 16.99 (0-85234-225-X, Pub. by Evangelical Pr) P & R Pubng.

— Ultimas Preguntas.Tr. of Ultimate Questions. (SPA.). 32p. 1987. pap. 0.99 (0-85234-237-3, 497715) Editorial Unilit.

— Ultimate Questions. (SPA.). 1991. pap. 1.95 (0-87552-770-1) P & R Pubng.

— What in the World Is a Christian? 1987. pap. 7.95 (0-310-20101-2, 11678P) Zondervan.

— Whatever Happened to Hell? LC 94-39192. 336p. 1995. pap. 14.99 (0-89107-837-1) Crossway Bks.

***Blanchard, John.** Why Y2K? What the Millennium is Really All About. 1999. mass mkt. 4.99 (0-85234-433-3) Evangelical Pr.

Blanchard, John. Will the Real Jesus Please Stand Up? 1989. pap. 8.99 (0-85234-258-6, Pub. by Evangelical Pr) P & R Pubng.

Blanchard, Jonathan. Debate on Slavery. LC 70-92419. 1845. 18.00 (0-403-00153-6) Scholarly.

Blanchard, Jonathan & Rice, N. L. Debate on Slavery: Is Slavery in Itself Sinful & the Relation Between Master & Slave a Sinful Relation. LC 72-82175. (Anti-Slavery Crusade in America Ser.). 1970. reprint ed. 37.95 (0-405-00614-4) Ayer.

Blanchard, Karen. Get Ready to Write. LC 97-7382. 112p. 1997. pap. text 16.73 (0-201-69517-0) Addison-Wesley.

Blanchard, Karen & Root, Christine B. For your Information One: A Thematic Reader. LC 95-41269. 1996. pap. text 20.30 (0-201-83409-X, Pub. by Addison-Wesley) Longman.

— For Your Information Two. LC 95-24397. 1995. pap. text 21.32 (0-201-82538-4) Longman.

Blanchard, Karen L. & Root, Christine B. For Your Information 4: Advanced Reading Skills LC 99-20124. 272p. 1999. 22.60 (0-201-34053-4) Addison-Wesley.

— For your Information Three: High-Intermediate Reading Skills. LC 96-19323. 1996. pap. text 21.32 (0-201-87798-8) Longman.

Blanchard, Karen L. & Root, Christine B. News for Now Book 1. 19.95 (0-534-83556-2, Pub. by Heinle & Heinle) Thomson Learn.

— News for Now Book 2. 19.95 (0-534-83548-1, Pub. by Heinle & Heinle) Thomson Learn.

— News for Now Student Book 3. 19.95 (0-534-83557-0, Pub. by Heinle & Heinle) Thomson Learn.

Blanchard, Karen L. & Root, Christine B. Ready to Write: A First Composition Text. 2nd ed. LC 93-21021. 1994. pap. text 18.38 (0-201-85999-8) Longman.

— Ready to Write More. LC 96-26254. 160p. 1996. pap. text 20.21 (0-201-87807-0) Addison-Wesley.

***Blanchard, Ken.** Road to Riches. 2000. pap. 13.00 (0-06-095843-X) HarpC.

***Blanchard, Ken & Bowles, Sheldon.** Big Bucks! Make Serious Money for Both You & Your Company. LC 00-25345. 224p. 2000. 20.00 (0-688-17035-8, Wm Morrow) Morrow Avon.

An Asterisk (*) at the beginning of an entry indicates that the title is appearing for the first time.

Blanchard, Kendall. The Anthropology of Sport: An Introduction. rev. ed. LC 95-6948. 352p. 1995. 72.95 (*0-89789-329-8*, Bergin & Garvey); pap. 22.95 (*0-89789-330-1*, Bergin & Garvey) Greenwood.

— The Economics of Sainthood: Religious Change among the Rimrock Navajos. LC 75-10141. (Illus.). 244p. 1976. 32.50 (*0-8386-1770-0*) Fairleigh Dickinson.

Blanchard, Kendall, ed. see Association for the Anthropological Study of Play, Meeting (9th: 1983: Baton Rouge, LA) Staff.

Blanchard, Kendall A. The Mississippi Choctaws at Play: The Serious Side of Leisure. LC 80-26527. 248p. 1981. text 24.95 (*0-252-00866-9*) U of Ill Pr.

Blanchard, Kenneth. Catch People Doing Something Right: Ken Blanchard on Empowerment. Date not set. 22.95 (*1-890009-64-4*) Exec Excell.

Blanchard, Kenneth. The Heart of a Leader: Insights on the Art of Influence. 1998. 12.99 (*1-56292-488-5*) Honor Bks OK.

— The One Minute Golfer: Enjoying the Great Game More. LC 99-17416. (One Minute Manager Library). 192p. 1999. pap. 9.95 (*0-688-16849-3*, Quil) HarperTrade.

— The One Minute Manager: Putting the One Minute Manager to Work, 2 vols. 1993. pap. text, boxed set 21.90 (*0-425-14074-1*) Berkley Pub.

— The One Minute Manager Balances Work & Life. 128p. 1999. pap. 9.95 (*0-688-16850-7*, Quil) HarperTrade.

— The One Minute Manager Builds High Performing Teams (revised Edition) rev. abr. ed. 128p. 2000. 20.00 (*0-688-17215-6*, Wm Morrow) Morrow Avon.

— One Minute Manager Meets the Monkey. 1991. pap. 10.00 (*0-688-10380-4*, Quil) HarperTrade.

— Putting the One-Minute Manager to Work. (Illus.). 110p. 1988. pap. 11.95 (*0-425-10425-7*) Berkley Pub.

— Understanding Business. (C). 1990. 42.67 (*0-13-935652-5*, Macmillan Coll) P-H.

Blanchard, Kenneth & Bowles, Sheldon. Gung Ho! Turn on the People in Any Organization. LC 97-21649. 256p. 1997. 20.00 (*0-688-15428-X*, Wm Morrow) Morrow Avon.

— Raving Fans: A Revolutionary Approach to Customer Service. LC 92-30255. 137p. 1993. 20.00 (*0-688-12316-3*, Wm Morrow) Morrow Avon.

Blanchard, Kenneth & Johnson, Spencer. The One Minute Manager. LC 82-8106. 112p. 1982. 20.00 (*0-688-01429-1*, Wm Morrow) Morrow Avon.

— The One-Minute Manager. 10th ed. 112p. 1993. pap. 12.95 (*0-425-09847-8*) Berkley Pub.

Blanchard, Kenneth & Peale, Norman Vincent. The Power of Ethical Management: Why the Ethical Way Is the Profitable Way - in Your Life & in Your Business. LC 87-24210. 136p. 1988. 17.95 (*0-688-07062-0*, Wm Morrow) Morrow Avon.

Blanchard, Kenneth & Waghorn, Terry. Mission Possible: Becoming a World Class Organization While There's Still Time. LC 96-77499. 220p. 1996. 22.00 (*0-07-005940-3*) McGraw.

Blanchard, Kenneth, et al. Empowerment Takes More Than a Minute. (Illus.). 125p. 1996. 20.00 (*1-881052-83-4*) Berrett-Koehler.

— Empowerment Takes More Than a Minute. (Illus.). 126p. 1998. reprint ed. pap. 12.00 (*1-57675-033-7*) Berrett-Koehler.

— Leadership & the One Minute Manager: Increasing Effectiveness Through Situational Leadership. 112p. 1999. reprint ed. pap. 10.00 (*0-688-16355-6*, Quil) HarperTrade.

— Leadership & the One Minute Manager: Increasing Effictiveness Through Situational Leadership. Golbitz, Pat, ed. LC 84-62389. (One Minute Manager Ser.). (Illus.). 112p. 1999. 20.00 (*0-688-03969-3*, Wm Morrow) Morrow Avon.

***Blanchard, Kenneth, et al.** Leadership by the Book: Tools to Transform Your Workplace. 240p. 1999. 20.00 (*1-57856-308-9*); audio 12.00 (*1-57856-313-5*) Waterbrook Pr.

— Leadership By the Book: Walking Your Faith in the Marketplace. LC 99-38109. (Illus.). 208p. 1999. 20.00 (*0-688-17239-3*, Wm Morrow) Morrow Avon.

Blanchard, Kenneth, et al. Managing by Values. LC 96-45613. (Illus.). 154p. 1997. 20.00 (*1-57675-007-8*) Berrett-Koehler.

— The One Minute Manager Builds High-Performing Teams. LC 91-18718. (Illus.). 128p. 1991. 18.50 (*0-688-10972-1*, Wm Morrow) Morrow Avon.

— The One-Minute Manager Meets the Monkey. 1988. 17.00 incl. audio (*0-671-66077-2*) S&S Audio.

— The One Minute Manager Meets The Monkey. 137p. 1989. 16.95 (*0-688-06767-0*, Quil) HarperTrade.

— The 3 Keys to Empowerment: Release the Power Within People for Astonishing Results. LC 99-12194. (Illus.). 286p. 1999. 20.00 (*1-57675-060-4*) Berrett-Koehler.

Blanchard, Kenneth, jt. auth. see Hersey, Paul.

Blanchard, Kenneth, jt. auth. see Shula, Don.

***Blanchard, Kenneth H. & Shula, Don.** The Little Book of Coaching: Motivating People to Be Winners. LC 00-40884. 2001. write for info. (*0-06-662103-8*) HarperTrade.

***Blanchard, Kenneth V.** High Five. 2001. write for info. (*0-688-17036-6*) Morrow Avon.

Blanchard, Laura, jt. auth. see Corson-Finnerty, Adam D.

Blanchard, Leah, et al. Guidelines & Documentation for Social Workers in Home Health Care. 25p. 1991. pap. 9.95 (*0-87101-181-6*) Natl Assn Soc Wkrs.

Blanchard, Leola H. Conquest of Southwest Kansas. 2nd ed. (Illus.). 410p. 1989. reprint ed. 19.95 (*0-9654410-4-0*); reprint ed. pap. 14.95 (*0-9654410-5-9*) Finney Cnty.

Blanchard, Marc, ed. On Leiris. (French Studies: No. 81). (Illus.). 164p. (C). 1992. pap. 18.00 (*0-300-05707-5*) Yale U Pr.

Blanchard, Marc E. Description: Sign, Self, Desire: Critical Theory in the Wake of Semiotics. (Approaches to Semiotics Ser.: No. 43). 300p. (C). 1980. 52.35 (*90-279-3488-6*); pap. 30.80 (*3-11-000317-1*) Mouton.

— In Search of the City: Engels, Baudelaire, Rimbaud. (Stanford French & Italian Studies: Vol. 37). 1985. pap. 56.50 (*0-915838-53-2*) Anma Libri.

Blanchard, Margaret. The Affairs of the Heart, Soul & 150p. 1999. pap. 11.95 (*1-881524-48-5*) Milligan Bks.

— The Birth of a Christian. LC 98-169317. 100p. 1998. pap. 9.95 (*1-881524-15-9*) Milligan Bks.

— Duet: Return to the Keys. (Illus.). 63p. (Orig.). 1995. pap. 14.95 (*0-913983-13-6*) M & A Edns.

— The Rest of the Deer: An Intuitive Study of Intuition. LC 89-82511. 300p. 1989. 14.95 (*0-9624626-7-5*) Astarte Shell Pr.

Blanchard, Margaret, ed. From the Listening Place: The Languages of Intuition. LC 96-39490. (Illus.). (Orig.). 1997. pap. 19.95 (*1-885349-05-X*) Astarte Shell Pr.

Blanchard, Margaret A., ed. History of the Mass Media in the United States: An Encyclopedia. LC 98-233183. 1000p. 1998. lib. bdg. 125.00 (*1-57958-012-2*) Fitzroy Dearborn.

Blanchard, Marjorie. The Sprouter's Cookbook: For Fast Kitchen Crops. LC 74-83147. (Illus.). 144p. 1983. pap. 5.95 (*0-88266-041-1*, Garden Way Pub) Storey Bks.

Blanchard, Marjorie P. Cater from Your Kitchen. 1981. pap. write for info. (*0-672-52688-3*) Macmillan.

Blanchard, Marlene. Wannabe, Wannabe, Wannabe. (Illus.). 40p. 1999. pap. 6.95 (*0-7392-0238-3*, PO3284) Morris Pubng.

Blanchard, Mary W. Oscar Wilde's America: Counterculture in the Gilded Age. LC 97-39628. (Illus.). 320p. 1998. 45.00 (*0-300-07460-3*) Yale U Pr.

***Blanchard, Melinda & Blanchard, Robert.** A Trip to the Beach. LC 00-29466. (Illus.). 256p. 2000. 25.00 (*0-609-60694-8*) C Potter.

Blanchard, Michael K. The Last Umbra: A Novel. (Illus.). 428p. 2001. pap. 19.95 (*1-883551-52-8*) Attic Studio Pub.

— Unsung Heroes: A Decade of Writings. LC 95-43135. (Illus.). 208p. 1995. pap. 10.00 (*1-883551-10-2*) Attic Studio Pub.

Blanchard, Nick P., et al. Effective Training: Systems, Strategies & Practices. LC 98-13480. 433p. 1998. 59.00 (*0-13-268160-9*) P-H.

Blanchard, Nina. The Look. 432p. 1996. mass mkt. 5.99 (*0-451-18034-8*, Sig) NAL.

Blanchard, Oliver J. Macroeconomics. 596p. (C). 1996. text 82.00 (*0-13-148099-5*) P-H.

Blanchard, Oliver J., et al, eds. Post-Communist Reform: Pain & Progress. 134p. 1993. 21.95 (*0-262-02362-8*) MIT Pr.

— Restoring Europe's Prosperity: Macroeconomic Papers from the Centre for European Policy Studies. 208p. 1986. 25.00 (*0-262-02249-4*) MIT Pr.

— The Transition in Eastern Europe, 2 vols., Set. LC 93-36585. (National Bureau of Economic Research Project Report Ser.). 384p. 1994. 39.95 (*0-226-05660-0*) U Ch Pr.

Blanchard, Oliver J. & Fischer, Stanley. Lectures on Macroeconomics. (Illus.). 656p. 1989. 50.00 (*0-262-02283-4*) MIT Pr.

Blanchard, Oliver J. & Fischer, Stanley, eds. NBER Macroeconomics Annual, 1989. 320p. (Orig.). 1989. pap. text 20.00 (*0-262-52145-8*) MIT Pr.

— NBER Macroeconomics Annual, 1990. 300p. 1990. pap. text 20.00 (*0-262-52155-5*) MIT Pr.

— NBER Macroeconomics Annual, 1991. (NBER Macroeconomics Annual Ser.). (Illus.). 350p. 1991. pap. text 20.00 (*0-262-52165-2*) MIT Pr.

— NBER Macroeconomics Annual, 1993. (Illus.). 360p. 1993. 40.00 (*0-262-02364-4*) MIT Pr.

— NBER Macroeconomics Annual, 1993. (Illus.). 360p. 1993. pap. text 20.00 (*0-262-52184-9*) MIT Pr.

Blanchard, Oliver J., et al. Reform in Eastern Europe. 128p. 1993. pap. text 11.00 (*0-262-52181-4*) MIT Pr.

Blanchard, Olivier. The Economics of Post-Communist Transition. LC 97-214707. (Clarendon Lectures in Economics). (Illus.). 162p. 1997. text 28.00 (*0-19-828926-X*, Clarendon Pr) OUP.

— The Economics of Post-Communist Transition. (Clarendon Lectures in Economics). (Illus.). 149p. 1999. pap. 17.95 (*0-19-829399-2*, Clarendon Pr) OUP.

***Blanchard, Olivier.** Macroeconomics. 2nd ed. LC 99-49531. (Illus.). 548p. 1999. 90.00 (*0-13-013306-X*) P-H.

Blanchard, Olivier J., et al, eds. NBER Macroeconomics Annual, 1992. 1992. pap. text 20.00 (*0-262-52174-1*) MIT Pr.

Blanchard, P., et al, eds. New Methods & Results in Non-Linear Field Equations. (Lecture Notes in Physics Ser.: Vol. 347). viii, 133p. 1989. 45.95 (*0-387-51977-7*) Spr-Verlag.

— Quantum Future: From Volta & Como to Present & Beyond. LC 99-12347. (Lecture Notes in Physics Ser.: Vol. 517). x, 257p. 1999. 73.00 (*3-540-65218-3*) Spr-Verlag.

Blanchard, P. & Bruning, E. Variational Methods in Mathematical Physics: A Unified Approach. Beiglbock, W. et al, eds. (Texts & Monographs in Physics). (Illus.). 300p. 1992. 97.95 (*0-387-16190-2*) Spr-Verlag.

Blanchard, P. & Streit, Ludwig, eds. Dynamics & Processes. (Lecture Notes in Mathematics Ser.: Vol. 1031). 213p. 1983. 35.95 (*0-387-12705-4*) Spr-Verlag.

Blanchard, P., et al. Mathematical & Physical Aspects of Stochastic Mechanics. (Lecture Notes in Physics Ser.: Vol. 281). 171p. 1987. 29.95 (*0-387-18036-2*) Spr-Verlag.

Blanchard, P., ed. see Albeverio, Sergio A.

Blanchard, P., ed. see Albeverio, Sergio A., et al.

Blanchard, Pamela. Modeling Highlights: Modeling Locally, Statewide & Nationally - Experience What Modeling Can Do for You. (Illus.). 100p. (Orig.). 1993. pap. 14.95 (*0-9638373-0-3*) Ritz Pubng.

***Blanchard, Pat & Suhr, Joanne.** Mi Caja de Insectas. Romo, Alberto, tr. (Books for Young Learners).Tr. of My Bug Box. (SPA., Illus.). 12p. (J). (gr. k-2). 1999. pap. text 5.00 (*1-57274-341-7*, A2877) R Owen Pubs.

Blanchard, Pat & Suhr, Joanne. My Bug Box. (Books for Young Learners). (Illus.). 12p. (J). (gr. k-2). 1999. pap. text 5.00 (*1-57274-273-9*) R Owen Pubs.

Blanchard, Patricia & Suhr, Joanne. Habia un Raton. Romo, Alberto, tr. (Books for Young Learners).Tr. of There Was a Mouse. (SPA., Illus.). 16p. (J). (gr. k-2). 1997. pap. text 5.00 (*1-57274-185-6*, A2865) R Owen Pubs.

— There Was a Mouse. (Books for Young Learners). (Illus.). 16p. (J). (gr. k-2). 1997. pap. text 5.00 (*1-57274-078-7*, A2210) R Owen Pubs.

***Blanchard, Paul.** Blue Guide to Southern Itlay. 9th ed. (Blue Guide Ser.). (Illus.). 608p. 1999. pap. 24.95 (*0-393-31946-6*) Norton.

Blanchard, Paul. Passport's Regional Guides of Italy: Venice & Northeastern Italy. LC 96-70352. (Illus.). 256p. 1997. pap. text 17.95 (*0-8442-9960-X*, 9960X) NTC Contemp Pub Co.

— Sicily & the Aeolian Islands. LC 98-65241. (Passport's Regional Guides of Italy Ser.). (Illus.). 256p. 1998. pap. 17.95 (*0-8442-9957-X*, 9957X, Passprt Bks) NTC Contemp Pub Co.

— Southern Italy. 8th ed. (Blue Guide Ser.). (Illus.). 416p. 1996. pap. 24.95 (*0-393-31418-9*, Norton Paperbks) Norton.

— Why Men Cheat & What to Do about It. 1996. pap. 6.95 (*1-884942-02-4*) Wrld Tampa.

Blanchard, Paul, jt. auth. see Berkey, Dennis D.

Blanchard, Paul, jt. ed. see Herz, Beatrice.

Blanchard, Paul, tr. see Bonsanti, Giorgio.

Blanchard, Paul, tr. see Bruzelius, Caroline, et al.

Blanchard, Paul, tr. see Santi, Bruno.

Blanchard, Paul H. Technology of Corn Wet Milling & Associated Processes. LC 92-14173. (Industrial Chemistry Library: Vol. 4). xxiv,536p. 1992. 305.50 (*0-444-88255-3*) Elsevier.

Blanchard, Peter. Grimoire Verum: Ancient Magick. (Illus.). 89p. 1997. 50.00 (*1-57179-060-8*) Intern Guild ASRS.

— The Law of Company Receiverships in Australia & New Zealand. 2nd ed. LC 95-141464. 1994. 168.00 (*0-409-31098-0*, AT, MICHIE) LEXIS Pub.

— Slavery & Abolition in Early Republican Peru. LC 92-4999. (Latin American Silhouettes Ser.). 248p. 1992. 45.00 (*0-8420-2400-X*, SR Bks); pap. text 17.95 (*0-8420-2429-8*, SR Bks) Scholarly Res Inc.

Blanchard, Peter, ed. see Markham, Clements R.

***Blanchard, Philippe, et al, eds.** Decoherence: Theoretical, Experimental & Conceptual Problems: Proceedings of a Workshop Held at Bielefeld, Germany, 10-14 November, 1998. LC 99-88828. (Lecture Notes in Physics Ser.: Vol. 538). xii, 345p. 2000. 69.95 (*3-540-66899-3*) Spr-Verlag.

Blanchard, Phyllis, jt. auth. see Paynter, Richard H.

Blanchard, Ralph. Becoming a Civilian Family. (Family Forum Library). 16p. 1994. 1.95 (*1-56688-164-1*) Bur For At-Risk.

— Family Readiness. (Family Forum Library). 16p. 1994. 1.95 (*1-56688-163-3*) Bur For At-Risk.

— How to Be a Successful Young Military Family. (Family Forum Library). 16p. 1994. 1.95 (*1-56688-165-X*) Bur For At-Risk.

— Protecting Children in Military Families: A Cooperative Response. 141p. (Orig.). (C). 1995. pap. text 35.00 (*0-7881-1827-7*) DIANE Pub.

***Blanchard, Richard.** High Traverse: A Novel. 192p. 2000. 24.00 (*0-942979-67-2*); pap. 11.00 (*0-942979-68-0*) Livingston AL.

Blanchard, Richard. Mounted in the City by the Bay. 1998. pap. 10.00 (*0-9663942-2-4*) Forever Fine Art.

Blanchard, Richard R. Spiritual Malpractice. (Illus.). 1998. pap. 29.95 (*0-9666636-1-6*, 0002) ACR Pub.

Blanchard, Robert. Ancient Grimoire of Dark Magick. Templar, Thorguard, ed. 105p. (Orig.). 1993. 50.00 (*1-883147-57-3*); 50.00 (*1-883147-58-1*) Intern Guild ASRS.

— Black Dragon. (Red Dragon Ser.: Pt. II). (Illus.). 125p. 1997. 65.00 (*1-57179-056-X*) Intern Guild ASRS.

— Doctor Johannes Faust Miracle & Magic Book: The Black Ravenor the Threefold Coercion of Hell. rev. ed. I.G.O.S. Society Staff, ed. LC 93-79454. (Illus.). 120p. (Orig.). (C). 1993. text 50.00 (*1-883147-21-2*) Intern Guild ASRS.

— Fian's Spellbook. Templar, James, ed. LC 93-79458. (Illus.). 115p. (Orig.). (C). 1993. pap. 50.00 (*1-883147-47-6*); text 50.00 (*1-883147-48-4*) Intern Guild ASRS.

— Gargoyle Magick. Templar, James, ed. LC 93-61066. 120p. (Orig.). 1993. 50.00 (*1-883147-42-5*); 50.00 (*1-883147-41-7*) Intern Guild ASRS.

— Graphiti, Bk. 1. rev. ed. (Illus.). 24p. (J). (gr. 2-4). 1976. pap. 5.95 (*0-918932-89-0*, A-1277) Activity Resources.

— Graphiti, Bk. 2. rev. ed. (Illus.). 24p. (J). (gr. 3-8). 1986. student ed. 5.95 (*0-918932-90-4*, A-1382) Activity Resources.

— Heptameron of Agrippa: Ancient Magick. (Illus.). 73p. 1997. 50.00 (*1-57179-061-6*) Intern Guild ASRS.

— The Lemegeton: King Solomon's Lesser Key. (Illus.). 76p. 1997. 55.00 (*1-57179-063-2*) Intern Guild ASRS.

— Magic & Sorcery in France: Sorcerers of Bygone. 155p. (Orig.). 1994. 45.00 (*1-57179-038-1*) Intern Guild ASRS.

— The Red Dragon: Grand Grimofre. Templar, Thor, ed. (Illus.). 325p. 1995. 89.00 (*1-57179-055-1*) Intern Guild ASRS.

— Rune Journey: Pathway to Yggdraszl. Templar, Thorguard, ed. (Illus.). 112p. 1994. 25.00 (*1-57179-030-6*) Intern Guild ASRS.

— Witchcraft Grimoire. LC 93-79457. 104p. (C). 1993. 45.00 (*1-883147-45-X*); text 45.00 (*1-883147-46-8*) Intern Guild ASRS.

Blanchard, Robert, tr. from FRE. Veritable Black Magic: Seals of Darkness. (Illus.). 270p. 1997. 45.00 (*1-57179-074-8*) Intern Guild ASRS.

Blanchard, Robert & Christ, William G. Media Education & the Liberal Arts: A Blueprint for the New Professionism. (Communication Ser.). 200p. (C). 1993. text 39.95 (*0-8058-0488-9*) L Erlbaum Assocs.

Blanchard, Robert & I.G.O.S. Society Staff. The Handbook of Honorius the Magus: A Medieval Grimoire. LC 93-79378. (Illus.). 120p. (Orig.). 1993. 50.00 (*1-883147-18-2*); 50.00 (*1-883147-17-4*) Intern Guild ASRS.

Blanchard, Robert, jt. auth. see Blanchard, Melinda.

Blanchard, Robert, jt. auth. see Sprinx.

Blanchard, Robert, jt. auth. see Templar, Thor.

Blanchard, Robert, tr. see Blandraex, Robert.

Blanchard, Robert O. & Tattar, Terry A. Field & Laboratory Guide to Tree Pathology. 2nd ed. LC 97-193894. (Illus.). 384p. 1997. text 79.95 (*0-12-103982-X*) Morgan Kaufmann.

Blanchard, Roberta R. Traditional Tole Painting: With Authentic Antique Designs & Working Diagrams for Stenciling & Brush-Stroke Painting. LC 77-78208. (Illus.). 96p. 1977. reprint ed. pap. 5.95 (*0-486-23531-9*) Dover.

— Traditional Tole Painting, with Authentic Antique Designs & Working Diagrams for Stenciling & Brush-Stroke Painting. 1990. 22.75 (*0-8446-5559-7*) Peter Smith.

Blanchard, Roderick D. Litigation & Trial Practice for the Legal Assistant. 3rd ed. Tubb, ed. 509p. (C). 1990. text 57.25 (*0-314-56995-2*) West Pub.

— Litigation/trial Prac F/legal Asst Hc 4e. 4th ed. LC 94-40807. (Paralegal). 692p. (C). 1995. pap. 85.95 (*0-314-04446-9*) West Pub.

Blanchard, Rufus. History of Du Page County, Illinois. (Illus.). 541p. 1997. reprint ed. lib. bdg. 57.50 (*0-8328-5736-X*) Higginson Bk Co.

Blanchard, Sarah, jt. auth. see Bean, Heike.

Blanchard-Smith, Beth. Essential Skills for the Workplace: Improving Workplace Performance. LC 93-23480. 1993. pap. 11.93 (*0-8092-3900-0*) NTC Contemp Pub Co.

Blanchard-Smith, Beth, jt. auth. see Strumpf, Lori.

Blanchard, Tamsin. Antonio Berardi: Sex & Sensibility. (Cutting Edge Ser.). (Illus.). 64p. 1999. 16.95 (*0-8230-1207-7*) Watsn-Guptill.

— Dressing Diana. (Illus.). 208p. 1998. 40.00 (*1-56649-293-9*) Welcome Rain.

***Blanchard, Tamsin.** Shoe: Sex, Seduction & Stiettos. 2000. 24.95 (*1-84222-066-7*) Carlton Bks Ltd.

Blanchard, Tim, et al. Managing Finance in Schools. Wragg, C. E., ed. (Education Matters Ser.). 144p. 1989. text 50.00 (*0-304-31707-1*) Continuum.

Blanchard, W. Scott. Scholars' Bedlam: Menippean Satire in the Renaissance. LC 94-19757. 208p. 1995. 35.00 (*0-8387-5281-0*) Bucknell U Pr.

Blanchard, William H. Neocolonialism American Style, 1960-2000, 372. LC 95-49673. (Contributions in Political Science Ser.: Vol. 372). 208p. 1996. 57.95 (*0-313-30013-5*, Greenwood Pr) Greenwood.

Blanchat, T. K. Experiments to Investigate Direct Containment Heating Phenomena with Scaled Models of the Calvert Cliffs Nuclear Power Plant. 196p. 1997. per. 18.00 (*0-16-062817-2*) USGPO.

— Performance Testing of Passive Autocatalytic Recombiners. 210p. 1998. per. 58.00 (*0-16-062930-6*) USGPO.

Blanche. Ecouter Pour S'Exprimer. 1995. 40.25 (*0-07-005858-X*) McGraw.

— Ecouter pour S'Exprimer. 1996. 40.25 (*0-07-911179-3*) McGraw.

Blanche, Claude-Pierre. Dictionnaire et Armorial des Noms de Famille de France. (FRE.). 312p. 1974. pap. 75.00 (*0-8288-6026-2*, M6038) Fr & Eur.

***Blanche, Cynthia.** Book of Energy. (gr. 11). 1999. pap. 9.95 (*0-7370-0070-8*) T-L Custom Pub.

Blanche, Cynthia. The Book of Energy: Invigorating Ways to Revitalize Your Life. LC 97-17383. (Illus.). 80p. (YA). (gr. 11). 1997. 12.95 (*0-7835-5255-6*) Time-Life.

— The Book of Love: Romantic Ways to Create Pleasure & Harmony. LC 97-28547. (Illus.). 96p. (YA). (gr. 11). 1999. 12.95 (*0-7835-5257-2*) Time-Life.

— The Book of Touch & Aroma: Sensual Ways with Massage & Aromatherapy. LC 97-34131. (Illus.). 96p. (YA). (gr. 11). 1999. 12.95 (*0-7835-5256-4*) Time-Life.

Blanche, Ella. Searching the Shadows. (Contemporary Poets Ser.: No. 1). 48p. (Orig.). 1983. pap. 2.95 (*0-916982-26-2*, RL226) CCR Pubns.

***Blanche, Erna I.** Combining Neuro-Developmental Treatment & Sensory Integration Principles: An Approach to Pediatr. 1998. pap. text 58.00 (*0-12-784570-4*) Acad Pr.

Blanche, Jacques-Emile, jt. auth. see Mauriac, Francois.

Blanche, Jerry. Native American Reader: Speeches, Poems & Stories of the American Indian. 302p. (Orig.). 1990. pap. 25.00 (*0-938737-20-1*) Denali Press.

Blanche, Margaret. Inspirations in Dough: Using a Sensational New Dough Recipe, Create Colourful Wall Plaques & Free-Standing Models. (Illus.). 48p. 1998. pap. 14.95 (*0-85532-837-1*, 8371, Pub. by Srch Pr) A Schwartz & Co.

Blanche, Martine. Poetique des Tableaux Chez Proust et Matisse. LC 96-68095.Tr. of Poetics of Painting in the Works of Proust & Matisse. (Illus.). 206p. 1996. 39.95 (*1-883479-10-X*) Summa Pubns.

B

Blanche, Patrick. Ecouter pour s'exprimer: Listening, Conversation & Composition in a Cultural Context - Student Tapes. 1996. write for info. incl. audio (*0-07-005861-X*) McGraw.

Blanche, R., jt. auth. see Alyea, Paul E.

Blancher, A. & Klein, Jan. Molecular Biology & Evolution of Blood Group & MHC Antigens in Primates. LC 97-369. 1997. text. write for info. (*3-540-61636-5*) Spr-Verlag.

Blanchet, Francis N. Historical Sketches of the Catholic Church in Oregon. 164p. 1983. 16.95 (*0-87770-306-X*) Ye Galleon.

Blanchet, Francis X. Ten Years on the Pacific Coast. 96p. 1982. 14.95 (*0-87770-281-0*) Ye Galleon.

Blanchet, Kevin D. AIDS: A Health Care Management Response. 319p. 1987. 75.00 (*0-87189-877-2*) Aspen Pub.

Blanchet, Kevin D. & Switlik, Mary M. The Handbook of Hospital Admitting Management. 350p. 1985. 102.00 (*0-87189-121-2*) Aspen Pub.

Blanchet, Louis-Emile. Comment Presenter un Texte Philosophique. LC B 0052.B55. (FRE.). 166p. reprint ed. pap. 51.50 (*0-608-30586-3*, 202266600029) Bks Demand.

Blanchet, M. Wylie. The Curve of Time. LC 92-43650. 170p. 1993. reprint ed. pap. 12.95 (*1-878067-27-3*) Seal Pr WA.

Blanchet, Philippe. Dictionnaire du Francais Regional de Provence. (FRE.). 157p. 1991. 50.00 (*0-8288-9481-7*) Fr & Eur.

Blanchet, Therese, et al. The Agreement on the European Economic Area (EEA) A Guide to the Free Movement of Goods & Competition Rules. 528p. 1994. 85.00 (*0-19-825892-5*); pap. text 39.95 (*0-19-825884-4*) OUP.

Blanchett, Chris, ed. Mintons Tiles. 1997. pap. 19.95 (*0-903685-50-7*, Pub. by R Dennis) Antique Collect.

Blanchett, Chris, jt. auth. see Van Lemmen, Hans.

Blanchett, Marie. Ella Nepa-llu.Tr. of Air a Sound. (ESK., Illus.). 20p. (J). (gr. k-3). 1998. pap. text 8.00 (*1-58084-043-4*) Lower Kuskokwim.

Blanchett, Suzanne S. & Flarey, Dominick L. Cardiovascular Outcomes: Collaborative, Path-Based Approaches. LC 98-13313. 350p. 1998. 59.00 (*0-8342-1138-6*, 11386) Aspen Pub.

— Health Care Outcomes: Collaborative, Path-Based Approaches. LC 98-9760. xviii, 403p. 1998. 59.00 (*0-8342-1137-8*, 11378) Aspen Pub.

Blanchette, Christopher J. God: In the Garden. Dowty, Daryl, ed. 100p. 1999. pap. 9.95 (*0-7392-0129-8*, PO3043) Morris Pubng.

Blanchette, Cornelia M. Tax Administration: IRS Can Do More to Collect Taxes Labelled "Currently Not Collectible" (Illus.). 52p. 1998. pap. text 20.00 (*0-7881-7209-3*) DIANE Pub.

Blanchette, Janis, ed. see Acret, James, et al.

Blanchette, Janis L., ed. see Akawie, Alice L., et al.

Blanchette, Janis L., ed. see Ankenmen, C. Gregg, et al.

Blanchette, Janis L., ed. see Bernhardt, Roger.

Blanchette, Janis L., ed. see Brown, Timothy N., et al.

Blanchette, Janis L., ed. see Chin, Llewellyn P., et al.

Blanchette, Janis L., ed. see Dean, Michael A., et al.

Blanchette, Janis L., ed. see Weir, William J. A., et al.

Blanchette, Janis L., ed. see Weller, Louis S. & Drucker, Cecily Ann.

Blanchette, Janis L., ed. see Weller, Louis S. & Todd, Ian D.

Blanchette, Janis LaRoche, ed. see Akawie, Alice L., et al.

Blanchette, Janis LaRoche, ed. see Weller, Louis S. & Drucker, Cecily Ann.

Blanchette, Jean-Francois, jt. auth. see Boily, Lise.

Blanchette, John. Welcome to Helmet Night: Dispatches from Mariner Nation, Cougar County & a Battered Tin Canoe. Higgins, Shaun O., ed. LC 98-146035. 271p. 1998. 22.95 (*0-923910-11-5*) NMV.

Blanchette, John & Bergum, Steve. Zagmania! The Story of the 1998-1999 Gonzaga Bulldog Basketball Team: WCC Champions & NCAA "Elite Eight" Higgins, Shaun O., ed. (Illus.). 66p. 1999. pap. 13.95 (*0-923910-16-6*) NMV.

***Blanchette, Joseph P.** The View from Shanty Pond: An Irish Immigrant's Look at Life in a New England Mill Town, 1875-1938. LC 99-90262. (Illus.). xviii, 200p. 1999. 24.95 (*0-9671537-5-1*) Shanty Pond.

Blanchette, Oliva. The Perfection of the Universe According to Aquinas: A Teleological Study. 328p. 1992. text 42.50 (*0-271-00797-4*) Pa St U Pr.

Blanchette, Oliva, et al. Philosophical Challenges & Opportunities of Globalization. LC 99-37510. (Cultural Heritage & Contemporary Change Ser.). Date not set. pap. write for info. (*1-56518-129-8*) Coun Res Values.

Blanchette, R. A. & Biggs, A. R., eds. Defense Mechanisms of Woody Plants Against Fungi. (Wood Science Ser.). (Illus.). 468p. 1992. 327.95 (*0-387-54643-X*) Spr-Verlag.

***Blanchette, Rick & LaScola, Jane N.** Growertalks on Crop Culture 2. LC 99-28399. 217p. 1999. 32.95 (*1-883052-21-1*) Ball Pub.

***Blanchette, Rick & VanderVelde, Jayne, eds.** Green Profit on Retailing. LC 99-57915. 225p. 2000. pap. 32.95 (*1-883052-22-X*, B041) Ball Pub.

Blanchette, Rick, ed. see Kah, Gary.

***Blanchfield, J. R.** Food Labelling. LC 00-31153. 2000. write for info. (*0-8493-0852-6*) CRC Pr.

***Blanchfield, J. Ralph.** Food Labelling. 512p. 2000. text 207.00 (*1-85573-496-6*, Pub. by Woodhead Pubng) Am Educ Systs.

Blanchfield, Lynne S., jt. auth. see Benson, C. David.

Blanchfield, Richard J. Gulf War Air Power Survey: Weapons, Tactics & Training & Space Operations, V. 4. 519p. 1994. per. 31.00 (*0-16-042927-7*) USGPO.

Blanchfield, Thomas, jt. auth. see Lenahan, Thomas.

Blanchfield, Thomas, jt. auth. see Snyder, Gerald.

Blanchflower, David G. & Oswald, Andrew J. The Wage Curve. (Illus.). 512p. 1995. 49.50 (*0-262-02375-X*) MIT Pr.

***Blanchflower, David G., et al.** Youth Employment & Joblessness in Advanced Countries LC 99-39694. (NBER Comparative Labor Markets Ser.). 2000. 70.00 (*0-226-05658-9*) U Ch Pr.

Blanchi. Lo Que Creen los Cristianos.Tr. of What Christians Believe?. (SPA.). 1994. pap. write for info. (*0-614-27075-8*) Editorial Unilit.

Blanchi, Ann. Italian Festival Food: Recipes & Traditions from Italy's Regional Country Food Fairs. (Illus.). 490p. 1999. 25.00 (*0-02-862332-0*, Pub. by Macmillan) S&S Trade.

Blanchi, John. Lo Que Creen los Cristianos. (Serie Guia - Bible Manuals Ser.).Tr. of What Christians Believe. (SPA.). 128p. 1986. pap. 5.99 (*0-8423-6269-X*, 490201) Editorial Unilit.

Blanchinus, Franciscus. De Tribus Generibus Instrumentorum Musicae Veterum Organicae Dissertation. fac. ed. (Monuments of Music & Music Literature in Facsimile Ser., Series II: Vol. 9). 1966. lib. bdg. 32.50 (*0-8450-2209-1*) Broude.

Blanchot, Francois. Le Chevalier Sur le Fleuve. (FRE.). 312p. 1990. pap. 16.95 (*0-7859-2141-9*, 2070382559) Fr & Eur.

Blanchot, Maurice. Arret de Mort. (Imaginaire Ser.). (FRE.). 126p. 1948. pap. 11.95 (*2-07-029699-7*) Schoenhof.

— Awaiting Oblivion. Gregg, John, tr. LC 96-273322. (French Modernist Library Series). 87p. 1997. text 35.00 (*0-8032-1257-7*) U of Nebr Pr.

— Awaiting Oblivion. LC 96-273322. (French Modernist Library Series). 87p. 1999. pap. 15.00 (*0-8032-6157-8*, Bison Books) U of Nebr Pr.

— Death Sentence. Davis, Lydia, tr. LC 98-19965. 86p. 1997. pap. text 12.95 (*1-886449-41-4*) Barrytown Ltd.

— L' Espace Litteraire. (FRE.). 1988. pap. 16.95 (*0-7859-2813-8*) Fr & Eur.

— L' Espace Litteraire. (Folio Essais Ser.: No. 89). (FRE.). 1988. pap. 12.95 (*2-07-032475-3*) Schoenhof.

— Friendship. Rottenberg, Elizabeth, tr. from FRE. LC 96-38201. 1997. write for info. (*0-8047-2758-9*); pap. 19.95 (*0-8047-2759-7*) Stanford U Pr.

— The Infinite Conversation. Hanson, Susan, tr. from FRE. (Theory & History of Literature Ser.: Vol. 82). 800p. (C). 1992. pap. 34.95 (*0-8166-1970-0*); text 49.95 (*0-8166-1969-7*) U of Minn Pr.

***Blanchot, Maurice.** Instant of My Death: Demeure: Fiction & Testimony. LC 99-462364. (Institute for Global Environmental Ser.). 2000. 29.50 (*0-8047-3325-2*) Stanford U Pr.

Blanchot, Maurice. The Last Man. Davis, Lydia, tr. (Twentieth-Century Continental Fiction Ser.). 1987. text 34.50 (*0-231-06244-3*) Col U Pr.

— Le Livre a Venir. (FRE.). 1986. pap. 17.95 (*0-7859-2803-0*) Fr & Eur.

— Le Livre a Venir. (Folio Essais Ser.: No. 48). (FRE.). 340p. 1959. pap. 14.95 (*2-07-032397-8*) Schoenhof.

— The Most High. Stoekl, Allan, tr. & intro. by. LC 95-31873. (French Modernist Library). xxxii, 258p. 1996. text 40.00 (*0-8032-1240-2*) U of Nebr Pr.

— The One Who Is Standing Apart from Me. 96p. 1997. pap. text 12.95 (*1-886449-42-2*) Barrytown Ltd.

— The One Who Was Standing Apart from Me. Quasha, George, ed. Davis, Lydia, tr. from FRE. Orig. Title: Celui Qui Ne M'Accompagnait Pas. 96p. (C). 1989. 25.00 (*0-88268-053-6*); pap. write for info. (*0-88268-140-0*) Station Hill Pr.

— Le Ressassement Eternel. (Reimpressions G & B Ser.). (FRE.). 150p. 1971. pap. text 72.00 (*0-677-50425-X*, PAP) Gordon & Breach.

— Sade et Restif de la Bretonne. (FRE.). 1986. pap. 23.95 (*0-7859-3308-5*, 2870271948) Fr & Eur.

— The Space of Literature: A Translation of "L'Espace Litteraire" Smock, Ann, tr. LC 82-2062. 279p. 1982. pap. text 16.50 (*0-8032-6092-X*, Bison Books) U of Nebr Pr.

— The Station Hill Maurice Blanchot Reader: Fiction & Literary Essays. Quasha, George, ed. Auster, Paul et al, trs. from FRE. LC 98-26242. 550p. 1999. pap. 29.95 (*1-886449-17-1*, P9171, Pub. by Barrytown Ltd) Consort Bk Sales.

— The Step Not Beyond. Nelson, Lycette, tr. from FRE. LC 91-13269. (SUNY Series, Intersections: Philosophy & Critical Theory). 139p. (C). 1992. pap. text 18.95 (*0-7914-0908-2*) State U NY Pr.

— The Step Not Beyond. Nelson, Lycette, tr. from FRE. & intro. by. LC 91-13269. (SUNY Series, Intersections: Philosophy & Critical Theory). 139p. (C). 1992. text 29.50 (*0-7914-0907-4*) State U NY Pr.

— Tres-Haut. (Imaginaire Ser.). (FRE.). pap. 13.95 (*2-07-071447-0*) Schoenhof.

— The Unavowable Community. Joris, Pierre, tr. LC 87-15996. 96p. 1988. 15.95 (*0-88268-043-9*) Station Hill Pr.

***Blanchot, Maurice.** Unavowable Community. 96p. 2000. pap. 14.95 (*1-58177-074-X*) Barrytown Ltd.

Blanchot, Maurice. Vicious Circles. Auster, Paul, tr. from FRE. LC 84-8437. Orig. Title: Le Resassement Eternel. 80p. 1985. 20.00 (*0-930794-98-2*) Station Hill Pr.

— When the Time Comes. Davis, Lydia, tr. from FRE. LC 84-12373. Orig. Title: Au Moment Voulu. 80p. 1984. 20.00 (*0-930794-96-6*) Station Hill Pr.

— The Work of Fire. Mandell, Charlotte, tr. from FRE. LC 94-32418. Orig. Title: Part de Feu. (ENG.). xi , 348p. 1995. 45.00 (*0-8047-2432-6*); pap. 16.95 (*0-8047-2493-8*) Stanford U Pr.

— The Writing of the Disaster. Smock, Ann, tr. from FRE. LC 85-8562. xvi, 151p. 1986. text 40.00 (*0-8032-1186-4*) U of Nebr Pr.

— The Writing of the Disaster. Smock, Ann, tr. LC 94-46856. (ENG & FRE.). xvi, 153p. 1995. pap. text 13.00 (*0-8032-6120-9*, Bison Books) U of Nebr Pr.

***Blanchot, Maurice & Derrida, Jacques.** The Instant of My Death/Demeure: Fiction & Testimony. LC 99-462364. 2000. pap. 12.95 (*0-8047-3326-0*) Stanford U Pr.

Blanchot, Maurice, jt. auth. see Foucault, Michel.

Blanchy, S. Dictionary Francais/Mahorais/Francais. (FRE & MAO.). 231p. 1996. 59.95 (*0-320-00957-2*) Fr & Eur.

Blanck-Cereijido, Fanny. La Vida, el Tiempo y la Muerte. (Ciencia para Todos Ser.). (SPA.). pap. 6.99 (*968-16-2710-5*, Pub. by Fondo) Continental Bk.

Blanck, Cheryl A. Understanding Helical Scanning. LC 97-48630. 1998. 24.95 (*0-683-30304-X*) Lppncott W & W.

Blanck, Dag. Becoming Swedish-American: The Construction of an Ethnic Identity in the Augustana Synod, 1860-1917. (Studia Historica Upsaliensia: No. 182). 240p. 1997. pap. 57.50 (*91-554-4027-4*, Pub. by Almqvist Wiksell) Coronet Bks.

Blanck, Dag, jt. ed. see Anderson, Philip J.

Blanck, Emily L., jt. auth. see Ewen, Ann J.

Blanck, Gertrude. How to Be a "Good Enough" Parent: The Subtle Seductions. LC 87-14339. Orig. Title: Subtle Seductions. 200p. 1996. pap. 30.00 (*0-87668-941-1*) Aronson.

***Blanck, Gertrude.** A Primer of Developmental Psychology. 2000. 40.00 (*0-7657-0286-X*) Aronson.

Blanck, Gertrude & Blanck, Rubin. Ego Psychology: Theory & Practice. 2nd ed. LC 93-15638. 322p. 1994. 43.50 (*0-231-08292-4*) Col U Pr.

— Ego Psychology Two: Developmental Psychology. LC 78-10956. (Illus.). 274p. 1979. text 44.00 (*0-231-04470-4*) Col U Pr.

Blanck, Gertrude, jt. auth. see Blanck, Rubin.

Blanck, Helen E. Rosemaling: Design Collection, No. II. (Illus.). 27p. 1991. spiral bd. 14.95 (*0-941016-67-6*) Penfield.

Blanck, Jacob. Bibliography of American Literature, Vol. 8. LC 54-5283. Vol. 8. 576p. (C). 1989. 95.00 (*0-300-03839-9*) Yale U Pr.

Blanck, Jacob, compiled by. Bibliography of American Literature, 7 vols. Incl. Vol. 4. Nathaniel Hawthorne to Joseph Holt Ingraham. LC 54-5283. xxii, 495p. 1963. 90.00 (*0-300-00313-7*); Vol. 5. Washington Irving to Henry Wadsworth Longfellow. LC 54-5283. xxii, 1969p. 1969. 90.00 (*0-300-01099-0*); LC 54-5283. (Illus.). write for info. (*0-318-56510-2*) Yale U Pr.

Blanck, Peter D. The Americans with Disabilities Act & the Emerging Work Force: Employment of People with Mental Retardation. Braddock, David L., ed. LC 98-10269. 303p. 1998. write for info. (*0-940898-52-7*) Am Assn Mental.

***Blanck, Peter D., ed.** Employment, Disability & the Americans with Disabilities Act: Issues in Law, Public Policy & Research. 472p. 1999. pap. 29.95 (*0-8101-1689-8*) Northwestern U Pr.

Blanck, Peter D., ed. Interpersonal Expectations: Theory, Research, & Applications. LC 92-36925. (Studies in Emotion & Social Interaction). (Illus.). 521p. (C). 1993. text 74.95 (*0-521-41783-X*); pap. text 32.95 (*0-521-42832-7*) Cambridge U Pr.

Blanck, Rubin & Blanck, Gertrude. Beyond Ego Psychology. LC 85-21356. 248p. 1986. text 40.50 (*0-231-06266-4*) Col U Pr.

— Marriage & Personal Development. LC 68-9577. 191p. 1968. text 52.50 (*0-231-03150-5*) Col U Pr.

Blanck, Rubin, jt. auth. see Blanck, Gertrude.

Blanck, T. J. & Wheeler, D. M., eds. Mechanisms of Anesthetic Action in Skeletal, Cardiac & Smooth Muscle. (Advances in Experimental Medicine & Biology Ser.: Vol. 301). (Illus.). 320p. (C). 1991. text 132.00 (*0-306-44011-3*, Kluwer Plenum) Kluwer Academic.

Blanck, Thomas J. Neuroprotection. 220p. 1997. write for info. (*0-683-18328-1*) Lppncott W & W.

***Blancke, Rolf.** Farbatlas Pflanzen der Karibik und Mittelamerikas (Color Atlas: Plants of the Caribbean & Central America) (GER., Illus.). 320p. 1999. 31.50 (*3-8001-3512-4*, Pub. by Eugen Ulmer) Balogh.

Blanckenhagen, P. V., jt. ed. see Schommers, W.

Blanckenhagen, P. Von, see Schommers, W. & Von Blanckenhagen, P., eds.

Blanckensee, Leni Von, see Von Blanckensee, Leni.

Blanco. Ahora Si! Level 1, Level 1. (College Spanish Ser.). (SPA.). (C). 1994. mass mkt. 61.95 (*0-8384-4782-1*) Heinle & Heinle.

— Ahora Si! Level 1, Level 1. annot. ed. (College Spanish Ser.). (SPA.). (C). 1994. mass mkt., teacher ed. 44.95 (*0-8384-4783-X*) Heinle & Heinle.

Blanco-Aguinaga, Carlos. A Time of Your Own. Moncy, Agnes, tr. from SPA. 1997. pap. text 10.00 (*0-9629903-3-7*) Jahbone Pr.

Blanco, Alberto. Angel's Kite (La Estrella de Angel) Bellm, Dan, tr. LC 93-42285. (ENG & SPA., Illus.). (J). 1994. 14.95 (*0-89239-121-9*) Childrens Book Pr.

— Angel's Kite (La Estrella de Angel) LC 93-42285. (ENG & SPA., Illus.). 32p. (YA). (gr. 1-4). 1998. pap. 7.95 (*0-89239-156-1*) Childrens Book Pr.

— Curso de Obligaciones y Contratos: Contratos en Especie (Explicaciones de Clase), Vol. III. 3rd ed. LC 77-4251. 1978. 9.60 (*0-8477-3010-7*); pap. 7.20 (*0-8477-3011-5*) U of PR Pr.

— Curso de Obligaciones y Contratos: Doctrina General de los Contratos, Vol. II. enl. ed. LC 77-4251. (SPA.). 1979. pap. 10.80 (*0-8477-3009-3*) U of PR Pr.

— Curso de Obligaciones y Contratos: Doctrina General de los Contratos, Vol. II. 3rd enl. ed. LC 77-4251. (SPA.). 1979. 12.00 (*0-8477-3008-5*) U of PR Pr.

— Dawn of the Senses: Selected Poems of Alberto Blanco. Acosta, Juvenal, ed. (Pocket Poets Ser.: No. 52). 180p. (Orig.). 1995. pap. 12.95 (*0-87286-309-3*) City Lights.

— The Desert Mermaid (La Sirena del Desierto) LC 92-1105. (Illus.). 32p. (YA). (gr. 1 up). 1992. 14.95 (*0-89239-106-5*) Childrens Book Pr.

— El Regimen de la Propiedad Privada en el Estado Libre Asociado de Puerto Rico (Intervencionismo, Dirigismo, Socializacion) LC 78-1748. (SPA.). 125p. 1978. pap. 2.80 (*0-8477-3016-6*) U of PR Pr.

Blanco, Alberto, tr. see Sawin, Martica.

Blanco, Alberto, tr. see Sheehy, William J.

***Blanco-Best, Mimi & Lovelace, Terry W.** PPC'S Eldercare Services Client Seminar, Vol. 1. 1998. ring bd. write for info. (*0-7646-0576-3*) Prctnrs Pub Co.

Blanco, Cheryl D. Doing More with Less: Approaches to Shortening Time to Degree. 1994. 10.00 (*0-614-13557-5*) SHEEO.

Blanco, D. & Canevari, P. Censo Neotropical De Aves Aquaticas, 1991. 62p. 1992. pap. text 10.00 (*1-883861-00-4*) Wetlnds Amer.

— Censo Neotropical De Aves Aquaticas, 1992. 75p. 1993. pap. text 10.00 (*1-883861-03-9*) Wetlnds Amer.

***Blanco, Evangeline & Platzes, Monika, eds.** Shaping the City: Modern Architecture in Central Europe, 1890-1937. (Illus.). 240p. 2000. 65.00 (*3-7913-2151-X*, Pub. by Prestel) te Neues.

Blanco, Hilda. How to Think about Social Problems: American Pragmatism & the Idea of Planning, 346. LC 94-876. 240p. 1994. 59.95 (*0-313-27775-3*) Greenwood.

Blanco, Hugo. Land or Death: The Peasant Struggle in Peru. LC 73-186689. 178p. 1972. reprint ed. pap. 14.95 (*0-87348-266-2*); reprint ed. lib. bdg. 45.00 (*0-87348-265-4*) Pathfinder NY.

Blanco, Jack, contrib. by. Clear Word. LC 98-120882. 1425p. 1996. pap. 19.99 (*0-8280-1006-4*) Review & Herald.

***Blanco, Jack, ed.** The Clear Word Bible. 1999. 49.99 (*0-8280-1002-1*); 49.99 (*0-8280-1003-X*); 79.99 (*0-8280-1005-6*) Review & Herald.

Blanco, Jodee. Complete Guide to Book Publicity. 288p. 1999. pap. text 19.95 (*1-58115-046-6*) Allworth Pr.

Blanco, Jodee, jt. auth. see Lunigan, Catherine.

Blanco, John D., tr. see Ramos, Julio.

Blanco, Jose. Mexico a Fines de Siglo I, II. (SPA.). 20.99 (*968-16-4051-9*, Pub. by Fondo) Continental Bk.

Blanco, Juan A. Reflections on the Third Millennium: An Alternative Vision to Postmodernism. 1997. pap. 15.95 (*1-876175-03-6*) Ocean Pr.

Blanco, Lazaro. Luces y Tiempos (Lights & Time) (SPA., Illus.). 64p. 1987. pap. 8.99 (*968-16-2639-7*, Pub. by Fondo) Continental Bk.

Blanco, Lobo. Balkan Thunder: WW II - the Balkan States-Free or Slave? unabridged ed. LC 96-90559. (Classic American Historical Novels: Vol. 2). 172p. 1996. pap. 12.50 (*1-890492-18-3*) Univ Pr of Copperas.

— Cairo to India: WW II Sean & Yvonne in the Orient. unabridged ed. LC 96-90560. (Classic American Historical Novels: Vol. 5). (Illus.). 164p. 1996. pap. 12.50 (*1-890492-39-6*) Univ Pr of Copperas.

— A Dangerous Sky: WWII: Terry & the Celtic Princess. unabridged ed. LC 97-90348. (Classic American Historical Novels: Vol. 3). (Illus.). 177p. 1997. pap. 12.50 (*1-890492-34-5*) Univ Pr of Copperas.

— Endgame: WWII: The Last Days of the German Luftwaffe. unabridged ed. LC 97-90351. (Classic American Historical Novels: Vol. 4). 169p. 1997. pap. 12.50 (*1-890492-26-4*) Univ Pr of Copperas.

— Jo Ellen: Princess of the Pirates. unabridged ed. Walker, Kerry, ed. LC 98-75202. (Classic American Historical Novels Ser.: Vol. 3). 192p. 1998. pap. write for info. (*1-890492-55-8*) Univ Pr of Copperas.

— The Pilot: WWII - From Hitler to Yon. unabridged ed. LC 96-90528. (Classic American Historical Novels: Vol. 1). (Illus.). 160p. (Orig.). 1996. pap. 12.50 (*1-890492-13-2*) Univ Pr of Copperas.

— Sea Hawks & Pirates: Freelance Gunslingers of the American Seas. unabridged ed. LC 96-90557. (Classic American Historical Novels Ser.: Vol. 2). 172p. 1997. pap. 12.50 (*1-890492-47-7*) Univ Pr of Copperas.

— Sea Rover: Adventuring in America in 1605, Fighting Pirates & Indians. unabridged ed. LC 96-90526. (Classic American Historical Novels Ser.: Vol. 1). ii, 142p. 1996. pap. 12.50 (*1-890492-05-1*) Univ Pr of Copperas.

***Blanco, Luis R., et al.** Employment Law Compliance for New Businesses - 1/99 Update. Hagelstein, Marie, ed. LC 97-77814. (California Business Start-Up Ser.). 392p. 1999. ring bd. 60.00 (*0-7626-0282-1*, BU-32911) Cont Ed Bar-CA.

Blanco, Osvaldo J., tr. see Sandhaus, Ellen.

Blanco, Ralph F. & Bogacki, David F. Prescriptions for Children with Learning & Adjustment Problems: A Consultant's Desk Reference. 3rd ed. 264p. 1988. 43.95 (*0-398-05390-1*); pap. 29.95 (*0-398-06022-3*) C C Thomas.

Blanco, Ralph F. & Rosenfeld, Joseph G. Case Studies in Clinical & School Psychology. (Illus.). 256p. 1978. 43.95 (*0-398-03807-4*); pap. 29.95 (*0-398-06021-5*) C C Thomas.

Blanco, Richard. City of a Hundred Fires. (Pitt Poetry Ser.). 60p. 1998. pap. 12.95 (*0-8229-5683-7*) U of Pittsburgh Pr.

Blanco, Richard L. Wellington's Surgeon General, Sir James McGrigor. LC 74-75477. 257p. reprint ed. pap. 79.70 (*0-608-13865-7*, 202375900033) Bks Demand.

Blanco, Richard L., ed. The American Revolution 1775-1783: An Encyclopedia, 2 vols. LC 92-42541. (Military History of the U. S. Ser.: Vol. 1). (Illus.). 1896p. 1993. text 193.00 (*0-8240-5623-X*, H926) Garland.

Blanco, T., tr. see Barrie, Joan.

An Asterisk (*) at the beginning of an entry indicates that the title is appearing for the first time.

Blanco, Tomas. El Prejuicio Racial en Puerto Rico. LC 85-80186. (Obras Completas de Tomas Blanco Ser.). (SPA.). 145p. 1985. pap. 7.50 (*0-940238-79-9*) Ediciones Huracan.
— El Prejuicio Racial en Puerto Rico: Racial Prejudice in Puerto Rico, Spanish Text. LC 74-14222. (Puerto Rican Experience Ser.). (Illus.). 90p. 1975. reprint ed. 13.95 (*0-405-06212-5*) Ayer.
— Prontuario Historico de Puerto Rico. LC 80-67412. (Obras Completas de Tomas Blanco Ser.). 166p. 1981. pap. 7.25 (*0-940238-34-9*) Ediciones Huracan.
— Los Vates. LC 80-67415. (Obras Completas de Tomas Blanco Ser.). 96p. 1981. pap. 7.50 (*0-940238-43-8*) Ediciones Huracan.
Blanco, Victor M. & Phillips, Mark M., eds. Progress & Opportunities in Southern Hemisphere Optical Astronomy: CTIO Twenty-Fifth Anniversary Symposium. (Astronomical Society of the Pacific Conference Ser.: Vol. 1). (Illus.). 438p. 1988. 34.00 (*0-937707-18-X*) Astron Soc Pacific.
Blanco, Walter & Roberts, Jennifer, trs. Herodotus: The Histories. (Critical Editions Ser.). 433p. (C). 1991. pap. text 13.25 (*0-393-95946-5*) Norton.
Blanco, Walter, tr. see Roberts, Jennifer T., ed.
Bland. Graded Exercises in Technical Drawing. Date not set. pap. text. write for info. (*0-582-65095-X*, Pub. by Addison-Wesley) Longman.
— Graphical Communication, Bk. 1. 1994. pap. text. write for info. (*0-582-22441-1*, Pub. by Addison-Wesley) Longman.
— Graphical Communication, Bk. 2. Date not set. pap. text. write for info. (*0-582-22445-4*, Pub. by Addison-Wesley) Longman.
— Sexology in Culture. LC 98-16625. 236p. 1999. pap. text 18.00 (*0-226-05667-8*); lib. bdg. 40.00 (*0-226-05665-1*) U Ch Pr.
— Sexology Uncensored. LC 98-16624. 261p. 1999. pap. text 18.00 (*0-226-05669-4*); lib. bdg. 45.00 (*0-226-05668-6*) U Ch Pr.
— Texas Government Today. 5th ed. (C). 1991. pap. text 28.00 (*0-534-15199-X*) Harcourt.
Bland & Daly. Surgical Oncology. 1999. pap. text 150.00 (*0-8385-8736-4*, Medical Exam) Appleton & Lange.
Bland, Alden. Behold a Cry. LC 73-18554. reprint ed. 37.50 (*0-404-11369-9*) AMS Pr.
Bland, Alexander. Observer of the Dance, 1958-1982. 250p. 1986. 49.95 (*0-903102-91-9*, Pub. by Dance Bks) Princeton Bk Co.
Bland, Bill. Yourowquains, a Wyandot Indian Queen: The Story of Caty Sage. Catron, Rhonda, ed. (Illus.). 288p. 1992. 19.95 (*0-9634133-0-9*) Hist Pubns VA.
Bland, C. C., tr. see Guibert.
Bland, C. E., jt. auth. see Deeter, D.
Bland, Carole J., et al, eds. Successful Faculty in Academic Medicine: Essential Skills & How to Acquire Them. LC 89-21921. (Medical Education Ser.: Vol. 12). 336p. 1989. 44.95 (*0-8261-6730-6*) Springer Pub.
Bland, Carole J., et al. The Vitality of Senior Faculty Members: Snow on the Roof - Fire in the Furnace. Fife, Jonathan D., ed. LC 97-75336. (ASHE-ERIC Higher Education Reports: Vol. 25-7). 123p. 1996. pap. 24.00 (*1-878380-79-6*) GWU Grad Schl E&HD.
Bland, Celia. The Conspiracy of the Secret Nine. (Mysteries in Time Ser.). (Illus.). 90p. (J). (gr. 4-6). 1995. text 14.95 (*1-881889-67-X*) Silver Moon.
— Exploring the Sea. LC 99-191508. (Eyes on Adventure Ser.). 28p. (J). 1998. write for info. (*1-56156-538-5*) Kidsbks.
— Exploring Unsolved Mysteries. LC 99-191421. (Eyes on Adventure Ser.). 28p. (J). 1998. write for info. (*1-56156-609-8*) Kidsbks.
Bland, Charles. A Vision of Unity: The Bland Family in England & America, 1555-1900. 610p. 1982. 79.95 (*0-9610804-0-X*) C L Bland.
Bland, Cynthia R. The Teaching of Grammar in Late Medieval England: An Edition with Commentary, of Oxford Lincoln College MS Latin 130. (Medieval Texts & Studies: No. 6). 235p. 1991. text 32.00 (*0-937191-16-7*) Mich St U Pr.
Bland, D. R. Wave Theory & Applications. (Oxford Applied Mathematics & Computing Science Ser.). (Illus.). 328p. 1988. 79.95 (*0-19-859654-5*); pap. 39.95 (*0-19-859669-3*) OUP.
Bland, D. R. & Sneddon, Ian N. Theory Linear Viscoelasticity. LC 59-14489. (International Series of Monographs on Pure & Applied Mathematics: Vol. 10). 1960. 58.00 (*0-08-009316-7*, Pub. by Pergamon Repr) Franklin.
Bland, David. Practical Poultry Keeping. (Illus.). 160p. 1996. 29.95 (*1-86126-010-5*, Pub. by Crolwood) Trafalgar.
Bland, David E. Managing Higher Education. 112p. 1990. pap. text 38.00 (*0-304-32275-X*) Continuum.
Bland, Douglas L. The Military Committee of the North Atlantic Alliance: A Study of Structure & Strategy. LC 90-7437. 288p. 1990. 65.00 (*0-275-93712-7*, C3712, Praeger Pubs) Greenwood.
Bland, Dwain. Turkey Hunter's Digest. rev. ed. LC 85-73743. (Illus.). 256p. 1994. pap. 17.95 (*0-87349-164-5*, THDR, DBI Bks) Krause Pubns.
Bland, Eleanor T. Done Wrong. 1996. mass mkt. 4.99 (*0-312-95794-7*, Pub. by Tor Bks) St Martin.
— Keep Still, Vol. 1. 240p. 1998. mass mkt. 5.99 (*0-312-96172-3*) St Martin.
— No Bones about It. (Dead Letter Mysteries Ser.). 1998. mass mkt. 5.99 (*0-312-96423-4*) St Martin.
***Bland, Eleanor T.** Scream in Silence: A Marti MacAlister Mystery. LC 99-54820. 290p. 2000. text 23.95 (*0-312-20378-0*) St Martin.
Bland, Eleanor T. See No Evil. LC 97-39642. 288p. 1998. text 22.95 (*0-312-16910-8*) St Martin.
— See No Evil. 288p. 1999. mass mkt. 5.99 (*0-312-96818-3*) St Martin.
— See No Evil. large type ed. LC 98-5508. (Core Ser.). 375p. 1998. 27.95 (*0-7838-0112-2*, G K Hall Lrg Type) Mac Lib Ref.
***Bland, Eleanor Taylor.** Scream in Silence. 2001. reprint ed. pap. write for info. (*0-312-97494-9*, St Martins Paperbacks) St Martin.
Bland, Eleanor Taylor. Tell No Tales. LC 98-46974. (Marti MacAlister Ser.). 288p. 1999. text 22.95 (*0-312-20067-6*) St Martin.
***Bland, Eleanor Taylor.** Tell No Tales: A Marti MacAlister Mystery. 288p. 2000. mass mkt. 5.99 (*0-312-97113-3*, Minotaur) St Martin.
Bland, Eleanor Taylor. Tell No Tales: A Marti MacAlister Mystery. LC 99-31989. 1999. write for info. (*1-56895-756-4*) Wheeler Pub.
Bland, Gary, jt. ed. see Tulchin, Joseph S.
Bland, Geneva F. Herman & the Mini-Bus with Soul. (Illus.). 22p. (J). 1994. 14.95 (*0-9638969-0-3*) GBL Pubng.
Bland, Glenn. The Legend of the Golden Scrolls: Ageless Secrets for Building Wealth. 144p. 1996. pap. text 12.00 (*0-7615-0666-7*) Prima Pub.
— The Legend of the Golden Scrolls: Ageless Secrets of Building Wealth. 144p. 1995. 15.95 (*1-55958-705-9*) Prima Pub.
— The Power of Thought: Ageless Secrets for Great Achievement. LC 95-36034. 176p. 1996. 16.95 (*0-7615-0341-2*) Prima Pub.
— Success: The Glenn Bland Method. 176p. 1983. mass mkt. 5.99 (*0-8423-6689-X*) Tyndale Hse.
— Trace Su Camino Al Exito. (Serie Guia de Bolsillo - Pocket Guides Ser.).Tr. of Chart Your Way to Success. (SPA.). 99p. 1990. pap. 2.79 (*1-56063-025-6*, 498057) Editorial Unilit.
Bland, Helen, et al. Life Is Too Short. 112p. (Orig.). 1994. mass mkt. 6.99 (*0-446-39523-4*, Pub. by Warner Bks) Little.
Bland, J. A. & Bretislav, Heinrich, eds. Ultrathin Magnetic Structures I: Introduction to the Electronic, Magnetic, & Structural Properties. LC 93-38679. (Illus.). 350p. 1994. 75.95 (*0-387-57407-7*) Spr-Verlag.
Bland, J. A. & Heinrich, B. Ultrathin Magnetic Structures II: Measurement Techniques & Novel Magnetic Properties. 368p. 1994. 86.95 (*0-387-57687-8*) Spr-Verlag.
Bland, J. O. Recent Events & Present Policies in China. (Illus.). 400p. 1998. text 60.00 (*0-7007-1019-1*, Pub. by Curzon Pr Ltd) UH Pr.
Bland, Jane. Houseplant Survival Manual. 1995. 14.98 (*0-7858-0390-4*) Bk Sales Inc.
Bland, Jeffrey. Choline, Lecithin, Inositol, Vol. 1. Passwater, Richard A., ed. (Good Health Guide Ser.). 30p. 1983. pap. 2.95 (*0-87983-277-0*, 32770K, Keats Publng) NTC Contemp Pub Co.
Bland, Jeffrey S. Intestinal Toxicity & Inner Cleansing. 31p. 1989. pap. 3.95 (*0-87983-433-1*, 34331K, Keats Publng) NTC Contemp Pub Co.
— The Keeping Healthy Plan for Successful Weight Management. Benum, Sara H., ed. (Keeping Healthy Ser.). (Illus.). 46p. (Orig.). 1989. pap. text 2.95 (*0-685-29810-8*) HealthComm Intl.
— The 20-Day Rejuvenation Diet Program. 240p. (Orig.). 1996. bds. 24.95 (*0-87983-760-8*, Keats Publng) NTC Contemp Pub Co.
— The 20-Day Rejuvenation Diet Program. 288p. (Orig.). 1999. pap. 16.95 (*0-87983-980-5*, 39805K, Keats Publng) NTC Contemp Pub Co.
— Vitamin C: The Future Is Now. Bensen, Don R., ed. (Good Health Guides Ser.). 48p. 1995. pap. 3.95 (*0-87983-685-7*, 36857K, Keats Publng) NTC Contemp Pub Co.
Bland, Jeffrey S. & Benum, Sara H. Genetic Nutritioneering. LC 98-33642. 288p. 1999. pap. 16.95 (*0-87983-921-X*, 3921XK, Keats Publng) NTC Contemp Pub Co.
Bland, Jeffrey S., jt. auth. see Mindell, Earl R.
Bland, Jim. For What It's Worth. (Illus.). 200p. 1997. 12.00 (*0-8059-4164-9*) Dorrance.
Bland, Joan, ed. The Pastoral Vision of John Paul II. 210p. 1982. pap. 7.50 (*0-8199-0839-8*, Frncscn Herld) Franciscan Pr.
Bland, Joellen. Stage Plays from the Classics. LC 87-14669. (Orig.). (YA). (gr. 7-12). 1987. pap. 15.95 (*0-8238-0281-7*) Kalmbach.
Bland, Joellen, ed. Playing Scenes from Classic Literature: Short Dramatizations of the World's Most Famous Literature. LC 96-36386. (YA). (gr. 9 up). 1996. pap. 14.95 (*1-56608-024-X*, B201) Meriwether Pub.
Bland, John & Colby, Jenna. The Complete Mall Walker's Handbook: Walking for Fun & Fitness. LC 98-39713. (Illus.). 160p. 1999. pap. 14.95 (*1-57749-042-8*, Pub. by Fairview Press) Natl Bk Netwk.
Bland, John H. Disorders of the Cervical Spine: Diagnosis & Medical Management. 2nd ed. LC 93-33171. 1994. text 105.00 (*0-7216-5015-5*, W B Saunders Co) Harcrt Hlth Sci Grp.
— Live Long, Die Fast: Playing the Aging Game to Win. LC 96-9430. (Illus.). 240p. (Orig.). 1997. pap. 14.95 (*1-57749-012-6*) Fairview Press.
Bland, John O. China, Japan & Korea. LC 77-160959. (Select Bibliographies Reprint Ser.). 1977. reprint ed. 35.95 (*0-8369-5826-8*) Ayer.
— Li Hung-Chang. LC 77-175688. (Select Bibliographies Reprint Ser.). 1977. reprint ed. 23.95 (*0-8369-6603-1*) Ayer.
Bland, Julia. The Bad & the Good: Childrens Sermons & Activity Pages for Lent & Easter. 28p. (Orig.). 1997. pap. 9.25 (*0-7880-0839-0*) CSS OH.
— Little Animal Sermons: Six Children's Sermons with Activity Pages. (Illus.). 28p. 1999. pap. 4.95 (*0-7880-1349-1*) CSS OH.
***Bland, Julia.** Simply Wonderful: 5 Children's Sermons & Activity Pages for Advent & Christmas. 24p. 1999. pap. 9.00 (*0-7880-1520-6*) CSS OH.
***Bland, Julia E.** The Honey Bee Dance: Six Children's Lessons & Activity Pages. (Illus.). (ps-3). 2000. pap. 6.95 (*0-7880-1592-3*) CSS OH.
Bland, Julia E. Rules for Happy Living: Children's Sermons with Activity Pages. 60p. 1998. pap. 6.95 (*0-7880-0766-1*) CSS OH.
Bland, Kalman P. Epistle on the Possibility of Conjunction with the Active Intellect. Rushd, Ibn, ed. & tr. by. (Moreshet Studies in Jewish History, Literature & Thought: No. 7). 35.00 (*0-87334-005-1*) Ktav.
Bland, Kirby I. & Cady, Blake. Atlas of Breast Surgery. (C). 1999. 135.00 (*0-8385-0442-6*) Appleton & Lange.
Bland, Kirby I. & Copeland, Edward M., III. The Breast: Comprehensive Management of Benign & Malignant Diseases. 2nd ed. LC 97-135. (Illus.). 1824p. (C). 1998. text 225.00 (*0-7216-6656-6*, W B Saunders Co) Harcrt Hlth Sci Grp.
Bland, Kirby I., et al. Atlas of Surgical Oncology. LC 93-40050. (Illus.). 688p. 1995. text 165.00 (*0-7216-4223-3*, W B Saunders Co) Harcrt Hlth Sci Grp.
***Bland, L. C., et al, eds.** Physics with a High Luminosity Polarized Electron-Ion Collider. 450p. 1999. 88.00 (*981-02-4052-X*) World Scientific Pub.
Bland, Larry I., et al, eds. The Papers of George Catlett Marshall Vol. 2: "We Cannot Delay" July 1, 1939 - December 6, 1941. LC 81-47593. 800p. 1986. text 55.00 (*0-8018-2553-9*) Johns Hopkins.
Bland, Larry I. & Hadsel, Fred L., eds. The Papers of George Catlett Marshall Vol. 1: "The Soldierly Spirit", December 1880-June 1939. LC 81-47593. (Illus.). 750p. 1981. text 55.00 (*0-8018-2552-0*) Johns Hopkins.
Bland, Larry I. & Stevens, Sharon R., eds. The Papers of George Catlett Marshall Vol. 4: "Aggressive & Determined Leadership" June 1, 1943-December 31, 1944. (Illus.). 840p. 1996. text 55.00 (*0-8018-5368-0*) Johns Hopkins.
Bland, Larry I., ed. see Marshall, George C.
Bland, Leland D. Sight Singing Through Melodic Analysis. LC 83-8184. 512p. (C). 1983. pap. text 34.95 (*0-88229-820-8*) Burnham Inc.
Bland, Linda, ed. see Quinlan, Jane.
Bland, Lucy. Banishing the Beast: Sexuality & the Early Feminists. 432p. 1995. 25.00 (*1-56584-307-X*, Pub. by New Press NY) Norton.
Bland, Lucy & Doan, Laura L. Sexology in Culture: Labelling Bodies & Desires LC 98-235238. ix, 236p. 1998. write for info. (*0-7456-1983-5*) Blackwell Pubs.
Bland, Martin. An Introduction to Medical Statistics. 2nd ed. (Illus.). 416p. 1995. pap. text 42.50 (*0-19-262428-8*) OUP.
***Bland, Martin.** An Introduction to Medical Statistics. 3rd ed. (Illus.). 416p. 2000. pap. text 35.00 (*0-19-263269-8*) OUP.
Bland, Michael & Theaker, Alison. Effective Media Relations. 1996. pap. 16.95 (*0-7494-1856-7*) Kogan Page Ltd.
Bland, P. E. Topics in Torsion Theory. 1999. pap. text 85.00 (*3-05-501805-2*) Akademie Verlag.
— Topics in Torsion Theory. LC 99-163027. 160p. 1998. pap. 94.95 (*3-527-40131-8*) Wiley.
Bland, Peter. Selected Poems. LC 99-203150. 144p. 1998. pap. 17.95 (*1-85754-357-2*, Pub. by Carcanet Pr) Paul & Co Pubs.
Bland, R. D. & Coalson, J. J. Chronic Lung Disease in Early Infancy. LC 99-37342. (Lung Biology in Health & Disease Ser.). (Illus.). 1062p. 1999. text 235.00 (*0-8247-9871-6*) Dekker.
Bland, Randall W. The Black Robe & the Bald Eagle: The Supreme Court & the Foreign Policy of the United States, 1789-1953. 336p. (Orig.). (C). 1996. pap. 44.95 (*1-880921-06-5*) Austin & Winfield.
— The Black Robe & the Bald Eagle: The Supreme Court & the Foreign Policy of the United States, 1789-1961. 2nd ed. LC 99-24835. 440p. (C). 1999. 64.50 (*1-880921-40-5*) Austin & Winfield.
— The Black Robe & the Bald Eagle: The Supreme Court & the Foreign Policy of the United States, 1954-Present. 288p. 1998. 74.95 (*1-57292-075-0*); pap. 54.95 (*1-57292-074-2*) Austin & Winfield.
— Constitutional Law in the United States: A Systematic Inquiry into the Change & Relevance of Supreme Court Decisions. LC 92-32142. 382p. 1994. 59.95 (*1-880921-08-1*); pap. 44.95 (*1-880921-07-3*) Austin & Winfield.
— Private Pressure on Public Law: The Legal Career of Justice Thurgood Marshall, 1934-1991. LC 92-34835. 250p. (C). 1993. reprint ed. pap. text 24.50 (*0-8191-8736-4*) U Pr of Amer.
— Problems of American Constitutionalism. 424p. 2000. 59.95 (*1-57292-133-1*); pap. 34.95 (*1-57292-132-3*) Austin & Winfield.
Bland, Randall W. & Brogan, Joseph. Constitutional Law in the United States: A Systematic Inquiry into the Change & Relevance of Supreme Court Decisions, 1999. 3rd ed. LC 98-54992. 464p. 1998. 74.95 (*1-57292-091-2*) Austin & Winfield.
Bland, Randall W., et al. Texas Government, 1999. 6th ed. 326p. 1999. pap. 24.95 (*1-57292-134-X*) Austin & Winfield.
— Texas Government Today. 5th ed. 528p. (C). 1991. pap. text 47.50 (*0-534-15198-1*) Harcourt.
Bland, Randall W., ed. see Corwin, Edward S.
Bland, Randall Walton & Brogan, Joseph V. Constitutional Law in the United States: A Systematic Inquiry into the Change & Relevance of Supreme Court Decisions. 3rd ed. LC 98-54992. 726p. 1999. pap. 74.95 (*1-57292-090-4*) Austin & Winfield.
Bland, Robert L. Revenue Guide for Local Government. 197p. (Orig.). 1989. pap. text 32.00 (*0-87326-080-5*) Intl City-Cnty Mgt.
Bland, Robert L., et al. Budgeting: A Guide for Local Governments. LC 97-216348. vi, 241 p. 1997. write for info. (*0-87326-151-8*) Intl City-Cnty Mgt.
Bland, Roger G., et al. Insects. 3rd ed. (Pictured Key Nature Ser.). 432p. (C). 1978. text. write for info. (*0-697-04752-0*, WCB McGr Hill) McGrw-H Hghr Educ.
Bland, Rosemary, ed. Developing Services for Older People & Their Families. LC 96-173331. (Research Highlights in Social Work Ser.: No. 29). 200p. 1996. pap. 29.95 (*1-85302-290-X*, Pub. by Jessica Kingsley) Taylor & Francis.
Bland, Salem G. The New Christianity: or The Religion of the New Age. LC 73-95815. (Social History of Canada Ser.). 118p. reprint ed. pap. 36.60 (*0-8357-8243-3*, 203407300088) Bks Demand.
Bland, Shirley T., et al. History of Martin County. Paige, Emeline K., ed. (Illus.). 538p. 1997. reprint ed. pap. 19.98 (*0-9630788-3-6*) Sewalls Pt.
Bland, Sidney R. Preserving Charleston's Past, Shaping Its Future: The Life & Times of Susan Pringle Frost. LC 98-40218. 192p. 1999. pap. 16.95 (*1-57003-290-4*) U of SC Pr.
— Preserving Charleston's Past, Shaping Its Future: The Life & Times of Susan Pringle Frost, 105. LC 94-17309. (Contributions in American Studies: No. 105). 256p. 1994. 55.00 (*0-313-29294-9*, Greenwood Pr) Greenwood.
***Bland, Sterling Lecater, Jr.** Voices of the Fugitives: Runaway Slave Stories & Their Fictions of Self-Creation. LC 99-55223. 2000. pap. write for info. (*0-275-96707-7*, Praeger Pubs) Greenwood.
— Voices of the Fugitives: Runaway Slave Stories & Their Fictions of Self-Creation, 199. LC 99-55223. (Contributions in Afro-American & African Studies: Vol. 199). 192p. 2000. 62.00 (*0-313-31169-2*, GM1169, Greenwood Pr) Greenwood.
***Bland, Sterling Lecater, ed.** African American Slave Narratives: An Anthology. 2001. lib. bdg. write for info. (*0-313-31168-4*) Greenwood.
— African American Slave Narratives: Anthology, Vol. 2001. lib. bdg. write for info. (*0-313-31717-8*); lib. bdg. write for info. (*0-313-31718-6*) Greenwood.
— African American Slave Narratives: Anthology, Vol. 1. 2001. lib. bdg. write for info. (*0-313-31716-X*) Greenwood.
Bland, Sue. Madame de Toucainville's Magnificent Hat. (Northern Lights Books for Children Ser.). (Illus.). 32p. (J). (ps-4). 1994. text 12.95 (*0-88995-115-2*, Pub. by Red Deer) Genl Dist Srvs.
Bland, Susan K. Intermediate Grammar: From Form to Meaning & Use. LC 93-44670. 544p. 1996. pap. text 19.95 (*0-19-434366-9*) OUP.
— Intermediate Grammar: From Form to Meaning & Use, Vol. B. (Illus.). 298p. 1996. pap. text, student ed. 11.95 (*0-19-435277-3*) OUP.
— Intermediate Grammar Student Book A: From Form to Meaning & Use, Vol. A. (Illus.). 296p. 1996. pap. text, student ed. 11.95 (*0-19-435276-5*) OUP.
Bland, Thomas A., Jr., ed. see Lolley, W. Randall, et al.
Bland, Valerie. Continuous Improvement in the Healthcare Manufacturing Industry: A Practical Guide for Implementing an Improvement Program. LC 99-37163. 1999. 149.00 (*1-57491-099-X*) Interpharm.
Bland, Will & Rolls, David. Weathering: An Introduction to the Basic Principles. LC 98-34261. (Arnold Publications). (Illus.). 288p. 1998. text 75.00 (*0-340-67745-7*); pap. text 24.95 (*0-340-67744-9*) OUP.
Bland, William B. Albania. (World Bibliographical Ser.: No. 94). 292p. 1988. lib. bdg. 65.00 (*1-85109-037-1*) ABC-CLIO.
Bland, William F. & Davidson, Robert L., eds. Petroleum Processing Handbook. LC 64-66366. (Illus.). 1114p. reprint ed. pap. 200.00 (*0-8357-3610-5*, AU0039500003) Bks Demand.
Bland, Yana M., ed. Nobody Can Imagine Our Longing: Addresses from the Association of Women of the Mediterranean Region, 1996 Conference. LC 96-72590. (Foundation Ser.). (Illus.). 136p. (Orig.). 1997. pap. 12.95 (*0-911051-93-7*) Plain View.
Blandamer, Michael J. Chemical Equilibria in Solution: Dependence of Rate & Equilibrium Constants on Temperature & Pressure. LC 92-22082. (Ellis Horwood Series in Liquid & Solution Chemistry). 152p. 1992. 72.00 (*0-13-131731-8*, Pub. by Tavistock-E Horwood) Routldge.
Blandau, Richard J., ed. The Biology of the Blastocyst. LC 70-128713. 574p. reprint ed. pap. 178.00 (*0-8357-3595-8*, 201995500015) Bks Demand.
Blandau, Richard J. & Moghissi, Kamran S., eds. The Biology of the Cervix. LC 72-91429. 463p. reprint ed. pap. 143.60 (*0-8357-7245-4*, 201995600015) Bks Demand.
Blandeau, R. J., ed. see International Symposium on Aging Gametes Staff.
Blander, Milton, ed. see International Symposium on Molten Salts Staff.
Blandford, Dick K. Digital Filter Analyzer. LC 87-1017. 1988. pap. 51.33 (*0-201-11663-4*) Addison-Wesley.
***Blandford, Edmund.** Fatal Decisions: Errors & Blunders in World War II. (Illus.). 272p. 2000. 34.95 (*1-55750-285-4*) Naval Inst Pr.

B

Blandford, Edmund. Under Hitler's Banner: Serving the Third Reich. LC 97-106271. (Illus.). 214p. 1996. 24.95 (0-7603-0268-5) MBI Pubg.

***Blandford, Edmund L.** SS Intelligence. 272p. 2000. 29.95 (1-84037-147-1, Pub. by Swan Hill Pr) Specialty Pr.

— Two Sides of the Beach: The Invasion & Defense of Europe in 1944. LC 99-488324. 296p. 2000. 29.95 (1-84037-074-2, Pub. by Swan Hill Pr) Voyageur Pr.

Blandford, Elisabeth. How to Write the Best Research Paper Ever. 112p. 1998. pap. 12.95 (1-880505-54-1, CLC0201) Pieces of Lrning.

Blandford, G. Fielding. Insanity & Its Treatment: Lectures on the Treatment, Medical & Legal, of Insane Patients. LC 75-16684. (Classics in Psychiatry Ser.). 1976. reprint ed. 39.95 (0-405-07416-6) Ayer.

Blandford, H. F. A List of the Ferns of Simla & North Western Himalaya. (Illus.). 22p. 1978. reprint ed. 2.00 (0-88065-065-6) Scholarly Pubns.

Blandford, Hugh. Hugh Blandford - Published Works & Notebooks. Roycroft, A. John, ed. 1998. pap. 12.95 (1-888690-03-8) Russell Ent.

Blandford, Percy W. Building Outdoor Furniture. 3rd ed. 320p. 1992. 24.95 (0-8306-4043-6, 4184); pap. 14.95 (0-8306-4044-4, 4184) McGraw-Hill Prof.

— Designing & Building Children's Furniture, with 61 Projects. 2nd ed. (Furniture Woodshop Ser.). (Illus.). 192p. 1988. 21.95 (0-8306-9264-9, 3064); pap. 12.95 (0-8306-9364-5, 3064) McGraw-Hill Prof.

— Designing & Building Outdoor Furniture With 57 Projects. 2nd ed. (Furniture Woodshop Ser.). (Illus.). 192p. 1988. 21.95 (0-318-32689-2, 3014H) McGraw-Hill Prof.

— Designing & Building Outdoor Furniture with 57 Projects. 2nd ed. (Furniture Woodshop Ser.). (Illus.). 192p. 1988. pap. 12.95 (0-318-32690-6, 3014P) McGraw-Hill Prof.

— Designing & Building Space-Saving Furniture, with 28 Projects. 2nd ed. (Furniture Woodshop Ser.). (Illus.). 192p. 1989. 21.95 (0-8306-1274-2, 3074); pap. 12.95 (0-8306-9374-2, 3074) McGraw-Hill Prof.

— Do-It-Yourselfer's Guide to Furniture Repair & Refinishing. 2nd ed. (Furniture Woodshop Ser.). (Illus.). 192p. 1988. 21.95 (0-8306-0994-6, 2994H) McGraw-Hill Prof.

— Fifty Practical & Decorative Knots You Should Know. (Illus.). 140p. 1988. pap. 8.95 (0-8306-9304-1, 3004) McGraw-Hill Prof.

— Home Full of Furniture: Seventy-Nine More Furniture Projects for Every Room. (Illus.). 360p. 1990. pap. 16.95 (0-8306-3500-9) McGraw-Hill Prof.

— Maps & Compasses. 2nd ed. 256p. 1991. 22.95 (0-8306-2141-5, 5007); pap. 14.95 (0-8306-2140-7) McGraw-Hill Prof.

— Maps & Compasses: A User's Handbook. (Illus.). 252p. (Orig.). 1984. pap. 12.95 (0-8306-1644-6) McGraw-Hill Prof.

— Netmaking. (C). 1987. 85.00 (0-85174-197-5) St Mut.

— The New Explorer's Guide to Maps & Compasses. 160p. 1992. 15.95 (0-8306-3915-2); pap. 7.95 (0-8306-3914-4) McGraw-Hill Prof.

— One Hundred One Kitchen Projects. 1991. 23.95 (0-8306-5324-4) McGraw-Hill Prof.

— One Hundred One Kitchen Projects for the Woodworker. (Illus.). 270p. 1987. 23.95 (0-8306-7884-0, 2884); pap. 14.95 (0-8306-2884-3) McGraw-Hill Prof.

— Percy Blandford's Complete Outdoor Buildings Book. 472p. 1992. 34.95 (0-8306-3608-0, 2803) McGraw-Hill Prof.

— Percy Blandford's Favorite Woodworking Projects. 800p. 1991. 39.95 (0-8306-2148-2) McGraw-Hill Prof.

— Playhouses, Gazebos & Sheds. 160p. 1992. pap. 9.95 (0-8306-3604-8) McGraw-Hill Prof.

— Practical Blacksmithing & Metalworking. 2nd ed. 368p. 1988. pap. 19.95 (0-07-155644-3) McGraw.

— Practical Blacksmithing & Metalworking. 2nd ed. (Illus.). 368p. 1988. 24.95 (0-8306-0394-8); pap. 17.95 (0-8306-2894-0) McGraw-Hill Prof.

— Puzzles, Boxes & Toys: Creative Scroll Saw Patterns. (Illus.). 200p. 1991. 19.95 (0-8306-6706-7, 3706); pap. 12.95 (0-8306-8706-8) McGraw-Hill Prof.

— Rope Splicing. (C). 1987. 50.00 (0-85174-268-8) St Mut.

— Seventy-Seven One-Weekend Woodworking Projects. (Illus.). 304p. (Orig.). 1987. pap. 18.95 (0-8306-2774-X) McGraw-Hill Prof.

— Traditional Furniture Projects. 1991. 22.95 (0-8306-2159-8); pap. 12.95 (0-8306-2158-X) McGraw-Hill Prof.

— Twenty-Four Router Projects. (Illus.). 120p. 1988. pap. 6.95 (0-8306-9062-X, 9062P) McGraw-Hill Prof.

— Twenty-Four Table Saw Projects. (Illus.). 128p. 1987. pap. 6.95 (0-8306-2964-5) McGraw-Hill Prof.

— Twenty-Four Table Saw Projects. 1991. 6.95 (0-8306-5309-0) McGraw-Hill Prof.

— Twenty-Four Woodturning Projects. (Illus.). 140p. 1990. 18.95 (0-8306-8334-8, 3334); pap. 9.95 (0-8306-3334-0) McGraw-Hill Prof.

— The Woodturner's Bible. enl. rev. ed. (Illus.). 1986. pap. 16.95 (0-8306-1954-2) McGraw-Hill Prof.

— Woodturner's Bible. 3rd ed. (Illus.). 272p. 1990. 26.95 (0-8306-8404-2, 3404); pap. 16.95 (0-8306-3404-5) McGraw-Hill Prof.

— Working in Canvas for Yachtsmen, Cadets & Sea Scouts. (C). 1987. 50.00 (0-85174-416-8) St Mut.

Blandford, Roger D., et al, eds. Pulsars As Physics Laboratories. LC 92-42239. (Illus.). 202p. 1994. text 55.00 (0-19-853983-5) OUP.

Blandford, Roger D., et al. Active Galactic Nuclei: Saas-Fee Advanced Course 20, Lecture Notes 1990, Swiss Society for Astrophysics & Astronomy. (Illus.). 308p. 1991. 49.50 (0-387-53285-4) Spr-Verlag.

Blandford, Roger D., jt. ed. see Riegler, Guenter R.

Blandford, Sonia. Managing Discipline in Schools. LC 97-43206. 208p. (C). 1998. pap. 24.99 (0-415-17491-0) Routledge.

***Blandford, Sonia.** Managing Professional Development in Schools. LC 99-41939. (Educational Management Ser.). 192p. 2000. pap. write for info. (0-415-19759-7) Routledge.

— Middle Management in Schools: How to Harmonize Managing & Teaching for an Effective School. 208p. 1998. pap. 54.50 (0-273-61608-0, Pub. by F T P-H) Trans-Atl Phila.

Blandford, Sonia, ed. see Poster, Cyril.

***Blandford, Steve, et al.** The Film Studies Dictionary. 228p. 2000. pap. 19.95 (0-340-74191-0, Pub. by E A); text 65.00 (0-340-74190-2, Pub. by E A) OUP.

Blandford, W. T. & Godwin-Austen, H. N. Mollusca: Testacelldae & Zonitidae, Vol. 1. (Fauna of British India Ser.). xxxii, 332p. 1978. reprint ed. 30.00 (0-685-04536-6) Scholarly Pubns.

Blandiana, Ana. The Hour of Sand: Selected Poems 1969-1989. 94p. 1990. pap. 14.95 (0-85646-225-X, Pub. by Anvil Press) Dufour.

Blandiana, Ana, et al. The Hour of Sand: Selected Poems, 1969-1989. 2nd ed. 104p. 1990. pap. 14.95 (0-85646-240-3, Pub. by Anvil Press) Dufour.

Blandin, Isabella M. History of Higher Education of Women in the South Prior to 1860. LC 75-37960. 1976. reprint ed. 30.00 (0-89201-024-X) Zenger Pub.

Blandin, Nanette M., jt. ed. see Fried, Edward R.

Blanding, A. L. McFaddin, 1730-1930. (Illus.). 99p. 1992. reprint ed. pap. 19.00 (0-8328-2689-8); reprint ed. lib. bdg. 29.00 (0-8328-2688-X) Higginson Bk Co.

Blanding, Don. Floridays. (Florida Classics Ser.). (Illus.). 1977. pap. 8.95 (0-912451-03-3) Florida Classics.

***Blanding, Don.** Floridays. (Illus.). 136p. 1999. 16.00 (1-883684-24-2) Peninsula MA.

Blanding, Don. Leaves from a Grass House. pap. 3.95 (0-681-26819-0) Booklines Hawaii.

— Leaves from a Grass House. 1972. reprint ed. pap. 3.95 (0-912180-17-X) Petroglyph.

***Blanding, Don.** Paradise Lost. (Illus.). 48p. 2000. reprint ed. pap. 5.95 (0-912180-55-2) Petroglyph.

Blanding, Don. Rest of the Road. Date not set. lib. bdg. 18.95 (0-8488-1894-6) Amereon Ltd.

— Vagabond House. 1992. reprint ed. lib. bdg. 21.95 (0-89968-294-4, Lghtyr Pr) Buccaneer Bks.

***Blanding, Douglass L.** Exact Constraint: Machine Design Using Kinematic Processing. LC 99-43043. 1999. write for info. (0-7918-0085-7) ASME Pr.

Blanding, Douglass L. Principles of Mechanical Constraint Design. (C). 1999. ring bd. 39.95 (0-201-37966-X) Addison-Wesley.

Blanding, Sharon L. Acquisitions: How to Create a Winning Advertising Program for Your Company. (Entrepreneur's Guide Ser.). 200p. 1991. pap. 24.95 (1-55738-202-6, Irwn Prfssnl) McGraw-Hill Prof.

***Blanding, Steven F.** Handbook of Enterprise Operations Management. 2nd ed. LC 99-39628. 672p. 1999. boxed set 95.00 (0-8493-9824-X) CRC Pr.

Blanding, Warren. Customer Service Operations: The Complete Guide. 350p. 1991. 75.00 (0-8144-5004-0) AMACOM.

— Customer Service Operations: The Complete Guide. (Illus.). 422p. 1998. reprint ed. text 40.00 (0-7881-5804-X) DIANE Pub.

Blandino, Betty. Coiled Pottery Revised Edition: Traditional & Contemporary Ways. 2nd ed. (Illus.). 128p. 1997. text. write for info. (90-5703-151-5, Harwood Acad Pubs) Gordon & Breach.

Blandino, James, ed. see Fitzpatrick, Mary.

Blandon, Peter R. Japan & World Trade Timber Markets. LC 98-56385. (CABI Publishing Ser.). 256p. 1999. text 75.00 (0-85199-327-3) OUP.

Blandon, Ronald. Portentous Tales: Views Through the Third Eye. LC 98-90896. 1999. pap. 9.95 (0-533-12975-3) Vantage.

Blandow, D. & Dyrenfurth, M., eds. Technology Education in School & Industry: Emerging Didactics for Human Resource Development. (NATO ASI Series F: Computer & Systems Science: Vol. 135). 367p. 1994. 93.95 (0-387-58250-9) Spr-Verlag.

Blandraex, Robert. Satanic Orgy. Templar, Thorguard, ed. Blanchard, Robert, tr. from FRE. 104p. (Orig.). 1993. 45.00 (1-883147-72-7); pap. 45.00 (1-883147-71-9) Intern Guild ASRS.

Blandy, Doug E. & Congdon, Kristin G., eds. Pluralistic Approaches to Art Criticism. LC 91-78362. 200p. (C). 1992. 29.95 (0-87972-543-5) Bowling Green Univ Popular Press.

Blandy, Douglas E. & Congdon, Kristin G., eds. Art in a Democracy. LC 87-18049. (Illus.). 221p. reprint ed. pap. 68.60 (0-608-08645-2, 206916800003) Bks Demand.

Blandy, John P. Lecture Notes on Urology. 5th ed. LC 97-23639. (Lecture Notes Ser.). (Illus.). 288p. 1998. pap. 34.95 (0-632-04022-8) Blackwell Sci.

Blandy, John P., et al. Urology. 2nd ed. (Illus.). 672p. 1995. 235.00 (0-632-03679-6, Pub. by Blckwll Scitfc UK) Blackwell Sci.

Blandy, Richard, et al, eds. Structured Chaos: Process of Productivity Advance. 120p. 1986. 24.95 (0-19-554687-3) OUP.

Blandy, Susan G., et al, eds. Assessment & Accountability in Reference Work. LC 92-26676. (Reference Librarian Ser.: No. 38). 266p. 1996. pap. 24.95 (0-7890-0070-9) Haworth Pr.

— Assessment & Accountability in Reference Work. LC 92-26676. (Reference Librarian Ser.: No. 38). (Illus.). 266p. 1992. reprint ed. 49.95 (1-56024-358-9) Haworth Pr.

Blandy, William. Castle or Picture of Policy. LC 71-38157. (English Experience Ser.: No. 436). 68p. 1972. reprint ed. 20.00 (90-221-0436-2) Walter J Johnson.

Blane, Andrew, ed. The Ecumenical World of Orthodox Civilization: Russia & Orthodoxy, Vol. 3. (Slavistic Printings & Reprintings Ser.: No. 260). 1974. text 86.15 (90-279-2610-7) Mouton.

— Georges Florovsky: Russian Intellectual & Orthodox Churchman. LC 93-34516. 1993. 29.95 (0-88141-140-X); pap. 19.95 (0-88141-137-X) St Vladimirs.

Blane, Howard T. & Chafetz, M. E., eds. Youth, Alcohol, & Social Policy. LC 79-9094. (Illus.). 450p. 1979. 65.00 (0-306-40253-X, Plenum Trade) Perseus Pubng.

Blane, Howard T., jt. ed. see Leonard, Kenneth E.

Blane, William N. Excursion Through the United States & Canada During the Years 1822-1823. LC 68-58049. (Illus.). 511p. 1969. reprint ed. lib. bdg. 69.50 (0-8371-4978-9, BLA&) Greenwood.

Blaner, William S., jt. ed. see Nau, Heinz.

Blanes Prieto, Joaquin. Dictionary of Accounting Terms. (ENG & SPA.). 430p. 1991. pap. 49.95 (0-8288-6359-8, S28549) Fr & Eur.

Blaney, Doris R. & Hobson, Charles J. Cost Effective Nursing Practice: Guidelines for Nurse Managers. LC 65-5559. (Nursing Management Ser.). (Illus.). 349p. 1988. text 44.50 (0-397-54649-1, Lippnctt) Lppncott W & W.

Blaney, Geoffrey W., jt. ed. see Batia, Shobha K.

Blaney, John W., ed. The Successor States to the U. S. S. R. LC 94-46162. 333p. (YA). (gr. 11). 1995. pap. text 34.95 (0-87187-978-6) Congr Quarterly.

***Blaney, Joseph L. & Benoit, William L.** The Clinton Scandals & the Politics of Image Restoration. 2001. write for info. (0-275-97106-6) Greenwood.

Blaney, Joseph R., jt. auth. see Benoit, William L.

***Blaney, Kathy D. & Howard, Paula R.** Applied Immunohematology. (Illus.). 464p. (C). 1999. text. write for info. (0-323-00165-3) Mosby Inc.

Blaney, Paul H., jt. ed. see Millon, Theodore.

Blaney, Retta, ed. Journalism: Stories from the Real World. 144p. (Orig.). (C). 1995. pap. text 16.95 (1-55591-935-9) Fulcrum Pub.

Blaney, Worth, jt. auth. see Provost, C. Antonio.

Blanford, D. W. DE Herculis Laborbvs. (Illus.). (C). 1982. pap. text 50.00 (0-900269-02-2, Pub. by Old Vicarage) St Mut.

Blanford, Percy W. Designing & Building Colonial & Early American Furniture-with 47 Projects. 2nd ed. (Furniture Woodshop Ser.). (Illus.). 192p. 1988. 21.95 (0-8306-0914-8, 3014H); pap. 12.95 (0-8306-9314-9, 3014P) McGraw-Hill Prof.

Blanford, Sonia. Resource Management in Schools: Effective & Practical Strategies for the Self-Managing School. (Illus.). 256p. 1997. pap. 62.50 (0-273-62411-3, Pub. by F T P-H) Trans-Atl Phila.

Blank. Rediscovering America. 400p. write for info. (0-471-35415-5) Wiley.

***Blank, Andreas & Koch, Peter, eds.** Historical Semantics & Cognition. LC 99-32695. (Cognitive Linguistics Research Ser.: No. 13). 312p. 1999. 124.00 (3-11-016614-3) De Gruyter.

***Blank, Andrew.** TCP/IP Jumpstart. 352p. 2000. pap. 19.99 (0-7821-2644-8) Sybex.

Blank, Antje, ed. see Smith, Charlotte.

Blank, Arthur, et al. Built from Scratch: How a Couple of Regular Guys Grew the Home Depot from Nothing to $30 Billion. LC 98-43326. 320p. 1999. 24.95 (0-8129-3058-4, Times Bks) Crown Pub Group.

Blank, Arthur E., jt. auth. see Caro, Francis G.

Blank, Arthur E., jt. ed. see Caro, Francis G.

Blank, Benjamin L. Esh: Genealogy of the Descendants of Christopher Esh. (Illus.). 201p. 1995. reprint ed. pap. 32.00 (0-8328-4872-7); reprint ed. lib. bdg. 42.00 (0-8328-4871-9) Higginson Bk Co.

Blank, Blanche D. The Not So Grand Jury: The Story of the Federal Grand Jury System. 108p. (Orig.). (C). 1993. pap. text 22.50 (0-8191-9101-9) U Pr of Amer.

— The Not So Grand Jury: The Story of the Federal Grand Jury System. 108p. (Orig.). (C). 1993. lib. bdg. 42.00 (0-8191-9100-0) U Pr of Amer.

Blank, Carla & Roberts, Jody. Live on Stage! Performing Arts for Middle School. Anderson, Catherine et al, eds. (Illus.). (Orig.). (YA). (gr. 6-8). 1996. pap., teacher ed. 35.00 (1-57232-209-8, 31500); pap., wbk. ed. 24.95 (1-57232-374-4, 31414) Seymour Pubns.

Blank, Carol. The Power Plant Writer: How to Put Power in Your Writing. LC 86-33578. 104p. (Orig.). 1987. pap. 14.95 (0-87683-888-3, A888-3) GP Courseware.

Blank, D. H., jt. auth. see Rogalla, H.

Blank, D. L., tr. & comment see Sextus Empiricus.

Blank, David. Ancient Philosophy & Grammar: The Syntax of Appolonius Dyscolus. LC 82-5751. (American Philological Association, American Classical Studies). 123p. 1983. pap. 15.95 (0-89130-580-7, 40 04 10) OUP.

Blank, David, tr. see Ammonius.

Blank, David, tr. see Ammonius, Hermiae.

Blank, David A. & Bock, Arthur E., eds. Introduction to Naval Engineering. 2nd ed. LC 85-18819. (Illus.). 545p. 1985. 35.00 (0-87021-320-2) Natl Inst Pr.

Blank, David E. Venezuela: Politics in a Petroleum Republic. LC 83-24469. (Politics in Latin America Ser.). 225p. 1984. 75.00 (0-275-91129-2, C1129, Praeger Pubs) Greenwood.

Blank, David M. The Volume of Residential Construction, 1889-1950. (Technical Papers: No. 9). 111p. 1954. reprint ed. 28.90 (0-87014-454-5) Natl Bur Econ Res.

Blank, David M. & Stigler, George J. The Demand & Supply of Scientific Personnel. (General Ser.: No. 62). 219p. 1957. reprint ed. 52.60 (0-87014-061-2) Natl Bur Econ Res.

Blank-Edelman, David. Perl for System Administration. Mui, Linda, ed. (Illus.). 250p. 2000. pap. 34.95 (1-56592-609-9) OReilly & Assocs.

Blank, Eugene. Pediatric Images: Casebook of Differential Diagnosis. LC 97-4093. (Illus.). 1100p. 1997. text 185.00 (0-316-09991-0) Lppncott W & W.

Blank, G. Kim. Wordsworth & Feeling: The Poetry of an Adult Child. LC 94-43068. 272p. 1995. 39.50 (0-8386-3600-4) Fairleigh Dickinson.

Blank, Glenn & Barnes, Robert. The Universal Machine: A Multimedia Approach to Computing. LC 97-22132. 556p. 1997. write for info. (0-256-21140-X, Irwn Prfssnl) McGraw-Hill Prof.

***Blank, Glenn & Barnes, Robert.** The Universal Machine: A Multimedia Introduction to Computing with CD. (C). 1998. 74.06 incl. cd-rom (0-07-561842-7) McGrw-H Hghr Educ.

Blank, Grace W. Jennie & Sue Visit a Kentucky Farm: Grace Delight's Second Book. LC 93-72946. (Illus.). 70p. (J). (gr. 3-6). 1994. 8.95 (0-9634122-5-6) Feather Fables.

Blank, Grant, et al, eds. New Technology in Sociology: Practical Applications in Research & Work. 170p. 1989. pap. 21.95 (0-88738-769-1) Transaction Pubs.

Blank, Gregor S. Systemorientiertes Controlling der Erfolgsfaktoren Zeit, Kosten Und Qualitat Auf Basis Eines Prozess-netzplan-modells (PNM) (Illus.). 357p. 1998. 56.95 (3-631-33761-2) P Lang Pubng.

***Blank, Hannah.** Brave Man Dead. (Alphonse Dantan Mystery Ser.: No. 2). 300p. 2000. 24.95 (0-9652778-3-6, Pub. by Prism Corp) Midpt Trade.

Blank, Hannah. A Murder of Convenience. 1999. 24.95 (0-9652778-1-X, Hightrees Bks) Prism Corp.

***Blank, Hanne.** Big Big Love: A Sourcebook on Sex for People of Size & Those Who Love Them. 280p. 2000. pap. 15.95 (1-890159-16-6) Greenery Pr.

Blank, Harrod. Wild Wheels. LC 92-62865. (Illus.). 112p. 1994. pap. 18.95 (1-56640-981-0) Pomegranate Calif.

Blank, Howard E. A Long Way from the Creek. LC 97-76068. 389p. 1998. 24.00 (0-9661751-1-5) Pikesville Pr.

***Blank, Hugo.** Rousseau -- Favart -- Mozart: Sechs Variationen Uber ein Libretto. (Studien und Dokumente Zur Geschichte der Romanischen Literaturen). 255p. 1999. 42.95 (3-631-35308-1) P Lang Pubng.

Blank, Jeanne W. The Death of an Adult Child: A Book for & about Bereaved Parents. LC 97-9835. (Death, Value & Meaning Ser.). 313p. 1998. text 44.95 (0-89503-178-7) Baywood Pub.

***Blank, Jeffery, et al.** Cooking Fearlessly: Recipes & Adventures from Hudson's on the Bend. (Illus.). 180p. 1999. 32.95 (0-9672323-0-9) Fearless Pr.

Blank, Joan. Give Your Whole Self. (Illus.). 96p. (Orig.). 1981. pap. 4.95 (0-941374-00-9) Grapetree Prods.

— Laugh Lines. (Illus.). 96p. (Orig.). 1982. pap. 4.95 (0-941374-01-7) Grapetree Prods.

Blank, Joan G. Key Biscayne: A History of Miami's Tropical Island & the Cape Florida Lighthouse. (Florida's History Through Its Places Ser.). (Illus.). 224p. 1996. 29.95 (1-56164-096-4); pap. 21.95 (1-56164-103-0) Pineapple Pr.

Blank, Joan W. & Voiers, Judith S. Fundamentals of Business English. 1990. text, wbk. ed. 25.15 (0-02-685580-1) Glencoe.

Blank, Joani. Good Vibrations: The Complete Guide to Vibrators. 3rd rev. ed. LC 89-34171. (Illus.). 72p. 1989. pap. 6.50 (0-940208-12-1) Down There Pr.

— A Kids' First Book about Sex. LC 89-14800. (Illus.). 48p. (Orig.). (J). (ps-3). 1983. pap. 6.00 (0-940208-07-5, Yes Pr) Down There Pr.

— The Playbook for Kids about Sex. (Illus.). 56p. (J). (gr. 2-6). 1980. pap. 5.00 (0-9602324-6-X, Yes Pr) Down There Pr.

— The Playbook for Men about Sex. rev. ed. (Illus.). 32p. 1981. pap. 4.50 (0-9602324-8-6) Down There Pr.

— The Playbook for Women about Sex. rev. ed. (Illus.). 32p. 1989. pap. 4.50 (0-940208-04-0) Down There Pr.

Blank, Joani, ed. Femalia. LC 93-2328. (Illus.). 72p. (Orig.). 1993. pap. 14.50 (0-940208-15-6) Down There Pr.

— First Person Sexual: Women & Men Write about Self-Pleasuring. LC 96-85336. 184p. (Orig.). 1996. pap. 14.50 (0-940208-17-2) Down There Pr.

— I Am My Lover: Women Pleasure Themselves. 2nd rev. ed. LC 97-5606. (Illus.). 108p. 1997. pap. 25.00 (0-940208-18-0) Down There Pr.

***Blank, Joani, ed.** Still Doing It: Women & Men Over Sixty Write about Their Sex Lives. 2000. pap. 12.50 (0-940208-27-X, Pub. by Down There Pr) LPC InBook.

***Blank, Joani & Whidden, Ann.** Good Vibrations: The New Complete Guide to Vibrators. 4th rev. ed. LC 00-23543. (Illus.). 88p. 2000. pap. 8.50 (0-940208-26-1) Down There Pr.

Blank, Joani, jt. ed. see Bright, Susie.

Blank, John S., III. Modern Towing. LC 87-47736. (Illus.). 607p. 1989. text 45.00 (0-87033-372-0) Cornell Maritime.

***Blank, Jonah.** Arrow of the Blue-Skinned God: Retracing the Ramayana Through India. 2000. pap. 14.00 (0-8021-3733-4, Grove) Grove-Atltic.

Blank, Jonah. Arrow of the Blue-Skinned God: Retracing the Ramayana Through India. LC 93-4739. 352p. 1993. reprint ed. pap. 12.00 (0-385-47203-X) Doubleday.

***Blank, Jonah.** Mullah on Mainframe. 2000. 32.50 (0-226-05676-7) U Ch Pr.

Blank, LeLand T. Engineering Economy: Solutions Manual to Accompany. 3rd ed. (C). 1989. text 28.12 (0-07-062983-8) McGraw.

Blank, Leland T. & Tarquin, Anthony J. Engineering Economy. 4th ed. LC 97-28589. (McGraw-Hill Series in Industrial Engineering & Management Science). 1997. 59.50 (0-07-063110-7) McGraw.

Blank, Leonard. Age of Shrinks. LC 79-52476. 1979. 10.95 (0-686-25248-9) Ewing Pubns.

— Changing Behavior in Individuals, Couples, & Groups: Identifying, Analyzing, & Manipulating the Elements

An Asterisk (*) at the beginning of an entry indicates that the title is appearing for the first time.

Involved in Change in Order to Promote or Inhibit Alteration of Behavior. (Illus.). 202p. 1996. 44.95 (*0-398-06656-6*); pap. 28.95 (*0-398-06657-4*) C C Thomas.

Blank, Les & Bogan, James, eds. Burden of Dreams. (Illus.). 338p. 1984. pap. 12.95 (*0-938190-17-2*) North Atlantic.

Blank, Louis. Alzheimer's Challenged & Conquered. 185p. 1996. 32.50 (*0-572-02196-8*, Pub. by W Foulsham) Trans-Atl Phila.

Blank, Marion, et al. Directing Early Discourse: Making the Transition to School Language. 349p. 1995. pap. text 99.00 (*0-7616-3211-5*) Commun Skill.

Blank, Martin. Bioelectrochemistry II: Membrane Phenomena. Milazzo, G., ed. LC 87-25761. (Ettore Majorana International Science Series, Life Sciences: Vol. 32). (Illus.). 556p. 1988. 135.00 (*0-306-42765-6*, Plenum Trade) Perseus Pubng.

Blank, Martin, ed. Bioelectrochemistry: Ions, Surfaces, Membranes. LC 80-18001. (Advances in Chemistry Ser.: No. 188). 527p. 1980. 65.95 (*0-8412-0473-X*) Am Chemical.

— Bioelectrochemistry: Ions, Surfaces, Membranes. LC 80-18001. (Advances in Chemistry Ser.: Vol. 188). 539p. 1980. reprint ed. pap. 167.10 (*0-608-03859-8*, 206430600008) Bks Demand.

— Critical Essays on Thornton Wilder. LC 95-2274. (Critical Essays on American Literature Ser.). 1996. 49.00 (*0-7838-0020-7*, G K Hall & Co) Mac Lib Ref.

— Electrical Double Layers in Biology. 326p. 1986. 79.50 (*0-306-42218-2*, Plenum Trade) Perseus Pubng.

— Electricity & Magnetism in Biology & Medicine. (Illus.). 1993. 50.00 (*0-911302-67-0*) San Francisco Pr.

— Electromagnetic Fields: Biological Interactions & Mechanisms. (Advances in Chemistry Ser.: No. 250). (Illus.). 550p. 1995. text 135.00 (*0-8412-3135-4*, Pub. by Am Chemical) OUP.

Blank, Martin, et al, eds. Thornton Wilder: New Essays. LC 98-48986. (Literary Studies: No. 26). 500p. 1999. lib. bdg. 55.00 (*0-933951-83-3*) Locust Hill Pr.

Blank, Martin & Findl, E., eds. Mechanistic Approaches to Interactions of Electric & Electromagnetic Fields with Living Systems. LC 87-7170. (Illus.). 454p. (C). 1987. text 156.00 (*0-306-42684-6*, Kluwer Plenum) Kluwer Academic.

Blank, Martin & Vodyanoy, Igor, eds. Biomembrane Electrochemistry. LC 93-24348. (Advances in Chemistry Ser.: No. 235). 616p. 1994. text 150.00 (*0-8412-2524-9*, Pub. by Am Chemical) OUP.

Blank, Martin, ed. see Markov, M. A.

Blank, Martin, jt. ed. see Milazzo, G.

Blank, Martin J., jt. auth. see Melaville, Atelia I.

Blank, Mary Ann & Kershaw, Cheryl. The Designbook for Building Partnerships. LC 97-62016. 440p. 1998. ring bd. 49.95 (*1-56676-619-2*) Scarecrow.

Blank, Michael. Discreteness & Continuity in Problems of Chaotic Dynamics. LC 97-551. (Translations of Mathematical Monographs: Vol. 161). 161p. 1997. text 89.00 (*0-8218-0370-0*, MMONO/161) Am Math.

— Wirtschaftliche Verflechtungen Deutscher Mittelstandischer Unternehmen mit der Republik Sudafrika Vol. XVIII: Betrachtungen vor dem Hintergrund Einer Theorie der Internationalen Produktion. (Europaische Hochshulschriften: Reihe 5: Bd. 2014). (GER., Illus.). XVIII, 330p. 1996. pap. 57.95 (*3-631-31107-9*) P Lang Pubng.

Blank, Norman. Chest Radiographic Analysis. (Illus.). 670p. 1989. text 205.00 (*0-443-08658-3*) Church.

Blank, Parthenia, jt. auth. see Adams, Cecilia.

Blank, Paula. Broken English. 224p. (C). 1996. 80.00 (*0-415-13779-9*) Routledge.

Blank, Peter. The First Spell of Winnefred Broomstock. (Illus.). 32p. (J). 1992. 7.95 (*1-56288-273-2*) Checkerboard.

Blank, Rebecca M. Do Justice: Linking Christian Faith & Modern Economic Life. LC 91-48104. 200p. (Orig.). (C). 1992. pap. 14.95 (*0-8298-0929-5*) Pilgrim OH.

— Is There a Trade-Off Between Unemployment & Inequality? (Public Policy Brief Highlights Ser.: Vol. 33A). 6p. 1997. write for info. (*0-941276-31-7*) J Levy.

— Is There a Trade-Off Between Unemployment & Inequality? No Easy Answers: Labor Market Problems in the United States Versus Europe. (Public Policy Briefs Ser.: Vol. 33). (Illus.). 28p. 1997. pap. 3.00 (*0-941276-28-7*) J Levy.

— It Takes a Nation: A New Agenda for Fighting Poverty. LC 96-8671. 400p. 1997. text 29.95 (*0-691-02675-0*, Pub. by Princeton U Pr); pap. text 17.95 (*0-691-00401-3*, Pub. by Princeton U Pr) Cal Prin Full Svc.

Blank, Rebecca M., ed. Social Protection vs. Economic Flexibility: Is There a Tradeoff? (National Bureau of Economic Research Comparative Labor Markets Ser.). (Illus.). 386p. 1994. 50.00 (*0-226-05678-3*) U Ch Pr.

***Blank, Rebecca M. & Card, David, eds.** Finding Jobs: Work & Welfare Reform. 512p. 2000. 42.50 (*0-87154-116-5*) Russell Sage.

Blank, Renee & Slipp, Sandra. Voices of Diversity: Real People Talk about Problems & Solutions in a Workplace Where Everyone Is Not Alike. LC 94-13517. 224p. 1994. 22.95 (*0-8144-0217-8*) AMACOM.

***Blank, Renee, et al.** From the Outside In: Seven Strategies for Success When You're Not a Member of the Dominant Group in Your Workplace. 208p. 2000. pap. 17.95 (*0-8144-7981-2*) AMACOM.

Blank, Robert H. Biomedical Policy. 1995. text 42.95 (*0-8304-1366-9*) Thomson Learn.

— Brain Policy: How the New Neuroscience Will Change Our Lives & Our Politics. LC 98-46088. 224p. 1999. text 60.00 (*0-87840-712-X*) Georgetown U Pr.

— Brain Policy: How the New Neuroscience Will Change Our Lives & Our Politics. LC 98-46088. (Illus.). 199p. 1999. pap. 21.95 (*0-87840-713-8*) Georgetown U Pr.

— Fertility Control: New Techniques, New Policy Issues, 32. LC 91-13115. (Contributions in Medical Studies: No. 32). 176p. 1991. 49.95 (*0-313-27640-4*, BKF, Greenwood Pr) Greenwood.

— Fetal Protection in the Workplace: Women's Rights, Business Interests & the Unborn. LC 92-42906. 1993. 38.50 (*0-231-07694-0*) Col U Pr.

— Individualism in Idaho: The Territorial Foundations. LC 88-21060. (Illus.). 110p. (C). 1988. pap. 9.00 (*0-87422-052-1*) Wash St U Pr.

— Life, Death & Public Policy. 187p. 1988. pap. 15.00 (*0-87580-540-X*) N Ill U Pr.

— Mother & Fetus: Changing Notions of Maternal Responsibility, 36. LC 91-38029. (Contributions in Medical Studies: No. 36). 224p. 1992. 55.00 (*0-313-27639-0*, BOF/, Greenwood Pr) Greenwood.

— New Zealand Health Policy: A Comparative Study. (Readings in New Zealand Politics Ser.). (Illus.). 160p. 1994. pap. text 39.95 (*0-19-558319-1*) OUP.

— The Price of Life: The Future of American Health Care. LC 96-3465. 352p. 1997. 31.00 (*0-231-10294-1*) Col U Pr.

— Rationing Medicine. (Illus.). 288p. 1988. text 52.50 (*0-231-06536-1*) Col U Pr.

— Rationing Medicine. 290p. 1989. pap. text 20.00 (*0-231-06537-X*) Col U Pr.

— Regulating Reproduction. 272p. (C). 1992. pap. text 19.00 (*0-231-07017-9*) Col U Pr.

Blank, Robert H. & Bonnicksen, Andrea L., eds. Debates over Medical Authority & Challenges in Biomedical Experimentation, Vol. II: Emerging Issues in Biomedical Policy: an Annual Review. 244p. 1993. 55.50 (*0-231-08016-6*) Col U Pr.

— Medicine Unbound: The Human Body & the Limits of Medical Intervention. LC 94-41829. 287p. 1994. 57.50 (*0-231-08148-0*) Col U Pr.

— Setting Allocation Priorities & Genetic & Reproductive Technologies. (Emerging Issues in Biomedical Policy Ser.: Vol. 1). 315p. 1993. pap. 23.00 (*0-231-07411-5*) Col U Pr.

Blank, Robert H. & Merrick, Janna. The Comedy of Democracy. LC 95-34411. 216p. 1996. 59.95 (*0-275-94979-6*, Praeger Pubs) Greenwood.

Blank, Robert H. & Merrick, Janna, eds. Encyclopedia of U. S. Biomedical Policy. LC 95-33969. 384p. 1996. lib. bdg. 95.00 (*0-313-28641-8*, Greenwood Pr) Greenwood.

Blank, Robert H. & Merrick, Janna C. Human Reproduction: Emerging Technologies & Conflicting Rights. LC 95-10455. 269p. (YA). (gr. 11). 1995. text 14.97 (*0-87187-938-7*) Congr Quarterly.

Blank, Robert H. & Mills, Miriam, eds. Biomedical Technologies & Health Policy. (Orig.). 1989. pap. 15.00 (*0-944285-07-4*) Pol Studies.

Blank, Robert H. & Mills, Miriam K., eds. Biomedical Technology & Public Policy, 26. LC 89-16899. (Contributions in Medical Studies: No. 26). 250p. 1989. 65.00 (*0-313-26629-8*, BBH/, Greenwood Pr) Greenwood.

Blank, Robert H., jt. ed. see Darrough, Masako N.

Blank, Robert H., jt. ed. see Merrick, Janna C.

Blank, Robert H., jt. ed. see Mills, Miriam K.

Blank, Rolf & Gruebel, Dorreen. State Indicators of Science & Mathematics Educations, 1997. LC 97-143912. 130p. 1995. pap. 18.00 (*1-884037-13-5*) Coun Chief St Schl Offs.

Blank, Rolf & Perryman, Ellen M. State Curriculum Frameworks in Mathematics & Science: How Are They Changing Across the States? LC 96-171434. 132p. 1995. pap. 18.00 (*1-884037-11-9*) Coun Chief St Schl Offs.

Blank, Rolf K. & Brathwaite, Barbara C. Key State Education Policies on K-12 Education: Content Standards, Graduation, Teacher Licensure, Time & Attendance, a 50-State Report, 1998. 60p. 1998. pap. 10.00 (*1-884037-52-6*) Coun Chief St Schl Offs.

***Blank, Rolf K., et al.** State Education Indicators with a Focus on Title 1, 1998. (Illus.). 128p. (Orig.). 1999. pap. write for info. (*1-884037-54-2*) Coun Chief St Schl Offs.

Blank, Rolf K., jt. auth. see Wilson, Linda D.

Blank, Ronald. The SPC Troubleshooting Guide. LC 97-45676. 80p. 1997. 15.00 (*0-527-76343-8*) Productivity Inc.

Blank, Sheldon H. Jeremiah: Man & Prophet. LC 61-14333. 272p. reprint ed. pap. 84.40 (*0-7837-3402-6*, 204336200008) Bks Demand.

— Prophetic Faith in Isaiah. LC 57-9887. (Wayne Bks.: No. WB24). 253p. reprint ed. pap. 78.50 (*0-7837-3646-0*, 204351500009) Bks Demand.

— Prophetic Thought: Essays & Addresses. LC 77-5898. (Jewish Perspectives Ser.: No. 2). 179p. reprint ed. pap. 55.50 (*0-7837-1398-3*, 204157900021) Bks Demand.

— Understanding the Prophets. 144p. (C). 1983. pap. text 5.00 (*0-8074-0250-8*, 382755) UAHC.

Blank, Shoshana, ed. see Ratcliff, Carter.

Blank, Shoshana, ed. see Westfall, Stephen.

Blank, Stephen. The Russian Military: Is Time Running Out? Colbert, James, ed. 88p. 1998. pap. 15.00 (*0-9644523-3-2*) Jewish Inst Nat Secur.

— The Sorcerer As Apprentice: Stalin As Commissar of Nationalities, 1917-1924, 145. LC 93-18148. (Contributions in Military Studies Ser.: No. 145). 312p. 1994. 69.50 (*0-313-28683-3*, BVK/) Greenwood.

Blank, Stephen & Haar, Jerry, eds. Making NAFTA Work: U. S. Firms & the New North American Business Environment. LC 98-5602. 112p. 1997. 16.95 (*1-57454-047-5*) U Miami N-S Ctr.

Blank, Stephen, et al. Responding to Low-Intensity Conflict Challenges. (Illus.). 332p. (Orig.). (C). 1993. pap. text 45.00 (*1-56806-436-5*) DIANE Pub.

— Seachange & Anxiety in the Advanced Economies. 160p. 1997. pap. 29.00 (*1-883223-11-3*) Pacific NY.

***Blank, Stephen J.** U. S. Military Engagement with Transcaucasia & Central Asia. 47p. 2000. pap. write for info. (*1-58487-023-0*) SSI US Army.

***Blank, Stephen J., ed.** Mediterranean Security into the Coming Millennium. 521p. 1999. pap. write for info. (*1-58487-003-6*) SSI US Army.

Blank, Stephen J. & Kipp, Jacob W., eds. The Soviet Military & the Future, 130. LC 92-14617. (Contributions in Military Studies Ser.: No. 130). 328p. 1992. 59.95 (*0-313-27506-8*, KSM, Greenwood Pr) Greenwood.

Blank, Stephen J. & Rubenstein, Alvin Z., eds. Imperial Decline: Russia's Changing Role in Asia. LC 96-30130. 272p. 1997. pap. text 16.95 (*0-8223-1897-0*); lib. bdg. 49.95 (*0-8223-1905-5*) Duke.

Blank, Stephen J., et al. Conflict, Culture & History: Regional Dimensions. LC 92-40526. (Illus.). 370p. 1991. pap. 17.00 (*1-58566-043-4*) Air Univ.

— European Security: Washington's Shaping Strategy in Action. 47p. 2000. pap. write for info. (*1-58487-017-6*) SSI US Army.

Blank, Steven C. The End of Agriculture in the American Portfolio. LC 97-21995. 232p. 1998. 65.00 (*1-56720-165-2*, Quorum Bks) Greenwood.

Blank, Susan, jt. auth. see McGee, Elizabeth A.

Blank, Thomas & Haber, Gilda M., eds. Building Design for Handicapped & Aged Persons. 256p. 1992. text 49.00 (*0-07-012533-3*) McGraw.

Blank, Thomas O. A Social Psychology of Developing Adults. LC 81-19835. (Wiley Series on Personality Processes). 343p. 1982. reprint ed. pap. 106.40 (*0-7837-2836-0*, 205763600006) Bks Demand.

Blank, Thomas O., ed. Topics in Gerontology: Selected Annotated Bibliographies, 22. LC 93-9311. (Bibliographies & Indexes in Gerontology Ser.: No. 22). 256p. 1993. lib. bdg. 69.50 (*0-313-28337-0*, BTY/, Greenwood Pr) Greenwood.

Blank, Uel. The Community Tourism Industry Imperative: The Necessity, the Opportunities, Its Potential. LC 89-50207. 224p. (C). 1989. 29.95 (*0-910251-31-2*) Venture Pub PA.

Blank, Warren. The Nine Natural Laws of Leadership. LC 95-33153. 288p. 1995. 27.95 (*0-8144-0309-3*) AMACOM.

Blank, William. Torah, Tarot & Tantra: A Guide to Jewish Spiritual Growth. 1991. pap. 16.95 (*0-904575-51-9*) Sigo Pr.

Blank, William E. Handbook for Developing Competency-Based Training Programs. (Illus.). 352p. (C). 1982. text 72.80 (*0-13-377416-3*) P-H.

Blanke & Smith. Cities in Transition. LC 99-18873. 272p. 1999. text 69.95 (*0-312-22215-7*) St Martin.

***Blanke, David.** Sowing the American Dream: How Consumer Culture Took Root in the Rural Midwest. 336p. (C). 2000. pap. text 21.95 (*0-8214-1348-1*) Ohio U Pr.

— Sowing the American Dream: How Consumer Culture Took Root in the Rural Midwest. 336p. (C). 2000. text 59.95 (*0-8214-1347-3*) Ohio U Pr.

Blanke, Gail. In My Wildest Dreams. LC 98-6262. 288p. 1998. 24.00 (*0-684-84113-4*) S&S Trade.

— In My Wildest Dreams: Living the Life You Long For. 1999. pap. 13.00 (*0-684-85308-6*, Fireside) S&S Trade Pap.

Blanke, Helmut, jt. auth. see Barth, Markus.

***Blanke, M., et al, eds.** Transportation Systems, Computer Control, Vol. Q. 560p. 1999. pap. 126.00 (*0-08-042755-3*) Elsevier.

Blanke, M. & Soderstrom, T. S. System Identification, 1994 (SYSID '94) LC 95-17156. (IPPV IFAC Ser.: 3-set). 1700p. 1995. pap. 305.00 (*0-08-042225-X*, Pergamon Pr) Elsevier.

Blanke, Richard. Orphans of Versailles: The German Minority in Western Poland, 1918-1939. LC 92-19216. 328p. (C). 1993. 39.95 (*0-8131-1803-4*) U Pr of Ky.

— Prussian Poland in the German Empire, 1871-1900. (East European Monographs: No. 86). 268p. 1981. text 52.50 (*0-914710-80-X*, Pub. by East Eur Monographs) Col U Pr.

Blanken, Gerhard, et al, eds. Linguistic Disorders & Pathologies: An International Handbook. LC 93-34475. (Handbooks of Linguistics & Communication Science: Vol. 8). xiv, 962p. (C). 1993. lib. bdg. 638.50 (*3-11-011324-4*) De Gruyter.

Blanken, Rhea L., jt. auth. see Liff, Allen.

Blankenbaker, E. Keith. Modern Plumbing. LC 96-19156. 384p. 1997. 39.96 (*1-56637-345-X*) Goodheart.

— Painting & Decorating: Skills & Techniques for Success. LC 98-51813. (Illus.). 2000. 39.96 (*1-56637-506-1*) Goodheart.

Blankenbaker, Frances & Mears, Henrietta C. What the Bible Is All about for Young Explorers: Based on the Best-Selling Classic by Henrietta Mears. rev. ed. LC 98-12360. (J). 1998. 15.99 (*0-8307-2364-1*); pap. 10.99 (*0-8307-2363-3*) Gospel Lght.

Blankenberg, Floris P. Appropriate Technologies for Rural Development in India. (C). 1991. 35.00 (*81-7022-371-7*, Pub. by Concept) S Asia.

Blankenberger, Anne. Resources for the Implementation of Total Quality Management (TQM) in Education, in Nonprofits, & in the Service Sector. annot. ed. Sullivan, Maureen, ed. 24p. 1992. pap. 10.00 (*0-918006-71-6*) ARL.

Blankenbuehler, William J., intro. Historical Magazine of Monongahela's Old Home Coming Week, September 6-13, 1908. (Illus.). 271p. 1993. reprint ed. lib. bdg. 33.50 (*0-8328-3118-2*) Higginson Bk Co.

Blankenhorn, D. H. Preventv Treatmnt Athers. (C). 1984. text 39.95 (*0-201-10638-8*, Health Sci) Addison-Wesley.

Blankenhorn, David. The American Idea: Dan Quayle, Murphy Brown, & the Rest of Us. 160p. (Orig.). 1997. pap. 22.00 (*0-465-01546-8*, Pub. by Basic) HarpC.

— Fatherless America: Confronting Our Most Urgent Social Problem. LC 94-40151. 336p. 1996. pap. 15.00 (*0-06-092683-X*) HarpC.

Blankenhorn, David, et al, eds. Rebuilding the Nest: A New Commitment to the American Family. LC 90-44116. 280p. 1990. pap. 21.95 (*0-87304-242-5*) Manticore Pubs.

Blankenhorn, David, jt. ed. see Glendon, Mary Ann.

Blankenhorn, David, et. see Glenn, Norval.

Blankenhorn, Heber. The Strike for Union. LC 75-89718. (American Labor, from Conspiracy to Collective Bargaining Ser., No. 1). 259p. 1974. reprint ed. 21.95 (*0-405-02104-6*) Ayer.

Blankenhorn, James C. Controlled Impedance Analysis Program. (C). 1992. 695.00 incl. disk (*1-882812-11-5*) SMT Plus.

— How to Do SMT - FPT Repair & Rework. 128p. (C). 1992. pap. text 99.95 (*1-882812-09-3*) SMT Plus.

— Professional SMT Component & Land Pattern Book, 2 vols., Set, Vols. 1 & 2. (C). 1992. text 299.95 (*1-882812-07-7*) SMT Plus.

— SMT Advance Design Techniques. 268p. (C). 1988. text 199.95 (*1-882812-01-8*) SMT Plus.

— SMT Area Analysis Program. (C). 1992. 295.00 incl. disk (*1-882812-10-7*) SMT Plus.

— SMT Design Rules & Standards. 175p. (C). 1991. text 299.95 (*1-882812-03-4*) SMT Plus.

— SMT Designing for Testability. 119p. (C). 1991. text 99.95 (*1-882812-02-6*) SMT Plus.

— SMT Fundamentals of Product Design. 235p. (C). 1990. text 99.95 (*1-882812-00-X*) SMT Plus.

Blankenhorn, James C., jt. auth. see Ritchey, Lee W.

Blankenhorn, Kathy & Richards, Joanne. Language Arts Folder Fun: Activities for Reinforcement & Enrichment. Britt, Leslie, ed. & intro. by. (Illus.). 80p. (J). (gr. 2-5). 1995. pap. text 9.95 (*0-86530-316-9*, 1P316-9) Incentive Pubns.

Blankenship. Your Research. Date not set. pap. text 24.00 (*0-314-01531-0*) West Pub.

— Your Research. 2nd ed. 1995. 41.95 (*0-314-08753-2*) West Pub.

Blankenship, Loyd. GURPS Cyberpunk: High-Tech, Low-Life Roleplaying Sourcebook. Jackson, Steve & Lambard, Creede, eds. (Illus.). 128p. 1990. pap. 19.95 (*1-55634-168-7*, Pub. by S Jackson Games) BookWorld.

— GURPS Supers: Super-Powered Roleplaying Meets the Real World. 2nd ed. Jackson, Steve & Punch, Sean, eds. (Illus.). 1993. pap. 19.95 (*1-55634-194-6*, 6017) S Jackson Games.

Blankenship, Loyd, ed. see Jackson, Steve & Ford, John M.

Blankenship, Loyd, ed. see McCubbin, Chris.

Blankenship, A. B., et al. State of the Art Marketing Research. 2nd ed. LC 97-29370. (Illus.). 464p. 1998. 49.95 (*0-8442-3443-5*, NTC Business Bks) NTC Contemp Pub Co.

Blankenship, A. B., jt. auth. see Beville, Hugh M.

Blankenship, A. B., jt. auth. see Breen, George.

Blankenship, Alan. The Appraisal Writing Handbook. LC 97-49263. 1997. 19.50 (*0-922154-46-5*) Appraisal Inst.

Blankenship, Albert B. Consumer & Opinion Research. Assael, Henry, ed. LC 78-234. (Century of Marketing Ser.). (Illus.). 1979. reprint ed. lib. bdg. 24.95 (*0-405-11177-0*) Ayer.

Blankenship, Bart & Blankenship, Robin. Earth Knack: Stone Age Skills for the 21st Century. (Illus.). 192p. 1996. pap. 14.95 (*0-87905-733-5*) Gibbs Smith Pub.

Blankenship, Bob. Cherokee Roots, 2 vols., Set. 2nd ed. 163p. 1992. pap. text 30.00 (*0-9633774-0-X*) Cherokee Roots.

— Cherokee Roots, 2 vols., Vol. I: Eastern Version. 2nd ed. 200p. 1992. pap. text 15.00 (*0-9633774-1-8*) Cherokee Roots.

— Cherokee Roots, 2 vols., Vol. II: Western Version. 2nd ed. 400p. 1992. pap. text 22.00 (*0-9633774-2-6*) Cherokee Roots.

— Dawes Plus. 217p. 1994. pap. text 30.00 (*0-9633774-3-4*) Cherokee Roots.

— Millel Plus. 276p. 1994. pap. text 35.00 (*0-9633774-4-2*) Cherokee Roots.

Blankenship, Frank J. The Prentice Hall Real Estate Appraisal Deskbook. 320p. 1986. 39.95 (*0-13-696378-1*) P-H.

Blankenship, G., et al, eds. Basic & Advanced in Vitreous Surgery. (FIDIA Research Ser.). x, 419p. 1986. 203.00 (*0-387-96330-8*) Spr-Verlag.

— Current Concepts in Diagnosis & Treatment of Vitreoretinal Diseases. (Developments in Ophthalmology Ser.: Vol. 2). (Illus.). xxviii, 408p. 1981. 256.75 (*3-8055-1672-X*) S Karger.

Blankenship, G. L., jt. auth. see Kwatny, Harry G.

Blankenship, G. Wesley. The Development of a Variable Center Distance Gear Noise Test Facility. (Nineteen Eighty-Eight Fall Technical Meeting Ser.: Vol. 88FTM13). (Illus.). 11p. 1988. pap. text 30.00 (*1-55589-518-2*) AGMA.

Blankenship, G. Wesley, jt. auth. see Renggli, Bernard J.

***Blankenship, John.** C Is for Control: A Laboratory Text for Hardware Interfacing with C & C++ LC 99-21067. (Illus.). 245p. 1999. pap. text 58.00 (*0-02-310742-1*) P-H.

Blankenship, John. The Gradebook System: Apple II-IIe. (Illus.). 80p. 1984. 33.95 (*0-13-362542-7*) P-H.

***Blankenship, John.** Sunshine & Shadows. 1999. pap. write for info. (*1-58235-192-9*) Watermrk Pr.

Blankenship, John H., jt. auth. see Thoreson, James D.

Blankenship, Laurel, ed. see Freel, Kenn.

Blankenship, Leroy. Papa Ob Long: The Animals' Great Journey. LC 97-44248. (Illus.). 32p. (J). 1998. 12.99 (0-8499-5824-5) Tommy Nelson.
— Somebody Bigger Than I. LC 98-46165. (Illus.). 22p. (J). (ps-k). 1999. 6.99 (0-8499-5884-9) Tommy Nelson.
Blankenship, Michael B., ed. Understanding Corporate Criminality. LC 93-18139. (Current Issues in Criminal Justice Ser.: Vol. 3). (Illus.). 296p. 1993. text 53.00 (0-8153-0883-3, SS845) Garland.
— Understanding Corporate Criminality. LC 93-18139. (Current Issues in Criminal Justice Ser.: Vol. 3). (Illus.). 296p. 1995. pap. text 24.95 (0-8153-1922-3, SS845) Garland.
Blankenship, R. E., ed. Anoxygenic Photosynthetic Bacteria. (Advances in Photosynthesis Ser.). 1368p. (C). 1995. pap. text 247.00 (0-7923-3682-8) Kluwer Academic.
Blankenship, R. E., et al, eds. Anoxygenic Photosynthetic Bacteria. (Advances in Photosynthesis Ser.). 1368p. (C). 1995. lib. bdg. 492.00 (0-7923-3681-X) Kluwer Academic.
***Blankenship, Robert E.** Photosynthesis. (Illus.). 2000. pap. 39.95 (0-632-04321-0) Blackwell Sci.
Blankenship, Robin, jt. auth. see Blankenship, Bart.
Blankenship, Scott. Figuring It Out Fast: The Family's Best Approaches to Nursing Homes. LC 95-46539. 2000. pap. 25.00 (1-56072-268-1, Nova Kroshka Bks) Nova Sci Pubs.
***Blankenship, Scott.** Handbook on Nursing Homes. 153p. 2000. 43.00 (1-56072-383-1) Nova Sci Pubs.
Blankenship, Sonja B. St. Michael the Archangel: Celestial Friends vs. Demonic Enemies. 2nd ed. (Illus.). 1997. pap. 11.00 (1-888516-03-8) Apostlte Our Lady.
***Blankenship, Steven.** The Word. 360p. 1999. pap. write for info. (0-7392-0439-4, PO3727) Morris Pubng.
Blankenship, William D. Time of the Wolf. 320p. 1998. 22.95 (1-55611-528-8) D I Fine.
— The Time of the Wolf. LC 98-22703. 1998. 22.95 (1-55611-548-2, Pub. by D I Fine) Penguin Putnam.
Blankenstein, M. E. Rotary in Baton Rouge, 1918-1970. 1970. 25.00 (1-57980-031-9) Claitors.
Blankenstein, T., ed. Gene Therapy: Principles & Applications. LC 98-37011. 400p. 1999. 132.00 (3-7643-5972-2) Birkhauser.
Blankenstein, Thomas. Gene Therapy: Principles & Applications. LC 98-37011. 1998. 129.00 (0-8176-5972-2) Birkhauser.
***Blankert, Albert.** Dutch Classicism: In 17th Century Painting. (Illus.). 2000. 59.95 (90-5662-120-3) NAi Uitgevers.
Blankert, Albert. Rembrandt: A Genius & His Impact. (Illus.). 450p. 1998. 59.00 (90-400-9981-2, Pub. by Waandrs) Consort Bk Sales.
Blankholm, Hans P. Intrasite Spatial Analysis in Theory & Practice. (Illus.). 406p. (C). 1991. text 40.00 (87-7288-329-4, Pub. by Aarhus Univ Pr) David Brown.
— On the Track of a Prehistoric Economy. Maglemosian Subsistence in Early Postglacial South Scandinavia. (Illus.). 320p. 1996. 40.00 (87-7288-439-8, Pub. by Aarhus Univ Pr) David Brown.
Blankholm, Robert F. Twenty-Six Friends: The Shape of the Alphabet Letters. 2nd ed. LC 90-71355. (Illus.). 64p. (J). 1990. reprint ed. pap. 7.95 (0-933499-02-7) Stagecoach Rd Pr.
Blankinship, A. B. State of the Art Marketing Research. (Illus.). 608p. 1994. 44.95 (0-8442-3457-5, NTC Business Bks) NTC Contemp Pub Co.
Blankinship, Khalid Y. The End of the Jihad State: The Reign of Hisham Ibn 'Abd al-Malik & the Collapse of the Umayyads. LC 93-26126. (SUNY Series in Medieval Middle East History). 399p. (C). 1994. text 74.50 (0-7914-1827-8); pap. text 24.95 (0-7914-1828-6) State U NY Pr.
— The End of the Jihad State: The Reign of Hisham Ibn Abd al-Malik & the Collapse of the Umayyids. 350p. 1996. pap. 19.95 (0-614-21109-3, 255) Kazi Pubns.
Blankinship, Khalid Y., tr. The History of al-Tabari Vol. 11: The Challenge to the Empires, A. D. 633-635, A. H. 12-13. LC 90-28420. (SUNY Series in Near Eastern Studies). 261p. (C). 1993. text 59.50 (0-7914-0851-5); pap. text 23.95 (0-7914-0852-3) State U NY Pr.
— The History of al-Tabari Vol. 25: The End of Expansion: The Caliphate of Hisham, A.D. 724-738-A.H. 105-120. LC 87-7125. (SUNY Series in Near Eastern Studies). 219p. (C). 1989. text 59.50 (0-88706-569-4); pap. text 21.95 (0-88706-570-8) State U NY Pr.
Blankinship, Khalid Y., tr. see Al-Tabari.
Blankinship, Marilyn, jt. auth. see Mitsch, Darelyn.
Blankley, Ron. John's Letters: Discovering Genuine Christianity. (LifeGuide Bible Studies). 63p. (Orig.). 1990. pap., wbk. ed. 4.99 (0-8308-1020-X, 1020) InterVarsity.
Blankman, Howard, jt. auth. see Rengier, John.
Blankman, Lynn. Ghost Beyond the Garden. 1996. 9.09 (0-606-10193-4, Pub. by Turtleback) Demco.
Blankman, Peter, et al. Union College: Celebrating Two Centuries, 1795-1995. LC 94-19426. (Illus.). 1994. write for info. (0-89865-906-X) Donning Co.
Blankmeyer, Eric, jt. auth. see Savage, V. Howard.
***Blanks, Billy.** The Tae-Bo Way. LC 99-42801. (Illus.). 264p. 1999. 25.00 (0-553-80100-7) Bantam.
Blanks, D. R. Addictive Disease: A Basic Primer on America's #1 Health Problems. Chapman, Thomas, ed. 180p. 1999. pap. write for info. (0-7392-0249-9, PO3303) Morris Pubng.
Blanks, D. Rodney. The Keeper of the Trees. 194p. (Orig.). 1996. pap. 10.00 (1-57502-326-1, P01096) Morris Pubng.
Blanks, David. Images of the Other: Europe & the Muslim World Before 1700. 140p. 1997. pap. 10.00 (977-424-388-9, Pub. by Am Univ Cairo Pr) Col U Pr.
Blanks, Henry S. Reliability in Procurement & Use: From Specification to Replacement. LC 92-10301. 368p. 1992. 235.00 (0-471-93488-7) Wiley.
Blanks, Mary L. & Holler, Anne. Fun with the Family in New York: Hundreds of Ideas for Day Trips with the Kids. 2nd ed. LC 98-27392. (Fun with the Family Ser.). (Illus.). 224p. 1999. pap. 12.95 (0-7627-0244-3) Globe Pequot.
Blanksby, Brian A., et al. Athletics, Growth, & Development in Children: The University of Western Australia Study. LC 93-47059. 288p. 1994. text 55.00 (3-7186-0578-3) Gordon & Breach.
Blankstein, K. R., jt. auth. see Hartman, L. M.
Blankstein, Kirk R., et al, eds. Self-Control & Self-Modification of Emotional Behavior. (Advances in the Study of Communication & Affect Ser.: Vol. 7). 216p. 1982. 42.50 (0-306-40945-3, Plenum Trade) Perseus Pubng.
Blanksten, George I. Peron's Argentina. LC F 2849.B55. (Midway Reprint Ser.). 494p. reprint ed. pap. 153.20 (0-608-12647-0, 202408300035) Bks Demand.
***Blankston, Carl L.** Sociology Basics. LC 00-36775. (Magill's Choice Ser.). 2000. write for info. (0-89356-207-6) Salem Pr.
Blann, Jack R. A Private's Diary: The Battle of Germany As Seen Through the Eyes of an 18 Year Old Infantry Rifleman. LC 97-93105. (Illus.). 196p. 1997. 24.95 (0-9654653-0-6) J & L Publng.
Blann, Robinson. Throwing the Scabbard Away: Byron's Battle Against the Censors of Don Juan. LC 90-19402. (American University Studies: English Language & Literature: Ser. IV, Vol. 126). VIII, 179p. (C). 1991. text 34.95 (0-8204-1437-9) P Lang Pubng.
Blanning. French Revolution: Aristocrats. 1996. text 11.95 (0-333-36304-3, Pub. by Macmillan) St Martin.
Blanning, T. C. French Revolution: Class War or Culture Clash. 2nd ed. LC 97-9606. 104p. 1998. pap. 11.95 (0-312-17521-3) St Martin.
Blanning, T. C., ed. The Oxford Illustrated History of Modern Europe. LC 98-10536. (Illus.). 372p. 1998. reprint ed. pap. 22.50 (0-19-285348-1) OUP.
Blanning, T. C. W. The French Revolutionary Wars, 1787-1802. (Modern Wars Ser.). (Illus.). 304p. 1996. pap. text 19.95 (0-340-56911-5) OUP.
***Blanning, T. C. W., ed.** The Eighteenth Century: Europe 1688-1815. (Short Oxford History of Europe Ser.). (Illus.). 253p. 2000. pap. 19.95 (0-19-873120-5); text 65.00 (0-19-873181-7) OUP.
— The Nineteenth Century: Europe 1789-1914. (Short Oxford History of Europe Ser.). (Illus.). 260p. 2000. pap. 19.95 (0-19-873135-3); text 65.00 (0-19-873136-1) OUP.
— The Oxford History of Modern Europe. 400p. 2000. pap. 16.95 (0-19-285371-6) OUP.
Blanning, Timothy C. W. Joseph II. LC 93-29516. (Profiles in Power Ser.). (C). 1994. text 50.95 (0-582-05273-4, Pub. by Addison-Wesley) Longman.
— Joseph II Profiles Power. LC 93-29516. (Profiles in Power Ser.). 228p. (C). 1995. pap. text 23.44 (0-582-05272-6, Pub. by Addison-Wesley) Longman.
— The Origins of the French Revolutionary Wars: Origins of Modern Wars. (Origins of Modern Wars Ser.). (Illus.). 226p. (C). 1986. pap. text 26.50 (0-582-49051-0, 73460) Longman.
Blanning, Timothy C. W., ed. The Oxford Illustrated History of Modern Europe. (Oxford Illustrated Histories Ser.). (Illus.). 372p. (C). 1996. 49.95 (0-19-820374-8) OUP.
— The Rise & Fall of the French Revolution. (Studies in European History from the Journal of Modern History). 476p. 1996. pap. 22.50 (0-226-05692-9); lib. bdg. 42.00 (0-226-05691-0) U Ch Pr.
Blanning, Timothy C. W. & Cannadine, David, eds. History & Biography: Essays in Honour of Derek Beales. 207p. (C). 1996. text 59.95 (0-521-47330-6) Cambridge U Pr.
***Blanning, Timothy C. W. & Wende, Peter, eds.** Reform in Great Britain & Germany, 1750-1850. (Proceedings of the British Academy Ser.: Vol. 100). 192p. 1999. text 35.00 (0-19-726201-5) OUP.
Blanpain. Law in Motion: Proceedings of the World Law Conference, Brussels, 1996. LC 97-2852. 1997. 192.00 (90-411-0386-4) Kluwer Law Intl.
— Workers' Participation. 1992. pap. text 84.50 (90-6544-600-1) Kluwer Academic.
Blanpain, Jan, et al. National Health Insurance & Health Resources: The European Experience. LC 77-25818. 320p. 1978. 29.95 (0-674-26955-1) HUP.
Blanpain, R. Comparative Labour Law & Industrial Relations in Industrialized Market Economies. 6th ed. LC 98-230724. 573 p. 1998. 143.00 (90-411-0487-9) Kluwer Law Intl.
— European Labour Law. 6th ed. LC 99-17098. 1999. 96.00 (90-411-1157-3) Kluwer Law Intl.
— Institutional Changes & European Social Policies after the Treaty of Amsterdam. LC 98-19000. (Studies in Social Policy). 1998. 165.00 (90-411-1018-6) Kluwer Law Intl.
Blanpain, R. & Engels, C., eds. Comparative Labour Law & Industrial Relations in Industrialized Market Economies. 6th ed. LC 99-167927. 573p. 1998. student ed. 54.00 (90-411-0556-5) Kluwer Law Intl.
Blanpain, R. & Engels, Christian. European Labour Law. 4th ed. LC 97-6819. 1997. 192.00 (90-411-0395-3) Kluwer Law Intl.
— European Labour Law. 5th ed. LC 98-16778. 1998. pap. 86.00 (90-411-0587-5) Kluwer Law Intl.
Blanpain, R., et al. Labour Law & Industrial Relations at the Turn of the Century: Liber Amicorum in Honour of Professor Roger Blanpain. LC 98-39644. 1998. 216.00 (90-411-1084-4) Kluwer Law Intl.
Blanpain, Roger. Employee Rights. 1994. pap. text 66.50 (90-6544-804-7) Kluwer Academic.
— Labour Law Industrial. 252p. 1998. pap. text 86.00 (90-411-0527-1) Kluwer Law Intl.
— The OECD Guidelines for Multinational Enterprises & Labour Relations: Experience & Mid-Term Report, 1979-1982. 244p. 1983. 75.50 (90-312-0194-4) Kluwer Law Intl.
— OECD Guidelines for Multinational Enterprises & Labour Relations: 1976-1979 Experience & Review. 366p. 1980. lib. bdg. 87.00 (90-312-0108-1) Kluwer Law Intl.
— Part Management. 1993. pap. text 66.50 (90-6544-769-5) Kluwer Academic.
— Public Employee Unionism in Belgium. LC 76-634393. (Comparative Studies in Public Employment Labor Relations Ser.). 1971. 10.00 (0-87736-003-0); pap. 5.00 (0-87736-004-9) U of Mich Inst Labor.
— Strikes & Lock Outs. 1994. pap. text 92.00 (90-6544-841-1) Kluwer Academic.
Blanpain, Roger, ed. Comparative Labour Law & Industrial Relations. 412p. 1982. 26.00 (90-312-0179-0) Kluwer Academic.
— Comparative Labour Law & Industrial Relations in Industrialised Market Economies: Industrial Relations, Vol. II. 4th rev. ed. 262p. 1990. pap. 48.00 (90-6544-495-5) Kluwer Law Intl.
— Comparative Labour Law & Industrial Relations in Industrialised Market Economies: Labour Law, Vol. I. 4th rev. ed. 400p. 1990. pap. 64.00 (90-6544-466-1) Kluwer Law Intl.
— Economic Restructuring & Industrial Relations in Industrialised Countries. (Bulletin of Comparative Labour Relations Ser.: Vol. 20). 240p. 1990. pap. 60.00 (90-6544-488-2) Kluwer Law Intl.
— Equity & Prohibition of Discrimination Employment, Vol. 14. 1985. lib. bdg. 91.00 (90-6544-215-4) Kluwer Academic.
— Flexibility in Wages. (Bulletin of Comparative Labour Relations Ser.: Vol. 19). 360p. 1990. pap. 82.00 (90-6544-461-0) Kluwer Law Intl.
— In Search of Inclusive Unionism. (Bulletin of Comparative Labour Relations Ser.: Vol. 18). 290p. 1990. pap. 54.00 (90-6544-439-4) Kluwer Law Intl.
— International Bibliography of Publications in English & French on Labour Law & Labour Relations in Those Countries Where English & French Are Not Official Languages. (Bulletin of Comparative Labour Relations Ser.: No. 6). 1976. 15.00 (90-312-0023-9) Kluwer Academic.
— The International Encyclopaedia for Labour Law & Industrial Relations, 21 vols., Set. 1989. ring bd. 2855.00 (90-6544-905-1) Kluwer Law Intl.
***Blanpain, Roger, ed.** International Encyclopaedia of Labour Law & Industrial Relations: European Works Council. 300p. 1999. ring bd. 180.00 (90-411-1132-8) Kluwer Law Intl.
— Multinational Enterprises & the Social Challenges of the XXIst Century: The ILO Declaration on Fundamental Principles at Work Public & Private Corporate Codes of Conduct. (Bulletin of Comparative Labour Relations Ser.: Vol. 37). 416p. 1999. pap. text 138.00 (90-411-1280-4) Kluwer Law Intl.
— Private Employment Agencies: The Impact of ILO Convention 181 (1997) & the Judgement of the European Court of Justice of 11 December 1997. (Bulletin of Comparative Labour Relations Ser.: Vol. 36). 414p. 1999. pap. 138.00 (90-411-1118-2) Kluwer Law Intl.
Blanpain, Roger, ed. Restructuring Labour in the Enterprise. (Bulletin of Comparative Labour Relations Ser.: Vol. 15). 152p. 1987. pap. 62.00 (90-6544-283-9) Kluwer Law Intl.
— Temporary Work & Labour Law of the European Community & Member States. LC 92-45138. 1993. 57.00 (90-6544-682-6) Kluwer Law Intl.
— Trade Union Democracy & Industrial Relations. (Bulletin of Comparative Labour Relations Ser.: Vol. 17). 220p. 1989. pap. 62.00 (90-6544-394-0) Kluwer Law Intl.
— Unions & Industrial Relations: Recent Trends & Prospects. (Bulletin of Comparative Labour Relations Ser.: Vol. 16). 220p. 1987. pap. 62.00 (90-6544-294-4) Kluwer Law Intl.
— Women & Labour. (Bulletin of Comparative Labour Relations Ser.: No. 9). 1978. 26.00 (90-312-0077-8) Kluwer Academic.
***Blanpain, Roger, et al, eds.** The Process of Industrialization & the Role of Labor Law in Asian Countries. (Bulletin of Comparative Labour Relations Ser.: Vol. 34). 172p. 1999. pap. 60.00 (90-411-1047-X) Kluwer Law Intl.
***Blanpain, Roger & Biagi, M., eds.** Non-Standard Work & Industrial Relations. (Bulletin of Comparative Labour Relations Ser.: Vol. 35). 200p. 1999. pap. 72.00 (90-411-1117-4) Kluwer Law Intl.
Blanpain, Roger & Engels, C., eds. Comparative Labour Law & Industrial Relations in Industrialised Market Economies. 5th rev. ed. LC 93-5969. 1993. 138.00 (90-6544-742-3) Kluwer Law Intl.
Blanpain, Roger & Engels, Chris. Labour Law & Industrial Relations of the European Community: Maastricht & Beyond. 2nd rev. ed. LC 93-5813. 1993. write for info. (90-6544-741-5) Kluwer Law Intl.
Blanpain, Roger & Kohler, E., eds. Legal & Contractual Limitations to Working-Time in the European Community Member States. 466p. 1988. 84.00 (90-6544-364-9) Kluwer Law Intl.
Blanpain, Roger & Nagy, Lajos. Labour Law & Industrial Relations in Central & Eastern Europe: From Planned to a Market Economy. LC 96-36287. (Bulletin of Comparative Labour Relations Ser.). 1996. pap. 78.50 (90-411-0298-1) Kluwer Law Intl.
Blanpain, Roger, jt. auth. see Hanami, T. A.
Blanpain, Roger, jt. ed. see Hanami, T. A.
Blanpied, John W. Time & the Artist in Shakespeare's English Histories. LC 82-40387. 280p. 1983. 38.50 (0-87413-230-4) U Delaware Pr.
Blanpied, M. L., jt. ed. see Marone, Chris J.
Blanpied, Pamela W. Dragons: The Modern Infestation. (Illus.). 168p. (Orig.). 1997. pap. 19.95 (0-85115-680-0) Boydell & Brewer.
Blanpied, W., jt. ed. see Holton, Gerald.
Blanquez. Diccionario Latino-Espanol, Espanol-Latino, 3 vols., Set. deluxe ed. (LAT & SPA.). 2703p. 395.00 (0-7859-0885-4, S50419) Fr & Eur.
Blansdorf, ed. see Morel & Buchner.
Blansett, Mary L. Put a Book in Their Hands: Whole Language Projects for Beginning Readers. (Illus.). 128p. (Orig.). (J). (ps). 1992. pap. text 12.95 (0-86530-151-4, 197-0) Incentive Pubns.
Blansett, Mary L. & Schimminger, Lorraine. Put a Frog in Your Pocket: Educational Art Activities for Young Children. (Illus.). 112p. (J). (gr. k-6). 1985. pap. text, student ed. 10.95 (0-86530-085-2, IP 85-2) Incentive Pubns.
Blansfeld, Joseph, et al. Resource Document for Nursing Care of the Trauma Patient. 2nd unabridged ed. Welton, Bob & Baker, Pam, eds. (Illus.). 226p. 1997. pap. 15.00 (0-935890-18-1) Emerg Nurses IL.
Blansfield, Karen C. Cheap Rooms & Restless Hearts. LC 87-72837. 143p. (C). 1988. 26.95 (0-87972-420-X) Bowling Green Univ Popular Press.
Blanshard, Audrey. The Blackoke Tyrant. large type ed. 320p. 1995. 27.99 (0-7089-3252-5) Ulverscroft.
— Countess Incognito. large type ed. 1994. 27.99 (0-7089-3162-6) Ulverscroft.
— The Ebford Foundlings. large type ed. 1994. 27.99 (0-7089-3198-7) Ulverscroft.
— The Fearns of Audley Street. 224p. 1980. pap. 1.75 (0-449-50035-7, Coventry) Fawcett.
— The Frensham Inheritance. large type ed. (Historical Romance Ser.). 384p. 1993. 27.99 (0-7089-2928-1) Ulverscroft.
— Granborough's Filly. large type ed. 304p. 1993. 27.99 (0-7089-2873-0) Ulverscroft.
— The Hipsley Reputation. large type ed. 1994. 27.99 (0-7089-3143-X) Ulverscroft.
— The Lydeard Beauty. large type ed. 336p. 1994. 27.99 (0-7089-3037-9) Ulverscroft.
— The Matchmakers. large type ed. (Dales Large Print Ser.). 259p. 1997. pap. 18.99 (1-85389-763-9, Dales) Ulverscroft.
— The Shy Young Denbury. large type ed. (General Ser.). 304p. 1993. 27.99 (0-7089-2835-8) Ulverscroft.
— A Singular Elopement. large type ed. (Romance Ser.). 1994. pap. 16.99 (0-7089-7613-1, Linford) Ulverscroft.
— A Virginian at Venncombe. large type ed. (Historical Romance Ser.). 336p. 1993. 27.99 (0-7089-2946-X) Ulverscroft.
***Blanshard, B.** On Philosophical Style, 1 Vol. 70p. 1999. pap. 18.95 (1-85506-598-3) Thoemmes Pr.
Blanshard, Brand. Four Reasonable Men: Marcus Aurelius, John Stuart Mill, Ernest Renan, Henry Sidgwick. LC 84-2195. 316p. 1984. reprint ed. pap. 98.00 (0-608-03015-5, 206346500006) Bks Demand.
***Blanshard, Brand.** On Philosophical Style. LC 99-49474. (Key Texts Ser.). 2000. pap. text 14.00 (1-890318-53-1) St Augustines Pr.
Blanshard, Brand. On Philosophical Style. LC 69-13830. 69p. 1969. reprint ed. lib. bdg. 55.00 (0-8371-1975-8, BLPS, Greenwood Pr) Greenwood.
— Reason & Belief: Based on Gifford Lectures at St. Andrews & Noble Lectures at Harvard. LC 75-301090. 620p. 1974. write for info. (0-04-230013-4) Allen & Unwin Pty.
— Reason & Belief: Based on Gifford Lectures at St. Andrews & Noble Lectures at Harvard. LC 75-301090. 626p. reprint ed. pap. 194.10 (0-8357-8755-9, 203367300087) Bks Demand.
Blanshard, Brand, ed. Education in the Age of Science. LC 70-142608. (Essay Index Reprint Ser.). 1977. 23.95 (0-8369-2144-5) Ayer.
Blanshard, Catherine. Children & Young People: Library Association Guidelines for Public Library. 2nd ed. 61p. 1997. pap. 35.00 (1-85604-209-X, LAP4209X, Pub. by Library Association) Bernan Associates.
— Providing Library Services to Children & Young People: A Practical Handbook. 192p. 1997. pap. 80.00 (1-85604-226-X, LAP226X, Pub. by Library Association) Bernan Associates.
Blanshard, Frances M. Retreat from Likeness in the Theory of Painting. 2nd ed. LC 72-37913. (Select Bibliographies Reprint Ser.). 1977. reprint ed. 23.95 (0-8369-6733-X) Ayer.
Blanshard, J. M., jt. ed. see Mitchell, J. R.
Blanshard, J. M. V., et al, eds. Chemistry & Physics of Baking Materials, Processes & Products. (Special Publication Ser.: No. 56). (Illus.). 300p. 1986. text. write for info. (0-85186-995-5, Pub. by Royal Soc Chem) Spr-Verlag.
Blanshard, J. M. V. & Lillford, P. J. The Glassy State in Foods. 542p. 1999. 160.00 (1-897676-20-4, Pub. by Nottingham Univ Pr) St Mut.
Blanshard, J. M. V. & Lillford, P., eds. Food Structure & Behaviour. 291p. 1987. text 104.00 (0-12-104230-8) Acad Pr.
Blanshard, J. M. V. & Mitchell, J. R. Food Structure - Its Creation & Evaluation. (Illus.). 504p. 1988. pap. text 299.00 (0-408-02950-1) Buttrwrth-Heinemann.
Blanshard, Paul. American Freedom & Catholic Power. LC 84-19141. 402p. 1984. reprint ed. lib. bdg. 79.50 (0-313-24620-3, BLAF, Greenwood Pr) Greenwood.
— Communism, Democracy, & Catholic Power. LC 75-156175. 350p. 1972. reprint ed. lib. bdg. 69.50 (0-8371-6118-5, BLCD, Greenwood Pr) Greenwood.

Blanshard, Paul, ed. Classics of Free Thought. rev. ed. LC 77-73846. (Skeptic's Bookshelf Ser.). 190p. 1977. pap. 19.95 (*0-87975-421-4*) Prometheus Bks.

Blanshei, J., ed. see Turkevich, John.

Blansit, Frankie C. Fitness Is Fun. (Illus.). 67p. 1980. pap. text 9.95 (*0-89641-035-8*) American Pr.

Blansitt, Edward L., ed. see Georgetown University Round Table Meeting on Lingu.

Blant, Edmont F. Le, see Le Blant, Edmont F.

***Blanthorn, Ouida.** A History of Tooele County. LC 98-61318. (Illus.). 1998. write for info. (*0-913738-44-1*) Utah St Hist Soc.

Blantom, Casey, jt. auth. see Nordstrom, Alison D.

Blanton. Travel Writing. LC 97-18791. Vol. 15. 1997. 33.00 (*0-8057-0967-3*, Twyne) Mac Lib Ref.

Blanton & Whimbey, Arthur. The Whimbey Writing Program: How to Analyze, Organize, & Write Effectively, Sample bklt. 1995. pap., student ed., wbk. ed. write for info. (*1-57004-029-X*) L Erlbaum Assocs.

Blanton & Whimbley, Arthur. The Whimbey Writing Program: How to Analyze, Organize, & Write Effectively, 10 bks., Set. 1995. pap., student ed., wbk. ed. 129.95 (*1-57004-030-3*) L Erlbaum Assocs.

— The Whimbey Writing Program: How to Analyze, Organize, & Write Effectively, 10 bks., Set incl. instr's. manual. 1995. pap., student ed., wbk. ed. 149.95 (*1-57004-026-5*) L Erlbaum Assocs.

***Blanton, Brad.** Practicing Radical Honesty. 2000. 25.00 (*0-9630921-3-8*); pap. 15.00 (*0-9630921-9-7*) Sparrowhawk.

Blanton, Brad. Radical Honesty. 1995. 24.00 (*0-9630921-4-6*) Sparrowhawk.

— Radical Honesty: How to Transform Your Life by Telling the Truth. LC 96-162551. 320p. 1996. pap. 14.95 (*0-440-50754-5*, Dell Trade Pbks) Dell.

— Radical Honesty: How to Transform Your Life by Telling the Truth. (Illus.). 292p. 1994. pap. 15.00 (*0-9630921-2-X*) Sparrowhawk.

— Telling the Truth: Growing Up to Intimacy & Freedom. 300p. 1991. 24.95 (*0-9630921-0-3*) Sparrowhawk.

Blanton, Casey, ed. see Edwards, Elizabeth, et al.

Blanton, Gail. And the Race Goes On. 87p. 1986. 8.99 (*0-8341-9174-1*, MP-637) Lillenas.

— Sarah Mae & Her Kin Folk: Monologues & Dialogues with a Mountain View Point. LC 99-218323. 1997. pap. 15.99 (*0-8341-9656-5*) Lillenas.

— Seniors Centerstage: Sketches Designed for Seniors. 1998. pap. 8.99 (*0-8341-9775-8*) Nazarene.

— The Sheople Incidents. 1995. pap. 8.99 (*0-8341-9438-4*, MP-767) Nazarene.

***Blanton, J. D.** Foundations of Differential Calculus. LC 99-43386. 224p. 2000. 59.95 (*0-387-98534-4*) Spr-Verlag.

Blanton, Linda L. Composition Practice, Bk. 4. 2nd ed. LC 92-41832. 188p. (J). 1993. pap. 20.95 (*0-8384-4075-4*) Heinle & Heinle.

— Composition Practice, Bks. 1 & 2. 2nd ed. 96p. (J). 1988. mass mkt. 20.95 (*0-8384-2943-2*); mass mkt. 20.95 (*0-8384-2942-4*) Heinle & Heinle.

— Composition Practice Bk. 3: A Text for English Language Learners. 2nd ed. LC 92-31028. 146p. (J). 1992. mass mkt. 20.95 (*0-8384-4076-2*, Newbury) Heinle & Heinle.

— Intermediate Composition Practice, Bk I. (C). 1981. mass mkt. 15.00 (*0-8384-2781-2*, Newbury) Heinle & Heinle.

— Intermediate Composition Practice, Bk. 2. (Illus.). 160p. (J). 1983. mass mkt. 15.00 (*0-8384-2987-4*, Newbury) Heinle & Heinle.

— The Multicultural Workshop: A Reading & Writing Program, Bk. 2. (College ESL Ser.). 192p. (J). 1994. mass mkt. 26.95 (*0-8384-4835-6*) Heinle & Heinle.

— The Multicultural Workshop: A Reading & Writing Program, Bk. 3. (College ESL Ser.). 266p. (J). 1995. mass mkt. 26.95 (*0-8384-5020-2*) Heinle & Heinle.

— Writing Workshop: Promoting College Success. LC 98-122219. 256p. (J). 1997. pap. 20.95 (*0-8384-7973-1*) Heinle & Heinle.

Blanton, Linda L. & Lee, Linda. The Multicultural Workshop: A Reading & Writing Program, Bk. 1. LC 93-39447. 192p. (J). 1994. mass mkt. 21.95 (*0-8384-4834-8*) Heinle & Heinle.

— The Reading Box: Multicultural Workshop. 200p. (J). 1995. pap. 291.95 (*0-8384-5021-0*) Heinle & Heinle.

Blanton, Linda P., et al. Teacher Education in Transition. 276p. (C). 1996. pap. text 39.95 (*0-89108-250-6*, 9701) Love Pub Co.

Blanton, Lowell D. The Long Night. rev. ed. (Read-along Radio Dramas Ser.). (J). (gr. 6-9). 1984. ring bd. 38.00 (*1-878298-08-9*) Balance Pub.

Blanton, Lynne & King, Dorothy F. English. LC 97-217622. (Illus.). 128p. 1997. write for info. (*0-7853-1953-0*) Pubns Intl Ltd.

Blanton, Melissa. Water Recycling & Reuse. McClurg, Sue, ed. (Layperson's Guide Ser.). (Illus.). 20p. 1992. pap. 5.00 (*1-893246-50-7*) Water Educ.

***Blanton, Nicholas & Capeille, Valerie.** French Renaissance Dances for the Hammered Dulcimer. 48p. 1998. pap. 19.95 incl. cd-rom (*0-7866-2555-4*) Mel Bay.

Blanton, Paul. The Las Vegas Nightfighters. 108p. 1998. pap. 9.95 (*0-9665355-0-2*) P Blanton.

Blanton, R. E. Houses & Households: A Comparative Study. LC 93-34651. (Interdisciplinary Contributions to Archaeology Ser.). (Illus.). 286p. (C). 1993. 42.50 (*0-306-44444-5*, Kluwer Plenum) Kluwer Academic.

Blanton, Richard, et al. Ancient Oaxaca. (Case Studies in Early Societies). (Illus.). 220p. (C). 1999. text 49.95 (*0-521-57114-6*); pap. text 17.95 (*0-521-57787-X*) Cambridge U Pr.

Blanton, Richard E., et al, eds. Economic Analysis Beyond the Local System. LC 96-14148. (Monographs in Economic Anthropology: No. 13). 330p. (C). 1996. pap. text 31.00 (*0-7618-0342-4*); lib. bdg. 67.50 (*0-7618-0341-6*) U Pr of Amer.

Blanton, Richard E., et al. Ancient Mesoamerica: A Comparison of Change in Three Regions. 2nd ed. (New Studies in Archaeology). (Illus.). 298p. (C). 1993. pap. text 22.95 (*0-521-44606-6*) Cambridge U Pr.

— Ancient Mesoamerica: A Comparison of Change in Three Regions. 2nd ed. (New Studies in Archaeology). (Illus.). 298p. (C). 1993. text 59.95 (*0-521-44053-X*) Cambridge U Pr.

— Monte Alban's Hinterland: The Prehispanic Settlement Patterns of the Central & Southern Parts of the Valley of Oaxaca, Mexico, Pt. 1. (Memoirs Series, Prehistory & Human Ecology of the Valley of Oaxaca: No. 15, Vol. 7). 1982. pap. 20.00 (*0-932206-91-3*) U Mich Mus Anthro.

Blanton, Robert. Defining the New World Order: Economic Regions & Patterns of Global Cooperation. rev. ed. LC 98-46215. (Transnational Business & Corporate Culture Ser.). (Illus.). 212p. 1998. 53.00 (*0-8153-3333-1*) Garland.

Blanton, Tom, ed. White House E-Mail: The Top-Secret Messages the Reagan/Bush White House Thought They Had Destroyed. 256p. (Orig.). 1995. pap. 14.95 (*1-56584-276-6*, Pub. by New Press NY) Norton.

Blanton, Tom, et al. Eyes on the President: History in Essays & Cartoons - George Bush Retrospective. Heagerty, Leo, ed. LC 92-75674. (Illus.). 288p. (Orig.). (YA). (gr. 8 up). 1993. 24.95 (*0-9633624-1-0*); pap. 16.95 (*0-9633624-0-2*) Chronos Pub.

***Blanton, William J.** Mill Hill Pilot. 193p. 1998. 23.95 (*1-57087-375-5*) Prof Pr NC.

Blanton, Wyndham B. Medicine in Virginia in the Eighteenth Century. LC 80-12669. reprint ed. 78.00 (*0-404-13238-3*) AMS Pr.

— Medicine in Virginia in the Seventeenth Century. LC 77-180556. (Medicine & Society in America Ser.). (Illus.). 430p. 1977. reprint ed. 28.95 (*0-405-03936-0*) Ayer.

Blantz, Thomas E. George N. Shuster: On the Side of Truth. LC 92-56867. (C). 1993. text 40.50 (*0-268-01028-5*) U of Notre Dame Pr.

Blanz, W., et al, eds. Machine Vision Applications in Character Recognition & Industrial Inspection. 1992. 20.00 (*0-8194-0815-8*, 1661) SPIE.

Blaricom, Robert Van, see Petersen, Marjorie.

Blarkstone, Harry. 200 Magic Tricks Anyone Can Do. (Illus.). 256p. 1999. pap. 12.00 (*0-8065-2100-7*, Citadel Pr) Carol Pub Group.

Blarney, Kathleen, tr. see Ricoeur, Paul.

Blas, C. & Wiseman, J. The Nutrition of the Rabbit. LC 98-7573. 352p. 1999. text 100.00 (*0-85199-279-X*) OUP.

Blas, Lynette, jt. auth. see Bankhead, Donna.

Blasband. Workbook for Today's Nursing Asstistant. 1998. pap. text, wbk. ed. 24.80 (*0-8359-4986-9*) P-H.

Blasband, Barbara A., jt. auth. see Grubbs, Peggy A.

Blasberg. Paradox 3.5 Einfuhrung und Leitfaden. (GER.). (C). 1991. text. write for info. (*0-201-55972-2*) Addison-Wesley.

Blasch, Bruce B., et al. Foundations of Orientation & Mobility. 2nd ed. 800p. 1997. text 68.95 (*0-89128-946-1*) Am Foun Blind.

Blaschek, Gunther. Object-Oriented Programming with Prototypes in Omega. LC 93-39557. (Illus.). 335p. 1994. 59.00 (*0-387-56469-1*) Spr-Verlag.

Blaschek, Gunther, jt. auth. see Pomberger, Gustav.

***Blaschke, David, et al, eds.** Understanding Deconfinement in QCD. 350p. 1999. 86.00 (*981-02-4063-5*) World Scientific Pub.

Blaschke, Monika. Die Entdeckung des Weiblichen Publikums: Presse Fur Deutsche Einwanderinnen in den U. S. A. 1890-1914. (GER., Illus.). 401p. 1997. 63.95 (*3-631-31028-5*) P Lang Pubng.

Blaschke, Robert P. Astrology - A Language of Life: Progressions. LC 98-94839. (Illus.). x, 150p. 1999. pap. 14.95 (*0-9668978-0-3*) Earthwalk Schl.

Blaschke, W. Projektive Geometrie. 3rd ed. (Mathematische Reihe Ser.: No. 17). (Illus.). 197p. 1980. 39.00 (*0-8176-0032-9*) Birkhauser.

Blaschke, Wieslaw, ed. New Trends in Coal Preparation Technologies & Equipment. (Recent Advances in Coal Processing Ser). 1016p. 1995. text 198.00 (*2-88449-139-2*) Gordon & Breach.

Blaschko, Thomas M., jt. auth. see Burlingame, Joan.

Blasco. Early Intervention. LC 99-49319. 432p. (C). 2000. 62.33 (*0-205-19443-5*) Allyn.

Blasco, Elmer A. The Sporting Goods Agent: A Vital Link. LC 91-157234. (Illus.). 168p. (Orig.). 1991. pap. 25.00 (*0-9630922-0-0*) Spt Gds Agents.

Blasco Ibanez, Vicente. The Four Horsemen of the Apocalypse. 512p. 1983. reprint ed. pap. 8.95 (*0-88184-016-5*) Carroll & Graf.

Blasco-Ibanez, Vicente. Reeds & Mud. Beberfall, Lester, tr. (Orig.). 1966. pap. 7.95 (*0-8283-1470-5*) Branden Bks.

Blasco Ibanez, Vicente, adapted by. Sangre y Arena, Level 4. (Leer en Espanol Ser.). (SPA.). (C). 1998. pap. 6.95 (*84-294-3439-9*) Santillana.

Blasco-Ibanez, Vincente. Arroz y Tartana. (SPA.). 300p. 1978. 10.00 (*0-8288-8560-5*) Fr & Eur.

— Barraca. (SPA.). 234p. 1978. write for info. (*0-8288-8583-4*) Fr & Eur.

— The Four Horsemen of the Apocalypse. 30.95 (*0-8488-0198-9*) Amereon Ltd.

— The Four Horsemen of the Apocalypse. 1982. reprint ed. lib. bdg. 29.95 (*0-89966-384-2*) Buccaneer Bks.

Blasco-Ibanez, Vincenti & Lorente, Mariano J. Last Lion & Other Stories. pap. 5.95 (*0-8283-1444-6*) Branden Bks.

Blasco, James J. How to Live Victoriously: Confessions of a Believing Warrior. LC 88-90660. 160p. (Orig.). 1989. pap. 15.95 (*0-929296-00-1*) Practical Defense Inst.

Blasco, Joaquin & Solis, Fernando L. Harrap's Mini Spanish. (ENG & SPA.). 640p. 1994. pap. 5.95 (*0-13-381005-4*, Harraps IN) Macmillan Gen Ref.

— Harrap's Pocket Spanish. (ENG & SPA.). 640p. 1992. pap. 10.00 (*0-13-381013-5*, Harraps IN) Macmillan Gen Ref.

Blasco, Paloma Gay y, see Gay y Blasco, Paloma.

Blasco Pascual, Francisco J., ed. see Jimenez, Juan Ramon.

Blascovich, Jim & Katkin, Edward S., eds. Cardiovascular Reactivity to Psychological Stress & Disease. (Illus.). 242p. 1993. pap. text 19.95 (*1-55798-337-2*) Am Psychol.

Blase, Betty E. De, see De Blase, Betty E.

Blase, Christoph. Hardware-Software-Artware. 1998. pap. 35.00 (*3-89322-928-0*, Pub. by Edition Cantz) Dist Art Pubs.

Blase, Jo & Blase, Joseph. Handbook of Instructional Leadership: How Really Good Principals Promote Teaching & Learning. LC 97-45258. (One-Off Ser.). (Illus.). 208p. 1998. 61.95 (*0-8039-6553-2*); pap. 27.95 (*0-8039-6554-0*) Corwin Pr.

Blase, Jo, jt. auth. see Blase, Joseph R.

Blase, Jo R., jt. auth. see Blase, Joseph R.

Blase, Jo Roberts, jt. auth. see Blase, Joseph.

***Blase, Joseph & Blase, Jo Roberts.** Empowering Teachers: What Successful Principals Do. 2nd ed. LC 00-8786. 2000. write for info. (*0-7619-7732-5*) Corwin Pr.

Blase, Joseph & Kirby, Peggy C. Bringing Out the Best in Teachers: What Effective Principals Do. 160p. 1992. 43.95 (*2-8106-6009-3*); pap. 18.95 (*2-8106-6010-7*) NEA.

***Blase, Joseph & Kirby, Peggy C.** Bringing Out the Best in Teachers: What Effective Principals Do. 2nd rev. ed. LC 99-6348. (One-Off Ser.). 166p. 1999. 51.95 (*0-8039-6861-2*) Corwin Pr.

— Bringing Out the Best in Teachers: What Effective Principals Do. 2nd rev. ed. LC 99-6348. (One-Off Ser.). 166p. 1999. pap. 22.95 (*0-8039-6862-0*) Corwin Pr.

Blase, Joseph, jt. auth. see Blase, Jo.

Blase, Joseph R., ed. The Politics of Life in Schools: Power, Conflict, & Cooperation. LC 91-13614. 288p. 1991. pap. 26.95 (*0-8039-3893-4*) Corwin Pr.

Blase, Joseph R. & Anderson, Gary L., eds. The Micropolitics of Educational Leadership: From Control to Empowerment. (Teacher Development Ser.). 176p. (C). 1995. pap. text 22.95 (*0-8077-3501-9*) Tchrs Coll.

Blase, Joseph R. & Blase, Jo. The Fire Is Back! Principals Sharing School Governance. LC 96-25240. (Illus.). 184p. 1996. pap. 24.95 (*0-8039-6332-7*) Corwin Pr.

— The Fire Is Back! Principals Sharing School Governance. LC 96-25240. (Illus.). 184p. 1996. 55.95 (*0-8039-6331-9*) Corwin Pr.

Blase, Joseph R. & Blase, Jo R. Empowering Teachers: What Successful Principals Do. LC 94-30531. 192p. 1994. 55.95 (*0-8039-6091-3*); pap. 24.95 (*0-8039-6092-1*) Corwin Pr.

Blase, Joseph R. & Kirby, Peggy C. Bringing Out the Best in Teachers: What Effective Principals Do. LC 91-32153. 160p. 1991. pap. 19.95 (*0-8039-6010-7*, D1478) Corwin Pr.

— Bringing Out the Best in Teachers: What Effective Principals Do. LC 91-32153. 160p. 1991. 45.95 (*0-8039-6009-3*, D1478) Corwin Pr.

Blase, Joseph R., et al. Democratic Principals in Action: Eight Pioneers. LC 94-45029. 192p. 1995. 55.95 (*0-8039-6131-6*); pap. 24.95 (*0-8039-6132-4*) Corwin Pr.

Blase, Melvin G., jt. auth. see Van Dyne, Donald L.

Blasecki, John W., ed. Mechanisms of Immunity to Virus-Induced Tumors. LC 81-163. (Immunology Ser.: No. 12). 368p. reprint ed. pap. 114.10 (*0-7837-0942-0*, 204124700019) Bks Demand.

Blaser, A., ed. Natural Language at the Computer. (Lecture Notes in Computer Science Ser.: Vol. 320). iii, 176p. 1988. 30.00 (*0-387-50011-1*) Spr-Verlag.

Blaser, A., et al, eds. Database Systems of the 90s: International Symposium Muggelsee, Berlin, FRG, November 5-7, 1990 Proceedings. (Lecture Notes in Computer Science Ser.: Vol. 466). viii, 334p. 1990. 38.00 (*0-387-53397-4*) Spr-Verlag.

Blaser, Arthur. Evolving Worlds of Human Rights: The International Nongovernmental Organizations. Date not set. pap. 26.50 (*0-8133-7727-7*) Westview.

Blaser, H. U. Symposium on Heterogeneous Catalysis, et al. Heterogeneous Catalysis & Fine Chemicals IV: Proceedings of the 4th International Symposium on Heterogeneous Catalysis & Fine Chemicals, Basel, Switzerland, September 8-12, 1996, Vol. 108. LC 97-3265. (Studies in Surface Science & Catalysis). 676p. 1997. 316.50 (*0-444-82390-5*) Elsevier.

Blaser, Jurgen, ed. see Goslesagentstvo Staff, et al.

Blaser, K., ed. Regulatory Process in Allergy & Asthma. (Journal: International Archives of Allergy & Applied Immunology: Vol. 90, Suppl. 1). (Illus.). iv, 76p. 1990. pap. text 33.25 (*3-8055-5152-5*) S Karger.

Blaser, Martin J., et al, eds. Infections of the Gastrointestinal Tract. LC 95-2610. (Illus.). 1616p. 1995. text 267.00 (*0-7817-0226-7*) Lppncott W & W.

Blaser, Martin J., jt. ed. see Nachamkin, Irving.

Blaser, Robin. The Holy Forest. LC 94-122933. 416p. 1993. pap. 26.95 (*0-88910-435-2*, Pub. by Talonbks) Genl Dist Srvs.

— Pell Mell. 128p. 1988. pap. 11.95 (*0-88910-339-9*, Pub. by Talonbks) Genl Dist Srvs.

— Syntax. (NFS Canada Ser.). 1993. pap. 8.95 (*0-88922-209-6*) Genl Dist Srvs.

***Blaser, Robin, et al.** Etruscan Reader Vol. VI: Robin Blaser/Barbara Guest/Lee Harwood. 134p. 1998. pap. 13.95 (*1-901538-08-7*, Pub. by etruscan bks) SPD-Small Pr Dist.

Blaser, Robin, ed. see Spicer, Jack.

***Blaser, Werner.** An Architect Meets Architects: English/german. (Illus.). 120p. 2000. pap. 35.00 (*3-7643-6314-2*) Birkhauser.

Blaser, Werner. Atrium. (Illus.). 205p. 1985. 49.00 (*3-85977-080-2*, Pub. by Wepf & Co) H B Fenn Co.

— Chagall Lithographe V, 1974-1979: Catalogue Raisonne. (FRE., Illus.). 252p. (gr. 9 up). 1984. 200.00 (*0-8150-0019-7*) Wittenborn Art.

— Courtyard House in China: Tradition & Present. 2nd ed. (Illus.). 128p. 1995. 39.50 (*3-7643-5227-2*, Pub. by Birkhauser) Princeton Arch.

— Filigree Architecture: Metal & Glass Construction. (ENG, FRE & GER., Illus.). 216p. 1980. pap. 19.00 (*0-89192-298-9*, Pub. by Wepf & Co) H B Fenn Co.

— Helmut Jahn Airports. (Illus.). 204p. 1991. 48.00 (*3-7643-2613-1*, Pub. by Birkhauser) Princeton Arch.

— Mies van der Rohe. 2nd ed. LC 97-13753. (Studio Paperback Ser.). (Illus.). 248p. 1997. pap. 29.95 (*3-7643-5619-7*, Pub. by Birkhauser) Princeton Arch.

***Blaser, Werner.** Mies Van der Rohe: Farnsworth House: Weekend House. LC 99-42388. (Illus.). 84p. 1999. pap. 29.95 (*3-7643-6089-5*) Birkhauser.

— Mies Van Der Rohe: Farnsworth House: Weekend House = Wochenendhaus. LC 99-42388. 1999. write for info. (*0-8176-6089-5*) Birkhauser.

— Mies van der Rohe: Lake Shore Drive Apartments: High Rise Building. LC 99-48031. (Illus.). 80p. 1999. pap. 29.95 (*3-7643-6090-9*) Birkhauser.

Blaser, Werner. Mies van der Rohe: The Art of Structure: Die Kunst Der Struktur. enl. rev. ed. LC 92-46540. xi, 227p. 1993. 45.70 (*0-8176-2848-7*, Pub. by Birkhauser) Princeton Arch.

— Mies Van Der Rohe: West Meets East. (Illus.). 132p. 1996. 50.00 (*3-7643-5430-5*, Pub. by Birkhauser) Princeton Arch.

— Richard Meier: Building for Art. (Illus.). 176p. 1990. 29.50 (*3-7643-2326-4*, Pub. by Birkhauser) Princeton Arch.

— Richard Meier: Details. LC 96-46684. (Illus.). 168p. 1996. 80.00 (*3-7643-5403-8*, Pub. by Birkhauser) Princeton Arch.

— Richard Meier: Weishaupt Forum. (Illus.). 96p. 1993. 65.00 (*3-7643-2847-9*, Pub. by Birkhauser) Princeton Arch.

— The Temple & the Teahouse in Japan. (ENG & GER.). 180p. 1988. 132.00 (*0-8176-1963-1*) Birkhauser.

— Transformation, Livio Vacchini. (Illus.). 168p. 1997. 98.00 (*3-7643-2987-4*, Pub. by Birkhauser) Princeton Arch.

— Werner Sobek: Art of Engineering. LC 99-11571. (Illus.). 176p. 1999. 75.00 (*3-7643-6001-1*, Pub. by Birkhauser) Princeton Arch.

— Werner Sobek: Art of Engineering - Ingenieur-Kunst. LC 99-11571. 1999. write for info. (*0-8176-6001-1*) Birkhauser.

— Wood Houses. (Illus.). 1985. 38.00 (*3-85977-079-9*, Pub. by Wepf & Co) H B Fenn Co.

— Wood Houses: Form in Rural Architecture. 2nd ed. (ENG, FRE & GER., Illus.). 216p. 1985. pap. 19.00 (*0-89192-300-4*, Pub. by Wepf & Co) H B Fenn Co.

Blaser, Werner, ed. Chicago Architecture: Holabird & Root, 1880-1992. (GER., Illus.). 192p. 1996. 65.00 (*3-7643-2787-1*, Pub. by Birkhauser) Princeton Arch.

— Helmut Jahn - Transparency. (Illus.). 204p. 1996. 80.00 (*3-7643-5154-3*, Pub. by Birkhauser) Princeton Arch.

— Norman Foster: Sketch Book. (Illus.). 112p. 1993. pap. 42.00 (*3-7643-2837-1*, Pub. by Birkhauser) Princeton Arch.

***Blaser, Werner & Muller, Lars, eds.** Christa de Carouge: Habit-Habitat. (Illus.). 160p. 2000. 85.00 (*3-907078-15-2*, Pub. by Lars Muller) Princeton Arch.

Blaser, Werner, ed. see Horden, Richard.

Blaser, Werner, ed. see Jahn, Helmut.

Blashaw, Brian, jt. auth. see Davis, Vance A.

Blashfield, Edwin H. & Wilbour, Evangeline. Italian Cities, 2 vols. 1976. lib. bdg. 250.00 (*0-8490-2085-9*) Gordon Pr.

Blashfield, Evangeline. Portraits & Backgrounds. LC 73-134054. (Essay Index Reprint Ser.). 1977. 30.95 (*0-8369-2103-8*) Ayer.

Blashfield, Jean. Villains of Volturnus. 1983. 2.00 (*0-394-71547-0*) Random.

Blashfield, Jean, jt. auth. see Star, Cima.

Blashfield, Jean F. Antarctica. LC 94-40911. (Wonders of the World Ser.). (Illus.). 64p. (J). 1995. lib. bdg. 25.64 (*0-8114-6366-4*) Raintree Steck-V.

— The Awesome Almanac: Illinois. LC 92-74707. 1993. 20.10 (*0-606-09019-3*, Pub. by Turtleback) Demco.

Blashfield, Jean F. The Awesome Almanac: Minnesota. LC 92-74710. 1994. 18.43 (*0-606-09022-3*, Pub. by Turtleback) Demco.

Blashfield, Jean F. Awesome Almanacs: Illinois. rev. ed. (J). (gr. 4-12). 1994. pap. 14.95 (*1-880190-50-8*) B&B Pub.

— Awesome Almanacs: Minnesota. (J). (gr. 4-12). 1993. pap. 12.95 (*1-880190-07-9*) B&B Pub.

— Calcium. LC 98-4518. (Sparks of Life Ser.). (J). 1999. 27.12 (*0-8172-5040-9*) Raintree Steck-V.

***Blashfield, Jean F.** The California Gold Rush. (We the People Ser.). (Illus.). 48p. (J). 2000. write for info. (*0-7565-0041-9*) Compass Point.

Blashfield, Jean F. Carbon. LC 98-4517. (Sparks of Life Ser.). (J). 1999. 27.12 (*0-8172-5041-7*) Raintree Steck-V.

— Colorado. LC 98-19855. (America the Beautiful Ser.). 144p. (YA). (gr. 5-8). 1999. 32.00 (*0-516-20684-2*) Childrens.

B

*Blashfield, Jean F. Delaware. LC 99-48164. (America the Beautiful Ser.). (J). 2000. 33.00 (0-516-21090-4) Childrens.
Blashfield, Jean F. Galapagos Islands. LC 94-3030. (Wonders of the World Ser.). (Illus.). 64p. (J). (gr. 4-7). 1994. lib. bdg. 25.64 (0-8114-6362-1) Raintree Steck-V.
— Horse Soldiers: Cavalry in the Civil War. LC 97-8525. (A First Book). 64p. (J). (gr. 5-7). 1998. 22.00 (0-531-20300-X) Watts.
— Hydrogen. LC 98-4524. (Sparks of Life Ser.). (J). 1999. 27.12 (0-8172-5038-7) Raintree Steck-V.
— Italy. LC 98-45227. (Enchantment of the World Ser.). 144p. (YA). (gr. 5-9). 1999. lib. bdg. 32.00 (0-516-20960-4) Childrens.
*Blashfield, Jean F. Leonard Bernstein: Conductor & Composer. LC 00-37580. (Career Biographies Ser.). 2000. write for info. (0-89434-337-8) Ferguson.
Blashfield, Jean F. Mines & Minie Balls: Weapons of the Civil War. LC 96-32157. (First Bks.). (J). 1997. lib. bdg. 22.00 (0-531-20273-9) Watts.
— Nitrogen. LC 98-4534. (Sparks of Life Ser.). (J). 1999. 27.12 (0-8172-5039-5) Raintree Steck-V.
— Norway. LC 99-21552. (Enchantment of the World Ser.). (Illus.). 144p. (gr. 5-9). 2000. 32.00 (0-516-20651-6) Childrens.
*Blashfield, Jean F. The Oregon Trail. (We the People Ser.). (Illus.). 48p. (J). 2000. write for info. (0-7565-0045-1) Compass Point.
Blashfield, Jean F. Oxygen. LC 98-4508. (Sparks of Life Ser.). (J). 1999. 27.12 (0-8172-5037-9) Raintree Steck-V.
*Blashfield, Jean F. The Santa Fe Trail. (We the People Ser.). (Illus.). 48p. (J). 2000. write for info. (0-7565-0047-8) Compass Point.
Blashfield, Jean F. Sodium. LC 98-15236. (Sparks of Life Ser.). (J). 1999. 27.12 (0-8172-5042-5) Raintree Steck-V.
— Sparks of Life. 1998. 113.88 (0-8172-5043-3) Raintree Steck-V.
— Virginia. LC 98-38560. (America the Beautiful Second Ser.). 144p. (YA). (gr. 5-8). 1999. 32.00 (0-516-20831-4) Childrens.
*Blashfield, Jean F. Washington. LC 00-29512. (America the Beautiful Ser.). (Illus.). (J). 2001. write for info. (0-516-21095-5) Childrens.
Blashfield, Jean F. Wisconsin. 2nd ed. LC 97-49198. (America the Beautiful Ser.). (J). 1998. 32.00 (0-516-20640-0) Childrens.
— Women at the Front: Their Changing Roles in the Civil War. LC 96-31319. (First Bks.). (J). 1997. lib. bdg. 22.00 (0-531-20275-5) Watts.
— Women Inventors 4. (Illus.). 48p. (J). (gr. 3-7). 1995. 19.00 (0-516-35277-6) Childrens.
— Women Inventors 1. (Illus.). 48p. (J). (gr. 3-7). 1995. 19.00 (0-516-35275-X) Childrens.
— Women Inventors 3. (Illus.). 48p. (J). (gr. 3-7). 1995. 19.00 (0-516-35274-1) Childrens.
— Women Inventors 2. (Illus.). 48p. (J). (gr. 3-7). 1995. 19.00 (0-516-35276-8) Childrens.
Blashfield, Jean F., jt. auth. see Black, Wallace B.
Blashfield, R. K. The Classification of Psychopathology: Neokraepelinian & Quantitative Approaches. LC 83-26871. (Illus.). 354p. (C). 1984. 80.00 (0-306-41405-8, Plenum Trade) Perseus Pubng.
Blashfield, Roger K., jt. auth. see Aldenderfer, Mark S.
Blashford-Snell, Victoria, jt. auth. see Treuille, Eric.
Blashill, Lorraine. Remembering the Fifties: Growing up in Western Canada. (Illus.). 144p. 1997. pap. 26.95 (1-55143-091-6) Orca Bk Pubs.
Blashko, H., et al. Reviews of Physiology, Biochemistry & Pharmacology, Vol. 98. (Illus.). 260p. 1983. 93.00 (0-387-12817-4) Spr-Verlag.
Blasi, Anthony J. Making Charisma: The Social Construction of Paul's Public Image. 170p. (C). 1991. 39.95 (0-88738-400-5) Transaction Pubs.
— Organized Religion & Seniors' Mental Health. LC 99-11322. 128p. 1999. 37.00 (0-7618-1347-0); pap. 22.50 (0-7618-1348-9) U Pr of Amer.
— A Sociology of Johannine Christianity. LC 96-41014. (Texts & Studies in Religion: Vol. 69). 456p. 1997. text 109.95 (0-7734-8753-0) E Mellen.
Blasi, Anthony J. & Cuneo, Michael W. The Sociology of Religion: An Organizational Bibliography. LC 90-40684. 490p. 1990. text 25.00 (0-8240-2584-9, SS612) Garland.
Blasi, F., jt. auth. see Allegra, L.
Blasi, F., jt. auth. see Allegra, Luigi.
Blasi, Gene. Louisville's Early Medicine Bottles. (Illus.). 95p. 1992. pap. write for info. (0-9645406-0-6) G Blasi.
— Postcard Views of Louisville from 1900 to 1920: A Picture Postcard History. (Illus.). 107p. 1994. pap. write for info. (0-9645406-1-4) G Blasi.
Blasi, Joseph R. Communal Experience of the Kibbutz. 275p. (C). 1986. 44.95 (0-88738-056-5); pap. 24.95 (0-88738-611-3) Transaction Pubs.
— Employee Ownership. 1990. pap. 18.95 (0-88730-443-5, HarpBusn) HarpInfo.
— Employee Ownership: Revolution or Ripoff? 352p. 1988. 29.95 (0-88730-065-0, HarpBusn) HarpInfo.
— The New Owners: The Mass Emergence of Employee Ownership & What It Means to American Business. LC 91-58513. 224p. 1991. 27.95 (0-88730-509-1, HarpBusn) HarpInfo.
Blasi, Joseph R., et al. Kremlin Capitalism: Privatizing the Russian Economy. LC 96-33557. (ILR Press Book Ser.). 160p. 1996. pap. 16.95 (0-8014-8396-4); text 45.00 (0-8014-3351-7) Cornell U Pr.
Blasi, Marlena De, see De Blasi, Marlena.
Blasi, Ronald W. 1999 Bank Tax Guide. rev. ed. Bond, Kris, ed. 850p. 1999. pap. 175.00 (0-8080-0340-2) CCH INC.
Blasi, Ronald W. 2000 Bank Tax Guide. Bond, Kris, ed. 1000p. pap. text 195.00 (0-8080-0487-5) CCH INC.
Blasi, Susan, jt. auth. see Delacenserie, Emily.
*Blasi, Vera. Woman on Top: A Sexy Delicious Fairytale. (Illus.). 80p. 2000. 18.95 (0-06-039396-3, ReganBks) HarperTrade.
Blasi, Vincent. The Burger Court: The Counter-Revolution That Wasn't. LC 83-5828. 320p. 1986. pap. 20.00 (0-300-03620-5) Yale U Pr.
— Law & Liberalism in the 1980s. 1991. text 46.00 (0-231-07198-1) Col U Pr.
Blasier, Clarence L. May I Share Something with You Someone Once Shared with Me? (Illus.). 96p. (Orig.). 1994. pap. 6.95 (0-9625444-2-6) Matthew OH.
Blasier, Clarence L., compiled by. My Book of Bible Promises. 303p. 1998. lthr. 4.97 (1-55748-154-7) Barbour Pub.
Blasier, Cole. The Hovering Giant: U. S. Responses to Revolutionary Change in Latin America, 1910-1985. rev. ed. LC 85-40335. (Latin American Ser.). (Illus.). 384p. (C). 1985. pap. 19.95 (0-8229-5372-2) U of Pittsburgh Pr.
Blasier, Stewart C., ed. Constructive Change in Latin America. LC 68-12724. 269p. reprint ed. pap. 83.40 (0-608-15647-7, 203190000077) Bks Demand.
Blasing, Mutlu K. American Poetry. LC 86-22395. 272p. 1987. 37.50 (0-300-03793-7) Yale U Pr.
— Politics & Form in Postmodern Poetry: O'Hara, Bishop, Ashbery, & Merrill. (Studies in American Literature & Culture: No. 94). 235p. (C). 1995. text 59.95 (0-521-49607-1) Cambridge U Pr.
Blasing, Randy. Double House of Life. 64p. 1989. pap. 9.95 (0-89255-143-7) Persea Bks.
— Graphic Scenes: Poems. 72p. (Orig.). 1994. pap. 10.00 (0-89255-202-6) Persea Bks.
— The Particles. LC 83-10052. 57p. (Orig.). 1983. pap. 8.00 (0-914278-40-1) Copper Beech.
— To Continue. 75p. (Orig.). (C). 1983. pap. 5.95 (0-89255-071-6) Persea Bks.
Blasing, Randy, tr. see Hikmet, Nazim.
*Blasing, Rebecca Ondov. The Once in a Blue Moon Boot Bus. LC 00-24226. (Illus.). (J). 2000. 10.99 (0-7814-3439-4) Cook Communs Minist.
*Blasing, T. J. Environmental Assessment Renewal of Material Licenses for Alaron Corp. Northeast Regional Service Facility, Wampum, Pennsylvania. 57p. 1998. pap. 5.00 (0-16-062981-0) USGPO.
*Blasingame, Gerry D. Treatment for Developmentally Disabled Persons with Sexual Behavior Problems: Community-Based Treatment, Management & Supervision of Sexual Behavior Problems among Developmentally Disabled Persons. 2001. pap. 29.95 (1-885473-45-1) Wood N Barnes.
Blasingame, Ike. Dakota Cowboy: My Life in the Old Days. LC 58-11667. (Illus.). 317p. Date not set. pap. 14.95 (0-8032-5015-0, Bison Books) U of Nebr Pr.
Blasio, Mary-Amm, jt. compiled by see Kyvig, David E.
Blasiola, George. The New Saltwater Aquarium Handbook. 144p. 1991. pap. 9.95 (0-8120-4482-7) Barron.
Blasiola, George C. Koi: Everything about Selection, Care, Nutrition, Diseases, Breeding, Pond Design & Maintenance, & Popular Aquatic Plants. LC 95-7036. 1995. pap. 6.95 (0-8120-3568-2) Barron.
*Blasiola, George C. & Vriends, Matthew M. The Saltwater Aquarium Handbook: Everything about Setting up a Marine Aquarium, Aquarium Conditioning & Maintenance, Selecting Fish & Invertebrates, Nutrition & Disease Control. rev. ed. LC 99-26660. (Pet Handbks.). 144p. 2000. pap. 9.95 (0-7641-1241-4) Barron.
Blasis, Celeste De, see De Blasis, Celeste.
Blasius, Chip & Blasius, Ralfie. Earning More Funds. 185p. 1992. spiral bd. 21.95 (0-9638524-0-X, TX 3627 707) B C Creations.
— Earning More Funds: Fundraising Strategies. 3rd rev. ed. (Illus.). 180p. 1995. pap. 19.95 (0-9638524-1-8) B C Creations.
*Blasius, Chip & Blasius, Ralphie. Fundraise Painlessly: How to Earn More Funds. (Illus.). 192p. 1999. reprint ed. pap. 19.95 (1-890394-18-1) Rhodes & Easton.
Blasius, Jorg & Greenacre, Michael L. Visualization of Categorical Data. LC 97-35782. (Illus.). 594p. 1998. text 74.95 (0-12-299045-5) Morgan Kaufmann.
Blasius, Jorg, jt. auth. see Greenacre, Michael.
Blasius, Karl H., et al, eds. Sorts & Types in Artificial Intelligence. (Lecture Notes in Artificial Intelligence Ser.: Vol. 418). viii, 307p. 1990. 36.00 (0-387-52337-5) Spr-Verlag.
Blasius, Karl H. & Burchert, Hans-Jurgen, eds. Deduction Systems in Artificial Intelligence. (Artificial Intelligence Ser.). 1989. text 39.95 (0-470-21550-X) P-H.
Blasius, Leslie D. The Music Theory of Godfrey Winham. LC 97-5562. 208p. 1997. text 35.00 (0-691-01227-X, Pub. by Princeton U Pr) Cal Prin Full Svc.
— Schenker's Argument & the Claims of Music Theory. (Cambridge Studies in Music Theory & Analysis: No. 9). 172p. (C). 1996. text 54.95 (0-521-55085-8) Cambridge U Pr.
Blasius, Mark. Gay & Lesbian Politics: Sexuality & the Emergence of a New Ethic. LC 93-40681. 240p. (C). 1994. text 69.95 (1-56639-173-3); pap. text 22.95 (1-56639-174-1) Temple U Pr.
*Blasius, Mark. Identity/Space/Power: Lesbian, Gay, Bisexual & Transgender Politics. (Illus.). 368p. 2001. 60.00 (0-691-05866-0); pap. 19.95 (0-691-05867-9) Princeton U Pr.
Blasius, Mark & Phelan, Shane, eds. We Are Everywhere: A Historical Sourcebook of Gay & Lesbian Politics. 600p. (C). (gr. 13). 1992. pap. 24.99 (0-415-90859-0, B2938) Routledge.
— We Are Everywhere: A Historical Sourcebook of Gay & Lesbian Politics. 600p. (C). (gr. 13). 1997. 80.00 (0-415-90858-2, B2934) Routledge.
Blasius, Ralfie, jt. auth. see Blasius, Chip.
Blasius, Ralphie, jt. auth. see Blasius, Chip.
Blaska, Joan K. Using Children's Literature to Learn about Disabilities & Illness. 168p. (C). 1996. pap. text 19.95 (1-886979-07-3) Practicl Pr.
*Blaskas, Janet. Easy Exercises for Pregnancy. (Illus.). 1999. pap. text 14.95 (0-7112-1048-9) F Lincoln.
Blaski, Steven. Keep the Killer Asleep. 83p. (Orig.). 1994. pap. 9.95 (0-932112-34-X) Carolina Wren.
Blasko, Andrew, ed. see Zviglyanich, Vladimir A.
Blaskovic, D., et al. Studies on Tick-Borne Encephalitis. (Bulletin of WHO Ser.: Suppl. No. 1 to Vol. 36). 94p. 1967. pap. 9.00 (92-4-068361-5, 1033601) World Health.
Blaskower, Pat. The Art of Doubles: Winning Tennis Strategies. LC 93-31933. (Illus.). 144p. 1994. pap. 14.99 (1-55870-330-6, Betrwy Bks) F & W Pubns Inc.
Blasowiak, S. & Kaczkowski, Z. Iterative Methods Structural Analysis. LC 63-12799. 1966. 258.00 (0-08-010015-5, Pub. by Pergamon Repr) Franklin.
Blasquiz, Klaus. The Fender Bass. 48p. 1991. per. 9.95 (0-7935-0757-X, 00183681) H Leonard.
Blass. Newtonian Casino. 1990. text. write for info. (0-582-05752-3, Pub. by Addison-Wesley) Longman.
— Reflection & Beyond. (J). 1993. student ed. 23.95 incl. audio (0-8384-4136-X) Heinle & Heinle.
Blass, ed. Dinarchi. (GRE.). 1967. reprint ed. pap. 17.95 (3-519-01270-7, T1270, Pub. by B G Teubner) U of Mich Pr.
Blass, A., jt. auth. see Scedrov, Andrej.
Blass, A. R., ed. Omega-Bibliography of Mathematical Logic, Vol. V. (Perspectives in Mathematical Logic Ser.). li, 790p. 1987. 355.00 (0-387-15525-2) Spr-Verlag.
Blass, Bill, jt. auth. see Molinsky, Steven J.
Blass, E. M. Developmental Psychobiology & Behavioral Ecology. LC 87-38501. (Handbook of Behavioral Neurobiology Ser.: Vol. 9). (Illus.). 476p. (C). 1988. text 115.00 (0-306-42728-1, Kluwer Plenum) Kluwer Academic.
— Developmental Psychobiology & Developmental Neurobiology. LC 85-19276. (Handbook of Behavioral Neurobiology Ser.: Vol. 8). (Illus.). 348p. (C). 1986. text 95.00 (0-306-42034-1, Kluwer Plenum) Kluwer Academic.
Blass, Elliott M. & Ciaramitaro, Vivian. A New Look at Some Old Mechanisms in Human Newborns: Taste & Tactile Determinants of State, Affect, & Action. (Monographs of the Society for Research in Child Development: No. 239). 112p. 1994. pap. text 15.00 (0-226-05699-6) U Ch Pr.
Blass, F. & Debrunner, A. Greek Grammar of the New Testament & Other Early Christian Literature. Funk, Robert W., tr. 1990. 54.99 (0-310-24780-2, 18076) Zondervan.
Blass, Friedrich. Die Attische Beredsamkeit, 3 vols. in 4, Set. 2321p. 1979. reprint ed. 480.00 (3-487-00305-8) G Olms Pubs.
— Die Griechische Beredsamkeit in Dem Zeitraum Von Alexander Bis Auf Augustus. (GER.). viii, 234p. 1977. reprint ed. 55.00 (3-487-06340-9) G Olms Pubs.
— Die Interpolationen in der Odyssee. 306p. 1973. reprint ed. 55.00 (3-487-04817-5) G Olms Pubs.
Blass, Gerhard A. Theoretical Physics. LC 62-8896. (ACC Series in Physics). 465p. reprint ed. pap. 144.20 (0-608-12393-5, 205568200030) Bks Demand.
*Blass, John P. & McDowell, Fletcher H., eds. Oxidative/Energy Metabolism in Neurodegenerative Disorders. 1999. write for info. (1-57331-209-6) NY Acad Sci.
Blass, John P., jt. ed. see Khachaturian.
Blass, Kimbery S., et al. Atlanta Scenes. (Images of America Ser.). (Illus.). 128p. 1998. pap. 16.99 (0-7524-0893-3) Arcadia Publng.
*Blass, Laurie. Quest: Listening & Speaking in the Academic World, Bk. 2. 288p. (C). 1999. pap. 22.50 (0-07-006252-8) McGrw-H Hghr Educ.
Blass, Laurie & Baky, Meredith P. Worldbeat: Current Readings for ESL Students. 176p. (C). 1991. 22.81 (0-07-005866-0) McGraw.
Blass, Laurie & Pike-Baky, Meredith. Mosaic Two: A Content-Based Writing Book. 3rd ed. LC 95-82405. xix, 242 p. 1996. write for info. (0-07-114513-3) McGraw.
Blass, Laurie, jt. auth. see Hartmann, Pamela.
Blass, Piotr & Lang, Jeffrey. Zariski Surfaces & Differential Equations in Characteristic P<O. (Pure & Applied Mathematics Ser.: Vol. 106). (Illus.). 456p. 1987. text 169.75 (0-8247-7637-2) Dekker.
Blass, Regina. Relevance Relations in Discourse: A Study with Special Reference to Sissala. (Cambridge Studies in Linguistics: No. 55). (Illus.). 296p. (C). 1990. text 69.95 (0-521-38515-6) Cambridge U Pr.
Blass, Rosanne J., jt. auth. see Jurenka, Nancy A.
Blass, Thomas, ed. Obedience to Authority: Current Perspectives on the Milgram Paradigm. LC 99-30504. 300p. 1999. write for info. (0-8058-2737-4) L Erlbaum Assocs.
Blass, Virginia A. Loaves & Fishes: From Faith Experience to Empowered Community. LC 95-30887. 128p. (Orig.). 1996. pap. 11.95 (0-8091-3614-7) Paulist Pr.
*Blassa, Peter. The Transfiguration of the Novel. (Studies in Modern Philology: No. 14). 176p. 1999. pap. 32.00 (963-05-7654-6, Pub. by Akade Kiado) Intl Spec Bk.
Blasse, G., et al, contrib. by. Complex Chemistry. (Structure & Bonding Ser.: Vol. 76). (Illus.). 208p. 1991. 111.95 (0-387-53499-7) Spr-Verlag.
Blasse, G. & Grabmaier, B. C. Luminescent Materials. LC 94-20336. 1994. 62.95 (0-387-58019-0) Spr-Verlag.
Blasser Riley, Gail. Miranda vs. Arizona: Rights of the Accused. LC 93-34380. (Landmark Supreme Court Cases Ser.). (Illus.). 128p. (YA). (gr. 6 up). 1994. lib. bdg. 20.95 (0-89490-504-X) Enslow Pubs.
Blassie, Dee & Wynn, Mychal. Building Dreams: Teacher Activity Book. Smith, Denise, ed. (Illus.). (Orig.). 1995. pap. 29.95 (1-880463-45-8) Rising Sun.
Blassie, Richard R. De, see De Blassie, Richard R.
Blassingame, Carol & Cross, Thomas S. Success in Bowling: Through Practical Fundamentals. 80p. 1993. per. 9.95 (0-8403-8570-6) Kendall-Hunt.
Blassingame, John W. Black New Orleans, 1860-1880. LC 72-97664. (Illus.). xviii, 302p. 1976. reprint ed. pap. text 4.95 (0-226-05708-9, P662) U Ch Pr.
— The Slave Community: Plantation Life in the Ante-Bellum South. 2nd enl. rev. ed. (Illus.). 432p. 1979. pap. text 23.95 (0-19-502563-6) OUP.
Blassingame, John W., ed. Slave Testimony: Two Centuries of Letters, Speeches, Interviews, & Autobiographies. LC 75-18040. (Illus.). lxvi, 777p. 1977. pap. text 19.95 (0-8071-0273-3) La State U Pr.
Blassingame, John W., et al. Antislavery Newspapers & Periodicals, Vol. II: Annotated Index of Letters in the Liberator, Anti-Slavery Record, Human Rights & Observer, 1846-1865. 1980. 95.00 (0-8161-8434-8, Hall Reference) Macmillan.
Blassingame, John W., jt. auth. see Berry, Mary F.
Blassingame, John W., ed. see Douglass, Frederick.
Blassingame, W. Doak. The Blassingame Families, Vol. 1. LC 73-92924. (Illus.). 1974. 28.85 (0-8418-4594-8) Blassingame Family.
— The Blassingame Families, Vol. 2. (Illus.). 555p. 1988. 47.82 (0-9620041-2-X) Blassingame Family.
Blassingame, Wyatt. His Kingdom for a Horse. LC 75-81263. (Short Story Index Reprint Ser.). (Illus.). 1977. 19.95 (0-8369-3015-0) Ayer.
Blassingame, Wyatt. Look-it-Up Book of Presidents. (J). 1996. 14.09 (0-606-11574-9, Pub. by Turtleback) Demco.
Blassingame, Wyatt. The Look-It-Up Book of Presidents. rev. ed. LC 89-10519. (Illus.). 176p. (J). (gr. 4-7). 1990. pap. 8.99 (0-679-80358-0, Pub. by Random Bks Yng Read) Random.
— The Look-It-Up Book of Presidents. rev. ed. LC 89-10519. (Illus.). (J). (gr. 5-9). 1990. lib. bdg. 14.99 (0-679-90353-4, Pub. by Random Bks Yng Read) Random.
Blassingame, Wyatt, jt. auth. see Cottman, Evans W.
Blassingname, John W. Black New Orleans, 1860-1880. LC 72-97664. (Illus.). 319p. Date not set. reprint ed. pap. 98.90 (0-608-20582-6, 205454700003) Bks Demand.
Blasutti, Dan. Spiritual Warrior. LC 98-13000. 105p. Date not set. write for info. (0-9681262-0-0) R B Luce.
Blaszak, Barbara J. George Jacob Holyoake & the Development of the British Cooperative Movement, 1817-1906. LC 88-9467. (Studies in British History: Vol. 13). 180p. 1989. lib. bdg. 79.95 (0-88946-454-5) E Mellen.
*Blaszak, Barbara J. The Matriarchs of England's Cooperative Movement: Female Leadership & Gender Politics Within the English Cooperative Movement, 56. LC 99-4303. (Contributions in Labor Studies: No. 56). 224p. 1999. 59.95 (0-313-30995-7, Greenwood Pr) Greenwood.
Blaszak, Maaiej & Mickiewicz, A. Multi-Hamiltonian Theory of Dynamical Systems. Balian, R. et al, eds. LC 98-22162. (Texts & Monographs in Physics). (Illus.). x, 353p. 1998. 59.95 (3-540-64251-X) Spr-Verlag.
Blaszak, Mike & Schafer, Mike. Railroad Photography: How to Shoot Like the Pros. (Illus.). 64p. (Orig.). 1993. pap. text 24.95 (0-944119-10-7) Andover Junction.
Blaszcynski, Alex, et al. The Road Ahead: A Self-Help Guide for Road Trauma Sufferers & Their Carers. 96p. 1998. pap. 19.95 (0-86840-688-0, Pub. by New South Wales Univ Pr) Intl Spec Bk.
*Blaszczak, Mike. Professional MFC with Visual C++ 6.0. 1203p. 1999. 64.99 (1-86100-015-4) Wrox Pr Inc.
Blaszczak, Mike. Revolutionary Guide to MFC 4 Programming with Visual C++ 2nd rev. ed. Dobson, Julian & Stockton, Alex, eds. LC 95-61789. 900p. (Orig.). 1996. pap. 49.95 (1-874416-92-3) Wrox Pr Inc.
*Blaszczyk, Regina Lee. Imagining Consumers: Design & Innovation from Wedgwood to Corning. LC 99-15428. (Studies in Industry & Society). 368p. 1999. 39.95 (0-8018-6193-4) Johns Hopkins.
Blatas, Arbit. An Artist's Venice. LC 96-3065. (Illus.). 136p. 1997. text 45.00 (0-86565-984-2) Vendome.
Blatch, Harriot S. Challenging Years: The Memoirs of Harriot Stanton Blatch. (American Biography Ser.). 347p. 1991. reprint ed. lib. bdg. 79.00 (0-7812-8026-5) Rprt Serv.
— Mobilizing Women-Power. LC 74-75231. (United States in World War I Ser.). (Illus.). iv, 195p. 1974. reprint ed. lib. bdg. 26.95 (0-89198-094-6) Ozer.
Blatch, Harriot S., jt. auth. see Stanton, Theodore.
Blatch, Mervyn. A Guide to London's Churches. (Illus.). 450p. 1998. 19.95 (0-09-474630-3, Pub. by Constable & Co) Trafalgar.
Blatchford, ed. History into Practice. 1992. pap. text. write for info. (0-582-08825-9, Pub. by Addison-Wesley) Longman.
Blatchford & Head, eds. Shakespeare: The Tempest. (Longman Literature Ser.). 1994. pap. text. write for info. (0-582-22583-3, Pub. by Addison-Wesley) Longman.
Blatchford, Barbara. Long Distance Walkers' Handbook. 6th ed. (Illus.). 288p. 1998. pap. 19.95 (0-7136-4835-X, 93301, Pub. by A & C Blk) Midpt Trade.
Blatchford, Claire. Friend of My Heart: Meeting Christ in Everyday Life. LC 98-54163. 160p. 1999. pap. 14.95 (0-940262-94-0, Lindisfarne) Anthroposophic.
Blatchford, Claire H. Going with the Flow. LC 97-10011. (First Person Ser.). (Illus.). 39p. (J). (gr. 2-3). 1997. lib. bdg. 19.93 (1-57505-069-2, Carolrhoda) Lerner Pub.
— Going with the Flow. (Illus.). 40p. (J). 1998. pap. 7.95 (1-57505-284-9, Carolrhoda) Lerner Pub.

An Asterisk (*) at the beginning of an entry indicates that the title is appearing for the first time.

B

— Nick's Mission. LC 95-856. (J). 1995. lib. bdg. 19.95 (*0-8225-0740-4*, Lerner Publctns) Lerner Pub.

***Blatchford, Claire H.** Nick's Secret. LC 00-8274. (Mysteries Ser.). (Illus.). 180p. (J). (gr. 4-7). 2000. 19.93 (*0-8225-0743-9*, Carolrhoda) Lerner Pub.

Blatchford, Clare. Full Face: A Correspondence about Becoming Deaf in Mid-Life. LC 97-179598. 1997. pap. 9.95 (*1-884362-21-4*) Butte Pubns.

Blatchford, E. Blatchford: Memorial II: A Genealogy Record of the Family of Rev. Samuel Blatchford. (Illus.). 123p. 1990. reprint ed. pap. 21.00 (*0-8328-1579-9*); reprint ed. lib. bdg. 31.00 (*0-8328-1578-0*) Higginson Bk Co.

Blatchford, John. Narrative of John Blatchford: Detailing His Sufferings in the Revolutionary War. (American Biography Ser.). 127p. 1991. reprint ed. lib. bdg. 59.00 (*0-7812-8027-3*) Rprt Serv.

— Narrative of John Blatchford: Detailing His Sufferings in the Revolutionary War While a Prisoner with the British. LC 70-140855. (Eyewitness Accounts of the American Revolution Ser.). (Illus.). 1971. reprint ed. 14.95 (*0-405-01216-0*) Ayer.

Blatchford, Peter. Social Life in School: Pupils' Experiences of Breaktime & Recess from 6 to 16. LC 98-179236. 1998. 79.00 (*0-7507-0743-7*, Falmer Pr); pap. 26.95 (*0-7507-0742-9*, Falmer Pr) Taylor & Francis.

— Warthog of Wartonia: A Play of Young People. limited unabridged ed. 36p. (J). (gr. 3-10). 1998. 8.00 (*1-56439-072-1*) Ridgeway.

Blatchford, Peter, jt. auth. see Pellegrini, Anthony.

Blatchford, Roy, ed. see Bronte, Emily Jane.

Blatchford, Roy, ed. see Shakespeare, William.

Blatchley, Jeremy, ed. see Silverman, Samuel.

Blatchley, Mary E., jt. auth. see Holle, Mary L.

Blatchly, John. The Town Library of Ipswich Provided for the Use of the Town Preachers in 1599: A History & Catalogue. (Illus.). 214p. 1989. 75.00 (*0-85115-517-0*) Boydell & Brewer.

Blate, Michael. Acupressure Handbook. 88p. 1995. pap. 9.95 (*0-8050-0146-8*) H Holt & Co.

Blate, Sam, ed. Tuesday Nights with Rosa Aurora: A Story Anthology. (Illus.). 194p. 1998. pap. 12.00 (*0-9666330-0-8*) Howlin Wolf.

Blatherwick, David E. The International Politics of Telecommunications. LC 87-3509. (Research Ser.: No. 68). viii, 109p. (C). 1987. pap. text 8.95 (*0-87725-168-1*) U of Cal IAS.

Blathwayt, Benedict. Kip - a Dog's Day. (Illus.). 32p. (J). (gr. k-2). 1996. 18.95 (*1-85681-592-7*, Pub. by Julia MacRae) Trafalgar.

— The Runaway Train. 32p. (J). (gr. 1-4). 1997. pap. 9.95 (*0-09-938571-6*) Trafalgar.

Blatner, Adam. Acting-In: Practical Applications of Psychodramatic Methods. 3rd rev. ed. LC 95-49848. (Illus.). 224p. 1996. pap. 32.95 (*0-8261-1402-4*) Springer Pub.

***Blatner, Adam.** Foundations of Psychodrama: History, Theory & Practice. 4th ed. LC 99-59299. 304p. 2000. pap. 42.95 (*0-8261-6041-7*) Springer Pub.

Blatner, Adam & Blatner, Allee. The Art of Play: Helping Adults Reclaim Imagination & Spontaneity. rev. ed. LC 96-49930. 208p. 1997. pap. 24.95 (*0-87630-844-2*) Brunner-Mazel.

— Foundations of Psychodrama: History, Theory & Practice. 3rd ed. 224p. 1988. pap. 33.95 (*0-8261-6040-9*) Springer Pub.

Blatner, Allee, jt. auth. see Blatner, Adam.

Blatner, David. The Joy of Pi. LC 97-23705. (Illus.). 160p. (gr. 9-12). 1997. 18.00 (*0-8027-1332-7*) Walker & Co.

— The Joy of Pi. (Illus.). 144p. 1999. reprint ed. pap. 12.00 (*0-8027-7562-4*) Walker & Co.

— The QuarkXPress 4 Book. Davis, Nancy, ed. LC 98-228953. 964p. (C). 1998. pap. 34.95 (*0-201-69695-9*, Pub. by Peachpit Pr) Addison-Wesley.

Blatner, David & Fraser, Bruce. Real World Photoshop 5. 3rd ed. LC 99-196875. (Real World Ser.). 736p. (C). 1998. pap. text 44.99 (*0-201-35375-X*, Pub. by Peachpit Pr) Addison-Wesley.

Blatner, David & Fraser, Bruce. Real World Photoshop 4. 2nd ed. LC 97-222190. 672p. (C). 1997. pap. text 44.95 (*0-201-68888-3*) Peachpit Pr.

Blatner, David & Weibel, Bob. The QuarkXPress Book for Windows. 2nd ed. (Illus.). 708p. (C). 1995. pap. text 29.95 (*1-56609-135-7*) Peachpit Pr.

Blatner, David, et al. QuarkXPress Tips & Tricks. 2nd ed. (Illus.). 456p. 1995. pap. 34.95 incl. cd-rom (*1-56609-137-3*) Peachpit Pr.

— Real World Scanning & Halftones. 2nd ed. 464p. (C). 1998. pap. text 29.95 (*0-201-69683-5*, Pub. by Peachpit Pr) Addison-Wesley.

Blatnica, Dorothy A. At the Altar of Their God: African American Catholics in Cleveland, 1922-1961. 9412th ed. LC 94-32943. (Studies in African American History & Culture). (Illus.). 272p. 1994. text 57.00 (*0-8153-1933-9*) Garland.

Blatnik, Andrej. Skinswaps. Soban, Tamara, tr. from SLV. LC 98-34133. (Writings from an Unbound Europe Ser.). 109p. 1998. 39.95 (*0-8101-1656-1*); pap. 14.95 (*0-8101-1657-X*) Northwestern U Pr.

Blaton, Victor H. & Van Steirteghem, A., eds. Plasma Isoenzymes: The Current Status. (Advances in Clinical Enzymology Ser.: Vol. 3). (Illus.). viii, 208p. 1986. 155.75 (*3-8055-4321-2*) S Karger.

***Blatt.** The French Defeat of 1940. 2000. 24.50 (*1-57181-226-1*) Berghahn Bks.

Blatt. Modern Physics. 1992. student ed. 20.62 (*0-07-005878-4*) McGraw.

— 100 Greatest Baseball Players of All Time. 1998. 10.00 (*0-671-01177-4*, Pocket Books) PB.

***Blatt & Tracy.** Petrology: Igneous Sedimentary & Metamorphic. 3rd ed. 2000. pap. text. write for info. (*0-7167-3743-4*) W H Freeman.

Blatt, jt. ed. see Diamond.

Blatt, A. H., ed. Organic Syntheses: Collective Volumes, Vol. 2. 644p. 1943. 135.00 (*0-471-07986-3*) Wiley.

Blatt, Burton & Kaplan, Fred. Christmas in Purgatory: A Photographic Essay on Mental Retardation. (Illus.). 1974. 12.25 (*0-937540-00-5*, HPP-3) Human Policy Pr.

***Blatt, Burton, et al.** In Search of the Promise Land: The Collected Papers of Burton Blatt. LC 99-21914. 181p. 1999. 34.95 (*0-940898-63-2*) Am Assn Mental.

Blatt, Charles, jt. auth. see Graboys, Thomas.

Blatt, Charles M., jt. auth. see Graboys, Thomas B.

Blatt, Ethal S., jt. auth. see Blatt, Sidney J.

Blatt, Frank J. Modern Physics. 517p. (C). 1992. 85.63 (*0-07-005877-6*) McGraw.

— Physics: For Scientists & Engineers - Solutions, Vol. 1. 4th ed. 1998. pap. write for info. (*1-57259-514-0*) Worth.

— Principles of Physics. 3rd ed. 912p. 1989. teacher ed. write for info. (*0-318-63881-9*, H17866); pap., student ed. 10.67 (*0-685-44214-4*, H19391); pap., student ed. 21.00 (*0-685-22014-1*, H17858); write for info. (*0-318-63882-7*, H19540); trans. write for info. (*0-318-63883-5*, H21546) P-H.

Blatt, Gloria T., ed. Once upon a Folktale: Capturing the Folktale Process with Children. LC 92-36897. 208p. (C). 1993. pap. text 18.95 (*0-8077-3232-X*) Tchrs Coll.

Blatt, Harvey. Laboratory Exercises in Environmental Geology. 192p. (C). 1993. spiral bd. write for info. (*0-697-17071-3*, WCB McGr Hill) McGrw-H Hghr Educ.

— Laboratory Exercises in Environmental Geology. 2nd ed. 224p. (C). 1997. text. write for info. (*0-697-28288-0*, WCB McGr Hill) McGrw-H Hghr Educ.

— Our Geologic Environment. LC 96-30973. 541p. 1997. pap. text 70.67 (*0-13-371022-X*) P-H.

Blatt, Harvey, jt. auth. see Ehlers, Ernest G.

Blatt, Howard. Dream Team III: Quest for the Gold. (J). 1996. mass mkt. 4.50 (*0-671-00369-0*) PB.

— Fast Breaks: The NBA's 10 Greatest Teams Ever. (Illus.). 96p. (J). (gr. 2-5). 1999. pap. 4.99 (*0-590-01090-5*) Scholastic Inc.

— Magic! Against the Odds. LC 97-134542. (J). 1996. mass mkt. 4.50 (*0-671-00301-1*) PB.

— NBA Fun Facts & Trivia LC 99-163139. 46p. (J). 1998. write for info. (*0-590-03271-2*) Scholastic Inc.

— This Championship Season: The Incredible Story of the 1998 New York Yankees 125 Win Season. (Orig.). 1998. mass mkt. 6.99 (*0-671-03596-7*) PB.

Blatt, Joel, ed. The French Defeat of 1940: Reassessments. LC 96-53856. 384p. 1998. 69.00 (*1-57181-109-5*) Berghahn Bks.

Blatt, John M. Dynamic Economic Systems: A Post-Keynesian Approach. LC 82-24013. 370p. (gr. 13). 1984. text 76.95 (*0-87332-215-0*); pap. text 40.95 (*0-87332-306-8*) M E Sharpe.

Blatt, John M. & Weisskopf, Victor F. Theoretical Nuclear Physics. (Illus.). 878p. 1991. reprint ed. pap. 19.95 (*0-486-66827-4*) Dover.

Blatt, Martin, ed. The Collected Works of Ezra H. Heywood. 392p. 1985. 35.00 (*0-87730-013-5*) M & S Pr.

Blatt, Martin, ed. see Eastern National Park Staff.

Blatt, Martin H. Free Love & Anarchism: The Biography of Ezra Heywood. LC 88-36734. (Illus.). 240p. 1989. text 26.95 (*0-252-01638-6*) U of Ill Pr.

***Blatt, Martin H., et al, eds.** Hope & Glory: Essays on the Legacy of the 54th Massachusetts Regiment. 2000. 34.95 (*1-55849-277-1*) U of Mass Pr.

Blatt, Martin H. & Norkunas, Martha K., eds. Work, Recreation, & Culture: Essays in American Labor History. LC 95-46207. (Labor in America Ser.: Vol. 02). 288p. 1996. text 55.00 (*0-8153-1650-X*, SS955) Garland.

Blatt, Marvin B. & Schwab, Norman. Seeing Double, the Autopen Guide. 80p. (Orig.). 1986. pap. 7.95 (*0-937991-00-7*) La La Ltd.

Blatt, Max, compiled by. Index to Monthly Review: May 1949-April 1981. LC 81-85233. 1983. 25.00 (*0-85345-585-6*, Pub. by Monthly Rev) NYU Pr.

Blatt, Sidney J. & Blatt, Ethal S. Continuity & Change in Art: The Development of Modes of Representation. 432p. (C). 1984. text 89.95 (*0-89859-342-5*) L Erlbaum Assocs.

Blatt, Sidney J. & Ford, R. Q. Therapeutic Change: An Object Relations Perspective. (Applied Clinical Psychology Ser.). (Illus.). 336p. (C). 1994. 49.50 (*0-306-44601-4*, Plenum Trade) Perseus Pubng.

Blatt, Sidney J., jt. ed. see Segal, Zindel V.

Blatt, Thomas T. From the Ashes of Sobibor: A Story of Survival. LC 97-5455. (Jewish Lives Ser.). 1997. 49.95 (*0-8101-1221-3*); pap. text 15.95 (*0-8101-1302-3*) Northwestern U Pr.

***Blatt, Thomas T.** Sobibor: The Forgotton Revolt. 5th ed. (Illus.). 240p. 2000. reprint ed. pap. 15.00 (*0-9649442-0-0*, Pub. by Holocaust Educ) Partners Pubs Grp.

Blatt, Warren. Resources for Jewish Genealogy in the Boston Area. (Illus.). 284p. 1996. text 25.00 (*0-9652151-0-5*) Jewish Geneal Soc.

Blatt, Warren, jt. auth. see Mokotoff, Gary.

Blattberg. Marketing Information Revolution. 1993. 39.95 (*0-07-103428-5*) McGraw.

***Blattberg, Charles.** From Pluralist to Patriotic Politics: Putting Practices First. LC 99-45062. 312p. 2000. text 85.00 (*0-19-829688-6*) OUP.

Blattberg, Robert C. Sales Promotion. 1995. pap. text 23.60 (*0-13-442302-X*) P-H.

Blattberg, Robert C., et al, eds. The Marketing Information Revolution. LC 93-15849. 384p. 1994. 35.00 (*0-87584-329-8*) Harvard Busn.

Blatteis, Clark M., ed. Physiology & Pathophysiology of Temperature Regulation. 120p. 1998. 18.00 (*981-02-3172-5*) World Scientific Pub.

— Thermoregulation Vol. 813: Tenth International Symposium on the Pharmacology of Thermoregulation. LC 97-329. 1997. 170.00 (*1-57331-088-3*) NY Acad Sci.

— Thermoregulation Vol. 813: 10th International Symposium on the Pharmacology of Thermoregulation. LC 97-329. xvi, 878 p. 1997. pap. 170.00 (*1-57331-089-1*) NY Acad Sci.

Blattel, Harry. International Dictionary Miniature Painters, Porcelain Printers, & Silhouettists. (Illus.). 1424p. 1997. 195.00 (*3-928263-11-0*, Pub. by Arts & Antiques) Seven Hills Bk.

— International Dictionary of Miniature Painters. (ENG, FRE & GER.). 1422p. 1992. 595.00 (*0-7859-9991-4*) Fr & Eur.

— International Dictionary of Miniature Painters: English-German-French. (ENG, FRE & GER.). 1422p. 1992. 495.00 (*0-7859-8570-0*, 3928263110) Fr & Eur.

— Wine & Price. 2nd ed. 1964p. 1997. 159.00 (*3-928263-22-6*, Pub. by Arts & Antiques) Seven Hills Bk.

Blattel, Harry & Stainless, Frank, eds. Wine & Price, 1997: International Auction Results Wine & Spirits. 1700p. 1997. 64.00 (*3-928263-21-8*, Pub. by Arts & Antiques) Seven Hills Bk.

Blattenberger, David E., 3rd. Rethinking 1 Corinthians 11:2-16 Through Archaeological & Moral-Rhetorical Analysis. LC 97-17799. (Studies in the Bible & Early Christianity: Vol. 36). 108p. 1997. text 59.95 (*0-7734-8562-7*) E Mellen.

Blattenberger, Ruth, ed. see Leach, Robert J.

Blatter, Alfred. Instrumentation - Orchestration. 427p. 1980. 35.00 (*0-02-873250-2*, Schirmer Books) Mac Lib Ref.

— Instrumentation Orchestration. 2nd ed. LC 96-33608. 1997. 40.00 (*0-02-864570-7*, Hall Reference) Macmillan.

Blatter, Andreas, jt. auth. see Von Allmen, Martin.

Blatter, Christian. Wavelets: A Primer. LC 98-29959. (Illus.). 212p. (C). 1998. text 32.00 (*1-56881-095-4*) AK Peters.

Blatter, E. Beautiful Flowers of Kashmir, Set. 1983. reprint ed. 395.00 (*0-7855-6635-X*, Pub. by Intl Bk Distr) St Mut.

— Beautiful Flowers of Kashmir, Vols. 1 & 2. 402p. 1984. reprint ed. pap. 750.00 (*81-7089-011-X*, Pub. by Intl Bk Distr) St Mut.

— The Ferns of Bombay. (C). 1978. text 95.00 (*0-89771-559-4*, Pub. by Intl Bk Distr) St Mut.

— The Ferns of Bombay. 1228p. 1978. reprint ed. 110.00 (*0-7855-6636-8*, Pub. by Intl Bk Distr) St Mut.

— The Palms of British India & Ceylon. (C). 1978. text 500.00 (*0-89771-557-8*, Pub. by Intl Bk Distr) St Mut.

— The Palms of British India & Ceylon. 600p. 1978. reprint ed. 300.00 (*0-7855-6637-6*, Pub. by Intl Bk Distr) St Mut.

— Records of the Botanical Survey of India Vol. 8, No. 1, Pt. 1: Flora Arabica, Rancinul. 69p. (C). 1978. 80.00 (*0-7855-3245-5*, Pub. by Scientific) St Mut.

Blatter, E., ed. Beautiful Flowers of Kashmir, Vols. 1-2. (C). 1984. 125.00 (*0-7855-2280-8*, Pub. by Scientific) St Mut.

Blatter, E. & Hallberg, F. The Flora of the Indian Desert. 125p. (C). 1984. 125.00 (*81-85046-09-3*, Pub. by Scientific) St Mut.

Blatter, E. & McCann, C. The Bombay Grasses. (Scientific Monograph - The Imperial Council of Agricultural Research Ser.: No. 5). 326p. (C). 1988. 250.00 (*0-7855-3252-8*, Pub. by Scientific) St Mut.

Blatter, George J., tr. see Agreda, Mary.

***Blatter, Joachim & Ingram, Helen, eds.** Reflections on Water: New Approaches to Transboundary Conflicts & Cooperation. (American & Comparative Environmental Policy Ser.). (Illus.). 356p. 2001. 62.00 (*0-262-02487-X*) MIT Pr.

— Reflections on Water: New Approaches to Transboundary Conflicts & Cooperation. (American & Comparative Environmental Policy Ser.). (Illus.). 356p. (C). 2001. pap. 25.00 (*0-262-52284-5*) MIT Pr.

Blatter, Joerg. Grothendieck Spaces in Approximation Theory. LC 52-42839. (Memoirs Ser.: No. 1/120). 121p. 1972. pap. 16.00 (*0-8218-1820-1*, MEMO/1/120) Am Math.

Blatti, Gloria, ed. The Pocket Guide to CPR for Infants & Children. LC 99-207577. 128p. 1998. per. 3.99 (*0-671-00975-3*) PB.

Blatti, Jo, compiled by. Women's History in Minnesota: A Survey of Published Sources & Dissertations. LC 93-15751. (Illus.). xv, 124p. (Orig.). 1994. pap. 14.95 (*0-87351-291-X*) Minn Hist.

Blatties, Clark M., jt. auth. see Fregly, Melvin J.

Blattmachr, Jonathan. Wealth Preservation for Closely Held Business Owners. 672p. 1998. 74.95 (*0-89526-352-1*) Regnery Pub.

***Blattmachr, Jonathan G.** Complete Guide to Wealth Preservation & Estate Planning. (Illus.). 2000. 165.00 (*0-89526-254-1*) Regnery Pub.

Blattmachr, Jonathan G. & Michaelson, Arthur M. Income Taxation of Estates & Trusts. 14th ed. 350p. 1995. ring bd. 135.00 (*0-614-17125-3*, J1-1473) PLI.

Blattman, George. The Sun: The Ancient Mysteries & a New Physics.Tr. of Die Sonne. 240p. 1985. pap. text 16.95 (*0-88010-148-2*) Anthroposophic.

Blattmann, Ekkehard. Heinrich Mann - Die Bildvorlagen Zum Henri Quatre-Roman. (GER., Illus.). 450p. 1997. 95.95 (*3-631-45932-7*) P Lang Pubng.

***Blattner, Don.** Seven Wonders of the World & More. (Illus.). 96p. (YA). (gr. 5). 1998. pap. text 10.95 (*1-58037-073-X*, Pub. by M Twain Media) Carson-Dellos.

— U. S. History Maps. (Illus.). 96p. (YA). (gr. 5). 1999. pap. text 10.95 (*1-58037-109-4*, Pub. by M Twain Media) Carson-Dellos.

***Blattner, Don & Blattner, Lisa.** Classroom Publishing. (Illus.). 112p. (YA). (gr. 5-8). 1998. pap. text 11.95 (*1-58037-034-9*, Pub. by M Twain Media) Carson-Dellos.

— Health, Wellness, & Physical Fitness. (Illus.). 96p. (YA). (gr. 5-8). 1997. pap. text 10.95 (*1-58037-022-5*, Pub. by M Twain Media) Carson-Dellos.

***Blattner, Don & Howerton, Lisa.** Disasters. (Illus.). 144p. (YA). (gr. 5-8). 1999. pap. text 12.95 (*1-58037-101-9*, Pub. by M Twain Media) Carson-Dellos.

Blattner, Don & Shireman, Myrl. Algebra Class Test. (Illus.). 112p. (YA). (gr. 5). 1996. pap. text 11.95 (*1-58037-057-8*, Pub. by M Twain Media) Carson-Dellos.

— Math in American History. (Illus.). 96p. 1997. pap. text 10.95 (*1-58037-117-5*, Pub. by M Twain Media) Carson-Dellos.

— Math in Geography. (Illus.). 96p. 1997. pap. text 10.95 (*1-58037-139-6*, Pub. by M Twain Media) Carson-Dellos.

— Math in Weather. (Illus.). 96p. 1997. pap. text 10.95 (*1-58037-113-2*, Pub. by M Twain Media) Carson-Dellos.

— Understanding Math Through Writing & Reading. (Illus.). 96p. 1997. pap. text 10.95 (*1-58037-118-3*, Pub. by M Twain Media) Carson-Dellos.

Blattner, E. Bosquejos Homileticos.Tr. of Sermon Outlines & Homileties. (SPA.). 192p. 1972. pap. 5.99 (*0-8297-0511-2*) Vida Pubs.

— Tabernaculo.Tr. of Tabernacle. (SPA.). 52p. 1964. pap. 1.99 (*0-8297-0601-1*) Vida Pubs.

Blattner, J. Wray. Clean Air Compliance Handbook. 2nd ed. (Environmental Compliance Handbook Ser.: Vol. 2). 136p. 1994. pap. 90.00 (*0-471-11261-5*) Wiley.

Blattner, Karl. Englische fur Kaufleute: English for Business Correspondence Guide. 17th ed. (ENG & GER.). 472p. 1980. reprint ed. 49.95 (*0-7859-5670-0*, 3468401205) Fr & Eur.

Blattner, Karl, et al. Langenscheidt German-Russian Pocket Dictionary: Langenscheidt Taschenwoerterbuch Deutsch-Russich. 10th ed. (GER & RUS.). 604p. 1981. 29.95 (*0-8288-1236-5*, F19670) Fr & Eur.

— Langenscheidt Russian-German Pocket Dictionary: Langenscheidt Taschenwoerterbuch Russisch-Deutsch. 13th ed. (GER & RUS.). 568p. 1981. 29.95 (*0-8288-1237-3*, F19680) Fr & Eur.

Blattner, Lisa, jt. auth. see Blattner, Don.

Blattner, N., et al, eds. Banking in Switzerland. (Studies in Contemporary Economics). vii, 329p. 1993. 71.95 (*0-387-91474-9*) Spr-Verlag.

— Competitiveness in Banking. (Studies in Contemporary Economics). (Illus.). 315p. 1992. pap. 59.00 (*0-387-91418-8*) Spr-Verlag.

Blattner, Patrick. Microsoft Excel 2000: Function Reference. 1999. pap. 29.99 (*0-7897-2045-0*) Que.

Blattner, Patrick, et al. Using Microsoft Word & Excel in Office 2000. (Special Edition Using... Que Ser.). (Illus.). 1344p. 1999. pap. 34.99 (*0-7897-1929-0*) Que.

Blattner, Teresa. People of Color Vol. 2: Black Genealogical Records & Abstracts from MO Sources. 170p. 1998. pap. 18.00 (*0-7884-0927-1*, B403) Heritage Bk.

Blattner, Teresa L. Gasconade County, Missouri, Marriage Records, Books A-C, 1821-1873. (Illus.). 152p. (Orig.). 1995. pap. text 16.50 (*0-7884-0174-2*) Heritage Bk.

Blattner, William A., ed. Human Retrovirology: HTLV. LC 90-8204. (Illus.). 500p. 1990. reprint ed. pap. 155.00 (*0-608-05789-4*, 205975400007) Bks Demand.

Blattner, William D. Heidegger's Temporal Idealism. LC 98-24491. (Modern European Philosophy Ser.). 336p. (C). 1999. 54.95 (*0-521-62067-8*) Cambridge U Pr.

Blatty, William P. The Exorcist. 1995. reprint ed. lib. bdg. 35.95 (*1-56849-609-5*) Buccaneer Bks.

— The Exorcist: 25th Anniversary Edition. aut. limited ed. 353p. 1997. 65.00 (*1-887368-09-4*) Gauntlet.

Blatty, William Peter. The Exorcist. 400p. 2000. mass mkt. 6.50 (*0-06-100722-6*, Harp PBks) HarpC.

Blatz, Iomogene & Zimmer, Alard. Threads from Our Tapestry: Benedictine Women in Central Minnesota. LC 94-8627. 1994. pap. 14.95 (*0-87839-085-5*) North Star.

Blatz, Perry K. Democratic Miners: Work & Labor Relations in the Anthracite Coal Industry, 1875-1925. LC 93-843. (SUNY Series in American Labor History). (Illus.). 368p. (C). 1994. pap. text 21.95 (*0-7914-1820-0*) State U NY Pr.

— Democratic Miners: Work & Labor Relations in the Anthracite Coal Industry, 1875-1925. LC 93-843. (SUNY Series in American Labor History). (Illus.). 368p. (C). 1994. text 64.50 (*0-7914-1819-7*) State U NY Pr.

Blatz, William E. Collected Studies on the Dionne Quintuplets. LC 74-21401. (Classics in Child Development Ser.). (Illus.). 294p. 1975. reprint ed. 42.95 (*0-405-06454-3*) Ayer.

— Human Security: Some Reflections. LC 66-486. 147p. reprint ed. pap. 45.60 (*0-608-30642-8*, 201413800089) Bks Demand.

Blau, Abram. The Master Hand: A Study of the Origin & Meaning of Right & Left Sidedness & Its Relation to Personality & Language. LC 78-72790. (Brainedness, Handedness, & Mental Abilities Ser.). reprint ed. 49.50 (*0-404-60854-X*) AMS Pr.

Blau, Aljoscha, jt. auth. see Bell, Anthea.

Blau, Bernard. Vest Pocket English. LC 89-15370.Tr. of Ingles en el Bolsillo. (ENG & SPA.). 1989. pap. 5.95 (*0-8489-5107-7*) Inst Lang Study.

Blau, Cyril, jt. auth. see Greer, Rita.

Blau, David M. The Economics of Child Care. LC 91-17321. 1991. 34.95 (*0-87154-118-1*) Russell Sage.

B

B

Blau, David M., ed. The Economics of Child Care. (Illus.). 192p. 1995. pap. 14.95 (*0-87154-119-X*) Russell Sage.

Blau, David M. & Freed, Anne O., eds. Mental Health in the Nursing Home: An Educational Approach for Staff. 138p. (Orig.). 1983. pap. 27.50 (*0-8236-3362-4*, 03362) Intl Univs Pr.

Blau, Diane S., jt. auth. see Kottler, Jeffrey A.

Blau, Douglas. Fictions. (Illus.). 88p. 1987. pap. 20.00 (*1-878607-13-8*) Kent Gallery.

— Jack Barth. Barth, Rochelle, ed. 20p. 1989. pap. 15.00 (*0-924008-05-9*) Blum Helman.

— Michael Byron: Mindfields: 100 Works on Paper. (Illus.). 20p. 1995. 65.00 (*91-630-2985-5*) Dist Art Pubs.

— Peter Waite. 12p. (Orig.). 1991. pap. text 5.00 (*0-914489-08-9*) Univ Miss-KC Art.

— The Times, the Chronicle & the Observer. (Illus.). 64p. 1990. pap. 20.00 (*1-878607-25-1*) Kent Gallery.

Blau DuPlessis, Rachel, jt. ed. see Snitow, Ann.

Blau, Eileen K., jt. auth. see Baker-Gonzalez, Joan.

Blau, Eric. Common Heroes: Facing a Life Threatening Illness. (Illus.). 96p. 1989. pap. 15.95 (*0-939165-12-0*) NewSage Press.

— The Hero of the Slocum Disaster. 250p. 1996. text 22.95 (*0-88962-615-4*) Mosaic.

— Stories of Adoption: Loss & Reunion. (Illus.). 132p. 1993. pap. 16.95 (*0-939165-17-1*) NewSage Press.

Blau, Esther, ed. Spice & Spirit Vol. 1: The Complete Kosher Jewish Cookbook. LC 89-8053. (Illus.). 1990. reprint ed. 34.95 (*0-8266-0238-X*) Bloch.

Blau, Esther & Deitsch, Cyrel, eds. Spice & Spirit of Kosher-Passover Cooking. LC 77-72116. (Lubavitch Women's Organization Ser.). 1981. 7.95 (*0-317-14690-4*) Lubavitch Women.

Blau, Esther, ed. see Lubavitch Women's Organization Staff.

Blau, Eve. The Architecture of Red Vienna, 1919-1934. LC 98-25675. (Illus.). 500p. 1999. 60.00 (*0-262-02451-9*) MIT Pr.

— Ruskinian Gothic: The Architecture of Deane & Woodard, 1845-1861. LC 81-7302. 313p. 1982. reprint ed. pap. 97.10 (*0-7837-9300-6*, 206003900004) Bks Demand.

Blau, Eve & Kaufman, Edward, eds. Architecture & Its Image: Four Centuries of Architectural Representation Works from the Collection of the Canadian Centre for Architecture. (Illus.). 400p. 1989. 75.00 (*0-262-02289-3*) MIT Pr.

Blau, Eve & Troy, Nancy J., eds. Architecture & Cubism. LC 96-49785. (Illus.). 364p. 1997. 42.00 (*0-262-02422-5*) MIT Pr.

Blau, Evelyne. Krishnamurti: 100 Years. LC 94-47595. (Illus.). 288p. 1995. 29.95 (*1-55670-407-0*) Stewart Tabori & Chang.

Blau, Evelyne, ed. see Krishnamurti, J.

Blau, Francine D. & Ehrenberg, Ronald G., eds. Gender & Family Issues in the Workplace. LC 96-46510. 336p. (C). 1997. text 42.50 (*0-87154-117-3*) Russell Sage.

Blau, Francine D. & Kahn, Lawrence M. Wage Inequality: International Comparisons of Its Sources. (AEI Studies on Understanding Inequality). 43p. (Orig.). 1996. pap. 9.95 (*0-8447-7074-4*, AEI Pr) Am Enterprise.

Blau, Francine D., et al. The Economics of Women, Men & Work. 3rd ed. LC 97-25554. 396p. (C). 1997. pap. text 59.00 (*0-13-565979-5*) P-H.

Blau, Gary. Trends in Productivity Quality & Worker Attitude. (Studies in Productivity: Highlights of the Literature Ser.: Vol. 3). 36p. 1978. pap. 55.00 (*0-318-41889-4*) Work in Amer.

Blau, Gary E., jt. auth. see Neely, W. Brock.

Blau, Gary E., jt. ed. see Neely, W. Brock.

Blau, Gary M. & Gullotta, Thomas P., eds. Adolescent Dysfunctional Behavior: Causes, Interventions, & Prevention. LC 95-35479. (Issues in Children's & Families' Lives Ser.: Vol. 3). 304p. 1995. 52.00 (*0-8039-5372-0*); pap. 25.50 (*0-8039-5373-9*) Sage.

Blau, George. Law & Mental Health Professionals: Wyoming. LC 97-32112. (Law & Mental Health Professionals Ser.). 541p. 1997. 59.95 (*1-55798-447-6*) Am Psychol.

Blau, George E., tr. German Campaigns in the Balkans (Spring 1941) (Center for Military History Publication German Report Series, DA Pam: No. 104-4). (Illus.). 170p. (Orig.). 1987. reprint ed. pap. 8.00 (*0-16-001953-2*, S/N 008-029-00151-9) USGPO.

Blau, Helen M., jt. ed. see Kelly, Alan M.

Blau, Herbert. The Audience. LC 89-30491. (Parallax: Re-Visions of Culture & Society Ser.). 432p. 1990. pap. text 19.95 (*0-8018-3845-2*) Johns Hopkins.

***Blau, Herbert.** Nothing in Itself: Complexions of Fashion. LC 99-19964. (Theories of Contemporary Culture Ser.). 352p. 1999. 49.95 (*0-253-33587-6*) Ind U Pr.

Blau, Herbert. Nothing in Itself: Complexions of Fashion. LC 99-19964. (Theories of Contemporary Culture Ser.). (Illus.). 352p. 1999. pap. 24.95 (*0-253-21333-9*) Ind U Pr.

***Blau, Herbert.** Sails of the Herring Fleet: Essays on Beckett. (Illus.). 248p. 2000. text 47.50 (*0-472-11149-3*, 11149) U of Mich Pr.

Blau, Herbert. Take up the Bodies: Theater at the Vanishing Point. LC 81-19774. (Illus.). 328p. 1985. pap. text 14.95 (*0-252-01245-3*) U of Ill Pr.

Blau, J. N. Migraine: Clinical & Research Aspects. LC 87-3801. (Series in Contemporary Medicine & Public Health). 680p. 1988. text 160.00 (*0-8018-3551-8*) Johns Hopkins.

Blau, J. R. Social Contracts & Economic Markets. (Illus.). 232p. (C). 1993. 39.50 (*0-306-44391-0*, Plenum Trade) Perseus Pubng.

Blau, Joel. Illusions of Prosperity: America's Working Families in an Age of Economic Insecurity. LC 98-30262. 288p. 1999. 30.00 (*0-19-508993-6*) OUP.

— The Visible Poor: Homelessness in the United States. 256p. (C). 1993. reprint ed. pap. 10.95 (*0-19-508353-9*, 6311) OUP.

Blau, Joseph L. Judaism in America: From Curiosity to Third Faith. LC 75-5069. (Chicago History of American Religion Ser.). 176p. 1976. lib. bdg. 6.00 (*0-226-05727-5*) U Ch Pr.

— Judaism in America: From Curiosity to Third Faith. 170p. 1998. pap. text 14.50 (*0-226-05728-3*) U Ch Pr.

— Judaism in America: From Curiosity to Third Faith. LC 75-5069. (Chicago History of American Religion Ser.). 170p. Date not set. reprint ed. pap. 52.70 (*0-608-20584-2*, 205454900003) Bks Demand.

— Modern Varieties of Judaism. LC 66-10732. (Lectures on the History of Religions Ser.). 217p. 1972. pap. text 20.00 (*0-231-08668-7*) Col U Pr.

Blau, Joseph L., jt. ed. see Baron, Salo W.

Blau, Joseph L., ed. see Wayland, Francis.

Blau, Joshua. The Renaissance of Modern Hebrew & Modern Standard Arabic: Parallels & Differences in the Revival of Two Semitic Languages. (Publications in Near Eastern Studies: Vol. 18). 1982. pap. 50.00 (*0-520-09548-0*, Pub. by U CA Pr) Cal Prin Full Svc.

— Topics in Hebrew & Semitic Linguistics. 372p. 1998. text 40.00 (*965-493-006-4*) Magnes Pr.

Blau, Joshua & Reif, Stefan C., eds. Genizah Research after Ninety Years: The Case of Judaeo-Arabic. (University of Cambridge Oriental Publications: No. 47). 190p. (C). 1992. text 59.95 (*0-521-41773-2*) Cambridge U Pr.

Blau, Judith R. Architects & Firms: A Sociological Perspective on Architectural Practices. 208p. 1984. reprint ed. 30.00 (*0-262-02209-5*) MIT Pr.

— Architects & Firms: A Sociological Perspective on Architectural Practices. 208p. 1987. reprint ed. pap. text 13.50 (*0-262-52128-8*) MIT Pr.

— The Shape of Culture: A Study of Contemporary Cultural Patterns in the United States. (American Sociological Assn. Rose Monographs). (Illus.). 219p. (C). 1992. pap. text 19.95 (*0-521-43793-8*) Cambridge U Pr.

Blau, Judith R. & Goodman, Norman, eds. Social Roles & Social Institutions: Essays in Honor of Rose Laub Coser. 296p. (C). 1994. pap. 24.95 (*1-56000-797-4*) Transaction Pubs.

Blau, Karl & King, Graham S., eds. Handbook of Derivatives for Chromatography. LC 78-310911. 592p. reprint ed. pap. 183.60 (*0-608-12330-7*, 202519500042) Bks Demand.

***Blau, Lisa.** Easy Math for the Overhead: 10 Transparencies, Punch-Out Numbers & Manipulatives & Fun Lessons. (Illus.). 32p. (J). 2000. pap. 11.95 (*0-439-08679-5*) Scholastic Inc.

Blau, Lisa. Fall Is Fabulous. (Reader's Theatre Resource Bks.). 96p. 1994. teacher ed. 10.95 (*0-9640333-1-3*) One Heart Educ.

— Favorite Folktales & Fabulous Fables. (Reader's Theatre Resource Bks.). 108p. 1994. 10.95 (*0-9640333-4-8*) One Heart Educ.

— Super Science! (Reader's Theatre Resource Bks.). 118p. 1994. 10.95 (*0-9640333-3-X*) One Heart Educ.

— Touching Hearts & Minds. 104p. 1992. teacher ed. 10.95 (*0-9640333-0-5*) One Heart Educ.

— Winter Is Wonderful. (Reader's Theatre Resource Bks.). 88p. 1994. teacher ed. 10.95 (*0-9640333-2-1*) One Heart Educ.

Blau, Lucie R., jt. auth. see Sommers, Albert T.

Blau, Melinda. Loving & Listening: A Parent's Book of Daily Inspirations for Rebuilding the Family after Divorce. LC 95-45918. 384p. (Orig.). 1996. pap. 13.00 (*0-399-52202-6*, Perigee Bks) Berkley Pub.

— Whatever Happened to Amelia Earhart? LC 77-22173. 48p. (gr. 4-7). 1992. pap. 4.95 (*0-8114-6868-2*) Raintree Steck-V.

Blau, Melinda, jt. auth. see Evers-Williams, Myrlie.

Blau, Melinda, jt. auth. see Taffel, Ron.

Blau, Peter. The Organization of Academic Work. 2nd ed. LC 94-7215. 312p. (C). 1994. pap. 24.95 (*1-56000-756-7*) Transaction Pubs.

Blau, Peter & Schwartz, Joseph E. Crosscutting Social Circles: Testing a Macrostructural Theory of Intergroup Relations. LC 96-38937. 262p. (Orig.). 1997. pap. text 21.95 (*1-56000-903-9*) Transaction Pubs.

Blau, Peter J. Friction Science & Technology. (Mechanical Engineering Series of Reference Books & Textbooks: Vol. 100). (Illus.). 416p. 1995. text 165.00 (*0-8247-9576-8*) Dekker.

Blau, Peter J. & Lawn, Brian R., eds. Microindentation Techniques in Materials Science & Engineering, STP 889. LC 85-28577. (Illus.). 300p. 1986. text 46.00 (*0-8031-0441-3*, STP889) ASTM.

Blau, Peter J., jt. ed. see Divakar, Ramesh.

Blau, Peter M. The Dynamics of Bureaucracy. 2nd rev. ed. LC 63-22822. xiv, 322p. 1973. pap. text 6.95 (*0-226-05726-7*, P500) U Ch Pr.

— The Dynamics of Bureaucracy: A Study of Interpersonal Relations in Two Government Agencies. 2nd ed. LC 63-22822. (Illus.). 336p. Date not set. reprint ed. pap. 104.20 (*0-608-20583-4*, 205454800003) Bks Demand.

— Exchange & Power in Social Life. 372p. 1986. pap. text 24.95 (*0-88738-628-8*) Transaction Pubs.

— Structural Contexts of Opportunities. LC 94-10313. 244p. 1994. 32.50 (*0-226-05729-1*) U Ch Pr.

— A Theory of Social Integration. (Reprint Series in Social Sciences). (C). 1993. reprint ed. pap. text 1.00 (*0-8290-2704-1*, S-30) Irvington.

Blau, Richard, et al. S Corporations: Federal Taxation. 1989. 130.00 (*0-685-44924-6*) West Group.

***Blau, Sheldon P.** How to Get Out of the Hospital Alive: A Guide to Patient Power. (Illus.). 2000. 21.95 (*0-7858-1209-1*) Bk Sales Inc.

Blau, Sheldon P. How to Get Out of the Hospital Alive: A Guide to Patient Power. LC 98-22861. 256p. 1998. pap. text 14.95 (*0-02-862363-0*) Macmillan.

— Living with Lupus: All the Knowledge You Need to Help Yourself. (Illus.). 224p. 1993. pap. 12.00 (*0-201-60809-X*) Addison-Wesley.

***Blau, Sheldon P. & Shimberg, Elaine F.** How to Get Out of the Hospital Alive: A Guide to Patient Power. 226p. 1999. reprint ed. text 22.00 (*0-7881-6661-1*) DIANE Pub.

***Blau, Tatjana.** Tibetan Mandalas. LC 99-45229. 2000. pap. 10.95 (*0-8069-2887-5*) Sterling.

Blau, Theodore H. The Forensic Documentation Sourcebook: A Comprehensive Collection of Forms & Records for Forensic Mental Health Practice. LC 98-16154. 224p. 1998. pap. text 75.00 incl. disk (*0-471-25459-2*) Wiley.

— The Psychological Examination of the Child. LC 90-39091. (Series on Personality Processes). 279p. 1991. 99.95 (*0-471-63559-6*) Wiley.

— Psychological Services for Law Enforcement. 464p. 1994. 125.00 (*0-471-55950-4*) Wiley.

— The Psychologist As Expert Witness. 2nd ed. LC 98-2523. 596p. 1998. 95.00 (*0-471-17870-5*) Wiley.

— Psychotherapy Tradecraft: The Technique & Style of Doing Therapy. LC 87-21786. 328p. 1988. text 38.95 (*0-87630-479-X*) Brunner-Mazel.

Blau, Ulrich. Die Dreiwertige Logik der Sprache Ihre Syntax, Semantik und Anwendung in der Sprachanalyse. (Grundlagen der Kommunikation & Kognition (Foundations of Communication & Cognition) Ser.). (C). 1977. 58.50 (*3-11-006989-X*) De Gruyter.

Blau, William. Momentum, Direction & Divergence. LC 94-38103. (Traders' Advantage Ser.). 160p. 1995. 55.00 (*0-471-02729-4*) Wiley.

Blau, Zena S., ed. Current Perspectives on Aging & the Life Cycle, Vol. 4. 249p. 1995. 73.25 (*1-55938-367-4*) Jai Pr.

— Current Perspectives on Aging & the Life Cycle, Vol. 5. Date not set. 73.25 (*0-7623-0033-7*) Jai Pr.

— Personal History Through the Life Course, Vol. 3. (Current Perspectives on Aging & the Life Cycle Ser.). 298p. 1990. 73.25 (*0-89232-739-1*) Jai Pr.

— Work, Retirement & Social Policy, Vol. 1. (Current Perspectives on Aging & the Life Cycle Ser.). 366p. 1986. 73.25 (*0-89232-296-9*) Jai Pr.

Blau, Zena S. & Kartzer, David I., eds. Family Relations in Life Course Perspective. (Current Perspectives on Aging & the Life Cycle Ser.: Vol. 2). 280p. 1986. 73.25 (*0-89232-522-4*) Jai Pr.

Blauberg, Alyssa. Teddy Bear Soap on a Rope. (Illus.). 4p. (J). (gr. 1-6). 1998. pap. 4.95 (*1-58295-016-4*, Pub. by Pace Prods) Andrews & McMeel.

Blauch, Lloyd E. Federal Cooperation in Agricultural Extension Work, Vocational Education, & Vocational Rehabilitation. LC 76-89150. (American Education: Its Men, Institutions, & Ideas. Series 1). 1978. reprint ed. 18.95 (*0-405-01388-4*) Ayer.

Blauer, Clinton E., ed. & intro. see Klint of Denmark.

Blauer, Ettagale. African Elegance. (Illus.). 176p. 50.00 (*0-8478-2224-9*, Pub. by Rizzoli Intl) St Martin.

— Ghana. LC 98-45226. (Enchantment of the World Ser.). 144p. (YA). (gr. 5-9). 1999. lib. bdg. 32.00 (*0-516-21053-X*) Childrens.

— South Africa in the 21st Century. 1999. pap. 17.99 (*0-525-45637-6*) Viking Penguin.

Blauer, Ettagale & Laure, Jason. Morocco. LC 98-17644. (Enchantment of the World Ser.). 144p. (YA). (gr. 5-9). 1999. 32.00 (*0-516-20961-2*) Childrens.

— South Africa. LC 97-26014. (Enchantment of the World Ser.). (Illus.). 144p. (YA). (gr. 5-9). 1998. 32.00 (*0-516-20606-0*) Childrens.

Blauer, Gideon & Sund, Horst, eds. Optical Properties & Structure of Tetrapyrroles: Proceedings of a Symposium, University of Konstanz, West Germany, August 12-17, 1984. (Illus.). xiv, 536p. 1985. 211.55 (*3-11-010054-1*) De Gruyter.

Blauer, Gideon, ed. see Protein-Ligand Interactions Symposium Staff.

Blauer, Stephen. The Juicing Book: A Complete Guide to the Juicing of Fruits & Vegetables for Maximum Health & Vitality. LC 89-6725. (Illus.). 176p. 1996. pap. 8.95 (*0-89529-253-X*, Avery) Penguin Putnam.

Blauert, Jens. Spatial Hearing: The Psychophysics of Human Sound Localization. rev. ed. Allen, John S., tr. from GER. LC 96-12637.Tr. of Raumliches Horen. (Illus.). 480p. (C). 1996. 41.50 (*0-262-02413-6*) MIT Pr.

Blauert, Jutta & Zadek, Simon, eds. Mediating Sustainability: Growing Policy from the Grassroots. LC 98-3325. 304p. 1998. 55.00 (*1-56549-082-7*); pap. 25.95 (*1-56549-081-9*) Kumarian Pr.

Blaufarb, Douglas, jt. auth. see Tanham, George K.

Blaufox, D., jt. auth. see Naqvi, N. H.

***Blaufox, M. D.** The Stethoscope - Its Place in Medical History. (Illus.). 150p. 2001. 78.00 (*1-85070-278-0*) Prthnon Pub.

Blaufox, M. Donald, ed. Evaluation of Renal Function & Disease with Radionuclides. 2nd rev. ed. (Illus.). xviii, 418p. 1989. 241.00 (*3-8055-4933-4*) S Karger.

— Radionuclides in Nephro-Urology. (Contributions to Nephrology Ser.: Vol. 79). (Illus.). xii, 232p. 1990. 29.75 (*3-8055-5073-1*) S Karger.

Blaufox, M. Donald & Langford, H. G., eds. Non-Pharmacologic Therapy of Hypertension. (Bibliotheca Cardiologica Ser.: No. 41). (Illus.). vi, 150p. 1987. 121.75 (*3-8055-4459-6*) S Karger.

Blaufox, M. Donald, jt. ed. see Bischof-Delaloye, A.

Blaug, Mark. Economic Theories, True or False? Essays in the History & Methodology of Economics. 256p. 1990. text 90.00 (*1-85278-376-1*) E Elgar.

— Economic Theory in Retrospect. 5th ed. 750p. (Orig.). (C). 1997. text 85.00 (*0-521-57153-7*); pap. text 36.95 (*0-521-57701-2*) Cambridge U Pr.

— Economics of Education. 3rd ed. 1966. 87.00 (*0-08-020627-1*, Pub. by Pergamon Repr) Franklin.

— Economics of Education: A Selected Annotated Bibliography. 3rd ed. (C). 1970. write for info. (*0-318-55158-6*, Pergamon Pr) Elsevier.

— The Economics of the Arts. (Modern Revivals in Economics Ser.). 272p. 1992. 72.95 (*0-7512-0099-9*, Pub. by Gregg Pub) Ashgate Pub Co.

— Education & the Employment Problem in Developing Countries. vii, 89p. 1997. 22.50 (*92-2-101005-8*) Intl Labour Office.

— Great Economists Before Keynes: An Introduction to the Lives & Works of One Hundred Great Economists of the Past. 304p. 1997. 90.00 (*1-85898-571-4*) E Elgar.

— Great Economists Before Keynes: An Introduction to the Lives & Works of the One Hundred Great Economists of the Past. (Illus.). 304p. (C). 1989. pap. text 23.95 (*0-521-36741-7*) Cambridge U Pr.

— Great Economists since Keynes: An Introduction to the Lives & Works of One Hundred Modern Economists. 2nd ed. LC 97-37217. 328p. 1998. 85.00 (*1-85898-692-3*) E Elgar.

— The Methodology of Economics: or How Economists Explain. 2nd ed. (Surveys of Economic Literature Ser.). 314p. (C). 1992. pap. text 21.95 (*0-521-43678-8*) Cambridge U Pr.

— Not Only an Economist: Recent Essays. LC 96-26479. 416p. 1997. 100.00 (*1-85898-455-6*) E Elgar.

— Ricardian Economics, 8--8. LC 73-9208. 269p. 1973. reprint ed. lib. bdg. 38.50 (*0-8371-6982-8*, BLRE, Greenwood Pr) Greenwood.

— Richard Cantillon (1680-1734) & Jacques Turgot (1727-1881) (Pioneers in Economics Ser.: Vol. 9). 320p. 1991. text 150.00 (*1-85278-471-7*) E Elgar.

Blaug, Mark, ed. Adam Smith, 1723-1790, 2 vols., Set. (Pioneers in Economics Ser.: No. 12). 592p. 1991. 245.00 (*1-85278-474-1*) E Elgar.

— Alfred Marshall (1842-1924) & Francis Edgeworth (1845-1926) (Pioneers in Economics Ser.: No. 29). 384p. 1992. 150.00 (*1-85278-492-X*) E Elgar.

— Aristotle (394-322 B.C.) (Pioneers in Economics Ser.: Vol. 2). 304p. 1991. 135.00 (*1-85278-464-4*) E Elgar.

— Arthur Pigou, 1877-1959. (Pioneers in Economics Ser.: Vol. 36). 208p. 1992. 100.00 (*1-85278-499-7*) E Elgar.

— Bertil Ohlin, 1899-1979. abr. ed. (Pioneers in Economics Ser.: Vol. 43). 224p. 1992. 110.00 (*1-85278-507-1*) E Elgar.

— Carl Menger (1840-1921) (Pioneers in Economics Ser.: No. 26). 256p. 1992. 120.00 (*1-85278-489-X*) E Elgar.

— David Hume (1711-1776) & James Steuart (1712-1780) (Pioneers in Economics Ser.: Vol. 11). 352p. 1991. text 150.00 (*1-85278-473-3*) E Elgar.

— David Ricardo (1772-1823) (Pioneers in Economics Ser.: No. 14). 272p. 1991. text 125.00 (*1-85278-476-8*) E Elgar.

— Dissenters: Charles Fourier, 1772-1837, Henri de St. Simon, 1760-1825, Pierre-Joseph Proudhon, 1809-1865, John Hobson, 1858-1940. LC 91-44996. (Pioneers in Economics Ser.: Vol. 31). 256p. 1992. 120.00 (*1-85278-494-6*) E Elgar.

— The Early Mercantilists: Thomas Mun (571-1641), Edward Misselden (1608-1634), Gerard de Mallynes (1586-1623) (Pioneers in Economics Ser.: Vol. 4). 320p. 1991. text 135.00 (*1-85278-466-0*) E Elgar.

— The Economic Value of Education: Studies in the Economics of Education. (International Library of Critical Writings in Economics: No. 17). 560p. 1992. text 215.00 (*1-85278-542-X*) E Elgar.

— Edward Chamberlin, 1899-1967. (Pioneers in Economics Ser.: No. 38). 264p. 1992. 120.00 (*1-85278-502-0*) E Elgar.

— Eugen von Bohm-Bawerk (1851-1914) & Friedrich von Weiser (1851-1926) (Pioneers in Economics Ser.: No. 27). 272p. 1992. 120.00 (*1-85278-490-3*) E Elgar.

— Francois Quesnay, (1694-1774), 2 vols., Vols. 1 & 2. (Pioneers in Economics Ser.: Vol. 10). 656p. 1991. text 280.00 (*1-85278-472-5*) E Elgar.

— Frank Knight, 1885-1972, Henry Simons, 1899-1946, & Joseph Schumpeter, 1883-1950. (Pioneers in Economics Ser.: Vol. 37). 464p. 1992. 180.00 (*1-85278-500-4*) E Elgar.

— George Scrope (1797-1876), Thomas Attwood (1783-1856), Edwin Chadwick (1800-1890), John Cairnes (1823-1875) (Pioneers in Economics Ser.: Vol. 20). 304p. 1991. text 135.00 (*1-85278-482-2*) E Elgar.

— Gustav Schmoller (1838-1917) & Werner Sombart (1863-1941) (Pioneers in Economics Ser.: Vol. 30). 256p. 1992. 120.00 (*1-85278-493-8*) E Elgar.

— Harold Hotelling, 1895-1973, Lionel Robbins, 1898-1984, Clark Warburton, 1896-1979, John Bates Clark, 1847-1938, & Ludwig von Mises, 1881-1973. (Pioneers in Economics Ser.: Vol. 40). 324p. 1992. 135.00 (*1-85278-504-7*) E Elgar.

— Harry Johnson, 1923-1977. (Pioneers in Economics Ser.: Vol. 42). 192p. 1992. 100.00 (*1-85278-506-3*) E Elgar.

— Henry George (1839-1897) (Pioneers in Economics Ser.: No. 34). 404p. 1992. 160.00 (*1-85278-497-0*) E Elgar.

— Henry Thorton (1760-1815), Jeremy Bentham (1748-1832), James Lauderdale (1759-1839), Simonde de Sismondi (1773-1842) (Pioneers in Economics Ser.: No. 13). 368p. 1991. text 150.00 (*1-85278-475-X*) E Elgar.

— The Historiography of Economics. (Pioneers in Economics Ser.: Vol. I). 256p. 1991. text 125.00 (*1-85278-463-6*) E Elgar.

— The History of Economic Thought. (International Library of Critical Writings in Economics Ser.: Vol. 6). 416p. 1990. text 175.00 (*1-85278-191-2*) E Elgar.

An Asterisk (*) at the beginning of an entry indicates that the title is appearing for the first time.

— Irving Fisher (1867-1947), Arthur Hadley (1856-1930), Ragnar Frisch (1895-1973), Friedrich von Hayek (1899-1992), Allyn Young (1876-1929), Ugo Mazzola (1863-1899) (Pioneers in Economics Ser.: Vol. 41). 242p. 1992. 120.00 (*1-85278-505-5*) E Elgar.

— James Mill, 1773-1836, John Rae, 1796-1872, Edward West, 1782-1828, Thomas Joplin, 1790-1847. (Pioneers in Economics Ser.: No. 21). 416p. 1991. text 165.00 (*1-85278-483-0*) E Elgar.

— James Wilson (1805-1860), Issac Butt (1813-1879), T.E. Cliffe Leslie (1827-1882) (Pioneers in Economics Ser.: No. 22). 384p. 1991. text 160.00 (*1-85278-484-9*) E Elgar.

— Jean-Baptiste Say, 1767-1832. (Pioneers in Economics Ser.: No. 15). 168p. 1991. text 100.00 (*1-85278-477-6*) E Elgar.

— Joan Robinson, 1903-1983 & George Shackle, 1903-1992. (Pioneers in Economics Ser.: Vol. 45). 192p. 1992. 100.00 (*1-85278-509-8*) E Elgar.

— Johan von Thunen (1783-1850), Augustin Cournot (1801-1877), Jules Dupuit (1804-1866) (Pioneers in Economics Ser.: No. 24). 516p. 1992. 190.00 (*1-85278-486-5*) E Elgar.

— John Maynard Keynes, 1883-1946, 2 vols., Set. (Pioneers in Economics Ser.: Vol. 46). 1104p. 1991. text 425.00 (*1-85278-510-1*) E Elgar.

— Karl Marx, 1818-1883. (Pioneers in Economics Ser.: No. 23). 416p. 1991. text 175.00 (*1-85278-485-7*) E Elgar.

Blaug, Mark, ed. Knut Wicksell (1851-1926) (Pioneers in Economics Ser.: Vol. 28). 448p. 1992. 175.00 (*1-85278-491-1*) E Elgar.

Blaug, Mark, ed. The Later Mercantilists: Josiah Child, 1603-1699 & John Locke, 1632-1704. (Pioneers in Economics Ser.: Vol. 5). 416p. 1991. text 180.00 (*1-85278-467-9*) E Elgar.

— Leon Walras, 1834-1910. (Pioneers in Economics Ser.: Vol. 25). 480p. 1992. 190.00 (*1-85278-488-1*) E Elgar.

— Michal Kalecki, 1899-1970. (Pioneers in Economics Ser.: Vol. 39). 208p. 1992. 100.00 (*1-85278-503-9*) E Elgar.

— Piero Sraffa, 1898-1983. (Pioneers in Economics Ser.: Vol. 44). 192p. 1992. 100.00 (*1-85278-508-X*) E Elgar.

— Pre-Classical Economists: Pierre le Pesant Boisguilbert (1645-1714), George Berkeley (1685-1753), Baron de Montesquieu (1689-1755), Ferdinando Galiani (1727-1787), James Anderson (1739-1808), Dugald Stewart (1753-1828) (Pioneers in Economics Ser.: Vol. 7). 192p. 1991. text 110.00 (*1-85278-469-5*) E Elgar.

— Pre-Classical Economists Vol. 1: Charles Davenant (1656-1714) & William Petty (1623-1687) (Pioneers in Economics Ser.: Vol. 6). 272p. 1991. text 125.00 (*1-85278-468-7*) E Elgar.

— Pre-Classical Economists Vol. 3: John Law (1671-1729), & Bernard Mandeville (1660-1733) (Pioneers in Economics Ser.: Vol. 8). 272p. 1991. text 135.00 (*1-85278-470-9*) E Elgar.

— Ramsay McCulloch (1978-1864), Nassau Senior (1790-1864), Robert Torrens (1780-1864) (Pioneers in Economics Ser.: No. 17). 320p. 1991. text 135.00 (*1-85278-479-2*) E Elgar.

— St. Thomas Aquinas (1225-1274) (Pioneers in Economics Ser.: Vol. 3). 320p. 1991. text 140.00 (*1-85278-465-2*) E Elgar.

Blaug, Mark, ed. Thomas Robert Malthus, 1766-1834 & John Stuart Mill, 1806-1873. (Pioneers in Economics Ser.: No. 16). 400p. 1991. text 165.00 (*1-85278-478-4*) E Elgar.

— Thomas Tooke (1774-1858), Mountifort Longfield (1802-1884), Richard Jones (1790-1855) (Pioneers in Economics Ser.: No. 18). 384p. 1991. text 160.00 (*1-85278-480-6*) E Elgar.

Blaug, Mark, ed. Thorstein Veblen, 1857-1929. (Pioneers in Economics Ser.: Vol. 32). 352p. 1992. 150.00 (*1-85278-495-4*) E Elgar.

— Vilfredo Pareto, 1848-1923. (Pioneers in Economics Ser.). 400p. 1992. 160.00 (*1-85278-498-9*) E Elgar.

— Wesley Mitchell (1874-1948), John Commons (1862-1945), Clarence Ayers (1891-1972) (Pioneers in Economics Ser.: Vol. 33). 288p. 1992. 125.00 (*1-85278-496-2*) E Elgar.

***Blaug, Mark, ed.** Who's Who in Economics. 3rd ed. LC 99-27513. 1104p. 1999. 350.00 (*1-85898-886-1*) E Elgar.

Blaug, Mark, ed. William Whewell 1794-1866, Dionysius Lardner 1793-1859, Charles Babbage 1792-1871. (Pioneers in Economics Ser.: No. 19). 288p. 1991. text 135.00 (*1-85278-481-4*) E Elgar.

Blaug, Mark, et al. The Quantity Theory of Money: From Locke to Keynes & Friedman. 160p. 1995. 80.00 (*1-85898-177-8*) E Elgar.

Blaug, Mark, jt. ed. see De Marchi, Neil.

Blaug, Ricardo. Democracy, Real & Ideal: Discourse Ethics & Radical Politics. LC 98-7751. (SUNY Series in Social & Political Thought). 256p. (C). 1999. text 65.50 (*0-7914-4107-5*); pap. text 21.95 (*0-7914-4108-3*) State U NY Pr.

Blaugher, Michael A. Guide to over 900 Aircraft Museums, U. S. A. & Canada. 19th ed. 139p. 1999. pap. 8.50 (*0-9640128-7-1*) Eight-Hund Aircraft.

Blaugrund, A., et al. American Watercolors, Pastels & Drawings. Date not set. 8.95 (*0-87273-098-0*) Bklyn Mus.

Blaugrund, Annette. Audubon. 112p. 1999. 12.95 (*0-7407-0291-2*) Andrews & McMeel.

Blauhut, B., jt. ed. see Lundsgaard-Hansen, P.

Blaukopf, Herta, ed. Gustav Mahler & Richard Strauss Correspondence, 1888-1911. Jephcott, Edmund, tr. from GER. LC 84-16473. (Illus.). 172p. 1985. reprint ed. 30.00 (*0-226-05767-4*) U Ch Pr.

Blaukopf, Herta, jt. auth. see Blaukopf, Kurt.

Blaukopf, Herta, jt. auth. see De La Grange, Henry L.

Blaukopf, Herta, ed. see Mahler, Gustav & Strauss, Richard.

Blaukopf, Kurt. Musical Life in a Changing Society: Aspects of Musical Sociology. Marinelli, David, tr. from GER. LC 92-17805. (Illus.). 328p. 1992. pap. 22.95 (*0-931340-55-1*, Amadeus Pr) Timber.

***Blaukopf, Kurt & Blaukopf, Herta.** Mahler: His Life, Work & World. LC 91-65994. (Illus.). 256p. 2000. pap. 27.50 (*0-500-28197-1*, Pub. by Thames Hudson) Norton.

Blaukopf, Kurt & Desmont, Mark, eds. The Cultural Behaviour of Youth: Towards a Cross-Cultural Survey in Europe & Asia. 1976. pap. 39.00 (*3-7024-0114-8*, UE26247) Eur-Am Music.

Blaum, Paul A. The Days of the Warlords: A History of the Byzantine Empire: A. D. 969 - 991. LC 94-27632. 142p. (Orig.). (C). 1994. pap. text 28.50 (*0-8191-9657-6*); lib. bdg. 46.50 (*0-8191-9656-8*) U Pr of Amer.

Blaunbaum. Foundations of College Geometry. 420p. 2000. 73.33 (*0-13-591405-1*) P-H.

Blauner, Bob. Black Lives, White Lives: Three Decades of Race Relations in America. 350p. (C). 1989. pap. 17.95 (*0-520-06950-1*, Pub. by U CA Pr) Cal Prin Full Svc.

— Our Mothers' Spirits: Great Writers on the Death of Mothers & the Grief of Men. (Illus.). 352p. 1999. pap. 12.00 (*0-06-098731-6*, ReganBks) HarperTrade.

Blauner, Laurie. Children of Gravity. 67p. 1995. pap. 12.00 (*0-937669-56-3*) Owl Creek Pr.

— Other Lives. (Poetry Chapbook Ser.). 64p. 1984. pap. 12.00 (*0-937669-13-X*) Owl Creek Pr.

— Self-Portrait with an Unwilling Landscape. 1990. pap. 12.00 (*0-937669-39-3*) Owl Creek Pr.

Blauner, Peter. Casino Moon. 320p. 1996. mass mkt. 5.99 (*0-380-72589-4*, Avon Bks) Morrow Avon.

— The Intruder. 1996. 23.00 (*0-614-19128-9*) S&S Trade.

— The Intruder. large type ed. LC 96-22488. 1996. 25.95 (*1-56895-348-8*) Wheeler Pub.

— The Intruder. 464p. 1997. reprint ed. mass mkt. 6.99 (*0-446-60505-0*, Pub. by Warner Bks) Little.

— The Intruder, Set. abr. ed. 192p. 1996. pap. 18.00 incl. audio (*0-671-57041-2*, 394045) S&S Trade.

— Man of the Hour. LC 98-31801. 432p. (gr. 8). 1999. 24.00 (*0-316-03817-2*) Little.

***Blauner, Peter.** Man of the Hour. 496p. 2000. mass mkt. 7.99 (*0-446-60541-7*, Pub. by Warner Bks) Little.

Blauner, Peter. Slow Motion Riot. 384p. 1992. mass mkt. 6.99 (*0-380-71306-3*, Avon Bks) Morrow Avon.

Blauner, Robert. Alienation & Freedom: The Factory Worker & His Industry. LC 64-15820. 1967. pap. text 9.95 (*0-226-05811-5*) U Ch Pr.

— Alienation & Freedom: The Factory Worker & His Industry. LC HD6961.B57. (Phoenix Bks.: Vol. P271). 238p. Date not set. reprint ed. pap. 73.80 (*0-608-20585-0*, 205455000003) Bks Demand.

— Alienation & Freedom: The Factory Worker & His Industry. LC 64-15820. (Illus.). 238p. reprint ed. pap. 73.80 (*0-608-09390-4*, 205413500004) Bks Demand.

Blaunstein, Nathan. Radio Propagation in Cellular Networks. LC 99-45836. 386p. 1999. 89.00 (*1-58053-067-2*) Artech Hse.

Blaurock, Donna. Life's Lessons: Cheat Notes from the Classroom of Life. Caton, Patrick, ed. LC 96-78973. 168p. 1997. pap. 5.95 (*1-56245-286-X*) Great Quotations.

Blaustein, Albert P. Constitutions of the World. LC 92-39039. (Philadelphia Constitution Foundation Bk.). xi, 86p. 1993. reprint ed. 22.50 (*0-8377-0362-X*, Rothman) W S Hein.

Blaustein, Albert P., ed. Bicentennial Concordance: Indexes to the Constitution of the United States of America. LC 92-9674. (Philadelphia Constitution Foundation Bk.). xiv, 202p. 1992. 45.00 (*0-8377-0361-1*, Rothman) W S Hein.

— Fiction Goes to Court. LC 77-2827. 288p. 1977. reprint ed. lib. bdg. 65.00 (*0-8371-9522-5*, BLFG, Greenwood Pr) Greenwood.

Blaustein, Albert P. & Epstein, Dana. Resolving Language Conflicts: A Study of the World's Constitution. LC 86-52465. 105p. 1986. 45.00 (*0-934833-01-X*) US English.

Blaustein, Albert P. & Ferguson, Clarence C. Desegregation & the Law: The Meaning & Effect of the School Segregation Cases. (Illus.). xiv, 333p. 1985. reprint ed. 32.50 (*0-8377-0344-1*, Rothman) W S Hein.

Blaustein, Albert P. & Mersky, Roy M. The First One Hundred Justices: Statistical Studies on the Supreme Court of the United States. 210p. 1978. 69.50 (*0-208-01290-7*) Elliots Bks.

Blaustein, Albert P. & O'Brien, James P. Religious Liberty in the World's Constitutions. (Religion Reference Ser.). 500p. 1998. text 75.00 (*0-8153-0798-5*) Garland.

Blaustein, Albert P. & Porter, Charles O. The American Lawyer: A Summary of the Survey of the Legal Profession. LC 72-5452. 360p. 1972. reprint ed. lib. bdg. 69.50 (*0-8371-6438-9*, BLAL, Greenwood Pr) Greenwood.

Blaustein, Albert P., et al. Framing the Modern Constitution: A Checklist. LC 93-41510. (Philadelphia Constitution Foundation Bk.). 48p. 1994. reprint ed. pap. 22.50 (*0-8377-0364-6*, Rothman) W S Hein.

Blaustein, Bernard D., et al, eds. New Approaches in Coal Chemistry. LC 81-12740. (ACS Symposium Ser.: No. 169). 1981. 46.95 (*0-8412-0659-7*) Am Chemical.

— New Approaches in Coal Chemistry. LC 81-12740. (ACS Symposium Ser.: No. 169). (Illus.). 475p. 1981. reprint ed. pap. 147.30 (*0-608-03252-2*, 206377100007) Bks Demand.

Blaustein, Bernard D., jt. ed. see Markuszewski, Richard.

Blaustein, Bernard H. Ocular Manifestations of Neurologic Disease. LC 95-50441. (Optometric Problem Solving Ser.). (Illus.). 304p. (C). (gr. 13). 1996. pap. text 39.95 (*0-8151-0507-X*, 24391) Mosby Inc.

Blaustein, David. Memoirs of David Blaustein: Educator & Communal Worker. LC 74-27966. (Modern Jewish Experience Ser.). (Illus.). 1975. reprint ed. 31.95 (*0-405-06696-1*) Ayer.

Blaustein, David I. & Heffez, Leslie B. Arthroscopic Atlas of the Temporomandibular Joint. LC 89-13158. (Illus.). 117p. 1989. 89.00 (*0-8121-1242-3*) Lppncott W & W.

— Arthroscopic Atlas of the Temporomandibular Joint. LC 89-13158. (Illus.). 117p. 1990. text 89.00 (*0-685-48046-1*) Lppncott W & W.

Blaustein, John. The Hidden Canyon: A River Journey. LC 98-29161. (Illus.). 144p. 1999. pap. 19.95 (*0-8118-2261-3*) Chronicle Bks.

— The Hidden Canyon: A River Journey. rev. ed. (Illus.). 144p. 1999. 35.00 (*0-8118-2453-5*) Chronicle Bks.

Blaustein, M. P., ed. Reviews of Physiology, Biochemistry & Pharmacology, Vol. 132. (Illus.). 86p. 1998. 79.95 (*3-540-63492-4*) Spr-Verlag.

Blaustein, M. P., et al, eds. Reviews of Physiology, Biochemistry & Pharmacology. (Illus.). v, 145p. 1999. 115.00 (*3-540-64779-1*) Spr-Verlag.

— Reviews of Physiology, Biochemistry & Pharmacology, Vol. 113. (Illus.). vi, 150p. 1989. 80.00 (*0-387-50948-8*) Spr-Verlag.

— Reviews of Physiology, Biochemistry & Pharmacology, Vol. 114. (Illus.). 272p. 1989. 113.00 (*0-387-51693-X*) Spr-Verlag.

— Reviews of Physiology, Biochemistry & Pharmacology, Vol. 118. (Illus.). v, 128p. 1991. 76.00 (*0-387-54211-6*) Spr-Verlag.

— Reviews of Physiology, Biochemistry & Pharmacology, Vol. 120. (Illus.). 200p. 1992. 140.00 (*0-387-55364-9*) Spr-Verlag.

— Reviews of Physiology, Biochemistry & Pharmacology, Vol. 122. (Illus.). 290p. 1993. 143.00 (*0-387-56380-6*) Spr-Verlag.

— Reviews of Physiology, Biochemistry & Pharmacology, Vol. 123. v, 266p. 1994. 133.00 (*0-387-57536-7*) Spr-Verlag.

— Reviews of Physiology, Biochemistry & Pharmacology, Vol. 125. 1994. 124.00 (*0-387-57930-3*) Spr-Verlag.

— Reviews of Physiology, Biochemistry & Pharmacology, Vol. 126. (Advances in Pharmacological Sciences Ser.: 126). 425p. 1994. 135.00 (*3-540-58477-3*) Spr-Verlag.

— Reviews of Physiology, Biochemistry & Pharmacology, Vol. 127. (Illus.). 272p. 1995. 152.00 (*3-540-60135-X*) Spr-Verlag.

— Reviews of Physiology, Biochemistry & Pharmacology, Vol. 128. (Illus.). vi, 268p. 1996. 116.00 (*3-540-61343-9*) Spr-Verlag.

— Reviews of Physiology, Biochemistry & Pharmacology, Vol. 129. (Illus.). 80p. 1996. 74.95 (*3-540-61435-4*) Spr-Verlag.

— Reviews of Physiology, Biochemistry & Pharmacology, Vol. 130. (Illus.). 260p. 1997. 116.00 (*3-540-61762-0*) Spr-Verlag.

— Reviews of Physiology, Biochemistry & Pharmacology, Vol. 133. (Illus.). 110p. 1998. 89.95 (*3-540-63945-4*) Spr-Verlag.

— Reviews of Physiology, Biochemistry & Pharmacology, Vol. 134. (Illus.). 230p. 1999. 149.00 (*3-540-64753-8*) Spr-Verlag.

— Reviews of Physiology, Biochemistry & Pharmacology, Vol. 137. (Illus.). iv, 165p. 1999. 115.00 (*3-540-65362-7*) Spr-Verlag.

— Reviews of Physiology, Biochemistry & Pharmacology, Vol. 138. (Illus.). 185p. 1999. 119.00 (*3-540-65484-4*) Spr-Verlag.

— Reviews of Physiology, Biochemistry & Pharmacology, Vol. 139. (Illus.). iv, 120p. 1999. 89.00 (*3-540-65694-4*) Spr-Verlag.

***Blaustein, M. P., et al, eds.** Reviews of Physiology, Biochemistry & Pharmacology, Vol. 140. (Illus.). iv, 142p. 2000. 92.00 (*3-540-66603-6*) Spr-Verlag.

Blaustein, M. P., et al, eds. Reviews of Physiology, Biochemistry & Pharmacology: Special Issue on Signal Transduction, Vol. 119, Pt. I. (Illus.). 264p. 1992. 147.00 (*0-387-55192-1*) Spr-Verlag.

— Reviews of Physiology, Biochemistry & Pharmacology: Special Issue on Signal Transduction II, Vol. 121. (Illus.). 216p. 1992. 140.00 (*0-387-55969-8*) Spr-Verlag.

— Special Issue on Novel Aspects of Membrane-Mediated Cellular Responses: The Roles of Reactive Oxygens, NO, CO II. (Reviews of Physiology, Biochemistry & Pharmacology Ser.: Vol. 131). (Illus.). xiv, 115p. 1997. 89.00 (*3-540-61992-5*) Spr-Verlag.

— Special Issue on Signal Transduction III. (Reviews of Physiology, Biochemistry & Pharmacology Ser.: Vol. 124). 140p. 1994. 113.00 (*0-387-57587-1*) Spr-Verlag.

Blaustein, M. P., ed. see Pette, D., et al.

Blaustein, Muriel. Bedtime, Zachary! LC 86-45772. (Illus.). 32p. (J). (ps-2). 1987. 7.95 (*0-694-00191-0*) HarpC Child Bks.

— Make Friends, Zachary! LC 88-6308. (Illus.). 32p. (J). (ps-2). 1990. 12.95 (*0-06-020545-8*) HarpC Child Bks.

— Play Ball, Zachary! LC 87-45274. (Illus.). 32p. (J). (ps-2). 1988. 11.95 (*0-06-020543-1*) HarpC Child Bks.

Blaustein, Paul H. Learned Hand on Patent Law. LC 82-63003. 350p. 1983. text 50.00 (*0-686-88645-3*); lib. bdg. 50.00 (*0-9610490-0-6*) Pineridge Pub.

Blaustein, Randy B. How to Do Business with the IRS. LC 82-5319. 342p. (C). 1982. text 54.95 (*0-13-396168-0*, Busn) P-H.

— How to Do Business with the IRS: Taxpayers Edition. 250p. 1986. 17.95 (*0-13-405507-1*) P-H.

Blaustein, Saul J. Job & Income Security for Unemployed Workers: Some New Directions. LC 81-10423. 127p. 1981. pap. text 9.00 (*0-911558-84-5*) W E Upjohn.

— Unemployment Insurance in the United States: The First Half Century. LC 93-13480. 367p. 1993. text 40.00 (*0-88099-136-4*); pap. text 22.00 (*0-88099-135-6*) W E Upjohn.

Blaustone, Jan. Every Family Is Special: Love Comes First. 190p. 1994. pap. 9.95 (*0-925190-72-1*) Fairview Press.

— Joy of Parenthood. 160p. 1993. pap. 7.00 (*0-671-86778-4*) S&S Trade.

— The Joy of Parenthood: Inspiration & Encouragement for Parents. LC 92-40271. (Illus.). 112p. 1993. pap. 6.00 (*0-88166-198-8*) Meadowbrook.

Blaut, J. M. The Colonizer's Model of the World: Geographical Diffusionism & Eurocentric History. LC 93-22346. 246p. 1993. pap. text 19.95 (*0-89862-348-0*); lib. bdg. 45.00 (*0-89862-349-9*) Guilford Pubns.

***Blaut, J. M.** Eight Eurocentric Historians. 222p. 2000. 41.95 (*1-57230-590-8*); pap. text 21.95 (*1-57230-591-6*, C0591) Guilford Pubns.

Blaut, James M. Fourteen Ninety-Two: The Debate on Colonialism, Eurocentrism, & History. LC 92-32975. 1992. 24.95 (*0-86543-369-0*); pap. 9.95 (*0-86543-370-4*) Africa World.

Blauton. Varied Voices. LC 98-128147. (College ESL Ser.). 160p. (C). 1998. mass mkt. 23.95 (*0-8384-7962-6*) Heinle & Heinle.

Blauvelt, Carolyn T. & Nelson, Fred. A Manual of Orthopaedic Terminology, No. 6. 6th ed. LC 98-10711. (Illus.). 475p. (C). (gr. 13). 1998. pap. text 36.95 (*0-8151-2787-1*, 31249) Mosby Inc.

Blauvelt, Euan & Durlacher, Jennifer, eds. Sources of African & Middle-Eastern Economic Information, 2 vols. LC 81-4125. 1982. lib. bdg. 250.00 (*0-313-23058-7*, BAF/) Greenwood.

— Sources of African & Middle-Eastern Economic Information, 2 vols., Vol. 1. LC 81-4125. 1982. lib. bdg. 250.00 (*0-313-23059-5*, BAF/01) Greenwood.

— Sources of African & Middle-Eastern Economic Information, 2 vols., Vol. 2. LC 81-4125. 1982. lib. bdg. 250.00 (*0-313-23060-9*, BAF/02) Greenwood.

— Sources of Asian Pacific Economic Information, 2 vols., Set. LC 80-28645. 1981. lib. bdg. 250.00 (*0-313-22963-5*, BLS/) Greenwood.

— Sources of Asian Pacific Economic Information, 2 vols., Vol. 1. LC 80-28645. 1981. lib. bdg. 250.00 (*0-313-22964-3*, BLS/1) Greenwood.

— Sources of Asian Pacific Economic Information, 2 vols., Vol. 2. LC 80-28645. 1981. lib. bdg. 250.00 (*0-313-22965-1*, BLS/2) Greenwood.

Blauvelt, Louis L. Blauvelt Family Genealogy: A Comprehensive Compilation of the Descendants of Gerrit Hendricksen (Blauvelt), 1620-1687, Who Came to America in 1638. (Illus.). 1064p. 1995. reprint ed. pap. 135.00 (*0-8328-4447-0*); reprint ed. lib. bdg. 145.00 (*0-8328-4446-2*) Higginson Bk Co.

— Blauvelt Family Genealogy: A Comprehensive Compilation of the Descendants of Gerrit Hendricksen (Blauvelt) (1620-1687) Who Came to America in 1638. (Illus.). 1064p. 1995. reprint ed. pap. 149.50 (*0-8328-4744-5*); reprint ed. lib. bdg. 159.50 (*0-8328-4743-7*) Higginson Bk Co.

Blauvelt, Peter D. Effective Strategies for School Security. LC 81-214117. (Illus.). 84p. reprint ed. pap. 30.00 (*0-608-18138-2*, 203279200081) Bks Demand.

— Making Schools Safe for Students: Creating a Proactive School Safety Plan. LC 99-6377. (One-Off Ser.). (Illus.). 192p. 1999. pap. 59.95 (*0-8039-6888-4*) Corwin Pr.

Blauwkamp, Christi. Fairway to Kitchen. (Illus.). 113p. 1998. pap. 9.95 (*0-9665045-1-8*) ClassicGolf.

— A Simple Guide to Lowering Your Golf Scores. (Illus.). 77p. 1984. pap. 9.95 (*0-9665045-0-X*) ClassicGolf.

Blavatsky, Helena P. Abridgement of the Secret Doctrine. Preston, Elizabeth & Humphreys, Christmas, eds. 1999. pap. 12.00 (*0-8356-0009-2*, Quest) Theos Pub Hse.

Blavatsky, Helena P. Collected Writings of H. P. Blavatsky, 15 vols. (Illus.). 435.00 (*0-8356-1930-3*, Quest) Theos Pub Hse.

Blavatsky, Helena P. Essays by Blavatsky: Fundamentals of Theosophy; Ancient Egyptian Magic; Spirits of Various Kinds; The Fall of Ideals; Spiritual Progress; My Books; The Origin of Evil; Star-Angel Worship in the Roman Catholic Church; The Kabacah & the Kabalah; Roots of Ritualism in Church & Masonry; Kosmic Mind; Magnetism; The Tidal Wave. 312p. 1992. reprint ed. pap. 24.95 (*1-56459-248-0*) Kessinger Pub.

— From the Caves & Jungles of Hindustan. De Zirkoff, Boris, ed. LC 74-26605. (Illus.). 750p. 1975. pap. 19.50 (*0-8356-0239-7*, Quest) Theos Pub Hse.

— Glossary of Theosophy: Glosario Teosofico. (SPA.). 903p. 1982. 43.95 (*0-8288-2200-X*, S35162) Fr & Eur.

— H. P. Blavatsky Collected Writings Vol. 15: Cumulative Index. Eklund, Dara, ed. 647p. 1991. 29.00 (*0-8356-0237-0*, Quest) Theos Pub Hse.

— H. P. Blavatsky to the American Conventions: 1888-1891, with a Historical Perspective. LC 78-74256. 86p. 1979. pap. 7.95 (*0-911500-88-X*) Theos U Pr.

— An Invitation to the Secret Doctrine. LC 89-50118. (Illus.). 112p. 1994. reprint ed. pap. 8.95 (*1-55700-009-3*) Theos U Pr.

— Isis Unveiled. 2 vols. LC 72-186521. 1471p. 1999. reprint ed. 41.95 (*0-911500-02-2*); reprint ed. pap. 29.95 (*0-911500-03-0*) Theos U Pr.

— Isis Unveiled: A Master-Key to the Mysteries of Ancient & Modern Science & Theology, 2 vols. in 1. (Illus.). 1300p. 1931. reprint ed. 20.00 (*0-938998-01-3*) Theosophy.

— Isis Unveiled: Collected Writings, 1877, 2 vols. De Zirkoff, Boris, ed. LC 94-164. 1656p. 1994. pap. 33.00 (*0-8356-0247-8*, Quest) Theos Pub Hse.

— Isis Unveiled: Secrets of the Ancient Wisdom Tradition, Madame Blavatsky's First Work. abr. ed. Gomes, Michael, ed. LC 97-17867. 286p. (Orig.). 1997. pap. 14.00 (*0-8356-0729-1*, Quest) Theos Pub Hse.

B

An Asterisk (*) at the beginning of an entry indicates that the title is appearing for the first time.

— The Key to Theosophy. xii, 310p. 1930. reprint ed. 7.00 (*0-938998-03-X*) Theosophy.
— The Key to Theosophy: An Abridgement. Mills, Joy, ed. LC 75-181716. 1992. pap. 10.00 (*0-8356-0427-6*, Quest) Theos Pub Hse.
— The Key to Theosophy: Verbatim with 1889 Edition. LC 72-95701. 442p. 1995. reprint ed. 22.95 (*0-911500-06-5*); reprint ed. pap. 14.95 (*0-911500-07-3*) Theos U Pr.
— The Key to Theosophy Simplified. Codd, Clare, ed. 11.50 (*81-7059-078-7*, 7060, Quest) Theos Pub Hse.
— The Key to Theosophy (1890) 370p. 1998. reprint ed. pap. 24.95 (*0-7661-0171-1*) Kessinger Pub.
— A Modern Panarion. 504p. 1981. reprint ed. 16.00 (*0-938998-22-6*) Theosophy.
— Nightmare Tales. 139p. 1971. reprint ed. spiral bd. 14.00 (*0-7873-1219-3*) Hlth Research.
— Nightmare Tales. 135p. 1992. reprint ed. pap. 12.95 (*1-56459-251-0*) Kessinger Pub.
— The Original Programme of the Theosophical Society. 1931. 3.00 (*0-8356-7150-X*, Quest) Theos Pub Hse.
— The People of the Blue Mountains. 227p. 1996. reprint ed. pap. 19.95 (*1-56459-619-2*) Kessinger Pub.
— Practical Occultism. 3rd ed. 1989. 4.95 (*81-7059-076-0*, Pub. by Theos Pub Hse) Natl Bk Netwk.
— The Secret Doctrine, 2 vols. LC 92-51049. 1972. 500.00 (*0-8490-1010-1*) Gordon Pr.
— The Secret Doctrine, 3 vols. LC 92-51049. 2310p. 1993. pap. 49.95 (*0-8356-0238-9*, Quest) Theos Pub Hse.
— The Secret Doctrine, 2 vols. fac. ed. LC 74-76603. 1571p. 1999. reprint ed. pap. 29.95 (*1-55700-002-6*) Theos U Pr.
— The Secret Doctrine, 2 vols., fac. ed. LC 74-76603. 1571p. 1999. reprint ed. 41.95 (*1-55700-001-8*) Theos U Pr.
— The Secret Doctrine: The Synthesis of Science, Religion, & Philosophy, 2 vols. in 1. xci, 1474p. 1925. reprint ed. 22.00 (*0-938998-00-5*) Theosophy.
— The Secret Doctrine: The Synthesis of Science, Religion & Philosophy. (Occultism (1897) Ser.: Vol. 3). 610p. 1993. reprint ed. pap. 49.95 (*1-56459-415-7*) Kessinger Pub.
— Secret Doctrine Commentary--Stanzas I-IV: Transactions of the Blavatsky Lodge. fac. ed. LC 94-7279. 120p. 1994. reprint ed. 14.95 (*1-55700-027-1*); reprint ed. pap. 8.95 (*1-55700-028-X*) Theos U Pr.
— Secret Instructions to Probators of an Esoteric Occult School. 122p. 1996. reprint ed. spiral bd. 25.00 (*0-7873-1218-5*) Hlth Research.
— The Self & Its Problems: The Blavatsky Lecture for 1919. Woods, Charlotte E., ed. 190p. 1992. reprint ed. pap. 19.95 (*1-56459-264-2*) Kessinger Pub.
— Studies in Occultism. LC 67-18822. 218p. (C). 1987. 16.95 (*0-911500-08-1*); pap. 10.95 (*0-911500-09-X*) Theos U Pr.
— Studies in Occultism, No. 2. 68p. 1996. reprint ed. spiral bd. 9.00 (*0-7873-0113-2*) Hlth Research.
— Studies in Occultism, Vol. 3. 2nd ed. 57p. 1996. reprint ed. spiral bd. 10.00 (*0-7873-1336-X*) Hlth Research.
— Studies in Occultism, 1910 Vol. 1, 2 & 3, Vol. 1. 200p. 1996. reprint ed. pap. 9.95 (*1-56459-781-4*) Kessinger Pub.
— The Theophysical Glossary. 1975. lib. bdg. 250.00 (*0-87968-487-9*) Krishna Pr.
— Theosophical Articles: Reprinted from the Theosophist, Lucifer & other Nineteenth-Century Journals, 3 vols. 1692p. 1982. 48.00 (*0-938998-26-9*) Theosophy.
— The Theosophical Glossary: A Photographic Reproduction of the Original Edition, As First Issued at London, England, 1892. Mead, G. R., ed. & intro. by. vi, 389p. 1930. reprint ed. 17.00 (*0-938998-04-8*) Theosophy.
— The Theosophist: Oct. Eighteen Seventy-Nine to Sept. Eighteen Eighty. 2nd ed. (Secret Doctrine Reference Ser.). (Illus.). 320p. 1979. pap. 14.00 (*0-913510-31-9*) Wizards.
— Transactions of the Blavatsky Lodge of the T. S. Reprinted Verbatum from the Original Edition. 150p. 1923. 7.00 (*0-938998-05-6*) Theosophy.
— Two Books of the Stanzas of Dzyan. 1986. 8.75 (*81-7059-006-X*, 7223, Quest) Theos Pub Hse.
— The Veda Commentaries of H. P. Blavatsky. Spierenburg, H. J., ed. 250p. (Orig.). 1996. pap. 14.95 (*0-913004-98-7*) Point Loma Pub.
— Voice of the Silence. 1989. pap. 21.75 (*0-88695-046-5*) Concord Grove.
— Voice of the Silence. 1998. 5.50 (*81-7059-116-3*, 7228, Quest) Theos Pub Hse.
— The Voice of the Silence. LC 91-50978. 174p. 1992. pap. text 8.00 (*0-8356-0680-5*, Quest) Theos Pub Hse.
— The Voice of the Silence. LC 76-25345. 112p. 1992. reprint ed. 12.95 (*0-911500-04-9*); reprint ed. pap. 7.95 (*0-911500-05-7*) Theos U Pr.
— The Voice of the Silence: Being Extracts from the Book of the Golden Precepts. LC 91-50978. 178p. 1992. 15.95 (*0-8356-0681-3*, Quest) Theos Pub Hse.
— The Voice of the Silence (1889) 98p. 1998. reprint ed. pap. 14.95 (*0-7661-0202-5*) Kessinger Pub.

Blavatsky, Helena P., compiled by. Gems from the East: A Birthday Book of Precepts & Axioms. LC 83-50510. (Illus.). 224p. 1983. reprint ed. 15.95 (*0-911500-12-X*) Theos U Pr.
Blavatsky, Helena P., tr. The Voice of the Silence: Chosen Fragments from the Book of the Golden Precepts. iv, 110p. 1928. reprint ed. 5.00 (*0-938998-06-4*) Theosophy.
Blavatsky, Helena P. & Judge, W. Q. Occult Tales. 226p. 1996. reprint ed. pap. 19.95 (*1-56459-694-X*) Kessinger Pub.
Blavatsky, Helena P. & Van Mater, John P. The Secret Doctrine: Index. LC 97-35589. 441p. 1997. 20.95 (*1-55700-003-4*); pap. 13.95 (*1-55700-004-2*) Theos U Pr.
Blavatsky, Helena P., et al. Theosophical Articles & Notes. 300p. 1985. reprint ed. 16.00 (*0-938998-29-3*) Theosophy.
Blavatsky, Helena P., jt. auth. see Besant, A.
Blavatsky, Helena P., jt. auth. see Hillard, Katherine.
Blavatsky, Helena P., ed. see Hartman, Franz.
Blavatsky, Helena Petrovna & Iyer, Raghavan N. The Mystery of the Avatar: The Divine Descent. (Theosophical Texts Ser.). 80p. 1987. pap. 12.75 (*0-88695-035-X*) Concord Grove.
Blavet, M. Sonata in D Major, Opus 2 No. 5: For Flute. 24p. 1992. pap. 9.95 (*0-7935-1584-X*) H Leonard.
— Sonata in E Minor, Opus 2 No. 3: For Flute. 16p. 1991. pap. 8.95 (*0-7935-1206-9*, 50488571) H Leonard.
— Sonata Number 6 in a Minor: For Flute. 16p. 1992. pap. 9.95 (*0-7935-1585-8*) H Leonard.
Blavier-Paquot. Lexicon of Economic & Commercial Terms (Lexique des Termes Economiques et Commerciaux) (FRE & SPA.). 225p. 1988. pap. 24.95 (*0-7859-4659-4*) Fr & Eur.
Blavin, Nehemiah. The Owner's Manual to the Soul: A Modern Guide to Spirituality from the Most Ancient Jewish Torah Sources. LC 99-23299. 2000. 30.00 (*0-7657-6107-6*) Aronson.
Blavo, Ebenezer Q. The Problems of Refugees in Africa: Boundaries & Borders. (University of North London Voices in Development Management Ser.). 186p. 1999. text 65.95 (*1-84014-999-X*, Pub. by Ashgate Pub) Ashgate Pub Co.
Blaw, Melinda. Families Apart: Ten Keys to Successful Co-Parenting. 352p. (Orig.). 1995. pap. 12.00 (*0-399-52150-X*, Perigee Bks) Berkley Pub.
Blawyn, Elrond, et al. Chakra Workout: The Alchemy of Breath & Movement for Health & Transformation. (Illus.). 256p. 1999. pap. 14.95 (*1-56718-074-4*) Llewellyn Pubns.
Blaxall, Martha, ed. Women & the Workplace: The Implications of Occupational Segregation. LC 76-10536. 336p. 1976. pap. text 13.50 (*0-226-05822-0*); lib. bdg. 24.95 (*0-226-05821-2*) U Ch Pr.
Blaxell, Gregory, jt. auth. see Winch, Gordon.
Blaxland De Lange, Simon, tr. see Smit, Jorgen.
Blaxland, G. Cuthbert. Mayflower Essays: On the Story of the Pilgrim Fathers, As Told in Governor Bradford's Ms. History of the Plymouth Plantation. LC 78-39713. (Essay Index Reprint Ser.). 1977. reprint ed. 16.95 (*0-8369-2748-6*) Ayer.
Blaxland, Kathleen. Creative Clothing & Accessories for Children. LC 99-162257. (Illus.). 128p. 1998. pap. text 14.95 (*1-86351-213-6*, Pub. by Sally Milner) Sterling.
Blaxter, David, jt. auth. see Baxter, Betty.
Blaxter, John H., et al, eds. Advances in Marine Biology, Vol. 26. 314p. 1990. text 104.00 (*0-12-026126-X*) Acad Pr.
— Advances in Marine Biology, Vol. 34. 416p. (C). 1998. boxed set 99.95 (*0-12-026134-0*) Harcourt.
— Advances in Marine Biology Vol. 33: The Biology of Calanoid Copepods. (Illus.). 720p. (C). 1998. pap. 69.95 (*0-12-105545-0*); text 99.95 (*0-12-026133-2*) Morgan Kaufmann.
Blaxter, John H. & Southward, Alan J., eds. Advances in Marine Biology, Vol. 24. (Serial Publication Ser.). 473p. 1988. text 104.00 (*0-12-026124-3*) Acad Pr.
— Advances in Marine Biology, Vol. 25. 274p. 1989. text 104.00 (*0-12-026125-1*) Acad Pr.
— Advances in Marine Biology, Vol. 28. (Illus.). 452p. 1992. text 104.00 (*0-12-026128-6*) Acad Pr.
— Advances in Marine Biology, Vol. 29. (Illus.). 352p. 1993. text 104.00 (*0-12-026129-4*) Acad Pr.
— Advances in Marine Biology, Vol. 30. (Illus.). 361p. 1994. text. write for info. (*0-12-026130-8*) Acad Pr.
— Advances in Marine Biology, Vol. 31. (Illus.). 368p. 1997. text 75.00 (*0-12-026131-6*) Morgan Kaufmann.
Blaxter, Kenneth A. & Robertson, Noel. From Dearth to Plenty: The Modern Revolution in Food Production. (Illus.). 314p. (C). 1995. text 74.95 (*0-521-40322-7*) Cambridge U Pr.
Blaxter, Kenneth L. People, Food & Resources. 132p. 1986. text 49.95 (*0-521-32300-2*) Cambridge U Pr.
Blaxter, Kenneth L., ed. Food Chains & Human Nutrition. (Illus.). 459p. 1980. 117.00 (*0-85334-863-4*) Elsevier.
Blaxter, Loraine, et al. The Academic Career Handbook. LC 97-43057. (Illus.). 240p. 1998. pap. 27.95 (*0-335-19827-9*) OpUniv Pr.
— How to Research. 256p. 1996. pap. 19.95 (*0-335-19452-4*) OpUniv Pr.
— How to Succeed in Academic Life. LC 97-43057. (Illus.). 230p. 1998. pap. 89.00 (*0-335-19828-7*) OpUniv Pr.
Blaxton, John. The English Usurer: Or, Usury Condemned. LC 73-6102. (English Experience Ser.: No. 578). 80p. 1973. reprint ed. 20.00 (*90-221-0578-4*) Walter J Johnson.
Blaxton, Teresa, jt. auth. see Westphal, Christopher.
Blay. Reasons of the Infinite. 216p. 1999. pap. text 15.00 (*0-226-05835-2*) U Ch Pr.
Blay, Chuck & Siemers, Robert. Kauai's Geologic History - A Simplified Guide. (Illus.). 33p. 1998. pap. 10.95 (*0-9664058-0-3*) Teok Invest.
Blay, Iliana L. Sonntag, see Sonntag Blay, Iliana L.
Blay, Michel. Reasons of the Infinite. Debevoise, M. B., tr. LC 97-49423. 232p. 1998. 30.00 (*0-226-05834-4*) U Ch Pr.
Blay, Raphael David & Sergel, Christopher. Mother is a Freshman. 78p. 1949. pap. 5.50 (*0-87129-633-0*, M34) Dramatic Pub.
Blay, Sam, et al. Public International Law: An Australian Perspective. LC 98-158255. 1997. write for info. (*0-19-550690-1*) OUP.
Blay, Sam, et al, eds. Public International Law: An Australian Perspective. LC 98-158255. (Illus.). 476p. 1998. pap. text 55.00 (*0-19-553993-1*) OUP.
Blaylock, Bruce K. & Kennedy, Kenneth F., eds. Personal Financial Planning for Local Government Employees. LC 87-2948. (Orig.). 1987. pap. text 9.95 (*0-318-39866-4*) Intl City-Cnty Mgt.
Blaylock, Carolyn. Blessings & Prayers for You. LC 98-42206. 1999. 7.99 (*1-56476-770-1*) Chariot Victor.
Blaylock, James L. The Fundamentals of Public Speaking for Beginners. 32p. (Orig.). 1995. pap., teacher ed. 14.95 (*0-9645970-0-4*) J L Blaylock.
Blaylock, James P. All the Bells on Earth. LC 95-7142. 384p. 1995. 21.95 (*0-441-00247-1*) Ace Bks.
— All the Bells on Earth. 1997. mass mkt. 6.50 (*0-441-00490-3*) Ace Bks.
— Digging Leviathan. Cover, Arthur B., ed. Date not set. pap. write for info. (*1-893475-19-0*) Alexander Pubg.
— Homunculus. Cover, Arthur B., ed. Date not set. pap. write for info. (*1-893475-18-2*) Alexander Pubg.
— The Last Coin. 336p. 1996. mass mkt. 5.99 (*0-614-96140-8*) Ace Bks.
— The Last Coin. limited ed. 1988. 60.00 (*0-929480-00-7*) Mark Ziesing.
— Lord Kelvin's Machine. LC 91-14048. (Illus.). 272p. 1992. 22.95 (*0-87054-163-3*) Arkham.
— Night Relics. LC 93-14261. 320p. 1994. pap. 18.95 (*0-441-00022-3*) Ace Bks.
***Blaylock, James P.** Old Curiosity Shop. 54p. 1999. 50.00 (*1-892011-10-7*) ASAP Pub.
— Old Curiosity Shop. deluxe ed. 1999. 125.00 (*1-892011-11-5*) ASAP Pub.
Blaylock, James P. The Paper Grail. 1992. mass mkt. 5.99 (*0-441-65127-5*) Ace Bks.
— The Rainy Season. LC 99-13410. 368p. 1999. 21.95 (*0-441-00618-3*) Ace Bks.
***Blaylock, James P.** Rainy Season. 368p. 2000. mass mkt. 6.99 (*0-441-00756-2*) Ace Bks.
Blaylock, James P. Winter Tides. LC 96-6548. 352p. 1997. pap. 21.95 (*0-441-00444-X*) Ace Bks.
— Winter Tides. 352p. 1998. reprint ed. pap. 6.50 (*0-441-00575-6*) Ace Bks.
Blaylock, Mark. Nina's People. Fischbach, Karen, ed. 216p. 1998. spiral bd. 13.50 (*0-9654440-4-X*) Ironwood Pr AZ.
Blaylock, Mary. Mischief. unabridged ed. Schmidt, Peter, ed. LC 97-178984. (Illus.). 216p. (YA). (gr. 9 up). 1997. 20.95 (*0-9654440-0-7*) Ironwood Pr AZ.
***Blaylock, Mike.** Right Way to Win. 2000. write for info. (*0-8024-8415-8*) Moody.
Blaylock, Pearle. What's Happening in Friendsville? (Illus.). 200p. 1997. pap. 11.95 (*0-9649394-4-4*) Paint Rock.
Blaylock, Robert J., et al. California Probate Practice, 5 vols. 1991. 510.00 (*0-8205-1015-7*) Bender.
Blaylock, Russell L. Excitotoxins: The Taste That Kills. LC 96-52323. (Illus.). 1996. pap. 17.95 (*0-929173-25-2*) Health Press.
Blaylock, Suzanne. Getaway. (Sapphire Ser.). 1999. pap. text 9.95 (*0-352-33443-6*) London Brdge.
Blayne, et al. Lords of the Night. 320p. 1997. mass mkt. 4.99 (*0-8217-5593-5*, Zebra Kensgtn) Kensgtn Pub Corp.
Blayne, Sara. Enticed. 352p. 1999. mass mkt. 4.99 (*0-8217-6203-6*) Kensgtn Pub Corp.
***Blayne, Sara.** His Scandalous Duchess. 352p. 2000. mass mkt. 5.99 (*0-8217-6694-5*, Zebra Kensgtn) Kensgtn Pub Corp.
Blayne, Sara. Noble Deception. 1995. pap. 4.50 (*0-8217-5173-5*) NAL.
***Blayne, Sara.** Noble Heart. (Regency Romance Ser.). 2000. mass mkt. 4.99 (*0-8217-6653-8*, Zebra Kensgtn) Kensgtn Pub Corp.
Blayne, Sara. A Noble Pursuit. 256p. 1997. mass mkt. 4.99 (*0-8217-5756-3*, Zebra Kensgtn) Kensgtn Pub Corp.
— A Noble Resolve. 256p. 1998. pap. 4.99 (*0-8217-5912-4*) Kensgtn Pub Corp.
— Sea Witch. 1988. mass mkt. 3.75 (*0-8217-2542-4*, Zebra Kensgtn) Kensgtn Pub Corp.
Blayney, Margaret S., ed. see Chartier, Alain.
Blayney, Molly D. Wedded Bliss: A Victorian Bride's Handbook. (Illus.). 128p. 1991. 9.95 (*1-55859-332-2*) Abbeville Pr.
Blayney, Peter W. The First Folio of Shakespeare. (Illus.). 1991. pap. 7.95 (*0-9629254-3-8*) Folger.
Blaz, Ben. Bisita Guam: A Special Place in the Sun. LC 98-93161. 176p. 1998. write for info. (*0-9665238-1-4*) Evers Pr.
Blaz, Deborah. Foreign Language Teacher's Guide to Active Learning. LC 99-12549. 220p. 1999. pap. 29.95 (*1-883001-75-7*) Eye On Educ.
— Teaching Foreign Languages in the Block. LC 97-49633. (Teaching in the Block Ser.). 220p. 1998. pap. 29.95 (*1-883001-52-8*) Eye On Educ.
***Blaze.** Quick Review on Civil Procedure. 4th ed. (Sum & Substance Quick Review Ser.). 1999. pap. 18.95 (*0-314-24287-2*) West Pub.
Blaze, jt. auth. see Lankford.
Blaze, Doug. Civil Procedure. 3rd rev. ed. (Quick Review Ser.). 160p. (C). 1996. pap. text 18.95 (*1-57793-000-2*) Sum & Substance.
Blaze, Douglas A., jt. auth. see Lankford, Jefferson L.
Blaze, Elzear. Military Life under Napoleon: The Memoirs of Captain Elzear Blaze. 1997. 29.50 (*1-883476-06-2*, Pub. by Emperors Pr) Combined Pub.
Blaze, Francois H. L' Academie Imperiale de Musique: Histoire Litteraire, Musicale, Politique et Galant de Ce Theatre, de 1645 a 1855, 2 vols. LC 80-2258. 1981. reprint ed. 95.00 (*0-404-18804-4*) AMS Pr.
Blaze, John. Colt Flame. large type ed. (Linford Western Library). 288p. 1993. pap. 16.99 (*0-7089-7313-2*) Ulverscroft.
— Desert Trails. large type ed. (Linford Western Library). 288p. 1994. pap. 16.99 (*0-7089-7497-X*, Linford) Ulverscroft.
— Frontier Murder. large type ed. (Dales Large Print Ser.). 215p. 1997. pap. 18.99 (*1-85389-766-3*, Dales) Ulverscroft.
— Hell-Bent Gents. large type ed. (Linford Western Library). 288p. 1994. pap. 16.99 (*0-7089-7489-9*, Linford) Ulverscroft.
— Joe Killer. large type ed. (Dales Large Print Ser.). 206p. 1997. pap. 18.99 (*1-85389-736-1*) Ulverscroft.
— Killer's Greed. large type ed. (Linford Western Library). 272p. 1996. pap. 16.99 (*0-7089-7824-X*, Linford) Ulverscroft.
— Kiowa Blood. large type ed. (Western Ser.). 1994. pap. 16.99 (*0-7089-7592-5*, Linford) Ulverscroft.
— Lawless Hideout. large type ed. (Linford Western Library). 256p. 1993. pap. 16.99 (*0-7089-7437-6*, Linford) Ulverscroft.
— Shard at Lynchburg. large type ed. LC 96-10451. (Nightingale Ser.). 184p. 1996. pap. 17.95 (*0-7838-1735-5*, G K Hall Lrg Type) Mac Lib Ref.
— Sheriff Sixsmith. large type ed. (Dales Large Print Ser.). 224p. 1997. pap. 18.99 (*1-85389-737-X*, Dales) Ulverscroft.
— Young Gunnies. large type ed. (Linford Western Library). 272p. 1996. pap. 16.99 (*0-7089-7946-7*, Linford) Ulverscroft.
Blazejak, Jack. Quality Resource Planning: How to Integrate & Automate Your Quality Management System. unabridged ed. LC 98-92986. (Illus.). 219p. 1998. pap. 27.95 (*0-9664918-0-7*) Elemental Pubns.
Blazejczyk-Okolewska, Barbara. Chaotic Mechanics in Systems with Impacts & Friction. 1999. 51.00 (*981-02-3716-2*) World Scientific Pub.
Blazek, C., jt. auth. see Kadich, H.
Blazek, Dean & Blazek, Michael. Neon: The Next Generation. (Illus.). 240p. 1995. pap. 34.95 (*0-944094-07-4*) ST Pubns.
Blazek, Douglas. Flux & Reflux. 1970. pap. 2.50 (*0-685-04668-0*) Oyez.
Blazek, Douglas, ed. A Charles Bukowski Sampler. 3rd ed. 1979. reprint ed. pap. 3.00 (*0-685-04197-2*) Quixote.
Blazek, Jody. Financial Planning for Nonprofit Organizations. LC 96-19863. 304p. 1996. 67.95 (*0-471-12589-X*) Wiley.
***Blazek, Jody.** Tax Planning & Compliance for Tax-Exempt Organizations: Forms, Checklists, Procedures. 3rd ed. LC 98-44950. (Wiley Nonprofit Law, Finance, & Management Ser.). (Illus.). 818p. 1999. text 135.00 (*0-471-29380-6*) Wiley.
— Tax Planning & Compliance for Tax-exempt Organizations: Forms, Checklists, Procedures, February 2000 Supplement. 3rd ed. 112p. 2000. pap. 60.00 (*0-471-36138-0*) Wiley.
Blazek, Jody, jt. auth. see Hopkins, Bruce R.
Blazek, LeeAnn. Psychiatric Home Care & Care Paths: Step by Step. (Orig.). 1995. pap. write for info. (*0-9649995-0-1*) L A Blazek.
Blazek, Mark. Pecan Lovers' Cook Book. LC 86-25812. 120p. (Orig.). 1986. ring bd. 6.95 (*0-914846-27-2*) Golden West Pub.
Blazek, Michael, jt. auth. see Blazek, Dean.
Blazek, Patrick A. Nighthawks: Insider's Guide to the Heraldry & Insignia of the Lockheed F-117A Stealth Fighter. LC 98-86279. (Illus.). 80p. (Orig.). 1999. pap. 24.95 (*0-7643-0681-2*) Schiffer.
Blazek, Ronald & Aversa, Elizabeth S. The Humanities: A Selective Guide to Information Sources. 4th ed. LC 94-40302. (Library Science Text Ser.). 525p. 1994. pap. text 42.00 (*1-56308-168-7*) Libs Unl.
***Blazek, Ronald & Aversa, Elizabeth S.** The Humanities: A Selective Guide to Information Sources. 5th ed. LC 99-89831. (Humanities Ser.). 2000. 75.00 (*1-56308-601-8*) Libs Unl.
— The Humanities: A Selective Guide to Information Sources. 5th ed. LC 99-89831. (Humanities Ser.). 2000. pap. 60.00 (*1-56308-602-6*) Libs Unl.
Blazek, Ronald & Perrault, Anna H. United States History: A Selective Guide to Information Sources. xxviii, 411p. 1994. lib. bdg. 60.00 (*0-87287-984-4*) Libs Unl.
***Blazek, Sarah K.** An Irish Hallowe'en. LC 99-18323. (Illus.). 32p. (C). (gr. k-3). 1999. 14.95 (*1-56554-413-7*) Pelican.
Blazek, Sarah K. A Leprechaun's St. Patrick's Day. LC 96-22490. (Illus.). 32p. (J). (gr. 1-4). 1997. 14.95 (*1-56554-237-1*) Pelican.
Blazen, Ivan T. A Call to Ministry: Paul's Second Letter to the Corinthians. LC 97-45640. 1998. 8.99 (*0-8163-1581-7*) Pacific Pr Pub Assn.
Blazen, Ivan T. The Gospel on the Street: Paul's First Letter to the Corinthians. LC 97-18421. 1997. pap. 4.97 (*0-8163-1411-X*) Pacific Pr Pub Assn.
Blazer, Dan. Emotional Problems in Later Life: Intervention Strategies for Professional Caregivers. 2nd ed. LC 97-39495. 280p. 1997. 39.95 (*0-8261-7561-9*) Springer Pub.
— Freud vs. God: How Psychiatry Lost Its Soul & Christianity Lost Its Mind. LC 97-43516. 253p. 1998. 22.99 (*0-8308-1547-3*, 1547) InterVarsity.
Blazer, Dan G. Intervention Strategies for Emotional Problems in Later Life. LC 94-72729. 272p. 1994. pap. 50.00 (*1-56821-220-8*) Aronson.
Blazer, Dan G. & Hays, Judith C. An Introduction to Clinical Research in Psychiatry. (Oxford Psychiatry Ser.). (Illus.). 248p. 1998. text 39.95 (*0-19-510213-4*) OUP.
Blazer, Dan G., jt. ed. see Busse, Ewald W.
Blazer, Dolores, ed. Faith Development in Early Childhood. LC 88-61855. 192p. (Orig.). (C). 1989. pap. 12.95 (*1-55612-212-8*) Sheed & Ward WI.
***Blazer, Don.** Healthy Horses Seldom Burp. Small, Meribah, ed. LC 98-91055. (Illus.). 192p. 1999. pap. 19.95 (*0-9660127-2-0*) Success is Easy.

Blazer, Don. Make Money with Horses: You Can Do It! LC 97-92440. (Illus.). 142p. 1998. pap. 19.95 (*0-9660127-0-4*) Success is Easy.
— Nine Secrets of Perfect Horsemanship. Small, Meribah, ed. LC 97-91294. 149p. 1998. pap. 19.95 (*0-9660127-1-2*) Success is Easy.
Blazer, Stuart. Ricochet. 58p. 1988. write for info. (*0-318-64090-2*) Poets Pr.
***Blazewicz, J., et al, eds.** Handbook of Parallel & Distributed Processing. LC 99-56742. (International Handbooks on Information Systems Ser.). (Illus.). x, 635p. 2000. 119.00 (*3-540-66441-6*) Spr-Verlag.
Blazewicz, Jacek. Scheduling Computer & Manufacturing Processes. LC 96-29227. 488p. 1996. 129.50 (*3-540-61496-6*) Spr-Verlag.
Blazewicz, Jacek, et al. Scheduling in Computer & Manufacturing Systems. LC 92-37487. 1992. 109.00 (*0-387-55958-2*) Spr-Verlag.
— Scheduling in Computer & Manufacturing Systems. 2nd rev. ed. LC 94-17909. 1994. 99.95 (*0-387-58049-2*) Spr-Verlag.
Blazey-Ayoub, P. J., et al. Concise Evidence Law. 262p. 1996. pap. 39.00 (*1-86287-192-2*, Pub. by Federation Pr) Gaunt.
Blazey, Mark, jt. auth. see Lipman, Henry.
Blazey, Mark L. Insights to Performance Excellence 1998: An Inside Look at the 1998 Baldrige Award Criteria. (Illus.). 266p. 1998. pap. 37.00 (*0-87389-431-6*, H0998) ASQ Qual Pr.
Blazey, Richard. The Saga of the Electric Fork. 1990. pap. text 5.00 (*1-879719-02-9*) Idea Connect.
— Tales of the Innovation Process. (Illus.). 1990. write for info. (*1-879719-03-7*) Idea Connect.
Blazhevich, Vladislav. Advanced Musical Etudes for Trombone & Euphonium: 112 Rhythmic & Melodic Etudes in Bass Clef. Fink, Reginald H., ed. 96p. (C). 1991. student ed. 19.50 (*0-918194-23-7*) Accura.
— Advanced Rhythm & Technic Etudes: 26 Melodic Studies in Bass Clef. Fink, Reginald H., ed. 64p. (C). 1991. student ed. 12.98 (*0-918194-22-9*) Accura.
— Clef Studies for Trombone. 88p. 1985. pap. 8.95 (*0-7935-3315-5*, 00120238) H Leonard.
— Symphonic Duets in Bass Clef: Thirty-Eight Pedagocical & Performance Duets in Bass Clef. Fink, Reginald H., ed. 94p. 1992. student ed. 19.95 (*0-918194-25-3*) Accura.
Blazier, Kenneth D. Una Escuela Biblica Creciente - A Growing Church School. (SPA.). 1981. pap. 6.00 (*0-8170-0928-0*) Judson.
— A Growing Church School. LC 77-26297. 64p. 1978. reprint ed. pap. 30.00 (*0-608-00216-X*, 206101000006) Bks Demand.
Blazier, Kenneth D. & Isham, Linda R., eds. The Teaching Church at Work: A Manual for the Board of Christian Education. rev. ed. LC 93-31239. 88p. 1993. pap. 13.00 (*0-8170-1191-9*) Judson.
Blazier, W., jt. auth. see Ebbing, C.
Blazina, Carol A. Ballroom Dance: A Step in the Right Direction. (Illus.). (Orig.). pap. 9.00 (*0-614-00085-8*) C A Blazina.
Blazostocki, J. Giovanni Lorenzo Bernini. 70p. 1981. 50.00 (*0-7855-1620-4*) St Mut.
Blazovich, Phil. Having Fun with Baseball Nicknames. (Illus.). vi, 281p. (Orig.). 1997. pap. 20.00 (*0-9657492-0-7*) MLC Pubns MN.
Blazquez, E., ed. Gut Regulatory Peptides: Their Role in Health & Disease. (Frontiers of Hormone Research Ser.: Vol. 16). (Illus.). viii, 236p. 1988. 161.00 (*3-8055-4520-7*) S Karger.
Blazquez, Ricardo. Neo-Catechumenal Communities. (C). 1988. 39.00 (*0-7855-3222-6*, Pub. by St Paul Pubns) St Mut.
— Neo-Catechumenal Communities. 110p. (C). 1990. 40.00 (*0-85439-280-7*, Pub. by St Paul Pubns) St Mut.
Blazquez, T. M. Manual de Historia de Espana Vol. 1: Prehistoria, y Edad Antigua. 562p. 1989. 125.00 (*84-239-5091-3*) Elliots Bks.
Blazucki, Joan, jt. auth. see Lawson, Harvey.
Blazwick, Iwona. Abigail Lane. (Illus.). 48p. 1996. 24.95 (*0-905263-74-X*) Dist Art Pubs.
***Blazwick, Iwona & Wilson, Simon, eds.** Tate Modern: The Handbook. (Illus.). 272p. 2000. pap. 29.95 (*0-520-22770-0*, Pub. by U CA Pr) Cal Prin Full Svc.
***Blazwick, Iwona & Wilson, Simon P., eds.** Tate Modern: The Handbook. (Illus.). 272p. 2000. 50.00 (*0-520-22769-7*, Pub. by U CA Pr) Cal Prin Full Svc.
Blazyca, George & Dubrowski, Janusz M. Monitoring Economic Transition: The Polish Case. 192p. 1995. text 68.95 (*1-85972-068-4*, Pub. by Avebry) Ashgate Pub Co.
Blazynski, T. Z. Applied Elasto-Plasticity of Solids. (Illus.). 272p. (C). 1984. text 60.00 (*0-333-34544-4*) Scholium Intl.
***Blbejer, Mario I. & International Monetary Fund Staff.** Inflation Targeting in Practice: Strategic & Operational Issues & Application to Emerging Market Economies. LC 00-35115. 2000. write for info. (*1-55775-889-1*) Intl Monetary.
Blbejer, Mario I. & Skreb, Marko. Balance of Payments, Exchange Rates & Competitiveness in Transition Economics. LC 99-26147. 1999. write for info. (*0-7923-8441-5*) Kluwer Academic.
***Blbejer, Mario I. & Skreb, Marko.** Balance of Payments, Exchange Rates & Competitiveness in Transition Economies. LC 99-26147. 1999. write for info. (*0-7923-8422-9*) Kluwer Academic.
Blea, Irene I. Bessemer: A Sociological Perspective of a Chicano Barrio. LC 87-45778. (Immigrant Communities & Ethnic Minorities in the U. S. & Canada Ser.: No. 13). (Illus.). 1991. 49.50 (*0-404-19423-0*) AMS Pr.
— La Chicana & the Intersection of Race, Class & Gender. LC 90-28075. 192p. 1991. 59.95 (*0-275-93980-4*, C3980, Praeger Pubs); pap. 16.95 (*0-275-93982-0*, B3982, Praeger Pubs) Greenwood.
— Researching Chicano Communities: Social-Historical, Physical, Psychological, & Spiritual Space. LC 95-2224. 176p. 1995. 59.95 (*0-275-94974-5*, Praeger Pubs); pap. 18.95 (*0-275-95219-3*, Praeger Pubs) Greenwood.
— Toward a Chicano Social Science. LC 88-6593. 173p. 1988. 42.95 (*0-275-92408-4*, C2408, Praeger Pubs); pap. 18.95 (*0-275-92531-5*, B2531, Praeger Pubs) Greenwood.
— U. S. Chicanas & Latinas Within a Global Context: Women of Color at the Fourth World Women's Conference. LC 97-12806. 200p. 1997. 59.95 (*0-275-95623-7*, Praeger Pubs); pap. 20.95 (*0-275-95624-5*, Praeger Pubs) Greenwood.
***Blea, Juan.** Under the Same Sky: A Santero's Journey. 87p. 2000. pap. 12.95 (*0-615-11156-4*) Redtail.
***Bleach, Kevan.** Induction & Mentoring of Newly Qualified Teachers: A New Deal for Teachers. (Illus.). 134p. 1999. pap. 29.95 (*1-85346-635-2*) David Fulton.
Bleach, Nigel, et al. Operative Otorhinolaryngology. LC 95-47084. (Illus.). 512p. 1997. 299.95 (*0-632-03747-4*) Blackwell Sci.
Bleach, Yvonne, jt. auth. see Miller, Stanford.
Bleackley, Horace. Ladies Fair & Frail. (Biographical Reference Works). xiv, 328p. 1985. reprint ed. 49.00 (*0-932051-26-X*) Rprt Serv.
— Trial of Jack Sheppard, No. 1. (Notable British Trials Ser.). vi, 260p. 1995. reprint ed. 81.00 (*1-56169-117-8*) Gaunt.
Bleackley, Horace, ed. Trial of Henry Fauntleroy, No. 1. (Notable British Trials Ser.). 269p. 1995. reprint ed. 84.00 (*1-56169-130-5*) Gaunt.
***Bleakley, Alan, contrib. by.** The Animalizing Imagination: Totemism, Textuality & Ecocriticism. LC 99-38751. 2000. text 59.95 (*0-312-22830-9*) St Martin.
Bleakley, Alasdair & Anselm, Marcus. Intellectual Property & Media Law Companion. 120p. 1997. pap. 33.00 (*1-85811-118-8*, Pub. by CLT Prof) Gaunt.
Bleakley, Ann & Carrigan, Jackie. Resource-Based Learning Activities: Information Literacy for High School Students. LC 94-13857. 1994. pap. 30.00 (*0-8389-3443-9*) ALA.
***Bleakley, David.** C. S. Lewis at Home in Ireland. LC 99-191219. 202 p. 1998. 9.99 (*1-898787-67-0*) Ambassador Prodns Ltd.
Bleakley, Kenneth. Economic Impact Analysis: Assessing a Project's Value to a Community. Kerrigan, Sheila, ed. 75p. (Orig.). 1993. pap. text 75.00 (*0-9616567-4-3*) Amer Econ Dev Council.
Bleakney, Darlene H. Ideas for Library Teachers. (Illus.). 170p. 1991. ring bd. 21.95 (*0-89420-274-X*, 343660) Natl Book.
Bleakney, Thomas P. Retirement Systems for Public Employees. (Pension Research Council Publications). 232p. (C). 1991. text 37.50 (*0-256-01407-8*) U of Pa Pr.
***Bleandonu, Gerard.** Wilfred Bion: His Life & Works, 1897-1979. LC 00-28346. (Illus.). 2000. write for info. (*1-892746-57-3*) Other Pr LLC.
Bleandonu, Gerard. Wilfred Bion: His Life & Works, 1897-1979. Pajaczkowska, Claire, tr. from FRE. (Illus.). 301p. 1998. reprint ed. 42.00 (*1-892746-09-3*, 46093) Other Pr LLC.
Bleaney, B. I. Electricity & Magnetism, Vol. 1. 3rd ed. (Illus.). 324p. 1989. pap. text 40.00 (*0-19-851172-8*) OUP.
Bleaney, B. I. Electricity & Magnetism, Vol. 2. 3rd ed. (Illus.). 470p. 1989. pap. text 40.00 (*0-19-851173-6*) OUP.
Bleaney, C. H. Israel & the West Bank & Gaza Strip. 2nd rev. ed. LC 96-192269. (World Bibliographical Ser.: Vol. 58). 390p. 1994. lib. bdg. 86.50 (*1-85109-176-9*) ABC-CLIO.
— Lebanon. 2nd rev. ed. LC 92-190447. (World Bibliographical Ser.). 264p. 1992. lib. bdg. 84.00 (*1-85109-150-5*) ABC-CLIO.
Bleaney, C. H., compiled by. Iraq. 2nd rev. ed. LC 96-192554. (World Bibliographical Ser.: Vol. 42). 264p. 1995. lib. bdg. 72.00 (*1-85109-229-3*) ABC-CLIO.
Bleaney, Michael F., jt. ed. see Greenaway, David.
Bleasdale, Alan. Boys from the Blackstuff. 281p. 1990. pap. 15.95 (*0-7487-0350-0*) Dufour.
Bleasdale, J. K. Molecular Mechanisms in Bioorganic Processes. Golding, Bernard T., ed. 1990. 142.00 (*0-85186-946-7*) CRC Pr.
Bleasdale, John E., et al, eds. Inositol & Phosphoinositides: Metabolism & Regulation. LC 84-131. (Experimental Biology & Medicine Ser.: Vol. 6). (Illus.). 698p. 1985. 125.00 (*0-89603-074-1*) Humana.
Bleasdell, Babsie. Babsie, Go Teach My People. 1998. pap. text 12.95 (*0-940535-96-3*) Franciscan U Pr.
Bleasdell, Ursula. Refresh Your Life in the Spirit: How the Holy Spirit Can Empower You Every Day. LC 97-22779. 180p. 1997. pap. text 10.99 (*1-56955-022-0*) Servant.
Blease, Derek. Evaluating Educational Software. 160p. 1986. 35.00 (*0-317-44653-3*, Pub. by C Helm) Routldge.
Blease, Kathleen. A Friend is Forever: Precious Poems That Celebrate the Beauty of Friendship. LC 98-31426. 144p. 1999. pap. 10.00 (*0-449-00381-7*) Fawcett.
— Love in Verse. LC 97-29400. 128p. 1999. pap. 10.00 (*0-449-00128-8*) Fawcett.
***Blease, Kathleen.** Love in Verse. 1999. pap. 10.00 (*0-449-45904-7*) Fawcett.
Blease, Kathleen. A Mother's Love: Classic Poems Celebrating the Maternal Heart. LC 98-51979. 144p. 1999. pap. 10.00 (*0-449-00545-3*) Fawcett.
***Blease, Kathleen.** One Dark Night: 13 Masterpieces of the Macabre. (Illus.). 144p. 2000. pap. 10.00 (*0-345-44044-7*, Ballantine) Ballantine Pub Grp.
Blease, Walter L. The Emancipation of English Women. LC 78-173103. 1972. reprint ed. 26.95 (*0-405-08274-6*, Pub. by Blom Pubns) Ayer.
Bleau, Barbara L. Forgotten Algebra. 2nd ed. 330p. 1994. pap. 12.95 (*0-8120-1942-3*) Barron.
— Forgotten Calculus: A Refresher Course with Applications to Economics & Business. 2nd ed. LC 94-4070. 400p. 1994. pap. 13.95 (*0-8120-1941-5*) Barron.
Bleau, Savannah. Greek Style. LC 98-90753. 1999. 22.95 (*0-533-12906-0*) Vantage.
Bleby, Henry. Josiah: The Maimed Fugitive. LC 76-89422. (Black Heritage Library Collection). 1977. 15.95 (*0-8369-8513-3*) Ayer.
***Blech, Benjamin.** The Compete Idiot's Guide to Understanding Judaism. 384p. 1999. pap. text 16.95 (*0-02-863191-9*, Pub. by Macmillan Gen Ref) S&S Trade.
Blech, Benjamin. More Secrets of Hebrew Words: Holy Days & Happy Days. LC 93-14636. 232p. 1993. 30.00 (*0-87668-223-9*) Aronson.
— The Secrets of Hebrew Words. LC 90-48735. 248p. 1991. 40.00 (*0-87668-610-2*) Aronson.
Blecha, A., jt. ed. see Courvoisier, T. J.
Blecharczyk & Lister. Investigating Human Development. (C). 1992. text 13.25 (*0-07-005872-5*) McGraw.
Blecher, Carol S., et al. Safe Handling Cytotoxic Drugs: An Independent Study Module. rev. ed. Welch, Jacqueline & Silveria, Joyce M., eds. (Illus.). 20p. 1997. pap. text 10.00 (*1-890504-00-9*) Oncology Nursing.
***Blecher, David P., et al.** Categories of Operator Modules: Morita Equivalence & Projective Modules. LC 99-54529. (Memoirs of the American Mathematical Society Ser.). 1999. write for info. (*0-8218-1916-X*) Am Math.
Blecher, Earl. Advocacy Planning for Urban Development: With Analysis of Six Demonstration Programs. LC 77-146890. (Special Studies in U. S. Economic, Social & Political Issues). 1971. 39.50 (*0-89197-650-7*) Irvington.
Blecher, George, jt. ed. see Blecher, Lone T.
Blecher, George, tr. see Larsen, Michael.
Blecher, George, tr. see Nilsson, Ulf.
Blecher, George, tr. see Tikkanen, Henrik.
Blecher, Lone T. & Blecher, George, eds. Swedish Folktales & Legends. (Illus.). 416p. 1995. pap. 17.00 (*0-679-75841-0*) Pantheon.
Blecher, Lone T., tr. see Larsen, Michael.
Blecher, Lone T., tr. see Nilsson, Ulf.
Blecher, Lone T., tr. see Tikkanen, Henrik.
Blecher, M. & Gotow, K., eds. Low Energy Tests of Conservation Laws in Particle Physics: Conference Proceedings, Blacksburg, Virginia, 1983. LC 84-71157. (AIP Conference Proceedings Ser.: No. 114, Subseries on Particles & Fields No. 33). 322p. 1984. lib. bdg. 40.50 (*0-88318-313-7*) Am Inst Physics.
Blecher, Marc. China. (Marxist Regimes Ser.). 252p. 1986. text 49.00 (*0-86187-402-1*); pap. text 17.50 (*0-86187-403-X*) St Martin.
— China Against the Tides: Iconoclasm & Innovation in Revolution & Reform. 224p. 1997. pap. 24.95 (*1-85567-227-8*) Bks Intl VA.
— China Against the Tides: Iconoclasm & Innovation in Revolution & Reform. 2nd ed. 272p. 1997. 85.00 (*1-85567-226-X*) Bks Intl VA.
Blecher, Marc J. Tethered Deer: Government & Economy in a Chinese County. LC 95-19174. 322p. 1996. 39.50 (*0-8047-2565-9*) Stanford U Pr.
Blecher, Melvin, ed. Methods in Receptor Research, 2 pts., Pt. 1. LC 75-40846. (Methods in Molecular Biology Ser.: No. 9). (Illus.). 403p. reprint ed. pap. 125.00 (*0-8357-6210-6*, 203451700001) Bks Demand.
— Methods in Receptor Research, 2 pts., Pt. 2. LC 75-40846. (Methods in Molecular Biology Ser.: No. 9). (Illus.). 396p. reprint ed. pap. 122.80 (*0-8357-6211-4*, 203451700002) Bks Demand.
Blecher, Sharon & Jaffee, Kathy. Weaving in the Arts, Widening the Learning Circle: Integrating the Fine Arts in the Classroom Curriculum. LC 97-51721. 211p. 1998. pap. 26.00 (*0-325-00032-8*) Heinemann.
Blechert, Siegfried, ed. see De Meijere, Armin.
Blechinger, C. J. & Sherif, S. A., eds. Devices for Flow Measurement & Control 1993. LC 93-71642. (FED Ser.: Vol. 159). 69p. 1993. pap. 25.00 (*0-7918-0967-6*, H00799) ASME.
Blechman, Barry L., et al. The American Military in the Twenty-First Century. LC 93-33963. 530p. 1993. text 55.00 (*0-312-10369-7*) St Martin.
Blechman, Barry M. The Case for Nuclear Arms Control. (CISA Working Papers: No. 47). 31p. (Orig.). 1985. pap. 15.00 (*0-86682-060-4*) Ctr Intl Relations.
— The Changing Soviet Navy. LC 73-2881. (Studies in Defense Policy). 51p. 1973. pap. 7.95 (*0-8157-0995-1*) Brookings.
— The Control of Naval Armaments: Prospects & Possibilities. LC 75-5153. (Brookings Institution Studies in Defense Policy). 110p. reprint ed. pap. 34.10 (*0-608-14527-0*, 202536200043) Bks Demand.
Blechman, Barry M., ed. Preventing Nuclear War: A Realistic Approach. LC 84-43115. (Illus.). 197p. reprint ed. pap. 61.10 (*0-608-09329-7*, 205407500002) Bks Demand.
Blechman, Barry M. & Ellis, W. Philip. The Politics of National Security: Congress & U. S. Defense Policy. 272p. 1992. reprint ed. pap. text 22.00 (*0-19-507705-9*) OUP.
Blechman, Barry M. & Fisher, Cathleen S. The Silent Partner: West Germany & Arms Control. 280p. 1988. 39.95 (*0-88730-316-1*, HarpBusn); pap. text 21.95 (*0-88730-320-X*, HarpBusn) HarpInfo.
Blechman, Barry M. & Nolan, Janne E. The U. S.-Soviet Conventional Arms Transfer Negotiations. (Pew Case Studies in International Affairs). 50p. (C). 1993. pap. text 3.50 (*1-56927-302-2*) Geo U Inst Dplmcy.
Blechman, Barry M., et al. The Soviet Military Buildup & U. S. Defense Spending. LC 77-86492. (Brookings Institution Studies in Defense Policy). 69p. reprint ed. pap. 30.00 (*0-608-14528-9*, 202536300043) Bks Demand.
Blechman, Bruce J. & Levinson, Jay C. Guerrilla Financing: Alternative Techniques to Finance Any Small Business. (Guerrilla Ser.). 352p. 1992. pap. 14.00 (*0-395-52264-1*) HM.
Blechman, Burt. How Much. 1961. 10.95 (*0-8392-1050-7*) Astor-Honor.
Blechman, Elaine A. Solving Child Behavior Problems at Home & at School. LC 85-61468. 296p. (Orig.). 1985. pap. text 18.95 (*0-87822-247-2*, 2472) Res Press.
Blechman, Elaine A., ed. Behavior Modification with Women. LC 82-15655. 560p. reprint ed. pap. 173.60 (*0-7837-0687-1*, 204102000019) Bks Demand.
— Emotions & the Family: For Better or for Worse. 248p. (C). 1990. text 69.95 (*0-8058-0136-7*) L Erlbaum Assocs.
Blechman, Elaine A. & Brownell, Kelly D., eds. Behavioral Medicine & Women: A Comprehensive Handbook. LC 97-36130. 876p. 1997. lib. bdg. 80.00 (*1-57230-218-6*, 0218) Guilford Pubns.
Blechman, Elaine A., jt. ed. see Hetherington, E. Mavis.
Blechman, Fred. Bent Wings. LC 98-83109. 365p. 1999. 25.00 (*0-7388-0345-6*); pap. 15.00 (*0-7388-0346-4*) Xlibris Corp.
— Simple, Low Cost Electronics Projects. LC 97-77994. (Illus.). 224p. 1998. pap. 19.95 (*1-878707-46-9*) LLH Tech Pub.
Blechman, Max, ed. Drunken Boat: Art, Rebellion & Anarchy. (Illus.). 288p. (Orig.). 1994. pap. 12.00 (*1-57027-002-3*) Left Bank.
***Blechman, Max, ed.** Revolutionary Romanticism: A Drunken Boat Anthology. LC 99-17522. 260p. 1999. pap. 15.95 (*0-87286-351-4*, Pub. by City Lights) SPD-Small Pr Dist.
***Blechman, Nicholas, et al.** Fresh Dialogue 1: New Voices in Graphic Design. LC 99-53585. (Illus.). 144p. 2000. pap. 24.95 (*1-56898-223-2*) Princeton Arch.
***Blechman, R. O.** The Juggler of Our Lady: A Medieval Legend. (Illus.). 122p. 2000. reprint ed. text. write for info. (*0-7881-9045-8*) DIANE Pub.
— The Life of Saint Nicholas. (Illus.). 120p. 2000. reprint ed. text 19.00 (*0-7881-9052-0*) DIANE Pub.
Blechman, Rachel S., jt. auth. see Goonan, Norma M.
Blechman, Samuel. Through My Eyes. 2nd ed. 136p. 1994. pap. 10.00 (*0-9615879-3-8*) Puddinhead Pr.
Blechner, Marc J. & White, Gordon. Micropolitics in Contemporary China: A Technical Unit During & after the Cultural Revolution. LC 79-67176. 149p. 1979. reprint ed. pap. 46.20 (*0-7837-9965-9*, 206069200006) Bks Demand.
Blechner, Mark J., ed. Hope & Mortality: Psychodynamic Approaches to AIDS & HIV. LC 97-13637. 288p. 1997. 45.00 (*0-88163-223-6*) Analytic Pr.
Bleck, Eugene E. Orthopedic Management of Cerebral Palsy. 2nd ed. LC 65-80559. (Clinics in Developmental Medicine Ser.: No. 99-100). (Illus.). 497p. (C). 1991. text 85.00 (*0-521-41218-8*) Mc Keith Pr.
Bleck, Linda. The Answer Is at School: Bringing Health Care to Our Students. 36p. (Orig.). 1993. pap. write for info. (*0-942054-07-5*) R W Johnson Found.
Bleck, Robert T., jt. auth. see Araoz, Daniel L.
Bleck, Thomas P., ed. Neurocritical Care. 352p. Date not set. text 65.00 (*0-07-005925-X*) McGraw-Hill HPD.
Bleck, Thomas P., jt. auth. see Mandell, Gerald L.
Bleck, Thomas P., jt. ed. see Mandell, Gerald L.
Blecker, Robert A. Are Americans on a Consumption Binge? The Evidence Reconsidered. 71p. 1990. 12.00 (*0-944826-22-9*) Economic Policy Inst.
— Beyond the Twin Deficits: A Trade Strategy for the 1990s. LC 92-9033. (Economic Policy Institute Ser.). 296p. (gr. 13). 1992. pap. text 35.95 (*1-56324-091-2*) M E Sharpe.
— Beyond the Twin Deficits: A Trade Strategy for the 1990s. LC 92-9033. (Economic Policy Institute Ser.). 296p. (C). (gr. 13). 1992. text 74.95 (*1-56324-090-4*) M E Sharpe.
Blecker, Robert A., ed. U. S. Trade Policy & Global Growth: New Directions in the International Economy. LC 95-9028. (Economic Policy Institute Ser.). 336p. (C). (gr. 13). 1995. text 74.95 (*1-56324-530-2*); pap. text 35.95 (*1-56324-531-0*) M E Sharpe.
Blecki, Catherine L. & Wulf, Karin A. Milcah Martha Moore's Book: A Commonplace Book of Early American Literature. LC 96-37555. 1997. 45.00 (*0-271-01690-6*); pap. 14.95 (*0-271-01691-4*) Pa St U Pr.
Bleckner, Ross, photos by. Ross Bleckner: Watercolor. (Illus.). 108p. 1998. bds. 55.00 (*0-9657280-9-9*) Arena Editions.
— Ross Bleckner Photographs. (Illus.). 124p. 1998. 60.00 (*0-944092-58-6*) Twin Palms Pub.
— Ross Bleckner Photographs. limited ed. (Illus.). 124p. 1998. 150.00 (*0-944092-59-4*) Twin Palms Pub.
Bleckner, Ross & Strassfield, Christina M. Ross Bleckner. (Illus.). 12p. 1993. pap. 5.00 (*0-933793-28-6*) Guild Hall.
Bleckner, Ross, jt. auth. see Ottmann, Klaus.
Blecua, Alberto, ed. see De Cervantes Saavedra, Miguel.
Bleddyn, Davies, jt. auth. see Bebbington, Andrew.
Bledsoe. Paramedic Emergency Care. 4th ed. 288p. 2000. 61.33 (*0-8359-5033-6*) P-H.
Bledsoe, jt. auth. see Porter.
Bledsoe, Albert T. Essay on Liberty & Slavery. LC 72-149864. (Black Heritage Library Collection). 1977. 28.95 (*0-8369-8746-2*) Ayer.

— An Examination of President Edwards' Inquiry into the Freedom of the Will. LC 75-3003. reprint ed. 55.00 (*0-404-59047-0*) AMS Pr.

— The Philosophy of Mathematics. LC 75-3004. (Philosophy in America Ser.). reprint ed. 49.50 (*0-404-59048-9*) AMS Pr.

Bledsoe, Bryan. Anatomy & Physiology for Emergency Care. (C). 1998. 36.00 (*0-8359-4992-3*) P-H.

***Bledsoe, Bryan & Porter, Robert.** Paramedic Careions Vol. 5: Principles & Practice. 448p. 2000. 51.93 (*0-13-021599-6*) P-H.

Bledsoe, Bryan, jt. auth. see Porter, Robert.

Bledsoe, Bryan E. Atlas of Paramedic Skills. (Illus.). 272p. 1987. pap. 60.00 (*0-89303-444-4*) P-H.

— Intermediate Emergency Care. 1994. pap., wbk. ed. 16.67 (*0-89303-024-4*) Mosby Inc.

— Prehospital Emergency Pharmacology. 2nd ed. (Illus.). 304p. 1988. pap. text 31.00 (*0-89303-797-4*) P-H.

Bledsoe, Bryan E. & Clayden, Dwayne E. Paramedic Pocket Reference. 2nd ed. LC 97-19809. 192p. 1997. pap. text 23.00 (*0-8359-5120-0*) P-H.

***Bledsoe, Bryan E. & Porter, Robert S.** Paramedic Care. 2000. pap., teacher ed. 46.60 (*0-13-021631-3*) P-H.

— Paramedic Care: Patient. 128p. 2000. wbk. ed. 31.33 (*0-13-021632-1*) P-H.

Bledsoe, Bryan E. & Porter, Robert S. Paramedic Emergency Care. 3rd ed. 1136p. 1996. 74.00 (*0-8359-4987-7*, Pub. by P-H) S&S Trade.

Bledsoe, Bryan E., et al. Intermediate Emergency Care. 2nd ed. LC 97-41364. 480p. 1997. pap. 57.00 (*0-8359-5160-X*) P-H.

— Prehospital Emergency Pharmacology. LC 83-15893. 336p. pap. text 19.95 (*0-89303-765-6*) P-H.

— Prehospital Emergency Pharmacology. 4th ed. LC 95-24665. 432p. 1995. 49.00 (*0-8359-6065-X*) P-H.

Bledsoe, Caroline, et al, eds. Fertility & the Male Life Cycle in the Era of Fertility Decline. (International Studies in Demography). (Illus.). 386p. 2000. text 85.00 (*0-19-829444-1*) OUP.

Bledsoe, Caroline & Pison, Gilles, eds. Nuptiality in Sub-Saharan Africa: Contemporary Anthropological & Demographic Perspectives. (International Studies in Demography). (Illus.). 342p. 1994. text 72.00 (*0-19-828761-5*) OUP.

Bledsoe, Caroline H. Women & Marriage in Kpelle Society. LC 78-66170. 233p. 1980. reprint ed. pap. 30.00 (*0-608-03817-2*, 206467200009) Bks Demand.

Bledsoe, Caroline H., ed. see Caroline H.\National Research Council Staff.

Bledsoe, Caroline H., ed. see National Research Council Staff.

Bledsoe, Christena, jt. auth. see Bailey, Cornelia.

Bledsoe, Dennis, jt. ed. see Cutino, Peter.

Bledsoe, Drew & Brown, Greg. Make the Right Call. LC 98-38629. (Illus.). 40p. (J). (gr. 2-7). 1998. 14.95 (*0-87833-215-4*) Taylor Pub.

***Bledsoe, Erik, ed.** Getting Naked with Harry Crews. LC 99-33902. 376p. 1999. 24.95 (*0-8130-1709-2*) U Press Fla.

Bledsoe, Erik, ed. see Burton, W. C.

Bledsoe, Erik, ed. see Burton, W. C. "Mutt".

Bledsoe, Glen. Creepy Classics III. (Classics Ser.). 128p. 1999. pap. 5.95 (*0-7373-0122-8*, 01228W) NTC Contemp Pub Co.

Bledsoe, Glen & Bledsoe, Karen, compiled by. Classic Sea Stories. (Illus.). 128p. (J). (gr. 4-7). 1999. pap. 5.95 (*0-7373-0041-8*, 00418W) NTC Contemp Pub Co.

Bledsoe, Glen & Bledsoe, Karen, eds. Classic Mysteries Vol. II: A Collection of Mind-Bending Masterpieces. (Roxbury Park Ser.). (Illus.). 128p. (J). (gr. 4-7). 1999. pap. 5.95 (*0-7373-0273-9*, 02739W, Pub. by Lowell Hse) NTC Contemp Pub Co.

***Bledsoe, Glen & Bledsoe, Karen E.** Ballooning Adventures. LC 00-24997. (Dangerous Adventures Ser.). (Illus.). 48p. (YA). (gr. 5 up). 2000. lib. bdg. 21.26 (*0-7368-0574-5*, Capstone Bks) Capstone Pr.

Bledsoe, Glen, ed. see Kiwak, Barbara.

Bledsoe, Helen W. Riverdale School, 1888-1988. LC 88-70297. (Illus.). 176p. 1988. pap. 17.00 (*0-8323-0462-X*) Binford Mort.

Bledsoe, Helen W., ed. see Newbegin, Wade.

Bledsoe, J. O. Right Angles. 200p. 1989. write for info. (*0-318-65356-7*) Nickajack Group.

Bledsoe, Jane K., ed. see Campbell, Lawrence, et al.

Bledsoe, Jane K., jt. ed. see Glenn, Constance W.

Bledsoe, Jerry. The Angel Doll: A Christmas Story. LC 96-85568. (Illus.). 125p. 1996. 14.95 (*1-878086-54-5*, Pub. by Down Home NC) Blair.

— The Angel Doll: A Christmas Story That Will Live in Your Heart Forever. 112p. 1999. mass mkt. 3.99 (*0-312-97189-3*, St Martins Paperbacks) St Martin.

— Before He Wakes. (Illus.). 448p. 1996. mass mkt. 6.99 (*0-451-40609-5*, Onyx) NAL.

— Bitter Blood: A True Story of Southern Family Pride, Madness, & Multiple Murder. 576p. 1989. mass mkt. 7.50 (*0-451-40210-3*, Onyx) NAL.

— Blood Games: A True Account of Family Murder. (Illus.). 448p. 1992. mass mkt. 6.99 (*0-451-40344-4*, Onyx) NAL.

— Blue Horizons: Faces & Places from a Bicycle Journey along the Blue Ridge Parkway. LC 93-71245. (Illus.). 150p. 1993. pap. 11.95 (*1-878086-05-7*, Pub. by Down Home NC) Blair.

— Death Sentence: The True Story of Velma Barfield's Life, Crimes & Execution. 432p. 1999. reprint ed. mass mkt. 6.99 (*0-451-40755-5*, Onyx) NAL.

***Bledsoe, Jerry.** A Gift of Angels. (Illus.). 150p. 1999. 16.95 (*1-878086-80-4*, Pub. by Down Home NC) Blair.

Bledsoe, Jerry. Just Folks: Visitin' with Carolina People. LC 90-80966. (Illus.). 208p. 1990. reprint ed. pap. 8.95 (*0-9624255-5-9*, Pub. by Down Home NC) Blair.

— North Carolina Curiosities: Jerry Bledsoe's Outlandish Guide to the Dadblamedest Things to See & Do in North Carolina. 3rd ed. Pitzer, Sara, ed. LC 98-32210. (Illus.). 288p. 1998. pap. 10.95 (*0-7627-0327-X*) Globe Pequot.

— Where's Mark Twain When We Really Need Him? 183p. 1992. 9.95 (*0-9610320-0-6*) Shipley Schl.

— The World's Number One, Flat-Out, All-Time Great, Stock Car Racing Book, 20th Anniversary Edition. rev. ed. 335p. 1995. pap. 13.95 (*1-878086-36-7*, Pub. by Down Home NC) Blair.

Bledsoe, Jerry, jt. auth. see Timberlake, Bob.

Bledsoe, Jerry, ed. see Browning, Wilt.

Bledsoe, Jerry, ed. see Carden, Gary & Anderson, Nina.

Bledsoe, Jerry, ed. see Gaillard, Frye.

Bledsoe, Jerry, ed. see Harkey, Hugh, Jr.

Bledsoe, Jerry, ed. see King, Henry.

Bledsoe, Jerry, ed. see Klinkenberg, Jeff.

Bledsoe, Jerry, ed. see Loftin, Glenda.

Bledsoe, Jerry, ed. see Morgan, Fred.

Bledsoe, Jerry, ed. see Newman, Bob.

Bledsoe, Jerry, ed. see Nicholson, Mary.

Bledsoe, Jerry, ed. see Powell, Lew.

Bledsoe, Jerry, ed. see Simpson, N. P.

Bledsoe, Jerry, ed. see Sturkey, Don.

Bledsoe, Jerry, ed. see Wineka, Mark & Lesley, Jason.

Bledsoe, Jerry, ed. see Young, Jane.

Bledsoe, John D. Roth to Riches: The Ordinary to Roth IRA Handbook. 208p. 1998. pap. 19.95 (*0-9629114-1-0*) Legacy TX.

— Successful Estimating Methods: From Concept to Bid. (Illus.). 250p. 1992. 64.95 (*0-87629-216-3*, 67287) R S Means.

Bledsoe, John D. & Lustig, Theodore S. Texas Living Trust: The Ultimate Estate Planning Technique for the 1990's. 1991. 21.95 (*0-9629114-0-2*) Legacy TX.

Bledsoe, John T. The Bledsoe Family. LC 73-75223. (Illus.). 298p. reprint ed. pap. 92.40 (*0-8357-7317-5*, 205041900078) Bks Demand.

Bledsoe, Karen, jt. compiled by see Bledsoe, Glen.

Bledsoe, Karen, jt. ed. see Bledsoe, Glen.

Bledsoe, Karen, ed. see Kiwak, Barbara.

Bledsoe, Karen E. & Norvell, Candyce. 365 Nature Crafts & Activities. (Craft & Project Books for Children Ser.). (Illus.). 240p. (J). (gr. 3-6). 1998. lib. bdg. 24.95 (*1-56674-227-7*, HTS Bks) Forest Hse.

Bledsoe, Karen E., jt. auth. see Bledsoe, Glen.

Bledsoe, Lucy J. The Big Bike Race. LC 95-7165. (Illus.). 96p. (J). (gr. 4-6). 1995. 15.95 (*0-8234-1206-7*) Holiday.

Bledsoe, Lucy J. The Big Bike Race. 96p. (J). 1997. mass mkt. 3.99 (*0-380-72830-3*, Avon Bks) Morrow Avon.

Bledsoe, Lucy J. The Big Bike Race. 1997. 9.19 (*0-606-10996-X*, Pub. by Turtleback) Demco.

— Sweat: Stories & a Novella. LC 95-16106. 164p. (Orig.). 1995. pap. 10.95 (*1-878067-64-8*) Seal Pr WA.

— Tracks in the Snow. LC 96-52915. 160p. (J). (gr. 3-7). 1997. pap. 15.95 (*0-8234-1309-8*) Holiday.

***Bledsoe, Lucy J.** Tracks in the Snow. LC 96-52915. 128p. (J). (gr. 3-7). 2000. mass mkt. 3.99 (*0-380-73230-0*, Avon Bks) Morrow Avon.

Bledsoe, Lucy J. Working Parts. LC 96-47425. 208p. (Orig.). 1997. pap. 12.00 (*1-878067-94-X*) Seal Pr WA.

Bledsoe, Lucy J., ed. Gay Travels: A Literary Companion. LC 98-19303. 238p. 1998. pap. 14.95 (*1-883513-06-5*) Whereabouts.

— Heatwave: Women in Love & Lust. 200p. (Orig.). 1995. pap. 11.95 (*1-55583-318-7*) Alyson Pubns.

— Lesbian Travels: A Literary Companion. LC 98-37807. 218p. 1998. pap. 14.95 (*1-883513-07-3*) Whereabouts.

Bledsoe, Michele. The Doggy Bone Cookbook. (Illus.). 13p. 1997. 9.95 (*0-9653042-0-5*) Come & Get It.

***Bledsoe, Michele.** The Kitty Treats Cookbook. 2nd ed. (Illus.). 13p. 1999. bds. 9.95 (*0-9653042-8-0*) Come & Get It.

— The Small Dogs Doggy Bone Bookbook. (Illus.). 13p. 1999. bds. 9.95 (*0-9653042-9-9*) Come & Get It.

Bledsoe, Michelle. Horse d'Oeurves. (Illus.). 14p. (J). (gr. 1 up). 1999. bds. 9.95 (*0-9653042-1-3*) Come & Get It.

Bledsoe, Robert. Henry Fothergill Chorley: A Study. LC 98-23743. 365p. 1998. text 78.95 (*1-84014-257-X*, ML423.C55B54, Pub. by Ashgate Pub) Ashgate Pub Co.

Bledsoe, Robert, et al, eds. Rethinking Germanistik: Canon & Culture. LC 90-6030. (Berkeley Insights in Linguistics & Semiotics Ser.: Vol. 6). XX, 214p. (C). 1991. text 46.95 (*0-8204-1373-9*) P Lang Pubng.

Bledsoe, Robert L. & Boczek, Boleslaw A. The International Law Dictionary. LC 86-32060. (Clio Dictionaries in Political Science Ser.: No. 11). 422p. 1987. pap. text 24.75 (*0-87436-489-2*) ABC-CLIO.

Bledsoe, Samuel T. Indian Land Laws. Bruchey, Stuart, ed. LC 78-53557. (Development of Public Land Law in the U. S. Ser.). 1979. reprint ed. lib. bdg. 52.95 (*0-405-11369-2*) Ayer.

Bledsoe, Sara. Colorado. LC 92-31054. (Hello U. S. A. Ser.). (Illus.). 72p. (J). (gr. 3-6). 1993. lib. bdg. 19.93 (*0-8225-2750-2*, Lerner Publctns) Lerner Pub.

— Colorado. (Illus.). 72p. (J). 1995. pap. 5.95 (*0-8225-9705-5*) Lerner Pub.

Bledsoe, Shirley, jt. auth. see MacKenzie, Joy.

Bledsoe, Timothy. Careers in City Politics: The Case for Urban Democracy. LC 92-36908. (Pitt Series in Policy & Institutional Studies). 254p. 1993. reprint ed. pap. 78.80 (*0-608-07895-6*, 206787600010) Bks Demand.

Bledsoe, Timothy, jt. auth. see Welch, Susan.

***Bledsoe, Vee.** Kenaf - An Alternative Crop. (Illus.). 200p. 1999. pap. 15.50 (*0-9645041-3-8*) Cntryside Pub.

Bledsoe, W. W. & Loveland, Donald, eds. Automated Theorem Proving: After 25 Years. LC 84-9226. (Contemporary Mathematics Ser.: Vol. 29). 360p. 1984. reprint ed. pap. 42.00 (*0-8218-5027-X*, CONM/29) Am Math.

Blee, Ben W. Battleship North Carolina. Conlon, Frank S. & Judd, Amo F., eds. (Illus.). 100p. 1982. 14.95 (*0-9608538-0-4*); pap. 8.95 (*0-9608538-1-2*) USS North Car.

***Blee, Jill.** Brigid. 262p. 1999. pap. 19.95 (*0-9585805-4-5*, Pub. by Indra Pubng) Intl Spec Bk.

Blee, Jill. The Pines Hold Their Secrets. 283p. 1998. pap. 19.95 (*0-9587718-8-X*, Pub. by Indra Pub) Intl Spec Bk.

Blee, Kathleen M. Women of the Klan: Racism & Gender in the 1920s. 1992. pap. 16.95 (*0-520-07876-4*, Pub. by U CA Pr) Cal Prin Full Svc.

Blee, Kathleen M., ed. No Middle Ground. LC 97-21111. 329p. 1998. text 55.00 (*0-8147-1279-7*); pap. text 19.00 (*0-8147-1280-0*) NYU Pr.

Blee, Kathleen M., jt. auth. see Billings, Dwight B.

Blee, Tony, jt. ed. see Kaye, Charles.

***Bleech, Mike.** Hiking Pennsylvania. LC 00-25312. (America's Best Day Hiking Ser.). (Illus.). 224p. 2000. pap. 19.95 (*0-7360-0166-2*) Human Kinetics.

Bleeck, Arthur H. Avesta: The Religious Books of the Parsees. 1974. lib. bdg. 300.00 (*0-87968-133-0*) Krishna Pr.

— Avesta: The Religious Books of the Parsees, from Professor Spiegel's German Translation. 1988. reprint ed. lib. bdg. 59.00 (*0-7812-0114-4*) Rprt Serv.

Bleecker, Ann E. Posthumous Works. LC 70-104419. 375p. reprint ed. lib. bdg. 32.00 (*0-8398-0167-X*) Irvington.

Bleecker, D. D., jt. auth. see Booss, B.

Bleecker, David. Basic Partial Differential Equations. 1992. text 49.95 (*0-442-01253-5*) Chapman & Hall.

Bleecker, David & Csordas, George. Basic Partial Differential Equations. (Illus.). 768p. (C). (gr. 13). 1992. pap. text 64.95 (*0-412-06761-7*) Chapman & Hall.

Bleecker, David & Csordas, George, eds. Basic Partial Differential Equations. (Undergraduate Texts Ser.). (Illus.). 756p. (C). 1997. 59.00 (*1-57146-036-5*) Intl Pr Boston.

Bleecker, Margit L. & Hansen, John A., eds. Occupational Neurology & Clinical Neurotoxicology. LC 93-13454. (Illus.). 384p. 1994. 75.00 (*0-683-00848-X*) Lppncott W & W.

Bleecker, Mary N. Ruffles, Drums, & Ragged Men. LC 96-95408. 242p. 1997. 19.95 (*0-9653132-1-2*) Gilderoy Publns.

Bleecker, Theodore. Staying on Top. LC 98-90102. 317p. 1998. write for info. (*0-9662819-0-X*) Virgin Pr.

Bleecker, Tom. Unsettled Matters: The Life & Death of Bruce Lee. LC 96-94563. 228p. (Orig.). 1996. pap. text 7.99 (*0-9653132-0-4*) Gilderoy Publns.

Bleed, Ann & Flowerday, Charles A., eds. An Atlas of the Sand Hills. 1990. 20.00 (*1-56161-000-3*) U NE Inst Agr & Nat Resc.

Bleed, Ann S. & Flowerday, Charles A., eds. An Atlas of the Sand Hills. 3rd rev. ed. LC 98-24716. (Illus.). 260p. 1998. pap. 25.00 (*1-56161-002-X*) U NE Inst Agr & Nat Resc.

Bleed, Peter. The Archaeology of Petaga Point: The Preceramic Component. LC 75-626260. (Publications of the Minnesota Historical Society). (Illus.). 65p. reprint ed. pap. 30.00 (*0-608-06688-5*, 206688500009) Bks Demand.

***Bleed, Peter.** National Treasure. LC 00-130486. (Antiquity Alive Ser.). 309p. 2000. pap. 19.95 (*0-9675798-1-3*) RKLOG Pr.

Bleedorn, Berenice D. Creative Leadership for a Global Future: Studies & Speculations. (American University Studies: Language: Ser. XIV, Vol. 12). XVI, 193p. (C). 1988. text 31.70 (*0-8204-0656-2*) P Lang Pubng.

— The Creativity Force in Education, Business & Beyond: An Urgent Message. LC 97-52788. 1998. pap. 19.95 (*1-880090-57-0*) Galde Pr.

Bleefeld, Bradley & Shook, Robert L. Saving the World Entire: And 100 Other Beloved Parables from the Talmud. LC 98-22127. 256p. 1998. pap. 11.95 (*0-452-27988-7*, Plume) Dutton Plume.

Bleehen, Norman M., ed. Investigational Techniques in Oncology. (Illus.). 240p. 1987. 97.95 (*0-387-17075-8*) Spr-Verlag.

Bleehen, Norman M., et al, eds. Radiation Therapy Planning. LC 82-22017. (Fundamentals of Cancer Management Ser.: Vol. 1). 734p. 1983. reprint ed. pap. 200.00 (*0-608-03815-6*, 206466500009) Bks Demand.

Bleek, Dorothea F. The Naron: A Bushman Tribe of the Central Kalahari. LC 76-44692. reprint ed. 37.50 (*0-404-15908-7*) AMS Pr.

Bleek, Whilhelm H. & Lloyd, Lucy C. Specimens of Bushman Folklore. LC 78-67687. (Folktale Ser.). (Illus.). reprint ed. 49.50 (*0-404-16056-5*) AMS Pr.

Bleek, Wilhelm, jt. auth. see Schleicher, August.

Bleek, Wilhelm H. Reynard the Fox in South Africa. LC 78-67686. (Folktale Ser.). reprint ed. 24.50 (*0-404-16055-7*) AMS Pr.

Bleeke, Joel & Ernst, David, eds. Collaborating to Compete: Using Strategic Alliances & Acquisitions in the Global Marketplace. LC 92-23933. 284p. 1993. 35.00 (*0-471-58009-0*) Wiley.

Bleeker, Ann E. Posthumous Works. 375p. (C). 1986. reprint ed. pap. text 7.95 (*0-8290-1888-3*) Irvington.

Bleeker, D. Basic Partial Differential Equation Solutions Manual. 1993. ring bd. 26.95 (*0-442-01521-6*, Chap & Hall CRC) CRC Pr.

Bleeker, G. M., et al, eds. Orbital Disorders. (Illus.). 1978. text 268.50 (*90-6193-570-9*) Kluwer Academic.

Bleeker, G. M., ed. see International Symposium on Orbital Disorders Staff.

Bleeker, Harry, et al. Boundary-Scan Test: A Practical Approach. LC 92-39160. 244p. (C). 1992. reprint ed. text 121.00 (*0-7923-9296-5*) Kluwer Academic.

Bleeker, J. A. & Hermsen, W., eds. X-Ray & Gamma-Ray Astronomy: Proceedings of Symposium 14 of the COSPAR 27th Plenary Meeting Held in Espoo, Finland, 18-29 July, 1988. (Advances in Space Research Ser.: Vol. 10). (Illus.). 324p. 1989. pap. 89.00 (*0-08-040158-9*, Pergamon Pr) Elsevier.

Bleekman & Fiedler. Looking at Biology. 5th ed. 200p. 1993. pap. text, lab manual ed. 33.80 (*0-536-58399-4*) Pearson Custom.

Bleezarde, Thomas W., ed. see Warren, Philip H.

Blegen, Carl W., et al, eds. The Palace of Nestor at Pylos in Western Messenia: Acropolis & Lower Town; Tholoi, Grave Circle, & Chamber Tombs; Discoveries Outside the Citadel, Vol. III. LC 65-17131. (Illus.). 364p. reprint ed. pap. 112.90 (*0-608-11403-0*, 201303200083) Bks Demand.

Blegen, Carl W., ed. see University of Cincinnati, Excavations in the Troad.

Blegen, Theodore C. The Kensington Rune Stone: New Light on an Old Riddle. LC 68-66739. (Illus.). viii, 213p. 1968. 7.50 (*0-87351-044-5*) Minn Hist.

— The Land Lies Open. LC 74-27727. 246p. 1975. reprint ed. lib. bdg. 35.00 (*0-8371-7912-2*, BLLO, Greenwood Pr) Greenwood.

— Minnesota: A History of the State. 2nd ed. LC 75-6116. (Illus.). xiv, 731p. 1975. 29.95 (*0-8166-0754-0*) U of Minn Pr.

— Norwegian Migration to America: The American Transition. LC 31-20308. 677p. reprint ed. pap. 200.00 (*0-8357-3438-2*, 203969500013) Bks Demand.

— Norwegian Migration to America: The American Transition. LC 68-31271. (Illus.). 655p. (C). 1969. reprint ed. lib. bdg. 75.00 (*0-8383-1215-2*) M S G Haskell Hse.

— Norwegian Migration to America, 1825-1860. LC 69-18759. (American Immigration Collection. Series 1). 1969. reprint ed. 20.95 (*0-405-00507-5*) Ayer.

— Norwegian Migration to America, 1825-1860. LC 68-31271. 413p. (C). 1969. reprint ed. lib. bdg. 75.00 (*0-8383-0325-0*) M S G Haskell Hse.

— Norwegian Migration to America, 1825-1860, 2 Vols. LC 68-31271. (American History & Americana Ser.: No. 47). 1969. reprint ed. lib. bdg. 150.00 (*0-8383-0330-7*) M S G Haskell Hse.

— Songs of the Voyageurs. 43p. 1998. 16.95 incl. audio (*0-87351-361-4*, 361-4) Minn Hist.

Blegen, Theodore C., ed. Norwegian-American Studies & Records, Vol. 4. 159p. 1929. 12.00 (*0-87732-008-X*) Norwegian-Am Hist Assn.

— Norwegian-American Studies & Records, Vol. 5. 152p. 1930. 12.00 (*0-87732-009-8*) Norwegian-Am Hist Assn.

— Norwegian-American Studies & Records, Vol. 6. 191p. 1932. 12.00 (*0-87732-010-1*) Norwegian-Am Hist Assn.

— Norwegian-American Studies & Records, Vol. 8. 176p. 1934. 12.00 (*0-87732-014-4*) Norwegian-Am Hist Assn.

— Norwegian-American Studies & Records, Vol. 9. 131p. 1936. 12.00 (*0-87732-017-9*) Norwegian-Am Hist Assn.

— Norwegian-American Studies & Records, Vol. 10. 202p. 1938. 12.00 (*0-87732-019-5*) Norwegian-Am Hist Assn.

— Norwegian-American Studies & Records, Vol. 11. 183p. 1940. 15.00 (*0-87732-022-5*) Norwegian-Am Hist Assn.

— Norwegian-American Studies & Records, Vol. 16. 218p. 1950. 15.00 (*0-87732-033-0*) Norwegian-Am Hist Assn.

— Norwegian-American Studies & Records, Vol. 17. 185p. 1952. 15.00 (*0-87732-035-7*) Norwegian-Am Hist Assn.

— Norwegian-American Studies & Records, Vol. 18. 252p. 1952. 15.00 (*0-87732-037-3*) Norwegian-Am Hist Assn.

— Norwegian-American Studies & Records, Vol. 19. 218p. 1956. 15.00 (*0-87732-039-X*) Norwegian-Am Hist Assn.

— Norwegian-American Studies & Records, Vol. 20. 246p. 1959. 15.00 (*0-87732-041-1*) Norwegian-Am Hist Assn.

— Peter Testman's Account of His Experiences in North America. 60p. 1927. 5.00 (*0-87732-004-7*) Norwegian-Am Hist Assn.

Blegen, Theodore C., et al, eds. Norwegian Emigrant Songs & Ballads. LC 78-15211. (Scandinavians in America Ser.). 1979. reprint ed. lib. bdg. 30.95 (*0-405-11633-0*) Ayer.

Blegen, Theodore C. & Davidson, Sarah A., eds. Iron Face. 1950. 25.00 (*0-940550-00-8*) Caxton Club.

Blegen, Theodore C., ed. see Heg, Hans C.

Blegen, Theodore C., ed. see Neill, Edward D.

Blegen, Theodore C., ed. & tr. see Rynning, Ole.

Bleger, Jose. Symbiosis & Ambiguity: The Psychoanalysis of Very Early Experience. 1998. pap. 28.95 (*1-899209-11-5*, Pub. by Process Pr) Intl Spec Bk.

***B'Leguad, Lenore.** Ana Banana y Yo. (SPA., Illus.). (J). 1999. 14.40 (*0-606-16025-6*) Turtleback.

Blegvad. Busu. LC 86-30610. (J). 1987. 12.95 (*0-13-108481-X*) P-H.

Blegvad, B. M., ed. European Yearbook in Law & Sociology. (European Studies in Law & Sociology). 1979. lib. bdg. 86.50 (*90-247-2158-X*) Kluwer Academic.

Blegvad, B. M., et al, eds. European Yearbook in Law & Sociology: 1977. 1977. pap. text 55.00 (*90-247-2017-6*) Kluwer Academic.

Blegvad, Erik. Self-Portrait. LC 84-43134. (J). (gr. 3 up). 1979. 12.95 (*0-201-00498-4*) HarpC Child Bks.

Blegvad, Erik, jt. auth. see Langton, Jane.

Blegvad, Erik, jt. illus. see Norton, Mary.

Blegvad, Lenore. Anna Banana & Me. (Illus.). (J). (gr. 1-3). 1988. pap. 15.95 incl. audio (*0-87499-103-X*) Live Oak Media.

— Anna Banana & Me. LC 84-547. (Illus.). 32p. (J). (gr. k-3). 1985. text, lib. bdg. 13.95 (*0-689-50274-5*) McElderry Bks.

— Anna Banana & Me. LC 86-22220. (Illus.). 32p. (J). (ps-3). 1987. reprint ed. pap. 4.99 (*0-689-71114-X*) Aladdin.

— Anna Banana & Me, Set. (Illus.). (J). (ps-4). 1988. pap. 33.95 incl. audio (*0-87499-105-6*) Live Oak Media.

— Once upon a Time & Grandma. LC 92-7407. (Illus.). 32p. (J). (ps-3). 1993. 14.95 (*0-689-50548-5*) McElderry Bks.

B

— Rainy Day Kate. LC 87-16805. (Illus.). 32p. (J). (gr. k-4). 1988. lib. bdg. 13.95 (*0-689-50442-X*) McElderry Bks.

Blegvad, Lenore. A Sound of Leaves. LC 94-46961. (Illus.). 64p. (J). (ps-3). 1996. pap. 15.00 (*0-689-80038-X*) McElderry Bks.

Blehar, Mary C., jt. ed. see Rosenthal, Norman E.

Blehaut, Jean-Francvois. Iban Baskets. LC 98-944552. 235 p. 1994. write for info. (*983-9115-03-0*) Sarawak Lit Soc.

Blehert, Dean. I Swear He Was Laughing: Poems about Dogs (Mostly) Who Only Think They Are People, but Aren't, So Can't Read This Book, So Will You Please Read It for Them? Graham, Alan, ed. LC 96-60835. (Illus.). 84p. 1996. pap. 8.95 (*0-9644857-4-5*) Wrds & Pict Pr.

— No Cats Have Been Maimed or Mutilated During the Making of This Book . . . But Some of Them Are Disappointed - Deeply Disappointed - In Me. Graham, Alan, ed. LC 96-60834. (Illus.). 84p. 1996. pap. 8.95 (*0-9644857-5-3*) Wrds & Pict Pr.

— Please, Lord, Make Me a Famous Poet: Or Everything You Always Wanted to Know about Poetry but Were Afraid If You Asked Someone Would Start Talking about Whatchamajigger Pentameter. LC 98-96522. (Illus.). 416p. 1999. pap. 19.95 (*1-892261-03-0*) Wrds & Pictres.

— Poems for Adults & Other Children. Bates, Jeff, ed. (Illus.). 55p. 1988. 5.95 (*0-938823-01-9*) Wrds & Pictres.

Blehert, M. Dean. Poems for Adults & Other Children. (Poetry Ser.: No. 1). (Illus.). 64p. 1988. pap. 5.95 (*0-685-23290-5*) Pogment Pr.

Blehl, Vincent F. The White Stone: The Spiritual Theology of John Henry Newman. LC 93-31998. 187p. 1993. pap. 19.95 (*1-879007-03-7*) St Bedes Pubns.

Blehl, Vincent F., ed. see Newman, John Henry.

Blehm, Gary. Penman: Modern Cartooning. LC 94-10479. 112p. 1995. pap. 9.00 (*0-15-600076-8*, Harvest Bks) Harcourt.

Blei. General, Organic & Biochemistry. 1999. write for info. (*0-7167-3581-4*) W H Freeman.

— General, Organic & Biological Chemistry. 1999. pap. text 24.95 (*0-7167-3579-2*) W H Freeman.

***Blei & Odian.** General Organic Biochemistry. 2000. pap. text, lab manual ed. 32.95 (*0-7167-3582-2*) W H Freeman.

***Blei, Ira & Odian, George G.** General Chemistry: Connecting Chemistry to Your Life: An Introduction to Chemistry. LC 00-39307. 2000. write for info. (*0-7167-4159-8*) W H Freeman.

Blei, Norbert. Adventures in an American's Literature. 224p. (Orig.). 1982. pap. 5.95 (*0-933180-41-1*) Ellis Pr.

— Chi Town. 384p. 1990. 19.95 (*0-944024-10-6*) Ellis Pr.

— Chronicles of a Rural Journalist in America. (Illus.). 474p. (Orig.). 1990. pap. 11.95 (*0-9626140-3-3*) Samizdat Pr.

— Door Steps: The Days, the Seasons. 288p. 1983. 14.95 (*0-933180-44-6*) Ellis Pr.

— Door Way. 320p. 1992. 19.95 (*0-933180-22-5*) Ellis Pr.

— The Ghost of Sandburg's Phizzog. 196p. 1987. pap. 8.95 (*0-944024-01-7*) Ellis Pr.

— The Ghost of Sandburg's Phizzog & Other Stories. 192p. 1986. 13.95 (*0-933180-87-X*) Ellis Pr.

— Neighborhood. (Illus.). 272p. 1998. pap. 14.95 (*0-944024-35-1*) Ellis Pr.

— Paint Me a Picture--Make Me a Poem. (Illus.). 108p. 1987. pap. 5.95 (*0-933180-97-7*) Spoon Riv Poetry.

Blei, Norbert, jt. auth. see Peterson, Charles.

Blei, Ron C. Fractional Dimensions & Bounded Fractional Forms. LC 85-13512. (Memoirs of the AMS Ser.: No. 57/331). 70p. 1985. pap. 17.00 (*0-8218-2332-9*, MEMO/57/331) Am Math.

Bleiberg, Edward. The Official Gift in Ancient Egypt. LC 96-20282. 192p. 1996. text 27.95 (*0-8061-2871-2*, 2871) U of Okla Pr.

Bleiberg, Edward & Freed, Rita, eds. Fragments of a Shattered Visage: Proceedings of the International Symposium on Ramesses II. viii, 270p. 1993. pap. text 30.00 (*0-9636816-0-5*) MSU Egyp Art.

Bleiberg, German. Diccionario de Historia de Espana. (SPA.). 1986. write for info. (*0-7859-5033-8*) Fr & Eur.

— Diccionario de Historia de Espana, Vol. 1. 3rd ed. (SPA.). 1368p. 1986. 105.00 (*0-7859-5724-3*, 8420652059) Fr & Eur.

— Diccionario de Historia de Espana, Vol. 2. (SPA.). 1192p. 1986. 105.00 (*0-7859-5725-1*, 8420652067) Fr & Eur.

— El Informe Secreto de Mateo Aleman Sobre el Trabajo Forzoso en las Minas de Almaden. (Monagrafias A Ser.: Vol. CVII). (SPA.). 150p. (C). 1985. 51.00 (*0-7293-0200-8*, Pub. by Tamesis Bks Ltd) Boydell & Brewer.

Bleiberg, German, et al, eds. Dictionary of the Literature of the Iberian Peninsula, 2 vols., Set. LC 90-2755. 1840p. 1993. lib. bdg. 195.00 (*0-313-21302-X*, BLD/, Greenwood Pr) Greenwood.

— Dictionary of the Literature of the Iberian Peninsula, Vol. 1. LC 90-2755. 928p. 1993. lib. bdg. 195.00 (*0-313-28731-7*, Greenwood Pr) Greenwood.

— Dictionary of the Literature of the Iberian Peninsula, Vol. 2. LC 90-2755. 936p. 1993. lib. bdg. 195.00 (*0-313-28732-5*, Greenwood Pr) Greenwood.

Bleiberg, M. L., ed. see International Conference Radiation Effects in Bree.

Bleibreu, John, ed. see Ichazo, Oscar.

Bleibtreu, John, ed. see Ichazo, Oscar.

Bleich, jt. auth. see Rosner, Fred.

Bleich, David. Know & Tell: Disclosure, Genre & Membership in the Teaching of Writing & Language. LC 98-12307. 248p. 1998. pap. 28.00 (*0-86709-446-X*, Pub. by Boynton Cook Pubs) Heinemann.

— Subjective Criticism. LC 77-12968. 315p. reprint ed. pap. 97.70 (*0-608-06100-X*, 206643200008) Bks Demand.

Bleich, David J. Bioethical Dilemmas: A Jewish Perspective. LC 98-28595. 1998. 29.50 (*0-88125-473-8*) Ktav.

— Utopia: The Psychology of a Cultural Fantasy. LC 84-2537. (Studies in Speculative Fiction: No. 5). 160p. reprint ed. pap. 49.60 (*0-8357-1574-4*, 207053000001) Bks Demand.

Bleich, J. David. Bi-Netivot HaHalakhah, No. 1. (HEB.). 1996. 25.00 (*0-88125-547-5*) Ktav.

— Contemporary Halakhic Problems. Date not set. pap. 14.95 (*0-88125-064-3*) Yeshiva Univ Pr.

— Contemporary Halakhic Problems, Vol. IV. (Library of Jewish Law & Ethics: Vol. 4). 1995. 35.00 (*0-88125-474-6*) Ktav.

— Judaism & Healing: Halakhic Perspectives. Date not set. pap. 9.95 (*0-87068-289-X*) Yeshiva Univ Pr.

Bleich, J. David, anno. With Perfect Faith: The Foundations of Jewish Belief. 1982. 29.50 (*0-87068-891-X*) Ktav.

Bleich, Ronald L. & Mandel, Hal W. WGL Tax Planning Checklists. annuals rev. ed. Orig. Title: Modern Tax Planning Checklists. 1991. suppl. ed. 125.00 (*0-7913-0974-6*) Warren Gorham & Lamont.

Bleicher, Fred & Hu, W. C. Temmoku: A Study of Pottery & Tea Aesthetics. write for info. (*0-89344-032-9*) Ars Ceramica.

Bleicher, Fred, et al. Highlights of Pewabic Pottery. LC 77-92628. 1977. pap. 9.95 (*0-89344-015-9*) Ars Ceramica.

Bleicher, Fred, jt. auth. see Swallow, Robert W.

Bleicher, Joseph. Contemporary Hermeneutics: Hermeneutics As Method, Philosophy & Critique. 224p. 1980. pap. 14.95 (*0-7100-0552-0*, Routledge Thoemms) Routledge.

— The Hermeneutic Imagination: Outline of a Positive Critique of Scientism & Sociology. 240p. 1982. pap. 10.95 (*0-7100-9257-1*, Routledge Thoemms) Routledge.

Bleichert, Peter von, see von Bleichert, Peter.

Bleichrodt, N. & Drenth, Pieter J., eds. Contemporary Issues in Cross-Cultural Psychology. viii, 464p. 1991. pap. 58.25 (*90-265-1117-5*) Swets.

Bleicken, Jochen. Lex Publica: Gesetz und Recht in der roemischen Republik. (C). 1975. 146.15 (*3-11-004584-2*) De Gruyter.

***Bleidner, Larry & Scott, Peter.** L. & L. Beancounter's Catalog: Get Ready for Your Career. 80p. 2000. pap. 9.71 (*1-56751-180-5*, Pub. by Common Courage) LPC InBook.

Bleidt, Barry, ed. Multicultural Pharmaceutical Education. LC 92-49896. (Journal of Pharmacy Teaching: Vol. 3, No. 2). (Illus.). 151p. 1992. 39.95 (*1-56024-356-2*) Haworth Pr.

— Multicultural Pharmaceutical Education. LC 92-49896. (Journal of Pharmacy Teaching: Vol. 3, No. 2). 151p. 1996. pap. 14.95 (*0-7890-0071-7*, Pharmctl Prods) Haworth Pr.

Bleidt, Barry & Montagne, Michael. Clinical Research in Pharmaceutical Development. LC 96-26648. (Drugs & the Pharmaceutical Sciences Ser.: Vol. 75). (Illus.). 368p. 1996. text 145.00 (*0-8247-9745-0*) Dekker.

Bleiel, Jeff, jt. auth. see Cunningham, Don.

Bleiel, Jeffrey. That's All: Bobby Darin on Record, Stage & Screen. LC 93-83934. (Rock & Roll Reference Ser.: No. 38). (Illus.). 304p. 1993. lib. bdg. 40.00 (*1-56075-031-6*) Popular Culture.

Bleier, Carol S., et al. L' Chaim - To Good Health & Life: A History of Montefiore Hospital Pittsburgh, PA, 1898-1990. LC 97-71894. (Illus.). viii, 286p. 1997. 50.00 (*0-945704-04-6*); pap. 35.00 (*0-945704-05-4*) Genesis Comns.

Bleier, Frank P. Fan Handbook: Selection, Application & Design. LC 97-23697. (Illus.). 640p. 1997. 89.95 (*0-07-005933-0*) McGraw.

Bleier, Ruth. The Hypothalamus of the Guinea Pig: A Cytoarchitectonic Atlas. LC 83-47756. 149p. 1983. reprint ed. pap. 46.20 (*0-608-01920-8*, 206257500003) Bks Demand.

— The Hypothalamus of the Rhesus Monkey: A Cytoarchitectonic Atlas. LC 84-40146. 136p. 1984. reprint ed. pap. 42.20 (*0-608-01921-6*, 206257600003) Bks Demand.

— Science & Gender: A Critique of Biology & Its Theories on Women. (Athene Ser.). (Illus.). 250p. 1984. text 45.00 (*0-08-030972-0*, Pergamon Pr); pap. text 18.95 (*0-08-030971-2*, Pergamon Pr) Elsevier.

— Science & Gender: A Critique of Biology & Its Theories on Women. LC 97-7367. (Athene Ser.). 240p. (C). 1984. pap. text 18.95 (*0-8077-6200-8*) Tchrs Coll.

Bleier, Ruth, ed. Feminist Approaches to Science. LC 85-28378. (Athene Ser.). 224p. 1986. text 36.50 (*0-08-032787-7*, K133, H110, R210, Pergamon Pr); pap. text 15.95 (*0-08-032786-9*, Pergamon Pr) Elsevier.

— Feminist Approaches to Science. (Athene Ser.). 224p. (C). pap. text 16.95 (*0-8077-6201-6*) Tchrs Coll.

***Bleier, Thomas E. & Steinert, Eric C.** Net.people: The Personalities & Passions Behind the Web Sites. LC 99-42511. (Illus.). 320p. 2000. pap. 19.95 (*0-910965-37-4*, CyberAge Bks) Info Today Inc.

Bleifeld, Maurice. Botany Projects for Young Scientists. (Projects for Young Scientists Ser.). (J). 1992. 12.05 (*0-606-02533-2*, Pub. by Turtleback) Demco.

— Experimenting with a Microscope. LC 88-14043. (Venture-Science Experiments & Projects Ser.). (Illus.). 128p. (YA). (gr. 7-12). 1988. lib. bdg. 22.50 (*0-531-10580-6*) Watts.

— How to Prepare for the SAT II: Biology. 12th rev. ed. LC 98-4473. 400p. 1998. pap. 13.95 (*0-7641-0461-6*) Barron.

Bleifeld, Stanley, et al. Stanley Bleifeld. LC 96-3191. 1996. write for info. (*1-56833-083-9*) Madison Bks UPA.

Bleifeld, W., et al, eds. Evaluation of Cardiac Function by Echocardiography. (Illus.). 210p. 1980. 53.00 (*0-387-10045-8*) Spr-Verlag.

***Bleifield, Erik, et al.** Programming with VisiBroker. LC 97-37943. 464p. 1998. pap. 49.99 incl. cd-rom, audio compact disk (*0-471-23901-1*) Wiley.

Bleifuss, William. Gold: How & Where to Find It Yourself. LC 80-679. 1981. pap. 7.95 (*0-672-52661-1*, Bobbs) Macmillan.

Bleikasten, Andre. The Ink of Melancholy: Faulkner's Novels from "The Sound & the Fury" to "Light in August" LC 89-45357. 416p. 1990. 39.95 (*0-253-31200-0*) Ind U Pr.

— The Most Splendid Failure: Faulkner's, The Sound & the Fury. LC 75-22638. 286p. reprint ed. pap. 88.70 (*0-608-17132-8*, 205621700056) Bks Demand.

Bleiker, Annemarie, jt. auth. see Bleiker, Hans.

Bleiker, Hans & Bleiker, Annemarie. Applied Maximizing. 1988. write for info. (*0-925368-03-2*) IPMP.

— The Augmentation - Meta-Process: Leadership in Guiding a Complex Problem-Solving & Decision Making Process. 1988. ring bd. write for info. (*0-925368-05-9*) IPMP.

— Citizen Participation Handbook for Public Officials & Other Professionals Serving the Public. 1990. ring bd. write for info. (*0-925368-00-8*) IPMP.

— Decision-Making under Uncertainty. 1988. ring bd. write for info. (*0-925368-01-6*) IPMP.

— Life-Fulfillment Planning & Personal Decision-Making. 1988. ring bd. write for info. (*0-925368-04-0*) IPMP.

— Quantifying Your Preferences for Qualitatively Different Outcomes. 1988. ring bd. write for info. (*0-925368-02-4*) IPMP.

Bleiker, Roland. Nonviolent Struggle & the Revolution in East Germany. (Monograph Ser.). 53p. 1993. 3.00 (*1-880813-07-6*) A Einstein Inst.

***Bleiker, Roland.** Popular Dissent, Human Agency & Global Politics. (Cambridge Studies in International Relations: No. 70). 313p. (C). 2000. text 59.95 (*0-521-77099-8*); pap. text 22.95 (*0-521-77829-8*) Cambridge U Pr.

Bleikher, V. M. Eponymic Dictionary of Psychiatric Terminology. 238p. 1980. 14.95 (*0-8288-1857-6*, M15372) Fr & Eur.

Bleil, D. F., ed. see International Conference on Nondestructive Evaluat.

Bleil, Ulrich & Thiede, Jorn, eds. Geological History of the Polar Oceans: Arctic vs. Antarctic. (C). 1990. text 372.50 (*0-7923-0739-9*) Kluwer Academic.

Bleile, Henry R. & Rodgers, Stephen. Marine Coatings. (Illus.). 28p. 1989. pap. 30.00 (*0-934010-29-3*) Fed Soc Coat Tech.

Bleile, Ken. New Strategies for Treating Children's Articulation & Phonological Disorders. 1998. 110.00 incl. VHS (*1-58041-017-0*, 0112092) Am Speech Lang Hearing.

Bleile, Ken M. Articulation & Phonological Disorders: A Book of Exercises. 2nd ed. LC 96-23808. (Illus.). 306p. (C). 1996. pap. 49.95 (*1-56593-688-4*, 1350) Thomson Learn.

— Manual of Articulation & Phonological Disorders: Infancy Through Adulthood. (Clinical Competence Ser.). (Illus.). 404p. (C). 1995. pap. 51.95 (*1-56593-343-5*, 0641) Thomson Learn.

Bleile, Ken M., ed. The Care of Children with Long-Term Tracheostomies. LC 93-3951. (Illus.). 300p. (Orig.). (C). 1993. pap. text 55.00 (*1-56593-094-0*, 0398) Thomson Learn.

Bleiler. Five Victorian Ghost Novels. 1998. pap. 12.95 (*0-486-22558-5*) Dover.

— Supernatural Fiction Writers, Vol. 1. 1985. 110.00 (*0-684-18621-7*) Simon & Schuster.

— Supernatural Fiction Writers, Vol. 2. 1985. 110.00 (*0-684-18622-5*) Macmillan.

Bleiler, David, ed. TLA Film & Video Guide, 2000-2001. (Illus.). 768p. 1999. pap. 18.95 (*0-312-24330-8*, St Martin Griffin) St Martin.

Bleiler, David, ed. see TLA Publication Staff.

Bleiler, E. F. Marmaduke Multiply's Merry Method of Making Minor Mathematicians. 103p. 1971. pap. 4.95 (*0-486-22773-1*) Dover.

Bleiler, Ellen H., ed. from ITA. Famous Italian Opera Arias: A Dual-Language Book. 144p. (Orig.). 1996. pap. text 7.95 (*0-486-29158-8*) Dover.

Bleiler, Ellen H., tr. see Mozart, Wolfgang Amadeus.

Bleiler, Ellen H., tr. see Verdi, Giuseppe.

Bleiler, Everett F. Collected Ghost Stories of Mrs. Riddell. 27.95 (*0-89190-696-7*) Amereon Ltd.

— Essential Japanese Grammar. 156p. (Orig.). (C). 1963. pap. 4.95 (*0-486-21027-8*) Dover.

— Science-Fiction: The Early Years. LC 90-4839. 1024p. 1991. 75.00 (*0-87338-416-4*) Kent St U Pr.

Bleiler, Everett F., ed. Supernatural Fiction Writers: Fantasy & Horror, 2 vols., Vol. 2. 1169p. 1985. 210.00 (*0-684-17808-7*) S&S Trade.

— Three Victorian Detective Novels. 320p. 1978. pap. 8.95 (*0-486-23668-4*) Dover.

Bleiler, Everett F., notes. Mother Goose Melodies. (Illus.). 128p. (J). (ps up). 1970. reprint ed. pap. 3.95 (*0-486-22577-1*) Dover.

***Bleiler, Everett F. & Bleiler, Richard J.** Science-Fiction: The Gernsback Years. LC 98-13374. 768p. 1998. text 65.00 (*0-87338-604-3*) Kent St U Pr.

Bleiler, Everett F., jt. auth. see Gardner, Alexander.

Bleiler, Everett F., jt. auth. see Stern, Guy.

Bleiler, Everett F., ed. see Bierce, Ambrose.

Bleiler, Everett F., ed. see Blackwood, Algernon.

Bleiler, Everett F., ed. see Donnelly, Ignatius.

Bleiler, Everett F., ed. see Doyle, Arthur Conan.

Bleiler, Everett F., ed. see Hoffmann, E. T. A.

Bleiler, Everett F., ed. see James, Montague R.

Bleiler, Everett F., ed. see Le Fanu, Joseph Sheridan.

Bleiler, Everett F., ed. see Lovecraft, H. P.

Bleiler, Everett F., ed. see Mother Goose Staff.

Bleiler, Everett F., ed. see Okakura, Kakuzo.

Bleiler, Everett F., ed. see Wells, H. G.

Bleiler, Richard. Reference Guide to Mystery & Detective Fiction. LC 99-19091. (Reference Sources in the Humanities Ser.). 415p. 1999. 65.00 (*1-56308-380-9*) Libs Unl.

— Science Fiction Writers: Critical Studies of the Major Authors from the Early Nineteenth Century to the Present Day. 2nd ed. LC 98-54321. 1009p. 1999. 125.00 (*0-684-80593-6*) Macmillan Gen Ref.

Bleiler, Richard & Van Tong, Dieu. Marcel Proust at UAB: A Checklist of Proust Holdings at the Mervyn H. Sterne Library. 59p. (C). 1988. pap. text 7.95 (*0-9620942-0-X*) M H Sterne Lib.

Bleiler, Richard J. The Annotated Index to The Thrill Book: Complete Indexes to & Descriptions of Everything Published in Street & Smith's the Thrill Book. (Starmont Reference Guide Ser.: Vol. 18). vii, 256p. (Orig.). 1991. lib. bdg. 37.00 (*1-55742-206-0*) Millefleurs.

Bleiler, Richard J., jt. auth. see Bleiler, Everett F.

Bleiler, S., jt. auth. see Casson, A.

Bleiman, ed. Five Modern Poets. (Longman Literature Ser.). 1993. pap. text. write for info. (*0-582-09713-4*, Pub. by Addison-Wesley) Longman.

***Bleiman, Jerry.** Organized Sports Betting: How to Even the Score with Your Bookmaker. 60p. 2000. pap. write for info. (*0-9701535-0-3*) J & J Pubng.

Bleiman, Joyce & Boisen, Kathleen. Love among the Wild Gods: Reclaiming True Power & Peace. LC 98-21177. 144p. 1998. 17.95 (*1-56474-277-6*) Fithian Pr.

Bleiman, Rita M., et al. From Valley Playwrights Theatre, Vol. 1. LC 86-90567. 183p. (Orig.). 1986. pap. write for info. (*0-9617282-0-5*) Playwrights Pr.

Bleistein, Norman & Handelsman, Richard A. Asymptotic Expansions of Integrals. 448p. 1986. reprint ed. pap. text 12.95 (*0-486-65082-0*) Dover.

***Bleistein, Norman, et al.** Mathematics of Multidimensional Seismic Inversion. LC 00-41971. (Interdisciplinary Applied Mathematics Ser.). 2000. write for info. (*0-387-95061-3*) Spr-Verlag.

Bleiwas, Howard. Ethernet Design, Implementing, & Maintaining. pap. 39.95 (*0-89435-448-5*) Wiley.

Bleiweis, Maxine. Helping Business - the Library's Role in Community Economic Development: A How-to-Do-It Manual for Public Librarians. LC 97-5291. (How-to-Do-It Manuals Ser.). 225p. 1997. pap. 45.00 (*1-55570-231-7*) Neal-Schuman.

Bleiweiss, Robert. Adventures in Prehistoric Archaeology: Differentiated Curriculum for Elementary & Intermediate Level Gifted Students. 1989. 16.00 (*0-910609-18-7*) Gifted Educ Pr.

Blejer, Mario I., et al, eds. Eastern Europe in Transition: From Recession to Growth? LC 93-14779. (Discussion Paper Ser.: No. 196). 217p. 1993. pap. 22.00 (*0-8213-2406-3*, 12406) World Bank.

— Financial Factors in Economic Stabilization & Growth. LC 95-16467. (Illus.). 288p. (C). 1996. text 57.95 (*0-521-48050-7*) Cambridge U Pr.

Blejer, Mario I. & Cheasty, Adrienne, eds. How to Measure the Fiscal Deficit: Analytical & Methodological Issues. LC 92-10723. x, 350p. 1992. 22.50 (*1-55775-192-7*) Intl Monetary.

Blejer, Mario I. & Chu, Ke-Young, eds. Fiscal Policy, Stabilization, & Growth in Developing Countries. LC 89-15237. ix, 387p. 1989. pap. 22.50 (*1-55775-034-3*) Intl Monetary.

— Measurement of Fiscal Impact: Methodological Issues. (Occasional Papers: No. 59). 70p. 1988. pap. 7.50 (*1-55775-016-5*) Intl Monetary.

Blejer, Mario I. & Coricelli, Fabrizio, eds. The Making of Economic Reform in Eastern Europe: Conversations with Leading Reformers in Poland, Hungary & the Czech Republic. (Studies of Communism in Transition). 168p. 1995. 80.00 (*1-85898-150-6*) E Elgar.

Blejer, Mario I. & Skreb, Marko. Macroeconomic Stabilization in Transition Economies. LC 96-46103. 347p. 1997. text 47.95 (*0-521-58177-X*) Cambridge U Pr.

Blejer, Mario I. & Skreb, Marko, eds. Financial Sector Transformation: Lessons from Economies in Transition. LC 98-20735. (Illus.). 300p. (C). 1999. text 59.95 (*0-521-64037-7*) Cambridge U Pr.

Blejer, Mario I. & Ter-Minassian, Teresa M., eds. Fiscal Policy & Economic Reform: Essays in Honour of Vito Tanzi. LC 95-497779. 328p. (C). 1997. 110.00 (*0-415-13739-X*) Routledge.

— Macroeconomic Dimensions of Public Finance: Essays in Honour of Vito Tanzi. LC 95-497779. (Studies in the Modern World Economy: Vol. 5). 528p. (C). 1997. 115.00 (*0-415-14111-7*) Routledge.

Blejer, Mario I., et al. China: Economic Reform & Macroeconomic Management. LC 90-27878. (Occasional Papers: No. 76). v, 38p. (Orig.). 1991. pap. 10.00 (*1-55775-202-8*) Intl Monetary.

— Optimum Currency Areas: New Analytical & Policy Developments. LC 97-13514. 1997. pap. write for info. (*1-55775-652-X*) Intl Monetary.

Blejwas, Stanislaus A. Realism in Polish Politics: Warsaw Positivism & National Survival in Nineteenth Century Poland. LC 83-51814. (Yale Russian & East European Publications: No. 5). xii, 312p. 1984. 27.50 (*0-936586-05-2*, Pub. by Yale Russian) Slavica.

— St. Stanislaus Parish, Meriden, Connecticut: A Century of Connecticut Polonia. 215p. 1991. 20.00 (*0-910179-01-8*) CCSU Polish.

Blekhman, I. I., ed. Synchronization in Science & Technology. 350p. 1988. 68.00 (*0-7918-0003-2*, 800032) ASME Pr.

***Blekhman, Iliya I.** Vibrational Mechanics: Nonlinear Dynamic Effects, General Approach, Applications. LC 99-57906. 1999. 90.00 (*981-02-3890-8*) WSC Inst MA Studies.

Blekhman, Samuel. Postal History & Stamps of Tuva. 2nd ed. Hogg, Ron, tr. from RUS. (Illus.). 104p. 1998. pap. 30.00 (*1-58490-017-2*) Scientific Consulting.

***Blell, Gabriele & Kruck, Brigitte.** Mediale Textvielfalt und Handlungskompetenz im Fremdsprachenunterricht: Zu Ehren Wilfried Gienows. 238p. 1999. 39.95 (*3-631-34458-9*) P Lang Pubng.

Blelloch, Giy E., et al, eds. Specification of Parallel Algorithms: DIMACS Workshop, May 9-11, 1994. LC 94-30810. (DIMACS Series in Discrete Mathematics & Theoretical Computer Science: 18). 399p. 1994. text 79.00 (*0-8218-0253-4*, DIMACS/18) Am Math.

Blelloch, Paola. Eccoci: Beginning Italian Student Text. 512p. 1997. text 55.00 incl. audio (*0-471-17711-3*) Wiley.

Blelloch, Paola & D'Angelo, Rosetta. Eccoci: Beginning Italian. LC 96-43941. (ITA.). 512p. 1997. text 80.95 (*0-471-30941-9*) Wiley.

— Eccoci! Beginning Italian Student Text & Cassette & Workbook & Laboratory Manual to Accompany Eccoci. 788p. 1997. text 112.90 (*0-471-19720-3*) Wiley.

Blelloch, Paola, jt. auth. see D'Angelo, Rosetta.

Bleloch, Andrew L., ed. see American Society of Mechanical Engineers Staff.

Blemenfeld, Yorick. 2099: A Eutopia. LC 99-70947. (Prospects for Tomorrow Ser.). 112p. 2000. pap. 12.95 (*0-500-28157-2*, Pub. by Thames Hudson) Norton.

Blench, R. M., jt. ed. see Crozier, D. H.

Blench, Roger & Briggs, Matt. Archaeology & Language, 1. LC 96-44969. 1996. write for info. (*0-415-10054-2*) Routledge.

Blench, Roger & Spriggs, Matthew, eds. Archaeology & Language I: Theoretical & Methodological Orientations. LC 96-44969. (One World Archaeology Ser.). (Illus.). 408p. (C). 1997. 115.00 (*0-415-11760-7*) Routledge.

— Archaeology & Language II: Archaeological Data & Linguistic Hypotheses. (One World Archaeology Ser.). (Illus.). 448p. (C). 1999. 125.00 (*0-415-11761-5*) Routledge.

***Blench, Roger & Spriggs, Matthew, eds.** Archaeology & Language IV: Language Change & Cultural Transformation. (One World Archaeology Ser.: Vol. 35). (Illus.). 256p. (Orig.). (C). 1999. text 125.00 (*0-415-11786-0*) Routledge.

***Blencoe, Gregory J.** The Art of Management: Insights from an Employee's Perspective. 112p. 1999. pap. 14.95 (*0-9675893-0-4*, Pub. by Mt Olympus CO) ACCESS Pubs Network.

Blencowe, Craig, jt. auth. see Hanify, Mary L.

Blend, Ellen Marie. Visual Encounters. (Illus.). 160p. 1999. per. 11.99 (*1-929219-00-8*) Image Ink.

Blend, Martha. A Child Alone. LC 95-8397. (Library of Holocaust Testimonies). 188p. 1995. pap. 16.00 (*0-85303-297-1*, Pub. by M Vallentine & Co) Intl Spec Bk.

***Blendinger, Doris E.** Park It Here! 2000: Parking Guide for New York City Streets. (Illus.). 320p. 2000. pap. 13.95 (*1-891160-44-3*) Alixa.

Blendinger, Jack G. QLM - Quality Leading & Managing: A Practical Guide for Improving Schools. 108p. (C). 1996. spiral bd. 25.95 (*0-7872-2883-4*, 41288301) Kendall-Hunt.

Blendinger-Jones. Reaching Out to Families: A Handbook for Teachers & Administration. 208p. (C). 1998. per. 26.95 (*0-7872-4841-X*, 41484101) Kendall-Hunt.

Blendis, Laurence M., jt. ed. see Bomzon, Arieh.

Blendon, E. G. & Nalepa, B. H. Quick Survey Course in Forms Typing. 1967. text 8.96 (*0-07-005892-X*) McGraw.

— Quick Survey Course in Forms Typing. fac. ed. 1967. pap. text 8.96 (*0-07-005891-1*) McGraw.

Blenerhasset, Thomas. A Revelation of the True Minerva. LC 42-5954. 84p. 1978. reprint ed. 50.00 (*0-8201-1196-1*) Schol Facsimiles.

Blenerhasset, Thomas, jt. auth. see Higgins, John.

Blengino, Tony, jt. ed. see Benson, John.

Blenk, Katie & Fine, Doris L. Making School Inclusion Work: A Guide to Everyday Practices. LC 94-38275. 254p. 1994. pap. 24.95 (*0-914797-96-4*) Brookline Bks.

Blenk, Werner, ed. Labour Relations in Caribbean Countries Proceedings of a Tripartite Caribbean Seminar on Labour Relations (Castries, St. Lucia, 1-4 November 1988) (Labour-Management Relations Ser.: No. 75). vi, 124p. (Orig.). 1990. pap. 15.75 (*92-2-107279-7*) Intl Labour Office.

Blenkhorn, David L., jt. auth. see Leenders, Michiel R.

Blenkhorn, David L., jt. ed. see Fleisher, Craig S.

Blenkin, Geva. Principles into Practice in Early Childhood Education. LC 97-221357. 1997. pap. text 26.95 (*1-85396-306-2*, Pub. by P Chapman) P H Brookes.

Blenkin, Geva M. & Kelly, A. V., eds. Assessment in Early Childhood Education. (One-Off Ser.). (Illus.). 200p. 1992. pap. (*1-85396-153-1*) Corwin Pr.

— Early Childhood Education: A Development Curriculum. 2nd ed. 272p. 1996. pap. 24.95 (*1-85396-315-1*, Pub. by P Chapman) Taylor & Francis.

— The National Curriculum & Early Learning: An Evaluation. 240p. 1994. pap. 25.00 (*1-85396-241-4*, Pub. by P Chapman) Taylor & Francis.

Blenkin, Geva M., et al. Change & the Curriculum. 160p. 1992. pap. 27.00 (*1-85396-154-X*, Pub. by P Chapman) Taylor & Francis.

Blenkinsop, Tom G. & Tromp, Paul L., eds. Sub-Saharan Economic Geology. (Illus.). 300p. (C). 1995. text 123.00 (*90-5410-610-7*, Pub. by A A Balkema) Ashgate Pub Co.

Blenkinsopp, Alison & Paxton, Paul. Symptoms in the Pharmacy: A Guide to the Management of Common Illness. 3rd ed. (Illus.). 304p. 1998. pap. 44.95 (*0-632-04941-3*) Blackwell Sci.

— Symptoms in the Pharmacy: A Guide to the Management of Common Symptoms. 2nd ed. LC 94-11238. 256p. 1994. pap. 39.95 (*0-632-03609-5*, Pub. by Blckwll Scitfc UK) Blackwell Sci.

***Blenkinsopp, Alison, et al.** Health Promotion for Pharmacists. 2nd ed. LC 99-40698. 256p. 2000. 42.50 (*0-19-263044-X*) OUP.

Blenkinsopp, Joseph. Ezekiel. (Interpretation: A Bible Commentary for Teaching & Preaching Ser.). 288p. 1990. 25.00 (*0-8042-3118-4*) Westminster John Knox.

— Gibeon & Israel: The Role of Gibeon & the Gibeonites in the Political & Religious History of Early Israel. LC 74-171672. (Society for Old Testament Studies.: No. 2). 164p. reprint ed. pap. 46.80 (*0-608-15694-9*, 2031621) Bks Demand.

— A History of Prophecy in Israel. rev. ed. LC 96-21402. 336p. (Orig.). 1996. pap. 28.95 (*0-664-25639-2*) Westminster John Knox.

***Blenkinsopp, Joseph.** Isaiah 1-39: A New Translation with Introduction & Commentary. LC 00-21326. (Anchor Bible Ser.). 2000. pap. 50.00 (*0-385-49716-4*) Doubleday.

Blenkinsopp, Joseph. The Pentateuch. 288p. 1992. 34.95 (*0-385-41207-X*) Doubleday.

***Blenkinsopp, Joseph.** The Pentateuch: An Introduction to the First Five Books of the Bible. 288p. 2000. pap. 20.00 (*0-385-49788-1*, Anchor Bib) Doubleday.

Blenkinsopp, Joseph. Prophecy & Canon: A Contribution to the Study of Jewish Origins. LC 76-22411. 206p. 1986. pap. 13.00 (*0-268-01559-7*) U of Notre Dame Pr.

— Sage, Priest, & Prophet: Religious & Intellectual Leadership in Ancient Israel. Knight, Douglas A., ed. LC 95-1792. (Library of Ancient Israel). 208p. 1995. 19.00 (*0-664-21954-3*) Westminster John Knox.

— Wisdom & Law in the Old Testament: The Ordering of Life in Israel & Early Judaism. 2nd ed. (Oxford Bible Ser.). 206p. (Orig.). 1995. pap. text 18.95 (*0-19-875504-X*) OUP.

Blenman, Jonathan. Remarks on Several Acts of Parliament Relating More Especially to the Colonies Abroad. LC 70-141127. (Research Library of Colonial Americana). 1972. reprint ed. 20.95 (*0-405-03331-1*) Ayer.

Blenn, Frank R. Easy & Elegant Entrees. LC 94-36830. (Healthy Selects Cookbook Ser.). (Illus.). 80p. 1996. pap. 8.95 (*0-945448-40-6*, 4609-01, Pub. by Am Diabetes) NTC Contemp Pub Co.

— Great Starts & Fine Finishes. LC 94-32299. (Healthy Selects Cookbook Ser.). (Illus.). 80p. 1996. pap. 8.95 (*0-945448-39-2*, 4607-01, Pub. by Am Diabetes) NTC Contemp Pub Co.

— Quick & Hearty Main Dishes. (Healthy Selects Cookbook Ser.). (Illus.). 80p. 1996. pap. 8.95 (*0-945448-46-5*, 00465Q, Pub. by Am Diabetes) NTC Contemp Pub Co.

— Savory Soups & Salads. (Healthy Selects Cookbook Ser.). (Illus.). 80p. 1996. pap. 8.95 (*0-945448-41-4*, 00414Q, Pub. by Am Diabetes) NTC Contemp Pub Co.

— Simple & Tasty. (Healthy Selects Cookbook Ser.). (Illus.). 72p. 1996. pap. 8.95 (*0-945448-45-7*, 00457Q, Pub. by Am Diabetes) NTC Contemp Pub Co.

Blennerhassett, Charlotte J. Sidelights. Gulcher, E., tr. LC 68-54329. (Essay Index Reprint Ser.). 1977. 19.95 (*0-8369-0216-5*) Ayer.

Blensly, Douglas L. & Plank, Tom M. Accounting Desk Book. 8th ed. LC 84-21102. 542p. 1984. text 59.50 (*0-87624-011-2*, Inst Busn Plan) P-H.

— Accounting Desk Book. 10th ed. 736p. (C). 1995. text 69.95 (*0-13-366980-7*) P-H.

Blenz, Beth. The Encyclopedia of Michigan: A Reference Guide to the Wolverine State. 2nd ed. (Encyclopedia of the United States Ser.). (Illus.). 693p. 1990. lib. bdg. 79.00 (*0-403-09973-0*) Somerset Pub.

Blenz-Clucas, Beth & Gribble, Gloria, eds. Recommended Videos for Schools. LC 91-13091. 300p. 1991. lib. bdg. 55.00 (*0-87436-644-5*) ABC-CLIO.

Bleoca, Liviu, jt. ed. see Sorkin, Adam J.

Blerk, A. Van, see Van Blerk, A.

Blerkom, Jonathan Van, see Van Blerkom, Jonathan, ed.

Bles, Adrien. Dictionnaire Historique des Rues de Marseilles. (FRE.). 442p. 1989. 250.00 (*0-8288-9531-7*) Fr & Eur.

Bles, Arthur, tr. see Weingartner, Felix.

Bles, Irene. Damn, Sam, I Want to Share My Life but I Need to Live Alone. (Minority Poet Ser.). (ENG & SPA.). 42p. 1987. pap. 4.00 (*1-880046-00-8*) Baculite Pub.

Bles, Mark. Child at War: The True Story of a Young Belgian Resistance Fighter. LC 90-23218. (Illus.). 301p. 1991. reprint ed. 20.95 (*1-56279-004-8*) Mercury Hse Inc.

— In Search of Limits: Climbing the Alpine 400-Metre. (Illus.). 224p. 1995. 39.95 (*0-340-59614-7*, Pub. by Hodder & Stought Ltd) Trafalgar.

Blesa, Miguel A., et al. Chemical Dissolution of Metal Oxides. 432p. 1993. lib. bdg. 149.95 (*0-8493-5943-0*, QD181) CRC Pr.

Bleser, Carol, ed. The Hammonds of Redcliffe. LC 97-40191. (Illus.). 445p. 1997. reprint ed. pap. 18.95 (*1-57003-221-1*) U of SC Pr.

— Secret & Sacred: The Diaries of James Henry Hammond, a Southern Slaveholder. LC 97-40192. (Illus.). 372p. 1997. reprint ed. pap. 16.95 (*1-57003-222-X*) U of SC Pr.

— Tokens of Affection: The Letters of a Planter's Daughter in the Old South. LC 94-40961. (Southern Voices from the Past Ser.). 1996. 45.00 (*0-8203-1727-6*) U of Ga Pr.

Bleser, Carol K., ed. In Joy & in Sorrow: Women, Family & Marriage in the Victorian South, 1830-1900. (Illus.). 384p. (C). 1992. pap. text 21.95 (*0-19-506048-2*) OUP.

Bleser, Nicholas J. Tumacacori: From Rancheria to National Monument. Priehs, T. J., ed. LC 89-61675. (Illus.). 48p. (Orig.). 1990. pap. 6.95 (*0-911408-84-3*) SW Pks Mnmts.

Blesh, Rudi. Classic Piano Rags. 364p. (Orig.). 1973. pap. 15.95 (*0-486-20469-3*) Dover.

— Combo, U. S. A. Eight Lives in Jazz. LC 79-12293. (Roots of Jazz Ser.). 1979. reprint ed. 29.50 (*0-306-79568-X*) Da Capo.

— Shining Trumpets: A History of Jazz. 2nd rev. ed. LC 74-28309. (Roots of Jazz Ser.). (Illus.). xxxii, 412p. 1975. reprint ed. lib. bdg. 39.50 (*0-306-70658-X*) Da Capo.

Blesie-Hicks, Sharon, jt. auth. see Judson, Karen.

Blesie, Sharon, jt. auth. see Judson, Karen.

Bless, Claire & Kathuria, Ravinder. Fundamentals of Social Statistics: An African Perspective. 367p. (C). 1993. pap. text 46.15 (*0-7021-2940-2*, Pub. by Juta & Co) Intl Spec Bk.

Bless, Diane M. Phonosurgery. Ford, Charles N., ed. (Illus.). 256p. 1991. text 108.00 (*0-88167-772-8*) Lppncott W & W.

Bless, Diane M., jt. auth. see Hirano, Minoru.

***Bless, Herbert.** Subjective Experience in Social Cognition & Behavior. LC 99-51588. 352p. 1999. 54.95 (*0-86377-690-6*) L Erlbaum Assocs.

Bless, Mark. Hearts & Minds. 400p. 1994. 26.95 (*0-450-61008-X*, Pub. by Hodder & Stought Ltd) Trafalgar.

Bless, Nancy, contrib. by. Notes from the Material World: Contemporary Photomontage. LC 92-44897. (Illus.). 36p. 1992. pap. 14.95 (*0-932718-34-5*) Kohler Arts.

Bless, Robert C. Discovering the Cosmos. LC 94-37452. (Illus.). 768p. (C). 1996. text 58.00 (*0-935702-67-9*) Univ Sci Bks.

Blesse, Frederick C. Check Six. 178p. 1987. 17.95 (*0-912173-15-7*) Champlin Museum.

Blessed, Brian. Nothing's Impossible. large type ed. 288p. 1996. 22.95 (*1-85695-113-8*, Pub. by ISIS Lrg Prnt) Transaction Pubs.

Blessed Theophylact. The Explanation of the Holy Gospel According to St. Luke. Stade, Christopher, tr. from GRE. LC 93-174571. (Blessed Theophylact's Explanation of the New Testament Ser.: Vol. 3). (Illus.). viii, 328p. 1997. per. 16.00 (*0-9635183-5-6*); boxed set 22.00 (*0-9635183-4-8*) Chrysostom Pr.

Blessin, Ann M. Sacred Dance with Physically & Mentally Handicapped. Adams, Doug, ed. 1982. pap. 3.00 (*0-941500-28-4*) Sharing Co.

Blessing, Airilee Ellyn, jt. auth. see Van Valkenburgh, Norman J.

Blessing, Buck. Selling the Big Ticket: How to Manage the Multiple Approval Sale. 2nd unabridged ed. (Illus.). v, 187p. (Orig.). 1994. pap. 23.95 (*0-9656474-0-4*) Buck Blessing.

Blessing, Christina. Adventure & Profit in the World's Bazaars. 237p. (Orig.). 1996. pap. 19.95 (*0-9648194-8-1*) Lost Cities.

***Blessing, Hedrich, photos by.** A View from the River: The Chicago Architecture Foundation's River Cruise. LC 00-130347. (Illus.). 96p. 2000. pap. 14.95 (*0-7649-1333-6*, A537) Pomegranate Calif.

Blessing, Jennifer, et al. Rrose Is a Rrose Is a Rrose: Gender Performance in Photography. (Illus.). 232p. 1997. 65.00 (*0-8109-6901-7*, Pub. by Abrams) Time Warner.

Blessing, Julia A., jt. auth. see Caspi, Mishael M.

Blessing, Kamila. It Was a Miracle: Stories of Ordinary People & Extraordinary Healing. LC 98-49504. 160p. 1999. pap. 11.99 (*0-8066-3732-3*, 9-3732, Augsburg) Augsburg Fortress.

Blessing, Lee. Cobb. 1991. pap. 5.25 (*0-8222-0224-7*) Dramatists Play.

— Down the Road. 1991. pap. 5.25 (*0-8222-0324-3*) Dramatists Play.

— Eleemosynary. 1987. pap. 5.25 (*0-8222-0354-5*) Dramatists Play.

— Fortinbras. 1992. pap. 5.25 (*0-8222-0421-5*) Dramatists Play.

— Independence. 1985. pap. 5.25 (*0-8222-0567-X*) Dramatists Play.

— Lake Street Extension. 1993. pap. 5.25 (*0-8222-1336-2*) Dramatists Play.

Blessing, Lee. Lee Blessing: Four Plays. LC 90-38989. 207p. (Orig.). (C). 1990. pap. 13.95 (*0-435-08601-4*, 08601) Heinemann.

Blessing, Lee. Nice People Dancing to Good Country Music. 1983. pap. 5.25 (*0-8222-0816-4*) Dramatists Play.

— Oldtimers Game. 1988. pap. 5.25 (*0-8222-0843-1*) Dramatists Play.

— Patient A. 1993. pap. 5.25 (*0-8222-1364-8*) Dramatists Play.

— Patient A & Other Plays: Five Plays by Lee Blessing. LC 95-2412. 255p. 1995. pap. 15.95 (*0-435-08662-6*, 08662) Heinemann.

— Riches. 1986. pap. 5.25 (*0-8222-1221-8*) Dramatists Play.

— Two Rooms. 1990. pap. 5.25 (*0-8222-1183-1*) Dramatists Play.

— A Walk in the Woods. 1988. pap. 5.25 (*0-8222-1220-X*) Dramatists Play.

Blessing, Lucienne, tr. see Pahl, Gerald & Beitz, Wolfgang.

***Blessing, Lusienne T. M. & Chakrabarti, Amaresh.** A Design Research Methodology LC 99-41994. 1999. 59.95 (*1-85233-625-0*) Spr-Verlag.

Blessing, Matt. The Changing Workforce: Teaching Labor History with City & County Directories. (Illus.). 20p. 1996. pap. 9.95 (*0-87020-288-X*, CHWO) State Hist Soc Wis.

Blessing-Moore, Joann, ed. see Rudoff, Carol.

Blessing, Patrick J. The Irish in America: A Guide to the Literature & the Manuscript Collections. LC 90-1667. 347p. 1992. text 49.95 (*0-8132-0731-2*) Cath U Pr.

Blessing, Peter H. Income Tax Treaties of the United States. 1904p. 1995. 265.00 (*0-7913-2585-7*) Warren Gorham & Lamont.

Blessing, Ralph J. Feelings - A Poetic Look Inside Friendship, Love & Deceit. 1999. pap. write for info. (*1-58235-026-4*) Watermrk Pr.

Blessing, Richard. Poems & Stories. LC 82-22177. 75p. 1983. 14.00 (*0-937872-12-1*); pap. 6.00 (*0-937872-13-X*) Dragon Gate.

— Winter Constellations. 3rd ed. Boyer, Dale, ed. LC 77-72388. (Ahsahta Press Modern & Contemporary Poets of the West Ser.). 52p. 1977. pap. 6.95 (*0-916272-05-2*) Ahsahta Pr.

Blessing, Richard, ed. see Oberg, Arthur.

Blessing, Richard A. Wallace Stevens: Whole Harmonium. LC 71-105612. 1970. 34.50 (*0-8156-2145-0*) Syracuse U Pr.

Blessing, Tim H., jt. auth. see Murray, Robert K.

Blessing, William W. The Lower Brainstem & Bodily Homeostasis. (Illus.). 592p. 1997. text 89.50 (*0-19-507511-0*) OUP.

Blessinger, Timothy L. Abraham Lincoln: An American, the Kentuckiana Years. 64p. 1997. pap. write for info. (*0-932970-91-5*) Prinit Pr.

Blessington, Francis. Lantskip. LC 87-1116. 67p. (Orig.). 1987. pap. 8.95 (*0-87233-090-7*) Bauhan.

— Lorenzo de Medici: A Verse Play. LC 92-11125. 66p. (Orig.). (C). 1992. pap. text 18.50 (*0-8191-8748-8*) U Pr of Amer.

***Blessington, Francis.** Wolf Howl: Poems. 2000. pap. write for info. (*1-886157-29-4*) BkMk.

Blessington, Francis C. Paradise Lost: Ideal & Tragic Epic. (Masterwork Studies: No. 12). 160p. 1988. 29.00 (*0-8057-7969-8*, Twyne) Mac Lib Ref.

— Paradise Lost & the Classical Epic. 1979. 19.95 (*0-7100-0160-6*, Routledge Thoemms) Routledge.

Blessington, H. K. Urban Transport. LC 95-221016. 152p. 1995. 57.00 (*0-7277-2084-8*) Am Soc Civil Eng.

Blessington, Marguerite P. The Works of Lady Blessington. LC 71-37681. (Women of Letters Ser.). reprint ed. 64.50 (*0-404-56717-7*) AMS Pr.

Blessington, Thomas M. & Collins, Pamela C. Foliage Plants: Prolonging Quality: Postproduction Care & Handling. LC 92-45172. (Postproduction Ser.). (Illus.). 203p. (C). 1993. pap. text 19.95 (*0-9626796-9-0*, B015) Ball Pub.

Blessitt, Arthur. Arthur A. Pilgrim. LC 85-71322. (Orig.). 1985. pap. 5.00 (*0-934461-00-7*, BP601) Blessitt Pub.

— Arthur-Peacemaker. LC 85-71322. (Orig.). 1986. pap. 5.00 (*0-934461-02-3*, BP603) Blessitt Pub.

— Glory. LC 88-70080. 59p. 1988. pap. 5.00 (*0-934461-06-6*) Blessitt Pub.

— Joy to the World. 2nd ed. (Orig.). 1987. pap. 5.00 (*0-934461-05-8*) Blessitt Pub.

— Simon. LC 87-7213. 128p. 1987. pap. 5.00 (*0-934461-04-X*) Blessitt Pub.

Blessley, Jane, ed. Constitutional Law. 200p. (C). 1990. pap. 100.00 (*1-85352-508-1*, Pub. by HLT Pubns) St Mut.

Blessman, T. Denise, ed. see Blackberry Castle Productions Staff, et al.

Blesso, John. Off to a Bad Start: Chicken Soup for the Sold. LC 96-92544. 170p. (Orig.). 1997. pap. 12.95 (*0-9654452-0-8*) Silk City Pr.

Blest Gana, Alberto. Martin Rivas. Whitham, Charles, tr. 1977. lib. bdg. 59.95 (*0-8490-2212-6*) Gordon Pr.

— Martin Rivas. Concho, Jaime, ed. O'Dwyer, Tess, tr. LC 99-47790. (Library of Latin America). 448p. 2000. 30.00 (*0-19-510713-6*); pap. 18.95 (*0-19-510714-4*) OUP.

***Blet, Pierre.** Pius XII & the Second World War: According to the Archives of the Vatican. Johnson, Lawrence J., tr. from FRE. LC 99-24020. 416p. 1999. 29.95 (*0-8091-0503-9*) Paulist Pr.

Blethen, Alden J. Genealogy of the Blethen Family. 108p. 1988. reprint ed. pap. 20.00 (*0-8328-0267-0*); reprint ed. lib. bdg. 28.00 (*0-8328-0266-2*) Higginson Bk Co.

Blethen, H. Tyler & Wood, Curtis, eds. Ulster & North America: Transatlantic Perspectives on the Scotch-Irish. LC 96-25002. 320p. 1997. text 39.95 (*0-8173-0823-7*) U of Ala Pr.

Blethen, H. Tyler & Wood, Curtis W., Jr. From Ulster to Carolina: The Migration of the Scotch-Irish to Southwestern North Carolina. rev. ed. (Illus.). xi, 71p. 1998. pap. 9.00 (*0-86526-279-9*) NC Archives.

Bletz, Frans & Praaning, Rip, eds. The Future of European Defence. 1986. pap. text 60.00 (*90-247-3290-5*) Kluwer Academic.

Bletzacker, Richard W., et al. Bletzacker's OBBC Study Guide. 2nd ed. 310p. 1990. 80.00 (*0-8322-0264-9*) Banks-Baldwin.

Bletzer, June G. The Encyclopedic Psychic Dictionary. 3rd ed. Orig. Title: Donning International Encyclopedic Psychic Dictionary. xiii, 875p. 1998. reprint ed. pap. 24.95 (*0-9627209-1-7*) New Leaf Dist.

***Bletzer, June G.** Self-Disclosure of a Soul Memory: A Study of Emotion. Sellen, Esther, ed. xii, 309p. 1999. pap. write for info. (*0-9674836-0-3*) J G Bletzer.

Bleuel, Hans P. Deutschlands Bekenner: German Men of Knowledge: the Professiate from the Rule of the Kaiser to the Rise of Hitler. Metzger, Walter P., ed. LC 76-55206. (Academic Profession Ser.). (GER., Illus.). 1977. reprint ed. lib. bdg. 21.95 (*0-405-10032-9*) Ayer.

Bleuel, William H. & Patton, Joseph D. Service Management: Principles & Practices. 2nd ed. LC 86-10682. 326p. 1986. reprint ed. pap. 101.10 (*0-7837-5131-1*, 204485900004) Bks Demand.

Bleuel, William H., jt. auth. see Patton, Joseph D.

Bleuer, Jeanne C., et al. Activities for Counseling Underachievers. Schilling, Dianne, ed. 128p. (J). (gr. 5-12). 1994. pap. text 14.95 (*1-56499-016-8*, IP9016) Innerchoice Pub.

***Bleuins, Dave.** 7 Angels, 7 Horns. 148p. 2000. spiral bd. 20.00 (*0-9672731-7-X*) David Blevins.

An Asterisk (*) at the beginning of an entry indicates that the title is appearing for the first time.

Bleuler, Eugen. Dementia Praecox: Or the Group of Schizophrenias. Zinkin, Joseph, tr. (Monograph Series on Schizophrenia: No. 1). 548p. 1966. 72.50 (*0-8236-1180-9*) Intl Univs Pr.

— Textbook of Psychiatry. LC 75-16685. (Classics in Psychiatry Ser.). (Illus.). 1977. reprint ed. 54.95 (*0-405-07417-4*) Ayer.

Bleuler, Manfred. The Schizophrenic Disorders: Long-Term Patient & Family Studies. Clemens, Siegfried M., tr. LC 75-43303. 553p. reprint ed. pap. 171.50 (*0-7837-3283-X*, 205768500006) Bks Demand.

Bleumer, Ria, tr. see Provoost, Anne.

Bleustein, Jeffrey L., ed. Mechanics & Sport: Papers of a Symposium Presented During the Winter Annual Meeting of the American Society of the Mechanical Engineers , Detroit , Nov. 11-15, 1973, (Sponsored by the Applied Mechanics Division, ASME) LC 73-89078. (AMD Ser.: Vol. 4). 320p. reprint ed. pap. 99.20 (*0-608-16199-3*, 205616000052) Bks Demand.

Bleutge, Peter. Product Liability - The New Pocket Liability Law in Germany: Tochtergesellschaften Deutscher Unternehmen in den U. S. A. 1994-95. (ENG & GER.). 80p. 1993. 25.00 (*0-86640-049-4*) German Am Chamber.

Bleuthmann, Horst & Ohashi, Pamela, eds. Transgenesis & Targeted Mutagenesis in Immunology. LC 93-43197. (Illus.). 316p. (C). 1994. text 34.95 (*0-12-105760-7*) Acad Pr.

Bleux, J. Lexington Industrial Automation. (FRE & ENG.). 157p. 1996. 37.95 (*0-320-02481-4*) Fr & Eur.

Blevgad, Lenore. First Friends. LC 99-63968. (Growing Tree Ser.). (Illus.). 24p. (YA). (ps up). 2000. 9.95 (*0-694-01273-4*, HarpFestival) HarpC Child Bks.

Blevi, Viktor & Sween, Gretchen. Aromatherapy. (Illus.). 176p. (Orig.). 1993. pap. 10.00 (*0-380-76429-6*, Avon Bks) Morrow Avon.

— The Complete Book of Beauty. 208p. (Orig.). 1993. pap. 10.00 (*0-380-76188-2*, Avon Bks) Morrow Avon.

Blevins, Audie L., jt. auth. see Jensen, Katherine.

Blevins, Brooks. Cattle in the Cotton Fields: A History of Cattle Raising in Alabama. LC 98-19778. 216p. 1998. text 34.95 (*0-8173-0940-3*) U of Ala Pr.

Blevins, Bruce H. A. K. A. Jackson Lake. unabridged ed. (Illus.). 24p. 1998. pap. 3.95 (*1-893771-00-8*) W I M.

— An Early History of Red Lodge, Montana. unabridged ed. (Illus.). 17p. 1998. pap. 2.98 (*1-893771-01-6*) W I M.

— Park County, Wyoming Facts & Maps Through Time. unabridged ed. (Illus.). 81p. 1999. pap. 14.95 (*1-893771-03-2*) W I M.

Blevins, Carolyn, ed. Women in Church History: A Bibliography. LC 95-24835. 200p. (C). 1995. text 30.00 (*0-86554-493-X*, MUP/H387) Mercer Univ Pr.

Blevins-Church, Adrian. The Man Who Went Out for Cigarettes. Rogers, Bertha, ed. (Award Chapbook Ser.). 26p. (Orig.). 1996. pap. 5.00 (*0-9646844-2-X*) Bright Hill.

Blevins, Clyde D. On the Wings of a Prayer. 159p. 1998. pap. 8.00 (*1-55630-880-9*) Brentwood Comm.

— Redemptions Great Story. 231p. 1998. pap. 10.00 (*1-55630-890-6*) Brentwood Comm.

Blevins, Dallas R. Internal Control: An Introduction. Campbell, Lee A., ed. 95p. 1991. pap. text, student ed. 130.00 (*0-89413-251-2*, A6048) Inst Inter Aud.

***Blevins, Dave.** The Doonesbury Trivia Book. 2nd ed. 64p. 2000. spiral bd. 15.00 (*0-9672731-6-1*) David Blevins.

— On This Day in Television History... 2nd ed. 48p. 2000. pap. 15.00 (*0-9672731-5-3*) David Blevins.

— On This Day in UFO History... 3rd ed. 77p. 2000. spiral bd. 20.00 (*0-9672731-9-6*) David Blevins.

— Random Thoughts as We Traverse the New Millennium. 45p. 2000. pap. 15.00 (*0-9672731-8-8*) David Blevins.

Blevins, David. The Doonesbury Trivia Book. 84p. 1999. pap. 15.00 (*0-9672731-4-5*) David Blevins.

***Blevins, David.** The Hall of Fame Directory. 120p. 1999. pap. 20.00 (*0-9672731-1-0*) David Blevins.

— Museums You Never Knew Existed. 72p. 1999. pap. 15.00 (*0-9672731-2-9*) David Blevins.

— On This Day in Television History... 60p. 1999. pap. 15.00 (*0-9672731-3-7*) David Blevins.

— On This Day in UFO History... 2nd rev. ed. 89p. 1999. pap. 15.00 (*0-9672731-0-2*) David Blevins.

***Blevins, Don.** Peculiar, Uncertain & Two Egg: The Unusual Origins of More Than 3,000 American Place Names. LC 00-27923. (Illus.). 352p. 2000. pap. 14.95 (*1-58182-094-1*, Cumberland Hearthside) Cumberland Hse.

Blevins, Edna L., et al. The Nursing Home & You: Partners in Caring for a Relative with Alzheimer's Disease. 48p. (Orig.). 1987. pap. text 8.95 (*0-943774-37-3*) Am Assn Homes.

Blevins, Gary D. Six Six Six the Final Warning. rev. ed. (Illus.). 512p. (Orig.). 1990. pap. 14.95 (*0-9626841-1-2*) Vision Res.

Blevins, Isabel F. & Richstatter, Thomas. Liturgy & Worship: A Course on Prayer & Sacraments, Parish Annotated Guide: Keystone Parish Edition. (Faith & Witness Program Ser.). (Illus.). (J). (gr. 7-9). 1998. pap. 15.00 (*0-8215-5665-7*) Sadlier.

— Liturgy & Worship - A Course on Prayer & Sacraments, School Guide: Keystone School Edition. annot. ed. (Faith & Witness Program Ser.). (Illus.). 272p. 1998. pap., teacher ed. 21.90 (*0-8215-5614-2*) Sadlier.

***Blevins, Richard.** The Collected Later Poems of Philip Marlowe. 28p. 1999. pap. 4.00 (*1-893032-15-9*, Pub. by Jensen Daniels) SPD-Small Pr Dist.

Blevins, Richard W. Franz Xaver Kroetz: The Emergence of a Political Playwright. Sander, Volkmar, ed. LC 83-48018. (New York University Ottendorfer Ser.: Vol. 18). 295p. (C). 1983. pap. text 28.40 (*0-8204-0013-0*) P Lang Pubng.

— Longplaying. Mycue, Edward, ed. (Took Modern Poetry in English Ser.: No. 43). 40p. 1994. pap. 5.00 (*1-879457-45-8*) Norton Coker Pr.

— Three Sleep: A Historomance. LC 91-77166. 118p. (Orig.). 1992. pap. text 10.00 (*0-9627891-3-5*) Igneus Pr.

Blevins, Richard W., ed. see Butterick, George.

Blevins, Richard W., ed. see Butterick, George F.

Blevins, Richard W., ed. see Olson, Charles & Creeley, Robert.

Blevins, Robert D. Applied Fluid Dynamics Handbook. LC 92-4247. 570p. 1992. reprint ed. lib. bdg. 86.50 (*0-89464-717-2*) Krieger.

— Flow-Induced Vibration. 2nd ed. LC 92-40221. 478p. (C). 1994. 68.50 (*0-89464-823-3*) Krieger.

— Formulas for Natural Frequency & Mode Shape 1995. 506p. 1994. 59.50 (*0-89464-894-2*) Krieger.

Blevins, T. F., ed. see Richardson, Robert M.

Blevins, W. Quick & Easy Phonics. 48p. (J). (gr. 1-3). 1997. pap. 8.95 (*0-590-96380-5*) Scholastic Inc.

Blevins, Wade. And Then the Feather Fell. (Cherokee Indian Legend Ser.). (Illus.). 48p. (J). (gr. k-8). 1993. text 11.95 (*1-56763-060-X*); pap. text 5.95 (*0-685-67465-7*) Ozark Pub.

— And Then the Feather Fell. (J). (gr. 4-7). 1996. pap. text 2.95 (*1-56763-061-8*) Ozark Pub.

— And Then the Feather Fell. LC 96-10304. (Cherokee Indian Legend Ser.: No. 1). (Illus.). 35p. (J). 1996. 12.95 (*1-56763-096-0*) Ozark Pub.

— Atagahi's Gift. LC 96-11123. (Cherokee Indian Legend Ser.: No. 6). (Illus.). 51p. (J). 1996. 12.95 (*1-56763-135-5*) Ozark Pub.

— Ganseti & the Legend of the Little People. LC 96-7032. (Cherokee Indian Legend Ser.: No. 4). (Illus.). 43p. (J). (gr. 2 up). 1993. lib. bdg. 12.95 (*1-56763-065-0*) Ozark Pub.

— Legend of Little Deer. LC 96-7033. (Cherokee Indian Legend Ser.: No. 3). (Illus.). 49p. (J). (gr. 2 up). 1993. lib. bdg. 12.95 (*1-56763-073-1*) Ozark Pub.

— Path of Destiny. LC 96-10308. (Cherokee Indian Legend Ser.: No. 2). (Illus.). 49p. (J). (gr. 2 up). 1993. lib. bdg. 12.95 (*1-56763-071-5*) Ozark Pub.

— Se-lu's Song. LC 96-6324. (Cherokee Indian Legend Ser.: Vol. 7). (Illus.). 53p. (J). 1996. 12.95 (*1-56763-133-9*) Ozark Pub.

— The Wisdom Circle. LC 96-10302. (Cherokee Indian Legend Ser.: Vol. 5). (Illus.). 45p. (J). (gr. k-8). 1993. lib. bdg. 12.95 (*1-56763-075-8*) Ozark Pub.

Blevins, Wiley. Phonics from A to Z: A Practical Guide. 112p. 1998. 14.95 (*0-590-31510-2*) Scholastic Inc.

***Blevins, Wiley.** Songs & Rhymes: Live Audio Tape, Reproducible Song & Rhyme Sheets & Easy Lessons That Prepare Kids for Phonics Instructions with Cassette(s) (Phonemic Awareness Ser.). (Illus.). (J). 1999. pap. 15.95 incl. audio (*0-590-64409-2*) Scholastic Inc.

Blevins, Wiley, jt. auth. see Stamper, Judith B.

Blevins, Wiley, jt. auth. see Stamper, Judith Bauer.

***Blevins, Win.** Ravenshadow. LC 99-38122. 448p. 1999. 25.95 (*0-312-86565-1*, Pub. by Forge NYC) St Martin.

— Ravenshadow. 432p. 2000. mass mkt. 6.99 (*0-8125-9017-1*) Tor Bks.

Blevins, Win. The Rock Child. 480p. 1999. mass mkt. 6.99 (*0-8125-4472-2*, Pub. by Forge NYC) St Martin.

Blevins, Winfred. Charbonneau: A Man of Two Dreams. 22.95 (*0-8488-0110-5*) Amereon Ltd.

— Charbonneau: A Man of Two Dreams. LC 85-14761. (Frontier Library). 280p. 1985. pap. 7.95 (*0-915463-16-4*) Jameson Bks.

— Give Your Heart to the Hawks: A Tribute to the Mountain Men. 328p. 1976. mass mkt. 5.50 (*0-380-00694-4*, Avon Bks) Morrow Avon.

— Give Your Heart to the Hawks: A Tribute to the Mountain Men. (Illus.). 360p. 1995. pap. 16.95 (*1-886609-01-2*) Tamarack Bks.

— The Misadventures of Silk & Shakespeare. LC 85-18207. (Frontier Library). 250p. 1985. 13.95 (*0-915463-26-1*, Frontier Libr) Jameson Bks.

— Stone Song. 400p. 1996. mass mkt. write for info. (*0-614-05528-8*); mass mkt. 6.99 (*0-8125-3369-0*, Pub. by Forge NYC) St Martin.

Blevins, Winfred. Stone Song, a Novel of the Life of Crazy Horse. 1996. 12.09 (*0-606-13818-8*, Pub. by Turtleback) Demco.

Blevins, Winfred, jt. auth. see Schmidt, Thomas.

Blevins, Winifred. Dictionary of the American West. (Illus.). 416p. 1993. pap. 17.95 (*0-8160-2858-3*) Facts on File.

Bleviss, Deborah L. The New Oil Crisis & Fuel Economy Technologies: Preparing the Light Transportation Industry for the Nineteen Nineties. LC 87-3260. 283p. 1988. 72.95 (*0-89930-311-0*, BVP/, Quorum Bks) Greenwood.

Bleviss, Deborah L. & Lide, Vanessa, eds. Energy Efficiency Strategies for Thailand: The Needs & the Benefits Report of a Conference Held on March 4-6, 1988, Pattaya, Thailand. LC 89-33664. (Illus.). 470p. (C). 1989. lib. bdg. 65.00 (*0-8191-7497-1*) U Pr of Amer.

Blew, George. Invasion Balkans: The German Campaign in the Balkans, Spring 1941. 2nd ed. LC 97-27879. 164p. 1998. reprint ed. 19.95 (*1-57249-070-5*, Burd St Pr) White Mane Pub.

***Blew, Mary Clearman.** Bone Deep in Landscape: Essays on Writing, Reading, & Place. LC 99-29878. (Literature of the American West Ser.). 208p. 1999. 22.95 (*0-8061-3177-2*) U of Okla Pr.

— Bone Deep in Landscape: Writing, Reading & Place. (Illus.). 208p. 2000. pap. 12.95 (*0-8061-3270-1*) U of Okla Pr.

— Sister Coyote: Montana Stories. 224p. 2000. 22.95 (*1-58574-071-3*) Lyons Pr.

— Written on Water: Essays on Idaho Rivers by Idaho Writers. LC 99-58474. 2000. write for info. (*0-89301-224-6*) U of Idaho Pr.

Blew, Robert W., ed. see Bose, Johanne C.

Blew, William, ed. Breviarium Aberdonense, 2 vols. LC 73-39874. (Bannatyne Club, Edinburgh. Publications: No. 96). reprint ed. 335.00 (*0-404-52844-9*) AMS Pr.

Blewer, Robert S. & McConica, Carol M., eds. Tungsten & Other Refractory Metals for VLSI Applications IV. 1989. text 17.50 (*0-931837-98-7*, Vol. V-4) Materials Res.

Blewett, Bert. The A-Z of World Boxing: An Authoritative & Entertaining Compendium of the Fight Game from Its Origins to the Present Day. LC 97-66437. (Illus.). 440p. 1997. 38.95 (*1-86105-004-6*, Robson-Parkwest) Parkwest Pubns.

Blewett, Craig, jt. auth. see Erwin, Geoff.

Blewett, Daniel K. American Military History: A Guide to Reference & Information Sources. (Reference Sources in the Social Sciences Ser.). xx, 295p. 1995. lib. bdg. 52.00 (*1-56308-035-4*) Libs Unl.

Blewett, David. Defoe's Art of Fiction: Robinson Crusoe, Moll Flanders, Colonel Jack & Roxana. LC 79-2827. 188p. reprint ed. pap. 58.30 (*0-608-15380-X*, 202932400060) Bks Demand.

— The Illustration of Robinson Crusoe: 1719-1920. LC 96-198275. (Illus.). 240p. 1996. text 75.00 (*0-901072-67-2*) OUP.

— The Illustration of Robinson Crusoe, 1719-1920. LC 94-43045. 1994. write for info. (*0-389-21013-7*) B&N Imports.

Blewett, David, ed. see Defoe, Daniel.

Blewett, David, ed. see Smollett, Tobias George.

Blewett, David, ed. & intro. see Defoe, Daniel.

Blewett, George J. The Christian View of the World. 1912. 69.50 (*0-685-89741-9*) Elliots Bks.

Blewett, John, ed. John Dewey: His Thought & Influence, No. 2--2. LC 72-8236. (Orestes Brownson Series on Contemporary Thought & Affairs). 242p. 1973. reprint ed. lib. bdg. 59.50 (*0-8371-6543-1*, BLJD, Greenwood Pr) Greenwood.

Blewett, John E., tr. see Calvez, Jean-Yves.

Blewett, Mary H. Constant Turmoil: The Politics of Industrial Life in 19th Century New England. LC 99-47848. (Illus.). 544p. 2000. text 40.00 (*1-55849-239-9*) U of Mass Pr.

— The Last Generation: Work & Life in the Textile Mills of Lowell, Massachusetts, 1910-1960. LC 89-77124. (Illus.). 352p. (C). 1990. pap. 19.95 (*0-87023-713-6*) U of Mass Pr.

— Men, Women, & Work: Class, Gender, & Protest in the New England Shoe Industry, 1780-1910. LC 87-19039. (Working Class in American History Ser.). 472p. 1988. text 34.95 (*0-252-01484-7*); pap. text 15.95 (*0-252-06142-X*) U of Ill Pr.

— We Will Rise in Our Might: Workingwomen's Voices from Nineteenth-Century New England. LC 91-55077. (Documents in American Social History Ser.). (Illus.). 224p. 1991. 39.95 (*0-8014-2246-9*); pap. text 15.95 (*0-8014-9537-7*) Cornell U Pr.

Blewett, Mary H., ed. Surviving Hard Times: The Working People of Lowell. LC 81-86362. (Illus.). xii, 176p. (Orig.). 1982. pap. 6.95 (*0-942472-05-5*) Lowell Museum.

Blewett, Mary H. & McKenna, Christine. To Enrich & to Serve: The Centennial History of the University of Massachusetts. McGauvran, Mary & Osborne, Gordon, eds. LC 94-42358. (Illus.). 1995. write for info. (*0-89865-925-6*) Donning Co.

Blewett, Stephen E. Smog: The Ozone Myth. LC 96-218119. (Illus.). 142p. (Orig.). 1996. pap. 15.00 (*0-9640565-0-X*) Ozone Resch.

— What's in the Air: Natural & Man-Made Air Pollution LC 98-70936. 140 p. 1998. write for info. (*0-9640565-2-6*) Ozone Resch.

Blewett, Steve & Stafford, Jeffrey. Hitting the Bricks. 92p. (C). 1995. spiral bd. 18.95 (*0-7872-1604-6*) Kendall-Hunt.

Blewitt, Mary & Bergel, Thomas. Celestial Navigation for Yachtsmen. 2nd ed. 1994. pap. 12.95 (*0-07-005928-4*) Intl Marine.

Blewitt, Phyllis, tr. see Doblin, Alfred.

Blewitt, Trevor, tr. see Doblin, Alfred.

Bley, Carol R., jt. auth. see Lansky, Melvin R.

Bley, Helmut. Namibia under German Rule: Studies on African History. 352p. 1997. pap. text 22.95 (*3-89473-225-3*) Transaction Pubs.

Bley, Nancy S. & Thornton, Carol A. Teaching Mathematics to Students with Learning Disabilities. 3rd ed. LC 94-6988. (Illus.). 486p. (C). 1995. pap. text 38.00 (*0-89079-603-3*, 6783) PRO-ED.

***Bley, Nancy S. & Thornton, Carol A.** Teaching Mathematics to Students with Learning Disabilities. 4th ed. LC 00-37457. (Illus.). 2000. write for info. (*0-89079-857-5*) PRO-ED.

Bley, Nancy S., jt. ed. see Thornton, Carol A.

Bley, Paul & Lee, David. Stopping Time: Paul Bley & the Transformation of Jazz. (Illus.). 224p. 1999. pap. 17.95 (*1-55065-111-0*, Pub. by Vehicule Pr) LPC Group.

***Bley, William B.** Thirty Days Hath April: Special Readers Edition. LC 99-61227. xi, 289p. 1999. write for info. (*0-9670217-4-X*) Zeugma.

Bleyer, Willard G. Main Currents in the History of American Journalism. LC 70-77720. (American Scene Ser.). (Illus.). v, 464p. 1973. reprint ed. lib. bdg. 39.50 (*0-306-71358-6*) Da Capo.

Bleyhl, Norris A. Three Military Posts in Northeastern California, 1849-1863. (ANCRR Occasional Publications: No. 9). 57p. 1984. 6.00 (*0-614-05677-2*) Assn NC Records.

Bleyker, Merle D., jt. auth. see Hendricks, William C.

Bleyker, Merle Den, see Den Bleyker, Merle.

Bleyleben, Maximilian, tr. see Chalfen, Israel.

Bleys, Rudi C. The Geography of Perversion: Male-to-Male Sexual Behavior Outside the West & the Ethnographic Imagination, 1750-1918. 328p. (C). 1995. text 50.00 (*0-8147-1262-2*) NYU Pr.

— The Geography of Perversion: Male-to-Male Sexual Behavior Outside the West & the Ethnographic Imagination, 1750-1918. 328p. (C). 1996. pap. text 19.50 (*0-8147-1265-7*) NYU Pr.

***Bleys, Rudi C.** Images of Ambiente: Homotextuality (Sic) & Latin (O/A) American Art, 1810-Today. LC 99-86252. (Illus.). 2000. 74.95 (*0-8264-4722-8*); pap. text 29.95 (*0-8264-4723-6*) Continuum.

Bleything, Dennis, jt. auth. see Button, Robert C.

Bleything, Willard, ed. see Maples, W. C.

Bleything, Willard, ed. see Schmitt, Earl P.

***Bleything, Willard B., ed.** Building a Dynamic Vision Therapy Practice. (Illus.). 152p. 1998. pap. 25.00 (*0-943599-27-X*) OEPF.

Blezard, Tracey, jt. auth. see Baddiel, Ivor.

Bleznick, Donald W. A Sourcebook for Hispanic Literature & Language: A Selected Annotated Guide to Spanish, Spanish-American, & United States Hispanic Bibliography, Literature, Linguistics, Journals, & Other Source Materials. 3rd ed. LC 94-47011. 322p. 1995. 60.00 (*0-8108-2981-9*) Scarecrow.

Bleznick, Donald W., ed. Studies on Don Quijote & Other Cervantine Works. LC 83-51090. 79p. 1984. 12.00 (*0-938972-07-3*) Spanish Lit Pubns.

— The Thought of Contemporary Spanish Essayists. LC 92-24203. 146p. (Orig.). (C). 1992. lib. bdg. 39.50 (*0-8191-8860-3*) U Pr of Amer.

Bleznick, Donald W., ed. from SPA. The Thought of Contemporary Spanish Essayists. LC 92-24203. 146p. (Orig.). (C). 1992. pap. text 23.50 (*0-8191-8861-1*) U Pr of Amer.

Bleznick, Donald W., jt. ed. see Pattison, Walter T.

Bleznick, Donald W., ed. see Vallejo, Antonio B.

Blezzard, Judith, ed. German Romantic Part Songs. 112p. (C). 1993. pap. 18.95 (*0-19-343512-8*, 1747) OUP.

— The Tudor Church Music of the Lumley Books. (Recent Researches in Music of the Renaissance Ser.: Vol. RRR65). (Illus.). xvii, 119p. 1985. pap. 45.00 (*0-89579-147-1*, RRR65) A-R Eds.

***Blhuhdorn, Ingolfur.** Post-Ecologist Politics: Social Theory & the Abdication of the Ecologist Paradigm. LC 00-32173. (Innovations in Political Theory Ser.). 2000. write for info. (*0-415-19203-X*) Routledge.

Bli, jt. auth. see Molinsky.

Blia. Nine-In-One, Grr! Grr! A Folktale From The Hmong People Of Laos. 1989. 12.15 (*0-606-05510-X*, Pub. by Turtleback) Demco.

Blicher, Adolph. Power Thyristor Physics. (Applied Physics & Engineering Ser.: Vol. 12). 1976. 96.00 (*0-387-90173-6*) Spr-Verlag.

Blicher, Steen S. The Diary of a Parish Clerk. 50p. 1991. pap. 5.95 (*1-880755-01-7*) Mermaid Pr.

— The Diary of a Parish Clerk & Other Stories. Hostrup-Jessen, Paula, tr. LC 96-15949. (Illus.). 185p. 1996. 35.00 (*0-485-04851-5*, Pub. by Athlone Pr) Humanities.

— The Diary of a Parish Clerk & Other Stories: Selected Short Stories. Hostrup-Jessen, Paula, tr. (Illus.). 224p. (C). 1996. 35.00 (*0-485-11500-X*, Pub. by Athlone Pr) Humanities.

Blick, Boris, et al. Rebels Against the Old Order: Essays in Honor of Morris Slavin. (Illus.). xiv, 213p. 1994. pap. 35.00 (*0-9623146-2-5*) Youngstown State Univ.

Blick, C. R., ed. Early Metallurgical Sites in Great Britain: BC2000 to AD1500. 112p. 1991. 20.00 (*0-901462-84-5*, Pub. by Inst Materials) Ashgate Pub Co.

Blick, Christie, ed. Late Proterozoic & Cambrian Tectonics, Sedimentation, & Record of Metazoan Radiation in the Western United States. (IGC Field Trip Guidebooks Ser.). 88p. 1989. 21.00 (*0-87590-657-5*, T331) Am Geophysical.

Blick, Edward F. Correlation of the Bible & Science. 50p. (Orig.). 1994. pap. 2.95 (*1-879366-70-3*) Hearthstone OK.

— 123 Engineering Math Handbook. 1991. pap. text 11.75 (*0-201-50607-6*) Addison-Wesley.

— A Scientific Analysis of Genesis. (Illus.). 126p. (Orig.). 1991. pap. 9.95 (*1-879366-12-6*) Hearthstone OK.

— Special Creation vs. Evolution. 38p. (Orig.). 1994. pap. 2.95 (*1-879366-65-7*) Hearthstone OK.

Blick, Frank W. A Walk to Walla Walla & the Anvil Chorus. LC 96-90441. (Orig.). 1996. pap. 8.95 (*0-533-12056-X*) Vantage.

Blick, Jeffrey P., tr. see Bove, Frederick J, et al, eds.

Blickem, Vic, jt. auth. see Hagard, Michele.

Blickensderfer, Jacob. Blickensderfer: History of the Blickensderfer Family in America. 56p. 1994. reprint ed. pap. 11.00 (*0-8328-4185-4*) Higginson Bk Co.

***Blickensdorfer, Hans.** North Wind in Your Spokes: A Novel of the Tour de France. Cambon, Marlis, tr. from GER.Tr. of Salz im Kaffee. 304p. 2000. 23.00 (*1-891369-18-0*, Pub. by Breakaway Bks) Consort Bk Sales.

Blickle, Frieder, jt. auth. see Auster, Paul.

Blickle, Peter. Communal Reformation: The Quest for Salvation in Sixteenth-Century Germany. Dunlap, Thomas J., tr. from GER. LC 91-33112. (Studies in Central European Histories). 240p. (C). 1992. text 49.95 (*0-391-03730-7*) Humanities.

— From the Communal Reformation to the Revolution of the Common Man. LC 98-18525. (Studies in Medieval & Reformation Thought: Vol. 65). x, 226p. 1998. 90.50 (*90-04-10770-3*) Brill Academic Pubs.

— Obedient Germans? A Rebuttal: A New View of German History. Brady, Thomas A., Jr., tr. from GER. LC

B

97-26222. (Studies in Early Modern German History Ser.).Tr. of Deutsche Untertanen. 145p. 1998. text 45.00 (*0-8139-1745-X*); pap. text 16.00 (*0-8139-1809-X*) U Pr of Va.

Blickle, Peter, ed. Resistance, Representation, & Community. LC 97-228620. (The Origins of the Modern State in Europe Ser.). (Illus.). 428p. 1997. text 98.00 (*0-19-820548-1*) OUP.

***Blickle, Peter & Moser, Rupert.** Traditionen der Republik - Wege Zur Demokratie: Herausgegeben im Auftrag des Collegium Generale der Universitat Bern. 256p. 1999. 35.95 (*3-906762-69-6*, Pub. by P Lang) P Lang Pubng.

Blickle, Peter, tr. see Berg, Maria.

***BLICKMAN.** Radiologia Pediatrica. 2nd ed. (C). 1999. text 47.91 (*84-8174-370-4*) Harcourt.

***Blickman, Hans.** Pediatric Imaging: Case Review. (Illus.). 224p. (C). 1999. text. write for info. (*0-323-00505-5*) Mosby Inc.

Blickman, Johan G. Pediatric Radiology. 2nd ed. LC 97-29332. (Requisites Ser.). (Illus.). 340p. (C). (gr. 13). 1997. text 79.00 (*0-8151-0993-8*, 29191) Mosby Inc.

Blickmann, H., jt. auth. see Ebel, K. D.

Blicksilver, Edith, ed. The Ethnic American Woman: Problems, Protests, Lifestyle. 5th ed. (Illus.). 471p. 1997. reprint ed. pap. 39.95 (*0-7872-3462-1*) E Blicksilver.

B

Blickstein, Hector H. Sex & Peyronie's Disease (Penile Induration, Strabismus) Index of New Information. rev. ed. 127p. 1998. 44.50 (*0-7883-1854-3*); pap. 39.50 (*0-7883-1855-1*) ABBE Pubs Assn.

***Blickstein, I. & Keith, L. G., eds.** Iatrogenic Multiple Pregnancy: Clinical Implications. (Illus.). 350p. 2000. 110.00 (*1-85070-726-X*) Prthnon Pub.

Blickstein, Steve. Bouts of Glory & Fields of Dreams: Great Stadiums & Ballparks of North America. (Illus.). 128p. 1995. 29.95 (*1-882933-05-2*) Cherbo Pub Grp.

Blicq & Moretto. Technically Write. 5th ed. LC 98-4239. 452p. (C). 1998. pap. text 56.00 (*0-13-081177-7*) P-H.

Blicq, Ron S. & Moretto, Lisa A. Guidelines for Report Writing. 3rd ed. (Illus.). 200p. 1995. pap. text 28.00 (*0-13-359803-9*) P-H.

Blicq, Ronald S. & Moretto, Lisa A. Writing Reports to Get Results: Quick, Effective Results Using the Pyramid Method. 2nd ed. LC 94-13312. 240p. 1994. pap. 29.95 (*0-7803-1019-5*, PP03673) Inst Electrical.

Blidstein, Gerald J. In the Rabbis' Garden: Adam & Eve in the Midrash. LC 97-408. 144p. 1997. pap. 25.00 (*0-7657-5987-X*) Aronson.

Blieberg, Harry, et al. Management of Colorectal Cancer. 408p. 1998. write for info. (*1-85317-377-0*, Pub. by Martin Dunitz) Mosby Inc.

Bliedtner, J. Potential Theory. (Universitext Ser.). xiv, 435p. 1986. 79.95 (*0-387-16396-4*) Spr-Verlag.

***Bliefeld, Horst.** Mice. (Complete Pet Owner's Manual Ser.). (Illus.). 2000. pap. text 6.95 (*0-7641-1450-6*) Barron.

Blier, Richard K. Hiking Trails II: Southeastern Vancouver Island. (Illus.). 136p. 1993. pap. 13.95 (*0-9690401-8-0*) Orca Bk Pubs.

— Island Backroads: Hiking, Camping & Paddling on Vancouver Island. (Illus.). 224p. 1998. pap. 14.95 (*1-55143-097-5*) Orca Bk Pubs.

— More Island Adventures: An Outdoors Guide to Vancouver Island. (Illus.). 176p. (Orig.). 1993. pap. 14.95 (*0-920501-91-5*) Orca Bk Pubs.

Blier, Susanne P. The Royal Arts of Africa: The Majesty of Form. LC 97-25456. (Perspectives Ser.). (Illus.). 272p. 1998. pap. 24.95 (*0-8109-2705-5*, Pub. by Abrams) Time Warner.

Blier, Suzanne P. African Vodun: Art, Psychology, & Power. LC 94-2180. 486p. 1995. 50.00 (*0-226-05858-1*) U Ch Pr.

— African Vodun: Art, Psychology, & Power. (Illus.). 476p. 1996. pap. text 34.95 (*0-226-05860-3*) U Ch Pr.

— The Anatomy of Architecture: Ontology & Metaphor in Batammaliba Architectural Expression. (Illus.). 334p. 1994. pap. text 17.95 (*0-226-05861-1*) U Ch Pr.

— Kingship & Art in Africa. LC 94-49648. (Perspectives Ser.). 1995. write for info. (*0-8109-2720-9*) Abrams.

— The Royal Arts of Africa: The Majesty of Form. LC 94-49648. (Perspectives Ser.). 1998. pap. text 18.67 (*0-13-440207-3*) P-H.

***Bliese, John.** Conservation for Conservatives. 2000. 27.00 (*0-8133-3802-6*, Pub. by Westview) HarpC.

Blieseuer, Klaus. My Village. 16p. (J). (gr. k-3). 1995. 20.00 (*1-56021-247-0*, 0099) W J Fantasy.

Blieszner, Rosemary, jt. auth. see Ramsey, Janet L.

Blieszner, Rosemary, jt. ed. see Adams, Rebecca G.

Blieszner, Rosemary H. Adult Friendship. (Series on Close Relationships). 160p. (C). 1992. text 42.00 (*0-8039-3672-9*) Sage.

Blieszner, Rosemary H. & Bedford, Victoria H., eds. Aging & the Family: Theory & Research. LC 94-17988. 536p. 1996. pap. 35.00 (*0-275-95697-0*, Praeger Pubs) Greenwood.

— Handbook of Aging & the Family. LC 94-17988. 536p. 1995. lib. bdg. 105.00 (*0-313-28395-8*, Greenwood Pr) Greenwood.

Blieszner, Rosemary H., jt. ed. see Adams, Rebecca.

Blieux, Dianna De, see De Blieux, Dianna.

Bliev, N. Generalized Analytic Functions in Fractional Spaces. Radok, R. & Begehr, Heinrich, trs. 1997. 62.95 (*0-582-28861-4*, Pub. by Addison-Wesley) Longman.

Bliffeld, Carlos A., tr. see Fleischman, Sid.

Bligh & Woodgate. Pickfords Guide to Business Removals. 1977. 25.00 (*0-85941-047-1*) St Mut.

***Bligh, Donald.** What's the Point in Discussion? 320p. 2000. pap. 34.95 (*1-871516-69-2*, Pub. by Intellect) Intl Spec Bk.

Bligh, Donald, ed. Accountability or Freedom for Teachers? SRHE Leverhulme VII. 137p. 1982. 28.00 (*0-900868-88-0*) OpUniv Pr.

***Bligh, Donald, et al.** Understanding Higher Education: An Introduction for Parents, Staff, Employers & Students. 224p. 1999. pap. 24.95 (*1-871516-74-9*, Pub. by Intellect) Intl Spec Bk.

***Bligh, Donald A.** What's the Use of Lectures? LC 99-6979. (Higher & Adult Education Ser.). 384p. 2000. pap. 29.95 (*0-7879-5162-5*, Pfffr & Co) Jossey-Bass.

Bligh, E. G., ed. Seafood Science & Technology. (Illus.). 416p. 1992. 125.00 (*0-85238-173-5*) Blackwell Sci.

Bligh, J. & Voigt, K., eds. Thermoreception & Temperature Regulation. (Illus.). 300p. 1990. 97.95 (*0-387-51711-1*) Spr-Verlag.

***Bligh, Joanna.** Mosby's Medical Assisting Examination Review. (Illus.). 320p. (C). 1999. text. write for info. (*0-323-00349-4*) Mosby Inc.

Bligh, John. Galatians. (C). 1988. 60.00 (*0-85439-006-5*, Pub. by St Paul Pubns) St Mut.

— The Sermon on the Mount. (C). 1988. 39.00 (*0-85439-118-5*, Pub. by St Paul Pubns) St Mut.

— The Sign of the Cross. (C). 1988. 39.00 (*0-85439-109-6*, Pub. by St Paul Pubns) St Mut.

Bligh, William. An Account of the Mutiny on H. M. S. Bounty. large type ed. Bowman, Robert, ed. 213p. 1990. 19.95 (*1-85089-405-1*, Pub. by ISIS Lrg Prnt) Transaction Pubs.

— The Mutiny on Board H. M. S. Bounty. (Illustrated Classics Collection 5). 64p. 1994. pap. 4.95 (*0-7854-0781-2*, 40562) Am Guidance.

— The Mutiny on Board H. M. S. Bounty. 486p. 1984. lib. bdg. 23.95 (*0-89968-256-1*, Lghtyr Pr) Buccaneer Bks.

— The Mutiny on Board H. M. S. Bounty. (Now Age Illustrated V Ser.). (Illus.). 64p. (J). (gr. 4-12). 1979. pap. text 2.95 (*0-88301-392-4*); student ed. 1.25 (*0-88301-416-5*) Pendulum Pr.

— The Mutiny on Board H. M. S. Bounty Readalong. (Illustrated Classics Collection 5). 64p. 1994. pap. 14.95 incl. audio (*0-7854-0797-9*, 40564) Am Guidance.

— Mutiny on the Bounty. Vogel, Malvina, ed. (Great Illustrated Classics Ser.: Vol. 19). (Illus.). 240p. (J). (gr. 3-6). 1992. 9.95 (*0-86611-970-1*) Playmore Inc.

— Mutiny on the H. M. S. Bounty. 24.95 (*0-8488-1278-6*) Amereon Ltd.

Blight. African American History. 2002. pap., teacher ed. write for info. (*0-312-19729-2*) St Martin.

Blight. Geotechnics in the African - 10th African, Vol. 1. 1991. 149.00 (*90-5410-008-7*) Ashgate Pub Co.

Blight, David W. Frederick Douglass' Civil War: Keeping Faith in Jubilee. LC 88-29200. 312p. 1989. reprint ed. pap. text 14.95 (*0-8071-1724-2*) La State U Pr.

***Blight, David W.** Race & Reunion: The Civil War in American Memory. 576p. 2001. 29.95 (*0-674-00332-2*) HUP.

Blight, David W. & Simpson, Brooks D., eds. Union & Emancipation: Essays on Politics & Race in the Civil War Era. LC 96-34978. 242p. 1997. 35.00 (*0-87338-565-9*) Kent St U Pr.

Blight, David W., jt. auth. see Bingham, Caleb.

Blight, David W., ed. see Brewster, Charles H.

Blight, David W., ed. see Du Bois, W. E. B.

Blight, G. E., ed. Mechanics of Residual Soils: A Guide to the Formation, Classification & Geotechnical Properties of Residual Soils, with Advice for Geotechnical Design. LC 99-496405. (Illus.). 248p. (C). 1997. text 110.00 (*90-5410-696-4*, Pub. by A A Balkema) Ashgate Pub Co.

Blight, G. E., et al, eds. Geotechnics in the African Environment: Proceedings of the 10th Regional Conference for Africa on Soil Mechanics & Foundation Engineering & the 3rd International Conference on Tropical & Residual Soils, Maseru, 23-27 September 1991, 2 vols. (Illus.). 600p. (C). 1991. text 272.00 (*90-5410-007-9*, Pub. by A A Balkema) Ashgate Pub Co.

Blight, James G. The Shattered Crystal Ball: Fear & Learning in the Cuban Missile Crisis. 224p. (C). 1990. pap. text 14.95 (*0-8226-3015-X*, R 7609) Littlefield.

— The Shattered Crystal Ball: Fear & Learning in the Cuban Missile Crisis. 224p. (C). 1990. lib. bdg. 52.50 (*0-8476-7609-9*, R 7609) Rowman.

Blight, James G. & Kornbluh, Peter. Politics of Illusion: The Bay of Pigs Invasion Reexamined. LC 97-23213. (Studies in Cuban History). 284p. 1997. 49.95 (*1-55587-783-4*) L Rienner.

***Blight, James G. & Kornbluh, Peter, eds.** Politics of Illusion: The Bay of Pigs Invasion Reexamined. (Studies in Cuban History). 284p. 1998. pap. 22.50 (*1-55587-822-9*) L Rienner.

Blight, James G., jt. ed. see Weiss, Thomas G.

Blight, John. John Blight: Selected Poems. 259p. 1992. pap. 19.95 (*0-7022-2425-1*, Pub. by Univ Queensland Pr) Intl Spec Bk.

Blight, Reynold E. Freemasonry at a Glance: Answers to 555 Questions (1928) 72p. 1998. reprint ed. pap. 14.95 (*0-7661-0717-5*) Kessinger Pub.

Blight, Richard C. An Exegetical Summary of 1 & 2 Thessalonians. 331p. 1989. pap. 16.60 (*0-88312-926-4*) S I L Intl.

Blignault, Karin. Successful Schooling: Train Your Horse with Empathy. 1997. 69.00 (*0-85131-628-X*, Pub. by J A Allen) Trafalgar.

Blij, Harm de, see De Blij, Harm.

Blik, Tyler. Trademarks of the '60s & '70s. LC 97-9340. 1997. pap. 16.95 (*0-8118-1698-2*) Chronicle Bks.

Blik, Tyler, jt. auth. see Baker, Eric.

Blikle, A. Metasoft Primer. (Lecture Notes in Computer Science Ser.: Vol. 288). xiii, 140p. 1987. 30.00 (*0-387-18657-3*) Spr-Verlag.

***Bliley, Tom.** The Tobacco Settlement: Views of Tobacco Industry Executives: Congressional Hearings. (Illus.). 339p. (C). 1999. pap. text 50.00 (*0-7881-8305-2*) DIANE Pub.

Blilie, Charles. The Image As Information: A General Theory of Sensors & Sense Data. LC 97-30080. 207p. 1997. lib. bdg. 85.00 (*1-56072-458-7*) Nova Sci Pubs.

Blim, Michael L. Made in Italy: Small-Scale Industrialization & Its Consequences. LC 89-16338. 304p. 1990. 65.00 (*0-275-93101-3*, C3101, Greenwood Pr) Greenwood.

Blim, Michael L., jt. auth. see Rothstein, Frances A.

Blimes, Michael E. & Sproat, Ron. More Dialing, More Dollars: Twelve Steps to Successful Telemarketing. LC 85-30682. (Illus.). 93p. (Orig.). 1986. pap. 9.95 (*0-915400-47-2*, ACA Bks) Am for the Arts.

Blimkie, Cameron J. & Bar-Or, Oded, eds. New Horizons in Pediatric Exercise Science. LC 95-7588. 264p. 1995. text 40.00 (*0-87322-528-7*, BBLI0528) Human Kinetics.

***Blimling, Gregory.** Instructor's Manual To Accompany The Resident: Applications & Strategies for Working with College Stud. 5th ed. 84p. (C). 1999. pap. text. write for info. (*0-7872-6333-8*) Kendall-Hunt.

— The Resident Assistant: Working with College Students in Residence. 5th ed. LC 99-180744. 592p. 1998. per. 34.95 (*0-7872-5104-6*, 41510401) Kendall-Hunt.

Blimling, Gregory S. The Experienced Resident Assistant: Readings, Case Studies & Structured Group Exercises for Advanced Training. 2nd ed. 320p. (C). 1993. pap., per. 39.95 (*0-8403-7610-3*, 40761001) Kendall-Hunt.

— Good Practice in Student Affairs: Principles to Foster Student Learning. LC 99-6119. 1999. 32.95 (*0-7879-4457-2*) Jossey-Bass.

— The Resident Assistant: Case Studies & Exercises. 256p. (C). 1994. per. 31.95 (*0-8403-9191-9*) Kendall-Hunt.

***Blin, A. H., et al, eds.** Hadron Physics: Effective Theories of Low Energy QCD. LC 00-100412. (AIP Conference Proceedings Ser.: Vol. 508). (Illus.). xi, 410p. 2000. 125.00 (*1-56396-927-0*) Am Inst Physics.

Blin, Jean, et al. Flexible Exchange Rates & International Business. LC 81-85396. (British-North American Committee Ser.). 112p. 1981. pap. 8.00 (*0-89068-058-2*) Natl Planning.

Blin-Stoyle, R. J. Eureka! Physics of Particles, Matter & the Universe. LC 97-19999. (Illus.). 226p. 1997. pap. 25.00 (*0-7503-0416-2*) IOP Pub.

Blin-Stoyle, R. J. Eureka! Physics of Particles, Matter & the Universe. LC 97-19999. (Illus.). 226p. 1997. 95.00 (*0-7503-0415-4*) IOP Pub.

Blin-Stoyle, R. J. & Hamilton, W. D., eds. Interactions & Structures in Nuclei: Proceedings of a Conference to Celebrate the 65th Birthday of Sir Denys Wilkinson. (Illus.). 216p. 1988. 110.00 (*0-85274-396-3*) IOP Pub.

Blinc, R. & Zeks, B. Ferroelectric & Antiferroelectric Liquid Crystals & Their Electro-Optic Applications. 400p. (C). 1998. text 86.00 (*981-02-0325-X*) World Scientific Pub.

Blinc, R., et al. Ferroelectric Liquid Crystals. 500p. 1984. pap. text 477.00 (*0-677-16595-1*) Gordon & Breach.

— Proceedings of the Fourth European Winter Conference on Liquid Crystals of Low Dimensional Order & Their Applications: A Special Issue of the Journal Molecular Crystals & Liquid Crystals, 2 vols., Set. 650p. 1984. 1101.00 (*0-685-47157-8*) Gordon & Breach.

Blinc, R., ed. see Clark, N. A., et al.

Blincoe, Colin. Down at Dinsmore. (Illus.). 60p. (Orig.). 1991. pap. write for info. (*0-9624673-4-0*) Picture This Bks.

Blincoe, Deborah, jt. auth. see Forrest, John.

Blincoe, Nicholas. Acid Casuals. (Mask Noir Title Ser.). 230p. (Orig.). 1997. pap. 12.99 (*1-85242-509-1*, Mask Noir) Serpents Tail.

— Jello Salad. (Mask Noir Title Ser.). 1997. pap. text 12.99 (*1-85242-567-9*) Serpents Tail.

Blincoe, Robert. Ethnic Realities & the Church: Lessons from Kurdistan. LC 97-69533. 208p. 1998. 16.95 (*0-9652533-2-5*) Presby Ctr Mission.

Blind, Adolphe, jt. auth. see Clarke, Sidney W.

Blind, M. George Eliot. LC 72-3623. (English Literature Ser.: No. 33). 1972. reprint ed. lib. bdg. 75.00 (*0-8383-1586-0*) M S G Haskell Hse.

Blind, Mary A. Managing Human Resources: HSM 385 Course. 356p. (C). 1993. student ed., ring bd. write for info. (*0-933195-49-4*) CA College Health Sci.

Blind, Mathilde, tr. see Strauss, David F.

Blind Melon. Soup. 112p. 1996. per. 19.95 (*0-7935-5999-5*) H Leonard.

Blinder, Alan S. Central Banking in Theory & Practice. LC 97-24961. (Lionel Robbins Lectures). (Illus.). 106p. 1997. 20.00 (*0-262-02439-X*) MIT Pr.

— Central Banking in Theory & Practice. (Lionel Robbins Lectures). (Illus.). 104p. 1999. reprint ed. pap. text 12.00 (*0-262-52260-8*) MIT Pr.

— Hard Heads, Soft Hearts: Tough-Minded Economics for a Just Society. 1988. pap. 16.00 (*0-201-14519-7*) Addison-Wesley.

— Hard Heads Soft Hearts: Tough-Minded Economics for a Just Society. 256p. 1987. pap. 10.95 (*0-685-18508-7*) Addison-Wesley.

— Macroeconomics under Debate. 216p. 1990. text 54.50 (*0-472-10140-4*, 10140) U of Mich Pr.

— Maintaining Competitiveness with High Wages. 20p. 1992. pap. 9.95 (*1-55815-171-0*) ICS Pr.

Blinder, Alan S., ed. Paying for Productivity: A Look at the Evidence. 275p. 1990. pap. 18.95 (*0-8157-0999-4*) Brookings.

— Paying for Productivity: A Look at the Evidence. fac. ed. LC 89-25328. (Illus.). 320p. 1990. pap. 99.20 (*0-7837-7678-0*, 204743100007) Bks Demand.

Blinder, Alan S., et al. Asking about Prices: A New Approach to Understanding Price Stickiness. LC 97-26536. (Illus.). 336p. 1998. 34.95 (*0-87154-121-1*) Russell Sage.

— The Economics of Public Finance. LC 74-276. (Studies of Government Finance). 435p. 1974. pap. 14.95 (*0-8157-0997-8*) Brookings.

Blinder, Alan S., jt. auth. see Baumol, William J.

Blinder, Caroline. A Self-Made Surrealist: Ideology & Aesthetics in the Works of Henry Miller. LC 99-38103. (European Studies in the Humanities). 164p. 1999. 55.00 (*1-57113-133-7*) Camden Hse.

Blinder, Martin. Fluke. LC 98-27860. 216p. 1999. 22.00 (*1-57962-017-5*) Permanent Pr.

— Psychiatry in the Everyday Practice of Law. 3rd ed. LC 92-74140. 1992. 135.00 (*0-685-59904-3*) West Group.

Blinder, Martin & Lynch, Carmen. Choosing Lovers: Ten Steps to a Happier Relationship. 192p. 1991. pap. 3.95 (*0-380-71201-6*, Avon Bks) Morrow Avon.

Blinderman, Abraham, ed. Critics on Upton Sinclair. LC 74-11470. (Readings in Literary Criticism Ser.: No. 24). 1975. 19.95 (*0-87024-263-6*) U of Miami Pr.

Blinderman, Barry. Signs of Life: Rebecca Howland, Cara Perlman, Christy Rupp, Kiki Smith. (Illus.). 72p. (Orig.). 1992. pap. 25.00 (*0-945558-19-8*) ISU Univ Galls.

Blinderman, Barry, contrib. by. Joseph Nechvatal, Paintings, 1986-1987. (Illus.). 20p. 1988. 5.00 (*0-945558-00-7*) ISU Univ Galls.

— Mark Innerst: Landscape & Beyond. (Illus.). 48p. 1988. 20.00 (*0-945558-02-3*) ISU Univ Galls.

— Synthetic Nuvism. (Illus.). 16p. 1995. 5.00 (*0-945558-14-7*) ISU Univ Galls.

Blinderman, Barry, et al. Keith Haring: Future Primeval. (Illus.). 128p. 1992. pap. 24.95 (*1-55859-378-0*) Abbeville Pr.

Blinderman, Charles. Biolexicon: A Guide to the Language of Biology. (Illus.). 380p. 1990. pap. 32.95 (*0-398-06023-1*) C C Thomas.

— Biolexicon: A Guide to the Language of Biology. (Illus.). 380p. (C). 1990. text 48.95 (*0-398-05671-4*) C C Thomas.

Blindheim, Martin. Norwegian Romanesque Decorative Sculpture, 1090-1210. (Illus.). 1966. 35.00 (*0-85458-170-7*) Transatl Arts.

— Painted Wooden Sculptures in Norway, 1100-1250. 160p. 1998. text 43.00 (*82-00-37681-8*) Scandnvan Univ Pr.

Bliney, E., ed. Crisis & Reform in China. 249p. (C). 1997. lib. bdg. 85.00 (*1-56072-416-1*) Nova Sci Pubs.

Bling, M., jt. auth. see Samec, E.

Blinka, Daniel D. & Adams, James A. Pretrial Motions in Criminal Prosecutions. 2nd ed. LC 98-87879. 886p. 1998. 110.00 (*0-327-00497-5*, 6003511) LEXIS Pub.

Blinka, Daniel D. & Imwinkelried, Edward A. Criminal Evidentiary Foundations, 1998 Supplement. 35p. 1998. suppl. ed. write for info. (*0-327-00494-0*, 6297910) LEXIS Pub.

Blinka, Daniel D., jt. auth. see Adams, James A.

Blinka, Daniel D., jt. auth. see Grenig, Jay.

Blinka, Daniel D., jt. auth. see Imwinkelried, Edward A.

Blinka, Deborah C. Frederic March: Craftsman First, Star Second, 65. LC 95-19584. (Contribution in Drama & Theatre Studies). 320p. 1996. 65.00 (*0-313-29802-5*, Greenwood Pr) Greenwood.

Blinken, Anthony J. Ally Versus Ally: America, Europe, & the Siberian Pipeline Crisis. LC 86-25222. 200p. 1987. 57.95 (*0-275-92410-6*, C2410, Praeger Pubs); pap. text 14.95 (*0-685-18009-3*, B2616, Praeger Pubs) Greenwood.

Blinkenberg, A. & Hoybye, P. Dansk-Fransk Ordbog. deluxe ed. (DAN & FRE.). 2058p. 1975. 295.00 (*0-8288-5795-4*, M1278) Fr & Eur.

Blinkenberg, C. The Thunderweapon in Religion & Folklore. xii, 122p. (C). 1987. reprint ed. lib. bdg. 30.00 (*0-89241-205-4*) Caratzas.

— Timachides: Chronicum Lindium. 80p. 1980. pap. 10.00 (*0-89005-353-7*) Ares.

Blinkenberg, Lars. India-Pakistan: The History of Unsolved Conflicts, 2 vols. LC 98-178084. (Illus.). 770p. 1998. pap. 61.50 (*87-7838-285-8*, Pub. by Odense Univ) Intl Spec Bk.

— India-Pakistan: The History of Unsolved Conflicts LC 98-178084. 1998. write for info. (*87-7838-286-6*); write for info. (*87-7838-287-4*) Odense Univ.

Blinkert, B. Herder-Lexikon Soziologie. (GER.). 240p. 35.00 (*3-451-16468-X*, M7452); 35.00 (*0-8288-7620-7*, M7452) Fr & Eur.

Blinkhorn, Anthony S. Treatment Planning for Pedodontic Patients. (Illus.). 152p. 1992. text 62.00 (*1-85097-014-9*) Quint Pub Co.

Blinkhorn, Anthony S., jt. auth. see Kent, G.

Blinkhorn, Anthony S., jt. ed. see Schou, Lone.

Blinkhorn, Martin. Democracy & Civil War in Spain, 1931-1939 LC 99-166052. (Lancaster Pamphlets Ser.). xvi, 60 p. 1996. write for info. (*0-415-00699-6*) Routledge.

— Fascism & the Right in Europe, 1891-1945. (C). 2000. pap. 12.67 (*0-582-07021-X*) Addison-Wesley.

— Mussolini & Fascist Italy. (Lancaster Pamphlets Ser.). 64p. 1984. pap. text 6.95 (*0-415-04022-1*, NO. 4164) Routledge.

— Mussolini & Fascist Italy. 2nd ed. LC 93-45640. (Lancaster Pamphlets Ser.). 80p. (C). 1994. pap. 11.99 (*0-415-10231-6*, B2466) Routledge.

Blinkin, Meir. Stories by Meir Blinkin. Rosenfeld, Max, tr. from YID. LC 83-15564. (SUNY Series in Literature & Culture). 166p. 1984. text 5.50 (*0-87395-818-7*) State U NY Pr.

Blinko, Janine. Mathematical Beginnings. 1995. pap. text 20.95 (*1-871098-00-9*, Pub. by Claire Pubns) Parkwest Pubns.

Blinko, Janine & Graham, Noel. Mathematics with Cubes: Problem Solving Activities for Older Children. 64p. (J). (gr. 3-7). pap. 12.50 (*1-871098-14-9*, Pub. by Claire Pubns) Parkwest Pubns.

— Pattern Block Circus. 1997. pap. 12.50 (*1-871098-32-7*, Pub. by Claire Pubns) Parkwest Pubns.

— Zero to Ninety-Nine. 96p. (J). (gr. k-3). pap. 17.50 (*1-871098-02-5*, Pub. by Claire Pubns) Parkwest Pubns.

Blinko, Nick. The Primal Screamer. (Illus.). 128p. (Orig.). 1995. pap. 12.95 (*0-9525744-0-3*, Pub. by Spare Change) AK Pr Dist.

Blinkov, Samuil Mikha'ilovich & Smirnov, N. A. Brain Displacements & Deformations. Lindsley, Donald B., ed. Onischenko, George T., tr. from RUS. LC 70-107532. 230p. reprint ed. pap. 71.30 (*0-8357-7375-2*, 202070500018) Bks Demand.

Blinks, William, et al. Memories of Early Michigan City. Lewis, Patricia, ed. (Little Bit of History Ser.: Bk. 4). (Orig.). (J). (gr. 6 up). 1990. pap. 2.00 (*0-935549-14-5*) MI City Hist.

Blinn, Bruce. Portable Shell Programming: An Extensive Collection of Bourne Shell Examples. LC 95-39657. 288p. 1995. pap. 48.00 (*0-13-451494-7*) P-H.

***Blinn, Charles R. & Thompson, Michael A., eds.** Planning & Implementing Forest Operations to Achieve Sustainable Forests: Proceedings (1996) (Illus.). 282p. (C). 2000. reprint ed. pap. text 45.00 (*0-7881-8613-2*) DIANE Pub.

Blinn, Cynthia L. Maternal Ties: A Selection of Programs for Female Offenders. LC 97-12521. 191p. 1997. 29.95 (*1-56991-068-5*) Am Correctional.

Blinn, D. W., jt. auth. see Czarnecki, D. B.

Blinn, Hansjuergen. Informationshandbuch Deutsche Literaturwissenschaft. (GER.). 496p. 1994. pap. 22.50 (*3-596-12588-X*, Pub. by Fischer Tasch) Intl Bk Import.

Blinn, J. A., et al. AP Biology. 592p. 2000. pap. 29.95 (*0-87891-316-5*) Res & Educ.

Blinn, Jim. Jim Blinn's Corner: A Trip down the Graphics Pipeline. LC 96-23163. 216p. 1996. pap. text 29.95 (*1-55860-387-5*) Morgan Kaufmann.

— Jim Blinn's Corner: Dirty Pixels. 2nd ed. LC 97-44811. 215p. 1998. pap. 29.95 (*1-55860-455-3*) Morgan Kaufmann.

Blinn, Lynn. Making Decisions. LC 79-54910. (C). 1980. teacher ed. 8.00 (*0-8273-1711-5*) Delmar.

Blinn, William. Brian's Song. (Illus.). 128p. (YA). (gr. 6 up). 1983. mass mkt. 5.50 (*0-553-26618-7*) Bantam.

— Brian's Song: Sreenplay. (Bantam Starfire Bks.). 1972. 10.09 (*0-606-02436-0*, Pub. by Turtleback) Demco.

Blinn, William, et al. Locator II Reference Manual. 82p. 1992. 50.00 (*1-880933-00-4*) Mgmt Comp Srvs.

Blinn, William, ed. see Painter, Jeff.

Blinov, A. Y., tr. see Bisnovatyi-Kogan, G. S.

Blinov, Lev M. Electro-Optical & Magneto-Optical Properties of Liquid Crystals. LC 82-24800. (Illus.). 363p. reprint ed. pap. 112.60 (*0-8357-8633-1*, 203505700092) Bks Demand.

Blinov, Lev M. & Chigriniv, Vladimir G. Electrooptic Effects in Liquid Crystal Materials: Partially Ordered Systems. (Illus.). 420p. 1993. write for info. (*3-540-94030-8*) Spr-Verlag.

Blinov, Lev M. & Chigrinov, Vladimir G. Electrooptic Effects in Liquid Crystal Materials. Orig. Title: Electro-Optic & Magneto-Optical Properties of Liquid Crystals. (Illus.). 488p. 1996. pap. 59.95 (*0-387-94708-6*) Spr-Verlag.

— Electrooptic Effects in Liquid Crystal Materials. rev. ed. LC 93-17485. (Partially Ordered Systems Ser.). Orig. Title: Electro-Optic & Magneto-Optical Properties of Liquid Crystals. 1993. reprint ed. 129.00 (*0-387-94030-8*) Spr-Verlag.

Blinov, Sergei, ed. see Postnikov, Sergei P.

Blinov, V. N., jt. auth. see Blinova, T. K.

Blinova, T. K. & Blinov, V. N. The Birds of Southern Transuralia: Forest-Steppe & Steppe, Vol. 1. (RUS.). 296p. 1998. 74.95 (*5-02-031238-X*, Pub. by Pensoft Pubs) Intl Scholars.

Blinovsky, Volodia. Asymptotic Combinatorial Coding Theory. LC 97-28666. (The Kluwer International Series in Engineering & Computer Science: No. 415). 128p. 1997. text 98.00 (*0-7923-9988-9*) Kluwer Academic.

Blintiff, John L., et al. Conceptual Issues in Environmental Archaeology. 300p. 1990. pap. 29.50 (*0-85224-546-7*, Pub. by Edinburgh U Pr) Col U Pr.

***Blintliff, John & Sbonias, Kostas, eds.** Reconstructing Past Population Trends in Mediterranean Europe (3000 BC - AD 1800) (Archaeology of the Mediterranean Landscape, Populus Monograph: Vol. 1). (Illus.). 288p. 2000. 99.95 (*1-900188-62-7*, Pub. by Oxbow Bks) David Brown.

Blinv, L. M. Physics Reviews: Non-centrosymmetric Langmuir-Blodgett Films, Vol. 12. Gol'danskii, V. I. et al, eds. (Soviet Scientific Reviews Ser.: Vol. 12, Pt. 1). ii, 90p. 1989. pap. text 96.00 (*3-7186-4906-3*) Gordon & Breach.

Bliokh, Pavel. Dusty & Self-Gravitational Plasmas in Space. (Astrophysics & Space Science Library). 268p. (C). 1995. text 132.50 (*0-7923-3022-6*) Kluwer Academic.

Bliokh, Pavel, et al. Dusty & Self-Gravitational Plasmas in Space, Vol. 204. LC 95-34350. (Astrophysics & Space Science Library). 1995. lib. bdg. write for info. (*0-7923-3675-5*) Kluwer Academic.

Bliquez, Lawrence J. Classical Vases & Containers in the Collection of the Seattle Art Museum. LC 85-50711. (Illus.). 32p. (Orig.). 1985. pap. 4.95 (*0-932216-19-6*) Seattle Art.

— Corpus of Cypriote Antiquities: Cypriote Objects in Washington State. (Studies in Mediterranean Archaeology: Vol. XX:6). (Illus.). 31p. (Orig.). 1978. pap. 20.50 (*91-85058-26-2*, Pub. by P Astroms) Coronet Bks.

— Roman Surgical Instruments & Minor Objects in the University of Mississippi. (Studies in Mediterranean Archaeology & Literature: No. 58). (Illus.). 87p. (Orig.). 1988. pap. 37.50 (*91-86098-61-6*, Pub. by P Astroms) Coronet Bks.

Blischke, Wallace R. & Murthy, D. N., eds. Product Warranty Handbook. (Illus.). 952p. 1995. text 225.00 (*0-8247-8955-5*) Dekker.

— Warranty Cost Analysis. (Illus.). 744p. 1993. text 250.00 (*0-8247-8911-3*) Dekker.

***Blischke, Wallace R. & Murthy, D. N. Prabhakar.** Reliability: Modeling, Prediction & Optimization. 712p. 2000. text 89.95 (*0-471-18450-0*, Wiley-Interscience) Wiley.

Blish, Carolyn. Drawing Closer: The Paintings & Personal Reflections of Carolyn Blish. Maclay, Elise, ed. LC 97-10708. (Illus.). 152p. 1997. 29.95 (*0-86713-041-5*, 88089) Greenwich Wrkshop.

Blish, J. K. Blish Family Genealogy, 1637-1905. (Illus.). 366p. 1990. reprint ed. pap. 58.50 (*0-8328-1443-1*); reprint ed. lib. bdg. 68.50 (*0-8328-1442-3*) Higginson Bk Co.

Blish, James. And All the Stars a Stage. LC 73-331155. 206 p. (J). 1972. write for info. (*0-571-10103-8*) Faber & Faber.

Blish, James. Black Easter. 160p. 1993. reprint ed. lib. bdg. 28.95 (*0-89968-392-4*, Lghtyr Pr) Buccaneer Bks.

***Blish, James.** A Case of Conscience. 256p. 2000. pap. 12.00 (*0-345-43835-3*) Ballantine Pub Grp.

Blish, James. A Case of Conscience. 1993. reprint ed. lib. bdg. 18.95 (*0-89968-330-4*, Lghtyr Pr) Buccaneer Bks.

***Blish, James.** Cities in Flight. LC 99-59586. 590p. 2000. 35.00 (*1-58567-008-1*, Pub. by Overlook Pr) Penguin Putnam.

Blish, James. Dusk of Idols. 224p. 1996. 22.00 (*0-7278-4967-0*) Severn Hse.

— Star Trek: Spock Must Die! (Star Trek Ser.). 128p. 1985. mass mkt. 5.50 (*0-553-24634-8*) Bantam.

— Star Trek 11. 188p. Date not set. 20.95 (*0-8488-2214-5*) Amereon Ltd.

— Star Trek 5. 18.95 (*0-8488-0741-3*) Amereon Ltd.

— Star Trek 4. 18.95 (*0-8488-0740-5*) Amereon Ltd.

— Star Trek 1. 18.95 (*0-8488-0431-7*) Amereon Ltd.

— Star Trek 7. 159p. Date not set. 18.95 (*0-8488-2212-9*) Amereon Ltd.

— Star Trek 10. 164p. Date not set. 19.95 (*0-8488-2213-7*) Amereon Ltd.

— Star Trek 3. 18.95 (*0-8488-0739-1*) Amereon Ltd.

— Star Trek 2. 18.95 (*0-8488-0738-3*) Amereon Ltd.

— The Tale That Wags the God. 296p. 1987. 18.00 (*0-911682-29-5*) Advent.

— With All of Love: Selected Poems. Daniels, Keith A., ed. LC 95-12340. 208p. 1995. 29.95 (*0-9631203-1-X*) Anamnesis Pr.

Blish, James & Roddenberry, Gene. The Star Trek Reader II LC 77-150066. 457 p. (J). 1977. 8.95 (*0-525-20960-3*, Dutton Child) Peng Put Young Read.

— The Star Trek Reader III LC 77-152626. 447 p. (J). 1977. 8.95 (*0-525-20961-1*, Dutton Child) Peng Put Young Read.

— The Star Trek Reader IV LC 78-102307. 472 p. (J). 1978. 9.95 (*0-525-20962-X*, Dutton Child) Peng Put Young Read.

Blishak, Sylvia. Improving Your Company Image: Creating a Positive First Impression. Keppler, Kay, ed. LC 91-76245. (Fifty-Minute Ser.). 90p. 1992. pap. 10.95 (*1-56052-136-8*) Crisp Pubns.

Blishen, Bernard R. Doctors in Canada: The Changing World of Medical Practice. 224p. 1991. text 50.00 (*0-8020-5926-0*); pap. text 19.95 (*0-8020-6866-9*) U of Toronto Pr.

Blishen, Edward. Science Fiction Stories. (Story Library). (J). 1993. 12.05 (*0-606-05581-9*, Pub. by Turtleback) Demco.

Blishen, Edward, ed. Children's Classics to Read Aloud. LC 92-53097. (Illus.). 256p. (J). (gr. 2 up). 1992. 18.95 (*1-85697-825-7*, Kingfisher) LKC.

Blishen, Edward, ed. Children's Classics to Read Aloud. LC 94-26070. (Illus.). 256p. 1995. pap. 8.95 (*1-85697-538-X*, Kingfisher) LKC.

Blishen, Edward & Blishen, Nancy, eds. A Treasury of Stories for Five Year Olds. LC 92-53107. (Treasury of Stories Ser.). (Illus.). 160p. (Orig.). (J). (ps-4). 1992. pap. 6.95 (*1-85697-827-3*) LKC.

— A Treasury of Stories for Seven Year Olds. LC 92-53109. (Treasury of Stories Ser.). (Illus.). 160p. (J). (ps-4). 1992. pap. 6.95 (*1-85697-829-X*) LKC.

— A Treasury of Stories for Six Year Olds. LC 92-53108. (Treasury of Stories Ser.). (Illus.). 160p. (J). (ps-4). 1992. pap. 6.95 (*1-85697-828-1*) LKC.

Blishen, Edward, jt. auth. see Blishen, Nancy.

Blishen, Nancy & Blishen, Edward. A Treasury of Stories for Four Year Olds. LC 94-2337. (Illus.). 160p. (J). (ps-4). 1994. pap. 6.95 (*1-85697-984-9*) LKC.

Blishen, Nancy, jt. ed. see Blishen, Edward.

Bliss. Elementry & Middle School Teachers In Midst of Reform. LC 99-46139. (Illus.). 180p. 1999. pap. text 24.00 (*0-13-716474-2*) P-H.

Bliss. Expressways Achv Test, Vol. 3A. 36p. 1992. pap. text 16.60 (*0-13-291766-1*) P-H.

Bliss. Quick Baby Knits. 80p. 1999. pap. 18.95 (*0-312-20251-2*) St Martin.

***Bliss & Demas, Corinne.** The Disappearing Island. LC 98-37733. (Illus.). 32p. (J). (ps-3). 2000. 16.00 (*0-689-80539-X*) S&S Bks Yung.

Bliss & Molinsky. Voices Freedom. 2nd ed. 1997. pap., teacher ed. 19.53 (*0-13-187824-7*) P-H.

Bliss & Molinsky, Steven J. Classmates: Level 3. 128p. (C). 2001. pap. text 15.93 (*0-13-350026-8*) P-H.

— Classmates Science. (C). 2001. pap. text 19.93 (*0-13-350042-X*) P-H.

Bliss, jt. auth. see Molinsky.

Bliss, jt. auth. see Molinsky, Steven J.

Bliss, Alan J. A Dictionary of Foreign Words & Phrases in Current English. 400p. 1983. pap. 14.95 (*0-415-05905-4*, 9521X) Routledge.

— A Dictionary of Foreign Words & Phrases in Current English. 400p. 1983. pap. 14.95 (*0-7100-9521-X* Routledge Thoemms) Routledge.

Bliss, Alan J. & Dunning, T. P., eds. The Wanderer. (Old English Ser.). 1969. pap. text 8.95 (*0-89197-572-1*) Irvington.

Bliss, Angelie. I Discovered the Ancient Secrets of the Fountain of Youth! The Golden Key to Unlock the Hidden Door of the Profound Treasure Within. LC 96-84089. (Illus.). 128p. (Orig.). 1996. pap. 12.95 (*0-9651438-3-X*, Forever Yng Club) Air & Water King.

— Learn & Understand the Magic of Sex Unity: We Are One. (Illus.). 170p. 2000. pap. 21.95 (*0-9651438-1-3*) Air & Water King.

— Tai Chi for Longevity with Polynesian & Alsharqi Techniques. LC 97-72122. (Illus.). 140p. 1998. per. 15.95 (*0-9651438-5-6*, Forever Yng Club) Air & Water King.

Bliss, Angelie, ed. & tr. see Abad, Amading S.

Bliss, Anne. North American Dye Plants. rev. ed. (Illus.). 288p. 1994. reprint ed. pap. 8.95 (*0-934026-89-0*) Interweave.

Bliss, Anne M. & Rigg, J. A., eds. Zambia. LC 85-149132. (World Bibliographical Ser.: No. 51). 254p. 1985. lib. bdg. 60.00 (*0-903450-88-7*) ABC-CLIO.

Bliss, Arthur. Bliss on Music: Selected Writings of Arthur Bliss, 1920-1975. Roscow, Gregory, ed. (Illus.). 304p. 1991. 55.00 (*0-19-816222-7*, 12065) OUP.

Bliss, B. P. & Johnson, A. G. Aims & Motives in Clinical Medicine: A Practical Approach to Medical Ethics. 150p. 1975. pap. 25.00 (*0-8464-0123-1*) Beekman Pubs.

Bliss, Beatrice L. Reluctant Pioneer: Mary Vowell Adams. (Illus.). 256p. 1992. reprint ed. pap. 13.95 (*0-9622738-4-8*) M Bliss.

***Bliss, Bill & Molinsky, Steven.** Word by Word Primary Phonics Picture Dictionary. 1999. pap. text 17.00 (*0-13-022171-6*) P-H.

Bliss, Bill & Molinsky, Steven J. Classmates, Level 2. 144p. 1996. pap. text 9.27 (*0-13-350018-7*) P-H.

— Classmates, Level 4. 144p. 2001. pap. text 15.93 (*0-13-350034-9*) P-H.

— Classmates Health. (C). 2001. pap. text 19.93 (*0-13-350075-6*) P-H.

— Classmates Math. 2001. pap. text 19.93 (*0-13-350067-5*) P-H.

— Classmates Social Studies. (C). 2001. pap. 19.93 (*0-13-350059-4*) P-H.

— Communicator I. LC 94-20249. 192p. 1994. pap. text 18.20 (*0-13-301649-8*) P-H.

— Expressways Foundations. (C). 1988. pap. text 9.60 (*0-13-297763-X*) P-H.

— Navigator 1. LC 95-514. 176p. 1995. pap. text 9.73 (*0-13-359563-3*) P-H.

— Side by Side, Bk. 1. 2nd ed. (C). 1989. pap. text, teacher ed. 25.40 (*0-13-811167-7*) P-H.

— Side by Side, Bk. 2. 2nd ed. (Illus.). 140p. (C). 1988. pap. text 15.53 (*0-13-811241-X*) P-H.

— Side by Side, Bk. 3. 2nd ed. (C). 1989. pap. text, teacher ed. 25.40 (*0-13-811779-9*) P-H.

— Side by Side, Bk. 4. 2nd ed. 1989. pap. text, teacher ed. 25.40 (*0-13-811829-9*) P-H.

— Voices of Freedom: English & Civics for the U. S. Citizenship Exam. 2nd ed. LC 93-7091. 192p. (C). 1993. pap. text 14.93 (*0-13-035684-0*) P-H.

Bliss, Bill, jt. auth. see Molinsky, Steven.

Bliss, Bill, jt. auth. see Molinsky, Steven H.

Bliss, Bill, jt. auth. see Molinsky, Steven J.

Bliss, C. J. & Stern, N. H. Palanpur: The Economy of an Indian Village. (Illus.). 352p. 1982. text 39.95 (*0-19-828419-5*) OUP.

Bliss, Carey S. Autos Across America: A Bibliography of Transcontinental Automobile Travel, 1903-1940. 83p. 1982. 25.00 (*0-8363-0169-2*, PA8-32-7506) Jenkins.

Bliss, Charles A. The Structure of Manufacturing Production: A Cross-Section View. (General Ser.: No. 36). 252p. 1939. reprint ed. 65.60 (*0-87014-035-3*) Natl Bur Econ Res.

Bliss, Christopher. Economic Theory & Policy for Trading Blocks. LC 93-50583. 1994. text 79.95 (*0-7190-4018-3*) Manchester Univ Pr.

Bliss, Christopher & De Macedo, Jorge B., eds. Unity with Diversity in the European Economy: The Community's Southern Frontier. (Illus.). 391p. (C). 1990. text 69.95 (*0-521-39520-8*) Cambridge U Pr.

Bliss, Corinne D. Daffodils or the Death of Love: Short Fiction. LC 82-11048. (Breakthrough Bks.: No.39). 112p. (Orig.). 1983. pap. 12.95 (*0-8262-0385-X*) U of Mo Pr.

— Electra & the Charlotte Russe. LC 96-80392. (Illus.). 32p. (J). (gr. 2). 1997. 14.95 (*1-56397-436-3*) Boyds Mills Pr.

— The Littlest Matryoshka. LC 98-36156. (Illus.). 32p. (J). (ps-3). 1999. lib. bdg. 16.49 (*0-7868-2125-6*, Pub. by Hyperion) Little.

— The Littlest Matryoshka. LC 98-36156. (Illus.). 32p. (J). (ps-2). 1999. 15.99 (*0-7868-0153-0*, Pub. by Hypm Child) Time Warner.

— Matthew's Meadow. LC 91-10840. (Illus.). 40p. 1997. pap. 7.00 (*0-15-201500-0*) Harcourt.

— The Shortest Kid in the World. LC 93-45421. (Step into Reading Ser.: A Step 2 Book). (Illus.). 48p. (J). (ps-3). 1995. pap. 3.99 (*0-679-85809-1*, Pub. by Random Bks Yng Read) Random.

— The Shortest Kid in the World. (Step into Reading Ser.: A Step 2 Book). (J). (gr. 1-3). 1994. 9.19 (*0-606-08461-5*, Pub. by Turtleback) Demco.

— Snow Day. LC 97-45810. (Step into Reading Ser.: A Step 2 Book). (Illus.). 47p. (J). (gr. k-3). 1998. pap. 3.99 (*0-679-88222-7*) Random.

— Snow Day. LC 97-45810. (Step into Reading Ser.: A Step 2 Book). (Illus.). 47p. (J). (gr. k-3). 1998. lib. bdg. 11.99 (*0-679-98222-1*) Random.

Bliss, Corinne Demas. Hurricane! LC 98-46891. (Illus.). 32p. (J). (gr. k-3). 2000. 15.95 (*0-7614-5052-1*, Cav Child Bks) Marshall Cavendish.

— Matthew's Meadow. 1997. 12.20 (*0-606-11604-4*, Pub. by Turtleback) Demco.

Bliss, Corrine D. Matthew's Meadow. LC 91-10840. (Illus.). 40p. (J). (gr. 1-5). 1992. 15.00 (*0-15-200759-8*, Harcourt Child Bks) Harcourt.

Bliss, Daniel. Jeshua: The Gospel According to Benjamin. LC 94-78469. 288p. 1995. 20.00 (*0-9628001-3-9*) Monmouth Pr.

— Letters from a New Campus. (Illus.). 256p. (Orig.). (C). 1997. 18.95 (*0-8156-6087-1*) Syracuse U Pr.

Bliss, Dave. Northwest Boat Dives: 60 Ultimate Dives in Puget Sound & Hood Canal. LC 96-50999. 184p. (Orig.). 1997. pap. 16.95 (*1-57061-090-8*) Sasquatch Bks.

Bliss, Debbie. Baby Knits. LC 88-12023. (Illus.). 80p. 1988. pap. 18.95 (*0-312-02061-9*) St Martin.

***Bliss, Debbie.** Baby Style. 2000. pap. write for info. (*0-312-26714-2*) St Martin.

Bliss, Debbie. Bright Knits for Kids: Over 25 Innovative Designs for Infants to Six-Year-Olds. (Illus.). 80p. 1996. 19.95 (*1-57076-025-X*, Trafalgar Sq Pub) Trafalgar.

— Bright Knits for Kids: Over 25 Innovative Designs for Infants to Six-Year-Olds. (Illus.). 80p. 1998. pap. 13.95 (*1-57076-113-2*, Trafalgar Sq Pub) Trafalgar.

***Bliss, Debbie.** Celtic Knits: Over 25 Designs for Babies, Children & Adults. (Illus.). 80p. 2000. 22.95 (*1-57076-140-X*) Trafalgar.

— Classic Knits for Kids. 2000. 25.50 (*0-8446-7112-6*) Peter Smith.

Bliss, Debbie. Classic Knits for Kids: 30 Traditional Aran & Guernsey Designs for 0-6 Years. (Illus.). 80p. 1995. pap. 13.95 (*1-57076-026-8*, Trafalgar Sq Pub) Trafalgar.

— Debbie Bliss Nursery Knits. LC 96-17878. 80p. 1996. pap. 17.95 (*0-312-14584-5*) St Martin.

— Family Knits: Over 25 Versatile Designs for Babies Children & Adults. LC 98-84288. (Illus.). 80p. 1998. 22.95 (*1-57076-123-X*, Trafalgar Sq Pub) Trafalgar.

— Great Knits for Kids: Over 25 Classic Designs for Infants to Ten-Year-Olds. LC 96-60984. (Illus.). 80p. 1997. 22.95 (*1-57076-076-4*, Trafalgar Sq Pub) Trafalgar.

Bliss, Debbie. Great Knits for Kids: Twenty-Five Classic Knits for Infants to Ten Year-Olds. (Illus.). 1997. pap. (*0-316-09979-1*) Little.

Bliss, Debbie. Great Knits for Kids: 27 Classic Designs for Infants to Ten-Year-Olds. (Illus.). 1999. pap. 14.95 (*1-57076-153-1*, Trafalgar Sq Pub) Trafalgar.

— How to Knit: The Definitive Knitting Course Complete with Step-by-Step Techniques, Stitch Library & Projects for Your Home & Family. LC 98-87458. (Illus.). 1999. 29.95 (*1-57076-145-0*) Trafalgar.

— Kids' Country Knits. LC 93-4033. 1993. pap. 18.95 (*0-312-09837-5*) St Martin.

— Kids' Knits for Heads, Hands, & Toes: More Than 40 Delightful Patterns for Kids' Hats, Scarves, Mittens, Gloves, Berets, Slippers, Socks & More. (Illus.). 104p. (Orig.). 1992. pap. 19.95 (*0-312-08038-7*) St Martin.

***Bliss, Debbie.** Nautical Knits. 1998. (*0-316-09386-6*) Little.

Bliss, Debbie. Nautical Knits for Kids: 25 Seashore Designs for Children up to Six Years Old. (Illus.). 80p. 1998. 22.95 (*1-57076-107-8*, Trafalgar Sq Pub) Trafalgar.

— New Baby Knits: 30 Original Designs for 0-3 Year Olds. 2nd ed. (Illus.). 104p. (Orig.). 1991. pap. 19.95 (*0-312-07397-6*) St Martin.

— Teddy Bears. LC 97-16671. 1997. pap. 18.95 (*0-312-17042-4*) St Martin.

Bliss, Doris. Dobie 'n' Me in Noot Owl Noller. 156p. 1998. pap. write for info. (*1-57502-930-8*, PO2563) Morris Pubng.

Bliss, Dorothy E. & Abele, Lawrence, eds. The Biology of Crustacea Vols. 1 & 2: Systematic Fossil & Biogeography Record, 1. 1982. text 142.00 (*0-12-106401-8*) Acad Pr.

Bliss, Dorothy E. & Atwood, Harold L., eds. The Biology of Crustacea Vol. 3: Structure & Function. 1982. text 142.00 (*0-12-106403-4*) Acad Pr.

Bliss, Dorothy E. & Mantel, Linda H., eds. The Biology of the Crustacea: Itegument, Pigments, & Hormonal Process, Vol. 9. 1985. text 142.00 (*0-12-106409-3*) Acad Pr.

***Bliss, Edward, Jr.** Beyond the Stone Arches: An American Medical Missionary in China, 1892-1932. 256p. 2000. 24.95 (*0-471-39759-8*) Wiley.

Bliss, Edward, Jr. Now the News: The Story of Broadcast Journalism. 575p. (C). 1992. pap. 25.50 (*0-231-04403-8*) Col U Pr.

Bliss, Edward, Jr. & Hoyt, James L. Writing News for Broadcast. 3rd ed. LC 93-29715. 161p. 1994. pap. 16.50 (*0-231-07973-7*) Col U Pr.

Bliss, Edward, Jr. & Patterson, John M. Writing News for Broadcast. 2nd ed. LC 93-29715. 216p. 1978. text 37.00 (*0-231-04372-4*) Col U Pr.

Bliss, Edward, Jr., jt. auth. see Murrow, Edward R.

Bliss, Elyse D. Apples of the Mummy's Eye: The Dickerson Sisters. expanded rev. ed. (Illus.). 276p. Date not set. pap. write for info. (*0-9638260-3-4*) E Bliss.

— Apples of the Mummy's Eye: The Dickerson Sisters. rev. exp. ed. 276p. pap. write for info. (*0-9638260-2-6*) E Bliss.

Bliss, Eugene F. Diary of David Zeisberger, 2 vols., Set. 1993. reprint ed. lib. bdg. 150.00 (*0-7812-5340-3*) Rprt Serv.

Bliss, Eugene F., ed. Diary of David Zeisberger: A Missionary among the Indians of Ohio, 2 vols., Set. LC 73-108557. 1972. reprint ed. 89.00 (0-403-00253-2) Scholarly.

Bliss, Eugene L. Multiple Personality, Allied Disorders & Hypnosis. 282p. 1986. text 45.00 (0-19-503658-1) OUP.

Bliss, F. A., ed. Enhancement of Biological Nitrogen Fixation of Common Bean in Latin America: Results from an FAD-IAEA Co-Ordinated Research Programme, 1985-1991. LC 93-26850. (Developments in Plant & Social Sciences Ser.). 160p. (C). 1993. text 112.00 (0-7923-2451-X) Kluwer Academic.

Bliss, Frederick. Catholic & Ecumenical: Why the Catholic Church Is Ecumenical & What She Is Doing about It. LC 99-12580. 224p. 1999. pap. 18.95 (1-58051-056-6) Sheed & Ward WI.

Bliss, Frederick J. The Development of Palestine Exploration: Being the Ely Lectures for 1903. Davis, Moshe, ed. LC 77-70676. (America & the Holy Land Ser.). 1977. reprint ed. lib. bdg. 33.95 (0-405-10228-3) Ayer.

— Religions of Modern Syria & Palestine. LC 76-39454. reprint ed. 39.50 (0-404-00897-6) AMS Pr.

Bliss, Frederick M. Understanding Reception. (Studies in Theology). 180p. (Orig.). 1993. pap. 20.00 (0-87462-625-0) Marquette.

Bliss, Geoffrey. My Path to Heaven: A Young Person's Guide to the Faith. LC 97-13452. Orig. Title: A Retreat with St. Ignatius: In Pictures for Children. (Illus.). 96p. (Orig.). (J). (gr. 4-6). 1997. reprint ed. pap. 12.95 (0-918477-48-4) Sophia Inst Pr.

Bliss, Gilbert A. Lectures on the Calculus of Variations. LC 46-5369. (Phoenix Bks.). 304p. reprint ed. pap. 94.30 (0-608-16521-2, 202676400052) Bks Demand.

— Logarithmic Potential, 3 vols. in 1. 2nd ed. Incl. Fundamental Existence Theorems. reprint ed. 25.00 (0-8284-0305-8) Chelsea Pub.

Bliss, Gill. Practical Solutions for Potters: Your Top 465 Questions with Thousands of Practical Solutions. LC 98-48456. (Illus.). 192p. 1998. 29.95 (0-8069-6307-7) Sterling.

Bliss, Harry. Bliss: Picture Book. 32p. (gr. 2-5). 5.95 (0-06-443593-8) HarpC.

Bliss, Isabel. Edward Young. LC 68-28488. (Twayne's English Authors Ser.). (C). 1969. text 20.95 (0-8057-1588-6) Irvington.

Bliss, J., ed. see Andrewes, Lancelot.

Bliss, James, et al. Rethinking Effective Schools. 224p. (C). 1990. pap. text 69.95 (0-13-778804-5) P-H.

Bliss, Joan, et al. Learning Sites: Social & Technological Resources for Learning. LC 99-24854. (Advances in Learning & Instruction Ser.). 352p. 1999. 82.00 (0-08-043350-2, Pergamon Pr) Elsevier.

Bliss, John H. Genealogy of the Bliss Family in America, from about the Year 1550 to 1880. (Illus.). 811p. 1988. reprint ed. pap. 121.50 (0-8328-0269-7); reprint ed. lib. bdg. 129.50 (0-8328-0268-9) Higginson Bk Co.

Bliss, Jonathan. Ace Defensemen. LC 93-38210. (Hockey Heroes Ser.). 48p. (J). (gr. 3-8). 1994. lib. bdg. 22.60 (1-55916-011-X) Rourke Bk Co.

— Aging. (Troubled Society Ser.: Set II). 64p. (J). 1991. lib. bdg. 17.95 (0-86593-114-3) Rourke Corp.

— Batting Champs. (Baseball Heroes Ser.). 48p. (J). (gr. 3-8). 1991. lib. bdg. 15.95 (0-86593-129-1) Rourke Corp.

— Centers. LC 93-42533. (Hockey Heroes Ser.). 48p. (J). (gr. 3-8). 1994. lib. bdg. 22.60 (1-55916-014-4) Rourke Bk Co.

— Child Abuse. (The Family Ser.). (Illus.). 64p. (J). (gr. 7 up). 1990. lib. bdg. 17.95 (0-86593-081-3) Rourke Corp.

— China. (World Partners Ser.). (Illus.). 64p. (YA). (gr. 7 up). 1990. lib. bdg. 18.95 (0-86593-090-2) Rourke Corp.

— Dynasties. LC 92-412. (Football Heroes Ser.). 48p. (J). (gr. 3-8). 1992. lib. bdg. 15.95 (0-86593-156-9) Rourke Corp.

— Great Goalies. LC 93-33591. (Hockey Heroes Ser.). 48p. (J). (gr. 3-8). 1994. lib. bdg. 22.60 (1-55916-010-1) Rourke Bk Co.

— Home Run Leaders. (Baseball Heroes Ser.). (J). 1991. lib. bdg. 16.67 (0-685-66094-X) Rourke Corp.

— Home Run Leaders. (Baseball Heroes Ser.). 48p. (J). (gr. 3-8). 1991. lib. bdg. 15.95 (0-86593-128-3) Rourke Corp.

— Legends. LC 93-42816. (Hockey Heroes Ser.). 48p. (J). (gr. 3-8). 1994. lib. bdg. 22.60 (1-55916-015-2) Rourke Bk Co.

— Merchants & Miners in Utah. 1984. 20.00 (0-914740-29-6) Western Epics.

— Wingmen Warriors. LC 93-39507. (Hockey Heroes Ser.). 48p. (J). (gr. 3-8). 1994. lib. bdg. 22.60 (1-55916-013-6) Rourke Bk Co.

Bliss, Joseph R. English Silver: Jerome & Rita Gans Collection of English Silver. 1992. pap. 34.95 (0-917046-53-6) Va Mus Arts.

Bliss, Joy V., jt. auth. see Dybwad, G. L.

Bliss, Laura C. Study Guide to Accompany Visual Merchandising & Display: The Business of Presentation. 3rd ed. 210p. 1995. pap. 15.00 (1-56367-045-3) Fairchild.

Bliss, Lawrence C., jt. auth. see Balbach, Margaret.

Bliss, Lee, ed. see Denez, Deeva.

Bliss, Lee, ed. see Shakespeare, William.

Bliss, Lynn S. Pragmatic Language Intervention: Interactive Activities. LC 93-25192. 1993. 51.00 (0-930599-85-3) Thinking Pubns.

Bliss, Marilyn, ed. The Compact Music Dictionary. 128p. (Orig.). 1996. pap. 5.95 (0-8256-1430-9, AM 92225, Amsco Music) Music Sales.

Bliss, Mary L., jt. ed. see Clapp, Jeanie J.

Bliss, Michael. Banting: A Biography. rev. ed. 336p. 1992. reprint ed. pap. text 19.95 (0-8020-7386-7) U of Toronto Pr.

— Brian de Palma. LC 83-3306. (Filmmakers Ser.: No. 6). 176p. 1983. 21.00 (0-8108-1621-0) Scarecrow.

— A Canadian Millionaire: The Life & Business Times of Sir Joseph Flavelle, Bart., 1858-1939. (Reprints in Canadian History Ser.). 582p. 1992. reprint ed. pap. text 24.95 (0-8020-7351-4) U of Toronto Pr.

— The Discovery of Insulin. 304p. 1996. pap. 19.99 (0-7710-1560-7) McCland & Stewart.

— The Discovery of Insulin. LC 82-50911. (Illus.). 304p. (C). 1984. pap. text 18.00 (0-226-05898-0) U Ch Pr.

***Bliss, Michael.** Dreams Within a Dream: The Films of Peter Weir. LC 99-27241. (Illus.). 240p. 2000. 39.95 (0-8093-2284-6) S Ill U Pr.

Bliss, Michael. Justified Lives: Morality & Narrative in the Films of Sam Peckinpah. LC 92-37684. (Illus.). 464p. 1993. 46.95 (0-8093-1823-7) S Ill U Pr.

— William Osler: A Life in Medicine. LC 99-32066. (Illus.). 632p. 1999. 35.00 (0-19-512346-8) OUP.

— The Word Made Flesh: Catholicism & Conflict in the Films of Martin Scorsese. LC 95-1156. (Filmmakers Ser.: no. 46). 131p. 1995. 31.00 (0-8108-3019-1) Scarecrow.

— The Word Made Flesh: Catholicism & Conflict in the Films of Martin Scorsese. Slide, Anthony, ed. (Scarecrow Filmmakers Ser.: No. 45). (Illus.). 160p. 1998. pap. 24.50 (0-8108-3589-4) Scarecrow.

Bliss, Michael, intro. Doing It Right: The Best Criticism on Sam Peckinpah's The Wild Bunch. LC 93-14502. (Illus.). 240p. (C). 1994. pap. 18.95 (0-8093-1863-6) S Ill U Pr.

Bliss, Michael & Banks, Christiana. What Goes Around Comes Around: The Films of Jonathan Demme. LC 94-41204. (Illus.). 184p. (C). 1996. 24.95 (0-8093-1983-7); pap. 14.95 (0-8093-1984-5) S Ill U Pr.

Bliss, Pamela & Lowe, Virginia. Contemporary's Foundations Writing. Fiene, Pat, ed. LC 93-16325. (Contemporary's Foundations Ser.). 197p. 1993. pap. 11.26 (0-8092-3829-2) NTC Contemp Pub Co.

Bliss, Patricia L. Christian Petersen Remembered. LC 86-21065. (Illus.). 233p. reprint ed. pap. 72.30 (0-608-00138-4, 206091900006) Bks Demand.

Bliss, Peter. Word by Word Songbook. (C). 1995. pap. text 25.00 (0-13-064767-5) P-H.

Bliss, Phil, et al. Velveteen Rabbit. LC 97-147157. (Illus.). 1997. write for info. (0-7853-2110-1) Pubns Intl Ltd.

Bliss, R. Voyage to the Stars. 1994. pap. 9.95 (0-932662-18-8) St Andrews NC.

Bliss, Richard B. Origins: Creation or Evolution. LC 92-190747. (Illus.). 80p. (YA). (gr. 6 up). 1988. pap. 9.95 (0-89051-132-2) Master Bks.

Bliss, Robert. ISO 9000 Video Seminar Workbook. 65p. 1993. pap. 24.95 (1-883495-03-2) Int Qual Systs.

Bliss, Robert, jt. auth. see Durand, Ian.

Bliss, Robert R., Jr., jt. auth. see Ronn, Ehud I.

***Bliss, Robert W.** A. N. G. E. L. S., Inc. 1998. 8.50 (0-07-229823-5) McGraw.

— Indigenous Art of the Americas, Collection of Robert Woods Bliss. (LC History-America-E). 159p. 1999. reprint ed. lib. bdg. 69.00 (0-7812-4279-7) Rprt Serv.

Bliss, Rodney & Wynne, Rebecca. Microsoft Exchange 5.0 Connectivity Guide. LC 96-36636. 400p. 29.95 (1-57231-220-3) Microsoft.

Bliss, Ronald, jt. auth. see Mears, Raymond.

Bliss, Ronald G. Eagle Trap. LC 82-71045. (Illus.). 108p. (J). (gr. 3-5). 1990. pap. 3.50 (0-943864-05-4) Davenport.

Bliss, Sands & Co. Staff. The Magic Moving Picture Book. Orig. Title: The Motograph Moving Picture Book. 32p. (J). (gr. 4 up). 1975. reprint ed. pap. 3.95 (0-486-23224-7) Dover.

Bliss, Steve. Buckeye Football Fitness: Fourth down & One Rep to Go. LC 83-81242. (Illus.). 368p. 1986. reprint ed. pap. 114.10 (0-608-06462-9, 206730000009) Bks Demand.

***Bliss, Steven & Masterson-Glen, Josie, eds.** Managing the Small Construction Business: A Hands-on-Guide. 2nd rev. ed. LC 99-75375. 336p. 1999. pap. 34.95 (1-928580-00-9, Jrnl Lght) Builderburg Grp.

Bliss, Steven & Wagner, John D., eds. Advanced Framing: Techniques, Troubleshooting & Structural Design. 3rd ed. (Illus.). 281p. 1998. pap. text 29.95 (0-9632268-6-X) Builderburg Grp.

Bliss, Steven, ed. see Faller, Timothy.

Bliss, Steven, ed. see JLC Staff.

Bliss, Steven, ed. see Journal of Light Construction Staff.

Bliss, Steven, ed. see Randall, Robert.

Bliss, Steven, ed. see Ransone, Gary.

Bliss, Steven, ed. & intro. see Journal of Light Construction Staff.

Bliss, Sylvester. Memoirs of William Miller. LC 72-134374. reprint ed. 62.50 (0-404-08422-2) AMS Pr.

Bliss, Sylvia H. Uncut Leaves Vol. I: Quests (1920) & Sea Level (1933) LC 89-14854. 212p. 1989. 15.00 (0-912362-07-3) Adamant Pr.

— Uncut Leaves Vol. II: Prose Writings. LC 89-14854. 367p. 1990. lib. bdg. 40.00 (0-912362-08-1) Adamant Pr.

Bliss, Terry. Stock Cleaning Technology: A Literature Review. 120p. 1997. pap. 120.00 (1-85802-144-8, Pub. by Pira Internatl) Bks Intl VA.

Bliss, Traci & Mazur, Joan. Secondary & Middle School Teachers in the Midst of Reform: Common Thread Cases. LC 97-35122. 170p. (C). 1997. pap. text 29.00 (0-13-716432-7) P-H.

Bliss, William & Wheeler, Sessions S. Tahoe Heritage: The Bliss Family of Glenbrook, Nevada. (Illus.). 176p. (Orig.). 1997. pap. 15.95 (0-87417-299-3) U of Nev Pr.

Bliss, William D., ed. The Encyclopedia of Social Reform: Including Political Economy, Political Science, Sociology & Statistics. LC 71-88519. 1439p. 1971. reprint ed. lib. bdg. 195.00 (0-8371-4974-6, BLSR, Greenwood Pr) Greenwood.

Bliss, William D. & Binder, Rudolph M., eds. New Encyclopedia of Social Reform. 3rd ed. LC 77-112524. (Rise of Urban America Ser.). 1970. reprint ed. 72.95 (0-405-02436-3) Ayer.

Bliss, William D., jt. ed. see Andrews, John B.

Bliss, William R. Side Glimpses from the Colonial Meeting House. 2000. reprint ed. 40.00 (1-55888-224-3) Omnigraphics Inc.

Blissett, Marlan. Energy in Texas: Electric-Power Generation. (Policy Research Project Report Ser.: No. 13). 125p. 1976. pap. 3.00 (0-89940-608-4) LBJ Sch Pub Aff.

— Energy in Texas: Policy Alternatives. (Policy Research Project Report Ser.: No. 7). 120p. 1976. pap. 3.00 (0-89940-603-3) LBJ Sch Pub Aff.

— High-Level Radioactive Waste & Spent Nuclear Fuel Disposal: An Assessment of Impact Evaluations & Decisionmaking Systems. (Policy Research Project Report Ser.: No. 84). 182p. 1987. pap. 12.00 (0-89940-688-2) LBJ Sch Pub Aff.

— Toward a Renewable Energy Future: The Urban Potential, Austin, Texas. LC 81-82253. (Policy Research Project Report Ser.: No. 44). 139p. 1982. pap. 7.00 (0-89940-646-7) LBJ Sch Pub Aff.

Blissett, Marlan & Odum, H. Ecology & Economy: "Emergy" Analysis & Public Policy in Texas. (Policy Research Project Report Ser.: No. 78). 194p. 1986. pap. 8.00 (0-89940-682-3) LBJ Sch Pub Aff.

Blissett, Marlan, jt. auth. see Redford, Emmette S.

Blissett, William, ed. Editing Illustrated Books: Papers Given at the Fifteenth Annual Conference on Editorial Problems, University of Toronto, 2-3 November 1979. LC 80-22003. (Conference on Editorial Problems Ser.: No. 15). 1987. 42.50 (0-404-63665-9) AMS Pr.

Blissett, William, ed. see MacCallum, Reid.

Blissmer, Robert H. Introducing Computers: Concepts, Systems, & Applications. 95th ed. 336p. 1995. pap. 34.95 (0-471-11360-3) Wiley.

Blissmer, Robert H. Introducing Computers: Concepts, Systems & Applications with Getting Started Set, 1990-1991. 19th ed. pap. 34.96 (0-471-52393-3) Wiley.

Blissmer, Robert H. Introducing Computers 1995/96 Edition & Wiley Getting Started with Microsoft Applications Integrating Microsoft Office Windows 3.1 Set. 1240p. 1996. pap. 104.80 (0-471-16956-0) Wiley.

— Working with Computers. (C). 1989. pap., teacher ed. 2.76 (0-395-50505-4) HM.

— Working with Excel. (C). 1995. pap. text 22.36 (0-395-71471-0) HM.

— Working with MS Access. (C). 1995. pap. text 22.36 (0-395-71472-9) HM.

— Working with MS Office. (C). 1995. pap. text 54.76 (0-395-71468-0) HM.

— Working with MS Word. (C). 1995. pap. text 22.36 (0-395-71470-2) HM.

— Working with MS Works 3.0, 2 vols. (C). 1994. pap. 5.96 (0-395-65536-6) HM.

— Working with Powerpoint. (C). 1995. pap. text 22.36 (0-395-71473-7) HM.

Blissmer, Robert H. & Alden, Roland. Blissmer Working W/MS Office W. 640p. (C). 1995. pap. text 57.56 (0-395-72111-3) HM.

— Working with Computers. LC 88-81324. 1989. teacher ed. 2.76 (0-318-36886-2) HM.

— Working with Computers. LC 88-81324. (C). 1989. pap. 61.16 (0-395-43301-0) HM.

— Working with Computers & Windows. 144p. (C). 1995. pap. text 22.36 (0-395-71469-9) HM.

— Working with Computers & Windows. (C). 1995. text, teacher ed. 11.96 (0-395-72112-1) HM.

Blissmer, Robert H., et al. Introducing Computers: Concepts Systems & Applications & Wiley Getting Started With WordPerfect 6.1 for Windows & Wiley Getting Started with Lotus 1-2-3 5.0 for Windows & Getting Started with Dbase IV. 880p. 1996. pap. 94.80 incl. 5.25 ld (0-471-17648-6) Wiley.

Blistein, Elmer H. Comedy in Action. LC 64-22154. 162p. reprint ed. pap. 50.30 (0-608-11944-X, 202336800032) Bks Demand.

Blistein, Elmer M., ed. The Drama of the Renaissance: Essays for Leicester Bradner. LC 72-91653. 213p. reprint ed. pap. 66.10 (0-608-15234-X, 202750000055) Bks Demand.

Blitch, Charles P. Allyn Young: The Peripatetic Economist. (Studies in the History of Economics). 224p. 1996. text 65.00 (0-312-12881-9) St Martin.

Blitchington, Peter & Cruise, Robert J. Understanding Your Temperament: A Self-Analysis with a Christian Viewpoint. 42p. (Orig.). 1979. pap. 3.99 (0-943872-67-7) Andrews Univ Pr.

Blitman, Joe. Barbie Doll & Her Mod Mod Mod Mod World of Fashion. LC 97-131152. (Illus.). 224p. 1996. 26.95 (0-87588-462-8) Hobby Hse.

— Francie & Her Mod, Mod, Mod, World of Fashions. LC 96-169684. (Illus.). 160p. 1996. pap. 19.95 (0-87588-449-0) Hobby Hse.

Blits, Jan H. The End of the Ancient Republic: Shakespeare's Julius Caesar. LC 92-13744. 104p. (C). 1992. reprint ed. pap. text 19.95 (0-8476-7760-5) Rowman.

— The Insufficiency of Virtue: Macbeth & the Natural Order. 296p. 1996. pap. text 24.95 (0-8476-8251-X); lib. bdg. 67.50 (0-8476-8250-1) Rowman.

Blitt, Casey D. Monitoring in Anesthesia. 3rd ed. 1994. text 156.00 (0-443-08912-4) Church.

Blitt, Jessica, jt. ed. see Homer-Dixon, Thomas.

***Blitt, Rita, contrib. by.** Rita Blitt: The Passionate Gesture. (Illus.). 168p. 2000. pap. write for info. (0-9630785-8-5) RAM Publications.

***Blitz, Amy.** The Contested State: American Foreign Policy & Regime Change in the Philippines. 256p. 2000. pap. 26.95 (0-8476-9935-8) Rowman.

— The Contested State: American Foreign Policy & Regime in the Philippines. 256p. 2000. 59.00 (0-8476-9934-X) Rowman.

Blitz, Bruce. Blitz - The Big Book of Cartooning: The Ultimate Guide to Hours & Hours of Fun Creating Funny Faces, Wacky Creatures, & Lots More! (Illus.). 320p. 1998. 14.98 (0-7624-0249-0, Courage) Running Pr.

— Blitz Cartooning Kit. (Illus.). 56p. (J). (gr. 3 up). 1991. 14.95 (1-56138-011-3) Running Pr.

— Drawing Cartoon Animals. (How to Draw & Paint Ser.). (Illus.). 48p. 1991. pap. 6.95 (1-56010-102-4, HT249) W Foster Pub.

— Drawing Cartoon Portraits. (How to Draw & Paint Ser.). (Illus.). 48p. (Orig.). 1994. pap. 6.95 (1-56010-145-8, HT246) W Foster Pub.

— Drawing Cartoons. (How to Draw & Paint Ser.). (Illus.). 48p. 1991. pap. 6.95 (1-56010-100-8, HT247) W Foster Pub.

***Blitz, Bruce.** The Fun Book of Cartoon Faces. LC 98-66889. (Illus.). 127p. (YA). (gr. 5 up). 1999. pap. 12.95 (0-7624-0452-3) Running Pr.

Blitz, Bruce. How to Draw. (How to Draw & Paint Ser.). (Illus.). 48p. 1991. pap. 6.95 (1-56010-099-0, HT251) W Foster Pub.

— How to Draw. rev. ed. (Illus.). 48p. 1997. mass mkt. 5.95 (1-889179-02-7, R610) Blitz Art.

— How to Draw Cartoon Animals. rev. ed. Orig. Title: Drawing Cartoon Animals. (Illus.). 48p. 1997. mass mkt. 5.95 (1-889179-03-5, R620) Blitz Art.

— How to Draw Cartoon Characters. rev. ed. Orig. Title: Drawing Cartoon Characters. (Illus.). 48p. 1997. mass mkt. 5.95 (1-889179-05-1, R630) Blitz Art.

— How to Draw Cartoon Portraits. rev. ed. Orig. Title: Drawing Cartoon Portraits. (Illus.). 48p. 1997. mass mkt. 5.95 (1-889179-01-9, R635) Blitz Art.

— How to Draw Cartoons. Orig. Title: Drawing Cartoons. (Illus.). 48p. 1997. mass mkt. 5.95 (1-889179-04-3, R625) Blitz Art.

— How to Draw Comic Strips. rev. ed. Orig. Title: Drawing Comic Strips. (Illus.). 48p. 1997. mass mkt. 5.95 (1-889179-00-0, R615) Blitz Art.

Blitz, David. Emergent Evolution: Qualitative Novelty & the Levels of Reality. (Episteme Ser.). 252p. (C). 1992. lib. bdg. 141.50 (0-7923-1658-4, Pub. by Kluwer Academic) Kluwer Academic.

Blitz, J. Electrical & Magnetic Methods of Nondestructive Testing. (Illus.). 248p. 1991. 124.00 (0-7503-0148-1) IOP Pub.

***Blitz, J. & Little, C. B., eds.** Fundamental & Applied Aspects of Chemically Modified Surfaces. (Special Publications: Vol. 235). 400p. 1999. write for info. (0-85404-714-X, Pub. by Royal Soc Chem) Spr-Verlag.

Blitz, John H. Ancient Chiefdoms of the Tombigbee. LC 92-28876. 232p. (Orig.). (C). 1993. pap. text 29.95 (0-8173-0672-2) U of Ala Pr.

— An Archaeological Study of the Mississippi Choctaw Indians. LC 85-620004. (Archaeological Report Ser.: No. 16). (Illus.). vi, 116p. (Orig.). 1985. pap. text 5.00 (0-938896-44-X) Mississippi Archives.

Blitz, L., ed. The Evolution of Interstellar Medium. (ASP Conference Series Proceedings: Vol. 12). 346p. 1990. 34.00 (0-937707-31-7) Astron Soc Pacific.

Blitz, Leo, ed. The Center, Bulge, & Disk of the Milky Way. LC 92-24067. (Astrophysics & Space Science Library: Vol. 180). 176p. (C). 1992. text 89.50 (0-7923-1913-3) Kluwer Academic.

Blitz, Leo & Lockman, F. J., eds. The Outer Galaxy. (Lecture Notes in Physics Ser.: Vol. 306). ix, 291p. 1988. 42.95 (0-387-19484-3) Spr-Verlag.

Blitz, Leo & Teuben, Peter, eds. Unsolved Problems of the Milky Way. 725p. 1996. lib. bdg. 208.00 (0-7923-4039-6) Kluwer Academic.

Blitz, Mark. Heidegger's Being & Time & the Possibility of Political Philosophy. LC 81-3253. 288p. 1981. text 42.50 (0-8014-1320-6) Cornell U Pr.

Blitz, Michael. Five Days in the Electric Chair. 40p. 1990. pap. 9.00 (0-916258-22-X) Left Hand Bks.

— Partitions. (Illus.). 50p. (Orig.). 1982. 11.00 (0-916258-13-0); pap. 7.50 (0-916258-12-2) Woodbine Pr.

— The Spacialist. 50p. 1986. 12.50 (0-916258-15-7); pap. 7.50 (0-916258-16-5) Woodbine Pr.

— Suction Files. 25p. 1995. pap. text 15.00 (0-916258-27-0) Woodbine Pr.

Blitz, Michael & Hurlbert, C. Mark. Letters for the Living: Teaching Writing in a Violent Age. LC 98-13637. (Refiguring English Studies). 181p. 1998. pap. 25.95 (0-8141-2803-3) NCTE.

Blitz, Michael, jt. ed. see Hurlbert, C. Mark.

Blitz, Rudolph C., tr. see Gossen, Hermann H.

Blitz, S. The Aleph Bet Word Book: A Pictorial Hebrew-English Dictionary for Children. (ArtScroll Youth Ser.). (Illus.). (J). (gr. k-2). 1995. 14.99 (0-89906-515-5) Mesorah Pubns.

Blitz, Stanley J. Bandstand, the Untold Story: The Years Before Dick Clark. (Illus.). 336p. (Orig.). 1997. pap. 19.95 (0-914207-14-8) Cornucopia Pubns.

— Bandstand, the Untold Story: The Years Before Dick Clark. (Illus.). 336p. (Orig.). 1997. 29.95 (0-914207-12-1) Cornucopia Pubns.

Blitzer. College Algebra. LC 97-22702. 859p. 1997. 86.00 (0-13-399940-8) P-H.

— Introduction to Algebra for College Students. 428p. 1998. pap. text 40.75 (0-536-01628-3) Pearson Custom.

An Asterisk (*) at the beginning of an entry indicates that the title is appearing for the first time.

B

— Liberal Arts. LC 99-88495. 740p. 1999. 86.00 (*0-13-948845-6*) P-H.

— Outpacing the Pros. 2000. 30.00 (*0-07-135586-3*) McGraw.

Blitzer, Andrew. Office-Based Surgery in Otolaryngology. LC 97-42732. 1998. 98.00 (*3-13-110511-9*) Thieme Med Pubs.

Blitzer, Andrew, et al, eds. Office-Based Surgery in Otolaryngology. LC 97-42732. (Illus.). 700p. 1997. 98.00 (*0-86577-739-X*) Thieme Med Pubs.

Blitzer, Andrew, et al. Management of Facial Lines & Wrinkles. 368p. 1999. text 99.00 (*0-7817-1551-2*) Lppncott W & W.

— Neurologic Disorders of the Larynx. (Illus.). 352p. 1992. text 82.00 (*0-86577-400-5*) Thieme Med Pubs.

— Surgery of the Paranasal Sinuses. 2nd ed. (Illus.). 480p. 1991. text 175.00 (*0-7216-3583-0*, W B Saunders Co) Harcrt Hlth Sci Grp.

Blitzer, Andrew, jt. auth. see Aviv, Jonathan E.

Blitzer, Barbara, jt. auth. see Benjamin, Alan.

Blitzer, Charles, ed. see Harrington, James.

Blitzer, David M. What's the Economy Trying to Tell You? Everyone's Guide to Understanding & Profiting from the Economy. (Illus.). 336p. 1999. pap. 14.95 (*0-07-007097-0*) McGraw.

Blitzer, Robert. Algebra For College Student: Student Solution Manual. LC 97-22702. 1024p. (C). 1997. text. write for info. (*0-13-660259-2*) P-H.

— Algebra For College Student: Student Solution Manual. 3rd ed. 560p. (C). 1997. pap. text, student ed. 30.80 (*0-13-752289-4*) P-H.

Blitzer, Robert. Algebra for College Students. 3rd ed. LC 97-22700. 969p. 1997. 83.00 (*0-13-700212-2*) P-H.

Blitzer, Robert. Algebra for College Students. 3rd ed. LC 97-22700. 1136p. (C). 1997. text, lab manual ed. 28.15 (*0-13-752370-X*) P-H.

— Intermediate Algebra for College Students. 2nd ed. LC 97-15279. 870p. 1997. 83.00 (*0-13-275181-X*) P-H.

— Introductory Algebra College Student. 2nd ed. 328p. (C). 1997. pap. text, student ed. 30.80 (*0-13-860594-7*) P-H.

— Introductory Algebra for College Students. 2nd ed. LC 97-15280. 744p. 1997. student ed. 83.00 (*0-13-275745-1*) P-H.

Blitzer, Robert F. & Gill, Jack C. College Mathematics Review. 4th ed. Hackworth, Robert & Davis, Karen, eds. (Illus.). 460p. (C). 1992. pap. text 39.95 (*0-943202-40-X*) H & H Pub.

Blitzer, Robert F., jt. auth. see Gill, Jack C.

Blitzer, Roy J. Office Smarts. LC 94-15873. 160p. 1994. pap. 6.95 (*1-56440-386-6*) Globe Pequot.

Blitzer, Roy J. & Reynolds-Rush, Jacquie. Find the Bathrooms First! Starting Your New Job on the Right Foot. Young, George, ed. LC 99-75056. (Illus.). 112p. 1999. pap. 11.95 (*1-56052-553-3*, Pub. by Crisp Pubns) Natl Bk Netwk.

Blitzstein, M. Regina: Vocal Score. Lefferts, Michael, ed. 256p. (C). 1992. per. 45.00 (*0-7935-1545-9*, 00311578) H Leonard.

Bliven, Bruce, Jr. American Revolution, 1760-1783. 1981. pap. 5.99 (*0-394-84696-6*) Random.

Bliven, Bruce. American Revolution, 1760-1783. (Landmark Bks.). (J). 1981. 11.09 (*0-606-02015-2*, Pub. by Turtleback) Demco.

Bliven, Bruce, Jr. Men Who Make the Future. LC 70-111816. (Essay Index Reprint Ser.). 1977. 23.95 (*0-8369-1643-3*) Ayer.

Bliven, Bruce, Jr. & Mezerik, Avrahm G., eds. What the Informed Citizen Needs to Know. LC 72-1244. (Essay Index Reprint Ser.). 1977. reprint ed. 26.95 (*0-8369-2833-4*) Ayer.

Bliven, Edmond. Book of Catholic Prayer. 422p. 1992. pap. 9.95 (*0-915531-02-X*) OR Catholic.

Bliven, Edmond E. Book of Catholic Prayer. deluxe ed. 422p. 1997. reprint ed. 24.95 (*0-915531-96-8*) OR Catholic.

Bliven, Neal, et al. Devising Policies to Help the Poor in South India. LC 97-913670. (C). 1997. 42.00 (*81-7018-929-2*, Pub. by BR Pub) S Asia.

Bliven, Roy B. Project: Earth. Bookcrafters Staff, ed. (Illus.). 128p. 1998. pap. 13.00 (*0-9663387-0-7*) I Am NY.

***Blix, Fay, et al.** California Durable Powers of Attorney: 3/98 Update. Gerber, Mary, ed. LC 96-83298. 414p. 1998. ring bd. 40.00 (*0-7626-0187-6*, ES-32662) Cont Ed Bar-CA.

Blix, Jacqueline & Heitmiller, David. Getting a Life: Real Lives Transformed by Your Money or Your Life. 364p. 1999. pap. 13.95 (*0-14-025877-9*) Viking Penguin.

Blixen-Finecke, Hans V. The Art of Training: Lessons from a Lifetime with Horses. LC 96-39851. (Masters of Horsemanship Ser.). 1996. 24.95 (*0-939481-48-0*) Half Halt Pr.

Blixen-Finecke, Hans Von, see Von Blixen-Finecke, Hans.

Blixseth, Edra D. Uncharged Battery. Hodgson, Cheryl, ed. 256p. 1988. text 16.95 (*0-945033-00-1*) PEP Pr.

— Uncharged Battery. 256p. 1990. mass mkt. 9.95 (*0-446-39059-3*, Pub. by Warner Bks) Little.

Blixt, Albert B., jt. auth. see Simon, Neil J.

Blixt, Janet, jt. auth. see Stanich, Susan.

Bliz, Einar. Trails to Timberline: In West Central British Columbia. rev. ed. (Illus.). 201p. (Orig.). 1989. pap. 17.50 (*0-88925-969-0*) Gordon Soules Bk.

Blizard, E. P., ed. see Chilton, Arthur B., et al.

Blizard, Lee, ed. The Diary of Benjamin Reynolds. 72p. (Orig.). (C). 1993. pap. text 12.00 (*1-55613-796-6*) Heritage Bk.

Blizard, Rosalie E. The First Rosalie of Philadelphia: Sequel to Diary of Benjamin Reynolds. (Illus.). 191p. (Orig.). 1994. pap. text 19.00 (*0-7884-0059-2*) Heritage Bk.

Bliznakov, Emile G. & Hunt, Gerry. The Miracle Nutrient: Coenzyme Q10. 256p. 1986. mass mkt. 6.99 (*0-553-26233-5*) Bantam.

Bliznetsova, Ina. Solea. LC 98-5217. 118p. 1998. 10.00 (*1-55779-107-4*) Hermitage Pubs.

— Vid na Nebo (A View to a Sky) LC 91-29079. (RUS.). 90p. (Orig.). 1991. pap. 8.00 (*1-55779-048-5*) Hermitage Pubs.

***Blizzard, Dennis F.** The Roster & Register of the General Society of the War of 1812, 4 vols. in 2. 3143p. 1999. reprint ed. 90.00 (*0-8063-4865-8*) Clearfield Co.

Blizzard, Gladys. Come Look with Me: Animals in Art. LC 92-5357. (Come Look with Me Ser.). 32p. (J). (gr. 1-8). 1992. 13.95 (*1-56566-013-7*) Lickle Pubng.

— Come Look with Me: Enjoying Art with Children. LC 90-19627. (Come Look with Me Ser.). (Illus.). 32p. 1991. 13.95 (*0-934738-76-9*) Lickle Pubng.

— Come Look with Me: Exploring Landscape Art with Children. LC 91-34320. (Come Look with Me Ser.). (Illus.). 32p. (J). (gr. 1-8). 1992. 13.95 (*0-934738-95-5*) Lickle Pubng.

— Come Look with Me: World of Play. LC 92-36263. (Come Look with Me Ser.). (Illus.). 32p. (J). (gr. 1-8). 1993. 13.95 (*1-56566-031-5*) Lickle Pubng.

Blizzard Publishing Staff. Prerogatives: Contemporary Plays by Women. LC 98-232149. 256p. 1998. pap. 24.95 (*0-921368-69-0*) Blizzard Publ.

Blizzard, Richard. Blizzard's Garden Woodwork: Stylish Outdoor Projects Made Easy. (Illus.). 128p. 1997. 24.95 (*0-7063-7511-4*, Pub. by WrLock) Sterling.

— Blizzard's Garden Woodwork: Stylish Outdoor Projects Made Easy. (Illus.). 128p. 1998. pap. text 19.95 (*0-7063-7742-7*, Pub. by WrLock) Sterling.

— Garden Woodwork in a Weekend. (Illus.). 128p. 1999. 27.95 (*0-7153-0820-3*, Pub. by D & C Pub) Sterling.

— Making Wooden Toys. (Illus.). 64p. (Orig.). 1994. pap. 15.95 (*0-7195-5296-6*, Pub. by John Murray) Trafalgar.

Blizzard, Roy B., jt. auth. see Bivin, David.

Blizzard, Samuel. The Protestant Parish Minister: A Behavioral Science Interpretation. LC 85-50402. (Monographs: No. 5). 1985. pap. 8.00 (*0-932566-04-9*) Soc Sci Stud Rel.

***Blizzard, Vicki, ed.** Guardian Angels: Transfer Book. (Illus.). 236p. 2001. pap. write for info. (*1-882138-66-X*) Hse White Birches.

— Teddy Bear Treasures Transfer Book. (Illus.). 224p. 2000. pap. 19.96 (*1-882138-57-0*) Hse White Birches.

Bljach, I. S. & Bagma, L. T. German-Russian Economics Dictionary: Deutsch-Russisches Oekonomisches Woerterbuch. (GER & RUS.). 663p. 1982. 95.00 (*0-8288-0820-1*, M9056) Fr & Eur.

Bljuger, Fiodor Ephroim. Design of Precast Concrete Structures. (Civil & Mechanical Engineering Ser.). 288p. 1988. text 83.95 (*0-470-21034-6*) P-H.

Blo-bzan-chos-kyi-rgyal-mtshan, jt. auth. see Tharchin.

Blob, Hans-Ulrich. Ertragsteuerliche Auswirkungen der Haftung im Einfach & Qualifiziert Faktischen Abhangigkeitsverhaltnis: Eine Abgrenzung zur Sogenannten Verunglückten Organschaft. (GER.). 188p. 1996. 42.95 (*3-631-30547-8*) P Lang Pubng.

Blobaum, Cindy. Geology Rocks! 50 Hands-on Activities to Explore the Earth. LC 98-53299. 96p. (J). (gr. 2-7). 1999. pap. 10.95 (*1-885593-29-5*) Williamson Pub Co.

Blobaum, Robert. Feliks Dzierzynski & the Sdkpil: A Study of the Origins of Polish Communism. 307p. 1984. text 92.50 (*0-88033-046-5*, Pub. by East Eur Monographs) Col U Pr.

Blobaum, Robert E. Rewoluja: Russian Poland, 1904-1907. (Illus.). 320p. 1995. text 39.95 (*0-8014-3054-2*) Cornell U Pr.

Bloch. Compressors & Expanders: Selection & Application for the Process Industry. (Chemical Industries Ser.: Vol. 8). (Illus.). 344p. 1982. text 165.00 (*0-8247-1854-2*) Dekker.

— High-Tech Jobs for Liberal Arts Grads. 1995. pap. 15.00 (*0-671-89889-2*) S&S Trade.

— Nutrition Facts Manual: A Quick Reference. 352p. 1996. pap. text 34.75 (*0-683-07719-8*) Lppncott W & W.

Bloch. Once around Bloch. 1995. mass mkt. 4.99 (*0-8125-2089-0*) Tor Bks.

Bloch. Strange Defeat. 204p. 1999. reprint ed. pap. 12.95 (*0-393-31911-3*) Norton.

— Twilight Zone. 1983. mass mkt. 2.95 (*0-446-32200-8*, Pub. by Warner Bks) Little.

Bloch & Shamim. Oil Mist Lubrication. 400p. 1998. 84.00 (*0-13-975210-2*) P-H.

Bloch, Abby S. Nutrition Management of the Cancer Patient: A Practical Guide for Professionals. 431p. (C). 1990. text 82.00 (*0-8342-0132-1*) Aspen Pub.

Bloch, Abraham P. A Book of Jewish Ethical Concepts: Biblical & Postbiblical. 1984. 25.00 (*0-88125-039-2*) Ktav.

— Midrashic Comments on the Torah: Torah Thoughts for Sabbaths & Holidays. 17.95 (*0-88125-377-4*) Ktav.

— One a Day: An Anthology of Jewish Historical Anniversaries for Every Day of the Year. 29.50 (*0-88125-108-9*) Ktav.

***Bloch, Alice & Levy, Carl.** Refugees, Citizenship & Social Policy in Europe. LC 98-35605. 288p. 1999. text 69.95 (*0-312-21724-2*) St Martin.

Bloch, Annette & Bloch, Richard. Fighting Cancer. rev. ed. (Illus.). 256p. 1989. reprint ed. pap. 3.95 (*0-685-30128-1*) R A Block Cancer.

Bloch, Anthony, ed. Hamiltonian & Gradient Flows, Algorithms, & Control. LC 94-28546. (Fields Institute Communications Ser.: Vol. 3). 155p. 1995. text 71.00 (*0-8218-0255-0*, FIC/3) Am Math.

***Bloch, Ariel & Bloch, Chana, trs.** The Song of Songs: A New Translation. 253p. 2000. 35.00 (*0-520-22675-5*) U CA Pr.

Bloch, Ariel, tr. see Ravikovitch, Dahlia.

***Bloch, Ariel A. & Bloch, Chana.** The Song of Songs: A New Translation with an Introduction & Commentary. LC 97-34743. (ENG & HEB.). 253p. 1998. pap. 17.95 (*0-520-21330-0*, Pub. by U CA Pr) Cal Prin Full Svc.

***Bloch, Arthur.** Murphy's Law. (J). 1999. pap. 10.99 (*0-8431-7485-4*, Price Stern) Peng Put Young Read.

— Murphy's Law: Doctors. LC 00-28281. (Illus.). 240p. (YA). 2000. pap. 7.99 (*0-8431-7581-8*, Price Stern) Peng Put Young Read.

— Murphy's Law: Lawyers. LC 00-28288. (Illus.). 240p. (YA). 2000. pap. 7.99 (*0-8431-7580-X*, Price Stern) Peng Put Young Read.

Bloch, Arthur. Murphy's Law 2000: What Else Can Go Wrong in the 21st Century! LC 98-48575. 96p. 1999. pap. 6.99 (*0-8431-7482-X*, Price Stern) Peng Put Young Read.

***Bloch, Arthur.** Murphy's Law 2001 Desk Calendar. 640p. 2000. pap. 10.99 (*0-8431-7570-2*) Peng Put Young Read.

Bloch, Barbara. A Little Jewish Cookbook. (Illus.). 60p. 1995. 7.95 (*0-8118-1016-X*) Chronicle Bks.

— A Little New England Cookbook. (Traditional Little Cookbooks of the World Ser.). (Illus.). 60p. 1991. 7.95 (*0-87701-879-0*) Chronicle Bks.

— A Little New York Cookbook. (Traditional Little Cookbooks of the World Ser.). (Illus.). 60p. 1991. 7.95 (*0-87701-876-6*) Chronicle Bks.

Bloch, Bernard. Bernard Bloch on Japanese. LC 72-99834. (Yale Linguistic Ser.). 230p. reprint ed. pap. 71.30 (*0-8357-8702-8*, 203367400087) Bks Demand.

Bloch, Bernice, jt. auth. see Kirn, Elaine.

Bloch, Bertram, jt. auth. see Brewer, George, Jr.

Bloch, Britt. Candidate Prep-Package. 24p. 1998. pap. 6.00 (*0-8059-4403-6*) Dorrance.

Bloch, C. America the Beautiful Activity Book. (Illus.). 48p. (J). (gr. k-6). 1993. reprint ed. pap. 2.95 (*1-879424-81-9*) Nickel Pr.

— Book of Dinosaurs. (Illus.). 64p. (Orig.). (J). (gr. k-6). 1993. pap. 3.95 (*1-879424-46-0*) Nickel Pr.

— Dinosaur Sticker Atlas. (Illus.). 32p. (J). (gr. k-6). 1993. reprint ed. pap. 3.95 (*1-879424-19-3*) Nickel Pr.

— Endangered Animals Sticker Book. (Illus.). 32p. (Orig.). (J). (gr. k-6). 1993. pap. 3.95 (*1-879424-62-2*) Nickel Pr.

— Ocean Life Sticker Book. (Illus.). 32p. (Orig.). (J). (gr. k-6). 1993. pap. 3.95 (*1-879424-61-4*) Nickel Pr.

— Planets: Outer Space Sticker Atlas. (Illus.). 32p. (J). (gr. k-6). 1993. reprint ed. pap. 3.95 (*1-879424-13-4*) Nickel Pr.

Bloch, Carol. Zoo Animal Sticker Atlas. (Illus.). 32p. (J). (gr. k-6). 1993. reprint ed. pap. 3.95 (*1-879424-18-5*) Nickel Pr.

Bloch, Chana. Mrs. Dumpty. 80p. (J). 1998. 18.95 (*0-299-16000-9*); pap. 11.95 (*0-299-16004-1*) U of Wis Pr.

— The Past Keeps Changing: Poems. LC 92-9628. 85p. (Orig.). 1992. pap. 12.95 (*1-878818-15-5*, Pub. by Sheep Meadow) U Pr of New Eng.

Bloch, Chana, jt. auth. see Bloch, Ariel A.

Bloch, Chana, tr. see Amichai, Yehuda.

Bloch, Chana, jt. tr. see Bloch, Ariel.

Bloch, Chana, tr. see Ravikovitch, Dahlia.

Bloch, Chayim. Golem: Legends of the Ghetto of Prague. 244p. 1997. reprint ed. pap. 11.95 (*0-7661-0111-8*) Kessinger Pub.

Bloch, D. & Enlander, Derek. Microcomputer Interpretation of Clinical Lab Results. 90p. 1984. 30.00 (*0-685-08623-2*) Med Software.

Bloch, Daniel, jt. ed. see Ducloy, Martial.

Bloch, David S. The Essence of This. (Illus.). 32p. 1992. pap. 5.95 (*1-882817-01-X*) J Bloch.

— Haunting Us with His Love. LC 97-176735. (Illus.). 32p. 1996. pap. 5.95 (*1-882817-04-4*) J Bloch.

— A Knock at the Gate. (Illus.). 32p. 1994. pap. 5.95 (*1-882817-03-6*) J Bloch.

— No Such Thing As Strangers. (Illus.). 32p. 1993. pap. 5.95 (*1-882817-02-8*) J Bloch.

Bloch, Deborah P. Have a Winning Job Interview. LC 97-33185. (Here's How Ser.). (Illus.). 192p. 1997. pap. 12.95 (*0-8442-2476-6*, 24766, NTC Learningworks) NTC Contemp Pub Co.

— How to Get a Good Job & Keep It. LC 92-23925. (Illus.). 184p. 1994. pap. 7.95 (*0-8442-4162-8*, 41628, VGM Career) NTC Contemp Pub Co.

— How to Get a Good Job & Keep It. 1993. 13.05 (*0-606-05363-8*, Pub. by Turtleback) Demco.

— How to Get & Get Ahead on Your First Job. 160p. 1993. pap. 7.95 (*0-8442-6691-4*, VGM Career) NTC Contemp Pub Co.

— How to Have a Winning Job Interview. 3rd ed. LC 98-25037. 144p. 1998. pap. 14.95 (*0-8442-8149-2*, 81492, VGM Career) NTC Contemp Pub Co.

— How to Make the Right Career Moves. (Illus.). 160p. 1994. pap. 7.95 (*0-8442-6664-7*, VGM Career) NTC Contemp Pub Co.

— How to Write a Winning Resume. 128p. 1993. pap. 6.95 (*0-8442-6639-6*, NTC Business Bks) NTC Contemp Pub Co.

— How to Write a Winning Resume. 4th ed. LC 98-20710. 128p. 1998. pap. 14.95 (*0-8442-6692-2*, 66922, VGM Career) NTC Contemp Pub Co.

— Make the Right Career Moves. LC 99-13607. (Here's How Ser.). 160p. 1999. pap. 12.95 (*0-8442-2076-0*, 20760, Natl Textbk Co) NTC Contemp Pub Co.

— Write a Winning Resume. LC 97-30754. (Here's How Ser.). (Illus.). 128p. 1997. pap. 12.95 (*0-8442-2475-8*, 24758, NTC Learningworks) NTC Contemp Pub Co.

Bloch, Deborah P. & Richmond, Lee J. SoulWork: Finding the Work You Love, Loving the Work You Have. LC 98-18576. 224p. 1998. pap. 18.95 (*0-89106-119-3*, 7790, Pub. by Consulting Psychol) Natl Bk Netwk.

Bloch, Deborah P. & Richmond, Lee J., eds. Connections Between Spirit & Work in Career Development: New Approaches & Practical Perspectives. LC 97-15339. 288p. 1997. 35.95 (*0-89106-105-3*, 7761, Davies-Black Pub) Consulting Psychol.

Bloch-Dermant, Janine. Guidargus de la Verrerie de l'Antiquite a Nos Jours: Argus Guide to Glassware from Antiquity to Present. (FRE.). 384p. 1992. 175.00 (*0-8288-7231-7*, 2859171150) Fr & Eur.

Bloch, Don. Face Value. 346p. (C). 1989. 18.95 (*0-941533-67-0*, NAB) I R Dee.

Bloch, Don, tr. see Willems, Wim.

Bloch, Dorothy. "So the Witch Won't Eat Me" Fantasy & the Child's Fear of Infanticide. LC 94-70895. 256p. 1994. pap. 40.00 (*1-56821-259-3*) Aronson.

Bloch, Douglas. I Am with You Always: A Treasury of Inspirational Quotations, Poems & Prayers. 207p. 1998. reprint ed. pap. 12.95 (*0-929671-01-5*, Pub. by Pallas Comns) New Leaf Dist.

— Listening to Your Inner Voice: Discover the Truth Within You & Let It Guide Your Way. 232p. pap. 9.95 (*1-56838-079-8*) Hazelden.

— When Going Through Hell... Don't Stop: A Survivor's Guide to Overcoming Anxiety & Clinical Depression. (Illus.). 270p. 1999. pap. 14.95 (*0-929671-02-3*, Pub. by Pallas Comns) Partners-West.

— Words That Heal. 128p. 1989. pap. 12.95 (*0-929671-00-7*, Pub. by Pallas Comns) New Leaf Dist.

Bloch, Douglas & Merritt, Jon. Positive Self-Talk for Children: Teaching Self-Esteem Through Affirmations - A Guide for Parents, Teachers, & Counselors. LC 93-21706. 352p. 1993. pap. 12.95 (*0-553-35198-2*) Bantam.

Bloch, Douglas, jt. auth. see George, Demetra.

Bloch, E. Scelomo Solomon Rhapsodie Hebraique: Violoncelle & Piano. 36p. 1986. pap. 18.95 (*0-7935-5213-3*, 50274500) H Leonard.

— Suite Hebraique: Viola or Violin & Piano. 16p. 1986. pap. 7.50 (*0-7935-5188-9*, 50286080) H Leonard.

— Visions et Propheties: Piano Solo. 16p. 1992. pap. 7.95 (*0-7935-1587-4*, 50328750) H Leonard.

Bloch, E. Maurice. Focusing on Nature: Landscape Drawings from the Collection of E. Maurice Bloch. (Illus.). 76p. 1991. pap. 12.00 (*0-87328-133-0*) Huntington Lib.

— The Paintings of George Caleb Bingham: A Catalogue Raisonne. LC 85-29013. (Illus.). 328p. 1986. text 64.00 (*0-8262-0461-9*) U of Mo Pr.

Bloch, Edmond C. Pediatric Anesthesia: A Pocket Companion. LC 94-30840. 352p. 1999. text 32.50 (*0-7506-9602-8*) Buttrwrth-Heinemann.

Bloch, Edmond C. & Ginsberg, Brian. Pediatric Anesthesia: A Quick Pocket Reference. 2nd ed. LC 99-19066. 365p. 1999. pap. text 35.00 (*0-7506-7142-4*) Buttrwrth-Heinemann.

Bloch, Ellin L., jt. auth. see Wainrib, Barbara R.

Bloch, Ernest, jt. auth. see Schwartz, Robert A.

Bloch, Ernst. Literary Essays. Joron, Andrew, tr. from ENG. LC 98-11401. (Meridian Ser.). 448p. 1998. 65.00 (*0-8047-2706-6*) Stanford U Pr.

— Literary Essays. Joron, Andrew, tr. from ENG. LC 98-11401. (Meridian Ser.). (Illus.). 448p. 1998. pap. 22.95 (*0-8047-2707-4*) Stanford U Pr.

— Natural Law & Human Dignity. Schmidt, Dennis J., tr. from GER. (Studies in Contemporary German Social Thought). 408p. 1986. 32.50 (*0-262-02221-4*) MIT Pr.

— Natural Law & Human Dignity. Schmidt, Dennis J., tr. from GER. (Studies in Contemporary German Social Thought). 408p. 1987. pap. text 24.00 (*0-262-52129-6*) MIT Pr.

— The Principle of Hope, 3 vols. Plaice, Neville, tr. 1995. pap. text 65.00 (*0-262-52204-7*) MIT Pr.

— The Principle of Hope, Vol. 1. Plaice, Neville et al, trs. Vol. 1. 488p. 1995. pap. text 24.00 (*0-262-52199-7*) MIT Pr.

— Principles of Hope, Vol. 3. Plaice, Neville et al, trs. 504p. 1995. pap. text 24.00 (*0-262-52201-2*) MIT Pr.

***Bloch, Ernst.** The Spirit of Utopia LC 99-38497. (Meridian Ser.). 2000. pap. 19.95 (*0-8047-3765-7*) Stanford U Pr.

Bloch, Ernst. The Utopian Function of Art & Literature: Selected Essays. Zipes, Jack D. & Mecklenburg, Frank, trs. from GER. (Studies on Contemporary German Social Thought). 360p. 1987. 30.00 (*0-262-02270-2*) MIT Pr.

— The Utopian Function of Art & Literature: Selected Essays. Zipes, Jack D. & Mecklenburg, Frank, trs. from GER. (Studies on Contemporary German Social Thought). 360p. 1989. pap. text 21.00 (*0-262-52139-3*) MIT Pr.

Bloch, Ernst, et al, eds. Heritage of Our Times. Plaice, Stephen, tr. & intro. by. LC 90-11013. (Weimar & Now: German Cultural Criticism Ser.: No. 1). 375p. 1991. 55.00 (*0-520-07057-7*, Pub. by U CA Pr) Cal Prin Full Svc.

Bloch, Ernst, et al. Aesthetics & Politics. 220p. 1985. pap. 18.00 (*0-86091-722-3*) Norton.

— Principles of Hope, Vol. 2. Plaice, Neville et al, trs. (Studies in Contemporary German Social Thought). 488p. 1995. pap. text 24.00 (*0-262-52200-4*) MIT Pr.

Bloch, Ernst, jt. auth. see Bruch, Max.

Bloch, Ethan D. A First Course in Geometric Topology & Differential Geometry. LC 96-15470. 421p. 1996. 59.50 (*0-8176-3840-7*) Birkhauser.

Bloch, Ethan D. Proofs & Fundamentals: A First Course in Abstract Mathematics. 432p. 1999. 49.50 (*0-8176-4111-4*) Birkhauser.

***Bloch, Ethan D.** Proofs & Fundamentals: A First Course in Abstract Mathematics. LC 00-23309. 2000. write for info. (*3-7643-4111-4*) Birkhauser.

B

B

Bloch, Farrell. Antidiscrimination Law & Minority Employment: Recruitment Practices & Regulatory Constraints. LC 93-44408. 148p. (C). 1994. 19.95 (*0-226-05983-9*) U Ch Pr.

Bloch, Farrell E. Statistics for Non-Statisticians: A Primer for Professionals. 2nd ed. (Illus.). 188p. 1993. pap. 30.00 (*0-916559-45-9*) EPF.

Bloch, Frank S. Disability Determination: The Administrative Process & the Role of Medical Personnel, 13. LC 91-33483. (Studies in Social Welfare Policies & Programs: No. 13). 248p. 1992. 55.00 (*0-313-27638-2*, BNP/, Greenwood Pr) Greenwood.

Bloch, George. Pablo Picasso: Catalogue of the Printed Graphic Work 1904-1972, 3 Vols. 911p. 1979. 600.00 (*1-55660-173-5*) A Wofsy Fine Arts.

— Pablo Picasso: Catalogue of the Printed Graphic Work 1904-1972, 4 vols., Set. 911p. 1979. 795.00 (*1-55660-044-5*) A Wofsy Fine Arts.

— Picasso Catalogue of the Printed Graphic Work, 4 vols. (Illus.). 1971. 795.00 (*0-8150-0026-X*) Wittenborn Art.

— Picasso Catalogue of the Printed Graphic Work, Vol. 1, 1904-1967. (Illus.). 1971. 175.00 (*0-8150-0467-2*) Wittenborn Art.

— Picasso Catalogue of the Printed Graphic Work, Vol. 2, 1967-1969. (Catalogue of the Printed Graphic Work Ser.: Vols. 1 & 2). (Illus.). 1971. 175.00 (*0-8150-0468-0*) Wittenborn Art.

— Picasso Catalogue of the Printed Graphic Work, Vol. 4, 1970-1972. (ENG, FRE & GER., Illus.). 253p. 1979. 175.00 (*3-85773-009-9*) Wittenborn Art.

— Picasso Ceramics. (Catalogue of the Printed Graphic Work Ser.: Vol. 3, Ceramiques 1949-1971). (Illus.). 1972. 195.00 (*0-8150-0646-2*) Wittenborn Art.

Bloch, Gordon B. How to Train for & Run Your Best Marathon: Valuable Coaching from a National Class Marathoner on Getting up for & Finishing the Popular 26.2 Mile Event. LC 93-18870. 272p. (Orig.). 1993. pap. 14.00 (*0-671-79727-1*, Fireside) S&S Trade Pap.

***Bloch, Gottfried R.** Unfree Associations. LC 98-89284. 320p. 1999. pap. 19.95 (*1-888996-12-9*, Red Hen Press) Valentine CA.

Bloch, H. Spencer. Adolescent Development, Psychopathology, & Treatment. 417p. 1995. 55.00 (*0-8236-0065-3*) Intl Univs Pr.

Bloch, Heinz. Process Plant Machinery. 2nd ed. LC 98-10447. 512p. 1998. 95.00 (*0-7506-7081-9*) Buttrwrth-Heinemann.

Bloch, Heinz & Geitner, Fred K. Machinery Failure Analysis & Troubleshooting. 3rd ed. LC 97-12229. (Practical Machinery Management for Process Plants Ser.: Vol. 2). 600p. 1997. 95.00 (*0-88415-662-1*, 5662) Gulf Pub.

Bloch, Heinz P. Handbook of Compressor & Steam Turbine Technology. 348p. 1995. 62.50 (*0-07-005924-1*) McGraw.

— Improving Machinery Reliability. 2nd ed. (Practical Machinery Management for Process Plants Ser.: Vol. 1). (Illus.). 438p. 1988. 95.00 (*0-87201-455-X*, 1455) Gulf Pub.

— A Practical Guide to Compressor Technology. LC 95-22898. 518p. 1995. 62.50 (*0-07-005937-3*) McGraw.

***Bloch, Heinz P.** Practical Lubrication for Industrial Facilities. LC 99-34016. 612p. 2000. 150.00 (*0-88173-296-6*) Fairmont Pr.

Bloch, Heinz P. Process Plant Machinery. (Illus.). 493p. 1989. text 125.00 (*0-409-90087-7*) Buttrwrth-Heinemann.

Bloch, Heinz P. & Geitner, Fred K. Machinery Component Maintenance & Repair, Vol. 3. 2nd rev. ed. LC 84-15738. (Practical Machinery Management for Process Plants Ser.). (Illus.). 370p. 1990. 95.00 (*0-87201-781-8*, 1781) Gulf Pub.

— Machinery Failure Analysis & Troubleshooting. fac. ed. LC 83-10731. (Practical Machinery Management for Process Plants Ser.: No. 2). (Illus.). 668p. pap. 200.00 (*0-7837-7429-X*, 204722400006) Bks Demand.

— Machinery Failure Analysis & Troubleshooting. 2nd ed. LC 93-4776. (Practical Machinery Management for Process Plants Ser.: Vol. 2). (Illus.). 726p. 1994. reprint ed. pap. 200.00 (*0-608-07293-1*, 206752100009) Bks Demand.

— Major Process Equipment & Repair. 2nd ed. (Practical Machinery Management for Process Plants Ser.: Vol. 4). 720p. 1997. 95.00 (*0-88415-663-X*, 5663) Gulf Pub.

Bloch, Heinz P. & Hoefner, John J. Reciprocating Compressors: Operating & Maintenance. (Illus.). 504p. 1996. 85.00 (*0-88415-525-0*, 5525) Gulf Pub.

Bloch, Heinz P. & Shamim, Abdus. Oil Mist Lubrication: Practical Applications. LC 97-53166. 280p. 1998. 84.00 (*0-88173-256-7*) Fairmont Pr.

Bloch, Henriette. Grand Dictionnaire Larousse de la Psychologie. (FRE.). 862p. 1991. 175.00 (*0-7859-7664-7*, 2035010306) Fr & Eur.

Bloch, Herbert. Monte Cassino in the Middle Ages, 3 vols. LC 80-39809. (Illus.). 1576p. 1988. 228.95 (*0-674-58655-7*) HUP.

Bloch, Herbert A. & Niederhoffer, Arthur. The Gang: A Study in Adolescent Behavior. LC 76-6517. 231p. 1976. reprint ed. lib. bdg. 65.00 (*0-8371-8865-2*, BLTG, Greenwood Pr) Greenwood.

Bloch, Howard. The British Barnum: The Life of William Holland. 256p. 1996. 26.95 (*1-874312-23-0*, Pub. by Hisarlik Pr) Intl Spec Bk.

Bloch, I. Odoratus Sexualis: Smell & Sex. (Studies in the Psychopathology of Sex). 1992. lib. bdg. 88.00 (*0-8490-5365-X*) Gordon Pr.

— The Physics of Oscillations & Waves: With Applications in Electricity & Mechanics. LC 97-15933. 328p. (C). 1997. text 89.50 (*0-306-45721-0*, Kluwer Plenum) Kluwer Academic.

Bloch, I. S. Is War Now Impossible? Being an Abridgement of the Future of War. (Modern Revivals in Military History Ser.). 460p. 1992. 61.95 (*0-7512-0041-7*, Pub. by Gregg Revivals) Ashgate Pub Co.

Bloch, Iwan. Anthropological Studies in the Strange Sexual Practices of All Races in All Ages, Ancient & Modern, Oriental & Occidental, Primitive & Civilized. Wallis, Keene, tr. from GER. LC 72-9615. reprint ed. 39.50 (*0-404-57410-6*) AMS Pr.

— Marquis de Sade: The Man & His Age. Bruce, James, tr. LC 72-9613. (Human Sexual Behavior Ser.). reprint ed. 45.00 (*0-404-57412-2*) AMS Pr.

— Odoratus Sexualis: A Scientific & Literary Study of Sexual Scents & Erotic Perfumes. LC 72-9620. reprint ed. 42.50 (*0-404-57414-9*) AMS Pr.

— The Sexual Life of Our Time in Its Relation to Modern Civilization. Paul, M. Eden, tr. LC 72-9619. reprint ed. 90.00 (*0-404-57415-7*) AMS Pr.

Bloch, James P. Assessment & Treatment of Multiple Personality & Dissociative Disorders. Smith, Harold H., Jr., ed. LC 91-52545. (Practitioner's Resource Ser.). 112p. 1991. pap. 17.45 (*0-943158-67-2*, ATMBP, Prof Resc Pr) Pro Resource.

Bloch, Jean-Richard, jt. auth. see Rolland, Romain.

Bloch, Jeff, compiled by. Frankly, My Dear: More Than Six Hundred Fifty of the Funniest, Smartest, Gutsiest, Nastiest, Sexiest & Simply Greatest Quotes in Celebration of Women in the Movies. (Illus.). 224p. 1993. pap. 9.95 (*0-8065-1446-9*, Citadel Pr) Carol Pub Group.

— Woman's Book of Movie Quotes. (Illus.). 240p. 1995. pap. 9.95 (*0-8065-1629-1*, Citadel Pr) Carol Pub Group.

***Bloch, Jon P.** Finding Your Leading Man: How to Create Male-To-Male Intimacy & Make Your Relationship a Block. 256p. 2000. pap. 13.95 (*0-312-26736-3*) St Martin.

Bloch, Jon P. New Spirituality, Self & Belonging: How New Agers & Neo-Pagans Talk about Themselves. LC 97-27929. (Religion in the Age of Transformation Ser.). 144p. 1998. 55.00 (*0-275-95957-0*, Praeger Pubs) Greenwood.

Bloch, Joseph S. My Reminiscences. LC 73-2188. (Jewish People; History, Religion, Literature Ser.). 1973. reprint ed. 48.95 (*0-405-05254-5*) Ayer.

Bloch, Julie H. Carving Stamps. (Illus.). 20p. 1997. pap. 5.95 (*1-882817-05-2*) J Bloch.

— Some Linocuts. (Illus.). 26p. 1998. pap. 5.95 (*1-882817-07-9*) J Bloch.

— They Say (Djed Sen) (EGY., Illus.). 16p. (J). 1997. pap. 2.95 (*1-882817-06-0*) J Bloch.

Bloch, Kalman. The Orchestral Clarinet. (Study of Symphonic Repertoire Ser.: Vol. 3). 75p. (Orig.). 1989. pap. text 14.00 (*0-9620014-1-4*) Clarion Music Assn.

— Orchestral Clarinet, Vol. I. (Study of Symphonic Repertoire Ser.). 1989. pap. text 17.95 (*0-317-94094-5*) Clarion Music Assn.

— Orchestral Clarinet, Vol. II. (Study of Symphonic Repertoire Ser.). 1989. pap. text 12.00 (*0-317-94095-3*) Clarion Music Assn.

Bloch, Kenneth D., jt. ed. see Zapol, Warren M.

Bloch, Konrad. Blondes in Venetian Paintings, the Nine-Banded Armadillo, & Other Essays in Biochemistry. (Illus.). 288p. 1997. pap. 17.00 (*0-300-07055-1*) Yale U Pr.

Bloch, Kurt. German Interests & Policies in the Far East. LC 75-30098. (Institute of Pacific Relations Ser.). reprint ed. 39.50 (*0-404-59507-3*) AMS Pr.

Bloch, Lawrence W., ed. see Farr, Naunerle C.

Bloch, Louis M., Jr. Overland to California in 1859: A Guide for Wagon Train Travelers. LC 83-71506. (Illus.). 64p. (J). (gr. 3-6). 1990. pap. 12.95 (*0-914276-04-2*) Bloch & Co OH.

Bloch, Lucille S., jt. auth. see Margulies, Harold.

Bloch, Marc. Feudal Society, 2 vols., Vol. 1. Manyon, L. A., tr. LC 61-4322. 299p. 1964. pap. 11.95 (*0-226-05978-2*, P156) U Ch Pr.

— Feudal Society, 2 vols., Vol. 2. Manyon, L. A., tr. LC 61-4322. 227p. 1964. pap. 11.00 (*0-226-05979-0*, P157) U Ch Pr.

— French Rural History: An Essay on Its Basic Characteristics. Sondheimer, Janet, tr. from FRE. LC 66-15483. (Illus.). 1966. pap. 18.95 (*0-520-01660-2*, Pub. by U CA Pr) Cal Prin Full Svc.

— Historian's Craft. 1964. pap. text 4.16 (*0-07-553696-X*) McGraw.

— Historian's Craft. 1964. pap. 6.36 (*0-394-70512-2*) Random.

Bloch, Marianne N., et al, eds. Women & Education in Sub-Saharan Africa: Power, Opportunities & Constraints. LC 98-9498. (Women & Change in the Developing World Ser.). 350p. 1998. lib. bdg. 59.95 (*1-55587-704-4*) L Rienner.

Bloch, Marianne N. & Pellegrini, Anthony D., eds. Ecological Context of Children's Play. LC 88-26756. 336p. (C). 1989. text 73.25 (*0-89391-520-3*) Ablx Pub.

Bloch, Marie H., ed. Ukrainian Folk Tales. (Hippocrene Folk Tale Ser.). (Illus.). 76p. (J). (gr. 2 up). 1999. 12.50 (*0-7818-0744-1*) Hippocrene Bks.

Bloch, Marie H., ed. see Dubovy, Andrew.

Bloch, Marie H., tr. see Dubovy, Andrew.

Bloch, Marilyn A., ed. see Bloch, Robert H.

Bloch, Maruice & Parry, Jonathan P., eds. Death & the Regeneration of Life. LC 82-9467. 248p. 1982. pap. text 19.95 (*0-521-27037-5*) Cambridge U Pr.

Bloch, Maurice. Marxist Analyses & Social Anthropology. 2nd ed. (ASA Studies). 256p. (C). 1984. pap. 15.95 (*0-422-79500-3*, 9278, Pub. by Tavistock) Routldge.

— Placing the Dead: Tombs, Ancestral Villages, & Kinship Organization in Madagascar. rev. ed. (Illus.). 241p. (C). 1994. reprint ed. pap. text 12.95 (*0-88133-766-8*) Waveland Pr.

— Prey into Hunter: The Politics of Religious Experience. (Lewis Henry Morgan Lectures). 131p. (C). 1991. text 54.95 (*0-521-41154-8*); pap. text 17.95 (*0-521-42312-0*) Cambridge U Pr.

— Ritual, History & Power: Selected Papers in Anthropology. LC 88-36611. (London School of Economics Monographs on Social Anthropology: Vol. 58). 288p. (C). 1989. pap. 22.50 (*0-485-19658-1*, Pub. by Athlone Pr); text 70.00 (*0-485-19558-5*, Pub. by Athlone Pr) Humanities.

Bloch, Maurice & Holcomb, Grant. Joyce Treiman: Friends & Strangers. LC 87-83075. 50p. (Orig.). 1988. pap. 15.00 (*0-9602974-9-9*) USC Fisher Gallery.

Bloch, Maurice & Parry, Jonathan P., eds. Money & the Morality of Exchange. 288p. (C). 1989. text 59.95 (*0-521-36597-X*) Cambridge U Pr.

Bloch, Maurice E. How We Think They Think: Anthropological Approaches to Cognition, Memory & Literacy. 216p. 1998. pap. text 18.00 (*0-8133-3374-1*, Pub. by Westview) HarpC.

Bloch, Michael. Duchess of Windsor. LC 96-30805. 1996. text 27.50 (*0-312-15115-2*) St Martin.

Bloch, Michael, ed. Wallis & Edward - Letters, 1931-1937: The Intimate Correspondence of the Duke & Duchess of Windsor. 368p. 1988. mass mkt. 4.95 (*0-380-70362-9*, Avon Bks) Morrow Avon.

Bloch, Nava. Israel on a Budget. LC 90-64268. 360p. (Orig.). 1995. pap. 12.95 (*0-8442-9538-8*, Passprt Bks) NTC Contemp Pub Co.

Bloch, Norman J. & Michaels, John G. Linear Algebra. (Illus.). 352p. (C). 1992. reprint ed. text 65.00 (*1-878907-59-X*) TechBooks.

Bloch, O. R. La Philosophie de Gassendi: Nominalisme, Materialisme & Metaphysique. (International Archives of the History of Ideas Ser.: No. 38). 555p. 1971. lib. bdg. 141.50 (*90-247-5035-0*) Kluwer Academic.

Bloch, Oscar & Von Wartburg, Walter. Dictionnaire Etymologique de la Langue Francaise. 10th ed. (FRE.). 720p. 1994. 135.00 (*0-8288-5855-1*, FC1016) Fr & Eur.

Bloch, P., comment. Reichenauer Evangelistar. fac. ed. (Glanzlichter der Buchkunst (Splendor of Book Craft) Ser.: Band 5). (GER.). 182p. 1995. reprint ed. 98.00 (*3-201-01643-8*, Pub. by Akademische Druck-und) Balogh.

Bloch, P., et al, eds. Fundamental Symmetries. LC 87-20228. (Ettore Majorana International Science Series, Life Sciences: Vol. 31). (Illus.). 372p. 1987. 95.00 (*0-306-42673-0*, Plenum Trade) Perseus Pubng.

Bloch, Peter C., et al, eds. Land & Agrarian Reform in the Kyrgyz Republic. (Research Paper Ser.: Vol. 128). (Illus.). vii, 130p. (C). 1996. pap. 7.00 (*0-934519-41-2*, RP128) U of Wis Land.

Bloch, Peter C., et al. Land Tenure Issues in Rural Haiti: Review of the Evidence. (Research Paper Ser.: Vol. 94). (Illus.). 94p. (C). 1988. pap. 7.00 (*0-934519-04-8*, RP94) U of Wis Land.

Bloch, Peter C., jt. auth. see Dickerman, Carol W.

Bloch, Phillip. Elements of Style. LC 97-41007. 272p. 1998. mass mkt. 21.99 (*0-446-67423-0*, Pub. by Warner Bks) Little.

Bloch, R. F., jt. ed. see Ingram, D.

Bloch, R. Howard. Etymologies & Genealogies: A Literary Anthropology of the French Middle Ages. LC 82-20036. xii, 296p. (C). 1983. lib. bdg. 30.00 (*0-226-05981-2*) U Ch Pr.

— Etymologies & Genealogies: A Literary Anthropology of the French Middle Ages. LC 82-20036. 294p. (C). 1986. pap. 14.95 (*0-226-05982-0*) U Ch Pr.

— God's Plagiarist: Being an Account of the Fabulous Industry & Irregular Commerce of the Abbe Migne. LC 93-31872. 162p. 1994. 24.95 (*0-226-05970-7*) U Ch Pr.

— God's Plagiarist: Being an Account of the Fabulous Industry & Irregular Commerce of the Abbe Migne. (Illus.). 152p. 1995. pap. text 10.95 (*0-226-05971-5*) U Ch Pr.

— Medieval Misogyny & the Invention of Western Romantic Love. LC 91-12699. 308p. 1992. pap. text 19.95 (*0-226-05973-1*) U Ch Pr.

— Medieval Misogyny & the Invention of Western Romantic Love. LC 91-12699. 304p. 1993. lib. bdg. 45.00 (*0-226-05972-3*) U Ch Pr.

— The Scandal of the Fabliaux. LC 85-16428. 1986. pap. text 8.95 (*0-226-05976-6*) U Ch Pr.

— The Scandal of the Fabliaux. LC 85-16428. 166p. 1986. lib. bdg. 27.00 (*0-226-05975-8*) U Ch Pr.

Bloch, R. Howard & Ferguson, Frances, eds. Misogyny, Misandry, & Misanthropy. (Representation Bks.: No. 3). 1989. pap. 14.95 (*0-520-06546-8*, Pub. by U CA Pr) Cal Prin Full Svc.

Bloch, R. Howard & Hesse, Carla, eds. Future Libraries. LC 94-29447. (Representation Bks.: Vol. 7). (Illus.). 165p. 1995. pap. 17.95 (*0-520-08811-5*, Pub. by U CA Pr) Cal Prin Full Svc.

Bloch, R. Howard & Nichols, Stephen G., eds. Medievalism & the Modernist Temper. (Parallax). (Illus.). 496p. 1996. text 60.00 (*0-8018-5086-X*); pap. text 19.95 (*0-8018-5087-8*) Johns Hopkins.

Bloch, Ricardo. Only Child. (Artists' Books Ser.). (Illus.). 48p. (Orig.). 1995. pap. 15.00 (*0-89822-112-9*) Visual Studies.

Bloch, Richard, jt. auth. see Bloch, Annette.

Bloch, Richard I., jt. auth. see Zack, Arnold M.

Bloch, Robert. Bitter Ends: The Selected Stories of Robert Bloch, Vol. 2. 1990. 12.95 (*0-8065-1201-6*, Citadel Pr) Carol Pub Group.

— Complete Stories of Robert Bloch: Last Rites, Vol. 3. 1991. pap. 12.95 (*0-8065-1227-X*, Citadel Pr) Carol Pub Group.

— The Early Fears. (Illus.). 480p. (C). 29.00 (*1-878252-12-7*) Fedogan & Bremer.

— The Early Fears. limited ed. (Illus.). 480p. (C). 60.00 (*1-878252-13-5*) Fedogan & Bremer.

— Flowers from the Moon & Other Lunacies. LC 98-10086. 296p. 1998. 22.95 (*0-87054-172-2*) Arkham.

***Bloch, Robert.** Hell on Earth. Schow, David J., ed. (Lost Bloch Ser.: Vol. 2). (Illus.). 300p. 2000. 40.00 (*1-892284-62-6*) Subtrrnean Pr.

— Hell on Earth: Lettered Edition. deluxe ed. Schow, David J., ed. (Lost Bloch Ser.: Vol. 2). (Illus.). 300p. 2000. 150.00 (*1-892284-63-4*) Subtrrnean Pr.

Bloch, Robert. Lost in Time & Space with Lefty Feep. Stanley, John, ed. LC 86-71608. (Lefty Feep Ser.: Vol. 1). (Illus.). 276p. 1987. pap. 12.95 (*0-940064-01-4*) Creatures at Large.

— Midnight Pleasures. 1991. pap. 3.95 (*0-8125-1574-9*, Pub. by Tor Bks) St Martin.

— The Opener of the Way. 1993. reprint ed. lib. bdg. 18.95 (*0-89968-421-1*, Lghtyr Pr) Buccaneer Bks.

— Psycho. 224p. 1991. mass mkt. 5.99 (*0-8125-1932-9*, Pub. by Tor Bks) St Martin.

— Psycho. reprint ed. lib. bdg. 21.95 (*0-88411-077-X*) Amereon Ltd.

— Psycho. 1993. reprint ed. lib. bdg. 18.95 (*0-89968-420-3*, Lghtyr Pr) Buccaneer Bks.

— Psycho House. 1991. mass mkt. 4.95 (*0-8125-0919-6*, Pub. by Tor Bks) St Martin.

— Psycho II. 1989. pap. 3.95 (*0-8125-0033-4*) Tor Bks.

— Psycho II. 320p. 1982. mass mkt. 3.50 (*0-446-90804-5*, Pub. by Warner Bks) Little.

— Psycho II. 224p. 1982. 16.00 (*0-918372-09-7*) Whispers.

— Psycho II. limited ed. 224p. 1982. boxed set 36.00 (*0-918372-08-9*) Whispers.

— Robert Bloch's Psychos. 400p. 1998. per. 6.99 (*0-671-88598-7*) PB.

— Strange Eons. LC 78-66962. (Illus.). 1979. 15.00 (*0-918372-30-5*) Whispers.

— There Is a Serpent in Eden. (Orig.). 1979. mass mkt. 2.25 (*0-89083-514-4*, Zebra Kensgtn) Kensgtn Pub Corp.

***Bloch, Robert, ed.** Monsters in Our Midst. 304p. 2000. pap. 13.95 (*0-312-86943-6*, Pub. by Tor Bks) St Martin.

Bloch, Robert, ed. Monsters in Our Mist. 1995. pap. 4.99 (*0-8125-0344-9*, Pub. by Tor Bks) St Martin.

— Psycho-Paths. 320p. 1993. mass mkt. 4.99 (*0-8125-0340-6*) Tor Bks.

— Robert Bloch's Psychos. 341p. 1998. 30.00 (*1-881475-26-3*) Cemetery Dance.

Bloch, Robert & Norton, Andre. The Jekyll Legacy. 1991. mass mkt. 4.99 (*0-8125-1583-8*, Pub. by Tor Bks) St Martin.

Bloch, Robert & Stanley, John. Lost in Time & Space with Lefty Feep. LC 86-71608. 1987. write for info. (*0-940064-03-0*) Creatures at Large.

Bloch, Robert, et al. Nyarlathotep Cycle: Stories about the God of a Thousand Forms. Price, Robert M., ed. (Call of Cthulhu Roleplaying Ser.). 256p. 1997. pap. 10.95 (*1-56882-092-5*) Chaosium.

Bloch, Robert H. Ready Sell Aim: Get Ready to Sell, Sell the Modern Way, Aim for Repeat Customers. Bloch, Marilyn A., ed. (Illus.). 136p. (Orig.). 1995. pap. 16.95 (*0-9650771-0-1*) Swiss Alp.

Bloch, S., et al, eds. Algebraic Geometry: Proceedings of the U. S.-U. S. S. R. Symposium Held in Chicago, June 20-July 14, 1989. (Lecture Notes in Mathematics Ser.: Vol. 1479). vii, 300p. 1991. pap. 41.00 (*0-387-54456-9*) Spr-Verlag.

Bloch, S. J., et al. Applications of Algebraic K-Theory to Algebraic Geometry & Number Theory, 2 pts., Pt. 1. LC 86-7904. (Contemporary Mathematics Ser.: Vol. 55). 406p. 1986. pap. 45.00 (*0-8218-5055-5*, CONM/55.1) Am Math.

— Applications of Algebraic K-Theory to Algebraic Geometry & Number Theory, 2 pts., Pt. 2. LC 86-7904. (Contemporary Mathematics Ser.: Vol. 55). 818p. 1986. pap. 46.00 (*0-8218-5056-3*, CONM/55.2) Am Math.

— Applications of Algebraic K-Theory to Algebraic Geometry & Number Theory, 2 pts., Set. LC 86-7904. (Contemporary Mathematics Ser.: Vol. 55). 856p. 1986. pap. 79.00 (*0-8218-5054-7*, CONM/55) Am Math.

Bloch, S. P. Algebraic Geometry-Bowdoin 1985, 2 pts., Pt. I. LC 87-12306. (PSPUM Ser.: Vol. 46). 481p. 1987. text 74.00 (*0-8218-1476-1*, PSPUM/46.1) Am Math.

— Algebraic Geometry-Bowdoin 1985, 2 pts., Pt. II. LC 87-12306. (PSPUM Ser.: Vol. 46). 513p. 1987. text 80.00 (*0-8218-1480-X*, PSPUM/46.2) Am Math.

— Algebraic Geometry-Bowdoin 1985, 2 pts., Set. LC 87-12306. (PSPUM Ser.: Vol. 46). 994p. 1987. text 146.00 (*0-8218-1481-8*, PSPUM/46) Am Math.

Bloch, Selwyn, jt. auth. see Brearley, Kate.

Bloch, Sidney. An Introduction to the Psychotherapies. 3rd ed. (Illus.). 361p. (C). 1996. text 75.00 (*0-19-262710-4*); pap. text 39.50 (*0-19-262709-0*) OUP.

Bloch, Sidney, ed. An Introduction to the Psychotherapies. 2nd ed. 250p. 1986. pap. 28.50 (*0-19-261469-X*) OUP.

Bloch, Sidney, et al, eds. Psychiatric Ethics. 3rd ed. LC 98-24779. (Illus.). 568p. 1999. pap. text 59.50 (*0-19-262899-2*) OUP.

Bloch, Sidney & Singh, Bruce. Understanding Troubled Minds: A Guide to Mental Illness & Its Treatment. LC 98-170613. 320p. 1997. pap. 17.95 (*0-522-84642-4*, Pub. by Melbourne Univ Pr) Paul & Co Pubs.

— Understanding Troubled Minds: A Guide to Mental Illness & Its Treatment. LC 99-24160. 1999. pap. 19.95 (*0-8147-9859-4*) NYU Pr.

Bloch, Sidney & Singh, Bruce, eds. Foundations of Clinical Psychiatry. LC 94-165714. 488p. (C). 1994. pap. 49.95 (*0-522-84531-2*, Pub. by Melbourne Univ Pr) Paul & Co Pubs.

Bloch, Sidney & Singh, Bruce S. Understanding Troubled Minds: A Guide to Mental Illness & Its Treatment. LC 99-24160. 2000. text 55.00 (*0-8147-9858-6*) NYU Pr.

An Asterisk (*) at the beginning of an entry indicates that the title is appearing for the first time.

Bloch, Sidney, et al. The Family in Clinical Psychiatry. LC 93-45494. (Medical Publications). (Illus.). 312p. 1994. 79.50 (*0-19-262311-7*); pap. text 36.50 (*0-19-262310-9*) OUP.

Bloch, Sidney, jt. auth. see Coady, Margaret.

Bloch-Smith, Elizabeth. Judahite Burial Practices & Beliefs about the Dead. (Journal for the Study of the Old Testament Supplement Ser.: No. 123). 314p. (C). 1992. 85.00 (*1-85075-335-0*, Pub. by Sheffield Acad) CUP Services.

Bloch, Sonny & Ahlert, Gary. Selling Your Idea or Invention: The Birthplace to Marketplace Guide. LC 94-19043. (Illus.). 240p. 1994. 19.95 (*1-55972-244-4*, Birch Ln Pr) Carol Pub Group.

Bloch, Sonny & Hollingsworth, Jerome L. Sonny Bloch's Cover Your Assets. LC 92-10939. 160p. (Orig.). 1992. pap. 9.95 (*0-399-51778-2*, Perigee Bks) Berkley Pub.

***Bloch, Spencer J.** Higher Regulators, Algebraic K-Theory & Zeta Functions of Elliptic Curves. (CRMM Ser.: Vol. 11). 97p. 2000. 24.00 (*0-8218-2114-8*) Am Math.

Bloch, Steven A., jt. auth. see Ungerleider, Steven.

Bloch, Stuart M. The Liability Game. 1988. pap. 59.95 (*0-318-42425-8*) Exec Ent Pubns.

Bloch, Stuart M., ed. Understanding R-41C: An Annotated Edition of the Federal Home Loan Bank Boards Standard on Appraisals. 31p. 1987. 4.95 (*0-318-22826-2*) Land Dev Inst.

— The Workout Game: Managing Non-Performing Real Estate Assets. LC 86-81722. 358p. 1987. 59.95 (*0-317-01444-7*) Land Dev Inst.

Bloch, Stuart M. & Ingersoll, William B. Florida Real Estate Timesharing Act: Annotated Edition, Including 1984 Supplement. 2nd ed. 150p. 1983. 34.95 (*0-318-19280-2*); write for info. (*0-318-60373-X*) Land Dev Inst.

— Interstate Land Sales Act: Annotated Edition. 33p. 1980. 12.95 (*0-318-19282-9*) Land Dev Inst.

— Regulation Z Handbook. 44p. 1982. 19.95 (*0-318-19283-7*) Land Dev Inst.

Bloch, Stuart M. & Ingersoll, William B., eds. Digest of State Land Sales Regulations. 200p. 150.00 (*0-318-19273-X*) Land Dev Inst.

— Land Development Law Reporter. 395.00 (*0-318-19272-1*) Land Dev Inst.

Bloch, Stuart M., ed. see Real Estate Timesharing & the Property Staff.

Bloch, Susan L. Supreme Court Politics: The Institution & Its Procedure. Krattenmaker, Thomas G., ed. LC 94-9272. 698p. (C). 1994. pap. 45.50 (*0-314-03492-7*) West Pub.

— Supreme Court Politics: The Institution & Its Procedure, Teacher's Manual to Accompany. Krattenmaker, Tom, ed. (American Casebook Ser.). 17p. 1994. pap. text. write for info. (*0-314-04153-2*) West Pub.

***Bloch, Sylvan C.** Excel for Engineers & Scientists. LC 99-58797. (Illus.). 280p. 1999. pap. 32.95 incl. cd-rom (*0-471-32169-9*) Wiley.

Bloch, Sylvan C. Introduction to Classical & Quantum Harmonic Oscillators. LC 96-44728. 384p. 1997. text 85.00 incl. audio compact disk (*0-471-14744-3*) Wiley.

— Spreadsheet Analysis for Engineers & Scientists. LC 95-10234. 336p. 1995. pap. 54.95 (*0-471-12683-7*, Wiley-Interscience) Wiley.

Bloch, Talia. Doing Business in Eastern Europe. (Doing Business in Regions & Countries Around the World Ser.). Date not set. write for info. (*1-882390-87-3*) Princeton Trng.

— Doing Business in North America. (Doing Business in Regions & Countries Around the World Ser.). Date not set. write for info. (*1-882390-85-7*) Princeton Trng.

Bloch, Talia & Rosenberg, Suzanna. Doing Business in France. (Doing Business in Regions & Countries Around the World Ser.). 80p. Date not set. write for info. (*1-882390-58-X*) Princeton Trng.

Bloch, Werner. Melancholie und Bestandigkeit: Humanistische Gelehrsamkeit und Individuelle Weltsicht Im Poetischen Werk Jean de Spondes. (Franzosische Sprache und Literatur Ser.: Bd. 220). (GER.). 239p. 1998. 39.95 (*3-631-47755-4*) P Lang Pubng.

Blocher. Cost Management: Study Guide. 352p. 1998. pap., student ed. 26.88 (*0-07-366253-4*) McGraw.

— Cost Management & Cases. 1998. text 70.25 (*0-07-561946-6*) McGraw.

Blocher & Chen. Cost Management. LC 98-8633. 1998. 70.25 (*0-07-005916-0*) McGraw.

Blocher, jt. auth. see Thomas.

***Blocher, Chris.** FrontPage 2000 - Advanced: Instructor Edition. 184p. (C). 1999. pap., teacher ed. write for info. (*1-58719-214-4*) Element K.

— FrontPage 2000 - Advanced: Student Manual. 182p. (C). 1999. pap., student ed. write for info. (*1-58719-213-6*) Element K.

Blocher, Donald H. Career Actualization & Life Planning. LC 88-82697. 212p. 1989. pap. text 19.95 (*0-89108-206-9*) Love Pub Co.

***Blocher, Donald H.** Counseling: A Developmental Approach. 4th ed. LC 99-43402. 400p. 2000. text 55.00 (*0-471-25462-2*) Wiley.

— The Evolution of Counseling Psychology. LC 00-20289. 2000. write for info. (*0-8261-1348-6*) Springer Pub.

***Blocher, Edward, et al.** Cases & Readings in Strategic Cost Management for Use with Cost Management: A Strategic Emphisis. 260p. (C). 1998. pap. 26.88 (*0-07-366252-6*) McGrw-H Hghr Educ.

— Cost Management: A Strategic Emphasis - Ready Notes. 208p. (C). 1998. pap. 14.38 (*0-07-366254-2*) McGrw-H Hghr Educ.

***Blocher, Edward J.** Cost Management: A Strategic Emphasis. 854p. 1999. 90.75 (*0-07-115970-3*) McGraw.

Blocher, Henri. Evil & the Cross. LC 94-39873. 153p. (Orig.). 1995. pap. 12.99 (*0-8308-1526-0*, 1526) InterVarsity.

— In the Beginning: The Opening Chapters of Genesis. Preston, David G., tr. from FRE. LC 84-12800. 240p. (Orig.). 1984. pap. 15.99 (*0-87784-325-2*, 325) InterVarsity.

— Original Sin: Illuminating the Riddle. LC 98-53406. (New Studies in Biblical Theology). 158p. 1999. pap. 18.00 (*0-8028-4411-1*) Eerdmans.

Blocher, John M., Jr., ed. see International Conference on Chemical Vapor Deposit.

Blocher, Larry, et al. Teaching Music Through Performance in Band, Vol. 2. Miles, Richard, ed. 665p. 1998. 39.50 (*1-57999-028-2*, G-4889) GIA Pubns.

Blocher, Larry R. & Miles, Richard B. Block Scheduling: Implications for Music Education. LC 96-61827. 201p. (Orig.). 1996. pap. 19.95 (*0-9655808-0-6*) Focus on Excell.

— Scheduling & Teaching Music. 1999. pap. 19.95 (*0-9655808-2-2*) Focus on Excell.

Blocher, Mark. The Right to Die? Caring Alternatives to Euthanasia. 212p. 1999. pap. 10.99 (*0-8024-7739-9*) Moody.

***Blocher, Wendy.** Happy Birthday, Vol. 2457. (Illus.). 32p. 1999. pap. 6.98 (*1-57471-629-8*, 2457) Creat Teach Pr.

Blocher, Wendy, ed. see Conrad, Marjorie.

Blocher, Wendy, ed. see Garcia, Adela.

Blocher, Wendy, ed. see Snyder, Juli & Graves, Kimberlee.

Blocher, Wendy, ed. see Throop, Sara.

Blochet, Edgar. Musulman Painting, 12th-17th Century. Binyon, C. M., tr. from FRE. (Illus.). 1975. reprint ed. lib. bdg. 50.00 (*0-87817-155-X*) Hacker.

Blochet, Edward. The Role of Analytical Procedures in Detecting Management Fraud. Barth, Claire, ed. 73p. (Orig.). 1993. pap. 20.00 (*0-86641-218-2*, 93280) Inst Mgmt Account.

Blochl, P. E., et al, eds. Computations for the Nano-Scale: Proceedings of the NATO Advanced Research Workshop, Aspet, France October 12-16, 1992. LC 93-8335. (NATO Advanced Science Institutes Series C: Mathematical & Physical Sciences). 304p. (C). 1993. text 250.00 (*0-7923-2360-2*) Kluwer Academic.

Blochle, Herbert. Luthers Stellung zum Heidentum im Spannungsfeld von Tradition, Humanismus und Reformation. (Europaische Hochschulschriften Ser.: Reihe 23, Bd. 531). (GER.). 534p. 1995. 74.95 (*3-631-48662-6*) P Lang Pubng.

Blochman, Lawrence G., jt. auth. see Callas, Evangelia.

Blochmann, Henry F. The Prosody of the Persians, According to Saifi, Jami & Other Writers. 1976. lib. bdg. 59.95 (*0-8490-2487-0*) Gordon Pr.

Block. Atlas of Implant Surgery. (C). 2001. text. write for info. (*0-7216-8317-7*, W B Saunders Co) Harcrt Hlth Sci Grp.

— The Changing World in Plays & Theatre. 1991. write for info. (*0-316-09972-4*) Little.

— Corporate Venturing. 1995. pap. 14.95 (*0-07-103631-8*) McGraw.

— Cps Bus 481 Mngrl Fin Revse Ed. 2nd ed. 1999. pap. text 40.00 (*0-07-236017-8*) McGraw.

— Design Essentials. 2nd ed. LC 99-43242. 130p. 1999. pap. text 26.60 (*0-13-502469-2*) P-H.

— Found. Finance Management Ready Notes. 8th ed. 1996. 67.00 (*0-256-23441-8*) McGraw.

— Foundations of Financial Management. 8th ed. 1998. 74.25 (*0-256-24382-4*) McGraw.

— Foundations of Financial Management. 9th ed. LC 99-31782. 1999. 67.00 (*0-07-228336-X*) McGraw.

— 101 Best Cover Letters. LC 99-19053. 1999. 11.95 (*0-07-134257-5*) McGraw.

— Perfect Nonprofit Boards. LC 99-160603. 168p. (C). 1998. pap. text 21.95 (*0-536-01184-2*) Pearson Custom.

— Safe Love. (J). (gr. 7 up). 14.95 (*0-06-028127-8*) HarpC.

— Sex over 50. LC 98-42503. (C). 1998. 27.95 (*0-13-080968-3*) P-H.

Block, A. G. & Buck, Claudia, eds. California Political Almanac, 1997-1998. (Illus.). 540p. (Orig.). 1997. 34.95 (*0-930302-46-X*) Cal Journal.

Block, A. Harvey. Impact Analysis & Local Area Planning: An Input-Output Study. 138p. 1977. pap. text 21.95 (*0-87855-774-1*) Transaction Pubs.

Block, Adrienne F. Amy Beach, Passionate Victorian: The Life & Works of the American Composer, 1867-1944. (Illus.). 448p. 1998. 45.00 (*0-19-507408-4*) OUP.

— The Early French Parody, Vol. 1. LC 83-1175. (Studies in Musicology: No. 36). 227p. reprint ed. pap. 70.40 (*0-8357-1437-3*, 207060200001) Bks Demand.

— The Early French Parody, Vol. 2. LC 83-1175. (Studies in Musicology: No. 36). 696p. reprint ed. pap. 200.00 (*0-8357-1438-1*, 207060200002) Bks Demand.

Block, Adrienne F. & Neuls-Bates, Carol, eds. Women in American Music: A Bibliography of Music & Literature. LC 79-7722. (Illus.). 302p. 1979. lib. bdg. 59.95 (*0-313-21410-7*, NBW/, Greenwood Pr) Greenwood.

***Block, Adrienne Fried.** Amy Beach, Passionate Victorian: The Life & Work of an American Composer, 1867-1944. (Illus.). 409p. 2000. pap. 19.95 (*0-19-513784-1*) OUP.

Block, Alan. East Side - West Side: Organizing Crime in New York, 1930-1950. LC 83-4773. 280p. 1995. reprint ed. pap. 24.95 (*0-87855-931-0*) Transaction Pubs.

Block, Alan A. Anonymous Toil: A Reevaluation of the American Radical Novel in the Twentieth Century. 152p. (Orig.). (C). 1992. pap. text 24.50 (*0-8191-8559-0*) U Pr of Amer.

— I'm Only Bleeding: Education As the Practice of Social Violence Against Children. LC 96-31810. (Counterpoints Studies in the Postmodern Theory of Education Ser.: Vol. 10). VI, 190p. (C). 1997. pap. 29.95 (*0-8204-2684-9*) P Lang Pubng.

— Occupied Reading: Critical Foundations for Ecological Theory. LC 94-22358. (Critical Education Practice Ser.: Vol. 3). 264p. 1995. pap. text 23.95 (*0-8153-1925-8*, SS860) Garland.

— Occupied Reading: Critical Foundations for Ecological Theory. LC 94-22358. (Critical Education Practice Ser.: Vol. 3). 264p. 1995. text 47.00 (*0-8153-0932-5*, SS860) Garland.

— Organizing Crime: Essays in Opposition. 254p. 1991. lib. bdg. 98.50 (*0-7923-1033-0*) Kluwer Academic.

— The Serious Crime Community & the Underground Economy: A Postscript. LC 97-20175. xii, 345p. 1998. pap. text 24.95 (*1-56000-971-3*) Transaction Pubs.

— Space, Time & Organized Crime. 2nd ed. 264p. (C). 1993. text 44.95 (*1-56000-104-6*) Transaction Pubs.

Block, Andrew. The English Novel, Seventeen Forty to Eighteen Fifty: A Catalogue Including Prose Romances, Short Stories, & Translations of Foreign Fiction. rev. ed. LC 81-17866. 349p. 1982. reprint ed. lib. bdg. 77.50 (*0-313-23224-5*, BLEN) Greenwood.

Block, Andrew R. Presurgical Psychological Screening in Chronic Pain Syndromes: A Guide for the Behavioral Health Practitioner. LC 96-18082. 150p. 1996. 49.95 (*0-8058-2407-3*); pap. 24.50 (*0-8058-2408-1*) L Erlbaum Assocs.

Block, Andrew R., et al, eds. Handbook of Pain Syndromes: Biopsychosocial Perspectives. LC 98-36687. 705p. 1998. 175.00 (*0-8058-2680-7*) L Erlbaum Assocs.

Block, Anita. The Changing World in Plays & Theatre. LC 73-77721. (Theatre, Film & Literature Ser.). 448p. 1971. reprint ed. lib. bdg. 55.00 (*0-306-71359-4*) Da Capo.

Block, Anita R. Love & Kisses. 1964. pap. 5.25 (*0-8222-0689-7*) Dramatists Play.

— Love Is a Four Letter Word. LC 73-116940. (Short Story Index Reprint Ser.). 1977. 21.95 (*0-8369-3442-3*) Ayer.

Block, Arlene, jt. auth. see WiseBooks Staff.

Block, Arthur R., jt. auth. see Rebell, Michael A.

Block, Barbara. Chutes & Adders. 1995. pap. 4.99 (*0-8217-4997-8*) NAL.

— Community Development Corporations. Segel, Michael, ed. 13p. (Orig.). 1977. pap. 8.00 (*0-317-04853-8*) Natl Coun Econ Dev.

— In Plain Sight: A Robin Light Mystery. LC 96-76016. 321p. 1996. 18.95 (*1-57566-059-8*, Knsington) Kensgtn Pub Corp.

— In Plain Sight: A Robin Light Mystery. 336p. 1997. mass mkt. 5.50 (*1-57566-199-3*, Knsington) Kensgtn Pub Corp.

— The Scent of Murder. LC 96-80067. 336p. 1997. 18.95 (*1-57566-195-0*, Knsington) Kensgtn Pub Corp.

— The Scent of Murder. 336p. 1998. pap. 5.99 (*1-57566-331-7*) Kensgtn Pub Corp.

— Twister. 304p. 1996. mass mkt. 4.99 (*1-57566-062-8*, Knsington) Kensgtn Pub Corp.

— Vanishing Act. LC 98-65136. 352p. 1998. 20.00 (*1-57566-326-0*, Knsington) Kensgtn Pub Corp.

Block, Barbara & Benjamin, Janice Y. How to Become Happily Employed in Phoenix: A Step-by-Step Guide to Finding the Job That is Right for You. LC 84-522. 208p. 1988. pap. 9.95 (*0-9613630-4-5*) Career Manage Pr.

Block, Barbara & Holbrook, Gail. The Bride's Little Instruction Book. 96p. 1995. mass mkt. 4.99 (*0-8217-0149-5*, Zebra Kensgtn) Kensgtn Pub Corp.

Block, Brian P. & Hostettler, John. Hanging in the Balance. LC 98-174702. 288 p. 1997. write for info. (*1-872870-47-3*) Waterside Pr.

Block, C. B., jt. auth. see Vandecasteele, C.

Block, Carolyn & Block, Richard, eds. Trends, Risks, & Interventions in Lethal Violence: Proceedings of the Third Annual Spring Symposium of the Homicide Research Working Group. (Illus.). 370p. (C). 1997. reprint ed. pap. text 50.00 (*0-7881-3494-9*) DIANE Pub.

Block, Carolyn R., et al, eds. Crime Analysis Through Computer Mapping. rev. ed. LC 94-70186. (Case Studies in Police Decision-Making: Vol. 1). (Illus.). 297p. (Orig.). 1995. pap. 29.00 (*1-878734-34-2*) Police Exec Res.

Block, Carolyn R. & Block, Richard L., eds. Questions & Answers in Lethal & Non-Lethal Violence: Proceeding of the Second Annual Workshop of the Homicide Research Working Group. (Illus.). 230p. (Orig.). (C). 1994. pap. text 50.00 (*0-7881-1422-0*) DIANE Pub.

— Questions & Answers in Lethal & Non-Lethal Violence: Proceedings of the First Annual Workshop of the Homicide Research Working Group. (Illus.). 141p. 1994. reprint ed. pap. text 35.00 (*0-7881-1474-3*) DIANE Pub.

Block, Carolyn R. & Green, Lynn A. The Geoarchive Handbook: A Guide for Developing a Geographic Database As an Information Foundation for Community Policing. (Illus.). 53p. 1998. pap. text 25.00 (*0-7881-4885-0*) DIANE Pub.

Block, Cathy C. Literacy Difficulties: Diagnosis & Instruction. LC 96-76564. 608p. (C). 1996. text 61.50 (*0-15-500364-X*, Pub. by Harcourt Coll Pubs) Harcourt.

Block, Cathy C. & Mangieri, John N. Power Thinking for Success. 238p. 1996. pap. text 16.95 (*1-57129-015-2*) Brookline Bks.

— Reason to Read Vol. 1: Thinking Strategies for Life Through Literature. LC 95-187327. 252p. (Orig.). 1995. pap. 25.49 (*0-201-49047-1*) Addison-Wesley.

— Reason to Read Vol. 1: Thinking Strategies for Life Through Literature. Fowkes, Lois & Farber, Rachel, eds. (Reason to Read Ser.). (Illus.). 282p. (Orig.). 1995. pap., teacher ed. 18.95 (*0-201-49048-X*) Supplementary Div.

Block, Cathy C. & Zinke, Jo A. Creating a Culturally Enriched Curriculum for Grades K-6. 256p. 1994. pap. text 34.99 (*0-205-14691-0*, Longwood Div) Allyn.

Block, Cathy C., et al. Literacy Difficulties: Diagnosis & Instruction. 2nd ed. 608p. (C). 1996. text 64.50 (*0-15-502841-3*, Pub. by Harcourt Coll Pubs) Harcourt.

Block, Cheryl, et al. Editor in Chief A1: Grammar Disasters & Punctuation Faux Pas. (Illus.). 68p. (Orig.). (J). (gr. 4-6). 1994. pap. 14.95 (*0-89455-515-4*) Crit Think Bks.

— Editor in Chief B1: Grammar Disasters & Punctuation Faux Pas. (Illus.). 86p. (Orig.). (YA). (gr. 6-8). 1995. pap. 15.95 (*0-89455-516-2*) Crit Think Bks.

— Editor in Chief C1: Grammar Disasters & Punctuation Faux Pas. 2nd expanded ed. (Illus.). 134p. (Orig.). (YA). (gr. 8 up). 1999. pap. 16.95 (*0-89455-517-0*) Crit Think Bks.

Block, Cheryl D. Corporate Taxation: Examples & Explanations. LC 97-38190. 484p. 1998. pap. text. write for info. (*1-56706-633-X*) Panel Pubs.

Block, Collins, et al. Reason to Read Vol. 1: Thinking Strategies for Life Through Literature, Vol. 3. (Reason to Read Ser.). (Illus.). 300p. (Orig.). (J). 1996. pap., teacher ed. 23.70 (*0-201-49049-8*) Addison-Wesley.

Block, Daniel I. The Book of Ezekiel: Chapters 25-48. (New International Commentary on the Old Testament Ser.: Vol. 2). 792p. 1998. 50.00 (*0-8028-2536-2*) Eerdmans.

— The Book of Ezekiel 1-24. (New International Commentary on the New Testament Ser.). 872p. 1997. 48.00 (*0-8028-2535-4*) Eerdmans.

— Judges - Ruth. LC 99-11089. (New American Commentary Ser.). 1999. 32.99 (*0-8054-0106-7*) Broadman.

Block, Darrell L., ed. Three Views on the Millennium & Beyond. LC 98-37483. (Counterpoints Ser.). 208p. 2000. pap. 16.99 (*0-310-20143-8*) Zondervan.

Block, Dave. MMS - No Laughing Matter: Male Menopausal Syndrome. (Illus.). 52p. 1993. pap. 1.50 (*0-9639812-0-X*) Laid Back Ent.

Block, David. Mission Culture on the Upper Amazon: Native Tradition, Jesuit Enterprise, & Secular Policy in Moxos, 1660-1880. LC 93-24620. (Illus.). xiii, 240p. 1994. text 40.00 (*0-8032-1232-1*) U of Nebr Pr.

Block, David, ed. SALALM & the Area Studies Community. xi, 235p. (Orig.). 1994. pap. 45.00 (*0-917617-39-8*) SALALM.

Block, David L. & Greenberg, J. Mayo, eds. New Extragalactic Perspectives in the New South Africa: Proceedings of International Conference on Cold Dust & Galaxy Morphology, Johannesburg, South Africa, 1996. LC 96-34039. (Astrophysics & Space Science Library: Vol. 209). 653p. 1996. text 242.50 (*0-7923-4223-2*) Kluwer Academic.

***Block, David L., et al.** Toward a New Millennium in Galaxy Morphology - From z=0 to the Lyman Break. 828p. 2000. 345.00 (*0-7923-6185-7*, Kluwer Plenum) Kluwer Academic.

Block, Deborah P. How to Have a Winning Job Interview. 1992. pap. 7.95 (*0-8442-6687-6*, VGM Career) NTC Contemp Pub Co.

Block, Dennis J. The Business Judgement Rule: Fiduciary Duties of Corporate Directors & Officers. write for info. (*0-318-66842-4*) P-H.

— New Strategies in Contests for Corporate Control 1999. LC 99-177620. (Corporate & Practice Course Handbook Ser.). 696 p. 1999. 99.00 (*0-87224-558-6*) PLI.

Block, Dennis J., et al, eds. The Corporate Counsellor's Desk Book. 2nd ed. 1985. 75.00 (*0-317-29398-2*, #H43848) Harcourt.

Block, Dennis J. & Epstein, Michael A. The Corporate Counsellor's Deskbook. 5th ed. LC 99-10341. 1999. ring bd. 220.00 (*0-7355-0381-8*) Panel Pubs.

Block, Dennis J. & Epstein, Michael A., eds. The Corporate Counsellor's Deskbook. 4th ed. 954p. 1992. ring bd. 125.00 (*0-13-225079-9*) Aspen Law.

Block, Dennis J. & Pitt, Harvey L. Contests for Corporate Control. 1432p. 1991. pap. text 35.00 (*0-685-49911-1*, B4-6954) PLI.

Block, Dennis J. & Solovy, Jerold S. Dealing with Hostile Takeover Threats. 35.00 (*0-317-29517-9*, #CO3697) Harcourt.

Block, Dennis J., et al. The Business Judgment Rule: Fiduciary Duties of Corporate..., 2 vols. 5th ed. LC 96-45452. xxvii, 2496p. 1998. boxed set 195.00 (*1-56706-327-6*) Aspen Law.

— The Business Judgment Rule: Fiduciary Duties of Corporate Directors. 4th ed. LC 93-39489. 1993. 150.00 (*0-13-299744-4*) Aspen Law.

— The Business Judgment Rule: Fiduciary Duties of Corporate Directors. 4th ed. 1100p. ring bd. 173.00 (*1-56706-171-0*, 1903X) Panel Pubs.

— The Corporate Counsellor's Deskbook. 2nd ed. LC 84-28913. 1984. 75.00 (*0-15-004384-8*) Harcourt.

Block, Diana R., ed. The Art of Whitfield Lovell: Whispers from the Walls. LC 99-39459. (Illus.). 88p. 1999. pap. 29.95 (*1-57441-075-X*, Pub. by UNTX Pr) Tex A&M Univ Pr.

— Charles T. Williams Retrospective with Friends: An Exhibition. LC 97-43251. (Illus.). 52p. 1998. pap. 25.00 (*1-57441-045-8*) UNTX Pr.

***Block, Dorian.** The Dori Story. 2000. pap. 18.00 (*0-7388-2224-8*) Xlibris Corp.

Block Drug Company, jt. auth. see American Dental Hygienists' Association Staff.

Block, E., ed. Heteratom Chemistry. 376p. 1990. 149.00 (*0-471-18731-3*) Wiley.

***Block Ediger, Tina.** Window to the World: Extraordinary Stories from a Century of Overseas Mission, 1900-2000. (Illus.). 180p. 1999. pap. 19.95 (*0-87303-396-5*) Faith & Life.

Block, Edwin. Ideas for the University: Proceedings of Marquette University's Mission Seminar & Conference. LC 95-41721. 231p. (Orig.). 1995. 25.00 (*0-87462-002-3*) Marquette.

Block, Edwin F., Jr. Rituals of Dis-Integration: Romance & Madness in the Victorian Psychomythic Tale. LC 93-2310. (Origins of Modernism Ser.). 264p. 1993. text 20.00 (*0-8153-1083-8*, H1650) Garland.

Block, Elizabeth. The Effects of Divine Manifestations on the Reader's Perspective in Virgil's "Aenead" rev. ed. Connor, W. R., ed. LC 80-2640. (Monographs in Classical Studies). 1981. lib. bdg. 42.95 (*0-405-14028-2*) Ayer.
— Ovid Ars Amatoria, Bk. 1. (Latin Commentaries Ser.). 83p. (Orig.). (C). 1984. pap. text 6.00 (*0-929524-45-4*) Bryn Mawr Commentaries.
Block, Eric. Heteroatom Chemistry. 376p. 1990. 95.00 (*0-89573-743-4*, Wiley-VCH) Wiley.
Block, Eric, ed. Advances in Sulfur Chemistry, Vol. 2. 1994. 109.50 (*0-7623-0074-4*) Jai Pr.
Block, Eugene B. Science vs. Crime. LC 79-21941. (Illus.). 1980. 12.95 (*0-89666-007-9*) Cragmont Pubns.
— Science vs. Crime. LC 79-21941. (Illus.). 208p. 1980. pap. 6.95 (*0-89666-010-9*) Cragmont Pubns.
— When Men Play God: The Fallacy of Capital Punishment. LC 81-15143. 1984. 14.95 (*0-89666-015-X*) Cragmont Pubns.
Block, Francesca Lia. Baby Be-Bop. LC 94-44314. (Joanna Cotler Bks.). 96p. (J). (gr. 7 up). 1995. lib. bdg. 13.89 (*0-06-024880-7*) HarpC Child Bks.
— Baby Be-Bop. LC 94-44314. (Illus.). 112p. (YA). (gr. 7 up). 1997. pap. 4.95 (*0-06-447176-4*, HarpTrophy) HarpC Child Bks.
— Baby Be-Bop. 1997. 9.60 (*0-606-11065-8*, Pub. by Turtleback) Demco.
Block, Francesca Lia. Block Book IV. (gr. 7 up). 4.95 (*0-06-440745-4*) HarpC Child Bks.
— Charm. (gr. 7 up). pap. 4.95 (*0-06-440744-6*) HarpC Child Bks.
Block, Francesca Lia. Cherokee Bat & the Goat Guys. LC 91-20706. (Trophy Keypoint Bk.). 128p. (YA). (gr. 7 up). 1993. pap. 4.95 (*0-06-447095-4*, HarpTrophy) HarpC Child Bks.
Block, Francesca Lia. Cherokee Bat & the Goat Guys. 1993. 9.60 (*0-606-05201-1*, Pub. by Turtleback) Demco.
— Dangerous Angels: The 5 Weetzie Bat Books. LC 97-40933. 496p. (YA). 1998. pap. 12.00 (*0-06-440697-0*, Perennial) HarperTrade.
Block, Francesca Lia. Girl Goddess #9: Nine Stories. LC 95-52050. Vol. 9. 192p. (YA). (gr. 7-12). 1996. 14.95 (*0-06-027211-2*) HarpC Child Bks.
— Girl Goddess #9: Nine Stories. LC 95-52050. (Girl Goddess Ser.). 192p. (YA). (gr. 7-12). 1998. pap. 4.95 (*0-06-447187-X*, HarpTrophy) HarpC Child Bks.
— Girl Goddess #9: Nine Stories. (YA). (gr. 7 up). 1998. 10.05 (*0-606-12944-8*, Pub. by Turtleback) Demco.
***Block, Francesca Lia.** The Hanged Man. LC 94-720. (Illus.). 160p. (J). 1999. mass mkt. 7.95 (*0-06-440832-9*) HarpC.
Block, Francesca Lia. The Hanged Man. LC 94-720. 144p. (YA). (gr. 7 up). 1994. lib. bdg. 15.89 (*0-06-024537-9*, J Cotler) HarpC Child Bks.
— I Was a Teenage Fairy. LC 98-14598. 192p. (J). (gr. 7 up). 1998. lib. bdg. 14.89 (*0-06-027748-3*) HarpC.
— I Was a Teenage Fairy. LC 98-14598. 192p. (YA). (gr. 7 up). 1998. 14.95 (*0-06-027747-5*) HarpC.
***Block, Francesca Lia.** I Was a Teenage Fairy. LC 98-14598. 192p. (YA). (gr. 7-12). 2000. mass mkt. 7.95 (*0-06-440862-0*, HarpTrophy) HarpC Child Bks.
— I Was a Teenage Fairy. (Illus.). (J). 2000. 13.30 (*0-606-18903-3*) Turtleback.
— Missing Angel Juan. LC 92-38299. (Illus.). 144p. (YA). (gr. 7 up). 1993. 14.89 (*0-06-023007-X*) HarpC Child Bks.
Block, Francesca Lia. Missing Angel Juan. LC 92-38299. (Trophy Bk.). 144p. (J). (gr. 12 up). 1995. pap. 4.95 (*0-06-447120-9*, HarpTrophy) HarpC Child Bks.
— Missing Angel Juan. (J). 1995. 9.60 (*0-606-08463-0*, Pub. by Turtleback) Demco.
***Block, Francesca Lia.** Nymph. 128p. 2000. 16.95 (*1-885865-30-9*) Circlet Pr.
— The Rose & the Beast: Fairy Tales Retold. 240p. (J). write for info. (*0-06-029342-X*) HarpC Child Bks.
— The Rose & the Beast: Fairy Tales Retold. LC 00-22444. 240p. (YA). (gr. 7-12). 2000. 14.95 (*0-06-028129-4*) HarpC Child Bks.
— The Rose & the Beast: Fairy Tales Retold. LC 00-22444. 240p. (YA). (gr. 7 up). 2000. 14.89 (*0-06-028130-8*) HarpC Child Bks.
— Safe Love. (J). (gr. 7 up). 2000. lib. bdg. 14.89 (*0-06-028128-6*) HarpC Child Bks.
Block, Francesca Lia. Violet & Claire. LC 99-23890. (Illus.). 176p. (YA). 1999. 14.95 (*0-06-027749-1*) HarpC.
— Violet & Claire. LC 99-23890. (Illus.). 176p. (YA). (gr. 7-12). 1999. lib. bdg. 14.89 (*0-06-027750-5*) HarpC.
***Block, Francesca Lia.** Violet & Claire. LC 99-23890. 176p. (J). 2000. mass mkt. 6.95 (*0-06-447253-1*, HarpTrophy) HarpC Child Bks.
Block, Francesca Lia. Weetzie Bat. LC 88-6214. (Charlotte Zolotow Bk.). 96p. (J). (gr. 7 up). 1991. pap. 4.50 (*0-06-447068-7*, HarpTrophy) HarpC Child Bks.
— Weetzie Bat. (J). 1991. 9.60 (*0-606-05688-2*, Pub. by Turtleback) Demco.
— Weetzie Bat: 10th Anniversary Edition. LC 88-6214. (Charlotte Zolotow Bk.). 128p. (YA). (gr. 7-k). 1999. 14.95 (*0-06-020534-2*) HarpC Child Bks.
— Weetzie Bat: 10th Anniversary Edition. 10th anniversary ed. LC 88-6214. 128p. (YA). (gr. 7-12). 1999. pap. 7.95 (*0-06-440818-3*) HarpC Child Bks.
— Witch Baby. LC 90-28916. (Charlotte Zolotow Bk.). 112p. (YA). (gr. 7 up). 1991. lib. bdg. 14.89 (*0-06-020548-2*) HarpC Child Bks.
— Witch Baby. LC 90-28916. (Charlotte Zolotow Bk.). 128p. (YA). (gr. 7 up). 1992. pap. 4.95 (*0-06-447065-2*, HarpTrophy) HarpC Child Bks.
— Zine Scene: Do It Yourself Guide to Zines. 120p. 1998. pap. 14.95 (*0-9659754-3-6*) Girl Pr.

Block, Fred. Revising State Theory: Essays in Politics & Postindustrialism. 256p. (C). 1987. pap. 22.95 (*0-87722-524-9*) Temple U Pr.
— The Vampire State. 1997. pap. 16.95 (*1-56584-194-8*, Pub. by New Press NY) Norton.
— The Vampire State: And Other Myths & Fallacies about the U. S. Economy. LC 96-4400. 320p. 1996. 23.00 (*1-56584-193-X*, Pub. by New Press NY) Norton.
Block, Fred L. The Origins of International Economic Disorder: A Study of United States International Monetary Policy from World War Two to the Present. LC 75-7190. 1977. pap. 16.95 (*0-520-03729-4*, Pub. by U CA Pr) Cal Prin Full Svc.
— Postindustrial Possibilities: A Critique of Economic Discourse. 1990. pap. 17.95 (*0-520-06988-9*, Pub. by U CA Pr) Cal Prin Full Svc.
Block, Gay & Drucker, Malka. Rescuers: Portraits of Moral Courage in the Holocaust. LC 91-31499. (Illus.). 272p. 1992. 49.95 (*0-8419-1322-6*); pap. 29.95 (*0-8419-1323-4*) Holmes & Meier.
— Rescuers: Portraits of Moral Courage in the Holocaust. LC 98-178304. (Illus.). 320p. 1998. pap. 19.95 (*1-57500-062-8*, Pub. by TV Bks) HarpC.
Block, Geoffrey. Enchanted Evenings: The Broadway Musical from Show Boat to Sondheim. LC 96-53477. (Illus.). 432p. 1997. 35.00 (*0-19-510791-8*) OUP.
Block, Geoffrey H. Charles Ives: A Bio-Bibliography, 14. LC 88-21316. (Bio-Bibliographies in Music Ser.: No. 14). (Illus.). 437p. 1988. lib. bdg. 69.50 (*0-313-25404-4*, BCV/, Greenwood Pr) Greenwood.
— Ives No. 2: Concord Sonata: Piano Sonata. LC 95-46934. (Cambridge Music Handbooks Ser.). 125p. (C). 1996. text 39.95 (*0-521-49656-X*) Cambridge U Pr.
— Ives No. 2: Concord Sonata: Piano Sonata. LC 95-46934. (Cambridge Music Handbooks Ser.). 125p. (C). 1997. pap. text 13.95 (*0-521-49821-X*) Cambridge U Pr.
Block, Geoffrey H. & Burkholder, J. Peter, eds. Charles Ives & the Classical Tradition. LC 95-31915. 192p. 1996. 32.00 (*0-300-06177-3*) Yale U Pr.
Block, George E. & Moosa, A. R. Operative Colorectal Surgery. LC 92-48340. (Illus.). 640p. 1994. text 155.00 (*0-7216-3366-8*, W B Saunders Co) Harcrt Hlth Sci Grp.
Block, Gertrude. Effective Legal Writing for Law Students & Lawyers. 101p. 1992. pap. text. write for info. (*0-88277-992-3*) Foundation Pr.
— Effective Legal Writing for Law Students & Lawyers. 4th ed. 290p. 1992. pap. text 19.50 (*0-88277-964-8*) Foundation Pr.
Block, Gwendoline H., jt. compiled by see Gifford, Edward W.
Block, Gwendoline H., jt. compiled by see Gifford, Edward W.
Block, H. W., et al, eds. Topics in Statistical Dependence. LC 91-71759. (IMS Lecture Notes - Monographs: Vol. 16). x, 522p. 1991. pap. 45.00 (*0-940600-23-4*) Inst Math.
Block, Haskell M. Mallarme & the Symbolist Drama. LC 63-9302. (Wayne State University Studies: Language & Literature: No. 14). 173p. reprint ed. pap. 49.40 (*0-7837-3818-8*, 2043638) Bks Demand.
— Mallarme & the Symbolist Drama, No. 14. Language and Literature--14. LC 77-9242. (Wayne State University Study of Language & Literature: No. 14). 164p. 1977. reprint ed. lib. bdg. 38.50 (*0-8371-9706-6*, BLMS, Greenwood Pr) Greenwood.
Block, Haskell M., ed. The Poetry of Paul Celan: Papers from the Conference at the State University of New York at Binghamton, October 28-29, 1988. LC 91-31335. (American University Studies: Comparative Literature: Ser. III, Vol. 42). 69p. (C). 1992. text 23.95 (*0-8204-1615-0*) P Lang Pubng.
Block, Haskell M., ed. see Gerber, Richard.
Block, Heinz P. Practical Machinery Management. 3rd ed. LC 98-26184. (Practical Machinery Management for Process Plants Ser.: No. 1). 600p. 1998. 95.00 (*0-88415-661-3*, 5661) Gulf Pub.
Block, Herbert. Bella & Me: Life in the Service of a Cat. (Illus.). 47p. 1995. 12.95 (*1-56625-052-8*) Bonus Books.
— Herblock: A Cartoonist's Life. 1998. pap. 16.00 (*0-8129-3054-1*, Times Bks) Crown Pub Group.
— Herblock: A Cartoonist's Life. (Illus.). 320p. 1993. 24.00 (*0-02-511895-1*, Lisa Drew) Scribner.
Block, Herman, jt. auth. see Lyon, Hastings.
Block, Howard, et al. Powerbuilder Foundation Class Library: Professional Reference. LC 97-22705. (Client/Server Computing Ser.). (Illus.). 448p. 1997. pap., pap. text 49.95 incl. cd-rom (*0-07-913267-7*) McGraw.
Block, Howard M. Silverstream: The Authorized Guide. LC 98-25957. 512p. 1998. pap. text 49.95 incl. cd-rom (*0-07-913719-9*) McGraw.
Block, Ira, photos by. University of Rochester. (First Edition Ser.). (Illus.). 112p. 1988. 39.00 (*0-916509-36-2*) Harmony Hse Pub.
Block, Ira, jt. auth. see Smith, Betty.
Block, Iris. Dass der Mensch Allein Nicht das Ganze Ist! Versuche Menschlicher Zweisamkeit Im Werk Max Frischs. (Beitrage Zur Literatur uns Litertaturwissenschaft des 20. Jahrhunderts Ser.: Bd. 17). (GER.). 368p. 1998. 51.95 (*3-631-33454-0*) P Lang Pubng.
Block, Irving. The Charter of the Heart Mountain Relocation Center, Wyoming. limited ed. (Santa Susana Press California Masters Ser.: No. 4). 56p. 1983. 36.00 (*0-937048-32-1*) Santa Susana.
Block, Irving J. A Rabbi & His Dream: Building the Brotherhood Synagogue: A Memoir. LC 99-18025. 359p. 1999. 29.50 (*0-88125-657-9*) Ktav.
Block, Issac I. Assault on God's Image: Domestic Abuse. 128p. 1992. pap. 15.95 (*1-895308-11-9*) Windflower Comns.

Block, J. C. Viruses in Water Systems: Detection & Identification. 136p. 1989. 89.95 (*0-471-18681-3*, Wiley-VCH) Wiley.
Block, J. Richard & Yuker, Harold. Can You Believe Your Eyes? (Illus.). 256p. 1990. pap. 9.95 (*0-452-26552-5*, Plume) Dutton Plume.
— Can You Believe Your Eyes? Over 250 Illusions & Other Visual Oddities. LC 89-11950. 254p. 1992. 19.95 (*0-87630-695-4*) Brunner-Mazel.
Block, J. Richard, jt. auth. see Yuker, Harold E.
Block, Jack. Lives Through Time. 313p. 1971. 24.95 (*0-685-53570-3*) Bancroft Bks.
— Lives Through Time. 312p. 1971. text 59.95 (*0-9600332-0-3*) L Erlbaum Assocs.
— Understanding Historical Research: A Search for Truth. (Illus.). 156p. 1971. pap. text 7.00 (*0-9600478-0-8*) Research Pubns.
Block, Jack, et al. Food Service Careers: A Handy Guidebook for Those Seeking a Career in the Hospitality Industry. LC 85-188023. (Illus.). 214p. (Orig.). 1985. pap. write for info. (*0-935423-00-1*) Educ Pubns.
Block, Jack, jt. auth. see Witzman, Joseph E.
Block, Jacqueline, jt. auth. see Martinez, Benjamin.
Block, James H. & King, Nancy R. School Play: A Source Book. LC 86-33491. (Source Books on Education: Vol. 10). 360p. 1987. text 58.00 (*0-8240-8632-5*) Garland.
Block, James H., et al. Comprehensive School Reform: A Program Perspective. 450p. (C). per. 69.95 (*0-7872-6334-6*) Kendall-Hunt.
Block, Jan. Die Wirtschaftspolitik In der Weltwierschaftskrise 1929 Bis 1932 Im Urteil der Nationalsozialisten. VIII, 192p. 1997. 41.95 (*3-631-32260-7*) P Lang Pubng.
Block, Jane. Les XX & Belgian Avant-Gardism, 1868-1894. Foster, Stephen, ed. LC 83-17981. (Studies in the Fine Arts: The Avant-Garde: No. 41). 201p. 1984. reprint ed. pap. 62.40 (*0-8357-1463-2*, 207044800093) Bks Demand.
Block, Jane, ed. Belgium: The Golden Decades, 1880-1914. LC 96-18596. (Belgian Francophone Library: No. 3). (Illus.). XXIV, 264p. (C). 1997. text 49.95 (*0-8204-2741-1*) P Lang Pubng.
Block, Janice. Locations Locations Locations: Ideal Settings for Your Special Event on the Monterey Peninsula. 168p. (Orig.). 1995. pap. 12.95 (*0-9632181-1-5*) Crits Choice.
Block, Janice & Rankine, David. Critic's Choice Recipe Collection: 145 Recipes from Monterey Peninsula's Best Restaurants. Carlson, Ticien & Kantro, Barbara, eds. (Illus.). 168p. (Orig.). 1992. pap. 15.95 (*0-9632181-0-7*) Crits Choice.
— Locations, Locations, Locations: Ideal Settings for Your Special Event on the Monterey Peninsula. 2nd rev. ed. Coe, Shirley, ed. 196p. 1999. pap. 15.95 (*0-9632181-2-3*) Crits Choice.
Block, Jay A. & Betrus, Michael. 101 Best Resumes: Endorsed by the Professional Association of Resume Writers. LC 96-49936. 197p. 1997. pap. 11.95 (*0-07-032893-5*) McGraw.
Block, Jay A., et al. 101 More Best Resumes. LC 99-18630. 208p. 1999. pap. 11.95 (*0-07-032969-9*) McGraw.
Block, Jean-Claude & Schwartzbrod, Louis. Viruses in Water Systems: Detection & Identification. LC 88-26124. 136p. 1989. lib. bdg. 55.00 (*0-89573-274-2*, Wiley-VCH) Wiley.
Block, Jean F. Hyde Park Houses: An Informal History, 1856-1910. LC 78-3174. (Illus.). 1978. 12.95 (*0-226-06000-4*) U Ch Pr.
— Hyde Park Houses: An Informal History, 1856-1910. LC 78-3174. (Illus.). 240p. Date not set. reprint ed. pap. 74.40 (*0-608-20586-9*, 205455100003) Bks Demand.
— The Uses of Gothic: Planning & Building the Campus of the University of Chicago, 1892-1932. LC 83-6545. (Illus.). 284p. 1985. pap. 23.95 (*0-226-06004-7*) U Ch Pr.
Block, Jean L., jt. auth. see Dufresne, Isabelle.
Block, Jeanne H. Sex Role Identity & Ego Development. LC 84-7918. (Jossey-Bass Social & Behavioral Science Ser.). 351p. reprint ed. pap. 108.90 (*0-7837-2516-7*, 204267500006) Bks Demand.
***Block, Jed.** The Best Year of My Life Bk. 1: Getting Diabetes. LC 99-90681. (Illus.). 28p. (J). (gr. 2-6). 1999. pap. 10.95 (*0-9672728-0-7*) J Block.
Block, Jennifer A., jt. auth. see Weiss, Vikki.
Block, Jill. Tying Shoelaces. (California Master Ser.: No. 8). (Illus.). 16p. 1989. text 96.00 (*0-937048-44-5*) Santa Susana.
Block, Joel. Secrets of Better Sex. (Illus.). 320p. (C). 1996. pap. text 14.95 (*0-13-621442-8*) P-H.
Block, Joel & Bakos, Susan Crain. Sex over 50. 320p. 1999. pap. 14.00 (*0-7352-0058-0*) PH Pr.
***Block, Joel D.** Broken Promises, Mended Hearts: Maintaining Trust in Love Relationships. LC 00-22723. 256p. 2000. 23.95 (*0-8092-2396-1*, Contemporary Bks) NTC Contemp Pub Co.
— Magic of Lasting Love: The Step-By-Step Program to Help You Make Love Last. 252p. 2000. pap. 12.95 (*1-58741-027-3*) Wellness Inst.
Block, Joel D. Romance of Sex. LC 97-36534. (Illus.). 160p. (C). 1997. text 12.95 (*0-13-644635-3*) P-H.
Block, Joel D. & Bakos. Secrets of Better Sex. 320p. (C). 1996. text 26.95 (*0-13-241613-1*) P-H.
Block, John. The Racer's Guide to Fabricating Shop Equipment. (Illus.). 56p. 1985. pap. text 16.95 (*0-936834-45-5*) S S Autosports.
Block, John D., et al. Sotheby's Art at Auction: The Art Market Review, 1994-1995. (Illus.). 312p. 1996. 65.00 (*1-85029-718-5*) Antique Collect.

Block, John H. Inorganic Medicinal & Pharmaceutical Chemistry. LC 73-19604. 481p. reprint ed. pap. 149.20 (*0-608-17755-5*, 205650200069) Bks Demand.
Block, John H., et al, eds. Probing Bioactive Mechanisms. LC 89-17998. (Symposium Ser.: No. 413). (Illus.). 400p. 1989. text 65.00 (*0-8412-1702-5*, Pub. by Am Chemical) OUP.
Block, Jonathan & Leisure, Jerry. Understanding Three Dimensions. (Illus.). 144p. (C). 1986. pap. text 39.33 (*0-13-937202-4*) P-H.
Block, Joseph S. Factional Politics & the English Reformation, 1520-1540. (Royal Historical Society: Studies in History: No. 66). 188p. (C). 1993. 75.00 (*0-86193-223-4*) Boydell & Brewer.
Block, Judith, ed. Lighting Listings: A Worldwide Guide to Lighting Publications, Research Organizations, Educational Opportunities & Associations. 2nd rev. ed. 223p. (Orig.). 1995. spiral bd. 37.00 (*1-885750-01-3*, LL-95) Visions Communs.
Block, Judy. Performance Appraisal on the Job. 1982. pap. 5.95 (*0-917386-52-3*) Exec Ent Pubns.
Block, Judy, jt. auth. see Carter, Carol.
Block, Julian. It's Not What You Make, It's What You Keep: Your Year-Round Tax Planning Guide for Keeping As Much As the Law Allows. LC 94-19863. 336p. 1994. pap. 14.95 (*1-55958-580-3*) Prima Pub.
— Julian Block's Tax Avoidance Secrets, 1996. 576p. 1995. 59.00 (*0-88723-112-8*) Boardroom.
— Julian Block's Year-Round Tax Strategies for the 40,000 Dollar Plus Household, 1994. 368p. 1993. pap. 14.95 (*1-55958-356-8*) Prima Pub.
— Julian Block's Year-Round Tax Strategies for the 40,000 Dollars-Plus Household. 1993rd ed. 336p. (Orig.). 1992. pap. 14.95 (*1-55958-264-2*) Prima Pub.
— Ten Forty Handbook, Incl. Suppl. 550p. 1989. 23.50 (*0-13-903535-4*, Busn) P-H.
Block, Julian & Robinson, Alan S. Ten-Forty Handbook: 1988 Special New Tax Law Edition. 550p. 1987. 21.50 (*0-13-903709-8*) P-H.
Block, Julius I. Mortal & Immortals: Life under the Last Three Czars. (Illus.). 257p. (Orig.). 1994. pap. 34.50 (*0-930329-57-0*) Kabel Pubs.
Block, K. S., ed. Ludus Coventriae. (EETS, ES Ser.: Vol. 120). 1969. reprint ed. 30.00 (*0-8115-3412-X*) Periodicals Srv.
— Ludus Coventriae: or The Place Called Corpus Christi. (ES 120 Ser.). 466p. 1970. reprint ed. 35.00 (*0-19-722560-8*) OUP.
Block, Kevin James. Without Shedding of Blood. LC 95-109988. 185p. 1994. pap. 9.99 (*1-895308-17-8*) Hyperion Pr.
Block, Larry. All about Frogs. 3rd ed. (Illus.). 48p. (J). (gr. 1-3). 1998. reprint ed. pap. 6.95 (*1-891929-13-5*, Manatee Publng) Four Seasons.
Block, Lawrence. After the First Death. 268p. 1994. 4.50 (*0-7867-0167-6*) Carroll & Graf.
Block, Lawrence. After the First Death. large type ed. (Nightingale Ser.). 291p. 1992. pap. 14.95 (*0-8161-5408-2*, G K Hall Lrg Type) Mac Lib Ref.
Block, Lawrence. Ariel. 288p. 1997. mass mkt. 4.95 (*0-7867-0385-7*) Carroll & Graf.
— Ariel. 273p. 1996. lib. bdg. 22.36 (*0-614-16125-8*) G & G Pubng.
— The Burglar in the Closet. 320p. 1997. mass mkt. 6.99 (*0-451-18074-7*, Sig) NAL.
— The Burglar in the Closet. large type ed. LC 95-47317. (Cloak & Dagger Ser.). 1996. 24.95 (*0-7862-0548-2*) Thorndike Pr.
— The Burglar in the Library. 366p. 1998. mass mkt. 6.99 (*0-451-40783-0*, Sig) NAL.
— The Burglar in the Library. large type ed. LC 97-32304. (Americana Series). 498p. 1998. 27.95 (*0-7862-1280-2*) Thorndike Pr.
— The Burglar in the Rye. LC 98-51326. (Bernie Rhodenbarr Mystery Ser.). 280p. 1999. 23.95 (*0-525-94500-8*, Dutt) Dutton Plume.
***Block, Lawrence.** The Burglar in the Rye. (Bernie Rhodenbarr Mystery Ser.). 320p. 2000. mass mkt. 6.99 (*0-451-19847-6*, Sig) NAL.
Block, Lawrence. The Burglar in the Rye. large type ed. LC 99-16640. 1999. 29.95 (*0-7862-2136-4*) Mac Lib Ref.
— The Burglar Who Liked to Quote Kipling: A Bernie Rhodenbarr Mystery. 320p. 1997. mass mkt. 6.99 (*0-451-18075-5*) NAL.
— The Burglar Who Liked to Quote Kipling: A Bernie Rhodenbarr Mystery. large type ed. LC 96-42398. (Cloak & Dagger Ser.). 319p. 1996. 25.95 (*0-7862-0895-3*) Thorndike Pr.
***Block, Lawrence.** The Burglar Who Painted Like Mondrian. LC 98-20568. (Bernie Rhodenbarr Mystery Ser.). 224p. 1998. 23.95 (*0-525-94382-X*) NAL.
— The Burglar Who Painted Like Mondrian. large type ed. LC 99-22151. (Large Print Book Ser.). 1999. 26.95 (*1-56895-726-2*) Wheeler Pub.
Block, Lawrence. The Burglar Who Painted Like Mondrian. 320p. 1999. reprint ed. mass mkt. 6.99 (*0-451-18076-3*, Sig) NAL.
***Block, Lawrence.** The Burglar Who Studied Spinoza. (Bernie Rhodenbarr Mystery Ser.). 320p. 1998. mass mkt. 6.99 (*0-451-19488-8*, Sig) NAL.
Block, Lawrence. The Burglar Who Studied Spinoza. large type ed. LC 98-22094. (Large Print Book Ser.). 1998. 25.95 (*1-56895-602-9*) Wheeler Pub.
— The Burglar Who Thought He Was Bogart. 1996. pap. 5.99 (*0-614-98080-1*, Onyx); mass mkt. 6.99 (*0-451-18634-6*, Onyx) NAL.
— The Burglar Who Traded Ted Williams. 384p. 1995. mass mkt. 6.99 (*0-451-18426-2*, Onyx) NAL.
— The Canceled Czech. 224p. 1999. mass mkt. 5.99 (*0-451-19404-7*, Sig) NAL.

An Asterisk (*) at the beginning of an entry indicates that the title is appearing for the first time.

— Chip Harrison Scores Again. 1996. lib. bdg. 22.36 (*0-614-16123-1*) G & G Pubng.
— Coward's Kiss. 160p. 1996. mass mkt. 3.95 (*0-7867-0334-2*) Carroll & Graf.
***Block, Lawrence.** Coward's Kiss. LC 99-35099. (Mystery Ser.). 1999. pap. 19.95 (*0-7862-2075-9*) Mac Lib Ref.
— A Dance at the Slaughterhouse: A Matthew Scudder Novel. (Matthew Scudder Mystery Ser.). 304p. 2000. pap. 13.00 (*0-380-81373-4*, Avon Bks) Morrow Avon.
Block, Lawrence. A Dance at the Slaughterhouse: A Matthew Scudder Novel. (Matthew Scudder Mystery Ser.). 320p. 1992. reprint ed. mass mkt. 6.99 (*0-380-71374-8*, Avon Bks) Morrow Avon.
— Deadly Honeymoon. 192p. 1995. 4.50 (*0-7867-0226-5*) Carroll & Graf.
***Block, Lawrence.** The Devil Knows You're Dead: A Matthew Scudder Novel. LC 99-94873. (Matthew Scudder Mystery Ser.). 288p. 1999. pap. 12.50 (*0-380-80759-9*, Avon Bks) Morrow Avon.
Block, Lawrence. The Devil Knows You're Dead: A Matthew Scudder Novel. (Matthew Scudder Mystery Ser.). 352p. 1994. reprint ed. mass mkt. 6.99 (*0-380-72023-X*, Avon Bks) Morrow Avon.
Block, Lawrence. Ehrengraf for the Defense. (Illus.). 168p. 1994. 125.00 (*1-892011-08-5*) ASAP Pub.
Block, Lawrence. Eight Million Ways to Die. LC 91-92136. (Matthew Scudder Mystery Ser.). 336p. 1993. reprint ed. mass mkt. 6.50 (*0-380-71573-2*, Avon Bks) Morrow Avon.
— Even the Wicked: A Matthew Scudder Novel. LC 96-23013. (Matthew Scudder Mystery Ser.). 1997. 23.00 (*0-688-14181-1*, Wm Morrow) Morrow Avon.
— Even the Wicked: A Matthew Scudder Novel. large type ed. (Matthew Scudder Mystery Ser.). 384p. 1998. mass mkt. 6.99 (*0-380-72534-7*, Avon Bks) Morrow Avon.
— Even the Wicked: A Matthew Scudder Novel. large type ed. LC 97-6333. (Cloak & Dagger Ser.). 546p. 1997. 26.95 (*0-7862-1093-1*) Thorndike Pr.
***Block, Lawrence.** Everybody Dies: A Matthew Scudder Novel. LC 98-10529. (Matthew Scudder Mystery Ser.). 336p. 1998. 25.00 (*0-688-14182-X*, Wm Morrow) Morrow Avon.
— Everybody Dies: A Matthew Scudder Novel. LC 98-10529. (Matthew Scudder Mystery Ser.). 384p. 1999. mass mkt. 6.99 (*0-380-72535-5*, Avon Bks) Morrow Avon.
Block, Lawrence. Everybody Dies: A Matthew Scudder Novel. large type ed. LC 98-48520. 1999. 30.00 (*0-7862-1706-5*) Thorndike Pr.
— The Girl with the Long Green Heart. 160p. 1994. mass mkt. 3.95 (*0-7867-0106-4*) Carroll & Graf.
***Block, Lawrence.** The Girl with the Long Green Heart. LC 98-56128. 1999. 21.95 (*0-7862-1812-6*) Thorndike Pr.
Block, Lawrence. The Girl with the Long Green Heart. large type ed. LC 92-18390. (Nightingale Ser.). 308p. 1992. pap. 14.95 (*0-8161-5409-0*, G K Hall Lrg Type) Mac Lib Ref.
***Block, Lawrence.** Hit List. 304p. 2000. 25.00 (*0-06-019833-8*, Wm Morrow) Morrow Avon.
— Hit List. large type ed. 2000. 25.00 (*0-06-019911-3*, HarpCollins) HarperTrade.
Block, Lawrence. Hit Man. 256p. 1998. 22.00 (*0-688-14179-X*, Wm Morrow) Morrow Avon.
— Hit Man. LC 97-20272. 352p. 1999. mass mkt. 6.99 (*0-380-72541-X*, Avon Bks) Morrow Avon.
— Hit Man. large type ed. LC 98-35823. 1998. 26.95 (*0-7862-1618-2*) Thorndike Pr.
— In the Midst of Death. (Matthew Scudder Mystery Ser.). 192p. 1992. mass mkt. 5.99 (*0-380-76362-1*, Avon Bks) Morrow Avon.
— In The Midst of Death. 164p. 1996. lib. bdg. 22.36 (*0-614-16126-6*) G & G Pubng.
— Like a Lamb to Slaughter. 272p. 1996. mass mkt. 5.99 (*0-380-78806-3*, Avon Bks) Morrow Avon.
— A Long Line of Dead Men: A Matthew Scudder Novel. (Matthew Scudder Mystery Ser.). 1996. mass mkt. 5.99 (*0-380-72024-8*, Avon Bks) Morrow Avon.
— A Long Line of Dead Men: A Matthew Scudder Novel. (Matthew Scudder Mystery Ser.). 304p. 1999. pap. 12.50 (*0-380-80604-5*, Avon Bks) Morrow Avon.
— A Long Line of Dead Men: A Matthew Scudder Novel. large type ed. LC 94-47382. (Cloak & Dagger Ser.). 479p. 1995. lib. bdg. 23.95 (*0-7862-0407-9*) Thorndike Pr.
— Mona. 144p. 1994. pap. 3.95 (*0-7867-0105-6*) Carroll & Graf.
— Mona. LC 98-31418. 1999. 21.95 (*0-7862-1705-7*, Five Star MI) Mac Lib Ref.
— No Score. 1996. lib. bdg. 22.36 (*0-614-16124-X*) G & G Pubng.
— Not Comin' Home to You. 224p. 1997. mass mkt. 4.95 (*0-7867-0388-1*) Carroll & Graf.
— Out on the Cutting Edge. (Matthew Scudder Mystery Ser.). 256p. 1990. reprint ed. mass mkt. 5.99 (*0-380-70993-7*, Avon Bks) Morrow Avon.
***Block, Lawrence.** Random Walk. 372p. 1999. pap. 18.95 (*1-58348-381-0*) iUniversecom.
— Ronald Rabbit Is a Dirty Old Man. (Illus.). 112p. 1995. 125.00 (*1-892011-09-3*) ASAP Pub.
— Ronald Rabbit is a Dirty Old Man. 3rd ed. 150p. 2000. reprint ed. pap. 16.00 (*1-892284-56-1*) Subtrrnean Pr.
Block, Lawrence. Sins of the Fathers. (Matthew Scudder Mystery Ser.). 192p. 1991. mass mkt. 5.99 (*0-380-76363-X*, Avon Bks) Morrow Avon.
— Some Days You Get the Bear. 304p. 1994. reprint ed. mass mkt. 5.99 (*0-380-71568-6*, Avon Bks) Morrow Avon.
— The Specialists. 160p. 1993. 3.95 (*0-7867-0046-7*) Carroll & Graf.
Block, Lawrence. The Specialists. Cahill, James, ed. (Illus.). 160p. 1996. 25.00 (*0-9640454-3-5*) J Cahill Pubng.
— The Specialists. deluxe limited ed. Cahill, James, ed. (Illus.). 160p. 1960. text 75.00 (*0-9640454-4-3*) J Cahill Pubng.
Block, Lawrence. Spider, Spin Me A Web: A Handbook for Fiction Writers. LC 96-14569. 243p. 1996. pap. 13.00 (*0-688-14690-2*, Quil) HarperTrade.
— A Stab in the Dark. (Matthew Scudder Mystery Ser.). 192p. 1992. reprint ed. mass mkt. 5.99 (*0-380-71574-0*, Avon Bks) Morrow Avon.
— Such Men Are Dangerous. 192p. 1993. mass mkt. 3.95 (*0-7867-0047-5*) Carroll & Graf.
— Tanner on Ice. LC 99-19133. 1999. 25.95 (*1-56895-701-7*) Wheeler Pub.
— Tanner on Ice. 320p. 1999. reprint ed. mass mkt. 6.99 (*0-451-19410-1*, Sig) NAL.
***Block, Lawrence.** Tanner's Twelve Swingers. 272p. 1999. mass mkt. 5.99 (*0-451-19833-6*, Sig) NAL.
Block, Lawrence. Telling Lies-Fun & P. LC 93-33749. 256p. 1994. reprint ed. pap. 13.00 (*0-688-13228-6*, Quil) HarperTrade.
— The Thief Who Couldn't Sleep. (Evan Tanner Novel Ser.). 1998. mass mkt. 5.99 (*0-451-19403-9*, Sig) NAL.
— A Ticket to the Boneyard. (Matthew Scudder Mystery Ser.). 352p. 1991. reprint ed. mass mkt. 5.99 (*0-380-70994-5*, Avon Bks) Morrow Avon.
— Time to Murder & Create: A Matthew Scudder Novel. (Matthew Scudder Mystery Ser.). 192p. 1991. mass mkt. 5.99 (*0-380-76365-6*, Avon Bks) Morrow Avon.
— The Topless Tulip Caper: A Chip Harrison Mystery. 272p. 1998. mass mkt. 5.99 (*0-451-18799-7*, Sig) NAL.
— The Triumph of Evil. 126p. 1994. mass mkt. 3.95 (*0-7867-0181-1*) Carroll & Graf.
***Block, Lawrence.** A Walk among the Tombstones: A Matthew Scudder Crime Novel. 304p. 2000. pap. 12.50 (*0-380-81118-9*, Avon Bks) Morrow Avon.
Block, Lawrence. A Walk among the Tombstones: A Matthew Scudder Crime Novel. large type ed. LC 93-16773. 431p. 1993. lib. bdg. 22.95 (*0-8161-5759-6*, G K Hall Lrg Type) Mac Lib Ref.
— A Walk among the Tombstones: A Matthew Scudder Crime Novel. 336p. 1993. reprint ed. mass mkt. 5.99 (*0-380-71375-6*, Avon Bks) Morrow Avon.
— When the Sacred Ginmill Closes. (Matthew Scudder Mystery Ser.). 1997. mass mkt. 5.99 (*0-614-27706-X*, Avon Bks); mass mkt. 5.99 (*0-380-72825-7*, Avon Bks) Morrow Avon.
— Writing the Novel: From Plot to Print. 218p. 1985. pap. 14.99 (*0-89879-208-8*, Wrtrs Digest Bks) F & W Pubns Inc.
— You Could Call It Murder. 240p. 1996. mass mkt. 4.95 (*0-7867-0342-3*) Carroll & Graf.
***Block, Lawrence, ed.** Death Cruise: Crime Stories on the Open Seas. LC 99-20020. 320p. 1999. 24.95 (*1-58182-007-0*) Cumberland Hse.
Block, Lawrence, ed. Master's Choice: Mystery Stories by Today's Top Writers & the Masters Who Inspired Them. LC 99-30270. 1999. 21.95 (*0-425-17031-4*, Prime Crime) Berkley Pub.
Block, Lawrence, jt. auth. see Adams Round Table Staff.
Block, Lawrence, jt. auth. see Bradway, Lauren C.
Block, Lawrence, ed. see Woolrich, Cornell.
Block, Leo. Diesel Engines: A Boat Owner's Guide to Operation & Maintenance. LC 90-55449. (Illus.). 143p. 1991. pap. 11.95 (*0-87033-418-2*) Cornell Maritime.
Block, Linda F. & Dubin, Debbie I. Chanukah on Noah's Ark. 72p. (Orig.). (J). (gr. 1-7). 1987. pap. 6.95 (*0-9619082-0-3*) Noahs Ark.
Block, Louis S. & Coppel, William A. Dynamics in One Dimension. LC 92-8152. (Lecture Notes in Mathematics Ser.: Vol. 1513). 1992. 62.00 (*3-540-55309-6*) Spr-Verlag.
Block, Louis S., et al. Dynamics in One Dimension. Dold, A. et al, eds. (Lecture Notes in Mathematics Ser.: Vol. 1513). 249p. 1995. 53.95 (*0-387-55309-6*) Spr-Verlag.
Block, M. M. & White, A. R. Multiparticle Dynamics: Proceedings of the XXIIIth International Symposium. 500p. 1994. text 109.00 (*981-02-1780-3*) World Scientific Pub.
Block, Marguerite. The New Church in the New World. LC 67-18752. 502p. 1984. 12.95 (*0-87785-126-3*) Swedenborg.
Block, Marian R., jt. auth. see Coulehan, John L.
***Block, Marilyn R.** Identifying Environmental Aspects & Impacts. LC 99-35572. 1999. write for info. (*0-87389-446-4*) ASQ Qual Pr.
Block, Marilyn R. Implementing ISO 14001. 247p. 1997. 45.00 (*0-87389-357-3*, H0916) ASQ Qual Pr.
Block, Marilyn R. & Marash, I. Robert. Integrating ISO 14001 into a Quality Management System. LC 98-52672. 270p. 1999. 35.00 (*0-87389-399-9*, H0991) ASQ Qual Pr.
Block, Martin. Gypsies: Their Life & Their Customs. Kuczynski, Barbara & Taylor, Duncan, trs. LC 75-3451. (Illus.). reprint ed. 31.50 (*0-404-16886-8*) AMS Pr.
— Die Zigeuner. Hohmann, Joachim S., ed. (Studien Zur Tsiganologie und Folkloristik Ser.: Vol. 20). (Illus.). 250p. 1997. pap. 51.95 (*3-631-30126-X*) P Lang Pubng.
Block, Martin & Totten, John C. Analyzing Sales Promotion. 2nd ed. 226p. 1994. pap. 34.95 (*0-85013-229-0*) Dartnell Corp.
Block, Martin H. A Teacher's Guide to Including Students with Disabilities in Regular Physical Education. LC 93-38428. 288p. 1994. reprint ed. pap. 39.00 (*1-55766-156-1*) P H Brookes.
Block, Martin P. & Block, Tamara S. Business-to-Business Market Research: Identifying, Qualifying & Understanding Your Customers. 300p. 1994. text 37.50 (*1-55738-559-9*, Irwn Prfssnl) McGraw-Hill Prof.
Block, Martin P., jt. auth. see Totten, John C.
Block, Mary & Leigh, Gallery Staff, compiled by. Graven Images: The Rise of Professional Printmaking in Antwerp & Haarlem, 1540-1640. LC 92-27840. 175p. 1993. 25.00 (*0-941680-11-8*) M&L Block.
***Block, Mary A.** No More Antibiotics: Preventing & Treating Ear & Respiratory Infections the Natural Way. 128p. 2000. mass mkt. 5.99 (*1-57566-500-X*) Kensgtn Pub Corp.
Block, Mary A. No More Ritalin. 144p. 1996. pap. 14.00 (*1-57566-126-8*, Knsington) Kensgtn Pub Corp.
Block, Mary Ann. No More Amoxicillin. LC 99-188647. 144p. 1998. pap. 12.00 (*1-57566-316-3*, Knsington) Kensgtn Pub Corp.
Block, Maxine, jt. auth. see Bieler, Henry G.
Block, May A. No More Ritalin. 160p. 1997. pap. 5.99 (*1-57566-239-6*) Kensgtn Pub Corp.
Block, Melissa, jt. auth. see Mindell, Earl.
Block, Mervin. Broadcast Newswriting: The RTNDA Reference Guide. LC 94-29925. 271p. 1994. 29.95 (*1-56625-017-X*) Bonus Books.
— Rewriting Network News: Wordwatching Tips from 345 TV & Radio Scripts. 221p. 1990. 24.95 (*0-929387-15-5*) Bonus Books.
— Writing Broadcast News - Shorter, Sharper, Stronger. 2nd expanded rev. ed. LC 97-6266. 314p. 1997. 29.95 (*1-56625-084-6*) Bonus Books.
Block, Mervin & Durso, Joe. Writing News for TV & Radio: The Interactive Cd & Handbook. LC 98-41024. 168p. 1998. pap. 59.95 (*1-56625-113-3*) Bonus Books.
Block, Michael K. & Lenard, Thomas M. Deregulating Electricity: The Federal Role. 85p. 1998. pap. 29.95 (*0-9659578-2-9*) Progress & Freedom.
Block, Michael S. & Kent, John N. Endosseous Implants for Maxillofacial Reconstruction. LC 94-21278. (Illus.). 624p. 1995. text 195.00 (*0-7216-3958-5*, W B Saunders Co) Harcrt Hlth Sci Grp.
Block, Michael S., et al. Implants in Dentistry. Fletcher, Judy, ed. LC 96-50087. 336p. 1997. text 65.00 (*0-7216-2174-0*, W B Saunders Co) Harcrt Hlth Sci Grp.
Block, Mickey. Before the Dawn. 1990. mass mkt. 4.99 (*0-671-72607-2*) PB.
Block, Mindy O. Lost Heritage. 152p. 1997. pap. 15.00 (*0-9663197-0-2*) Sustaining Systs.
Block, Nancy R., ed. see Gullick, Michael.
Block, Ned J., ed. Readings in Philosophy of Psychology, Vol. 1. (Language & Thought Ser.). 318p. 1983. pap. 18.50 (*0-674-74876-X*) HUP.
— Readings in Philosophy of Psychology, Vol. 2. (Language & Thought Ser.). (Illus.). 372p. 1985. pap. 16.95 (*0-674-74878-6*) HUP.
— Readings in the Philosophy of Psychology, Vol. 2. LC 79-25593. (Language & Thought Ser.). (Illus.). 372p. 1981. 41.50 (*0-674-74877-8*) HUP.
Block, Ned J., et al, eds. The Nature of Consciousness: Philosophical Debates. LC 96-17500. (Illus.). 608p. 1997. 65.00 (*0-262-02399-7*, Bradford Bks) MIT Pr.
— The Nature of Consciousness: Philosophical Debates. LC 96-17500. (Illus.). 608p. 1997. pap. text 32.95 (*0-262-52210-1*, Bradford Bks) MIT Pr.
Block, Paula M., jt. auth. see Erdmann, Terry J.
Block, Penny. A Banquet of Health. (Illus.). 224p. (Orig.). 1994. pap. 17.95 (*1-879260-28-X*) Evanston Pub.
Block, Peter. California Vocational Rehabilitation Toolkit (Post-'94 Injury Version) A Worker's Guide to Successful Vocational Rehabilitation in California with Tips for Winning the Right Job & Thriving the Rest of Your Working Life. (Toolkit Ser.). (Illus.). 186p. (Orig.). 1994. 14.95 (*0-9642766-1-5*) Quest Vocat.
— California Vocational Rehabilitation Toolkit (Pre-1994 Injury Version) A Worker's Guide to Successful Vocational Rehabilitation in California with Tips for Winning the Right Job & Thriving the Rest of Your Working Life. (Toolkit Ser.). (Illus.). 186p. (Orig.). 1994. 14.95 (*0-9642766-0-7*) Quest Vocat.
— The Empowered Manager: Positive Political Skills at Work. LC 86-45619. (Management Ser.). 226p. 1987. 32.95 (*1-55542-019-2*) Jossey-Bass.
— The Empowered Manager: Positive Political Skills at Work. LC 86-45619. (Management Ser.). 214p. 1991. reprint ed. mass mkt. 20.00 (*1-55542-265-9*) Jossey-Bass.
Block, Peter. The Empowered Manager Audio Program: Positive Political Skills at Work. 1989. 26.95 incl. audio (*1-55542-907-6*) Jossey-Bass.
Block, Peter. Flawless Consulting: A Guide to Getting Your Expertise Used. LC 81-4283. (Illus.). 214p. 1981. text 39.95 (*0-89384-052-1*, Pfffr & Co) Jossey-Bass.
***Block, Peter.** Flawless Consulting: A Guide to Getting Your Expertise Used. 2nd ed. LC 99-6430. 400p. 1999. text 39.95 (*0-7879-4803-9*) Jossey-Bass.
— Flawless Consulting Fieldbook & Companion: Practical Strategies for Getting Your Expertise Used. 2000. pap. 39.95 (*0-7879-4804-7*) Jossey-Bass.
— Managing in the Media. (Illus.). 300p. 2000. pap. 47.95 (*0-240-51599-4*, Focal) Buttrwrth-Heinemann.
Block, Peter. Stewardship: Choosing Service over Self-Interest. LC 93-6597. (Illus.). 256p. 1993. 27.95 (*1-881052-28-1*) Berrett-Koehler.
— Stewardship: Choosing Service over Self-Interest. LC 93-6597. 288p. 1996. pap. 16.95 (*1-881052-86-9*) Berrett-Koehler.
Block, Polly. The Crossing, Beneath a Prairie Bush. LC 96-68805. (Nurturing the Spirit Ser.: Vol. I). (Illus.). 266p. 1996. reprint ed. pap. 10.95 (*1-57636-016-4*) SunRise Pbl.
— Polly's Birth Book: Obstetrics for the Home. LC 96-68998. (Illus.). 563p. 1996. reprint ed. pap. 21.95 (*1-57636-019-9*) SunRise Pbl.
— She Carried Me All the Way, the Fastest Buggy Horse in Alpine. LC 96-68805. (Nurturing the Spirit Ser.: Vol. II). (Illus.). 266p. 1996. reprint ed. pap. 10.95 (*1-57636-017-2*) SunRise Pbl.
— Tell Me: Twenty-Four Heartwarming Stories. 286p. 1995. pap. text 14.95 (*1-57636-008-3*) SunRise Pbl.
Block, R. A., ed. Cognitive Models of Psychological Time. 304p. 1990. text 89.95 (*0-8058-0359-9*) L Erlbaum Assocs.
Block, Ralph & Hobbs, Rodney. Tax Administration: IRS' Partnership Compliance Activities Could Be Improved. (Illus.). 33p. (C). 1996. reprint ed. pap. text 15.00 (*0-7881-3273-3*) DIANE Pub.
***Block, Ralph & Seymour, Kathleen D.** Tax Administration: Alternative Filing Systems. 51p. 2000. pap. text 20.00 (*0-7881-8913-1*) DIANE Pub.
Block, Ralph L. Investing in REITs: Real Estate Investment Trusts. LC 98-24139. (Bloomberg Personal Bookshelf Ser.). (Illus.). 256p. 1998. 21.95 (*1-57660-055-6*, Pub. by Bloomberg NJ) Norton.
Block, Ralph T. Tax Credits: Opportunities to Improve Oversight of the Low-Income Housing Program. (Illus.). 175p. 1998. pap. text 35.00 (*0-7881-3871-5*) DIANE Pub.
***Block, Richard & Fenves, Peter, eds.** The Spirit of Poesy: Essays in Honor of Geza Von Molnar. 336p. 1999. 59.95 (*0-8101-1681-2*) Northwestern U Pr.
Block, Richard, jt. ed. see Block, Carolyn.
Block, Richard A. Discover Rain Forests. (Discover Ser.). (Illus.). 48p. (J). (gr. 3-6). 1992. lib. bdg. 15.95 (*1-56674-030-4*, HTS Bks) Forest Hse.
— MET Publication 516: Port State Control. 420p. 1997. pap. 85.00 (*1-879778-65-3*, BK-0722) Marine Educ.
Block, Richard A., ed. Able Seaman & Lifeboatman, Bk. 1. rev. ed. (Illus.). 528p. 1996. pap. text 68.00 (*1-879778-57-2*, BK-105-01) Marine Educ.
— Able Seaman & Lifeboatman, Bk. 2. rev. ed. (Illus.). 550p. 1996. pap. text 52.00 (*1-879778-58-0*, BK-105-02) Marine Educ.
***Block, Richard A., ed.** Ballast Water Record Book. 64p. 1999. pap. 15.00 (*1-879778-83-1*) Marine Educ.
Block, Richard A., ed. Lifeboatman. rev. ed. (Illus.). 212p. 1997. pap. text 42.50 (*1-879778-63-7*, BK-105-1) Marine Educ.
— Limited Master, Mate & Operator License Study Course, Bk. 1. rev. ed. (Illus.). 630p. 1996. pap. text 67.00 (*1-879778-49-1*, BK-001) Marine Educ.
— Limited Master, Mate & Operator License Study Course, Bk. 2. rev. ed. 672p. 1996. pap. text 66.00 (*1-879778-52-1*, BK-002) Marine Educ.
— Limited Master, Mate & Operator License Study Course, Bk. 3. rev. ed. 620p. 1996. pap. text 65.00 (*1-879778-53-X*, BK-003) Marine Educ.
— Limited Master, Mate & Operator License Study Course, Bk. 4. rev. ed. 450p. 1996. pap. text 48.00 (*1-879778-54-8*, BK-004) Marine Educ.
— Limited Master, Mate & Operator License Study Course, Bk. 5. rev. ed. 296p. 1996. pap. text 36.00 (*1-879778-55-6*, BK-005) Marine Educ.
***Block, Richard A., ed.** M. E. T. Publication No. 515: Rules & Regulations for Foreign Vessels Operating in the United States, Bks. 1 & 2. 6th rev. ed. 794p. 1999. pap. 146.00 (*1-879778-84-X*) Marine Educ.
— R. B.-169 - Navigation Rules for International & Inland Waters Including the Great Lakes & Western Rivers: Edition "F" rev. ed. (Illus.). 252p. 1999. pap. 30.00 (*1-879778-85-8*) Marine Educ.
Block, Richard A., ed. Radar Observer Manual. 5th ed. (Illus.). 141p. 1983. pap. text 27.50 (*0-934114-42-0*, BK-112) Marine Educ.
— The T-Boat Handbook: A Guide to the Operation of Small Inspected Passenger Vessels. 2nd rev. ed. (Illus.). 266p. 1996. pap. 35.00 (*1-879778-61-0*, BK-115) Marine Educ.
— Tankerman. rev. ed. (Illus.). 352p. 1997. pap. text 70.00 (*1-879778-67-X*, BK-106) Marine Educ.
— Victimization & Fear of Crime: World Perspectives. (Illus.). 102p. (Orig.). (C). 1995. pap. text 25.00 (*0-7881-2065-4*) DIANE Pub.
— Western Rivers License Primer. (Illus.). 382p. (Orig.). 1994. pap. text 45.00 (*1-879778-34-3*, BK-0364) Marine Educ.
Block, Richard A., ed. see Gianelloni, V. J., III.
Block, Richard A., ed. see Sutton, John R.
Block, Richard A., ed. see Vandegrift, John F., Sr.
Block, Richard A., ed. see Ward, Robert J.
Block, Richard J., Memorial Symposium (1962: Atlan. Amino Acids & Serum Proteins: Based on the Richard J. Block Memorial Symposium Sponsored by the Division of Biological Chemistry at the 142nd Meeting of the American Chemical Society, Atlantic City, NJ, September 11, 1962. LC 64-16321. (Advances in Chemistry Ser.: Vol. 44). (Illus.). 180p. 1964. reprint ed. pap. 55.80 (*0-608-06917-5*, 206712500009) Bks Demand.
Block, Richard L., jt. ed. see Block, Carolyn R.
Block, Richard N., et al. Labor Law, Industrial Relations & Employee Choice: The State of the Workplace in the 1990's. Kruger, Daniel H., ed. LC 96-17405. 116p. (C). 1996. text 34.00 (*0-88099-164-X*); pap. text 15.00 (*0-88099-163-1*) W E Upjohn.
Block, Richard N., jt. auth. see Wolkinson, Benjamin W.
Block, Robert. Marbles. 2nd expanded rev. ed. LC 98-143835. (Illus.). 160p. 1998. pap. 19.95 (*0-7643-0454-2*) Schiffer.
— Marbles: Identification & Price Guide. 3rd rev. ed. LC 99-31912. (Illus.). 160p. 1999. pap. 19.95 (*0-7643-0888-2*) Schiffer.
— Marbles Illustrated: Prices at Auction. (Illus.). 160p. 1999. pap. 16.95 (*0-7643-0970-6*) Schiffer.

B

An Asterisk (*) at the beginning of an entry indicates that the title is appearing for the first time.

Block, Robert W. & Rash, Francis C. Handbook of Behavioral Pediatrics. LC 81-11665. 245p. reprint ed. pap. 76.00 (*0-608-15904-2*, 203083900071) Bks Demand.

Block, Roger R. The "Grounds" for Lightning & EMP Protection. 2nd ed. (Illus.). 100p. (Orig.). (C). 1993. pap. text 22.95 (*0-9644493-1-5*) PolyPhaser.

Block, Ron. The Dirty Shame Hotel: And Other Short Stories. LC 97-69843. (Minnesota Voices Project Ser.: Vol. 87). 160p. 1998. pap. 14.95 (*0-89823-187-6*) New Rivers Pr.

Block, Ronald. Dismal River. (Minnesota Voices Project Ser.: Vol. 38). 88p. 1990. pap. 6.00 (*0-89823-112-4*) New Rivers Pr.

Block, Rudolph E. Children of Men. LC 76-103496. (Short Story Index Reprint Ser.). 1977. 21.95 (*0-8369-3238-2*) Ayer.

Block, Russell, tr. see Trotsky, Leon.

Block, Seymor S., ed. Disinfection, Sterilization & Preservation. 4th ed. LC 90-22653. (Illus.). 1162p. 1991. text 198.50 (*0-8121-1364-0*) Lppncott W & W.

***Block, Seymour S.** Disinfection, Sterilization & Preservation. 5th ed. LC 00-41221. (Illus.). 2000. write for info. (*0-683-30740-1*) Lppncott W & W.

Block, Sharon, ed. see McDaniel, Nello & Thorn, George.

Block, Sharon, ed. see Schiller, Sherry.

Block, Shira. Step-by-Step Miracles: A Practical Guide to Achieving Your Dreams. LC 96-107656. 93p. 1995. pap. 11.00 (*0-8217-4990-0*, Zebra Kensgtn) Kensgtn Pub Corp.

***Block, Shira.** The Way Home. Ward, Mike, ed. (Illus.). 72p. 2000. pap. text 10.95 (*0-9676650-0-0*) Mantic Arts.

***Block, Simon.** Chimps. 1999. pap. 5.60 (*0-87129-915-1*, C98) Dramatic Pub.

Block, Simon. Chimps. (Nick Hern Bks.). 96p. 1998. pap. 13.95 (*1-85459-373-0*) Theatre Comm.

— Not a Game for Boys. 64p. (Orig.). 1996. pap. 13.95 (*1-85459-234-3*, Pub. by N Hern Bks) Theatre Comm.

***Block, Simon.** Place at the Table. 72p. 2000. pap. 16.95 (*1-85459-488-5*) Theatre Comm.

Block, Stanley. Marble Mania. LC 98-18146. 192p. 1998. 34.95 (*0-7643-0014-8*) Schiffer.

***Block, Stanley & Hirt, Geoffrey.** Foundations Of Financial Management. 9th ed. (C). 1999. pap., student ed. 85.63 incl. cd-rom (*0-07-231933-X*) McGrw-H Hghr Educ.

Block, Stanley & Hirt, Geoffrey. Foundations of Financial Management (Canadian) 2nd ed. 896p. (C). 1991. text 55.95 (*0-256-09762-3*, Irwn McGrw-H) McGrw-H Hghr Educ.

— Foundations of Financial Management (Canadian) 3rd ed. LC 93-61415. 976p. (C). 1994. text 55.95 (*0-256-12632-1*, Irwn McGrw-H) McGrw-H Hghr Educ.

Block, Stanley B., ed. Mechanisms of Phase Transitions. (Transactions of the American Crystallographic Association Ser.: Vol. 7). 154p. 1971. pap. 25.00 (*0-686-60378-8*) Polycrystal Bk Serv.

Block, Stanley B. & Hirt, Geoffrey A. CPS - Select Material Foundations of Financial Management. 7th ed. 392p. (C). 1995. text 29.95 (*0-256-20442-X*, Irwn McGrw-H) McGrw-H Hghr Educ.

— Foundations of Financial Management. 6th ed. 704p. (C). 1991. text 66.95 (*0-256-08355-X*, Irwn McGrw-H) McGrw-H Hghr Educ.

— Foundations of Financial Management. 7th ed. 800p. (C). 1993. text 71.75 (*0-256-14407-9*, Irwn McGrw-H) McGrw-H Hghr Educ.

— Foundations of Financial Management. 8th ed. LC 96-10499. (Series in Finance). (Illus.). 728p. (C). 1996. text 71.75 (*0-256-14615-2*, Irwn McGrw-H) McGrw-H Hghr Educ.

— Foundations of Financial Management. 8th annot. ed. LC 96-10499. (Series in Finance). (Illus.). 1996. teacher ed. write for info. (*0-256-14623-3*, Irwn McGrw-H) McGrw-H Hghr Educ.

— Foundations of Financial Management: CPCU Special Edition. 1993. text 29.83 (*0-7863-0177-5*, Irwn Prfssnl) McGraw-Hill Prof.

— Foundations of Financial Management Casebook. 8th ed. 96p. (C). 1996. text 14.95 (*0-256-14616-0*, Irwn McGrw-H) McGrw-H Hghr Educ.

— Foundations of Financial Management Package: With Ready Notes. 8th ed. (C). 1996. text, student ed. 82.95 (*0-256-24478-2*, Irwn McGrw-H) McGrw-H Hghr Educ.

— Foundations of Financial Management Ready Notes. 8th ed. (C). 1996. text 10.00 (*0-256-14621-7*, Irwn McGrw-H) McGrw-H Hghr Educ.

— Foundations of Financial Management Study Guide. 8th ed. 264p. (C). 1996. text 27.50 (*0-256-14617-9*, Irwn McGrw-H) McGrw-H Hghr Educ.

Block, Stanley B., et al. CPS - Foundations of Financial Management & Cases in Finance: Select Chapters. 7th ed. 456p. (C). 1995. text 30.50 (*0-256-20020-3*, Irwn McGrw-H) McGrw-H Hghr Educ.

— Foundations of Financial Management (Canadian) 4th ed. 928p. (C). 1997. per. 47.21 (*0-256-18672-3*, Irwn McGrw-H) McGrw-H Hghr Educ.

Block, Stanley B., jt. auth. see Hirt, Geoffrey A.

Block, Stephan M. On Foot in Arizona's Red Rock Country: Seven Spectacular Hikes with Interpretive Guide. 2nd rev. ed. 24p. 1994. pap. text 3.95 (*0-9641888-0-5*) Kokopelli Pr.

Block, Sue. Aerobix Plus: How to Sweat with Class. LC 81-80789. (Illus.). 240p. (Orig.). 1982. reprint ed. pap. 74.40 (*0-608-04284-6*, 206506300012) Bks Demand.

Block, Susan. The Ten Commandments of Pleasure: Erotic Keys to the Best Sex of Your Life. 1996. 16.95 (*0-614-97012-1*) St Martin.

Block, Susan M. Ten Commandments of Pleasure: Erotic Keys to a Healthy Sex Life, Set. abr. ed. 1996. audio 18.00 (*0-694-51740-2*, CPN 2602) HarperAudio.

Block, Susan Taylor. Along the Cape Fear. (Images of America Ser.). (Illus.). 128p. 1998. pap. 16.99 (*0-7524-0965-4*) Arcadia Publng.

***Block, Susan Taylor.** Cape Fear Beaches. (Images of America Ser.). 128p. 2000. pap. 18.99 (*0-7385-0578-1*) Arcadia Publng.

— Cape Fear Lost. (Images of America Ser.). (Illus.). 128p. 1999. pap. 18.99 (*0-7385-0192-1*) Arcadia Publng.

Block, T., et al. Innovations in Antiviral Development & the Detection of Virus Infection. (Advances in Experimental Medicine & Biology Ser.: Vol. 312). (Illus.). 240p. (C). 1992. text 89.50 (*0-306-44209-4*, Kluwer Plenum) Kluwer Academic.

Block, Tamara S., ed. The Only Sales Promotion Techniques You'll Ever Need. (Illus.). 267p. 1996. 39.95 (*0-85013-255-X*) Dartnell Corp.

Block, Tamara S., jt. auth. see Block, Martin P.

Block, Thomas, jt. auth. see DeMille, Nelson.

Block, Thomas A. & Frame, J. Davidson. The Project Office: A Key to Managing Projects Effectively. Christopher, Bill, ed. LC 97-68245. (Management Library: No. 12). 88p. 1997. pap. text 12.95 (*1-56052-443-X*) Crisp Pubns.

Block, Thomas H., jt. auth. see DeMille, Nelson.

Block, Timothy A., jt. auth. see Rhoads, Ann F.

Block, Valerie. Was It Something I Said? 359p. 1998. per. 14.00 (*0-671-02586-4*, WSP) PB.

— Was It Something I Said? LC 97-16735. 368p. 1998. 24.00 (*1-56947-109-6*) Soho Press.

Block, W. Annotated Bibliography of Antarctic Invertebrates (Terrestrial & Freshwater) 204p. 1992. pap. 50.00 (*0-85665-148-6*, Pub. by Brit Antarctic Surv) Balogh.

Block, W. T. Cotton Bales, Keelboats, & Sternwheelers: A History of the Sabine River & Trinity River Cotton Trades, 1837-1900. 256p. (Orig.). 1995. pap. 15.00 (*0-9646846-9-1*) Dogwood TX.

— Early Saw Mill Towns of the Louisiana-Texas Border Lands. (Illus.). 282p. 1996. reprint ed. pap. 15.00 (*1-887745-00-3*) Dogwood TX.

Block, W. T. Sawmills of East Texas. 408p. 35.00 (*1-878096-31-1*, Epigram Pr) Best E TX Pubs.

— Sawmills of East Texas, Vol. II. 408p. 35.00 (*1-878096-35-4*, Epigram Pr) Best E TX Pubs.

— Sawmills of East Texas, Vol. III. 408p. 35.00 (*1-878096-42-7*, Epigram Pr) Best E TX Pubs.

Block, W. T. Schooner Sail to Starboard: Confederate Blockade-Running on the Louisiana-Texas Coast Lines. large type ed. (Illus.). 258p. (Orig.). (C). 1997. pap. 15.00 (*1-887745-08-4*) Dogwood TX.

Block, Walter. Defending the Undefendable: The Pimp, Prostitute, Scab, Slumlord, Libeler, Moneylender & Other Scapegoats in the Rogues Gallery of American Society. 2nd ed. 232p. 1991. reprint ed. pap. 12.95 (*0-930073-05-3*) Fox & Wilkes.

Block, Will, jt. auth. see Valentine, Gail.

***Block, William M. & Finch, Deborah M., eds.** Songbird Ecology on Southwestern Ponderosa Pine Forests: A Literature Review. 152p. 2000. pap. text 30.00 (*0-7881-8582-9*) DIANE Pub.

Block, Zenas & MacMillan, Ian C. Corporate Venturing: Creating New Businesses Within the Firm. LC 92-28830. 272p. 1993. 35.00 (*0-87584-321-2*) Harvard Busn.

— Corporate Venturing: Creating New Businesses within the Firm. 384p. 1995. pap. 14.95 (*0-87584-641-6*) Harvard Busn.

— Corporate Venturing: New Business Creation from Within. 1992. text 35.00 (*0-07-103387-4*) McGraw.

Blockbuster Entertainment Staff. The Blockbuster Entertainment Guide to Movies & Videos: 1999 Edition. 1589p. 1998. mass mkt. 7.99 (*0-440-22598-1*) Doubleday.

— Blockbuster Entertainment Guide to Television on Video. LC 96-231749. 1996. mass mkt. 6.99 (*0-671-52902-1*) PB.

Blockcolsk. 40,000 Selected Words. 1998. pap. text 29.50 (*0-12-784551-8*) Acad Pr.

Blocker. World Philosophy: An East-West Comparative Introduction to Philosophy. LC 98-33926. 304p. (C). 1998. pap. text 38.60 (*0-13-862012-1*) P-H.

Blocker, ed. Introduction to Ethics. 600p. 1986. pap. 65.00 (*0-930586-42-5*) Haven Pubns.

Blocker, Anne K. Baby Basics: A Guide for New Parents. LC 98-231265. 276p. (Orig.). 1997. pap. 12.95 (*1-56561-090-3*) Wiley.

Blocker, Anne K. Baby Basics: A Guide for New Parents. 304p. (Orig.). 1997. pap. 12.95 (*0-471-34660-8*) Wiley.

Blocker, Anne K., jt. auth. see Behrens, Rosemary.

Blocker, Carolyn S. H-2 A Agricultural Guestworker Program: Changes Could Improve Services to Employers & Better Protect Workers. (Illus.). 148p. (C). 1998. pap. text 30.00 (*0-7881-7447-9*) DIANE Pub.

Blocker, David J. The Art of Emotions. large type ed. LC 97-95004. (Illus.). 254p. 1997. 39.97 (*0-9661694-0-9*, 1971) Hidden Thghts.

Blocker, Deborah E., jt. auth. see Dashman, Theodore.

Blocker, Francis A. History of Palmer, Texas. Palmer Preservation Society Staff, ed. LC 94-187125. (Illus.). 328p. 1994. reprint ed. text 60.00 (*0-88107-243-5*) Curtis Media.

Blocker, H., et al, eds. Chemical Synthesis in Molecular Biology: Biological Macromolecules. LC 87-8131. (GBF Monographs: Vol. 8). (Illus.). 222p. 1987. 105.00 (*3-527-26564-3*, Wiley-VCH) Wiley.

Blocker, H. Gene. The Aesthetics of Primitive Art. (Illus.). 342p. (Orig.). (C). 1994. pap. text 48.00 (*0-8191-9317-8*) U Pr of Amer.

Blocker, H. Gene & Bender, John W. Contemporary Philosophy of Art: Readings in Analytic Aesthetics. LC 92-30165. 672p. (C). 1992. text 41.20 (*0-13-018086-6*) P-H.

Blocker, H. Gene, jt. auth. see Jeffers, Jennifer M.

Blocker, H. Gene, jt. auth. see Parsons, Michael J.

Blocker, H. Gene, jt. auth. see Stewart, David.

Blocker, H. Gene, jt. compiled by see Smith, Elizabeth.

Blocker, H. Gene, jt. ed. see Liyuan, Zhu.

Blocker, Jack S., Jr. American Temperance Movements: Cycles of Reform. (Social Movements Past & Present Ser.). 264p. (C). 1988. 26.95 (*0-8057-9727-0*, Twyne) Mac Lib Ref.

— Give to the Winds Thy Fears: The Women Temperance Crusade, 1873-1874, 55. LC 84-15718. (Contributions in Women's Studies: No. 55). (Illus.). 280p. 1985. 59.95 (*0-313-24556-8*, BGW/, Greenwood Pr) Greenwood.

— Retreat from Reform: The Prohibition Movement in the United States, 1890-1913, 51. LC 76-5325. (Contributions in American History Ser.: No. 51). 263p. 1976. 38.50 (*0-8371-8899-7*, BRR/, Greenwood Pr) Greenwood.

Blocker, Jack S., Jr., ed. Alcohol, Reform & Society: The Liquor Issue in Social Context, 83. LC 78-73800. (Contributions in American History Ser.: No. 83). (Illus.). 289p. 1979. 65.00 (*0-313-20889-1*, BLA/, Greenwood Pr) Greenwood.

Blocker, Jane & Mendieta, Ana. Where Is Ana Mendieta? Identity, Performativity, & Exile. LC 98-30341. (Orig.). 1999. write for info. (*0-8223-2304-4*); pap. 17.95 (*0-8223-2324-9*) Duke.

Blocker, William, Jr. & Cardus, David, eds. Rehabilitation in Ischemic Heart Disease. LC 80-22840. (Illus.). 500p. 1983. text 80.00 (*0-88331-194-1*) R B Luce.

Blockley, Ann. Countryside with Color. pap. 14.95 (*0-00-412287-9*, Pub. by HarpC) Trafalgar.

Blockley, John. Creative Watercolour Techniques. (Leisure Arts Ser.: No. 7). (Illus.). 32p. pap. 4.95 (*0-85532-406-6*, 406-6, Pub. by Srch Pr) A Schwartz & Co.

— Pastels. (Learn to Paint Ser.). (Illus.). 1999. pap. 15.95 (*0-00-413346-3*, Pub. by HarpC) Trafalgar.

***Blockley, Mary.** Aspects of Old English Poetic Syntax: Where Clauses Begin. (Illinois Medieval Studies). 288p. 2001. text 39.95 (*0-252-02606-3*) U of Ill Pr.

Blockmans, W., jt. auth. see Berting, Jan.

Blockmans, Willem P. & Prevenier, Walter. The Promised Lands: The Low Countries under Burgundian Rule, 1369-1530. LC 98-48565. 1999. 19.95 (*0-8122-1382-3*) U of Pa Pr.

Blockmans, Wim. A History of Power in Europe: People, Markets, States. LC 98-111002. (Illus.). 400p. 1997. 60.00 (*0-8109-6347-7*, Pub. by Abrams) Time Warner.

— Promised Lands The Low Countries Under Burgundian Rule, 1369-1530. LC 98-48565. 1999. 42.50 (*0-8122-3130-9*) U of Pa Pr.

Blocknel, Eric, tr. see Berg, Alban.

***Blocksidge, Martin.** Teaching Literature 11-18. 2000. pap. 21.95 (*0-8264-4818-6*) Continuum.

Blocksma. Spaceships that Really Fly. 7.95 (*0-13-824318-2*) P-H.

Blocksma, Mary. Yoo Hoo, Moon! (Illus.). 32p. (J). 1992. pap. 4.50 (*0-553-35212-1*) Bantam.

***Blocksom, Jonathon T.** Golly Gee Blocks. (J). (gr. 3-8). 2000. cd-rom 25.00 (*0-9701391-0-1*) GollyGee.

Blocksom, Rita H. Nurturing Early Promise: Creative Thinking & Doing Activities for Young Children. LC 89-62690. (Illus.). 112p. (Orig.). 1989. pap. 10.95 (*0-939705-03-6*) Pinnaroo.

Blockson, Charles L. African Americans in Pennsylvania. LC 93-74114. 230p. (Orig.). 1994. pap. 14.95 (*0-933121-85-7*) Black Classic.

— Black Genealogy. LC 90-82688. 233p. 1992. reprint ed. pap. 14.95 (*0-933121-53-9*); reprint ed. text 24.95 (*0-933121-54-7*) Black Classic.

— Catalog of the Charles L. Blockson Afro-American Collection. (Illus.). 900p. 1991. 79.95 (*0-87722-749-7*) Temple U Pr.

— A Commented Bibliography of One Hundred & One Influential Books by & about People of African Descent (1556-1982). A Collector's Choice. (Illus.). 74p. 1989. text 60.00 (*90-70775-03-4*) Oak Knoll.

— Damn Rare: Memoirs of an African-American Bibliophile. unabridged ed. Hope, Barbara, ed. LC 98-86709. (Illus.). 356p. 1998. 24.95 (*1-892697-00-9*, 1-892697-cc-9) QLP CA.

— The Journey of John W. Mosley. (Illus.). 192p. 1992. 35.00 (*0-9627161-7-0*) QLP CA.

— Underground Railroad: Dramatic Firsthand Accounts of Daring Escapes to Freedom. 304p. 1994. pap. 10.00 (*0-425-14136-5*) Berkley Pub.

Blockton, Rita. Don't Call Me Rover: 5,001 Names to Call Your Pet. LC 95-94306. 256p. (Orig.). 1997. pap. 12.00 (*0-380-79224-9*, Avon Bks) Morrow Avon.

— 5001 Names for Your Pet. 256p. (Orig.). 1995. mass mkt. 4.99 (*0-380-78040-2*, Avon Bks) Morrow Avon.

Blodget, Samuel. Economica: A Statistical Manual for the United States of America. LC 64-17403. (Reprints of Economic Classics Ser.). viii, 202p. 1964. reprint ed. 35.00 (*0-678-00037-9*) Kelley.

Blodgett. Manual of Respiratory Care Procedures. 2nd ed. LC 65-8782. 1987. text 19.50 (*0-397-50714-3*, Lippnctt) Lppncott W & W.

Blodgett, Audrey H., jt. auth. see Wheelwright, Joseph B.

Blodgett, E. D. D. G. Jones & His Works. (Canadian Author Studies). 46p. (C). 1985. pap. text 9.95 (*0-920802-92-3*, Pub. by ECW) Genl Dist Srvs.

Blodgett, E. D., ed. from PRO. The Romance of Flamenca. LC 95-12161. (Library of Medieval Literature: Vol. 101A). Orig. Title: Flamenca. (Illus.). 504p. 1995. text 105.00 (*0-8240-5169-6*) Garland.

Blodgett, E. D., ed. see Wiebe, Rudy, et al.

Blodgett, Geoffrey. Oberlin Architecture, College & Town: A Guide to Its Social History. LC 84-18987. (Illus.). 260p. 1985. pap. 11.00 (*0-87338-309-5*) Kent St U Pr.

Blodgett, George B., ed. Records of Deaths in First Church of Rowley, Massachusetts, 1696-1777. Orig. Title: Copy of the Records of the Deaths of the First Church of Rowley, Massachusetts. 56p. 1996. reprint ed. pap. 15.00 (*1-878545-21-3*) ACETO Bookmen.

Blodgett, Harold W. Walt Whitman in England. 1972. 59.95 (*0-8490-1274-0*) Gordon Pr.

Blodgett, Harold W., ed. see Whitman, Walt.

Blodgett, Harriet. Capacious Hold-All: An Anthology of English-Women's Diary Writings. LC 91-16187. (Feminist Issues Ser.). 447p. reprint ed. pap. 138.60 (*0-608-20053-0*, 207132500011) Bks Demand.

— Centuries of Female Days: Englishwomen's Private Diaries. 304p. (C). 1988. text 45.00 (*0-8135-1314-6*) Rutgers U Pr.

Blodgett, Harriet E. Mentally Retarded Children: What Parents & Others Should Know. LC 72-152301. 175p. reprint ed. pap. 54.30 (*0-608-14092-9*, 205584500039) Bks Demand.

Blodgett, Harriet E. & Warfield, Grace J. Understanding Mentally Retarded Children. LC 59-12295. (Illus.). (Orig.). 1959. pap. text 8.95 (*0-89197-457-1*) Irvington.

Blodgett, I. D. Blodgett: Asahel Blodgett of Hudson & Dorchester, N. H. (Illus.). 144p. 1990. reprint ed. pap. 23.00 (*0-8328-1581-0*); reprint ed. lib. bdg. 33.00 (*0-8328-1580-2*) Higginson Bk Co.

Blodgett, Jan. Land of Bright Promise: Advertising the Texas Panhandle & South Plains, 1870-1917. LC 87-2531. (M. K. Brown Range Life Ser.: No. 17). (Illus.). 165p. 1988. 17.95 (*0-292-73037-3*) U of Tex Pr.

— Protestant Evangelical Literary Culture & Contemporary Society, 51. LC 96-53517. (Contributions to the Study of Religion Ser.: No. 51). 192p. 1997. 59.95 (*0-313-30395-9*, GM0395, Greenwood Pr) Greenwood.

Blodgett, Mark S., jt. auth. see Litka, Michael P.

***Blodgett, Peter J.** Land of Golden Dreams: California in the Gold Rush Decade 1848-1858. LC 99-39377. 144p. 1999. pap. 14.95 (*0-87328-182-9*) Huntington Lib.

— Land of Golden Dreams: California in the Gold Rush Decade, 1848-1858. LC 99-39377. (Illus.). 144p. 1999. 20.95 (*0-87328-183-7*) Huntington Lib.

Blodgett, Richard. Federal Paper Board at Seventy Five: The Intimate History of an American Enterprise. Robbins, Cella D., ed. (Illus.). 224p. 1991. text. write for info. (*0-944641-01-6*) Greenwich Pub Group.

— Johnson & Higgins at 150 Years. Robbins, Ceila D., ed. LC 94-80243. (Illus.). 160p. 1995. write for info. (*0-944641-11-3*) Greenwich Pub Group.

***Blodgett, Richard.** Menasha Corporation: An Odyssey of Five Generations. LC 99-60003. (Illus.). 168p. 1999. write for info. (*0-944641-35-0*) Greenwich Pub Group.

Blodgett, Richard, jt. auth. see Blount, Winton M.

Blodgett, Terrell. City Government That Works: The History of Council-Manager Government in Texas. unabridged ed. LC 98-61044. (Illus.). 300p. 1998. text 50.00 (*0-9665314-0-X*); lthr. 75.00 (*0-9665314-1-8*) TX City Mgmt Assn.

— Contracting Selected State Government Functions: Legislation & Implementation. (Policy Research Project Report Ser.: No. 81). 213p. 1987. pap. 12.00 (*0-89940-685-8*) LBJ Sch Pub Aff.

— An Institutional & Legal Assessment of an Instream Aeration Project in the Houston Ship Channel. (Policy Research Institute Ser.: No. 3). 200p. 1987. pap. 10.00 (*0-89940-152-X*) LBJ Sch Pub Aff.

— Management Review of the Texas State Preservation Board & the Office of the Architect. (Special Project Reports). 24p. 1988. pap. 5.00 (*0-89940-860-5*) LBJ Sch Pub Aff.

— Management Study of the American Educational Complex College District, Killeen, Texas. (Special Project Reports). 350p. 1989. pap. 10.00 (*0-89940-863-X*) LBJ Sch Pub Aff.

— Management Study of the Texas State Auditor's Office. 167p. 1984. pap. 3.00 (*0-89940-807-9*) LBJ Sch Pub Aff.

— Senior Management Service for Texas State Government. (Special Project Reports). 103p. 1989. pap. 7.00 (*0-89940-862-1*) LBJ Sch Pub Aff.

Blodgett, Terrell & Chapman, Jerome. Contracting Selected State Government Functions: Issues & Next Steps. (Policy Research Project Report Ser.: No. 75). 216p. 1987. pap. 10.00 (*0-89940-677-7*) LBJ Sch Pub Aff.

Blodgett, Terrell & Jordan, Barbara. Local Government Election Systems. LC 84-81908. (Policy Research Project Report: No. 62). 174p. 1984. pap. 8.95 (*0-89940-664-5*) LBJ Sch Pub Aff.

Blodgett, Timothy B., jt. ed. see Bursk, Edward C.

Blodgette, George B. & Jewett, Amos E. Early Settlers of Rowley. 472p. 1995. reprint ed. lib. bdg. 47.50 (*0-8328-4673-2*) Higginson Bk Co.

— Early Settlers of Rowley, Massachusetts. LC 81-83875. (Illus.). 472p. 1997. reprint ed. 45.00 (*0-89725-027-3*, 1235) Picton Pr.

Blodi, Frederic C., et al, eds. Surgical Ophthalmology Two. (Illus.). 728p. 1992. 298.00 (*0-387-52107-0*) Spr-Verlag.

Blodi, Frederic C., et al. Surgical Ophthalmology One. (Illus.). 592p. 1991. 327.00 (*0-387-52105-4*) Spr-Verlag.

Blodi, Frederick C., tr. see Bec, Pierre.

Blodi, Frederick C., tr. see Hollwich, Fritz.

Blodi, Frederick C., tr. see Pau, H.

Blodi, Frederick C., tr. see Richard, Gisbert.

Blodi, Frederick C., tr. see Richard, G., et al.

Blodinger, Anat. Intangible Assets in Germany & Great Britain: An Accounting Comparison. (European University Studies: Vol. 2376). 262p. 1998. 48.95 (*3-631-33993-3*) P Lang Pubng.

— Intangible Assets in Germany & Great Britain: An

B

An Asterisk (*) at the beginning of an entry indicates that the title is appearing for the first time.

Accounting Comparison. (European University Studies: Vol. 2376). 262p. (C). 1998. pap. text 48.95 (*0-8204-3636-4*) P Lang Pubng.

Blodnieks, Adolfs. Undefeated Nation. 1959. 15.00 (*0-8315-0019-0*) Speller.

Blodorn, Niels. Integriertes Rechnungswesen von Leasinggesellschaften. (GER., Illus.). 620p. 1996. 95.95 (*3-631-50065-3*) P Lang Pubng.

Bloebaum. Implant Retrieval & Analysis. 1995. 234.00 (*0-8493-6940-1*, CRC Reprint) Franklin.

Bloechl, Jeffrey. Liturgy of the Neighbor: Emmanuel Levinas & the Religion of Responsibility. LC 99-6670. 325p. 2000. text 55.00 (*0-8207-0311-7*) Duquesne.

***Bloechl, Jeffrey, ed.** The Face of the Other & the Trace of God: Essays on the Philosophy of Emmanuel Levinas. LC 99-49540. (Perspectives in Continental Philosophy Ser.: No. 10). 336p. (C). 2000. 39.95 (*0-8232-1965-8*, Pub. by Fordham); pap. 19.95 (*0-8232-1966-6*, Pub. by Fordham) BookMasters.

***Bloed, A.** Protection of Minority Rights Through Bilateral Treaties: The Case of Central & Eastern Europe. LC 99-40298. 1999. 130.00 (*90-411-1270-7*) Kluwer Law Intl.

Bloed, Arie. The Changing Functions of the Western European Union (WEU) Introduction & Basic Documents. LC 94-24130. 260p. (C). 1994. lib. bdg. 111.00 (*0-7923-3221-0*, Pub. by M Nijhoff) Kluwer Academic.

— The External Relations of the Council for Mutual Economic Assistance. (C). 1988. lib. bdg. 104.50 (*90-247-3783-4*) Kluwer Academic.

Bloed, Arie, ed. The Challenges of Change: The Helsinki Summit of the CSCE & Its Aftermath. LC 94-30591. 1994. lib. bdg. 142.50 (*0-7923-3089-7*) Kluwer Academic.

— Monitoring Human Rights in Europe: Comparing International Procedures & Mechanisms. (International Helsinki Federation for Human Rights Studies). 352p. (C). 1993. lib. bdg. 117.00 (*0-7923-2383-1*) Kluwer Academic.

Bloed, Arie & Conference on Security & Cooperation in Europe (Or. The Conference on Security & Co-Operation in Europe: Basic Documents, 1993-1995. LC 97-2274. 924p. 1997. 257.50 (*90-411-0372-4*) Kluwer Law Intl.

Bloed, Arie & Van Dijk, P., eds. The Human Dimension of the Helsinki Process: The Vienna Follow-up Meeting & Its Aftermath. (International Studies in Human Rights). 364p. (C). 1991. lib. bdg. 128.00 (*0-7923-1337-2*) Kluwer Academic.

Bloede, Louis W. The Effective Pastor: A Guide to Successful Ministry. 144p. 1996. pap. 15.00 (*0-8006-2787-3*, 1-2787, Fortress Pr) Augsburg Fortress.

Bloedel, James R., et al, eds. Acquisition of Motor Behavior in Vertebrates. (Illus.). 480p. 1996. 65.00 (*0-262-02404-7*, Bradford Bks) MIT Pr.

Bloedel, James R., jt. ed. see Davis, Ross.

Bloeh & Isacoff. Piano Repertoire. 1999. 40.00 (*0-02-864748-3*, Schirmer Books) Mac Lib Ref.

Bloem, Diane. Growing Godly. pap. 3.95 (*0-310-23141-8*) Zondervan.

Bloem, Diane B. Bible Hidden Word Puzzles. 96p. (J). 1992. reprint ed. pap. 3.99 (*0-310-21332-0*) Zondervan.

— Challenging Bible Crossword Puzzles. 96p. (J). 1992. pap. 3.99 (*0-310-21342-8*) Zondervan.

— Classic Bible Crossword Puzzles. 96p. (J). 1992. pap. 3.99 (*0-310-21382-7*) Zondervan.

— Into the Midst of Suffering: A Woman's Workshop on Job. (Woman's Workshop Ser.). (Orig.). 1986. pap. 5.95 (*0-310-42771-1*, 11213P); pap. 3.95 (*0-310-42781-9*, 11214P) Zondervan.

— A Woman's Workshop on Proverbs. 1978. teacher ed. 5.95 (*0-310-21371-1*, 10684P) Zondervan.

— A Woman's Workshop on the Beautitudes. (Orig.). 1981. pap. 5.95 (*0-310-42641-3*, 11216P); pap. 4.99 (*0-310-42651-0*, 11217P) Zondervan.

— Woman's Workshop on the Sermon on the Mount. 1987. pap. 5.99 (*0-310-42701-0*, 10739P) Zondervan.

Bloem, Diane B. & Bloem, Robert C. A Women's Workshop on Bible Marriages. (Woman's Workshop Ser.). 128p. (Orig.). 1980. pap. 5.99 (*0-310-21391-6*, 10687P); pap. 5.95 (*0-310-21401-7*, 10688P) Zondervan.

Bloem, J. L. Liber Amicorum Presented to Prof. Dr. J. D. Mulder: Journal: Diagnostic Imaging in Clinical Medicine, Vol. 55, Nos. 4 & 5. (Illus.). 100p. 1986. pap. 61.75 (*3-8055-4480-4*) S Karger.

Bloem, John L. & Satoris, David J. MRI & CT of the Musculoskeletal System. (Illus.). 672p. 1991. 150.00 (*0-683-00875-7*) Lppncott W & W.

Bloem, Martin W., jt. ed. see Semba, Richard.

Bloem, Maurice & Wolffers, Ivan, eds. The Impact of Injections on Daily Medical Practice. 130p. 1993. pap. 25.00 (*90-5383-147-9*, Pub. by VU Univ Pr) Paul & Co Pubs.

Bloem, Patricia L., jt. auth. see Klooster, David J.

Bloem, Robert C., jt. auth. see Bloem, Diane B.

Bloembergen, Nicolaas. Encounters in Magnetic Resonance: Selected Papers of Nicolaas Bloembergen, with Commentary. 1996. pap. text 36.00 (*981-02-2590-3*) World Scientific Pub.

— Encounters in Nonlinear Optics: Selected Papers of Nicolaas Bloembergen, with Commentary. (World Scientific Series in 20th Century Mathematics: Vol. 16). 600p. 1996. write for info. (*981-02-2549-0*); pap. write for info. (*981-02-2591-1*) World Scientific Pub.

— Nonlinear Optics. 4th ed. LC 96-215048. 1996. 32.00 (*981-02-2598-9*); pap. text 18.00 (*981-02-2599-7*) World Scientific Pub.

Bloembergen, Nicolaas, ed. Encounters in Magnetic Resonances: Selected Papers of Nicolaas Bloembergen. LC 95-45777. (Series in 20th Century Physics: Vol. 15). 560p. 1996. write for info. (*981-02-2505-9*) World Scientific Pub.

— Nonlinear & Quantum Optics, 10 vols., Set. LC 96-77141. (Research Trends in Physics Ser.). (Illus.). 620p. (C). 1996. 85.00 (*1-889545-00-7*) Stefan Univ Pr.

Bloeme, Peter. Frisbee Dogs: How to Raise, Train & Compete. LC 94-92094. 192p. (Orig.). 1994. pap. text 14.95 (*0-9629346-2-3*) Skyhoundz.

— Frisbee Dogs: How to Raise, Train & Compete (Packaged with Frisbee Disc) (Illus.). 192p. 1994. pap. 18.95 (*0-9629346-4-X*) Skyhoundz.

— Skyhoundz Images. LC 98-90124. 80p. 1999. 19.95 (*0-9629346-7-4*) Skyhoundz.

Bloemen, Hans, ed. The Interstellar Disk-Halo Connection in Galaxies. (C). 1991. pap. text 69.00 (*0-7923-1256-2*); lib. bdg. 157.50 (*0-7923-1255-4*) Kluwer Academic.

***Bloemendaal, Leon.** Humanual. 2000. pap. 25.00 (*0-9664100-6-8*) Razorfish Studios.

Bloemertz, Gunther. Heaven Next Stop: A Luftwaffe Fighter Pilot at War. (Illus.). 192p. 1997. 29.95 (*1-57427-070-2*) Howell Pr VA.

— Heaven Next Stop: A Luftwaffe Fighter Pilot at War. (Illus.). 192p. 1996. 31.95 (*0-7509-1328-2*, Pub. by Sutton Pub Ltd) Intl Pubs Mktg.

— Heaven Next Stop: A Luftwaffe Fighter Pilot at War. (Illus.). 189p. 1998. pap. 21.95 (*0-7509-2054-8*) Sutton Pub Ltd.

Bloemheuvel, Marente, jt. ed. see Guidemond, Jaap.

Bloemheuvel, Marente, ed. see Mol, Pieter L.

Bloemink, Barbara. Georgia O'Keeffe: Canyon Suite. pap. 20.00 (*0-8076-1469-6*, Pub. by Braziller) Norton.

Bloemink, Barbara. Georgia O'Keeffe: Canyon Suite. (Illus.). 104p. 1995. 35.00 (*0-8076-1375-4*); pap. 20.00 (*0-8076-1376-2*) Braziller.

— A Natural Order: The Experience of Landscape in Contemporary Sculpture. (Illus.). 44p. (Orig.). 1990. pap. 7.50 (*0-943651-23-9*) Hudson Riv.

Bloemink, Barbara J. The Life & Art of Florine Stettheimer. LC 95-30528. (Illus.). 320p. 1995. 50.00 (*0-300-06340-7*) Yale U Pr.

Bloemink, Barbara J. & Self, Dana. Reality Bites: Realism in Contemporary Art. (Illus.). 42p. 1996. pap. 15.00 (*1-891246-00-3*) Kemper Mus.

Bloesch, Daniel W., tr. see Bonhoeffer, Dietrich.

Bloesch, Donald G. Christian Foundations, 4 vols. 97.96 (*0-8308-8140-9*) InterVarsity.

— Christian Foundations, 4 vols., Set. 1994. 94.96 (*0-8308-1410-8*, 1410) InterVarsity.

— The Christian Life & Salvation. 168p. 1991. reprint ed. pap. 17.95 (*0-939443-24-4*) Helmers Howard Pub.

— The Crisis of Piety: Essays Toward a Theology of the Christian Life. 2nd ed. LC 88-10989. 180p. 1988. pap. 17.95 (*0-939443-05-8*) Helmers Howard Pub.

— Crumbling Foundations: Death & Rebirth in an Age of Upheaval. 160p. (Orig.). (C). 1984. pap. 2.95 (*0-310-29821-0*, 12740P) Zondervan.

— Essentials of Evangelical Theology Vol. I: God, Authority, Salvation. LC 77-15872. 288p. 1982. pap. 19.00 (*0-06-060802-1*, RD 386, Pub. by Harper SF) HarpC.

— The Future of Evangelical Christianity: A Call for Unity amid Diversity. 2nd rev. ed. LC 88-11187. 228p. 1988. reprint ed. pap. 17.95 (*0-939443-10-4*) Helmers Howard Pub.

— God the Almighty: Power, Wisdom, Love, Holiness. LC 95-40450. (Christian Foundations Ser.: Vol. 3). 380p. (Orig.). 1995. 24.99 (*0-8308-1413-2*, 1413) InterVarsity.

— The Ground of Certainty. 212p. 1993. reprint ed. ring bd. 17.95 (*1-57383-010-0*) Regent College.

— Holy Scripture: Revelation, Inspiration & Interpretation. LC 93-47018. (Christian Foundations Ser.: Vol. 2). 384p. 1994. 24.99 (*0-8308-1412-4*, 1412) InterVarsity.

***Bloesch, Donald G.** Holy Spirit: Works & Gifts. (Illus.). 400p. 2000. 24.99 (*0-8308-1415-9*) InterVarsity.

Bloesch, Donald G. Jesus Christ: Savior & Lord. LC 97-30225. (Christian Foundations Ser.: Vol. 4). 216p. 1997. 22.99 (*0-8308-1414-0*, 1414) InterVarsity.

***Bloesch, Donald G.** The Reform of the Church. 200p. 1998. pap. 20.00 (*1-57910-174-7*) Wipf & Stock.

Bloesch, Donald G. The Struggle of Prayer. LC 87-23764. 192p. (C). 1988. pap. 17.95 (*0-939443-04-X*) Helmers Howard Pub.

— Theological Notebook, Vol. I. LC 88-24566. 256p. 1989. pap. 18.95 (*0-939443-12-0*) Helmers Howard Pub.

— Theological Notebook, Vol. 2. LC 88-24566. (Spiritual Journals of Donald G. Bloesch). 219p. 1991. pap. 18.95 (*0-939443-13-9*) Helmers Howard Pub.

— A Theology of Word & Spirit: Authority & Method in Theology. LC 92-20688. (Christian Foundations Ser.: Vol. 1). 400p. 1992. 24.99 (*0-8308-1411-6*, 1411) InterVarsity.

***Blofeld, John.** Taoism. 208p. 2000. pap. 15.95 (*1-57062-589-1*, Pub. by Shambhala Pubns) Random.

Blofeld, John E. Bodhisattva of Compassion: The Mystical Tradition of Kuan Yin. LC 87-28524. (Dragon Editions Ser.). (Illus.). 158p. 1988. pap. 15.00 (*0-87773-126-8*, Pub. by Shambhala Pubns) Random.

— The Chinese Art of Tea. (Illus.). 224p. (Orig.). 1997. pap. 19.95 (*1-57062-279-5*, Pub. by Shambhala Pubns) Random.

— Mantras Sacred Word of Power. 106p. 1977. 11.95 (*0-04-294097-4*) Asia Bk Corp.

— The Tantric Mysticism of Tibet. 256p. 1992. reprint ed. pap. 13.95 (*0-14-019336-7*, Arkana) Viking Penguin.

— The Zen Teaching of Huang Po: On the Transmission of the Mind. 144p. 1959. pap. 12.00 (*0-8021-5092-6*, Grove) Grove-Atltic.

Blofeld, John E., ed. I Ching: The Book of Change. 228p. 1991. pap. 12.95 (*0-14-019335-9*, Arkana) Viking Penguin.

Blogg, Colin E., jt. auth. see Boulton, Thomas B.

Bloggett, Helen N. Cancer Care - Aid & Facilities: Index of New Information & Resources. 160p. 1997. 47.50 (*0-7883-1532-3*); pap. 44.50 (*0-7883-1533-1*) ABBE Pubs Assn.

Blohincev, D. I., et al. Probability & Physical Problems. (Translations Ser.: Series 1, Vol. 11). 390p. 1962. reprint ed. pap. 35.00 (*0-8218-1611-X*, TRANS1/11) Am Math.

Blohm, Hans, jt. auth. see Hass, Rudi.

Blohm, Judith M. Where in the World Are You Going? (Illus.). 64p. (Orig.). (J). (gr. 1-5). 1996. pap. 9.95 (*1-877864-44-7*) Intercult Pr.

Blohnik, Joel, jt. auth. see Smisek, Anita.

Blohowiak, Don. Lead Your Staff to Think Like Einstein, Create Like DaVinci, & Invent Like Edison: Powerful Real World Techniques That Work! 2nd ed. LC 94-44810. 125p. 1995. 15.95 (*0-7863-0424-3*, Irwn Prfssnl) McGraw-Hill Prof.

— Your People Are Your Product: How to Hire the Best So You Can Stay the Best. LC 97-77507. 256p. 1998. 22.95 (*1-886284-10-5*, Pub. by Chandler Hse) Natl Bk Netwk.

Blohowiak, Don, et al. Complete Idiot's Guide to Great Customer Service. LC 97-73148. 352p. 1997. 16.95 (*0-02-861953-6*) Macmillan Gen Ref.

Blohowiak, Donald W. No Comment! An Executive's Guide to the News Media. LC 87-15831. 237p. 1987. 59.95 (*0-275-92820-9*, C2820, Praeger Pubs) Greenwood.

Bloice, Carl. Israel: Image & Reality: a Journalist's First-Hand Report. 48p. 1973. pap. 0.65 (*0-87898-103-9*) New Outlook.

Blois, Beverly. History Civil Combin, Vol. 2. 9th ed. 1996. pap. text, student ed. 19.33 (*0-13-228412-X*) P-H.

Blois, John T. Gazetteer of the State of Michigan. LC 75-87. (Mid-American Frontier Ser.). 1975. reprint ed. 34.95 (*0-405-06855-7*) Ayer.

— Gazetteer of the State of Michigan. 418p. 1993. reprint ed. lib. bdg. 45.00 (*0-8328-3498-X*) Higginson Bk Co.

— Michigan Gazetteer, 1838. 418p. 1979. 19.75 (*0-686-27820-8*) Bookmark.

Blois, Lukas De, see De Blois, Lukas.

Bloise, Patricia Anne. Dancing with the Serpent: Diary of Madness. 1998. pap. 12.00 (*1-889131-36-9*) CasAnanda.

***Blok, Aleksandr.** Selected Poems. 128p. 2000. 14.95 (*1-85754-473-0*, Pub. by Carcanet Pr) Paul & Co Pubs.

***Blok, Anton.** Honor & Violence. 240p. 1999. 26.95 (*0-7456-0449-8*, Pub. by Polity Pr) Blackwell Pubs.

Blok, Anton. The Mafia of a Sicilian Village, 1860-1960: A Study of Violent Peasant Entrepreneurs. (Illus.). 293p. (C). 1988. reprint ed. pap. text 13.95 (*0-88133-325-5*) Waveland Pr.

Blok, Arie W., tr. see Dathenus, Petrus.

Blok, C. Illustrated Automobile Dictionary Polish-French-English-German-Italian-Russian. (ENG, FRE, GER, ITA & POL.). 680p. 1987. 62.00 (*83-206-0234-3*, Pub. by Komunikacji Lacz) IBD Ltd.

Blok, Czeslaw, et al. Dictionnaire Illustre Technique Automobile en 6 Langues. (DUT, ENG, FRE, GER & ITA.). 680p. 1981. 195.00 (*0-8288-0050-2*, M9475) Fr & Eur.

— Different Elements of a General Science of Culture. 110p. 1990. text 72.95 (*1-85628-065-9*, Pub. by Avebry) Ashgate Pub Co.

Blok, D. P., ed. Proceedings of the Eighth International Congress of Onomastic Sciences, Amsterdam, 1963. (Janua Linguarum, Series Major: No. 17). 1966. 176.95 (*90-279-0609-2*) Mouton.

Blok, F. F., ed. Seventy-Seven Neo-Latin Letters: An Anthology. (Illus.). ix, 256p. 1985. 50.00 (*90-6088-091-9*, Pub. by Boumas Boekhuis) Gen Publ ON.

Blok, Frits. I Ching: A Spiritual Guide. (Illus.). 144p. 1997. 24.95 (*1-55670-590-5*) Stewart Tabori & Chang.

***Blok, H. & Van Den Berg, P. M.** Electromagnetic Waves: An Introductory Course. (Illus.). 258p. 1999. pap. 37.50 (*90-407-1836-9*, Pub. by Delft U Pr) Coronet Bks.

Blok, Josine H. The Early Amazons: Modern & Ancient Perspectives on a Persistent Myth. LC 94-36310. (Religions in the Graeco-Roman World Ser.: Vol. 120). xxiii, 473p. 1994. 171.00 (*90-04-10077-6*) Brill Academic Pubs.

Blok, Petrus J. History of the People of the Netherlands, 5 vols. Bierstadt, O. A. & Putnam, Ruth, trs. LC 76-109911. (Illus.). reprint ed. 345.00 (*0-404-00900-X*) AMS Pr.

— The Life of Admiral De Ruyter. Renier, G. J., tr. LC 74-9393. (Illus.). 338p. 1975. reprint ed. lib. bdg. 55.00 (*0-8371-7666-2*, BLAR, Greenwood Pr) Greenwood.

Blok, W. J. & Pigozzi, D. L. Algebraizable Logics. LC 88-8130. (MEMO Ser.: Vol. 77-396). 78p. 1990. pap. 16.00 (*0-8218-2459-7*, MEMO/77/396) Am Math.

Blok, W. J. & Pigozzi, Don. Algebraizable Logics. LC 88-8130. (American Mathematical Society Ser.: Vol. 396). (Illus.). 87p. 1989. reprint ed. pap. 30.00 (*0-608-07978-2*, 205267300001) Bks Demand.

Blokdijk, Andre & Blokdijk, Paul, eds. Planning & Design of Information Systems. (Illus.). 578p. 1991. pap. text 65.00 (*0-12-107071-9*) Acad Pr.

Blokdijk, Paul, jt. ed. see Blokdijk, Andre.

Blokh, A. G. Heat Transfer in Steam Boiler Furnaces. 350p. 1987. 160.00 (*0-89116-626-2*) Hemisp Pub.

Blokhin, A. M. Differential Equation Theory. 207p. (C). 1996. lib. bdg. 125.00 (*1-56072-311-4*) Nova Sci Pubs.

— Mathematical Modelling & Differential Equations. 217p. (C). 1996. lib. bdg. 135.00 (*1-56072-310-6*) Nova Sci Pubs.

— Strong Discontinuities in Magnetohydrodynamics. Zakharov, A. V., tr. 167p. 1994. lib. bdg. 145.00 (*1-56072-144-8*) Nova Sci Pubs.

Blokhin, A. M. & Dorovsky, V. N. Mathematical Modelling in the Theory of Multivelocity Continuum. 192p. (C). 1995. lib. bdg. 165.00 (*1-56072-240-1*) Nova Sci Pubs.

Blokhin, A. M. & Tkachev, D. L. Mixed Problems for the Wave Equation in Coordinate Domains. LC 98-28355. 1998. 95.00 (*1-56072-592-3*) Nova Sci Pubs.

Blokhin, M. & Curzon, F. Methods of X-Ray Spectroscopic Research. LC 63-10112. 1965. 203.00 (*0-08-010016-3*, Pub. by Pergamon Repr) Franklin.

Blokhin, N. N. & Trapeznikov. Soviet Medical Reviews Section F Oncology Reviews, Vol. 1. xii, 222p. 1987. text 389.00 (*3-7186-0313-6*) Gordon & Breach.

— Soviet Medical Reviews Section F Oncology Reviews, Vol. 2. ix, 130p. 1987. text 237.00 (*3-7186-0436-1*) Gordon & Breach.

Blokhintsev, D. I. The Philosophy of Quantum Mechanics. LC 68-22439. 132p. 1968. text 122.00 (*90-277-0105-9*) Kluwer Academic.

— Quantum Mechanics. Sykes, J. B. & Kearsley, M. J., trs. from RUS. 535p. 1964. text 137.50 (*90-277-0104-0*) Kluwer Academic.

— Space & Time in the Microworld. Smith, Z., tr. from RUS. LC 72-77871. Orig. Title: Prostranstuo I Uremja V Micromire. 330p. 1973. text 184.00 (*90-277-0240-3*) Kluwer Academic.

Blokhintsev, D. I. & Weinstein, Jack B. Law & Administration: Nuclear Liability. LC 59-8165. (Progress in Nuclear Energy Ser.: Vol. 10). 1962. 221.00 (*0-08-009703-0*, Pub. by Pergamon Repr) Franklin.

Blokker, Bill. What the Other Eye Sees. (Chapbook Ser.: Series 6). 32p. 1991. 5.00 (*0-933573-14-6*) Wayland Pr.

— What Will Happen to the Children? A Macabre View of the Future - or Today? Orig. Title: A Pocketful of Wry. 14p. 1998. reprint ed. pap. 3.25 (*0-88680-434-5*, C4345) I E Clark.

Blokker, Bill, jt. auth. see Smith, Barbara.

Blokker, Bill, ed. see Glaes, Jan.

Blokker, Niels. International Regulation of World Trade in Textiles. (C). 1989. lib. bdg. 139.50 (*0-7923-0560-4*) Kluwer Academic.

— Towards More Effective Supervision by International Organizations: Essays in Honour of Henry G. Schermers, Vol. I. 372p. (C). 1994. lib. bdg. 169.50 (*0-7923-3159-1*, Pub. by M Nijhoff) Kluwer Academic.

Blokker, Niels, et al, eds. The European Union after Amsterdam: A Legal Analysis. LC 98-43825. 364p. 1998. 135.00 (*90-411-1131-X*) Kluwer Academic.

Blokker, Roy & Dearling, Robert. The Music of Dmitri Shostakovich. LC 78-68623. 192p. 1979. 32.50 (*0-8386-1948-7*) Fairleigh Dickinson.

Blokland, A. F. D. In Search of the Text Syntax: Toward a Syntactic Text-Segmentation Model for Biblical Hebrew. (Applicatio Ser.: Vol. 14). 318p. 1995. pap. 35.00 (*90-5383-388-9*) Paul & Co Pubs.

Blokland, Hans T. Roads to Freedom: Freedom, Autonomy & Culture in Western Society. LC 96-30128. 336p. (C). 1997. 85.00 (*0-415-15000-0*) Routledge.

Blokland, J. Continuous Consumer Equivalence Scales. 1976. pap. text 78.50 (*90-247-1847-3*) Kluwer Academic.

Blokland, R. Elasticity & Structure of Polyurethane Networks. 118p. 1968. 24.00 (*0-677-61200-1*) Gordon & Breach.

Bloksberg, Robin. Alexander Ant Cools Off: Big Book. large type ed. (Little Books & Big Bks.). (Illus.). 8p. (J). (gr. k-2). 1997. pap. text 19.47 (*0-8215-0921-7*) Sadlier.

Bloland, Harland G. Associations in Action: The Washington, D. C. Higher Education Community. Fife, Jonathan D., ed. & frwd. by. LC 85-72833. (ASHE-ERIC Higher Education Reports: No. 85-2). 135p. (Orig.). 1985. pap. 24.00 (*0-913317-21-7*) GWU Grad Schl E&HD.

— Creating Chea: Building a New National Organization on Accrediting. (Ace/Oryx Series on Higher Education). 200p. 2000. text 34.95 (*1-57356-233-5*) Oryx Pr.

Bloland, Harland G. & Bloland, Sue M. American Learned Societies in Transition: The Impact of Dissent & Recession. LC 74-1339. 150p. reprint ed. pap. 46.50 (*0-8357-5380-8*, 202948800061) Bks Demand.

Bloland, Sue M., jt. auth. see Bloland, Harland G.

***Blom, Ansuya.** Let Us See, Is This Real? 112p. 2000. 35.00 (*90-5662-137-8*) NAi Uitgevers.

Blom-Cooper, Louis, ed. Progress in Penal Reform. 1975. 59.00 (*0-19-825325-7*) OUP.

Blom, Dorothea. Art & the Changing World: Uncommon Sense in the Twentieth Century. LC 72-80094. (Illus.). 32p. (Orig.). (C). 1972. pap. 4.00 (*0-87574-183-5*) Pendle Hill.

— Art Imagery & the Mythic Process. LC 77-91636. (Illus.). 31p. (Orig.). 1977. pap. 4.00 (*0-87574-215-7*) Pendle Hill.

— Art Responds to the Bible. LC 74-24006. (Illus.). 32p. (Orig.). 1974. pap. 4.00 (*0-87574-197-5*) Pendle Hill.

Blom, Dorothea. Encounters with Art. LC 63-15300. (C). 1963. pap. 1.00 (*0-87574-128-2*) Pendle Hill.

— Life Journey of a Quaker Artist. LC 80-80916. 32p. (Orig.). 1980. 1.00 (*0-87574-232-7*) Pendle Hill.

Blom, Dorothea. The Prophetic Element in Modern Art. LC 66-28100. (C). 1966. pap. 4.00 (*0-87574-148-7*) Pendle Hill.

Blom, Edward C. Radio & Electric Power Supply Equipment for Schools. LC 77-176571. (Columbia University. Teachers College. Contributions to Education Ser.: No. 409). reprint ed. 37.50 (*0-404-55409-1*) AMS Pr.

Blom, Eirik A. T. Teaching Kids about Birds: A Special Publication from Bird Watcher's Digest. Thompson, William, III & Bowers, Mary B., eds. LC 96-206353. (Illus.). 32p. (Orig.). 1996. pap. write for info. (*1-880241-09-9*) Bird Watchers.

B

An Asterisk (*) at the beginning of an entry indicates that the title is appearing for the first time.

Blom, Eric. Beethoven's Pianoforte Sonatas Discussed. (Music Book Index Ser.). 251p. 1992. reprint ed. lib. bdg. 79.00 (*0-7812-9488-6*) Rprt Serv.
— Classics: Major & Minor. LC 74-166098. 212p. 1972. reprint ed. lib. bdg. 29.50 (*0-306-70293-2*) Da Capo.
— The Limitations of Music: A Study in Aesthetics. LC 72-80139. 1972. reprint ed. 20.95 (*0-405-08275-4*, Pub. by Blom Pubns) Ayer.
— Mozart: Music Book Index. 387p. 1993. reprint ed. lib. bdg. 89.00 (*0-7812-9610-2*) Rprt Serv.
— Music in England. 1988. reprint ed. lib. bdg. 49.00 (*0-317-90766-2*) Rprt Serv.
— Music in England. LC 71-181112. 220p. 1942. reprint ed. 49.00 (*0-403-01511-1*) Scholarly.
— Romance of the Piano. LC 69-15608. (Music Ser.). (Illus.). 1969. reprint ed. 32.50 (*0-306-71060-9*) Da Capo.
— Stepchildren of Music. LC 67-28731. (Essay Index Reprint Ser.). 1977. 20.95 (*0-8369-0217-3*) Ayer.
— Tchaikovsky: Orchestral Works. 51p. 1990. reprint ed. lib. bdg. 59.00 (*0-7812-9162-3*) Rprt Serv.
Blom, Eric, tr. see Deutsch, Otto E.
Blom, Eric D., et al. Tracheoesophageal Voice Restoration Following Total Laryngectomy. LC 98-14671. (Illus.). 250p. 1998. pap. 191.95 (*1-56593-908-5*, 1798) Thomson Learn.
Blom, Frans, et al, compiled by. English Catholic Books, 1701-1800: A Bibliography. LC 95-36772. 400p. 1996. 104.95 (*1-85928-148-6*, Pub. by Scolar Pr) Ashgate Pub Co.
Blom, G. Probability & Statistics. (Texts in Statistics Ser.). (Illus.). 375p. 1989. 84.95 (*0-387-96852-0*) Spr-Verlag.
Blom, Gaston E., et al. Stress in Childhood: An Intervention Model for Teachers & Other Professionals. LC 85-14825. (Special Education Ser.). 219p. reprint ed. pap. 67.90 (*0-7837-4627-X*, 204435000002) Bks Demand.
Blom, Gertrude D. Gertrude Blom: Bearing Witness. Harris, Alex & Sartor, Margaret, eds. LC 83-23272. (Illus.). 160p. 1984. pap. 49.60 (*0-608-05215-9*, 206575200001) Bks Demand.
Blom, Gunilla, jt. auth. see Graves, Peter.
Blom, Gunnar, et al. Problems & Snapshots from the World of Probability. LC 93-31828. (Illus.). 240p. 1994. 43.95 (*0-387-94161-4*) Spr-Verlag.
Blom, Hans H. A Revision of the Schistidium Apocarpum Complex in Norway & Sweden. Gradstein, S. R., ed. (Bryophytorum Bibliotheca: Vol. 49). (GER., Illus.). 334p. 1996. pap. 83.00 (*3-443-62021-3*, DM 140, Pub. by Gebruder Borntraeger) Balogh.
Blom, Hans W., ed. see Sidney, Algernon.
***Blom, Ida, et al, eds.** Gendered Nations: Nationalisms & Gender Order in the Nineteenth Century. (Illus.). 256p. 2000. 65.00 (*1-85973-259-3*, Pub. by Berg Pubs); pap. 19.50 (*1-85973-264-X*, Pub. by Berg Pubs) NYU Pr.
***Blom, J. C., et al, eds.** The History of the Jews in the Netherlands. (Illus.). 450p. 1999. 55.00 (*1-874774-51-X*) Intl Spec Bk.
Blom, J. C. & Lamberts, E., eds. History of the Low Countries. Kennedy, James C., tr. from DUT. LC 98-22708. Orig. Title: Geschiedenis van de Nederlanden. (Illus.). 504p. 1999. 85.00 (*1-57181-084-6*); pap. 29.95 (*1-57181-085-4*) Berghahn Bks.
Blom, John, jt. auth. see Hayes, Allan.
Blom, Lynne A. & Chaplin, L. Tarin. The Moment of Movement: Dance Improvisation. LC 88-1332. (Illus.). 256p. (Orig.). (C). 1988. pap. 14.95 (*0-8229-5405-2*); text 29.95 (*0-8229-3586-4*) U of Pittsburgh Pr.
Blom, Lynne A., et al. The Intimate Act of Choreography. LC 82-2056. (Illus.). 252p. (C). 1982. pap. 14.95 (*0-8229-5342-0*) U of Pittsburgh Pr.
Blom, M. L. Depicted Deities: Painters' Model Books in Nepal. (Groningen Oriental Studies: Vol. IV). vii, 92p. (Orig.). 1989. pap. 46.00 (*90-6980-029-2*, Pub. by Egbert Forsten) Hod1der & Stoughton.
Blom, Margaret. Charlotte Bronte. (English Authors Ser.: No. 203). 176p. 1977. 21.95 (*0-8057-6673-1*, Twyne) Mac Lib Ref.
Blom, Oivind. Hugo Norwegian in Three Months: Simplified Language Course. LC 98-48007. (Hugo Ser.). (NOR & ENG.). 1999. 29.95 incl. audio (*0-7894-4437-2*) DK Pub Inc.
— Norwegian in Three Months. LC 98-48007. (Hugo Ser.). 240p. 1999. pap. 14.95 (*0-7894-4428-3*) DK Pub Inc.
***Blom, Phillipp.** Wines of Austria. (Illus.). 192p. 2000. pap. 17.00 (*0-571-19533-4*, Pub. by Faber & Faber) Penguin Books.
Blom, Raimo, et al, eds. Between Plan & Market: Social Change in the Baltic State & Russia. (Societies in Transition Ser.: No. 6). x, 182p. (C). 1996. text 52.95 (*3-11-015017-4*) De Gruyter.
***Blom, Susanne Alles.** Inca. 352p. 2001. text 24.95 (*0-312-87434-0*) Forge NYC.
Blomain, et al. The Rainbow. 2nd ed. 80p. (C). 1997. spiral bd. 18.50 (*0-7872-4618-2*) Kendall-Hunt.
Blomain, Karen. Black Diamond. 28p. 1987. pap. 3.50 (*0-963465-7-4*) Great Elm.
— Borrowed Light. Zarucchi, Roy, ed. (Poetry Bks.). (Illus.). 64p. (Orig.). 1992. pap. 10.00 (*1-879205-32-7*) Nightshade Pr.
— Normal Avenue. (Poetry Ser.). 48p. 1998. pap. 10.00 (*1-879205-78-5*) Nightshade Pr.
— The Slap. 2nd ed. Zarucchi, Roy, ed. (Illus.). 32p. (Orig.). 1993. pap. 5.00 (*1-879205-40-8*) Nightshade Pr.
***Blomain, Karen, ed.** Potato Eyes, No. 19. (Illus.). 128p. 1999. pap. 9.95 (*1-879205-79-3*) Nightshade Pr.
Blomback, Birger & Hanson, Lars A., eds. Plasma Proteins. Hogg, Desmond, tr. from SWE. LC 78-10126. (Illus.). 419p. reprint ed. pap. 129.90 (*0-8357-8619-6*, 203504200091) Bks Demand.
Blomback, M. & Brakman, P., eds. Synthetic Substrates & Synthetic Inhibitors: The Use of Chromogenic Substrates in Studies of the Haemostatic Mechanism. (Haemostasis Ser.: Vol. 7, Nos. 2-3). (Illus.). 1978. pap. 33.25 (*3-8055-2907-4*) S Karger.
Blomberg, C. The Barbier Reaction & Related One-Step Processes. LC 93-34011. (Reactivity & Structure, Concepts in Organic Chemistry Ser.: Vol. 31). (Illus.). 196p. 1994. 162.95 (*0-387-57169-8*) Spr-Verlag.
Blomberg, Catharina. The Heart of the Warrior: Origins & Religious Background of the Samurai System in Feudal Japan. LC 93-190707. (Japan Library). (Illus.). 240p. (C). 1996. pap. text 25.00 (*1-873410-13-1*, Pub. by Curzon Pr Ltd) UH Pr.
Blomberg, Craig L. I Corinthians. LC 94-21472. (NIV Application Commentary Ser.). 352p. 1995. 24.99 (*0-310-48490-1*) Zondervan.
— The Historical Reliability of the Gospels. LC 87-2946. 268p. 1987. reprint ed. pap. 15.99 (*0-87784-992-7*, 992) InterVarsity.
— Interpreting the Parables. LC 89-38811. 334p. (Orig.). (C). 1990. pap. 21.99 (*0-8308-1271-7*, 1271) InterVarsity.
— Jesus & the Gospels: An Introduction & Survey. LC 97-5288. 384p. 1997. text 24.99 (*0-8054-1058-9*) Broadman.
— Matthew. LC 92-13777. (New American Commentary Ser.: Vol. 22). 1992. 27.99 (*0-8054-0122-9*) Broadman.
— Neither Poverty nor Riches: A Biblical Theology of Material Possessions. LC 99-14691. (New Studies in Biblical Theology). 300p. 1999. pap. 20.00 (*0-8028-4401-4*) Eerdmans.
Blomberg, Craig L. & Robinson, Stephen E. How Wide the Divide? A Mormon & an Evangelical in Conversation. LC 96-51534. 228p. (Orig.). 1997. pap. 11.99 (*0-8308-1991-6*, 1991) InterVarsity.
Blomberg, David. Gross Pathology. 1994. text 400.00 (*1-56815-027-X*) Mosby Inc.
***Blomberg, Dianne L.** Sam & Gram & the First Day of School. LC 98-31516. (Illus.). 32p. (J). (ps-1). 1999. 14.95 (*1-55798-562-6*, 441-5626, Magination Press) Am Psychol.
Blomberg, Erik, jt. auth. see Menzinsky, George.
Blomberg, Nancy J. Navajo Textiles: The William Randolph Hearst Collection. LC 88-4794. (Illus.). 257p. 1994. reprint ed. pap. 36.00 (*0-8165-1467-4*) U of Ariz Pr.
Blomberg, Peter E. On Corinthian Iconography: The Bridled Winged Horse & the Helmeted Female Head in the Sixth Century B. C. LC 97-156619. (Uppsala Studies in Ancient Mediterranean & Near Eastern Civilizations: No. 25). (Illus.). 109p. (Orig.). 1996. pap. 37.50 (*91-554-3702-8*, Pub. by Uppsala Univ Acta Univ Uppsaliensis) Coronet Bks.
Blomberg, Stefan. A Pragmatic Approach to Low-Back Pain Including Manual Therapy & Steroid Injections: A Multicentre Study in Primary Health Care. 146p. (Orig.). 1993. pap. 45.00 (*91-554-3030-9*) Coronet Bks.
Blomberg, Thomas G. & Cohen, Stanley, eds. Punishment & Social Control. (Social Institutions & Social Change Ser.). 328p. 1995. lib. bdg. 49.95 (*0-202-30497-3*) Aldine de Gruyter.
***Blomberg, Thomas G. & Lucken, Karol.** American Penology: A History of Control. (New Lines in Criminology Ser.). 400p. 2000. pap. text 23.95 (*0-202-30638-0*); lib. bdg. 49.95 (*0-202-30637-2*) Aldine de Gruyter.
Blombery, Alec M. The Flowers of Central Australia. (Illus.). 64p. (Orig.). reprint ed. pap. 7.95 (*0-86417-244-3*, Pub. by Kangaroo Pr) Seven Hills Bk.
— The Living Centre of Australia: A Complete Field Guide to the Area. 2nd ed. (Illus.). 80p. reprint ed. pap. 14.95 (*0-86417-234-6*, Pub. by Kangaroo Pr) Seven Hills Bk.
Blombery, Alec M. & Maloney, Betty. Guide to Kosciusko. (Illus.). (Orig.). 1993. pap. 9.95 (*0-86417-498-5*, Pub. by Kangaroo Pr) Seven Hills Bk.
— Propagating Australian Plants. (Illus.). 120p. (Orig.). 1995. pap. 14.95 (*0-86417-613-9*) Seven Hills Bk.
— Proteaceae of the Sydney Region. (Illus.). 216p. 1993. 37.50 (*0-86417-433-0*, Pub. by Kangaroo Pr) Seven Hills Bk.
Blome, C. D. Bulletins of American Paleontology Vol. 85: Upper Triassic Radiolaria & Radiolarian Zonation from Western North America. 88p. 1984. 25.00 (*0-87710-394-1*) Paleo Res.
Blome, Gotz. Advanced Bach Flower Therapy: A Scientific Approach to Diagnosis & Treatment. LC 99-30201. 400p. 1999. pap. 19.95 (*0-89281-828-X*, Heal Arts VT) Inner Tradit.
Blomen, L. J. & Mugerwa, M. N. Fuel Cell Systems. (Illus.). 636p. (C). 1994. text 135.00 (*0-306-44158-6*, Kluwer Plenum) Kluwer Academic.
Blomenberg, Paula, ed. Graduate Programs & Faculty in Reading. 4th ed. LC 81-13704. 381p. reprint ed. pap. 118.20 (*0-608-17965-5*, 202795100057) Bks Demand.
Blomeyer, Robert L., Jr. & Martin, C. Dianne, eds. Case Studies of Computer Aided Learning. 270p. 1991. pap. 34.95 (*1-85000-647-4*, Falmer Pr) Taylor & Francis.
Blomfield, Adelaide. The Sound of Breathing. 1977. 7.25 (*0-941490-15-7*) Solo Pr.
Blomfield, Reginald T. Formal Garden in England. 3rd ed. LC 77-181912. (BCL Ser. I). reprint ed. 48.50 (*0-404-00898-4*) AMS Pr.
— Six Architects. LC 78-99682. (Essay Index Reprint Ser.). 1977. 18.95 (*0-8369-1340-X*) Ayer.
— Three Hundred Years of French Architecture, 1494-1794. LC 70-124233. (Select Bibliographies Reprint Ser.). 1977. 18.95 (*0-8369-5414-9*) Ayer.
Blomgren, Paige. Beading: From Necklaces to Napkin Rings, 20 Easy & Creative Projects to Make in a Weekend. LC 98-45007. (Weekend Crafter Ser.). (Illus.). 80p. 1999. pap. 14.95 (*1-57990-091-7*, Pub. by Lark Books) Random.
Blomgren, David K., et al, eds. Restoring Praise & Worship to the Church. 220p. (Orig.). (C). 1989. pap. text 7.95 (*0-317-94072-4*) Trumpet Pubns.
***Blomgren, Mary.** Recipe for Recovery: Group Process for Women's Addictions to Violence, Self Destruction & Abuse. 96p. 1999. 15.95 (*1-55691-164-5*) Learning Pubns.
Blomgren, Paige. Making Paths & Walkways: Creative Ideas & Simple Techniques Stone, Brick, Bark, Pebbles, Grass & More. LC 99-12166. (Illus.). 144p. 1999. 24.95 (*1-57990-108-5*, Pub. by Lark Books) Random.
Blomgren, Paige G., ed. see Morgan, Aaron.
Blomhoff, Rune. Vitamin A in Health & Disease. (Antioxidants in Health & Disease Ser.: Vol. 1). (Illus.). 704p. 1994. text 215.00 (*0-8247-9120-7*) Dekker.
Blomkamp, P. J., jt. auth. see Gracie, N. C.
Blomley, Nicholas K. Law, Space, & the Geographies of Power. LC 94-18264. (Mappings). 259p. 1994. lib. bdg. 35.00 (*0-89862-496-7*, C2496) Guilford Pubns.
Blommaert, A., et al. Financial Decision Making: An Introduction To Managerial & Financial Accounting & Financial Management. LC F5657.4.B56 1991 9. 1991. 36.30 (*0-13-318262-2*) P-H.
***Blommaert, Jan, ed.** Language-Ideological Debates. LC 99-32848. 1999. pap. 24.95 (*3-11-016349-7*) De Gruyter.
— Language-Ideological Debates. LC 99-32848. (Language, Power & Social Process Ser.: No. 2). 447p. 1999. 93.00 (*3-11-016350-0*) De Gruyter.
Blommaert, Jan & Verschueren, Jef. Debating Diversity: Analysing the Rhetoric of Tolerance. LC 98-15143. (Illus.). 240p. (C). 1998. 75.00 (*0-415-19137-8*); pap. 22.99 (*0-415-19138-6*) Routledge.
Blommaert, Jan & Verschueren, Jef, eds. Pragmatics at Issue, 3 vols., Set. 900p. 1991. 236.00 (*1-55619-101-4*) J Benjamins Pubng Co.
— The Pragmatics of Intercultural & International Communication Vol. 3: Selected Papers of the International Pragmatics Conference, Antwerp, August 17-22, 1987. LC 91-22067. (Pragmatics & Beyond New Ser.: Vol. 6: 3). viii, 249p. 1991. 80.00 (*1-55619-108-1*) J Benjamins Pubng Co.
Blomme, Jan, jt. ed. see Van der Wee, Herman.
Blommer, Peter. Biking on Bike Trails Between Chicago & Milwaukee. 1998. pap. text 14.95 (*0-9662259-0-2*) Blommer Bks.
Blommers, John. Architecting Enterprise Solutions with Unix Networking. LC 98-38706. 352p. 1998. pap. text 44.99 (*0-13-792706-1*) P-H.
***Blommers, John.** Openview Network Node Manager. 2000. pap. 49.00 (*0-13-019849-8*) P-H.
Blommers, Paul J. & Forsyth, Robert A. Elementary Statistical Methods in Psychology & Education. 2nd ed. LC 83-6978. (Illus.). 584p. (C). 1983. reprint ed. pap. text 26.50 (*0-8191-2684-5*) U Pr of Amer.
— Elementary Statistical Methods in Psychology & Education: Study Manual. 2nd ed. (Illus.). 268p. 1984. reprint ed. pap. text 20.25 (*0-8191-4122-4*) U Pr of Amer.
Blommestein, Eva T., ed. The New Banking Landscape in Central & Eastern Europe: Country Experience & Policies for the Future. 380p. 1997. pap. 25.00 (*92-64-15683-6*, 14-97-10-1, Pub. by Org for Econ) OECD.
Blommestein, Hendrikus J., ed. Government & Markets: Establishing a Democratic Constitutional Order & a Market Economy in Former Socialist Countries. (International Studies in Economics & Econometrics). 340p. (C). 1994. lib. bdg. 153.00 (*0-7923-3059-5*) Kluwer Academic.
Blomquist, Ake, ed. Wave Propagation, Antennas & Systems: Nordic Radio Symposium 13-16 March, 1989. (Illus.). 312p. (Orig.). 1989. pap. 120.00 (*91-7056-075-7*) Coronet Bks.
***Blomquist, Ann K. & Taylor, Robert A., eds.** This Cruel War: The Civil War Letters of Grant & Malinda Taylor. LC 99-42544. 320p. 1999. 32.95 (*0-86554-654-1*) Mercer Univ Pr.
Blomquist, David. Weekends Like Other People. 1983. pap. 5.25 (*0-8222-1229-3*) Dramatists Play.
Blomquist, Geraldine M. & Blomquist, Paul B. Zachary's New Home: A Story for Foster & Adopted Children. LC 90-41914. (Illus.). 32p. (J). (ps-2). 1990. 11.95 (*0-945354-28-2*); pap. 8.95 (*0-945354-27-4*) Am Psychol.
Blomquist, Glenn, et al. The Economic Value of Visibility. (Studies in Urban & Resource Economics). (Illus.). xii, 312p. 1988. 46.00 (*0-943893-07-0*); pap. 26.00 (*0-943893-06-2*) Blackstone.
Blomquist, Glenn C. The Regulation of Motor Vehicle & Traffic Safety. (C). 1988. lib. bdg. 91.00 (*0-89838-280-7*) Kluwer Academic.
Blomquist, Hugo L., jt. auth. see Greene, Wilhelmina F.
Blomquist, Karin, jt. ed. see Ostenfeld, Erik.
Blomquist, Paul & Bloomquist, Geraldine M. Hiking the Gunnison River Basin, Western Section. 120p. (Orig.). 1996. pap. 11.95 (*0-943727-20-0*) Wayfinder Pr.
Blomquist, Paul B., jt. auth. see Blomquist, Geraldine M.
Blomquist, Thomas W. & Mazzaoui, Maureen F., eds. The "Other Tuscany" Essays in the History of Lucca, Pisa, & Siena During the Thirteenth, Fourteenth & Fifteenth Centuries. LC 94-4664. (Studies in Medieval Culture: Vol. 34). 1994. pap. 15.00 (*1-879288-42-7*); boxed set 35.00 (*1-879288-41-9*) Medieval Inst.
***Blomquist, Tina Haettner.** Gates & Gods: Cults & City Gates of Iron Age Palestine - An Investigation of the Archaeological & Biblical Sources. (Coniectanea Biblica Old Testament Ser.: Vol. 46). 246p. 1999. pap. 52.50 (*91-22-01860-3*, Pub. by Almqvist) Coronet Bks.
Blomquist, William A. Dividing the Waters: Governing Groundwater in Southern California. LC 92-24878. 416p. 1992. 34.95 (*1-55815-200-8*) ICS Pr.
— Making the Commons Work: Theory, Practice, & Policy. Bromley, Daniel W., ed. LC 92-24880. 339p. 1992. pap. 21.95 (*1-55815-217-2*) ICS Pr.
***Blomqvist, E. Maria, et al.** Biological, Physical & Geochemical Features of Enclosed & Semi-Enclosed Marine Systems. LC 99-15352. (Developments in Hydrobiology Ser.). 1999. write for info. (*0-7923-5784-1*) Kluwer Academic.
Blomqvist, Gun & Persson, Elwy. Tatting: Patterns & Designs. 1990. 21.75 (*0-8446-6392-1*) Peter Smith.
— Tatting Patterns & Designs. (Illus.). 96p. 1988. pap. 5.95 (*0-486-25813-0*) Dover.
Blomqvist, Hans C. Economic Interdependence & Development in East Asia. LC 96-44676. 160p. 1997. 59.95 (*0-275-95583-4*, Praeger Pubs) Greenwood.
Blomqvist, Karin. The Tyrant in Aristotle's Politics: Theoretical Assumptions & Historical Background. (Scripta Minora 1997-1998 1: Vol. 1). 55p. 1998. pap. 29.50 (*91-22-01805-0*) Coronet Bks.
Blomqvist, Lars E., jt. auth. see Arvidsson, Claes.
Blomstrom, David. Fossils of the Great Plains States. LC 96-18867. (First Impressions Ser.). (J). 1997. lib. bdg. write for info. (*0-8225-1947-X*, Lerner Publctns) Lerner Pub.
— Fossils of the Northeastern States. LC 96-18792. (First Impressions Ser.). (J). 1997. lib. bdg. write for info. (*0-8225-1944-5*, Lerner Publctns) Lerner Pub.
— Fossils of the Northwest & Pacific States. LC 96-41209. (First Impressions Ser.). (J). 1997. lib. bdg. write for info. (*0-8225-1948-8*, Lerner Publctns) Lerner Pub.
— Fossils of the Southern States. LC 96-18866. (First Impressions Ser.). (J). 1997. lib. bdg. write for info. (*0-8225-1945-3*, Lerner Publctns) Lerner Pub.
— Fossils of the Southwestern States. LC 96-21239. (First Impressions Ser.). (J). 1997. lib. bdg. write for info. (*0-8225-1949-6*, Lerner Publctns) Lerner Pub.
— (Ir)Rational Parks: An Offbeat Look at Wilderness, Tourism & America. LC 95-94662. (Illus.). 240p. (Orig.). 1995. pap. 13.95 (*0-9646777-0-9*) Geobopological.
— Teacher with an Attitude: Only You Prevent Education! Lane, Jay, ed. LC 96-94827. (Illus.). 324p. (Orig.). 1996. pap. 15.95 (*0-9646777-1-7*) Geobopological.
Blomstrom, Magnus. Foreign Investment & Spillovers. 128p. 1989. 47.50 (*0-415-03073-0*) Routledge.
Blomstrom, Magnus & Meller, Patricio, eds. Diverging Paths: Comparing a Century of Scandinavian & Latin American Economic Development. 286p. 1991. 21.00 (*0-940602-36-9*) IADB.
***Blomstrom, Magnus, et al.** Foreign Direct Investment: Firm & Host Country Strategies. LC 99-55732. 2000. 69.95 (*0-312-23141-5*) St Martin.
***Blonchek, Robert M. & O'Neil, Martin F.** Act Like an Owner: Building an Ownership Culture. LC 98-44675. 256p. 1999. 29.95 (*0-471-32285-7*) Wiley.
Bloncourt-Herselin, Jacqueline, ed. Dictionnaire Italien-Francais, Francais-Italien. (FRE & ITA.). 1969. write for info. (*0-7859-8617-0*, 208070009X) Fr & Eur.
***Blond, Anthony.** A Scandalous History of the Roman Emperors. (Illus.). 256p. 2000. pap. 11.95 (*0-7867-0759-3*, Pub. by Carroll & Graf) Publishers Group.
***Blond, Barbara A.** A Murder of Crows. LC 99-72791. 2000. 18.95 (*1-881636-82-8*, Pub. by Windsor Hse Pub Grp) Baker & Taylor.
Blond, Georges. La Grande Armee. (Illus.). 560p. 1997. pap. 24.95 (*1-85409-411-4*, Pub. by Arms & Armour) Sterling.
Blond, Neil, et al. Blond's Civil Procedure. rev. ed. (Blond's Law Guides Ser.). (Illus.). 352p. (Orig.). 1996. pap. 16.99 (*0-945819-35-8*) Sulzburger & Graham Pub.
— Blond's Constitutional Law. 3rd ed. (Blond's Law Guides Ser.). (Illus.). 440p. (Orig.). (C). 1993. pap. 16.99 (*0-945819-44-7*) Sulzburger & Graham Pub.
— Blond's Property. 3rd rev. ed. (Blond's Law Guides Ser.). (Illus.). 336p. (Orig.). (C). 1992. pap. 16.99 (*0-945819-31-5*) Sulzburger & Graham Pub.
— Blond's Torts. 3rd rev. ed. (Blond's Law Guides Ser.). (Illus.). 272p. (Orig.). (C). 1992. pap. 16.99 (*0-945819-24-2*) Sulzburger & Graham Pub.
Blond, Neil C. Blond's Evidence. 3rd ed. (Blond's Law Guides Ser.). 456p. (Orig.). (C). pap. 16.99 (*0-945819-56-0*) Sulzburger & Graham Pub.
— Criminal Procedure. 4th ed. 284p. 1992. pap. 16.99 (*0-945819-89-7*) Sulzburger & Graham Pub.
— International Law. 2nd ed. 312p. 1995. pap. 16.99 (*0-945819-81-1*) Sulzburger & Graham Pub.
Blond, Neil C., et al. Blond's Administrative Law. rev. ed. (Blond's Law Guides Ser.). (Illus.). 280p. (C). 1998. pap. 16.99 (*0-945819-52-8*) Sulzburger & Graham Pub.
— Blond's Civil Procedure. 4th rev. ed. (Blond's Law Guides Ser.). (Illus.). 330p. (Orig.). (C). 1995. pap. text 16.99 (*0-945819-85-4*) Sulzburger & Graham Pub.
— Blond's Civil Procedure for Yeazel. (Blond's Law Guides Ser.). (Illus.). 196p. (Orig.). (C). 1993. pap. 16.99 (*0-945819-45-5*) Sulzburger & Graham Pub.
— Blond's Contracts. 5th rev. ed. (Blond's Law Guides Ser.). (Illus.). 433p. (C). 1995. pap. text 16.99 (*0-945819-84-6*) Sulzburger & Graham Pub.
— Blond's Contracts for Farnsworth. (Blond's Law Guides Ser.). (Illus.). 208p. (Orig.). (C). 1994. pap. 16.99 (*0-945819-27-7*) Sulzburger & Graham Pub.
— Blond's Corporate Tax. (Blond's Law Guides Ser.). 284p. (C). 1991. pap. 14.99 (*0-945819-13-7*) Sulzburger & Graham Pub.
— Blond's Corporations. 2nd rev. ed. (Blond's Law Guides Ser.). (Illus.). 349p. (C). 1995. pap. text 16.99 (*0-945819-82-X*) Sulzburger & Graham Pub.
— Blond's Criminal Law. 4th rev. ed. (Blond's Law Guides Ser.). (Illus.). 349p. (Orig.). (C). 1995. pap. text 16.99 (*0-945819-83-8*) Sulzburger & Graham Pub.

An Asterisk (*) at the beginning of an entry indicates that the title is appearing for the first time.

— Blond's Family Law. 2nd rev. ed. (Blond's Law Guides Ser.). (Illus.). 355p. (C). 1994. pap. text 16.99 (*0-945819-67-6*) Sulzburger & Graham Pub.

— Blond's Income Tax (Personal) rev. ed. (Blond's Law Guides Ser.). (Illus.). 296p. (C). 1993. pap. 16.99 (*0-945819-51-X*) Sulzburger & Graham Pub.

— Blond's International Law. (Blond's Law Guides Ser.). 312p. (C). 1991. pap. 14.99 (*0-945819-12-9*) Sulzburger & Graham Pub.

— Blond's Multistate. 4th ed. (Blond's Law Guides Ser.). 508p. (C). 1992. pap. 29.99 (*0-945819-17-X*) Sulzburger & Graham Pub.

— Blond's Property for Dukeminier. (Blond's Law Guides Ser.). (Illus.). 192p. (Orig.). 1992. pap. 14.99 (*0-945819-30-7*) Sulzburger & Graham Pub.

— Blond's Torts for Henderson. (Blond's Law Guides Ser.). (Illus.). 186p. (Orig.). (C). 1993. pap. 16.99 (*0-945819-47-1*) Sulzburger & Graham Pub.

— Blond's Torts for Prosser. (Blond's Law Guides Ser.). (Illus.). 256p. (Orig.). (C). 1992. disk 27.99 (*0-945819-26-9*) Sulzburger & Graham Pub.

— Blond's Torts (Wade Edition) rev. ed. (Blond's Law Guides Ser.). 235p. (C). 1994. pap. text 16.99 (*0-945819-66-8*) Sulzburger & Graham Pub.

Blond, Philip E. A Tribute to the Group Settlers. (Staples South West Region Publications). pap. 9.95 (*0-85564-279-3*, Pub. by Staples) Intl Spec Bk.

Blond, Phillip. Post-Secular Philosophy: Between Philosophy & Theology. LC 97-8952. 392p. (C). 1998. 85.00 (*0-415-09777-0*); pap. 25.99 (*0-415-09778-9*) Routledge.

Blondal, Gisli. Fiscal Policy in the Smaller Industrial Countries, 1972-82. ix, 232p. 1986. 24.00 (*0-939934-36-1*); pap. 12.50 (*0-939934-53-1*) Intl Monetary.

— Fiscal Policy in the Smaller Industrial Countries, 1972-82. LC 86-15210. 242p. reprint ed. pap. 75.10 (*0-608-17950-7*, 202909000058) Bks Demand.

***Blondal, Jon & Organisation for Economic Co-operation & Development Staff.** User Charging for Government Services: Best Practice Guidelines & Case Studies. LC 98-201231. (Public Management Occasional Papers). 100 p. 1998. write for info. (*92-64-16042-6*) Org for Econ.

Blonde, Allan. The Complete Guide to Researching & Writing the English Term Paper. LC 78-63036. (Orig.). 1978. pap. text 5.50 (*0-87936-013-5*) Scholium Intl.

Blonde, Concrete. Walking in London (Piano - Vocal) Okun, Milton, ed. (Illus.). 56p. (Orig.). 1992. pap. text 14.95 (*0-89524-750-X*, Pub. by Cherry Lane) H Leonard.

Blondel. Comparative Government. 2nd ed. 384p. 1997. pap. 39.60 (*0-13-433905-3*) P-H.

Blondel, Alain. Tamara de Lempicka: Catalogue Raisonne, 1921-1979. 1998. 295.00 (*2-940033-28-5*) Acatos Edit.

Blondel, Eric. Nietzsche: The Body & Culture: Philosophy As a Philological Genealogy. Hand, Sean, tr. from FRE. LC 89-51665. 296p. 1991. 47.50 (*0-8047-1551-3*); pap. 17.95 (*0-8047-1906-3*) Stanford U Pr.

***Blondel, Jacques & Aronson, James.** Biology & Wildlife of the Mediterranean. LC 99-26200. (Illus.). 352p. 1999. text 50.00 (*0-19-850036-X*); pap. text 35.00 (*0-19-850035-1*) OUP.

Blondel, Jean. World Leaders: Heads of Government in the Postwar Period. LC 79-63826. (Political Executives in Comparative Perspective: A Cross-National Empirical Study: No. 1). (Illus.). 291p. reprint ed. pap. 90.30 (*0-8357-8478-9*, 203474300091) Bks Demand.

Blondel, Jean, et al, eds. Population Biology of Passerine Birds: An Integrated Approach. (NATO ASI Series G: Ecological Sciences: Vol. 24). xv, 496p. 1991. 216.95 (*0-387-51759-6*) Spr-Verlag.

Blondel, Jean & Cotta, M., eds. Party & Government. 260p. 1996. text 65.00 (*0-312-15917-X*) St Martin.

***Blondel, Jean & Cotta, Maurizio.** The Nature of Party Government: A Comparative European Perspective. LC 00-33337. 2000. write for info. (*0-312-23762-6*) St Martin.

Blondel, Jean & Muller-Rommel, Ferdinand, eds. Governing Together: The Extent & Limits of Joint Decision-Making in Western European Cabinets. LC 93-17276. 1993. text 59.95 (*0-312-09990-8*) St Martin.

Blondel, Jean, et al. People & Parliament in the European Union: Participation, Democracy & Legitimacy. LC 98-12093. (Illus.). 304p. 1998. text 70.00 (*0-19-829308-9*) OUP.

Blondel, Jean, jt. auth. see Curtis, Michael.

Blondel, Nathalie. Mary Butts: Scenes from the Life. LC 97-41973. (Illus.). 600p. 1998. 35.00 (*0-929701-55-0*) McPherson & Co.

Blondel, Phillippe, jt. auth. see Murton, Bramley J.

Blondel, V. Simultaneous Stabilation of Linear Systems. (Lecture Notes in Control & Information Sciences: Vol. 191). (Illus.). 216p. 1993. 45.95 (*0-387-19862-8*) Spr-Verlag.

***Blondel, Vincent.** Open Problems in Mathematical Systems & Control Theory. LC 98-38067. (Communications & Control Engineering Ser.). 1999. 99.00 (*1-85233-044-9*) Spr-Verlag.

***Blondell, Anthony J.** Honor & Sacrifice: The Montagnards of Ba Cat, Vietnam. 225p. 2000. 21.95 (*1-55571-533-8*, Pub. by PSI Resch) Midpt Trade.

Blondell, Ruby, ed. see Euripides.

Blonder, Ellen & Low, Annabel. Every Grain of Rice: A Taste of Our Chinese Childhood in America. LC 97-26276. 208p. 1998. 25.00 (*0-609-60102-4*) C Potter.

Blondheim, Menahem. News over the Wires: The Telegraph & the Flow of Public Information in America 1844-1897. LC 93-28731. (Studies in Business History: No. 42). 216p. 1994. text 39.95 (*0-674-62212-X*) HUP.

Blondheim, S. H., et al, eds. Recent Advances in Obesity Research, Vol. V. 416p. 1987. 74.00 (*0-917678-22-2*) Food & Nut Pr.

Blondheim, S. H., ed. see International Congress of Internal Medicine Staff.

Blondin, Antoine. Les Enfants du Bon Dieu. (FRE.). 1973. pap. 10.95 (*0-7859-1762-4*, 2070364747) Fr & Eur.

— L' Europe Buissonniere. (FRE.). 528p. 1979. pap. 12.95 (*0-7859-1883-3*, 2070370674) Fr & Eur.

— L' Humeur Vagabonde. (FRE.). 1979. pap. 10.95 (*0-7859-1891-4*, 2070371115) Fr & Eur.

— Monsieur Jadis Ou l'Ecole du Soir. (FRE.). 1972. pap. 10.95 (*0-7859-1688-1*, 2070360296) Fr & Eur.

— Quat'Saisons. (FRE.). 212p. 1977. pap. 10.95 (*0-7859-1860-4*, 2070369730) Fr & Eur.

— Un Singe en Hiver. (FRE.). 224p. 1987. pap. 10.95 (*0-7859-1739-X*, 2070363597) Fr & Eur.

Blondin, George. Yamoria the Lawmaker: Stories of the Dene. (Northwest Passage Ser.). (Illus.). 263p. 1997. pap. 17.95 (*1-896300-20-0*) NeWest Pubs.

Blondin, Pam & Blackburn, Charles, eds. International Cooperation in Science & Technology. (Illus.). 1999. pap. text. write for info. (*0-914446-13-4*) Sigma Xi.

Blondin, Robert & King, Hedley. The Solitary Slocum: Captain Joshua Slocum. 196p. 1992. reprint ed. pap. 14.95 (*1-55109-026-0*) Nimbus Publ.

Blong, Adele M., et al. Welfare Myths: Fact or Fiction? Exploring the Truth about Welfare. (Illus.). 48p. 1996. pap. 8.00 (*0-9653488-0-6*) Ctr Soc Welfare.

Blong, R. J. Volcanic Hazards: A Sourcebook on the Effects of Eruptions. 440p. 1984. text 162.00 (*0-12-107180-4*) Acad Pr.

Blong, Russell, jt. auth. see Henderson-Sellers, Ann.

Blonigen, Julie A. Biking for a Better Voice. (Illus.). 48p. (J). (gr. k-8). 1992. student ed. 43.95 (*0-937857-26-2*, 1597) Speech Bin.

***Blonigen, Julie A.** The Blonigen Fluency Program. (Illus.). 116p. 2000. pap. 19.95 (*0-937857-85-8*, 1492) Speech Bin.

Blonigen, Julie A. Concepts for Learning. (Illus.). 172p. (ps-2). 1989. teacher ed. 22.95 (*0-937857-08-4*, 1565) Speech Bin.

***Blonigen, Julie A.** Is the Child Really Stuttering: Questions & Answers about Preschool Disfluency. 12p. 1999. pap. text 9.95 (*0-937857-83-1*, 1516) Speech Bin.

Blonigen, Julie A. Rewarding Speech. (Illus.). 32p. 1993. 12.95 (*0-937857-40-8*, 1542) Speech Bin.

— Stuttering: Helping the Disfluent Preschool Child. (Illus.). 40p. 1996. pap. text 10.95 (*0-937857-64-5*, 1489) Speech Bin.

— What Is Vocal Hoarseness? 24p. 1995. pap. text 16.95 (*0-937857-55-6*, 1547) Speech Bin.

***Blonna, Richard.** Coping with Stress in a Changing World 2nd ed. LC 99-27552. 2000. write for info. (*0-07-289111-4*) McGrw-H Hghr Educ.

Blonna, Richard, ed. Readings Plus with WebLinks: Issues in Human Sexuality, 98-99. 226p. (C). 1998. pap. text 14.95 (*0-89582-388-8*) Morton Pub.

Blonna, Richard & Levitan, Jean E. Human Sexuality. (Illus.). 624p. (C). 1999. pap. text 59.95 (*0-89582-410-8*) Morton Pub.

Blonnigen, Christoph. Der Griechische Ursprung der Judisch-Hellenistischen Allegorese und Ihre Rezeption in der Alexandrinischen Patristik. (Europaische Hochschulschriften Ser.: Reihe 15, Bd. 59). (GER.). 370p. 1992. 65.80 (*3-631-45175-X*) P Lang Pubng.

Blonshine, Susan, jt. auth. see Brown, Robert.

Blonsky, Marshall. ABCs for Millenium. 1999. pap. 11.95 (*0-14-024133-7*, Viking) Viking Penguin.

— American Mytholgies. 512p. 1999. pap. 12.95 (*0-14-023781-X*) Viking Penguin.

— American Mythologies. (Illus.). 560p. 1992. 35.00 (*0-19-505062-2*) OUP.

Blonsky, Marshall, ed. On Signs. LC 84-47952. (Illus.). 576p. 1985. pap. 21.95 (*0-8018-3007-9*) Johns Hopkins.

Blonstein, A. D. & King, P. J., eds. A Genetic Approach to Plant Biochemistry. (Plant Gene Research Ser.). (Illus.). 1987. 103.95 (*0-387-81912-6*) Spr-Verlag.

Blonston, Gary. William Morris: Artifacts/Glass. (Illus.). 128p. 1996. 40.00 (*0-7892-0167-4*) Abbeville Pr.

Blonz, Ed. Nutrition Doctor's A to Z Food Counter. LC 99-182511. 288p. 1999. mass mkt. 6.50 (*0-451-19587-6*, Sig) NAL.

— Power Nutrition: How to Live Longer, Prevent Illness & Be Healthier with Good Nutrition. LC 99-171536. 272p. 1998. mass mkt. 5.99 (*0-451-19726-7*, Sig) NAL.

Blonz, Edward R. Fiber & Fat Counter. 1996. mass mkt. 3.99 (*0-451-18487-4*, Sig) NAL.

— What's in your Food. 1999. pap. 12.95 (*0-452-27437-0*, Plume) Dutton Plume.

Blood. Madam Secretary. 320p. 1999. pap. 16.95 (*0-312-19505-2*) St Martin.

— Saunders Comprehensive Veterinary Dictionary. 2nd ed. (C). 1998. text 55.00 (*0-7020-2442-2*, Pub. by W B Saunders) Saunders.

Blood, Arlie J. Only Angels Have Wings. LC 98-116756. 234 p. 1997. write for info. (*0-9658016-0-8*) A Blood.

Blood, Benjamin P. The Anaesthetic Revelation & the Gist of Philosophy. LC 75-3051. reprint ed. 24.50 (*0-404-59050-0*) AMS Pr.

— The Philosophy of Justice Between God & Man. LC 75-3056. reprint ed. 20.50 (*0-404-59054-3*) AMS Pr.

— Pluriverse: An Essay in the Philosophy of Pluralism. LC 75-3057. reprint ed. 20.50 (*0-404-59055-1*) AMS Pr.

— Pluriverse: An Essay in the Philosophy of Pluralism. LC 75-36829. (Occult Ser.). 1976. reprint ed. 25.95 (*0-405-07941-9*) Ayer.

— The Poetical Alphabet. (Surrealist Research & Development Monographs). 24p. 1972. pap. 10.00 (*0-941194-04-3*) Black Swan Pr.

Blood, Charles L. & Link, Martin. The Goat in the Rug. 1990. 11.19 (*0-606-03387-4*, Pub. by Turtleback) Demco.

Blood, Charles L. & Link, Martin. The Goat in the Rug. LC 89-77701. (Illus.). 40p. (J). (ps-3). 1990. reprint ed. mass mkt. 5.99 (*0-689-71418-1*) Aladdin.

Blood, Charles L., jt. auth. see Boyle, George E.

Blood, D. C. Bailliere's Comprehensive Veterinary Dictionary. 1312p. 1988. text 82.95 (*0-7020-1195-9*, W B Saunders Co) Harcrt Hlth Sci Grp.

— Veterinary Dictionary. 2nd ed. (C). 1998. pap. text 39.95 (*0-7020-2034-6*, W B Saunders Co) Harcrt Hlth Sci Grp.

— Veterinary Information Management. 1989. text 66.00 (*0-7020-1328-5*, W B Saunders Co) Harcrt Hlth Sci Grp.

— Veterinary Medicine: Pocket Companion. (Illus.). 743p. 1994. pap. text 37.95 (*0-7020-1695-0*, Pub. by W B Saunders) Saunders.

Blood, Ernie. The Pocket Ad Writer: For Real Estate Professionals. unabridged ed. 241p. 1986. reprint ed. pap. 29.95 (*1-893572-00-5*) Carmel Pubg.

— The Pocket Assistant's Guide: For Real Estate Professionals. unabridged ed. 191p. 1997. reprint ed. pap. 29.95 (*1-893572-05-6*) Carmel Pubg.

— The Pocket Call Conversation Guide: For Real Estate Professionals. unabridged ed. 130p. 1989. reprint ed. pap. 29.95 (*1-893572-01-3*) Carmel Pubg.

— The Pocket Internet Guide: For Real Estate Professionals. unabridged ed. 130p. 1996. reprint ed. pap. 29.95 (*1-893572-06-4*) Carmel Pubg.

— The Pocket Library of Letters: For Real Estate Professionals. unabridged ed. 283p. 1989. reprint ed. pap. 29.95 (*1-893572-02-1*) Carmel Pubg.

— The Pocket Library of Letters II: For Real Estate Professionals. unabridged ed. 1999. reprint ed. pap. 29.95 (*1-893572-08-0*) Carmel Pubg.

— The Pocket Property Management Guide: For Real Estate Professionals. unabridged ed. 1999. reprint ed. pap. 29.95 (*1-893572-09-9*) Carmel Pubg.

— The Pocket Prospecting Guide: For Real Estate Professionals. unabridged ed. 219p. 1988. reprint ed. pap. 29.95 (*1-893572-03-X*) Carmel Pubg.

— The Pocket Self Promotion, Marketing, & Advertising Guide: For Real Estate Professionals. unabridged ed. 233p. 1994. reprint ed. pap. 29.95 (*1-893572-07-2*) Carmel Pubg.

— The Pocket Selling & Closing Guide: For Real Estate Professionals. unabridged ed. 231p. 1992. reprint ed. pap. 29.95 (*1-893572-04-8*) Carmel Pubg.

Blood, F. R., ed. Essays in Toxicology, Vols. 1-7. Incl. Vol. 1. 1969. pap. 24.00 (*0-12-107651-2*); Vol. 2. 1970. 50.00 (*0-12-107602-4*); Vol. 2. 1970. pap. 24.00 (*0-12-107652-0*); Vol. 3. Hayes, Wayland J., Jr. 1972. 35.00 (*0-12-107603-2*); Vol. 3. Hayes, Wayland J., Jr. 1972. pap. 24.00 (*0-12-107653-9*); Vol. 4. 1973. 50.00 (*0-12-107604-0*); Vol. 5. 1974. 49.00 (*0-12-107605-9*); Vol. 6. 1975. 50.00 (*0-12-107606-7*); Vol. 7. 1976. 60.00 (*0-12-107607-5*); pap. write for info. (*0-318-50263-1*) Acad Pr.

Blood, Henry A. The History of Temple, NH. (Illus.). 352p. 1993. reprint ed. lib. bdg. 39.50 (*0-8328-3186-7*) Higginson Bk Co.

Blood-Horse, Inc. Staff. Thoroughbred Champions: The Top 100 Racehorses of the 20th Century. 1999. pap. text 24.95 (*1-58150-024-6*, Pub. by Blood-Horse) IPG Chicago.

***Blood-Horse Staff.** Thoroughbred Champions: Top 100 Racehorses of the 20th Century. limited ed. Duke, Jacqueline, ed. (Illus.). 256p. 1999. 195.00 (*1-58150-034-3*) Blood-Horse.

Blood, Jennifer. One Stop Hallelujah Coffee Shop. Holst, Richard, ed. (Illus.). 150p. (Orig.). 1997. pap., per. write for info. (*0-9643280-3-8*) Cape Elizabeth.

Blood, Marje. Exploring the Oregon Coast by Car. 2nd ed. LC 85-81529. (Illus.). 210p. 1986. reprint ed. pap. 9.95 (*0-9615233-3-6*) Image Imprints.

— Morning Song-Mourning Song: Narcissa: Her Story, Bk. II. 285p. 1987. write for info. (*0-318-61951-2*); pap. 10.95 (*0-9615233-5-2*) Image Imprints.

— A Song Heard in a Strange Land: Narcissa Her Story, Bk. 1. LC 85-81462. 220p. 1985. pap. 9.95 (*0-9615233-1-X*) Image Imprints.

Blood, Peter, ed. Rise up Singing: The Group Singing Songbook. rev. ed. (Illus.). 288p. reprint ed. pap. 17.95 (*0-9626704-9-9*) Sing Out.

— Rise up Singing: The Group Singing Songbook. rev. ed. (Illus.). 288p. 1988. reprint ed. spiral bd. 17.95 (*0-9626704-7-2*) Sing Out.

— Rise up Singing: The Group Singing Songbook. rev. ed. (Illus.). 288p. 1988. reprint ed. lib. bdg. 39.95 (*0-9626704-8-0*) Sing Out.

***Blood, Peter, et al, eds.** Physics & Simulation of Optoelectronic Devices VII. 840p. 1999. pap. text 136.00 (*0-8194-3095-1*) SPIE.

Blood, Peter, jt. auth. see Orton, J. W.

Blood, Peter, ed. see Seeger, Pete.

Blood, Peter R., ed. Pakistan: A Country Study. LC 95-17247. (Area Handbook Ser.). 1995. 22.00 (*0-8444-0834-4*, 008020013773) Lib Congress.

— Pakistan: A Country Study. 6th ed. (Illus.). 398p. 1996. reprint ed. text 45.00 (*0-7881-3631-3*) DIANE Pub.

***Blood, Philip.** Return Fire 2: Official Strategies & Secrets. LC 98-88089. 256p. 1998. pap. 19.99 (*0-7821-2458-5*) Sybex.

Blood, Robert O. & Wolfe, Donald M. Husbands & Wives: The Dynamics of Married Living. LC 78-5734. 293p. 1978. reprint ed. lib. bdg. 35.00 (*0-313-20453-5*, BLHW, Greenwood Pr) Greenwood.

Blood-Ryan, H. W., tr. see Goering, H. W.

Blood, Susan. Baudelaire & the Aesthetics of Bad Faith. LC 96-27397. 1997. write for info. (*0-8047-2809-7*) Stanford U Pr.

Blood, Thomas. Madam Secretary: A Biography of Madeleine Albright. LC 97-16521. (Illus.). 320p. 1997. text 24.95 (*0-312-17180-3*) St Martin.

Bloodgood, R. A. Ciliary & Flagellar Membranes. LC 89-23227. (Illus.). 450p. (C). 1990. text 115.00 (*0-306-43279-X*, Kluwer Plenum) Kluwer Academic.

Bloodroot Collective Staff. Addendum to the Political Palate Series. 85p. 1997. pap. 9.95 (*0-9605210-4-6*) Sanguinaria.

— The Political Palate: A Feminist Vegetarian Cookbook. LC 80-53521. (Illus.). 325p. (Orig.). 1980. pap. 12.95 (*0-9605210-0-3*) Sanguinaria.

— The Second Seasonal Political Palate. LC 84-52064. 200p. 1984. pap. 12.95 (*0-9605210-2-X*) Sanguinaria.

Bloodroot Collective Staff, et al. The Perennial Political Palate: A Feminist Vegetarian Cookbook. LC 82-83994. (Illus.). 320p. (Orig.). 1993. pap. 16.95 (*0-9605210-3-8*) Sanguinaria.

Bloodstein, Oliver. A Handbook on Stuttering. 5th ed. (Illus.). 596p. (C). 1995. pap. 62.95 (*1-56593-395-8*, 0859) Thomson Learn.

— Stuttering: The Search for a Cause & Cure. LC 92-11153. 216p. 1992. 69.00 (*0-205-13845-4*, H38458) Allyn.

Bloodworth, Bertha E. & Morris, Alton C. Places in the Sun: The History & Romance of Florida Placenames. LC 77-13754. (University of Florida Bk.). 251p. reprint ed. pap. 77.90 (*0-7837-0594-8*, 204094200019) Bks Demand.

Bloodworth, Bryan & Cushman, Roger. 100 Years of Illinois State Redbird Basketball. Mossman, Kenny & Lamonica, Tom, eds. LC 98-38461. (Illus.). 160p. 1998. 29.99 (*1-56478-158-5*) Dalkey Arch.

Bloodworth, Dennis, ed. The Profile of an Opportunity: The Risks & Rewards of Investing in China. LC 95-948213. 296p. 1995. pap. 22.50 (*981-210-076-8*, Pub. by Times Academic) Intl Spec Bk.

Bloodworth, Jessie A. & Greenwood, Elizabeth J. Personal Side. LC 71-137156. (Poverty U. S. A. Historical Record Ser.). 1971. reprint ed. 29.95 (*0-405-03094-0*) Ayer.

Bloodworth, Trey & Raley, Mike. Hidden in Plain Sight: A Practical Guide to Concealed Handgun Carry. 2nd ed. LC 98-193049. (Illus.). 176p. 1998. pap. 40.00 (*0-87364-990-7*) Paladin Pr.

Bloodworth, Venice. Key to Yourself. 1986. pap. 9.95 (*0-87516-296-7*) DeVorss.

Bloodworth, William A., Jr. Max Brand. (Twayne's United States Authors Ser.). 208p. 1993. 22.95 (*0-8057-7646-X*, Twyne) Mac Lib Ref.

Bloom. Brain, Mind & Behavior. 2000. teacher ed. write for info. (*0-7167-2758-7*) W H Freeman.

— Creepers: British Horror & Fantasy in the Twentieth Century. LC 92-36706. 190p. (C). 44.95 (*0-7453-0664-0*, Pub. by Pluto GBR); pap. 14.95 (*0-7453-0665-9*, Pub. by Pluto GBR) Stylus Pub VA.

***Bloom.** Early Islamic Art. (Illus.). 500p. 2000. 156.00 (*0-86078-705-2*) Ashgate Pub Co.

Bloom. Mind, Brain & Behavior. 2000. pap. text, student ed. write for info. (*0-7167-2802-8*) W H Freeman.

— Power Data: Solving Business Problems with Microsoft Access. (C). 1996. pap. text. write for info. (*0-201-48325-4*) Addison-Wesley.

— Synergistic Approach Stuttering Therapy. LC 98-50995. 288p. 1999. text 40.00 (*0-7506-9527-7*) Buttrwrth-Heinemann.

Bloom & Young. Brain Browser (International Edition) A Spinnaker PLUS Based Hypertext Application for Microsoft Windows. 227p. 1994. 105.00 (*0-12-107260-6*) Acad Pr.

Bloom, jt. auth. see Rosson.

***Bloom, Abby.** Health Reform in Australia & New Zealand. 320p. 2000. pap. text 39.95 (*0-19-550860-2*) OUP.

Bloom, Abigail B., ed. see Ritchie, Anne Thackeray.

***Bloom, Abigail Burnham.** Nineteenth-century British Women Writers: A Bio-bibliographical Critical Sourcebook. LC 99-43163. 472p. 2000. lib. bdg. 95.00 (*0-313-30439-4*) Greenwood.

Bloom, Adrian. Adrian Bloom's Year-Round Garden. LC 98-20545. (Illus.). 287p. 1998. 39.95 (*0-88192-457-1*) Timber.

— Conifers for Your Garden. (Illus.). 144p. 1972. reprint ed. 25.95 (*0-903001-01-2*, Pub. by Burall Floraprint) J Markham Assocs.

— Making the Most of Conifers & Heathers. 2nd ed. (Illus.). 78p. 1989. pap. 12.95 (*0-903001-61-6*, Pub. by Burall Floraprint) J Markham Assocs.

Bloom, Alan. Come You Here Boy! Autobiography of a Gardener. large type ed. 20.95 (*1-85695-129-4*, Pub. by ISIS Lrg Prnt) Transaction Pubs.

— Garden Alpines. (Illus.). 1994. 24.95 (*0-85628-254-5*, Pub. by Aidan Ellis Pub) Antique Collect.

— Hardy Plants & Alpines. (Illus.). 252p. 1990. reprint ed. 27.95 (*0-903001-62-4*, Pub. by Burall Floraprint) J Markham Assocs.

— Mistress of Melthorpe. large type ed. (Ulverscroft Large Print Ser.). 352p. 1997. 27.99 (*0-7089-3859-0*) Ulverscroft.

Bloom, Alan, ed. Steam Alive: The Story of Bressingham Steam Museum. 208p. 1990. 60.00 (*0-948251-56-5*, Pub. by Picton) St Mut.

Bloom, Alexander & Breines, Winifred, eds. Takin' It to the Streets: A Sixties Reader. 656p. 1995. text 59.95 (*0-19-506623-5*); pap. text 29.95 (*0-19-506624-3*) OUP.

Bloom, Alfed. Shoshinge: The Heart of Shin Buddhism. Nagatani, T. & Tabrah, Ruth, trs. LC 86-26379. 108p. 1986. pap. 8.95 (*0-938474-06-5*) Buddhist Study.

Bloom, Alfred. The Life of Shinram Shonin: The Journey of Self Acceptance. rev. ed. (Institute of Buddhist Studies). 80p. 1994. pap. 6.95 (*0-940583-00-3*) Inst Buddhst Studies Pr.

— Shinran's Gospel of Pure Grace. 8th ed. LC 64-8757. (Monographs: No. 20). xiv, 97p. 1991. reprint ed. pap. 10.00 (*0-8165-0405-9*) Assn Asian Studies.

B

— Tannisho: A Resource for Modern Living. LC 80-39523. 112p. (Orig.). (C). 1981. pap. 8.95 (*0-938474-00-6*) Buddhist Study.

***Bloom, Alfred, ed.** Yemyo Imamura: Pioneer American Buddhist. Takeshita, Tsuneichi, tr. from JPN. 120p. 2000. pap. write for info. (*0-938474-21-9*) Buddhist Study.

Bloom, Alfred & Snyder, Gary. Strategies for Modern Living: A Commentary with the Text of Tannisleo. LC 91-61704. 188p. (C). 1992. pap. 11.95 (*0-9625618-1-9*) Heian Intl.

Bloom, Alfred H. Linguistic Shaping of Thought: A Study in the Impact of Language on Thinking in China & the West. 128p. 1981. text 29.95 (*0-89859-089-2*) L Erlbaum Assocs.

Bloom, Allan. Closing of the American Mind. 400p. 1988. pap. 13.00 (*0-671-65715-1*, Touchstone) S&S Trade Pap.

— Confronting the Constitution: The Challenge to Locke, Montesquieu, Jefferson, & the Federalists from Utilitarianism, Historicism, Marxism, Freudianism. 180p. (C). 1991. pap. 19.95 (*0-8447-3700-3*) Am Enterprise.

— Giants & Dwarfs: Essays, 1960-1990. 400p. 1991. pap. 11.00 (*0-671-74726-6*, Touchstone) S&S Trade Pap.

— Love & Friendship. 592p. 1994. pap. 15.00 (*0-671-89120-0*, Touchstone) S&S Trade Pap.

Bloom, Allan & Jaffa, Harry V. Shakespeare's Politics. x, 150p. 1981. pap. text 12.50 (*0-226-06041-1*) U Ch Pr.

Bloom, Allan, ed. see Strauss, Leo.

Bloom, Allan, ed. & pref. see Strauss, Leo.

Bloom, Allan, tr. see Plato.

Bloom, Allan, tr. see Rousseau, Jean-Jacques.

***Bloom, Allan David.** Shakespeare on Love & Friendship. LC 99-55777. 160p. 1999. pap. 12.00 (*0-226-06045-4*) U Ch Pr.

Bloom, Allen & Jaffa, Harry V. Shakespeare's Politics. LC 81-10342. x, 160p. 1987. pap. text 15.95 (*0-226-06040-3*, Midway Reprint) U Ch Pr.

***Bloom, Amy.** A Blind Man Can See How Much I Love You: Stories. LC 99-55153. 208p. 2000. 22.95 (*0-375-50268-8*) Random.

Bloom, Amy. Come to Me: Stories. 192p. 1994. reprint ed. pap. 12.00 (*0-06-099514-9*, Perennial) HarperTrade.

— Love Invents Us. LC 97-21966. 224p. 1998. pap. 12.00 (*0-375-75022-3*) Vin Bks.

Bloom, Anthony. Beginning to Pray. LC 70-169613. 114p. 1982. pap. 6.95 (*0-8091-1509-3*) Paulist Pr.

— Beginning to Pray. large type ed. (Large Print Inspirational Ser.). 160p. 1986. pap. 8.95 (*0-8027-2517-1*) Walker & Co.

— Meditations. 1970. pap. 11.95 (*0-87193-010-2*) Dimension Bks.

Bloom, Anthony & LeFebvre, George. Courage to Pray. 3rd ed. Livingstone, Dinah, tr. from FRE. 123p. (Orig.). 1984. reprint ed. pap. text 8.95 (*0-88141-031-4*) St Vladimirs.

Bloom, Arnold & Bloom, Stephen. Toohey's Medicine for Nurses. 14th ed. (Illus.). 335p. 1986. text 34.00 (*0-443-03076-6*) Church.

Bloom, Arthur D. & De Serres, Frederick J., eds. Ecotoxicity & Human Health: A Biological Approach to Environmental Remediation. 336p. 1995. lib. bdg. 85.00 (*1-56670-141-4*, L1141) Lewis Pubs.

Bloom, Arthur D. & James, L. S., eds. The Fetus & the Newborn. (Alan R. Less, Inc. Ser.: Alan R Liss., Inc. Ser.). 1981. 36.00 (*0-686-37765-6*) March of Dimes.

Bloom, Arthur D., jt. ed. see Spatz, Lawrence.

Bloom, Arthur L. Geomorphology: A Systematic Analysis of Late Cenozoic Landforms. 3rd ed. LC 97-29109. 482p. (C). 1997. 97.00 (*0-13-505496-6*) P-H.

Bloom, Arthur L., et al, eds. Haemostasis & Thrombosis, 2 vols. 3rd ed. LC 93-10621. (Illus.). 1152p. 1993. text 336.00 (*0-443-04521-6*) Church.

Bloom, Arthur L. & Thomas, Duncan P., eds. Haemostasis & Thrombosis. 2nd ed. (Illus.). 1040p. 1987. 230.00 (*0-443-03190-8*) Church.

Bloom, Arthur W. Joseph Jefferson: Dean of the American Theatre. LC 99-21148. (Illus.). 528p. 2000. 35.00 (*0-913720-55-0*) Beil.

Bloom, Audrey E., jt. auth. see Bader, Gloria E.

Bloom, Barbara. Access to Health Care, Vol. 2. 51p. 1997. pap. 5.00 (*0-16-049121-5*) USGPO.

Bloom, Barbara. Esprit De l'Escalier. (Artists' Bks.). (FRE., Illus.). 36p. 1988. 5.00 (*0-936739-14-2*) Hallwalls Inc.

Bloom, Barbara, et al. Access to Health Care: Children, Working-Age Adults, & Older Adults. (Illus.). 125p. (C). 1998. pap. text 35.00 (*0-7881-7371-5*) DIANE Pub.

Bloom, Barbara H. Index to the Journal of Sedimentary Petrology, Volumes 1-26: Nineteen Thirty-One to Nineteen Fifty-Six. LC QE0420J69. (Society of Economic Paleontologists & Mineralogists, Special Publication Ser.: No. 6). 55p. reprint ed. pap. 30.00 (*0-608-12927-5*, 202473300038) Bks Demand.

Bloom, Barbara L. & Cohen, Garry W. Romance of Waterfalls: Northwest Oregon & Southwest Washington. LC 98-11992. (Illus.). 252p. 1998. pap. 16.95 (*0-9662756-0-8*, 1001) Outdoor Romance.

Bloom, Barry. Sandy & Roberto Alomar: Baseball Brothers. Rains, Rob, ed. (Super Star Ser.). (Illus.). 96p. (J). 1999. pap. 4.95 (*1-58261-054-1*) Sprts Pubng.

— Tony Gwynn: Mr. Padre. Rains, Rob, ed. (Super Star Ser.). 96p. (J). 1999. pap. 4.95 (*1-58261-049-5*) Sprts Pubng.

Bloom, Barry R., ed. Tuberculosis: Pathogenesis, Protection & Control. LC 94-2932. (Illus.). 500p. 1994. 99.95 (*1-55581-072-1*) ASM Pr.

***Bloom, Becky.** Mice Make Trouble. LC 99-37708. (Illus.). 32p. (J). (ps-2). 2000. 15.95 (*0-531-30253-9*); lib. bdg. 16.99 (*0-531-33253-5*) Orchard Bks Watts.

Bloom, Becky. Mr. Cuckoo. LC 97-43650. (Illus.). 32p. (J). (gr. k-4). 1998. 15.95 (*1-57255-626-9*) Mondo Pubng.

— Wolf! LC 98-42421. (Illus.). 32p. 1999. 15.95 (*0-531-30155-9*) Orchard Bks Watts.

Bloom, Benjamin S., et al. INTRO EDUCATNL PSYCH BK1. LC 64-12369. 207p. (C). 1989. reprint ed. pap. text 45.00 (*0-582-28010-9*, 71079) Longman.

Bloom, Bernard L. Planned Short-Term Psychotherapy: A Clinical Handbook. 2nd ed. LC 96-48082. 309p. 1997. pap. text 47.00 (*0-205-19344-7*) Allyn.

Bloom, Bernard M. & O'Brien, Maureen E. Wills Law of NY. 250p. (C). ring bd. 34.95 (*0-87526-404-2*) Gould.

Bloom, Beth-Ann & Selijeskog, Edward L. A Parent's Guide to Spina Bifida. LC 88-10784. (Guides to Birth & Childhood Disorders Ser.). (Illus.). 96p. 1988. 16.95 (*0-8166-1486-5*) U of Minn Pr.

Bloom, Bruce J. Fast Track to the Best Job: How to Launch a Successful Career Right Out of College. 160p. 1991. pap. 9.95 (*0-9628965-2-7*) Blazer Bks.

Bloom, Carol, ed. Insights on Diversity. LC 94-4955. 48p. (Orig.). 1994. pap. 10.00 (*0-912099-09-7*, 502) Kappa Delta Pi.

Bloom, Carol A. Nifty, Thrifty, No-Sew Costumes & Props: Make Costumes for a Wide Variety of Characters, & Animals. LC 97-209832. (Illus.). 208p. 1997. pap. text 14.95 (*0-673-36372-4*, GoodYrBooks) Addson-Wesley Educ.

— Playing with Print. LC 97-198274. 1997. pap. text 14.95 (*0-673-36326-0*) Addson-Wesley Educ.

— The Secret of the Locked Trunk. (Magic Mansion Mystery Ser.: No. 1). 125p. (J). (gr. 4-6). 1998. pap. 9.99 (*0-88092-475-6*, 4756) Royal Fireworks.

Bloom, Carole. All about Chocolate. LC 98-20895. 352p. 1998. pap. 17.00 (*0-02-862283-9*) Macmillan.

— Truffles, Candies, & Confections: Elegant Candy Making in the Home. (Illus.). 208p. 1996. pap. 14.95 (*0-89594-833-8*) Crossing Pr.

Bloom, Charles P. & Loftin, R. Bowen, eds. Facilitating the Development & Use of Interactive Learning Environments. LC 97-44903. (Computers, Cognition, & Work Ser.). 225p. 1997. pap. write for info. (*0-8058-1851-0*); text. write for info. (*0-8058-1850-2*) L Erlbaum Assocs.

Bloom, Claire, et al. Celebration of Christmas Classics. unabridged ed. 1994. audio 29.95 (*0-694-51491-8*, BGS 005) HarperAudio.

Bloom, Claire. Leaving a Doll's House: A Memoir. (Illus.). 288p. 1998. pap. 13.95 (*0-316-09383-1*) Little.

Bloom, Claire. These Are Women. LC 84-740018. 1988. audio 22.00 (*0-694-50790-3*, SWC 243, Caedmon) HarperAudio.

Bloom, Claire, jt. see Anderson, Judith.

Bloom, Clive. Cult Fiction: Popular Reading & Pulp Theory. 272p. 1998. pap. 17.95 (*0-312-21356-5*) St Martin.

— Gothic Horror: A Reader's Guide from Poe to King & Beyond. LC 97-32057. 320p. 1998. pap. 19.95 (*0-312-21239-9*); text 59.95 (*0-312-21238-0*) St Martin.

***Bloom, Clive.** Literature & Culture in Modern Britain, 1956-1990. 2000. pap. 23.95 (*0-582-07552-1*) Addison-Wesley.

Bloom, Clive, ed. American Drama. LC 94-3782. 1995. text 45.00 (*0-312-12387-6*) St Martin.

— LIT& CULTURE MOD BRIT V1, Vol. 1. LC 93-932. (C). 1993. text 72.95 (*0-582-07549-1*, 79858) Longman.

Bloom, Clive, et al, eds. Nineteenth Century Suspense: From Poe to Conan Doyle. 192p. 1988. 24.95 (*0-317-66555-3*) St Martin.

***Bloom, Clive & Day, Gary.** Literature & Culture in Modern Britain, 1956 - 1990: Supplement, Vol. 3. 288p. 2000. 85.95 (*0-582-07553-X*) Longman.

Bloom, Clive & Docherty, Brian. American Poetry: The Modernist Ideal. LC 94-3770. 1995. text 45.00 (*0-312-12388-4*) St Martin.

Bloom, Clive, jt. auth. see McCue, Greg S.

Bloom, Clive, ed. see Cohen, Derek.

Bloom, Clive, jt. ed. see Simons, John.

Bloom, Dale F., et al. The Ph.D. Process: A Student's Guide to Graduate School in the Sciences. LC 97-37159. 224p. 1999. pap. 16.95 (*0-19-511900-2*); text 35.00 (*0-19-511889-8*) OUP.

Bloom, Daniel. Stories & Songs of Hanukkah Audio. abr. ed. (J). 1987. audio 11.95 (*0-89845-746-7*, CPN 1815, Caedmon) HarperAudio.

Bloom, Daniel H. The Man from Galilee. (Illus.). 32p. 1987. 9.95 (*0-915361-90-6*) Lambda Pubs.

Bloom, David. Paradise Forks Rock Climbing. (Illus.). 50p. (Orig.). 1995. pap. 12.95 (*0-934641-98-6*) Falcon Pub Inc.

***Bloom, David.** The Quality of Life in Rural Asia. (A Study of Rural Asia: Vol. 4). 496p. 2000. pap. 29.95 (*0-19-592454-1*); text 55.00 (*0-19-592453-3*) OUP.

Bloom, David E. & Godwin, Peter, eds. The Economics of HIV & AIDS: The Case of South & South East Asia. LC 97-900366. (Illus.). 270p. (C). 1997. text 21.95 (*0-19-564150-7*) OUP.

Bloom, David E. & Trahan, Jane T. Flexible Benefits & Employee Choice. (Studies in Productivity: No. 46). 50p. 1986. pap. text 55.00 (*0-08-029518-5*) Work in Amer.

Bloom, Dwila. Africa, Europe & Asia: Ready-to-Use Interdisciplinary Lessons & Activities. LC 97-25321. Vol. 2. (Illus.). 400p. 1997. pap. text 34.95 (*0-87628-590-6*) Ctr Appl Res.

— America: Ready-to-Use Interdisciplinary Lessons & Activities. LC 97-25321. 400p. 1997. spiral bd. 34.95 (*0-87628-589-2*) Ctr Appl Res.

— Multicultural Art Activities Kit. (Illus.). 384p. 1994. pap. text 59.95 (*0-87628-587-6*) Ctr Appl Res.

Bloom, Edgar B. It All Starts with Counting: A Short Guide to Old-Fashioned Arithmetic & Other Mathematical Concepts. Holliman, Mary C., ed. LC 93-9567. 130p. (Orig.). (YA). (gr. 6-12). 1993. pap. 10.00 (*0-936015-26-8*) Pocahontas Pr.

Bloom, Edward, ed. Drafting in Massachusetts. LC 94-73529. 1996. ring bd. 145.00 (*0-944490-81-6*) Mass CLE.

Bloom, Edward & Bloom, Lillian. Addison & Steele: The Critical Heritage. (Critical Heritage Ser.). 1980. 65.00 (*0-7100-0375-7*, 03757, Routledge Thoemms) Routledge.

Bloom, Edward A., ed. Shakespeare, 1564-1964: A Collection of Modern Essays by Various Hands. LC 64-17777. (Brown University Bicentennial Publications). 240p. reprint ed. pap. 74.40 (*0-7837-2618-X*, 204295300006) Bks Demand.

Bloom, Edward A. & Bloom, Lillian D. Joseph Addison's Sociable Animal: In the Market Place, on the Hustings, in the Pulpit. LC 73-111455. 290p. reprint ed. pap. 89.90 (*0-608-15373-7*, 202924900059) Bks Demand.

— The Piozzi Letters: Correspondence of Hester Lynch Piozzi, 1784-1821, Vol. 4: 1805-1810, Vol. 4. LC 87-40231. (Illus.). 360p. 1996. 52.50 (*0-87413-393-9*) U Delaware Pr.

Bloom, Edward A. & Bloom, Lillian D., eds. The Piozzi Letters: Correspondence of Hester Lynch Piozzi, 1784-1791, Vol. 1. LC 87-40231. (Illus.). 424p. 1989. 75.00 (*0-87413-115-4*) U Delaware Pr.

— The Piozzi Letters: Correspondence of Hester Lynch Piozzi, 1784-1821 (Formerly Mrs. Thrale), Vol. 3: 1799-1804. LC 87-40231. (Illus.). 536p. 1992. 75.00 (*0-87413-392-0*) U Delaware Pr.

Bloom, Edward A., ed. see Burney, Fanny.

Bloom, Edward A., ed. see Piozzi, Hester Lynch.

Bloom, Edward A., ed. & intro. see Burney, Fanny.

Bloom, Elise M. Handling Your First Employment Discrimination Case. LC 99-161606. (New York Practice Skills Course Handbook Ser.). 376p. 1998. 129.00 (*0-87224-545-4*) PLI.

Bloom, Elizabeth, jt. auth. see Letinsky, Laura.

Bloom, Eric & Soybel, Jeremy G. Turbo Pascal Trilogy. 1991. 29.95 (*0-8306-6667-2*) McGraw-Hill Prof.

— Turbo Pascal Trilogy: Version 5.0 & 5. 1991. 24.95 (*0-8306-6737-7*); 24.95 (*0-8306-7738-0*) McGraw-Hill Prof.

Bloom, Eric P. The C Trillogy: A Complete Library for C Programmers. 600p. 1987. 34.95 (*0-8306-7890-5*, 2890H) McGraw-Hill Prof.

— Turbo C++ Trilogy. 1991. 29.95 incl. 3.5 hd (*0-8306-6759-8*) McGraw-Hill Prof.

— Turbo C++ Trilogy, Version 2.0. 1991. 29.95 (*0-8306-6733-4*) McGraw-Hill Prof.

— The Turbo C Trilogy. 1991. 29.95 (*0-8306-6674-5*) McGraw-Hill Prof.

Bloom, Eric P. & Soybel, Jeremy G. Turbo Pascal Trilogy: A Complete Library for Programmers, Featuring Versions 5.0 & 5.5. 1990. pap. 24.95 (*0-07-156865-4*) McGraw.

Bloom, F. Ill-Posed Problems for Integrodifferential Equations in Mechanics & Electromagnetic Theory. LC 80-53713. (Studies in Applied Mathematics: No. 3). ix, 222p. 1981. text 58.50 (*0-89871-171-1*) Soc Indus-Appl Math.

Bloom, F. E., ed. The Primate Nervous System Pt. II, Pt. 1. LC 97-3750. (Handbook of Chemical Neuroanatomy Ser.: 14). 552p. 1997. 264.50 (*0-444-82558-4*) Elsevier.

***Bloom, F. E., et al, eds.** The Primate Nervous System, Part III. 1999. write for info. (*0-444-50043-X*, Excerpta Medica) Elsevier.

Bloom, F. E., et al. The Primate Nervous System Pt. II. (Handbook of Chemical Neuroanatomy Ser.: Vol. 14). 1998. write for info. (*0-444-82912-1*) Elsevier.

Bloom, Floyd E., ed. Handbook of Physiology: Section 1, The Nervous System, Vol. IV: Intrinsic Regulatory Systems of the Brain. (American Physiological Society Book). (Illus.). 850p. 1988. text 258.00 (*0-19-520661-4*) OUP.

— Neuroscience: From the Molecular to the Cognitive. LC 94-12298. (Progress in Brain Research Ser.: Vol. 100). 300p. 1994. 266.00 (*0-444-81678-X*) Elsevier.

Bloom, Floyd E., et al, eds. Peptides: Integrators of Cell & Tissue Function. LC 79-65140. (Society of General Physiologists Ser.: No. 35). 271p. 1980. reprint ed. pap. 84.10 (*0-7837-9524-6*, 206027300005) Bks Demand.

Bloom, Floyd E. & Lazerson, Arlyne. Brain, Mind & Behavior. 2nd ed. LC 87-30598. (Illus.). 394p. (C). 1988. pap. text 50.95 (*0-7167-1863-4*) W H Freeman.

— Brain, Mind & Behavior. 2nd ed. LC 87-30598. (Illus.). 142p. (C). 1988. teacher ed. 4.00 (*0-7167-1895-2*); pap. text, student ed. 21.95 (*0-7167-1894-4*) W H Freeman.

Bloom, Floyd E., et al. Brain Browser. 220p. 1989. text, student ed. 314.00 incl. disk (*0-12-107250-9*) Acad Pr.

Bloom, Floyd E., jt. ed. see Kupfer, David J.

Bloom, Floyd F. & Young, Warren G. Brain Browser: A Spinnaker Plus Based HyperText Application for Microsoft Windows. 227p. 1994. spiral bd. 104.00 (*0-12-107240-1*) Acad Pr.

***Bloom, Gert Jan, et al.** Evaporative Air-Conditioning: Applications for Environmentally Friendly Cooling. LC 98-31273. 87p. 1999. 22.00 (*0-8213-4334-3*) World Bank.

Bloom, Gilbert D., jt. auth. see Newton, Grant.

Bloom, Gilbert D., jt. auth. see Newton, Grant W.

Bloom, Gordon F. & Northrup, Herbert R. The Economics of Labor Relations. 8th ed. (C). 1977. 19.50 (*0-256-01910-X*, Irwn McGrw-H) McGrw-H Hghr Educ.

Bloom, Gunnar, ed. International Symposium on Protection Against Chemical Warfare Agents (2nd, 1986) Proceedings. (Illus.). 440p. (C). 1998. reprint ed. pap. text 60.00 (*0-7881-7062-7*) DIANE Pub.

— International Symposium on Protection Against Chemical Warfare Agents (2nd, 1986) Proceedings - Supplement. (Illus.). 88p. (C). 1998. reprint ed. pap. text 30.00 (*0-7881-7063-5*) DIANE Pub.

— International Symposium on Protection Against Chemical Warfare Agents (3rd, 1989) Proceedings. (Illus.). 416p. (C). 1998. reprint ed. pap. text 60.00 (*0-7881-7060-0*) DIANE Pub.

— International Symposium on Protection Against Chemical Warfare Agents (3rd, 1989) Proceedings - Supplement. (Illus.). 247p. (C). 1998. reprint ed. pap. text 40.00 (*0-7881-7061-9*) DIANE Pub.

— International Symposium on Protection Against Chemical Warfare Agents (4th, 1992) Proceedings. (Illus.). 380p. (C). 1998. reprint ed. pap. text 60.00 (*0-7881-7064-3*) DIANE Pub.

Bloom, H. Book on Freud. 1999. text. write for info. (*0-670-80462-2*) Viking Penguin.

Bloom, H. J. G. & Larzen. Brain, Mind & Behavior. 3rd ed. (C). 2000. pap. text. write for info. (*0-7167-2389-1*) W H Freeman.

Bloom, H. J. G., ed. see Cromwell Hospital International Conference on Mult.

***Bloom, Harold.** Agatha Christie. (Modern Critical Views Ser.). 2000. 36.95 (*0-7910-5921-9*) Chelsea Hse.

Bloom, Harold. The Age of Innocence. LC 98-13286. (Bloom's Notes Ser.). 90p. 1998. pap. 4.95 (*0-7910-4918-3*) Chelsea Hse.

— Agon: Towards a Theory of Revisionism. 350p. 1983. pap. text 13.95 (*0-19-503354-X*) OUP.

— Alex Hailey & Malcolm X's The Autobiography of Malcolm X. 1998. pap. text 4.95 (*0-7910-4111-5*) Chelsea Hse.

***Bloom, Harold.** Alexander Solzhenitsyn. (Modern Critical Views Ser.). 2000. 36.95 (*0-7910-5918-9*) Chelsea Hse.

— Alice Walker. LC 99-14577. (Bloom's Major Novelists Ser.). 120p. (YA). (gr. 8 up). 1999. 19.95 (*0-7910-5250-8*) Chelsea Hse.

— Alice Walker's the Color Purple. LC 99-52024. (Modern Critical Interpretations Ser.). 176p. 2000. 34.95 (*0-7910-5666-X*) Chelsea Hse.

— All Quiet on the Western Front. (Modern Critical Interpretations Ser.). 2000. 36.95 (*0-7910-5923-5*) Chelsea Hse.

Bloom, Harold. The American Religion: The Emergence of the Post-Christian Nation. 288p. 1993. pap. 12.00 (*0-671-86737-7*, Touchstone) S&S Trade Pap.

***Bloom, Harold.** Amy Tan. (Modern Critical Views Ser.). 300p. 1999. 34.95 (*0-7910-5658-9*) Chelsea Hse.

Bloom, Harold. Animal Farm. (Bloom's Notes Ser.). (J). 1998. pap. 4.95 (*0-7910-4110-7*) Chelsea Hse.

— Anna Karenina. (Major Literary Characters Ser.). 1996. 29.95 (*0-7910-0943-2*) Chelsea Hse.

— Anton Chekhov. LC 87-27819. (Modern Critical Views Ser.). 1988. 27.50 (*1-55546-293-6*) Chelsea Hse.

***Bloom, Harold.** Anton Chekhov. LC 99-15683. 120p. 1999. 19.95 (*0-7910-5243-5*) Chelsea Hse.

— Anton Chekhov. (Major Short Story Writers Ser.). 2000. 19.95 (*0-7910-5942-1*) Chelsea Hse.

Bloom, Harold. The Anxiety of Influence: A Theory of Poetry. 2nd ed. 208p. 1997. pap. 13.95 (*0-19-511221-0*) OUP.

— Arthur Miller. LC 99-26951. 120p. 1999. 19.95 (*0-7910-5246-X*) Chelsea Hse.

— The Awakening. LC 98-17600. (Bloom's Notes Ser.). 88 p. 1999. 4.95 (*0-7910-4919-1*) Chelsea Hse.

— Becky Sharp. 1996. 29.95 (*0-7910-0946-7*) Chelsea Hse.

— Beowulf. (Bloom's Reviews Ser.). 1999. pap. 4.95 (*0-7910-4112-3*) Chelsea Hse.

— The Best of the Best American Poetry: 1988-1997. (American Poetry Ser.). 384p. 1998. per. 15.00 (*0-684-84779-5*) Scribner.

— Billy Budd, Benito Carano & Bartleby. (Bloom's Notes Ser.). 1998. pap. 4.95 (*0-7910-4113-1*) Chelsea Hse.

— Bloom of Mice & Men. 1996. pap. text 4.95 (*0-7910-4143-3*) Chelsea Hse.

— Bloom Pride & Prejudice. 1999. pap. text 4.95 (*0-7910-4147-6*) Chelsea Hse.

— Bloom's Major Poets Set, 12. 1998. 227.40 (*0-7910-5129-3*) Chelsea Hse.

— Bloom's Oedipus the King: Opedipus at Colonus & Antigone. LC 95-43496. 1999. pap. 4.95 (*0-7910-4142-5*) Chelsea Hse.

— Bloom's Romeo & Juliet. 1998. pap. text 4.95 (*0-7910-4149-2*) Chelsea Hse.

— Bloom's Short Story Writers Set, 12 vols. 1998. 227.40 (*0-7910-5130-7*) Chelsea Hse.

— The Book of J. Rosenberg, David, tr. LC 91-50220. 352p. 1991. pap. 14.00 (*0-679-73624-7*) Vin Bks.

— Brave New World. 1999. pap. text 4.95 (*0-7910-4114-X*) Chelsea Hse.

— The Breaking of the Vessels. LC 81-12975. (Wellek Library Lectures). (C). 1982. lib. bdg. 10.00 (*0-226-06043-8*) U Ch Pr.

— The Breaking of the Vessels. LC 81-12975. (Wellek Library Lectures). (C). 1983. pap. text 7.95 (*0-226-06044-6*) U Ch Pr.

— Brontes. LC 99-31887. 120p. 1999. 19.95 (*0-7910-5257-5*) Chelsea Hse.

— Caribbean Women Writers. LC 97-4276. (Women Writers & Their Works Ser.). 180p. (C). 1997. 29.95 (*0-7910-4476-9*); pap. 16.95 (*0-7910-4492-0*) Chelsea Hse.

***Bloom, Harold.** Catch-22. (Modern Critical Interpretations Ser.). 2000. 36.95 (*0-7910-5927-8*) Chelsea Hse.

— Catcher in the Rye. LC 99-49612. 176p. 1999. 34.95 (*0-7910-5664-3*) Chelsea Hse.

Bloom, Harold. Charles Dickens. LC 99-29506. 120p. 1999. 19.95 (*0-7910-5251-6*) Chelsea Hse.

— The Crucible. 1998. pap. 4.95 (*0-7910-4117-4*) Chelsea Hse.

***Bloom, Harold.** D. H. Lawrence. (Major Short Story Writers Ser.). 2000. 19.95 (*0-7910-5947-2*) Chelsea Hse.

— Dante. (Major Poets Ser.). 2000. 19.95 (*0-7910-5939-1*) Chelsea Hse.

An Asterisk (*) at the beginning of an entry indicates that the title is appearing for the first time.

— Death of a Salesman. (Bloom's Notes Ser.). 1998. pap. 4.95 (*0-7910-4118-2*) Chelsea Hse.
— Don Quixote. (Modern Critical Interpretations Ser.). 2001. 36.95 (*0-7910-5922-7*) Chelsea Hse.
Bloom, Harold. Edgar Allan Poe. LC 98-41380. (Bloom's Short Story Writers Ser.). 112p. (YA). (gr. 8 up). 1999. lib. bdg. 18.95 (*0-7910-5117-X*); lib. bdg. 18.95 (*0-7910-5113-7*) Chelsea Hse.
— Edmund Spenser's "The Faerie Queene" LC 87-30391. (Modern Critical Interpretations Ser.). 1988. 24.50 (*1-55546-326-6*) Chelsea Hse.
— Emily Dickinson. LC 98-41763. (Bloom's World Poets Ser.). 112p. (YA). (gr. 8 up). 1999. lib. bdg. 18.95 (*0-7910-5106-4*) Chelsea Hse.
— Ernest Hemingway. LC 98-42029. (Bloom's Short Story Writers Ser.). 112p. (YA). (gr. 8 up). 1999. lib. bdg. 18.95 (*0-7910-5121-8*) Chelsea Hse.
— Eudora Welty. (Bloom's Short Story Writers Ser.). 112p. (YA). (gr. 8 up). 1999. lib. bdg. 18.95 (*0-7910-5126-9*) Chelsea Hse.
— Eugene O'Neill. LC 99-36815. 120p. 1999. 19.95 (*0-7910-5245-1*) Chelsea Hse.
— F. Scott Fitzgerald. LC 98-33276. (Bloom's Short Story Writers Ser.). 112p. (YA). (gr. 11 up). 1999. lib. bdg. 18.95 (*0-7910-5122-6*) Chelsea Hse.
— F. Scott Fitzgerald. LC 99-27013. 120p. 1999. 19.95 (*0-7910-5254-0*) Chelsea Hse.
***Bloom, Harold.** Fahrenheit 451. (Modern Critical Interpretations Ser.). 2000. 36.95 (*0-7910-5929-4*) Chelsea Hse.
Bloom, Harold. Flannery O'Connor. LC 98-31662. (Bloom's Short Story Writers Ser.). 112p. (YA). (gr. 11 up). 1999. lib. bdg. 18.95 (*0-7910-5119-6*) Chelsea Hse.
— Geoffrey Chaucer. (Bloom's World Poets Ser.). 112p. (YA). (gr. 8 up). 1999. lib. bdg. 18.95 (*0-7910-5115-3*) Chelsea Hse.
— George B. Shaw. LC 99-27601. 120p. 1999. 19.95 (*0-7910-5237-0*) Chelsea Hse.
***Bloom, Harold.** Great Expectations. LC 99-51594. (Modern Critical Interpretations Ser.). 176p. 1999. 34.95 (*0-7910-5661-9*) Chelsea Hse.
— Gwendolyn-Brooks. (Modern Critical Views Ser.). 300p. 2000. 34.95 (*0-7910-5656-2*) Chelsea Hse.
— Handmaid's Tale. (Modern Critical Interpretations Ser.). 2000. 36.95 (*0-7910-5926-X*) Chelsea Hse.
Bloom, Harold. Heart of Darkness: And, The Secret Sharer. (Bloom's Notes Ser.). 1999. mass mkt. 4.95 (*0-7910-4127-1*) Chelsea Hse.
— Henrik Ibsen. LC 99-15682. (Illus.). 120p. 1999. 19.95 (*0-7910-5239-7*) Chelsea Hse.
***Bloom, Harold.** Henry James. (Major Short Story Writers Ser.). 2000. 19.95 (*0-7910-5943-X*) Chelsea Hse.
Bloom, Harold. Herman Melville. (Bloom's Short Story Writers Ser.). 112p. (YA). (gr. 8 up). 1999. lib. bdg. 18.95 (*0-7910-5118-8*) Chelsea Hse.
***Bloom, Harold.** Homer. (Major Poets Ser.). 2000. 19.95 (*0-7910-5938-3*) Chelsea Hse.
— How to Read & Why. 288p. 2000. 25.00 (*0-684-85906-8*) Scribner.
— How to Read & Why. large type ed. 384p. 2000. 25.00 (*0-7432-0428-X*) S&S Trade.
— Italo Calvino. LC 00-31422. (Modern Critical Views Ser.). 2000. 36.95 (*0-7910-5919-7*) Chelsea Hse.
Bloom, Harold. J. D. Salinger. LC 98-41379. (Bloom's Short Story Writers Ser.). 112p. (YA). (gr. 8 up). 1999. lib. bdg. 18.95 (*0-7910-5120-X*) Chelsea Hse.
***Bloom, Harold.** J. R. R. Tolkien. LC 99-51326. (Modern Critical Views Ser.). 300p. 2000. 34.95 (*0-7910-5660-0*) Chelsea Hse.
— Jack London. (Major Short Story Writers Ser.). 2000. 19.95 (*0-7910-5945-6*) Chelsea Hse.
Bloom, Harold. James Joyce. (Bloom's Short Story Writers Ser.). 112p. (YA). (gr. 8 up). 1999. lib. bdg. 18.95 (*0-7910-5127-7*) Chelsea Hse.
— Jane Austen. LC 99-29497. (Illus.). 120p. 1999. 19.95 (*0-7910-5260-5*) Chelsea Hse.
— Jane Eyre: Comprehensive Research Study Guides. (Bloom's Reviews Ser.). 1998. pap. 4.95 (*0-7910-4132-8*) Chelsea Hse.
***Bloom, Harold.** Jean-Paul Sartre. (Modern Critical Views Ser.). 2000. 36.95 (*0-7910-5917-0*) Chelsea Hse.
Bloom, Harold. John Donne. LC 98-53871. (Bloom's World Poets Ser.). 112p. (YA). (gr. 8 up). 1999. lib. bdg. 18.95 (*0-7910-5116-1*) Chelsea Hse.
***Bloom, Harold.** John Irving. (Modern Critical Views Ser.). 2000. 36.95 (*0-7910-5920-0*) Chelsea Hse.
— John Keats. (Major Poets Ser.). 2000. 19.95 (*0-7910-5934-0*) Chelsea Hse.
— John Knowles' a Separate Peace. LC 99-49120. (Modern Critical Interpretations Ser.). 176p. 1999. text 34.95 (*0-7910-5663-5*) Chelsea Hse.
Bloom, Harold. John Milton. (Bloom's World Poets Ser.). 112p. (YA). (gr. 8 up). 1999. lib. bdg. 18.95 (*0-7910-5111-0*) Chelsea Hse.
— John Steinbeck. LC 98-49209. (Bloom's Short Story Writers Ser.). 112p. (YA). (gr. 11 up). 1999. lib. bdg. 18.95 (*0-7910-5125-0*) Chelsea Hse.
— John Steinbeck. LC 99-22479. (Bloom's Major Novelists Ser.). 120p. 1999. 19.95 (*0-7910-5252-4*) Chelsea Hse.
***Bloom, Harold.** John Updike. (Major Short Story Writers Ser.). 2000. 19.95 (*0-7910-5946-4*) Chelsea Hse.
— Joseph Conrad. LC 00-24062. (Bloom's Major Short Story Writers Ser.). 2000. pap. 19.95 (*0-7910-5940-5*) Chelsea Hse.
Bloom, Harold. Kabbalah & Criticism. LC 75-12820. 128p. (C). 1983. pap. 15.95 (*0-8264-0242-9*) Continuum.
***Bloom, Harold.** Katherine Anne Porter. LC 00-24064. 2000. 19.95 (*0-7910-5941-3*) Chelsea Hse.
Bloom, Harold. King Lear. (Bloom's Notes Ser.). 1998. pap. 4.95 (*0-7910-4134-4*) Chelsea Hse.
***Bloom, Harold.** Kurt Vonnegut. LC 99-49119. (Modern Critical Views Ser.). 300p. 2000. 34.95 (*0-7910-5655-4*) Chelsea Hse.
Bloom, Harold. Langston Hughes. (Bloom's World Poets Ser.). 112p. (YA). (gr. 8 up). 1999. lib. bdg. 18.95 (*0-7910-5110-2*) Chelsea Hse.
— A Map of Misreading. 218p. 1980. pap. 13.95 (*0-19-502809-0*) OUP.
***Bloom, Harold.** Margaret Atwood. LC 99-52023. (Modern Critical Views Ser.). 300p. 2000. 34.95 (*0-7910-5659-7*) Chelsea Hse.
Bloom, Harold. Mark Twain. LC 98-54082. (Bloom's Short Story Writers Ser.). 112p. (YA). (gr. 8 up). 1999. lib. bdg. 18.95 (*0-7910-5124-2*) Chelsea Hse.
— Mark Twain. LC 99-33402. 120p. 1999. 19.95 (*0-7910-5256-7*) Chelsea Hse.
***Bloom, Harold.** Maya Angelou. (Major Poets Ser.). 2000. 19.95 (*0-7910-5937-5*) Chelsea Hse.
— Nathaniel Hawthorne. (Major Short Story Writers Ser.). 2000. 19.95 (*0-7910-5949-9*) Chelsea Hse.
— Night. (Modern Critical Interpretations Ser.). 2000. 36.95 (*0-7910-5924-3*) Chelsea Hse.
Bloom, Harold. Nineteen Eighty-Four. (Bloom's Notes Ser.). 1998. pap. 4.95 (*0-7910-4140-9*) Chelsea Hse.
— The Old Man & the Sea. (Bloom's Notes Ser.). 1998. pap. 4.95 (*0-7910-4144-1*) Chelsea Hse.
— Omens of the Millennium: The Gnosis of Angels, Dreams & Resurrection. 272p. 1997. reprint ed. pap. 13.00 (*1-57322-629-7*, Riverhd Trade) Berkley Pub.
— Percy Bysshe Shelley's Major Lyrics. LC 87-37509. (Modern Critical Interpretations Ser.). 1988. 19.95 (*1-55546-960-4*) Chelsea Hse.
— Percy Bysshe Shelley's "The Triumph of Life" LC 87-33846. (Modern Critical Interpretations Ser.). 1988. 24.50 (*1-55546-973-6*) Chelsea Hse.
***Bloom, Harold.** Percy Shelley. 2000. 19.95 (*0-7910-5930-8*) Chelsea Hse.
Bloom, Harold. The Poetics of Influence: New & Selected Criticism of Harold Bloom. Hollander, John, ed. & intro. by. 500p. 1988. 49.95 (*0-939681-00-5*); pap. 24.95 (*0-939681-01-3*) H R Schwab.
***Bloom, Harold.** Poets of WWI. (Major Poets Ser.). 2000. 19.95 (*0-7910-5932-4*) Chelsea Hse.
Bloom, Harold. Ralph Waldo Emerson's Nature. LC 87-30400. (Modern Critical Interpretations Ser.). 1988. 24.50 (*1-55546-329-0*) Chelsea Hse.
***Bloom, Harold.** Ray Bradbury. LC 00-22682. 2000. 36.95 (*0-7910-5914-6*) Chelsea Hse.
Bloom, Harold. The Ringers in the Tower: Studies in Romantic Tradition. LC PR0447.B6. 364p. Date not set. reprint ed. pap. 112.90 (*0-608-20587-7*, 205455200003) Bks Demand.
***Bloom, Harold.** Robert Browning. (Major Poets Ser.). 2000. 19.95 (*0-7910-5931-6*) Chelsea Hse.
Bloom, Harold. Robert Frost. LC 98-35358. (Bloom's World Poets Ser.). 80p. (YA). (gr. 8 up). 1999. lib. bdg. 18.95 (*0-7910-5105-6*) Chelsea Hse.
— Ruin the Sacred Truths: Poetry & Belief from the Bible to the Present. LC 88-21651. (Charles Eliot Norton Lectures). 216p. 1989. 36.50 (*0-674-78027-2*) HUP.
— Ruin the Sacred Truths: Poetry & Belief from the Bible to the Present. (Charles Eliot Norton Lectures). 216p. (C). 1991. pap. text 12.95 (*0-674-78028-0*) HUP.
***Bloom, Harold.** Samuel Taylor Coleridge. (Major Poets Ser.). 2000. 16.62 (*0-7910-5933-2*) Chelsea Hse.
— Shakespeare: The Invention of the Human. LC 98-21325. 800p. 1998. 35.00 (*1-57322-120-1*, Riverhead Books) Putnam Pub Group.
Bloom, Harold. Shakespeare: The Invention of the Human. 745p. (C). 2000. reprint ed. pap. 15.95 (*1-57322-751-X*) R Books.
— Shakespeare's Comedies. LC 99-15681. 120p. 1999. 19.95 (*0-7910-5238-9*) Chelsea Hse.
— Shakespeare's Histories. LC 99-36774. (Illus.). 120p. 1999. 19.95 (*0-7910-5241-9*) Chelsea Hse.
— Shakespeare's Poems & Sonnets. (Bloom's World Poets Ser.). 112p. (YA). (gr. 8 up). 1999. lib. bdg. 18.95 (*0-7910-5107-2*) Chelsea Hse.
— Shakespeare's Romances. LC 99-29303. 120p. 1999. 19.95 (*0-7910-5244-3*) Chelsea Hse.
***Bloom, Harold.** Shakespeare's Romances. LC 99-49611. (Modern Critical Views Ser.). 300p. 1999. 34.95 (*0-7910-5657-0*) Chelsea Hse.
Bloom, Harold. Shakespeare's Tragedies. LC 99-29302. 120p. 1999. 19.95 (*0-7910-5242-7*) Chelsea Hse.
***Bloom, Harold.** Shirley Jackson. (Major Short Story Writers Ser.). 2000. 19.95 (*0-7910-5948-0*) Chelsea Hse.
— Slaughterhouse-Five. (Modern Critical Interpretations Ser.). 2000. 36.95 (*0-7910-5925-1*) Chelsea Hse.
— Stephen Crane. LC 00-35849. (Bloom's Major Short Story Writers Ser.). 2000. pap. 19.95 (*0-7910-5944-8*) Chelsea Hse.
— Stranger. (Modern Critical Interpretations Ser.). 2000. 36.95 (*0-7910-5928-6*) Chelsea Hse.
— Sylvia Plath. (Major Poets Ser.). 2000. 19.95 (*0-7910-5935-9*) Chelsea Hse.
Bloom, Harold. T. S. Eliot. LC 98-39703. (Bloom's World Poets Ser.). 87p. (YA). (gr. 8 up). 1999. lib. bdg. 18.95 (*0-7910-5109-9*) Chelsea Hse.
— Tennessee Williams. LC 99-21422. (Bloom's Major Dramatists Ser.). (Illus.). 120p. (YA). (gr. 8 up). 1999. 19.95 (*0-7910-5240-0*) Chelsea Hse.
— Theodore Dreiser. LC 87-33858. (Modern Critical Views Ser.). 1988. 19.95 (*1-55546-409-2*) Chelsea Hse.
— To Kill a Mockingbird. (Bloom's Notes Ser.). 1998. pap. 4.95 (*0-7910-4168-9*) Chelsea Hse.
— To the Tally of My Soul: Whitman's Image of Voice. (Chapbooks in Literature Ser.). 36p. (Orig.). 1980. pap. text 5.00 (*0-9614940-4-2*) Bennington Coll.
***Bloom, Harold.** Tom Wolfe. (Modern Critical Views Ser.). 2000. 36.95 (*0-7910-5916-2*) Chelsea Hse.
— Toni Morrison. LC 99-34234. (Bloom's Major Novelists Ser.). 120p. 1999. 19.95 (*0-7910-5258-3*) Chelsea Hse.
— Toni Morrison's "Beloved" LC 98-39619. (Bloom's Notes Ser.). 1999. pap. 4.95 (*0-7910-5223-0*) Chelsea Hse.
Bloom, Harold. Twentieth-Century American Literature, 15 bks. (Modern Critical Interpretations Ser.). 1988 469.25 (*0-7910-3576-X*) Chelsea Hse.
— The Visionary Company: A Reading of English Romantic Poetry. rev. ed. LC 73-144032. 506p. 1971. pap. text 17.95 (*0-8014-9117-7*) Cornell U Pr.
***Bloom, Harold.** W. E. B. DuBois. (Modern Critical Views Ser.). 2000. 36.95 (*0-7910-5915-4*) Chelsea Hse.
Bloom, Harold. Wallace Stevens: The Poems of Our Climate. 416p. 1980. pap. text 18.95 (*0-8014-9135-1*) Cornell U Pr.
— Walt Whitman. (Bloom's World Poets Ser.). 112p. (YA). (gr. 8 up). 1999. lib. bdg. 18.95 (*0-7910-5108-0*) Chelsea Hse.
— The Western Canon: The Books & School of the Ages. LC 95-1680. 560p. 1995. pap. 15.00 (*1-57322-514-2*, Riverhd Trade) Berkley Pub.
— The Western Canon: The Books & School of the Ages. LC 93-43542. 1994. 29.95 (*0-15-195747-9*) Harcourt.
— The Western Canon: The Books & School of the Ages. 608p. 1994. 29.95 (*0-15-100133-2*) Harcourt.
***Bloom, Harold.** Willa Cather. LC 99-15164. 120p. 1999. 19.95 (*0-7910-5261-3*) Chelsea Hse.
— William Butler Yeats. (Major Poets Ser.). 2000. 19.95 (*0-7910-5936-7*) Chelsea Hse.
Bloom, Harold. William Faulkner. LC 98-46689. (Bloom's Short Story Writers Ser.). 112p. (YA). (gr. 11 up) 1999. lib. bdg. 18.95 (*0-7910-5128-5*) Chelsea Hse.
— William Faulkner. 120p. 1999. 19.95 (*0-7910-5255-9*) Chelsea Hse.
— William Shakespeare's Macbeth. LC 98-38964. 1998. pap. 4.95 (*0-7910-4136-0*) Chelsea Hse.
***Bloom, Harold.** William Shakespeare's Romeo & Juliet. LC 99-49118. (Modern Critical Interpretations Ser.). 176p. 2000. 34.95 (*0-7910-5662-7*) Chelsea Hse.
Bloom, Harold. William Wordsworth. (Bloom's World Poets Ser.). 112p. (YA). (gr. 8 up). 1999. lib. bdg. 18.95 (*0-7910-5114-5*) Chelsea Hse.
— Yeats. 512p. 1972. reprint ed. pap. text 17.95 (*0-19-501603-3*) OUP.
***Bloom, Harold.** Zora Neale Hurston's Their Eyes Were Watching God. LC 98-19255. (Bloom's Notes Ser.). 1998. pap. 4.95 (*0-7910-4568-4*) Chelsea Hse.
Bloom, Harold, ed. American Women Fiction Writers 1900-1960, 3. (Women Writers of English Ser.: Vol. 3). 200p. (YA). (gr. 9 up). 1999. 29.95 (*0-7910-4652-4*); pap. 16.95 (*0-7910-4653-2*) Chelsea Hse.
— American Women Fiction Writers, 1900-1960, Vol. 1. LC 97-6310. (Women Writers & Their Works Ser.). (Illus.). 180p. (C). 1997. 29.95 (*0-7910-4480-7*); pap. 16.95 (*0-7910-4496-3*) Chelsea Hse.
— American Women Fiction Writers, 1900-1960, Vol. 2. (Women Writers & Their Works Ser.). (Illus.). 180p. (C). 1997. 29.95 (*0-7910-4481-5*); pap. 16.95 (*0-7910-4497-1*) Chelsea Hse.
Bloom, Harold, ed. Antiquity to Enlightenment. 26p. (YA). (gr. 5-8). 1996. 287.20 (*0-7910-4507-2*) Chelsea Hse.
Bloom, Harold, ed. Anton Chekhov. LC 98-6614. (Modern Critical Views Ser.). 300p. (YA). (gr. 8 up). 1999. 34.95 (*0-7910-4783-0*) Chelsea Hse.
— Asian American Women Writers. LC 97-9166. (Women Writers & Their Works Ser.). 180p. (C). 1997. 29.95 (*0-7910-4475-0*); pap. 16.95 (*0-7910-4491-2*) Chelsea Hse.
— Asian-American Writers. LC 98-15463. (Modern Critical Views Ser.). 300p. (YA). 1999. 34.95 (*0-7910-4787-3*) Chelsea Hse.
Bloom, Harold, ed. Bloom's Notes: 20th Century Literature. 26p. 1996. 412.85 (*0-7910-4509-9*) Chelsea Hse.
Bloom, Harold, ed. British Women Fiction Writers of the 19th Century: Women Writers of Fiction & Their Works. LC 97-50561. (Women Writers & Their Works Ser.). (Illus.). 180p. (YA). (gr. 9 up). 1998. lib. bdg. 29.95 (*0-7910-4482-3*) Chelsea Hse.
— British Women Fiction Writers, 1900-1960, Vol. 1. LC 97-20282. (Women Writers & Their Works Ser.). (Illus.). 180p. (C). 1997. 29.95 (*0-7910-4483-1*) Chelsea Hse.
— British Women Fiction Writers, 1900-1960, Vol. 1. LC 97-20282. (Women Writers & Their Works Ser.). (Illus.). 180p. (C). 1997. pap. 14.95 (*0-7910-4499-8*) Chelsea Hse.
— British Women Fiction Writers, 1900-1960, Vol. 2. LC 97-20282. (Women Writers & Their Works Ser.). (Illus.). 227p. (YA). (gr. 10 up). 1997. 29.95 (*0-7910-4484-X*) Chelsea Hse.
— British Women Fiction Writers, 1900-1960, Vol. 2. LC 97-20282. (Women Writers & Their Works Ser.). (Illus.). 227p. (YA). (gr. 10 up). 1997. pap. 16.95 (*0-7910-4500-5*) Chelsea Hse.
— The Catcher in the Rye. (Bloom's Reviews Ser.). 69p. 1998. pap. text 4.95 (*0-7910-4115-8*) Chelsea Hse.
— Charles Dickens's A Tale of Two Cities: Comprehensive Research & Study Guides. 1997. pap. 4.95 (*0-7910-4166-2*) Chelsea Hse.
***Bloom, Harold, ed.** Ernest Hemingway. LC 99-15165 120p. 1999. 19.95 (*0-7910-5259-1*) Chelsea Hse.
Bloom, Harold, ed. Henrik Ibsen. LC 98-30508. (Modern Critical Views Ser.). 300p. (YA). 1999. 34.95 (*0-7910-4784-9*) Chelsea Hse.
— Hispanic-American Writers. LC 97-53071. (Modern Critical Views Ser.). 300p. (YA). 1999. 34.95 (*0-7910-4786-5*) Chelsea Hse.
***Bloom, Harold, ed.** The Iliad. 1999. pap. 4.95 (*0-7910-4130-1*) Chelsea Hse.
Bloom, Harold, ed. Implementation of the Indian Gaming Regulatory Act: Survey Report & Audit Report. (Illus.). 62p. (C). 1998. pap. text 25.00 (*0-7881-7254-9*) DIANE Pub.
— Invisible Man. LC 98-6615. (Modern Critical Interpretations Ser.). 259p. (YA). (gr. 9 up). 1998. lib. bdg. 34.95 (*0-7910-4776-8*) Chelsea Hse.
— Jamaica Kincaid. LC 98-14078. (Modern Critical Views Ser.). 300p. (YA). 1999. 34.95 (*0-7910-4781-4*) Chelsea Hse.
— Jewish Women Fiction Writers. LC 97-32468. (Women Writers & Their Works Ser.). 180p. 1997. 29.95 (*0-7910-4477-7*) Chelsea Hse.
— Jewish Women Fiction Writers. LC 97-32468. (Women Writers & Their Works Ser.). 180p. (C). (gr. 5 up). 1997. pap. 16.95 (*0-7910-4493-9*) Chelsea Hse.
— Lesbians & Bisexual Fiction Writers. LC 97-4113. (Women Writers & Their Works Ser.). (Illus.). 180p. (C). 1997. 29.95 (*0-7910-4478-5*); pap. 16.95 (*0-7910-4494-7*) Chelsea Hse.
— Library of Literary Criticism. Incl. Beaumont & Fletcher to Sir Thomas Browne. 650p. 1986. 75.00 (*0-87754-792-0*); Critical Perspective Bibliographical Supplement & Index. Joshi, S. T., ed. 200p. 1989. text 50.00 (*1-55546-774-1*); Fanny Burney to Walter Savage Landor. 650p. 1988. 75.00 (*0-87754-796-3*); Izaak Walton to Henry Fielding. 650p. 1987. 75.00 (*0-87754-793-9*); Mary Wollstonecraft to William Godwin. 650p. 1988. 75.00 (*0-87754-795-5*); Nathaniel Hawthorne to Edward FitzGerald. 650p. 1989. 75.00 (*0-87754-797-1*); Vol. 1. Beowulf to Christopher Marlowe. 650p. 1985. 75.00 (*0-87754-790-4*); Vol. 1. Walter Abish to William S. Burroughs. 650p. 1985. 75.00 (*0-87754-801-3*); Vol. 2. Edmund Spenser & William Shakespeare. 650p. 1986. 75.00 (*0-87754-791-2*); Vol. 5. Jonathan Edwards to Edmund Burke. 650p. 1987. 75.00 (*0-87754-794-7*); Vol. 9. Emily Dickinson to Lewis Carroll. 650p. 1989. 75.00 (*0-87754-798-X*); 1988. Set pap. text 2600.00 (*0-7910-3592-1*) Chelsea Hse.
***Bloom, Harold, ed.** Lord of the Rings. LC 99-52464. (Modern Critical Interpretations Ser.). 300p. 1999. 34.95 (*0-7910-5665-1*) Chelsea Hse.
Bloom, Harold, ed. Maya Angelou. LC 97-50357. (Modern Critical Views Ser.). 300p. (YA). 1999. 34.95 (*0-7910-4782-2*) Chelsea Hse.
— Modern Critical Views. (Illus.). 144-300p. (J). 279.60 (*0-7910-5220-6*) Chelsea Hse.
— Native American Women Writers. LC 97-40088. (Women Writers & Their Works Ser.). (Illus.). 180p. (YA). (gr. 10 up). 1998. 29.95 (*0-7910-4479-3*); pap. 16.95 (*0-7910-4495-5*) Chelsea Hse.
— Native-American Writers. LC 97-51447. (Modern Critical Views Ser.). 300p. (YA). 1999. 34.95 (*0-7910-4785-7*) Chelsea Hse.
***Bloom, Harold, ed.** 19th Century. 26p. (YA). 1998. 323.10 (*0-7910-4508-0*) Chelsea Hse.
Bloom, Harold, ed. The Romantic Tradition in American Literature, 33 bks. 1972. reprint ed. 891.00 (*0-405-04620-0*) Ayer.
— Romanticism & Consciousness. 405p. (Orig.). (C). 1970. pap. text 16.75 (*0-393-09954-7*) Norton.
— A Scholarly Look at The Diary of Anne Frank. LC 98-49479. 176p. 1999. 34.95 (*0-7910-5192-7*) Chelsea Hse.
— Science Fiction Writers of the Golden Age. (Writers of English Ser.). 180p. 1995. pap. text 14.95 (*0-7910-2198-X*) Chelsea Hse.
— Science Fiction Writers of the Golden Age. LC 94-4322. (Writers of English Ser.). 180p. 1995. 14.95 (*0-7910-2199-8*) Chelsea Hse.
— The Sound & the Fury. LC 98-2807. (Bloom's Notes Ser.). 90p. (YA). 1998. pap. 4.95 (*0-7910-4569-2*) Chelsea Hse.
— Stephen King. LC 97-49605. (Modern Critical Views Ser.). 300p. (YA). 1999. 34.95 (*0-7910-4780-6*) Chelsea Hse.
— To Kill a Mockingbird. LC 98-23258. (Modern Critical Interpretations Ser.). 176p. (YA). 1999. 34.95 (*0-7910-4779-2*) Chelsea Hse.
— Women Memoirists. LC 97-35879. (Women Writers of English Ser.: Vol. 1). (Illus.). 158p. (YA). (gr. 10 up). 1997. pap. 16.95 (*0-7910-4501-3*) Chelsea Hse.
— Women Memoirists. LC 97-35879. (Women Writers of English Ser.: Vol. 2). 200p. (YA). (gr. 9 up). 1999. pap. 29.95 (*0-7910-4654-0*) Chelsea Hse.
— Women Memoirists. LC 97-35879. (Women Writers of English Ser.: Vol. 1). (Illus.). 200p. (YA). (gr. 10 up). 1999. 29.95 (*0-7910-4485-8*) Chelsea Hse.
— Women Memoirists, 2. LC 97-35879. (Women Writers of English Ser.: Vol. 2). 200p. (YA). (gr. 9 up). 1999. pap. 16.95 (*0-7910-4655-9*) Chelsea Hse.
— Women Writers of Children's Literature. LC 97-28610. (Women Writers & Their Works Ser.). (Illus.). 180p. (C). 1997. 29.95 (*0-7910-4486-6*); pap. 16.95 (*0-7910-4502-1*) Chelsea Hse.
Bloom, Harold, ed. The Critical Cosmos, 3 vols. Incl. American Fiction 1914-1945. 1987. 69.95 (*0-87754-962-1*); British Modernist Fiction 1920-1945. 375p. 1987. 59.95 (*0-87754-987-7*); 1987. 199.85 (*0-87754-950-8*) Chelsea Hse.
— Edith Wharton's "The Age of Innocence" LC 98-13286. (Bloom's Notes Ser.). 90p. (YA). (gr. 8 up). 1999. lib. bdg. 16.95 (*0-7910-4515-3*) Chelsea Hse.
— Henry James's "The Portrait of a Lady" large type ed. LC 98-23885. (Bloom's Notes Ser.). 90p. (YA). (gr. 8-12). 1999. lib. bdg. 16.95 (*0-7910-4514-5*) Chelsea Hse.
— Kate Chopin's "The Awakening" LC 98-17600. (Bloom's Notes Ser.). 90p. (YA). (gr. 8 up). 1999. lib. bdg. 16.95 (*0-7910-4512-9*) Chelsea Hse.
— Modern Critical Interpretations. (Illus.). 144-176p. (J). 1999. 419.40 (*0-7910-5221-4*) Chelsea Hse.

B

B

— Toni Morrison's "Beloved" LC 98-39619. (Bloom's Notes Ser.). 90p. (YA). (gr. 8 up). 1999. lib. bdg. 17.95 (0-7910-4516-1) Chelsea Hse.

— William Faulkner's "The Sound & the Fury" LC 98-2807. (Bloom's Notes Ser.). 90p. (YA). (gr. 8 up). 1999. lib. bdg. 16.95 (0-7910-4519-6) Chelsea Hse.

— Zora Neale Hurston's "Their Eyes Were Watching God" LC 98-19255. (Bloom's Notes Ser.). 90p. (YA). (gr. 8-12). 1999. lib. bdg. 16.95 (0-7910-4520-X) Chelsea Hse.

Bloom, Harold, intro. George Bernard Shaw. (Modern Critical Views Ser.). 222p. 1987. 29.95 (0-87754-649-5) Chelsea Hse.

— George Orwell. (Modern Critical Views Ser.). 222p. 1987. 29.95 (0-87754-648-7) Chelsea Hse.

— Gerard Manley Hopkins. (Modern Critical Views Ser.). 179p. 1986. 29.95 (0-87754-691-6) Chelsea Hse.

— Herman Melville. 222p. 1986. 29.95 (0-87754-670-3) Chelsea Hse.

— Jane Austen. (Modern Critical Views Ser.). 222p. 1986. 34.95 (0-87754-682-7) Chelsea Hse.

— John Keats. (Modern Critical Views Ser.). 222p. 1985. 34.95 (0-87754-608-8) Chelsea Hse.

— Mark Twain. (Modern Critical Views Ser.). 222p. 1986. 29.95 (0-87754-698-3) Chelsea Hse.

— Stephen Crane. (Modern Critical Views Ser.). 222p. 1987. 34.95 (0-87754-694-0) Chelsea Hse.

— Virginia Woolf. (Modern Critical Views Ser.). 222p. 1986. 34.95 (0-87754-673-8) Chelsea Hse.

Bloom, Harold & Joyce, James. James Joyce's "A Portrait of the Artist As a Young Man" LC 98-16607. (Bloom's Notes Ser.). 82 p. 1999. pap. 4.95 (0-7910-4566-8) Chelsea Hse.

Bloom, Harold & Lehman, David. The Best of the Best American Poetry: 1988-1997. (American Poetry Ser.). 384p. 1998. 29.50 (0-684-84279-3) Scribner.

Bloom, Harold & Trilling, Lionel, eds. Romantic Poetry & Prose. (Anthology of English Literature Ser.). (Illus.). 830p. 1973. pap. text 32.95 (0-19-501615-7) OUP.

Bloom, Harold, et al. Deconstruction & Criticism. LC 93-38427. 256p. 1979. pap. 17.95 (0-8264-0010-8) Continuum.

Bloom, Harold, ed. see Angelou, Maya.

Bloom, Harold, ed. see Bronte, Emily.

Bloom, Harold, ed. see Ellison, Ralph.

Bloom, Harold, ed. see Emerson, Ralph Waldo.

Bloom, Harold, ed. see Golding, William.

Bloom, Harold, ed. see Hawthorne, Nathaniel.

Bloom, Harold, ed. see Hemingway, Ernest.

Bloom, Harold, jt. ed. see Hollander, Joan.

Bloom, Harold, ed. see Miller, Arthur.

Bloom, Harold, ed. see Morrison, Toni.

Bloom, Harold, ed. see Orwell, George.

Bloom, Harold, ed. see Shakespeare, William.

Bloom, Harold, ed. see Tennyson, Alfred Lord.

Bloom, Harold, jt. ed. see Trilling, Lionel.

Bloom, Harold, ed. & intro. see Angelou, Maya.

Bloom, Harold, ed. & intro. see Henry, O.

Bloom, Harold, ed. & intro. see Joyce, James.

Bloom, Harold, ed. & intro. see Pater, Walter.

Bloom, Harold, ed. & selected by see Ruskin, John.

Bloom, Harrison G. & Shlom, Elizabeth A. Drug Prescribing for the Elderly. 320p. 1993. pap. text 37.00 (0-88167-989-5) Lppncott W & W.

Bloom, Harry. Transvaal Episode. 24.95 (0-8488-0918-1) Amereon Ltd.

— Transvaal Episode. LC 81-51098. 363p. 1981. reprint ed. 22.00 (0-933256-24-8); reprint ed. pap. 16.00 (0-933256-25-6) Second Chance.

Bloom, Helen, et al. Euromanagement. 1997. pap. text 19.95 (0-7494-1207-0) Kogan Pg.

***Bloom, Howard.** Global Brain: The Evolution of Mass Mind from the Big Bang to the 21st Century. LC 99-85976. 384p. 2000. 27.95 (0-471-29584-1) Wiley.

Bloom, Howard. The Lucifer Principle: A Scientific Expedition into the Forces of History. LC 94-11464. 480p. 1997. reprint ed. pap. 15.00 (0-87113-664-3, Atlntc Mnthly) Grove-Atltic.

Bloom, Howard S. Back to Work: Testing Reemployment Services for Displaced Workers. LC 90-12909. 192p. 1990. 35.00 (0-88099-097-X); pap. 17.00 (0-88099-098-8) W E Upjohn.

Bloom, Ira M. & Solomon, Lewis D. Federal Taxation of Estates, Trusts & Gifts: Cases, Problems & Materials, 2 vols., set. 2nd ed. LC 98-14635. (Casebook Ser.). 1998. 56.50 (0-8205-3123-5) Bender.

***Bloom, Ira Mark.** Federal Taxation of Estates, Trusts & Gifts: Cases, Problems & Materials 1998. annuals 2nd ed. 1998. text 56.00 (0-8205-4182-6) Bender.

Bloom, Irene. Religious Diversity & Human Rights. LC 96-18261. (Illus.). 368p. 1996. pap. 19.50 (0-231-10417-0) Col U Pr.

Bloom, Irene, ed. Knowledge Painfully Acquired: The K'Un-Chih Chi of Lo Ch'In-Shun. 235p. 1995. pap. 22.00 (0-231-06409-8) Col U Pr.

Bloom, Irene, tr. Knowledge Painfully Acquired: The K'un-Chin Shi of Lo Ch'in-Shun. (Neo-Confucian Studies). 328p. 1987. text 68.50 (0-231-06408-X) Col U Pr.

Bloom, Irene & Fogel, Joshua A., eds. Meeting of Minds: Intellectual & Religious Interaction in East Asian Traditions of Thought. 384p. 1996. 52.00 (0-231-10352-2) Col U Pr.

Bloom, Irene, jt. ed. see De Bary, William T.

Bloom, Irene, jt. ed. see Debary, William T.

Bloom, Irene, jt. ed. see DeBary, William T.

Bloom, J. Siting Hazardous Waste Management Facilities. 71p. 1983. 3.00 (0-318-20482-7) Natl Resources Defense Coun.

Bloom, J., jt. auth. see Gordon, W.

***Bloom, J. C.** Toxicology of the Hematopoietic System, 13 vols. (Comprehensive Toxicology Ser.: Vol. 4). 402p. 1999. 157.50 (0-08-042969-6) Elsevier.

Bloom, J. Don. Married Cooperators. LC 97-71454. (Illus.). 160p. 1997. text 59.95 (1-85972-691-7, Pub. by Ashgate Pub) Ashgate Pub Co.

Bloom, J. M. & Ekvall, J. C., eds. Probabilistic Fracture Mechanics & Fatigue Methods: Applications for Structural Design & Maintenance - STP 798. LC 82-83518. 215p. 1983. text 36.00 (0-8031-0242-9, STP798) ASTM.

Bloom, Jack H. By the Power Vested in Me. Date not set. write for info. (0-7657-6171-8) Aronson.

Bloom, Jack M. Class, Race, & the Civil Rights Movement: The Changing Political Economy of Southern Racism. LC 85-45983. (Blacks in the Diaspora Ser.). 278p. 1987. pap. 14.95 (0-253-20407-0, MB 407) Ind U Pr.

Bloom, James. Ashes & Tears. Sherer, Michael L., ed. (Orig.). 1987. pap. 5.95 (1-55673-018-7, 8802) CSS OH.

— Caterpillars, Cocoons & Butterflies. (Orig.). 1988. pap. 2.25 (1-55673-052-7, 8823) CSS OH.

Bloom, James D. Left Letters: The Culture Wars of Mike Gold & Joseph Freeman. 160p. 1992. text 44.00 (0-231-07690-8) Col U Pr.

— The Literary Bent: In Search of High Art in Contemporary American Writing. LC 96-36882. (Penn Studies in Contemporary American Fiction). 168p. 1997. 34.95 (0-8122-3375-1); pap. text 14.95 (0-8122-1598-2) U of Pa Pr.

— The Stock of Available Reality: R. P. Blackmur & John Berryman. LC 83-45489. 216p. 1984. 32.50 (0-8387-5066-4) Bucknell U Pr.

Bloom, James H. Shakespeare's Church. LC 73-116790. (Studies in Shakespeare: No. 24). 1971. reprint ed. lib. bdg. 49.95 (0-8383-1032-X) M S G Haskell Hse.

Bloom, James M. & Sherer, Michael L. A Festival of Lights. (Orig.). 1986. pap. 2.95 (0-89536-833-1, 6847) CSS OH.

Bloom, Jennifer. Paintings of Manuel Ocampo, Virgin Destroyer. 96p. 1996. pap. 30.00 (0-945367-17-1) Hardy Marks Pubns.

Bloom, Jill. The Sky's the Limit. 1986. per. 2.25 (0-373-25205-6) Harlequin Bks.

Bloom, Jill, jt. auth. see Berk, Susan.

***Bloom, Jim.** Living It up on the Way Out. 1999. pap. 10.00 (0-7880-1402-1) CSS.

Bloom, Joel A. Principles of Intermediate Swimming. (Illus.). 111p. 1978. spiral bd. 9.95 (0-89641-002-1); per. 9.95 (0-89641-010-2) American Pr.

Bloom, John. A House of Cards: Baseball Card Collecting & Popular Culture. LC 96-32883. (American Culture Ser.). 1997. pap. 14.95 (0-8166-2871-8); text 37.95 (0-8166-2870-X) U of Minn Pr.

***Bloom, John.** To Show What an Indian Can Do: Sports at Native American Boarding Schools. 2000. 24.95 (0-8166-3651-6); pap. write for info. (0-8166-3652-4) U of Minn Pr.

Bloom, John, ed. Comprehensive Competency-Based Guidance CCBG. 85p. (C). 1997. ring bd. 15.00 (1-56109-068-9, EC206) CAPS Inc.

***Bloom, John & Walz, Garry.** Cybercounseling & Cyberlearning: Strategies & Resources for the Millennium. LC 99-88958. 473p. 2000. pap. text 41.95 (1-55620-180-X, 72693) Am Coun Assn.

Bloom, John W. Credentialing Professional Counselors for the 21st Century. 109p. (C). 1996. pap. text 18.95 (1-56109-070-0, EC210) CAPS Inc.

Bloom, John W., jt. auth. see Barbee, Robert A.

Bloom, Jonathan. The Kutubiyya Mosque Minbar. LC 98-9277. 114p. 1998. 40.00 (0-87099-854-4) Metro Mus Art.

***Bloom, Jonathan & Blair, Sheila S.** Islam: A Thousand Years of Power & Faith. (Illus.). 336p. 2000. 28.00 (1-57500-092-X, Pub. by TV Bks) HarpC.

Bloom, Jonathan & Blair, Sheila S. Islamic Arts. (Arts & Ideas Ser.). (Illus.). 448p. 1997. pap. 22.95 (0-7148-3176-X, Pub. by Phaidon Press) Phaidon Pr.

Bloom, Jonathan M. Minaret: Symbol of Islam. (Oxford Studies in Islamic Art: Vol. VII). (Illus.). 216p. 1990. text 65.00 (0-19-728013-7) OUP.

Bloom, Jonathan M., jt. auth. see Blair, Sheila S.

Bloom, Joseph D., et al, eds. Sexual Misconduct in Physicians. LC 98-27810. 1999. 51.95 (0-88048-706-2, 8706) Am Psychiatric.

Bloom, Jotice, ed. see Bloom, Maude Elizabeth.

Bloom, Kaled J. Mississippi Valley's Great Yellow Fever Epidemic of 1878. LC 93-2965. 296p. (C). 1993. text 40.00 (0-8071-1824-9) La State U Pr.

Bloom, Kathleen, ed. Prospective Issues in Infancy Research. LC 80-17479. 208p. 1981. text 39.95 (0-89859-059-0) L Erlbaum Assocs.

Bloom, Katya & Shreeves, Rosa. Moves: A Sourcebook of Ideas for Body Awareness & Creative Movement. (Performing Arts Studies). (Illus.). 136p. 1998. text 25.00 (90-5702-132-3, Harwood Acad Pubs); pap. text 23.00 (90-5702-133-1, Harwood Acad Pubs) Gordon & Breach.

Bloom, Ken. Hollywood Song: The Complete Film & Musical Companion, 3 vols., Set. 1552p. 1995. 225.00 (0-8160-2002-7) Facts on File.

— Standard Practices: Reliquaries for America. (Illus.). 8p. 1998. 7.50 (0-9650808-3-8) Landmark Arts.

Bloom, Kenneth. American Song Vol. 2: The Complete Musical Theatre Companion. LC 84-24728. 628p. reprint ed. pap. 194.70 (0-8357-3499-4, 203976000002) Bks Demand.

Bloom, Lary. Something Personal: True & Intimate Tales of Connecticut. Winburn, Jan & Hochberg, Judith H., eds. 128p. (Orig.). 1988. pap. 7.95 (0-685-22572-0) NE Press.

— The Writer Within: A Guide to Creative Nonfiction. 216p. 1997. reprint ed. pap. 14.95 (0-939883-01-5) Bibliopola Pr.

Bloom, Lary, et al. Twain's World: Essays on Hartford's Cultural Heritage. Date not set. pap. write for info. (0-9646638-3-X) Hartford Courant.

Bloom, Leonard. Identity & Ethnic Relations in Africa: Towards Collective & Individual Psychotherapy. LC 98-73507. (Interdisciplinary Research Series in Ethnic, Gender & Class Relations). 214p. 1998. text 59.95 (1-84014-529-3, Pub. by Ashgate Pub) Ashgate Pub Co.

Bloom, Leonard & Riemer, Ruth. Removal & Return: The Socio-Economic Effects of the War on Japanese Americans. LC 49-9867. (University of California Publications in Social Welfare: Vol. 4). 276p. reprint ed. pap. 85.60 (0-608-13943-2, 202139300022) Bks Demand.

Bloom, Leslie. Barbeque: Sizzling Fireside Know-How. Levine, Marian, ed. (Collector's Ser.: Vol. 20). 64p. (Orig.). 1987. pap., per. 5.95 (0-942320-26-3) Am Cooking.

— Chicken on the Run, Vol. 24. 64p. 1988. pap., per. 3.95 (0-942320-31-X) Am Cooking.

Bloom, Leslie B. & Ver Ploeg, Marcie. Seafood Cooking for Dummies. (For Dummies Ser.). (Illus.). 384p. 1999. pap. 19.99 (0-7645-5177-9, Dummies Trade Pr) IDG Bks.

Bloom, Leslie R. Under the Sign of Hope: Feminist Methodology & Narrative Interpretation. LC 97-50232. (Series, Identities in the Classroom Ser.). 188p. (C). 1998. text 59.50 (0-7914-3917-8); pap. text 19.95 (0-7914-3918-6) State U NY Pr.

Bloom, Lillian, jt. auth. see Bloom, Edward.

Bloom, Lillian D., jt. auth. see Bloom, Edward A.

Bloom, Lillian D., jt. ed. see Bloom, Edward A.

Bloom, Lillian D., ed. see Burney, Fanny.

Bloom, Lillian D., ed. see Piozzi, Hester Lynch.

Bloom, Lisa. Gender on Ice: American Ideologies of Polar Expeditions. LC 92-40916. (American Culture Ser.: Vol. 10). 176p. 1993. pap. 15.95 (0-8166-2093-8); text 39.95 (0-8166-2091-1) U of Minn Pr.

Bloom, Lisa, ed. With Other Eyes: Looking at Race & Gender in Visual Culture. LC 99-29675. 336p. 1999. pap. 19.95 (0-8166-3223-5, Pub. by U of Minn Pr); lib. bdg. 49.95 (0-8166-3222-7, Pub. by U of Minn Pr) Chicago Distribution Ctr.

Bloom, Lloyd. Poems for Jewish Holidays. LC 85-27179. 32p. (J). (gr. k-3). 1986. lib. bdg. 15.95 (0-8234-0606-7) Holiday.

Bloom, Lois. One Word at a Time: The Use of Single Word Utterances Before Syntax. LC 72-94445. (Janua Linguarum, Ser. Minor: No. 154). 262p. 1973. pap. text 27.70 (90-279-3375-8) Mouton.

— The Transition from Infancy to Language: Acquiring the Power of Expression. (Illus.). 364p. (C). 1995. pap. text 19.95 (0-521-48379-4) Cambridge U Pr.

Bloom, Lois, et al. Advances in Infancy Research, Vol. 8. 376p. 1993. text 78.50 (0-89391-827-X) Ablx Pub.

Bloom, Lois A. Mourning after Suicide. (Looking up Ser.). 24p. 1986. pap. 1.95 (0-8298-0588-5) Pilgrim OH.

Bloom, Lora, jt. auth. see Campbell, Jeanine.

Bloom, Louise, et al. Victorian Arkansans: How They Lived, Played & Worked. Daggett, Mala, ed. LC 81-67251. (Illus.). 208p. 1981. 17.00 (0-686-30547-7) AR Commemorative.

Bloom, Lynn Z. Composition Studies As a Creative Art: Teaching, Writing, Scholarship, Administration. LC 98-8968. x, 269 p. 1998. pap. 19.95 (0-87421-246-4) Utah St U Pr.

— The Easy Connection. 491p. (C). 1984. pap. text 31.96 (0-669-04476-8) HM Trade Div.

— The Essay Connection. 2nd ed. LC 86-83170. 544p. (C). 1987. teacher ed. 2.66 (0-669-14205-0); pap. text 31.16 (0-669-14204-2) HM Trade Div.

— The Essay Connection: Readings for Writers. (C). 1995. text, teacher ed. 31.56 (0-669-34118-5) HM Trade Div.

— The Essay Connection: Readings for Writers. 3rd ed. LC 90-81521. 753p. (C). 1991. pap. text 31.16 (0-669-20472-2) HM Trade Div.

— The Essay Connection: Readings for Writers. 4th ed. 752p. (C). 1995. pap. text 30.36 (0-669-34117-7) HM Trade Div.

— Fact & Artifact: Writing Nonfiction. 2nd ed. LC 93-21424. 343p. 1993. pap. text 38.40 (0-13-338807-7) P-H.

— The Lexington Reader. 828p. (C). 1987. teacher ed. 2.66 (0-669-09559-1) HM Trade Div.

— Writing. 400p. (C). 2001. pap. 21.00 (0-02-311121-6, Macmillan Coll) P-H.

Bloom, Lynn Z., et al, eds. Composition in the Twenty-First Century: Crisis & Change. LC 96-1147. 320p. 1997. pap. 19.95 (0-8093-2128-9) S Ill U Pr.

— Composition in the 21st Century: Crisis & Change. LC 95-1147. 320p. (C). 1996. 39.95 (0-8093-1878-4) S Ill U Pr.

Bloom, Lynn Z. & White, Edward M. Inquiry: A Cross-Curricular Reader. LC 92-29509. 732p. 1992. pap. text 39.20 (0-13-466137-0) P-H.

Bloom, Lynn Z., ed. see Sams, Margaret.

Bloom, M. H., ed. see Computers in Aerodynamics Symposium Staff.

Bloom, Marc. Runner's Bible. LC 82-46075. (Outdoor Bible Ser.). (Illus.). 208p. 1985. pap. 12.95 (0-385-18874-9) Doubleday.

Bloom, Marc, jt. auth. see Scott, Steve.

Bloom, Margaret, tr. see Sand, George.

Bloom, Marjorie W. & Galton, Grace C. Estimate! Calculate! Evaluate! Calculator Activities for the Middle Grades. (J). (gr. 4-7). 1995. pap. 10.95 (0-201-48032-8) Addison-Wesley.

— Estimate! Calculate! Evaluate! Calculator Activities for the Middle Grades. (Illus.). 88p. (J). (gr. 5-8). 1990. pap. text 10.95 (0-938587-12-9) Cuisenaire.

Bloom, Mark V., et al. Instructors Prepara. LC 95-35419. 371p. (C). 1995. pap. 51.00 (0-8053-3040-2) Benjamin-Cummings.

Bloom, Mark Vincent, jt. auth. see Tagliaferro, Linda.

Bloom, Martin. Accommodating the Lively Arts: An Architect's View. LC 97-34439. (Career Development Ser.). (Illus.). 112p. 1998. pap. 16.95 (1-57525-128-0) Smith & Kraus.

— Business Buying Basics. 180p. (Orig.). 1992. pap. 12.95 (0-945339-54-2) Columbine Communs.

Bloom, Martin. Controversial Issues in Human Behavior in Social Environments. LC 96-20610. 297p. 1996. pap. text 35.00 (0-205-19339-0) P-H.

Bloom, Martin. Primary Prevention Practices. (Issues in Children's & Families' Lives Ser.: Vol. 5). (Illus.). 512p. 1996. 58.00 (0-8039-7151-6); pap. 27.95 (0-8039-7152-4) Sage.

Bloom, Martin, ed. Single-System Research Designs. (Journal of Social Service Research: Vol. 3, No. 1). 134p. 1979. pap. text 14.95 (0-917724-70-4) Haworth Pr.

Bloom, Martin, intro. Single-System Designs in the Social Services: Issues & Options for the 1990s. LC 93-40395. (Journal of Social Service Research). (Illus.). 190p. 1994. lib. bdg. 39.95 (1-56024-574-3) Haworth Pr.

Bloom, Martin, et al. Evaluating Practice: Guidelines for the Accountable Professional. 3rd ed. LC 98-16475. 715p. 1998. pap. text 69.00 (0-205-27930-9) Allyn.

Bloom, Martin, jt. auth. see Germain, Carol B.

Bloom, Martin, jt. auth. see Klein, Waldo C.

Bloom, Matt. Blue Paradise: A Novel. LC 97-42784. 280p. 1998. pap. 12.95 (1-57826-002-7, Pub. by Hatherleigh) Norton.

Bloom, Maude Elizabeth. History of the Mesilla Valley 1903. Bloom, Jotice, ed. LC 98-61626. 1999. pap. text 8.95 (1-881325-33-4) Yucca Tree Pr.

Bloom, Melvin R. Letters to Bridgie. (Illus.). 88p. (Orig.). 1996. pap. 6.95 (1-886203-95-4) Pubs Paradigm.

Bloom, Metropolitan A. Living Prayer. LC 68-16522. 126p. 1968. pap. 9.95 (0-87243-054-5) Templegate.

— Metropolitan Anthony. Wybrew, Hugh, ed. (Modern Spirituality Ser.). 96p. 1987. pap. 4.95 (0-87243-167-3) Templegate.

Bloom, Michael. Adolescent-Parental Separation. LC 79-13928. 1980. text 24.95 (0-89876-035-6) Gardner Pr.

— The Pretzel As a Strategic Weapon: A Humor Anthology. 32p. 1997. pap. 7.00 (0-8059-4131-2) Dorrance.

Bloom, Michael D., et al. Analyzing Financial Statements. 3rd ed. (Illus.). 361p. (C). 1988. text 46.00 (0-89982-352-1) Am Bankers.

Bloom, Michael J., ed. Domestic Tranquility & the Common Defence: How the Joint Chiefs of Staff, the National Security Council, & the U. S. Treasury Department Used Scenario & Strategic Planning to Uphold the Constitution of the United States. (Illus.). 288p. (Orig.). 1995. pap. write for info. (0-9648554-0-2) Prior Plning.

— Law Enforcement Policy Analysis: A Sampler. (Illus.). 362p. (Orig.). 1995. pap. write for info. (0-9648554-1-0) Prior Plning.

Bloom, Miriam. Understanding Sickle Cell Disease. LC 94-44275. (Understanding Health & Sickness Ser.). 128p. 1995. pap. 11.95 (0-87805-745-5) U Pr of Miss.

Bloom, Murray T., et al, eds. ASJA Handbook: A Writer's Guide to Ethical & Economic Issues. 2nd rev. ed. 90p. 1992. pap. 12.95 (1-880832-00-3) Am Soc Jrnl & Auth.

Bloom, Naomi. Favorite Pedal Tours of California. 1992. pap. 12.95 (0-938665-12-X) Fine Edge Prods.

***Bloom, Neil, ed.** 411 Digital North America: North America's Professional Reference Guide for Visual Effects & Post Production. 432p. 2000. pap. 49.00 (1-879930-17-X, Pub. by LA Four-Eleven) SCB Distributors.

Bloom, Norman & Beattie, Edward J. Atlas of Cancer Surgery. (Illus.). 510p. 2000. text. write for info. (0-7216-6199-8, W B Saunders Co) Harcrt Hlth Sci Grp.

Bloom, Norman, jt. auth. see Baumann, Ernst F.

Bloom, Pamela. The Amazon up Close. 2nd ed. Orig. Title: Fielding's The Amazon. (Illus.). 230p. (Orig.). 1997. pap. 14.95 (1-55650-780-1) Hunter NJ.

— Brazil - Up Close. (Illus.). 550p. (Orig.). 1996. pap. 19.95 (1-55650-755-0) Hunter NJ.

***Bloom, Pamela, ed.** Buddhist Acts of Compassion. 170p. 2000. pap. 11.95 (1-57324-523-2) Conari Press.

***Bloom, Paul.** How Children Learn the Meanings of Words. LC 99-23901. (Learning, Development & Conceptual Change Ser.). (Illus.). 569p. 2000. 39.95 (0-262-02469-1) MIT Pr.

Bloom, Paul, ed. Language Acquisition: Core Readings. LC 93-27417. 624p. 1993. pap. text 29.50 (0-262-52187-3) MIT Pr.

Bloom, Paul, et al, eds. Language & Space. LC 95-36427. (Language, Speech & Communication Ser.). (Illus.). 672p. 1996. 55.00 (0-262-02403-9, Bradford Bks) MIT Pr.

Bloom, Paul, et al. Language & Space. (Language, Speech & Communication Ser.). 616p. 1999. reprint ed. pap. 29.50 (0-262-52266-7, Bradford Bks) MIT Pr.

Bloom, Paul N. Advances in Marketing & Public Policy, Vol. 2. 277p. 1991. 73.25 (0-89232-923-8) Jai Pr.

***Bloom, Paul N. & Gundlach, Gregory T.** Handbook of Marketing & Society. LC 00-9055. 2000. write for info. (0-7619-1626-1) Sage.

Bloom, Paula J. Avoiding Burnout: Managing Time, Space, & People in Early Childhood Education. (Illus.). 291p. (C). 1994. pap. text 14.95 (0-9621894-0-5) New Horzns Lake Forest.

An Asterisk (*) at the beginning of an entry indicates that the title is appearing for the first time.

*Bloom, Paula J. Circle of Influence: Implementing Shared Decision Making & Participative Management. (Director's Toolbox Ser.). (Illus.). 2000. write for info. (0-9621894-3-X) New Horzns Lake Forest.
Bloom, Paula J., et al. Blueprint for Action: Achieving Center-Based Change Through Staff Development. (Illus.). 300p. (Orig.). (C). 1991. pap. text 28.95 (0-9621894-2-1) New Horzns Lake Forest.
*Bloom, Paula Jorde. Workshop Essentials: Planning & Presenting Dynamic Workshops. 2000. pap. 24.95 (0-9621894-4-8) New Horzns Lake Forest.
Bloom, Peter. The Life of Berlioz. LC 98-3050. (Musical Lives Ser.). (Illus.). 208p. (C). 1998. pap. 14.95 (0-521-48548-7) Cambridge U Pr.
Bloom, Peter, ed. Berlioz Studies. (Illus.). 299p. (C). 1992. text 69.95 (0-521-41286-2) Cambridge U Pr.
*Bloom, Peter, ed. The Cambridge Companion to Berlioz. (Cambridge Companions to Music Ser.). (Illus.). 324p. (C). 2000. Price not set. (0-521-59388-3); pap. Price not set. (0-521-59638-6) Cambridge U Pr.
Bloom, Peter, ed. Papers from the International Conference on Music in Paris in the Eighteen Thirties (Smith College, April 1982) Sponsored by the National Endowment for the Humanities. LC 87-2248. (Musical Life in Nineteenth-Century France Ser.: No. 4). (Illus.). 1987. lib. bdg. 62.00 (0-918728-71-1) Pendragon NY.
Bloom, Peter, jt. auth. see Fetis, Francis J.
*Bloom, Phil. Hiking Indiana. (Illus.). 272p. 2000. pap. 16.95 (1-56044-720-6) Falcon Pub Inc.
*Bloom, Poppy. Best Friends: A Special Book of True Friendship! (Illus.). 96p. (YA). (gr. 3 up). 1999. pap. 4.95 (1-902618-47-5, Pub. by Element Childrns) Penguin Putnam.
Bloom, Richard L. Victims: A Survival Guide for the Age of Crime. Eaves, Richard W., ed. 160p. (Orig.). 1993. pap. 9.95 (0-9632355-1-6) Guardian Pr.
Bloom, Richard L., ed. see Eaves, Richard W.
Bloom, Robert. Anatomies of Egotism: A Reading of the Last Novels of H. G. Wells. LC 76-47559. 206p. reprint ed. pap. 63.90 (0-7837-1816-0, 204201600001) Bks Demand.
*Bloom, Robert. Unlikely Adversaries. LC 99-91434. 243p. 2000. 25.00 (0-7388-0770-2); pap. 18.00 (0-7388-0771-0) Xlibris Corp.
Bloom, Robert & Bebessay, Araya. Inflation Accounting: Reporting of General & Specific Price Changes. LC 83-26973. 316p. 1984. 59.95 (0-275-91130-6, C1130, Praeger Pubs) Greenwood.
Bloom, Robert & Elgers, Pieter T. Foundations of Accounting Theory & Policy: A Reader. 602p. (C). 1994. pap. text 46.50 (0-03-010422-X) Dryden Pr.
— Issues in Accounting Policy. 95th ed. 384p. (C). 1995. pap. text 46.50 (0-03-097924-2) Dryden Pr.
Bloom, Robert, et al. The Schism in Accounting. LC 93-5445. 168p. 1994. 55.00 (0-89930-699-3, Quorum Bks) Greenwood.
Bloom, Robert, jt. auth. see Heyman, H. G.
Bloom, Robert, jt. auth. see Heymann, H. G.
Bloom, Robert M. & Brodin, Mark S. Criminal Procedure: Examples & Explanations. 2nd ed. LC 95-82176. (Examples & Explanations Ser.). 416p. 1996. pap. text 30.95 (0-316-09931-7, 99317) Aspen Law.
Bloom, Robert M. & Brodin, Mark S. Criminal Procedure: Examples & Explanations. 2nd ed. 416p. 1996. pap. 30.95 (0-7355-0630-2) Panel Pubs.
— Criminal Procedure: Examples & Explanations. 3rd rev. ed. (Examples & Explanations Ser.). 410p. 2000. pap. write for info. (0-7355-1318-X, 1318X) Panel Pubs.
Bloom, Ronald L., et al, eds. Discourse Analysis & Applications: Studies in Adult Clinical Populations. 264p. 1994. text 55.00 (0-8058-1365-9) L Erlbaum Assocs.
Bloom, Ronald L., jt. auth. see Ferrand, Carole T.
Bloom, S. R. & Burstock, G. Peptides: A Target for New Drug Development. 160p. (C). 1991. 350.00 (1-85271-056-X, Pub. by IBC Tech Srvs) St Mut.
Bloom, S. R. & Farthing, M. J., eds. Gastro-Entero-Pancreatic Tumors, Proceedings of Somatostatin Analogues - Peptide Therapy in Action Symposium, Session I, January 1989 & Perspectives in Gastroenterology, Proceedings of Somatostatin Analogues - Peptide Therapy in Action Symposium, Session II, January 1989, Vol. 45, Suppl. 1, 1990. (Illus.). 88p. 1990. pap. 38.50 (3-8055-5202-5) S Karger.
Bloom, Sandra. Creating Sanctuary: Toward the Evolution of Sane Societies. LC 96-37298. 320p. 1997. pap. 20.99 (0-415-91858-8) Routledge.
*Bloom, Sandra, ed. Violence: A Public Health Menace & a Public Health Approach. 144p. 2000. pap. 24.00 (1-85575-192-5, Pub. by H Karnac Bks Ltd) Other Pr LLC.
Bloom, Sandra L. & Reichert, Michael. Bearing Witness: Violence & Collective Responsibility. LC 98-29059. 334p. (C). 1998. lib. bdg. 59.95 (0-7890-0477-1) Haworth Pr.
— Bearing Witness: Violence & Collective Responsibility. LC 98-29059. 348p. (C). 1998. pap. text 29.95 (0-7890-0478-X) Haworth Pr.
Bloom, Saul, et al, eds. Hidden Casualties: The Environmental, Health, & Political Consequences of the Persian Gulf War. LC 93-5473. 436p. (Orig.). 1994. pap. 20.00 (1-55643-163-5) North Atlantic.
Bloom, Sherman. Diagnostic Criteria in Cardiovascular Pathology. LC 96-32121. 400p. 1996. text 82.00 (0-397-51630-4) Lppncott W & W.
Bloom, Sol. Autobiography of Sol Bloom. (American Autobiography Ser.). 345p. 1995. reprint ed. lib. bdg. 89.00 (0-7812-8460-0) Rprt Serv.
— History of the Formation of the Union under the Constitution Vol. I: With Liberty Documents & Report of the Commission. 895p. 1999. reprint ed. 225.00 (1-56169-443-6) Gaunt.
— The Story of the Constitution. LC 86-12666. (Illus.). 192p. 1986. reprint ed. pap. text 8.95 (0-911333-45-2, 200046) National Archives & Recs.
Bloom, Stephen, jt. auth. see Bloom, Arnold.
Bloom, Stephen, jt. auth. see Lynn, John.
*Bloom, Stephen G. Postville: A Clash of Cultures in Heartland America. (Illus.). 324p. 2000. 25.00 (0-15-100652-0) Harcourt.
Bloom, Stephen L. & Esik, Zoltan, eds. Iteration Theories: Equational Logic of Iterative Processes. LC 93-18445. (EATCS Monographs on Theoretical Computer Science). 1993. 107.95 (0-387-56378-4) Spr-Verlag.
Bloom, Stephen R., ed. Toohey's Medicine: A Textbook for Students in the Health Care Professions. 15th ed. 377p. 1994. pap. text 35.95 (0-443-04704-9) Church.
Bloom, Stephen R., jt. ed. see Grundemar, Lars.
Bloom, Steve. In Praise of Primates. (Illus.). 202p. 1999. 29.95 (3-8290-1556-9, 520974) Konemann.
Bloom, Steve, ed. Revolutionary Marxism & Social Reality in the 20th Century: Collected Essays of Ernest Mandel. LC 92-33943. (Revolutionary Studies). 224p. (C). 1994. pap. 18.50 (0-391-03800-1) Humanities.
Bloom, Steven. No New Jokes: A Novel. LC 96-28799. 187p. 1997. 23.00 (0-393-04047-X) Norton.
Bloom, Steven M. & Brucker, Alexander J. Laser Surgery of the Posterior Segment. 2nd ed. LC 96-47103. 432p. 1996. text 98.00 (0-397-58423-7) Lppncott W & W.
Bloom, Susan & Ronzani, Maggie. Geography LC 97-224714. (Handy Homework Helper Ser.). (Illus.). 128 p. (YA). 1997. write for info. (0-7853-1954-9) Pubns Intl Ltd.
— U. S. History Writers. LC 97-209226. (Illus.). 128p. 1997. write for info. (0-7853-1952-2) Pubns Intl Ltd.
Bloom, Susan P. & Mercier, Cathyrn M. Presenting Zibby Oneal. (Twayne's Young Adult Authors Ser.: No. 585). 128p. (C). 1991. 20.95 (0-8057-8216-8, Twyne) Mac Lib Ref.
Bloom, Susan P., jt. auth. see Mercier, Cathyrn M.
Bloom, Thomas. The Nova Affair. unabridged ed. LC 99-93050. 216p. 1999. pap. 9.95 (0-9659845-2-4) Ravenhaus Pub.
*Bloom, Thomas. The Plains of Heaven. 2000. 24.95 (0-9659845-5-9, Pub. by Ravenhaus Pub) Seven Hills Bk.
Bloom, Thomas, et al, eds. Modern Methods in Complex Analysis. LC 95-40840. (Annals of Mathematics Studies: No. 137). (Illus.). 360p. 1996. pap. text 35.00 (0-691-04428-7, Pub. by Princeton U Pr) Cal Prin Full Svc.
Bloom, Thomas A. Kenneth Macgowan & the Aesthetic Paradigm for the New Stagecraft in America. LC 94-14063. (New Studies in Aesthetics: Vol. 20). (Illus.). XII, 184p. (C). 1997. text 43.95 (0-8204-2308-4) P Lang Pubng.
Bloom, Thomas A., jt. auth. see Sweet, O. Robin.
Bloom, Thomas S. Surplus Lines Insurance Principles & Issues. 2nd ed. Feldhaus, William R., ed. LC 97-72954. 265p. (Orig.). (C). 1997. pap. text 41.00 (0-89462-111-4, 16102) IIA.
Bloom, Tom. Children's Letters to God: The New Collection. 3rd ed. LC 90-21211. 96p. 1991. 7.95 (0-89480-999-7, 1999) Workman Pub.
Bloom, Tom, jt. auth. see Charles, Jill.
Bloom, Ursula. The Great Tomorrow. 1978. mass mkt. 1.95 (0-89083-361-3, Zebra Kensgtn) Kensgtn Pub Corp.
— Lovely Shadow. large type ed. (Lythway Ser.). 265p. 1992. 15.95 (0-7451-1613-2, G K Hall Lrg Type) Mac Lib Ref.
— Theatre Sister in Love. large type ed. 248p. 1990. 19.95 (0-7451-1156-4, G K Hall Lrg Type) Mac Lib Ref.
— Young Kangaroos Prefer Riding. large type ed. 1989. 22.95 (0-7451-0946-2, G K Hall Lrg Type) Mac Lib Ref.
Bloom, Ursula & Burns, Sheila. The Nurse Who Shocked the Matron. large type ed. 264p. 1989. 22.95 (0-7451-0983-7, G K Hall Lrg Type) Mac Lib Ref.
Bloom, Valerie. Fruits: A Caribbean Counting Poem. LC 96-28890. (Illus.). 32p. 1997. 15.95 (0-8050-5171-6) H Holt & Co.
— Fruits: A Caribbean Counting Poem. (Illus.). 32p. (J). 1997. pap. 11.95 (0-333-65312-2, Pub. by Pan) Trans-Atl Phila.
Bloom, Walter R. & Heyer, Herbert. Harmonic Analysis of Probability Measures on Hypergroups, Vol. 20. LC 94-37375. 607p. (C). 1994. lib. bdg. 144.95 (3-11-012105-0) De Gruyter.
Bloom, Wendy. Coordinating English at Key Stage 1. LC 99-51894. (Subject Leaders Handbks.). 1998. pap. 23.95 (0-7507-0685-6, Falmer Pr) Taylor & Francis.
Bloom, William. The Christ Sparks: The Inner Dynamics of Group Consciousness. (Orig.). 1995. pap. 9.95 (1-899171-15-0, Pub. by Findhorn Pr) Words Distrib.
— First Steps: An Introduction to Spiritual Practice. (Orig.). 1993. pap. 10.95 (0-905249-85-2, Pub. by Findhorn Pr) Words Distrib.
— The Healing Spirit of Plants. LC 99-15818. (Illus.). 192p. 1999. 24.95 (0-8069-7072-3) Sterling.
— Money, Heart & Mind: Financial Well-Being for People & Planet. Turner, Philip, ed. LC 96-20594. 288p. 1996. 24.00 (1-56836-153-X) Kodansha.
— Psychic Protection: Creating Positive Energies for People & Places. LC 97-18271. 1997. pap. text. write for info. (0-7499-1603-6) S&S Trade.
— Psychic Protection: Creating Positive Energies for People & Places. LC 97-18271. 176p. 1997. per. 10.00 (0-684-83519-3) S&S Trade Pap.
— Sacred Times: A New Approach to Festivals. 144p. (Orig.). 1990. pap. 11.95 (0-905249-76-3, Pub. by Findhorn Pr) Words Distrib.
*Bloom, William. Working with Angels, Fairies & Nature Spirits. 192p. 2000. pap. 9.95 (0-7499-1904-3, Pub. by Piatkus Bks) London Brdge.
Bloom, William H. Songs of the Sea & the Shore. LC 98-86798. 48p. 1999. pap. 6.95 (1-56167-504-0) Am Literary Pr.
Bloombaum, Milton, jt. auth. see Gugelyk, Ted.
BloomBecker, Jay J. Computer Crime Law, 1 vol. 1992. ring bd. 125.00 (0-685-68849-6) West Group.
BloomBecker, Jay J., ed. Computer Crime, Computer Security, Computer Ethics. 32p. (Orig.). 1986. pap. 28.00 (0-933561-02-4) Natl Ctr Computer Crime.
Bloombecker, Jay J., ed. Introduction to Computer Crime. 391p. (Orig.). 1985. pap. 28.00 (0-933561-01-6) Natl Ctr Computer Crime.
*Bloomberg. The Jewish World in the Middle Ages. 2000. 17.95 (0-88125-684-6) Ktav.
*Bloomberg, Beverly. The Last Hollywood Romance. 240p. 2000. 22.95 (1-882593-36-7) Bridge Wrks.
Bloomberg, David J., ed. Western Illinois University 13th Annual Spring Transportation-Physical Distribution Seminar Proceedings: Just in Time: New Dimensions in Logistics. 100p. 1986. pap. 10.50 (0-931497-03-5) WIU CBER.
Bloomberg, Gerri & Holden, Margaret. Women's Job Search Handbook: With Issues & Insights Into the Workplace. LC 90-26614. 264p. 1991. pap. 12.95 (0-913589-49-7) Williamson Pub Co.
Bloomberg, Karen & Johnson, Hilary. Communication Without Speech: A Guide for Parents & Teachers. (C). 1991. pap. 15.95 (0-86431-092-7, Pub. by Aust Council Educ Res) Stylus Pub VA.
Bloomberg, Lawrence N. The Investment Value of Goodwill. LC 78-64172. (Johns Hopkins University. Studies in the Social Sciences. Thirtieth Ser. 1912: 3). 1983. reprint ed. 47.50 (0-404-61281-4) AMS Pr.
Bloomberg, Mark & Mohlie, Steven, eds. Physicians in Managed Care: A Career Guide. LC 94-70991. 152p. (Orig.). 1994. pap. text 25.00 (0-924674-25-3) Am Coll Phys Execs.
Bloomberg, Mark S., et al. Canine Sports Medicine & Surgery. LC 96-24186. (Illus.). 496p. (C). 1998. text 95.00 (0-7216-5022-8, W B Saunders Co) Harcrt Hlth Sci Grp.
Bloomberg, Marty & Barrett, Buckley B. The Jewish Holocaust: An Annotated Guide to Books in English. 2nd expanded rev. ed. Clark, Boden et al, eds. LC 94-29741. (Studies in Judaica & the Holocaust: No. 1). 312p. 1995. pap. 29.00 (0-8095-1406-0) Millefleurs.
— Stalin: An Annotated Guide to Books in English. Burgess, Michael & Seldis, Paul D., eds. LC 92-43368. (Borgo Reference Guides Ser.: No. 1). 128p. 1993. pap. 17.00 (0-8095-1701-9) Millefleurs.
Bloomberg, Michael. Bloomberg. LC 96-53327. (Illus.). 261p. 1997. 24.95 (0-471-15545-4) Wiley.
*Bloomberg, Michael & Winkler, Matthew. Bloomberg. 261p. 1998. pap. 16.95 (0-471-25149-6) Wiley.
Bloomberg, Morton, ed. Creativity: Theory & Research. 1973. 24.95 (0-8084-0347-8); pap. 16.95 (0-8084-0348-6) NCUP.
Bloomberg, Warner & Schmandt, Henry J., eds. Power, Poverty & Urban Policy. LC 68-24710. (Urban Affairs Annual Reviews Ser.: Vol. 2). 604p. reprint ed. pap. 172.20 (0-608-09935-X, 2021871) Bks Demand.
Bloomberg, Warner, Jr., jt. ed. see Schmandt, Henry J.
Bloome, David, ed. Classrooms & Literacy. LC 88-36906. 432p. (C). 1989. text 78.50 (0-89391-506-8) Ablx Pub.
— Literacy & Schooling. LC 86-20642. 416p. (C). 1987. text 78.50 (0-89391-331-6) Ablx Pub.
Bloome, David, et al, eds. Alternative Perspectives in Assessing Children's Language & Literacy. 240p. (C). 1994. pap. 39.50 (0-89391-914-4); text 73.25 (0-89391-864-4) Ablx Pub.
Bloome, David, jt. ed. see Egan-Robertson, Ann.
Bloome, Mark. Sometimes the Shepherd Sometimes the Wolf. 32p. 1998. pap. 5.00 (1-881168-36-0) Red Danceflr.
Bloomenthal, Harold S. Going Public & the Public Corporation, 4 vols., Set. LC 86-11386. (Securities Law Ser.). 1986. ring bd. 495.00 (0-87632-511-8) West Group.
— Going Public Handbook 1992. 1993. pap. 97.50 (0-87632-886-9) West Group.
— International Capital Markets & Securities Regulation, 5 vols., Set. LC 82-12959. (Securities Law Ser.). 1982. ring bd. 795.00 (0-87632-357-3) West Group.
— Securities & Federal Corporate Law, 6 vols., Set. LC 72-90956. (Securities Law Ser.). 1972. ring bd. 795.00 (0-87632-086-8) West Group.
Bloomenthal, Harold S. & Wolff, Samuel L. Securities & Federal Corporate Law 2nd ed. LC 98-43367. 1998. write for info. (0-8366-1285-X) West Group.
Bloomenthal, Jules & Wyvill, Brian, eds. Introduction to Implicit Surfaces: Theory & Application in Computer Graphics. LC 97-219220. 400p. 1998. text 69.95 (1-55860-233-X) Morgan Kaufmann.
Bloomer. Witchcraft in the Pews. rev. ed. LC 98-168772. 1997. pap. 9.99 (1-56229-120-3) Pneuma Life Pub.
Bloomer, Anne. Activity Math: Using Manipulatives in the Classroom Grades K Through 3. (J). (gr. k-3). 1992. pap. 32.00 (0-201-45505-6) Addison-Wesley.
— Activity Math: Using Manipulatives in the Classroom Grades 4 Through 6. (J). (gr. 4-6). 1992. 32.00 (0-201-45506-4) Addison-Wesley.
Bloomer, Anne M. Getting into Area: Hands-on Problem-Solving Activities. 2nd ed. Apple, Mali, ed. LC 94-220581. 102p. (Orig.). Date not set. pap. text 12.95 (0-86651-833-9, DS21337) Seymour Pubns.
Bloomer, Carolyn M. Principles of Visual Perception. 2nd ed. (Illus.). 192p. 1989. 29.95 (0-8306-1704-3) McGraw-Hill Prof.
Bloomer, D. C. Life & Writings of Amelia Bloomer. LC 72-78650. 1895. reprint ed. 49.00 (0-403-01994-X) Somerset Pub.
*Bloomer, George. I'm Not Who You've Heard I Am. iv, 32p. 1998. mass mkt. 2.99 (1-892352-00-1, Blooming Hse Pubs) Blooming Bks.
— Oppressionless. 94p. 1998. pap. 9.99 (1-892352-01-X) Blooming Bks.
— The Witching Craft: Exposing the Subtleties of Satan. v, 102p. 1999. pap. 9.99 (1-892352-08-7, Blooming Hse Pubs) Blooming Bks.
Bloomer, George G. 101 Most Asked Questions by Women. 1997. pap. text 8.99 (1-56229-118-1) Pneuma Life Pub.
— When Loving You Is Wrong: But I Want to be Right. LC 97-24811. 188p. 1997. pap. 12.99 (0-88368-504-3) Whitaker Hse.
Bloomer, J. J. Practical Fluid Mechanics for Engineering Applications. LC 99-39935. (Mechanical Engineering Ser.). 392p. 1999. 150.00 (0-8247-9575-X) Dekker.
Bloomer, Jennifer. Architecture & the Text: The Scrypts of Joyce & Piranesi. LC 92-31624. (Theoretical Perspectives in Architectural History & Criticism Ser.). 248p. (C). 1993. 42.50 (0-300-04927-7) Yale U Pr.
Bloomer, John. Power Programming with RPC. (Computer Science). 522p. (Orig.). 1992. pap. write for info. (0-937175-77-3) Thomson Learn.
Bloomer, Kent. The Nature of Ornament: Rhythm & Metamorphosis In Architecture. 256p. 1999. 45.00 (0-393-73036-0) Norton.

B

Bloomer, Kent C. & Moore, Charles W. Body, Memory & Architecture. LC 77-76304. (Illus.). 147p. 1977. pap. 20.00 (0-300-02142-9) Yale U Pr.
Bloomer, M. Curriculum Making in Post 16 Education: The Social Conditions of Studentship. LC 97-6438. 240p. (C). 1997. 85.00 (0-415-12022-5); pap. 24.99 (0-415-12023-3) Routledge.
Bloomer, M. & Shaw, K. E. Challenge of Education Change: The Content & Organization of Schooling. 1979. 112.00 (0-08-022994-8, Pub. by Pergamon Repr) Franklin.
Bloomer, Mary H., ed. see Tucker, Melba L.
Bloomer, O. T. Measurement of Gas Law Deviations with Bean & Burnett Apparatus. (Research Bulletin Ser.: No. 13). iv, 12p. 1952. pap. 25.00 (1-58222-030-1) Inst Gas Tech.
— Physical-Chemical Properties of Methane-Nitrogen Mixtures. (Research Bulletin Ser.: No. 17). iv, 35p. 1952. pap. 25.00 (1-58222-036-0) Inst Gas Tech.
Bloomer, O. T. & Rao, K. N. Thermodynamic Properties of Nitrogen. (Research Bulletin Ser.: No. 18). iv, 28p. 1952. pap. 25.00 (1-58222-052-2) Inst Gas Tech.
Bloomer, O. T., et al. Physical-Chemical Properties of Methane-Ethane Mixtures. (Research Bulletin Ser.: No. 22). iv, 39p. 1953. pap. 25.00 (1-58222-035-2) Inst Gas Tech.
Bloomer, O T., et al. Thermodynamic Properties of Methane-Nitrogen Mixtures. (Research Bulletin Ser.: No. 21). iv, 51p. 1955. pap. 25.00 (1-58222-051-4) Inst Gas Tech.
Bloomer, Peter L., photos by. Timeless Trees: The U. S. National Bonsai Collection. (Illus.). 109p. 1986. 44.95 (0-87358-415-5) Horizons West.
Bloomer, Peter L., ed. see Tucker, Melba L.
Bloomer, Robert J. The Bloomer Family in America, 1655-1988. LC 88-71048. (Illus.). 300p. 1988. 53.50 (0-9620012-0-1); lib. bdg. 42.50 (0-9620012-1-X) R J Bloomer.
Bloomer, W. Martin. Latinity & Literary Society at Rome. LC 96-45632. 336p. 1997. text 39.95 (0-8122-3390-5) U of Pa Pr.
— Valerius Maximus & the Rhetoric of the New Nobility. LC 92-53628. viii, 288p. (C). 1992. 55.00 (0-8078-2047-4) U of NC Pr.
Bloomfield. Basic & Intermediate Algebra. 1993. pap. 26.00 (0-314-11118-2) Brooks-Cole.
— Basic Mathematics Study Guide. (Math). 1994. 32.75 (0-314-11105-0) Brooks-Cole.
Bloomfield. Basic Mathematics & Introduction Algebra. 1994. pap. 34.75 (0-314-11096-8) West Pub.
— How Things Work. 2nd ed. pap. write for info. (0-471-38151-9) Wiley.
Bloomfield. Intermediate Algebra. 1994. mass mkt., student ed. 14.25 (0-314-04167-2) Wadsworth Pub.
— Introductory Algebra. 3rd ed. (Mathematics). 1994. mass mkt., suppl. ed. 5.25 (0-314-04147-8) Wadsworth Pub.
— Managing Conflict. LC 95-73316. 229p. 1996. pap. text 35.95 (0-312-13675-7) St Martin.
Bloomfield, ed. The Soviet Revolution. (C). 1989. pap. 19.50 (0-85315-713-8, Pub. by Lawrence & Wishart) NYU Pr.
Bloomfield & Effendi, Shoghi. Ascension of Abdu'l-Baha. 32p. 1986. pap. 4.95 (0-900125-60-8) Bahai.
Bloomfield, et al. Microbial Quality Assurance in Pharmaceuticals: Cosmetics & Toiletries. (Pharmaceutical Technology Ser.). 264p. 1988. text 62.95 (0-470-21122-9) P-H.
Bloomfield, Andrew. Learning Practical Tibetan. rev. ed. Tsering, Yanki, tr. LC 98-9465. Orig. Title: The Tibetan Phrasebook. 186p. 1998. pap. 16.95 (1-55939-098-0) Snow Lion Pubns.
Bloomfield, Andrew & Tshering, Yanki. Tibetan, Survival, Set. 145p. (YA). 1991. pap. 24.95 incl. audio (0-88432-738-8, AFTB10) Audio-Forum.
Bloomfield, Arthur. Arthur Bloomfield's Restaurant Book: A Celebration of Dining in the Bay Area & Beyond. (Illus.). 225p. 1987. pap. 10.95 (0-317-60779-0) Aris Bks.
*Bloomfield, Arthur. How to Recognize the Antichrist: What Bible Prophecy Says about the Great Deceiver. 160p. 2000. pap. 8.99 (0-7642-2409-3) Bethany Hse.
Bloomfield, Arthur E. Before the Last Battle - Armageddon. 24p. 1998. pap. 9.99 (0-7642-2192-2) Bethany Hse.

— End of the Days. 288p. 1998. pap. 9.99 (*0-7642-2193-0*) Bethany Hse.

— Preludio al Armagedon.Tr. of Before the Last Battle. 192p. 1977. 8.99 (*0-88113-003-6*) Caribe Betania.

Bloomfield, Arthur I. Capital Imports & the American Balance of Payments, 1934-39: A Study in Abnormal International Capital Transfers. LC 66-23017. (Reprints of Economic Classics Ser.). (Illus.). xvii, 340p. 1966. reprint ed. 45.00 (*0-678-00165-0*) Kelley.

— Essays in the History of International Trade Theory. 288p. 1994. 90.00 (*1-85278-834-8*) E Elgar.

— Monetary Policy under the International Gold Standard. Wilkins, Mira, ed. LC 78-3899. (International Finance Ser.). 1979. reprint ed. lib. bdg. 17.95 (*0-405-11204-1*) Ayer.

Bloomfield, B. C., ed. Theses on Asia Accepted by Universities in the United Kingdom & Ireland: 1877-1964. 127p. 1967. 35.00 (*0-7146-1093-3*, Pub. by F Cass Pubs) Intl Spec Bk.

Bloomfield, Barb. Fabulous Beans. LC 94-18045. 144p. (Orig.). 1994. pap. 12.95 (*0-913990-17-5*) Book Pub Co.

***Bloomfield, Barb.** Flax the Super Food: Delicious Recipes for Better Health. LC 00-24071. 2000. pap. write for info. (*1-57067-099-4*) Book Pub Co.

Bloomfield, Barb. Soups On! Vegetarian Soups, Muffins & Accompaniments. LC 97-17644. (Illus.). 128p. 1997. pap. 10.95 (*1-57067-047-1*) Book Pub Co.

Bloomfield, Brian, et al, eds. Information Technology & Organizations: Strategies, Networks, & Integration. LC 96-46458. (Illus.). 194p. 1997. text 58.00 (*0-19-828939-1*) OUP.

Bloomfield, Brian P., ed. The Question of Artificial Intelligence: Philosophical & Sociological Perspectives. 256p. 1988. lib. bdg. 59.00 (*0-7099-3957-4*, Pub. by C Helm) Routldge.

Bloomfield, Brian P., et al, eds. Information Technology & Organizations: Strategies, Networks & Integration. LC 99-58633. (Illus.). 200p. 2000. pap. text 27.50 (*0-19-829611-8*) OUP.

Bloomfield, Brynna C. & Moskowitz, Jane M. The Traveling Jewish in America: The Complete Guide for 1986 for Business & Pleasure. 407p. (Orig.). 1986. pap. 9.95 (*0-9617104-0-3*) Wandering You Pr.

Bloomfield, Brynna C., et al. The Traveling Jewish in America: For Business & Pleasure. rev. ed. 472p. 1987. pap. 9.95 (*0-9617104-1-1*) Wandering You Pr.

Bloomfield, Christopher A. Presenting Financing Proposals to Banks. 2nd ed. 135p. 1991. pap. 57.00 (*0-406-00282-7*, U.K., MICHIE) LEXIS Pub.

Bloomfield, Clara D. Adult Leukemias. 1982. text 226.00 (*90-247-2478-3*) Kluwer Academic.

Bloomfield, Clara D., ed. Chronic & Acute Leukemias in Adults. (Cancer Treatment & Research Ser.). 1985. text 186.00 (*0-89838-702-7*) Kluwer Academic.

Bloomfield, David. Political Dialogue in Northern Ireland: The Brooke Initiative, 1989-92. LC 97-22915. 1998. text 59.95 (*0-312-17726-7*) St Martin.

Bloomfield, Dennis A., ed. Dye Curves: The Theory & Practice of Indicator Dilution. LC 77-356568. 466p. reprint ed. pap. 144.50 (*0-608-12374-9*, 205206700033) Bks Demand.

Bloomfield, Derek I. Basic Math. Date not set. pap. text, teacher ed. write for info. (*0-314-02881-1*); pap. text, teacher ed. write for info. (*0-314-03321-1*) West Pub.

— Elementary Algebra. Pullins, ed. LC 93-8666. 525p. (C). 1994. mass mkt. 47.50 (*0-314-02259-7*) West Pub.

— Intermediate Algebra. Date not set. pap. text, teacher ed. write for info. (*0-314-03323-8*) West Pub.

— Intermediate Algebra. Pullins, ed. LC 93-42966. 525p. (C). 1994. mass mkt. 46.25 (*0-314-02892-7*) West Pub.

— Introduction to Algebra. Date not set. pap. text, teacher ed. write for info. (*0-314-03322-X*) West Pub.

— Introduction to Algebra. 1994. mass mkt., student ed. 15.75 (*0-314-03729-2*) West Pub.

— Successful Math. Date not set. pap. text. write for info. (*0-314-04234-2*) West Pub.

Bloomfield, Derek I., jt. auth. see Ebersole, Dennis.

Bloomfield, Diana. Engraver's Cut, Diana Bloomfield: Twenty-Six Wood Engravings Chosen by the Artist with an Autobiographical Note & Bibliography. LC 97-43355. 1998. 5.95 (*1-884718-47-7*) Oak Knoll.

Bloomfield, Harold. Think Safe, Be Safe: The Only Guide to Inner Peace. LC 98-13633. 304p. 1998. pap. 14.00 (*0-609-80190-2*) Crown Pub Group.

Bloomfield, Harold, jt. auth. see McWilliams, Peter.

Bloomfield, Harold H. Healing Anxiety Naturally. 368p. 1999. pap. 13.00 (*0-06-093035-7*) HarpC.

***Bloomfield, Harold H.** Healing Anxiety with Herbs: Bloomfield,&Harold, Set. unabridged ed. 1998. audio 18.00 (*0-694-51999-5*) HarperAudio.

Bloomfield, Harold H. How to Heal Depression. 1995. pap. text 5.95 (*0-931580-61-7*) Prelude Press.

— Hypericum & Depression: Can Depression Be Sucessfully Treated with a Safe, Inexpensive, Medically Proven Herb Available Without a Prescription? LC 97-168746. 1996. 19.95 (*0-931580-38-2*) Prelude Press.

— Making Peace with Your Parents. LC 96-96686. 1996. pap. 10.00 (*0-345-41047-5*) Ballantine Pub Grp.

— Making Peace With your Past 13.00 (*0-06-093314-3*) HarpC.

— Making Peace with Your Past: The 6 Essential Steps to Enjoying a Great Future. LC 99-89719. 288p. 2000. 24.00 (*0-06-019528-2*, HarpCollins) HarperTrade.

— Making Peace with Yourself. LC 96-96696. (Orig.). 1996. pap. 10.00 (*0-345-41011-4*) Ballantine Pub Grp.

— The Power of 5: Hundreds of 5-Second to 5-Minute Techniques to Improve All of Your Life Without Wasting Any of Your Time. LC 94-33084. 1994. 24.95 (*0-87596-201-7*) Rodale Pr Inc.

Bloomfield, Harold H. & Cooper, Robert K. Power of Five: Hundreds of 5-Second to 5-Minute Scientific Shortcuts to Ignite Your Energy, Burn Fat, Stop Aging & Revitalize Your Love Life. 524p. 1996. pap. 12.95 (*0-87596-363-3*) Rodale Pr Inc.

Bloomfield, Harold H. & Kory, Robert B. Making Peace in Your Stepfamily: Surviving & Thriving As Parents & Stepparents. LC 92-35074. 304p. 1993. 19.45 (*1-56282-885-1*, Pub. by Hyperion) Time Warner.

Bloomfield, Harold H. & McWilliams, Peter. How to Heal Depression. 240p. 1994. 14.95 (*0-931580-39-0*) Prelude Press.

Bloomfield, Harold H. & Vettese, Sirah. Lose Weight: Vettese,&Sirah. abr. ed. 1991. audio 9.95 (*1-55994-466-8*, CPN 5013) HarperAudio.

***Bloomfield, John.** Flip Flop. 1999. 24.95 (*0-9669007-0-7*) Fish On Co.

Bloomfield, John, ed. Science & Medicine in Sport. 2nd ed. 648p. 1995. pap. 69.95 (*0-86793-321-6*) Blackwell Sci.

Bloomfield, John, et al. Applied Anatomy & Biomechanics in Sport. (Illus.). 304p. (Orig.). 1994. pap. text 40.00 (*0-86793-305-4*, BBLO0305, Pub. by Blckwll Scitfc UK) Human Kinetics.

Bloomfield, Judy, et al, eds. Too Darn Hot: Writing about Sex since Kinsey. LC 98-5293. 288p. 1998. pap. 15.00 (*0-89255-233-6*) Persea Bks.

Bloomfield, Ken. Stormont Crisis: A Memoir. LC 94-184560. 295p. 1995. pap. 25.00 (*0-85640-525-6*, Pub. by Blackstaff Pr) Dufour.

Bloomfield, Leonard. Cree-English Lexicon, 2 vols., Set. (Language & Literature Ser.). 1984. 44.00 (*0-317-37051-0*) HRAFP.

— Fox-English Lexicon. (Language & Literature Ser.). 1984. 22.00 (*0-317-37052-9*) HRAFP.

— Introduction to the Study of Language. (Classics in Psycholinguistics Ser.: 3). xxxviii, x, 335p. 1983. reprint ed. 78.00 (*90-272-1891-9*); reprint ed. pap. 34.95 (*90-272-1892-7*) J Benjamins Pubng Co.

— Language. (C). 1994. text 22.00 (*81-208-1195-X*, Pub. by Motilal Bnarsidass) S Asia.

— Language. LC 84-8439. x, 580p. 1984. pap. text 29.00 (*0-226-06067-5*) U Ch Pr.

— A Leonard Bloomfield Anthology. Hockett, Charles F., ed. xii, 328p. (C). 1987. pap. text 17.95 (*0-226-06071-3*) U Ch Pr.

— A Leonard Bloomfield Anthology. Hockett, Charles F., ed. LC 78-98981. (Indiana University Studies in the History & Theory of Linguistics). 585p. reprint ed. pap. 181.40 (*0-608-18475-6*, 205673500081) Bks Demand.

— Menomini Texts. LC 73-3548. (American Ethnological Society Publications: No. 12). reprint ed. 92.50 (*0-404-58162-5*) AMS Pr.

— Plains Cree Texts. LC 73-3552. (American Ethnological Society Publications: No. 16). reprint ed. 47.50 (*0-404-58166-8*) AMS Pr.

— Sacred Stories of the Sweet Grass Cree. LC 74-7933. reprint ed. 67.50 (*0-404-11821-6*) AMS Pr.

— Spoken Dutch. LC 75-15107. (Spoken Language Ser.). 266p. 1975. pap. 15.00 (*0-87950-054-9*); pap., student ed. 90.00 incl. audio (*0-87950-061-1*); audio 75.00 (*0-87950-060-3*) Spoken Lang Serv.

Bloomfield, Leonard & Barnhart, Clarence L. Let's Read, a Linguistic Approach. LC 61-9080. (Illus.). 474p. 1961. 21.95 (*0-8143-1115-6*) Wayne St U Pr.

Bloomfield, Leonard, et al. Spoken Russian, Bk. I. 1971. pap. 95.00 incl. audio (*0-87950-197-9*) Spoken Lang Serv.

— Spoken Russian, Bk. I, Units 1-12. 481p. 20.00 (*0-87950-190-1*) Spoken Lang Serv.

— Spoken Russian, Bk. II, Units 13-30. 398p. 20.00 (*0-87950-191-X*) Spoken Lang Serv.

— Spoken Russian, Pt. 1. Incl. Bk. IE. Spoken Russian. pap. 135.00 incl. audio (*0-87950-202-9*); Bk. IIE. Spoken Russian. pap. 130.00 incl. audio (*0-87950-203-7*); Bks. I & II. Spoken Russian. pap. 265.00 incl. audio (*0-87950-204-5*); Pt. 1E. Spoken Russian. audio 115.00 (*0-87950-200-2*); Pt. 2E. Spoken Russian. audio 110.00 (*0-87950-201-0*); 1971. Set audio 75.00 (*0-87950-196-0*) Spoken Lang Serv.

Bloomfield, Lincoln P. The Power to Keep Peace, Today & in a World Without War. 1971. pap. 2.95 (*0-912018-12-7*) World Without War.

Bloomfield, Lincoln P., ed. Outer Space. rev. ed. LC 68-27433. 1968. reprint ed. pap. 2.50 (*0-317-02959-2*, 64511) Am Assembly.

Bloomfield, Lincoln P. & Yost, Charles W. What Future for the U. N.? 40p. (C). 1977. pap. 18.95 (*0-87855-741-5*) Transaction Pubs.

Bloomfield, Lincoln P., ed. see American Assembly Staff.

Bloomfield, Lincoln P., jt. ed. see Cleveland, Harlan.

Bloomfield, Lisa. War Comics. (Illus.). 32p. (Orig.). 1989. pap. 3.00 (*0-917061-28-4*) Top Stories.

Bloomfield, Louis, ed. see Gallagher.

Bloomfield, Louis A. How Things Work: The Physics of Everyday Life. LC 96-14288. 720p. 1996. pap. 64.95 (*0-471-59473-3*) Wiley.

Bloomfield, Mark A., jt. ed. see Walker, Charles E.

Bloomfield, Masse. The Automated Society: What the Future Will Be & How We Will Get It That Way. LC 95-94348. viii, 139p. (Orig.). (C). 1995. pap. text 19.95 (*1-879981-02-5*) Jarren Pr.

— How to Publish Your Own Book for Less Than $575. LC 95-95120. 80p. 1996. pap. text 14.95 (*1-879981-03-3*) Jarren Pr.

— How to Reduce Crime, Revitalize Education & Shrink the Welfare Rolls. LC 97-92896. v, 163p. 1996. pap. text 24.95 (*1-879981-04-1*) Jarren Pr.

— How to Use a Guide to Literature Searching. 2nd ed. LC 91-90354. vi, 89p. (Orig.). (C). 1991. pap. 24.95 (*1-879981-00-9*) Jarren Pr.

— Mankind in Transition: A View of the Distant Past, the Present & the Far Future. LC 91-90359. vi, 187p. (C). 1993. 29.95 (*1-879981-01-7*) Jarren Pr.

Bloomfield, Maureen. Error & Angels: Poems by Maureen Bloomfield. LC 97-4724. 90p. 1997. text 15.95 (*1-57003-193-2*) U of SC Pr.

— Error & Angels: Poems by Maureen Bloomfield. LC 97-4724. 90p. 1997. pap. 9.95 (*1-57003-194-0*) U of SC Pr.

Bloomfield, Maurice. Religion of the Veda. LC 70-94310. (BCL Ser. II). reprint ed. 34.50 (*0-404-00912-3*) AMS Pr.

— Vedic Concordance. (C). 1990. 58.00 (*81-85418-53-5*, Pub. by Low Price) S Asia.

Bloomfield, Maurice, tr. Hymns of the Atharva-Veda: Together with Extracts from the Ritual Books & the Commentaries. LC 69-14131. 716p. 1970. reprint ed. lib. bdg. 38.50 (*0-8371-1879-4*, VEHA, Greenwood Pr) Greenwood.

Bloomfield, Maurice & Garbe, Richard V. The Kashmirian Atharva-veda (School of the Phaippaleadas) 1979. 62.95 (*0-405-10582-7*) Ayer.

Bloomfield, Maxwell. American Lawyers in a Changing Society, 1776-1876. (Studies in Legal History). 425p. 1976. 45.00 (*0-674-02910-0*) HUP.

***Bloomfield, Maxwell H.** Peaceful Revolution: Constitutional Change & American Culture from Progressivism to the New Deal. LC 00-26108. (Illus.). 224p. 2000. 35.00 (*0-674-00304-7*) HUP.

Bloomfield, Meyer. Vocational Guidance of Youth. LC 70-89151. (American Education: Its Men, Institutions, & Ideas. Series 1). 1975. reprint ed. 16.95 (*0-405-01389-2*) Ayer.

Bloomfield, Micah, jt. auth. see Lynn, Theodore S.

***Bloomfield, Michael & Summerville, Scott.** Me & Big Joe. (Illus.). 60p. 1999. reprint ed. pap. 5.99 (*1-889307-05-X*, Pub. by RE Search) Subterranean Co.

Bloomfield, Michaela, jt. auth. see Mcallister, Angela.

Bloomfield, Molly M. & Stephens, Lawrence J. Chemistry & the Living Organism. 6th ed. LC 95-32172. 704p. 1995. text 89.95 (*0-471-10777-8*) Wiley.

— Chemistry & the Living Organism. 6th ed. 336p. 1995. pap., student ed. 28.95 (*0-471-12078-2*) Wiley.

— Chemistry & the Living Organism. 6th ed. 400p. 1996. pap., lab manual ed. 49.95 (*0-471-12077-4*) Wiley.

— Chemistry & the Living Organism. 6th ed. 992p. 1996. text, student ed. 109.90 (*0-471-17551-X*) Wiley.

Bloomfield, Morton W., ed. Allegory, Myth, & Symbol. (English Studies: No. 9). 400p. 1982. 32.50 (*0-674-01640-8*) HUP.

Bloomfield, Morton W. & Dunn, Charles W. The Role of the Poet in Early Societies. (Illus.). 176p. (C). 1992. pap. 22.95 (*0-85991-347-3*) Boydell & Brewer.

Bloomfield, Morton W., et al. Incipits of Latin Works on the Virtues & Vices, 1100-1500 A. D. LC 75-36481. (Medieval Academy Bks.: No. 88). 1979. 75.00 (*0-910956-65-0*) Medieval Acad.

Bloomfield, Morton W., jt. auth. see Newmark, Leonard D.

Bloomfield, Morton W., jt. ed. see Haugen, Einar.

Bloomfield, Paul. Oriental Party Food. 160p. 1995. 8.95 (*0-316-09923-6*) Little.

Bloomfield, Peter & Steiger, William, eds. Applications of Least Absolute Deviations. (Progress in Probability & Statistics Ser.: Vol. 6). 400p. 1983. 69.00 (*0-8176-3157-7*) Birkhauser.

Bloomfield, R., et al, eds. VDM '88 - VDM: The Way Ahead. (Lecture Notes in Computer Science Ser.: Vol. 328). ix, 499p. 1988. 53.00 (*0-387-50214-9*) Spr-Verlag.

Bloomfield, R. M. Poole: Harbour, Health & Islands. 108p. 1984. 30.00 (*0-7212-0664-6*, Pub. by Regency Pr GBR) St Mut.

Bloomfield, Richard J., ed. Regional Conflict & U. S. Policy: Angola & Mozambique. LC 88-23461. (Illus.). (C). 1988. text 29.00 (*0-917256-45-X*) Ref Pubns.

Bloomfield, Richard J., ed. Regional Conflict & U. S. Policy: Angola & Mozambique. LC 88-23461. (Illus.). (C). 1988. pap. 16.00 (*0-917256-46-8*) Ref Pubns.

Bloomfield, Robert. Collected Poems, 1800-1822, 5 vols. in 1. Lawson, Jonathan N., ed. & intro. by. LC 79-161927. 704p. 1971. 90.00 (*0-8201-1088-4*) Schol Facsimiles.

— The Farmer's Boy. 122p. 1986. 50.00 (*0-948697-00-8*, Pub. by Lark Pubns) St Mut.

Bloomfield, Robert & Chandler, Ted. Pocket Mnemonics for Practitioners. abr. ed. 1983. pap. 4.95 (*0-9612242-2-3*) Harbinger Med Pr NC.

Bloomfield, Robert L., et al, eds. Hypertension: A Multidisciplinary Clinical Approach. LC 93-72953. 398p. 1995. boxed set 85.00 (*0-89089-545-7*) Carolina Acad Pr.

Bloomfield, Robert L. & Chandler, Ted. Mnemonics Rhetoric & Poetics for Medics, Vol. I. 1983. pap. 11.50 (*0-9612242-1-5*) Harbinger Med Pr NC.

Bloomfield, Robert L. & Pedley, Carolyn F. Mnemonics Rhetoric & Poetics for Medics, Vol. III. (Illus.). 165p. 1990. pap. 9.75 (*0-9612242-6-6*) Harbinger Med Pr NC.

Bloomfield, Robert L., jt. auth. see Chandler, E. Ted.

Bloomfield, S., jt. auth. see Baird, R.

Bloomfield, Valerie. Commonwealth Elections, 1945-1970: A Bibliography. LC 76-24992. 306p. 1977. lib. bdg. 59.95 (*0-8371-9067-3*, BCE/, Greenwood Pr) Greenwood.

Bloomfield, Victor A., et al. Nucleic Acids: Structures, Properties, & Functions. LC 98-45268. (Illus.). 794p. (C). 2000. text 85.00 (*0-935702-49-0*) Univ Sci Bks.

Bloomfield, William. Career Action Plan: Implementation Guide. (YA). (gr. 9 up). 1989. pap. 12.95 (*0-936007-16-8*, 3301) Meridian Educ.

Bloomfield, William M. Career Action Plan. 1989. pap. 9.95 (*0-936007-15-X*, 3300) Meridian Educ.

Bloomfield, Yvonne, jt. auth. see Kerr, Gillian.

Bloomgarden, David, ed. Divorce Lawyers of Los Angeles County, Vol. 1. 84p. 1996. pap. 14.95 (*0-9651716-5-5*, LA396) Peoples Gde CA.

Bloomgarden, Yehoash. The Feet of the Messenger. Davis, Moshe, ed. LC 77-70682. (America & the Holy Land Ser.). 1977. reprint ed. lib. bdg. 29.95 (*0-405-10229-1*) Ayer.

Bloomingdale Brothers Staff. Bloomingdale's Illustrated Eighteen Eighty-Six Catalog: Fashions, Dry Goods & Housewares. (Illus.). 160p. 1988. pap. 10.95 (*0-486-25780-0*) Dover.

Bloomingdale, Lewis M., ed. Attention Deficit Disorder: New Research in Attention, Treatment & Psychopharmacology, Vol. 3. 220p. 1988. 97.00 (*0-08-036466-7*, Pub. by Pergamon Repr) Franklin.

Bloomingdale, Lewis M. & Sergeant, Joseph A., eds. Attention Deficit Disorder, Vol. 5. 234p. 1988. 56.50 (*0-08-036509-4*, Pergamon Pr) Elsevier.

Bloomingdale, Lewis M. & Swanson, James, eds. Attention Deficit Disorder, Vol. 4. 360p. 1990. 114.50 (*0-08-036508-6*, Pergamon Pr) Elsevier.

Bloomquist, Dale S., et al. Surgical Complications: A Self-Instructional Guide, Bk. 4. 3rd rev. ed. Hooley, James R. & Whitacre, James R., eds. (Illus.). 64p. 1983. pap. 7.95 (*0-89939-041-2*) Stoma Pr.

Bloomquist, Geraldine M., jt. auth. see Blomquist, Paul.

Bloomquist, Jane, jt. auth. see Rickert, William E.

Bloomquist, Karen L. & Stumme, John R., eds. The Promise of Lutheran Ethics. LC 98-34165. 256p. 1998. pap. 18.00 (*0-8006-3132-3*, 1-3132) Augsburg Fortress.

Bloomquist, L. Gregory. The Function of Suffering in Philippians. (Journal for the Study of the New Testament, Supplement Ser.: No. 78). 235p. 1993. 70.00 (*1-85075-383-0*, Pub. by Sheffield Acad) CUP Services.

***Bloomquist, L. Gregory & Carey, Greg, eds.** Vision & Persuasion: Rhetorical Dimensions of Apocalyptic Discourse. LC 99-48416. 1999. 22.99 (*0-8272-4005-8*) Chalice Pr.

Bloomquist, Michael L. Skills Training for Children with Behavior Disorders: A Parent & Therapist Guidebook. LC 96-27. 272p. 1996. pap. text 29.95 (*1-57230-080-9*, 0080) Guilford Pubns.

Bloomquist, R., et al. Number-Key Practice for Use on Typewriter, Ten-Key & Keypunch Keyboards. (C). 1975. text 12.24 (*0-07-006105-X*) McGraw.

***Bloomquist, Tom.** Which Way from Here. LC 99-64736. 304p. 1999. 23.95 (*0-9674119-0-4*) Noslo Pubng.

Bloomsberg, G., ed. see Hatch, Mike.

Bloomsbury Review Editorial Staff. The Colorado Book Guide: A Directory of the Colorado Book Community. 4th rev. ed. 172p. 1998. pap. 10.95 (*0-9631589-6-1*) Bloomsbury Rev.

Bloomstein, Charles, ed. see Nesbitt, William A. & Abramowitz, Norman.

Bloor, jt. auth. see Barnes.

Bloor, Colin M. & Liebow, Averill A. The Pulmonary & Bronchial Circulations in Congenital Heart Disease. LC 79-25988. (Topics in Cardiovascular Disease Ser.). (Illus.). 296p. 1980. reprint ed. pap. 91.80 (*0-608-05448-8*, 206591700006) Bks Demand.

Bloor, D., jt. auth. see Hann, Richard.

Bloor, D., jt. ed. see Hann, R. A.

Bloor, D. M. & Chance, R. R., eds. Polydiacetylenes: Synthesis, Structure & Electronic Properties. 1985. text 233.00 (*90-247-3251-4*) Kluwer Academic.

Bloor, D. M. & Wyn-Jones, E., eds. The Structure, Dynamics & Equilibrium Properties of Colloidal Systems. (NATO Advanced Science Institutes Series C: Mathematical & Physical Sciences). 900p. 1990. text 372.50 (*0-7923-0993-6*) Kluwer Academic.

Bloor, David. Knowledge & Social Imagery. 2nd ed. 216p. 1991. pap. text 16.00 (*0-226-06097-7*) U Ch Pr.

— Knowledge & Social Imagery. 2nd ed. 216p. 1999. lib. bdg. 38.50 (*0-226-06096-9*) U Ch Pr.

— Wittgenstein on Rules & Institutions. LC 97-1475. (Illus.). 192p. (C). 1997. 70.00 (*0-415-16147-9*) Routledge.

Bloor, David, et al, eds. Encyclopedia of Advanced Materials, 4 vols. 2500p. 1994. 1811.25 (*0-08-040606-8*, Pergamon Pr) Elsevier.

Bloor, David, jt. ed. see Ashwell, Geoffrey J.

Bloor, Edward. Crusader. LC 99-6293. 384p. (YA). (gr. 7 up). 1999. 17.00 (*0-15-201944-8*, Harcourt Child Bks) Harcourt.

— Tangerine. LC 96-34182. 304p. (YA). (gr. 6 up). 1997. 17.00 (*0-15-201246-X*) Harcourt.

— Tangerine. 304p. (YA). (gr. 6-12). 1998. pap. 4.99 (*0-590-43277-X*, Pub. by Scholastic Inc) Penguin Putnam.

Bloor, I. G. Reference Guide to Management Techniques & Activities. LC 86-30266. 114p. 1987. 48.00 (*0-08-034268-X*, Pub. by Pergamon Repr) Franklin.

Bloor, Liz. Woolcraft. 1996. pap. 14.95 (*0-563-36794-6*, BBC-Parkwest) Parkwest Pubns.

Bloor, M. J., et al. One Foot in Eden. (Sociological Study of the Range of Therapeutic Community Practice). 256p. (C). 1988. lib. bdg. 55.00 (*0-415-00254-0*) Routledge.

Bloor, Meriel, jt. auth. see Bloor, Thomas.

Bloor, Michael. A Sociology of HIV Transmission. 176p. 1995. 69.95 (*0-8039-8749-8*); pap. 26.95 (*0-8039-8750-1*) Sage.

Bloor, Michael, ed. Selected Writings in Medical Sociological Research. LC 97-73458. (Cardiff Papers in Qualitative Research). 224p. 1997. text 69.95 (*1-85972-676-3*, Pub. by Ashgate Pub) Ashgate Pub Co.

Bloor, Michael & Taraborrelli, Patricia, eds. Qualitative Studies in Health & Medicine. (Cardiff Papers in Qualitative Research). 139p. 1994. 66.95 (*1-85628-579-0*, Pub. by Avebry) Ashgate Pub Co.

Bloor, Mike & Wood, Fiona, eds. Issues in Problem Drug Use & the Addictions: Behavior, Policy & Practice. 208p. 1997. pap. 28.95 (*1-85302-594-1*, Pub. by Jessica Kingsley) Taylor & Francis.

***Bloor, Robin.** The Electronic B@zaar: From the Silk Road to the Eroad. LC 00-20316. (Illus.). 338p. 2000. 27.50 (*1-85788-258-X*, Pub. by Nicholas Brealey) Natl Bk Netwk.

Bloor, Susan & Owen, Jon. Product Data Exchange. LC 94-42780. 320p. 1994. 49.95 (*1-85728-279-5*, Pub. by UCL Pr Ltd) Taylor & Francis.

Bloor, Thomas & Bloor, Meriel. The Functional Analysis of English: A Hallidayan Approach. LC 95-11092. 288p. 1995. pap. text 19.95 (*0-340-60012-8*, Pub. by E A) OUP.

Bloore, Carolyn, jt. auth. see Seiberling, Grace.

Bloothooft, Gerrit, jt. ed. see Young, Steve.

***Blore, Shawn.** Frommer's Vancouver & Victoria 2001. (Illus.). 2000. pap. 15.99 (*0-7645-6192-8*, Frommer) Macmillan Gen Ref.

— Vancouver: Secrets of the City. 175p. 1999. pap. 12.95 (*1-55152-062-1*, Pub. by Arsenal Pulp) LPC InBook.

Blos. Bringing Jackson Home. (J). 1997. 16.00 (*0-689-80357-5*) Atheneum Yung Read.

— Brothers of the Heart. (J). 1998. pap. 3.95 (*0-87628-338-5*) Ctr Appl Res.

Blos, Joan. A Gathering of Days: A New England Girl's Journey, 1830-1832, Vol. 1. 1999. pap. 2.99 (*0-689-82991-4*) Aladdin.

Blos, Joan W. Bedtime! (J). 1998. 13.00 (*0-689-80868-2*) S&S Bks Yung.

— Bedtime! LC 96-42100. 32p. (J). (ps-4). 1998. 12.00 (*0-689-81031-8*) S&S Childrens.

— Brooklyn Doesn't Rhyme. LC 93-31589. (Illus.). 96p. (J). (gr. 3-6). 1994. pap. 16.00 (*0-684-19694-8*) Scribner.

— Brothers of the Heart: A Story of the Old Northwest, 1837-1838. (J). 1993. 9.05 (*0-606-12203-6*, Pub. by Turtleback) Demco.

— Brothers of the Heart: A Story of the Old Northwest, 1837-1838. 2nd ed. LC 92-39668. 176p. (J). (gr. 5 up). 1993. reprint ed. mass mkt. 3.95 (*0-689-71724-5*) Aladdin.

— A Gathering of Days: A New England Girl's Journal, 1830-1832. 2nd ed. LC 90-32. 160p. (J). (gr. 3-7). 1990. reprint ed. mass mkt. 3.95 (*0-689-71419-X*) Aladdin.

— A Gathering of Days: A New England Girl's Journal, 1830-32. LC 79-16898. 144p. (J). (gr. 4-7). 1979. 15.00 (*0-684-16340-3*) Scribner.

— Gathering of Days: A Novel. 1990. 9.05 (*0-606-00471-8*, Pub. by Turtleback) Demco.

— The Grandpa Days. LC 88-19801. (J). (ps-3). 1994. pap. 3.95 (*0-671-88244-9*, Half Moon Paper) S&S Childrens.

— Hello, Shoes! LC 98-16796. (Illus.). 32p. (J). (ps). 1999. per. 13.00 (*0-689-81441-0*) S&S Childrens.

— The Heroine of the Titanic: A Tale Both True & Otherwise of the Life of Molly Brown. LC 90-35369. (Illus.). 40p. (J). (gr. 1 up). 1991. 16.00 (*0-688-07546-0*, Wm Morrow) Morrow Avon.

— Nellie Bly's Monkey: His Remarkable Story in His Own Words. LC 95-13713. (Illus.). (J). (ps-3). 1996. 15.00 (*0-688-12677-4*, Wm Morrow) Morrow Avon.

— Old Henry. LC 86-21745. (Illus.). 32p. (J). (ps-4). 1987. lib. bdg. 15.93 (*0-688-06400-0*, Wm Morrow) Morrow Avon.

— Old Henry. LC 86-21745. (Illus.). 32p. (J). (ps-3). 1990. mass mkt. 6.95 (*0-688-09935-1*, Wm Morrow) Morrow Avon.

— Old Henry. (J). 1990. 11.15 (*0-606-04761-1*, Pub. by Turtleback) Demco.

— One Very Best Valentine's Day. (Illus.). 32p. (J). (ps-2). 1992. pap. 2.50 (*0-671-75297-9*) Litle Simon.

— One Very Best Valentine's Day. 32p. (J). (ps-2). 1998. per. 4.99 (*0-689-81944-7*) S&S Childrens.

— One Very Best Valentine's Day. (J). 1998. 10.19 (*0-606-13008-X*, Pub. by Turtleback) Demco.

Blos, Joan W. & Schutzer, Dena. The Hungry Little Boy. (Illus.). 32p. (J). (ps up). 1995. 14.00 (*0-671-88128-0*) S&S Bks Yung.

Blos, Joan W., ed. see Brown, Margaret Wise.

Blos, Peter. The Adolescent Passage: Developmental Issues. LC 78-61245. 538p. (Orig.). 1979. 80.00 (*0-8236-0095-5*) Intl Univs Pr.

— On Adolescence: A Psychoanalytic Interpretation. LC 61-14110. 1966. pap. 14.95 (*0-02-904330-1*) Free Pr.

Blos, Sarah I. & Davis, Julie N. Katsu & the Kite. (Illus.). 14p. (J). 1988. pap. 0.96 (*0-912303-43-3*) Michigan Mus.

Blose, Lois B. Keep the Home Fires Moving: The Life of a Military Wife. LC 96-69277. 192p. (Orig.). 1996. pap. 12.95 (*1-884570-53-4*) Research Triangle.

Blose, Nora & Lovejoy, Sharon. Herb Drying Handbook: Includes Complete Microwave Drying Instructions. Cusick, Dawn, ed. LC 92-41410. (Illus.). 96p. 1993. pap. 9.95 (*0-8069-0281-7*) Sterling.

***Blosil, Georgia Jensen.** Where Was Mary. 17p. 1999. mass mkt. 3.95 (*1-56684-576-9*) Evans Bk Dist.

Bloss. Physical Geology. 1999. 33.74 (*0-697-21689-6*) McGraw.

Bloss, Bob. Baseball Managers: Stats, Stories, & Strategies. LC 98-25276. (Baseball in America Ser.). (Illus.). 400p. 1999. 29.50 (*1-56639-661-1*) Temple U Pr.

Bloss, Donald F. The Spindle Stage: Principles & Practice. LC 80-21488. (Illus.). 392p. 1981. text 95.00 (*0-521-23292-9*) Cambridge U Pr.

Bloss, Esther. Labor Legislation in Czechoslovakia. LC 79-76641. (Columbia University. Studies in the Social Sciences: No. 446). reprint ed. 20.00 (*0-404-51446-4*) AMS Pr.

Bloss, F. Donald. Crystallography & Crystal Chemistry. rev. ed. (Illus.). 545p. (C). 1994. pap. text 32.00 (*0-939950-37-5*) Mineralogical Soc.

— An Introduction to the Methods of Optical Crystallography. LC 61-6759. (Illus.). 302p. (C). 1990. reprint ed. text 88.00 (*1-878907-01-8*, RAN) TechBooks.

***Bloss, F. Donald.** Optical Crystallography. (Monograph Ser.). (Illus.). 239p. 1999. 32.00 (*0-939950-49-9*) Mineralogical Soc.

Bloss, F. Donald. Physical Geology. (Illus.). 640p. 1991. 37.95 (*0-8016-0787-6*) Mosby Inc.

Bloss, F. Donald & Kensler, Andrew. Sammy Seahorse Teaches Chess: A Light-Hearted Introduction. (Illus.). 192p. (Orig.). 1995. pap. 11.95 (*0-936015-61-6*) Pocahontas Pr.

Bloss, Julie L. The Church Guide to Employment Law. 152p. (Orig.). (C). 1993. pap. text 12.95 (*1-880562-05-7*) Christ Minist.

— QDROs: A Guide for Plan Administration. 2nd ed. Brzezinski, Mary Jo, ed. LC 97-70271. 132p. 1997. pap. 38.00 (*0-89154-511-5*) Intl Found Employ.

Bloss, Margaret V. & Hales, R. Stanton. Badminton. 7th ed. 144p. (C). 1993. text. write for info. (*0-697-12600-5*) Brown & Benchmark.

Bloss, Margaret Varner. Badminton. 8th ed. 144p. 2000. pap. 13.13 (*0-697-34534-3*) McGraw.

Bloss, W. H. & Grassi, G., eds. E. C. Photovoltaic Solar Energy Conference, 4th. 1982. text 310.00 (*90-277-1463-0*) Kluwer Academic.

Bloss, W. H. & Pfisterer, F. Advances in Solar Energy Technology: Proceedings of the Biennial Congress of the International Solar Energy Society, Hamburg, FRG, 13-18 September 1987, 4 vols., Set. LC 88-17824. 4070p. 1988. 1767.00 (*0-08-034315-5*, Pub. by Pergamon Repr); pap. 75.00 (*0-08-034316-3*, Pub. by Pergamon Repr) Franklin.

Blosser, Betsy J. English for Adult Living: Competency-Based "Survival Skills" ESL, Bk. 1. Ragan, Lise B., ed. (English for Adult Living Ser.). 1987. pap. text 11.95 (*0-8325-0650-8*, Natl Textbk Co) NTC Contemp Pub Co.

— English for Adult Living: Competency-Based "Survival Skills" ESL Book 2. Ragan, Lise B. & Weinstein, Amy, eds. (English for Adult Living Ser.). (YA). (gr. 9-12). 1987. pap. text 11.95 (*0-8325-0651-6*, Natl Textbk Co) NTC Contemp Pub Co.

— Living in English. (Illus.). 160p. 1994. pap. 15.95 (*0-8442-7437-2*, 74372, Natl Textbk Co) NTC Contemp Pub Co.

— Living in English, 2 cass. 160p. 1992. pap. 39.95 incl. audio (*0-8442-7378-3*, 73783, Natl Textbk Co) NTC Contemp Pub Co.

Blosser, Fred. Primer on Occupational Safety & Health. LC 91-43769. 374p. 1992. trans. 55.00 (*0-87179-741-0*, 0741) BNA Books.

Blosser, Jean L. Pediatric Traumatic Brain Injury 2nd ed. 2000. pap. 36.00 (*0-7693-0055-3*) Singular Publishing.

Blosser, Jean L & DePompei, Roberta. Pediatric Traumatic Brain Injury: Proactive Intervention. LC 94-11315. (Neurogenic Communication Disorders Ser.). (Illus.). 280p. (Orig.). (C). 1994. pap. text 45.00 (*1-56593-168-8*, 0479) Thomson Learn.

Blosser, Jean L, jt. auth. see Neidecker, Elizabeth A.

Blosser, Jody L. Everybody Wins! Non-Competitive Party Games & Activities for Children. LC 95-39394. (Illus.). 144p. 1996. 16.95 (*0-8069-6102-3*) Sterling.

— Everybody Wins! Non-Competitive Party Games & Activities for Children. (Illus.). 144p. (J). (ps up). 1997. pap. 7.95 (*0-8069-6103-1*) Sterling.

Blosser, Patricia E. How to Ask the Right Questions. (Illus.). 16p. 1991. pap. text 5.00 (*0-87355-102-8*) Natl Sci Tchrs.

Blosser, Philip. Scheler's Critique of Kant's Ethics. LC 94-45367. (Continental Thought Ser.: No. 22). 237p. (C). 1995. text 39.95 (*0-8214-1108-X*) Ohio U Pr.

Blosser, Philip, et al, eds. Japanese & Western Phenomenology. LC 92-39095. (Contributions to Phenomenology Ser.: Vol. 12). 468p. (C). 1993. text 200.50 (*0-7923-2075-1*) Kluwer Academic.

Blosser, Philip & Bradley, Marshell C., eds. Friendship: Philosophical Reflections on a Perennial Concern. 2nd ed. LC 97-21695. 422p. (C). 1997. pap. 39.50 (*0-7618-0818-3*) U Pr of Amer.

Blosseville, J. M., ed. see IFAC Symposium on Transportation Systems (1994: Ti.

Blossfeld, Hans-Peter & Hakim, Catherine, eds. Between Equalization & Marginalization: Women Working Part-Time in Europe & the United States of America. LC 97-8953. (Illus.). 354p. 1997. text 85.00 (*0-19-828086-6*) OUP.

Blossfeld, Hans-Peter & Hamerle, Alfred M. Event History Analysis: Statistical Theory & Application in the Social Sciences. Mayer, Karl U., ed. 304p. 1989. text 69.95 (*0-8058-0126-X*) L Erlbaum Assocs.

Blossfeld, Hans-Peter & Prein, Gerald, eds. Rational Choice Theory & Large-Scale Data Analysis. LC 97-35715. (Social Inequality Ser.). 336p. (C). 1998. pap. 65.00 (*0-8133-9027-3*, Pub. by Westview) HarpC.

Blossfeld, Hans-Peter & Rohwer, Gotz. Techniques of Event History Modeling: New Approaches to Casual Analysis. LC 95-23513. 304p. 1995. 59.95 (*0-8058-1959-2*); pap. 32.50 (*0-8058-1960-6*) L Erlbaum Assocs.

Blossfeldt, Karl. Art Forms in the Plant World. (Illus.). 128p. 1986. reprint ed. pap. 9.95 (*0-486-24990-5*) Dover.

— Karl Blossfeldt. (Illus.). 160p. 1997. pap. 40.00 (*3-89322-408-4*) Dist Art Pubs.

— Karl Blossfeldt: Photography. 1996. pap. text 35.00 (*3-89322-638-9*, Pub. by Edition Cantz) Dist Art Pubs.

— Karl Blossfeldt: The Alphabet of Plants. Wild, Ann & Wild, Jurgen, eds. (Illus.). 80p. 1998. 19.95 (*3-8238-0364-6*) te Neues.

— Natural Art Forms: 120 Classic Photographs. (Illus.). 128p. 1998. pap. 10.95 (*0-486-40003-4*) Dover.

Blossom, Bonnie & Ford, Fran. Physical Therapy in Public Schools Vol. 1: A Related Service. LC 91-62293. (Illus.). 182p. (Orig.). (C). 1991. pap. text 45.00 (*0-9630294-0-1*) Rehab P & T.

Blossom, Bonnie, et al. Physical Therapy & Occupational Therapy in Schools Vol. 2: A Related Service. (Illus.). 317p. (C). 1996. pap. text 65.00 (*0-9630294-1-X*) Rehab P & T.

Blossom, Jonathan. Engines of Creation: Programming Virtual Reality on the Macintosh. 350p. 1995. pap. 29.95 (*1-878739-90-5*) Sams.

Blossom, Laurel, ed. Many Lights in Many Windows: Twenty Years of Great Fictions & Poetry from the Writers Community. LC 97-11722. 324p. (Orig.). 1997. pap. 16.95 (*1-57131-218-8*) Milkweed Ed.

Blossom, Thomas. Narino, Hero of Colombian Independence. LC 66-20661. 241p. reprint ed. pap. 74.80 (*0-608-13685-9*, 205537400017) Bks Demand.

Blostein, David A., ed. see Marston, John.

Blostein, Fay. Invitations, Celebrations: Ideas & Techniques for Promoting Reading in Junior & Senior High Schools. enl. rev. ed. LC 93-36976. 226p. 1993. pap. 32.95 (*1-55570-202-3*) Neal-Schuman.

Blot, David. Many Steps. 96p. (Orig.). (C). 1984. pap. text 4.50 (*0-317-93601-8*) D Blot Pubns.

— Starting Lines. (College ESL Ser.). (J). 1995. mass mkt., suppl. ed. 6.95 (*0-8384-5259-0*) Heinle & Heinle.

— Who or What Are You Referring To? 64p. (Orig.). (C). 1987. pap. text 4.00 (*0-317-93604-2*) D Blot Pubns.

— Write from the Start. 2nd ed. (College ESL Ser.). (J). 1994. mass mkt., suppl. ed. 7.95 (*0-8384-4849-6*) Heinle & Heinle.

Blot, David & Davidson, David. Put It in Writing: Writing Activities for Students of ESL. (Illus.). 104p. (Orig.). (C). 1981. mass mkt. 8.50 (*0-8384-2782-0*, Newbury) Heinle & Heinle.

— Starting Lines: A Beginning Writing Text. LC 94-39153. 144p. (J). 1995. mass mkt. 21.95 (*0-8384-5258-2*) Heinle & Heinle.

Blot, David, jt. auth. see Davidson, David M.

Blot, David, jt. auth. see De Jesus, Socorro.

Blot, David, jt. auth. see Kreppel, Beatrice.

Blot, Jean-Yves. Underwater Archaeology: Exploring the World Beneath the Sea. Campbell, Alexandra, tr. (Discoveries Ser.). (Illus.). 176p. 1996. pap. 12.95 (*0-8109-2859-0*, Pub. by Abrams) Time Warner.

Blot, Pierre. Handbook of Practical Cookery, for Ladies & Professional Cooks. LC 72-9789. (Cookery Americana Ser.). 1973. reprint ed. 17.95 (*0-405-05042-9*) Ayer.

— Karate for Beginners. (Illus.). 144p. 1997. pap. 12.95 (*0-8069-3873-0*) Sterling.

Blotcky, Mark J., jt. auth. see Lewis, Jerry M., 3rd.

Blotevogal, Hans H., jt. auth. see Fielding, Anthony J.

***Blotkamp, Carel.** Van Gogh to Mondrian: Dutch Works on Paper. (Illus.). 184p. 2000. pap. 50.00 (*90-400-9414-4*) U of Wash Pr.

Blotkamp, Carel, jt. ed. see Bionda, Richard.

Blotner, ed. see Faulkner, William.

Blotner, J., ed. see Faulkner, William.

Blotner, Joseph, jt. auth. see Faulkner, William.

Blotner, Joseph, jt. auth. see Gwynn, Frederick L.

Blotner, Joseph, ed. see Faulkner, William.

Blotner, Joseph, jt. ed. see Gwynn, Frederick L.

Blotner, Joseph L. The Political Novel. LC 78-9868. 100p. 1979. reprint ed. lib. bdg. 55.00 (*0-313-21228-7*, BLPN, Greenwood Pr) Greenwood.

Blotnick, Elihu. Blue Turtle Moon Queen. (Illus.). 120p. (YA). (gr. 6-12). Date not set. pap. 6.95 (*0-915090-29-1*) Calif Street.

— California Street No. 1. (Illus.). 1980. pap. 11.00 (*0-915090-21-X*) Calif Street.

— The Canyon Kids: Seedlings: Growing up Redwood. (Illus.). 80p. 2000. pap. 11.00 (*0-915090-16-3*) Firefall.

— The Fog Line. (Mr. Blot Ser.: No. 3). (Illus.). 72p. (YA). (gr. 6 up). 2000. pap. 5.95 (*0-915090-12-0*) Calif Street.

— Glimmins: Children of the Western Woods. (Illus.). 72p. (J). (gr. 1 up). 2001. pap. 11.95 (*0-915090-18-X*) Calif Street.

— Never Distrust an Asparagus. (Complete Blot Ser.). (Illus.). 1979. pap. 4.95 (*0-915090-10-4*) Calif Street.

— Rio Arriba. (Illus.). 342p. (Orig.). Date not set. pap. 17.95 (*0-915090-24-4*) Calif Street.

— Russian Hill: Storm Year. Fragment, Ariel, ed. 64p. 1983. pap. 7.25 (*0-915090-17-1*) Calif Street.

— Saltwater Flats: A Silent Film. LC 74-18166. (Illus.). 64p. 1975. pap. 17.00 (*0-915090-00-7*) Calif Street.

Blotnick, Elihu & Robinson, Barbara. Mysterious Mr. Blot. Fragment, Ariel, ed. LC 79-51994. (Illus.). 1979. 5.00 (*0-915090-09-0*) Calif Street.

Blotnick, Srully. Ambitious Men: Their Drives, Dreams, & Delusions. 448p. 1988. pap. 4.95 (*0-14-008818-0*, Penguin Bks) Viking Penguin.

— Otherwise Engaged: The Private Lives of Successful Career Women. LC 84-28708. 310p. reprint ed. pap. 96.10 (*0-608-16043-1*, 203317000084) Bks Demand.

Blottenberger, Mike W. Morsels of Manna. LC 95-3922. 68p. 1996. pap. 14.95 (*0-7734-2721-X*, Mellen Poetry Pr) E Mellen.

Blotter, P. Thomas. Introduction to Engineering. LC 91-13256. 60p. (C). 1981. pap. text, teacher ed. 5.00 (*0-471-09947-3*) Krieger.

— Introduction to Engineering. LC 91-13256. 304p. (C). 1991. reprint ed. 46.00 (*0-89464-604-4*) Krieger.

***Blottner, Gene.** Universal-International Westerns, 1947-1963: The Complete Filmography. (Illus.). 376p. 2000. lib. bdg. 55.00 (*0-7864-0791-3*) McFarland & Co.

Blotzer, Mary Ann & Ruth, Richard. Sometimes You Just Want to Feel Like a Human Being: Case Studies of Empowering Psychotherapy with People with Disabilities. 288p. 1995. pap. 26.95 (*1-55766-196-0*) P H Brookes.

Blouch, Christine, ed. see Haywood, Eliza.

Blouch, Ralph I., ed. International Association of Fish & Wildlife Agencies, 69th Convention: Proceedings. (Orig.). 1980. 15.00 (*0-932108-04-0*) IAFWA.

Blouet. New World Orders. 1997. pap. text 29.00 (*0-02-311081-3*) P-H.

Blouet, Brian. Halford Mackinder: A Biography. LC 86-23013. 248p. 1987. 24.95 (*0-89096-292-8*) Tex A&M Univ Pr.

Blouet, Brian W. & Blouet, Olwyn M. Latin America & the Caribbean: A Systematic & Regional Survey. 3rd ed. LC 96-9925. 512p. 1996. pap. 81.95 (*0-471-13570-4*) Wiley.

Blouet, Brian W. & Lawson, Merlin P., eds. Images of the Plains: The Role of Human Nature in Settlement. LC 74-76130. (Illus.). xiv, 214p. 1975. text 50.00 (*0-8032-0839-1*) U of Nebr Pr.

Blouet, Brian W., ed. see Cultural Heritage of the Plains Symposium Staff.

Blouet, Olwyn M., jt. auth. see Blouet, Brian W.

Blough, Carman G. Practical Applications of Accounting Standards: A Decade of Comment on Accounting & Auditing Problems. Brief, Richard P., ed. LC 80-1472. (Dimensions of Accounting Theory & Practice Ser.). 1980. reprint ed. lib. bdg. 49.95 (*0-405-13502-5*) Ayer.

Blough, Glenn O. & Schwartz, Julius. Elementary School Science & How to Teach It. 8th ed. 640p. (C). 1990. text 72.50 (*0-03-031312-0*, Pub. by Harcourt Coll Pubs) Harcourt.

Blough, Joan, et al. The Parent Leadership Program Training Manual. (Illus.). 151p. 1996. pap. 20.00 (*0-9642014-3-7*) Inst Fmly Ctr.

Blouin, Barbara, et al, eds. The Legacy of Inherited Wealth: Interviews with Heirs. rev. ed. LC 95-232932. 185p. 1995. pap. 17.95 (*0-9699195-0-6*) Trio Pr.

Blouin, Barbara & Gibson, Katherine. Inheritors & Work: The Search for Purpose: A Guide for Inheritors & Wealthy Parents. 50p. 1996. pap. 16.50 (*0-9699195-3-0*) Trio Pr.

Blouin, Francis X., Jr., ed. Vatican Archives: An Inventory & Guide to Historical Documents of the Holy See. LC 97-29248. 640p. 1998. text 175.00 (*0-19-509552-9*) OUP.

Blouin, Glen. Weeds of the Woods: Small Trees & Shrubs of the Eastern Forest. 125p. 1992. per. 11.95 (*0-86492-127-6*, Pub. by Goose Ln Edits) Genl Dist Srvs.

***Blouin, Lenora P.** May Sarton: A Biography. 2nd ed. LC 99-87233. (Scarecrow Author Bibliography Ser.: No. 104). (Illus.). 448p. 2000. 85.00 (*0-8108-3687-4*) Scarecrow.

***Blouin, Nicole.** Mountain Biking Albuquerque. LC 99-22407. (Illus.). 120p. 1999. pap. 10.95 (*1-56044-746-X*) Falcon Pub Inc.

Blouin, Nicole, et al. Waterfalls of the Blue Ridge: A Guide to the Blue Ridge Parkway & Great Smokey Mountains National Park. 2nd ed. 172p. 1997. pap. text 14.95 (*0-89732-190-1*) Menasha Ridge.

Blouke, Morley M., ed. Solid State Sensor Arrays Vol. 3019: Development & Applications. 294p. 1997. 59.00 (*0-8194-2430-7*) SPIE.

— Solid State Sensor Arrays Vol. 3301: Development & Applications II. LC 98-184979. 206p. 1998. 59.00 (*0-8194-2741-1*) SPIE.

Blouke, Morley M., et al, eds. High-Resolution Sensors & Hybrid Systems. 1992. 20.00 (*0-8194-0810-7*, 1656) SPIE.

***Blouke, Morley M. & Williams, George M., eds.** Sensors, Cameras & Systems for Scientific/Industrial Applications. 250p. 1999. pap. text 72.00 (*0-8194-3120-6*) SPIE.

Blount, jt. auth. see Price.

Blount & Co. Staff, ed. Visual Elements Four: World Folk Patterns. (Design Sourcebook Ser.). (Illus.). 120p. 1989. pap. 19.99 (*0-935603-12-3*, 30143) Rockport Pubs.

Blount, Alexander, ed. Integrated Primary Care: The Future of Medical & Mental Health Collaboration. LC 97-44806. 320p. 1998. 40.00 (*0-393-70253-7*) Norton.

Blount, Ben G., ed. Language, Culture, & Society: A Book of Readings. 2nd rev. ed. LC 96-133955. 608p. (C). 1995. pap. text 23.95 (*0-88133-850-8*) Waveland Pr.

Blount, Ben G., jt. ed. see Gragson, Ted L.

Blount, Brian K. Cultural Intrepretation: Reorienting New Testament Criticism. 224p. 1995. pap. 21.00 (*0-8006-2859-4*, 1-2859) Augsburg Fortress.

— Go Preach! Mark's Kingdom Message & the Black Church Today. LC 98-48668. (Bible & Liberation Ser.). 240p. (Orig.). 1998. pap. 20.00 (*1-57075-171-4*) Orbis Bks.

***Blount, Brian K.** Making Room at the Table: An Invitation to Multicultural Worshop. 176p. 2000. pap. 15.95 (*0-664-22202-1*) Westminster John Knox.

Blount Day & Assoc. Staff. Georgia Stories I & II: A Fourth Grade Teacher's Guide. (Illus.). 73p. 1996. pap. text, teacher ed. 10.00 (*1-892720-23-X*) GA Public Brdcstng.

Blount, Edward. Memoirs of Sir Edward Blount. Wilkins, Mira & Reid, Stuart J., eds. LC 76-29985. (European Business Ser.). (Illus.). 1977. reprint ed. lib. bdg. 28.95 (*0-405-09717-4*) Ayer.

***Blount, Georgia Y.** The Realness of God in My Life. 263p. 1999. reprint ed. pap. 12.95 (*0-9672255-0-7*) G Y Blount.

Blount, Henry. A Voyage into Levant. LC 77-6850. (English Experience Ser.: No. 850). 1977. reprint ed. lib. bdg. 25.00 (*90-221-0850-3*) Walter J Johnson.

Blount, Henry C. Looking for Honey. (Illus.). (Orig.). 1984. 5.00 (*0-9614047-0-1*) McArthur Pub.

Blount, Henry C., Jr. Soul Sounds: Reflections on the Higher Self. Waters, Marlen, ed. (Illus.). 107p. (Orig.). 1988. pap. 6.95 (*0-9614047-1-X*) McArthur Pub.

B

Blount, Jackie M. Destined to Rule the Schools: Women & the Superintendency, 1873-1995. LC 97-25555. (SUNY Series, Educational Leadership). 244p. (C). 1998. pap. text 21.95 (*0-7914-3730-2*) State U NY Pr.
— Destined to Rule the Schools: Women & the Superintendency, 1873-1995. LC 97-25555. (SUNY Series, Educational Leadership). 244p. (C). 1998. text 65.50 (*0-7914-3729-9*) State U NY Pr.
Blount, Lucy D. Lenten Love Letters. LC 98-232050. 215p. 1998. write for info. (*0-9630017-9-5*) Light-Bearer.
— Letters from a Candidate's Wife: or It Looks Like a Rough Ride but There's a Rainbow in Sight. (Illus.). 294p. (Orig.). 1994. pap. text. write for info. (*0-9630017-4-4*) Light-Bearer.
— Letters from a Candidate's Wife: or It Looks Like a Rough Ride but There's a Rainbow in Sight. (Illus.). 294p. (Orig.). 1995. write for info. (*0-9630017-6-0*) Light-Bearer.
— Letters to the Precious Group. (Illus.). 176p. 1990. 19.95 (*0-9630017-1-X*) Light-Bearer.
— Letters to the Precious Group. LC 91-90462. (Illus.). 176p. 1991. 13.98 (*0-9630017-0-1*) Light-Bearer.
— The Story of Lucy What's-Her-Name! And Your Name Too! (Illus.). 48p. (J). 1992. spiral bd. 12.00 (*0-9630017-2-8*) Light-Bearer.
Blount, Marcellus & Cunningham, George P. Representing Black Men. 288p. (C). (gr. 13). 1995. pap. 17.99 (*0-415-90759-4*, Pub. by Tavistock) Routldge.
***Blount, Roy, Jr.** Be Sweet: A Conditional Love Story. LC 99-15146. 336p. 1999. pap. 13.00 (*0-15-600682-0*, Harvest Bks) Harcourt.
Blount, Roy, Jr. Be Sweet: A Conditional Love Story. LC 97-49352. 320p. 1998. 24.00 (*0-679-40054-0*) Villard Books.
Blount, Roy, Jr. Crackers. 1982. mass mkt. 3.95 (*0-345-29805-5*) Ballantine Pub Grp.
Blount, Roy, Jr. Crackers. LC 98-3852. 304p. 1998. reprint ed. pap. 14.95 (*0-8203-2060-9*, Brown Thrasher) U of Ga Pr.
— If Only You Knew How Much I Smell You: Time Portraits of Dogs. LC 97-77747. (Illus.). 112p. 1998. 19.95 (*0-8212-2497-2*, Pub. by Bulfinch Pr) Little.
— Now, Where Were We? Back to Basic Truths That We Have Lost Sight of Through No Fault of My Own. 1989. 17.95 (*0-685-24552-7*) Villard Books.
Blount, Roy, Jr., ed. Roy Blount's Book of Southern Humor. LC 94-18611. 672p. 1994. 27.50 (*0-393-03695-2*) Norton.
Blount, Steve & Walker, Lisa. Lonely Planet Diving & Snorkeling Guide to Bahamas: Nassau & New Providence Island. 2nd ed. (Pisces Diving & Snorkeling Guides Ser.). 1990. pap. 14.95 (*1-55992-040-8*, Pisces Books) Lonely Planet.
Blount, Steve & Walker, Lisa, eds. Designs for Marketing No. 1: Primo Angeli. (Illus.). 144p. 1991. reprint ed. pap. 19.95 (*0-935603-65-4*, 30304) Rockport Pubs.
Blount, Steve, jt. auth. see Walker, Lisa.
Blount, Thomas P. De Re Poetica: or Remarks upon Poetry. (Anglistica & Americana Ser.: No. 32, 1). x, 377p. 1969. reprint ed. 160.00 incl. 3.5 hd (*0-685-66433-3*, 05102305) G Olms Pubs.
— Glossographia. (Anglistica & Americana Ser.: No. 32, 2). 688p. 1972. reprint ed. 185.00 (*3-487-04332-7*) G Olms Pubs.
Blount, Tricia. Model & Talent 2000: The International Directory of Model & Talent Agencies & Schools. 200p. 2000. 29.95 (*0-87314-143-1*, Pub. by Peter Glenn) SCB Distributors.
***Blount, Tricia, ed.** Model & Talent 2001: The International Directory of Model & Talent Agencies & Schools. 240p. 2001. pap. 29.95 (*0-87314-144-X*, Pub. by Peter Glenn) SCB Distributors.
— New York City Model Agency Directory, Vol. 10. 80p. 2000. pap. 13.95 (*0-87314-132-6*, Pub. by Peter Glenn) SCB Distributors.
Blount, Veronica. Heaven Help Us! (C). 1988. 39.00 (*0-7855-3227-7*, Pub. by St Paul Pubns) St Mut.
Blount, Walter P. Fractures in Children. LC 76-11. 294p. 1977. reprint ed. 33.50 (*0-88275-392-4*) Krieger.
Blount, Willie. How to Become Power Partners. 100p. 1998. pap. 10.00 (*1-57502-820-4*, PO2256) Morris Pubng.
Blount, Winton M. & Blodgett, Richard. Doing It My Way. (Illus.). 224p. 1996. write for info. (*0-944641-19-9*) Greenwich Pub Group.
Blouse, Ann, ed. see Sullivan, Rick & Gaffikin, Lynne.
Bloustein, Edward J. Individual & Group Privacy. LC 77-28972. 100p. 1978. 24.95 (*0-87855-286-3*) Transaction Pubs.
Blout, Elkan, ed. The Power of Boldness: Ten Master Builders of American Industry Tell Their Success Stories. 224p. 1996. pap. 18.95 (*0-309-05445-1*, Joseph Henry Pr) Natl Acad Pr.
Bloveld, John, tr. see Hai, Hui.
Blovin, Nicole. Mountain Biking South Carolina. LC 98-11814. (Illus.). 128p. 1998. pap. 12.95 (*1-56044-684-6*) Falcon Pub Inc.
Blovits, Larry. Pastel for the Serious Beginner: Basic Lessons in Becoming a Good Painter. (Illus.). 144p. 1996. pap. text 19.95 (*0-8230-3907-2*) Watsn-Guptill.
Blow, Christopher J. Airport Terminals. 2nd ed. (Illus.). 176p. 1996. text 125.00 (*0-7506-2585-6*) Buttrwrth-Heinemann.
Blow, D. M., jt. auth. see Holmes, K. C.
Blow, David, ed. see Balzac, Honore de.
Blow, David, ed. see Huysmans, J. K.
Blow, David, ed. see Raspe, Erich R.
***Blow, Frederic C., ed.** Substance Abuse among Older Adults: Treatment Improvement Protocol. 173p. (C). 1999. pap. text 35.00 (*0-7881-8071-1*) DIANE Pub.
Blow, J. J., ed. Eukaryotic DNA Replication No. 15. LC 96-331. (Frontiers in Molecular Biology Ser.: No. 15). (Illus.). 252p. (C). 1996. text 105.00 (*0-19-963586-2*) OUP.
Blow, J. Julian, ed. Eukaryotic DNA Replication. LC 96-331. (Frontiers in Molecular Biology Ser.: No. 15). (Illus.). 252p. 1996. pap. text 55.00 (*0-19-963585-4*) OUP.
Blow, John. Amphion Anglicus. fac. ed. (Monuments of Music & Music Literature in Facsimile Ser., Series I: Vol. 2). 1964. lib. bdg. 70.00 (*0-8450-2002-1*) Broude.
Blow, John. A Blow Anthology: 8 Anthems. King, Deborah S., ed. 72p. 1996. pap. 19.95 (*0-19-353058-9*) OUP.
***Blow, Jonathon.** Internet Game Programming. 500p. 2000. pap. 54.95 (*1-884777-88-0*, Pub. by Manning Pubns) IPG Chicago.
Blow, Larry E., Jr. & Askenas, Rich. Golf for Fun & Profit. large type ed. (For Fun & Profit Ser.). 350p. 1999. pap. 24.95 (*1-56559-907-1*) HGI-Over Fifty.
Blow Molding Technical Conference (2nd: 1985: Itas. High Performance Container Technology: 2nd Blow Molding Technical Conference Sponsored by the Chicago Section & the Blow Molding Division of the Society of Plastics Engineers Inc. LC TP0986.5.H5. 277p. reprint ed. pap. 85.90 (*0-608-17120-4*, 202770100056) Bks Demand.
Blow, Suzanne. Old Forunatus: The Pleasant Comedy of Old Fortunatus by Thomas Dekker, London 1600. LC 86-72942. 160p. (C). 1987. pap. text 20.00 (*0-938991-05-1*) Colonial Pr AL.
Blow, Thomas, ed. Build with Living Stones: Comprehensive Course on the Franciscan Mission Charism. Date not set. pap. write for info. (*1-57659-134-4*) Franciscan Inst.
— Build with Living Stones: Comprehensive Course on the Franciscan Mission Charism, Lesson 1. Date not set. pap. write for info. (*1-57659-135-2*) Franciscan Inst.
— Build with Living Stones: Comprehensive Course on the Franciscan Mission Charism, Lesson 2. Date not set. pap. write for info. (*1-57659-136-0*) Franciscan Inst.
— Build with Living Stones: Comprehensive Course on the Franciscan Mission Charism, Lesson 3. Date not set. pap. write for info. (*1-57659-137-9*) Franciscan Inst.
— Build with Living Stones: Comprehensive Course on the Franciscan Mission Charism, Lesson 4. Date not set. pap. write for info. (*1-57659-138-7*) Franciscan Inst.
— Build with Living Stones: Comprehensive Course on the Franciscan Mission Charism, Lesson 5. Date not set. pap. write for info. (*1-57659-139-5*) Franciscan Inst.
— Build with Living Stones: Comprehensive Course on the Franciscan Mission Charism, Lesson 6. Date not set. pap. write for info. (*1-57659-140-9*) Franciscan Inst.
— Build with Living Stones: Comprehensive Course on the Franciscan Mission Charism, Lesson 7. Date not set. pap. write for info. (*1-57659-141-7*) Franciscan Inst.
— Build with Living Stones: Comprehensive Course on the Franciscan Mission Charism, Lesson 8. Date not set. pap. write for info. (*1-57659-142-5*) Franciscan Inst.
— Build with Living Stones: Comprehensive Course on the Franciscan Mission Charism, Lesson 9. Date not set. pap. write for info. (*1-57659-143-3*) Franciscan Inst.
— Build with Living Stones: Comprehensive Course on the Franciscan Mission Charism, Lesson 10. Date not set. pap. write for info. (*1-57659-144-1*) Franciscan Inst.
— Build with Living Stones: Comprehensive Course on the Franciscan Mission Charism, Lesson 11. Date not set. pap. write for info. (*1-57659-145-X*) Franciscan Inst.
— Build with Living Stones: Comprehensive Course on the Franciscan Mission Charism, Lesson 12. Date not set. pap. write for info. (*1-57659-146-8*) Franciscan Inst.
— Build with Living Stones: Comprehensive Course on the Franciscan Mission Charism, Lesson 13. Date not set. pap. write for info. (*1-57659-147-6*) Franciscan Inst.
— Build with Living Stones: Comprehensive Course on the Franciscan Mission Charism, Lesson 14. Date not set. pap. write for info. (*1-57659-148-4*) Franciscan Inst.
— Build with Living Stones: Comprehensive Course on the Franciscan Mission Charism, Lesson 15. Date not set. pap. write for info. (*1-57659-149-2*) Franciscan Inst.
— Build with Living Stones: Comprehensive Course on the Franciscan Mission Charism, Lesson 16. Date not set. pap. write for info. (*1-57659-150-6*) Franciscan Inst.
— Build with Living Stones: Comprehensive Course on the Franciscan Mission Charism, Lesson 17. Date not set. pap. write for info. (*1-57659-151-4*) Franciscan Inst.
— Build with Living Stones: Comprehensive Course on the Franciscan Mission Charism, Lesson 18. Date not set. pap. write for info. (*1-57659-152-2*) Franciscan Inst.
— Build with Living Stones: Comprehensive Course on the Franciscan Mission Charism, Lesson 19. Date not set. pap. write for info. (*1-57659-153-0*) Franciscan Inst.
— Build with Living Stones: Comprehensive Course on the Franciscan Mission Charism, Lesson 20. Date not set. pap. write for info. (*1-57659-154-9*) Franciscan Inst.
— Build with Living Stones: Comprehensive Course on the Franciscan Mission Charism, Lesson 21. Date not set. pap. write for info. (*1-57659-155-7*) Franciscan Inst.
— Build with Living Stones: Comprehensive Course on the Franciscan Mission Charism, Lesson 22. Date not set. pap. write for info. (*1-57659-156-5*) Franciscan Inst.
— Build with Living Stones: Comprehensive Course on the Franciscan Mission Charism, Lesson 23. Date not set. pap. write for info. (*1-57659-157-3*) Franciscan Inst.
— Build with Living Stones: Comprehensive Course on the Franciscan Mission Charism, Lesson 24. Date not set. pap. write for info. (*1-57659-158-1*) Franciscan Inst.
— Build with Living Stones: Comprehensive Course on the Franciscan Mission Charism, Lesson 25. Date not set. pap. write for info. (*1-57659-159-X*) Franciscan Inst.
Blowdryer, Jennifer. Where's My Wife. 24p. (Orig.). 1989. pap. 3.00 (*0-929730-15-1*) Zeitgeist Pr.
— White Trash Debutante. (Illus.). 94p. 1997. pap. 9.95 (*0-9640300-3-9*) Galhattan Pr.
— Wrong Wrong Wrong. 20p. (Orig.). 1991. pap. 3.00 (*0-929730-34-8*) Zeitgeist Pr.
Blowen, Martha, ed. see Ledoux, Denis.
Blowen, Martha, ed. see Schawlow, A. L. & Ledour, Denis.
Blower, Arye, tr. see Fell, Alison.
Blower, Arye, tr. see Fell, Alison, ed.
Blower, James G. Athens County, Ohio: Trimble Township History 1797-1960. 211p. 1974. reprint ed. 25.00 (*1-885463-00-6*) Ohio Genealogy.
Blower, W. E. MG Workshop Manual: Complete Turning & Maintenance for All Models from "M" Type to "T. F. 1500": 1929-1955. LC 75-33494. (Illus.). 608p. (Orig.). 1975. pap. 60.00 (*0-8376-0117-7*) Bentley Pubs.
Blowers, Andrew. Something in the Air: Corporate Power in the Environment. 372p. (C). 1984. 40.00 (*0-7855-2382-0*) St Mut.
Blowers, Andrew, ed. Planning Sustainable Environment. 240p. (Orig.). 1992. 34.00 (*1-85383-145-X*, Pub. by Escan Pubns) Island Pr.
Blowers, Andrew & Glasbergen, Pieter. Environmental Policy in an International Context: Prospects for Environmental Change. (International Environmental Studies Ser.: Vol. 3). 256p. 1996. pap. text 44.95 (*0-470-23585-3*) Halsted Pr.
Blowers, Andrew, jt. auth. see Glasbergen, Pieter.
Blowers, Andrew, jt. auth. see Sloep, Peter.
Blowers, Andy & Evans, Bob, eds. Town Planning in the 21st Century. LC 98-204434. 208p. (C). 1997. pap. 25.99 (*0-415-10526-9*) Routledge.
— Town Planning in the 21st Century. LC 98-204434. 208p. (C). 1998. 85.00 (*0-415-10525-0*) Routledge.
Blowers, Paul M. Exegesis & Spiritual Pedagogy in Maximus the Confessor: An Investigation of the Quaestiones ad Thalassium. LC 90-50973. (Christianity & Judaism in Antiquity Ser.: Vol. 7). (C). 1991. text 34.50 (*0-268-00927-9*) U of Notre Dame Pr.
Blowers, Paul M., tr. The Bible in Greek Christian Antiquity. LC 97-13525. Vol. 1. 464p. 1997. pap. 40.00 (*0-268-00702-0*) U of Notre Dame Pr.
Blowes, David W., jt. ed. see Alpers, Charles N.
Blowey, R. W. A Veterinary Book for Dairy Farmers. 2nd ed. (Illus.). 496p. 1988. 38.95 (*0-85236-179-3*, Pub. by Farming Pr) Diamond Farm Bk.
Blowey, R. W. & Weaver, A. D. A Color Atlas of Diseases & Disorders of Cattle. LC 90-85771. (Illus.). 224p. (C). 1990. text 92.95 (*0-7234-1597-8*) Iowa St U Pr.
Blowey, Roger. Cattle Lameness & Hoofcare. (Illus.). 96p. 1993. text 36.95 (*0-85236-252-8*, Pub. by Farming Pr) Diamond Farm Bk.
Blowey, Roger & Edmondson, Peter. Mastitis Control in Dairy Herds. (Illus.). 208p. 1995. 44.95 (*0-85236-314-1*, Pub. by Farming Pr) Diamond Farm Bk.
Blowfield, M. The Allocation of Labour to Perennial Crops: Decision-Making by African Smallholders. 1993. pap. 25.00 (*0-85954-360-9*, Pub. by Nat Res Inst) St Mut.
Blows, Johanna M. Eagle & Crow: An Exploration of an Australian Aboriginal Myth. LC 94-36191. (Folklore Library: Vol. 1671, Vol. 9). (Illus.). 240p. 1995. text 15.00 (*0-8153-1258-X*, H1691) Garland.
Blowsnake, Sam. Crashing Thunder: The Autobiography of an American Indian. Radin, Paul, ed. LC 83-6894. (Native American Autobiography Ser.). (Illus.). 251p. 1983. reprint ed. pap. 77.90 (*0-608-08001-2*, 2067966) Bks Demand.
***Bloxham, Frederick.** Lycanthropia. LC 99-67824. 288p. 2000. 25.00 (*1-885003-40-4*, Pub. by R D Reed Pubs) Midpt Trade.
Bloy, Duncan. Criminal Law. (Lecture Notes Ser.). 279p. 1994. pap. write for info. (*1-874241-60-0*, Pub. by Cavendish Pubng) Gaunt.
— Criminal Law. 2nd ed. (Lecture Notes Ser.). 326p. 1996. pap. 30.00 (*1-85941-168-1*, Pub. by Cavendish Pubng) Gaunt.
— SWOT Family Law. 240p. (C). 1990. 85.00 (*1-85431-031-3*) St Mut.
— SWOT Family Law. 4th ed. 250p. 1995. pap. 22.00 (*1-85431-341-X*, Pub. by Blackstone Pr) Gaunt.
Bloy, Duncan & Parry, Philip. Principles of Criminal Law. 3rd ed. (Principles of Law Ser.). xxxix, 410p. 1997. pap. 29.00 (*1-85941-373-0*, Pub. by Cavendish Pubng) Gaunt.
Bloy, Duncan J. Child Law. (Lecture Notes Ser.). 254p. 1996. pap. 30.00 (*1-874241-59-7*, Pub. by Cavendish Pubng) Gaunt.
Bloy, Leon. La Femme Pauvre. (FRE.). 1980. pap. 11.95 (*0-7859-1914-7*, 2070371948) Fr & Eur.
Bloyd, Sunni. Animal Rights. LC 90-6197. (Overview Ser.). (Illus.). 96p. (J). (gr. 5-8). 1990. lib. bdg. 22.45 (*1-56006-114-6*) Lucent Bks.
— Travel Tips for Teachers. 132p. (Orig.). 1991. pap. 8.95 (*0-929923-43-X*) Lowell Hse.
Bloyer, Christen T., jt. auth. see Makar, Ragai N.
Bloze, Vytautas. Smoke from Nothing. Zdanys, Jonas, tr. from LIT. 32p. 1998. pap. 10.00 (*0-930502-35-3*) Pine Pr.
Blpes. International Bibliography of Social Sciences: Anthropology, 1995, Vol. 41. 420p. (C). 1997. 250.00 (*0-415-15214-3*) Routledge.
— International Bibliography of Social Sciences: Political Science, 1995, Vol. 44. 588p. (C). 1997. 250.00 (*0-415-15217-8*) Routledge.
— International Bibliography of Social Sciences: Sociology, 1995, Vol. 45. 636p. (C). 1997. 250.00 (*0-415-15216-X*) Routledge.
Blu, Karen I. The Lumbee Problem: The Making of an American Indian People. LC 79-12908. (Cambridge Studies in Cultural Systems: No. 5). 292p. pap. 83.30 (*0-608-15695-7*, 2031622) Bks Demand.
Blu, Susan. Word of Mouth: A Guide to Commercial Voice-Over Excellence. 1998. pap. 19.95 incl. audio (*0-938817-47-7*) Pomegranate Pr.
Blu, Susan & Mullin, Molly A. Word of Mouth: A Guide to Commercial Voice-over Excellence. 1998. audio 11.95 (*0-938817-09-4*) Pomegranate Pr.
— Word of Mouth: A Guide to Commercial Voice-over Excellence. 2nd ed. LC 87-61591. (Illus.). 176p. 1999. pap. 11.95 (*0-938817-32-9*) Pomegranate Pr.
Bluche, Francois. Dictionnaire des Citations et des Mots Historiques. (FRE.). 1997. pap. write for info. (*0-7859-9509-9*) Fr & Eur.
— Dictionnaire des Mots Historiques de Cesar a Churchill. (FRE.). 401p. 1992. pap. 45.00 (*0-7859-8180-2*, 2877061493) Fr & Eur.
Bluchel, Kurt G. Game & Hunting. 2 Vols. (Illus.). 640p. 1997. boxed set 49.95 (*3-89508-471-9*, 520168) Konemann.
Bluck, John. Beyond Neutrality: A Christian Critique of the Media. LC 80-505714. (Illus.). 70p. reprint ed. pap. 30.00 (*0-7837-5997-5*, 204580700008) Bks Demand.
Blucker, Judith & Graf, Joanne. Championship Slowpitch Softball: A Complete Handbook for Coaches, Teachers & Players. (Illus.). 131p. (Orig.). 1984. pap. 12.00 (*0-9614446-0-6*) Jugs.
Bludman, S. A., et al, eds. Supernovae: Proceedings of the Les Houches Summer School, Course LIV, 31 July-1 September, 1990. (Houches Summer School Proceedings Ser.: Vol. 54). 878p. 1994. 305.00 (*0-444-81474-4*, North Holland) Elsevier.
Blue. Pilgrim Hymnal. LC 58-1015. 1958. 12.95 (*0-8298-0460-9*) Pilgrim OH.
Blue, jt. auth. see Harpham.
Blue, jt. auth. see Scott, Arthur G.
Blue & Gray Magazine Editors. Blue & Gray Magazine's History & Tour Guide of the Atlanta Campaign. Davis, Stephen & McMurry, Richard M., eds. 352p. 1996. pap. text 19.95 (*0-9626034-6-5*) Generals Bks.
— Guide to Haunted Places of the Civil War. 176p. 1996. pap. text 12.95 (*0-9626034-7-3*) Generals Bks.
Blue & Gray Magazine Staff. Guide to the Battle for South Mountain & Jackson's Seige of Harper's Ferry. 1997. pap. text 12.95 (*0-9626034-8-1*) Generals Bks.
***Blue & the Crew Publishers Staff.** My Name Is Blue, from Me to You, All about PTSD, Vol. 2. Rain & the Crew Publishers Staff, ed. 16p. 2000. pap. 6.00 (*1-929396-01-5*) Rain Blue.
Blue, Adrianne. Martina: The Lives & Times of Martina Navratilova. 240p. 1995. 19.95 (*1-55972-300-9*, Birch Ln Pr) Carol Pub Group.
— On Kissing: Travels in an Intimate Landscape. LC 97-2763. 208p. 1997. 22.00 (*1-56836-173-4*) Kodansha.
— On Kissing: Travels in an Intimate Landscape. 224p. 1999. pap. 15.00 (*1-56836-261-7*, Kodansha Globe) Kodansha.
— Queen of the Track: The Liz McColgan Story. (Illus.). 224p. 1994. pap. 13.95 (*0-85493-232-1*) Trafalgar.
— Queen of the Track: The Liz McColgan Story. (Illus.). 224p. 1993. 29.95 (*0-85493-223-2*, Pub. by V Gollancz) Trafalgar.
Blue, Alex. Judge Ye Not. LC 99-61555. 350p. 1999. pap. 6.99 (*1-893181-17-0*, Simon & Northrop) Le Gesse Stevens.
Blue, Anthony D. The Complete Book of Mixed Drinks: Over One Thousand Alcoholic & Non-Alcoholic Cocktails. LC 92-54840. 336p. 1993. pap. 18.00 (*0-06-095007-2*, Perennial) HarperTrade.
Blue Bird Circle Members. The Gathering: A Collection of Recipes. (Illus.). 224p. 1987. spiral bd. 12.95 (*0-9617897-0-0*) Blue Bird Cir.
***Blue, Brenda.** Life's Passages. 1999. pap. write for info. (*1-58235-294-1*) Watermrk Pr.
Blue Cliff Editions Staff, tr. see Zehetmair, Helmut & Steinschaden, Bruno.
Blue Cloud, Peter. Back Then Tomorrow. (Illus.). 1978. pap. 5.00 (*0-942396-27-8*) Blackberry ME.
Blue, Dana, ed. see Grant, Cheri B.
Blue, Daniel. Thrilling Narrative of the Adventures, Sufferings & Starvation of Pike's Peak Gold Seekers on the Plains of the West in the Winter & Spring of 1859. 23p. 1968. reprint ed. pap. 5.95 (*0-87770-032-X*) Ye Galleon.
Blue, Denise, ed. see Powers, Alexis.
Blue Evening Star Staff. Tipis & Yurts: Authentic Designs for Circular Shelters. Dierks, Leslie, ed. LC 95-6219. (Illus.). 128p. 1995. 24.95 (*0-937274-88-7*, Pub. by Lark Books) Random.
***Blue Evening Star Staff.** Tipis & Yurts: Authentic Designs for Circular Shelters. (Illus.). 2000. pap. 16.95 (*1-887374-69-8*) Lark Books.
Blue Feather, Milina. Heaven in My Pocket. 100p. 1995. pap. write for info. (*1-887135-01-4*) Jewell Pub NC.
Blue Feather, Milina, jt. auth. see A'aragon d'Ar Satumi.
Blue, Frederick J. Charles Sumner & the Conscience of the North. Kraut, Alan M. & Wakelyn, Jon L., eds. (American Biographical History Ser.). (Illus.). 150p. (C). 1994. pap. text 12.95 (*0-88295-911-5*) Harlan Davidson.
— The Free Soilers: Third Party Politics 1848-54. LC 72-86408. 364p. reprint ed. pap. 112.90 (*0-608-13813-4*, 202023100016) Bks Demand.
— Salmon P. Chase: A Life in Politics. LC 86-27664. 408p. 1987. 28.00 (*0-87338-340-0*) Kent St U Pr.
Blue, Frederick J., et al. Mahoning Memories: A History of Youngstown & Mahoning County. 1995. write for info. (*0-89865-944-2*) Donning Co.
Blue, Gabriel, ed. see Schmidt, Rosemary J.
Blue, George M. & Mitchell, Rosamond, eds. Language & Education. (British Studies in Applied Linguistics: No. 11). 140p. 1996. pap. 39.95 (*1-85359-370-2*, Pub. by Multilingual Matters) Taylor & Francis.
Blue, Gregory, jt. ed. see Brook, Timothy.

An Asterisk (*) at the beginning of an entry indicates that the title is appearing for the first time.

Blue, Gwendolyn, ed. see Ogbankwa-Stevens, Michelle.

Blue, Helen M., ed. Sierra Valley Memories: With Artie Strang, Frank Dotta & Rita Bradley. (Illus.). 122p. 1990. lib. bdg. 35.50 (*1-56475-348-4*); fiche. write for info. (*1-56475-349-2*) U NV Oral Hist.

Blue, Helen M. & Coughtry, Jamie, eds. Clarence Ray: Black Politics & Gaming in Las Vegas, 1920s-1980s. (History of Las Vegas Black Community Ser.). (Illus.). 122p. 1991. lib. bdg. 34.50 (*1-56475-002-7*) U NV Oral Hist.

Blue, Helen M. & King, R. T., eds. Albina Redner: A Shoshone Life. (Illus.). 162p. 1990. lib. bdg. 39.50 (*1-56475-346-8*); fiche. write for info. (*1-56475-347-6*) U NV Oral Hist.

— Barbara Bennett: Mayor of Reno & Community Activist. (Illus.). 144p. 1989. 9.95 (*1-56475-340-9*); lib. bdg. 34.00 (*1-56475-339-5*); fiche. write for info. (*1-56475-341-7*) U NV Oral Hist.

— Clarence K. Jones: From Paperboy to Philanthropist. (Illus.). 210p. 1988. 20.00 (*1-56475-337-9*); lib. bdg. 45.50 (*1-56475-336-0*); fiche. write for info. (*1-56475-338-7*) U NV Oral Hist.

Blue, Helen M., jt. intro. see Gash, Karen R.

Blue, Herbert T. Centennial History of Hardin County, Ohio. (Illus.). 180p. 1993. reprint ed. lib. bdg. 28.00 (*0-8328-3227-8*) Higginson Bk Co.

***Blue Highway Staff.** Blue Highway, 2 vols. 1999. pap. 15.97 (*5-550-10697-3*) Nairi.

— Blue Highway, Vol. 4. 1999. pap. 9.98 (*5-550-10698-1*) Nairi.

Blue, Jane. Now That I Am in the Light I See. (Orig.). 1996. pap. write for info. (*0-914134-11-6*) Konocti Bks.

— Sacrament. (Illus.). 32p. (Orig.). 1986. pap. 4.00 (*0-914485-08-3*) Trill Pr.

***Blue, Jean A.** Time to Talk. 120p. 1999. pap. 8.00 (*0-7392-0368-1*, PO3576) Morris Pubng.

Blue, John, ed. see Knote, Charlie & Knote, Ruthie.

Blue, John S. History & Tales of a Pioneer. (Illus.). 194p. 1980. 25.00 (*0-9604474-0-7*) Jasper County.

— Hoosier Tales & Proverbs. (Illus.). 93p. 1982. 15.00 (*0-9604474-1-5*) Jasper County.

— Hoosier Wit & Wisdom, Vol. I. Kriebel, Robert C., ed. (Illus.). 137p. 1985. 20.00 (*0-9604474-3-1*) Jasper County.

— Hoosier Wit & Wisdom, Vol. II. (Illus.). 131p. 1987. 20.00 (*0-9604474-2-3*) Jasper County.

Blue, Judy, jt. auth. see Blue, Ron.

Blue, Ken. Alien Alert: Bible Baptism vs. Baptist Bride Baptism. 64p. 1991. pap. 3.25 (*1-930452-06-3*) Local Church.

Blue, Ken. Authority to Heal. LC 87-22575. 168p. (Orig.). (C). 1987. pap. 10.99 (*0-8308-1700-X*, 1700) InterVarsity.

Blue, Ken. Baptist Briders Boloney. 27p. 1997. pap. 3.25 (*1-930452-07-1*) Local Church.

— A Dispensational Bible Study. 43p. 1991. pap. 3.25 (*1-930452-05-5*) Local Church.

— Dispensationalism Misunderstood. 18p. 1997. pap. 3.25 (*1-930452-04-7*) Local Church.

— Having the Right Bait: A Fishermen's Guide to Soul Wining. pap. 3.25 (*1-930452-08-X*) Local Church.

Blue, Ken. Healing Spiritual Abuse: How to Break Free from Bad Church Experiences. LC 93-21558. 168p. (Orig.). 1993. pap. 9.99 (*0-8308-1660-7*, 1660) InterVarsity.

Blue, Ken. How to Assist Your Pastor. 47p. 1991. pap. 3.25 (*1-930452-03-9*) Local Church.

— Parables of Matthew 13. 51p. 1997. pap. 3.25 (*1-930452-02-0*) Local Church.

— A Study on the Book of Acts. Obrastoff, Sharon, ed. (Illus.). 269p. 1996. pap. 11.95 (*1-930452-00-4*) Local Church.

— A Study on the Book of Job. 328p. 1998. pap. 16.95 (*1-930452-01-2*) Local Church.

Blue, L. My Affair with Christianity. text 35.00 (*0-340-66906-3*, Pub. by Hodder & Stought Ltd) Trafalgar.

— Tales of Body & Soul. 1995. mass mkt. 15.95 (*0-340-64955-0*, Pub. by Hodder & Stought Ltd) Trafalgar.

Blue Lake-Deerhaven Cookbook Staff. A Texas Hill Country Cookbook. (Illus.). 406p. 1983. reprint ed. pap. 12.95 (*0-9609210-0-1*) RAR Enterprises.

Blue Lantern Studio Staff. Baby Days: A Baby Record Book. (Illus.). 96p. 1999. 35.95 (*1-883211-19-0*) Laughing Elephant.

Blue, Lionel. Lionel Blue. Marshall, Gordian & Richardson, Daphne, eds. (Modern Spirituality Ser.). 96p. 1987. pap. 4.95 (*0-87243-168-1*) Templegate.

Blue, Lisa & Saginaw, Jane. Jury Selection: Strategy & Science. 1989. 130.00 (*0-318-42408-8*); suppl. ed. write for info. (*0-318-65003-7*) West Group.

***Blue, Martha.** Indian Trader: The Life & Times of J. L. Hubbell. LC 00-24704. (Illus.). 2000. write for info. (*1-885772-21-1*) Kiva Pubng.

— Indian Trader: The Life & Times of J. L. Hubbell. LC 00-24704. (Illus.). 356p. 2000. 32.50 (*1-885772-17-3*) Kiva Pubng.

Blue, Martha. The Witch Purge of 1878: Oral & Documentary History in the Early Navajo Reservation Years. 1988. pap. 4.75 (*0-912586-66-4*) Dine College Pr.

***Blue Moon Book Staffs, ed.** Lustful Memoirs. 2000. mass mkt. 7.95 (*1-56201-199-5*) Blue Moon Bks.

***Blue Moon Books Staff.** Lascivious Scenes in the Convent. 2000. mass mkt. 7.95 (*1-56201-202-9*) Blue Moon Bks.

Blue Mountain College Alumnae Association Cookbook, ed. Blue Mountain College Cookbook: Presidential Edition. (Illus.). 304p. (Orig.). 1989. 12.00 (*0-9624097-0-7*) Blue Mntn Coll.

Blue Mountain Ranch Commune Staff. January Thaw: People at Blue Mt. Ranch Write about Living Together in the Mountains. LC 74-79106. (Illus.). 160p. (Orig.). 1974. 14.50 (*0-87810-530-1*); pap. 7.25 (*0-87810-030-X*) Times Change.

***Blue, Nelson A.** Machiavelli's "The Republican" The Best Possible America & How to Achieve It. 176p. 2000. pap. 14.95 (*1-880849-19-4*) Chapel Hill NC.

Blue Oyster Cult. Blue Oyster Cult: Cult Classics. 112p. 1996. per. 19.95 (*0-7935-6130-2*) H Leonard.

Blue, Patt. Living on a Dream: A Marriage Tale. LC 97-39452. (Illus.). 200p. 1998. 28.00 (*1-57806-057-5*) U Pr of Miss.

***Blue, R.** Halle Berry. (Black Americans of Achievement Ser.). 2000. 19.95 (*0-7910-5802-6*) Chelsea Hse.

— Halle Berry. (Black Americans of Achievement Ser.). (Illus.). 2001. pap. 9.95 (*0-7910-5803-4*) Chelsea Hse.

— Wesley Snipes. (Black Americans of Achievement Ser.). 2000. 19.95 (*0-7910-5800-X*) Chelsea Hse.

— Wesley Snipes. (Black Americans of Achievement Ser.). (Illus.). 2001. pap. 9.95 (*0-7910-5801-8*) Chelsea Hse.

Blue Ridge Bicycle Club Staff. Road Bike Asheville, North Carolina: Favorite Rides of the Blue Ridge Bicycle Club. LC 97-7823. (Illus.). 96p. (Orig.). 1997. pap. 9.95 (*1-889596-00-0*) Milestone NC.

Blue, Ron. Avoiding Common Financial Mistakes. 24p. 1991. pap. 2.50 (*0-89109-312-5*) NavPress.

— Generous Living. 1997. pap. 12.99 (*0-614-28129-6*) Zondervan.

— Generous Living: Finding Contentment Through Giving. LC 97-21287. 192p. 1997. pap. 12.99 (*0-310-21090-9*) Zondervan.

— Master Your Money: A Step-by-Step Plan for Financial Freedom Revised & Updated for the Financial Realities of the 90s. LC 97-27076. 1997. pap. 10.99 (*0-7852-7061-2*) Nelson.

— Master Your Money Workbook. 1993. pap., wbk. ed. 16.99 (*0-8407-3393-3*) Nelson.

— Sobreponiendose Problemas Financieros - Avoiding Common Financial Problems. (SPA.). 119p. 1995. write for info. (*0-7899-0005-X*) Editorial Unilit.

— Taming the Money Monster. LC 93-10563. 1993. pap. 9.99 (*1-56179-168-7*) Focus Family.

***Blue, Ron.** Taming the Money Monster: Five Steps to Conquering Debt. 220p. 2000. mass mkt. 6.99 (*1-56179-587-9*) Focus Family.

Blue, Ron & Berndt, Jodie. Money Talks & So Can We: How Couples Can Communicate about Spending & Giving, Getting Out of Debt, Investing, Planning for Retirement, & Other Money Matters. LC 98-39128. 1999. 17.99 (*0-310-22461-6*); pap. 12.99 (*0-310-22266-4*) Zondervan.

Blue, Ron & Blue, Judy. Raising Money-Smart Kids. 256p. 1992. pap. 10.99 (*0-8407-3195-7*) Nelson.

— A Woman's Guide to Financial Peace of Mind. 1991. pap. 8.99 (*1-56179-053-2*) Focus Family.

— A Woman's Guide to Financial Peace of Mind. 1991. 13.99 (*1-56179-026-5*) Focus Family.

Blue, Rose. Bring Me a Memory. LC 95-16015. (Illus.). 93p. (Orig.). (J). (gr. 4-6). 1995. pap. 9.95 (*0-931625-28-9*) DIMI Pr.

Blue, Rose. Colin Powell: Straight to the Top. (Gateway Biography Ser.). (Illus.). (J). 1997. 13.40 (*0-606-18282-9*) Turtleback.

Blue, Rose. First Americans Story. Date not set. pap. 7.95 (*0-448-11101-2*) Putnam Pub Group.

— Good Yontif: A Picture Book of the Jewish Year. LC 96-31054. (Illus.). 32p. (J). 1997. 16.95 (*0-7613-0142-9*) Millbrook Pr.

— Me & Einstein: Breaking Through the Reading Barrier. (Illus.). (J). (gr. 3 up). 1984. 16.95 (*0-87705-388-X*, Kluwer Acad Hman Sci); pap. 10.95 (*0-89885-185-8*, Kluwer Acad Hman Sci) Kluwer Academic.

— Staying Out of Trouble in a Troubled Family. LC 98-15625. 112p. (YA). (gr. 7 up). 1998. 21.40 (*0-7613-0365-0*) TFC Bks NY.

— Whoopi Goldberg: Entertainer. Huggins, Nathan I., ed. (Black Americans of Achievement Ser.). (Illus.). 124p. (YA). (gr. 5 up). 1994. lib. bdg. 19.95 (*0-7910-2152-1*) Chelsea Hse.

— Whoopi Goldberg: Entertainer. Huggins, Nathan I., ed. (Black Americans of Achievement Ser.). (Illus.). 124p. (YA). (gr. 5 up). 1995. pap. 8.95 (*0-7910-2153-X*) Chelsea Hse.

— Wishful Lying. LC 79-21806. (Illus.). 32p. (J). (ps-3). 1980. 16.95 (*0-87705-473-8*, Kluwer Acad Hman Sci) Kluwer Academic.

Blue, Rose & Nadan, Corrine J. Madeleine Albright: U. S. Secretary of State. LC 98-13723. (Library of Famous Women). (Illus.). 64p. (J). (gr. 4-7). 1998. lib. bdg. 17.95 (*1-56711-253-6*) Blackbirch.

Blue, Rose & Naden, Corinne J. Andes Mountains. LC 94-3028. (Wonders of the World Ser.). (Illus.). 64p. (J). (gr. 4-7). 1994. lib. bdg. 25.64 (*0-8114-6363-X*) Raintree Steck-V.

— Barbara Jordan: Politician. Huggins, Nathan I., ed. (Black Americans of Achievement Ser.). (Illus.). 124p. (YA). (gr. 5 up). 1992. lib. bdg. 19.95 (*0-7910-1131-3*) Chelsea Hse.

— The Black Sea. LC 94-40912. (Wonders of the World Ser.). (Illus.). 64p. (J). 1995. lib. bdg. 25.64 (*0-8114-6371-0*) Raintree Steck-V.

***Blue, Rose & Naden, Corinne J.** Chris Rock, Comedian. LC 99-39931. (Illus.). 144p. 1999. 9.95 (*0-7910-5278-8*) Chelsea Hse.

Blue, Rose & Naden, Corinne J. Colin Powell: Straight to the Top. LC 96-39006. (Gateway Biographies Ser.). (Illus.). 48p. (J). (gr. 2-4). 1997. lib. bdg. 20.90 (*0-7613-0256-5*) Millbrook Pr.

— Colin Powell: Straight to the Top. large type ed. 1993. 13.50 (*0-614-09818-1*, L-34130-00) Am Printing Hse.

— Colin Powell: Straight to the Top. rev. ed. LC 96-39006. (Gateway Biographies Ser.). (Illus.). 48p. (J). (gr. 2-4). 1997. pap. 7.95 (*0-7613-0242-5*) Millbrook Pr.

— Colin Powell: Straight to the Top. 94th ed. 1994. text 22.20 (*0-15-302263-9*) Harcourt.

— The Expansion Years, 1857-1901. LC 97-15038. (Who's That in the White House? Ser.). 96p. (J). (gr. 7-8). 1998. lib. bdg. 28.55 (*0-8172-4302-X*) Raintree Steck-V.

— The Formative Years: Jackson to Pierce, 1829-1857. LC 97-15727. (Who's That in the White House? Ser.). 96p. (J). 1998. 28.55 (*0-8172-4301-1*) Raintree Steck-V.

— The Founding Years, 1789-1829. LC 97-14218. (Who's That in the White House? Ser.). 96p. (J). 1998. 28.55 (*0-8172-4300-3*) Raintree Steck-V.

— The Modern Years: Nixon to Clinton, 1969 to the Present. LC 97-15039. (Who's That in the White House? Ser.). 96p. 1998. 28.55 (*0-8172-4305-4*) Raintree Steck-V.

— People of Peace. LC 93-30547. (Illus.). 80p. (J). (gr. 4-6). 1994. lib. bdg. 25.90 (*1-56294-409-6*) Millbrook Pr.

— The Progressive Years, 1901 to 1933. LC 97-14710. (Who's That in the White House? Ser.). 96p. (J). (gr. 7-8). 1998. lib. bdg. 28.55 (*0-8172-4303-8*) Raintree Steck-V.

— The Turbulent Years: F. D. Roosevelt to L. Johnson, 1933-1969. LC 97-19104. (Who's That in the White House? Ser.). 96p. (J). 1998. lib. bdg. 28.55 (*0-8172-4304-6*) Raintree Steck-V.

— The White House Kids. (Illus.). 80p. (J). (gr. 5-8). 1995. lib. bdg. 24.90 (*1-56294-447-9*) Millbrook Pr.

Blue, Rose, jt. auth. see Nadan, Corinne J.

Blue, Rose, jt. auth. see Naden, Corinne.

Blue, Rose, jt. auth. see Naden, Corinne J.

Blue, Rose, jt. auth. see Naden, Corinne J.

Blue, Sharkmeat, pseud. King Death: And Other Poems. Richey, Joseph, ed. (Illus.). 64p. 1992. pap. 8.00 (*1-882775-02-3*) Selva Edit.

Blue Sky Software Corporation Staff. Mastering Windows 95 Help: A Preview of Law School & Legal Processing. 3rd rev. ed. LC 95-81226. 192p. 1996. pap. 24.95 incl. disk (*0-9647236-1-1*) Blue Sky Sftware.

Blue, Steven. Wordsongs. 48p. (Orig.). 1993. pap. 7.95 (*0-9635499-0-1*) Arrowcloud Pr.

Blue, Ted. Delphi Database Development: With CD. 1997. pap. text 49.95 (*1-55851-566-6*, M&T Bks) IDG Bks.

Blue, Tyson. The Unseen King. LC 88-1074. (Starmont Studies in Literary Criticism: No. 26). viii, 200p. 1989. pap. 23.00 (*1-55742-072-6*) Millefleurs.

Blue, William R. Comedia: Art & History. (University of Kansas Humanistic Studies: Vol. 2). 212p. (C). 1989. text 40.30 (*0-8204-0644-9*) P Lang Pubng.

— The Development of Imagery in Calderons Comedias. LC 82-60939. 222p. 1983. 18.00 (*0-938972-05-7*) Spanish Lit Pubns.

— Spanish Comedy & Contexts in the 1620s. 1996. 45.00 (*0-271-01546-2*) Pa St U Pr.

Bluebond-Langner, Myra. In the Shadow of Illness: Parents & Siblings of Ill Children. LC 96-6800. 328p. 1996. text 29.95 (*0-691-02783-8*, Pub. by Princeton U Pr) Cal Prin Full Svc.

***Bluebond-Langner, Myra.** In the Shadow of Illness: Parents & Siblings of the Chronically Ill Child. (Illus.). 328p. 2000. pap. text 14.95 (*0-691-05079-1*, Pub. by Princeton U Pr) Cal Prin Full Svc.

Bluebond-Langner, Myra. The Private Worlds of Dying Children. LC 77-85529. 298p. 1978. pap. text 15.95 (*0-691-02820-6*, Pub. by Princeton U Pr) Cal Prin Full Svc.

***Bluebonnets.** Journeys: An Intimate Interlude. 140p. 2000. pap. 18.00 (*0-7388-2200-0*) Xlibris Corp.

Bluefarb, Sam. Reunion. LC 97-67670. 304p. 1998. pap. 14.50 (*0-88739-164-8*) Creat Arts Bk.

Blueford, ed. Mesozoic & Cenozoic Siliceous Sediments of California, No. T109. (IGC Field Trip Guidebooks Ser.). 56p. 1989. 21.00 (*0-87590-605-2*) Am Geophysical.

Blueford, J. R. Rock Cycle - Understanding the Earth's Crust. 1992. 22.95 (*1-56638-103-7*) Math Sci Nucleus.

Blueford, J. R., et al. Applied Science - Our Technological World. 1992. 24.95 (*1-56638-000-6*) Math Sci Nucleus.

— Life Cycle - A Diversity in a Balance. (J). (gr. k-6). 1992. 24.95 (*1-56638-157-6*) Math Sci Nucleus.

— Universe Cycle - Search for Our Beginning. (J). (gr. k-6). 1992. 20.95 (*1-56638-055-3*) Math Sci Nucleus.

— Water Cycle - The Earth's Gift. (J). (gr. k-6). 1992. 19.95 (*1-56638-146-0*) Math Sci Nucleus.

Blueford, Joyce E., ed. Kreyenhagen Formation & Related Rocks. (Illus.). 98p. (Orig.). 1984. pap. 2.00 (*1-878861-35-2*) Pac Section SEPM.

***Bluege, Wilor.** The Golden Bough: A Fairytale Ballet for Children. LC 99-68849. (Illus.). 28p. (J). (ps-12). 2000. pap. 25.00 (*1-883477-39-5*) Lone Oak MN.

Bluegrass Chapter, Society of Professional Journal. 1995 Kentucky Media Guide. 94p. 11.50 (*1-883589-22-3*) Clark Pub KY.

— 1994 Kentucky Media Guide. 94p. 1994. 10.00 (*1-883589-18-5*) Clark Pub KY.

***Bluegrass Group Sierra Club Members.** Hiking the Red: A Complete Trail Guide to Kentucky's Red River Gorge. Strode, W. H., ed. (Illus.). 104p. 2000. pap. 12.95 (*1-56469-066-0*) Harmony Hse Pub.

Bluehorse, Elizabeth. The View from the Hill. LC 97-90675. 81p. 1998. 14.95 (*0-533-12454-9*) Vantage.

Bluejay, Jana. It's Time: A Nuclear Novel. 206p. (Orig.) 1987. reprint ed. pap. 7.95 (*0-9615129-0-3*) Tough Dove.

Blueme, Keith. Original Ferrari V12, 1965-73: The Restorers Guide to Front Engined Road Cars. LC 99-56957. (Illus.). 128p. 1999. text 35.95 (*1-901432-22-X*, 128276AE) Motorbooks Intl.

Bluemel, Keith. Ferrari: The Road Cars. LC 99-187741. (Illus.). 160p. 2000. 39.95 (*0-7509-1919-1*, Pub. by Sutton Publng) Intl Pubs Mktg.

***Bluemel, Keith.** Ferrari: The Road Cars. (Illus.). 160p. 2000. pap. 21.95 (*0-7509-2483-7*) Sutton Publng.

Bluemel, Keith. Original Ferrari V8: Restoration Guide for All Models 1974-1994, Vol. 8. (Original Ser.). (Illus.). 128p. 1996. 35.95 (*1-870979-78-8*, Bay View Bks) MBI Pubg.

Bluemel, W. D., ed. Geowissenschaftliche Spitzbergen - Expedition, 1990-92 (SPE 90-92) - Liefde-, Wood- und Bockfjord/NW-Spitzbergen (Geoscientific Spitsbergen - Expedition, 1990-1992 (SPE 90-92) - Lifde-, Wood- & Bockfiord NW-Spitsbergen) (Zeitschrift fuer Geomorphologie - Annals of Geomorphology Ser.: Supplementband 97). (GER., Illus.). viii, 274p. 1994. pap. 105.00 (*3-443-21097-X*, Pub. by Gebruder Borntraeger) Balogh.

Bluemel, Wolf-Dieter, ed. Aeolische Dynamik - Formen und Prozesse - Eolian Dynamics, Landforms & Processes: Proceedings of the 2nd Middle-European Conference on Geomorphology, Stuttgart 1996. (Zeitschrift fuer Geomorphologie - Annals of Geomorphology Ser.: Supplementband 111). (Illus.). vi, 174p. 1998. pap. 67.20 (*3-443-21111-9*, Pub. by Gebruder Borntraeger) Balogh.

***Bluemer, Keith.** Ferrari: The Racing Cars. (Illus.). 2001. 27.95 (*0-7509-2487-X*, Pub. by Sutton Publng) Intl Pubs Mktg.

***Bluemer, R. G.** Fate of the Phoenix. (Illus.). 208p. 1999. pap. 12.00 (*0-9673680-0-6*) Grand Village.

Bluemond, James. The Job Hunter's Word Finder. 224p. (Orig.). 1996. pap. 12.95 (*1-56079-600-6*) Petersons.

Blueprint Collective Staff, jt. ed. see Muller, Lauren.

Blueprint Publishing Limited Staff. Desktop Publishing: Design Basics. (Illus.). 128p. 1991. mass mkt. 40.95 (*0-948905-42-5*) Chapman & Hall.

— The Print & Production Manual. 5th rev. ed. 348p. 1991. 129.95 (*0-948905-48-4*) Chapman & Hall.

***Blues, Mary.** The Blues Lover's Cookbook for Kids. (Illus.). 72p. (J). 1999. 15.00 (*0-9676216-0-7*) N R Etc.

Bluestein, Abe, tr. see Casas, Juan G.

***Bluestein, Barry.** Express Cooking: Make Healthy Meals Fast in Today's Quiet, Safe Pressure Cookers. LC 99-47353. (Illus.). 288p. 2000. 24.95 (*1-55788-326-2*, HP Books) Berkley Pub.

Bluestein, Barry. Guilt-Free Frying: All of Your Favorite "Fried" Foods with No Muss, No Fuss & Almost No Fat! LC 99-35635. 320p. 1999. 23.95 (*1-55788-318-1*, HP Books) Berkley Pub.

Bluestein, Barry & Morrissey, Kevin. The Complete Cookie. 336p. 1996. 25.00 (*0-385-47773-2*) Doubleday.

— Light Sauces: Delicious Low-Calorie, Low-Fat, Low-Cholesterol Recipes. 112p. (Orig.). 1991. pap. 9.95 (*0-8092-4063-7*) NTC Contemp Pub Co.

— 99Fat-Free Italian Cooking: All Your Favorite Dishes with Less Than 1 Gram of Fat. LC 98-41251. (Illus.). 288p. 1999. 27.50 (*0-385-48545-X*) Doubleday.

— Quick Breads. 128p. 1991. pap. 11.95 (*0-8092-3973-6*, 397360, Contemporary Bks) NTC Contemp Pub Co.

Bluestein, Bernard R. & Hilton, Clifford, eds. Amphoteric Surfactants. LC 82-12999. (Surfactant Science Ser.: No. 12). 351p. reprint ed. pap. 108.90 (*0-8357-4257-1*, 203704600007) Bks Demand.

Bluestein-Davis, Susan, jt. auth. see De Vries, Hilary.

Bluestein, Frayda S. A Legal Guide to Purchasing & Contracting for North Carolina Local Governments. LC 99-185173. (C). 1998. ring bd. 28.00 (*1-56011-330-8*) Institute Government.

Bluestein, Frayda S., jt. auth. see Wicker, Warren J.

Bluestein, Gene. Anglish Yinglish: Yiddish in American Life & Literature. 2nd expanded rev. ed. LC 98-10943. 164p. 1998. pap. 12.00 (*0-8032-6147-0*) U of Nebr Pr.

— Anglish/Yinglish: Yiddish in American Life & Literature. 2nd expanded rev. ed. LC 98-10943. xxxiii, 164p. 1998. text 40.00 (*0-8032-1225-9*) U of Nebr Pr.

— Poplore: Folk & Pop in American Culture. LC 93-43614. 184p. 1994. 35.00 (*0-87023-903-1*); pap. 15.95 (*0-87023-904-X*) U of Mass Pr.

Bluestein, Gene, tr. see Bisberg-Youkelson, Feigl & Youkelson, Rubin, eds.

Bluestein, Howard B. Synoptic-Dynamic Meteorology in Midlatitudes: Observations & Theory of Weather Systems, Vol. 2. (Illus.). 608p. (C). 1993. text 82.00 (*0-19-506268-X*) OUP.

— Synoptic-Dynamic Meteorology in Midlatitudes: Principles of Kinematics & Dynamics, Vol. 1. (Illus.). 448p. (C). 1992. text 77.95 (*0-19-506267-1*) OUP.

— Tornado Alley: Monster Storms of the Great Plains. LC 97-48265. (Illus.). 192p. 1999. 35.00 (*0-19-510552-4*) OUP.

Bluestein, Jane. Mentors, Masters & Mrs. MacGregor: Stories of Teachers Making a Difference. 260p. (Orig.). 1995. 22.00 (*1-55874-336-7*, 3367); pap. 11.95 (*1-55874-337-5*, 3375) Health Comm.

— Parents in a Pressure Cooker: Win-Win Classroom Teachers Workbook. 60p. (Orig.). 1990. pap. 5.00 (*0-935493-25-5*, RRB415) Modern Learn Pr.

— The Parent's Little Book of Lists: Do's & Dont's of Effective Parenting. LC 97-29511. 200p. 1997. pap. 10.95 (*1-55874-512-2*) Health Comm.

— Parents, Teens & Boundaries: How to Draw the Line. 200p. 1993. pap. 8.95 (*1-55874-279-4*) Health Comm.

Bluestein, Jane & Colling, Lynn. Parents in a Pressure Cooker, Parent Workbook: A Guide to Responsible & Loving Parent-Child Relationships. Sklakal, Linda, ed. 60p. 1990. pap. 5.00 (*0-935493-24-7*) Modern Learn Pr.

Bluestein, Jane & Collins, Lynn. Parents in a Pressure Cooker: A Guide to Responsible & Loving Parent-Child Relationships. rev. ed. (Illus.). 181p. 1989. reprint ed. pap. 10.95 (*0-935493-20-4*, RRB 413) Modern Learn Pr.

Bluestein, Jane, et al. Daily Riches: A Gratitude Journal. LC 98-6264. 200p. 1998. pap. text 10.95 (*1-55874-592-0*) Health Comm.

B

Bluestein, Jane, ed. see Gerrard, Tamara L.

Bluestein, Jane E. Rx: Handwriting; An Individualized, Prescriptive System for Painless Managing Handwriting Instruction. (Illus.). 48p. 1983. pap. 8.95 (*0-915817-01-2*) ISS Pubns.

Bluestein, Janet. Being a Successful Teacher. 1988. pap. 28.99 (*0-8224-6791-7*) Fearon Teacher Aids.

Bluestein, Sheldon. Exploring Idaho's High Desert. (Illus.). 176p. (Orig.). 1988. pap. 10.95 (*0-9608120-1-6*) Challenge Exp.

Bluestone & Stool. Earache in Children: A Guide for Parents. (Pediatrics Ser.). (Illus.). 24p. 1995. pap. 2.95 (*1-885274-10-6*) Health InfoNet Inc.

Bluestone, Barbara, tr. see Stangerup, Henrik.

Bluestone, Barry & Bluestone, Irving. Negotiating the Future: A Labor Perspective on American Business. LC 91-59007. 352p. 1994. pap. 13.00 (*0-465-04918-4*, Pub. by Basic) HarpC.

Bluestone, Barry & Ghilarducci, Teresa. Making Work Pay: Wage Insurance for the Working Poor. (Public Policy Briefs Ser.: Vol. 28). (Illus.). 40p. (Orig.). 1996. pap. text 3.00 (*0-941276-20-1*) J Levy.

***Bluestone, Barry & Harrison, Bennett.** Growing Prosperity: Striving for Growth with Equity in the Twenty-First Century. LC 99-46647. 352p. 2000. 24.00 (*0-395-82286-6*) HM.

Bluestone, Barry & Rose, Stephen. The Unmeasured Labor Force. (Public Policy Brief Highlights Ser.: No. 39A). 6p. 1998. pap. write for info. (*0-941276-46-5*) J Levy.

— The Unmeasured Labor Force: The Growth in Work Hours. (Public Policy Brief Ser.: No. 39). (Illus.). 64p. 1998. pap. write for info. (*0-941276-45-7*) J Levy.

***Bluestone, Barry & Stevenson, Mary Huff.** The Boston Renaissance: Race, Space & Economic Changes in an American Metropolis. 430p. 2000. 45.00 (*0-87154-125-4*) Russell Sage.

Bluestone, Barry, et al. Aircraft Industry Dynamics. LC 81-2118. 223p. 1981. 57.95 (*0-86569-053-7*, Auburn Hse) Greenwood.

— Low Wages & the Working Poor. LC 73-620152. (Policy Papers in Human Resources & Industrial Relations Ser.: No. 22). 215p. 1973. pap. 5.00 (*0-87736-127-4*) U of Mich Inst Labor.

***Bluestone, Barry, et al.** The Prosperity Gap: Why Americans Are Falling Behind: A Posterbook. (Illus.). 64p. 1999. pap. 16.95 (*1-56584-479-3*, Pub. by New Press NY) Norton.

Bluestone, Barry, et al. The Retail Revolution: Market Transformation, Investment, & Labor in the Modern Department Store. LC 80-26036. (Illus.). 175p. 1980. 52.95 (*0-86569-052-9*, Auburn Hse) Greenwood.

***Bluestone, Carol.** Washington, D. C. Guidebook for Kids. 7th ed. 64p. (YA). (gr. 4-9). 2000. pap. 8.95 (*0-9601022-5-6*) Noodle Pr.

Bluestone, Carol & Irwin, Susan. Washington, D. C. Guidebook for Kids. rev. ed. LC 87-50322. (Illus.). 64p. (YA). (gr. 4-9). 1995. pap. 7.95 (*0-9601022-4-8*) Noodle Pr.

***Bluestone, Charles D.** Conquering Otitis Media. 90p. 1999. 9.95 (*1-896998-05-4*, Empowering Pr) Decker.

— The Eustachian Tube: Structure, Function, & Role in the Middle Ear. 240p. 2000. boxed set 129.00 (*1-55009-066-6*) DEKR.

Bluestone, Charles D. & Klein, Jerome O. Otitis Media in Infants & Children. 2nd ed. LC 93-40646. (Illus.). 310p. 1994. text 69.00 (*0-7216-4818-5*, W B Saunders Co) Harcrt Hlth Sci Grp.

Bluestone, Charles D. & Stool, Sylvan E. Atlas of Pediatric Otolaryngology. LC 93-40737. (Illus.). 1994. text. write for info. (*0-7216-3711-6*, W B Saunders Co) Harcrt Hlth Sci Grp.

Bluestone, Charles D., et al. Pediatric Otoloaryngology, 2 vols., Set. 3rd ed. LC 95-17701. (Illus.). 1504p. 1995. text 350.00 (*0-7216-5246-8*, W B Saunders Co) Harcrt Hlth Sci Grp.

Bluestone, Charles D., jt. auth. see Rosenfeld, Richard M.

Bluestone, Daniel. Constructing Chicago. (Illus.). 288p. (C). 1991. 50.00 (*0-300-04848-3*) Yale U Pr.

— Constructing Chicago. (Illus.). 235p. (C). 1993. pap. 30.00 (*0-300-05750-4*) Yale U Pr.

Bluestone, G. Journeys on Mind Mountain. LC 89-7052. 1990. pap. 7.95 (*0-89087-577-4*) Celestial Arts.

Bluestone, Harry. Easy Solos for Clarinet. 52p. 1989. pap. 6.95 (*0-87166-835-1*, 94197) Mel Bay.

— Easy Solos for Flute. 55p. 1989. pap. 6.95 (*0-87166-834-3*, 94196) Mel Bay.

— Easy Solos for Trumpet. 52p. 1989. pap. 6.95 (*0-87166-833-5*, 94195) Mel Bay.

— Easy Solos for Violin. 52p. 1989. pap. 6.95 (*0-87166-836-X*, 94198) Mel Bay.

Bluestone, Harvey, et al, eds. Psychiatric-Legal Decision Making by the Mental Health Practitioner: The Clinician As de Facto Magistrate. (Publication Series of the Department of Psychiatry Albert Einstein College of Medicine of Yeshiva University: Vol. 9). 310p. 1994. 135.00 (*0-471-00431-6*) Wiley.

Bluestone, Irving, et al, eds. The Aging of the American Work Force: Problems, Programs, Policies. LC 89-5572. (Labor Economics & Policy Ser.). (Illus.). 434p. (C). 1990. pap. text 24.95 (*0-8143-2175-5*) Wayne St U Pr.

Bluestone, Irving, jt. auth. see Bluestone, Barry.

Bluestone, Jeffrey A., ed. Immunology: A University of Chicago Perspective, Vol. 13, No. 4. (Journal Ser.: Vol. 13, No. 4, 1994). (Illus.). 104p. 1995. pap. 36.50 (*3-8055-6142-3*) S Karger.

Bluestone, Max. From Story to Stage: The Dramatic Adaptation of Prose Fiction in the Period of Shakespeare & His Contemporaries. (Studies in English Literature: No. 70). 1974. pap. 52.35 (*90-279-2697-2*) Mouton.

Bluestone, Morton D. & Mautner, Richard. How to Program Computers in COBOL. LC 74-6061. xii, 164 p. 1974. write for info. (*0-02-008080-8*) CMCI.

— How to Program Computers in COBOL. LC 73-19045. xii, 164p. 1974. write for info. (*0-02-511870-6*) Macmillan.

Bluestone, Natalie H. Women & the Ideal Society: Plato's "Republic" & Modern Myths of Gender. LC 87-6002. 248p. (C). 1987. pap. text 17.95 (*0-87023-581-8*); lib. bdg. 32.50 (*0-87023-580-X*) U of Mass Pr.

Bluestone, Natalie H., ed. Double Vision: Perspectives on Gender & the Visual Arts. LC 92-55110. 1995. 49.50 (*0-8386-3540-7*) Fairleigh Dickinson.

Bluestone, Rodney, et al. Straight Talk on Spondylitis. 2nd ed. Swezey, Robert L. et al, eds. LC 92-36216. 1993. write for info. (*1-881941-01-9*) Spondylitis Assn.

Bluestone, Stephen. The Laughing Monkeys of Gravity. LC 94-27079. 63p. 1994. pap. 10.95 (*0-86554-452-2*, MUP/P112) Mercer Univ Pr.

Bluett, Anthony. Ireland in Love. LC 96-140132. 1997. pap. 10.95 (*1-85635-139-4*, Pub. by Mercier Pr) Irish Amer Bk.

— Things Irish: A Compendium of Irish Life. 156p. 1997. pap. 11.95 (*1-85635-079-7*, Pub. by Mercier Pr) Irish Amer Bk.

BlueWolf, James Don. Sitting by His Bones. Greenlee, Carolyn W. & Worley, Daniel, eds. LC 99-24019. (Illus.). 75p. 1999. pap. 12.95 (*1-887400-23-0*, EVB-1019) Earthen Vessel Prodns.

***BlueWolf, James Don & Lupe, Nathan S.** Grandpa Says--Stories for a Seventh Generation. LC 00-35353. 2000. write for info. (*1-887400-24-9*) Earthen Vessel Prodns.

BlueWolf, James Don, ed. see Wing, Thomas W. & Greenlee, Carolyn Wing.

Bluffstone, Randall & Larson, Bruce A., eds. Controlling Pollution in Transition Economies: Theories & Methods. LC 97-25020. (New Horizons in Environmental Economics Ser.). 304p. 1997. 85.00 (*1-85898-452-1*) E Elgar.

Bluger, A. Virology Reviews Vol. 5, Pt. 1: Viral Hepatitis, Vol. 5. (Soviet Medical Reviews Ser.: Section E). 148p. 1992. pap. text 235.00 (*3-7186-5356-7*, Harwood Acad Pubs) Gordon & Breach.

Bluger, Marianne. Gathering Wild. 48p. 1987. pap. 7.50 (*0-919626-35-1*, Pub. by Brick Bks) Genl Dist Srvs.

— On Nights Like This. 40p. 1984. pap. 6.95 (*0-919626-25-4*, Pub. by Brick Bks) Genl Dist Srvs.

— Summer Grass. 80p. 1992. pap. 10.95 (*0-919626-59-9*, Pub. by Brick Bks) Genl Dist Srvs.

Bluh, Bonnie. The Eleanor Roosevelt Girls. LC 98-66696. 225p. 1999. pap. 12.00 (*0-9664820-1-8*, Pub. by LyreBird Bks) IPG Chicago.

Bluhm, Andreas, et al. The Colour of Sculpture: 1840-1910. (Illus.). 280p. 1997. 85.00 (*90-400-9847-6*, Pub. by Waanders) U of Wash Pr.

Bluhm, Annika, compiled by. The Methuen Audition Book for Women. 101p. (Orig.). (C). 1990. pap. 11.95 (*0-413-61300-3*, A0405, Methuen Drama) Methn.

Bluhm, Annika, ed. The Methuen Audition Book for Men. 100p. (Orig.). (C). 1990. pap. 11.95 (*0-413-62300-9*, A0404, Methuen Drama) Methn.

Bluhm, Jeremy S., jt. auth. see Roberts, Marc J.

Bluhm, Lothar. Die Bruder Grimm und der Beginn der Deutschen Philologie. (Spolia Berolinensia Ser.: Bd. 11). (Illus.). 420p. 1997. 80.00 (*3-615-00187-7*, Pub. by Weidmann) Lubrecht & Cramer.

— Grimm-Philologie. (GER.). xi, 198p. 1995. write for info. (*3-487-09860-1*) G Olms Pubs.

Bluhm, Raymond K., Jr. & Motley, James B. The Soldier's Guidebook. 2nd rev. ed. (Association of the U. S. Army Book Ser.). (Illus.). 424p. 1999. 24.95 (*1-57488-070-5*); pap. 7.20 (*1-57488-081-0*) Brasseys.

Bluhm, Raymond K., jt. auth. see Motley, James B.

Bluhm, William. Building an Austrian Nation: The Political Integration of a Western State. LC 72-91288. 278p. reprint ed. pap. 86.20 (*0-8357-7463-5*, 202198100024) Bks Demand.

Bluhm, William F., ed. Group Insurance. 2nd ed. LC 92-31337. 887p. (C). 1996. text 84.00 (*1-56698-244-8*) Actex Pubns.

Bluhm, William J., et al. Science Methods for Elementary & Middle School Teachers. 1995. spiral bd. 24.40 (*0-87563-579-2*) Stipes.

Bluhm, William T. Force or Freedom? The Paradox in Modern Political Thought. LC 83-51293. 339p. reprint ed. pap. 105.10 (*0-7837-3285-6*, 205768700006) Bks Demand.

Blum. The Book of Runes: Tenth Anniversary Edition. 10th ed. 1993. text 19.95 (*0-312-10819-2*) St Martin.

— Debit/Credit Law. 592p. (C). 1993. 25.95 (*0-316-10143-5*, Aspen Law & Bus) Aspen Pub.

— Everyday Fashions of the Twenties as Pictured in Sears & Other Catalogs. (Illus.). 156p. pap. 12.95 (*0-486-24134-3*) Dover.

***Blum.** Man Who Called It Love. 2000. pap. 27.00 (*0-7382-0278-9*, Pub. by Perseus Pubng) HarpC.

Blum. Mathamusements. LC 98-7678. 1998. pap. 5.95 (*0-8069-9784-2*) Sterling.

— Psychobiology of Alcohol. (Substance & Alcohol Actions & Misuse). 1983. pap. 46.00 (*0-08-030949-6*, Pergamon Pr) Elsevier.

Blum, et al, eds. Pharmaceuticals & Health Policy: International Perspectives on Provision & Control of Medicines. LC 80-26498. 387p. 1981. 44.50 (*0-8419-0682-3*) Holmes & Meier.

Blum & Manzo. Neurotoxicology. (Drug & Chemical Toxicology Ser.: Vol. 3). (Illus.). 704p. 1985. text 255.00 (*0-8247-7283-0*) Dekker.

Blum, A. E., jt. ed. see Nagy, K. R.

Blum, A. L., et al. Almanach des Dyspepsies. LC 92-28887. 1992. 57.95 (*0-387-55674-5*) Spr-Verlag.

Blum, Abraham. Plant Breeding for Stress Environments. LC 87-23855. 208p. 1988. 135.00 (*0-8493-6388-8*, SB123, CRC Reprint) Franklin.

Blum, Adam. Active X Web Programming: ISAPI, Controls, & Scripting. LC 96-44768. 402p. 1996. pap. 24.95 (*0-471-16177-2*) Wiley.

— Building Business Web Sites. 89p. 1995. pap. 39.95 incl. cd-rom (*1-55828-431-1*) IDG Bks.

— Neural Networks Programming in C++ An Object-Oriented Framework for Building Connectionist Systems. Ep. 1992. pap. 34.95 (*0-471-55202-X*) Wiley.

— Neural Networks Programming in C++ An Object-Oriented Framework for Building Connectionist Systems. 224p. 1992. pap., pap. text 69.90 incl. disk (*0-471-55201-1*) Wiley.

— Neural Networks in C++ An Object-Oriented Framework for Building Connectionist Systems. LC 91-39648. 224p. 1992. pap. 34.95 (*0-471-53847-7*) Wiley.

Blum, Alan & McHugh, Peter, eds. Friends, Enemies & Strangers: Theorizing in Art, Science & Everyday Life. LC 79-11397. (Modern Sociology Ser.). 232p. 1979. text 73.25 (*0-89391-007-4*) Ablx Pub.

Blum, Albert. Government-Sponsored Manpower Research: Its History & Implications. (Working Paper Ser.: No. 3). 48p. 1976. pap. 2.50 (*0-89940-510-X*) LBJ Sch Pub Aff.

Blum, Albert A. The Arts: Years of Development, Time of Decision. (Symposia Ser.). 142p. 1976. pap. 3.50 (*0-89940-403-0*) LBJ Sch Pub Aff.

Blum, Albert A., ed. International Handbook of Industrial Relations: Contemporary Developments & Research. LC 79-8586. (Illus.). 698p. 1981. lib. bdg. 145.00 (*0-313-21303-8*, BLH/, Greenwood Pr) Greenwood.

Blum, Albert A., jt. ed. see Form, William H.

Blum, Albert A., jt. ed. see Rahim, M. Afzalur.

Blum, Andre. The Origin & Early History of Engraving in France. LC 77-73881. (Illus.). 1978. reprint ed. lib. bdg. 60.00 (*0-87817-216-5*) Hacker.

Blum, Ann, et al. An Introduction to Law in Georgia. 3rd ed. LC 97-26306. (Illus.). 313p. (YA). 1998. text 24.45 (*0-89854-187-5*) U of GA Inst Govt.

— Using Law-Related Education in Georgia Studies Curriculum Supplement. LC 93-31320. 290p. 1993. ring bd. 22.50 (*0-89854-169-7*) U of GA Inst Govt.

Blum, Arlene. Annapurna: A Woman's Place. 20th ed. 1998. pap. 16.00 (*1-57805-022-7*, Pub. by Sierra) Random.

Blum, Arthur, jt. auth. see Biegel, David E.

Blum, Arthur, jt. ed. see Biegel, David E.

Blum, B., et al, eds. Sensory to Motor Transformation: Pre-Motor Mechanisms. (Journal: Brains, Behavior & Evolution: Vol. 33, Nos. 2-3, 1989). (Illus.). 136p. 1989. pap. 81.75 (*3-8055-5061-8*) S Karger.

Blum, B. I., jt. auth. see Timmers, T.

Blum, Barbara L. Psychological Aspects of Pregnancy, Birthing, & Bonding. LC 80-14227. (New Directions in Psychotherapy Ser.: Vol. IV). 380p. 1980. 49.00 (*0-87705-210-7*, Kluwer Acad Hman Sci) Kluwer Academic.

Blum, Barry, jt. auth. see Blum, Gloria.

Blum, Bernard, tr. I Was Born in a Siberian Prison. 176p. 1999. pap. text 14.95 (*1-886388-06-7*, Pub. by Flower Valley Pr) LPC InBook.

Blum, Bill. The Face of Justice. 384p. 1998. mass mkt. 6.99 (*0-451-40803-9*, Onyx) NAL.

— The Face of Justice. 1999. pap. 19.95 (*0-525-93906-7*) NAL.

— Prejudicial Error. 368p. 1996. mass mkt. 5.99 (*0-451-18309-6*, Sig) NAL.

Blum, Brian A. Bankruptcy & Debtor, Creditor: Examples & Explanations. 2nd ed. LC 98-55955. 576p. 1999. pap. text 33.95 (*0-7355-0032-0*) Panel Pubs.

— Contracts: Examples & Explanations. LC 97-48593. 772p. 1998. pap. text 32.00 (*1-56706-634-8*) Panel Pubs.

— Mechanics & Construction Liens in Alaska, Oregon & Washington. 510p. 1993. ring bd. 75.00 (*0-409-20008-5*, MICHIE) LEXIS Pub.

— Mechanics & Construction Liens in Alaska, Oregon & Washington. 1994. suppl. ed. 57.50 (*0-685-73841-8*, MICHIE) LEXIS Pub.

— Oregon Debtor-Creditor Law. 2nd ed. 570p. 1992. ring bd. 95.00 (*0-88063-996-2*, MICHIE) LEXIS Pub.

Blum, Bruce I. Beyond Programming: To a New Era of Design. (Johns Hopkins Applied Physics Laboratory Series in Science & Engineering). (Illus.). 448p. 1996. text 45.00 (*0-19-509160-4*) OUP.

Blum, Bruce I. Software Engineering: A Holistic View. (Johns Hopkins Applied Physics Laboratory Series in Science & Engineering). (Illus.). 608p. (C). 1992. text 71.00 (*0-19-507159-X*) OUP.

Blum, Bruce I. & Duncan, Karen. History of Medical Informatics. (ACM Press History Ser.). (Illus.). 496p. (C). 1990. 58.95 (*0-201-50128-7*) Addison-Wesley.

Blum, Bruce I., ed. see Kuperman, G. J., et al.

Blum, Carol. Rousseau & the Republic of Virtue: The Language of Politics in the French Revolution. 1989. pap. text 16.95 (*0-8014-9557-1*) Cornell U Pr.

Blum, Cinzia, et al. La Futurista: Benedetta Cappa Marinetti. LC 98-71577. (Illus.). 64p. 1998. pap. 30.00 (*1-58442-019-7*) Galleries at Moore.

Blum, Cinzia S. The Other Modernism: F. T. Marinetti's Futurist Fiction of Power. LC 96-3604. (Illus.). 250p. (C). 1996. 50.00 (*0-520-20048-9*, Pub. by U CA Pr); pap. 17.95 (*0-520-20049-7*, Pub. by U CA Pr) Cal Prin Full Svc.

Blum-Condon & Gasparis. Pediatric Nursing. LC 91-5214. (Nursetest: A Review Ser.). 384p. 1991. pap. 21.95 (*0-87434-305-4*) Springhouse Corp.

Blum, D. Steven. Walter Lippmann: Cosmopolitanism in the Century of Total War. LC 84-7041. 208p. 1984. 37.50 (*0-8014-1676-0*) Cornell U Pr.

Blum, Daniel. Screen World, 10 vols. 1949, 1951-1959, Set. LC 70-84068. (Illus.). 1969. 200.00 (*0-8196-0255-8*) Biblo.

Blum, Daniel J. Understanding Active Directory Services. LC 99-23386. (Strategic Technologies Ser.). 1999. pap. text 24.99 (*1-57231-721-3*) Microsoft.

Blum, Daniel J. & Litwack, David M. The E-Mail Frontier: Emerging Markets & Evolving Technologies. (Illus.). 496p. (C). 1994. 49.95 (*0-201-56860-8*) Addison-Wesley.

Blum, David. The Art of Quartet Playing: The Guarneri Quartet in Conversation with David Blum. LC 86-479677. (Illus.). 246p. 1987. pap. text 16.95 (*0-8014-9456-7*) Cornell U Pr.

— Casals & the Art of Interpretation. LC 77-1444. 1996. pap. 17.95 (*0-520-04032-5*, Pub. by U CA Pr) Cal Prin Full Svc.

***Blum, David.** Quintet: Five Journeys Toward Musical Fulfillment. LC 99-47562. 208p. 1999. 25.00 (*0-8014-3731-8*) Cornell U Pr.

Blum, David Y. Managing by the Law of the Sphere: How to Organize a Business for Maximum Profitability. (Illus.). 134p. 1999. 17.95 (*1-58244-014-X*) Rutledge Bks.

Blum, Deborah. The Monkey Wars. (Illus.). 334p. 1995. pap. 14.95 (*0-19-510109-X*) OUP.

— Sex on the Brain: The Biological Differences Between Men & Women. LC 96-52034. 352p. 1998. pap. 13.95 (*0-14-026348-9*) Viking Penguin.

Blum, Deborah & Knudson, Mary, eds. A Field Guide for Science Writers. LC 96-25466. 304p. 1997. 25.00 (*0-19-510068-9*) OUP.

— A Field Guide for Science Writers. 304p. 1998. reprint ed. pap. 14.95 (*0-19-512494-4*) OUP.

Blum, Dilys, jt. auth. see Philadelphia Museum of Art Staff.

Blum, Dilys E., et al. Best Dressed: Fashion from the Birth of Couture to Today. LC 97-31268. 87p. 1997. pap. 35.00 (*0-87633-118-5*) Phila Mus Art.

Blum, Dilys E., jt. auth. see Philadelphia Museum of Art Staff.

Blum, Dorothy J. School Counselor's Book of Lists. LC 97-31496. 370p. 1997. spiral bd. 32.95 (*0-87628-129-3*) Ctr Appl Res.

Blum, E. B., et al. Micro Bunches Workshop: AIP Conference Proceedings. (AIP Press Conference Proceedings Ser.: No. 367). (Illus.). 536p. 1996. 145.00 (*1-56396-555-0*, CP 367, AIP Pr) Spr-Verlag.

Blum, E. K., et al, eds. Mathematical Studies of Information Processing: Proceedings, International Conference, Kyoto, Japan, August 23-26, 1978. (Lecture Notes in Computer Science Ser.: Vol. 75). 1979. 46.00 (*0-387-09541-1*) Spr-Verlag.

Blum, Edward K. Numerical Analysis & Computation Theory & Practice. LC 79-150574. (Addison-Wesley Series in Mathematics). 624p. reprint ed. pap. 193.50 (*0-608-15178-5*, 205608000046) Bks Demand.

***Blum, Edwin A.** Revelation. LC 98-48092. 1999. pap. text 5.95 (*0-8054-9017-5*) Broadman.

Blum, Eleanor. Basic Books in the Mass Media: An Annotated, Selected Booklist Covering General Communications, Book Publishing, Broadcasting, Editorial Journalism, Film, Magazines, & Advertising. LC 71-151998. 264p. reprint ed. pap. 81.90 (*0-8357-5975-X*, 201905200010) Bks Demand.

— Basic Books in the Mass Media: An Annotated, Selected Booklist Covering General Communications, Book Publishing, Broadcasting, Editorial Journalism, Film, Magazines, & Advertising. 2nd ed. LC 80-11289. 439p. 1980. text 34.95 (*0-252-00814-6*) U of Ill Pr.

Blum, Eleanor & Wilhoit, Frances M. Mass Media Bibliography: An Annotated Guide to Books & Journals for Research & Reference. 352p. 1990. text 49.95 (*0-252-01706-4*) U of Ill Pr.

Blum, Erhard. Studien Zur Komposition des Pentateuch. (Beiheft zur Zeitschrift fuer die Alttestamentliche Wissenschaft Ser.: Band 189). x, 433p. (C). 1990. lib. bdg. 113.85 (*3-11-012027-5*) De Gruyter.

Blum, Ethel. Miami Alive. (SPA.). 1981. pap. 5.95 (*0-935572-06-6*) Alive Pubns.

— Total Traveler by Ship. 12th ed. 476p. 1993. pap. 16.95 (*1-55868-158-2*) Gr Arts Ctr Pub.

— The Total Traveler Guide to Worldwide Cruising. 13th rev. ed. LC 98-65585. Orig. Title: Total Traveler by Ship. 584p. (Orig.). 1998. pap. 24.95 (*0-9663309-0-0*) Onboard Media.

Blum, Eva M. & Blum, Richard H. Alcoholism: Modern Psychological Approaches to Treatment. LC 67-13278. (Jossey-Bass Behavioral Science Ser.). 391p. reprint ed. pap. 121.30 (*0-8357-4967-3*, 203790000009) Bks Demand.

Blum, Evan, jt. auth. see Blum, Leslie.

Blum, Fred. Depth Psychology & the Healing Ministry. (C). 1990. pap. 35.00 (*0-85305-302-2*, Pub. by Arthur James) St Mut.

Blum, Fred H. Toward a Democratic Work Process. LC 73-11840. 229p. 1974. reprint ed. lib. bdg. 15.00 (*0-8371-7063-X*, BLDW, Greenwood Pr) Greenwood.

Blum, George P. The Rise of Fascism in Europe. LC 97-43867. (Greenwood Press Guides to Historic Events of the Twentieth Century Ser.). 232p. 1998. 39.95 (*0-313-29934-X*, Greenwood Pr) Greenwood.

Blum, Gil. Life is for the Living: Recovering & Rebuilding after Spousal Loss: Recovering & Rebuilding After Spousal Loss. LC 98-90344. 1998. pap. text 12.95 (*0-9663921-0-8*) Timed Resources.

Blum, Gloria & Blum, Barry. Feeling Good about Yourself: A Guide for People Working with People Who Have Disabilities or Low Self-Esteem. 3rd rev. ed. 80p. 1986. 9.95 (*0-9615412-0-2*) Feeling Good Assocs.

— I Can Say "No" 22p. 1984. teacher ed. 39.00 (*0-9615412-1-0*) Feeling Good Assocs.

Blum, H. E., et al, eds. Gut & Liver. LC 98-146171. (Falk Symposium Ser.). 448p. 1998. 225.00 (*0-7923-8736-8*) Kluwer Academic.

— Molecular Diagnosis & Gene Therapy: Proceedings of the

An Asterisk (*) at the beginning of an entry indicates that the title is appearing for the first time.

88th Falk Symposium (Part III of the Basel Liver Week), Held in Basel, Switzerland, October 22-23, 1995. LC 96-17381. 160p. 1996. text 88.00 (*0-7923-8702-3*) Kluwer Academic.

Blum, Harold F. Time's Arrow & Evolution. 3rd ed. LC 68-31676. 250p. reprint ed. pap. 77.50 (*0-8357-2786-6*, 203991200014) Bks Demand.

Blum, Harold P. Reconstruction in Psychoanalysis: Childhood Revisited & Recreated. LC 93-38933. 1994. 32.00 (*0-8236-5783-3*) Intl Univs Pr.

Blum, Harold P., ed. Defense & Resistance: Historical Perspectives & Current Concepts. LC 85-18028. 429p. 1985. 65.00 (*0-8236-1157-4*, 01157) Intl Univs Pr.

— Female Psychology: Contemporary Psychoanalytic Views. 454p. 1977. pap. 37.50 (*0-8236-1901-X*) Intl Univs Pr.

— Psychoanalytic Explorations of Technique: Discourse on the Theory of Therapy. LC 79-22349. 468p. 1980. 70.00 (*0-8236-5053-7*) Intl Univs Pr.

Blum, Harold P., et al, eds. Fantasy, Myth, & Reality: Essays in Honor of Jacob A. Arlow. LC 88-12766. 520p. 1988. 75.00 (*0-8236-1887-0*, BN 01887) Intl Univs Pr.

— The Psychoanalytic Core: Essays in Honor of Leo Rangell, M. D. LC 89-36104. 550p. 1989. 70.00 (*0-8236-4409-X*) Intl Univs Pr.

Blum, Herwig. Die Antike Mnemotechnik. (GER.). 219p. 1970. 40.00 (*0-318-70620-2*) G Olms Pubs.

Blum, Howard. Brigade. 26.00 (*0-06-019486-3*) HarpC.

Blum, Howard. Brigade. 14.00 (*0-06-093283-X*) HarpC.

— Gangland. 2. abr. ed. audio 17.00 (*0-671-88297-X*, Audioworks) S&S Trade.

Blum, Howard. Gangland. Todd, Rebecca, ed. 432p. 1995. reprint ed. per. 6.99 (*0-671-90015-3*) PB.

— The Gold Exodus. 1999. mass mkt. 6.99 (*0-671-02732-8*) PB.

— The Gold of Exodus: The Discovery of the True Mount Sinai. LC 97-33296. 368p. 1998. 24.50 (*0-684-80918-4*) S&S Trade.

— I Pledge Allegiance. 496p. 1989. mass mkt. 6.50 (*0-671-66717-3*) PB.

— I Pledge Allegiance: The True Story of an American Spy Family. (Illus.). 304p. 1987. 17.95 (*0-317-63133-0*) S&S Trade.

— Out There. Rubenstein, Julie, ed. 352p. 1991. reprint ed. mass mkt. 6.99 (*0-671-66261-9*, Pocket Star Bks) PB.

Blum, Ivon B. River of Souls: A Novel of the American Myth. Smith, James C., ed. LC 98-46848. 320p. 1999. 28.95 (*0-86534-281-4*) Sunstone Pr.

Blum, Jack, jt. auth. see Winterowd, W. Ross.

Blum, Jakub & Rich, Vera. The Image of the Jew in Soviet Literature. LC 84-12196. 276p. 1985. 35.00 (*0-88125-062-7*) Ktav.

Blum, James D. Profitable Coexistence: A New Strategy in Foreign Affairs. LC 97-69937. 58p. 1998. 12.95 (*1-887750-74-6*) Rutledge Bks.

Blum, James D., ed. see American Institute of Certified Public Accountants.

Blum, Jared O., ed. Beyond Washington: An Association Guide to Shaping a State Government Affairs Program. 82p. (Orig.). 1990. pap. 24.00 (*0-88034-042-8*) Am Soc Assn Execs.

Blum, Jeanne E. Woman Heal Thyself: An Ancient Healing System for Contemporary Women. LC 94-46764. (Illus.). 192p. 1995. 24.95 (*0-8048-3045-2*) Tuttle Pubng.

— Woman Heal Thyself: An Ancient Healing System for Contemporary Women. rev. ed. LC 96-8886. (Illus.). 328p. 1996. pap. text 16.95 (*0-8048-3101-7*) Tuttle Pubng.

Blum, Jeffrey. Pseudoscience & Mental Ability: The Origins & Fallacies of the IQ Controversy. LC 77-81371. 240p. 1979. pap. 10.00 (*0-85345-496-5*, Pub. by Monthly Rev) NYU Pr.

Blum, Jerome. The End of the Old Order in Rural Europe. LC 77-85530. 523p. reprint ed. pap. 162.20 (*0-7837-1423-8*, 204177800023) Bks Demand.

— Noble Landowners & Agriculture in Austria, 1815-1848: A Study in the Origins of the Peasant Emancipation of 1848. LC 78-64204. (Johns Hopkins University. Studies in Historical & Political Science: Extra Volumes; New Ser.: No. 2 1947). reprint ed. 42.50 (*0-404-61310-1*) AMS Pr.

Blum, John. The National Experience, Vol. 1. 8th ed. (C). 1993. pap. text, student ed. 22.50 (*0-15-500732-7*, Pub. by Harcourt Coll Pubs) Harcourt.

Blum, John B. & Cannon, W. Roger, eds. Multilayer Ceramic Devices. LC 86-32080. (Advances in Ceramics Ser.: No. 19). 240p. reprint ed. pap. 74.40 (*0-7837-1382-7*, 204155800021) Bks Demand.

Blum, John M. The National Experience. 8th ed. (C). 1993. text 75.50 (*0-15-500366-6*, Pub. by Harcourt Coll Pubs) Harcourt.

— The Progressive Presidents: Theodore Roosevelt, Woodrow Wilson, Franklin D. Roosevelt, Lyndon B. Johnson. 224p. (C). 1982. pap. 14.00 (*0-393-00063-X*) Norton.

— Republican Roosevelt. 2nd ed. LC 54-5182. 177p. 1977. pap. 14.95 (*0-674-76302-5*) HUP.

— V Was for Victory: Politics & American Culture During World War II. LC 77-3426. 384p. 1977. pap. 15.00 (*0-15-693628-3*, Harvest Bks) Harcourt.

— Woodrow Wilson Politics. (Library of American Biography). 215p. (C). 1997. pap. 20.20 (*0-673-39321-6*) Addson-Wesley Educ.

— Years of Discord: American Politics & Society, 1961-1974. (Illus.). 608p. 1991. 25.00 (*0-393-02969-7*) Norton.

— Years of Discord: American Politics & Society, 1961-1974. 544p. 1992. pap. 19.95 (*0-393-30910-X*) Norton.

Blum, John M., et al. The National Experience, Pt. 1. 8th ed. (Illus.). 885p. (C). 1993. pap. text 61.00 (*0-15-500730-0*, Pub. by Harcourt Coll Pubs) Harcourt.

— The National Experience: A History of the United States. 7th ed. 920p. (C). 1988. student ed. write for info. (*0-318-64537-8*); write for info. (*0-318-64538-6*); disk. write for info. (*0-318-64539-4*) Harcourt Coll Pubs.

— The National Experience: A History of the United States since 1865, Pt. 2. 7th ed. 560p. (C). 1989. disk. write for info. (*0-318-64536-X*) Harcourt Coll Pubs.

— The National Experience: A History of the United States to 1877, Pt. 1. 7th ed. 450p. (C). 1989. disk. write for info. (*0-318-64531-9*) Harcourt Coll Pubs.

Blum, Jonathan. Seeing I. (Doctor Who Ser.). 1998. pap. 5.95 (*0-563-40586-4*) BBC.

Blum, Joseph J. Introduction to Analog Computation. 175p. (Orig.). (C). 1969. 0.50 (*0-15-541554-9*) Harcourt Coll Pubs.

Blum, Joshua, et al. The United States of Poetry. LC 95-6263. (Illus.). 176p. 1998. 29.95 (*0-8109-3927-4*, Pub. by Abrams) Time Warner.

Blum, Karl. Density Matrix Theory & Applications. LC 81-268. (Physics of Atoms & Molecules Ser.). 230p. 1981. 75.00 (*0-306-40684-5*, Plenum Trade) Perseus Pubng.

— Density Matrix Theory & Applications. 2nd ed. LC 96-21443. (Physics of Atoms & Molecules Ser.). (Illus.). 319p. (C). 1996. text 107.00 (*0-306-45341-X*, Kluwer Plenum) Kluwer Academic.

***Blum, Kenneth.** Black Ink/The Book. (Illus.). 280p. 1998. reprint ed. 95.00 (*0-9675181-0-5*) Butrfly Pub OH.

Blum, Kenneth. Disease "Precept" of "The Reward Deficiency Syndrome" A Biogenic Model. 1996. pap. text 24.95 (*0-89876-232-4*) Gardner Pr.

— Handbook of Abusable Drugs. (Illus.). 721p. 1996. pap. text, suppl. ed. 69.95 (*0-89876-196-4*) Gardner Pr.

— Handbook of Abusable Drugs. 1996. pap. text 79.95 (*0-89876-227-8*) Gardner Pr.

Blum, Kenneth, et al, eds. Handbook of Psychiatric Genetics. LC 96-19053. 512p. 1996. boxed set 139.95 (*0-8493-4486-7*) CRC Pr.

Blum, Kenneth & Payne, James E. Alcohol & the Addictive Brain: New Hope for Alcoholics from Biogenetic Research. 300p. 1991. 29.95 (*0-02-903701-8*) Free Pr.

Blum, Kenneth, et al. Steroid Receptors & Disease: Cancer, Autoimmune, Bone & Circulatory Disorders. Sheridan, Peter J. & Trachtenberg, Michael C., eds. 672p. 1988. text 195.00 (*0-8247-7954-1*) Dekker.

Blum, Kenneth, jt. auth. see Miller, Dave.

Blum, Kristen Raub. The Greater Evergreen Area Guide: Including the Communities: Bailey, Conifer, Evergreen, Genesee, Indian Hills, Kittredge, Lookout Mountain, Morrison, & Pine. Wagers, Tracy, ed. LC 98-96544. (Illus.). 192p. 1999. pap. 14.95 (*0-9667085-0-4*) Wanderlust.

Blum-Kulka, Shoshana. Dinner Talk: Cultural Patterns of Sociability & Socialization in Family Discourse. LC 96-46362. 288p. 1997. 69.95 (*0-8058-1775-1*) L Erlbaum Assocs.

— Dinner Talk: Cultural Patterns of Sociability & Socialization in Family Discourse. LC 96-46362. 288p. 1997. pap. 34.50 (*0-8058-1776-X*) L Erlbaum Assocs.

Blum-Kulka, Shoshana, et al, eds. Cross-Cultural Pragmatics - Requests & Apologies. LC 88-22176. (Advances in Discourse Processes Ser.: Vol. 31). 320p. (C). 1989. text 78.50 (*0-89391-513-0*) Ablx Pub.

Blum-Kulka, Shoshana, jt. ed. see Kasper, Gabriele.

Blum, L. & Malik, F. B. Condensed Matter Theories, Vol. 8. (Illus.). 694p. (C). 1993. text 179.50 (*0-306-44405-4*, Kluwer Plenum) Kluwer Academic.

Blum, L., et al. Community Assessment of Natural Food Sources of Vitamin A. LC 97-900050. 220p. 1997. pap. 20.00 (*0-88936-767-1*, Pub. by IDRC Bks) Stylus Pub VA.

Blum, L., jt. ed. see Halley, J. W.

Blum, Laura & Rubin, Barry. The May 1983 Agreement over Lebanon. (Pew Case Studies in International Affairs). 50p. (C). 1992. pap. text 3.50 (*1-56927-312-X*) Geo U Inst Dplmcy.

***Blum, Laurence.** Force under Pressure: How Police Officers Cope with Stress. 192p. 2000. pap. 20.00 (*1-930051-12-3*) Lantern Bks.

Blum, Laurie. The Complete Guide to Getting a Grant: How to Turn Your Ideas into Dollars. rev. ed. LC 96-16543. 368p. 1996. 29.95 (*0-471-15509-8*) Wiley.

— Financial Resources for Older Americans: Funding & Support Services for Caregivers. 544p. 1994. 75.00 (*0-8342-0525-4*, 20525) Aspen Pub.

— Free Money & Services for Seniors & Their Families. LC 94-40816. 341p. 1995. pap. 14.95 (*0-471-11489-8*) Wiley.

— Free Money for Athletic Scholarships. 224p. 1995. 35.00 (*0-8050-2659-2*); pap. 14.95 (*0-8050-2660-6*) H Holt & Co.

— Free Money for College. 272p. 1991. reprint ed. pap. 14.95 (*0-8160-2342-5*) Facts on File.

— Free Money for College. 4th ed. LC 96-11496. 240p. 1996. pap. 14.95 (*0-8160-3498-2*) Facts on File.

— Free Money for College. 4th rev. ed. LC 96-11496. 240p. 1996. 27.95 (*0-8160-3497-4*) Facts on File.

— Free Money for College: A Guide to More Than 1,000 Grants & Scholarships for Undergraduate Study. 5th ed. LC 98-39651. 240p. 1999. 25.95 (*0-8160-3947-X*); pap. 14.95 (*0-8160-3948-8*) Facts on File.

— Free Money for College: A Guide to More Than 1,000 Grants & Scholarships for Undergraduates. rev. ed. LC 92-10053. 1992. pap. 14.95 (*0-8160-2850-8*) Facts on File.

— Free Money for College: A Guide to More Than 1,000 Grants & Scholarships for Undergraduates. 3rd ed. LC 93-45553. 272p. 1994. 25.95 (*0-8160-3101-0*); pap. 15.95 (*0-8160-3102-9*) Facts on File.

— Free Money for College from the Government. LC 93-13486. (Reference Bks.). 224p. 1995. pap. 14.95 (*0-8050-2662-2*) H Holt & Co.

— Free Money for Diseases of Aging. large type ed. 450p. (Orig.). 1993. lib. bdg. 12.95 (*1-56054-927-0*) Thorndike Pr.

— Free Money for Diseases of Aging. large type ed. 450p. (Orig.). 1992. reprint ed. lib. bdg. 16.95 (*1-56054-473-2*) Thorndike Pr.

— Free Money for Foreign Study. 272p. 1992. reprint ed. pap. 14.95 (*0-8160-2710-2*) Facts on File.

— Free Money for Graduate School. rev. ed. 224p. 1995. 35.00 (*0-8050-2655-X*); pap. 14.95 (*0-8050-2656-8*) H Holt & Co.

— Free Money for Graduate School: A Guide to More Than 1,000 Grants & Scholarships for Graduate Study. 3rd ed. LC 96-35426. 304p. 1996. 29.95 (*0-8160-3562-8*); pap. 15.95 (*0-8160-3563-6*) Facts on File.

***Blum, Laurie.** Free Money for Graduate School: A Guide to More Than 1,000 Grants & Scholarships for Graduate Study. 4th ed. LC 00-26355. (Illus.). 304p. 2000. 53.00 (*0-8160-4278-0*) Facts on File.

— Free Money for Graduate School: A Guide to More Than 1,000 Grants & Scholarships for Graduates. 4th ed. 2000. pap. write for info. (*0-8160-4279-9*) Facts on File.

Blum, Laurie. Free Money for Health Care: A Financial Aid Directory for Patient Care & Patient Services. LC 93-18151. 711p. 1993. 75.00 (*0-8342-0361-8*, 20361) Aspen Pub.

— Free Money for Heart Disease & Cancer Care. large type ed. 450p. (Orig.). 1993. lib. bdg. 11.95 (*1-56054-928-9*) Thorndike Pr.

— Free Money for Heart Disease & Cancer Care. large type ed. 450p. (Orig.). 1992. reprint ed. lib. bdg. 16.95 (*1-56054-472-4*) Thorndike Pr.

— Free Money for People in the Arts. expanded rev. ed. 256p. Date not set. pap. 15.95 (*1-55783-256-0*) Applause Theatre Bk Pubs.

— Free Money for Small Businesses & Entrepreneurs. 4th ed. 293p. 1995. 39.95 (*0-471-10388-8*); pap. 16.95 (*0-471-10387-X*) Wiley.

— Free Money from Colleges & Universities. LC 92-44655. 224p. 1995. 35.00 (*0-8050-2657-6*); pap. 14.95 (*0-8050-2658-4*) H Holt & Co.

— Free Money from the Federal Government for Small Businesses & Entrepreneurs. 2nd ed. 368p. 1996. pap. 18.95 (*0-471-13009-5*) Wiley.

— Free Money When You're Unemployed. 2nd ed. 330p. 1996. pap. 16.95 (*0-471-13011-7*) Wiley.

— How to Invest in Real Estate Using Free Money. LC 90-35675. 296p. 1991. 89.95 (*0-471-52488-3*) Wiley.

***Blum, Laurie.** Pocket Gatronomical Dictionary. 2001. pap. 12.95 (*0-9666899-3-3*) Mariposa Pr NM.

Blum, Laurie. Theplete Guide to Getting a Grant: How to Turn Your Ideas into Dollars. rev. ed. 368p. 1996. pap. 18.95 (*0-471-15508-X*) Wiley.

***Blum, Laurie, et al, eds.** International Yellow Pages: Barcelona/Madrid. 2000. pap. 16.95 (*0-9666899-2-5*) Mariposa Pr NM.

Blum, Lawrence A. Friendship, Altruism & Morality. (International Library of Philosophy). 256p. 1980. pap. 12.95 (*0-7100-9332-2*, Routledge Thoemms) Routledge.

— Moral Perception & Particularity. 285p. (C). 1994. text 69.95 (*0-521-43028-3*) Cambridge U Pr.

Blum, Lawrence A. & Seidler, Victor J. A Truer Liberty: Simone Weil & Marxism. 200p. 1989. pap. 17.95 (*0-415-90195-2*, A3570) Routledge.

— A Truer Liberty: Simone Weil & Marxism. 200p. 1989. 49.50 (*0-415-90046-8*) Routledge.

Blum, Lenore, et al. Complexity & Real Computation. LC 97-22859. 432p. 1997. 39.95 (*0-387-98281-7*) Spr-Verlag.

Blum, Leon. For All Mankind. Pickles, W., tr. 1990. 16.50 (*0-8446-0499-2*) Peter Smith.

— Marriage. Wells, Warre B., tr. from FRE. LC 72-9703. (Illus.). reprint ed. 42.50 (*0-404-57416-5*) AMS Pr.

Blum, Leslie & Blum, Evan. Irreplaceable Artifacts: Decorating the Home with Architectural. LC 97-219240. 1997. 35.00 (*0-517-70486-2*) Random.

Blum, Lila. Tuning in to Spoken Messages. 1990. pap. text 16.31 (*0-8013-0164-5*, 75826) Longman.

***Blum, Linda M.** At the Breast. 296p. 2000. pap. 18.00 (*0-8070-2141-5*) Beacon Pr.

Blum, Linda M. At the Breast: Breastfeeding & Motherhood in the Contemporary United States. LC 98-46108. 304p. 1999. 30.00 (*0-8070-2140-7*) Beacon Pr.

— Between Feminism & Labor: The Significance of the Comparable Worth Movement. LC 90-37561. 215p. 1991. pap. 16.95 (*0-520-07259-6*, Pub. by U CA Pr) Cal Prin Full Svc.

Blum, Loic J. & Coulet, Pierre R., eds. Biosensor Principles & Applications. (Bioprocess Technology Ser.: No. 15). (Illus.). 376p. 1991. text 185.00 (*0-8247-8546-0*) Dekker.

Blum, Lucille H. Reading Between the Lines. LC 79-182040. 183p. 1972. 28.50 (*0-8236-5770-1*); pap. 24.95 (*0-8236-8268-4*, 25770) Intl Univs Pr.

Blum, Lucille H., et al. Rorschach Workbook. rev. ed. LC 74-10227. 193p. 1975. spiral bd. 25.00 (*0-8236-5961-1*) Intl Univs Pr.

***Blum, Marcy.** Wedding Kit for Dummies. (For Dummies Ser.). (Illus.). 384p. 2000. pap. 24.99 incl. cd-rom (*0-7645-5263-5*) IDG Bks.

Blum, Marcy & Kaiser, Laura Fisher. Weddings for Dummies. LC 97-80697. (For Dummies Ser.). (Illus.). 432p. 1997. pap. 19.99 (*0-7645-5055-1*) IDG Bks.

Blum, Mark. Amphibians & Reptiles in 3-D. LC 99-18128. (Illus.). 96p. 1999. 18.95 (*0-8118-2509-4*) Chronicle Bks.

— Beneath the Sea in 3-D. LC 96-27578. (Illus.). 96p. 1997. 18.95 (*0-8118-1412-2*) Chronicle Bks.

— Bugs in 3-D. LC 97-41594. (Illus.). 96p. (J). (gr. 1 up). 1998. 18.95 (*0-8118-1945-0*) Chronicle Bks.

***Blum, Mark Laurence.** The Origins & Development of Pure Land Buddhism: A Study & Translation of Gyonen's Jodo Homon Genrusho. LC 99-49558. (Illus.). 336p. 2000. text 45.00 (*0-19-512524-X*) OUP.

***Blum, Martha.** The Walnut Tree. 316p. 1999. pap. 14.95 (*1-55050-154-2*, Pub. by Coteau) Genl Dist Srvs.

Blum, Matthew S., jt. auth. see Garlock, David C.

Blum, Miriam D. The Silent Speech of Politicians: Body Language in Government. Rathbone, Lee, ed. (Illus.). 128p. (Orig.). 1988. pap. 7.95 (*0-929535-00-6*) Brenner Info Group.

Blum, Murray S. Fundamentals of Insect Physiology. LC 84-26936. 616p. 1985. 160.00 (*0-471-05468-2*) Wiley.

Blum, Murray S., ed. Chemistry & Toxicology of Diverse Classes of Alkaloids. LC 95-80642. (Illus.). 386p. (C). 1996. text 99.50 (*1-880293-06-4*) Alaken.

— The Toxic Action of Marine & Terrestrial Alkaloids. (Illus.). 328p. (C). 1995. text 89.95 (*1-880293-04-8*) Alaken.

Blum, Odette. Addendum to Modern Dance Fundamentals. 74p. 1991. spiral bd. 17.95 (*0-87127-195-8*) Princeton Bk Co.

Blum, Owen, tr. see Peter Damian, St.

Blum, Owen J., tr. see Damian, Peter.

Blum, Owen J., tr. see St. Peter Damien.

Blum, Pamela Z. Early Gothic Saint-Denis: Restorations & Survivals. (C). 1992. 60.00 (*0-520-07371-1*, Pub. by U CA Pr) Cal Prin Full Svc.

— Early Gothic Saint-Denis: Restorations & Survivals. (Illus.). 199p. (C). 1994. pap. 32.50 (*0-520-07373-8*, Pub. by U CA Pr) Cal Prin Full Svc.

Blum, Pamela Z., ed. see Crosby, Sumner M.

Blum, Paul. Surviving & Succeeding in Difficult Classrooms. LC 97-49214. 160p. (C). 1998. pap. 17.99 (*0-415-18523-8*) Routledge.

Blum, Paul C., tr. see Matsumoto, Seicho.

Blum, Paul Von, see Von Blum, Paul.

Blum, Peter. Everybody Counts: A T. A. Self-Help Book for Math Aversion. LC 81-80247. 54p. (Orig.). 1981. pap. 6.95 (*0-9605756-0-X*) Math Counsel Inst.

Blum, Peter, ed. Herzog & De Meuron Zeichnangen Drawings. (Illus.). 416p. 1997. 75.00 (*0-935875-15-8*) P Blum Edit.

Blum, Peter, ed. see Franz, Erich.

Blum, Peter H. Brewed in Detroit: Breweries & Beers since 1830. LC 99-14013. (Illus.). 304p. 1999. 34.95 (*0-8143-2661-7*, Great Lks Bks) Wayne St U Pr.

Blum, Peter J. Model Soldier Manual. (Illus.). (Orig.). 1971. pap. 6.00 (*0-912364-03-3*) Imrie-Risley.

Blum, Ralph. The Book of Runes: A Handbook for the Use of an Ancient & Contemporary Oracle. (Illus.). 112p. (Orig.). 1982. pap. 24.95 (*0-943434-00-9*) Oracle Bks CA.

— Rune Play. 1997. pap. text 10.95 (*0-88079-499-2*, BK96) US Games Syst.

Blum, Ralph, et al. The Serenity Runes. LC 99-168794. 48p. 2000. 19.95 (*0-312-19329-7*, Thomas Dunne) St Martin.

Blum, Ralph H. The Book of Runes: A Handbook for the Use of an Anceint Oracle: The Viking Runes With Stones. 10th anniversary ed. (Illus.). 159p. 1993. text 29.95 (*0-312-09758-1*) St Martin.

— Rune Play. LC 90-36874. 226p. 1991. pap. 12.95 (*0-312-05150-6*) St Martin.

— Runecards, 7 vols. 2nd ed. LC 97-14666. 224p. 1997. text 29.95 (*0-312-16992-2*) St Martin.

— Serenity Runes Kit. 1998. 119.70 (*0-312-19701-2*) St Martin.

Blum, Ralph H. & Loughan, Susan. The Healing Runes: Tools for the Recovery of Body, Mind, Heart, & Soul. 160p. 1995. text 29.95 (*0-312-13507-6*) St Martin.

Blum, Raymond. Math Tricks, Puzzles & Games. LC 93-46750. (Illus.). 128p. (J). 1994. 14.95 (*0-8069-0582-4*) Sterling.

— Math Tricks, Puzzles & Games. (Illus.). 128p. 1995. pap. 5.95 (*0-8069-0583-2*) Sterling.

— Mathamusements. (J). Date not set. 5.95 (*0-8069-3190-6*) Sterling.

— Mathamusements. LC 96-49196. (Illus.). 96p. (J). 1997. 14.95 (*0-8069-9783-4*) Sterling.

— Mathemagic. LC 91-22523. (Illus.). 128p. (YA). (gr. 8 up). 1991. pap. 4.95 (*0-8069-8355-8*) Sterling.

Blum, Renon. California Wax Museum. LC 94-30507. 16p. (J). (gr. 4-8). 1994. pap. 5.00 (*0-88734-518-2*) Players Pr.

Blum, Renon. Explore Your Dream. LC 96-32004. 55p. (Orig.). (J). (gr. k-12). 1996. pap. 6.00 (*0-88734-528-X*) Players Pr.

***Blum, Richard.** The Fat Man Can't Swim. LC 99-65729. 384p. 2000. pap. 16.95 (*0-88739-309-8*) Creat Arts Bk.

— Sendmail for Linux with CD-ROM. LC 99-66163. (Illus.). 544p. 2000. 34.99 (*0-672-31834-2*) Sams.

Blum, Richard & Golitsin, Alexander. The Sacred Athlete: On the Mystical Experience & Dionysios - Its Westernworld Fountainhead. 510p. (Orig.). (C). 1991. pap. text 40.00 (*0-8191-8183-8*); lib. bdg. 59.00 (*0-8191-8182-X*) U Pr of Amer.

Blum, Richard & Heinrichs, LeRoy. Helping Women Keep Well: A Guide to Health Promotion & Illness Prevention for the Health Professional. LC 88-2752. 487p. 1988. text 52.50 (*0-8290-1793-3*) Irvington.

Blum, Richard A. American Film Acting: The Stanislavski Heritage. Kirkpatrick, Diane, ed. LC 84-8778. (Studies in Cinema: No. 28). 131p. 1984. reprint ed. pap. 40.70 (*0-8357-1590-6*, 207062800009) Bks Demand.

B

— Television & Screen Writing: From Concept to Contract. 3rd ed. (Illus.). 272p. 1995. pap. 29.95 (*0-240-80194-6*, Focal) Buttrwrth-Heinemann.

***Blum, Richard A.** Television & Screen Writing: From Concept to Contract. 4th ed. 336p. 2000. pap. 34.95 (*0-240-80397-3*, Focal) Buttrwrth-Heinemann.

Blum, Richard A. Working Actors: The Craft of Television, Film, & Stage Performance. 153p. 1989. pap. text 34.95 (*0-240-80004-4*, Focal) Buttrwrth-Heinemann.

Blum, Richard A. & Lindheim, Richard D. Inside Television Producing. (Illus.). 336p. 1991. 47.95 (*0-240-80019-2*, Focal) Buttrwrth-Heinemann.

Blum, Richard H. Drug Dealers - Taking Action. LC 76-187065. (Jossey-Bass Behavioral Science Ser.). 336p. reprint ed. pap. 104.20 (*0-608-30948-6*, 201385800087) Bks Demand.

— Nausea & Vomiting: New Perspectives & Practical Treatments. 1998. 80.00 (*1-86156-079-6*) Whurr Pub.

— Offshore Haven Banks, Trusts & Companies: The Business of Crime in the Euromarket. LC 83-27059. 310p. 1984. 55.00 (*0-275-91732-0*, C1732, Praeger Pubs) Greenwood.

— Offshore Haven Banks, Trusts & Companies: The Business of Crime in the Euromarket. LC 83-27059. 1984. 29.95 (*0-03-069629-1*) Holt R&W.

Blum, Richard H., et al. The Dream Sellers: Perspectives on Drug Dealers. LC 79-184960. (Jossey-Bass Science Ser.). 406p. reprint ed. pap. 125.90 (*0-8357-9316-8*, 201378900087) Bks Demand.

— Horatio Alger's Children: The Role of the Family in the Origin & Prevention of Drug Risk. LC 72-186580. (Jossey-Bass Behavioral Science Ser.). 345p. reprint ed. 107.00 (*0-8357-9325-7*, 201386000087) Bks Demand.

— Society & Drugs: Social & Cultural Observations. LC 73-75936. (Jossey-Bass Behavioral Science Ser.). 416p. reprint ed. pap. 129.00 (*0-8357-4697-6*, 205235200008) Bks Demand.

— Students & Drugs: College & High School Observations. LC 73-75936. (Jossey-Bass Behavioral Science Ser. & Series in Higher Education). 419p. reprint ed. pap. 129.90 (*0-8357-4968-1*, 203790100009) Bks Demand.

Blum, Richard H., jt. auth. see Blum, Eva M.

Blum, Robert, ed. Cultural Affairs & Foreign Relations. rev. ed. LC 68-20455. 1968. reprint ed. 3.95 (*0-317-02952-5*, C-19557); reprint ed. pap. 2.95 (*0-317-02953-3*) Am Assembly.

Blum, Robert E. & Arter, Judith A., eds. A Handbook for Student Performance Assessment in an Era of Restructuring. LC 96-5657. 802p. 1996. ring bd. 140.00 (*0-87120-267-0*, 196020) ASCD.

Blum, Ronald, jt. auth. see Roller, Duane.

Blum, Rudolf. Kallimachos: The Alexandrian Library & the Origins of Bibliography. Wellisch, Hans H., tr. LC 91-28997. (Studies in Classics). 282p. (C). 1991. 39.95 (*0-299-13170-X*) U of Wis Pr.

Blum, Ruth C. Von, see Von Blum, Ruth C.

Blum, Sandra J. Designing Direct Mail That Sells. LC 98-39467. (Illus.). 144p. 1999. 28.99 (*0-89134-827-1*, North Lght Bks) F & W Pubns Inc.

***Blum, Shane.** Hotel Operations: Theories & Applications. 88p. (C). 2000. spiral bd. 49.95 (*0-7872-7294-9*) Kendall-Hunt.

Blum, Solomon. Labor Economics. LC 79-89719. (American Labor, from Conspiracy to Collective Bargaining Ser., No. 1). 579p. 1977. reprint ed. 33.95 (*0-405-02105-4*) Ayer.

Blum-Spicker, Helen. Helmut Hahn: Textile Art. (Illus.). 224p. 75.00 (*3-925369-35-X*, Pub. by Arnoldsche Art Pubs) Antique Collect.

Blum, Stella. Eighteenth Century French Fashion Plates in Full Color: 64 Engravings from the "Galerie des Modes", 1778-1787. (Antiques Ser.). (Illus.). 79p. (Orig.). 1982. pap. 13.95 (*0-486-24331-1*) Dover.

— Fashions & Costumes from Godey's Lady's Book: Eight Plates in Full Color. (Antiques Series: Costume). (Illus.). 136p. 1985. pap. 9.95 (*0-486-24841-0*) Dover.

— Victorian Fashions & Costumes from Harper's Bazaar, 1898-1967. (Illus.). 320p. (Orig.). 1974. pap. 14.95 (*0-486-22990-4*) Dover.

Blum, Stella, ed. Everyday Fashions of the Thirties As Pictured in Sears Catalogs. (Illus.). 144p. (Orig.). 1986. pap. 11.95 (*0-486-25108-X*) Dover.

— Paris Fashions of the 1890's: A Picture Source Book with 450 Designs, Including 24 in Full Color. (Antiques Ser.). 88p. (Orig.). 1984. pap. 9.95 (*0-486-24534-9*) Dover.

Blum, Stella, ed. see Ackermann, Rudolph.

Blum, Stephen, et al. Ethnomusicology & Modern Music History. 336p. 1990. pap. text 18.95 (*0-252-06343-0*) U of Ill Pr.

Blum, Stephen, jt. ed. see Kartomi, Margaret J.

Blum, Susan. The Ministry of Evangelization. (Ministry Ser.). 80p. (C). 1988. pap. 1.95 (*0-8146-1599-6*) Liturgical Pr.

***Blum, Susan D.** Portraits of "Primitives" Ordering Human Kinds in the Chinese Nation. 256p. 2000. 69.00 (*0-7425-0091-8*); pap. 24.95 (*0-7425-0092-6*) Rowman.

Blum, Terry C. & Roman, Paul M. Cost-Effectiveness & Preventive Implications of Employee Assistance Programs. 45p. (C). 1998. reprint ed. pap. text 15.00 (*0-7881-3897-9*) DIANE Pub.

Blum, U. & Schmid, J., eds. Demographic Processes, Occupation & Technological Change: Symposium Held at the University of Bamberg from the 17th to 18th of November 1989. (Illus.). xii, 123p. 1991. 49.00 (*0-387-91398-X*) Spr-Verlag.

Blum, V. Vertebrate Reproduction. Whittle, A. C., tr. from GER. (Illus.). 400p. 1986. pap. 69.00 (*0-387-16314-X*) Spr-Verlag.

Blum, V. O. Equator: The Story & the Letters. LC 88-50892. 275p. (Orig.). 1989. pap. 7.95 (*0-9620886-0-9*) Times Eagle Bks.

— Sunbelt Stories. LC 94-60575. (Illus.). 150p. (Orig.). 1994. pap. 7.95 (*0-9620886-1-7*) Times Eagle Bks.

Blum, Vicki. The Trouble with Spitt. LC 96-73. 108p. (Orig.). (J). (gr. 4-8). 1996. pap. 5.95 (*1-57345-147-9*) Deseret Bk.

Blum, Virgil C. Catholic Parents--Political Eunuchs. LC 72-89553. (Paperback Ser.). 66p. 1972. pap. text. write for info. (*0-87839-013-8*) North Star.

Blum, Virgil C., ed. see Graham, Robert A. & Lichten, Joseph L.

Blum, Virginia L. Hide & Seek: The Child Between Psychoanalysis & Fiction. LC 94-37896. 304p. 1995. text 39.95 (*0-252-02157-6*); pap. text 17.95 (*0-252-06458-5*) U of Ill Pr.

Blum, Walter & Yerian, C. Theo. Personal Shorthand for the Journalist. 176p. (Orig.). (C). 1980. pap. text 13.95 (*0-89420-214-6*, 242032); audio 237.20 (*0-89420-225-1*, 242000) Natl Book.

Blum, Walter J. & Kalven, Harry. The Uneasy Case for Progressive Taxation. LC HJ2327.U5K3. (Phoenix Bks.: P130). 135p. reprint ed. pap. 41.90 (*0-608-16522-0*, 202676500052) Bks Demand.

Blum, Werner, et al, eds. Gesammelte Werke - Collected Works: Original Scientific Papers - Wissenschaftliche Originalarbeiten. (Series A & B: Pt. 3). 476p. 1993. 185.95 (*0-387-13848-X*) Spr-Verlag.

Blum, Werner & Roland, L. Particle Detection with Drift Chambers. LC 94-32036. 1994. 76.95 (*0-387-58322-X*) Spr-Verlag.

Blum, Werner & Rolandi, L. Particle Detection with Drift Chambers. LC 93-13632. (Illus.). xv, 346p. 1993. 119.00 (*0-387-56425-X*) Spr-Verlag.

— Particle Detection with Drift Chambers. LC 94-32036. 1994. write for info. (*3-540-58322-X*) Spr-Verlag.

Blum, Werner, et al. Modelling, Applications & Applied Problem Solving: Teaching Mathematics in Real Context. 1989. text 59.95 (*0-470-21570-4*) P-H.

Blum, Werner, ed. see Heisenberg, Werner.

Blum, William, Sr. Baylis Family of Virginia: With Supplements on the Chunn, Fawcett, Hawkins & Turner Families & a Baylis Family in England. (Illus.). 669p. 1993. reprint ed. pap. 99.00 (*0-8328-3642-7*); reprint ed. lib. bdg. 109.00 (*0-8328-3641-9*) Higginson Bk Co.

Blum, William. Killing Hope: U. S. Global Interventions since World War II. 500p. 1995. text 39.95 (*1-56751-053-1*) Common Courage.

— Killing Hope: U. S. Global Interventions since World War II. 500p. 1995. pap. text 19.95 (*1-56751-052-3*) Common Courage.

***Blum, William.** Rogue State: A Guide to the World's Only Superpower. LC 00-21558. 2000. pap. 16.95 (*1-56751-194-5*, Pub. by Common Courage); lib. bdg. 29.95 (*1-56751-195-3*, Pub. by Common Courage) Login Brothers Bk Co.

Blum, Yehuda Z. Eroding the United Nations Charter. LC 92-41378. (Law & International Organizations Ser.). 304p. 1993. lib. bdg. 111.00 (*0-7923-2069-7*) Kluwer Academic.

— For Zion's Sake. LC 86-47797. (Illus.). 248p. 1987. 24.50 (*0-8453-4809-4*, Cornwall Bks) Assoc Univ Prs.

***Bluman.** Critical Think Elementary Study Behavior. 80p. 1999. pap., wbk. ed. 18.75 (*0-07-236945-0*) McGraw.

Bluman. Elementary Statistics. 2nd ed. 1994. 44.06 (*0-697-17171-X*); teacher ed. 35.31 (*0-697-17166-3*) McGraw.

— Elementary Statistics. 3rd ed. 1997. pap. 30.00 (*0-256-26927-0*); pap. 82.25 (*0-07-561052-3*) McGraw.

— Elementary Statistics. 4th ed. 2000. 60.74 (*0-07-231694-2*) McGraw.

Bluman, Allan G. Elementary Statistics: A Step by Step Approach. 624p. (C). 1991. text, student ed. 19.38 (*0-697-06980-X*, WCB McGr Hill) McGrw-H Hghr Educ.

— Elementary Statistics: A Step by Step Approach. 624p. (C). 1992. text, student ed. 18.13 (*0-697-16862-X*, WCB McGr Hill) McGrw-H Hghr Educ.

— Elementary Statistics: A Step by Step Approach. 2nd ed. 180p. (C). 1994. student ed., spiral bd. 21.00 (*0-697-17168-X*, WCB McGr Hill); student ed., spiral bd. 22.75 (*0-697-17169-8*, WCB McGr Hill) McGrw-H Hghr Educ.

— Elementary Statistics: A Step by Step Approach. 2nd ed. 704p. (C). 1994. text 64.45 (*0-697-17165-5*, WCB McGr Hill); text, student ed. 23.95 (*0-697-17167-1*, WCB McGr Hill) McGrw-H Hghr Educ.

***Bluman, Allan G.** Elementary Statistics: A Step by Step Approach. 4th ed. LC 00-28272. 2000. write for info. (*0-07-237593-0*) McGraw.

Bluman, Allan G. Elementary Statistics: Critical Thinking Challenges & Data Analysis Projects: A Step by Step Approach. 2nd ed. 80p. (C). 1995. text 26.87 (*0-697-29225-8*, WCB McGr Hill) McGrw-H Hghr Educ.

— Elementary Statistics Stat-Star. 166p. (C). 1992. spiral bd., wbk. ed., lab manual ed. 39.37 (*0-697-17435-2*) Brown & Benchmark.

— Elementary Statistics with Stat-Star. 624p. (C). 1992. pap. text 58.75 incl. 5.25 hd (*0-697-20009-4*) Brown & Benchmark.

Bluman, G. W. Problem Book for First Year Calculus. (Problem Books in Mathematics). (Illus.). 350p. 1984. 69.95 (*0-387-90920-6*) Spr-Verlag.

Bluman, G. W. & Kumei, S. Symmetries & Differential Equations. (Applied Mathematical Sciences Ser.: Vol. 81). (Illus.). xiii, 412p. 1996. 64.95 (*0-387-96996-9*) Spr-Verlag.

Bluman-Robinson. Elementary Statistics. 3rd ed. 1997. student ed. 24.00 (*0-256-26910-6*) McGraw.

***Blumb, Jon, ed.** S. P. Dinsmoor's Garden of Eden & Cabin Home, Lucas, Kansas: A Photographic Portfolio. deluxe ed. (Illus.). 100p. 2000. 600.00 (*0-615-11450-4*) J Blumb.

Blumberg. Bankruptcy: 1994 Supplement. 1994. 90.00 (*0-316-10151-6*, Aspen Law & Bus) Aspen Pub.

— LCG: St Statlaw. 1995. 155.00 (*0-316-09990-2*, Aspen Law & Bus) Aspen Pub.

Blumberg, et al. Supplement to Bankruptcy, 1995: 1995 Supplement. 1995. suppl. ed. 100.00 (*0-316-10189-3*) Little.

Blumberg, A. E., tr. see Schlick, Moritz.

Blumberg, Abraham S., ed. Law & Order: The Scales of Justice. rev. ed. LC 72-87667. 188p. 1970. pap. text 18.95 (*0-87855-543-9*) Transaction Pubs.

Blumberg, Alan F., jt. auth. see Spaulding, Malcolm L.

Blumberg, Arnold. A Carefully Planned Accident: The Italian War of 1859. LC 88-43296. (Illus.). 240p. 1990. 39.50 (*0-945636-07-5*) Susquehanna U Pr.

— The History of Israel. LC 97-45659. (The Greenwood Histories of the Modern Nations Ser.). 264p. 1998. 35.00 (*0-313-30224-3*, Greenwood Pr) Greenwood.

— A View from Jerusalem, 1849-1958: The Consular Diaries of James & Elizabeth Anne Finn. 1990. write for info. (*0-318-66861-0*) Fairleigh Dickinson.

— A View from Jerusalem, 1849-1958: The Consular Diary of James & Elizabeth Anne Finn. (Illus.). 352p. 1970. 45.00 (*0-8386-2271-2*) Fairleigh Dickinson.

— Zion Before Zionism, 1838-1880. LC 85-17287. (Illus.). 250p. reprint ed. pap. 77.50 (*0-608-07593-0*, 205990800010) Bks Demand.

Blumberg, Arnold, ed. Great Leaders, Great Tyrants? Contemporary Views of World Leaders Who Made History. LC 94-16066. 368p. (YA). (gr. 9 up). 1995. 49.95 (*0-313-28751-1*, Greenwood Pr) Greenwood.

Blumberg, Arnold B. Zion Before Zionism: Eighteen Thirty-Eight to Eighteen Eighty. LC 85-17287. (Illus.). 240p. 1985. text 39.95 (*0-8156-2336-4*) Syracuse U Pr.

Blumberg, Arthur. Sensitivity Training: Processes, Problems & Applications. LC 74-157409. (Notes & Essays Ser.: No. 68). 1971. pap. 2.50 (*0-87060-040-0*, NES 68) Syracuse U Cont Ed.

— Supervisors & Teachers: A Private Cold War. 2nd ed. LC 79-89771. 192p. 1980. 36.00 (*0-8211-0133-1*) McCutchan.

Blumberg, Barach S., ed. Hepatitis B & the Prevention of Cancer of the Liver - Selected Publications of Baruch S. Blumberg. 600p. 1997. text 92.00 (*981-02-3217-9*) World Scientific Pub.

Blumberg, Barbara. The New Deal & the Unemployed: The View from New York City. 332p. 1979. 32.50 (*0-685-19073-0*) Bucknell U Pr.

Blumberg, Donald F. Managing Service As a Strategic Profit Center. 232p. 1991. 22.95 (*0-07-006189-0*) McGraw.

Blumberg, Esterita C. Remember the Catskills: Tales by a Recovering Hotelkeeper. LC 96-9570. (Illus.). 293p. 1996. reprint ed. pap. 19.50 (*0-935796-80-0*, 80) Purple Mnt Pr.

Blumberg, Grace Ganz. Community Property in California. 2nd ed. 928p. 1993. 54.00 (*0-316-10107-9*, 01079); teacher ed. write for info. (*0-316-10149-4*, 01494) Aspen Law.

— Community Property in California. 3rd ed. LC 98-55945. 880p. 1999. boxed set 58.00 (*0-7355-0022-3*) Panel Pubs.

Blumberg, Harry & Lewittes, Mordecai H. Modern Hebrew: Ivrit Hayah, Vol. 1. 3rd ed. 449p. 1982. pap. 13.95 (*0-88482-718-6*) Hebrew Pub.

Blumberg, Harry, ed. see Averroes.

Blumberg, Harry, tr. see Averroes.

Blumberg, Herbert H., et al, eds. Small Groups & Social Interaction, Vol. 1. LC 82-8558. 477p. reprint ed. pap. 147.90 (*0-8357-7541-0*, 203626400001) Bks Demand.

— Small Groups & Social Interaction, Vol. 2. LC 82-8558. 609p. reprint ed. pap. 188.80 (*0-8357-7542-9*, 203626400002) Bks Demand.

Blumberg, Herbert H. & French, Christopher C., eds. Peace: Abstracts of Psychological & Behavioral Literature, 1967-1990. (Bibliographies in Psychology Ser.: No. 10). 229p. 1992. pap. text 19.95 (*1-55798-137-X*) Am Psychol.

— The Persian Gulf War: Views from the Social & Behavioral Sciences. 638p. (Orig.). (C). 1993. pap. text 46.50 (*0-8191-9253-8*); lib. bdg. 78.00 (*0-8191-9252-X*) U Pr of Amer.

Blumberg, Herbert H., jt. auth. see Hare, A. Paul.

Blumberg, Jane. Mary Shelley's Early Novels: This Child of Imagination & Misery. LC 92-61803. 269p. 1993. text 27.95 (*0-87745-397-7*) U of Iowa Pr.

Blumberg, Janice R. One Voice: Rabbi Jacob M. Rothschild & the Troubled South. LC 84-22723. (Illus.). xi, 240p. 1985. 19.95 (*0-86554-150-7*, MUP H141) Mercer Univ Pr.

Blumberg, Leda. Breezy. 96p. (J). (gr. 3-7). 1988. pap. 2.50 (*0-380-89942-6*, Avon Bks) Morrow Avon.

Blumberg, Leonard U., et al. Liquor & Poverty: Skid Row As a Human Condition. LC 76-620080. (Monographs: No. 13). 1978. 12.00 (*0-911290-46-X*) Rutgers Ctr Alcohol.

Blumberg-Lorenzana, Shelley, tr. see Weor, Samael A.

Blumberg, Louis & Gottlieb, Robert. War on Waste: Can America Win Its Battle with Garbage? LC 89-11169. (Illus.). 303p. 1989. text 40.00 (*0-933280-92-0*); pap. text 24.95 (*0-933280-91-2*) Island Pr.

Blumberg, Margie. Is There Life after Chocolate? A 1990 Desk Calendar & Recipe Collection. (Illus.). 1989. 10.00 (*0-9624166-0-6*) MB Prodns Inc.

Blumberg, Margie, jt. auth. see Aagesen, Colleen.

Blumberg, Mark. AIDS: The Impact on the Criminal Justice System. 336p. (C). 1990. pap. text 20.60 (*0-675-21183-2*, Merrill Coll) P-H.

Blumberg, Mike, jt. auth. see Blair, Matt.

Blumberg, Morris B. In Soul. LC 84-28229. 1986. pap. 14.95 (*0-87949-258-9*) Ashley Bks.

Blumberg, Nathaniel. The Afternoon of March 30: A Contemporary Historical Novel. LC 84-90141. 378p. 1984. 27.00 (*0-9613338-0-4*) Wood Fire.

Blumberg, P. I. Corporate Group Spec. 1992. boxed set 170.00 (*0-316-10093-5*, Aspen Law & Bus) Aspen Pub.

Blumberg, Paul. The Predatory Society: Deception in the American Marketplace. 272p. 1990. reprint ed. pap. text 19.95 (*0-19-506654-5*) OUP.

Blumberg, Phillip I. Corporate Groups: Procedural Law. 1983. 155.00 (*0-316-10025-0*, Aspen Law & Bus) Aspen Pub.

— The Law of Corporate Groups: Problems in Bankruptcy or Reorganization of Parent & Subsidiary Corporations, Including the Law of Corporate Guarantees. LC 84-81755. 1985. 155.00 (*0-316-10033-1*, Aspen Law & Bus) Aspen Pub.

— The Law of Corporate Groups: Problems in Bankruptcy or Reorganization of Parent & Subsidiary Corporations, Including the Law of Corporate Guaranties. 860p. 1998. boxed set 170.00 (*0-316-10041-2*, Aspen Law & Bus) Aspen Pub.

— The Law of Corporate Groups: Problems of Parent & Subsidiary Corporations under State Statutory Law. (Law of Corporate Groups Ser.). 878p. 1998. boxed set 170.00 (*0-316-10226-1*, 02261) Aspen Law.

— The Law of Corporate Groups: Problems of Parent & Subsidiary Corporations under Statutory Law Specifically Applying Enterprise Principles. (Law of Corporate Groups Ser.). 1090p. boxed set 155.00 (*0-316-10139-7*, 01397) Aspen Law.

— The Law of Corporate Groups: Procedural Problems in the Law of Parent & Subsidiary Corporations. 527p. 1998. boxed set 170.00 (*0-316-10036-6*, Aspen Law & Bus) Aspen Pub.

— The Law of Corporate Groups: Substantive Law. LC 86-80930. (Law of Substantive Groups Ser.). 687p. 1987. 155.00 (*0-316-10038-2*, Aspen Law & Bus) Aspen Pub.

— The Multinational Challenge to Corporation Law: The Search for a New Corporate Personality. LC 92-25046. 336p. 1993. text 70.00 (*0-19-507061-5*) OUP.

— Problems of Parent & Subsidiary Corporations under Statutory Law of General Application. 1168p. 1989. 155.00 (*0-316-10047-1*, Aspen Law & Bus) Aspen Pub.

— Statistical Law Set. 110932p. 1998. boxed set 170.00 (*0-316-10074-9*, Aspen Law & Bus) Aspen Pub.

— Supplement Substant '90. 1990. 40.00 (*0-316-10077-3*, Aspen Law & Bus) Aspen Pub.

— Tort, Contract, & Other Common Law Problems in the Substansive Law of Parent & Subsidiary Corporations. (Law of Corporate Groups Ser.). 816p. 1988. suppl. ed. 30.00 (*0-685-27093-9*, Aspen Law & Bus) Aspen Pub.

— Tort, Contract & Other Common Law Problems in the Substansive Law of Parent & Subsidiary Corporations. 753p. 1998. boxed set 170.00 (*0-316-10055-2*, Aspen Law & Bus) Aspen Pub.

Blumberg, Phillip I. & Strasser, Kurt A. Enterprise Liability in Commercial Relationships: Including Franchising, Licensing, Health Care Enterprises, Successor Liability, Lender Liability, & Inherent Agency. LC 97-38004. (Law of Corporate Groups Ser.). 1998. boxed set 165.00 (*1-56706-627-5*) Aspen Law.

— Problems of Parent & Subsidiary Corporations under Complex Statutory Law Using a Standard of "Control". 1989. write for info. (*0-318-65447-4*, Aspen Law & Bus) Aspen Pub.

Blumberg, Rae L. Women, Development, & the Wealth of Nations: Making the Case for the Gender Variable. (C). 1929. text 30.00 (*0-8133-1098-9*); pap. text 13.95 (*0-8133-1099-7*) Westview.

Blumberg, Rae L., et al, eds. Engendering Wealth & Well-Being: Empowerment for Global Change. (Latin America in Global Perspective Ser.). 311p. (C). 1995. pap. 28.00 (*0-8133-2107-7*, Pub. by Westview) HarpC.

Blumberg, Raphael, tr. see Nachshoni, Yehuda.

Blumberg, Rhoda. Bloomers! LC 92-27154. (Illus.). (J). (gr. k-3). 1996. pap. 5.95 (*0-689-80455-5*) Aladdin.

— Bloomers! LC 92-27154. (Illus.). 32p. (J). (gr. k-5). 1993. lib. bdg. 14.95 (*0-02-711684-0*, Bradbury S&S) S&S Childrens.

Blumberg, Rhoda. Bloomers! LC 92-27154. 1993. 11.15 (*0-606-09088-6*, Pub. by Turtleback) Demco.

Blumberg, Rhoda. Commodore Perry in the Land of the Shogun. LC 84-21800. (Illus.). 128p. (J). (gr. 4 up). 1985. 17.00 (*0-688-03723-2*) Lothrop.

— Full Steam Ahead: The Race to Build a Transcontinental Railroad. LC 94-34979. (Illus.). 160p. (J). (gr. 7 up). 1996. 18.95 (*0-7922-2715-8*, Pub. by Natl Geog) S&S Trade.

— Full Steam Ahead: The Race to Build the Transcontinental Railroad. (J). 1995. 23.00 (*0-689-80320-6*) S&S Bks Yung.

— Incredible Journey of Lewis & Clark. 1995. 15.15 (*0-606-07705-7*, Pub. by Turtleback) Demco.

***Blumberg, Rhoda.** The Incredible Journey of Lewis & Clark. 1999. 23.50 (*0-8446-7030-8*) Peter Smith.

Blumberg, Rhoda. Perry in Toyland. pap. write for info. (*0-688-16678-4*, Wm Morrow) Morrow Avon.

***Blumberg, Rhoda.** Shipwrecked! (J). 2001. lib. bdg. 16.89 (*0-06-029365-9*) Morrow Avon.

— Shipwrecked! 64p. (J). (gr. 3 up). 2001. 16.95 (*0-688-17484-1*, Wm Morrow) Morrow Avon.

Blumberg, Rhoda. What's the Deal? Jefferson, Napoleon & the Louisiana Purchase. (Illus.). 144p. (YA). (gr. 7 up). 1998. 18.95 (*0-7922-7013-4*, T07013C, Pub. by Natl Geog) S&S Trade.

Blumberg, Rhoda L. Civil Rights: The 1960's Freedom Struggle. rev. ed. (Twayne's Social Movements Past & Present Ser.: No. 248). 248p. (C). 1991. 29.95 (*0-8057-9733-5*, Twyne); pap. 20.00 (*0-8057-9734-3*, Twayne) Mac Lib Ref.

An Asterisk (*) at the beginning of an entry indicates that the title is appearing for the first time.

Blumberg, Rhoda L. & Dwarki, Leela. India's Educated Women: Options & Constraints. 172p. 1980. 19.95 (*0-940500-36-1*) Asia Bk Corp.

Blumberg, Rhoda L., jt. ed. see West, Guida.

Blumberg, Rhoda R. The Incredible Journey of Lewis & Clark. LC 87-4235. (Illus.). 144p. (J). (gr. 4-7). 1995. pap. 9.95 (*0-688-14421-7*, Wm Morrow) Morrow Avon.

Blumberg, Sherry H. Rooftop Secrets: And Other Stories of Anti-Semitism. LC 86-1362. (Illus.). 144p. (J). (gr. 7-9). 1987. pap., teacher ed. 5.00 (*0-8074-0326-1*, 201441) UAHC.

Blumberg, Stanley & Owens, Guinn. The Survival Factor. 1998. lib. bdg. write for info. (*1-56723-023-7*) Yestermorrow.

Blumberg, Stephen K. Win-Win Administration. 1983. pap. text 12.95 (*0-913878-26-X*) T Horton & Dghts.

Blumberg, Stephen M. & Baughman, Willis S. Preventing Legal Malpractice: California Case Studies on Legal Malpractice. 200p. (Orig.). (C). 1989. pap. write for info. (*0-318-64461-4*) Lawyers Mutual Insur.

Blume, Bernhard. A Life in Two Worlds: An Experiment in Autobiography. Hannum, Hildegarde, tr. from GER. LC 91-37695. (Literature & the Sciences of Man Ser.: Vol. 3). (Illus.). XII, 240p. 1993. 47.95 (*0-8204-1765-3*) P Lang Pubng.

Blume, C. & Jakob, W. Programming Language for Industrial Robots. rev. ed. (Symbolic Compilation - Artificial Intelligence Ser.). 330p. 1986. 91.00 (*0-387-16319-0*) Spr-Verlag.

Blume, C., et al. Pasro: Pascal & C for Robots. 2nd ed. (Illus.). 240p. 1987. pap. 53.00 (*0-387-18093-1*) Spr-Verlag.

Blume, Clemens. Repertorium Repertorii. 315p. 1971. reprint ed. 80.00 (*3-487-04209-6*) G Olms Pubs.

Blume, Dan. Making It in Radio: Your Future in the Modern Medium. LC 83-71022. (Illus.). 176p. (Orig.). 1983. pap. 9.95 (*0-912349-00-X*) Continent Media.

Blume, Dorothy M., jt. auth. see Cornett, Emily F.

Blume, E. Sue. Secret Survivors: Uncovering Incest & It's Aftereffects in Women. LC 89-34113. 352p. 1991. mass mkt. 5.99 (*0-345-36979-3*) Ballantine Pub Grp.

***Blume, E. Sue.** You're Still Standin' 65p. 2000. pap. 24.95 (*0-9701627-0-7*) Incest.

Blume, F., ed. Musik in Geschichte und Gegenwart: Allegemeine Enzyklopaedie der Musik, 17 vols., Set. write for info. (*3-7618-0641-8*); write for info. (*3-7618-5913-9*) Adlers Foreign Bks.

Blume, Friedrich. Classic & Romantic Music. Norton, M. D., tr. LC 78-77390. (C). 1970. pap. text 14.75 (*0-393-09868-0*) Norton.

— Renaissance & Baroque Music: A Comprehensive Survey. Norton, M. Herter, tr. (Illus.). (Orig.). (C). 1967. pap. text 14.75 (*0-393-09710-2*) Norton.

Blume, Glendon W. & Nicely, Robert F., Jr., eds. A Guide for Reviewing School Mathematics Programs. LC 91-18724. 65p. 1991. pap. 10.95 (*0-87353-334-8*) NCTM.

Blume, Helmut. Color Atlas of the Surface Forms of the Earth. Gardner, Rita & Goudie, Andrew S., eds. Wygrala, Bjorn, tr. from GER. (Illus.). 144p. (C). 1992. 79.00 (*0-674-14306-X*) HUP.

Blume, Henning H., ed. see Midha, Kamal K.

Blume, James D., ed. see Better Homes & Gardens.

***Blume, James M.** Illegal Aliens: Changes in the Process of Denying Aliens Entry into the United States. (Illus.). 109p. (C). 2000. reprint ed. pap. text 20.00 (*0-7881-8595-0*) DIANE Pub.

Blume, Jason. 6 Steps to Songwriting Success: The Comprehensive Guide to Writing & Marketing Hit Songs. LC 99-47003. (Illus.). 288p. 1999. pap. 19.95 (*0-8230-8422-1*) Watsn-Guptill.

Blume, Jim, ed. see Godwin, Sara.

Blume, Jim, ed. see Godwin, Sara & Smith, Linda J.

Blume, John A., as told by. John A. Blume. LC 94-39697. (Connections: The EERI Oral History Ser.). 1994. pap. 15.00 (*0-943198-44-5*) Earthquake Eng.

Blume, Judy. Are You There God? It's Me, Margaret. 149p. (J). (gr. 4-6). pap. 3.50 (*0-8072-1421-3*) Listening Lib.

— Are You There God? It's Me, Margaret. 149p. (YA). (gr. 5 up). pap. 4.99 (*0-8072-1508-2*) Listening Lib.

— Are You There God? It's Me, Margaret. 160p. (J). (gr. 4-6). 2000. 16.00 (*0-689-84158-2*) Atheneum Yung Read.

Blume, Judy. Are You There God? It's Me, Margaret. 160p. (J). (gr. 4-8). 1971. pap. 4.99 (*0-440-40419-3*, YB BDD) BDD Bks Young Read.

— Are You There God? It's Me, Margaret. 160p. (J). (gr. 4-7). 1991. mass mkt. 4.99 (*0-440-90419-6*, YB BDD) BDD Bks Young Read.

— Are You There God? It's Me, Margaret. (Illus.). (J). 1993. mass mkt. 3.99 (*0-440-90047-6*) BDD Bks Young Read.

Blume, Judy. Are You There God? It's Me, Margaret. (J). 1970. 9.60 (*0-606-02123-X*, Pub. by Turtleback) Demco.

— Are You There God? It's Me, Margaret. 2nd ed. LC 90-44484. 160p. (J). (gr. 4-6). 1990. reprint ed. lib. bdg. 16.00 (*0-02-710991-7*, Bradbury S&S) S&S Childrens.

Blume, Judy. Blubber. 153p. (J). (gr. 4-7). 1976. pap. 4.99 (*0-440-40707-9*, YB BDD) BDD Bks Young Read.

— Blubber. LC 73-94116. 160p. (J). (gr. 4-7). 1982. lib. bdg. 16.00 (*0-02-711010-9*, Bradbury S&S) S&S Childrens.

— Blubber. (J). 1974. 9.09 (*0-606-00673-7*, Pub. by Turtleback) Demco.

Blume, Judy. Blubber. unabridged ed. (Soundways to Reading Ser.). (J). (gr. 4-6). 1983. pap. 15.98 incl. audio (*0-8072-1102-8*, SWR32SP) Listening Lib.

— Bubber. 153p. (J). (gr. 4-6). pap. 3.99 (*0-8072-1404-3*) Listening Lib.

Blume, Judy. Deenie. 144p. (YA). (gr. 7 up). 1991. mass mkt. 4.99 (*0-440-93259-9*, LLL BDD) BDD Bks Young Read.

Blume, Judy. Deenie. 143p. (YA). (gr. 7 up). pap. 3.99 (*0-8072-1360-8*) Listening Lib.

Blume, Judy. Deenie. LC 73-80197. 192p. (J). (gr. 6-8). 1982. lib. bdg. 16.00 (*0-02-711020-6*, Bradbury S&S) S&S Childrens.

— Deenie. (J). 1974. 9.60 (*0-606-03014-X*, Pub. by Turtleback) Demco.

— Estas Ahi Dios? Soy Yo, Margaret. Ada, Alma F., tr. LC 83-2730. (SPA.). 160p. (J). (gr. 4-6). 1983. mass mkt. 15.00 (*0-02-710950-X*, Bradbury S&S) S&S Childrens.

— Forever. LC 74-22850. (YA). 1989. per. 6.50 (*0-671-69530-4*) PB.

— Forever. LC 74-28850. 216p. (YA). (gr. 7 up). 1982. lib. bdg. 16.00 (*0-02-711030-3*, Bradbury S&S) S&S Childrens.

Blume, Judy. Forever. (J). 1975. 11.09 (*0-606-01696-1*, Pub. by Turtleback) Demco.

Blume, Judy. Freckle Juice. LC 85-280. (Illus.). 48p. (J). (gr. 1-3). 1978. pap. 4.50 (*0-440-42813-0*, YB BDD) BDD Bks Young Read.

— Freckle Juice. (Illus.). (J). (gr. 4). 1995. 9.00 (*0-395-73238-7*) HM.

Blume, Judy. Freckle Juice. 47p. (J). (gr. 1-3). pap. 4.50 (*0-8072-1330-6*) Listening Lib.

Blume, Judy. Freckle Juice. (J). 1971. 9.19 (*0-606-03017-4*, Pub. by Turtleback) Demco.

— Freckle Juice. large type ed. (Illus.). 50p. (J). (gr. 4). 12.50 (*0-614-20591-3*, L-38179-00 APHB) Am Printing Hse.

— Freckle Juice. LC 85-280. (Illus.). 40p. (J). (gr. 1-3). 1984. reprint ed. text 15.00 (*0-02-711690-5*, Four Winds Pr) S&S Childrens.

— Fudge-a-Mania. LC 90-39627. 160p. (J). (gr. 3-7). 1991. pap. 4.99 (*0-440-40490-8*, YB BDD) BDD Bks Young Read.

— Fudge-a-Mania. LC 90-39627. 128p. (J). (gr. 3-7). 1990. 14.99 (*0-525-44672-9*, Dutton Child) Peng Put Young Read.

— Fudge-a-Mania. (J). 1990. 9.60 (*0-606-00451-3*, Pub. by Turtleback) Demco.

Blume, Judy. Fudge-a-Mania. unabridged ed. (J). (gr. 4-6). 1992. pap. 21.98 incl. audio (*0-8072-7378-3*, YA 841 SP) Listening Lib.

Blume, Judy. Fudge-a-Mania, 3 vols., Set. (J). (gr. 4-7). 1992. boxed set 14.00 (*0-440-36051-X*) Dell.

— Here's to You, Rachel Robinson. 208p. (YA). (gr. 5 up). 1995. mass mkt. 4.99 (*0-440-21974-4*, LLL BDD) BDD Bks Young Read.

— Here's to You, Rachel Robinson. 208p. (J). 1994. pap. 5.50 (*0-440-40946-2*) Dell.

— Here's to You, Rachel Robinson. LC 93-9631. 208p. (YA). (gr. 5 up). 1993. 15.95 (*0-531-06801-3*) Orchard Bks Watts.

Blume, Judy. Here's to You, Rachel Robinson. 1993. 9.60 (*0-606-07004-4*, Pub. by Turtleback) Demco.

Blume, Judy. Iggie's House. 128p. (J). (gr. 3-6). 1975. pap. 4.50 (*0-440-44062-9*, YB BDD) BDD Bks Young Read.

— Iggie's House. LC 70-104340. 128p. (J). (gr. 4-6). 1982. lib. bdg. 16.00 (*0-02-711040-0*, Bradbury S&S) S&S Childrens.

— Iggie's House. (J). 1970. 9.09 (*0-606-03015-8*, Pub. by Turtleback) Demco.

Blume, Judy. Iggie's House, Vol. 1. (J). 1980. 8.95 (*0-87888-017-8*, Bradbury S&S) S&S Childrens.

Blume, Judy. It's Not the End of the World. 176p. (J). (gr. k-6). 1986. pap. 4.99 (*0-440-44158-7*, YB BDD) BDD Bks Young Read.

— It's Not the End of the World. (YA). 1979. mass mkt. 1.95 (*0-553-13628-3*) Bantam.

— It's Not the End of the World. 176p. (YA). (gr. k-6). 1982. mass mkt. 4.99 (*0-440-94140-7*) Dell.

Blume, Judy. It's Not the End of the World. 174p. (YA). (gr. 5 up). pap. 4.50 (*0-8072-1365-9*) Listening Lib.

Blume, Judy. It's Not the End of the World. LC 70-181739. 176p. (J). (gr. 5-7). 1982. lib. bdg. 16.00 (*0-02-711050-8*, Bradbury S&S) S&S Childrens.

— It's Not the End of the World. (J). 1986. 9.60 (*0-606-03964-3*, Pub. by Turtleback) Demco.

— Judy Blume. Incl. Are You There God? It's Me, Margaret. 1983. pap. Blubber. 1983. pap. Otherwise Known As Sheila the Great. 1983. pap. Tales of a Fourth Grade Nothing. 1983. pap. (J). 1983. Set boxed set 13.00 (*0-440-44348-2*) Dell.

— Judy Blume, 4 vols., Set. (J). (gr. 4-7). 1992. boxed set 14.00 (*0-440-36053-6*) Dell.

— Judy Blume: Judy Blume & You, Friends for Life, 4 vols. (J). (gr. 4-7). 1991. boxed set 13.50 (*0-440-36013-7*) Dell.

— Judy Blume Collection, 5 bks., Set. Incl. Are You There God? It's Me, Margaret. 1986. Otherwise Known As Sheila the Great. Starring Sally J. Freedman As Herself. 1986. Tales of a Fourth Grade Nothing. pap. (J). (gr. 3-8). 1986. Set boxed set 16.25 (*0-440-44356-3*) Dell.

— Jugo de Pecas.Tr. of Freckle Juice. (SPA.). (J). 6.95 (*84-372-3050-0*) Santillana.

— Jugo de Pecas.Tr. of Freckle Juice. (SPA.). 1995. pap. text 4.50 (*84-372-1929-9*) Santillana.

— Jugo de Pecas.Tr. of Freckle Juice. 1996. 13.70 (*0-606-10430-5*, Pub. by Turtleback) Demco.

— Just As Long As We're Together. 304p. (J). (gr. k-6). 1988. pap. 5.50 (*0-440-40075-9*, YB BDD) BDD Bks Young Read.

— Just As Long As We're Together. 304p. (YA). (gr. 4-7). 1991. mass mkt. 5.50 (*0-440-21094-1*, YB BDD) BDD Bks Young Read.

Blume, Judy. Just As Long As We're Together. (J). 1987. 10.09 (*0-606-04063-3*, Pub. by Turtleback) Demco.

Blume, Judy. Letters to Judy: What Your Kids Wish They Could Tell You. 320p. 1987. mass mkt. 4.50 (*0-671-62696-5*) PB.

Blume, Judy. Letters to Judy: What Your Kids Wish They Could Tell You. (J). 1987. 9.60 (*0-606-03246-0*, Pub. by Turtleback) Demco.

Blume, Judy. The One in the Middle Is the Green Kangaroo. (Illus.). 48p. (J). (gr. k-2). 1982. pap. 3.99 (*0-440-46731-4*, YB BDD) BDD Bks Young Read.

— The One in the Middle Is the Green Kangaroo. (Illus.). 32p. (J). (ps-3). 1992. pap. 5.99 (*0-440-40668-4*, YB BDD) BDD Bks Young Read.

Blume, Judy. The One in the Middle Is the Green Kangaroo. 39p. (J). (gr. k-3). pap. 3.99 (*0-8072-1337-3*) Listening Lib.

Blume, Judy. The One in the Middle is the Green Kangaroo. 1991. 11.19 (*0-606-00918-3*, Pub. by Turtleback) Demco.

— The One in the Middle Is the Green Kangaroo. 2nd ed. LC 80-29664. (Illus.). 32p. (J). (gr. k-2). 1991. reprint ed. text 16.00 (*0-02-711055-9*, Bradbury S&S) S&S Childrens.

— Otherwise Known As Sheila the Great. 128p. (J). (gr. 4-7). 1976. pap. 4.99 (*0-440-46701-2*, YB BDD) BDD Bks Young Read.

Blume, Judy. Otherwise Known As Sheila the Great. 166p. pap. 4.99 (*0-8072-1497-3*) Listening Lib.

Blume, Judy. Otherwise Known As Sheila the Great. (J). (gr. 3-6). 1972. 15.99 (*0-525-36455-2*, Dutton Child) Peng Put Young Read.

— Otherwise Known As Sheila the Great. (J). 1972. 9.50 (*0-606-00739-3*, Pub. by Turtleback) Demco.

***Blume, Judy.** Otherwise Known as Sheila the Great. (Illus.). (J). (gr. 4-7). 2000. mass mkt. 2.99 (*0-375-80679-2*, Pub. by Random Bks Yng Read) Random.

Blume, Judy. The Pain & the Great One. (Illus.). 32p. (J). (ps-3). 1985. pap. 6.99 (*0-440-40967-5*) Dell.

Blume, Judy. The Pain & the Great One. 28p. (J). (gr. k-3). pap. 5.99 (*0-8072-1265-2*) Listening Lib.

Blume, Judy. The Pain & the Great One. LC 84-11005. (Illus.). 32p. (J). (gr. k-3). 1984. 16.00 (*0-02-711100-8*, Bradbury S&S) S&S Childrens.

— The Pain & the Great One. 1984. 11.19 (*0-606-00365-7*, Pub. by Turtleback) Demco.

— Quiza No Lo Haga. 1992. 16.05 (*0-606-10494-1*, Pub. by Turtleback) Demco.

— Sally J. Freedman. (J). 1996. pap. 5.99 (*0-440-91189-3*) BDD Bks Young Read.

— Sheila la Magnifica. Salazar-Alonso, Olvido, tr.Tr. of Sheila the Great. (SPA.). 151p. (J). (gr. 5-8). 1991 pap. 8.50 (*84-204-4577-0*) Santillana.

— Sheila la Magnifica.Tr. of Sheila the Great. 1988. 15.60 (*0-606-10507-7*, Pub. by Turtleback) Demco.

— Smart Women. 1990. per. 6.50 (*0-671-72758-3*) PB.

— Starring Sally J. Freedman As Herself. 304p. (J). (gr. 4 up). 1986. pap. 4.99 (*0-440-48253-4*, LLL BDD) BDD Bks Young Read.

— Starring Sally J. Freedman As Herself. LC 76-57805. 296p. (J). (gr. 4-7). 1982. lib. bdg. 17.00 (*0-02-711070-2*, Bradbury S&S) S&S Childrens.

***Blume, Judy.** Starring Sally J. Freedman as Herself. (J). (gr. 4-7). 2000. per. 17.99 (*0-689-84089-6*) S&S Trade.

Blume, Judy. Starring Sally J. Freedman as Herself. (YA). 1991. 9.09 (*0-606-01243-5*, Pub. by Turtleback) Demco.

— Summer Sisters: A Novel. LC 98-9911. 416p. 1998. 21.95 (*0-385-32405-7*) Delacorte.

***Blume, Judy.** Summer Sisters: A Novel. 416p. 1999. mass mkt. 7.50 (*0-440-22643-0*) Dell.

— Summer Sisters: A Novel. large type ed. LC 98-25149. 441p. 1998. write for info. (*0-7540-1203-4*) Chivers N Amer.

Blume, Judy. Summer Sisters: A Novel. large type ed. LC 98-25149. 564p. 1998. 30.00 (*0-7862-1536-4*) Thorndike Pr.

— Superfudge. 176p. (J). (gr. 3-7). 1986. pap. 4.99 (*0-440-48433-2*, YB BDD) BDD Bks Young Read.

— Superfudge. (J). 1994. pap. 4.99 (*0-440-91028-5*) BDD Bks Young Read.

— Superfudge. (J). write for info. (*0-318-62400-1*) Dell.

— Superfudge. (J). 1983. pap. write for info. (*0-318-57249-4*) Dell.

Blume, Judy. Superfudge. 166p. (J). (gr. 2-4). pap. 4.99 (*0-8072-1457-4*) Listening Lib.

Blume, Judy. Superfudge. LC 80-10439. 176p. (J). (gr. 4-7). 1980. 14.99 (*0-525-40522-4*, Dutton Child) Peng Put Young Read.

— Superfudge. LC 49-127440. (SPA.). (J). (gr. 4-7). 1996. pap. text 12.95 (*1-56014-665-6*) Santillana.

— Superfudge. (SPA.). (J). (gr. 6-10). 1996. pap. 9.95 (*0-614-20254-X*) Santillana.

— Superfudge. (J). 1980. 9.09 (*0-606-02659-2*, Pub. by Turtleback) Demco.

— Superfudge. (J). 1996. 18.05 (*0-606-10512-3*, Pub. by Turtleback) Demco.

***Blume, Judy.** Superfudge. large type ed. (LRS Large Print Cornerstone Ser.). 216p. (YA). (gr. 5-10). 2000. lib. bdg. 28.95 (*1-58118-061-6*, 23475) LRS.

Blume, Judy. Superfudge. unabridged ed. (J). (gr. 3-5). 1993. pap. 21.98 incl. audio (*0-8072-7407-0*, YA842SP) Listening Lib.

Blume, Judy. Supersheila. 6th ed. 1997. pap. 17.95 (*2-211-01612-X*) Distribks Inc.

Blume, Judy. Tales of a Fourth Grade Nothing. LC 76-171594. (Illus.). 128p. (J). (gr. 3-7). 1976. pap. 4.99 (*0-440-48474-X*, YB BDD) BDD Bks Young Read.

Blume, Judy. Tales of a Fourth Grade Nothing. 120p. (J). (gr. 3-5). pap. 4.99 (*0-8072-1496-5*) Listening Lib.

Blume, Judy. Tales of a Fourth Grade Nothing. LC 70-179050. (Illus.). 128p. (J). (gr. 4-7). 1972. 15.99 (*0-525-40720-0*, Dutton Child) Peng Put Young Read.

— Tales of a Fourth Grade Nothing. (J). 1972. 9.09 (*0-606-02286-4*, Pub. by Turtleback) Demco.

— Tales of a Fourth Grade Nothing. unabridged ed. (J). (gr. 3-6). 1996. 21.98 incl. audio (*0-8072-7760-6*, YA911) Listening Lib.

— Then Again, Maybe I Won't. 128p. (YA). (gr. 6 up). 1975. mass mkt. 4.99 (*0-440-98659-1*, LLL BDD) BDD Bks Young Read.

— Then Again, Maybe I Won't. 176p. (J). (gr. 5-8). 1986. pap. 4.99 (*0-440-48659-9*, YB BDD) BDD Bks Young Read.

Blume, Judy. Then Again, Maybe I Won't. 125p. pap. 3.99 (*0-8072-1445-0*) Listening Lib.

Blume, Judy. Then Again, Maybe I Won't. LC 77-156548. 176p. (J). (gr. 5-7). 1982. mass mkt. 16.00 (*0-02-711090-7*, Bradbury S&S) S&S Childrens.

Blume, Judy. Then Again, Maybe I Won't, Set. unabridged ed. (YA). (gr. 7 up). 1990. pap. 28.98 incl. audio (*0-8072-7306-6*, YA827SP) Listening Lib.

— Then Again, Maybe I Won't: A Novel. (J). 1971. 9.60 (*0-606-05069-8*, Pub. by Turtleback) Demco.

Blume, Judy. Tiger Eyes. 224p. (YA). (gr. 7 up). 1982. mass mkt. 4.99 (*0-440-98469-6*, LLL BDD) BDD Bks Young Read.

— Tiger Eyes. (YA). (gr. 8-12). 14.95 (*0-87888-185-9*, 128826, Bradbury S&S) S&S Childrens.

— Tiger Eyes. LC 81-6152. 256p. (YA). (gr. 7 up). 1982. mass mkt. 16.00 (*0-02-711080-X*, Bradbury S&S) S&S Childrens.

— Tiger Eyes. (J). 1981. 10.09 (*0-606-00712-1*, Pub. by Turtleback) Demco.

Blume, Judy. Wifey. 276p. 1989. per. 6.99 (*0-671-69381-6*) PB.

Blume, Judy, ed. Are You There God? It's Me, Margaret, Set. unabridged ed. (YA). (gr. 5 up). 1997. write for info. incl. audio (*0-8072-7869-6*, YA937CX) Listening Lib.

Blume, Judy, ed. Places I Never Meant to Be: Original Stories by Censored Writers. LC 98-30343. 208p. (YA). (gr. 7 up). 1999. per. 16.95 (*0-689-82034-8*) S&S Bks Yung.

***Blume, Judy, et al.** Author Talk: Conversations with Judy Blume... [et al]. Marcus, Leonard S., ed. & compiled by. by. LC 99-39777. (J). 2000. per. 19.95 (*0-689-81383-X*) S&S Childrens.

— It's Fine to Be Nine. (Illus.). 144p. (J). (gr. 3-6). 2000. pap. 4.99 (*0-590-38604-2*, Little Apple) Scholastic Inc.

— It's Heaven to Be Seven. (Illus.). 128p. (J). (gr. 2-5). 2000. pap. 4.99 (*0-439-11675-9*, Little Apple) Scholastic Inc.

Blume, K. L. Catalogus van Eenige der Merkwaardigste Zoo in- Als Witheemsche Gewassen: Te Winden in's Land Plantentium te Buitenzorg. 1946. pap. 10.00 (*0-934454-20-5*) Lubrecht & Cramer.

Blume, Karin & Pokornik, Brigitte. Circus. (Funny Fingers Ser.). (Illus.). 16p. (J). 1996. 6.95 (*0-7892-0179-8*, Abbeville Kids) Abbeville Pr.

— My New Friends: A Funny Fingers Book. (Funny Fingers Ser.). (Illus.). 16p. (J). (ps-1). 1996. 6.95 (*0-7892-0180-1*, Abbeville Kids) Abbeville Pr.

Blume, Keith. The Presidential Election Show: Campaign '84 & Beyond on the Nightly News. LC 85-13472. 363p. 1985. 39.95 (*0-89789-080-9*, Bergin & Garvey) Greenwood.

Blume, Lawrence E., jt. auth. see Simon, Carl P.

Blume, Mary. A French Affair: The Paris Beat, 1965-1998. LC 99-17142. (Illus.). 304p. 1999. 23.50 (*0-684-86301-4*) S&S Trade.

***Blume, Mary.** French Affair: The Paris Beat, 1965-1998. 2000. pap. 13.00 (*0-452-28203-9*) Penguin Books.

Blume, Randy. Crazy in the Cockpit. LC 98-27419. 256p. 1999. text 21.95 (*0-7894-2572-6*, D K Ink) DK Pub Inc.

Blume, Sheila B. Alcohol/Drug Dependant Women: New Insights into Their Problems, Treatment, & Recovery. 1988. pap. 4.95 (*0-935908-45-5*, 3273, HazeldenJohnson Inst) Hazelden.

— Alcoholism & Depression. 32p. 1984. pap. 3.50 (*0-935908-25-0*, 3256, HazeldenJohnson Inst) Hazelden.

— What You Can Do to Prevent Fetal Alcohol Syndrome: A Professional's Guide. LC 92-15315. 64p. 1992. pap. 7.75 (*1-56246-043-9*, 3133, HazeldenJohnson Inst) Hazelden.

Blume, Simon. Mathematics for Economist Problems. pap. text 0.00 (*0-393-95734-9*) Norton.

Blume, Stuart S. Insight & Industry: On the Dynamics of Technological Change in Medicine. (Inside Technology Ser.). (Illus.). 356p. 1991. 38.50 (*0-262-02332-6*) MIT Pr.

Blume, Stuart S., ed. Perspectives in the Science of Sociology. LC 76-30827. 245p. reprint ed. pap. 69.90 (*0-685-20695-5*, 2030484) Bks Demand.

Blume, Sue E. Secret Survivors. 1998. pap. 12.95 (*0-345-41945-6*) Ballantine Pub Grp.

Blume, U., ed. Hair Research. (Journal: Skin Pharmacology: Vol. 7, No. 1-2, 1994). (Illus.). 108p. 1993. pap. 94.00 (*3-8055-5858-9*) S Karger.

Blume, Warren T. & Kaibara, Masako. Atlas of Adult Electroencephalography. LC 94-31100. (Illus.). 292p. 1994. text 110.00 (*0-7817-0162-7*) Lppncott W & W.

— Atlas of Pediatric Electroencephalography. 2nd ed. LC 98-29865. 1998. 129.00 (*0-7817-1434-6*) Lppncott W & W.

Blumel, R. & Reinhardt, W. P. Chaos in Atomic Physics. (Cambridge Monographs on Atomic, Molecular, & Chemical Physics Ser.: Vol. 10). (Illus.). 341p. (C). 1997. text 85.00 (*0-521-45502-2*) Cambridge U Pr.

Blumen, A., et al, eds. Dynamical Processes in Condensed Molecular Systems. 464p. (C). 1990. text 141.00 (*981-02-0277-6*) World Scientific Pub.

Blumen, A., jt. ed. see Richert, R.

Blumen, Karen. The Friendly Beasts. LC 97-28193. (Illus.). (J). 1997. pap. 6.99 (*0-8066-3330-1*, 9-3330, Augsburg) Augsburg Fortress.

B

— One More River. LC 95-21209. (Illus.). (J). (ps). 1995. pap. 6.99 (*0-8066-2759-X*, 9-2759) Augsburg Fortress.

Blumen, William, ed. Atmospheric Processes over Complex Terrain. (Meteorological Monograph: No. 45). (Illus.). 394p. 1990. 60.00 (*1-878220-01-2*) Am Meteorological.

Blumenaner, Margaret, ed. see Kobett, Beth M. & Stillman, Meg M.

Blumenau, Ralph, tr. see Kotek, Joel.

Blumenberg, Hans. The Genesis of the Copernican World. Wallace, Robert M., tr. from GER. (Studies in Contemporary German Social Thought). 848p. 1989. pap. text 22.00 (*0-262-52144-X*) MIT Pr.

— The Legitimacy of the Modern Age. McCarthy, Tom, ed. Wallace, Robert M., tr. from GER. (German Social Thought Ser.). 728p. 1985. pap. text 32.50 (*0-262-52105-9*) MIT Pr.

— Shipwreck with Spectator: Paradigm of a Metaphor for Existence. (Studies in Contemporary German Social Thought). (Illus.). 112p. 1996. 10.00 (*0-262-02411-X*) MIT Pr.

Blumenberg, M., jt. ed. see Darmon, Michel.

Blumenberg, Werner. Karl Marx: An Illustrated History. (Illus.). 210p. 1998. 25.00 (*1-85984-705-6*, Pub. by Verso) Norton.

***Blumenberg, Werner & Jones, Gareth Stedman.** Karl Marx: An Illustrated History. (Illus.). 210p. 2000. pap. 18.00 (*1-85984-254-2*, Pub. by Verso) Norton.

Blumenbrg & Kury. Herder-Lexikon Psychologie. 2nd ed. (GER.). 239p. 1976. pap. 35.00 (*0-8288-5705-9*, M7451) Fr & Eur.

Blumenfeld, Aaron. The Blues, Boogie & Barrelhouse Piano Workbook. 232p. (YA). pap. 19.95 (*0-943748-56-9*, PF0798) Ekay Music.

— How to Play Blues & Boogie Piano Styles. 176p. 1995. pap. 19.95 (*0-943748-70-4*) Ekay Music.

Blumenfeld, David, jt. ed. see Bell, Linda A.

Blumenfeld, Erwin. Eye to I: The Autobiography of a Photographer. Mitchell, Mike & Murdoch, Brian, trs. LC 98-75140. (Illus.). 384p. 1999. 29.95 (*0-500-01907-X*, Pub. by Thames Hudson) Norton.

Blumenfeld, Esther & Alpern, Lynne. Oh, Lord, It's Monday Again. (Illus.). 128p. 1991. pap. 6.95 (*1-56145-026-X*) Peachtree Pubs.

Blumenfeld, Esther & Alpers, Lynne. The Smile Connection: How to Use Humor in Dealing with People. 300p. 1985. 14.95 (*0-13-525783-2*); pap. 7.95 (*0-13-525775-1*) P-H.

Blumenfeld, Esther, jt. auth. see Alpern, Lynne.

Blumenfeld, Hans. The Modern Metropolis: Its Origins, Growth, Characteristics, & Planning - Selected Essays by Hans Blumenfeld. fac. ed. Spreiregen, Paul D., ed. LC 67-13391. (Illus.). 395p. pap. 122.50 (*0-7837-7547-4*, 204692200005) Bks Demand.

— The Modern Metropolis: Its Origins, Growth, Characteristics, & Planning, Selected Essays. Spreiregen, Paul D., ed. LC 76-31874. 1971. pap. text 15.50 (*0-262-52028-1*) MIT Pr.

Blumenfeld, Hans & Spreiregen, Paul D. Metropolis & Beyond: Selected Essays. LC 78-17955. 436p. reprint ed. pap. 135.20 (*0-608-12411-7*, 205571400032) Bks Demand.

Blumenfeld, Harold, tr. see Praetorius, Michael.

Blumenfeld, Helaine, jt. auth. see Upson, Nicola.

Blumenfeld, J. & Scherr, J., eds. Four in '94: Assessing National Actions to Implement Agenda 21--A Country by Country Progress Report. 230p. 1994. pap. text 15.00 (*0-9644661-0-4*) Earth Summit Watch.

Blumenfeld, Jesmond, ed. South Africa in Crisis. 312p. 1987. lib. bdg. 45.00 (*0-7099-4252-4*, A0408, Pub. by C Helm) Routldge.

Blumenfeld, Jon D. & Laragh, John H. Congestive Heart Failure: Pathophysiology, Diagnosis & Treatment. 215p. 1994. pap. 17.95 (*0-9632400-6-4*) Prof Comms.

Blumenfeld-Kosinski, Renate. Not of Woman Born: Representations of Caesarean Birth in Medieval & Renaissance Culture. LC 89-17421. (Illus.). 216p. 1991. reprint ed. pap. text 14.95 (*0-8014-9974-7*) Cornell U Pr.

— Reading Myth: Classical Mythology & Its Interpretations in Medieval French Literature. LC 97-718. (Figurae Ser.). 322p. 1997. 45.00 (*0-8047-2810-0*) Stanford U Pr.

— The Writings of Margaret of Oingt: Medieval Prioress & Mystic. (Library of Medieval Women). 96p. 1997. 19.95 (*0-85991-442-9*, DS Brewer) Boydell & Brewer.

Blumenfeld-Kosinski, Renate, ed. The Selected Writings of Christine de Pizan: New Translations, Criticism. LC 96-12764. (C). 1997. pap. text 14.75 (*0-393-97010-8*) Norton.

Blumenfeld-Kosinski, Renate & Szell, Timea, eds. Images of Sainthood in Medieval Europe. LC 90-55889. (Illus.). 320p. 1991. text 49.95 (*0-8014-2507-7*); pap. text 17.95 (*0-8014-9745-0*) Cornell U Pr.

Blumenfeld, L. A. Physics of Bioenergetics Processes. Haken, H., ed. (Springer Series in Energetics: Vol. 16). (Illus.). 150p. 1983. 57.95 (*0-387-11417-3*) Spr-Verlag.

Blumenfeld, Lev A. & Tikhonov, Alexander N. Biophysical Thermodynamics of Intracellular Processes: Molecular Machines of the Living Cell. LC 93-35826. (Illus.). 200p. 1994. 79.95 (*0-387-94179-7*) Spr-Verlag.

Blumenfeld, Mark. Conducting an Environmental Audit. (Environmental Audit Handbook Ser.: Vol. 1). 1991. pap. 49.95 (*0-7816-0072-3*) Exec Ent Pubns.

Blumenfeld, Phyllis C. & Anderson, Linda, eds. Teaching Educational Psychology: A Special Issue of Educational Psychologist. 88p. 1996. pap. 20.00 (*0-8058-9920-0*) L Erlbaum Assocs.

Blumenfeld, Robert. Accents: A Manual for Actors. LC 98-19867. 320p. 1998. pap. 22.50 (*0-87910-269-1*) Limelight Edns.

***Blumenfeld, Rodica & Testaferri, Ada.** The Pleasure of Writing: Critical Essays on Dacia Maraini. LC 99-89306. (Studies in Romance Literatures: Vol. 20). 2000. 43.95 (*1-55753-197-8*) Purdue U Pr.

Blumenfeld, Samuel L. Alpha-Phonics: A Primer for Beginning Readers. 8th ed. LC 82-12873. 169p. 1991. reprint ed. pap. 29.95 (*0-941995-00-3*) Paradigm ID.

— Homeschooling: A Parents Guide to Teaching Children. LC 97-17000. 176p. 1997. write for info. (*0-8065-1911-8*) Carol Pub Group.

— Homeschooling: A Parents Guide to Teaching Children. 230p. 1999. reprint ed. 30.95 (*0-7351-0087-X*) Replica Bks.

— How to Tutor. 2nd ed. LC 73-10834. 304p. 1988. pap. 24.95 (*0-941995-01-1*) Paradigm ID.

— How to Tutor Large Size Type Student Lesson Book. 175p. (J). (gr. k-2). 1998. pap. 19.95 (*0-941995-11-9*) Paradigm ID.

— Is Public Education Necessary? 4th ed. LC 85-16721. 263p. 1989. pap. 19.95 (*0-941995-04-6*) Paradigm ID.

— NEA: Trojan Horse in American Education. 7th ed. LC 84-16546. 284p. (Orig.). 1993. pap. 19.95 (*0-941995-07-0*) Paradigm ID.

— The Whole Language/OBE Fraud. LC 95-26059. 351p. (Orig.). 1996. pap. 19.95 (*0-941995-09-7*) Paradigm ID.

Blumenfeld, Samuel L., jt. auth. see Simkus, Barbara.

Blumenfeld, Warren J. AIDS & Your Religious Community: A Hands-On Guide for Local Programs. Alexander, Scott W., ed. 108p. 1994. 15.00 (*1-55896-243-3*, Skinner Hse Bks) Unitarian Univ.

Blumenfeld, Warren J., ed. Homophobia: How We All Pay the Price. LC 91-36287. 324p. 1992. pap. 20.00 (*0-8070-7919-7*) Beacon Pr.

Blumenfeld, Warren J. & Raymond, Diane. Looking at Gay & Lesbian Life. rev. ed. LC 92-30483. 448p. 1992. pap. 19.00 (*0-8070-7923-5*) Beacon Pr.

***Blumenfeld, Yorick.** The Naked & the Veiled: The Photographic Nudes of Erwin Blumenfeld. LC 98-61830. (Illus.). 144p. 1999. 50.00 (*0-500-54230-9*, Pub. by Thames Hudson) Norton.

Blumenfeld, Yorick. Towards the Millennium: Optimistic Visions for Change, 1. 1997. pap. text 25.00 (*0-9531526-0-X*) Chimera Pr.

Blumenfeld, Yorick, ed. Scanning the Future: 20 Eminent Thinkers Write about the World of Tomorrow. LC 98-60037. (Prospects for Tomorrow Ser.). 304p. 1999. pap. 16.95 (*0-500-28045-2*, Pub. by Thames Hudson) Norton.

Blumenfrucht, Israel, et al. HBJ Federal Tax Course, 1990 - 1991. 76p. (C). 1990. pap. text 4.00 (*0-15-535287-3*) Harcourt Coll Pubs.

Blumenhagen, Wilhelm. Wanderungen Durch den Harz. (Malerische und Romantische Deutscheland Ser.: Vol. IV). (GER.). ii, 256p. 1996. reprint ed. 25.00 (*3-487-08049-4*) G Olms Pubs.

Blumenkopf, Todd A., jt. auth. see Woods, Michael.

Blumenreich, Julia. Meeting Tessie. 40p. (Orig.). 1994. pap. 6.00 (*0-935162-14-3*) Singing Horse.

Blumenreich, Patricia E. & Lewis, Susan, eds. Managing the Violent Patient: A Clinician's Guide. LC 93-12563. 176p. 1993. text 24.95 (*0-87630-707-1*) Brunner-Mazel.

Blumenson. Massachusetts Criminal Practice, 2 vols., Vols. 1 & 2. 2nd ed. Incl. Vol. 1. Massachusetts Criminal Practice. 2nd ed. LC 98-89802. 1998. (*0-327-00759-1*); Vol. 2. Massachusetts Criminal Practice. 2nd ed. 1998. (*0-327-00760-5*); LC 98-89802. 1500p. 1998. 195.00 (*0-327-00639-0*, 8145911) LEXIS Pub.

Blumenson, Eric D. Massachusetts Criminal Defense, 2 vols., Set. 1600p. 1993. ring bd., wbk. ed. 140.00 (*0-614-05896-1*, MICHIE) LEXIS Pub.

Blumenson, Eric D. & Fisher, Stanley Z. Massachusetts Criminal Practice, Student Edition 1998. 800p. 1999. write for info. (*0-327-01013-4*, 1062611) LEXIS Pub.

Blumenson, Eric D., et al. Massachusetts Criminal Defense. 270p. 1994. pap., student ed. 45.00 (*0-88063-727-7*, 10626-10, MICHIE) LEXIS Pub.

— Massachusetts Criminal Defense, 2 vols., Set. 1600p. 1990. boxed set 140.00 (*0-88063-202-X*, 81459-10, MICHIE) LEXIS Pub.

Blumenson, John J. Identifying American Architecture. rev. ed. 1990. pap. 12.95 (*0-393-30610-0*) Norton.

— Identifying American Architecture: A Pictorial Guide to Styles & Terms, 1600-1945. LC 95-49370. (American Association for State & Local History Book Ser.). (Illus.). 128p. 1981. reprint ed. pap. 12.95 (*0-7619-9143-3*) AltaMira Pr.

Blumenson, Martin. Anzio: The Gamble That Failed. LC 77-26027. (Great Battles of History). (Illus.). 212p. 1978. reprint ed. lib. bdg. 35.00 (*0-313-20093-9*, BLAN, Greenwood Pr) Greenwood.

— Bloody River: The Real Tragedy of the Rapido. LC 98-19281. (Texas A&M University Military History Ser.: No. 63). (Illus.). 166p. 1998. pap. 14.95 (*0-89096-852-7*) Tex A&M Univ Pr.

***Blumenson, Martin.** The Duel for France 1944: The Men & Battles That Changed the Fate of Europe. 480p. 2000. pap. 18.00 (*0-306-80938-9*) Da Capo.

— Kasserine Pass: Rommel's Bloody, Climactic Battle for Tunisia. (Illus.). 2000. reprint ed. pap. 19.95 (*0-8154-1099-9*, Pub. by Cooper Sq) Natl Bk Netwk.

Blumenson, Martin. Patton: The Man Behind the Legend, 1885-1945. (Illus.). 320p. 1994. pap. 16.00 (*0-688-13795-4*, Quil) HarperTrade.

— The Patton Papers, 1885-1940. (Illus.). 1048p. 1998. reprint ed. pap. 24.50 (*0-306-80862-5*) Da Capo.

— Patton Papers, 1885-1940, Vol. I. (Illus.). 1010p. 1999. reprint ed. lib. bdg. 53.95 (*0-7351-0076-4*) Replica Bks.

— Patton Papers, 1940-1945, Vol. II. 914p. 1999. reprint ed. lib. bdg. 53.95 (*0-7351-0048-9*) Replica Bks.

Blumenson, Martin & Stokesbury, James L. Masters of the Art of Command. (Quality Paperbacks Ser.). (Illus.). 410p. 1990. reprint ed. pap. 14.95 (*0-306-80403-4*) Da Capo.

Blumenson, Martin, ed. see Patton, George S.

Blumenstein, Lili W. Let Him Go! (Illus.). 240p. 1996. 13.00 (*0-8059-3904-0*) Dorrance.

Blumenstock, David I. The Ocean of Air. LC 59-7509. 471p. reprint ed. pap. 146.10 (*0-608-11660-2*, 205047200083) Bks Demand.

Blumenstock, Dorothy, jt. auth. see Lasswell, Harold D.

Blumental, Joshua, ed. see Calderone, Tony.

Blumenthal. Ans Key-alt Tests Eng 3200,4e College Ed. 4th ed. (C). 1994. pap. text 8.50 (*0-15-501785-3*) Harcourt Coll Pubs.

— Answer Key-english 2600,6e (college Ed)+ 6th ed. (C). 1993. pap. text 8.00 (*0-15-500863-3*) Harcourt Coll Pubs.

— Answer Key-english 3200,4e (college Ed)+ 4th ed. (C). 1994. pap. text 8.00 (*0-15-500866-8*) Harcourt.

— Asparas. 1998. 21.95 (*0-684-19179-2*) Simon & Schuster.

— English 2200: Answer Key. 4th ed. (C). 1994. pap. text 8.00 (*0-15-500860-9*, Pub. by Harcourt Coll Pubs) Harcourt.

— English 2600 with Writing Applications: Alternate Tests. 6th ed. (C). 1994. pap. text 15.50 (*0-15-502123-0*, Pub. by Harcourt Coll Pubs) Harcourt.

— English 2600 with Writing Applications: Answer Key to Alternate Tests. 6th ed. (C). 1994. pap. text 8.00 (*0-15-502124-9*, Pub. by Harcourt Coll Pubs) Harcourt.

— English 3200: Alternate Tests. 4th ed. (C). 1994. pap. text 8.00 (*0-15-501784-5*, Pub. by Harcourt Coll Pubs) Harcourt.

— Last Days of the Sicilians. 1994. per. 4.95 (*0-671-89461-7*) PB.

Blumenthal, Aaron H. If I Am Only for Myself: The Story of Hillel. 1973. 3.75 (*0-8381-0219-0*) USCJE.

Blumenthal, Andrea K., jt. auth. see Blumenthal, Jay.

Blumenthal, Anita, jt. auth. see Lindeman, Eric D.

Blumenthal, Arthur L. Language & Psychology: Historical Aspects of Psycholinguistics. LC 80-12611. 262p. 1980. reprint ed. 69.50 (*0-89874-167-X*) Elliots Bks.

Blumenthal, Ben, ed. The All-American Stamp Album. rev. ed. (Illus.). 500p. 1992. 49.95 (*0-912236-34-5*, Minkus Pubns) Novus Debut.

Blumenthal, Betsy & Kreider, Kathryn. Hands on Dyeing. LC 88-12260. (Illus.). 111p. (Orig.). 1988. pap. 12.95 (*0-934026-36-X*) Interweave.

Blumenthal, Bob. Jazz: Photographs of the Masters. LC 95-24546. (Illus.). 252p. 1995. 40.00 (*1-885183-25-9*) Artisan.

Blumenthal, Brad, et al, eds. Human-Computer Interaction: Selected Papers of the Fourth International Conference, EWHCI '94, St. Petersburg, Russia, August 2-5, 1995. (Lecture Notes in Computer Science Ser.: Vol. 876). 1994. write for info. (*0-387-58648-2*); 39.95 (*3-540-58648-2*) Spr-Verlag.

— Human-Computer Interaction: 5th International Conference, EWHCI '95, Moscow, Russia, July 3-7, 1995: Selected Papers. LC 95-46342. (Lecture Notes in Computer Science Ser.: Vol. 1015). 203p. 1995. 43.00 (*3-540-60614-9*) Spr-Verlag.

Blumenthal, Caroline, jt. auth. see Logan, Beatrice.

Blumenthal, Daniel S. & Ruttenber, James, eds. Introduction to Environmental Health. 2nd rev. ed. 392p. (C). 1995. 43.95 (*0-8261-3901-9*) Springer Pub.

Blumenthal, Dannielle. Women & Soap Operas: A Cultural Feminist Perspective. LC 97-18721. 152p. 1997. 49.95 (*0-275-96039-0*, Praeger Pubs) Greenwood.

Blumenthal, David. Understanding Jewish Mysticism: The Philosophic-Mystical Tradition & the Hasidic Tradition, Vol.II. 25.00 (*0-87068-205-9*); pap. 16.95 (*0-87068-225-3*) Ktav.

Blumenthal, David, et al, eds. Renewing the Promise: Medicare & Its Reform. (Illus.). 238p. 1988. text 37.95 (*0-19-504304-9*) OUP.

Blumenthal, David R. The Banality of Good & Evil: Moral Lessons from the Shoah & Jewish Tradition. LC 98-43090. (Moral Traditions & Moral Arguments Ser.). 336p. 1999. pap. 23.95 (*0-87840-715-4*); text 65.00 (*0-87840-714-6*) Georgetown U Pr.

— God at the Center: Meditations on Jewish Spirituality. LC 94-27785. 290p. 1996. pap. 30.00 (*1-56821-348-4*) Aronson.

Blumenthal, David R., ed. And Bring Them Closer to Torah: The Life & Works of Rabbi Aaron H. Blumenthal. 235p. 1986. text 9.95 (*0-88125-082-1*) Ktav.

— Emory Studies on the Holocaust. LC 84-52494. 178p. (Orig.). (C). 1985. pap. 5.00 (*0-912313-01-3*) Witness Holocaust.

Blumenthal, David R. & Hanover, Sue M., eds. Emory Studies on the Holocaust: An Interfaith Inquiry, Vol. 2. LC 84-52494. 205p. (Orig.). 1988. pap. 7.50 (*0-912313-02-1*) Witness Holocaust.

***Blumenthal, Deborah.** Aunt Claire's Yellow Beehive Hair. LC 99-86366. (J). 2001. write for info. (*0-8037-2509-4*, Dial Yng Read) Peng Put Young Read.

Blumenthal, Deborah. The Chocolate-Covered-Cookie Tantrum. (Illus.). 32p. (J). (ps-1). 1996. 15.00 (*0-395-68699-7*, Clarion Bks) HM.

— The Chocolate-Covered-Cookie Tantrum. (Illus.). 32p. (J). (ps-1). 1999. pap. 5.95 (*0-395-70028-0*) HM.

Blumenthal, Eileen & Taymor, Julie. Julie Taymor: Playing with Fire: Theater, Opera, Film. LC 94-48321. (Illus.). 200p. 1995. 49.50 (*0-8109-3879-0*, Pub. by Abrams) Time Warner.

— Julie Taymor: Playing with Fire: Theater, Opera, Film. LC 99-30225. 1999. pap. 35.95 (*1-881390-22-5*) OSU Wexner Ctr.

***Blumenthal, Eileen & Taymor, Julie.** Julie Taymor Updated Edition: Playing with Fire. expanded ed. LC 99-30225. (Illus.). 240p. 1999. 49.50 (*0-8109-3517-1*, Pub. by Abrams) Time Warner.

Blumenthal, Erik. Believeing in Yourself: A Practical Guide to Building Self Confidence. LC 98-187151. 160p. 1997. pap. 10.95 (*1-85168-135-3*, Pub. by Onewrld Pubns) Penguin Putnam.

— Peace with Your Partner: A Practical Guide to Happy Marriage. 160p. 1997. pap. 10.95 (*1-85168-136-1*, Pub. by Onewrld Pubns) Penguin Putnam.

— To Understand & Be Understood. 160p. (Orig.). 1994. pap. 7.50 (*1-85168-004-7*, Pub. by Onewrld Pubns) Penguin Putnam.

— To Understand & Be Understood: A Practical Guide to Successful Relationships. LC 98-28977. 160p. 1998. reprint ed. pap. 12.95 (*1-56838-229-4*) Hazelden.

— The Way to Inner Freedom: A Practical Guide to Personal Development. 144p. (Orig.). 1994. pap. 7.50 (*1-85168-011-X*, Pub. by Onewrld Pubns) Penguin Putnam.

— The Way to Inner Freedom: A Practical Guide to Personal Development. LC 98-28982. 160p. (Orig.). 1998. reprint ed. pap. 12.95 (*1-56838-227-8*) Hazelden.

Blumenthal, Erik & Dreikurs, Rudolf. Friend or Foe: A Practical Guide to Parent-Child Relationships. 1998. pap. 11.95 (*1-85168-159-0*, Pub. by Element MA) Penguin Putnam.

Blumenthal, Gerda. Thresholds: A Study of Proust. 112p. 1984. 13.95 (*0-917786-49-1*) Summa Pubns.

Blumenthal, H. J. Aristotle & Neoplatonism in Late Antiquity: Interpretations of the "De Anima" LC 96-24573. 288p. 1996. text 59.95 (*0-8014-3336-3*) Cornell U Pr.

— Plotinus Psychology: His Doctrines of the Embodied Soul. 170p. 1971. text 65.00 (*90-247-5037-7*) Kluwer Academic.

— Soul & Intellect: Studies in Plotinus & Later Neoplatonism. (Collected Studies: No. CS 426). 352p. 1993. 115.95 (*0-86078-392-8*, Pub. by Variorum) Ashgate Pub Co.

Blumenthal, H. T., ed. The Regulatory Role of the Nervous System in Aging. (Interdisciplinary Topics in Gerontology Ser.: Vol. 7). 1970. 45.25 (*3-8055-0508-6*) S Karger.

Blumenthal, Harriet. Pordage's Mundorum Explicatio. rev. ed. LC 91-31758. (Renaissance Imagination Ser.: No. 2). 688p. 1991. text 20.00 (*0-8153-0451-X*) Garland.

Blumenthal, Henry. American & French Culture, 1800-1900: Interchanges in Art, Science, Literature, & Society. fac. ed. LC 74-27187. 572p. 1975. reprint ed. pap. 163.10 (*0-7837-7936-4*, 2047692) Bks Demand.

— A Reappraisal of Franco-American Relations, Eighteen Thirty to Eighteen Seventy-One. LC 79-25197. 255p. 1980. reprint ed. lib. bdg. 65.00 (*0-313-22138-3*, BLRA, Greenwood Pr) Greenwood.

Blumenthal, Henry & Robinson, Howard, eds. Aristotle & the Later Tradition. 288p. 1991. text 80.00 (*0-19-823965-3*) OUP.

Blumenthal, Howard. Blues CD Listener's Guide: The Best on CD. 208p. 1998. 14.95 (*0-8230-7610-5*) Watsn-Guptill.

— Classical Music CD Listener's Guide: The Best on CD. 208p. 1998. pap. text 14.95 (*0-8230-8268-7*) Watsn-Guptill.

— The Jazz CD Listeners Guide: The Best on CD. LC 97-40493. (Illus.). 208p. 1998. pap. 14.95 (*0-8230-7662-8*, Billboard Bks) Watsn-Guptill.

— The World Music CD Listener's Guide: The Best on CD. LC 97-40492. (Illus.). 208p. 1998. pap. 14.95 (*0-8230-7663-6*, Billboard Bks) Watsn-Guptill.

Blumenthal, Howard J. & Goodenough, Oliver. This Business of Television. 672p. 1991. 32.50 (*0-8230-7762-4*) Watsn-Guptill.

Blumenthal, Howard J. & Goodenough, Oliver R. This Business of Television. LC 98-4860. 688p. 1998. 35.00 (*0-8230-7704-7*) Watsn-Guptill.

Blumenthal, Ira. Ready, Blame, Fire! Myths & Misses in Marketing. 192p. 1998. pap. 19.95 (*1-882180-95-X*) Griffin CA.

Blumenthal, Ivan. Child Abuse: A Handbook for Health Care Practitioners. LC 96-126567. 160p. 1994. pap. text 29.95 (*0-340-60141-8*, Pub. by E A) OUP.

— Child Abuse: A Handbook for Health Care Practitioners. (Illus.). 160p. 1994. pap. text 39.95 (*1-56593-505-5*, 1168) Singular Publishing.

Blumenthal, James A. & McKee, Daphne C., eds. Applications in Behavioral Medicine & Health Psychology: A Clinician's Source Book. LC 86-62715. 616p. 1987. 39.45 (*0-943158-18-4*, ABMBP) Pro Resource.

Blumenthal, James A., jt. ed. see Krantz, David S.

Blumenthal, Jay & Blumenthal, Andrea K. A Parent's Guide to College Entrance Exams: How You Can Help Your College-Bound Student Succeed. LC 99-38552. 240p. 2000. pap. 14.95 (*1-57685-266-0*) LrningExprss.

Blumenthal, John. The Tinseltown Murders: A Mac Slade Mystery. 1985. pap. 2.95 (*0-671-55539-1*, Fireside) S&S Trade Pap.

***Blumenthal, John.** What's Wrong with Dorfman? LC 00-101031. 230p. 2000. pap. 11.95 (*0-9679444-0-6*) Farmer St.

Blumenthal, Joseph. Bruce Rogers, a Life in Letters 1870-1957. (Illus.). 232p. 1989. pap. 30.00 (*0-935072-16-0*, 42171) Oak Knoll.

— The Printed Book in America. LC 88-40520. (Illus.). 266p. 1989. reprint ed. pap. 29.95 (*0-87451-480-0*) U Pr of New Eng.

— Robert Frost & His Printers. 112p. 1985. 45.00 (*0-614-24482-X*, 18950) Oak Knoll.

— Robert Frost & His Printers. 85.00 (*0-935072-06-3*) W T Taylor.

— Typographic Years: A Printer's Journey Through a Half Century. LC 82-71904. (Illus.). 153p. 1982. 26.50 (*0-913720-38-0*) Beil.

An Asterisk (*) at the beginning of an entry indicates that the title is appearing for the first time.

B

An Asterisk (*) at the beginning of an entry indicates that the title is appearing for the first time.

Blundell, B. G., et al. An Introductory Guide to Silvar Lisco & Hilo Simulators. (Computer Science Ser.). (Illus.). 208p. (C). 1987. pap. text 35.00 (*0-333-44848-0*) Scholium Intl.

Blundell, Barry. Volumetric Three-Dimensional Display Systems. LC 99-30124. 330p. 2000. 110.00 (*0-471-23928-3*) Wiley.

***Blundell, Brian, et al.** Learning at Work: The Learning Organization in Practice. 288p. 2000. pap. 37.50 (*0-7494-2788-4*, Pub. by Kogan Page Ltd) Stylus Pub VA.

Blundell, D. J., et al, eds. A Continent Revealed: The European Geotraverse. (Illus.). 287p. (C). 1992. pap. text 39.95 (*0-521-42948-X*) Cambridge U Pr.

— A Continent Revealed: The European Geotraverse. (Illus.). 287p. (C). 1993. boxed set 90.00 (*0-521-41923-9*) Cambridge U Pr.

Blundell, D. J. & Gibbs, A. D., eds. Tectonic Evolution of the North Sea Rifts. (Illus.). 290p. 1991. 125.00 (*0-19-854595-9*) OUP.

Blundell, D. J., jt. ed. see Hall, R.

Blundell, David S. Masks Anthropology on the Sinhalese Belief System. LC 91-36067. (American University Studies: Theology & Religion: Ser. VII, Vol. 88). XVII, 197p. (C). 1994. text 46.95 (*0-8204-1427-1*) P Lang Pubng.

Blundell, Geoff, jt. auth. see William, David L.

Blundell, Gillian & Graham, Noel. Creative Connections. 1997. pap. 12.50 (*1-871098-33-5*, Pub. by Claire Pubns) Parkwest Pubns.

— Problem Solving Activities with Mottik. 64p. (J). (gr. k-4). pap. 12.50 (*1-871098-21-1*, Pub. by Claire Pubns) Parkwest Pubns.

***Blundell, John & Robinson, Colin.** Regulation Without the State. (Occasional Paper Ser.: No. 109). 44p. 1999. pap. 11.95 (*0-255-36426-1*, Pub. by Inst Economic Affairs) Coronet Bks.

***Blundell, John E.** Out of the Desert. 1999. 25.00 (*1-56311-536-0*) Turner Pub KY.

Blundell, John E., jt. ed. see Carruba, Michele O.

***Blundell-Jones.** Modern Architecture Through Case Studies. 2000. text 69.95 (*0-7506-3805-2*) Buttrwrth-Heinemann.

Blundell, Jude, ed. see Dreishpoon, Douglas.

Blundell, Judy, jt. auth. see Watson, Jude.

Blundell, K. & Taylor, Jenny. Maze Puzzles. (Maze Fun Ser.). (Illus.). 72p. (J). (gr. k-2). 1994. pap. 10.95 (*0-7460-1327-2*, Usborne) EDC.

Blundell, Kim & Tyler, Jenny. Animal Mazes. (Maze Puzzles Ser.). (Illus.). 24p. (J). (gr. k-2). 1993. pap. 4.50 (*0-7460-1323-X*, Usborne) EDC.

— Monster Mazes. (Maze Fun Ser.). (Illus.). 24p. (J). (gr. k-2). 1994. pap. 4.50 (*0-7460-1325-6*, Usborne) EDC.

Blundell, Kim, jt. auth. see Hawthorn, P.

Blundell, M. Collins Photo Guide: Wild Flowers of East Africa. 464p. 1994. 35.95 (*0-00-219812-6*, Pub. by HarpC) Whitman Dist Co.

Blundell, Mary W. Helping Friends & Harming Enemies: A Study in Sophocles & Greek Ethics. 310p. (C). 1991. pap. text 22.95 (*0-521-42390-2*) Cambridge U Pr.

— Pastorals of Dorset. LC 73-160931. (Short Story Index Reprint Ser.). (Illus.). 1977. reprint ed. 23.95 (*0-8369-3910-7*) Ayer.

— Sophocles' Antigone. (Classical Library). 118p. 1998. pap. text 7.95 (*0-941051-25-0*) Focus Pub-R Pullins.

Blundell, Mary W., et al. Women on the Edge: Four Plays by Euripides. (New Classical Canon Ser.). 512p. (C). (gr. 13). 1998. pap. 22.99 (*0-415-90774-8*, B0561) Routledge.

Blundell, Mary W., jt. auth. see Cumming, Ann.

Blundell, Mary W., tr. see Sophocles.

Blundell, N. Ancient England. 144p. 1997. 14.98 (*0-7858-0765-9*) Bk Sales Inc.

Blundell, Nigel. Beer. 1998. 6.99 (*0-7858-0929-5*) Bk Sales Inc.

— Boy Who Would Be King. 1999. 14.99 (*0-7858-1108-7*) Bk Sales Inc.

— Cigars. 1998. 6.99 (*0-7858-0930-9*) Bk Sales Inc.

— Encyclopedia of Serial Killers, Vol. 2. 192p. 1996. 14.99 (*1-57215-144-7*, JG1143) World Pubns.

— Grandes Ladrones y Estafores del Mundo. 1997. pap. text 13.98 (*968-890-149-0*) Edit Diana.

— A Pictorial History of Adolf Hitler. (Illus.). 96p. 1995. write for info. (*1-57215-137-4*) World Pubns.

— A Pictorial History of Franklin Delano Roosevelt. (Illus.). 96p. 1996. 10.99 (*1-57215-139-0*, JG1138) World Pubns.

— A Pictorial History of Joseph Stalin. (Illus.). 96p. 1996. write for info. (*1-57215-138-2*) World Pubns.

— A Pictorial History of Winston Churchill. (Illus.). 96p. 1996. 10.99 (*1-57215-140-4*, JG1139) World Pubns.

— Scotch Whisky. 1998. 6.99 (*0-7858-0928-7*) Bk Sales Inc.

***Blundell, Nigel.** Scotland. (Illus.). 256p. 2000. 19.98 (*1-58663-101-2*) M Friedman Pub Grp Inc.

Blundell, Nigel. Shipwrecks. LC 99-27208. (Illus.). 144p. 1999. 15.98 (*1-57145-159-5*, Thunder Bay) Advantage Pubs.

— Windsor vs. Windsor. 1996. mass mkt. 6.99 (*1-85782-115-7*, Pub. by Blake Publng) Seven Hills Bk.

Blundell, R. H. & Seaton, R. E., eds. Trial of Jean Pierre Vaquier, No. 1. (Notable British Trials Ser.). xxiv, 208p. 1995. reprint ed. 70.00 (*1-56169-172-0*, 15116) Gaunt.

Blundell, R. H. & Wilson, G. Haswell, eds. Trial of Buck Ruxton, No. 1. 2nd ed. (Notable British Trials Ser.). lxxxvii, 457p. 1995. reprint ed. 165.00 (*1-56169-181-X*) Gaunt.

Blundell, Richard & Salter, Graham. Effective Business Communication. 288p. 1997. pap. 32.00 (*0-13-742701-8*) P-H.

Blundell, Richard W., et al, eds. The Measurement of Household Welfare. LC 93-5717. (Illus.). 293p. (C). 1994. text 59.95 (*0-521-45195-7*) Cambridge U Pr.

Blundell, Sue. Women in Ancient Greece. LC 93-36217. (Illus.). 288p. 1995. pap. 19.95 (*0-674-95473-4*, BLUWOX) HUP.

Blundell, Sue & Williamson, Margaret. The Sacred & the Feminine in Ancient Greece. LC 97-25099. (Illus.). 208p. (C). 1998. 75.00 (*0-415-12662-2*); pap. 20.99 (*0-415-12663-0*) Routledge.

***Blundell, Susan.** Women in Classical Athens. LC 99-225206. (Classical World Ser.). (Illus.). 148p. (C). 1998. pap. text 18.95 (*1-85399-543-6*, Pub. by Brist Class Pr) Focus Pub-R Pullins.

Blundell, T. L. & Johnson, Louise. Protein Crystallography. (Molecular Biology Ser.). 1976. text 264.00 (*0-12-108350-0*) Acad Pr.

Blundell, T. L., jt. auth. see Noble, D.

Blundell, T. L., jt. ed. see Noble, D.

Blundell, Thalia. On the Way. 1999. pap. text 10.99 (*1-85792-407-X*) Christian Focus.

Blundell, Tony. Beware of Boys. LC 90-24299. (J). (ps-3). 1996. mass mkt. 4.95 (*0-688-14739-9*, Wm Morrow) Morrow Avon.

— Beware of Boys. 1996. 10.15 (*0-606-08697-8*, Pub. by Turtleback) Demco.

Blundell, Tony. Funny Stories. LC 92-26447. (Story Library). 260p. (J). (gr. 1 up). 1993. 7.95 (*1-85697-883-4*, Kingfisher) LKC.

Blundell, William E. The Art & Craft of Feature Writing: The Wall Street Journal Guide. 288p. 1988. pap. 14.95 (*0-452-26158-9*, Plume) Dutton Plume.

Blunden, Allan, tr. see Mann, Thomas.

Blunden, Caroline & Elvin, Mark. Cultural Atlas of China. (Cultural Atlas Ser.). (Illus.). 240p. 1983. 45.00 (*0-87196-132-6*) Facts on File.

— Cultural Atlas of China. rev. ed. LC 98-34322. (Cultural Atlas Ser.). (Illus.). 240p. 1998. 50.00 (*0-8160-3814-7*, Checkmark) Facts on File.

Blunden, E. Shelley & Keats As They Struck Their Contemporaries. LC 70-174689. (English Literature Ser.: No. 33). 1971. reprint ed. lib. bdg. 75.00 (*0-8383-1341-8*) M S G Haskell Hse.

Blunden, Edmund. Edmund Blunden (1896-1974) Selected Poems. Marsack, Robyn, ed. 1982. pap. 8.50 (*0-85635-425-2*) Carcanet Pr.

— English Villages. (Writers' Britain Ser.). (Illus.). 96p. 1997. 11.95 (*1-85375-247-9*) Prion.

— Wayside Sonnets, 1750-1850: An Anthology Gathered by Edmund Blunden & Bernard Mellor. LC 73-170371. 181p. 1971. reprint ed. pap. 56.20 (*0-608-02389-2*, 206303000004) Bks Demand.

Blunden, Edmund C. After the Bombing, & Other Short Poems. LC 70-164589. (Select Bibliographies Reprint Ser.). 1977. reprint ed. 12.95 (*0-8369-5873-X*) Ayer.

— Edmund Blunden. LC 76-117761. (Essay Index Reprint Ser.). 1977. 26.95 (*0-8369-1743-X*) Ayer.

— Leigh Hunt & His Circle. (BCL1-PR English Literature Ser.). 402p. 1992. reprint ed. lib. bdg. 99.00 (*0-7812-7570-9*) Rprt Serv.

— Mind's Eye: Essays. LC 67-28745. (Essay Index Reprint Ser.). 1977. 20.95 (*0-8369-0218-1*) Ayer.

— On the Poems of Henry Vaughan: Characteristics & Intimations. (BCL1-PR English Literature Ser.). 64p. 1992. reprint ed. lib. bdg. 59.00 (*0-7812-7416-8*) Rprt Serv.

— Votive Tablets: Studies Chiefly Appreciative of English Authors & Books. LC 67-26716. (Essay Index Reprint Ser.). 1977. 23.95 (*0-8369-0219-X*) Ayer.

Blunden, Edmund C. & Mellor, Bernard. Wayside Poems of the Early Eighteenth Century: An Anthology. LC 64-54686. 174p. reprint ed. pap. 54.00 (*0-608-13791-X*, 202077300018) Bks Demand.

Blunden, Gerald, jt. ed. see Guiry, M. D.

Blunden, John & Curry, Nigel. A Future for Our Countryside. (Illus.). 256p. 1993. pap. 26.95 (*0-631-16272-0*) Blackwell Pubs.

***Blunden, John & Curry, Nigel, eds.** A People's Charter? Forty Years of the National Parks & Access to the Countryside Act 1949 (U. K.) (Illus.). 299p. 1999. reprint ed. pap. text 25.00 (*0-7881-6662-X*) DIANE Pub.

Blunden, John, jt. ed. see Sarre, Philip.

Blunden, John R., jt. ed. see McGlashan, Neil.

Blunden, Margaret & Dando, Malcom, eds. Rethinking Public Policy-Making: Questioning Assumptions, Challenging Beliefs. 240p. 1995. 55.00 (*0-8039-7602-X*) Sage.

Blunden, S. J., et al. The Industrial Uses of Tin Chemicals. 346p. 1985. text 38.00 (*0-85186-927-0*, Pub. by Royal Soc Chem) Spr-Verlag.

Blunden, W. E. C. I. I. Financial Aspects of Life Business, No. 140-081. (C). 1987. 245.00 (*0-7855-4295-7*, Pub. by Witherby & Co) St Mut.

Blunden, W. R. & Black, J. A. The Land Use-Transport System. 2nd ed. (Urban & Regional Planning Ser.: Vol. 2). (Illus.). 264p. 1984. text 56.00 (*0-08-029836-2*, Pergamon Pr); pap. text 27.00 (*0-08-029841-9*, Pergamon Pr) Elsevier.

Blundetto, Sandra G. Werbel's New York Law Addendum: Property & Casualty Insurance. rev. ed. 138p. (C). 1999. pap. text 12.95 (*1-884803-01-6*) Werbel Pub.

Blundeville, Thomas. A Briefe Description of Universal Mappes & Cardes. LC 79-38159. (English Experience Ser.: No. 438). 44p. 1972. reprint ed. 20.00 (*90-221-0438-9*) Walter J Johnson.

— M. Blundeville, His Exercises Containing Sixe Treatises. LC 78-171736. (English Experience Ser.: No. 361). (Illus.). 718p. 1971. reprint ed. 75.00 (*90-221-0361-7*) Walter J Johnson.

— A Newe Booke, Containing the Arte of Ryding. LC 75-25640. (English Experience Ser.: No. 118). (Illus.). 232p. 1969. reprint ed. 55.00 (*90-221-0118-5*) Walter J Johnson.

— The True Order & Method of Wryting & Reading Hystories. LC 79-84088. (English Experience Ser.: No. 908). 68p. 1979. reprint ed. lib. bdg. 20.00 (*90-221-0908-9*) Walter J Johnson.

Blundo, James V. Moments of Selfhood: Three Plays by Luigi Pirandello. LC 90-36613. (American University Studies: Romance Languages & Literature: Ser. II, Vol. 135). 208p. (C). 1991. text 38.95 (*0-8204-1205-8*) P Lang Pubng.

Blunk & Gudas, J. P. Cancer Rehabilitation Continuing Care. 1999. write for info. (*0-7506-9538-2*) Buttrwrth-Heinemann.

Blunk, Merrie, jt. ed. see Lampert, Magdalene.

Blunk, Tim & Levasseur, Raymond L. Hauling up the Morning: Writings & Art by Political Prisoners & Prisoners of War in the U. S. Jacobin Books Staff et al, eds. LC 90-61145.Tr. of Izando la Manana. (ENG & SPA., Illus.). 350p. (C). 1990. 39.95 (*0-932415-59-8*); pap. 15.95 (*0-932415-60-1*) Red Sea Pr.

Blunk, Timothy. The Risks Worth Taking: Poetry & Art from a Decade of Imprisonment. (Illus.). 90p. (Orig.). 1997. pap. text 14.95 (*0-9657912-0-3*) Puffin Found.

Blunn, O., jt. auth. see Demyanyuk, F.

Blunsden, John & Phipps, David. The Story of the Ford Grand Prix Engine: Its Design & Development. LC 74-163124. 224p. 1971. write for info. (*0-8376-0052-9*) Bentley Pubs.

— Such Sweet Thunder: The Story of the Ford Grand Prix Engine. LC 72-179316. 224p. 1971. write for info. (*0-900549-12-2*) CE69.

Blunt, Alfred W., jt. auth. see Hamilton, Mary A.

Blunt, Alison. Travel, Gender & Imperialism: Mary Kingsley & West Africa. LC 94-2306. (Mappings). 190p. 1994. pap. text 18.95 (*0-89862-546-7*) Guilford Pubns.

Blunt, Alison & Rose, Gillian, eds. Writing Women & Space: Women's Colonial & Postcolonial Geographies. LC 94-11691. (Mappings Ser.). 268p. 1994. pap. text 18.95 (*0-89862-498-3*, 2498) Guilford Pubns.

***Blunt, Alison & Wills, Jane.** Dissident Geographies: An Introduction to Radical Ideas & Practice. LC 99-52128. 224p. 2000. write for info. (*0-582-29489-4*) P-H.

Blunt, Anne. Bedouin Tribes of the Euphrates, 2 vols. in 1. (Illus.). xxviii, 629p. reprint ed. write for info. (*0-318-71490-6*) G Olms Pubs.

— Pilgrimage to Neid, 2 vols. (Illus.). 1968. reprint ed. 135.00 (*0-7146-1979-5*, Pub. by F Cass Pubs) Intl Spec Bk.

— A Pilgrimage to Nejd. 632p. 1984. 350.00 (*1-85077-016-6*, Pub. by Darf Pubs Ltd) St Mut.

Blunt, Anthony. Art & Architecture in France, 1500-1700. rev. ed. LC 98-23229. (Yale University Press Pelican History of Art Ser.). 1998. pap. 35.00 (*0-300-07748-3*) Yale U Pr.

— Art & Architecture in France, 1500-1700. 5th ed. LC 98-23229. (Pelican History of Art Ser.). (Illus.). 304p. 1998. 70.00 (*0-300-07735-1*) Yale U Pr.

Blunt, Anthony. Artistic Theory in Italy, 1450-1600. LC 94-3411. (Illus.). 178p. 1962. reprint ed. pap. 19.95 (*0-19-881050-4*) OUP.

— Baroque Rome: The Churches. (Illus.). 2000. pap. 34.95 (*1-873429-18-5*) Pallas Athene.

Blunt, Anthony. Borromini. (Studies in Art History Paperbacks). (Illus.). 240p. 1989. pap. text 19.95 (*0-674-07926-4*) Belknap Pr.

— Francois Mansart: Origin of French Classical Architecture. LC 90-34883. (Illus.). 152p. 1990. reprint ed. lib. bdg. 49.00 (*1-878592-12-2*) Native Amer Bk Pubs.

— Francois Mansart & the Origins of French Classical Architecture. LC 42-1541. 1941. reprint ed. 59.00 (*0-403-07230-1*) Somerset Pub.

Blunt, Anthony, ed. Diary of the Cavaliere Bernini's Visit to France. LC 85-42680. 412p. 1985. reprint ed. pap. 127.80 (*0-7837-9314-6*, 206005400004) Bks Demand.

Blunt, Anthony, jt. ed. see Friedlaender, Walter.

Blunt, C. E., et al. Coinage in Tenth-Century England: From Edward the Elder to Edgar's Reform. (British Academy Ser.). (Illus.). 408p. 1989. 130.00 (*0-19-726060-8*) OUP.

Blunt, D. Incredible Benefits. 1997. pap. 7.95 (*1-888103-12-4*) Trophy Pubng.

Blunt, David M. The Characteristics of a Plodder. 24p. 1998. 1.99 (*1-893716-00-7*) Church Rk.

— The Characteristics of a Plodder. 40p. 1999. 1.99 (*1-893716-06-6*) Church Rk.

— Gods Benefit: Healing. 128p. 1998. pap. 7.99 (*1-893716-03-1*) Church Rk.

— How to Get Answers from God. 56p. 1998. 1.99 (*1-893716-04-X*) Church Rk.

— One Minute Motivators. 64p. 1998. 1.00 (*1-893716-01-5*) Church Rk.

— The Power of Expectation. 56p. 1998. pap. write for info. (*1-893716-05-8*) Church Rk.

— This Life's for You! 40p. 1998. 1.00 (*1-893716-02-3*) Church Rk.

Blunt, Edna M. Margie the Cat. pap. 6.95 (*0-681-02740-1*) Booklines Hawaii.

***Blunt, Frank.** Frank Blunt's Office Bits. 1998. pap. text 12.95 (*0-9643986-5-6*) Leapin Lizard.

— Frank Blunt's Sporting Bits. 1998. pap. text 12.95 (*0-9643986-6-4*) Leapin Lizard.

Blunt, Giles. Cold Eye. 288p. 1990. pap. 3.95 (*0-380-70876-0*, Avon Bks) Morrow Avon.

***Blunt, Giles.** Forty Words for Sorrow. 2000. write for info. (*0-679-31057-6*) Random.

Blunt, Hugh F. Great Magdelens. LC 71-86731. (Essay Index Reprint Ser.). 1977. 21.95 (*0-8369-1122-9*) Ayer.

— Great Penitents. LC 67-30198. (Essay Index Reprint Ser.). 1977. 19.95 (*0-8369-0220-3*) Ayer.

Blunt, J. H., ed. The Myroure of Our Lady. (EETS, ES Ser.: No. 19). 1974. reprint ed. 54.00 (*0-527-00232-1*) Periodicals Srv.

Blunt, Jane & Gainger, Stan. Engineering Coatings: Design & Application. 2nd ed. 250p. 1998. 170.00 (*1-85573-369-2*, Pub. by Woodhead Pubng) Am Educ Systs.

Blunt, Jerry. A Gap in Generations. 110p. (YA). (gr. 10 up). 1970. pap. 5.50 (*0-87129-841-4*, G11) Dramatic Pub.

— More Stage Dialects. 140p. 1996. pap. 19.95 (*0-87129-603-9*, M92) Dramatic Pub.

— Stage Dialects. 1994. pap. 19.95 (*0-87129-331-5*, SA5) Dramatic Pub.

Blunt, John H., ed. Dictionary of Sects, Heresies, Ecclesiastical Parties, & Schools of Religious Thought. LC 89-29543. 647p. 1990. reprint ed. lib. bdg. 75.00 (*1-55888-903-5*) Omnigraphics Inc.

Blunt, Lady A. A Pilgrimage to the Nejd, the Cradle of the Arab RAce, 2 pts. in 1 vol. (Documenta Arabica Ser.). (Illus.). xlvi, 556p. 1983. reprint ed. 95.00 (*3-487-07407-9*) G Olms Pubs.

Blunt, Peter & Jones, Merrick L. Managing Organisations in Africa. (Studies in Organization: No. 40). xiv, 356p. (C). 1992. lib. bdg. 113.85 (*3-11-012646-X*) De Gruyter.

Blunt, Peter & Warren, Michael D. Indigenous Organizations & Development. LC 97-182196. (Studies in Indigenous Knowledge & Development). 166p. 1996. pap. 29.95 (*1-85339-321-5*, Pub. by Intermed Tech) Stylus Pub VA.

Blunt, Peter, et al. Managing Organizations in Africa: Readings, Cases & Exercises. LC 93-6796. (Studies in Organization: No. 49). xii, 219p. (Orig.). (C). 1993. pap. text 32.00 (*3-11-013671-6*) De Gruyter.

Blunt, Phyllis. Bursting the Cherry. 1998. pap. text 10.95 (*1-874509-54-9*, Pub. by X Pr) LPC InBook.

Blunt, Reginald. The Carlyle's Chelsea Home. LC 75-30875. (Studies in Carlyle: No. 53). 1975. lib. bdg. 75.00 (*0-8383-2079-1*) M S G Haskell Hse.

Blunt, Richard. Waldorf Education: Theory & Practice. LC 95-190042. pap. 21.95 (*0-9583885-4-7*, 2006, Pub. by Novalis Trust) Anthroposophic.

Blunt, Ronald L. The Smoking Gun. LC 98-66617. 307p. 1998. text 21.00 (*1-890622-36-2*) Leathers Pub.

***Blunt, Roscoe C., Jr.** Foot Soldier. 2000. 24.95 (*1-885119-72-0*) Sarpedon.

Blunt, Stavia. Shaping Up During & After Pregnancy. 1998. pap. text 19.95 (*1-84024-013-X*, Pub. by Summers) Howell Pr VA.

— Working Mother: Balancing Childcare & Career, 1. LC 99-490306. 1998. pap. text 19.95 (*1-84024-060-1*, Pub. by Summers) Seven Hills Bk.

Blunt, Wilfred. The Art of Botanical Illustration: An Illustrated History. unabridged ed. (Illus.). 372p. 1993. reprint ed. pap. 14.95 (*0-486-27265-6*) Dover.

Blunt, Wilfred S. The Land War in Ireland. LC 75-28808. (Celtic Ser.). 528p. reprint ed. 57.50 (*0-404-13801-2*) AMS Pr.

Blunt, Wilfrid. The Art of Botanical Illustration. Stearn, William T., ed. (Illus.). 320p. 1995. 59.50 (*1-85149-177-5*) Antique Collect.

— The Stage Lighting Handbook. 5th ed. (Theatre Production Ser.). 224p. 1968. pap. 3.75 (*0-87830-064-3*) Routledge.

Blunt, Wilfrid S. The Poetical Works of Wilfrid Scawen Blunt, 2 vols. (BCL1-PR English Literature Ser.). 1992. reprint ed. lib. bdg. 150.00 (*0-7812-7448-6*) Rprt Serv.

— The Poetical Works of Wilfrid Scawen Blunt, 2 vols. LC 14-22324. 1968. reprint ed. 59.00 (*0-403-00110-2*) Scholarly.

Bluntschli, Johann C. Geschichte des Alligemeinen Staatsrechts & der Politik. Mayer, J. P., ed. LC 78-67333. (European Political Thought Ser.). (GER.). 1980. reprint ed. lib. bdg. 50.95 (*0-405-11679-9*) Ayer.

Bluntschli, Johann K. Theory of the State. LC 77-152975. (Select Bibliographies Reprint Ser.). 1977. reprint ed. 31.95 (*0-8369-5727-X*) Ayer.

Blurton, T. Richard. Hindu Art. LC 92-11157. (Illus.). 240p. (C). 1993. 49.95 (*0-674-39188-8*) HUP.

— Hindu Art. LC 92-11157. (Illus.). 240p. (C). 1994. pap. 28.00 (*0-674-39189-6*) HUP.

Blurton, T. Richard, jt. auth. see Isaacs, Ralph.

Blusse, L. & Gaastra, F., eds. Companies & Trade: Essays on Overseas Trading During the Ancient Regime. 272p. 1981. lib. bdg. 118.00 (*90-6021-473-0*) Kluwer Academic.

Blusse, Leonard & Gaastra, Femme S., eds. On the Eighteenth Century As a Category of Asian History: Van Leur in Retrospect. LC 98-17321. (Illus.). 313p. 1998. text 83.95 (*1-84014-610-9*, Pub. by Ashgate Pub) Ashgate Pub Co.

Blusse, Leonard & Zurndorfer, Harriet T., eds. Conflict & Accommodation in Early Modern East Asia: Essays in Honour of Erik Zurcher. LC 92-46561. 1993. 121.00 (*90-04-09775-9*) Brill Academic Pubs.

Blust, Robert A. Austronesian Root Theory: An Essay on the Limits of Morphology. LC 87-34137. (Studies in Language Companion Ser.: Vol. 19). xi, 190p. (C). 1988. 47.00 (*90-272-3020-X*) J Benjamins Pubng Co.

Blustain, Harvey. Resource Management & Agricultural Development in Jamaica: Lessons for a Participatory Approach. (Special Series on Resource Management: No. 2). 151p. (Orig.). (C). 1982. pap. text 9.00 (*0-86731-083-9*) Cornell CIS RDC.

Blustain, Harvey & LaFranc, Elsie, eds. Organizational Strategies for Small Farm Development in Jamaica. (RDC Bks.). 200p. 1982. 8.00 (*0-86731-119-3*) Cornell CIS RDC.

Blustain, Harvey & LeFranc, Elsie, eds. Organizational Strategies for Small-Farm Agriculture in Jamaica. 217p. (Orig.). (C). 1981. pap. text 8.00 (*0-86731-013-8*) Cornell CIS RDC.

Blustein, Bonnie E. Educating for Health & Prevention: A History of the Department of Community & Preventive Medicine of the (Woman's) Medical College of

An Asterisk (*) at the beginning of an entry indicates that the title is appearing for the first time.

Pennsylvania. LC 93-5822. (Illus.). 160p. (C). 1993. 15.00 (*0-88135-148-2*, Sci Hist); pap. text 9.95 (*0-88135-185-7*, Sci Hist) Watson Pub Intl.
— Preserve Your Love for Science: Life of William Hammond, American Neurologist. (History of Medicine Ser.). (Illus.). 301p. (C). 1991. text 74.95 (*0-521-39262-4*) Cambridge U Pr.

Blustein, Jeffrey. Care & Commitment: Taking the Personal Point of View. 288p. (C). 1991. text 50.00 (*0-19-506799-1*) OUP.

Blustein, Jeffrey, et al, eds. The Adolescent Alone: Decision Making in Health Care in the United States. LC 98-48330. (Illus.). 280p. 1999. 59.95 (*0-521-65240-5*); pap. 19.95 (*0-521-65891-8*) Cambridge U Pr.

Blustein, Lotte & Geary, Rosemary J. Writing the Research Paper. (Illus.). 62p. (gr. 7 up). 1985. pap. text 6.50 (*0-9605248-2-7*) Blustein-Geary.
— Writing the Research Paper. 70p. (YA). (gr. 9 up). 1992. pap. text 7.50 (*0-9605248-3-5*) Blustein-Geary.

Bluteau, Ralphael. Vocabulario Portuguez e Latino, 5 vols. cclxiv, 7085p. write for info. (*0-318-71076-5*) G Olms Pubs.

Bluth, Christoph. The Collapse of Soviet Military Power. LC 95-19401. (Illus.). 320p. 1995. text 79.95 (*1-85521-482-2*, Pub. by Dartmth Pub) Ashgate Pub Co.

***Bluth, Christoph.** The Nuclear Challenge. 184p. 2000. 69.95 (*1-85521-896-8*) Ashgate Pub Co.

Bluth, Christoph. Soviet Strategic Arms Policy Before SALT. (Cambridge Russian, Soviet & Post-Soviet Studies: No. 83). (Illus.). 331p. (C). 1992. text 69.95 (*0-521-40372-3*) Cambridge U Pr.

Bluth, Christoph, jt. ed. see Allison, Roy.

Bluth, Christopher. Britain, Germany & Western Nuclear Strategy. (Nuclear History Program Ser.: No. 3). 334p. 1995. text 75.00 (*0-19-828004-1*) OUP.

***Bluth, Edward I.** Ultrasound. (Illus.). 768p. 1999. 159.00 (*0-86577-861-2*) Thieme Med Pubs.
— Ultrasound: A Practical Approach to Clinical Problems. LC 99-40816. 1999. write for info. (*0-86577-895-7*) Thieme Med Pubs.

Bluth, Ephraim. The Pocketbook Shaliach: Aliyah Advice for the Pragmatic Idealist. LC 96-36973. 78p. 1996. pap. 12.95 (*965-229-168-4*, Pub. by Gefen Pub Hse) Gefen Bks.

Bluthenthal, Diana Cain. Matilda the Moocher. LC 96-42288. (Illus.). 32p. (J). (ps-2). 1997. 15.95 (*0-531-30003-X*); lib. bdg. 16.99 (*0-531-33003-6*) Orchard Bks Watts.

Bly, Amy S. How to Sell Your House, Condo, Co-Op. 1993. pap. 15.95 (*0-89043-357-7*) Consumer Reports.

Bly, Bob. Quick Tips for Better Business-to-Business Marketing Communications. 200p. (Orig.). 1997. pap. write for info. (*0-9656965-1-0*) Busn Mktging.

Bly, Carol. An Adolescent's Christmas, 1944. unabridged ed. LC 99-28414. 64p. 2000. 15.00 (*1-890434-18-3*) Afton Hist Soc.
— Backbone: Short Stories. LC 84-61733. (Illus.). 126p. (Orig.). (C). 1983. pap. 10.95 (*0-915943-36-0*) Milkweed Ed.

***Bly, Carol.** Letters from the Country. LC 98-53291. 208p. 1999. pap. 14.95 (*0-8166-3322-3*) U of Minn Pr.
— My Lord Bag of Rice: New & Selected Stories. LC 99-47930. 326p. 2000. pap. 16.95 (*1-57131-031-2*) Milkweed Ed.

Bly, Carol. The Passionate, Accurate Story: Making Your Hearts Truth into Literature. 216p. 1998. reprint ed. pap. 13.95 (*1-57131-219-6*) Milkweed Ed.

Bly, Carol, ed. Changing the Bully Who Rules the World: Reading & Thinking about Ethics. 584p. 1996. pap. 18.95 (*1-57131-205-6*) Milkweed Ed.

Bly, Gisela. Harvest of Riches. 30p. 1989. write for info. (*0-9613989-8-1*) E R Kaltovich.

Bly, Herman O. Communism, the Cold War, & the FBI Connection: Special Agent for the FBI. LC 98-71671. 224p. 1998. pap. 12.99 (*1-56384-149-5*) Huntington Hse.

Bly, Janet. Awakening Your Sense of Wonder: Discovering God Through the Ordinary. LC 96-44860. 256p. (Orig.). 1997. pap. 12.99 (*1-57293-018-7*) Discovery Hse Pubs.
— God Is Good All the Time. LC 98-39563. 168p. 1999. pap. 12.99 (*1-57293-045-4*) Discovery Hse Pubs.

***Bly, Janet.** Hope Lives Here. LC 00-34624. 2000. write for info. (*1-57293-060-8*) Discovery Hse Pubs.

Bly, Janet. The Island Mansion Mysteries. (Making Choices Ser.). (Illus.). 160p. (J). (gr. 3-6). 1995. pap. 4.99 (*0-7814-0191-7*) Chariot Victor.

Bly, Janet, jt. auth. see Bly, Stephen.

Bly, Janet C. The Heart of a Runaway: Hope & Understanding for the Woman Who Longs to Escape. LC 95-34024. 224p. (Orig.). 1995. pap. 12.99 (*0-929239-95-4*) Discovery Hse Pubs.

Bly, John. Discovering English Furniture. 1989. pap. 25.00 (*0-85263-359-9*, Pub. by Shire Pubns) St Mut.
— Discovering Hall Marks on English Silver. 1989. pap. 25.00 (*0-85263-796-9*, Pub. by Shire Pubns) St Mut.
— Discovering Hallmarks on English Silver. (Handbook Ser.: No. 38). (Illus.). 72p. 1999. pap. 9.50 (*0-7478-0349-8*, Pub. by Shire Pubns) Parkwest Pubns.
— Miller's Silver & Sheffield Plate Marks: Including a Guide to Makers & Styles. Miller, Judith & Miller, Martin, eds. (Illus.). 192p. 1993. pap. 12.95 (*1-85732-096-4*, Pub. by Millers Pubns) Antique Collect.

Bly, John, ed. Heirloom. 144p. (C). 1990. 65.00 (*1-85283-246-0*, Pub. by Boxtree) St Mut.

Bly, Leon. An Analysis of Leadership & How to Be a Better Leader. 117p. (Orig.). (YA). (gr. 9). 1988. text, student ed. 24.95 (*0-9621505-0-9*) Schwarz Pauper.
— An Analysis of Leadership & How to Be a Better Leader: A Textbook. 60p. (Orig.). 1989. student ed. 12.95 (*0-9621505-2-5*) Schwarz Pauper.

Bly, Leon. An Analysis of Leadership & How to Be a Better Leader: A Textbook. 60p. (Orig.). 1989. pap. text 12.95 (*0-9621505-1-7*) Schwarz Pauper.

Bly, Leon. Jenny Turnbull Vol. 1: Risk Taker. LC 94-7859. 160p. (Orig.). pap. 9.00 (*0-9621505-3-3*) Schwarz Pauper.
— Jenny Turnbull Vol. 2: Kurdistan Mission. 180p. (YA). pap. 9.00 (*0-9621505-4-1*) Schwarz Pauper.

Bly, Lois. The Components of Normal Movement During the First Year of Life & Abnormal Motor Development. (Illus.). 52p. (C). 1983. pap. 25.00 (*0-9621991-0-9*) NDTA.

***Bly, Lois.** Facilitation Techniques Based on NDT Principles. 1998. pap. text 79.00 (*0-12-784581-X*) Acad Pr.

Bly, Lois. Motor Skills Acquisition in the First Year: An Illustrated Guide to Normal Development. (Illus.). 1998. pap. text 67.00 (*0-12-784552-6*) Acad Pr.

Bly, Margaret A., jt. auth. see Garrison, Mark.

Bly, Margaret Ann, jt. auth. see Garrison, Mark.

***Bly, Mark.** Production Notebooks Vol. 2: Theatre in Process. Vol. 2. (Illus.). 268p. 2001. pap. 17.95 (*1-55936-189-1*) Theatre Comm.

Bly, Mark, ed. The Production Notebooks: Theatre in Process, Vol. 1. LC 95-45987. (Illus.). 280p. (Orig.). 1995. pap. 16.95 (*1-55936-110-7*) Theatre Comm.

***Bly, Mary.** Queer Virgins & Virgin Queens on the Early Modern Stage. 224p. 2000. text 55.00 (*0-19-818699-1*) OUP.

Bly, Nellie. Barbra Streisand: Untold Story. 1994. mass mkt. 4.99 (*0-7860-0051-1*, Pinncle Kensgtn) Kensgtn Pub Corp.
— The Kennedy Men: Three Generations of Sex, Scandal & Secrets. LC 95-81479. 368p. 1996. 22.95 (*1-57566-015-6*) Kensgtn Pub Corp.
— The Kennedy Men: Three Generations of Sex, Scandal & Secrets. (Illus.). 432p. 1996. mass mkt. 5.99 (*1-57566-106-3*, Knsington) Kensgtn Pub Corp.
— Marlon Brando: Larger Than Life. 320p. 1994. mass mkt. 4.99 (*0-7860-0086-4*, Pinncle Kensgtn) Kensgtn Pub Corp.
— Oprah! Up Close & down Home. 400p. 1994. mass mkt. 4.99 (*0-8217-4613-8*, Zebra Kensgtn) Kensgtn Pub Corp.
— Reckless. 1996. pap. 22.95 (*0-8217-5223-5*) NAL.

Bly, Nellie, jt. auth. see Peck, Ira.

***Bly, Robert.** Angels of Pompeii. (Illus.). 40p. 1999. reprint ed. text 20.00 (*0-7881-6828-2*) DIANE Pub.

Bly, Robert. The Apple Found in the Plowing. (Illus.). 28p. (Orig.). 1989. pap. 20.00 (*0-9621666-4-2*) Haw River Bk.

***Bly, Robert.** Best American Poetry 1999. (Illus.). (J). 1999. 21.35 (*0-606-18620-4*) Turtleback.

Bly, Robert. Business to Business Direct Marketing: Proven Direct Response Methods to Generate More Leads & Sales. (Illus.). 280p. 1994. 39.95 (*0-8442-3472-9*, NTC Business Bks) NTC Contemp Pub Co.
— Comic Book Heroes: One Thousand One Trivia Questions about America's Favorite Superheroes, from the Atom to the X-Men. LC 94-20250. (Illus.). 256p. 1994. 9.95 (*0-8065-1571-6*, Citadel Pr) Carol Pub Group.
— The Complete Idiot's Guide to Getting the Job You Want. 350p. 1995. 24.95 incl. disk (*1-56761-608-9*, Alpha Ref) Macmillan Gen Ref.
— The Copywriter's Handbook. LC 89-38563. 368p. 1995. pap. 13.95 (*0-8050-1194-3*, Owl) H Holt & Co.
— Eating the Honey of Words: New & Selected Poems. 288p. 2000. pap. 13.00 (*0-06-093069-1*) HarpC.
— Fairy Tales for Men & Women. 1996. write for info. (*0-201-40647-0*) Addison-Wesley.
— Four Ramages. (Illus.). 16p. (Orig.). 1983. pap. 3.95 (*0-935306-11-0*) Barnwood Pr.
— Getting Your Book Published: Inside Secrets of a Successful Author. 2nd rev. ed. LC 98-138326. (Illus.). 224p. 1997. pap. 14.95 (*0-934968-10-1*) Roblin Pr.
— Gratitude to Old Teachers. (Pamphlet Ser.: Vol. 8). 21p. 1993. 7.00 (*1-880238-01-2*) BOA Edns.
— Holes the Crickets Have Eaten in Blankets. (BOA Pamphlets Ser.: No. 9). 22p. 1997. pap. 7.50 (*1-880238-58-6*) BOA Edns.
— Holes the Crickets Have Eaten in Blankets. limited ed. (Pamphlet Ser.: No. 9). 20p. 1997. 35.00 (*1-880238-57-8*) BOA Edns.
— Iron John: A Book about Men. 1992. pap. 13.00 (*0-679-73119-9*) Vin Bks.
— Jumping Out of Bed. 48p. 1991. pap. 7.00 (*0-934834-08-3*) White Pine.
— A Little Book on the Human Shadow. Booth, William C., ed. LC 87-45687. 96p. 1988. pap. 11.00 (*0-06-254847-6*, PL 4255, Pub. by Harper SF) HarpC.
— Maiden Czar. 1999. pap. write for info. (*0-679-76856-4*) Knopf.
— The Maiden King: The Reunion of Masculine & Feminine. 1999. pap. 12.95 (*0-8050-5778-1*, Owl) H Holt & Co.
— The Man in the Black Coat Turns. LC 88-45108. 80p. 1991. reprint ed. pap. 10.00 (*0-06-097186-X*, PL 7186, Perennial) HarperTrade.
— Morning Poems. LC 97-1502. 128p. 1997. 23.00 (*0-06-018251-2*) HarpC.
— Morning Poems. 128p. 1998. pap. 12.00 (*0-06-092873-5*) HarpC.

***Bly, Robert.** 100 Best Careers in Media & Communications. 304p. 1999. pap. 15.95 (*0-02-862178-6*) Macmillan.

Bly, Robert. Point Reyes Poems. (Orig.). 1989. pap. 6.00 (*0-912449-32-2*) Floating Island.
— Point Reyes Poems. (Orig.). 1989. 10.00 (*0-941220-15-X*) Jungle Garden.
— Point Reyes Poems. rev. ed. 32p. (Orig.). 1993. pap. 6.00 (*0-912449-46-2*) Floating Island.
— Remembering James Wright. 44p. 1991. pap. 6.00 (*0-915408-44-9*) Ally Pr.

***Bly, Robert.** Saturday Nights in Marietta. limited ed. (Winter Book Ser.: Vol. 11). (Illus.). 34p. 1999. 195.00 (*1-879832-30-5*) MN Ctr Book Arts.
— Saturday Nights in Marietta: Chapbook Edition. limited ed. (Winter Book Ser.: Vol. 11). (Illus.). 20p. 1999. 20.00 (*1-879832-29-1*) MN Ctr Book Arts.

Bly, Robert. Secrets of a Freelance Writer: How to Make 85,000 Dollars a Year. LC 89-38564. (Owl Bks.). 288p. 1995. pap. 10.95 (*0-8050-1192-7*) H Holt & Co.
— The Sibling Society. LC 96-36867. 1997. pap. 13.00 (*0-679-78128-5*) Vin Bks.
— The Sibling Society. limited ed. 288p. 1996. 100.00 (*0-201-46133-1*) Addison-Wesley.
— Silence in the Snowy Fields: Poems. LC 62-18340. (Wesleyan Poetry Program Ser.: Vol. 15). 60p. 1962. pap. 12.95 (*0-8195-1015-7*, Wesleyan Univ Pr) U Pr of New Eng.
— Soul Is Here For It's Own Joy. 288p. 1999. reprint ed. pap. 15.00 (*0-88001-475-X*) HarpC.
— Talking All Morning. (Poets on Poetry Ser.). 316p. 1980. pap. 18.95 (*0-472-15760-4*, 15760) U of Mich Pr.
— Ten Poems by Issa. (Illus.). 32p. 1992. pap. 6.00 (*0-912449-41-1*) Floating Island.
— We Have Tasted Heaven Many Times: New & Selected Poems. LC 98-51152. 288p. 1999. 25.00 (*0-06-017562-1*) HarpC.
— What's Your Frasier IQ? 501 Questions & Answers for Fans. LC 95-19778. (Illus.). 160p. 1995. pap. 8.95 (*0-8065-1732-8*, Citadel Pr) Carol Pub Group.

Bly, Robert, ed. Leaping Poetry: An Idea with Poems & Translations. LC 73-6243. 112p. 1978. reprint ed. pap. 12.00 (*0-8070-6393-2*) Beacon Pr.

Bly, Robert, ed. The Soul Is Here For It's Own. LC 95-16868. 280p. 1995. 20.00 (*0-88001-355-9*) HarpC.
— Ten Love Poems. 1981. pap. 3.50 (*0-915408-24-4*) Ally Pr.

Bly, Robert, et al, eds. The Rag & Bone Shop of the Heart: A Poetry Anthology. LC 91-50460. 560p. 1993. reprint ed. pap. 17.00 (*0-06-092420-9*, Perennial) HarperTrade.

***Bly, Robert, frwd.** Rumi the Path of Love. (Illus.). 96p. 1999. text 24.95 (*1-86204-633-6*, Pub. by Element MA) Penguin Putnam.

Bly, Robert, intro. News of the Universe: Poems of Twofold Consciousness. LC 79-12812. 320p. 1995. pap. 12.00 (*0-87156-368-1*, Pub. by Sierra) Random.

Bly, Robert & Duffy, William, eds. The Fifties, No. 1. 1982. reprint ed. pap. 5.95 (*0-934888-03-5*) Hobart & Wm Smith.
— The Fifties, No. 2. 1982. reprint ed. pap. 5.95 (*0-934888-04-3*) Hobart & Wm Smith.
— The Fifties, No. 3. 1982. reprint ed. pap. 5.95 (*0-934888-05-1*) Hobart & Wm Smith.
— The Fifties & the Sixties, 10 vols., Set. 1982. pap. 40.00 (*0-934888-13-2*) Hobart & Wm Smith.

Bly, Robert & Duffy, William, eds. The Sixties, No. 4. 1982. reprint ed. pap. 5.95 (*0-934888-06-X*) Hobart & Wm Smith.
— The Sixties, No. 5. 1982. reprint ed. pap. 5.95 (*0-934888-07-8*) Hobart & Wm Smith.
— The Sixties, No. 6. 1982. reprint ed. pap. 5.95 (*0-934888-08-6*) Hobart & Wm Smith.
— The Sixties, No. 7. 1982. reprint ed. pap. 5.95 (*0-934888-09-4*) Hobart & Wm Smith.
— The Sixties, No. 8. 1982. reprint ed. pap. 5.95 (*0-934888-10-8*) Hobart & Wm Smith.
— The Sixties, No. 9. 1982. reprint ed. pap. 5.95 (*0-934888-11-6*) Hobart & Wm Smith.
— The Sixties, No. 10. 1982. reprint ed. pap. 5.95 (*0-934888-12-4*) Hobart & Wm Smith.

Bly, Robert & Ponge, Francis. Ten Poems of Francis Ponge. (Owl's Head Translation Ser.). 1995. per. 9.95 (*0-920635-04-0*) Genl Dist Srvs.

Bly, Robert & Woodman, Marion. The Maiden King: The Reunion of Masculine & Feminine. LC 98-21706. 256p. 1998. 24.00 (*0-8050-5777-3*) H Holt & Co.

***Bly, Robert, et al.** Internet Direct Mail: The Complete Guide to Successful E-Campaigns. 2000. 39.95 (*0-658-00136-1*, Natl Textbk Co) NTC Contemp Pub Co.

Bly, Robert, jt. auth. see Tannen, Deborah.

Bly, Robert, ed. see Jacosen, Rolf.

Bly, Robert, ed. see Kabir.

Bly, Robert, ed. & intro. see Stafford, William.

Bly, Robert, ed. & tr. see Neruda, Pablo & Vallejo, Cesar.

Bly, Robert, tr. see Ekelof, Gunnar.

Bly, Robert, tr. see Ghalib, Mirza A.

Bly, Robert, tr. see Hamsun, Knut.

Bly, Robert, tr. see Hauge, Olav H.

Bly, Robert, tr. see Hernandez, Miguel.

Bly, Robert, tr. see Kabir.

Bly, Robert, tr. see Machado, Antonio.

Bly, Robert, tr. see Maulana, Jalal al-Din Rumi.

Bly, Robert, tr. see Neruda, Pablo.

Bly, Robert, tr. see Rumi, Jalal Al-Din.

Bly, Robert, tr. & comment see Rilke, Rainer Maria.

Bly, Robert, tr. & compiled by see Garcia Lorca, Federico, et al.

Bly, Robert W. The Advertising Manager's Handbook. 2nd ed. LC 98-29618. 800p. (C). 1998. 79.95 (*0-13-757188-7*) P-H.
— Business to Business Direct Marketing: Proven Direct Response Methods to Generate More Leads & Sales. 2nd ed. LC 97-29941. (Illus.). 416p. 1998. 44.95 (*0-8442-3243-2*, NTC Business Bks) NTC Contemp Pub Co.
— Careers for Writers: And Others Who Have a Way with Words. (Careers for You Ser.). (Illus.). 208p. 1995. 14.95 (*0-8442-4333-7*, 43337, VGM Career) NTC Contemp Pub Co.
— Careers for Writers: And Others Who Have a Way with Words. LC 95-23253. (Careers for You Ser.). (Illus.). 208p. 1995. pap. 9.95 (*0-8442-4334-5*, 43345, VGM Career) NTC Contemp Pub Co.
— Create the Perfect Sales Piece: How To Produce Brochures, Catalogs, Fliers & Pamphlets. LC 85-12457. 243p. 1985. pap. 17.95 (*0-471-82525-5*) Wiley.
— The Encyclopedia of Business Letters, Fax Memos, & E-Mail. 288p. 1999. pap. 18.99 (*1-56414-375-9*) Career Pr Inc.

***Bly, Robert W.** Getting Started in Speaking, Training or Seminar Consulting. (Getting Started in Ser.). 256p. 2000. pap. 19.95 (*0-471-38882-3*) Wiley.
— How to Get Your Book Published. 224p. 2000. pap. 14.95 (*0-934968-14-4*, 494-008, Pub. by Roblin Pr) BookWorld.

Bly, Robert W. The Lead Generation Handbook: How to Generate All the Sales Leads You'll Ever Need-Quickly, Easily & Inexpensively. LC 98-6003. 320p. 1998. 59.95 (*0-8144-0363-8*) AMACOM.

***Bly, Robert W.** 101 Ways to Make Every Second Count: Time Management Tips & Techniques for More Success with Less Stress. LC 99-25026. 224p. 1999. pap. 14.99 (*1-56414-406-2*) Career Pr Inc.

Bly, Robert W. The Perfect Sales Piece: A Complete Do-It-Yourself Guide to Creating Brochures, Catalogs, Fliers. LC 94-11311. 237p. 1994. pap. 14.95 (*0-471-00411-1*) Wiley.
— The Perfect Sales Piece: A Complete Do-It-Yourself Guide to Creating Brochures, Catalogs, Fliers, & Pamphlets. (Small Business Editions Ser.). 237p. 1994. 49.95 (*0-471-00403-0*) Wiley.
— Power-Packed Direct Mail: How to Get More Leads & Sales by Mail. LC 94-32821. 1995. 25.00 (*0-8050-3505-2*) H Holt & Co.
— Power-Packed Direct Mail: How to Get More Leads & Sales by Mail. 1995. pap. 14.95 (*0-8050-3506-0*) H Holt & Co.
— Secrets of a Freelance Writer. 2nd rev. ed. LC 97-2229. 1995. pap. 12.95 (*0-8050-4760-3*) H Holt & Co.
— Secrets of Successful Telephone Selling. LC 96-40389. 224p. 1995. pap. 14.95 (*0-8050-4098-6*, Owl) H Holt & Co.
— Selling Your Services: Proven Strategies for Getting Clients to Hire You (Or Your Firm) 368p. 1995. pap. 14.95 (*0-8050-2041-1*, Owl) H Holt & Co.
— The Six Figure Consultant: How to Start (or Jump-Start) Your consulting Career & Earl $100,000+ a Year. LC 98-28295. 256p. 1998. 29.95 (*1-57410-120-X*, 56158801) Dearborn.
— Start & Run a Profitable Mail-Order Business: Getting Started for under $500: Your Step-by-Step Business Plan. 176p. (Orig.). 1997. pap. 14.95 (*1-55180-065-9*) Self-Counsel Pr.
— Targeted Public Relations: How to Get Thousands of Dollars of Free Publicity for Your Product, Service, Organization, or Idea. 352p. 1995. pap. 14.95 (*0-8050-1974-X*) H Holt & Co.
— The Ultimate Unauthorized Stephen King Trivia Challenge. LC 97-224828. 304p. 1997. pap. 14.00 (*1-57566-228-0*, Knsington) Kensgtn Pub Corp.

***Bly, Robert W.** Ultimate Unauthorized Stephen King Trivia Challenge. 240p. 1998. 8.95 (*1-56731-288-8*, MJF Bks) Fine Comms.

Bly, Robert W. Write More, Sell More. LC 98-15816. 240p. 1998. 17.99 (*0-89879-816-7*, Wrtrs Digest Bks) F & W Pubns Inc.

***Bly, Robert W., ed.** The Best American Poetry, 1999. 224p. 1999. per. 14.00 (*0-684-86003-1*) Scribner.

Bly, Robert W. & Lehman, David, eds. Best American Poetry, 1999. 224p. 1999. 29.50 (*0-684-84280-7*) Scribner.

Bly, Robert W., jt. auth. see Blake, Gary.

Bly, Stephen. False Claims at the Little Stephen Mine. large type ed. LC 94-12085. 269p. 1994. lib. bdg. 18.95 (*0-8161-7405-9*, G K Hall Lrg Type) Mac Lib Ref.
— Hard Winter at Broken Arrow Crossing. large type ed. LC 93-19643. 234p. 1993. lib. bdg. 18.95 (*0-8161-5822-3*, G K Hall Lrg Type) Mac Lib Ref.

***Bly, Stephen.** Hidden Treasure. (Chronicles of the Golden Frontier Ser.: Bk. 2). 272p. 2000. pap. 11.99 (*1-58134-199-7*) Crossway Bks.

Bly, Stephen. I'm Off to Montana for to Throw the Hoolihan. LC 97-17736. (Code of the West Ser.: Vol. 6). 208p. 1997. pap. 9.99 (*0-89107-953-X*) Crossway Bks.
— I'm Off to Montana for to Throw the Hoolihan. large type ed. LC 98-34801. 255p. 1998. 22.95 (*0-7838-0338-9*, G K Hall Lrg Type) Mac Lib Ref.
— It's Your Misfortune & None of My Own. large type ed. LC 96-11957. (West-Hall Ser.: Bk. 1). 280p. (Orig.). 1997. lib. bdg. 22.95 (*0-7838-1787-8*, G K Hall Lrg Type) Mac Lib Ref.
— The Kill Fee of Cindy LaCoste. LC 97-18925. (Austin-Stoner Files Ser.: Bk. 3). 384p. 1997. pap. 11.99 (*0-89107-954-8*) Crossway Bks.
— Last Swan in Sacramento. LC 99-21425. (Old California Ser.: Vol. 2). 224p. 1999. pap. 10.99 (*1-58134-109-1*) Crossway Bks.
— The Lost Manuscript of Martin Taylor Harrison. LC 95-2613. (Austin-Stoner Files Ser.: Bk. 1). 352p. 1995. pap. 11.99 (*0-89107-852-5*) Crossway Bks.

***Bly, Stephen.** Marthellen & the Major. 260p. 2000. pap. 10.99 (*1-56955-159-6*) Servant.

Bly, Stephen. Miss Fontenot. LC 98-46369. (Heroines of the Golden West Ser.: No. 3). 224p. 1999. pap. 10.99 (*1-58134-074-5*) Crossway Bks.

B

An Asterisk (*) at the beginning of an entry indicates that the title is appearing for the first time.

B

***Bly, Stephen.** Miss Fontenot. large type ed. LC 99-33512. 1999. 24.95 (*0-7838-8729-9*, G K Hall Lrg Type) Mac Lib Ref.

— Proud Quail of the San Joaquin. LC 99-49704. (Old California Ser.: Vol. 3). 240p. 2000. pap. 10.99 (*1-58134-152-0*) Crossway Bks.

— Roberta & the Renegade, 3. (Carson City Chronicles Ser.). 2000. pap. 10.99 (*1-56955-123-5*) Servant.

Bly, Stephen. Son of an Arizona Legend. LC 94-360. (Stuart Brannon Western Adventure Ser.: Vol. 6). 192p. 1994. pap. 8.99 (*0-89107-770-7*) Crossway Bks.

— Stay Away from That City...They Call It Cheyene. large type ed. LC 97-50408. (Western Ser.). 293p. 1998. 24.95 (*0-7838-8414-1*, G K Hall & Co) Mac Lib Ref.

— Time Warp Tunnel. (Making Choices Ser.). (Illus.). 160p. (J). (gr. 3-6). 1995. pap. 4.99 (*0-7814-0187-9*) Chariot Victor.

— Where the Deer & the Antelope Play. large type ed. LC 96-11959. (West-Hall Ser.: Bk. 3). 280p. (Orig.). 1997. lib. bdg. 22.95 (*0-7838-1789-4*, G K Hall Lrg Type) Mac Lib Ref.

Bly, Stephen & Bly, Janet. Fox Island. large type ed. LC 98-42035. (Christian Fiction Ser.). 1999. 24.95 (*0-7862-1679-4*) Thorndike Pr.

Bly, Stephen A. Beneath a Dakota Cross. LC 99-18878. (Fortune of the Black Hills Ser.: Vol. 1). 224p. 1999. pap. 9.99 (*0-8054-1659-5*) Broadman.

— Columbia Falls. large type ed. LC 99-32535. 351p. 1999. pap. 23.95 (*0-7862-2055-4*) Mac Lib Ref.

— Copper Hill. large type ed. LC 98-53620. 1999. 23.95 (*0-7862-1805-3*) Thorndike Pr.

— Danger at Deception Pass. LC 97-32231. (Lewis & Clark Squad Adventure Ser.: Vol. 5). 160p. (J). (gr. 8-12). 1998. pap. 4.99 (*0-89107-985-8*) Crossway Bks.

— The Final Chapter of Chance McCall. LC 96-11176. (Austin-Stoner Files Ser.: Bk. 2). 368p. 1996. pap. 11.99 (*0-89107-903-3*) Crossway Bks.

— Final Justice at Adobe Wells. LC 93-14185. (Stuart Brannon Western Adventure Ser.: No. 5). 192p. 1993. pap. 8.99 (*0-89107-744-8*) Crossway Bks.

***Bly, Stephen A.** Fool's Gold. LC 99-89568. (Skinners of Goldfield: Bk. 1). 272p. 2000. pap. 11.99 (*1-58134-155-5*) Crossway Bks.

Bly, Stephen A. Hard Winter at Broken Arrow Crossing. LC 91-11345. (Stuart Brannon Western Adventure Ser.: No. 1). 192p. 1991. pap. 8.99 (*0-89107-620-4*) Crossway Bks.

— Hawks Don't Say Goodbye, No. 6. LC 94-20255. (Nathan T. Riggins Adventure Ser.: Vol. 6). 128p. (J). (gr. 4-7). 1994. pap. 4.99 (*0-89107-782-0*) Crossway Bks.

— Hazards of the Half-Court Press. LC 97-32230. (Lewis & Clark Squad Adventure Ser.: Vol. 6). 160p. (J). (gr. 8-12). 1998. pap. 4.99 (*0-89107-986-6*) Crossway Bks.

— Intrigue at the Rafter B Ranch. LC 96-40083. (Lewis & Clark Squad Adventure Ser.: Vol. 1). 160p. (J). (gr. 4-9). 1997. pap. 4.99 (*0-89107-939-4*) Crossway Bks.

— It's Your Misfortune & None of My Own. LC 94-15386. (Code of the West Ser.: Vol. 1). 192p. 1994. pap. 9.99 (*0-89107-797-9*) Crossway Bks.

***Bly, Stephen A.** Judith & the Judge. (Carson City Chronicles Ser.). 260p. 2000. pap. 10.99 (*1-56955-158-8*) Servant.

Bly, Stephen A. Just Because They've Left Doesn't Mean They're Gone. LC 93-1318. 1993. 14.99 (*1-56179-140-7*) Focus Family.

— Last Hanging at Paradise Meadow. LC 92-13085. (Stuart Brannon Western Adventure Ser.: Vol. 3). 192p. 1992. pap. 8.99 (*0-89107-672-7*) Crossway Bks.

— The Last Stubborn Buffalo in Nevada, No. 4. LC 93-8654. (Nathan T. Riggins Western Adventure Ser.: Vol. 4). 128p. (J). (gr. 4-9). 1993. pap. 4.99 (*0-89107-746-4*) Crossway Bks.

***Bly, Stephen A.** The Last Swan in Sacramento. LC 00-33461. (Old California Ser.). 2000. write for info. (*0-7838-9127-X*, G K Hall & Co) Mac Lib Ref.

— The Long Trail Home. 2001. pap. 12.99 (*0-8054-2356-7*) Broadman.

Bly, Stephen A. The Lost Manuscript of Martin Taylor Harrison. large type ed. 465p. (Orig.). 1996. 21.95 (*0-7838-1596-4*, G K Hall Lrg Type) Mac Lib Ref.

— The Marquesa. LC 98-33717. (Heroines of the Golden West Ser.). 1998. pap. text 10.99 (*1-58134-025-7*) Crossway Bks.

— The Marquesa. LC 99-22371. (Heroines of the Golden West Ser.). 1999. 23.95 (*0-7838-8608-X*, G K Hall & Co) Mac Lib Ref.

— My Foots in the Stirrup - My Pony Won't Stand. large type ed. LC 98-18672. (Code of the West Ser.). 316p. 1998. 21.95 (*0-7838-0177-7*, G K Hall Lrg Type) Mac Lib Ref.

— My Foot's in the Stirrup--My Pony Won't Stand, No. 5. LC 96-31445. (Code of the West Ser.: Vol. 5). 192p. 1996. pap. 9.99 (*0-89107-898-3*) Crossway Bks.

— One Went to Denver & the Other Went Wrong. LC 94-38680. (Code of the West Ser.: Bk. 2). 192p. (gr. 8 up). 1995. pap. 9.99 (*0-89107-834-7*) Crossway Bks.

— The Red Dove of Monterey. LC 98-16580. (Old California Ser.: Vol. 1). 224p. 1998. 10.99 (*1-58134-004-4*) Crossway Bks.

***Bly, Stephen A.** Red Dove of Monterey. large type ed. LC 99-59551. (G. K. Hall Western Ser.). 2000. 25.95 (*0-7838-8944-5*, G K Hall Lrg Type) Mac Lib Ref.

Bly, Stephen A. Revenge on Eagle Island. LC 97-32232. (Lewis & Clark Squad Adventure Ser.: Vol. 4). 160p. (J). (gr. 8-12). 1998. pap. 4.99 (*0-89107-984-X*) Crossway Bks.

— The Secret of the Old Rifle. LC 96-40081. (Lewis & Clark Squad Adventure Ser.: No. 2). 160p. (J). (gr. 4-9). 1997. pap. 4.99 (*0-89107-940-8*) Crossway Bks.

***Bly, Stephen A.** Shadow of Legends. LC 99-16673. (Fortunes of the Black Hills Ser.: No. 2). 224p. 2000. pap. 12.99 (*0-8054-2174-2*) Broadman.

Bly, Stephen A. Standoff at Sunrise Creek. LC 92-33517. (Stuart Brannon Western Ser.: Vol. 4). 192p. 1993. pap. 8.99 (*0-89107-695-6*) Crossway Bks.

— Stay Away from That City They Call It Cheyenne. LC 95-26675. (Code of the West Ser.: Vol. 4). 192p. 1996. pap. 9.99 (*0-89107-890-8*) Crossway Bks.

— Sweet Carolina. LC 97-49183. (Heroines of the Golden West Ser.: Vol. 1). 224p. (gr. 7-12). 1998. pap. 10.99 (*0-89107-973-4*) Crossway Bks.

— Sweet Carolina. large type ed. LC 98-31301. 1999. 30.00 (*0-7838-0410-5*) Mac Lib Ref.

— Treachery at the River Canyon. LC 96-40088. (Lewis & Clark Squad Adventure Ser.: No.3). 160p. (J). (gr. 4-9). 1997. pap. 4.99 (*0-89107-941-6*) Crossway Bks.

— Where the Deer & the Antelope Play. large type ed. LC 95-14510. (Code of the West Ser.: Bk. 3). 192p. 1995. pap. 9.99 (*0-89107-850-9*) Crossway Bks.

Bly, Steven. Surprising Side of Grace: Appreciating God's Loving Anger. LC 94-11149. 192p. 1994. pap. 9.99 (*0-929239-89-X*) Discovery Hse Pubs.

Bly, William. The Crucible (Miller) (Barron's Book Notes Ser.). (C). 1984. pap. 3.95 (*0-8120-3408-2*) Barron.

Blyden, Edward W. African Life & Customs. LC 93-74113. 96p. 1993. reprint ed. pap. 8.95 (*0-933121-43-1*) Black Classic.

— African Life & Customs. (African Studies). 1993. reprint ed. 15.00 (*0-938818-31-7*) ECA Assoc.

— Christianity, Islam & the Negro Race. LC 93-74112. 441p. 1993. reprint ed. pap. 14.95 (*0-933121-41-5*) Black Classic.

— Christianity, Islam & the Negro Race. (African Heritage Classical Research Studies). 407p. reprint ed. 40.00 (*0-938818-36-8*) ECA Assoc.

— Christianity, Islam & the Negro Race. 408p. (C). 1990. reprint ed. 34.95 (*0-685-45610-2*); reprint ed. pap. 21.95 (*0-685-45611-0*) J Richardson.

***Blyden, Nemata.** West Indians in West Africa, 1808-1880: The African Diaspora in Reverse. (Rochester Studies in the History of the African Diaspora: Vol. 1092-5228). 320p. 2000. 75.00 (*1-58046-046-1*) Univ Rochester Pr.

Blye, Richard P., jt. ed. see Gregoire, A. T.

Blyenburgh, Hans Van, see Van Blyenburgh, Hans.

Blyle, Nancy Roundy, jt. auth. see Perkins, Jane.

Blyler, D. A. Shared Solitude. (Illus.). 68p. (Orig.). 1995. pap. 7.95 (*0-9645655-1-X*) BurnhillWolf.

Blyler, John E. & Ray, Gary A. What's Size Got to Do with It? Understanding Rightsizing. LC 97-24334. 416p. 1997. pap. 44.95 (*0-7803-1096-9*, PP4499) Inst Electrical.

Blyler, Nancy & Thralls, Charlotte. Professional Communication: The Social Perspective. (Illus.). 320p. (C). 1992. 46.00 (*0-8039-3934-5*); pap. 19.95 (*0-8039-3935-3*) Sage.

Blyler, Nancy R. Strategies for Technical Communication. fac. ed. LC 84-26134. (Illus.). 441p. 1985. reprint ed. pap. 136.80 (*0-7837-8215-2*, 204791500008) Bks Demand.

Blylock, Robert C., jt. auth. see Anstall, Harold B.

Blymyer Engineering, Inc. Staff. Environmental Compliance Manual for Land Transportation. LC 98-23054. (Illus.). 408p. 1998. 138.95 (*0-07-006896-8*) McGraw-Hill Prof.

***Blymyer, Ginger Sugar.** Hairdresser to the Stars: A Memoir. LC 99-69436. 2000. 25.00 (*0-7388-1268-4*); pap. 18.00 (*0-7388-1269-2*) Xlibris Corp.

Blystone, Jasper. The Pragmatics of the Human Heritage. 92p. (Orig.). 1997. 19.95 (*0-941910-13-X*) Long Beach Pubns.

Blyth & Kelton. Paralleles Interactive MAC. (C). 1996. 66.67 (*0-13-242140-2*) P-H.

Blyth, Alan. Opera on CD: The Essential Guide to the Best Recordings of 100 Operas. 3rd ed. 192p. 1995. pap. 19.95 (*1-85626-139-5*, Pub. by Cathie Kyle) Trafalgar.

— Opera on Video: The Essential Guide. 246p. 1996. pap. 19.95 (*1-85626-175-1*, Pub. by Cathie Kyle) Trafalgar.

Blyth, Alan, ed. Choral Music on Record. 317p. (C). 1991. text 47.95 (*0-521-36309-8*) Cambridge U Pr.

— Song on Record, Vol. 2. 296p. 1988. text 49.95 (*0-521-33155-2*) Cambridge U Pr.

***Blyth, Alastair & Worthington, John.** Managing the Brief for Better Design. LC 00-33908. 2000. pap. write for info. (*0-419-24470-0*, E & FN Spon) Routledge.

Blyth, Carl. Untangling the Web: A Beginner's Guide to Language & Culture on the Internet. LC 97-80140. (Illus.). 160p. 1997. pap. text 14.95 (*0-312-18254-6*) St Martin.

— Untangling the Web, 1999 Edition: Nonce's Guide to Language & Culture on the Internet. LC 99-209865. (Illus.). 160p. 1998. pap. text 12.00 (*1-893022-50-1*) Nonce Pubs.

***Blyth, Carl S.** Untangling the Web: Nonce's Guide to Language & Culture on the Internet. 2000. pap. write for info. (*0-471-39247-2*) Wiley.

Blyth, Charles R., ed. Thomas Hoccleve: The Regiment of Princes. (Teams). viii, 278p. (C). pap. text 18.00 (*1-58044-023-1*) Medieval Inst.

Blyth, Dale A. & Karnes, Elizabeth L., compiled by. Philosophy, Policies & Programs for Early Adolescent Education: An Annotated Bibliography. LC 81-4237. 689p. 1981. lib. bdg. 89.50 (*0-313-22687-3*, BEA/, Greenwood Pr) Greenwood.

Blyth, Dale A. & Saito, Rebecca N. Understanding Mentoring Relationships. 62p. 1992. pap. text 8.00 (*1-57482-316-7*) Search Inst.

Blyth, Dale A., et al. Making the Case: Measuring the Impact of Youth Development Programs. (Illus.). 28p. (Orig.). 1996. pap. 6.95 (*1-57482-721-9*) Search Inst.

Blyth, Dale A., jt. auth. see Roehlkepartain, Eugene C.

Blyth, Dale A., jt. auth. see Simmons, Roberta G.

Blyth, Derek. Amsterdam Explored. (Pallas for Pleasure Ser.). (Illus.). 274p. 1997. pap. 14.95 (*1-873429-63-0*, XC3711) Cimino Pub Grp.

***Blyth, Derek.** Belgium. 9th ed. (Blue Guide Ser.). (Illus.). 448p. 2000. pap. 24.95 (*0-393-32012-X*) Norton.

Blyth, Derek. Brussels Explored. (Illus.). 320p. 1998. pap. text 19.95 (*1-873429-14-2*, Pub. by Pallas Athene) Cimino Pub Grp.

***Blyth, Derek.** Flemish Cities Explored: Bruges, Ghent, Leuven, Mechelen, Antwerp & Ostend. 4th ed. (Illus.). 2000. pap. 24.95 (*1-873429-30-4*) Pallas Athene.

Blyth, Eric & Milner, Judith. Improving School Attendance. LC 98-38000. 1999. 85.00 (*0-415-17871-1*); pap. 27.99 (*0-415-17872-X*) Routledge.

— Social Work with Children: The Educational Perspective. LC 97-25031. x, 164p. 1997. write for info. (*0-582-29308-1*) Longman.

Blyth, Joan. History in Primary Schools: A Practical Approach for Teachers of 5 to 11 Year Old Children. 224p. 1989. pap. 31.95 (*0-335-15829-3*) OpUniv Pr.

Blyth, John. Farm Woodland Management. 2nd ed. (Illus.). 208p. 1991. 34.95 (*0-85236-219-6*, Pub. by Farming Pr) Diamond Farm Bk.

Blyth, Juliet. The Parfit Knight. 1987. reprint ed. pap. 3.50 (*0-317-64583-8*) St Martin.

Blyth, Kenneth K. Cradle Crew: Royal Canadian Air Force World War II. LC 98-120470. (Illus.). 197p. 1997. pap. 19.95 (*0-89745-217-8*) Sunflower U Pr.

Blyth, Laureli. The Numerology of Names. 152p. (Orig.). 1996. pap. 9.95 (*0-7137-2636-9*, Pub. by Blandford Pr) Sterling.

Blyth, Mary M. & Blyth, W. John. Telecommunications: Concepts, Development & Management. 352p. (C). 1985. teacher ed. write for info. (*0-672-97992-6*); text. write for info. (*0-672-97991-8*) Macmillan.

Blyth, Mary M., jt. auth. see Blyth, W. John.

Blyth, Pamela L. OSHA's Final Bloodborne Pathogens Standard: Implications for Health Care Environmental Services. 96p. (Orig.). 1993. pap. 40.00 (*0-87258-632-4*, 057014) Am Hospital.

Blyth, Pamela L., ed. Health Care Environmental Services: Staffing the Department - Key Considerations & Options. LC 93-1311. (Illus.). 96p. (Orig.). 1993. pap. 75.00 (*0-87258-640-5*, 057015) Am Hospital.

— Health Care Finishes: Problems & Solutions - an Environmental Services Perspective. 92p. (Orig.). 1993. pap. 60.00 (*0-87258-643-X*, 057016) Am Hospital.

Blyth, R. H. Haiku: Autumn - Winter, Index. (Illus.). 330p. 1997. pap. 32.95 (*4-590-00575-1*, Pub. by Hokuseido Pr) Book East.

— Haiku: Spring. (Illus.). 300p. 1997. pap. 32.95 (*4-590-00573-5*, Pub. by Hokuseido Pr) Book East.

— Haiku: Summer-Autumn. (Illus.). 340p. 1997. pap. 32.95 (*4-590-00574-3*, Pub. by Hokuseido Pr) Book East.

— Haiku Vol. 1: Eastern Culture. (Illus.). 350p. 1997. pap. 32.95 (*4-590-00572-7*, Pub. by Hokuseido Pr) Book East.

— A History of Haiku Vol. 1: From the Beginning up to Issa. rev. ed. (Illus.). 440p. 1997. pap. 32.95 (*0-9647040-2-1*, Pub. by Hokuseido Pr) Book East.

— A History of Haiku Vol. 2: From Issa up to the Present. (Illus.). 430p. 1998. reprint ed. pap. 32.95 (*0-9647040-3-X*, Pub. by Hokuseido Pr) Book East.

— Senryu: Japanese Satirical Verses. LC 72-98820. 230p. 1971. reprint ed. lib. bdg. 35.00 (*0-8371-2958-3*, BLSE, Greenwood Pr) Greenwood.

— Zen in English Literature & Oriental Classics. (Illus.). 302p. 1942. reprint ed. pap. 27.95 (*0-9647040-1-3*) Book East.

Blyth, Sally & Wotherspoon, Ian, eds. Hong Kong Remembers. (Illus.). 296p. 1997. text 45.00 (*0-19-587768-3*) OUP.

Blyth, T. S. Mathematical Terms in Computer Science: A Glossary. 200p. 1993. 20.00 (*0-387-19611-0*) Spr-Verlag.

Blyth, T. S. & Janowitz, M. F. Residuation Theory. LC 77-142177. 380p. (C). 1972. 170.00 (*0-08-016408-0*, Pub. by Pergamon Repr) Franklin.

Blyth, T. S. & Robertson, E. F. Algebra Thru Practice, Bk. 1. 112p. 1984. pap. text 14.95 (*0-521-27285-8*) Cambridge U Pr.

— Algebra Thru Practice, Bk. 2. 112p. 1984. pap. text 14.95 (*0-521-27286-6*) Cambridge U Pr.

— Algebra Thru Practice, Bk. 6. 112p. 1985. pap. text 14.95 (*0-521-27291-2*) Cambridge U Pr.

— Basic Linear Algebra. LC 97-28661. (Undergraduate Mathematics Ser.). (Illus.). xi, 201p. 1998. pap. 29.95 (*3-540-76122-5*) Spr-Verlag.

— Essential Student Algebra, 5 vols., 1. 128p. 1986. pap. text 12.95 (*0-412-27880-4*, 9989) Chapman & Hall.

— Essential Student Algebra, 5 vols., 2. 128p. 1986. pap. text 12.95 (*0-412-27870-7*, 9995) Chapman & Hall.

— Essential Student Algebra, 5 vols., 3. 128p. 1986. pap. text 12.95 (*0-412-27860-X*, 9999) Chapman & Hall.

— Essential Student Algebra, 5 vols., 4. 128p. 1986. pap. text 12.95 (*0-412-27850-2*, 8012) Chapman & Hall.

— Essential Student Algebra, 5 vols., Vol. 5. 128p. (C). (gr. 13). 1986. ring bd. 35.95 (*0-412-27840-5*, 1000) Chapman & Hall.

Blyth, T. S. & Varlet, J. C. Ockham Algebras. (Illus.). 250p. 1994. text 115.00 (*0-19-859938-2*) OUP.

Blyth, W. John & Blyth, Mary M. Telecommunications: Concepts, Development, & Management. 2nd ed. 1990. text 46.12 (*0-02-680841-2*) Glencoe.

Blyth, W. John, jt. auth. see Blyth, Mary M.

Blyth, Wynter. Butterflies of the Indian Region. (Illus.). 523p. 1982. 75.00 (*0-88065-247-0*, Pub. by Today Tomorrow) Scholarly Pubns.

Blythe, A. Complete Guide to Liberty Seated Half Dimes. (Illus.). 1992. pap. 30.00 (*1-880731-07-X*) S J Durst.

***Blythe, Anne, et al.** Best Program. 2000. pap. 29.95 (*0-86431-336-5*, Pub. by Aust Council Educ Res) Stylus Pub VA.

Blythe, Anne, ed. & intro. see Pringle, Elizabeth A.

Blythe, Betty J. & Tripodi, Tony. Measurement in Direct Practice. (Human Services Guides Ser.: Vol. 59). 160p. (C). 1989. pap. text 18.95 (*0-8039-3080-1*) Sage.

Blythe, Betty J., et al. Direct Practice Research in Human Service Agencies. LC 94-24325. (Illus.). 240p. 1995. 57.50 (*0-231-07366-6*); pap. 26.50 (*0-231-07367-4*) Col U Pr.

Blythe, Daniel. Dr. Who Handbook: The First Doctor. (Dr. Who New Adventures Ser.). (Illus.). 1995. mass mkt. 5.95 (*0-426-20430-1*, Pub. by Virgin Bks) London Brdge.

Blythe, G. German-English Glossary of Pyschiatric Terms. (ENG & GER.). 95p. 1987. lib. bdg. 95.00 (*0-8288-3409-1*, F79921) Fr & Eur.

Blythe, G., tr. see Kroger, Fred, et al.

Blythe, H. J., ed. see International Symposium on the Decontamination of.

Blythe, Hal & Sweet, Charlie. It Works for Me: Shared Tips for Teaching. 94p. (C). 1998. pap. 15.95 (*0-913507-95-4*) New Forums.

Blythe, Hal, et al. Private Eyes: A Writer's Guide to Private Investigators. (Howdunit Ser.). 208p. (Orig.). 1993. pap. 15.99 (*0-89879-549-4*, Wrtrs Digest Bks) F & W Pubns Inc.

Blythe, Hal T., et al. Competencies in Materials Development & Machine Operation: Self Directive Activities, a Functional Approach. 2nd ed. (Illus.). 173p. 1982. pap. text 11.95 (*0-89641-114-1*) American Pr.

Blythe, Helen S. Knights of the Oblong Table. (Illus.). 128p. 1996. pap. 16.00 (*0-933380-21-6*) Olive Pr Pubns.

Blythe, Hy, ed. see Pioneer Museum Staff.

Blythe, James M. Ideal Government & the Mixed Constitution in the Middle Ages. 365p. 1992. text 59.50 (*0-691-03167-3*, Pub. by Princeton U Pr) Cal Prin Full Svc.

Blythe, James M., tr. see Bartholomew of Lucca.

Blythe, Jim. Essence of Consumer Behaviour. 150p. (C). 1997. pap. text 19.95 (*0-13-573122-4*) P-H.

— Essentials of Marketing. 320p. 2000. pap. write for info. (*0-273-63021-0*) F T P H.

— Marketing Communications. LC 99-25715. 356p. 2000. 42.50 (*0-273-63960-9*) F T P H.

Blythe, LeGette. William Henry Belk: Merchant of the South. LC 58-14574. xvi, 271p. 1950. 29.95 (*0-8078-0729-X*) U of NC Pr.

Blythe-Lord, Robin. Captions & Graphics for Low Budget Video. (Illus.). 123p. 1992. 44.95 (*0-240-51312-6*, Focal) Buttrwrth-Heinemann.

— Captions & Graphics for Low Budget Video. LC 92-770. (Illus.). 129p. reprint ed. pap. 40.00 (*0-608-06251-0*, 206658000008) Bks Demand.

Blythe, Martin. Naming the Other: Images of the Maori in New Zealand Film & Television. LC 94-495. (Illus.). 342p. 1994. 45.00 (*0-8108-2741-7*) Scarecrow.

Blythe, Ronald. Characters & Their Landscapes. LC 83-7890. (Helen & Kurt Wolff Bk.). Orig. Title: From the Headlands. 224p. 1983. 14.95 (*0-15-116792-3*) Harcourt.

***Blythe, Ronald.** Divine Landscapes: A Pilgrimage Through Britain's Sacred Places. (Illus.). 256p. 2000. pap. 23.95 (*1-85311-194-5*) Canterbury Press Norwich.

Blythe, Ronald. The Visitors: The Stories of Ronald Blythe. LC 85-8527. (Helen & Kurt Wolff Bk.). 256p. 1985. 16.95 (*0-15-193912-8*) Harcourt.

Blythe, Ronald, ed. see Hardy, Thomas.

Blythe, Ronald, ed. & intro. see James, Henry.

Blythe, Tina. Teaching for Understanding. LC 97-33735. 208p. 1997. pap., wbk. ed. 27.95 (*0-7879-0993-9*) Jossey-Bass.

Blythe, Tina, et al. Looking Together at Students' Work: A Companion Guide to Assessing Student Learning. LC 99-22561. 21. 64p. 1999. pap. 11.95 (*0-8077-3855-7*) Tchrs Coll.

— Teaching Practical Intelligence: What Research Tells Us. LC 95-32138. (What Research Tells Us Ser.). 16p. 1995. pap. 1.50 (*0-912099-31-3*, 402) Kappa Delta Pi.

Blythe, Will, ed. Why I Write: Thoughts on the Craft of Fiction. LC 98-21419. 256p. (gr. 8). 1998. 23.00 (*0-316-10229-6*, Back Bay) Little.

— Why I Write: Thoughts on the Craft of Fiction. 256p. 1999. pap. 13.95 (*0-316-11592-4*, Back Bay) Little.

Blytheway, Bill, jt. auth. see Bryar, Rosamund.

Blythin, Evan. Huei Tlatoani: The Mexican Speaker. 110p. (Orig.). (C). 1990. pap. text 15.00 (*0-8191-7934-5*); lib. bdg. 33.00 (*0-8191-7933-7*) U Pr of Amer.

— The Universe of Discourses: Issues & Features. LC 94-22106. 1994. 29.50 (*0-8191-9638-X*) U Pr of Amer.

***Blythman, Joanna.** Food We Eat. 320p. 1998. pap. 13.95 (*0-14-027366-2*, Pub. by Pnguin Bks Ltd) Trafalgar.

***Blyton, Enid.** El Bebe Entre los Juncos. (SPA.). 1999. pap. 4.99 (*0-8254-1063-0*) Kregel.

— Best Stories for 5-Year-Olds. (Enid Blyton's Best Stories Ser.). (Illus.). 128p. (J). (gr. k). 2000. pap. 6.95 (*0-7475-3225-7*, Pub. by Blmsbury Pub) Trafalgar.

— Best Stories for 7-Year-Olds. (Enid Blyton's Best Stories Ser.). (Illus.). 128p. (J). (gr. 2). 2000. pap. 6.95 (*0-7475-3227-3*, Pub. by Blmsbury Pub) Trafalgar.

— Best Stories for 6-Year-Olds. (Enid Blyton's Best Stories Ser.). (Illus.). 128p. (J). (gr. 1). 2000. pap. 6.95 (*0-7475-3226-5*, Pub. by Blmsbury Pub) Trafalgar.

Blyton, Enid. Bible Stories. (Religious Stories Ser.). 128p. (J). (gr. 3 up). 1998. 6.95 (*1-901881-42-3*, Pub. by Element MA) Penguin Putnam.

***Blyton, Enid.** Bimbo & Topsy. (Enid Blyton's Happy Days Ser.). (Illus.). 96p. (J). (gr. 1-4). 2000. pap. 6.95 (*0-7475-3220-6*, Pub. by Blmsbury Pub) Trafalgar.

— Binkle & Flip Misbehave. (Enid Blyton's Happy Days Ser.). (Illus.). 96p. (J). (gr. 1-4). 1999. pap. 6.95 (*0-7475-4350-X*, Pub. by Blmsbury Pub) Trafalgar.

— Christmas Story. (Orig.). (J). 1992. 8.95 (*0-09-987840-2*, Pub. by Random) Trafalgar.

— David, el Nino Pastor. (SPA.). 1999. pap. 4.99 (*0-8254-1064-9*, Edit Portavoz) Kregel.

— The Famous Five: Five Have a Mystery to Solve. large type ed. (Illus.). (J). 2000. pap. write for info. (*0-7540-6094-2*) Chivers N Amer.

Blyton, Enid. The First Christmas. LC 98-37941. (Religious Stories Ser.). 96p. (J). (gr. 3 up). 1998. 6.95 (*1-901881-32-6*, Pub. by Element MA) Penguin Putnam.

***Blyton, Enid.** Five Go to Demon's Rocks. large type ed. (Illus.). (J). 1999. pap. write for info. (*0-7540-6082-9*, Galaxy Child Lrg Print) Chivers N Amer.

Blyton, Enid. Five Have Plenty of Fun. large type ed. (Illus.). (J). 1998. pap. 16.95 (*0-7540-6012-8*, Galaxy Child Lrg Print) Chivers N Amer.

— Five on a Secret Trail. large type ed. (J). 1998. pap. 16.95 (*0-7540-6024-1*, Galaxy Child Lrg Print) Chivers N Amer.

***Blyton, Enid.** Five on Finniston Farm. 1999. 16.95 (*0-7540-6065-9*) Chivers N Amer.

— The Knights of the Round Table. LC 98-36321. (Myths & Legends Ser.). (Illus.). 96p. (J). (gr. 3 up). 1998. pap. 4.95 (*1-901881-72-5*, Pub. by Element MA) Penguin Putnam.

Blyton, Enid. The Land of Far Beyond. (Religious Stories Ser.). 128p. (J). (gr. 3 up). 1998. 6.95 (*1-901881-22-9*, Pub. by Element MA) Penguin Putnam.

***Blyton, Enid.** Last Term at Malory Towers. (J). 1999. mass mkt. 7.50 (*1-84032-061-3*, Pub. by HOD2) Ulverscroft.

Blyton, Enid. Learn the Alphabet with Noddy. (Illus.). 32p. (J). (ps-k). 1999. pap. 3.99 (*0-06-102017-6*, HarpEntertain) Morrow Avon.

— Learn to Count with Noddy. (Illus.). 32p. (J). (ps-k). 1999. pap. 3.99 (*0-06-102018-4*, HarpEntertain) Morrow Avon.

***Blyton, Enid.** Mr Pink-Whistle Has Some Fun. (Enid Blyton's Happy Days Ser.). (Illus.). 96p. (J). (gr. 1-4). 2000. pap. 6.95 (*0-7475-4345-3*, Pub. by Blmsbury Pub) Trafalgar.

— Mr Twiddle in Trouble Again. (Enid Blyton's Happy Days Ser.). (Illus.). 96p. (J). (gr. 1-4). 2000. pap. 6.95 (*0-7475-4355-0*, Pub. by Blmsbury Pub) Trafalgar.

— El Nino con los Panes y los Peces. (SPA.). 1999. pap. 4.99 (*0-8254-1065-7*, Edit Portavoz) Kregel.

— El Nino en el Templo. (SPA.). 1999. pap. 4.99 (*0-8254-1066-5*, Edit Portavoz) Kregel.

— El Nino Jesus. (SPA.). 1999. pap. 4.99 (*0-8254-1067-3*, Edit Portavoz) Kregel.

Blyton, Enid. Noddy & the Great Cake Bake-Off. (Illus.). 32p. (J). (ps-k). 1999. pap. 3.99 (*0-06-102016-8*, HarpEntertain) Morrow Avon.

***Blyton, Enid.** Noddy Gives a Birthday Party. (Lift-the-Flap Bk.: No. 1). 32p. (ps up). 2000. mass mkt. 4.50 (*0-06-107366-0*) HarpC Child Bks.

— Noddy Hardcover Storybook, No. 2. 2001. write for info. (*0-06-107365-2*, HarpEntertain) Morrow Avon.

— Noddy Makes a Friend. (Lift-the-Flap Bk.: No. 2). 32p. (ps up). 2000. mass mkt. 4.50 (*0-06-107367-9*) HarpC Child Bks.

Blyton, Enid. Noddy Meets Santa. (Illus.). 32p. (ps-1). 1999. 13.95 (*0-06-107363-6*) HarpC.

— Noddy's Super Busy Day. 32p. 1999. pap. 3.99 (*0-06-102015-X*) HarpC.

***Blyton, Enid.** La Pequena Jija de Jairo. (SPA.). 1999. pap. 4.99 (*0-8254-1068-1*, Edit Portavoz) Kregel.

Blyton, Enid. Robin Hood. (Myths & Legends Ser.). (Illus.). 96p. (YA). (gr. 3 up). 1998. pap. 4.95 (*1-901881-77-6*, Pub. by Element MA) Penguin Putnam.

***Blyton, Enid.** Secret Seven. 1998. 24.95 (*0-7540-6203-1*) Chivers N Amer.

— The Secret Seven: Secret Seven Mystery. large type ed. (Illus.). (J). 2000. pap. write for info. (*0-7540-6098-5*) Chivers N Amer.

Blyton, Enid. Secret Seven Adventure. large type ed. (Illus.). (J). 1998. pap. 16.95 (*0-7540-6015-2*, Galaxy Child Lrg Print) Chivers N Amer.

***Blyton, Enid.** Secret Seven Win Through: A Secret Seven Mystery. (J). 1999. 16.95 (*0-7540-6068-3*) Chivers N Amer.

Blyton, Enid. A Story Book of Jesus. (Religious Stories Ser.). 128p. (J). (gr. 3 up). 1998. 6.95 (*1-901881-52-0*, Pub. by Element MA) Penguin Putnam.

— Tales from the Arabian Nights. (Myths & Legends Ser.). (Illus.). 96p. (J). (gr. 3 up). 1998. pap. 4.95 (*1-901881-62-8*, Pub. by Element MA) Penguin Putnam.

— Tales of Ancient Greece. (Myths & Legends Ser.). (Illus.). 96p. (J). (gr. 3 up). 1998. pap. 4.95 (*1-901881-67-9*, Pub. by Element MA) Penguin Putnam.

***Blyton, Enid.** Third Year at Malory Towers. abr. ed. 1999. mass mkt. 7.50 incl. audio (*1-84032-059-1*, Pub. by HOD2) Ulverscroft.

— Three Cheers, Secret Seven. large type ed. (Illus.). (J). 1999. pap. write for info. (*0-7540-6085-3*) Chivers N Amer.

Blyton, Enid. Well Done, Secret Seven. large type ed. (J). 1998. pap. 16.95 (*0-7540-6027-6*, Galaxy Child Lrg Print) Chivers N Amer.

***Blyton, Enid.** You're a Nuisance Mr Meddle. (Enid Blyton's Happy Days Ser.). (Illus.). 96p. (J). (gr. 1-4). 2000. pap. 6.95 (*0-7475-4360-7*, Pub. by Blmsbury Pub) Trafalgar.

Blyton, Paul & Morris, Jonathan, eds. A Flexible Future? Prospects for Employment & Organization. (Studies in Organization: No. 30). xvi, 365p. (C). 1991. lib. bdg. 97.15 (*3-11-012434-3*) De Gruyter.

Blyton, Paul & Turnbull, Peter. Reassessing Human Resource Management. (Illus.). 272p. (C). 1992. 62.00 (*0-8039-8697-1*); pap. 22.95 (*0-8039-8698-X*) Sage.

BMC Staff. MGA 1600 Twin Cam Wor., 58-60. (Illus.). 204p. 1994. 50.00 (*0-8376-0501-6*) Bentley Pubs.

BMCC COOP Staff. Interview Handbook. 2nd ed. 48p. 1995. 9.95 (*0-8403-8494-7*) Kendall-Hunt.

— Resume Handbook. 2nd ed. 48p. 1995. 9.71 (*0-8403-8493-9*) Kendall-Hunt.

BMR-Delmar Staff. Instant Nursing Assessment: Gerontologic. LC 95-21192. (Instant Nursing Education Ser.). 192p. (C). 1995. pap. 31.95 (*0-8273-7101-2*) Delmar.

BMR-Delmar Staff. Instant Nursing Assessment: Respiratory. LC 95-371. (Nursing Education Ser.). 224p. (C). 1995. mass mkt. 21.50 (*0-8273-7099-7*) Delmar.

BMR-Delmar Staff, et al. Instant Nursing Assessment: Women's Health. (Instant Nursing Assessment Ser.). 224p. (C). 1995. mass mkt. 21.50 (*0-8273-7100-4*) Delmar.

BMW Car Club of America Staff. BMW Enthusiast's Companion: Owner Insights on Service, Performance, & Driving. LC 95-34083. (Illus.). 328p. 1995. 29.95 (*0-8376-0321-8*) Bentley Pubs.

BNA Editores. Civil Trial Practice Deskbook: 1997 Edition. LC 96-53325. 1018p. 1997. pap. 250.00 (*1-57018-006-7*, 1006-PR7) BNA Books.

BNA Editorial Staff. Grievance Guide. 9th ed. LC 95-35630. 474p. 1995. pap. 35.00 (*1-57018-003-2*) BNA Books.

***BNA Editorial Staff.** Grievance Guide. 10th ed. (Policy & Practice Ser.). 2000. pap. 55.00 (*1-57018-217-5*, 1217-PRYY) BNA Books.

BNA Library Staff. BNA's Directory of State & Federal Courts, Judges & Clerks: 1998. 610p. 1998. pap. 125.00 (*1-57018-088-1*) BNA Books.

BNA PLUS Staff. Corporate Compliance: A BNA Plus Information Package. 1998. ring bd. 50.00 (*1-55871-376-X*) BNA PLUS.

— Drug Testing: A BNA PLUS Information Package. 1998. ring bd. 50.00 (*1-55871-377-8*) BNA PLUS.

— Employee Morale: A BNA Plus Information Package. 1998. ring bd. 50.00 (*1-55871-378-6*) BNA PLUS.

— Employee vs. Independent Contractor: A BNA Plus Information Package. 1998. ring bd. 50.00 (*1-55871-382-4*) BNA PLUS.

— Ergonomics: A BNA Plus Information Package. 1998. ring bd. 50.00 (*1-55871-379-4*) BNA PLUS.

— Family & Medical Leave Act: A BNA Plus Information Package. 1998. ring bd. 50.00 (*1-55871-380-8*) BNA PLUS.

— Fifty-State Environment & Safety Monitoring Service. 1988. write for info. (*1-55871-070-1*) BNA PLUS.

— Hiring Issues: A BNA Plus Information Package. 1998. ring bd. 50.00 (*1-55871-381-6*) BNA PLUS.

— National Labor Relations Board Election Statistics. 1989. write for info. (*1-55871-077-9*) BNA PLUS.

— Sexual Harassment: A BNA Plus Information Package. 1998. ring bd. 50.00 (*1-55871-383-2*) BNA PLUS.

— State Recordkeeping Requirements. 1993. 95.00 (*1-55871-295-X*) BNA PLUS.

— Telecommuting: A BNA Plus Information Package. 1998. ring bd. 50.00 (*1-55871-384-0*) BNA PLUS.

— Termination Procedures: A BNA Plus Information Package. 1998. ring bd. 50.00 (*1-55871-385-9*) BNA PLUS.

— Work & Family: A BNA PLUS Information Package. 1998. ring bd. 50.00 (*1-55871-386-7*) BNA PLUS.

— Workplace Privacy: A BNA Plus Information Package. 1998. ring bd. 50.00 (*1-55871-387-5*) BNA PLUS.

— Workplace Violence: A BNA Plus Information Package. 1998. ring bd. 50.00 (*1-55871-388-3*) BNA PLUS.

BNA PLUS Staff, compiled by. Environment & Safety Compliance Calendar. LC 92-31353. 1992. write for info. (*1-55871-284-4*) BNA PLUS.

BNA Staff, jt. auth. see UNESCO Staff.

BNA's Business & Human Resources Services Staff. EEOC Compliance Manual. 1975. ring bd. 263.00 (*0-87179-940-5*) BNA.

— Employment Guide. 1986. ring bd. 499.00 (*0-87179-508-6*) BNA.

— Individual Employment Rights. (Labor Relations Reporter Ser.). 1986. ring bd. 829.00 (*0-87179-911-1*) BNA.

— Labor Arbitration & Dispute Settlements. (Labor Relations Reporter Ser.). 1937. ring bd. 1099.00 (*1-55871-036-1*) BNA.

BNA's Collective Bargaining Negotiations & Contrac. Calendar of Negotiations, 1998. 1998. 25.00 (*1-55871-370-0*) BNA.

BNA's Environment & Safety Services Staff. Index to Chemical Regulations. (Chemical Regulation Reporter Ser.). 1980. ring bd. 774.00 (*0-87179-996-0*) BNA.

BNA's Legal Services Staff. Corporate Practice Series. 1978. ring bd. 1600.00 (*1-55871-247-X*) BNA.

BNC Staff. Mirror of Our Times: More Than a Century. 1997. per. 22.95 (*1-57571-003-X*) Birm News.

Bnder, Lionel. Los Inventos. 1995. 18.95 (*84-372-3760-2*) Santillana.

Bndges, Mark, jt. ed. see Dineen, Joe.

BNF Metals Technology Centre Staff. Critical Survey of Available High Temperature Mechanical Property Data for Copper & Copper Alloys. (INCRA Monographs). 328p. 1983. 30.00 (*0-943642-12-4*) Intl Copper.

— Gaseous & Gas-Forming Elements in Copper & Copper Alloys. (INCRA Monographs). 203p. 1983. 30.00 (*0-943642-11-6*) Intl Copper.

***BNI BUILDING NEWS.** Code Finder For Building & Construction. 1999. pap. 69.95 (*0-13-087500-7*) P-H.

BNI BUILDING NEWS. Remodeling Cost Book 99. 1999. pap. text 69.95 (*0-13-022646-7*) S&S Trade.

BNI Building News Staff. ADA Accessibility Guidelines Checklist for Buildings & Facilities: With ADA Technical Assistance Manuals. 350p. 1996. ring bd. 69.95 (*1-55701-153-2*) BNI Pubns.

— Building Air Quality: A Guide for Building Owners & Facilities Managers. 250p. 1996. ring bd. 59.95 (*1-55701-152-4*) BNI Pubns.

— Building News Construction Dictionary & Reference. 500p. 1997. pap. text 49.95 (*1-55701-151-6*) BNI Pubns.

— 1996 National Electrical Code Interpretive Diagrams. 270p. 1996. pap. text 34.95 (*1-55701-147-8*) BNI Pubns.

— Standard Plans for Public Construction, 1997: Metric Edition. 375p. 1996. pap. text 59.95 (*1-55701-149-4*) BNI Pubns.

***BNI Building News Staff.** Standard Specifications for Public Works Construction: 2000 Metric Edition. 730p. 1999. 59.95 (*1-55701-314-4*) BNI Pubns.

BNI Buildings New Staff. Construction Dictionary Pocket Edition. 1997. pap. text 14.95 (*1-55701-181-8*) BNI Pubns.

BNI Publications Staff. State of California Construction Safety Orders: Cal/OSHA. 1999. pap. 64.95 (*1-55701-264-4*) BNI Pubns.

***Bnita, Qumry.** Lian's Lie. LC 99-96467. (Qumry Bnita's Scripts Ser.: Bk. II). (Illus.). 48p. (J). (gr. 3-9). 1999. pap. 6.50 (*1-891339-02-8*) Akebulan Ctr.

— Wuuf Wuuf the Champs. LC 99-96468. (Qumry Bnita's Scripts Ser.: Bk. I). (Illus.). 48p. (J). (ps-3). 1999. pap. 6.50 (*1-891339-03-6*) Akebulan Ctr.

Bo. How to Succeed with Women. LC 76-4236. 1976. 5.95 (*0-87212-064-3*) Libra.

Bo, Ben. The Edge. LC 99-20027. 139p. (YA). (gr. 7-13). 1999. lib. bdg. 14.95 (*0-8225-3307-3*, LernerSports) Lerner Pub.

***Bo, Ben.** Skullcrack. LC 99-47395. (Young Adult Novel Ser.). 160p. (YA). (gr. 9 up). 2000. 14.95 (*0-8225-3308-1*, LernerSports) Lerner Pub.

Bo Chen, Lan, et al, eds. Advances in Molecular & Cell Biology Vol. 8: Organelles in Vivo. 208p. 1994. 128.50 (*1-55938-636-3*) Jai Pr.

Bo, Domenico. Le Principali Problematiche del Dialogus de Oratoribus. (Spudasmata Ser.: Bd. 51). (GER.). 462p. 1993. 75.00 (*3-487-09687-0*) G Olms Pubs.

Bo, Domenico, ed. Horatius - Lexicon Horatianum, 2 vols. (Alpha Omega, Reihe A Ser.: Vol. I). xii, 694p. 1966. 198.00 (*3-487-00955-2*) G Olms Pubs.

— Musaeus: Musaei Lexicon. 96p. 1966. 25.00 (*0-318-71967-3*) G Olms Pubs.

— Persius Flaccus, Aulus: Auli Persii Flacci Lexicon. xiii, 199p. 1967. 50.00 (*0-318-71970-3*) G Olms Pubs.

Bo, Domenico, ed. see Musaeus, J. K.

Bo, Domenico, ed. see Persius.

Bo, Walter J., et al. Basic Atlas of Sectional Anatomy with Correlated Imaging. 3rd ed. LC 97-26180. (Illus.). 560p. 1998. text 120.00 (*0-7216-3265-3*, W B Saunders Co) Harcrt Hlth Sci Grp.

Bo Yang. Secrets: A Collection of Short Stories. Deterding, David, tr. (CHI.). 175p. 1985. pap. 8.95 (*0-88727-051-4*) Cheng & Tsui.

Bo Yin Ra. About My Books, Concerning My Name & Other Texts. Reichenbach, Bodo A., tr. from GER. LC 76-27910. 1977. pap. 3.00 (*0-915034-00-X*) Kober Pr.

— The Book on Happiness. Reichenbach, Bodo A., tr. from GER. 133p. 1995. pap. 10.95 (*0-915034-04-2*) Kober Pr.

— The Book on Life Beyond. Reichenbach, Bodo A., tr. from GER. LC 78-51633. 1978. pap. 5.00 (*0-915034-02-6*) Kober Pr.

— The Book on Solace. Reichenbach, Bodo A., tr. from GER. LC 96-76167. 51p. 1996. 12.00 (*0-915034-05-0*) Kober Pr.

— The Book on the Living God. Reichenbach, B. A., tr. from GER. LC 90-63676. (ENG.). 352p. (Orig.). 1992. pap. 10.95 (*0-915034-03-4*) Kober Pr.

— The Wisdom of St. John. Reichenbach, Bodo A., tr. from GER. LC 74-15272. 112p. 1975. 8.00 (*0-915034-01-8*) Kober Pr.

Boa, E. & Lenne, J. M. Diseases of Nitrogen Fixing Trees in Developing Countries. annot. ed. 82p. 1994. pap. 38.00 (*0-85954-375-7*, Pub. by Nat Res Inst) St Mut.

Boa, Elizabeth. Kafka: Gender, Class & Race in the Letters & Fictions. 320p. (C). 1996. text 75.00 (*0-19-815919-X*) OUP.

Boa, Fraser. The Way of the Dream: Conversations on Jungian Dream Interpretation with Marie-Louise Franz. LC 94-6184. 192p. 1994. pap. 19.95 (*1-57062-035-9*, Pub. by Shambhala Pubns) Random.

Boa, Karen, jt. auth. see Boa, Ken.

Boa, Karen, jt. auth. see Boa, Kenneth.

Boa, Ken & Boa, Karen. Simple Prayers: A Daybook of Conversation with God. LC 98-127262. 336p. 1997. 17.99 (*1-56292-367-6*) Honor Bks OK.

Boa, Kenneth. Cultos, Religiones del Mundo y Usted: Un Analisis de Cultos Religiosos a la Luz del Christianismo. Bravo-Guzman, Pedro, tr. from ENG. (SPA.). 350p. 1988. reprint ed. write for info. (*0-318-64256-5*) His Pub Works.

— Cults, World Religions, & the Occult. 240p. 1990. pap. 9.99 (*0-89693-823-9*, 6-1823, Victor Bks) Chariot Victor.

— Handbook to Prayer: Praying Scripture Back to God. 480p. 1993. text 22.95 (*1-884330-00-2*) Trnty House.

— Handbook to Renewal: Renewing Your Mind with Affirmations from Scripture. unabridged ed. LC 97-221821. 474p. 1996. lthr. 39.95 incl. audio (*1-884330-04-5*) Trnty House.

***Boa, Kenneth.** The Psalms: A Journal: Spiritual Formation Through Personal Encounters with. LC 00-30517. 2001. write for info. (*1-57683-251-1*) NavPress.

— Romans. (Holman New Testament Commentary Ser.: Vol. 6). 2000. 16.99 (*0-8054-0207-1*) Broadman.

Boa, Kenneth. That I May Know God: Pathways to Spiritual Formation. LC 98-18708. 224p. 1998. 18.99 (*1-57673-281-9*) Multnomah Pubs.

Boa, Kenneth, adapted by. Face to Face: Praying the Scriptures for Intimate Worship, 2 vols., Vol. 1. LC 97-60198. 1997. pap. 6.99 (*0-310-92550-9*) Zondervan.

— Face to Face: Praying the Scriptures for Spiritual Growth, 2 vols., Vol. 2. LC 97-60198. 402p. 1997. pap. 6.99 (*0-310-92552-5*); bond lthr. 16.99 (*0-310-92553-3*) Zondervan.

Boa, Kenneth & Boa, Karen. Simple Prayers for Graduates. (Simple Prayers Ser.). 155p. 1999. pap. 6.99 (*1-56292-600-4*) Honor Bks OK.

— Simple Prayers for Women: Facing the Future with God. 160p. 1999. pap. 6.99 (*1-56292-601-2*) Honor Bks OK.

Boa, Kenneth & Burnett, Gail. The Art of Living Well: A Biblical Approach from Proverbs. 139p. 1999. pap. 8.00 (*1-57683-122-1*) NavPress.

— Pursuing Wisdom: A Biblical Approach from Proverbs. 128p. 1999. pap. 8.00 (*1-57683-121-3*) NavPress.

***Boa, Kenneth & Burnett, Gail.** Wisdom at Work: A Biblical Approach to the Workplace. 2000. pap. 8.00 (*1-57683-197-3*) NavPress.

***Boa, Kenneth & Kruidenier, William.** Living What You Believe. 2000. pap. 8.00 (*1-57683-198-1*) NavPress.

Boa, Kenneth & Livgren, Kerry. Seeds of Change: The Spiritual Quest of Kerry Livgren. 2nd rev. ed. 230p. reprint ed. pap. 9.95 (*0-917143-03-5*) Sparrow TN.

Boa, Kenneth & Moody, Larry. I'm Glad You Asked. 204p. 1995. pap. 10.99 (*1-56476-387-0*, 6-3387, Victor Bks) Chariot Victor.

Boa, Kenneth & Proctor, William. The Return of the Star of Bethlehem. 224p. (Orig.). 1985. pap. 6.95 (*0-310-33631-7*, 12770P) Zondervan.

Boa, Kenneth, jt. auth. see Wilkinson, Bruce.

Boa, Kenneth D. Seasons of Prayer: In Word & Image. 96p. 1999. 19.99 (*1-56292-541-5*) Honor Bks OK.

Boa, Kenneth D. & Bowman, Robert M., Jr. An Unchanging Faith in a Changing World: Understanding & Responding to Critical Issues That Christians Face Today. LC 97-28966. 416p. 1998. 22.99 (*0-7852-7352-2*, Oliver-Nelson) Nelson.

Boackle, K. F. Real Estate Closing Deskbook. LC 97-18900. 1997. pap. write for info. (*1-57073-449-6*) Amer Bar Assn.

Boad, Bob, jt. auth. see Blackett, Tom.

Boada, Ana M. Asentamientos Indigenas en el Valle de la Laguna. (SPA., Illus.). 197p. 1987. pap. 8.50 (*1-877812-17-X*, BR007) UPLAAP.

Boadella, David. Lifestreams: An Introduction to Biosynthesis. 256p. (Orig.). 1987. pap. 13.95 (*0-7102-1145-7*, Routledge Thoemms) Routledge.

— The Spiral Flame: A Study in the Meaning of D. H. Lawrence. Efron, Arthur & Hoerner, Dennis, eds. (Illus.). 1977. reprint ed. pap. 6.00 (*0-9602478-2-3*) Paunch.

Boadella, David, ed. In the Wake of Reich. LC 77-75314. 424p. 1978. 24.95 (*0-87949-103-5*) Ashley Bks.

— In the Wake of Reich. 1991. 14.95 (*0-904576-58-2*) Sigo Pr.

Boaden, Ann, ed. The Masks of Comedy. LC 79-57417. (Augustana College Library Publications: No. 34). 102p. (Orig.). 1980. pap. 9.00 (*0-910182-40-X*) Augustana Coll.

Boaden, James. An Inquiry into the Authenticity of Various Pictures & Prints Which, from the Decease of the Poet to Our Own Times Have Been Offered to the Public As Portraits of Shakespeare. LC 70-39458. (Illus.). reprint ed. 39.50 (*0-404-00915-8*) AMS Pr.

— Letter to George Steevens. LC 74-39459. reprint ed. 31.50 (*0-404-00916-6*) AMS Pr.

— Memoirs of the Life of John Philip Kemble, 2 vols. LC 77-89713. 1972. 60.95 (*0-405-08276-2*, Pub. by Blom Pubns) Ayer.

— Memoirs of the Life of John Philip Kemble, Vol. 1. 1972. 30.95 (*0-405-18119-1*) Ayer.

— Memoirs of the Life of John Philip Kemble, Vol. 2. 1972. 30.95 (*0-405-18120-5*) Ayer.

Boaden, Noel, et al. Public Participation in Local Services. LC 81-14269. 200p. reprint ed. pap. 62.00 (*0-7837-1605-2*, 204189700024) Bks Demand.

Boaden, P. Primary Care Making Connection: Making Connections. LC 97-13905. (State of Health Ser.). 1997. 98.00 (*0-335-19749-3*); pap. 31.95 (*0-335-19748-5*) OpUniv Pr.

Boadt. Book of Job. 1999. text 26.95 (*0-312-22512-1*) St Martin.

— The Book of Job. LC 99-28745. (Classic Bible Ser.). 120p. 1999. pap. 12.95 (*0-312-22107-X*) St Martin.

— Genesis 1999. text. write for info. (*0-312-22515-6*) St Martin.

— Sayings of the Wise 1999. text. write for info. (*0-312-22516-4*) St Martin.

***Boadt.** Stories from the Old Testament. 1999. text 26.95 (*0-312-22509-1*) St Martin.

Boadt. Stories of the Old Testament. LC 99-28746. 240p. 1999. pap. 14.95 (*0-312-22108-8*) St Martin.

Boadt & Updike, John. Song of Solomon: Love Poetry of the Spirit. 64p. 1999. text 24.95 (*0-312-22212-2*) St Martin.

Boadt, Bruce. Psalms 1999. text. write for info. (*0-312-22517-2*) St Martin.

Boadt, Lawrence. Song of Solomon: Love Poetry of the Spirit. LC 99-23290. 64p. 1999. pap. 10.95 (*0-312-22079-0*) St Martin.

— Stories from the Old Testament, Vol. VII. LC 99-28746. (Classic Bible Ser.). 336p. 1999. pap. 12.95 (*0-312-22110-X*, St Martins Paperbacks) St Martin.

Boadt, Lawrence, ed. Genesis: The Book of Beginnings. LC 99-28741. 192p. 1999. pap. 12.95 (*0-312-22104-5*, St Martins Paperbacks) St Martin.

— Hebrew Prophets: Visionaries of the Ancient World. 224p. 1999. text 26.95 (*0-312-22210-6*) St Martin.

B

— Sayings of the Wise: The Legacy of King Solomon. LC 99-28742. 112p. 1999. pap. 11.95 (*0-312-22105-3*, St Martins Paperbacks) St Martin.

Boadt, Lawrence & Bruce, F. F., eds. The Psalms: Ancient Poetry of the Spirit. LC 99-28743. 192p. 1999. pap. 12.95 (*0-312-22109-6*, St Martins Paperbacks) St Martin.

***Boadt, Lawrence & Hunt, Michael J.** Why I Am a Priest: Thirty Success Stories. LC 99-48306. 144p. 2000. pap. 7.95 (*0-8091-3910-3*) Paulist Pr.

Boadt, Lawrence E. Introduction to Wisdom Literature, Proverbs. (Collegeville Bible Commentary - Old Testament Ser.). 104p. 1986. pap. 4.95 (*0-8146-1475-2*) Liturgical Pr.

— Reading the Old Testament: An Introduction. LC 84-60723. 416p. (Orig.). (C). 1984. pap. 14.95 (*0-8091-2631-1*) Paulist Pr.

***Boadway, R. & Raj, B., eds.** Advances in Public Economics. (Studies in Empirical Economics Ser.). (Illus.). viii, 170p. 2000. 64.00 (*3-7908-1283-8*, Pub. by Spr-Verlag) Spr-Verlag.

Boadway, Robin W., jt. auth. see Stiglitz, Joseph E.

Boag, David. The Changing River. 1996. pap. 17.95 (*0-7459-3176-6*, Pub. by Lion Pubng) Trafalgar.

Boag, David. The Kingfisher. (Orig.). 1989. pap. 25.00 (*0-85263-831-0*, Pub. by Shire Pubns) St Mut.

Boag, David. Secret Woods. 1996. pap. 17.95 (*0-7459-3175-8*, Pub. by Lion Pubng) Trafalgar.

— Wild Coast. 1996. pap. 17.95 (*0-7459-3173-1*, Pub. by Lion Pubng) Trafalgar.

Boag, J. W., et al, eds. Kapitza in Cambridge & Moscow: Life & Letters of a Russian Physicist. xviii, 430p. 1990. pap. 60.50 (*0-444-98749-5*, North Holland) Elsevier.

Boag, Peter G. Environment & Experience: Settlement Culture in Nineteenth-Century Oregon. LC 92-12931. 1992. 45.00 (*0-520-07719-9*, Pub. by U CA Pr) Cal Prin Full Svc.

Boagno, Marina. Corelli: The Man, the Voice. unabridged ed. Schiavone, Mark, tr. from ITA. LC 96-50939. (Great Voices Ser.: No. 5). Orig. Title: Franco Corelli: Un Uomo, Una Voce. 1996. 38.00 (*1-880909-50-2*) Baskerville.

Boahen, A. Adu. African Perspectives on Colonialism. LC 87-2769. 144p. 1989. reprint ed. pap. text 13.95 (*0-8018-3931-9*) Johns Hopkins.

Boahen, A. Adu, et al. Topics in West African History. 2nd ed. 202p. (C). 1989. pap. 41.40 (*0-582-58504-X*, 74457) Longman.

Boahen, A. Adu, jt. auth. see Webster, J. B.

Boahen, A. Adu, ed. see UNESCO Staff.

Boak, George. The Complete Guide to Learning Contracts. LC 97-20723. 173p. 1997. text 74.95 (*0-566-07927-5*, Pub. by Gower) Ashgate Pub Co.

Boake, Christine R. B., ed. Quantitative Genetic Studies of Behavioral Evolution. LC 93-33824. 400p. 1994. pap. text 24.95 (*0-226-06216-3*); lib. bdg. 66.00 (*0-226-06215-5*) U Ch Pr.

Boakes, R. A., jt. ed. see Dickinson, A.

Boakes, Robert A., et al, eds. Eating Habits: Food, Physiology, & Learned Behavior. fac. ed. LC 86-15776. (Illus.). 237p. 1987. reprint ed. pap. 73.50 (*0-608-00965-2*, 206181300011) Bks Demand.

Boal, Augusto. Games for Actors & Non-Actors. Jackson, Adrian, tr. from FRE. LC 91-43612.Tr. of Jeux pour Acteurs et Non-Acteurs. (Illus.). 288p. (gr. 13). 1992. reprint ed. pap. 21.99 (*0-415-06155-5*, A5337) Routledge.

— Games for Actors & Non-Actors. 7th ed. Jackson, Adrian, tr. from FRE. LC 91-43612.Tr. of Jeux pour Acteurs et Non-Acteurs. (Illus.). 176p. (C). (gr. 13). 1992. reprint ed. text 52.95 (*0-415-06154-7*, A5333) Routledge.

— Legislative Theatre: Using Performance to Make Politics. LC 98-37221. (Illus.). 224p. (C). (gr. 13). 1998. 75.00 (*0-415-18240-9*, D6202) Routledge.

— Legislative Theatre: Using Performance to Make Politics. Jackson, Adrian, tr. LC 98-37221. xiv, 254 p. 1999. pap. 22.99 (*0-415-18241-7*, D6206) Routledge.

— The Rainbow of Desire: The Boal Method of Theatre & Therapy. Jackson, Adrian, tr. LC 94-13955. 216p. (C). (gr. 13). 1995. pap. 22.99 (*0-415-10349-5*, B3152) Routledge.

— Theatre of the Oppressed. 208p. 1985. pap. 12.95 (*0-930452-49-6*) Theatre Comm.

Boal, Dean. Interlochen: A Home for the Arts. LC 98-9014. (Illus.). 248p. 1998. 29.95 (*0-472-10882-4*, 10882) U of Mich Pr.

Boal, Ellis. Teamster Rank & File Legal Defense Handbook. 312p. 1984. pap. 8.00 (*0-614-29601-3*) Assn Union Demo.

***Boal, Frederick W., ed.** Ethnicity Housing: Accommodating the Differences. LC 99-75557. (Research in Ethic Relations Ser.). 318p. 2000. text 74.95 (*1-85972-596-1*, Pub. by Ashgate Pub) Ashgate Pub Co.

Boal, Frederick W. & Royle, Stephen, eds. North America: A Geographical Mosaic. (Illus.). 352p. 2000. text 75.00 (*0-340-69262-6*) OUP.

— North America: Environment Society. (Illus.). 352p. 2000. pap. 24.95 (*0-340-69261-8*) OUP.

Boal, Iain, jt. ed. see Brook, James.

Boal, John T. Be a Global Force of One! 202 Common Sense, Portable & Human Ways to Restore Our Communities, Our Schools & Ourselves. 261p. 1998. pap. 14.95 (*0-9626617-2-4*) PacRim Pub.

Boal, Rick. So You Want to Be a Comics Retailer: A Step-by-Step Guide on Opening & Operating a Successful & Profitable Comic Book Store. 208p. (Orig.). 1995. pap. text 12.95 (*0-9645094-0-7*) RBM Pr.

Boalch, Donald H. Makers of the Harpischord & Clavichord, 1440-1840. 3rd ed. Mould, Charles, ed. (Illus.). 820p. 1995. text 160.00 (*0-19-318429-X*) OUP.

Boaler, Jo. Experiencing School Mathematics: Teaching Styles, Sex, & Setting. LC 97-36144. 1997. 94.00 (*0-335-19963-1*); pap. 27.95 (*0-335-19962-3*) OpUniv Pr.

***Boaler, Jo.** Multiple Perspectives on Mathematics Teaching & Learning. LC 00-35567. (International Perspectives on Mathematics Education Ser.). 2000. write for info. (*1-56750-535-X*) Ablx Pub.

***Boaler, Jo, ed.** Multiple Perspectives on Mathematics Teaching & Learning: International Perspectives on Mathematics Education Ser. Vol. V.1. 2000. lib. bdg. write for info. (*1-56750-534-1*) Greenwood.

***Boales, Kevin.** Racing Kart Performance Handbook: The Ultimate Guide for Tuning. (Illus.). 160p. 2000. pap. 21.95 (*0-7603-0843-8*, 130525AP, Pub. by MBI Pubg) Motorbooks Intl.

Boalt, Gunnar. Competing Belief Systems. 164p. 1984. text 54.00 (*91-22-00678-8*) Coronet Bks.

Boalt, Siv B. Autonomy Coping & Defense in Small Work Groups. 202p. (Orig.). 1983. pap. text 35.00 (*91-22-00628-1*) Coronet Bks.

Boam, R. & Sparrow, P. Designing & Achieving Competency: A Competency Based Approach. 204p. (C). 1992. pap. 68.85 (*0-07-707572-2*, Pub. by IPM Hse) St Mut.

Boamah-Wiafe, Daniel. The Black Experience in Contemporary America. 2nd rev. ed. 453p. (C). 1993. text. write for info. (*0-9624567-4-8*); pap. text. write for info. (*0-9624567-8-0*) Wisdom NE.

— The Black Experience in Contemporary America. 3rd ed. (Illus.). 480p. 1998. write for info. (*0-614-30114-9*); pap. write for info. (*0-614-30115-7*) Wisdom NE.

— The Land, People & Cultural Institutions. (Illus.). 380p. (C). 1993. pap. write for info. (*0-9624567-5-6*) Wisdom NE.

***Boan, Jim.** Rising Sun Sinking: Okinawa. LC 99-16653. 2000. pap. write for info. (*1-57168-327-5*, Eakin Pr) Sunbelt Media.

Boand, Nicole. Just Beneath the Surface. Jaeger, Joseph, ed. LC 93-61854. 200p. 1994. pap. 12.95 (*1-880254-14-X*) Vista.

Boanes, Phyllis, ed. see Abrams, Irving.

Boar, Bernard H. Abend Debugging for COBOL Programmers. LC 75-42457. 335p. 1976. reprint ed. pap. 103.90 (*0-7837-3429-8*, 205775000008) Bks Demand.

— Application Prototyping: A Requirements Definition Strategy for the '80's. LC 83-16934. 210p. 1984. 55.00 (*0-471-89317-X*) Wiley.

— The Art of Strategic Planning for Information Technology: Crafting Strategy for the 90's. LC 93-9880. 384p. 1993. 49.99 (*0-471-59918-2*) Wiley.

— Constructing Blueprints for Enterprise IT Architectures. LC 98-8272. 352p. 1998. 49.99 (*0-471-29620-1*) Wiley.

— Practical Steps for Aligniny Information Technology with Business Strategy: How to Achieve a Competitive Analysis. 368p. 1994. 59.99 (*0-471-07637-6*) Wiley.

— Strategic Thinking for Information Technology. LC 96-27114. 288p. 1996. pap. 59.99 (*0-471-15881-X*) Wiley.

Boar, Gerard. Sketches for Thirteen Sonnets. 1969. pap. 1.00 (*0-685-04673-7*) Oyez.

Board, D. B., jt. auth. see Drago, Raymond J.

***Board for Certification of Genealogists Staff, ed.** The BCG Genealogical Standards Manual. LC 00-23694. 113p. 2000. 16.95 (*0-916489-92-2*) Ancestry.

Board, J. A., Jr., ed. Transputer Research & Applications 2: Proceedings of the Second North American Transputer Users Group Meeting, Durham, NC, October 18-19, 1989. (Transputer & Occam Engineering Ser.). 462p. (gr. 12). 1990. pap. 115.00 (*90-5199-027-8*, Pub. by IOS Pr) IOS Press.

Board, John C. Special Relationship: Our Teachers & How We Learn. 1991. 28.95 (*0-916366-68-5*, Pub. by Pushcart Pr) Norton.

Board, Joseph B., tr. see Stinissen, Wilfrid.

Board, K., jt. auth. see Morgan, D. V.

Board, Kjersti, tr. see Sundvall, Viveca L.

Board, Kjersti, tr. see Wallenberg, Raoul.

Board of Aldermen Staff. Police in New York City: An Investigation. LC 79-154565. (Police in America Ser.). 1971. reprint ed. 29.95 (*0-405-03382-6*) Ayer.

Board of Bar Overseers, Superior Judicial Court St. Massachusetts Attorney Discipline Reports, 14 vols., Set. 2370p. 1980. boxed set 420.00 (*0-88063-027-2*, 81427-10, MICHIE) LEXIS Pub.

Board of Practice Consultants Staff. California Real Estate Reporter. text 290.00 (*0-8205-2104-3*) Bender.

Board of Proprietor Staff. The Minutes of the Board of Proprietors of the Eastern Division of New Jersey from 1685-1705, Vol. I. 280p. 1985. reprint ed. 30.00 (*0-614-30724-4*) NJ Hist Soc.

Board of Reviewers. Florida Torts, 5 vols. 1988. ring bd. 730.00 (*0-8205-1565-5*) Bender.

Board of Reviewers Staff. Indiana Estate Planning & Probate Practice, 4 vols., Set. 1990. 600.00 incl. cd-rom (*0-8205-1493-4*, 493) Bender.

Board of Scholars Staff, ed. English-Hebrew, Hebrew-English Dictionary. (ENG & HEB.). 783p. 1992. 49.95 (*0-8288-6977-4*) Fr & Eur.

Board of Scholars Staff, tr. from SAN. The Natya Sastra of Bharatamuni. (Raga Nrtya Ser.: No. 2). 537p. (C). 1996. 34.00 (*81-7030-134-3*, Pub. by Sri Satguru Pubns) S Asia.

Board of St. Paul Editorial Staff. Celibacy Myth. (C). 1989. 55.00 (*0-85439-295-5*, Pub. by St Paul Pubns) St Mut.

— Fathers of the Church. (C). 1989. 30.00 (*0-85439-301-3*, Pub. by St Paul Pubns) St Mut.

— Forty-Six Christian Assemblies. (C). 1989. 80.00 (*0-85439-315-3*, Pub. by St Paul Pubns) St Mut.

— The Hour of Jesus: The Passion & Resurrection of Jesus According to John: The Text & Spirit. De Poetterie, Ignace, ed. 233p. (C). 1996. pap. 39.95 (*0-85439-285-8*, Pub. by St Paul Pubns) St Mut.

— Servants of the People. (C). 1989. 75.00 (*0-85439-318-8*, Pub. by St Paul Pubns) St Mut.

— Through the Eye of a Needle. (C). 1989. 40.00 (*0-85439-313-7*, Pub. by St Paul Pubns) St Mut.

Board of St. Paul Editorial Staff, jt. auth. see Cantalamessa, Raniero.

Board of St. Paul Editorial Staff, jt. auth. see Carretto, Carlo.

Board of St. Paul Editorial Staff, jt. auth. see Cox, Dermot.

Board of St. Paul Editorial Staff, jt. auth. see Dominian, Jack.

Board of St. Paul Editorial Staff, jt. auth. see Dubois-Dumee, Jean P.

Board of St. Paul Editorial Staff, jt. auth. see Martini, Carlo-Maria.

Board of St. Paul Editorial Staff, jt. auth. see Ratzinger, Joseph.

Board of Student Advisers Staff. Introduction to Advocacy: Research, Writing, & Argument. 6th ed. LC 96-8774. 190p. 1996. pap. text. write for info. (*1-56662-351-0*) Foundation Pr.

Board on Agriculture Staff & National Research Council Staff. Rangeland Health: New Methods to Classify, Inventory, & Monitor Rangelands. 200p. (Orig.). (C). 1993. pap. text 26.00 (*0-309-04879-6*) Natl Acad Pr.

Board on Agriculture Staff, National Research Coun, ed. Toward Sustainability: A Plan for Collaborative Research on Agriculture & Natural Resource Management. 164p. 1991. pap. text 19.00 (*0-309-04540-1*) Natl Acad Pr.

Board on Children, Youth, & Families Staff, et al. Paying Attention to Children in a Changing Health Care System: Summaries of Workshops. LC 96-230003. 104p. (Orig.). 1996. pap. text 26.00 (*0-309-05588-1*, Joseph Henry Pr) Natl Acad Pr.

Board, Prudy T. & Colcord, Esther B. The Belleview Mido Resort Hotel: A Century of Hospitality. LC 96-43081. 1996. write for info. (*0-89865-981-7*) Donning Co.

— Mending Lives, Healing Hearts: The Florida Sheriffs' Youth Ranches - The First 40 Years. LC 97-15320. 1997. write for info. (*0-89865-988-4*) Donning Co.

— Venice Through the Years: A Pictorial History. LC 95-6483. (Illus.). 1995. write for info. (*0-89865-931-0*) Donning Co.

Board, R. G. & Lovelock, D. W., eds. Sampling: Microbiological Monitoring of Environments. (Society for Applied Bacteriology Technical Ser.: No. 7). 1973. text 132.00 (*0-12-108250-4*) Acad Pr.

— Some Methods for Microbiological Assay. 1975. text 152.00 (*0-12-108240-7*) Acad Pr.

Board, R. G., jt. ed. see Dillon, V. M.

Board, Russell A. First Things First. 1991. pap. 5.95 (*0-911866-12-4*) LifeSprings Res.

Board, Sherri. Boat Cosmetics Made Simple: How to Improve & Maintain a Boat's Appearance. 2nd ed. 1996. pap. text 12.95 (*0-07-006216-1*) McGraw.

— Boat Cosmetics Made Simple: How to Improve & Maintain a Boat's Appearance. 2nd rev. ed. Ayers, James A., ed. (Illus.). 131p. 1993. pap. 12.95 (*0-9634767-8-5*) Tug Pr CA.

Board, Sherri L. Ambrosia & the Coral Sun. Board, Timothy A., ed. LC 93-61236. (Illus.). 249p. (Orig.). (J). 1994. pap. 12.95 (*0-9634767-7-7*) Tug Pr CA.

— Angels of Anguish. LC 99-72159. (Katlin Lamar Mystery Ser.). 304p. 1999. pap. 11.95 (*0-9634767-5-0*) Crime-Zone Bks.

***Board, Stephen.** Ecclesiastes. (Fisherman Bible Studyguides Ser.). 2000. pap. 4.99 (*0-87788-206-1*, H Shaw Pubs) Waterbrook Pr.

Board, Stephen. Great Doctrines of the Bible. (Fisherman Bible Studyguide Ser.). (Orig.). 1992. pap. 4.99 (*0-87788-356-4*, H Shaw Pubs) Waterbrook Pr.

Board, Timothy A., ed. see Board, Sherri L.

Boardingham, Robert. Impressionist Masterpieces in American Museums. 1996. 35.00 (*0-88363-156-3*) H L Levin.

— Young Picasso. 1997. 19.95 (*0-7893-0093-1*, Pub. by Universe) St Martin.

Boardman. Holt Music Grade Kindergarten. 1988. teacher ed. 75.75 (*0-03-005249-1*) Harcourt Schl Pubs.

— Holt Music Grade 1. 1988. pap., teacher ed. 75.75 (*0-03-005262-9*) Harcourt Schl Pubs.

— Holt Music Grade 3. 1988. teacher ed. 75.75 (*0-03-005287-4*) Harcourt Schl Pubs.

— Holt Music Grade 4. 1988. teacher ed. 75.75 (*0-03-005294-7*) Harcourt Schl Pubs.

— Holt Music Grade 5. 1988. teacher ed. 82.50 (*0-03-005303-X*) Harcourt Schl Pubs.

— Holt Music Grade 6. 1988. teacher ed. 82.50 (*0-03-005312-9*) Harcourt Schl Pubs.

— Holt Music Grade 7. 1988. teacher ed. 89.25 (*0-03-005319-6*) Harcourt Schl Pubs.

— Holt Music Grade 8. 1988. teacher ed. 89.25 (*0-03-005328-5*) Harcourt Schl Pubs.

— Music. (J). (gr. 1-2). 1988. 40.00 (*0-03-005268-8*) Harcourt Schl Pubs.

— Music 1988. 1988. 75.00 (*0-03-005269-6*) Harcourt Schl Pubs.

— Music 1988. (J). (gr. k-2). 1988. student ed. 43.25 (*0-03-005302-1*) Harcourt Schl Pubs.

— Music 1988. (J). (gr. k-6). 1988. student ed. 43.25 (*0-03-005309-9*) Harcourt Schl Pubs.

— Music 1988. (J). (gr. k-8). 1989. student ed. 52.50 (*0-03-005327-7*) Harcourt Schl Pubs.

— Music, 1988: Holiday Songbook. (J). 1988. pap., teacher ed. 21.75 (*0-03-005253-X*) Harcourt Schl Pubs.

— The Shining Mountain. 1985. 8.95 (*0-07-544743-6*) McGraw.

— Texas Heritage Songbook: Grade 7-8. (J). (gr. 7-8). 1988. pap. 23.25 (*0-03-014058-7*) Harcourt Schl Pubs.

— Texas Teacher Edition for Music: Grade 7. 1988. pap., teacher ed. 99.00 (*0-03-014054-4*) Harcourt Schl Pubs.

— Texas Teacher Edition for Music: Grade 8. 1988. pap., teacher ed. 99.00 (*0-03-014057-9*) Harcourt Schl Pubs.

Boardman & Sandomir. Foundations of Business Thought. 3rd ed. 464p. 1998. pap. text 32.75 (*0-536-01441-8*) Pearson Custom.

Boardman, jt. auth. see Sandomir.

Boardman, A. D., et al. Advanced Photonics with Second-Order Optically Nonlinear Processes. LC 98-31124. (NATO ASI Ser.). 1998. 214.00 (*0-7923-5315-3*) Kluwer Academic.

Boardman, A. W. The Battle of Towton. (Illus.). 192p. 1996. pap. 19.95 (*0-7509-1245-6*, Pub. by Sutton Pub Ltd) Intl Pubs Mktg.

Boardman, Alan D. Physics Programs: Optics. LC 80-40123. 131p. reprint ed. pap. 40.70 (*0-608-12335-8*, 202437500037) Bks Demand.

Boardman, Alan D., ed. Applied Physics. LC 80-40121. (Physics Programs Ser.: No. 4). (Illus.). 134p. reprint ed. pap. 41.60 (*0-8357-5683-1*, 203045100069) Bks Demand.

— Electromagnetic Surface Modes. LC 81-14777. 786p. reprint ed. pap. 200.00 (*0-8357-3467-6*, 203972900013) Bks Demand.

— Magnetism. LC 80-40124. (Physics Programs Ser.: Vol. 2). (Illus.). 104p. reprint ed. pap. 32.30 (*0-608-17605-2*, 203045500069) Bks Demand.

— Solid State & Quantum Physics. LC 80-40125. (Physics Programs Ser.: Vol. 3). (Illus.). 142p. reprint ed. pap. 44.10 (*0-608-17606-0*, 203045600069) Bks Demand.

Boardman, Alan D., et al, eds. Nonlinear Waves in Solid State Physics. LC 90-25112. (NATO ASI Ser.: Vol. 247). (Illus.). 508p. (C). 1991. text 174.00 (*0-306-43811-9*, Kluwer Plenum) Kluwer Academic.

***Boardman, Andrew W.** The Battle of Towton. 320p. 2000. pap. 16.95 (*0-7509-2479-9*) Sutton Publng.

Boardman, Andrew W. The Medieval Soldier: The Men Who Fought the Wars of the Roses. LC 99-159663. (Fifteenth Century Ser.). (Illus.). 224p. 1998. 36.95 (*0-7509-1465-3*, Pub. by Sutton Pub Ltd) Intl Pubs Mktg.

Boardman, Anthony, et al. Cost Benefit Analysis: Concepts & Practices. LC 95-37859. 493p. 1996. text, boxed set 73.33 (*0-13-519968-9*) P-H.

Boardman, Bob. Red Hot Peppers: Book, Audio, & Speed Rope. (Illus.). 64p. (J). (gr. 2 up). 1994. 18.95 incl. audio (*1-57061-002-9*) Sasquatch Bks.

Boardman, Bob. Red Hot Peppers: The Skookum Book of Jump Rope Games, Rhymes, & Fancy Footwork. (Illus.). 64p. (Orig.). (J). (gr. 3 up). 1993. pap. 8.95 (*0-912365-74-9*) Sasquatch Bks.

Boardman, Brigid. Between Heaven & Charing Cross: The Life of Francis Thompson. LC 87-37243. (C). 1988. 55.00 (*0-300-04143-8*) Yale U Pr.

Boardman, Calvin M. Foundations of Business Thought. 2nd ed. 334p. (C). 1996. text 41.00 (*0-536-59804-5*) Pearson Custom.

Boardman, Calvin M. & Sandomir, Alan. Foundations of Business Thought. 398p. (C). 1995. text 38.60 (*0-536-58751-5*) Pearson Custom.

Boardman, Edna. All Things Decently & in Order: And Other Writings on Germans from Russia Heritage. LC 96-71119. (Illus.). 156p. 1997. pap. 11.95 (*0-942323-24-6*) N Amer Heritage Pr.

— Growing on the Job: Professional Development for the School Librarian. (Professional Growth Ser.). (Illus.). 81p. 1991. pap. text 17.95 (*0-938865-10-2*) Linworth Pub.

Boardman, Edna N. Censorship: The Problem That Won't Go Away. (Professional Growth Ser.). 80p. 1993. pap. text 17.95 (*0-938865-18-8*) Linworth Pub.

Boardman, Eunice, ed. Dimensions of Musical Thinking. (Illus.). 128p. (C). 1989. pap. 15.50 (*0-940796-62-7*, 1081) MENC.

Boardman, George D. The Problem of Jesus. 32p. 1984. pap. 7.00 (*0-8170-1059-9*) Judson.

Boardman, Gerre, ed. see Bolger, Janie, et al.

Boardman, Gregory D., ed. Hazardous & Industrial Wastes Vol. 29: Proceedings of the Twenty-Ninth Mid-Atlantic Industrial & Hazardous Waste Conference. 656p. 1997. pap. 119.95 (*1-56676-592-7*, 765927) Technomic.

Boardman, James. America, & the Americans. LC 73-13120. (Foreign Travelers in America, 1810-1935 Ser.). 446p. 1974. reprint ed. 34.95 (*0-405-05443-2*) Ayer.

Boardman, John. Athenian Black Figure Vases. (World of Art Ser.). (Illus.). 252p. 1985. pap. 14.95 (*0-500-20138-2*, Pub. by Thames Hudson) Norton.

— Athenian Red Figure Vases. (World of Art Ser.). (Illus.). 252p. 1985. pap. 14.95 (*0-500-20143-9*, Pub. by Thames Hudson) Norton.

— Athenian Red Figure Vases: The Classical Period. LC 89-50539. (World of Art Ser.). (Illus.). 1989. pap. 14.95 (*0-500-20244-3*, Pub. by Thames Hudson) Norton.

— Classical Art in Eastern Translation: The Seventeenth J. L. Myres Memorial Lecture - Ashmolean Museum, Oxford, 27 May 1993. (Illus.). 27p. 1993. pap. 9.00 (*0-904920-30-5*, Pub. by Leopards Head Pr) David Brown.

— The Diffusion of Classical Art in Antiquity. LC 94-16269. (A. W. Mellon Lectures in the Fine Arts: Vol. XXXV, 42). 352p. 1994. text 55.00 (*0-691-03680-2*, Pub. by Princeton U Pr) Cal Prin Full Svc.

— Early Greek Vase Painting: 11th to 6th Centuries B. C. LC 97-61112. (World of Art Ser.). (Illus.). 288p. 1998. pap. 14.95 (*0-500-20309-1*, Pub. by Thames Hudson) Norton.

— Engraved Gems: The Ionides Collection. LC 68-17325. (Illus.). 114p. reprint ed. pap. 35.40 (*0-608-11326-3*, 201528300094) Bks Demand.

— The Great God Pan: The Survival of an Image. LC 97-61345. (Walter Neurath Memorial Lectures). (Illus.). 48p. 1998. 16.95 (*0-500-55030-1*, Pub. by Thames Hudson) Norton.

— Greek Art. 4th rev. ed. LC 96-60184. (World of Art Ser.). (Illus.). 304p. 1996. pap. 16.95 (*0-500-20292-3*, Pub. by Thames Hudson) Norton.

***Boardman, John.** Greek Gems & Finger Rings: Early Bronze to Late Classical. 2nd ed. LC 00-101391. (Illus.). 474p. 2001. reprint ed. 95.00 (*0-500-23777-8*, Pub. by Thames Hudson) Norton.

Boardman, John. Greek Sculpture: The Archaic Period. LC 84-51303. (World of Art Ser.). (Illus.). 252p. 1985. pap. 14.95 (*0-500-20163-3*, Pub. by Thames Hudson) Norton.

— Greek Sculpture: The Archaic Period. LC 84-51303. (World of Art Ser.). (Illus.). 252p. 1985. 19.95 (*0-500-18166-7*, Pub. by Thames Hudson) Norton.

— Greek Sculpture: The Classical Period. LC 84-51303. (World of Art Ser.). (Illus.). 252p. (Orig.). 1985. pap. 14.95 (*0-500-20198-6*, Pub. by Thames Hudson) Norton.

— Greek Sculpture: The Late Classical Period & Sculpture in Colonies & Overseas. LC 95-60279. (World of Art Ser.). (Illus.). 248p. 1995. pap. 14.95 (*0-500-20285-0*, Pub. by Thames Hudson) Norton.

— The Greeks Overseas: Their Early Colonies & Trade. 4th rev. ed. LC 98-61437. (Illus.). 304p. 1999. reprint ed. pap. 22.50 (*0-500-28109-2*, Pub. by Thames Hudson) Norton.

***Boardman, John.** Persia & the West: An Archaeological Investigation of the Genesis of Achaemenid Persian Art. LC 99-66194. (Illus.). 272p. 2000. 60.00 (*0-500-05102-X*, Pub. by Thames Hudson) Norton.

Boardman, John. The Persian Empire & the West. 2nd ed. (Cambridge Ancient History Ser.: Vol. 4). 960p. 1988. text 150.00 (*0-521-22804-2*) Cambridge U Pr.

Boardman, John, ed. Assyrian Empire: The Assyrian & Babylonian Empires & Other States of the New East, 8th-6th Centuries B. C. LC 75-85719. (Cambridge Ancient History Ser.: Vol. 3, Pt. 2). (Illus.). 926p. 1992. text 150.00 (*0-521-22717-8*) Cambridge U Pr.

— The Cambridge Ancient History: Volume of Plates, Vols. 5-6. (Illus.). 220p. (C). 1995. text 80.00 (*0-521-23349-6*) Cambridge U Pr.

— The Oxford History of Classical Art. LC 96-38850. (Illus.). 416p. 1997. reprint ed. pap. 24.95 (*0-19-285337-6*) OUP.

— The Oxford History of the Classical World: Greece & the Hellenistic World, Vol. 1. (Illus.). 454p. 1988. pap. text 22.50 (*0-19-282165-2*) OUP.

— The Oxford History of the Classical World: The Roman World, Vol. 2. (Illus.). 466p. 1988. pap. text 22.50 (*0-19-282166-0*) OUP.

— The Oxford Illustrated History of Classical Art. LC 93-6835. (Illus.). 416p. 1993. 55.00 (*0-19-814386-9*) OUP.

— Soils & Quaternary Landscape Evolution. LC 84-20994. (Illus.). 401p. reprint ed. pap. 124.40 (*0-7837-6369-7*, 204608100010) Bks Demand.

Boardman, John, et al, eds. Assyrian Empire: Prehistory of the Balkans, & the Middle East & the Aegean World, 10th-8th Centuries B. C. 2nd ed. LC 75-85719. (Cambridge Ancient History Ser.: Vol. 3, Pt. 1). (Illus.). 1088p. 1982. text 160.00 (*0-521-22496-9*) Cambridge U Pr.

— The Oxford History of Greece & the Hellenistic World. (Illus.). 528p. 1991. pap. text 16.95 (*0-19-285247-7*) OUP.

— The Oxford History of the Classical World. (Illus.). 892p. 1986. 60.00 (*0-19-872112-9*) OUP.

— The Oxford History of the Roman World. (Illus.). 526p. 1991. pap. text 16.95 (*0-19-285248-5*) OUP.

Boardman, John & Favis-Mortlock, David, eds. Climate Change & Soil Erosion. (Series on Environmental Science & Management). 400p. 1999. 68.00 (*1-86094-180-X*) World Scientific Pub.

Boardman, John & Hammond, Nicholas G., eds. Assyrian Empire: The Expansion of the Greek World, 8th-6th Centuries B. C. 2nd ed. (Cambridge Ancient History Ser.: Vol. 3, Pt. 3). (Illus.). 544p. 1982. text 105.00 (*0-521-23447-6*) Cambridge U Pr.

Boardman, John & Vaphopoulou-Richardson, C. E., eds. Chios: A Conference at the Homereion in Chios, 1984. 300p. 1987. 105.00 (*0-19-814864-X*) OUP.

Boardman, John, et al. Modelling Soil Erosion by Water. LC 98-10582. (NATO ASI Ser.: Vol. 55). (Illus.). 542p. 1998. 199.00 (*3-540-64034-7*) Spr-Verlag.

Boardman, John, jt. ed. see Bell, Martin.

***Boardman, Jonathan.** Rome: A Cultural & Literary Companion. (Illus.). 2000. pap. 15.00 (*1-56656-361-5*) Interlink Pub.

***Boardman, Liz.** Amelia's Meltdown. Williams, Lori, ed. 170p. 1999. pap. 9.99 (*1-58365-755-X*, Timeless Romance) BT Pub.

Boardman, Lynda T. First Impressions: A Complete Guide for Ministry in the Church Nursery. 68p. 1995. pap. 14.99 (*0-8341-1566-2*) Beacon Hill.

— The Ministry of Teaching Toddlers. 96p. (Orig.). 1983. pap. 7.99 (*0-8341-0820-8*) Beacon Hill.

Boardman, Lynda T. Tending & Teaching Babies. 84p. (Orig.). 1985. pap. 6.99 (*0-8341-1063-6*) Beacon Hill.

Boardman, Mark & Carney, Cindy. Pigeon Creek & Tidal Delta: A Field Trip Guide. (Illus.). 8p. (C). 1996. pap. text 2.00 (*0-935909-59-1*) Bahamian.

Boardman, Mark R., ed. Proceedings of the Seventh Symposium on the Geology of the Bahamas. (Illus.). 74p. (Orig.). (C). 1995. pap. text 16.00 (*0-935909-55-9*) Bahamian.

Boardman, Mark R., et al. Field Trip Guidebook: The Sixth Symposium on the Geology of the Bahamas. (Illus.). 56p. (Orig.). (C). 1992. pap. text 12.00 (*0-935909-39-7*) Bahamian.

Boardman, Mark R., jt. auth. see Anderson, C. B.

***Boardman, Michael.** Teach Sailing the Fun Way. 2nd rev. ed. 51p. 2000. pap. 12.00 (*1-882502-84-1*) US Sail Assn.

Boardman, Michael M. Narrative Innovation & Incoherence: Ideology in Defoe, Goldsmith, Austen, Eliot, & Hemingway. LC 92-3785. 237p. 1992. text 34.95 (*0-8223-1239-5*) Duke.

***Boardman, Mike, et al.** Legends Vol. 4: Outstanding Quarter Horse Stallions & Mares. (Legends Ser.). (Illus.). 216p. 2000. pap. 17.95 (*0-911647-49-X*) Western Horseman.

Boardman, Nancy A. Aviation Safety: Opportunities Exist for FAA to Refine the Controller Staffing Process. (Illus.). 63p. (Orig.). (C). 1997. pap. text 20.00 (*0-7881-4637-8*) DIANE Pub.

Boardman, Peter & Tasker, Joe. The Boardman Tasker Omnibus. 890p. 1995. 38.00 (*0-89886-436-4*) Mountaineers.

Boardman, Philip. Enduring Legacies: Ancient & Medieval Culture. 246p. (C). 1995. text 33.20 (*0-536-59011-7*) Pearson Custom.

Boardman, Phillip C., ed. The Legacy of Language: A Tribute to Charlton Laird. LC 86-30840. 224p. 1987. 24.95 (*0-87417-121-0*) U of Nev Pr.

Boardman, R., et al. Fossil Invertebrates. 720p. 1987. 69.95 (*0-86542-302-4*) Blackwell Sci.

Boardman, Richard S. Reflections on the Morphology, Anatomy, Evolution & Classification of the Class Stenolaemata (Bryozoa) LC 98-9732. (Smithsonian Contributions to Paleobiology Ser.: Vol. 86). (Illus.). 63p. reprint ed. pap. 30.00 (*0-608-10499-X*, 207114100009) Bks Demand.

Boardman, Richard S., et al. Morphology, Anatomy, & Systematics of the Cinctiporidae, New Family, Bryozoa, Stenolaemata. LC 91-38765. (Smithsonian Contributions to Paleobiology Ser.: No. 70). 85p. reprint ed. pap. 30.00 (*0-7837-3160-4*, 204282200006) Bks Demand.

Boardman, Robert. Canadian Environmental Policy: Ecosystems, Politics & Process. (Illus.). 324p. 1992. pap. text 35.00 (*0-19-540774-1*) OUP.

— Post-Socialist World Orders: Russia, China & the U. N. System. LC 93-31242. 1994. text 65.00 (*0-312-10671-8*) St Martin.

— Unforgettable Men in Unforgettable Times. LC 97-62568. (Illus.). 272p. (C). 1998. pap. 12.99 (*1-57921-093-7*, Pub. by WinePress Pub) BookWorld.

Boardman, Robert B. Savior of Fire. LC 91-75804. 294p. (Orig.). 1991. pap. 5.95 (*1-878398-11-3*) Blue Note Pubns.

Boardman, Roy, jt. auth. see McRae, John.

Boardman, Susan K., jt. auth. see Harrington, Charles C.

***Boardman, Ted.** Inside 3D Studio Max 3: Modeling, Materials & Rendering. LC 99-64953. (Illus.). 752p. 1999. cd-rom 54.99 (*0-7357-0085-0*) New Riders Pub.

Boardman, Ted. Inside 3D Studio Max 2: Modeling & Materials. 1998. pap. text 59.99 (*1-56205-864-9*) New Riders Pub.

Boardman, Terry, tr. see Nimura, Kazuo.

Boardman, Terry, tr. see Nimura, Kazuo & Gordon, Andrew.

Boardman, Terry, tr. see Reuveni, Amnon.

***Boardman, Terry M.** Mapping the Millennium: Behind the Plans of the New World Order. (Illus.). 192p. 1998. pap. 10.95 (*0-904693-97-X*, Pub. by Temple Lodge) Anthroposophic.

Boardman, William F. The Ancestry of William Francis Joseph Boardman, Hartford, Conn. (Illus.). 419p. 1988. reprint ed. pap. 66.00 (*0-8328-0273-5*); reprint ed. lib. bdg. 76.00 (*0-8328-0272-7*) Higginson Bk Co.

Boardroom Classics. Healing Unlimited. LC 97-162315. 1997. write for info. (*0-88723-142-X*) Boardroom.

Boardroom Reports, Inc. The Complete Book of Money Secrets. LC 97-165528. 1997. write for info. (*0-88723-143-8*) Boardroom.

Boardroom's Experts & Editors Staff. The Big Black Book. rev. ed. 512p. 1996. 59.00 (*0-88723-124-1*) Boardroom.

— The Complete Book of Retirement Secrets. LC 96-138484. 352p. 1995. 59.00 (*0-88723-121-7*) Boardroom.

— The Great Book of Business Secrets. 2nd rev. ed. LC 98-135086. 512p. 1994. 59.00 (*0-88723-086-5*) Boardroom.

— Healing Unlimited. 3rd rev. ed. LC 96-145075. 512p. 59.00 (*0-88723-119-5*) Boardroom.

— More Secrets: More Inside Information. 352p. 1994. 59.00 (*0-88723-087-3*) Boardroom.

— Tax Loopholes: Everything the Law Allows. rev. ed. LC 86-30967. 352p. 1996. 59.00 (*0-614-14887-1*) Boardroom.

***Boardt.** Stories from the Old Testament. 1999. text 26.95 (*0-312-22510-5*) St Martin.

***Boarnet, Marlon & Crane, Randall.** Travel by Design: The Influence of Urban Form on Travel. (Spatial Information Systems Ser.). (Illus.). 240p. 2000. text 60.00 (*0-19-512395-6*) OUP.

Boart, Jeff, ed. see Richards, R. W.

Boas. Mathematical Methods in the Physical Sciences. 3rd ed. text (*0-471-19826-9*) Wiley.

Boas & Chamberlain. Kutenai Tales. (Bureau of American Ethnology Bulletins Ser.). 387p. 1995. lib. bdg. 99.00 (*0-7812-4059-X*) Rprt Serv.

Boas, Adrian. Crusader Archaeology: The Material Culture of the Latin East. LC 98-41042. 1999. 50.00 (*0-415-17361-2*) Routledge.

Boas, F. S., ed. see Lee, Sidney.

Boas, Franz. Anthropology & Modern Life. 255p. 1986. reprint ed. pap. 8.95 (*0-486-25245-0*) Dover.

— Anthropology & Modern Life. LC 83-22694. 255p. 1984. reprint ed. lib. bdg. 59.50 (*0-313-24370-0*, BANM Greenwood Pr) Greenwood.

— Bella Bella Texts. (Columbia University. Contributions to Anthropology Ser.: No. 5). reprint ed. 47.50 (*0-404-50555-4*) AMS Pr.

— The Central Eskimo. LC 64-63593. (Bison Book Ser.). (Illus.). 283p. reprint ed. pap. 87.80 (*0-608-05992-7*, 206632000008) Bks Demand.

— Chinook Texts. (Smithsonian Institution, Bureau of Ethnology Ser.: Bulletin 20). 280p. (C). 1994. pap. 23.50 (*1-55567-658-8*) Coyote Press.

— Chinook Texts. (Bureau of American Ethnology Bulletins Ser.). 178p. 1995. lib. bdg. 79.00 (*0-7812-4020-4*) Rprt Serv.

— Contributions to the Ethnology of the Kwakiutl. LC 77-82353. (Columbia Univ. Contributions to Anthropology Ser.: Vol. 3). reprint ed. 54.00 (*0-404-50553-8*) AMS Pr.

— The Decorative Art of the Indians of the North Pacific Coast. LC 74-7936. (Illus.). reprint ed. 27.50 (*0-404-11823-2*) AMS Pr.

— The Entnography of Franz Boas. Parker, Hedy, tr. LC 70-77152. 361p. Date not set. reprint ed. pap. 112.00 (*0-608-20589-3*, 205455400003) Bks Demand.

Boas, Franz. The Eskimo of Baffin Land & Hudson Bay, 2 pts. in 1. LC 74-5828. reprint ed. 79.50 (*0-404-11631-0*) AMS Pr.

Boas, Franz. Facial Paintings of the Indians of Northern British Columbia. LC 73-3509. (Jesup North Pacific Expedition. Publications: Vol. 1, Pt. 1). reprint ed. 32.50 (*0-404-58101-3*) AMS Pr.

— Franz Boas among the Inuit of Baffin Island, 1883-1884 (Franz Boas Bei den Inuit in Baffinland, 1883-1884) Journals & Letters (Tagebucher und Briefe) Muller-Wille, Ludger, ed. Barr, William, tr. from GER. LC 99-216117. (Illus.). 312p. 1998. text 50.00 (*0-8020-4150-7*) U of Toronto Pr.

— A Franz Boas Reader: The Shaping of American Anthropology, 1883-1911. Stocking, George W., ed. LC 81-21851. xiv, 354p. (C). 1982. pap. text 12.00 (*0-226-77490-2*) U Ch Pr.

— A Franz Boas Reader: The Shaping of American Anthropology, 1883-1911. Stocking, George W., Jr., ed. xiv, 368p. 1989. pap. text 28.00 (*0-226-06243-0*, Midway Reprint) U Ch Pr.

— Geographical Names of the Kwakiutl Indians. fac. ed. (Columbia University Contributions to Anthropology Ser.: Vol. 20). (Illus.). 124p. (C). 1934. reprint ed. pap. text 13.75 (*1-55567-684-7*) Coyote Press.

— Geographical Names of the Kwakiutl Indians. LC 77-82361. (Columbia Univ. Contributions to Anthropology Ser.: No. 20). 1969. reprint ed. 37.50 (*0-404-50570-8*) AMS Pr.

— Handbook of the American Indian Languages, 4 vols., Set. 1988. reprint ed. lib. bdg. 360.00 (*0-7812-5040-4*) Rprt Serv.

— Handbook of the American Indian Languages, 4 vols., Set. reprint ed. 395.00 (*0-403-08964-6*) Scholarly.

— The Huntington California Expedition Vol. XVII, Pt. IV: Anthropology of Central California. (Publications of American Museum in Natural History: Vol. XVII, Pt. IV). (Illus.). 44p. (C). 1905. reprint ed. pap. text 5.00 (*1-55567-428-3*) Coyote Press.

— Introduction to the Handbook of American Indian Languages. 83p. 1986. reprint ed. pap. 10.00 (*0-8466-4023-6*, I-23, Shorey Pubns) Shoreys Bkstore.

— Kathlamet Texts. (Bureau of American Ethnology Bulletins Ser.). 261p. 1995. lib. bdg. 89.00 (*0-7812-4026-3*) Rprt Serv.

— Kathlamet Texts. reprint ed. 49.00 (*0-403-03624-0*) Scholarly.

— Keresan Texts, Set, Vols. 1 & 2. LC 73-3543. (American Ethnological Society Publications: No. 8). reprint ed. 77.50 (*0-404-58158-7*) AMS Pr.

— Kwakiutl Grammar - With a Glossary of Suffixes. LC 74-7939. reprint ed. 38.50 (*0-404-11826-7*) AMS Pr.

— The Kwakiutl of Vancouver Island. LC 73-3526. (Jesup North Pacific Expedition. Publications: Vol. 5, Pt. 2). reprint ed. 64.50 (*0-404-58124-2*) AMS Pr.

— Kwakiutl Tales. LC 70-82343. (Columbia University. Contributions to Anthropology Ser.: No. 2). reprint ed. 49.50 (*0-404-50552-X*) AMS Pr.

— Kwakiutl Tales: New Series, 2 vols. LC 79-82367. (Columbia Univ. Contributions to Anthropology Ser.: Vol. 26). 1969. reprint ed. 49.00 (*0-404-50576-7*) AMS Pr.

— Materials for the Study of Inheritance in Man. LC 71-82349. (Columbia Univ. Contributions to Anthropology Ser.: No. 6). 1969. reprint ed. 49.50 (*0-404-50556-2*) AMS Pr.

— The Mind of Primitive Man. rev. ed. LC 83-10869. 254p. (C). 1983. reprint ed. lib. bdg. 77.50 (*0-313-24004-3*, BOMP, Greenwood Pr) Greenwood.

— The Mythology of the Bella Coola Indians. LC 73-3510. (Jesup North Pacific Expedition. Publications: Vol. 1, Pt. 2). reprint ed. 40.00 (*0-404-58113-7*) AMS Pr.

— Notes on the Tillamook. fac. ed. (University of California Publications in American Archaeology & Ethnology: Vol. 20: 1). 14p. (C). 1923. reprint ed. pap. text 1.88 (*1-55567-237-X*) Coyote Press.

— Primitive Art. (Illus.). 378p. 1955. pap. 9.95 (*0-486-20025-6*) Dover.

— Primitive Art. (Illus.). 1962. 23.50 (*0-8446-1695-8*) Peter Smith.

— Race & Democratic Society. 15.00 (*0-685-71709-7*) J J Augustin.

— Race & Democratic Society. LC 70-86641. 1969. reprint ed. 30.00 (*0-8196-0248-5*) Biblo.

— Race, Language & Culture. xx, 668p. 1994. pap. text 23.95 (*0-226-06242-2*, Midway Reprint) U Ch Pr.

— Race, Language & Culture. LC 81-21998. (Illus.). xx, 648p. (C). 1982. reprint ed. pap. text 22.50 (*0-226-06241-4*) U Ch Pr.

— Religion of the Kwakiutl Indians, 2 vols. LC 72-82368. (Columbia Univ. Contributions to Anthropology Ser.: No. 10). reprint ed. 60.00 (*0-404-50560-0*) AMS Pr.

Boas, Franz. The Social Organization & the Secret Societies of the Kwakiutl indians. (Smithsonian Institution, Annual Reports of the Board of Regents). (Illus.). 532p. (C). pap. text 55.00 (*1-55567-888-2*) Coyote Press.

Boas, Franz. Tsimshian Texts. (Bureau of American Ethnology Bulletins Ser.). 244p. 1995. lib. bdg. 89.00 (*0-7812-4027-1*) Rprt Serv.

— Tsimshian Texts. LC 90-44636. 244p. 1990. reprint ed. pap. 29.00 (*1-878592-16-5*); reprint ed. lib. bdg. 49.00 (*1-878592-15-7*) Native Amer Bk Pubs.

Boas, Franz, ed. Bella Bella Tales. LC 34-11630. (American Folklore Society Memoirs Ser.: Vol. 25). 1972. reprint ed. 30.00 (*0-527-01077-4*) Periodicals Srv.

Boas, Franz, et al, eds. The Jesup North Pacific Expedition: Publications, 27 vols., Vols.1-11, & Suppl. Album. (Illus.). reprint ed. 1764.00 (*0-404-58100-5*) AMS Pr.

Boas, Franz & Deloria, Ella. Dakota Grammar. LC 74-7942. reprint ed. write for info. (*0-404-11829-1*) AMS Pr.

Boas, Franz & Hunt, George. Kwakiutl Texts. LC 73-3523. (Jesup North Pacific Expedition. Publications: No. 3). reprint ed. 97.50 (*0-404-58103-X*) AMS Pr.

— Kwakiutl Texts--Second Series. LC 73-3662. (Jesup North Pacific Expedition. Publications: Vol. 10, Pt. 1). reprint ed. 64.50 (*0-404-58110-2*) AMS Pr.

Boas, Franz & Powell, J. W. Introduction to Handbook of American Indian Languages & Indian Linguistic Families of America North of Mexico. Holder, Preston, ed. 221p. Date not set. pap. text 12.00 (*0-8032-5017-7*, Bison Books) U of Nebr Pr.

Boas, Franz, jt. auth. see Hyatt, Marshall.

Boas, Franz, jt. auth. see Swanton, John R.

Boas, Franz, jt. auth. see Teit, James.

Boas, Franz, ed. see Teit, James A.

Boas, Frederick S. Five Pre-Shakespearean Comedies: Early Tudor Period. LC 86-4629. 361p. 1986. reprint ed. lib. bdg. 69.50 (*0-313-25203-3*, BOFI, Greenwood Pr) Greenwood.

— From Richardson to Pinero: Some Innovators & Idealists. LC 69-17563. (Essay Index Reprint Ser.). 1977. 40.95 (*0-8369-0063-4*) Ayer.

— An Introduction to Tudor Drama. LC 75-41032. (BCL Ser.: II). reprint ed. 32.50 (*0-404-14509-4*) AMS Pr.

— Marlowe & His Circle: A Biographical Survey. (BCL1-PR English Literature Ser.). 159p. 1992. reprint ed. lib. bdg. 69.00 (*0-7812-7249-1*) Rprt Serv.

— Marlowe & His Circle: A Biographical Survey. (BCL1-PR English Literature Ser.). 159p. 1992. reprint ed. lib. bdg. 69.00 (*0-7812-7260-2*) Rprt Serv.

— Ovid & the Elizabethans. (Studies in Shakespeare: No. 24). 1970. reprint ed. pap. 19.95 (*0-8383-0008-1*) M S G Haskell Hse.

— Queen Elizabeth in Drama & Related Studies. LC 78-119954. (Select Bibliographies Reprint Ser.). 1977. 21.95 (*0-8369-5397-5*) Ayer.

— Queen Elizabeth in Drama & Related Studies. (Select Bibliographies Reprint Ser.). 212p. 1982. reprint ed. lib. bdg. 14.00 (*0-8290-0828-4*) Irvington.

— Rossetti & His Poetry. LC 75-22072. (English Literature Ser.: No. 33). 1975. lib. bdg. 59.00 (*0-8383-2074-0*) M S G Haskell Hse.

— Shakespeare & His Predecessors. LC 68-59404. 564p. 1968. reprint ed. 75.00 (*0-87752-011-9*) Gordian.

— Shakespeare & His Predecessors. LC 69-13831. 555p. 1969. reprint ed. lib. bdg. 75.00 (*0-8371-0316-9*, BOSH, Greenwood Pr) Greenwood.

— Shakespeare & His Predecessors. LC 68-24898. (Studies in Shakespeare: No. 24). 1969. reprint ed. lib. bdg. 75.00 (*0-8383-0914-3*) M S G Haskell Hse.

— Shakespeare & His Predecessors. (BCL1-PR English Literature Ser.). 555p. 1992. reprint ed. lib. bdg. 99.00 (*0-7812-7278-5*) Rprt Serv.

— Shakespeare & His Predecessors. 1969. reprint ed. 13.00 (*0-403-00109-9*) Scholarly.

— University Drama in the Tudor Age. LC 65-20049. (Illus.). 1979. 30.95 (*0-405-08277-0*, Pub. by Blom Pubns) Ayer.

— University Drama in the Tudor Age. (BCL1-PR English Literature Ser.). 414p. 1992. reprint ed. lib. bdg. 99.00 (*0-7812-7101-0*) Rprt Serv.

Boas, Frederick S., ed. Songs & Lyrics. LC 77-14508. 1978. reprint ed. lib. bdg. 65.00 (*0-8371-9842-9*, BOMO, Greenwood Pr) Greenwood.

— Songs & Lyrics from the English Masques & Light Operas. 175p. 1949. reprint ed. 15.00 (*0-403-03693-3*) Scholarly.

— Songs & Lyrics from the English Playbooks. reprint ed. 15.00 (*0-403-04290-9*) Somerset Pub.

Boas, Frederick S., ed. see Lee, Sidney.

Boas, Frederick S., ed. see Marlowe, Christopher.

Boas, G. The Hieroglyphics of Horapollo. (Bollingen Ser.: No. XXIII). (Illus.). 148p. 1993. pap. text 14.95 (*0-691-00092-1*, Pub. by Princeton U Pr) Cal Prin Full Svc.

***Boas, Gary.** Starstruck! Photographs from a Fan. 1999. pap. text 27.95 (*0-9664272-5-4*) Dilettante Pr.

Boas, George. Critical Analysis of the Philosophy of Emile Meyerson. LC 70-109616. (Select Bibliographies Reprint Ser.). 1977. 19.95 (*0-8369-5224-3*) Ayer.

— The Cult of Childhood. LC 90-33312. (Dunquin Ser.: No. 18). 122p. 1966. reprint ed. pap. 13.50 (*0-88214-218-6*) Spring Pubns.

B

An Asterisk (*) at the beginning of an entry indicates that the title is appearing for the first time.

— The Heaven of Invention. LC 63-8810. (Illus.). 412p. 1962. reprint ed. pap. 127.80 (*0-608-05928-5*, 206626400008) Bks Demand.
— The Mind's Road to God: Bonaventura. 72p. (C). 1953. pap. text 7.33 (*0-02-311250-6*, Macmillan Coll) P-H.
— Primer for Critics. LC 68-55100. (Illus.). 153p. 1968. reprint ed. lib. bdg. 55.00 (*0-8371-0318-5*, BOPC, Greenwood Pr) Greenwood.
— Primitivism & Related Ideas in the Middle Ages. LC 96-29536. 240p. 1997. reprint ed. pap. text 16.95 (*0-8018-5610-8*) Johns Hopkins.
— Rationalism in Greek Philosophy. LC 61-15638. 514p. reprint ed. pap. 159.40 (*0-608-10025-0*, 201317300086) Bks Demand.
— Vox Populi: Essays in the History of an Idea. LC 69-13538. (Seminars in the History of Ideas Ser.). (Illus.). 308p. reprint ed. pap. 95.50 (*0-608-14667-6*, 202583300046) Bks Demand.
— Wingless Pegasus: A Handbook for Critics. 1979. 16.95 (*0-405-10584-3*) Ayer.
Boas, George, tr. see Michaud, Regis.
Boas-Hall, Marie. Promoting Experimental Learning: Experiment & the Royal Society, 1660-1727. 215p. (C). 1991. text 69.95 (*0-521-40503-3*) Cambridge U Pr.
Boas, Harold P., tr. see Kytmanov, Alexander M.
Boas, Henrietta O. Rossetti & His Poetry. LC 74-120979. (Poetry & Life Ser.). reprint ed. 16.00 (*0-404-52504-0*) AMS Pr.
Boas, Henriette. Aeneas' Arrival in Latium. 263p. write for info. (*0-318-71077-3*) G Olms Pubs.
Boas, Jacob. We Are Witnesses: Five Diaries of Teenagers Who Died in the Holocaust. (YA). (gr. 8 up). 1996. pap. 3.99 (*0-590-84475-X*) Scholastic Inc.
— We Are Witnesses, Five Diaries of Teenagers Who Died in the Holocaust. (J). 1996. 9.09 (*0-606-12052-1*, Pub. by Turtleback) Demco.
Boas, Jacob, ed. We Are Witnesses: The Diaries of Five Teenagers Who Died in the Holocaust. LC 94-43889. (J). (gr. 7 up). 1995. 15.95 (*0-8050-3702-0*, Bks Young Read) H Holt & Co.
Boas, Keith, jt. auth. see Doeffinger, Derek.
Boas, Louise, jt. auth. see Boas, Ralph P.
Boas, Louise S. Harriet Shelley: Five Long Years. LC 78-12350. 237p. 1979. reprint ed. lib. bdg. 55.00 (*0-313-21143-4*, BOHF, Greenwood Pr) Greenwood.
— Woman's Education Begins: The Rise of the Women's Colleges. LC 74-165705. (American Education, Ser, No. 2). 1974. reprint ed. 20.95 (*0-405-03694-9*) Ayer.
Boas, Mary L. Mathematical Methods in the Physical Sciences. 2nd ed. LC 83-1226. 816p. 1983. text 102.95 (*0-471-04409-1*) Wiley.
— Mathematical Methods in the Physical Sciences. 2nd ed. 616p. (C). 1984. pap., teacher ed. 49.95 (*0-471-09920-1*) Wiley.
Boas, Nancy. The Society of Six: California Colorists. LC 96-37048. (Illus.). 1997. 68.00 (*0-520-21054-9*, Pub. by U CA Pr); pap. 39.95 (*0-520-21055-7*, Pub. by U CA Pr) Cal Prin Full Svc.
***Boas, Norman F., ed.** The Battle of Groton Heights: A Collection of Narratives, Official Reports Records, Etc. 3rd ed. LC 99-75802. (Illus.). 400p. 1999. reprint ed. pap. 30.00 (*0-9672626-1-5*) Boas & Meyer.
Boas, Ralph P. Collected Works of Hidehiko Yamabe. xii, 142p. 1967. text 192.00 (*0-677-00610-1*) Gordon & Breach.
Boas, Ralph P., Jr. Lion Hunting & Other Mathematical Pursuits: A Collection of Mathematics, Verse & Stories. Alexanderson, Gerald L. & Mugler, Dale H., eds. LC 94-78313. 320p. 1995. pap. text 25.00 (*0-88385-323-X*, DOL-15) Math Assn.
— A Primer of Real Functions. 4th rev. ed. LC 96-77785. (Carus Mathematical Monograph: No. 13). 314p. (C). 1996. text 43.95 (*0-88385-029-X*, CAM-13R) Math Assn.
Boas, Ralph P. & Boas, Louise. Cotton Mather, Keeper of the Puritan Conscience. (BCL1 - United States Local History Ser.). 271p. 1991. reprint ed. lib. bdg. 79.00 (*0-7812-6265-8*) Rprt Serv.
Boas, Ralph P., ed. see Polya, George.
Boas, Ralph P., tr. see Levin, Boris J.
Boas, Ralph P., tr. see Shiriaev, Albert N.
Boas, Ralph P., tr. see Shiryayev, A. N., Jr.
Boas, Ralph P., tr. see Steickin, S. B., ed.
Boas, Ralph P., tr. see Vorobyev, Nicolai N.
Boas, Rollo M., jt. auth. see White, Mary C.
Boas, Sarah, jt. auth. see Baldwin, Shirley.
Boas, Simone B., tr. see Archimault, Charles.
Boasberg, T., et al. Historic Preservation Law & Taxation, 3 vols., Set. 3000p. 1986. 110.00 (*0-929179-80-3*) Juris Pubng.
Boasdottir, Solveig A. Violence, Power, & Justice: A Feminist Contribution to Christian Sexual Ethics. LC 98-171909. (Uppsala Studies in Social Ethics: Vol. 20). 202p. 1998. pap. 47.50 (*91-554-4165-3*) Coronet Bks.
Boase, Joan P. Shifting Sands: Government-Group Relationships in the Health Care Sector. LC 93-90659. (Canadian Public Administration Ser.). 240p. 1994. 55.00 (*0-7735-1158-X*, Pub. by McG-Queens Univ Pr) CUP Services.
Boase, Leonard S. Prayer of Faith. 126p. 1985. reprint ed. pap. 5.95 (*0-8294-0493-7*) Loyola Pr.
Boase, Petra. Applique. (New Craft Ser.). (Illus.). 96p. 1997. 15.95 (*1-85967-530-1*, Lorenz Bks) Anness Pub.
***Boase, Petra.** Christmas Crafts for Kids: Practical Decorations & Gift Ideas for Festive Fun. (Illus.). 96p. 1999. 11.98 (*1-84038-422-0*) Hermes Hse.
Boase, Petra. Decorating Makeovers: More Than 150 Easy Projects For Furniture, Floors And Walls, Lighting And Accessories. LC 99-42885. 160p. 2000. 25.00 (*0-688-17235-0*, Wm Morrow) Morrow Avon.
***Boase, Petra.** How to Throw the Best Kids' Party Ever. (Illus.). 192p. 2000. pap. 16.95 (*0-7548-0286-8*, Lorenz Bks) Anness Pub.
— I Can Play Games. (Illus.). 40p. (J). 2000. pap. 7.95 (*0-7548-0225-6*, Lorenz Bks) Anness Pub.
Boase, Petra. Nail Art for Kids. 1999. pap. text 14.95 (*1-85868-662-8*, Pub. by Carlton Bks Ltd) Natl Bk Netwk.
— Rainy Day Projects for Kids. (Illus.). 96p. (J). (gr. 2-7). 1997. pap. 9.95 (*1-85967-544-1*, Lorenz Bks) Anness Pub.
— T-Shirt Fun: Fabulous T-Shirt Designs & Creations. (Creative Fun Ser.). (Illus.). 64p. (J). (gr. 3-7). 1997. 7.95 (*1-85967-508-5*, Lorenz Bks) Anness Pub.
Boase, T. S. Kingdoms & Strongholds of the Crusaders. LC 73-157118. 1971. 15.00 (*0-672-51606-3*, Bobbs) Macmillan.
***Boase, Tony.** Bowl Turning: Techniques Masterclass. (Illus.). 2000. pap. 17.95 (*1-86108-117-0*) Guild Master.
Boase, Tony. Woodturning Masterclass. (Illus.). 144p. 1996. pap. 18.95 (*0-946819-84-X*, Pub. by Guild Master) Sterling.
Boase, Wendy. Tres Chivos Testarudos. (Primeros Cuentos Ser.). 1994. 13.70 (*0-606-10518-2*, Pub. by Turtleback) Demco.
Boashash. Time Frequency Signal Analysis. Date not set. pap. text. write for info. (*0-582-71286-6*, Pub. by Addison-Wesley) Longman.
Boashash, Bouaelem, et al, eds. Higher Order Statistical Signal Processing. LC 94-23195. 560p. 1996. 168.00 (*0-470-23458-X*) Wiley.
Boashash, Boualem, ed. Signal Processing - Theories, Implementation & Applications: ISSPA 87: Proceedings IASTED Symposium, Brisbane, Australia, August 24-28, 1987 (Co-Sponsored by IEEE, IREE, IE Australia), 2 vols., 1. 907p. 1988. write for info. (*0-85814-141-8*) Acta Pr.
— Signal Processing - Theories, Implementation & Applications: ISSPA 87: Proceedings IASTED Symposium, Brisbane, Australia, August 24-28, 1987 (Co-Sponsored by IEEE, IREE, IE Australia), 2 vols., 2. 907p. 1988. write for info. (*0-85814-142-6*) Acta Pr.
— Signal Processing - Theories, Implementation & Applications: ISSPA 87: Proceedings IASTED Symposium, Brisbane, Australia, August 24-28, 1987 (Co-Sponsored by IEEE, IREE, IE Australia), 2 vols., Set. 907p. 1988. 98.00 (*0-85814-143-4*, 120) Acta Pr.
Boasson, Charles & Nurock, Max, eds. The Changing International Community: Some Problems of Its Laws, Structures, & Peace Research & the Middle East Conflict. (New Babylon Studies in the Social Sciences: No. 18). 1973. text 49.25 (*90-279-7292-3*) Mouton.
Boassy, Gay. A Romantic Treasury of Love: Sweet Words to Win the Heart. 32p. 1999. 16.99 (*0-7369-0007-1*) Harvest Hse.
Boassy, Gay T. A Forever Friend. LC 99-168560. 48p. 1998. pap. 9.99 (*1-56507-949-3*) Harvest Hse.
***Boassy, Gay Talbott.** The Key to My Heart: Your Friendship Opens Treasures of Love. 48p. 2000. pap. 7.99 (*0-7369-0098-5*) Harvest Hse.
Boast, jt. auth. see Foster, Lynn.
Boast, jt. auth. see Nyberg, Cheryl.
Boast, Clare. The Ancient Olympics. LC 95-39282. (Olympic Library). (Illus.). (J). 1998. 18.50 (*1-57572-034-5*) Heinemann Lib.
— Australia. LC 97-53108. (Next Stop! Ser.). (J). 1998. 19.92 (*1-57572-675-0*) Heinemann Lib.
— Field. LC 95-39284. (Olympic Library). (J). 1998. (*1-57572-038-8*) Heinemann Lib.
— France. LC 97-16748. (Next Stop! Ser.). (J). (gr. 2-4). 1998. 19.92 (*1-57572-565-7*) Heinemann Lib.
— Germany. LC 97-16747. (Next Stop! Ser.). (J). 1998. 19.92 (*1-57572-566-5*) Heinemann Lib.
— Indonesia. LC 97-42534. (Next Stop! Ser.). (J). 1998. 19.92 (*1-57572-676-9*) Heinemann Lib.
— Italy. LC 97-16743. (Next Stop! Ser.). (Illus.). 32p. (J). 1998. 19.92 (*1-57572-567-3*) Heinemann Lib.
— Japan. LC 97-19805. (Next Stop! Ser.). (J). 1998. 19.92 (*1-57572-568-1*) Heinemann Lib.
— Kenya. LC 97-53234. (Next Stop! Ser.). (J). 1998. (*1-57572-677-7*) Heinemann.
— Russia. LC 97-16745. (Next Stop! Ser.). 32p. (J). (gr. 2-4). 1998. 19.92 (*1-57572-569-X*) Heinemann Lib.
— South Korea. LC 97-42535. (Next Stop! Ser.). (J). 1998. 19.92 (*1-57572-678-5*) Heinemann Lib.
— Spain. LC 97-16744. (Next Stop! Ser.). (J). 1998. 19.92 (*1-57572-570-3*) Heinemann Lib.
Boast, D. & Coveney, V. A., eds. Finite Element Analysis of Elastomers. 283p. 1999. 131.00 (*1-86058-171-4*) Prof Eng Pubng.
Boast, Philip. City. 576p. 1995. mass mkt. 8.95 (*0-7472-4726-9*, Pub. by Headline Bk Pub) Trafalgar.
— Deus. (Illus.). 1998. pap. 8.95 (*0-7472-5380-3*, Pub. by Headline Bk Pub) Trafalgar.
— The Foundling. 608p. 1996. pap. 10.95 (*0-7472-4882-6*, Pub. by Headline Bk Pub) Trafalgar.
— Gloria. 576p. 1996. mass mkt. 11.95 (*0-7472-4555-X*, Pub. by Headline Bk Pub) Trafalgar.
— London's Daughter. 608p. 1994. mass mkt. 13.95 (*0-7472-4023-X*, Pub. by Headline Bk Pub) Trafalgar.
— London's Millionaire. 496p. 1995. mass mkt. 11.95 (*0-7472-4216-X*, Pub. by Headline Bk Pub) Trafalgar.
***Boast, Philip.** Pride. 1999. pap. 11.00 (*0-7472-3629-1*, Pub. by Headline Bk Pub) Trafalgar.
Boast, Philip. Resurrection. 480p. 1998. pap. 8.95 (*0-7472-5379-X*, Pub. by Headline Bk Pub) Trafalgar.
***Boast, Philip.** Watersmeet. 1999. pap. 11.00 (*0-7472-3446-9*, Pub. by Headline Bk Pub) Trafalgar.
Boast, Philip. Watersmeet. large type ed. 1993. 39.95 (*0-7066-1023-7*, Pub. by Remploy Pr) St Mut.
Boast, William M. & Martin, Benjamin. Masters of Change: How Great Leaders in Every Age Thrived in Turbulent Times. 168p. 1997. 22.95 (*1-890009-07-5*) Exec Excell.
Boat, Thomas F., jt. auth. see Chernick, Victor.
Boateng, Charles. Nkrumah's Consciencism. 188p. (C). 1995. pap. text, per. 35.95 (*0-7872-1396-9*, 41139601) Kendall-Hunt.
Boateng, E. A. A Geography of Ghana. 2nd ed. LC 65-22922. 270p. reprint ed. pap. 77.00 (*0-608-16915-3*, 2027254) Bks Demand.
Boateng, Faustine A. Asante, 56 vols. (Heritage Library of African Peoples). (Illus.). 64p. (YA). (gr. 7-12). 1996. lib. bdg. 16.95 (*0-8239-1975-7*) Rosen Group.
Boateng, Yaw A. The Young Detectives. (Junior African Writers Ser.). (Illus.). 80p. (J). (gr. 3 up). 1992. pap. 4.95 (*0-7910-2918-2*) Chelsea Hse.
Boatfield, Graham. Calculations for Agriculture & Horticulture. Hamilton, Iar, ed. (Illus.). 120p. 1984. pap. 18.95 (*0-85236-145-9*, Pub. by Farming Pr) Diamond Farm Bk.
— Farm Crops. 2nd ed. (Illus.). 144p. 1983. pap. 18.95 (*0-85236-129-7*, Pub. by Farming Pr) Diamond Farm Bk.
— Farm Livestock. 3rd ed. (Illus.). 144p. 1994. pap. 18.95 (*0-85236-274-9*, Pub. by Farming Pr) Diamond Farm Bk.
Boatman, Alec C. The Pacific Appointment: Two Lives That Met at Pearl Harbor. (Illus.). 128p. (Orig.). 1996. pap. 9.95 (*1-56474-155-9*) Fithian Pr.
Boatman, Dennis, ed. see Aaron, Chester.
Boatman, John. Jane's U. S. Military R&D Special Report: Find Out about the Latest Defense-Critical Technologies. 1997. 695.00 (*0-7106-1644-9*) Janes Info Group.
— My Elders Taught Me: Aspects of Western Great Lakes American Indian Philosophy. 73p. (Orig.). (C). 1992. text 32.50 (*0-8191-8691-0*); pap. text 17.50 (*0-8191-8692-9*) U Pr of Amer.
— North American Intelligent Transportation. (Transportation - Related Special Reports). 1996. 695.00 (*0-7106-1500-0*) Janes Info Group.
Boatman, John. A Survey of the United States Ethnic Experience: Africans, Asians & Immigrants, Vol. 2. 272p. (C). 1996. pap. text 30.95 (*0-7872-2862-1*) Kendall-Hunt.
— A Survey of the United States Ethnic Experience: American Indians, Hispanics & Immigrants from Northern & Western Europe, Vol. 1. 232p. (Orig.). (C). 1996. pap. text 30.95 (*0-7872-2861-3*) Kendall-Hunt.
Boatman, John. U. S. Conventional Munitions. (Military Systems - Related Special Reports). 1996. 695.00 (*0-7106-1499-3*) Janes Info Group.
— U. S. Information Warfare. (Military Systems - Related Special Reports). 1996. 695.00 (*0-7106-1640-6*) Janes Info Group.
Boatman, Russell. The End Time. 3rd ed. LC 79-56542. (What the Bible Says Ser.). 422p. (C). 1991. pap. text 10.99 (*0-89900-370-2*) College Pr Pub.
Boatman, Thomas, jt. auth. see Ferguson, Paul.
Boatner, Mark A., III. Biographical Dictionary of World War II. LC 96-13437. 736p. 1996. 50.00 (*0-89141-548-3*) Presidio Pr.
Boatner, Mark M., III. The Biographical Dictionary of World War II. 736p. 1999. pap. 24.95 (*0-89141-624-2*) Presidio Pr.
— The Civil War Dictionary. LC 91-50013. (Vintage Civil War Library). 1008p. 1991. pap. 20.00 (*0-679-73392-2*) Vin Bks.
— The Civil War Dictionary. rev. ed. (Illus.). 974p. 1987. write for info. (*0-8129-1726-X*, Times Bks) Crown Pub Group.
— Encyclopedia of the American Revolution. 1974. 9.98 (*0-679-50440-0*) McKay.
— Encyclopedia of the American Revolution. (Illus.). 1312p. 1994. 34.95 (*0-8117-0578-1*) Stackpole.
Boatner, Mark M. Landmarks of the American Revolution: People & Places Vital to the Quest for Independence. rev. ed. LC 91-27501. 608p. 1992. reprint ed. pap. 188.50 (*0-608-00477-4*, 206129600007) Bks Demand.
Boatner, Mark M., III. Military Customs & Traditions. LC 75-17189. (Illus.). 176p. 1976. reprint ed. lib. bdg. 35.00 (*0-8371-8299-9*, BOMCT, Greenwood Pr) Greenwood.
Boatness, Marie E. Travel Games for the Family. Westheimer, Mary, ed. LC 93-90005. (Illus.). 144p. (Orig.). (J). (gr. 1-8). 1993. pap. 6.95 (*0-9635619-0-1*) Canyon Creek.
***Boatright.** Job Search Skills. 258p. 1999. pap. text, wbk. ed. 19.95 (*0-536-02311-5*) Pearson Custom.
Boatright, Daniel T., et al. Risk Communication: A Bibliography of Risk Communication & Environmental Health Risk Literature. 139p. (Orig.). 1996. pap. 55.00 (*0-944111-14-9*) Natl Environ Health.
***Boatright, Jeffry S.** Journey of Truth. 144p. 1999. pap. 9.95 (*1-892937-03-4*) Spec Pubns.
Boatright, John R. Cases in Ethics & the Conduct. LC 94-379. 336p. 1994. pap. text 45.00 (*0-13-120601-X*) P-H.
Boatright, John R., ed. Ethics in Finance. LC 98-33146. (Foundations of Business Ethics Ser.). 224p. 1999. 54.95 (*0-631-21426-7*); pap. 19.95 (*0-631-21427-5*) Blackwell Pubs.
Boatright, Kevin, ed. see Stetson, Daniel E.
Boatright, Kevin, ed. see Stetson, Daniel E. & Shamen, Sanford S.
Boatright, Kevin, ed. see Stetson, Daniel E. & Threlfall, Tim.
Boatright, Kevin, ed. see Stetson, Daniel E., et al.
Boatright, Mody C. Folklore of the Oil Industry. LC 63-21186. (Illus.). 228p. 1984. reprint ed. pap. 9.95 (*0-87074-204-3*) SMU Press.
— Gib Morgan: Minstrel of the Oil Fields. LC 46-815. (Texas Folklore Society Publications: No. 20). (Illus.). 104p. 1965. reprint ed. 11.95 (*0-87074-008-3*) UNTX Pr.
Boatright, Mody C., ed. Mexican Border Ballads & Other Lore. LC 48-7407. (Texas Folklore Society, Publication Ser.: No. 21). 151p. reprint ed. pap. 46.90 (*0-608-17197-2*, 202700300053) Bks Demand.
— The Sky Is My Tipi. LC 49-1690. (Texas Folklore Society Publications: No. 22). (Illus.). 243p. 1966. reprint ed. 13.95 (*0-87074-010-5*) UNTX Pr.
Boatright, Mody C., et al, eds. And Horns on the Toads. LC 59-15694. (Texas Folklore Society Publications: No. 29). 237p. 1959. 12.95 (*0-87074-013-X*) UNTX Pr.
— The Best of Texas Folk & Folklore, 1916-1954. LC 54-11200. (Texas Folklore Society Publications: Vol. XXVI). (Illus.). 356p. 1998. pap. 18.95 (*1-57441-055-5*) UNTX Pr.
— Folk Travelers: Ballads, Tales, & Talk. LC 53-12578. (Texas Folklore Society Publications: No. 25). 261p. 1953. 13.95 (*0-87074-014-8*) UNTX Pr.
— Golden Log. LC 61-17184. (Texas Folklore Society Publications: No. 31). 168p. 1962. 12.95 (*0-87074-015-6*) UNTX Pr.
— A Good Tale & a Bonnie Tune. LC 63-10979. (Texas Folklore Society Publications: No. 32). 274p. 1964. 14.95 (*0-87074-016-4*) UNTX Pr.
— Madstones & Twisters. LC 58-9269. (Texas Folklore Society Publications: No. 28). 169p. 1958. 12.95 (*0-87074-017-2*) UNTX Pr.
— Mesquite & Willow. LC 56-12566. (Texas Folklore Society Publications: No. 27). 203p. 1957. 12.95 (*0-87074-018-0*) UNTX Pr.
— Singers & Storytellers. LC 60-15894. (Texas Folklore Society Publications: No. 30). 304p. 1961. 14.95 (*0-87074-019-9*) UNTX Pr.
Boatright, Mody C. & Day, Donald, eds. Backwoods to Border. LC 48-18054. (Texas Folklore Society Publications: No. 18). (Illus.). 247p. 1967. reprint ed. 12.95 (*0-87074-011-3*) UNTX Pr.
— From Hell to Breakfast. LC 68-4642. (Texas Folklore Society, Publication Ser.: No. 19). 222p. reprint ed. pap. 68.90 (*0-608-17200-6*, 202700500053) Bks Demand.
***Boatright, Robert G. & American Judicature Society Staff.** Improving Citizen Response to Jury Summonses: A Report with Recommendations. LC 98-74667. xv, 144p. 1998. pap. 25.00 (*0-938870-88-2*) Am Judicature.
Boatsman, James R., et al. Advanced Accounting. 7th ed. LC 93-10648. 1136p. (C). 1993. text 75.40 (*0-256-10819-6*, Irwn McGrw-H) McGrw-H Hghr Educ.
— CPS - Advanced Accounting Select Chapters. 7th ed. 356p. (C). 1995. text 29.95 (*0-256-20385-7*, Irwn McGrw-H) McGrw-H Hghr Educ.
— Financial Reporting Research Cases: A Multi-Company Approach. 7th ed. 56p. (C). 1994. text 21.25 (*0-256-17034-7*, Irwn McGrw-H) McGrw-H Hghr Educ.
Boatswain, T. & Nicolson, C. A Traveller's History of Greece. 3rd ed. LC 89-15341. (Traveller's History Ser.). (Illus.). 336p. 1998. pap. 14.95 (*1-56656-229-5*) Interlink Pub.
Boatwright, Alice, ed. see Biestman, Margot S. & Bieshman, Margot S.
Boatwright, Becki H., et al. Getting Equipped to Stop Bullying: A Kid's Survival Kit for Understanding & Coping with Violence in the Schools. LC 98-74456. (Illus.). 80p. (YA). (gr. 5-8). 1998. pap. 12.95 (*0-932796-84-2*) Ed Media Corp.
Boatwright, Donna D. PPM Industrial Technology. 2nd rev. ed. 64p. 1996. pap. text, teacher ed. 12.00 (*0-8273-6975-1*) Delmar.
— Practical Problems in Mathematics for Industrial Technology. LC 95-37205. (Practical Problems in Mathematics Ser.). 288p. 1996. mass mkt. 25.95 (*0-8273-6974-3*) Delmar.
Boatwright, Eleanor M. Status of Women in Georgia, 1783-1860. LC 94-16767. (Scholarship in Women's History Ser.: Vol. 2). 1994. 50.00 (*0-926019-63-5*) Carlson Pub.
Boatwright, Howard. Chromaticism: Theory & Practice. (Illus.). 300p. (C). 1994. text 56.00 (*0-8156-8118-6*) Syracuse U Pr.
Boatwright, Howard, ed. see Ives, Charles.
Boatwright, James, ed. Shenandoah: An Anthology. LC 85-60719. 1986. 28.00 (*0-916366-33-2*, Pub. by Pushcart Pr) Norton.
Boatwright, Mary T. Hadrian & the City of Rome. (Illus.). 315p. 1987. pap. text 35.00 (*0-691-00218-5*, Pub. by Princeton U Pr) Cal Prin Full Svc.
Boatwright, Mary T., jt. ed. see Evans, Harry B.
Boaz. Essential Biological Anthropology. LC 98-25732. 393p. 1998. pap. 59.00 (*0-13-080793-1*) P-H.
— Mystery at Dragon Bone Hill: Beijing. 1997. 25.00 (*0-02-903711-5*) Free Pr.
Boaz, David. The Libertarian Reader. LC 96-48122. 458p. 1997. 27.00 (*0-684-83200-3*) Free Pr.
— Libertarianism: A Primer. LC 96-46012. 320p. 1997. 22.50 (*0-684-83198-8*) Free Pr.
— Libertarianism: The Newest Oldest Movement in America & Why You Should Join. 1997. 21.00 (*0-614-20400-3*) Free Pr.
Boaz, David, ed. Left, Right, & Babyboom: America's New Politics. 119p. 1986. pap. 2.00 (*0-932790-57-7*) Cato Inst.
Boaz, David & Crane, Edward H., eds. Beyond the Status Quo: Policy Proposals for America. 292p. 1985. 5.00 (*0-932790-46-1*); pap. 3.00 (*0-932790-49-6*) Cato Inst.
— Market Liberalism: A Paradigm for the 21st Century. LC 92-42550. 352p. 1993. 25.95 (*0-932790-98-4*) Cato Inst.
Boaz, David, jt. ed. see Crane, Edward H.
Boaz, Doniella C. Embrace You Child-Self: Change Your Life. (Illus.). 100p. (Orig.). 1995. pap. 11.95 (*1-883573-00-9*) Pride & Imprints.

***Boaz, Franz.** Tsimshian Texts. fac. ed. (Smithsonian Institution, Bureau of American Ethnology, Bulletins Ser.: No. 27). 244p. (C). 2002. reprint ed. pap. text 25.63 (*1-55567-788-6*) Coyote Press.

Boaz, Franz. A Wealth of Thought: Franz Boaz on Native American Art. Jonaitis, Aldona, ed. LC 94-15180. (Illus.). 352p. 1994. pap. 24.95 (*0-295-97384-6*) U of Wash Pr.

Boaz, John K., ed. The Adlai Stevenson Memorial Lecture Series: The First Twenty-Five Years, 1966-1991. 228p. (C). 1994. pap. text 24.00 (*0-8191-9629-0*); lib. bdg. 54.50 (*0-8191-9628-2*) U Pr of Amer.

Boaz, John K., jt. auth. see Staniford, David J.

Boaz Jones-Fulwylic, Christine. In Whom We Trust. 92p. (Orig.). 1987. pap. 5.00 (*1-885742-00-2*) Boaz-Fulwylic.

— In Whom We Trust. rev. ed. (Illus.). 97p. (Orig.). 1994. pap. 7.00 (*1-885742-01-0*) Boaz-Fulwylic.

Boaz, Martha. Librarian-Library Educator: An Autobiography & Planning for the Future. LC 87-4349. 322p. 1987. 31.00 (*0-8108-1988-0*) Scarecrow.

Boaz, Noel T. Biological Anthropology. (C). 1996. pap. text. write for info. (*0-15-502998-3*); pap. text, teacher ed. write for info. (*0-15-502999-1*) Harcourt Coll Pubs.

— Eco Homo: How the Human Being Emerged from the Cataclysmic History of the Earth. 1998. pap. 14.00 (*0-465-01804-1*, Pub. by Basic) HarpC.

— Quarry: Closing in on the Missing Link. 268p. 1993. 24.95 (*0-02-904501-0*) Free Pr.

Boaz, Noel T., ed. Evolution of Environments & Hominidae in the African Western Rift Valley. (Illus.). 356p. (Orig.). 1990. pap. 39.95 (*0-9625801-0-4*) VA Mus Natl Hist.

Boaz, Noel T. & Almquist, Alan J. Biological Anthropology: A Synthetic Approach to Human Evolution. LC 95-37820. 595p. 1996. pap. text 66.67 (*0-13-369208-6*) P-H.

Boaz, Noel T. & Wolfe, Linda D., eds. Biological Anthropology: The State of the Science. 264p. (Orig.). 1995. pap. text 39.95 (*0-614-04085-X*) Intl Inst Human Evol.

— Biological Anthropology: The State of the Science. 2nd ed. (Illus.). vi, 277p. (Orig.). (C). 1997. pap. text 39.95 (*0-9644248-1-9*) Intl Inst Human Evol.

Boaz, Thomas. For the Glory of the Marines! 2nd ed. (Illus.). 163p. 1993. pap. text 14.95 (*0-9635269-0-1*) Dockyard Pr.

— Guns for Cotton: England Arms the Confederacy. LC 95-53817. 86p. 1996. pap. 9.95 (*1-57249-004-7*, Burd St Pr) White Mane Pub.

Boaz, Thomas M. Libby Prison & Beyond: A Union Staff Officer in the East, 1862-1865. LC 99-11789. 225p. 1999. 24.95 (*1-57249-123-X*, Burd St Pr) White Mane Pub.

Boaz, Yakin. A Price above Rubies. (Illus.). 160p. (Orig.). 1999. pap. 14.00 (*0-571-19644-6*) Faber & Faber.

Bob & Candland, Elanor. A New Owner's Guide to Boston Terriers. (New Owner's Guide to Ser.). (Illus.). 160p. 12.95 (*0-7938-2802-3*) TFH Pubns.

Bob, B. Sam. Participation of the Poor in Rural Development Programmes: Selected Case Studies. LC 98-903262. x, 112p. 1998. 21.00 (*81-7141-409-5*, Pub. by Discovery Pub Hse) Nataraj Bks.

Bob, Castello. Meet Shaquille O'Neal: An Unauthorized Biography. (J). 1993. 9.09 (*0-606-05923-7*, Pub. by Turtleback) Demco.

Bob, Daniel E., jt. auth. see SRI International Staff.

Bob, Joe. 50 Ways to Get Even with Your Lover. (Illus.). 78p. 1994. pap. 6.95 (*0-9625593-2-6*) B R Pub Co TN.

***Bob Jones University Staff.** Up the Ladder. 2000. pap. 11.95 (*0-89084-950-1*) Bob Jones Univ.

Bob, Murray L. A Contrarian's Dictionary: 2000 Damnable Definitions for the Year 2000. LC 97-92494. (Illus.). 208p. 1997. pap. 14.95 (*0-9660154-0-1*) Contrarian Pr.

Bob, Skipper. Cruising the New York Canal System. 2nd rev. ed. LC 98-92425. (Illus.). 55p. 1998. pap. 10.00 (*0-9662208-5-4*, EC) Skip Bob.

— The Great Circle Route. LC 98-92423. (Illus.). 103p. 1998. pap. 18.00 (*0-9662208-4-6*, GCR) Skip Bob.

Bob, Tom B. How to Be a Successful Corporate So-&-So. (Illus.). 125p. (Orig.). 1996. pap. 12.95 (*1-884363-10-5*) Odenwald Pr.

Bobadilla, Jose L., et al, eds. Premature Death in the New Independent States. LC 97-67217. 408p. (Orig.). 1997. pap. 59.00 (*0-309-05734-5*, Joseph Henry Pr) Natl Acad Pr.

Bobadilla, Jose-Luis, jt. auth. see Lee, Haeduck.

Bobak. Very Large Databases. (ITCP-US Computer Science Ser.). 320p. 1997. pap. 44.99 incl. cd-rom (*1-85032-888-9*) ITCP.

Bobak, Angelo R. Data Modeling & Design for Today's Architectures. LC 97-33150. 500p. 1997. 79.00 (*0-89006-877-1*) Artech Hse.

— Distributed & Multi-Database Systems. LC 95-42035. 476p. 1995. 69.00 (*0-89006-614-0*, QA76.9) Artech Hse.

Bobak, Cathy. Poetry from A to Z: A Guide for Young Writers. LC 94-10528. 176p. (J). (gr. 4-8). 1994. mass mkt. 16.00 (*0-02-747672-3*, Mac Bks Young Read) S&S Childrens.

Bobak, Irene M. NurseNotes: Maternal-Newborn Nursing. LC 96-9117. 304p. 1997. pap. text 29.95 (*0-7817-1128-2*) Lppncott W & W.

— Quick Reference for Maternity & Gynecologic Nursing. 93p. (C). (gr. 13). 1992. pap. text 8.95 (*0-8016-6666-X*, 06666) Mosby Inc.

Bobak, Irene M., et al. Little, Brown's Maternal-Newborn Nursing Review. LC 96-9117. 1997. pap. text 22.95 (*0-316-10209-1*) Lppncott W & W.

— Little, Brown's NCLEX-RN Examination Review. rev. ed. Lagerquist, Sally L., ed. LC 95-49688. (Illus.). 680p. 1996. pap. text 34.95 (*0-316-51279-6*, Little Brwn Med Div) Lppncott W & W.

— Maternity & Gynecologic Care: The Nurse & the Family. 4th ed. (Illus.). 1408p. (C). 1988. trans. 75.00 (*0-8016-0470-2*) Mosby Inc.

— Maternity Nursing. 4th ed. (Illus.). teacher ed. write for info. (*0-8151-0615-7*) Mosby Inc.

Bobak, Irene M., jt. auth. see Lowdermilk, Deitra L.

Bobala, Daniel. The Complete Idiot's Guide to Word 97. 2nd ed. LC 98-84857. 394p. 1998. 19.99 (*0-7897-1697-6*) Que.

Boban, Jose K. Tribal Ethnomedicine: Continuity & Change. LC 98-909143. 1998. 62.00 (*81-7648-027-4*, Pub. by Ashish Pub Hse) S Asia.

Bobango, Gerald J. Religion & Politics: Bishop Valerian Trifa & His Times. (East European Monographs: No. 92). 294p. 1981. text 68.50 (*0-914710-86-9*, Pub. by East Eur Monographs) Col U Pr.

Bobath, jt. auth. see Eggers, Ortrud.

Bobath, Berta. Adult Hemiplegia: Evaluation & Treatment. 3rd ed. 208p. 1990. pap. text 40.00 (*0-7506-0168-X*) Buttrwrth-Heinemann.

Bobath, Karel. A Neurophysiological Basis for the Treatment of Cerebral Palsy. 2nd ed. (Clinics in Developmental Medicine Ser.: No. 75). (Illus.). 98p. (C). 1991. text 29.95 (*0-521-41202-1*) Mc Keith Pr.

Bobb, Dilip & Raina, Ashok. The Great Betrayal: Assassination of Indira Gandhi. 100p. 1985. text 13.95 (*0-89891-008-0*) Advent Bks Div.

Bobb, F. Scott. Historical Dictionary of Democratic Republic of the Congo (Zaire) rev. ed. LC 98-34189. (African Historical Dictionaries Ser.: No. 76). (Illus.). 632p. 1999. 75.00 (*0-8108-3571-1*) Scarecrow.

— Historical Dictionary of Zaire. LC 88-11410. (African Historical Dictionaries Ser.: No. 43). (Illus.). 385p. 1989. 37.50 (*0-8108-2109-5*) Scarecrow.

Bobb, Glenn. 1990 Marketer's Handbook Vol. II: Pennsylvania Zip Code Data. 183p. 1995. pap. 45.00 (*1-885925-06-9*) Penn State Data Ctr.

Bobb, June D. Beating a Restless Drum: The Poetics of Kamau Brathwaite & Derek Walcott. LC 98-6594. 280p. 1997. 79.95 (*0-86543-599-5*); pap. 21.95 (*0-86543-600-2*) Africa World.

Bobb-Semple, Colin. Sourcebook on Criminal Litigation & Sentencing. (Sourcebook Ser.). 800p. 1996. pap. write for info. (*1-85941-101-0*, Pub. by Cavendish Pubng) Gaunt.

***Bobb-Semple, Colin, et al.** Advanced Criminal Litigation in Practice. 4th ed. (Inns of Court School of Law Ser.). 207p. 2000. pap. 46.00 (*1-84174-004-7*, Pub. by Blackstone Pr) Gaunt.

Bobb-Semple, Colin, et al. Criminal Law in Practice. 2nd ed. 199p. 1998. pap. 48.00 (*1-85431-717-2*, Pub. by Blackstone Pr) Gaunt.

***Bobb-Semple, Colin, et al.** Criminal Law in Practice. 3rd ed. 201p. 1999. pap. 50.00 (*1-85431-901-9*, Pub. by Blackstone Pr) Gaunt.

Bobba, Vittorio. Parabellum: A Technical History of Swiss Lugers. (Illus.). 224p. 1996. 100.00 (*88-8068-052-8*) Safari Pr.

Bobbe, Dorothie. De Witt Clinton. 308p. 1993. reprint ed. lib. bdg. 89.00 (*0-7812-5168-0*) Rprt Serv.

Bobber, Robert J. Underwater Electroacoustic Measurements. LC 87-63303. 341p. 1989. reprint ed. 43.95 (*0-932146-19-8*) Peninsula CA.

Bobbett, David G., ed. World Radio TV Handbook, 1999. (Illus.). 608p. 1998. pap. 24.95 (*0-8230-5931-6*) Watsn-Guptill.

***Bobbett, David G., ed.** World Radio TV Handbook 2000. 640p. 1999. pap. text 24.95 (*0-8230-5932-4*, Rotovision) Watsn-Guptill.

— World Radio TV Handbook, 2001. 632p. 2000. pap. 24.95 (*0-8230-7796-9*) Watsn-Guptill.

Bobbett, Victor M., ed. see Jacobs, Russell F.

Bobbi. Affairs of the Heart. (Illus.). 120p. (Orig.). 1990. pap. 9.95 (*0-9626608-0-9*) Magik NY.

— Beyond Within. 96p. 1984. 8.95 (*0-9626608-2-5*) Magik NY.

— Feelings from Within. 86p. 1980. text 6.95 (*0-9626608-1-7*) Magik NY.

— Grandma's Teapot. (Illus.). 37p. (J). 1992. pap. 3.95 (*0-9626608-3-3*) Magik NY.

— Matthew's Dream. (Illus.). 51p. (J). 1993. pap. 5.95 (*0-9626608-6-8*) Magik NY.

— T-Neck. 63p. (J). 1992. pap. 5.95 (*0-9626608-4-1*) Magik NY.

Bobbin, Toni. Being on Top of the World. (Illus.). 96p. (Orig.). 1995. pap. 12.95 (*0-86417-684-8*, Pub. by Kangaroo Pr) Seven Hills Bk.

Bobbio, Norberto. The Age of Rights. rev. ed. 200p. 1996. pap. 27.95 (*0-7456-1595-3*) Blackwell Pubs.

— Democracy & Dictatorship. 216p. 1989. pap. 15.95 (*0-8166-1813-5*) U of Minn Pr.

***Bobbio, Norberto.** Electrodynamics of Materials. (C). 1999. text 79.95 (*0-12-108260-1*) Acad Pr.

Bobbio, Norberto. Estado, Gobierno y Sociedad. (Breviarios Ser.). (SPA.). pap. 8.99 (*968-16-3142-0*, Pub. by Fondo) Continental Bk.

— Ideological Profile of Twentieth-Century Italy. Cochrane, Lydia G., tr. from ITA. LC 94-42287. (Giovanni Agnelli Foundation Series in Italian History).Tr. of Profilo Ideologico del Novecento. 288p. 1995. text 32.50 (*0-691-04352-3*, Pub. by Princeton U Pr) Cal Prin Full Svc.

***Bobbio, Norberto.** In Praise of Meekness. 2000. 59.95 (*0-7456-2308-5*, Pub. by Polity Pr); pap. 24.95 (*0-7456-2309-3*, Pub. by Polity Pr) Blackwell Pubs.

Bobbio, Norberto. Left & Right. LC 96-26392. 1996. pap. text 14.95 (*0-226-06246-5*); lib. bdg. 34.95 (*0-226-06245-7*) U Ch Pr.

— Thomas Hobbes & the Natural Law Tradition. Gobetti, Daniela, tr. 246p. (C). 1993. pap. text 16.95 (*0-226-06248-1*) U Ch Pr.

— Thomas Hobbes & the Natural Law Tradition. Gobetti, Daniela, tr. 248p. (C). 1994. lib. bdg. 35.00 (*0-226-06247-3*) U Ch Pr.

Bobbio, Norberto & Matteucci, N. Diccionario de Politica, Vol. 1, A-J. (SPA.). 896p. 1982. 105.00 (*0-7859-5903-3*, 8432304301) Fr & Eur.

— Diccionario de Politica, Vol. 2, K-Z. (SPA.). 884p. 1983. 105.00 (*0-7859-5904-1*, 8432304611) Fr & Eur.

— Dictionary of Politics: Diccionario de Politica, 2 vols. (ENG & SPA.). 1751p. 1983. 225.00 (*0-8288-2266-2*, S40514) Fr & Eur.

Bobbit, Malcom. The London Taxi. (Illus.). 160p. 1998. 24.95 (*1-874105-99-5*, Pub. by Vloce Pub) Motorbooks Intl.

Bobbitt, Charles & Bobbitt, Ladonna. Peoria: A Postcard History. LC 98-86603. (Postcard History Ser.). (Illus.). 128p. 1998. pap. 16.99 (*0-7524-1284-1*) Arcadia Publng.

***Bobbitt, Charles & Bobbitt, Ladonna.** Peoria Revisited: In Vintage Postcards. (Postcard History Ser.). (Illus.). 128p. 2000. pap. 18.99 (*0-7385-0711-3*) Arcadia Publng.

Bobbitt, Charles E., Jr. Ssri Supp Mold Compound. LC 92-23857. (Six Sigma Research Institute Ser.). 1992. pap. text 10.95 (*0-201-63433-3*) Addison-Wesley.

Bobbitt, Franklin. Curriculum. LC 78-165706. (American Education, Ser.). 1979. reprint ed. 30.95 (*0-405-03695-7*) Ayer.

Bobbitt, Ladonna, jt. auth. see Bobbitt, Charles.

***Bobbitt, Malcolm.** Citroen DS. (Illus.). 160p. 2000. pap. 19.95 (*0-7509-2282-6*) Sutton Publng.

Bobbitt, Malcolm. Fiat & Abarth 500 - 600. (Illus.). 144p. 1998. pap. 24.95 (*1-901295-22-2*, Pub. by Vloce Pub) Motorbooks Intl.

— Rolls-Royce & Bentley: From Aero Engines to Motor Cars. 1999. 44.95 (*0-7509-1623-0*) A Sutton.

***Bobbitt, Malcolm.** Rolls-Royce Silver Shadow & Bentley T-Series. 2nd ed. (Illus.). 160p. 2000. 39.95 (*1-901295-84-2*, 129987AE, Pub. by Vloce Pub) Motorbooks Intl.

— Rolls-Royce Silver Spirit, Silver Spur & Bentley Mulsanne. (Illus.). 160p. 2000. 49.95 (*1-901295-77-X*, 129986AE, Pub. by Vloce Pub) Motorbooks Intl.

— VW Bus Type 2: Bus, Camper & Van. (Illus.). 160p. 2000. pap. 24.95 (*1-901295-37-0*, 130737AE, Pub. by Vloce Pub) Motorbooks Intl.

Bobbitt, Malcolm. VW Transporter Type 2, Bus, Camper & Van. (Illus.). 160p. 1997. 29.95 (*1-874105-74-X*, Pub. by Vloce Pub) Motorbooks Intl.

Bobbitt, Philip. Constitutional Fate: Theory of the Constitution. 298p. 1984. pap. text 22.95 (*0-19-503422-8*) OUP.

Bobbitt, Philip, jt. auth. see Calabresi, Guido.

Bobbitt, Sharon A., et al. Qualifications of the Public School Teacher Workforce, 1988 & 1991. LC 95-137286. (Statistical Analysis Report National Center for Education Statistics Reports). ii, 31 p. 1994. write for info. (*0-16-045436-0*) USGPO.

Bobbitt, Steve. The Road to Real Wealth: Genuine Success Stories from the Subscribers of the Real Estate Digest. 1988. pap. write for info. (*0-318-64321-9*) Real Estate Digest.

Bobboyi, Hamidu, et al, eds. Arabic Literature of Africa: The Writings of Central Sudanic Africa, 2. (Handbook of Oriental Studies. Part 1 Middle East Ser.: Vol. 2). (Illus.). Xxvi, 732p. 1995. text 251.00 (*90-04-10494-1*) Brill Academic Pubs.

Bobde, P. V., tr. Garland of Divine Flowers: Selected Devotional Lyrics of Saint Jnanesvara. (C). 1987. 11.00 (*81-208-0390-6*, Pub. by Motilal Bnarsidass) S Asia.

— Poet Moropanta's Kekavali: A Series of the Peacock's Screams. LC 94-900471. (C). 1994. 18.00 (*81-208-1115-1*, Pub. by Motilal Bnarsidass) S Asia.

Bobee, Bernard & Ashkar, Fahim. The Gamma Family & Derived Distributions Applied in Hydrology. LC 90-70598. 203p. 1991. pap. 42.00 (*0-918334-68-3*); disk 85.00 (*0-685-59074-7*) WRP.

Bobel, Peg. Trail Guide Handbook: Cuyahoga Valley National Recreation Area. 2nd rev. ed. Bobel, Rob, ed. & illus. by. LC 92-114089. 190p. 1997. pap. 14.95 (*0-9630416-1-4*) Cuyahoga Valley.

Bobel, Rob, ed. & illus. see Bobel, Peg.

***Bobel, Robert.** Active Core Essentials of Microsoft Word 2000 MOUS Exam. (Active Books & Video CD-ROM Ser.). (Illus.). 365p. 2000. pap. 49.95 incl. cd-rom (*1-58612-016-6*) Active Curriculum.

— Active Essentials of Microsoft Word 2000. (Illus.). 369p. 1999. student ed., wbk. ed. 34.95 incl. vdisk (*1-58612-001-8*) Active Curriculum.

— Active Intermediate Microsoft Word 2000. (Active Books & Video CD-ROM Ser.). (Illus.). 184p. 2000. pap. 39.95 incl. cd-rom (*1-58612-055-7*) Active Curriculum.

— Active Introduction to Microsoft Windows 98. (Active Books & Video CD-ROM Ser.). (Illus.). 186p. 2000. pap. 39.95 incl. cd-rom (*1-58612-054-9*) Active Curriculum.

— Active Introduction to Microsoft Word 2000. (Active Books & Video CD-ROM Ser.). 190p. 2000. pap 39.95 incl. cd-rom (*1-58612-056-5*) Active Curriculum.

Bobenhausen, William. Simplified Design of HVAC Systems. (Parker Simplified Design Guides Ser.). 448p. 1994. 79.00 (*0-471-53280-0*) Wiley.

Bobenhausen, William, jt. auth. see Fitch, James Marston.

Bobenko, A. I. & Seiler, Ruedi, eds. Discrete Integrable Geometry & Physics. LC 98-51827. (Oxford Lecture Series in Mathematics & Its Applications: No. 16). (Illus.). 398p. 1999. text 75.00 (*0-19-850160-9*) OUP.

Bober, Harry. The Book of Trades of Jan Van Vliet. LC 81-69221. (Illus.). 39p. 1981. 8.00 (*0-317-64496-3*) Early Am Indus.

Bober, Harry, ed. see Male, Emile.

Bober, Jonathan, contrib. by. Charles Clark in Memoriam: European & American Prints since 1960. (Illus.). 40p. 1991. pap. 12.00 (*0-935213-20-1*) J S Blanton Mus.

Bober, Jonathan & Hale, Kenneth J., intros. Guest Artists in Printmaking. (Illus.). 70p. (Orig.). 1989. pap. 12.00 (*0-935213-19-8*) J S Blanton Mus.

Bober, Natalie. Countdown to Independence. LC 99-27086. (J). 2001. 18.00 (*0-689-81329-5*) S&S Childrens.

— Thomas Jefferson: Man on a Mountain. LC 97-193563. 288p. (YA). (gr. 7 up). 1997. per. 12.00 (*0-689-81523-9*) Aladdin.

Bober, Natalie S. Abigail Adams: Witness to a Revolution. (Illus.). 272p. (YA). (gr. 7 up). 1998. per. 8.99 (*0-689-81916-1*) Aladdin.

— Abigail Adams: Witness to a Revolution. LC 94-19259. (Illus.). 272p. (YA). (gr. 5 up). 1995. 18.00 (*0-689-31760-3*) Atheneum Yung Read.

— Abigail Adams: Witness to a Revolution. 1998. 14.09 (*0-606-13106-X*, Pub. by Turtleback) Demco.

— Marc Chagall: Painter of Dreams. LC 91-25463. (Illus.). 124p. (J). (gr. 4-8). 1991. 14.95 (*0-8276-0379-7*) JPS Phila.

— Restless Spirit: The Story of Robert Frost. (J). (gr. 4-12). 1998. pap. 16.95 (*0-8050-6075-8*) H Holt & Co.

Bober, Patricia A. & Corbett, Sandra L. Occupational Therapy & Physical Therapy: A Resource & Planning Guide. 204p. (Orig.). (C). 1996. pap. text 27.00 (*1-57337-035-5*, 7040) WI Dept Pub Instruct.

Bober, Phyllis P. Art, Culture, & Cuisine: Ancient & Medieval Gastronomy. LC 98-36867. (Illus.). 480p. (C). 1993. 50.00 (*0-226-06253-8*) U Ch Pr.

Bober, Robert, jt. auth. see Perec, Georges.

***Bober, Stanley.** Alternative Principles of Economics. (Illus.). 336p. 2000. text 68.95 (*0-7656-0553-8*) M E Sharpe.

Bober, Stanley. Modern Macroeconomics: A Post-Keynesian Perspective. 288p. 1987. lib. bdg. 62.50 (*0-7099-5080-2*, Pub. by C Helm) Routldge.

— Pricing & Growth: A Neo-Ricardian Approach. LC 91-6972. 168p. (C). (gr. 13). 1992. text 61.95 (*0-87332-856-6*); pap. text 32.95 (*0-87332-857-4*) M E Sharpe.

— Recent Developments in Non-Neoclassical Economics. LC 96-79840. 496p. 1997. 101.95 (*1-85972-338-1*, Pub. by Avebry) Ashgate Pub Co.

Bober, William & Kenyon, R. A. Fluid Mechanics. (Illus.). 574p. (C). 1991. reprint ed. 115.00 (*1-878907-24-7*) TechBooks.

Boberfeld, Wilhelm O. Von, see Klapp, Ernst & Von Boberfeld, Wilhelm O.

Boberg, Dorothy K. Evolution & Reason. deluxe ed. Hicks, Lyn H., ed. (Illus.). 640p. 1994. lib. bdg. 45.00 (*1-881804-14-3*) Clarion Pacific.

— Evolution & Reason: Beyond Darwin. deluxe limited ed. Hicks, Lyn H., ed. (Illus.). 640p. 1993. 48.00 (*1-881804-07-0*) Clarion Pacific.

Boberg, F., jt. auth. see Czogalla, C. D.

***Boberg, Jill.** Woodfuel Markets in Developing Countries: A Case Study of Tanzania. (Studies in Environmental Policy & Practice). 236p. 1999. text 65.95 (*1-85972-448-5*, Pub. by Ashgate Pub) Ashgate Pub Co.

Boberg, P. Q. Law of Delict Vol. 1: Aquilian Liability. rev. ed. 958p. 1989. reprint ed. 90.00 (*0-7021-2315-3*, Pub. by Juta & Co) Gaunt.

— The Law of Persons & the Family. 820p. 1976. write for info. (*0-7021-0714-X*, Pub. by Juta & Co); pap. 36.00 (*0-7021-0715-8*, Pub. by Juta & Co) Gaunt.

Boberg, Scott, ed. see Kohl, Jeanette, et al.

Boberg, Scott, ed. see Moss, Karen.

Bobes, Toby. The Crowded Bed: An Effective Framework for Doing Couple Therapy. LC 98-22639. 208p. 1999. 27.00 (*0-393-70280-4*) Norton.

Bobeth, Johannes. Die Zeitschriften der Romantik. x, 431p. 1970. reprint ed. 115.00 (*0-318-71741-7*) G Olms Pubs.

Bobgan, Deidre, jt. auth. see Bobgan, Martin.

Bobgan, Deidre, jt. auth. see Bobgan, Martin M.

Bobgan, Deidre N., jt. auth. see Bobgan, Martin.

Bobgan, Deidre N., jt. auth. see Bobgan, Martin M.

Bobgan, Deidre N., jt. auth. see Bobgan, Martin N.

Bobgan, Martin & Bobgan, Deidre. CRI (Christian Research Institute) Guilty of Psychoheresy? LC 98-92420. 152p. 1998. pap. 10.00 (*0-941717-13-5*) EastGate Pubs.

— The End of "Christian Psychology" LC 97-94482. 1997. pap. 14.00 (*0-941717-12-7*) EastGate Pubs.

— James Dobson's Gospel of Self-Esteem & Psychology. rev. ed. LC 98-93727. 248p. 1998. pap. 15.00 (*0-941717-16-X*) EastGate Pubs.

— Larry Crabb's Gospel. LC 98-93330. 1998. pap. 12.00 (*0-941717-14-3*) EastGate Pubs.

***Bobgan, Martin & Bobgan, Deidre.** Missions & Psychoheresy. LC 00-190743. 168p. 2000. pap. 10.00 (*0-941717-17-8*) EastGate Pubs.

Bobgan, Martin & Bobgan, Deidre N. 12 Steps to Destruction: Codependency Recovery Heresies. LC 91-72638. 256p. 1991. pap. 12.00 (*0-941717-05-4*) EastGate Pubs.

Bobgan, Martin M. & Bobgan, Deidre. Four Temperaments, Astrology & Personality Testing. LC 92-81219. 214p. (Orig.). 1992. pap. 12.00 (*0-941717-07-0*) EastGate Pubs.

Bobgan, Martin M. & Bobgan, Deidre N. Competent to Minister: The Biblical Care of Souls. LC 96-86500. 256p. (Orig.). 1996. pap. 14.00 (*0-941717-11-9*) EastGate Pubs.

— PsychoHeresy: The Psychological Seduction of Christianity. LC 87-80001. 272p. (Orig.). 1987. pap. 15.00 (*0-941717-00-3*) EastGate Pubs.

B

***Bobgan, Martin M. & Bobgan, Deidre N.** TheoPhostic Counseling: Divine Revelation of Psychoheresy? LC 99-91321. 144p. 1999. pap. 10.00 (*0-941717-15-1*) EastGate Pubs.

Bobgan, Martin N. & Bobgan, Deidre N. Against Biblical Counseling: For the Bible. LC 94-92307. 200p. (Orig.). 1994. pap. 12.00 (*0-941717-09-7*) EastGate Pubs.

Bobia, Rosa. The Critical Reception of James Baldwin in France. 2nd ed. (American University Studies: Vol. 68, No. XXIV). XII, 191p. (C). 1998. reprint ed. pap. text 24.95 (*0-8204-4415-4*) P Lang Pubng.

Bobik, Joseph. Aquinas on Matter & Form & the Elements: A Translation & Interpretation of the De Principiis Naturae & the De Mixtione Elementorum of St. Thomas Aquinas. LC 97-26521. (LAT.). 264p. 1998. pap. 19.00 (*0-268-02000-0*) U of Notre Dame Pr.

— Aquinas on Matter & Form & the Elements: A Translation & Interpretation of the De Principiis Naturae & the De Mixtione Elementorum of St. Thomas Aquinas. LC 97-26521. (C). 1998. 39.00 (*0-268-00653-9*) U of Notre Dame Pr.

Bobik, Joseph, tr. from LAT. The Commentary of Conrad of Prussia on de Unitate et Uno of Dominicus Gundissalinus. LC 89-12769. (Studies in the History of Philosophy: Vol. 12). (ENG & LAT.). 264p. 1990. lib. bdg. 89.95 (*0-88946-302-6*) E Mellen.

Bobilin, Robert. Revolution from Below: Buddhist & Christian Movements for Justice in Asia: Four Case Studies from Thailand & Sri Lanka. 190p. (Orig.). (C). 1988. pap. text 20.00 (*0-8191-7038-0*) U Pr of Amer.

Bobillier, Marie. Haydn. Leese, C. Leonard, tr. LC 79-39688. (Select Bibliographies Reprint Ser.). 1977. reprint ed. 15.95 (*0-8369-9930-4*) Ayer.

Bobillier, Marie, see Brenet, Michel, pseud.

Bobin, Christian. Secret of Francis of Assisi: A Meditation. Kohn, Michael H., tr. from FRE. LC 96-41013. 1997. 15.00 (*1-57062-295-7*, Pub. by Shambhala Pubns) Random.

— Secret of Francis of Assisi: A Meditation. 112p. 1999. pap. 12.00 (*1-57062-368-6*, Pub. by Shambhala Pubns) Random.

Bobin, Christopher A. Agricultural Options: Trading, Risk Management & Hedging. LC 89-70468. 272p. 1990. 49.95 (*0-471-52429-8*) Wiley.

Bobis, Merlinda. Summer Was a Fast Train Without Terminals. 1999. pap. 13.95 (*1-875559-76-0*) SpiniFex Pr.

***Bobit, Bonnie.** Death Row: The Encyclopedia of Capital Punishment, 2000 Edition. 296p. 2000. pap. 24.95 (*0-9624857-0-5*, Pub. by Bobit Pubng) IPG Chicago.

Bobit, Bonnie. Death Row Book: Roster of All 3,526 Death Row Inmates. 10th ed. 1999. pap. text 24.95 (*0-9624857-8-0*) Bobit Pubng.

Bobker, Joe. The Jewish Festivals. LC 99-34347. Date not set. 35.00 (*0-7657-6113-0*) Aronson.

Bobker, Lee R. Elements of Film. 3rd ed. 302p. (Orig.). (C). 1979. pap. text 41.50 (*0-15-522096-9*, Pub. by Harcourt Coll Pubs) Harcourt.

Bobko. Correlate Regress Industry Organization. 3rd ed. 1995. 25.94 (*0-07-042788-7*) McGraw.

Bobko, Philip. Correlation & Regression in Industrial & Organizational Psychology & Management. LC 94-4096. (C). 1994. pap. text 70.50 (*0-07-006223-4*) McGraw.

Bobkov, Serguei G. & Houdre, Christian. Some Connections Between Isoperimetric & Sobolev-Type Inequalities. LC 97-21758. (Memoirs of the American Mathematical Society Ser.: Vol. 129, No. 616). 111p. 1997. pap. 38.00 (*0-8218-0642-4*) Am Math.

Bobley, Phyllis & Kimche, Joan. Alfie & the Four Seasons. (Illus.). 50p. (Orig.). (J). (gr. k-6). 1996. write for info. (*0-9653050-0-7*) P Bobley.

Boblitt, Brenda, jt. auth. see Wiegand, Ronn.

Bobnak, Paul, ed. 1998 Directory of Major Mailers & What They Mail: The Most Powerful Database on Direct Mail Ever Created. 1312p. 1998. pap. 395.00 (*1-888576-37-5*) North Am Pub Co.

Bobo, Betty, jt. auth. see Embry, Lynn.

Bobo, Connie C. On Eagle's Wings: A Practical Guide for the Care of Terminally Ill Loved Ones. LC 98-93065. (Illus.). 136p. 1998. pap. 19.95 (*0-9665418-0-4*) Freefall Fact.

***Bobo, Gwendolyn.** Okra Soup: A Soulful Dish of Reasoning & Poetry. vii, 166p. 1999. pap. 9.95 (*0-9675627-0-8*, 010991) Bobo.

Bobo, J. B. Modern Coin Magic. (Illus.). 358p. 1982. reprint ed. pap. 8.95 (*0-486-24258-7*) Dover.

Bobo, Jacqueline. Black Women As Cultural Readers. LC 94-25317. 224p. 1995. pap. 18.50 (*0-231-08395-5*) Col U Pr.

— Black Women Film & Video Artists. LC 97-32062. (Afi Film Readers Ser.). 288p. (C). 1998. 80.00 (*0-415-92041-8*); pap. 20.99 (*0-415-92042-6*) Routledge.

***Bobo, Jacqueline, ed.** Black Feminist Cultural Criticism. 2001. 59.95 (*0-631-22239-1*); pap. 26.95 (*0-631-22240-5*) Blackwell Pubs.

Bobo, Jana, jt. auth. see Bobo, Richard.

Bobo, Kimberley A., jt. auth. see Institute for World Order Staff.

Bobo, Kimberly A., et al. Organizing for Social Change: A Manual for Activists in the 1990s. LC 90-47467. 271p. 1991. pap. 19.95 (*0-932020-93-3*) Seven Locks Pr.

—Organizing for Social Change: A Manual for Activists in the 1990s. 2nd ed. LC 90-47467. 1996. pap. text 19.95 (*0-929765-41-9*) Seven Locks Pr.

***Bobo, Lawrence, et al, eds.** City of Dreams, City of Pain: Analyzing Inequality in Los Angeles. 500p. 2000. 45.00 (*0-87154-129-7*) Russell Sage.

— Urban Inequality: Evidence from Four Cities. 496p. 2000. 45.00 (*0-87154-650-7*) Russell Sage.

Bobo, Mike & Dykes, Spike. Principles of Coaching Football. LC 97-29510. 287p. 1997. pap. text 29.00 (*0-205-26253-8*) P-H.

Bobo, Richard & Bobo, Jana. Pianists' Guide to Progressive Finger Fitness. 1994. 24.95 (*0-9633819-5-4*) Prescott Pub.

Bobo, Sharlynn, ed. see Hicks, H. Beecher, Jr.

Bobo, Sheilah A. & Thompson, Pearl M. Teaching English to Speakers of ESD, ESL & EFL. 216p. (C). 1990. lib. bdg. 49.00 (*0-8191-7868-3*) U Pr of Amer.

Bobo, Thomas. Alexander & Mister Bobo. 1995. pap. text 12.95 (*0-9638776-9-0*) Pea Pod Tree.

Bobok, Elemer. Fluid Mechanics for Petroleum Engineers. LC 92-21858. (Developments in Petroleum Science Ser.: No. 32). 412p. 1993. 211.25 (*0-444-98668-5*) Elsevier.

Bobola, Dan. The Complete Idiot's Guide to Microsoft Money. (Illus.). (Orig.). 1996. pap. 19.99 (*0-7897-0678-4*) Que.

— The Complete Idiot's Guide to Networking. (Illus.). 324p. (Orig.). 1995. 19.99 (*1-56761-590-2*, Alpha Ref) Macmillan Gen Ref.

— Complete Idiot's Guie to Microsoft Word 2000. LC 98-86979. (Complete Idiot's Guide Ser.). (Illus.). 341p. 1999. pap. 16.99 (*0-7897-1860-X*) Que.

— TMG to Windows NT. 1996. 14.99 (*0-7897-0683-0*) Que.

Bobon, D. P., et al, eds. AMDP System in Pharmacopsychiatry. (Modern Problems of Pharmacopsychiatry Ser.: Vol. 20). (Illus.). vi, 234p. 1983. 115.00 (*3-8055-3637-2*) S Karger.

— The Neuroleptics. (Modern Problems of Pharmacopsychiatry Ser.: Vol. 5). 1970. 41.00 (*3-8055-0530-2*) S Karger.

Bobonis, Clemente. Oracion de Una Oracion. (SPA.). 97p. 1996. pap. write for info. (*0-929441-01-X*) Pubns Puertorriquenas.

Bobosh, Theodore. Am I Saved? The Eastern Orthodox Way to Salvation. 1984. pap. 3.95 (*0-937032-38-7*) Light&Life Pub Co MN.

— The Divine Liturgy According to St. John Chrysostom with Scripture References & Commentary. 1989. pap. 5.95 (*0-937032-70-0*) Light&Life Pub Co MN.

Bobri, Vladimir. Complete Study of Tremolo for the Classic Guitar. Stang, Aaron, ed. 28p. (C). 1985. pap. text 7.95 (*0-7692-1295-6*, FC03046) Wrner Bros.

Bobri, Vladimir, et al. The Segovia Technique. 2nd ed. (Illus.). 98p. 1990. reprint ed. pap. 21.95 (*0-933224-49-4*, T038) Bold Strummer Ltd.

Bobrick, Benson. Angel in the Whirlwind: The Triumph of the American Revolution. LC 97-11320. 608p. 1997. 29.50 (*0-684-81060-3*) S&S Trade.

— Angel in the Whirlwind: The Triumph of the American Revolution. LC 97-11320. 560p. 1998. pap. 15.95 (*0-14-027500-2*) Viking Penguin.

— East of the Sun: The Epic Conquest & Tragic History of Siberia. (Illus.). 544p. 1995. pap. 18.95 (*0-8050-2981-8*) H Holt & Co.

— East of the Sun: The Epic Conquest & Tragic History of Siberia. (Illus.). 560p. 1992. 28.00 (*0-671-66755-6*) S&S Trade.

— East of the Sun: The Epic Conquest & Tragic History of Siberia. (Illus.). 542p. 1997. reprint ed. text 28.00 (*0-7881-5139-8*) DIANE Pub.

— Knotted Tongues: Stuttering in History & the Quest for a Cure. Baker, Deborah, ed. LC 95-25881. (Kodansha Globe Ser.). 240p. 1996. pap. 14.00 (*1-56836-121-1*, Kodansha Globe) Kodansha.

— Labyrinths of Iron: Subways in History, Myth, Art, Technology, & War. LC 93-41460. (Illus.). 352p. 1995. pap. 16.95 (*0-8050-3109-X*) H Holt & Co.

Bobrick, Elizabeth A. Theophrastus Characters. (Greek Commentaries Ser.). 44p. (C). 1991. pap. text 6.00 (*0-929524-69-1*) Bryn Mawr Commentaries.

Bobrick, Sam. Hamlet II: Better Than the Original : A New Comedy. LC 86-198427. 82 p. 1985. write for info. (*0-573-61983-2*) S French Trade.

Bobrinskoy, Boris. The Mystery of the Trinity: Trinitarian Experience & Vision in the Biblical & Patristic Tradition. Gythiel, Anthony P., tr. from FRE. LC 98-50071. 1999. write for info. (*0-88141-182-5*) St Vladimirs.

Bobrinskoy, George V., jt. auth. see Bond, Otto F.

Bobrinskoy, Tania. How to Pronounce Russian. 72p. 1988. pap. 13.95 (*0-8442-4285-3*) NTC Contemp Pub Co.

Bobroff, Alvin & Krishnamurti, U. G. Mystique of Enlightenment. 190p. 1985. pap. 9.95 (*0-87418-020-1*, 156) Coleman Pub.

Bobroff-Hajal, Anne. Working Women in Russia under the Hunger Tsars: Political Activism & Daily Life. LC 94-20199. (Scholarship in Women's History Ser.: Vol. 3). 300p. 1994. 60.00 (*0-926019-64-3*) Carlson Pub.

Bobroff, Norman & Estler, W. Tyler, eds. Proceedings from ASPE Spring Topical Meeting on Precision Interferometric Metrology. 103p. 1992. pap. write for info. (*1-887706-07-0*) Am Soc Prec Engr.

Bobrov, E. G. & Chapepanov, S. K., eds. Compositae, Tribes Cynareae & Mutisieae, Vol. 28. (Flora of the USSR Ser.). (Illus.). (C). 1996. text. write for info. (*1-886106-45-2*) Science Pubs.

Bobrov, E. G. & Tsvelev, M. N., eds. Compositae, Tribe Cichorieae, Vol. 29. (Flora of the USSR Ser.). (Illus.). (C). 2000. text. write for info. (*1-886106-46-0*) Science Pubs.

Bobrov, E. G., jt. ed. see Shishkin, B. K.

Bobrov, Nicholas, tr. see Grinius, Leonas.

Bobrov, Nicholas, tr. see Kryzhanovsky, G. N.

Bobrov, Nicholas, tr. see Meerson, Felix Z.

Bobrov, Nicholas, tr. see Raikov, I. B.

Bobrov, Nicholas N., tr. see Belousov, V. P.

Bobrov, Sergei, jt. auth. see Pasternak, Boris.

Bobrov, V., tr. see Babayan, Edward A. & Gonopolsky, M. W.

Bobrov, Vladimi, tr. see Collet's Holdings, Ltd. Staff, ed.

Bobrovich, Mildred & Kurdylo, Kevin, eds. The Literature of the Nonprofit Sector: A Bibliography with Abstracts, Vol. 3. 1991. pap. text 45.00 (*0-87954-386-8*) Foundation Ctr.

Bobrovnikoff, N. Astronomy Before the Telescope, Part II: The Solar System. (History of Astronomy Ser.: Vol. 4). 1990. pap. 38.00 (*0-88126-226-9*) Pachart Pub Hse.

***Bobrow.** Cliffs ACT Quick Review. (Quick Reference Ser.). 288p. 1999. pap. 9.95 (*0-7645-8533-9*) IDG Bks.

Bobrow. Cliff's GMAT CAT Preparation Guide. LC HF1118.B58 1997. 101p. 1980. pap. 12.95 (*0-8220-2062-9*) IDG Bks.

***Bobrow.** Cliffs SAT I Quick Review. (Cliffs Notes Ser.). 288p. 1999. pap. 9.95 (*0-7645-8536-3*) IDG Bks.

Bobrow. Representation & Understanding. 1975. text 65.00 (*0-12-108550-3*) Acad Pr.

Bobrow, Daniel G., ed. Artificial Intelligence in Perspective. LC 93-21601. (Special Issues of Artificial Intelligence Ser.). 472p. 1994. pap. text 42.50 (*0-262-52186-5*, Bradford Bks) MIT Pr.

— Qualitative Reasoning about Physical Sciences. 504p. 1985. 35.00 (*0-262-02218-4*, Bradford Bks) MIT Pr.

Bobrow, Daniel G., ed. see Ristad, Eric Sven.

***Bobrow, Davis B., ed.** Prospecting International Relations: Conjectures at the Millennium International Studies Review Millennium Special Issue. 172p. 1999. pap. text 32.95 (*0-631-21829-7*) Blackwell Pubs.

Bobrow, Davis B. & Dryzek, John S. Policy Analysis by Design. LC 87-5974. (Political Science Ser.). (Illus.). 256p. 1987. pap. 16.95 (*0-8229-5392-7*) U of Pittsburgh Pr.

Bobrow, Edwin E. Creating New Products. LC 97-70166. 1997. pap. 16.95 (*0-02-861489-5*) Macmillan Gen Ref.

— My Say: A Mentor's Guide to Success. LC 98-89738. 304p. 1999. 15.95 (*1-886284-36-9*, Pub. by Chandler Hse) Natl Bk Netwk.

— 10 Minute Guide to Planning. 160p. 1997. pap. text 10.95 (*0-02-861818-1*, Pub. by Macmillan) S&S Trade.

Bobrow, Ella. Autumnal Cadenza: Ballads, Poems, Translations. (Illus.). 96p. 1994. pap. 8.95 (*0-88962-281-7*) Mosaic.

— Irina Odoevtseva. 160p. 1997. 14.95 (*0-88962-600-6*) Mosaic.

***Bobrow, Jerry.** ACT Preparation Guide. 6th ed. (Cliffs Preparation Guides Ser.). (Illus.). 360p. 2000. pap. 16.99 (*0-7645-8613-0*) IDG Bks.

Bobrow, Jerry. Algebra I. (Cliffs Quick Reviews Ser.). (Illus.). 172p. 1994. pap. 7.95 (*0-8220-5302-0*, Cliff) IDG Bks.

— Basic Math & Pre-Algebra Quick Review. (Cliffs Quick Reviews Ser.). (Illus.). 184p. (Orig.). 1995. pap. text 7.95 (*0-8220-5304-7*, Cliff) IDG Bks.

— Basic Math & Pre-Algebra Quick Review. (Illus.). 180p. (Orig.). 1997. pap. text 9.95 (*0-8220-5307-1*, Cliff) IDG Bks.

***Bobrow, Jerry.** CBEST Preparation Guide. 6th ed. (Cliffs Preparation Guides Ser.). 360p. 2000. pap. 17.99 (*0-7645-8608-4*) IDG Bks.

Bobrow, Jerry. Cliff Praxis I: PPST Preparation Guide: Pre-Professional Skills Test. 2nd rev. ed. (Cliffs Test Preparation Ser.). (Illus.). 101p. (C). 1996. pap. text 9.95 (*0-8220-2052-1*, Cliff) IDG Bks.

— ELM Review: Entry Level Mathematics Test for California. (Cliffs Test Preparation Ser.). 422p. (Orig.). 1987. pap. text 8.95 (*0-8220-2071-8*, Cliff) IDG Bks.

***Bobrow, Jerry.** GMAT CAT Preparation Guide. 8th ed. (Cliffs Preparation Guides Ser.). 360p. 2000. pap. 16.99 (*0-7645-8610-6*) IDG Bks.

— GRE CBT Preparation Guide. 6th ed. (Cliffs Preparation Guides Ser.). 360p. 2000. pap. 16.99 (*0-7645-8612-2*) IDG Bks.

— How to Prepare for the Civil Service Examinations for Stenographer, Typist, Clerk & Office Manager. 4th ed. LC 99-17933. 384p. 2000. pap. 13.95 (*0-7641-0777-1*) Barron.

Bobrow, Jerry. SAT I Preparation Guide: Scholastic Assessment Test. (Cliffs Test Preparation Ser.). (Illus.). 446p. (Orig.). 1979. pap. text 9.95 (*0-8220-2074-2*, Cliff) IDG Bks.

***Bobrow, Jerry.** Test Prep SAT I/PSAT Preparation Guide. 360p. 2000. pap. 16.99 (*0-7645-8611-4*) IDG Bks.

Bobrow, Jerry. You Can Pass the GED. 2nd rev. ed. (Cliffs Test Preparation Ser.). (Illus.). 602p. 1989. pap. text 11.95 (*0-8220-2077-7*, Cliff) IDG Bks.

Bobrow, Jerry & Fisher, Stephen. MSAT Preparation Guide: Multiple Subjects Assessment for Teachers. (Cliffs Test Preparation Ser.). (Illus.). 580p. (Orig.). (C). 1995. pap. text 24.95 (*0-8220-2048-3*, Cliff) IDG Bks.

Bobrow, Jerry & Orton, Peter Z. Writing Proficiency Examinations Preparation Guide: For California State Universities Graduation Writing Assessment Requirement. (Cliffs Test Preparation Ser.). (Illus.). 338p. (C). 1990. pap. text 8.95 (*0-8220-2043-2*, Cliff) IDG Bks.

Bobrow, Jerry, et al. ACT Preparation Guide. 5th rev. ed. (Test Preparation Guides Ser.). (Illus.). 342p. 1995. pap. text 8.95 (*0-8220-2078-5*, Cliff) IDG Bks.

— California Basic Educational Skills Test. 5th ed. (Cliffs Test Preparation Ser.). (Illus.). 101p. (C). 1983. pap. 10.95 (*0-8220-2094-7*, Cliff) IDG Bks.

— Cliff Praxis II: NTE Core Battery Preparation Guide: National Teacher's Examinations. (Cliffs Test Preparation Ser.). (Illus.). 101p. (C). 1984. 16.95 (*0-8220-2058-0*, Cliff) IDG Bks.

— How to Prepare for Civil Service Examinations: Stenographer, Typist, Clerk, & Office Machine Operator. 3rd ed. LC 93-36439. 320p. 1994. pap. 12.95 (*0-8120-1440-5*) Barron.

***Bobrow, Jerry, et al.** How to Prepare for the LSAT: Law School Admission Test. 9th rev. ed. 608p. (YA). 1999. pap. 14.95 (*0-7641-0467-5*) Barron.

Bobrow, Jerry, et al. How to Prepare for the LSAT - Law School Admission Test: Law School Admission Test. 9th rev. ed. (Illus.). 608p. 1999. pap. 29.95 incl. cd-rom (*0-7641-7288-3*) Barron.

— Math Review for Standardized Tests. (Cliffs Test Preparation Ser.). (Illus.). 422p. (Orig.). (C). 1985. pap. text 8.95 (*0-8220-2033-5*, Cliff) IDG Bks.

— Pass Key to the LSAT: Law School Admission Test. 3rd ed. LC 98-37111. 390p. 1999. pap. 7.95 (*0-7641-0468-3*) Barron.

— Postal Examinations Preparation Guide. rev. ed. (Cliffs Test Preparation Ser.). (Illus.). 312p. 1991. pap. 10.95 (*0-8220-2076-9*, Cliff) IDG Bks.

— TASP Preparation Guide: Texas Academic Skills Program. 2nd ed. LC 94-221798. (Cliffs Test Preparation Ser.). 330p. (Orig.). 1989. pap., student ed. 8.95 (*0-8220-2072-6*, Cliff) IDG Bks.

Bobrow, Jill. In the Spirit of Tradition: Old & New Classic Yachts. LC 97-22128. (Illus.). 256p. 1997. 60.00 (*0-393-04556-0*) Norton.

Bobrow, Jill R. Classic Yacht Interiors: A Reissue. 5th ed. (Illus.). 192p. 1993. reprint ed. 50.00 (*0-393-03274-4*) Concepts Pub.

— St. Vincent & the Grenadines: A Plural Country. 4th ed. (Illus.). 130p. 1985. reprint ed. 35.00 (*0-393-03309-0*) Concepts Pub.

— The World's Most Extraordinary Yachts. 4th ed. (Illus.). 234p. 1992. reprint ed. 50.00 (*0-393-03314-7*) Concepts Pub.

Bobrow, Jill R., ed. see Mitchell, James F.

Bobrow, Joseph, ed. see Hanh, Thich Nhat.

Bobrow, Judy, ed. see Portnoy, Lynn.

Bobrow, Leonard S. Elementary Linear Circuit Analysis: International Student Edition. 2nd ed. LC 96-30994. 736p. 1995. student ed. 28.50 (*0-19-511373-X*) OUP.

— Fundamentals of Electrical Engineering. LC 84-15829. 926p. (C). 1985. teacher ed. write for info. (*0-03-070631-9*) SCP.

— Fundamentals of Electrical Engineering. 2nd ed. (Electrical & Computer Engineering Ser.). (Illus.). 1184p. (C). 1996. text 89.95 (*0-19-510509-5*) OUP.

— Fundamentals of Electrical Engineering. 2nd ed. (The Oxford Series in Electrical & Computer Engineering). 324p. 1996. pap., teacher ed. write for info. (*0-19-511124-9*) OUP.

***Bobrow, Louise.** History in the Making: The Easiest Way to Preserve Your Family History. 100p. 2000. pap. 24.95 incl. audio (*0-9665319-6-5*) Grnlf Ent.

Bobrow, Mitch. Views from the Tightrope: Living Wisely in an Uncertain World. 144p. (Orig.). 1997. pap. 12.95 (*0-943914-84-1*) Larson Pubns.

***Bobrow, Thomas & Associates Staff, et al.** Building Type Basics for Healthcare Facilities. 368p. 1999. 69.95 (*0-471-35672-7*) Wiley.

Bobrowaky. Geoenvironmental Mapping. 95.00 (*90-5410-487-2*) Ashgate Pub Co.

Bobrowski. Mass Land, Set. 928p. 1994. 145.00 (*0-316-10185-0*) Little.

— Massachusetts Land Use. 1993. 145.00 (*0-316-10150-8*, Aspen Law & Bus) Aspen Pub.

Bobrowski, Johannes. Boehlendorff: A Short Story & Seven Poems. Golffing, Francis, tr. from GER. 44p. 1989. 25.00 (*0-930126-26-2*) Typographeum.

— Darkness & a Little Light. Vennewitz, Leila, tr. from GER. LC 94-20543. 112p. 1994. 19.95 (*0-8112-1259-9*, Pub. by New Directions) Norton.

— Levin's Mill. Cropper, Janet, tr. from GER. Orig. Title: Levins Muhle. 240p. 1988. 16.95 (*0-7145-0020-8*) M Boyars Pubs.

— Levin's Mill. Cropper, Janet, tr. from GER. LC 95-47598. (A New Directions Classic Ser.). Orig. Title: Levins Muhle. 230p. 1996. pap. 12.00 (*0-8112-1329-3*, Pub. by New Directions) Norton.

— Shadow Lands: Selected Poems. Mead, Ruth & Mead, Matthew, trs. from GER. LC 94-9979. 208p. (Orig.). 1994. pap. 10.95 (*0-8112-1276-9*, NDP788, Pub. by New Directions) Norton.

— The White Mirror. Hunting, Constance, ed. Nagel, Muska, tr. 100p. 1993. pap. 12.95 (*0-913006-55-6*) Puckerbrush.

Bobrowski, Robert. Rediscovering the Woodburning Cookstove: Cooking with Wood. LC 76-4680. (Illus.). 98p. 1976. pap. 9.95 (*0-85699-130-9*) Chatham Pr.

Bobrowski, Steve M. Mastering Oracle7 & Client/Server Computing. 2nd ed. 752p. 1996. pap. 39.99 incl. disk (*0-7821-1840-2*) Sybex.

***Bobrowski, Steve M.** Oracle8i for Linux Starter Kit. 528p. 2000. 49.99 (*0-07-212442-3*, Oracle Press) Osborne-McGraw.

— Oracle81 for Windows NT Starter Kit. 481p. 2000. pap. 49.99 incl. cd-rom (*0-07-212248-X*) McGraw.

Bobrowski, Steven M. Oracle 8 Architecture. LC 97-220323. 356p. 1997. pap. text 34.99 (*0-07-882274-2*) Osborne-McGraw.

Bobrowsky, P. T. Aggregate Resources: A Global Perspective. (Illus.). 480p. (C). 1997. text 99.00 (*90-5410-675-1*, Pub. by A A Balkema) Ashgate Pub Co.

Bobylev. Banking & Stock Exchange Six Languages Dictionary. (ENG, FRE, GER, ITA & RUS.). 288p. 1992. pap. 49.95 (*0-7859-1086-7*, 5870120071) Fr & Eur.

Bobylev, Iu A. Dictionary of Banking & Stock Exchange in Six Languages. 286p. (C). 1992. text 75.00 (*0-569-17111-3*, Pub. by Collets) St Mut.

***Bobylev, N. A., et al.** Geometrical Methods in Variational Problems. LC 99-15353. (Mathematics & Its Applications Ser.). 1999. write for info. (*0-7923-5780-9*) Kluwer Academic.

Bobylev, Nikolai A., et al. Approximation Procedures in Nonlinear Oscillation Theory. LC 94-16854. (Series in Nonlinear Analysis & Applications: Vol. 2). 283p. (C). 1994. lib. bdg. 89.95 (*3-11-014132-9*) De Gruyter.

An Asterisk (*) at the beginning of an entry indicates that the title is appearing for the first time.

Bobzien, Susanne. Determinism & Freedom in Stoic Philosophy. LC 98-26373. 454p. 1999. text 85.00 (*0-19-823794-4*) OUP.

Bobzin, Hagen. Indivisibilities: Microeconomic Theory with Respect to Indivisible Goods & Factors. LC 98-25047. (Contributions to Economics Ser.). (Illus.). x, 364p. 1998. pap. 73.00 (*3-7908-1123-8*, AIP Pr) Spr-Verlag.

Boc Limited Research University, ed. Membranes in Gas Separation & Enrichment, No. 62. (Illus.). 414p. (Orig.). (C). 1987. pap. text 72.00 (*0-85186-676-X*, Pub. by Royal Soc Chem) Spr-Verlag.

Boc, Victor. How to Solve All Your Money Problems Forever: Creating a Positive Flow of Money into Your Life. LC 97-16805. 288p. 1998. pap. 14.95 (*0-399-52378-2*, Perigee Bks) Berkley Pub.

Bocaccio. The Falcon & Other Tales. (Little Blue Bk.). 1990. pap. 10.00 (*0-936128-79-8*) De Young Pr.

Bocacho, Manuel M. De Barrosa Du, see De Barrosa Du Bocacho, Manuel M.

Bocage, Aaron A. & Waters, George E., Jr. Making Money the Old-Fashioned Way: A Story of Black Entrepreneurship. (Illus.). iii, 110p. 1997. pap. text 13.95 (*0-9661712-0-9*) EDTEC.

Bocanegra, Suzanne, ed. see Heartney, Eleanor & Middlebury College Staff.

Bocardo, Claire. Sweet Nothings. 544p. 1993. mass mkt. 4.50 (*0-8217-4366-X*, Zebra Kensgtn) Kensgtn Pub Corp.

— To Love Again: Lovers & Friends. 512p. 1995. mass mkt. 4.99 (*0-8217-4839-4*, Zebra Kensgtn) Kensgtn Pub Corp.

Bocatius, Ionnes & Csonka, eds. Opera Quae Exstant Omnia Poetica, Vols. 1 & 2. (FRE.). 1990. pap. 445.00 (*963-05-5376-7*, Pub. by Akade Kiado) St Mut.

Bocca, Geoffrey. Best-Seller: A Nostalgic Celebration of the Less Than Great Books You Have Always Been Afraid to Admit You Loved. 1981. 12.95 (*0-671-61071-6*) S&S Trade.

Boccacci, P., jt. auth. see Bertero, M.

Boccaccin, Gabriele. Beyond the Essene Hypothesis: The Parting of the Ways Between Qunuran & Enocic Judaism. LC 97-41870. 229p. 1998. pap. 25.00 (*0-8028-4360-3*) Eerdmans.

Boccaccio. Andreuccio da Perugia Level A. text 7.95 (*0-88436-049-0*) EMC-Paradigm.

Boccaccio, Giovanni. Amorosa Visione. Hollander, Robert et al, trs. LC 85-40488. (ENG & ITA.). 285p. 1986. reprint ed. pap. 88.40 (*0-7837-8194-6*, 204789900008) Bks Demand.

— Amorous Fiammetta. Yong, Bartholomew, tr. LC 76-98821. 356p. 1970. reprint ed. lib. bdg. 69.50 (*0-8371-3026-3*, BOAF, Greenwood Pr) Greenwood.

— Chaucer's Boccaccio: Sources for Troilus & the Knight's & Franklin's Tales. Havely, Nick R., tr. (Chaucer Studies: Vol. 5). 231p. (C). 1992. pap. 29.95 (*0-85991-349-X*) Boydell & Brewer.

— Chichibo & the Crane. (Illus.). (J). (gr. 1-6). 1961. 8.95 (*0-8392-3004-4*) Astor-Honor.

— The Corbaccio: Giovanni Boccaccio: Or, The Labyrinth of Love. Cassell, Anthony K., ed. & tr. by. LC 92-42698. 120p. 1993. pap. 9.95 (*0-86698-154-3*, P14) Pegasus Pr.

— De Casibus Illustrium Virorum. LC 62-7017. 256p. 1962. reprint ed. 50.00 (*0-8201-1005-1*) Schol Facsimiles.

— De Casibus Illustrium Virorum: Here Begynneth the Boke Calledde Ioh. Bochas Descriuinge the Falle of Princis. Ludgate, John, tr. LC 76-57358. (English Experience Ser.: No. 777). 1977. reprint ed. lib. bdg. 95.00 (*90-221-0777-9*) Walter J Johnson.

— The Decameron. 1982. mass mkt. 7.99 (*0-451-62746-6*) NAL.

— The Decameron. Musa, Mark & Bondanella, Peter E., eds. LC 77-5664. (Critical Editions Ser.). 334p. (C). 1977. pap. text 12.50 (*0-393-09132-5*) Norton.

— The Decameron. Musa, Mark & Bondanella, Peter E., trs. from ITA. 1983. 29.95 (*0-393-01754-0*) Norton.

— The Decameron. Usher, Jonathan, ed. Waldman, Guideo, tr. (Oxford World's Classics Ser.). 752p. 1999. pap. 11.95 (*0-19-283691-9*) OUP.

— The Decameron. McWilliam, G. H., tr. & intro. by. (Illus.). 992p. 1996. pap. 13.95 (*0-14-044629-X*) Penguin Putnam.

— The Decameron: A Diplomatic Edition. Singleton, Charles S., ed. LC 72-8892. (ITA., Illus.). 688p. 1974. 150.00 (*0-8018-1465-0*) Johns Hopkins.

— Decameron: Preserved to Posterity, 4 vols. Hutton, Edward, tr. LC 10-4801. (Tudor Translations, First Ser.: Nos. 41-44). reprint ed. 230.00 (*0-404-51960-1*) AMS Pr.

***Boccaccio, Giovanni.** The Decameron: Selected Tales. LC 99-56149. 2000. pap. 2.00 (*0-486-41113-3*) Dover.

Boccaccio, Giovanni. Decameron: The John Payne Translation, 3 vols. Payne, John, tr. from ITA. LC 77-83112. (Illus.). 444p. 1983. pap. 47.50 (*0-520-05872-0*, Pub. by U CA Pr) Cal Prin Full Svc.

Boccaccio, Giovanni. Diana's Hunt - Caccia Di Diana: Boccaccio's First Fiction. Cassell, Anthony K. & Kirkham, Victoria, eds. & trs. by. from ITA. LC 90-45815. (Middle Ages Ser.). (Illus.). 288p. (C). 1991. text 37.50 (*0-8122-8219-1*) U of Pa Pr.

Boccaccio, Giovanni. Early English Versions of the Tales of Guiscardo & Ghismonda & Titus Gisippus from the Decameron. Wright, H. G. et al, eds. (EETS, OS Ser.: No. 205). 1972. reprint ed. 63.00 (*0-527-00205-4*) Periodicals Srv.

— The Elegy of Lady Fiammetta. Mauch, Thomas, ed. & tr. by. Causa-Steindler, Mariangela, tr. LC 90-11057. xxvi, 208p. 1990. pap. 14.95 (*0-226-06276-7*) U Ch Pr.

— The Elegy of Lady Fiammetta. Causa-Steindler, Mariangela & Mauch, Thomas, eds. & trs. by. LC 90-11057. xxvi, 208p. 1996. lib. bdg. 33.00 (*0-226-06275-9*) U Ch Pr.

— The Elegy of Madonna Fiammetta Sent by Her to Women in Love. Payne, Roberta L. & Olsen, Alexandra Hennessey, trs. from ITA. LC 91-47749. (Studies in Italian Culture: Literature in History: Vol. 9). 149p. 1993. 34.95 (*0-8204-1837-4*) P Lang Pubng.

— The Filostrato of Giovanni Boccaccio. LC 67-25164. 1929. pap. 25.00 (*0-8196-0187-X*) Biblo.

— Giovanni Boccaccio, the Decameron. 30.00 (*0-916379-37-X*) Scripta.

— On Poetry. Osgood, Charles G., tr. 1956. pap. 5.80 (*0-672-60265-2*, LLA82, Bobbs) Macmillan.

— A Pleasant Disport of Divers Noble Personages Entitled Philocopo. LC 71-25579. (English Experience Ser.: No. 277). 116p. 1970. reprint ed. 35.00 (*90-221-0277-7*) Walter J Johnson.

Boccaccio, Giovanni & Aretino, Lionardo B. Earliest Lives of Dante. Smith, James R., tr. LC 74-7168. (Studies in Dante: No. 9). 1974. lib. bdg. 55.00 (*0-8383-1974-2*) M S G Haskell Hse.

Boccaccio, Giovanni, jt. auth. see Anderson, David.

Boccaccio, Giovanni, jt. auth. see Cartier, N. R.

Boccaccio, Mary. Pitt County, North Carolina: Eastern Reflections. LC 98-86002. (Images of America Ser.). (Illus.). 128p. 1998. pap. 14.99 (*0-7524-0974-3*) Arcadia Publng.

***Boccafogli, Roberto.** F1 '99: Behind the Scenes. (Illus.). 208p. 2000. 29.95 (*88-87110-17-4*, 129686AE, Pub. by SEP Editrice) Motorbooks Intl.

Boccafogli, Roberto. Ferrari Century: The Story of the Prancing Horse from 1898 until Today. LC 98-34965. (Illus.). 166p. 1998. pap. text 24.95 (*0-7603-0550-1*) MBI Pubg.

Boccafogli, Roberto, jt. auth. see D'Alessio, Paolo.

Boccagna, David. Musical Terminology: A Practical Compendium in Four Languages. LC 99-31743. (Illus.). 243p. 1999. pap. 9.99 (*1-57647-015-6*) Pendragon NY.

***Boccagna, David L.** Inside the World of Investment Fraud, Scams & Deceptive Practices & Mastering the World of Investment Fraud, Scams & Deceptive Practices, 2 vols., Vols. I & II, set. 270p. (C). 2000. pap. write for info. (*0-9701224-0-3*) I E S C Pr.

Boccaletti, D. Theory of Orbits: Perturbative & Geometrical Methods, Vol. 2. (Theory of Orbits Ser.). 350p. 1999. 69.00 (*3-540-60355-7*) Spr-Verlag.

Boccaletti, D. & Pucacco, G. Theory of Orbits: Integrable Systems & Non-perturbative Methods. LC 96-140412. (Astronomy & Astrophysics Library: Vol.1). 392p. 1996. 69.00 (*3-540-58963-5*) Spr-Verlag.

Boccara, Nino. Functional Analysis: An Introduction for Physicists. 327p. 1990. text 73.00 (*0-12-108810-3*) Acad Pr.

Boccara, Nino, jt. ed. see Conte, Robert.

Boccara, Nino, ed. see Meunier, J.

Boccardo, L. & Tesei, A. Nonlinear Parabolic Equation. 1987. pap. text. write for info. (*0-582-99459-4*, Pub. by Addison-Wesley) Longman.

Boccato, Alessandra. Churches of Venice. 191p. 1999. pap. 9.95 (*88-7743-201-2*) Arsenale Editrice.

Boccato, P., jt. auth. see Ravetto, Carlo.

Boccato, Paolo, jt. auth. see Ravetto, Carlo.

Boccazzi-Varotto, Attilio. Paris 360 Degrees. LC 99-17755. 144p. 1999. 75.00 (*0-679-44285-5*) Random Hse Value.

Boccazzi-Varotto, Attilio & Filaferro, Marco. Rome 360 Degrees. LC 97-3971. 144p. 1998. 75.00 (*0-679-44286-3*) Random Hse Value.

Bocchi, Gianluca & Ceruti, Mauro. Solidarity or Barbarism: A Europe of Diversity Against Ethnic Cleansing. Montuori, Alfonso, tr. from ITA. LC 97-20826. (Conflict & Consciousness: Vol. 3). X, 155p. (C). 1998. pap. text 24.95 (*0-8204-3147-8*) P Lang Pubng.

***Bocchi, Joseph, et al.** Making Connections, Achieving Success, Understanding Others. 2nd ed. 368p. (C). 1999. per. 32.95 (*0-7872-6351-6*, 41635101) Kendall-Hunt.

Bocchicchio, Rebecca P., jt. ed. see Saxton, Kirsten T.

***Bocchieri, Barry.** Things That Work: A No-Nonsense Guide to Recovery by One Who Knows. 154p. 2000. pap. 16.95 (*1-55691-176-9*, 769) Learning Pubns.

Bocchina, Anthony J. & Beal, Ronald L. McLain vs. Barber. 2nd ed. 200p. 1997. pap. 22.95 (*1-55681-540-9*) Natl Inst Trial Ad.

Bocchino, Anthony J. Donavan v. Barkley: Legal Malpractice. 82p. 1991. pap. 22.95 (*1-55681-262-0*) Natl Inst Trial Ad.

— Donavan v. Barkley (Pretrial Case File) 66p. 1994. pap. 22.95 (*1-55681-453-4*) Natl Inst Trial Ad.

— Drury Plumbing Construction Company v. Gordon Plastics, Inc. Contract Dispute. 2nd ed. 61p. 1991. pap. 22.95 (*1-55681-171-3*) Natl Inst Trial Ad.

— Federal Rules of Evidence with Objections. 1994. 15.95 (*0-614-06015-X*, 41213) Natl Prac Inst.

***Bocchino, Anthony J.** Federal Rules of Evidence with Objections: Reflects Changes Made to the Federal Rules of Evidence Through December 1, 1998. 4th ed. LC 99-462513. 1998. 25.95 (*1-55681-641-3*) Natl Inst Trial Ad.

Bocchino, Anthony J. In Re: Cooperman: NITA Programs Edition. 88p. 1993. pap. 22.95 (*1-55681-359-7*) Natl Inst Trial Ad.

— In Re: Cooperman: Professional Responsibility. 64p. 1993. pap. 22.95 (*1-55681-257-4*) Natl Inst Trial Ad.

— In Re: Masters: Professional Responsibility. 58p. 1991. pap. 22.95 (*1-55681-258-2*) Natl Inst Trial Ad.

***Bocchino, Anthony J.** North Carolina Rules of Evidence with Objections. 2nd ed. 187p. 2000. pap. 25.95 (*1-55681-492-5*) Natl Inst Trial Ad.

— Pennsylvania Rules of Evidence with Objections. LC 99-209365. 293p. 1998. 25.95 (*1-55681-621-9*) Natl Inst Trial Ad.

— A Practical Guide to Pennsylvania Evidence: Objections, Responses, Rules & Practice Commentary. LC 99-189425. 241 p. 1998. 39.95 (*1-55681-622-7*) Natl Inst Trial Ad.

Bocchino, Anthony J. & Beal, Ronald L. McLain v. Barber (Pretrial Edition) 120p. 1994. pap. 22.95 (*1-55681-393-7*) Natl Inst Trial Ad.

Bocchino, Anthony J. & Beskind, Donald H. BMI v Minicom, Inc. (Casefile/Contract Action) 6th ed. 182p. 1995. pap. 22.95 (*1-55681-374-0*) Natl Inst Trial Ad.

— BMI v. Minicom (Pretrial Casefile) LC 96-134682. 80p. 1995. pap. 22.95 (*1-55681-456-9*) Natl Inst Trial Ad.

— Developing Deposition Skills: BMI Vs. Minicom, Materials for the Advocates. 142p. 1993. pap. 22.95 (*1-55681-385-6*) Natl Inst Trial Ad.

— Developing Deposition Skills: BMI Vs. Minicom, Materials for the Barristers. 3rd ed. 142p. 1993. pap. 22.95 (*1-55681-386-4*) Natl Inst Trial Ad.

— State vs. Burns: Criminal Case File - Armed Robbery Felony Murder. 5th rev. ed. 140p. 1992. pap. 18.95 (*1-55681-297-3*) Natl Inst Trial Ad.

Bocchino, Anthony J. & Natali, Louis M. NITA Fire & Casualty Co. vs. Anthony Rubino, d. b. a. Rubino & Son. 321p. 1982. pap. 22.95 (*1-55681-064-4*) Natl Inst Trial Ad.

Bocchino, Anthony J. & Sonenshein, David A. Developing Deposition Skills: Polisi Vs. Clark & Parker & Gould, Materials for the Defendant. 116p. 1993. pap. 22.95 (*1-55681-391-0*) Natl Inst Trial Ad.

— Developing Deposition Skills: Polisi Vs. Clark & Parker & Gould, Materials for the Plaintiff. 134p. 1993. pap. 22.95 (*1-55681-390-2*) Natl Inst Trial Ad.

***Bocchino, Anthony J. & Sonenshein, David A.** Polisi vs. Clark & Parker & Gould: Sexual Harassment. 188p. 1998. pap. 22.95 (*1-55681-629-4*) Natl Inst Trial Ad.

— A Practical Guide to Federal Evidence: Objections, Responses, Rules & Practice Commentary. 4th ed. 2000. 39.95 (*1-55681-650-2*) Natl Inst Trial Ad.

Bocchino, Anthony J. & Sonenshein, David A. Problems & Materials in Civil Procedure: Polisi v. Clark & Parker & Gould - Law School Edition. LC 96-155305. Orig. Title: Materials for a Motion Practice Workshop. 525p. 1994. 34.95 (*1-55681-465-8*) Natl Inst Trial Ad.

— Problems & Materials in Civil Procedure: Polisi v. Clark & Parker & Gould - Library of Cases. Orig. Title Materials for a Motion Practice Workshop. 585p. 1997. 29.95 (*1-55681-514-X*) Natl Inst Trial Ad.

Bocchino, Anthony J., et al. Indiana State Rules of Evidence with Objections. 202p. 1994. pap. 25.95 (*1-55681-394-5*) Natl Inst Trial Ad.

— Maryland State Rules of Evidence with Objections. 227p. 1995. pap. 25.95 (*1-55681-466-6*) Natl Inst Trial Ad.

— Michigan State Rules of Evidence with Objections. 193p. 1995. pap. 25.95 (*1-55681-459-3*) Natl Inst Trial Ad.

— Minnesota State Rules of Evidence with Objections. 208p. 1994. pap. 22.95 (*1-55681-399-6*) Natl Inst Trial Ad.

— Oregon Evidence Code with Objections. 231p. 1997. pap. 25.95 (*1-55681-551-4*) Natl Inst Trial Ad.

— Problems & Cases in Interviewing, Counseling & Negotiation. 3rd ed. 248p. 1986. pap. 26.95 (*1-55681-071-7*, FBPCICN) Natl Inst Trial Ad.

— Rhode Island State Rules of Evidence with Objections. 199p. 1994. pap. 22.95 (*1-55681-401-1*) Natl Inst Trial Ad.

— Trial Evidence: Making & Meeting Objections. 2nd ed. 190p. 1990. pap. 29.95 (*1-55681-233-7*) Natl Inst Trial Ad.

— Wisconsin State Rules of Evidence with Objections. 247p. 1995. pap. 25.95 (*1-55681-460-7*) Natl Inst Trial Ad.

Bocchino, Anthony J., jt. auth. see Carey, James P.

Bocchino, Anthony J., jt. auth. see Greenberg, Mark S.

Bocchino, Peter, jt. auth. see Geisler, Norman.

***Bocchino, Rob.** Emotional Literacy: To Be a Different Kind of Smart. LC 99-6179. (One-Off Ser.). (Illus.). 160p. 1999. pap. 22.95 (*0-8039-6824-8*); lib. bdg. 51.95 (*0-8039-6823-X*) Sage.

Boccia, Edward. Moving the Still-Life. 26p. 1995. pap. 7.95 (*0-944754-18-X*) Pudding Hse Pubns.

— No Matter How Good the Light Is: Poems by a Painter. LC 97-50548. 77p. 1998. 22.00 (*1-56809-044-7*); pap. 14.50 (*1-56809-045-5*) Time Being Bks.

Boccia, Michael. Form As Content & Rhetoric in the Modern Novel. (American University Studies: English Language & Literature: Ser. IV, Vol. 77). VIII, 191p. (C). 1988. text 31.50 (*0-8204-0676-7*) P Lang Pubng.

***Boccia, Vincent.** A Momentary Lapse of Reason. LC 00-190996. 247p. 2000. 25.00 (*0-7388-2185-3*); pap. 18.00 (*0-7388-2186-1*) Xlibris Corp.

Boccialetti, Gene. It Takes Two: Manage Yourself When Working with Bosses & Other Authority Figures. (The Management Ser.). 380p. 1995. text 29.95 (*0-7879-0088-5*) Jossey-Bass.

***Boccio, John L., ed.** Safety Engineering & Risk Analysis. (SERA Ser.: Vol. 9). 125p. 1999. 70.00 (*0-7918-1657-5*) ASME Pr.

Boccon-Gibod, Laurent, ed. New Avenues & Perspectives in the Management of Advanced Prostate Cancer: Paris, September 1996. (European Urology Ser.: Vol. 31, Suppl. 1997). (Illus.). iv, 40p. 1997. pap. 21.75 (*3-8055-6487-2*) S Karger.

Boccon-Gibod, Laurent, et al, eds. European Association of Urology: 12th Congress, Paris, September 1996 - Abstracts. (Journal: European Urology: Vol. 30, Suppl. 2, 1996). (Illus.). 310p. 1996. pap. 135.00 (*3-8055-6387-6*) S Karger.

***Bocelli, Andrea.** Scenes from My Life: An Autobiography. (Illus.). 288p. 2000. 24.95 (*0-446-52682-7*) Warner Bks.

Boch-Isaacson, Joel M., ed. Architecture & Construction Management in the Highland & Remote Areas of Nepal. 166p. (C). 1987. 125.00 (*0-89771-095-9*, Pub. by Ratna Pustak Bhandar) St Mut.

Boch, R., ed. Il Nuovo Boch: Dizionario Francese-Italiano/ Italiano-Francese. (FRE & ITA.). 2178p. 1992. 125.00 (*0-913298-54-9*) S F Vanni.

Boch, Ron, ed. Directory of College & University Foodservice, 1992-1993. 462p. 1992. pap. 249.00 (*0-86730-562-2*) Lebhar Friedman.

Bocharon, A. V., et al. Symmetries & Conservation Laws for Differential Equations of Mathematical Physics. LC 98-53018. (GER.). 333p. 1999. write for info. (*0-8218-0958-X*) Am Math.

Bocharov, A. P., ed. A Description of Devices Used in the Study of Wind Erosion of Soils. Dhamija, S. C., tr. from RUS. (ENG.). 98p. (C). 1984. text 116.00 (*90-6191-426-4*, Pub. by A A Balkema) Ashgate Pub Co.

Bocharov, Gennady. Russian Roulette: Afghanistan Through Russian Eyes. 187p. 1997. reprint ed. text 19.00 (*0-7881-5109-6*) DIANE Pub.

— Russkaya Ruletka (Russian Roulette) LC 94-60801. (Illus.). 144p. (Orig.). 1994. pap. 12.00 (*1-885563-01-9*) VIA Press MD.

Boche. Relay: An Information Management Workflow. (KM - Office Procedures Ser.). 1990. 455.00 (*0-538-25530-7*) S-W Pub.

Boche, Cheryl. Easy Reference Guide: Microsoft Works, Macintosh. 1993. mass mkt. 7.95 (*0-538-62519-8*) S-W Pub.

Bochel, Catherine, jt. auth. see Bochel, Hugh M.

Bochel, Hugh M. Parliament & Welfare Policy. 164p. 1992. 72.95 (*1-85521-279-X*, Pub. by Dartmth Pub) Ashgate Pub Co.

Bochel, Hugh M. & Bochel, Catherine. Careers of Councillors. LC 99-76652. 145p. 69.95 (*1-84014-096-8*) Ashgate Pub Co.

Bochel, J. M., et al, eds. The Referendum Experience, Scotland 1979. (Illus.). 224p. 1981. text 26.00 (*0-08-025734-8*, R120, Pergamon Pr) Elsevier.

***Bochen, Christine M., selected by.** Thomas Merton: Writings. (Modern Spiritual Masters Ser.). 144p. 2000. pap. 14.00 (*1-57075-331-8*) Orbis Bks.

Bochen, Christine M., jt. auth. see Merton, Thomas.

Bochen, Christine M., ed. see Merton, Thomas.

Bochenski. Filosofía Actual. (Breviarios Ser.). (SPA.). pap. 8.99 (*968-16-0245-5*, Pub. by Fondo) Continental Bk.

Bochenski, I. M., ed. Logisches Philosophieren - Festschrift Fuer Albert Menne Zum 60. (GER.). xii, 208p. 1988. write for info. (*3-487-07421-4*) G Olms Pubs.

Bochenski, Innocentius. Contemporary European Philosophy. Nicholl, Donald & Aschenbrenner, Karl, trs. from GER. LC 82-2987. Orig. Title: Europaische Philosophie der Gegenwart. 326p. 1982. reprint ed. lib. bdg. 38.50 (*0-313-23490-6*, BOCY) Greenwood.

Bochenski, J. M. A Precis of Mathematical Logic. Bird, Otto, tr. from FRE. (Snthese Library: No.1). 110p. 1960. text 113.00 (*90-277-0073-7*, D Reidel) Kluwer Academic.

— Soviet Russian Dialectical Materialism. rev. ed. Sollohub, Nicholas, tr. from GER. 185p. 1963. text 137.50 (*90-277-0043-5*, D Reidel) Kluwer Academic.

Bochenski, J. M. & Blakeley, Thomas J., eds. Studies in Soviet Thought. (Sovietica Ser.: No. 7). 141p. 1970. lib. bdg. 81.00 (*90-277-0051-6*) Kluwer Academic.

Bochenski, Joseph M. Autoritat, Freiheit, Glaube Sozialphilosophische Studien. (Introductiones Ser.). 213p. 1988. 39.00 (*3-88405-062-1*); pap. 30.00 (*3-88405-074-5*) Philosophia Pr.

Bochenski, Michael I. Theology from Three Worlds: Liberation & Evangelization for the New Europe. LC 97-14480. (Regent's Study Guides Ser.). 224p. 1997. pap. 17.00 (*1-57312-168-1*) Smyth & Helwys.

Bochert-Kimmig, Reinhold, jt. auth. see Schuster, Ekkehard.

Bochin, Hal W. Richard Nixon: Rhetorical Strategist, 6. LC 89-17193. (Great American Orators: Critical Studies, Speeches & Sources: No. 6). 237p. 1990. lib. bdg. 55.00 (*0-313-26108-3*, BCQ/, Greenwood Pr) Greenwood.

Bochin, Hal W., jt. auth. see Weatherson, Michael A.

Bochinski, Julianne B. The Complete Handbook of Science Fair Projects. 2nd rev. ed. LC 95-22791. (Illus.). 240p. (YA). (gr. 7 up). 1996. pap. 14.95 (*0-471-12377-3*) Wiley.

— The Complete Handbook of Science Fair Projects. 2nd rev. ed. LC 95-22791. (Illus.). 240p. 1996. 29.95 (*0-471-12378-1*) Wiley.

Bochius, Johannes & Van Der Borcht, Pieter. Descriptio Publicae Gratulationis Spectaculorum Et Ludorum, in Adventu: Ernesti Archiducis Austriae Antiverpiae. LC 68-21207. (LAT., Illus.). 1972. reprint ed. 54.95 (*0-405-08278-9*, Pub. by Blom Pubns) Ayer.

Bochkarev, M. N., et al. Organoderivatives of Rare Earth Elements. LC 94-31169. (Topics in F-Element Chemistry Ser.: Vol. 3). 556p. (C). 1995. text 254.00 (*0-7923-3153-2*) Kluwer Academic.

Bochkov, A. E. & Zaikov, G. E. Chemistry of the O-Glycosidic Bond: Formation & Cleavage. 1979. 95.00 (*0-08-022949-2*, Pub. by Pergamon Repr) Franklin.

Bochkov, A. F., et al. Carbohydrates. (Illus.). 154p. 1991. 110.00 (*90-6764-118-9*, Pub. by VSP) Coronet Bks.

Bochman, Alexander, tr. see Orevkov, V. P.

Bochmann, G. V. & Probst, D. K., eds. Computer Aided Verification: Fourth International Workshop, CAC 92, Montreal, Canada, 1992. LC 93-9405. (Lecture Notes in Computer Science Ser.: Vol. 663). 1993. 61.95 (*0-387-56496-9*) Spr-Verlag.

Bochmann, Klaus, ed. Sprachpolitik in der Romania: Zur Geschichte Sprachpolitischen Denkens und Handelns Von der Franzoesischen Revolution Bis Zur Gegenwart. (GER.). xvi, 528p. 1993. lib. bdg. 206.15 (*3-11-013614-7*) De Gruyter.

Bochmann, Manfred. Organometallics 1: Complexes with Transition Metal-Carbons-Bonds. (Oxford Chemistry Primers Ser.: Vol. 12). (Illus.). 96p. (C). 1994. pap. text 12.95 (*0-19-855750-7*, 7848) OUP.

B

— Organometallics 2: Complexes with Transition Metal-Carbon p-Bonds. (Oxford Chemistry Primers Ser.: No. 13). (Illus.). 96p. (C). 1994. text 29.95 (*0-19-855814-7*); pap. text 12.95 (*0-19-855813-9*) OUP.

Bochnak, J., et al. Real Algebraic Geometry. Bombieri, E. et al, eds. LC 98-29344. (Ergebnisse der Mathematik und Ihrer Grenzgebiete Ser.). (Illus.). xi, 430p. 1998. 119.00 (*3-540-64663-9*) Spr-Verlag.

Bochnak, Peter M. Fire Loss Control: A Management Guide. 2nd ed. (Occupational Safety & Health Ser.: Vol. 22). (Illus.). 344p. 1991. text 160.00 (*0-8247-8413-8*) Dekker.

Bochner, Arthur Berg, jt. auth. see Berg, Adriane G.

Bochner, Arthur P., jt. ed. see Ellis, Carolyn.

Bochner, Bruce S., ed. Adhesion Molecules in Allergic Disease. LC 97-7152. (Illus.). 440p. 1997. text 190.00 (*0-8247-9836-8*) Dekker.

***Bochner, Daniel.** The Therapists Use of Self in Family Therapy. LC 99-55415. 2000. 45.00 (*0-7657-0248-7*) Aronson.

Bochner, Felix, et al. Handbook of Clinical Pharmacology. 2nd ed. 352p. 1983. 30.95 (*0-316-10064-1*, Little Brwn Med Div) Lppncott W & W.

Bochner, Harry. Simplicity in Generative Morphology. LC 92-28365. (Publications in Language Sciences: Vol. 37). vi, 247p. 1992. pap. 98.50 (*3-11-013594-9*) Mouton.

Bochner, Jay. Blaise Cendrars: Discovery & Re-Creation. LC 77-2580. (University of Toronto Romance Ser.: No. 32). (Illus.). 332p. reprint ed. pap. 103.00 (*0-8357-6395-1*, 203575100096) Bks Demand.

***Bochner, Jay & Edwards, Justin D., eds.** American Modernism Across the Arts. LC 98-25597. (Studies on the Themes & Motifs in Literature: Vol. 46). (Illus.). 309p. (C). 1999. text 58.00 (*0-8204-4143-0*) P Lang Pubng.

Bochner, Mel, jt. auth. see Schwabsky, Barry.

Bochner, S. The Psychology of the Dentist-Patient Relationship. (Contributions to Psychology & Medicine Ser.). (Illus.). 200p. 1988. 112.00 (*0-387-96642-0*) Spr-Verlag.

Bochner, S. & Chandrasekharan, K. Fourier Transforms. (Annals of Mathematics Studies: No. 19). 1949. 25.00 (*0-527-02735-9*) Periodicals Srv.

Bochner, Salomon. Lectures on Fourier Integrals: With an Author's Supplement on Monotonic Functions, Stieltjes Integrals, & Harmonic Analysis. Tenenbaum, Morris & Pollard, Harry, trs. LC 59-5589. (Annals of Mathematics Studies: No. 42). 343p. reprint ed. pap. 106.40 (*0-608-06637-0*, 206683400009) Bks Demand.

— The Role of Mathematics in the Rise of Science. LC 66-10550. 396p. reprint ed. pap. 122.80 (*0-8357-7012-5*, 205228700085) Bks Demand.

Bochner, Salomon, jt. auth. see Gunning, Robert.

Bochner, Sandra, et al. Child Language Development. 150p. 1997. 39.95 (*1-56593-885-2*, 1734) Singular Publishing.

Bochner, Stephen, ed. The Mediating Person: Bridges Between Cultures. 323p. 1982. pap. text 13.25 (*0-87073-893-3*) Schenkman Bks Inc.

Bochner, Stephen, jt. auth. see Furnham, Adrian F.

***Bochner, Steven E., et al.** Capitalizing & Protecting New Businesses: February 2000 Update. Kronenberg, Hale, ed. LC 97-65861. (California Business Start-Up Ser.). 318p. 2000. 60.00 (*0-7626-0406-9*, BU-32943) Cont Ed Bar-CA.

Bochnovic, David A., jt. auth. see Masson, D. J.

Bochnovic, John. The Inventive Step: Its Evolution in Canada, the United Kingdom, & the United States. Beier, Freidrich-Karl et al, eds. (IIC Studies Ser.). 90p. 1982. pap. 45.00 (*3-527-25699-7*, Wiley-VCH) Wiley.

Bochorishvili. My Name Is Nina, Bk. 2. (Play & Say Ser.). 48p. 1995. pap. text 13.23 (*0-201-83260-7*) Addison-Wesley.

Bochorishvili, Natalia & Palkus, Vitalij. My Name Is Nina!, Bk. 2. (C). 1996. text, teacher ed. 18.17 (*0-201-83264-X*) Addison-Wesley.

Bochorisvili. My Name Is Nina, BK. 1. (Play & Say Ser.). 48p. 1995. pap. text 13.23 (*0-201-60973-8*) Addison-Wesley.

Bochove, Thomas E. Van, see Van Bochove, Thomas E.

Bochsler, Katharina. Ich Han da Inne Ungehortu Ding Gesehen: Die Jenseitsvisionen Mechthilds von Magdeburg in der Tradition der Mittelalterlichen Visionsliteratur. (Deutsche Literatur von den Aufangen bis 1700 Ser.: Bd. 23). (GER.). x, 193p. 1997. 33.95 (*3-906756-56-4*, Pub. by P Lang) P Lang Pubng.

Bochuan, He. China on the Edge: Crisis of Ecology & Development in China. China Books & Periodicals, Inc. Staff, tr. from CHI. LC 91-70073. 200p. 1992. pap. 16.95 (*0-8351-2448-7*) China Bks.

Bocij, Paul. Introduction to CD-Rom & Multimedia. (Orig.). 1996. pap. 34.95 (*1-898307-28-8*, Pub. by Capall Bann Pubng) Holmes Pub.

— Making Money with Your Computer. (Orig.). 1996. pap. 29.95 (*1-898307-29-6*, Pub. by Capall Bann Pubng) Holmes Pub.

***Bocij, Paul & Chaffey, Dave.** Business Information: Technology, Systems & Management. (Systems ser.). 640p. (Orig.). 1999. pap. 57.50 (*0-273-63849-1*, Pub. by F T P-H) Trans-Atl Phila.

Bociurkiw, Bohdan R. Ukrainian Churches under Soviet Rule: Two Case Studies. 63p. 1994. write for info. (*0-9609822-3-X*) Ukrainian Studies Fund.

Bociurkiw, Marusya. The Woman Who Loved Airports: Stories & Narratives. LC PR9199.3.B558W66 199. 168p. 1994. pap. 12.95 (*0-88974-035-6*, Pub. by Press Gang Pubs) LPC InBook.

Bock & Heiko. Vocabulaire Allemand de Base. 420p. 1992. 20.00 (*3-468-49402-5*) Langenscheidt.

Bock & Muller. Basic German Vocabulary. 322p. 1992. student ed. 17.50 (*3-468-49401-7*) Langenscheidt.

— Vocabulaire Allemand de Base. 328p. 1992. student ed. 17.50 (*3-468-49403-3*) Langenscheidt.

Bock, jt. auth. see Carroll, Charles R.

Bock, jt. auth. see Heiko.

***Bock, Alan.** Waiting to Inhale: The Politics of Medical Marijuana. 224p. 2000. pap. 18.95 (*0-929765-82-6*) Seven Locks Pr.

Bock, Alan W. Ambush at Ruby Ridge. (Illus.). 94p. 1995. 22.00 (*1-880741-48-2*) Dickens Pr.

Bock, Alan W. Ambush at Ruby Ridge: How Government Agents Set Randy Weaver up & Took His Family Down. LC 96-209092. 1996. mass mkt. 6.99 (*0-425-15729-6*) Berkley Pub.

Bock, Angela. Die Sala Regia im Vatikan als Beispiel der Selbstdarstellung des Papsttums in der 2. Halfte des 16. Jahrhunderts. (Studien Zur Kunstgeschichte: Bd. 112). (Illus.). 260p. 1997. 80.00 (*3-487-10297-8*) G Olms Pubs.

Bock, Arthur E., jt. ed. see Blank, David A.

Bock, Audie E., tr. see Kurosawa, Akira.

Bock, B. R. & Kelley, K. R. Predicting N Fertilizer Needs for Corn in Humid Regions: Proceedings of Soil Science Society of America Symposium on the Same Title, Denver, Nov. 1991. (Bulletin Y-226 Ser.). 1992. write for info. (*0-87077-007-1*) TVA.

Bock, B. R. & Kissel, D. E., eds. Ammonia Volitilization from Urea Fertilizer. (Illus.). 189p. 1989. 15.00 (*0-87077-003-9*) TVA.

***Bock, Barbara.** Munuscula Mesopotamica: Frestschrift fur Johannes Renger. Cancik-Kirschbaum, Eva C. & Richter, Thomas, eds. (Alter Orient und Altes Testament Ser.: No. 267). (GER.). xxix, 704p. 1999. text 135.00 (*3-927120-81-2*, Pub. by Ugarit-Verlag) Eisenbrauns.

Bock, Becky S. & Cage, Cheryl A. Welcome Aboard! Your Career as a Flight Attendant. LC 97-78405. 89p. 1998. pap. 14.95 (*0-9642839-3-X*) Cage Consult.

Bock, Betty. You Can Make a Difference: Changing Situations That Hurt Others. Edwards, Judy, ed. 116p. 1993. pap. text 6.95 (*1-56309-060-0*, W935102) Womans Mission Union.

Bock, Carl A. The Head-Hunters of Borneo: A Narrative of Travel up the Mahakkam & Down the Barito. 2nd ed. LC 77-86966. reprint ed. 125.00 (*0-404-16698-9*) AMS Pr.

Bock, Carl E. Credit - Get It! 1994. pap. text 29.95 (*1-883000-01-7*) Derrymore West.

— Credit - Get It! How to Get the Credit You Deserve, Handle Debt Wisely & Build a Secure Financial Future. LC 93-72605. 320p. (Orig.). 1994. pap. 29.95 (*1-884000-01-0*) Action Pubng.

***Bock, Carl E. & Bock, Jane H.** The View from Bald Hill. LC 99-47507. (Organisms & Environments Ser.: Vol. 1). 228p. 2000. pap. 16.95 (*0-520-22184-2*, Pub. by U CA Pr) Cal Prin Full Svc.

Bock, Carol. Charlotte Bronte & the Storyteller's Audience. LC 92-13446. (Illus.). 204p. 1992. text 34.95 (*0-87745-363-2*) U of Iowa Pr.

***Bock, Darrell L.** Blasphemy & Exaltation in Judaism: The Charge Against Jesus in Mark 14:53p65. (Biblical Studies Library). 300p. (C). (gr. 13 up). 2000. pap. 26.99 (*0-8010-2236-3*) Baker Bks.

Bock, Darrell L. Luke, 2. (Baker Exegetical Commentary on the New Testament Ser.). 2,150p. 1993. 80.00 (*0-8010-1051-9*) Baker Bks.

— Luke. (NIV Application Commentary Ser.). 608p. 1996. 27.99 (*0-310-49330-7*) Zondervan.

— Luke Vol. 1: 1: 1-9:50, 1. LC 94-33507. (Baker Exegetical Commentary on the New Testament Ser.: Vol. 1). 988p. (J). 1994. 44.99 (*0-8010-1053-5*) Baker Bks.

— Luke Vol. 2: 9:51-24:53, 2. LC 94-33507. (Baker Exegetical Commentary on the New Testament Ser.). 1,162p. 1996. 44.99 (*0-8010-1052-7*) Baker Bks.

Bock, Darrell L. Proclamation from Prophecy & Pattern: Lucan Old Testament Christology. (JSNT Supplement Ser.: No. 12). 413p. 1987. 85.00 (*1-85075-000-9*, Pub. by Sheffield Acad) CUP Services.

Bock, Darrell L., jt. auth. see Blaising, Craig A.

Bock, Darrell L., jt. ed. see Zuck, Roy B.

Bock, Dennis. Olympia. 272p. 1999. 22.95 (*1-58234-023-4*) Bloomsbury Pubg.

— Olympia. 256p. 1998. mass mkt. write for info. (*0-385-25698-1*) Doubleday.

Bock, Dorothy, et al, eds. Korone: A Collection of Women's Poetry & Prose, Vol. VI. 136p. (Orig.). 1990. pap. 9.95 (*0-945595-02-6*) Womanspace.

— Korone: Women's Voices, Vol. VIII. 119p. (Orig.). 1994. pap. 8.00 (*0-945595-04-2*) Womanspace.

— Korone: Women's Voices, Vol. IX. 112p. (Orig.). 1996. pap. 8.00 (*0-945595-05-0*) Womanspace.

Bock, Dorothy & Hirschenberger, Elaine, eds. Korone: Women's Voices, Vol. VII. 120p. (Orig.). 1992. pap. 8.00 (*0-945595-03-4*) Womanspace.

Bock, Douglas G. & Perkins, Terry M. Intro Speech Communication. 3rd ed. 96p. (C). 1996. pap. text, spiral bd. 8.95 (*0-7872-0455-2*) Kendall-Hunt.

Bock, Duncan, ed. The Little Book of Opera. LC 96-28051. (Illus.). 176p. 1996. 20.00 (*0-87113-649-X*, Atlntc Mnthly) Grove-Atltic.

Bock, Elfried. Adolph Menzel: The Graphic Work. rev. ed. (ENG & GER., Illus.). 576p. 1991. reprint ed. 150.00 (*1-55660-124-7*) A Wofsy Fine Arts.

Bock, Emil. The Apocalypse of Saint John. 208p. 1990. 27.50 (*0-86315-045-4*, 212, Pub. by Floris Bks) Anthroposophic.

— The Childhood of Jesus: Christ & Jesus, Mary & John the Evangelist. LC 97-221636. 1998. pap. 24.95 (*0-86315-257-0*, Pub. by Floris Bks) Gryphon Hse.

— Genesis: Creation & the Patriarchs. 188p. 1990. 27.50 (*0-86315-000-4*, 398, Pub. by Floris Bks) Anthroposophic.

— Moses: From the Mysteries of Egypt to the Judges of Israel. 224p. 1990. pap. 12.95 (*0-89281-117-X*, 1162, Pub. by Floris Bks) Anthroposophic.

***Bock, Emil.** Rhythm of the Christian Year. 2000. 26.00 (*0-86315-308-9*) Floris Bks.

Bock, Emil. Saint Paul. 31.95 (*0-86315-130-2*, 976, Pub. by Floris Bks) Anthroposophic.

— The Three Years: The Life of Christ Between Baptism & Ascension. 290p. 1990. 27.50 (*0-86315-060-8*, 1307, Pub. by Floris Bks) Anthroposophic.

Bock, Felicia G. Classical Learning & Taoist Practices in Early Japan, with Translation of Books XVI & XX of the Engi-Shiki. LC 82-84464. (Occasional Paper Arizona State Univ., Center for Asian Studies: No. 17). 102p. 1985. pap. 10.00 (*0-939252-13-9*) ASU Ctr Asian.

Bock, Frances, jt. auth. see Oliver, Rose.

Bock, Fred. Bock's Best, Vol. 1. 152p. 1997. spiral bd. 24.95 (*0-7935-9391-3*) H Leonard.

Bock, Fred. Charlie Brown's Favorite Sunday School Songs. (Peanuts Piano Course Ser.). (Illus.). 24p. (Orig.). (J). (gr. 1-6). 1992. pap. 7.95 (*1-56516-012-6*) H Leonard.

Bock, Fred. From This Day Forward Vocal. 1997. pap. 20.95 (*0-634-00344-5*) H Leonard.

— Here Comes the Bride Organ. 1997. pap. 10.95 (*0-634-00345-3*) H Leonard.

— Hymns & Gospel Songs. (Bock's Best Piano Solos Ser.: Vol. 4). 148p. 1997. pap. 24.95 (*0-7935-9392-1*) H Leonard.

— Hymns & Gospel Songs. (Bock's Best Piano Solos Ser.: Vol. 5). 148p. 1997. pap. 24.95 (*0-7935-9393-X*) H Leonard.

— The Organ Music of Fred Bock, Vol. 1. 1997. pap. 10.95 (*0-634-00357-7*) H Leonard.

— Organ Praise & Worship Organ. 1997. pap. 10.95 (*0-634-00360-7*) H Leonard.

— Piano. (Bock's Best Ser.: Vol. 2). 1997. pap. 24.95 (*0-7935-9394-8*) H Leonard.

— Piano Praise & Worship. (Piano Collection Ser.). 1997. pap. 10.95 (*0-7935-9990-3*) H Leonard.

— Piano Praise & Worship. (Piano Collection Ser.: No. 3). 1997. pap. 10.95 (*0-7935-9991-1*) H Leonard.

— Praise & Worship Piano. (Piano Collection Ser.: No. 2). 1997. pap. 10.95 (*0-7935-9992-X*) H Leonard.

— 25 Christmas Piano Solos. (Bock's Best Ser.: Vol. 3). 1997. 12.95 (*0-7935-9395-6*) H Leonard.

— Whom God Hath Joined Together. (Wedding Ser.). 1997. pap. 10.95 (*0-634-00349-6*) H Leonard.

Bock, Fred & Leech, Bryan J., eds. The Hymnal Companion. 1979. 12.95 (*0-89477-004-7*) Paragon Benson.

— Hymns for the Family of God. 1976. 7.95 (*0-89477-000-4*); pap. 7.95 (*0-89477-001-2*); ring bd. 6.95 (*0-89477-002-0*) Paragon Benson.

Bock, Fred, jt. auth. see Bock, Lois.

Bock, Fred G., jt. ed. see Gori, Gio B.

Bock, Geoffrey E. BIB Net from Michelin North America. (Illus.). 15p. 1997. pap. 295.00 (*1-892815-16-8*) Patricia Seybold.

***Bock, Geoffrey E.** Heineken's Operational Planning System: Replenishing Beer Through the Web. (Illus.). 15p. 1998. pap. write for info. (*1-892815-09-5*) Patricia Seybold.

— The Wall Street Journal Interactive Edition, 1997. (Illus.). 25p. 1998. pap. 295.00 (*1-892815-19-2*) Patricia Seybold.

Bock, Geoffrey E., jt. auth. see Marca, David A.

Bock, Gisela & James, Susan, eds. Beyond Equality & Difference: Citizenship, Feminist Politics & Female Subjectivity. 240p. (C). 1992. pap. 24.99 (*0-415-07989-6*, A7948) Routledge.

— Beyond Equality & Difference: Citizenship, Feminist Politics & Female Subjectivity. 288p. (C). (gr. 13). 1992. text 59.95 (*0-415-07988-8*, A7944) Routledge.

Bock, Glenn H., et al. A Parent's Guide to Kidney Disorders. LC 92-35697. (Guides to Birth & Childhood Disorders Ser.). (Illus.). 188p. (C). 1993. 18.95 (*0-8166-1745-7*) U of Minn Pr.

Bock, Gregory & Goode, Jamie. Novartis Foundation Symposium 215: Immunological Tolerance, Vol. 215. LC 98-14471. (Novartis Foundation Symposium Ser.). 248p. 1998. 128.00 (*0-471-97843-4*) Wiley.

— Sensory Guidance of Movement, Vol. 218. LC 98-38056. (Novartis Foundation Symposium Ser.). 354p. 1998. 128.00 (*0-471-98262-8*) Wiley.

***Bock, Gregory, et al.** The Limits of Reductionism in Biology. LC 98-2779. (Novartis Foundation Symposium Ser.: Vol. 213). 238p. 1998. 128.00 (*0-471-97770-5*) Wiley.

Bock, Gregory, et al. Plasminogen-Related Growth Factors, Vol. 212. LC 97-34811. (Ciba Foundation Symposium Ser.). 268p. 1998. 128.00 (*0-471-97456-0*) Wiley.

Bock, Gregory R. & Ackrill, Kate, eds. The Origins & Development of High Ability: Symposium No. 178. LC 93-29488. (CIBA Foundation Symposium Ser.: Vol. 178). 266p. 1993. 134.95 (*0-471-93945-5*) Wiley.

Bock, Gregory R. & Cardew, Gail, eds. Olfaction in Mosquito-Host Interactions - Symposium No. 200. LC 96-15908. (Ciba Foundation Symposium Ser.: Vol. 200). 342p. 1996. 128.00 (*0-471-96362-3*) Wiley.

Bock, Gregory R. & Goode, Jamie. The Molecular Basis of Cellular Defence Mechanisms. LC 96-43728. (Ciba Foundation Symposium Ser.: Vol. 204). 260p. 1997. 128.00 (*0-471-96567-7*) Wiley.

Bock, Gregory R. & Goode, Jamie A., eds. Growth Factors As Drugs for Neurological & Sensory Disorders. LC 95-48131. (Ciba Foundation Symposium Ser.: Vol. 196). 264p. 1996. 128.00 (*0-471-95721-6*) Wiley.

— Higher-Order Processing in the Visual System, No. 29-6. LC 94-13268. (Ciba Foundation Symposium Ser.: Vol. 184). 256p. 1994. 135.00 (*0-471-94412-2*) Wiley.

Bock, Gregory R. & Widdows, Kate, eds. Polyfunctional Cytokines: IL-6 & LIF. LC 92-5732. (CIBA Foundation Symposium Ser.: Vol. 167). 290p. 1992. 128.00 (*0-471-93439-9*) Wiley.

Bock, H. The HMO Model & Its Application, 3 vols. Incl. Vol. 1. Basis & Manipulation. Heilbronner, E. 454p. 1976. 50.00 (*3-527-25654-7*, Wiley-VCH); Vol. 2. Problems with Solutions. Heilbronner, E. 449p. 1976. 44.00 (*3-527-25655-5*, Wiley-VCH); Vol. 3. Tables of Huckel Molecular Orbitals. Heilbronner, Edgar. 190p. 1976. 28.00 (*3-527-25656-3*, Wiley-VCH); 1976. 50.00 (*0-685-05247-8*, Wiley-VCH) Wiley.

Bock, H. D., et al, eds. Protein Metabolism in Farm Animals: Evaluation, Digestion, Absorption, & Metabolism. (Illus.). 464p. 1990. 115.00 (*0-19-854251-8*) OUP.

***Bock, H. H. & Diday, E., eds.** Analysis of Symbolic Data: Exploratory Methods for Extracting Statistical Information from Complex Data. LC 99-89233. (Studies in Classification, Data Analysis & Knowledge Organization). xviii, 425p. 2000. pap. 82.95 (*3-540-66619-2*) Spr-Verlag.

Bock, Hal. David Robinson. LC 96-34637. (Basketball Legends Ser.). (Illus.). 64p. (J). (gr. 3 up). 1997. lib. bdg. 15.95 (*0-7910-4387-8*) Chelsea Hse.

— Steve Young. LC 95-18222. (Football Legends Ser.). (Illus.). 96p. (J). (gr. 3 up). 1996. lib. bdg. 15.95 (*0-7910-2499-7*) Chelsea Hse.

Bock, Hans G., et al, eds. Enumath 97: Proceedings of the 2nd European Conference on Numerical Mathematics & Advanced Applications. 800p. 1998. 128.00 (*981-02-3546-1*) World Scientific Pub.

Bock, Hans-Hermann, et al, eds. Information Systems & Data Analysis: Prospects, Foundations, Applications. LC 94-17910. (Studies in Classification, Data Analysis, & Knowledge Organization). 1994. 99.00 (*0-387-58057-3*) Spr-Verlag.

Bock, Hans-Hermann & Polasek, Wolfgang, eds. Data Analysis & Information Systems: Statistical & Conceptual Approaches: Proceedings of the 19th Annual Conference of the Gesellschaft fur Klassifikation E. V., University of Basel, March 8-10, 1995. LC 96-33740. (Studies in Classification, Data Analysis, & Knowledge Organization Ser.). (Illus.). 548p. 1996. pap. text 127.00 (*3-540-60774-9*) Spr-Verlag.

Bock, Hans-Manfred, jt. ed. see Grunewald, Michel.

Bock, Hans-Michael. Lexikon Filmschauspieler International. (GER.). 850p. 1994. 135.00 (*0-7859-8549-2*, 3894871997) Fr & Eur.

Bock, Harold De, see Weaver, David H. & Wilhoit, G. Cleveland.

Bock, Harold De, see Wilhoit, G. Cleveland.

Bock, Harold De, see Weaver, David & Wilhoit, G. Cleveland.

Bock, Hedwig & Wertheim, Albert, eds. Essays on Contemporary British Drama. 310p. (C). 1981. pap. 29.95 (*3-19-002214-3*) Adlers Foreign Bks.

Bock, Hedwig & Werthrim, Albert, eds. Essays on Contemporary American Drama. 302p. (Orig.). (C). 1981. pap. 36.95 (*3-19-002232-1*) Adlers Foreign Bks.

Bock, I. R., et al. Elsevier's Dictionary of European Community Company, Business, Financial Law. (DAN, ENG & GEH.). 552p. 1997. 187.00 (*0-444-81783-2*) Elsevier.

Bock, Jane H. Evolutionary Ecology of Plants. 600p. (C). 1990. pap. 750.00 (*81-7089-131-0*, Pub. by Intl Bk Distr) St Mut.

Bock, Jane H., jt. auth. see Bock, Carl E.

Bock, Jason. Visual Basic 6 Win 32 API Tutorial. 450p. 1998. pap. 49.99 (*1-86100-243-2*, Pub. by Wrox Press) Wrox Pr Inc.

Bock, Joanne. Ethnic Vision: A Romanian American Inheritance. LC 96-54007. (Illus.). 384p. 1997. 49.95 (*0-87081-396-X*) Univ Pr Colo.

— Pop Wiener: Naive Painter. LC 72-90409. (Illus.). 176p. 1974. lib. bdg. 25.00 (*0-87023-122-7*) U of Mass Pr.

Bock, John C. & Papagiannis, George J. The Demystification of Nonformal Education. (Issue Paper Ser.: No. 1). 35p. (Orig.). (C). 1976. pap. 3.00 (*0-932288-37-5*) Ctr Intl Ed U of MA.

Bock, John C. & Papagiannis, George J., eds. Nonformal Education & National Development: A Critical Assessment of Policy, Research, & Practice. LC 83-4031. (Praeger Studies in Comparative Education). 390p. 1983. 38.95 (*0-275-90949-2*, C0949, Praeger Pubs) Greenwood.

Bock, Joseph G. The White House Staff & The National Security Assistant: Friendship & Friction at the Water's Edge. LC 86-29619. (Contributions in Political Science Ser.: No. 170). 226p. 1987. 59.95 (*0-313-25698-5*, BFF, Greenwood Pr) Greenwood.

Bock, Judy & Kranz, Rachel. Scholastic Encyclopedia of the United States. LC 96-39774. (Illus.). 144p. (J). (gr. 3-7). 1997. 17.95 (*0-590-94747-8*) Scholastic Inc.

Bock, K. W., et al, eds. Hepatic Metabolism & Disposition of Endo- & Xenobiotics. (Falk Symposium Ser.). xii, 324 p. (C). 1991. text 225.50 (*0-7923-8953-0*) Kluwer Academic.

Bock, Kenneth. Human Nature Mythology. LC 93-24318. 144p. 1994. text 27.95 (*0-252-02072-3*); pap. text 12.95 (*0-252-06365-1*) U of Ill Pr.

Bock, Kenneth & Sabin, Nellie. The Road to Immunity: How to Survive & Thrive in a Toxic World. LC 97-18169. 1997. per. 14.00 (*0-671-54507-8*, PB Trade Paper) PB.

Bock, Lois & Bock, Fred. Creating Four-Part Harmony. LC 89-81184. 208p. 1989. pap. 14.95 (*0-916642-40-2*, 964) Hope Pub.

Bock, Lynn N., jt. auth. see Daniel, Larry J.

Bock, M. Technology Essentials. 106p. (C). 1998. pap. text 24.00 (*1-58076-049-X*) Que Educ & Trng.

Bock, Martin. Crossing the Shadow-Line: The Literature of Estrangement. LC 88-25075. 180p. reprint ed. pap. 55.80 (*0-608-09655-5*, 206977000006) Bks Demand.

An Asterisk (*) at the beginning of an entry indicates that the title is appearing for the first time.

— Ihr aber, wer sgt ihr, dafs ich sei? (Mark 8, 29) (Beitra Zur Theologischen Urteilsbildung Ser.: Vol. 4). 328p. 1998. 51.95 (*3-631-31895-2*) P Lang Pubng.

Bock, Michael, jt. ed. see Rickheit, Gert.

***Bock, Nadine.** Rechtliche Voraussetzungen der Organentnahme von Lebenden und Verstorbenen: Eine Juristische Untersuchung, Basierend Auf Den Medizinischen Grundlagen der Organtransplantation, Unter Besonderer Berucksichtigung der Aktuellen Rechtspolitischen und Rechtsethischen Diskussion. (Europaische Hochschulschriften Ser: Bd. 2625). 308p. 1999. 52.95 (*3-631-34812-6*) P Lang Pubng.

Bock, P. The Emergence of Artificial Cognition: An Introduction to Collective Learning. 344p. 1994. text 74.00 (*981-02-1169-4*); pap. text 37.00 (*981-02-1170-8*) World Scientific Pub.

Bock, Philip K. Handbook of Psychological Anthropology. LC 93-43434. 432p. 1994. lib. bdg. 105.00 (*0-313-28433-4*, Greenwood Pr) Greenwood.

Bock, Philip K. Rethinking Psychological Anthropology: Continuity & Change in the Study of Human Action. 2nd ed. LC 99-234450. 309p. (C). 1999. pap. 17.95 (*1-57766-055-2*) Waveland Pr.

Bock, Philip K., et al, eds. Psychological Anthropology. LC 93-43434. 432p. 1994. pap. 32.50 (*0-275-94956-7*) Greenwood.

Bock, R. Darrell. Multivariate Statistical Methods in Behavioral Research. 2nd ed. 1985. pap. 40.00 (*0-89498-014-9*) Sci Ware.

Bock, R. Darrell, ed. Multilevel Analysis of Educational Data. 354p. 1989. text 94.95 (*0-12-108840-5*) Acad Pr.

Bock, R. Darrell & Moore, Elsie G. Advantage & Disadvantage: A Profile of American Youth. 240p. (C). 1986. text 49.95 (*0-89859-686-6*) L Erlbaum Assocs.

Bock, R. Darrell, et al. AUXAL: Auxological Analysis of Longitudinal Measurements of Human Sature. 1994. 30.00 (*0-89498-036-X*) Sci Ware.

Bock, R. Darrell, jt. auth. see Finn, Jeremy D.

Bock, R. Darrell, jt. auth. see Mislevy, Robert.

Bock, R. Darrell, jt. auth. see Muraki, Eiji.

***Bock, R. K.** Data Analysis Techniques for High-Energy Physics. 2nd ed. LC 99-20207. 2000. write for info. (*0-521-63219-6*) Cambridge U Pr.

Bock, R. K. & Krischer, W. The Data Analysis BriefBook. (Accelerator Physics Ser.). (Illus.). iv, 180p. 1998. 29.95 (*3-540-64119-X*) Spr-Verlag.

Bock, R. K. & Vasilescu, A. The Particle Detector BriefBook. (Accelerator Physics Ser.). (Illus.). v, 126p. 1998. 29.95 (*3-540-64120-3*) Spr-Verlag.

Bock, Richard. Tu-16 Badger in Action. (Aircraft in Action Ser.). (Illus.). 50p. 1990. pap. 9.95 (*0-89747-252-7*, 1108) Squad Sig Pubns.

Bock, Richard D. & Jones, Lyle V. The Measurement & Prediction of Judgment & Choice. LC 66-17897. (Holden-Day Series in Psychology). 384p. reprint ed. pap. 119.10 (*0-608-13403-1*, 205574300034) Bks Demand.

Bock, S. Allan. Food Allergy: A Primer for People. LC 83-72531. 72p. 1983. pap. 5.00 (*0-9612332-0-6*) AJ Pub Co.

Bock, Steven J., et al. Natural Relief for Your Child's Asthma: A Guide to Controlling Asthma & Reducing Your Child's. LC 98-43771. (Illus.). 304p. 1999. pap. 13.95 (*0-06-095289-X*) HarpC.

Bock, Steven J., jt. auth. see Mitchell, Deborah.

***Bock, Susan.** Through a Child's Eyes: Creative Resources for the Whole Church. 112p. 2000. pap. 13.95 (*0-8192-1840-5*, 6285) Morehouse Pub.

Bock, T. A., et al. Hematopoietic Stem Cells, Vol. 15, Supplement 1. LC 97-73748. 308p. 1997. 69.00 (*1-880854-23-6*) AlphaMed Pr.

Bock, Wally. Getting on the Information Superhighway: Benefitting from on-Line Services. Henry, Carol, ed. LC 95-68991. (On-Line Ser.). 134p. (Orig.). 1995. pap. 12.95 (*1-56052-327-1*) Crisp Pubns.

Bock, Wally & Senne, Jeff. Net Income: Cut Costs, Boost Profits, & Enhance Operations Online. LC 97-216306. 250p. 1997. pap. 29.95 (*0-442-02558-0*, VNR) Wiley.

Bock, Wally & Senne, Jeff. Net Income: Cut Costs, Boost Profits, & Enhance Operations Online. 320p. 1997. pap. 29.95 (*0-471-28839-X*, VNR) Wiley.

Bock, Walter J., jt. auth. see Richards, Lawrence P.

Bock-Weiss, Catherine C. Henri Matisse: A Guide to Research. Freitag, Wolfgang, ed. LC 96-19440. (Artist Resource Manuals Ser.: Vol. 1). 792p. 1996. text 95.00 (*0-8153-0086-7*, H1424) Garland.

Bock, William, jt. auth. see Carroll, Charles.

Bock, William Sauts. The First Americans Coloring Book. (Illus.). 64p. (J). pap. 4.95 (*0-912608-04-8*) Mid Atlantic.

Bock, Y., et al, eds. Global Positioning System: An Overview. (International Association of Geodesy Symposia Ser.: Vol. 102). xii, 447p. 1990. pap. 64.00 (*0-387-97266-8*) Spr-Verlag.

Bockanov, Alexander. The Romanovs: Love, Power & Tragedy. (Illus.). 321p. 1996. 69.95 (*0-9521644-0-X*, Pub. by Leppi Pubns) BookWorld.

Bockarev, S. V. Method of Averaging in the Theory of Orthogonal Series, & Some Problems in the Theory of Bases. LC 80-26300. (Proceedings of the Steklov Institute of Mathematics Ser.: No. 146). 92p. 1980. pap. 47.00 (*0-8218-3045-7*, STEKLO/146) Am Math.

Bockelman, Karen. Gathered & Sent: An Introduction to Worship, Participant Book Edition. 64p. 1999. pap. 5.99 (*0-8066-3844-3*, 3-80, Augsburg) Augsburg Fortress.

Bockelman, Wilfred. Finding the Right Words: Offering Care & Comfort When You Don't Know What to Say. LC 89-14975. 80p. 1990. pap. 5.99 (*0-8066-2444-2*, 9-2444, Augsburg) Augsburg Fortress.

— For Such a Time As This: Commemorating Seventy-Five Years of God's Activity at Mount Olivet Lutheran Church. 144p. 1994. 24.30 (*0-9642005-0-3*) Mt Olivet Lutheran.

***Bockelman, Wilfred & Minnesota Center for Corporate Responsibility Staff.** Culture of Corporate Citizenship: Minnesota's Business Legacy for the Global Future. LC 99-38725. 1999. write for info. (*1-880090-92-9*) Galde Pr.

Bockelmann, Christine, jt. auth. see Norris, Floyd.

Bockemuehl, Eugene D. On the Road with the Jimmy Dorsey Aggravation: 1947-1949. Kader, Don, ed. LC 96-77334. (Illus.). v, 135p. (Orig.). 1996. pap. 14.95 (*0-9653272-0-5*) Gray Castle.

Bockemuehl, Joyce M., ed. & frwd. see Holmes, Anne L.

Bockemuhl, Erich. Niederrheinisches Sagenbuch. (GER.). 286p. 1997. reprint ed. write for info. (*3-487-05972-X*) G Olms Pubs.

Bockemuhl, Jochen. In Partnership with Nature. (Illus.). 84p. pap. 19.00 (*0-938250-17-5*) Bio-Dynamic Farm.

— Metamorphosis of Plants. 1997. pap. text 10.95 (*0-9583885-2-0*, Pub. by Novalis Trust) Anthroposophic.

Bockemuhl, Jochen, et al. Toward a Phenomenology of the Etheric World: Investigations into the Life of Nature & Man. Gardner, Malcolm & Davy, John, eds. Meeks, John, tr. from GER. (Illus.). 200p. 1985. pap. 16.95 (*0-88010-115-6*) Anthroposophic.

Bockemuhl, M. Turner. 1994. pap. 9.99 (*3-8228-0554-8*) Taschen Amer.

Bockemuhl, Michael. Turner. (SPA.). 1996. pap. 9.99 (*3-8228-0669-2*) Taschen Amer.

Bockemuhl, U. Rembrandt. 1994. pap. 9.99 (*3-8228-0559-9*) Taschen Amer.

Bocken, Hubert & Ryckbost, D. Codification of Environmental Law Draft Decree on Environmental Policy: Prepared by Interuniversity Commission for the Revision of Environmental Law in the Flemish Region. LC 96-9506. (Nijhoff Law Specials Ser.). 1996. pap. 150.00 (*90-411-0911-0*) Kluwer Law Intl.

Bockenforde, Ernst-Wolfgang. State, Society & Liberty: Studies in Political Theory & Constitutional Law. Underwood, J. A., tr. from GER. LC 90-37046. (State, Law & Society Ser.). 266p. 1991. 19.95 (*0-85496-595-5*) Berg Pubs.

***Bocker, Manfred.** Antisemitismus ohne Juden: Die Zweite Republik, die antirepublikanische Rechte und die Juden. Spanien 1931 bis 1936. 2000. 52.95 (*3-631-36152-1*) P Lang Pubng.

Bocker, Martin. The Social Psychological Analysis of Attitudes Towards the European Community. LC 92-10902. (European University Studies: Psychology: Ser. 6, Vol. 367). (Illus.). XII, 461p. 1992. 72.00 (*3-631-44940-2*) P Lang Pubng.

Bocker, P. ISDN - The Integrated Services Digital Network. (Illus.). 260p. 1988. 79.00 (*0-387-17446-X*) Spr-Verlag.

— ISDN - The Integrated Services Digital Network. 2nd ed. (Illus.). 280p. 1992. 118.95 (*0-387-54819-X*) Spr-Verlag.

Bocker, Paul. Lost Illusions: Latin American's Struggle for Democracy, as Recounted by Its Leaders. Boeker, Paul H., ed. 360p. 1990. pap. text 12.95 (*1-55876-024-5*) Wiener Pubs Inc.

Bocker, W., jt. auth. see Schmid, Kurt W.

Bockhoff, Esther. Africa, Land of Diversity: An Ethnographic Exhibit at the Cleveland Museum of Natural History, March 4-October 31, 1977. (Illus.). 64p. (Orig.). 1977. pap. 3.50 (*1-878600-02-8*) Cleve Mus Nat Hist.

Bockhoff, Esther & Fleming, Nancy I. Tribal Traditions of Kenya: Kenyan Arts from the Collection of Irene Sedgwick Briedis. Ireland, Lucy & Platt, Carolyn, eds. (Illus.). 40p. (Orig.). 1986. pap. 7.50 (*1-878600-04-4*) Cleve Mus Nat Hist.

Bockhoff, K. H., ed. Nuclear Data for Science & Technology. 1983. text 389.50 (*90-277-1560-2*) Kluwer Academic.

Bockholt, A. J. World Food & Fiber Crops. 1975. spiral bd. 14.00 (*0-88252-037-7*) Paladin Hse.

Bockholts, P. & Heidebrink, I., eds. Chemical Spills & Emergency Management at Sea. (C). 1989. text 292.50 (*0-7923-0052-1*) Kluwer Academic.

Bockhorn, Henning, ed. Soot Formation in Combustion: Mechanisms & Models. LC 94-40218. (Chemical Physics Ser.: Vol. 59). 1994. 108.95 (*3-540-58398-X*) Spr-Verlag.

Bockhoven, Georgia. The Beach House. LC 99-18703. 1999. 25.95 (*1-57490-178-8*) T T Beeler.

— Things Remembered. LC 99-18705. 1999. 25.95 (*1-57490-195-8*, Beeler LP Bks) T T Beeler.

Bockie, Simon. Death & the Invisible Powers: The World of Kongo Belief. LC 92-30614. 176p. 1993. 35.00 (*0-253-31564-6*); pap. 14.95 (*0-253-20808-4*) Ind U Pr.

Bocking, Brian. The Little Book of Confucian Wisdom. LC 98-20067. (Little Bks.). (Illus.). 48p. 1998. 5.95 (*1-86204-230-6*, Pub. by Element MA) Penguin Putnam.

— Nagarjuna in China: A Translation of the Middle Treatise. LC 94-48168. (Studies in Asian Thought & Religion: Vol. 18). 512p. 1995. text 119.95 (*0-7734-8981-9*) E Mellen.

— A Popular Dictionary of Shinto. LC 97-21947. (Illus.). 288p. 1997. pap. 14.95 (*0-8442-0425-0*, 04250) NTC Contemp Pub Co.

Bocking, Richard C. Mighty River: A Portrait of the Fraser. LC 97-23760. (Illus.). 304p. 1998. 29.95 (*0-295-97670-5*) U of Wash Pr.

Bocking, Stephen. Ecologists & Environmental Politics: A History of Contemporary Ecology. LC 96-3407. 296p. 1997. 35.00 (*0-300-06763-1*) Yale U Pr.

Bocking, Stephen, ed. Biodiversity in Canada: An Introduction to Environmental Ethics. 400p. 2000. pap. 24.95 (*1-55111-238-8*) Broadview Pr.

Bockisch, Michael, ed. Fats & Oils Handbook: Nahrungsfette und Ole. LC 98-11974. Orig. Title: Nahrungsfette und-Ole: Handbuch der Lebensmittel-Technologie. (Illus.). 848p. 1998. lib. bdg. 180.00 (*0-935315-82-9*, PC115) Am Oil Chemists.

Bockl, George. God Beyond Religion: Personal Journeyings from Religiosity to Spirituality. LC 88-51337. 184p. (Orig.). 1989. pap. 10.95 (*0-87516-612-1*) DeVorss.

— How to Find Something Big to Live for: A Spirital Odyssey. 193p. (Orig.). 1984. pap. 7.95 (*0-942494-83-0*) Coleman Pub.

— Living Beyond Success: Balancing the Secular & Spiritual Aspects of Life. 160p. (Orig.). 1993. pap. 10.95 (*0-87516-662-8*) DeVorss.

***Bockl, George.** Where Did We Come from & Where Are We Going? In Search of a Road to Universal Spirituality. LC 99-76973. 250p. 2000. pap. 12.95 (*0-87516-732-2*) DeVorss.

Bockle, Gunther. Exploitation of Fine-Grain Parallelism. Goos, G. & Hartmanis, J., eds. LC 95-30348. (Lecture Notes in Computer Science Ser.: Vol. 942). ix, 188p. 1995. pap. 36.00 (*3-540-60054-X*) Spr-Verlag.

Bockman, Gwen & Fitting, Jana. Hey Babysitter, Let's Play! A Guide to Fun & Games for Babysitters. (Illus.). 128p. (J). 1990. pap. 11.95 (*0-923889-57-4*); spiral bd. 12.95 (*0-923889-64-7*) Inquisitors Pub.

Bockman, John F. Secular Humanism: An Orthodox Perspective. LC 90-63251. iv, 84 p. (Orig.). 1991. pap. 8.00 (*0-913026-73-5*) St Nectarios.

Bockman, Marc, jt. auth. see Pennington, Randy.

***Bockmiller, Stephen R. & Bopp, Lawrence J.** USS Constellation: An Illustrated History. (Civil War History Ser.). (Illus.). 128p. 2000. pap. 18.99 (*0-7385-0582-X*) Arcadia Publng.

Bockmon, Guy A. Madison Station. LC 97-74195. (Illus.). 192p. 1997. 29.95 (*1-57736-057-5*, Hillsboro Pr) Providence Hse.

Bockmuehl, Klaus. Books: God's Tools in the History of Salvation. 45p. 1992. 3.00 (*1-882840-00-3*) Comm Christian.

— The Christian Way of Living: An Ethics of the Ten Commandments. 147p. 1994. reprint ed. pap. 15.95 (*1-57383-023-2*) Regent College.

— Listening to the God Who Speaks: Reflections on God's Guidance from Scripture & the Lives of God's People. 176p. (Orig.). 1990. pap. 15.95 (*0-939443-18-X*) Helmers Howard Pub.

— The Unreal God of Modern Theology: Bultmann, Barth, & the Theology of Atheism: a Call to Recovering the Truth of God's Reality. Bromiley, Geoffrey W., tr. from GER. LC 88-24679. 192p. (Orig.). 1988. pap. 18.95 (*0-939443-11-2*) Helmers Howard Pub.

Bockmuehl, Klaus E. The Challenge of Marxism. 190p. (C). 1986. reprint ed. pap. 15.95 (*0-939443-00-7*) Helmers Howard Pub.

— Living by the Gospel: Christian Roots of Confidence & Purpose. LC 86-27124. 120p. (C). 1986. 17.95 (*0-939443-01-5*) Helmers Howard Pub.

Bockmuehl, Markus. Epistle to the Philippians. LC 98-11562. (Black's New Testament Commentary Ser.: Vol. 11). 328p. 1998. 24.95 (*1-56563-350-4*) Hendrickson MA.

— This Jesus: Martyr, Lord, Messiah. LC 96-11251. 252p. 1996. pap. 17.99 (*0-8308-1875-8*) InterVarsity.

Bockmuehl, Markus & Thompson, Michael, eds. A Vision for the Church: Studies in Early Christian Ecclesiology. 1997. 45.95 (*0-567-08573-2*, Pub. by T & T Clark) Bks Intl VA.

Bockmuehl, Markus & Thompson, Michael B., eds. A Vision for the Church: Studies in Early Christian Ecclesiology. 262p. pap. 29.95 (*0-567-08579-1*) T&T Clark Pubs.

Bockmuehl, Markus, tr. see Stemberger, Gunter.

Bocknath, Mark F., jt. auth. see Yount, Sylvia.

Bocknek, Gene. Ego & Self in Weekly Psychotherapy. LC 90-4923. 360p. 1991. 55.00 (*0-8236-1545-6*) Intl Univs Pr.

— The Young Adult: Development after Adolescence. LC 85-29202. 232p. 1986. pap. 19.95 (*0-89876-129-5*) Gardner Pr.

Bocknek, Jonathan, ed. see Bullard, Jean.

Bockol, Leslie. Victorian Majolica: With Price Guide. LC 95-45611. (Books for Collectors Ser.). (Illus.). 192p. 1996. 39.95 (*0-88740-953-9*) Schiffer.

— Willow Ware: Ceramics in the Chinese Tradition: With Price Guide. LC 94-42662. (Illus.). 160p. (Orig.). 1995. pap. 29.95 (*0-88740-720-X*) Schiffer.

Bockol, Leslie, jt. auth. see Snyder, Jeffrey B.

Bockol, Leslie, tr. see Kjellberg, Pierre.

Bockoras, Betty. Listen... Dad's Calling. iv, 126p. 1998. pap. 5.75 (*0-9669213-0-5*) Joy of Life.

Bockoven, Georgia. The Beach House. 432p. 1997. mass mkt. 6.50 (*0-06-108440-9*, Harp PBks) HarpC.

***Bockoven, Georgia.** Disguised Blessing. 400p. 2000. mass mkt. 6.50 (*0-06-103020-1*) HarpC.

— Disguised Blessing. large type ed. LC 00-40423. (Large Print Book Ser.). 2000. write for info. (*1-56895-913-3*) Wheeler Pub.

— Far from Home. LC 99-54227. 1999. 26.95 (*1-57490-246-6*, Beeler LP Bks) T T Beeler.

Bockrat, Mark, jt. auth. see Foster, Kathleeen A.

Bockrath, Joseph T. Contracts & the Legal Environment for Engineers & Architects. 5th ed. 672p. (C). 1994. 97.50 (*0-07-018239-6*) McGraw.

***Bockrath, Joseph T.** Contracts & the Legal Environment for Engineers & Architects. 6th ed. LC 99-15562. 2000. write for info. (*0-07-039363-X*) McGrw-H Hghr Educ.

Bockrath, Tina, ed. see Truman, Karol K.

Bockris, J. O. & Khan, S. U. Surface Electrochemistry: A Molecular Level Approach. (Illus.). 1046p. (C). 1993. text 47.50 (*0-306-44339-2*, Kluwer Plenum) Kluwer Academic.

Bockris, J. O. & Khan, S. U. Surface Electrochemistry: A Molecular Level Approach. (Illus.). 1046p. (C). 1993. 85.00 (*0-306-44298-1*, Plenum Trade) Perseus Pubng.

Bockris, J. O. & Reddy, A. K. Modern Electrochemistry: An Introduction to an Interdisciplinary Area, Vol. 2. LC 68-19518. (Illus.). 810p. (C). 1970. text 47.00 (*0-306-25002-0*, Kluwer Plenum) Kluwer Academic.

— Modern Electrochemistry 1: Ionics. 2nd ed. LC 97-24151. (Illus.). 666p. (C). 1998. 95.00 (*0-306-45554-4*, Plenum Trade) Perseus Pubng.

Bockris, J. O., et al. Comprehensive Treatise of Electrochemistry, Vol. 9. (Illus.). 467p. (C). 1984. text 156.00 (*0-306-41570-4*, Kluwer Plenum) Kluwer Academic.

— Comprehensive Treatise of Electrochemistry Vol. 7: Kinetics & Mechanisms of Electrode Processes. LC 83-17831. (Illus.). 806p. (C). 1983. text 180.00 (*0-306-41152-0*, Kluwer Plenum) Kluwer Academic.

— Comprehensive Treatise of Electrochemistry Vol. 8: Experimental Methods in Electrochemistry. (Illus.). 638p. (C). 1984. text 168.00 (*0-306-41448-1*, Kluwer Plenum) Kluwer Academic.

— Comprehensive Treatise of Electrochemistry Vol. 10: Bioelectrochemistry. (Illus.). 566p. (C). 1985. text 156.00 (*0-306-41541-0*, Kluwer Plenum) Kluwer Academic.

— Modern Aspects of Electrochemistry, Vol. 22. (Illus.). 566p. (C). 1992. text 138.00 (*0-306-44061-X*, Kluwer Plenum) Kluwer Academic.

— Modern Aspects of Electrochemistry, Vol. 25. (Illus.). 336p. (C). 1994. text 110.00 (*0-306-44375-9*, Kluwer Plenum) Kluwer Academic.

— Modern Aspects of Electrochemistry, Vol. 29. (Illus.). 453p. (C). 1996. text 132.00 (*0-306-45162-X*, Kluwer Plenum) Kluwer Academic.

— Modern Aspects of Electrochemistry, Vol. 31. (Illus.). 364p. (C). 1998. text 132.00 (*0-306-45650-8*, Kluwer Plenum) Kluwer Academic.

Bockris, John O., ed. Modern Aspects of Electrochemistry, Vol. 2. LC 54-12732. (Modern Aspect Series of Chemistry). 426p. reprint ed. pap. 132.10 (*0-608-08103-5*, 202576500002) Bks Demand.

— Modern Aspects of Electrochemistry, Vol. 3. LC 54-12732. 465p. reprint ed. pap. 144.20 (*0-608-08104-3*, 202576500003) Bks Demand.

Bockris, John O., et al, eds. Comprehensive Treatise of Electrochemistry Vol. 1: The Double Layer. LC 80-21493. (Illus.). 472p. (C). 1980. text 156.00 (*0-306-40275-0*, Kluwer Plenum) Kluwer Academic.

— Comprehensive Treatise of Electrochemistry Vol. 2: Electrochemical Processing. LC 80-24836. 638p. 1981. 139.50 (*0-306-40503-2*, Plenum Trade) Perseus Pubng.

— Comprehensive Treatise of Electrochemistry Vol. 3: Electrochemical Energy Conversion & Storage. LC 81-2175. (Illus.). 562p. (C). 1981. text 156.00 (*0-306-40590-3*, Kluwer Plenum) Kluwer Academic.

— Comprehensive Treatise of Electrochemistry Vol. 6: Electrodics-Transport. LC 82-13144. (Illus.). 546p. (C). 1982. text 156.00 (*0-306-40942-9*, Kluwer Plenum) Kluwer Academic.

— Modern Aspects of Electrochemistry, Vol. 14. LC 54-12732. 678p. (C). 1982. 125.00 (*0-306-40845-7*, Plenum Trade) Perseus Pubng.

— Modern Aspects of Electrochemistry, Vol. 17. LC 54-12732. 508p. 1986. 115.00 (*0-306-42149-6*, Plenum Trade) Perseus Pubng.

— Modern Aspects of Electrochemistry, Vol. 20. (Illus.). 532p. (C). 1989. text 138.00 (*0-306-43127-0*, Kluwer Plenum) Kluwer Academic.

Bockris, John O. & Conway, B. E., eds. Modern Aspects of Electrochemistry, Vol. 1. LC 54-12732. (Modern Aspect Series of Chemistry). 354p. reprint ed. pap. 109.80 (*0-608-08102-7*, 202576500001) Bks Demand.

— Modern Aspects of Electrochemistry, Vol. 4. LC 54-12732. (Modern Aspect Series of Chemistry). 325p. reprint ed. pap. 100.80 (*0-608-08105-1*, 202576500004) Bks Demand.

— Modern Aspects of Electrochemistry, Vol. 5. LC 54-12732. (Modern Aspect Series of Chemistry). 509p. reprint ed. pap. 157.80 (*0-608-08106-X*, 202576500005) Bks Demand.

— Modern Aspects of Electrochemistry, Vol. 6. LC 54-12732. (Modern Aspect Series of Chemistry). 395p. reprint ed. pap. 122.50 (*0-608-08107-8*, 202576500006) Bks Demand.

— Modern Aspects of Electrochemistry, Vol. 7. LC 54-12732. (Modern Aspect Series of Chemistry). 424p. reprint ed. pap. 131.50 (*0-608-08108-6*, 202576500007) Bks Demand.

— Modern Aspects of Electrochemistry, Vol. 8. LC 54-12732. (Modern Aspect Series of Chemistry). 357p. reprint ed. pap. 110.70 (*0-608-08109-4*, 202576500008) Bks Demand.

Bockris, John O. & Fredlein, Ronald A. A Workbook of Electrochemistry. LC 72-83606. 187p. 1973. reprint ed. pap. 58.00 (*0-608-05409-7*, 206587800006) Bks Demand.

Bockris, John O. & Reddy, Amulya K. Modern Electrochemistry 1: Ionics. 2nd ed. LC 97-24151. (Illus.). 824p. (C). 1998. pap. text 49.50 (*0-306-45555-2*, Kluwer Plenum) Kluwer Academic.

Bockris, John O. & White, J. L., eds. Physicochemical Measurements at High Temperatures. LC QD0515.P54. 402p. reprint ed. pap. 124.70 (*0-608-10166-4*, 205133200001) Bks Demand.

Bockris, John O., jt. auth. see McGown, Linda B.

Bockris, John O., jt. ed. see White, Ralph E.

B

*__Bockris, Victor.__ Beat Punks. (Illus.). 2000. pap. 16.00 (*0-306-80939-7*) Da Capo.

Bockris, Victor. Keith Richards: The Biography. LC 97-49994. (Illus.). 416p. 1998. reprint ed. pap. 15.95 (*0-306-80815-3*) Da Capo.

— The Life & Death of Andy Warhol: The Biography. LC 97-16881. (Illus.). 570p. 1997. reprint ed. pap. 17.95 (*0-306-80795-5*) Da Capo.

*__Bockris, Victor.__ Muhammad Ali: In Fighter's Heaven. (Illus.). 2000. pap. write for info. (*0-8154-1062-X*, Pub. by Cooper Sq) Natl Bk Netwk.

Bockris, Victor & Bayley, Roberta. Patti Smith: An Unauthorized Biography. LC 99-29435. (Illus.). 336p. 1999. 24.50 (*0-684-82363-2*) S&S Trade.

Bockris, Victor & Malanga, Gerard. Uptight: The Velvet Underground Story. (Illus.). 208p. pap. 16.95 (*0-7119-5223-X*, OP 47794) Omnibus NY.

Bockris, Victor, ed. see Harry, Debbie.

Bocks, P. & Prasad, B., eds. Engineering Data Management: Integrating the Engineering Enterprise: Proceedings of the ASME Database Symposium, Minneapolis, MN, 1994. 163p. 1994. pap. 163.00 (*0-7918-1281-2*) ASME.

Bockstael, Eric, ed. Handicap & Politics. (Studies in Pedagogy, Andragogy & Gerontagogy: Vol. 26). xiv, 225p. 1995. pap. 44.95 (*3-631-48763-0*) P Lang Pubng.

Bockstiegel, Karl H., jt. auth. see Institute of International Business Law & Practice.

Bockstiegel, Karl-Heinz. Space Law: Basic Legal Documents - Installment 5. 416p. (C). 1993. lib. bdg. 205.00 (*0-7923-2060-3*) Kluwer Academic.

— Space Law: Changes & Expectations at the Turn to Commercial Space Activities. (Forum Internationale Ser.: No. 8). 1987. 24.00 (*90-6544-256-1*) Kluwer Law Intl.

Bockstiegel, Karl-Heinz, ed. Space Law: Basic Legal Documents - Third Supplement. (C). 1991. lib. bdg. 210.00 (*0-7923-0556-6*) Kluwer Academic.

Bockstiegel, Karl-Heinz & Benko, Marietta. Space Law: Basic Legal Documents - First Supplement. (C). 1990. pap. text 165.00 (*0-7923-0554-X*) Kluwer Academic.

Bockstiegel, Karl-Heinz & Benko, Marietta, eds. Space Law: Basic Legal Documents - Basic Works. (C). 1990. pap. text 427.50 (*0-7923-0091-2*) Kluwer Academic.

— Space Law: Basic Legal Documents - Second Supplement. (C). 1990. pap. text 324.00 (*0-7923-0555-8*) Kluwer Academic.

Bockstoce, John. The Archaeology of Cape Nome, Alaska. (University Museum Monographs: No. 38). (Illus.). xiii, 133p. (Orig.). (C). 1979. pap. 25.00 (*0-934718-27-X*) U Museum Pubns.

Bockstoce, John R. Whales, Ice, & Men: The History of Whaling in the Western Arctic. LC 85-91266. (Illus.). 400p. 1995. pap. 29.95 (*0-295-97447-8*) U of Wash Pr.

*__Bockstoce, John R. & History Bank Staff.__ Arctic Discoveries: Images from Voyages of Four Decades in the North. LC 00-30236. (Illus.). 128p. 2000. pap. 29.95 (*0-295-98015-X*) U of Wash Pr.

Bockstoce, John R., jt. auth. see Maguire, Rochfort.

Bockstruck, Lloyd D. Research in Texas. LC 92-10706. (Research in the States Ser.). 1992. 6.50 (*0-915156-70-9*) Natl Genealogical.

Bockstruck, Lloyd DeWitt, see DeWitt Bockstruck, Lloyd.

Bockting, Ineke. Character & Personality in the Novels of William Faulkner: A Study in Psychostylistics. 312p. (C). 1995. lib. bdg. 44.00 (*0-8191-9849-8*) U Pr of Amer.

Bockus, Dennis. Insects & Spiders. (Eye to Eye Bks.). (Illus.). 32p. (J). (gr. 1-7). 1998. pap. 9.99 (*1-895897-27-0*) Somerville Hse.

— Insects & Spiders. (Eye To Eye Ser.). (Illus.). 32p. (J). (gr. 4-7). 1999. reprint ed. pap. 9.99 (*1-58184-021-7*) Somerville Hse.

— Snakes & Lizards. (Eye To Eye Ser.). (Illus.). 32p. (J). (gr. 1-7). 1999. pap. 9.99 (*1-58184-022-5*) Somerville Hse.

— Snakes & Lizards. (Eye to Eye Bks.). (Illus.). 32p. (J). (gr. 1-7). 1998. pap. 9.99 (*1-895897-28-9*) Somerville Hse.

Bockus, Frank. Couple Therapy. LC 80-66923. 396p. 1980. 50.00 (*0-87668-412-6*) Aronson.

— Couple Therapy. LC 80-66920. 392p. 1993. pap. 50.00 (*1-56821-101-5*) Aronson.

Bockus, William, Jr. "Boys" LC 95-69380. (Illus.). 192p. (Orig.). (J). (gr. 5-12). 1995. pap. 6.95 (*0-9647151-0-4*) Print Place.

— The Universe: Theoretical Physics & Astronomy for the Young Adult. LC 95-92361. (Illus.). 212p. (J). (gr. 6-12). 1999. pap. 12.00 (*0-9647151-1-2*, Pub. by Print Place) Quality Bks IL.

Bockwinkel, Susan R. The Divine Dance: Prayers from the Heart. Lavitt, Ben, ed. & photos by by. (Illus.). 44p. (Orig.). 1996. pap. 19.95 (*0-9655685-0-4*) Good Medicine.

— Rhiannon: Truth Seeker. Neimark, Paul, ed. 293p. 1996. 25.00 (*0-87418-320-0*) Coleman Pub.

Bocock, Jean & Watson, David, eds. Managing the University Curriculum: Making Common Cause. LC 94-28082. 160p. (Orig.). 1994. 132.00 (*0-335-19340-4*); pap. 34.95 (*0-335-19339-0*) OpUniv Pr.

Bocock, Maclin. A Citizen of the World. LC 98-54309. 208p. 1999. 22.00 (*1-58195-000-4*, Pub. by Zoland Bks) Consort Bk Sales.

— Heaven Lies About: Southern Stories. LC 93-13136. 72p. (Orig.). 1993. pap. 9.00 (*1-880284-02-2*) J Daniel.

Bocock, Peter, jt. auth. see Cortes, Mariluz.

Bocock, Robert. Consumption. LC 93-3444. (Key Ideas Ser.). 144p. (C). 1993. pap. 16.99 (*0-415-06962-9*) Routledge.

Bocock, Robert, ed. Sigmund Freud. (Key Sociologists Ser.). 128p. 1983. pap. 6.95 (*0-85312-580-5*, NO. 3754, Pub. by Tavistock-E Horwood) Routldge.

*__Bocola, Sandro.__ The Art of Modernism: Art, Culture & Society from Goya to the Present Day. (Illus.). 624p. 2000. 35.00 (*3-7913-2146-3*, Pub. by Prestel) te Neues.

Bocola, Sandro, ed. African Seats. LC 96-219783. (Illus.). 208p. 1995. 65.00 (*3-7913-1426-2*, Pub. by Prestel) te Neues.

Bocquet, Gilbert. Revisio Physolychnidum: Silene Subg. Physolychnis. (Phanerogamarum Monographiae: Vol. 1). (Illus.). 1969. 120.00 (*3-7682-0624-6*) Lubrecht & Cramer.

Bocquet, J. L., jt. auth. see Limoge, Y.

Bocsa, Ivan & Karus, Michael. The Cultivation of Hemp: Botany, Varieties, Cultivation & Harvesting.Tr. of Der Hanfanbau: Botanik, Sorten, Anbau & Ernte. (Illus.). 186p. Date not set. pap. 18.95 (*1-886874-03-4*) HEMPTECH.

Boctor, David. Microsoft Office 97-Visual Basic Step by Step. LC 97-8039. 384p. 1997. pap. text 34.99 (*1-57231-389-7*) Microsoft.

*__Boctor, David.__ Microsoft Office 2000 Programming/ mastering Set. 1999. pap. text 99.99 (*0-7356-0815-6*) Microsoft.

Boctor, David. Microsoft Office 2000 Visual Basic Fundamentals. LC 99-20167. 1999. pap. text 39.99 (*0-7356-0594-7*) Microsoft.

Boctor, S. A. Electrical Concepts & Applications. LC 96-33614. (C). 1997. mass mkt. 106.95 (*0-314-20202-1*) West Pub.

Bocuse, Paul. Bocuse's Regional French Cooking. 1997. 19.95 (*0-614-28086-9*, Pub. by Flammarion) Abbeville Pr.

— Bocuse's Regional French Cooking. Curtis, Stephanie, tr. LC 96-51640. (Illus.). 192p. 1997. pap. text 19.95 (*2-08-013641-0*, Pub. by Flammarion) Abbeville Pr.

Boczek, B., ed. The Transfer of Marine Technology to Developing Nations in International Law No. 32: Occasional Paper. 79p. 1982. 3.75 (*0-911189-04-1*) Law Sea Inst.

Boczek, Boleslaw A. Historical Dictionary of International Tribunals. LC 94-15331. (International Organizations Ser.: No. 5). 389p. 1994. 54.00 (*0-8108-2903-7*) Scarecrow.

— Scandinavia: New Focus of Soviet Pressures. (C). 1990. 50.00 (*0-907967-99-X*, Pub. by Inst Euro Def & Strat) St Mut.

Boczek, Boleslaw A., jt. auth. see Bledsoe, Robert L.

Boczko, Faerella & Santo Pietro, Mary J. The Breakfast Club. 64p. (Orig.). 1997. pap. text 25.00 (*0-937857-74-2*) Speech Bin.

Boczko, Faerella, jt. auth. see Santo Pietro, Mary J.

Bod. Beyond Grammar: An Experience-Based Theory of Language. LC 98-26880. (Lecture Notes Ser.: No. 88). 144p. (C). 1998. 59.95 (*1-57586-151-8*, Pub. by CSLI) Cambridge U Pr.

— Beyond Grammar: An Experience-Based Theory of Language: Data Oriented Parsing. LC 98-26880. (Lecture Notes Ser.: No. 88). 144p. (C). 1998. pap. 22.95 (*1-57586-150-X*) CSLI.

Boda, D. & Turi, S., eds. Paediatric Nephrology: A Research Update. (Contributions to Nephrology Ser.: Vol. 67). (Illus.). x, 238p. 1988. 29.75 (*3-8055-4689-0*) S Karger.

Boda, K., ed. Nonconventional Feedstuffs in the Nutrition of Farm Animals. (Developments in Animal & Veterinary Science Ser.: No. 23). 260p. 1990. 154.50 (*0-444-98780-0*) Elsevier.

*__Boda, Mark J.__ Praying the Tradition. LC 99-47146. 1999. 108.35 (*3-11-016433-7*) De Gruyter.

Boda, Yang. Essence of Qing Jades. Gusun, Lu, tr. (CHI., Illus.). 392p. (Orig.). 1994. write for info. (*1-883662-00-1*) Chinese Arts.

*__Bodah, Paula M.__ Rhode Island. (Illus.). 96p. 2000. 12.95 (*0-8109-5569-5*, Pub. by Abrams) Time Warner.

Bodai, Balazs I., ed. Synopsis of Common Surgical Procedures. LC 92-49577. (Illus.). 200p. 1993. pap. text 29.95 (*0-8121-1220-2*) Lppncott W & W.

Bodall, Howard, jt. contrib. by see Allen, Renata.

*__Bodanis, David.__ E=mc2: A Biography of the World's Most Famous Equation. (Illus.). 224p. 2000. 23.00 (*0-8027-1352-1*) Walker & Co.

Bodanis, David. The Secret Family. LC 97-14809. 224p. 1997. 27.00 (*0-684-81019-0*) S&S Trade.

Bodanis, David & Daniel. Secret Family: Twenty Four Hours Inside the Mysterious World of Our Minds & Bodies. 224p. 1999. per. 15.00 (*0-684-84593-8*) S&S Trade.

Bodansky, David. Nuclear Energy: Principles, Practices & Prospects. (Illus.). 416p. 1996. text 65.00 (*1-56396-244-6*) Am Inst Physics.

*__Bodansky, Steve.__ Extended Massive Orgasm: How You Can Give & Receive Intense Sexual Pleasure. 2000. pap. 13.95 (*0-89793-289-7*) Hunter Hse.

*__Bodansky, Yossef.__ Bin Laden: The Man Who Declared War on America. LC 99-30318. 384p. 1999. 27.95 (*0-7615-1968-8*) Prima Pub.

Bodanszky, Agnes, jt. auth. see Bodanszky, Miklos.

Bodanszky, M. Peptide Chemistry. (Illus.). 240p. 1988. pap. 33.00 (*0-387-18984-X*) Spr-Verlag.

— Principles of Peptide Synthesis. (Reactivity & Structure Ser.: Vol. 16). (Illus.). 240p. 1991. 89.00 (*0-387-12395-4*) Spr-Verlag.

— Principles of Peptide Synthesis. 2nd rev. ed. (Illus.). 320p. 1993. pap. write for info. (*3-540-56431-4*) Spr-Verlag.

Bodanszky, M., et al. The Practice of Peptide Synthesis. (Reactivity & Structure, Concepts in Organic Chemistry Ser.: Vol. 21). 240p. 1992. 113.00 (*0-387-13471-9*) Spr-Verlag.

Bodanszky, M., jt. auth. see Wieland, T.

Bodanszky, Miklos. Peptide Chemistry: A Practical Textbook. rev. ed. LC 93-26806. (Illus.). 220p. 1993. pap. text. write for info. (*3-540-56675-9*) Spr-Verlag.

— Peptide Chemistry: A Practical Textbook. 2nd rev. ed. LC 93-26806. (Illus.). 220p. 1993. 38.95 (*0-387-56675-9*) Spr-Verlag.

— Principles of Peptide Synthesis. 2nd rev. ed. LC 93-3332. (Illus.). 330p. 1993. 54.95 (*0-387-56431-4*) Spr-Verlag.

Bodanszky, Miklos & Bodanszky, Agnes. The Practice of Peptide Synthesis. 2nd rev. ed. Trost, Barry M., ed. LC 94-890. (Laboratory Ser.). (Illus.). 280p. (C). 1994. 49.00 (*0-387-57505-7*) Spr-Verlag.

Bodanszky, Miklos, et al. Peptide Synthesis. 2nd ed. LC 76-16099. (Illus.). 224p. reprint ed. pap. 69.50 (*0-7837-3430-1*, 205775100008) Bks Demand.

Bodard, Lucien. L' Aventure. (Guerre d'Indochine Ser.: Vol. IV). (FRE.). 544p. 1973. pap. 10.95 (*0-7859-1723-3*, 2070362981) Fr & Eur.

— L' Epuisement. (Guerre d'Indochine Ser.). (FRE.). 1973. pap. 10.95 (*0-7859-2199-0*, 207036299X) Fr & Eur.

— L' Humiliation. (Guerre d'Indochine Ser.: Vol. III). (FRE.). 1973. pap. 10.95 (*0-7859-1722-5*, 2070362973) Fr & Eur.

— L' Illusion. (Guerre d'Indochine Ser.: Vol. II). (FRE.). 1973. pap. 10.95 (*0-7859-1721-7*, 2070362965) Fr & Eur.

Bodart-Bailey, Beatrice, ed. see Kaempfer, Engelbert.

Bodart-Bailey, Beatrice M. & Massarella, Derek, eds. The Furthest Goal: Engelbert Kaempfer's Encounter with Tokugawa Japan. (Japan Library). 192p. (C). 1996. text 40.00 (*1-873410-37-9*, Pub. by Curzon Pr Ltd) UH Pr.

Bodart, F. & Vanderdonckt, J., eds. Design, Specification & Verification of Interactive Systems '96: Proceedings of the Eurographics Workshop in Namur, Belgium, June 5-7, 1996. (Illus.). 383p. 1996. text 99.00 (*3-211-82900-8*) Spr-Verlag.

Bodart, Joni R. Booktalk! Two: Booktalking for All Ages & Audiences. LC 85-14223. 408p. 1985. 32.00 (*0-8242-0716-5*) Wilson.

— Booktalking the Award Winners: Children's Retrospective Volume. LC 97-8202. 350p. 1997. 32.00 (*0-8242-0901-X*) Wilson.

— Booktalking the Award Winners: Young Adult Retrospective Volume. 210p. (Orig.). (YA). 1996. pap. 32.00 (*0-8242-0877-3*) Wilson.

— One Hundred World-Class Thin Books: or What to Read When Your Book Report Is Due Tomorrow. xviii, 206p. (YA). (gr. 6-12). 1993. lib. bdg. 27.50 (*0-87287-986-0*) Libs Unl.

*__Bodart, Joni R.__ What to Read When Your Book Report Is Due Tomorrow: The World's Best Thin Books. rev. ed. LC 99-38615. 256p. (gr. 8-12). 2000. pap. 16.95 (*1-57886-007-5*, Pub. by Scarecrow) Natl Bk Netwk.

Bodart, Joni R., ed. The Book Talker, Vol. 2. 141p. 1995. 24.95 (*0-9651269-2-7*) BkHooks Pubng.

— Booktalk! Five: Booktalks!, No. 5. LC 92-14017. 294p. 1993. 32.00 (*0-8242-0836-6*) Wilson.

— Booktalk! Four: Selections from the Booktalker. LC 92-13556. 320p. 1992. 32.00 (*0-8242-0835-8*) Wilson.

— Booktalking the Award Winners: 1992-1993. 224p. 1995. 32.00 (*0-8242-0866-8*) Wilson.

— Booktalking the Award Winners 4. 176p. 1998. 32.00 (*0-8242-0923-0*) Wilson.

— Booktalking the Award Winners, 1994-1995. 192p. (Orig.). 1996. pap. 32.00 (*0-8242-0898-6*) Wilson.

— Index to the Wilson Booktalking Series: A Guide to Talks from Nine Volumes. LC 97-10800. 248p. 1997. pap. 27.00 (*0-8242-0905-2*) Wilson.

Bodart-Talbot, Joni. Booktalk! Three. 386p. 1988. 32.00 (*0-8242-0764-5*) Wilson.

*__Boday, Arlene.__ The Journey to Fruition: The Continuation of the Third Time Is Now. 1999. pap. 11.50 (*1-878406-21-3*, Paintbrsh) Parker Dstb.

*__Bodde, Albert.__ Reincarnation & Karma. 2000. pap. 15.95 (*0-85207-326-7*) C W Daniel.

Bodde, D. Shakespeare & the Ireland Forgeries. LC 75-22073. (Studies in Shakespeare: No. 24). 1975. lib. bdg. 49.00 (*0-8383-2084-8*) M S G Haskell Hse.

Bodde, D., tr. see Ssu-Ma, Ch'Ien.

Bodde, Derk. China's Gifts to the West. LC 43-3077. (Asiatic Studies in American Education: No. 1). 47p. reprint ed. pap. 30.00 (*0-608-10948-7*, 201450700093) Bks Demand.

— Chinese Ideas in the West. LC 48-8567. (Asiatic Studies in American Education: No. 3). 50p. reprint ed. pap. 30.00 (*0-608-10952-5*, 201450000093) Bks Demand.

— Chinese Thought, Society & Science: The Intellectual & Social Background of Science & Technology in Pre-Modern China. LC 91-4437. 456p. 1991. text 42.00 (*0-8248-1334-0*) UH Pr.

Bodde, Derk, intro. A Short History of Chinese Philosophy. abr. ed. Orig. Title: History of Chinese Philosophy. 1966. pap. 18.95 (*0-02-910980-9*) Free Pr.

Bodde, Derk, tr. History of Chinese Philosophy, 2 vols. 812p. 1953. pap. text 39.95 (*0-691-02022-1*, Pub. by Princeton U Pr) Cal Prin Full Svc.

Bodde, Derk, tr. see Fung, Yu-Lan.

Bodde, Derk, tr. & anno. see Jun Li-Ch'en.

Boddekker, Karl W., jt. ed. see Crespo, Joao G.

Bodden, Donna, jt. ed. see Lang, Eleanor R.

Bodden, Marlene, ed. see Bodden, Tom.

Bodden, Mary-Catherine, ed. from ANG. Old English Finding of the True Cross. (Illus.). 144p. 1987. 75.00 (*0-85991-198-5*) Boydell & Brewer.

Bodden, Tom. Heat Pumps: Operation & Service. 2nd ed. Bodden, Marlene, ed. (Illus.). 100p. 1998. pap., ring bd. 30.00 (*0-9659322-3-0*) MarTom Pub.

Bodden, Tom. Heat Pumps: Operation & Service. 2nd rev. ed. (Illus.). 100p. 1997. 30.00 (*0-9659322-1-4*) MarTom Pub.

Bodden, Tom. HVAC - Operation & Service. rev. ed. (Illus.). 130p. 1999. 30.00 (*0-9659322-5-7*) MarTom Pub.

*__Boddenberg, Jill.__ Seeds of Inspiration: Motivating Quotes for You & Your Students. 1999. 7.95 (*1-56245-373-4*) Great Quotations.

Boddewyn, J. J. Advertising Self-Regulation: Sixteen Advanced Systems. 105p. 1986. 65.00 (*0-318-22260-4*) Intl Advertising Assn.

— Barriers to Trade & Investment in Advertising: Government Regulation & Industry Self-Regulation in 53 Countries. 1989. 70.00 (*0-317-02006-4*) Intl Advertising Assn.

— The Case for Advertising Self-Regulation: An Essay. 1991. 10.00 (*0-685-64975-X*) Intl Advertising Assn.

— Juvenile Smoking Initiation & Advertising: A 16-Country Survey of the Perceived Role of Advertising & Other Factors Bearing on Juvenile Smoking Initiation. 1989. 40.00 (*0-317-02007-2*) Intl Advertising Assn.

— Premiums, Gifts & Competitions & Other Promotions: Regulation & Self-Regulation in 42 Countries. 160p. 1988. 60.00 (*0-317-02008-0*) Intl Advertising Assn.

— Sexism & Decency in Advertising: Government Regulation & Industry Self Regulation in 47 Countries. 70p. 1989. 70.00 (*0-317-02009-9*) Intl Advertising Assn.

Boddewyn, J. J., ed. Tobacco Advertising Bans & Consumption in 16 Countries. 31p. 1986. 15.00 (*0-317-01314-9*) Intl Advertising Assn.

Boddewyn, Jean J. Advertising Self-Regulation & Outside Participation: A Multinational Comparison. LC 87-24939. 384p. 1988. 75.00 (*0-89930-295-5*, BAV/, Quorum Bks) Greenwood.

— Global Perspectives on Advertising Self-Regulation: Principles & Practices in Thirty-Eight Countries. LC 91-47662. 272p. 1992. 62.95 (*0-89930-723-X*, BYV, Quorum Bks) Greenwood.

Boddewyn, Jean J., ed. European Industrial Managers: West & East. LC 76-10916. 568p. reprint ed. pap. 176.10 (*0-608-14932-2*, 202612500048) Bks Demand.

Boddie, Caryn & Boddie, Peter. Hiking Colorado. LC 97-1392. (Guide Ser.). (Illus.). 300p. 1996. reprint ed. pap. 15.95 (*1-56044-377-4*) Falcon Pub Inc.

— Hiking in Colorado, Vol. II. (Illus.). 304p. (Orig.). 1999. pap. 15.95 (*1-56044-714-1*) Falcon Pub Inc.

Boddie, Hillary. The Herbal Beauty & Health Book: Safe & Natural Ways to Enhance Your Beauty. LC 94-31160. (Illus.). 256p. 1995. pap. 12.95 (*1-55958-693-1*) Prima Pub.

Boddie, John, jt. auth. see Metzger, Philip W.

Boddie, John B. The Albemarle Parish Register of Surry & Sussex Counties, Virginia: Births, Deaths & Sponsors, 1717-1778. LC 64-22294. 167p. 1998. reprint ed. pap. 22.00 (*0-8063-0024-8*) Clearfield Co.

— Colonial Surry, Virginia. 249p. 1997. reprint ed. 25.00 (*0-8063-0026-4*, 498) Clearfield Co.

— Historical Southern Families, Vol. XVII. 248p. 1994. pap. 22.50 (*0-8063-0525-8*) Clearfield Co.

— Historical Southern Families, Vol. I. LC 67-29833. (Illus.). 385p. 1998. reprint ed. pap. 30.00 (*0-8063-0027-2*) Clearfield Co.

*__Boddie, John B.__ Historical Southern Families, Vol. XIV. 240p. 1998. pap. 22.00 (*0-8063-0450-2*) Clearfield Co.

Boddie, John B. Historical Southern Families, Vol. XVI. 288p. 1994. reprint ed. pap. 25.00 (*0-8063-0524-X*) Clearfield Co.

— Historical Southern Families, Vol. XVIII. 240p. 1994. pap. 22.00 (*0-8063-0565-7*) Clearfield Co.

— Historical Southern Families, Vol. XIX. 204p. 1995. reprint ed. pap. 21.00 (*0-8063-0626-2*) Clearfield Co.

Boddie, John B. Historical Southern Families, Vol. XX. 201p. 1995. pap. 21.00 (*0-8063-0672-6*) Clearfield Co.

— Historical Southern Families, Vol. XXII. 246p. 1995. pap. 22.50 (*0-8063-4524-1*) Clearfield Co.

— Historical Southern Families, Vol. XXIII. 212p. 1995. pap. 21.00 (*0-8063-4525-X*) Clearfield Co.

Boddie, John B. Seventeenth Century Isle of Wight County, Virginia. (Illus.). 768p. 1993. reprint ed. pap. text 43.00 (*1-55613-887-3*) Heritage Bk.

— Southside Virginia Families, Vol. 1. LC 66-28239. (Illus.). 422p. 1999. reprint ed. pap. 32.50 (*0-8063-0040-X*) Clearfield Co.

*__Boddie, John B.__ Southside Virginia Families, Vol. 2. 286p. 1999. pap. 29.50 (*0-8063-0041-8*) Clearfield Co.

*__Boddie, John B. & Boddie, Mrs. John B.__ Historical Southern Families, Vol. II. 315p. 1998. pap. 25.00 (*0-8063-0028-0*) Clearfield Co.

Boddie, John B. & Boddie, Mrs. John B. Historical Southern Families, Vol. III. (Illus.). 255p. 1998. reprint ed. pap. 22.50 (*0-8063-0029-9*, 503) Clearfield Co.

— Historical Southern Families, Vol. IV. 259p. 1998. reprint ed. pap. 23.00 (*0-8063-0030-2*, 504) Clearfield Co.

*__Boddie, John B. & Boddie, Mrs. John B.__ Historical Southern Families, Vol. V. 320p. 1998. pap. 26.00 (*0-8063-0031-0*) Clearfield Co.

Boddie, John B. & Boddie, Mrs. John B. Historical Southern Families, Vol. VI. 275p. 1998. reprint ed. pap. 24.00 (*0-8063-0032-9*, 506) Clearfield Co.

— Historical Southern Families, Vol. VII. 282p. 1995. reprint ed. pap. 35.00 (*0-8063-0033-7*, 507) Clearfield Co.

— Historical Southern Families, Vol. VIII. (Illus.). 254p. 1998. reprint ed. pap. 22.50 (*0-8063-0034-5*, 508) Clearfield Co.

— Historical Southern Families, Vol. IX. (Illus.). 302p. 1998. reprint ed. pap. 26.00 (*0-8063-0035-3*, 509) Clearfield Co.

— Historical Southern Families, Vol. X. (Illus.). 275p. 1995. reprint ed. pap. 24.00 (*0-8063-0036-1*, 510) Clearfield Co.

— Historical Southern Families, Vol. XI. (Illus.). 287p. 1995. reprint ed. pap. 25.00 (*0-8063-0037-X*, 511) Clearfield Co.

— Historical Southern Families, Vol. XII. (Illus.). 289p. 1995. reprint ed. pap. 25.00 (*0-8063-0038-8*, 512) Clearfield Co.

— Historical Southern Families, Vol. XIII. (Illus.). 256p. 1998. reprint ed. pap. 22.50 (*0-8063-0039-6*, 513) Clearfield Co.

Boddie, John Bennett. Virginia Historical Genealogies. (Illus.). 384p. 1999. reprint ed. pap. 32.50 (*0-8063-0042-6*, 535) Clearfield Co.

Boddie, Mrs. John B., jt. auth. see Boddie, John B.

Boddie, Peter, jt. auth. see Boddie, Caryn.

Boddie, William W. History of Williamsburg: Something about the People of Williamsburg County, South Carolina, from the First Settlement by Europeans about 1705 until 1923. LC 80-17789. (Illus.). 620p. 1995. reprint ed. pap. 45.00 (*0-8063-4563-2*) Clearfield Co.

***Boddiger, George.** Getting People to Work Together Effectively. 184p. 2000. pap. 18.95 (*1-56167-548-2*) Am Literary Pr.

Bodding, P. O. A Santal Dictionary, 7 pts. in 5 vols. 3560p. 1998. pap. 1800.00 (*81-212-0423-2*, Pub. by Print Hse) St Mut.

Boddington, C. American Hunting Rifles: Their Application in the Field for Practical Shooting. (Illus.). 1995. boxed set 85.00 (*1-57157-030-6*) Safari Pr.

— American Hunting Rifles: Their Application in the Field for Practical Shooting. (Illus.). 300p. 1995. 35.00 (*1-57157-016-0*) Safari Pr.

— Shots at Big Game. (Illus.). 198p. 1993. pap. 15.95 (*0-940143-89-5*) Safari Pr.

Boddington, C. T. Safari Rifles. 2nd ed. (Illus.). 423p. 1990. 37.50 (*0-940143-49-6*) Safari Pr.

Boddington, Craig. Make It Accurate: Get the Maximum Performance from Your Hunting Rifle. (Illus.). 224p. Date not set. 24.95 (*1-57157-150-7*) Safari Pr.

— Safari Rifles. (Illus.). 423p. 1997. pap. 24.95 (*1-57157-108-6*) Safari Pr.

— Where Lions Roar: Ten More Years of African Hunting. 2nd ed. (Illus.). 347p. 1998. 35.00 (*1-57157-069-1*) Safari Pr.

— Whitetail Medicine. LC 97-176646. (Whitetail Secrets Ser.: No. 6). (Illus.). 196p. 1995. 19.95 (*1-56416-156-0*) Derrydale Pr.

Boddington, Craig, ed. America: The Men & Their Guns That Made Her Great. 200p. 1981. 19.95 (*0-8227-3022-7*) Petersen Pub.

Boddington, Craig, ed. see Bynum, Bill.

Boddington, Craig, ed. see Fears, J. Wayne.

Boddington, Craig, ed. see Knight, Harold & Hale, David.

Boddington, Craig, ed. see Morris, David.

Boddington, Craig, ed. see Roy, Jim.

Boddington, Craig, ed. see Thornberry, Russell.

Boddington, Craig, ed. see Wensel, Gene & Wensel, Barry.

Boddington, Craig, ed. see Winke, Bill.

Boddington, Craig, ed. see Wootters, John.

Boddington, D. Radio Control Model Manual. (Illus.). 192p. 1996. 32.95 (*1-85260-480-8*, Pub. by J H Haynes & Co) Motorbooks Intl.

Boddington, David. Building & Flying Radio Controlled Model Aircraft. 3rd ed. (Illus.). 242p. 1996. pap. 28.50 (*1-85486-135-2*) Nexus Special Interests.

— Radio Control Primer. 3rd ed. (Illus.). 132p. (Orig.). 1986. pap. 21.50 (*0-85242-899-5*) Nexus Special Interests.

Boddington, M. J., et al, eds. Chlorinated Dioxins & Related Compounds 1984: Proceedings of the Fourth International Conference held at Ottawa, Canada, October 16-18, 1984. (Illus.). 420p. 1985. pap. 51.00 (*0-08-032608-0*, Pub. by PPL) Elsevier.

Boddington, Michael M., jt. auth. see Spriggs, Arthur I.

Boddy, jt. auth. see Wimpenny.

Boddy, Alexander A. To Kairwan the Holy. 320p. 1985. 250.00 (*1-85077-069-7*, Pub. by Darf Pubs Ltd) St Mut.

Boddy, Bill. Aero-Engined Racing Cars. (Illus.). 160p. 1992. 39.95 (*0-85429-867-3*) Haynes Manuals.

— Brooklands Giants. (Illus.). 160p. 1995. 44.95 (*0-85429-960-2*, Pub. by J H Haynes & Co) Motorbooks Intl.

— Vintage Motor Cars. 1989. pap. 25.00 (*0-85263-776-4*, Pub. by Shire Pubns) St Mut.

Boddy, David, et al, eds. The New Management Challenge: Information Systems for Improved Performance. 160p. 1988. lib. bdg. 57.50 (*0-7099-5084-5*) Routledge.

Boddy, David & Paton, Rob. Management: An Introduction. LC 97-32792. 1998. 39.99 (*0-13-257098-X*) P-H.

Boddy, David, jt. auth. see Gunson, Nicky.

Boddy, Janice. Wombs & Alien Spirits: Women, Men & the Zar Cult in Northern Sudan. LC 89-40250. (New Directions in Anthropological Writing Ser.). 384p. 1989. pap. text 25.95 (*0-299-12314-6*) U of Wis Pr.

Boddy, Janice, jt. auth. see Barnes, Virginia L.

Boddy, Joe. Ultimate Hidden Picture Puzzle Book. 32p. (J). 1990. pap. 2.95 (*0-486-26297-9*) Dover.

Boddy, John. Brain Systems & Psychological Concepts. LC 77-21203. 477p. reprint ed. pap. 147.90 (*0-8357-7378-7*, 203102200073) Bks Demand.

Boddy, Kasia & Sillars, Jane, eds. Original Prints: New Writing from Scottish Women, Vol. II. LC 87-63209. 156p. (Orig.). 1988. pap. 9.95 (*0-948275-30-8*) Dufour.

Boddy, L., et al, eds. Nitrogen, Phosphorus & Sulphur Utilisation by Fungi. (British Mycological Society Symposium Ser.: No. 15). 316p. (C). 1989. text 110.00 (*0-521-37405-7*) Cambridge U Pr.

Boddy, Marlys. ABC Book of Feelings. (Illus.). 32p. (J). (ps-3). 1991. 8.99 (*0-570-04190-2*, 56-1649) Concordia.

Boddy, Martin, et al. Sunbelt City? A Study of Economic Change in Britain's M4 Growth Corridor. (Inner City in Context Ser.). (Illus.). 240p. 1986. pap. 16.95 (*0-19-823265-9*) OUP.

Boddy, William. Fifties Television: The Industry & Its Critics. (Illinois Studies in Communications). (Illus.). 304p. (Orig.). 1990. pap. text 14.95 (*0-252-06299-X*) U of Ill Pr.

— Volkswagen Beetle Type 1 & the New Generation. (Illus.). 160p. 1999. pap. 19.95 (*1-85532-885-2*, Pub. by Osprey) Motorbooks Intl.

Bode. The Accordion Family. (J). 2001. mass mkt. 16.00 (*0-689-81945-5*) S&S Childrens.

Bode & Broere. Could You Leave the Light On? (J). 1997. write for info. (*0-237-51753-1*) EVN1 UK.

— Tomorrow I Will Feel Better. (J). 1997. write for info. (*0-237-51752-3*) EVN1 UK.

— You Will Always Be My Dad. 1997. write for info. (*0-237-51756-6*) EVN1 UK.

***Bode, Adrian, et al.** Where We Live. (Adventures in Architecture Ser.). (Illus.). 30p. (YA). (gr. 3-10). 1999. 14.95 (*3-7913-2104-8*, Pub. by Prestel) te Neues.

Bode, Arndt. Parallel Virtual Machine, EuroPVM '96: Third European PVM Conference, Munchen, Germany, October 7-9, 1996 Proceedings, Vol. 115. LC 96-43299. (Lecture Notes on Computer Science Ser.). xiv, 362p. 1996. 62.00 (*3-540-61779-5*) Spr-Verlag.

Bode, Arndt, ed. Distributed Memory Computing: 2nd European Conference, EDMCC2 Munich, FRG, April 22-24, 1991 Proceedings. (Lecture Notes in Computer Science Ser.: Vol. 487). xv, 506p. 1991. 53.95 (*0-387-53951-4*) Spr-Verlag.

Bode, Arndt, et al, eds. PARLE '93: Proceedings of the 5th International PARLE Conference, Munich, Germany, June 14-17, 1993. (Lecture Notes in Computer Science Ser.: Vol. 694). xvii, 770p. 1993. 108.95 (*0-387-56891-3*) Spr-Verlag.

Bode, Arndt & Cin, Mario D., eds. Parallel Computer Architectures: Theory, Hardware, Software, Applications. LC 93-35538. (Lecture Notes in Computer Science Ser.: Vol. 732). 1993. 54.00 (*0-387-57307-0*) Spr-Verlag.

Bode, Boyd H. Progressive Education at the Crossroads. LC 71-165707. (American Education Ser, No. 2). 1972. reprint ed. 17.95 (*0-405-03696-5*) Ayer.

Bode, Bruce W., et al. The Insulin Dump Therapy Book: Insights from the Experts. 157p. (Orig.). 1995. pap. text 19.00 (*0-9647837-0-3*) MiniMed Tech.

Bode, Carl. The Anatomy of American Popular Culture, 1840-1861. LC 83-5643. (Illus.). 292p. 1983. reprint ed. lib. bdg. 65.00 (*0-313-24005-1*, BOAN, Greenwood Pr) Greenwood.

Bode, Carl, ed. see Emerson, Ralph Waldo.

Bode, Carl, ed. see Mencken, H. L.

Bode, Carl, ed. see Thoreau, Henry David.

Bode, Caroline L. The Franklin & Malinda Barton Family. (Illus.). 229p. 1981. 20.00 (*0-89015-289-6*) C L Riley.

Bode, Charles G. Wines of Italy. (Illus.). 135p. 1974. reprint ed. pap. 3.95 (*0-486-23003-1*) Dover.

Bode, Christian, et al, eds. Fachhochschulen: Specialist Technical Colleges in Germany. (ENG & GER.). 320p. 1997. 55.00 (*3-7913-1844-6*, Pub. by Prestel) te Neues.

Bode, Diane. Skiing Is for Kids Coloring Book. (Illus.). 84p. (J). 1993. pap. 6.95 (*1-56861-000-9*) Swift Lrn Res.

***Bode, E. A.** A Dose of Frontier Soldiering: The Memoirs of Corporal E. A. Bode, Frontier Regular Infantry, 1877-1882. Smith, Thomas T., ed. LC 93-26155. (Illus.). 250p. 1999. pap. 14.95 (*0-8032-6160-8*, Bison Books) U of Nebr Pr.

Bode, E. A. A Dose of Frontier Soldiring: The Memoirs of Corporal E. A. Bode, Frontier Regular Infantry, 1877-1882. Smith, Thomas T., ed. LC 93-26155. (Illus.). 250p. (C). 1994. text 40.00 (*0-8032-4232-8*, Bison Books) U of Nebr Pr.

— The Queen of Sheba & Her Only Son Menyelek, Vol. I. Obaba, Al I., ed. (Illus.). 196p. 1922. pap. text 27.00 (*0-916157-59-8*) African Islam Miss Pubns.

Bode, Elroy. Home Country: An Elroy Bode Reader. LC 96-61727. 1997. 30.00 (*0-87404-244-5*) Tex Western.

— This Favored Place: The Texas Hill Country. (Illus.). 124p. 1983. 13.95 (*0-940672-09-X*) Shearer Pub.

Bode, Frederick A. Protestantism & the New South: North Carolina Baptists & Methodists in Political Crisis, 1894-1903. LC 75-1289. 184p. reprint ed. pap. 57.10 (*0-8357-2705-X*, 203981800013) Bks Demand.

Bode, Georg H., ed. Scriptores Rerum Mythicarum, Latini Tres Romae Nuper Reperti, 2 vols. in 1. xlvi, 472p. 1967. reprint ed. 120.00 (*0-318-71225-3*) G Olms Pubs.

Bode, H. Pediatric Applications of Transcranial Doppler Sonography. (Illus.). 150p. 1988. 49.95 (*0-387-82073-6*) Spr-Verlag.

***Bode, H., ed.** Metal-Supported Automotive Catalytic Converters. 220p. 1999. 145.00 (*3-527-29925-4*) Wiley.

Bode, Harold. James Brindley. (Lifelines Ser.: No. 14). (Illus.). 48p. 1989. pap. 25.00 (*0-85263-485-4*, Pub. by Shire Pubns) Parkwest Pubns.

Bode, James. Food Fight: A Guide to Eating Disorders for Preteens & Their Parents. (J). (gr. 3-7). 1997. 16.00 (*0-614-29064-3*) S&S Childrens.

Bode, Janet. Beating the Odds. large type ed. 165p. 1993. reprint ed. lib. bdg. 15.95 (*1-56054-591-7*) Thorndike Pr.

— The Colors of Freedom: Immigrant Stories. LC 98-29608. (J). 1999. 24.00 (*0-531-11530-5*) Watts.

***Bode, Janet.** Colors of Freedom: Immigrant Stories. (Illus.). (J). 2000. 15.30 (*0-606-18146-6*) Turtleback.

— Colors of Freedom: Immigrant Stories. (Illus.). (J). 2000. pap. 9.95 (*0-531-15961-2*) Watts.

Bode, Janet. Death Is Hard to Live With: Teenagers Talk about How They Cope with Loss. 1995. 9.60 (*0-606-07426-0*, Pub. by Turtleback) Demco.

— Food Fight. LC 96-29186. 160p. (J). (gr. 3-7). 1997. per. 16.00 (*0-689-80272-2*) S&S Childrens.

***Bode, Janet.** Hard Time: A Real Life Look at Juvenile Crime & Violence. 1998. 10.09 (*0-606-13457-3*, Pub. by Turtleback) Demco.

— Heartbreak & Roses: Real Life Stories of Troubled Love. rev. ed. (Illus.). (YA). 2000. pap. 8.95 (*0-531-16464-0*) Watts.

Bode, Janet. Heartbreak & Roses Real Life Stories of Troubled Love. 1996. 10.09 (*0-606-08542-4*, Pub. by Turtleback) Demco.

— Kids Still Having Kids: People Talk about Teen Pregnancy. 1999. pap. text 9.95 (*0-531-15973-6*) Watts.

***Bode, Janet.** Kids Still Having Kids: Talking about Teen Pregnancy. rev. ed. LC 98-45477. (YA). (gr. 9-12). 1999. 25.00 (*0-531-11588-7*) Watts.

Bode, Janet. New Kids in Town: Oral Histories of Immigrant Teens. 128p. (J). 1991. pap. 3.50 (*0-590-44144-2*) Scholastic Inc.

— Truce: Ending the Sibling War. 112p. (YA). (gr. 8-12). 1991. lib. bdg. 24.00 (*0-531-10996-8*) Watts.

— Trust & Betrayal. (J). 1996. 20.95 (*0-385-30990-2*) BDD Bks Young Read.

— Trust & Betrayal, Real Life Stories of Friends & Enemies. 1997. 10.09 (*0-606-12831-X*, Pub. by Turtleback) Demco.

— Voices of Rape. LC 97-41225. (YA). (gr. 9-12). 1998. 22.50 (*0-531-11518-6*) Watts.

— Voices of Rape. (Illus.). 160p. (J). 1999. pap. text 9.95 (*0-531-15932-9*) Watts.

Bode, Janet & Mack, Stan. Hard Time: A Real Life Look at Juvenile Crime & Violence. (Illus.). 224p. (YA). (gr. 7 up). 1996. 16.95 (*0-385-32186-4*, Delacorte Pr Bks) BDD Bks Young Read.

***Bode, Janet & Mack, Stanely.** Heartbreak & Roses rev. ed. LC 99-38550. 2000. 25.00 (*0-531-11776-6*) Watts.

Bode, Kenneth A. The South Dakota Poll: A Critical Analysis. 1970. 1.00 (*1-55614-001-0*) U of SD Gov Res Bur.

Bode, L. E., et al, eds. Pesticide Formulations & Application Systems, Vol. 10. (Special Technical Publication Ser.: No. 1078). (Illus.). 260p. 1990. text 39.00 (*0-8031-1388-9*, STP1078) ASTM.

Bode, Loren E. & Chasin, David G., eds. Pesticide Formulations & Application Systems, Vol. 11. (Special Technical Publication Ser.: No. 1112). (Illus.). 310p. 1992. text 38.00 (*0-8031-1414-1*, STP1112) ASTM.

Bode, M. F., ed. RS Opiuchi (1985) & the Recurrent Nova Phenomenon. 270p. 1986. lib. bdg. 98.00 (*90-6764-074-3*, Pub. by VSP) Coronet Bks.

Bode, Mabel H. The Pali Literature of Burma. LC 77-87008. reprint ed. 37.50 (*0-404-16796-9*) AMS Pr.

Bode, Mabel H., jt. tr. see Geiger, Wilhelm.

Bode, Richard. Beachcombing at Miramar: The Quest for an Authentic Life. 208p. 1997. reprint ed. mass mkt. 10.99 (*0-446-67276-9*, Pub. by Warner Bks) Little.

— First You Have to Row a Little Boat: Reflections on Life & Living. 224p. 1995. reprint ed. mass mkt. 11.99 (*0-446-67003-0*, Pub. by Warner Bks) Little.

Bode, Sharon, et al. Listening in & Speaking Out: Intermediate. (Listening in & Speaking Out Ser.). (Illus.). 128p. (Orig.). 1980. pap. text 32.57 (*0-582-79736-5*, 74992) Longman.

— Listening in & Speaking Out Advanced Pack: Book & Cassette. (English As a Second Language Bk.). 1989. pap. text 43.09 (*0-582-79780-2*, 75034) Longman.

Bode-Snyder, Barbara. Practical Math for the Technician: The Basics. 592p. 1990. pap. text 100.00 (*0-13-251513-X*) P-H.

Bode, Ulrike, tr. see Heider, Ulrike.

Bode, Ursula. Botero (Fernand) The Sculpture. (GER., Illus.). 60p. 1978. 125.00 (*1-55660-097-6*) A Wofsy Fine Arts.

Bode, Vaughn. The Bode Sketchbook Diaries, Vol. 1. Groth, Gary, ed. (Illus.). 64p. 1990. 9.95 (*1-56097-028-6*) Fantagraph Bks.

— The Bode Sketchbook Diaries, Vol. 2. (Illus.). 64p. 1990. pap. 12.95 (*1-56097-044-8*) Fantagraph Bks.

— The Bode Sketchbook Diaries, Vol. 3. (Illus.). 72p. 1991. pap. 10.95 (*1-56097-053-7*) Fantagraph Bks.

— Bode's Erotica, Vol. 1. 48p. (Orig.). 1996. pap. 12.95 (*1-56097-307-2*) Fantagraph Bks.

— Bode's Erotica, Vol. 2. (Collected Vaughn Bode Ser.). (Illus.). 48p. (Orig.). 1996. pap. 12.95 (*0-930193-55-5*) Fantagraph Bks.

Bode, Vaughn. Bodes Erotica, Vol. 3. pap. 12.95 (*1-56097-267-X*, Pub. by Fantagraph Bks) Seven Hills Bk.

Bode, Vaughn. Cheech Wizard, Vol. 1. (Illus.). 64p. 1990. pap. 12.95 (*1-56097-042-1*, Pub. by Fantagraph Bks) Seven Hills Bk.

— Cheech Wizard, Vol. 2. (Illus.). 64p. 1991. pap. 12.95 (*1-56097-054-5*) Fantagraph Bks.

— Junkwaffel, Vol. 1. Boyd, Robert, ed. (Illus.). 96p. (Orig.). 1992. pap. 12.95 (*1-56097-086-3*) Fantagraph Bks.

— Junkwaffel, Vol. 2. Boyd, Robert, ed. (Illus.). 80p. (Orig.). 1996. pap. 12.95 (*1-56097-110-X*, Pub. by Fantagraph Bks) Seven Hills Bk.

— Lizard Zen. 1998. pap. 9.95 (*1-56097-309-9*) Fantagraph Bks.

Bode, W. K. European Gastronomy: The Story of Man's Food & Eating Customs. (Illus.). 262p. 1995. pap. 54.95 (*0-470-23572-1*) Wiley.

Bode, Wilhelm. The Italian Bronze Statuettes of the Renaissance. Draper, James D., ed. Gretor, William, tr. LC 80-82165. (Illus.). 1980. 395.00 (*0-937370-00-2*) Polymath Pr.

Bode, William. Reason Plays at War: The American Liberal Vision & Revolutionary Warfare. 150p. (C). pap. text 24.00 (*0-8191-9572-3*); lib. bdg. 46.00 (*0-8191-9571-5*) U Pr of Amer.

Bodea, Cornelia, jt. ed. see Michelson, Paul E.

Bodea, Sorin A. Information Technology & Economic Performance: Is Measuring Productivity Still Useful? 41p. (Orig.). 1994. pap. text. write for info. (*1-879716-18-6*, P-94-8) Ctr Info Policy.

Bodeau, J. Katmai National Park. (Illus.). 206p. 1995. pap. 14.95 (*0-936425-16-4*) Alaska Natural.

Bodechtel, J., jt. ed. see Toselli, F.

***Bodecker, N. M.** Hurry, Hurry, Mary Dear! LC 97-17350. (Illus.). 32p. (J). (gr. 2-4). 1998. per. 16.00 (*0-689-81770-3*) McElderry Bks.

Bodecker, N. M. I'm Sad Dad. (J). Date not set. 12.95 (*0-689-50372-5*) McElderry Bks.

— King with the Blooming Umbrella. (J). Date not set. 12.95 (*0-689-50374-1*) McElderry Bks.

— Our House. (J). Date not set. 12.95 (*0-689-50375-X*) McElderry Bks.

— Pigeon Toes & Colicos. (J). Date not set. 12.95 (*0-689-50373-3*) McElderry Bks.

Bodeen, DeWitt, jt. auth. see Ringgold, Gene.

Bodeen, Donald V., jt. auth. see Jensen, Bernard.

Bodeen, Jim. Impulse to Love. (Illus.). 108p. 1998. pap. 13.00 (*0-911287-27-2*) Blue Begonia.

— Our Mother Blooming. (Illus.). 24p. (Orig.). 1986. pap. 5.00 (*0-911287-09-4*) Blue Begonia.

***Bodeen, Jim.** This House. 1999. pap. 15.00 (*0-9644440-6-2*) Tsunami.

Bodeen, Jim. Whole Houses Shaking. (Illus.). 88p. 1993. pap. 10.00 (*0-912887-30-3*) Blue Begonia.

Bodeen, Jim, ed. see Andrews, Linda.

Bodeen, Jim, ed. see Skillman, Judith.

Bodeen, Jim, ed. see Vargas, Javier & Mexican Writers Staff.

Bodega, Bobby. The Street Smart Guide to Blue Collar Secrets for Finding & Getting a Good Job. (Illus.). 150p. (Orig.). 1992. pap. 11.95 (*0-9632079-0-3*) Cisco Pr.

Bodega de la Familia Staff, contrib. by. La Cocina de la Familia: Recipes from Alphabet City. LC 98-43879. 224p. 1998. pap. text 15.00 (*1-885492-77-4*) City & Co.

Bodega Land Trust Committee Staff, ed. The Potluck Cookbook: Bodega Cooks for the Bodega Land Trust. (Illus.). 179p. (Orig.). 1997. pap. 13.50 (*0-614-29919-5*) Tannery Creek.

Bodegom, Volker. Bicycling Vancouver. pap. 11.95 (*1-55105-012-9*) Lone Pine.

Bodek, Itamar, et al. Environmental Inorganic Chemistry. LC 88-25281. (Society of Environmental Toxicology & Chemistry Ser.). (Illus.). 1280p. 1988. 564.00 (*0-08-036833-6*, CRC Reprint) Franklin.

Bodek, Ralph. Miami Poppycock: The First 100 Years. LC 93-80955. (Illus.). 1995. pap. 14.95 (*0-9646914-0-X*); pap. 7.95 (*0-9646914-1-8*) Hallmark Pubs.

Bodek, Richard. Proletarian Performance in Weimar Berlin: Agitprop, Chorus, & Brecht. LC 97-15691. (GERM Ser.). 210p. 1998. 55.00 (*1-57113-126-4*) Camden Hse.

Bodel, Jean. Jeu de Saint Nicolas. (FRE.). 91p. 1966. 9.95 (*0-8288-7493-X*) Fr & Eur.

Bodel, John. Roman Brick Stamps in the Kelsey Museum. (Kelsey Museum of Archaeology Ser.). (Illus.). 136p. 1983. pap. text 32.50 (*0-472-08039-3*, 08039) U of Mich Pr.

Bodel, John & Tracy, Stephen. Greek & Latin Inscriptions in the U. S. A. A Checklist. LC 98-235084. (Orig.). (C). 1997. pap. 29.00 (*1-879549-05-0*) Am Acad Rome.

Bodell, Dorothy H. Montgomery White Sulphur Springs: A History of the Resort, Hospital, Cemeteries, Markers, & Monument. LC 93-5005. (Illus.). 98p. (Orig.). 1993. pap. 7.95 (*0-936015-43-8*) Pocahontas Pr.

Bodelle, J., et al. Les Universites Americaines: Dynamismes et Traditions. (FRE.). 416p. (Orig.). 1985. pap. 30.00 (*0-318-18948-8*, Pub. by Technique et Documentation) IBD Ltd.

Bodelsen, C. A., jt. auth. see Vinterberg, H.

Bodemann, Y. Michael, ed. Jews, Germans, Memory: Reconstruction of Jewish Life in Germany. LC 95-79368. (Social History, Popular Culture & Politics in Germany Ser.). 304p. (C). 1996. text 57.50 (*0-472-10584-1*, 10584) U of Mich Pr.

Boden. Sheep & Goat Practice 2. 2nd ed. 1997. pap. text 55.00 (*0-7020-2330-2*, W B Saunders Co) Harcrt Hlth Sci Grp.

Boden, Anthony. F.W. Harvey: Soldier, Poet. (Illus.). 368p. 1998. pap. 17.95 (*0-7509-1904-3*) Sutton Pub Ltd.

Boden, Arthur & Woodside, John. Boden's Beasts. (Illus.). (J). (gr. 1-5). 1964. 8.95 (*0-8392-3045-1*) Astor-Honor.

Boden, Daryl G. & Larson, Wiley J. Cost-Effective Space Mission Operations. (Space Technology Ser.). (Illus.). 714p. (C). 1996. 45.00 (*0-07-006379-6*) McGraw.

— Cost-Effective Space Mission Operations. (Space Technology Ser.). (Illus.). 714p. (C). 1996. pap. 38.43 (*0-07-006382-6*) McGraw.

Boden, Deirdre, ed. The Business of Talk: Organizations in Action. 280p. (C). 1994. pap. text 26.95 (*0-7456-1356-X*) Blackwell Pubs.

Boden, Dierdre & Zimmerman, Don H., eds. Talk & Social Structure. 315p. 1991. 47.50 (*0-520-07506-4*, Pub. by U CA Pr) Cal Prin Full Svc.

Boden, Dierdre, jt. ed. see Friedland, Roger.

Boden, Edward, ed. Black's Veterinary Dictionary. 19th ed. (Illus.). 608p. 1998. 99.50 (*0-389-21017-X*) U Pr of Amer.

Boden, Leslie I. The AMA Guides in Maryland: An Assessment. LC 92-28509. 1992. 35.00 (*0-935149-35-X*, WC-92-5) Workers Comp Res Inst.

— Medicolegal Fees in California: An Assessment. LC 93-50720. 1994. 50.00 (*0-935149-45-7*, WC-94-1) Workers Comp Res Inst.

— Permanent Partial Disability in Tennessee: Similar Benefits for Similar Injuries? LC 97-45625. 40p. 1997. pap. 50.00 (*0-935149-70-8*, WC-97-5) Workers Comp Res Inst.

— Reducing Litigation: Evidence from Wisconsin. 1988. 35.00 (*0-935149-16-3*, WC-88-7) Workers Comp Res Inst.

— Use of Medical Evidence: Low-Back Permanent Partial Disability Claims in Maryland. 60p. (Orig.). 1986. pap. 35.00 (*0-935149-02-3*, SP-86-1) Workers Comp Res Inst.

B

— Use of Medical Evidence: Low-Back Permanent Partial Disability Claims in New Jersey. LC 87-31628. 1987. 35.00 (*0-935149-07-4*, WC-87-2) Workers Comp Res Inst.

Boden, Leslie I. & Fleischman, Charles A. Medical Costs in Workers' Compensation: Trends & Interstate Comparisons. LC 89-24975. 70p. 1989. 35.00 (*0-935149-22-8*, WC-89-5) Workers Comp Res Inst.

Boden, Leslie I., et al. Reducing Litigation: Using Disability Guidelines & State Evaluators in Oregon. LC 91-33586. 1991. 35.00 (*0-935149-29-5*, WC-91-3) Workers Comp Res Inst.

Boden, Margaret A. Artificial Intelligence & Natural Man. 2nd exp. ed. 1987. pap. text 19.95 (*0-262-52123-7*) MIT Pr.

— Artificial Intelligence & Natural Man. 2nd expanded ed. 1987. 37.50 (*0-262-02259-1*) MIT Pr.

— Artificial Intelligence in Psychology: Interdisciplinary Essays. (Explorations in Cognitive Science Ser.). 172p. 1989. 25.00 (*0-262-02285-0*, Bradford Bks) MIT Pr.

— Artificial Intelligence in Psychology: Interdisciplinary Essays. (Explorations in Cognitive Science Ser.). 172p. 1989. pap. text 14.00 (*0-262-52140-7*, Bradford Bks) MIT Pr.

— Computer Models of Mind: Computational Approaches in Theoretical Psychology. (Problems in the Behavioral Sciences Ser.: No. 6). (Illus.). 304p. 1988. pap. text 24.95 (*0-521-27033-2*) Cambridge U Pr.

— Purposive Explanation in Psychology. LC 73-169858. 422p. reprint ed. pap. 130.90 (*0-7837-3843-9*, 204366500010) Bks Demand.

Boden, Margaret A., ed. Artificial Intelligence. 2nd ed. (Handbook of Perception & Cognition Ser.). (Illus.). 376p. 1996. text 59.95 (*0-12-161964-8*) Acad Pr.

— Dimensions of Creativity. (Illus.). 420p. 1994. 40.00 (*0-262-02368-7*, Bradford Bks) MIT Pr.

— Dimensions of Creativity. (Illus.). 256p. 1996. pap. text 20.00 (*0-262-52219-5*, Bradford Bks) MIT Pr.

— The Philosophy of Artificial Intelligence. (Oxford Readings in Philosophy Ser.). 460p. 1990. pap. text 22.00 (*0-19-824854-7*) OUP.

— The Philosophy of Artificial Life. (Oxford Readings in Philosophy Ser.). (Illus.). 414p. 1996. text 65.00 (*0-19-875154-0*); pap. text 19.95 (*0-19-875155-9*) OUP.

***Boden, Mark & Miles, Ian.** Services & the Knowledge-Based Economy. LC 00-29521. (Science, Technology & the International Political Economy Ser.). 2000. pap. write for info. (*0-8264-4953-0*) Continuum.

Boden, Mikael B., jt. ed. see Niklasson, Lars.

Boden, R. & Corden, A. Measuring Low Incomes: Self-Employment & Family Credit. 134p. 1994. pap. 25.00 (*0-11-701787-6*, HM17876, Pub. by Statnry Office) Bernan Associates.

Boden, Scott D. & Bohlman, Henry H. The Failed Spine Surgery Patient: Evaluation, Imaging & Management. 450p. text 165.00 (*0-7817-1760-4*) Lppncott W & W.

***Boden, Tanya.** Five-Minute Beautiful Nails. (Illus.). 76p. 1999. reprint ed. text 18.00 (*0-7881-6821-5*) DIANE Pub.

Boden, William E. Bovine Practice. 1991. pap. text 48.00 (*0-7020-1556-3*, W B Saunders Co) Harcrt Hlth Sci Grp.

— Bovine Practice 2. 2nd ed. 1997. pap. text 55.00 (*0-7020-2331-0*, W B Saunders Co) Harcrt Hlth Sci Grp.

— Canine Practice. 1991. pap. text 44.95 (*0-7020-1522-9*, W B Saunders Co) Harcrt Hlth Sci Grp.

— Equine Practice. 1991. pap. text 48.00 (*0-7020-1521-0*, W B Saunders Co) Harcrt Hlth Sci Grp.

— Equine Practice 3. 3rd ed. 1997. pap. text 55.00 (*0-7020-2332-9*, W B Saunders Co) Harcrt Hlth Sci Grp.

— Feline Practice. 1991. pap. text 39.00 (*0-7020-1523-7*, W B Saunders Co) Harcrt Hlth Sci Grp.

Boden, William E. & Capone, Robert J. Coronary Care. (Blue Bk.). (Illus.). 224p. 1984. pap. text 38.00 (*0-7216-1072-2*, W B Saunders Co) Harcrt Hlth Sci Grp.

Bodendiek, R. & Henn, R., eds. Topics in Combinatorics & Graph Theory: Essays in Honour of Gerhard Ringel. (Illus.). xx, 792p. 1992. 140.95 (*0-387-91373-4*) Spr-Verlag.

Bodenhamer, Bob & Hall, L. Michael. Adventures with Time Lines. LC 98-66555. 302p. 1998. pap. 19.95 (*0-916990-42-7*) META Pubns.

— Figuring Out People: Design Engineering with Meta Programmes. 291p. 1997. pap. 24.95 (*1-899836-10-1*, Pub. by Crown Hse) LPC Group.

Bodenhamer, Bob G. & Hall, L. Michael. Time-Lining: Patterns for Adventuring in "Time" 283p. 1997. pap. 24.95 (*1-899836-12-8*, Pub. by Crown Hse) LPC Group.

***Bodenhamer, Bob G. & Hall, L. Michael.** The User's Manual for the Brain: The Complete Manual for Neuro-Linguistic Programming Practitioner Certification. 422p. 2000. 44.95 (*1-899836-32-2*, Pub. by Crown Hse) LPC Group.

Bodenhamer, Bobby, jt. auth. see Hall, L. Michael.

Bodenhamer, Bobby G., jt. auth. see Hall, L. Michael.

Bodenhamer, David J. Fair Trial: Rights of the Accused in American History. (Bicentennial Essays on the Bill of Rights Ser.). 192p. (C). 1991. pap. text 19.95 (*0-19-505559-4*) OUP.

Bodenhamer, David J. & Barrows, Robert G., eds. The Encyclopedia of Indianapolis. LC 94-16665. 928p. 1994. 59.95 (*0-253-31222-1*) Ind U Pr.

Bodenhamer, David J. & Ely, James W., Jr., eds. The Bill of Rights in Modern America: After 200 Years. LC 92-15815. 256p. (C). 1993. 35.00 (*0-253-31223-X*); pap. 15.95 (*0-253-20767-3*, MB 767) Ind U Pr.

Bodenhamer, David J., ed. see Slutz, Ted.

Bodenhamer, Gregory. Back in Control. 132p. 1984. per. 10.00 (*0-671-76165-X*) S&S Trade.

— Drug Free: The Back in Control Program for Keeping Your Kids off Drugs. 144p. 1998. pap. 7.95 (*0-13-055336-0*) P-H.

— Parent in Control: Restore Order in Your Home & Create a Loving Relationship with Your Adolescent. LC 95-535. 192p. 1995. per. 10.00 (*0-684-80777-7*, Fireside) S&S Trade Pap.

Bodenheim, Maxwell. Returning to Emotion. LC 73-18552. (BCL Ser.: I). reprint ed. 20.00 (*0-404-11367-2*) AMS Pr.

— Sixty Seconds. LC 73-18549. (BCL Ser.: I). reprint ed. 20.00 (*0-404-11364-8*) AMS Pr.

Bodenheimer, Aron-Ronald. Doris: The Story of a Disfigured Deaf Child. LC 72-11341. 139p. reprint ed. pap. 43.10 (*0-7837-3813-7*, 204363300010) Bks Demand.

Bodenheimer, Edgar. Jurisprudence: The Philosophy & Method of the Law. rev. ed. LC 74-77182. 585p. 1974. 47.50 (*0-674-49001-0*) HUP.

— Philosophy of Responsibility. x, 147p. 1980. text 18.50 (*0-8377-0309-3*, Rothman) W S Hein.

Bodenheimer, Edgar, et al. Readings & Cases on an Introduction to the Anglo-American Legal System: Introduction, Readings & Cases. 2nd ed. (American Casebook Ser.). 166p. (C). 1988. reprint ed. pap. 25.50 (*0-314-36662-8*) West Pub.

***Bodenheimer, Hans S.** From Bad Nauheim to Bloomfield: My Journey of Faith. (Illus.). 64p. 1999. pap. 10.95 (*0-916897-36-2*) Andrew Mtn Pr.

Bodenheimer, Henriette H. Max Bodenheimer (1865-1940) 125p. (C). 1989. text 39.00 (*0-946270-86-4*, Pub. by Pentland Pr) St Mut.

Bodenheimer, Rosemarie. The Politics of Story in Victorian Social Fiction. LC 87-17313. 264p. 1988. 39.95 (*0-8014-2099-7*) Cornell U Pr.

— The Politics of Story in Victorian Social Fiction. LC 87-17313. 264p. 1990. reprint ed. pap. text 16.95 (*0-8014-9920-8*) Cornell U Pr.

— The Real Life of Mary Ann Evans: George Eliot, Her Letters & Fiction. (Illus.). 320p. 1996. pap. text 16.95 (*0-8014-8184-8*) Cornell U Pr.

Bodenheimer, Thomas & Gould, Robert. Rollback! Right-Wing Power in U. S. Foreign Policy. LC 88-29479. 272p. (Orig.). (C). 1989. 30.00 (*0-89608-346-2*); pap. 12.00 (*0-89608-345-4*) South End Pr.

Bodenheimer, Thomas S. Understanding Health Policy: A Clinical Approach. 2nd ed. (Illus.). 322p. (C). 1998. pap. 34.95 (*0-8385-9075-6*, Apple Lange Med) McGraw.

Bodenhorn, Diran, jt. auth. see Graham, Pearson.

***Bodenhorn, Howard.** A History of Banking in Antebellum America: Financial Markets & Economic Development in an Era of Nation-Building. LC 99-13089. (Studies in Macroeconomic History). (Illus.). 280p. (C). 2000. 59.95 (*0-521-66285-0*); pap. 22.95 (*0-521-66999-5*) Cambridge U Pr.

Bodenmechanik, jt. ed. see Lehrstuhl, Grundbau.

Bodensieck, E. J. A Stress-Life-Reliability Rating System for Gear & Rolling-Element Bearing Compressive Stress & Gear Root Bending Stress. (Technical Papers: Vol. P229.19). (Illus.). 44p. 1974. pap. text 30.00 (*1-55589-286-8*) AGMA.

***Bodensiek, Paul.** Electrify Your Web Site in a Weekend. 1999. pap. 24.99 (*0-7615-2505-X*); pap. 24.99 (*0-7615-2479-7*) Prima Pub.

Bodenstab, Charles J. Information Breakthrough: How to Turn Mountains of Confusing Data into Gems of Useful Information. LC 97-39492. (Illus.). 130p. (Orig.). 1997. pap. 22.95 (*1-55571-413-7*, Oasis Pr) PSI Resch.

— A New Era in Inventory Management: For the Distribution Industry. (Illus.). 133p. 1993. 40.00 (*0-9639358-0-1*) Hilta Pr.

Bodenstein, E. Langenscheidts Euroworterbucher: Danisch. (DAN.). 1997. pap. write for info. (*3-468-12100-8*) Langenscheidt.

Bodenstein, Joe F. Der Bildhauer Kurt Arentz. (Illus.). 144p. 1984. text 30.00 (*0-914301-29-2*, Pub. by Marco) West-Art.

Bodenstein, Marco, ed. see Zavrel, B. John.

Bodenstein, Max, jt. auth. see Wolfrum, J.

Bodensteiner, Ivan E. & Levinson, Rosalie B. State & Local Government Civil Rights Liability, 2 vols. 1992. 185.00 (*0-318-36193-0*) West Group.

Bodensteiner, Ivan E., jt. auth. see Levinson, Rosalie.

Bodensteiner, Luke. Endless Winter: An Olympian's Journal. 212p. (Orig.). 1994. pap. text 12.95 (*0-9643927-0-4*) Alta Press.

Bodepuci, Prasad. The Revolutionary Guide to PowerBuilder 4.0. 860p. 1995. pap. 49.95 incl. cd-rom (*1-874416-60-5*) Wrox Pr Inc.

Boder, Elena. Further Studies on the Etiology & Significance of Congenital Cranial Osteoporosis. (SRCD M Ser.: Vol. 13, No. 2). 1948. pap. 25.00 (*0-527-01544-X*) Periodicals Srv.

Bodet, B., jt. ed. see Court, L.

Bodet, Jose Novoa. Como Formar Buenos Hijos. (SPA., Illus.). 150p. 1997. pap. text 12.98 (*968-13-2811-6*) Edit Diana.

Bodett, Tom. As Far As You Can Go Without a Passport: Views from the End of the Road. 160p. 1986. pap. 13.00 (*0-201-10673-6*) Addison-Wesley.

— The Big Garage on Clear Shot: Gossip, Tall Tales & Local News from the Folks at the End of the Road. 256p. 1992. mass mkt. 4.99 (*0-380-71642-9*, Avon Bks) Morrow Avon.

— The Free Fall of Webster Cummings. LC 95-25694. 384p. (J). 1996. 22.45 (*0-7868-6209-2*, Pub. by Hyperion) Little.

— Small Comforts: More Comments & Comic Pieces. 160p. 1988. pap. 13.00 (*0-201-13689-9*) Addison-Wesley.

Bodett, Tom. Williwaw! LC 98-36108. 192p. (J). (gr. 4-7). 1999. lib. bdg. 17.99 (*0-679-99030-5*) Knopf.

— Williwaw! LC 98-36108. 192p. (YA). (gr. 5-9). 1999. 16.00 (*0-679-89030-0*) Knopf.

***Bodett, Tom.** Williwaw! (Illus.). (J). 2000. pap. 4.99 (*0-375-80687-3*) Knopf.

***Bodett, Tom, reader.** Wiliwaw! 2000. audio 30.00 (*0-8072-8225-1*) Listening Lib.

Bodeu, Cornelia, ed. see Berry, Burton Y.

***Bodeus, Richard.** Aristotle & the Theology of the Living Immortals. Garrett, Jan, tr. (C). 2000. pap. text 19.95 (*0-7914-4728-6*) State U NY Pr.

— Aristotle & the Theology of the Living Immortals. Garrett, Jan, tr. (C). 2000. text 59.50 (*0-7914-4727-8*) State U NY Pr.

Bodeus, Richard. The Political Dimensions of Aristotle's Ethics. Garrett, Jan, tr. LC 92-34024. (SUNY Series in Ancient Greek Philosophy). 250p. (C). 1993. pap. text 19.95 (*0-7914-1610-0*) State U NY Pr.

— The Political Dimensions of Aristotle's Ethics. Garrett, Jan, tr. LC 92-34024. (SUNY Series in Ancient Greek Philosophy). 250p. (C). 1993. text 59.50 (*0-7914-1609-7*) State U NY Pr.

Bodewitz, H. W., tr. from SAN. The Jyotistoma Ritual No. I, 66-364: Jaiminiya Brahmana. LC 89-48913. (Orientalia Rheno-Traiectina Ser.: Vol. 34). x, 334p. 1990. 88.50 (*90-04-09120-3*) Brill Academic Pubs.

Bodey, Gerald P., ed. Candidiasis. fac. ed. LC 84-22342. (Illus.). 293p. pap. 90.90 (*0-7837-7283-1*, 204702300005) Bks Demand.

— Candidiasis: Pathogenesis, Diagnosis, & Treatment. 2nd ed. LC 92-21810. (Illus.). 435p. 1993. reprint ed. pap. 134.90 (*0-608-05837-8*, 205980300007) Bks Demand.

Bodey, Gerald P. & Rodriguez, Victorio, eds. Hospital-Associated Infections in the Compromised Host. LC 78-31462. (Handbook on Hospital-Associated Infections Ser.: No. 2). (Illus.). 279p. reprint ed. pap. 86.50 (*0-7837-0795-9*, 204110900019) Bks Demand.

Bodey, J. Bulgarian-Hungarian Pocket Dictionary. (BUL & HUN.). 560p. 1985. pap. 30.00 (*963-205-132-7*, Pub. by Akade Kiado) St Mut.

— Bulgarian-Hungarian Pocket Dictionary. (BUL & HUN.). 560p. (C). 1985. 39.00 (*0-7855-2647-1*, Pub. by Akade Kiado) St Mut.

— Hungarian-Bulgarian & Bulgarian-Hungarian Dictionary for Tourists. 342p. (C). 1990. 35.00 (*963-205-246-3*, Pub. by Akade Kiado) St Mut.

— Hungarian-Bulgarian & Bulgarian-Hungarian Dictionary for Tourists. 2nd ed. (BUL & HUN.). 475p. 1986. 14.95 (*0-8288-1652-2*, M11162) Fr & Eur.

— Hungarian-Bulgarian Pocket Dictionary. 3rd ed. (BUL & HUN.). 584p. 1986. 14.95 (*0-8288-1653-0*, F102250) Fr & Eur.

***Bodey, John.** When Darkness Falls. 2000. pap. 19.95 (*0-7022-2994-6*, Pub. by Univ Queensland Pr) Intl Spec Bk.

Bodey, Oliver O. Embryo Research-Development, Uses, Storage, Ethics & Legal Decisions: Index of New Information. (Illus.). 150p. 1997. 47.50 (*0-7883-1392-4*); pap. 44.50 (*0-7883-1393-2*) ABBE Pubs Assn.

Bodey, Richard A., ed. see Macartney, Clarence E.

***Bodey, Richard Allen.** Voice from the Cross: Classic Sermons on the Seven Last Words of Christ. 2000. pap. 7.99 (*0-8254-2064-4*) Kregel.

Bodfish, Waldo, Sr. Kusiq: An Eskimo Life History from the Arctic Coast of Alaska. LC 90-11246. (Oral Biography Ser.: No. 2). (Illus.). 330p. 1991. pap. 21.00 (*0-912006-44-7*) U of Alaska Pr.

Bodge, George M. Soldiers in King Philip's War. (New World Ser.: Vol. 1). (Illus.). 496p. 1997. 34.95 (*1-58057-050-X*, SKPW001B) Digital Antiq.

— Soldiers in King Philip's War: Being a Critical Account of that War with a Concise History of the Indian Wars of New England from 1620-1677. 3rd ed. (Illus.). 502p. 2000. reprint ed. pap. 40.00 (*0-8063-0043-4*, 545) Genealog Pub.

— Soldiers in King Philip's War, Containing Lists of the Soldiers of Massachusetts Colony Who Served in the Indian War of 1675-1677. 369p. 1992. reprint ed. lib. bdg. 39.00 (*0-8328-2369-4*) Higginson Bk Co.

Bodger, Alan, tr. see Tsivian, Yuri.

Bodger, Carole. Healing Back Pain. LC 99-29977. (Smart Guides Ser.). 230p. 1999. pap. 12.95 (*0-471-35649-2*) Wiley.

— Smart Guide to Getting Strong & Fit. LC 98-33833. (Smart Guides Ser.). 181p. 1998. pap. 10.95 (*0-471-29635-X*) Wiley.

***Bodger, Carole.** Smart Guide to Relieving Stress. LC 99-11246. 192p. 1999. pap. 10.95 (*0-471-31858-2*) Wiley.

Bodger, Joan. Clever-Lazy. LC 97-60507. 208p. (J). (gr. 3-6). 1997. pap. 7.95 (*0-88776-418-5*) Tundra Bks.

— The Forest Family. LC 99-70968. (Illus.). 112p. (J). (gr. 4-7). 1999. 16.95 (*0-88776-485-1*) Tundra Bks.

***Bodger, Joan.** How the Heather Looks: A Joyous Journey to the British Sources of Children's Books. 249p. 1999. 23.95 (*0-7710-1118-0*) McCland & Stewart.

***Bodger, Keith, et al.** Clinical Economics in Gastroenterology. LC 99-26447. (Illus.). 1999. 125.00 (*0-632-05033-0*) Blackwell Sci.

Bodger, Lorraine. Chocolate Cookies. LC 98-11978. 144p. 1998. pap. 7.95 (*0-312-18707-6*) St Martin.

***Bodger, Lorraine.** For You My Friend, I Wish... 350 Kind, Funny, Wise & Wonderful Wishes. 2000. 7.95 (*0-7407-0990-9*) Andrews & McMeel.

— For Your Birthday, I Wish... 350 Wishes for the Happiest of Birthdays. 2000. 7.95 (*0-7407-0991-7*) Andrews & McMeel.

— Four-Sided Cookie: 55 Recipes for Squares & Bars. LC 99-52614. (Illus.). 126p. 2000. pap. 10.95 (*0-312-20675-5*) St Martin.

Bodger, Lorraine. Great American Cakes. LC 87-40173. 176p. 1988. 15.45 (*0-446-51364-4*); mass mkt. 9.95 (*0-446-38666-9*, Pub. by Warner Bks) Little.

— Sweet & Savory Sauces: More than 60 Recipes that Make Any Meal a Special Occasion. LC 95-23391. (Illus.). 128p. 1995. 15.00 (*0-684-81157-X*) Simon & Schuster.

— 2,001 Ways to Pamper Yourself, 1. LC 99-33119. 1999. pap. 8.95 (*0-7407-0022-7*) Andrews & McMeel.

— A Year of Cookies: 52 Recipes for Everyday & Holiday Cookies to Bake & Enjoy Year-Round. LC 98-37528. 144p. 1998. pap. 9.95 (*0-312-19964-3*) St Martin.

Bodha, Daji, ed. see Da Free John.

Bodhi, jt. auth. see Nyanaponika.

Bodhi, Bhikkha, ed. & intro. see Thera, Nyanaponika, et al.

Bodhi, Bhikkhu. A Comprehensive Manual of Abhidhamma. 432p. 1993. 24.00 (*955-24-0103-8*, Pub. by Buddhist Pub Soc) Vipassana Res Pubns.

— Maha Kaccana: Master of Doctrinal Exposition. 56p. 1995. 3.75 (*955-24-0138-0*, Pub. by Buddhist Pub Soc) Vipassana Res Pubns.

— The Noble Eightfold Path. 144p. 1994. 6.00 (*955-24-0116-X*, Pub. by Buddhist Pub Soc) Vipassana Res Pubns.

— Nourishing the Roots. 64p. 1990. 3.75 (*955-24-0072-4*, Pub. by Buddhist Pub Soc) Vipassana Res Pubns.

***Bodhi, Bhikkhu.** Numerical Discourses of the Buddha: An Anthology of Suttas from the Anguttara Nikaya. 352p. 2000. pap. 19.95 (*0-7425-0405-0*) AltaMira Pr.

Bodhi, Bhikkhu, ed. Dana: The Practice of Giving. 80p. 1990. 3.75 (*955-24-0077-5*, Pub. by Buddhist Pub Soc) Vipassana Res Pubns.

***Bodhi, Bhikkhu, tr.** The Connected Discourses of the Buddha: A New Translation of the Samyutta Nikaya, 2 vols., Set. 2080p. 2000. 120.00 (*0-86171-168-8*) Wisdom MA.

Bodhi, Bhikkhu, tr. from PLI. The Discourse on the Fruits of Recluseship: The Samannaphala Sutta & Its Commentaries. 200p. (Orig.). (C). 1989. 12.00 (*955-24-0045-7*, Pub. by Buddhist Pub Soc) Vipassana Res Pubns.

— The Discourse on the Root of Existence: The Mulapariyaya Sutta & Its Commentaries. 90p. 1992. 7.20 (*955-24-0064-3*, Pub. by Buddhist Pub Soc) Vipassana Res Pubns.

— The Great Discourse on Causation: The Mahanidana Sutta & Its Commentaries. LC 97-900540. 160p. 1995. 12.00 (*955-24-0117-8*, Pub. by Buddhist Pub Soc) Vipassana Res Pubns.

***Bodhi, Bhikkhu & Anuruddha, Acariya.** A Comprehensive Manual of Abhidhamma: The Abhidhammattha Sangaha of Acariya Anuruddha. LC 99-53412. (Illus.). 2000. 24.00 (*1-928706-02-9*) Vipassana Res Pubns.

***Bodhi, Bhikkhu & Thera, Nyanaponika, eds.** Numerical Discourses of the Buddha: An Anthology of Suttas from the Anguttara Nikaya. LC 99-21076. (Sacred Literature Ser.). 344p. 2000. 65.00 (*0-7619-4808-2*) AltaMira Pr.

— Numerical Discourses of the Buddha: An Anthology of Suttas from the Anguttara Nikaya. LC 99-21076. (Sacred Literature Ser.). 344p. 2000. pap. 24.95 (*0-7619-4809-0*) AltaMira Pr.

Bodhi, Bhikkhu, jt. auth. see Thera, Nyanaponika.

Bodhi, Bhikkhu, tr. see Buddha, Gautama.

Bodhi, Bhikkhu, jt. tr. see Namamoli, Bhikkhu.

Bodhidharma & Broughton, Jeffrey L. The Bodhidharma Anthology: The Earliest Records of Zen. LC 98-18245. 197p. 1999. 45.00 (*0-520-21200-2*, Pub. by U CA Pr) Cal Prin Full Svc.

Bodhisattva Ma Deva Barkha, ed. see Osho.

Bodhisattva Ma Nisango, ed. see Osho.

Bodi, Daniel. The Book of Ezekiel & the Poem of Erra. (Orbis Biblicus et Orientalis Ser.: Vol. 104). 324p. 1991. text 61.75 (*3-7278-0731-8*, Pub. by Presses Univ Fribourg) Eisenbrauns.

Bodian, Miriam. Hebrews of the Portuguese Nation: Conversos & Community in Early Modern Amsterdam. LC 96-48373. (Modern Jewish Experience Ser.). (Illus.). 240p. 1998. lib. bdg. 39.95 (*0-253-33292-3*) Ind U Pr.

***Bodian, Miriam.** Hebrews of the Portuguese Nation: Conversos & Community in Early Modern Amsterdam. (Modern Jewish Experience Ser.). (Illus.). 219p. 1999. pap. 15.95 (*0-253-21351-7*) Ind U Pr.

Bodian, Nat. The Joy of Publishing. 256p. 1996. 19.95 (*0-912411-47-3*) Open Horizons.

Bodian, Nat G. Book Marketing Handbook: Tips & Techniques for the Sale & Promotion of Scientific, Technical, Professional, & Scholarly Books & Journals, Vol. I. 482p. 1980. 64.95 (*0-8352-1286-6*) Bowker.

— Book Marketing Handbook: Tips & Techniques for the Sale & Promotion of Scientific, Technical, Professional, & Scholarly Books & Journals, Vol. II. 607p. 1983. 64.95 (*0-8352-1685-3*) Bowker.

— Direct Marketing Rules of Thumb: 1,000 Practical & Profitable Ideas to Help You Improve Response, Save Money, & Increase Efficiency in Your Direct Program. 448p. 1995. 59.95 (*0-07-006340-0*) McGraw.

— How to Choose a Winning Title: A Guide for Writers, Editors, & Publishers. LC 88-25235. 192p. 1989. pap. 25.00 (*0-89774-540-X*) Oryx Pr.

— NTC's Dictionary of Mailing List Terminology & Techniques. (Illus.). 320p. 1994. 49.95 (*0-8442-3188-6*, Natl Textbk Co) NTC Contemp Pub Co.

— The Publisher's Direct Mail Handbook. LC 86-27471. 288p. 1987. 42.50 (*0-89495-079-7*) Oryx Pr.

Bodian, Nat G. & Luedtke, Robert. Beyond Lead Generation: Merchandising Through Card Packs. Bauer, Lawrence M. & Marcus, Ruth E., eds. 32p. 1986. pap. 9.95 (*0-9616785-0-X*) Solar Pr.

***Bodian, Stephan.** Meditation for Dummies: A Reference for the Rest of Us. LC 99-60185. 384p. 1999. pap. 19.99 (*0-7645-5116-7*) IDG Bks.

Bodian, Stephan, ed. see Ardagh, Arjuna N.

B

An Asterisk (*) at the beginning of an entry indicates that the title is appearing for the first time.

Bodie. Essentials of Investing. 2nd ed. 1996. teacher ed., student ed. 142.50 (*0-256-22810-8*) McGraw.
— Financial Economics. LC 99-31591. (Illus.). 479p. 1999. 86.67 (*0-13-310897-X*) P-H.
— Investments. 4th ed. LC 98-8117. 992p. 1998. 90.94 (*0-256-24626-2*) McGraw.
— Investments. 4th ed. 992p. 1998. 107.50 (*0-256-26192-X*) McGraw.

Bodie & Kane. Essentials of Investments. 4th ed. 2000. 68.00 (*0-07-231859-7*); 9.74 (*0-07-231867-8*) McGraw.

Bodie, Avi & Kane, Alex. Investments: Student Solutions Manual. 3rd ed. 224p. (C). 1996. text 11.25 (*0-256-19736-9*, Irwn McGrw-H) McGrw-H Hghr Educ.

Bodie, Avi, et al. Investments: The Wall Street Journal Edition. 3rd ed. 1088p. (C). 1995. text 84.00 (*0-256-21366-6*, Irwn McGrw-H) McGrw-H Hghr Educ.

Bodie, Charles A. & Seiner, William H., compiled by. A Guide to Gloucester County, Virginia, Historical Manuscripts, 1651-1865. xvii, 109p. 1976. pap. 7.95 (*0-88490-070-3*) Library of VA.

Bodie, Idella. Carolina Girl: A Writer's Beginning. (Illus.). 225p. (J). 1998. 16.95 (*0-87844-143-3*) Sandlapper Pub Co.
— Carolina Girl: A Writer's Beginning. LC 97-40937. (Illus.). 225p. (J). 1998. pap. 10.95 (*0-87844-140-9*) Sandlapper Pub Co.

***Bodie, Idella.** The Fighting Gamecock. LC 00-22289. (Heroes & Heroines of the American Revolution Ser.). 2000. 6.95 (*0-87844-151-4*) Sandlapper Pub Co.

Bodie, Idella. The Revolutionary Swamp Fox. LC 98-54635. 1999. pap. 6.95 (*0-87844-147-6*) Sandlapper Pub Co.
— The Secret Message. LC 98-6715. (Heroes & Heroines of the American Revolution Ser.: Vol. 2). (Illus.). 45p. (J). 1998. pap. 5.95 (*0-87844-145-X*) Sandlapper Pub Co.

***Bodie, Idella.** Spunky Revolutionary War Heroine. LC 00-36578. (Heroes & Heroines of the American Revolution Ser.). (Illus.). (YA). 2000. write for info. (*0-87844-154-9*) Sandlapper Pub Co.

Bodie, Idella F. Ghost in the Capitol. LC 86-6702. (Illus.). 116p. (J). (gr. 5-7). 1986. pap. 6.95 (*0-87844-072-0*) Sandlapper Pub Co.
— Ghost Tales for Retelling. Stone, Barbara, ed. LC 94-34761. (Illus.). 78p. (Orig.). (J). (gr. 5-8). 1994. pap. 6.95 (*0-87844-125-5*) Sandlapper Pub Co.
— The Man Who Loved the Flag. LC 96-41692. (Illus.). 48p. (Orig.). (J). (gr. 3-5). 1997. pap. 5.95 (*0-87844-135-2*) Sandlapper Pub Co.
— The Mystery of Edisto Island. Stone, Barbara, ed. LC 94-618. (Illus.). 157p. (Orig.). (J). (gr. 5-7). 1994. pap. 9.95 (*0-87844-123-9*) Sandlapper Pub Co.
— The Mystery of the Pirate's Treasure. LC 84-5451. (Illus.). 136p. (J). (gr. 5 up). 1984. reprint ed. pap. 6.95 (*0-87844-059-3*) Sandlapper Pub Co.
— South Carolina Women. rev. ed. Pettus, Louise & Benefield, Linda, eds. LC 90-48424. Orig. Title: South Carolina Women: They Dared to Lead. (Illus.). 1990. pap. 12.95 (*0-87844-102-6*) Sandlapper Pub Co.
— Stranded! LC 84-14098. (Illus.). 132p. (Orig.). (J). (gr. 5-7). 1984. pap. 6.95 (*0-87844-060-7*) Sandlapper Pub Co.
— Trouble at Star Fort. (Illus.). (J). (gr. 5-7). 1992. 14.95 (*0-87844-118-2*); pap. 9.95 (*0-87844-119-0*) Sandlapper Pub Co.
— Whopper! LC 88-36243. (Illus.). (J). (gr. 4-7). 1989. pap. 6.95 (*0-87844-086-0*) Sandlapper Pub Co.

Bodie, Neil & Bodie, Renee. Red R Y. A. N. Caso, Adolph, ed. LC 99-18277. 260p. 1999. pap. 16.95 (*0-8283-2041-1*) Branden Bks.

Bodie, Renee, jt. auth. see Bodie, Neil.

Bodie, Scott & Browne, Corinne. Confessions of a Fish Doctor. 1977. 7.95 (*0-911104-83-6*) Workman Pub.

Bodie, Thomas J. Politics & the Emergence of an Activist International Court of Justice. LC 94-37739. 128p. 1995. 49.95 (*0-275-95014-X*, Praeger Pubs) Greenwood.

***Bodie, Warren.** American War Eagles, 1939-1941. (America's Arsenal of Democracy Ser.: Vol. 1). (Illus.). 196p. 2000. 39.95 (*0-9629359-4-8*, 130745AE, Pub. by Widewing Pubns) Motorbooks Intl.

Bodie, Warren, jt. auth. see Ethell, Jeff.

Bodie, Warren, jt. auth. see Ethell, Jeffrey L.

Bodie, Z. Essentials of Investments, Second Edition. Essentials Of Investments Solutions Manual With Introduction Letter. 2nd ed. (C). 1996. text 20.50 (*0-256-22839-6*) McGraw.

***Bodie, Zvi.** Finance. 1999. 86.67 (*0-13-015102-5*) P-H.

Bodie, Zvi. Investments. 5th ed. 2001. 69.74 (*0-07-233916-0*) McGraw.
— Investments: 1995-1996 User's Manual. 3rd ed. (C). 1995. text 81.90 incl. 3.5 ld (*0-256-19456-4*, Irwn McGrw-H) McGrw-H Hghr Educ.

Bodie, Zvi, et al, eds. Issues in Pension Economics. LC 86-19346. (National Bureau of Economic Research Project Report Ser.). (Illus.). viii, 384p. 1987. lib. bdg. 54.00 (*0-226-06284-8*) U Ch Pr.
— Securing Employer-Based Pensions: An International Perspective. (Illus.). 388p. 1996. text 44.95 (*0-8122-3334-4*) U of Pa Pr.

***Bodie, Zvi & Davis, E. P.** The Foundations of Pension Finance, 2 vols. LC 00-37673. (Elgar Mini Ser.). 1252p. 2000. text 400.00 (*1-84064-186-X*) E Elgar.

Bodie, Zvi & Munnell, Alicia H., eds. Pensions & the Economy: Sources, Uses, & Limitations of Data. LC 91-45276. (Pension Research Council Publications). (Illus.). 304p. (C). 1992. text 45.00 (*0-8122-3118-X*) U of Pa Pr.

Bodie, Zvi, et al. Essentials of Investments. 2nd ed. LC 94-18527. (Finance Ser.). 558p. (C). 1994. text 69.65 (*0-256-13559-2*, Irwn McGrw-H) McGrw-H Hghr Educ.
— Essentials of Investments. 3rd ed. LC 97-13806. 1997. 72.80 (*0-256-16459-2*, Irwn Prfssnl) McGraw-Hill Prof.
— Financial Aspects of the United States Pension System. LC 83-9119. (National Bureau of Economic Research Project Report Ser.). 464p. 1984. lib. bdg. 62.50 (*0-226-06281-3*) U Ch Pr.
— Investments. 3rd ed. LC 95-23345. 1088p. (C). 1995. text 72.75 (*0-256-14638-1*, Irwn Prfssnl) McGraw-Hill Prof.
— Pensions in the U. S. Economy. (National Bureau of Economic Research Project Report Ser.). (Illus.). 208p. 1988. lib. bdg. 34.00 (*0-226-06285-6*) U Ch Pr.

Bodiford, William M. Soto Zen in Medieval Japan. LC 92-37843. (Studies in East Asian Buddhism: No. 8). 400p. (C). 1993. text 37.00 (*0-8248-1482-7*) UH Pr.

Bodig, Jozsef, ed. Reliability-Based Design of Engineered Wood Structures: Proceedings of the NATO Advanced Research Workshop, Florence, Italy 3-5 June 1991. LC 92-15408. 208p. (C). 1992. text 127.50 (*0-7923-1801-3*) Kluwer Academic.

Bodig, Jozsef & Jayne, Benjamin A. Mechanics of Wood & Wood Composites. 736p. (C). 1993. reprint ed. lib. bdg. 89.50 (*0-89464-777-6*) Krieger.

Bodig, Richard, ed. Diphona Amoena et Florida: A Collection of Bicinia, 2 vols., Vols. I & II. Incl. Vol. I. Diphona Amoena et Florida: A Collection of Bicinia. vi, 76p. 1996. pap. text 27.00 (*1-56571-140-8*); Vol. II. Diphona Amoena et Florida: A Collection of Bicinia. ii, 76p. 1996. pap. text 27.00 (*1-56571-141-6*); (Renaissance Ser.). 1996. Set pap. text 27.00 (*0-614-23619-3*) PRB Prods.

Bodigheimer, Carl-Freidrich & Hain, Richard M., eds. Mapping Class Groups & Moduli Spaces of Reimann Surfaces: Proceedings of Workshops Held June 24-28, 1991 & August 6-10, 1991 in Gottingen, Germany & Seattle, Washington. LC 93-14150. (Contemporary Mathematics Ser.: Vol. 150). 372p. 1993. pap. 51.00 (*0-8218-5167-5*, CONM/150) Am Math.

Bodilly, Susan. Lessons from New American Schools Development Corporation's Demonstration. LC 96-19822. 150p. 1996. pap. text 15.00 (*0-8330-2369-1*, MR-729-NASDC) Rand Corp.

Bodilly, Susan & Mitchell, Karen. Evaluating Challenge Grants for Technology in Education: A Sourcebook. LC 97-8973. (Illus.). xvii, 194p. 1997. pap. text 13.00 (*0-8330-2487-6*, MR-839-ED) Rand Corp.

Bodilly, Susan, et al. Designing New American Schools: Baseline Observations on Nine Design Teams. 115p. 1995. pap. 15.00 (*0-8330-2323-3*, MR-598-NASDC) Rand Corp.

Bodilly, Susan J., et al. Lessons from New American Schools' Scale-Up Phase: Prospects for Bringing Designs to Multiple Schools. LC 98-20629. (Illus.). 140p. 1998. pap. 15.00 (*0-8330-2632-1*) Rand Corp.

Bodily, Jolene, jt. auth. see Kreiswirth, Kinny.

Bodily, Samuel, et al. Cases in Quantitative Business Analysis. 288p. (C). 1996. text 28.00 (*0-256-14714-0*, Irwn McGrw-H) McGrw-H Hghr Educ.
— Quantitative Business Analysis: Text & Cases. LC 97-24214. 672p. (C). 1997. text 57.50 (*0-256-14713-2*, Irwn McGrw-H) McGrw-H Hghr Educ.

Bodin. Routing & Scheduling. (Computers & Operations Research). 1983. pap. 47.00 (*0-08-030227-0*, Pergamon Pr) Elsevier.

Bodin, Jean. Colloquium of the Seven about Secrets of the Sublime: Colloquium Heptaplomeres de Rerum Sublimium Arcanis Abditis. Kuntz, Marion L., tr. & anno. by. LC 73-2453. 592p. reprint ed. pap. 183.60 (*0-8357-3302-5*, 203952500013) Bks Demand.
— De la Demonomanie des Sorciers. (GER.). xiv, 251p. 1988. reprint ed. write for info. (*3-487-07931-3*) G Olms Pubs.
— On Sovereignty. Franklin, Julian H., ed. (Cambridge Texts in the History of Political Thought Ser.). 188p. (C). 1992. text 54.95 (*0-521-34206-6*); pap. text 17.95 (*0-521-34992-3*) Cambridge U Pr.
— Paradoxes. xiv, 128p. write for info. (*0-318-71322-5*) G Olms Pubs.
— Response to the Paradoxes of Malestroit. Tudor, Henry, ed. & tr. by. (Primary Sources in Political Thought Ser.). 160p. 1997. 48.00 (*1-85506-532-0*); pap. 18.00 (*1-85506-533-9*) Thoemmes Pr.
— The Six Bookes of Commonweale. Mayer, J. P., ed. LC 78-67335. (European Political Thought Ser.). 1980. reprint ed. lib. bdg. 73.95 (*0-405-11680-2*) Ayer.

Bodin, Jeanne, jt. auth. see Kava, Beth M.

Bodin, Lynn. The Boxer Rebellion. (Men-at-Arms Ser.: No. 95). (Illus.). 48p. pap. 11.95 (*0-85045-335-6*, 9031, Pub. by Ospry) Stackpole.

Bodin, Madeline. Maximizing Call Center Performance: 136 Innovative Ideas for Increasing Productivity & Customer Satisfaction. (Illus.). 110p. 1998. per. 19.95 (*1-57820-026-1*) Telecom Bks.

***Bodin, Madeline & Dawson, Keith.** The Call Center Dictionary: The Complete Guide to Call Center Help Desk Technology & Operations. 2nd ed. 224p. 1999. pap. 19.95 (*1-57820-043-1*, Pub. by Telecom Bks) Publishers Group.

Bodin, Madeline & Dawson, Keith. The Call Center Dictionary: The Complete Guide to Call Center Technology & Operations. 350p. 1996. per. 19.95 (*0-936648-79-1*) Telecom Bks.

Bodin, Philippe, tr. see Ryan, Perry T.

Bodin, Ron. Voodoo, Past & Present. LC 90-82516. (Louisiana Life Ser.: No. 5). 101p. 1990. pap. 5.00 (*0-940984-60-1*) Univ LA Lafayette.

Bodinat, Henri De, see De Bodinat, Henri.

Bodine, Echo. Echoes of the Soul: The Soul's Journey Beyond the Light- Through Life, Death, & Life after Death. LC 98-42956. 224p. 1999. pap. 12.95 (*1-57731-076-4*) New Wrld Lib.
— Hands That Heal. 2nd ed. 136p. 1997. pap. 12.95 (*0-935127-55-0*) ACS Pubns.

***Bodine, Echo.** Relax, It's Only a Ghost: My Adventures with Spirits, Hauntings & Things That Go Bump in the Night. 160p. 2000. 18.95 (*1-86204-819-3*, Pub. by Element MA) Penguin Putnam.

Bodine, Jay F., jt. ed. see Probst, Gerhard F.

Bodine, John J. Taos Pueblo: A Walk Through Time. LC 77-73460. (Illus.). 64p. (Orig.). 1996. pap. 6.95 (*1-887896-00-7*, Rio Nuevo) Treas Chest Bks.

Bodine, Laurence. Trial Manual for Proving Hedonic Damages. LC 92-74523. 325p. 1993. 85.00 (*0-915544-23-7*) Lawpress CA.

Bodine, Marian M., jt. auth. see Rhodes, Ron.

Bodine, Richard, jt. auth. see Crawford, Donna.

Bodine, Richard J. & Crawford, Donna K. Developing Emotional Intelligence: A Guide to Behavior Management & Conflict Resolution in Schools. 220p. 1999. pap. text 19.95 (*0-87822-421-1*) Res Press.

Bodine, Richard J., et al. Creating the Peaceable School: A Comprehensive Program for Teaching Conflict Resolution. LC 94-67020. 376p. (Orig.). 1994. pap. text, teacher ed. 35.95 (*0-87822-346-0*, 4763); pap. text, student ed. 14.95 (*0-87822-350-9*, 4764) Res Press.

Bodine, Richard J., jt. auth. see Crawford, Donna.

Bodine, Walter R. The Greek Text of Judges: Recensional Developments. LC 80-12578. (Harvard Semitic Monographs: No. 23). 218p. reprint ed. pap. 67.60 (*0-7837-5405-1*, 204516900005) Bks Demand.

Bodine, Walter R., ed. Linguistics & Biblical Hebrew. LC 92-29716. x, 285p. 1992. text 39.50 (*0-931464-55-2*) Eisenbrauns.

Bodinger-de Uriarte, Christina. Hate Crime. 150p. 1991. pap. 18.95 (*1-56602-046-8*) Research Better.

Bodington, Joan, jt. auth. see Benn, Tony.

Bodington, Stephen. Computers & Socialism. 245p. 1987. 50.00 (*0-7855-1006-0*) St Mut.
— The Cutting Edge of Socialism: Working People Against Transnational Capital. 87p. 1982. pap. 14.95 (*0-85124-332-0*, Pub. by Spkesman) Coronet Bks.

Bodini, Vittorio. The Hands of the South. Feldman, Ruth & Swann, Brian, trs. LC 80-68879. 1980. 7.50 (*0-910350-02-7*) Charioteer.

Bodinier, Gilbert. Dictionnaire des Officiers de l'Armee Royale Qui Ont Combattu Aux Etats-Unis Pedant la Guerre D'Independence. (FRE.). 498p. 1982. pap. 55.00 (*0-7859-8133-0*, 2863230158) Fr & Eur.

Bodinski, Lois H. The Nurse's Guide to Diet Therapy. 2nd ed. 1989. pap. text 33.50 (*0-8273-4209-8*) Delmar.

Bodio, Gene, jt. auth. see Ruff, Barry.

Bodio, Stephen. On the Edge of the Wild: Passions & Pleasures of a Naturalist. LC 97-28147. 208p. 1998. 25.00 (*1-55821-648-0*) Lyons Pr.
— A Rage for Falcons. LC 92-8003. (Illus.). 135p. 1992. pap. 12.95 (*0-87108-826-6*) Pruett.

Bodio, Stephen J. Aloft: A Meditation on Pigeons & Pigeon Flying. 128p. 1990. 15.95 (*1-55821-054-7*) Lyons Pr.
— Aloft: A Meditation on Pigeons & Pigeon-Flying. LC 93-9819. (Illus.). 84p. 1993. pap. 12.95 (*0-87108-837-1*) Pruett.
— Good Guns Again: A Celebration of Fine Sporting Arms. LC 95-141604. (Illus.). 183p. 1994. 29.00 (*1-885106-05-X*) Wild Adven Pr.
— Good Guns Again: A Celebration of Fine Sporting Arms. limited ed. LC 95-141604. (Illus.). 192p. 1994. lthr. 95.00 (*1-885106-06-8*) Wild Adven Pr.

Bodio, Steve. Querencia. LC 89-82474. 176p. 1990. pap. 12.95 (*0-944439-15-2*) Clark City Pr.

Bodio, Steven. Querencia. 2nd ed. LC 89-82474. 176p. 1996. reprint ed. 19.95 (*0-944439-75-6*) Clark City Pr.

***Bodisch, Robert J., Sr.** Multi-Year Statewide Strategy for Drugs & Violent Crime Control: State of Texas. (Illus.). 51p. (C). 1999. pap. text 25.00 (*0-7881-7212-3*) DIANE Pub.

Bodker, Susanne. Through the Interface: A Human Activity Approach to User Interface Design. 192p. (C). 1990. pap. 32.50 (*0-8058-0571-0*); text 65.00 (*0-8058-0570-2*) L Erlbaum Assocs.

Bodkin, Larry E., jt. auth. see Harris, Robert C.

Bodkin, M. McDonnell. Famous Irish Trials. 142p. 1997. reprint ed. 34.00 (*1-901658-08-2*); reprint ed. pap. 22.00 (*1-901658-03-1*) Gaunt.
— Recollections of an Irish Judge: Press, Bar & Parliament. 388p. 1996. reprint ed. 97.00 (*1-56169-196-8*) Gaunt.

Bodkin, Odds. The Banshee Train. LC 93-39635. (Illus.). 32p. (J). 1995. 14.95 (*0-395-69426-4*, Clarion Bks) HM.
— Banshee Train. (Illus.). 32p. 1996. pap. 6.95 (*0-395-79722-5*) HM.

Bodkin, Odds. Banshee Train. 1995. 11.15 (*0-606-10749-5*, Pub. by Turtleback) Demco.

Bodkin, Odds. The Christmas Cobweb. LC 97-25626. (Illus.). (J). 2000. 16.00 (*0-15-201459-4*) Harcourt.
— The Crane Wife. LC 96-35488. (Illus.). 32p. (J). (gr. k-4). 1998. 16.00 (*0-15-201407-1*) Harcourt.
— The Crane Wife. 1998. 24.26 (*0-8172-5767-5*) Raintree Steck-V.
— Ghost of the Southern Belle: A Sea Tale. LC 98-15778. (Illus.). 32p. (J). (gr. k-3). 1999. 15.95 (*0-316-02608-5*) Little.

Bodkin, Robin O., tr. see Desquiron, Lilas.

Bodkin, Ronald, et al. A History of Macroeconometric Model-Building. (Illus.). 592p. 1991. text 150.00 (*1-85278-369-9*) E Elgar.

Bodkin, Thomas. Four Irish Landscape Painters. (Illus.). 1920. 14.95 (*0-7165-2405-8*, Pub. by Irish Acad Pr) Intl Spec Bk.

Bodky, Erwin. The Interpretation of Bach's Keyboard Works. LC 75-44101. (Illus.). 421p. 1976. reprint ed. lib. bdg. 35.00 (*0-8371-8720-6*, BOBK, Greenwood Pr) Greenwood.

Bodle, David W., et al. Characterization of the Electrical Environment. LC 76-22886. 335p. reprint ed. pap. 103.90 (*0-608-15387-7*, 202932500060) Bks Demand.

Bodleian Library Staff, jt. auth. see Kiessling, Nicolas K.

Bodley, John H. Anthropology & Contemporary Human Problems. 3rd ed. LC 95-23596. xii, 244p. (C). 1996. pap. text 28.95 (*1-55934-522-5*, 1522) Mayfield Pub.
— Cultural Anthropology: Tribes, States, & the Global System. (Illus.). 480p. 1999. reprint ed. pap. text 20.00 (*0-7881-6025-7*) DIANE Pub.
— Cultural Anthropology: Tribes, States & the Global System. 3rd ed. LC 99-12137. 528p. 1999. pap. text 52.95 (*0-7674-1194-3*) Mayfield Pub.
— Tribal Peoples & Development Issues: A Global Overview. LC 87-12508. 421p. (C). 1988. pap. text 40.95 (*0-87484-786-9*, 786) Mayfield Pub.
— Victims of Progress. 4th ed. LC 98-20615. 304p. 1998. pap. text 28.95 (*0-7674-0505-6*, 0505-9) Mayfield Pub.

Bodley, Ronald V. Messenger: The Life of Mohammed. LC 70-92296. 368p. 1970. reprint ed. lib. bdg. 65.00 (*0-8371-2423-9*, BOTM, Greenwood Pr) Greenwood.

Bodley, Seoirse. Mass of Glory. 1989. pap. 30.00 (*0-86217-050-8*, Pub. by Veritas Pubns); pap. 30.00 (*0-86217-049-4*, Pub. by Veritas Pubns) St Mut.
— Mass of Joy: In Honour of St. John of God. 1989. pap. 30.00 (*0-905092-78-3*, Pub. by Veritas Pubns) St Mut.

Bodley, Temple. George Rogers Clark: His Life & Public Services. (BCL1 - U. S. History Ser.). 425p. 1991. reprint ed. lib. bdg. 99.00 (*0-7812-6103-1*) Rprt Serv.

Bodley, Temple, ed. Littell's Political Transactions in & Concerning Kentucky. LC 70-146375. (First American Frontier Ser.). 322p. 1971. reprint ed. 33.95 (*0-405-02826-1*) Ayer.

Bodman, D., jt. auth. see Fairbanks, Ellen.

Bodman, Ellen & Fairbanks, D. Critical Guide to Documentary Films of the Islamic World. (C). 1998. pap. 59.00 (*0-8133-8490-7*) Westview.

Bodman, Herbert L. & Tahidi, Nayereh, eds. Women in Muslim Societies: Diversity Within Unity. LC 97-40395. 312p. 1998. 55.00 (*1-55587-558-0*); pap. 22.00 (*1-55587-578-5*) L Rienner.

Bodman, Jean W. Spaghetti Forever. (J). 1991. mass mkt. 18.95 (*0-8384-3351-0*) Heinle & Heinle.

Bodman, Jean W. & Lanzano, Michael. No Hot Water Tonight. 2nd ed. (J). 1991. mass mkt. 18.95 (*0-8384-3231-X*) Heinle & Heinle.

Bodman, Manoah. A Matter of Infinite Moment. 32p. 1998. reprint ed. pap. 4.00 (*1-893032-00-0*) Jensen Daniels.

Bodman, Nicholas C. Spoken Amoy Hokkien. (Spoken Language Ser.). 630p. 1987. pap. text 170.00 incl. audio (*0-87950-452-8*) Spoken Lang Serv.

Bodman, Nicholas C. Spoken Amoy Hokkien. (Spoken Language Ser.). 630p. 1987. audio 125.00 (*0-87950-451-X*) Spoken Lang Serv.

Bodman, Nicholas C. Spoken Amoy Hokkien: Vocabulary Units 1-30. (Spoken Language Ser.). 630p. 1987. pap. text 45.00 (*0-87950-450-1*) Spoken Lang Serv.

Bodman, Nicholas C. & Su-Chu, Wu. Spoken Taiwanese. (Spoken Language Ser.). (CHI.). 208p. 1980. pap. 15.00 (*0-87950-460-9*); pap. 120.00 incl. audio (*0-87950-462-5*) Spoken Lang Serv.

Bodman, Nicholas C. & Su-Chu, Wu. Spoken Taiwanese. (Spoken Language Ser.). (CHI.). 208p. 1980. audio 105.00 (*0-87950-461-7*) Spoken Lang Serv.

Bodman, Richard W., tr. see Xiaokang, Su & Luxiang, Wang.

Bodmer, Beatriz P. The Armature of Conquest: Spanish Accounts of the Discovery of America, 1492-1589. Hunt, Lydia L., tr. from SPA. LC 91-39494. 344p. (C). 1992. 49.50 (*0-8047-1977-2*) Stanford U Pr.
— The Armature of Conquest: Spanish Accounts of the Discovery of America, 1492-1589. Hunt, Lydia L., tr. from SPA. 340p. 1995. pap. 16.95 (*0-8047-2470-9*) Stanford U Pr.

***Bodmer, Frederick.** The Loom of Language. 669p. 1999. reprint ed. pap. 19.95 (*0-85036-350-0*, Pub. by MRLN) Paul & Co Pubs.

Bodmer, Frederick. The Loom of Language. Hogben, Lancelot, ed. (Illus.). 720p. 1985. reprint ed. pap. 19.95 (*0-393-30034-X*) Norton.

Bodmer, Johann J. & Breitinger, Johann J., eds. Der Mahler der Sitten, Bd. 2. (GER.). 1285p. 1972. reprint ed. write for info. (*3-487-04242-8*) G Olms Pubs.

***Bodmer, Judy.** What's in the Bible for... Mothers. Richards, Larry, ed. LC 99-69038. (What's in the Bible for... Ser.: No. 2). (Illus.). 336p. 2000. pap. 16.95 (*1-892016-26-5*, Pub. by Starburst) Natl Bk Netwk.
— When Love Dies: How to Save a Hopeless Marriage. LC 99-24421. 196p. 1999. pap. 12.99 (*0-8499-3714-0*) Word Pub.

Bodmer, Karl. Karl Bodmer's America. annot. ed. LC 83-27391. (Illus.). xii, 376p. 1984. text 125.00 (*0-8032-1185-6*) U of Nebr Pr.

Bodmer, Kerri & Fuchs, Nan K. The Giant Book of Women's Health Secrets. Kroening, Steven E., ed. 448p. 1998. pap. 24.95 (*1-885385-00-5*) Soundview Pubns.

Bodmer, Mark W., jt. ed. see Henderson, Brian.

Bodmer-Turner, Jeffrey, jt. auth. see Gil, Eliana M.

Bodmer, W. F. & Owen, M. J., eds. Molecular Mechanisms of the Immune Response. (Cancer Surveys Ser.: Vol. 22). (Illus.). 190p. (C). 1994. 56.25 (*0-87969-442-4*) Cold Spring Harbor.

Bodmer, W. F., jt. auth. see Cavalli-Sforza, L. L.

Bodmer, W. F., jt. ed. see McMichael, A. J.

Bodmer, Walter. Book of Man. 1995. 25.00 (*0-684-80102-7*) S&S Trade.

Bodmer, Walter & McKie, Robin. The Book of Man: The Human Genome Project & the Quest to Discover Our Genetic Heritage. LC 96-37423. (Illus.). 272p. 1997. reprint ed. pap. 13.95 (*0-19-511487-6*) OUP.

Bodmer, Walter F., jt. auth. see Terasaki, Paul I.

B

An Asterisk (*) at the beginning of an entry indicates that the title is appearing for the first time.

*__Bodnabr, Judit.__ Fin de Millenaire Budapest: Metamorphoses of Urban Life. LC 00-9538. (Globalization & Community Ser.). 2001. pap. write for info. (*0-8166-3585-4*) U of Minn Pr.

*__Bodnar, Bohdan, ed.__ Applied Telecommunication Symposium 1998. 188p. 1998. 40.00 (*1-56555-146-X*) Soc Computer Sim.

*__Bodnar, Bohdan & Sharon, Ariel, eds.__ Applied Telecommunications Symposium. (Simulation Ser.: Vol. 31, No. 4). 272p. 1999. 100.00 (*1-56555-165-6*) Soc Computer Sim.

__Bodnar, Cecily K.__ Speaking Statistics. LC 95-45. 1995. pap. 12.50 (*0-13-030180-9*) P-H.

__Bodnar, Cecily K. & Hopwood, William S.__ Accounting Information Systems. 4th ed. (C). write for info. incl. 5.25 hd (*0-318-68770-4*); write for info. incl. 3.5 hd (*0-318-68771-2*) P-H.

__Bodnar, Don.__ How to Write an RFP for a Telecommunications Cabling System. (Illus.). 150p. 1997. pap. 34.95 (*1-57820-001-6*) Telecom Bks.

__Bodnar, Edward W. & Mitchell, Charles, eds.__ Vita Viri Clarissimi et Famosissimi Kyriaci Anconitani. LC 94-78512. (Transactions Ser.: Vol. 86, Pt. 4). 278p. (Orig.). 1996. pap. 25.00 (*0-87169-864-1*, T864-boe) Am Philos.

__Bodnar, Endre & Frater, Robert W.__ Replacement Cardiac Valves. (Illus.). 480p. 1991. 94.50 (*0-08-035773-3*, Pub. by PPI) McGraw.

__Bodnar, George & Hopwood, William S.__ Accounting Information Systems. 7th ed. LC 97-38248. 686p. (C). 1997. 100.00 (*0-13-750978-2*) P-H.

*__Bodnar, George H. & Hopwood, William S.__ Accounting Information Systems. 8th ed. LC 00-26208. 688p. 2000. 82.67 (*0-13-086177-4*) P-H.

__Bodnar, Janet.__ Dollars & Sense for Kids: What They Need to Know about Money - And How to Tell Them. 308p. 1999. pap. 17.95 (*0-938721-67-4*, Pub. by Kiplinger Bks) Natl Bk Netwk.

__Bodnar, John.__ Anthracite People: Families, Unions & Work, 1900-1940. (Illus.). 100p. 1983. pap. text 6.95 (*0-89271-023-3*) Pa Hist & Mus.

— Immigration & Industrialization: Ethnicity in an American Mill Town, 1870-1940. LC 77-74549. 233p. 1977. reprint ed. pap. 72.30 (*0-608-05324-4*, 201915000010) Bks Demand.

— Remaking America: Public Memory, Commemoration, & Patriotism in the Twentieth Century. 318p. (C). 1992. pap. text 18.95 (*0-691-03495-8*, Pub. by Princeton U Pr) Cal Prin Full Svc.

__Bodnar, John, ed.__ Bonds of Affection: Americans Define Their Patriotism. 352p. 1996. text 57.50 (*0-691-04397-3*, Pub. by Princeton U Pr); pap. text 16.95 (*0-691-04396-5*, Pub. by Princeton U Pr) Cal Prin Full Svc.

__Bodnar, John, et al.__ Lives of Their Own: Blacks, Italians, & Poles in Pittsburgh, 1900-1960. LC 81-3382. (Working Class in American History Ser.). (Illus.). 302p. 1981. text 29.95 (*0-252-00880-4*) U of Ill Pr.

— Lives of Their Own: Blacks, Italians, & Poles in Pittsburgh, 1900-1960. LC 81-3382. (Working Class in American History Ser.). (Illus.). 302p. 1983. pap. text 15.95 (*0-252-01063-9*) U of Ill Pr.

__Bodnar, John E.__ Steelton: Immigration & Industrialization, 1870-1940. LC 90-33284. (Pittsburgh Series in Social & Labor History). 237p. 1990. pap. 73.50 (*0-608-05087-3*, 206564100005) Bks Demand.

— The Transplanted: A History of Immigrants in Urban America. LC 84-48041. (Interdisciplinary Studies in History). (Illus.). 320p. 1985. pap. 13.95 (*0-253-20416-X*) Ind U Pr.

— The Transplanted: A History of Immigrants in Urban America. LC 84-48041. (Interdisciplinary Studies in History). (Illus.). 320p. 1985. 35.00 (*0-253-31347-3*) Ind U Pr.

__Bodnar, John E., ed.__ The Ethnic Experience in Pennsylvania. LC 72-3257. (Illus.). 330p. 1973. 39.50 (*0-8387-1155-3*) Bucknell U Pr.

*__Bodnar, Judit.__ Tale of a Tail. LC 93-19046. (Illus.). 40p. (J). (ps-3). 1998. 15.89 (*0-688-12175-6*, Wm Morrow) Morrow Avon.

__Bodnar, Judit, ed. see Alexander, Nina.__

__Bodnar, Judit, ed. see Engle, Marion.__

__Bodnar, Judit, ed. see Korman, Susan.__

__Bodnar, Judit, ed. see Lewis, Zoe.__

__Bodnar, Judit, ed. see Sinykin, Sheri Cooper.__

__Bodnar, Judit, ed. see Williams, L. E.__

__Bodnar, Judit Z.__ Tale of a Tail. LC 93-19046. (Illus.). 40p. (J). (ps-3). 1998. 16.00 (*0-688-12174-8*, Wm Morrow) Morrow Avon.

— A Wagonload of Fish. LC 93-19047. (Illus.). 32p. (J). (gr. k-2). 1996. lib. bdg. 14.93 (*0-688-12173-X*) Lothrop.

— A Wagonload of Fish. LC 93-19047. (Illus.). 32p. (J). (ps-3). 1996. 15.00 (*0-688-12172-1*) Lothrop.

__Bodnar, Szilvia.__ The Museum of Fine Arts. 144p. 1989. pap. 85.00 (*963-13-3897-5*, Pub. by Corvina Bks) St Mut.

__Bodnarchuk, Kari.__ Rwanda: A Country Torn Apart. LC 96-43424. (World in Conflict Ser.). 96p. (YA). (gr. 7-10). 1999. lib. bdg. 25.26 (*0-8225-3557-2*, Lerner Publctns) Lerner Pub.

__Bodnarchuk, Kari J.__ Kurdistan: Region under Siege. LC 99-19500. (World in Conflict Ser.). (Illus.). 104p. (YA). (gr. 7-10). 2000. lib. bdg. 25.26 (*0-8225-3556-4*, Lerner Publctns) Lerner Pub.

__Bodner.__ Chemistry: Prelim. Edition Core Test & Modular Chapters. ed. 1051p. 1995. pap. text 80.90 (*0-471-14949-7*) Wiley.

— Chemistry: Structure & Dynamics. 370p. 1996. pap. text, teacher ed. 36.95 (*0-471-14759-1*) Wiley.

__Bodner, Allen J.__ When Boxing Was a Jewish Sport. LC 97-14469. 248p. 1997. 24.95 (*0-275-95353-X*, Praeger Pubs) Greenwood.

__Bodner, Elizabeth L.__ Uncompromising Vol. 1: Family Style. LC 97-90128. 235p. (Orig.). 1997. pap. 14.95 (*0-9657162-0-1*) EBW Assocs.

__Bodner, G. M.__ Chemistry: An Experimental Science. 2nd ed. 780p. 1994. pap., student ed. 36.95 (*0-471-59877-1*) Wiley.

— Chemistry Solutions Manual: An Experimental Science. 2nd ed. 200p. 1994. pap. 36.95 (*0-471-59876-3*) Wiley.

__Bodner, George M. & Pardue, Harry L.__ Chemistry: An Experimental Science. 2nd ed. 1104p. 1994. text 103.95 (*0-471-59386-9*) Wiley.

__Bodner, George M., et al.__ Chemistry: Structure & Dynamics. alternate ed. LC 95-23042. 784p. (C). 1995. pap. 48.95 (*0-471-12815-5*) Wiley.

— Chemistry, Structure & Dynamics: Modular Chapters. alternate ed. 368p. 1995. pap. 31.95 (*0-471-14278-6*) Wiley.

__Bodner, Michael S.__ Micro-to-Mainframe Data (3.5) 2nd ed. 1991. 49.95 (*0-8306-6743-1*) McGraw-Hill Prof.

__Bodner, Pinchas.__ Halachos of Muktzah. 1985. 23.95 (*0-87306-856-4*) Feldheim.

__Bodner, S. R. & Liebowitz, H., eds.__ Mechanics of Damage & Fracture: Proceedings of the IUTAM Symposium, Haifa, Israel, 1-4 June 1985. (JEFM Ser.: No. 25). (Illus.). 300p. 1988. 115.00 (*0-08-034931-5*, Pergamon Pr) Elsevier.

__Bodner, Yisroel.__ Halachos of Brochos. 1997. 29.95 (*0-87306-832-7*); pap. 25.95 (*0-87306-835-1*) Feldheim.

*__Bodney, John A.__ Bodney's California Insurance Digest. 1999. write for info. (*1-58012-039-3*) James Pub Santa Ana.

— Bodney's California Insurance Digest. 1999. write for info. (*1-58012-045-8*) James Pub Santa Ana.

__Bodo, Gianluigi, jt. ed. see Massaglia, Silvano.__

__Bodo, Imre, jt. ed. see Alderson, Lawrence.__

__Bodo, John, et al, contrib. by.__ SourceBook of Funerals. 234p. 1998. text 43.00 (*0-930921-13-5*, FNR) Comm Res OH.

__Bodo, John, et al.__ Sourcebook of Worship Resources, Vol. 2. Purdum, Stan, ed. 243p. 1996. 39.00 (*0-930921-08-9*, SBWR2) Comm Res OH.

__Bodo, John R.__ Prophet on the Payroll: When Pulpit & Pew Clash. LC 98-46475. 188p. 1999. pap. 19.95 (*1-57249-156-6*, Burd St Pr) White Mane Pub.

— Protestant Clergy & Public Issues, Eighteen Twelve to Eighteen Forty-Eight. LC 79-12849. (Perspectives in American History Ser.: No. 52). xiv, 291p. 1980. reprint ed. lib. bdg. 45.00 (*0-87991-854-3*) Porcupine Pr.

*__Bodo, John R.__ Who They Really Were: Preaching on Biblical Personalities. 2000. pap. 13.25 (*0-7880-1540-0*) CSS OH.

__Bodo, Martin.__ The Hard Drive Bible. 8th ed. Moorehead, Harold, ed. & photos by. (Illus.). 500p. 1996. write for info. incl. cd-rom (*0-9641503-1-X*) Corp Systs Ctr.

__Bodo, Murray.__ The Almond Tree Speaks: New & Selected Writings 1974-1994. 150p. 1995. pap. 7.95 (*0-86716-237-6*) St Anthony Mess Pr.

— Clare: A Light in the Garden. enl. rev. ed. 126p. 1992. pap. 7.95 (*0-86716-122-1*) St Anthony Mess Pr.

— Francis: The Journey & the Dream. rev. ed. (Illus.). 119p. 1988. pap. 5.95 (*0-86716-116-7*) St Anthony Mess Pr.

— Francisco: El Viaje y el Sueno. Sarre, Alicia, tr. (SPA.). 133p. 1994. pap. 6.95 (*0-86716-205-8*) St Anthony Mess Pr.

— Tales of an Endishodi: Father Berard Haile & the Navajos, 1900-1961. LC 97-30841. 263p. 1998. 45.00 (*0-8263-1829-0*); pap. 24.95 (*0-8263-1879-7*) U of NM Pr.

— Tales of St. Francis: Ancient Stories for Contemporary Times. 191p. 1992. pap. 8.95 (*0-86716-195-7*) St Anthony Mess Pr.

*__Bodo, Murray.__ The Threefold Way of Saint Francis. (IlluminationBook Ser.). 2000. pap. 5.95 (*0-8091-4003-9*) Paulist Pr.

__Bodo, Murray.__ Through the Year with Francis of Assisi: Daily Meditations from his Words & Life. 240p. 1993. pap. 9.95 (*0-86716-196-5*) St Anthony Mess Pr.

— The Way of St. Francis: The Challenge of Franciscan Spirituality for Everyone. 160p. 1995. pap. 8.95 (*0-86716-244-9*) St Anthony Mess Pr.

__Bodo, Murray & Sing, Susan S.__ A Retreat with Francis & Clare of Assisi: Following Our Pilgrim Hearts. 112p. (Orig.). 1996. pap. 7.95 (*0-86716-238-4*, B2384) St Anthony Mess Pr.

__Bodo, Peter.__ The Atlantic Salmon Handbook: An Atlantic Salmon Federation Book. LC 97-8223. (Illus.). 224p. 1997. 25.00 (*1-55821-510-7*); pap. 16.95 (*1-55821-511-5*) Lyons Pr.

— The Courts of Babylon: Tales of Greed & Glory in the Harsh New High-Stakes World of Professional Tennis. 320p. 1995. 25.00 (*0-684-81296-7*) S&S Trade.

__Bodo, Peter, jt. auth. see McEnroe, Patrick.__

__Bodoczky, Caroline, jt. auth. see Malderez, Angi.__

__Bodoh, John J., et al.__ An Index of Greek Verb Forms. (Alpha-Omega Band Ser.: No. XIV). x, 481p. 1984. 105.00 (*3-487-03035-7*) G Olms Pubs.

__Bodomo, Adams.__ The Structure of Dagaare. LC 96-37999. (Stanford Monographs in African Languages). 168p. (C). 1997. 39.95 (*1-57586-077-5*) CSLI.

__Bodomo, Adams, jt. ed. see Garry, Jane.__

__Bodoni.__ Elements Of Motion Pictures. 1998. 47.00 (*0-07-233502-5*) McGraw.

__Bodoni, Giam Battista.__ Il Cimelio of Bodoni. 252p. 1991. write for info. (*0-87923-924-7*) Godine.

__Bodor, Adam.__ The Euphrates at Babylon. 1992. pap. 12.95 (*0-7486-6055-0*, Pub. by Edinburgh U Pr) Col U Pr.

__Bodor, Geza.__ Structural Investigation of Polymers. 477p. 1991. 125.00 (*963-05-5606-5*, Pub. by Akade Kiado) St Mut.

__Bodourian, Marilyn.__ Conservation for Children: All Levels Guide. (Illus.). 116p. 1994. pap. text, teacher ed. 13.95 (*1-57035-013-2*, 17CCALL) Sopris.

— Conservation for Children: Crafty Ideas. (Illus.). 56p. 1994. pap. text, teacher ed. 6.50 (*1-57035-026-4*, 17CCRAFT) Sopris.

— Conservation for Children: Level 1 Guide. (Conservation for Children Ser.). (Illus.). 158p. 1994. pap. text, teacher ed. 13.95 (*1-57035-007-8*, 17CC1) Sopris.

— Conservation for Children: Level 2 Guide. (Conservation for Children Ser.). (Illus.). 158p. 1994. pap. text, teacher ed. 13.95 (*1-57035-008-6*, 17CC2) Sopris.

— Conservation for Children: Level 3 Guide. (Conservation for Children Ser.). (Illus.). 158p. 1994. pap. text, teacher ed. 13.95 (*1-57035-009-4*, 17CC3) Sopris.

— Conservation for Children: Level 4 Guide. (Conservation for Children Ser.). (Illus.). 158p. 1994. pap. text, teacher ed. 13.95 (*1-57035-010-8*, 17CC4) Sopris.

— Conservation for Children: Level 5 Guide. (Illus.). 158p. 1994. pap. text, teacher ed. 13.95 (*1-57035-011-6*, 17CC5) Sopris.

— Conservation for Children: Level 6 Guide. (Illus.). 158p. 1994. pap. text, teacher ed. 13.95 (*1-57035-012-4*, 17CC6) Sopris.

— Conservation for Children Program Kit, 8 publications, Set. (Illus.). 1120p. 1994. pap. text, teacher ed. 90.00 (*1-57035-033-7*, C17CCSET) Sopris.

__Bodow, Steven.__ Sitting Bull. LC 92-16518. (American Troublemakers Ser.). (Illus.). 128p. (J). (gr. 7-10). 1992. lib. bdg. 27.11 (*0-8114-2328-X*) Raintree Steck-V.

*__Bodri, William, tr.__ The Means to Win: Strategies for Success in Business & Politics. 176p. 2000. pap. 15.00 (*0-87573-083-3*) Jain Pub Co.

__Bodri, William & Shu-Mei, Lee.__ Twenty-Five Doors to Meditation: A Handbook for Entering Samadhi. LC 97-51639. (Illus.). 176p. 1998. pap. 14.95 (*1-57863-035-5*) Weiser.

__Bodrogligeti, A. J., jt. ed. see Decsy, Gyula.__

__Bodrova, Elena, jt. auth. see Leong, Deborah J.__

__Bodrova, Valentina & Anker, Richard, eds.__ Working Women in Socialist Countries: The Fertility Connection (WEP Study) xvi, 234p. (Orig.). 1987. pap. 24.75 (*92-2-103910-2*) Intl Labour Office.

__Bodry-Sanders, Penelope.__ African Obsession: The Life & Legacy of Carl Akeley. 2nd rev. ed. Orig. Title: Carl Akeley, Africa's Collector, Africa's Savior. (Illus.). 298p. 1998. pap. 14.95 (*0-9629759-9-0*) Batax Mus.

__Bodshotz, Mike.__ Stripper Photos of Aussie Lads. (Illus.). 1999. pap. text 25.00 (*0-85449-289-5*) Gay Mens Pr.

__Bodshotz, Mike, photos by.__ Stripper: Photos of Aussie Lads. (Illus.). 64p. 1999. pap. 25.00 (*0-85449-276-3*) LPC InBook.

__Bodson, Gerard.__ Secrets of the Apocalypse: The Prophecies of the Last Book of the Bible: Revelation. 2000. 24.95 (*1-86204-730-8*, Pub. by Element MA) Penguin Putnam.

__Bodson, Herman.__ Agent for the Resistance: A Belgian Saboteur in World War II. LC 94-25762. (Military History Ser.: No. 35). (Illus.). 262p. 1994. 29.95 (*0-89096-607-9*) Tex A&M Univ Pr.

__Bodsworth, Colin.__ The Extraction & Refining of Metals. 368p. 1994. boxed set 104.95 (*0-8493-4433-6*) CRC Pr.

__Bodsworth, Colin & Appleton, A. S.__ Problems in Applied Thermodynamics. LC 66-78638. 223p. reprint ed. pap. 69.20 (*0-608-30459-X*, 200363600038) Bks Demand.

__Bodsworth, Fred.__ The Last of the Curlews. 136p. 1996. pap. text 5.95 (*0-7710-9874-X*) McCland & Stewart.

— The Last of the Curlews. 1993. reprint ed. lib. bdg. 18.95 (*1-56849-179-4*) Buccaneer Bks.

__Bodsyth, Charles W.__ The Ultra Dry Basement: A Basic Guide to Understanding & Correcting Foundation Water Problems. 2nd rev. ed. (Illus.). 1998. spiral bd. 29.95 (*0-9672330-0-3*) Best Basement.

__Bodt, Saskia De, see Museum Boijmans Van Beuningen Staff.__

__Bodtke, Leslie C., ed. see Suggs, Jackie.__

__Boduszynski, Mieczyslaw H., jt. ed. see Altgelt, Klaus H.__

__Bodwell, C. E. & Erdman, John W.__ Nutrient Interactions. (IFT Basic Symposium Ser.: Vol. 3). (Illus.). 408p. 1988. text 125.00 (*0-8247-7868-5*) Dekker.

*__Body-Gendrot, Sophie.__ The Social Control of Cities? LC HT321.B65 1999. (Studies in Urban & Social Change). 320p. 1999. 62.95 (*0-631-20520-9*); pap. text 28.95 (*0-631-20521-7*) Blackwell Pubs.

*__Body-Gendrot, Sophie & Martiniello, Marco.__ Minorities in European Cities: The Dynamics of Social Integration & Social Exclusion at the Neighborhood Level. LC 99-54922. 2000. 65.00 (*0-312-23132-6*) St Martin.

__Body, Jacques.__ Jean Giraudoux: The Legend & the Secret. Norwood, James, tr. LC 89-46424. 152p. 1991. 32.50 (*0-8386-3407-9*) Fairleigh Dickinson.

__Body, Jacques, jt. auth. see Giraudoux, Jean.__

__Body, Jacques, ed. see Giraudoux, Jean.__

*__Body, Jean J.__ Tumor Bone Diseases & Osteoporosis in Cancer Patients. LC 99-39513. (Illus.). 561p. 1999. text 195.00 (*0-8247-6399-8*) Dekker.

__Body, Jerry C., Jr.__ Indian Draft Spirit. LC 98-86647. 64p. 1998. pap. text 11.00 (*1-56167-416-8*) Am Literary Pr.

__Body, Paul.__ Hungarian Statesmen of Destiny, 1876-1956. (Atlantic Studies on Society in Change, East European Monographs: No. 262). 209p. 1989. text 52.00 (*0-88033-159-3*, Pub. by East Eur Monographs) Col U Pr.

— Joseph Eotvos & the Modernization of Hungary, 1840-1870. 1985. text 48.50 (*0-88033-066-X*, 174, Pub. by East Eur Monographs) Col U Pr.

__Body, Sean.__ Wish the World Away: Mark Eitzel & the American Music Club. (Illus.). 246p. 1998. pap. 18.95 (*0-946719-20-9*, Pub. by Helter Skelter) Interlink Pub.

__Body Shop International Staff.__ The Body Shop Book. 1999. pap. 14.95 (*0-452-27403-6*, Plume) Dutton Plume.

__Body Surface Mapping of Cardiac Fields Symposium S.__ Body Surface Mapping of Cardiac Fields: Proceedings of the Symposium, Burlington, Vermont, 1972. Lepeschkin, E. & Rush, S., eds. (Advances in Cardiology Ser.: Vol. 10). (Illus.). 344p. 1974. 123.50 (*3-8055-1566-9*) S Karger.

__Bodycombe, David J.__ The Mammoth Book of Brainstorming Puzzles. (Mammoth Book Ser.). (Illus.). 560p. 1996. pap. 10.95 (*0-7867-0299-0*) Carroll & Graf.

— The Mammoth Puzzle Carnival. LC 97-18975. (Mammoth Book Ser.). (Illus.). 512p. 1997. pap. 10.95 (*0-7867-0427-6*) Carroll & Graf.

__Bodziak, William J.__ Footwear Impression Evidence. LC 95-13582. (Elsevier Series in Practical Aspects of Criminal & Forensic Investigations). 448p. 1992. reprint ed. boxed set 87.95 (*0-8493-9500-3*) CRC Pr.

— Footwear Impression Evidence: Detection, Recovery & Examination. 2nd ed. LC 99-28347. (Practical Aspects of Criminal & Forensic Investigations Ser.). 528p. 1999. boxed set 89.95 (*0-8493-1045-8*) CRC Pr.

__Boe, Alf.__ From Gothic Revival to Functional Form. 233p. (C). 1997. text 34.00 (*82-00-42741-2*) Scandnvan Univ Pr.

— From Gothic Revival to Functional Form. LC 78-31194. (Architecture & Decorative Art Ser.). 1979. reprint ed. 29.50 (*0-306-77544-1*) Da Capo.

__Boe, Anne.__ Networking Success: How to Turn Business & Financial Relationships into Fun & Profit. 250p. 1995. pap. 12.95 (*1-55874-365-0*, 3650) Health Comm.

__Boe, Anne & Youngs, Bettie B.__ Is Your "Net" Working? A Complete Guide to Building Contacts & Career Visibility. LC 88-28086. 250p. 1989. 27.95 (*0-471-61547-1*) Wiley.

__Boe, Beverly, jt. auth. see Philcox, Phil.__

__Boe, Brian D. & Collingwood, David H.__ Enright-Shelton Theory & Vogan's Problem for Generalized Principal Series. LC 92-38215. (Memoirs Ser.: No. 486). 107p. 1993. pap. 30.00 (*0-8218-2547-X*) Am Math.

__Boe, Deborah.__ Mojave. LC 87-334. 1987. 15.00 (*0-914610-47-3*); pap. 7.00 (*0-914610-44-9*) Hanging Loose.

__Boe, Deen.__ Outdoor Recreation in Economic Development. (New Alliances for Rural America Ser.). (Orig.). 1988. pap. text 6.00 (*1-55877-021-6*) Natl Governor.

__Boe, Erling E. & Church, Russell M., eds.__ Punishment: Issues & Experiments. LC 68-23894. (Century Psychology Ser.). (Illus.). (Orig.). (C). 1968. pap. text 13.95 (*0-89197-367-2*) Irvington.

__Boe, Erling E., ed. see National Research Council Staff.__

__Boe, Eugene.__ Friendship with God: A Study of the Christian Life. Rinden, David, ed. 66p. 1997. pap. text 4.95 (*0-943167-38-8*) Faith & Fellowship Pr.

— Identity in Christ: A Study on Justification. 38p. (Orig.). 1992. pap. 4.95 (*0-943167-18-3*) Faith & Fellowship Pr.

__Boe, Eugene, jt. auth. see Demko, George.__

__Boe, John.__ Life Itself: "Messiness Is Next to Goddessness" & Other Essays. LC 94-19711. 184p. (Orig.). 1994. pap. 14.95 (*0-933029-86-1*) Chiron Pubns.

__Boe, John & Planchart, Alejandro, eds.__ Beneventanum Troporum Corpus: Essays, Commentary, & Preface Chants. (Recent Researches in Music of the Middle Ages & Early Renaissance Ser.: Vol. RRM 25). (Illus.). lxxxix, 130p. 1996. pap. 75.00 (*0-89579-336-9*) A-R Eds.

— Beneventanum Troporum Corpus: Gloria: Essays & Commentary. (Recent Researches in Music of the Middle Ages & Early Renaissance Ser.: Vol. RRM 22). (Illus.). xxi, 51p. 1990. pap. 30.00 (*0-89579-369-5*) A-R Eds.

— Beneventanum Troporum Corpus: Gloria: Music. (Recent Researches in Music of the Middle Ages & Early Renaissance Ser.: Vol. RRM 23-24). (Illus.). 217p. 1990. pap. 70.00 (*0-89579-370-9*) A-R Eds.

— Beneventanum Troporum Corpus: Kyrie: Essays & Commentary. (Recent Researches in Music of the Middle Ages & Early Renaissance Ser.: Vol. RRM 19). (Illus.). xxxix, 89p. 1989. pap. 45.00 (*0-89579-344-X*) A-R Eds.

— Beneventanum Troporum Corpus: Kyrie: Music. (Recent Researches in Music of the Middle Ages & Early Renaissance Ser.: Vol. RRM 20-21). (Illus.). 219p. 1989. pap. 75.00 (*0-89579-345-8*) A-R Eds.

— Beneventanum Troporum Corpus: Sanctus Chants & Tropes. (Recent Researches in Music of the Middle Ages & Early Renaissance Ser.: Vol. RRM 26). (Illus.). 135p. 1996. pap. 50.00 (*0-89579-368-7*) A-R Eds.

— Beneventanum Troporum Corpus: Tropes of the Proper of the Mass: Essays & Commentary. (Recent Researches in Music of the Middle Ages & Early Renaissance Ser.: Vol. RRM16). (Illus.). liv, 95p. 1994. pap. 50.00 (*0-89579-343-1*) A-R Eds.

— Beneventanum Troporum Corpus: Tropes of the Proper of the Mass: Music. (Recent Researches in Music of the Middle Ages & Early Renaissance Ser.: Vol. RRM 17-18). (Illus.). 250p. 1994. pap. 85.00 (*0-89579-304-0*) A-R Eds.

__Boe, John D. & Kahn, Alice.__ Your Joke Is in the E-Mail: Cyberlaffs from Mousepotatoes. LC 97-40737. (Illus.). 181p. 1997. pap. 7.95 (*0-89815-988-1*) Ten Speed Pr.

__Boe, Kathryn L., et al.__ Franchise Option: How to Expand Your Business Through Franchising. 2nd ed. (Illus.). 153p. 1987. 24.00 (*0-942209-00-1*); pap. 24.00 (*0-685-25527-1*) Intl Franchise Assn.

__Boe, Susan.__ The Parent Connection: A Health Resource for Parents of Teens. Mackin, David, ed. (Parent Connection for Total Health Ser.). (Illus.). 313p. 1997. spiral bd., wbk. ed. 11.95 (*0-9646843-5-7*) RiversEdge Pub.

— Total Health: Choices for a Winning Lifestyle. Wright, Barbara, ed. (Illus.). 464p. (YA). (gr. 9-12). 1995. text 27.95 (*0-9646843-4-9*); text, teacher ed. 34.95 (*0-9646843-1-4*); pap. text 22.95 (*0-9646843-0-6*) RiversEdge Pub.

An Asterisk (*) at the beginning of an entry indicates that the title is appearing for the first time.

— Total Health: Choices for a Winning Lifestyle Test & Quiz Book. Wright, Barbara, ed. (Illus.). (YA). (gr. 9-12). 1995. pap. text 14.95 (*0-9646843-3-0*) RiversEdge Pub.

Boece, Hector. Hectoris Boetii Murthlacensium Et Aberdonensium Episcoporum Vitae, Iterum in Lucem Editae. LC 76-39462. (Bannatyne Club, Edinburgh. Publications: No. 11). reprint ed. 44.50 (*0-404-52711-6*) AMS Pr.

Boeck, George, jt. auth. see Esau, Erika.

Boeck, George A., Jr. Texas Livestock Auctions: A Folklife Ethnography. LC 89-45369. (Studies in Anthropology: No. 8). 1990. 49.50 (*0-404-62608-4*, HD 9433) AMS Pr.

Boeck, Monika, jt. auth. see Rao, Aparna.

Boeck, P. The Paraganglia. (Handbuch der Mikroskopischen Anatomie Des Menschen Ser.: Vol. 1-8). (Illus.). 400p. 1982. 228.00 (*0-387-10978-1*) Spr-Verlag.

Boeck, P., et al. Peroxisomes & Related Particles in Animal Tissues. (Cell Biology Monographs: Vol. 7). (Illus.). 250p. 1980. 121.00 (*0-387-81582-1*) Spr-Verlag.

Boeck, Tammy L. Connections. (C). 2000. pap. text. write for info. (*0-321-04431-2*) Addson-Wesley Educ.

Boecker, Alexander. Probable Italian Source of Shakespeare's Julius Caesar. reprint ed. 29.50 (*0-404-00918-2*) AMS Pr.

Boecker, Heinz-Dieter, et al, eds. Interactive Problem Solving Using LOGO. 568p. (C). 1991. pap. 55.00 (*0-8058-0306-8*); text 120.00 (*0-8058-0305-X*); disk 14.95 (*1-56321-069-X*); disk 14.95 (*1-56321-068-1*) L Erlbaum Assocs.

Boeckh, A., ed. Pindarus: Interpretatio Epiniciorum Latina Cum Commentario Perpetuo, Fragmenta et Indices. 862p. 1963. reprint ed. 225.00 (*0-318-72066-3*) G Olms Pubs.

Boeckh, A., et al, eds. Corpus Inscriptionum Graecarum, 5 vols. in 4, Set. (Subsidia Epigraphica Ser.). (GER.). lxxii, 4090p. 1977. reprint ed. 1345.00 incl. 3.5 hd (*3-487-06286-0*) G Olms Pubs.

Boeckh, August. Enzyklopaedie und Methodenlehre der Philologischen Wissenschaften. 3rd ed. (GER.). 247p. 1966. 69.95 (*0-8288-6715-1*, M7079) Fr & Eur.

Boeckh, Augustus. The Public Economy of Athens: To Which Is Added a Dissertation on the Silver Mines of Laurion. 2nd rev. ed. Lewis, George C., tr. LC 75-13364. (History of Ideas in Ancient Greece Ser.). (ENG.). 1976. reprint ed. 61.95 (*0-405-07299-6*) Ayer.

Boecking, Stefan. Boecking's Object Oriented Network Protocols. 448p. (C). 1999. 49.95 (*0-201-17789-7*) Addison-Wesley.

***Boeckl, Christine.** Images of Plague & Pestilence: Iconography & Iconology. (Sixteenth Century Essays & Studies: 53). 2000. 45.00 (*0-943549-72-8*); pap. text 30.00 (*0-943549-85-X*) Truman St Univ.

Boeckman, Charles. When the Devil Came to Endless. LC 95-96224. 192p. 1996. 18.95 (*0-8034-9171-9*, Avalon Bks) Bouregy.

Boeckman, Patti. Captive Heart. 1980. pap. 1.50 (*0-373-58003-7*) Harlequin Bks.

Boeckman, Robert K., ed. Organic Synthesis, Vol. 73. LC 21-17747. (Organic Synthesis Ser.). 353p. 1996. 44.95 (*0-471-14701-X*) Wiley.

***Boeckmann, Cathy.** A Question of Character: Scientific Racism & the Genres of American Fiction, 1892-1912. LC 99-6765. (Studies in American Literary Realism & Naturalism). 256p. 2000. 39.95 (*0-8173-1021-5*) U of Ala Pr.

***Boeckmann, Susie.** Caviar: The Definitive Guide. (Illus.). 160p. 2000. 40.00 (*0-470-39299-1*) Wiley.

***Boeckmann, Susie & Rebeiz-Nielsen, Natalie.** Caviar: A True Delicacy. (Illus.). 64p. 1999. reprint ed. text 13.00 (*0-7881-6644-1*) DIANE Pub.

Boeckmann, Tore, jt. auth. see Rand, Ayn.

Boeckner, Keith, jt. auth. see Brown, P. Charles.

Boed, Viktor. Controls & Automation for Facilities Managers: Applications Engineering. LC 97-46785. 1998. lib. bdg. 89.95 (*0-8493-9872-X*) Lewis Pubng.

Boed, Viktor & Goldschmidt, Ira. Network & Integration of Facilities Automation Systems LC 99-15538. 264p. 1999. boxed set 69.95 (*0-8493-0699-X*) CRC Pr.

Boeddicker, H., tr. see Fsrstner, Ulrich.

Boedecker, Kenneth J., Jr., jt. auth. see Brockenbrough, Roger L.

Boedecker, Ray F. Eleven Conditions for Excellence: The IBM Total Quality Improvement Process. LC 88-83584. 461p. 1989. ring bd. 187.00 (*0-935517-02-2*) Amer Inst Mgnt.

Boedeker, Deborah. Descent from Heaven: Images of Dew in Greek Poetry & Religion. (American Philological Association, American Classical Studies: No. 13). 146p. (C). 1985. pap. 15.95 (*0-89130-807-5*, 40 04 13) OUP.

Boedeker, Deborah D. & Raaflaub, Kurt A. Democracy, Empire & the Arts in Fifth-Century Athens. LC 98-17113. viii, 504 p. 1999. write for info. (*0-674-19769-0*) HUP.

Boedeker, Edgar C., ed. Attachment of Organisms to the Gut Mucosa, Vol. I. 240p. 1984. 137.00 (*0-8493-5286-X*, QR171, CRC Reprint) Franklin.

— Attachment of Organisms to the Gut Mucosa, Vol. II. 272p. 1984. 150.00 (*0-8493-5287-8*, CRC Reprint) Franklin.

Boeder. Thinking about Imps. 12.95 (*0-939460-76-9*, 0795) Devyn Pr.

***Boeder, Bob.** Hardrock Feaver: Running100 Miles in Colorado's San Juan Mountains. LC 00-190206. (Illus.). 179p. 2000. pap. 12.95 (*1-884778-84-4*) Old Mountain.

Boeder, Heribert. Seditions: Heidegger & the Limit of Modernity. Brainard, Marcus, ed. & tr. by. from GER. LC 97-12835. (SUNY Series in Contemporary Continental Philosophy). 359p. (C). 1997. text 59.50 (*0-7914-3531-8*); pap. text 19.95 (*0-7914-3532-6*) State U NY Pr.

Boeder, Maria. Visa est Vox: Sprache und Bild in der Spatantiken Literatur. (Europaische Hochschulschriften, Reihe 28: Bd. 268). (GER.). 200p. 1996. 42.95 (*3-631-30402-1*) P Lang Pubng.

Boeder, Paul. Paul Boeder, PhD: Teacher of Physiological Optics. (Ophthalmology Oral History Ser.). (Illus.). xxix, 194p. 1992. pap. 35.00 (*0-926866-04-4*) FAAO.

Boeder, Robert B. Beyond the Marathon: The Grand Slam of Trail Ultrarunning. (Illus.). 142p. (Orig.). 1996. pap. text 10.95 (*1-884778-15-1*) Old Mountain.

— Malawi. (Profiles of Africa Ser.). 1996. text 26.50 (*0-86531-777-1*) Westview.

Boeder, Steven M. & Repetitive Manufacturing S. I. G. Staff. Backflushing Training Aid. 60p. (Orig.). 1995. pap. 35.00 (*1-55822-122-0*) Am Prod & Inventory.

Boedigheimer, Michael & Stevens, Flumo. Cost/Managerial Accounting. 120p. (C). 1995. pap. text 11.25 (*1-56226-278-5*) CAT Pub.

***Boeding, Conrad.** The Love Disorder. Champion, Judith, ed. (Illus.). 170p. 1998. per. 17.00 (*0-9668302-0-2*, Pub. by Human Pass Inst) Herveys Bklink.

Boeding, Conrad J., jt. auth. see McKelvey, Carole Conner.

Boedtker, A. T., ed. Partonopeus de Blois. (EETS, ES Ser.: No. 109). 1974. reprint ed. 65.00 (*0-527-00312-3*) Periodicals Srv.

Boef, Walter De, see De Boef, Walter.

Boef, Walter De, see Almekinder, Connie & De Boef, Walter.

Boeft, J. Den, et al, eds. Philological & Historical Commentary on Ammianus Marcellinus XX. xv, 338p. (C). 1987. 63.00 (*90-6980-012-8*, Pub. by Egbert Forsten) Hod1der & Stoughton.

Boeft, J. Den & Van Poll, M. L. The Impact of Scripture in Early Christianity. LC 98-51547. (Supplements to Vilgilae Christianae Ser.). 1999. write for info. (*90-04-11143-3*) Brill Academic Pubs.

Boeft, J. Den, et al. Archh: A Collection of Patristic Studies. LC 97-40208. Vol. 41. (FRE & GER., Illus.). Xiv, 332p. 1997. text 124.50 (*90-04-10834-3*) Brill Academic Pubs.

Boeft, J. Den, et al. Philological & Historical Commentary on Ammianus Marcellinus XXI. xiv, 310p. 1991. 63.00 (*90-6980-044-6*, Pub. by Egbert Forsten) Hod1der & Stoughton.

— Philological & Historical Commentary on Ammianus Marcellinus XXII. xiv, 392p. 1996. lib. bdg. 82.00 (*90-6980-086-1*, Pub. by Egbert Forsten) Hod1der & Stoughton.

Boeft, J. Den, see Den Boeft, J.

Boeft, J. Den, jt. ed. see Hilhorst, A.

Boeft, Jan D., et al, eds. Denken over dichten: Dertig eeuwen poeticale reflectie. (Illus.). (C). 1994. pap. text 34.50 (*90-5356-091-2*, Pub. by Amsterdam U Pr) U of Mich Pr.

Boege, Steven, jt. auth. see Benson, Barry W.

Boegehold, Alan L. The Lawcourts at Athens: Sites, Buildings, Equipment, Procedure, & Testimonia. LC 95-18926. (Athenian Agora Ser.: Vol. 28). (Illus.). 1995. 100.00 (*87661-228-1*) Am Sch Athens.

— When a Gesture Was Expected: A Selection of Examples from Archaic & Classical Greek Literature. LC 99-14574. 176p. 1999. 32.50 (*0-691-00263-0*, Pub. by Princeton U Pr) Cal Prin Full Svc.

Boegehold, Alan L. & Scafuro, Adele C., eds. Athenian Identity & Civic Ideology. LC 92-46746. 264p. (C). 1993. text 42.50 (*0-8018-4578-5*) Johns Hopkins.

***Boegehold, Betty.** Hurray for Christmas. (Jellybean Bks.). (Illus.). 24p. (J). (ps-k). 1999. 1.99 (*0-375-80148-0*, Pub. by Random Bks Yng Read); lib. bdg. 7.99 (*0-375-90148-5*, Pub. by Random Bks Yng Read) Random.

Boegehold, Betty. A Pet for Pippa Mouse. (J). 1999. lib. bdg. 7.99 (*0-679-99340-1*) Random.

— A Pet for Pippa Mouse. (Illus.). (J). 2000. 2.99 (*0-679-89340-7*, Pub. by Random Bks Yng Read) Random.

— Pippa Mouse's House. (J). 1998. lib. bdg. 7.99 (*0-679-99191-3*, Pub. by Random Bks Yng Read) Random.

Boegehold, Betty D. Education Before Five. 203p. 1977. pap. 16.95 (*0-8077-2557-9*) Tchrs Coll.

Boegehold, Betty D., jt. auth. see Hooks, William H.

Boegehold, Lindley, ed. The Perfect Thanksgiving Book: Delicious Recipes for a Fabulous Family Feast. (Illus.). 64p. 1995. 9.95 (*1-85967-121-7*, Lorenz Bks) Anness Pub.

Boeghold, Betty. Pippa Mouse's House. 24p. (J). (ps-k). 1998. 1.99 (*0-679-89191-9*) Random.

Boegler, Susan & Abruzzini, Debbie. Scissors, Glue, & Concepts, Too! Interactive Activities for Practicing Basic Concepts. 199p. 1992. spiral bd. 37.95 (*1-55999-237-9*) LinguiSystems.

Boegler, Susan, jt. auth. see Abruzzini, Debbie.

Boegli, Emily H. Surgical Technology Review Book. LC 94-6785. 320p. 1994. pap. 50.00 (*0-13-034703-5*) P-H.

***Boehi, Dave.** I Still Do: Stories of Lifelong Love & Marriage. 192p. 2000. 14.99 (*0-8054-2374-5*) Broadman.

Boehi, Dave, jt. auth. see Rainey, Dennis.

Boehler, J. P., ed. Failure Criteria of Structured Media: Proceedings of the CNRS International Colloquium, No. 351, Villard de Lans, June 1993. (Illus.). 470p. (C). 1993. text 149.00 (*90-6191-179-6*, Pub. by A A Balkema) Ashgate Pub Co.

— Mechanical Behavior of Anisotropic Solids. 1983. text 389.50 (*90-247-2813-4*) Kluwer Academic.

Boehler, Ted, jt. auth. see Galbraith, Robert.

Boehlert, George & Yamada, Juro, eds. Rockfishes of the Genus Sebastes: Their Reproduction & Early Life History. (Developments in Environmental Biology of Fishes Ser.). (C). 1991. text 257.50 (*0-7923-0962-6*) Kluwer Academic.

Boehlert, Robert, jt. auth. see Martin, Fenton S.

***Boehlert, Sherwood L., ed.** The Future of the Tennessee Valley Authority & Its Non-Power Programs: Congressional Hearing. (Illus.). 180p. (C). 1999. reprint ed. pap. text 30.00 (*0-7881-8330-3*) DIANE Pub.

Boehles, H. Infusionstherapie und klinische Ernaehrung in der Kinderheilkunde. (Handbuch der Infusionstherapie und Klinischen Ernaehrung Ser.: Band 6). (Illus.). x, 166p. 1983. 61.75 (*3-8055-3719-0*) S Karger.

Boehlich, Walter, ed. The Letters of Sigmund Freud to Eduard Silberstein, 1871-1881. Pomerans, Arnold J., tr. 204p. 1994. 32.50 (*0-317-03028-0*) Belknap Pr.

— The Letters of Sigmund Freud to Eduard Silberstein, 1871-1881. Pomerans, Arnold J., tr. LC 90-39119. (Illus.). 204p. 1990. text 39.00 (*0-674-52827-1*) HUP.

— The Letters of Sigmund Freud to Eduard Silberstein, 1871-1881. Pomerans, Arnold J., tr. (Illus.). 240p. 1992. pap. 17.50 (*0-674-52828-X*) HUP.

Boehlig, Alexander & Markschies, Christoph. Gnosis und Manichaeismus: Forschungen und Studien Zu den Texten Von Valentin und Mani Sowie Zu den Bibliotheken Von Nag Hammadi und Medinet Madi. (Beiheft zur Zeitschrift fuer die Neuetestamentliche Wissenschaft Ser.: Vol. 72). (GER.). xi, 316p. (C). 1994. lib. bdg. 113.85 (*3-11-014294-5*) De Gruyter.

Boehlig, Gertrud, ed. Ioannis Caminiatae de Expugnatione Thessalonicae. LC 72-83054. (Corpus Fontium Historiae Byzantinae Ser.: Berolinensis Vol. 4). (C). 1973. 70.00 (*3-11-002286-9*) De Gruyter.

Boehling, Rebecca. A Question of Priorities: Democratic Reform & Economic Recovery in Postwar Germany. LC 96-24204. (Monographs in German History Ser.: Vol. 2). (Illus.). 312p. 1996. 59.95 (*1-57181-035-8*) Berghahn Bks.

— A Question of Priorities: Democratic Reform & Economic Recovery in Postwar Germany. LC 96-24204. (Monographs in German History Ser.: Vol. 2). (Illus.). 312p. 1998. pap. 24.00 (*1-57181-159-1*) Berghahn Bks.

Boehlje, Michael D. & Eidman, Vernon R. Farm Management. 832p. 1984. text 108.95 (*0-471-04688-4*) Wiley.

Boehlke, Frederick J., Jr. From Generation to Generation: A History of Southern Baptists in Pennsylvania/South Jersey. LC 96-70300. 496p. (Orig.). 1996. pap. 29.95 (*1-57736-007-9*) Providence Hse.

Boehlke, LeRoy & Silldorff, Donald. Freistadt & the Lutheran Imigration. Trinity of Freistadt Historical Society Staff, ed. Suelflow, Harry & Ruedt, Lucy W., trs. (Illus.). 141p. 1989. pap. 8.00 (*0-9622699-0-5*) TECOF.

Boehlke, Paul, et al, eds. Discovering God's Creation: A Guidebook to Hands-on Science. (Illus.). 425p. 1997. teacher ed., ring bd. 35.00 (*1-890600-01-6*) M L College.

Boehlke, Robert R., ed. & tr. see Aritonang, Jan S.

Boehm. World Regional Geography. (Earth Science Ser.). write for info. (*0-534-52722-1*) Wadsworth Pub.

Boehm, jt. auth. see Eden.

Boehm, A., ed. see Kraus, K.

Boehm, Ann E. & Slater, Barbara R. Cognitive Skills Assessment Battery. 2nd ed. 1981. 51.95 (*0-8077-5975-9*) Tchrs Coll.

Boehm, Ann E. & Weinberg, Richard A. The Classroom Observer: Developing Observation Skills in Early Childhood Settings. 3rd ed. LC 96-28688. 168p. (C). 1996. pap. text 19.95 (*0-8077-3570-1*) Tchrs Coll.

Boehm, Arlene P. A Cheerful Note for Jack. (Illus.). 32p. (J). (gr. 2-5). 1996. 14.95 (*1-57098-081-0*) Roberts Rinehart.

— Jack in Search of Art. LC 98-13995. (Illus.). 32p. (J). (ps-3). 1998. 16.95 (*1-57098-244-9*) Roberts Rinehart.

— Jack in Search of Art. LC 98-13995. (Illus.). 32p. (J). (ps-6). 1998. pap. 7.95 (*1-57098-234-1*) Roberts Rinehart.

Boehm, Arthur, jt. auth. see Brown, Edward.

Boehm, Arthur, jt. auth. see Goldman, Katja.

Boehm, Arthur, jt. auth. see Tsai, Ming.

Boehm, Barbara D., et al. Enamels of Limoges: 1100-1350. (Illus.). 480p. 1996. pap. 29.95 (*0-87099-759-5*) Metro Mus Art.

***Boehm, Barry W.** Software Cost Estimation with Cocomo Ii. 450p. 2000. pap. text 47.00 incl. cd-rom (*0-13-026692-2*) P-H.

Boehm, Barry W. Software Engineering Economics. (Illus.). 768p. (C). 1981. 97.00 (*0-13-822122-7*) P-H.

— Software Risk Management. LC 89-80295. 508p. 1989. 62.00 (*0-8186-8906-4*, 1906) IEEE Comp Soc.

Boehm, C. Montenegrin Social Organization & Values. (Studies in Anthropology: No. 1). 1983. 29.50 (*0-404-62601-7*) AMS Pr.

Boehm, C., jt. ed. see Astesiano, E.

Boehm, C., jt. ed. see Ausiello, G.

Boehm, Christopher. Blood Revenge: The Enactment & Management of Conflict in Montenegro & Other Tribal Societies. 2nd ed. LC 86-24904. (Ethnohistory Ser.). (Illus.). 282p. (C). 1986. pap. text 19.95 (*0-8122-1241-X*) U of Pa Pr.

— Hierarchy in the Forest: The Evolution of Egalitarian Behavior. LC 99-24035. 320p. 1999. 39.95 (*0-674-39031-8*) HUP.

— Montenegrin Social Organization & Values: Political Ethnography of a Refuge Area Tribal Adaptation. LC 77-87156. (Studies in Anthropology: No. 1). 1983. 29.50 (*0-404-16895-7*) AMS Pr.

Boehm, Deborah. Ceremonies of Escape: A Zen Romance. 288p. 25.00 (*4-7700-1979-3*) FS&G.

Boehm, Deborah, tr. see Takagi, Akimisu.

***Boehm, Deborah B.** Ghost of a Smile. 2001. 25.00 (*4-7700-2531-9*) Kodansha.

Boehm, Deborah B. A Zen Romance: One Woman's Adventures in a Monastery. Floyd, Elizabeth, ed. 288p. 1996. 25.00 (*4-7700-2032-5*) Kodansha.

— A Zen Romance: One Woman's Adventures in a Monastery. 1998. pap. text 14.00 (*4-7700-2177-1*, Pub. by Kodansha Intl) Kodansha.

Boehm, Ellen, jt. auth. see Toole, Amy L.

Boehm, Erika & Berd, Malcolm, eds. Passage V-VI. LC 74-1564. 1980. 3.95 (*0-931672-01-5*) Triton Coll.

— Passage Four. LC 74-1564. (Passage Ser.). (Illus.). 1978. pap. 3.95 (*0-931672-03-1*) Triton Coll.

Boehm, Erika & Semelroth, W. Darrell, eds. Ariel. (Poetry Anthology Ser.). 1983. 2.95 (*0-931672-05-8*) Triton Coll.

— Ariel III. (Poetry Anthology Ser.). 1984. 3.95 (*0-931672-07-4*) Triton Coll.

Boehm, Erika, jt. ed. see Semelroth, W. Darrell.

Boehm, F. & Vogel, Paul. Physics of Massive Neutrinos. 2nd ed. (Illus.). 259p. (C). 1992. text 99.95 (*0-521-41824-0*); pap. text 37.95 (*0-521-42849-1*) Cambridge U Pr.

Boehm, Frank H., jt. auth. see Eden, Robert D.

Boehm, G., jt. ed. see Leuschner, R.

Boehm, Gero Von, see Pei, I. M. & Von Boehm, Gero.

Boehm, Gottfried, et al. Canto d'Amore: Classicism in Modern Art & Music 1914-1935. (Illus.). 496p. 1997. 75.00 (*1-85894-035-4*, Pub. by Merrell Holberton) U of Wash Pr.

Boehm, Helen F. With a Little Luck: An American Odyssey. limited ed. (Illus.). 1985. 35.00 (*0-89256-291-9*) E M Boehm.

***Boehm, Joan.** Never Diet Again Workbook. (Illus.). 146p. 1999. pap. 12.95 (*0-9672084-0-8*, 119) Pers Train Cons.

Boehm, Margaret D., tr. see Maine De Biran, Pierre.

Boehm, Max H. Natur und Sittlichkeit Bei Fichte. (Abhandlungen Zur Philosophie und Ihrer Geschichte Ser.: Bd. 46). (GER.). 40p. 1981. reprint ed. write for info. (*3-487-06793-5*) G Olms Pubs.

Boehm, Philip, tr. see Bachmann, Ingeborg.

Boehm, Philip, tr. see Fink, Ida.

Boehm, Philip, tr. see Hein, Christoph.

Boehm, Philip, tr. see Schneider, Peter.

Boehm, R. Kritik der Grundlagen des Zeitalters. (GER.). 318p. 1975. pap. text 121.50 (*90-247-1663-2*, Pub. by M Nijhoff) Kluwer Academic.

Boehm, R. F., ed. Thermodynamics & the Design, Analysis, & Improvement of Energy Systems. (AES Series, Vol. 27: HTD Ser.: Vol. 228). 392p. 1992. 67.50 (*0-7918-1073-9*, G00717) ASME.

Boehm, Randolph, et al. Records of The American Committee on Africa. LC 97-223643. (Black Studies Research Sources). 51p. 1992. write for info. (*1-55655-432-X*) U Pubns Amer.

— Records of the British Colonial Office, Class 5. LC 92-953091. 53p. 1983. write for info. (*0-89093-410-X*) U Pubns Amer.

— Records of the Immigration & Naturalization Service: Editorial Advisor, Alan Kraut. LC 93-16315. (Research Collections in American Immigration). 1992. write for info. (*1-55655-160-6*) U Pubns Amer.

— Records of the Southern Christian Leadership Conference, 1954-1970. LC 95-24346. (Black Studies Research Sources). 82 p. 1995. write for info. (*1-55655-555-5*) U Pubns Amer.

Boehm, Randolph, jt. auth. see Goggin, Jacqueline A.

Boehm, Randolph H., compiled by. Mary McLeod Bethune Papers: The Bethune-Cookman College Collection, 1922-1955. LC 95-30841. (Black Studies Research Sources). (C). 1995. 1790.00 (*1-55655-554-7*) U Pubns Amer.

Boehm, Randolph H. & Heldman, Dan C. Public Employees, Unions, & the Erosion of Civic Trust: A Study of San Francisco in the 1970s. LC 82-51294. 265p. 1982. pap. 24.95 (*0-313-27094-5*, P7094); lib. bdg. 59.95 (*0-313-27070-8*, U7070) Greenwood.

Boehm, Richard G. & Petersen, James F., eds. The First Assessment: Research in Geographic Education. 293p. 1997. pap. 45.00 (*0-9660862-0-1*) SW TX St Univ.

Boehm, Richard G. & Visser, Sent, eds. Latin America: Case Studies. LC 84-80211. (National Council for Geographic Education, Pacesetter Ser.). (Illus.). 310p. 1984. reprint ed. pap. 96.10 (*0-7837-9722-2*, 206045300005) Bks Demand.

Boehm, Robert F. Design Analysis of Thermal Systems. LC 86-32609. 288p. 1987. text 106.95 (*0-471-83204-9*) Wiley.

Boehm, Robert F., ed. Developments in the Design of Thermal Systems. (Illus.). 304p. (C). 1997. text 69.95 (*0-521-46204-5*) Cambridge U Pr.

Boehm, Robert F., jt. ed. see Kreith, Frank.

Boehm, Roy. First Seal. 1997. 23.00 (*0-671-53625-7*, PB Hardcover) PB.

Boehm, Roy & Sasser, Charles. First Seal. 1998. per. 6.99 (*0-671-53626-5*) PB.

***Boehm, Roy & Sasser, Charles W.** First Seal. (Illus.). 308p. 1999. text 23.00 (*0-7881-6046-X*) DIANE Pub.

Boehm, Rudolph. Vom Gesichtspunkt der Phanomenologie, No. II. (Phaenomenologica Ser.: No. 83). vii, 262p. 1981. lib. bdg. 135.00 (*90-247-2415-5*, Pub. by M Nijhoff) Kluwer Academic.

— Vom Gesichtspunkt der Phanomenologie Husserl - Studien. (Phaenomenologica Ser.: No. 26). 1968. pap. text 55.00 (*90-247-0258-5*) Kluwer Academic.

Boehm, Sarah, jt. auth. see Koch, Deborah.

Boehm, Stephan & Frowen, Stephen F., eds. Economics As a Way of Thinking: Essays in Memory of G. L. S. Shackle. 288p. (C). 1999. 65.00 (*0-415-10162-X*) Routledge.

Boehm, Stephan, jt. ed. see Caldwell, Bruce J.

B

Boehm, Theobold. Flute & Flute-Playing in Acoustical, Technical & Artistic Aspects. Miller, Dayton C., tr. (Illus.). 197p. (C). 1998. pap. 7.95 (*0-486-21259-9*) Dover.

Boehm, Thomas, ed. see Devienne, Francois.

Boehm, Toni G. The Spiritual Intrapreneur: Awakening the Power & Potential Within You. 104p. 1996. pap. 12.00 (*0-8059-3983-0*) Dorrance.

***Boehm, Toni G.** A Wise Woman Initiation & Crowning Ceremony: Celebrating the Menopausal Metamorphosis & the Years over 40! (Women's Wisdom Ser.: Bk. II). (Illus.). 140p. 2000. pap. write for info. (*0-9701537-1-6*, Inner Visioning Pr) Awakening Hrts Min.

Boehm, Ullrich & Lenhart, Volker. Technology Education in Trinidad & Tobago. LC 92-479. 120p. 1992. 27.00 (*3-631-44869-4*) P Lang Pubng.

Boehm, Werner W. Gut Gezielt, Schuetze. (GER., Illus.). 180p. Date not set. write for info. (*3-487-08395-7*) G Olms Pubs.

Boehm, William B. From Barren Desert to Thriving Community: A Social History of White Sands Missile Range, 1945-1954. unabridged ed. LC 97-74732. (Illus.). 86p. 1997. pap. 10.00 (*1-887523-12-X*) Human Systs Res.

Boehm, Wolfgang. Methods of Studying Root Systems. LC 79-9706. (Ecological Studies: Vol. 33). (Illus.). 1987. 94.95 (*0-387-09329-X*) Spr-Verlag.

Boehm, Wolfgang & Prautzsch, Hartmut. Geometric Concepts for Geometric Design. LC 93-20666. (Illus.). 424p. (C). 1993. text 59.00 (*1-56881-004-0*) AK Peters.

— Numerical Methods. (Illus.). 196p. (C). 1993. pap. text 39.95 (*1-56881-020-2*) AK Peters.

Boehme. Improving Upper Body Control. (C). 1998. pap. text 58.00 (*0-12-784579-8*) Acad Pr.

Boehme, Ann J. Planning Successul Meetings & Events. LC 98-35089. 174p. 1998. pap. 18.95 (*0-8144-7995-2*) AMACOM.

Boehme, Audrey M. Stars in God's Drama on Planet Earth. LC 97-60417. 352p. 1997. write for info. (*1-57921-009-0*) WinePress Pub.

Boehme-Brown, M., tr. see Hirt, Franz J.

Boehme, Jacob. The Aurora. 723p. (Orig.). 1992. reprint ed. pap. 33.00 (*1-56459-115-8*) Kessinger Pub.

— Aurora: The Dayspring, or Dawning of the Day in the East. Barker, C. J., ed. Sparrow, John, tr. 1992. reprint ed. pap. text 19.95 (*1-55818-181-4*, Sure Fire) Holmes Pub.

— The Clavis: or Key: An Exposition of Some Principal Matters & Words in the Writings of Jacob Boehme. Sparrow, John, tr. 63p. 1992. reprint ed. pap. 5.95 (*1-56459-267-7*) Kessinger Pub.

— The Clavis, or Key: Being an Exposition of Some Principal Matters & Words in the Writings of Jacob Boehme. Barker, C. J., ed. 1996. pap. 9.95 (*1-55818-107-5*) Holmes Pub.

— The Confessions of Jacob Boehme. 188p. 1992. reprint ed. pap. 19.95 (*1-56459-214-6*) Kessinger Pub.

— Dialogues on the Supersensual Life. Law, William, tr. 144p. 1992. reprint ed. pap. 17.95 (*1-56459-216-2*) Kessinger Pub.

— Discourse Between a Soul Hungry & Thirsty & a Soul Enlightened. 1984. pap. 4.95 (*0-916411-89-3*, Sure Fire) Holmes Pub.

— The Forty Questions of the Soul. Sparrow, John, tr. 363p. 1992. reprint ed. pap. 24.95 (*1-56459-266-9*) Kessinger Pub.

— Forty Questions of the Soul & the Clavis. Sparrow, John, tr. 1992. text 45.00 (*1-55818-180-6*, Sure Fire) Holmes Pub.

— Fundamental Statement Concerning the Earthly & Heavenly Mysteries. 1989. pap. 3.95 (*1-55818-114-8*, Sure Fire) Holmes Pub.

— How a Man May Find Himself & So Finding Come to All Mysteries, Even to the Ninth Number, Yet No Higher. 1990. reprint ed. pap. 5.95 (*1-55818-127-X*, Sure Fire) Holmes Pub.

— The Image of the Soul & of the Turba Which Is the Destroyer of the Image. 1988. reprint ed. pap. 3.95 (*1-55818-111-3*, Sure Fire) Holmes Pub.

— The Incarnation of Jesus Christ. Earle, John R., tr. 290p. 1993. reprint ed. pap. 19.95 (*1-56459-378-9*) Kessinger Pub.

— Jacob Boehme's "The Way to Christ" Stoudt, John J., tr. LC 78-13976. 254p. 1979. reprint ed. lib. bdg. 35.00 (*0-313-21075-6*, BOTW, Greenwood Pr) Greenwood.

— Mysterium Magnum or an Exposition of the First Book of Moses Called Genesis. Sparrow, John, ed. 1030p. 1992. reprint ed. pap. 50.00 (*1-56459-212-X*) Kessinger Pub.

— Of Heaven & Hell: A Dialogue Between Junius, a Scholar & Theophorus, His Master. 1986. pap. 4.95 (*0-916411-53-2*, Sure Fire) Holmes Pub.

— On the Election of Grace & Theosophic Questions. 327p. 1992. reprint ed. pap. 27.00 (*1-56459-146-8*) Kessinger Pub.

— The Signature of All Things; of the Supersensual Life; of Heaven & Hell; Discourse Between Two Souls. 300p. 1992. reprint ed. pap. 27.00 (*1-56459-215-4*) Kessinger Pub.

— Six Mystical Points. 1989. pap. 5.95 (*1-55818-113-X*) Holmes Pub.

— Six Theosophic Points (an Open Gate of All the Secrets of Life Wherein the Causes of All Beings Become Known) Six Mystical Points on the Earthly & Heavenly Mystery on the Divine Intuition. Earle, John R., tr. 220p. 1992. reprint ed. pap. 19.95 (*1-56459-240-5*) Kessinger Pub.

— Spiritual Thoughts of Jacob Boehme. Sire, Evelyn, ed. & tr. by. 1994. pap. 7.95 (*1-55818-301-9*, Sure Fire) Holmes Pub.

— Supersensual Life. 1985. reprint ed. pap. 5.95 (*0-916411-90-7*, Sure Fire) Holmes Pub.

— Theoscopia, or the Highly Precious Gate of the Divine Intuition. 1989. pap. 8.95 (*1-55818-112-1*, Sure Fire) Holmes Pub.

— Thoughts on the Spiritual Life, 1896. Rainy, Charlotte A., tr. 88p. 1996. reprint ed. pap. 7.95 (*1-56459-905-1*) Kessinger Pub.

— The Threefold Life of Man: The High & Deep Searching Out of the Three Principles. Sparrow, John, tr. 670p. 1992. reprint ed. pap. 33.00 (*1-56459-224-3*) Kessinger Pub.

— The Tree of the Christian Faith. 1993. reprint ed. pap. 8.95 (*1-55818-190-3*, Sure Fire) Holmes Pub.

— True Resignation. 57p. 1992. reprint ed. pap. 12.00 (*1-56459-217-0*) Kessinger Pub.

— The Way to Christ: Of True Repentance; of True Resignation; of Regeneration; of the Supersensual Life. 159p. 1992. reprint ed. pap. 12.95 (*1-56459-218-9*) Kessinger Pub.

— The Wellspring of Light. Sire, Evelyn, tr. (Orig.). 1997. pap. 6.95 (*1-55818-390-6*) Holmes Pub.

Boehme, Jacob & Sparrow, John. Concerning the Three Principles of the Divine Essence: Of the Eternal, Dark, Light, & Temporary World. 809p. 1992. reprint ed. pap. 45.00 (*1-56459-213-8*) Kessinger Pub.

Boehme, Jacob, et al. The Key of Jacob Boehme. LC 90-47418. (Magnum Opus Hermetic Sourceworks Ser.: Vol. 9).Tr. of The/Clavis. (Illus.). 84p. 2000. reprint ed. pap. 12.50 (*0-933999-94-1*) Phanes Pr.

Boehme, Jakob. The Confessions. 1975. 250.00 (*0-87968-258-2*) Gordon Pr.

— Works of Jakob Boehme, 4 vols. 1974. lib. bdg. 2900.00 (*0-87968-465-8*) Gordon Pr.

Boehme, Kate A. New Thought Healing Made Plain. 142p. 1997. pap. 12.00 (*0-89540-272-6*, SB-272) Sun Pub.

Boehme, Manfred. JG 7: The World's First Jet Fighter Unit, 1944-1945. Johnson, David, tr. from GER. LC 92-60364. (Illus.). 280p. 1992. text 29.95 (*0-88740-395-6*) Schiffer.

Boehme, Regi. Myofascial Release & It's Application to Neuro-Developmental Treatment. (Illus.). 87p. (Orig.). (C). 1991. pap. text 20.00 (*1-879801-00-0*) Boehme Wkshps.

Boehme, Ron. If God Has a Plan for My Life, Why Can't I Find It? You Have a Destiny. 156p. 1992. pap. 8.99 (*0-927545-41-1*) YWAM Pub.

— Leadership for the 21st Century: Changing Nations Through the Power of Serving. 231p. 1989. pap. 9.99 (*0-9615534-8-0*) YWAM Pub.

— Restoring America's Conscience. 256p. (Orig.). 1996. pap. 12.99 (*0-529-10696-5*, RAC) World Publng.

Boehme, S., ed. Astronomy & Astrophysics Abstracts: Literature, Vol. 32; 1982, Pt. 2. 848p. 1983. 118.95 (*0-387-12516-7*) Spr-Verlag.

— Astronomy & Astrophysics Abstracts Vol. 3: Literature 1970, Pt. 1. x, 490p. 1970. 62.95 (*0-387-05314-X*) Spr-Verlag.

— Astronomy & Astrophysics Abstracts Vol. 4: Literature 1970, Pt. 2. x, 562p. 1971. 62.95 (*0-387-05514-2*) Spr-Verlag.

— Astronomy & Astrophysics Abstracts Vol. 5: Literature 1971, Pt. 1. x, 505p. 1971. 62.95 (*0-387-05701-3*) Spr-Verlag.

— Astronomy & Astrophysics Abstracts Vol. 6: Literature 1971, Pt. 2. x, 560p. 1972. 62.95 (*0-387-05888-5*) Spr-Verlag.

— Astronomy & Astrophysics Abstracts Vol. 29: Literature 1981,, Pt. 1. 853p. 1981. 94.95 (*0-387-11264-2*) Spr-Verlag.

Boehme, S., et al, eds. Astronomy & Astrophysics Abstacts Vol. 23-24: Literature 1969, Part 1. vii, 435p. 1969. 62.95 (*0-387-04421-3*) Spr-Verlag.

— Astronomy & Astrophysics Abstracts, Vol. 37. Schmadel, Lutz D., tr. (Literature 1984 Ser.: Pt. 1). 920p. 1985. 151.95 (*0-387-13937-0*) Spr-Verlag.

— Astronomy & Astrophysics Abstracts: Literature 1979, Pt. 2, Vol. 26. 794p. 1980. 94.95 (*0-387-10134-9*) Spr-Verlag.

— Astronomy & Astrophysics Abstracts Vol. 2: Literature 1969, Pt. 2. x, 516p. 1970. 62.95 (*0-387-04773-5*) Spr-Verlag.

— Astronomy & Astrophysics Abstracts Vol. 7: Literature 1972, Pt. 1. x, 526p. 1972. 62.95 (*0-387-06072-3*) Spr-Verlag.

— Astronomy & Astrophysics Abstracts Vol. 8: Literature 1972, Pt. 2. x, 594p. 1973. 62.95 (*0-387-06352-8*) Spr-Verlag.

— Astronomy & Astrophysics Abstracts Vol. 9: Literature 1973, Pt. 1. vii, 610p. 1973. 62.95 (*0-387-06560-1*) Spr-Verlag.

— Astronomy & Astrophysics Abstracts Vol. 10: Literature 1973, Pt. 2. viii, 661p. 1974. 63.95 (*0-387-06795-7*) Spr-Verlag.

— Astronomy & Astrophysics Abstracts Vol. 21: Literature 1978, Pt. 1. viii, 834p. 1978. 65.00 (*0-685-07582-6*) Spr-Verlag.

— Astronomy & Astrophysics Abstracts Vol. 22: Literature 1978, Pt. 2. viii, 849p. 1979. 76.95 (*0-387-09464-4*) Spr-Verlag.

— Astronomy & Astrophysics Abstracts Vol. 23-24. 1127p. 1980. 94.95 (*0-387-09830-5*) Spr-Verlag.

— Astronomy & Astrophysics Abstracts Vol. 25: Literature 1979, Pt. 1. x, 871p. 1979. 94.95 (*0-387-09831-3*) Spr-Verlag.

— Astronomy & Astrophysics Abstracts Vol. 27: Literature 1980, Pt. 1. 939p. 1980. 94.95 (*0-387-10479-8*) Spr-Verlag.

— Astronomy & Astrophysics Abstracts Vol. 28: Literature 1980, Pt. 2. 841p. 1981. 94.95 (*0-387-10799-1*) Spr-Verlag.

— Astronomy & Astrophysics Abstracts, Vol. 30: Literature, 1981. 792p. 1982. 118.95 (*0-387-11721-0*) Spr-Verlag.

— Literature, 1983, Pt. 1. (Astronomy & Astrophysics Abstracts Ser.: Vol. 33). 815p. 1983. 118.95 (*0-387-13017-9*) Spr-Verlag.

Boehme, S., et al. Astronomy & Astrophysics Abstracts Vol. 31: Literature 1982, Pt. 1. x, 776p. 1982. 118.95 (*0-387-12072-6*) Spr-Verlag.

Boehme, Sarah. Whitney Gallery of Western Art. (Illus.). 76p. 1998. pap. 9.95 (*0-931618-60-6*) Buffalo Bill Hist Ctr.

Boehme, Sarah, et al. Powerful Images: Portrayals of Native America. (Illus.). 160p. 1998. 50.00 (*0-295-97697-7*) U of Wash Pr.

Boehme, Sarah E. Absarokee Hut: The Joseph Henry Sharp Cabin. (Illus.). 64p. 1992. pap. 14.95 (*0-614-09461-5*) Buffalo Bill Hist Ctr.

— Rendezvous to Roundup: The First One Hundred Years of Art in Wyoming. LC 90-82510. (Illus.). 56p. 1992. pap. 16.95 (*0-931618-30-4*) Buffalo Bill Hist Ctr.

Boehme, Sarah E. & Conaty, Gerald T. Powerful Images: Portrayals of Native America. LC 97-40098. (Illus.). 160p. 1998. pap. text 30.00 (*0-295-97675-6*) U of Wash Pr.

***Boehme, Sarah E., et al.** John James Audubon in the West: The Last Expedition: Mammals of North America. (Illus.). 208p. 2000. 45.00 (*0-8109-4210-0*, Pub. by Abrams) Time Warner.

Boehme, Sarah E., et al. Seth Eastman: A Portfolio of North American Indians. LC 95-77591. (Illus.). 168p. 1995. 75.00 (*0-9639338-4-1*) Afton Hist Soc.

Boehme, Wolfgang & Klaver, Charles J. Das Tierreich - The Animal Kingdom Pt. 112: Chamaeleonidae: A Characterization & Compilation of the Recent Animal Groups. LC 97-29347. (ENG & GER., Illus.). 112p. (C). 1997. lib. bdg. 135.00 (*3-11-015187-1*) De Gruyter.

Boehmer-Christiansen, S. & Skea, Jim. Acid Politics: Environmental & Energy Policies in Britain & Germany. 256p. 1992. text 41.95 (*1-85293-116-7*, Pub. by P P Pubs) CRC Pr.

Boehmer-Christiansen, Sonja & Weidner, Helmut. Environmental Regulations in Britain & Germany: The Case of Vehicle Emissions. 200p. 1994. 35.00 (*0-8386-3601-2*) Fairleigh Dickinson.

Boehmer, Elleke. Colonial & Postcolonial Literature: Migrant Metaphors. (Illus.). 314p. 1995. pap. text 17.95 (*0-19-289232-0*) OUP.

Boehmer, Elleke, ed. Empire Writing: An Anthology of Colonial Literature 1870-1918. (Oxford World's Classics Ser.). (Illus.). 564p. 1998. pap. 14.95 (*0-19-283265-4*) OUP.

Boehmer, H. The Jesuits. 1975. 250.00 (*0-87968-199-3*) Gordon Pr.

Boehmer, Heinrich. Luther & the Reformation in the Light of Modern Research. LC 83-45639. reprint ed. 67.50 (*0-404-19823-6*) AMS Pr.

Boehmer, Konrad, ed. Schonberg & Kandinsky: An Historic Encounter. (Contemporary Music Studies). (Illus.). 233p. 1998. text 54.00 (*90-5702-046-7*, Harwood Acad Pubs); pap. text 15.00 (*90-5702-047-5*, Harwood Acad Pubs) Gordon & Breach.

Boehmer, M. C. The Micro in Your Library. 50p. (Orig.). (C). 1984. pap. 5.00 (*0-914677-00-4*) Contemp Issues.

***Boehmer, Raquel.** 10-Minute Scrapbook Pages: Hundreds of Easy Innovative Designs. (Illus.). 2000. 24.95 (*0-8069-1971-X*) Sterling.

Boehmer, Raquel D. Raquel's Main Guide to New England Seafoods. (Illus.). (Orig.). 1988. pap. 4.95 (*0-685-22580-1*) Seafood Soundings Pr.

Boehmer, Ulrike. The Personal & the Political: Women's Activism in Response to the Breast Cancer & AIDS Epidemics. LC 99-41118. 224p. (C). 2000. text 57.50 (*0-7914-4549-6*) State U NY Pr.

***Boehmer, Ulrike.** The Personal & the Political: Women's Activism in Response to the Breast Cancer & AIDS Epidemics. LC 99-41118. 224p. (C). 2000. pap. text 18.95 (*0-7914-4550-X*) State U NY Pr.

Boehn, Andreas. Vollendende Mimesis: Wirklichkeitsdarstellung & Selbsbezueglichkeit in Theorie & Literarischer Praxis. (Quellen und Forschungen zur Sprach und Kulturgeschichte der Germanischen Voelker: NF Bd. 101). (GER.). xii, 215p. (C). 1992. lib. bdg. 84.65 (*3-11-013685-6*) De Gruyter.

Boehn, Erika C., ed. Passage VII-VIII. LC 74-1564. 1982. 3.95 (*0-931672-04-X*) Triton Coll.

Boehn, Max. Dolls. (Illus.). 269p. 1972. pap. 6.95 (*0-486-22847-9*) Dover.

Boehn, Max Von. Miniatures & Silhouettes: Modes & Manners Supplement. LC 70-145772. (Illus.). 224p. 1972. reprint ed. 21.95 (*0-405-08279-7*, Pub. by Blom Pubns) Ayer.

— Modes & Manners: From the Middle Ages to the End of the Eighteenth Century, 4 vols., 2 bks. LC 68-56493. (Illus.). 1972. reprint ed. 55.95 (*0-405-08280-0*, Pub. by Blom Pubns) Ayer.

— Ornaments: Lace, Fans, Gloves, Walking-Sticks, Parasols, Jewelry, & Trinkets. Modes & Manners Supplement. LC 70-148467. (Illus.). 293p. 1972. reprint ed. 30.95 (*0-405-08286-X*, Pub. by Blom Pubns) Ayer.

Boehn, Max Von & Fischel, Oskar. Modes & Manners of the Ninteenth Century, 4 vols., 2 bks., 2. enl. rev. ed. LC 68-56493. (Illus.). 1972. reprint ed. 27.95 (*0-405-08282-7*, Pub. by Blom Pubns) Ayer.

— Modes & Manners of the Ninteenth Century, 4 vols., 2 bks., Set. enl. rev. ed. LC 68-56493. (Illus.). 747p. 1972. reprint ed. 55.95 (*0-405-08283-5*, Pub. by Blom Pubns) Ayer.

— Modes & Manners of the Ninteenth Century, 4 vols., 2 bks., Vol. 1. enl. rev. ed. LC 68-56493. (Illus.). 1972. reprint ed. 27.95 (*0-405-08281-9*, Pub. by Blom Pubns) Ayer.

Boehn, Max von, see Von Boehn, Max.

***Boehner, John A., ed.** Erisa: A Quarter Century of Providing Workers Health Insurance: Congressional Hearingt. (Illus.). 155p. 2000. pap. text 35.00 (*0-7567-0102-3*) DIANE Pub.

Boehner, Philotheus. Conferences for Franciscan Religious. (Spirit & Life Ser.). vi, 106p. 1966. 2.00 (*1-57659-087-9*) Franciscan Inst.

— Walter Burleigh De Puritate Artis Logicae Tractus Langios. Incl. Tractatus Brevior. 1955. lib. bdg. (Text Ser.). 1955. 6.00 (*0-686-17965-X*) Franciscan Inst.

Boehner, Philotheus, ed. Walter Burleigh. De Puritate Artis Logicae Tractatus Longior. (Text Ser.). xvi, 264p. 1955. 6.00 (*1-57659-057-7*) Franciscan Inst.

Boehner, Philotheus & Buytaert, Eligius M. Collected Articles on Ockham. (Philosophy Ser.). x, 482p. 1958. pap. 23.00 (*1-57659-101-8*) Franciscan Inst.

Boehner, Philotheus, tr. see St. Bonaventure.

Boehner, Philotheus, tr. see William of Ockman.

Boehner, Philotheus, tr. & intro. see William of Ockham.

Boehnke, D. Neal & Delumyea, R. Del. Environmental Chemistry Laboratory Experiments. LC 99-24941. 279p. (C). 1999. pap. text 50.00 (*0-13-917171-1*, Macmillan Coll) P-H.

Boehnke, Klaus. Political Psychology: A Special Issue of the Journal of Applied Psychology: An International Review. 126p. 1998. 24.95 (*0-86377-969-7*, Pub. by Psychol Pr) Taylor & Francis.

***Boehnlein, James K.** Psychiatry & Religion. LC 99-40826. (Issues in Psychiatry Ser.). 2000. 29.00 (*0-88048-920-0*) Am Psychiatric.

Boehnlein, James M. The Sociocognitive Rhetoric of Meridel le Sueur: Feminist Discourse & Reportage of the Thirties. LC 93-50868. 172p. 1994. text 79.95 (*0-7734-9136-8*) E Mellen.

Boehnlein, John. The High Performance Marshall Handbook: A Guide to Great Marshall Amplifier Sounds. (Illus.). 1994. pap. 13.95 (*0-933224-80-X*, T400) Bold Strummer Ltd.

Boehnlein, Mary M. & Hager, Beth H. Children, Parents, & Reading: An Annotated Bibliography. LC 85-167. 98p. reprint ed. pap. 30.40 (*0-8357-2634-7*, 204012200014) Bks Demand.

***Boehr, Karren.** Graduation Is Not for Angels: Contemporary Christian Dramas. LC 99-55449. 2000. pap. 17.50 (*0-7880-1587-7*) CSS OH.

Boehr, Karren. In Him Was Life: Four Dramas for Lent & Easter. 24p. 1997. pap. 4.50 (*0-7880-1130-8*) CSS OH.

Boehrer, Bruce T. The Fury of Men's Gullets: Ben Jonson & the Digestive Canal. LC 97-11661. (C). (gr. 13). 1997. text 38.50 (*0-8122-3408-1*) U of Pa Pr.

— Monarchy & Incest in Renaissance England: Literature, Culture, Kinship, & Kingship. LC 91-46228. (New Cultural Studies). 224p. (C). 1992. text 29.95 (*0-8122-3134-1*) U of Pa Pr.

***Boehrer, Stephen L.** Dead Men's Bones. LC 00-132996. 279p. 2000. pap. 14.95 (*0-9660607-1-7*) Wind-borne Pubns.

Boehrer, Stephen L. Unless a Grain of Wheat. LC 97-91102. 270p. 1997. pap. 14.95 (*0-9660607-0-9*) Wind-borne Pubns.

Boehringer, Christof. Zur Chronologie Mittelhellenistischer Muenzserien 220-160 vor Chr. (Antike Muenzen und Geschnittene Steine Ser.: Vol. 5). (Illus.). 240p. (C). 1972. 136.95 (*3-11-001763-6*) De Gruyter.

***Boehringer, Michael.** The Telling Tactics of Narrative Strategies in Tieck, Kleist, Stifter & Storm. (North American Studies in Nineteenth-Century German Literature: Vol. 24). 216p. 1999. 48.95 (*0-8204-4439-1*) P Lang Pubng.

Boeing Commercial Airplane Group Staff & Institute of Noise Control Engineering Staff. Noise-Con, '96, 2 vols. 974p. write for info. (*0-931784-35-2*) Noise Control.

Boeing, Gunther. Herder Economics Dictionary: Herder-Lexikon Wirtschaft. 5th ed. (GER.). 254p. 1981. pap. 35.00 (*0-8288-1275-6*, M7462) Fr & Eur.

Boeing, Gunther & Haeusgen. Herder-Lexikon Kunst. (GER.). 240p. 1974. pap. 35.00 (*0-8288-6049-1*, M7458) Fr & Eur.

***Boeing, H., ed.** EPIC Study - German Part: European Prospective Investigation into Cancer & Nutrition. (Annals of Nutrition & Metabolism Ser.: Vol. 43, No. 4). (Illus.). 76p. 1999. pap. 25.25 (*3-8055-7016-3*) S Karger.

Boeing-Haeusgen, Ursula. Diccionario Rioduero: Arte, Vol. 1. (SPA.). 312p. 1978. pap. 14.95 (*0-8288-5153-0*, S50170) Fr & Eur.

— Diccionario Rioduero, Arte, Vol. 2. (SPA.). 352p. 1980. pap. 14.95 (*0-7859-5737-5*, 8422009331) Fr & Eur.

Boeing, Robert. Chaucer & the Mystics: The Canterbury Tales & the Genre of Devotional Prose. LC 94-33130. 1995. 37.50 (*0-8387-5288-8*) Bucknell U Pr.

Boek, Walter E. The Evolution of a Democracy: This Is Our Country, the United States of America. LC 90-37111. (Illus.). 448p. 1991. 19.95 (*1-880469-00-6*) Col Democracy.

— How to Establish a Democracy or Improve the One You Now Have: A Practical Guide for Developing Essential Government & Business Structures & Personal Systems of Values. LC 92-37111. (Illus.). 448p. (C). 1993. text 19.95 (*1-880469-01-4*) Col Democracy.

***Boekaerts, Monique.** Handbook of Self-Regulation. 783p. (C). 1999. text 99.95 (*0-12-109890-7*) Acad Pr.

Boeke, Julius H. Economics & Economic Policy of Dual Societies, As Exemplified by Indonesia. LC 75-30045. (Institute of Pacific Relations Ser.). reprint ed. 55.00 (*0-404-59508-1*) AMS Pr.

— The Structure of the Netherlands Indian Economy. LC 75-30047. (Institute of Pacific Relations Ser.). 1983. reprint ed. 39.50 (*0-404-59509-X*) AMS Pr.

Boeke, Karin, et al. Politische Leitvokabeln in der Adenauer-Aera. (Sprache, Politik, Oeffentlichkeit Ser.: Vol. 8). (GER.). xii, 496p. (C). 1996. lib. bdg. 161.50 (*3-11-014236-8*) De Gruyter.

Boeke, W. R., et al, eds. Intermediate Uveitis. (Developments in Ophthalmology Ser.: Vol. 23). (Illus.). viii, 290p. 1991. 248.00 (*3-8055-5436-2*) S Karger.

Boeke, W. R., ed. see International Symposium on Immunology & Immunopath.

Boeke, Wanda, tr. see Dorrestein, Renate.

Boeke, Wanda, tr. see Dudevszky, Szabinka.

Boeke, Wanda, tr. see Hofmann, Helga.

Boeke, Wanda, tr. see Holtwijk, Ineke.

Boeke, Wanda, tr. see Kraan, Hanna.

Boeke, Wanda, tr. see Mikes, Petr.

***Boekelheide, K., et al.** Reproductive & Endocrine Toxicology, 13 vols. (Comprehensive Toxicology Ser.: Vol. 10). 761p. 1999. 200.50 (*0-08-042975-0*) Elsevier.

Boekelheide, Robert J., jt. ed. see Ainley, David G.

Boekels, Joachim. Schleiermacher als Kirchengeschichtler: Mit Edition der Nachschrift Karl Rudolf Hagenbachs von 1821-22. (Schleiermacher-Archiv Ser.: Vol. 13). (GER.). xii, 488p. (C). 1994. lib. bdg. 183.10 (*3-11-014203-1*) De Gruyter.

Boeker, Egbert. Environmental Physics. 2nd ed. 1978. text. write for info. (*0-471-99779-X*) Wiley.

Boeker, Egbert & Van Grondelle, Rienk. Environmental Physics. LC 94-9542. 462p. 1995. pap. 64.95 (*0-471-95110-2*) Wiley.

— Environmental Physics. LC 94-9542. 462p. 1995. 155.00 (*0-471-93931-5*) Wiley.

Boeker, M. Status of the Beginning Calculus Students in Pre-Calculus College Mathematics: Study Carried Out with Students in Brooklyn College & City College of New York. LC 76-176690. (Columbia University. Teachers College. Contributions to Education Ser.: No. 922). reprint ed. 37.50 (*0-404-55922-0*) AMS Pr.

Boeker, Paul H., ed. Latin America's Turnaround: The Paths to Privatization & Foreign Investment. 250p. (Orig.). 1993. pap. 19.95 (*1-55815-247-4*) ICS Pr.

Boeker, Paul H., ed. see Bocker, Paul.

***Boekestein, A.** Towards an Agenda for Agriculture Research in Europe. 320p. 2000. pap. 72.00 (*90-74134-80-7*) Wageningen Pers.

***Boekhoff, P. M.** The Scarlet Letter. LC 00-9234. (Understanding Great Literature Ser.). 2000. write for info. (*1-56006-812-4*) Lucent Bks.

Boekholt, R. Welding Mechanization & Automation in World Shipbuilding: Production Methods & Trends Based on Yard Capacity. 352p. 1996. pap. 135.00 (*1-85573-219-X*, Pub. by Woodhead Pubng) Am Educ Systs.

— Welding Workplace, 2000. 200p. 2000. boxed set 153.00 (*1-85573-445-1*) Am Educ Systs.

Boekhorst, Peter te, jt. auth. see Poll, Roswitha.

Boekstein, A. & Pavicevic, M. K., eds. Electron Microbeam Analysis: Mikrochimaxa Acta - Supplementum 12. 200p. 1992. 143.95 (*0-387-82359-X*) Spr-Verlag.

Boelaert, Edmond. Nsong' a Lianja: L'Epopee Nationale des Nkundo. (B. E. Ser.: No. 126). 1949. pap. 18.00 (*0-8115-3054-X*) Periodicals Srv.

Boelan, Jacobus. A Merchant's Perspective: Captain Jacobus Boelen's Narrative of His Visit to Hawai'i in 1828. Broeze, Frank J., ed. & tr. by. 150p. (C). 1988. text 24.00 (*0-945048-00-9*) HI Hist Soc.

Boelcke, Jurgen. Commercial Correspondence in German: La Correspondance Commerciale en Allemand. (FRE & GER.). 1988. pap. 14.95 (*0-8288-1558-5*, M508) Fr & Eur.

— Dictionary of German Economic Terms: Dictionnaire de l'Allemand Economique. (FRE & GER.). 1988. 65.00 (*0-8288-0810-4*, M590) Fr & Eur.

— Wirtschaftsworterbuch, Vol. 1. 2nd ed. (FRE & GER.). 440p. 1990. lib. bdg. 135.00 (*0-8288-3895-X*, F131470) Fr & Eur.

— Wirtschaftsworterbuch, Vol. 2. (FRE & GER.). 381p. 1990. lib. bdg. 135.00 (*0-8288-3896-8*, F131190) Fr & Eur.

Boelcke, Jurgen, et al. Dictionnaire Comptable et Financier: French-German, German-French. (FRE & GER.). 196p. 1993. pap. 75.00 (*0-7859-7940-9*, 2712704045) Fr & Eur.

— Dictionnaire de l'Allemand Economique et Commercial. (FRE & GER.). 482p. 1982. pap. 29.95 (*0-7859-4737-X*) Fr & Eur.

Boelcke, Oswald. An Aviator's Field Book. (Great War Ser.: No. 14). (Illus.). 219p. reprint ed. 29.95 (*0-89839-163-6*) Battery Pr.

Boele-Woelki, K., et al, eds. Comparability & Evaluation: Essays on Comparative Law, Private International Law, & International Commercial Arbitration in Honour of Dimitra Kokkini-Iatridou. LC 94-35315. 432p. (C). 1994. lib. bdg. 129.50 (*0-7923-3157-5*, Pub. by M Nijhoff) Kluwer Academic.

Boele-Woelki, Katharina. Die Effektivitatsprufung der Staatsangehorigkeiten im Niederlandischen Internationalen Familienrecht. 206p. 1983. pap. 34.00 (*90-6544-117-4*) Kluwer Academic.

Boeles. Fair Immigration Proceedings in Europe. 1997. 172.00 (*90-411-0324-4*) Kluwer Law Intl.

Boelhouwer, P. & Papa, O. A. Housing Systems in Europe: A Comparative Study, 2 vols., 1. 539p. (Orig.). 1992. 49.50 (*90-6275-769-3*) Coronet Bks.

— Housing Systems in Europe: A Comparative Study, 2 vols., 2. 539p. (Orig.). 1992. 49.50 (*90-6275-770-7*) Coronet Bks.

Boelhouwer, P. J., ed. Financing the Social Rented Sector in Western Europe. LC 97-190641. (Housing & Urban Policy Studies: Vol. 13). 115p. 1997. pap. 25.00 (*90-407-1433-9*, Pub. by Delft U Pr) Coronet Bks.

Boelhouwer, P. J. & Menkveld, A. J. Housing Expenditure in Western Europe: Macro & Micro Housing Quotas. (Housing & Urban Policy Studies: Vol. 11). 49p. (Orig.). 1996. pap. 22.50 (*90-407-1327-8*, Pub. by Delft U Pr) Coronet Bks.

Boelhower, William, ed. see Iannace, Carmine Biagio.

Boelhower, William, tr. see Gramsci, Antonio.

Boelhower, William Q., tr. see Goldmann, Lucien.

Boelk, Mary P. C++ Lab Manual for Computer Science: An Overview. 5th ed. 304p. (C). 1997. pap. text 21.20 (*0-201-31545-9*) Addison-Wesley.

Boella, M. J. Human Resource Management in the Hospitality Industry. 6th ed. 336p. 1996. pap. 47.50 (*0-7487-2256-4*, Pub. by S Thornes Pubs) Trans-Atl Phila.

***Boella, M. J.** Human Resource Management in the Hospitality Industry. 7th ed. (Illus.). 368p. 2000. pap. 59.50 (*0-7487-5466-0*, Pub. by S Thornes Pubs) Trans-Atl Phila.

Boella, Michael & Pannett, Alan. Principles of Hospitality Law. 416p. 1998. pap. 32.95 (*0-304-70472-5*) Continuum.

Boella, Michael, jt. auth. see Pannett, Alan.

Boels, D., et al, eds. Soil Degradation: Proceedings of the Land Use Seminar on Soil Degradation, Wageningen, 13-15th October 1980. 286p. (C). 1982. text 123.00 (*90-6191-220-2*, Pub. by A A Balkema) Ashgate Pub Co.

Boelts, Darwin, jt. auth. see Boelts, Maribeth.

***Boelts, Maribeth.** Big Daddy, Frog Wrestler. LC 99-16677. (Illus.). 32p. (J). (ps-3). 2000. lib. bdg. 14.95 (*0-8075-0717-2*) A Whitman.

Boelts, Maribeth. Dry Days, Wet Nights. LC 93-28674. (Illus.). 32p. (J). (ps-1). 1994. lib. bdg. 14.95 (*0-8075-1723-2*) A Whitman.

— Dry Days, Wet Nights. LC 93-28674. 1994. 11.15 (*0-606-10174-8*, Pub. by Turtleback) Demco.

— Dry Days, Wet Nights. LC 93-28674. (Concept Book Ser.). (Illus.). 32p. (J). (ps-1). 1996. reprint ed. pap. 5.95 (*0-8075-1724-0*) A Whitman.

— Grace & Joe. Tucker, Kathy, ed. LC 93-45920. (Illus.). 32p. (J). (ps-1). 1994. lib. bdg. 14.95 (*0-8075-3019-0*) A Whitman.

— A Kid's Guide to Staying Safe Around Fire. LC 96-47918. (Kid's Library of Personal Safety). (J). (gr. k-3). 1997. lib. bdg. 15.93 (*0-8239-5077-8*, PowerKids) Rosen Group.

— A Kid's Guide to Staying Safe at Playgrounds. LC 96-30003. (Kid's Library of Personal Safety). (J). (gr. k-3). 1997. lib. bdg. 15.93 (*0-8239-5081-6*, PowerKids) Rosen Group.

— A Kid's Guide to Staying Safe at School. LC 96-30001. (Kid's Library of Personal Safety). (J). (gr. k-3). 1997. lib. bdg. 15.93 (*0-8239-5079-4*, PowerKids) Rosen Group.

— A Kid's Guide to Staying Safe on Bikes. LC 96-48942. (Kid's Library of Personal Safety). (J). (gr. k-3). 1997. lib. bdg. 15.93 (*0-8239-5076-X*, PowerKids) Rosen Group.

— A Kid's Guide to Staying Safe on the Streets. LC 96-54271. (Kid's Library of Personal Safety). (J). (gr. k-3). 1997. lib. bdg. 15.93 (*0-8239-5080-8*, PowerKids) Rosen Group.

— A Kid's Guide to Water Safety. LC 96-48944. (Kid's Library of Personal Safety). 24p. (J). (gr. k-3). 1997. lib. bdg. 15.93 (*0-8239-5078-6*, PowerKids) Rosen Group.

— Little Bunny's Cool Tool Set. LC 96-54862. (Concept Bks.). (Illus.). 32p. (J). (ps-1). 1997. lib. bdg. 14.95 (*0-8075-4584-8*) A Whitman.

— Little Bunny's Cool Tool Set. (Illus.). 32p. (J). (ps-1). 1999. pap. 6.95 (*0-8075-4585-6*) A Whitman.

— Little Bunny's Pacifier Plan. LC 98-35244. (Illus.). (J). (ps-k). 1999. lib. bdg. 14.95 (*0-8075-4581-3*) A Whitman.

— Little Bunny's Preschool Countdown. (Illus.). 32p. (J). (ps-1). 1996. lib. bdg. 14.95 (*0-8075-4582-1*) A Whitman.

— Little Bunny's Preschool Countdown. (Illus.). 32p. (J). (ps-1). 1999. pap. 6.95 (*0-8075-4583-X*) A Whitman.

— Summer's End. LC 94-14837. (Illus.). 32p. (J). (gr. k-3). 1995. 14.95 (*0-395-70559-2*) HM.

Boelts, Maribeth & Boelts, Darwin. Kids to the Rescue! First-Aid Techniques for Kids. LC 91-50666. (Illus.). 72p. (Orig.). (J). (ps-6). 1992. pap. 7.95 (*0-943990-82-3*); lib. bdg. 17.95 (*0-943990-83-1*) Parenting Pr.

Boelza, Igor F. Handbook of Soviet Musicians. 1988. reprint ed. lib. bdg. 49.00 (*0-7812-0201-9*) Rprt Serv.

— Handbook of Soviet Musicians. Bush, Alan, ed. LC 74-166221. (Illus.). 101p. 1972. reprint ed. 29.00 (*0-403-01348-8*) Scholarly.

Boeman, John S. Investigation of "Brainstorming" in the USAF. 116p. 1996. pap. text 29.95 (*0-89126-197-4*) MA-AH Pub.

— Morotai: A Memoir of War. 2nd rev. ed. (Illus.). 284p. 1989. pap. 14.95 (*0-89745-124-4*) Sunflower U Pr.

— Peace, from War to War. 450p. 1991. pap. text 57.95 (*0-89126-170-2*) MA-AH Pub.

Boeman, Meg, ed. Feminist Classics: Women's Words That Changed the World. 181p. (Orig.). 1994. pap. 7.95 (*0-940483-09-2*) Hot Flash Pr.

Boemeke, Manfred E., ed. The Treaty of Versailles: A Reassessment after 75 Years. LC 98-36611. (Publications of the German Historical Insitute, Washington, D.C.). (Illus.). 770p. (C). 1998. text 85.00 (*0-521-62132-1*) Cambridge U Pr.

Boemeke, Manfred F., et al, eds. Anticipating Total War: The German & American Experiences, 1871-1914. (Publications of the German Historical Institute, Washington, D. C.). 512p. (C). 1999. text 59.95 (*0-521-62294-8*) Cambridge U Pr.

Boemer, Marilyn L. The Children's Hour: Radio Programs for Children, 1929-1956. LC 89-24133. 230p. 1989. 30.00 (*0-8108-2270-9*) Scarecrow.

Boemus, Joannes. The Fardle of Facions Conteining the Aunciente Maners of Affrike & Asia. LC 76-25836. (English Experience Ser.: No. 227). 368p. 1970. reprint ed. 28.00 (*90-221-0227-0*) Walter J Johnson.

Boen, F. S., ed. see International Symposium on Peritoneal Dialysis Staff.

Boenau, A. Bruce & Niiro, Katsuyuki, eds. Post-Industrial Society. 508p. (Orig.). (C). 1984. pap. text 37.00 (*0-8191-3613-1*) U Pr of Amer.

Boenau, A. Bruce, jt. ed. see McCardle, Arthur W.

Boener, Peter, ed. see Von Wolzogen, Caroline.

Boenig, Herman V. Plasma Science & Technology. LC 81-15200. (Illus.). 304p. 1982. text 57.50 (*0-8014-1356-7*) Cornell U Pr.

Boenig, Pierre. Waiting & After. 128p. (Orig.). 1989. pap. 9.95 (*0-945819-01-3*) Sulzburger & Graham Pub.

Boenig, Robert. The Acts of Andrew in the Country of the Cannibals: Translations from the Greek, Latin, & Old English. LC 90-19952. (Library of Medieval Literature: Vol. 70B). 176p. 1991. text 11.00 (*0-8240-7088-7*) Garland.

— Saint & Hero: Andreas & Medieval Doctrine. LC 89-46401. 136p. 1991. 32.50 (*0-8387-5187-3*) Bucknell U Pr.

Boenig, Robert, et al, eds. Studia Mystica, Vol. XVI. (Illus.). 260p. 1995. text 89.95 (*0-7734-9045-0*) E Mellen.

***Boenig, Robert, tr.** Anglo-Saxon Spirituality: Selected Writings. LC 00-31386. (Classics of Western Spirituality Ser.). 2001. 37.95 (*0-8091-0515-2*); pap. 27.95 (*0-8091-3950-2*) Paulist Pr.

***Boenig, Robert & Davis, Kathleen.** Manuscript, Narrative, Lexicon: Essays on Literary & Cultural Transmission in Honor of Whitney F. Bolton. LC 99-55721. (Illus.). 264p. 2000. 44.50 (*0-8387-5440-6*) Bucknell U Pr.

Boenig, Robert & Pollard, William F., eds. Mysticism & Spirituality in Medieval England. LC 97-10759. (Illus.). 272p. 1997. 60.00 (*0-85991-516-6*, DS Brewer) Boydell & Brewer.

Boenig, Robert, jt. auth. see Giles, Mary E.

Boenig, Robert W. Research in Science Education, 1938-1947. LC 69-12581. (Reviews of Research in Science Education Ser.: Vol. 1: 1938-1947). 306p. reprint ed. pap. 94.90 (*0-608-14888-1*, 202599300048) Bks Demand.

Boenig, Robert W. & Swift, Nathan J. Research in Science Education, 1948-1952. LC 69-12581. (Reviews of Research in Science Education Ser.: Vol. 2). 203p. reprint ed. pap. 63.00 (*0-608-15092-4*, 202607300048) Bks Demand.

Boening, John, ed. The Reception of Classical German Literature in England, 1760-1860: A Documentary History from Contemporary Periodicals, 10 vols. Incl. Vol. 1. General Introduction & Reviews from 1760 to 1813. 1977. lib. bdg. 120.00 (*0-8240-0990-8*); Vol. 2. Reviews from 1813 to 1835. 1977. lib. bdg. 120.00 (*0-8240-0991-6*); Vol. 3. Reviews from 1835 to 1860. 1977. lib. bdg. 120.00 (*0-8240-0992-4*); Vol. 4. Authors from Bodmer to Klopstock. 1977. lib. bdg. 120.00 (*0-8240-0993-2*); Vol. 5. Authors from Lavater to Novalis. 1977. lib. bdg. 120.00 (*0-8240-0994-0*); Vol. 6. Reception of Early German Romantics: Richter, the Brothers Schlegel, Tieck & Hoffmann. Boening, John, intro. 1977. lib. bdg. 120.00 (*0-8240-0995-9*); Vol. 7. General Critical Articles on Goethe & Reviews Which Discuss Goethe & Schiller Together, Arranged in Order of Appearance. 1977. lib. bdg. 120.00 (*0-8240-0996-7*); Vol. 8. Reviews of Werther, Goethe's Early Works, His Poems & Faust. 1977. lib. bdg. 120.00 (*0-8240-0997-5*); Vol. 9. Works of Goethe's Midcareer: Wilhelm Meister & Such Works As Dichtung und Wahrheit, Etc. Boening, John, intro. 1977. lib. bdg. 120.00 (*0-8240-0998-3*); Vol. 10. English Reception of Specific Works of Schiller, from the Early Plays to the Historical Works. 1977. lib. bdg. 120.00 (*0-8240-0999-1*); 1977. lib. bdg. write for info. (*0-686-77265-2*) Garland.

Boenisch, Edmond W. & Haney, Michele. The Stress Owner's Manual: Meaning, Balance & Health in Your Life. LC 96-26977. 208p. (Orig.). 1996. pap. 14.95 (*0-915166-84-4*) Impact Pubs CA.

Boenke, Heidi M., compiled by. Flute Music by Women Composers: An Annotated Catalog, 16. LC 88-21317. (Music Reference Collection: No. 16). 211p. 1988. lib. bdg. 55.00 (*0-313-26019-2*, BFE/, Greenwood Pr) Greenwood.

Boenke, Mary, ed. Transforming Families. LC 98-89291. (Illus.). 160p. 1999. pap. 11.95 (*0-9663272-1-7*) W Trook Pubg.

Boenzi, Joe, tr. see Aubry, Joseph.

Boer & Pingree, eds. Heliodori. (GRE.). 1962. 34.50 (*3-322-00836-3*, T1424, Pub. by B G Teubner) U of Mich Pr.

Boer, jt. auth. see Ellis.

Boer, jt. ed. see Lammert.

Boer, Andrew. Small Business Management--Level 3: A Resource-Based Approach for the Hospitality & Tourism Industries. (Hospitality, Travel & Tourism Ser.). 1997. pap. 19.95 (*0-304-33441-3*) Continuum.

Boer, Andrew, jt. ed. see Teare, Richard.

***Boer-Ashworth, Elizabeth de & Tausch, Arno.** The Global Political Economy & Post-1989 Change: The Place of the Central European Transition. LC 00-23345. 2000. write for info. (*0-312-23463-5*) St Martin.

Boer, B. W. & Gleeson, V. B. The Law of Education. 210p. 1982. 55.00 (*0-409-30923-0*, AT, MICHIE) LEXIS Pub.

Boer, Ben, et al, eds. Environmental Outlook: Law & Policy. 350p. 1994. pap. 49.00 (*1-86287-140-X*, Pub. by Federation Pr) Gaunt.

— Environmental Outlook No. 2: Law & Policy. 300p. 1996. pap. 54.00 (*1-86287-204-X*, Pub. by Federation Pr) Gaunt.

Boer, Ben, et al. International Environmental Law in the Asia Pacific. LC 98-139822. 432p. 1998. text 218.00 (*90-411-0706-1*) Kluwer Law Intl.

Boer, Bertil H. Van, see Van Boer, Bertil H.

Boer, C. De, see Chretien de Troyes & De Boer, C.

***Boer, C. R., et al, eds.** Parallel Kinematic Machines: Theoretical Aspects & Industrial Requirements. LC 99-37640. (Advanced Manufacturing Ser.). (Illus.). 458p. 1999. pap. 119.00 (*1-85233-613-7*, Pub. by Spr-Verlag) Spr-Verlag.

Boer, C. R., et al. Process Modelling for Metal Forming & Thermomechanical Treatment. (Materials Research & Engineering Ser.). (Illus.). xv, 410p. 1986. 131.95 (*0-387-16401-4*) Spr-Verlag.

Boer, Charles. Charles Olson in Connecticut. LC 91-62199. 1991. pap. 12.95 (*0-933598-28-9*) NC Wesleyan Pr.

***Boer, Charles, ed.** Lost Souls. (Spring Journal Ser.: Vol. 65). 2000. pap. 17.50 (*1-882670-17-5*, Pub. by Spring Jrnl) Continuum.

Boer, Charles, ed. Mom & the Kids. (Spring Journal Ser.: Vol. 63). 166p. 1998. pap. 17.50 (*1-882670-13-2*, Pub. by Spring Jrnl) Continuum.

Boer, Charles, et al, eds. Disillusionment. (Spring Journal: Vol. 58). 176p. (Orig.). 1995. pap. 17.50 (*1-882670-06-X*) Spring Jrnl.

Boer, Charles, tr. from GRE. The Homeric Hymns. rev. ed. LC 87-6530. (Dunquin Ser.: No. 10). 182p. 1970. reprint ed. pap. 17.00 (*0-88214-210-0*) Spring Pubns.

— Ovid's Metamorphoses. LC 89-4223. (Dunquin Ser.: No. 17). ix, 342p. (Orig.). 1989. pap. 22.00 (*0-88214-217-8*) Spring Pubns.

Boer, Charles, jt. auth. see Hillman, James.

Boer, Charles, ed. see Hillman, James & Giegerich, Wolfgang.

Boer, Charles, jt. ed. see Hillman, James.

Boer, Charles, ed. see Hillman, James, et al.

Boer, Charles, ed. see Livernois, Jay & Pollack, Rachel.

Boer, Charles, tr. see Ficino, Marsilio.

Boer, E. De, see De Boer, E., ed.

Boer, Esther De, see De Boer, Esther.

Boer, F. Peter. The Valuation of Technology: Business & Financial Issues in R&D. LC 98-39117. (Operations Management Series for Professionals). 432p. 1999. 60.00 incl. cd-rom, disk (*0-471-31638-5*) Wiley.

Boer, Fritz & Dunn, Judith F., eds. Children's Sibling Relationships: Developmental & Clinical Issues. 184p. 1992. text 49.95 (*0-8058-1107-9*) L Erlbaum Assocs.

***Boer, G. Den & Stoelhorst, D., eds.** Challenges for Concrete in the Next Millenium: Proceedings of the XIII FIP Congress, Amsterdam, 23-29 May 1998. (Illus.). 1106p. 1998. 178.00 (*90-5410-945-9*, Pub. by A A Balkema) Ashgate Pub Co.

Boer, G. F. De, see De Boer, G. F., ed.

Boer, G. J., jt. auth. see Gash, D. M.

Boer, Germain. Use of Expert Systems in Management Accounting. Barth, Claire, ed. 55p. (Orig.). 1989. pap. 20.00 (*0-86641-173-9*, 89230) Inst Mgmt Account.

Boer, H. H., jt. ed. see Lever, J. L.

Boer, Harry. Organising Innovative Manufacturing Systems. (Business School Library). 284p. 1991. text 82.95 (*1-85628-273-2*, Pub. by Avebry) Ashgate Pub Co.

***Boer, Harry, et al, eds.** CI Changes from Suggestion Box to Organisational Learning: Continuous Improvement in Europe & Australia. 352p. 2000. text 78.95 (*0-7546-1190-6*, Pub. by Ashgate Pub) Ashgate Pub Co.

Boer, Harry R. The Doctrine of Reprobation in the Christian Reformed Church. LC 83-1602. 94p. reprint ed. 30.00 (*0-608-16658-8*, 202753700055) Bks Demand.

— A Short History of the Early Church. LC 75-25742. 1990. pap. 14.00 (*0-8028-1339-9*) Eerdmans.

Boer, Inge, jt. auth. see Bal, Meike.

Boer, J. A. Den, see Den Boer, J. A.

Boer, J. A. Den, see Westenberg, H. G.

Boer, J. De, see De Boer, J., ed.

Boer, James Den, see Olson, Charles & Den Boer, James.

Boer, James Den, see Den Boer, James.

Boer, Jaques A. Den, see Vlaardingerbroek, Marinus T.

Boer, Jaques A. Den, see Vlaardingerbroek, Marinus T. & Den Boer, Jaques A.

Boer, John A. Den, see Den Boer, John A., ed.

Boer, John J. De, see De Boer, John J.

Boer, K., jt. ed. see Goswami, Y.

Boer, K. W. Advances in Solar Energy: An Annual Review of Research & Development, Vol. 4. LC 85-646250. (Illus.). 534p. (C). 1988. 155.00 (*0-306-42810-5*, Plenum Trade) Perseus Pubng.

— Advances in Solar Energy: An Annual Review of Research & Development, Vol. 5. (Illus.). 470p. (C). 1989. 155.00 (*0-306-43323-0*, Plenum Trade) Perseus Pubng.

— Advances in Solar Energy: An Annual Review of Research & Development, Vol. 6. LC 85-646250. (Illus.). 630p. (C). 1990. 155.00 (*0-306-43727-9*, Plenum Trade) Perseus Pubng.

Boer, Karl W. Joint Conference American Section International Solar Energy Society Winnipeg 8/76, 10 vols., Set. (Sharing the Sun Solar Technology in the Seventies Ser.). reprint ed. 1774.00 (*0-08-021707-9*, Pub. by Pergamon Repr) Franklin.

— Solar Heating & Cooling of Buildings: Contains Sections 3 4.1 4.3. (Sharing the Sun Solar Technology in the Seventies Ser.: Vol. 3). reprint ed. 187.00 (*0-08-021699-4*, Pub. by Pergamon Repr) Franklin.

— Survey of Semiconductor Physics Vol. II: Barriers, Junctions, Surfaces & Devices. (Illus.). 1488p. 1992. text 89.95 (*0-442-00672-1*, VNR) Wiley.

B

Boer, Karl W., ed. Advances in Solar Energy, Vol. 11. 11th ed. (Illus.). 547p. 1996. text 125.00 (*0-89553-254-9*) Am Solar Energy.

— Advances in Solar Energy: An Annual Review of Research & Development, Vol. 12. (Illus.). 516p. 1998. 125.00 (*0-89553-255-7*) Am Solar Energy.

Boer, Karl W. & Duffie, John A., eds. Advances in Solar Energy: An Annual Review of Research & Development in 1981, Vol. I. (Illus.). 1982. pap. text 125.00 (*0-89553-040-6*) Am Solar Energy.

Boer, Karl W., ed. see Awerbuch, Shimon, et al.

Boer, Karl W., ed. see International Solar Energy Society, American Secti.

Boer, Karl W., ed. see International Solar Energy Society Staff.

Boer, Leobert E. De, see De Boer, Leobert E., ed.

Boer, Martinus C. De, see De Boer, Martinus C., ed.

Boer, Marvin E. De, see De Boer, Marvin E., ed.

Boer, Monica Den, see Anderson, Malcolm & Den Boer, Monica.

Boer, N. C. den, et al, eds. Clinical Chemistry: An Overview. (Illus.). 874p. 1989. 155.00 (*0-306-43093-2*, Plenum Trade) Perseus Pubng.

Boer, P. De, see Searle, A. G. & De Boer, P., eds.

Boer, Paul M. De, see De Boer, Paul M.

Boer, Pim D. History As a Profession: The Study of History in France (1818-1914) Pomerans, Arnold J., tr. from DUT. LC 97-39415. 496p. 1998. text 65.00 (*0-691-03339-0*, Pub. by Princeton U Pr) Cal Prin Full Svc.

Boer, Pim Den, see Den Boer, Pim, ed.

Boer, R. De. Porous Media: Theory & Experiments LC 99-20352. 1999. write for info. (*0-7923-5692-6*) Kluwer Academic.

Boer, Roland. Knockin' on Heaven's Door: Hebrew Bible & Cultural Criticism. LC 98-55198. 1999. text. write for info. (*0-415-19410-5*) Routledge.

***Boer, Roland.** Knockin' on Heaven's Door: Hebrew Bible & Cultural Criticism. LC 98-55198. 1999. pap. 27.99 (*0-415-19411-3*) Routledge.

Boer, Roland. Novel Histories: The Fiction of Biblical Criticism. (Playing the Texts Ser.: Vol. 2). 224p. 1997. 74.00 (*1-85075-835-2*, Pub. by Sheffield Acad); pap. 24.50 (*1-85075-836-0*, Pub. by Sheffield Acad) CUP Services.

Boer, S. P. De, see De Boer, S. P.

Boer, Steven E. & Lycan, William G. Knowing Who. 232p. (C). 1985. 27.50 (*0-262-02228-1*, Bradford Bks) MIT Pr.

Boer, T. W. De, see De Boer, T. W.

Boer, Theodore De. The Development of Husserl's Thought. Plantinga, Theodore, tr. (Phaenomenologica Ser.: No. 76). 1978. pap. text 115.50 (*90-247-2124-5*); lib. bdg. 194.00 (*90-247-2039-7*) Kluwer Academic.

Boer, Theodore De, see De Boer, Theodore.

Boer, Tjitze J. De, see De Boer, Tjitze J.

Boer, W. Den. The Art of Memory & Its Mnemotechnical Traditions. (Mededelingen der Koninklijke Nederlandse Akademie van Wetenschappen, Afd. Letterkunde Ser.: No. 49(3)). 1986. pap. text 18.75 (*0-444-85655-2*) Elsevier.

Boer, W. Den, see Den Boer, W.

Boerckel, Catharina. Ideal und Realitat. (Anglo-Amerikanische Studien Ser.: No. 10). VIII, 142p. 1997. 35.95 (*3-631-31706-9*) P Lang Pubng.

***Boerefijn, I.** The Reporting Procedure under the Covenant on Civil & Political Rights: Practice & Procedures of the Human Rights Committee. (School of Human Rights Research Ser.: Vol. 2). 417p. 1999. 80.00 (*90-5095-074-4*, Pub. by Intersentia Uitgevers) Intl Spec Bk.

Boeren, P. C. Rorgo Fretellus de Nazareth et Sa Description de la Terre Sainte. 108p. pap. 56.25 (*0-7204-8492-8*) Elsevier.

Boerens, Patrice. Two-Hour Cross-Stitch: 515 Fabulous Designs. LC 94-30301. (Illus.). 144p. 1995. 24.95 (*0-8069-0952-8*, Chapelle) Sterling.

— Two Hour Cross-Stitch: 515 Fabulous Designs. (Illus.). 144p. 1997. pap. text 14.95 (*0-8069-0953-6*, Chapelle) Sterling.

Boerens, Trice. Stringing Along. (Illus.). 96p. 1996. pap. text 7.95 (*0-486-29467-6*) Dover.

***Boerens, Trice & Beesley, Terrece.** Fun with Sunbonnet Sue. LC 99-10299. (Illus.). 128p. 1999. 24.95 (*1-56477-268-3*, B390) Martingale & Co.

Boerens, Trice, jt. auth. see Beesley, Terrece.

Boerger, E., et al. The Classical Decision Problem. (Perspectives in Mathematical Logic Ser.: Vol. 7). 482p. 1996. 129.00 (*0-387-57073-X*) Spr-Verlag.

Boerger, Egon, et al. The Classical Decision Problem. LC 96-44426. (Perspectives in Mathematical Logic Ser.). 482p. 1996. 129.00 (*3-540-57073-X*) Spr-Verlag.

Boerger, James A. The Car Buyer's Handbook! rev. ed. (Illus.). 128p. 1989. pap. 9.95 (*0-685-26554-4*) CAR Ltd.

Boergesen, Frederik. The Marine Algae of the Danish West Indies, 3 pts. in 1. (Dansk Botanisk Arkiv Ser.: Bind 1-3). (Illus.). 726p. 1985. reprint ed. 200.00 (*3-87429-253-3*, 001419, Pub. by Koeltz Sci Bks) Lubrecht & Cramer.

Boerhave Beekman, W., ed. Elsevier's Wood Dictionary, 3 Vols., Set. (University Casebook Ser.). (DUT, ENG, FRE, GER & ITA.). 1968. write for info. (*0-686-43878-7*) Elsevier.

— Elsevier's Wood Dictionary Vol. 1: Commercial & Botanical Nomenclature of World Timbers, Sources of Supply. (University Casebook Ser.: 1). (DUT, ENG, FRE, GER & ITA.). 502p. 1964. 209.00 (*0-444-40063-X*) Elsevier.

— Elsevier's Wood Dictionary Vol. 2: Production, Transport, Trade. (University Casebook Ser.: 3). (DUT, ENG, FRE, GER & ITA.). 470p. 1968. 209.00 (*0-444-40053-2*) Elsevier.

— Elsevier's Wood Dictionary Vol. 3: Research, Manufacture, Utilization. (University Casebook Ser.). (DUT, ENG, FRE, GER & ITA.). 470p. 1981. 209.00 (*0-444-40713-8*) Elsevier.

***Boeri, Tito.** Structural Change, Welfare Systems & Labour Reallocation: Lessons from the Transition of Formerly Planned Economies. (Illus.). 256p. 2000. text 65.00 (*0-19-829365-8*) OUP.

Boeri, Tito, et al. Mediating the Transition: Labour Markets in Central & Eastern Europe. (EPI Forum Report: No. 4). 135p. 1998. pap. 14.95 (*1-898128-32-4*, Pub. by Ctr Econ Policy Res) Brookings.

Boericke, William. A Compend of the Principles of Homeopathy. 160p. 1996. reprint ed. spiral bd. 14.00 (*0-7873-0114-0*) Hlth Research.

— Materia Medica with Repertory. 1982. 25.00 (*0-685-76567-9*) Formur Intl.

Boericke, William & Dewey, Willis. The Twelve Tissue Remedies of Schuessler. 10.95 (*0-89378-065-0*) Formur Intl.

Boericke, William & Dewey, Willis A. The Twelve Tissue Remedies of Schuessler. 303p. 1994. reprint ed. spiral bd. 19.50 (*0-7873-1220-7*) Hlth Research.

Boeringer, James. Morning Star: The Life & Works of Francis Florentine Hagen. LC 84-62100. (Illus.). 176p. 1986. 29.50 (*0-941642-01-1*) Morav Music Found.

— Organa Britannica: Organs Built in England, 1660-1860, 3 vols., 1. LC 78-72492. (Illus.). 1200p. 1983. 95.00 (*0-8387-1894-9*) Bucknell U Pr.

— Organa Britannica: Organs Built in England, 1660-1860, 3 vols., 2. LC 78-72492. (Illus.). 1200p. 1987. 95.00 (*0-8387-5043-5*) Bucknell U Pr.

— Organa Britannica: Organs Built in England, 1660-1860, 3 vols., 3. LC 78-72492. (Illus.). 1200p. 1990. 125.00 (*0-8387-5044-3*) Bucknell U Pr.

Boeringer, James, ed. Choral Buch: A Facsimile of the First Edition of 1784. LC 83-62496. (Illus.). 336p. 1984. 30.00 (*0-941642-00-3*) Morav Music Found.

Boerio-Goates, Juliana, jt. auth. see Ott, J. Bevan.

***Boerjars, Kersti & Burridge, Kate.** Introducing English Grammar. (An Arnold Publication). 256p. 2000. pap. 19.95 (*0-340-69173-5*); text 60.00 (*0-340-69172-7*) OUP.

***Boerma, W. G. W. & Fleming, D. M.** The Role of General Practice in Primary Health Care. 121p. 1998. 65.00 (*0-11-322098-7*, Pub. by Statnry Office) Balogh.

Boerncke, Frank, ed. see Wittgenstein, Ludwig Josef Johann.

Boerne, Ludwig. La Balance. (Revue Allemande et Francaise Ser.). 168p. 1973. reprint ed. 50.00 (*3-487-04610-5*) G Olms Pubs.

Boerner, F. Taschenwoerterbuch der Botanischen Pflanzennamem. 2nd ed. (GER.). 435p. 1966. 75.00 (*0-8288-6728-3*, M7631) Fr & Eur.

— Taschenwoerterbuch der Botanischen Pflanzennamen fuer Gaertner, Garten- und Pflanzenfreunde, Land- und Forstwirte (Dictionary of Plant Names for Gardeners, Nature Lovers, Land & Forest Workers) 4th rev. ed. 468p. 1989. 32.00 (*3-8263-2960-0*, Pub. by Blckwell Wissenschafts) Balogh.

Boerner, G., et al. Astrophysics. LC 25-9130. (Tracts in Modern Physics Ser.: Vol. 69). (Illus.). iv, 120p. 1973. 58.95 (*0-387-06376-5*) Spr-Verlag.

***Boerner, Michael, et al.** Professional Linux Deployment. (Professional Ser.). 1000p. 1999. pap. 49.99 (*1-86100-287-4*) Wrox Pr Inc.

Boerner, Peter, ed. Concepts of National Identity: An Interdisciplinary Dialogue. 262p. 1986. 71.25 (*3-7890-1304-8*, Pub. by Nomos Verlags) Intl Bk Import.

Boerner, Wolfgang M. Modern Problems in Radar Target Imaging. LC 94-8274. (Wave Phenomena Ser.: Vol. 13). 1994. 131.95 (*0-387-57791-2*) Spr-Verlag.

Boerner, Wolfgang M., ed. Direct & Inverse Methods in Radar Polarimetry, 2 vols., Set. (C). 1992. lib. bdg. 545.50 (*0-7923-1498-0*) Kluwer Academic.

Boerner, Wolfgang M., et al, eds. Inverse Methods in Electromagnetic Imaging, 2 vols., Set. 1985. lib. bdg. 395.50 (*90-277-1890-3*) Kluwer Academic.

Boerner, Wolfgang M., jt. ed. see Mott, Harold.

Boernstein, Henry. Memoirs of a Nobody: The Missouri Years of an Austrian Radical, 1849-1866. Rowan, Steve, ed. & tr. by. from GER. LC 97-20637. (GER., Illus.). 412p. (Orig.). 1997. 27.95 (*1-883982-20-0*) MO Hist Soc.

— Memoirs of a Nobody: The Missouri Years of an Austrian Radical, 1849-1866. Rowan, Steven, tr. from GER. LC 97-20637. (GER., Illus.). 412p. (Orig.). 1997. pap. 19.95 (*1-883982-21-9*) MO Hist Soc.

— Memoirs of a Nobody: The Missouri Years of an Austrian Radical, 1849-1866. 432p. (Orig.). 1997. 34.95 (*0-8143-2725-7*) Wayne St U Pr.

— The Mysteries of St. Louis. Rowan, Steven & Sims, Elizabeth, eds. Munch, Freidrich, tr. from GER. (Foreign-Language American Left Ser.). (Illus.). 320p. (C). 1990. reprint ed. 35.00 (*0-88286-169-7*); reprint ed. pap. 18.00 (*0-88286-168-9*) C H Kerr.

Boero, Gianna & Silberston, Aubrey, eds. Environmental Economics: Conference Proceedings of the Confederation of European Economic Associations at Oxford, 1993. LC 94-46183. (Confederation of European Economic Associations Conference Volumes Ser.). 1995. text 85.00 (*0-312-12579-8*) St Martin.

***Boero, Patricia.** Career Counseling Over the Internet: An Emerging Model for Trusting & Responding to Online Clients. 208p. 2001. write for info. (*0-8058-3744-2*); pap. write for info. (*0-8058-3745-0*) L Erlbaum Assocs.

Boers, Arthur. Justice That Heals: A Biblical Vision for Victims & Offenders. LC 92-71357. 166p. 1992. pap. 12.95 (*0-87303-184-9*) Faith & Life.

Boers, Arthur P. Lord, Teach Us to Pray: A New Look at the Lord's Prayer. LC 92-71102. 192p. (Orig.). 1992. pap. 11.99 (*0-8361-3583-0*) Herald Pr.

— On Earth As in Heaven: Justice Rooted in Spirituality. LC 90-85237. 216p. (Orig.). 1991. pap. 10.99 (*0-8361-3545-8*) Herald Pr.

Boers, David. Happy Classrooms: The Cartie Model for Behavioral - Academic Success K-12. 230p. 1995. pap. text 14.95 (*1-886790-03-5*) WISC Publ.

— Making the Difference: Journal Writing for at-Risk Youth. 80p. (J). (gr. k-12). 1993. pap. text 10.00 (*1-886790-01-9*) WISC Publ.

Boers, David, et al. The History of Wisconsin Through Integrated Student Creations. 80p. (J). (gr. 3-10). 1992. pap. text 25.95 incl. audio (*1-886790-00-0*) WISC Publ.

Boers, G. H. Homocystinuria: A Risk Factor of Premature Vascular Disease. (Clinical Research Ser.: No. 3). vii, 166p. (Orig.). (C). 1986. pap. text 42.30 (*3-11-013366-0*) Mouton.

Boers, Hendrikus. The Justification of the Gentiles: Paul's Letters to the Galatians & Romans. LC 93-47042. 334p. 1994. 24.95 (*1-56563-011-4*) Hendrickson MA.

Boers, Jane, et al, eds. Writers Who Cook: A Tasty Assortment of Prose, Poetry & Recipes. 83p. (Orig.). 1995. pap. 12.95 (*0-9634813-0-4*) Herringbone.

Boers, P. C., et al, eds. Proceedings of the Third International Workshop on Phosphorus in Sediments. LC 92-46549. (Developments in Hydrobiology Ser.: Vol. 84). 416p. (C). 1993. text 289.50 (*0-7923-2126-X*) Kluwer Academic.

Boersema, Jan J., jt. ed. see Zweers, W.

Boersema, Raymond. Calculus for Management & the Life & Social Sciences. 144p. (C). 1988. text, student ed. 16.50 (*0-256-06302-8*, Irwn McGrw-H) McGrw-H Hghr Educ.

Boersema, Raymond, jt. auth. see Doran, Edward.

Boersma, B. J. Elecromagnetic Effects in Cylindrical Pipe Flow. (Illus.). 113p. 1997. pap. 43.50 (*90-407-1530-0*, Pub. by Delft U Pr) Coronet Bks.

Boersma, F. J., jt. auth. see Wilton, K. M.

Boersma, Hans. Eating God's Words: The Life of Jeremiah. LC 98-45125. (Revelation Ser.). 64p. 1998. pap., student ed. 4.95 (*1-56212-380-7*, 1312-0200) CRC Pubns.

***Boersma, Hans.** Jeremiah: Eating God's Words Leader. (Revelation Ser.). 64p. 1999. pap. 6.75 (*1-56212-381-5*, 1312-0240) CRC Pubns.

— The Vision of Zechariah: Leader Guide. (Revelation Ser.). 1999. pap., teacher ed. 6.75 (*1-56212-406-4*, 150055) CRC Pubns.

— The Visions of Zechariah: Student Guide. LC 99-52292. (Revelation Ser.). (Illus.). 48p. 1999. pap., student ed. 4.95 (*1-56212-405-6*, 150050) CRC Pubns.

Boersma, J. S. Oria & Valesio: Dutch Archaeological Investigations in the Brindisi Region of Southern Italy. (Mededelingen der Koninklijke Nederlandse Akademie van Wetenschappen, Afd. Letterkunde Ser.: No. 53(3)). 56p. 1990. pap. text 22.50 (*0-444-85717-6*) Elsevier.

Boersma, Jeanette. Grace in the Gulf. Bruggink, Donald J., ed. (Historical Series of the Reformed Church in America). xx, 292p. (Orig.). 1991. pap. 17.00 (*0-8028-0603-1*) Eerdmans.

Boersma, Johannes. Mutatio Valentia: The Late Roman Baths at Valesio, Salento. (Scrinium IX). (Illus.). 424p. 1995. 157.00 (*90-5170-337-6*, Pub. by Thesis Pubs) D Brown Bk Co.

***Boerst, William.** Time Machine: The Story of H. G. Wells. LC 99-41832. (World Writers Ser.). (Illus.). 112p. (YA). (gr. 5 up). 1999. lib. bdg. 19.95 (*1-883846-40-4*) M Reynolds.

***Boerst, William J.** Edgar Rice Burroughs: Creator of Tarzan. (World Writers Ser.). (Illus.). 112p. (YA). (gr. 5 up). 2000. lib. bdg. 19.95 (*1-883846-56-0*) M Reynolds.

Boerst, William J. Isaac Isimov: Writer of the Future. LC 98-29407. (World Writers Ser.). (Illus.). 112p. (YA). (gr. 5 up). 1999. lib. bdg. 18.95 (*1-883846-32-3*) M Reynolds.

Boerstler, Richard W., et al. Life to Death: Harmonizing the Transition: A Holistic & Meditative Approach for Care-Givers & the Dying. LC 95-38850. 256p. (Orig.). 1995. pap. 14.95 (*0-89281-329-6*, Heal Arts VT) Inner Tradit.

***Boertlein, John.** Howdunit: How Crimes Are Committed & Solved. (Illus.). 416p. 2000. pap. 19.99 (*1-58297-015-7*, Wrtrs Digest Bks) F & W Pubns Inc.

Boerwalst, Wayne, et al. Memories of Overdevelopment: Philippine Diaspora in Contemporary Art. (Illus.). 228p. 1997. pap. 25.00 (*0-921381-16-6*, Pub. by Plug In Editions) RAM Publications.

Boes, Don. The Eighth Continent. LC 93-30711. (Samuel French Morse Poetry Prize Ser.: Vol. 1993). 64p. 1993. pap. text 11.95 (*1-55553-178-4*) NE U Pr.

Boes, Duane C. Economic Theory of Public Enterprise. (Lecture Notes in Economics & Mathematical Systems Ser.: Vol. 188). (Illus.). 142p. 1981. 27.00 (*0-387-10567-0*) Spr-Verlag.

Boes, Lars & Scandinavian Philatelic Foundation Staff. AFA Iceland Specialized Catalog 1997: Pre-Republic Stamp Issues, 1870-1944. Smith, Jay, tr. from DAN. LC 96-72530. (Illus.). 94p. 1997. 44.50 (*0-936493-18-6*) Scand Philatelic.

Boes, M., ed. Environmental Law. (International Encyclopedia of Laws Ser.). 1991. ring bd. 170.00 (*0-685-58992-7*) Kluwer Law Intl.

Boes, Marc, ed. Environmental Law. (International Encyclopedia of Laws Ser.). 1992. ring bd. 147.00 (*90-6544-945-0*) Kluwer Law Intl.

Boesak, Allan A. Black & Reformed: Apartheid, Liberation, & the Calvinist Tradition. Sweetman, Leonard, ed. LC 84-7212. 187p. (Orig.). 1984. reprint ed. pap. 58.00 (*0-7837-9805-9*, 206053400005) Bks Demand.

— Farewell to Innocence: A Socio-Ethical Study on Black Theology & Black Power. LC 77-5578. 197p. (Orig.). reprint ed. pap. 61.10 (*0-7837-5523-6*, 204529300005) Bks Demand.

— The Finger of God: Sermons on Faith & Socio-Political Responsibility. Randall, Peter, tr. from AFR. LC 81-16943. 112p. 1982. reprint ed. pap. 34.80 (*0-7837-9803-2*, 206053200005) Bks Demand.

— If This Is Treason: I Am Guilty. LC 87-15512. 144p. reprint ed. pap. 44.70 (*0-7837-3195-7*, 204279900006) Bks Demand.

— If This Is Treason, I Am Guilty. 192p. (Orig.). (C). 1987. pap. 7.95 (*0-86543-055-1*) Africa World.

— Walking on Thorns: The Call to Christian Obedience. LC 84-13782. 75p. (Orig.). reprint ed. pap. 30.00 (*0-8357-4355-1*, 203718300007) Bks Demand.

Boesch-Achermann, Hedwige, jt. auth. see Boesch, Christophe.

Boesch, Axel, ed. Provisional Remedies in International Commercial Arbitration: A Practitioner Handbook. LC 94-27891. 830p. (C). 1994. lib. bdg. 290.80 (*3-11-012377-0*) De Gruyter.

***Boesch, Christophe & Boesch-Achermann, Hedwige.** The Chimpanzees of the Tai Forest: Behavioural Ecology & Evolution. (Illus.). 320p. 2000. text 95.00 (*0-19-850508-6*); pap. text 39.50 (*0-19-850507-8*) OUP.

Boesch, D. F. & Rabalais, Nancy N., eds. Long-Term Environmental Effects of Offshore Oil & Gas Development. 720p. 1987. mass mkt. 271.50 (*1-85166-094-1*) Elsevier.

Boesche, Roger. Theories of Tyranny. LC 94-42591. 544p. 1995. 19.95 (*0-271-01458-X*) Pa St U Pr.

— Theories of Tyranny. LC 94-42591. 544p. 1996. 70.00 (*0-271-01457-1*) Pa St U Pr.

Boeschen, John. How to Work at Home & Prosper: A Father's View. (Illus.). 183p. (Orig.). 1989. pap. 12.95 (*0-9625052-0-X*) J Boeschen.

Boeschenstein, Hermann. Zur Deutschen Literatur und Philosophie: Ausgewahlte Aufsatze. Symington, Rodney, ed. (Kanadische Studien zur deutschen Sprache und Literatur: Vol. 35). 320p. 1986. text 34.00 (*0-8204-0383-0*) P Lang Pubng.

Boeschenstein, Warren. Historic American Towns Along the Atlantic Coast. LC 99-10688. (Creating the North American Landscape Ser.). (Illus.). 320p. 1999. 39.95 (*0-8018-6144-6*) Johns Hopkins.

Boeschoten, Hendrik, tr. Stories of the Prophets: Qisas al-Anbiya: an Eastern Turkish Version, 2 vols. 832p. 1996. 322.75 (*0-614-21095-X*, 1415) Kazi Pubns.

Boeschoten, Hendrik & Verhoeven, Ludo T., eds. Turkish Linguistics Today. LC 90-28654. (Illus.). ix, 194p. 1991. 71.50 (*90-04-09375-3*) Brill Academic Pubs.

Boeschoten, Riki Van, see Van Boeschoten, Riki.

Boeschoten, W. C. & Fase, M. M. G. The Volume of Payments & the Informal Economy in the Netherlands, 1965. 1984. pap. text 48.50 (*90-247-3095-3*) Kluwer Academic.

***Boese, Ann.** Hidden Florida. 7th ed. (Illus.). 2000. pap. 17.95 (*1-56975-223-0*) Ulysses Pr.

Boese, Dierdre D., ed. Nun Better: Tastes & Tales from Around a Cajun Table. (Illus.). 288p. 1996. 18.95 (*0-9655106-0-3*) St Cecilia Schl.

Boese, Jane. A Lifetime of Rhyme. 80p. 1995. pap., per. 9.95 (*1-883852-02-1*) Sagest Pr OK.

Boese, Johannes. Altmesopotamische Weihplatten: Eine Sumerische Denkmalsgattung des Dritten Jahrtausends v. Chr. (Untersuchungen zur Assyriologie und Vorderasiatischen Archaeologie Ser.: Vol. 6). (Illus.). 232p. (C). 1971. 184.65 (*3-11-002484-5*) De Gruyter.

Boese, John T. Civil False Claims & Qui Tam Actions. 724p. 1993. ring bd. 126.00 (*0-13-241204-7*) Aspen Law.

Boese, M. & Kozarski, S., eds. Last Ice Sheet Dynamics & Deglaciation in the North European Plain: International Symposium Poznan, Berlin, May 1992. (Zeitschrift fuer Geomorphologie - Annals of Geomorphology Ser.: Supplementband 95). (Illus.). vi, 149p. 1994. pap. 52.00 (*3-443-21095-3*, Pub. by Gebruder Borntraeger) Balogh.

Boese, Neal R. Spiritual Gifts. LC 95-60997. 1995. pap. 7.95 (*0-7880-0615-0*, 6150, Fairway Pr) CSS OH.

***Boesel, David, et al.** Educational & Labor Market Performances of GED Recipients: Research Synthesis. (Illus.). 147p. 2000. reprint ed. pap. text 35.00 (*0-7881-8522-5*) DIANE Pub.

Boeselager, Amy, ed. Sheet Metal Punching: Collected Articles & Technical Papers. (Illus.). 210p. (Orig.). (C). 1993. pap. 33.00 (*1-881113-03-5*) Croydon Grp.

— Tube Producing: Collected Articles & Technical Papers. 176p. 1992. pap. 28.00 (*1-881113-01-9*) Croydon Grp.

Boeselager, Amy, ed. see Jones, Ed.

Boeselager, Amy, ed. see Nicks, J. E.

Boeselager, Wolfhard Von, see Von Boeselager, Wolfhard.

Boesen, Jannik & Mohele, A. T. The Success Story of Peasant Tobacco Production in Tanzania. (Centre for Development Research Publications: No. 2). 169p. 1980. write for info. (*91-7106-163-0*, Pub. by Nordic Africa) Transaction Pubs.

Boesen, Jannik, et al. Ujamaa - Socialism from Above. 183p. 1977. write for info. (*91-7106-125-8*, Pub. by Nordic Africa) Transaction Pubs.

Boesen, Jannik, ed. see Scandinavian Institute for African Studies.

Boesen, Victor, jt. auth. see Graybill, Florence Curtis.

Boeser, Knut. Nostradamus. Brownjohn, John, tr. from GER. LC 95-37244. 1996. 7.99 (*0-517-14910-9*) Random Hse Value.

An Asterisk (*) at the beginning of an entry indicates that the title is appearing for the first time.

B

Boffi, S., et al. Perspectives in Nuclear Physics. 596p. 1995. text 122.00 (*981-02-1688-2*) World Scientific Pub.

Boffi, Sigfrido, et al, eds. Perspectives in Hadronic Physics: Proceedings of the Conference ICTP, Trieste, Italy 12-16 May, 1997. 562p. 1998. 138.00 (*981-02-3321-3*) World Scientific Pub.

Boffi, Sigfrido, et al. Electromagnetic Response of Atomic Nuclei. LC 97-151536. (Oxford Studies in Nuclear Physics: No. 20). (Illus.). 518p. 1996. text 150.00 (*0-19-851774-2*) OUP.

Boffi, V. C., et al. Nonlinear Kinetic Theory & Mathematical Aspects of Hyperbolic Systems. Bampi, Franco & Toscani, Giuseppe, eds. LC 92-33361. (Advances in Mathematics Ser.: Vol. 9). 284p. 1993. text 95.00 (*981-02-1087-6*) World Scientific Pub.

Boffin, Tessa, ed. Stolen Glances: Lesbians Take Photographs. (Illus.). 256p. 1991. pap. 21.95 (*0-04-440707-6*) NYU Pr.

Boffin, Tessa, jt. ed. see Gupta, Sunil.

Boffo, Nancy Otto & Tomblin, Linda. The Tie That Binds: Devotions for Mothers & Daughters. LC 99-11985. 224p. 1999. pap. 13.00 (*0-570-05339-0*, 12-3387GJ) Concordia.

Boffo-Stetter, Iris. Luise Reichardt Als Musikpadagogin und Komponistin: Untersuchungen zu den Bedingungen Beruflicher Musikausubung Durch Frauen im Fruhen 19, Jahrhundert. (Beitrage zur Geschichte der Musikpadagogik Ser.: Bd. 4). (GER., Illus.). 179p. 1996. 42.95 (*3-631-30123-5*) P Lang Pubng.

Bofill, Francesc. Jack & the Beanstalk (Juan y los Frijoles Magicos) Alejando, Alis, tr. 32p. (J). (gr. k-2). 1998. 12.95 (*0-8118-2062-9*) Chronicle Bks.

Bofill, Ricardo. El Tiempo es el Diablo. (Biblioteca Cubana Contemporanea Ser.). (SPA.). 106p. (Orig.). 1985. pap. 6.00 (*84-359-0397-4*) Ediciones.

Bofill, Ricardo & Andre, Jean. Spaces of a Life. 192p. 2000. pap. 14.95 (*0-06-430213-X*, Icon Edns) HarpC.

Bofinger, Eve, et al, eds. The Frontiers of Modern Statistical Inference Procedures, Proceedings & Discussions of the Ipasras-II Conference (Second International Conference on Inference Procedures Associated with Statistical Ranking & Selection, University of Sydney, Australia, August 1987) LC 91-74124. (American Sciences Press Series in Mathematical & Management Sciences: Vol. 28). 500p. 1992. 195.00 (*0-935950-30-3*) Am Sciences Pr.

Bofinger, Peter & Portes, Richard, eds. Economic Transformation: The Next Stage in Central Europe. 208p. (C). 1995. pap. 21.95 (*1-898128-20-0*) Brookings.

Bofman, Theodora H. The Poetics of the Ramakian. (Special Reports: No. 21). 258p. (C). 1984. pap. 16.95 (*1-877979-71-6*) SE Asia.

Boga, Steve. Cyclists: How the World's Most Daring Riders Train & Compete. (Illus.). 227p. 1997. reprint ed. pap. text 15.00 (*0-7881-5114-2*) DIANE Pub.

— On Their Own: Adventure Athletes in Solo Sports, 3 bks. Kratoville, Betty Lou, ed. (Illus.). (J). (gr. 3-9). 1992. student ed. 14.00 (*0-87879-929-X*) High Noon Bks.

— On Their Own: Adventure Athletes in Solo Sports, 3 bks., Set. Kratoville, Betty Lou, ed. (Illus.). (J). (gr. 3-9). 1992. pap. text 12.00 (*0-87879-928-1*) High Noon Bks.

— Risk! An Exploration into the Lives of Athletes on the Edge. 2nd ed. (Illus.). 173p. (Orig.). 1988. pap. 9.95 (*1-55643-042-6*) North Atlantic.

Boga, Steve, jt. auth. see Bensman, Bobbi.

Boga, Steve, jt. auth. see Kelty, Nena.

Boga, Steven. Archery. LC 96-53457. (Backyard Games Ser.). (Illus.). 96p. 1997. pap. 10.00 (*0-8117-2486-7*) Stackpole.

— Badminton. (Games Ser.). (Illus.). 112p. 1996. pap. 10.00 (*0-8117-2487-5*) Stackpole.

— Camping & Backpacking with Children. LC 94-23013. (Illus.). 256p. 1995. pap. 16.95 (*0-8117-2522-7*) Stackpole.

— Caving. LC 96-29881. (Illus.). 208p. 1997. pap. 19.95 (*0-8117-2710-6*) Stackpole.

— Climbers: Scaling the Heights with the Sport's Elite. (Adventure Athletes Ser.). (Illus.). 240p. 1994. pap. 14.95 (*0-8117-2415-8*) Stackpole.

— Croquet. LC 94-45855. (Games Ser.). (Illus.). 96p. 1995. pap. 10.00 (*0-8117-2489-1*) Stackpole.

— Horseshoes. LC 96-23096. (Backyard Games Ser.). (Illus.). 96p. 1996. pap. 10.00 (*0-8117-2490-5*) Stackpole.

— Orienteering: The Sport of Navigating with Map & Compass. LC 96-24380. (Illus.). 208p. 1997. pap. 17.95 (*0-8117-2870-6*) Stackpole.

— Volleyball. LC 96-21976. (Illus.). 112p. 1997. pap. 10.00 (*0-8117-2491-3*) Stackpole.

Boga, Steven & Corbett, Mike. Aid Climbing with Mike Corbett. LC 94-47517. (Illus.). 96p. 1995. pap. 10.95 (*0-8117-2417-4*) Stackpole.

Boga, Steven & Lowe, Alex. Ice Climbing with Alex Lowe. LC 96-53458. (Climbing Specialists Ser.). (Illus.). 96p. 1997. pap. 14.95 (*0-8117-2806-4*) Stackpole.

Boga, Steven, jt. auth. see Bachar, John.

Boga, Steven, jt. auth. see Croft, Peter.

Boga, Steven, jt. auth. see Erbesfield, Robyn.

Boga, Steven A. Adventure Athletes: Runners & Walkers: Keeping Pace with the World's Best. LC 92-34536. (Illus.). 240p. (Orig.). 1993. pap. 14.95 (*0-8117-2414-X*) Stackpole.

Boga, Steven A. & Wright, Bob. Scoreboard Series: Fast Break, The Lunch Bowl, Side Kick, Strike Zone, In the Running, 5 bks., Set. Kratoville, Betty Lou, ed. (Illus.). 48p. (J). (gr. 2 up). 1994. pap. text 17.00 (*0-87879-989-3*) Acad Therapy.

Bogaard, Paul A. & Treash, Gordon, eds. Metaphysics As Foundation: Essays in Honor of Ivor Leclerc. LC 91-43054. 358p. (C). 1992. pap. text 21.95 (*0-7914-1258-X*) State U NY Pr.

Bogaards, Paul. Robert & Van Dale Dictionnaire Francais-Neerlandais, Neerlandais-Francais. 1400p. 1994. 125.00 (*0-7859-9201-4*) Fr & Eur.

Bogach, Susan V. Wood As Fuel: Energy for Developing Countries. LC 84-26640. 176p. 1985. 45.00 (*0-275-90062-2*, C0062, Praeger Pubs) Greenwood.

Bogach, V. Susan, jt. auth. see Piscitello, E. Scott.

Bogach, V. Susan, jt. auth. see Taylor, Robert P.

Bogachev, Vladimir I. Gaussian Measures. LC 98-27239. (Mathematical Surveys & Monographs). 433p. 1998. 95.00 (*0-8218-1054-5*) Am Math.

Bogachev, Yury. The Master's Minstrel: The Christian Confession of a Soviet Singer. Stronge, Barry, tr. from RUS. LC 95-158613. 144p. (Orig.). 1995. pap. 8.95 (*1-883893-03-8*) WinePress Pub.

Bogacki, Anatole C. A Polish Paradox. 1991. text 50.00 (*0-88033-200-X*, Pub. by East Eur Monographs) Col U Pr.

Bogacki, David F., jt. auth. see Blanco, Ralph F.

Bogacki, Tomasz. Cat & Mouse in the Night. LC 97-30160. 32p. (J). (ps-1). 1998. 15.00 (*0-374-31190-0*) FS&G.

— The Story of a Blue Bird. LC 97-10875. (Illus.). 32p. (J). (ps-k). 1998. 15.00 (*0-374-37197-0*) FS&G.

Bogacki, Tomek. Cat & Mouse. LC 95-44018. (Illus.). 32p. (J). (ps-3). 1996. 14.00 (*0-374-31225-7*) FS&G.

— Cat & Mouse in the Rain. LC 96-27937. (Illus.). 32p. (J). (ps-k). 1997. 15.00 (*0-374-31189-7*) FS&G.

*__Bogacki, Tomek.__ Cat & Mouse in the Snow. LC 98-36165. (Illus.). 32p. (J). (ps-k). 1999. 16.00 (*0-374-31192-7*, Frances Foster) FS&G.

— Circus Girl. 2001. text. write for info. (*0-374-31291-5*) FS&G.

Bogacki, Tomek. I Hate You! I Like You! LC 96-5291. (Illus.). 32p. (J). (ps-k). 1997. 14.00 (*0-374-33544-3*) FS&G.

— My First Garden. LC 99-24503. (Illus.). 40p. (YA). (ps-3). 2000. 16.00 (*0-374-32518-9*) FS&G.

Bogacz, Stephen J. New York Juvenile Delinquency Practice. LC 98-87339. 1122p. 1998. 99.00 (*0-327-00341-3*, 6012010) LEXIS Pub.

Bogaeri, Maurice P. Diccionario Enciclopedico de la Biblia. (SPA.). 1998. 149.95 (*0-8245-2152-8*) Crossroad NY.

Bogaert, G. Van Den, see Gautier, Theophile & Van Den Bogaert, G.

Bogaert, Harmen M. A Journey into Mohawk & Oneida Country, 1634-1635: The Journal of Harmen Meyndertsz Van Den Bogaert. Gehring, Charles T. & Starna, William A., eds. LC 88-2219. (Iroquois Bks.). (Illus.). 104p. 1988. reprint ed. pap. 32.30 (*0-608-06962-0*, 206717000009) Bks Demand.

*__Bogaert, Harmen M., et al.__ Early Vocabularies of Mohawk. LC 99-51922. (American Language Reprints Ser.: Vol. 16). 47p. 1999. 16.00 (*1-889758-14-0*) Evol Pubng & Manuf.

Bogaert, J., et al, eds. Magnetic Resonance of the Heart & Great Vessels: Clinical Applications. LC 98-24570. (Medical Radiology Ser.). (Illus.). 433p. 1999. 189.00 (*3-540-63448-7*) Spr-Verlag.

*__Bogaert, J., et al, eds.__ Magnetic Resonance of the Heart & Great Vessels: Clinical Applications. (Medical Radiology Ser.). (Illus.). xii, 286p. 2000. 75.00 (*3-540-67217-6*) Spr-Verlag.

*__Bogaert, Rita Flores.__ Pesto, Loose Ends & Other Love Poems. 36p. 1999. pap. 5.00 (*0-9674775-0-6*) Coral Bell Pr.

Bogaert-Tullis, Marjorie & Samuels, Sarah. A Resource Guide for Nutrition Management for Older Persons. 101p. 1986. write for info. (*0-318-61578-9*) US HHS.

Bogaerts, Anthony M. Chesterton & the Victorian Age. 189p. (C). 1966. reprint ed. lib. bdg. 75.00 (*0-8383-0510-5*) M S G Haskell Hse.

Bogaevski, V. N. & Povzner, A. Y. Algebraic Methods in Nonlinear Perturbation Theory. (Applied Mathematical Sciences Ser.: Vol. 88). (Illus.). 263p. 1991. 89.95 (*0-387-97491-1*) Spr-Verlag.

Bogan & Uline. Teaching Teaching: Experiencing the Other Side of the Desk. 124p. (C). 1997. per. 25.95 (*0-7872-4462-7*) Kendall-Hunt.

Bogan, Arthur E., jt. auth. see Parmalee, Paul W.

Bogan, Christopher E. Benchmarking for Best Practices. 312p. 1994. 29.95 (*0-07-006375-3*) McGraw.

Bogan, Dallas R. Warren County, Ohio & Beyond. LC 97-211841. xvi, 418p. 1997. pap. 29.50 (*0-7884-0678-7*, B520) Heritage Bk.

Bogan, Elizabeth C. & Kiernan, Joseph J. Macroeconomics: Theories & Applications. LC 86-24643. (Illus.). 569p. (C). 1987. pap. text, student ed. 20.00 (*0-314-34713-5*) West Pub.

Bogan, Gretchen. Genesis. 1958. pap. 3.50 (*0-87129-218-1*, G12) Dramatic Pub.

Bogan, James. Ozark Meandering. 91p. 1999. pap. 12.00 (*0-944048-13-7*) Timberline Missouri.

Bogan, James & Goss, Fred, eds. Sparks of Fire: William Blake in a New Age. (Io Ser.: No. 29). (Illus.). 484p. (Orig.). 1982. 35.00 (*0-913028-89-4*); pap. 12.95 (*0-913028-90-8*) North Atlantic.

Bogan, James, jt. ed. see Blank, Les.

Bogan, Joseph A. Criminal Justice & Violations of Your Civil Rights. 2nd ed. 172p. (C). 1994. pap. text 19.95 (*0-8403-9134-X*) Kendall-Hunt.

Bogan, Kathleen, jt. auth. see Coffey, Marilyn.

Bogan, Louise. The Blue Estuaries. LC 95-20822. 136p. 1995. pap. 12.00 (*0-374-52461-0*) FS&G.

Bogan, Louise, tr. see Goethe, Johann Wolfgang Von.

Bogan, Margaret. Creating Environmentally Literature Citizens: A Curriculum Guide. LC 98-125022. 164p. (C). 1997. per. 32.95 (*0-7872-4419-8*) Kendall-Hunt.

Bogan, Mary I., tr. see Augustine, Saint.

Bogan, Mary Inez. Vocabulary & Style of the Soliloquies & Dialogues of St. Augustine, Vol. 42. (Patristic Studies). 238p. 1984. reprint ed. 40.00 (*0-939738-27-9*) Zubal Inc.

Bogan, Mary Inez, tr. see Augustine, Saint.

Bogan, Paulette. Spike. LC 96-45328. (Illus.). 32p. (J). 1998. 12.99 (*0-399-23163-3*, G P Putnam) Peng Put Young Read.

*__Bogan, Paulette.__ Spike in the City. LC 99-31108. (Illus.). 32p. (J). (ps-1). 2000. 12.99 (*0-399-23442-X*, G P Putnam) Peng Put Young Read.

Bogan, Paulette, jt. auth. see Zoehfeld, Kathleen W.

Bogan, Robert V. Angelica, Belmont, & Wellsville. (Images of America Ser.). 1998. pap. 16.99 (*0-7524-0821-6*) Arcadia Publng.

Bogan, Samuel D. & Hinders, Mark K. Interface Effects in Elastic Wave Scattering. LC 93-51046. (Lecture Notes in Physics, New Series M, Monographs: No. M19). xii, 182p. 1994. 51.95 (*0-387-57657-6*) Spr-Verlag.

*__Bogarad.__ Legacies 2nd ed. (C). 2001. pap. text. write for info. (*0-15-506953-5*) Harcourt.

Bogarad. Legacies: Fiction, Poetry, Drama. (C). 1994. pap. text 49.00 (*0-15-500213-9*, Pub. by Harcourt Coll Pubs) Harcourt.

— Legacies: Fiction, Poetry, Drama. (C). 1994. pap. text, teacher ed. 4.00 (*0-15-500215-5*) Harcourt Coll Pubs.

Bogard. Statistic Radiation Protection. 1994. 85.00 (*0-07-105441-3*) McGraw.

Bogard, Lawrence J. & Neville, Peterson & Williams Staff, eds. Customs Law & Administration: Commentary, 2 vols. 3rd ed. 1983. ring bd. 400.00 (*0-379-20802-4*) Oceana.

Bogard, Mary, jt. auth. see Hagen, George Griffen.

*__Bogard, Michael.__ The Bold & the Dutiful: The Book of James. (Generation Why Ser.: No. 5, Pt. 3). 37p. (YA). (gr. 9-12). 2000. pap. 12.95 (*0-87303-389-2*) Faith & Life.

Bogard, Mike. 41 Ways to Build a Better Youth Group. LC 95-61921. 180p. 1996. pap. 12.95 (*0-87303-226-8*) Faith & Life.

Bogard, Travis. Eugene O'Neill at Tao House. Priehs, T. J., ed. LC 88-63080. (Illus.). 16p. (Orig.). 1989. pap. 3.95 (*0-911408-80-0*) SW Pks Mnmts.

— The Eugene O'Neill Songbook. LC 93-71672. xii, 249p. 1993. pap. 49.95 (*0-930997-03-4*) East Bay Bks.

— From the Silence of Tao House: Essays about Eugene & Carlotta O'Neill & the Tao House Plays. (Illus.). 198p. (Orig.). 1993. 100.00 (*0-9637215-0-X*); pap. 24.95 (*0-9637215-1-8*) E ONeill Fnd.

Bogard, Travis, et al. Revels History of Drama in English, Vol. 8: American Drama. (Illus.). 1978. 59.95 (*0-416-13090-9*, NO. 2101); pap. 27.50 (*0-416-81400-X*, NO. 2102) Routledge.

Bogard, Travis, ed. see O'Neill, Eugene.

Bogard, Travis, ed. & comment see O'Neill, Eugene.

Bogard, Vicki, tr. from FRE. Monkeys, Apes & Other Primates. LC 89-5378. (Young Discovery Library). (Illus.). 38p. (J). (ps-3). 1989. 5.95 (*0-944589-26-X*, 026) Young Discovery Lib.

Bogard, Vicki, tr. see Barbey, Dorine.

Bogard, Vicki, tr. see Brice, Raphaelle.

Bogard, Vicki, tr. see Busuttil, Joelle.

Bogard, Vicki, tr. see Costa de Beauregard, Diane.

Bogard, Vicki, tr. see Courtault, Martine.

Bogard, Vicki, tr. see De Beauregard, Diane C.

Bogard, Vicki, tr. see Dievart, Roger.

Bogard, Vicki, tr. see Fontanel, Beatrice.

Bogard, Vicki, tr. see Gandiol-Coppin, Brigitte.

Bogard, Vicki, tr. see Henry-Biabaud, Chantal.

Bogard, Vicki, tr. see Krafft, Maurice.

Bogard, Vicki, tr. see Laurencin, Genevieve.

Bogard, Vicki, tr. see Lazier, Christine.

Bogard, Vicki, tr. see Limousin, Odile & Neumann, Daniele.

Bogard, Vicki, tr. see Morel, Gaud.

Bogard, Vicki, tr. see Pfeffer, Pierre.

Bogard, Vicki, tr. see Prot, Viviane A.

Bogard, Vicki, tr. see Riquier, Aline.

Bogard, Vicki, tr. see Tordjman, Nathalie.

Bogard, Vicki, tr. see Verdat, Jean-Pierre.

Bogard, William. The Simulation of Surveillance: Hyper-Control in Telematic Societies. (Cultural Social Studies). 217p. (C). 1996. text 59.95 (*0-521-55081-5*); pap. text 19.95 (*0-521-55561-2*) Cambridge U Pr.

Bogarde, Dirk. Cleared for Take Off. (Illus.). 232p. 1995. text. write for info. (*0-670-86505-2*, Viking) Viking Penguin.

*__Bogarde, Dirk.__ For the Time Being. LC 99-205215. 288p. 1998. text. write for info. (*0-670-88005-1*) Viking.

Bogardi, I. & Kuzelka, R. D., eds. Nitrate Contamination: Exposure, Consequences & Control. (NATO ASI Series G: Ecological Sciences: Vol. 30). xii, 520p. 1991. 288.95 (*0-387-53088-6*) Spr-Verlag.

Bogardi, John L. Sediment Transport in Alluvial Streams. 826p. (C). 1978. 150.00 (*963-05-1826-0*, Pub. by Akade Kiado) St Mut.

Bogardus, A. H. Field, Cover & Trap Shooting. (Library Classics). (Illus.). 500p. 1987. reprint ed. 43.00 (*0-935632-48-4*) Wolfe Pub Co.

Bogardus, Carl R., Jr. The Clinical Applications of the Physics of Radiology & Nuclear Medicine. LC 67-26010. (Illus.). 248p. 1969. 15.00 (*0-87527-002-6*) Green.

Bogardus, Edgar. Various Jangling Keys. LC 70-144756. (Yale Series of Younger Poets: No. 50). reprint ed. 18.00 (*0-404-53850-9*) AMS Pr.

Bogardus, Emory S. The Development of Social Thought. 4th ed. LC 79-9741. 689p. 1979. reprint ed. lib. bdg. 45.50 (*0-313-21261-9*, BODS, Greenwood Pr) Greenwood.

— Fundamentals of Social Psychology. LC 73-2963. (Classics in Psychology Ser.). 1974. reprint ed. 29.95 (*0-405-05136-0*) Ayer.

— Mexican in the United States. LC 70-129389. (American Immigration Collection. Series 2). 1974. reprint ed. 12.95 (*0-405-00575-X*) Ayer.

Bogardus, Emory S., ed. see American Sociological Society Staff.

Bogardus, George F., tr. see Hereth, Michael.

Bogardus, Ralph F. Pictures & Texts: Henry James, A. L. Coburn, & New Ways of Seeing in Literary Culture. LC 84-8844. (Studies in Photography: No. 2). (Illus.). 265p. reprint ed. pap. 82.20 (*0-8357-1471-3*, 207049500097) Bks Demand.

Bogardus, Ralph F. & Hobson, Fred, eds. Literature at the Barricades: Essays on the American Writers in the 1930's. LC 81-3015. 247p. 1982. pap. 76.60 (*0-7837-8364-7*, 205917300009) Bks Demand.

Bogardus, William B. Dear Cousin: A Charted Genealogy of the Descendants of Anneke Jans Bogardus (1605-1663) to the 5th Generation. 192p. (C). 1996. 29.50 (*0-9621897-2-3*) W B Bogardus.

— Directory of Genealogical & Historical Articles Published in "de Halve Maen" from 1923 to 1991. iv, 27p. (C). 1992. pap. 8.00 (*0-9621897-1-5*) W B Bogardus.

Bogart. Introduction to Digital Circ. 42.95 (*0-02-819941-3*) Glencoe.

— Introductory Combinatorics. 3rd ed. (C). 1995. pap. text, teacher ed. write for info. (*0-03-097353-8*) Harcourt Coll Pubs.

— Introductory Combinatorics. 3rd ed. (C). 1999. text 63.50 (*0-03-097352-X*) Harcourt Coll Pubs.

— Ten for Dinner. large type ed. (J). (ps-2). 1989. 19.95 (*0-590-73173-4*) Scholastic Inc.

Bogart, Barbara A. In Place: Stories of Landscape & Identity from the American West. (Illus.). 128p. (Orig.). 1994. pap. 10.95 (*0-931271-27-4*) Hi Plains Pr.

Bogart, Carolyn, jt. auth. see Terry, Patricia.

Bogart, Charles H. Controlled Mines: A History of Their Use by the United States. 2nd rev. ed. (Military History Monograph: Vol. 50). (Illus.). 54p. 1997. 19.95 (*1-57638-080-7*, M50H); pap. 9.95 (*1-57638-036-X*, M50S) Merriam Pr.

Bogart, Emma H. Hoffman. Some Notes on the History of the Hoffman & Schermerhorn Family in Canada, with Genealogical Record of My Parents Isaiah Hoffman & Susanah Schermerhorn Hoffman. (Illus.). 64p. 1997. reprint ed. pap. 13.00 (*0-8328-9160-6*); reprint ed. lib. bdg. 23.00 (*0-8328-9159-2*) Higginson Bk Co.

Bogart, Ernest L. & Leffingwell, Russell C. War Costs & Their Financing: A Study of the Financing of the War & the After-War Problems of Debt & Taxation. LC 74-75232. (United States in World War I Ser.). xxiv, 510p. 1974. reprint ed. lib. bdg. 59.95 (*0-89198-095-4*) Ozer.

Bogart, Frank & Bogart, Mary. Till War Do Us Part. LC 95-68068. (Illus.). 160p. (Orig.). 1995. pap. 17.00 (*0-913337-24-2*) Southfarm Pr.

Bogart, Geoffrey S., jt. auth. see Manchester, Lydia.

Bogart, Greg. Finding Your Life's Calling: Spiritual Dimensions of Vocational Choice. LC 94-93938. 192p. (Orig.). 1995. pap. 14.95 (*0-9639068-4-4*) Dawn Mtn Pr.

— The Nine Stages of Spiritual Apprenticeship: Understanding the Student-Teacher Relationship. 250p. (Orig.). 1997. pap. 17.95 (*0-9639068-5-2*) Dawn Mtn Pr.

— Therapeutic Astrology: Using the Birth Chart in Psychotherapy & Spiritual Counseling. (Illus.). 240p. (Orig.). 1996. pap. 17.95 (*0-9639068-6-0*) Dawn Mtn Pr.

Bogart, Gregory C. Astrology & Spiritual Awakening. LC 93-73696. (Illus.). 244p. (Orig.). 1994. pap. 19.95 (*0-9639068-3-6*) Dawn Mtn Pr.

Bogart, J. A. Bogart: The Bogart Family: Tunis Gysbert Bogaert & His Descendents. (Illus.). 280p. 1992. reprint ed. pap. 44.00 (*0-8328-2306-6*); reprint ed. lib. bdg. 54.00 (*0-8328-2305-8*) Higginson Bk Co.

Bogart, J. E., jt. ed. see Rabas, T. J.

Bogart, James P., ed. Evolution & Ecology of Unisexual Vertebrates. (Bulletin Ser.: No. 466). (Illus.). 302p. (Orig.). (C). 1989. pap. text 30.00 (*1-55557-179-4*) NYS Museum.

Bogart, Jeff, ed. see Richards, R. W.

Bogart, Jeffrey, ed. see Richards, R. W.

Bogart, Jo E. & Reid, Barbara. Cadeaux.Tr. of Gifts. (Illus.). 32p. (J). mass mkt. 8.99 (*0-590-24682-8*) Scholastic Inc.

Bogart, Jo Ellen. Gifts. LC 94-23651. (Illus.). 44p. (J). (ps-2). 1996. 15.95 (*0-590-55260-0*) Scholastic Inc.

— Jeremiah Learns to Read. LC 98-54913. (Illus.). 32p. (J). (gr. k-4). 1999. lib. bdg. 16.99 (*0-531-33190-3*) Orchard Bks Watts.

*__Bogart, Jo Ellen.__ Jeremiah Learns to Read. LC 98-54913. (Illus.). 32p. (J). (gr. k-4). 1999. 15.95 (*0-531-30190-7*) Orchard Bks Watts.

— Tomas Aprende A Leer. (SPA., Illus.). (ps-k). 1998. 16.95 (*84-261-3066-6*) Juventud Edit.

Bogart, John W. Van, see Van Bogart, John W.

Bogart, K., et al. The Dilworth Theorems: Selected Papers of R. P. Dilworth. (Contemporary Mathematicians Ser.). 450p. 1990. 80.50 (*0-8176-3434-7*) Birkhauser.

Bogart, Kenneth P. Introductory Combinatorics. 2nd ed. 622p. (C). 1989. text 91.00 (*0-15-541576-X*) SCP.

— Introductory Combinatorics. 2nd ed. 622p. (C). 1990. pap. text 20.75 (*0-15-541577-8*) SCP.

*__Bogart, Kenneth P.__ Introductory Combinatorics. 3rd ed. (Illus.). 650p. 1999. 77.95 (*0-12-110830-9*) Acad Pr.

Bogart, Kenneth R. Discrete Mathematics. LC 87-80567. 658p. (C). 1988. text 74.76 (*0-669-08665-7*); pap. text 18.36 (*0-669-16975-7*); pap. text, teacher ed. 2.66 (*0-669-08666-5*) HM Trade Div.

An Asterisk (*) at the beginning of an entry indicates that the title is appearing for the first time.

B

Bogen, David. Order Without Rules: Critical Theory & the Logic of Conversation. LC 98-7242. (SUNY Series in the Philosophy of the Social Sciences). 192p. (C). 1999. text 59.50 (*0-7914-4055-9*); pap. text 19.95 (*0-7914-4056-7*) State U NY Pr.

***Bogen, Deborah.** California Courts & Judges Handbook: 2000 Edition. 1999. pap. write for info. (*1-58012-054-7*) James Pub Santa Ana.

— Paralegal Success: Going from Good to Great in the New Century. LC 99-12032. (Illus.). 320p. (C). 1999. pap. text 32.20 (*0-13-095193-5*) P-H.

Bogen, Don. The Known World. LC 96-38589. (Wesleyan Poetry Ser.). 79p. 1997. pap. 12.95 (*0-8195-2237-6*, Wesleyan Univ Pr); text 25.00 (*0-8195-2233-3*, Wesleyan Univ Pr) U Pr of New Eng.

Bogen, Elizabeth. Immigration in New York. LC 87-15073. 281p. 1987. 65.00 (*0-275-92199-9*, C2199, Praeger Pubs) Greenwood.

Bogen, Ellen. Clinical Cardiac Pacing & Defibrillation. 2nd ed. LC RC684.P3C54 2000. 1999. text. write for info. (*0-7216-7683-9*, W B Saunders Co) Harcrt Hlth Sci Grp.

Bogen, Ellen, et al. Clinical Cardiac Pacing. (Illus.). 736p. 1994. text 188.00 (*0-7216-5462-2*, W B Saunders Co) Harcrt Hlth Sci Grp.

Bogen, Hyman. The Luckiest Orphans: A History of the Hebrew Orphan Asylum of New York. LC 91-28913. (Illus.). 304p. (C). 1992. 34.95 (*0-252-01887-7*) U of Ill Pr.

Bogen, James & McGuire, James E. How Things Are. 519p. 1984. text 154.50 (*90-277-1583-1*, D Reidel) Kluwer Academic.

Bogen, Jules I. & Nadler, Marcus. The Banking Crisis: The End of an Epoch. Bruchey, Stuart, ed. LC 80-1179. (Rise of Commercial Banking Ser.). 1981. reprint ed. lib. bdg. 20.95 (*0-405-13670-6*) Ayer.

Bogen, Jules I., jt. auth. see Willis, Henry P.

Bogen, Kenneth T. Uncertainty in Environmental Health Risk Assessment. LC 90-3766. (Environment: Problems & Solutions Ser.). 219p. 1990. text 15.00 (*0-8240-0407-8*) Garland.

Bogen, Laurel A. Fission. (Illus.). 32p. 1998. pap. 35.00 (*1-881168-26-3*) Red Danceflr.

— The Last Girl in the Land of the Butterflies. 64p. (Orig.). 1996. pap. 10.00 (*1-889504-00-9*) Red Wind Bks.

Bogen, Mark D. What Every Condo Owner Should Know. 90p. pap. 4.95 (*0-9641154-0-9*) M D Bogen.

Bogen, Nancy. Bagatelle - Guinevere by Felice Rothman. LC 94-4038. (Illus.). 328p. 1995. 22.95 (*0-936726-05-9*); pap. 14.95 (*0-936726-06-7*) Twickenham Pr.

— Bobe Mayse: A Tale of Washington Square. LC 92-63378. 1993. 21.95 (*0-936726-03-2*); pap. 15.95 (*0-936726-04-0*) Twickenham Pr.

— How to Write Poetry. 2nd ed. LC 94-4341. 160p. 1994. pap. 8.00 (*0-671-89567-2*) P-H.

— Klytaimnestra, Who Stayed at Home. LC 80-51052. 240p. (Orig.). 1980. pap. 10.95 (*0-936726-00-8*) Twickenham Pr.

— Klytaimnestra, Who Stayed at Home. 2nd ed. 256p. (Orig.). 1988. 17.95 (*0-931642-22-1*) Lintel.

Bogen, Nancy, ed. see Blake, William.

Bogeng, Gustav A., et al. Einfuhrung in die Bibliophilie. (Buchkunliche Arbeiten Ser.: Vol. III). vii, 251p. 1984. reprint ed. 55.00 (*3-487-02336-9*) G Olms Pubs.

— Geschichte der Buchdruckerkunst, Set. (Buchkundliche Arbbeiten Ser.: Vols. VI-VII). 1973. reprint ed. 400.00 (*3-487-04420-X*) G Olms Pubs.

— Die Groben Bibliophilen: Geschichte der Buchersammler und Ihrer Sammlungen, 3 vols. in 2, Set. (Buchkundliche Arbeiten Ser.: Vols. I & II). (GER.). 1984. reprint ed. 240.00 (*3-487-07510-5*) G Olms Pubs.

— Kleine Schriften. write for info. (*0-318-71742-5*) G Olms Pubs.

— Streifzuge eines Bucherfreundes. (Buchkundliche Arbeiten Ser.: Vol. VIII). 452p. 1985. reprint ed. 75.00 (*3-487-07519-9*) G Olms Pubs.

— Umrib Einer Fachkunde fur Buchersammler. (Buchkunliche Arbeiten Ser.: Vol. IV). 436p. 1978. reprint ed. 75.00 (*3-487-06479-0*) G Olms Pubs.

***Bogenhold, D. & Schmidt, D.** Eine neue Grunderzeit? Die Wiederentdeckung kleiner Unternehmen in Theorie und Praxis. Vol. 1.Tr. of New Times to Invest? The Rediscovery of Smaller Enterprises in Theory & Practice. (GER.). 304p. 1999. pap. text 35.00 (*90-5708-056-7*, Verlag Fakultas) Gordon & Breach.

Bogenn, Tim. Legacy of Kain. (Brady Games Strategy Guides Ser.). (Illus.). 191p. 1999. pap. 7.99 (*1-56686-874-2*, BradyGAMES) Brady Pub.

— 1080 Degree Snowboarding: Prima's Unauthorized Game Secrets. LC 98-65659. 80p. 1998. per. 12.99 (*0-7615-1592-5*) Prima Pub.

Bogenschuetz, A. Fachwoerterbuch Fuer Batterien und Energie-Direktumwandlung. (ENG & GER.). 200p. 1968. 39.95 (*0-8288-6644-9*, M7395, Pub. by O Brandstetter Verlag) Trafalgar.

Bogenschutz, A. F. & George, V. Analysis & Testing in Production of Circuit Boards & Plated Plastics. 210p. 1991. 265.00 (*0-904477-08-8*, Pub. by FMJ Intl) St Mut.

Boger, Amy, jt. auth. see Humbad, Sunetra.

Boger-Brown, Uta, jt. auth. see Brown, Robert.

Boger, D. V. & Walters, K. Rheological Phenomena in Focus. (Rheological Ser.: Vol. 4). 166p. 1993. 153.00 (*0-444-89473-X*) Elsevier.

Boger, Gordon, jt. auth. see Mull, J. Alexander.

Boger, Jane & Boger, Phillip. Our Geologic Environment. 244p. (C). 1996. ring bd. 31.95 (*0-7872-2718-8*, 41271801) Kendall-Hunt.

Boger, John C. & Wegner, Judith W., eds. Race, Poverty, & American Cities. LC 95-45056. 528p. (C). 1996. pap. text 29.95 (*0-8078-4578-7*) U of NC Pr.

— Race, Poverty, & American Cities. LC 95-45056. 528p. (C). (gr. 13). 1996. lib. bdg. 69.95 (*0-8078-2274-4*) U of NC Pr.

Boger, Karl. Postwar Industrial Policy in Japan: An Annotated Bibliography. LC 87-26535. 218p. 1988. 35.00 (*0-8108-2080-3*) Scarecrow.

Boger, Karl, compiled by. Japanese Direct Foreign Investments: An Annoted Bibliography, 8. LC 89-7488. (Bibliographies & Indexes in Economics & Economic History Ser.: No. 8). 229p. 1989. lib. bdg. 69.50 (*0-313-26318-3*, Greenwood Pr) Greenwood.

Boger, Louise A. The Complete Guide to Furniture Styles. enl. ed. (Illus.). 500p. (C). 1997. reprint ed. pap. text 32.95 (*0-88133-939-3*) Waveland Pr.

Boger, Michael B., jt. auth. see Link, Albert N.

Boger, Peter & Sandmann, Gerhard, eds. Target Assays for Modern Herbicides & Related Phytotoxic Compounds. LC 92-26381. 320p. 1992. lib. bdg. 119.00 (*0-87371-539-X*, QK753, CRC Reprint) Franklin.

Boger, Peter H. & Sandmann, Gerhard, eds. Target Sites of Herbicide Action. 304p. 1989. lib. bdg. 259.00 (*0-8493-4985-0*, QK753) CRC Pr.

Boger, Phillip, jt. auth. see Boger, Jane.

Boger, R. P., jt. auth. see Griffore, R. J.

Boger, Robert P., et al, eds. Child Nurturance Vol. 4: Child Nurturing in the 1980s. LC 83-20373. 204p. 1984. 69.50 (*0-306-41505-4*, Plenum Trade) Perseus Pubng.

Bogers, K., et al, eds. The Phonological Representation of Suprasegmentals: Studies on African Languages Offered to J. M. Stewart on His 60th Birthday. (Publications in African Languages & Linguistics). x, 379p. 1986. pap. 90.80 (*90-6765-158-3*) Mouton.

***Bogershausen, Ulli.** Fingerstyle Guitar Made Easy Bk/CD. 84p. 2000. pap. 19.95 (*0-7866-5705-7*, 99140BCD) Mel Bay.

Bogert & Martin del Campo. Gila Monster & Allies. LC 93-83047. 1993. write for info. (*0-916984-31-1*) SSAR.

Bogert, George G., et al. The Law of Trusts, Cases & Text On. 6th ed. (University Casebook Ser.). 695p. 1991. text 39.95 (*0-88277-883-8*) Foundation Pr.

— The Law of Trusts, Manual for Teachers to Accompany Cases & Text. 6th ed. (University Casebook Ser.). 90p. (C). 1991. pap. text. write for info. (*0-88277-946-X*) Foundation Pr.

Bogert, George T. Trusts. (Hornbook Ser.). (C). 1987. text. write for info. (*0-314-35140-X*) West Pub.

— Trusts. 6th ed. (Hornbook Ser.). 794p. (C). 1987. student ed. 37.00 (*0-314-35139-6*) West Pub.

Bogert, Judith B. & Worley, Karla. Managing Business Communications. (C). 1987. pap. text 36.80 (*0-13-548629-7*) P-H.

Bogert, Judith B. & Worley, Rebecca B. Managing Business Communications: An Applied Process Approach. (Illus.). 480p. (C). 1988. pap. text. write for info. (*0-318-62138-X*) P-H.

Bogert, Ralph. The Writer As Naysayer: Miroslav Krleza & the Aesthetic of Interwar Central Europe. (UCLA Slavic Studies: Vol. 20). 266p. 1991. 27.95 (*0-89357-212-8*) Slavica.

Bogert, Ralph, tr. see Tasic, Vladimir.

Bogetic, Zeljko & Hillman, Arye, eds. Financing Government in the Transition: Bulgaria: The Political Economy of Tax Policies, Tax Bases, & Tax Evasion. (World Bank Ser.). 272p. 1996. 77.95 (*1-85972-329-2*, Pub. by Avebry) Ashgate Pub Co.

Bogetic, Zeljko, jt. ed. see Hillman, Arye L.

Bogetoft, Peter. Non-Cooperative Planning Theory. LC 94-22845. 1994. write for info. (*0-387-58361-0*) Spr-Verlag.

***Bogetoft, Peter.** Planning with Multiple Criteria: Investigation, Communication & Choice. 2nd ed. LC 98-115551. 1999. 38.00 (*87-16-13386-2*) Mksgaard.

Bogetto, Filippo, ed. see Ravizza, Luigi.

Bogg, John S. A Glossary of Terms & Phrases Used by Swedenborg. 188p. 1994. 17.50 (*1-883270-02-2*) Swedenborg Assn.

Boggan. Developing Online Help for Windows. 1993. 39.95 incl. disk (*0-672-30230-6*) Sams.

Boggan, Debra & Versteeg, Anna. Confessions of an Unmanager: How Managing Less & Employee Teams Saved Our Company. LC 97-65287. 220p. 1997. 24.95 (*0-85013-272-X*) Dartnell Corp.

Boggan, Debra, et al. Empowering Business Teams: Been There, Done That, It Works! (Illus.). 184p. (Orig.). 1996. pap. 19.95 (*0-9649920-0-0*) Comp Solutions.

Boggan, Jim, ed. see Forsythe, Max A.

Boggan, Scott, jt. auth. see Zubak, Cheryl Lockett.

Boggan, William E. Safe Sex. 358p. 1998. pap. 17.95 (*1-85702-506-7*) Trafalgar.

Bogger, Tommy L. Free Blacks in Norfolk, Virginia, 1790-1860: The Darker Side of Freedom. LC 96-23403. (Carter G. Woodson Institute Series in Black Studies). 264p. 1997. text 35.00 (*0-8139-1690-9*) U Pr of Va.

Bogger, Tommy L. & Wiggins, William B. Open Shutters: Photographic Impressions by African-Americans in Hampton Roads. Reiss, Donna, ed. (Illus.). 72p. 1995. pap. 15.00 (*1-885163-02-9*) Virginia Beach Ctr.

Boggess, Albert. Calclabs with Maple V. (Mathematics Ser.). 1994. mass mkt., lab manual ed. 19.25 (*0-534-25590-6*) Brooks-Cole.

— CR Manifolds & the Tangential Cauchy Riemann Complex. (Illus.). 330p. 1991. lib. bdg. 79.95 (*0-8493-7152-X*, QA) CRC Pr.

Boggess, Arthur C. The Settlement of Illinois, 1778-1830. LC 71-128873. (Select Bibliographies Reprint Ser.). 1977. 28.95 (*0-8369-5493-9*) Ayer.

— The Settlement of Illinois, 1778-1830. 267p. 1997. reprint ed. lib. bdg. 32.50 (*0-8328-6636-9*) Higginson Bk Co.

Boggess, Bill & Boggess, Louise. Identifying American Brilliant Cut Glass. 3rd ed. (Illus.). 284p. 1996. pap. 19.95 (*0-7643-0169-1*) Schiffer.

— Reflections on American Brilliant Cut Glass. LC 95-5450. 256p. (Orig.). 1995. 59.95 (*0-88740-722-6*) Schiffer.

Boggess, Dawnalyn & Sundberg, John P. Systematic Approach to Evaluation of Mouse Mutations. LC 99-14308. 216p. 1999. boxed set 99.95 (*0-8493-1905-6*) CRC Pr.

Boggess, Laurence. Everyone's Guide to Job Searching in Private Schools. LC 92-85334. 256p. (Orig.). 1992. pap. 10.00 (*0-9634083-6-4*) Ryanna Bks.

Boggess, Louise & Boggess, William. Collecting American Brilliant Cut Glass. LC 91-67002. (Illus.). 320p. 1992. text 59.95 (*0-88740-383-2*) Schiffer.

Boggess, Louise, jt. auth. see Boggess, Bill.

Boggess, William, jt. auth. see Boggess, Louise.

Boggiano, Ann K. & Pittman, Thane S., eds. Achievement & Motivation: A Social-Developmental Perspective. (Illus.). 303p. (C). 1993. text 49.95 (*0-521-32220-0*) Cambridge U Pr.

Boggiano, Antonio. International Standard Contracts: The Price of Fairness. (C). 1991. lib. bdg. 205.50 (*0-7923-0709-7*) Kluwer Academic.

Boggiano, H. F. Orthopedic Surgery: Elastic Compression. 2nd rev. ed. (Illus.). 650p. 1996. 85.00 (*0-9654469-0-5*) H F Boggiano.

Boggiatto, P., et al. Global Hypoellipticity & Spectral Theory. LC 97-102285. (Mathematical Research Ser.: Vol. 92). 170p. 1996. pap. text 73.45 (*3-05-501724-2*, Pub. by Akademie Verlag) Wiley.

Boggio, Giorgio & Gallimore, R., eds. Evaluation of Research & Development. 1982. lib. bdg. 119.00 (*90-277-1425-8*) Kluwer Academic.

Boggio, Giorgio & Spachis-Papazois, Eleni, eds. Evaluation of Research & Development, Methodologies for R & D Evaluation in the European Community Member States, the United States of America & Japan. 1984. lib. bdg. 90.50 (*90-277-1759-1*) Kluwer Academic.

Boggis. Global Past. 1998. pap. text 0.01 (*0-312-18442-5*) St Martin.

— Western Trade, Sem. 1. 2nd ed. 280p. 1996. pap., student ed. 34.20 (*0-13-601956-0*) P-H.

Boggis, A. Western Trade, Sem. 2. 2nd ed. 280p. 1996. pap. text, student ed. 36.00 (*0-13-601949-8*) P-H.

Boggis, Carol & Marsh, Jayne D., eds. From the Heart: On Being the Mother of a Child with Special Needs. LC 95-2356. (Illus.). 150p. (C). 1995. pap. 14.95 (*0-933149-79-4*) Woodbine House.

— From the Heart: Stories by Mothers of Children with Special Needs. 152p. (Orig.). 1994. pap. text 12.00 (*0-939561-22-0*) Univ South ME.

Boggis, Jay. Western Tradition Administrative & Faculty: Semester II. 2nd ed. 200p. (C). 1996. pap. text 25.60 (*0-13-496787-9*, Prentice Hall) P-H.

— Western Tradition Administrative Handbook & Faculty Guide, Semester I. 2nd ed. 208p. (C). 1996. pap. text 25.60 (*0-13-496779-8*, Prentice Hall) P-H.

Boggs, et al. Livestock & Carcasses Evaluation. 5th ed. 256p. 1998. per. 37.95 (*0-7872-4569-0*, 41456901) Kendall-Hunt.

Boggs, jt. auth. see Tesch.

Boggs, Ardith G. Goshen, Maryland: A History & It's People. LC 94-187954. (Illus.). 127p. (Orig.). 1994. pap. text 22.00 (*1-55613-987-X*) Heritage Bk.

Boggs, Bernard C. Succeeding with Pointing Dogs, Field Trials & Hunting Tests. 500p. 1989. 39.95 (*0-9608838-1-9*) Glenbrier Pub.

Boggs, Bruce A. Rebels with a Cause: Adam & Eve in Modern Spanish Literature. (Iberica Ser.: Vol. 24). XII, 130p. (C). 1998. text 36.95 (*0-8204-3484-1*) P Lang Pubng.

***Boggs, Carl.** The End of Politics: Corporate Power & the Decline of the Public Sphere. LC 99-48588. (Critical Perspectives Ser.). 310p. 1999. lib. bdg. 23.95 (*1-57230-496-0*, CO496) Guilford Pubns.

Boggs, Carl. Gramsci's Marxism. (C). 1980. pap. text 14.50 (*0-904383-03-2*) Westview.

— Intellectuals & the Crisis of Modernity. LC 92-31368. (SUNY Series in Radical, Social & Political Theory). 222p. (C). 1993. text 20.50 (*0-7914-1543-0*) State U NY Pr.

— Social Movements & Political Power: Emerging Forms of Radicalism in the West. LC 86-6045. 304p. 1989. pap. 22.95 (*0-87722-622-9*) Temple U Pr.

— The Socialist Tradition: From Crisis to Decline. (Revolutionary Thought & Radical Movements Ser.). 320p. (C). 1994. pap. 18.99 (*0-415-90670-9*, B0751) Routledge.

— The Two Revolutions: Gramsci & the Dilemmas of Western Marxism. LC 84-50943. 311p. 1984. 35.00 (*0-89608-226-1*); pap. 9.50 (*0-89608-225-3*) South End Pr.

Boggs, Carl & Plotke, David, eds. Politics of Euro-Communism. 479p. write for info. (*0-919618-32-4*); pap. write for info. (*0-919618-31-6*) Black Rose.

Boggs, Cary. W. D. the Wonder Dog. LC 96-44990. (Illus.). 32p. (J). (gr. 1-3). 1998. 16.00 (*0-689-81376-7*) Aladdin.

Boggs, Charles W., Jr. Marine Aviation in the Philippines. (Elite Unit Ser.: No. 30). (Illus.). 184p. reprint ed. 34.95 (*0-89839-168-7*) Battery Pr.

Boggs, David L. Adult Civic Education. 152p. 1991. pap. 26.95 (*0-398-06024-X*) C C Thomas.

— Adult Civic Education. 152p. (C). 1991. text 36.95 (*0-398-05724-9*) C C Thomas.

***Boggs, Denis.** Getting There: Departures & Arrivals. 94p. 2000. 17.95 (*0-7541-1085-0*, Pub. by Minerva Pr) Unity Dist.

Boggs, Donald L. & Merkel, Robert A. Live Animal Carcass Evaluation & Selection Manual. 4th ed. 256p. 1995. per. 31.95 (*0-8403-7609-X*) Kendall-Hunt.

Boggs, E. B. Hammer: The Hammers & Allied Families, with Their Family Circles Centering in Pendleton Co., W.V. (Illus.). 176p. 1992. reprint ed. pap. 28.00 (*0-8328-2663-4*); reprint ed. lib. bdg. 38.00 (*0-8328-2662-6*) Higginson Bk Co.

Boggs, Glenn H. Business Law in Florida. 3rd ed. Date not set. pap. text 26.00 (*0-314-47367-X*) West Pub.

Boggs, Grace L. Living for Change: An Autobiography. LC 97-27296. 1998. pap. 18.95 (*0-8166-2955-2*) U of Minn Pr.

— Living for Change: An Autobiography. LC 97-27296. 1998. 47.95 (*0-8166-2954-4*) U of Minn Pr.

Boggs, Grace L., jt. auth. see Boggs, James.

Boggs, J. Robert. I'll Move Over: The Story of A Great Love. 1995. 16.50 (*0-9648880-2-5*) Boggs Bks.

— I'll Move Over - The Story of a Great Love: How One Family Is Coping with Alzheimer's. 3rd ed. (Illus.). 152p. (Orig.). 1996. pap. 9.95 (*0-9648880-1-7*) Boggs Bks.

Boggs, James. The American Revolution. fac. ed. LC 63-20103. 93p. pap. 30.00 (*0-7837-6969-5*, 2056417300054) Bks Demand.

— Racism & the Class Struggle: Further Pages from a Black Worker's Notebook. LC 74-105314. 188p. reprint ed. pap. 58.30 (*0-7837-3916-8*, 204376400010) Bks Demand.

Boggs, James & Boggs, Grace L. Revolution & Evolution in the Twentieth Century. LC 73-90076. 288p. 1975. reprint ed. pap. 11.00 (*0-85345-353-5*, Pub. by Monthly Rev) NYU Pr.

Boggs, James, et al. Conversations in Maine: Exploring Our Nation's Future. LC 78-55014. (Illus.). 299p. 1978. 30.00 (*0-89608-009-9*); pap. 8.50 (*0-89608-008-0*) South End Pr.

Boggs, Jay. Tucker Knob Mountain: The Old Sorghum Sopper. 257p. (YA). (gr. 4-12). 1995. write for info. (*1-888423-00-5*); pap. write for info. (*1-888423-01-3*) Echoes Tucker Knob.

Boggs, Jean S. Degas: The Art Institute of Chicago, Artists in Focus. Rossen, Susan F., ed. LC 96-85474. (Artists in Focus Ser.). (Illus.). 112p. 1996. 19.95 (*0-8109-6324-8*) Art Inst Chi.

— Degas at the Races. (Illus.). 288p. 1998. 50.00 (*0-300-07517-0*) Yale U Pr.

Boggs, Jean S., et al. Degas at the Races. LC 97-43580. 1998. 32.00 (*0-89468-273-3*) Natl Gallery Art.

Boggs, Jean S., jt. auth. see Feigenbaum, Gail.

Boggs, Jessie, ed. see MacPhee, Ross.

Boggs, Johnny D. The Courtship of Hannah & the Horseman. LC 97-94276. (Hannah & the Horseman Western Ser.: Bk. 2). 192p. 1997. 18.95 (*0-8034-9270-7*, Avalon Bks) Bouregy.

***Boggs, Johnny D.** The Curse of Dunbar's Gold. LC 98-96851. 192p. 1999. lib. bdg. 18.95 (*0-8034-9340-1*, Avalon Bks) Bouregy.

Boggs, Johnny D. Hannah & the Horseman. LC 96-95479. (Hannah & the Horseman Western Ser.: Bk. 1). 192p. 1997. 18.95 (*0-8034-9230-8*, Avalon Bks) Bouregy.

— Hannah & the Horseman at the Gallows Tree. LC 98-96339. 192p. 1998. lib. bdg. 17.95 (*0-8034-9320-7*, Avalon Bks) Bouregy.

— Hannah & the Horseman on the Western Trail. LC 99-90150. 192p. 1997. lib. bdg. 18.95 (*0-8034-9360-6*, Avalon Bks) Bouregy.

***Boggs, Johnny D.** Pampered Cowboy. (Illus.). 250p. 2000. pap. 18.95 (*1-55622-782-5*, Rep of TX Pr) Wordware Pub.

Boggs, Johnny D. Riding with Hannah & the Horseman. LC 98-96074. 192p. 1998. 18.95 (*0-8034-9300-2*, Avalon Bks) Bouregy.

***Boggs, Johnny D.** Ten & Me. LC 99-90985. 182p. 1999. 18.95 (*0-8034-9390-8*, Avalon Bks) Bouregy.

— That Terrible Texas Weather. LC 99-49503. 1999. pap. 18.95 (*1-55622-727-2*) Wordware Pub.

Boggs, Johnny D. This Man Colter. LC 97-93733. 192p. 1997. lib. bdg. 18.95 (*0-8034-9251-0*, Avalon Bks) Bouregy.

Boggs, Joseph M. & Petrie, Dennis W. The Art of Watching Films. 5th ed. LC 99-22859. xxii, 570p. 1999. pap. text 41.95 (*0-7674-0532-3*) Mayfield Pub.

Boggs, Kathleen, jt. auth. see Arnold, Elizabeth.

***Boggs, Kathleen U.** Instructor's Manual for Interpersonal Relationships: Professional Communication Skills for Nurses. 3rd ed. Wood, Terri, ed. (Illus.). 95p. 1999. teacher ed. write for info. (*0-7216-8104-2*, W B Saunders Co) Harcrt Hlth Sci Grp.

Boggs, Kathleen U., jt. auth. see Arnold, Elizabeth N.

Boggs, Kathleen U., jt. ed. see Arnold, Elizabeth.

Boggs, Larry, ed. see Solana, Tambor.

Boggs, Lesley P., jt. auth. see McNutt, John.

Boggs, Lindy. Washington Through a Purple Veil: Memoirs of a Southern Woman. (Illus.). 400p. 1994. 24.95 (*0-15-193106-2*) Harcourt.

— Washington Through a Purple Veil: Memoirs of a Southern Woman. large type ed. (Niagara Large Print Ser.). 501p. 1995. 29.50 (*0-7089-5816-8*) Ulverscroft.

Boggs, Marcia, ed. see Rapp, Augustus.

Boggs, Marian, ed. see Mason, Marian.

Boggs, Marion A. The Alexander Letters, 1787-1900. (American Biography Ser.). 387p. 1991. reprint ed. lib. bdg. 79.00 (*0-7812-8028-1*) Rprt Serv.

Boggs, Marlene, ed. see Noehring, Jeanne.

Boggs, Michael D., jt. auth. see Boggs, Wendy.

Boggs, Patton, jt. auth. see National Institute of Construction Law Inc.

Boggs, Paul T., et al, eds. Numerical Optimization, 1984. LC 85-50611. (Proceedings in Applied Mathematics Ser.: No. 20). xi, 287p. 1985. text 38.75 (*0-89871-054-5*) Soc Indus-Appl Math.

An Asterisk (*) at the beginning of an entry indicates that the title is appearing for the first time.

Boggs, Peter B. Sneezing Your Head Off? Learning to Live with Your Allergic Nose. (Illus.). 274p. 1994. pap. 10.00 (*0-9642569-0-8*) Patient Ed Pubns.

Boggs, R. F. Radiological Safety Aspects of the Operation of Neutron Generators. (Safety Ser.: No. 42). (Illus.). 42p. 1976. pap. 15.00 (*92-0-123076-1*, ISP427, Pub. by IAEA) Bernan Associates.

Boggs, R. S. Basic Spanish Pronunciation. (C). 1987. pap. text 9.45 (*0-13-069360-X*) P-H.

Boggs, Ralph S. Basic Spanish Pronunciation. (SPA.). (Orig.). (YA). (gr. 9-11). 1969. pap. 3.75 (*0-88345-012-7*, 17442) Prentice ESL.

Boggs, Ralph S. & Dixon, J. I. Everyday Spanish Idioms. (SPA.). (YA). (gr. 9-12). 1978. pap. text 5.95 (*0-88345-326-6*, 18426) Prentice ESL.

Boggs, Ralph S. & Dixson, Lolita. English Step by Step with Pictures. (gr. 4-12). 1987. pap. text 7.25 (*0-13-282963-0*, 18186) Prentice ESL.

— English Step by Step with Pictures. 3rd ed. (Illus.). 224p. (C). 1990. pap. text 18.53 (*0-13-277104-7*) P-H.

Boggs, Ralph S., et al. Everyday Spanish Idioms. (C). 1987. pap. text 13.65 (*0-13-292913-9*) Prentice ESL.

Boggs, Rochelle L., ed. see American Association for Critical Care Nurses Staff.

Boggs, S. A., et al, eds. Gas-Insulated Substations: Technology & Practice: Proceedings of the International Symposium on Gas-Insulated Substations: Technology & Practice, Toronto, Canada 9-12 September 1985. (Illus.). 600p. 1986. 230.00 (*0-08-031864-9*, A120, A115, B11, Pergamon Pr) Elsevier.

Boggs, S. A., ed. see Symposium on Underground Cable Thermal Backfill, T.

Boggs, Sam, Jr. Petrology of Sedimentary Rocks. (Illus.). 720p. (C). 1991. text 63.80 (*0-02-311790-7*, Macmillan Coll) P-H.

— Principles of Sedimentology & Stratigraphy. 2nd ed. (Illus.). 774p. (C). 1994. 99.00 (*0-02-311792-3*, Macmillan Coll) P-H.

Boggs, Samuel W. The Polar Regions: Geographical & Historical Data for Consideration in a Study of Claims to Sovereignty in the Arctic & Antarctic Regions. LC 89-85449. (Illus.). 138p. 1990. reprint ed. lib. bdg. 37.50 (*0-89941-726-4*, 306380) W S Hein.

Boggs, Stephen T. Speaking, Relating, & Learning: A Study of Hawaiian Children at Home & at School. LC 85-7388. 216p. (C). 1986. text 73.25 (*0-89391-330-8*) Ablx Pub.

Boggs, Sue H. All Mine to Give. 1984. pap. 4.35 (*0-89137-433-7*) Quality Pubns.

— Is a Job Really Worth It? 1979. pap. 5.80 (*0-89137-522-8*) Quality Pubns.

— The Secret of Hind's Feet. 1982. 4.35 (*0-89137-537-6*) Quality Pubns.

Boggs, Suzanne, ed. Nebraska Championship Season. (Illus.). 160p. pap. text 14.95 (*1-886830-00-2*) Athlon Sports.

Boggs, Thomas, Jr. Corporate Political Activity. Vol. C4. text 82.00 (*0-8205-2394-1*) Bender.

Boggs, Thomas. Tokyo Vanilla. 256p. 1997. pap. 14.95 (*0-85449-255-0*, Pub. by Gay Mens Pr) LPC InBook.

Boggs, Timothy. The Eye of the Ram. (Hercules: The Legendary Journeys Ser.: No. 3). 1997. mass mkt. 5.99 (*1-57297-224-6*) Blvd Books.

— Hercules: The Legendary Journeys: By the Sword. 1996. mass mkt. 5.99 (*1-57297-198-3*) Blvd Books.

— Serpent's Shadow. (Hercules: The Legendary Journeys Ser.: No. 2). (J). 1996. mass mkt. 5.99 (*1-57297-214-9*) Blvd Books.

Boggs, Vernon W. Salsiology: Afro-Cuban Music & the Evolution of Salsa in New York City. 26. LC 91-43983. (Contributions to the Study of Music & Dance Ser.: No. 26). 400p. 1992. 69.50 (*0-313-28468-7*, BSP/, Greenwood Pr) Greenwood.

Boggs, Vernon W., et al. The Apple Sliced: Sociological Studies of New York City. LC 82-22763. (Illus.). 352p. 1983. 49.95 (*0-275-91716-9*, C1716, Praeger Pubs) Greenwood.

Boggs, Wendy & Boggs, Michael D. Mastering UML with Rational Rose. (Mastering Ser.). (Illus.). 957p. 1999. pap. 49.99 incl. cd-rom (*0-7821-2453-4*) Sybex.

Boggs, William O. The Man Who Never Comes Back. 40p. (Orig.). 1992. pap. 5.00 (*0-9628478-3-6*) North Star OH.

— Swimming in Clear Water. 1989. 3.50 (*0-941127-08-7*) Dacotah Terr Pr.

Bogguss, Suzy. Something up My Sleeve. 40p. 1995. pap. 14.95 (*0-7935-5811-5*) H Leonard.

***Boghanni, Ashok & Brown, Andrew.** Technology Management Challenges in the Automotive Industry. LC 99-54208. 132p. 2000. 25.00 (*0-7680-0532-9*, R-258) Soc Auto Engineers.

Boghigian, Apo & Apelian, Edward, eds. Artsakian Darekroutioun, 1988. (ARM.). 1989. pap. text 10.00 (*0-317-93970-X*) Asbarez Pub.

Bogholm, N. Milton & Paradise Lost. LC 74-7116. (Studies in Milton: No. 22). 1974. lib. bdg. 75.00 (*0-8383-1968-8*) M S G Haskell Hse.

Boghosian, Paula J., et al. Sacramento's Memorial Auditorium: Seven Decades of Memories. (Illus.). 176p. (Orig.). 1997. pap. 24.00 (*0-9657354-0-0*) Sacramento Heritage.

***Boghossian, Paul & Peacocke, Christopher, eds.** New Essays on the a Priori. 40p. 2000. pap. 24.95 (*0-19-924127-9*); text 70.00 (*0-19-924126-0*) OUP.

Boghurst, William. Loimographia: An Account of the Great Plague of London in 1665. Payne, J. F., ed. LC 75-23686. reprint ed. 44.50 (*0-404-13239-1*) AMS Pr.

Bogie, Mord. Churchill's Horses & the Myths of American Corporations: Power, Stakeholders & Governance. LC 97-21855. 232p. 1998. 59.95 (*1-56720-073-7*, Quorum Bks) Greenwood.

Bogin. Growth Of Humanity. 320p. pap. write for info. (*0-471-35448-1*) Wiley.

Bogin, Barry. Patterns of Human Growth. (Cambridge Studies in Biological Anthropology: No. 3). (Illus.). 280p. 1988. pap. text 32.95 (*0-521-34690-8*) Cambridge U Pr.

***Bogin, Barry.** Patterns of Human Growth. 2nd ed. (Studies in Biological Anthropology: No. 23). (Illus.). 350p. (C). 1999. pap. text 39.95 (*0-521-56438-7*) Cambridge U Pr.

Bogin, Barry, jt. ed. see Mascie-Taylor, C. G.

Bogin, Frederick D., ed. American Jewish Committee, New York. LC 89-16915. (Archives of the Holocaust Ser.: Vol. 17). 464p. 1993. text 124.00 (*0-8240-5499-7*) Garland.

Bogin, George. In a Surf of Strangers: Poems. LC 80-23965. (Contemporary Poetry Ser.). 66p. reprint ed. pap. 30.00 (*0-7837-5036-6*, 204470900004) Bks Demand.

Bogin, Magda, tr. see Allende, Isabel.

Bogin, Magda, tr. see Espriu, Salvador.

Bogin, Meg. The Women Troubadours. (Illus.). 192p. 1980. reprint ed. pap. 10.95 (*0-393-00965-3*) Norton.

Bogin, Ruth. Abraham Clark & the Quest for Equality in the Revolutionary Era, 1774 - 1794. LC 81-65872. 219p. 1982. 30.00 (*0-8386-3100-2*) Fairleigh Dickinson.

Bogin, Ruth, jt. ed. see Loewenberg, Bert J.

***Bogitsch, Burt J. & Cheng, Thomas C.** Human Parasitology. 2nd ed. LC 98-84421. (Illus.). 496p. (C). 1999. text 59.95 (*0-12-110870-8*) Morgan Kaufmann.

Bogitsh. Human Parasitology. (C). 1990. text. write for info. (*0-15-540381-8*) Harcourt Coll Pubs.

***Boglar, Luiz.** Orinoco-Parima: Indian Societies in Venezuela. (Cisneros Collections). (Illus.). 2000. 55.00 (*3-7757-0873-1*) Gerd Hatje.

Bogle, Donald. Blacks in American Film & Television: An Encyclopedia. LC 87-29241. 700p. 1988. text 95.00 (*0-8240-8715-1*, H604) Garland.

— Brown Sugar: Eighty Years of America's Black Female Superstars. (Quality Paperbacks Ser.). (Illus.). 208p. 1990. pap. 17.95 (*0-306-80380-1*) Da Capo.

— Dorothy Dandridge: A Biography. (Illus.). 613p. 1998. pap. 17.00 (*1-57297-292-0*) Blvd Books.

***Bogle, Donald.** Dorothy Dandridge: A Biography. (Illus.). 1999. pap. 17.00 (*0-425-17578-2*) Blvd Books.

Bogle, Donald. Dorothy Dandridge: A Biography. LC 97-16478. (Illus.). 400p. 1997. 27.95 (*1-56743-034-1*, Amistad) HarperTrade.

***Bogle, Donald.** Primetime Blues: African Americans on Network Television. (Illus.). 512p. 2000. 27.00 (*0-374-23720-4*) FS&G.

Bogle, Donald. Toms, Coons, Mulattoes, Mammies & Bucks: A History of Blacks in American Films from Birth of a Nation to Malcolm X. 3rd ed. (Illus.). 412p. 1994. reprint ed. pap. 19.95 (*0-8264-0578-9*) Continuum.

Bogle, Donald, ed. Black Arts Annual: 1988-89. LC 10-427104. (Illus.). 266p. 1990. text 20.00 (*0-8240-4943-8*, 1206) Garland.

Bogle, Emory C. Islam: Origin & Belief. LC 97-33934. 208p. 1998. 30.00 (*0-292-70861-0*, BOGISL); pap. 14.95 (*0-292-70862-9*, BOGISP) U of Tex Pr.

— The Modern Middle East: From Imperialism to Freedom, 1880-1958. LC 95-15863. 528p. (C). 1995. pap. text 52.00 (*0-13-206509-6*) P-H.

Bogle, James G., jt. auth. see Cohen, Stan.

Bogle, Joanna. A Book of Feasts & Seasons. 3rd ed. 206p. 1993. pap. 12.95 (*0-85244-217-3*, 917, Pub. by Gra1cewing) Morehouse Pub.

Bogle, Joanna, ed. Families for Tomorrow. 1992. pap. 24.95 (*0-85244-172-X*, 6339, Pub. by Gra1cewing) Morehouse Pub.

Bogle, John C. Bogle on Mutual Funds: New Perspectives for the Intelligent Investor. 352p. 1994. pap. 16.95 (*0-440-50682-4*) Dell.

— Bogle on Mutual Funds: New Perspectives for the Intelligent Investor. LC 93-22697. 320p. 1993. text 25.00 (*1-55623-860-6*, Irwn Prfssnl) McGraw-Hill Prof.

Bogle, John C. Common Sense on Mutual Funds: New Imperatives for the Intelligent Investor. 496p. 1999. pap. 16.95 (*0-471-39228-6*) Wiley.

Bogle, John C. Common Sense on Mutual Funds: New Imperatives for the Intelligent Investor. LC 98-55377. 496p. 1999. 24.95 (*0-471-29543-4*) Wiley.

Bogle, Michael. Design in Australia. LC 98-129679. (Illus.). 192p. 1997. text 80.00 (*90-5703-461-1*) Gordon & Breach.

— Modern Australian Furniture: Profiles of Contemporary Designer-Makers. (Illus.). 160p. 1990. text 35.00 (*0-947131-26-4*) Gordon & Breach.

***Bogle, Michael.** Off the Beaten Path. 2000. write for info. (*1-58235-535-5*) Watermrk Pr.

Bogler, Helmut, tr. see Aharoni, Zvi.

Bogler, Helmut, tr. see Kieser, Egbert.

Bogler, Philip L. Radar Principles with Applications to Tracking Systems. LC 89-34215. 319p. 1990. 135.00 (*0-471-50192-1*) Wiley.

Bogles, John. An Insider's Guide to Government. 1996. pap. 23.95 (*1-884350-56-9*) Alpha Pubng.

Bognanno, Mario F. & Coleman, Charles J., eds. Labor Arbitration in America: The Profession & Practice. LC 92-399. 200p. 1992. 49.95 (*0-275-94375-5*, C4375, Praeger Pubs) Greenwood.

Bognanno, Mario F. & Ready, Kathryn J., eds. The North American Free Trade Agreement: Labor, Industry, & Government Perspectives. LC 93-19113. 272p. 1993. 69.50 (*0-89930-849-X*, Q849, Quorum Bks); pap. 27.95 (*0-275-94675-4*, B4675, Praeger Pubs) Greenwood.

Bognar, Botond. The Japan Guide. (Illus.). 336p. (Orig.). 1995. pap. 24.95 (*1-878271-33-4*) Princeton Arch.

***Bognar, Botond.** Nikken Sekkel: Building Future Japan, 1900-2000. (Illus.). 352p. 2000. text 65.00 (*0-8478-2246-X*) Rizzoli Intl.

Bognar, Botond. Tokyo. (World Cities Ser.: Vol. IV). (Illus.). 368p. 1997. 95.00 (*1-85490-485-X*) Academy Ed UK.

— Tokyo. 368p. 1998. 135.00 (*0-471-97689-X*) Wiley.

Bognar, Botond & Maki, Fumihiko. Togo Murano: Master Architect of Japan. LC 95-46479. (Illus.). 160p. 1996. 40.00 (*0-8478-1887-X*, Pub. by Rizzoli Intl) St Martin.

Bognar, Botund. Japanese Architecture II: Architectural Design Profile 99. 1992. pap. 26.95 (*0-312-08105-X*) St Martin.

***Bognar, David.** Cancer: Increasing Your Odds for Survival. 300p. 2000. reprint ed. pap. 16.00 (*0-7881-9236-1*) DIANE Pub.

Bognar, David. Cancer-Increasing Your Odds for Survival: A Resource Guide for Integrating Mainstream, Alternative & Complementary Therapies. LC 98-34440. (Illus.). 352p. 1998. pap. 15.95 (*0-89793-247-1*) Hunter Hse.

— Cancer-Increasing Your Odds for Survival: A Resource Guide for Integrating Mainstream, Alternative & Complementary Therapies. LC 98-34440. (Illus.). 352p. 1998. 25.95 (*0-89793-248-X*) Hunter Hse.

Bognar, David. Human Operator's Manual: How Feelings Work, a Psychological Primer. (Illus.). 88p. 1991. reprint ed. pap. 8.95 (*1-929860-03-X*) New Way Prods.

***Bognar, Desi K.** International Dictionary of Broadcasting & Film. 2nd ed. LC 99-27781. (Illus.). 316p. 1999. pap. 34.95 (*0-240-80376-0*, Focal) Buttrwrth-Heinemann.

Bognar, Desi K. & Szentpaly, Katalin, eds. Hungarians in America: A Biographical Directory of Professionals of Hungarian Origin. LC 72-97113. (East-Central European Biographies & Studies Ser.: Nos. 4 & 5). 240p. 1972. 16.50 (*0-912460-01-6*) Media Forum.

Bognar, J. Economic Policy & Planning in Developing Countries. 628p. 1975. 100.00 (*0-7855-2765-6*, Pub. by Akade Kiado) St Mut.

— Economic Policy & Planning in Developing Countries. 628p. (C). 1975. 92.00 (*963-05-1001-4*, Pub. by Akade Kiado) St Mut.

Bognar, J. & Szoekelalvi-Nagy, J. Indefinite Inner Product Spaces. LC 73-10669. (Ergebnisse der Mathematik und Ihrer Grenzgebiete Ser.: Vol. 78). 236p. 1974. 49.00 (*0-387-06202-5*) Spr-Verlag.

Bognar, Matyas. Foundations of Linking Theory. 163p. (C). 1992. pap. 80.00 (*963-05-6264-2*, Pub. by Akade Kiado) St Mut.

Bognasian, Eric. Sex, Drugs, Rock & Roll. LC 96-36475. 136p. (Orig.). 1996. pap. 10.95 (*1-55936-124-7*) Theatre Comm.

Bogner, Jerry L. Facts about AIDS & Other Sexually Transmitted Diseases: Sexual Decisions of Responsible Adults. LC 87-13208. 108p. (Orig.). 1987. 14.95 (*0-943323-00-2*); pap. 6.95 (*0-943323-01-0*) Bogners Limited.

Bogner, Jerry L., jt. auth. see Bogner's Limited Staff.

Bogner, Marilyn S., ed. Human Error in Medicine. 424p. 1994. pap. 45.00 (*0-8058-1386-1*) L Erlbaum Assocs.

— Human Error in Medicine. 424p. 1994. text 89.95 (*0-8058-1385-3*) L Erlbaum Assocs.

Bogner, Marilyn S., et al, eds. Surgical-Assist Systems. LC 98-227294. (Proceedings of SPIE Ser.: Vol. 3262). 316p. 1998. 99.00 (*0-8194-2701-2*) SPIE.

***Bogner, Norman.** Honor Thy Wife. LC 99-26077. 448p. 1999. 25.95 (*0-312-86808-1*, Pub. by Forge NYC) St Martin.

— Honor Thy Wife. 536p. 2000. mass mkt. 6.99 (*0-8125-7556-3*, Pub. by Forge NYC) St Martin.

— The Madonna Complex. 352p. 2000. 25.95 (*0-312-87519-3*, Pub. by Forge NYC) St Martin.

Bogner, Norman. Seventh Avenue. 1998. mass mkt. 6.99 (*0-8125-7570-9*, Pub. by Tor Bks) St Martin.

— To Die in Provence. LC 98-23592. 391p. 1999. mass mkt. 6.99 (*0-8125-9044-9*, Pub. by Forge NYC) St Martin.

— To Die in Provence. LC 98-23592. 384p. 2000. 24.95 (*0-312-86628-3*, Pub. by Forge NYC) St Martin.

Bogner, Phyllis. Handbook of Pharmacologic Therapeutics: A Disease-Oriented Review. (Illus.). 379p. 1987. pap. 30.95 (*0-316-10088-9*, Little Brwn Med Div) Lppncott W & W.

Bogner, R. E. & Constantinides, A. G., eds. Introduction to Digital Filtering. LC 74-4924. 210p. reprint ed. pap. 65.10 (*0-608-15853-4*, 203146600074) Bks Demand.

Bogner, W. C. & Thomas, H. Drugs to Market: Creating Value & Advantage in Pharmaceutical Industries. (Technology, Innovation, Entrepreneurship, & Competitive Strategy Ser.). 208p. 1996. text 62.50 (*0-08-042559-3*, Pergamon Pr) Elsevier.

Bogner's Limited Staff & Bogner, Jerry L. Bogner's Complete Professional Bartender's Guide. LC 87-50919. (Illus.). 150p. 1987. 30.95 (*0-943323-02-9*); pap. 14.95 (*0-943323-03-7*) Bogners Limited.

Bognmo, Joe Eoueme. Madoulina. LC 99-61826. 32p. (J). (gr. k-3). 1999. pap. 6.95 (*1-56397-822-9*) Boyds Mills Pr.

— Madoulina. LC 99-61826. 32p. (J). (ps-3). 1999. 14.95 (*1-56397-769-9*) Boyds Mills Pr.

Bogo, Marion Do Carmo, see Do Carmo Bogo, Maria.

Bogo, Marion & Vayda, Elaine. The Practice of Field Instruction in Social Work: Theory & Process. 2nd ed. (Illus.). 288p. 1998. pap. text 18.95 (*0-8020-7979-2*) U of Toronto Pr.

— The Practice of Field Instruction in Social Work Theory & Process. 176p. (C). 1987. pap. text 17.95 (*0-8020-6689-5*) U of Toronto Pr.

***Bogo, Marion & Vayda, Elaine J.** Practice Field Instruction in Social Work: Theory & Process: Theory & Practice. 2nd ed. LC 97-48592. 288p. 1998. pap. 24.50 (*0-231-11319-6*) Col U Pr.

Bogoch, Samuel, ed. The Future of the Brain Sciences: Proceedings of a Conference Held at the New York Academy of Medicine, May 2-4, 1968. LC 75-79571. 643p. reprint ed. pap. 199.40 (*0-608-30230-9*, 202070400018) Bks Demand.

Bogoda, Robert. A Simple Guide to Life. 56p. 1994. 3.75 (*955-24-0125-9*, Pub. by Buddhist Pub Soc) Vipassana Res Pubns.

Bogojavlensky, Marianne. Russian Review Grammar. xviii, 450p. (Orig.). (C). 1982. pap. text 19.95 (*0-89357-096-6*) Slavica.

Bogojavlensky, Marrianne. Reflections on Nikolai Gogol. 69p. 1968. pap. 3.00 (*0-317-30452-6*) Holy Trinity.

Bogoliubov, N. N. Lectures on Quantum Statistics, 2 vols., Vol. 2. viii, 232p. 1970. text 249.00 (*0-677-20570-8*) Gordon & Breach.

Bogoliubov, N. N., ed. Theory of Superconductivity, Vol. 4. (International Science Review Ser.). (Illus.). xiv, 356p. 1968. text 274.00 (*0-677-00080-4*) Gordon & Breach.

Bogoliubov, N. N. & Mitropolsky, Y. A. Asymptotic Methods in the Theory of Non-Linear Oscillations. 548p. 1961. text 527.00 (*0-677-20050-1*) Gordon & Breach.

Bogolub, Ellen. Helping Families Through Divorce: An Eclectic Approach. 272p. 1995. 39.95 (*0-8261-9060-X*) Springer Pub.

Bogolubov, N. N., Jr. An Introduction to Quantum Statistical Mechanics. 308p. 1982. text 47.00 (*9971-950-31-6*); pap. text 28.00 (*9971-950-04-9*) World Scientific Pub.

Bogolubov, N. N. N. N. Bogolubov: Selected Works, 2. vols., Vol. 2. 1990. text 414.00 (*2-88124-771-7*) Gordon & Breach.

Bogolubov, N. N., Jr. N. N. Bogolubov Pt. IV: Selected Works: Quantum Field, Vol. 2. (Classics of Soviet Mathematics Ser.). 464p. 1995. text 180.00 (*2-88124-926-4*) Gordon & Breach.

Bogolubov, N. N. N. N. Bugolubov: Selected Works, 4 vols., Vol. 2. 1995. text 785.00 (*2-88449-068-X*) Gordon & Breach.

Bogolubov, N. N., Jr. Some Aspects of Polaron Theory. (Lecture Notes in Physics Ser.: Vol. 4). 132p. 1988. text 37.00 (*9971-978-98-9*); pap. text 21.00 (*9971-978-99-7*) World Scientific Pub.

Bogolubov, N. N., ed. N. N. Bogolubov: Selected Works: Dynamical Theory, Vol. 2. (Classics of Soviet Mathematics Ser.: Vol. 1). x, 386p. 1990. text 211.00 (*2-88124-752-0*) Gordon & Breach.

— N. N. Bogolubov, Selected Works: Quantum & Classical Statistical Mechanics. (Classics of Soviet Mathematics Ser.: Vol. 2). x, 420p. 1990. text 226.00 (*2-88124-768-7*) Gordon & Breach.

Bogolubov, N. N., Jr., et al, eds. High Temperature Superconductivity. 620p. (C). 1990. text 166.00 (*981-02-0003-X*) World Scientific Pub.

— Interaction of Electromagnetic Field with Condensed Matter. (Series in Directions in Modern Condensed Matter Physics: Vol. 7). 336p. (C). 1990. text 99.00 (*981-02-0043-9*); pap. text 53.00 (*981-02-0044-7*) World Scientific Pub.

Bogolubov, N. N. & Bogolubov, N. N., Jr. An Introduction to Quantum Statistical Mechanics. Ermilov, A. N., tr. LC 92-30354. (RUS.). 1992. write for info. (*2-88124-879-9*) Gordon & Breach.

Bogolubov, N. N., Jr., et al. General Principles of Quantum Field Theory. (C). 1990. text 447.00 (*0-7923-0540-X*) Kluwer Academic.

Bogolubov, N. N., Jr., jt. auth. see Bogolubov, N. N.

Bogolyubov, N. N., Jr., ed. Statistical Mechanics & the Theory of Dynamical Systems: Collection of Papers. LC 92-16440. (Proceedings of the Steklov Institute of Mathematics Ser.: Vol. 191). 243p. 1992. pap. 160.00 (*0-8218-3144-5*, STEKLO/191) Am Math.

Bogolyubov, N. N., et al, eds. Analytic Number Theory, Mathematical Analysis & Their Applications: Proceedings of the Steklov Institute of Math, No. 143. LC 80-14363. (Proceedings of the Steklov Institute of Mathematics Ser.). 220p. 1980. pap. 96.00 (*0-8218-3044-9*, STEKLO/143) Am Math.

— Collection of Articles II: Dedicated to Academician I. M. Vinogradov on the Eightieth Anniversary of His Birth. LC 73-6783. (Proceedings of the Steklov Institute of Mathematics Ser.: No. 128). 303p. 1974. pap. 92.00 (*0-8218-3028-7*, STEKLO/128) Am Math.

— Theory of Numbers, Mathematical Analysis & Their Applications. LC 79-20552. (Proceedings of the Steklov Institute of Mathematics Ser.: No. 142). 289p. 1979. pap. 113.00 (*0-8218-3042-2*, STEKLO/142) Am Math.

Bogolyubov, N. N. & Mardzhanishvili, K. K. Theory of Numbers, Mathematical Analysis & Their Applications. LC 83-22405. (Proceedings of the Steklov Institute of Mathematics Ser.: Vol. 157). 248p. 1983. pap. 96.00 (*0-8218-3076-7*, STEKLO/157) Am Math.

Bogolyubov, N. N., et al. Analytic Number Theory, Mathematical Analysis & Their Applications. LC 84-265. (Trudy Steklov Ser.: No.158). 247p. 1984. pap. 101.00 (*0-8218-3077-5*, STEKLO/158) Am Math.

Bogolyubov, N. N., ed. see Steklov Institute of Mathematics, Academy of Scien.

Bogolyubov, Nikolai N., ed. Structure of Complex Nuclei. LC 69-12510. 225p. reprint ed. pap. 69.80 (*0-608-10296-2*, 202067900018) Bks Demand.

Bogolyubov, V. S., jt. ed. see Bratukhin, A. G.

***Bogomilsky.** Vedibarta Bam: Megilat Esther. 206p. 2000. 18.95 (*1-880880-38-5*) Israeli Trad.

— Vedibarta Bam - And You Shall Speak of Them: Pirkei Avot - Ethics of Our Fathers. 353p. 2000. text 18.95 (*1-880880-36-9*) Israeli Trad.

Bogomilsky, Moshe. Vedibarta Bam: And You Shall Speak of Them: A Compilation of Selected Torah Insights, Thought-Provoking Ideas, Homilies & Explanations of Torah Passages. LC 98-121485. 1995. write for info. (*1-880880-22-9*) Israeli Trad.

— Vedibartha Bam: And You Shall Speak of Them. Kaplan, Philip, ed. (Moshe Ser.: Bogomilsky). 247p. (C). 1995. 16.95 (*1-880880-14-8*) Israeli Trad.

— Vedibartha Bam: And You Shall Speak of Them. Kaplan, Philip, ed. (Exodus (Shemot) Ser.). 247p. (C). 1996. 16.95 (*1-880880-15-6*) Israeli Trad.

B

B

Bogomilsky, Rabbi. Vedibarta Bam - And You Should Speak of Them Vol. 4: Numbers. Kaplan, Phillip, ed. 245p. 1997. 16.95 (*1-880880-20-2*) Israeli Trad.

— Vedibarta Bam - And You Should Speak of Them Vol. 5: Deuteronomy (Devarim) Kaplan, Phillip, ed. 250p. 1997. 16.95 (*1-880880-21-0*) Israeli Trad.

***Bogomilsky, Rabbi M.** Ki Yishalcha Bincha: Passover Haggadah - When a Child Asks. 221p. 1999. 15.00 (*1-880880-28-8*) Israeli Trad.

Bogomolny, Abby. The Millennium Journal: Once Every Thousand Years. 144p. 1998. wbk. ed. 12.95 (*0-9650665-1-7*) Burning Bush CA.

Bogomolny, Abby, ed. New to North America: Writing by Immigrants, Their Children & Grandchildren. LC 97-24186. 400p. 1997. pap. 24.95 (*0-9650665-9-2*) Burning Bush CA.

Bogomolny, Abby L. Black of Moonlit Sea: Poetry from the Mist. 60p. 1991. pap. 6.00 (*0-939821-02-8*) HerBooks.

Bogomolny, Abbylynn. People Who Do Not Exist, Vol. 1. LC 96-51185. (Series 2B: Vol. 2B). 60p. (Orig.). 1997. pap. 13.95 (*0-934172-45-5*) WIM Pubns.

Bogomolny, Robert L., ed. see Symposium on Human Experimentation Staff.

Bogomolov, N. A., jt. auth. see Malmstad, John E.

Bogomolov, Yu. G., et al. Hydrogeological Studies in Soil Percolation & Land Reclamation. x, 290p. 1985. text 358.00 (*2-88124-031-3*) Gordon & Breach.

Bogoras, Naum. The Soviet Machine-Tool Industry: An Assessment. Gullant, Jonathan, ed. Saigent, Peter, tr. from RUS. (Illus.). 121p. (Orig.). 1989. pap. text 75.00 (*1-55831-098-3*) Delphic Associates.

Bogoraz, Vladimir G. The Chukchee. LC 73-3527. (Jesup North Pacific Expedition. Publications: No. 7). reprint ed. 172.50 (*0-404-58107-2*) AMS Pr.

— Chukchee Mythology. LC 73-3528. (Jesup North Pacific Expedition. Publications: Vol. 8, Pt. 1). reprint ed. 52.50 (*0-404-58108-0*) AMS Pr.

— The Eskimo of Siberia. LC 73-3530. (Jesup North Pacific Expedition. Publications: Vol. 8, Pt. 3). reprint ed. 32.50 (*0-404-58126-9*) AMS Pr.

— Koryak Texts. LC 73-3540. (American Ethnological Society Publications: No. 5). reprint ed. 32.50 (*0-404-58155-2*) AMS Pr.

— Tales of Yukaghir, Lamut & Russianized Natives of Eastern Siberia. LC 78-67689. (Folktale Ser.). reprint ed. 37.50 (*0-404-16057-3*) AMS Pr.

Bogorodsky, V. V., et al. Ice Destruction: Methods & Technology. 1987. text 193.50 (*90-277-2229-3*) Kluwer Academic.

— Radioglaciology. 1985. text 191.50 (*90-277-1893-8*) Kluwer Academic.

Bogosian, Eric. The Essential Bogosian: Talk Radio, Drinking in America, FunHouse, & Men Inside. LC 93-51493. 240p. 1994. reprint ed. pap. 12.95 (*1-55936-082-8*) Theatre Comm.

***Bogosian, Eric.** Mall: A Novel. 256p. 2000. 22.50 (*0-684-85727-8*) S&S Trade.

Bogosian, Eric. Notes from Underground. LC 97-40724. 176p. 1997. pap. text 11.95 (*1-55936-142-5*) Theatre Comm.

— Pounding Nails in the Floor with My Forehead. 80p. (Orig.). 1994. pap. 8.95 (*1-55936-096-8*) Theatre Comm.

— Suburbia. 1995. pap. 5.25 (*0-8222-1428-8*) Dramatists Play.

— Suburbia. LC 96-6555. 1997. pap. 12.95 (*0-312-16615-X*) St Martin.

Bogosian, Eric, et al, contrib. by. Love's Fire: Seven New Plays Inspired by Seven Shakespearean Sonnets. LC 98-14725. 128p. 1998. pap. 16.00 (*0-688-16172-3*, Quil) HarperTrade.

Bogosian, Wayne G. & Lee, Dee. The Complete Idiot's Guide to 401 (k) Plans. LC 97-73165. 368p. 1997. 17.95 (*0-02-861948-X*) Macmillan Gen Ref.

Bogoslovskaya, Lyudmila, jt. auth. see Freeman, Milton M.

Bogossian, Ben, jt. auth. see Wiegand, Ingrid.

Bogot, Howard. Becky & Benny Thank God. (Illus.). 20p. (J). (ps-1). 1995. 9.95 (*0-88123-065-0*) Central Conf.

***Bogot, Howard & Orkand, Robert.** Gates of Wonder: A Prayerbook for Very Young Children. (Illus.). 47p. 2000. pap. 9.95 (*0-88123-098-7*) Central Conf.

Bogot, Howard, et al. Gates of Awe. LC 91-7413. (Illus.). 62p. (J). (ps-8). 1991. 9.95 (*0-88123-014-6*) Central Conf.

— Gates of Wonder: A Prayerbook for Very Young Children. (Illus.). 47p. (J). (ps-8). 1990. 9.95 (*0-88123-009-X*) Central Conf.

Bogot, Howard I. My First 100 Hebrew Words: A Young Person's Dictionary of Judaism. (Illus.). (J). (gr. k-3). 1993. 11.95 (*0-8074-0509-4*, 101716) UAHC.

***Bogot, Howard I.** Shalom, Salaam, Peace: Special Edition for Educational Use. Or, Amir & Jarrar, Faruk, trs. from HEB. (Illus.). 2000. 2.25 (*0-88123-094-4*) Central Conf.

— Shalom, Salaam, Peace: The Long & Winding Road to Peace in the Middle East. Or, Amir & Jarrar, Faruk, trs. from ARA. LC 98-43112. (Illus.). 36p. 2000. pap. 9.95 (*0-88123-083-9*, Pub. by Central Conf) Natl Bk Netwk.

— Shalom, Salaam, Peace: The Long & Winding Road to Peace in the Middle East. Or, Amir & Jarrar, Faruk, trs. from ARA. LC 98-43112. (Illus.). 36p. (J). (ps-6). 2000. 18.00 (*0-88123-082-0*, Pub. by Central Conf) Natl Bk Netwk.

Bogot, Howard I. & Bogot, Mary K. Seder with the Animals. LC 95-38778. 32p. (J). (ps up). 1995. pap. 10.95 (*0-88123-067-7*) Central Conf.

— Seven Animal Stories from the Bible. (Illus.). 45p. (J). (ps-3). 1997. pap. 9.95 (*0-943706-41-6*) Pitspopany.

— Seven Animal Stories from the Bible, Vol. 1. (Illus.). 48p. (J). (ps-1). 1997. 16.95 (*0-943706-40-8*) Pitspopany.

Bogot, Howard I. & Syme, Daniel B. Books Are Treasures. (Illus.). 32p. 1982. pap. text 4.00 (*0-8074-0160-9*, 101033) UAHC.

— I Learn about God. (Illus.). 32p. (J). (ps). 1982. pap. 4.00 (*0-8074-0159-5*, 101970) UAHC.

— My Body Is Something Special. (Illus.). (J). (ps). 1982. pap. 4.00 (*0-8074-0152-8*, 101715) UAHC.

Bogot, Howard I. & Yedwab, Paul M. Learn Hebrew Today: Alef-Bet for Adults. (C). 1992. pap. text 7.95 (*0-8074-0483-7*, 101093) UAHC.

Bogot, Howard I., jt. auth. see Kipper, Lenore C.

Bogot, Howard I., jt. auth. see Magnus, Joann.

Bogot, Howard I., jt. auth. see Syme, Daniel B.

Bogot, Mary K., jt. auth. see Bogot, Howard I.

Bogot, Mary K., ed. see Tiersky, Kathryn.

Bogousslausky, Julien, jt. auth. see Fisher, Marc.

Bogousslavsky, Julien, jt. auth. see Biller, Jose.

***Bogousslavsky, J., ed.** Stroke Prevention by the Practitioner. (Cerebrovascular Diseases Ser.: Vol. 9, Suppl. 4, 1999). (Illus.). vi, 70p. 1999. pap. 25.25 (*3-8055-6881-9*) S Karger.

Bogousslavsky, J., et al, eds. Trials for Acute Stroke Therapy. (Journal Ser.: Vol. 5, Suppl. 1, 1995). (Illus.). iv, 34p. 1995. pap. 15.75 (*3-8055-6228-4*) S Karger.

— World Stroke Congress & European Stroke Conference: 3rd Congress & 5th Conference, Munich, September 1996 - Abstracts. (Journal: Cerebrovascular Diseases Ser.: Vol. 6, Suppl. 2, 1996). (Illus.). ii, 192p. 1996. pap. 59.25 (*3-8055-6370-1*) S Karger.

Bogousslavsky, J. & Adams, H. P., eds. Strategies for Stroke Prevention: Sanofi Wintrop Symposium to the Third European Stroke Conference, Stockholm, May 1994. (Journal: Chemotherapy: Vol. 4, Suppl. 4, 1994). (Illus.). iv, 38p. 1995. pap. 21.75 (*3-8055-6073-7*) S Karger.

Bogousslavsky, J. & Easton, J. D., eds. Update in Stroke Prevention: Problems of the Stroke Recurrence: Sanofi Winthrop Symposium to the 3rd World Stroke Congress & the 5th European Stroke Conference, Munich, September 1996. (Journal Ser.: Vol. 7, Supplement 1, 1997). (Illus.). iv, 28p. 1997. pap. 21.75 (*3-8055-6462-7*) S Karger.

***Bogousslavsky, J. & Fieschi, C., eds.** Recovery after Acute Stroke: Symposium to the 8th European Stroke Conference, Venice, April 7-10, 1999. (Cerebrovascular Diseases Ser.). iv, 32p. 1999. write for info. (*3-8055-6955-6*) S Karger.

Bogousslavsky, J. & Wang, X. D., eds. Cerebral Ischemia: From Pharmacology to Modern Techniques & Clinical Implications. Value of Almitrine-Raubasine: International Symposium, Hangzhou, People's Republic of China, May 14, 1994. (Journal Ser.: Vol. 35, Suppl. 1, 1995). (Illus.). iv, 48p. 1995. pap. 22.75 (*3-8055-6232-2*) S Karger.

Bogousslavsky, Julien, ed. Emerging Treatments in Neurology: Centenary Issues, 1897-1997. (European Neurology Ser.: Vol. 38, No. 3, 1997). 120p. 1997. pap. 60.00 (*3-8055-6612-3*) S Karger.

Bogousslavsky, Julien & Caplan, Louis, eds. Stroke Syndromes. (Illus.). 532p. (C). 1995. text 135.00 (*0-521-45397-6*) Cambridge U Pr.

***Bogousslavsky, Julien & Cummings, Jeffrey L., eds.** Behavior & Mood Disorders in Focal Brain Lesions. (Illus.). 400p. (C). 2000. pap. 69.95 (*0-521-77482-9*) Cambridge U Pr.

Bogousslavsky, Julien & Fisher, Marc. Textbook of Neurology. LC 98-21166. 896p. 1998. text 75.00 (*0-7506-9918-3*) Buttrwrth-Heinemann.

Bogousslavsky, Julien, jt. auth. see Fisher, Marc.

Bogousslavsky, Julien, jt. auth. see Ginsberg, Myron D.

Bogousslavsky, Julien, jt. ed. see Fisher, Marc.

Bogovski, P., ed. see International Agency for Research on Cancer Staff.

Bogoyavlensky, O. I. Methods in the Qualitative Theory of Dynamical Systems in Astrophysics & Gas Dynamics. Gokhman, Dimitri, tr. from RUS. (Soviet Mathematics Ser.). (Illus.). 320p. 1985. 125.95 (*0-387-13614-2*) Spr-Verlag.

Bograd, Larry. The Better Angel. LC 85-42613. 256p. (YA). (gr. 7 up). 1985. 12.95 (*0-397-32126-0*); lib. bdg. 12.89 (*0-397-32127-9*) HarpC Child Bks.

— Travelers. LC 85-45172. 192p. (YA). (gr. 7 up). 1986. 11.95 (*0-397-32128-7*); lib. bdg. 11.89 (*0-397-32129-5*) HarpC Child Bks.

Bograd, Mark D. & Singleton, Theresa A., eds. The Archaeology of the African Diaspora in the Americas. (Columbian Quincentenary Ser.: No. 2). (Illus.). 87p. (Orig.). 1995. pap. 10.00 (*1-886818-00-2*) Society Hist Arch.

Bograd, Michele, ed. Feminist Approaches for Men in Family Therapy. (Journal of Feminist Family Therapy: Vol. 2 Nos. 3 & 4). 279p. 1991. pap. text 19.95 (*1-56023-000-2*, Harrington Park) Haworth Pr.

— Feminist Approaches for Men in Family Therapy. (Journal of Feminist Family Therapy: Vol. 2 Nos. 3 & 4). 279p. 1991. text 49.95 (*1-56024-128-4*) Haworth Pr.

Bograd, Michele, jt. ed. see Yllo, Kersti.

Bograd, Michele L., jt. ed. see Weingarten, Kathy.

Bogtucki, Peter. The Origins of Human Society. LC 98-56285. (History of the World Ser.). (Illus.). 352p. 1999. text 62.95 (*1-55786-349-0*) Blackwell Pubs.

***Bogucki, Peter.** The Origins of Human Society. (History of the World Ser.). (Illus.). 352p. 1999. pap. 29.95 (*1-57718-112-3*) Blackwell Pubs.

Bogucki, Peter I., ed. Iron Age Europe. 336p. 1993. boxed set 69.95 (*0-8493-8882-1*, GN503) CRC Pr.

Bogue. The Population of the United States. 1996. 150.00 (*0-02-903712-3*) Free Pr.

Bogue, Allan G. The Congressman's Civil War. (Interdisciplinary Perspectives on Modern History Ser.). 224p. (C). 1989. text 64.95 (*0-521-35405-6*); pap. text 16.95 (*0-521-35705-5*) Cambridge U Pr.

— Frederick Jackson Turner: Strange Roads Going Down. LC 97-43149. (Illus.). xviii, 576p. 1998. 34.95 (*0-8061-3039-3*) U of Okla Pr.

— From Prairie to Corn Belt: Farming on the Illinois & Iowa Prairies in the Nineteenth Century. LC 94-7080. (Illus.). 336p. (C). 1994. text 41.95 (*0-8138-2218-1*) Iowa St U Pr.

Bogue, Allan G. & Taylor, Robert, eds. The University of Wisconsin: 125 Years. LC 74-27306. (Illus.). 301p. 1975. reprint ed. pap. 93.40 (*0-608-07466-7*, 206769300009) Bks Demand.

Bogue, Carl, ed. see Butler, R. Will.

Bogue, Carole. Studying in the Content Areas, Social Science. 2nd ed. LC 93-79043. (Illus.). 309p. (C). 1993. pap. text 26.95 (*0-943202-43-4*) H & H Pub.

— Studying in the Content Areas, the Sciences. 2nd ed. LC 93-79042. (Illus.). 309p. (C). 1993. pap. text 26.95 (*0-943202-38-8*) H & H Pub.

— Studying the Content Areas: Mathematics & Business. Davis, Karen H., ed. LC 88-81386. (Illus.). 467p. (C). 1988. pap. 28.00 (*0-943202-28-0*) H & H Pub.

Bogue, Donald J. The Ecological Impact of Population Aging. (Essays in Human Ecology Ser.: No. 4). (Illus.). 83p. 1999. pap. 7.50 (*1-884211-06-2*) Soc Develop.

Bogue, Donald J., ed. Demographic Implications of NAFTA: Toward an Integrated Demography of America. 68p. 1995. pap. 6.30 (*1-884211-01-1*) Soc Develop.

Bogue, Donald J., jt. ed. see Burgess, Ernest W.

Bogue, E. Grady. A Journey of the Heart: The Call to Teaching. LC 91-60523. 98p. (Orig.). 1991. 8.00 (*0-87367-449-9*) Phi Delta Kappa.

— Leadership by Design: The Governing Ideals of Effective Leadership. (Higher & Adult Education Ser.). 185p. 1994. text 30.95 (*0-7879-0034-6*) Jossey-Bass.

Bogue, E. Grady & Aper, Jeffrey. Exploring the Heritage of American Higher Education: The Evolution of Philosophy & Policy. LC 99-49294. 272p. 1999. boxed set 34.95 (*1-57356-310-2*) Oryx Pr.

Bogue, Gary. Isis. (Illus.). 48p. (Orig.). 1990. pap. 9.95 (*0-9623012-1-3*) Lesher Commns.

— It's a Wild Life. (Illus.). 123p. (Orig.). 1989. pap. 15.95 (*0-9623012-0-5*) Lesher Commns.

Bogue, Jeanne, ed. see Pencak, Richard.

Bogue, Lois. Winds over Saddle Creek. Leih, Janet, ed. LC 94-60966. (Illus.). 56p. (Orig.). 1994. pap. 6.00 (*1-877649-23-6*) Tesseract SD.

Bogue, Lucile. Dancers on Horseback: The Perry-Mansfield Story. (Illus.). 240p. (Orig.). 1984. pap. 9.95 (*0-89407-058-4*) Strawberry Hill.

— Miracle on a Mountain: The Story of a College. LC 87-17947. (Illus.). 166p. (Orig.). 1987. pap. 9.95 (*0-89407-086-X*) Strawberry Hill.

— One Woman, One Ranch, One Summer. LC 97-18921. (Illus.). 128p. (Orig.). 1997. pap. 10.95 (*0-89407-121-1*, 1211) Strawberry Hill.

Bogue, Margaret B. Around the Shores of Lake Michigan: A Guide to Historic Sites. LC 84-40490. (Illus.). 400p. 1985. pap. text 21.95 (*0-299-10004-9*) U of Wis Pr.

— Patterns from the Sod. Bruchey, Stuart, ed. LC 78-56691. (Management of Public Lands in the U. S. Ser.). (Illus.). 1979. reprint ed. lib. bdg. 26.95 (*0-405-11318-8*) Ayer.

***Bogue, Margaret Beattie.** Fishing the Great Lakes: An Environmental History, 1783-1933. 2000. 65.00 (*0-299-16760-7*) U of Wis Pr.

— Fishing the Great Lakes: An Environmental History, 1783-1933. LC 00-8601. (Illus.). 2000. pap. 27.95 (*0-299-16764-X*) U of Wis Pr.

Bogue, Merwyn & Reilly, Gladys B. Ish Kabibble: The Autobiography of Merwyn Bogue. LC 88-29213. (Illus.). 264p. 1989. 29.95 (*0-8071-1498-7*) La State U Pr.

Bogue, Richard J. & Hall, Claude H. Health Network Innovations: How 20 Communities Are Improving Their Systems Through Collaboration. LC 97-6224. 1997. pap. 55.00 (*1-55648-198-5*) AHPI.

Bogue, Ronald. Deleuze & Guattari. (Critics of the Twentieth Century Ser.). 192p. 1989. 42.50 (*0-415-02017-4*) Routledge.

— Deleuze & Guattari. (Critics of the Twentieth Century Ser.). 192p. (C). 1989. pap. 22.99 (*0-415-02443-9*) Routledge.

Bogue, Ronald, ed. Mimesis, Semiosis & Power: Mimesis in Contemporary Theory: An Interdisciplinary Approach, Vol. 2. LC 84-14494. (Cultura Ludens Ser.: Vol. 1: 2). viii, 210p. 1991. 59.00 (*1-55619-150-2*) J Benjamins Pubng Co.

Bogue, Ronald, et al, eds. Violence & Mediation in Contemporary Culture. LC 95-2451. (SUNY Series, The Margins of Literature). 207p. (C). 1995. text 54.50 (*0-7914-2719-6*) State U NY Pr.

Bogue, Ronald, tr. from FRE. Contestatory Visions: Five Plays by Georges Astalos. LC 90-53302. 208p. 1991. 38.50 (*0-8387-5199-7*) Bucknell U Pr.

Bogue, Ronald & Cornis-Pope, Marcel, eds. Violence & Mediation in Contemporary Culture. LC 95-2451. (SUNY Series, The Margins of Literature). 224p. (C). 1995. pap. text 17.95 (*0-7914-2720-X*) State U NY Pr.

Bogue, Ronald & Spariosu, Mihai I., eds. The Play of the Self. LC 93-43552. (SUNY Series, The Margins of Literature). 268p. (C). 1994. text 59.50 (*0-7914-2079-5*); pap. text 19.95 (*0-7914-2080-9*) State U NY Pr.

Bogues, Anthony. Caliban's Freedom, Vol. 1. 216p. (C). pap. text 19.95 (*0-7453-0614-4*, Pub. by Pluto GBR) Stylus Pub VA.

— Caliban's Freedom, Vol. 1. LC 96-34395. 216p. (C). 1997. text 49.95 (*0-7453-0613-6*, Pub. by Pluto GBR) Stylus Pub VA.

Bogulavsky, M. M. Copyright in International Relations. Catterns, David, ed. Poulet, N., tr. from RUS. 224p. 1979. reprint ed. 30.00 (*0-9595513-0-1*) W S Hein.

Bogumil, Mary L. Understanding August Wilson. LC 98-40219. (Understanding Contemporary American Literature Ser.). 128p. 1999. 24.95 (*1-57003-252-1*) U of SC Pr.

Bogumil, M.L., jt. auth. see Bogumil, Walter.

***Bogumil, Walter & Bogumil, M.L.** A Biography of Florida Union Organizer Frank E'Dalgo. LC 00-32456. (Studies in American History: Vol. 27). 104p. 2000. 59.95 (*0-7734-7751-9*) E Mellen.

Boguraev, Bran & Briscoe, Ted, eds. Computational Lexicography for Natural Language Processing. LC 88-18077. 326p. 1989. reprint ed. pap. 101.10 (*0-608-03582-3*, 206440500009) Bks Demand.

Boguraev, Branimir & Pustejovsky, James, eds. Corpus Processing for Lexical Acquisition: Language, Speech & Communication. LC 95-26557. (Bradford Bk.). 245p. 1996. 38.50 (*0-262-02392-X*, Bradford Bks) MIT Pr.

Boguraev, Branimir, jt. ed. see Pustejovsky, James.

Bogus. New Age Reader: Readings for an Educated New Millenium. 2nd ed. 536p. 1998. pap. text 41.00 (*0-536-59591-7*) Pearson Custom.

Bogus, Ronald, jt. auth. see Landau, Sidney I.

Bogus, Ronald, ed. see Wood, Clement.

Bogus, Ronald J., jt. ed. see Landau, Sidney I.

Bogus, Ronald J., jt. ed. see Landau, Sidney M.

Bogus, S. Diane, ed. The Poetry Workbook: A Poet's Workbook. 3rd ed. 25p. (YA). (gr. 11-12). 1995. reprint ed. pap. 10.00 (*0-934172-20-X*) WIM Pubns.

Bogus, SDiane A. The Chant of the Women of Magdalena: A Narrative Poem. LC 88-50837. (Illus.). 119p. 1990. pap. 20.00 (*0-934172-16-1*) WIM Pubns.

— Dyke Hands & Sutras: Erotic Lyric. 2nd ed. LC 88-51697. 960p. 1992. pap. text 15.00 (*0-934172-21-8*) WIM Pubns.

— For the Love of Men: Shikata Gai Nai. 2nd ed. (Illus.). 96p. 1991. pap. 15.00 (*0-934172-30-7*) WIM Pubns.

— I'm off to See the Goddamn Wizard, Alright! 3rd ed. LC 95-10389. (Illus.). 48p. (Orig.). (C). 1995. reprint ed. pap. text 15.00 (*0-934172-00-5*, 00-5) WIM Pubns.

— Woman in the Moon. 2nd ed. LC 93-14298. (Illus.). 96p. (C). 1996. reprint ed. pap. 15.00 (*0-934172-37-4*) WIM Pubns.

Bogus, Sdiane A., ed. The (Studenthood) New Age Reader: Anthology of Educational Essays with Appendix. 268p. (C). 1995. pap. text 64.00 (*0-536-58729-9*) Pearson Custom.

Bogush, Alfred J. Radar & the Atmosphere. LC 88-35003. (Artech House Radar Library). (Illus.). 470p. reprint ed. pap. 145.70 (*0-7837-5395-0*, 204515900005) Bks Demand.

***Boguslavskaya, Suetlana.** Pozdnie Ztoety.Tr. of Late Flowers. (RUS., Illus.). 1999. text. write for info. (*0-9673753-3-9*) Gelany.

Boguslavski, Mark M. Joint Ventures in the U. S. S. R. A Guide to Soviet Law. 192p. 1992. text 149.50 (*1-85043-200-7*, Pub. by I B T) St Martin.

— The Soviet Approach. Winter, David & Simons, William B., trs. (C). 1988. lib. bdg. 126.50 (*90-247-3629-3*) Kluwer Academic.

Boguslavski, P. S. German-Russian Dictionary of Measurements: Deutsch-Russisches Woerterbouk der Messtechnik. (GER & RUS.). 556p. 1984. 95.00 (*0-8288-2135-6*, M1985) Fr & Eur.

Boguslavskij, I. A. Filtering & Control. Balakrishnan, A. V., ed. LC 88-38090. (Translations Series in Mathematics & Engineering).Tr. of Prikladnye zadachi fil'tratsii i upravleniia. 400p. 1988. text 85.00 (*0-911575-21-9*) Optimization Soft.

Boguslavsky, M. M. & Smirnov, P. S. The Reorganization of Soviet Foreign Trade: Legal Aspects. Levitsky, Serge L., ed. LC 88-26348. 232p. (C). (gr. 13). 1989. text 119.95 (*0-87332-508-7*) M E Sharpe.

Boguslaw, Robert. New Utopians: A Study of System Design & Social Change. enl. ed. LC 80-18602. 1981. pap. text 17.95 (*0-8290-0115-8*) Irvington.

— Systems Analysis & Social Planning: Human Problems of Post-Industrial Society. 1982. text 32.50 (*0-8290-0111-5*) Irvington.

— Systems Analysis & Social Planning: Human Problems of Post Industrial Society. (C). 1986. reprint ed. pap. text 14.95 (*0-8290-2011-X*) Irvington.

Boguslaw, Robert, jt. auth. see Berg, William M.

Boguslawski, A. Illustrated Russian-Polish, Polish-Russian Dictionary. (POL & RUS., Illus.). 1992. write for info. (*0-8288-7275-9*) Fr & Eur.

Boguslawski, Albrecht Von, see Von Boguslawski, Albrecht.

Boguslawski, Dorothy B. Guide for Establishing & Operating Day Care Centers for Young Children. rev. ed. LC 66-18695. 1991. pap. 14.95 (*0-87868-032-2*, 0322) Child Welfare.

Bogusz, Wladyslaw & Jakubowski, Waclaw, eds. Systems with Fast Ionic Transport-IV. (Solid State Phenomena Ser.: Vols. 39-40). (Illus.). 350p. (C). 1995. 200.00 (*3-908450-07-1*, Pub. by Trans T Pub) Enfield Pubs NH.

Bogutz, Allan D., jt. auth. see Hegland, Kenney F.

Bogzaran, Fariba, jt. auth. see Miedzinski, Charles.

Boh, Katja, et al, eds. Changing Patterns of European Family Life: A Comparative Analysis of 14 European Countries. LC 88-39976. 331p. reprint ed. pap. 102.70 (*0-608-20312-2*, 207156500002) Bks Demand.

— Cross-Cultural Perspectives on Families, Work & Change. LC 89-20092. (Marriage & Family Review Ser.: Vol. 14, Nos. 1-2). 292p. 1990. text 49.95 (*0-86656-961-8*) Haworth Pr.

Boh, Larry E. Clinical Clerkship Manual. 2nd ed. 512p. (Orig.). pap. text. write for info. (*0-7817-2541-0*) Lppncott W & W.

An Asterisk (*) at the beginning of an entry indicates that the title is appearing for the first time.

Boh, Larry E., ed. Clinical Clerkship Manual. LC 92-71899. 416p. (Orig.). (C). 1993. pap. text 38.50 (*0-915486-17-2*) Applied Therapeutics.

Bohac, Janet. Evidence of the Outer World. LC 92-61206. 180p. (Orig.). 1992. pap. 8.95 (*0-9628595-5-9*) Paradigm San Diego.

Bohac, Jennifer. Career Game Plan for Student Athletes. LC 99-14675. (Illus.). 194p. 1999. pap. text 30.00 (*0-13-082278-7*) P-H.

Bohac, Stephen, et al. Passport Evaluation of Popular Outdoor Antennas. (Radio Database International White Paper). (Illus.). 34p. (Orig.). 1993. pap. 6.95 (*0-914941-31-3*) IBS PA.

***Bohach, Carolyn.** Lab Manual for Introductory Biology of Bacteria & Viruses. 2nd ed. 222p. (C). 1998. spiral bd. 33.95 (*0-7872-5565-3*, 41556501) Kendall-Hunt.

Bohachevsky-Chomiak, Martha. Political Communities & Gendered Ideologies in Contemporary Ukraine: The Petryshyn Memorial Lecture, Harvard University, 26 April 1994. (Harvard Papers in Ukrainian Studies). (Illus.). 27p. 1994. pap. text 5.00 (*0-916458-72-5*) Harvard Ukrainian.

Bohachevsky-Chomiak, Martha, jt. ed. see Glatzer, Bernice Rosenthal.

Bohacs, K. M., jt. auth. see Schwalbach, J. R.

Bohaczyk, Pete. The Student, News Watcher & Couch Potato Guide to the Constitution. 174p. (Orig.). (C). 1991. pap. text 21.50 (*0-8191-8313-X*) U Pr of Amer.

Bohan, Brian. Capital Acquisitions Tax. 1993. pap. text 121.00 (*1-85475-607-9*, IE, MICHIE) LEXIS Pub.

***Bohan, Edmund.** Blest Madman: Fitzgerald of Canterbury. (Illus.). 369p. (Orig.). 1998. pap. 49.95 (*0-908812-77-9*, Pub. by Canterbury Univ) Accents Pubns.

Bohan, James F. The House of Atreus: Abortion as a Human Rights Issue. LC 98-38280. 256p. 1999. 39.95 (*0-275-96282-2*, Praeger Pubs) Greenwood.

Bohan, Janis. Conversations about Psychology & Sexual Orientation. LC 99-6333. 1999. pap. text 20.00 (*0-8147-1325-4*) NYU Pr.

— Psychology & Sexual Orientation: Coming to Terms. LC 96-2187. 256p. (C). 1996. pap. 19.99 (*0-415-91514-7*) Routledge.

— Psychology & Sexual Orientation: Coming to Terms. 2nd ed. LC 96-2187. 256p. (C). 1996. 65.00 (*0-415-91513-9*) Routledge.

— Re-Placing Women in Psychology. 160p. (C). 1995. pap. text 28.95 (*0-7872-1036-6*) Kendall-Hunt.

Bohan, Janis, et al. Conversations about Psychology & Sexual Orientation. LC 99-6333. 224p. 1999. text 55.00 (*0-8147-1324-6*) NYU Pr.

Bohan, Patrick. Money Sense: A Commonsense Road to Financial Security & Early Retirement. LC 97-40892. 175p. 2000. pap. 18.95 (*1-56072-519-2*, Nova Kroshka Bks) Nova Sci Pubs.

Bohan, Thomas L. & Damask, Arthur C., eds. Forensic Accident Investigation: Motor Vehicles, 2 Vols. 175.00 (*1-55834-254-0*) LEXIS Pub.

Bohan, Thomas L. & Damask, Arthur C., eds. Forensic Accident Investigation: Motor Vehicles. 800p. 1995. 175.00 (*1-55834-240-0*, 60596, MICHIE) LEXIS Pub.

Bohanan, Ana, ed. & des. see Cohen, Stewart C.

Bohanan, Donna. Old & New Nobility in Aix-en-Provence, 1600-1695: Portrait of an Urban Elite. LC 92-6707. 200p. (C). 1992. text 30.00 (*0-8071-1624-6*) La State U Pr.

***Bohanan, Jennifer L.** The Art of Scott Jacobs. Stieglitz, Cliff, ed. (Illus.). 120p. 2000. 39.95 (*0-9637336-2-1*) Airbrush Act.

Bohannan, Laura & Bohannan, Paul. The Tiv of Central Nigeria. LC DT0515.B66. (Ethnographic Survey of Africa Ser.; Western Africa). 103p. reprint ed. pap. 32.00 (*0-608-11779-X*, 205538200017) Bks Demand.

Bohannan, Laura, jt. auth. see Bohannan, Paul.

Bohannan, Paul. How Culture Works. LC 94-31733. 1994. 24.95 (*0-02-904505-3*) Free Pr.

— Justice & Judgment among the Tiv. rev. ed. (Illus.). 221p. (C). 1989. reprint ed. pap. text 12.50 (*0-88133-459-6*) Waveland Pr.

— We, the Alien: An Introduction to Cultural Anthropology. (Illus.). 344p. (C). 1992. pap. text 30.95 (*0-88133-637-8*) Waveland Pr.

Bohannan, Paul & Bohannan, Laura. Tiv Economy. LC 66-17013. (Northwestern University African Studies Ser.: No. 20). 279p. reprint ed. pap. 86.50 (*0-608-13177-6*, 201528800093) Bks Demand.

Bohannan, Paul & Curtin, Philip De Armond. Africa & Africans. 4th rev. ed. (Illus.). 301p. (C). 1995. pap. text 17.95 (*0-88133-840-0*) Waveland Pr.

Bohannan, Paul & Glazer, Mark. High Points in Anthropology. 2nd ed. 480p. (C). 1988. pap. 50.31 (*0-07-553977-2*) McGraw.

Bohannan, Paul & Van Der Elst, Dirk. Asking & Listening: Ethnography As Personal Adaptation. LC 99-182090. (Illus.). 107p. (C). 1998. pap. text 9.95 (*0-88133-987-3*) Waveland Pr.

Bohannan, Paul, jt. auth. see Bohannan, Laura.

Bohannon, Cynthia & George, Ted. Your Solar Return: A Living Diary of Life Through the Annual Solar Revolutions. LC 96-78499. 90p. 1997. pap. 13.00 (*0-932782-07-8*) Arthur Pubns.

***Bohannon, Jim.** America in Crisis: Making Things Right in a Nation Gone Wrong. 2000. 24.95 (*1-879706-93-8*) Paper Chase.

Bohannon-Kaplan, Margaret. Another Way: Solving Social Problems Without Raising Taxes. LC 97-60850. 100p. (Orig.). 1997. pap. 8.00 (*0-915915-34-0*) Wellington Pubns.

— Another Way: Step by Step. 120p. 1999. pap. 8.00 (*0-915915-37-5*) Wellington Pubns.

Bohannon-Kaplan, Margaret, ed. Excerpts from the 1998 Harry Singer Foundation National High School Essay Contests: Responsibility: Who Has It & The Budget Process, The National Debt. LC 98-61700. 130p. 1998. pap. 8.00 (*0-915915-36-7*) Wellington Pubns.

— Excerpts from the 1995 Harry Singer Foundation High School Essay Contest: Should Government Intervene to Help Children or Teens in Trouble? LC 97-222619. 80p. (Orig.). 1996. pap., per. 6.95 (*0-915915-32-4*) Wellington Pubns.

— Excerpts from the 1997 Harry Singer Foundation National High School Essay Contests. 100p. (Orig.). 1997. pap. 8.00 (*0-915915-33-2*) Wellington Pubns.

— Responsibility: Who Has It & Who Doesn't & What That Means to the Nation: Excerpts from the 1997 Harry Singer Foundation Essay Contest. 1997. pap. 8.00 (*0-915915-35-9*) Wellington Pubns.

— Responsibility - Who Has It & Who Doesn't & What That Means to the Nation: Excerpts from the 1994 Harry Singer Foundation Essay Contest. LC 94-60871. 160p. (Orig.). 1994. pap. 8.00 (*0-915915-27-8*) Wellington Pubns.

— What If Any Should Government's Role Be in Health Care: Selected Essays from the 1992 Harry Singer Foundation Essay Contest. 128p. 1992. pap. 8.00 (*0-915915-22-7*) Wellington Pubns.

— What Role Does & What Role Should the Media Play in Choosing Our Candidates for National Office? Excerpts from the 1993 Harry Singer Foundation Essay Contest. 1993. pap. 8.00 (*0-915915-23-5*) Wellington Pubns.

Bohannon-Kaplan, Margaret, ed. see Harry Singer Foundation Staff.

Bohannon-Kaplan, Margaret, jt. ed. see Zachman-Navarro, Ann.

Bohannon, Keith S. The Giles, Allegheny & Jackson Artillery. (Virginia Regimental Histories Ser.). (Illus.). 130p. 1990. 19.95 (*0-930919-94-7*) H E Howard.

Bohannon, Keith S., jt. ed. see Allen, Randall.

***Bohannon, Lisa Frederiksen.** Women's Rights & Nothing Less: The Story of Elizabeth Cady Stanton. LC 00-25565. (Notable Americans Ser.). 2000. lib. bdg. write for info. (*1-883846-66-8*) M Reynolds.

Bohannon, Mike, et al. The New Right in the States: The Groups, the Issues, & the Strategies. 92p. 1983. 7.95 (*0-89788-079-X*) CPA Washington.

Bohannon, Paul, jt. ed. see Gruter, Margaret.

Bohannon, Paul M. Bohannon's New Mexico Environmental Law Handbook, 1990-93. 420p. 1993. ring bd. 95.00 (*0-409-25533-5*, MICHIE); ring bd., suppl. ed. 65.00 (*0-250-42722-2*, MICHIE) LEXIS Pub.

Bohannon, Richard, et al. Food for Life. LC 98-15348. 336p. 1998. pap. 16.95 (*0-8092-2845-9*, 284590, Contemporary Bks) NTC Contemp Pub Co.

Bohanon, Cecil. Principles of Microeconomics. 224p. (C). 1994. pap. text 15.50 (*1-57074-101-8*) Greyden Pr.

Bohanon, Thomas C., ed. see Hayes, Karen E.

Bohart, Arthur C. & Greenberg, Leslie S., eds. Empathy Reconsidered: New Directions in Psychotherapy. LC 97-3398. 477p. 1997. text 49.95 (*1-55798-410-7*, 431-7860) Am Psychol.

Bohart, Arthur C. & Tallman, Karen. How Clients Make Therapy Work: The Process of Active Self-Healing. LC 98-48623. (Illus.). 347p. 1999. 39.95 (*1-55798-571-5*) Am Psychol.

Bohart, George E. & Gressitt, J. Linsley. Filth-Inhabiting Flies of Guam. (BMB Ser.: No. 204). (Illus.). 1951. 25.00 (*0-527-02312-4*) Periodicals Srv.

Bohart, R. M. & Kimsey, Lynn S. A Synopsis of the Chrysididae in America North of Mexico. (Memoir Ser.: No.33). (Illus.). 266p. 1982. 35.00 (*1-56665-031-3*) Assoc Pubs FL.

Bohart, R. M. & Washino, R. K. Mosquitoes of California. 3rd ed. LC 77-84551. 164p. 1978. pap. 6.00 (*0-931876-15-X*, 4084) ANR Pubns CA.

Bohart, Richard M. & Gillaspy, J. E. California Sand Wasps of the Subtribe Stictiellina. (Bulletin of the California Insect Survey Ser.: Vol. 27). 1986. pap. 48.00 (*0-520-09697-5*, Pub. by U CA Pr) Cal Prin Full Svc.

Bohart, Richard M., jt. auth. see Kimsey, Lynn S.

Bohatta, Hanns. Katalog der Liturgischen Drucke des 15 und 16: Jahrhunderts in der Herzogl. Parma'schen Bibliothek in Schwarzau am Steinfeld, 2 vols. xvi, 910p. reprint ed. write for info. (*0-318-71743-3*) G Olms Pubs.

— Liturgische Bibliographie des XV: Jahrhunderts. 79p. 1960. reprint ed. 25.00 (*0-318-71744-1*) G Olms Pubs.

Bohatta, Hanns, jt. auth. see Holzmann, Michael.

Bohatta, Hanns, jt. auth. see Weale, W. H.

***Bohaychuk, Wendy & Ball, Graham.** Conducting GCP Compliant Clinical Research: A Practical Guide. LC 98-54676. 226p. 1999. 120.00 (*0-471-98824-3*) Wiley.

Bohdan, Michael. What's Buggin' You? Michael Bohdan's Guide to Home Pest Control. LC 98-5210. (Illus.). 256p. 1998. pap. 12.95 (*1-891661-01-9*, 1-01-9) Snta Monica.

Bohdanowicz, Janet & Clamp, Liz. Fashion Marketing. LC 94-4446. 192p. (C). 1994. pap. 20.95 (*0-415-05940-2*) Thomson Learn.

— Fashion Marketing. LC 94-4446. 192p. (C). (gr. 13). 1994. pap. 60.95 (*0-415-05939-9*) Thomson Learn.

Bohec, Yann Le, see Le Bohec, Yann.

Boheemen-Saaf, Christine Van, see Van Boheemen-Saaf, Christine.

Bohei, D. Pearl, jt. auth. see Hockenberry, Ingrid P.

Boheler, K. R., jt. ed. see Wobus, A. M.

Bohensky, Fred. Photo Manual & Dissection Guide of the Cat: With Sheep Heart, Brain, Eye. 2nd ed. (Illus.). 176p. 1979. student ed. 10.95 (*0-89529-019-7*, Avery) Penguin Putnam.

— Photo Manual & Dissection Guide of the Fetal Pig: With Sheep Heart, Brain, Eye. (Illus.). 128p. 1978. student ed. 10.95 (*0-89529-058-8*, Avery) Penguin Putnam.

— Photo Manual & Dissection Guide of the Frog. (Avery's Anatomy Ser.). (Illus.). 88p. (C). 1982. student ed. 10.95 (*0-89529-162-2*, Avery) Penguin Putnam.

— Photo Manual & Dissection Guide of the Rat: With Sheep Eye. (Avery's Anatomy Ser.). (Illus.). 154p. (C). 1986. student ed. 10.95 (*0-89529-213-0*, Avery) Penguin Putnam.

— Photo Manual & Dissection Guide of the Shark. (Avery's Anatomy Ser.). (Illus.). 120p. (Orig.). (C). 1981. pap. text 10.95 (*0-89529-140-1*, Avery) Penguin Putnam.

Bohere, G. Profession Journalist: A Study on the Working Conditions of Journalists. Orig. Title: Fr.. ix, 177p. 1984. pap. 22.50 (*92-2-103531-X*) Intl Labour Office.

Bohi, Charles. Canadian National's Western Depots. (Illus.). 128p. 20.00 (*0-919130-28-3*, Pub. by Boston Mills) Genl Dist Srvs.

Bohi, Douglas R. Energy Price Shocks & Macroeconomic Performance. LC 89-10722. 93p. 1989. pap. 11.95 (*0-915707-51-9*) Resources Future.

Bohi, Douglas R. & Montgomery, W. David. Oil Prices, Energy Security, & Import Policy. LC 82-15083. 203p. 1982. 25.00 (*0-8018-2821-X*) Resources Future.

Bohi, Douglas R. & Quandt, William B. Energy Security in the 1980s: Economic & Political Perspectives. LC 84-72355. 52p. 1984. pap. 7.95 (*0-8157-1001-1*) Brookings.

Bohi, Douglas R & Russell, Milton. Limiting Oil Imports: An Economic History & Analysis. LC 77-18881. 356p. 1978. 30.50 (*0-8018-2106-1*) Resources Future.

Bohi, Douglas R. & Russell, Milton. U. S. Energy Policy: Alternatives for Security. LC 75-4209. 141p. reprint ed. pap. 40.20 (*0-608-18477-2*, 2032988) Bks Demand.

— U. S. Energy Policy: Alternatives for Security. LC 75-4209. 141p. 1975. reprint ed. pap. 43.80 (*0-608-10381-0*, 203298800082) Bks Demand.

Bohi, Douglas R. & Toman, Michael A. Analyzing Nonrenewable Resource Supply. LC 83-43264. 159p. 1984. pap. text 12.95 (*0-915707-06-3*); lib. bdg. 25.00 (*0-915707-05-5*) Resources Future.

— The Economics of Energy Security. LC 95-49387. 168p. (C). 1996. lib. bdg. 97.00 (*0-7923-9685-5*) Kluwer Academic.

Bohidar, H. B. Novel Applications of Lasers: Proceedings of a Symposium, 9-10 January 1992, New Delhi. (C). 1994. 22.00 (*81-224-0627-0*, Pub. by Wiley Estrn) Franklin.

Bohidar, N. R. Optimization Statistics & Designs in Pharmaceutics. 465p. 1999. 73.95 (*0-8493-9421-X*) CRC Pr.

Bohidar, Nabesh. Sterling Dictionary of Sports. (C). 1997. pap. write for info. (*81-7359-065-6*) Sterling Pubs.

Bohigas, Joaquin. Genesis y Transfiguraciones de las Estrellas. (Ciencia para Todos Ser.). (SPA.). pap. 6.99 (*968-16-3440-3*, Pub. by Fondo) Continental Bk.

Bohigas, Oriol. Espinet & Ubach. (Current Architecture Catalogues Ser.). (Illus.). 96p. 1996. pap. text 29.95 (*84-252-1673-7*) Watsn-Guptill.

Bohigas, Oriol, et al. Miguel Angel Roca. 2nd rev. ed. (Academy Architecture Ser.). (Illus.). 176p. 1986. pap. 24.95 (*0-312-53229-6*) St Martin.

***Bohigian, George M. & Vallum, Shailaja.** Handbook of Ocular Infections & External Diseases. 208p. (C). 2000. pap. text 33.00 (*1-55642-436-1*) SLACK Inc.

Bohigian, Haig E. The Foundations & Mathematical Models of Operations Research with Extensions to the Criminal Justice System. LC 75-186274. (Illus.). xxiii, 282p. (Orig.). 1972. pap. 24.95 (*0-933390-01-7*) Valian Assocs.

— Master Track & Field Ranking Book, 1980: Men & Women Ages 30-89, U. S. A., Canada & Mexico. 104p. (Orig.). 1981. pap. 4.00 (*0-933390-07-6*) Valian Assocs.

— Track & Field Masters Ranking Book 1981: Men & Women Ages 30-89; U. S. A., Canada & Mexico. 96p. (Orig.). 1982. pap. 15.00 (*0-933390-06-8*) Valian Assocs.

— Track & Field Masters Ranking Book 1982: Men & Women Ages 30-89, U. S. A., Canada & Mexico. 96p. (Orig.). 1981. pap. 10.00 (*0-686-91816-9*) Valian Assocs.

— Track & Field Masters Ranking Book 1982: Men & Women Ages 30-89, U. S. A., Canada & Mexico. 96p. (Orig.). 1983. pap. 15.00 (*0-933390-05-X*) Valian Assocs.

Bohigian, Valerie. Ladybucks: Why Certain Women Turn Work into Wealth. 246p. (Orig.). 1987. 24.95 (*0-396-08852-X*) Valian Assocs.

Bohinski. Modern Concepts in Biochemistry. 5th ed. 750p. 1986. teacher ed. write for info. (*0-318-61496-0*, H88537); teacher ed. 3.00 (*0-685-17393-3*, H88545) P-H.

Bohinski, Robert C. Bioquimica. 2nd ed. 1987. pap. 41.75 (*0-201-64017-1*) Addison-Wesley.

Bohjalian, Christopher A. Hangman. LC 91-4506. 301p. 1991. 18.95 (*0-88184-685-6*) Carroll & Graf.

Bohjalian, Christopher A. The Law of Similars. LC 98-15807. 275p. 1998. 23.00 (*0-517-70586-9*) Harmony Bks.

***Bohjalian, Christopher A.** The Law of Similars, 1 vol. 320p. 2000. pap. 13.00 (*0-679-77147-6*) Vin Bks.

— The Law of Similars. large type ed. LC 99-30647. (Large Print Book Ser.). 1999. write for info. (*1-56895-723-8*) Wheeler Pub.

Bohjalian, Christopher A. Midwives: A Novel. 1998. 24.00 (*0-609-60497-X*) Crown Pub Group.

***Bohjalian, Christopher A.** Midwives: A Novel. 372p. 1998. pap. 13.00 (*0-375-70677-1*) Knopf.

Bohjalian, Christopher A. Midwives: A Novel. 400p. 1998. pap. 13.00 (*0-679-77146-8*) Vin Bks.

— Midwives: A Novel. large type ed. (Niagara Large Print Ser.). 1997. lib. bdg. 29.50 (*0-7089-5880-X*) Ulverscroft.

***Bohjalian, Christopher A.** Trans-Sister Radio. LC 99-49250. 368p. 2000. 24.00 (*0-609-60407-4*) Harmony Bks.

Bohjalian, Christopher A. Water Witches. LC 97-2112. 340p. 1997. pap. 13.00 (*0-684-82612-7*) Scribner.

— Water Witches. LC 94-9816. (Hardscrabble Bks.). 351p. 1995. 24.95 (*0-87451-687-0*) U Pr of New Eng.

Bohl, A. H., ed. Computer Aided Formulation: A Manual for Implementation. 298p. 1990. 105.00 (*0-471-18789-5*) Wiley.

Bohl, Al. Guide to Cartooning. LC 96-44340. (Illus.). 176p. (J). 1997. pap. 9.95 (*1-56554-177-4*) Pelican.

— Guide to Cartooning: Teacher's Guide. (Illus.). 64p. 1997. pap., teacher ed. 9.95 (*1-56554-178-2*) Pelican.

Bohl, Franz M. Akkadian Chrestomathy Vol. 1: Selected Cuneiform Texts. xvi, 166p. 1947. pap. text 28.00 (*0-614-03990-8*, Pub. by Netherlands Inst) Eisenbrauns.

Bohl, Marilyn & Rynn, Maria. Tools for Structured Design: An Introduction to Programming Logic. (Illus.). 320p. (C). 1992. teacher ed. write for info. (*0-318-69282-1*) Macmillan.

— Tools for Structured Design: An Introduction to Programming Logic. 4th ed. LC 97-3743. 336p. 1997. pap. 82.00 (*0-13-626466-2*) P-H.

***Bohl, Marilyn & Rynn, Maria.** Tools for Structured Design: An Introduction to Programming Logic. 5th ed. LC 99-57566. (Illus.). 368p. (C). 2000. pap. 77.00 (*0-13-020037-9*) P-H.

B

Bohl, Martin. Molecular Structure: Biological Activity of Steroids. 495p. 1992. lib. bdg. 229.00 (*0-8493-6955-X*, QP752) CRC Pr.

Bohl, Winfried. Standards In der Psychiatrie: Eine Untersuchung Zur Zivilrechtlichen Verantwortlichkeit des Klinikpsychiaters Bei der Behandlung Psychisch Kranker. 304p. 1998. 56.95 (*3-631-34110-5*) P Lang Pubng.

***Bohlander, et al.** Web Tutor On Webct to Accompany Human Resource Management. 12th ed. 2000. pap. 19.00 (*0-324-06454-3*) Sth-Wstrn College.

Bohlander, jt. auth. see Sherman.

Bohlander, George W. Impact of Third-Party Payors on Collective Bargaining in the Health Care Industry. (Monograph & Research Ser.: No. 26). 106p. 1980. 6.50 (*0-89215-109-9*) U Cal LA Indus Rel.

— Managing Human Resources. 11th ed. (Miscellaneous/Catalogs Ser.). 1997. mass mkt., student ed. 18.95 (*0-538-87078-8*) S-W Pub.

Bohlander, George W., et al. Managing Human Resources. 10th ed. LC 95-8634. (C). 1995. pap. 70.95 (*0-538-83925-2*) S-W Pub.

Bohlander, George W., et al. Managing Human Resources. 11th ed. LC 97-16115. (Miscellaneous/Catalogs Ser.). 1997. mass mkt. 87.95 (*0-538-87075-3*) S-W Pub.

Bohlander, George W., jt. auth. see Sherman, Arthur W., Jr.

Bohlander, George W., jt. auth. see Sherman, Arthur W.

Bohlander, John E. A Boy Named John. (Illus.). 280p. (Orig.). 1996. pap. 10.00 (*0-9650521-0-9*) Oak Branch.

Bohlander, Richard E., ed. World Explorers & Discoverers. LC 97-41566. (Illus.). 544p. 1998. reprint ed. pap. 25.95 (*0-306-80824-2*) Da Capo.

***Bohle, A., ed.** BCG - The Optimal Approach in Superficial Bladder Cancer: Proceedings of the Symposium Held at the 14th European Association of Urology Congress, Stockholm, April, 1999. (European Urology Ser.: Vol. 37, Suppl. 1). (Illus.). iv, 40p. 1999. pap. 25.25 (*3-8055-7019-8*) S Karger.

Bohle, F. The Design of Gear Teeth. (Technical Papers: Vol. P255). (Illus.). 19p. 1944. pap. text 30.00 (*1-55589-456-9*) AGMA.

— Toward More Economical Gear Inspection. (Technical Papers: Vol. P239.05). (Illus.). 14p. 1957. pap. text 30.00 (*1-55589-302-3*) AGMA.

Bohle, F. & Saari, O. Spiroid Gears. (Technical Papers: Vol. P389.01). (Illus.). 14p. 1955. pap. text 30.00 (*1-55589-398-8*) AGMA.

***Bohle, Philip & Quinlan, Michael.** Managing Occupational Health & Safety a Multidisciplinary Approach. 512p. 2000. pap. 54.95 (*0-7329-4078-8*, Pub. by Macmill Educ) Paul & Co Pubs.

Bohle, S., jt. auth. see Adhikari, S.

Bohlemann, Peter. Jesus und der Taufer: Schlussel Zur Theologie und Ethik des Lukas. (Society for New Testament Studies Monograph Ser.: Vol. 99).Tr. of Jesus & the Baptist: Key to the Theology & Ethics of Luke. (GER.). 393p. (C). 1997. text 74.95 (*0-521-59421-9*) Cambridge U Pr.

Bohlen, Janet T. For the Wild Places: Profiles in Conservation. LC 92-38118. (Illus.). 240p. 1993. 27.50 (*1-55963-125-2*) Island Pr.

***Bohlen, Janet Trowbridge.** Braided River: A Collection of Poetry. iii, 48p. 2000. 14.50 (*0-615-11273-0*) J T Bohlen.

***Bohlen, Jim.** Making Waves: The Origins & Future of Greenpeace. 235p. 2000. 48.99 (*1-55164-167-4*); pap. 19.99 (*1-55164-166-6*) Black Rose.

Bohlen, John R. The Cult of Cannibals. (Illus.). 314p. 1987. pap. 9.95 (*0-9607702-1-6*) Kingdom God.

— How to Rule the World: Seek First the Kingdom of God. LC 81-90513. (Illus.). 271p. 1982. pap. 9.95 (*0-9607702-0-8*) Kingdom God.

— The King's Greatest Secret. (Illus.). 64p. 1993. pap. 3.95 (*0-9607702-4-0*) Kingdom God.

Bohlen, John R. & Bohlen, Karen. How to Raise "Perfect" Kids. (Illus.). 215p. 1987. pap. 8.95 (*0-9607702-3-2*) Kingdom God.

— The Sexual Ministry: A Modern Sex Manual. (Illus.). 345p. 1987. pap. 9.95 (*0-9607702-2-4*) Kingdom God.

Bohlen, Karen, jt. auth. see Bohlen, John R.

An Asterisk (*) at the beginning of an entry indicates that the title is appearing for the first time.

B

***Bohlen, M. H., et al, eds.** Spatio-Temporal Database Management: Proceedings, International Workshop STDBM'99, Edinburgh, Scotland, September 10-11, 1999. LC 99-40186. (Lecture Notes in Computer Science Ser.: Vol. 1678). x, 243p. 1999. pap. 52.00 (*3-540-66401-7*) Spr-Verlag.

Bohler, Carolyn S. Chips & Salsa! Children (Youth) in Plays: Short & Lively Sacred Action. LC 98-20731. 85p. (YA). (gr. 6-12). 1998. 12.95 (*1-57895-064-3*) Bridge Resources.

— God Is Like a Mother Hen & Much, Much More. 32p. (Orig.). (J). (ps-1). 1996. 15.00 (*1-57153-200-5*) Curriculm Presbytrn KY.

— Opening to God: Guided Imagery Meditation on Scripture. LC 95-62356. 192p. 1996. pap. 13.00 (*0-8358-0768-1*) Upper Room Bks.

Bohler, Christian. Practical CAD Training, CAD 3D Pt. 2: Introduction to Three-Dimensional Design. 212p. 1990. pap. 19.95 (*1-56990-005-1*) Hanser-Gardner.

Bohler, Christian & Frommer, Hans. CAD Training Handbook Series. (C). 1990. pap. text 175.50 (*1-56990-122-8*) Hanser-Gardner.

Bohler, Dieter. Die Heilige Stadt in Esdras a und Esra-Nehemia: Zwei Konzeptionen der Wiederherstellung Israels. (Orbis Biblicus et Orientalis Ser.: Vol. 158). (GER.). xiii, 435p. 1997. text 89.75 (*3-7278-1147-1*, Pub. by Ed Univ Fri) Eisenbrauns.

Bohler, Liette. Der Mythos der Weiblichkeit im Werke Max Frischs. (Studies on the Themes & Motifs in Literature: Vol. 36). (GER.). VII, 237p. (C). 1998. 46.95 (*0-8204-3886-3*) P Lang Pubng.

Bohler, Michael, ed. see Weber, Paul.

Bohlin, Diane D., jt. ed. see Bohn, Babbette.

Bohlin, Erik & Grandstrand, Ove, eds. The Race to European Eminence: Who are the Coming Tele-service Multinationals? LC 94-3800. 572p. 1994. 139.50 (*0-444-81961-4*) Elsevier.

Bohlin, Henrik. Groundless Knowledge: A Humean Solution to the Problem of Skepticism. LC 97-223762. (Stockholm Studies in Philosophy: Vol. 19). 231p. 1997. pap. 49.50 (*91-22-01773-9*, Pub. by Almqvist Wiksell) Coronet Bks.

Bohlin, Karen E., jt. auth. see Ryan, Kevin A.

Bohlin, Lars. Bioassay Methods in Natural Product Research & Drug Development. LC 98-47446. 1998. write for info. (*0-7923-5480-X*) Kluwer Academic.

Bohlin, Raymond G., jt. auth. see Lester, Lane P.

Bohlin, Roy M., jt. auth. see Clemente, Rebecca.

Bohlin, T., et al. Interactive System Identification: Prospects & Pitfalls. Dickinson, B. W. et al, eds. (Communications & Control Engineering Ser.). (Illus.). 384p. 1991. 99.95 (*0-387-53636-1*) Spr-Verlag.

Bohling, Corey A. It's about Time: The Theory of Evolution Is Impossible. (Illus.). 250p. (Orig.). 1998. pap. write for info. (*0-614-28368-X*) C Bohling Pub.

— On the Monday Side of the Street: A Text on Alcoholism for Professional & Lay People. Fieser, Virginia, tr. (Illus.). 100p. (Orig.). (C). 1989. pap. 5.95 (*0-9625478-3-2*, TXU-368-156) C Bohling Pub.

Bohlinger, Maryanne S. Merchandise Buying. 3rd ed. 550p. 1989. text 46.00 (*0-205-12196-9*, H21967) Allyn.

— Merchandise Buying. 3rd ed. 550p. 1989. teacher ed. write for info. (*0-318-66368-6*, H21975) P-H.

Bohlke, Dorothee. Cokolina & the Wild Island. Max, Jill & Bradford, Elizabeth, eds. Verlag, Mangold, tr. LC 91-24337. (Magic Mountain Fables Ser.). (Illus.). 24p. (J). (gr. k-3). 1991. lib. bdg. 14.60 (*1-56074-032-9*) Garrett Ed Corp.

Bohlke, Eugenia B. Catalog of Type Specimens in the Ichthyological Collection of the Academy of Natural Sciences of Philadelphia. (Special Publication: No. 14). 246p. 1984. pap. 10.00 (*0-910006-41-5*) Acad Nat Sci Phila.

Bohlke, James E. & Chaplin, Charles C. Fishes of the Bahamas & Adjacent Tropical Waters. 2nd rev. ed. LC 92-20389. (Illus.). 857p. (C). 1993. 125.00 (*0-292-70792-4*) U of Tex Pr.

Bohlke, L. Brent, ed. see Cather, Willa.

Bohlken-Zumpe, Elizabeth. Torches Extinguished: Memories of a Communal Bruderhof Childhood in Paraguay, Europe & the U. S. A. Huntington, Gertrude E., ed. LC 93-72237. (Women from Utopia Ser.). (Illus.). 330p. (Orig.). 1993. pap. 17.00 (*1-882260-01-5*) Carrier Pigeon.

Bohlman, Henry H., jt. auth. see Boden, Scott D.

Bohlman, Herbert M. Legal Environment. 3rd ed. 1996. pap., student ed. 21.75 (*0-314-09634-5*) West Pub.

— Legal, Ethical & Regulatory Environment of Business. 4th ed. LC 98-19537. (SWC-Business Law Ser.). 1998. pap. 98.95 (*0-538-88492-4*) S-W Pub.

Bohlman, Herbert M. & Dundas, Mary J. The Legal, Ethical & International Environment of Business. 2nd ed. Perlee, Clyde, ed. LC 92-15448. 680p. (C). 1993. text 68.50 (*0-314-00905-1*) West Pub.

— The Legal, Ethical & International Environment of Business. 3rd ed. LC 95-35003. 620p. (C). 1996. pap. 69.75 (*0-314-06456-7*) West Pub.

Bohlman, Otto, ed. Human Rights Watch World Report, 1998. 424p. 1998. pap. 25.00 (*0-300-07482-4*) Yale U Pr.

Bohlman, Philip V. Central European Folk Music: An Annotated Bibliography of Sources in German. Porter, James, ed. LC 96-14970. (Library of Music Ethnology: Vol. 3). 344p. 1996. text 55.00 (*0-8153-0304-1*, H1448) Garland.

— The Land Where Two Streams Flow: Music in the German-Jewish Community of Israel. LC 88-25902. (Illus.). 280p. 1989. text 24.95 (*0-252-01596-7*) U of Ill Pr.

— The Study of Folk Music in the Modern World. LC 87-45401. 182p. 1988. 35.00 (*0-253-35555-9*); pap. 15.95 (*0-253-20464-X*, MB 464) Ind U Pr.

— The World Centre for Jewish Music in Palestine, 1936-1940: Jewish Musical Life on the Eve of World War II. (Illus.). 328p. 1992. text 79.00 (*0-19-816237-5*) OUP.

Bohlman, Philip V., jt. auth. see Nettl, Bruno.

Bohlman, Philip V., jt. auth. see Radano, Ronald M.

Bohlman, Philip V., jt. ed. see Bergeron, Katherine.

Bohlman, Philip V., ed. see Weill, Kurt & Milhaud, Darius.

***Bohlmann, Barney F.** Human Behavior & Reactions in Various Living Conditions: Index of New Information with Authors, Subjects & Bibliography. rev. ed. 153p. 1999. 47.50 (*0-7883-1994-9*); pap. 44.50 (*0-7883-1995-7*) ABBE Pubs Assn.

Bohlmann, Paul A., jt. auth. see Muto, Lisa M.

***Bohlmark, Marta, tr. from DUT.** Tusenskonan. unabridged ed. (Listen & Learn Language Audio Ser.: Vol. LL1098).Tr. of Daisy. (ENG & SWE., Illus.). 28p. (J). (gr. 3 up). 1998. pap. 15.95 incl. audio (*1-892623-00-5*, 001) Intl Book.

Bohlmark, Marta, tr. Kejsarens Nya Klader, Vol. 2. 2nd ed. (Listen & Learn Language Audio Ser.: Vol. LL0399).Tr. of The Emperor's New Clothes. (ENG & SWE.). 28p. 1999. pap. 9.95 (*1-892623-03-X*) Intl Book.

***Bohlmark, Marta, tr.** Kejsarens Nya Klader: The Emperor's New Clothes, Vol. 2. 2nd unabridged ed. (Listen & Learn Language Audio Ser.: Vol. LL0399). (ENG & SWE.). 28p. 1999. pap. 15.95 incl. audio, cd-rom (*1-892623-02-1*) Intl Book.

Bohlmark, Marta, jt. auth. see Lang, Ingrid, ed.

Bohlmeijer, Arno. Something Very Sorry. LC 95-30208. 176p. (Orig.). (J). (gr. 5-9). 1996. 15.00 (*0-395-74679-5*) HM.

— Something Very Sorry. (Orig.). 1997. 11.05 (*0-606-13032-2*, Pub. by Turtleback) Demco.

Bohlmg, B. Studien Zur Landschaftsoekologischen Raumgliederung Auf der Mediterranen Insel Naxos (Griechenland) Unter Besonderer Beruecksichtigung Von Zeigerpflanzen. (Dissertationes Botanicae Ser.: Band 230). (Illus.). vii, 247p. 1994. pap. 83.00 (*3-443-64142-3*, Pub. by Gebruder Borntraeger) Balogh.

Bohlool, Janet. Library Orientation: Syllabus. 2nd ed. 1975. pap. text 9.50 (*0-89420-080-1*, 216788); audio 101.70 (*0-89420-161-1*, 140800) Natl Book.

Bohls, Elizabeth A. Women Travel Writers & the Language of Aesthetics, 1716-1818. (Studies in Romanticism: No. 13). (Illus.). 320p. (C). 1995. text 59.95 (*0-521-47458-2*) Cambridge U Pr.

Bohm. Carlo Baumschlager & Dietmar Eberle. (Portraits of Austrian Architects Ser.: Vol. 3). (Illus.). 150p. 1996. 52.00 (*3-211-82725-0*) Spr-Verlag.

— Woerterbuch Paedegogik. 13th ed. (GER.). 646p. 1988. 59.95 (*0-7859-7442-3*, 3520094134) Fr & Eur.

Bohm & MacDonald. Power: Mechanics of Energy Control. 2nd ed. 1983. teacher ed. 11.16 (*0-02-672470-7*) Glencoe.

Bohm, A. Dinoflagellates of the Coastal Waters of the Western Pacific. (BMB Ser.). 1936. pap. 25.00 (*0-527-02243-8*) Periodicals Srv.

— Distribution & Variability of Ceratium in the Northern & Western Pacific. (BMB Ser.). 1931. pap. 25.00 (*0-527-02193-8*) Periodicals Srv.

Bohm, A., et al, eds. Irreversibility & Causality: Semigroups & Rigged Hilbert Spaces. LC 98-18096. (Lecture Notes in Physics Ser.: Vol. 504). xix, 385p. 1998. 95.00 (*3-540-64305-2*) Spr-Verlag.

Bohm, Andreas. Metaphysica in Usum Auditorii Sui Ordine Scientifico Bd. 42. 674p. 1998. write for info. (*3-487-10657-4*) G Olms Pubs.

Bohm, Andreas, jt. auth. see Wolff, Christian.

Bohm, Arno. Quantum Mechanics. 2nd enl. ed. LC 85-4710. (Texts & Monographs in Physics). (Illus.). 550p. 1986. pap. 75.50 (*0-387-13985-0*) Spr-Verlag.

— Quantum Mechanics: Foundations & Applications. 3rd enl. rev. ed. LC 92-44947. (Texts & Monographs in Physics). (Illus.). 688p. 1994. 69.95 (*0-387-97944-1*) Spr-Verlag.

Bohm, Arno & Gadella, M. Dirac Kets, Gamow Vectors & Gel'fand Triplets. (Lecture Notes in Physics Ser.: Vol. 348). (Illus.). vii, 119p. 1989. 34.95 (*0-387-51916-5*, 3730) Spr-Verlag.

Bohm, B. & Punzo, L. F., eds. Economic Performance: A Look at Austria & Italy. (Contributions to Economics Ser.). (Illus.). vi, 323p. 1995. 70.00 (*3-7908-0811-3*) Spr-Verlag.

Bohm, Bartholomaus, jt. auth. see Milsom, Jeffrey W.

Bohm-Bawerk. Capital & Interest, 3 vols. in 1. 1959. 47.50 (*0-910884-08-0*) Libertarian Press.

Bohm-Bawerk, Eugen Von. Capital & Interest, 3 vols., Set. Incl. Vol. 1. History & Critique of Interest Theories. LC 58-5555. 490p. 1959. (*0-910884-09-9*); Vol. 2. Positive Theory of Capital. LC 58-5555. 466p. 1959. (*0-910884-10-2*); Vol. 3. Further Essays on Capital & Interest. LC 58-5555. 246p. 1959. (*0-910884-11-0*); LC 58-5555. 1202p. 1959. 57.50 (*0-910884-07-2*) Libertarian Press.

— The Positive Theory of Capital. Smart, William, tr. LC 70-175689. (Select Bibliographies Reprint Ser.). 1977. reprint ed. 29.95 (*0-8369-6604-X*) Ayer.

— Shorter Classics. 370p. 1962. pap. 12.95 (*0-910884-12-9*) Libertarian Press.

Bohm-Bawerk, Eugen Von & Hilferding, Rudolph. Karl Marx & the Close of His System: Bohm-Bawerk's Criticism of Marx. Sweezy, Paul M., ed. xxx, 224p. 1984. reprint ed. pap. 14.95 (*0-87991-250-2*) Porcupine Pr.

Bohm, Bettina. Internationales Produkt-Design. (Europaische Hochschulschriften: Reibe 5: Reihe 5, Bd. 2262). (Illus.). XVII, 312p. 1998. pap. 56.95 (*3-631-32963-6*) P Lang Pubng.

Bohm, Bruce A. Introduction to Flavonoids. (Chemistry & Biochemistry of Organic Natural Products Ser.: Vol. 2). (Illus.). 496p. 1999. text 145.00 (*90-5702-353-9*, Harwood Acad Pubs) Gordon & Breach.

Bohm, C., et al. Theoretical Computer Science: Proceedings - 3rd Italian Conference. 436p. 1989. text 113.00 (*981-02-0070-6*) World Scientific Pub.

Bohm, Daivd. Wholeness & the Implicate Order. 240p. 1996. pap. 17.99 (*0-415-11966-9*) Routledge.

Bohm, David. Causality & Chance in Modern Physics. LC 57-28894. 128p. 1971. reprint ed. pap. 16.95 (*0-8122-1002-6*) U of Pa Pr.

— Quantum Theory. 655p. 1998. pap. 14.95 (*0-486-65969-0*) Dover.

***Bohm, David.** Science, Order & Creativity. 2nd ed. 320p. 2000. pap. 17.95 (*0-415-17183-0*); text 60.00 (*0-415-17182-2*) Routledge.

Bohm, David. The Special Theory of Relativity. LC 96-27226. 256p. 1996. pap. 18.99 (*0-415-14809-X*) Routledge.

— The Special Theory of Relativity. LC 96-27226. 256p. (C). 1996. 65.00 (*0-415-14808-1*) Routledge.

— The Special Theory of Relativity: Its Origins, Meanings, & Implications. 1979. text. write for info. (*0-8053-1001-0*) Addison-Wesley.

— Thought As a System. 272p. (C). 1994. 70.00 (*0-415-11980-4*); pap. 17.99 (*0-415-11030-0*, B4699) Routledge.

— Unfolding Meaning. 192p. 1996. pap. 17.99 (*0-415-13638-5*) Routledge.

— Wholeness & the Implicate Order. Date not set. pap. 14.95 (*0-7448-0000-5*) Routledge.

Bohm, David, reader. An Interview with David Bohm. unabridged ed. 1995. 10.95 incl. audio (*1-56176-913-4*, MYS-76913) Mystic Fire.

Bohm, David & Biederman, Charles. Bohm Biederman Correspondence: Creativity & Science, Vol. 1. LC 98-24759. (Illus.). 253p. 1999. 40.00 (*0-415-16225-4*) Routledge.

Bohm, David & Hiley, Basil. The Undivided Universe. 416p. (C). 1995. pap. 22.99 (*0-415-12185-X*) Routledge.

Bohm, David & Nichol, Lee. On Creativity. LC 97-29460. 160p. (C). 1998. 60.00 (*0-415-17395-7*); pap. 17.99 (*0-415-17396-5*) Routledge.

— On Dialogue. LC 96-20527. xviii, 101p. 1996. pap. 17.99 (*0-415-14912-6*) Routledge.

— On Dialogue. LC 96-20527. 128p. (C). 1996. 60.00 (*0-415-14911-8*) Routledge.

Bohm, David, jt. auth. see Krishnamurti, J.

Bohm, David, jt. auth. see Krishnamurti, Jiddu.

Bohm, Dieter, jt. ed. see Overbeck, Werner.

Bohm-Duchen, Monica. After Auschwitz: Responses to the Holocaust in Contemporary Art. (Illus.). 160p. 1995. pap. 39.95 (*0-85331-666-X*, Pub. by Lund Humphries) Antique Collect.

— Chagall. LC 98-229702. (Illus.). 352p. 1998. pap. 19.95 (*0-7148-3160-3*) Phaidon Pr.

— The Nude. (Artists & Themes Ser.). (Illus.). 64p. (Orig.). 1992. pap. 9.95 (*1-85759-004-X*) Scala Books.

— Walls & Windows: Colour Photographs by Dorothy Bohm. (Illus.). 1998. 30.00 (*0-85331-718-6*, Pub. by Lund Humphries) Antique Collect.

Bohm-Duchen, Monica, ed. Rubies & Rebels: Jewish Female Identity in Contemporary British Art. (Illus.). 96p. 1996. pap. 29.95 (*0-85331-703-8*, Pub. by Lund Humphries) Antique Collect.

Bohm, F. & Willumeit, H. P., eds. Tyre Models for Vehicle Dynamic Analysis: Proceedings of the 2nd International Colloquium, Held at the Technical University of Berlin, Germany, February 20-21, 1997, Germany. (Supplement Vehicle System Dynamics (VSD) Ser.: Vol. 27). 356p. 1997. 91.00 (*90-265-1488-3*) Swets.

Bohm, Fred C. & Swartout, Robert R., Jr., eds. Naval Surgeon in Yi Korea: The Journal of George W. Woods. LC 84-80605. (Korea Research Monographs: No. 10). (Illus.). 137p. (Orig.). 1984. pap. 12.00 (*0-912966-68-8*) IEAS.

Bohm, G. J., et al, eds. Pressure Vessels & Piping: Design & Analysis - A Decade of Progress, 4 vols. 1972. write for info. (*0-685-00843-6*, G00020) ASME.

Bohm, J. Akronyme und Abbreviata, Abkuerzungen Aus Naturwissenschaft und Technik---Acronyms & Abbreviations in Natural Science & Technology, Tiel 1. (Boden in Niedersachsen Ser.). (DUT & ENG.). vi, 65p. 1992. pap. 17.00 (*3-510-65151-0*, Pub. by E Schweizerbartsche) Balogh.

Bohm, Kristie & Council, Aaron. Greenville: An Economic Celebration. (Illus.). 240p. 1998. 39.00 (*1-885352-31-X*) Community Comm.

Bohm, M., et al, eds. From Hypertension to Heart Failure. LC 98-17988. (Illus.). 100p. 1998. pap. 60.00 (*3-540-63542-4*) Spr-Verlag.

Bohm, M. & Erdmann, Erland. Chronic Heart Failure. Riecker, G. et al, eds. LC 97-41344. (Illus.). 255p. 1998. pap. 54.00 (*3-540-63579-3*) Spr-Verlag.

Bohm, M. C. One-Dimensional Organometallic Materials. (Lecture Notes in Chemistry Ser.: Vol. 45). v, 180p. 1987. 32.95 (*0-387-17216-5*) Spr-Verlag.

Bohm, Maria. Angelus Silesius' "Cherubinischer Wandersmann" A Modern Reading with Selected Translations. LC 96-53918. (Renaissance & Baroque Studies & Texts: Vol. 22). (Illus.). XVI, 174p. (C). 1997. text 42.95 (*0-8204-3734-4*) P Lang Pubng.

Bohm, P., jt. ed. see Doerfler, W.

Bohm, Peter. Deposit-Refund Systems: Theory & Applications to Environmental, Conservation, & Consumer Policy. LC 81-47617. 175p. 1981. 29.95 (*0-8018-2706-X*) Resources Future.

— The Economics of Environmental Protection: Theory & Demand Revelation. LC 96-48050. (New Horizons in Environmental Economics Ser.). 400p. 1997. 100.00 (*1-85898-124-7*) E Elgar.

Bohm, Ralph C. & MacDonald. Power: Mechanics of Energy Control. 2nd ed. 1983. 39.47 (*0-02-672460-X*) Glencoe.

Bohm, Richard D., jt. auth. see Perkins, Roswell B.

Bohm, Robert. Kali Yuga. 13p. 1976. pap. 3.00 (*0-89924-003-8*) Lynx Hse.

— Notes on India. LC 81-51390. 244p. 1982. pap. 7.50 (*0-89608-125-7*) South End Pr.

Bohm, Robert A., ed. see Energy, Environment, & Resources Center, the Unive, et al.

Bohm, Robert M. Deathquest: An Introduction to the Theory & Practice of Capital Punishment in the United States. LC 98-50466. 1999. pap. 31.95 (*0-87084-212-9*) Anderson Pub Co.

Bohm, Robert M. A Primer on Crime & Delinquency. LC 96-21953. (Contemporary Issues in Crime & Justice Ser.). 180p. 1996. 32.95 (*0-534-50711-5*) Wadsworth Pub.

Bohm, Robert M. & Haley, Keith N. Introduction to Criminal Justice. 1996. teacher ed. write for info. (*0-02-800913-4*); student ed. 54.95 (*0-02-800911-8*) Glencoe.

Bohm, Robert M. & Haley, Keith N. Introduction to Criminal Justice. 2nd ed. LC 98-24208. 1998. 57.50 (*0-02-802823-6*); write for info. (*0-02-802824-4*) Glencoe.

***Bohm, Robert M. & Haley, Keith N.** Introduction to Criminal Justice. 2nd ed. LC 98-24208. xxv, 517p. 1999. write for info. (*0-02-805063-0*); text 52.00 incl. cd-rom (*0-02-802830-9*) Glencoe.

Bohm, Ronald J. & Templeton, Lee B. The Executive Guide to Video Teleconferencing. LC 84-45201. 156p. reprint ed. pap. 48.40 (*0-7837-3020-9*, 204292000006) Bks Demand.

Bohm-Vitense, Erika. Introduction to Stellar Astrophysics: Stellar Structure & Evolution. (Illus.). 285p. (C). 1992. pap. 30.95 (*0-521-34871-4*) Cambridge U Pr.

— Introduction to Stellar Astrophysics Vol. 1: Basic Stellar Observations & Data. (Illus.). 256p. (C). 1989. text 69.95 (*0-521-34402-6*); pap. text 30.95 (*0-521-34869-2*) Cambridge U Pr.

— Introduction to Stellar Astrophysics Vol. 2: Stellar Atmospheres. (Illus.). 264p. (C). 1989. pap. text 30.95 (*0-521-34870-6*) Cambridge U Pr.

— Introduction to Stellar Astrophysics Vol. 2: Stellar Atmospheres. (Illus.). 264p. (C). 1990. text 69.95 (*0-521-34403-4*) Cambridge U Pr.

— Introduction to Stellar Astrophysics Vol. 3: Stellar Structure & Evolution. (Illus.). 301p. (C). 1992. text 69.95 (*0-521-34404-2*) Cambridge U Pr.

Bohm, Werner. Chakras, Yoga & Consciousness: Balancing Your Life. LC 97-32879. Orig. Title: Chakras: Roots of Power. (Illus.). 144p. 1998. pap. 12.95 (*1-57863-041-X*) Weiser.

— Ross und Reiter. (Documenta Hippologica Ser.). (GER., Illus.). 254p. 1996. write for info. (*3-487-08373-6*) G Olms Pubs.

Bohm, Wolfgang. Biographisches Handbuch Zur Geschichte des Pflanzenbaus (Biographical Handbook of the History of Plant Cultivation) ix, 398p. 1997. write for info. (*3-598-11324-2*) K G Saur Verlag.

Bohman, James. New Philosophy of Social Science: Problems of Indeterminacy. 288p. 1993. pap. text 17.50 (*0-262-52183-0*) MIT Pr.

— Public Deliberation: Pluralism, Complexity, & Democracy. LC 96-599. (Studies in Contemporary German Social Thought). (Illus.). 320p. (C). 1996. 35.50 (*0-262-02410-1*) MIT Pr.

***Bohman, James.** Public Deliberation: Pluralism, Complexity & Democracy. LC 96-599. (Studies in Contemporary German Social Thought). (Illus.). 320p. 2000. reprint ed. pap. 17.00 (*0-262-52278-0*) MIT Pr.

Bohman, James, et al, eds. Deliberative Democracy: Essays on Reason & Politics. LC 97-8350. (Illus.). 480p. 1997. pap. text 25.00 (*0-262-52241-1*) MIT Pr.

Bohman, James & Lutz-Bachmann, Matthias, eds. Perpetual Peace: Essays on Kant's Cosmopolitan Ideal. LC 96-37739. (Studies in Contemporary German Social Thought). (Illus.). 272p. 1997. 38.50 (*0-262-02428-4*) MIT Pr.

Bohman, James & Lutz-Bachmann, Matthias, eds. Perpetual Peace: Essays on Kant's Cosmopolitan Ideal. LC 96-37739. (Studies in Contemporary German Social Thought). (Illus.). 272p. 1997. pap. text 19.50 (*0-262-52235-7*) MIT Pr.

Bohman, James & Rehg, William, eds. Deliberative Democracy: Essays on Reason & Politics. LC 97-8350. (Illus.). 480p. 1997. 50.00 (*0-262-02434-9*) MIT Pr.

Bohman, James, tr. see Peukert, Helmut.

Bohman, Jenny, tr. see Sjoman, Vilgot.

Bohman, Svante. The Problems of the Innermost Self: A Psychological & Conceptanalytical Study Along with Some Parapsychological Reflections. 114p. (Orig.). 1988. pap. 28.50 (*91-22-01270-2*) Coronet Bks.

— What Is Concept Analysis? 79p. (Orig.). 1992. pap. 33.00 (*91-22-01479-9*) Coronet Bks.

— What Is Intelligence? 148p. (Orig.). 1980. pap. 33.00 (*91-22-00404-1*) Coronet Bks.

Bohman, Sven-Olof, jt. ed. see Mandal, Anil K.

***Bohme, Caroline & Wharton, Rona B.** Women's Health under 40: What You Should Know. (Your Health). (Illus.). 196p. 2000. pap. 6.99 (*1-55870-554-6*, Betrwy Bks) F & W Pubns Inc.

***Bohme, Caroline, et al.** Women's Health over 40: What You Should Know. (Your Health). (Illus.). 196p. 2000. pap. 6.99 (*1-55870-555-4*, Betrwy Bks) F & W Pubns Inc.

Bohme, Diethard K. & Herbst, Eric, eds. Chemistry & Spectroscopy of Interstellar Molecules. (Illus.). 310p. 1990. 100.00 (*0-86008-465-5*, Pub. by U of Tokyo) Col U Pr.

Bohme, E., et al, eds. Astronomy & Astrophysics Abstracts, Vol. 42: Literature, 1986, Pt. 2. 1130p. 1987. 182.95 (*0-387-17898-8*) Spr-Verlag.

Bohme, Franz M., jt. auth. see Erk, Ludwig.

Bohme, Frederick G. A History of the Italians in New Mexico. LC 74-17920. (Italian American Experience Ser.). (Illus.). 304p. 1975. 57.00 (*0-405-06393-8*) Ayer.

Bohme, G. Non-Newtonian Fluid Mechanics. (North-Holland Series in Applied Mathematics & Mechanics: Vol. 31). xii, 352p. 1987. 162.60 (*0-444-70186-9*, North Holland) Elsevier.

Bohme, Gernot & Stehr, Nico, eds. The Knowledge Society. 1986. pap. text 73.50 (*90-277-2306-0*); lib. bdg. 110.00 (*90-277-2305-2*) Kluwer Academic.

Bohme, H., et al. Zur Chemie Durch Halogene, Stickstoff Oder Sauerstoff Substituierter Organischer Schwefelverbindungen, Vol. 6. Senning, Alexander, ed. (Sulfer Reports: Vol. 6, No. 4). (GER.). 120p. 1986. pap. text 110.00 (*3-7186-0365-9*) Gordon & Breach.

Bohme, Klaus-Richard. The Defense Policies of the Nordic Countries, 1918-1939. Krosby, H. Peter, tr. from SWE. 80p. (Orig.). 1979. pap. text 25.95 (*0-89126-073-0*) MA-AH Pub.

— Growth of the Swedish Aircraft Industry, 1918-1945. 200p. 1987. pap. text 12.00 (*0-89745-098-1*) Sunflower U Pr.

Bohme, R. Inventory of World Topographic Mapping: South America, Central America & Africa, Vol. 2. (International Cartographic Association Ser.). 524p. 1991. 360.00 (*1-85166-661-3*, Pergamon Pr) Elsevier.

Bohme, R., compiled by. Inventory of World Topographic Mapping: The International Cartographic Association, 3 vols. 1993. 781.50 (*0-08-042414-7*, Pergamon Pr) Elsevier.

— Inventory of World Topographic Mapping: Western Europe, North America & Australasia, Vol. 1. 196p. 1989. 228.50 (*1-85166-357-6*) Elsevier.

Bohme, Robert. Orpheus - Das Alter der Kitharoden. 140p. write for info. (*3-296-10900-5*) G Olms Pubs.

Bohme, S., et al, eds. Literature, 1985, Pt. 1. (Astronomy & Astrophysics Abstracts Ser.: Vol. 39). 1048p. 1985. 158.95 (*0-387-16032-9*) Spr-Verlag.

— Literature, 1985, Pt. 2. (Astronomy & Astrophysics Abstracts Ser.: Vol. 40). 1100p. 1986. 158.95 (*0-387-16655-6*) Spr-Verlag.

— Literature, 1984, Pt. 2. Zech, G., tr. (Astronomy & Astrophysics Abstracts Ser.: Vol. 38). 920p. 1985. 151.95 (*0-387-15562-7*) Spr-Verlag.

— Literature, 1987, Pt. 1. (Astronomy & Astrophysics Abstracts Ser.). 1200p. 1988. 182.95 (*0-387-18640-9*) Spr-Verlag.

— Literature, 1987, Pt. 2. (Astronomy & Astrophysics Abstracts Ser.: Vol. 44). 1300p. 1988. 206.95 (*0-387-19283-2*) Spr-Verlag.

— Literature, 1986, Part 1. (Astronomy & Astrophysics Abstracts Ser.: Vol. 41). 1100p. 1986. 158.95 (*0-387-17252-1*) Spr-Verlag.

— Literature, 1983, Pt. 2. (Astronomy & Astrophysics Abstracts Ser.: Vol. 34). 960p. 1984. 151.95 (*0-387-13485-9*) Spr-Verlag.

Bohme, Ulrich. Evangelischer Religionsunterricht in Hilfsschulen und Anstalten des 19. und Beginnenden 20. Jahrhunderts Im Nordlichen Deutschland. (Europaische Hochschulschriften Ser.: Reihe 23, Bd. 384). (GER., Illus.). 268p. 1990. 56.80 (*3-631-40759-9*) P Lang Pubng.

Bohmer, C. W. Gear Lubrication. (Technical Papers: Vol. P176). (Illus.). 19p. (Orig.). 1938. pap. text 30.00 incl. audio compact disk (*1-55589-355-4*) AGMA.

***Bohmer, Carol.** The Wages of Seeking Help: Sexual Exploitation by Professionals. LC 99-45991. 224p. 2000. write for info. (*0-275-96793-X*) Greenwood.

***Bohmer, John.** How to Buy a Forklift, Forklift 101. (Illus.). 150p. 1999. pap. 39.95 (*0-9643958-4-3*) Assoctd W Palm Bch.

Bohmer, K. & Stetter, H. J., eds. Defect Correction Methods. (Computing Ser.: Suppl. 5). (Illus.). 240p. 1985. 59.95 (*0-387-81832-4*) Spr-Verlag.

Bohmer, M., jt. auth. see Kuzvart, M.

Bohmer, M., jt. ed. see Becker, Martin.

Bohmer, V., jt. ed. see Vicens, Jacques.

***Bohmer, Whitney & Collier-Stone, Kay.** Singular Spirituality. 128p. 1999. pap. 11.95 (*0-8192-1764-6*, 2507) Morehouse Pub.

Bohmerova, Ada. Slovak for You: Slovak for Speakers of English. LC 96-15124. (SLO., Illus.). 143p. 1996. pap. 30.00 (*0-86516-331-6*) Bolchazy-Carducci.

Bohmert, Heinz. Plastic & Reconstructive Surgery of the Breast: A Surgical Atlas. LC 96-33255. (Illus.). 2388p. 1996. text 199.00 (*0-86577-628-8*) Thieme Med Pubs.

Bohmert, Heinz, et al. Breast Cancer. (Illus.). 535p. 1989. text 139.00 (*0-86577-326-2*) Thieme Med Pubs.

Bohmisch, Franz & Tagliacarne, ierfelice, eds. Gunter Krinetzki: Rechtsprechung und Amt Im Deuteronomium. (GER.). 300p. 1993. 55.95 (*3-631-46472-X*) P Lang Pubng.

Bohmont. Standard Pesticide User's Guide. 5th ed. LC 98-51775. 544p. 1999. 98.00 (*0-13-679192-1*) P-H.

Bohn & MacDonald. Energy Technology: Power & Transportation. 4th ed. (Illus.). 288p. (YA). (gr. 6-12). 1999. student ed., wbk. ed. 8.87 (*0-02-675402-9*) Glencoe.

— Energy Technology: Power & Transportation, Instructor's Resource Guide. 4th ed. 304p. 1999. teacher ed. 44.40 (*0-02-676500-4*) Glencoe.

Bohn, Babbette. The Illustrated Bartsch Vol. 39-1 Commentary: Italian Masters of the Sixteenth Century. 1996. lib. bdg. 149.00 (*0-89835-138-3*) Abaris Bks.

Bohn, Babbette, ed. The Illustrated Bartsch Vol. 39-2, Commentary: Italian Masters of the Sixteenth Century. 1997. lib. bdg. 149.00 (*0-89835-280-0*) Abaris Bks.

Bohn, Babbette & Bohlin, Diane D., eds. The Illustrated Bartsch Vol. 39-1: Italian Masters of the Sixteenth Century. 1980. lib. bdg. 149.00 (*0-89835-039-5*) Abaris Bks.

Bohn, Carole R., jt. ed. see Brown, Joanne C.

Bohn, Cynthia N., ed. see Leach, Nicky.

Bohn, Dave. East of These Golden Shores: Architecture of the Earlier Days in Contra Costa & Alameda Counties. (Illus.). 124p. 1971. pap. 7.50 (*0-937106-00-3*) Ross Valley.

Bohn, Dave & Petschek, Rodolfo. Kinsey, Photographer: A Half Century of Negatives by Darius & Tabitha May Kinsey. (Illus.). 320p. 1975. boxed set 150.00 (*0-685-52668-2*) Ross Valley.

— Kinsey, Photographer: A Half Century of Negatives by Darius & Tabitha May Kinsey, 1. (Illus.). 320p. 1975. write for info. (*0-937106-01-1*) Ross Valley.

— Kinsey, Photographer: A Half Century of Negatives by Darius & Tabitha May Kinsey, 2. (Illus.). 320p. 1975. write for info. (*0-937106-02-X*) Ross Valley.

— Kinsey, Photographer: The Locomotive Portraits. (Illus.). 144p. 1997. 19.98 (*1-884822-65-7*) Blck Dog & Leventhal.

— Kinsey, Photographer: The Locomotive Portraits. (Illus.). 320p. 1984. 40.00 (*0-87701-319-5*) Chronicle Bks.

— Kinsey, Photographer: The Locomotive Portraits. (Illus.). 320p. 1988. pap. 22.95 (*0-87701-558-9*) Chronicle Bks.

Bohn, Dave, jt. auth. see Millman, Mary.

Bohn, Dave, ed. see Cramer, T. Dudley.

Bohn, Diana. Who Was Jesus? (Great Big Bks.). (Illus.). 16p. (J). (gr. k-1). 1995. pap. 14.95 (*0-687-07067-8*) Abingdon.

Bohn, Diana M. Islands of the Rainbow: An Indonesian Adventure. LC 98-5339. (J). 1998. 5.90 (*0-377-00323-9*) Friendship Pr.

— Teacher's Guide to "Islands of the Rainbow" An Indonesian Adventure. (Illus.). 32p. 1998. pap., teacher ed. 4.95 (*0-377-00324-7*) Friendship Pr.

Bohn, Diana M. Who Was Jesus? Leader's Guide. (J). (gr. k-1). 1.50 (*0-687-05387-0*) Abingdon.

Bohn, Dieora & Schneider, Jill L., eds. Alaska's Mineral Resources: Annual Report 1992. (Illus.). 65p. (Orig.). (C). 1993. pap. text 25.00 (*1-56806-571-X*) DIANE Pub.

Bohn, Dorothy, jt. auth. see Schumacher, Alice.

Bohn, Earl, jt. auth. see Marcello, Beth.

Bohn, Emil. Bibliographie der Musik-Druckwerke Bis 1700. vii, 450p. 1969. reprint ed. 130.00 (*0-318-71745-X*) G Olms Pubs.

***Bohn, Frank.** Monetary Union & Fiscal Stability: A New Approach. LC 99-87533. (Contributions to Economics Ser.). (Illus.). xiv, 225p. 2000. pap. 63.00 (*3-7908-1266-8*, Pub. by Physica-Verlag) Spr-Verlag.

Bohn, Greg. Slip Bobbering. 3rd ed. (Secrets of a Northwoods Walleye Guide Ser.). (Illus.). 64p. 1990. 6.95 (*0-685-48129-8*) Fishing Hot.

— Weeds 'n Walleyes. LC 92-74158. (Secrets of a Northwoods Walleye Guide Ser.: Vol. 3). 1989. write for info. (*0-939314-51-7*) Fishing Hot.

— Workin' the Wood. (Secrets of a Northwoods Walleye Guide Ser.). (Illus.). 64p. 1989. pap. 6.95 (*0-939314-50-9*) Fishing Hot.

Bohn, Henry G. Biography & Bibliography of Shakespeare. LC 74-38033. reprint ed. 49.50 (*0-404-00920-4*) AMS Pr.

— A Catalogue of Books: The Famous "Guinea Catalogue" LC 74-8717. reprint ed. 205.00 (*0-404-11610-8*) AMS Pr.

— Handbook of Proverbs. LC 68-55795. (Bohn's Antiquarian Library). reprint ed. 27.50 (*0-404-50003-X*) AMS Pr.

— Polyglot of Foreign Proverbs. LC 68-55796. (Bohn's Antiquarian Library). reprint ed. 27.50 (*0-404-50004-8*) AMS Pr.

Bohn, Henry G., tr. see Schiller, Friedrich.

Bohn, Henry G., tr. see Von Humboldt, Alexander.

Bohn, Hinrich L., et al. Soil Chemistry. 2nd ed. LC 85-3221. 360p. 1985. 110.00 (*0-471-82217-5*) Wiley.

Bohn, John T. & Jefferson, James W. Lithium & Manic Depression: A Guide. rev. ed. 31p. 1999. pap. 4.95 (*1-890802-18-2*) Madison Inst of Med.

Bohn, John T., jt. auth. see Polmar, Norman.

Bohn, Joyce, ed. see Tiner, John.

***Bohn, Parker, III & Brunswick Pro Staff.** Bowling: How to Master the Game. 2000. pap. 29.95 (*0-7893-0494-5*) Universe.

Bohn, Paul T. A Charging Rhino Will Make Your Heart Sing. 233p. 1999. pap. 8.95 (*0-7880-1445-5*, Fairway Pr) CSS OH.

Bohn, Rainer & Schreiter, Ina. Sprachspielereien Fur Deutschlernende. 168p. 1993. 15.95 (*3-324-00483-7*) Langenscheidt.

Bohn, Ralph C. Energy Technology Power & Transportation. 1991. 28.98 (*0-02-675401-0*) Glencoe.

Bohn, Ralph Paul. "C'mon God, Let's Have a Little Wind" And Other Theological Strories. LC 98-93105. 108p. (Orig.). 1998. pap. 10.95 (*0-9664472-0-4*) AMBI Pr.

Bohn, Richard N. Sales Automation Software Compendium. 330p. (Orig.). 1995. pap. text 97.00 (*1-885413-00-9*) Denali Grp.

Bohn, Robert, et al. Archiv und Geschichte im Ostseeraum: Festschrift fur Sten Korner. (Studia Septemtrionalia: Bd. 3). (GER., Illus.). 343p. 1997. 57.95 (*3-631-31231-8*) P Lang Pubng.

Bohn, Ronald C., jt. auth. see Jakoi, Emma R.

Bohn, Thomas W. An Historical & Descriptive Analysis of the Why We Fight Series: With a New Introduction. 1977. 20.95 (*0-405-09885-5*, 11480) Ayer.

Bohn, Thomas W. & Stromgren, Richard L. Light & Shadows: A History of Motion Pictures. 3rd ed. LC 86-61131. xlv, 427p. (C). 1987. pap. text 51.95 (*0-87484-702-8*, 702) Mayfield Pub.

Bohn, U. & Neuhausl, R., eds. Vegetation & Flora of Temperate Zones. (Illus.). viii, 83p. 1990. pap. 35.00 (*90-5103-034-7*, Pub. by SPB Acad Pub) Balogh.

Bohn, Willard. The Aesthetics of Visual Poetry, 1914-1928. (Illus.). 240p. 1986. text 69.95 (*0-521-30697-3*) Cambridge U Pr.

— The Aesthetics of Visual Poetry, 1914-1928. (Illus.). 248p. 1993. pap. text 14.95 (*0-226-06325-9*) U Ch Pr.

— Apollinaire & the Faceless Man: The Creation & Evolution of a Modern Motif. LC 90-55161. (Illus.). 176p. 1991. 32.50 (*0-8386-3416-8*) Fairleigh Dickinson.

— Apollinaire & the International Avant-Garde. LC 96-11930. (SUNY Series, The Margins of Literature). 320p. (C). 1997. text 75.50 (*0-7914-3195-9*); pap. text 24.95 (*0-7914-3196-7*) State U NY Pr.

— Apollinaire, Visual Poetry, & Art Criticism. LC 91-59059. (Illus.). 272p. 1993. 42.50 (*0-8387-5226-8*) Bucknell U Pr.

***Bohn, Willard.** Modern Visual Poetry. LC 99-55924. 2000. write for info. (*0-87413-710-1*) U Delaware Pr.

Bohn, Willard, tr. The Dada Market: An Anthology of Poetry. LC 91-45283. (Illus.). 224p. (C). 1993. 35.95 (*0-8093-1818-0*); pap. 16.95 (*0-8093-1819-9*) S Ill U Pr.

Bohnaker, Joseph J. Of Arms I Sing: A Novel. Smith, James C., Jr., ed. LC 89-34611. (Illus.). 260p. (Orig.). 1989. pap. 10.95 (*0-86534-136-2*) Sunstone Pr.

Bohne, Harald & VanIerssel, Harry. Publishing: The Creative Business. LC 72-96455. 100p. reprint ed. pap. 31.00 (*0-608-18596-5*, 202045600018) Bks Demand.

Bohnecke, G. The Principles of Measuring Currents. 28p. 1955. write for info. (*0-318-61387-5*) Intl Assoc Phys Sci Ocean.

Bohnecke, Gunther. Temperature, Salinity & Density of the Surface Waters of the Atlantic Ocean Vol. 5: Scientific Results of the German Atlantic Expedition of the Research Vessel "Meteor", 1925-1927, Atlas, Vol. 5. Date, N. P., tr. from GER.Tr. of Temperatur, Salzgehalt und Dichte an der Oberflache des Atlantischen Ozeans. (Illus.). 172p. 1992. 149.00 (*90-5410-238-1*, Pub. by A A Balkema) Ashgate Pub Co.

Bohnen, Michael J. & Coggins, Dana. Massachusetts Corporate Forms, 2 vols. 1260p. 1994. suppl. ed. 35.00 (*0-318-71301-2*, MICHIE) LEXIS Pub.

— Massachusetts Corporate Forms, 2 vols., Set. 1260p. 1989. ring bd. 290.00 incl. disk (*0-8342-0043-0*, 81450-10, MICHIE) LEXIS Pub.

Bohnen, Michael J., jt. auth. see Coggins, Dana C.

***Bohnenblust, Stephen E.** Basic Statistics for the Health Sciences. 4th ed. LC 00-38006. 2000. pap. write for info. (*0-7674-1752-6*) Mayfield Pub.

Bohnenkamp, Gwen. From the Cat's Point of View: The Complete Book on Cat Behavior. 48p. 1991. pap. text 11.95 (*0-9644601-1-4*) Perfect Paws.

— Help! My Dog Has an Attitude. 192p. 1994. pap. 17.95 (*0-9644601-2-2*) Perfect Paws.

— Manners for the Modern Dog. 34p. 1990. pap. text 9.95 (*0-9644601-0-6*) Perfect Paws.

Bohnenkamp, Klaus E. Die Horazische Strophe. Studien Zur "Lex Meinekiana" (Spudasmata Ser.: Bd. XXX). (GER.). ix, 385p. 1972. 65.00 (*3-487-04204-5*) G Olms Pubs.

Bohner, Charles. Bold Journey: West with Lewis & Clark. LC 84-19328. (Illus.). 171p. (J). (gr. 5 up). 1985. pap. 6.95 (*0-395-54978-7*) HM.

— Robert Penn Warren. rev. ed. (United States Authors Ser.). 176p. (C). 1981. 22.95 (*0-8057-7345-2*, Twyne) Mac Lib Ref.

Bohner, Charles H. Bold Journey: West with Lewis & Clark: A Novel. (J). 1985. 12.05 (*0-606-04618-6*, Pub. by Turtleback) Demco.

— John Pendleton Kennedy: Gentleman from Baltimore. LC 61-10735. (Illus.). 282p. reprint ed. pap. 87.50 (*0-608-14665-X*, 202583200046) Bks Demand.

Bohner, Charles H. & Dougherty, Dean. Short Fiction: Classic & Contemporary. 4th ed. LC 98-18939. 1264p. 1998. pap. text 49.00 (*0-13-460049-5*) P-H.

Bohner, H. O., ed. Light Metals, 1985: Proceedings of the Technical Sessions. LC 84-29479. (Illus.). 1543p. reprint ed. pap. 200.00 (*0-608-17838-1*, 203259900080) Bks Demand.

Bohner, Jean A., jt. auth. see Hoffmeir, Patricia A.

***Bohner, Olivine Nadeau.** 27 Reasons Why We Don't Have to Be Afraid. LC 99-91080. 1999. 25.00 (*0-7388-0604-8*); pap. 18.00 (*0-7388-0605-6*) Xlibris Corp.

Bohner, Shawn, jt. auth. see Arnold, Robert.

Bohnert, Joachim. Grundrib des Ordnungswidrigkeitenrechts. x,128p. 1996. write for info. (*3-11-014678-9*) De Gruyter.

***Bohnet, Jeanne.** Living Between Heaven & Earth: And Other Everyday Miracles. Carnahan, Martha, ed. (Illus.). 99p. 1999. pap. 18.00 (*0-9665926-0-3*, 1001, Pub. by Rising Phoenix) ACCESS Pubs Network.

Bohnhoff, James. The Walker's Log: Calendar & Journal. 96p. 1998. spiral bd. 9.95 (*1-885061-05-6*) Adventure Pubns.

Bohnhoff, Maya K. The Spirit Gate. 352p. 1996. per. 5.99 (*0-671-87712-7*) Baen Bks.

Bohnhorst, Ben. Desent from the Cross. 24p. (Orig.). 1995. pap. text 6.00 (*1-56439-048-9*) Ridgeway.

— Perfume & Tears. 24p. (Orig.). 1995. pap. text 6.00 (*1-56439-050-0*) Ridgeway.

— Raking the Gravel. 32p. (Orig.). 1992. pap. text 5.00 (*1-56439-024-1*) Ridgeway.

***Bohnhorst, Ben.** Rolling Home & Entering the Valley Bk. II: And Other Poems. LC 99-91223. 1999. 25.00 (*0-7388-0682-X*); pap. 18.00 (*0-7388-0683-8*) Xlibris Corp.

***Bohnhorst, Jill.** Gentechnologie in der Haftpflichtversicherung. (Versicherungsrechtliche Studien. : Bd. 61). 205p. 1999. 37.95 (*3-631-35405-3*) P Lang Pubng.

***Bohning, D.** Computer Assisted Analysis of Mixtures. LC 99-10833. 260p. 1999. boxed set 69.95 (*0-8493-0385-0*, Chap & Hall CRC) CRC Pr.

***Bohning, Dankmar.** Computer Assisted Analysis of Mixtures & Applications: Meta Analysis, Disease Mapping & Others. (Monographs on Statistics & Applied Probability). 248p. 1999. boxed set 69.95 (*1-58488-179-8*, Chap & Hall CRC) CRC Pr.

Bohning, I., ed. Autonome Architekur und Partizipatorisches Bauen. (GER.). 356p. (C). 1981. 65.00 (*0-8176-1260-2*) Birkhauser.

Bohning, W. R. Employing Foreign Workers: A Manual on Policies & Procedures of Special Interest to Middle- & Low-Income Countries. LC 97-109777. xi, 97p. 1996. pap. 18.00 (*92-2-109453-7*) Intl Labour Office.

***Bohnke, F., ed.** Cochlear Mechanics. (ORL Ser.: Vol. 61, No. 5). (Illus.). 88p. 1999. pap. 34.00 (*3-8055-6988-2*) S Karger.

Bohnsack, Bill. Fables of Joseph Cole. 100p. (Orig.). (J). 1996. pap. 7.00 (*1-57502-193-5*, D0821) Morris Pubng.

— I Knew Them...Well! Two Short Novels. 130p. (Orig.). 1997. pap. 5.95 (*1-57502-426-8*, PO1305) Morris Pubng.

Bohnsack, Bill, jt. auth. see Helgeson, Lars J.

Bohnsack, G. The Solubility of Magnetite in Water & in Aqueous Solutions of Acid & Alkali. 161p. 1988. 106.00 (*0-89116-831-1*) Hemisp Pub.

Bohnsack, William H. Now! with Emotion. 80p. (Orig.). 1996. pap. 5.95 (*1-57502-327-X*, P01098) Morris Pubng.

Boholin, E., ed. Telecommunications Transformation: Technology, Strategy & Policy. LC 97-77020. 396p. Date not set. 99.00 (*90-5199-366-8*, 366-8) IOS Press.

Boholm, Asa. The Doge of Venice: The Symbolism of State Power in the Renaissance. (University of Gothenburg Institute for Advanced Studies in Social Anthropology). (Illus.). 298p. (Orig.). 1990. pap. 99.50 (*91-630-0135-7*) Coronet Bks.

Bohon, Serenity. Pearly Days - Oyster Days. (Fresh Perspective Ser.: Vol. 2). 23p. 1998. pap. 3.50 (*0-9660886-3-8*) Scribbles & Scribes.

***Bohon, Stephanie.** Latinos in Ethnic Enclaves: Immigrant Workers & the Competition for Jobs. LC 00-39314. (Latino Communities Ser.). 2000. pap. write for info. (*0-8153-3765-5*) Garland.

Bohor, Bruce F. & Triplehorn, Don M. Tonsteins: Altered Volcanic Ash Layers in Coal-Bearing Sequences. LC 93-17797. (Special Papers: No. 285). 1993. pap. 12.00 (*0-8137-2285-3*) Geol Soc.

Bohr, Aage & Mottelson, Ben R. Nuclear Structure. LC 97-51929. 1998. 86.00 (*981-02-3979-3*); 86.00 (*981-02-3980-7*) World Scientific Pub.

— Nuclear Structure: Single-Particle Motion, Nuclear Deformations. LC 97-51929. 1256p. 1997. text 86.00 (*981-02-3197-0*) World Scientific Pub.

Bohr, Annette. Uzbekistan: Politics & Foreign Policy. 60p. 1998. pap. 12.95 (*1-86203-081-2*, Pub. by Royal Inst Intl Affairs) Brookings.

Bohr, D. F., ed. see U. S. - Japan Cooperative Symposium Staff.

Bohr, David. Catholic Moral Tradition: "In Christ, a New Creation" 2nd rev. ed. LC 98-67324. 368p. 1999. pap. 19.95 (*0-87973-931-2*) Our Sunday Visitor.

Bohr, David F., et al, eds. Handbook of Physiology: Section 2, The Cardiovascular System, Vol. II: Vascular Smooth Muscle. (American Physiological Society Book). (Illus.). 694p. 1988. text 110.00 (*0-19-520664-9*) OUP.

Bohr, Deborah, jt. ed. see Longo, Daniel R.

Bohr, H. & Brunak, Soren. Protein Structure by Distance Analysis. LC 94-75946. (YA). (gr. 12). 1994. 82.00 (*90-5199-161-4*) IOS Press.

Bohr, Harald. Almost Periodic Functions. LC 47-5500. 1980. 12.00 (*0-8284-0027-X*) Chelsea Pub.

***Bohr, Harry J.** Teenage Hobos: A Memoir. LC 97-91151. (Illus.). 1998. write for info. (*0-932970-87-7*) Prinit Pr.

Bohr, Heather K. Realife, 4 bks., Set. unabridged ed. Unterseher, Thomas & Unterseher, Thomas E., eds. (JPN.). 127p. (Orig.). 1993. pap., pap. text 89.99 incl. audio (*1-57237-045-9*); pap., pap. text 89.99 incl. audio (*1-57237-046-7*); pap. text 89.99 incl. audio (*1-57237-044-0*); pap. text 89.99 incl. audio (*1-57237-047-5*) Cultural Designs.

— Realife Business. unabridged ed. Unterseher, Thomas & Unterseher, Thomas E., eds. (SPA.). 32p. 1993. pap., pap. text 22.99 incl. audio (*1-57237-026-2*); pap., pap. text 22.99 incl. audio (*1-57237-030-0*); pap., pap. text 22.99 incl. audio (*1-57237-034-3*); pap., pap. text 22.99 incl. audio (*1-57237-038-6*); pap., pap. text 22.99 incl. audio (*1-57237-042-4*) Cultural Designs.

— Realife Business: With Cantonese CD. unabridged ed. Unterseher, Thomas & Unterseher, Thomas E., eds. 32p. 1993. pap. text 29.99 incl. audio compact disk (*1-57237-009-2*) Cultural Designs.

— Realife Business: With Japanese CD. unabridged ed. Unterseher, Thomas & Unterseher, Thomas E., eds. (JPN.). 32p. 1993. pap. text 29.99 incl. audio compact disk (*1-57237-005-X*) Cultural Designs.

— Realife Business: With Korean CD. unabridged ed. Unterseher, Thomas & Unterseher, Thomas E., eds. (KOR.). 32p. 1993. pap. text 29.99 incl. audio compact disk (*1-57237-021-1*) Cultural Designs.

— Realife Business: With Mandarin CD. unabridged ed. Unterseher, Thomas & Unterseher, Thomas E., eds. 32p. 1993. pap. text 29.99 incl. audio compact disk (*1-57237-013-0*) Cultural Designs.

B

— Realife Business: With Spanish CD. unabridged ed. Unterseher, Thomas & Unterseher, Thomas E., eds. (SPA.). 32p. 1993. pap. text 29.99 incl. audio compact disk (*1-57237-001-7*) Cultural Designs.

— Realife Entertainment. unabridged ed. Unterseher, Thomas & Unterseher, Thomas E., eds. (SPA.). 32p. 1993. pap., pap. text 22.99 incl. audio (*1-57237-025-4*); pap., pap. text 22.99 incl. audio (*1-57237-029-7*); pap., pap. text 22.99 incl. audio (*1-57237-033-5*); pap., pap. text 22.99 incl. audio (*1-57237-037-8*); pap., pap. text 22.99 incl. audio (*1-57237-041-6*) Cultural Designs.

— Realife Entertainment: With Cantonese CD. unabridged ed. Unterseher, Thomas & Unterseher, Thomas E., eds. 32p. 1993. pap. text 29.99 incl. audio compact disk (*1-57237-008-4*) Cultural Designs.

— Realife Entertainment: With Japanese CD. unabridged ed. Unterseher, Thomas & Unterseher, Thomas E., eds. (JPN.). 32p. 1993. pap. text 29.99 incl. audio compact disk (*1-57237-004-1*) Cultural Designs.

— Realife Entertainment: With Korean CD. unabridged ed. Unterseher, Thomas & Unterseher, Thomas E., eds. (KOR.). 32p. 1993. pap. text 29.99 incl. audio compact disk (*1-57237-020-3*) Cultural Designs.

— Realife Entertainment: With Mandarin CD. unabridged ed. Unterseher, Thomas & Unterseher, Thomas E., eds. 32p. 1993. pap. text 29.99 incl. audio compact disk (*1-57237-012-2*) Cultural Designs.

— Realife Entertainment: With Spanish CD. unabridged ed. Unterseher, Thomas & Unterseher, Thomas E., eds. (SPA.). 32p. 1993. pap. text 29.99 incl. audio compact disk (*1-57237-000-9*) Cultural Designs.

— Realife Etiquette. unabridged ed. Unterseher, Thomas & Unterseher, Thomas E., eds. (SPA.). 31p. 1993. pap., pap. text 22.99 incl. audio (*1-57237-027-0*); pap., pap. text 22.99 incl. audio (*1-57237-031-9*); pap., pap. text 22.99 incl. audio (*1-57237-035-1*); pap., pap. text 22.99 incl. audio (*1-57237-039-4*); pap., pap. text 22.99 incl. audio (*1-57237-048-3*) Cultural Designs.

— Realife Etiquette: With Cantonese CD. unabridged ed. Unterseher, Thomas & Unterseher, Thomas E., eds. 31p. 1993. pap. text 29.99 incl. audio compact disk (*1-57237-010-6*) Cultural Designs.

— Realife Etiquette: With Japanese CD. unabridged ed. Unterseher, Thomas & Unterseher, Thomas E., eds. (JPN.). 31p. 1993. pap. text 29.99 incl. audio compact disk (*1-57237-006-8*) Cultural Designs.

— Realife Etiquette: With Korean CD. unabridged ed. Unterseher, Thomas & Unterseher, Thomas E., eds. (KOR.). 31p. 1993. pap. text 29.99 incl. audio compact disk (*1-57237-022-X*) Cultural Designs.

— Realife Etiquette: With Mandarin CD. unabridged ed. Unterseher, Thomas & Unterseher, Thomas E., eds. 31p. 1993. pap. text 29.99 incl. audio compact disk (*1-57237-014-9*) Cultural Designs.

— Realife Etiquette: With Spanish CD. unabridged ed. Unterseher, Thomas & Unterseher, Thomas E., eds. (SPA.). 31p. 1993. pap. text 29.99 incl. audio compact disk (*1-57237-002-5*) Cultural Designs.

— Realife Relationships. unabridged ed. Unterseher, Thomas & Unterseher, Thomas E., eds. (SPA.). 32p. 1993. pap., pap. text 22.99 incl. audio (*1-57237-028-9*); pap., pap. text 22.99 incl. audio (*1-57237-032-7*); pap., pap. text 22.99 incl. audio (*1-57237-036-X*); pap., pap. text 22.99 incl. audio (*1-57237-040-8*); pap., pap. text 22.99 incl. audio (*1-57237-049-1*) Cultural Designs.

— Realife Relationships: With Cantonese CD. unabridged ed. Unterseher, Thomas & Unterseher, Thomas E., eds. 32p. 1993. pap. text 29.99 incl. audio compact disk (*1-57237-011-4*) Cultural Designs.

— Realife Relationships: With Japanese CD. unabridged ed. Unterseher, Thomas & Unterseher, Thomas E., eds. (JPN.). 32p. 1993. pap. text 29.99 incl. audio compact disk (*1-57237-007-6*) Cultural Designs.

— Realife Relationships: With Korean CD. unabridged ed. Unterseher, Thomas & Unterseher, Thomas E., eds. (KOR.). 32p. 1993. pap. text 29.99 incl. audio compact disk (*1-57237-023-8*) Cultural Designs.

— Realife Relationships: With Mandarin CD. unabridged ed. Unterseher, Thomas & Unterseher, Thomas E., eds. 32p. 1993. pap. text 29.99 incl. audio compact disk (*1-57237-015-7*) Cultural Designs.

— Realife Relationships: With Spanish CD. unabridged ed. Unterseher, Thomas & Unterseher, Thomas E., eds. (SPA.). 32p. 1993. pap. text 29.99 incl. audio compact disk (*1-57237-003-3*) Cultural Designs.

Bohr, Henrik, ed. Characterising Complex Systems. 210p. (C). 1990. pap. 23.00 (*981-02-0182-6*); text 74.00 (*981-02-0181-8*) World Scientific Pub.

Bohr, Henrik & Brunak, Soren, eds. Protein Folds: A Distance Based Approach. 336p. 1995. boxed set 179.95 (*0-8493-4009-8*, 4009) CRC Pr.

Bohr, Niels. Atomic Theory & the Description of Nature. LC 75-41033. 1976. reprint ed. 20.00 (*0-404-14737-2*) AMS Pr.

— Atomic Theory & the Description of Nature. LC 87-7779. (Philosophical Writings of Niels Bohr Ser.: Vol. I). viii, 119p. 1987. reprint ed. 30.00 (*0-918024-51-X*); reprint ed. pap. 16.00 (*0-918024-50-1*) Ox Bow.

— Causality & Complementarity: Supplementary Papers. Faye, Jan & Folse, Henry J., eds. LC 98-12467. (Philosophical Writings of Niels Bohr Ser.: Vol. IV). viii, 192p. 1999. 40.00 (*1-881987-14-0*); pap. 20.00 (*1-881987-13-2*) Ox Bow.

— The Correspondence Principle, 1918-1923. Nielsen, J. Rud, ed. (Niels Bohr Collected Works: Vol. 3). xii, 702p. 1976. 327.25 (*0-7204-1803-8*, North Holland) Elsevier.

— Early Work, 1905-1911 Vol. 1. Nielsen, J. Rud, ed. (Niels Bohr Collected Works: Vol. 1). 608p. 1973. 270.75 (*0-444-10003-2*, North Holland) Elsevier.

— Early Works, 1905-1911. Nielsen, J. Rud, ed. (Niels Bohr Collected Works: Vol. 1). xviii, 608p. 1986. reprint ed. 295.25 (*0-7204-1801-1*, North Holland) Elsevier.

— The Emergence of Quantum Mechanics (Mainly 1924-1926) Stolzenburg, K. & Rudinger, E., eds. (Niels Bohr Collected Works: Vol. 5). xxii, 528p. 1984. 236.00 (*0-444-86501-2*, North Holland) Elsevier.

— Essays, 1933-1957 on Atomic Physics & Human Knowledge. LC 87-7772. (Philosophical Writings of Niels Bohr Ser.: Vol. II). Orig. Title: Atomic Physics & Human Knowledge. viii, 101p. 1987. reprint ed. 30.00 (*0-918024-53-6*); reprint ed. pap. 16.00 (*0-918024-52-8*) Ox Bow.

— Essays, 1958-1962 on Atomic Physics & Human Knowledge. LC 87-7771. (Philosophical Writings of Niels Bohr Ser.: Vol. III). x, 100p. 1987. reprint ed. 30.00 (*0-918024-55-2*); reprint ed. pap. 16.00 (*0-918024-54-4*) Ox Bow.

— The Periodic System, 1920-1923. Nielsen, J. Rud, ed. (Niels Bohr Collected Works: Vol. 4). x, 766p. 1977. 350.75 (*0-7204-1804-6*, North Holland) Elsevier.

— Physique Atomique et Connaissance Humaine. (FRE.). 641p. 1991. pap. 18.95 (*0-7859-1676-8*, 2070326195) Fr & Eur.

— Works on Atomic Physics, 1912-1917. Hoyer, V., ed. (Niels Bohr Collected Works: Vol. 2). 648p. 1982. 262.00 (*0-444-86132-7*, North Holland) Elsevier.

Bohr, Paul R. Famine in China & the Missionary: Timothy Richard As Relief Administrator & Advocate of National Reform, 1876-1884. LC 72-75828. (East Asian Monographs: No. 48). (Illus.). 301p. 1972. pap. 25.00 (*0-674-29425-4*) HUP.

Bohr, Sarah H. & Harrington, Chantal. Bohr's Social Security Issues Annotated. 1998. 95.00 (*1-58012-019-9*) James Pub Santa Ana.

Bohr, Tomas, et al. Dynamical Systems Approach to Turbulence. LC 97-10933. (Nonlinear Science Ser.: Vol. 8). (Illus.). 370p. (C). 1998. text 85.00 (*0-521-47514-7*) Cambridge U Pr.

Bohren. Absorption & Scattering of Light. 544p. 1998. pap. 49.95 (*0-471-29340-7*) Wiley.

Bohren, Craig F. What Light Through Yonder Window Breaks: More Experiments in Atmospheric Physics. LC 00-90. 190p. 1991. pap. 12.95 (*0-471-52915-X*) Wiley.

Bohren, Craig F., ed. Selected Papers on Scattering in the Atmosphere. (Milestone Ser.). 648p. 1989. pap. 50.00 (*0-8194-0240-0*, VOL. MS07(S)) SPIE.

Bohren, Craig F. & Albrecht, Bruce A. Atmospheric Thermodynamics. LC 97-19688. (Illus.). 416p. (C). 1998. text 71.95 (*0-19-509904-4*) OUP.

***Bohrer, Brian L.** Winning on the Inside: The Road to Recovery. Price, Marilyn L., ed. 154p. 1999. pap. 10.00 (*1-893019-50-0*) Vic Christian Living.

Bohrer, David. America's Special Forces: Weapons Missions, Training. LC 97-52218. (Illus.). 128p. 1998. 21.95 (*0-7603-0366-5*) MBI Pubg.

Bohrer, Dick. Lion of God: A Biography of John G. Mitchell, D. D. LC 94-75841. 480p. (Orig.). 1994. pap. 11.95 (*0-9640330-0-3*) Multnomah Bible.

Bohrer, Dick, jt. auth. see Newton, John.

***Bohrer, Frederick N., ed.** Sevruguin & the Persian Image: Photographs of Iran, 1870-1930. LC 99-28447. (Illus.). 120p. 1999. pap. 24.95 (*0-295-97845-7*) U of Wash Pr.

Bohrer, John D., jt. auth. see Stoutzenberger, Joseph.

Bohrer, Karl H. Suddenness: On the Moment of Aesthetic Appearance. Crowley, Ruth, tr. LC 93-29695. (European Perspectives Ser.). 253p. (C). 1994. 61.00 (*0-231-07524-3*) Col U Pr.

Bohrer, Robert A., ed. From Research to Revolution: Scientific, Business & Legal Perspectives on the New Biotechnology. LC 87-9634. xi, 131p. 1987. reprint ed. 35.00 (*0-8377-0355-7*, Rothman) W S Hein.

Bohrer, Stanley P. & Alavi, Abass. Bone Ischaemia & Infarction in Sickle Cell Disease. LC 79-50182. (Illus.). 347p. (C). 1981. 44.50 (*0-87527-188-X*) Green.

Bohringer, Christoph. Allgemeine Gleichgewichtsmodelle als Instrument der Energie- und Umweltpolitischen Analyse: Theoretische Grundlagen und Empirische Anwendung. (GER., Illus.). 221p. 1996. pap. 42.95 (*3-631-30399-8*) P Lang Pubng.

Bohringer, Hans, et al, eds. Seventeenth Texas Symposium on Relativistic Astrophysics & Cosmology, Vol. 759. LC 95-34165. (Annals of the New York Academy of Sciences Ser.). 1995. write for info. (*0-89766-941-X*); pap. 190.00 (*0-89766-942-8*) NY Acad Sci.

Bohringer, Richard. C'Est Beau une Village la Nuit. (FRE.). 316p. 1989. pap. 10.95 (*0-7859-2112-5*, 2070381161) Fr & Eur.

Bohrmann, Hans, ed. NS-Presseanweisungen der Vorkriegszeit Edition und Dokumentation 1933-1939, Vol. 2, 1934. xxvi, 694p. 1985. lib. bdg. 90.00 (*3-598-10553-3*) K G Saur Verlag.

— NS-Presseanweisungen der Vorkriegszeit Edition und Dokumentation 1935-1939, 2 vols., Vol.3, 1935. 1112p. 1987. lib. bdg. 190.00 (*3-598-10554-1*) K G Saur Verlag.

— NS-Presseanweisungen der Vorkriegszeit, 1936, Bd. 4. (NS-Presseanweisungen der Vorkriegszeit Edition und Dokumentation Ser.). (GER.). 1993. lib. bdg. 286.00 (*3-598-11004-9*) K G Saur Verlag.

Bohrmann, Hans & Toepser-Ziegert, Gabriele. NS-Presseanweisungen der Vorkriegszeit Edition und Dokumentation 1933-1939, Vol. 1, 1933. 351p. 1984. lib. bdg. 60.00 (*3-598-10552-5*) K G Saur Verlag.

***Bohrmann, Peter.** Bartender's Guide. 1999. pap. text 14.99 (*1-84100-301-8*) Quadrillion Pub.

Bohrnstedt, George W. & Knoke, David. Statistics for Social Data Analysis. 3rd ed. LC 93-86174. 574p. (C). 1994. teacher ed., boxed set 55.00 (*0-87581-381-X*, SSDA3) F E Peacock Pubs.

***Bohrnstedt, Jennifer Cain, ed.** Soldiering with Sherman: Civil War Letters of George F. Cram. LC 99-89803. (Illus.). 250p. 2000. 32.00 (*0-87580-261-3*, 261-3) N Ill U Pr.

Bohs, Lynn. Cyphomandra (Solanaceae) (Flora Neotropica Monographs: Vol. 63). (Illus.). 172p. 1994. pap. text 24.50 (*0-89327-385-6*) NY Botanical.

Bohsali, Mary Lou. Langley School: The First Fifty Years. LC 93-24211. 1993. write for info. (*0-89865-875-6*) Donning Co.

Bohss, Von G. German-English--English German Dictionary of Printed Circuit Boards & Interconnection Technology. 2nd ed. (ENG & GER.). 272p. 1992. 79.00 (*0-7859-8900-5*) Fr & Eur.

Bohstedt, John. Riots & Community Politics in England & Wales, 1790-1810. (Illus.). 320p. 1983. 39.95 (*0-674-77120-6*) HUP.

***Bohtlingk, Otto.** Panini's Grammatik, 2 pts. 480, 357p. 1998. pap. 500.00 (*81-208-1025-2*, Pub. by Motilal Bnarsidass) St Mut.

***Bohun, W.** The Law of Tithes. 2nd rev. ed. iv, 472p. 2000. reprint ed. 147.00 (*1-56169-608-0*) Gaunt.

Bohusch, Otmar. Lexikon der Grammatischen Terminologie: Lexicon of Grammar Technology. (GER.). 1972. 35.00 (*0-8288-6408-X*, M7254) Fr & Eur.

Boi, L., et al, eds. A Century of Geometry, 1830-1930: Epistemology, History, & Mathematics. LC 92-12537. (Lecture Notes in Physics Ser.: Vol. 402). (Illus.). viii, 304p. 1992. 55.00 (*3-540-55408-4*) Spr-Verlag.

Boia, Eugene. Romania's Diplomatic Relations with Yugoslavia in the Interwar Period 1919-1941. 450p. (C). 1993. text 69.50 (*0-88033-253-0*, 356, Pub. by East Eur Monographs) Col U Pr.

***Boia, Lucian.** History & Myth in Romanian Consciousness. 270p. (C). 2000. 49.95 (*963-9116-96-3*); pap. 21.95 (*963-9116-97-1*) Ctrl Europ Univ.

Boia, Lucian, ed. Great Historians from Antiquity to 1800: An International Dictionary. LC 88-25089. 440p. 1989. lib. bdg. 85.00 (*0-313-24517-7*, BGH/, Greenwood Pr) Greenwood.

Boia, Lucian, et al, eds. Great Historians of the Modern Age: An International Dictionary. LC 89-26009. 868p. 1991. lib. bdg. 115.00 (*0-313-27328-6*, BMX/, Greenwood Pr) Greenwood.

Boiangiu, Suri, jt. auth. see Keylin, Arleen.

Boiardo, Matteo M. Orlando Innamorato. Ross, Charles S., tr. & intro. by. (World's Classics Ser.). (Illus.). 454p. 1995. pap. 13.95 (*0-19-282438-4*) OUP.

Boiarsky, Carolyn & Soven, Margot I. Writings from the Workplace: Documents, Models, Cases. (C). 1994. pap. text, teacher ed. write for info. (*0-205-16536-2*, H6536-0) Allyn.

Boiarsky, Carolyn R. Technical Writing: Contexts, Audiences, & Communities. LC 92-35635. 640p. 1992. pap. text 60.00 (*0-205-13932-9*) Allyn.

Boiarsky, Carolyn R. Technical Writing: Contexts, Audiences, & Communities. (C). 1993. pap. text, teacher ed. write for info. (*0-205-14860-3*, H4860-6) Allyn.

Boiarsky, Carolyn R. & Soven, Margot K. Writings from the Workplace: Documents, Models, & Cases. LC 94-32252. 450p. 1994. pap. text 38.00 (*0-205-15012-8*) Allyn.

***Boica, Roman.** Theoretical Foundations of Molecular Magnetism LC 99-38267. (Current Methods in Inorganic Chemistry Ser.). 1999. write for info. (*0-444-50229-7*) Elsevier.

Boice. Handbook for New Faculty Members. LC 99-51610. 288p. 2000. pap. text 28.00 (*0-205-28159-1*) Allyn.

Boice, Daniel. The Mitchell Kennerley Imprint: A Bibliography. (Pittsburgh Series in Bibliography). (Illus.). 272p. 1996. 75.00 (*0-8229-3948-7*) U of Pittsburgh Pr.

Boice, J. M. Los Fundamentos de la Fe Cristiana.Tr. of Foundations of the Christian Faith. (SPA.). 742p. 1996. 21.99 (*0-7899-0239-7*, 491041) Editorial Unilit.

— King Has Come. 9.99 (*1-85792-006-6*, Pub. by Christian Focus) Spring Arbor Dist.

— Sure I Believe! So What? 10.99 (*1-85792-095-3*, Pub. by Christian Focus) Spring Arbor Dist.

Boice, Jack. The Captive of Truth. LC 95-72731. 259p. 1996. pap. 16.95 (*1-57197-014-2*) Pentland Pr.

Boice, James M. Acts: An Expositional Commentary. LC 97-5128. 456p. (YA). (gr. 10). 1997. text 29.99 (*0-8010-1137-X*) Baker Bks.

***Boice, James M.** Awakening to God: Chinese Edition. Kao, David, tr. (Foundations of the Christian Faith Ser.: No. III). (CHI.). 204p. 1999. pap. 12.00 (*1-56582-134-3*) Christ Renew Min.

Boice, James M. Christ's Call to Discipleship. LC 98-15294. 168p. 1998. pap. text 10.99 (*0-8254-2074-1*) Kregel.

— Dealing with Bible Problems. 49p. 1999. mass mkt. 4.99 (*0-87508-478-8*, 478) Chr Lit.

— Ephesians: An Expositional Commentary. LC 97-35514. 304p. 1997. reprint ed. 24.99 (*0-8010-1153-1*) Baker Bks.

Boice, James M. The Epistles of John: An Expositional Commentary. 224p. 1983. reprint ed. mass mkt. 17.99 (*0-310-21531-5*, 10421P) Zondervan.

Boice, James M. Foundations of the Christian Faith. 2nd ed. LC 86-2736. 740p. 1986. 31.99 (*0-87784-991-9*, 991) InterVarsity.

Boice, James M. Genesis, 1. 1988. mass mkt. 19.99 (*0-310-21541-2*) Zondervan.

Boice, James M. Genesis, Vol. I. 352p. 1982. 20.95 (*0-310-21540-4*, 10486) Zondervan.

— Genesis: An Expositional Commentary, 3. 1392p. 1998. 79.95 (*0-8010-1160-4*) Baker Bks.

— Genesis: An Expositional Commentary, Vol. 2. 352p. 1986. 20.95 (*0-310-21560-9*, 10487) Zondervan.

— Genesis Vol. 1: An Expositional Commentary, (Creation & Fall, Genesis 1-11), 1. LC 98-16993. 464p. 1998. 29.99 (*0-8010-1161-2*) Baker Bks.

— Genesis Vol. 2: An Expositional Commentary, (a New Beginning, Genesis 12-36), 2. 464p. 1998. 29.99 (*0-8010-1162-0*) Baker Bks.

— Genesis Vol. 3: An Expositional Commentary, Genesis Thirty-Seven thru Fifty Twenty-Six. 368p. 1987. text 20.95 (*0-310-21590-0*, 10488) Zondervan.

— Genesis Vol. 3: An Expositional Commentary, (Living by Faith, Genesis 37-50), 3. 464p. 1998. 29.99 (*0-8010-1163-9*) Baker Bks.

— God the Redeemer - Chinese Edition. Feng, Wang & Ou-Yang, Geng Hau, trs. (Foundations of the Christian Faith Ser.: No. II). (CHI.). 228p. 1997. pap. 12.00 (*1-56582-110-6*) Christ Renew Min.

— The Gospel of John. 1985. 59.99 (*0-310-21570-6*, 10429) Zondervan.

— Living by the Book: The Joy of Loving & Trusting God's Word. LC 96-47820. 176p. (Orig.). 1997. pap. 11.99 (*0-8010-5758-2*) Baker Bks.

— The Minor Prophets, 1. 1988. pap. 17.99 (*0-310-21551-X*) Zondervan.

— The Minor Prophets, Vol. 2. 1988. pap. 17.99 (*0-310-21581-1*) Zondervan.

— The Minor Prophets: An Expositional Commentary, 2 vols. in 1. LC 96-40998. 544p. 1996. reprint ed. pap. 21.99 (*0-8254-2148-9*) Kregel.

— The Minor Prophets: An Expositional Commentary (Hosea-Jonah), Vol. 1. 272p. 1984. 17.95 (*0-310-21550-1*, 10423) Zondervan.

— The Minor Prophets: An Expositional Commentary (Micah-Malachi), Vol. 2. 1986. 17.95 (*0-310-21580-3*, 10424) Zondervan.

— Ordinary Men Called by God: A Study of Abraham, Moses & David. LC 97-47515. 144p. 1998. pap. 9.99 (*0-8254-2075-X*) Kregel.

— Parables of Jesus. pap. 10.99 (*0-8024-0163-5*, 243) Moody.

***Boice, James M.** Philippians: An Expositional Commentary. LC 99-59700. 320p. 2000. 25.99 (*0-8010-1190-6*) Baker Bks.

— Philippians: An Expositional Commentary. 320p. 1982. reprint ed. mass mkt. 19.99 (*0-310-21501-3*, 10310P) Zondervan.

Boice, James M. Psalms: An Expositional Commentary (Psalms 42-106), 2. LC 93-36246. 544p. 1996. 29.99 (*0-8010-1118-3*) Baker Bks.

— Psalms Vol. 1: An Expositional Commentary (Psalms 1-41), 1. LC 93-36246. 394p. 1994. 29.99 (*0-8010-1077-2*) Baker Bks.

— Psalms Vol. 3: An Expositional Commentary Psalms 107-150, 3. 480p. 1998. 29.99 (*0-8010-1164-7*) Baker Bks.

— Romans - An Expositional Commentary Vol. 3: God & History (Romans 9-11), 3. LC 91-7204. 544p. 1993. 32.99 (*0-8010-1058-6*) Baker Bks.

— Romans - An Expositional Commentary Vol. 4: The New Humanity (Romans 12-16), 4. LC 91-7204. 512p. 1995. 32.99 (*0-8010-1039-X*) Baker Bks.

— Romans: An Expositional Commentary, 4. 2,104p. 1995. 119.95 (*0-8010-1109-4*) Baker Bks.

— Romans: An Expositional Commentary: The Reign of Grace (Romans 5-8), 2. LC 91-7204. 536p. 1992. 32.99 (*0-8010-1003-9*) Baker Bks.

— Romans: An Expositional Commentary Vol. 1: Justification by Faith (Romans 1-4), 1. LC 91-7204. 512p. (Orig.). 1991. 32.99 (*0-8010-1002-0*) Baker Bks.

— The Sovereign God - Chinese Edition. Liu, John, tr. (Foundations of the Christian Faith Ser.: No. 1). (CHI.). 208p. 1997. pap. 8.50 (*1-56582-095-9*) Christ Renew Min.

***Boice, James M.** Standing on the Rock: Upholding Biblical Authority in a Secular Age. LC 98-44653. 200p. 1999. pap. 11.99 (*0-8254-2073-3*) Kregel.

Boice, James M. Two Cities, Two Loves: Christian Responsibility in a Crumbling Culture. LC 96-8115. 280p. 1996. 19.99 (*0-8308-1987-8*, 1987) InterVarsity.

— What Makes a Church Evangelical. LC 99-11515. (Today's Issues Ser.). 48p. 1999. pap. 4.99 (*1-58134-049-4*) Crossway Bks.

Boice, James M. & Sasse, Benjamin S., eds. Here We Stand! A Call from Confessing Evangelicals. LC 96-26128. 208p. (YA). (gr. 10). 1996. 16.99 (*0-8010-1134-5*) Baker Bks.

Boice, James M., et al. Christ in Christmas: A Family Advent Celebration. LC 89-62891. 80p. 1989. pap. 8.00 (*0-89109-605-1*) NavPress.

Boice, James M., jt. auth. see Ryken, Philip G.

***Boice, James Montgomery.** Foundations of God's City: Christians in a Crumbling Culture. 1999. pap. 14.99 (*0-8308-2225-9*) InterVarsity.

— The Gospel of John: Christ & Judaism, John 5-8, Vol. 2. LC 99-22764. (Expositional Commentary Ser.). 331p. 1999. 24.99 (*0-8010-1073-X*) Baker Bks.

— The Gospel of John: The Coming of the Light, John 1-4, Vol. 1. LC 99-22764. (Expositional Commentary Ser.). 365p. 1999. 24.99 (*0-8010-1182-5*) Baker Bks.

Boice, James Montgomery. The Gospel of John Vol. 5: Triumph Through Tragedy, John 18-21, Vol. 5. LC 99-22764. 352p. 1999. 24.99 (*0-8010-1183-3*) Baker Bks.

***Boice, James Montgomery.** The Gospel of John Vol.4: Peace in Storm, John 13-17. LC 99-22764. (Gospel of John Ser.). 400p. 1999. 24.99 (*0-8010-1106-X*) Baker Bks.

Boice, James Montgomery. Psalms: An Expositional Commentary, 3. 1998. 79.95 (*0-8010-1174-4*) Baker Bks.

Boice, John D. & Fraumeni, Joseph F., eds. Radiation Carcinogenesis: Epidemiology & Biological Significance. LC 83-21247. (Progress in Cancer Research & Therapy Ser.: No. 26). (Illus.). 509p. reprint ed. pap. 157.80 (*0-7837-7127-4*, 204695600004) Bks Demand.

Boice, John D., jt. auth. see National Council on Radiation Protection & Measure.

An Asterisk (*) at the beginning of an entry indicates that the title is appearing for the first time.

Boice, John M. The Sermon on the Mount: An Exposition. 328p. (Orig.). (C). 1981. pap. 19.99 (*0-310-21511-0*, 10360P) Zondervan.

***Boice, Judith.** But My Doctor Never Told Me That! Secrets for Creating Lifelong Health. (Illus.). 253p. 1999. pap. 18.95 (*0-9670453-1-2*, 001) Althea Pr.

Boice, Judith. Pocket Guide to Naturopathic Medicine. (Crossing Press Pocket Ser.). (Illus.). 128p. (Orig.). 1996. pap. 6.95 (*0-89594-821-4*) Crossing Pr.

Boice, L. Peter. Encountering a City: The Spatial Learning Process of Urban Newcomers. 1977. 5.00 (*0-686-19119-6*, 1264, Sage Prdcls Pr) Sage.

Boice, Martha H. Maps of the Shaker West: A Journey of Discovery. LC 97-197398. (Illus.). 140p. 1997. pap. write for info. (*0-9655018-1-7*, Pub. by Knot Grdn Pr) Partners Bk Dist.

Boice, Robert. First-Order Principles for College Teachers: Ten Basic Ways to Improve the Teaching Process. LC 97-118449. 200p. (C). 1996. 24.95 (*1-882982-12-6*) Anker Pub.

— How Writers Journey to Comfort & Fluency: A Psychological Adventure. LC 94-2984. 280p. 1994. 59.95 (*0-275-94907-9*, Praeger Pubs) Greenwood.

— The New Faculty Member: Supporting & Fostering Professional Development. LC 91-37579. (Higher & Adult Education Ser.). 396p. (C). 1992. text 38.95 (*1-55542-423-6*) Jossey-Bass.

— Procrastination & Blocking: A Novel, Practical Approach. LC 96-20684. 240p. 1996. 57.95 (*0-275-95657-1*, Praeger Pubs) Greenwood.

— Professors As Writers: A Self-Help Guide to Productive Writing. LC 89-63465. 180p. 1989. pap. 19.95 (*0-913507-13-X*) New Forums.

Boice, Robert, jt. ed. see Gainen, Joanne.

Boice, Suessa L. Dart Family in America. (Illus.). 119p. 1997. reprint ed. pap. 18.00 (*0-8328-8214-3*); reprint ed. lib. bdg. 28.00 (*0-8328-8213-5*) Higginson Bk Co.

Boice, Tara. If You Find a Baby Bird: How to Protect & Care for Wild Baby Birds. (Educational Ecology Ser.). 36p. (J). (gr. 4-9). 1992. pap. 7.95 (*0-9631916-0-8*) Seawind Pub.

Boicelli, A., jt. ed. see Rescigno, A.

Boichel, Margery R., jt. ed. see Simpson, Smith.

Boichenko, M. S., et al. Continuous Casting of Steel in the Soviet Union. LC 58-25475. 20p. reprint ed. pap. 30.00 (*0-608-11293-3*, 202064500018) Bks Demand.

Boichuk, Irv, jt. auth. see Weisenburger, E.

Boidin, Jacques & Lanquetin, Paule. Le Genre Scytinostroma Donk: Basidiomycetes, Lachnocladiaceae. (Bibliotheca Mycologica: Vol. 114). (GER., Illus.). 130p. 1987. 36.00 (*3-443-59015-2*, Pub. by Gebruder Borntraeger) Balogh.

Boie, Kirsten. Todo Cambio Con Jakob.Tr. of Everything Changed with Jakob. (Orig.). (J). (gr. 4-7). 1998. pap. text 8.95 (*84-204-4764-1*) Santillana.

Boieau, J., jt. ed. see Rico, A. G.

Boies, Bob, ed. see Coleman, George.

Boies, Henry M. Prisoners & Paupers: A Study of the Abnormal Increase of Criminals & the Public Burden of Pauperism in the United States; the Causes & Remedies. LC 72-5478. (Select Bibliographies Reprint Ser.). 1977. reprint ed. 27.95 (*0-8369-6897-2*) Ayer.

Boies, John L. Buying for Armageddon: Society, Economy, & the State since the Cuban Missile Crisis. LC 93-41777. (Arnold & Caroline Rose Monograph Series of the American Sociological Association). 200p. (C). 1994. text 40.00 (*0-8135-2082-7*) Rutgers U Pr.

Boies, Robert B., Sr. Genealogy of the Boies Family of Pennsylvania & Adjoining Counties in Eastern Ohio & James Boies of Milton Mass. (Illus.). 156p. (Orig.). 1986. 49.95 (*0-9616981-2-8*); pap. 38.95 (*0-9616981-0-1*) R B Boies.

***Boiffier, J. L.** The Dynamics of Flight: The Equations, Vol. 1. LC 98-17337. 390p. 1998. pap. 90.00 (*0-471-94237-5*) Wiley.

Boigon, Brian. Culture Lab. (Illus.). 256p. (Orig.). 1993. pap. 17.95 (*1-878271-77-6*) Princeton Arch.

Boik, Goodwin, et al. Sandplay Therapy: A Step-by-Step Manual for Psychotherapists of Diverse Orientations. LC 99-32765. 2000. 35.00 (*0-393-70319-3*) Norton.

Boik, John C. Cancer & Natural Medicine: A Textbook of Basic Science & Clinical Research. LC 95-69639. (Illus.). 332p. (Orig.). 1996. pap. 28.00 (*0-9648280-0-6*) OR Med Pr.

***Boik, John C.** Natural Compounds in Cancer Therapy. (Illus.). 685p. 2000. pap. 28.00 (*0-9648280-1-4*) OR Med Pr.

Boikess, Olga, ed. see Zagat, Eugene H., Jr. & Zagat, Nina S.

Boikess, Robert. Solutions Manual to Accompany Chemical Principles. 3rd ed. 224p. (C). 1994. per. 20.95 (*0-8403-7964-1*) Kendall-Hunt.

Boikess, Robert S. & Edelson, Edward. Chemical Principles. 3rd ed. 944p. (C). 1994. per. 49.95 (*0-8403-8773-3*) Kendall-Hunt.

Boiko, Claire. Children's Plays for Creative Actors. LC 81-19180. 384p. (J). (gr. 3-7). 1985. reprint ed. pap. 16.95 (*0-8238-0267-1*) Kalmbach.

— Children's Plays for Creative Actors: A Collection of Royalty-Free Plays for Boys & Girls. (J). 1985. 20.10 (*0-606-04398-5*, Pub. by Turtleback) Demco.

Boilard, Steve D. Russia at the Twenty-First Century: Politics & Social Changes in the Post-Soviet Era. LC 96-78842. 224p. (C). 1997. pap. text 29.50 (*0-15-505317-5*, Pub. by Harcourt Coll Pubs) Harcourt.

Boilard, Steven D. Reinterpreting Russia: An Annotated Bibliography of Books on Russia, the Soviet Union & the Russian Federation, 1991-1996. LC 96-38095. (Magill Bibliographies Ser.). 1997. 47.00 (*0-8108-3298-4*) Scarecrow.

Boilat, P. D. Esquisses Senegalaises, Physiognomie du Pays, Peuplades, Commerce, Religions, Passe et Avenir, Recits et Legendes. (B. E. Ser.: No. 167). (FRE.). 1853. 55.00 (*0-8115-3080-9*) Periodicals Srv.

Boileau, David A. Principles of Catholic Social Teaching. LC 97-45330. (Studies in Philosophy). 1998. 25.00 (*0-87462-638-2*) Marquette.

Boileau-Despreaux, Nicolas. Le Lutrin: An Heroick Poem. LC 92-22030. (Augustan Reprints Ser.: No. 126). 1967. reprint ed. 14.50 (*0-404-70126-4*, PQ1721) AMS Pr.

— Selected Criticism. Dilworth, Ernest N., tr. from FRE. LC 65-26530. 1965. pap. text 8.95 (*0-672-60471-X*) Irvington.

***Boileau, Kevin Craig.** Genuine Reciprocity & Group Authenticity: (Foucault's Developments or Satre's Ontology) 192p. 2000. 38.50 (*0-7618-1725-5*) U Pr of Amer.

Boileau, Linda. Loaded Pen. LC 95-17768. (Editorial Cartoonists Ser.). (Illus.). 160p. 1995. pap. 8.95 (*1-56554-115-4*) Pelican.

Boileau, Michele, tr. see Zeman, Ludmila.

Boileau-Narcejac. Carte Vermeil. (FRE.). 224p. 1987. pap. 10.95 (*0-7859-2218-0*, 207037212X) Fr & Eur.

— A Coeur Perdu: Meurtre a 45 Tours. (FRE.). 1987. pap. 10.95 (*0-7859-3990-3*) Fr & Eur.

— Le Contrat. (FRE.). 187p. 1988. pap. 18.95 (*0-7859-2242-3*, 220723522X) Fr & Eur.

— Les Diaboliques. (Celle Qui N'etait Plus Ser.). (FRE.). 1973. pap. 10.95 (*0-7859-1731-4*, 2070363260) Fr & Eur.

— L' Ingenieur Aimait Trops - Les Chiffres. (FRE.). 216p. 1986. pap. 10.95 (*0-7859-2029-3*, 2070377237) Fr & Eur.

— J'ai Ete un Fantome. (FRE.). 186p. 1991. pap. 10.95 (*0-7859-2157-5*, 2070383334) Fr & Eur.

— Les Louves. (FRE.). 1973. pap. 10.95 (*0-7859-1744-6*, 2070363856) Fr & Eur.

— Les Magiciennes. (FRE.). 192p. 1972. pap. 10.95 (*0-7859-1708-X*, 2070361780) Fr & Eur.

— Malefices. (FRE.). 213p. 1985. pap. 11.95 (*0-7859-2016-1*, 2070376621) Fr & Eur.

— Manigances. (FRE.). 373p. 1986. pap. 11.95 (*0-7859-2037-4*, 2070377431) Fr & Eur.

— Le Mauvais Oeil Suivi de au Bois Dormant. (FRE.). 1978. pap. 10.95 (*0-7859-1823-X*, 2070367819) Fr & Eur.

— Sueurs Froides (D'Entre les Morts) (FRE.). 192p. 1973. pap. 10.95 (*0-7859-2201-6*, 207036366X) Fr & Eur.

— Terminus. (FRE.). 1982. pap. 10.95 (*0-7859-2222-9*, 207037386X) Fr & Eur.

— Les Untouchables. (FRE.). 256p. 1984. pap. 10.95 (*0-7859-2000-5*, 2070375951) Fr & Eur.

— Les Visages de L'Ombre. (FRE.). 214p. 1985. pap. 11.95 (*0-7859-2013-7*, 2070376532) Fr & Eur.

Boileau, Nicolas. Art Poetique: Univers des Lettres Bordas. (FRE., Illus.). 128p. 1984. pap. 6.95 (*0-7859-0919-2*, F35304) Fr & Eur.

— Oeuvre Vol. 1: Satires; Le Lutrin. (FRE.). 1969. pap. 10.95 (*0-7859-3396-4*) Fr & Eur.

— Oeuvres Vol. 2: Epitres; L'Art Poetique; Oeuvres Diverses. (FRE.). 1969. pap. 10.95 (*0-7859-2965-7*) Fr & Eur.

— Oeuvres Completes. Escal, Marcelle, ed. (FRE.). 1360p. 1966. lib. bdg. 105.00 (*0-7859-3743-9*, 2070100693) Fr & Eur.

— Satires, Epitres, Art Poetique. (Poesie Ser.). (FRE.). pap. 15.95 (*2-07-032293-9*) Schoenhof.

— Satires, Epitres, l'Art Poetique. (FRE.). 1985. pap. 19.95 (*0-7859-2794-8*) Fr & Eur.

Boileau, P., jt. ed. see Walch, G.

Boileau, Pierre & Narcejac, Thomas. Diaboliques. (Folio Ser.: No. 326). (FRE.). 185p. 1952. pap. 6.95 (*2-07-036326-0*) Schoenhof.

— Manigances. (Folio Ser.: No. 1743). (FRE.). 373p. 1971. pap. 10.95 (*2-07-037743-1*) Schoenhof.

— Terminus. (Folio Ser.: No. 1386). (FRE.). (Orig.). pap. 8.95 (*2-07-037386-X*) Schoenhof.

Boileau, Pierre, ed. see Narcejac, Thomas.

***Boileau, Ray.** ABCs of Collecting Online. 2nd rev. ed. (Illus.). 128p. 1999. pap. 12.95 (*0-87588-559-4*) Hobby Hse.

— The ABCs of Collecting Online 3. 3rd ed. 144p. 2000. pap. 12.95 (*0-87588-583-7*) Hobby Hse.

— The ABCs of Making Money Online. 144p. 1999. pap. 12.95 (*0-87588-555-1*) Hobby Hse.

Boileau, Richard A., ed. see Advances in Pediatric Sport Sciences Staff.

Boiles, Charles L., tr. see Leon-Portilla, Miguel.

Boiling, Chris. The Jet Ski Book. 96p. (C). 1990. text 59.00 (*0-906754-65-8*, Pub. by Fernhurst Bks) St Mut.

Boillat, G., et al. Recent Mathematical Methods in Nonlinear Wave Propagation: Lectures Given at the 1st Session of the Centro Internazionale Matematico Estivo (C.I.M.E.), Held in Montecatini Terme, Italy, May 23-31, 1994. LC 96-36819. (Lecture Notes in Mathematics Ser.: Vol. 1640). 142p. 1996. pap. 29.00 (*3-540-61907-0*) Spr-Verlag.

Boillot & Settle. Developing Computer Skills Using PFS: First Choice. 1990. pap. 51.00 (*0-314-68135-3*) Thomson Learn.

Boillot, Michel H., et al. Essentials of Flowcharting. LC 74-77927. vii, 114 p. 1975. write for info. (*0-697-08110-9*) Brown & Benchmark.

Boillot, Michel H., et al. Essentials of Flowcharting LC 78-55766. viii, 145p. 1979. write for info. (*0-697-08129-X*, WCB McGr Hill) McGrw-H Hghr Educ.

***Boillot, Gilbert & Coulon, Christian.** La Dechirure Continentale et L'ouverture Oceanique: Geologie Des Marges Passives. (FRE., Illus.). 208p. 1998. pap. text 35.00 (*90-5699-188-4*) Gordon & Breach.

Boillot, Michel. BASIC: Concepts & Structured Problem-Solving. 2nd ed. 442p. (C). 1988. text 50.75 (*0-314-65461-5*) West Pub.

— Basic Concepts. 2nd ed. Date not set. pap. text 53.25 (*0-314-65463-1*) West Pub.

— Understanding FORTRAN 77 with Structured Problem Solving. LC 86-26662. (Illus.). 527p. (C). 1987. pap. text, teacher ed. write for info. (*0-314-34720-8*) West Pub.

— Understanding Structural Cobol. 2nd ed. Date not set. pap. text, teacher ed. 21.95 (*0-314-96598-X*) West Pub

— Understanding Structured COBOL. 2nd ed. LC 85-22719. (Illus.). 622p. (C). 1986. pap. text 52.00 (*0-314-93155-4*) West Pub.

Boillot, Michel & Settle, Mickey G. Programming in Turbo & Apple Pascal. LC 86-19098. (Illus.). 571p. (Orig.). (C). 1987. text 50.75 (*0-314-28510-5*); pap. text 49.75 (*0-314-34801-8*); pap. text, student ed. 26.00 (*0-314-34839-5*) West Pub.

— Turbo Pascal: Programming & Problem Solving (HC) 535p. (C). 1988. mass mkt. 45.50 (*0-314-62309-4*) West Pub.

Boillot, Michel, et al. Essentials of Flowcharting. 4th ed. 200p. (C). 1985. pap. text. write for info. (*0-697-00420-1*, WCB McGr Hill) McGrw-H Hghr Educ.

— Essentials of Flowcharting. 5th ed. LC 94-71691. 160p. (C). 1994. text 28.75 (*0-697-25418-6*) Bus & Educ Tech.

Boillot, Michel, jt. auth. see Horn, L. Wayne.

Boilly, B., jt. ed. see Taban, C. H.

Boilly-Widmer, Yvette, jt. auth. see Mermier, Guy R.

Boily, Chad, jt. auth. see LoPresti, Vincent.

Boily, Lise. Bread Ovens of Quebec. 1979. pap. 8.95 (*0-226-56284-0*) U Ch Pr.

Boily, Lise & Blanchette, Jean-Francois. The Bread Ovens of Quebec. (Illus.). 128p. 1979. pap. 8.95 (*0-660-00120-9*, 56284-0, Pub. by CN Mus Civilization) U of Wash Pr.

Boily, Robert, et al. Donnees Sur le Quebec. 2nd ed. LC 75-501941. (FRE., Illus.). 270p. reprint ed. pap. 83.70 (*0-7837-6945-8*, 204677400003) Bks Demand.

Boim, L. & Morgan, G. G., eds. The Soviet Procuracy Protests, 1937-1973. (Law in Eastern Europe Ser.: No. 21). 324p. 1978. lib. bdg. 221.00 (*90-286-0138-4*) Kluwer Academic.

Boime, Albert. Art & the French Commune: Imagining Paris after War & Revolution. LC 94-5324. (Princeton Ser. in Nineteenth-Century Art, Culture, & Society). 200p. 1995. text 49.50 (*0-691-02962-8*, Pub. by Princeton U Pr) Cal Prin Full Svc.

— Art & the French Commune: Imagining Paris after War & Revolution. (Illus.). 250p. 1995. pap. text 19.95 (*0-691-01555-4*, Pub. by Princeton U Pr) Cal Prin Full Svc.

— Art in the Age of Revolution, 1750-1800. (Illus.). 552p. (C). 1987. 35.00 (*0-226-06332-1*) U Ch Pr.

— The Art of the Macchia & the Risorgimento: Representing Culture & Nationalism in Nineteenth-Century Italy. LC 92-17169. (Illus.). 360p. (C). 1993. 60.00 (*0-226-06330-5*) U Ch Pr.

— Hollow Icons: The Politics of Sculpture in Nineteenth-Century France. LC 87-4247. (Illus.). 175p. 1987. 18.00 (*0-87338-346-X*) Kent St U Pr.

— A Social History of Modern Art: Art in an Age of Bonapartism, 1800-1815, Vol. 2. LC 89-20201. (Illus.). 736p. 1990. 59.95 (*0-226-06335-6*) U Ch Pr.

— A Social History of Modern Art: Art in an Age of Bonapartism, 1800-1815, Vol. 2. LC 89-20201. (Illus.). xxviii, 734p. (C). 1993. pap. text 40.00 (*0-226-06336-4*) U Ch Pr.

— A Social History of Modern Art Vol. 1: Art in the Age of Revolution, 1750-1800. LC 87-5944. (Illus.). xxx, 550p. 1990. pap. text 28.00 (*0-226-06334-8*) U Ch Pr.

— Thomas Couture & the Eclectic Vision. LC 79-23507. (Illus.). 707p. reprint ed. pap. 200.00 (*0-7837-4529-X*, 208019900003) Bks Demand.

— The Unveiling of the National Icons: A Plea for Patriotic Iconoclasm in a Nationalist Era. LC 97-3471. (Studies in American Visual Culture). (Illus.). 446p. (C). 1997 text 59.95 (*0-521-57067-0*) Cambridge U Pr.

Boime, Albert, ed. Violence & Utopia: The Work of Jerome Boime. 176p. 1996. pap. text 28.00 (*0-7618-0324-6*); lib. bdg. 48.50 (*0-7618-0323-8*) U Pr of Amer.

Boime, Irving, jt. ed. see Chin, William W.

Boin, S., jt. tr. see Lamotte, E.

Boine, Giovanni. Carteggio Boine-Amici de "La Voce" (1904-1917) Vol. IV: Edizioni di Storia e Letteratura. (ITA.). 690p. 1979. pap. 40.00 (*0-614-10124-7*) Am Inst Ital Stud.

— Carteggio Boine-Amici del "Rinnovamento" Vol. III: Tome 1 (1905-1910); Tome 2 (1911-1917) Edizioni di Storia e Letteratura. (ITA.). 1130p. 1977. pap. 40.00 (*0-614-10123-9*) Am Inst Ital Stud.

— Carteggio Boine-Cecchi (1911-1917) Vol. II: Edizioni di Storia e Letteratura. (ITA.). 233p. 1982. pap. 30.00 (*0-614-10122-0*) Am Inst Ital Stud.

— Carteggio Boine-Prezzolini (1908-1915) Vol. I: Edizioni di Storia e Letteratura. (ITA.). 264p. 1981. pap. 30.00 (*0-614-10121-2*) Am Inst Ital Stud.

Boinski, Sue & Garber, Paul A. On the Move: How & Why Animals Travel in Groups. LC 99-13382. 2000. pap. text 35.00 (*0-226-06340-2*) U Ch Pr.

***Boinski, Sue & Garber, Paul Alan.** On the Move: How & Why Animals Travel in Groups. LC 99-13382. 2000. lib. bdg. 95.00 (*0-226-06339-9*) U Ch Pr.

Boire, Gary. Morley Callaghan: Literary Anarchist. LC 95-138552. (Illus.). 130p. 1994. pap. 9.95 (*1-55022-185-X*, Pub. by ECW) LPC InBook.

— Morley Callaghan & His Works. (Canadian Author Studies). 70p. (C). 1990. pap. text 9.95 (*1-55022-029-2*, Pub. by ECW) Genl Dist Srvs.

Boire, Richard G. Marijuana Law: A Comprehensive Legal Manual. 2nd rev. ed. (Illus.). 288p. (Orig.). 1996. pap. 15.95 (*0-914171-86-0*) Ronin Pub.

— Sacred Mushrooms & the Law. 2nd ed. 72p. 1997. pap., per. 9.95 (*1-890425-00-1*) Spectral Mindustries.

Boire, Richard G., tr. see Sociedad Para La Preservation de las Plantas Del M.

***Boire, Richard Glen.** The Complete Entheogen Law Reporter Vol. 1: Issues 1-10 of TELR: The Journal of Law, Policy & Commentary. 100p. 1999. pap. 28.50 (*1-890425-02-8*) Spectral Mindustries.

— The Complete Entheogen Law Reporter Vol. 2: Issues 1-10 of TELR: The Journal of Law, Policy & Commentary. 125p. 1999. pap. 35.50 (*1-890425-03-6*) Spectral Mindustries.

Boire, Suzanne, ed. see Anthony, Thomas A.

Boireau. Drama on Drama. LC 96-36456. 344p. 1997. text 49.95 (*0-312-16541-2*) St Martin.

Boireau, Nicole & Lippke, Wolfgang, eds. Beyond Taboos: Images of Outrageousness in Recent English-Speaking Drama. (Contemporary Theatre Review Ser.: Vol. 5, Pt. 1). 148p. 1995. pap. text 16.00 (*3-7186-5845-3*, ECU21, Harwood Acad Pubs) Gordon & Breach.

Bois, C., jt. auth. see Pinet, B.

Bois, Charles G. Du, see Du Bois, Charles G.

Bois, David A. Du, see Gadbow, Nancy F. & Du Bois, David A.

Bois, E., et al, eds. Interactions Between Physics & Dynamics of Solar System Bodies: Proceedings of the International Astronomical Symposium Held in Pleneuf-Val-Andre (France) from June 21 to June 28, 1992. LC 93-33792. 1993. lib. bdg. 144.00 (*0-7923-2556-7*) Kluwer Academic.

Bois, Gary, jt. auth. see Moses, James.

Bois, Guy. The Transformation of the Year One Thousand: The Village of Lournand from Antiquity to Feudalism. Birrell, Jean, tr. LC 92-1488. 1992. text 27.95 (*0-7190-3566-X*, Pub. by Manchester Univ Pr) St Martin.

Bois, Ive-Alain, et al. Ellsworth Kelly: The Years in France, 1948-1954. LC 92-15853. (Illus.). 216p. 1992. 35.00 (*3-7913-1189-1*, Pub. by Prestel) te Neues.

Bois, J. Samuel. The Art of Awareness. 4th rev. ed. David, Gary, ed. LC 97-130918. (Illus.). 382p. (Orig.). 1996. pap. 22.50 (*0-9651037-0-6*) Philosphere Pubs.

— Epistemics: The Science-Art of Innovating. LC 71-93028. (Illus.). 200p. 1972. pap. 15.95 (*0-9651037-2-2*) Philosphere Pubs.

— Explorations in Awareness. LC 56-12233. (Illus.). 212p. 1957. pap. 13.50 (*0-9651037-1-4*) Philosphere Pubs.

Bois, Mario. Iannis Xenakis, the Man & His Music: A Conversation with the Composer & a Description of His Works. LC 80-12638. (Illus.). 40p. 1980. reprint ed. lib. bdg. 45.00 (*0-313-22415-3*, BOIX, Greenwood Pr) Greenwood.

Bois, Paul M. Du, see Lappe, Frances M. & Du Bois, Paul M.

Bois, Pierre-Andre, et al, eds. Les Lettres Francises dans les Revues Allemandes du XVIIIe Siecle: Die Franzosische Literatur in Den Deutschen Zeitschriften des 18. Jahrhunderts. (Convergences Ser.: Vol. 4). (FRE.). xii, 388p. 1997. 51.95 (*3-906758-14-1*, Pub. by P Lang) P Lang Pubng.

***Bois, Pierre-Andre, et al, eds.** Voix Conservatrices et Reactionnaires dans les Periodiques Allemands De La Revolution Francaise A La Restauration. (Convergences Ser.). xvi, 431p. 1999. 59.95 (*3-906762-97-1*, Pub. by P Lang) P Lang Pubng.

Bois-Reymond, Emil H. Du, see Du Bois-Reymond, Emil H.

Bois, Thomas J., II & Luther, Bernard J. California Groundwater & Soil Contamination: Technical Preparation & Litigation Management, 1. (Environmental Law Library). 608p. 1994. boxed set 155.00 (*0-471-01996-8*) Wiley.

Bois, William P. Du, see Du Bois, William P.

Bois, William P. Du, see Bowen, Otis R. & Du Bois, William P.

Bois, William P. Du, see Du Bois, William P.

Bois, William Pene Du, see Pene Du Bois, William.

Bois, William Pene Du, see Caudill, Rebecca & Pene Du Bois, William.

Bois, Yve-Alain. Abstraction Gesture Ecriture: Painting from The Daros Collection. 1999. 49.95 (*3-908247-99-3*) Scalo Pubs.

— Ellsworth Kelly: The Early Drawings, 1948-1955. LC 98-53905. 264p. 1999. pap. 45.00 (*1-891771-07-8*, Pub. by Harvard Art Mus) U Ch Pr.

— Matisse & Picasso. LC 98-44307. (Illus.). 272p. 1999. 50.00 (*2-08-013548-1*, Pub. by Flammarion) Abbeville Pr.

— Painting As a Model. (Illus.). 357p. (C). 1993. pap. text 25.00 (*0-262-52180-6*) MIT Pr.

— Pompidou/Guggenheim: A Rendezvous. (Illus.). 550p. 1998. 75.00 (*0-8109-6916-5*, Pub. by Abrams) Time Warner.

Bois, Yve-Alain & Kimbell Art Museum Staff. Matisse & Picasso. LC 98-44307. 1998. write for info. (*0-912804-34-3*) Kimbell Art.

***Bois, Yve-Alain & Krauss, Rosalind E.** Formless: A User's Guide. Orig. Title: L'Informe: Mode d'Emploi. (Illus.). 304p. (C). 2000, reprint ed. pap. 30.00 (*0-942299-44-2*, Pub. by Zone Bks) MIT Pr.

Bois, Yve-Alain, et al. Ellsworth Kelly: The Early Drawings, 1948-1955. LC 98-53905. (Illus.). 263p. 2000. lib. bdg. 65.00 (*1-891771-09-4*, Pub. by Harvard Art Mus) U Ch Pr.

Bois, Yve-Alain, jt. auth. see Duthuit, Claude.

Bois, Yve-Alain, jt. auth. see Krauss, Rosalind E.

B

Boisard, M. A., et al, eds. Multilateral Diplomacy: The United Nations System at Geneva: A Working Guide - La Diplomatie Multilaterale: Le Systeme des Nations UNIES a Geneve: Guide de Travail. LC 97-32488. 524p. 1998. 171.00 (*90-411-0524-7*) Kluwer Law Intl.

Boisard, Marcel A. Humanism in Islam. Al-Jarrahi, Abdussamad, tr. from FRE. LC 82-70456. 200p. (Orig.). 1987. 18.95 (*0-89259-035-1*) Am Trust Pubns.

— Jihad: A Commitment to Universal Peace.Tr. of L'Humanisme De L'Islam. 57p. (Orig.). 1988. pap. 5.00 (*0-89259-073-4*) Am Trust Pubns.

Boisard, Marcel A., tr. see Michel, Albin.

Boisclaire, Larry, ed. see Leenbouts, Keith J.

Boisclaire, Yvonne. In the Shadow of the Rising Sun. 2nd rev. ed. LC 97-220417. (Illus.). 224p. 1997. pap. 14.95 (*0-9649997-3-0*) Clearwood Pubs.

Boisclaire, Yvonne R. The Flag of Yoshihara. unabridged ed. LC 96-83318. (Illus.). 112p. (Orig.). 1996. pap. 8.95 (*0-9649997-1-4*) Clearwood Pubs.

Boisde, Gilbert E. & Harmer, Alan. Chemical & Biochemical Sensing with Optical Fibers & Waveguides. LC 96-20964. 389p. 1996. 103.00 (*0-89006-737-6*) Artech Hse.

Boise, Otis B. Music & Its Masters. LC 73-39464. (Illus.). reprint ed. 32.50 (*0-404-08367-6*) AMS Pr.

Boise, Ruth. The Lord Will Keep You Going. Lane, Barry, ed. (Opening Doors Ser.: No. 1). (Illus.). 32p. (Orig.). 1989. pap. 4.00 (*1-877829-04-8*) Homegrown Bks.

Boise State University Staff. College Chemistry, Vol. C-134. 136p. (C). 1996. pap. text, spiral bd., lab manual ed. 15.95 (*0-7872-3384-6*, 41338401) Kendall-Hunt.

— College Chemistry C-132 Laboratory Manual. 112p. (C). 1996. pap. text, ring bd. 17.95 (*0-7872-2597-5*, 41259701) Kendall-Hunt.

— Concepts of Biology Lab Manual. 2nd ed. 128p. (C). 1998. spiral bd., lab manual ed. 12.95 (*0-7872-5068-6*, 41506801) Kendall-Hunt.

— Concepts of Biology Laboratory Manual. 126p. (C). 1996. pap. text, spiral bd. 8.95 (*0-7872-2730-7*) Kendall-Hunt.

Boiselle, Arthur H., et al. Test File Using Math Bus. LC 80-16710. (Illus.). 384p. (C). 1981. 3.00 (*0-201-00041-5*) Addison-Wesley.

— Using Mathematics in Business. LC 80-16710. (Illus.). 384p. (C). 1981. pap. 18.25 (*0-201-00098-9*) Addison-Wesley.

Boisen, Kathleen, jt. auth. see Bleiman, Joyce.

Boisen, M., jt. auth. see Gibbs, G. V.

Boisgontier, Jacques. Dictionnaire du Francais Regional des Pays Aquitaines. (FRE.). 157p. 1991. 50.00 (*0-8288-9482-5*) Fr & Eur.

— Dictionnaire du Francais Regional du Midi Touloussain et Pyreneen. (FRE.). 157p. 1992. 50.00 (*0-8288-9484-1*) Fr & Eur.

Boisits, Edward K., jt. auth. see Maibach, Howard I.

Boismard, Marie-Emile, ed. Our Victory over Death: Resurrection? Beaumont, Madeleine, tr. from ENG. LC 98-29486. 168p. 1999. pap. 16.95 (*0-8146-2458-8*) Liturgical Pr.

Boismier, W. A., jt. ed. see Gamble, C. S.

Boismont, Alexandre-Jacques-Francois Brierre De, see Brierre De Boismont, Alexandre-Jacques-Francois.

Boisnard, Luc. Dictionnaire des Anciennes Familles de Touraine. (FRE.). 464p. 1992. 250.00 (*0-7859-8101-2*, 2855540542) Fr & Eur.

Boisot, Max, ed. The East-West Business Collaboration: The Challenge of Governance in Post-Socialist Enterprises. LC 93-24227. (Centre for Organizational Studies). 176p. (C). 1993. pap. 29.95 (*0-415-10270-7*, B3801) Thomson Learn.

— The East-West Business Collaboration: The Challenge of Governance in Post-Socialist Enterprises. LC 93-24227. (Bus Press-Previous Routledge). 176p. (C). (gr. 13). 1993. mass mkt. 57.95 (*0-415-10269-3*, B3797) Thomson Learn.

Boisot, Max H. Knowledge Assests: Securing Competetive Advantage in the Information Economy. LC 97-42642. (Illus.). 306p. 1998. text 39.95 (*0-19-829086-1*) OUP.

— Knowledge Assets: Securing Competitive Advantage in the Information Economy. LC 99-27820. (Illus.). 312p. 1999. pap. text 19.95 (*0-19-829607-X*) OUP.

Boisot, Max H., ed. Information Space: A Framework for Learning in Organizations, Institutions, & Culture. LC 94-48389. 560p. (C). (gr. 13). 1995. pap. 30.99 (*0-415-11490-X*) Thomson Learn.

Boissard, Janine. Cecile. Feeny, Mary, tr. from FRE. 250p. 1988. 17.95 (*0-316-10103-6*) Little.

— Christmas Lessons. Feeney, Mary, tr. from FRE. 252p. 1984. 15.95 (*0-316-10097-8*) Little.

— A Different Woman: A Novel. Feeney, Mary, tr. from FRE. 224p. 1989. 17.95 (*0-316-10104-4*) Little.

Boissard, Janine. L'Esprit de Famille: Level B. text 8.95 (*0-8219-1065-5*) EMC-Paradigm.

Boissard, Janine. A New Woman. large type ed. 304p. 1984. 27.99 (*0-7089-1154-4*) Ulverscroft.

Boisseau, Joyce. You Can Live in Divine Health. 302p. 1993. pap. 6.95 (*0-914984-02-0*) Starburst.

Boisseau, Marc. An Introduction to ATM Technology. 144p. 1995. mass mkt. 29.95 (*1-85032-140-X*) ITCP.

Boisseau, Marc, et al. An Introduction to ATM Technology. 2nd ed. (ITCP-UK Computer Science Ser.). (Illus.). 128p. 1996. pap. 29.95 (*1-85032-304-6*) ITCP.

Boisseau, N., et al. High-Speed Networks. LC 94-10084. (Series in Communication & Distributed Systems). 204p. 1995. pap. 99.95 (*0-471-95109-9*) Wiley.

Boisseau, T. Sultan to Sultan: Adventures among the Masai & Other Tribes of East Africa. LC 97-33349. (Illus.). 192p. 1998. 69.95 (*0-7190-5113-4*, Pub. by Manchester Univ Pr) St Martin.

Boissel, J. P., jt. ed. see Bellanti, J. A.

Boisselier, Jean. Trends in Khmer Art. Eilenberg, Natasha, ed. Elliott, Melvin, tr. from FRE. (Studies on Southeast Asia: No. 6). (Illus.). 124p. 1989. pap. text 15.00 (*0-87727-705-2*) Cornell SE Asia.

— The Wisdom of the Buddha. (Discoveries Ser.). (Illus.). 192p. 1994. pap. 12.95 (*0-8109-2807-8*, Pub. by Abrams) Time Warner.

Boisselier, June. The Ministry of a Wife. LC 89-92037. 316p. (Orig.). 1993. pap. 11.95 (*0-9625705-4-0*) Revival Pubns.

Boisselle, Berangere, ed. see West Pasco County Genealogical Society Staff.

Boisser, Jean-Louis, et al. ArtIntAct: A CD ROM Magazine. 112p. 1995. text 49.95 (*3-89322-675-3*) Dist Art Pubs.

Boisset, Caroline. The Garden Source Book: The Essential Guide to Planning & Planting. LC 99-195082. 360 p. 1994. write for info. (*1-85732-986-4*) Mitchell Beazley.

— Pumpkins & Squashes. LC 97-4070. (Illus.). 120p. 1997. 19.95 (*0-89577-957-9*, Pub. by RD Assn) Penguin Putnam.

Boisset, Caroline, jt. ed. see Best, Clare.

Boissevain, Andrea L., et al. Corporate Health & Safety: Managing Environmental Issues in the Workplace. (Illus.). 300p. 1996. 89.00 (*0-9648570-0-6*) Ergonomics.

Corporate Health & Safety is a comprehensive resource for industrial hygienists, safety officers/personnel & management on several of the most important environmental considerations facing the business community. Subjects of emphasis: Risk Analysis: Assessment, Management & Communication; Assessment & Management of Air Quality in the Workplace; Measurement & Control of Sound & Vibration; Magnetic & Electric Field Measurements, Dosimetric Techniques & Proactive Measures; Bioaerosols & Indoor Air Quality; Asbestos & Lead Management; & Managing Ergonomic Risks. The special capabilities of seven companies have been brought together into one book. The authors were chosen for their own expertise & for the expertise of their firms. Each author is actively involved with field work & writes from his or her experiences. Corporate Health & Safety provides contemporary insight on the state of technology with a focus on current measurement & mitigation methods. Informed perspectives on complex health & safety issues & how to develop strong assessment & management techniques are given. The charts, graphs & drawings illustrate the covered concepts & quantity & reseller discounts available are of great value to any manager faced with the pressing issues of liability, productivity & work environment quality. Applications include use as a college/university &/or seminar text. To order: Ergonomics Inc., P.O. Box 964, Southampton, PA 18966. 1-800-862-0102, 215-357-5124, or FAX 215-364-7582, Web Site: www.ergonomicsusa.com, e-mail: info@ergonomicsusa.com. *Publisher Paid Annotation.*

Boissevain, Jeremy. The Italians of Montreal. LC 74-17921. (Italian American Experience Ser.). (Illus.). 104p. 1975. reprint ed. 14.95 (*0-405-06394-6*) Ayer.

Boissevain, Jeremy, ed. Coping with Tourists: European Reactions to Mass Tourism. LC 95-37305. (New Directions in Anthropology Ser.: Vol. I). (Illus.). 240p. 1996. 59.95 (*1-57181-878-2*); 19.95 (*1-57181-900-2*) Berghahn Bks.

Boissevain, Jeremy & Mitchell, J. Clyde, eds. Network Analysis: Studies in Human Interaction. LC 72-77471. (Change & Continuity in Africa Ser.). 1973. 32.35 (*90-279-7187-0*) Mouton.

Boissevain, Philipp, ed. see Dio Cocceianus, Cassius.

Boissier, A. Dictionary Dromois/Francais/Dromois. (FRE.). 115p. 1992. reprint ed. 35.00 (*0-320-00899-1*) Fr & Eur.

Boissier, Edmond. Diagnoses Orientalium Plantarum Novarum, 3 vols. fac. ed. (GER.). 2326p. 1969. reprint ed. 310.00 (*3-201-00719-6*, Pub. by Akademische Druck-und) Balogh.

Boissier, Gaston. Ciceron Et Ses Amis: Etude Sur La Societe Romaine Du Temps De Cesar. 523p. 1976. reprint ed. 105.00 incl. 3.5 hd (*3-487-05614-3*) G Olms Pubs.

— La Fin du Paganisme, 2 vols., Set. 978p. 1987. reprint ed. 210.00 (*3-487-06392-1*) G Olms Pubs.

— Madame de Sevigne. Williams, Henry L., tr. LC 79-38341. (Select Bibliographies Reprint Ser.). 1977. 17.95 (*0-8369-6794-1*) Ayer.

— Le Religion Romaine d'Auguste aux Antonins, 2 vols. in 1. xi, 917p. 1979. reprint ed. lib. bdg. 190.00 (*3-487-06702-1*) G Olms Pubs.

— Rome & Pompeii: Archaeological Rambles. Fisher, D. Havelock, tr. LC 77-39193. (Select Bibliographies Reprint Ser.). (Illus.). 1977. 31.95 (*0-8369-6795-X*) Ayer.

— Rome & Pompeii: Archaeological Rambles. Fisher, D. Havelock, tr. LC 77-39193. (Select Bibliographies Reprint Ser.). (Illus.). 435p. reprint ed. lib. bdg. 28.00 (*0-8290-0505-6*) Irvington.

Boissier, J. R., et al, eds. Differential Psychopharmacology on Anxiolytics & Sedatives. (Modern Problems of Pharmacopsychiatry Ser.: Vol. 14). (Illus.). 1979. 47.00 (*3-8055-2777-2*) S Karger.

Boissiere, Olivier. European Contemporary Houses. 1998. pap. 24.95 (*2-7450-0026-8*) Telleri Edit.

— Jean Nouvel. (Illus.). 208p. 1997. 27.50 (*2-87939-105-9*) Stewart Tabori & Chang.

— Jean Nouvel. 2nd ed. (Studio Paperback Ser.). (Illus.). 208p. 1996. pap. 29.95 (*3-7643-5356-2*, Pub. by Birkhauser) Princeton Arch.

***Boissiere, Olivier.** Los Angeles. (Illus.). 160p. 1999. (*2-7450-0061-6*) Telleri Edit.

— Outstanding Hotel Designs. (Illus.). 160p. 24.95 (*2-7450-0031-4*) Telleri Edit.

Boissiere, Olivier. Twentieth-Century Houses: Europe. (Illus.). 208p. 1998. pap. text 27.50 (*2-87939-185-7*, Pub. by Pierre Terrail) Rizzoli Intl.

Boissiere, Robert. The Hopi Way: An Odyssey. LC 84-16256. 96p. (Orig.). 1985. pap. 8.95 (*0-86534-055-2*) Sunstone Pr.

— Meditations with the Hopi. LC 86-70257. (Meditations with Ser.). (Illus.). 144p. (Orig.). 1986. pap. 9.95 (*0-939680-27-0*) Bear & Co.

— Po Pai Mo: The Search for White Buffalo Woman. LC 83-4668. (Illus.). 96p. (Orig.). 1983. pap. 8.95 (*0-86534-024-2*) Sunstone Pr.

Boissieu, Christian De, see Fair, Donald E. & De Boissieu, Christian, eds.

Boissieu, Marc De, see De Boissieu, Marc.

Boisson De Chazournes, Laurence, jt. ed. see Salman, Salman M. A.

Boissonade, Jean F. Anecdota Graeca. lxii, 2881p. 1962. reprint ed. 640.00 (*0-318-70879-5*) G Olms Pubs.

Boissonade, Jean F., ed. see Tzetza.

Boissonnade, Auguste, tr. see Lagrange, J. L.

Boissonnade, Prosper. Life & Work in Medieval Europe: The Evolution of Medieval Economy from the Fifth to the Fifteenth Century. Power, Eileen E. & White, Lynn, Jr., trs. from FRE. LC 82-11818. (Illus.). 395p. 1982. reprint ed. lib. bdg. 79.50 (*0-313-23566-X*, BOLW) Greenwood.

Boissonnas, J. & Omenetto, P., eds. Mineral Deposits Within the European Community. (Special Publications of the Society for General Microbiology). (Illus.). 530p. 1988. 161.00 (*0-387-18201-2*) Spr-Verlag.

Boissonnat, Jean-Daniel & Yvinec, Mariette. Algorithmic Geometry. Bronnimann, Herve, tr. LC 97-19739. (Illus.). 540p. (C). 1998. text 95.00 (*0-521-56322-4*); pap. text 40.95 (*0-521-56529-4*) Cambridge U Pr.

Boissonnat, L. D. & Laumond, J. P., eds. Geometry & Robotics. (Lecture Notes in Computer Science Ser.: Vol. 391). vi, 413p. 1989. 59.00 (*0-387-51683-2*) Spr-Verlag.

Boissonnault, William G., ed. Examination in Physical Therapy Practice: Screening for Medical Disease. LC 91-26796. (Illus.). 385p. 1991. reprint ed. pap. 119.40 (*0-7837-9751-6*, 206047900005) Bks Demand.

— Examination in Physical Therapy Practice: Screening for Medical Disease. 2nd ed. 1995. text 44.00 (*0-443-08956-6*) Church.

Boister, Neil, ed. South African Human Rights Yearbook, 1993. 1993. pap. 25.00 (*1-86840-106-5*, Pub. by Univ Natal Pr) Intl Spec Bk.

Boisuert, Bernie & Eick, Chuck. ASNT Level III Study Guide: Liquid Penetrant Method. (Illus.). 102p. (Orig.). (C). 1998. ring bd. 39.00 (*0-931403-79-0*, 2255) Am Soc Nondestructive.

Boisvert, Bernie. Principles & Applications of Liquid Penetrant Testing: A Classroom Training Text. (Illus.). 156p. (C). 1994. pap. 53.50 (*0-931403-49-9*, 2004) Am Soc Nondestructive.

Boisvert, Clotilde. Herbes et Epices: Petit Dictionnaire de Sorcellerie. (FRE.). 207p. 1977. pap. 22.95 (*0-7859-7834-8*, 2226004300) Fr & Eur.

Boisvert, Conrad J. Bay Area Mountain Bike Trails: 45 Mountain Bike Trails Throughout the San Francisco Bay Area. (Bay Area Bike Trails Ser.). (Illus.). 160p. (Orig.). 1995. pap. 13.95 (*0-9621694-5-5*) Penngrove Pubns.

— East Bay Bike Trails: Road & Mountain Bicycle Rides Through Alameda & Contra Costa Counties. (Bay Area Bike Trails Ser.). (Illus.). 128p. (Orig.). 1993. pap. 12.95 (*0-9621694-4-7*) Penngrove Pubns.

— San Francisco Peninsula Bike Trails: Road & Mountain Bicycle Rides Through San Francisco & San Mateo Counties. rev. ed. (Bay Area Bike Trails Ser.). (Illus.). 128p. (Orig.). 1993. pap. 11.95 (*0-9621694-3-9*) Penngrove Pubns.

— South Bay Bike Trails: Road & Mountain Bicycle Rides Through Santa Clara & Santa Cruz Counties. 2nd rev. ed. (Bay Area Bike Trails Ser.). 128p. 2000. pap. 13.95 (*0-9621694-8-X*) Penngrove Pubns.

***Boisvert, Donald L.** Queering the Sacred: Meditations on Gay Spirituality. LC 99-54448. 160p. 2000. pap. 19.95 (*0-8298-1369-1*) Pilgrim OH.

Boisvert, Mathieu. The Five Aggregates: Understanding Theravada Psychology & Soteriology. (Bibliotheca Indo-Buddhica Ser.). (C). 1997. 24.00 (*81-7030-562-4*, Pub. by Sri Satguru Pubns) S Asia.

— The Five Aggregates: Understanding Theravada Psychology & Soteriology. LC 96-111592. xii, 166p. (C). 1995. pap. 24.95 (*0-88920-257-5*) W Laurier U Pr.

Boisvert, Paul O., contrib. by. Vermont: A Seasonal Celebration. LC 98-28735. 132p. 1998. 40.00 (*1-881535-30-4*) New Eng Pr VT.

Boisvert, Paul O., photos by. Lake Champlain: A Photographic Discovery. LC 95-67532. (Illus.). 88p. (Orig.). 1995. 25.00 (*1-881535-15-0*); pap. text 16.95 (*1-881535-14-2*) New Eng Pr VT.

Boisvert, R. F., jt. auth. see Rice, J.

Boisvert, Raymond D. Dewey's Metaphysics. LC 88-80074. xii, 227p. 1988. pap. 17.00 (*0-8232-1197-5*) Fordham.

— John Dewey: Rethinking Our Time. LC 96-52291. (SUNY Series, the Philosophy of Education). 189p. (C). 1997. text 54.50 (*0-7914-3529-6*); pap. text 17.95 (*0-7914-3530-X*) State U NY Pr.

Boisvert, Robin & Mahaney, C. J. How Can I Change: Biblical Hope for Lasting Change. Somerville, Greg, ed. 112p. 1993. pap. 6.99 (*1-881039-03-X*) PDI Ministries.

— This Great Salvation: Unmerited Favor, Unmatched Joy. 112p. 1992. pap. 6.99 (*1-881039-01-3*) PDI Ministries.

Boit, H. G., ed. see Beilstein Institut fur Literatur der Organischen Chemie.

Boit, John. The Log of the Union: John Boit's Remarkable Voyage to the Northwest Coast & Around the World 1794-1976. Hayes, Edmund, Sr., ed. LC 80-83181. (North Pacific Studies: No. 6). (Illus.). 176p. 1981. pap. 12.95 (*0-87595-089-2*) Oregon Hist.

Boit, R. Boit: Chronicles of the Boit Family & Their Descendants. (Illus.). 260p. 1990. reprint ed. pap. 39.00 (*0-8328-1583-7*); reprint ed. lib. bdg. 49.00 (*0-8328-1582-9*) Higginson Bk Co.

Boitani. Antarctic & Patagonia. 1989. lib. bdg. 23.75 (*0-8172-3349-0*) Raintree Steck-V.

***Boitani, Luigi & Fuller, Todd.** Research Techniques in Animal Ecology: Controversies & Consequences. LC 99-52230. (Illus.). 464p. 1999. 75.00 (*0-231-11340-4*); pap. 32.00 (*0-231-11341-2*) Col U Pr.

Boitani, Piero. The Bible & its Rewritings. LC 99-36578. 248p. 1999. text 60.00 (*0-19-818487-5*) OUP.

— The Shadow of Ulysses: Figures of a Myth. 210p. (C). 1994. text 45.00 (*0-19-812268-3*) OUP.

Boitani, Piero, ed. The European Tragedy of Troilus. (Illus.). 330p. 1989. text 72.00 (*0-19-812970-X*) OUP.

Boitani, Piero & Mann, Jill, eds. The Cambridge Chaucer Companion. 272p. 1986. pap. text 18.95 (*0-521-31689-8*) Cambridge U Pr.

Boitani, Piero & Torti, Anna, eds. The Body & the Soul in Medieval Literature. LC 99-22580. (J. A. W. Bennett Memorial Lectures: Vol. 1361-7621). (Illus.). 224p. 1999. 72.00 (*0-85991-545-X*) Boydell & Brewer.

— Intellectuals & Writers in Fourteenth Century Europe: The J. A. W. Bennett Memorial Lectures, Perugia 1984. 280p. 1986. 75.00 (*0-85991-223-X*) Boydell & Brewer.

— Interpretation: Medieval & Modern: The J. A. W. Bennett Memorial Lectures Eight Series. 224p. (C). 1993. 60.00 (*0-85991-382-1*) Boydell & Brewer.

Boitano, Brian & Harper, Suzanne. Boitano's Edge: Inside the Real World of Figure Skating. LC 97-29498. (Illus.). 144p. (J). (gr. 3 up). 1997. pap. 25.00 (*0-689-81915-3*) S&S Trade.

Boitard, Christian. B Cells & Autoantibody Production in Autoimmune Diseases. LC 95-22862. (Medical Intelligence Unit Ser.). 270p. 1996. 99.00 (*1-57059-209-8*) Landes Bioscience.

Boiten, Theo. Bristol Blenheim. (Illus.). 192p. 1998. 44.95 (*1-86126-115-2*, Pub. by Cro1wood) Motorbooks Intl.

— Nachtjagd. (Illus.). 256p. 1997. 44.95 (*1-86126-086-5*, Pub. by Cro1wood) Motorbooks Intl.

***Boiten, Theo.** Night Airwar: Personal Recollections of the Conflict over Europe, 1939-45. (Illus.). 192p. 2000. 44.95 (*1-86126-298-1*, 129770AE, Pub. by Cro1wood) Motorbooks Intl.

***Boiten, W.** Hydrometry. (IHE Delft Lecture Note Ser.). (Illus.). 282p. (C). 2000. text 85.00 (*90-5410-419-8*, Pub. by A A Balkema); pap. text 60.00 (*90-5410-423-6*, Pub. by A A Balkema) Ashgate Pub Co.

Boiteux, Henri, jt. auth. see Mavrodineanu, Radu.

Boiti, M., et al, eds. Nonlinear Evolution Equations & Dynamical Systems, '91: Proceedings of the Workshop. 600p. 1992. text 143.00 (*981-02-0856-1*) World Scientific Pub.

Boito, Camillo. Senso: And Other Stories. 2nd ed. Morris, Roderick C., ed. Donougher, Christine, tr. from ITA. (Decadence Ser.). 208p. 1999. reprint ed. pap. 11.95 (*0-946626-83-9*) Dedalus.

Boito, Camilo, ed. The Basilica of St. Mark in Venice Illustrated from the Points of View of Art & History by Venetian Writers. Scott, William, tr. 1976. lib. bdg. 125.95 (*0-8490-1477-8*) Gordon Pr.

Boitos, Myra E. Designer Music: A Study of Harmonization. Meisenheimer, Adel & Zeeman, Mark, eds. (Illus.). 17p. 1987. 15.00 (*0-944582-01-X*) Song Crafters.

Boivie, Jorgen, et al, eds. Touch, Temperature, & Pain in Health & Disease: Mechanisms & Assessments. LC 94-36236. (Progress in Pain Research & Management Ser.: 3). (Illus.). 548p. 1994. 27.00 (*0-931092-08-6*, PPRM3) Intl Assn Study Pain.

Boivin, Gilles. French - English - Latin Lexicon of Vegetables. (ENG, FRE & LAT.). 61p. 1992. pap. 29.95 (*0-8288-9405-1*) Fr & Eur.

Boivin, Gilles. Lex of Machine Assembling Tools. (FRE & ENG.). 82p. 1994. pap. 24.95 (*0-320-02953-0*) Fr & Eur.

Boivin, Gilles. Lexique de la Restaurant Chinoise. (ENG & FRE.). 58p. 1984. pap. 7.95 (*0-8288-1297-7*, M9587) Fr & Eur.

Boivin, Gilles & Duquet-Picard, Diane. English French Software Vocabulary. (ENG & FRE.). 63p. 1991. pap. 29.95 (*0-8288-9417-5*) Fr & Eur.

Boivin, Gilles & Michel, France. Lexicon of Building & Several Other Related Fields. (ENG & FRE.). 51p. 1992. pap. 29.95 (*0-8288-9392-6*) Fr & Eur.

Boivin, Jacques, tr. & illus. see Rancourt, Sylvie.

Boivin, Kelly. What's in a Box? LC 91-4062. (Rookie Readers Ser.). (Illus.). 32p. (J). (ps-3). 1991. lib. bdg. 17.00 (*0-516-02010-2*) Childrens.

Boivin, Michel. Renovation du Shi'isme Ismaelien en Inde et au Pakistan: D'apres les Ecrits et les Discours de Sultan Muhammad Shah Aga Khan. 492p. 1997. 110.00 (*0-7103-0535-4*, Pub. by Kegan Paul Intl) Col U Pr.

Boix, Carles. Political Parties, Growth & Equality: Conservative & Social Democratic Economic Strategies in the World Economy. LC 97-27896. (Cambridge Studies in Comparative Politics). (Illus.). 272p. (C). 1998. pap. 19.95 (*0-521-58595-3*); text 59.95 (*0-521-58446-9*) Cambridge U Pr.

An Asterisk (*) at the beginning of an entry indicates that the title is appearing for the first time.

Boix, Esther. Europa & Norteamerica: De los Totalitarismos Politicos a las Artes Conceptuales. (Del Arte Moderno Ser.: Vol. III). (SPA., Illus.). 128p. 1993. 100.00 (*84-343-0733-2*) Elliots Bks.
— Razon y el Sueno: Del Cubismo Al Surrealismo. (Del Arte Moderno Ser.: Vol. II). (SPA., Illus.). 128p. 1993. 100.00 (*84-343-0545-3*) Elliots Bks.
— Revolucion Del Arte Moderno: Del Impresionismo Al Expresionismo. (Del Arte Moderno Ser.: Vol. I). (SPA., Illus.). 128p. 1993. 100.00 (*84-343-0500-3*) Elliots Bks.
Boix, Esther & Creus, Ricard. Arte en la Escuela: Expresion Plastica. (SPA., Illus.). 116p. 1993. 100.00 (*84-343-0465-1*) Elliots Bks.
Boixados, Alberto. Myths of Modern Art. 144p. (Orig.). (C). 1990. pap. text 20.00 (*0-8191-7953-1*); lib. bdg. 37.00 (*0-8191-7952-3*) U Pr of Amer.
Boixados, Maria D. Balada de un Musico. 2nd ed. 228p. 1985. 5.00 (*0-8477-3518-4*) U of PR Pr.
Bojaciuk, George. Building & Detailing Scale Model Muscle Cars. LC 98-165844. (Illus.). 88p. 1998. pap. 15.95 (*0-89024-566-5*, 12180, Kalmbach Books) Kalmbach.
Bojadziev, George & Bojadziev, Maria. Fuzzy Sets, Fuzzy Logic, Applications. LC 95-45806. (Advances in Fuzzy Systems Ser.: Vol. 5). 240p. 1996. text 42.00 (*981-02-2388-9*) World Scientific Pub.
Bojadziev, Maria, jt. auth. see Bojadziev, George.
Bojanczyk, Adam & Cybenko, George, eds. Linear Algebra for Signal Processing. LC 95-2605. (IMA Volumes in Mathematics & Its Applications Ser.: Vol. 69). (Illus.). 200p. 1995. 59.95 (*0-387-94491-5*) Spr-Verlag.
Bojanic, Ivan & Pecina, Marko M. Overuse Injuries of the Musculoskeletal System. LC 93-8061. 384p. 1993. boxed set 136.95 (*0-8493-4492-1*, RD97) CRC Pr.
Bojanov, B. & Wozniakowski, H., eds. Optimal Recovery. 292p. 1992. 175.00 (*1-56072-016-6*) Nova Sci Pubs.
Bojanov, B. D. Spline Functions & Multivariate Interpolations. (Mathematics & Its Applications Ser.). 292p. (C). 1993. text 188.00 (*0-7923-2229-0*) Kluwer Academic.
Bojanowski, John. Fest - Pass, '98 No. II: The Only Guide to Europe from Festival to Festival. 160p. 1998. pap. 25.00 (*0-9663082-0-4*) Europ Fest Ntwrk.
Bojar, E. J., ed. Last Dangerous Christmas. (Illus.). 48p. 1997. pap. 5.95 (*1-883847-31-1*) MU Press.
Bojar, Robert M. Manual of Perioperative Care in Cardiac & Thoracic Surgery. 2nd ed. LC 93-31153. (Illus.). 512p. 1994. pap. 44.95 (*0-86542-347-4*) Blackwell Sci.
Bojar, Robert M. & Warner, Kenneth G. Manual of Perioperative Care in Cardiac Surgery. 3rd ed. LC 98-33471. (Illus.). 1998. pap. 51.95 (*0-632-04365-2*) Blackwell Sci.
Bojarevics, V., et al. Electrically Induced Vortical Flows. (C). 1988. text 304.50 (*90-247-3712-5*) Kluwer Academic.
Bojarska, Brigitte, tr. see Urs von Balthasar, Hans.
Bojarski, Richard. The Complete Films of Bela Lugosi. 1992. pap. 15.95 (*0-8065-0808-6*, Citadel Pr) Carol Pub Group.
Bojczuk, William. Evidence. 260p. (C). 1991. 80.00 (*1-85352-877-3*, Pub. by HLT Pubns); 72.00 (*1-85352-388-7*, Pub. by HLT Pubns) St Mut.
Bojczuk, William, ed. Evidence. rev. ed. 260p. (C). 1991. pap. 72.00 (*1-85352-860-9*, Pub. by HLT Pubns) St Mut.
Boje, David M., et al, eds. Postmodern Management & Organization Theory. 320p. 1995. 52.00 (*0-8039-7004-8*); pap. 25.00 (*0-8039-7005-6*) Sage.
Boje, Shirley. When the Drums Speak of Love. (Heartbeats Ser.). 112p. (YA). (gr. 7 up). 1995. pap. 5.95 (*0-7910-2931-X*) Chelsea Hse.
Boje, Thomas, et al. European Societies: Fusion or Fission? LC 98-26301. (ESA Studies in European Society). 1999. 85.00 (*0-415-19843-7*) Routledge.
***Boje, Thomas P. & Leira, Arnlaug.** Gender, Welfare State & the Market: Towards a New Division of Labour. LC 00-30428. (Research in Gender & Society Ser.). 2000. pap. write for info. (*0-415-23531-6*) Routledge.
Bojer, Johan. The Emigrants. Jayne, A. G., tr. LC 73-21338. 351p. 1974. reprint ed. lib. bdg. 35.00 (*0-8371-6194-0*, BOTE, Greenwood Pr) Greenwood.
— The Emigrants. LC 91-22742. xii, 351p. 1991. reprint ed. pap. 12.95 (*0-87351-260-X*, Borealis Book) Minn Hist.
— The Great Hunger. 24.95 (*0-88411-064-8*) Amereon Ltd.
Bojkov, R. D. & Fabian, P., eds. Ozone in the Atmosphere: Proceedings of Quadrennial Ozone Symposium, 1988. LC 89-77829. (Illus.). 822p. 1990. 87.00 (*0-937194-15-8*) A Deepak Pub.
Bojkovic, Z. S., jt. auth. see Rao, K. R.
Bojnansky, V. & Fargasova, A. Dictionary of Plant Virology. (ENG, FRE, GER, RUS & SPA.). 494p. 1991. 174.50 (*0-444-98740-1*) Elsevier.
— Dictionary of Plant Virology in English, Russian, German, French & Spanish. (ENG, FRE, GER, RUS & SPA.). 472p. 1991. 250.00 (*0-8288-9202-4*) Fr & Eur.
Bojnicic, J. Adel von Kroatien und Slavonien. (CRO & GER.). 258p. 1990. reprint ed. 150.00 (*0-317-03844-3*) Szwede Slavic.
Bojnicic, J., jt. auth. see Rosenfeld, F. H.
Bojo, Jan, et al. Environment & Development: An Economic Approach. (C). 1990. lib. bdg. 102.00 (*0-7923-0802-6*) Kluwer Academic.
— Environment & Development: An Economic Approach. LC 92-21700. (Economy & Environment Ser.: No. 6). 224p. (C). 1992. lib. bdg. 127.50 (*0-7923-1878-1*) Kluwer Academic.
Bojomisky, Moshe. Vedebarta Bam: And You Shall Speak of Them. (Vayikra Ser.: Vol. III). 205p. 1996. 19.95 (*1-880880-17-2*) Israeli Trad.
Bojorge, Horacio. The Image of Mary: According to the Evangelists. Owen, Aloysius, tr. from SPA. LC 77-15516. (Illus.). 1978. pap. 4.00 (*0-8189-0362-7*) Alba.
Bojrab, M. Joseph, et al, eds. Pathophysiology in Small Animal Surgery. LC 80-25780. 928p. reprint ed. pap. 200.00 (*0-7837-1480-7*, 205717500023) Bks Demand.
Bojrab, M. Joseph & Tholen, Mark A., eds. Small Animal Oral Medicine & Surgery. LC 88-32647. (Illus.). 1271p. 1993. text 79.50 (*0-8121-1205-9*) Lppncott W & W.
Bojrab, M. Joseph, et al. Current Techniques in Small Animal Surgery. 3rd ed. LC 89-13005. (Illus.). 950p. 1989. text 105.00 (*0-8121-1193-1*) Lppncott W & W.
— Current Techniques in Small Animal Surgery. 4th ed. LC 97-22997. (Illus.). 1300p. 1998. 99.95 (*0-683-00890-0*) Lppncott W & W.
— Disease Mechanisms in Small Animal Surgery. 2nd ed. (Illus.). 1000p. 1992. text 105.00 (*0-8121-1491-4*) Lppncott W & W.
Bojtar, Endre. East European Avant-Garde Literature. (Studies in Modern Philology: Vol. 10). 156p. (C). 1996. pap. 65.00 (*963-05-6297-9*, Pub. by Akade Kiado) St Mut.
— Foreward to the Past: A Cultural History of the Baltic People. LC 00-27577. (Illus.). 350p. 2000. 49.95 (*963-9116-42-4*) Ctrl Europ Univ.
— Slavic Structuralism. LC 85-4291. (Linguistic & Literary Studies in Eastern Europe: No. 11). 160p. 1985. 55.00 (*90-272-1507-3*) J Benjamins Pubng Co.
Boju, V., ed. see Smarandache, Florentin.
Bojunga-Nunes, Lygia. Companions. 64p. 1989. 11.95 (*0-374-31465-9*) FS&G.
— My Friend the Painter. LC 90-46043. (J). 1995. 10.10 (*0-606-09649-3*, Pub. by Turtleback) Demco.
Bok. Secrets. 1984. 8.95 (*0-07-544545-X*) McGraw.
— Secrets. 1998. 7.95 (*0-07-006537-3*) McGraw.
Bok, Bart J. & Bok, Priscilla F. The Milky Way. 5th ed. LC 80-22544. (Harvard Books on Astronomy). (Illus.). 364p. (C). 1981. 46.50 (*0-674-57503-2*) HUP.
Bok, Bart J. & Jerome, Lawrence E. Objections to Astrology. LC 75-29798. (Science & the Paranormal Ser.). 62p. 1975. 8.95 (*0-87975-059-6*) Prometheus Bks.
Bok-Bennema, Reineke. Case & Agreement in Inuit. LC 91-34845. (Studies in Generative Grammar: No. 38). xx, 308p. (C). 1991. lib. bdg. 98.50 (*3-11-013025-4*) Mouton.
Bok-Bennema, Reineke & Coopmans, Peter. Linguistics in the Netherlands, 1990. 164p. 1990. pap. 38.50 (*3-11-013036-X*) Mouton.
Bok, Curtis. Star Wormwood. LC 84-45877. (Capital Punishment Ser.). 1983. reprint ed. 30.00 (*0-404-62402-2*, 8675) AMS Pr.
Bok, Derek C. Beyond the Ivory Tower: Social Responsibilities of the Modern University. LC 81-20278. 328p. 1982. 29.95 (*0-674-06899-8*) HUP.
— Beyond the Ivory Tower: Social Responsibilities of the Modern University. LC 81-20278. 328p. 1984. pap. text 20.50 (*0-674-06898-X*) HUP.
— The Cost of Talent: How Executives & Professionals Are Paid & How It Affects America. 320p. 1993. 24.95 (*0-02-903755-7*) Free Pr.
— Higher Learning. 208p. 1986. 29.50 (*0-674-39175-6*) HUP.
— Higher Learning. 208p. 1988. reprint ed. pap. 15.50 (*0-674-39176-4*) HUP.
— State of the Nation. 496p. 1998. pap. text 18.95 (*0-674-29211-1*) HUP.
— The State of the Nation: Government & the Quest for a Better Society, 1960-1995. LC 96-22881. 480p. 1998. 35.00 (*0-674-29210-3*) HUP.
— Universities & the Future of America. LC 89-49196. 128p. (C). 1990. text 18.95 (*0-8223-1036-8*) Duke.
Bok, Derek C., jt. auth. see Bowen, William G.
Bok, Edward. The Americanization of Edward Bok. 28.95 (*0-8488-0199-7*) Amereon Ltd.
— The Americanization of Edward Bok. 1993. reprint ed. lib. bdg. 89.00 (*0-7812-5428-0*) Rprt Serv.
— Man from Maine. 1993. reprint ed. lib. bdg. 89.00 (*0-7812-5429-9*) Rprt Serv.
Bok, Edward W. America's Taj Mahal: The Singing Tower of Florida. 2nd ed. (Illus.). 48p. 1989. reprint ed. 15.95 (*0-9623313-0-9*) Bok Tower.
Bok, Gordon. Time & the Flying Snow. LC 77-80648. 88p. 1977. pap. 10.95 (*0-938702-03-3*) Folk-Legacy.
Bok, Hannes, jt. auth. see Merritt, Abraham.
Bok, Hilary. Freedom & Responsibility. LC 98-21288. 248p. 1998. text 39.50 (*0-691-01566-X*, Pub. by Princeton U Pr) Cal Prin Full Svc.
Bok, Julien, et al, eds. The Gap Symmetry & Fluctuations in High-Tc Superconductors: Proceedings of a NATO ASI Held in Cargese, France, September 1-13, 1997. (NATO ASI Series B: Vol. 371). (Illus.). xiii, 560 p. (C). 1998. text. write for info. (*0-306-45934-5*) Plenum.
Bok, Lee T. The Forbidden Zone. 66p. 1990. pap. 10.95 (*0-912159-05-7*) Center Pr CA.
Bok, Marcia. Civil Rights & the Social Programs of the 1960s: The Social Justice Functions of Social Policy. LC 91-46996. 200p. 1992. 55.00 (*0-275-93654-6*, C3654, Praeger Pubs) Greenwood.
Bok, Marcia, ed. Multicultural Human Services for AIDS Treatment & Prevention: Policy, Perspectives, & Planning. LC 92-48833. (Journal of Multicultural Social Work: Vol. 2, No. 3). (Illus.). 134p. 1993. 39.95 (*1-56024-414-3*); pap. 12.95 (*1-56023-038-X*, Harrington Park) Haworth Pr.
Bok, Marten J., jt. auth. see Schwartz, Gary.
Bok, Priscilla F., jt. auth. see Bok, Bart J.
Bok, S., jt. auth. see Callahan, D.
Bok, Sissela. Alva Myrdal: A Daughter's Memoir. 375p. 1991. 22.95 (*0-201-57086-6*) Addison-Wesley.
— Common Values. (C). 1995. 27.50 (*0-8262-1038-4*) U of Mo Pr.
— Lying: Moral Choice in Public & Private Life. 1989. pap. 14.00 (*0-679-72470-2*) Vin Bks.
***Bok, Sissela.** Lying Updated Edition. 1999. pap. 14.00 (*0-375-70528-7*) Knopf.
Bok, Sissela. Mayhem: Violence As Public Entertainment. LC 97-48620. 208p. 1998. 32.00 (*0-201-48979-1*) Perseus Pubng.
— Mayhem: Violence As Public Entertainment. 208p. 1999. pap. text 13.00 (*0-7382-0145-6*, Pub. by Perseus Pubng) HarpC.
— Secrets: On the Ethics of Concealment & Revelation. 1989. pap. 13.00 (*0-679-72473-7*) Vin Bks.
Bokat, Nicole S. The Novels of Margaret Drabble: "this Freudian family nexus" LC 97-44504. (Sexuality & Literature Ser.: Vol. 7). 274p. (C). 1998. 51.95 (*0-8204-3980-0*) P Lang Pubng.
***Bokat, Nicole S.** Redeeming Eve. LC 99-30773. 264p. 2000. 24.00 (*1-57962-064-7*) Permanent Pr.
Bokat, Stephen A. & Thompson, Horace A., 2nd. Occupational Safety & Health Law, Cumulative Supplement 2. LC 88-7252. 1995. text, suppl. ed. 65.00 (*0-87179-882-4*) BNA Books.
— Occupational Safety & Health Law, 1988, includes the 1999 supplement. LC 88-7252. 1034p. 1988. suppl. ed. 100.00 incl. trans. (*0-87179-527-2*, 9147-PR9) BNA Books.
Bokemeier, Janet. Harvest of Hope: Farming Family. 1996. text 37.50 (*0-8133-1181-0*) Westview.
— Harvest of Hope: Farming Family. (C). 1996. pap. text 14.00 (*0-8133-1184-5*) Westview.
Boken, Julia B. Carolyn Heilbrun & Amanda Cross. LC 96-20002. 1996. 32.00 (*0-8057-4030-9*, Twyne) Mac Lib Ref.
Bokenham's. Lives of Holy Women. (EETS, OS Ser.: No. 206). 1969. reprint ed. 63.00 (*0-527-00206-2*) Periodicals Srv.
Bokenkamp, Stephen R. Early Daoist Scriptures. 520p. 1999. pap. 19.95 (*0-520-21931-7*, Pub. by U CA Pr) Cal Prin Full Svc.
Bokenkotter, Thomas. Church & Revolution. 1997. pap. 15.00 (*0-385-48735-5*) Doubleday.
— Church & Revolution: The Quest for Social Justice in the Catholic Church. LC 97-49429. (Illus.). 592p. 1998. pap. 15.95 (*0-385-48754-1*, Image Bks) Doubleday.
— A Concise History of the Catholic Church. 512p. 1990. pap. 14.95 (*0-385-41147-2*) Doubleday.
— Dynamic Catholicism: Dynamics of Faith & Belief. LC 86-4390. 464p. 1985. pap. 14.95 (*0-385-23243-8*, Image Bks) Doubleday.
Boker, Carol, ed. Homemade Christmas: Holiday Recipes, Gifts, Decorations & Memories to Treasure. (Illus.). 224p. 1995. spiral bd. 15.95 (*1-879958-27-9*, Tradery) Wimmer Cos.
Boker, Carol, ed. see Bedwell, Randall.
Boker, Carol, ed. see Epstein, Bob T.
Boker, Carol, ed. see Memphis Herb Society Staff.
Boker, Carol, ed. see National Wild Turkey Federation Staff.
Boker, George H. Plays & Poems, 2 vols. reprint ed. 84.50 (*0-404-00930-1*) AMS Pr.
— Plays & Poems, 2 vols. (Anglistica & Americana Ser.: No. 40). 1969. reprint ed. 200.00 (*0-685-66434-1*, 05102518) G Olms Pubs.
— Poems of the War. LC 72-4949. (Romantic Tradition in American Literature Ser.). 204p. 1980. reprint ed. 28.95 (*0-405-04623-5*) Ayer.
Boker, Pamela A. The Grief Taboo in American Literature. 1998. pap. text 20.00 (*0-8147-1314-9*) NYU Pr.
— The Grief Taboo in American Literature: Loss & Prolonged Adolescence in Twain, Melville, & Hemingway. (Literature & Psychoanalysis Ser.). 416p. (C). 1995. text 50.00 (*0-8147-1228-2*) NYU Pr.
Bokey & Shell. Stomal Therapy. 1985. 33.00 (*0-08-029865-6*); pap. 20.00 (*0-08-029862-1*, Pergamon Pr) Elsevier.
***Bokforlag, Sanduik.** Amadeus "Best Friends" (Illus.). 9p. (J). 1999. bds. 11.98 (*1-58048-067-5*) Sandvik Pub.
— Amadeus Is Happy. (Illus.). 8p. (J). 1999. 12.98 (*1-58048-090-X*) Sandvik Pub.
— Amadeus Photo Album. (Illus.). 12p. (J). (ps-5). 1998. bds. 6.99 (*1-58048-052-7*) Sandvik Pub.
— At Nursery School. (Illus.). 11p. 1998. bds. 5.99 (*1-58048-012-8*) Sandvik Pub.
Bokforlag, Sanduik. Baby Panda. (Illus.). 6p. (J). 1995. 9.99 (*1-881445-48-8*) Sandvik Pub.
***Bokforlag, Sanduik.** Elly the Elephant. (Illus.). 6p. (J). 1999. 12.98 (*1-58048-092-6*) Sandvik Pub.
Bokforlag, Sanduik. Faces. (Illus.). (J). 1998. 12.98 (*1-58048-024-1*) Sandvik Pub.
— In the Zoo. (Illus.). 10p. (J). 1994. pap. 8.98 (*1-881445-29-1*) Sandvik Pub.
***Bokforlag, Sanduik.** Leo the Lion. (Illus.). 6p. (J). 1999. 12.98 (*1-58048-093-4*) Sandvik Pub.
Bokforlag, Sanduik. Little Rabbit. (Illus.). 9p. (J). (ps). 1994. 19.99 (*1-881445-38-0*) Sandvik Pub.
— Little Spotted Calf. (Illus.). 10p. (J). 1992. pap. 5.25 (*1-881445-05-4*) Sandvik Pub.
— Little Woolly Lamb. (Illus.). 10p. (J). 1992. 5.25 (*1-881445-04-6*) Sandvik Pub.
***Bokforlag, Sanduik.** Mother & Child. 120p. 1998. pap. 11.95 (*1-58048-051-9*) Sandvik Pub.
— My Family. (Illus.). 11p. 1998. bds. 5.99 (*1-58048-013-6*) Sandvik Pub.
— My Favorite Things. (Illus.). 5p. (J). 1998. pap. 4.99 (*1-58048-050-0*) Sandvik Pub.
Bokforlag, Sanduik. My First Book of Animals. (Illus.). (J). 1998. bds. 12.98 (*1-58048-008-X*) Sandvik Pub.
— My Little Huggy Pup. (Illus.). (J). 1997. 5.99 (*1-58048-015-2*) Sandvik Pub.
— My Toys. (Illus.). 12p. (J). (ps). 1992. pap. 7.99 (*1-881445-10-0*) Sandvik Pub.
Bokforlag, Sanduik. Noise & Smell. (Illus.). 1997. pap. 9.99 (*1-58048-006-3*) Sandvik Pub.
— Nursery Treasury. (Illus.). 1997. pap. 12.98 (*1-58048-004-7*) Sandvik Pub.
— Piano Song Book. (Illus.). 1998. pap. 9.99 (*1-58048-026-8*) Sandvik Pub.
Bokforlag, Sanduik. Roger the Puppy. (Illus.). 8p. (J). (ps). 1992. 5.99 (*1-881445-46-1*) Sandvik Pub.
— The Sooty Little Mouse. (Illus.). 16p. (J). (ps). 1994. pap. 9.99 (*1-881445-30-5*) Sandvik Pub.
— Teddy's Day. (Illus.). 6p. (J). 1993. 16.99 (*1-881445-18-6*) Sandvik Pub.
— Teddy's Day. (Illus.). (J). 1997. 11.99 (*1-58048-016-0*) Sandvik Pub.
— The Wheels on the Bus. (Illus.). (J). 1998. 11.98 (*1-58048-007-1*) Sandvik Pub.
Bokforlag, Sandviks. Bus Trip. (Illus.). 8p. (J). 1993. 11.99 (*1-881445-23-2*) Sandvik Pub.
— Jilly Rabbit. (Illus.). 8p. (J). (ps). 1992. 7.99 (*1-881445-02-X*) Sandvik Pub.
Bokhari, Imiaz H. & Thornton, Thomas P. The Nineteen Seventy-Two Simla Agreement: An Asymmetrical Negotiation. (Pew Case Studies in International Affairs). 51p. (Orig.). (C). 1988. pap. text 3.50 (*1-56927-420-7*) Geo U Inst Dplmcy.
Bokhari, Imtiaz H. Management of Third World Crisis in Adverse Partnership: Theory & Practice. LC 98-119438. 356p. 1997. 45.00 (*0-19-577757-3*) OUP.
Bokhari, Shahid H. Assignment Problems in Parallel & Distributed Computing. (C). 1987. text 84.00 (*0-89838-240-8*) Kluwer Academic.
Bokhoven, Wim M. Van, see Leenaerts, Domine M.
Bokhoven, Wim M. Van, see Leenaerts, Domine M. & Van Bokhoven, Wim M.
Bokich, Obren. Christmas Card for Mr. McFizz. (J). 1998. 10.95 (*0-671-75181-6*) S&S Bks Yung.
Bokides, Dessa, jt. auth. see Taylor, Lonn.
Bokina, John. Political Ideas in Opera: From Monteverdi to Henze. LC 96-53455. 264p. 1997. 30.00 (*0-300-06935-9*) Yale U Pr.
Bokina, John & Lukes, Timothy J., eds. Marcuse: From the New Left to the Next Left. LC 93-40249. 256p. 1994. 35.00 (*0-7006-0658-0*); pap. 16.95 (*0-7006-0659-9*) U Pr of KS.
Bokkon, Pauline H. Footprints in the Coal Dust. 117p. (Orig.). 1994. pap. 8.95 (*0-9641169-0-1*) Gds In The Woods.
***Boklan, Kent D.** Prometheus in Bondage: or All the Girls I Should Have Kissed. 2000. pap. 14.95 (*1-929613-21-0*) Avid MI.
Boklund, Gunnar. The Duchess of Malfi: Sources, Themes, Characters. LC 62-19212. 199p. 1962. reprint ed. pap. 61.70 (*0-7837-1673-7*, 205720500024) Bks Demand.
— The Sources of the White Devil. (Essays & Studies on English Language & Literature: Vol. 17). 1974. reprint ed. pap. 25.00 (*0-8115-0215-5*) Periodicals Srv.
— The Sources of the White Devil, John Webster. LC 68-1396. (Studies in Comparative Literature: No. 35). 1969. reprint ed. lib. bdg. 75.00 (*0-8383-0648-9*) M S G Haskell Hse.
Boklund-Lagopoulou, Karin, jt. auth. see Lagopoulos, Alexandros P.
Bokonyi, S. History of Domestic Mammals in Central & Eastern Europe. 596p. (C). 1988. 168.00 (*963-05-5216-7*, Pub. by Akade Kiado) St Mut.
Bokonyi, Sandor. Mecklenburg Collection Pt. I: Data on Iron Age Horses of Central & Eastern Europe & Human Skeletal Materials from Slovenia. LC 68-22588. (American School of Prehistoric Research Bulletins Ser.: No. 25). (Illus.). 116p. 1968. pap. 8.00 (*0-87365-526-5*) Peabody Harvard.
Bokor, J., jt. ed. see Attwood, D. T.
Bokor-Szego, H. Questions of International Law: Hungarian Perspectives, Vol. 4. Simon, Sandor, tr. from HUN. 265p. (C). 1988. 78.00 (*963-05-4689-2*, Pub. by Akade Kiado) St Mut.
— Questions of International Law: Hungarian Perspectives, Vol. 5. 225p. (C). 1991. 100.00 (*963-05-6015-1*, Pub. by Akade Kiado) St Mut.
Bokor-Szego, Hanna, ed. Questions on International Law-Hungarian Perspectives. 1987. lib. bdg. 99.00 (*90-247-3293-X*) Kluwer Academic.
Bokoske, Sharon, jt. auth. see Davidson, Margaret.
Bokov, Nikolai. Nobody. Fitzlyon, April, tr. from RUS. 1979. pap. 11.95 (*0-7145-3551-6*) Riverrun NY.
Bokova, Hildegard. Der Schreibstand der Deutschsprachigen Urkunden und Stadtbucheintragungen Suedboehmens aus Vorhussitischer Zeit (1300-1419) (GER., Illus.). 415p. 1998. pap. 56.95 (*3-631-32251-8*) P Lang Pubng.
Bokovoy, Douglas, tr. see Wolffsohn, Michael.
Bokovoy, Melissa K. Peasants & Communists: Politics & Ideology in the Yugoslav Countryside, 1941-53. LC 97-33877. (Pitt Series in Russian & East European Studies). 286p. 1998. text 40.00 (*0-8229-4061-2*) U of Pittsburgh Pr.
Bokros, Lajos & Dethier, Jean-Jacques, eds. Public Finance Reform During the Transition: The Expeirence of Hungary. 596p. 1998. pap. 60.00 (*0-8213-4252-5*, 14252) World Bank.
Boksenberg, Alec & Wall, Jaspar, eds. Modern Technology & Its Influence on Astronomy. (Illus.). 335p. 1990. text 90.00 (*0-521-34313-5*) Cambridge U Pr.
Bokser, Baruch M. History of Judaism: The Next Ten Years. LC 80-25501. (Brown Judaic Studies: No. 21). 175p. reprint ed. pap. 54.30 (*0-7837-5421-3*, 204518500005) Bks Demand.
— Post Mishnaic Judaism in Transition: Samuel on Berakhot

B

An Asterisk (*) at the beginning of an entry indicates that the title is appearing for the first time.

& the Beginnings of Gemara. LC 80-19702. (Brown Judaic Studies: No. 17). 575p. reprint ed. pap. 178.30 (0-7837-5418-3, 204518200005) Bks Demand.

Bokser, Baruch M., tr. see Neusner, Jacob, ed.

Bokser, Ben Z. Hasiddur: The Prayer Book. 842p. 1957. 14.00 (0-88482-069-6) Hebrew Pub.

— The Passover Haggadah. 120p. 1974. 8.00 (0-88482-354-7) Hebrew Pub.

— Pharisaic Judaism in Transition. LC 73-2189. (Jewish People; History, Religion, Literature Ser.). 1979. reprint ed. 20.95 (0-405-05255-3) Ayer.

Bokser, Ben Z., comment. Siddur: The Prayer Book. 15.00 (0-317-70173-8); pap. 15.00 (0-317-70174-6) Behrman.

Bokser, Ben Z., tr. Minhah & Maariv Service. 45p. 1958. pap. 3.00 (0-88482-125-0) Hebrew Pub.

— The Prayer Book. 430p. 1983. 18.00 (0-87441-368-0); pap. 15.00 (0-87441-372-9) Behrman.

Bokser, Ben Zion. Abraham Isaac Kook. 216p. (Orig.). 1990. pap. 13.95 (0-916349-15-2, Pub. by Element MA) Penguin Putnam.

— The Essential Writings of Abraham Isaac Kook. 216p. 1990. 24.95 (0-916349-17-9, Pub. by Element MA) Penguin Putnam.

Bokser, Ben Zion, tr. Abraham Isaac Kook: The Lights of Penitence, Lights of Holiness. the Moral Principles. Essays, Letters & Poems. LC 78-70465. (Classics of Western Spirituality Ser.). 448p. 1978. pap. 22.95 (0-8091-2159-X) Paulist Pr.

B

Bokser, Daniel. The Directory of M&A Intermediaries, 1997. 666p. 1996. 295.00 (0-914470-82-5) SD Pub.

— The Merger Yearbook, 1997: U. S./International Edition. 19th ed. (Illus.). 1036p. 1997. 550.00 (0-914470-85-X) SD Pub.

— Pratt's Guide to Venture Capital Sources, 1997. 21st ed. 968p. 1997. 325.00 (0-914470-84-1) SD Pub.

Bokser, Daniel, ed. The Directory of Buyout Financing Sources, 1997. 744p. 1996. 295.00 (0-914470-81-7) SD Pub.

Bokser, Daniel & Weissberg, Ted, eds. Directory of Buyout Financing Sources. 712p. 1995. 275.00 (0-914470-76-0) Venture Econ.

— Directory of M&A Intermediaries. 651p. 1995. 275.00 (0-914470-77-9) Venture Econ.

— Pratt's Guide to Venture Capital Sources. 18th ed. 900p. 1996. 295.00 (0-914470-70-1) Venture Econ.

Bokshtein, B. S. Thermodynamics & Kinetics of Diffusion of Solids. (C). 1985. 37.50 (81-205-0027-X, Pub. by Oxford IBH) S Asia.

Bokstein, B. & Balandina, N., eds. Grain Boundary Diffusion & Grain Boundary Segregation. (Defect & Diffusion Forum Ser.: Vol. 156). (Illus.). 292p. (C). 1998. text 98.00 (3-908450-31-4, Pub. by Scitec Pubns) Enfield Pubs NH.

Bokstein, M. F., et al. Four Papers on Topology. LC 51-5559. (Translations Ser.: Series 2, Vol. 11). 385p. 1959. reprint ed. text 44.00 (0-8218-1711-6, TRANS2/11) Am Math.

Bokun, Branko. Spy in the Vatican. 224p. (Orig.). 1988. pap. 9.95 (0-9510525-2-7) Riverrun NY.

Bokut, I., et al. First Siberian School - "Algebra & Analysis" Proceedings. LC 90-23506. (Translations Ser.: Series 2, Vol. 148). 112p. 1991. text 66.00 (0-8218-3700-1, TRANS2/148) Am Math.

Bokut, L., ed. Second Siberian Winter School "Algebra & Analysis" Proceedings of the Second Siberian School, Tomsk State University, Tomsk. 1989. LC 92-15960. (Translations Ser.: Series 2, Vol. 151). 145p. 1992. text 130.00 (0-8218-3142-9, TRANS2/151) Am Math.

Bokut, L. A., et al, eds. Proceedings of the International Conference on Algebra Dedicated to the Memory of A. I. Mal'cev, 3 vols., Pt. 1. LC 92-9983. (Contemporary Mathematics Ser.: Vol. 131). 712p. 1992. pap. 80.00 (0-8218-5136-5, CONM/131.1) Am Math.

— Proceedings of the International Conference on Algebra Dedicated to the Memory of A. I. Mal'cev, 3 vols., Pt. 2. LC 92-9983. (Contemporary Mathematics Ser.: Vol. 131). 704p. 1992. pap. 79.00 (0-8218-5137-3, CONM/131.2) Am Math.

— Proceedings of the International Conference on Algebra Dedicated to the Memory of A. I. Mal'cev, 3 vols., Pt. 3. LC 92-9983. (Contemporary Mathematics Ser.: Vol. 131). 666p. 1992. pap. 70.00 (0-8218-5138-1, CONM/131.3) Am Math.

— Proceedings of the International Conference on Algebra Dedicated to the Memory of A. I. Mal'cev, 3 vols., Set. LC 92-9983. (Contemporary Mathematics Ser.: Vol. 131). 2176p. 1992. pap. 206.00 (0-8218-5134-9, CONM/131) Am Math.

— Second International Conference on Algebra. LC 94-47104. (Contemporary Mathematics Ser.: Vol. 184). 449p. 1995. pap. 65.00 (0-8218-0295-X, CONM/184) Am Math.

Bokut, L. A. & Kukin, G. P. Algorithmic & Combinatorial Algebra. Berzevich, A. Z. et al, trs. from RUS. LC 93-13343. (Mathematics & Its Applications Ser.: Vol. 255). 472p. (C). 1994. text 272.50 (0-7923-2313-0) Kluwer Academic.

Bokx, H. Dutch-English Laboratory Vocabulary. (DUT & ENG.). 143p. 1993. 38.00 (0-7859-8768-1) Fr & Eur.

Bokx, K. Dutch-English Vocabulary of the Laboratory. (DUT & ENG.). 143p. 1993. 39.95 (0-7859-7466-0, 9020127683) Fr & Eur.

Bol, G., et al, eds. Risk Measurement, Econometrics & Neural Networks: Selected Articles of the 6th Econometric-Workshop in Karlsruhe, Germany. LC 98-43065. (Contributions to Economics Ser.). (Illus.). xii, 306p. 1999. pap. 73.00 (3-7908-1152-1) Spr-Verlag.

Bol, Marsha C. North, South, East, West: American Indians & the Natural World. LC 98-5094. (Illus.). 176p. 1998. 40.00 (1-57098-094-2); pap. 24.95 (1-57098-197-3) Roberts Rinehart.

Bol, Marsha C. & Carnegie Museum of Natural History Staff, eds. The Stars above, the Earth Below: American Indians & Nature. LC 98-5747. (Illus.). 276p. 1998. pap. 19.95 (1-57098-198-1, R Rinehart Intl) Roberts Rinehart.

Bol, Peter C. Argivische Schilde. (Olympische Forschungen Ser.: Vol. XVII). xi, 176p. (C). 1989. lib. bdg. 152.35 (3-11-011587-5) De Gruyter.

— Grossplastik aus Bronze in Olympia. (Olympische Forschungen Ser.: Vol. 14). (GER.). (C). 1978. 111.55 (3-11-006701-3) De Gruyter.

Bol, Peter K. This Culture of Ours: Intellectual Transitions in T'ang & Sung China. LC 91-16004. 532p. 1992. 57.50 (0-8047-1920-9) Stanford U Pr.

— This Culture of Ours: Intellectual Transitions in T'ang & Sung China. (Transitions in T'ang & Sung China). xii, 520p. 1994. pap. 22.50 (0-8047-2361-3) Stanford U Pr.

Bol, Peter R. The Winner's Guide on Retail Selling. LC 84-72669. 128p. (Orig.). 1985. pap. text 6.95 (0-9613917-0-7) Dynamic Comm.

Bolaane, Maitseo, et al. Batswana. LC 96-50255. (Heritage Library of African Peoples: Set 4). (Illus.). 64p. (YA). (gr. 7-12). 1996. lib. bdg. 16.95 (0-8239-2008-9, D2008-9) Rosen Group.

***Bolam, Emily.** Chunky Farm Cow. (Illus.). 14p. (ps-k). 2000. 3.95 (0-7641-5319-6) Barron.

— Chunky Farm Horse. (Illus.). 14p. (ps-k). 2000. 3.95 (0-7641-5322-6) Barron.

— Chunky Farm Pig. (Illus.). 14p. (ps-k). 2000. 3.95 (0-7641-5323-4) Barron.

— Chunky Farm Sheep. (Illus.). 14p. (ps-k). 2000. 3.95 (0-7641-5321-8) Barron.

Bolam, Emily. Mother Goose Math. 32p. 1999. pap. 5.99 (0-14-056393-8, PuffinBks) Peng Put Young Read.

***Bolam, Emily.** Peephole Rhymes. (Illus.). (J). (ps-3). 2000. 7.99 (0-8431-7594-X, Price Stern) Peng Put Young Read.

Bolam, Emily. Sleepy, Sleepy! 8p. 1999. pap. 12.99 (0-8431-7532-X, Price Stern) Peng Put Young Read.

Bolam, Emily. The Little Red Hen, Level 2, Red. LC 95-11149. (Easy-to-Read Bks.). 32p. (J). (ps-k). 1995. pap. 3.99 (0-14-037817-0, PuffinBks) Peng Put Young Read.

— Mother Goose Math. LC 96-61716. 32p. (J). 1997. 14.99 (0-670-87569-4) Viking Penguin.

— The Princess & the Pea. (Easy-to-Read Classics Ser.). 32p. (J). (ps-3). 1996. 13.99 (0-670-86054-9, Viking Child) Peng Put Young Read.

— The Twelve Days of Christmas: A Song Rebus. LC 96-25147. 32p. (J). 1997. 16.00 (0-689-81101-2) Atheneum Yung Read.

Bolam, Emily, jt. auth. see Ziefert, Harriet.

Bolam, Emily, jt. illus. see Ziefert, Harriet.

Bolam, F., jt. auth. see Witts, A.

Bolam, J. P., ed. Experimental Neuroanatomy: A Practical Approach. LC 90-49818. (Practical Approach Ser.). (Illus.). 296p. 1993. pap. text 60.00 (0-19-963325-8) OUP.

Bolam, K. Folksongs from Eastern Europe. 1992. pap. 9.95 (0-571-51308-5) H Leonard.

Bolan, James, et al. Ethical Lawyering: A Practical Guide for Massachusetts Lawyers. LC 90-63091. 400p. 1992. ring bd. 75.00 (0-944490-39-5) Mass CLE.

Bolan, James S. & Massachusetts Continuing Legal Education, Inc. Sta. The New Rules of Professional Conduct: The Impact on Ethical Practice in Massachusetts. LC 97-76381. xxii, 508p. 1998. write for info. (1-57589-076-3) Mass CLE.

Bolan, James S., et al. Ethical Lawyering in Massachusetts, 1996 Supplement. LC 90-63091. 462p. 1995. ring bd., suppl. ed. 39.50 (1-57589-010-0, 96-18.10-SP) Mass CLE.

— Ethical Lawyering in Massachusetts, 1997 Supplement. LC 90-63091. 744p. 1997. ring bd., suppl. ed. 39.50 (1-57589-069-0, 97-18.06-SP) Mass CLE.

Bolan, Mack. Combat Stretch, No. 152. 1991. mass mkt. 3.50 (0-373-61152-8) Harlequin Bks.

***Bolan, Mack.** Conflagration. (Superbolan Ser.: No. 72). 352p. 2000. per. 5.99 (0-373-61472-1, Gold Eagle) Harlequin Bks.

Bolan, Mack. Executioner. 1989. write for info. (0-318-64943-8) S&S Trade.

***Bolan, Mack.** Storm Front. (Superbolan Ser.: Bk. 73). 352p. 2000. per. 5.99 (0-373-61473-X, 1-61473-4, Wrldwide Lib) Harlequin Bks.

Bolan, Mark. Blockade. (Superbolan Ser.: No. 22). 1991. per. 4.50 (0-373-61422-5) Harlequin Bks.

***Boland, Barbara.** Prosecutors & Computers: Automating Major Operations - What a Prosecutor Needs to Know. (Illus.). 79p. (Orig.). (C). 1994. pap. text 25.00 (0-7881-1486-7) DIANE Pub.

Boland, Barbara, jt. auth. see Healey, Kerry M.

Boland, Bob. Thistles & Docks. 160p. 1997. pap. 12.95 (1-85635-131-9, Pub. by Mercier Pr) Irish Amer Bk.

Boland, Bridget. The Prisoner. 1998. pap. 5.25 (0-8222-0916-0) Dramatists Play.

Boland, Bridget, jt. auth. see Boland, Maureen.

Boland, Bridget, jt. ed. see Byrne, Muriel S.

Boland, Brien. Windows 95 Manager's Handbook. 1995. pap. text 29.95 (1-56276-267-2, Ziff-Davis Pr) Que.

Boland, C. Richard, ed. Gastroenterology & Hepatology: The Comprehensive Visual Reference, Vol. II: Colon, Rectum & Anus. LC 95-32010. (Gastroenterology & Hepatology Ser.: Vol. 2). (Illus.). 248p. 1996. text 85.00 (1-878132-79-2) Current Med.

Boland, Carol. Reinsurance Office Practice. (DYP Textbook Ser.). 230p. 1993. pap. 155.00 (1-870255-86-0) LLP.

Boland, D. J. Trees for the Tropics: Growing Australian Multipurpose Trees & Shrubs in Developing Countries. (Illus.). 247p. (Orig.). 1988. pap. 156.00 (0-949511-87-0) St Mut.

Boland, D. J., et al. Eucalyptus Leaf Oils: Use, Chemistry, Distillation & Marketing. 252p. (C). 1991. text 260.00 (0-909605-69-6, Pub. by ACIAR) St Mut.

— Forest Trees of Australia. (Illus.). 687p. 1992. text 89.95 (0-643-05423-5, Pub. by CSIRO) Accents Pubns.

Boland, Dara. How to Eat Like a Tree. 1999. pap. 14.95 (0-89087-945-1) Celestial Arts.

***Boland, Dara.** How to Sleep Like a Bear: Putting Insomnia to Bed. (Illus.). 112p. 2001. 12.95 (0-89087-975-3) Celestial Arts.

Boland, Dean M. Rock & Roll Call: The History & Mystery Behind Rock Names. (Illus.). 131p. 1997. pap. 8.95 (0-9646452-9-7, DO10040, Pub. by Dowling Pr) Music Sales.

Boland, Eavan. In a Time of Violence: Poems. 80p. 1995. pap. 10.00 (0-393-31298-4) Norton.

— A Kind of Scar: The Woman Poet. (C). 1989. 35.00 (0-946211-79-5) St Mut.

***Boland, Eavan.** Limitations. 8p. 2000. pap. 50.00 (1-891472-18-6) Dim Gray.

Boland, Eavan. The Lost Land: Poems. LC 98-3214. 96p. 1998. 21.00 (0-393-04663-X) Norton.

***Boland, Eavan.** The Lost Land: Poems. 72p. 1999. pap. 11.00 (0-393-31951-2) Norton.

Boland, Eavan. Object Lessons: The Life of the Woman & the Poet in Our Time. LC 94-32195. 254p. 1995. 23.00 (0-393-03716-9) Norton.

— Object Lessons: The Life of the Woman & the Poet in Our Time. 254p. 1996. pap. 13.00 (0-393-31437-5, Norton Paperbks) Norton.

— An Origin Like Water: Collected Poems, 1967-1987. 206p. 1997. pap. 12.00 (0-393-31601-7) Norton.

— Outside History: Selected Poems. 160p. 1991. pap. 10.95 (0-393-30822-7) Norton.

***Boland, Eavan, et al.** The Wake Forest Book of Irish Women's Poetry, 1967-2000. O'Brien, Peggy, ed. 314p. 1999. pap. 17.95 (0-916390-88-8) Wake Forest.

Boland, Eavan, jt. auth. see Mac Liammoir, Micheal.

Boland, Eavan, jt. auth. see Strand, Mark.

Boland, Emily. When You Were Young: A Memory Book for the Toddler Years. (Illus.). 72p. 1991. 14.95 (1-55859-164-8) Abbeville Pr.

Boland, Emily. When You Were Young: A Memory Book for the First Two Years. 64p. 1985. 14.95 (0-89659-603-6) Abbeville Pr.

Boland, Faye. Anglo-American Insanity Defence Reform: The War Between Law & Medicine. LC 98-36009. 9p. (C). 1998. text 70.95 (1-84014-716-4, KF9242.B65, Pub. by Ashgate Pub) Ashgate Pub Co.

***Boland, Gerry.** Top 15 Walks in Dublin. (Illus.). 160p. 2000. pap. 14.95 (0-658-00076-4, 000764) NTC Contemp Pub Co.

Boland, Gerry & Plunkett, Myles. This Is Dublin Pocket Guide. (Illus.). 112p. 1999. pap. 14.95 (1-56554-683-0) Pelican.

Boland, J. J., et al, eds. Environmental in Frastructure Management. LC 97-43086. 224p. 1998. lib. bdg. 130.50 (0-7923-4866-4) Kluwer Academic.

Boland, Jack & Caldwell, David E. And That's the Way It Really Is! Transforming Your Desires into Reality. LC 97-169991. xi, 191p. 1997. write for info. (0-88152-064-0) Master Mind.

Boland, James N. & FitzGerald, J. D. Defects & Processes in the Solid State: Geoscience Applications. (Developments in Petrology Ser.: Vol. 14). 494p. 1993. pap. 96.00 (0-444-81701-8) Elsevier.

Boland, James N. & FitzGerald, John D., eds. Defects & Processes in the Solid State: Geoscience Applications, the McLaren Volume. LC 93-26347. 494p. 1993. 192.50 (0-444-81700-X) Elsevier.

Boland, Janice. El Animal Mas Fuerte. Torres, Raquel, tr. (Books for Young Learners).Tr. of Strongest Animal. (SPA., Illus.). 12p. (J). (gr. k-2). 1996. pap. text 5.00 (1-57274-034-5, A2820) R Owen Pubs.

— Breakfast with John. (Books for Young Learners). (Illus.). 8p. (J). (gr. k-2). 1997. pap. text 5.00 (1-57274-109-0, A2130) R Owen Pubs.

***Boland, Janice.** Los Cuervos de la Senora Murphy. Romo, Alberto, tr. (Books for Young Learners).Tr. of Mrs. Murphy's Crows. (SPA., Illus.). 12p. (J). (gr. k-2). 1999. pap. text 5.00 (1-57274-339-5, A2844) R Owen Pubs.

Boland, Janice. El Desayuno con Juan. Romo, Alberto, tr. (Books for Young Learners).Tr. of Breakfast with John. (SPA., Illus.). 8p. (J). (gr. k-2). 1998. pap. text 5.00 (1-57274-198-8, A2847) R Owen Pubs.

— Dog Named Sam. (Puffin Easy-to-Read Ser.). (J). 1998. 9.19 (0-606-12917-0, Pub. by Turtleback) Demco.

— The Fox. (Books for Young Learners). (Illus.). 8p. (J). (gr. k-2). 1996. pap. text 5.00 (1-57274-023-X, A2150) R Owen Pubs.

— Girasoles. Romo, Alberto, tr. (Books for Young Learners).Tr. of Sunflowers. (SPA., Illus.). 8p. (J). (gr. k-2). 1998. pap. text 5.00 (1-57274-203-8, A2860) R Owen Pubs.

— Mrs. Murphy's Crows. (Books for Young Learners). (Illus.). 12p. (J). (gr. k-2). 1999. pap. text 5.00 (1-57274-141-4) R Owen Pubs.

— The Pond. (Books for Young Learners). (Illus.). 8p. (J). (gr. k-2). 1997. pap. text 5.00 (1-57274-070-1, A2185) R Owen Pubs.

— The Strongest Animal. (Books for Young Learners). (Illus.). 12p. (J). (gr. k-2). 1996. pap. text 5.00 (1-57274-024-8, A2510) R Owen Pubs.

— Sunflowers. (Books for Young Learners). (Illus.). 8p. (J). (gr. k-2). 1998. pap. text 5.00 (1-57274-136-8, A2200) R Owen Pubs.

— Zippers. (Books for Young Learners). (Illus.). 8p. (J). (gr. k-2). 1997. pap. text 5.00 (1-57274-116-3, A2220) R Owen Pubs.

— El Zorro. Torres, Raquel, tr. (Books for Young Learners).Tr. of The Fox. (SPA., Illus.). 8p. (J). (gr. k-2). 1996. pap. text 5.00 (1-57274-037-X, A2920) R Owen Pubs.

Boland, Janice D. Method for the One-Keyed Flute. LC 97-49641. 236p. 1998. pap. 24.95 (0-520-21447-1, Pub. by U CA Pr) Cal Prin Full Svc.

Boland, John, jt auth. see Marino, Manuel.

Boland, John C. The Seventh Bearer. Isaacson, Dana, ed. 256p. (Orig.). 1993. mass mkt. 4.99 (0-671-74100-4) PB.

Boland, K. T., jt. auth. see Schiemer, F.

Boland, Katie. I Got Pregnant, You Can Too! How Healing Yourself Physically, Mentally & Spiritually Leads to Fertility. LC 98-9477. 185p. (Orig.). 1998. pap. 12.00 (1-887424-38-5) Underwood Bks.

Boland, Kevin. Speaking Your Best: The Beginners Guide to Public Speaking. Computype, Inc. Staff & Hansell, Karen, eds. 144p. (Orig.). 1996. pap. 12.95 (0-9645364-0-4) Great Bks.

Boland, Lawrence A. Critical Economic Methodology: A Personal Odyssey. LC 96-291. (Illus.). 320p. (C). 1997. 80.00 (0-415-13607-5) Routledge.

— The Foundations of Economic Method. 200p. (C). 1982. pap. text 19.95 (0-04-330329-3) Routledge.

— A Methodology for a New Microeconomics: The Critical Foundations. 208p. 1987. pap. text 18.95 (0-04-330407-9) Routledge.

— The Methodology of Economic Model Building: Model Building after Samuelson. (New Library of Economics). 208p. (C). 1991. pap. 27.99 (0-415-06462-7, A5685) Routledge.

— Principles of Economics. LC 91-31008. 256p. (C). (gr. 13). 1992. 90.00 (0-415-06433-3) Routledge.

— The Principles of Economics: Some Lies My Teachers Told Me. LC 95-21630. 256p. (Orig.). (C). 1995. pap. 29.99 (0-415-13208-8) Routledge.

Boland, Margaret. Architectural Structure in the Lais of Marie de France. LC 93-34617. (Currents in Comparative Romance Languages & Literatures Ser.: Vol. 21). X, 226p. (C). 1995. text 44.95 (0-8204-2224-X) P Lang Pubng.

Boland, Margaret M. Cleomades: A Study in Architectonic Patterns. LC 74-19101. (Romance Monographs: No. 11). 1975. pap. 17.00 (84-399-2791-6) Romance.

Boland, Mary L. Crime Victim's Guide to Justice. LC 97-12716. (Legal Survival Guides Ser.). 224p. 1997. pap. 19.95 (1-57071-166-6, Sphinx Pubng) Sourcebks.

— Your Right to Child Custody, Visitation & Support. LC 99-35179. (Legal Survival Guides Ser.). 336p. 2000. pap. 19.95 (1-57248-097-1, Sphinx Pubng) Sourcebks.

***Boland, Maureen & Boland, Bridget.** Old Wives' Lore for Gardeners. (Illus.). 64p. 2000. 9.95 (1-85479-409-4, Pub. by M OMara) Trafalgar.

Boland, Mechtilde. Die Wind-Atem-Lehre in den Alteren Upanishaden. (Forschungen Zur Ahtropologie & Religionsgeschichte Ser.: Vol. 31). (GER.). xix, 157p. 1997. pap. 21.50 (3-927120-52-9, Pub. by Ugarit-Verlag) Eisenbrauns.

Boland, Peter. The Capitation Sourcebook: A Practical Guide to Managing at Risk Arrangements. LC 96-85011. (Illus.). 664p. 1996. 65.00 (0-9652717-0-6) Aspen Pub.

Boland, Peter. Making Managed Healthcare Work: A Practical Guide to Strategies & Solutions. 620p. 1992. 99.00 (0-8342-0391-X) Aspen Pub.

— Redesigning Health Care Delivery: A Practical Guide to Reengineering, Restructuring & Renewal. (Illus.). 926p. 1996. 65.00 (0-9652717-1-4, 71714) Aspen Pub.

Boland, Peter, ed. The New Healthcare Market: A Guide to PPOs for Purchasers, Payors, & Providers. (Health Care Administration Ser.). 1152p. 1988. 115.00 (0-87094-534-3) Aspen Pub.

Boland, Peter, jt. auth. see Goldfield, Norbert.

Boland, Philip, jt. ed. see Alden, Jeremy.

Boland, Reed. Promoting Reproductive Rights: A Global Mandate. unabridged ed. Rahman, Anika, ed. 48p. 1997. pap. text 10.00 (1-890671-11-8) Center Reprod.

Boland, Robert & Argentini, Paul. Musicals! Directing School & Community Theatre. LC 97-11996. (Illus.). 208p. 1997. pap. 29.50 (0-8108-3323-9) Scarecrow.

Boland, Rosita. Muscle Creek. 1996. pap. 10.95 (1-85186-087-8) Dufour.

— Sea Legs: Hitch-Hiking the Coast of Ireland Alone. 272p. 1992. pap. 15.95 (1-874597-00-6) Dufour.

***Boland, Roy C.** Culture & Customs of El Salvador. LC 00-33124. (Culture & Customs of Latin America & the Caribbean Ser.). 2000. write for info. (0-313-30620-6, Greenwood Pr) Greenwood.

Boland, T. P. Thomas Carr: Archbishop of Melbourne. LC 97-189165. 450p. 1997. 49.95 (0-7022-2967-9, Pub. by Univ Queensland Pr); pap. 39.95 (0-7022-2944-X, Pub. by Univ Queensland Pr) Intl Spec Bk.

Boland, Tim. Government Open Systems Interconnection Profile User's Guide. (Illus.). 143p. (Orig.). (C). 1993. pap. text 35.00 (1-56806-525-6) DIANE Pub.

Boland, Vivian. Ideas in God According to Saint Thomas Aquinas: Sources & Synthesis. LC 95-53243. (Studies in the History of Christian Thought, 0081-8607: Vol. 69). 1996. 128.00 (90-04-10392-9) Brill Academic Pubs.

Boland, Wilfried & Van Woerden, Hugo, eds. Birth & Evolution of Massive Stars & Stellar Groups. 1985. text 184.00 (90-277-2135-1) Kluwer Academic.

Bolande. Sorensen's Basic Nursing. 3rd ed. 1994. 75.00 (0-7216-5217-4) Harcourt.

Bolande, Robert P. Cellular Aspects of Developmental Pathology. LC 67-19136. (Illus.). 383p. reprint ed. 118.80 (0-8357-9398-2, 201452600094) Bks Demand.

Bolande, Robert P., jt. ed. see Rosenberg, Harvey S.

Bolander. Sorensen & Luckmann's Basic Nursing: Performing Checklist. 3rd ed. 1994. wbk. ed. 15.95 (0-7216-5216-6) Harcourt.

An Asterisk (*) at the beginning of an entry indicates that the title is appearing for the first time.

***Bolander, Anne M. & Renning, Adair N.** I Was #87: A Deaf Woman's Ordeal of Misdiagnosis, Institutionalization, & Abuse. LC 00-28788. 232p. 2000. 24.95 (*1-56368-092-0*) Gallaudet Univ Pr.

Bolander, Donald O., ed. Instant Legal Handbook: Paralegal Guide - Spelling Dictionary Latin Words & Phrases. LC 92-72105. (Instant Reference Library). 320p. (C). 1992. 6.95 (*0-911744-00-2*) Career Pub IL.

Bolander, Donald O. & Bisdorf, Rita, eds. Instant Medical Spelling Dictionary: 20,000 Medical, Biological & Pharmaceutical Words. 1986. 6.95 (*0-911744-35-5*) Career Pub IL.

Bolander, Donald O., et al. The Instant Quotation Dictionary: 4800 Quotations on More Than 600 Subjects. LC 74-104786. 320p. 1990. 6.95 (*0-911744-05-3*) Career Pub IL.

— Instant Synonyms & Antonyms: 5,100 Maru Word Entries, 52,000 Synonyms, 31,000 Antonyms. LC 75-113518. 320p. 1992. 6.95 (*0-911744-06-1*) Career Pub IL.

— The New Webster's Desk Reference. 1991. mass mkt. 5.99 (*0-425-12884-9*) Berkley Pub.

Bolander, Donald O., jt. auth. see Semmelmeyer, Madeline.

Bolander, Franklyn F. Molecular Endocrinology. 2nd ed. LC 94-10458. (Illus.). 601p. 1994. text 74.00 (*0-12-111231-4*) Acad Pr.

Bolander, James. Essence. 425p. 1998. mass mkt. 7.99 (*1-57532-197-1*) Press-Tige Pub.

Bolander, Pine, jt. auth. see Bolander, Varner.

Bolander, Steven F., et al, eds. Manufacturing Planning & Control in Process Industries. LC 81-68512. 162p. 1981. pap. 20.00 (*0-935406-04-2*) Am Prod & Inventory.

Bolander, Steven F. & Taylor, Sam G. Process Flow Scheduling. 1994. pap. 26.00 (*1-55822-109-3*) Am Prod & Inventory.

Bolander, Varner & Bolander, Pine. Instant Synonyms & Antonyms. 400p. 1990. reprint ed. mass mkt. 5.99 (*0-440-20536-0*, LE) Dell.

Bolander, Verolyn B. Examaster to Accompany Sorensen & Luckmann's Basic Nursing: A Psychophysiologic Approach. 3rd ed. 1994. text. write for info. (*0-7216-5253-0*, W B Saunders Co) Harcrt Hlth Sci Grp.

— Sorensen & Luckmann's Basic Nursing: A Psychophysiologic Approach. 3rd ed. 379p. 1994. write for info. (*0-7216-5237-9*, W B Saunders Co) Harcrt Hlth Sci Grp.

— Student Study Guide for Sorensen & Luckmann's Basic Nursing: A Psychophysiologic Approach. 3rd ed. (Illus.). 380p. 1994. pap. text 19.00 (*0-7216-4327-2*, W B Saunders Co) Harcrt Hlth Sci Grp.

— Transparencies to Accompany Sorensen & Luckmann's Basic Nursing: A Psychophysiologic Approach. 3rd ed. 160p. 1994. write for info. incl. trans. (*0-7216-4745-6*, W B Saunders Co) Harcrt Hlth Sci Grp.

Bolander, Verolyn B., ed. Sorensen & Luckmann's Basic Nursing: A Psychophysiologic Approach, Study Guide/Checklist Package. 3rd ed. (Illus.). 1994. student ed. 87.00 (*0-7216-5218-2*, W B Saunders Co) Harcrt Hlth Sci Grp.

Bolander, Verolyn R., ed. Sorensen & Luckmann's Basic Nursing: A Psychophysiologic Approach. 3rd ed. LC 93-21589. (Illus.). 1664p. 1994. text 61.00 (*0-7216-4013-3*, W B Saunders Co) Harcrt Hlth Sci Grp.

***Bolanos, Harry & Lewis, David.** Entrepreneurship & Small Business. (Illus.). 144p. 2000. pap. 29.95 (*0-9676613-1-5*) Big Purr Pr.

Bolanos, Laura. Chiapas: Los Indios de Verdad. 1997. pap. text 14.98 (*970-661-012-X*) EDAM.

Bolanowski, S. J. & Gescheider, George A., eds. Ration Scaling of Psychological Magnitude: In Honor of the Memory of S. S. Stevens. 336p. (C). 1990. text 69.95 (*0-8058-0710-1*) L Erlbaum Assocs.

***Bolante, Anthony.** Premiere 5.1 for Macintosh & Windows: Visual QuickStart Guide. 352p. (C). 1999. pap. text 19.99 (*0-201-35475-6*) Peachpit Pr.

***Bolante, Antony.** Visual Quickpro Guide. 344p. 2000. pap. 29.99 (*0-201-70281-9*) Addison-Wesley.

Bolar, Daniel R., jt. auth. see Jennings, Michael N.

Bolar, Jerry L. The Best of J. L. Bolar. 130p. (Orig.). 1995. pap. write for info. (*1-57502-031-9*, P00436) Morris Pubng.

Bolar, L. J. The One They Called "Quiet" LC 94-90383. 269p. 1998. 16.95 (*0-533-11208-7*) Vantage.

— Quartermaster Rangers. 1992. 13.95 (*0-533-08931-X*) Vantage.

Bolaria, B. Singh & Bolaria, Rosemary V., eds. International Labour Migrations. LC 97-900360. 224p. 1998. 22.95 (*0-19-564166-3*) OUP.

Bolaria, L. Politics of Cultural Diversity. 1993. pap. text. write for info. (*0-7730-5174-0*) Addison-Wes.

Bolaria, Rosemary V., jt. ed. see Bolaria, B. Singh.

Bolarsky, C. The Art of Workplace English: A Curriculum for All Students. LC 97-38281. 1997. pap. text 23.50 (*0-86709-426-5*) Heinemann.

Bolas, Gerald D., ed. An Illustrated Checklist of the Collection: Washington University Gallery of Art, St. Louis. LC 81-51198. (Illus.). 80p. 1981. pap. 5.00 (*0-936316-01-2*) Wash U Gallery.

Bolas, Mark T., et al, eds. Steroscopic Displays & Virtual Reality Systems V, Vol. 3295. 462p. 1998. 89.00 (*0-8194-2735-7*) SPIE.

Bolc. Time & Logic: A Computational Approach. 367p. 1994. 70.00 (*1-85728-233-7*, Pub. by UCL Pr Ltd) Taylor & Francis.

Bolc, L. & Borowik, P. Many-Valued Logics 2: Automated Reasoning & Practical Applications. xvi, 282p. 1998. 59.95 (*3-540-64507-1*) Spr-Verlag.

Bolc, Leonard. Cooperative Interfaces to Information Systems. Jarke, Matthias, ed. (Topics in Information Systems Ser.). (Illus.). 400p. 1986. 69.00 (*0-387-16599-1*) Spr-Verlag.

— Natural Language Parsing Systems. (Symbolic Computation Ser.). (Illus.). 335p. 1987. 77.95 (*0-387-17537-7*) Spr-Verlag.

Bolc, Leonard, ed. Computational Models of Learning. (Symbolic Computation Ser.). (Illus.). 240p. 1987. 79.00 (*0-387-16318-2*) Spr-Verlag.

— The Design of Interpreters, Compilers, & Editors, for Augmented Transition Networks. (Symbolic Computation Ser.). (Illus.). 214p. 1985. 71.95 (*0-387-12789-5*) Spr-Verlag.

— Natural Language Communication with Pictorial Information Systems. (Symbolic Computation - Artificial Intelligence Ser.). (Illus.). 340p. 1984. 71.95 (*0-387-13478-6*) Spr-Verlag.

Bolc, Leonard & Borowik, P. Many-Valued Logics, Vol. 1. LC 92-34076. 1992. write for info. (*3-540-55926-4*); 69.95 (*0-387-55926-4*) Spr-Verlag.

Bolc, Leonard & Coombs, M. J., eds. Expert System Applications. (Symbolic Computation Ser.). 530p. 1988. 106.95 (*0-387-18722-7*) Spr-Verlag.

Bolc, Leonard, jt. ed. see McDonald, D. D.

Bolch, Ben W. & Lyons, Harold. Apocalypse Not: Science, Economics & Environmentalism. LC 93-19348. 139p. 1993. 19.95 (*1-882577-05-1*) Cato Inst.

Bolch, Gunter, et al. Queueing Networks & Markov Chains: Modeling & Performance Evaluation with Computer Science Applications. LC 98-11959. 744p. 1998. 98.95 (*0-471-19366-6*) Wiley.

Bolch, Judy, ed. see Snow, A. C.

Bolchazy, Ladislaus J. Hospitality in Antiquity. LC 95-9701. iv, 135p. 1994. pap. 20.00 (*0-89005-212-3*) Ares.

Bolchazy, Ladislaus J. & Sweeny, J. M., eds. Ausonius: Concordantia in Ausonium, with Indices to Proper Nouns & Greek Forms. (Alpha-Omega, Reihe A Ser.: Bd. XLV). 908p. 1982. 190.00 (*3-487-07156-8*) G Olms Pubs.

Bolchazy, Ladislaus J., ed. see More, Thomas.

Bolchover, Richard. British Jewry & the Holocaust. LC 92-20409. 220p. (C). 1993. text 54.95 (*0-521-43234-0*) Cambridge U Pr.

Bolcom & Kenyon. Briefly it Enters Vocal Pianocycle: Songs from Poems by Jane Kenyon. 36p. 1997. pap. 8.95 (*0-7935-9132-5*) H Leonard.

Bolcom, Weins. Cabaret Songs Vols. 1 & 2: For Medium Voice & Piano. 64p. 1986. pap. 14.95 (*0-7935-2078-9*, 8273) H Leonard.

— Capriccio: For Violoncello & Piano. 36p. 1995. pap. 9.95 (*0-7935-4255-3*, 00841003) H Leonard.

— Gospel Preludes, Bk. 3. 20p. 1994. pap. 8.95 (*0-7935-1598-X*, 00009242) H Leonard.

— Gospel Preludes, Bk. 4. 24p. 1994. pap. 8.95 (*0-7935-1599-8*, 00009243) H Leonard.

— I Will Breathe a Mountain: A Song Cycle from American Women Poets. 48p. 1995. pap. 12.50 (*0-7935-4239-1*, 00740011) H Leonard.

— Recuerdos 2 Pianos 4 Hands. 48p. 1993. pap. 15.00 (*0-7935-1948-9*, 00008707) H Leonard.

— Sonata Violoncello & Piano. 40p. 1993. pap. 28.00 (*0-7935-1238-7*, 00009240) H Leonard.

— Third Sonata for Violin & Piano. 48p. 1994. pap. 22.50 (*0-7935-3027-X*, 00008708) H Leonard.

— Three Dance Portraits. 24p. 1991. pap. 8.95 (*0-7935-0969-6*, 00009642) H Leonard.

— 12 New Etudes for Piano, Vol. 2. 64p. 1988. pap. 12.95 (*0-7935-2801-1*, 00009221) H Leonard.

***Bolcom, William.** Complete Rags for Piano. 128p. 2000. otabind 16.95 (*0-634-00182-5*) H Leonard.

— First Sonata: For Violin & Piano. 48p. 1999. pap. 14.95 (*0-634-00106-X*) H Leonard.

— Fourth Sonata: For Violin & Piano. 44p. 1999. pap. 14.95 (*0-634-00107-8*) H Leonard.

— Second Sonata: For Violin & Piano. 1985. pap. text 17.50 (*0-634-00863-3*) H Leonard.

Bold, Alan. The Edge of the Wood. 1989. write for info. (*0-946487-08-1*) Luath Pr Ltd.

— MacDiarmid: A Critical Biography. LC 89-20452. (Illus.). 504p. (C). 1990. lib. bdg. 40.00 (*0-87023-714-4*) U of Mass Pr.

— Scotland Yes. 64p. 1978. pap. 11.95 (*0-8464-1292-6*) Beekman Pubs.

Bold, Alan, ed. Smollett: Author of the First Distinction. (Critical Studies). 240p. 1982. text 44.00 (*0-389-20240-1*, 07097) B&N Imports.

— W. H. Auden: The Far Interior. LC 85-7358. (Critical Studies). 224p. 1985. 58.50 (*0-389-20573-7*, N8132) B&N Imports.

Bold, Alan, jt. auth. see Murray, Keith, Publishing Staff.

Bold, Alan N. Longman Dictionary of Poets: The Lives & Works of 1001 Poets in the English Language. LC 86-129123. 320p. reprint ed. pap. 99.20 (*0-8357-6195-9*, 203448500090) Bks Demand.

— Muriel Spark. (Contemporary Writers Ser.). 96p. 1986. pap. 7.50 (*0-416-40360-3*, 9733) Routledge.

— Scotland: A Literary Guide. 384p. 1989. 75.00 (*0-415-00731-3*) Routledge.

— Summoned by Knox: Poems in Scots. 84p. 1985. pap. 12.95 (*0-905075-20-X*, Pub. by Wilfion Bks) Dufour.

Bold, Benjamin. Famous Problems of Geometry & How to Solve Them. (Illus.). 128p. 1982. reprint ed. pap. 4.95 (*0-486-24297-8*) Dover.

***Bold, Christine.** Progression in Primary Design & Technology. 1999. pap. text 27.95 (*1-85346-605-0*) David Fulton.

Bold, Christine. The WPA Guides: Mapping America. LC 99-26871. (Illus.). 224p. 1999. 48.00 (*1-57806-194-6*); pap. 20.00 (*1-57806-195-4*) U Pr of Miss.

Bold, F. C., jt. auth. see Tawil, Jack J.

Bold, Harold C. & La Claire, John. The Plant Kingdom. 5th ed. (Illus.). 320p. (C). 1986. pap. text 39.80 (*0-13-680398-9*) P-H.

Bold, Harold C. & Wynne, Michael J. Introduction to the Algae. 2nd ed. (Illus.). 736p. (C). 1985. text 58.60 (*0-13-477746-8*) P-H.

Bold, Harold C., et al. Morphology of Plants & Fungi. 5th ed. 928p. (C). 1997. pap. 126.00 (*0-06-040839-1*) Addison-Wesley Educ.

Bold, Harold C., jt. auth. see Chantanachat, S.

Bold, Harold C., jt. auth. see Cox, Elenor R.

Bold, Harold C., jt. auth. see Deason, Temd R.

Bold, Harold C., jt. auth. see Mattox, Karl R.

Bold, Harold C., jt. ed. see Bischoff, Harry W.

Bold, John. John Webb: Architectural Theory & Practice in the Seventeenth Century. (Clarendon Studies in the History of Art). (Illus.). 216p. 1990. 105.00 (*0-19-817503-5*) OUP.

Bold, John & Chaney, Edward, eds. English Architecture, Public & Private: Essays for Kerry Downes. LC 93-13308. 336p. 1993. 75.00 (*1-85285-095-7*) Hambledon Press.

Bold, W. A. Van Den, see Van den Bold, W. A., ed.

Bold, W. A. Vanden. Bulletins of American Paleontology Vol. 79: Distribution of Ostracoda in the Neogene of Central Haiti. 1981. 25.00 (*0-87710-382-8*) Paleo Res.

Boldea, I. Reluctance Synchronous Machines & Drives. LC 97-108433. (Monographs in Electrical & Electronic Engineering: No. 38). (Illus.). 240p. 1996. text 115.00 (*0-19-859391-0*) OUP.

Boldea, I. & Nasar, Syed A. Electric Machines: Steady State Operation. 250p. 1990. 95.00 (*0-89116-991-1*) Hemisp Pub.

— Electric Machines Vol. 2: Dynamics & Control. 250p. 1991. write for info. (*0-89116-992-X*) CRC Pr.

— Linear Electric Actuators & Generators. (Illus.). 247p. (C). 1997. text 64.95 (*0-521-48017-5*) Cambridge U Pr.

Boldea, Ion & Nasar, Syed A. Electric Drives. LC 98-22209. 432p. 1998. boxed set 84.95 (*0-8493-2521-8*) CRC Pr.

Boldea, Ion, jt. auth. see Nasar, Syed A.

***Bolden, Jr.** Psychological Science. 304p. 1999. pap. text 21.00 (*0-536-02814-1*) Pearson Custom.

Bolden, B. J. Urban Rage in Bronzeville: Social Commentary in the Poetry of Gwendolyn Brooks, 1945-1960. LC 97-30831. 224p. 1997. 39.95 (*0-88378-194-8*); pap. 16.95 (*0-88378-195-6*) Third World.

Bolden, Frank E., et al. A Legacy in Bricks & Mortar: African-American Landmarks in Allegheny County. Sturgess, Louise, ed. LC 95-67169. (Illus.). 84p. 1995. pap. text 8.95 (*0-916670-17-1*) Pitt Hist & Landmks Found.

Bolden, John. The Rickety-Run-Down House. unabridged ed. 20p. 1994. spiral bd. 5.00 (*1-929326-43-2*) Ha Bar Pubg.

Bolden, K. J., et al. Practice Management. (Illus.). 144p. 1992. pap. 32.95 (*0-632-03319-3*) Blackwell Sci.

Bolden, Millicent A. & Jimenez, Luis A., eds. Studies in Honor of Maria A. Salgado. (Homenajes Ser.: Vol. 10). 181p. 1995. 22.50 (*0-936388-67-6*) Juan de la Cuesta.

Bolden, Tonya. And Not Afraid to Dare. LC 96-7320. 244p. (J). (gr. 4-9). 1998. 16.95 (*0-590-48080-4*) Scholastic Inc.

— Book of African-American Women: 150 Crusaders, Creators & Uplifters. 1996. 16.00 (*1-55850-647-0*) Adams Media.

— Doing It for Yourself: A Tammy & Owen Adventure with Madame C. J. Walker. LC 97-65041. (America's Family Bks.). (Illus.). 48p. (J). (gr. 2-5). 1997. 15.95 (*1-885053-01-0*) Corp Cult Lit.

Bolden, Tonya. Rites of Passage: Stories about Growing up by Black Writers from Around the World. 1995. 12.80 (*0-606-08858-X*, Pub. by Turtleback) Demco.

Bolden, Tonya. Rock of Ages. (J). 1999. 17.00 (*0-679-89485-3*); lib. bdg. 18.99 (*0-679-99485-8*) Knopf.

— Strong Men Keep Coming: The Book of African American Men. LC 98-41699. 307p. (C). 1999. 24.95 (*0-471-25202-6*) Wiley.

***Bolden, Tonya.** Strong Men Keep Coming: The Book of African American Men. 308p. 1999. pap. 15.95 (*0-471-34873-2*) Wiley.

— 33 Things Every Girl Should Know: Stories, Songs, Poems & Smart Talk by 33 Extraordinary Women. 1998. 18.10 (*0-606-13948-6*, Pub. by Turtleback) Demco

Bolden, Tonya. Through Loona's Door: A Tammy & Owen Adventure with Carter G. Woodson. LC 94-69224. (America's Family Bks.). (Illus.). 48p. (J). (gr. k-5). 1997. 15.95 (*1-885053-00-2*) Corp Cult Lit.

Bolden, Tonya, ed. Rites of Passage: Stories about Growing up by Black Writers from Around the World. LC 93-31304. 240p. (YA). (gr. 5 up). 1994. 16.95 (*1-56282-688-3*, Pub. by Hyprn Child) Time Warner.

— 33 Things Every Girl Should Know: Stories, Songs, Poems & Smart Talk by 33 Extraordinary Women. LC 97-29431. 159p. (YA). (gr. 6 up). 1998. pap. 13.00 (*0-517-70936-8*, Crown); lib. bdg. 17.99 (*0-517-70999-6*) Crown Pub Group.

Bolden, Tonya, jt. auth. see Higginsen, Vy.

Bolden, Tonya, jt. auth. see Love, Mother.

Bolden, Tonya, ed. & abr. see Mother Love.

Boldereff, Frances, jt. auth. see Olson, Charles.

Bolderson, H. & Gains, F. Crossing National Frontiers. (DSS Research Report Ser.). 1993. 35.00 (*0-11-762131-5*, Pub. by Statnry Office) Bernan Associates.

Bolderson, H. & Mabbett, D. Delivering Social Security: A Cross-National Study. LC 99-175612. (DSS Research Report Ser.). 1997. write for info. (*0-11-762447-0*, Pub. by Statnry Office) Bernan Associates.

Bolderson, Helen. Social Security, Disability & Rehabilitation: Conflicts in the Development of Social Policy 1914-1946. 280p. 1991. 75.00 (*1-85302-517-8*) Taylor & Francis.

Boldin, M. V., et al. Sign-Based Methods in Linear Statistical Models. LC 97-3452. (Translations of Mathematical Monographs: Vol. 162). 234p. 1997. text 99.00 (*0-8218-0371-9*, MMONO/162) Am Math.

Boldin, Valery. Ten Years That Shook the World: The Gorbachev Era As Witnessed by His Chief of Staff. Rossiter, Evelyn, tr. 310p. 1998. reprint ed. text 25.00 (*0-7881-5178-9*) DIANE Pub.

Bolding, Kevin, ed. see PCRCW '94 Staff.

Boldis, Hector A. Laser Plasma Theory & Simulation. (Laser Science & Technology Ser.). 121p. 1994. pap. text 61.00 (*3-7186-5489-X*, Harwood Acad Pubs) Gordon & Breach.

Boldman, Craig & Matthews, Pete. Every Excuse in the Book: 714 Ways to Say, "It's Not My Fault!" LC 97-39094. 1998. pap. 8.95 (*0-8362-5195-4*) Andrews & McMeel.

Boldman, Craig, jt. auth. see Matthews.

Boldorini, Maria G. Christmas Eve. (Illus.). 12p. (J). 1995. 7.99 (*0-679-87691-X*) Random.

Boldorini, Maria G. The First Christmas. 6p. (J). (ps-1). 1994. 7.99 (*0-679-86706-6*, Pub. by Random Bks Yng Read) Random.

Boldrey, Richard. Guide to Operatic Duets. 114p. (Orig.). 1994. pap. 35.00 (*1-877761-65-6*) Pst.

— Guide to Operatic Roles & Arias. 554p. (Orig.). 1994. pap. 65.00 (*1-877761-64-8*) Pst.

Boldrey, Richard, et al. Singer's Edition: Operatic Arias - Light Lyric Soprano. 358p. 1992. pap. 49.95 (*1-877761-02-8*) Pst.

— Singer's Edition: Operatic Arias - Soubrette. 328p. 1992. pap. 49.95 (*1-877761-03-6*) Pst.

Boldrick, Lorrie & Hale, Lydia. Pygmy Goats: Management & Veterinary Care. LC 96-85589. (Illus.). 238p. (Orig.). 1996. pap. 19.95 (*0-9624531-3-7*) All Pub.

Boldrick, Lorrie B. The Illustrated Standard of the Pygmy Goat. 2nd ed. Hale, Lydia, ed. (Illus.). 140p. 1990. reprint ed. pap. 9.95 (*0-9624531-1-0*) All Pub.

— Veterinary Care of Pot Bellied Pet Pigs. 130p. (Orig.). 1993. pap. 20.00 (*0-9624531-2-9*) All Pub.

Boldrick, Lorrie B., jt. auth. see Mull, Kayla.

Boldrini, M. Scientific Truth & Statistical Method. 1972. 35.00 (*0-85264-197-4*) Lubrecht & Cramer.

Boldt, Anita Z., tr. see Baierlain, E. R.

Boldt, Annette. Das Fursorgewesen der Stadt Braunschweig in Spatmittelalter und Fruher Neuzeit. (Braunschweiger Werkstucke Ser.: Reihe A). (GER.). xii, 428p. 1988. write for info. (*3-487-09127-5*) G Olms Pubs.

Boldt, Christine, ed. AIS New Car Cost Guide, 1986. 6th ed. 1986. 73.00 (*0-88098-076-1*, H M Gousha) Prntice Hall Bks.

Boldt, David H. Update on Hemostasis. (Contemporary Management in Internal Medicine Ser.: Vol. 1, No. 2). (Illus.). 240p. 1990. text 35.00 (*0-443-08823-3*) Church.

Boldt-Irons, Leslie A., ed. On Bataille: Critical Essays. LC 94-22405. (SUNY Series, Intersections). 338p. (C). 1995. text 59.50 (*0-7914-2455-3*); pap. text 21.95 (*0-7914-2456-1*) State U NY Pr.

Boldt, Jeanine, jt. ed. see Jones, Michael P.

Boldt, Larry. Manifest Your Destiny: Life Planning with Punch. rev. ed. Grant, Kim, ed. LC 87-80391. (Illus.). 346p. 1987. pap. 24.95 (*0-9617762-0-X*); ring bd. 149.95 (*0-9617762-9-3*) Lightning Pr.

— Your Life's Work: How to Find It & Do It. LC 88-83515. (Illus.). 96p. (Orig.). 1989. pap. 5.95 (*0-9617762-2-6*) Lightning Pr.

— Your Life's Work Book: A Practical Guide to Creating the Work You Love. Grant, Kim, ed. LC 88-83516. (Illus.). 320p. (Orig.). 1989. pap. 19.95 (*0-9617762-3-4*) Lightning Pr.

Boldt, Laurence G. How to Find the Work You Love. 154p. 1996. pap. 10.95 (*0-14-019524-6*, Arkana) Viking Penguin.

***Boldt, Laurence G.** The Tao of Abundance: Eight Ancient Principles for Living Abundantly. LC 99-27726. (Illus.). 353p. 1999. pap. 15.95 (*0-14-019606-4*, Penguin Bks) Viking Penguin.

Boldt, Laurence G. Zen & the Art of Making a Living: A Practical Guide to Creative Career Design. LC 98-55070. (Illus.). 640p. 1999. pap. 17.95 (*0-14-019599-8*) Viking Penguin.

— Zen Soup: Tasty Morsels of Wisdom from Great Minds East & West. LC 97-5190. 190p. 1997. pap. 10.95 (*0-14-019560-2*) Viking Penguin.

Boldt, Leslie A., tr. & intro. see Bataille, Georges.

Boldt, Mark. U-Do Book: "Awareness Is Doing Something" large type ed. LC 98-93592. (Illus.). 32p. (J). (gr. k-8). 1998. pap. write for info. (*0-9662556-2-3*, U-DO 03) Boldt Ent.

***Boldt, Mark.** U-Do Book "CC & the Cool Rule!" A Burnsafe Educational U-Do Book, 6. LC 00-91889. (Illus.). 32p. (J). (gr. k-8). 2000. write for info. (*0-9662556-5-8*, U-Do, 06) Bold Ent.

Boldt, Mark. U-Do Book "It's a MADD House Here", Vol. 2. large type ed. LC 98-92697. (Illus.). 24p. (J). (gr. k-6). 1998. pap. write for info. (*0-9662556-1-5*, U-DO, 02) Boldt Ent.

— U-Do Book "Morning Matters", Vol. 5. large type ed. LC 99-94632. (Illus.). 24p. (Orig.). (J). (gr. k-6). 1999. pap. write for info. (*0-9662556-4-X*, U-DO, 05) Boldt Ent.

— U-Do Book "The Force B with U" A Fundsafe U-Do Book. LC 98-94885. (Illus.). 92p. (J). (gr. k-8). 1998. pap. write for info. (*0-9662556-3-1*) Boldt Ent.

— U-Do Book, "The Rules of Safety" large type ed. (Illus.). 24p. (J). (gr. k-6). 1997. pap. write for info. (*0-9662556-0-7*, U-DO,01) Boldt Ent.

B

Boldt, Menno. Surviving as Indians: The Challenge of Self-Government. LC 93-215302. 384p. 1994. pap. text 19.95 (0-8020-7767-6) U of Toronto Pr.

Boldt, Menno & Long, J. Anthony, eds. The Quest for Justice: Aboriginal Peoples & Aboriginal Rights. LC 86-157870. 416p. reprint ed. pap. 129.00 (0-7837-1227-8, 204136300020) Bks Demand.

Boldt, Menno, et al. The Quest for Justice: Aboriginal Peoples & Aboriginal Rights. 416p. 1985. pap. text 22.95 (0-8020-6589-9) U of Toronto Pr.

***Bolduc, Dylan.** Moth & the Flame. LC 99-56241. (Publish-a-Book Ser.). (Illus.). 24p. (ps-3). 2000. pap. text 8.50 (0-7398-2369-8) Raintree Steck-V.

Bolduc, Ed. The Face of God Music Collection. 1999. pap. 13.00 (1-58459-005-X, 7446) Wrld Lib Pubns.

Bolduc, Henry L. The Journey Within: Past Life & Channeling. 304p. (Orig.). 1993. pap. 12.95 (0-9601302-3-3) Adventures Time.

— Life Patterns: Soul Lessons & Forgiveness. 3rd ed. Reynolds, Majorie, ed. LC 94-68926. (Illus.). 300p. 1994. pap. 14.95 (0-9601302-4-1) Adventures Time.

— Self-Hypnosis: Creating Your Own Destiny. 165p. 1993. pap. 9.95 (0-9601302-2-5) Adventures Time.

***Bolduc, Henry Leo.** Self-Hypnosis: Scripts & Suggestions for Your Subconscious. Chadwick, Gloria, ed. LC 00-130512. 140p. 2000. pap. 12.95 (1-883717-02-7) Myst Mndscapes.

Bolduc, Jean B. Mission of the Columbia. 144p. 1979. 19.95 (0-87770-216-0) Ye Galleon.

Bolduc, Kathleen D. His Name Is Joel: Searching for God in a Son's Disability. LC 99-25594. 134p. 1999. write for info. (1-57895-034-1) Curriculm Presbytrn KY.

Boldue, Ed. We Are Faithful Songbook. 28p. 1998. pap. 7.00 (0-937690-59-7, 7441) Wrld Lib Pubns.

***Boldurian, Anthony T. & Cotter, John L.** Clovis Revisited: New Perspectives on Paleoindian Adaptations from Blackwater Draw, New Mexico. LC 99-6020. (Illus.). 1999. write for info. (0-924171-67-7) U Museum Pubns.

— Clovis Revisited: New Perspectives on Paleoindian Adaptations from Blackwater Draw, New Mexico. LC 99-6020. (University Museum Monographs). 2p. 1999. write for info. (0-924171-68-5) U Museum Pubns.

Boldy, Adrian P. & Radha Krishna, Hari C., eds. Hydraulic Design of Hydraulic Machinery. LC 96-85968. (Hydraulic Machinery Bks.). 608p. 1997. 119.95 (0-291-39851-0, Pub. by Avebury Technical) Ashgate Pub Co.

Boldy, Adrian P., jt. auth. see Swaffield, J. A.

***Boldy, Duncan P.** Empowering Frail Elderly People: Opportunities & Impediments in Housing, Health & Support Service Delivery. Heumann, Leonard F. & McCall, Mary E., eds. LC 00-25465. 272p. 2000. 64.00 (0-275-96651-8, C6651, Praeger Pubs) Greenwood.

Boldy, Duncan P., jt. ed. see Heumann, Leonard F.

Boldy, S. A., ed. Permian & Triassic Rifting in Northwest Europe. (Geological Society Special Publication Ser.: No. 91). (Illus.). 263p. 1995. 100.00 (1-897799-33-0, 332, Pub. by Geol Soc Pub Hse) AAPG.

Boldy, S. A., jt. ed. see Fleet, A. J.

Boldy, Steven, ed. see Fuentes, Carlos.

***Boldyrev.** Reactivity Of Molecular Solids, Vol. 3. 340p. 1999. 249.00 (0-471-99907-5) Wiley.

Boldyrev, A., jt. auth. see Simmons, J.

Boldyrev, V. V. Reactivity in Solids: Past, Present, & Future. (Chemistry for the 21st Century Monograph). (Illus.). 320p. 1996. text 79.50 (0-86542-687-2) Blackwell Sci.

Bole, A. G. & Dineley, W. O. Radar & Arpa Manual. (Illus.). 432p. 1993. pap. 69.95 (0-7506-0818-8) Buttrwrth-Heinemann.

Bole, A. G., et al. The Navigation Control Manual. 2nd ed. (Illus.). 314p. 1992. pap. 79.95 (0-7506-0542-1) Buttrwrth-Heinemann.

Bole-Becker, Luanne. A Scrap of Pride: How to Use Quilting As a Tool to Bring People Together. (Illus.). ii, 30p. (Orig.). (YA). (gr. k-12). 1996. pap., wbk. ed. 35.00 incl. VHS (0-9654560-0-5) BB Sound.

Bole, John A. The Harmony Society: A Chapter in German American Culture History. 1976. lib. bdg. 59.95 (0-8490-1933-8) Gordon Pr.

Bole, Thomas J., III & Bondeson, William B. Rights to Health Care. 318p. (C). 1991. lib. bdg. 155.00 (0-7923-1137-X, Pub. by Kluwer Academic) Kluwer Academic.

Bole, William, jt. auth. see Higgins, George G.

Bolea, Patricia Stow, jt. auth. see Harold, Rena D.

Boleij, J. S., et al. Occupational Hygiene of Chemical & Biological Agents. 298p. 1995. 161.50 (0-444-81997-5) Elsevier.

Bolek, Catherine S. & Niemcryk, Steve J., eds. Ethnic & Multicultural Drug Abuse: Perspectives on Current Research. LC 92-23858. (Drugs & Society Ser.: Vol. 6, Nos. 1-4). (Illus.). 520p. 1993. pap. 29.95 (1-56023-023-1, Harrington Park); lib. bdg. 59.95 (1-56024-321-X) Haworth Pr.

Bolek, Francis, ed. Who's Who in Polish America: A Biographical Directory of Polish-American Leaders & Distinguished Poles Resident in the Americas. LC 75-129390. (American Immigration Collection. Series 2). 1970. reprint ed. 34.95 (0-405-00545-8) Ayer.

Bolek, Raymond W., et al. Touche Ross Government Executives' Guide to Selecting a Small Computer. LC 84-4726. 244p. 1984. 49.95 (0-13-925611-3, Busn) P-H.

Bolek, Raymond W., jt. auth. see Berkery, Michael J.

Boleman. Physics. 3rd ed. 1995. pap. text, teacher ed. write for info. (0-13-164121-2) Allyn.

Bolemon, ed. College Physics. (C). 2002. pap. text, student ed. write for info. (0-673-99907-6) Addison-Wesley.

Bolen, Dianna W., jt. auth. see Rosenfeld, Nancy.

***Bolen, Barbara Bradley.** Breaking the Bonds of Irritable Bowel Syndrome: A Psychological Approach to Regaining Control of Your Life. (Illus.). 175p. 2000. pap. 14.95 (1-57224-188-8) New Harbinger.

Bolen, Cheryl. A Duke Deceived. (Historical Ser.). 1998. per. 4.99 (0-373-29006-3, 1-29006-3) Harlequin Bks.

Bolen, David B., II. The Essence of Living: Reaching Beyond Global Insanity. LC 94-67371. (Illus.). 180p. (Orig.). 1995. pap. 11.95 (0-9641909-0-7) New Verity.

Bolen, David B., 2nd. How You See It, How You Don't: Discover the Magic & Power of Your Own Beliefs. LC 96-92044. 126p. (Orig.). (C). 1997. pap. 11.95 (0-9641909-1-5) New Verity.

Bolen, Dennis E. Stand in Hell. 208p. 1995. 22.91 (0-394-22402-7) Random.

Bolen, Eric, jt. auth. see Baldassarre, Guy A.

Bolen, Eric G. Ecology of North America. (Illus.). 464p. 1998. 85.00 (0-471-13156-3) Wiley.

Bolen, Eric G. & Flores, Dan. The Mississippi Kite. LC 93-3657. (Corrie Herring Hooks Ser.: No. 25). (Illus.). 128p. (C). 1993. 17.95 (0-292-75148-6) U of Tex Pr.

Bolen, Eric G. & Robinson, William L. Wildlife Ecology & Management. 4th ed. LC 98-7009. 605p. 1998. 90.00 (0-13-840422-4) P-H.

Bolen, Eric G. & Rylander, Michael K. Whistling-Ducks: Zoogeography, Ecology, Anatomy. (Special Publications: No. 20). (Illus.). 67p. 1983. pap. 12.00 (0-89672-111-6) Tex Tech Univ Pr.

Bolen, Eric G., jt. auth. see Rodiek, Jon E.

Bolen, Jean S. Close to the Bone. 1996. 21.50 (0-614-20405-4, Scribners Ref) Mac Lib Ref.

— Close to the Bone: Life-Threatening Illness & the Search for Meaning. 224p. 1996. 22.50 (0-684-82237-7) S&S Trade.

— Close to the Bone: Life-Threatening Illness & the Search for Meaning. 224p. 1998. per. 11.00 (0-684-83530-4, Touchstone) S&S Trade Pap.

— Crossing to Avalon: A Woman's Midlife Pilgrimage. LC 90-55174. 320p. 1995. pap. 15.00 (0-06-250272-7, Perennial) HarperTrade.

— Goddesses In Every Woman Reissue: New Psychology of Women, A. LC 83-48990. 352p. 1993. pap. 14.00 (0-06-091291-X, PL 1291, Perennial) HarperTrade.

— Gods In Everyman Reissue: New Psychology of Men's Lives & Loves, A. LC 88-45663. 352p. 1993. reprint ed. pap. 13.00 (0-06-097280-7, Perennial) HarperTrade.

— The Tao of Psychology: Synchronicity & the Self. LC 79-1778. 128p. 1982. pap. 13.00 (0-06-250081-3, Pub. by Harper SF) HarpC.

***Bolen, Jean Shinoda.** Goddesses in Older Women. 2001. write for info. (0-06-019152-X) HarpC.

— Goddesses in Older Women. 2002. pap. write for info. (0-06-092923-5, Perennial) HarperTrade.

— The Millionth Circle: How to Change Ourselves & the World. LC 99-23769. 168p. 1999. 14.95 (1-57324-176-8) Conari Press.

Bolen, Jean Shinoda. Ring of Power: Symbols & Themes, Love vs. Power in Wagner's Ring Cycle & in Us - A Jungian Feminist Perspective. rev. ed. LC 98-45627. Orig. Title: Ring of Power: The Abandoned Child, the Authoritarian Father & the Disempowered Feminine. (Illus.). 272p. 1999. reprint ed. pap. 18.95 (0-89254-043-5) Nicolas-Hays.

Bolen, Steven J. A Legacy for Our Children. Lewis, Lynne E., ed. & intro. by. LC 93-85582. 239p. (Orig.). 1995. pap. write for info. (1-885487-07-X) Brownell & Carroll.

Bolen, Val, jt. auth. see Humesky, Assya.

Bolendas, Joa. So That You May Be One: From the Visions of Joa Bolendas. Hill, John, tr. from GER. & intro. by. Schroeder-Shecker, Therese et al, intros. LC 96-40526. 416p. 1997. pap. 24.95 (0-940262-85-1, Lindisfarne) Anthroposophic.

Bolender, John, jt. auth. see Arman, Mike.

Bolender, Joyce, jt. auth. see Martinsen, Emily C.

Bolens, Lucie. L' Andalousie du Quotidien au Sacre (XIe-XIIIe Siecles) (Collected Studies: No. CS 337). 320p. 1991. 113.95 (0-86078-290-5, Pub. by Variorum) Ashgate Pub Co.

Boler, Megan. Feeling Power: Emotions & Education. LC 98-27448. 224p. (C). 1999. pap. 22.99 (0-415-92104-X, D5782) Routledge.

— Feeling Power: Emotions & Education. LC 98-27448. 224p. (C). (gr. 13). 1999. 75.00 (0-415-92103-1, D5778) Routledge.

***Boler, Olivia J.** Year of the Smoke Girl. 213p. 2000. pap. 14.95 (1-883938-78-3) Dry Bones Pr.

***Boles.** Resource Guide on Right. 2001. pap. 49.95 (0-7693-0034-0) Thomson Learn.

Boles, Anita B. & Patterson, John C. Improving Community Response to Victims of Crime: An Eight-Step Model for Developing Protocol. 224p. 1996. 45.00 (0-8039-7244-X, 7244X) Sage.

Boles, Dan. The Snow Birds & Other Stories. 302p. (Orig.). 1994. pap. 12.95 (0-938711-23-7) Tecolote Pubns.

Boles, Daniel N. Alfie, a Leg up & Other Stories. 260p. (Orig.). 1995. pap. 9.95 (0-938711-34-2) Tecolote Pubns.

Boles, Daralice, jt. auth. see Doubilet, Susan.

Boles, David. Windows 95 Communication & Online Secrets. LC 96-75007. 696p. 1996. pap. 39.99 (1-56884-837-4) IDG Bks.

Boles, Donald E. Mr. Justice Rehnquist, Judicial Activist: The Early Years. LC 87-3295. 161p. 1987. reprint ed. pap. 50.00 (0-608-00049-3, 206081500006) Bks Demand.

Boles, Frank & Young, Julia M. Archival Appraisal. 155p. 1991. pap. text 49.95 (1-55570-064-0) Neal-Schuman.

Boles, H. Leo. The Holy Spirit: His Personality, Nature & Work. 2nd ed. (Classics Ser.). 313p. 1999. reprint ed. pap. 14.99 (0-89225-384-3) Gospel Advocate.

Boles, Janet K., ed. The Egalitarian City: Issues of Rights, Distribution, Access & Power. LC 85-22371. 224p. 1985. 45.00 (0-275-92029-1, C2029, Praeger Pubs) Greenwood.

Boles, Janet K., et al. From the Goddess to the Glass Ceiling: A Dictionary of Feminism. LC 95-42618. 448p. 1996. pap. text 19.95 (1-56833-072-3) Madison Bks UPA.

— Historical Dictionary of Feminism. (Historical Dictionaries of Religions, Philosophies, & Movements Ser.: Vol. 6). 478p. 1996. 49.50 (0-8108-3042-6) Scarecrow.

Boles, John B. Black Southerners, 1619-1869. LC 83-10177. (New Perspectives on the South Ser.). 256p. 1983. reprint ed. pap. text 17.00 (0-8131-0161-1) U Pr of Ky.

— The Great Revival: Beginnings of the Bible Belt. rev. ed. LC 95-25319. (Religion in the South Ser.: No. 1). (Illus.). 256p. 1996. pap. 17.00 (0-8131-0862-4) U Pr of Ky.

— The Great Revival, 1787-1805: The Origins of the Southern Evangelical Mind. LC 77-183349. 252p. reprint ed. pap. 78.20 (0-608-12690-X, 202435800037) Bks Demand.

— The Irony of Southern Religion. LC 94-11508. (Rockwell Lectures: Vol. 3). 118p. (Orig.). 1994. 31.95 (0-8204-2584-2) P Lang Pubng.

— The Irony of Southern Religion. (The Rockwell Lecture Ser.: Vol. 5). 128p. (Orig.). (C). 1994. pap. text 31.95 (0-8402-2584-9) P Lang Pubng.

— Masters & Slaves in the House of the Lord: Race & Religion in the American South, 1740-1870. LC 88-6525. 264p. 1990. pap. 17.00 (0-8131-0187-5) U Pr of Ky.

— Religion in Antebellum Kentucky. LC 95-12711. 160p. 1995. pap. 12.50 (0-8131-0844-6) U Pr of Ky.

— The South Through Time: A History of an American Region. LC 94-3343. 640p. 1994. text 51.00 (0-13-825050-2) P-H.

— The South Through Time: A History of An American Region, Vol. 1. 2nd ed. LC 98-7710. 386p. (C). 1998. pap. text 36.80 (0-13-095915-4) P-H.

— The South Through Time: A History of an American Region, vol. 2. 2nd ed. LC 98-7710. (South Through Time Ser.). 252p. 1998. pap. text 36.80 (0-13-095914-6) P-H.

Boles, John B. & Nolen, Evelyn T., eds. Interpreting Southern History: Historiographical Essays in Honor of Sanford W. Higginbotham. LC 86-10662. 624p. 1987. pap. text 24.95 (0-8071-1361-1) La State U Pr.

Boles, Keith E., jt. auth. see Neumann, Bruce R.

Boles, Kenny. Heaven: What a Wonderful Place. (Small Group Studies). 90p. 1999. pap. 5.99 (0-89900-830-5) College Pr Pub.

Boles, Laurence H. The Huguenots, the Protestant Interest, & the War of the Spanish Succession, 1702-1714. LC 95-39352. (American University Studies IX: Vol. 181). XIII, 287p. (C). 1997. text 46.95 (0-8204-3070-6) P Lang Pubng.

Boles, Margo Smith, jt. ed. see Morphy, Howard.

Boles, Mark A., et al. Nuclear Medicine: Principles & Practice, 2 Vols. Henkin, Robert E., ed. (Illus.). 1852p. (C). (gr. 13). 1995. text 309.00 (0-8016-7701-7, 07701) Mosby Inc.

Boles, Martha & Newman, Rochelle. The Surface Plane. (Orig.). 1996. reprint ed. pap. text 40.00 (0-697-35578-0) Pythagorean Pr.

Boles, Michael A., jt. auth. see Cengel, Unus.

Boles, Michael A., jt. auth. see Cengel, Yanus A.

Boles, Michael A., jt. auth. see Cengel, Yunis A.

Boles, Michael A., jt. auth. see Cengel, Yunus A.

Boles, Richard, ed. see Hogan, Donald F.

Boleslavski, R. Les Lanciers. (FRE.). 376p. 1986. pap. 12.95 (0-7859-2032-3, 2070377296) Fr & Eur.

Boleslavsky, Richard. Acting: The First Six Lessons. 134p. 1987. 17.99 (0-87830-000-7, Thtre Arts Bks) Routledge.

Bolesta, Karen, ed. Amish. (Classic American Quilt Collection). (Illus.). 128p. 1996. text 19.95 (0-87596-725-6) Rodale Pr Inc.

Bolet, S. Dios Usa a Personas Que No Son Perfectas.Tr. of God Uses People Who Are Not Perfect. (SPA.). 1996. 4.50 (0-7899-0140-4, 493037) Editorial Unilit.

Boley, Bruno A. & Weiner, Jerome H. Theory of Thermal Stresses. LC 96-49597. (Illus.). 502p. 1997. reprint ed. pap. text 15.95 (0-486-69579-4) Dover.

Boley, Bruno A., ed. see International Union of Theoretical & Applied Mecha.

***Boley, Farrell M.** West of the Cimarron: With Betsy & Peek-A-Boo. LC 00-190994. 2000. 25.00 (0-7388-2175-6) Xlibris Corp.

— West of the Cimarron: With Betsy & Peek-a-Boo. LC 00-190994. 2000. pap. 18.00 (0-7388-2176-4) Xlibris Corp.

***Boley, H.** A Tight, Practical Integration of Relations & Functions. (Lecture Notes in Artificial Intelligence Ser.: Vol. 1712). xi, 169p. 1999. pap. 45.00 (3-540-66644-3) Spr-Verlag.

Boley, H., et al, eds. Processing Declarative Knowledge: International Workshop PDK '91 Kaiserslautern, Germany, July 1-3, 1991 Proceedings. (Lecture Notes in Artificial Intelligence Ser.: Vol. 567). xii, 427p. 1991. 58.95 (0-387-55033-X) Spr-Verlag.

Boley, Robert E. Industrial Districts: Principles in Practice. LC HD0058.. (Urban Land Institute, Technical Bulletin Ser.: No. 44). 200p. reprint ed. pap. 62.00 (0-8357-8182-8, 203394900087) Bks Demand.

Boleyn, Thomas, jt. auth. see Honari, Morteza.

Bolfarine, H. & Zacks, S. Prediction Theory for Finite Populations. Berger, J. O. et al, eds. (Series in Statistics). 224p. (C). 1992. 72.95 (0-387-97785-6) Spr-Verlag.

Bolfert, Tom. The Big Book of Harley-Davidson. rev. ed. (Illus.). 288p. 1991. 39.95 (0-9624113-1-0) Harley-Davidson.

Bolgan, Anne C. What the Thunder Really Said: A Retrospective Essay on the Making of the Waste Land. LC 73-79500. 202p. reprint ed. pap. 62.70 (0-7837-6936-9, 204676500003) Bks Demand.

Bolger, jt. auth. see Parenteau.

Bolger, Bruce & Stoller, Gary. Fodor's Short Escapes to Britain: 25 Country Getaways for People Who Love to Walk. 2nd ed. (Illus.). 256p. 1996. pap. 13.00 (0-679-03072-7) Fodors Travel.

— Fodor's Short Escapes to France: 25 Country Getaways for People Who Like to Walk. 2nd ed. 256p. 1996. pap. 13.00 (0-679-03071-9) Fodors Travel.

***Bolger, Daniel G.** Thirteen. Schaefer, George, ed. 14p. 1999. pap. 3.00 (1-930160-03-8) Across The Universe.

Bolger, Daniel P. The Battle for Hunger Hill: The 1st Battalion, 327th Infantry Regiment at the Joint Readiness Center. LC 96-47564. (Illus.). 384p. 1997. 24.95 (0-89141-453-3) Presidio Pr.

Bolger, Daniel P. Death Ground: Today's American Infantry in Battle. (Illus.). 384p. 1999. 29.95 (0-89141-671-4, Pub. by Presidio Pr) Natl Bk Netwk.

***Bolger, Daniel P.** Death Ground: Today's American Infantry in Battle. 384p. 2000. pap. 19.95 (0-89141-720-6) Presidio Pr.

Bolger, Dermot. April Bright & Blinded by the Light. (Nick Hern Bks.). 160p. 1997. pap. 16.95 (1-85459-362-5, Pub. by N Hern Bks) Theatre Comm.

***Bolger, Dermot.** Dermot Bolger Plays, Vol. 1. 2000. pap. 14.95 (0-413-74500-7) Methn.

Bolger, Dermot. Internal Exiles. 1986. pap. 11.95 (0-85105-445-5, Pub. by Smyth) Dufour.

— Invisible Dublin. 178p. 1991. pap. 14.95 (1-85186-089-4) Dufour.

— Invisible Dublin. 1996. pap. 12.95 (1-85186-016-9) Dufour.

— Ireland in Exile: Irish Writers Abroad. 176p. (Orig.). 1993. reprint ed. pap. 11.95 (1-874597-55-3, Pub. by New Island Books) Irish Bks Media.

***Bolger, Dermot.** Ladies' Night at Finbars Hotel. 2000. write for info. (0-15-100608-3) Harcourt.

Bolger, Dermot. Leinster Street Ghosts. 32p. 1990. pap. 7.95 (1-85186-067-3) Dufour.

***Bolger, Dermot.** Passion of Jerome. 2000. pap. 10.95 (0-413-73880-9, Methuen Drama) Methn.

— Taking My Letters Back: New & Selected Poems LC 98-215049. 128 p. :p. 1998. 14.95 (1-874597-98-7) New Island Books.

Bolger, Dermot. The Vintage Book of Contemporary Irish Fiction. LC 95-11104. 1995. pap. 14.00 (0-679-76546-8) Vin Bks.

Bolger, Dermot, adapted by. A Dublin Bloom. 112p. 1995. pap. 16.95 (1-874597-26-X) Dufour.

— A Dublin Bloom. 112p. 1996. pap. 14.95 (1-85459-214-9, Pub. by New Island Books) Irish Bks Media.

Bolger, Dermot, ed. Bright Wave/An Tonn Gheal: Poetry in Irish Now. (ENG & IRI.). 200p. 1986. pap. 14.95 (1-85186-008-8) Dufour.

— Greatest Hits. LC 97-184004. (Nick Hern Bks.). 160p. 1997. pap. 16.95 (1-85459-352-8, Pub. by N Hern Bks) Theatre Comm.

— Sixteen on Sixteen: Irish Writers on the Easter Rising. 48p. 1988. pap. 7.95 (1-85186-051-7) Dufour.

Bolger, Dermot & Carty, Ciaran, eds. The Hennessy Book of Irish Fiction: A Celebration of New Irish Writing from "The Sunday Tribune" 172p. (Orig.). 1995. pap. 11.95 (1-874597-28-6, Pub. by New Island Books) Irish Bks Media.

Bolger, Dermot, ed. see Binchy, Maeve, et al.

Bolger, Dermot, ed. see Ledwidge, Francis.

Bolger, Dermot, ed. see Toibin, Colm & Doyle, Roddy.

Bolger, Doreen, et al. American Pastels in the Metropolitan Museum of Art. (Illus.). 256p. 1989. 60.00 (0-8109-1895-1, Pub. by Abrams) Time Warner.

— American Pastels in the Metropolitan Museum of Art. 1989. 25.00 (0-87099-547-2, 0-8109-1895-1) Metro Mus Art.

— Thomas Eakins & the Swimming Picture. LC 95-45967. (Illus.). 176p. 1996. pap. 30.00 (0-88360-085-4) Amon Carter.

— William M. Harnett. unabridged ed. LC 91-26675. (Illus.). 352p. 1992. pap. 10.00 (0-88360-069-2) Amon Carter.

Bolger, Dorita E., jt. compiled by see Wolcott, Roger T.

Bolger, F., jt. auth. see Wright, G.

Bolger, Francis William Pius. The Years Before "Anne" LC 92-161625. (Illus.). v, 229p. 1991. pap. 12.95 (0-921054-77-7) Nimbus Publ.

Bolger, Francis William Pius, ed. & selected by see Montgomery, L. M., et al.

Bolger, Janie, et al. Xeriscape for Central Texas: A Water-Wise Approach to Home Landscaping. Boardman, Gerre, ed. Orig. Title: Xeriscape Landscaping in the Austin Area Handbook. (Illus.). 242p. 1998. pap. 20.00 (0-9668649-0-5) Xeriscape Garden.

Bolger, Nancy, ed. see Bolger, Stuart.

Bolger, Niall, et al, eds. Persons in Context: Developmental Processes. (Human Development in Cultural & Historical Contexts Ser.). (Illus.). 280p. 1989. text 49.95 (0-521-35577-X) Cambridge U Pr.

Bolger, Philip C. Boats with an Open Mind: Seventy-Five Uninhibited Designs & Concepts. LC 94-19978. 1994. pap. write for info. (0-07-006376-1) Intl Marine.

Bolger, Philip H. & Draper, C. Stark, eds. Space Rescue & Safety, 1975. (Science & Technology Ser.: Vol. 41). (Illus.). 230p. 1976. 25.00 (0-87703-077-4) Univelt Inc.

Bolger, Philip H. & Richards, Paul B., eds. Skylab & Pioneer Report, 12th Goddard Memorial Symposium, Mar. 8, 1974, Washington, D.C. 12th Goddard Memorial

B

An Asterisk (*) at the beginning of an entry indicates that the title is appearing for the first time.

Symposium, Washington, D. C., Mar. 8, 1974. (Science & Technology Ser.: Vol. 36). (Illus.). 160p. 1975. 20.00 (*0-87703-071-5*, Am Astronaut Soc) Univelt Inc.

Bolger, Stephen G. The Irish Character in American Fiction, 1830-1860. LC 76-6323. (Irish Americans Ser.). 1976. 21.95 (*0-405-09320-9*) Ayer.

Bolger, Stuart. Genesee Country Museum: Scenes from Town & Country. LC 85-81337. (Illus.). 102p. (Orig.). 1985. 13.50 (*0-685-34770-2*); pap. 5.95 (*0-931535-04-2*) Genesee Ctry Mus Pr.

— Genesee Country Village: Scenes of Town & Country in the Nineteenth Century. 2nd ed. Bolger, Nancy, ed. LC 93-72617. (Illus.). 112p. 1993. 19.95 (*0-931535-05-0*); pap. 12.95 (*0-931535-06-9*) Genesee Ctry Mus Pr.

Bolger, William F., intro. All about Letters. rev. ed. LC 82-600601. (Illus.). 64p. (J). (gr. 9-12). 1982. pap. 2.50 (*0-685-06202-3*, 01135) USPS.

— P. S. Write Soon! All about Letters. LC 82-600641. (Illus.). 64p. (Orig.). (J). (gr. 4-8). 1982. pap. 2.50 (*0-8141-3796-2*, 37962) USPS.

Bolgiano, Chris. Appalachian Forest: A Search for Roots & Renewal. LC 98-17747. (Illus.). 288p. 1998. 25.00 (*0-8117-0126-3*) Stackpole.

— Mountain Lion: An Unnatural History of Pumas & People. LC 95-10063. (Illus.). 224p. 1995. 19.95 (*0-8117-1044-0*) Stackpole.

Bolhuis, Johan J., jt. ed. see Hogan, Jerry A.

Bolhuis, John J. & Hogan, Jerry A. Development of Animal Behavior: A Reader. LC 98-16168. 352p. 1998. 64.95 (*0-631-20707-4*); pap. 34.95 (*0-631-20708-2*) Blackwell Pubs.

Bolhuis, John L. & Wolff, Roger K. The Financial Ingredient in Foodservice Management. Educational Foundation of the National Restaurant, ed. LC 76-9243. 211p. 1976. student ed. 32.50 (*0-915452-28-6*) Educ Found.

— The Financial Ingredient in Foodservice Management. Educational Foundation of the National Restaurant, ed. LC 76-9243. 211p. 1976. reprint ed. text 16.95 (*0-669-00009-4*) Educ Found.

Boli, J. & Altbach, P. G. New Citizens for a New Society: The Institutional Origins of Mass Schooling in Sweden. LC 88-26571. (Pergamon Comparative & International Education Ser.: Vol. 9). (Illus.). 300p. 1989. 141.00 (*0-08-036461-6*, Pub. by Pergamon Repr) Franklin.

Boli, John & Thomas, George M., eds. Constructing World Culture: International Nongovernmental Organizations since 1875. LC 98-35017. 376p. 1998. 55.00 (*0-8047-3421-6*); pap. 18.95 (*0-8047-3422-4*) Stanford U Pr.

Boli, John, jt. ed. see Lechner, Frank.

Bolia, Inge. Rituals of Respect: The Secret of Survival in the High Peruvian Andes. LC 98-8930. (Illus.). 304p. 1998. pap. 16.95 (*0-292-70867-X*) U of Tex Pr.

Bolian, Charles E., jt. auth. see Starbuck, David R.

Bolian, Charles E., jt. ed. see Starbuck, David R.

Bolibruch, A. A., et al. Mathematics in St. Petersburg. LC 91-640741. (American Mathematical Society Translations Ser.: Series 2, Vol. 174). 273p. 1996. text 99.00 (*0-8218-0559-2*, TRANS2/174) Am Math.

Bolibrukh, A. A. The 21st Hilbert Problem for Linear Fuchsian Systems. (Proceedings of the Steklov Institute of Mathematics Ser.: Vol. 206). 145p. 1996. 116.00 (*0-8218-0466-9*, STEKLO/206C) Am Math.

Bolick, Clint. The Affirmative Action Fraud: Can We Restore the American Civil Rights Vision? 176p. 1996. 19.95 (*1-882577-27-2*); pap. 10.95 (*1-882577-28-0*) Cato Inst.

— Changing Course: Civil Rights at the Crossroads. 192p. 1988. 39.95 (*0-88738-179-0*) Transaction Pubs.

— Grassroots Tyranny: The Limits of Federalism. 195p. 1993. 21.95 (*1-882577-01-9*) Cato Inst.

Bolick, Clint. Protecting Civil Rights Should be an Urgent Conservative Issue. (Issue Paper #5-88 Ser.). 3p. 1988. pap. text 8.00 (*1-57655-025-7*) Independ Inst.

Bolick, Clint. Transformation: The Promise of Politics & Empowerment. LC 98-15506. 200p. 1998. 21.95 (*1-55815-506-6*) ICS Pr.

— Unfinished Business: A Civil Rights Strategy for America's Third Century. LC 90-7332. 220p. (Orig.). (C). 1990. 24.95 (*0-936488-35-2*); pap. 12.95 (*0-936488-36-0*) PRIPP.

Bolick, Gary. A Snowman in July. LC 97-78453. 225p. 1998. 24.50 (*0-88739-179-6*); pap. 14.50 (*0-88739-202-4*) Creat Arts Bk.

Bolick, James H. Sermon Outlines from the Word. (Sermon Outline Ser.). 64p. 1959. pap. 4.99 (*0-8010-0528-0*) Baker Bks.

Bolick, Jann, ed. see Connor, Tim.

Bolick, Nancy O. How to Survive Your Parents' Divorce. LC 94-15075. (Changing Family Ser.). (Illus.). 128p. (YA). (gr. 7-12). 1994. lib. bdg. 24.00 (*0-531-11054-0*) Watts.

Bolick, Nancy O. & Randolph, Sallie G. Shaker Villages. LC 92-34587. (Illus.). 96p. (J). (gr. 5 up). 1993. 12.95 (*0-8027-8209-4*); lib. bdg. 13.85 (*0-8027-8210-8*) Walker & Co.

Bolick, Nancy O., jt. auth. see Randolph, Sallie.

***Bolik, Sibylle, et al.** Medienfiktionen: Illusion - Inszenierung - Simulation Festschrift Fur Helmut Schanze Zum 60. Geburtstag. 472p. 1999. 63.95 (*3-631-34613-1*) P Lang Pubng.

Bolin, Anne. In Search of Eve: Transsexual Rites of Passage. LC 87-13702. 222p. 1987. 47.95 (*0-89789-082-5*, Bergin & Garvey); pap. 16.95 (*0-89789-115-5*, Bergin & Garvey) Greenwood.

Bolin, Anne & Whelehan, Patricia. Perspectives on Human Sexuality. LC 98-38210. (Illus.). 416p. (C). 1999. text 92.50 (*0-7914-4133-4*) State U NY Pr.

— Perspectives on Human Sexuality. LC 98-38210. (Illus.). 503p. (C). 1999. pap. text 34.95 (*0-7914-4134-2*) State U NY Pr.

Bolin, Bert, ed. The Atmosphere & the Sea in Motion. LC 59-14858. (Illus.). 512p. 1960. 10.00 (*0-87470-000-0*) Rockefeller.

Bolin, Bert, et al, eds. The Greenhouse Effect, Climatic Change, & Ecosystems. LC 86-1319. (SCOPE Ser.). 574p. 1986. 550.00 (*0-471-91012-0*) Wiley.

Bolin, Bert & Doos, Bo R. The Greenhouse Effect, Climatic Change & Ecosystems. LC 86-1319. (Scientific Committee on Problems of the Environment Ser.: No. 29). 574p. 1990. pap. 225.00 (*0-471-92635-3*) Wiley.

Bolin, Carole A., jt. auth. see Brown, Corrie.

Bolin, Cay & Trent, Cindy. How to Be Your Husband's Best Friend. 160p. (Orig.). 1995. mass mkt. 6.00 (*0-89109-874-7*) Pinon Press.

Bolin, Cong, ed. see Tsung, Po-Lin.

Bolin, Dan. Hole in One: And Other Life lessons from Golf. 112p. 1999. 10.00 (*1-57683-141-8*) NavPress.

— How to Be Your Daughter's Daddy: Three Hundred Sixty-Five Ways to Show Her You Care. LC 92-63218. 160p. 1993. pap. 6.00 (*0-89109-727-9*) Pinon Press.

— How To Be Your Wife's Husband's Best Friend: 365 Ways To Express Your Love-12 Copy Display. 1994. pap. text. write for info. (*0-89109-889-5*) Pinon Press.

— The One That Got Away. LC 99-190194. 1998. pap. 10.00 (*1-57683-074-8*) NavPress.

— Winning Run: And Other Lifelessons from Baseball. 112p. 1999. 10.00 (*1-57683-136-1*) NavPress.

Bolin, Dan & Trent, John. How to Be Your Wife's Best Friend. 160p. (Orig.). 1995. mass mkt. 6.00 (*0-89109-875-5*) Pinon Press.

Bolin, Danny, photos by. Lincoln's Doctor's Dog: A Collection of Grace Notes. 2nd ed. LC 98-92699. (Illus.). xv, 357p. 1997. reprint ed. pap. 19.95 (*0-9663086-0-3*) G M Brown.

Bolin, Frances S., ed. Emily Dickinson: Poetry for Young People. LC 94-13809. (Illus.). 48p. (J). 1994. 14.95 (*0-8069-0635-9*) Sterling.

Bolin, Frances S., ed. see Sandburg, Carl.

Bolin, Francis S. & McConnell-Falk, Judith, eds. Teacher Renewal: Professional Issues, Personal Choices. 240p. (C). 1986. pap. 19.95 (*0-8077-2822-5*) Tchrs Coll.

Bolin, Goran, jt. auth. see Fornas, Johan.

Bolin, Inge. Rituals of Respect: The Secret of Survival in the High Peruvian Andes. LC 98-8930. (Illus.). 304p. 1998. 35.00 (*0-292-70866-1*) U of Tex Pr.

Bolin, J. J. Yankee Doodle & the Secret Society. LC 98-228529. (Cover-to-Cover Chapter Bks.). (Illus.). 54p. (J). 1997. write for info. (*0-7807-6715-2*) Perfection Learn.

***Bolin, James D.** Bossism & Reform in a Southern City: Lexington, Kentucky, 1880-1940. LC 99-49405. (Illus.). 224p. 2000. 24.95 (*0-8131-2150-7*) U Pr of Ky.

Bolin, John, jt. auth. see Haggard, Ted.

Bolin, Kirsten, jt. auth. see Noland, Dianne A.

Bolin, M. C. Armageddon. 224p. (J). 1998. mass mkt. 4.99 (*0-7868-8938-1*, Pub. by Hyperion) Time Warner.

— Enemy of the State. (J). 1998. mass mkt. 5.99 (*0-7868-8951-9*) Hyperion.

***Bolin, M. C.** Gone in 60 Seconds. LC 00-20142. 208p. 2000. mass mkt. 5.99 (*0-7868-8989-6*, Pub. by Hyperion) Time Warner.

Bolin, Richard L., ed. The Changing World of Free Zones. 1999. pap. 40.00 (*0-945951-20-5*) Flagstaff Inst.

Bolin, Richard L, ed. Export Processing Zones Move to High Technology: How Can Government Assist? LC 97-149305. 105p. 1997. pap. 40.00 (*0-945951-16-7*) Flagstaff Inst.

Bolin, Richard L., ed. Free Zones & Export Processing Zones in Central Europe/CIS to Speed Trade with Western Europe. LC 96-211743. 122p. 1996. pap. text 40.00 (*0-945951-15-9*) Flagstaff Inst.

— Free Zones in the New Europe. 97p. 1992. pap. 40.00 (*0-945951-08-6*) Flagstaff Inst.

— The Global Network of Export Processing Zones. 125p. (Orig.). (C). 1989. pap. text 40.00 (*0-945951-01-9*) Flagstaff Inst.

— The Global Network of Free Zones in the 21st Century. 117p. 1998. pap. 40.00 (*0-945951-19-1*) Flagstaff Inst.

— Impact of 57 New Export Processing Zones in Mercosur. 92p. (Orig.). 1996. pap. 40.00 (*0-945951-12-4*) Flagstaff Inst.

— Linking the Export Processing Zone to Local Industry. 174p. (C). 1990. pap. text 40.00 (*0-945951-04-3*) Flagstaff Inst.

— Mainline Free Zones, Mediterranean, Gulf, Indian Subcontinent. LC 95-185882. 101p. (C). 1995. pap. text 40.00 (*0-945951-11-6*) Flagstaff Inst.

— The New Zones: East-West Europe & North-South America. 84p. 1992. pap. 40.00 (*0-945951-07-8*) Flagstaff Inst.

— The Privatization of WEPZA. LC 97-198263. 1997. pap. 40.00 (*0-945951-18-3*) Flagstaff Inst.

— Production Sharing: A Conference with Peter Drucker. LC 77-649702. 156p. (C). 1988. reprint ed. pap. text 40.00 (*0-945951-00-0*) Flagstaff Inst.

— Public vs. Private Free Zones. 84p. 1993. pap. 40.00 (*0-945951-09-4*) Flagstaff Inst.

— Reaching the Global Market Through Free Zones. 142p. 1991. pap. 40.00 (*0-945951-06-X*) Flagstaff Inst.

— Technology Transfer & Management in Export Processing Zones. 127p. 1990. pap. 40.00 (*0-945951-05-1*) Flagstaff Inst.

— The World Impact of NAFTA. LC 94-210506. 83p. (Orig.). 1994. pap. text 40.00 (*0-945951-10-8*) Flagstaff Inst.

Bolin, Richard L., jt. auth. see Haywood, Robert C.

Bolin, Robert, ed. The Loma Prieta Earthquake: Studies of Short-Term Impacts. (Monograph: No. 50). 116p. (Orig.). 1990. pap. 20.00 (*1-877943-02-9*) Natural Hazards.

Bolin, Robert C. Household & Community Recovery After Earthquakes. LC 93-38641. (Program on Environment & Behavior Monograph Ser.: No. 56). 1993. 20.00 (*1-877943-11-8*) Natural Hazards.

— Long-Term Family Recovery from Disaster. (Program on Environment & Behavior Monograph Ser.: No. 36). 280p. (Orig.). (C). 1982. pap. 20.00 (*0-685-28110-8*) Natural Hazards.

Bolin, Robert C. & Bolton, Patricia. Race, Religion, & Ethnicity in Disaster Recovery. (Program on Environment & Behavior Monograph Ser.: No. 42). 400p. (Orig.). (C). 1986. pap. 20.00 (*0-685-28116-7*) Natural Hazards.

Bolin, Robert C. & Stanford, Lois. The Northridge Earthquake: Vulnerability & Disaster. LC 98-11059. (Illus.). 288p. (C). 1998. 110.00 (*0-415-17897-5*) Routledge.

Bolin, Sheila A., et al. Disabled Offenders (Stop, Search & Arrest) 200p. 1997. ring bd. 29.95 (*0-87526-542-1*) Gould.

Bolin, Sheila A., et al. Use of Force (Reasonable & Deadly) For Educators, Law Enforcement, Public Safety & Security. 150p. pap. 24.95 (*0-87526-553-7*) Gould.

Bolin, Thomas M. Freedom Beyond Forgiveness: The Book of Jonah Re-Examined. (JSOTS Ser.: Vol. 236). 217p. 1997. 60.00 (*1-85075-642-2*, Pub. by Sheffield Acad) CUP Services.

Bolinder, E. Folke, ed. see Riesz, Marcel.

Boling, Bobby. A Dancer's Manual: A Motivational Guide to Professional Dancing. Sellon-Wright, Keith & Mirault, Don, eds. 188p. 2000. pap. 19.95 (*0-9637864-9-0*, Pub. by Rafter Pub) SCB Distributors.

Boling, Carolyn. Julie Warren Martin: Sculptor of Stone. 168p. 1993. 75.00 (*0-9636618-0-9*) C Boling.

Boling, Douglas. Programming Windows CE. LC 98-29279. 650p. 49.99 incl. cd-rom (*1-57231-856-2*) Microsoft.

Boling, Fredrick W. Incident at Crazy Woman Creek: A Historical Western Novel. 273p. 1999. pap. 16.95 (*0-7414-0046-4*) Buy Books.

Boling, Guo & Dadi, Yang, eds. Nonlinear Partial Differential Equations & Applications: Proceedings of the Conference Chongqing University, Pr China 25 - 31 May 1997. 260p. 58.00 (*981-02-3659-X*) World Scientific Pub.

Boling, Joseph E., jt. auth. see Schwan, C. Frederick.

Boling, Katharine. A Piece of the Fox's Hide. LC 72-86903. 376p. 1998. reprint ed. pap. 9.95 (*0-87844-054-2*) Sandlapper Pub Co.

Boling, Muzzy Vance. A Children's Guide to Worship. LC 98-100249. 1997. pap. 6.95 (*0-664-50015-3*) Geneva Press.

Boling, Patricia. Privacy & the Politics of Intimate Life. 240p. 1996. text 39.95 (*0-8014-3271-5*); pap. text 15.95 (*0-8014-8351-4*) Cornell U Pr.

Boling, Peter. The Physician's Role in Home Health Care. LC 97-13704. 328p. 1997. 46.95 (*0-8261-9700-0*) Springer Pub.

Boling, R. G. The Early Biblical Community in Transjordan. (Social World of Biblical Antiquity Ser.: Vol. 6). 80p. 1988. 25.00 (*1-85075-094-7*, Pub. by Sheffield Acad) CUP Services.

Boling, Robert G. The Early Biblical Community in Transjordan. (Social World of Biblical Antiquity Ser.: Vol. 6). 80p. 1988. pap. 13.00 (*1-85075-093-9*, Pub. by Sheffield Acad) CUP Services.

Boling, Robert G., tr. Judges, Vol. 6A. LC 72-96229. (Illus.). 376p. 1974. 35.00 (*0-385-01029-X*) Doubleday.

Boling, Robert G. & Wright, Ernest. Joshua, Vol. 6. LC 79-6583. (Illus.). 432p. 1982. 42.50 (*0-385-00034-0*) Doubleday.

***Boling, Ruth.** Come Worship with Me: A Journey Through the Church Year. (Mouse Bks.: Vol. 2). (Illus.). 48p. (J). (ps-3). 2000. 19.95 (*0-664-50045-5*) Geneva Press.

Bolingbroke, Henry. Historical Writings. Kramnick, Isaac, ed. LC 72-75608. (Classics of British Historical Literature Ser.). 397p. Date not set. reprint ed. pap. 123.10 (*0-608-20590-7*, 205455500003) Bks Demand.

— Political Writings. Armitage, David, ed. (Cambridge Texts in the History of Political Thought Ser.). 352p. (C). 1997. text 69.95 (*0-521-44393-8*); pap. text 25.95 (*0-521-58697-6*) Cambridge U Pr.

Bolingbroke, Henry S. Political Writings. Kramnick, Isaac, ed. (Crofts Classics Ser.). 112p. 1970. pap. text 4.95 (*0-88295-015-0*) Harlan Davidson.

Bolingbroke, Henry S., jt. auth. see Warburton, William.

Bolingbroke, Viscount & Jackman, Sydney W., eds. The Ideas of a Patriot King. LC 64-66066. 1965. pap. [illegible].45 (*0-672-60433-7*, Bobbs) Macmillan.

Bolinger, Athalie, ed. see Petterson, Steve D.

Bolinger, Bonnie F. Madison County Folklore. Fancher, Burr E., ed. & intro. by. 80p. (Orig.). (J). (gr. 4 up). 1995. pap. 5.00 (*1-887335-00-5*) Fancher & Assocs.

Bolinger, Camille. The Edge of Christmas: Carving Christmas Whimsies. LC 98-87455. (Illus.). 64p. (Orig.). 1999. pap. 14.95 (*0-7643-0687-1*) Schiffer.

Bolinger, Camille, jt. auth. see Bolinger, Paul.

Bolinger, Camille, jt. auth. see Bolinger, Paul F.

Bolinger, Camille J. The Forever Wreath. LC 92-81305. (Illus.). 40p. (J). (ps-4). 1993. 17.95 (*0-9632777-6-6*) Dutch Run Pub.

Bolinger, Camille J., jt. auth. see Bolinger, Paul F.

Bolinger, Don & Bronson, Tan. Applying RCS & SCCS: From Source Control to Project Control. Loukides Mike, ed. (Illus.). 500p. (Orig.). 1995. pap. 29.95 (*1-56592-117-8*) Thomson Learn.

Bolinger, Dwight. Essays on Spanish: Words & Grammar. Silverman, Joseph, ed. (Estudios Linguisticos Ser.: Vol. 3). 352p. 1991. pap. 10.00 (*0-936388-44-7*) Juan de la Cuesta.

— Intonation & Its Parts: Melody in Spoken English. LC 83-40698. 440p. 1986. 49.50 (*0-8047-1241-7*) Stanford U Pr.

— Intonation & Its Uses: Melody in Grammar & Discourse. LC 88-35572. 488p. 1989. 49.50 (*0-8047-1535-1*) Stanford U Pr.

— Language: The Loaded Weapon: The Use & Abuse of Language Today. (Longman Linguistics Library). (Illus.). 240p. 1989. pap. text 22.55 (*0-582-29108-9*, 71746) Longman.

— That's That. (Janua Linguarum, Ser. Minor: No. 155). 79p. (Orig.). 1972. pap. text 23.10 (*90-279-2319-1*) Mouton.

Bolinger, Dwight & Sears, Donald A. Aspects of Language. 3rd ed. 352p. (C). 1981. pap. text 37.00 (*0-15-503872-9*, Pub. by Harcourt Coll Pubs) Harcourt.

Bolinger, Dwight L. Interrogative Structures of American English (the Direct Question) (Publications of the American Dialect Society: No. 28). 184p. 1957. pap. text 15.00 (*0-8173-0628-5*) U of Ala Pr.

Bolinger, Loren, jt. ed. see Ossorio, Nelson A.

Bolinger, Paul & Bolinger, Camille. Carving Seasonal Decorations for Windows & Door Frames. LC 98-89439. (Illus.). 64p. 1999. pap. 14.95 (*0-7643-0715-0*) Schiffer.

***Bolinger, Paul & Bolinger, Camille.** Snowmen Are Cool: Woodcarving Winter Creations. (Illus.). 64p. 1999. pap. 14.95 (*0-7643-0976-5*) Schiffer.

Bolinger, Paul, jt. auth. see Nicastro, Nicholas.

Bolinger, Paul F. & Bolinger, Camille. Halloween Carving. 64p. 1998. pap. 14.95 (*0-7643-0608-1*) Schiffer.

Bolinger, Paul F. & Bolinger, Camille J. Carving & Painting an Heirloom Santa. LC 96-70301. (Illus.). 64p. 1997. pap. 12.95 (*0-7643-0194-2*) Schiffer.

— Carving Humorous Santas. LC 97-80148. (Illus.). 64p. 1998. pap. 14.95 (*0-7643-0423-2*) Schiffer.

Bolinger, Taree & Seeman, Cary. First Steps to Story Writing. (Writing Ser.). (Illus.). 32p. (J). (gr. 1-3). 1994. pap. text 4.95 (*1-55799-288-6*, EMC 289) Evan-Moor Edu Pubs.

Bolino, August C. From Depression to War: American Society in Transition, 1939. LC 97-38542. 312p. 1998. 59.95 (*0-275-96064-1*, Praeger Pubs) Greenwood.

Bolinske, Janet L., ed. Hansel & Gretel. LC 87-61670. (Children's Classics Ser.). (Illus.). 32p. (Orig.). (J). (gr. 1-3). 1987. pap. text 3.95 (*0-88335-575-2*) Milliken Pub Co.

— Henny Penny. LC 87-61674. (Children's Classics Ser.). (Illus.). 32p. (Orig.). (J). (gr. 1-3). 1987. pap. text 4.95 (*0-88335-571-X*) Milliken Pub Co.

— Little Red Riding Hood. LC 87-61673. (Children's Classics Ser.). (Illus.). 32p. (Orig.). (J). (gr. 1-3). 1987. pap. text 4.95 (*0-88335-573-6*) Milliken Pub Co.

— The Tale of Peter Rabbit. LC 87-61672. (Children's Classics Ser.). (Illus.). 32p. (J). (gr. 1-3). 1987. pap. text 4.95 (*0-88335-572-8*) Milliken Pub Co.

— Thumbelina. LC 87-61669. (Children's Classics Ser.). (Illus.). 32p. (J). (gr. 1-3). 1987. pap. text 4.95 (*0-88335-576-0*) Milliken Pub Co.

— The Ugly Duckling. LC 87-61671. (Children's Classics Ser.). (Illus.). 32p. (J). (gr. 1-3). 1987. pap. text 4.95 (*0-88335-574-4*) Milliken Pub Co.

Bolinske, Janet L., ed. see Kaplan, Carol B.

Bolioli, Oscar, ed. The Caribbean: Culture of Resistance, Spirit of Hope. LC 92-43635. 1993. pap. 7.95 (*0-377-00254-2*) Friendship Pr.

Bolioli, Oscar L. Hope & Justice for All in the Americas: Discerning God's Mission. LC 98-2656. 1998. 7.95 (*0-377-00325-5*) Friendship Pr.

Bolis, C. L., et al, eds. Water & Life: Comparative Analysis of Water Relationships at the Organismic, Cellular & Molecular Level. (Illus.). 404p. 1992. 181.95 (*0-387-54112-8*) Spr-Verlag.

Bolis, Liana, ed. see International Conference on Biological Membranes S.

Bolis, Liana, jt. ed. see Nistico, Giuseppe.

Bolitho, Harold & Wallace-Crabbe, Chris. Approaching Australia: Papers from the Harvard Australian Studies Symposium. LC 98-26221. 1998. pap. 24.95 (*0-674-04190-9*) HUP.

— Approaching Australia: Papers from the Harvard Australian Studies Symposium. LC 98-26221. 1998. write for info. (*0-674-04189-5*) HUP.

Bolitho, Hector, ed. Twelve Jews. LC 67-23179. (Essay Index Reprint Ser.). 1977. 23.95 (*0-8369-0223-8*) Ayer.

Bolitho, Hector & Mulgan, John. Emigrants. LC 70-108635. (Essay Index Reprint Ser.). 1977. 20.95 (*0-8369-1547-X*) Ayer.

Bolitho, Janie. Dangerous Deceit. large type ed. (Dales Large Print Ser.). 286p. 1997. pap. 18.99 (*1-85389-731-0*) Ulverscroft.

— Kindness Can Kill. LC 96-7357. (Mystery Ser.). 252p. 1996. per. 4.99 (*0-373-26193-4*, 1-26193-2, Wrldwide Lib) Harlequin Bks.

— Ripe for Revenge. 1996. per. 4.99 (*0-373-26220-5*, 1-26220-3, Wrldwide Lib) Harlequin Bks.

***Bolitho, Janie.** Snapped in Cornwall. 2000. pap. 9.95 (*0-7490-0469-X*, Pub. by Allison & Busby) Intl Pubs Mktg.

Bolitho, Janie. Sweets for My Sweet. 224p. 1996. 22.00 (*0-7278-4883-6*) Severn Hse.

***Bolitho, Janie.** Sweets for My Sweet. large type ed. 320p. 1999. pap. 20.99 (*1-85389-923-2*, Dales) Ulverscroft.

Bolitho, Janie. Wound for Wound. 224p. 1995. 20.00 (*0-7278-4739-2*) Severn Hse.

— Wound for Wound. large type ed. (Dales Large Print Ser.). (Illus.). 329p. 1996. pap. 18.99 (*1-85389-632-2*) Ulverscroft.

Bolitho, Rod, jt. ed. see Rossner, Richard.

Bolitho, William, jt. ed. see Millet, George.

Bolitnikov, Alexander & Wahlen, Gina. True Believer. (Orig.). 1997. pap. 8.99 (*0-8280-1301-2*) Review & Herald.

Bolivar, Josefa V., ed. see Bolivar, Jossy Ann.

B

An Asterisk (*) at the beginning of an entry indicates that the title is appearing for the first time.

Bolivar, Jossy Ann. With Love, from Jo. Bolivar, Josefa V., ed. LC 80-13999. (Illus.). 120p. (Orig.). 1980. pap. 7.95 (*0-914598-01-5*) Padre Prods.

Bolivar Plaza Staff, tr. see Marin, Antonio R.

Boljar, Boris. Das Doktor Schiwago Kochbuch. (GER., Illus.). 64p. (C). 1995. 15.00 (*3-8170-0024-3*, Pub. by Knstvrlag Weingrtn) Intl Bk Import.

Bolk, Dick, ed. Lord of Light, Prince of Peace. 1986. 6.99 (*0-685-68482-2*, MC-58) Lillenas.

Bolke, Stefan. Die Marineschule Murwik: Architekturmonographische Untersuchung Eines Repraesentationsbaues der Kaiserlichen Marine. (Europaische Hochschulschriften Ser.: Reihe 28, Band 328). (GER., Illus.). 380p. 1998. pap. 67.95 (*3-631-33386-2*) P Lang Pubng.

Bolker, Ethan D. Using Algebra. LC 90-50000. 305p. (C). 1990. pap. text 20.00 (*1-55605-134-4*) Wyndham Hall.

Bolker, Henry I. Natural & Synthetic Polymers: An Introduction. LC 72-97483. (Illus.). 706p. reprint ed. pap. 200.00 (*0-7837-0816-5*, 204113100019) Bks Demand.

Bolker, Joan. The Art of the Dissertation. 1997. 22.50 (*0-8050-4890-1*) H Holt & Co.

— World's Best Writing Advice. 1996. 22.50 (*0-8050-4892-8*) H Holt & Co.

— World's Best Writing Advice. LC 96-49810. 1997. pap. 14.95 (*0-8050-4893-6*) H Holt & Co.

— Writing Your Dissertation in Fifteen Minutes a Day. LC 98-5262. 256p. 1998. pap. 15.95 (*0-8050-4891-X*) H Holt & Co.

Bolkestein, A. M., et al, eds. Predicates & Terms in Functional Grammar. (Functional Grammar Ser.: No. 2). 304p. 1985. pap. 65.40 (*90-6765-104-4*) Mouton.

Bolkestein, A. Machtelt, jt. ed. see Hannay, Mike.

Bolkestein, Hendrik. Wonnltatigkeit und Armenpflege Im Vorchristlichen Altertum. Vlastos, Gregory, ed. LC 78-15858. (Morals & Law in Ancient Greece Ser.). 1979. reprint ed. lib. bdg. 40.95 (*0-405-11531-8*) Ayer.

Bolkestein, Hendrik, jt. auth. see Bolkestein, Johanna C.

Bolkestein, Johanna C. & Bolkestein, Hendrik. Hosios en Eusebes & Thecphrastes' Charakter der Deisidaimonia ais Religionsgeschichtliche, 2 vols. Vlastos, Gregory, ed. LC 78-14605. (Morals & Law in Ancient Greece Ser.). (DUT, FRE, GER & GRE.). 1979. reprint ed. lib. bdg. 28.95 (*0-405-11575-X*) Ayer.

Bolkestein, M., et al, eds. Syntax & Pragmatics in Functional Grammar. (Functional Grammar Ser.). xiv, 223p. 1985. pap. 50.00 (*90-6765-097-8*) Mouton.

Bolkey, Lorna, et al, eds. Dog in the Manger. LC 95-19046. (Illus.). 160p. (Orig.). 1995. pap. 12.95 (*1-57090-021-3*) Alexander Dist.

Bolkey, Lorna, ed. see Lucas, David.

Bolkey, Lorna, ed. see McCready, Jack.

Bolkey, Lorna, ed. see Milner, Cinthia & Sexton, Robin.

Bolkey, Lorna, ed. see Terrell, Bob.

Bolkhovitinov, N. N. & Hartgrove, J. Dane. Russia & the United States: An Analytical Survey of Archival Documents & Historical Studies. LC 86-27955. 88p. (gr. 13). 1986. text 52.95 (*0-87332-414-5*) M E Sharpe.

Bolkhovitinov, Nikolai. Russia & the American Revolution. Smith, C. Jay & Len Sen, George A., trs. from RUS. LC 74-42220. 277p. 1976. 29.70 (*0-910512-20-5*) Diplomatic IN.

Bolkhovitinov, Nikolai N. Russian-American Relations & the Sale of Alaska, 1834-1867. Pierce, Richard A., tr. LC 97-16077. (Alaska History Ser.: No. 45). (RUS & ENG., Illus.). 394p. 1997. 35.00 (*1-895901-06-5*) Limestone Pr.

Bolko, Claire. Elementary School Plays: Three Plays, Vol. 1. 71p. (J). 1986. pap. 8.95 (*1-57514-009-8*, 4023) Encore Perform Pub.

Bolkosky, Sidney, jt. auth. see Lipson, Great B.

Bolkosky, Sidney M. Harmony & Dissonance: Voices of Jewish Identity in Detroit, 1914-1967. LC 91-17287. (Illus.). 544p. 1991. 30.00 (*0-8143-1933-5*) Wayne St U Pr.

Boll. Als der Drieg Ausbrach. (GER.). (C). 1965. 14.95 (*0-8442-2719-6*, X2719-6) NTC Contemp Pub Co.

— Das Brot der Fruhen Jahre. (GER.). (C). 1986. 12.95 (*0-8442-2780-3*, X2780-3) NTC Contemp Pub Co.

Boll. Erzahlungen: Level D. text 8.95 (*0-88436-108-X*) EMC-Paradigm.

Boll, Darlene. Olive. (Illus.). 201p. (J). (ps-2). 1983. pap. 6.90 (*0-7399-0073-0*, 2338) Rod & Staff.

Boll, Deborah, et al. Albuquerque '50s. (Illus.). 60p. (Orig.). 1989. pap. 10.00 (*0-944282-06-7*) UNM Art Mus.

Boll, Eleanor S., jt. auth. see Bossard, James H.

Boll, Eleanor S., jt. ed. see Bossard, James H.

Boll, Franz. Sphaera. xiv, 564p. 1967. reprint ed. 135.00 (*0-318-70880-9*) G Olms Pubs.

Boll, Heinrich. Absent Without Leave: Two Novellas. Vennewitz, Leila, tr. LC 95-12350. (European Classics Ser.). 148p. 1995. pap. 13.95 (*0-8101-1209-4*); text 39.95 (*0-8101-1231-0*) Northwestern U Pr.

— And Never Said a Word. Vennewitz, Leila, tr. from GER. (European Classics Ser.). 204p. (C). 1994. 29.95 (*0-8101-1153-5*); pap. text 10.95 (*0-8101-1147-0*) Northwestern U Pr.

— And Where Were You, Adam? Vennewitz, Leila, tr. from GER. (European Classics Ser.). 156p. 1994. reprint ed. 35.00 (*0-8101-1179-9*); reprint ed. pap. 10.95 (*0-8101-1164-0*) Northwestern U Pr.

— Billiards at Half-Past Nine. 288p. 1994. pap. 13.95 (*0-14-018724-3*, Penguin Classics) Viking Penguin.

— The Bread of Those Early Years. Vennewitz, Leila, tr. from GER. LC 94-10923. (European Classics Ser.). 133p. 1994. reprint ed. 35.00 (*0-8101-1178-0*); reprint ed. pap. 10.95 (*0-8101-1163-2*) Northwestern U Pr.

— The Casualty. 189p. 1989. pap. 8.95 (*0-393-30599-6*) Norton.

— The Clown. Vennewitz, Leila, tr. 272p. 1994. pap. 13.95 (*0-14-018726-X*, Penguin Classics) Viking Penguin.

— End of a Mission. Vennewitz, Leila, tr. from GER. (European Classics Ser.). 220p. (C). 1994. 29.95 (*0-8101-1154-3*); pap. 10.95 (*0-8101-1148-9*) Northwestern U Pr.

— Group Portrait with Lady. 1976. mass mkt. 4.95 (*0-380-00020-2*, Avon Bks) Morrow Avon.

— Irish Journal. Vennewitz, Leila, tr. from GER. (European Classics Ser.). 140p. (C). 1994. 29.95 (*0-8101-1155-1*) Northwestern U Pr.

— Irish Journal. Vennewitz, Leila, tr. from ENG. LC 98-6903. (Marlboro Travel Ser.). 144p. 1998. pap. 12.95 (*0-8101-6062-5*, Marlboro) Northwestern U Pr.

— The Lost Honor of Katharina Blum. Vennewitz, Leila, tr. 160p. 1994. pap. 12.95 (*0-14-018728-6*, Penguin Classics) Viking Penguin.

***Boll, Heinrich.** The Lost Honour of Katharina Blum. large type ed. LC 99-46762. 259p. 1999. 24.95 (*1-56000-463-0*) Transaction Pubs.

Boll, Heinrich. The Mad Dog: Stories. Mitchell, Breon, tr. LC 97-16104. 144p. 1997. text 19.95 (*0-312-16757-1*) St Martin.

— The Mad Dog: Stories. 176p. 1998. pap. 12.00 (*0-312-19549-4*) St Martin.

— Missing Persons & Other Essays. Vennewitz, Leila, tr. from GER. LC 94-10930. (European Classics Ser.). 290p. 1994. reprint ed. 39.95 (*0-8101-1177-2*); reprint ed. pap. 13.95 (*0-8101-1162-4*) Northwestern U Pr.

— The Safety Net. Vennewitz, Leila, tr. from GER. LC 95-20769. (European Classics Ser.). 314p. 1995. pap. 15.95 (*0-8101-1210-8*) Northwestern U Pr.

— The Silent Angel: A Novel. Mitchell, Breon, tr. from GER. LC 95-16219. 192p. 1995. pap. 12.00 (*0-312-13171-2*) St Martin.

— A Soldier's Legacy. Vennewitz, Leila, tr. from GER. (European Classics Ser.). 131p. 1994. reprint ed. 35.00 (*0-8101-1198-5*); reprint ed. pap. 10.95 (*0-8101-1202-7*) Northwestern U Pr.

— The Stories of Heinrich Boll. Vennewitz, Leila, tr. from GER. LC 95-38263. (European Classics Ser.). 690p. (C). 1995. pap. 19.95 (*0-8101-1207-8*) Northwestern U Pr.

— Tomorrow & Yesterday. LC 95-54204. 250p. (C). 1996. pap. 16.95 (*0-8101-1206-X*) Northwestern U Pr.

— Le Train Etait a 1;Heure Suivi de Quatorze Nouvelles. (FRE.). 1983. pap. 11.95 (*0-7859-1971-6*, 2070374599) Fr & Eur.

— The Train Was on Time. Vennewitz, Leila, tr. from GER. (European Classics Ser.). 120p. (C). 1994. 29.95 (*0-8101-1156-X*); pap. 9.95 (*0-8101-1123-3*) Northwestern U Pr.

— What's to Become of the Boy? or Something to Do with Books. Vannewitz, Leila, tr. LC 95-51551. 82p. (C). 1996. pap. 13.95 (*0-8101-1208-6*) Northwestern U Pr.

— Women in a River Landscape: A Novel in Dialogues & Soliloquies. McLintock, David, tr. from GER. LC 95-12352. (European Classics Ser.). 208p. 1995. pap. 14.95 (*0-8101-1205-1*) Northwestern U Pr.

Boll, John J., ed. Reader Services in Libraries: A Day in Honor of Margaret E. Monroe. 64p. 1982. pap. 4.00 (*0-936442-09-3*) U Wis Sch Lib.

Boll, Lawrence L. Relation of Diu Krone to La Mule Sanz Frain. LC 77-140018. (Catholic University Studies in German: No. 2). reprint ed. 37.50 (*0-404-50222-9*) AMS Pr.

Boll, Mary Jane. Mother's Little Helper Cookbook. (Illus.). 42p. (J). 1996. pap. 4.40 (*0-7399-0246-6*, 2357) Rod & Staff.

Boll, Michael M. The American Mission in the Allied Control Commission for Bulgaria 1944-1947. 1985. text 64.50 (*0-88033-068-6*, 176, Pub. by East Eur Monographs) Col U Pr.

— Cold War in the Balkans: American Foreign Policy & the Emergence of Communist Bulgaria, 1943-1947. LC 84-7438. 264p. 1984. 34.95 (*0-8131-1527-2*) U Pr of Ky.

Boll, Richard & Overshott, K. J. Magnetic Sensors. LC 89-25053. (Sensors Ser.). xii, 513p. 1989. pap. write for info. (*0-89573-677-2*, Wiley-VCH) Wiley.

Boll, Richard H. Tables of Light-Scattering Functions: Relative Indices of Less Than Unity & Infinity. LC 57-7175. reprint ed. pap. 93.00 (*0-608-30490-5*, 2011234) Bks Demand.

— Tables of Light-Scattering Functions: Relative Indices of Less Than Unity & Infinity. LC 57-7175. 372p. 1958. reprint ed. pap. 115.40 (*0-608-10348-9*, 205107400074) Bks Demand.

Boll, Shirley. At Every Gate a Pearl. 1986. pap. 3.25 (*0-87813-525-1*) Christian Light.

Boll, Stephan. Intergenerationale Umverteilungswirkungen der Fiskalpolitik in der Bundesrepublik Deutschland: Ein Ansatz mit Hilfe des Generational Accounting. (GER., Illus.). 241p. 1994. 39.95 (*3-631-48004-0*) P Lang Pubng.

Boll, Theophilus E. M. Miss May Sinclair: A Biographical & Critical Introduction. LC 72-414. 332p. 1973. 45.00 (*0-8386-1156-7*) Fairleigh Dickinson.

Boll, Thomas J. & Bryant, Brenda K., eds. Clinical Neuropsychology & Brain Function: Research, Measurement, & Practice. LC 88-14558. (Master Lectures: Vol. 7). 202p. (Orig.). 1988. pap. 24.95 (*1-55798-038-1*) Am Psychol.

Bolla, Alexander J. & McDorman, Ted L. Comparative Asian Environmental Law Anthology. LC 99-22361. 576p. 1999. pap. text 60.00 (*0-89089-674-7*) Carolina Acad Pr.

Bolla, M., ed. Endometrial Cancers. (Illus.). x, 270p. 1986. 128.75 (*3-8055-4211-9*) S Karger.

Bolla, Peter De, see De Bolla, Peter.

Bollacher, Martin, ed. see Oh, Seong-Kyun.

***Bollacher, Olivier M.** Geistiges Aristokratentum Im Dienste der Demokratie: Thomas Mann und Paul Valery. (GER.). 722p. 1999. 85.95 (*3-631-34457-0*) P Lang Pubng.

Bollack, C. G. & Cinqualbre, J., eds. Recent Advances in Renal Cell Carcinoma. (Progress in Surgery Ser.: Vol. 17). (Illus.). viii, 160p. 1983. ring bd. 113.25 (*3-8055-3621-6*) S Karger.

Bollack, C. G. & Clavert, A., eds. Epididymis & Fertility: Biology & Pathology. (Progress in Reproductive Biology & Medicine Ser.: Vol. 8). (Illus.). x, 174p. 1981. 103.50 (*3-8055-2157-X*) S Karger.

— Seminal Vesicles & Fertility. (Progress in Reproductive Biology & Medicine Ser.: Vol. 12). (Illus.). x, 182p. 1984. 129.75 (*3-8055-3907-X*) S Karger.

Bollag & Stotzky, eds. Soil Biochemistry, Vol. 6. (Books in Soils, Plants & the Environment: Vol. 15). (Illus.). 584p. 1990. text 137.50 (*0-8247-8232-1*) Dekker.

— Soil Biochemistry, Vol. 7. (Books in Soils, Plants & the Environment: Vol. 22). (Illus.). 432p. 1991. text 137.50 (*0-8247-8575-4*) Dekker.

— Soil Biochemistry, Vol. 8. (Books in Soils, Plants & the Environment: Vol. 27). (Illus.). 432p. 1993. text 137.50 (*0-8247-9044-8*) Dekker.

Bollag, Daniel M., et al. Protein Methods. 2nd ed. LC 96-14083. 432p. 1996. pap. 59.99 (*0-471-11837-0*, Wiley-Liss) Wiley.

Bollag, Jean-Marc, jt. ed. see Stotzky, G.

Bolland, B., jt. auth. see Barr, M.

***Bolland, Beverly J.** The Fruits of the Spirit. LC 99-97760. 2000. pap. 7.95 (*0-533-13477-3*) Vantage.

Bolland, Brian, jt. auth. see Barr, Mike W.

Bolland, David. Guide to Kathakali: With the Stories of 35 Plays. 1996. pap. write for info. (*0-614-25270-9*) Sterling Pubs.

Bolland, Eric J. & Hofer, Charles W. Future Firms: How America's High Technology Companies Work. (Illus.). 416p. 1998. 35.00 (*0-19-510436-6*) OUP.

Bolland, H. R., et al. World Catalogue of the Spider Mite Family (Acari: Tetranychidae) LC 98-6449. xii, 380p. 1998. 156.00 (*90-04-11087-9*) Brill Academic Pubs.

Bolland, John H., jt. auth. see Herson, Lawrence J.

Bolland, William C. A Manual of Yearbook Studies. LC 85-81801. (Cambridge Studies in English Legal History). 184p. 1986. reprint ed. 48.00 (*0-912004-40-1*) Gaunt.

— Year Books: Lectures Delivered in the University of London at the Request of the Faculty of Laws. xi, 84p. 1986. reprint ed. 30.00 (*0-8377-1937-2*, Rothman) W S Hein.

Bollans, Sue, tr. see Fischer, Hermann.

***Bollansee, J.** Hermippos of Smyrna & His Biographical Writings: A Reappraisal. xxxvi, 256p. 1999. 69.00 (*90-429-0779-7*, Pub. by Peeters Pub) Bks Intl VA.

Bollansee, Jan. Felix Jacoby Pt. 4: Fragmente der Griechischen Historiker Continued: Biography & Antiquarian Literature IV A: Hermippos of Smyrna. (Biography & Antiquarian Literature Ser: No. 3). 672p. 1999. 209.00 (*90-04-11303-7*) Brill Academic Pubs.

Bollard, Alan. Just for Starters: A Handbook of Small-Scale Business Opportunities. 208p. 1984. pap. 29.50 (*0-903031-94-9*, Pub. by Intermed Tech) Stylus Pub VA.

— New Zealand, 1984-1991: Economic Reforms, 1984-1991. LC 92-8467. 52p. 1992. pap. 9.95 (*1-55815-214-8*) ICS Pr.

Bollard, Alan, jt. ed. see Savage, John.

Bollard, Joe. Out of Sight. (Illus.). 176p. 1998. pap. 12.95 (*0-86327-623-7*, Pub. by Wolfhound Press) Irish Amer Bk.

Bollard, John. Pronouncing Dictionary of Proper Names: Pronounciations of the Names of Notable People, Places & Things. 2nd ed. LC 97-23664. 1997. lib. bdg. 110.00 (*0-7808-0098-2*) Omnigraphics Inc.

Bollard, John K. Scholastic Children's Thesaurus. LC 97-25049. (Illus.). 256p. (J). (gr. 4-8). 1998. 15.95 (*0-590-96785-1*) Scholastic Inc.

Bollard, Thomas & Turner, Lisa R. Mom's Search for Sanity: A Survival Kit. LC 95-70528. (Illus.). 158p. (Orig.). 1995. pap. text 9.95 (*0-9644552-4-2*) SunRise Pbl.

Bollard, Thomas S. Divine Compassion: Healing the Heart. Adams, Linda H. et al, eds. LC 96-60449. 120p. 1996. 12.95 (*1-57636-013-X*) SunRise Pbl.

Bollas, Christopher. Being a Character: Psychoanalysis & Self-Experience. 294p. 1994. pap. 11.00 (*0-8090-1569-2*) Hill & Wang.

— Cracking Up: The Work of Unconscious Experience. 174p. 1996. pap. text 13.00 (*0-8090-1590-0*) Hill & Wang.

***Bollas, Christopher.** Hysteria. LC 99-38081. 208p. 1999. pap. 29.95 (*0-415-22033-5*) Routledge.

Bollas, Christopher. The Shadow of the Object: Psychoanalysis of the Unthought Known. 274p. 1989. pap. text 19.50 (*0-231-06627-9*) Col U Pr.

Bollas, Christopher & Sundelson, David. The New Informants: The Betrayal of Confidentiality in Psychoanalysis & Psychotherapy. LC 95-14299. 232p. 1995. 35.00 (*1-56821-595-9*) Aronson.

Bollback, Anthony G. Capture of the Twin Dragon. LC 97-215106. 153p. (J). (gr. 4-9). 1997. pap. 7.95 (*1-885729-14-6*) Toccoa Falls.

— Mystery of the Counterfeit Money. LC 98-226248. 127p. (J). (gr. 4-9). 1997. pap. 7.95 (*1-885729-15-4*) Toccoa Falls.

***Bollback, Anthony G.** Rescue at Cripple Creek, Vol. 4. (Jack & Jill Mysteries Ser.). 135p. 1999. pap. 7.95 (*1-885729-18-9*) Toccoa Falls.

Bollback, Anthony G. Smugglers in Hong Kong. LC 97-214663. 158p. (J). (gr. 4-9). 1997. pap. 7.95 (*1-885729-13-8*) Toccoa Falls.

— To China & Back. LC 90-86214. (Jaffray Collection of Missionary Portraits: Bk. 4). (Illus.). 130p. 1991. pap. 9.99 (*0-87509-444-9*) Chr Pubns.

Bolle de Bal, Marcel. The Double Games of Participation: Pay, Performance & Culture. Shayler, Irene, tr. LC 92-33198. (Studies in Organization: No. 43). (ENG & FRE.). xii, 265p. 1993. lib. bdg. 72.95 (*3-11-012972-8*) De Gruyter.

Bolle, Eric. Die Kunst der Differenz: Philosophische Untersuchungen zur Bestimmung der Kunst bei Martin Heidegger, Friedrich Holderlin, Paul Celan und Bram van Velde. (Schriften Zur Philosophie der Differenz Ser.: No. 2). (GER.). 120p. 1988. 31.00 (*90-6032-305-X*, Pub. by B R Gruner) Humanities.

Bolle, H. J., ed. Remote Sounding of the Atmosphere from Space: Proceedings of the Committee on Space Research, 21st Plenary Meeting, Innsbruck, Austria, 1978. (Illus.). 1979. 76.00 (*0-08-023419-4*, Pergamon Pr) Elsevier.

Bolle, H. J., jt. ed. see Ohring, G.

Bolle, Jeff, ed. Lay Mission Handbook. 100p. ring bd. 20.00 (*0-318-21725-2*) Intl Liaison.

Bolle, Kees W. The Freedom of Man in Myth. LC 68-8564. 216p. 1993. reprint ed. pap. 16.95 (*0-8265-1248-8*) Vanderbilt U Pr.

Bolle, Kees W., ed. Mythology Series, 39 vols., Set. (Illus.). 1978. lib. bdg. 1807.50 (*0-405-10529-0*); lib. bdg. 669.00 (*0-405-18984-2*) Ayer.

— Reading in Mythology: An Original Anthology. LC 77-139. (Mythology Ser.). (FRE & GER.). 1978. lib. bdg. 17.95 (*0-405-10573-8*) Ayer.

— Studies of A. J. Wensinck: An Original Arno Press Anthology. LC 77-82275. (Mythology Ser.). 1978. lib. bdg. 19.95 (*0-405-10567-3*) Ayer.

Bolle, Kees W., ed. see Creuzer, Georg F.

Bolle, Kees W., ed. see David-Neel, Alexandra & Yongden, Lama.

Bolle, Kees W., ed. see De Gubernatis, Angelo.

Bolle, Kees W., ed. see De Rebecque, Constant & Benjamin, Henri.

Bolle, Kees W., ed. see De Vries, Jan.

Bolle, Kees W., ed. see Dumezil, Georges.

Bolle, Kees W., ed. see Ehrenreich, Paul.

Bolle, Kees W., ed. see Gorres, Joseph.

Bolle, Kees W., ed. see Jensen, Adolf E.

Bolle, Kees W., jt. ed. see Jensen, Adolf E.

Bolle, Kees W., ed. see Krappe, Alexandre H.

Bolle, Kees W., ed. see Langer, Fritz.

Bolle, Kees W., ed. see Leenhardt, Maurice.

Bolle, Kees W., ed. see Lessmann, Heinrich.

Bolle, Kees W., ed. see Liebert, Arthur.

Bolle, Kees W., ed. see Lipps, Gottlob F.

Bolle, Kees W., ed. see Mannhardt, Wilhelm.

Bolle, Kees W., ed. see Meyer, Richard M.

Bolle, Kees W., ed. see Muller, Friedrich M.

Bolle, Kees W., ed. see Muller, Karl O.

Bolle, Kees W., ed. see Mus, Paul.

Bolle, Kees W., ed. see Nestle, Wilhelm.

Bolle, Kees W., ed. see Oppert, Gustav.

Bolle, Kees W., ed. see Otto, Walter F.

Bolle, Kees W., ed. see Pettazzoni, Raffaele.

Bolle, Kees W., jt. ed. see Pettazzoni, Raffaele.

Bolle, Kees W., ed. see Pigott, Grenville.

Bolle, Kees W., ed. see Preller, Ludwig.

Bolle, Kees W., ed. see Siecke, Ernst.

Bolle, Kees W., ed. see Vignoli, Tito.

Bolle, Kees W., ed. see Wirz, Paul.

Bolle, Kees W., ed. see Zeitlin, Ida.

Bolle, Kees W., ed. see Ziegler, Leopold.

Bolle-Kleinbub, Ingrid. West Highland White Terriers. (Barron's Pet Owner's Manuals Ser.). (Illus.). 96p. (Orig.). 1994. pap. 6.95 (*0-8120-1950-4*) Barron.

Bollee, W. B., tr. from PLI. Kunala-jataka. (C). 1970. 25.50 (*0-86013-050-9*, Pub. by Pali Text) Elsevier.

Bollella, Greg, jt. auth. see Gosling, James.

Bollen, Colleen F. Shorts: A Gateway into New Markets. 80p. (Orig.). 1996. pap. 8.95 (*0-9654384-0-6*) Turtle Isl WA.

Bollen, J., jt. auth. see Tan, Lee M.

Bollen, Kenneth A. & Long, J. Scott, eds. Testing Structural Equation Models. (Focus Editions Ser.: Vol. 154). (Illus.). 280p. (C). 1993. text 59.95 (*0-8039-4506-X*); pap. text 26.00 (*0-8039-4507-8*) Sage.

Bollen, M. The Structure & Regulation of Type-1 Protein Phosphataese Involved in Hepatic Glycogen Matabolism. No. 49. 79p. (Orig.). 1991. pap. 28.00 (*90-6186-481-X*, Pub. by Leuven Univ) Coronet Bks.

***Bollen, Math H. J.** Solving Power Quality Problems: Voltage Sags & Interruptions LC 99-23546. (Series on Power Engineering). 1999. 79.95 (*0-7803-4713-7*) IEEE Standards.

Bollen, Peter D. The Best of Dear Bureaucrat: The Selected Letters of Peter Bollen. LC 88-82942. (Illus.). 128p. (Orig.). 1988. pap. 6.95 (*0-9611350-2-6*) Highland Hillside.

***Bollen, Peter D.** Great Labor Quotations: Sourcebook & Reader. 2000. pap. 19.95 (*0-929349-06-7*) Red Eye Pr.

Bollen, Peter D. A Handbook of Great Labor Quotations. LC 83-90292. (Illus.). 128p. (Orig.). 1983. pap. 5.95 (*0-9611350-0-X*) Highland Hillside.

***Bollen, Peter J. A., et al.** The Laboratory Swine. LC 99-57595. (Laboratory Animal Pocket References Ser.). 152p. 1999. spiral bd. 44.95 (*0-8493-1035-0*) CRC Pr.

Bollen, Roger, jt. auth. see Sadler, Marilyn.

Bollen, William. Structual Equations with Latent Variables. LC 88-27272. (Probability & Mathematical Statistics Ser.). 528p. 1989. 94.95 (*0-471-01171-1*) Wiley.

Bollenbacher, George. Commercial Banks in Securities Business: Practice Guide. (C). 1990. 45.00 (*0-13-151549-7*, Macmillan Coll) P-H.

B

An Asterisk (*) at the beginning of an entry indicates that the title is appearing for the first time.

Bollenbacher, George M. The New Business of Banking: Surviving & Thriving in Times of Unparalleled Consolidation & Competition. 250p. 1992. text 32.50 (*1-55738-331-6*, Irwn Prfssnl) McGraw-Hill Prof.
— New Business of Banking: Transforming Challenges into Opportunities in Today's Financial Services Marketplace. (Illus.). 278p. 1998. reprint ed. lib. bdg. 35.00 (*0-7351-0038-1*) Replica Bks.
— The New Business of Banking: Transforming Challenges into Opportunities in Today's Financial Services Marketplace. 2nd rev. ed. 250p. 1995. text 35.00 (*1-55738-771-0*, Irwn Prfssnl) McGraw-Hill Prof.
Bollenback, G. N., jt. auth. see Hoynak, P. X.
Bollenbaugh, Mick, ed. see Alder, George, et al.
Bollendorf, Susan, jt. auth. see Johnston, Sona K.
Bollens, John C. Appointed Executive Local Government: The California Experience. LC 52-12988. (Illus.). 233p. 1970. reprint ed. lib. bdg. 65.00 (*0-8371-8068-6*, BOAE, Greenwood Pr) Greenwood.
— Special District Governments in the United States. LC 77-26250. 280p. 1978. reprint ed. lib. bdg. 59.75 (*0-313-20065-3*, BOSD, Greenwood Pr) Greenwood.
***Bollens, Scott A.** On Narrow Ground: Urban Policy & Conflict in Jerusalem & Belfast. LC 99-39693. (SUNY Series in Urban Public Policy). (Illus.). 448p. (C). 2000. text 73.50 (*0-7914-4413-9*); pap. text 24.95 (*0-7914-4414-7*) State U NY Pr.
Bollens, Scott A. Urban Peacebuilding in Divided Societies: Belfast & Johannesburg. LC 98-29197. 360p. 1998. 69.00 (*0-8133-3541-8*, Pub. by Westview) HarpC.
Boller. Perfect Union, 4 vols. 4th ed. (C). 1995. pap. text 29.56 (*0-395-74524-1*) HM.
— Perfect Union, 4 vols., Vol. 2. 4th ed. (C). 1995. pap. text 29.56 (*0-395-74525-X*) HM.
Boller, C. & Seeger, T. Material Data for Cyclic Loading, 5 vols., Set. (Materials Science Monographs: No. 42 A-E). xxxvi,1856p. 1987. 824.00 (*0-444-42875-5*) Elsevier.
Boller, David. Kaos Moon: Full Circle. (Illus.). 64p. 1997. pap. 5.95 (*0-941613-98-4*, Caliber Comics) Stabur Pr.
Boller, F., et al, eds. Handbook of Neuropsychology, Vol. 1. (Handbook of Neuropsychology Ser.: I). xvi,436p. 1988. reprint ed. pap. 91.50 (*0-444-81215-6*) Elsevier.
— Heterogeneity of Alzheimer's Disease. LC 92-48751. (Research & Perspectives in Alzheimer's Disease Ser.). 1992. write for info. (*3-540-55918-3*); 98.95 (*0-387-55918-3*) Spr-Verlag.
Boller, F. & Grafman, J. Handbook of Neuropsychology, Vol. 10. 510p. pap. 106.25 (*0-444-82766-8*, North Holland) Elsevier.
— Handbook of Neuropsychology, Vol. 11. 448p. 1997. pap. 97.50 (*0-444-82763-3*) Elsevier.
Boller, F. & Grafman, J., eds. Handbook of Neuropsychology. (Handbook of Neuropsychology Ser.: Vol. 11). 448p. 1997. 224.00 (*0-444-82467-7*) Elsevier.
— Handbook of Neuropsychology, 10. 510p. 1995. 246.50 (*0-444-89979-0*) Elsevier.
Boller, F., et al. Handbook of Neuropsychology, Vol. 9. 448p. pap. 92.00 (*0-444-82765-X*, North Holland) Elsevier.
— Handbook of Neuropsychology, Vol. 9. (Handbook of Neuropsychology Ser.: 9). 448p. 1994. 285.00 (*0-444-89966-9*) Elsevier.
Boller, F., jt. auth. see Spinnler, H.
Boller, F., jt. ed. see Spinnler, H.
Boller, F. Richard. Woodworking & Cabinetmaking. 400p. 1986. text 18.95 (*0-02-512800-0*) Macmillan.
Boller, Francois & Frank, Ellen. Sexual Dysfunction in Neurological Disorders: Diagnosis, Management & Rehabilitation. LC 81-85165. (Illus.). 108p. 1982. reprint ed. pap. 33.50 (*0-608-00602-5*, 206118900007) Bks Demand.
Boller, Paul, Jr. Presidential Wives: An Anecdotal History. 2nd ed. 576p. 1998. 30.00 (*0-19-512702-1*) OUP.
— Presidential Wives: An Anecdotal History. 2nd ed. LC 98-3480. 576p. 1999. pap. 14.95 (*0-19-512142-2*) OUP.
Boller, Paul F., Jr. American Thought in Transition: The Impact of Evolutionary Naturalism, 1865-1900. LC 80-6210. 285p. 1981. reprint ed. pap. text 22.00 (*0-8191-1551-7*) U Pr of Amer.
— Congressional Anecdotes. 368p. 1992. pap. 14.95 (*0-19-507706-7*) OUP.
— Freedom & Fate in American Thought: From Edwards to Dewey. LC 78-5813. 316p. 1978. 17.50 (*0-87074-169-1*) SMU Press.
Boller, Paul F. George Washington & Religion. LC 63-9755. 247p. reprint ed. pap. 76.60 (*0-8357-8888-1*, 203341100086) Bks Demand.
— Memoirs of an Obscure Professor. LC 91-30356. (Illus.). 258p. 1992. 24.95 (*0-87565-097-X*) Tex Christian.
Boller, Paul F., Jr. Not So! Popular Myths about America from Columbus to Clinton. 288p. 1996. reprint ed. pap. 12.95 (*0-19-510972-4*) OUP.
— Not So! Popular Myths About America's Past from Columbus to Clinton. 288p. 1995. text 30.00 (*0-19-509186-8*) OUP.
— Presidential Anecdotes. rev. ed. 472p. 1996. pap. 14.95 (*0-19-509731-9*) OUP.
— Presidential Anecdotes. rev. ed. 472p. 1996. text 30.00 (*0-19-510715-2*) OUP.
— Presidential Campaigns. rev. ed. 480p. 1996. pap. 15.95 (*0-19-509730-0*) OUP.
— Presidential Wives. 544p. 1989. reprint ed. pap. 12.95 (*0-19-505976-X*) OUP.
Boller, Paul F., Jr. & George, John. They Never Said It: A Book of Fake Quotes, Misquotes, & Misleading Attributions. 192p. 1989. reprint ed. text 30.00 (*0-19-505541-1*) OUP.
Bollerman, Jeff. Dixie Highway: The Eye of the Beholder. (Illus.). 128p. 1992. pap. 19.95 (*1-880680-02-5*) Sand Dllr Fl.
Bolles, A. Lynn. Sister Jamaica: A Study of Women, Work, & Households in Kingston. LC 95-46006. 150p. (C). 1996. lib. bdg. 32.50 (*0-7618-0211-8*) U Pr of Amer.
— We Paid Our Dues: Women Trade Union Leaders of the Caribbean. LC 95-50954. (C). 1996. pap. 21.95 (*0-88258-085-X*) Howard U Pr.
Bolles, Albert S. Financial History of the United States, 3 vols., Set. LC 68-22371. (Library of Money & Banking History). 1969. 175.00 (*0-678-00465-X*) Kelley.
— Financial History of the United States Vol. 1: 1774-1789. 4th ed. LC 68-22371. xii, 371p. 1969. reprint ed. 65.00 (*0-678-04033-8*) Kelley.
— Financial History of the United States Vol. 2: From 1789 to 1860. 4th ed. LC 68-22371. ix, 621p. 1969. reprint ed. 65.00 (*0-678-04034-6*) Kelley.
— Financial History of the United States Vol. 3: From 1861 to 1885. 2nd ed. LC 68-22371. xi, 585p. 1969. reprint ed. 65.00 (*0-678-04035-4*) Kelley.
— The National Bank Act & Its Judicial Meaning. Bruchey, Stuart, ed. LC 80-1135. (Rise of Commercial Banking Ser.). 1981. reprint ed. lib. bdg. 41.95 (*0-405-13635-8*) Ayer.
— Pennsylvania Province & State, 1609-1790, 2 vols., Set. 1993. reprint ed. lib. bdg. 150.00 (*0-7812-5430-2*) Rprt Serv.
— Practical Banking. Bruchey, Stuart, ed. LC 80-1136. (Rise of Commercial Banking Ser.). 1981. reprint ed. lib. bdg. 30.95 (*0-405-13636-6*) Ayer.
Bolles, Blair. Tyrant from Illinois. LC 73-16641. 248p. 1974. reprint ed. lib. bdg. 35.00 (*0-8371-7205-5*, BOTI, Greenwood Pr) Greenwood.
Bolles, David, jt. ed. see Gubler, Ruth.
Bolles, DeVallon, et al. United States Foreign Policy Regarding Greece, Turkey & Cyprus: The Rule of Law & American Interests. 127p. (Orig.). 1989. 15.00 (*0-941882-00-4*) Amer Hellenic Inst.
Bolles, Edmund B. Free Yourself from Chronic Backache. 144p. 1990. mass mkt. 5.99 (*0-440-20571-9*) Dell.
— Galileo's Commandment: An Anthology of Great Science Writing. 1999. pap. text 16.95 (*0-7167-3693-4*) W H Freeman.
— The Ice Finders: How a Poet, a Professor & a Politician Discovered the Ice Age. LC 99-35799. 272p. 1999. text 24.00 (*1-58243-030-6*, Pub. by Counterpt DC) HarpC.
***Bolles, Edmund Blair.** The Ice Finders. 2000. pap. 13.00 (*1-58243-101-9*, Pub. by Counterpt DC) HarpC.
Bolles, Frank. A Collection of Important English Statutes. 3rd ed. 189p. 1978. reprint ed. lib. bdg. 60.00 (*0-89941-141-X*, 300090) W S Hein.
Bolles, Julia & Wilson, Peter. Bolles - Wilson: New Buildings & Projects. LC 97-41668. (GER., Illus.). 128p. 1997. 55.00 (*3-7643-5610-3*, Pub. by Birkhauser) Princeton Arch.
Bolles, M. Marjorie, jt. auth. see Landis, Carney.
Bolles, R. C., et al, eds. Intelligent Robots: Sensing, Modeling, & Planning. LC 97-33096. (Series in Machine Perception & Artificial Intelligence: Vol. 27). 500p. 1997. 86.00 (*981-02-3185-7*) World Scientific Pub.
Bolles, Richard. How to Find Your Mission in Life. abr. ed. 1995. 9.95 incl. audio (*0-89815-702-1*) Audio Lit.
— What Color Is Your Parachute? abr. ed. 1995. 50.00 incl. audio (*0-89815-700-5*) Audio Lit.
Bolles, Richard & Christen, Carol. An Introduction & Overview of "What Color Is Your Parachute?" abr. ed. 1995. 9.95 incl. audio (*0-89815-701-3*) Audio Lit.
Bolles, Richard Nelson. How to Find Your Mission in Life. gif. ed. (Illus.). 64p. Date not set. 12.95 (*0-89815-859-1*) Ten Speed Pr.
— Job-Hunting on the Internet. 2nd rev. ed. (Illus.). 244p. 1999. pap. 8.95 (*1-58008-078-2*) Ten Speed Pr.
— The New Quick Job-Hunting Map. rev. ed. 64p. 1985. pap. 4.95 (*0-89815-387-5*) Ten Speed Pr.
— The Three Boxes of Life: And How to Get Out of Them. LC 78-17000. (Illus.). 466p. 1981. pap. 18.95 (*0-913668-58-3*) Ten Speed Pr.
— What Color Is Your Parachute? 2000: The Best-Selling Job-Hunting Book in the World. 30th anniversary ed. LC 84-649334. (Illus.). 368p. 1999. pap. 16.95 (*1-58008-123-1*) Ten Speed Pr.
***Bolles, Richard Nelson.** What Color is Your Parachute? 2001: A Practical Manual for Job-Hunters & Career-Changers. 2000. 24.95 (*1-58008-241-6*); pap. 16.95 (*1-58008-242-4*) Ten Speed Pr.
— The What Color Is Your Parachute Workbook. rev. ed. (Illus.). 48p. 1998. pap. 9.95 (*0-89815-880-X*) Ten Speed Pr.
***Bolles, Richard Nelson & Brown, Dale Susan.** Job-Hunting for the So-Called Handicapped. rev. expanded ed. (Illus.). 160p. 2000. pap. 12.95 (*1-58008-195-9*) Ten Speed Pr.
***Bolles, Richard Nelson & Figler, Howard.** The Career Counselor's Handbook. 320p. 1999. pap. 17.95 (*1-58008-157-6*) Ten Speed Pr.
Bolles, Robert C. The Story of Psychology: A Thematic History. (C). 1993. mass mkt. 55.75 (*0-534-19668-3*) Brooks-Cole.
— The Story of Psychology: A Thematic History. 1993. mass mkt., teacher ed. write for info. (*0-534-19670-5*) Brooks-Cole.
Bolles, Robert C., ed. Hedonics of Taste. 224p. 1991. 49.95 (*0-8058-0366-1*) L Erlbaum Assocs.
Bolles, Robert C. & Beecher, Michael D., eds. Evolution & Learning. 224p. 1987. 49.95 (*0-89859-542-8*) L Erlbaum Assocs.
Bolles, Simeon. Early History of the Town of Bethlehem. (Illus.). 108p. 1997. reprint ed. pap. 15.00 (*0-8328-5977-X*) Higginson Bk Co.
Bolles, William H., jt. auth. see Geyer, Alan R.
Bollet, Alfred J. Mosby's USMLE Step 2 Reviews: General Clinical Sciences. LC 96-4742. (Ace the Boards Ser.). (Illus.). 552p. (C). (gr. 13). 1996. pap. text 37.00 (*0-8151-0723-4*, 27048) Mosby Inc.
— Plagues & Poxes: The Rise & Fall of Epidemic Disease. LC 87-71319. 208p. 1987. pap. text 39.95 (*0-939957-06-X*) Demos Medical.
Bollet, Alfred J. & Bruckheim, Allan H., eds. Mediquiz, Vol. 2. (Illus.). 344p. 50.00 (*0-935466-04-5*) Pierson Pubs.
Bollett, Alfred Jay. Ace Clinical Sciences. (Illus.). 522p. 1996. text 37.00 (*0-8151-1054-5*, 28976) Mosby Inc.
— Civil War Medicine. (Illus.). 375p. 2000. pap. write for info. (*1-883620-03-1*) Galen AZ.
***Bollettieri, Nick & Gruppo, Anthony C.** Under Construction: From the First Ball to the Last Ball. (Illus.). 170p. 1999. pap. 12.95 (*0-9660315-9-8*) Cutter Ent.
Bollettieri, Nick & Maher, Charles A. The Mental Efficiency Program: Positive Self Development for Tennis, Sport, & Life. (Mental Efficiency & Sport Psychology Ser.). (Orig.). pap. text. write for info. (*1-878843-11-7*) Intl Merc OH.
— Nick Bollettieri's Mental Efficiency Program for Playing Great Tennis. (Illus.). 248p. 1996. pap. 12.95 (*0-8092-3282-0*, 328200, Contemporary Bks) NTC Contemp Pub Co.
Bolli, Hans M., et al. Benthic Formaniniferal Biostratigraphy of the South Caribbean. (Illus.). 420p. (C). 1994. text 160.00 (*0-521-41521-7*) Cambridge U Pr.
Bolli, Richard. Revision of the Genus Sambucus. (Dissertationes Botanicae Ser.: Band 223). (Illus.). ii, 256p. 1994. pap. 42.00 (*3-443-64135-0*, Pub. by Gebruder Borntraeger) Balogh.
Bollich, Celia F., jt. auth. see Bollich, James T.
Bollich, James J. Missing in Action, Ww Ii: Mission No. 70. LC 98-93703. 229 p. 1998. write for info. (*0-9643275-4-6*) J J Bollich.
— A Soldier's Journal. 2nd ed. LC 97-94823. (Illus.). 176p. 1998. reprint ed. 20.00 (*0-9643275-3-8*) J J Bollich.
— White Cotton over Black Gold. LC 97-94794. (Illus.). 220p. 1998. 20.00 (*0-9643275-2-X*) J J Bollich.
— Young James of Acadiana. (Illus.). 300p. 1994. 20.00 (*0-9643275-0-3*) J J Bollich.
Bollich, James T. & Bollich, Celia F. Young James to Jim. unabridged ed. (Illus.). 275p. (Orig.). 1997. pap. 20.00 (*0-9643275-1-1*) J J Bollich.
Bollier, David. The Future of Community & Personal Identity in the Coming Electronic Culture. (Communications & Society Program Book Ser.). 47p. 1996. pap. 10.00 (*0-89843-166-2*) The Aspen Inst.
— The Future of Electronic Commerce. (Communications & Society Program Book Ser.). 53p. 1996. pap. 10.00 (*0-89843-188-3*) The Aspen Inst.
Bollier, David. The Global Wave of Entrepreneurialism: Harnessing the Synergies of Personal Initiative, Digital Technologies & Global Commerce. (Communications & Society Ser.). 42p. pap. write for info. (*0-89843-264-2*) The Aspen Inst.
Bollier, David. How to Appraise & Improve Your Daily Newspaper. 1980. pap. 5.00 (*0-686-36550-X*) Ctr Responsive Law.
— Work & Future Society: Where Are the Economy & Technology Taking Us? LC 98-164509. iii, 52 p. 1998. 10.00 (*0-89843-232-4*) The Aspen Inst.
Bollier, David, et al. Pioneers of Progress: Policy Entrepreneurs & Community Development, Vol. 1. 1991. pap. 20.00 (*1-887410-53-8*) Jobs for Future.
Bollier, David, jt. auth. see Cohn, Henry.
Bollier, Renee B., et al. Stephenson's Connecticut Civil Procedure. 310p. 1997. text 145.00 (*1-878698-38-9*) Atlantic Law.
Bollig, Jeff, ed. see Kerkhoff, Blair.
Bolliger, Barbara E., et al. The Journal of Decorative & Propaganda Arts No. 19/1993: Swiss Theme Issue. (Illus.). 200p. (Orig.). 1993. pap. 25.00 (*0-9631601-2-5*) Wolfson Fnd D&P Arts.
Bolliger, C. T. & Fagerstrom, K. O., eds. The Tobacco Epidemic. LC 97-29285. (Progress in Respiratory Research Ser.: No. 28). (Illus.). x, 266p. 1997. 82.75 (*3-8055-6531-3*) S Karger.
***Bolliger, C. T. & Mathur, P. N., eds.** Interventional Bronchoscopy. (Progress in Respiratory Research Ser.: Vol. 30). (Illus.). X, 298p. 1999. 172.25 (*3-8055-6851-7*) S Karger.
Bolliger, Hans. Dokumetations - Bibliothek Zur Kunst des 20 Jahrhunderts: Bibliography of Twentieth Century Art Publications. (GER., Illus.). 608p. 1991. 150.00 (*1-55660-079-8*) A Wofsy Fine Arts.
Bolliger, Hans, intro. Picasso's Vollard Suite. LC 85-50441. (Illus.). 120p. 1994. reprint ed. pap. 15.95 (*0-500-27100-3*, Pub. by Thames Hudson) Norton.
Bolliger, Markus. Die Gattung Pulmonaria in Westeuropa. (Phanerogamarum Monographiae: No. VIII). (GER.). 250p. (Orig.). 1982. text 80.00 (*3-7682-1338-2*) Lubrecht & Cramer.
Bolliger, Max. Three Little Bears. (Illus.). (J). (ps-3). 1987. 12.95 (*1-55774-006-2*) Lambda Pubs.
Bollin, S. K. My Cat's Book: The Who, What, When & Where of My Cat's Life - An Essential Book for All Cat Owners. 32p. 1992. pap. 4.95 (*0-914846-63-9*) Golden West Pub.
— My Dog's Book: The Who, What, When & Where of My Dog's Life - An Essential Book for All Dog Owners. 32p. 1992. pap. 4.95 (*0-914846-62-0*) Golden West Pub.
— My Horse's Book: The Who, What, When & Where of My Horse's Life - An Essential Book for All Horse Owners. 32p. 1992. pap. 4.95 (*0-914846-64-7*) Golden West Pub.
Bollin, Susan K. Chip & Dip Lovers Cook Book: More Than 150 Delectable Dip Recipes for Chips, Crackers. LC 93-36756. 128p. 1993. ring bd. 5.95 (*0-914846-93-0*) Golden West Pub.
— Quick-n-Easy Mexican Recipes: Marvelous Mexican Meals, in Minutes! LC 93-21427. 128p. 1993. ring bd. 5.95 (*0-914846-85-X*) Golden West Pub.
— Sedona Cook Book: Recipes from Red Rock Country. LC 94-12950. 1994. ring bd. 7.95 (*0-914846-98-1*) Golden West Pub.
Bollin, Susan K., ed. see Fischer, Lee & Fischer, Bruce.
Bolling, C. California Suite. 1990. 5.00 (*0-685-32125-8*, SHAT65) Hansen Ed Mus.
— Concerto for Classic Guitar & Jazz Piano: Drum Part. 1990. 5.00 (*0-685-32227-0*, SIL29) Hansen Ed Mus.
— Jazz a la Francaise. 60p. 1987. pap. 14.95 (*0-7935-2201-3*, 00357026) H Leonard.
— Main Theme: C. Bolling's California Suite for Flute-Jazz Piano-Bass & Drums. 1990. 10.00 (*0-685-32228-9*, SHAT60) Hansen Ed Mus.
— Philosophy & Literature. 210p. 1986. 65.00 (*0-930586-22-0*) Haven Pubns.
— Picnic Suite: Solo Flute. 1990. 7.00 (*0-685-32121-5*, SIL41) Hansen Ed Mus.
— Picnic Suite for Flute, Guitar, & Jazz Piano Trio. 1991. pap. text 40.00 (*0-7935-0842-8*, 00673218) H Leonard.
— Sonata for Two Pianists. 1990. 7.50 (*0-685-32229-7*, SIL50) Hansen Ed Mus.
— Sonata for Two Pianists No. 1: Pianist No. 1 - Classical; Pianist No. 2 - Jazz String Bass, Percussion. 68p. 1992. pap. 35.00 (*0-7935-0054-0*, 00490343) H Leonard.
— Sonata for Two Pianists No. 2: Pianist No. 2 - Bass, Drums. 1992. pap. text 35.00 (*0-7935-1198-4*, 00490534) H Leonard.
— Suite for Cello & Jazz Piano Trio: Bass & Drums. 1990. 10.00 (*0-685-32232-7*, SHAT73) Hansen Ed Mus.
— Suite for Flute & Jazz Piano. 1990. pap. text 40.00 (*0-7935-0097-4*, 00490508) H Leonard.
— Suite for Flute & Jazz Piano: Solo Flute. 1990. 8.00 (*0-685-32124-X*, SIL8) Hansen Ed Mus.
— Suite for Flute & Piano. 1990. 8.00 (*0-685-32230-0*, SIL6) Hansen Ed Mus.
— Suite for Violin & Jazz Piano. 1990. 8.00 (*0-685-32239-4*, SIL36) Hansen Ed Mus.
— Suite Jazz Flute Solos. 1990. 10.00 (*0-685-32118-5*, SHAT061) Hansen Ed Mus.
— Toot Suite for Trumpet & Jazz Piano. 1991. pap. text 40.00 (*0-7935-0840-1*, 00673217) H Leonard.
— Toot Suite for Trumpet & Jazz Piano. 1990. 8.00 (*0-685-32183-5*, SIL55) Hansen Ed Mus.
Bolling, Claude. Sonate pour Guitare. 20p. 1996. pap. 9.95 (*0-7935-6527-8*) H Leonard.
Bolling, David. How to Save a River: A Handbook for Citizen Action. LC 93-50690. 1994. pap. 21.95 (*1-55963-250-X*); text 40.00 (*1-55963-249-6*) Island Pr.
Bolling, G. Fredric. Art of Achieving Quality. 171p. 1995. 56.95 (*0-566-07462-1*, Pub. by Gower) Ashgate Pub Co.
— The Art of Forecasting. LC 95-40202. 200p. 1996. 56.95 (*0-566-07764-7*, Pub. by Gower) Ashgate Pub Co.
— The Art of Manufacturing Development. 144p. 1995. 56.95 (*0-566-07463-X*, Pub. by Gower) Ashgate Pub Co.
— Leadership & Immensity. 200p. 1996. 56.95 (*0-566-07763-9*, Pub. by Gower) Ashgate Pub Co.
Bolling, G. Fredric & Withington, Valerie A. The Graphic Work of Dame Laura Knight: Including a Catalogue Raisonne of Her Prints. 160p. 1993. 121.95 (*0-85967-939-X*, Pub. by Scolar Pr) Ashgate Pub Co.
Bolling, Rick, tr. see Happel, Lioba, et al.
Bolling, Ruben. Tom the Dancing Bug: Everything I Ever Needed to Know I Learned from My Golf-Playing Cats. (Illus.). 80p. 1997. pap. 1.49 (*1-56163-183-3*) NBM.
Bolling, Steven F. Endocarditis: A Multidisciplinary Approach to Modern Treatment. Vlessis, Angelo A., ed. LC 99-26873. (Illus.). 440p. 1999. 98.00 (*0-87993-433-6*) Futura Pub.
Bollinger, A., jt. ed. see Allegra, C.
Bollinger, A., jt. ed. see Reneman, R. S.
Bollinger, Alfred & Fagrell, Bengt, eds. Clinical Capillaroscopy: A Guide to Its Use in Clinical Research & Practice. LC 90-5052. (Illus.). 168p. 1990. text 64.00 (*0-88937-048-6*) Hogrefe & Huber Pubs.
Bollinger, Don. Hardwood Floors: Laying, Sanding & Finishing. LC 90-11065. (Illus.). 144p. (C). 1990. pap. 19.95 (*0-942391-62-4*, 070103) Taunton.
Bollinger, Donald E. Band Director's Complete Handbook. (Illus.). 1979. text 24.95 (*0-13-055442-1*, Parker Publishing Co) P-H.
Bollinger, Edward E. On the Threshold of the Closed Empire: Mid-Nineteenth Century Missionaries in Okinawa. LC 91-73083. 249p. (Orig.). (C). 1991. pap. text 14.95 (*0-87808-230-1*, WCL230-1) William Carey Lib.
Bollinger, G. A. Blast Vibration Analysis. LC 79-22421. (Illus.). 149p. 1980. reprint ed. pap. 9.95 (*0-8093-0951-3*) S Ill U Pr.
***Bollinger, Gil.** A Chronology of the Indian War Battles & Other Important Events in the Bozeman Trail: Powder River Country for the Frontier Period - 1840 Through 1900. (Illus.). 25p. 2000. pap. 4.95 (*0-9670560-3-9*) Gatchell Museum.
— Jim Gatchell - The Man & the Museum. 432p. 1999. 48.95 (*0-9670560-0-4*); pap. 16.95 (*0-9670560-1-2*) Gatchell Museum.
Bollinger, J. Michael. Aviation Security: Implementation of Recommendations Is under Way, but Completion Will Take Several Years. (Illus.). 68p. 1999. pap. text 20.00 (*0-7881-8025-8*) DIANE Pub.
Bollinger, John G. & Duffie, Neil A. Computer Control of Machines & Processes. LC 87-14019. (Mechanical Engineering Ser.). (Illus.). 620p. (C). 1988. 105.00 (*0-201-10645-0*) Addison-Wesley.

***Bollinger, John J., et al, eds.** Non-Neutral Plasma Physics III. LC 99-68554. (AIP Conference Proceeding Ser.). (Illus.). 487p. 1999. 130.00 (*1-56396-913-0*) Am Inst Physics.

Bollinger, Kristie. Create Your Own Goldilocks & the Three Bears Sticker Picture: With 30 Reusable Stickers. (Illus.). (J). (gr. k-3). 1994. pap. 2.95 (*0-486-27946-4*) Dover.

Bollinger, Lee C. Images of a Free Press. LC 90-27740. 222p. 1991. 25.95 (*0-226-06348-8*) U Ch Pr.

— Images of a Free Press. 222p. 1994. pap. text 14.95 (*0-226-06349-6*) U Ch Pr.

— The Tolerant Society. 320p. 1988. pap. text 21.00 (*0-19-505430-X*) OUP.

Bollinger, Linda. Jack Russell Terriers: A New Owner's Guide. 1998. 12.95 (*0-7938-2799-X*) TFH Pubns.

Bollinger, Lorenz, ed. Cannabis Science - From Prohibition to Human Right (Cannabis-Wissenschaft - Von der Prohibition zum Recht auf Genub. (Illus.). 335p. 1997. 38.95 (*3-631-49279-0*) P Lang Pubng.

— Cannabis Science - From Prohibition to Human Right (Cannabis-Wissenschaft - Von der Prohibition zum Recht auf Genub. (Illus.). 335p. 1997. 38.95 (*0-8204-3238-5*) P Lang Pubng.

Bollinger, Marilyn. The Hunchback of Notre Dame: Quasimodo Finds a Friend. LC 97-221250. (Magic Touch Talking Bks.). (Illus.). 22p. (J). (ps-2). 1996. 19.99 (*1-888208-16-3*) Hasbro.

— Mickey's Safari Park Adventure. (Magic Touch Talking Bks.). (Illus.). 22p. (J). (ps-2). 1996. 19.99 (*1-888208-13-9*) Hasbro.

— Monkeytalia: Monkeying Around with the ABCs. (Magic Touch Talking Bks.). (Illus.). 22p. (J). (ps-2). 1996. 19.99 (*1-888208-05-8*) Hasbro.

— 101 Dalmatian's Cruise Caper. LC 97-162941. (Magic Touch Talking Bks.). (Illus.). 22p. (J). (ps-2). 1996. 19.99 (*1-888208-14-7*) Hasbro.

— Pooh's Surprise Party Surprise. LC 97-202427. (Magic Touch Talking Bks.). (Illus.). 22p. (J). (ps-2). 1996. 19.99 (*1-888208-15-5*) Hasbro.

— Team Tonka Saves the Day. (Magic Touch Talking Bks.). (Illus.). 22p. (J). (ps-2). 1996. 19.99 (*1-888208-06-6*) Hasbro.

Bollinger, Oran E. God Without Fear: An Experience of Exploration into the Nature of God. 160p. 1991. text 8.95 (*0-9630982-0-9*) Orchid Pubs.

Bollinger, R. F. American Admiralty Bureau's Guide to Seaman's Rights & Legal Remedies. LC 95-224001. 52p. (C). 1995. pap. 24.95 (*1-879778-39-4*, BK-0494) Marine Educ.

Bollinger, R. F., jt. ed. see Wilson, James A.

Bollinger, Raymond F. American Admiralty Bureau's Commentator, Vol. 1. 28p. (Orig.). 1994. pap. text 150.00 (*1-879778-27-0*, BK-0409-1) Marine Educ.

— American Admiralty Bureau's Commentator, Vol. 3. 58p. (Orig.). 1997. pap. text 35.75 (*1-879778-59-9*, BK-0409-3) Marine Educ.

— American Admiralty Bureau's Guide to Marine Nomenclature & Terminology. (Illus.). 154p. (Orig.). 1995. pap. text 40.00 (*1-879778-37-8*, BK-0458) Marine Educ.

— American Admiralty Bureau's Guide to the Enduring Principles of International Maritime Law. 86p. (Orig.). 1996. pap. text 15.95 (*1-879778-28-9*, BK-0631) Marine Educ.

— American Admiralty Bureau's Harbor Notebook - New Orleans. 16p. (Orig.). 1995. pap. text 17.95 (*1-879778-44-0*, BK-0203) Marine Educ.

Bollinger, Raymond F., ed. American Admiralty Bureau's Guide to Maritime Training Programs: Admiralty Bureau's Guide to Maritime Training Programs. (Illus.). 130p. (Orig.). 1993. pap. 19.95 (*1-879778-19-X*, BK-0277) Marine Educ.

— American Admiralty Bureau's Lawyers Guide to the Navigational Rules. 212p. (Orig.). 1993. pap. text 37.80 (*1-879778-17-3*, BK-0245) Marine Educ.

Bollinger, Raymond F., et al. American Admiralty Bureau's Commentator, Vol. 2. 20p. (Orig.). 1995. pap. text 35.00 (*1-879778-38-6*, BK-0409-2) Marine Educ.

Bollinger, Raymond R. American Admiralty Bureau's Introductory Guide to Ocean Cargo Claims. 70p. (Orig.). 1993. pap. 23.50 (*1-879778-18-1*, BK-0273) Marine Educ.

Bollinger, Rick & Hardiman, Carole J. Rating Scale of Communication in Cognitive Decline RSCCD. 50p. 1996. pap. 30.00 (*0-937857-66-1*, 1655) Speech Bin.

Bollinger, Robert E. & Crowl, Daniel A. Inherently Safer Chemical Processes: A Life Cycle Approach. LC 96-41370. (CCPS Concept Bks.). 154p. 1996. 79.00 (*0-8169-0703-X*, G-41) Am Inst Chem Eng.

Bollinger, Taree & Seeman, Cary. Chalk It Up! Outdoor Blacktop Activities & Games Across the Curriculum. Clark Editorial & Design Staff, ed. (Illus.). 136p. 1997. pap. 12.95 (*0-88160-276-0*, LW346) Learning Wks.

Bollinger, Theresa & Cramer, Patricia. The Baby Gear Guide: How to Make Smart Choices in Essential Baby Equipment. (Illus.). 320p. 1985. pap. 12.95 (*0-201-10636-1*) Addison-Wesley.

Bollinger, Thomas. Samenanalytische Untersuchung der Fruehjungsteinzeitlichen Siedlung Egolzwil 3. (Dissertationes Botanicae Ser.: Band 221). (Illus.). x, 190p. 1994. pap. 53.00 (*3-443-64133-4*, Pub. by Gebruder Borntraeger) Balogh.

Bollinger, William H., et al. Project Design & Recommendations for Watershed Reforestation & Fuelwood Development in Sri Lanka. (Illus.). 122p. 1979. pap. 15.00 (*0-936130-03-2*) Intl Sci Tech.

Bollington, Rob, et al. An Introduction to Teacher Appraisal. (School Development Ser.). 160p. 1991. pap. text 33.95 (*0-304-31982-1*) Continuum.

Bollington, Rob, jt. auth. see Craft, Anna.

Bollioud-Mermet, Louis. De la Corruption du Goust dans la Musique Francaise. LC 76-43907. (Music & Theatre in France in the 17th & 18th Centuries Ser.). reprint ed. 31.50 (*0-404-60150-2*) AMS Pr.

Bollis, Christopher. Mystery of Things. LC 98-53607. 1999. pap. 29.99 (*0-415-21232-4*); text. write for info. (*0-415-21231-6*) Routledge.

Bollman, Don. Cat with Nine Lives: A Year Memoir of the Minor Leaguer of Canadian Lakes. LC 97-75723. (Illus.). 400p. 1998. 22.95 (*0-9662583-0-4*) Canadian Lakes.

Bollman, Ivana F. Westminster Colony, California, 1869-1879. LC 83-82983. (Illus.). 152p. 1983. 13.50 (*0-943480-56-6*) Friis-Pioneer Pr.

Bollman, James F., jt. auth. see Gura, Philip F.

Bollman, Kathryn L. Intentional Forgiveness: A Compassionate Approach to Counseling. Knispel, Julia S., ed. (Illus.). 125p. 1996. pap. 10.95 (*0-9651746-0-3*) Evergreen Leaves.

Bollman, Ray D. & Bryden', John, eds. Rural Employment: An International Perspective. LC 97-8471. (A CAB International Publication). 480p. (C). 1997. 100.00 (*0-85199-198-X*) OUP.

Bollmann, W. Crystal Lattices, Interfaces, Matrices: An Extension of Crystallography. (Illus.). 360p. 1982. 56.00 (*2-88105-000-X*) Polycrystal Bk Serv.

Bollmer, Jennifer. Architecture & the Text: The (S)crypts of Joyce & Piranesi. 1995. pap. 19.00 (*0-300-06302-4*) Yale U Pr.

Bollobas, Bela. Combinatorics. 190p. 1986. pap. text 22.95 (*0-521-33703-8*) Cambridge U Pr.

— Extremal Graph Theory with Emphasis on Probabilistic Method. LC 85-30670. (CBMS Regional Conference Series in Mathematics: Vol. 62). 64p. 1986. pap. 18.00 (*0-8218-0712-9*, CBMS/62) Am Math.

— Graph Theory: An Introductory Course. (Graduate Texts in Mathematics Ser.: Vol. 63). (Illus.). 1994. 54.95 (*0-387-90399-2*) Spr-Verlag.

***Bollobas, Bela.** Linear Analysis: An Introductory Course. 2nd ed. LC 99-11614. 245p. (C). 1999. pap. text 27.95 (*0-521-65577-3*) Cambridge U Pr.

Bollobas, Bela. Littlewood's Miscellany. 208p. 1986. pap. text 22.95 (*0-521-33702-X*) Cambridge U Pr.

— Probabilistic Combinatorics & Its Applications. LC 91-33123. (Proceedings of Symposia in Applied Mathematics Ser.). 196p. 1991. text 43.00 (*0-8218-5500-X*, PSAPM/44) Am Math.

Bollobas, Bela & Thomason, A. G. Combinatorics, Geometry & Probability: In Memory of Paul Erdos. 583p. (C). 1997. text 105.00 (*0-521-58472-8*) Cambridge U Pr.

Bollobas, E. Tradition & Innovation in American Free Verse: Whitman to Duncan. (Studies in Modern Philology: Vol. 3). 328p. (C). 1986. pap. 48.00 (*963-05-4139-4*, Pub. by Akade Kiado) St Mut.

Bollobas, Eniko. Charles Olson. (Twayne's United States Authors Ser.: No. 590). 190p. (C). 1992. 22.95 (*0-8057-7629-X*, Twyne) Mac Lib Ref.

***Bolloch, Ivan.** Games. rev. ed. (Action Math Ser.). (Illus.). (J). 2000. pap. 4.95 (*1-58728-050-7*) Two Can Pub.

Bollon, Arthur P. Recombinant DNA Products: Insulin, Interferon & Growth Hormone. 208p. 1985. 118.00 (*0-8493-5542-7*, QH442, CRC Reprint) Franklin.

Bollone, Pierluigi B. The Shroud under the Microscope. 1996. pap. 39.95 (*0-85439-533-4*, Pub. by St Paul Pubns) St Mut.

Bolloten, Burnett. The Spanish Civil War: Revolution & Counterrevolution. LC 89-77911. xxxiii, 1074p. (C). 1991. 80.00 (*0-8078-1906-9*) U of NC Pr.

Bollow, Janet, ed. see Arrigoni, Patricia.

Bollow, Ludmillow. One Acts & Monologues for Women. (Illus.). 96p. 1983. pap. 6.95 (*0-88145-008-1*) Broadway Play.

***Bolls, Imogene.** Advice for the Climb: Poems. (Midwest Poets Ser.). 76p. 1999. pap. 9.95 (*0-933087-55-1*) Bottom Dog Pr.

Bolluyt, James E. Design Modeling with Pro/Engineer. (Illus.). 206p. 1997. pap. text 49.95 (*1-887503-58-7*) Schroff Dev Corp.

Bolluyt, James E. Modeling for Design Using Silverscreen. (Engineering Ser.). 28.95 (*0-534-93336-X*) PWS Pubs.

***Bollweg, Jutta.** Vorderasiatische Wagentypen: Im Spiegel der Terracottaplastik Bis Zur Altbabylonischen Zeit. (Orbis Biblicus et Orientalis Ser.: Vol. 167). (GER.). viii, 206p. 1999. text 45.00 (*3-7278-1254-0*, Pub. by Ed Univ Fri) Eisenbrauns.

Bolman, Lee B. & Deal, Terrence E. Reframing Organizations: Artistry, Choice & Leadership. 2nd ed. LC 96-53592. (Jossey-Bass Higher & Adult Education Ser.). 1997. 36.95 (*0-7879-0822-3*) Jossey-Bass.

Bolman, Lee G. Organizacion & Liderazgo. (SPA.). 512p. (C). 1995. pap. text 13.33 (*0-201-60106-0*) Addison-Wesley.

Bolman, Lee G. & Deal, Terrence E. Becoming a Teacher Leader: From Isolation to Collaboration. LC 93-36370. 96p. 1993. pap. text 14.95 (*0-8039-6087-5*) Corwin Pr.

***Bolman, Lee G. & Deal, Terrence E.** Escape from Cluelessness: A Guide for the Organizationally Challenged. LC 00-20156. (Illus.). 272p. 2000. 25.00 (*0-8144-7071-8*) AMACOM.

Bolman, Lee G. & Deal, Terrence E. Leading with Soul: An Uncommon Journey of Spirit. LC 94-9277. (The Management Ser.). 206p. 1995. mass mkt. 20.00 (*1-55542-707-3*) Jossey-Bass.

— Modern Approaches to Understanding & Managing Organizations. LC 83-49257. (Management Ser.). 345p. 1984. 36.45 (*0-87589-592-1*) Jossey-Bass.

— The Path to School Leadership: A Portable Mentor. LC 92-38985. (Road Maps to Success Ser.). 80p. 1992. pap. 14.95 (*0-8039-6052-2*) Corwin Pr.

— Reframing Organizations: Artistry, Choice & Leadership. LC 90-46853. (Management-Social & Behavioral Science Ser.). 520p. 1991. text 40.95 (*1-55542-299-3*) Jossey-Bass.

— Reframing Organizations: Artistry, Choice & Leadership. 2nd ed. LC 96-53592. (Jossey-Bass Higher & Adult Education Ser.). 1997. pap. 28.95 (*0-7879-0821-5*) Jossey-Bass.

Bolman, Lee G., et al. Becoming a School Board Member. LC 94-45030. 86p. reprint ed. pap. 30.00 (*0-608-10490-6*, 207111900009) Bks Demand.

Bolme, Ed. Rache Bartmoss' Guide to the Net. (Illus.). 152p. (Orig.). 1993. pap. 16.00 (*0-937279-39-0*, CP3241) Talsorian.

Bolme, Ed, et al. Bastille Day. (Cyberpunk Ser.). (Illus.). 48p. (Orig.). 1993. pap. 6.00 (*0-937279-41-2*, CP3261) Talsorian.

Bolme, Ed, jt. auth. see Ackerman, David.

Bolme, Edward, et al. VirtualFront. (Cyberpunk Ser.). (Illus.). 88p. (Orig.). 1995. pap. 12.00 (*0-937279-75-7*, CP3441) Talsorian.

Bolmen, Richard A., Jr., ed. Semiconductor Safety Handbook: Safety & Health in the Semiconductor Industry. LC 97-24032. (Illus.). 610p. 1998. 125.00 (*0-8155-1418-2*) Noyes.

Bolner, Mary, ed. Planning & Developing a Library Orientation Program: Proceedings. LC 75-676. (Library Orientation Ser.: No. 3). 1975. 25.00 (*0-87650-061-0*) Pierian.

Bolner, Myrtle & Poirier, Gayle. The Research Process: Books & Beyond. 346p. (C). 1996. pap. text, per. 28.95 (*0-7872-1915-0*) Kendall-Hunt.

Bolnick, Bruce. Economics of Development: Study Guide & Workbook. 4th ed. (C). 1996. pap. text, student ed., wbk. ed. write for info. (*0-393-96852-9*) Norton.

Bolnick, Bruce, et al. Waterfalls of the White Mountains: 30 Hikes to 100 Waterfalls. 2nd rev. ed. LC 99-11110. (Illus.). 320p. 1999. pap. 18.00 (*0-88150-464-5*, Pub. by Countryman) Norton.

Bolnick, Jamie Pastor, jt. auth. see Bolnick, Tina S.

Bolnick, Jay. Cellasene Revolution: Living Without Cellulite, Vol. 1. 1999. 23.00 (*0-7871-2176-2*, Dove Audio) NewStar Media.

***Bolnick, Tina S. & Bolnick, Jamie Pastor.** Living at the End of the World: A Teenager's Survival in the Tunnels of Grand Central Station. 288p. 2000. 24.95 (*0-312-20047-1*) St Martin.

Bolocan, David. Advanced Appleworks. 256p. 1986. pap. 16.95 (*0-8306-0148-1*, 2648P) McGraw-Hill Prof.

— Advanced Excel. (Illus.). 224p. 1986. 26.95 (*0-8306-0368-9*, 2668H) McGraw-Hill Prof.

— Excel Simplified for the IBM. (Illus.). 260p. 1988. pap. 19.95 (*0-8306-2968-8*, 2968P) McGraw-Hill Prof.

— Lotus 1-2-3 Simplified: Including Version 2.0. 2nd ed. (Illus.). 272p. 1986. pap. 16.95 (*0-8306-2748-0*) McGraw-Hill Prof.

— Lotus 1-2-3 Simplified, Release 3.1. (Illus.). 368p. 1991. pap. 19.95 (*0-8306-3772-9*, 3772) McGraw-Hill Prof.

— Mastering Symphony. (Illus.). 224p. 1985. pap. 16.95 (*0-8306-1948-8*, 1948P) McGraw-Hill Prof.

— Mastering Symphony. 2nd ed. (Illus.). 240p. 1986. 22.95 (*0-8306-1318-8*, NO. 2718) McGraw-Hill Prof.

— Mastering Symphony. 3rd ed. (Illus.). 260p. 1989. pap. 22.95 (*0-8306-9368-8*, 3068) McGraw-Hill Prof.

— The WORD Book. LC 85-2528. (Illus.). 240p. (Orig.). 1985. 24.95 (*0-8306-0958-X*, 1958H); pap. 16.95 (*0-8306-1958-5*, 1958P) McGraw-Hill Prof.

Bolocan, David & Bixby, Robert. Microsoft Word 5.0 Simplified for the IBM PC. (Illus.). 368p. 1993. pap. 19.95 (*0-685-47250-7*, 3318) McGraw-Hill Prof.

Bolocan, David & Tow, Tim. Advanced AppleWorks. 2nd ed. (Illus.). 260p. 1988. pap. 17.95 (*0-8306-9348-3*, 3048) McGraw-Hill Prof.

Bolofsky, Glen. Cheap Parking in NYC: Park Cheap & Save Money. 96p. (Orig.). 1991. pap. write for info. (*0-931579-18-X*) J F Caroll Pub.

Bolofsky, Glen, ed. see Peskoff, Joel.

Bologna Center Staff. Monetary Reform & the Price of Gold: Alternative Approaches. Hinshaw, Randall, ed. LC 67-24630. (Illus.). 192p. 1967. reprint ed. pap. 59.60 (*0-608-04029-0*, 206476500011) Bks Demand.

Bologna-Claremont International Monetary Conference. Key Issues in International Monetary Reform: Proceedings. Hinshaw, Randall W., ed. LC 75-18963. (Business Economics & Finance Ser.: No. 4). 175p. reprint ed. pap. 54.30 (*0-7837-0704-5*, 204103600019) Bks Demand.

Bologna, G. Jack & Lindquist, Robert J. Fraud Auditing & Forensic Accounting: New Tools & Technique. 2nd ed. LC 95-5510. 272p. 1995. 85.00 (*0-471-10646-1*) Wiley.

Bologna, G. Jack & Walsh, Anthony M. The Accountant's Handbook of Information Technology. LC 96-31996. 384p. 1997. 125.00 (*0-471-30473-5*) Wiley.

Bologna, G. Jack, et al. The Accountant's Handbook of Fraud & Commercial Crime. LC 92-14510. 352p. 1992. 165.00 (*0-471-52642-8*) Wiley.

— The Accountant's Handbook of Fraud & Commercial Crime 1996. LC 92-14510. 359p. 1996. pap., suppl. ed. 65.00 (*0-471-14033-3*) Wiley.

— Avoiding Cyber Fraud in Small Businesses: What Auditors & Owners Need to Know. LC 99-89705. 256p. 2000. text 39.95 (*0-471-37297-8*) Wiley.

Bologna, Jack & Shaw, Paul. Corporate Crime Investigation. LC 96-42951. 208p. 1996. 49.95 (*0-7506-9659-1*) Buttrwrth-Heinemann.

Bologna, Jack, jt. auth. see Shaw, Paul.

Bologna, Joseph, jt. auth. see Taylor, Renbee.

Bolognani-Fantin, Anna M., jt. auth. see Manfredi-Romanini, Maria G.

Bolognese, Don. A Circus Adventure. (How to Draw Your Own Story Ser.: No. 6). 1996. mass mkt. 3.50 (*0-8125-6723-4*, Pub. by Tor Bks) St Martin.

— Demolition Derby. (How to Draw Your Own Story Ser.: No. 5). 1996. mass mkt. 3.50 (*0-8125-6722-6*, Pub. by Tor Bks) St Martin.

— The Dragon, the Knight & the Princess. (How to Draw Your Own Story Ser.: No. 3). 1996. mass mkt. 3.50 (*0-8125-4313-0*, Pub. by Tor Bks) St Martin.

— Little Hawk's New Name. LC 93-40723. (Hello Reader! Ser.). (Illus.). 48p. (J). (ps-3). 1995. 3.99 (*0-590-48292-0*, Cartwheel) Scholastic Inc.

— Little Hawk's New Name. (Hello Reader! Level 4 Ser.). (J). 1995. 9.19 (*0-606-07795-2*, Pub. by Turtleback) Demco.

— A Safari Adventure. (How to Draw Your Own Story Ser.: No. 4). 1996. mass mkt. 3.50 (*0-8125-4314-9*, Pub. by Tor Bks) St Martin.

Bolognese, Don, jt. auth. see Raphael, Elaine.

Bolognese, Raphael, et al. Pocahontas: Princess of the River Tribes. 32p. (J). (ps-3). 1995. pap. 4.95 (*0-590-44372-0*) Scholastic Inc.

Bolognesi, Dani P., jt. auth. see Putney, Scott D.

Bolognesi, Kitti, ed. see Goldbeck, Eugene O.

Bolognesi, Tommaso, et al, eds. LOTOSphere: Software Development with LOTOS. LC 94-39291. 524p. (C). 1995. text 139.00 (*0-7923-9529-8*) Kluwer Academic.

Bolomey, J. C., jt. auth. see Roubine, E.

Bolomey, Jean-Charles, jt. ed. see Miyakawa, Michio.

Bolon, Carol R. Forms of the Goddess Lajja Gauri in Indian Art. (College Art Association Monographs: Vol. 44). (Illus.). 184p. 1992. lib. bdg. 55.00 (*0-271-00761-3*) Pa St U Pr.

Bolon, Carol R., et al, eds. The Nature of Frank Lloyd Wright. (Illus.). 192p. (C). 1994. 29.95 (*0-226-06351-8*) U Ch Pr.

— The Nature of Frank Lloyd Wright. LC 87-13764. (Illus.). 215p. Date not set. reprint ed. pap. 66.70 (*0-608-20591-5*, 205455600003) Bks Demand.

Bolon, Meredith & Weber, Amy. Benchmarking: A Manager's Guide. (Monographs). 104p. 1995. pap. 12.95 (*0-944533-44-2*) Coopers Total Qlty.

Bolondi, L., et al, eds. Intraoperative Ultrasonography in Hepato-Biliary & Pancreatic Surgery: A Practical Guide. (Series in Radiology). (C). 1989. text 191.50 (*0-7923-0261-3*) Kluwer Academic.

Bolondi, L., et al. Diagnostic Ultrasound in Gastroenterology: Instrumentation, Clinical Problems & Atlas. 544p. 1984. text 64.00 (*1-57235-054-7*) Piccin Nuova.

***Boloni, Lotsi & Genereaux, Tom.** Programming KDE 2.0: Creating Linux Desktop Applicatons. 432p. 2000. pap. 49.95 incl. cd-rom (*1-929629-13-3*, Pub. by C M P Books) Publishers Group.

Bolonik, Kera & Griffin, Jennifer. Frugal Indulgents: How to Cultivate Decadence When Your Age & Salary Are under 30. LC 96-45270. 1995. pap. 12.95 (*0-8050-4718-2*) H Holt & Co.

Bolooki, Hooshang, ed. Clinical Applications of the Intra-Aortic Balloon Pump. 3rd rev. ed. LC 98-6276. (Illus.). 484p. 1998. 98.00 (*0-87993-401-8*) Futura Pub.

Bolotin, David. An Approach to Aristotle's Physics: With Particular Attention to the Role of His Manner of Writing. LC 96-38143. 156p. (C). 1997. text 44.50 (*0-7914-3551-2*); pap. text 14.95 (*0-7914-3552-0*) State U NY Pr.

— Plato's Dialogue on Friendship: An Interpretation of the "Lysis", with a New Translation. LC 88-43323. (Agora Paperback Editions Ser.). 232p. 1989. pap. text 13.95 (*0-8014-9561-X*) Cornell U Pr.

Bolotin, Fredric N., ed. International Public Policy Sourcebook Vol. 2: Education & Environment, Vol. 2. LC 88-16290. 390p. 1989. lib. bdg. 150.00 (*0-313-26613-1*, DEI02, Greenwood Pr) Greenwood.

***Bolotin, Norman.** Civil War A To Z. (J). (gr. 4-7). 2000. 17.99 (*0-525-46268-6*, Dutton Child) Peng Put Young Read.

— Growing up in West. (J). 2000. 16.99 (*0-525-67531-0*, Dutton Child) Peng Put Young Read.

Bolotin, V. V. Random Vibrations of Elastic Systems. (Mechanics of Elastic Stability Ser.: No. 8). 480p. 1984. text 278.00 (*90-247-2981-5*) Kluwer Academic.

Bolotin, Vladimir V. Mechanics of Fatigue. LC 98-29151. (Mechanical Engineering Ser.). 480p. 1999. boxed set 89.95 (*0-8493-9663-8*) CRC Pr.

— Stability Problems in Fracture Mechanics. LC 95-17501. (Nonlinear Science Ser.). (Illus.). 188p. 1996. 95.00 (*0-471-12546-6*, Wiley-Interscience) Wiley.

Bolotina, A. German/Russian/German Dictionary Medicine. (GER & RUS.). 773p. 1993. 250.00 (*0-320-00594-1*) Fr & Eur.

Bolotina, A. I. & Linnik, E. F. Dictionary Biology, English to German Plus 2000 Plant Names Latin. (ENG & GER.). 452p. 1996. 120.00 (*0-320-00517-8*) Fr & Eur.

Bolotina, A. I. & Yakusheva, E. O. English-Russian & Russian-English Medical Dictionary. 544p. (C). 1998. 37.50 (*0-8285-5486-2*) Firebird NY.

Bolotina, I. Still Life in Russian Art. (Illus.). (C). 1987. text 130.00 (*0-7855-5821-7*, Pub. by Collets) St Mut.

Bolotine, A., et al. French-Russian Engineering Dictionary: Dictionnaire Francais-Russe Technique. (FRE & RUS.). 590p. 1985. 95.00 (*0-7859-4962-3*) Fr & Eur.

Bolotine, Leonid. The Classic Guitar Collection. (Illus.). 96p. 1977. pap. 15.95 (*0-8256-2268-9*, AM32657) Music Sales.

— The Classic Guitar Collection, Vol. 2. (Illus.). 128p. 1977. pap. 15.95 (*0-8256-2269-7*, AM32665) Music Sales.

— The Classic Guitar Collection, Vol. 3. Vol. 3. (Illus.). 96p. 1977. pap. 15.95 (*0-8256-2270-0*, AM32673) Music Sales.

An Asterisk (*) at the beginning of an entry indicates that the title is appearing for the first time.

Bolotnikova, V. Byelorussian Cuisine. (Illus.). 119p. 1979. 6.95 (*0-8285-1551-4*) Firebird NY.

Bolotovskii, B. M. & Frenkel, V. Ya., eds. I. E. Tamm Selected Papers. (Illus.). 336p. 1991. 99.95 (*0-387-50972-0*) Spr-Verlag.

Bolouri, Hamid, jt. auth. see Bower, James M.

***Bolovan, Margaret M.** A Mazing of the Text: The Search for Signification in the Labyrinth of French Poetics. LC 98-48969. (Currents in Comparative Romance Languages & Literatures Ser.: Vol. 75). 208p. (C). 1999. text 48.95 (*0-8204-4069-8*) P Lang Pubng.

Boloyan, D. S., jt. auth. see Payen, Louis A.

Boloyan, David S., jt. auth. see Payen, Louis A.

Boloz, Autumn C., ed. see Boloz, Sigmund A.

Boloz, Sigmund A. Be Dangerous! Boloz, Autumn C., ed. (Illus.). 36p. 1998. pap. 6.00 (*1-886635-14-5*) Wooded Hill AZ.

— The Clouds Before the Storm. Muri, Donna, ed. (Illus.). 36p. (Orig.). 1994. pap. text 6.00 (*1-886635-02-1*) Wooded Hill AZ.

— Diarrhea, Diarrhea: And Other School Poems for Children. Boloz, Autumn C., ed. (Illus.). 36p. (J). (gr. 3-12). 1998. pap. 6.00 (*1-886635-15-3*) Wooded Hill AZ.

— The Distance Across One's Heart: Poetry for the Writer. Snow, Karen, ed. (Illus.). 36p. (Orig.). (J). (gr. 3-12). 1997. 6.00 (*1-886635-12-9*) Wooded Hill AZ.

— From Daybooks to Night Logs: Journeying with Journals. 3rd rev. ed. 36p. (Orig.). 1999. pap. text 10.00 (*1-886635-11-0*) Wooded Hill AZ.

***Boloz, Sigmund A.** Marinating the Soul: Writing Poetry with Aspiring Writers. Moriarty, Patricia, ed. (Illus.). 64p. 1999. pap. 10.00 (*1-886635-16-1*) Wooded Hill AZ.

Boloz, Sigmund A. Odious Mud. Stropko, Susan, ed. (Illus.). 36p. (Orig.). 1995. pap. text 6.00 (*1-886635-09-9*) Wooded Hill AZ.

— Prairie Dog Dreams: And Other Poems from Navajoland. Snow, Karen, ed. (Illus.). 36p. (Orig.). (J). (gr. 4-12). 1995. pap. text 6.00 (*1-886635-00-5*) Wooded Hill AZ.

— Recess Chaos: And Other School Poems for Children. (Illus.). 36p. (J). (gr. 3-12). 1997. 6.00 (*1-886635-13-7*) Wooded Hill AZ.

— A Wondrous Ride: And Other Poems for Children. Snow, Karen, ed. (Illus.). 32p. (Orig.). (J). (gr. k-6). 1995. pap. 5.00 (*1-886635-01-3*) Wooded Hill AZ.

Bolozky, S. 501 Hebrew Verbs. LC 95-83209. (HEB.). 1996. pap. 16.95 (*0-8120-9468-9*) Barron.

Bolozky, Shmuel. Measuring Productivity in Word Formation: The Case of Israeli Hebrew. LC 98-36385. (Studies in Semitic Languages & Linguistics). 1999. 54.50 (*90-04-11252-9*) Brill Academic Pubs.

Bols, Mikael. Carbohydrate Building Blocks. LC 95-16543. 182p. 1995. 69.95 (*0-471-13339-6*) Wiley.

Bolsche, Wilhelm. The Evolution of Man. Untermann, Ernest, tr. from GER. (Science for the Workers Ser.). (Illus.). 160p. 1984. lib. bdg. 17.95 (*0-88286-084-4*) C H Kerr.

— The Triumph of Life. Simons, May W., tr. from GER. (Science for the Workers Ser.). (Illus.). 157p. 1984. 17.95 (*0-88286-085-2*) C H Kerr.

Bolsenga, Stanley J. & Herdendorf, Charles E., eds. Lake Erie & Lake St. Clair Handbook. LC 93-10208. (Great Lakes Bks.). (Illus.). 484p. 1993. pap. 24.95 (*0-8143-2470-3*) Wayne St U Pr.

Bolshakoff, Serge. Father Michael: Recluse of Uusi Valamo. (Illus.). 56p. (Orig.). 1992. pap. 6.00 (*1-880364-09-3*) New Sarov.

— Konevitsa: And Northern Paradise. 68p. 1991. pap. 8.00 (*1-880364-04-2*) New Sarov.

***Bolshakoff, Serge.** Wisdom for the Journey: Conversations with Spiritual Fathers of the Christian East. Pennington, M. Basil, ed. LC 99-59478. (Illus.). 2000. pap. 14.95 (*0-8189-0836-X*) Alba.

Bolshakoff, Serge N. Elder Melchisidek: Hermit of the Roslavl Forest. LC 88-63915. (Acquisition of the Holy Spirit in Russia Ser.). (Illus.). 70p. (Orig.). 1988. pap. 5.00 (*0-938635-28-X*) St Herman Pr.

Bolshakoff, Sergius. Russian Mystics. (Cistercian Studies: No. 26). Orig. Title: I Mistici Russi. 303p. 1981. reprint ed. pap. 11.95 (*0-87907-926-6*) Cistercian Pubns.

Bolshakoff, Sergius & Pennington, M. Basil. In Search of True Wisdom: Visits to Eastern Spiritual Fathers. LC 91-17585. 190p. 1991. pap. 9.95 (*0-8189-0616-2*) Alba.

Bolshakov. Organic Sulfur Compounds of Petroleum, Vol. 5. 290p. 1986. text 277.00 (*3-7186-0355-1*) Gordon & Breach.

Bolsinger, Charles L. Shrubs of California's Chaparral, Timberland, & Woodland: Area, Ownership, & Stand Characteristics. (Illus.). 60p. 1998. reprint ed. 13.00 (*0-89904-544-8*, Ecosytems Resrch); reprint ed. pap. 7.00 (*0-89904-545-6*, Ecosytems Resrch) Crumb Elbow Pub.

***Bolsinov, A. V. & Fomenko, A. T.** Integrable Geodesic Flows on Two-Dimensional Surfaces. LC 99-52201. 332p. 2000. write for info. (*0-306-11065-2*, Kluwer Plenum) Kluwer Academic.

Bolsky, Morris & Korn, David G. The New KornShell Command & Programming Language. 2nd ed. 416p. 1995. pap. 55.00 (*0-13-182700-6*) P-H.

Bolsover, Stephen R., et al. From Genes to Cells. LC 96-28603. 440p. 1997. pap. 54.95 (*0-471-59792-9*) Wiley.

Bolstad, Owen C. Dear Folks...A Dog-Faced Infantryman in World War II. (Illus.). 241p. 1993. 25.00 (*0-9649759-3-9*) Greasewood.

Bolstad, Owen C., intro. Leslie Moren: Fifty Years an Eldo County Doctor. (Great Basin History of Medicine Ser.: No. 2). (Illus.). 182p. 1992. lib. bdg. 42.00 (*1-56475-353-0*) U NV Oral Hist.

Bolstein, M. Joel. The First Amendment in the Information Age: Regulation & the Video-Teletext Industry. 62p. (Orig.). 1987. pap. 9.95 (*0-937790-36-2*, 4280) Media Institute.

Bolster. Mathematics Grade 3: Pupil Edition. (Illus.). (J). pap. 6.59 (*0-673-11812-6*) Addson-Wesley Educ.

Bolster, Alice. Motherwise! 101 Tips for a New Mother. LC 97-73188. (Illus.). 120p. 1997. pap. 7.50 (*0-912500-23-9*) La Leche.

— Motherwise! 101 Tips for a New Mother. Vallejo, Cecilia, tr. from ENG. LC 99-63633. (SPA., Illus.). 127p. 1999. pap. 7.50 (*0-912500-57-3*) La Leche.

Bolster, Paul. The Wall Street Journal Applications in Finance, 1993. 2nd ed. 32p. (C). 1992. text 6.95 (*0-256-11900-7*, Irwn McGrw-H) McGrw-H Hghr Educ.

***Bolster, Richard.** Marie D'Agoult: The Rebel Countess. LC 99-55838. (Illus.). 256p. 2000. 25.00 (*0-300-08246-0*) Yale U Pr.

Bolster, Richard, ed. Histoire D'Eleonore de Parme: Source Perdue de "La Chartreuse de Parme" (Exeter French Texts Ser.: Vol. XCVIII). (FRE.). 70p. 1997. pap. 21.95 (*0-85989-536-X*, Pub. by Univ Exeter Pr) Northwestern U Pr.

Bolster, Stephanie. Two Bowls of Milk. LC 99-203463. 88p. 2000. pap. 12.95 (*0-7710-1557-7*) McCland & Stewart.

— White Stone: The Alice Poems. 76p. 1998. reprint ed. pap. 12.00 (*1-55065-099-8*, Pub. by Vehicule Pr) LPC Group.

***Bolster, Stephanie & Carroll, Lewis Society of Canada Staff.** Portraits of Alice. (Illus.). 1998. pap. 8.00 (*1-55246-039-8*) Battered Silicon.

Bolster, W. Jeffrey. Black Jacks: African American Seamen in the Age of Sail. LC 96-44928. (Illus.). 320p. 1997. 27.00 (*0-674-07624-9*) HUP.

— Black Jacks: African American Seamen in the Age of Sail. (Illus.). 360p. 1998. pap. 14.95 (*0-674-07627-3*) HUP.

Bolsterli, Margaret J., ed. A Remembrance of Eden: Harriet Bailey Bullock Daniel's Memories of a Frontier Plantation in Arkansas, 1849-1872. LC 93-6787. (Illus.). 160p. 1993. text 26.00 (*1-55728-290-0*) U of Ark Pr.

Bolsterli, Margaret J., ed. see Jackson, Nannie Stillwell.

Bolt. Earthquakes. 4th ed. LC 99-29955. 1999. 32.95 incl. cd-rom (*0-7167-3396-X*) W H Freeman.

— Earthquakes & Volcanoes. 3rd ed. 1997. 34.40 (*0-7167-3306-4*) W H Freeman.

— Exploring Social Psychology. 1993. teacher ed. 31.25 (*0-07-044302-5*) McGraw.

— Read In International Politics. 1998. pap. 9.50 (*0-07-233320-0*) McGraw.

Bolt, jt. auth. see Dykgraaf.

Bolt, Ben. Classical Guitar for the Rock Guitarist. 1995. vdisk 19.95 (*0-7866-0547-2*, 94700VX) Mel Bay.

— Favorite Classics Acoustic Guitar: Beginning to Intermediate Level. 1995. vdisk 24.95 (*0-7866-0453-0*, 95102VX) Mel Bay.

— Favorite Classics Acoustic Guitar: Beginning to Intermediate Level. 48p. 1998. 17.95 incl. audio compact disk (*0-7866-2497-3*, 95102BCD) Mel Bay.

***Bolt, Ben.** Guitar Classics in Tab. 48p. 1998. 9.95 (*0-7866-3517-7*, 96845BCD) Mel Bay.

— Mozart for Acoustic Guitar. 128p. 1997. pap. 22.95 incl. audio compact disk (*0-7866-0597-9*, 95526BCD) Mel Bay.

Bolt, Ben. Music Theory for the Rock Guitarist. 40p. 1996. 9.95 incl. audio compact disk (*0-7866-2720-4*, 94525BCD) Mel Bay.

***Bolt, Ben.** Note Reading for the Rock Guitarist. 32p. 1998. pap. 9.95 (*0-7866-3463-4*, 94813BCD) Mel Bay.

— Tarrega in Tablature: Intermediate Level. (SPA, FRE, ENG & JPN.). 128p. 1997. spiral bd. 22.95 incl. audio compact disk (*0-7866-1641-5*, 95689BCD) Mel Bay.

— Thirty-Nine Progressive Solos for Classical Guitar, Bk. 2. pap. 14.95 (*0-89524-688-0*, Pub. by Cherry Lane); pap. 17.95 (*0-89524-742-9*, Pub. by Cherry Lane) H Leonard.

— Thirty-Nine Progressive Solos for Classical Guitar, Bk. 1. pap. 14.95 (*0-89524-682-1*, Pub. by Cherry Lane); pap. 17.95 (*0-89524-741-0*, Pub. by Cherry Lane) H Leonard.

Bolt, Brian. The Amazing Mathematical Amusement Arcade. (Illus.). 136p. 1984. pap. 18.95 (*0-521-26980-6*) Cambridge U Pr.

— Mathematical Activities. 224p. 1982. pap. 20.95 (*0-521-28518-6*) Cambridge U Pr.

— Mathematical Cavalcade. (Illus.). 130p. (C). 1992. pap. 19.95 (*0-521-42617-0*) Cambridge U Pr.

— The Mathematical Funfair. (Illus.). 128p. (C). 1990. pap. 18.95 (*0-521-37743-9*) Cambridge U Pr.

— A Mathematical Jamboree. (Illus.). 111p. (C). 1995. pap. 19.95 (*0-521-48589-4*) Cambridge U Pr.

— A Mathematical Pandora's Box. LC 92-45680. (Illus.). 126p. (C). 1993. pap. 18.95 (*0-521-44619-8*) Cambridge U Pr.

Bolt, Brian & Hobbs, David. A Mathematical Dictionary for Schools. 160p. (C). 1998. pap. 10.95 (*0-521-55657-0*) Cambridge U Pr.

— 101 Mathematical Projects. 168p. 1991. pap. 20.95 (*0-521-34759-9*) Cambridge U Pr.

Bolt, Bruce A. Discover Volcanoes & Earthquakes. (Discover Ser.). (Illus.). 48p. (J). (gr. 3-6). 1992. lib. bdg. 15.95 (*1-56674-031-2*, HTS Bks) Forest Hse.

— Earthquakes & Geological Discovery. LC 93-12636. (Scientific American Library). 1993. pap. text 32.95 (*0-7167-5040-6*) W H Freeman.

— Inside the Earth. (Illus.). 205p. (C). 1991. reprint ed. text 67.00 (*1-878907-55-7*) TechBooks.

Bolt, Bruce A., intro. Earthquakes & Volcanoes: Readings from Scientific American. LC 79-21684. (Illus.). 154p. (C). 1995. text 13.60 (*0-7167-1164-8*) W H Freeman.

Bolt, Carol. The Book of Answers. LC 99-12910. 400p. 1999. text 14.95 (*0-7868-6566-0*, Pub. by Hyperion) Time Warner.

***Bolt, Carol.** The Literary Book of Answers. 704p. 2000. 14.95 (*0-7868-6699-3*, Pub. by Hyperion) Time Warner.

Bolt, Carol, et al. Class Acts: Six Plays for Children. rev. ed. LC 93-101228. 376p. (Orig.). 1992. pap. 18.95 (*0-88754-487-8*) Playwrights.

Bolt, Christine. American Indian Policy & American Reform: Case Studies of the Campaign to Assimilate the American Indians. 228p. (C). 1990. pap. text 34.95 (*0-04-445719-7*) Routledge.

— Feminist Ferment: "The Woman Question" in the U. S. A. & Britain, 1870-1940. 96p. 1996. pap. 12.50 (*1-85728-382-1*, Pub. by UCL Pr Ltd) Taylor & Francis.

— The Women's Movements in the United States & Britain from the 1790s to the 1920s. LC 93-1316. 400p. (Orig.). 1993. pap. 20.95 (*0-87023-867-1*) U of Mass Pr.

Bolt, Clarence R. Thomas Crosby & the Tsimshian: Small Shoes for Feet Too Large. 160p. 1992. 39.95 (*0-7748-0430-0*) U of Wash Pr.

***Bolt, David.** Digital Divide: Computers & Our Children's Future. LC 99-88058. (Illus.). 208p. 1999. 25.00 (*1-57500-086-5*, Pub. by TV Bks) HarpC.

Bolt, Ernest C. Ballots Before Bullets: The War Referendum Approach to Peace in America, 1914-1941. LC 77-680. 227p. reprint ed. pap. 70.40 (*0-8357-3277-0*, 203950000013) Bks Demand.

Bolt, G. H., et al, eds. Interactions at the Soil Colloid: Soil Solution Interface. (NATO Advanced Science Institutes Series C: Mathematical & Physical Sciences). (C). 1990. text 309.00 (*0-7923-1066-7*) Kluwer Academic.

Bolt, Gordon. Market & Sales Forecasting. 3rd ed. (Marketing & Sales Ser.). 1994. pap. 29.95 (*0-7494-0913-4*) Kogan Page Ltd.

Bolt, H. M., et al, eds. Use of Mechanistic Information in Risk Assessment: Proceedings of the 1993 EUROTOX Congress Meeting Held in Uppsala, Sweden, June 30-July 3, 1993. LC 93-44609. (Archives of Toxicology Ser.: Suppl. 16). 1994. write for info. (*3-540-57442-5*); 122.00 (*0-387-57442-5*) Spr-Verlag.

Bolt, James F. Executive Development: A Strategy for Corporate Competitiveness. 240p. 1989. 24.95 (*0-88730-274-2*, HarpBusn) HarpInfo.

— Executive Development: A Strategy for Corporate Competitiveness. 1991. pap. 15.95 (*0-88730-493-1*, HarpBusn) HarpInfo.

Bolt, Jeffery A., jt. auth. see Jwing-Ming, Yang.

Bolt, Jeffrey A., jt. auth. see Yang, Jwing-Ming.

Bolt, John, ed. see Bavinck, Herman.

Bolt, John Clifford. The Religious World of Kirti Sri: Buddhism, Art & Politics of Late Medieval Sri Lanka. (Illus.). 192p. 1996. pap. text 22.00 (*0-19-510757-8*) OUP.

Bolt, Jonathan. Threads. 1982. pap. 5.25 (*0-8222-1137-8*) Dramatists Play.

Bolt, Laurence G. Zen & the Art of Making a Living in the Post-Modern World: A Career Guide for Dharma Bums, Social Activists & Reformed Yuppies. Grant, Kim, ed. (Illus.). 480p. (Orig.). 1991. pap. 24.95 (*0-685-47819-X*) Lightning Pr.

Bolt, Martin. Exploring Psychology: Instructor's Resources. 3rd ed. 1996. teacher ed., ring bd. write for info. (*1-57259-052-1*); teacher ed., ring bd. write for info. (*1-57259-053-X*) Worth.

— Exploring Psychology: Lecture Guides. 3rd ed. 1996 write for info. (*1-57259-057-2*) Worth.

— Psychology: Instructor's Resources. 5th ed. 1998. teacher ed. write for info. (*1-57259-209-5*) Worth.

— Psychology: Lecture Guides. 5th ed. 1998. write for info. (*1-57259-548-5*) Worth.

Bolt, Nancy & Stephan, Sandy. Strategic Planning for Multitype Library Cooperatives: A Planning Process. (ASCLA Changing Horizons Ser.: Vol. 2). 153p. 1998. pap. 28.00 (*0-8389-7926-2*) ALA.

Bolt, Nancy De, see De Bolt, Nancy.

***Bolt, Paul J.** China & Southeast Asia's Ethnic Chinese: State & Diaspora in Contemporary Asia. LC 00-22347. 232p. 2000. 57.00 (*0-275-96647-X*, C6647, Praeger Pubs) Greenwood.

***Bolt, Peter.** Coaching for Growth: How to Bring Out the Best in Your Team & Yourself. 160p. 2000. pap. 14.95 (*1-86076-169-0*, Pub. by Oak Tr) Midpt Trade.

***Bolt, Peter & Payne, Tony.** Mark: The Beginning of the Gospel. (Faith Walk Bible Studies). 80p. 2000. 4.99 (*1-58134-147-4*) Crossway Bks.

Bolt, Ranjit, tr. Hercules. (Oberon Bks.). (Illus.). 96p. 1998. 16.95 (*1-870259-89-0*, Pub. by Theatre Comm) Consort Bk Sales.

— School for Wives. 112p. 1997. pap. 12.95 (*1-84002-004-0*) Theatre Comm.

— The Venetian Twins/Mirandolina. 144p. 1995. pap. 14.95 (*0-948230-63-0*, Pub. by Absolute Classics) Theatre Comm.

Bolt, Ranjit, tr. Tartuffe (The Sisterhood) 128p. 1989. pap. 12.95 (*0-948230-50-9*, Pub. by Absolute Classics) Theatre Comm.

Bolt, Ranjit, tr. see Rostand, Edmond.

Bolt, Robert. A Man for All Seasons. rev. ed. 1999. pap. 5.95 (*0-333-58052-4*) St Martin.

— A Man for All Seasons: A Play in Two Acts. 1962. 14.10 (*0-606-01664-3*, Pub. by Turtleback) Demco.

— A Man for All Seasons: A Play in Two Acts. LC 89-40518. (Vintage International Ser.). 95p. 1990. pap. 9.00 (*0-679-72822-8*) Vin Bks.

Bolt, Robert, jt. auth. see Center for Learning Network Staff.

Bolt, Rod. Bavaria. 2nd ed. 1999. pap. text 17.95 (*1-86011-916-6*) Cadgn Bks.

— Madeira 2nd ed. 2nd ed. (Orig.). 1999. pap. text 14.95 (*1-86011-901-8*) Cadgn Bks.

***Bolt, Rodney.** Amsterdam. 3rd ed. 256p. 1999. pap. text 14.95 (*1-86011-954-9*) Globe Pequot.

— Amsterdam & the Randstad: Rotterdam, Leiden & the Hague. (City Guides Ser.). (Illus.). 2000. pap. 14.95 (*1-86011-941-7*) Cadgn Bks.

— Holland. 2000. pap. 19.95 (*1-86011-961-1*, Pub. by Cadgn Bks) Globe Pequot.

— Take the Kids to Amsterdam: With Trips Around Holland. (Take the Kids Ser.). (Illus.). 2000. pap. 19.95 (*1-86011-990-5*) Cadgn Bks.

— The Xenophobe's Guide to the Dutch. (Xenophobe's Guides Ser.). 64p. 1999. pap. 5.95 (*1-902825-25-X*) Oval Bks.

***Bolt, Stephen R.** Money for Life: How You Can Create a Financial Plan for Life. 256p. 2000. 20.00 (*0-9677356-0-2*, 931-001, Pub. by Values Finan Net) BookWorld.

Bolt, Steven. Roofing the Right Way. 2nd ed. (Illus.). 240p. 1990. pap. 14.95 (*0-8306-3387-1*) McGraw-Hill Prof.

— Roofing the Right Way. 3rd ed. LC 96-41056. (Illus.). 416p. 1996. 34.95 (*0-07-006649-3*); pap. 24.95 (*0-07-006650-7*) McGraw.

— Roofing the Right Way: A Step-by-Step Guide for the Homeowner. (Illus.). 192p. 1986. 19.95 (*0-8306-0367-0*, 2667); pap. 11.95 (*0-8306-0467-7*) McGraw-Hill Prof.

Bolt, Thomas. Out of the Woods. LC 88-30313. 80p. (C). 1989. 18.00 (*0-300-04469-0*) Yale U Pr.

Boltanski, Christian. Diese Kinder Suchen Ihre Eltern. (GER., Illus.). 88p. 1998. pap. 24.95 (*3-929078-04-X*, Kehayoff) te Neues.

— Kaddish: Kaddish. (Illus.). 1160p. 1998. 65.00 (*3-929078-83-X*, Kehayoff) te Neues.

— Ost - West. LC 98-180816. (Illus.). 64p. 1998. pap. 19.95 (*3-929078-33-3*, Kehayoff) te Neues.

— Sterblich. LC 97-153101. (Illus.). 48p. 1998. pap. 14.95 (*3-929078-58-9*, Kehayoff) te Neues.

— Zeit. (Illus.). 64p. Date not set. pap. 19.95 (*3-929078-57-0*, Kehayoff) te Neues.

Boltanski, Christian, photos by. Christian Boltanski. (Illus.). 200p. pap. 45.00 (*88-8158-117-5*, 720014, Pub. by Charta) Dist Art Pubs.

Boltanski, Christian & Gumpert, Lynn, contrib. by. Christian Boltanski: Lessons of Darkness. LC 86-60663. (Illus.). 119p. 1988. pap. 40.00 (*0-914357-15-8*) New Mus Contemp Art.

Boltanski, Luc. Distant Suffering: Morality, Media & Politics. (Cultural Social Studies). 275p. (C). 1999. text 64.95 (*0-521-57389-0*); pap. text 24.95 (*0-521-65953-1*) Cambridge U Pr.

Bolte, Chuck & McCusker, Paul. Quick Skits & Discussion Starters: Skits to Involve Your Youth Group in Meaningful, Action-Packed Discussions. (Illus.). 109p. 1989. pap. 14.99 (*0-931529-68-9*) Group Pub.

— Short Skits for Youth Ministry: Tigger Faith-Building Discussions in Your Group. LC 93-11233. 1993. 14.99 (*1-55945-173-4*) Group Pub.

— 60-Second Skits: Discussion Starters for Youth Groups. (Illus.). 95p. 1991. pap. 14.99 (*1-55945-036-3*, Group Bks) Group Pub.

Bolte, H. D. Myocardial Biopsy: Diagnostic Significance. (Illus.). 180p. 1980. 43.00 (*0-387-10063-6*) Spr-Verlag.

Bolte, Johannes & Polivka, Georg. Anmerkungen Zu Den Kinder-und Hausmarchen der Bruder Grimm, 4 vols. (GER.). xxxix, 2538p. 1994. reprint ed. write for info. (*3-487-05364-0*) G Olms Pubs.

Bolte, Johannes, ed. see Wickram, Georg.

Bolte-Luthey, Christene. Window to My Soul, Vol. I. LC 89-90753. (Illus.). 120p. 1989. lib. bdg. 12.95 (*0-317-93861-4*) Luthey Assocs.

Bolte, Mary. Amelia Bedella. 1997. pap. text 7.95 (*1-55734-818-9*) Tchr Create Mat.

***Bolte, Mary.** Brown Bear, Brown Bear, What Do You See? (Illus.). 48p. 1999. pap., teacher ed. 7.95 (*1-57690-625-6*, TCM2625) Tchr Create Mat.

— A Guide for Using Bedtime for Frances & Other Frances Books in the Classroom. (Illus.). 48p. 1999. pap., teacher ed. 7.95 (*1-57690-593-4*, TCM 2593) Tchr Create Mat.

— Guide for Using the Clifford Series in the Classroom. (Illus.). 48p. 1999. pap., teacher ed. 7.95 (*1-57690-336-2*, TCM2336) Tchr Create Mat.

— How to Solve Word Problems: Grades 1-2. (Illus.). 48p. 2000. pap., teacher ed. 7.95 (*1-57690-941-7*, TCM 2941) Tchr Create Mat.

— How to Solve Word Problems Grades 2-3: Primary. 48p. 2000. pap. 7.95 (*1-57690-948-4*) Tchr Create Mat.

Bolte, Mary. Nate the Great: A Guide for Using Nate the Great in the Classroom. (Literature Unit Ser.). (Illus.). 48p. (J). 1998. pap., teacher ed. 7.95 (*1-57690-346-X*, TCM2346) Tchr Create Mat.

Bolten, Ernst. Managing Time & Space in the Modern Warehouse: Practices & Procedures in Warehousing - with Ready to Use Forms, Checklists. LC 97-3843. 240p. 1997. spiral bd. 40.00 (*0-8144-7956-1*) AMACOM.

Bolten, Jaap. Dutch Banknote Design. 1988. lib. bdg. 487.50 (*90-247-3752-4*, Pub. by M Nijhoff) Kluwer Academic.

Bolten, Juergen. Marktchance Wirtschaftsdeutsch Level 2: Begleitheft. (GER.). 46p. (C). 1993. pap. text 23.25 (*3-12-675142-3*, Pub. by Klett Edition) Intl Bk Import.

— Marktchance Wirtschaftsdeutsch Level 2: Lehrbuch. (GER.). 160p. (C). 1993. pap. text 25.25 (*3-12-675140-7*, Pub. by Klett Edition); audio 29.75 (*3-12-675141-5*, Pub. by Klett Edition) Intl Bk Import.

***Bolten, Steven E.** Stock Market Cycles: Practical Explanation. LC 99-46054. 184p. 2000. write for info. (*1-56720-320-5*, Quorum Bks) Greenwood.

Bolter, J. The Writing Space: The Computer Hypertext, & the History of Writing. 272p. (C). 1990. pap. 34.50 (*0-8058-0428-5*) L Erlbaum Assocs.

— The Writing Space: The Computer Hypertext, & the History of Writing. 272p. (C). 1991. text 75.00 (*0-8058-0427-7*); disk 12.95 (*1-56321-067-3*) L Erlbaum Assocs.

B

Bolter, J. David. Turing's Man: Western Culture in the Computer Age. LC 83-6942. (Illus.). xii, 264p. 1984. pap. 17.95 (*0-8078-4108-0*) U of NC Pr.

***Bolter, Jay David.** Writing Space: Computers, Hypertext & the Remediation of Print. 2nd ed. 272p. 2000. write for info. (*0-8058-2918-0*) L Erlbaum Assocs.

— Writing Space: Computers, Hypertext & the Remediation of Print. 2nd ed. 272p. 2000. pap. write for info. (*0-8058-2919-9*) L Erlbaum Assocs.

***Bolter, Jay David & Grusin, Richard.** Remediation: Understanding New Media. LC 98-25672. (Illus.). 307p. 2000. reprint ed. pap. 17.95 (*0-262-52279-9*) MIT Pr.

Bolter, Walter G., et al. Telecommunications Policy for the 1990s & Beyond: New Markets, Technology & Global Competitive Trends. LC 89-10803. 454p. (C). (gr. 13). 1990. text 106.95 (*0-87332-586-9*) M E Sharpe.

Bolthausen, Erwin, et al, eds. Proceedings of Seminar on Stochastic Analysis, Random Fields & Applications Held 1993, Ascona, Switzerland: Centro Stefano Francini, Ascona, 1993. LC 95-21846. (Progress in Probability Ser.: Vol. 36). 391p. 1995. 132.00 (*0-8176-5241-8*) Birkhauser.

Boltho, Andrea. Japan: An Economic Survey, 1953-1973. (Economies of the World Ser.). (Illus.). 1976. 34.50 (*0-19-877036-7*) OUP.

Boltianskii, V. G. Geometric Methods & Optimization Problems. LC 98-45185. 13p. 1999. 2.40 (*0-7923-5454-0*) Kluwer Academic.

Bolto, B. A. & Pawlowski, L. Wastewater Treatment by Ion Exchange. 250p. 1987. 69.95 (*0-419-13320-8*, 2968, E & FN Spon) Routledge.

Bolton. Control Engineering. 1993. pap. text. write for info. (*0-582-09729-0*, Pub. by Addison-Wesley) Longman.

— Electrical & Magnetic Properties of Materials. 1992. pap. text. write for info. (*0-582-07025-2*, Pub. by Addison-Wesley) Longman.

— Engineering Instrumentation & Control. 160p. 1996. pap. 27.95 (*0-7506-2725-5*) Buttrwrth-Heinemann.

— Engineering Materials Technology. 3rd ed. 480p. 1998. pap. text 39.95 (*0-7506-3917-2*) Buttrwrth-Heinemann.

— Industrial Control & Instrumentation. 1991. pap. text. write for info. (*0-582-06802-9*, Pub. by Addison-Wesley) Longman.

— Materials & Their Uses. 192p. 1996. pap. text 24.95 (*0-7506-2726-3*) Buttrwrth-Heinemann.

***Bolton.** Newnes Engineering Materials Pocket Book. 2000. 28.95 (*0-7506-4974-7*, Newnes) Buttrwrth-Heinemann.

Bolton. Quality Management Systems for the Food Industry. (Food Science & Technology Ser.). 1996. text 64.95 (*0-7514-4030-2*) Chapman & Hall.

— Technician Science. 1988. pap. text. write for info. (*0-582-01656-8*, Pub. by Addison-Wesley) Longman.

Bolton, jt. ed. see Wrenn.

Bolton, A. R. The Six Brides of Dilston. 100p. (C). 1988. 35.00 (*0-7212-0745-6*, Pub. by Regency Pr GBR) St Mut.

Bolton, A. T. The Architecture of Robert & James Adam, 1758-1794, 2 vols., Set. (Illus.). 880p. 1984. reprint ed. 195.00 (*0-907462-49-9*) Antique Collect.

Bolton, Alan, jt. auth. see Flynn, Douglas.

Bolton, Alan H., jt. auth. see Flynn, Douglas H.

***Bolton, Allan.** Managing the Academic Unit LC 99-16160. (Managing Universities & Colleges Ser.). 2000. 29.95 (*0-335-20403-1*) Taylor & Francis.

Bolton, Andrew. Quality Management Systems for the Food Industry: A Guide To Iso 9001/2. 193p. 1997. 95.00 (*0-8342-1333-8*) Aspen Pub.

Bolton, Angela. Dear Mr. Henshaw. (Literature Unit Ser.). (Illus.). 48p. 1995. pap., teacher ed. 7.95 (*1-55734-541-4*) Tchr Create Mat.

— How to Manage Your Multi Age Classroom. 1997. pap. text 12.95 (*1-55734-328-4*) Tchr Create Mat.

Bolton, Arthur. Structural Dynamics in Practice: Guide for Professional Engineers. LC 93-1511. (International Series in Civil Engineering). 256p. 1993. 49.00 (*0-07-707813-6*) McGraw.

Bolton, Barbara, jt. auth. see Brunson, Dorothy.

Bolton, Barry. Identification Guide to the Ant Genera of the World. LC 93-41270. 224p. 1994. 75.95 (*0-674-44280-6*) HUP.

— A New General Catalogue of the Ants of the World. LC 95-12908. 512p. (C). 1995. 140.50 (*0-674-61514-X*) HUP.

Bolton, Bill. Control Engineering. 2nd ed. 416p. (C). 1998. pap. text 73.33 (*0-582-32773-3*, Prentice Hall) P-H.

***Bolton, Bill.** Programmable Logic Controllers. 3rd ed. 192p. 2000. pap. 32.95 (*0-7506-4746-9*, Newnes) Buttrwrth-Heinemann.

Bolton, Bill, jt. auth. see Thompson, John.

Bolton, Brenda. Innocent III: Studies on Papal Authority & Pastoral Care. LC 95-3349. (Collected Studies: Vol. 490). 336p. 1995. 106.95 (*0-86078-489-4*, Pub. by Variorum) Ashgate Pub Co.

Bolton, Brett. An Edgar Cayce Encyclopedia of Foods for Health & Healing. LC 96-53991. 514p. 1997. pap. 14.95 (*0-87604-378-3*, 511) ARE Pr.

Bolton, Brett, ed. Edgar Cayce Speaks. 672p. 1976. mass mkt. 4.95 (*0-380-00553-0*, Avon Bks) Morrow Avon.

***Bolton, Brian.** Handbook of Measurement & Evaluation in Rehabilitation. 3rd ed. 352p. 2000. 55.00 (*0-8342-1819-4*) Aspen Pub.

Bolton, Brian, jt. auth. see Hinman, Suki.

Bolton, C. A. Church Reform in the 18th Century Italy: The Synod of Pistoia, 1786. (International Archives of the History of Ideas Ser.: No. 29). 171p. 1969. lib. bdg. 73.50 (*90-247-0208-9*) Kluwer Academic.

Bolton, Catherine, tr. see Vismara, Clement.

Bolton, Charles. Marriage Notices for the Whole United States, 1785-1794. 139p. 1989. reprint ed. lib. bdg. 18.00 (*1-56012-104-1*, 96) Kinship Rhinebeck.

Bolton, Charles C. Poor Whites of the Antebellum South: Tenants & Laborers in Central North Carolina & Northeast Mississippi. LC 93-25978. (Illus.). 272p. 1994. text 49.95 (*0-8223-1428-2*); pap. text 18.95 (*0-8223-1468-1*) Duke.

Bolton, Charles C. & Culclasure, Scott P., eds. The Confessions of Edward Isham: A Poor White Life of the Old South. LC 98-4359. 216p. 1998. 40.00 (*0-8203-2021-8*) U of Ga Pr.

— The Confessions of Edward Isham: A Poor White Life of the Old South. 820th ed. LC 98-4359. 216p. 1998. pap. 18.00 (*0-8203-2073-0*) U of Ga Pr.

Bolton, Charles C., jt. auth. see McMillen, Neil R.

Bolton, Charles D. & Kammeyer, Kenneth C. The University Student: A Study of Behavior & Values. 1967. pap. 19.95 (*0-8084-0308-7*) NCUP.

Bolton, Charles F., jt. auth. see Brown, William F.

Bolton, Charles K. The Boltons of Old & New England. (Illus.). 98p. 1988. reprint ed. pap. 19.50 (*0-8328-0275-1*); reprint ed. lib. bdg. 29.50 (*0-8328-0274-3*) Higginson Bk Co.

— Marriage Notices, 1785-1794, for the Whole United States from the Massachusetts Centinel & the Columbian Centinel. LC 65-28304. 139p. 1985. reprint ed. 15.00 (*0-8063-0045-0*) Genealog Pub.

— The Private Soldier under Washington. (American Revolution Ser.: Vol. 2). 96p. 1997. 10.95 (*1-58057-017-8*, PSUW001B) Digital Antiq.

— The Private Soldier under Washington. 3rd unabridged ed. (Illus.). 265p. 1997. reprint ed. pap. 15.95 (*0-87928-117-0*) Corner Hse.

— Scotch Irish Pioneers in Ulster & America. (Illus.). 412p. 1989. reprint ed. pap. 21.50 (*1-55613-235-2*) Heritage Bk.

Bolton, Charles S. Southern Anglicanism: The Church of England in Colonial South Carolina, 5. LC 81-6669. (Contributions to the Study of Religion Ser.: No. 5). (Illus.). 220p. 1982. 55.00 (*0-313-23090-0*, BOS/, Greenwood Pr) Greenwood.

Bolton, Chelsea L. Eyes of the Heart. 56p. 1999. pap. 8.00 (*0-8059-4745-0*) Dorrance.

Bolton, Clyde. The Alabama Gang. 1994. pap. 9.95 (*0-9635413-3-1*) Birm News.

— Crimson Tide: The Story of Alabama Football. rev. ed. (College Sports Bks.). (Illus.). 328p. 1987. pap. 11.95 (*0-87397-301-1*, Strode Pubs) Circle Bk Service.

— Ivy: A Personal Story Behind the Civil Rights Struggle. 384p. (J). 1986. mass mkt. 3.95 (*0-87067-832-9*, BH832) Holloway.

— The Lost Sunshine. LC 93-7775. 190p. 1994. 20.00 (*1-881320-06-5*, Black Belt) Black Belt Communs.

***Bolton, Clyde.** Nancy Swimmer: A Story of the Cherokee Nation. LC 99-37204. 272p. 1999. 24.95 (*0-9630273-3-6*, Southern Treas) Highland AL.

— Nancy Swimmer: A Story of the Cherokee Nation. deluxe aut. ed. LC 99-37204. 272p. 1999. lthr. 75.00 (*0-9630273-2-8*, Southern Treas) Highland AL.

Bolton, Clyde. War Eagle: The Story of Auburn Football. rev. ed. (College Sports Bks.). (Illus.). 358p. 1987. pap. 11.95 (*0-87397-302-X*, Strode Pubs) Circle Bk Service.

Bolton, Dale. Selection & Evaluation of Teachers. LC 72-10648. 234p. 1973. 34.00 (*0-8211-0123-4*) McCutchan.

Bolton, Derek. Mind, Meaning, & Mental Disorder: The Nature of Causal Explanation in Psychology & Psychiatry. 416p. 1996. pap. text 45.00 (*0-19-262936-0*) OUP.

Bolton, Derek & Hill, Jonathan. Mind, Meaning & Mental Disorder: The Nature of Causal Explanation in Psychology & Psychiatry. (Illus.). 406p. (C). 1996. text 89.50 (*0-19-261504-1*) OUP.

Bolton Discourse Network Staff, jt. auth. see Parker, Ian.

Bolton, Dorothy G., jt. auth. see Bolton, Robert.

Bolton, Douglas. Garden or Wilderness. 202p. 1980. 22.95 (*0-87073-890-9*); pap. 13.95 (*0-87073-882-8*) Schenkman Bks Inc.

Bolton Drinnon, Janis. In HIS Care. 1998. pap. write for info. (*1-57553-842-3*) Watermrk Pr.

Bolton, E. S. A History of the Stanwood Family in America. (Illus.). 317p. 1989. reprint ed. pap. 47.50 (*0-8328-1113-0*); reprint ed. lib. bdg. 55.50 (*0-8328-1112-2*) Higginson Bk Co.

Bolton, Edmund. The Cities Advocate: Whether Apprentiship Extinguisheth Gentry? LC 74-28834. (English Experience Ser.: No. 715). 1975. reprint ed. 15.00 (*90-221-0715-9*) Walter J Johnson.

— The Elements of Armories. LC 73-38160. (English Experience Ser.: No. 363). 356p. 1971. reprint ed. 45.00 (*90-221-0363-3*) Walter J Johnson.

Bolton, Edward R. Oils, Fats & Fatty Foods: Their Practical Examination. 4th ed. Williams, K. A., ed. LC 67-73132. 496p. reprint ed. pap. 153.80 (*0-608-10838-3*, 200459400044) Bks Demand.

Bolton, Eileen. Lichens for Vegetable Dyeing. 1991. 12.50 (*1-56659-001-9*) Robin & Russ.

Bolton, Elizabeth. Case of the Wacky Cat. LC 84-8725. (Easy-to-Read Mystery Ser.). (Illus.). 48p. (J). (gr. 2-4). 1999. pap. 3.50 (*0-8167-0401-5*) Troll Communs.

Bolton, Elizabeth, ed. see Oregon Writers Colony Staff.

Bolton, Ethel S. Immigrants to New England, 1700-1775. LC 66-28669. 235p. 1997. reprint ed. 15.00 (*0-8063-0047-7*) Genealog Pub.

— Shirley, Massachusetts, Uplands & Intervale. (Illus.). 394p. 1993. reprint ed. lib. bdg. 42.00 (*0-8328-2906-4*) Higginson Bk Co.

Bolton, Ethel S., ed. see Topliff, Samuel.

Bolton, Faye & Snowball, Diane. Ideas for Spelling. LC 93-2542. Orig. Title: Springboards. 120p. (YA). 1993. pap. text 21.00 (*0-435-08801-7*, 08801) Heinemann.

— Teaching Spelling: A Practical Resource. LC 93-8989. 120p. (YA). 1993. pap. text 19.50 (*0-435-08802-5*, 08802) Heinemann.

Bolton, Faye, jt. auth. see Snowball, Diane.

Bolton, Frank G. The Pregnant Adolescent: Problems of Premature Parenthood. LC 79-27082. (Sage Library of Social Research: No. 100). 247p. reprint ed. pap. 76.60 (*0-8357-4769-7*, 203770600009) Bks Demand.

Bolton, Frank G., Jr. When Bonding Fails: Clinical Assessment of High-Risk Families. LC 83-4425. (Sage Library of Social Research: No. 151). 224p. 1983. reprint ed. pap. 69.50 (*0-608-01521-0*, 205956500002) Bks Demand.

Bolton, Frank G. & Bolton, Susan R. Working with Violent Families. 400p. (C). 1987. text 55.00 (*0-8039-2586-7*); pap. text 26.00 (*0-8039-2587-5*) Sage.

Bolton, Frank G., Jr., et al. Males at Risk: The Other Side of Child Sexual Abuse. 224p. (C). 1989. text 52.00 (*0-8039-3236-7*) Sage.

***Bolton, Gavin & Heathcote, Dorothy.** So You Want to Use Role Play? 204p. 2000. pap. 25.00 (*1-85856-196-5*) Stylus Pub VA.

Bolton, Gavin, jt. auth. see Heathcote, Dorothy.

***Bolton, Gavin M.** Acting in Classroom Drama: A Critical Analysis. LC 99-40619. 330p. 1999. pap. text 25.00 (*1-893056-03-1*, 056031) Calendar Islands.

Bolton, Geoffrey. Daphne Street: The Biography of an Australian Community. 1997. pap. 19.95 (*1-86368-167-1*, Pub. by Fremantle Arts) Intl Spec Bk.

— A Fine Country to Starve In. LC 94-223884. 1994. pap. 29.95 (*1-875560-36-X*, Pub. by Univ of West Aust Pr) Intl Spec Bk.

— The Oxford History of Australia, 1942-1988 Vol. 5: The Middle Way. (Illus.). 52p. (C). 1993. reprint ed. pap. 21.00 (*0-19-553520-0*) OUP.

Bolton, Geoffrey, ed. The Oxford History of Australia Vol. 5: 1942 - 1988: The Middle Way. (Illus.). 360p. 1990. text 45.00 (*0-19-554613-X*) OUP.

Bolton, Geoffrey, et al, eds. The Wollaston Journals, 1842-1844, Vol. 2. 45.00 (*1-875560-02-5*, Pub. by Univ of West Aust Pr) Intl Spec Bk.

***Bolton, Geoffrey & Gregory, Jenny.** Claremont: A History. 264p. 1999. 39.95 (*1-876268-38-7*, Pub. by Univ of West Aust Pr); pap. 29.95 (*1-876268-39-5*, Pub. by Univ of West Aust Pr) Intl Spec Bk.

Bolton, Geoffrey, jt. ed. see Hudson, Wayne.

Bolton, Gerlinde. George Eliot & Goethe: An Elective Affinity. LC 98-189758. (Text Studies in Comparative Literature: Vol. 13). 290p. 1998. pap. 50.00 (*90-420-0359-6*) Editions Rodopi.

Bolton, Gillie. Therapeutic Potential of Creative Writing: Writing Myself. LC 99-192236. 252p. 1998. pap. text 28.95 (*1-85302-599-2*, Pub. by Jessica Kingsley) Taylor & Francis.

Bolton, Gregory L. Randy & Nightcap's Journey Through... The Bible... Using 123s & ABCs. (J). (gr. 5-7). 1998. pap. 6.95 (*0-533-12399-2*) Vantage.

Bolton, Guy, et al. Girl Crazy. 1930. 5.50 (*0-87129-573-3*, G23) Dramatic Pub.

Bolton, H. C. A Select Bibliography of Chemistry. Incl. First Supplement, 1492-1897: Section 7. 1999. 45.00 (*0-527-09420-X*); First Supplement, 1492-1897 Sect. 8: Academic Dissertations. reprint ed. 40.00 (*0-527-09426-9*); Second Supplement, 1492-1902. 1904. 40.00 (*0-527-09432-3*); (Smithsonian Miscellaneous Collections: No. 36). 1974. write for info. (*0-318-54037-1*) Periodicals Srv.

Bolton, H. C. & Bolton, R. P. The Family of Bolton in England & America, 1100-1894: A Study in Genealogy. (Illus.). 540p. 1988. reprint ed. pap. 89.00 (*0-8328-0277-8*); reprint ed. lib. bdg. 99.00 (*0-8328-0276-X*) Higginson Bk Co.

Bolton, H. Philip. Dickens Dramatized. 532p. 1987. 70.00 (*0-8161-8924-2*, Hall Reference) Macmillan.

— Scott Dramatized. (Novels on Stage Ser.). 608p. 1992. text 200.00 (*0-7201-2060-8*) Continuum.

***Bolton, H. Philip.** Women Writers Dramatized: A Calendar of Performances from Narrative Works Published in English to 1900. LC 99-40059. (Novels on Stage Ser.). 1999. 140.00 (*0-7201-2117-5*) Mansell Pub.

Bolton, H. Suzanne & Magoon, Orville T., eds. Coastal Wetlands. LC 91-4240. (Coastlines of the World Ser.). 168p. 1991. pap. text 51.00 (*0-87262-840-X*) Am Soc Civil Eng.

Bolton, Harry E., jt. auth. see Denison, E. Glenn.

Bolton, Herbert E. Anza's California Expeditions, 5 vols., Set. (BCL1 - United States Local History Ser.). 1991. reprint ed. lib. bdg. 375.00 (*0-7812-6337-9*) Rprt Serv.

— Fray Juan Crespi, Missionary Explorer on the Pacific Coast, 1769-1774. LC 78-158616. reprint ed. 37.50 (*0-404-01838-6*) AMS Pr.

— Guide to Materials for the History of the United States in the Principal Archives of Mexico. (Carnegie Institute Ser.: Vol. 18). 1913. 55.00 (*0-527-00698-X*) Periodicals Srv.

— The Hasinais: The Southern Caddoans As Seen by the Earliest Europeans. LC 86-40525. (Civilization of the American Indian Ser.: Vol. 182). (Illus.). 200p. 1987. 29.95 (*0-8061-2060-6*) U of Okla Pr.

— History of the Americas. LC 79-15343. (Illus.). 365p. 1980. reprint ed. lib. bdg. 65.00 (*0-8371-5273-9*, BOHA, Greenwood Pr) Greenwood.

— Rim of Christendom: A Biography of Eusebio Francisco Kino, Pacific Coast Pioneer. LC 84-8814. 644p. 1984. reprint ed. 60.95 (*0-8165-0863-1*) U of Ariz Pr.

— The Spanish Borderlands. 1993. reprint ed. lib. bdg. 75.00 (*0-7812-5918-5*) Rprt Serv.

— The Spanish Borderlands: A Chronicle of Old Florida & the Southwest. LC 95-24340. (Historians of the Frontier & American West Ser.). (Illus.). 320p. (C). 1996. pap. 22.50 (*0-8263-1681-6*) U of NM Pr.

— Spanish Exploration in the Southwest, 1542-1706. (BCL1 - United States Local History Ser.). 487p. 1991. reprint ed. lib. bdg. 99.00 (*0-7812-6333-6*) Rprt Serv.

— Spanish Exploration in the Southwest, 1542-1706. 1992. reprint ed. lib. bdg. 75.00 (*0-7812-5009-9*) Rprt Serv.

— Spanish Exploration in the Southwest, 1542-1706. 1993. reprint ed. lib. bdg. 75.00 (*0-7812-5867-7*) Rprt Serv.

— Texas in the Middle Eighteenth Century. 1993. reprint ed. lib. bdg. 75.00 (*0-7812-5868-5*) Rprt Serv.

Bolton Institute Staff, jt. ed. see Horrocks, A. R.

Bolton, Iris. My Son... My Son: A Guide to Healing after Death, Loss or Suicide. rev. ed. 120p. 1995. pap. 32.50 incl. audio (*0-9616326-4-X*) Bolton Pr.

Bolton, Iris. My Son... My Son: A Guide to Healing after Death, Loss or Suicide. rev. ed. 120p. 1995. 39.00 incl. audio (*0-9616326-5-8*) Bolton Pr.

Bolton, Iris & Mitchell, Curtis. My Son... My Son: A Guide to Healing after Death, Loss or Suicide. rev. ed. 120p. 1983. pap. 12.95 (*0-9616326-0-7*) Bolton Pr.

— My Son... My Son: A Guide to Healing after Death, Loss or Suicide. 12th rev. ed. 120p. 1983. 17.95 (*0-9616326-1-5*) Bolton Pr.

Bolton, Isabel. New York Mosaic: Do I Wake or Sleep; The Christmas Tree; Many Mansions. LC 97-18480. 401p. 1997. 35.00 (*1-883642-28-0*) Steerforth Pr.

— New York Mosaic: Do I Wake or Sleep; The Christmas Tree; Many Mansions. LC 97-18480. (Illus.). 401p. 1998. reprint ed. pap. 18.00 (*1-883642-89-2*) Steerforth Pr.

— Under Gemini: A Memoir. LC 98-31406. 131p. 1999. reprint ed. pap. 12.00 (*1-883642-68-X*) Steerforth Pr.

Bolton, James, jt. auth. see de Bay, Philip.

Bolton, James R., et al, eds. Electron Transfer in Inorganic, Organic, & Biological Systems. LC 91-12841. (Advances in Chemistry Ser.: No. 228). (Illus.). 295p. 1991. 110.00 (*0-8412-1846-3*, Pub. by Am Chemical) OUP.

— Electron Transfer in Inorganic, Organic, & Biological Systems: Developed from a Symposium Sponsored by the International Chemical Congress of Pacific Basin Societies, Honolulu, HI, December 17-22, 1989. LC 91-12841. (Advances in Chemistry Ser.: No. 228). 304p. reprint ed. pap. 94.30 (*0-608-06813-6*, 206701000009) Bks Demand.

Bolton, Janet. Folk Art Quilts. Date not set. write for info. (*1-897954-54-9*, Pub. by Mus Quilts Pub) Sterling.

— In a Patchwork Garden: Garden Designs in Applique. LC 96-22657. (Illus.). 112p. 1996. 27.95 (*0-8442-2624-6*, Quilt Dgst Pr) NTC Contemp Pub Co.

— Mrs. Noah's Patchwork Quilt. (Illus.). 22p. (J). 1995. 17.95 (*0-8362-4250-5*) Andrews & McMeel.

Bolton, Janet, jt. auth. see Leebow, Ken.

Bolton, Janet, ed. see Leebow, Ken & Lupus, Peter.

Bolton, Jess. The Love of Highland Mary. 288p. 1994. pap. write for info. (*1-874640-01-7*, Pub. by Argyll Pubng) St Mut.

Bolton, Joe. Days of Summer Gone. 75p. (Orig.). 1990. pap. 9.95 (*0-913123-30-7*) Galileo.

***Bolton, Joe.** Last Nostalgia: Poems, 1982-1990. LC 99-10535. 1999. pap. 24.00 (*1-55728-558-6*) U of Ark Pr.

Bolton, John R., ed. see Browning, Elizabeth Barrett.

Bolton, Jonathan. Personal Landscapes. LC 97-12380. 244p. 1997. text 39.95 (*0-312-17350-4*) St Martin.

Bolton, Jonathan W. & Wilson, Claire M. Scholars, Writers, & Professionals. LC 93-31683. (American Indian Lives Ser.). (Illus.). 160p. (YA). (gr. 5-12). 1994. 19.95 (*0-8160-2896-6*) Facts on File.

Bolton, Ken & Jenkins, John. The Ferrara Poems. (C). 1990. 50.00 (*0-949836-21-4*, Pub. by Pascoe Pub) St Mut.

Bolton, Kim. Conversations at the Girlville Diner. LC 99-37033. 150p. 1999. pap. 11.99 (*0-87788-171-5*, H Shaw Pubs) Waterbrook Pr.

Bolton, L. D. Twenty Six Spirituals. spiral bd. 28.00 (*0-9616326-7-4*) Bolton Pr.

Bolton Landing Conference Staff, et al. Ordered Alloys. 3rd ed. 1970. 45.00 (*0-87511-600-0*) Claitors.

Bolton, Linda. Art in Focus: Paris. (Illus.). 128p. 1995. pap. 12.95 (*0-8212-2155-8*, Pub. by Bulfinch Pr) Little.

***Bolton, Linda.** Cubism. (Art Revolutions Ser.). (Illus.). 32p. 2000. 16.95 (*0-87226-613-3*, 66133B, P Bedrick Books) NTC Contemp Pub Co.

Bolton, Linda. History & Techniques of the Masters: Gauguin. 1997. 8.98 (*0-7858-0795-0*) Bk Sales Inc.

***Bolton, Linda.** Impressionism. LC 99-86942. (Art Revolutions Ser.). 2000. 16.95 (*0-87226-611-7*, 66117B, P Bedrick Books) NTC Contemp Pub Co.

— Pop Art. LC 99-86941. (Art Revolutions Ser.). 32p. 2000. 16.95 (*0-87226-614-1*, 66141B, P Bedrick Books) NTC Contemp Pub Co.

— Surrealism. (Art Revolutions Ser.). (Illus.). 2000. 16.95 (*0-87226-612-5*, 66125B, P Bedrick Books) NTC Contemp Pub Co.

Bolton, Lyndon. An Introduction to the Theory of Relativity. 1976. lib. bdg. 250.00 (*0-8490-2075-1*) Gordon Pr.

Bolton, Mac. Assessment & Development in Europe: Adding Value to Individuals & Organizations. LC 95-2230. (Training Ser.). 1995. write for info. (*0-07-707928-0*) McGraw.

Bolton, Martha. Childhood Is a Stage: Sketches & Monologues for Kids. 1993. pap. text 8.99 (*0-00-546376-9*) Lillenas.

— Childhood Is a Stage: Sketches & Monologues for Kids. 48p. Date not set. pap. 8.99 (*0-8341-9796-0*) Nazarene.

— Club Family. 1996. pap. 8.99 (*0-8341-9528-3*, MP-772) Nazarene.

***Bolton, Martha.** Didn't My Skin Used to Fit? Living, Laughing, Loving Life after Forty! LC 00-8485. 192p. 2000. pap. 9.99 (*0-7642-2184-1*) Bethany Hse.

Bolton, Martha. Don't Jump to Conclusions Without a Bungee Cord... And Other Wise Advice from the Book of Proverbs. 1999. pap. 10.99 (*1-56955-080-8*) Servant.

***Bolton, Martha.** Don't Wake Me till after Lunch! 2nd ed. LC 00-24264. (Illus.). 160p. (gr. 7-12). 2000. pap. 4.99 (*0-8007-5730-0*, The Cafeteria L) Chosen Bks.

— Funny Thing Happened on My Way Through the Bible. (Illus.). 160p. 2000. pap. 6.99 (*1-56292-579-2*) Honor Bks OK.

Bolton, Martha. A Funny Thing Happened to Me on My Way Through the Bible. 70p. 1984. 15.99 (*0-8341-9084-2*, MP-628) Lillenas.

— Home, Home on the Stage. 1991. pap. 8.99 (*0-00-150867-9*) Lillenas.

— Home, Home on the Stage: A Master of Ceremonies' Guide to All Occasions. 64p. 1991. pap. 8.99 (*0-8341-9828-2*) Nazarene.

— The How'd I Get to Be in Charge of the Program? Help Book: An Almanac of Programming Resources for the Local Church. 93p. 1988. 8.99 (*0-8341-9091-5*, MP-648) Lillenas.

***Bolton, Martha.** I Love You... Still, Bk. 2. 2001. 14.99 (*0-8007-1780-5*) Revell.

— I Still Do: A Humorous Celebration of Marriage. LC 00-29118.Tr. of Rel 022000. 256p. (gr. 13 up). 2000. 14.99 (*0-8007-1774-0*) Revell.

— If Mr. Clean Calls, Tell Him I'm Not In! 2nd rev. ed. LC 00-24263. (Illus.). 96p. (gr. 7-12). 2000. pap. 4.99 (*0-8007-5729-7*) Revell.

Bolton, Martha. If the Pasta Wiggles, Don't Eat It! Wise Words to Tickle Your Funny Bone & Make You Think. 200p. 1995. pap. 10.99 (*0-89283-852-3*, Vine Bks) Servant.

— If You Can't Stand the Smoke, Get Out of My Kitchen. 120p. 1990. pap. 8.99 (*0-8341-1361-9*) Beacon Hill.

— Journey to the Center of the Stage: And Other Monologues with Mirth & Message. 47p. 1990. 9.99 (*0-8341-9176-8*, MP-658) Lillenas.

— Let My People Laugh. 58p. 1989. 15.99 (*0-8341-9009-5*, MP-653) Lillenas.

— Never Ask Delilah for a Trim . . . And Other Good Advice. LC 98-8573. 220p. (YA). 1998. pap. 10.99 (*1-56955-048-4*) Servant.

— On the Loose . . . the Cafeteria Lady. LC 94-16857. (J). 1994. pap. 6.99 (*1-56179-280-2*) Focus Family.

— Sermon on the Stage: More Sketches/Monologues Based on Familiar Bible Stories. LC 99-218639. 1998. 8.99 (*0-8341-9789-8*) Nazarene.

— These Truths Were Made for Walking: Comedy Sketches about Walking the Talk. 64p. 1992. 15.99 (*0-8341-9310-8*, MP-674) Lillenas.

— A View from the Pew. 72p. 1985. 15.99 (*0-8341-9180-6*, MP-633) Lillenas.

— Walk a Mile in His Truths: More Comedy Sketches on Walking the Talk. 62p. 1994. 15.99 (*0-8341-9124-5*, MP-751) Lillenas.

— Walk a Mile in His Truths: More Comedy Sketches on Walking the Talk. 1994. pap. text 8.99 (*0-00-504825-7*) Lillenas.

— What's Growing under Your Bed? A Collection of Sketches & Monologues for Children & Young Teens. 75p. 1986. 15.99 (*0-8341-9621-2*, MP-634) Lillenas.

— What's Growing under Your Bed? A Collection of Sketches & Monologues for Children & Young Teens. 1986. pap. 8.99 (*0-00-656471-2*) Lillenas.

— When the Going Gets Tough, the Tough Start Laughing. LC 97-147253. pap. 9.99 (*0-8024-9185-5*, 324) Moody.

— When the Meat Loaf Explodes, It's Done! 72p. (Orig.). 1993. pap. 6.99 (*0-8341-1509-3*) Beacon Hill.

***Bolton, Martha.** When You Walk Through Green Pastures...Stick to the Path: Real Life Insights from the Book of Psalms. 2000. pap. text 10.99 (*1-56955-170-7*) Servant.

Bolton, Martha & Allen, Dennis. A Lamb's Tale: A Christmas Musical for Kids. Date not set. pap. 9.99 (*0-8341-9653-0*) Lillenas.

Bolton, Martha & Parks, Marty. The Gospel Never Changes. 1996. pap. 5.50 (*0-8341-9476-7*, MB-728) Nazarene.

Bolton, Martha, jt. auth. see Lowry, Mark.

Bolton, Martha, jt. auth. see Perret, Gene.

***Bolton, Mary.** Behold Your God. LC 99-62939. 384p. 1999. pap. 12.99 (*1-57921-184-4*) WinePress Pub.

Bolton, Michael. Michael Bolton Greatest Hits, 1985-1995. 1997. pap. 22.95 (*1-57623-817-2*) Wrner Bros.

Bolton, Michael. The Secret of the Lost Kingdom. LC 96-46838. (Illus.). 48p. (J). 1997. 15.95 (*0-7868-0286-3*, Pub. by Hyprn Child) Time Warner.

***Bolton, Michele.** The Third Shift: Managing Hard Choices in Our Careers, Homes & Lives as Women. 2000. 25.00 (*0-7879-4854-3*) Jossey-Bass.

Bolton, Mike. The Complete Alabama Outdoorsman. (Illus.). 180p. (Orig.). 1996. pap. 14.95 (*1-878561-50-2*) Seacoast AL.

— Mike Bolton's Favorite Alabama Jokes. 3rd ed. (Illus.). 64p. 1992. pap. 5.00 (*1-878561-11-1*) Seacoast AL.

— Mike Bolton's Favorite Auburn Jokes. 3rd ed. (Illus.). 64p. (Orig.). 1992. pap. 5.00 (*1-878561-12-X*) Seacoast AL.

— Preparing & Cooking Alabama's Wild Game. (Illus.). 160p. (Orig.). 1992. pap. 10.00 (*1-878561-07-3*) Seacoast AL.

Bolton, Mike & Bailey, Tom. The Complete Alabama Fisherman. (Illus.). 360p. (Orig.). 1990. pap. text 16.95 (*1-878561-46-4*) Seacoast AL.

Bolton, Mike, jt. auth. see Price, Elizabeth.

Bolton, Neal. The Handbook of Landfill Operations: A Practical Guide for Landfill Engineers, Owners, & Operators. LC 95-83887. (Illus.). 600p. (Orig.). 1995. pap. 79.95 (*0-9646956-0-X*) Blue Rdge Servs.

Bolton, P. A., et al. Land Use Planning for Earthquake Hazard Mitigation: A Handbook for Planners. (Special Publications: No. 14). 123p. (Orig.). (C). 1986. pap. 20.00 (*0-685-28095-0*) Natural Hazards.

Bolton, Patricia, jt. auth. see Bolin, Robert C.

Bolton, Patrick, jt. auth. see Baron-Cohen, Simon.

Bolton, R., ed. The AIDS Pandemic: A Global Emergency. xii, 118p. 1989. pap. text 43.00 (*2-88124-374-6*) Gordon & Breach.

Bolton, R. P., jt. auth. see Bolton, H. C.

Bolton, Ralph, ed. The Content of Culture: Constants & Variants. LC 87-80184. (Anthology Ser.). 567p. 1989. 35.00 (*0-87536-118-8*) HRAFP.

Bolton, Ralph & Singer, Merrill, eds. Rethinking AIDS Prevention: Cultural Approaches. LC 92-13820. 367p. 1992. pap. text 36.00 (*2-88124-552-8*) Gordon & Breach.

Bolton, Reg. Circus in a Suitcase. (Illus.). 94p. 1982. pap. 8.95 (*0-932720-08-0*) New Plays Inc.

— Showtime! 75 Ways to Put on a Show. LC 98-22801. 48p. (J). 1998. 14.95 (*0-7894-3433-4*) DK Pub Inc.

Bolton, Reginald P., jt. auth. see Calver, William L.

***Bolton, Richard.** Creative Watercolour Techniques No. 7: Step-by-Step Leisure Arts. Vol. 7. 48p. 2001. pap. 10.95 (*0-85532-847-9*, Pub. by Srch Pr) Midpt Trade.

Bolton, Richard. Culture Wars: Documents from the Recent Controversies in the Arts. 1992. pap. 19.95 (*1-56584-011-9*, Pub. by New Press NY) Norton.

— How to Paint with Brush-Tipped Felt Pens. (Illus.). 48p. 1996. pap. 11.95 (*0-85532-801-0*, 28010, Pub. by Srch Pr) A Schwartz & Co.

— Painting Detail in Watercolour. (Leisure Arts Ser.: No. 9). (Illus.). 32p. pap. 4.95 (*0-85532-440-6*, 440-6, Pub. by Srch Pr) A Schwartz & Co.

— Texture & Detail in Watercolour. LC 96-41746. (Illus.). 128p. 1997. reprint ed. pap. text 14.95 (*0-486-29509-5*) Dover.

Bolton, Richard, ed. Contest of Meaning: Critical Histories of Photograph. (Illus.). 407p. 1992. reprint ed. pap. text 35.00 (*0-262-52169-5*) MIT Pr.

— The Contest of Meaning: Critical Histories of Photography. (Illus.). 456p. 1989. 65.00 (*0-262-02288-5*) MIT Pr.

Bolton, Richard, et al. Sant Khalsa: Of a Personal Nature. LC 98-14789. 1998. write for info. (*0-945486-13-8*) CSU SBRVFAM.

Bolton, Richard, jt. auth. see Brooklyn Museum Staff.

Bolton, Richard L. Wisconsin Discovery Law & Practice. 2nd ed. LC 97-11700. 520p. 1997. ring bd. 95.00 (*0-945574-98-3*) State Bar WI.

Bolton, Rick. No Fear: Don't Let Your Fears Stand in the Way of Your Dreams. 64p. 1995. 12.95 (*0-446-52026-8*, Pub. by Warner Bks) Little.

Bolton, Robert. Bolton. Genealogical & Biographical Account of the Family of Bolton in England & America, Deduced from an Early Period & Continued to the Present Time (1862) 223p. 1996. reprint ed. pap. 35.00 (*0-8328-5268-6*); reprint ed. lib. bdg. 45.00 (*0-8328-5267-8*) Higginson Bk Co.

— A Discourse about the State of True Happinesse. LC 79-84089. (English Experience Ser.: No. 909). 184p. 1979. reprint ed. lib. bdg. 30.00 (*90-221-0909-7*) Walter J Johnson.

— The Four Last Things: Death, Judgment, Hell & Heaven. 144p. 1994. 18.95 (*1-877611-89-1*) Soli Deo Gloria.

— General Directions for a Comfortable Walking with God. 450p. 1991. reprint ed. 27.95 (*1-877611-26-3*) Soli Deo Gloria.

— The History of Several Towns, Manors & Patents of the County of Westchester from the First Settlement to the Present Time. (Illus.). 1759p. 1996. pap. 98.00 (*0-7884-0444-X*, B547) Heritage Bk.

— History of Westchester County, N. Y., 2 vols. (Illus.). 786p. 1993. reprint ed. lib. bdg. 149.00 (*0-8328-6545-1*) Higginson Bk Co.

— People Skills: How to Assert Yourself, Listen to Others, & Resolve Conflicts. 300p. 1986. pap. 12.00 (*0-671-62248-X*, Touchstone) S&S Trade Pap.

Bolton, Robert & Bolton, Dorothy G. People Styles at Work: Making Bad Relationships Good & Good Relationships Better. 176p. 1996. pap. text 16.95 (*0-8144-7723-2*) AMACOM.

— Social Style/Management Style. LC 83-45959. 192p. 1984. pap. 15.95 (*0-8144-7617-1*) AMACOM.

Bolton, Robert & Goodwin, Thomas. The Carnal Professor - Christ Set Forth. 480p. 1992. reprint ed. 23.95 (*1-877611-47-6*) Soli Deo Gloria.

Bolton, Robert, jt. ed. see Lewis, Frank.

Bolton, Ruth P. Lab Experiments: Action Chemistry. 1979. text 26.50 (*0-03-044446-2*) Holt R&W.

Bolton, Ruthie M. Gal: A True Life. 288p. 1999. pap. 10.95 (*0-452-27481-8*, Plume) Dutton Plume.

— Gal: A True Life. LC 93-43705. 1994. 19.95 (*0-15-100104-9*) Harcourt.

— Gal: A True Life. 352p. 1995. mass mkt. 6.99 (*0-451-40627-3*, Onyx) NAL.

— Gal: A True Life. 1998. 3.99 (*0-681-06919-8*) Waldenbooks Co Inc.

Bolton, S., jt. auth. see Albers, H. G.

Bolton, S. Charles. Arkansas, 1800-1860: Remote & Restless. West, Elliott, ed. LC 98-16180. (Histories of Arkansas Ser.: No. 2). (Illus.). 224p. 1998. pap. 16.00 (*1-55728-519-5*) U of Ark Pr.

— Arkansas, 1800-1860: Remote & Restless. West, Elliott, ed. LC 98-16180. (Histories of Arkansas Ser.: No. 2). (Illus.). 224p. 1998. 28.00 (*1-55728-518-7*) U of Ark Pr.

***Bolton, Samuel.** The Arraignment of Error. 2nd ed. Kistler, Don, ed. 460p. 1999. reprint ed. 35.00 (*1-57358-098-8*) Soli Deo Gloria.

Bolton, Samuel. True Bounds of Christian Freedom. (Puritan Paperbacks Ser.). 1978. pap. 8.50 (*0-85151-083-3*) Banner of Truth.

Bolton, Samuel, et al. The Puritans on Conversion. Kistler, Don, ed. 211p. 1990. 16.95 (*1-877611-11-5*) Soli Deo Gloria.

Bolton, Sanford. Pharmaceutical Statistics: Practical & Clinical Applications. 3rd ed. LC 96-49907. (Drugs & the Pharmaceutical Sciences Ser.). (Illus.). 768p. 1997. text 150.00 (*0-8247-9812-0*) Dekker.

Bolton, Sarah K. Famous English Statesmen: Of Queen Victoria's Reign. LC 78-39705. (Essay Index Reprint Ser.). 1977. reprint ed. 30.95 (*0-8369-2749-4*) Ayer.

— Famous European Artists. LC 74-39676. (Essay Index Reprint Ser.). 1977. reprint ed. 22.95 (*0-8369-2750-8*) Ayer.

— Famous Givers & Their Gifts. LC 76-37129. (Essay Index Reprint Ser.). 1977. reprint ed. 30.95 (*0-8369-2484-3*) Ayer.

— Famous Leaders among Women. LC 76-38745. (Essay Index Reprint Ser.). 1977. reprint ed. 22.95 (*0-8369-2639-0*) Ayer.

— Famous Types of Womanhood. LC 74-37123. (Essay Index Reprint Ser.). 1977. reprint ed. 25.95 (*0-8369-2485-1*) Ayer.

— Famous Voyagers & Explorers. LC 70-39659. (Essay Index Reprint Ser.). 1977. reprint ed. 36.95 (*0-8369-2751-6*) Ayer.

— How Success Is Won. 1977. 18.95 (*0-8369-7209-0*, 8008) Ayer.

— Social Studies in England. 1977. 13.95 (*0-8369-7210-4*, 8009) Ayer.

— Successful Women: With Portraits. LC 74-936. (Essay Index Reprint Ser.). (Illus.). 1977. reprint ed. 18.95 (*0-518-10143-6*) Ayer.

Bolton-Smith, Robin. Portrait Miniatures in the National Museum of American Art. LC 84-2692. (Chicago Visual Library: No. 46). (Illus.). 92p. 1984. lib. bdg. 72.00 (*0-226-68857-7*) U Ch Pr.

Bolton, Stuart, ed. Noise-Con, '88: Proceedings - National Conference on Noise Control Engineering, Purdue University, June 20-22, 1988. 1988. 60.00 (*0-931784-17-4*) Noise Control.

Bolton, Stuart, jt. ed. see Bernhard, Robert J.

Bolton, Susan Oakander & Dashiell, Sallie. INCH: INteractive CHecklist for Augmentative Communication. 1988. 35.95 (*1-883315-30-1*) Imaginart Intl.

Bolton, Susan R., jt. auth. see Bolton, Frank G.

Bolton, Susanne. Probleme der Leistungsmessung. (Fernstudienangebot Ser.). (GER.). 200p. 1996. 11.25 (*3-468-49670-2*) Langenscheidt.

Bolton, Susie. Venice. (Illustrated Travel Guides from Thomas Cook Ser.). (Illus.). 192p. 1995. 12.95 (*0-8442-9083-1*, Passprt Bks) NTC Contemp Pub Co.

Bolton, T. Geological Maps: Their Solution & Interpretation. (Illus.). 160p. (C). 1989. text 69.95 (*0-521-36158-3*) Cambridge U Pr.

— Geological Maps: Their Solution & Interpretation. (Illus.). 160p. (C). 1993. pap. text 27.95 (*0-521-36705-0*) Cambridge U Pr.

Bolton, T. B. & Tomita, Tadao, eds. Smooth Muscle Excitation. (Illus.). 560p. 1996. text 120.00 (*0-12-112360-X*) Acad Pr.

Bolton, Theodore. Early American Portrait Draughtsmen in Crayons. LC 74-77724. (Library of American Art). (Illus.). 1970. reprint ed. lib. bdg. 35.00 (*0-306-71362-4*) Da Capo.

Bolton, Thomas E., jt. auth. see Copeland, M. J.

***Bolton, Tim & Capps, Clive.** Current Practice in Environmental Reporting: The Chemical Industry. 352p. 2000. ring bd. 530.00 (*1-85573-471-0*, Pub. by Woodhead Pubng) Am Educ Systs.

— Current Practice in Environmental Reporting: The International Pulp & Paper Industry. 352p. 2000. ring bd. 890.00 (*1-85573-470-2*, Pub. by Woodhead Pubng) Am Educ Systs.

Bolton, Tom. International Paper Trade. 192p. 1998. 170.00 (*1-85573-252-1*, Pub. by Woodhead Pubng) Am Educ Systs.

— Vibrations for Health & Happiness: Everyone's Easy Guide to Stress Free Living. 250p. 1998. pap. 14.95 (*1-899836-16-0*, Pub. by Crown Hse) LPC Group.

Bolton, Trevor. Human Resource Management: An Introduction. LC 96-9236. 300p. (Orig.). (C). 1997. pap. text 39.95 (*0-631-19626-9*) Blackwell Pubs.

Bolton, W. Basic Engineering. LC 95-32695. 386p. 1995. text. write for info. (*0-7506-2584-8*) Buttrwrth-Heinemann.

— Complex Numbers. 1996. pap. 14.95 (*0-582-23741-6*) Addison-Wesley.

Bolton, W. Electrical Circuit Principles. (Illus.). 432p. (Orig.). (C). 1997. pap. 49.95 (*0-582-08802-X*, Pub. by Addison-Wesley) Trans-Atl Phila.

Bolton, W. Engineering Science. 3rd ed. LC 98-159128. 336p. 1998. pap. text 29.95 (*0-7506-3916-4*) Buttrwrth-Heinemann.

— Essential Mathematics for Engineering. LC 97-191949. 656p. 2000. pap. text 37.95 (*0-7506-3621-1*, TA330) Buttrwrth-Heinemann.

— Fourier Series. 1995. pap. 14.95 (*0-582-23934-6*) Addison-Wesley.

***Bolton, W.** Higher Engineering Science. (Illus.). 275p. 1999. pap. 37.95 (*0-7506-4235-1*, Newnes) Buttrwrth-Heinemann.

— Materials for Engineering. 2nd ed. 192p. 2000. pap. 28.95 (*0-7506-4855-4*) Buttrwrth-Heinemann.

— Mathematics for Engineering. 2nd ed. 352p. 2000. pap. 28.95 (*0-7506-4931-3*) Buttrwrth-Heinemann.

Bolton, W. Mechatronics: Electronic Control Systems in Mechanical Engineering. 2nd ed. 390p. 1998. pap. 97.00 (*0-582-35705-5*, Prentice Hall) P-H.

***Bolton, W.** Motion Picture Camera Data. 2nd ed. 352p. 2001. pap. 49.95 (*0-240-51598-6*, Focal) Buttrwrth-Heinemann.

Bolton, W. Newnes Control Engineering Pocket Book. (Illus.). 304p. 1998. text 29.95 (*0-7506-3928-8*, Newnes) Buttrwrth-Heinemann.

— Pneumatic & Hydraulic Systems. LC 97-222388. 248p. 1997. pap. text 34.95 (*0-7506-3836-2*) Buttrwrth-Heinemann.

Bolton, w., ed. CRC Engineering Materials Pocketbook. 1989. 22.00 (*0-8493-7134-1*, TA4403) CRC Pr.

Bolton, W. F. & Wrenn, C. L., eds. Beowulf. 303p. 1997. pap. 11.95 (*0-85989-518-1*, Pub. by Univ Exeter Pr) Northwestern U Pr.

Bolton, W. F., ed. see Jonson, Ben.

Bolton, Whitney F. The Language of 1984: Orwell's English & Ours. LC 83-21671. 252p. 1984. reprint ed. pap. 78.20 (*0-608-02609-3*, 206326700004) Bks Demand.

Bolton, William. Engineering Materials Pocketbook. 2nd ed. LC 96-36327. (Illus.). 256p. 1996. text 29.95 (*0-7506-2886-3*) Buttrwrth-Heinemann.

— Engineering Science. (Illus.). 213p. (C). 1990. pap. text 22.95 (*0-8311-3007-5*) Indus Pr.

— Materials for Engineering. 2nd ed. LC 93-51083. 2000. pap. text 29.95 (*0-7506-1838-8*) Buttrwrth-Heinemann.

— Mechanical Science. LC 93-49. (Illus.). 344p. 1993. pap. 39.95 (*0-632-03579-X*) Blackwell Sci.

— Newnes Instrumentation & Measurement Pocket Book. 240p. 1991. text 32.95 (*0-7506-0039-X*) Buttrwrth-Heinemann.

— Newnes Instrumentation & Measurement Pocket Book. 2nd ed. LC 96-47098. (Illus.). 320p. 1996. 29.95 (*0-7506-2885-5*) Buttrwrth-Heinemann.

— Ordinary Differential Equations. 1996. pap. 15.95 (*0-582-23399-2*) Addison-Wesley.

— Production Planning & Control. (Illus.). 192p. (Orig.). 1994. pap. 39.50 (*0-582-22820-4*, Pub. by Addison-Wesley) Trans-Atl Phila.

— Technician Science. LC 88-7274. (Illus.). 148p. reprint ed. pap. 45.90 (*0-608-08057-8*, 206902200002) Bks Demand.

Boltovskoy, Demetrio, ed. South Atlantic Zooplanton, 2 vols. (Illus.). xvi, 1706p. 1999. 500.00 (*90-5782-035-8*, Pub. by Backhuys Pubs) Balogh.

Boltovskoy, E., et al, eds. Atlas of Benthic Shelf Foraminifera of the Southwest Atlantic. (Illus.). v, 153p. 1980. text 171.00 (*90-6193-604-7*) Kluwer Academic.

Boltuck, Richard & Litan, Robert E., eds. Down in the Dumps: Administration of the Unfair Trade Laws. 360p. 1991. 39.95 (*0-8157-1020-8*); pap. 18.95 (*0-8157-1019-4*) Brookings.

Boltwood, Bertram B., jt. auth. see Rutherford, Ernest.

Boltwood, Edw. History of Pittsfield, Ma., from the Year 1876 to 1916. (Illus.). 387p. 1995. reprint ed. lib. bdg. 42.00 (*0-8328-4467-5*) Higginson Bk Co.

Boltwood, Geoff. The Messenger: The Journey of a Spiritual Healer. 240p. 1995. pap. 14.95 (*0-7499-1458-0*, Pub. by Piatkus Bks) London Brdge.

Boltwood, L. M. History & Genealogy of the Family of Thomas Noble of Westfield, Mass., with Genealogical Notes of Other Families by the Name of Noble. (Illus.). 870p. 1989. reprint ed. pap. 130.50 (*0-8328-0905-5*); reprint ed. lib. bdg. 138.50 (*0-8328-0904-7*) Higginson Bk Co.

Boltwood, Lucius M., jt. auth. see Judd, Sylvester.

Boltyanski, Vladimir & Soifer, Alexander. Geometric Etudes in Combinatorial Mathematics. (Illus.). xii, 236p. (Orig.). (YA). (gr. 9-12). 1991. pap. 27.95 (*0-940263-02-5*) Ctr Excel Math.

Boltyanskii, V., jt. auth. see Pontryagin, Lev S.

Boltyanskii, V. G. & Postnikov, M. M. Two Papers on Homotopy Theory of Continuous Mappings. LC 51-5559. (Translations Ser.: Series 2, Vol. 7). 321p. 1957. reprint ed. text 38.00 (*0-8218-1707-8*, TRANS2/7) Am Math.

Boltyanskii, V. G., et al. Topology & Topological Algebra. (Translations Ser.: Series 1, Vol. 8). 455p. 1962. 35.00 (*0-8218-1608-X*, TRANS1/8) Am Math.

— Twenty Papers on Analytic Functions & Ordinary Differential Equations. (Translations Ser.: Series 2, Vol. 18). 382p. 1961. 42.00 (*0-8218-1718-3*, TRANS2/18) Am Math.

Boltyanskii, Vladimir G. & Gokhberg, Izrail T. The Decomposition of Figures into Smaller Parts. Christoffers, Henry & Branson, Thomas P., trs. from RUS. LC 79-10382. (Popular Lectures in Mathematics). 84p. 1980. pap. text 10.00 (*0-226-06357-7*) U Ch Pr.

Boltz, Jean H. Information Security: Serious Weaknesses Place Critical Federal Operations & Assets at Risk. 94p. (C). 1999. pap. text 20.00 (*0-7881-7634-X*) DIANE Pub.

Boltz, David F. Colorimetric Determination of Nonmetals. 2nd ed. LC 77-12398. (Chemical Analysis Ser.: No. 8). (Illus.). 563p. reprint ed. pap. 174.60 (*0-608-18202-8*, 205660600078) Bks Demand.

Boltz, Howard O. & Dombroff, Mark A. Federal Trial Evidence. 2nd ed. 352p. 1996. ring bd. 89.98 (*0-938065-84-X*) James Pub Santa Ana.

Boltz, Judith M. & University of California Staff. A Survey of Taoist Literature, Tenth to Seventeenth Centuries. LC 87-61572. (China Research Monographs). xiii, 417 p. 1987. pap. write for info. (*0-912966-88-2*) IEAS.

Boltz, William G. The Origin & Early Development of the Chinese Writing System. (American Oriental Ser.: Vol. 78). ix, 205p. 1994. 47.50 (*0-940490-78-1*) Am Orient Soc.

Boltz, William G. & Shapiro, Michael C., eds. Studies in the Historical Phonology of Asian Languages. LC 91-34227. (Current Issues in Linguistic Theory Ser.: No. 77). viii, 249p. 1991. 65.00 (*1-55619-132-4*) J Benjamins Pubng Co.

Boltzmann, Ludwig. Lectures on Gas Theory. Brush, Stephen G., tr. LC 94-41221. (Illus.). 512p. 1995. pap. text 12.95 (0-486-68455-5) Dover.

— Theoretical Physics & Philosophical Problems: Selected Writings. McGuinness, Brian F., ed. Foulkes, Paul, tr. from GER. LC 74-79571. (Vienna Circle Collection: No. 5). 296p. 1974. pap. text 73.50 (90-277-0250-0, D Reidel) Kluwer Academic.

Boluch, Kathleen A. Julia's World Pt. 1: Better Times. (Illus.). 58p. (YA). 1990. 14.95 (0-9626365-0-9) Swarovski Amer Ltd.

Bolukbasi, Suha. The Superpowers & the Third World: Turkish-American Relations & Cyprus. LC 88-10343. (Exxon Education Foundation Series on Rhetoric & Political Discourse: Vol. 15). 288p. (Orig.). (C). 1988. pap. text 25.00 (0-8191-6978-1, Pub. by White Miller Center); lib. bdg. 49.00 (0-8191-6977-3, Pub. by White Miller Center) U Pr of Amer.

Bolus, J. Brooklyn: Lessons about Young Lives in Chaos. Thornton, Susan, ed. LC 97-76360. xvi, 334p. 1999. pap. 14.50 (0-9671294-0-0) R Bolus.

Bolus, Jim. Derby Dreams. LC 95-49534. (Illus.). 264p. 1996. 18.95 (1-56554-207-X) Pelican.

Bolus, Jim. Derby Dreams. LC 95-49534. (Illus.). 264p. 1996. pap. 18.95 (1-56554-522-2) Pelican.

Bolus, Jim. Derby Fever. LC 94-41492. (Illus.). 256p. 1995. 18.95 (1-56554-124-3) Pelican.

— Derby Magic. LC 96-52479. 256p. 1997. pap. text 14.95 (1-56554-466-8) Pelican.

— Kentucky Derby Stories. LC 92-36082. (Illus.). 212p. 1993. 18.95 (0-88289-984-8) Pelican.

— Kentucky Derby Stories, 1. 212p. 1998. pap. 14.95 (1-56554-465-X) Pelican.

— Remembering the Derby. LC 93-34923. (Illus.). 256p. 1994. 18.95 (1-56554-040-9) Pelican.

B

***Bolus, Jim & Reed, Billy.** Louisville Cardinal Football. (Illus.). 160p. 1999. 24.95 (1-58382-048-5, Pub. by Sports Masters) Partners-West.

Bolus, Jim, ed. see Faulconer, J. B.

Bolus, Suzanne, ed. see Faulconer, J. B.

Bolvia, Lila, tr. see Holmes, Ernest.

Bolweg, Joep F. Job Design & Industrial Democracy. (Studies in the Quality of Working Life: No. 3). 1976. lib. bdg. 78.50 (90-207-0634-9) Kluwer Academic.

***Bolwell, Brian J., ed.** Current Controversies in Bone Marrow Transplantation. LC 99-38948. (Current Clinical Oncology Ser.). 336p. 1999. 125.00 (0-89603-782-7) Humana.

Bolwell, Christine. The Directory of Educational Software for Nursing: Addendum. 229p. (C). 1995. 39.95 (1-888418-00-1) FITNE.

Bolwell, Robert W. Life & Works of John Heywood. LC 21-22336. reprint ed. 20.00 (0-404-00934-4) AMS Pr.

Bolwig, Tom G., jt. ed. see Trimble, Michael R.

Boly, Aliou, et al. Guide de Formation des Comites de Gestion des Associations de Parents d'Eleves.Tr. of Training Guide in French for Parents Associations. (FRE.). 72p. 1995. pap. 16.00 (0-914262-15-7) World Educ.

Boly, Craig S. The Road to Lonergan's Method in Theology: The Ordering of Theological Ideas. 294p. (C). 1991. lib. bdg. 52.50 (0-8191-7741-5) U Pr of Amer.

Boly, John R. Reading Auden: The Returns of Caliban. LC 91-6948. 256p. 1991. 37.50 (0-8014-2565-4) Cornell U Pr.

— Reading Auden: The Returns of Caliban. LC 91-6948. 255p. reprint ed. pap. 79.10 (0-608-20875-2, 207197400003) Bks Demand.

***Bolyanatz, Alexander H.** Mortuary Feasting on New Ireland: The Activation of Matriliny among the Sursurunga. LC 99-59735. 208p. 2000. 59.95 (0-89789-721-8, Bergin & Garvey) Greenwood.

Bolyog, Michael E. & Young, Allen R. Aiden's Cauldron. LC 98-90511. (Aiden's Cauldron Trilogy Ser.). 252p. 1998. pap. 11.95 (0-9656684-1-X) Sendraaks Writing.

Bolz. The Counter Terrorism Handbook Tactics Procedures & Techniques. 256p. 1992. boxed set 73.95 (0-8493-9501-I) CRC Pr.

Bolz, F., et al. Counter-Terrorism Handbook: Tactics, Procedures, & Techniques. (Practical Aspects of Criminal & Forensic Investigations Ser.). 1992. lib. bdg. 57.95 (0-444-01524-8, HV6431) CRC Pr.

Bolz, Frank, et al. Anti-Terrorism Defense Tactics. 1989. write for info. (0-318-66282-5) Elsevier.

Bolz, J. Arnold. Portage into the Past: By Canoe along the Minnesota-Ontario Boundary. LC 60-15895. (Illus.). 199p. reprint ed. pap. 61.70 (0-8357-3298-3, 203955400013) Bks Demand.

Bolz, Margaret, jt. auth. see Sevaly, Karen.

Bolz, Norbert & Van Reijen, Willem. Walter Benjamin. Mazzarins, Laimdota, tr. LC 95-9006. 128p. (C). 1996. pap. 12.50 (0-391-03942-3); text 39.95 (0-391-03941-5) Humanities.

***Bolz, Peter & Sanner, Hans-Ulrich.** Native American Art: The Collections of the Ethnological Museum Berlin. (Illus.). 240p. 2000. pap. 40.00 (0-295-97954-2) U of Wash Pr.

Bolz, Ray E. & Tuve, George L., eds. Handbook of Tables for Applied Engineering Science. 2nd ed. (Handbook Ser.). 1184p. 1973. boxed set 135.95 (0-8493-0252-8, TA) CRC Pr.

Bolz, Roger W. Production Processes: The Productivity Handbook. 5th ed. LC 81-6494. 1089p. 1981. 60.00 (0-8311-1088-0) Indus Pr.

Bolz, Roger W., jt. auth. see Tver, David F.

Bolza, Oskar. Lectures on the Calculus of Variations. 3rd ed. LC 73-16324. 14.95 (0-8284-0145-4) Chelsea Pub.

— Vorlesungen Ueber Variationsrechnung. LC 62-8228. (GER.). ix, 715p. (C). reprint ed. text 29.50 (0-8284-0160-8, 160) Chelsea Pub.

Bolza, Oskar, et al. Festschrift Schwarz. LC 73-20209. Orig. Title: Mathematische Abhandlungen. viii, 451p. 1974. reprint ed. text 25.00 (0-8284-0275-2) Chelsea Pub.

Bolzak, Jerry R., ed. see Sullivan, Gordon R.

Bolze, Dorene A. Alaskan Wildlife Species & Habitats That Are Sensitive to Offshore Oil & Gas Development. (Illus.). 47p. (Orig.). 1987. pap. text. write for info. (0-930698-25-8) Natl Audubon.

Bolzern, Mark, ed. see Poduska, Paul, et al.

Bolzern, Mark, ed. see Welsh, Matt, et al.

Bom, H. B., jt. auth. see Das, Arup K.

Bom, Hans M. & Zuiderwijk, Johan C., eds. Global Estate Planning: Practical Guide to the Principles of Estates, Inheritance, & Gift Taxes. LC 96-12263. 1996. ring bd. 205.00 (90-411-0754-1) Kluwer Law Intl.

Bom, Lee S. South Korea Environmental Report: A Resource for Business. LC 95-49406. (International Environemental Report Ser.). 284p. 1996. pap. text 495.00 (0-86587-508-1) Gov Insts.

Bom, N. Echocardiology. 1977. text 155.50 (90-247-2009-5) Kluwer Academic.

Bom, N. & Roelandt, Jos R., eds. Intravascular Ultrasound: Techniques, Developments, Clinical Perspectives. (C). 1989. text 106.00 (0-7923-0387-3) Kluwer Academic.

Bom, Philip C. The Coming Century of Commonism: The Beauty & the Beast of Global Governance. 400p. 1992. pap. text 13.95 (0-9632148-0-2) Policy Bks.

BOMA International Staff. The ADA Answer Book: Answers to the 146 Most Critical Questions about the ADA, Title III. unabridged ed. (Illus.). 82p. 1992. pap. 60.00 (0-614-31139-X, 072-WYNTK) Build Own & Man.

Boma Staff. Boma's Guide to Writing a Commercial Real Estate Lease. rev. ed. 140p. (C). 1994. pap. 140.00 (0-943130-08-5) Build Own & Man.

Boman, M., et al, eds. Multi-Agent Rationality: 8th European Workshop on Modelling Autonomous Agents in a Multi-Agent World, MAAMAW'97, Ronneby, Sweden, May 13-16, 1997, Proceedings. LC 97-14896. (Lecture Notes in Artificial Intelligence Ser.: No. 1237). xii, 254p. 1997. pap. 49.00 (3-540-63077-5) Spr-Verlag.

Boman, Magnus. Models, Concepts & Information. (International Series in Computer Science). 304p. 1997. pap. 52.00 (0-13-514879-0, Prentice Hall) P-H.

Boman, Magnus, jt. ed. see Garijo, Francisco J.

***Boman, Monica.** Helena Hernmarck: Tapestry Weaver. (Illus.). 128p. 1999. 40.00 (91-7988-172-6) Byggforlaget.

Bomani, Asake & Rooks, Belvie, eds. Paris Connections: African American Artists in Paris. Rand, Lydia & Timmons, Nellie, trs. LC 92-50057. (ENG & FRE., Illus.). 96p. 1992. pap. 30.00 (0-936609-25-7) QED Ft Bragg.

— Paris Connections: African & Caribbean Artists in Paris. Rand, Lydia, tr. LC 92-5235. (ENG & FRE., Illus.). 64p. 1992. pap. 14.95 (0-936609-26-5) QED Ft Bragg.

Bomani, Paul, jt. auth. see Ensminger, Douglas.

Bomann, Ann H. The Private Chapel in Ancient Egypt: A Study of the Chapels in the Workmen's Village a el Amarna with Special Reference to Deir el Medina & other Sites. 300p. 1990. 79.95 (0-7103-0346-7) Routledge.

***Bomann, Rebecca P.** Faith in the Barrios: The Pentecostal Poor in Bogota. LC 98-44958. 150p. 1999. lib. bdg. 37.00 (1-55587-827-X) L Rienner.

Bomans, Godfried. Eric in the Land of the Insects. Kornblith, Regina L., tr. from DUT. LC 93-24071. 208p. (J). 1994. 14.95 (0-395-65231-6) HM.

Bomar, Elaine M. Cooking with Mrs. Claus. (Illus.). 128p. 1998. pap., spiral bd. 8.95 (0-9658807-1-0, Pub. by Dragonfire) Partners Pubs Grp.

Bomar, George W., rev. Texas Weather. 2nd rev. ed. LC 93-48572. (Illus.). 288p. (C). 1994. pap. 21.95 (0-292-70811-4); text 37.50 (0-292-70810-6) U of Tex Pr.

Bomar, Perri J., ed. Nurses & Family Health Promotion: Concepts, Assessment & Interventions. 2nd ed. LC 95-19486. (Illus.). 429p. 1995. pap. text 38.95 (0-7216-3795-7, W B Saunders Co) Harcrt Hlth Sci Grp.

Bomar, Wayne. Chronicles of the Christmas Reindeer. Anders, Isabel, ed. (Illus.). 250p. (Orig.). 1996. pap. 14.95 (1-886371-51-2) Dragonfire.

Bomar, Wayne H. Chronicles of the Christmas Reindeer, Vol. 2. (Illus.). ix, 270p. (J). 1997. pap. 14.95 (0-9658807-0-2) Dragonfire.

Bomar, William T. Postal Markings of U. S. Expositions. 2nd ed. (Illus.). 300p. 1996. pap. 45.00 (1-880065-20-7) Machine Cancel Soc.

Bomar, Willie M. The Education of Homemakers for Community Activities. LC 78-176574. (Columbia University. Teachers College. Contributions to Education Ser.: No. 477). reprint ed. 37.50 (0-404-55477-6) AMS Pr.

Bomareto, LaMarr. Focus...for Life: Nine Steps to Wellness. LC 92-90205. 152p. 1990. 15.00 (0-9642747-0-1) L B Assocs.

***Bomba, Bernard.** Rags & Again Rags. 120p. 2000. pap. 12.00 (1-892657-14-7) Town Bk Pr.

Bomba, John G., ed. Pipeline Research Needs: Proceedings of the Workshop on Pipeline Needs; March 28-29, 1996, Held at the Lansdowne Resort & Conventionn Center, Leesburg, Virginia. LC 97-16680. 160p. 1997. 18.00 (0-7844-0246-9) Am Soc Civil Eng.

Bombal, Maria L. House of Mist & The Shrouded Woman: Novels by Maria Luisa Bombal. LC 94-27110. (Texas Pan American Ser.). 264p. 1995. pap. 19.95 (0-292-70830-0) U of Tex Pr.

— New Islands & Other Stories. Cunningham, Richard & Cunningham, Lucia, trs. from SPA. LC 88-47764. 112p. 1988. reprint ed. pap. text 10.95 (0-8014-9538-5) Cornell U Pr.

— La Ultima Niebla. (SPA.). 8.50 (0-8288-2554-8, S655) Fr & Eur.

Bombard, Brent, et al. Management & Supervision. 278p. (C). 1991. pap. text 35.42 (1-56226-060-X) CAT Pub.

Bombard, Richard J., jt. auth. see El-Kareh, Badid.

Bombarde, Odile. The Barbarians. LC 87-34092. (Illus.). 38p. (J). (gr. k-5). 1988. 5.95 (0-944589-10-3, 103) Young Discovery Lib.

Bombarde, Odile & Moatti, Claude. Living in Ancient Rome. Matthews, Sarah, tr. from FRE. LC 87-37113. (Illus.). 38p. (J). (gr. k-5). 1988. 5.95 (0-944589-08-1, 081) Young Discovery Lib.

Bombaugh, Ruth. Science Fair Success. expanded rev. ed. LC 98-3297. (Science Fair Success Ser.). 128p. (YA). (gr. 6 up). 1999. lib. bdg. 20.95 (0-7660-1163-1) Enslow Pubs.

Bombay, Cal. Let My People Go: The True Story of Present-Day Persecution & Slavery. LC 98-226464. 170p. 1998. pap. 12.99 (1-57673-459-5) Multnomah Pubs.

Bombeck, Erma. All I Know About Animal Behavior: Bombeck,&Erma, Set. abr. ed. 1995. audio 17.00 (0-694-51578-7, 393200, Pub. by HarperAudio) Lndmrk Audiobks.

Bombeck, Erma. All I Know about Animal Behavior I Learned in Loehmann's Dressing Room. large type ed. LC 95-50030. (Large Print Bks.). 1996. 25.95 (1-56895-285-6) Wheeler Pub.

— At Wit's End. 1986. mass mkt. 5.99 (0-449-21184-3, Crest) Fawcett.

— Aunt Erma's Cope Book. 1985. mass mkt. 5.99 (0-449-20937-7) Fawcett.

— Best of Bombeck. 544p. 1987. 11.99 (0-88365-721-X) Galahad Bks.

— Erma's Suburban Field Guide: A Four in One Collection Consisting of: The Grass Is Always... 624p. 1996. 11.98 (0-88365-959-X) Galahad Bks.

— Family, the Ties That Bind & Gag. 1988. mass mkt. 5.95 (0-449-21529-6, Crest) Fawcett.

***Bombeck, Erma.** Forever, Erma. 288p. 2000. 7.98 (1-56731-365-5, MJF Bks) Fine Comms.

Bombeck, Erma. Forever, Erma: Best-Loved Writing from America's Favorite Humorist. LC 98-119859. (Illus.). 273p. 1997. pap. 10.95 (0-8362-3673-4) Andrews & McMeel.

— The Grass Is Always Greener over the Septic Tank. 1985. mass mkt. 5.99 (0-449-20759-5, Crest) Fawcett.

— I Lost Everything in the PostNatal Depression. LC 84-106. 1986. mass mkt. 5.99 (0-449-21118-5, Crest) Fawcett.

— If Life Is a Bowl of Cherries, What Am I Doing in the Pits? 1985. mass mkt. 5.99 (0-449-20839-7) Fawcett.

— A Marriage Made in Heaven: Or Too Tired for an Affair. 304p. 1994. mass mkt. 6.99 (0-06-109202-9, Harp PBks) HarpC.

Bombeck, Erma. Marriage Made in Heaven--Or Too Tired to Have an Affair: Bombeck,&Erma. abr. ed. 1993. audio 18.00 (1-55994-741-1, CPN 2352) HarperAudio.

Bombeck, Erma. A Marriage Made in Heaven: or Too Tired for an Affair. large type ed. LC 93-39610. 1993. 24.95 (1-56895-024-1) Wheeler Pub.

— Motherhood: The Second Oldest Profession. 192p. 1987. mass mkt. 5.99 (0-440-15901-6) Dell.

— When You Look Like Your Passport Photo, It's Time to Go Home. 288p. 1992. mass mkt. 6.99 (0-06-109981-3, Harp PBks) HarpC.

Bombeck, Erma. When You look Like Your Passport Photo, It's Time to Go Home: Bombeck,&Erma, Set. 1994. audio 18.00 (0-694-51478-0) HarperAudio.

Bombeck, Erma & Keane, Bill. Just Wait till You Have Children of Your Own! 1985. mass mkt. 5.99 (0-449-20834-6, Crest) Fawcett.

Bombeck, Stefan. Das Althebraische Verbalsystem Aus Aramaischer Sicht: Masoretischer Text, Targume und Peschitta. (Europaische Hochschulschriften Ser.: Reihe 23, Bd. 591). (GER.). 251p. 1996. 51.95 (3-631-30674-1) P Lang Pubng.

Bombeli, Karin. Modern & Healthy Body Care: Recipes for Professional, Natural Skin & Hair Care Products. unabridged ed. Ansdell, Peter, ed. LC 97-92195. (Illus.). ix, 105p. (Orig.). 1997. pap. 19.90 (0-9658528-0-6, B01-97) Somerset Bks.

Bombelli, Renato. Structure & Function in Normal & Abnormal Hips: How to Rescue Mechanically Jeopardized Hips. 3rd enl. rev. ed. LC 93-18576. 1993. 298.00 (0-387-56266-4) Spr-Verlag.

— Structure & Function in Normal & Abnormal Hips: How to Rescue Mechanically Jeopardized Hips. 3rd rev. ed. (Illus.). 235p. 1993. write for info. (3-540-56266-4) Spr-Verlag.

Bomberg, Elizabeth E. Green Parties & Politics in the European Union. LC 97-30845. (Illus.). 240p. (C). 1998. 90.00 (0-415-10264-2); pap. 27.99 (0-415-10265-0) Routledge.

Bomberg, Elizabeth E., jt. auth. see Peterson, John.

Bomberg, Hy. Workflow-Workspace. 83p. 1986. pap. text 7.50 (0-936658-24-X) H Miller Res.

Bomberg, Hyman, jt. auth. see Petter, Constance.

Bomberg, Mark & Trechsel, Heinz R., eds. Water Vapor Transmission Through Building Materials & Systems: Mechanisms & Measurement. LC 89-34778. (Special Technical Publication Ser.: No. STP 1039). (Illus.). 180p. 1989. text 24.00 (0-8031-1254-8, STP1039) ASTM.

Bomberg, Mark T. & Lstiburek, Joseph W. Spray Polyurethane Foam in External Envelopes of Buildings. LC 98-86273. 344p. 1998. pap. text 89.95 (1-56676-707-5) Technomic.

Bomberger, Bruce, jt. auth. see Waddell, Louis M.

Bomberger, Bruce D. Preservation & Repair of Historic Log Buildings. 16p. 1992. pap. 1.00 (0-16-061647-6) USGPO.

Bomberger, E. Douglas, ed. Brainard's Biographies of American Musicians, 79. LC 99-22686. (Music Reference Collection: No. 79). 352p. 1999. lib. bdg. 85.00 (0-313-30782-2, Greenwood Pr) Greenwood.

Bomberger, Jane. Benny Gets a Bully-Ache. (Illus.). 40p. (J). (gr. 1-4). 1997. pap. 12.95 (0-9638152-4-5) Freedom Pubng.

— Benny's Coloring Book from A to Z. (Illus.). 32p. (J). (gr. 1-4). 1997. pap. 5.95 (0-9638152-5-3) Freedom Pubng.

Bomberger, Russell Z. The Right to Live. Gottshall, Dorothy B., ed. LC 89-90328. 104p. (Orig.). 1989. pap. 4.00 (0-9623880-0-9) Tussy B Zug Pubs.

Bombieri, E., ed. see Bochnak, J., et al.

Bombieri, E., ed. see Fulton, W.

Bombieri, E., jt. ed. see Turan, Paul.

Bombieri, Enrico. An Introduction to Minimal Currents & Parametric Variational Problems, Vol. 2. (Mathematical Reports: Vol. 2 Pt. 3). viii, 100p. 1985. text 82.00 (3-7186-0299-7) Gordon & Breach.

***Bomda, Justin.** Determinants de l'Epargne Et Du Credit, Et Leurs Implications Pour le Developpement Du Systeme Financier Rural Au Cameroun. Heidhues, Franz, ed. (Development Economics & Policy Ser.: Volume 10). (Illus.). XXXII, 215p. 1998. 48.95 (3-631-33688-8) P Lang Pubng.

Bomely, Steven B. In His Steps - The Stations of the Cross. 1991. pap. 3.95 (1-55673-286-4, 9119) CSS OH.

Bomer, John M. The Presence of Montaigne in the Lettres Persanes. LC 88-62882. (ENG & FRE.). 193p. 1989. lib. bdg. 26.95 (0-917786-68-8) Summa Pubns.

Bomer, Katherine, jt. auth. see Bomer, Randy.

Bomer, Norm. Willow. LC 97-39857. (Illus.). 32p. (J). (ps-3). 1998. 14.99 (0-8010-4362-X) Baker Bks.

Bomer, Randy. Time for Meaning: Crafting Literate Lives in Middle & High School. LC 95-12089. 234p. 1995. pap. text 25.00 (0-435-08849-1, 08849) Heinemann.

***Bomer, Randy & Bomer, Katherine.** Reading & Writing for Social Action. 2000. pap. text. write for info. (0-325-00263-0, Pub. by Boynton Cook Pubs) Heinemann.

Bomers, Gerald B. & Peterson, Richard B. Conflict Management & Industrial Relations. 1982. lib. bdg. 97.50 (0-89838-068-5) Kluwer Academic.

Bomford, C. K., et al. Walter & Miller's Textbook of Radiotherapy: Radiation Physics, Therapy & Oncology. 5th ed. LC 92-48182. 624p. 1993. pap. text 88.00 (0-443-02873-7) Church.

Bomford, David. Colour. (Illus.). 80p. 1999. pap. text 10.00 (0-300-07922-2) Yale U Pr.

— Conservation of Paintings. LC 97-67665. (National Gallery Pocket Guides Ser.). 80p. 1997. pap. text 10.00 (0-300-07318-6) Yale U Pr.

Bomford, David & Finaldi, Gabriele. Venice Through Canaletto's Eyes. LC 98-66511. (Illus.). 64p. 1998. pap. 16.00 (0-300-07696-7) Yale U Pr.

Bomford, David, et al. Impressionism: Art in the Making. (Illus.). 215p. (Orig.). (C). 1991. 65.00 (0-300-05035-6); pap. 30.00 (0-300-05036-4) Yale U Pr.

Bomford, David, jt. auth. see Whistler, Catherine.

Bomford, Janette. That Dangerous & Persuasive Woman: Vida Goldstein. 208p. 1994. pap. 29.95 (0-522-84542-8) J M Bomford.

***Bomford, Rodney.** The Symmetry of God. 200p. 1999. 55.00 (1-85343-437-X); pap. 25.00 (1-85343-438-8) Free Assoc Bks.

Bomhard, Alan R. Toward Proto-Nostratic: A New Approach to the Comparison of Proto-Indo-European & Proto-Afroasiatic. (Current Issues in Linguistic Theory Ser.: Vol. 27). xi, 356p. 1984. 71.00 (90-272-3519-8) J Benjamins Pubng Co.

Bomhard, Allan R. Indo-European & the Nostratic Hypothesis. (Studia Nostratica Ser.: Vol. 1). (Illus.). v, 265p. (Orig.). (C). 1996. pap. text 30.00 (0-9652294-0-8) Signum Desktop.

Bomhard, Allan R. & Kerns, John C. The Nostratic Macrofamily: A Study in Distant Linguistic Relationship. LC 93-45587. (Trends in Linguistics, Studies & Monographs: No. 74). xii, 932p. (C). 1994. lib. bdg. 229.25 (3-11-013900-6) Mouton.

Bomhard, Allan R., jt. ed. see Arbeitman, Yoel L.

Bomhoff. Financial Forecasting For Business & Economics. 1998. pap. 32.95 (1-86152-423-4) Thomson Learn.

Bomhoff, Eduard J. Financial Forecasting for Business & Economics. 224p. 1995. pap. text 34.95 (0-12-112890-3) Acad Pr.

Bomm, Jack & Bomm, Nancy. Roseville: In All Its Splendor with Price Guide. LC 99-167651. (Illus.). 424p. 1998. 39.95 (0-89538-095-1) L-W Inc.

Bomm, Marian D. Beyond Prison Walls: From the Terror of War to Triumph in Service. (Illus.). 151p. (Orig.). 1987. pap. text 8.95 (1-888796-04-9) ABWE Pubng.

Bomm, Nancy, jt. auth. see Bomm, Jack.

Bomm, Urbanus. Der Wechsel der Modalitatsbestimmungen. 197p. 1975. reprint ed. 40.00 (3-487-05716-6) G Olms Pubs.

Bommarito, James W., jt. auth. see Johnson, Orval G.

Bommarito, Patricia S. & Ramsey, James L. What about Mom & Dad? Leader's Guide. 95p. (Orig.). 1988. pap. 49.95 (0-941697-02-9) ABT Inc.

— What about Mom & Dad? Participant. 75p. (Orig.). 1988. pap. 10.95 (0-941697-03-7) ABT Inc.

Bommer, Allan, jt. auth. see Aalam, Bryan O.

Bommer, Michael R. & Chorba, Ronald W. Decision Making for Library Management. LC 81-17160. (Professional Librarian Ser.). 178p. 1982. 35.00 (0-86729-000-5, Hall Reference) Macmillan.

An Asterisk (*) at the beginning of an entry indicates that the title is appearing for the first time.

Bommer, Rolf. Economic Integration & the Environment: A Political-Economic Perspective. LC 98-17087. (New Horizons in Environmental Economics Ser.). 192p. 1998. 75.00 (*1-85898-912-4*) E Elgar.

Bommer, William, jt. auth. see Vecchio, Robert P.

***Bommes, Michael & Geddes, Andrew.** Immigration & Welfare: Challenging the Borders of the Welfare State. LC 00-42468. 2000. write for info. (*0-415-22372-5*) Routledge.

Bommino, Antonietta. I Send You Your Angel Gabriel: A Family's Journey Through Faith. Embree, Mary, ed. 163p. 1998. 16.95 (*0-9664510-0-7*) GA Press.

Bompa, Tudor. Periodization Training for Sports. LC 98-48169. (Illus.). 248p. 1999. pap. 19.95 (*0-88011-840-7*, PBOM0840) Human Kinetics.

***Bompa, Tudor.** Total Training for Young Champions. LC 99-46655. (Illus.). 224p. 1999. pap. 19.95 (*0-7360-0212-X*, PBOM0212) Human Kinetics.

Bompa, Tudor O. Periodization: Theory & Methodology of Training. 4th rev. ed. LC 98-54460. (Illus.). 424p. 1999. pap. 33.00 (*0-88011-851-2*, PBOM0851) Human Kinetics.

— Power Training for Sport: Plyometrics for Maximum Power Development. rev. ed. LC 96-932270. 1998. pap. 14.95 (*0-88962-629-4*) Mosaic.

Bompa, Tudor O. & Cornacchia, Lorenzo J. Serious Strength Training. LC 98-12309. (Illus.). 312p. 1998. pap. 19.95 (*0-88011-834-2*, PBOM0834) Human Kinetics.

Bompas, Cecil H., tr. see Dorson, Richard M.

Bompey, Stuart H., et al. Wrongful Termination Claims: A Preventive Approach. 765p. 1991. text 40.00 (*0-87224-014-2*, H1-3000) PLI.

Bompiani. Diccionario de Autores Bompiani, 5 vols., Set. (SPA.). 3122p. 1988. 395.00 (*0-7859-3371-9*, 8485950534) Fr & Eur.

Bompiani, Valentino. Diccionario De Autores Bompiani, Vol. 1. (SPA.). 630p. 1987. 80.00 (*0-7859-6383-9*, 8485950542) Fr & Eur.

— Diccionario De Autores Bompiani, Vol. 2. (SPA.). 612p. 1988. 80.00 (*0-7859-6384-7*, 8485950550) Fr & Eur.

— Diccionario De Autores Bompiani, Vol. 3. (SPA.). 624p. 1988. 80.00 (*0-7859-6385-5*, 8485950569) Fr & Eur.

— Diccionario De Autores Bompiani, Vol. 4. (SPA.). 620p. 1988. 80.00 (*0-7859-6386-3*, 8485950577) Fr & Eur.

— Diccionario De Autores Bompiani, Vol. 5. 636p. 1988. 80.00 (*0-7859-6387-1*, 8485950585) Fr & Eur.

— Diccionario Literario Obras Personajes Bompiani, 12 vols., Set. (SPA.). 1987. 2795.00 (*0-7859-6369-3*, 8485950356) Fr & Eur.

— Diccionario Literario Obras Personajes Bompiani, Vol. 1. (SPA.). 585p. 1987. 195.00 (*0-7859-6370-7*, 8485950364) Fr & Eur.

— Diccionario Literario Obras Personajes Bompiani, Vol. 2. (SPA.). 920p. 1987. 195.00 (*0-7859-6371-5*, 8485950372) Fr & Eur.

— Diccionario Literario Obras Personajes Bompiani, Vol. 3. (SPA.). 944p. 1987. 195.00 (*0-7859-6372-3*, 8485950380) Fr & Eur.

— Diccionario Literario Obras Personajes Bompiani, Vol. 4. (SPA.). 976p. 1987. 195.00 (*0-7859-6373-1*, 8485950399) Fr & Eur.

— Diccionario Literario Obras Personajes Bompiani, Vol. 5. (SPA.). 1987. 195.00 (*0-7859-6374-X*) Fr & Eur.

— Diccionario Literario Obras Personajes Bompiani, Vol. 6. (SPA.). 920p. 1987. 195.00 (*0-7859-6375-8*, 8485950410) Fr & Eur.

— Diccionario Literario Obras Personajes Bompiani, Vol. 7. (SPA.). 960p. 1987. 195.00 (*0-7859-6376-6*, 8485950429) Fr & Eur.

— Diccionario Literario Obras Personajes Bompiani, Vol. 8. (SPA.). 790p. 1987. 195.00 (*0-7859-6377-4*, 8485950437) Fr & Eur.

— Diccionario Literario Obras Personajes Bompiani, Vol. 9. (SPA.). 888p. 1987. 195.00 (*0-7859-6378-2*, 8485950445) Fr & Eur.

— Diccionario Literario Obras Personajes Bompiani, Vol. 10. (SPA.). 840p. 1987. 195.00 (*0-7859-6379-0*, 8485950453) Fr & Eur.

— Diccionario Literario Obras Personajes Bompiani, Vol. 11. (SPA.). 1987. 195.00 (*0-7859-6380-4*, 8485950461) Fr & Eur.

— Diccionario Literario Obras Personajes Bompiani, Vol. 12. (SPA.). 648p. 1987. 195.00 (*0-7859-6501-7*) Fr & Eur.

— Diccionario Literario Obras Personajes Bompiani, Appendix 1. (SPA.). 776p. 1987. 195.00 (*0-7859-6381-2*, 8485950488) Fr & Eur.

— Diccionario Literario Obras Personajes Bompiani, Appendix 2. (SPA.). 792p. 1987. 195.00 (*0-7859-6382-0*, 8485950496) Fr & Eur.

— Diccionario Literario Obras Personajes Bompiani, Appendix 3. (SPA.). 550p. 1989. 195.00 (*0-7859-6389-8*, 8485950607) Fr & Eur.

Bompiani, Valentino, jt. auth. see Laffont, Robert.

Bompois, H. F. Examen Chronologique des Monnais Frappes par la Communaute des Macedoniens Avant, Pendant et Apes la Conquete Romaine. (FRE., Illus.). 102p. 1980. 20.00 (*0-916710-77-7*) Obol Intl.

Bompois, Michelle, tr. see Baul, Lee K.

Bomse, Marguerite D. Practical Spanish Dictionary & Phrasebook. (SPA.). 1978. pap. text 18.00 (*0-08-023020-2*, Pergamon Pr) Elsevier.

— Practical Spanish Grammar. 1978. pap. text 18.00 (*0-08-021859-8*, Pergamon Pr) Elsevier.

Bomse, Marguerite D. & Alfaro, Julian H. Practical Spanish for Medical & Hospital Personnel. 2nd ed. 1978. pap. text 16.00 (*0-08-023001-6*, Pergamon Pr) Elsevier.

— Practical Spanish for School Personnel, Firemen, Policemen & Community Agencies. 2nd ed. 1978. pap. text 16.00 (*0-08-023002-4*, Pergamon Pr) Elsevier.

Bomze, Henry D. Txt/fly Pro Digitals Pc: Basic. (C). 1984. pap. text 2.00 (*0-03-069427-2*) Harcourt Coll Pubs.

Bomze, Immanuel M. A Functional Analytic Approach to Statistical Experiments. LC 90-6105. (Pitman Research Notes in Mathematics Ser.: Vol. 237). 128p. 1990. reprint ed. pap. 39.70 (*0-608-03604-8*, 206442700009) Bks Demand.

Bomze, Immanuel M., ed. Developments in Global Optimization. LC 96-49521. (Nonconvex Optimization & Its Applications Ser.). 360p. (C). 1997. text 160.50 (*0-7923-4351-4*) Kluwer Academic.

Bomzon, Arieh & Blendis, Laurence M., eds. Cardiovascular Complications of Liver Disease. 384p. 1990. lib. bdg. 202.00 (*0-8493-4735-1*, RC848) CRC Pr.

Bon, jt. auth. see Bien.

***Bon Appetit Editors.** Bon Appetit: Outdoor Entertaining. (Illus.). 192p. 2000. 29.95 (*0-375-40767-7*) Pantheon.

Bon Appetit Editors. Bon Appetit Holidays. LC 97-173644. 160p. 1998. 29.95 (*0-679-44278-2*) Knopf.

— Bon Appetit Weekend Entertaining. LC 98-209954. (Illus.). 192p. 1999. 29.95 (*0-375-40250-0*) Pantheon.

— Flavors of Bon Appetite, Vol. 4. 224p. 1997. 27.50 (*0-679-44277-4*) Pantheon.

Bon Appetit Magazine Editorial Staff. Bon Appetit Christmas: Entertaining, Holiday Baking, Gifts from the Kitchen. LC 95-14877. 1995. 27.50 (*0-679-43977-3*) Pantheon.

Bon Appetit Magazine Editorial Staff. Bon Appetit 30-Minute Main Courses: Over 200 Simple & Sophisticated Recipes. 1996. 25.00 (*0-679-44220-0*) Pantheon.

Bon Appetit Magazine Editorial Staff. The Flavors of Bon Appetit. (Illus.). 224p. 1994. 27.50 (*0-679-43960-9*) Pantheon.

— The Flavors of Bon Appetit, Vol. 2. (Bon Appetit Ser.). (Illus.). 224p. 1995. 25.00 (*0-679-43994-3*) Pantheon.

— The Flavors of Bon Appetit Vol. 3: Featuring the Best Recipes for Entertaining Friends & Family Throughout the Year, Vol. 3. (Illus.). 224p. 1996. 25.00 (*0-679-44236-7*) Pantheon.

***Bon Appetit Staff.** The Flavors of Bon Appetit 2000. LC 99-89040. (Illus.). 224p. 2000. 29.95 (*0-609-60714-6*) C Potter.

***Bon Appetit Staff, ed.** Bon Appetit the Christmas Season. (Illus.). 224p. 2000. 29.95 (*0-609-60725-1*) C Potter.

— The Flavors of Bon Appetit, Vol. 6. 224p. 1999. 29.95 (*0-375-40628-X*) Pantheon.

Bon Appetit Staff & Mitchell, Carolyn B. Bon Appetite Entertaining with Style. 1997. 27.50 (*0-679-44268-5*) Pantheon.

Bon Appetite Magazine Editorial Staff. Bon Appetite Christmas. 1996. 27.50 (*0-676-51792-7*) Pantheon.

Bon, Gustav Le, see Le Bon, Gustav.

Bon, Gustave Le, see Le Bon, Gustave.

Bon Jovi, Jon. These Days. 96p. 1996. pap. 16.95 (*0-7935-5943-X*) H Leonard.

Bon, Leo Le, see Le Bon, Leo.

Bon, Marcel. Cortinarius. (Fungorum Rariorum Icones Coloratae Ser.: Pars XV). (FRE., Illus.). 25p. 1986. pap. 27.00 (*3-443-69001-7*, Pub. by Gebruder Borntraeger) Balogh.

— Pareys Buch der Pilze (Parey's Book of Mushroom) (Illus.). 362p. 1988. pap. 22.00 (*3-8263-8169-6*, Pub. by Blckwell Wissenschafts) Balogh.

Bon, Ottaviano. The Sultan's Seraglio: An Intimate Portrait of Life at the Ottoman Court. LC 96-148430. 160p. 1996. 39.95 (*0-86356-215-9*) Intl Spec Bk.

Bon, Pilar O. & Sola, Jorge. Se Esta Divorciando Sin Saberlo. Editorial Concepts Staff, ed. (SPA.). 152p. 1985. pap. 4.95 (*0-939193-07-8*) Edit Concepts.

***Bon, Ranko.** Economic Structure & Maturity: Collected Papers in Input-Output Modelling & Applications. 392p. 2000. text 83.95 (*1-84014-543-9*, Pub. by Ashgate Pub) Ashgate Pub Co.

Bon, Roger L. Large Mine Permits & Plants in Utah. (Public Information Ser.: 33). (Illus.). 1996. pap. 2.70 (*1-55791-372-2*, PI33) Utah Geological Survey.

Bon, Roger L., et al. 1996 Summary of Mineral Activity in Utah. LC 97-199806. (Circular of the Utah Geological Survey Ser.: Vol. 98). (Illus.). 12p. 1997. pap. 3.40 (*1-55791-610-1*, C-98) Utah Geological Survey.

— Utah Mineral Activity Summary for 1995. (Circular of the Utah Geological Survey Ser.: Vol. 91). (Illus.). 15p. (Orig.). 1996. pap. 4.60 (*1-55791-377-3*, C91) Utah Geological Survey.

Bon Vivant Press Staff, jt. auth. see Fish, Kathleen D.

Bon Vokal, Debi. Suburban Saints: New Religious Icons for Everyday Secular Lives. (Illus.). 208p. 2000. pap. 16.95 (*0-9672304-1-1*) Chrome Deco.

Bona & Barlett. Tibet. (C). 1981. 180.00 (*0-7855-7576-6*) St Mut.

Bona, Constantin A. Biological Applications of Anti-Idiotypes, 2 vols., Vol. I. 224p. 1988. 120.00 (*0-8493-6941-X*, QR186, CRC Reprint) Franklin.

— Biological Applications of Anti-Idiotypes, 2 vols., Vol. II. 224p. 1988. 114.00 (*0-8493-6942-8*, QR186, CRC Reprint) Franklin.

— Immunology for Medical Students. x, 250p. 1990. text 147.00 (*3-7186-0507-4*, Harwood Acad Pubs); pap. text 64.00 (*3-7186-0508-2*, Harwood Acad Pubs) Gordon & Breach.

— Textbook of Immunology. 2nd ed. LC 99-461715. 300p. 1996. text 52.00 (*3-7186-0596-1*, Harwood Acad Pubs); pap. text 18.00 (*3-7186-0597-X*, Harwood Acad Pubs) Gordon & Breach.

Bona, Constantin A., et al, eds. The Molecular Pathology of Autoimmune Disease. LC 92-49272. 795p. 1993. text 234.00 (*3-7186-0555-4*) Gordon & Breach.

Bona, Damien. Opening Shots: The Unusual, Unexpected, Potentially Career-Threatening First Roles That Launched the Careers of 70 Hollywood Stars. LC 93-21493. (Illus.). 288p. (Orig.). 1994. pap. 11.95 (*1-56305-279-2*, 3279) Workman Pub.

— Starring John Wayne As Genghis Khan: Hollywood's All-Time Worst Casting Blunders. LC 95-48048. (Illus.). 192p. 1996. pap. 12.95 (*0-8065-1797-2*, Citadel Pr) Carol Pub Group.

Bona, Damien, jt. auth. see Wiley, Mason.

Bona, Damien. Starring Demi Moore As Hester Prynne: Hollywood's All-Time Worst Casting Bounders. LC 95-48047. (Illus.). 192p. 1996. pap. 12.95 (*0-8065-1802-2*, Citadel Pr) Carol Pub Group.

Bona, Dominique. Argentina. (FRE.). 374p. 1986. pap. 12.95 (*0-7859-2034-X*, 2070377342) Fr & Eur.

Bona, E., et al. Future Research in Hungary. 383p. (C). 1983. 75.00 (*963-05-3475-4*, Pub. by Akade Kiado) St Mut.

Bona, Gabor, ed. The Hungarian Revolution & War of Independence, 1848-1849: A Military History. 700p. 1999. 81.00 (*0-88033-433-9*, 535, Pub. by East Eur Monographs) Col U Pr.

Bona, Giovanni. Guidance to Heaven. 195p. 1995. pap. 8.00 (*0-89555-520-4*) TAN Bks Pubs.

Bona, J. L., et al, eds. Dynamical Problems in Continuum Physics. (IMA Volumes in Mathematics & Its Applications Ser.: Vol. 4). (Illus.). 325p. 1986. 59.95 (*0-387-96463-0*) Spr-Verlag.

***Bona, Jerry, et al, eds.** Nonlinear PDE's, Dynamics & Continuum Physics. (CONM Ser.: Vol. 255). 264p. 2000. 65.00 (*0-8218-1052-9*) Am Math.

Bona, Luke Dalla, see Carlson, Roy & Dalla Bona, Luke, eds.

Bona, M. An Introduction to Wool Fabric Finishing. 1994. pap. 72.00 (*1-870812-59-X*, Pub. by Textile Inst) St Mut.

— Modern Control Techniques in Textile Finishing & Making-Up. 1990. pap. 42.00 (*0-7855-2810-5*, Pub. by Textile Inst) St Mut.

— Statistical Methods for the Textile Industry. 1993. pap. 81.00 (*1-870812-57-3*, Pub. by Textile Inst) St Mut.

— Textile Quality. 1994. pap. 110.00 (*1-870812-60-3*, Pub. by Textile Inst) St Mut.

***Bona, Mary J.** Claiming a Tradition: Italian American Women Writers. LC 99-21410. (Feminam - Women & Literature Ser.). 224p. 2000. 39.95 (*0-8093-2258-7*) S Ill U Pr.

Bona, Mary J. & Tamburri, Anthony J., eds. Through the Looking Glass: Italian & Italian/American Images in the Media: Selected Essays for the 27th Annual Conference of the American Italian Historical Association, 10-12 November 1994, Chicago, Illinois. LC 96-3654. 1996. write for info. (*0-934675-36-8*); pap. write for info. (*0-934675-35-X*) Am Italian.

Bona, Mary J., et al. Taking Parts: Ingredients for Leadership, Participation, & Empowerment. Buker, Eloise A. et al, eds. LC 93-45519. 284p. (Orig.). (C). 1994. pap. text 34.00 (*0-8191-9397-6*) U Pr of Amer.

Bona, Mary Jo, ed. The Voices We Carry: Recent Italian-American Women's Fiction. 376p. 1994. pap. 18.00 (*0-920717-84-5*) Guernica Editions.

Bona, P. Rhythmical Articulation: Complete Vocal Method. 76p. 1986. pap. 8.95 (*0-7935-0501-1*) H Leonard.

Bonabeau, Eric, et al. From Natural to Artificial Swarm Intelligence. LC 98-49821. (Santa Fe Institute Studies on the Sciences of Complexity). (Illus.). 320p. 1999. 65.00 (*0-19-513158-4*); pap. 29.95 (*0-19-513159-2*) OUP.

***Bonac, V. A.** Communicative Psychoanalysis with Children, 1. 1999. pap. text 19.95 (*1-86156-142-3*) Whurr Pub.

Bonaca, Jeanne R., tr. see Fabbri, Marcello.

Bonacci, Mary B. Real Love: The Ultimate Dating, Marriage & Sex Question Book. LC 96-76165. 322p. 1996. pap. text 12.95 (*0-89870-613-0*) Ignatius Pr.

— We're on a Mission from God: The Generation X Guide to John Paul II & the Real Meaning of Life. LC 95-78279. 216p. (Orig.). 1996. pap. 11.95 (*0-89870-567-3*) Ignatius Pr.

Bonacci, Nick. Aircraft Sheet Metal. LC 92-24394. (Illus.). 130p. (C). 1987. pap. 18.65 (*0-89100-296-0*, JS312633) Jeppesen Sanderson.

Bonacci, O. Karst Hydrology. (Physical Environment Ser.: Vol. 2). (Illus.). 210p. 1987. 120.95 (*0-387-18105-9*) Spr-Verlag.

Bonaccini, Domenico & Tyson, Robert K., eds. Adaptive Optical System Technologies. (Proceedings of SPIE Ser.: Vol. 3353). 1264p. 1998. 166.00 (*0-8194-2800-0*) SPIE.

***Bonaccorso, Frank J.** Bats of Papua New Guinea. (Illus.). 2000. pap. 40.00 (*1-881173-26-7*, Pub. by Conser Intl) U Ch Pr.

Bonachea, Ramon L. & Martin, Marta S. The Cuban Insurrection, 1952-1959. LC 72-94546. 450p. 1995. pap. 29.95 (*0-87855-576-5*) Transaction Pubs.

Bonacic-Koutecky, Vlasta, jt. auth. see Michl, Josef.

***Bonacich, E.** Capitalism & Racism. 275p. 2000. text 55.00 (*0-8133-2455-6*); pap. text 16.95 (*0-8133-2456-4*) Westview.

***Bonacich, Edna.** Behind the Label: Exploitation in the Los Angeles Apparel industry. LC 99-88415. (Illus.). 424p. 2000. pap. text 19.95 (*0-520-22506-6*, Pub. by U CA Pr) Cal Prin Full Svc.

— Behind the Label; Expolitation in the Los Angeles Apparel Industry. LC 99-88415. (Illus.). 424p. 2000. 50.00 (*0-520-21769-1*, Pub. by U CA Pr) Cal Prin Full Svc.

Bonacich, Edna, et al, eds. Global Production: The Apparel Industry in the Pacific Rim. LC 93-36974. (C). 1994. text 69.95 (*1-56639-168-7*) Temple U Pr.

— The New Asian Immigration in Los Angeles & Global Restructuring. LC 93-49863. (Asian American History & Culture Ser.). 336p. (C). 1994. text 69.95 (*1-56639-217-9*); pap. text 24.95 (*1-56639-218-7*) Temple U Pr.

Bonacich, Edna, jt. auth. see Light, Ivan H.

Bonacina, Conrad M., tr. see Von Lefort, Gertrud F.

Bonacker, Wilhelm. Karten-Woerterbuch. fac. ed. (GER.). 276p. 1971. 39.95 (*0-8288-6541-8*, M7493) Fr & Eur.

Bonacorda, Karen, ed. see Faragasso, Jack.

Bonacuse, Peter J., jt. ed. see Kalluri, Sreeramesh.

Bonadeo, Alfredo. D'Annunzio & the Great War. LC 94-33728. (Illus.). 176p. 1995. 32.50 (*0-8386-3587-3*) Fairleigh Dickinson.

— Mark of the Beast: Death & Degradation in the Literature of the Great War. LC 88-27645. 184p. 1989. 24.95 (*0-8131-1680-5*) U Pr of Ky.

Bonadies, John & Boudreau, Michael. DesignTutor: Typographic Primer. 1996. write for info. incl. disk (*1-55923-023-1*) Wicklow Ltd.

Bonadies, Michael. Sip by Sip: An Insider's Guide to Learning All about Wine. LC 98-16924. (Illus.). 224p. 1998. pap. 12.95 (*0-385-48750-9*) Doubleday.

Bonadio, Felice A. A. P. Giannini: Banker of America. LC 93-25768. (C). 1995. 40.00 (*0-520-08249-4*, Pub. by U CA Pr) Cal Prin Full Svc.

Bonadio, George R. Air Pollutants: Medical Subject Analysis with Bibliography. LC 87-47919. 150p. 1987. 39.50 (*0-88164-520-6*); pap. 34.50 (*0-88164-521-4*) ABBE Pubs Assn.

— Air Pollution of Humans with Bacteria, Fungus & Molds in Homes, Offices & Hospitals: Index of New Information with Authors & Subjects. rev. ed. 157p. 1995. 47.50 (*0-7883-0404-6*); pap. 44.50 (*0-7883-0405-4*) ABBE Pubs Assn.

— Fires: Index of Modern Information. rev. ed. LC 88-47562. 150p. 1991. 47.50 (*1-55914-488-2*); pap. 44.50 (*1-55914-489-0*) ABBE Pubs Assn.

***Bonadio, William.** Julia's Mother: Life Lessons in the Pediatric Emergency Room. LC 99-86893. 192p. 2000. text 22.95 (*0-312-25251-X*) St Martin.

Bonadles, John & Boudreau, Michael. Design Tutor User's Guide: For MacIntosh. 10p. (C). 1996. pap. text 26.95 (*1-55934-023-1*, 1023) Mayfield Pub.

Bonadonna, Gianni, ed. Breast Cancer, Diagnosis & Management. LC 83-6898. (Wiley Series on Cancer Investigation & Management: No. 1). 359p. reprint ed. pap. 111.30 (*0-8357-3468-4*, 203973000013) Bks Demand.

Bonadonna, Gianni, et al. Textbook of Breast Cancer: A Clinical Guide to Therapy. 368p. 1998. write for info. (*1-85317-348-7*) Martin Dunitz.

Bonafe, J. L. Dictionary of Pediatric Dermatology: Dictionnaire de Dermatologie Pediatrique. (ENG & FRE.). 1985. 175.00 (*0-8288-1790-1*, M15583) Fr & Eur.

Bonaffini, Luigi, ed. see Italian Poetry in Translation Staff.

Bonaffini, Luigi, tr. see Campana, Dino.

Bonaffini, Luigi, tr. see Cirese, Eugenio.

Bonaffini, Luigi, tr. see Jovine, Giuseppe.

Bonaffini, Luigi, tr. see Luzi, Mario.

Bonaffini, Luigi, tr. see Pierro, Albino.

Bonaffini, Luigi, tr. see Rimanelli, Giose.

Bonaffini, Luigi, tr. see Rimanelli, Giose & Serrao, Achille.

Bonaffini, Luigi, tr. see Sereni, Vittorio.

Bonaffini, Luigi, tr. see Serrao, Achille.

Bonafoux, Luis. Literatura de Bonafoux. Giron, Socorro, ed. LC 89-38004. (Coleccion Puertorriquena Ser.). 325p. (Orig.). 1990. pap. 10.95 (*0-8477-3642-3*) U of PR Pr.

Bonafoux, Pascal. Rembrandt: Master of the Portrait. Campbell, Alexandra, tr. (Discoveries Ser.). (Illus.). 176p. 1992. pap. 12.95 (*0-8109-2813-2*, Pub. by Abrams) Time Warner.

— Van Gogh: The Passionate Eye. (Discoveries Ser.). (Illus.). 176p. 1992. pap. 12.95 (*0-8109-2828-0*, Pub. by Abrams) Time Warner.

— A Weekend with Rembrandt. LC 91-40507. (Weekend with...Ser.). (Illus.). 64p. (J). (gr. 1-6). 1992. 19.95 (*0-8478-1441-6*, Pub. by Rizzoli Intl) St Martin.

Bonagura, John D. Kirk's Current Veterinary Therapy No. XII: Small Animal Practice. 12th ed. (Illus.). 1632p. 1995. text 92.00 (*0-7216-5188-7*, W B Saunders Co) Harcrt Hlth Sci Grp.

***Bonagura, John D.** Kirk's Current Veterinary Therapy XII: Small Animal Practice. Kersey, Ray, ed. (Illus.). 1435p. 1999. text 85.00 (*0-7216-5523-8*, W B Saunders Co) Harcrt Hlth Sci Grp.

***Bonair-Agard, Roger, et al.** Burning down the House: Selected Poems from the Nuyorican Poets Cafe National Poetry Slam Champions. 200p. 2000. pap. 13.50 (*1-887128-48-4*) Soft Skull Pr.

Bonaiuti, Andrea. A Critical & Historical Corpus of Florentine Painting Section IV: Richard Offneri, Vol. VI. LC 58-15756. 1979. 180.00 (*0-685-71939-1*) J J Augustin.

Bonal, Denise. Family Portrait. Johns, Timothy, tr. from FRE. (New French Plays Ser.). 110p. (Orig.). 1992. reprint ed. pap. 7.95 (*0-913745-36-7*) Ubu Repertory.

Bonal, Denise, et al. Plays by Women Vol. 3: An International Anthology, Vol. III. Kourilsky, Francoise, ed. MacDougall, Jill et al, trs. 440p. (Orig.). 1996. pap. 19.95 (*0-913745-46-4*) Ubu Repertory.

***Bonal, J.** Variable Speed Electric Drives Vol. 1: Reminders of Electrical & Mechanical Theory, Methods of Speed Control. (Illus.). 424p. 2000. pap. 89.00 (*1-898298-66-1*, Pub. by Intercept UK) Spr-Verlag.

***Bonal, J. & Seguier, G.** Variable Speed Electric Drives Vol. 2: Reminders on Power & Control Electronics. Electronics Variable Speed Drives. (Illus.). 462p. 2000. 89.00 (*1-898298-69-6*, Pub. by Intercept UK) Spr-Verlag.

Bonal, Jean. Methode de Guitare Jazz. Lefferts, Michael, ed. (FRE.). 72p. (Orig.). (C). 1997. pap. text 40.95 incl. audio compact disk (*0-7692-1321-9*, 01010314) Wrner Bros.

B

Bonald, Louis De, see De Bonald, Louis.

Bonaldo, Nadia. The Birthday of Baby Jesus. Wickenhiser, Mary D., tr. (Illus.). 16p. (Orig.). (J). (gr. 1-4). 1995. pap. 4.95 (*0-8198-1146-7*) Pauline Bks.

— My First Communion: A Day to Remember. Alampi, Janet & Alampi, Frank, trs. from ITA. (Illus.). 114p. (J). (gr. 2). 1993. reprint ed. 14.95 (*0-8198-4770-4*) Pauline Bks.

Bonami, Francesco, ed. Echoes: Contemporary Art at the Age of Endless Conclusions. LC 96-24487. (Illus.). 256p. 1996. pap. 35.00 (*1-885254-36-9*, Pub. by Monacelli Pr) Penguin Putnam.

Bonamy, David. English Tecnical Student. 1985. pap. text 6.95 (*0-582-74885-2*) Longman.

Bonanate, Luigi. Ethics & International Politics. Kegley, Charles W. & Puchala, Donald J., eds. Irving, John, tr. from ITA. LC 95-13017. (Studies in International Relations).Tr. of Etica e Politica Internazionale. 198p. 1995. text 49.95 (*1-57003-076-6*) U of SC Pr.

Bonander, Jane. Dancing on Snowflakes. Tolley, Carolyn, ed. 352p. (Orig.). 1995. mass mkt. 5.50 (*0-671-50110-0*) PB.

— Scent of Lilacs. 1984. per. 1.50 (*0-671-00916-8*) PB.

— Warrior Heart. 1997. per. 5.99 (*0-671-52981-1*, Pocket Books) PB.

— Wild Heart. 1995. mass mkt. 5.99 (*0-671-52983-8*) PB.

— Winter Heart. 303p. 1996. mass mkt. 5.99 (*0-671-52982-X*, PB Trade Paper) PB.

Bonander, Jane, et al. Avon Books Presents: A Christmas Together. 400p. (Orig.). 1994. mass mkt. 4.99 (*0-380-77740-1*, Avon Bks) Morrow Avon.

— Avon Books Presents: To Have & to Hold. 368p. (Orig.). 1994. mass mkt. 4.99 (*0-380-77691-X*, Avon Bks) Morrow Avon.

***Bonann, Gregory J.** Baywatch: Rescued from Prime Time. (Illus.). 2000. 27.95 (*1-893224-09-0*, New Millenn Pr) New Millenn Enter.

Bonanni. Falcon 4.0. LC 97-69342. 1998. 19.99 (*0-7615-0108-8*) Prima Pub.

Bonanni, Filippo. Antique Musical Instruments & Their Players. rev. ed. (Illus.). 301p. 1964. pap. 8.95 (*0-486-21179-7*) Dover.

Bonanni, Pete. Jetfighter II: The Ultimate Combat Strategy Guide. (Illus.). 224p. (Orig.). 1992. pap. 18.95 (*1-55958-187-5*) Prima Pub.

Bonanni, Peter A. Falcon 4.0 Checklist. 240p. 1998. pap. text 16.99 (*0-7821-2246-9*) Sybex.

Bonanni, Victoria, ed. see Barnum, William J.

Bonanni, Victoria-Ann. A Blue Perfume: A Collection of Poetry. (Illus.). 52p. (Orig.). 1993. pap. 8.95 (*0-9636942-9-4*) VB Document.

Bonanni, Victoria-Ann, ed. see Fiore, Dolores.

Bonanni, Victoria-Ann, ed. see Hicks, Gary.

Bonanni, Victoria-Ann, ed. & illus. see Fletcher, Ann M.

Bonanni, Victoria-Ann, ed. & illus. see Woolf, Rafael.

Bonanno. Visual Merchandising. (C). 1998. 26.95 (*1-56253-351-7*) Milady Pub.

Bonanno, Alessandro. Agricultural & Food Sector in the New Global Era. 1993. 28.00 (*81-7022-464-0*, Pub. by Concept) S Asia.

Bonanno, Alessandro, et al, eds. From Columbus to ConAgra: The Globalization of Agriculture & Food. LC 93-46569. (Rural America Ser.). 336p. 1994. 40.00 (*0-7006-0660-2*); pap. 17.95 (*0-7006-0661-0*) U Pr of KS.

Bonanno, Alessandro & Constance, Douglas. Caught in the Net: The Global Tuna Industry, Environmentalists, & the State. LC 95-31617. (Illus.). 346p. (C). 1996. 40.00 (*0-7006-0738-2*); pap. 19.95 (*0-7006-0739-0*) U Pr of KS.

Bonanno, Anthony. Archaeology & Fertility Cult in the Ancient Mediterranean: Papers Presented at the First International Conference on Archaeology of the Ancient Mediterranean. (Illus.). xii, 356p. (Orig.). 1986. pap. 55.00 (*90-6032-288-6*, Pub. by B R Gruner) Humanities.

Bonanno, Anthony, ed. Laurea Corona: Studies in Honour of Edward Coleiro. (ENG, FRE, ITA, LAT & SPA.). xxiii, 232p. (Orig.). (C). 1987. pap. 71.00 (*90-6032-300-9*, Pub. by B R Gruner) Humanities.

Bonanno, Antonio C., jt. auth. see Matlins, Antoinette L.

Bonanno, Antonio C., jt. auth. see Matlins, Antoinette Leonard.

***Bonanno, Bill.** Bound by Honor: A Mafioso's Story. (Illus.). 352p. 1999. pap. 6.99 (*0-312-97147-8*) St Martin.

Bonanno, Bill. Bound by Honor: A Mafioso's Story. 2nd ed. LC 99-14049. (Illus.). 282p. 1999. 24.95 (*0-312-20388-8*) St Martin.

— Sins of Honor. (Illus.). 352p. 1999. pap. 24.95 (*0-525-94203-3*) NAL.

Bonanno, Giacomo & Brandolini, Dario, eds. Industrial Structure in the New Industrial Economics. (Illus.). 184p. 1990. 45.00 (*0-19-828645-7*) OUP.

Bonanno, Joseph & Lalli, Sergio. A Man of Honor: The Autobiography of Joseph Bonanno. 1999. reprint ed. 49.95 (*1-56849-722-9*) Buccaneer Bks.

Bonanno, Joseph T., Jr. The Firehouse Grilling Cookbook: 150 Great Grilling Recipes Plus Safety Tips. LC 97-47507. (Illus.). 240p. 1998. 23.00 (*0-7679-0098-7*) Broadway BDD.

— The Healthy Firehouse Cookbook: Low-Fat Recipes from America's Fire Fighters. (Illus.). 288p. 1995. 20.00 (*0-688-12755-X*, Hearst) Hearst Commns.

Bonanno, Margaret W. Dwellers in the Crucible. (Star Trek Ser.: No. 25). 320p. 1991. mass mkt. 4.95 (*0-671-74147-0*) PB.

— Preternatural. 23.95 (*0-614-26957-1*) Tor Bks.

— Preternatural, Vol. 1. 1997. mass mkt. 5.99 (*0-8125-6764-1*, Pub. by Tor Bks) St Martin.

— Probe. Stern, Dave, ed. (Star Trek Ser.). 352p. 1993. reprint ed. mass mkt. 5.99 (*0-671-79065-X*) PB.

— Strangers from the Sky. (Star Trek Ser.). 1990. per. 5.99 (*0-671-73481-4*) PB.

***Bonanno, Margaret Wander.** Preternatural Too: Gyre. LC 99-89847. 320p. 2000. 23.95 (*0-312-86671-2*, Pub. by Tor Bks) St Martin.

Bonanno, Massimo. The Rolling Stones Chronicle: The First Thirty-Five Years. 2nd ed. 240p. 1997. pap. text 19.95 (*0-85965-237-8*, Pub. by Plexus) Publishers Group.

Bonanno, Rosalie & Donofrio, Beverly. Mafia Marriage: My Story. 240p. 1991. mass mkt. 4.99 (*0-380-70536-2*, Avon Bks) Morrow Avon.

Bonansea, Berbardine, ed. see Bettoni, Efrem.

Bonansea, Bernardine M., ed. see Ryan, John K.

Bonansinga, Jay. Head Case. LC 97-36464. 1998. 23.00 (*0-684-82514-7*); 22.50 (*0-684-84931-3*) S&S Trade.

— Head Case. large type ed. LC 98-15760. (Core Ser.). 1998. 26.95 (*0-7838-0168-8*) Thorndike Pr.

Bonansinga, Jay R. The Black Mariah. 352p. (Orig.). 1994. mass mkt. 5.99 (*0-446-36515-7*, Pub. by Warner Bks) Little.

— The Killer's Game. large type ed. LC 97-16229. (Americana Series). 621p. 1997. 25.95 (*0-7862-1132-6*) Thorndike Pr.

— Sick. 336p. (Orig.). 1995. mass mkt. 5.99 (*0-446-36516-5*, Pub. by Warner Bks) Little.

***Bonansinga, Kate.** New Icons: Three Japanese Artists Begin in the West: Tetsuji Aono, Kazuhito Kobayashi, Ren Sakurai. Hopkins, Terri M., ed. (Illus.). 12p. 2000. pap. 5.00 (*0-914435-34-5*) Marylhurst Art.

Bonaparte, Felicia. The Gypsy-Bachelor of Manchester: The Life of Mrs. Gaskell's Demon. LC 92-292. (Victorian Literature & Culture Ser.). 322p. reprint ed. pap. 99.90 (*0-608-20045-X*, 207131700011) Bks Demand.

Bonaparte, Marie. Female Sexuality. 225p. (Orig.). 1971. pap. 24.95 (*0-8236-8050-9*, 021900) Intl Univs Pr.

— Topsy: The Story of a Golden-Haired Chow. LC 93-26306. (Illus.). 193p. (C). 1993. text 29.95 (*1-56000-127-5*) Transaction Pubs.

***Bonaparte, N. Anthony.** Humorous Sceptic: or Is it Just Me? An Irreverent Collection of Political Cartoons. (Illus.). 175p. 1999. pap. 19.99 (*1-55164-158-5*, Pub. by Black Rose) Consort Bk Sales.

Bonaparte, N. Anthony. Humorous Sceptic or, Is It Just Me? An Irreverent Collection of Political Cartoons. 1999. 48.99 (*1-55164-159-3*, Pub. by Black Rose) Consort Bk Sales.

Bonaparte, Napoleon. How to Make War. unabridged ed. Cloarec, Yann, ed. Orig. Title: Comment Faire la Guerre. (Illus.). 155p. 1999. pap. 12.95 (*0-9642284-2-4*, EC3) Ediciones La Calavera.

— The Military Maxims of Napoleon. 256p. 1993. 24.95 (*0-947898-64-6*, 5553) Stackpole.

— Military Maxims of Napoleon. Chandler, David G. & Cairnes, William E., eds. D'Aguilar, George C., tr. from FRE. (Illus.). 253p. 1995. reprint ed. pap. 13.95 (*0-306-80618-5*) Da Capo.

— Napoleon's Letters. Thompson, J. M., ed. (Lost Treasure Ser.). 331p. 1998. pap. 19.95 (*1-85375-269-X*) Prion.

— Napoleon's Memoirs. De Chair, Somerset, ed. & tr. by. from FRE. (Illus.). 605p. 1986. reprint ed. pap. 19.95 (*0-948166-10-X*, Pub. by Soho Bk Co) Dufour.

Bonaparte, Rudolph, ed. Waste Containment Systems: Construction, Regulation & Performance. LC 90-49336. 272p. 1990. pap. text 31.00 (*0-87262-787-X*) Am Soc Civil Eng.

Bonar, A. A. Robert Murray McCheyne: A Biography. 224p. 1983. reprint ed. pap. 4.95 (*0-310-44701-1*, 12374P) Zondervan.

Bonar, Andrew A. Andrew Bonar Life & Diary: Diary & Life. 535p. 1984. reprint ed. 23.99 (*0-85151-432-4*) Banner of Truth.

— Heavenly Springs. 211p. (Orig.). 1986. reprint ed. pap. 7.99 (*0-85151-479-0*) Banner of Truth.

— Leviticus. (Banner of Truth Geneva Series Commentaries). 1978. 25.99 (*0-85151-086-8*) Banner of Truth.

— The Life of R. M. M'Cheyne. 1978. pap. 5.99 (*0-85151-085-X*) Banner of Truth.

— Memoir & Remains of R. M. M'Cheyne. 1978. 35.99 (*0-85151-084-1*) Banner of Truth.

Bonar, Andrew A., jt. auth. see Tyler, Bennet.

Bonar, Ann. The Complete Guide to Conservatory Plants. LC 95-34603. (Illus.). 192p. 1996. 29.95 (*0-87951-610-0*, Pub. by Overlook Pr) Penguin Putnam.

— The Complete Guide to Conservatory Plants. (Illus.). 192p. pap. 22.95 (*1-85585-120-2*) Trafalgar.

— The Complete Guide to Conservatory Plants. (Illus.). 192p. 1992. 34.95 (*1-85585-084-2*) Trafalgar.

Bonar, Ann. Fragrance. (Illus.). 64p. 1993. 4.98 (*1-55859-553-8*, Canopy Bks) Abbeville Pr.

Bonar, Ann. Garden Plant Survival Manual. (Illus.). 192p. 14.99 (*1-57215-232-X*, JG232X) World Pubns.

— How to Book of Flower Gardening. Daniels, Gilbert, ed. 1983. pap. 3.95 (*0-7137-1289-9*) Sterling.

Bonar, Clayton. Beacon Small-Group Bible Studies, Deuteronomy: Words to Live By. Wolf, Earl C., ed. 100p. (Orig.). 1986. pap. 4.99 (*0-8341-0959-X*) Beacon Hill.

Bonar, Eulalie H., ed. Woven by the Grandmothers: Nineteenth-Century Navajo Textiles from the National Museum of the American Indian. (Illus.). 240p. (Orig.). 1996. pap. 34.95 (*1-56098-728-6*) Smithsonian.

Bonar, H. Follow the Lamb. 1988. pap. 5.99 (*0-906731-63-1*, Pub. by Christian Focus) Spring Arbor Dist.

— Longing for Heaven. large type ed. 6.99 (*1-85792-011-2*, Pub. by Christian Focus) Spring Arbor Dist.

Bonar, Horatius. The Everlasting Righteousness. 211p. 1993. reprint ed. pap. 7.99 (*0-85151-655-6*) Banner of Truth.

— The Everlasting Righteousness. rev. ed. Robbins, John W., ed. & intro. by. 122p. 1994. pap. 8.95 (*0-940931-41-9*) Trinity Found.

— God's Way of Holiness. 1979. pap. 4.99 (*0-85234-130-X*, Pub. by Evangelical Pr) P & R Pubng.

— God's Way of Peace. 1989. reprint ed. pap. 4.99 (*0-85234-265-9*, Pub. by Evangelical Pr) P & R Pubng.

— Night of Weeping: When God's Children Suffer. 1999. pap. text 7.99 (*1-85792-441-X*) Christian Focus.

— Words Old & New. 386p. 1994. pap. 7.99 (*0-85151-643-2*) Banner of Truth.

— Words to Winners of Souls. 72p. 1995. pap. 3.99 (*0-87552-164-9*) P & R Pubng.

Bonar, James. Moral Sense: 1930 Edition. 300p. 1996. reprint ed. 64.00 (*1-85506-148-1*) Bks Intl VA.

— Philosophy & Political Economy. 420p. (C). 1991. text 49.95 (*0-88738-438-2*) Transaction Pubs.

— Philosophy & Political Economy, 1909. 452p. 1996. reprint ed. 68.00 (*1-85506-149-X*) Bks Intl VA.

— The Tables Turned. LC 70-107918. (Reprints of Economic Classics Ser.). vii, 135p. 1970. reprint ed. 29.50 (*0-678-00633-4*) Kelley.

— Theories of Population from Raleigh to Arthur Young: 1931 Edition. 252p. 1996. reprint ed. 64.00 (*1-85506-156-2*) Bks Intl VA.

Bonar, James, ed. A Catalogue of the Library of Adam Smith: Prepared for the Royal Economic Society. 2nd ed. LC 66-15561. (Reprints of Economic Classics Ser.). xxxiv, 218p. 1966. reprint ed. 39.50 (*0-678-00188-X*) Kelley.

Bonar, James, tr. see Knapp, Georg F.

***Bonar, Marjory.** Andrew Bonar: The Good Pastor. (Classic Biographies Ser.). (Illus.). 1999. pap. 10.99 (*1-84030-045-0*) Ambassador Prodns Ltd.

Bonar, Megg, ed. see Schildt, Herbert.

Bonar, Samantha. Asteroids. LC 98-25109. (Watts Library: Space). 63p. (J). (gr. 4-6). 1999. 24.00 (*0-531-20367-0*) Watts.

***Bonar, Samantha.** Asteroids. (Watts Library). (Illus.). (J). 2000. pap. 8.95 (*0-531-16418-7*) Watts.

Bonar, Samantha. Comets. LC 96-53502. (First Bk.). 63p. (J). (gr. 3-5). 1998. 22.00 (*0-531-20301-8*) Watts.

— Comets. (First Bks.). (Illus.). 64p. 1998. pap. 6.95 (*0-531-15907-8*) Watts.

Bonarini, Andrea. New Trends in Fuzzy Logic: Proceedings of the WILK, '95 Italian Workshop on Fuzzy Logic, 21-22 September 1995, Naples, Italy. LC 96-22862. 400p. 1996. write for info. (*981-02-2794-9*) World Scientific Pub.

Bonarrigo, Merrill. The Ultimate Wine & Food Pairing Cookbook. 125p. 1997. pap. 14.99 (*0-9662886-1-0*) Messina Hof Wine.

Bonars, Stephen G. & Moore, Carol. Incentive Pay, Information, & Earnings: Evidence from the National Longitudinal Survey of Youth. (Illus.). 79p. (C). 1998. reprint ed. pap. text 30.00 (*0-7881-3915-0*) DIANE Pub.

Bonasco, Beatriz, see Alexandria, Betty, pseud.

Bonasia, J. American Politics in the 20th Century. 1998. pap. 9.95 (*0-912517-36-0*) Bluewood Bks.

Bonasoni, Paolo. Algebra Geometrica. Schmidt, Robert, ed. & tr. by. from LAT. LC 85-80178. (Illus.). 202p. 1985. lib. bdg. 36.00 (*0-931267-01-3*) Golden Hind Pr.

Bonasoro, F., jt. ed. see Carnavali, M. D. Candia.

Bonasso, Pete & Miller, David, eds. Instantiating Real-World Agents: Papers from the 1993 Fall Symposium. (Technical Reports). (Illus.). 125p. (Orig.). 1994. spiral bd. 25.00 (*0-929280-52-0*) AAAI Pr.

***Bonate, Peter L.** Analysis of Pretest-Posttest Designs. LC 00-27509. 224p. (C). 2000. boxed set 69.95 (*1-58488-173-9*, Chap & Hall CRC) CRC Pr.

Bonati, Gina A. Ressurection. 6p. 1994. pap. 3.00 (*1-886206-10-4*) Venom Pr.

Bonatsos, Dennis. Interacting Boson Models of Nuclear Structure. (Oxford Studies in Nuclear Physics: No. 10). (Illus.). 330p. 1988. text 49.95 (*0-19-851727-0*) OUP.

Bonatti, Luigi. Uncertainty: Studies in Philosophy, Economics & Socio-Political Theory. (Bochumer Studien zur Philosophie Ser.: Vol. 2). xii, 132p. 1984. 35.00 (*90-6032-230-4*, Pub. by B R Gruner) Humanities.

Bonatti, M., et al, eds. Integrated Broadband Communications: Views from RACE. (North Holland Studies in Telecommunication: No. 16). xxii,470p. 1991. 157.50 (*0-444-89247-8*, North Holland) Elsevier.

***Bonatti, Walter.** Mountains of My Life. (Exploration Ser.). 2000. pap. 14.95 (*0-375-75640-X*) Modern Lib NY.

Bonatus, Guido. The Astrologer's Guide: Being the One Hundred & Forty-Six Considerations of the Famous Astrologer, Guido Bonatus. Lilly, William, ed. Coley, Henry, tr. from LAT. 1993. reprint ed. 37.50 (*1-55818-211-X*) Holmes Pub.

Bonatus, Guido & Coley, Henry, trs. The Astrologer's Guide. 105p. 1996. spiral bd. 12.00 (*0-7873-0115-9*) Hlth Research.

Bonaventura, Michael P. Why Can't a Woman Be More Like a Man? A Woman's Guide to Revitalizing Her Natural Sex Drive. 240p. 1996. pap. 16.95 (*1-56530-184-6*) Summit TX.

Bonavero, Piero, et al, eds. The Italian Urban System: Towards European Integration. 206p. 1999. text 65.95 (*1-85972-286-5*, Pub. by Ashgate Pub) Ashgate Pub Co.

Bonavia, David. China Guides: Beijing. 3rd ed. 208p. 1995. pap. 15.95 (*0-8442-9986-3*, Passprt Bks) NTC Contemp Pub Co.

— China's Warlords. (Oxford in Asia Paperbacks Ser.). (Illus.). 232p. 1995. pap. text 26.00 (*0-19-586179-5*) OUP.

— Deng: A Biography. (C). 1996. text 38.75 (*0-8133-1045-8*) Westview.

Bonavia, Duccio. Mural Painting in Ancient Peru. Lyon, Patricia J., tr. from SPA. LC 84-47883. (Illus.). 240p. 1985. 26.95 (*0-253-33940-5*) Ind U Pr.

Bonavia, E. The Flora of the Assyrian Monuments. (Illus.). 241p. 1998. reprint ed. spiral bd. 19.00 (*1-885395-46-9*) Book Tree.

Bonavia, Ferruccio. Verdi: Music Book Index. 120p. 1993. reprint ed. lib. bdg. 69.00 (*0-7812-9628-5*) Rprt Serv.

Bonavia-Hunt, Noel. The Church Organ. 140p. 1991. reprint ed. text 69.00 (*0-7812-9327-8*) Rprt Serv.

Bonavia-Hunt, Noel A. Modern Organ Stops. (Illus.). 1974. pap. 20.00 (*0-913746-05-3*) Organ Lit.

***Bonavia, Judy.** Silk Road: From Xian to Kashgar. rev. ed. (Odyssey Passport Ser.). (Illus.). 1998. pap. 19.95 (*962-217-606-2*) China Guides.

Bonavia, Judy. The Yangzi River. 4th ed. (China Guides Ser.). (Illus.). 208p. 1997. pap. 19.95 (*0-8442-4774-X*, 4774X, Passprt Bks) NTC Contemp Pub Co.

— Yangzi River. 5th ed. (Odyssey Passport Ser.). 1999. pap. text 19.95 (*962-217-607-0*) Norton.

Bonavia, Judy & Hurst, William. The Yangzi River. 3rd ed. (Illustrated Travel Guides from Thomas Cook Ser.). 220p. 1994. pap. 15.95 (*0-8442-9681-3*, Passprt Bks) NTC Contemp Pub Co.

Bonavia, Judy & Passport Books Staff. Essential Hong Kong. LC 93-85619. (Essential Travel Guides Ser.). (Illus.). 128p. 1994. pap. 7.95 (*0-8442-8913-2*, Passprt Bks) NTC Contemp Pub Co.

Bonavida, B., et al, eds. Tumor Necrosis Factor: Structure, Mechanism of Action, Role in Disease & Therapy. (Illus.). x, 254p. 1990. 172.25 (*3-8055-4966-0*) S Karger.

— Tumor Necrosis Factor-Cachectin & Related Cytokines. (Illus.). viii, 276p. 1988. 172.25 (*3-8055-4755-2*) S Karger.

Bonavida, B. & Golup, S., eds. NK Cells & Natural Immunity. (Journal Ser.: Vol. 14, 2, 1995). (Illus.). 60p. 1995. pap. 47.00 (*3-8055-6263-2*) S Karger.

Bonavida, B., jt. ed. see Lo, S-Y.

Bonavida, B., jt. ed. see Osawa, T.

Bonaviri, Giuseppe. Dolcissimo. Mariani, Umberto, tr. from ITA. & intro. by. LC 89-46224. 166p. (Orig.). 1991. pap. 12.50 (*0-934977-21-6*) Italica Pr.

— Nights on the Heights. Bussino, Giovanni R., tr. from ITA. LC 90-40033. XIV, 204p. (C). 1991. text 42.95 (*0-8204-1355-0*) P Lang Pubng.

Bonavita, John. Mego Action Figure Toys. (Illus.). 192p. 1996. pap. 19.95 (*0-7643-0025-3*) Schiffer.

Bonavita, Mark & Roberts, Brendan, eds. Hockey Register: 1998-99 Edition. 472p. 1998. 15.95 (*0-89204-598-1*) Sporting News.

— Official NBA Register: 1998-99 Edition. 684p. 1998. 15.95 (*0-89204-601-5*) Sporting News.

— Pro Football Register: 1998 Edition. annuals 904p. 1998. 15.95 (*0-89204-597-3*) Sporting News.

Bonavoglia, Rosario. Amalfi: Italy's Divine Coast. 128p. 1998. 29.95 (*0-7893-0344-2*, Pub. by Universe) St Martin.

— Rhythm & Colors of Manhattan. 1999. 35.00 (*0-8478-5787-5*, Pub. by Rizzoli Intl) St Martin.

***Bonavoglia, Rosario, photos by.** Sicily. (Illus.). 128p. 2000. text 29.95 (*0-7893-0410-4*) Universe.

Bonavolonta, Jules. The Good Guys. 1997. per. 6.50 (*0-671-01007-7*) S&S Trade.

Bonazountas, Marc, et al, eds. SESOIL in Environmental Fate & Risk Modeling. LC 97-185762. (Illus.). 686p. (C). 1997. text 59.95 (*1-884940-05-6*) Amherst Sci Pubs.

Bonazzi. Software Engineering with Oracle: Best Practices for Mission-Critical Systems. 784p. (C). 1999. pap. text 49.99 incl. audio compact disk (*0-13-020091-3*) P-H.

Bonazzi, Robert. Fictive Music. deluxe ed. 1979. pap. 10.00 (*0-930324-12-9*) Wings Pr.

— Man in the Mirror: John Howard Griffin & the Story of "Black Like Me" LC 97-18711. (Illus.). 180p. (Orig.). 1997. pap. 14.00 (*1-57075-118-8*) Orbis Bks.

Bonazzi, Robert, ed. see Griffin, John H.

Bonbright, James C. Public Utilities & the National Power Policies. LC 73-172007. (FDR & the Era of the New Deal Ser.). 1972. reprint ed. lib. bdg. 19.50 (*0-306-70424-2*) Da Capo.

— Railroad Capitalization. LC 70-78003. (Columbia University. Studies in the Social Sciences: No. 215). reprint ed. 47.50 (*0-404-51215-1*) AMS Pr.

Boncek, Raymond K., jt. ed. see Pirich, Andrew R.

Bonch-Osmolovsky, A. G. Physics of New Methods of Charged Particle Acceleration. 156p. 1994. text 61.00 (*981-02-1238-0*) World Scientific Pub.

Bonche, P., et al, eds. Heavy Ion Collisions: Cargese 1984. LC 85-24403. (NATO ASI Series B, Physics: Vol. 130). 418p. 1986. 105.00 (*0-306-42089-9*, Plenum Trade) Perseus Pubng.

Bonchek, Avigdor. Studying the Torah: A Guide to In-Depth Interpretation. LC 95-38538. 208p. 1996. 25.00 (*1-56821-504-5*) Aronson.

— Studying the Torah: A Guide to In-Depth Interpretation. LC 95-38538. 208p. 1997. pap. 25.00 (*0-7657-9964-2*) Aronson.

Bonchek, Mark S., jt. auth. see Shepsle, Kenneth A.

***Bonchev, D. & Rouvray, D. H., eds.** Chemical Topology: Introduction & Fundamentals. (Illus.). 336p. 1999. text 125.00 (*90-5699-174-4*) Gordon & Breach.

Bonchev, Danail. Information Theoretic Indices for Characterization of Chemical Structures. LC 82-16696. (Chemometrics Ser.: No. 5). (Illus.). 263p. reprint ed. pap. 81.60 (*0-8357-6157-6*, 203421600089) Bks Demand.

Bonchev, Danail, ed. Chemical Group Theory: Techniques & Applications. (Mathematical Chemistry Ser.). 259p. 1995. text 132.00 (*2-88449-034-5*) Gordon & Breach.

— Graph Theoretical Approaches to Chemical Reactivity. (Understanding Chemical Reactivity Ser.). 296p. (C). 1994. text 166.50 (*0-7923-2837-X*) Kluwer Academic.

Bonchev, Danail & Rouvray, D. H., eds. Chemical Graph Theory: Reactivity & Kinetics. (Mathematical Chemistry Ser.: Vol. 2). xii, 266p. 1992. text 176.00 (*0-85626-515-2*) Gordon & Breach.

An Asterisk (*) at the beginning of an entry indicates that the title is appearing for the first time.

Bonchev, Danail & Rouvray, Dennis H., eds. Chemical Group Theory: Introduction & Fundamentals. LC 93-38653. (Mathematical Chemistry Ser.: Vol. 3). xiii, 262p. 1994. text 146.00 (*2-88124-959-0*) Gordon & Breach.

***Bonchev, Danail & Rouvray, Dennis H., eds.** Chemical Topology Vol. 6: Applications & Techniques. (Illus.). 410p. 2000. 125.00 (*90-5699-240-6*, G & B Science) Gordon & Breach.

Boncompagno da Signa. Rota Veneris. Purkart, Josef, ed. LC 74-18250. 128p. 1975. reprint ed. lib. bdg. 50.00 (*0-8201-1137-6*) Schol Facsimiles.

Bonczek, Lindy, ed. see Pentz, Jane.

Bond. Bond's Franchise Guide. (Illus.). 520p. Date not set. pap. text 29.95 (*1-887137-01-7*) Source Bk Pubns.

***Bond.** Contested Terrains & Constructed. 224p. 2000. pap. 60.00 (*0-8133-3678-3*, Pub. by Westview) HarpC.

— Eleven Vests & Tuesday. LC 98-162566. 1997. pap. 10.95 (*0-413-72120-5*) Methn.

Bond. Encyclopedia of Civil Rights in the United States, 2 vols., Vol. 2. Martin, Waldo E., Jr. & Sullivan, Patricia, eds. LC 99-57548. 851p. 2000. 200.00 (*0-02-864765-3*) S&S Trade.

Bond. Handbook of Cognitive Behaviour: Brief. text. write for info. (*0-471-49107-1*) Wiley.

Bond. An Introduction to Abstract Mathematics. (Mathematics Ser.). 1999. pap. 87.95 (*0-534-95050-7*) PWS Pubs.

— Modern Polargraphic Methods in Analytical Chemistry. (Monographs in Electroanalytical Chemistry & Electrochemistry: Vol.4). (Illus.). 536p. 1980. text 225.00 (*0-8247-6849-3*) Dekker.

— Sociology/Health Care. 3rd ed. 1999. pap. text 29.95 (*0-443-05530-0*, W B Saunders Co) Harcrt Hlth Sci Grp.

— Xmas in the Chicken Coop. (J). 1983. 4.70 (*0-690-04332-5*) HarpC Child Bks.

Bond & Martin. Encyclopedia of Civil Rights in the United States, Vol. 1. LC 99-57548. 1999. 100.00 (*0-02-864763-7*) S&S Trade.

— Encyclopedia of Civil Rights in the United States, Vol. 2. 1999. 100.00 (*0-02-864764-5*) S&S Trade.

Bond & Smith. Social Psychology Across Cultures. 2nd ed. 401p. 1998. pap. text 44.00 (*0-205-28522-8*) Allyn.

Bond & Straub. Handbook on Environmental Control of Solid Waste. 1973. 324.00 (*0-87819-272-7*, CRC Reprint) Franklin.

Bond, jt. auth. see Bajpai, Avi C.

Bond, jt. auth. see Castillo.

***Bond & Pecaro, Inc. Staff.** CyberValuation: Internet Business Valuation, Trends & Analysis. 126p. 1999. pap. 695.00 (*0-9673111-0-1*) Bond & Pecaro.

Bond, A. C. & Faget, M. A. Technologies of Manned Space Systems. x, 122p. 1965. text 235.00 (*0-677-01250-0*) Gordon & Breach.

Bond, A. M. Modern Voltammetric Methods in Analytic Chemistry. Date not set. write for info. (*0-8247-9443-5*) Dekker.

Bond, Adrienne. Sugarcane House & Other Stories about Mr. Fat. LC 96-50026. (Illus.). 86p. (J). (gr. k-3). 1997. 16.00 (*0-15-201446-2*) Harcourt.

Bond, Adrienne. The Voice of the Poet: The Shape & Sound of Southern Poetry Today. (Georgia Humanities Council Publications). (Illus.). 60p. 1991. pap. 11.95 (*0-8203-1318-1*) U of Ga Pr.

Bond, Adrienne M. Time Was, She Declares: Selected Poems. LC 96-35540. 84p. 1996. 19.95 (*0-86554-538-3*, MUP/H411) Mercer Univ Pr.

Bond, Adrienne Moore. Eugene W. Stetson. LC 83-8292. x, 200p. 1983. text 12.95 (*0-86554-069-1*, MUP\H065) Mercer Univ Pr.

— Sugarcane House. LC 96-50026. 1997. pap. 5.00 (*0-15-201447-0*) Harcourt.

Bond, Alan. Over 300 Successful Business Letters for All Occasions. LC 97-33521. 224p. 1998. pap. 14.95 (*0-7641-0322-9*) Barron.

— The Sevenfold Path to Peace. 1986. 4.75 (*0-89536-774-2*, 6801) CSS OH.

Bond, Alan & Bond, Jill, eds. Our Planet, His Creation. (Kids Write Ser.). (Illus.). 112p. (Orig.). (J). (gr. k-12). 1992. pap. 5.00 (*0-9631992-2-6*) Bonding Place.

Bond, Alan & Gasser, Les, eds. Readings in Distributed Artificial Intelligence. 650p. 1988. pap. text 54.95 (*0-934613-63-X*) Morgan Kaufmann.

Bond, Alan B., jt. auth. see Diamond, Judy.

Bond, Alan B., ed. see Bond, C. Lawrence.

Bond, Alec. North of Sioux Falls. 24p. 1983. pap. 3.00 (*0-933180-58-6*) Spoon Riv Poetry.

— Phebus Lane. 89p. 1987. pap. 5.95 (*0-317-69927-X*) Spoon Riv Poetry.

***Bond, Allen M.** Always, Allen: Letters Home from the Pacific Theatre, January-May 1945. 2000. pap. 17.95 (*1-887137-24-6*) Source Bk Pubns.

Bond, Alma, et al. Dream Portrait: A Study of Nineteen Sequential Dreams As Indicators of Pretermination. LC 91-35421. 200p. (C). 1992. 30.00 (*0-8236-1438-7*) Intl Univs Pr.

Bond, Alma H. The Autobiography of Maria Callas: A Novel. LC 97-77319. 224p. 1998. 27.95 (*0-913559-49-0*) Birch Brook Pr.

— The Autobiography of Maria Callas: A Novel. 2nd ed. LC 97-77319. 224p. 1998. pap. 17.95 (*0-913559-48-2*) Birch Brook Pr.

— On Becoming a Grandparent: A Diary of Family Discovery. LC 94-9051. 176p. 1994. 19.95 (*1-882593-08-1*) Bridge Wrks.

— Who Killed Virginia Woolf? A Psychobiography. (Insight Bk.). (Illus.). 194p. 1989. 23.95 (*0-89885-427-X*, Kluwer Acad Hman Sci) Kluwer Academic.

Bond, Alyson J. & Lader, Malcolm H. Understanding Drug Treatment in Mental Health Care. LC 96-1090. (Series in Clinical Psychology). 1999. pap. text 51.95 (*0-471-96171-X*) Wiley.

Bond, Andrew H., et al. Metal Ion Separation & Preconcentration: Progress & Opportunities. 716. 12p. 1999. text 130.00 (*0-8412-3594-5*, Pub. by Am Chemical) OUP.

Bond, Anita W. & Mordarski, Sheila W. Dental Hygiene Care of the Special Needs Patient. 66p. 1983. write for info. (*0-318-17797-8*); 30.00 (*0-318-17798-6*) Am Dental Hygienists.

Bond, Ann. A Guide to the Harpsichord. LC 96-41086. (Illus.). 268p. 1997. 29.95 (*1-57467-027-1*, Amadeus Pr) Timber.

Bond, Ann S. Adam & Noah & the Cops, 001. LC 82-21181. (Illus.). 160p. (J). (gr. 3-6). 1983. 8.95 (*0-395-33225-7*) HM.

Bond, Aylson. Aggression: Individual Differences, Alcohol & Benzodiazephines. LC 97-202984. (Maudsley Monographs). 176p. 1997. 39.95 (*0-86377-482-2*) L Erlbaum Assocs.

Bond, Beverley W., Jr. Civilization of the Old Northwest. LC 73-124226. (Select Bibliographies Reprint Ser.). 1977. 23.95 (*0-8369-5415-7*) Ayer.

— Civilization of the Old Northwest. 1993. reprint ed. lib. bdg. 89.00 (*0-7812-5341-1*) Rprt Serv.

Bond, Beverley W. The Monroe Mission to France, 1794-1796. LC 78-63920. (Johns Hopkins University. Studies in the Social Sciences. Thirtieth Ser. 1912: 2-3). reprint ed. 42.50 (*0-404-61171-0*) AMS Pr.

— The Quit-Rent System in the American Colonies. 1919. 16.50 (*0-8446-1082-8*) Peter Smith.

Bond, Bob. The Handbook of Sailing. rev. ed. 1992. pap. 27.00 (*0-679-74063-5*) McKay.

— Solving the Mystery of Daniel's Unnamed Kingdom - Finishing the Puzzle of the Last Days: Daniel's Unnamed Kingdom. Ellis, Joyce K., ed. (Illus.). 148p. (Orig.). 1991. pap. 10.99 (*0-9628613-0-8*) Lrn to Discern.

***Bond, Bob, et al.** The Complete Book of Sailing. 192p. 1999. pap. text 19.95 (*0-600-59946-9*) Hamlyn Publishing Group Ltd.

Bond, Bradley G. Political Culture in the 19th-Century South: Mississippi, 1830-1900. LC 95-11134. 392p. 1995. text 40.00 (*0-8071-1976-8*) La State U Pr.

Bond, Brian. Britain, France, Belgium, 1939-1940. 2nd rev. ed. (Illus.). 136p. 1990. 35.00 (*0-08-037700-9*, Pub. by Brasseys) Brasseys.

— France & Belgium, Nineteen Thirty-Nine to Nineteen Forty. Frankland, Noble & Dowling, Christopher, eds. LC 79-52237. (Politics & Strategy of the Second World War Ser.). 208p. 1979. 18.50 (*0-87413-157-X*) U Delaware Pr.

— Liddell Hart: A Study of His Military Thought. (Modern Revivals in Military History Ser.). 300p. 1992. 63.95 (*0-7512-0029-8*, Pub. by Gregg Revivals) Ashgate Pub Co.

— The Pursuit of Victory: From Napoleon to Saddam Hussein. (Illus.). 272p. (C). 1996. 29.95 (*0-19-820497-3*) OUP.

— The Pursuit of Victory: From Napoleon to Saddam Hussein. (Illus.). 250p. 1998. reprint ed. pap. text 19.95 (*0-19-820735-2*) OUP.

— War & Society in Europe, 1870-1970. 256p. 1998. pap. 19.95 (*0-7735-1763-4*, Pub. by McG-Queens Univ Pr) CUP Services.

— War & Society in Europe, 1870-1970. 256p. 1986. pap. 21.95 (*0-19-520502-2*) OUP.

Bond, Brian, ed. see British Commission for Military History Staff.

Bond, Bruce. The Anteroom of Paradise. (QRL Poetry Bks.: Vol. XXX). 1991. 20.00 (*0-614-06434-1*) Quarterly Rev.

— Money Thoughts: The Abc of Money Management. 2nd ed. LC 94-181333. 184 p. 1990. write for info. (*0-85091-413-2*) Lothian Pub.

— The Possible. 32p. 1995. pap. 6.00 (*1-878851-06-3*) Silverfish Rev Pr.

— Radiography. LC 97-72083. (American Poets Continuum Ser.: No. 44). 79p. 1997. pap. 12.50 (*1-880238-51-9*) BOA Edns.

Bond, Bryce. Higher Techniques to Inner Perfection. 1991. 9.95 (*0-685-64740-4*) Inner Light.

Bond, C. Lawrence. Native Names of New England Towns & Villages: Translating 199 Names Derived from Native American Words. rev. ed. 84p. 1993. pap. 5.00 (*0-9638180-1-5*) A B Bond.

***Bond, C. Lawrence.** Native Names of New England Towns & Villages: Translating 199 Names Derived from Native American Words. 3rd rev. ed. Bond, Alan B., ed. (Illus.). 88p. 2000. mass mkt. 9.50 (*0-9638180-2-3*) A B Bond.

Bond, Carl E. Biology of Fishes. 2nd ed. LC 95-67414. (C). 1996. text 90.50 (*0-03-070342-5*) Harcourt Coll Pubs.

Bond, Carol T. A Book of Famous Black Americans: Complete Units for Teachers of Children, Ages 4-8. 1989. pap. 16.95 (*0-933212-38-0*) Partner Pr.

— Fee Fie Fo Fun: Enchanting Fairy Tale Units for Busy Teachers of Young Children. 1989. pap. 12.95 (*0-933212-34-8*) Partner Pr.

— Marmalade Days: Fall - Complete Units for Busy Teachers of Young Children. 1987. pap. 27.95 (*0-933212-35-6*) Partner Pr.

— Marmalade Days: Spring - Complete Units for Busy Teachers of Young Children. 1988. pap. 27.95 (*0-933212-37-2*) Partner Pr.

— Marmalade Days: Winter - Complete Units for Busy Teachers of Young Children. 1987. pap. 27.95 (*0-318-35167-6*) Partner Pr.

Bond, Catherine, jt. auth. see Grayson, Edward.

Bond, Cecil J. The Complete Book of Collection Letters, Telephone Scripts, & Faxes. LC 93-49991. 1994. text 69.95 (*0-07-006605-1*) McGraw.

Bond, Charles R., Jr. & Anderson, Terry H. A Flying Tiger's Diary. LC 83-40497. (Centennial Series of the Association of Former Students: No. 15). (Illus.). 264p. 1993. pap. 16.50 (*0-89096-408-4*) Tex A&M Univ Pr.

— A Flying Tiger's Diary. limited ed. LC 83-40497. (Centennial Series of the Association of Former Students: No. 15). (Illus.). 264p. 1993. 40.00 (*0-89096-576-5*) Tex A&M Univ Pr.

***Bond, Christopher S., ed.** Education Success = Business Success: Congressional Hearing. (Illus.). 149p. 2000. pap. text 25.00 (*0-7567-0142-2*) DIANE Pub.

— Environmental Compliance Tools for Small Business: Congressional Hearing. 230p. (C). 1999. reprint ed. pap. text 40.00 (*0-7881-8414-8*) DIANE Pub.

Bond, Christopher S., ed. Keeping up with the Trend Issues Affecting Home-Based Business Owners: Hearing Before the Committee on Small Business, U. S. Senate. 92p. (C). 1998. pap. text 25.00 (*0-7881-4955-5*) DIANE Pub.

— Women-Owned & Home-Based Businesses: Hearing Before the Committee on Small Business, U. S. Senate. (Illus.). 267p. (C). 1999. pap. text 40.00 (*0-7881-8009-6*) DIANE Pub.

Bond Clunie, Gloria. North Star. 103p. 1998. pap. 5.50 (*0-87129-831-7*, N47) Dramatic Pub.

Bond, Courtney C. Ottawa: Where Rivers Meet - An Illustrated History. LC 84-19571. 192p. 1984. 24.95 (*0-89781-111-9*) Am Historical Pr.

Bond, Creina, ed. Okavango: Sea of Land, Land of Water. (Illus.). 192p. (C). 1988. 180.00 (*0-685-32437-0*, Pub. by New5 Holland) St Mut.

Bond, Creina, jt. auth. see Siegfried, Roy.

Bond, Cynthia D., ed. The Pen Is Ours: A Listing of Writings by & about African-American Women Before 1910 with Secondary Bibliography to the Present. (Schomburg Library of Nineteenth-Century Black Women Writers). (Illus.). 400p. 1991. text 49.95 (*0-19-506203-5*) OUP.

Bond, D. A., ed. Vicia Faba: Feeding Value, Processing & Viruses. (World Crops: Production, Utilization & Description Ser.: Vol. 3). x, 424p. 1980. text 179.50 (*90-247-2362-0*) Kluwer Academic.

Bond, Dan. Following the Good Shepherd, Lord Teach Us How To Rest: Practical Expositions on Psalm 23. 170p. (Orig.). (C). 1990. pap. 6.95 (*1-877654-03-5*) Word Transfer.

— Lord Teach Us How to Fight: Practical Expositions on Ephesians 6: 10-18. 135p. 1989. write for info. (*1-877654-01-9*) Word Transfer.

Bond, Daniel. Stage Management: A Gentle Art. 2nd ed. LC 97-44377. 160p. 1998. pap. 20.99 (*0-87830-067-8*, Thtre Arts Bks) Routledge.

***Bond, Danny.** Clothed to Conquer: Putting on the Whole Armor of God. 142p. 1999. pap. 6.99 (*0-9676661-6-3*) Calvary Dist.

Bond, Danny. Overcoming Sin & Enjoying God. Smith, Chuck, ed. (Calvary Basics Ser.). 83p. 1996. pap. 3.50 (*0-936728-69-8*) Word for Today.

Bond, David J. Jacques Chessex: Calvinism & the Text. (Romance Ser.). 193p. (C). 1994. text 60.00 (*0-8020-0555-1*) U of Toronto Pr.

Bond, Dixie D. Oral Histories of Rural Utah: Generations Sanpete, 16 vols., Set. 230p. (Orig.). 1989. pap. 200.00 (*0-685-28902-8*) Violet Pr UT.

Bond, Dixie D., pref. Generations Sanpete Index: Oral Histories of Rural Utah. 230p. (Orig.). 1989. 49.95 (*0-9624396-0-6*) Violet Pr UT.

Bond, Donald & Bond, Vivian. La Familia Cristiana. (TEE Ser.). (SPA.). 233p. 1983. 6.95 (*1-879892-18-9*) Editorial Bautista.

Bond, Donald F. Age of Dryden. LC 72-118855. (Goldentree Bibliographies Series in Language & Literature). 120p. (C). 1970. pap. text 13.95 (*0-88295-502-0*) Harlan Davidson.

Bond, Donald F., ed. The Spectator, 5 vols., Vol. 1. (Illus.). 628p. 1987. 140.00 (*0-19-818610-X*) OUP.

— The Spectator, 5 vols., Vol. 2. (Illus.). 608p. 1987. text 140.00 (*0-19-818611-8*) OUP.

— The Spectator, 5 vols., Vol. 3. (Illus.). 608p. 1987. 140.00 (*0-19-818612-6*) OUP.

— The Spectator, 5 vols., Vol. 4. (Illus.). 608p. 1987. 140.00 (*0-19-818613-4*) OUP.

— The Spectator, 5 vols., Vol. 5. (Illus.). 512p. 1987. 140.00 (*0-19-818614-2*) OUP.

Bond, Donald F., ed. see Steele, Richard.

Bond, Donna, jt. auth. see Bond, Mel.

Bond, Donna, jt. auth. see Ringsven, Mary K.

Bond, Dorothy. Blest Be the Quilts: That Bind...Our Hearts in Christian Love. (Illus.). 52p. 1992. pap. 12.00 (*0-9606086-1-3*) D Bond.

— Crazy Quilt Stitches. (Illus.). 112p. (Orig.). 1981. pap. 12.00 (*0-9606086-0-5*) D Bond.

***Bond, Douglas.** Mr. Pipes & the British Hymn Makers. (Illus.). 236p. (YA). (gr. 7-12). 1999. pap. text 9.95 (*1-930092-12-1*) Christian Liberty.

Bond, Douglas. Sometimes, Seeing Is Believing. 1993. spiral bd. 23.35 (*0-88252-164-0*) Paladin Hse.

Bond, E. J. Ethics & Human Well-Being: An Introduction to Moral Philosophy. LC 96-4573. (Introducing Philosophy Ser.). 270p. (C). 1996. 55.95 (*0-631-19549-1*); pap. 23.95 (*0-631-19551-3*) Blackwell Pubs.

Bond, Earl D. & Komora, Paul O. Thomas W. Salmon: Psychiatrist. Grob, Gerald N., ed. LC 78-22550. (Historical Issues in Mental Health Ser.). (Illus.). 1980. reprint ed. lib. bdg. 19.95 (*0-405-11904-6*) Ayer.

Bond, Edward. A-A-America! & Stone. rev. ed. (Methuen Modern Plays Ser.). 115p. (C). 1982. pap. write for info. (*0-413-48320-7*, A0001, Methuen Drama) Methn.

— At the Inland Sea. LC 97-223555. 1996. pap. 13.95 (*0-413-70630-3*, Methuen Drama) Methn.

— Bingo. 76p. 1976. pap. 5.95 (*0-87129-685-3*, B20) Dramatic Pub.

— Bond: Plays Four. (Methuen World Dramatists Ser.). 411p. (Orig.). (C). 1992. pap. 13.95 (*0-413-64830-3*, A0628, Methuen Drama) Methn.

— Bond: Plays Two. (Methuen World Dramatists Ser.). 253p. (Orig.). (C). 1978. pap. 14.95 (*0-413-39270-8*, A0357, Methuen Drama) Methn.

Bond, Edward. Bond Plays, Bk. 3. 1987. pap. 14.95 (*0-413-33890-8*) Methn.

— Bond Plays, No. 6. 1998. pap. 14.95 (*0-413-70400-9*) Methn.

— Bond-Plays One. (Methuen World Dramatists Ser.). 312p. (C). 1983. pap. 9.95 (*0-413-45410-X*, A0035) Heinemann.

Bond, Edward. The Bundle. 98p. (C). 1978. pap. write for info. (*0-413-39360-7*, A0042, Methuen Drama) Methn.

— Coffee. (Methuen Plays Ser.). 1995. pap. 11.95 (*0-413-69710-X*, A0749) Heinemann.

***Bond, Edward.** Crime of the Twenty-First Century. 2000. pap. 10.95 (*0-413-73830-2*, Methuen Drama) Methn.

Bond, Edward. Derek & Choruses from after the Assassinations. (Methuen New Theatrescripts Ser.). 48p. (C). 1984. pap. write for info. (*0-413-54700-0*, A0072, Methuen Drama) Methn.

— The Fool & We Come to the River. (Methuen Modern Plays Ser.). 122p. (C). 1988. pap. 9.95 (*0-413-34770-2*, A0108) Heinemann.

— Human Cannon. (Methuen New Theatrescripts Ser.). 42p. (Orig.). (C). 1988. pap. write for info. (*0-413-57250-1*, A0129, Methuen Drama) Methn.

Bond, Edward. Lear. LC 73-153068. 1972. pap. 10.95 (*0-413-28770-X*) Methn.

Bond, Edward. Olly's Prison. 88p. (C). 1993. pap. 10.95 (*0-413-67610-2*, A0671, Methuen Drama) Methn.

— Edward Bond Plays: Five, Vol. 5. 1996. pap. 15.95 (*0-413-70390-8*, Methuen Drama) Methn.

— Restoration & the Cat. 2nd ed. 201p. (C). pap. 8.95 (*0-413-49920-0*, A0238) Heinemann.

— Saved. 123p. 1983. pap. 5.95 (*0-87129-099-5*, S64) Dramatic Pub.

— Saved. (Methuen Modern Plays Ser.). 123p. (C). 1988. pap. 10.95 (*0-413-31360-3*, A0254, Methuen Drama) Methn.

— The Sea. 80p. 1974. pap. 5.95 (*0-87129-759-0*, S19) Dramatic Pub.

— Tuesday. 208p. 1994. pap. 11.95 (*0-413-68220-X*, A0693, Methuen Drama) Methn.

— Two Post-Modern Plays: Jackets & In the Company of Men. (Methuen Modern Plays Ser.). 244p. (Orig.). (C). 1990. pap. write for info. (*0-413-62650-4*, A0464, Methuen Drama) Methn.

— The War Plays. (Methuen New Theatrescripts Ser.). 51p. (Orig.). (C). 1988. pap. write for info. (*0-413-57240-4*, A0310, Methuen Drama) Methn.

— The War Plays. (Methuen Modern Plays Ser.). 363p. (Orig.). (C). 1991. pap. write for info. (*0-413-64600-9*, A0558, Methuen Drama) Methn.

— The Woman. 148p. 1981. pap. 5.95 (*0-87129-081-2*, W44) Dramatic Pub.

— The Worlds. 176p. (C). 1988. pap. 8.95 (*0-413-46610-8*, A0321) Heinemann.

Bond, Edward, tr. see Wedekind, Frank.

Bond, Edward, tr. & adapted by see Wedekind, Frank.

Bond, Edward A., ed. Chronica Monasterii de Melsa, a Fundatione Usque ad Annum, 1396: Auctiore Thoma de Burton, Abbate, 3 vols. (Rolls Ser.: No. 43). 1972. reprint ed. 210.00 (*0-8115-1102-2*) Periodicals Srv.

***Bond, Edward L.** Damned Souls in a Tobacco Colony: Religion in Seventeenth-Century Virginia. 2000. 35.00 (*0-86554-708-4*, H526) Mercer Univ Pr.

Bond, Elden A. Tenth-Grade Abilities & Achievements. LC 79-176577. (Columbia University. Teachers College. Contributions to Education Ser.: No. 813). reprint ed. 37.50 (*0-404-55813-5*) AMS Pr.

Bond, Elias A. The Professional Treatment of the Subject Matter of Arithmetic for Teacher-Training Institutions. LC 75-176576. (Columbia University. Teachers College. Contributions to Education Ser.: No. 525). reprint ed. 37.50 (*0-404-55525-X*) AMS Pr.

Bond, Elizabeth. Incentive Compensation for Commercial Loan Officers: State of the Art. Behr, Joan H., ed. LC 92-12779. 64p. (Orig.). 1992. pap. 45.00 (*0-936742-87-9*, 35001) Robt Morris Assocs.

Bond, Elsie. Public Relief in New York State. 64p. 1993. reprint ed. lib. bdg. 69.00 (*0-7812-5244-X*) Rprt Serv.

Bond, Enriqueta C. Genetic Influences on Responses to the Environment: Report of a Conference on Implications of Environmental - Genetic Interactions. LC RB0155.G46. 125p. reprint ed. pap. 38.80 (*0-608-17958-2*, 201505200004) Bks Demand.

Bond, Evagene H., ed. La Comunidad: Design, Development, & Self-Determination in Hispanic Communities. LC 81-83365. (Illus.). 64p. 1982. pap. 9.00 (*0-941182-02-9*) Partners Livable.

Bond, Felicia. Big Red Barn. (Illus.). (J). (ps up). 1997. 21.95 (*0-694-01105-3*, HarpFestival) HarpC Child Bks.

Bond, Felicia. 4 Valentines In A Rainstorm. LC 82-45586. (Trophy Picture Bk.). (Illus.). 32p. (J). (gr. k-3). 1990. reprint ed. pap. 5.95 (*0-06-443216-5*, HarpTrophy) HarpC Child Bks.

Bond, Felicia. The Halloween Performance. LC 82-45920. (Illus.). 32p. (J). (ps-3). 1983. lib. bdg. 11.89 (*0-690-04309-0*) HarpC Child Bks.

— Halloween Performance. LC 82-45920. (Trophy Picture Bk.). (Illus.). 32p. (J). (ps-3). 1987. pap. 4.95 (*0-06-443155-X*, HarpTrophy) HarpC Child Bks.

B

An Asterisk (*) at the beginning of an entry indicates that the title is appearing for the first time.

*Bond, Felicia. The Halloween Play. LC 99-22741. (Illus.). 32p. (J). (ps-1). 1999. 8.95 (0-06-028684-9) HarpC Child Bks.

Bond, Felicia. Make Your Own Valentines! (Illus.). 32p. (J). (ps-3). 1999. 9.95 (0-694-01259-9) HarpC Child Bks.

— Mary Betty Lizzie McNutt's Birthday. (Illus.). (J). 1983. 4.70 (0-690-04255-8) HarpC Child Bks.

— Poinsettia & Firefighters. (J). 1984. 12.95 (0-690-04400-3) HarpC Child Bks.

— Poinsettia & Her Family. LC 81-43035. (Trophy Picture Bk.). (Illus.). 32p. (J). (ps-3). 1985. reprint ed. pap. 4.95 (0-06-443076-6, HarpTrophy) HarpC Child Bks.

— Poinsettia & the Firefighters. LC 83-46169. (Illus.). 32p. (J). (ps-3). 1984. lib. bdg. 16.89 (0-690-04401-1) HarpC Child Bks.

— Tumble Bumble. LC 96-14417. (Illus.). 32p. (J). (gr. k-2). 1996. 13.95 (1-886910-15-4, Front Street) Front Str.

— Tumble Bumble. 32p. (J). (ps-3). 2000. pap. 5.95 (0-06-443585-7, HarpTrophy) HarpC Child Bks.

— Tumble Bumble Board Book. (Illus.). 34p. (J). (ps-k). 1999. 7.95 (0-694-01344-7, HarpFestival) HarpC Child Bks.

Bond, Felicia, jt. auth. see Numeroff, Laura J.

Bond, Felicia, jt. auth. see Slate, Joseph.

Bond, Frances A. Darling Lady. large type ed. 656p. 1993. 27.99 (0-7505-0485-4) Ulverscroft.

— Return of the Swallow. large type ed. 648p. 1992. 27.99 (0-7505-0189-8) Ulverscroft.

*Bond, Frances Anne. Old Acquaintances. 288p. 2000. 26.00 (0-7278-2289-6, Pub. by Severn Hse) Chivers N Amer.

Bond, Francis. Gothic Architecture in England. LC 70-39656. (Select Bibliographies Reprint Ser.). 1977. reprint ed. 78.95 (0-8369-9931-2) Ayer.

Bond, Frank W., jt. auth. see Bruch, Michael.

Bond, Fred G. Flatboating on the Yellowstone, 1877. LC 96-10178. (Illus.). 64p. (YA). (gr. 6 up). 1998. 19.95 (1-886747-03-2) Ward Hill Pr.

Bond, Frederic D. Stock Movements & Speculation. 2nd ed. LC 75-871. (Wall Street & the Security Market Ser.). 1975. reprint ed. 25.95 (0-405-07248-1) Ayer.

Bond, Frederick B. Gate of Remembrance (1918) 198p. 1999. reprint ed. pap. 16.95 (0-7661-0779-5) Kessinger Pub.

Bond, Frederick W. The Negro & the Drama: The Direct & Indirect Contribution Which the American Negro Has Made to Drama & the Legitimate Stage. 26.95 (0-405-18492-1) Ayer.

Bond, G. C. Catalysis, Vol. 8. 1989. 186.00 (0-85186-594-1) CRC Pr.

Bond, G. C., jt. ed. see Che, M.

Bond, Garnett. The Good Green Witch from Ipswitch. (Illus.). 16p. (J). (ps-5). 1997. pap. 9.95 (1-886225-29-X) Dageforde Pub.

— The Inventions of Mr. Tinkers-a-Lot. Dageforde, Linda J., ed. LC 96-84223. (Illus.). 16p. (J). (ps-4). 1996. pap. 11.95 (1-886225-14-1) Dageforde Pub.

Bond, Garnett Tremain. Tickley Tiger. LC 95-70940. (Illus.). 12p. (Orig.). (J). 1995. pap. 9.95 (1-886225-05-2) Dageforde Pub.

*Bond, Geoffrey C. Natural Eating: Nutritional Anthropology: Eating in Harmony with Our Genetic. (Illus.). 256p. 2000. pap. 19.95 (1-58000-054-1) Griffin CA.

Bond, Geoffrey C., jt. auth. see Ponec, Vladimir.

Bond, George, ed. AIDS in Africa & the Caribbean. LC 97-9642. (C). 1997. pap. 26.00 (0-8133-2879-9, Pub. by Westview) HarpC.

Bond, George, ed. see Adeleke, Tuude.

Bond, George, ed. see Adinoyi-ojo, Onukaba.

Bond, George, ed. see Anda, Michael O.

Bond, George, ed. see Azuonye, Chukwuma.

Bond, George, ed. see Ifemesia, Chieka.

Bond, George, ed. see Nduwke, Pat I.

Bond, George, ed. see Nwanunibu, C. O.

Bond, George, ed. see Okeke, Chika.

Bond, George, ed. see Sallah, Tijan M.

Bond, George C. The Politics of Change in a Zambian Community. LC 75-12228. (Illus.). 189p. Date not set. reprint ed. pap. 58.60 (0-608-20592-3, 205455700003) Bks Demand.

Bond, George C. & Gilliam, Angela, eds. Social Construction of the Past: Representation as Power. LC 93-40053. (One World Archaeology Ser.). (Illus.). 176p. (C). (gr. 13). 1994. 85.00 (0-415-09045-8, B4676) Routledge.

— Social Construction of the Past: Representation As Power. (One World Archaeology Ser.). (Illus.). 256p. (C). 1997. pap. 25.99 (0-415-15224-0) Routledge.

Bond, George D. The Pearl Poem: An Introduction & Interpretation. LC 90-6163. (Studies in Medieval Literature: Vol. 6). 150p. 1991. lib. bdg. 69.95 (0-88946-309-3) E Mellen.

Bond, George D., jt. ed. see Kieckhefer, Richard.

Bond, Gerald A. The Loving Subject: Desire, Eloquence, & Power in Romanesque France. LC 95-17882. (Middle Ages Ser.). 296p. 1995. text 39.95 (0-8122-3322-0) U of Pa Pr.

Bond, Geri, jt. auth. see Spivack, Doris.

*Bond, Gilbert I. Diasporic Community, Cerole Consciousness & the Religious Life of Paul: A Phenomenology of Reconciliation. 208p. 2000. 39.95 (0-664-22271-4) Westminster John Knox.

Bond, Guy L. The Auditory & Speech Characteristics of Poor Readers. LC 72-176578. (Columbia University. Teachers College. Contributions to Education Ser.: No. 657). reprint ed. 37.50 (0-404-55657-4) AMS Pr.

Bond, Guy L., et al. Reading Difficulties. 7th ed. LC 93-6583. 384p. 1993. pap. 72.00 (0-205-15091-8) Allyn.

Bond, H. Lawrence, tr. Nicholas of Cusa: Selected Spiritual Writings. LC 96-44466. (Classics of Western Spirituality Ser.: No. 89). 384p. (Orig.). 1997. 34.95 (0-8091-0482-2); pap. 24.95 (0-8091-3698-8) Paulist Pr.

Bond, H. Lawrence, jt. ed. see Biechler, James E.

Bond, H. R. Autobiographical Reminiscences of Rev. Alvan Bond, D. D., 1793-1882. 214p. 1988. reprint ed. pap. 32.00 (0-8328-0279-4); reprint ed. lib. bdg. 42.00 (0-8328-0278-6) Higginson Bk Co.

Bond, Hallie E. Boats & Boating in the Adirondacks. LC 95-8603. (Illus.). 334p. 1995. pap. 34.95 (0-8156-0374-6) Syracuse U Pr.

— Boats & Boating in the Andirondacks. 1996. text 39.95 (0-07-006654-X) McGraw.

Bond, Harold. The Way It Happens to You. LC 79-50730. 1979. 6.95 (0-933706-08-1); pap. 3.95 (0-933706-09-X) Ararat Pr.

Bond, Helen J. & Kay, Peter. Business Law. 332p. (C). 1990. text 35.00 (1-85431-110-7, Pub. by Blackstone Pr) Gaunt.

— Business Law. 2nd ed. 378p. 1995. pap. 32.00 (1-85431-437-8, Pub. by Blackstone Pr) Gaunt.

Bond, Helen J., jt. auth. see Blake, Allan.

Bond, Helen K. Pontius Pilate in History & Interpretation. LC 97-45970. (Society for New Testament Studies Monograph Ser.: No. 100). 276p. (C). 1998. text 59.95 (0-521-63114-9) Cambridge U Pr.

*Bond, Henry. Point & Shoot. 2000. pap. 39.95 (3-7757-0894-4) Gerd Hatje.

Bond, Horace M. Black American Scholars: A Study of Their Beginnings. LC 72-78234. 210p. 1972. 8.95 (0-913642-01-0); pap. 3.95 (0-913642-04-5) Balamp Pub.

Bond, Horace M. & Bond, Julia W. The Star Creek Papers. Fairclough, Adam, ed. LC 96-48851. 1997. 19.95 (0-8203-1904-X) U of Ga Pr.

Bond, Horace M., et al. The Horace Mann Bond Papers. LC 90-12366. (Black Studies Research Sources). 98p. 1988. write for info. (1-55655-081-2) U Pubns Amer.

Bond, Horatio, ed. Fire & the Air War. 139p. 1946. reprint ed. pap. text 35.00 (0-89126-004-8) MA-AH Pub.

Bond, Howard. White Motif: The Cyclades Islands of Greece. (Illus.). 84p. 1991. 32.00 (0-9612734-2-9) Goodrich Pr.

Bond-Howard, Barbara. Introduction to Stroke. (Therapy Enhancement Ser.). (Illus.). 94p. (Orig.). (C). 1993. ring bd. 16.00 (1-882883-04-7, 275) Idyll Arbor.

Bond, I. D. The Syndicated Credits Market. LC HG1641. (Bank of England Economics Division Discussion Papers: 22). 97p. reprint ed. pap. 30.10 (0-608-15093-2, 202576800046) Bks Demand.

Bond, Ian. Guide to the RICS Members Account Regulations. 1995. pap. 60.00 (0-85406-683-7, Pub. by R-I-C-S Bks) St Mut.

Bond, Ian, et al. Potential Credit Exposure on Interest Rate Swaps. LC HG6024.5. (Bank of England, Economics Division. Working Paper Ser.: No. 25). (Illus.). 45p. reprint ed. pap. 30.00 (0-608-20163-4, 207142700011) Bks Demand.

Bond, J. The Hazards of Life & All That. LC 96-28766. (Illus.). 244p. 1996. 32.00 (0-7503-0360-3) IOP Pub.

Bond, J. A. Comprehensive Toxicology, 13 vols. Incl. General Principles., 13 vols. 354p. 1997. 149.50 (0-08-042966-1); LC 96-33052. (Illus.). 7482p. 1997. 3563.50 (0-08-042301-9, Pergamon Pr) Elsevier.

Bond, J. S. & Barrett, A. J., eds. Proteolysis & Protein Turnover. (Portland Press Proceedings Ser.: Vol. 6). (Illus.). 290p. (C). 1994. text 110.50 (1-85578-039-9, Pub. by Portland Pr Ltd) Ashgate Pub Co.

Bond, J. T., et al. Ypsilanti Perry Preschool Project: Preschool Years & Longitudinal Results Through Fourth Grade. LC 77-92916. (Monographs of the High/Scope Educational Research Foundation: No. 3). 142p. (Orig.). 1978. pap. 12.95 (0-931114-02-0, R1023) High-Scope.

Bond, Jack W. How EU & World Bank Policies Are Destroying Agriculture & the Environment. (Illus.). 168p. 1996. 65.00 (981-00-7101-9, Pub. by AgBe Pub); pap. 45.00 (981-00-7102-7, Pub. by AgBe Pub) Balogh.

Bond, James, III & Tiller, Kate, eds. Blenheim: Landscape for a Palace. 2nd ed. (Illus.). 176p. 1997. pap. 22.95 (0-7509-1589-7, Pub. by Sutton Pub Ltd) Intl Pubs Mktg.

Bond, James E. The Art of Judging. 110p. 1987. 34.95 (0-912051-13-2); pap. 24.95 (0-912051-14-0) Transaction Pubs.

— No Easy Walk to Freedom: Reconstruction & the Ratification of the Fourteenth Amendment. LC 96-42481. 312p. 1997. 65.00 (0-275-95703-9, Praeger Pubs) Greenwood.

Bond, James T., et al. The 1997 National Study of the Changing Workforce. (National Study of the Changing Workforce Ser.: Vol. 2). 176p. 1998. pap. 49.00 (1-888324-09-0, W98-01) Families & Work.

Bond, James T., jt. auth. see Galinsky, Ellen.

Bond, Jan. Through My Looking Glass: A View from the Beach. Lent, Penny, ed. LC 95-80731. 192p. (Orig.). 1995. pap. 9.95 (1-885371-14-4) Kldoscope Pr.

Bond, Jeff. The Music of Star Trek. LC 98-31903. (Illus.). 250p. 1999. pap. 21.95 incl. audio compact disk (1-58065-012-0, Pub. by Lone Eagle Pub) Natl Bk Netwk.

Bond, Jeffrey M., jt. auth. see Bond, Robert E.

Bond, Jennifer S. Science & Engineering Indicators (1998) (Illus.). 765p. (C). 1999. pap. text 50.00 (0-7881-7513-0) DIANE Pub.

Bond, Jennifer Sue. Science & Engineering Indicators, 1996. 648p. 1996. per. 66.00 (0-16-061861-4) USGPO.

— Science & Engineering Indicators, 1998. 808p. 1998. per. 79.00 (0-16-061863-0) USGPO.

Bond, Jill. Dinner's in the Freezer! More Mary & Less Martha. 300p. Date not set. pap. 14.99 (1-888306-54-8) Holly Hall.

— Dinner's in the Freezer! More Mary & Less Martha. 3rd ed. (Illus.). 256p. 1995. pap., student ed. 19.99 (0-9645396-0-8) Holly Hall.

*Bond, Jill. Mega Cooking: A Revolutionary New Plan for Quantity Cooking. (Illus.). 512p. 2000. pap. 24.95 (1-58182-096-8, Cumberland Hearthside) Cumberland Hse.

Bond, Jill. Writing to God's Glory: A Comprehensive Creative Writing Course from Crayon to Quill. LC 97-196791. 337p. 1997. lib. bdg. 39.99 (1-888306-15-7, Home School Pr) Holly Hall.

Bond, Jill, jt. ed. see Bond, Alan.

Bond, Joey. See Man Jump... See God Fall: Tai Chi vs. Technology. 236p. 1999. pap. 19.95 (1-57901-001-6, Pub. by Tai Chi INNERWAVE) ACCESS Pubs Network.

Bond, John. Sources of Ignition: Flammability Characteristics of Chemical & Products. 200p. 1991. text 59.95 (0-7506-1180-4) Buttrwrth-Heinemann.

Bond, John & Bond, Senga. Sociology & Health Care: An Introduction for the Health Care Professionals. 2nd ed. (Illus.). 280p. 1995. pap. text 29.95 (0-443-04059-1) Church.

Bond, John & Coleman, Peter, eds. Aging in Society: An Introduction to Social Gerontology. (Illus.). 338p. (C). 1990. text 45.00 (0-8039-8282-8); pap. text 19.95 (0-8039-8283-6) Sage.

*Bond, John W. The History of Elkhorn Tavern. (Illus.). 24p. 2000. pap. 2.80 (1-888213-54-X) Eastern National.

*Bond, Jon R. & Fleisher, Richard. Polarized Politics: Congress & the President in a Partisan Era. LC 99-59253. 2000. 24.95 (1-56802-493-2) Congr Quarterly.

Bond, Jon R. & Fleisher, Richard. The President in the Legislative Arena. (Illus.). 272p. 1990. pap. text 19.95 (0-226-06410-7) U Ch Pr.

— The President in the Legislative Arena. (Illus.). 272p. 1998. lib. bdg. 56.50 (0-226-06409-3) U Ch Pr.

Bond, Jonathan. Shadowrun Vol. 34: Terminus Report, 34. 1999. mass mkt. 5.99 (0-451-45704-8, ROC) NAL.

Bond, Jonathan & Kirshenbaum, Richard. Under the Radar: Talking to Today's Cynical Consumer. LC 97-24519. (Adweek Magazine Ser.). 256p. 1997. 27.95 (0-471-17469-6) Wiley.

Bond, Judith S., jt. auth. see Beynon, R. J.

Bond, Judith S., jt. ed. see Suzuki, Koichi.

Bond, Julia W., jt. auth. see Bond, Horace M.

*Bond, Julian & Wilson, Sondra Kathryn, eds. Lift every Voice & Sing: A Celebration of the Negro National Anthem 100 Years, 100 Voices. 256p. 2000. 29.95 (0-679-46315-1) Random.

Bond, Julika, tr. see Reiffenstuhl, Gunther, et al.

Bond, Katherine L. Garden of Eden. 1998. pap. 10.95 (1-892896-98-2) Buy Books.

Bond, Kathleen, jt. ed. see Ory, Marcia G.

Bond, Kris, ed. see Austin, Douglas V.

Bond, Kris, ed. see Blasi, Ronald W.

Bond, Kris, ed. see Pachkowski, John.

Bond, Kris, ed. see Turner, Dana.

Bond, L. Susan. Trouble with Jesus: Women, Christology & Preaching. LC 99-38564. 1999. 18.99 (0-8272-3635-2) Chalice Pr.

Bond, Larry. Cauldron. 1999. 9.98 (0-671-04411-7) S&S Trade.

— Cauldron. 768p. 1994. mass mkt. 7.50 (0-446-60026-1, Pub. by Warner Bks) Little.

— Day of Wrath. LC 97-32317. 496p. 1998. 25.00 (0-446-51677-5, Pub. by Warner Bks) Little.

— Day of Wrath. 528p. 1999. mass mkt. 7.99 (0-446-60705-3, Pub. by Warner Bks) Little.

— Day of Wrath. large type ed. LC 98-34898. 732p. 1999. 30.00 (0-7862-1616-6, G K Hall Lrg Type) Mac Lib Ref.

— Desert Storm. 1992. mass mkt. 15.99 (0-446-39397-5) Warner Bks.

*Bond, Larry. The Enemy Within. 1999. 12.98 (0-671-04632-2) S&S Trade.

Bond, Larry. The Enemy Within. 528p. 1997. mass mkt. 7.50 (0-446-60385-6, Pub. by Warner Bks) Little.

— The Enemy Within, Set. abr. ed. 192p. 1996. pap. 23.00 incl. audio (0-671-57054-4, 493929) S&S Trade.

— Red Phoenix. LC 88-40602. 736p. 1990. reprint ed. mass mkt. 7.99 (0-446-35968-8, Pub. by Warner Bks) Little.

— Vortex: A Novel. 944p. 1992. mass mkt. 7.99 (0-446-36304-9, Pub. by Warner Bks) Little.

Bond, Larry K. & Bond, Lois B. How to Make Money with a Home Computer. LC 86-72041. 96p. (Orig.). 1986. pap. 5.95 (0-940419-00-9) Bond Ent UT.

Bond, Lawrence, jt. auth. see Hopman, Ellen E.

Bond, Linda Thorsen, et al. Swingtime Canteen. LC 98-213917. 64 p. 1998. write for info. (0-573-62333-3) S French Trade.

Bond, Lois B., jt. auth. see Bond, Larry K.

Bond, Lynn A., et al. Promoting Successful & Productive Aging. LC 94-42212. (Primary Prevention of Psychopathology Ser.: Vol. 16). (Illus.). 360p. 1995. pap. text 26.50 (0-8039-7172-9) Sage.

Bond, Lynn E. A., et al. Promoting Successful & Productive Aging. LC 94-42212. (Primary Prevention of Psychopathology Ser.: Vol. 16). (Illus.). 360p. 1995. text 56.00 (0-8039-7171-0) Sage.

Bond, Lynne A. & Compas, Bruce E., eds. Primary Prevention & Promotion in the Schools. (Primary Prevention of Psychopathology Ser.: Vol. 12). 440p. (C). 1989. text 49.95 (0-8039-3526-9) Sage.

— Primary Prevention & Promotion in the Schools. LC 89-10130. (Primary Prevention of Psychopathology Ser.: Vol. 12). 452p. 1989. reprint ed. pap. 140.20 (0-608-03007-4, 206345700006) Bks Demand.

Bond, Lynne A. & Wagner, Barry M., eds. Families in Transition: Primary Prevention Programs That Work. LC 86-29795. (Primary Prevention of Psychopathology Ser.: No. 11). 376p. 1988. reprint ed. pap. 116.60 (0-608-01136-3, 205943700001) Bks Demand.

Bond, Lynne A., et al. Psychology, 4 bks. Biddle, Arthur W., ed. LC 86-82608. (Writer's Guide Ser.). 222p. (C). 2000. pap. text 24.36 (0-669-12004-9) HM Trade Div.

Bond, Lynne A., jt. auth. see Rothblum, Esther D.

Bond, M. Skills Clinical Supervision: A Practical Guide for Supervisees, Clinical Supervisors & Managers. LC 97-15164. (Supervision in Context Ser.). 1997. pap. 28.95 (0-335-19660-8) OpUniv Pr.

— Skills Clinical Supervision: A Practical Guide for Supervisees, Clinical Supervisors & Managers. 192p. 1997. 89.95 (0-335-19661-6) OpUniv Pr.

Bond, M. G., et al, eds. Clinical Diagnosis of Atherosclerosis: Quantitative Methods of Evaluation. (Illus.). 586p. 1983. 65.00 (0-387-90780-7) Spr-Verlag.

Bond, Margaret N., jt. auth. see Wauchope, Robert.

Bond, Margaret N., jt. auth. see Waxman, Jan LaMartina.

*Bond, Mark & Bond, Rita. International Relocation--A Practical Guide to Living & Working Overseas. (Special Publication Ser.). (Illus.). xii, 460p. 2000. pap. 50.00 (0-89181-821-9, 501) AAPG.

Bond, Mark, jt. auth. see Conran, Sebastian.

Bond, Mary. Balancing Your Body: A Self-Help Approach to Rolfing Movement. LC 96-16999. (Illus.). 224p. 1996. reprint ed. pap. 14.95 (0-89281-642-2, Heal Arts VT) Inner Tradit.

Bond, Mary E. & Caron, Martine M. Canadian Reference Sources: An Annotated Bibliography. LC 96-178990. 1076p. 225.00 (0-7748-0565-X) U of Wash Pr.

Bond, Mary W. Far Afield in the Caribbean. LC 75-140150. (Illus.). 1971. 6.95 (0-915180-13-8) Harrowood Bks.

— To James Bond with Love. LC 80-17134. (Illus.). 224p. 1980. 17.95 (0-915010-28-3) Sutter House.

Bond, Marybeth. Gutsy Mamas: Travel Tips & Wisdom for Mothers on the Road. (Travelers' Tales Guides Ser.). 139p. 1997. pap. 7.95 (1-885211-20-1, 20-1) Trvlers Tale.

Bond, Marybeth. Gutsy Women: Travel Tips & Wisdom for the Road. 25.00 (1-885211-17-1) Trvlers Tale.

Bond, Marybeth. Gutsy Women: Travel Tips & Wisdom for the Road. 123p. 1996. pap. 7.95 (1-885211-15-5, 15-5) Trvlers Tale.

Bond, Marybeth, ed. A Woman's World. (Travelers' Tales Ser.). (Illus.). 475p. 1995. pap. 17.95 (1-885211-06-6) Trvlers Tale.

Bond, Marybeth & Michael, Pamela, eds. A Woman's Passion for Travel: More Stories from a Woman's World. LC 99-35889. 298p. 1999. pap. 17.95 (1-885211-36-8, 36-8, Pub. by Trvlers Tale) OReilly & Assocs.

Bond, Marybeth, jt. ed. see Michael, Pamela.

Bond, Meg, jt. auth. see Hart, Elizabeth.

Bond, Mel. Understanding Your Worst Enemy. Cox, Gale, ed. 130p. (Orig.). 1991. pap. 6.00 (1-882318-00-5) Agape Wrd Minist.

Bond, Mel & Bond, Donna. Unimaginable Love. 1995. pap. write for info. (1-882318-01-3) Agape Wrd Minist.

Bond, Michael. A Bear Called Paddington. LC 60-9096. (Paddington Ser.). (Illus.). 128p. (J). (gr. 2-5). 1968. pap. 4.99 (0-440-40483-5, YB BDD) BDD Bks Young Read.

— A Bear Called Paddington. (Paddington Ser.). (Illus.). (J). (gr. 2-5). 1958. 9.60 (0-606-02273-2, Pub. by Turtleback) Demco.

*Bond, Michael. A Bear Called Paddington. rev. ed. LC 60-9096. (Paddington Ser.). (Illus.). 144p. (J). (gr. 2-5). 1998. 15.00 (0-395-92951-2) HM.

Bond, Michael. Halloween Performance. (J). 1983. 4.70 (0-690-04308-2) HarpC Child Bks.

— Here Comes Thursday! 128p. (J). 1994. pap. write for info. (1-85479-937-1, Pub. by M OMara) Trafalgar.

— The Hilarious Adventures of Paddington, 5 bks., Set. Incl. Bear Called Paddington. (Illus.). (J). (gr. 2-5). 1986. More about Paddington. (Illus.). (J). (gr. 2-5). 1986. Paddington at Large. (Illus.). (J). (gr. 2-5). 1986. Paddington at Work. (Illus.). (J). (gr. 2-5). 1986. Paddington Helps Out. (Illus.). (J). (gr. 2-5). 1986. (Illus.). (J). 1986. Set boxed set 14.75 (0-440-43668-0) Dell.

— Michael Bond's Book of Bears. 144p. (J). 1992. write for info. (1-85479-111-7, Pub. by M OMara) Assoc Pubs Grp.

— Monsieur Pamplemousse. large type ed. (Nightingale Series Large Print Bks.). 240p. 1991. pap. 14.95 (0-8161-5111-3, G K Hall Lrg Type) Mac Lib Ref.

*Bond, Michael. Monsieur Pamplemousse Afloat. 1999. pap. 9.95 (0-7490-0347-2) Allison & Busby.

Bond, Michael. Monsieur Pamplemousse & the Secret Mission: A Gastronomic Mystery. large type ed. (Nightingale Ser.). 280p. 1991. pap. 14.95 (0-8161-5110-5, G K Hall Lrg Type) Mac Lib Ref.

*Bond, Michael. Monsieur Pamplemousse Omnibus, Vol. 2. 1999. pap. text 9.95 (0-7490-0410-X) Allison & Busby.

— Monsieur Pamplemousse Omnibus, Vol. 3. 1999. pap. 9.95 (0-7490-0442-8) Allison & Busby.

— Monsieur Pamplemousse on Probation. 2000. pap. 9.95 (0-7490-0463-0, Pub. by Allison & Busby) Intl Pubs Mktg.

Bond, Michael. Monsieur Pamplemousse Rests His Case. 1993. mass mkt. 4.50 (0-449-22045-1) Fawcett.

— Monsieur Pamplemousse Stands Firm. 1994. mass mkt. 4.99 (0-449-22201-2) Fawcett.

— Monsieur Pamplemousse Takes the Cure. large type ed. (Nightingale Ser.). 288p. 1990. pap. 14.95 (0-8161-4893-7, G K Hall Lrg Type) Mac Lib Ref.

— More about Paddington, (Paddington Ser.). (Illus.). 144p. (J). (gr. 2-5). 1979. 15.00 (0-395-06640-9) HM.

B

An Asterisk (*) at the beginning of an entry indicates that the title is appearing for the first time.

B

Cohen, D. Bernard, ed. LC 79-7967. (Three Centuries of Science in America Ser.). (Illus.). 1980. reprint ed. lib. bdg. 56.95 (*0-405-12548-8*) Ayer.

Bond, William H. & Amory, Hugh, eds. Printed Catalogues of the Harvard College Library, 1723-1790. 738p. 1996. 75.00 (*0-9620737-3-3*, 44060) Oak Knoll.

Bond, William J. Going Solo: Developing a Home-Based Consulting Business from the Ground Up. (Illus.). 272p. 1997. pap. 14.95 (*0-07-006642-6*) McGraw.

— Home-Based Catalogue Marketing: A Success Guide for Entrepreneurs. (Illus.). 242p. 1998. reprint ed. lib. bdg. 29.95 (*0-7351-0029-2*) Replica Bks.

— Home-Based Mail Order: A Success Guide for Entrepreneurs. 232p. 1990. pap. 14.95 (*0-07-155920-5*) McGraw.

— Home-based Newsletter Publishing: A Success Guide for Entrepreneurs. 191p. 1991. pap. 14.95 (*0-07-006557-8*) McGraw.

— Managing Your Priorities from Start to Success. (Briefcase Bks.). 156p. 1996. text 16.95 (*0-7863-0387-5*, Irwn Prfssnl) McGraw-Hill Prof.

*__Bond, William J.__ Powerful Positive Pep Talks to Live By. (YA). (gr. 9). 1999. pap. 5.99 (*0-918694-05-1*) Career Pub MA.

— Powerful Positive Pep Talks to Live By. 1999. 12.99 (*0-918694-04-3*) Career Pub MA.

Bond, William J. You Can Do It - Just Try. 120p. (Orig.). 1993. 12.95 (*0-918694-02-7*); pap. 5.95 (*0-918694-03-5*) Career Pub MA.

*__Bond, Zinny.__ Slips of the Ear. (Illus.). 192p. 1999. 49.95 (*0-12-113340-0*) Acad Pr.

Bonda, Jan. The One Purpose of God: An Answer to the Doctrine of Eternal Punishment. LC 97-33626. 288p. (Orig.). 1997. pap. 25.00 (*0-8028-4186-4*) Eerdmans.

Bondad, Murthy V. & Wayson, Roger L., eds. High Speed Ground Transportation Systems I - Planning & Engineering: Proceedings of the First International Conference on High Speed Ground Transportation (HSGT) Systems. LC 93-11166. 798p. 1993. 62.00 (*0-87262-927-9*) Am Soc Civil Eng.

Bondada, Murthy V., ed. see American Society of Civil Engineers Staff.

Bondada, Murthy V., jt. ed. see Neumann, Edward S.

*__Bondada, Murthy V. A., et al.__ Urban Public Transporation Systems: Implementing Efficient Urban Transit Systems & Enhancing Transit Usage. LC 00-38953. 2000. pap. write for info. (*0-7844-0498-4*) Am Soc Civil Eng.

Bondanelia, Peter. Italian Cinema: From Neorealism to the Present. enl. ed. (Illus.). 510p. 1989. pap. 22.95 (*0-8264-0426-X*) Continuum.

*__Bondanella, J.__ Microworld Simulations for Command & Control Training of Theater Logistics & Support Staffs: A Curriculum Strategy. LC 98-49149. 1998. pap. 13.00 (*0-8330-2671-2*) Rand Corp.

Bondanella, Julia C. The Italian Renaissance Reader. 1987. pap. 15.95 (*0-452-01013-6*, Plume) Dutton Plume.

Bondanella, Julia C., et al, eds. The Life of Titian by Carlo Ridolfi. Bondanella, Peter, tr. (Illus.). 168p. 1996. pap. 22.50 (*0-271-01627-2*) Pa St U Pr.

Bondanella, Julia C., ed. see Ridolfi, Carlo.

Bondanella, Julia C., tr. see Rousseau, Jean-Jacques.

Bondanella, Julia Conway, tr. see Machiavelli, Niccolo.

Bondanella, Julia Conway, tr. see Vasari, Giorgio.

Bondanella, Peter. The Cinema of Federico Fellini. (Illus.). 392p. 1992. pap. text 19.95 (*0-691-00875-2*, Pub. by Princeton U Pr) Cal Prin Full Svc.

— Umberto Eco & the Open Text: Semiotics, Fiction, Popular Culture. LC 96-3099. 234p. (C). 1997. text 44.95 (*0-521-44200-1*) Cambridge U Pr.

Bondanella, Peter, et al, eds. La Strada. (Films in Print Ser.). (Illus.). 200p. 1987. pap. text 17.00 (*0-8135-1237-9*) Rutgers U Pr.

Bondanella, Peter, ed. & tr. see Machiavelli, Niccolo.

Bondanella, Peter, intro. see Vasari, Giorgio.

Bondanella, Peter, tr. see Bondanella, Julia C., et al, eds.

Bondanella, Peter, tr. see Machiavelli, Niccolo.

Bondanella, Peter, tr. see Ridolfi, Carlo.

Bondanella, Peter C., et al, eds. Dictionary of Italian Literature. expanded rev. ed. LC 95-33077. 736p. 1996. lib. bdg. 99.50 (*0-313-27745-1*, Greenwood Pr) Greenwood.

Bondanella, Peter E. The Eternal City: Roman Images in the Modern World. LC 86-30847. 304p. 1987. pap. 94.30 (*0-608-05202-7*, 206573900001) Bks Demand.

— The Films of Roberto Rossellini. LC 92-11012. (Cambridge Film Classics Ser.). (Illus.). 199p. (C). 1993. text 52.95 (*0-521-39236-5*); pap. text 14.95 (*0-521-39866-5*) Cambridge U Pr.

Bondanella, Peter E. & Degli-Esposti, Cristina, eds. Critical Essays on Federico Fellini. LC 92-43472. (Critical Essays on Film Ser.). 326p. 1993. 55.00 (*0-8161-7330-3*, G K Hall & Co) Mac Lib Ref.

Bondanella, Peter E., ed. see Boccaccio, Giovanni.

Bondanella, Peter E., tr. see Boccaccio, Giovanni.

Bondanella, Peter E., tr. see Machiavelli, Niccolo.

Bondar, Barbara. Fire! Raging Destruction. LC 98-128790. (Cover-To-Cover Bks.). 56 p. 1997. write for info. (*0-7807-6114-6*, Covercraft) Perfection Learn.

— On the Shuttle: Eight Days in Space. 1993. 15.15 (*0-606-05961-X*, Pub. by Turtleback) Demco.

— Volcano! Dome of Fire LC 98-196551. (Cover-to-cover Bks.). 56 p. 1997. write for info. (*0-7807-6148-0*) Perfection Learn.

Bondar, Barbara & Bondar, Roberta. On the Shuttle: Eight Days in Space. (Illus.). 64p. (YA). (gr. 4 up). 1995. 16.95 (*1-895688-12-4*, Pub. by Owl Bks); pap. 8.95 (*1-895688-10-8*, Pub. by Owl Bks) Firefly Bks Ltd.

Bondar, Roberta. Touching the Earth. (Illus.). 144p. 1994. pap. 19.95 (*1-55013-657-7*) Firefly Bks Ltd.

Bondar, Roberta, jt. auth. see Bondar, Barbara.

Bondarev, V. N., jt. auth. see Samsonov, G. V.

Bondarevsky, G. L., ed. Caucasian Archaeographical Commission, Proceedings 1866-1904. 14000p. 1996. 1495.00 (*1-85207-975-4*) N Ross.

Bondarko, Alexander V. Functional Grammar: A Field Approach. LC 91-7761. (Linguistic & Literary Studies in Eastern Europe: Vol. 35). viii, 207p. 1991. 65.00 (*1-55619-260-6*) J Benjamins Pubng Co.

Bondarowicz, Marv. Snapshots. (Illus.). 1977. pap. 5.00 (*0-89439-000-7*) Printed Matter.

Bondarvesky, Grigor. Boundary Issues in Central Asia. 60p. 1996. pap. text 12.95 (*1-899658-21-1*, Pub. by Royal Inst Intl Affairs) Brookings.

*__Bondaryk, J. E.__ Feasibility of High Frequency Acoustic Imaging for Inspection of Containments. 55p. 1998. pap. 5.50 (*0-16-062952-7*) USGPO.

Bondav, I., ed. Chronological Atlas of the Bulgarian Medicinal Plants. (Illus.). 272p. 1998. pap. 84.95 (*954-430-036-8*) Intl Scholars.

Bonde, Kurt. Birds of Lesotho. (Illus.). 120p. 1993. pap. text 29.95 (*0-86980-881-8*, Pub. by Univ Natal Pr) Intl Spec Bk.

Bonder, Bette. Psychopathology & Function. 2nd ed. (Illus.). 304p. 1995. pap. 30.00 (*1-55642-270-9*, 32709) SLACK Inc.

Bonder, Bette & Wagner, Marilyn B., eds. Functional Performance in Older Adults. LC 94-1427. (Illus.). 398p. (C). 1994. text 47.00 (*0-8036-0964-7*) Davis Co.

Bonder, Bette, et al. Care in Multicultural Settings: A Guide for Therapists. 250p. (C). Date not set. pap. text 33.00 (*1-55642-459-0*) SLACK Inc.

Bonder, Bette R. & Wagner, Marilyn B. Functional Performance in Order Adults. (Illus.). 425p. 2000. text 45.00 (*0-8036-0543-9*) Davis Co.

Bonder, N. The Kabbalah of Food. LC 97-42940. 1998. 18.00 (*1-57062-347-3*, Pub. by Shambhala Pubns) Random.

Bonder, Nilton. The Kabbalah of Money: Insights on Livelihood, Business, & All Forms of Economic Behavior. 192p. 1996. 18.00 (*1-57062-214-0*, Pub. by Shambhala Pubns) Random.

*__Bonder, Nilton.__ Yiddishe Kop: The Way of Creative Problem Solving in Jewish Learning, Lore, & Humor. LC 98-54851. 112p. 1999. pap. 12.95 (*1-57062-448-8*, Pub. by Shambhala Pubns) Random.

Bonder, Saniel. While Jesus Weeps. 177p. 1998. pap. 14.95 (*0-9662304-1-8*) Mt Tam Awakenings.

Bondeson, Jan. Buried Alive. 23.95 (*0-393-04906-X*) Norton.

Bondeson, Jan. A Cabinet of Medical Curiosities. LC 97-20749. (Illus.). 250p. 1997. text 29.95 (*0-8014-3431-9*) Cornell U Pr.

— A Cabinet of Medical Curiosities. (Illus.). 250p. 1999. pap. 14.00 (*0-393-31892-3*) Norton.

*__Bondeson, Jan.__ The Feejee Mermaid: And Other Essays in Natural & Unnatural History. LC 98-38295. (Illus.). 336p. 1999. 29.95 (*0-8014-3609-5*) Cornell U Pr.

— The London Monster: A Sanguinary Tale. 2000. 29.95 (*0-8122-3576-2*) U of Pa Pr.

— The Two-Headed Boy & Other Medical Marvels. LC 00-20902. (Illus.). 320p. 2000. 29.95 (*0-8014-3767-9*) Cornell U Pr.

Bondeson, Ulla V. Prisoners in Prison Societies. 356p. 1988. 44.95 (*0-88738-205-3*) Transaction Pubs.

Bondeson, William B., et al, eds. New Knowledge in the Biomedical Sciences. 242p. 1982. text 106.00 (*90-277-1319-7*, D Reidel) Kluwer Academic.

Bondeson, William B., et al. Abortion & the Status of the Fetus. 383p. 1983. text 111.00 (*90-277-1493-2*, D Reidel) Kluwer Academic.

Bondeson, William B., jt. auth. see Bole, Thomas J., III.

Bondesson, Lennart. Generalized Gamma Convolutions & Related Classes of Distributions & Densities. LC 92-16277. (Lecture Notes in Statistics Ser.: Vol. 76). (Illus.). 184p. 1992. 45.95 (*0-387-97866-6*) Spr-Verlag.

Bondeux, Monique, ed. Sailing Through the Storm to the Ocean of Peace. LC 95-94951. (Illus.). 40p. (J). (gr. k-6). 1996. 14.95 (*1-887494-08-1*) Kidsail.

Bondhus, Sandra V. Quimper Pottery: A French Folk Art Faience. (Illus.). 242p. 1995. reprint ed. 65.00 (*0-9640855-0-X*) S V Bondhus.

Bondi, A., et al, eds. Urogenital Infections. LC 87-14209. (Advances in Experimental Medicine & Biology Ser.: Vol. 224). (Illus.). 146p. 1988. 65.00 (*0-306-42799-0*, Plenum Trade) Perseus Pubng.

Bondi, Andrea H. & Hudson, Colin A. Lloyd's Introductory Test Textbook. 104p. 1986. 110.00 (*0-948691-05-0*, Pub. by Witherby & Co) St Mut.

Bondi, Aron A. Animal Nutrition: In Partial Collaboration with David Drori. LC 85-26376. 568p. reprint ed. pap. 176.10 (*0-8357-6935-6*, 203799400009) Bks Demand.

Bondi, Edward, et al. Dermatology: Clinical Manual. (Illus.). 422p. (C). 1992. pap. 32.95 (*0-8385-1274-7*, A1274-8, Apple Lange Med) McGraw.

Bondi, Hermann. Relativity & Common Sense: A New Approach to Einstein. (Illus.). 177p. (C). 1980. reprint ed. pap. 6.95 (*0-486-24021-5*) Dover.

Bondi, Hermann. Science, Churchill & Me: The Autobiogrpahy of Hermann Bondi Sir Hermann Bondi, KCB, FRS. (Illus.). 154p. 1990. 54.50 (*0-08-037235-X*, Pergamon Pr) Elsevier.

Bondi, Hermann & Weston-Smith, Elizabeth M., eds. The Universe Unfolding. LC 97-14899. (Illus.). 416p. (C). 1998. text 35.00 (*0-19-851188-4*) OUP.

Bondi, Joseph, jt. auth. see Wiles, Jon.

Bondi, Joseph, jt. auth. see Wiles, Jon W., Jr.

Bondi, Joseph W., jt. auth. see Wiles, Jon W.

Bondi, L. & Matthews, M. H., eds. Education & Society: Studies in the Politics, Sociology & Geography of Education. 272p. (C). 1988. lib. bdg. 57.50 (*0-415-00451-9*) Routledge.

*__Bondi, Richard.__ Cryptography for Visual Basic: A Programmer's Guide to the Microsoft CryptoAPI. 640p. 2000. pap. 49.99 incl. cd-rom (*0-471-38189-6*) Wiley.

Bondi, Roberta C. In Ordinary Time: Healing the Wounds of the Heart. 208p. 1996. 16.95 (*0-687-27326-9*) Abingdon.

— Memories of God: Theological Reflection on a Life. LC 94-37755. 224p. (Orig.). 1995. pap. 16.95 (*0-687-03892-8*) Abingdon.

*__Bondi, Roberta C.__ Night on the Flint River. LC 99-19063. 1999. 17.00 (*0-687-02455-2*) Abingdon.

Bondi, Roberta C. A Place to Pray. LC 98-35200. 208p. 1998. 18.95 (*0-687-02574-5*) Abingdon.

— To Love As God Loves: Conversations with the Early Church. LC 86-46421. 112p. 1987. pap. 13.00 (*0-8006-2041-0*, 1-2041, Fortress Pr) Augsburg Fortress.

— To Pray & to Love: Conversations on Prayer with the Early Church. LC 91-3026. 128p. 1991. pap. 14.00 (*0-8006-2511-0*, 1-2511, Fortress Pr) Augsburg Fortress.

— To Pray & to Love: Conversations with the Deserts Fathers. 160p. 1994. pap. 30.00 (*0-86012-195-X*, Pub. by Srch Pr) St Mut.

Bondo, P., jt. auth. see Thoma, J.

Bondoc, Anna. Direct Address. 1998. pap. write for info. (*0-201-31134-8*) Addison-Wesley.

*__Bondoc, Anna & Daly, Meg.__ Letters Of Intent: Women Cross the Generations to Talk About Family, Work, Sex, Love, & the Future of Feminism. LC 98-51896. 256p. 1999. 23.00 (*0-684-85624-7*) S&S Trade.

Bondor, Rebecca. The Little Mermaid: Flounder's Gift. LC 93-78806. (Golden Little Super Shape Bks.). (Illus.). 24p. (J). (ps-3). 1994. 1.79 (*0-307-10560-1*, 10560, Goldn Books) Gldn Bks Pub Co.

Bondorew, Ray. Stripers & Streamers. LC 97-101918. (Illus.). 120p. 1996. pap. 19.95 (*1-57188-072-0*) F Amato Pubns.

Bondow, Susan G. & Kelm, Paul. Through the Looking Glass & Back: Your Passport to Identity-Self-Image. LC 93-84288. 96p. 1993. 11.99 (*0-8100-0489-5*, 15N2000) Northwest Pub.

Bonds, Charles W., jt. auth. see Bonds, Lella G.

Bonds, Christopher N. The Musical Impulse. 2nd ed. LC 95-120081. 368p. 1994. pap., per. 60.95 (*0-8403-9802-6*, 40980201) Kendall-Hunt.

*__Bonds, Lawrence E.__ Daniel. (Berit Olam (The Everlasting Covenant) Ser.). 2000. 0.00 (*0-8146-5063-5*) Liturgical Pr.

Bonds, Lella G. & Bonds, Charles W. Teachers of the Year in the United States. 1998. 54.95 (*1-55630-829-9*) Brentwood Comm.

Bonds, Mark E. After Beethoven: Imperatives of Originality in the Symphony. (Illus.). 208p. 1996. 36.50 (*0-674-00855-3*) HUP.

— Wordless Rhetoric: Musical Form & the Metaphor of the Oration. (Studies in the History of Music). 248p. (C). 1991. 51.95 (*0-674-95602-8*) HUP.

Bonds, Parris A. For All Time. large type ed. LC 94-33997. 1996. 22.95 (*1-56895-124-8*) Wheeler Pub.

— Made for Each Other - Ravished, 2 bks. in 1. 304p. 1993. mass mkt. 4.99 (*0-505-51915-1*, Love Spell) Dorchester Pub Co.

*__Bonds, Ray.__ Vietnam War; The Illustrated History of the Conflict in Southeast Asia. 1999. 29.95 (*1-84065-108-3*) Salamander.

*__Bonds, Tim, et al.__ Employing Commercial Satellite Communications: Wideband Investment Options for the Department of Defense. (Illus.). xxiii, 145p. 2000. pap. 15.00 (*0-8330-2827-8*, MR-1192) Rand Corp.

Bonds, Tim, et al. A Tool for Evaluating Force Modernization Options. LC 98-22192. (Illus.). 59p. 1998. pap. 7.50 (*0-8330-2628-3*, MR-905-OSD) Rand Corp.

Bondur, Tom, ed. see Rozenshtein, David, et al.

Bondurant, Bob. Bob Bondurant on High Performance Driving. 4th ed. LC 98-24293. (Illus.). 144p. 1998. pap. 15.95 (*0-7603-0603-6*) MBI Pubg.

*__Bondurant, Bob & Sanow, Ed.__ Bob Bondurant on Police & Pursuit Driving. LC 99-49023. (Illus.). 160p. 2000. pap. 19.95 (*0-7603-0686-9*, 129990AP, Pub. by MBI Pubg) Motorbooks Intl.

Bondurant, Joan V. Conquest of Violence: The Gandhian Philosophy of Conflict. 296p. 1988. reprint ed. pap. text 15.95 (*0-691-02281-X*, Pub. by Princeton U Pr) Cal Prin Full Svc.

Bondurant, R. M., ed. see Thomas-Trautman.

Bondurant, Stuart, ed. see Institute of Medicine Staff.

Bondy. Graph Theory. text. write for info. (*0-471-36324-3*) Wiley.

Bondy, Andrew, ed. The Pyramid Approach to Education. 80p. 1996. ring bd. 25.00 (*1-928598-00-5*) Pyramid Educ.

Bondy, Andrew S. & Frost, Lori. Pecs - The Picture Exchange Communication System. (Illus.). 71p. 1996. 45.00 (*1-928598-01-3*) Pyramid Educ.

Bondy, Carolyn, jt. ed. see Le Roith, Derek.

Bondy, Carolyn, jt. ed. see LeRoith, Derek.

Bondy, Chris, et al. Color Copier/Printer Assessment. (Illus.). 119p. 1997. pap. 495.00 (*0-9658222-0-6*, CCPA-1) TPR Group.

Bondy, Jeffrey S., jt. auth. see Guzzo, Richard A.

Bondy, Philip K. & Rosenberg, Leon E. Metabolic Control of Disease. 8th ed. LC 78-52722. (Illus.). 1980. text 225.00 (*0-7216-1844-8*, W B Saunders Co) Harcrt Hlth Sci Grp.

Bondy, Sebastian S., et al. Theatre from Nigeria, 5 vols. in 1. (B. E. Ser.: No. 109). 1967. 25.00 (*0-8115-3040-X*) Periodicals Srv.

Bondy, Stephen C., ed. Metal Neurotoxicity. 198p. 1987. 117.00 (*0-8493-4941-9*, RC347, CRC Reprint) Franklin.

Bondy, Valerie C. Florida Bed & Breakfast Guide. De Mitchell, Lisa A., ed. (Illus.). 160p. (Orig.). 1995. pap. 10.95 (*0-9645336-0-X*) Queen of Hearts.

*__Bondy, Valerie Moore.__ Florida Bed & Breakfast Guide. 3rd rev. ed. Demitchell, Lisa A., ed. (Illus.). 96p. 2000. pap. 11.95 (*0-9645336-2-6*) Queen of Hearts.

Bondy, William. Separation of Governmental Powers in History, in Theory, & in the Constitutions. LC 04-1845. (Columbia University. Studies in the Social Sciences: No. 14). reprint ed. 34.50 (*0-404-51014-0*) AMS Pr.

*__Bondy, William.__ Separation of Governmental Powers in History, in Theory, & in the Constitutions, 1896. LC 98-44994. 185p. 1999. reprint ed. 65.00 (*1-886363-65-X*) Lawbk Exchange.

Bondzi-Simpson, P. Ebow. Legal Relations Between Transnational Corporations & Host States. LC 90-8389. 240p. 1990. 69.50 (*0-89930-590-3*, BZL, Quorum Bks) Greenwood.

Bondzi-Simpson, P. Ebow, ed. The Law & Economic Development in the Third World. LC 91-28004. 200p. 1992. 59.95 (*0-275-93925-1*, C3925, Praeger Pubs) Greenwood.

Bone. Designing for Safe Building: Avoiding Health & Safety Hazard. 96p. 1999. pap. text 29.95 (*0-7506-3085-X*) Buttrwrth-Heinemann.

Bone, Arthur H., ed. see Pierce, Walter M.

Bone, B. E. C. I. I. Management Eleven Insurance Broking, No. 311. (C). 1983. suppl. ed. 240.00 (*0-7855-4281-7*, Pub. by Witherby & Co) St Mut.

Bone, Bob. Discover the Good Life in Rural America: The City Slicker's Guide to Buying Country Real Estate Without Losing Your Shirt. Ross, Marilyn, ed. & frwd. by. Ross, Tom, frwd. 1994. pap. 12.95 (*0-918880-36-X*) Comm Creat.

Bone, Chi. Atlanta Color Tour Book. (Illus.). 72p. (Orig.). (C). 1989. pap. text 7.95 (*0-936672-78-1*) Aerial Photo.

Bone, Christopher. The Disinherited Children: A Study of the New Left & the Generation Gap. LC 74-19086. 192p. 1977. reprint ed. pap. 59.60 (*0-608-05346-5*, 206505100012) Bks Demand.

Bone, David L. & Scifres, Mary J. Music & Worship Planner, 1996-97. 144p. 1996. pap. text, spiral bd. 15.95 (*0-687-10961-2*) Abingdon.

— Prepare! A Weekly Worship Planbook for Pastors & Musicians, 1998-1999. Orig. Title: Music & Worship Planner. 144p. 1998. pap. 16.95 (*0-687-18999-3*) Abingdon.

*__Bone, David L. & Scifres, Mary J.__ Prepare! A Weekly Worship Planbook for Pastors & Musicians, 1999-2000. 1999. 17.00 (*0-687-07401-0*) Abingdon.

Bone, David L. & Scifres, Mary J. United Methodist Music & Worship Planner, 1998-99. 1998. pap. 16.95 (*0-687-19009-6*) Abingdon.

Bone, Diane. The Business of Listening: A Practice Guide to Effective Listening. rev. ed. Crisp, Michael, ed. LC 93-74408. (Fifty-Minute Ser.). (Illus.). 88p. (Orig.). 1994. pap. 10.95 (*1-56052-286-0*) Crisp Pubns.

Bone, Diane & Griggs, Rick. Quality at Work: A Personal Guide to Professional Standards. LC 88-72252. (Fifty-Minute Ser.). (Illus.). 88p. (Orig.). 1989. pap. 10.95 (*0-931961-72-6*) Crisp Pubns.

Bone, Diane, jt. auth. see Hicks, Robert.

Bone, Edith, tr. see Lukacs, Georg.

Bone, Edith, tr. see Tolstoy, Leo.

Bone, G. Days in Old Spain. 1976. lib. bdg. 59.95 (*0-8490-1702-5*) Gordon Pr.

Bone, Gavin D. Anglo-Saxon Poetry. LC 75-128874. (Select Bibliographies Reprint Ser.). 1977. 12.95 (*0-8369-5494-7*) Ayer.

— Anglo-Saxon Poetry. LC 79-161951. 1950. reprint ed. 39.00 (*0-403-01347-X*) Scholarly.

Bone, Hugh A., jt. auth. see Ogden, Daniel M., Jr.

Bone, Ian, ed. Class War: A Decade of Disorder. (Illus.). 160p. (gr. 13). 1991. pap. 17.00 (*0-86091-558-1*, A6245, Pub. by Verso) Norton.

Bone, Ian, jt. auth. see Lindsay, Kenneth W.

Bone, J. J. Going Native. (Illus.). 276p. (Orig.). 1989. pap. 14.95 (*0-9620069-0-4*) Pygmy Pr.

— How to Self-Publish or Perish: What the Other Guides Won't Tell You So They Can Sell You Their Book. 140p. (Orig.). 1996. pap. 9.95 (*0-9620069-1-2*) Pygmy Pr.

Bone, J. P. Illegals. LC 96-94555. 214p. (Orig.). 1996. pap. 12.95 (*0-9651921-0-5*) Mindfld Pubns.

Bone, Jan. Opportunities in Cable Television. (Illus.). 160p. 1986. 13.95 (*0-8442-6258-7*, VGM Career) NTC Contemp Pub Co.

— Opportunities in Cable Television. (Illus.). 160p. 1988. pap. 10.95 (*0-8442-6259-5*, VGM Career) NTC Contemp Pub Co.

— Opportunities in Cable Television Careers. LC 92-18317. (Opportunities in...Ser.). (Illus.). 160p. 1994. 14.95 (*0-8442-4026-5*, VGM Career) NTC Contemp Pub Co.

— Opportunities in Computer Aided Design & Computer Aided Manufacturing Careers (CAD-CAM) LC 93-17885. (Opportunities in...Ser.). (Illus.). 160p. 1994. 14.95 (*0-8442-4084-2*, 40842, VGM Career) NTC Contemp Pub Co.

— Opportunities in Film. (Opportunities In . . . Ser.). (Illus.). 160p. pap. 12.95 (*0-8442-8622-2*, 297OIF, VGM Career) NTC Contemp Pub Co.

— Opportunities in Film Careers. LC 97-32180. (Opportunities in...Ser.). (Illus.). 160p. 1998. 14.95 (*0-8442-2337-9*, 23379, VGM Career); pap. 11.95 (*0-8442-2339-5*, 23395, VGM Career) NTC Contemp Pub Co.

— Opportunities in Laser Technology Careers. (Opportunities In . . . Ser.). (Illus.). 160p. pap. 12.95 (*0-8442-6515-2*, 297OILT, VGM Career) NTC Contemp Pub Co.

An Asterisk (*) at the beginning of an entry indicates that the title is appearing for the first time.

— Opportunities in Laser Technology Careers. (Illus.). 160p. 1991. 14.95 (*0-8442-6514-4*, VGM Career) NTC Contemp Pub Co.

*Bone, Jan.** Opportunities in Laser Technology Careers. rev. ed. LC 99-52563. (Opportunities in... Ser.). 160p. 2000. 14.95 (*0-658-00203-1*, 002031); pap. 11.95 (*0-658-00204-X*, 00204X) NTC Contemp Pub Co.

Bone, Jan. Opportunities in Plastics Careers. LC 90-50732. (Opportunities In . . . Ser.). (Illus.). 160p. (YA). (gr. 7-12). pap. 12.95 (*0-8442-8674-5*, 297OIPLA, VGM Career) NTC Contemp Pub Co.

— Opportunities in Robotics Careers. 160p. 1993. pap. 10.95 (*0-8442-6021-5*, VGM Career) NTC Contemp Pub Co.

— Opportunities in Robotics Careers. 160p. 1994. text 13.95 (*0-8442-6020-7*, VGM Career) NTC Contemp Pub Co.

— Opportunities in Robotics Careers. (Opportunities in...Ser.). (Illus.). 160p. 1994. 14.95 (*0-8442-4057-5*, 40575, VGM Career) NTC Contemp Pub Co.

— Opportunities in Telecommunications. (Illus.). 160p. 1992. 13.95 (*0-8442-8654-0*, VGM Career) NTC Contemp Pub Co.

— Opportunities in Telecommunications. (Illus.). 160p. 1993. pap. 10.95 (*0-8442-8655-9*, VGM Career) NTC Contemp Pub Co.

— Opportunities in Telecommunications Careers. rev. ed. LC 95-24092. (Opportunities In . . . Ser.). 160p. pap. 12.95 (*0-8442-4588-7*, 297OITEL, VGM Career) NTC Contemp Pub Co.

— Opportunities in Telecommunications Careers. rev. ed. LC 95-24092. (VGM Opportunities Ser.). 160p. 1995. 14.95 (*0-8442-4587-9*, VGM Career) NTC Contemp Pub Co.

Bone, Jan & Johnson, Ron. Understanding the Film: An Introduction to Film Appreciation. 5th rev. ed. LC 96-13299. (Illus.). 352p. 1996. pap. 33.95 (*0-8442-5797-4*, 57974) NTC Contemp Pub Co.

Bone, Jan, jt. auth. see Johnson, Ron.

Bone, Jesse F. Animal Anatomy & Physiology. 3rd ed. (C). 1988. text 71.25 (*0-8359-0099-1*) P-H.

— Animal Anatomy & Physiology. 3rd ed. (Illus.). 560p. (C). 1988. text 25.00 (*0-685-19514-7*) P-H.

Bone, John H. The Indian Captive: A Narrative of the Adventures & Suffering of Matthew Brayton, In His Thirty-Four Years of Captivity Among the Indians of Northwestern America. 65p. 1982. 16.95 (*0-87770-265-9*) Ye Galleon.

Bone, Kevin. New York Waterfront. LC 96-53253. 280p. 1997. pap. 35.00 (*1-885254-54-7*, Pub. by Monacelli Pr) Penguin Putnam.

Bone, M., et al. Plans & Provisions for the Mentally Handicapped. 1972. 50.00 (*0-7855-0582-2*, Pub. by Natl Inst Soc Work) St Mut.

Bone, Neil. Meteors. (Sky & Telescope's Observer's Guides Ser.). (Illus.). 176p. (Orig.). 1993. pap. 18.95 (*0-933346-67-0*) Sky Pub.

— Meteors, Comets, Supernovae: Observing Transient Pehenomena. LC 98-18112. (Practical Astronomy Ser.). 1998. pap. 29.95 (*1-85233-017-1*) Spr-Verlag.

*Bone, Patrick.** Bloody Mary: The Mystery of Amanda's Magic Mirror. 105p. 1999. pap. text 9.95 (*1-57072-093-2*) Overmountain Pr.

Bone, Philip J. Guitar & Mandolin: Biographies of Celebrated Players & Composers. 1988. reprint ed. lib. bdg. 69.00 (*0-7812-0739-8*) Rprt Serv.

Bone, Q., ed. The Biology of Pelagic Tunicates. (Illus.). 354p. 1998. text 175.00 (*0-19-854024-8*) OUP.

Bone, Q., et al, eds. The Biology of Chaetognaths. (Illus.). 184p. 1991. 95.00 (*0-19-857715-X*) OUP.

Bone, Q., et al. Biology of Fishes. 2nd ed. (Illus.). 341p. 1995. pap. 72.50 (*0-7487-4498-3*, Pub. by S Thornes Pubs) Trans-Atl Phila.

Bone, Quentin B. Henrietta Maria: Queen of the Cavaliers. LC 70-172250. 297p. reprint ed. pap. 92.10 (*0-608-13780-4*, 202021400016) Bks Demand.

Bone, Robert. Down Home: A History of Afro-American Short Fiction from Its Beginning to the End of the Harlem Renaissance. (Morningside Bk.). 350p. 1988. pap. text 21.00 (*0-231-06859-X*) Col U Pr.

Bone, Robert C. The Dynamics of the Western New Guinea (Irian Barat) Problem. LC DU0744.5.B6. (Cornell University, Modern Indonesian Project, Interim Report Ser.). 182p. reprint ed. pap. 56.50 (*0-608-14825-3*, 202589700047) Bks Demand.

Bone, Robert M. The Geography of the Canadian North: Issues & Challenges. (Illus.). 284p. 1992. pap. text 35.00 (*0-19-540772-5*) OUP.

Bone, Robert W. Maverick Guide to Hawaii. 20th ed. (Maverick Guides Ser.). 432p. 1998. pap. text 15.95 (*1-56554-312-2*) Pelican.

*Bone, Robert W.** Maverick Guide to New Zealand. 11th ed. 368p. 2000. pap. text 17.95 (*1-56554-778-0*) Pelican.

Bone, Roger C. Critical Care Medicine: Principles & Management. (Illus.). 1800p. (C). (gr. 13). 1994. text 210.00 (*0-8016-7005-5*, 07005) Mosby Inc.

— Pulmonary & Critical Care Medicine: Update 5. 5th ed. (Illus.). 950p. (C). (gr. 13). 1997. text 128.00 (*0-8151-1371-4*, 29725) Mosby Inc.

— Pulmonary & Critical Care Medicine on CD-ROM, 1999. rev. ed. (C). (gr. 13). 1998. spiral bd. 125.00 (*0-8151-2083-4*) Mosby Inc.

Bone, Roger C., ed. Current Practice of Medicine, 4 vols., Set. (Illus.). 2792p. 1996. text 195.00 (*0-443-07894-7*) Current Med.

Bone, Roger C., et al, eds. Acute Respiratory Failure. (Illus.). 473p. 1987. 73.00 (*0-443-08366-5*) Church.

Bone, Roger C. & Rosen, Robert L., eds. Quick Reference to Internal Medicine. LC 93-25286. (Illus.). 1568p. 1994. 49.50 (*0-89640-229-0*) Igaku-Shoin.

Bone, Roger C., et al. Bone's Atlas of Pulmonary & Critical Care Medicine. LC 98-4009. 1998. write for info. (*0-683-30486-0*) Lppncott W & W.

Bone, Roger C., jt. ed. see Eubanks, David.

Bone, Stanley, jt. auth. see Glick, Robert A.

Bone, Stanley, jt. ed. see Oldham, John M.

Bone, Stephen & Zaba, B. N. Bioelectronics. (Series in Biotechnology). 158p. 1992. 137.95 (*0-471-93296-5*, Wiley-Interscience) Wiley.

*Bone, Thomas H., III.** Pee Wee Pipes & the Wing Thing. LC 00-91370. (Pee Wee Pipes Adventure Ser.: Vol. 1). 32p. (J). (ps-2). 2000. 15.00 (*0-9674602-1-2*) Blue Marlin Pubns.

*Bone, Thomas H.** Why Can't I Spray Today: A PeeWee Pipes Adventure. 32p. (J). (ps). 1999. 15.00 (*0-9674602-0-4*) Blue Marlin Pubns.

Bone, Tim. Pedaling Coast to Coast. LC 98-8960. 110p. 1999. pap. 9.95 (*1-884778-60-7*) Old Mountain.

Bone, William J. Pre-Nineteen Hundred Dog License Tags. LC 93-90483. (Illus.). 218p. 1993. pap. text 27.50 (*0-9638012-0-1*) W J Bone Ent.

Bonebakker, S. A. Hatimi & His Encounter with Mutanabbi: A Biographical Sketch. (Verhandelingen der Koninklijke Nederlandse Akademie van Wetenschappen, Afd. Letterkunde, Nieuwe Reeks Ser.: No. 122). 62p. 1984. pap. 43.75 (*0-444-85568-8*) Elsevier.

— Nihil Obstat in Story Telling. (Mededelingen der Koninklijke Nederlandse Akademie van Wetenschappen, Afd. Letterkunde Ser.: No. 55(8)). 1992. pap. 15.00 (*0-444-85756-7*) Elsevier.

Bonebakker, Seeger A., jt. auth. see Rowson, Everett K.

Bonebrake, Lorraine. Colorado's Scenic Ghost Towns. LC 97-46483. (Littlebook Ser.). (Illus.). 64p. 1998. 14.95 (*1-56579-287-4*) Westcliffe Pubs.

— Santa Fe: Dancing Ground of the Sun. (Illus.). 64p. 1997. 14.95 (*1-56579-239-4*) Westcliffe Pubs.

Bonebrake, Robert. Voices in the Air: The Fascination of Radio. unabridged ed. LC 97-91675. (Illus.). 150p. (Orig.). 1997. pap. 12.95 (*0-9656902-2-9*) RAD Pub IL.

Bonebreak, Robert L. Practical Techniques of Electronic Circuit Design. LC 81-11394. (Illus.). 324p. reprint ed. pap. 100.50 (*0-7837-3526-X*, 205786200008) Bks Demand.

Bonechi. Masterpieces of Heeresgeschich. 64p. text 11.95 (*88-7009-505-3*, Pub. by Bonechi) Eiron.

— Masterpieces of Kunsthistorisc. 64p. text 14.95 (*88-7009-500-2*, Pub. by Bonechi) Eiron.

— Naples. 96p. 1999. pap. text 15.95 (*88-8029-773-2*) Bonechi.

Bonechi. Sorrento & the Amalfi Coast. (Illus.). 96p. 1999. pap. 12.95 (*88-8029-936-0*) Bonechi.

Bonechi, Casa. All of Burgundy. 128p. pap. text 14.95 (*88-7009-222-4*, Pub. by Bonechi) Eiron.

— All of Mont Saint Michel. 64p. text 9.95 (*88-7009-186-4*, Pub. by Bonechi) Eiron.

— All of Turkey: English Edition. 160p. pap. text 15.95 (*88-7009-271-2*, Pub. by Bonechi) Eiron.

— All Versailles: English Edition. 128p. pap. text 14.95 (*88-7009-375-1*, Pub. by Bonechi) Eiron.

— Archaeological Mexico. 128p. pap. text 14.95 (*88-7009-485-5*, Pub. by Bonechi) Eiron.

— Art & History of Capri: English Edition. pap. text 14.95 (*88-7009-281-X*, Pub. by Bonechi) Eiron.

— Art & History of Florence. 192p. pap. text 16.95 (*88-7009-422-7*, Pub. by Bonechi) Eiron.

— Art & History of Pompeii. 128p. pap. text 14.95 (*88-7009-454-5*, Pub. by Bonechi) Eiron.

— Art & History of Venice: English Edition. 174p. pap. text 17.95 (*88-7009-302-6*, Pub. by Bonechi) Eiron.

— Avignon: English Edition. 64p. pap. text 10.95 (*88-7009-107-4*, Pub. by Bonechi) Eiron.

— Bahamas. 64p. text 10.95 (*88-7009-213-5*, Pub. by Bonechi) Eiron.

— Cairo. 64p. pap. text 10.95 (*88-7009-231-3*, Pub. by Bonechi) Eiron.

— Cathedral of Cologne. 64p. pap. text 9.95 (*88-7009-126-0*, Pub. by Bonechi) Eiron.

— Chateau of Amboise. 48p. pap. text 7.95 (*88-7009-225-9*, Pub. by Bonechi) Eiron.

— Gold Guide to Florence. 96p. pap. text 10.95 (*88-7009-438-3*, Pub. by Bonechi) Eiron.

— Golden Book Chateaux: The Loire. 128p. text 14.95 (*88-7009-380-8*, Pub. by Bonechi) Eiron.

— Golden Book Cordova: English Edition. 48p. pap. text 9.95 (*88-7009-266-6*, Pub. by Bonechi) Eiron.

— Golden Book Madrid & Toledo: English Edition. 128p. pap. text 12.95 (*88-7009-317-4*, Pub. by Bonechi) Eiron.

— Golden Book of Bangkok. 96p. pap. text 11.95 (*88-7009-475-8*, Pub. by Bonechi) Eiron.

— Golden Book of Florence. 128p. pap. text 12.95 (*88-7009-426-X*, Pub. by Bonechi) Eiron.

— Golden Book of Paris. 128p. pap. text 14.95 (*88-7009-191-0*, Pub. by Bonechi) Eiron.

— Golden Book of Rome. 128p. pap. text 12.95 (*88-7009-444-8*, Pub. by Bonechi) Eiron.

— Golden Book of Vienna. 96p. text 14.95 (*88-7009-490-1*, Pub. by Bonechi) Eiron.

— Holland: English Edition. 128p. pap. text 14.95 (*88-7009-286-0*, Pub. by Bonechi) Eiron.

— Italy: Amalfi. 128p. text 15.95 (*88-7009-758-7*, Pub. by Bonechi) Eiron.

— Italy: Venice. 96p. text 9.95 (*88-8029-500-4*, Pub. by Bonechi) Eiron.

— Jamaica. 96p. pap. text 12.95 (*88-7009-478-2*, Pub. by Bonechi) Eiron.

— Jerusalem: English Edition. 64p. pap. text 8.95 (*88-7009-253-4*, Pub. by Bonechi) Eiron.

— Lake Garda: English Edition. 128p. pap. text 12.95 (*88-7009-261-5*, Pub. by Bonechi) Eiron.

— Lake Powell Monument Valley. 64p. text 10.95 (*88-7009-215-1*, Pub. by Bonechi) Eiron.

— Masterpieces of Pinacoteca. 96p. text 12.95 (*88-7009-465-0*, Pub. by Bonechi) Eiron.

— Mississippi River. 128p. text 14.95 (*88-8029-420-2*, Pub. by Bonechi) Eiron.

— Nimes Pont du Gard. 32p. pap. text 8.95 (*88-7009-397-2*, Pub. by Bonechi) Eiron.

— Paris: English Edition. 64p. pap. text 11.95 (*88-7009-204-6*, Pub. by Bonechi) Eiron.

— Practical Guide to Three Days in Paris: English Edition. 96p. text 10.95 (*88-7009-368-9*, Pub. by Bonechi) Eiron.

— Practical Guide to Visiting Vienna. 96p. text 10.95 (*88-7009-495-2*, Pub. by Bonechi) Eiron.

— Principality of Monaco. 128p. pap. text 14.95 (*88-7009-418-9*, Pub. by Bonechi) Eiron.

— Saint Paul de Vence. 48p. pap. text 9.95 (*88-7009-413-8*, Pub. by Bonechi) Eiron.

— Sicilian Cookery. 1999. pap. text. write for info. (*88-8029-596-9*) Bonechi.

— Tuscany. 160p. pap. text 15.95 (*88-7009-469-3*, Pub. by Bonechi) Eiron.

Bonechi, Casa. U. S. A. San Francisco. 64p. text 10.95 (*88-8029-478-4*, Pub. by Bonechi) Eiron.

*Bonechi Staff.** Rome, Florence, Venice, Naples. (Illus.). 2000. pap. 18.95 (*88-476-0037-5*) Bonechi.

Boneck, Lenora. Morning Light. (Illus.). 270p. (Orig.). 1986. pap. 12.95 (*0-940415-00-3*) B&K Pub Hse.

— Sons of the Morning. LC 88-92285. 112p. 1989. pap. 8.95 (*0-940415-08-9*) B&K Pub Hse.

— Terra-Phaza. (Illus.). 182p. 1988. pap. 8.95 (*0-940415-07-0*) B&K Pub Hse.

Boneck, Lenora & Self, L. B. Return to Paradise. 328p. 1987. pap. 12.95 (*0-940415-01-1*) B&K Pub Hse.

Bonefeld. Open Marxism, Vol. 1. (C). 54.95 (*0-7453-0424-9*, Pub. by Pluto GBR) Stylus Pub VA.

— Open Marxism, Vol. 2. (C). 54.95 (*0-7453-0425-7*, Pub. by Pluto GBR) Stylus Pub VA.

Bonefeld. Open Marxism Vol. 1: Dialectics & History. Vol. 1. LC 91-8323. 179p. (C). pap. 20.95 (*0-7453-0590-3*, Pub. by Pluto GBR) Stylus Pub VA.

— Open Marxism Vol. 2: Theory & Practice, Vol. 2. LC 91-8323. 172p. (C). pap. 20.95 (*0-7453-0591-1*, Pub. by Pluto GBR) Stylus Pub VA.

Bonefeld, et al. Emancipating Marx Vol. III: Emancipating Marx, Vol. 3. (C). 63.00 (*0-7453-0863-5*, Pub. by Pluto GBR); pap. 17.95 (*0-7453-0864-3*, Pub. by Pluto GBR) Stylus Pub VA.

Bonefeld, Werner. Open Marxism: Theory & Practice, 2. 1993. pap. 16.95 (*0-7453-0690-X*) LPC InBook.

— The Recomposition of the British State During the 1980s. 290p. 1993. 72.95 (*1-85521-377-X*, Pub. by Dartmth Pub) Ashgate Pub Co.

Bonefeld, Werner & Holloway, John, eds. Global Capital, National State & the Politics of Money. LC 94-35570. 232p. 1995. text 75.00 (*0-312-12466-X*) St Martin.

*Bonefeld, Werner & Psychopedis, Kosmas.** The Politics of Change: Globalization, Ideology & Critique. LC 00-42063. 2000. write for info. (*0-312-23559-3*) St Martin.

Bonefeld, Werner, et al. A Major Crisis? The Politics of Economic Policy in Britain in the 1990s. LC 95-19398. (Illus.). 256p. 1995. pap. 29.95 (*1-85521-550-0*, Pub. by Dartmth Pub); text 82.95 (*1-85521-544-6*, Pub. by Dartmth Pub) Ashgate Pub Co.

Boneham, Margaret, jt. auth. see Blakemore, Ken.

Boneham, Sheila W. Breed Rescue: How to Start & Run a Successful Program. LC 98-26041. (Illus.). 216p. 1998. pap. 24.95 (*1-57779-008-1*) Alpine Pubns.

Bonekeeper, Edward H., III. How Robert E. Lee Lost the Civil War. LC 97-18213. (Illus.). 280p. 1998. 29.95 (*1-887901-15-9*) Sergeant Kirk.

*Bonekemper, Edward H.** How Robert E. Lee Lost the Civil War. Seagrave, Pia S., ed. (Illus.). 248p. 1999. pap. 18.95 (*1-887901-33-7*) Sergeant Kirk.

*Bonel, Paul & Liindon, Jennie.** Playwork: A Guide to Good Practice. 2nd ed. (Illus.). 268p. 2000. pap. 39.50 (*0-7487-5496-2*, Pub. by S Thornes Pubs) Trans-Atl Phila.

Bonel, Paul & Lindon, Jennie. Good Practice in Playwork. 192p. (Orig.). 1996. pap. 29.50 (*0-7487-2227-0*, Pub. by S Thornes Pubs) Trans-Atl Phila.

Bonell, E., ed. see Quintilianu.

Bonell, E. Frank. Creating a Criminal. 56p. 1998. pap. 8.00 (*0-8059-4342-0*) Dorrance.

*Bonell, M. J., ed.** A New Approach to International Commercial Contracts: The UNIDROIT Principles of International Contracts. 456p. 1999. text 138.00 (*90-411-1254-5*) Kluwer Law Intl.

Bonell, Michael, et al, eds. Hydrology & Water Management in the Humid Tropics: Hydrological Research Issues & Strategies for Water Management. (Illus.). 610p. (C). 1993. text 120.00 (*0-521-45268-6*) Cambridge U Pr.

Bonell, Michael J. An International Restatement of Contract Law: The Unidroit Principles of International Commercial Contracts. 2nd ed. LC 97-39369. 1997. 115.00 (*1-57105-074-4*) Transnatl Pubs.

— UNILEX - International Case Law & Bibliography on the United Nations Convention on Contracts for the Sale of Goods & on the Unidroit Principles: CISG, 3 vols. LC 95-39727. 1995. ring bd. 450.00 (*1-57105-022-1*) Transnatl Pubs.

*Bonelli, Sabra.** Step Aerobics. (Illus.). 75p. 2000. pap. 14.95 (*1-890720-02-X*) Am Coun Exer.

Bonello, Frank J., jt. auth. see Swartz, Thomas R.

Bonello, Frank J., jt. ed. see Swartz, Thomas R.

Bonello, Kurt L. When Pappy Goes Hunting. LC 94-72497. (Illus.). 24p. (J). (ps-3). 1994. 12.95 (*0-9642248-0-1*) Bonello Studios.

Bonem, Gilbert W., jt. auth. see Wollman, Nathaniel.

Bonem, Rena M., jt. auth. see Strykowski, Joe.

*Bonenberger, Paul R.** The First Snap-Fit Handbook Creating Attachments for Plastics Parts. LC 00-35080. (Illus.). 2000. write for info. (*1-56990-279-8*) Hanser-Gardner.

Boneparth, Ellen. Women, Power & Policy. (Policy Studies on Social Policy). 300p. 1982. text 72.00 (*0-08-028048-X*, Pergamon Pr); pap. text 20.00 (*0-08-028047-1*, Pergamon Pr) Elsevier.

Boneparth, Ellen & Stoper, Emily, eds. Women, Power & Policy: Toward the Year 2000. 2nd ed. (Government & Politics Ser.). 320p. 1988. text 45.00 (*0-08-034486-0*, Pergamon Pr); pap. text 18.50 (*0-08-034485-2*, Pergamon Pr) Elsevier.

Boner, Alice. Principles of Composition in Hindu Sculpture: Cave Temple Period. (Illus.). 290p. 1992. 115.00 (*0-7103-0443-9*, A6782) Routledge.

Boner, Alice, et al. Vastusutra Upanisad: The Essence of Form in Sacred Art. 3rd rev. ed. 192p. (C). 1996. 28.00 (*81-208-0090-7*, Pub. by Motilal Bnarsidass) S Asia.

*Boner, Dave.** Fist of Dick. 217p. 1998. pap. 25.00 (*0-9675881-0-3*) Faloopnik.

Boner, Georgette, ed. Alice Boner Diaries: India 1934-1967. (C). 1993. 32.00 (*81-208-1121-6*, Pub. by Motilal Bnarsidass) S Asia.

Boner, R. E. & Talaske, Richard H., eds. Theatres for Drama Performance: Recent Experiences in Acoustical Design. LC 86-72934. 167p. 1987. pap. 26.00 (*0-88318-516-4*) Acoustical Soc Am.

Bonerjee, B. N. Environmental Pollution & Bhopal Killings. (C). 1987. 25.00 (*81-212-0119-5*, Pub. by Gian Publng Hse) S Asia.

Bones, Chris. The Self-Reliant Manager. LC 93-16828. (Self-Development for Managers Ser.). 130p. (C). 1994. pap. 12.95 (*0-415-07928-4*) Routledge.

Bones, Frances. Fostoria Glassware, 1887-1982: 95 Years of Glassmaking, Identification & Values. 384p. 1999. 24.95 (*1-57432-108-0*) Collector Bks.

Bones, Frances M. American Silverplate: The Standard Encyclopedia of Flatware & Hollow Ware. LC 98-153011. 1998. pap. text 24.95 (*1-57432-061-0*, 5058) Collector Bks.

*Bones, Jan.** Lingerie Secrets: Sew a Perfect Fit for Every Body. LC 99-69481. (Illus.). 128p. 2000. pap. 21.95 (*0-87341-852-2*, BLIN) Krause Pubns.

Bones, Jim. Texas Earth Surfaces: A Photographic Essay. (Illus.). 1970. 17.50 (*0-88426-016-X*) Encino Pr.

Bones, Jim & Giovan, Tria, photos by. The Smithsonian Guides to Natural America the South Central States: Texas, Oklahoma, Arkansas, Louisana, Mississippi. (Illus.). 1996. pap. 19.95 (*0-679-76479-8*) Random.

Bones, Jim, Jr. & Graves, John. Texas Heartland: A Hill Country Year. LC 75-16352. (Illus.). 104p. 1982. 32.95 (*0-89096-002-X*) Tex A&M Univ Pr.

Bonesteal, Michael, jt. auth. see Smith, Kent J.

Bonesteel, Georgia. Bright Ideas for Lap Quilting. 160p. 1991. 24.95 (*0-8487-1003-7*) Oxmoor Hse.

— Bright Ideas for Lap Quilting. LC 90-61776. 160p. 1994. pap. 14.95 (*0-8487-1184-X*) Oxmoor Hse.

— Easy Does It! Quilts. 160p. 1995. pap. 19.95 (*0-8487-1468-7*) Oxmoor Hse.

— Georgia Bonesteel's Spinning Spools Sampler. 64p. pap. 9.95 (*0-8487-1158-0*, 100315) Oxmoor Hse.

*Bonesteel, Georgia.** Lap Quilting Lives. LC 99-44337. (Illus.). 112p. 1999. pap. 26.95 (*1-56477-259-4*, B376, That Patchwrk Pl) Martingale & Co.

Bonesteel, Georgia. Lap Quilting with Georgia Bonesteel. LC 81-83054. (Illus.). 122p. 1982. 24.95 (*0-8487-0524-6*) Oxmoor Hse.

— More Lap Quilting with Georgia Bonesteel. LC 84-60287. (Illus.). 132p. 1985. 19.95 (*0-8487-0634-X*) Oxmoor Hse.

— New Ideas for Lap Quilting. (Illus.). 160p. 1987. 19.95 (*0-8487-0704-4*) Oxmoor Hse.

Bonesteel, Michael. Artist - Lee Godie: A Twenty-Year Retrospective. Matsumoto, Pat, ed. (Illus.). 34p. (Orig.). 1993. pap. 10.00 (*0-938903-16-0*) Cty of Chicago.

Bonet, Diana. Clear Writing: A Step by Step Guide. Brett, Elaine, ed. LC 90-84924. (Fifty-Minute Ser.). 110p. (Orig.). 1991. pap. 10.95 (*1-56052-094-9*) Crisp Pubns.

— Easy English. Brett, Elaine, ed. LC 92-74206. 168p. (Orig.). 1993. pap. 13.95 (*1-56052-198-8*) Crisp Pubns.

— Punctuation & Spelling. 128p. 1997. pap. 12.95 (*1-56052-360-3*) Crisp Pubns.

— Spelling. 1998. pap. 10.95 (*1-56052-500-2*) Crisp Pubns.

— Vocabulary Improvement. Gerould, Philip, ed. LC 91-76246. (Fifty-Minute Ser.). 134p. (Orig.). 1992. pap. 10.95 (*1-56052-124-4*) Crisp Pubns.

Bonet, Eugeni. Videospain. (Illus.). 16p. (Orig.). 1988. pap. 10.00 (*0-913263-22-2*) Exit Art.

Bonet, Javier & Wood, Richard D. Nonlinear Continuum Mechanics for Finite Element Analysis. LC 97-11366. (Illus.). 266p. (C). 1997. text 52.95 (*0-521-57272-X*) Cambridge U Pr.

Bonet, Juan M., jt. auth. see Baldeweg, Juan N.

Bonet-Maury, G. L' Islamisme et le Christianisme en Afrique. (B. E. Ser.: No. 172). (FRE.). 1906. 35.00 (*0-8115-3083-3*) Periodicals Srv.

Bonet, Pilar. Figures in a Red Landscape. (Woodrow Wilson Center Press Ser.). 128p. 1993. 18.95 (*0-943875-45-5*) Johns Hopkins.

— Figures in a Red Landscape. Di Giovanni, Norman T. & Ashe, Susan, trs. from SPA. LC 93-16722. 166p. reprint ed. pap. 51.50 (*0-608-08810-2*, 206944900004) Bks Demand.

Bonet, Rafael H., tr. see Singer, Peter Albert David.

Bonett, Colin. Transportion Questions & Answers on Freight Loss & Damage. Hunter, Ann A., ed. 560p. 1999. 79.95 (*0-9630797-8-6*) Loft Pr.

Bonett, Douglas. Business Statistics: A Computer-Assisted Workbook. 260p. (C). 1995. pap. text, per. 30.95 (*0-8403-9657-0*) Kendall-Hunt.

Bonetti, A., et al, eds. Evolution of Interstellar Dust & Related Topics: Proceedings of the International School of Physics, "Enrico Fermi," Course CI, Varenna, Italy,

B

22 July-1 August 1986. (Enrico Fermi International Summer School of Physics Ser.: Vol. 101). 473p. 1990. 213.75 (*0-685-34639-0*, North Holland) Elsevier.

Bonetti, E. & Fiorani, D., eds. Nanophase Materials. (Materials Science Forum Ser.: Vol. 195). (Illus.). 240p. 1996. text 106.00 (*0-87849-709-9*, Pub. by Trans T Pub) Enfield Pubs NH.

Bonetti, Kay, et al, eds. Conversations with American Novelists: The Best Interviews from the Missouri Review & the American Audio Prose Library. LC 97-33393. 272p. 1997. pap. 19.95 (*0-8262-1136-4*) U of Mo Pr.

Bonetti, Lee, jt. auth. see Melyan, Wesley R.

Bonevac. Simple Logic. LC 98-71176. (C). 1998. text 53.50 (*0-15-503171-6*) Harcourt Coll Pubs.

— Simple Logic. (C). 1998. pap. text, student ed. 19.50 (*0-15-503173-2*) Harcourt Coll Pubs.

Bonevac, Daniel & Phillips, Stephen. Understanding Non-Western Philosophy: Introductory Readings. LC 92-39700. 350p. (C). 1993. pap. text 26.95 (*1-55934-077-0*, 1077) Mayfield Pub.

Bonevac, Daniel, et al. Beyond the Western Tradition: Readings in Moral & Political Philosophy. LC 91-33102. 372p. (C). 1992. pap. text 26.95 (*1-55934-075-4*, 1075) Mayfield Pub.

***Bonevac, Daniel, et al.** Logic, Sets & Functions. 296p. (C). 1999. per. 56.95 (*0-7872-6355-9*, 41635501) Kendall-Hunt.

Bonevac, Daniel A. Reduction in the Abstract Sciences. vi, 180p. (C). 1982. lib. bdg. 24.00 (*0-915145-14-6*) Ridgeview.

— Today's Moral Issues: Classic & Contemporary Perspectives. 3rd ed. LC 98-4869. 704p. 1998. pap. text 44.95 (*0-7674-0011-9*) Mayfield Pub.

Bonewit-West, Kathy. Administration Procedures for Medical Assistant. (C). 2000. pap. text 21.95 (*0-7216-3178-9*) Harcrt Hlth Sci Grp.

— Clinical Procedures for Medical Assistants. 4th ed. (Illus.). 1995. teacher ed. write for info. (*0-7216-5414-2*, W B Saunders Co) Harcrt Hlth Sci Grp.

— Clinical Procedures for Medical Assistants. 4th ed. (Illus.). 1995. pap. text, student ed. 17.95 (*0-7216-5337-5*, W B Saunders Co) Harcrt Hlth Sci Grp.

— Clinical Procedures for Medical Assistants. 4th ed. (Illus.). 708p. 1995. text, student ed. 48.00 (*0-7216-6104-1*, W B Saunders Co) Harcrt Hlth Sci Grp.

— Clinical Procedures for Medical Assistants. 5th ed. (Illus.). 735p. text. write for info. (*0-7216-8406-8*, W B Saunders Co) Harcrt Hlth Sci Grp.

— Clinical Procedures for the Medical Assistant. 4th ed. LC 94-10991. (Illus.). 708p. 1995. text 36.50 (*0-7216-5413-4*, W B Saunders Co) Harcrt Hlth Sci Grp.

— Computer Concepts & Applications for the Medical Office. 296p. 1993. pap. text 34.00 (*0-7216-4945-9*, W B Saunders Co) Harcrt Hlth Sci Grp.

Bonewits, Isaac. Authentic Thaumaturgy. Jackson, Steve, ed. (Illus.). 144p. 1998. pap. 20.95 (*1-55634-360-4*, 3004, Pub. by S Jackson Games) BookWorld.

— Real Magic: An Introductory Treatise on the Basic Principles of Yellow Magic. LC 88-13099. (Illus.). 304p. 1989. reprint ed. pap. 14.95 (*0-87728-688-4*) Weiser.

Bonewitz, R. A. Cosmic Crystal Spiral. 1993. pap. 9.95 (*0-906540-94-1*, Pub. by Element MA) Penguin Putnam.

***Bonewitz, Ron.** Pyramids. (Guides for Beginners Ser.). (Illus.). 96p. 2000. pap. 11.95 (*0-340-75383-8*, Pub. by Headway) Trafalgar.

— Timeless Wisdom of the Maya. (Guides for Beginners Ser.). (Illus.). 96p. 2000. pap. 11.95 (*0-340-77257-3*, Pub. by Headway) Trafalgar.

***Bonewitz, Ronald A.** Maya Prophecy. (Guides Ser.). 144p. 2000. pap. 6.95 (*0-7499-1959-0*, Pub. by Piatkus Bks) London Brdge.

***Bonewitz, Ronald A. & Verner-Bonds, Lilian.** New Cosmic Crystals: The Definitive Guide. 2000. pap. 19.95 (*0-7225-3973-8*, Pub. by Thorsons PA) HarpC.

***Boney, F. N.** A Pictorial History of the University of Georgia. 2nd ed. LC 99-49011. (Illus.). 2000. 34.95 (*0-8203-2198-2*) U of Ga Pr.

Boney, F. N. Rebel Georgia. LC 97-431. 112p. (Orig.). 1997. 24.95 (*0-86554-545-6*, H416); pap. 15.95 (*0-86554-551-0*, P156) Mercer Univ Pr.

Boney, F. N. A Walking Tour of the University of Georgia. LC 88-25997. (Illus.). 112p. (Orig.). 1989. pap. 9.95 (*0-8203-1081-6*) U of Ga Pr.

Boney, F. N., et al, eds. God Made Man, Man Made the Slave: The Autobiography of George Teamoh. LC 90-26719. 219p. (C). 1991. text 24.95 (*0-86554-368-2*, MUP/H305) Mercer Univ Pr.

***Boney, James.** Cisco IOS in a Nutshell. (Illus.). 700p. 2000. pap. text 39.95 (*1-56592-942-X*) OReilly & Assocs.

Bonfadini, John. Educational Research Tutorial. 1998. pap. text 24.00 (*0-13-997719-8*) P-H.

Bonfante, Larissa. Etruscan. (Reading the Past Ser.). (Illus.). 64p. 1990. pap. 13.95 (*0-520-07118-2*, Pub. by U CA Pr) Cal Prin Full Svc.

— Etruscan Dress. LC 75-11344. (Illus.). 256p. reprint ed. pap. 79.40 (*0-608-15524-1*, 202970500063) Bks Demand.

Bonfante, Larissa, ed. Etruscan Life & Afterlife: A Handbook of Etruscan Studies. LC 86-5457. (Illus.). 320p. 1986. pap. 26.95 (*0-8143-1813-4*) Wayne St U Pr.

— Etruscan Life & Afterlife: A Handbook of Etruscan Studies. LC 86-5457. (Illus.). 320p. reprint ed. pap. 99.20 (*0-608-10550-3*, 2071170) Bks Demand.

Bonfante, Larissa & Bonfante-Warren, Alexandra, trs. from LAT. The Plays of Hrotswitha of Gandersheim. LC 79-90053. 1986. reprint ed. pap. 18.00 (*0-86516-178-X*) Bolchazy-Carducci.

Bonfante-Warren, Alexandra. Country Life: Celebrations in Art. 72p. 1995. 12.98 (*1-56799-166-1*, MetroBooks) M Friedman Pub Grp Inc.

— Currier & Ives: Portaits of a Nation. LC 98-8206. (Illus.). 128p. 1998. 19.98 (*1-56799-589-6*, MetroBooks) M Friedman Pub Grp Inc.

— Doors. LC 97-52232. 1998. 15.00 (*1-56799-618-3*, Friedman-Fairfax) M Friedman Pub Grp Inc.

***Bonfante-Warren, Alexandra.** Doors. (Illus.). 72p. 2000. 6.98 (*1-58663-063-6*) M Friedman Pub Grp Inc.

— The Louvre. (Illus.). 320p. 2000. 75.00 (*0-88363-501-1*, Pub. by H L Levin) Publishers Group.

— The Louvre & the Musee d'Orsay, 2 vols. 2000. boxed set 100.00 (*0-88363-503-8*, Pub. by H L Levin) Publishers Group.

Bonfante-Warren, Alexandra. Love. (Celebrations in Art Ser.). 72p. 1995. 12.98 (*1-56799-167-X*, MetroBooks) M Friedman Pub Grp Inc.

***Bonfante-Warren, Alexandra.** Moroccan Style. LC 99-57931. (Architecture & Design Library Ser.). (Illus.). 96p. 2000. 17.95 (*1-56799-956-5*, Friedman-Fairfax) M Friedman Pub Grp Inc.

— The Musee d'Orsay. (Illus.). 320p. 2000. 75.00 (*0-88363-502-X*, Pub. by H L Levin) Publishers Group.

— Mythical Beasts. (Illus.). 176p. 2000. 19.98 (*1-56799-985-9*) M Friedman Pub Grp Inc.

Bonfante-Warren, Alexandra. Saints. LC 97-43537. (Illus.). 128p. 1998. 16.98 (*1-56799-651-5*, MetroBooks) M Friedman Pub Grp Inc.

***Bonfante-Warren, Alexandra.** Saints: Seventy Stories of Faith. 128p. (YA). 2000. 19.98 (*0-7624-0684-4*, Courage) Running Pr.

Bonfante-Warren, Alexandra. Timeless Places Provence. LC 99-13790. (Timeless Places Ser.). (Illus.). 96p. 2000. text 17.95 (*1-56799-751-1*) M Friedman Pub Grp Inc.

— Tuscany. LC 99-13791. (Timeless Places Ser.). (Illus.). 96p. 2000. text 17.95 (*1-56799-752-X*) M Friedman Pub Grp Inc.

***Bonfante-Warren, Alexandra.** Venice. LC 99-56401. (Timeless Places Ser.). (Illus.). 96p. 2000. 17.95 (*1-56799-788-0*, Friedman-Fairfax) M Friedman Pub Grp Inc.

Bonfante-Warren, Alexandra, tr. see Allen, Peter.

Bonfante-Warren, Alexandra, jt. tr. see Bonfante, Larissa.

Bonfante-Warren, Alexandra, tr. see Flamarion, Edith.

Bonfante-Warren, Alexandra, tr. see Lemoine, Bertrand.

Bonfante-Warren, Alexandra, tr. see Mormorio, Diego.

Bonfanti, Mario, jt. auth. see Pereni, Angelo.

Bonfield, Arthur E. State Administrative Rule Making. 704p. 1986. 145.00 (*0-316-10122-2*, Aspen Law & Bus) Aspen Pub.

— State Administrative Rule Making of Books & Supplies, Set. 1988. 145.00 (*0-316-10124-9*, Aspen Law & Bus) Aspen Pub.

Bonfield, Arthur E. & Asimow, Michael R. Administrative Law, State & Federal, Teacher's Manual to Accompany Cases & Materials On. (American Casebook Ser.). 488p. (C). 1989. pap. text. write for info. (*0-314-66576-5*) West Pub.

— State & Federal Administrative Law: Cases & Materials. (American Casebook Ser.). 826p. (C). 1989. reprint ed. text 44.00 (*0-314-50388-9*) West Pub.

— State & Federal Administrative Law: 1993 Supplement. (American Casebook Ser.). 185p. 1993. pap. text 12.00 (*0-314-02697-5*) West Pub.

Bonfield, Charles, jt. ed. see Kritchevsky, David.

Bonfield, Lloyd. Marriage Settlements, 1601-1740. LC 85-82331. (Cambridge Studies in English Legal History). 154p. 1986. reprint ed. 48.00 (*0-912004-55-X*) Gaunt.

Bonfield, Lynn A. & Morrison, Mary C. Roxana's Children: The Biography of a Nineteenth-Century Vermont Family. LC 95-2417. (Illus.). 288p. 1995. pap. 19.95 (*0-87023-981-3*); text 50.00 (*0-87023-972-4*) U of Mass Pr.

***Bonfield, W.** Overseas Mission on Biomaterials to Japan '98. 88p. 1998. pap. 70.00 (*1-86125-067-3*) Institute of Management Consultants.

Bonfiglio, Michael, jt. auth. see Cohen, Jonathan.

Bonfiglio, Michael, jt. ed. see Clark, Charles R.

Bonfiglio, Thomas a. & Erozan, Yener S., eds. Gynecologic Cytopathology. LC 96-15640. 288p. 1996. text 143.00 (*0-397-51501-4*) Lppncott W & W.

Bonfiglio, Thomas A., jt. ed. see Erozan, Yener S.

Bonfiglioli Riduttori SAP Staff, ed. Gear Motor Handbook. LC 95-9911. 1995. write for info. (*0-387-58988-0*) Spr-Verlag.

Bonfil Batalla, Guillermo. Mexico Profundo: Reclaiming a Civilization. Dennis, Philip A., tr. from SPA. (Translations from Latin America Ser.). 216p. (Orig.). 1996. pap. 16.95 (*0-292-70843-2*); text 30.00 (*0-292-70844-0*) U of Tex Pr.

Bonfil, Robert. Jewish Life in Renaissance Italy. Oldcorn, Anthony, tr. LC 93-11424. (Illus.). 336p. 1994. 40.00 (*0-520-07350-9*, Pub. by U CA Pr) Cal Prin Full Svc.

Bonfil, Robert, ed. Rabbis & Jewish Communities in Renaissance Italy. (Illus.). 380p. 1993. reprint ed. pap. 24.95 (*1-874774-17-X*) Intl Spec Bk.

Bonfills, Bolette. Peter Joins the Circus. LC 94-24501. (Crocodile Lift-The-Flap Bk.). (Illus.). 24p. (J). (ps-2). 1994. 9.95 (*1-56656-154-X*, Crocodile Bks) Interlink Pub.

Bonfils, Bolette. Peter's Christmas. LC 94-24500. (Crocodile Life-the-Flap Bk.). (Illus.). 24p. (J). (ps-2). 1994. 9.95 (*1-56656-162-0*, Crocodile Bks) Interlink Pub.

— Peter's Package. LC 94-24492. (Crocodile Lift-The-Flap Bk.). (Illus.). 24p. (J). (ps-2). 1994. 9.95 (*1-56656-155-8*, Crocodile Bks) Interlink Pub.

Bonfils, Marie, ed. Seattle & Eastside Private School Guide. 480p. 1995. pap. 29.95 (*0-9631102-3-3*) Cap Hill WA.

Bonforte, Lisa. Birds Coloring Book. (Illus.). (J). 1993. pap. 1.00 (*0-486-27356-3*) Dover.

— Farm Animals Coloring Book. (Illus.). 64p. (J). 1997. pap. 1.00 (*0-486-29781-0*) Dover.

— Fifty Favorite Birds-Coloring Book. (J). 1983. pap. 2.95 (*0-486-24261-7*) Dover.

— I Can Draw Dinosaurs. (Illus.). 64p. (J). (gr. 1-4). 1997. 4.99 (*0-689-81453-4*) Atheneum Yung Read.

Bonforte, Lisa. I Can Draw Dinosaurs. (I Can Draw Bks.). (J). 1997. 10.19 (*0-606-11496-3*, Pub. by Turtleback) Demco.

Bonforte, Lisa. Puppies. (Illus.). 32p. (J). 1998. pap. 1.00 (*0-486-40350-5*) Dover.

Bonforte, Lisa. Rain Forest Animal Stickers. (Illus.). (J). 1996. pap. 3.95 (*0-486-28886-2*) Dover.

Bonforte, Lisa. Sea Animals Coloring Book. (Illus.). (J). (gr. k-3). 1993. pap. 1.00 (*0-486-27729-1*) Dover.

Bong, Gayle. Thirtysomething: A Patchwork Pattern. (Illus.). 60p. (Orig.). 1997. pap. 19.00 (*0-9654580-1-6*) P L Publns.

Bong, Park H. The Poor Fisherman. (Illus.). 88p. (Orig.). 1995. pap. text 9.95 (*0-9639999-3-1*) Jay St Pubs.

Bonga, Dieuwke W. Eight Prison Camps: A Dutch Familiy in Japanese Java. LC 96-33722. (Monographs in International Studies, Southeast Asia Ser.: No. 97). (Illus.). 233p. (Orig.). (C). 1996. pap. text 18.00 (*0-89680-191-8*) Ohio U Pr.

Bonga, J. M. & Durzan, Don J. Tissue Culture in Forestry. 1982. text 195.50 (*90-247-2660-3*) Kluwer Academic.

Bonga, J. M. & Durzan, Don J., eds. Cell & Tissue Culture in Forestry, 3 vols. (Forestry Sciences Ser.). 1986. lib. bdg. 156.50 (*90-247-3430-4*) Kluwer Academic.

— Cell & Tissue Culture in Forestry, 3 vols., Set. (Forestry Sciences Ser.). 1987. lib. bdg. 93.00 (*90-247-3433-9*) Kluwer Academic.

Bonga, J. M. & Von Aderkas, P. In Vitro Culture of Trees. LC 91-38182. 236p. 1992. text 113.00 (*0-7923-1540-5*) Kluwer Academic.

Bongaarts, John, et al, eds. Family Demography: Methods & Their Application. (International Studies in Demography). 384p. 1991. reprint ed. pap. 32.00 (*0-19-828366-0*) OUP.

Bongaarts, John & Potter, Robert G., eds. Fertility, Biology & Behavior: An Analysis of the Proximate Determinants (Monograph) (Studies in Population). 216p. 1983. text 70.00 (*0-12-114380-5*) Acad Pr.

Bongaarts, P. J. & Martini, R., eds. Complex Differential Geometry & Supermanifolds in Strings & Fields. (Lecture Notes in Physics Ser.: Vol. 311). v, 252p. 1988. 45.95 (*0-387-50324-2*) Spr-Verlag.

Bongaerts, Jan, jt. ed. see Newland, Amy.

Bongaerts, Theo, et al, eds. Computer Applications in Language Learning. viii, 172p. (Orig.). (C). 1988. pap. 52.35 (*90-6765-400-0*) Mouton.

Bongaerts, Theo & De Bot, Kees, eds. Perspectives on Foreign Language Policy: Studies in Honor of Theo van Els. LC 97-9930. viii, 224p. 1997. lib. bdg. 54.00 (*1-55619-518-4*) J Benjamins Pubng Co.

Bongar, Bruce. The Suicidal Patient: Clinical & Legal Standards of Care. LC 91-4568. 311p. 1991. 39.95 (*1-55798-109-4*) Am Psychol.

Bongar, Bruce, et al, eds. Risk Management with Suicidal Patients. LC 97-48981. 240p. 1997. lib. bdg. 35.00 (*1-57230-302-6*, C0302) Guilford Pubns.

— Risk Management with Suicidal Patients. 197p. 1999. pap. text 20.00 (*1-57230-498-7*, C0320) Guilford Pubns.

Bongar, Bruce & Beutler, Larry E., eds. Foundations of Psychotherapy: Theory & Practice. (Textbooks in Clinical Psychology Ser.). (Illus.). 520p. (C). 1995. text 57.95 (*0-19-508215-X*) OUP.

Bongard. Surgery: A Clinical Approach. LC 96-41027. 1996. pap. text 49.00 (*0-443-08994-9*, W B Saunders Co) Harcrt Hlth Sci Grp.

Bongard, Fred, et al. Vascular Injuries in Surgical Practice. (Illus.). 339p. (C). 1991. text 85.00 (*0-8385-9383-6*, A9383-9, Apple Lange Med) McGraw.

Bongard, Frederick S. & Sue, Darryl Y. Current Critical Care Diagnosis & Treatment. 2nd ed. (C). 1999. pap. text 45.00 (*0-8385-1454-5*) Appleton & Lange.

Bongard, Frederick S. & Sue, Darryl Y., eds. Current Critical Care Diagnosis & Treatment. (Illus.). 787p. (C). 1996. pap. text 54.95 (*0-8385-1443-X*, A1443-9, Apple Lange Med) McGraw.

***Bongard, Gerald.** Near-Birth Experience: A Journey to the Center of Self. 2000. pap. 13.95 (*1-56924-602-5*) Marlowe & Co.

Bongard-Levin, G. The Image of India: The Study of Ancient Indian Civilization in the U. S. S. R. 270p. 1986. 15.00 (*0-8364-1807-7*, Pub. by Abhinav) S Asia.

Bongard-Levin, G. M. A Complex Study of Ancient India. 1986. 39.95 (*81-202-0141-8*) Asia Bk Corp.

— The Great Russian Historian M. I. Rostovtsev in the U. S. A. The Years of Exile. LC 99-15144. (Russian Studies in the Humanities: Vol. 3). (RUS.). 600p. 1999. text 119.95 (*0-7734-3226-4*) E Mellen.

Bongard, Tim & Coulter, Bill. Richard Petty: Cars of King: Race Cars. (Illus.). 261p. 1997. 34.95 (*1-57167-174-9*) Sports Pub.

Bongartz, Heinz, ed. see Bhargava, Kant K.

Bongco, Mila. Reading Comics: Language, Culture & the Concept of the Superhero in Comic Books. LC 99-46175. (Garland Studies in American Popular History & Culture). 250p. 1999. 50.00 (*0-8153-3344-7*) Garland.

Bonge, Lyle. The Photographs of Lyle Bonge. 1982. 32.50 (*0-912330-53-8*) Jargon Soc.

Bonge, Steve. Tattoo'd with Attitude. (Illus.). 128p. 1995. pap. 19.95 (*0-86369-935-9*, Pub. by Virgin Bks) London Brdge.

Bongenaar, A. C. Neo-Babylon Ebabbar Temple at Sippar: Its Administration & Its Prosopography. LC 97-211764. (Illus.). xvi, 559p. 1997. pap. text 52.25 (*90-6258-081-5*, Pub. by Netherlands Inst) Eisenbrauns.

Bonger, Willem A. Race & Crime. Hordyk, Margaret M., tr. LC 69-14912. (Criminology, Law Enforcement, & Social Problems Ser.: No. 34). 1969. reprint ed. 23.00 (*0-87585-034-0*); reprint ed. pap. 12.00 (*0-87585-907-0*) Patterson Smith.

Bongers. Local Government & 1992. 1990. pap. text. write for info. (*0-582-07570-X*, Pub. by Addison-Wesley) Longman.

Bongers, C. Standardization: Mathematical Methods in Assortment Determination. 265p. 1980. lib. bdg. 85.50 (*0-89838-029-4*) Kluwer Academic.

***Bongi, Salvatore.** Annali di Gabriel Giolito de' Ferrari. 1076p. 2000. 125.00 (*1-57898-167-0*) Martino Pubng.

Bongianni, Murizio. Simon & Schuster's Guide to Horses & Ponies. 256p. 1988. pap. 14.00 (*0-671-66068-3*, Fireside) S&S Trade Pap.

Bongie, Chris. Exotic Memories: Literature, Colonialism & the Fin de Siecle. xiii, 262p. 1991. 42.50 (*0-8047-1876-8*); pap. 15.95 (*0-8047-1900-4*) Stanford U Pr.

— Islands & Exiles: The Creole Identities of Post Colonial Literature. LC 98-16325. 600p. 1998. 65.00 (*0-8047-3280-9*); pap. 24.95 (*0-8047-3281-7*) Stanford U Pr.

Bongie, Elizabeth B., tr. see Pseudo-Athanasius.

Bongie, Laurence L. David Hume: Prophet of the Counter-Revolution. LC 99-25723. 2000. 18.00 (*0-86597-209-5*) Liberty Fund.

***Bongie, Laurence L.** David Hume: Prophet of the Counter-Revolution. LC 99-25723. 2000. pap. 10.00 (*0-86597-208-7*) Liberty Fund.

— Sade: A Biographical Essay. LC 98-25227. 326p. 1998. 29.00 (*0-226-06420-4*) U Ch Pr.

***Bongie, Laurence L.** Sade: A Biographical Essay. (Illus.). 2000. pap. 16.00 (*0-226-06421-2*) U Ch Pr.

Bongielo, Max. In the Islands. Schumake, John P., ed. (Orig.). (C). 1992. 12.95 (*0-9616789-6-8*) Earnest Pubns.

— A Life in the Day of Gordon Freewalker. Schumake, John P., ed. (Orig.). 1992. pap. 12.00 (*0-9616789-4-1*) Earnest Pubns.

Bongio, Enrico P. Principles of Industrial Welding. 1978. text 6.50 (*0-686-24289-0*); text 5.85 (*0-686-26120-8*) Lincoln Arc Weld.

Bongiorni, Kevin, jt. ed. see Bell, Darnetta.

Bongiorno, Andrew, tr. see Pareto, Vilfredo.

Bongiorno, Frank. The People's Party: Victorian Labor & the Radical Tradition 1875-1914. LC 96-231084. 240p. 1997. pap. 24.95 (*0-522-84738-2*, Pub. by Melbourne Univ Pr) Paul & Co Pubs.

Bongiorno, Joseph A. Fascist Italy & the Disarmament Question, 1928-1934. LC 91-22149. (Modern European History II Ser.). 232p. 1991. text 20.00 (*0-8153-0478-1*) Garland.

***Bongiorno, Linda, ed.** Landmines: Exploring the Hidden Crisis, 3 vols. Incl. Landmines: Exploring the Hidden Crisis: A Standards Based Curriculum Unit for the Middle Grades. Johnson, Jacquelyn S. (Illus.). 100p. 1999. pap. (*0-943804-44-2*); Landmines: Exploring the Hidden Crisis: A Standards Based Curriculum Unit for the Secondary Grades (9-12) Hurt, J. P. Antony. (Illus.). 120p. 1999. pap. (*0-943804-43-4*); Landmines: Exploring the Hidden Crisis: A Standards Based Curriculum Unit for the Upper Elementary Grades. Duncan, Elizabeth. (Illus.). 35p. 1999. pap. (*0-943804-45-0*); (Illus.). 255p. 1999. pap. write for info. (*0-943804-48-5*) U of Denver Teach.

Bongiorno, Linda, ed. see Martens, Mert & Anderson, Marilyn.

Bongiorno, Linda, ed. see Meier, Marcie.

***Bongiovanni.** Medical Spanish. 3rd ed. (SPA.). 176p. 1999. pap. 24.95 (*0-07-134550-7*) McGraw.

Bongiovanni, Alfred M., ed. Adolescent Gynecology: A Guide for Clinicians. LC 82-22396. 276p. 1983. 55.00 (*0-306-41203-9*, Kluwer Plenum) Kluwer Academic.

***Bongiovanni, G., et al, eds.** Algorithms & complexity: 4th Italian Conference, CIAC 2000, Rome, Italy, March 1-3, 2000, Proceedings. (Lecture Notes In Computer Science: 1767). viii, 317p. 2000. pap. text (*3-540-67159-5*) Spr-Verlag.

Bongiovanni, Gail L. & Teitel, Ariel D. Medical Spanish. 2nd ed. 1991. pap. 18.95 (*0-07-064489-6*) McGraw.

Bongiovanni, Giancarlo, et al. Algorithms & Complexity: Third Italian Conference, CIAC '97, Rome, Italy, March 12-14, 1997: Proceedings, Vol. 120. LC 97-6970. (Lecture Notes in Computer Science Ser.). 1997. pap. write for info. (*3-540-62592-5*) Spr-Verlag.

BonGiovanni, Guy. Depression. 17p. (Orig.). (C). 1983. pap. 2.00 (*0-912981-04-0*) Hse BonGiovanni.

— Depression: Ten Days to a New You. 40p. (Orig.). (C). 1983. pap. 3.95 (*0-912981-02-4*) Hse BonGiovanni.

— In My Lifetime: An Odyssey of Supernatural Happenings. LC 95-94084. 188p. 1995. pap. 7.99 (*0-912981-24-5*) Hse BonGiovanni.

— The Ministry of Reconciliation in the Christian Church of North America. 23p. (Orig.). (C). 1983. pap. 2.00 (*0-912981-03-2*) Hse BonGiovanni.

— The Seed Royale. 21p. 1988. pap. 1.00 (*0-912981-19-9*) Hse BonGiovanni.

— Water Baptism. 24p. (Orig.). (C). 1983. pap. 1.00 (*0-912981-05-9*) Hse BonGiovanni.

BonGiovanni, Guy, ed. see Miucco, Barbara A.

Bongiovanni, Joseph N. & Bender's Editors. Pennsylvania Transaction Guide: Legal Forms, 16 vols. 1974. ring bd. 1340.00 (*0-8205-1436-5*) Bender.

Bongiovanni, Joseph N., jt. auth. see Skylar, S. Jay.

Bongiovanni, Marie. How to Sell Your Carvings: Advice from the Pros. LC 98-5702. 144p. 1998. pap. 12.95 (*0-8117-2798-X*) Stackpole.

Bongrand, P., et al, eds. Studying Cell Adhesion. LC 94-36098. 1994. 114.95 (*0-387-57590-1*) Spr-Verlag.

An Asterisk (*) at the beginning of an entry indicates that the title is appearing for the first time.

Bongrand, Pierre, ed. Physical Basis of Cell-Cell Adhesion. 280p. 1988. 158.00 (*0-8493-6554-6*, QH623, CRC Reprint) Franklin.

Bonham, Alan, jt. auth. see Langdon, Ken.

Bonham-Carter. Geographic Information Systems for Geologists: Modelling with GIS. LC 94-28315. (Computer Methods in the Geosciences Ser.: No. 13). 414p. 1995. pap. text 47.00 (*0-08-042420-1*, Pergamon Pr) Elsevier.

Bonham-Carter, Graeme. Geographic Information Systems for Geologists: Modelling with GIS. LC 94-28315. (Computer Methods in the Geosciences Ser.: No. 13). (Illus.). 414p. 1995. text 117.00 (*0-08-041867-8*, Pergamon Pr) Elsevier.

Bonham-Carter, Victor. Land & Environment: The Survival of the English Countryside. LC 72-3522. (Illus.). 240p. 1973. 34.50 (*0-8386-1195-8*) Fairleigh Dickinson.

Bonham, Charles. Measurements for Terrestrial Vegetation. LC 88-14269. 352p. 1989. 125.00 (*0-471-04880-1*) Wiley.

***Bonham, Christine E.** Credit Reform: Greater Effort Needed to Overcome Persistent Cost Estimation Problems. (Illus.). 120p. (C). 2000. reprint ed. pap. text 25.00 (*0-7881-8584-5*) DIANE Pub.

***Bonham, Christine E. & McClarin, Elizabeth A.** Accrual Budgeting: Experiences of Other Nations & Implications for the United States. (Illus.). 217p. 2000. pap. text 35.00 (*0-7567-0077-9*) DIANE Pub.

Bonham, Christine E., et al. Budget Issues: Budgeting for Federal Capital. (Illus.). 119p. (Orig.). (C). 1997. pap. text 40.00 (*0-7881-4143-0*) DIANE Pub.

— Budget Issues: Budgeting for Federal Insurance Programs. (Illus.). 224p. (C). 1998. pap. text 45.00 (*0-7881-7043-0*) DIANE Pub.

Bonham, Frank. The Best Western Stories of Frank Bonham. Pronzini, Bill & Greenberg, Martin H., eds. LC 89-11263. (Western Writers Ser.). 288p. 1989. 24.95 (*0-8040-0929-5*) Swallow.

— The Best Western Stories of Frank Bonham. Pronzini, Bill & Greenberg, Martin H., eds. LC 89-11263. (Western Writers Ser.). 288p. 1990. pap. 15.95 (*0-8040-0930-9*) Swallow.

— Blood on the Land. large type ed. LC 94-11945. 339p. 1994. lib. bdg. 18.95 (*0-8161-7400-8*, G K Hall Lrg Type) Mac Lib Ref.

— Bold Passage. large type ed. (Sagebrush Large Print Westerns Ser.). 228p. 1995. lib. bdg. 18.95 (*1-57490-006-4*) T T Beeler.

— Break for the Border. LC 99-19639. 1999. 20.95 (*0-7838-8578-4*, G K Hall & Co) Mac Lib Ref.

— Break for the Border. 144p. 1990. pap. 2.95 (*0-380-70852-3*, Avon Bks) Morrow Avon.

***Bonham, Frank.** Break for the Border. large type ed. LC 00-40276. 2000. write for info. (*1-57490-286-5*, Sagebrush LP West) T T Beeler.

Bonham, Frank. The Canon of Maverick Brands: A Western Trio. LC 97-6781. 213p. 1997. lib. bdg. 17.95 (*0-7862-0746-9*) Five Star.

— The Canon of Maverick Brands: A Western Trio. large type ed. LC 98-24420. 1999. 18.95 (*0-7862-0769-8*) Thorndike Pr.

***Bonham, Frank.** Cast a Long Shadow. large type ed. LC 99-41393. 1999. pap. 22.95 (*0-7838-8754-X*, G K Hall & Co) Mac Lib Ref.

— Defiance Mountain. large type ed. LC 99-39437. 2000. 30.00 (*0-7838-8732-9*, G K Hall Lrg Type) Mac Lib Ref.

— Durango Street. 187p. (YA). (gr. 7 up). pap. 4.99 (*0-8072-1549-X*) Listening Lib.

Bonham, Frank. Durango Street. LC 99-461905. 192p. (gr. 7 up). 1999. pap. 4.99 (*0-14-130309-3*, PuffinBks) Peng Put Young Read.

***Bonham, Frank.** Gunflame. LC 99-54891. 2000. 19.95 (*1-57490-251-2*) T T Beeler.

— Last Stage West. large type ed. 237p. 2000. pap. 20.95 (*0-7838-9013-3*) Mac Lib Ref.

Bonham, Frank. Logan's Choice. 128p. 1989. pap. 2.95 (*0-380-70851-5*, Avon Bks) Morrow Avon.

— Lost Stage Valley. 1998. 17.50 (*0-7540-8022-6*, Gunsmoke) Chivers N Amer.

— Lost Stage Valley. large type ed. LC 97-44872. (Nightingale Ser.). 294p. 1998. pap. 18.95 (*0-7838-8377-3*, G K Hall & Co) Mac Lib Ref.

— One Ride Too Many & Twelve Other Action Stories of the Wild West. Greenberg, Martin H. & Pronzini, Bill, eds. LC 94-46919. 270p. 1995. pap. 12.00 (*1-56980-034-0*) Barricade Bks.

— Snaketrack. large type ed. LC 93-31599. 268p. 1994. lib. bdg. 16.95 (*0-8161-5854-1*, G K Hall Lrg Type) Mac Lib Ref.

— Snaketrack. 160p. 1989. reprint ed. pap. 2.95 (*0-380-70845-0*, Avon Bks) Morrow Avon.

— Sound of Gunfire. large type ed. LC 94-42788. (Nightingale Ser.). 232p. 1995. pap. 16.95 (*0-7838-1150-0*, G K Hall Lrg Type) Mac Lib Ref.

— That Bloody Bozeman Trail & Stagecoach West. 1990. pap. 3.50 (*0-8125-0534-4*, Pub. by Tor Bks) St Martin.

Bonham, Frank, jt. auth. see Hinton, S. E.

Bonham, Gary. Ideology & Interests in the German State. LC 91-17759. (Modern European History Outstanding Studies & Dissertations). 464p. 1991. text 25.00 (*0-8153-0473-0*) Garland.

Bonham, Hilledge L. British Consuls in the Confederacy. LC 11-31660. (Columbia University. Studies in the Social Sciences: No. 111). reprint ed. 32.50 (*0-404-51111-2*) AMS Pr.

Bonham, John. The Middle Class Vote. LC 74-11985. (Illus.). 210p. 1974. reprint ed. lib. bdg. 59.50 (*0-8371-7709-X*, BOMI, Greenwood Pr) Greenwood.

***Bonham, Margaret H.** Introduction to Dog Agility. 144p. 2000. pap. write for info. (*0-7641-1439-5*, Pub. by Barron) Prodn Assocs.

— Soft Coated Wheaten Terriers: A Complete Pet Owner's Manual. LC 99-35914. (Complete Pet Owner's Manuals Ser.). (Illus.). 104p. 2000. 6.95 (*0-7641-1312-7*) Barron.

Bonham, Tad D. The Treasury of Clean Children's Jokes. 2nd rev. ed. LC 96-53374. 144p. (J). 1997. pap. 5.99 (*0-8054-6364-X*) Broadman.

— The Treasury of Clean Church Jokes. 2nd rev. ed. LC 96-29826. 144p. 1997. pap. 5.99 (*0-8054-6363-1*) Broadman.

Bonham, Tal D. & Gulledge, Jack. The Treasury of Clean Seniors' Jokes. 2nd rev. ed. LC 96-53375. 144p. (Orig.). 1997. pap. 5.99 (*0-8054-6365-8*) Broadman.

Bonham, Ted H., jt. auth. see Hedgepeth, Tommy O.

Bonham, Thomas. The Chyrgeons: Or, an Antidotarie Chyrurgicall. Poeton, E., ed. LC 68-54619. (English Experience Ser.: No. 31). 360p. 1968. reprint ed. 49.00 (*90-221-0031-6*) Walter J Johnson.

Bonheim, Helmut. Literary Systematics. (Illus.). 392p. (C). 1990. 75.00 (*0-85991-298-1*) Boydell & Brewer.

— The Narrative Modes: Techniques of the Short Story. 208p. (C). 1992. 75.00 (*0-85991-086-5*) Boydell & Brewer.

Bonheim, Jalaja. Aphrodite's Daughters: Women's Sexual Stories & the Journey of the Soul. LC 96-53615. 1997. per. 13.00 (*0-684-83080-9*) Simon & Schuster.

***Bonheim, Jalaja.** The Hunger for Ecstasy. 2001. 19.95 (*1-57954-116-X*, Daybrk) Rodale Pr Inc.

Bonheim, Jalaja. The Serpent & the Wave: A Guide to Movement Meditation. (Illus.). 320p. (Orig.). 1995. pap. 14.95 (*0-89087-657-6*) Celestial Arts.

Bonheim, Jalaja, ed. Goddess: A Celebration in Art & Literature. LC 97-8432. (Illus.). 240p. 1997. 50.00 (*1-55670-621-9*) Stewart Tabori & Chang.

Bonheur, Albert Le, see Le Bonheur, Albert.

Bonheur, Gaston. Qui a Casse la Vase Se Soisons?, Tome I. (FRE.). 1976. pap. 11.95 (*0-7859-1814-0*, 2070367290) Fr & Eur.

— Qui a Casse la Vasse de Soisons?, Tome II. (FRE.). 1976. pap. 11.95 (*0-7859-1815-9*, 2070367304) Fr & Eur.

Bonhoeffer, Dietrich. Act & Being. Floyd, Wayne W., ed. Rumscheidt, H. Martin, tr. (Dietrich Bonhoeffer Works: Vol. 2). 224p. 1996. 32.00 (*0-8006-8302-1*, 1-8302, Fortress Pr) Augsburg Fortress.

— Christ the Center. 128p. 1978. pap. 12.00 (*0-06-060811-0*, Pub. by Harper SF) HarpC.

— The Cost of Discipleship. 1983. 24.00 (*0-8446-5960-6*) Peter Smith.

— The Cost of Discipleship. LC 95-22223. 320p. 1995. per. 11.00 (*0-684-81500-1*, Touchstone) S&S Trade Pap.

— Creation & Fall: A Theological Exposition of Genesis 1-3. De Gruchy, John W., ed. Bax, Douglas S., tr. LC 97-36937. (Dietrich Bonhoeffer Works Ser.: Vol. 3). 208p. 1997. 30.00 (*0-8006-8303-X*, Fortress Pr) Augsburg Fortress.

— Creation & Fall: Temptation. 1983. 23.50 (*0-8446-5962-2*) Peter Smith.

— Creation & Fall & Temptation. LC 96-47034. 144p. 1997. per. 9.00 (*0-684-82587-2*) S&S Trade Pap.

— Dietrich Bonhoeffer. (Modern Spirituality Ser.). 96p. 1992. pap. 4.95 (*0-87243-198-3*) Templegate.

***Bonhoeffer, Dietrich.** Discipleship. (Dietrich Bonhoeffer Works). 2000. pap. 48.00 (*0-8006-8304-8*, Fortress Pr) Augsburg Fortress.

Bonhoeffer, Dietrich. Ethics. Bethge, Eberhard, ed. Smith, Neville H., tr. from GER. LC 95-20402. 384p. 1995. per. 11.00 (*0-684-81501-X*, Touchstone) S&S Trade Pap.

— Letters & Papers from Prison. 1981. 17.95 (*0-02-513110-9*) Macmillan.

— Letters Papers from Prison. 1997. per. 13.00 (*0-684-83827-3*) S&S Trade.

— Life Together. LC 54-6901. 128p. 1976. reprint ed. pap. 7.95 (*0-06-060851-X*, RD292) Harper SF.

— Life Together: A Discussion of Christian Fellowship. 128p. 1978. pap. 12.00 (*0-06-060852-8*, Pub. by Harper SF) HarpC.

— Life Together: The Classic Exploration of Faith in Community. Doberstein, John W., tr. & intro. by. LC 92-54665. 128p. 1993. reprint ed. 16.00 (*0-06-060853-6*, Pub. by Harper SF) HarpC.

— Life Together & Prayerbook of the Bible. Kelly, Geffrey B., ed. Bloesch, Daniel W. & Burtness, James H., trs. (Dietrich Bonhoeffer Works: Vol. 5). 232p. 1996. 32.00 (*0-8006-8305-6*, 1-8305, Fortress Pr) Augsburg Fortress.

— Meditating on the Word. large type ed. (Orig.). 1988. pap. 9.95 (*0-8027-2591-0*) Walker & Co.

— The Mystery of Easter. Weber, Manfred, ed. LC 97-69106. (Illus.). 48p. 1997. 14.95 (*0-8245-1722-9*, Crsrd) Crossroad NY.

— The Mystery of Holy Night. Weber, Manfred, ed. LC 96-85500. (Illus.). 48p. 1996. 14.95 (*0-8245-1591-9*) Crossroad NY.

— Psalms: The Prayer Book of the Bible. 2nd ed. Burtness, James H., tr. from GER. LC 73-101111.Tr. of Das/Gebetbuch der Bibel. 88p. 1970. pap. 6.99 (*0-8066-1439-0*, 10-5321, Augsburg) Augsburg Fortress.

— Sanctorum Communio: A Theological Study of the Sociology of the Church. Green, Clifford J., ed. Kraus, Reinhard & Lukens, Nancy, trs. LC 98-29640. (Dietrich Bonhoeffer Works Ser.: No. 1). 340p. 1998. 35.00 (*0-8006-8301-3*, 1-8301) Augsburg Fortress.

— Spiritual Care. Rochelle, Jay C., tr. LC 85-47711. 128p. 1985. pap. 14.00 (*0-8006-1874-2*, 1-1874, Fortress Pr) Augsburg Fortress.

— Temptation. 1965. write for info. (*0-318-54207-2*) Macmillan.

— A Testament to Freedom: The Essential Writings of Dietrich Bonhoeffer. rev. ed. LC 94-42563. 592p. 1995. pap. 23.00 (*0-06-064214-9*, Pub. by Harper SF) HarpC.

— Voices in the Night. LC 99-29099. 128p. 1999. 14.99 (*0-310-22874-3*) HarpC.

Bonhoeffer, Dietrich & Weber, Manfred. Meditations on the Cross. Stott, Douglas W., tr. from GER. LC 97-29636. 128p. 1998. pap. 12.00 (*0-664-25755-0*) Westminster John Knox.

***Bonhoff, Karla.** Standing Right Here Next to Me. 1999. pap. 7.98 incl. audio (*0-7601-2885-5*) Brentwood Music.

***Bonhoffer, Adolf Friedrich.** The Ethics of the Stoic Epictetus: An English Translation. Stephens, William O., tr. from GER. (Revisioning Philosophy Ser.: Vol. 2). 360p. 2000. pap. text 37.95 (*0-8204-5139-8*) P Lang Pubng.

Bonhotal, Jean F. & Krasny, Marianne E. Composting: Wastes to Resources: Experience 4-H Natural Resources. 2nd ed. (Illus.). 72p. 1994. reprint ed. 8.50 (*1-57753-038-1*, 147CWRF) Corn Coop Ext.

Bonhotal, Jean F., et al. What about Waste? Experience 4-H Natural Resources. (Four-H Ser.). (Illus.). 24p. (J) (gr. 3-7). 1990. pap. 3.25 (*1-57753-198-1*, 147WAW) Corn Coop Ext.

Bonhote, J. M. Samuel Mareschal: Melodiae Suaves. (Wissenschaftliche Abhandlungen-Musicological Studies: Vol. 25). (FRE.). 36p. 1976. pap. 8.00 (*0-912024-77-1*) Inst Mediaeval Mus.

Boni, Ada. Talisman Italian Cook Book. La Rosa, Matilde, tr. (International Cookbook Ser.). 1950. 12.00 (*0-517-50387-5*) Harmony Bks.

Boni, Albert, ed. Photographic Literature: An International Bibliographic Guide to General & Specialized Literature on Photographic Processes. 346p. 1996. reprint ed. 50.00 (*1-888262-39-7*) Martino Pubng.

Boni, Franco, ed. Rhubarb-O-Rama! Plays & Playwrights from the Rhubarb! Festival. 2nd ed. LC 98-162307. 336p. 1998. pap. 18.95 (*0-921368-78-X*) Genl Dist Srvs.

Boni, M., jt. ed. see Fontbote, L.

Boni, Pat, ed. see Freidman, Maurice.

Boni, Simone, et al. Bible Stories: A Treasury for Young Readers. LC 94-72598. (Children's Classics Ser.). 56p. (J). (ps-3). 1995. 9.98 (*1-56138-485-2*, Courage) Running Pr.

***Boni, William C. & Kovacich, Gerald L.** Netspionage: The Global Threats to Information. 224p. 2000. pap. 29.95 (*0-7506-7257-9*, Newnes) Buttrwrth-Heinemann.

***Boni, William F. & Kovacich, Gerald L.** I-Way Robbery: Crime on the Internet. LC 99-11320. 224p. 1999. pap. text 34.95 (*0-7506-7029-0*) Buttrwrth-Heinemann.

Boni, William F., jt. auth. see Kovacich, Gerald L.

Bonica, Diane. Hand-Shaped Art. (Illus.). 112p. (J). (ps-2). 1989. student ed. 12.99 (*0-86653-474-1*, GA1079, Good Apple.

— Hand-Shaped Gifts. 144p. (J). (ps-4). 1991. 13.99 (*0-86653-612-4*, GA1331) Good Apple.

— Little Kids Can Write Books Too! Making Classroom Books with Young Children. (Illus.). 112p. 1994. 12.99 (*0-86653-784-8*, GA1478) Good Apple.

Bonica, Diane. Writing & Art Go Hand in Hand. 80p. (J). (gr. 2-6). 1988. pap. text 9.95 (*0-86530-068-2*, IP 13-2) Incentive Pubns.

Bonica, John J., ed. The Management of Pain, 2 vols. 2nd ed. LC 88-8983. (Illus.). 2195p. 1990. 295.00 (*0-8121-1122-2*) Lppncott W & W.

— Pain. LC 79-5214. (Association for Research in Nervous & Mental Disease Research Publications: No. 58). (Illus.). 419p. 1980. reprint ed. pap. 129.90 (*0-608-00598-3*, 206118500007) Bks Demand.

Bonica, John J., et al, eds. Management of Superior Pulmonary Sulcus Syndrome (Pancoast Syndrome) LC 82-5337. 254p. 1982. reprint ed. pap. 78.80 (*0-608-04679-5*, 206540000004) Bks Demand.

Bonica, John J. & McDonald, John S. Principles & Practice of Obstetric Analgesia & Anesthesia. 2nd ed. (Illus.). 1344p. 1994. text 175.00 (*0-683-00930-3*, Lppncott W & W.

Bonica, John J., ed. see World Congress on Pain Staff.

Bonicatto, Marsha. Christmas Song of the North. LC 97-60279. (Illus.). 32p. (J). (ps-6). 1997. 14.95 (*1-57025-145-2*) Pfeifer-Hamilton.

Boniecki, Adam. Herbarz Polski, 16 vols., Set. 1985. reprint ed. 2100.00 (*0-318-23364-9*) Szwede Slavic.

***Boniecki, Adam.** The Making of the Pope of the Millennium: Kalendarium of the Life of Karol Wojtyla. LC 00-102005. (Illus.). 938p. 2000. 45.00 (*0-944203-49-3*) Marian Pr.

Boniello, Rose M., ed. Preserving Our Italian Heritage: A Cookbook. 222p. 1998. text 15.00 (*0-7881-5748-5*) DIANE Pub.

Bonier, Marie L. The Beginnings of the Franco-American Colony in Woonsocket, Rhode Island. rev. ed. Quintal, Claire, ed. & tr. by. from FRE. LC 98-125715. (Illus.). 560p. 26.95 (*1-880261-04-9*) Fl Assump Coll.

— Debuts De la Colonie Franco-Americaine De Woonsocket.Tr. of French Settlers of Woonsocket. (FRE., Illus.). 342p. 1997. reprint ed. lib. bdg. 39.50 (*0-8328-6493-5*) Higginson Bk Co.

***Boniface, Brian G.** Geography of Travel & Tourism. 3rd ed. 1999. pap. 39.95 (*0-7506-4231-9*) Buttrwrth-Heinemann.

Boniface, Brian G. & Cooper, Chris. The Geography of Travel & Tourism. 2nd ed. 270p. 1994. pap. 36.95 (*0-7506-1670-9*) Buttrwrth-Heinemann.

Boniface, Brian G. & Cooper, Chris P. The Geography of Travel & Tourism. 240p. 1990. pap. 26.95 (*0-7506-0531-6*) Buttrwrth-Heinemann.

Boniface, David R. Experiment Design & Statistical Methods for Behavioral & Social Research. LC 94-70924. 272p. (gr. 13). 1994. per. 41.95 (*0-412-54230-7*, Chap & Hall CRC) CRC Pr.

Boniface, Douglas M. Microelectronics: The Structure & Operation of Microprocessor-Based Systems. LC 97-153703. 208p. 1997. pap. text 24.95 (*1-898563-32-2*, Pub. by Horwood Pub) Paul & Co Pubs.

Boniface, Priscilla. Managing Quality Cultural Tourism. LC 95-7782. 144p. (C). (gr. 13). 1995. 60.00 (*0-415-09985-4*) Routledge.

Boniface, Priscilla & Fowler, Peter. Heritage & Tourism in the Global Village: Heritage: Care-Preservation-Management Program Ser. LC 92-14577. (Illus.). 200p. (C). 1993. pap. 32.99 (*0-415-07237-9*, A7874) Routledge.

— Northumberland & Newcastle upon Tyne. (Country Guide Ser.: No. 30). (Illus.). 64p. pap. 8.50 (*0-85263-998-8*, Pub. by Shire Pubns) Parkwest Pubns.

Boniface, Priscilla, jt. auth. see Robinson, Mike.

***Boniface, Russell P., ed.** Our Call to Serve Others: Award-Winning, Student Initiated Service Projects - A Resource for Schools. (Illus.). 1999. write for info. (*0-88210-333-4*) Natl Assn Principals.

Boniface, William. The Adventures of Max the Minnow. LC 97-25157. (Illus.). 32p. (J). 1997. pap. 15.95 (*0-939251-95-7*) Accord CO.

— Mystery in Bugtown. LC 96-49312. (Illus.). (J). 1997. 15.95 (*0-939251-90-6*) Accord CO.

— Studs. 356p. 1996. 18.95 (*0-9654573-0-3*) W Boniface.

***Boniface, William.** Trim the Tree for Christmas. (Illus.). (J). (ps-1). 2000. 9.99 (*0-8431-7558-3*, G & D) Peng Put Young Read.

***Bonifacino, Juan S., et al, eds.** Current Protocols in Cell Biology. LC 98-36334. 700p. 1999. pap. text 395.00 (*0-471-24108-3*) Wiley.

Bonifacio, P. The Psychological Effects of Police Work: A Psychodynamic Approach. (Criminal Justice & Public Safety Ser.). (Illus.). 220p. (C). 1991. 42.50 (*0-306-43955-7*, Plenum Trade) Perseus Pubng.

Bonifacio, Rodalfo, ed. Mysteries, Puzzles & Paradoxes in Quantum Mechanics. LC 99-60523. (AIP Conference Proceedings Ser.). (Illus.). 362p. 1999. 95.00 (*1-56396-852-5*) Am Inst Physics.

Bonifacio, Rodolfo & Barletta, William A., eds. Towards X-Ray Free Electron Lasers: Workshop on Single Pass, High Gain FELs Starting from Noise, Aiming at Coherent X-Rays. LC 97-77194. (AIP Conference Proceedings Ser.: Vol. 413). (Illus.). 352p. 1998. 90.00 (*1-56396-744-8*) Am Inst Physics.

Bonifas, Aime. Prisoner 20-801: A French National in the Nazi Labor Camps. Foster, Claude R. & Van Sice, Mildred M., trs. 143p. 1987. pap. 20.00 (*1-887732-10-1*) West Chester Univ.

Bonifaz, Oscar. Remembering Rosario: A Personal Glimpse into the Life & Works of Rosario Castellanos. Allgood, Myralyn F., ed. & tr. by. 1990. 27.50 (*0-916379-72-8*) Scripta.

Bonifaz, Ruben. Del Templo de Su Cuerpo. (SPA.). pap. 7.99 (*968-16-3927-8*, Pub. by Fondo) Continental Bk.

Bonifer & Weaver. Out of Bounds: An Anecdotal History of Notre Dame Football. LC 78-60060. (Illus.). 1978. 15.00 (*0-87832-043-1*) Piper.

Bonifield, Ruth. Keeping the Glow: Kassie's Story. LC 96-61275. 312p. (Orig.). 1996. pap. 7.00 (*1-57502-305-9*, P1047) Morris Pubng.

Bonikowska, Halina. Dzien Jak Co Dzien (Day As Any Other) (POL.). 72p. (Orig.). 1989. pap. 7.00 (*0-930401-21-2*) Artex Pub.

— Dziennik Pisany na Wyspie: Diary Written on an Island.Tr. of Memoirs Written on the Island. 76p. (Orig.). 1987. pap. write for info. (*0-318-61881-8*); pap. 7.95 (*0-930401-08-5*) Artex Pub.

— Island Diary. Karesek, Jan, tr. from POL.Tr. of Dziennik pisany na Wyspie. (Illus.). 80p. 1989. pap. 8.00 (*0-930401-25-5*) Artex Pub.

— Pod Sztandarem Z Gwiazd. LC 85-61376. (POL.). 112p. (Orig.). 1985. pap. text 8.00 (*0-930401-01-8*) Artex Pub.

Bonilla, Alejandro Vargas, jt. auth. see Funston, James.

Bonilla, Alejandro Vargas, jt. auth. see Funston, James H.

Bonilla, Alvaro. History of the Revenue Stamps of Costa Rica. Washburn, Richard A. et al, eds. (Illus.). viii, 272p. (Orig.). 1996. pap. 30.00 (*0-9645247-3-2*) SCRC.

Bonilla, Antulio P. Cooperativismo: Teoria y Practica. 2nd ed. Bauza, Carmen M., ed. (Cooperatives Ser.). 352p. 1985. 11.95 (*0-934885-00-1*) Edit Nosotros.

***Bonilla, C. F. & Lauderdale, Katherine, eds.** Hello Parents, Where Are You? The Teachers' Call for Involvement. LC 98-72646. (Illus.). viii, 79p. 1998. pap. 19.95 (*1-879774-16-X*) ICA Pub Co.

Bonilla, C. F., ed. see Symposium on Thermophysical Properties.

Bonilla, Carlos A. A Skeptic's Guide to Alternative Medicine: The Holistic Approach to Well Being. Lauderdale, Katherine, ed. LC 97-74916. (Illus.). 64p. 1998. pap. 19.95 (*1-879774-13-5*) ICA Pub Co.

Bonilla, Carlos A., ed. Perspectives in Multicultural Education: The Diverse Classroom. (Illus.). 210p. (Orig.). (C). 1996. pap. text 19.95 (*1-879774-10-0*) ICA Pub Co.

Bonilla, Carlos A., et al, eds. Chaotic Conversation: A Foray into the Complex World of Communication. LC 98-72172. (Illus.). 125p. 1998. pap. 19.95 (*1-879774-08-9*) ICA Pub Co.

— Our Educational Melting Pot: Have We Reached the Boiling Point? LC 97-71584. (Illus.). 100p. (Orig.). 1997. pap. text 19.95 (*1-879774-07-0*) ICA Pub Co.

Bonilla, Carlos A. & Brazda, Jana L. School Dropouts: The Tragedy of America's Undereducated Youth. LC 91-70837. (Illus.). 224p. (Orig.). 1993. per. 29.95 (*1-879774-00-3*) ICA Pub Co.

Bonilla, Carlos A. & Goss, Joyce L., eds. Public (K-12) Education's Hot Jalapenos: Topics Picantes in Special Education. LC 96-79027. (Illus.). 58p. (Orig.). 1997. pap. 19.95 (*1-879774-03-8*) ICA Pub Co.

— Teaching to Ethnicity, Gender & Race: The Quest for Equality. LC 97-74911. (Illus.). 74p. 1997. pap. 19.95 (*1-879774-12-7*) ICA Pub Co.

Bonilla, Carlos A., et al. Students At-Risk: Poverty, Pregnancy, Violence, Depression & the Demise of the Traditional Family. 2nd rev. ed. LC 97-71123. (Illus.). 92p. 1999. pap. 19.95 (*1-879774-25-9*) ICA Pub Co.

— Students At-Risk: The Teachers Call to Action. LC 97-71123. (Illus.). 114p. (Orig.). 1997. pap., teacher ed. 19.95 (*1-879774-09-7*) ICA Pub Co.

Bonilla, Carlos A., jt. auth. see Lauderdale, Kathi.

Bonilla, Carlos A., ed. see Goss, Joyce L. & Fisicaro, Maria.

***Bonilla, Denise M.** School Violence. LC 00-24137. (The Reference Shelf Ser.). 2000. pap. write for info. (*0-8242-0982-6*) Wilson.

Bonilla, Denise M. & Levy, Beth. The Power of the Press: The Birth of American Political Reporting. LC 99-21172. (Reference Shelf Ser.). 1999. write for info. (*0-8242-0962-1*) Wilson.

Bonilla, Frank, et al, eds. Borderless Borders: U. S. Latinos, Latin Americans, & the Paradox of Interdependence. LC 97-41270. (Illus.). 336p. (C). 1998. pap. text 22.95 (*1-56639-620-4*) Temple U Pr.

— Borderless Borders: U. S. Latinos, Latin Americans, & the Paradox of Interdependence. LC 97-41270. (Illus.). 336p. (C). 1998. text 69.95 (*1-56639-619-0*) Temple U Pr.

Bonilla, Frank & Campos, Ricardo. Industry & Idleness. Rodriguez, Camille & Brand-Gomez, Olga, eds. 106p. 1986. pap. 7.00 (*1-878483-08-0*) Hunter Coll CEP.

Bonilla, Frank, jt. auth. see Morales, Rebecca.

Bonilla, Hector. Astrogeology: Origin & Destiny of the Earth. (Illus.). 144p. 1999. pap. 15.95 (*0-7414-0054-5*) Buy Books.

Bonilla, Jayne. If Hurricanes Were Candy Canes. (Nicebreaker Ser.). (Illus.). 16p. (Orig.). (J). (gr. k-6). 1992. pap. 4.95 (*0-9635105-0-9*) J R Bonilla.

***Bonilla, M., et al, eds.** Financial Modelling. (Contributions to Management Science Ser.). xii, 428p. 2000. pap. (*3-7908-1282-X*) Spr-Verlag.

Bonilla, Ruth M., et al. Hay Amores Que Matan: La Violencia Contra las Mujeres en la Vida Conyugal. LC 90-61437. 116p. 1996. pap. 7.50 (*0-929157-09-5*) Ediciones Huracan.

Bonilla-Santiago, Gloria. Breaking Ground & Barriers: Hispanic Women Developing Effective Leadership. (Illus.). 345p. (Orig.). (C). 1992. pap. 22.00 (*0-927065-08-8*) Marin Chula Vista.

Bonime, Andrew & Pohlmann, Ken C. Writing for New Media: The Essential Guide to Writing for Interactive Media, CD-ROMS, & the Web. LC 97-25193. (Books for Writers Ser.). (Illus.). 236p. 1997. pap. 16.95 (*0-471-17030-5*) Wiley.

Bonime-Blanc, Andrea R., ed. Commercial & Investment Law: Latin America, 3 vols. 1995. 165.00 (*1-57105-028-0*) Transnatl Pubs.

Bonime, Walter. The Clinical Use of Dreams. (Psychoanalysis: Examined & Re-Examined Ser.). 343p. (C). 1982. reprint ed. lib. bdg. 35.00 (*0-306-79710-0*) Da Capo.

— Collaborative Psychoanalysis: Anxiety, Depression, Dreams & Personality Change. LC 86-46161. 416p. 1989. 55.00 (*0-8386-3298-X*) Fairleigh Dickinson.

Bonin, jt. auth. see DuBuisson-Hamel, Melany A.

Bonin, jt. auth. see Hinds.

Bonin, Adelyn. Allegiances. (Illus.). 352p. 1993. pap. 12.95 (*1-56474-036-6*) Fithian Pr.

Bonin, Albert M., jt. auth. see Hinds, Robert T.

Bonin, Helene, tr. see Champsaur, Paul & Milleron, Jean-Claude.

Bonin, Helene, tr. see Laffont, Jean-Jacques.

Bonin, J. & Golterman, H. L., eds. Fluxes Between Trophic Levels & Through the Water-Sediment Interface. (Developments in Hydrobiology Ser.). (C). 1991. text 285.00 (*0-7923-0961-8*) Kluwer Academic.

Bonin, J. J. & Stevenson, D. E., eds. Risk Assessment in Setting National Priorities. (Advances in Risk Analysis Ser.: Vol. 7). (Illus.). 698p. (C). 1989. text 210.00 (*0-306-43246-3*, Kluwer Plenum) Kluwer Academic.

Bonin, Jean. Les Machines a Papier. (FRE., Illus.). 298p. 1988. pap. text (*2-9800538-3-X*) CA66.

Bonin, Jean M. Piano - Beds & Music by Steam: An Index with Abstracts to Musical-Related United States Patent Records, 1790-1874. LC 92-93191. (Reference Books in Music: No. 24). xxii, 236p. 1993. 39.50 (*0-914913-17-4*, Fallen Lef Pr) Scarecrow.

Bonin, John P. & Putterman, Louis. Economics of Cooperation & the Labor-Managed Economy. (Fundamentals of Pure & Applied Economics Ser.: Vol. 14). viii, 188p. 1987. pap. text 68.00 (*3-7186-0358-6*) Gordon & Breach.

Bonin, John P. & Szekely, Istvan P., eds. The Development & Reform of Financial Systems in Central & Eastern Europe. 384p. 1994. 95.00 (*1-85898-024-0*) E Elgar.

Bonin, John P., et al. Banking in Transition Economies: Developing Market Oriented Banking Sectors in Eastern Europe. LC 97-41480. 208p. (C). 1998. 85.00 (*1-85898-604-4*) E Elgar.

Bonin, John P., tr. see Champsaur, Paul & Milleron, Jean-Claude.

Bonin, John P., tr. see Laffont, Jean-Jacques.

Bonin, Joseph E., et al, eds. Matroid Theory: AMS-IMS-SIAM Joint Summer Research Conference on Matroid Theory, July 2-6, 1995, University of Washington, Seattle. LC 96-18251. (Contemporary Mathematics Ser.: Vol. 196). 418p. 1996. pap. 72.00 (*0-8218-0508-8*, CONM/197) Am Math.

Bonin, P., tr. see Pikulik, Ivan I. & Leger, Francois, eds.

Bonin, Serge. Le Traitement Graphique D'une Information Hydrometeorologique Relative a L'espace Maritime Du Nord Sovietique, 2 vols., Set. Incl. Vol. 1. Documents Graphiques. (Illus.). 1974. pap. text Vol. 2. Analyses et Commentaires. 2200p. 1974. pap. text (Contributions du Centre d'Etudes Antiques Ser.: No. 11). (FRE., Illus.). 1974. Set pap. text 52.75 (*0-686-22587-2*) Mouton.

***Bonin, Theraese M. & Albertus Magnus.** Creation as Emanation: The Origin of Diversity in Albert the Great's On the Causes & the Procession of the Universe. LC 00-32591. (Publications in Medieval Studies: Vol. 29). 248p. 2000. 45.00 (*0-268-02351-4*) U of Notre Dame Pr.

Bonin, W. Dictionary of Parapsychology: Diccionario de Parapsicologia, 2 vols. (ENG & SPA.). 1983. pap. 25.95 (*0-8288-2201-8*, S15803) Fr & Eur.

Bonin, Werner F. Dicc. de los Grandes Psicologos. (SPA.). pap. 20.99 (*968-16-3346-6*, Pub. by Fondo) Continental Bk.

Bonin, William. Doing Time. (Stories from the Mind of a Death Row Prisoner: Bk. 1). 74p. 1991. 10.00 (*1-879027-04-6*) Eagle Red Bluff.

Bonine, John E. & McGarity, Thomas O. The Law of Environmental Protection: Cases, Legislation, Policies. 2nd ed. (American Casebook Ser.). 1042p. (C). 1991. 62.50 (*0-314-92198-2*) West Pub.

Bonine, Michael E., ed. Population, Poverty, & Politics in Middle East Cities. LC 96-21377. 384p. 1997. 49.95 (*0-8130-1474-3*) U Press Fla.

Bonine, Michael E. & Keddie, Nikki R., eds. Modern Iran: The Dialectics of Continuity & Change. LC 80-19463. (Illus.). 474p. reprint ed. pap. 147.00 (*0-8357-6579-2*, 203597400097) Bks Demand.

Boning, Holger. Franzosische Revolution und Deutsche Offentlichkeit. (Deutsche Presseforschung Ser.: Vol. 28). (GER.). 280p. 1992. lib. bdg. 65.00 (*3-598-21629-7*) K G Saur Verlag.

Boning, Thomas. Metaphysik, Kunst und Sprache beim Fruhen Nietzche. (Monographien und Texte zur Nietzsche-Forschung Ser.: Vol. 20). (GER.). xiv, 518p. (C). 1988. lib. bdg. 192.35 (*3-11-011463-1*) De Gruyter.

Bonington. Climbing Everest. 1992. pap. text. write for info. (*0-17-556006-4*) Addison-Wesley.

***Bonington, Chris.** Boundless Horizons: The Autobiography of Chris Bonington. (Illus.). 672p. 2000. 32.00 (*0-89886-755-X*) Mountaineers.

Bonington, Chris. Heroic Climbs: A Celebration of World Mountaineering. LC 96-189031. 192p. 1996. pap. text 29.95 (*0-89886-496-8*) Mountaineers.

— Mountaineer: Thirty Years of Climbing on the World's Great Peaks. LC 89-38267. (Sierra Club Guides to the Natural Areas Ser.). 1990. 29.95 (*0-87156-618-4*, Pub. by Sierra) Random.

— Mountaineer: Thirty Years of Climbing on the World's Great Peaks. (Illus.). 192p. 1996. pap. 30.00 (*0-87156-905-1*, Pub. by Sierra) Random.

***Bonington, Chris.** Quest for Adventure. 2000. 35.00 (*0-7922-7953-0*) Natl Geog.

***Bonington, Chris & Clarke, Charles.** Tibet's Secret Mountain: The Triumph of Sepu Kangri. (Illus.). 200p. 2000. 29.95 (*0-297-81984-4*, Pub. by Weidenfeld & Nicolson) Trafalgar.

Bonini, William E., et al, eds. The Caribbean-South America Plate Boundry & Regional Tectonics. LC 84-5947. (Geological Society of America, Memoir Ser.: No. 162). (Illus.). 470p. Date not set. reprint ed. pap. 145.70 (*0-608-20648-2*, 207208500003) Bks Demand.

— The Caribbean-South American Plate Boundary & Regional Tectonics. (Memoir Ser.: No. 162). (Illus.). 432p. 1984. 10.00 (*0-8137-1162-2*) Geol Soc.

Bonino, Jose M. Faces of Latin American Protestantism. 160p. 1997. pap. 16.00 (*0-8028-4225-9*) Eerdmans.

Bonino, Maddalena. Fast & Fresh Entertaining: Delicious Recipes to Make in under 30 Minutes. (Illus.). 96p. 1996. pap. 22.95 (*1-85626-130-1*, Pub. by Cathie Kyle) Trafalgar.

Bonino, Maddalena, jt. auth. see Schwartz, Oded.

Bonior, David E., et al. The Vietnam Veteran: A History of Neglect. LC 84-15154. 220p. 1984. 57.95 (*0-275-91733-9*, C1733, Praeger Pubs) Greenwood.

— The Vietnam Veteran: A History of Neglect. LC 84-15154. 222p. 1985. pap. 18.95 (*0-275-92026-7*, B2026, Praeger Pubs) Greenwood.

Bonire, Josiah. Insights for Living. Dunham, Steve, ed. (Illus.). 140p. (Orig.). 1992. 11.95 (*1-879420-04-X*); pap. 7.95 (*1-879420-05-8*) Covenant Pubs.

Bonis, Eva M. Sensuous Hungarian-American Desserts: 52 Tempting Recipes, Each Less Than 300 Calories Per Serving. LC 97-76201. (Illus.). 68p. (Orig.). 1998. pap. 17.95 (*0-9653718-4-0*) Mayreni Pubng.

Bonis, J. Nicholas De, see Peterson, Roger S.

Bonis, L. J., ed. see Fundamental Phenomena in the Materials Science Sym.

Bonis, L. J., ed. see Symposium on Fundamental Phenomena in the Material.

Bonis, L. J., ed. see Symposium on Fundamental Phenomena in the Materials Sciences (4th: 1966: Boston, MA) Staff.

Bonis, M., et al, eds. International Progress in Precision Engineering. 576p. 1995. 196.00 (*0-444-10000-8*) Elsevier.

Bonis, Maria T. Teatros y Vida Teatral en Tudela, 1563-1750: 1563-1750. (Fuentes Ser.: No. XVII). (SPA., Illus.). 224p. 1991. pap. 53.00 (*1-85566-003-2*, Pub. by Tamesis Bks Ltd) Boydell & Brewer.

Bonisch, Susanne. Natural Healing for Dogs. LC 96-19222. (Illus.). 96p. 1996. pap. 10.95 (*0-8069-8120-2*) Sterling.

***Bonisteel, Roy.** All Things Considered. 264p. 1998. pap. 14.00 (*0-385-25728-7*) BDD Bks Young Read.

Bonisteel, Roy. There Was a Time . . . 272p. 1991. 24.95 (*0-385-25298-6*) Doubleday.

— There Was a Time. 272p. 1992. pap. 15.00 (*0-385-25363-X*) Doubleday.

Boniszewski, Tad. Self-Shielded Arc Welding. (Illus.). 240p. 1992. 135.00 (*1-85573-063-4*, Pub. by Woodhead Pubng) Am Educ Systs.

Bonita, Ruth. Women, Aging & Health: Achieving Health Across the Life Span, WHO/HRH/AHE/HPD/96.1. 58p. (Orig.). 1996. pap. text 10.80 (*0-614-19509-8*, 1930086) World Health.

Bonita, Ruth, jt. auth. see Beaglehole, Robert.

Bonitace, William. The Treasure Hunter. LC 98-27416. (Illus.). 24p. (J). 1998. 15.95 (*0-939251-97-3*) Accord CO.

Bonito Oliva, Achile, ed. see Cucchi, Enzo.

Bonitsis, Theologos H. & Brown, Chamberlain, eds. Quantity & Quality in Economic Research: Studies in Applied Business Research, Vol. IV. 272p. 1997. text 59.95 (*1-85972-682-8*, Pub. by Avebry) Ashgate Pub Co.

Bonitsis, Theologos H., jt. ed. see Arize, Augustine C.

Bonitz, Hermann. Aristotelische Studien, 5 vols. in 1. (GER.). 363p. 1969. reprint ed. 95.00 (*0-318-70451-X*) G Olms Pubs.

— Commentarius in Aristotelis Metaphysicam. viii, 596p. 1992. reprint ed. 145.00 incl. 3.5 hd (*3-487-05376-4*) G Olms Pubs.

— Platonische Studien. (GER.). xii, 323p. 1968. reprint ed. 90.00 (*0-318-70452-8*) G Olms Pubs.

Boniva, E. Orange & Lemons of India & Ceylon Text. (C). 1988. text 750.00 (*0-89771-561-6*, Pub. by Intl Bk Distr) St Mut.

Bonivento, C., et al, eds. Fuzzy Logic Control: Advances in Methodology: Proceedings of the Summer School Ferrara, Italy 16 - 20 June 1998. LC 98-213116. 280p. 1998. 64.00 (*981-02-3506-2*) World Scientific Pub.

Bonivento, C., ed. see Nicolo, F.

Bonivento, Claudio, et al. Colloquium on Automatic Control, Vol. 51. LC 96-21785. (Lecture Notes in Control & Information Sciences). 226p. 1996. pap. 54.00 (*3-540-76060-1*) Spr-Verlag.

Bonjean, Charles M. & Foss, Donald J., eds. Mental Health Research in Texas: Retrospect & Prospect. 400p. (Orig.). 1990. pap. 8.50 (*0-943463-09-2*) Hogg Found.

Bonjean, Charles M., jt. ed. see Schneider, Louis.

Bonjour, Edgar, et al. A Short History of Switzerland. LC 84-25253. 388p. 1985. reprint ed. lib. bdg. 52.50 (*0-313-24675-0*, BOSZ, Greenwood Pr) Greenwood.

Bonjour, Jean-Philippe & Tsang, Reginald C. Nutrition & Bone Development. LC 98-22556. 240p. 1998. text. write for info. (*0-7817-1753-1*) Lppncott W & W.

BonJour, Laurence. In Defense of Pure Reason: A Rationalist Account of "A Priori" Justification. LC 97-6563. (Studies in Philosophy). 246p. (C). 1998. text 59.95 (*0-521-59236-4*); pap. text 19.95 (*0-521-59745-5*) Cambridge U Pr.

Bonjour, Laurence. The Structure of Empirical Knowledge. 312p. (C). 1985. pap. 16.50 (*0-674-84381-9*) HUP.

Bonk, Kathy, et al. The Jossey-Bass Guide to Strategic Communications for Nonprofits: A Step-by-Step Guide to Working with the Media to Generate Publicity, Enhance Fundraising, Build Membership, Change Public Policy, Handle Crises & More. LC 98-40285. (Jossey-Bass Nonprofit & Public Management Ser.). 256p. 1999. 27.95 (*0-7879-4373-8*) Jossey-Bass.

Bonk, Alice J. W. A. T. 'S Manual. 96p. 1998. pap. 6.95 (*0-89228-113-8*) Impact Christian.

Bonk, Curtis J. & King, Kira S., eds. Electronic Collaborators: Learner-Centered Technologies for Literacy, Apprenticeship, & Discourse. LC 98-9394. 304p. 1998. 89.95 (*0-8058-2796-X*); pap. write for info. (*0-8058-2797-8*) L Erlbaum Assocs.

Bonk, Ecke, et al, contrib. by. Joseph Cornell - Marcel Duchamp: In Resonance. LC 98-87794. (Illus.). 343p. 1998. pap. 46.00 (*0-939594-47-1*) Menil Found.

— Joseph Cornell/Duchamp... In Resonance. LC 98-87794. (Illus.). 343p. 1998. 70.00 (*3-89322-431-9*, Pub. by Edition Cantz) Dist Art Pubs.

Bonk, Ecke, et al. Jacqueline Matisse: Kitetail Cocktail. Longhauser, Elsa, ed. LC 98-75477. (Illus.). 20p. 1999. pap. 20.00 (*1-58442-048-0*) Galleries at Moore.

Bonk, H. A., et al. English Language Textbook. (ENG & RUS.). 639p. 1991. 21.95 (*0-7859-1089-1*, 5339006360) Fr & Eur.

Bonk, Jon. The World at War - The Church at Peace: Studies in Biblical Peacemaking. 128p. (C). 1988. pap. 4.95 (*0-919797-87-3*); teacher ed. 1.50 (*0-919797-89-X*) Kindred Prods.

Bonk, Jonathan. The Theory & Practice of Missionary Identification, 1860-1920. LC 88-32579. (Studies in History of Missions: Vol. 2). 384p. 1990. lib. bdg. 99.95 (*0-88946-071-X*) E Mellen.

Bonk, Jonathan J. Missions & Money: Affluence As a Western Missionary Problem. LC 90-48231. (American Society of Missiology Ser.). xxi, 170 p. 1991. pap. 20.00 (*0-88344-718-5*) Orbis Bks.

Bonk, Mary R., ed. International Acronyms, Initialisms & Abbreviations Dictionary, Vol. 1. 4th ed. 1260p. 1997. 230.00 (*0-8103-7437-4*) Gale.

— Reverse Acronyms, Initialisms & Abbreviations Dictionary, Vol. 2. 4th ed. 1230p. 1997. 210.00 (*0-8103-7438-2*) Gale.

Bonk, Melinda. Controlling Hormones Naturally: My Journey for Solutions to PMS Menopause & Osteoporosis with... Aesoph, Lauri M. & Fraser, Laura K., eds. Orig. Title: Control Menopause Naturally. (Illus.). 240p. (Orig.). 1996. pap. 12.95 (*0-9650827-0-9*) MB Pubs.

Bonk, Melinda, ed. Alternative Medicine Yellow Pages: The Comprehensive Guide to the New World of Health. LC 94-179114. 225p. (Orig.). 1994. pap. 12.95 (*0-9636334-2-2*) AlternMed Bks.

Bonk, N. A. Textbook of the English Language. 2nd ed. 639p. 1993. 95.00 (*0-7859-9100-X*) Fr & Eur.

Bonk, Robert J. Medical Writing in Drug Development: A Practical Guide for Pharmaceutical Research. LC 97-18243. (Illus.). 139p. (C). 1998. 42.00 (*0-7890-0174-8*, Pharmctl Prods); pap. 19.95 (*0-7890-0449-6*, Pharmctl Prods) Haworth Pr.

— Pharmacoeconomics in Perspective: A Primer on Research, Techniques & Information. LC 98-47909. (Illus.). 116p. 1999. lib. bdg. 49.95 (*0-7890-0561-1*, Pharmctl Prods) Haworth Pr.

Bonk, Sigmund. We See God: George Berkeley's Philosophical Theology. (European University Studies, Series 20: Vol. 528). 109p. 1996. pap. 29.95 (*0-8204-3252-0*) P Lang Pubng.

— We See God: George Berkeley's Philosophical Theology. (European University Studies, Series 20: Vol. 528). 109p. 1997. pap. 29.95 (*3-631-31409-4*) P Lang Pubng.

Bonk, U. E. Biopsie und Operationspraeparat. (Illus.). viii, 134p. 1983. pap. 19.25 (*3-8055-3702-6*) S Karger.

Bonk, U. E., ed. Aktuelle Klinische Zytologie. (Beitraege Zur Onkologie, Contributions to Oncology Ser.: Vol. 38). (GER., Illus.). x, 350p. 1990. 68.75 (*3-8055-5230-0*) S Karger.

Bonkalo, Alexander & Krafeik, Patricia, eds. The Rusyns. 1990. text 46.50 (*0-88033-190-9*, Pub. by East Eur Monographs) Col U Pr.

Bonke, Benno, et al. Memory & Awareness in Anaesthesia. 396p. 1990. 37.25 (*90-265-1020-9*) Swets.

Bonke, Felix I. The Sinus Node: Structure, Function, & Clinical Relevance. 1978. text 199.50 (*90-247-2064-8*) Kluwer Academic.

Bonkovsky, Frederick, ed. The Built Environment: Present & Future Values. (Illus.). 76p. (Orig.). 1986. pap. 5.95 (*1-55630-000-X*) Brentwood Comm.

Bonkovsky, Frederick O. International Norms & National Policy. LC 79-21206. 234p. reprint ed. pap. 72.60 (*0-608-30533-2*, 202083900019) Bks Demand.

Bonkowski, Sara. Teens Are Nondivorceable: A Workbook for Divorced Parents & Their Children (Ages 12-18) LC 90-62137. (Illus.). 160p. 1990. pap. 8.95 (*0-915388-36-7*, 179) ACTA Pubns.

— Tots are Nondivorceable: A Workbook for Divorced Parents & Their Children, Ages Birth-5 Years. LC 97-77685. 1998. pap. text 8.95 (*0-87946-178-0*) ACTA Pubns.

Bonn, B., jt. auth. see Schilling, H. D.

Bonn, Bernadine A. & Rounds, Stewart A. Dream: Analytical Ground Water Flow Programs. (Illus.). 115p. 1990. lib. bdg. 119.00 incl. disk (*0-87371-271-4*, L271) Lewis Pubs.

Bonn, Charles. Le Roman Algerien De Langue Francaise: Vers un Espace De Communication Litteraire Decolonise? LC 85-172737. (FRE.). 359p. reprint ed. pap. 111.30 (*0-7837-6943-1*, 204677200003) Bks Demand.

Bonn, Ernie. Fifty Two Steps Underground. 225p. 1999. write for info. (*0-918616-27-1*); pap. write for info. (*0-918616-28-X*) Northern Mich.

Bonn, G., jt. auth. see Jandik, P.

Bonn, G., jt. auth. see Scherz, H.

Bonn, Gisela. The Indian Challenge. (C). 1992. 32.00 (*81-7023-370-4*, Pub. by Allied Pubs) S Asia.

***Bonn International Center for Conversion Staff.** Conversion Survey 1998: Global Disarmament, Defense Industry Consolidation & Conversion. (Illus.). 320p. 1998. pap. text 29.95 (*0-19-829448-4*) OUP.

Bonn International Center for Conversion Staff. Conversion Survey, 1998: Global Disarmament, Defense Industry Consolidation & Conversion. (Illus.). 320p. 1998. text 85.00 (*0-19-829449-2*) OUP.

Bonn International Center for Conversion Staff. Conversion Survey, 1997: Global Disarmament & the Disposal of Surplus Weapons. (Illus.). 320p. 1997. pap. text 38.00 (*0-19-829294-5*) OUP.

— Conversion Survey, 1997: Global Disarmament & the Disposal of Surplus Weapons. (Illus.). 320p. (C). 1997. text 85.00 (*0-19-829295-3*) OUP.

— Conversion Survey, 1996: Global Disarmament, Demilitarization, & Demobilization. (Illus.). 288p. 1996. text 80.00 (*0-19-828085-8*) OUP.

Bonn International Center for Conversion Staff. 3Conversion Survey, 1996: Global Disarmament, Demilitarization, & Demobilization. (Illus.). 282p. 1996. pap. text 35.00 (*0-19-828087-4*) OUP.

Bonn International Center for Conversion Staff, jt. auth. see Kingma, Kees.

Bonn, John. Taxation of Partnerships, 1987-1991, 2 vols. 240.00 (*0-685-24503-9*) West Group.

***Bonn, John R., et al.** Advising California Partnerships. 3rd ed. Peyerwold, David, ed. LC 99-64743. 904p. 1999. ring bd. 139.00 (*0-7626-0306-2*, BU-32880) Cont Ed Bar-CA.

Bonn, Keith E. The Army Officer's Guide. 48th ed. 1999. pap. text 22.95 (*0-8117-2659-2*) Stackpole.

— When the Odds Were Even: The Vosges Mountains Campaign, October 1944-January 1945. LC 94-5062. (Illus.). 320p. 1996. pap. 16.95 (*0-89141-602-1*) Presidio Pr.

***Bonn, Keith E. & Baker, Anthony E.** Guide to Military Operations Other Than War: Tactics, Techniques & Procedures for Stability & Support Operations: Domestic & International. LC 99-50040. 368p. 2000. 19.95 (*0-8117-2939-7*) Stackpole.

***Bonn, Klaus.** Entgegnungen - Erzahlungen Zur Literatur. 150p. 1999. 31.95 (*3-631-34542-9*) P Lang Pubng.

Bonn, Lauri. Coffee Cakes: 105 Wonderful Recipes. (Illus.). 147p. 1998. spiral bd. 15.00 (*0-9665450-5-2*) Maren Pubg.

Bonn, Linda. Work of the Worship Committee. LC 98-25913. 65p. 1998. pap. 9.00 (*0-8170-1294-X*) Judson.

Bonn, Ron, jt. auth. see McCue, Kathleen.

Bonn, Thomas L. Heavy Traffic & High Culture: New American Library As Literary Gatekeeper. LC 88-18517. (Illus.). 240p. (C). 1989. 21.95 (*0-8093-1478-9*) S Ill U Pr.

An Asterisk (*) at the beginning of an entry indicates that the title is appearing for the first time.

Bonnabeau, Richard F. The Promise Continues: Empire State College - the First Twenty-Five Years. LC 96-4381. 1996. write for info. (0-89865-966-3) Donning Co.

Bonnafous, Giles. Renault Technocentre. 1999. pap. text 39.95 (2-85025-630-7) Hazan.

Bonnafy, Francon. Management Accounting with Sap R/3. (C). 2000. 52.95 (0-201-61912-1) Addison-Wesley.

Bonnans, J. Frederic & Shapiro, A. Perturbation Analysis of Optimization Problems. LC 00-20825. (Springer Series in Operations Research). 624p. 2000. 79.95 (0-387-98705-3) Spr-Verlag.

Bonnar. Recent Advances in Obstetrics & Gynecology, Vol. 18. 18th ed. 1995. pap. text 65.00 (0-443-04870-3, W B Saunders Co) Harcrt Hlth Sci Grp.

— Recent Advances in Obstetrics & Gynecology, Vol. 19. 19th ed. 1996. pap. text 77.00 (0-443-05253-0, W B Saunders Co) Harcrt Hlth Sci Grp.

Bonnar, J., ed. Natural Conception Through Personal Hormone Monitoring. (Illus.). 68p. 1996. 25.00 (1-85070-718-9) Prthnon Pub.

Bonnar, J., et al, eds. Research in Family Planning. (Studies in Fertility & Sterility). 1984. lib. bdg. 163.50 (0-85200-813-9) Kluwer Academic.

Bonnar, John, ed. Recent Advances in Obstetrics & Gynaecology 17. 17th ed. (Illus.). 244p. (Orig.). 1992. pap. text 51.00 (0-443-04402-3) Church.

— Recent Advances in Obstetrics & Gynecology, No. 16. 16th ed. (Illus.). 278p. 1990. pap. text 39.95 (0-443-04117-2) Church.

Bonnard, B., et al, eds. Analysis of Controlled Dynamical Systems: Proceedings of a Conference in Lyon, France, July 1990, Vol. 8. (Progress in Systems & Control Theory Ser.). viii, 403p. 1991. 127.50 (0-8176-3576-9) Birkhauser.

Bonnard, Brian. Alderney at War. (Illus.). 192p. 1993. 26.95 (0-7509-0343-0, Pub. by Sutton Pub Ltd) Intl Pubs Mktg.

Bonnard, C., ed. Instability Phenomena in the Zone of the Alpine Arc: Extracts from the Proceedings of the 5th International Symposium on Landslides, Lausanne, 10-15 July 1988. 144p. 1990. pap. 78.00 (90-6191-841-3, Pub. by A A Balkema) Ashgate Pub Co.

Bonnard, Chantal, et al. Brachial Plexus Lessions: Drawings of Explorations & Reconstructions by Algimantas Otonas Narakas, m ☐. LC 98-50980. (Illus.). 1999. 225.00 (3-540-63428-2) Spr-Verlag.

Bonnard, Christophe, ed. Landslides: Glissements de Terrain: Proceedings of the Fifth International Symposium, Lausanne, 10-15 July 1988, 3 vols. 1800p. (C). 1988. text 505.00 (90-6191-837-5, Pub. by A A Balkema) Ashgate Pub Co.

***Bonnard, Marc.** The Viagra Alternative: The Complete Guide to Overcoming Impotence Naturally. LC 99-40743. (Illus.). 224p. 1999. pap. 14.95 (0-89281-789-5) Inner Tradit.

Bonnard, Pierre, jt. auth. see Terrasse, Antoine.

Bonnarens. Market Action. 2nd ed. 1995. 32.50 (0-256-19867-5) McGraw.

Bonnaud, O., ed. see Strunk, H. P., et al.

Bonne, A., jt. auth. see D'Allessandro, M.

Bonne, Alfred. State & Economics in the Middle East. LC 72-11325. (Illus.). 452p. 1973. reprint ed. lib. bdg. 79.50 (0-8371-6661-6, BOSE, Greenwood Pr) Greenwood.

Bonne, Dick. Florida Saltwater Fishing: A Visitor's Guide. Poley, Sue, ed. LC 97-61149. (Illus.). 60p. Date not set. pap. write for info. (0-9648461-3-6) Ebert Desgn.

Bonne-Tamir, Batsheva. New Perspectives on Genetic Markers & Diseases among Jewish People. (Illus.). 488p. 1992. text 69.50 (0-19-506817-3) OUP.

Bonneau. Sunday Lectionary: Ritual Word, Paschal Shape. LC 97-27349. 1998. pap. text 14.95 (0-8146-2457-X) Liturgical Pr.

Bonneau, Danielle. Le Regime Administratif de l'Eau du Nil: Dans l'Egypte Grecque, Romaine & Byzantine. (Probleme der Agyptologie Ser.: No. 8). (FRE.). xxii, 336p. 1993. 107.00 (90-04-09687-6) Brill Academic Pubs.

Bonneau, Dorothea H. To Destroy You Is No Loss. 37p. 1992. pap. 3.50 (0-87129-150-9, T86) Dramatic Pub.

Bonneau, E., jt. auth. see Bonneau, M.

Bonneau-Kramer, Helen. Taming Your Mental Lions: A Safari to Health. 176p. 1998. pap. 14.95 (1-890622-39-7) Leathers Pub.

Bonneau, M. & Bonneau, E. A la Decouverte de la France. (C). 1981. 30.00 (0-7175-0904-4, Pub. by S Thornes Pubs) St Mut.

Bonneau, M. & Hennessen, W., eds. Herpes Virus of Man & Animal: Standardization of Immunological Procedures. (Developments in Biological Standardization Ser.: Vol. 52). (Illus.). x, 574p. 1983. pap. 61.00 (3-8055-3636-4) S Karger.

Bonneau, M., jt. ed. see Landmann, G.

Bonneau, Norman. Preparing the Table of the Word. (Preparing for Liturgy Ser.). 48p. (Orig.). 1997. pap. 3.95 (0-8146-2499-5) Liturgical Pr.

Bonnecarrere, Paul. The Golden Triangle. large type ed. 433p. 1982. 27.99 (0-7089-0808-X) Ulverscroft.

Bonnechose, Emile de. The Reformers Before the Reformation, Set. Mackenzie, Campbell, tr. LC 78-63194. (Heresies of the Early Christian & Medieval Era Ser.: Second Ser.). reprint ed. 44.50 (0-404-16190-1) AMS Pr.

Bonnefil, Vivienne I. Parallel in the Heartland. LC 95-72009. (Illus.). 256p. (YA). (gr. 11-12). 1996. 21.95 (1-56167-233-5) Noble Hse MD.

Bonnefis, Philippe. Celine: The Recall of the Birds. Weidmann, Paul, tr. from FRE. 184p. (C). 1996. text 44.95 (0-8166-2646-4) U of Minn Pr.

Bonnefoi, Alexandre. Woerterbuch des Arbeits und Sozialrechtd. (FRE & GER.). 1975. 85.00 (0-8288-5969-8, M6938) Fr & Eur.

***Bonnefoi, Alice R., tr.** En Busca de Dios: Preceptos para el Derarrollo Espiritual Segun Edgar Cayce. LC 98-43132. (SPA.). 182p. 1998. pap. 12.95 (0-87604-418-6) ARE Pr.

Bonnefoi, Sarah L., tr. see Roger, Jacques.

Bonnefoy, N. Rue Traversiere, et Autres Recits sur Reve. (FRE.). 1992. pap. 16.95 (0-7859-2829-4) Fr & Eur.

Bonnefoy, Yves. The Act & the Place of Poetry: Selected Essays. 196p. 1989. 32.50 (0-226-06449-2) U Ch Pr.

— Beginning & End of Snow. Sapinkopf, tr. from FRE. (QRL Poetry Bks.: Vol. XXXI) 702p. 1992. 20.00 (0-614-06452-X) Quarterly Rev.

— Concordance Poemes: (Concordance de Poemes) LC 88-37734. (Studies in French Literature: Vol. 3). 360p. 1990. lib. bdg. 99.95 (0-88946-574-6) E Mellen.

— Dictionary of Mythology & the Religions of Traditional Societies: Dictionnaire des Mythologie & des Religions des Societes Tradionnelles. (ENG & FRE.). 1232p. 1981. 350.00 (0-8288-2304-9, M15214) Fr & Eur.

— Dictionnaire Mythologie, Religions Monde Traditionnale, Antique. (FRE.). 1998. 195.00 (0-320-00175-X) Fr & Eur.

— Early Poems, 1947-1959. Kinnell, Galway & Pevear, Richard, trs. from FRE. LC 89-72172. 303p. 1990. text 29.95 (0-8214-0966-2) Ohio U Pr.

Bonnefoy, Yves. Early Poems, 1947-1959. Kinnell, Galway & Pevear, Richard, trs. from FRE. LC 89-72172. 303p. (C). 1993. reprint ed. pap. text 16.95 (0-8214-1048-2) Ohio U Pr.

Bonnefoy, Yves. In the Shadow's Light. Naughton, John T., tr. from FRE. LC 90-38229. 192p. 1990. pap. 13.95 (0-226-06448-4) U Ch Pr.

— In the Shadow's Light. Naughton, John T., tr. from FRE. LC 90-38229. 192p. 1991. 29.95 (0-226-06447-6) U Ch Pr.

— The Lure & the Truth of Painting: Selected Essays on Art. Stamelman, Richard, ed. & afterword by by. LC 94-49686. (Illus.). 256p. 1995. 40.00 (0-226-06444-1) U Ch Pr.

— New & Selected Poems. Naughton, John T. & Rudolf, Anthony, eds. 252p. 1995. pap. 14.95 (0-226-06460-3) U Ch Pr.

— New & Selected Poems. Naughton, John T., ed. & tr. by. from FRE. Rudolf, Anthony, ed. LC 95-10350. 252p. 1995. lib. bdg. 39.00 (0-226-06458-1) U Ch Pr.

— Poemes: De Mouvement et de l'Immobilitie de Douve, Hier Regnant Desert, Pierre Ecrit, Dans le Leurre du Seuil. (FRE.). 1982. pap. 10.95 (0-8288-3814-3, F88690) Fr & Eur.

— Poemes: Du Mouvement et de l'Immobilite de Douve; Hier Regnant Desert; Pierre Ecrite, etc. (Poesie Ser.). (FRE.). pap. 13.95 (2-07-032221-1) Schoenhof.

Bonnefoy, Yves, ed. Mythologies, 2 vols. Doniger, Wendy, tr. LC 90-46982. 1312p. 1991. lib. bdg. 300.00 (0-226-06453-0) U Ch Pr.

Bonnel, Roland & Rubinger, Catherine, eds. Femmes Savantes et Femmes D'Esprit: Women Intellectuals of the French Eighteenth Century. 2nd ed. LC 93-812. (Eighteenth-Century French Intellectual History Ser.: Vol. 1). XIV, 449p. (C). 1997. reprint ed. pap. text 45.95 (0-8204-3937-1) P Lang Pubng.

Bonnel, Roland G. Ethique et Esthetique Du Retour A Campagne Au XVIIIe Siecle: L'Oeuvre Litteraire et Utopique De Lezay - Marnesia, 1735-1800. (Eighteenth Century French Intellectual History Ser.: Vol. 4). (FRE.). XIV, 500p. (C). 1995. text 79.95 (0-8204-2628-8) P Lang Pubng.

Bonnell, Allen T., ed. see American Association for the Advancement of Science Staff.

Bonnell, D. A., ed. Scanning Tunneling Microscopy & Spectroscopy: Theory, Techniques & Applications. 436p. 1993. 169.00 (0-471-18735-6) Wiley.

Bonnell, D. A. & Tien, T. Y., eds. Silicon Nitride: Preparation & Properties. (Materials Science Forum Ser.). 320p. 1989. text 78.00 (0-87849-593-2, Pub. by Trans T Pub) Enfield Pubs NH.

***Bonnell, Dawn A.** Scanning Probe Microscopy & Spectroscopy: Theory, Techniques & Applications. 2nd ed. LC 00-36821. (Illus.). 2000. write for info. (0-471-24824-X) Wiley.

Bonnell, Dawn A., ed. Scanning Tunneling Microscopy & Spectroscopy: Theory, Techniques & Applications. LC 92-46997. 400p. 1993. 125.00 (0-89573-768-X, Wiley-VCH) Wiley.

Bonnell, Dawn A., et al, eds. Structure & Properties of Interfaces in Ceramics. (MRS Symposium Proceedings Ser.: Vol. 357). 468p. 1995. 67.00 (1-55899-258-8) Materials Res.

Bonnell, Eduard. Lexicon Quintilianeum. lxxxiv, 1043p. 1962. reprint ed. 240.00 (0-318-71078-1) G Olms Pubs.

Bonnell, F. C., jt. auth. see Bonnell, Florence W.

Bonnell, Florence W. & Bonnell, F. C. Conrad Aiken, a Bibliography 1902-1978. LC 82-9241. 303p. 1982. reprint ed. pap. 94.00 (0-608-03464-9, 206416900008) Bks Demand.

Bonnell, John C., Jr. Sabres in the Shenandoah: The 21st New York Cavalry, 1862-1866. LC 96-31752. (Illus.). 377p. 1996. 34.95 (1-57249-012-8, Burd St Pr) White Mane Pub.

Bonnell, Kimberly. What to Wear LC 99-37557. 192p. 1999. pap. 12.95 (0-312-20944-4) St Martin.

Bonnell, Paula. The Birth of Color: Sarah Sutro/May 1997. 2nd rev. ed. (Illus.). 1997. pap. 12.00 (1-928668-02-X, Flying Univ Gallery) MillCreek Pr.

— Haiku Madness: An Essay & Haiku. 58p. 1997. pap. 10.00 (1-928668-01-1, Dragon of Wantly) MillCreek Pr.

— Japan in Duxbury. 20p. 1998. pap. 10.00 (1-928668-03-8) MillCreek Pr.

— Message. 64p. 1999. 20.00 (1-928668-04-6) MillCreek Pr.

— Sarah Sutro - May 1997. 24p. 1997. pap. 10.00 (1-928668-00-3, Flying Univ Gallery) MillCreek Pr.

Bonnell, Victoria, et al. Can Gorbachev's Reforms Succeed? 136p. (Orig.). (C). 1990. pap. 12.95 (0-9622629-1-9) UCB CFSEES.

Bonnell, Victoria E. Iconography of Power: Soviet Political Posters under Lenin & Stalin. LC 96-36252. (Studies on the History of Society & Culture). 385p. 1997. 48.00 (0-520-08712-7, Pub. by U CA Pr) Cal Prin Full Svc.

***Bonnell, Victoria E.** Iconography of Power: Soviet Political Posters Under Lenin & Stalin. Vol. 27. 395p. 1999. pap. 22.50 (0-520-22153-2, Pub. by U CA Pr) Cal Prin Full Svc.

— Russia in the New Century: Stability or Disorder? 384p. 2000. pap. 28.00 (0-8133-9041-9) Westview.

Bonnell, Victoria E., ed. The Russian Worker: Life & Labor under the Tsarist Regime. LC 83-47856. 240p. (C). 1983. pap. 16.95 (0-520-05059-2, Pub. by U CA Pr) Cal Prin Full Svc.

— The Russian Worker: Life & Labor under the Tsarist Regime. LC 83-47856. (Illus.). 234p. reprint ed. pap. 72.60 (0-7837-4760-8, 204450700003) Bks Demand.

Bonnell, Victoria E., et al, eds. Russia at the Barricades: Eyewitness Accounts of the August 1991 Coup. LC 93-27944. (Illus.). 392p. (gr. 13). 1994. text 77.95 (1-56324-271-0); pap. text 36.95 (1-56324-272-9) M E Sharpe.

***Bonnell, Victoria E., et al.** Beyond the Cultural Turn: New Directions in the Study of Society & Culture. LC 98-33118. (Studies on the History of Society & Culture). 318p. 1999. 45.00 (0-520-21678-4, Pub. by U CA Pr); pap. 16.95 (0-520-21679-2, Pub. by U CA Pr) Cal Prin Full Svc.

***Bonnell Werth, Karen & Mirel, James L.** Stepping Stones to Jewish Spiritual Living: Walking the Path Morning, Noon & Night. 240p. 2000. pap. 16.95 (1-58023-074-1) Jewish Lights.

Bonnelle, J. P., et al, eds. Surface Properties & Catalysis by Non-Metals. 1983. text 226.00 (90-277-1607-2) Kluwer Academic.

Bonnello, Joe. Supercross. LC 97-3069. (Enthusiast Color Ser.). (Illus.). 96p. 1997. pap. 13.95 (0-7603-0329-7) MBI Pubg.

Bonnello, Joe, jt. auth. see Thompson, John F.

Bonnem, Shirley. The Children's Hospital of Philadelphia 1974-1994: An Informal Report. (Illus.). 1995. write for info. (0-9617370-3-4); pap. write for info. (0-9617370-2-6); text. write for info. (0-9617370-1-8) Childrens Hospital of Philadelphia.

Bonnemains, Jacqueline, et al, eds. Baudin in Australian Waters: The Artwork of the French Voyage of Discovery to the Southern Lands, 1800-1804. (Illus.). 360p. 1988. 195.00 (0-19-554787-X) OUP.

Bonnemaison, Joel. The Tree & the Canoe: History & Ethnogeography of Tanna. Penot-Demetry, Josee, tr. from FRE. LC 94-14319. (Illus.). 392p. (C). 1994. reprint ed. text 36.00 (0-8248-1525-4) UH Pr.

Bonnemaison, Joel, et al, eds. Arts of Vanuatu. LC 96-53569. 1997. text 79.00 (0-8248-1956-X) UH Pr.

Bonnen, John J., jt. ed. see Chernenkoff, Russell A.

Bonner. Communicating in Business: Key to Success. 9th ed. 1999. pap., student ed. 24.95 (0-87393-702-3) Dame Pubns.

— Communicating in Business: The Key to Success. 9th ed. LC 97-67093. (SWC-Business Communication). 1999. 67.95 (0-87393-701-5) Dame Pubns.

Bonner. God's Decree & Man's Destiny. 1987. 109.95 (0-86078-203-4) Ashgate Pub Co.

Bonner. Human Resource Management in Real Estate. 306p. (C). 1997. pap. 19.20 (0-13-778127-X, Macmillan Coll) P-H.

— Power & Parenting. LC 97-38324. 177p. 1998. text 65.00 (0-312-21002-7) St Martin.

— Soc Stud Content Pic Dictionary-wkbk. (Global ESL). (Illus.). (J). 1997. mass mkt., wbk. ed. 12.95 (0-8384-6693-1) Heinle & Heinle.

— Studysmart. 1996. 25.94 (0-07-552888-6) McGraw.

Bonner, jt. auth. see Martin, Kieran.

Bonner, Adrian, jt. ed. see Waterhouse, James M.

Bonner, Amy, et al, eds. Poetry Society of America Anthology. LC 76-75709. (Granger Index Reprint Ser.). 1977. 23.95 (0-8369-6003-3) Ayer.

Bonner, Andrea, jt. auth. see Woollard, Rex.

Bonner, Ann & Bonner, Roger. Earlybirds...Earlywords. LC 72-89449. (Illus.). 32p. (J). (ps-2). 1973. 11.95 (0-87592-013-6) Scroll Pr.

Bonner, Anthony, ed. Doctor Illuminatus: A Ramon Llull Reader. Bonner, Eve, tr. LC 93-13696. (Mythos The Princeton - Bollingen Series in World Mythology). (Illus.). 512p. 1993. text 75.00 (0-691-03406-0, Pub. by Princeton U Pr); pap. text 17.95 (0-691-00091-3, Pub. by Princeton U Pr) Cal Prin Full Svc.

Bonner, Anthony, tr. see Kerrigan, Anthony, ed.

Bonner, Arthur. Alas! What Brought Thee Hither? The Chinese in New York, 1800-1950. LC 96-35536. 216p. 1996. 49.50 (0-8386-3704-3) Fairleigh Dickinson.

— Among the Afghans. LC 87-22260. xvi, 366p. 1987. text 38.95 (0-8223-0783-9) Duke.

— Averting the Apocalypse: Social Movements in India Today. LC 89-28006. 475p. (Orig.). (C). 1990. text 64.95 (0-8223-1029-5); pap. text 23.95 (0-8223-1048-1) Duke.

— Jerry McAuley & His Mission. LC 90-31906. 123p. 1991. 16.99 (0-87213-060-6) Loizeaux.

Bonner, Arthur, et al. Democracy in India: A Hollow Shell. LC 94-19522. 300p. (Orig.). 1994. lib. bdg. 66.00 (1-879383-25-X) Am Univ Pr.

— Democracy in India: A Hollow Shell. LC 94-19522. 300p. (Orig.). 1994. pap. text 27.50 (1-879383-26-8) Am Univ Pr.

Bonner, B. E. & Miettinen, H. E., eds. The Rice Meeting: 1990 Meeting of the Division of Particles & Fields of the American Physical Society. 1136p. (C). 1990. text 161.00 (981-02-0258-X) World Scientific Pub.

Bonner, B. E., jt. auth. see Augenstein, B. W.

Bonner, Barbara, ed. Sacred Ground: Writings about Home. LC 96-34814. 385p. (Orig.). 1996. pap. 17.95 (1-57131-010-X) Milkweed Ed.

Bonner, C. E. Index Hepaticarum: An Index to the Liverworts of the World. Incl. Pt. 2. Achiton to Balantiopsis. 1966. 48.00 (3-7682-0092-2); Pt. 3. Barbilophozia to Ceranthus. 1966. 48.00 (3-7682-0093-0); Pt. 4. Ceratolejeunea to Crystolejeunea. 1966. 48.00 (3-7682-0094-9); Pt. 5. Delavayella to Geothallus. 1966. 65.00 (3-7682-0095-7); Pt. 6. Goebelliella to Jubula. 1966. 48.00 (3-7682-0096-5); 1966. write for info. (0-318-54141-6) Lubrecht & Cramer.

— Index Hepaticarum, Index to the Liverworts of the World Part 7A: Supplement, Additions & Corrections to Parts 2-4. 1977. pap. text 60.00 (3-7682-0097-3) Lubrecht & Cramer.

Bonner, C. E. B. Index Hepaticarum: Lembidium to Mytilopsis, Vol. 10. Geissler, P. & Bischler, H., eds. 352p. 1985. lib. bdg. 90.00 (3-7682-1100-2) Lubrecht & Cramer.

Bonner, Cindy. Lily. 350p. 1992. 17.95 (0-945575-95-5) Algonquin Bks.

— Lily: A Novel. large type ed. LC 93-3766. 365p. 1993. lib. bdg. 17.95 (1-56054-743-X) Thorndike Pr.

— Looking after Lily. LC 93-33730. 336p. 1999. 18.95 (1-56512-045-0) Algonquin Bks.

— The Passion of Dellie O'Barr. 362p. 1996. 18.95 (1-56512-103-1, 72103) Algonquin Bks.

***Bonner, Cindy.** Right from Wrong. LC 98-44870. 336p. 1999. 21.95 (1-56512-104-X, 72104) Algonquin Bks.

Bonner, Cindy. Right from Wrong: A Novel, Vol. 1. LC 99-14978. 1999. 27.95 (0-7862-1990-4) Thorndike Pr.

Bonner, Crosby T. How to Reach the Unreached: A Practical Guide to Increase Your Life & Ministry. Harris, Patricia, ed. 132p. 1998. pap. 16.95 (1-878898-16-7) CAP Pub.

Bonner, Deborah, tr. see Valenzuela, Luisa.

***Bonner, Derrick.** Alley Katt. 516p. 1999. pap. write for info. (0-7392-0370-3, PO3585) Morris Pubng.

Bonner, Erin. Buying & Selling Coin Laundries: The Best Kept Secret in Small Business. Date not set. pap. write for info. (1-58599-017-5) E Bks & Scrnplays.

Bonner, Eugene. The Club in the Opera House: The Story of the Metropolitan Opera Club. 95p. 1993. 20.00 (1-883390-00-1) Metrop Opera.

Bonner, Eve, tr. see Bonner, Anthony, ed.

Bonner, Gerald. Church & Faith in the Pastristic Tradition: Augustine, Pelagianism, & Early Christian Northumbria. LC 95-45631. (Variorum Collected Studies: Vol. CS521). 336p. 1996. 92.95 (0-86078-557-2, Pub. by Variorum) Ashgate Pub Co.

Bonner, Gerald, et al, eds. St. Cuthbert, His Cult & His Community to AD 1200. (Illus.). 540p. 1995. 110.00 (0-85115-510-3, Boydell Pr) Boydell & Brewer.

— St. Cuthbert, His Cult & His Community to AD 1200. (Illus.). 540p. 1998. reprint ed. pap. 55.00 (0-85115-610-X, Boydell Pr) Boydell & Brewer.

Bonner, Gerald I. St. Augustine of Hippo: Life & Controversies. 430p. 1995. pap. 19.95 (0-907547-52-4, 859, Pub. by Canterbury Press Norwich) Morehouse Pub.

— St. Augustine of Hippo: Life & Controversies. LC 82-45807. (Orthodoxies & Heresies in the Early Church Ser.). 1985. reprint ed. 42.50 (0-404-62376-X) AMS Pr.

Bonner, Gerd, ed. Vasodepressor Hormones in Hypertension: Prostaglandins & Kallikrein-Kinins. (Agents & Actions Supplements Ser.: No. 22). 380p. 1987. 94.50 (0-8176-1922-4) Birkhauser.

Bonner, Gerd & Rahn, K. H. Prostacyclin & Hypertension. (Illus.). xii, 90p. 1990. 17.95 (0-387-52140-2) Spr-Verlag.

Bonner, Harold. When God Speaks: Tuning in to Our Talkative God. LC 99-24252. 64p. 1999. pap. text 6.99 (0-8341-1812-2) Beacon Hill.

Bonner, Helen. The Laid Daughter: A True Story. Huebsch, Jan, ed. 256p. 1995. pap. 16.95 (1-884178-23-5) Kairos Ctr.

***Bonner, Hilary.** A Fancy to Kill For. large type ed. 448p. 1999. 31.99 (0-7089-4083-8) Ulverscroft.

— For Death Comes Softly. 480p. 2000. 31.99 (0-7089-4201-6) Ulverscroft.

Bonner, Hilary, jt. auth. see Gunnell, Clive.

Bonner, Jack. The Cattle Drive. large type ed. (Linford Western Library Ser.). 272p. 1997. pap. 16.99 (0-7089-5143-0) Ulverscroft.

Bonner, James & Varner, Joseph, eds. Plant Biochemistry. 3rd ed. 1976. text 94.00 (0-12-114860-2) Acad Pr.

Bonner, James, jt. auth. see McMahon, Thomas.

Bonner, Joey. Wang Kuo-wei: An Intellectual Biography. (East Asian Monographs: No. 101). (Illus.). 336p. 1986. 45.95 (0-674-94594-8) HUP.

Bonner, John. Economic Efficiency & Social Justice: The Development of Utilitarian Ideas in Economics from Bentham to Edgeworth. LC 95-19606. 224p. 1995. 85.00 (1-85278-295-1) E Elgar.

— Introduction to the Theory of Social Choice. LC 85-19840. 208p. 1986. text 35.00 (0-8018-3304-3) Johns Hopkins.

Bonner, John L. The Daily Discipleship Journal - Focusing on the Word. (Illus.). 434p. (Orig.). 1996. pap. 24.99 (1-890241-01-6); ring bd. 29.95 (1-890241-21-0) Parousia Pub.

Bonner, John T. Cells & Societies. LC 55-5002. 240p. 1955. reprint ed. pap. 74.40 (0-608-02927-0, 206399300008) Bks Demand.

B

An Asterisk (*) at the beginning of an entry indicates that the title is appearing for the first time.

Bonner, John T., Jr. The Evolution of Culture in Animals. LC 79-3190. (Illus.). 216p. 1980. pap. 14.95 (*0-691-02373-5*, Pub. by Princeton U Pr) Cal Prin Full Svc.

Bonner, John T. Life Cycles. 222p. 1993. pap. text 14.95 (*0-691-00151-0*, Pub. by Princeton U Pr) Cal Prin Full Svc.

— Life Cycles: Reflections of an Evolutionary Biologist. (Illus.). 192p. 1993. text 39.50 (*0-691-03319-6*, Pub. by Princeton U Pr) Cal Prin Full Svc.

— On Development: The Biology of Form. LC 73-88053. (Commonwealth Fund Publications). 224p. 1977. pap. 15.50 (*0-674-63412-8*) HUP.

— Sixty Years of Biology: Essays on Evolution & Development. LC 95-25638. 168p. 1996. text 24.95 (*0-691-02130-9*, Pub. by Princeton U Pr) Cal Prin Full Svc.

— Size & Cycle: An Essay on the Structure of Biology. LC 65-14306. (Illus.). 265p. 1965. reprint ed. pap. 82.20 (*0-7837-8162-8*, 204786700008) Bks Demand.

Bonner, John T., ed. see Thompson, D'Arcy W.

***Bonner, John Tyler.** First Signals: The Evolution of Multicellular Development. LC 00-39976. 2001. pap. write for info. (*0-691-07038-5*) Princeton U Pr.

***Bonner, Kermit H.** The Cold War at Sea: An Illustrated History. LC 99-52624. (Illus.). 160p. 2000. pap. 24.95 (*0-7603-0732-6*, 129837AP, Pub. by MBI Pubg) Motorbooks Intl.

Bonner, Kermit H. Final Voyages. (Illus.). 208p. Date not set. 34.95 (*1-56311-289-2*) Turner Pub KY.

— Great Naval Disasters: U. S. Naval Accidents in the 20th Century. LC 98-36675. (Illus.). 144p. 1998. pap. 19.95 (*0-7603-0594-3*) Motorbooks Intl.

Bonner, Kevin J. Furniture Restoration: Practical Crafts Ser. (Illus.). 160p. 1996. pap. 10.95 (*1-86108-012-3*, Pub. by Guild Master) Sterling.

— Furniture Restoration & Repair for Beginners. (Illus.). 192p. 1995. pap. 24.95 (*0-946819-64-5*) Sterling.

Bonner, Kevin Jan. Furniture Restoration Workshop. (Illus.). 144p. 1999. pap. 19.95 (*1-86108-048-4*, Pub. by Guild Master) Sterling.

Bonner, Kieran. A Great Place to Raise Kids: Interpretation, Science & the Rural-Urban Debate. 256p. 1997. text 55.00 (*0-7735-1613-1*, Pub. by McG-Queens Univ Pr) CUP Services.

Bonner, Laurie & Bonner, Steve. Searching for Cyber-Roots: A Step-by-Step Guide to Genealogy on the World Wide Web. LC 97-15558. 160p. 1997. pap. 16.95 (*0-916489-78-7*) Ancestry.

Bonner, Lonnice B. Good Hair. LC 93-42027. 1994. reprint ed. pap. 10.00 (*0-517-88151-9*) Crown Pub Group.

— The Kitchen Beautician: For Colored Girls Who've Missed the Beauty Standard When It Became Too Ruff. 1997. pap. 12.00 (*0-614-27350-1*, Crown) Crown Pub Group.

— Plaited Glory: For Colored Girls Who've Considered Braids, Locks & Twists. (Illus.). 128p. 1996. pap. 12.00 (*0-517-88498-4*) Crown Pub Group.

Bonner, M., jt. auth. see Mitruka, B.

Bonner, Margaret. Focus on Grammar: High-Intermediate. 240p. 1995. pap. text, teacher ed. 26.97 (*0-201-65690-6*) Addison-Wesley.

— Step into Writing: A Basic Writing Text. LC 93-34652. 144p. (YA). 1994. pap. text 18.08 (*0-201-59265-7*) Addison-Wesley.

Bonner, Margaret, jt. auth. see Fuchs, Marjorie.

Bonner, Michael, Jr. Aristocratic Violence & Holy War Vol. 1: Studies in the Jihad & the Arab-Byzantine Frontier. LC 96-180355. (American Oriental Ser.: Vol. 80). xv, 221p. 1996. 45.00 (*0-940490-11-0*) Am Orient Soc.

Bonner, Michael, tr. see Halm, Heinz.

Bonner, Michael, tr. see Noth, Albrecht & Conrad, Lawrence I.

Bonner, Mickey. Brokenness, the Forgotten Factor of Prayer. LC 95-115141. (Brokenness Ser.). 255p. 1996. pap. 12.95 (*1-878578-12-X*) M Bonner Evan Assn.

— Brokenness, the Forgotten Factor of Prayer, Vol. 1. 154p. 1997. pap., student ed., wbk. ed. 11.95 (*1-878578-16-2*) M Bonner Evan Assn.

— Deliverance, the Children's Bread. LC 95-139824. 90p. 1992. pap. 7.00 (*1-878578-04-9*) M Bonner Evan Assn.

— God's Answer to the Critical Christian: KYMS - Keep Your Mouth Shut! 110p. 1992. pap. 7.00 (*1-878578-03-0*) M Bonner Evan Assn.

— Hearing God's Voice from Within. LC 98-169929. 224p. 1998. pap. 12.95 (*1-878578-17-0*) M Bonner Evan Assn.

— Prayer is Warfare. LC 96-122443. 105p. 1987. pap. 7.00 (*1-878578-00-6*) M Bonner Evan Assn.

— Spiritual Warfare Manual. 1983. pap. 5.00 (*1-878578-02-2*) M Bonner Evan Assn.

— Spiritual Warfare Prayer. 1987. pap., student ed. 11.95 (*1-878578-13-8*) M Bonner Evan Assn.

Bonner, Mike. Collecting Football Cards: A Complete Guide with Prices. LC 95-8016. (Illus.). 224p. 1995. pap. 15.95 (*0-87069-737-4*, Wllce-Homestd) Krause Pubns.

***Bonner, Mike.** The Composite Guide to Strongman Competition. LC 00-21258. (J). 2000. 16.95 (*0-7910-5868-9*) Chelsea Hse.

Bonner, Mike. Jeremy Mayfield. LC 99-23254. (Illus.). 64p. 1999. 16.95 (*0-7910-5412-8*) Chelsea Hse.

— Jeremy Mayfield. (Race Car Legends Ser.). (Illus.). 64p. (gr. 4-7). 1999. pap. 7.95 (*0-7910-5678-3*) Chelsea Hse.

— Paul Kariya. (Ice Hockey Legends Ser.). (Illus.). 64p. (YA). (gr. 3 up). 1999. lib. bdg. 16.95 (*0-7910-5015-7*) Chelsea Hse.

***Bonner, Mike.** Strongman Competition. (Composite Guides Ser.). (Illus.). 2000. pap. 5.95 (*0-7910-5877-8*) Chelsea Hse.

Bonner, N. & Walton, D., eds. Key Environments: Antarctica. (Key Environment Ser.). (Illus.). 350p. 1985. 23.50 (*0-685-11856-8*, Pub. by PPL) Elsevier.

Bonner, Nigel. The Natural History of Seals. (Natural History Ser.). (Illus.). 240p. 1990. 29.95 (*0-8160-2336-0*) Facts on File.

— Polar Regions. (Habitats Ser.). (Illus.). 48p. (J). (gr. 4-6). 1995. lib. bdg. 24.26 (*1-56847-386-9*) Raintree Steck-V.

— Seals & Sea Lions of the World. LC 92-46594. (Illus.). 224p. 1994. 29.95 (*0-8160-2955-5*) Facts on File.

— Whales of the World. (Illus.). 192p. 1998. pap. 17.95 (*0-7137-2369-6*, Pub. by Blandford Pr) Sterling.

— Whales of the World. (Illus.). 191p. 1989. 29.95 (*0-8160-1734-4*) Facts on File.

Bonner, Nigel W. Seals & Sea Lions of the World. 192p. 1999. pap. text 19.95 (*0-7137-2788-8*) Blandford Pr.

Bonner, Patrice. Network Programming with Windows Sockets. LC 95-40773. 512p. (C). 1995. pap. 39.95 incl. disk (*0-13-230152-0*) P-H.

Bonner, Paul. PC - Computing Customizing Windows 3.1. (Illus.). 560p. 1992. pap. 34.95 incl. disk (*1-56276-018-1*, Ziff-Davis Pr) Que.

— PC Magazine Visual BASIC Utilities. (Techniques & Utilities Ser.). 480p. 1993. pap. 29.95 incl. disk (*1-56276-106-4*, Ziff-Davis Pr) Que.

Bonner, Philip, et al, eds. Apartheid's Genesis, 1935-1962. 465p. (Orig.). (C). 1994. pap. text 24.95 (*0-86975-440-8*, Pub. by Ravan Pr) Ohio U Pr.

— Holding Their Ground: Class, Locality, & Culture in Nineteenth & Twentieth-Century South Africa. (History Workshop Topic Ser.: No. 4). 224p. (Orig.). 1990. pap. 28.95 (*0-86975-398-3*, Pub. by Ravan Pr) Ohio U Pr.

Bonner, R., et al. The Visually Limited Child. 1970. pap. text 12.95 (*0-8422-0061-4*) Irvington.

Bonner, R. I., jt. auth. see Whitney, W. A.

Bonner, Raymond. At the Hand of Man: Peril & Hope for Africa's Wildlife. 322p. 1998. text 24.00 (*0-7881-5480-X*) DIANE Pub.

Bonner, Raymond E., et al, eds. Computerized Interpretation of the Electrocardiogram VI. LC 82-82657. 224p. 1982. pap. 30.00 (*0-939204-16-9*, 81-12) Eng Found.

Bonner, Robert J. Lawyers & Litigants in Ancient Athens: The Genesis of the Legal Profession. LC 68-57185. 288p. 1972. reprint ed. 28.95 (*0-405-19013-1*, Pub. by Blom Pubns) Ayer.

— Lawyers & Litigants in Ancient Athens: The Genesis of the Legal Profession. LC 94-75664. xii, 276p. 1994. reprint ed. 75.00 (*1-56169-091-0*, 18183) Gaunt.

Bonner, Robert J. & Harrell, Hansen C. Evidence in Athenian Courts & Public Arbitration in Athenian Law, 2 vols. Vlastos, Gregory, ed. LC 78-14610. (Morals & Law in Ancient Greece Ser.). (ENG & GRE.). 1979. reprint ed. lib. bdg. 17.95 (*0-405-11586-5*) Ayer.

Bonner, Robert J. & Smith, Gertrude S. The Administration of Justice from Homer to Aristotle, 2 vols. LC 70-101917. (BCL Ser.: I). reprint ed. 79.50 (*0-404-00650-7*) AMS Pr.

Bonner, Roger, jt. auth. see Bonner, Ann.

Bonner, Sherwood. Dialect Tales. LC 70-38640. (Black Heritage Library Collection). 1977. reprint ed. 23.95 (*0-8369-8998-8*) Ayer.

— Dialect Tales & Suwannee River Tales. Frank, William L., ed. (Masterworks of Literature Ser.). 1991. pap. 13.95 (*0-8084-0427-X*) NCUP.

— Like unto Like. LC 96-51295. 220p. 1997. pap. 14.95 (*1-57003-184-3*) U of SC Pr.

— Suwanee River Tales. LC 73-38641. (Black Heritage Library Collection). (Illus.). 1977. reprint ed. 30.95 (*0-8369-8999-6*) Ayer.

Bonner, Simon H. Sex & Sexual Harassment: Index of New Information. LC 95-14593. 1995. 47.50 (*0-7883-0422-4*); pap. 44.50 (*0-7883-0423-2*) ABBE Pubs Assn.

— Sexology Encyclopedia Vol. 21: Sexual Harassment: Index & Reference Book of New Information. (Illus.). 143p. 1996. 49.50 (*0-7883-0890-4*); pap. 39.95 (*0-7883-0891-2*) ABBE Pubs Assn.

Bonner, Staci. Sports: Careers in Sports. LC 93-9887. (Now Hiring Ser.). (Illus.). 48p. (J). (gr. 5-6). 1994. lib. bdg. 14.95 (*0-89686-789-7*, Crstwood Hse) Silver Burdett Pr.

Bonner, Stephen. Angelo Benedetto Ventura, His Biography, Inventions & Compositions. (Illus.). 79p. 1970. 29.50 (*0-900998-08-3*) Theodore Front.

Bonner, Steve, jt. auth. see Bonner, Laurie.

Bonner, T., et al. Hazardous Waste Incineration Engineering. LC 81-14223. (Pollution Technology Review Ser.: No. 88). (Illus.). 432p. 1982. 45.00 (*0-8155-0877-8*) Noyes.

Bonner, T. D. The Life & Adventures of James P. Beckwourth, 2 vols. 537p. 1985. reprint ed. lib. bdg. 79.00 (*0-932051-88-X*) Rprt Serv.

— The Life & Adventures of James P. Beckwourth. rev. ed. (Illus.). 400p. 1977. reprint ed. 31.95 (*0-87928-085-9*) Corner Hse.

— The Life & Adventures of James P. Beckwourth: Mountainman. 1965. reprint ed. 25.00 (*0-87018-003-7*) Ross.

Bonner, T. D., ed. Life & Adventures of James P. Beckwourth, Mountaineer, Scout & Pioneer & Chief of the Crow Nation of Indians. LC 69-18563. (American Negro: His History & Literature. Series 2). 1968. reprint ed. 40.95 (*0-405-01850-9*) Ayer.

Bonner, Thomas, Jr The Kate Chopin Companion: With Chopin's Translations from French Fiction. LC 88-15463. 262p. 1988. lib. bdg. 49.95 (*0-313-25550-4*, BKP/, Greenwood Pr) Greenwood.

Bonner, Thomas, Jr. & Falcon, Guillermo N. William Faulkner, the William B. Wisdom Collection: A Descriptive Catalog. LC 79-26556. (Illus.). 1980. pap. 13.00 (*0-9603212-2-5*) Tulane Univ.

Bonner, Thomas, Jr. & Skinner, Robert E., eds. Immortelles: Poems of Life & Death by New Southern Writers. (Xavier Review Occasional Publications: No. 5). (Illus.). 94p. (Orig.). 1995. pap. 8.95 (*1-883275-04-0*) Xavier Rev.

Bonner, Thomas N. Becoming a Physician: Medical Education in Great Britain, France, Germany & the United States, 1750-1945. 424p. 1996. text 55.00 (*0-19-506298-1*) OUP.

— Medicine in Chicago: A Chapter in the Social & Scientific Development of a City, 1850- 1950. 2nd ed. 352p. 1991. text 42.50 (*0-252-01760-9*) U of Ill Pr.

— To the Ends of the Earth: Women's Search for Education in Medicine. (Illus.). 264p. (C). 1992. 44.00 (*0-674-89303-4*) HUP.

— To the Ends of the Earth: Women's Search for Education in Medicine. (Illus.). 264p. 1995. pap. text 18.50 (*0-674-89304-2*, BONENX) HUP.

***Bonner, Thomas Neville.** Becoming a Physician: Medical Education in Britain, France, Germany & the United States, 1750-1945. LC 00-20534. 424p. 2000. pap. 17.95 (*0-8018-6482-8*) Johns Hopkins.

Bonner, Vance. The Vance Stance. LC 92-50281. (Illus.). 176p. 1993. pap. 12.95 (*1-56305-311-X*, 3311) Workman Pub.

Bonner, W. N. & Walton, D. W., eds. Antarctica: Antarctica. LC 84-10973. (Key Environments Ser.: No. 4). (Illus.). 350p. 1985. 177.00 (*0-08-028881-2*, Pub. by Pergamon Repr) Franklin.

Bonner, William H. Contemporary Business English: Instructor's Guide. 2nd ed. pap. text 8.00 (*1-56118-526-4*) EMC-Paradigm.

— Contemporary Business English: Text. 2nd ed. 196p. text 15.95 (*1-56118-525-6*) EMC-Paradigm.

Bonner, William L., jt. auth. see William L. Bonner Literary Committee.

Bonnerjea, Biren, ed. Index to Bulletins One-One Hundred of the Bureau of American Ethnology, with Index to Contributions to North American Ethnology, Introductions, & Miscellaneous Publications. (Bureau of American Ethnology Bulletins Ser.). 716p. 1995. lib. bdg. 179.00 (*0-7812-4178-2*) Rprt Serv.

***Bonners, Susan.** Edwina Victorious. LC 00-24229. (Illus.). 144p. (gr. 2-5). 2000. text 16.00 (*0-374-31968-5*) FS&G.

— Making Music. 2002. text (*0-374-34732-8*) FS&G.

Bonners, Susan. A Penguin Year. 1981. 9.43 (*0-440-00170-6*) Delacorte.

— The Silver Balloon. (Illus.). 80p. (J). (gr. 2-4). 1997. 14.00 (*0-374-36913-5*) FS&G.

***Bonners, Susan.** The Silver Balloon. (Illus.). 80p. (J). (gr. 2-4). 1999. pap. 4.95 (*0-374-46647-5*, Sunburst Bks) FS&G.

Bonners, Susan. Why Does the Cat Do That? LC 97-38297. (Illus.). (J). (gr. 2-4). 1998. text 15.95 (*0-8050-4377-2*) St Martin.

— The Wooden Doll. (Illus.). (J). (ps-3). 1991. 13.95 (*0-688-08280-7*); lib. bdg. 13.88 (*0-688-08282-3*) Lothrop.

Bonnes, Mirilia & Secchiaroli, Gianfranco. Environmental Psychology: An Introduction. 240p. (C). 1995. 42.50 (*0-8039-7905-3*); pap. 15.99 (*0-8039-7906-1*) Sage.

Bonnesen, T. & Fenchel, W. Theorie der Konvexen Koerper. LC 49-29452. 8.95 (*0-8284-0054-7*) Chelsea Pub.

— Theory of Convex Bodies. Boron, Leo F. et al, trs. from GER. LC 86-71997. (Illus.). 182p. (Orig.). 1987. pap. 30.00 (*0-914351-02-8*) BCS Assocs.

Bonnet, ed. see Breton, Andre.

Bonnet, Alfred, tr. see Pareto, Vilfredo.

Bonnet, Alfred, tr. see Salvioli, G.

Bonnet, Anne-Marie, jt. auth. see Rodin, Auguste.

Bonnet, Bob. Physics. LC 99-33938. 1999. 17.95 (*0-8069-0707-X*) Strlng Pub CA.

— Science Fair Project in Energy. LC 97-33088. (Illus.). 95p. (J). (gr. 4-6). 1997. 16.95 (*0-8069-9793-1*) Sterling.

— Science Fair Projects in Flight, Space & Astronomy. (Illus.). 96p. (J). 1998. 8.95 (*0-8069-9482-7*) Sterling.

Bonnet, Bob. Science Fair Projects with Electricity & Electronics. 1997. 14.05 (*0-606-12806-9*, Pub. by Turtleback) Demco.

Bonnet, Bob & Keen, Dan. Science Fair Projects: Energy. (Illus.). 96p. (J). (gr. 3-7). pap. 8.95 (*0-8069-9794-X*) Sterling.

— Science Fair Projects with Electricity & Electronics. LC 95-51492. (Illus.). 96p. (J). 1996. 16.95 (*0-8069-1300-2*) Sterling.

— Science Fair Projects with Electricity & Electronics. (Illus.). 96p. (J). 1997. pap. 8.95 (*0-8069-1301-0*) Sterling.

Bonnet, Bob, jt. auth. see Keen, Dan.

Bonnet, Charles. Essai Analytique Sur les Facultes de l'Ame. (FRE.). xxxii, 552p. 1973. reprint ed. 110.00 (*3-487-04588-5*) G Olms Pubs.

— Essai de Psychologie. (FRE.). xlii, 390p. 1978. reprint ed. 95.00 (*3-487-06526-6*) G Olms Pubs.

Bonnet, Corinne & Xella, Paolo. Great Biblical Characters: Illustrated Profiles of People in the Bible. 160p. 1996. 27.50 (*88-7301-050-4*, Pub. by Gremese Intl) Natl Bk Netwk.

Bonnet, F. P. Adipose Tissue in Childhood. 192p. 1981. 108.00 (*0-8493-5771-3*, QP88, CRC Reprint) Franklin.

Bonnet, Hans. Reallexikon der aegyptischen Religionsgeschichte. 2nd ed. (GER., Illus.). (C). 1971. 176.95 (*3-11-003365-8*) De Gruyter.

Bonnet, J. P., ed. Eddy Structure Identification. (CISM International Centre for Mechanical Sciences Ser.: Vol. 353). (Illus.). 364p. 1996. pap. 92.00 (*3-211-82802-8*) Spr-Verlag.

Bonnet, J. P. & Glauser, M. N., eds. Eddy Structure Identification in Free Turbulence Shear Flows: Selected Papers from the IUTAM Symposium, Poitiers, 12-14 October 1992. LC 93-26851. (Fluid Mechanics & Its Applications Ser.: Vol. 21). 532p. (C). 1993. text 264.50 (*0-7923-2449-8*) Kluwer Academic.

Bonnet, Jacques. Lorenzo Lotto. (Illus.). 208p. 1997. 55.00 (*2-87660-190-7*, Pub. by Art Bks Intl) Partners Pubs Grp.

Bonnet, James. Stealing Fire from the Gods: A Dynamic New Story Model for Writers & Filmmakers. LC 99-23166. 300p. 1999. 26.95 (*0-941188-65-5*) M Wiese.

Bonnet, Jim. A Guide to Gambling. (C). 1989. 50.00 (*0-7223-2263-1*, Pub. by A H S Ltd) St Mut.

Bonnet, L. & Schroeder, A. Epistolas de Pablo Vol. 1. Cativiela, A., tr. (Comentario del Nuevo Testamento Ser.: Vol. 3).Tr. of Paul's Epistles. (SPA.). 538p. 1986. reprint ed. pap. 24.99 (*0-311-03052-1*) Casa Bautista.

Bonnet, L., jt. auth. see Schroeder, A.

Bonnet, L., jt. auth. see Schrolder, A.

Bonnet, M., ed. see Breton, Andre.

Bonnet, M. J. V., jt. auth. see Gutierrez, R.

Bonnet, Marc. Boundary Integral Equations Methods. 412p. 1999. 75.00 (*0-471-97184-7*) Wiley.

Bonnet, Marguerite, ed. see Breton, Andre.

***Bonnet, Matthew.** Christopher & Miguel. LC 99-91967. 190p. 2000. 25.00 (*0-7388-1448-2*); pap. 18.00 (*0-7388-1449-0*) Xlibris Corp.

Bonnet, Max. Le Latin de Gregoire de Tours. viii, 787p. 1968. reprint ed. 160.00 (*0-318-71079-X*) G Olms Pubs.

Bonnet, Max, ed. see Lipsius, Richard A.

Bonnet, Mireille. Microsurgery Retinal Detachment. 2nd ed. 1989. 120.00 (*0-938607-12-X*) Field & Wood Inc Medical.

***Bonnet-Rampersaud, Louise.** My Nose Is Running. LC 99-14242. 1999. 12.95 (*1-886388-14-8*) Flower Valley Pr.

Bonnet, Robert L. Computers: Forty-Nine Science Fair Projects. (Illus.). 160p. (J). (gr. 6-9). 1990. pap. 9.95 (*0-8306-3524-6*) McGraw-Hill Prof.

— Environmental Science: Forty-Nine Science Fair Projects. (Illus.). 160p. (YA). 1990. pap. 9.95 (*0-8306-3369-3*) McGraw-Hill Prof.

Bonnet, Robert L. & Dupree, A. K., eds. Solar Phenomena in Stars & Stellar Systems. 1981. text 191.50 (*90-277-1275-1*) Kluwer Academic.

Bonnet, Robert L. & Keen, Dan. Science Fair Projects: Flight, Space & Astronomy. LC 96-39281. (Illus.). 96p. (J). (gr. 4-6). 1997. 16.95 (*0-8069-9450-9*) Sterling.

Bonnet, Robert L. & Keen, G. Daniel. Botany: Forty-Nine More Science Fair Projects. (Illus.). 170p. (J). (gr. 4-7). 1990. pap. 9.95 (*0-8306-3416-9*) McGraw-Hill Prof.

— Botany: Forty Nine Science Fair Projects. 160p. 1989. pap. 10.95 (*0-07-157522-7*) McGraw.

— Earth Science: Forty-Nine Science Fair Projects. 160p. 1990. pap. 10.95 (*0-07-155083-6*) McGraw.

— Environmental Science: Forty-Nine Science Fair Projects. 140p. 1990. pap. 10.95 (*0-07-156104-8*) McGraw.

— Space & Astronomy: Forty-Nine Science Fair Projects. 144p. (J). 1991. 16.95 (*0-8306-3939-X*) McGraw-Hill Prof.

Bonnet, Robert L. & Keen, G. Daniel. Space & Astronomy: Forty-Nine Science Fair Projects. (Illus.). 144p. (J). 1991. pap. 9.95 (*0-8306-3938-1*) McGraw-Hill Prof.

***Bonnet, Robert L., et al.** Science Fair Projects: Chemistry. LC 99-87099. (Illus.). 2000. 17.95 (*0-8069-7771-X*) Sterling.

Bonnet, Robert L., jt. auth. see Keen, Dan.

Bonnet, Roger M. & Manno, Vittorio. International Cooperation in Space: The Example of the European Space Agency. LC 94-16206. (Frontiers of Space Ser.). (Illus.). 224p. 1994. text 43.50 (*0-674-45835-4*, BONINT) HUP.

Bonnet, Theodore. The Mudlark. 24.95 (*0-88411-063-X*) Amereon Ltd.

Bonneton Staff. Dictionnaire de la Cuisine de Nord-Pas-de-Calais. (FRE.). 160p. 1993. 39.95 (*0-7859-5661-1*, 2862531413) Fr & Eur.

Bonnett. Telewars in the States: Telecommunications Issues in a New Era of Competition. 1996. pap. 22.95 (*0-8058-2822-2*) L Erlbaum Assocs.

***Bonnett.** White Identities: An Introduction. LC 99-51417. 224p. 1999. pap. 25.95 (*0-582-35627-X*) Longman.

***Bonnett, Alastair.** Anti-Racism. LC 99-32882. (Key Ideas Ser.). 1999. pap. write for info. (*0-415-17120-2*) Routledge.

Bonnett, Clifford F. Railway Engineering. 300p. 1996. 42.00 (*1-86094-012-9*) World Scientific Pub.

Bonnett, D. The CdTe Thin Film Solar Energy. 357p. 1993. pap. text 476.00 (*3-7186-5345-1*) Gordon & Breach.

Bonnett, H. W. & Bonnett, M. B., eds. Marine Computing Directory. 2nd ed. 1996. text 35.00 (*0-07-006653-1*) McGraw.

Bonnett, Harold. Farming with Steam. (History in Camera Ser.: No. 3). (Illus.). 88p. pap. 10.50 (*0-85263-285-1*, Pub. by Shire Pubns) Parkwest Pubns.

— Traction Engines. (Album Ser.: No. 143). (Illus.). 32p. write for info. (*0-85263-738-1*, Pub. by Shire Pubns) Lubrecht & Cramer.

Bonnett, Kendra. The IBM Guide to Doing Business on the Internet. LC 99-86111. (Illus.). 261p. 2000. 24.95 (*0-07-031846-8*) McGraw.

Bonnett, M. B., jt. ed. see Bonnett, H. W.

Bonnett, Michael. Children's Thinking: Promoting Understanding in the Primary School. LC 93-44086. (Children, Teachers & Learning Ser.). (Illus.). 192p. 1995. 100.00 (*0-304-32939-8*); pap. 33.95 (*0-304-32937-1*) Continuum.

Bonnett, O. T. Confessions of a Healer: The Truth from an Unconventional Family Doctor. LC 94-26287. (Illus.). 228p. 1994. 18.95 (*1-878448-61-7*) MacMurray & Beck.

— Why Healing Happens. 209p. (Orig.). 1996. pap. 14.95 (*1-878448-70-6*) MacMurray & Beck.

Bonnett, Penelope, jt. auth. see Gill, Don.

An Asterisk (*) at the beginning of an entry indicates that the title is appearing for the first time.

*__Bonnett, Raymond.__ Chemical Aspects of Photodynamic Therapy, Vol. 1. Vol. 1. 451p. 2000. 48.00 (*90-5699-248-1*, G & B Science) Gordon & Breach.

Bonnett, Thomas W. A New Vocabulary for Governing in the 1990s: A Lexicon for Governors' Policy Advisors. LC 94-43274. 60p. (Orig.). 1995. pap. 8.95 (*0-934842-14-0*) CSPA.

— Strategies for Rural Competitiveness: Policy Options for State Governments. LC 93-11723. 1993. 19.95 (*0-934842-71-X*) CSPA.

— Telewars in the States: Telecommunications Issues in a New Era of Competition. LC 96-28061. 165p. 1996. pap. 22.95 (*0-934842-16-7*) CSPA.

Bonnett, Thomas W. & Olson, Robert L. Scenarios of State Government in the Year 2010: Thinking about the Future. LC 92-41392. 1992. 10.00 (*0-934842-72-8*) CSPA.

Bonnett, Wayne. Pacific Coast Seafaring: Photographic Collection, 1850's to 1950's. (Illus.). 218p. 1988. 55.00 (*0-915269-07-4*) Windgate Pr.

Bonnett, Wayne, ed. Victorian Classics of San Francisco, 1887. (Illus.). 120p. 1987. 32.00 (*0-915269-05-8*) Windgate Pr.

Bonnett, Wayne, ed. see DeNevi, Don & Moulin, Thomas.

Bonnett, Wayne, ed. see Shumate, Albert.

Bonnett, Wayne, ed. see Tracy, Jack.

Bonnette, Amy L., tr. & anno. see Xenophon.

Bonnette, Charlotte A., ed. see Dennie, Joseph C. & Weathers, Joseph.

Bonnette, Jeanne. Three Friends. 23p. (J). (gr. k-4). 1982. pap. 4.95 (*0-89992-066-7*) Coun India Ed.

Bonnetti, E., et al, eds. A Physicist's Outlook on New Materials. 200p. 1991. text 100.00 (*0-87849-615-7*, Pub. by Trans T Pub) Enfield Pubs NH.

Bonneuil, Noel. Transformation of the French Demographic Landscape, 1806-1906. LC 97-164752. (Illus.). 232p. 1997. text 55.00 (*0-19-823340-X*) OUP.

Bonnevie, Paul. Dictionnaire Hachette Juniors Encyclopedie, Noms Propres. (FRE.). 1990. write for info. (*0-7859-7609-4*, 2010164636) Fr & Eur.

— Dictionnaire Hachette Juniors Langue Francaise. (FRE.). 1990. write for info. (*0-7859-7608-6*) Fr & Eur.

Bonnevie, Paul & Amiel, Philippe, eds. Dictionnaire Hachette Juniors. (FRE.). write for info. (*0-7859-7606-X*, 2010143981) Fr & Eur.

Bonneville, Douglas, ed. & illus. see Masure, Myrle T.

Bonneville, Douglas A. Diderot's Vie de Seneque: A Swan Song Revised. LC 66-63483. (University of Florida Humanities Monographs: No. 19). 59p. reprint ed. pap. 30.00 (*0-7837-5016-1*, 204468300004) Bks Demand.

Bonneville, Georges, jt. auth. see Beaumarchais, Pierre De.

Bonneville, J. F., et al. Computed Tomography of the Pituitary Gland. (Illus.). 256p. 1986. 301.00 (*0-387-15324-1*) Spr-Verlag.

— Radiology of the Sella Turcica. (Illus.). 262p. 1980. 181.00 (*0-387-10319-8*) Spr-Verlag.

*__Bonneville, Victor.__ Attleboro. (Images of America Ser.). 1999. pap. 16.99 (*0-7524-1352-X*) Arcadia Publng.

Bonneviot, L. & Kaliaguine, S., eds. Zeolites: A Refined Tool for Designing Catalytic Sites: Proceedings of the International Zeolite Symposium, Quebec, Canada, 15-20 October 1995. LC 95-221621. (Studies in Surface Science & Catalysis: Vol. 97). 584p. 1995. text 272.50 (*0-444-82130-9*) Elsevier.

Bonneviot, Laurent. Mesoporous Molecular Sieves 1998: Proceedings of the First International Symposium, Baltimore, Md, U.S.A., July 10-12, 1998, Vol. 117. LC 98-22444. (Studies in Surface Science & Catalysis). 1998. write for info. (*0-444-82826-5*) Elsevier.

Bonney, Barbara. Fundamentals of Soccer. LC 97-8099. (Play It Like a Pro Ser.). (J). 1997. 17.27 (*1-57103-138-3*) Rourke Pr.

— Soccer: Attacking. LC 97-8096. (Play It Like a Pro Ser.). (J). 1997. lib. bdg. 17.27 (*1-57103-135-9*) Rourke Pr.

— Soccer: Defending. LC 97-8097. (Play It Like a Pro Ser.). (J). 1997. lib. bdg. 17.27 (*1-57103-136-7*) Rourke Pr.

— Soccer: Rules of the Game. LC 97-8101. (Play It Like a Pro Ser.). (J). 1997. lib. bdg. 17.27 (*1-57103-140-5*) Rourke Pr.

— Soccer Equipment. LC 97-8098. (Play It Like a Pro Ser.). (J). 1997. lib. bdg. 17.27 (*1-57103-137-5*) Rourke Pr.

— Soccer Skills. LC 97-8100. (Play It Like a Pro Ser.). (J). 1997. lib. bdg. 17.27 (*1-57103-139-1*) Rourke Pr.

— Softball: Batting. LC 98-11083. (Softball Ser.). (J). 1998. (*0-86593-476-2*) Rourke Corp.

— Softball: Field & Equipment. LC 98-11087. (Softball Ser.). (J). 1998. (*0-86593-480-0*) Rourke Corp.

— Softball: Pitching. LC 98-11088. (Softball Ser.). (J). 1998. (*0-86593-478-9*) Rourke Corp.

— Softball: Rules of the Game. LC 98-11086. (Softball Ser.). (J). 1998. (*0-86593-481-9*) Rourke Corp.

— Softball: Run, Throw & Catch. LC 98-11085. (Softball Ser.). (J). 1998. (*0-86593-477-0*) Rourke Corp.

— Softball: The Positions. LC 98-11084. (Softball Ser.). (J). 1998. (*0-86593-479-7*) Rourke Corp.

Bonney, Bruce F. & Drury, Jack K. The Backcountry Classroom. LC 92-26151. (Illus.). 288p. 1992. pap. 29.95 (*0-934802-18-1*) Globe Pequot.

Bonney, Charles C., jt. auth. see Dole, George F.

*__Bonney, Jo.__ Extreme Exposure: An Anthology of Solo Performance Texts from the 20th Century. LC 98-49391. (Illus.). 423p. 2000. pap. 18.95 (*1-55936-155-7*, Pub. by Theatre Comm) Consort Bk Sales.

Bonney, Lorraine G. Bonney's Guide to Jackson's Hole & Grand Teton National Park. 2nd ed. LC 94-76321. (Illus.). 268p. 1995. pap. 14.95 (*0-943972-32-9*) Homestead WY.

Bonney, Lorraine G., jt. auth. see Bonney, Orrin H.

Bonney, Merl E., et al, eds. Social Psychological Foundations for School Services. 318p. (C). 1986. 45.95 (*0-89885-282-X*, Kluwer Acad Hman Sci); pap. 24.95 (*0-89885-283-8*, Kluwer Acad Hman Sci) Kluwer Academic.

Bonney, Orrin H. & Bonney, Lorraine G. Field Book. Incl. Big Horn Range. 172p. 1977. pap. 7.95 (*0-8040-0536-2*); Teton Range & the Gros Ventre Range: Climbing Routes & Back Country. 2nd rev. ed. 263p. 1977. pap. 7.95 (*0-8040-0578-8*); Yellowstone Park: Absaroka Range. 2nd rev ed. 162p. 1977. pap. 7.95 (*0-8040-0579-6*); (Illus.). 1977. pap. write for info. (*0-318-55895-5*) Swallow.

— The Grand Controversy: Pioneer Climbs in the Teton Range & the Controversial First Ascent of the Grand Teton. (Illus.). 458p. 1992. pap 28.50 (*0-930410-45-9*) Amer Alpine Club.

Bonney, Richard. The European Dynastic States, 1494-1660. (Short Oxford History of the Modern World Ser.). (Illus.). 692p. 1992. pap. text 29.95 (*0-19-873023-3*) OUP.

Bonney, Richard. The Limits of Absolutism in Ancient Regime France: Collected Essays. LC 94-37035. (Collected Studies: No. CS491). 352p. 1995. 109.95 (*0-86078-482-7*, Pub. by Variorum) Ashgate Pub Co.

— Political Change in France under Richelieu & Mazarin, 1624-1661. (Illus.). 1978. text 69.00 (*0-19-822537-7*) OUP.

Bonney, Richard, ed. Economic Systems & State Finance: Thirteenth to Eighteenth Centuries: Economic Systems & State Finance. (The Origins of the Modern State in Europe Ser.: 2). (Illus.). 674p. 1995. text 110.00 (*0-19-820545-7*) OUP.

*__Bonney, Richard, ed.__ The Rise of the Fiscal State in Europe, C. 1200-1815. LC 98-49345. 544p. 1999. 110.00 (*0-19-820402-7*) OUP.

Bonney, Richard E. Beekeeping: A Practical Guide. Webb, Sandra, ed. LC 92-56145. (Illus.). 192p. 1993. pap. 18.95 (*0-88266-861-7*, Garden Way Pub) Storey Bks.

— Hive Management: A Seasonal Guide for Beekeepers. LC 90-55606. (Illus.). 160p. (Orig.). 1991. pap. 16.95 (*0-88266-637-1*) Storey Bks.

Bonney, Richard E., Jr., et al. Understanding Predation & Northeastern Birds of Prey. (Illus.). 49p. 1981. pap. 5.75 (*1-57753-196-5*, 147 1B 175) Corn Coop Ext.

Bonney, Robert J., ed. Inflammatory Disease Therapy: Preclinical & Clinical Developments. LC 93-17038. (Agents & Actions Supplements Ser.: Vol. 41). ix, 209p. 1993. 89.50 (*0-8176-2859-2*) Birkhauser.

Bonney, Sean, jt. auth. see Jones, Angier.

Bonney, William W. Thorns & Arabesques: Contexts for Conrad's Fiction. LC 80-13308. 256p. 1980. reprint ed. pap. 79.40 (*0-608-03641-2*, 206446700009) Bks Demand.

Bonnice. Essentials of Business Law. 4th ed. 1989. 25.71 (*0-07-006527-6*) McGraw.

Bonnice, Joseph G. Developing Consumer Attitudes. (HM - Consumer Education Ser.). 1986. pap., wbk. ed. 15.95 (*0-538-32401-5*) S-W Pub.

Bonnice, Joseph G. & Rosenberg, R. Robert. Business Law-Thirty. 3rd ed. 1982. text 14.88 (*0-07-006472-5*) McGraw.

Bonnichsen, Bill, jt. ed. see Breckenridge, Roy M.

Bonnichsen, Robson & Sorg, Marcella H., eds. Bone Modification. 535p. 1989. 72.00 (*0-912933-06-2*) Ctr Study First Am.

Bonnichsen, Robson & Steele, D. Gentry, eds. Method & Theory for Investigating the Peopling of the Americas. (Illus.). 264p. (Orig.). (C). 1994. pap. text 33.00 (*0-912933-11-9*) Ctr Study First Am.

— Method & Theory for Investigating the Peopling of the Americas, Vol. 1. (Illus.). 264p. (Orig.). (C). 1994. 42.00 (*0-912933-09-7*) Ctr Study First Am.

Bonnichsen, Robson & Turnmire, Karen L., eds. Ice Age Peoples of North America. LC 99-23496. (Illus.). 536p. 1999. 49.95 (*0-87071-458-9*) Oreg St U Pr.

Bonnici, John S. Person to Person: Friendship & Love in the Life & Theology of Hans Urs von Balthasar. LC 98-51510. 160p. 1999. pap. 9.95 (*0-8189-0858-0*) Alba.

Bonnici, John S., jt. auth. see Giandurco, Joseph R.

Bonnici, Peter. Layout. 1999. pap. 35.00 (*2-88046-397-1*, Rotovision) Watsn-Guptill.

— Visual Language. (Design Fundamentals Ser.). 1998. pap. text 35.00 (*2-88046-388-2*, Rotovision) Watsn-Guptill.

*__Bonnici, Roberta.__ Christians in the Workplace. (Spiritual Discovery Ser.). 96p. 1998. pap., teacher ed. 9.95 (*0-88243-227-3*, 02-0227); pap., student ed. 4.95 (*0-88243-127-7*, 02-0127) Gospel Pub.

Bonnick, Allan. Vehicle Electronic Systems & Fault Diagnosis. LC 98-85174. 200p. 1999. 24.95 (*0-7680-0241-9*, RS-001) Soc Auto Engineers.

Bonnick, Bertrand. Bighead. Ornest, Noemi, ed. (Orig.). 1994. pap. 10.95 (*1-885778-02-3*) Seaburn.

Bonnick, Gladstone G. Zambia Country Assistance Review: Turning an Economy Around. (Operations Evaluation Department Studies). (Illus.). 176p. 1997. pap. 22.00 (*0-8213-3879-X*, 13879) World Bank.

Bonnick, Sydney L. The Osteoporosis Handbook. 2nd ed. LC 97-204669. (Illus.). 216p. (Orig.). 1997. pap. 14.95 (*0-87833-978-7*) Taylor Pub.

Bonnick, Sydney Lou. Bone Densitometry in Clinical Practice: Application & Interpretation. LC 98-12447. (Current Clinical Practice Ser.). (Illus.). 280p. 1998. 89.50 (*0-89603-513-1*) Humana.

Bonnicksen, Andrea L. In Vitro Fertilization: Building Policy from Laboratories to Legislatures. 1991. pap. 18.50 (*0-231-06905-7*) Col U Pr.

Bonnicksen, Andrea L., jt. ed. see Blank, Robert H.

Bonnicksen, Thomas M. America's Ancient Forests: From the Ice Age to the Age of Discovery. LC 98-24396. 592p. 2000. 75.00 (*0-471-13622-0*) Wiley.

Bonnie, Fred. Detecting Metal: Stories. LC 98-73125 144p. 1999. reprint ed. 19.95 (*0-942979-54-0*); reprint ed. pap. 9.95 (*0-942979-53-2*) Livingston U Pr.

— Displaced Persons: Stories. LC 83-219911. 133p. 1982. write for info. (*0-88750-466-3*) Oberon Pr.

— Food Fights. LC 97-924. 1997. 24.00 (*1-881320-73-1*, Black Belt) Black Belt Communs.

— Squatter's Rights: Stories. LC 80-463710. (Illus.). 129 p. (J). 1979. write for info. (*0-88750-328-4*) Oberon Pr.

*__Bonnie, Fred.__ Thanh Ho Delivers. 448p. 2000. 24.95 (*1-880216-51-5*, Black Belt) Black Belt Communs.

— Widening the Road: Stories. 192p. 2000. 24.00 (*0-942979-66-4*); pap. 11.00 (*0-942979-65-6*) Livingston AL.

Bonnie, Richard J. & Monahan, John, eds. Mental Disorder, Work Disability, & the Law. LC 96-10971. (John D. & Catherine T. MacArthur Foundation Series on Mental Health & Development). (Illus.). 308p. 1996. 27.50 (*0-226-06450-6*) U Ch Pr.

Bonnie, Richard J. & Whitebread, Charles H. The Marihuana Conviction: A History of Marihuana Prohibition in the United States. LC 73-89907. 334p. reprint ed. pap. 119.10 (*0-608-13912-2*, 202032200017) Bks Demand.

Bonnie, Richard J. & Whitebread, Charles H., II. Marijuana Conviction: History of Marijuana Prohibition. LC 99-15034. 368p. 1999. pap. text 14.95 (*1-891385-06-2*, Pub. by Open Soc Inst) BookWorld.

Bonnie, Richard J., et al. Criminal Law. LC 97-2064. (University Casebook Ser.). 962p. 1997. text 40.75 (*1-56662-448-7*) Foundation Pr.

— Criminal Law, Teacher's Manual For. (University Casebook Ser.). 128p. 1997. pap. text. write for info. (*1-56662-537-8*) Foundation Pr.

— Reducing the Burden of Injury: Advancing Prevention & Treatment. LC 98-40288. 336p. 1999. 34.95 (*0-309-06566-6*) Natl Acad Pr.

Bonnie, Richard J., ed. see Institute of Medicine Staff.

Bonnier, Gaston & Douin, Robert. La Grande Flore en Couleurs de Gaston Bonnier. France, Suisse, Belgique et Pays Voisins (The Grand Flora As Illustrated by Gaston Bonnier. France, Switzerland, Belgium & Vicinities), 2 vols. (Illus.). 959p. 1990. 365.00 (*3-8263-2971-6*, Pub. by Blckwell Wissenschafts) Balogh.

Bonniffet, Pierre, jt. ed. see Bouquet-Boyer, Marie-Therese.

Bonnin, Heather. Hours to Remember: Life in South Australia 1889-1929. 180p. (C). 1989. pap. text 90.00 (*0-89771-026-6*, Pub. by Bob Mossel) St Mut.

Bonnin, J., et al, eds. Seismic Hazard in Mediterranean Regions. (C). 1988. lib. bdg. 175.00 (*90-277-2779-1*) Kluwer Academic.

Bonning, Tony. Another Fine Mess. LC 98-27025. (Illus.). 32p. (J). (ps-4). 1998. 14.95 (*1-888444-43-6*) Little Tiger.

Bonnington, C. Paul & Little, Charles H. The Foundations of Topological Graph Theory. LC 95-30507. (Illus.). 192p. 1995. 59.95 (*0-387-94557-1*) Spr-Verlag.

Bonnington, Christian. I Chose to Climb. large type ed. 432p. 1985. 27.99 (*0-7089-1346-6*) Ulverscroft.

Bonnington, S. T., jt. auth. see Bain, A. G.

*__Bonniwell, George B.__ The Bonniwells - 1000 Years. LC 99-73608. (Illus.). x, 170p. 1999. write for info. (*0-9673991-0-6*) G B Bonniwell.

Bonniwell, William R. The Life of Blessed Margaret of Castello. LC 83-70524. 113p. (J). (gr. 8). 1993. reprint ed. pap. 7.50 (*0-89555-213-2*) TAN Bks Pubs.

Bonnke, Reinhard. Beyond '99: Time to Turn! From Minus to Plus. 2nd rev. ed. Orig. Title: From Minus to Plus. (Illus.). 32p. 1998. pap. write for info. (*1-882729-09-9*) R Bonnke Minist.

— Evangelism. LC 99-46141. (Orig.). 1999. pap. 12.99 (*0-8307-2466-4*) Gospel Lght.

— Evangelism by Fire: Igniting Your Passion for Evangelism. 288p. 1992. pap. text 12.99 (*1-882729-00-5*) R Bonnke Minist.

— Faith: The Link with God's Power. LC 98-20603. 252p. 1998. pap. 12.99 (*0-7852-7469-3*) Nelson.

Bonno, Chris, jt. auth. see Deschaine, Scott.

Bonnot de Condillac, Etienne. La Logique. Albury, W. R., tr. (Janus Ser.).Tr. of Logic. 354p. 1980. lib. bdg. 25.00 (*0-913870-38-2*) Abaris Bks.

*__Bonnstetter, Bill J.__ What I Know Now. 1999. 19.95 (*0-8281-1420-X*) Forb Custom Pub.

Bonnvillain, Nancy. The Santee Sioux. (Indians of North America Ser.). 120p. (YA). (gr. 5 up). 1996. pap 9.95 (*0-7910-3482-8*) Chelsea Hse.

*__Bony, Clive.__ Business Writing Pocketbook. 112p. 1999. pap. 8.95 (*1-870471-22-9*, Pub. by Mngmnt Pocketbks) Stylus Pub VA.

*__Bony, Helen L.__ Music & Consciousness: My Life's Work. (C). 2000. pap. text. write for info. (*1-891278-10-X*) Barcelona Pubs.

Bony, Helen L. Music & Your Mind: Listening with a New Consciousness. 1990. pap. 10.95 (*0-88268-094-2*) Station Hill Pr.

Bony, Oscar. At Home in the Universe: From the Siberian Steppes to Baltimore. Diorio, David, ed. LC 89-80519. (Illus.). 160p. (Orig.). 1989. pap. 11.95 (*0-944806-01-5*) Icarus Press.

Bonnyay, Ene T. Westport & Weston. (Illus.). 80p. 1997. 24.95 (*0-9655360-0-9*) Drumgarth LLC.

Bonnycastle, Stephen. In Search of Authority: An Introductory Guide to Literary Theory. 2nd rev. ed. 190p. 1996. pap. 16.95 (*1-55111-083-0*) Broadview Pr.

Bonnyman, D. & Oberheid, K. Sprungbrett. (Teacher's Books ser.). (C). 1990. teacher ed. 32.00 (*0-7487-0490-6*, Pub. by S Thornes Pubs) Trans-Atl Phila.

— Sprungbrett. (C). 1990. 47.50 (*0-7487-0489-2*, Pub. by S Thornes Pubs) Trans-Atl Phila.

*__Bono.__ Psalms. LC 99-482758. (Books of the Bible). 144p. 1999. pap. 2.95 (*0-8021-3675-3*, Pub. by Grove-Atltic) Publishers Group.

Bono, ed. Critical Essays on Shakespeare's Macbeth. 1996. 47.00 (*0-7838-0002-9*, G K Hall & Co) Mac Lib Ref.

Bono, Agostino, tr. see Theological-Historical Commission for the Great Ju.

Bono, Chastity & Fitzpatrick, Billie. Family Outing: A Guide to the Coming-Out Process for Gays, Lesbians & Their Families. LC 98-7348. 272p. (gr. 8). 1998. 24.00 (*0-316-10233-4*, Back Bay) Little.

*__Bono, Chastity & Fitzpatrick, Billie.__ Family Outing: A Guide to the Coming-Out Process for Gays, Lesbians & Their Families. 272p. 1999. pap. 14.95 (*0-316-11596-7*, Back Bay) Little.

Bono, Diane M. Cultural Diffusion of Spanish Humanism in New Spain: Francisco Cervantes De Salazar's Dialogo De la Dignidad Del Hombre. LC 91-3909. (American University Studies: Romance Languages & Literature: Ser. II, Vol. 161). 161p. (C). 1992. text 38.00 (*0-8204-1622-3*) P Lang Pubng.

Bono, Edward De, see De Bono, Edward.

Bono, Edward de, see De Bono, Edward.

Bono, Edward De, see De Bono, Edward.

Bono, F. English Cathedrals. 1976. lib. bdg. 234.95 (*0-8490-1771-8*) Gordon Pr.

Bono, James. Medicine in the Life Sciences 1450 Through 1700. 1999. 22.95 (*0-8057-9513-8*, Twyne) Mac Lib Ref.

Bono, James J. The Word of God & the Languages of Man: Interpreting Nature in Early Modern Science & Medicine. LC 95-15652. (Science & Literature Ser.). (Illus.). 332p. 1995. 50.00 (*0-299-14790-8*); pap. 22.95 (*0-299-14794-0*) U of Wis Pr.

Bono, James V., et al, eds. Revision Total Hip Arthroplasty. LC 97-42562. (Illus.). 560p. 1998. 179.00 (*0-387-98391-0*) Spr-Verlag.

Bono, Michael. Consumer's Guide to Permanent Hair Removal, Vol. 4. (Illus.). 150p. 1999. pap. 15.00 (*0-9642682-2-1*) Tortoise Press.

— Real World Electrology: The Blend Method: The Illustrated Manual of the Blend Method of Electrolysis. LC 94-90332. (Illus.). 368p. (Orig.). (C). 1994. pap. text 50.00 (*0-9642682-0-5*) Tortoise Press.

— Telangiectasia: Procedure to Remove Dilated Blood Vessels Using the Blend Method. (Illus.). 100p. 1996. pap. text 40.00 (*0-9642682-1-3*) Tortoise Press.

Bono, Michael, ed. see Zaffuto, Angelo A.

Bono, Nicholas, jt. ed. see Gellis, Willard.

Bono, P. R., jt. auth. see Arnold, D. B.

Bono, Pam. More Quick Rotary-Cutter Quilts. LC 95-72637. 160p. 1996. pap. 19.95 (*0-8487-1514-4*) Oxmoor Hse.

— Quick Rotary Cutter Quilts. 1994. pap. 19.95 (*0-8487-1412-1*) Oxmoor Hse.

Bonoan, Raul J., ed. The Rizal-Pastells Correspondence. 240p. 1997. pap. text 16.00 (*971-550-124-9*, Pub. by Ateneo de Manila Univ Pr) UH Pr.

*__Bonocore, Joseph.__ Commanding Communications: Navigating Emerging Trends in Telecommunications. 224p. 2000. 29.95 (*0-471-38821-1*) Wiley.

Bonogura, jt. auth. see Darke, Peter G. G.

Bonola, Roberto. Non-Euclidean Geometry. Carslaw, H. S., ed. 431p. (C). 1955. pap. 10.95 (*0-486-60027-0*) Dover.

*__Bonoli, Giuliano.__ The Politics of Pension Reform: Institutions & Policy Change in Western Europe. LC 99-87065. (Illus.). 204p. 2000. write for info. (*0-521-77232-X*); pap. write for info. (*0-521-77606-6*) Cambridge U Pr.

*__Bonoli, Giuliano, et al.__ European Welfare Futures: Towards a Theory of Retrenchment. LC 99-39727. 192p. 2000. text 59.95 (*0-7456-1810-3*, Pub. by Polity Pr); pap. text 26.95 (*0-7456-1811-1*, Pub. by Polity Pr) Blackwell Pubs.

Bonoma. Marketing Performance Assesment. 218p. 1988. pap. 15.16 (*0-07-103211-8*) McGraw.

Bonoma, Thomas V. Managing Marketing: Text Cases & Reading. 512p. (C). 1984. 45.00 (*0-02-903720-4*) Free Pr.

— The Marketing Edge: Making Strategies Work. 240p. 1985. 32.95 (*0-02-904200-3*) Free Pr.

Bonometto, S. & Primack, J., eds. Dark Matter in the Universe. LC 96-78118. (International School of Physics Enrico Fermi Ser.: Vol. 132). 716p. (gr. 12). 1997. 195.00 (*90-5199-294-7*, 294-7) IOS Press.

Bonomi, Antonia. Universal Astrologer: 8-System World Horoscope Kit. 128p. 1997. pap. 24.95 (*88-7301-148-9*, Pub. by Gremese Intl) Natl Bk Netwk.

Bonomi, G. & Erseus, C., eds. Aquatic Oligochaeta. (Developments in Hydrobiology Ser.). 1984. text 232.00 (*90-6193-775-2*) Kluwer Academic.

Bonomi, Giorgio. Joseph Beuys: Diary of Seychelles. 1996. pap. 35.00 (*88-8158-089-6*, Pub. by Charta) Dist Art Pubs.

Bonomi, Ivanoe. From Socialism to Fascism: A Study of Contemporary Italy. LC 78-63652. (Studies in Fascism: Ideology & Practice). 168p. reprint ed. 37.50 (*0-404-16907-4*) AMS Pr.

Bonomi, Kathryn & Schlank, Christine. Italy: Major World Nations. (Major World Nations Ser.). (Illus.). 144p. (YA). (gr. 5 up). 1999. lib. bdg. 19.95 (*0-7910-4760-1*) Chelsea Hse.

Bonomi, L. & Orzalesi, N., eds. Glaucoma - Concepts in Evolution: Morphometric & Functional Parameters in the Diagnosis & Follow-Up of Management Glaucoma. LC 91-35342. (Illus.). 160p. 1991. lib. bdg. 51.50 (*90-6299-081-9*, Pub. by Kugler) Kugler Pubns.

Bonomi, Patricia U. The Lord Cornbury Scandal: The Politics of Reputation in British America. LC 97-40318. (Published for the Omohundro Institute of Early American History & Culture Ser.). (Illus.). 304p. 1998. 29.95 (*0-8078-2413-5*) U of NC Pr.

B

***Bonomi, Patricia U.** The Lord Cornbury Scandal: The Politics of Reputation in British America. LC 97-40318. (Published for the Omohundro Institute of Early American History & Culture, Williamsburg, Virginia Ser.). (Illus.). 304p. 2000. pap. 19.95 (*0-8078-4869-7*) U of NC Pr.

Bonomi, Patricia U. Under the Cope of Heaven: Religion, Society, & Politics in Colonial America. (Illus.). 304p. 1988. pap. text 19.95 (*0-19-505417-2*) OUP.

Bonomi, Patricia U., et al, eds. The American Constitutional System under Strong & Weak Parties. LC 80-39659. 142p. 1981. 47.95 (*0-275-90585-3*, C0585, Praeger Pubs) Greenwood.

Bonomini, V., ed. Dialysis Membranes: Structure & Predictions. (Contributions to Nephrology Ser.: Vol. 113). (Illus.). viii, 140p. 1994. 128.00 (*3-8055-6061-3*) S Karger.

Bonomini, V., et al, eds. Biotechnology in Renal Replacement Therapy. (Contributions to Nephrology Ser.: Vol. 70). (Illus.). xiv, 346p. 1989. 216.75 (*3-8055-4893-1*) S Karger.

Bonomini, V. & Chang, T. M., eds. Hemoperfusion. (Contributions to Nephrology Ser.: Vol. 29). (Illus.). vi, 150p. 1982. pap. 71.25 (*3-8055-3421-3*) S Karger.

Bonomini, V., jt. ed. see Giovannetti, Sergio.

Bonomo, James L., jt. auth. see Lempert, Robert J.

Bonomo, Joe. Vanishings from That Neighborhood. LC 95-38198. (Wick Poetry Chapbook Ser.: No. 9). 47p. (Orig.). 1996. pap. 4.75 (*0-87338-544-6*) Kent St U Pr.

Bonomo, Luca & Higginson, A. E., eds. International Overview on Solid Waste Management: A Report from the International Solid Wastes & Public Cleansing Association (ISWA) 253p. 1988. text 104.00 (*0-12-114975-7*) Acad Pr.

Bonomo, Perry & Seldler, Daniel. ErgAerobics: Why Does Working at My Computer Hurt So Much? LC 99-163013. (Illus.). 128p. 1998. pap. 14.95 (*0-9664090-0-0*) Erg Aerobics.

Bononcini, Giovanni M. Musico Prattico. (Illus.). 164p. 1969. reprint ed. 65.00 (*0-318-71581-3*) G Olms Pubs.

Bononcini, Antonio. Antonio Bononcini: Complete Sonatas for Violoncello & Basso Continuo. Lindgren, Lowell E., ed. (Recent Researches in Music of the Baroque Era Ser.: Vol. RRB77). (Illus.). xxiii, 157p. 1996. pap. 60.00 (*0-89579-333-4*) A-R Eds.

***Bononi, Alberto.** Optical Networking. LC 99-34588. xiv, 402p. 1999. pap. 119.00 (*1-85233-641-2*, Pub. by Spr-Verlag) Spr-Verlag.

Bononno, Robert, tr. see Guibert, Herve.

Bononno, Robert, tr. see Levy, Pierre.

Bononno, Robert, tr. see Lorme, Anna.

Bonora. France & the Algerian Conflict. 70.95 (*1-84014-751-2*) Ashgate Pub Co.

Bonora, L., et al. Integrable Quantum Field Theories. (NATO ASI Ser.: Vol. 310). (Illus.). 342p. (C). 1993. text 110.00 (*0-306-44534-4*, Kluwer Plenum) Kluwer Academic.

Bonora, P. L., jt. ed. see Fedrizzi, L.

Bonora, Pier L. & Deflorian, Flavio, eds. Electrochemical Methods in Corrosion Research, No. VI. (Materials Science Forum Ser.: Vols. 289-292). (Illus.). 1400p. (C). 1998. text 315.00 (*0-87849-819-2*, Pub. by Trans T Pub) Enfield Pubs NH.

Bonosky, Phillip. A Bird in Her Hair. Bean, Adelaide, ed. LC 87-3432. (Illus.). 180p. (Orig.). 1987. pap. 5.95 (*0-7178-0661-8*) Intl Pubs Co.

— Burning Valley. LC 97-18470. (Radical Novel Reconsidered Ser.). 320p. 1997. 15.95 (*0-252-06684-7*) U of Ill Pr.

— Devils in Amber: The Baltics. Steffan, Dieterich, ed. LC 91-45096. 305p. (Orig.). 1992. pap. 9.95 (*0-7178-0699-5*) Intl Pubs Co.

— Washington's Secret War Against Afghanistan. LC 84-19139. 264p. (Orig.). reprint ed. pap. 81.90 (*0-7837-0585-9*, 204092900019) Bks Demand.

Bonovitz, Jeffrey S. The Facilitating Partnership: A Winnicottian Approach for Social Workers & Other Helping Professionals. LC 94-49143. 1995. pap. text 30.00 (*0-7657-0201-0*) Aronson.

Bonovitz, Jennifer M., jt. auth. see Applegate, Jeffrey S.

Bonpland, Aime, jt. auth. see Von Humboldt, Alexander.

Bons, N., et al, eds. A Stereotaxic Atlas of the Grey Lesser Mouse Lemur Brain (Microcebus Murinus) LC 99-180360. 152p. 1998. 100.50 (*0-444-50098-7*) Elsevier.

Bons-Storm, Riet. The Incredible Woman: Listening to Women's Silences in Pastoral Care & Counseling. LC 96-3019. 160p. 1996. pap. 16.95 (*0-687-00652-X*) Abingdon.

Bonsal, Stephen. The American Mediterranean. 1977. lib. bdg. 69.95 (*0-8490-1415-8*) Gordon Pr.

Bonsall, Clive. The Mesolithic in Europe: The Third International Symposium. (Illus.). 500p. (C). 1996. 165.00 (*0-85976-205-X*, Pub. by J Donald) St Mut.

Bonsall, Crosby, jt. auth. see Bonsall, Peter.

Bonsall, Crosby N. The Amazing the Incredible Super Dog. LC 85-45811. (Illus.). 32p. (J). (gr. k-3). 1986. 11.95 (*0-06-020590-3*) HarpC Child Bks.

— And I Mean It, Stanley. (I Can Read Bks.). (Illus.). 32p. (J). (ps-1). 1974. lib. bdg. 15.89 (*0-06-020568-7*) HarpC Child Bks.

— And I Mean It, Stanley. LC 73-14324. (I Can Read Bks.). (Illus.). 32p. (J). (ps-3). 1984. pap. 3.95 (*0-06-444046-X*, HarpTrophy) HarpC Child Bks.

— And I Mean It, Stanley. (I Can Read Bks.). 32p. (J). (ps-1). 1990. pap. 8.95 incl. audio (*1-55994-265-7*) HarperAudio.

Bonsall, Crosby N. And I Mean It, Stanley. (I Can Read Bks.). (J). (ps-1). 1974. 8.95 (*0-606-03368-8*, Pub. by Turtleback) Demco.

Bonsall, Crosby N. The Case of the Cat's Meow. (I Can Read Bks.). (Illus.). 64p. (J). (gr. 1-3). 1965. lib. bdg. 15.89 (*0-06-020561-X*) HarpC Child Bks.

— The Case of the Cat's Meow. LC 65-11451. (I Can Read Bks.). (Illus.). 64p. (J). (ps-3). 1978. pap. 3.95 (*0-06-444017-6*, HarpTrophy) HarpC Child Bks.

— The Case of the Cat's Meow. (I Can Read Bks.). (Illus.). (J). (gr. 1-3). 1965. 8.95 (*0-606-02020-9*, Pub. by Turtleback) Demco.

— The Case of the Double Cross. (I Can Read Bks.). (Illus.). 64p. (J). (gr. 1-3). 1980. 11.89 (*0-06-020602-0*) HarpC Child Bks.

— The Case of the Double Cross. (I Can Read Bks.). (Illus.). 64p. (J). (gr. 1-3). 1980. lib. bdg. 15.89 (*0-06-020603-9*) HarpC Child Bks.

— The Case of the Double Cross. LC 80-7768. (I Can Read Bks.). (Illus.). 64p. (J). (ps-3). 1982. pap. 3.95 (*0-06-444029-X*, HarpTrophy) HarpC Child Bks.

— The Case of the Double Cross. (I Can Read Bks.). (Illus.). (J). (gr. 1-3). 1980. 8.95 (*0-606-00407-6*, Pub. by Turtleback) Demco.

— The Case of the Dumb Bells. (I Can Read Bks.). (Illus.). 64p. (J). (gr. 1-3). 1966. lib. bdg. 15.89 (*0-06-020624-1*) HarpC Child Bks.

— The Case of the Dumb Bells. LC 66-8267. (I Can Read Bks.). (Illus.). 64p. (J). (ps-3). 1982. pap. 3.95 (*0-06-444030-3*, HarpTrophy) HarpC Child Bks.

— The Case of the Dumb Bells. (I Can Read Bks.). (Illus.). (J). (gr. 1-3). 1966. 8.95 (*0-606-00408-4*, Pub. by Turtleback) Demco.

— El Caso del Forastero Hambriento. (I Can Read Bks.). Orig. Title: Case of the Hungry Stranger. (J). (gr. 1-3). 1996. 10.15 (*0-606-08733-8*, Pub. by Turtleback) Demco.

— The Case of the Hungry Stranger. (I Can Read Bks.). (Illus.). 64p. (J). (gr. 1-3). 1963. lib. bdg. 15.89 (*0-06-020571-7*) HarpC Child Bks.

— The Case of the Hungry Stranger. LC 91-14365. (I Can Read Bks.). (Illus.). 64p. (J). (ps-3). 1980. pap. 3.95 (*0-06-444026-5*, HarpTrophy) HarpC Child Bks.

— The Case of the Hungry Stranger. (I Can Read Bks.). (Illus.). (J). (gr. 1-3). 1963. 8.95 (*0-606-02056-X*, Pub. by Turtleback) Demco.

— The Case of the Hungry Stranger. abr. ed. (I Can Read Bks.). (Illus.). (J). (gr. 1-3). 1990. 8.95 incl. audio (*1-55994-223-1*, TBC 2231) HarperAudio.

— The Case of the Scaredy Cats. LC 75-159039. (I Can Read Bks.). (Illus.). 64p. (J). (ps-3). 1971. lib. bdg. 15.89 (*0-06-020566-0*) HarpC Child Bks.

— The Case of the Scaredy Cats. LC 75-159039. (I Can Read Bks.). (Illus.). 64p. (J). (ps-3). 1984. pap. 3.95 (*0-06-444047-8*, HarpTrophy) HarpC Child Bks.

— The Case of the Scaredy Cats. (I Can Read Bks.). (Illus.). (J). (gr. 1-3). 1984. 8.95 (*0-606-03376-9*, Pub. by Turtleback) Demco.

— The Case of the Scaredy Cats. abr. ed. (I Can Read Bks.). (Illus.). 64p. (J). (gr. 1-3). 1991. audio 8.95 (*1-55994-434-X*, TBC 434X) HarperAudio.

— The Day I Had to Play with My Sister. (Illus.). (J). (ps-3). 1972. 6.93 (*0-06-020575-X*, 133404) HarpC Child Bks.

Bonsall, Crosby N. The Day I Had to Play with My Sister. (My First I Can Read Bks.). (J). (ps-k). 1988. 8.95 (*0-606-03563-X*, Pub. by Turtleback) Demco.

Bonsall, Crosby N. The Day I Had to Play With My Sister. LC 98-20342. (My First I Can Read Bks.). (Illus.). 32p. (J). (ps-k). 1999. pap. 3.95 (*0-06-444253-5*, HarpTrophy) HarpC Child Bks.

— Mine's the Best. (My First I Can Read Bks.). (Illus.). (J). (ps-k). 1973. 14.89 (*0-06-020577-6*, 133480) HarpC Child Bks.

— Mine's the Best. (My First I Can Read Bks.). (Illus.). 32p. (J). (ps-k). 1973. lib. bdg. 14.89 (*0-06-020578-4*) HarpC Child Bks.

Bonsall, Crosby N. Mine's the Best. (My First I Can Read Bks.). (J). (ps-k). 1997. 8.95 (*0-606-11627-3*, Pub. by Turtleback) Demco.

Bonsall, Crosby N. Mine's the Best. LC 95-12405. (My First I Can Read Bks.). (Illus.). 32p. (J). (ps-k). 1997. reprint ed. pap. 3.95 (*0-06-444213-6*, HarpTrophy) HarpC Child Bks.

— Mine's the Best. rev. ed. (My First I Can Read Bks.). (Illus.). 32p. (J). (ps-k). 1996. lib. bdg. 15.89 (*0-06-027091-8*) HarpC Child Bks.

— Piggle. (I Can Read Bks.). (Illus.). (J). (gr. 1-3). 1973. 14.89 (*0-06-020579-2*, 133490) HarpC Child Bks.

— Piggle. LC 73-5478. (I Can Read Bks.). (Illus.). 64p. (J). (ps-3). 1973. lib. bdg. 15.89 (*0-06-020580-6*) HarpC Child Bks.

— Who's a Pest? LC 62-13310. (I Can Read Bks.). (Illus.). 64p. (J). (ps-3). 1962. lib. bdg. 15.89 (*0-06-020621-7*) HarpC Child Bks.

Bonsall, Crosby N. Who's a Pest? LC 62-13310. (I Can Read Bks.). (Illus.). 64p. (J). (ps-3). 1986. pap. 3.95 (*0-06-444099-0*, HarpTrophy) HarpC Child Bks.

Bonsall, Crosby N. Who's a Pest? (I Can Read Bks.). (Illus.). (J). (gr. 1-3). 1992. 6.93 (*0-06-020620-9*, 133597) HarpC Child Bks.

Bonsall, Crosby N. Who's a Pest? (I Can Read Bks.). (J). (gr. 1-3). 1986. 8.70 (*0-606-01966-9*, Pub. by Turtleback) Demco.

Bonsall, Crosby N. Who's Afraid of the Dark? (I Can Read Bks.). (Illus.). 32p. (J). (gr. 1-3). 2001. 14.95 (*0-06-020598-9*) HarpC Child Bks.

— Who's Afraid of the Dark? LC 79-2700. (I Can Read Bks.). (Illus.). 32p. (J). (ps-3). 2001. lib. bdg. 15.89 (*0-06-020599-7*) HarpC Child Bks.

— Who's Afraid of the Dark? (I Can Read Bks.). (Illus.). 32p. (J). (gr. 1-3). 2001. reprint ed. pap. 3.95 (*0-06-444071-0*, HarpTrophy) HarpC Child Bks.

Bonsall, Crosby N. & Siebel, Fritz. Tell Me Some More. LC 61-5773. (I Can Read Bks.). (Illus.). 64p. (J). (ps-3). 1961. lib. bdg. 15.89 (*0-06-020601-2*, 133507) HarpC Child Bks.

Bonsall, Crosby Newell. Who's Afraid of the Dark? (I Can Read Bks.). (J). (gr. 1-3). 1985. 8.95 (*0-606-00885-3*, Pub. by Turtleback) Demco.

Bonsall, David, ed. Securitisation. 335p. 1990. boxed set 170.00 (*0-406-11722-5*, UK, MICHIE) LEXIS Pub.

Bonsall, Donald G., jt. auth. see Chesebro, James W.

Bonsall, Joseph S. Brewster. LC 98-48019. (Molly the Cat Book Ser.). (J). 1999. 14.95 (*1-57102-149-3*, Ideals Child) Hambleton-Hill.

— The Home. LC 97-12847. (Molly Book Ser.). (Illus.). 32p. (J). (gr. 1-4). 1997. 14.95 (*1-57102-123-X*, Ideals Child) Hambleton-Hill.

— Molly. LC 97-10889. (Molly the Cat Book Ser.). (Illus.). 32p. (J). (gr. 1-4). 1997. 14.95 (*1-57102-122-1*, Ideals Child) Hambleton-Hill.

— Outside. LC 98-13303. (Molly the Cat Book Ser.). (Illus.). (J). 1998. 14.95 (*1-57102-130-2*, Ideals Child) Hambleton-Hill.

Bonsall, P. & Bell, M., eds. Information Technology Applications in Transport. (Topics in Transportation Ser.). 394p. 1987. 115.00 (*90-6764-066-2*, Pub. by VSP) Coronet Bks.

Bonsall, Penny. The Irish RMs. LC 98-132165. 240p. 1998. boxed set 45.00 (*1-85182-331-X*, Pub. by Four Cts Pr) Intl Spec Bk.

Bonsall, Peter. The Day I Had to Play With My Sister. LC 98-20342. (My First I Can Read Bks.). (Illus.). 32p. (J). (ps-k). 1999. lib. bdg. 12.89 (*0-06-028181-2*) HarpC Child Bks.

Bonsall, Peter & Bonsall, Crosby. The Day I Had to Play with My Sister. rev. ed. LC 98-20342. (My First I Can Read Bks.). (Illus.). 32p. (J). (ps-k). 1999. 12.95 (*0-06-028180-4*) HarpC Child Bks.

Bonsall, Thomas E. Guide to GM Muscle Cars. (Illus.). 208p. (Orig.). 1991. pap. 17.95 (*1-55788-003-4*, HP Books) Berkley Pub.

***Bonsall, Thomas E.** More Than They Promised: The Studebaker Story. 376p. 1999. 45.00 (*0-8047-3586-7*) Stanford U Pr.

Bonsangue, N. J. & Flatley, S. G. The Teddy Bear Express! A Phonological Development Program. LC 93-78926. 1994. pap. 24.95 (*0-89108-232-8*, 9308) Love Pub Co.

Bonsanti, G. Giotto. 314p. 1986. 800.00 (*1-57235-055-5*) Piccin Nuova.

Bonsanti, Giorgio. Basilica of St. Francis of Assisi: Glory & Destruction. LC 97-78102. (Illus.). 100p. 1998. pap. 24.95 (*0-8109-2767-5*, Pub. by Abrams) Time Warner.

— Caravaggio. (Grandes Maestros del Arte Ser.). (SPA., Illus.). 80p. 1992. pap. 12.99 (*1-878351-24-9*) Riverside NY.

— Caravaggio. Blanchard, Paul, tr. from ITA. (Library of Great Masters). (Illus.). 80p. 1990. reprint ed. pap. 14.99 (*1-878351-07-9*) Riverside NY.

— The Galleria Della Accademia Florence: Guide to the Gallery & Complete Catalogue. (Illus.). 96p. 1992. 19.95 (*0-8161-0609-6*, G K Hall & Co) Mac Lib Ref.

Bonsanti, Giorgio, et al. The Basilica of St. Francis of Assisi: Glory & Destruction. LC 97-78102. 99p. 1998. 7.10 (*0-8109-4024-8*, Pub. by Abrams) Time Warner.

***Bonse-Rohmann, Mathias.** Gesundheitsverhalten Und Gesundheitsbildung Von Auszuildenden: Ein Empirischer Beitrag Aus Berufs- Und Wirtschaftspadagogischer Perspektive. (Illus.). 402p. 1999. 56.95 (*3-631-34642-5*) P Lang Pubng.

Bonse, U. & Rauch, H., eds. Neutron Interferometry. (Illus.). 1980. 69.00 (*0-19-851947-8*) OUP.

Bonse, Ulrich, ed. Developments in X-Ray Tomography. 276p. 1997. 59.00 (*0-8194-2571-0*) SPIE.

Bonser, Carol & Miskimins, R. W. Mountain Biking North Lake Tahoe's Best Trails. LC 97-15307. (Illus.). 140p. (Orig.). 1997. pap. 14.95 (*0-938665-40-5*) Fine Edge Prods.

— Mountain Biking South Lake Tahoe's Best Trails. LC 97-46182. (Illus.). 144p. 1998. pap. 14.95 (*0-938665-52-9*, Mtn Biking Pr) Fine Edge Prods.

***Bonser, Charles F., et al.** American Public Policy Problems: An Introductory Guide. 2nd ed. LC 99-30857. 394p. 1999. pap. text 49.00 (*0-13-022361-1*) P-H.

Bonser, Frederick G. The Reasoning Ability of Children in the Fourth, Fifth, & Sixth School Grades. LC 70-176580. (Columbia University. Teachers College. Contributions to Education Ser.: No. 37). reprint ed. 37.50 (*0-404-55037-1*) AMS Pr.

Bonser, W. & Stephens, T. A. Proverb Literature. 1972. 59.95 (*0-8490-0908-1*) Gordon Pr.

Bonser, Wilfred, ed. see Stephens, Thomas A.

Bonsey, Lynn & Healey, Lorna. Memories & Memorabilia: More Than 600 Easy Ways to Preserve Them. (Illus.). 203p. (Orig.). 1995. pap. text 15.00 (*0-7884-0208-0*) Heritage Bk.

Bonsib, Sandy. Folk Art Quilts: A Fresh Look. Reikes, Ursula, ed. LC 98-4502. (Illus.). 128p. 1998. pap. 24.95 (*1-56477-218-7*, B329, That Patchwrk Pl) Martingale & Co.

***Bonsib, Sandy.** Quilting More Memories: More Inspiration for Designing with Image Transfer. (Illus.). 80p. 2001. pap. 22.95 (*1-56477-349-3*) Martingale & Co.

Bonsib, Sandy. Quilting Your Memories: Inspirations for Designing with Image Transfers. LC 98-42874. (Illus.). 112p. 1999. pap. 24.95 (*1-56477-251-9*, B360, That Patchwrk Pl) Martingale & Co.

Bonsignore. Before the Law, 6 vols. 6th ed. (C). 1998. pap. text 44.36 (*0-395-87070-4*) HM.

Bonsignore, A. T. The Effect of Cutter Diameter on Spiral Bevel Tooth Proportions. (Technical Papers: Vol. P124.20). (Illus.). 13p. 1976. pap. text 30.00 (*1-55589-184-5*) AGMA.

Bonsignore, John J. Before the Law, 5 vols. 5th ed. LC 93-89687. (C). 1993. pap. text 44.36 (*0-395-67588-X*) HM.

Bonson, Enrique, jt. ed. see Vasarhelyi, Miklos A.

Bonson, James, et al. Pennsylvania Folk Art of Samuel L. Plank. 68p. 1994. text 29.95 (*0-9643721-0-X*) Kishacoquillas.

Bonsor, Jack A. Athens & Jerusalem: The Role of Philosophy in Theology. LC 93-14771. 192p. 1993. pap. 11.95 (*0-8091-3398-9*) Paulist Pr.

Bonsor, Jack A. & Fiorenza, Francis S. Rahner, Heidegger, & Truth: Karl Rahner's Notion of Christian Truth, The Influence of Heidegger. 226p. (Orig.). (C). 1987. lib. bdg. 44.50 (*0-8191-6159-4*) U Pr of Amer.

Bonsor, N. C. Transportation Rates & Economic Development in Northern Ontario. LC 77-369766. (Ontario Economic Council Research Studies: No. 7). (Illus.). 99p. reprint ed. pap. 30.70 (*0-8357-4016-1*, 203670600005) Bks Demand.

Bonsor, N. R. Guernsey Railway: The German Occupation Lines in Guernsey & the Alderney Railway. 60p. (C). 1985. 50.00 (*0-85361-329-X*) St Mut.

— Jersey Railway. (C). 1985. 60.00 (*0-85361-344-3*) St Mut.

***Bonsteel, Alan.** Forever Young: A Doctor's Guide to More Energy, Less Stress & Better Sex. 256p. 2000. 25.00 (*0-89087-969-9*) Celestial Arts.

Bonsteel, Alan. Forever Young: Fitness, Sexual Fulfillment & Well-Being for the Best Years of Your Life. Raab, Fred, ed. (Illus.). Date not set. 24.95 (*0-9669210-0-3*, 001) Forever Young Pr.

***Bonsteel, Alan.** Stay Young, Start Now. (Illus.). 2000. pap. 16.95 (*0-89087-974-5*) Celestial Arts.

Bonsteel, Alan, et al. A Choice for Our Children: Curing the Crisis in America's Schools. LC 97-5230. (Illus.). 272p. (Orig.). 1997. pap. 19.95 (*1-55815-496-5*) ICS Pr.

Bonstetten, Karl V. Von, see Von Bonstetten, Karl V.

Bonstetten, Karl Viktor von, see von Bonstetten, Karl Viktor.

Bonstetter, Karl. Bonstettiana Band I/1-2: Briefkorrespondenzen Karl Viktor von Bonstetten und Seines Kreises, 1753-1773. lxxxi, 988p. 1996. 88.95 (*3-906756-76-9*, Pub. by P Lang) P Lang Pubng.

— Bonstettiana Band II: Briefkorrespondenzen Karl Viktor von Bonstettens und Seines Kreises, 1773-1776. 630p. 1997. 65.95 (*3-906756-77-7*, Pub. by P Lang) P Lang Pubng.

— Bonstettiana Band VI: Briefkorrespondenzen Karl Viktor von Bonstettens und Seines Kreises, 1787-1793. 700p. 67.95 (*3-906756-78-5*, Pub. by P Lang) P Lang Pubng.

Bonstingl, John J. Schools of Quality: An Introduction to Total Quality Management in Education. 2nd ed. LC 96-12294. 150p. 1996. pap. 20.95 (*0-87120-263-8*, 196019) ASCD.

Bont. Mirad, Boy from Bosnia. (Longman Literature Ser.). 1995. pap. text. write for info. (*0-582-24949-X*, Pub. by Addison-Wesley) Longman.

Bont, L. G. De, see Stegenga, B.

Bont, L. G. De, see Stegenga, B. & De Bont, L. G.

Bont, L. G. De, see Stegenga, B.

Bont, L. G. De, see Stegenga, B. & De Bont, L. G.

Bont, Petra De, see De Bont, Petra.

Bonta, Bruce D. Peaceful Peoples: An Annotated Bibliography. 301p. 1993. 40.00 (*0-8108-2785-9*) Scarecrow.

Bonta, Bruce D. & Neal, James G., eds. The Role of the American Academic Library in International Programs. LC 92-4314. (Foundations in Library & Information Science: Vol. 27). 283p. 1992. 78.50 (*1-55938-383-6*) Jai Pr.

Bonta, I. L., ed. Recent Developments in the Pharmacology of Inflammatory Mediators. (Agents & Actions Supplements Ser.: No. 2). 178p. 1980. 50.00 (*0-8176-0914-8*) Birkhauser.

Bonta, I. L., et al, eds. Inflammation Mechanisms & Their Impact on Therapy. (Agents & Actions Supplements Ser.: No. 3). (Illus.). 192p. 1980. 106.50 (*0-8176-0913-X*) Birkhauser.

Bonta, James, jt. auth. see Andrews, D. A.

Bonta, Juan P. American Architects & Texts: A Computer-Aided Analysis of Architectural Discourse. LC 95-380. (Illus.). 296p. 1996. 55.00 (*0-262-02400-4*) MIT Pr.

— Eladio Dieste: Buildings & Projects. (Illus.). 1997. pap. text 35.00 (*0-8230-1601-3*) Watsn-Guptill.

Bonta, Marcia. Appalachian Autumn. (Pitt Series in Nature & Natural History). 256p. (C). 1994. pap. 15.95 (*0-8229-5534-2*); text 34.95 (*0-8229-3784-0*) U of Pittsburgh Pr.

— Appalachian Spring. LC 90-12478. (Illus.). 198p. (C). 1991. pap. 15.95 (*0-8229-5442-7*) U of Pittsburgh Pr.

— Appalachian Summer. 236p. 1999. text 34.95 (*0-8229-4095-7*) U of Pittsburgh Pr.

— Appalachian Summer. (Illus.). 236p. 1999. pap. 15.95 (*0-8229-5693-4*) U of Pittsburgh Pr.

— More Outbound Journeys in Pennsylvania: A Guide to Natural Places for Individual & Group Outings. LC 94-23946. (Illus.). 176p. 1995. 32.50 (*0-271-01444-X*); pap. 14.50 (*0-271-01445-8*) Pa St U Pr.

— Outbound Journeys in Pennsylvania: A Guide to Natural Places for Individual & Group Outings. LC 86-43283. (Illus.). 216p. 1987. pap. 14.95 (*0-271-00606-4*) Pa St U Pr.

Bonta, Marcia M. Women in the Field: America's Pioneering Women Naturalists. LC 90-20729. 320p. 1992. pap. 16.95 (*0-89096-489-0*) Tex A&M Univ Pr.

Bonta, Marcia M., ed. American Women Afield: Writings by Pioneering Women Naturalists. LC 94-3664. (Louise Lindsey Merrick Natural Environment Ser.: No. 20). (Illus.). 272p. (C). 1995. 35.00 (*0-89096-633-8*); pap. 16.95 (*0-89096-634-6*) Tex A&M Univ Pr.

An Asterisk (*) at the beginning of an entry indicates that the title is appearing for the first time.

Bonta, Stephen, ed. The Instrumental Music of Giovanni Legrenzi. (Publications in Music: No. 14). 224p. 1985. pap. 39.95 (*0-674-45620-3*) HUP.
— The Instrumental Music of Giovanni Legrenzi: La Cetra: Sonate a Due Tre e Quattro Stromenti Libro Quattro, Opus 10 (1673) (Publications in Music). 164p. 1992. text 39.95 (*0-674-45621-1*) HUP.
Bonta, Vanna. Flight: A Quantum Fiction Novel. LC 96-75987. 397p. 1996. pap. 14.95 (*0-912339-17-9*) Meridian Hse.
Bontadelli, James A., jt. auth. see Sullivan, William G.
***Bontadina, Nadja.** Alexander Herzen und die Schweiz: Das Verhaltnis des Russischen Publizisten und Aristokraten Zur Einzigen Republik Im Europa Seiner Zeit. 511p. 1999. 62.95 (*3-906762-28-9*) P Lang Pubng.
***Bontatibus, Donna.** The Seduction Novel of the Early Nation. LC 99-6796. (Illus.). 126p. 1999. pap. 16.95 (*0-87013-509-0*) Mich St U Pr.
Bonte, B. Jaw Reflexes of Periodontal Origin. No. 66. 125p. (Orig.). 1993. pap. 33.50 (*90-6186-549-2*, Pub. by Leuven Univ) Coronet Bks.
Bonte, J., jt. auth. see Van Damme, J. P.
Bonte, P. Dictionnaire de l'Ethnologie et de l'Anthropologie. (FRE.). 1991. lib. bdg. 195.00 (*0-8288-3830-5*, F112720) Fr & Eur.
Bontecou, Eleanor. The Federal Loyalty-Security Program. LC 73-17628. 377p. 1974. reprint ed. lib. bdg. 75.00 (*0-8371-7256-X*, BOFL, Greenwood Pr) Greenwood.
Bontekoe, Ron & Stepaniants, Marietta, eds. Justice & Democracy: Cross-Cultural Perspectives. LC 97-5096. 424p. 1997. pap. text 28.00 (*0-8248-1926-8*) UH Pr.
Bontekoe, Ron, jt. ed. see Deutsch, Eliot.
Bontekoe, Ronald. Dimensions of the Hermeneutic Circle. LC 95-32208. 272p. (C). 1996. text 49.95 (*0-391-03933-4*) Humanities.
Bontekoe, W. Y. Memorable Description of the East Indian Voyage, 1618-1625. Hodgkinson, C. B., tr. from DUT. (C). 1992. reprint ed. 26.00 (*81-206-0791-0*, Pub. by Asian Educ Servs) S Asia.
Bontekoe, Willem Y. Die Vier und Zwantzigste Schiffahrt. Veenendaal, Augustus J., ed. LC 93-28793. 120p. 1993. reprint ed. 75.00 (*0-8201-1485-5*) Schol Facsimiles.
***Bontekoning, Y. M. & Kreutzberger, E., eds.** Concepts of New-Generation Terminal & Terminal Nodes. (TRAIL Reports in Transportation Planing). (Illus.). 176p. 1999. pap. 37.50 (*90-407-1905-5*, Pub. by Delft U Pr) Coronet Bks.
Bontemp, Nicole, ed. The Vortex State: Proceedings of the NATO ASI Vortices in Superfluids, Cargese, Corsica (France, July 19-31 1993) LC 94-21076. (NATO ASI Series, Series C, Mathematical & Physical Science: 438). 1994. text 220.50 (*0-7923-2971-6*) Kluwer Academic.
Bontempelli, Bruno. The Traveler's Tree. Coverdale, Linda, tr. from FRE. 256p. 1994. 20.00 (*1-56584-150-6*, Pub. by New Press NY) Norton.
***Bontempelli, Massimo.** Separations: Two Novels of Mothers & Children. Gilson, Estelle, tr. & pref. by. LC 99-88837. 315p. 2000. 28.00 (*0-929701-61-5*) McPherson & Co.
Bontempi, Francisco, et al. The Game of Truth: A Humorous Guide to Self-Discovery. 168p. 2000. pap. 14.95 (*0-9668876-0-3*, Pub. by Educ Dynamics) IPG Chicago.
Bontempo, Charles J. & Saracco, Cynthia M. Database Management: Principles & Products. LC 95-16652. (C). 1995. text 56.00 (*0-13-380189-6*) Prntice Hall Bks.
Bontempo, John A., ed. Development of Biopharmaceutical Parenteral Dosage Forms. LC 97-15956. (Drugs & the Pharmaceutical Sciences Ser.: Vol. 85). (Illus.). 264p. 1997. text 135.00 (*0-8247-9981-X*) Dekker.
Bontemps, Arna. American Negro Poetry. (American Century Ser.). 1996. 16.10 (*0-606-04387-X*, Pub. by Turtleback) Demco.
Bontemps, Arna. Black Thunder: Gabriel's Revolt: Virginia, 1800. LC 91-34123. 254p. 1992. pap. 16.50 (*0-8070-6337-1*) Beacon Pr.
— Bubber Goes to Heaven. LC 98-35830. (Iona & Peter Opie Library of Children's Literature). (Illus.). 96p. (J). (gr. 1-7). 1998. 17.95 (*0-19-512365-4*) OUP.
Bontemps, Arna, ed. Golden Slippers. 1941. 10.00 (*0-06-010395-7*) HarpC.
— Great Slave Narratives. LC 77-84792. 1969. pap. 19.50 (*0-8070-5473-9*) Beacon Pr.
Bontemps, Arna, intro. American Negro Poetry: An Anthology. 973p. 1995. 11.00 (*0-8090-1564-1*) Hill & Wang.
Bontemps, Arna & Conroy, Jack. Anyplace but Here. LC 96-45508. 384p. 1997. pap. 19.95 (*0-8262-1116-X*) U of Mo Pr.
Bontemps, Arna & Hughes, Langston. The Pasteboard Bandit. LC 97-11626. (Iona & Peter Opie Library of Children's Literature). (Illus.). 96p. (J). (gr. 3-7). 1997. 16.95 (*0-19-511476-0*) OUP.
***Bontemps, Arna & Hughes, Langston.** Popo & Fifina: Children of Haiti. (The Iona & Peter Opie Library of Children's Literature). (Illus.). 128p. (YA). 2000. pap. 8.95 (*0-19-513939-9*) OUP.
Bontemps, Arna, ed. see Handy, W. C.
Bontemps, Arna W. God Sends Sunday. LC 74-148531. reprint ed. 15.00 (*0-404-00137-8*) AMS Pr.
— One Hundred Years of Negro Freedom. LC 80-10828. 276p. 1980. reprint ed. lib. bdg. 59.50 (*0-313-22218-5*, BOOY, Greenwood Pr) Greenwood.
Bontemps, Arna W. & Hughes, Langston. Popo & Fifina. (Iona & Peter Opie Library of Children's Literature). (Illus.). 128p. (YA). (gr. 3 up). 1993. 16.95 (*0-19-508765-8*) OUP.
Bonthous, Jean-Marie. Revealing the American Language of Intelligence. 83p. 1996. pap. 35.00 (*0-9621241-3-3*) SCIP.
Bonthron. Clinical Genetics. 1997. pap. text 32.00 (*0-7020-2351-5*) Bailliere Tindall.
Bonting, Sjoerd L. Advances in Space Biology & Medicine, Vol. 1. 352p. 1991. 128.50 (*1-55938-296-1*) Jai Pr.
Bonting, Sjoerd L., ed. Advances in Space Biology & Medicine, Vol. 2. 320p. 1992. 128.50 (*1-55938-409-3*) Jai Pr.
— Advances in Space Biology & Medicine, Vol. 4. 296p. 1995. 128.50 (*1-55938-411-5*) Jai Pr.
— Advances in Space Biology & Medicine, Vol. 6. 336p. 1997. 128.50 (*0-7623-0147-3*) Jai Pr.
— Advances in Space Biology & Medicine Vol. 3: European Isolation & Confinement Study. 288p. 1993. 128.50 (*1-55938-410-7*) Jai Pr.
— Advances in Space Biology & Medicine Vol. 5: European Isolation & Confinement Study: EXEMSI. 424p. 1996. 128.50 (*1-55938-970-2*) Jai Pr.
Bonting, Sjoerd L. & Cogoli, Augusto, eds. Advances in Space Biology & Medicine, Vol. 7. Date not set. 128.50 (*0-7623-0393-X*) Jai Pr.
Bontly, Susan W. & Sheridan, Carol J. Enchanted Journeys Beyond the Imagination: An Annotated Bibliography of Fantasy, Futuristic, Supernatural & Time Travel Romance, Vol. 2. annot. ed. 176p. 1996. spiral bd. 24.95 (*0-9647291-1-3*, RBV2) Blue Diamond Pubns.
— Enchanted Journeys Beyond the Imagination: An Annotated Bibliography of Fantasy, Futuristic, Supernatural, & Time Travel Romances, Vol. 1. LC 95-214180. 149p. 1995. spiral bd. 24.95 (*0-9647291-0-5*) Blue Diamond Pubns.
— Enchanted Journeys Beyond the Imagination: An Annotated Bibliography of Fantasy, Futuristic, Supernatural, & Time Travel Romances, Vol. 3. annot. ed. 329p. 1997. spiral bd. 24.95 (*0-9647291-4-8*, RBV3) Blue Diamond Pubns.
— Enchanted Journeys Beyond the Imagination: An Annotated Bibliography of Fantasy, Futuristic, Supernatural, & Time Travel Romances, Vol. 4. annot. ed. 350p. 1999. spiral bd. 24.95 (*0-9647291-5-6*, RBV4) Blue Diamond Pubns.
— Enchanted Journeys Beyond the Imagination: An Annotated Bibliography of Fantasy, Futuristic, Supernatural, & Time Travel Romances, Vols. 1 & 2. annot. ed. LC 96-227965. 352p. 1996. pap. text 39.95 (*0-9647291-3-X*, RBS2) Blue Diamond Pubns.
— Enchanted Journeys Beyond the Imagination: Master Index for Volumes 1-3. 77p. 1997. spiral bd. 9.95 (*0-9647291-2-1*, MI01) Blue Diamond Pubns.
— Enchanted Journeys Beyond the Imagination: Master Index for Volumes 1-4, Vol. 5. annot. ed. 100p. 1999. spiral bd. 9.95 (*0-9647291-6-4*, MI02) Blue Diamond Pubns.
Bontolotti, Paola, jt. auth. see Loon, James van.
Bontoux, J. & Bebin, J. Wastewater Management in Coastal Areas. (Water Science & Technology Ser.: Vol. 25). (Illus.). 304p. 1993. 156.50 (*0-08-042191-1*, Pergamon Pr) Elsevier.
Bontrager. Anatomy & Positioning, Nos. 1-18. 2nd ed. 1995. student ed. write for info. (*0-8016-6283-4*) Mosby Inc.
— Anatomy & Positioning, Nos. 19-25. 2nd ed. 1995. student ed. write for info. (*0-8016-6282-6*) Mosby Inc.
— Introduction to X-Ray Physics & Techniques. 90p. (C). (gr. 13). 1985. text, student ed. 23.95 (*0-8016-5721-0*, 05721) Mosby Inc.
— Radiographic Anatomy & Positioning Instructor's Ma... 1985. spiral bd. 21.95 (*0-8016-4505-0*) Mosby Inc.
— Radiographic Anatomy & Positioning Instructor's Ma... 1985. spiral bd. 60.00 (*0-8016-4494-1*) Mosby Inc.
— Radiographic Anatomy & Positioning Instructor's Manual. 1985. spiral bd. 23.95 (*0-8016-4524-7*) Mosby Inc.
— Radiologic A & P: A Self-Paced Multimedia Learning S. 1995. write for info. (*0-8016-6851-4*); write for info. (*0-8016-6852-2*) Mosby Inc.
— Textbook of Radiographic Positioning & Related Anatomy. 4th ed. LC 97-147908. (Illus.). 784p. (gr. 13). 1996. text 110.00 (*0-8151-0947-4*, 28893) Mosby Inc.
Bontrager, G. Edwin & Showalter, Nathan. It Can Happen Today! Principles of Church Growth from the Book of Acts. LC 86-15036. 96p. (Orig.). 1986. pap. 6.99 (*0-8361-3419-2*) Herald Pr.
Bontrager, G. Edwin, jt. auth. see Van Dyck, Nicholas B.
Bontrager, Goldie. Favorite Amish Recipes, Vol. 1. (Illus.). 32p. (Orig.). 1980. pap. 3.95 (*0-9651112-0-2*, Fav Amish Recipes) Bontrager Ent.
— Favorite Amish Recipes, Vol. 2. (Illus.). 42p. (Orig.). 1993. pap. 3.95 (*0-9651112-1-0*, Fav Amish Recipes) Bontrager Ent.
Bontrager, Ida B. Ozark Parson. 1978. pap. 5.50 (*0-87813-512-X*) Christian Light.
Bontrager, Jennifer, ed. see Lewis, Carla & Bertolino, Angela.
Bontrager, Kenneth L. Handbook of Radiographic Positioning & Techniques: Pocket Atlas. 3rd ed. (CHI & POR., Illus.). 296p. (C). 1998. pap. text 27.75 (*0-9641723-2-1*) Bontrager Pub.
— Pocket Handbook: Radiographic Positioning & Techniques. 2nd ed. (Illus.). 294p. 1995. pap. text 27.75 (*0-9641723-1-3*) Bontrager Pub.
— Pocket Handbook, Radiographic Positioning & Techniques: Student Edition. (Illus.). 290p. (Orig.). (C). 1994. pap. text 24.00 (*0-9641723-0-5*) Bontrager Pub.
— Radiographic Positioning & Related Anatomy Slide Set & IM, Vols. 1 & 2. 1997. write for info. (*0-8151-4377-X*) Mosby Inc.
Bontrager, Kenneth L. & Lampignano, John P. Radiographic Positioning & Related Anatomy, Vol. 1. (Illus.). 1997. wbk. ed. write for info. (*1-55664-403-5*) Mosby Inc.
— Radiographic Positioning & Related Anatomy, Vol. 2. (Illus.). 1997. wbk. ed. write for info. (*1-55664-404-3*) Mosby Inc.
Bontrager, Kenneth L. & Lampignano, John P. Radiographic Positioning & Related Anatomy Workbook & Laboratory Manual. 4th ed. (Illus.). 624p. 1997. wbk. ed., lab manual ed. write for info. (*0-8151-1373-0*) Mosby Inc.
Bontrager, Lisa, jt. auth. see Anderson, Paul.
Bontrager, Rhonda. God Gives Me a Family. LC 98-171845. (Illus.). 20p. (J). (ps-k). 1998. pap. 5.95 (*0-87813-959-1*) Christian Light.
Bonuccelli, M., et al, eds. Algorithms & Complexity: Proceedings of the Second Italian Conference, CIAC '94, Rome, Italy, February 23-25, 1994. LC 94-3186. (Lecture Notes in Computer Science Ser.: Vol. 778). viii, 222p. 1994. 39.95 (*0-387-57811-0*) Spr-Verlag.
Bonuccelli, U. & Rabey, J. M., eds. Old & New Dopamine Agonists in Parkinson's Disease. LC 95-37404. (Journal of Neural Transmission: No. 45). 1995. write for info. (*0-387-82717-X*) Spr-Verlag.
— Old & New Dopamine Agonists in Parkinson's Disease. LC 95-37404. (Journal of Neural Transmission: No. 45). 300p. 1996. pap. 105.00 (*3-211-82717-X*) Spr-Verlag.
Bonucci, E., ed. Bone Pathology. (Journal: Applied Pathology: Vol. 5, No. 3, 1987). (Illus.). 56p. 1987. pap. 32.25 (*3-8055-4655-6*) S Karger.
Bonucci, E. & Motta, P. M., eds. Ultrastructure of Skeletal Tissue. (Electron Microscopy in Biology & Medicine Ser.). (C). 1990. text 320.00 (*0-7923-0373-3*) Kluwer Academic.
Bonucci, Ermanno, ed. Calcification in Biological Systems. 432p. 1992. lib. bdg. 249.00 (*0-8493-5735-7*, QP535) CRC Pr.
Bonura, Larry S. The Art of Indexing. (Technical Communication Library). (Illus.). 256p. 1994. 39.99 (*0-471-01449-4*) Wiley.
— Indexing Technical Documents. (Illus.). 138p. (Orig.). 1992. pap. 34.95 (*0-9620415-0-5*); ring bd. 99.95 (*0-9620415-1-3*) Word Workers.
Bonus, Anna K. Astrology Theologized: The Spiritual Hermeneutics of Astrology & Holy Writ Being a Treatise upon the Influence of the Stars on Man & on the Art of Ruling Them by the Law of Grace (1835) 121p. 1993. reprint ed. pap. 16.95 (*1-56459-409-2*) Kessinger Pub.
***Bonus, Rick.** Locating Filipino Americans: Ethnicity & Cultural Politics of Space. (Asian American History & Culture Ser.). (Illus.). 248p. 2000. 69.50 (*1-56639-778-2*); pap. 19.95 (*1-56639-779-0*) Temple U Pr.
Bonutto, Osvaldo. A Migrant's Story: The Struggle & Success of an Italian-Australian, 1920s-1960s. LC 94-185740. 99p. 1995. pap. 16.95 (*0-7022-2660-2*, Pub. by Univ Queensland Pr) Intl Spec Bk.
***Bonvalot, Gabriel.** Across Tibet: Being Translation of "De Paris au Tonkin a Travers le Tibet Inconnu", 2 vols. Pitman, C. B., tr. LC 98-902753. 1998. 82.00 (*81-206-1049-0*, Pub. by Asian Educ Servs) S Asia.
Bonvalot, Marie. Le Vocabulaire Medical de Base, 2 vols., Set. (FRE.). 447p. 1989. pap. 59.95 (*0-7859-4808-2*) Fr & Eur.
Bonventre, Enzo, tr. see Clements, Arthur L.
Bonventre, Joseph V., jt. ed. see Schlondorff, Detlef.
Bonventre, Peter, jt. auth. see Cosell, Howard.
Bonventura, Enzo, tr. see De Caro, Andrea T.
Bonvenure, Peter, jt. auth. see Cosell, Howard.
Bonvicini, Gianni & Istituto Affari Internazionali Staff. A Renewed Partnership for Europe: Tackling European Security Challenges by Eu-NATO Interaction. LC 96-135547. (Aktuelle Materialien zur Internationalen Politik Ser.). 337p. 1995. write for info. (*3-7890-4129-7*) Nomos Verlags.
Bonvicini, Giovanni, ed. QED Structure Functions: AIP Conference Proceedings, No. 201. LC 90-80229. (Particles & Fields Ser.: No. 39). (Illus.). 456p. 1990. lib. bdg. 85.00 (*0-88318-671-3*) Am Inst Physics.
***Bonvicino, Regis.** Sky-Eclipse: Selected Poems. Palmer, Michael, tr. (Green Integer Bks.: No. 44). 128p. 1999. pap. 9.95 (*1-892295-34-2*, Pub. by Green Integer) SPD-Small Pr Dist.
Bonvicino, Regis, et al, eds. Nothing the Sun Could Not Explain: New Brazilian Poetry. (Sun & Moon Classics Ser.: Vol. 82). 200p. 1998. pap. 15.95 (*1-55713-366-2*) Sun & Moon CA.
Bonvillain, Nancy. The Cheyennes: People of the Plains. LC 95-49929. (Native Americans Ser.). (Illus.). 64p. (J). (gr. 4-6). 1996. lib. bdg. 21.90 (*0-7613-0015-5*) Millbrook Pr.
***Bonvillain, Nancy.** Language, Culture & Communication: The Meaning of Messages. 3rd ed. LC 99-38023. 405p. 1999. pap. text 39.80 (*0-13-010429-9*) P-H.
Bonvillain, Nancy. Native American Medicine: Indians of North America. LC 97-11427. 120p. (YA). (gr. 5 up). 1997. lib. bdg. 19.95 (*0-7910-4041-0*) Chelsea Hse.
— Studies on Iroquoian Culture. (Occasional Publications in Northeastern Anthropology: No. 6). 1980. 6.00 (*0-318-19885-1*) Fund Anthrop.
— Women & Men: Cultural Constructs of Gender. 2nd ed. LC 96-49654. 312p. 1997. pap. text 35.20 (*0-13-651076-0*) P-H.
***Bonvillain, Nancy.** Women & Men: Cultural Constructs of Gender. 3rd ed. LC 00-25060. 320p. 2000. pap. 32.00 (*0-13-025973-X*) P-H.
Bonville, W. J. Footnotes to a Fairytale: A Study in the Nature of Expression in the Arts. LC 79-50183. 192p. 1979. 15.00 (*0-87527-192-8*) Green.
Bonvillian, Gary & Murphy, Robert. The Liberal Arts College Adapting to Change: The Survival of Small Schools. LC 95-45053. (Studies in Higher Education: Vol. 09). (Illus.). 272p. 1996. text 50.00 (*0-8153-1946-0*, SS1011) Garland.
Bonvin, D., ed. Advanced Control of Chemical Processes 1994: A Postprint Volume from the IFAC Symposium, Kyoto, Japan, 25-27 May, 1994. LC 94-43037. (IFAC Postprint Ser.). 560p. (Orig.). 1994. pap. 111.00 (*0-08-042229-2*, Pergamon Pr) Elsevier.
Bonwell, Charles C. & Eison, James A. Active Learning: Creating Excitement in the Classroom. Fife, Jonathan D., ed. LC 91-65608. (ASHE-ERIC Higher Education Reports: No. 91-1). 98p. 1991. pap. 24.00 (*1-878380-08-7*) GWU Grad Schl E&HD.
Bonwetsch, Bernd, jt. auth. see Thurston, Robert W.
Bonwick, Colin. The American Revolution. 315p. (C). 1991. pap. text 18.00 (*0-8139-1347-0*) U Pr of Va.
Bonwick, James. Egyptian Belief & Modern Thought. (African Heritage Classical Research Studies). 460p. reprint ed. 30.00 (*0-938818-33-3*) ECA Assoc.
— Irish Druids & Old Irish Religions. LC 75-36830. (Occult Ser.). 1976. reprint ed. 28.95 (*0-405-07942-7*) Ayer.
***Bonwit, Delores.** Colors. (My Little Wipe-Off Board Bks.). (Illus.). 8p. (J). (ps-1). 2000. bds. 4.99 (*0-7681-0224-3*, McClanahan Book) Learn Horizon.
Bony, J. M. & Morimoto, M., eds. New Trends in Microlocal Analysis, Vol. VIII. (Illus.). 244p. 1997. 74.95 (*4-431-70192-3*) Spr-Verlag.
Bony, J. M., jt. ed. see Cattabriga, L.
Bony, Jean. French Gothic Architecture of the Twelfth & Thirteenth Centuries. LC 74-82842. (California Studies in the History of Art: No. XX). (Illus.). 640p. (C). 1982. pap. 65.00 (*0-520-05586-1*, Pub. by U CA Pr) Cal Prin Full Svc.
Bonyhady, Tim. The Colonial Image Australian Painting 1800-1880. 112p. 1988. text 67.50 (*0-7103-0320-3*) Routledge.
— Images in Opposition: Australian Landscape Painting, 1801-1890. 216p. 1992. pap. 35.00 (*0-19-553259-7*) OUP.
— Law & the Countryside. 290p. 1987. 96.00 (*0-86205-256-4*, U.K., MICHIE); pap. 48.00 (*0-86205-257-2*, U.K., MICHIE) LEXIS Pub.
— Places Worth Keeping: Conservationists, Politics & Law in Australia. 208p. 1994. pap. 19.95 (*1-86373-448-1*, Pub. by Allen & Unwin Pty) Paul & Co Pubs.
Bonyhady, Tim, ed. The Skottowe Manuscript, Vols. I & II. 190p. 1989. 385.00 (*0-7103-0362-9*, A3936) Routledge.
Bonyhady, Tim & Griffiths, Tom. Prehistory to Politics: John Mulvaney, the Humanities & the Public Intellectual. LC 97-205478. (Illus.). 284p. 1997. pap. 29.95 (*0-522-84748-X*, Pub. by Melbourne Univ Pr) Paul & Co Pubs.
***Bonynge, Richard.** A Collector's Guide to Theatrical Postcards. (Illus.). 117p. 2000. 25.00 (*0-7881-9402-X*) DIANE Pub.
Bonynge, Richard. Joan Sutherland & Richard Bonynge: With the Australian Opera. (Illus.). 173p. 1990. text 19.00 (*0-947131-37-X*) Gordon & Breach.
Bonynge, Richard, jt. auth. see Walsh, Basil.
Bonyun, David. Security for Open Systems. (C). 1995. text. write for info. (*0-201-54875-5*) Addison-Wesley.
***Bonz, Marianne.** The Past as Legacy. LC 99-56275. 2000. write for info. (*0-8006-3225-7*) Augsburg Fortress.
Bonzales De Leon, Teadoro, pref. Gonzales de Leon: Architecture As Art. LC 98-196038. (I Talenti Ser.). (FRE, ITA & KOR., Illus.). 144p. 1998. pap. write for info. (*88-7838-033-4*) Rockport Pubs.
Bonzek, Debra B. Rocky Mountain Snowflakes. 3rd ed. (Illus.). 28p. 1993. reprint ed. pap. 7.95 (*0-9661572-0-6*) Dream Bee Pubns.
— Rocky Mountain Snowflakes 2. (Illus.). 56p. (YA). (gr. 3 up). 1998. pap. 8.95 (*0-9661572-1-4*) Dream Bee Pubns.
Bonzi, Susan, ed. ASIS '93: "Integrating Technologies, Converging Professions," Proceedings of the 56th Annual Meeting of the American Society for Information Science. 334p. 1993. pap. 47.50 (*0-938734-78-4*) Info Today Inc.
Bonzini, C., et al. Semigroups - Algebraic Theory & Applications to Formal Languages & Codes. 348p. 1993. text 109.00 (*981-02-1521-5*) World Scientific Pub.
Bonzon, Jessica. Trend's Who's Who in Recycling Worldwide (WIW) Vol. 1: Plastics & Others. rev. ed. xxxvii, 400p. (C). 1996. 99.00 (*1-889370-00-2*) Trend Assocs.
— Trend's Who's Who in Recycling Worldwide (WIW) Vol. 2: Textiles & Others. 5th rev. ed. xxxvii, 400p. (C). 1996. 99.00 (*1-889370-01-0*) Trend Assocs.
— Trend's Who's Who in Recycling Worldwide (WIW) Vol. 3: Glass & Others. rev. ed. xxxvii, 400p. (C). 1996. 99.00 (*1-889370-02-9*) Trend Assocs.
— Trend's Who's Who in Recycling Worldwide (WIW) Vol. 4: Paper & Others. rev. ed. xxxvii, 400p. (C). 1996. write for info. (*1-889370-03-7*) Trend Assocs.
— Trend's Who's Who in Recycling Worldwide (WIW) Vol. 5: Metals & Others. rev. ed. xxxvii, 400p. (C). 1996. 99.00 (*1-889370-04-5*) Trend Assocs.
Bonzon, Paul-Jacques. The Runaway Flying Horse. (J). 1976. 5.99 (*0-689-81905-6*) S&S Childrens.
***Bonzon, Pierre, et al.** Formal Aspects of Context. LC 00-30181. (Applied Logic Ser.). 2000. write for info. (*0-7923-6350-7*) Kluwer Academic.
Boo, Elizabeth. Ecotourism: The Potentials & Pitfalls, Vol. 1. LC 89-70735. 95p. (Orig.). 1990. reprint ed. pap. 30.00 (*0-608-04236-6*, 206499300001) Bks Demand.
— Ecotourism: The Potentials & Pitfalls, Vol. 2. LC 89-70735. 183p. (Orig.). 1990. reprint ed. pap. 56.80 (*0-608-04237-4*, 206499300002) Bks Demand.
Boo, Mary R., jt. auth. see Decker, Larry E.
Boo, Max De, see De Boo, Max.
Boo, Michael. The Story of Figure Skating. LC 99-161147. 1998. mass mkt. 7.95 (*0-688-15821-8*, Wm Morrow) Morrow Avon.

B

B

***Boo, Michael.** The Story of Figure Skating. LC 98-13569. (Illus.). 224p. (gr. 5-9). 1998. 16.00 (*0-688-15820-X*, Wm Morrow) Morrow Avon.

Boo, Michael, ed. see Geddes, Les & Geddes, LaNelle.

Boobbyer, Philip. S. L. Frank: The Life & Work of a Russian Philosopher, 1877-1950. LC 94-34209. (Illus.). 304p. (C). 1995. text 45.00 (*0-8214-1110-1*) Ohio U Pr.

***Boobbyer, Philip.** The Stalin Era. LC 00-32171. (Sources in History Ser.). 2000. pap. write for info. (*0-415-18298-0*) Routledge.

Boobyer, C., ed. Leasing Finance. 3rd ed. 1997. pap. 200.00 (*1-85564-553-X*, Pub. by Euromoney) Am Educ Systs.

Booch, Grady. The Best of Booch: Designing Strategies for Object Technology. Eykholt, Ed, ed. (SIGS Referency Library: No. 7). 252p. (C). 1996. pap. 44.95 (*0-13-739616-3*) Cambridge U Pr.

***Booch, Grady.** The Complete UML Training Course. 470p. 2000. pap. text, student ed. 108.00 (*0-13-087013-7*) P-H.

Booch, Grady. Diseno Orientado a Objetos. (SPA.). 672p. (C). 1995. pap. text 26.66 (*0-201-60122-2*) Addison-Wesley.

— Object Oriented Analysis Design & Application. 2nd ed. 608p. (C). 1993. 62.95 (*0-8053-5340-2*) Benjamin-Cummings.

— Object Solutions: Managing the Object-Oriented Project. LC 95-24671. 669p. (C). 1995. pap. 36.95 (*0-8053-0594-7*) Addison-Wesley.

***Booch, Grady, et al.** The Complete UML Training Course. 2000. 129.99 incl. cd-rom (*0-13-087014-5*) P-H.

Booch, Grady, et al. Object-Oriented Analysis & Design with Applications. 3rd ed. (Object Technology Ser.). 704p. 2001. 64.95 (*0-201-89551-X*) Addison-Wesley.

— Software Engineering with Ada. 3rd rev. ed. LC 93-5093. (Series in Object-Oriented Software Engineering). 576p. (C). 1994. pap. 54.95 (*0-8053-0608-0*) Benjamin-Cummings.

— The Unified Modeling Language User Guide. LC 98-30436. (Addison-Wesley Object Technology Ser.). 512p. (C). 1998. 47.95 (*0-201-57168-4*) Addison-Wesley.

Boochny, Etty. The Footsteps of Jesus in the Holy Land. Capes, David B. & Markos, Louis, eds. (Illus.). 256p. Date not set. 29.95 (*0-9662775-0-3*, Dror Intl); pap. write for info. (*0-9662775-1-1*, Dror Intl); mass mkt. 24.95 (*0-9662775-3-8*, Dror Intl) N M Intl.

Boock, Gregory D., jt. auth. see Stuart, Kirk S.

Boock, Paula. Dare Truth or Promise. LC 98-51981. 170p. (YA). (gr. 9 up). 1999. 15.00 (*0-395-97117-9*) HM.

Boockholdt, James L. Accounting Information Systems. 3rd ed. 896p. (C). 1992. text 72.50 (*0-256-10841-2*, Irwn McGrw-H) McGrw-H Hghr Educ.

— Accounting Information Systems: Transaction Processing & Controls. 4th ed. LC 95-12099. (Undergraduate Accounting Ser.). 864p. (C). 1995. text 72.50 (*0-256-16680-3*, Irwn McGrw-H) McGrw-H Hghr Educ.

— Accounting Information Systems: Transaction Processing & Controls. 5th ed. LC 98-6855. 922p. 1998. 89.06 (*0-256-21885-4*) McGraw.

— Accounting Information Systems, International. 3rd ed. (C). 1994. text, student ed. 35.50 (*0-256-11415-3*, Irwn McGrw-H) McGrw-H Hghr Educ.

Boockholdt, James L., et al. CPS Accounting Information Systems Select Material. 2nd ed. 360p. (C). 1995. text 32.50 (*0-256-21124-8*, Irwn McGrw-H) McGrw-H Hghr Educ.

Boockholdt, James L., jt. auth. see O'Brien, James.

Boockmeier, Barbara, ed. see Tracy, Denise D.

Boocock, Colin. The Heyday of Nine Elms & Its Locomotives. 23.95 (*0-7110-2067-1*) Spec Mkting Intl.

Boocock, Sarane S. & Schild, E. O., eds. Simulation Games in Learning. LC 68-21913. 279p. 1968. reprint ed. pap. 86.50 (*0-608-01474-5*, 205951800001) Bks Demand.

Boocock, Sarane S., jt. ed. see Barnett, W. Steven.

Boodabugah Brothers Staff. Crash Bandicoot 3: Prima's Official Strategy Guide. LC 98-67668. (Games Ser.). 96p. 1998. per. 12.99 (*0-7615-1861-4*) Prima Pub.

***Boodakian, Florence Dee.** Tormenting Angel: A Psychoaesthetic Theory of Imagination. LC 99-35008. (Sexuality & Literature Ser.: Vol. 9). 144p. 1999. 41.95 (*0-8204-4553-3*) P Lang Pubng.

Boodey, David M., jt. auth. see Moseley, Lonnie E.

Boodhoo, I. J. Between Two Seasons Caribbean Writrs Series. LC 93-36168. (Longman Caribbean Writers Ser.). 314p. (C). 1995. pap. 16.80 (*0-582-22869-7*) Addison-Wesley.

Boodin, John E. God & Creation, 2 vols., Set. LC 75-3058. reprint ed. 67.50 (*0-404-59057-8*) AMS Pr.

— Time & Reality. LC 75-3064. (Philosophy in America Ser.). reprint ed. 39.50 (*0-404-59063-2*) AMS Pr.

Boodley. The Commercial Greenhouse. 2nd ed. 32p. 1997. pap. text, teacher ed. 13.95 (*0-8273-7312-0*) Delmar.

— The Commercial Greenhouse. 2nd ed. 32p. 1997. pap. text, teacher ed., lab manual ed. 12.75 (*0-8273-8234-0*) Delmar.

Boodley, James W. The Commercial Greenhouse. LC 78-74806. (Agriculture Ser.). 568p. (C). 1981. text 41.50 (*0-8273-1719-0*) Delmar.

— The Commercial Greenhouse. 2nd ed. LC 96-5396. 624p. 1996. mass mkt. 68.95 (*0-8273-7311-2*) Delmar.

— The Commercial Greenhouse. 2nd ed. (Agriculture Ser.). (C). 1997. pap. text, lab manual ed. 18.75 (*0-8273-8099-2*) Delmar.

Boodman, Terryl C., jt. auth. see Bridges, Herb.

Boodry, Bertie H., ed. see Russell, Thomas J.

Boodry, Sharon, ed. see Cooley, Chris.

Boody, Bertha M. A Psychological Study of Immigrant Children at Ellis Island. LC 79-129391. (American Immigration Collection. Series 2). 1970. reprint ed. 16.95 (*0-405-00546-6*) Ayer.

Boody, Charles G., ed. see Music Educators National Conference Staff.

***Boody, Manchester.** Thinking & Living. LC 99-66632. 75p. 2000. pap. 5.99 (*1-893181-30-8*) Le Gesse Stevens.

Boog, et al. Lesespass. 88p. 1989. text 19.25 (*3-468-49467-X*); text, teacher ed. 11.25 (*3-468-49468-8*) Langenscheidt.

Boog, Bob. Selling Homes 1 - 2 - 3: Insider Advice on Becoming A Surprisingly Better Part-Time or Full-Time Real Estate Agent. Quinn, Robin, ed. LC 98-96509. (Illus.). 200p. 1998. pap. 19.95 (*0-9666130-1-5*) T H S Intl.

***Boog, Hornst, et al, eds.** Germany & The Second World War. Osers, Ewald, tr. (Illus.). 1300p. 2000. text 220.00 (*0-19-822888-0*) OUP.

Boog, Horst, ed. The Conduct of the Air War in the Second World War: An International Comparison. LC 90-19960. (Studies in Military History). 784p. 1992. 47.50 (*0-85496-697-8*) Berg Pubs.

Boog, Horst, et al. Germany & the Second World War: The Attack on the Soviet Union, Vol. IV. McMurray, Dean S. et al, trs. from GER. LC 99-223914. (Illus.). 1,400p. 1999. text 225.00 (*0-19-822886-4*) OUP.

***Boogaart, Pieter.** A272. 2000. pap. 24.95 (*1-873429-29-0*) Pallas Athene.

***Boogaert, John F.** No Feet in Concrete Volume 1: Leadership in an Entrepreneurial World. LC 00-103862. (Illus.). 128p. 2000. 21.95 (*0-9700981-5-4*) Panagraph Inc.

Boogerd, P. Dynamic Compaction of Ceramics: New Models to Determine the Shock Wave States of Solids & Powders. 240p. 1995. pap. 97.50 (*90-407-1116-X*, Pub. by Delft U Pr) Coronet Bks.

Boogert, Bob Van den, see Van den Boogert, Bob.

Boogher, William F. Gleanings of Virginia History. 443p. 1993. reprint ed. pap. text 38.00 (*1-55613-871-7*) Heritage Bk.

— Gleanings of Virginia History: An Historical & Genealogical Collection, Largely from Original Sources. 443p. 1995. pap. 35.00 (*0-8063-0048-5*, 605) Clearfield Co.

Boogieman, D. A. Gabriel's Song. 44p. 1996. pap. 11.95 (*1-881786-90-0*, OPC Lyrical Tongue Twister) Ohio PC.

— I Can't Believe It's Not Butta. 1996. pap. 9.95 (*1-881786-91-9*, OPC Lyrical Tongue Twister) Ohio PC.

— A Word Is Worth a Thousand Pictures: Memories. 28p. 1996. pap. 6.95 (*1-881786-92-7*, OPC Lyrical Tongue Twister) Ohio PC.

Booher. Personal Letters for Living. (C). 1997. text 34.95 (*0-13-264078-3*); pap. text 15.95 (*0-13-264060-0*) P-H.

Booher, Diana D. Winning Sales Letters: A Handbook of Model Sales & Marketing Letters. 331p. 1989. 51.95 (*0-669-20876-0*) Jossey-Bass.

Booher, Dianna. Communicate with Confidence! How to Say It Right the First Time & Every Time. 432p. 1994. 39.95 (*0-07-006455-5*) McGraw.

— Communicate with Confidence! How to Say It Right the First Time & Every Time. 413p. 1994. pap. 14.95 (*0-07-006606-X*) McGraw.

— Como Hablar En Publico Sin Temor.Tr. of Confident Communicater. (SPA.). 144p. 1994. pap. 7.99 (*0-8297-1844-3*) Vida Pubs.

***Booher, Dianna.** E-Writing. 2001. pap. write for info. (*0-7434-1258-3*, PB Trade Paper) PB.

Booher, Dianna. First Thing Monday Morning: Keeping Your Appointment with God. LC 98-66299. 1998. pap. text 12.99 (*0-89221-420-1*) New Leaf.

— Fresh Cut Flower for a Friend. LC 98-111090. (Illus.). 96p. 1997. 9.99 (*0-8499-5274-3*) Word Pub.

— Get a Life Without Sacrificing Your Career: How to Make More Time for What's Really Important. 1996. text 24.95 (*0-07-006646-9*) McGraw.

— Get a Life Without Sacrificing Your Career: How to Make More Time for What's Really Important. 295p. 1996. pap. 12.95 (*0-07-006647-7*) McGraw.

— Get Ahead, Stay Ahead! Learn the 70 Most Important Career Skills, Traits & Attitudes to: Stay Employed! Get Promoted! Get a Better Job! LC 97-9261. 192p. 1997. pap. 12.95 (*0-07-006648-5*) McGraw.

— Great Personal Letters for Busy People: 300 Ready-To-Use Letters for Every Occasion. LC 97-9027. 391p. 1997. pap. 19.95 (*0-07-006656-6*) McGraw.

— Love Notes: From My Heart to Yours. LC 98-131733. (Illus.). 7p. 1997. 9.99 (*0-8499-5263-8*) Word Pub.

— Ten Smart Moves Women Make to Succeed in Love & Life. LC 99-218942. 208p. 1997. 14.99 (*1-57757-016-2*) Honor Bks OK.

— Would You Put That in Writing? How to Write Your Way to Success in Business. rev. ed. (Illus.). 160p. 1992. 18.95 (*0-8160-2765-X*) Facts on File.

Booher, Dianna D. Complete Letterwriter's Almanac. LC 91-23491. 368p. (C). 1991. text 39.95 (*0-13-155904-4*, Busn) P-H.

— Cutting Paperwork in the Corporate Culture. LC 85-31204. 191p. reprint ed. pap. 59.30 (*0-7837-1360-6*, 204150800021) Bks Demand.

— The Executive's Portfolio of Model Speeches for All Occasions. 352p. (C). 1991. text 39.95 (*0-13-296989-0*) P-H.

— The Executive's Portfolio of Model Speeches for All Occasions. 352p. (C). 1992. pap. text 18.95 (*0-13-293317-9*) P-H.

— Good Grief, Good Grammar. 272p. 1989. mass mkt. 4.99 (*0-449-21681-0*, Crest) Fawcett.

— The New Secretary: How to Handle People As Well As You Handle Paper. LC 85-15864. 352p. 1985. reprint ed. pap. 109.20 (*0-608-02820-7*, 206388700007) Bks Demand.

— Rape: What Would You Do If? rev. ed. 160p. (J). (gr. 7 up). 1991. pap. 6.95 (*0-671-74546-8*, Julian Messner); lib. bdg. 13.95 (*0-671-74538-7*, Julian Messner) Silver Burdett Pr.

— To the Letter: A Handbook of Model Letters for the Busy Manager. LC 97-7628. (Business & Management Ser.). 528p. 1998. reprint ed. pap. 25.95 (*0-7879-4479-3*) Jossey-Bass.

Booher, Dianna Daniels. Little Book of Big Questions, 1. 1999. 9.99 (*0-8499-5482-7*) Word Pub.

***Booher, Dianna Daniels.** Mother's Gifts to Me. 1999. 12.99 (*0-8499-5509-2*) J Countryman.

— Well Connected: Power Your Own Soul by Plugging into Others. 2000. pap. write for info. (*0-8499-3736-1*) Word Pub.

Booher, Dianna Daniels. Worth of a Woman's Words: The Power of What We Say to Build or Destroy, Heal or Hurt, Inspire or, 1. LC 99-30236. 1999. pap. text 12.99 (*0-8499-3735-3*) Word Pubng.

Booher, Harold R. The Manprint: Approach to Systems Integration. 1990. text 59.95 (*0-442-00383-8*, VNR) Wiley.

— Origins, Icons & Illusions. LC 98-159250. 17p. 1997. pap. 29.95 (*0-87527-515-X*) Green.

Booher, James M. Prevention & Care of Athletic Injuries. 3rd ed. 202p. 1995. pap. 18.95 (*0-945483-40-6*) E Bowers Pub.

Booher, Jerry, jt. auth. see Roberts, Judy G.

Booher, Jerry, ed. see Roberts, Judy G.

Booher, Jery & Roberts, Judy G. Making Collector Plates on Your Scroll Saw. (Illus.). 50p. (Orig.). 1994. pap. 12.95 (*1-56523-050-7*) Fox Chapel Pub.

Booher, Ned, jt. auth. see Howard County Historical Society Staff.

Booij, C. J. & Den Nijs, Loes, eds. Arthropod Natural Enemies in Arable Land II: II. Survival, Reproduction & Enhancement. (Acta Jutlandica, 71:2; Natural Science Ser.: No. 10). 275p. 1996. pap. 27.00 (*87-7288-672-2*, Pub. by Aarhus Univ Pr) David Brown.

Booij, Geert. The Phonology of Dutch. (Phonology of the World's Languages Ser.: Vol. 2). (Illus.). 216p. 1995. text 55.00 (*0-19-824027-9*) OUP.

— The Phonology of Dutch. (The Phonology of the World's Languages Ser.). (Illus.). 218p. 1999. pap. text 29.95 (*0-19-823869-X*) OUP.

— Yearbook of Morphology 1997. 316p. 1998. 116.00 (*0-7923-5092-8*) Kluwer Academic.

Booij, Geert, ed. Yearbook of Morphology, 1992. 300p. (C). 1993. text 189.50 (*0-7923-1937-0*) Kluwer Academic.

— Yearbook of Morphology, 1993. 288p. (C). 1994. text 205.50 (*0-7923-2494-3*) Kluwer Academic.

— Yearbook of Morphology, 1994. (Yearbook of Morphology Ser.). 320p. (C). 1995. text 199.00 (*0-7923-3244-X*) Kluwer Academic.

Booij, Geert & Van Marle, Jaap. Yearbook of Morphology, 1989. 300p. 80.00 (*90-6765-444-2*); pap. 57.70 (*90-6765-445-0*) Mouton.

Booij, Geert & Van Marle, Jaap, eds. Yearbook of Morphology. viii, 328p. (Orig.). (C). 1988. pap. 73.10 (*90-6765-376-4*) Mouton.

***Booij, Geert & Van Marle, Jaap, eds.** Yearbook of Morphology 1998. 320p. 1999. 128.00 (*0-7923-6035-4*, Kluwer Acad) Kluwer Academic.

Booij, Geert & Van Marle, Jaap, eds. Yearbook of Morphology, 1990. vi, 241p. (Orig.). (C). 1991. pap. text 53.85 (*3-11-013374-1*) Mouton.

— Yearbook of Morphology, 1991. (Yearbook of Morphology Ser.). 268p. (C). 1992. text 125.00 (*0-7923-1416-6*) Kluwer Academic.

— Yearbook of Morphology, 1996. 1997. text 125.50 (*0-7923-4563-0*) Kluwer Academic.

***Booij, Herausgegeben von Geert, et al, eds.** Morphology/Morphologie, 2 vols. 1999. 441.00 (*3-11-011128-4*) De Gruyter.

Boojamra, John. The Church & Social Reform: The Policies of the Patriarch Athanasios of Constantinople. x, 181p. 1993. 30.00 (*0-8232-1334-X*); pap. 19.95 (*0-8232-1335-8*) Fordham.

Boojamra, John L. Foundations for Christian Education. LC 89-6075. 245p. (Orig.). 1989. pap. 11.95 (*0-88141-050-0*) St Vladimirs.

Boojamra, Lee, ed. see Grey, Leslie.

Boojamra, Lee, ed. see Leonhard, Gwen & Mast, Jennie.

Boojamra, Lee, ed. see Williams, Karen.

Book. Encyclopedia of Origami & Papercraft Techniques. 1995. 19.98 (*0-7858-0441-2*) Bk Sales Inc.

Book & Workbooks, Corporation Staff, jt. auth. see Concato, Cynthia.

Book, Albert C. Fundamentals of Copy & Layout: A Manual. 2nd ed. 256p. 1994. pap. 19.95 (*0-8442-3030-8*, NTC Business Bks) NTC Contemp Pub Co.

Book, Albert C. & Schick, C. Dennis. Fundamentals of Copy & Layout. 2nd ed. 256p. 1995. 39.95 (*0-8442-3028-6*) NTC Contemp Pub Co.

— Fundamentals of Copy & Layout. 3rd ed. (Illus.). 240p. 1996. 47.95 (*0-8442-3022-7*, NTC Business Bks); pap. 24.95 (*0-8442-3024-3*, NTC Business Bks) NTC Contemp Pub Co.

Book, Albert C., et al. The Radio & Television Commercial. 232p. 1994. pap. 19.95 (*0-8442-3097-9*) NTC Contemp Pub Co.

— The Radio & Television Commercial. 3rd rev. ed. (Illus.). 232p. 1995. pap. 19.95 (*0-8442-3013-8*, NTC Business Bks) NTC Contemp Pub Co.

Book, Beverley C. & Music, David H. Half a Sixpence - Musical. 151p. 1967. pap. 5.95 (*0-87129-178-9*, H01) Dramatic Pub.

Book Builders, Inc. Staff. Macmillan Encyclopedia of the Environment, Vol. 1. LC 96-29045. 1997. 50.00 (*0-02-897382-8*) Mac Lib Ref.

— Macmillan Encyclopedia of the Environment, Vol. 2. LC 96-29045. 1997. 50.00 (*0-02-897383-6*) Mac Lib Ref.

— Macmillan Encyclopedia of the Environment, Vol. 3. LC 96-29045. 1997. 50.00 (*0-02-897384-4*) Mac Lib Ref.

— Macmillan Encyclopedia of the Environment, Vol. 5. LC 96-29045. 1997. 50.00 (*0-02-897386-0*) Mac Lib Ref.

— Macmillan Encyclopedia of the Environment, Vol. 6. LC 96-29045. 1997. 50.00 (*0-02-897387-9*) Mac Lib Ref.

— Storytelling Encyclopedia: Historical, Cultural, & Multiethnic Approaches to Oral Traditions Around the World. Leeming, David A., ed. LC 97-23081. 543p. 1997. boxed set 69.95 (*1-57356-025-1*) Oryx Pr.

Book Builders, Incorporated Staff. Macmillan Encyclopedia of the Environment. LC 96-29045. 1997. 50.00 (*0-02-897385-2*) S&S Trade.

Book, C. L. Irish Birthday Book. 160p. 1995. 12.99 (*0-7858-0378-5*) Bk Sales Inc.

Book, Cassandra, jt. auth. see Galvin, Kathleen M.

***Book, Chris.** K Foundation Burn a Million Quid. 1998. pap. 22.50 (*1-899858-37-7*, Pub. by Ellipsis) Norton.

Book Company Paperblank Staff. Iris. (Wildflowers Ser.). 160p. 1999. 14.95 (*1-55156-016-X*) Paperblank.

Book, David L. Problems for Puzzlebusters. LC 92-90284. (Illus.). 358p. (YA). (gr. 7-12). 1992. 24.95 (*0-9633217-0-6*) Enigmatics.

Book Division Staff. Crossing America: National Geographic's Guide to the Interstates. LC 94-16464. 1995. pap. 21.95 (*0-87044-984-2*) Natl Geog.

Book, Doyle C. The Threshold Is High: The Brethren in Christ in Japan. (Illus.). xii, 209p. 1986. pap. 7.95 (*0-916035-15-8*) Evangel Indiana.

Book for Teens Staff. Book for Teens. LC 99-35041. 1999. 21.99 (*0-8423-3490-4*); pap. text 14.99 (*0-8423-3491-2*) Tyndale Hse.

Book, Fredrik. Hans Christian Andersen: A Biography. Schoolfield, George C., tr. LC 62-10765. 284p. reprint ed. pap. 88.10 (*0-608-30802-1*, 200474800046) Bks Demand.

Book, Howard, jt. auth. see Stein, Steven.

Book, Howard E. How to Practice Brief Psychodynamic Psychotherapy: The Core Conflictual Relationship Theme Method. LC 97-35592. 181p. 1997. text 39.95 (*1-55798-465-4*) Am Psychol.

Book Industry Study Group Staff & Publishers Marketing Association Staff. The Rest of Us: The First Study of America's 53,000 Independent, Smaller Book Publishers. (Illus.). 92p. 1999. pap. write for info. (*0-940016-73-7*) Bk Indus Study.

Book, Lana, et al. Coming Full Circle. Bright, Susan, ed. LC 96-69453. (New Voices Ser.: Vol. 10). (Illus.). 116p. (Orig.). 1997. pap. 12.95 (*0-911051-85-6*) Plain View.

Book, Leon, jt. auth. see McAlpine, David.

Book, Linda. A Frog's Tale. (Illus.). 32p. (Orig.). (J). (gr. k-6). 1990. lib. bdg. 5.00 (*0-9626294-0-5*) Words & Muse Prodns.

— The Overall Collection: Songs by Linda Book. (Illus.). 87p. (J). (gr. k-6). 1994. spiral bd. 14.00 (*0-9626294-1-3*) Words & Muse Prodns.

Book of the Dead Staff. The Chapters of Coming Forth by Day, 3 vols., Set. LC 73-18833. reprint ed. 125.00 (*0-404-11303-6*) AMS Pr.

Book, R. V., ed. see Van Breugel, F.

Book, Randall. Bama & the Bear. 199p. 1983. 19.95 (*0-934126-33-X*) CFI Dist.

Book Report & Library Talk Staff, compiled by. Elementary Author/Illustrator Profiles. LC 95-52743. 170p. 1996. ring bd. 29.95 (*0-938865-47-1*) Linworth Pub.

Book, Rick. Necking With Louise. 168p. (YA). (gr. 9-12). 1999. pap. 7.95 (*0-88995-194-2*, Pub. by Red Deer) Genl Dist Srvs.

Book, Rita. Big Questions Little Kids Ask: Answers to the 100 Most Asked Questions by Kids. 144p. (Orig.). 1994. pap. 7.00 (*0-380-77184-5*, Avon Bks) Morrow Avon.

Book, Ronald V., ed. Rewriting Techniques & Applications: 4th International Conference, RTA-91 Como, Italy, April 10-12, 1991 Proceedings. (Lecture Notes in Computer Science Ser.: Vol. 488). vii, 458p. 1991. 47.95 (*0-387-53904-2*) Spr-Verlag.

Book, Ronald V. & Otto, Friedrich. String-Rewriting Systems. LC 92-37370. (Texts & Monographs in Computer Science). 189p. 1993. 58.95 (*0-387-97965-4*) Spr-Verlag.

Book, Ronald V., ed. see Yongging, Liu & Zhaoshu, Feng.

Book Sales. Roses. 1998. pap. text 4.99 (*0-7858-0976-7*) Bk Sales Inc.

***Book Sales, Inc. Staff.** Heavy Equipment: Giants of Construction & Mining. (Illus.). 2000. 19.99 (*0-7858-1171-0*) Bk Sales Inc.

Book Sales, Inc. Staff. Illustrated Encyclopedia of Aquarium Fish. 1993. 12.98 (*1-55521-879-2*) Bk Sales Inc.

Book Sales, Inc. Staff. Illustrated Encyclopedia of the World's Aircraft. 19.98 (*0-89009-771-2*) Bk Sales Inc.

Book Sales, Inc. Staff. Introduction to Painting the Nude. 128p. 1993. 14.98 (*1-55521-902-0*) Bk Sales Inc.

— Luxury Trains. 1995. 17.98 (*0-7858-0225-8*) Bk Sales Inc.

***Book Sales, Inc. Staff.** MacMillan Dictionary of Quotations. 2000. 17.99 (*0-7858-1191-5*) Bk Sales Inc.

Book Sales, Inc. Staff. Mensa Logic Puzzles. 1996. 7.98 (*0-7858-0592-3*) Bk Sales Inc.

— Mensa Mind Power. 1996. 7.98 (*0-7858-0591-5*) Bk Sales Inc.

Book Sales, Inc. Staff. Mexican Main Dishes. 80p. 1996. 10.98 (*0-7858-0383-1*) Bk Sales Inc.

Book Sales, Inc. Staff. Mexican Snacks & Salsas. 80p. 1996. 10.98 (*0-7858-0385-8*) Bk Sales Inc.

— Special Forces. 1990. 12.98 (*1-55521-575-0*) Bk Sales Inc.

— Step by Step Art of Dried Flowers. 1993. 12.98 (*1-55521-886-5*) Bk Sales Inc.

— Step by Step Art of Papier Mache. 1993. 12.98 (*1-55521-885-7*) Bk Sales Inc.

— Thirty-Five Millimeter Camera Handbook. 1994. 17.98 (*0-7858-0019-0*) Bk Sales Inc.

An Asterisk (*) at the beginning of an entry indicates that the title is appearing for the first time.

Book Sales Incorporated, Staff. A Century of Gay Erotica. 1998. 10.99 (*0-7858-0890-6*) Bk Sales Inc.
— A Century of Lesbian Erotica. 1998. 10.99 (*0-7858-0891-4*) Bk Sales Inc.
— Identifying Spiders. 1998. 7.99 (*0-7858-0884-1*) Bk Sales Inc.
Book Sales Incorporated Staff. Simple Stenciling. 32p. 1997. pap. text 9.98 (*0-7858-0806-X*) Bk Sales Inc.
Book Sales Staff. Ancient Egyptian Culture. 1998. pap. text 6.99 (*0-7858-0996-1*) Bk Sales Inc.
— Art Deco Fashion & Jewelry. 1998. pap. text 6.99 (*0-7858-0987-2*) Bk Sales Inc.
— Art Deco Furniture & Metalwork. 1998. pap. text 6.99 (*0-7858-0986-4*) Bk Sales Inc.
— Art Nouveau Glass & Ceramics. 1998. pap. text 6.99 (*0-7858-0990-2*) Bk Sales Inc.
— Assess Yourself. 1998. pap. text 7.99 (*0-7858-0957-0*) Bk Sales Inc.
— Batik. 1998. 8.99 (*0-7858-1006-4*) Bk Sales Inc.
— Bead Work. 1998. 8.99 (*0-7858-1003-X*) Bk Sales Inc.
— Blues: Keeping the Faith. 1998. 29.99 (*0-7858-0900-7*) Bk Sales Inc.
— Bonsai. 1998. pap. text 4.99 (*0-7858-0974-0*) Bk Sales Inc.
— Brazilian Cooking. 1998. 12.99 (*0-7858-0888-4*) Bk Sales Inc.
— Cacti. 1998. pap. text 4.99 (*0-7858-0978-3*) Bk Sales Inc.
— Cadillac Century. 1998. 17.99 (*0-7858-0917-1*) Bk Sales Inc.
— Cats. 1998. 4.99 (*0-7858-0965-1*) Bk Sales Inc.
— Celtic Myths & Beliefs. 1998. pap. text 6.99 (*0-7858-0997-X*) Bk Sales Inc.
— Celts-Artists & Storytellers. 1998. pap. text 6.99 (*0-7858-0998-8*) Bk Sales Inc.
— Christmas Crafts. 1998. 8.99 (*0-7858-1004-8*) Bk Sales Inc.
— Complete Book of Sportfishing: Spinning & Baitcasting. 1998. 19.99 (*0-7858-0919-8*) Bk Sales Inc.
— Contemporary Flower Arranger. 1998. 19.99 (*0-7858-1020-X*) Bk Sales Inc.
— Decoupage. 1998. 8.99 (*0-7858-1001-3*) Bk Sales Inc.
— Dogs. 1998. pap. text 4.99 (*0-7858-0964-3*) Bk Sales Inc.
— Exotic Birds. 1998. pap. text 4.99 (*0-7858-0969-4*) Bk Sales Inc.
— Fossils. 1998. pap. text 4.99 (*0-7858-0970-8*) Bk Sales Inc.
— Freshwater Aquarium Fish. 1998. pap. text 4.99 (*0-7858-0968-6*) Bk Sales Inc.
— Gemstones. 1998. pap. text 4.99 (*0-7858-0972-4*) Bk Sales Inc.
— Giant Book of the Cat. 1998. 29.99 (*0-7858-0946-5*) Bk Sales Inc.
— Giant Book of the Dog. 1998. 29.99 (*0-7858-0947-3*) Bk Sales Inc.
— Gods & Pharaohs of Ancient Egypt. 1998. pap. text 6.99 (*0-7858-0999-6*) Bk Sales Inc.
— Herbs. 1998. pap. text 4.99 (*0-7858-0975-9*) Bk Sales Inc.
— Horses. 1998. pap. text 4.99 (*0-7858-0966-X*) Bk Sales Inc.
— Houseplants. 1998. pap. text 4.99 (*0-7858-0977-5*) Bk Sales Inc.
— Identifying Pocket Knives. 1998. pap. text 7.99 (*0-7858-1026-9*) Bk Sales Inc.
— Jazz: Legends of Style. 1998. 29.99 (*0-7858-0899-X*) Bk Sales Inc.
— Lateral Thinking. 1998. pap. text 7.99 (*0-7858-0956-2*) Bk Sales Inc.
— Marine Aquarium Fish. 1998. pap. text 4.99 (*0-7858-0967-8*) Bk Sales Inc.
— Mask Making. 1998. 8.99 (*0-7858-1008-0*) Bk Sales Inc.
— Pre-Raphaelites. 1998. pap. text 6.99 (*0-7858-0988-0*) Bk Sales Inc.
— Puppet Making. 1998. 8.99 (*0-7858-1007-2*) Bk Sales Inc.
— Pyramids. 1998. pap. text 6.99 (*0-7858-1000-5*) Bk Sales Inc.
— Rocks & Minerals. 1998. pap. text 4.99 (*0-7858-0971-6*) Bk Sales Inc.
— Shells. 1998. pap. text 4.99 (*0-7858-0973-2*) Bk Sales Inc.
— Stained Glass. 1998. 8.99 (*0-7858-1005-6*) Bk Sales Inc.
— Tie-Dyeing. 1998. 8.99 (*0-7858-1002-1*) Bk Sales Inc.
— Tiffany Glass. 1998. pap. text 6.99 (*0-7858-0989-9*) Bk Sales Inc.
— Turkish Cooking. 1998. 12.99 (*0-7858-0918-X*) Bk Sales Inc.
— Watches. 1998. pap. text 6.99 (*0-7858-0991-0*) Bk Sales Inc.
***Book Sales Staff, ed.** Nevermore: The Poems of E. A. Poe. 2000. 8.99 (*0-7858-1213-X*) Bk Sales Inc.
Book, Stephen A. Essentials of Statistics. (Illus.). 1978. student ed. 8.95 (*0-07-006466-0*) McGraw.
Book Store Staff. Learning to Deny Self. (Truth in Life Adult Study Work Bks.). 52p. 1998. pap., wbk. ed. write for info. (*0-9620615-3-0*) Guardian Truth Found.
Book, Tony. Soccer. (Skills of the Game Ser.). (Illus.). 144p. 1995. pap. 19.95 (*1-85223-557-8*, Pub. by Crolwood) Trafalgar.
Book, Wayne J., ed. see American Society of Mechanical Engineers Staff.
Book, Wayne J., jt. ed. see Hardt, D. E.
Book, William F. & Bryan, William L. The Psychology of Skill: Three Studies. LC 73-3029. (Classics in Psychology Ser.). 1977. reprint ed. 24.95 (*0-405-05157-3*) Ayer.
Bookbinder, Albert I. Computer-Assisted Investment Handbook. LC 82-61048. (Illus.). 220p. 1983. pap. text 119.95 incl. disk (*0-916106-03-9*) Prog Pr.
— Investment Decision Making. LC 67-29760. (Illus.). 145p. 1968. 9.95 (*0-916106-00-4*) Prog Pr.
— Security Options Strategy. LC 76-46120. 201p. 1976. 15.00 (*0-916106-01-2*) Prog Pr.
Bookbinder, Bernie. Long Island: People & Places, Past & Present. rev. ed. LC 98-21839. (Illus.). 280p. 1998. 39.95 (*0-8109-4255-0*, Pub. by Abrams) Time Warner.
— Out at the Old Ball Game: A Novel. LC 94-37578. 278p. 1995. 21.95 (*1-882593-09-X*) Bridge Wrks.
Bookbinder, David. Housing Options for Older People. (C). 1989. 35.00 (*0-86242-055-5*, Pub. by Age Concern Eng) St Mut.
— Housing Options for Older People. 120p. (C). 1991. 50.00 (*0-86242-108-X*, Pub. by Age Concern Eng) St Mut.
Bookbinder, David J. LOTUS GD 1 2 3 RELEASE 3. 512p. 1988. pap. 22.95 (*0-201-15038-7*) Addison-Wesley.
Bookbinder, J., jt. ed. see Giampapa, M.
Bookbinder, Jay A., jt. ed. see Donahue, Robert A.
Bookbinder, Paul. Weimar Germany. LC 95-47914. 160p. 1997. pap. 16.95 (*0-7190-4287-9*) St Martin.
Bookbinder, Robert. Amusing & Unorthodox Definitions. LC 99-94623. 115p. 1999. pap. 6.95 (*0-7392-0089-5*, PO2961) Morris Pubng.
— Classic Gangster Films. (Illus.). 256p. 1993. pap. 16.95 (*0-8065-1467-1*, Citadel Pr) Carol Pub Group.
— The Films of Bing Crosby. (Illus.). 1977. 14.95 (*0-8065-0598-2*, Citadel Pr) Carol Pub Group.
— The Films of the Seventies. (Illus.). 288p. 1984. reprint ed. pap. 16.95 (*0-8065-0927-9*, Citadel Pr) Carol Pub Group.
— Funny School Excuses. LC 99-95349. (Illus.). 100p. 1999. pap. 6.95 (*0-7392-0309-6*, PO3429) Morris Pubng.
— Witty Remarks & Epigrams. LC 99-94711. 110p. 1999. pap. 6.95 (*0-7392-0131-X*, PO3050) Morris Pubng.
***Bookbinder, Robert M.** A Cornucopia of Concise Quotations. LC 99-95201. 126p. 1999. pap. 6.95 (*0-7392-0275-8*, PO3363) Morris Pubng.
Bookbinder, Robert M. A Treasury of Noteworthy Proverbs. LC 99-94375. 118p. 1999. pap. 6.95 (*0-7392-0208-1*, PO3219) Morris Pubng.
Bookchin, Murray. Anarchism, Marxism & the Future of the Left: Essays & Interviews, 1993-1998. 400p. 1998. pap. 19.95 (*1-873176-35-X*, AK Pr San Fran) AK Pr Dist.
— The Ecology of Freedom: The Emergence & Dissolution of Hierarchy. rev. ed. LC 90-83628. 385p. 1991. 48.99 (*0-921689-73-X*, Pub. by Black Rose); pap. 19.99 (*0-921689-72-1*, Pub. by Black Rose) Consort Bk Sales.
— From Urbanization to Cities: Toward a New Politics of Citizenship. (Global Issues Ser.). 288p. 1996. pap. 24.95 (*0-304-32842-1*) Continuum.
— From Urbanization to Cities: Toward a New Politics of Citizenship. (Global Issues Ser.). 288p. 1997. 75.00 (*0-304-32840-5*) Continuum.
— The Limits of the City. 2nd rev. ed. 194p. 1986. 46.99 (*0-920057-34-9*, Pub. by Black Rose); pap. 17.99 (*0-920057-64-0*, Pub. by Black Rose) Consort Bk Sales.
— The Modern Crisis. 2nd rev. ed. 194p. 1987. write for info. (*0-920057-61-6*); pap. write for info. (*0-920057-62-4*) Black Rose.
— The Philosophy of Social Ecology. 2nd rev. ed. 183p. 1995. 48.99 (*1-55164-019-8*, Pub. by Black Rose); pap. 19.99 (*1-55164-018-X*, Pub. by Black Rose) Consort Bk Sales.
— The Philosophy of Social Ecology: Essays on Dialectical Naturalism. LC 90-81639. 199p. (Orig.). (C). 1990. 37.95 (*0-921689-69-1*, Pub. by Black Rose) Consort Bk Sales.
— Post-Scarcity Anarchism. rev. ed. 265p. 1986. pap. 19.99 (*0-920057-39-X*, Pub. by Black Rose) Consort Bk Sales.
— Post-Scarcity Anarchism. 2nd rev. ed. 265p. 1986. 48.90 (*0-920057-41-1*, Pub. by Black Rose) Consort Bk Sales.
— Re-Enchanting Humanity: A Defense of the Human Spirit Against Antihumanism, Misanthropy, Mysticism & Primitivism. LC 96-143573. (Global Issues Ser.). 288p. 1996. pap. 24.95 (*0-304-32839-1*) Continuum.
— Reenchanting Humanity: A Defense of the Human Spirit Against Antihumanism, Misanthropy & Primitivism. LC 96-143573. 1996. 65.00 (*0-304-32843-X*, Pub. by Cassell) LPC InBook.
— Remaking Society. 208p. 1989. write for info. (*0-921689-03-9*); pap. write for info. (*0-921689-02-0*) Black Rose.
— Social Anarchism or Lifestyle Anarchism: An Unbridgeable Chasm. 96p. (Orig.). 1996. pap. 7.95 (*1-873176-83-X*, AK Pr San Fran) AK Pr Dist.
— The Spanish Anarchists: The Heroic Years 1868-1936. (Illus.). 384p. 1996. pap. 19.95 (*1-873176-04-X*, AK Pr San Fran) AK Pr Dist.
— The Third Revolution: Popular Movements in the Revolutionary Era. 420p. 1998. 75.00 (*0-304-33595-9*); pap. 24.95 (*0-304-33596-7*) Continuum.
— The Third Revolution Vol. 1: Popular Movements in the Revolutionary Era, Vol. 1. (Global Issues Ser.). 384p. 1996. 85.00 (*0-304-33593-2*, Pub. by Cassell); pap. 19.95 (*0-304-33594-0*, Pub. by Cassell) LPC InBook.
— Toward an Ecological Society. 315p. 1980. 47.99 (*0-919618-99-5*, Pub. by Black Rose); pap. 18.99 (*0-919618-98-7*, Pub. by Black Rose) Consort Bk Sales.
— Urbanization Without Cities: The Rise & Decline of Citizenship. rev. ed. LC 91-72980. 316p. 1996. 48.99 (*1-895431-01-8*, Pub. by Black Rose) Consort Bk Sales.
— Which Way for the Ecology Movement? LC 93-40416. 76p. (Orig.). 1994. pap. 6.00 (*1-873176-26-0*, AK Pr San Fran) AK Pr Dist.
Bookchin, Murray, ed. To Remember Spain: The Anarchist & Syndicalist Revolution of 1936. LC 94-1376. 1994. 6.00 (*1-873176-87-2*, AK Pr San Fran) AK Pr Dist.
Bookchin, Murray & Biehl, Janet. The Murray Bookchin Reader. LC 97-7413. 1997. 70.00 (*0-304-33873-7*); pap. 24.95 (*0-304-33874-5*) Continuum.
Bookchin, Murray, et al. Hip Culture: Six Essays on Its Revolutionary Potential. 64p. (Orig.). 1970. pap. 2.95 (*0-87810-010-5*) Times Change.
Bookcrafters Staff, ed. see Bliven, Roy B.
Booker. The African Novel in English: An Introduction. LC 97-31166. (Studies in African Literature). 1998. text. write for info. (*0-435-07426-1*) Heinemann.
— Salman Rushdie. LC 99-20986. (Critical Essays Ser.). 1999. 49.00 (*0-7838-0429-6*) Mac Lib Ref.
Booker, Bruce R. A Call to Holiness: A Cry for Believers in Jesus to Come Out of Harlot Babylon. LC 97-94237. (Illus.). 176p. 1997. pap. 8.95 (*0-9660041-0-8*) Booker Educ.
— The Lie: Exposing the Satanic Plot Behind Anti-Semitism. LC 94-183266. vi, 73p. 1993. pap. 8.00 (*0-916573-05-2*) Brentwood Comm.
Booker, C. J., jt. auth. see Ashworth, V.
Booker-Canfield, Suzanne, jt. auth. see Canfield Reisman, Rosemary M.
***Booker, Christopher.** African-Americans & the Presidency: A History of Broken Promises. (Illus.). (YA). 2000. 25.00 (*0-531-11882-7*) Watts.
***Booker, Christopher B.** "I Will Wear No Chain!" A Social History of African American Males. LC 99-86221. 272p. 2000. 65.00 (*0-275-95637-7*, C5637, Praeger Pubs) Greenwood.
Booker, Gladys J. The Sun Never Stops Shining. 100p. (Orig.). 1991. 10.95 (*0-9629641-0-7*) E L Booker.
Booker, H. G. Energy in Electromagnetism. (Electromagnetic Waves Ser.: No. 13). 384p. 1982. boxed set 115.00 (*0-906048-59-1*, EW013) INSPEC Inc.
Booker, Henry G. Cold Plasma Waves. LC 84-9018. 1984. text 211.50 (*90-247-2977-7*) Kluwer Academic.
Booker, J. D., jt. auth. see Swift, K. G.
Booker, Jacqueline L., ed. see Toney-Brooks, Paula.
Booker, Jane, jt. auth. see Meyer, Mary.
Booker, Janice L. Philly Firsts: The Famous, Infamous, & Quirky of the City of Brotherly Love. LC 98-56026. (Illus.). 224p. 1999. pap. 9.95 (*0-940159-44-9*) Camino Bks.
Booker, Jean. Mystery House. unabridged ed. 112p. (J). (gr. 3-6). 1996. mass mkt. 4.95 (*0-7736-7448-9*) STDK.
Booker, Joan. A Newbury Childhood. 128p. 1987. pap. 30.00 (*0-9506044-3-7*) St Mut.
Booker, John. Temples of Mammon: The Architecture of Banking. (Illus.). 361p. 1991. 76.50 (*0-7486-0198-8*, Pub. by Edinburgh U Pr) Col U Pr.
Booker, John, jt. auth. see Arnsberger, David.
Booker, John T. & Pasco, Allan H. Play of Terror in France. LC 96-12771. (Illus.). 280p. 1996. 34.50 (*0-87413-589-3*) U Delaware Pr.
***Booker, Jon A., et al.** Financial Accounting: Ready Notes. 272p. (C). 1999. pap. 15.94 (*0-07-234706-6*) McGrw-H Hghr Educ.
Booker, Julian, jt. auth. see Swift, Ken.
Booker, Karen M. Languages of the Aboriginal Southeast: An Annotated Bibliography. LC 90-28779. (Native American Bibliography Ser.: No. 15). 265p. 1991. 37.50 (*0-8108-2401-9*) Scarecrow.
Booker, Karmen A., ed. see Harris, Claudia.
Booker, Keith. Critical Essays on Salman Rushdie. 1999. 47.00 (*0-7838-0056-8*) Mac Lib Ref.
Booker, M. Keith. The African Novel in English: An Introduction. LC 97-31166. (Studies in African Literature). 227p. 1998. pap. 24.00 (*0-325-00030-1*) Heinemann.
— Colonial Power, Colonial Texts: India in the Modern British Novel. LC 96-49590. 248p. (C). 1997. text 49.50 (*0-472-10780-1*, 10780) U of Mich Pr.
— The Dystopian Impulse in Modern Literature: Fiction as Social Criticism, 58. LC 93-40174. (Contributions to the Study of Science Fiction & Fantasy Ser.: Vol. 58). 208p. 1994. 55.00 (*0-313-29092-X*, Greenwood Pr) Greenwood.
— Dystopian Literature: A Theory & Research Guide. LC 93-40173. 424p. 1994. lib. bdg. 85.00 (*0-313-29115-2*, Greenwood Pr) Greenwood.
— Film & the American Left: A Research Guide. LC 99-11268. 440p. 1999. lib. bdg. 89.50 (*0-313-30980-9*, GR0980, Greenwood Pr) Greenwood.
— Flann O'Brien, Bakhtin, & Menippean Satire. LC 95-2468. (Irish Studies). 200p. 1995. 39.95 (*0-8156-2665-7*) Syracuse U Pr.
— Joyce, Bakhtin, & the Literary Tradition: Toward a Comparative Cultural Poetics. 288p. (C). 1997. pap. text 20.95 (*0-472-08521-2*, 08521) U of Mich Pr.
— Literature & Domination: Sex, Knowledge, & Power in Modern Fiction. LC 92-41442. 224p. 1993. 49.95 (*0-8130-1195-7*) U Press Fla.
— The Modern American Novel of the Left: A Research Guide. LC 98-55349. 424p. 1999. lib. bdg. 85.00 (*0-313-30470-X*) Greenwood.
— The Modern British Novel of the Left: A Research Guide. LC 97-43861. 424p. 1998. lib. bdg. 89.50 (*0-313-30343-6*, Greenwood Pr) Greenwood.
— A Practical Introduction to Literacy Theory & Criticism. LC 95-20852. 512p. (C). 1995. pap. 41.40 (*0-8013-1765-7*) Longman.
— Techniques of Subversion in Modern Literature: Transgression, Abjection, & the Carnivalesque. 352p. (C). 1991. 49.95 (*0-8130-1065-9*) U Press Fla.
***Booker, M. Keith.** Ulysses, Capitalism & Colonialism: Reading Joyce after the Cold War, 98. LC 99-43505. (Contributions to the Study of World Literature Ser.). 240p. 2000. 59.95 (*0-313-31243-5*, Greenwood Pr) Greenwood.
Booker, M. Keith. Vargas Llosa among the Postmodernists. LC 93-34788. 256p. (C). 1994. 49.95 (*0-8130-?248-1*) U Press Fla.
Booker, M. Keith & Juraga, Dubravka. Bakhtin, Stalin & Modern Russian Fiction: Carnival, Dialogism, & History, 58. LC 94-24572. (Contributions to the Study of World Literature Ser.: Vol. 58). 200p. 1995. 57.95 (*0-313-29526-3*, Greenwood Pr) Greenwood.
***Booker, M. Keith & Juraga, Dubravka.** The Caribbean Novel in English: An Introduction. (Studies in African Literature). 2000. write for info. (*0-325-00212-6*); lib. bdg. 60.00 (*0-325-00252-5*) Greenwood.
Booker, Margaret, tr. see Chekhov, Anton.
Booker, Marilyn F. & Ignatavicius, Donna D. Infusion Therapy: Techniques & Medications. LC 95-17700. (Illus.). 846p. 1996. pap. text 31.00 (*0-7216-4923-8*, W B Saunders Co) Harcrt Hlth Sci Grp.
Booker, Mark D., ed. Containers-Condition Law & Practice of Carriage & Use, 2 vols., Set. 1993. 395.00 (*0-907591-04-3*, Pub. by Witherby & Co) St Mut.
Booker, Mary. Music in the 20th Century. 1981. 30.00 (*0-7223-1397-7*, Pub. by A H S Ltd) St Mut.
— Music-Making in the British Isles from 1890 to 1990. (C). 1993. 65.00 (*0-7223-2745-5*) St Mut.
— The Work of Women Composers from 1150 to 1995. 1995. 59.95 (*0-7223-2975-X*, Pub. by A H S Ltd) St Mut.
Booker, Mary, jt. auth. see Abley, Sean.
Booker, Philip H., et al, eds. Powder Injection Molding Symposium - 1992: Proceedings of the 1992 Powder Injection Molding Symposium Sponsored by the Metal Powder Industries Federation & the American Powder Metallurgy Institute, June 21-26, 1992, San Francisco, California. LC 92-29757. 1992. 135.00 (*1-878954-18-0*) Metal Powder.
Booker, Randy, jt. auth. see Ruiz, Michael.
Booker, Richard. Blow the Trumpet in Zion. 216p. (Orig.). 1985. pap. 10.99 (*1-56043-009-5*) Destiny Image.
— Come & Dine. 210p. (Orig.). 1983. pap. 10.99 (*1-56043-019-2*) Destiny Image.
— Fast Start in Christian Living. 72p. (Orig.). 1992. wbk. ed. 9.95 (*0-9615302-9-4*) Sounds of Trumpet Inc.
— Here Comes the Bride. 41p. (Orig.). 1995. pap. 5.95 (*0-9615302-4-3*) Sounds of Trumpet Inc.
— How the Cross Became a Sword. 47p. (Orig.). 1994. pap. 5.95 (*0-9615302-3-5*) Sounds of Trumpet Inc.
— How to Prepare for the Coming Revival. 126p. (Orig.). 1990. pap. 9.99 (*1-56043-010-9*) Destiny Image.
— Islam, Christianity & Israel. 31p. (Orig.). 1994. pap. 5.95 (*0-9615302-2-7*) Sounds of Trumpet Inc.
— Jesus in the Feasts of Israel. 126p. 1987. pap. 9.99 (*0-914903-98-5*) Destiny Image.
— The Miracle of the Scarlet Thread. (Illus.). 168p. 1991. reprint ed. pap. 10.99 (*0-914903-26-8*) Destiny Image.
— Pressing Toward the Mark. 72p. (Orig.). 1994. wbk. ed. 9.95 (*0-9615302-8-6*) Sounds of Trumpet Inc.
— Radical Christian Living. 126p. 1985. pap. 9.99 (*1-56043-018-4*) Destiny Image.
— Seated in Hevenly Places. 154p. 1986. pap. 9.99 (*0-914903-73-X*) Destiny Image.
— Shabbat Shalom: A Guide for Christians to Understand the Sabbath. 48p. 1998. pap. 5.95 (*0-9615302-6-X*) Sounds of Trumpet Inc.
— The Time to Favor Zion Has Come. 47p. (Orig.). 1996. pap. 5.95 (*0-9615302-5-1*) Sounds of Trumpet Inc.
Booker, Robert J. And There Was Light! The 120 Year History of Knoxville College, Knoxville, Tennessee, 1875-1995. LC 94-28493. 1994. write for info. (*0-89865-907-8*) Donning Co.
— Two Hundred Years of Black Culture in Knoxville, Tennessee, 1791 to 1991. LC 93-45411. 1994. write for info. (*0-89865-890-X*) Donning Co.
Booker, Robert L., ed. see Toney-Brooks, Paula.
Booker, Rosemary H. Human Longevity - Analysis, Influences, Measures, Risks, Varieties & Maintenance: Index of New Information with Authors & Subjects. rev. ed. 164p. 1997. 47.50 (*0-7883-1512-9*); pap. 44.50 (*0-7883-1513-7*) ABBE Pubs Assn.
Booker, Stephen T. Tug. LC 94-1306. (Wesleyan Poetry Ser.). (Illus.). 62p. 1994. 14.95 (*0-8195-2212-0*, Wesleyan Univ Pr) U Pr of New Eng.
— Waves & Licence. (Illus.). 65p. (Orig.). 1983. pap. 4.00 (*0-912678-55-0*, Greenfld Rev Pr) Greenfld Rev Lit.
Booker, Trent, ed. see Bedwell, Randall.
Booker, Warren E., ed. Historical Notes, Jamaica: Windham County. (Illus.). 244p. 1997. reprint ed. lib. bdg. 31.50 (*0-8328-6929-5*) Higginson Bk Co.
Booker, William Riley. Bloody Hill: The Civil War Battle of Wilson's Creek. 2000. 17.95 (*1-57488-205-8*) Brasseys.
***Bookes, Sasha & Hodson, Pauline, eds.** The Invisible Matrix: An Exploration of Professional Relationships in the Service of Psychotherapy. 225p. 2000. pap. 19.99 (*1-900877-27-9*, Pub. by Rebus Pr Ltd) Intl Spec Bk.
Bookhardt, D. Eric & Newlin, Jon. Geopsychic Wonders of New Orleans. (Illus.). 70p. (Orig.). 1992. pap. 15.95 (*0-9639525-2-8*) Temperance Hall.
Bookheim, Louis W., Jr. Understanding the Bible: You Can Without Cant. LC 98-168802. 160p. 1998. text 19.00 (*0-929808-02-9*) PennUltimate Pubs.
***Bookhout, Mark R. & Greenman, Philip E.** Principles of Exercise Prescription. (Illus.). 368p. 2000. 49.50 (*0-7506-9885-3*) Buttrwrth-Heinemann.
Bookhout, Mark R., jt. auth. see Isaacs, Edward R.
Bookhout, T. A., ed. Research & Management Techniques for Wildlife & Habitats. 5th ed. 740p. 1994. 40.00 (*0-935868-81-X*) Wildlife Soc.
Bookides, Nancy & Stroud, Ronald S. The Sanctuary of Demeter & Kore: Topography & Architecture. LC 97-34629. (Corinth: Vol. 18, Pt. 3). (Illus.). 520p. (C). 1997. text 125.00 (*0-87661-183-8*) Am Sch Athens.
Bookidis, Nancy & Stroud, Ronald. Demeter & Persephone in Ancient Corinth. (American Excavations in Old Corinth, Corinth Notes Ser.: No. 2). (Illus.). 32p. 1987. pap. 3.00 (*0-87661-671-6*) Am Sch Athens.
Bookin-Weiner, Hedy, jt. auth. see Piani, Judith A.
Bookless, George, ed. see Sanford, M. G. & Shannon, James P.
Bookless, George, ed. see Sanford, Monard G.

B

Bookless, William A., ed. State of the Laboratory: Lawrence Livermore National Laboratory. (Illus.). 106p. (Orig.). (C). 1995. pap. text 30.00 (*0-7881-2614-8*) DIANE Pub.

Booklet Committee of the Chapel Hill Historical So. Historic Buildings & Landmarks of Chapel Hill, N. C. unabridged ed. LC 74-150976. (Illus.). 40p. 1975. reprint ed. pap. 1.25 (*0-940715-04-X*) Chapel Hill Hist.

Bookma, Ken, jt. auth. see Schloss, Andrew.

Bookmaker & Raquin, Michele. My First French Vocabulary. (Illus.). 48p. 1991. pap. 12.00 (*0-13-377607-7*, Harraps IN) Macmillan Gen Ref.

— My First German Vocabulary. (Illus.). 48p. 1991. pap. 11.00 (*0-13-377599-2*, Harraps IN) Macmillan Gen Ref.

— My First Spanish Vocabulary. (Illus.). 48p. 1991. pap. 11.00 (*0-13-377581-X*, Harraps IN) Macmillan Gen Ref.

Bookman, Terry, jt. auth. see Ferris, Monica.

Bookman, Ann & Morgen, Sandra, eds. Women & the Politics of Empowerment. LC 87-6504. (Women in the Political Economy Ser.). 352p. (C). 1987. pap. 22.95 (*0-87722-525-7*) Temple U Pr.

Bookman, Barbara, jt. auth. see Chapman, Betsy.

Bookman, Charles A., ed. Marine Salvage: Proceedings of the Third International Symposium. 188p. 1985. pap. text 21.00 (*0-933957-01-7*) Marine Tech Soc.

Bookman, Harvey. Cobol No. II: Programming Techniques, Efficiency Considerations, Debugging Techniques. (IBM McGraw-Hill Ser.). 1990. 55.00 (*0-07-006533-0*) McGraw.

Bookman, Ken, jt. auth. see Schloss, Andrew.

Bookman, Ken, ed. see Gerhard, Esther.

Bookman, Ken, ed. see Marsh, Bill.

B

Bookman, Lawrence A. Trajectories Through Knowledge Space: A Dynamic Framework for Machine Comprehension. (Kluwer International Series in Engineering & Computer Science). 296p. (C). 1994. text 127.00 (*0-7923-9487-9*) Kluwer Academic.

Bookman, Mark. Protecting Your Organization's Tax-Exempt Status: A Guide for Nonprofit Managers. LC 91-36572. (Nonprofit Sector-Public Administration Ser.). 295p. 1992. text 51.95 (*1-55542-432-5*) Jossey-Bass.

Bookman, Milica Z. The Demographic Struggle for Power: The Political Economy of Demographic Engineering in the Modern World. LC 96-38905. 288p. (C). 1997. 57.50 (*0-7146-4732-2*, Pub. by F Cass Pubs); pap. 26.50 (*0-7146-4282-7*, Pub. by F Cass Pubs) Intl Spec Bk.

— Economic Decline & Nationalism in the Balkans. 320p. 1994. text 49.95 (*0-312-09999-1*) St Martin.

— The Political Economy of Discontinuous Development: Regional Disparities & Inter-Regional Conflict. LC 91-10659. 288p. 1991. 59.95 (*0-275-93777-1*, C3777, Praeger Pubs) Greenwood.

*__Bookman, Milica Zarkovic.__ The Third Career: Revisiting the Home vs. Work Choice in Middle Age. LC 99-45992. 217p. 2000. 59.95 (*0-275-96811-1*, Praeger Pubs) Greenwood.

*__Bookman, Murray.__ Call Center Technology Architecture. (Illus.). 240p. 2000. pap. 34.95 (*1-57820-052-0*) Telecom Bks.

Bookman, Susan, jt. auth. see Sobel, Betty.

Bookman, Terry. The Busy Soul: Ten-Minute Spiritual Workouts Drawn from Jewish Tradition. LC 98-32327. 246p. 1999. pap. 14.00 (*0-399-52486-X*, Perigee Bks) Berkley Pub.

Bookmasters, Inc. Staff, ed. see Daniel, Thesina C.

Bookmiller, W. H. Selection & Design of Gear Generating Tools. (Technical Papers: Vol. P129.02). (Illus.). 20p. 1950. pap. text 30.00 (*1-55589-153-5*) AGMA.

Bookont, Melanie. Complanetus & All. 37p. 1998. 7.00 (*0-937013-89-7*, Pub. by Potes Poets) SPD-Small Pr Dist.

Bookout, Lloyd W., Jr., et al. Residential Development Handbook. 2nd ed. LC 90-70875. 1990. 64.95 (*0-87420-705-3*, R22) Urban Land.

Bookout, Lloyd W., et al. Value by Design: Landscape, Site Planning, & Amenities. LC 94-61233. 154p. 1994. pap. text 32.95 (*0-87420-763-0*, V05) Urban Land.

Bookout, Lloyd W., jt. ed. see Wentling, James W.

Books, C. L. Little Book of Creative Papercrafts. 1995. 4.98 (*0-7858-0283-5*) Bk Sales Inc.

— Little Book of Garlands & Festive Decorations. 1995. 4.98 (*0-7858-0285-1*) Bk Sales Inc.

Books, Coleman & Moyne, John, trs. This Longing. 96p. 1996. pap. 9.00 (*0-614-21371-1*, 1230) Kazi Pubns.

— Unseen Rain. 96p. 1996. pap. 9.00 (*0-614-21375-4*, 1273) Kazi Pubns.

Books, Coleman, jt. tr. see Moyne, John.

Books, Cyrus, tr. see Kastner, Erich.

Books, Emma K. Frosty the Snowman Board Book. (Musical Board Bk.). (Illus.). 12p. (J). (ps up). 1994. 5.95 (*0-694-00655-6*, HarpFestival) HarpC Child Bks.

Books Honor Staff. If I Really Wanted to Grow Closer to God, I Would... 2000. pap. 6.99 (*1-56292-568-7*) Honor Bks OK.

*__Books Honor Staff.__ If I Really Wanted to Lose Weight, I Would... 2000. pap. 6.99 (*1-56292-566-0*) Honor Bks OK.

Books Honor Staff. If I Really Wanted to Simplify My Life, I Would... 2000. pap. 6.99 (*1-56292-569-5*) Honor Bks OK.

— Treasury of Love & Romance: A Classic Collection of Stories, Quotes, Ballads, Verses & Poem. 464p. 1999. 24.99 (*1-56292-560-1*) Honor Bks OK.

Books, John W. & Prysby, Charles L. Political Behavior & the Local Context. LC 91-429. 184p. 1991. 52.95 (*0-275-93629-5*, C3629, Praeger Pubs) Greenwood.

Books, Kathryn J., ed. see Zola, John.

Books Nippan Editorial Staff, ed. Housing Developments. Date not set. 85.00 (*4-938812-35-5*, Pub. by Nihon Geijutsu) Bks Nippan.

Books Nippan Staff. Business Publication Graphics. 1997. 79.95 (*4-89444-038-5*, Pub. by PIE Bks) Bks Nippan.

Books Nippan Staff & Broadcast Dessign Assoc. Staff. 16th Annual BDA International Design Awards. (Illus.). viii, 208p. 1995. 45.00 (*0-9644038-1-1*) Design Ed.

Books Nippan Staff, jt. auth. see Thoth Publishers Editorial Staff.

Books, Reed. Make Your Own Fairy Tale. 24p. (J). (gr. k-3). 1999. pap. 9.95 (*0-316-85564-2*) Little.

Books Staff, Bent. Bent Guide to Gay-Lesbian Canada, 95-96. (Illus.). 204p. 1995. pap. 9.95 (*1-55022-253-8*, Pub. by ECW) LPC InBook.

Books, Sue, ed. Invisible Children in the Society & Its Schools. LC 97-33966. 208p. 1998. pap. 24.50 (*0-8058-2368-9*) L Erlbaum Assocs.

Books Victor Staff. Inspirational for Couples. (Heart for God Ser.). 128p. 1997. pap. text 5.99 (*1-56476-626-8*, Victor Bks) Chariot Victor.

Booksales Inc. Staff. Insects Pocket Companion. (Pocket Companion Ser.). 1999. pap. text 4.99 (*0-7858-0983-X*) Bk Sales Inc.

Booksales Staff. One Thousand & One Country Hints. 1994. 4.98 (*0-7858-0110-3*) Bk Sales Inc.

Bookspan, Jolie. Health & Fitness in Plain English. x, 357p. 1998. pap. 14.00 (*1-57566-288-4*, Knsington) Kensgtn Pub Corp.

Bookspan, Rochelle, ed. Santa Barbara by the Sea. (Illus.). 236p. pap. 10.00 (*0-87461-036-2*) McNally & Loftin.

Bookspan, Shelley. A Germ of Goodness: The California State Prison System, 1851-1944. LC 90-28876. (Law in the American West Ser.: Vol. 3). (Illus.). xx, 151p. 1991. text 45.00 (*0-8032-1216-X*) U of Nebr Pr.

Bookstaber, Richard M. Option Pricing & Investment Strategies. 3rd ed. 1991. text 45.00 (*1-55738-145-3*, Irwn Prfssnl) McGraw-Hill Prof.

— Option Pricing & Strategies in Investing. LC 80-15013. 256p. 1981. text 24.95 (*0-201-00123-3*) Addison-Wesley.

Bookstein, Abraham, et al, eds. Prospects for Change in Bibliographic Control: Proceedings of the 38th Annual Conference of the Graduate Library School, November 8-9, 1976. LC 77-23767. (University of Chicago Studies in Library Science). 138p. Date not set. reprint ed. pap. 42.80 (*0-608-20593-1*, 205455800003) Bks Demand.

Bookstein, Abraham, ed. see Chicago University, Graduate Library School Staff.

Bookstein, Abraham, jt. ed. see Koerig, Michael E.

Bookstein, Fred L. The Measurement of Biological Shape & Shape Change. LC 78-15923. (Lecture Notes in Biomathematics Ser.: Vol. 24). 1978. pap. 28.00 (*0-387-08912-8*) Spr-Verlag.

— Morphometric Tools for Landmark Data: Geometry & Biology. 455p. (C). 1992. text 100.00 (*0-521-38385-4*) Cambridge U Pr.

— Morphometric Tools for Landmark Data: Geometry & Biology. 455p. 1997. pap. text 36.95 (*0-521-58598-8*) Cambridge U Pr.

Bookstein, Fred L., ed. Proceedings of the Michigan Morphometrics Workshop. (Special Publications: No. 2). viii, 380p. (C). 1990. pap. text 17.50 (*0-9628499-0-1*); pap. text 25.00 incl. disk (*0-685-38831-X*) U MI Mus Zool.

Bookstein, Ken. Medical Student's Desk Reference: 1999 Edition. large type ed. 226p. (C). 1999. pap. 18.95 (*0-9660645-1-8*) Bookstein Pub.

— Medical Student's Pocket Reference. vi, 259p. 1996. pap. text 10.95 (*0-9660645-0-X*) Bookstein Pub.

— Medical Student's Pocket Reference: 1999 Edition. rev. ed. 322p. 1999. pap. 12.50 (*0-9660645-2-6*) Bookstein Pub.

*__Bookworld Services Staff.__ U. S. Constitution: And Fascinating Facts about It. 7th ed. 1999. pap. 2.95 (*1-881473-00-7*) Oak Hill Pub Co.

BookWorld Staff, ed. see Young, James A.

Booky, Albert R. Apache Shadows: A Novel. LC 85-30435. 144p. (Orig.). 1986. pap. 10.95 (*0-86534-084-6*) Sunstone Pr.

— The Buckskins: A Novel. LC 90-33902. 312p. (Orig.). 1990. pap. 12.95 (*0-86534-125-7*) Sunstone Pr.

— Hacienda: A Novel. LC 96-31644. 160p. (Orig.). 1997. pap. 16.95 (*0-86534-251-2*) Sunstone Pr.

— Son of Manitou: A Novel. LC 86-23169. 144p. 1987. pap. 10.95 (*0-86534-097-8*) Sunstone Pr.

*__Bool, Hilary & Lufford, Philip, trs.__ Academic Standards & Expectations: The Role of EAP. 161p. 1999. pap. 90.00 (*1-897676-69-7*, Pub. by Nottingham Univ Pr) St Mut.

Boolarong Publications Staff. Best of Mick Mayoh: Poems of Australia. 143p. (C). 1990. 48.00 (*0-7316-7609-2*, Pub. by Boolarong Pubns) St Mut.

— The Charater of Townsville: A Community Photography Book. (C). 1990. pap. 48.00 (*0-86439-141-2*, Pub. by Boolarong Pubns) St Mut.

— A Community Self Portrait of Brisbane. 90p. (C). 1990. pap. 75.00 (*0-86439-100-5*, Pub. by Boolarong Pubns) St Mut.

— Kenneth Jack: World War II Paintings & Drawings. 104p. (C). 1990. 90.00 (*0-86439-096-3*, Pub. by Boolarong Pubns) St Mut.

— Natasha's Dream. (YA). 1990. pap. 35.00 (*0-7316-3901-4*, Pub. by Boolarong Pubns) St Mut.

— The Railway Art of Kenneth Bowen. 128p. (C). 1990. 120.00 (*0-86439-021-1*, Pub. by Boolarong Pubns) St Mut.

— Spring Hill Resprung. 64p. (C). 1990. 44.00 (*0-908175-13-2*, Pub. by Boolarong Pubns) St Mut.

Boolchand, Punit. Insulating & Semiconducting Glasses. (Series on Directions in Condensed Matter Physics). 600p. 1999. 96.00 (*981-02-3673-5*) World Scientific Pub.

Boole, George. Laws of Thought. 424p. (C). 1958. pap. 10.95 (*0-486-60028-9*) Dover.

— Logical Works, 2 vols. Incl. Vol. 1. Studies in Logic & Probability. 500p. 1952. 29.95 (*0-87548-038-1*); Vol. 2. Laws of Thought. 464p. 1952. 31.95 (*0-87548-039-X*); 1952. write for info. (*0-318-54786-4*) Open Court.

— The Mathematical Analysis of Logic: Being an Essay Towards a Calculus of Deductive Reasoning. (Key Issues Ser.). 82p. 1998. reprint ed. pap. 14.00 (*1-85506-583-5*) Thoemmes Pr.

Boole, George, et al. George Boole: Selected Manuscripts on Logic & Its Philosophy. LC 97-4305. (Science Networks Historical Studies). 1997. write for info. (*0-8176-5456-9*); write for info. (*3-7643-5456-9*) Birkhauser.

Booley, Ruth, tr. see Kastner, Erich.

Booley, Ted, tr. see Kastner, Erich.

Boolootian, Richard A. Zoology: An Introduction to the Study of Animals. (Illus.). (C). 1979. teacher ed. write for info. (*0-318-54253-6*); student ed. write for info. (*0-318-54254-4*); student ed. write for info. (*0-318-54255-2*) Macmillan.

Boolootian, Richard A. & Heyneman, Donald. An Illustrated Laboratory Text in Zoology. 4th ed. (Illus.). 448p. (C). 1991. pap. text, student ed. 49.00 (*0-03-033369-5*, Pub. by SCP) Harcourt.

Boolos, George. Logic, Logic & Logic. 448p. 1999. pap. 22.95 (*0-674-53767-X*) HUP.

— The Logic of Provability. 314p. 1995. pap. text 25.95 (*0-521-48325-5*) Cambridge U Pr.

Boolos, George & Burgess, John P. Logic, Logic, & Logic. Jeffrey, Richard C., ed. LC 97-37668. 448p. 1999. text 45.00 (*0-674-53766-1*) HUP.

Boolos, George S. & Jeffrey, Richard C. Computability & Logic. 3rd ed. (Illus.). 320p. (C). 1989. pap. text 26.95 (*0-521-38923-2*) Cambridge U Pr.

*__Boolware, Chris & Noble, Jean E., eds.__ A Message to a Black Man. rev. ed. (Illus.). 81p. 1999. pap. 9.95 (*1-887653-12-0*) Papito.

Boom, B. M. Ethnobotany of the Chacobo Indians, Beni, Bolivia. LC 86-31248. (Advances in Economic Botany Ser.: Vol. 4). (Illus.). 68p. 1987. pap. 15.00 (*0-89327-312-0*) NY Botanical.

Boom, Rob, et al. Cohesion in Metals: Transition Metal Alloys. Mattens, W. C., ed. (Cohesion & Structure Ser.: Vol. 1). xvi, 758p. 1988. 214.50 (*0-444-87098-9*, North Holland) Elsevier.

Boome. The Brachial Plexus. LC 97-204554. 1996. text 60.00 (*0-443-04838-X*, W B Saunders Co) Harcrt Hlth Sci Grp.

Boomer, Garth. Fair Dinkum Teaching & Learning: Reflections on Literacy & Power. LC 84-21670. 204p. (Orig.). (C). 1985. pap. text 21.00 (*0-86709-139-8*, 0139, Pub. by Boynton Cook Pubs) Heinemann.

— Metaphors & Meanings: Essays on English Teaching. Green, Bill, ed. 240p. 1998. pap. text 17.50 (*0-909955-82-4*, 955824) Calendar Islands.

Boomer, Garth, et al, eds. Negotiating the Curriculum. 224p. 1992. 89.95 (*1-85000-931-7*, Falmer Pr); pap. 29.95 (*1-85000-937-6*, Falmer Pr) Taylor & Francis.

*__Boomer, L. Gary.__ Successful Technology Consulting: The Boomer Advantage. 200p. 1999. pap. 49.95 (*0-87051-286-2*, 093014) Am Inst CPA.

Boomer, L. Gary, et al. Guide to Creating a Technology Budget. 1997. spiral bd. 140.00 (*0-7646-0209-8*) Prctnrs Pub Co.

— Guide to Creating a Technology Plan & Budget. 1997. spiral bd. 495.00 (*0-7646-0204-7*) Prctnrs Pub Co.

Boomer, Percy. On Learning Golf. (Illus.). 1946. 20.00 (*0-394-41008-4*) Knopf.

— On Learning Golf. rev. ed. (Illus.). 220p. 1989. reprint ed. 28.00 (*0-940889-22-6*) Classics Golf.

Boomershine, Thomas E. Story Journey. LC 88-19038. 220p. 1988. pap. 17.95 (*0-687-39662-X*) Abingdon.

Boomgaard, Peter, et al, eds. Health Care in Java, Past & Present. LC 97-145593. (KITLV Proceedings Ser.). vi, 197p. (Orig.). 1996. pap. 33.50 (*90-6718-104-8*, Pub. by KITLV Pr) Cellar.

Boomgaarden, Wesley. Preservation Planning Program Resource Guides: Staff Training & User Awareness in Preservation Management. 89p. 1993. pap. 15.00 (*0-918006-64-3*) ARL.

Boomhower, Ray. The Country Contributor: The Life & Times of Juliet V. Strauss. LC 98-72782. 250p. 1998. 24.95 (*1-57860-064-2*) Guild Pr IN.

Boomhower, Ray E. Jacob Piatt Dunn, Jr. A Life in History & Politics, 1855-1924. LC 97-23545. (Illus.). xlii, 174p. 1997. text 24.95 (*0-87195-119-3*) Ind Hist Soc.

*__Boomhower, Ray E. & Jones, Darryl L.__ Destination Indiana: Travels Through Hoosier History. LC 00-32018. (Illus.). 2000. write for info. (*0-87195-147-9*) Ind Hist Soc.

Boomsma, Sylvia. Comfort: Study Guide. (Discover Your Bible Ser.). 39p. pap., student ed. 2.95 (*1-56212-234-7*) CRC Pubns.

— DYB - Esther Study Guide. 30p. 1991. pap., student ed. 2.45 (*1-56212-184-7*) CRC Pubns.

— DYB - Jesus in John Study Guide: Why He Came. 46p. 1993. pap., student ed. 3.95 (*1-56212-686-5*) CRC Pubns.

— DYB - Ruth. 32p. 1991. pap., teacher ed. 3.75 (*1-56212-148-0*) CRC Pubns.

— DYB James: Leader Guide. 57p. 1999. pap., teacher ed. 3.95 (*1-56212-505-2*, 152525) CRC Pubns.

— DYB James: Study Guide. 30p. 1999. pap., student ed. 2.75 (*1-56212-506-0*, 152520) CRC Pubns.

— DYB Ruth Study Guide. 20p. 1991. pap., student ed. 2.45 (*1-56212-150-2*) CRC Pubns.

— 1st Corinthians: Leader Guide. (Discover Your Bible Ser.). 88p. 1995. pap., teacher ed. 4.75 (*1-56212-113-8*) CRC Pubns.

Boon. Montaigne, Gentilhomme et Essayiste. 18.40 (*0-685-34192-5*) Fr & Eur.

— River Conservation. text 179.00 (*0-471-96062-4*) Wiley.

*__Boon, Andrew & Levin, Jennifer.__ The Ethics & Conduct of Lawyers in England & Wales. LC 99-224828. 418p. 1999. 54.00 (*1-84113-018-4*) Hart Pub.

Boon, Andy. Advocacy. Macfarlane, Julie, ed. (Legal Skills Ser.). 220p. 1994. pap. 22.00 (*1-874241-42-2*, Pub. by Cavendish Pubng) Gaunt.

*__Boon, Andy.__ Advocacy. 2nd ed. 228p. 1999. pap. 23.50 (*1-85941-485-0*, Pub. by Cavendish Pubng) Gaunt.

Boon, Debbie. My Gran. LC 97-31892. 32p. (J). (gr. k-2). 1998. lib. bdg. 19.90 (*0-7613-0312-X*) Millbrook Pr.

Boon, Emilie, jt. auth. see Ziefert, Harriet.

Boon, Fay. Picture Framing. 1995. 7.98 (*0-7858-0316-5*) Bk Sales Inc.

Boon, Gerard K. Technology & Employment in Footwear Manufacturing: A Study Prepared for the International Labour Office Within the Framework of the World Employment Programme. LC 80-50458. 232p. 1980. lib. bdg. 90.00 (*90-286-0170-8*) Kluwer Academic.

— Technology & Sector Choice in Economic Development. 324p. 1978. lib. bdg. 80.00 (*90-286-0068-X*) Kluwer Academic.

— Technology Transfer in Fibres, Textile & Apparel. 600p. 1981. lib. bdg. 233.00 (*90-286-0520-7*) Kluwer Academic.

Boon, Heather & Smith, Michael. The Botanical Pharmacy: The Pharmacology of Common Herbs. (Illus.). 320p. 1999. 39.95 (*1-55082-230-6*) Rockport Pubs.

Boon, James A. Affinities & Extremes: Crisscrossing the Bittersweet Ethnology of East Indies History, Hindu-Balinese Culture & Indo-European Allure. LC 89-20326. (Illus.). 264p. 1990. lib. bdg. 54.00 (*0-226-06461-1*) U Ch Pr.

— Affinities & Extremes: Crisscrossing the Bittersweet Ethnology of East Indies History, Hindu-Balinese Culture & Indo-European Allure. LC 89-20326. (Illus.). 264p. 1990. pap. text 17.95 (*0-226-06463-8*) U Ch Pr.

— Verging on Extra-Vagance: Anthropology, History, Religion, Literature, Arts . . . Showbiz. LC 98-35712. 1999. pap. 24.95 (*0-691-01631-3*, Pub. by Princeton U Pr) Cal Prin Full Svc.

*__Boon, James A.__ Verging on Extra-Vagance: Anthropology, History, Religion, Literature, Arts . . . Showbiz. LC 98-35712. 4p. 1999. 55.00 (*0-691-01632-1*, Pub. by Princeton U Pr) Cal Prin Full Svc.

Boon, Jean P. & Yip, Sidney. Molecular Hydrodynamics. (Illus.). 432p. 1992. reprint ed. pap. 13.95 (*0-486-66949-1*) Dover.

Boon, June A. Manual of Veterinary Echocardiography. LC 97-43333. 478p. 1998. 79.00 (*0-683-00938-9*) Lppncott W & W.

Boon, Kevin A. Absolute Zero. 1999. write for info. (*0-9670328-0-6*) Fort Schuyler Pr.

— Chaos Theory & the Interpretation of Literary Texts: The Case of Kurt Vonnegut. LC 97-37565. (Studies in American Literature: Vol. 27). viii, 191 p. 1997. text 79.95 (*0-7734-8553-8*) E Mellen.

— An Interpretive Reading of Virginia Woolf's The Waves. LC 98-21573. (Studies in British Literature: Vol. 37). 132p. 1998. text 69.95 (*0-7734-8370-5*) E Mellen.

Boon, Mathilde E. & Suurmeijer, Albert J. The Pap Smear. 3rd ed. 384p. 1996. text 54.00 (*3-7186-5857-7*) Gordon & Breach.

Boon, P. I. & Brock, M., eds. Plants & Processes in Wetlands. (Illus.). 180p. 1995. 50.00 (*0-643-05698-X*, Pub. by CSIRO) Accents Pubns.

Boon, Richard & Plastow, Jane, eds. Theatre Matters: Performance & Culture on the World Stage. LC 97-46774. (Cambridge Studies in Modern Theatre). 235p. (C). 1998. 54.95 (*0-521-63054-1*); pap. text 19.95 (*0-521-63443-1*) Cambridge U Pr.

Boon, Suzette & Draijer, Nel. Multiple Personality Disorders in the Netherlands: A Study on Reliability & Validity of the Diagnosis. 262p. 1993. pap. 46.00 (*90-265-1361-5*) Swets.

*__Boon-Thong, Lee, et al.__ Vanishing Borders: The New International Order of the 21st Century. (Illus.). 274p. 1998. text 65.95 (*1-84014-363-0*) Ashgate Pub Co.

Boondas, Jennifer, et al. Encyclopedia of Home Care for the Elderly. Romaine-Davis, Ada, ed. LC 94-17989. 456p. 1995. lib. bdg. 99.50 (*0-313-28532-2*, Greenwood Pr) Greenwood.

Boone. Business. 2nd ed. (C). 1997. text. write for info. (*0-03-024666-0*) Harcourt Coll Pubs.

— Business. 2nd ed. (C). 1997. pap. text, teacher ed. 40.00 (*0-03-024717-9*); pap. text, student ed. 21.50 (*0-03-024712-8*) Holt R&W.

— Cave: Contemporary Business. 7th ed. (C). 1993. write for info. (*0-03-006289-6*) Harcourt Coll Pubs.

— Contempoary Personal Finance. (C). 1996. text 60.00 (*0-03-018067-8*, Pub. by Harcourt Coll Pubs) Harcourt.

— Contempoary Personal Finance. (C). 1996. pap. text, student ed. 28.00 (*0-03-018422-3*, Pub. by Harcourt Coll Pubs) Harcourt.

— Contemporary Business. 8th ed. (C). 1995. pap. text, teacher ed. 33.75 (*0-03-015163-5*) Harcourt Coll Pubs.

— Contemporary Business. 8th ed. (C). 1995. pap. text, teacher ed. 31.75 (*0-03-015162-7*); pap. text, teacher ed., suppl. ed. 35.50 (*0-03-015157-0*, Pub. by Harcourt Coll Pubs) Harcourt.

— Contemporary Business. 8th ed. (C). 1995. pap. text, teacher ed. 29.75 (*0-03-015169-4*) Harcourt Coll Pubs.

— Contemporary Business. 8th ed. (C). 1996. audio compact disk 46.00 (*0-03-019222-6*) Harcourt Coll Pubs.

— Contemporary Business. 9th ed. (C). 1998. pap. text, student ed. 18.00 (*0-03-021759-8*) Harcourt Coll Pubs.

— Contemporary Business: Alternate Study Guide. 8th ed. (C). 1995. 3.5 hd 222.25 (*0-03-015153-8*) Harcourt Coll Pubs.

An Asterisk (*) at the beginning of an entry indicates that the title is appearing for the first time.

— Contemporary Business: Alternate Study Guide. 9th ed. (C). 1998. pap. text, student ed. write for info. (*0-03-021758-X*) Harcourt Coll Pubs.
— Contemporary Business: An Atlas Learning Guide. 8th ed. (C). 1996. pap. text, lab manual ed. 21.00 (*0-03-015158-9*) Harcourt Coll Pubs.
— Contemporary Business: Learning Guide. 8th ed. (C). 1995. pap. text, student ed. 29.00 (*0-03-015159-7*) Harcourt Coll Pubs.
— Contemporary Business with Learning Guide 96. 8th ed. (C). 1996. 89.00 (*0-03-017217-9*) Harcourt.
— Contemporary Marketing. 8th ed. (C). 1994. 65.25 incl. 5.25 hd (*0-03-015768-4*) Harcourt Coll Pubs.
— Contemporary Marketing. 9th ed. (C). 1997. pap. text, teacher ed. 33.50 (*0-03-019028-2*, Pub. by Harcourt Coll Pubs) Harcourt.
— Contemporary Marketing. 9th ed. 1997. 99.00 (*0-03-024214-2*, Pub. by Harcourt Coll Pubs) Harcourt.
— Contemporary Marketing. 9th ed. 1997. student ed. 28.00 (*0-03-019032-0*, Pub. by SCP) Harcourt.
— Contemporary Marketing, Vol. 1. 9th ed. (C). 1997. pap. text, teacher ed. 28.00 (*0-03-019044-4*) Harcourt Coll Pubs.
— Contemporary Marketing, Vol. 2. 9th ed. (C). 1997. pap. text, teacher ed. 28.00 (*0-03-019043-6*) Harcourt Coll Pubs.
— Contemporary Marketing 1999. LC 98-86928. (1999 The Dryden Press Series in Marketing). (C). 1998. pap. text 57.50 (*0-03-022313-X*) Harcourt Coll Pubs.
— Electronic Instructors Library. 8th ed. (C). 1995. 185.25 (*0-03-017593-3*) Harcourt Coll Pubs.
— L' Entreprise d'Aujourd'Hui. (FRE.). (C). 1989. pap. write for info. (*0-03-998265-3*) Harcourt Coll Pubs.
— A Little Math with Your Business. 8th ed. (C). 1995. pap. text 11.50 (*0-03-017807-X*) Harcourt Coll Pubs.
— Media Contemporary Marketing. 9th ed. (C). 1997. pap. text, teacher ed. 28.00 (*0-03-019038-X*) Harcourt.
— Organic Polymer Chemistry: A Primer : Supplement to Organic Chemistry. (C). 1994. pap. text, suppl. ed. 12.50 (*0-03-010633-8*) Harcourt Coll Pubs.
— Planning Your Financial Future. (C). 1996. pap. text, teacher ed. 42.00 (*0-03-018419-3*) Harcourt Coll Pubs.
— Planning Your Financial Future. 2nd ed. LC 99-72431. (C). 1999. text. write for info. (*0-03-021042-9*) Harcourt Coll Pubs.
— SELF-STUDY SFWR TA/CONT BUS '9. 97th ed. (C). 1997. pap. text 246.00 (*0-03-020618-9*) Harcourt Coll Pubs.
— Sexuality & Narrative. LC 97-30717. 528p. (C). 1997. lib. bdg. 54.00 (*0-226-06466-2*) U Ch Pr.
Boone & Kurtz. Instructor's Manual & Test Bank to Accompany Business 1995. 95th ed. 960p. (C). 1995. pap. text, teacher ed. 58.50 (*0-03-015423-5*) Dryden Pr.
Boone, jt. auth. see Amberg.
Boone & Crockett Club Staff. Hunting Trails on Three Continents: A Book of the Boone & Crocket Club. Gray, Printis N. et al, eds. (Fifty Greatest Bks.). (Illus.). 302p. 1992. reprint ed. 50.00 (*1-56416-039-4*) Derrydale Pr.
Boone, Barbara Z. Tools for Writing: Creating Writer's Workshops for Grades 2-8. LC 96-16600. 144p. 1996. 49.95 (*0-8039-6456-0*); pap. 21.95 (*0-8039-6457-9*) Corwin Pr.
Boone, Barry. JAVA Certification for Programmers & Developers. LC 97-202562. (Illus.). 704p. 1997. 54.95 incl. cd-rom (*0-07-913657-5*) McGraw.
— Java for C & C++ Programmers. 336p. (C). 1996. pap. text 19.95 (*0-201-47946-X*) Addison-Wesley.
Boone, Barry. Magic Cap Programmer's Cookbook. 384p. 1995. pap. 44.95 (*0-201-40953-4*) Addison-Wesley.
Boone, Barry & Mark, Dave. Learn Java on the Macintosh. 496p. 1996. pap. text 34.95 (*0-201-19157-1*) Addison-Wesley.
Boone, Barry & Stanek, William Robert. Java 2 All - In - One Certification: Exam Guide. 2nd ed. 900p. 1999. 59.99 incl. cd-rom (*0-07-913740-7*) McGraw.
Boone, Bradley G. Signal Processing Using Optics: Fundamentals, Devices, Architectures & Applications. LC 97-6961. (Johns Hopkins Applied Physics Laboratory Series in Science & Engineering). (Illus.). 416p. (C). 1997. text 97.00 (*0-19-508424-1*) OUP.
Boone, Bruce, jt. tr. see Gluck, Robert.
Boone, Catherine. Merchant Capital & the Roots of State Power in Senegal, 1930-1985. (Cambridge Studies in Comparative Politics). (Illus.). 317p. (C). 1992. text 74.95 (*0-521-41078-9*) Cambridge U Pr.
Boone County Bicentennial Committe, ed. see Warner, Jennifer S.
Boone County Historical Society Staff, ed. Boone County History, 1871-1985. (Illus.). 758p. 1986. text 75.00 (*0-88107-056-4*) Curtis Media.
Boone, Daniel. Cerebral Palsy. LC 76-190708. (Studies in Communicative Disorders). (C). 1972. pap. text. write for info. (*0-672-61290-9*, Bobbs) Macmillan.
— Critical Thinking: An Applied Approach. 200p. (C). 1996. pap. text, per. 28.95 (*0-7872-2767-6*) Kendall-Hunt.
Boone, Daniel & Hawks, Francis L. Daniel Boone, His Own Story & the Adventures of Daniel Boone. LC 95-77901. 128p. (YA). (gr. 10 up). 1995. pap. 12.95 (*1-55709-426-8*) Applewood.
Boone, Daniel R. Is Your Voice Telling on You? How to Find & Use Your Natural Voice. 2nd ed. LC 96-2934. (Illus.). 200p. 1997. pap. 35.00 (*1-56593-811-9*, 1588) Thomson Learn.
***Boone, Daniel R.** Voice & Voice Therapy. 6th ed. LC 99-22921. 308p. 1999. text 67.00 incl. audio compact disk (*0-205-30843-0*, Prentice Hall) P-H.
Boone, David B., Jr. & Castenholz, Richard W. Bergey's Manual of Systematic Bacteriology: The Archea, Cyanobacteria, Phototrophs & Deeply Branching General, Vol. 1. 2nd ed. 850p. text 125.00 (*0-683-30498-4*) Lppncott W & W.
Boone, Debby. Bedtime Hugs for Little Ones. LC 87-81035. (Illus.). 64p. (J). (ps-1). 1988. 14.99 (*0-89081-616-6*) Harvest Hse.
— Nightlights. LC 97-12443. (Illus.). 40p. (Orig.). (J). 1997. 14.99 (*1-56507-734-2*) Harvest Hse.
— Welcome to This World: A Love Letter to Little Ones. (Illus.). (Orig.). (J). 1995. 14.99 (*1-56507-302-9*) Harvest Hse.
Boone, Debby & Ferrar, Gabri. Counting Blessings. (Illus.). 32p. (J). 1998. 12.99 (*0-7369-0026-8*) Harvest Hse.
Boone, Debby & Ferrer, Gabriel. Welcome to This World: Baby Book. (Illus.). 25-30p. 1995. 22.99 (*1-56507-413-0*) Harvest Hse.
Boone, Don. Alternatives to Alcoholism's Grand Conspiracy. Roberts, Ralph, ed. (Illus.). 64p. 1992. pap. 6.95 (*1-56664-001-6*) WorldComm.
— Creative Loving. 64p. (Orig.). 1994. pap. 9.95 (*1-56664-064-4*) WorldComm.
— The Myth That Kills. (Illus.). 76p. 1997. pap. 9.95 (*1-56664-117-9*) WorldComm.
Boone, Don & Boone, Laura. You Chi: The Healing Spirit. 80p. (Orig.). 1993. pap. 9.95 (*1-56664-048-2*) WorldComm.
Boone, Don & Martin, Donna. Personal Options for Organizational Change: Surviving or Thriving Change Is Inevitable, Growth Is Optional, Stress Is a Choice. 64p. 1996. pap. 9.95 (*1-56664-096-2*) WorldComm.
Boone, Don & Martin, Donna B. Family Business in the Family Business. (Illus.). 76p. 1997. pap. 9.95 (*1-56664-115-2*) WorldComm.
Boone, Don, et al. The Courage to Manage: From the Top Down. 2nd ed. Dillingham, Nancy, ed. (Illus.). 100p. (Orig.). 1996. pap. 9.95 (*1-56664-090-3*) WorldComm.
— Run & Shoot Management: Generation X Managerial Excitement & Growth. (Illus.). 68p. 1998. pap. 9.95 (*1-56664-132-2*) WorldComm.
Boone, Donald. Chess Influences. 1997. spiral bd. 10.00 (*0-86690-466-2*, B3667-014) Am Fed Astrologers.
— Simple Boat Projects. O'Connor, John P., ed. LC 99-73127. (Illus.). 136p. 1999. spiral bd. 24.95 (*1-892216-19-1*) Bristol Fash.
Boone, Donald L. Engine Medicine. (Illus.). 60p. 1993. pap. text 12.50 (*1-882896-00-9*) Itchy Feet.
Boone, Donna L. & McDonald, R. Michael. Sacred Relationships: The Psychospiritual Path to Love, Intimacy & Happiness. iv, 327p. (Orig.). 1997. wbk. ed. 60.00 (*0-9658841-1-2*); pap. 19.95 (*0-9658841-0-4*) Benthall Hall.
***Boone, Douglas Paul.** Death in Madison. LC 00-190643. 199p. 2000. 25.00 (*0-7388-1890-9*); pap. 18.00 (*0-7388-1891-7*) Xlibris Corp.
Boone, Edgar J. Developing Programs in Adult Education. (Illus.). 244p. (C). 1992. reprint ed. pap. text 24.95 (*0-88133-689-0*) Waveland Pr.
Boone, Edgar J., et al, eds. Community-Based Programming in Action: The Experiences of Five Community Colleges. LC 98-227906. 278p. 1998. pap. 33.00 (*0-87117-318-2*, 1419) Comm Coll Pr Am Assn Comm Coll.
— Serving Personal & Community Needs Through Adult Education. LC 79-9664. (Jossey-Bass Series in Higher Education). 360p. reprint ed. pap. 111.60 (*0-8357-4836-7*, 203777300009) Bks Demand.
Boone, Edgar S., ed. see Plank, Donald M.
Boone, Edward. The Romance of Redemption: Studies in the Book of Ruth. 2nd ed. 208p. 1997. pap. 10.99 (*0-907927-87-4*) Emerald House Group Inc.
Boone, Elizabeth, jt. auth. see Barclay, Kathy.
Boone, Elizabeth H. The Aztec World. LC 94-9830. (Exploring the Ancient World Ser.). (Illus.). 176p. 1996. text 24.95 (*0-89599-040-7*) Smithsonian.
Boone, Elizabeth H., ed. Andean Art at Dumbarton Oaks, 2 vols., Set. LC 95-32235. 1996. 150.00 (*0-88402-225-0*, Dumbarton Rsch Lib) Dumbarton Oaks.
— The Aztec Templo Mayor: Symposium at Dumbarton Oaks, October 8 & 9, 1983. LC 86-4539. (Illus.). 520p. 1987. 40.00 (*0-88402-149-1*, BOAT) Dumbarton Oaks.
— Collecting the Pre-Columbian Past: A Symposium at Dumbarton Oaks, 6th & 7th October 1990. LC 92-12125. (Illus.). 368p. 1993. 30.00 (*0-88402-208-0*, BOCP, Dumbarton Rsch Lib) Dumbarton Oaks.
— Painted Architecture & Polychrome Monumental Sculpture in Mesoamerica. LC 85-4514. (Illus.). 201p. 1985. 24.00 (*0-88402-142-4*) Dumbarton Oaks.
— Ritual Human Sacrifice in Mesoamerica: A Conference at Dumbarton Oaks, October 13 & 14, 1979. LC 83-14059. (Illus.). 256p. 1984. 20.00 (*0-88402-120-3*) Dumbarton Oaks.
Boone, Elizabeth H., et al, eds. Southeast Classic Maya Zone: Symposium at Dumbarton Oaks. LC 87-22290. (Illus.). 420p. 1988. 40.00 (*0-88402-170-X*) Dumbarton Oaks.
Boone, Elizabeth H. & Cummins, Tom, eds. Native Traditions in the Postconquest World: A Symposium at Dumbarton Oaks, 2nd Through 4th October 1992. LC 96-11704. (C). 1998. 30.00 (*0-88402-239-0*) Dumbarton Oaks.
Boone, Elizabeth H. & Mignolo, Walter D., eds. Writing Without Words: Alternative Literacies in Mesoamerica & the Andes. LC 93-4531. (Illus.). 352p. 1994. text 54.95 (*0-8223-1377-4*); pap. text 18.95 (*0-8223-1388-X*) Duke.
***Boone, Elizabeth Hill.** Stories in Red & Black. LC 99-6214. (Illus.). 336p. 1999. 55.00 (*0-292-70876-9*) U of Tex Pr.
Boone, Gene. Name Your Pet. 20p. (Orig.). 1986. pap. 2.95 (*0-930865-05-7*) RSVP Press.
— Writing to Be Published. 1984. pap. 4.95 (*0-317-11581-2*, Pub. by Exploits Pub Ltd) Sterling.
— Writing to Be Published. 2nd ed. 40p. 1986. pap. 4.00 (*0-930865-00-6*) RSVP Press.
Boone, Graeme, ed. Essays on Medieval Music in Honor of David G. Hughes. LC 94-48626. (Harvard Music Department Ser.). (Illus.). 352p. 1994. text 39.95 (*0-674-26706-0*, BOOESS) HUP.
Boone, Graeme, jt. ed. see Covach, John.
Boone, Graeme M. Patterns in Play: A Model for Text Setting in the Early French Songs of Guillaume Dufay. LC 98-14767. (American Musicological Society Monographs). (Illus.). 466p. 1998. text 75.00 (*0-8032-1235-6*) U of Nebr Pr.
Boone, J. Letters to Strongheart. 1980. pap. 10.00 (*0-933062-19-2*) R H Sommer.
— You Are the Adventure. 1980. pap. 9.00 (*0-933062-20-6*) R H Sommer.
Boone, J. Allen. Kinship with All Life: Simple, Challenging, Real-Life Experiences Showing How Animals Communicate with. LC 54-6901. 160p. 1976. pap. 12.00 (*0-06-060912-5*, RD128, Pub. by Harper SF) HarpC.
Boone, J. Allen & Leonard, Paul H. Adventures in Kinship with All Life. 3rd ed. 128p. 1994. pap. text 12.00 (*0-930852-27-3*) Tree Life Pubns.
Boone, Jack W. Autumn Reflections. 221p. 1997. pap. 14.95 (*1-880719-03-7*) Grafco Prods.
***Boone, Jack W.** Billy Box. 367p. 1999. pap. 14.95 (*1-880719-07-X*, Grafco Bks) Grafco Prods.
Boone, Jack W. The Eagle Society. 355p. 1998. pap. 14.95 (*1-880719-04-5*) Grafco Prods.
***Boone, Jack W.** The Estonia System. 371p. 1999. pap. 14.95 (*1-880719-09-6*, Grafco Bks) Grafco Prods
Boone, Jack W. Miss Emma's Way. 292p. 1998. pap. 14.95 (*1-880719-06-1*) Grafco Prods.
— The Nation's Party Concept. 229p. 1993. pap. 9.95 (*1-880719-01-0*) Grafco Prods.
— A Plan to Kill. 347p. 1997. pap. 14.95 (*1-880719-02-9*, Grafco Bks) Grafco Prods.
Boone, James C. Remington No. 1: West of the Pecos. 176p. 1987. pap. 2.50 (*0-380-75265-4*, Avon Bks) Morrow Avon.
— Remington No. 6: Border Trouble. 176p. 1988. pap. 2.75 (*0-380-75271-9*, Avon Bks) Morrow Avon.
— Remington No. 7: Red River Revenge. 160p. 1988. pap. 2.75 (*0-380-75559-9*, Avon Bks) Morrow Avon.
— Remington No. 8: Six-Guns at Spanish Peak. 176p. 1988. pap. 2.75 (*0-380-75560-2*, Avon Bks) Morrow Avon.
Boone, Jerry R. The Safety Line: Evidence of Things Not Seen. LC 97-52241. 112p. 1998. pap. 9.95 (*1-57249-109-4*, Ragged Edge) White Mane Pub.
Boone, Joan. Interfacing Smalltalk Applications to Relational Databases: A Practical Guide. (C). 2001. pap. text 35.00 (*0-13-230251-9*) P-H.
***Boone, John M. & Dobbins, James T., eds.** Physics of Medical Imaging. 1032p. 1999. pap. text 145.00 (*0-8194-3131-1*) SPIE.
Boone, John M., jt. ed. see Dobbins, James T.
Boone, Joseph A. Libidinal Currents. LC 97-30717. 528p. 1997. pap. text 18.95 (*0-226-06467-0*) U Ch Pr.
— Queer Frontiers: Millennial Geographies, Genders, & Generations. LC 98-48151. (Illus.). 392p. 1999. pap. text 24.95 (*0-299-16094-7*) U of Wis Pr.
— Queer Frontiers: Politics, Polemics & Possibilities for the Millennium. LC 98-48151. 1999. 59.95 (*0-299-16090-4*) U of Wis Pr.
— Tradition Counter Tradition: Love & the Form of Fiction. LC 86-30911. (Women in Culture & Society Ser.). 408p. (C). 1993. 27.50 (*0-226-06464-6*) U Ch Pr.
— Tradition Counter Tradition: Love & the Form of Fiction. LC 86-30911. (Women in Culture & Society Ser.). 406p. (C). 1996. pap. text 17.95 (*0-226-06465-4*) U Ch Pr.
— Tradition Counter Tradition: Love & the Form of Fiction. LC 86-30911. (Women in Culture & Society Ser.). 404p. Date not set. reprint ed. pap. 125.30 (*0-608-20594-X*, 205455900003) Bks Demand.
***Boone, Kevin Alexander, ed.** At the Millennium's End: New Essays on the Work of Kurt Vonnegut. (C). 2001. pap. text. write for info. (*0-7914-4930-0*) State U NY Pr.
— At the Millennium's End: New Essays on the Work of Kurt Vonnegut. (C). 2001. text. write for info. (*0-7914-4929-7*) State U NY Pr.
***Boone, Kristina, et al.** Agricultural Communications: Changes & Challenges. (Illus.). 120p. 2000. 34.95 (*0-8138-2157-6*) Iowa St U Pr.
Boone, Kurt B. Looking for Myself. 40p. 1995. pap. 5.00 (*0-8059-3570-3*) Dorrance.
Boone, L. V., et al. Producing Farm Crops. 4th ed. 392p. 1991. 44.95 (*0-8134-2874-2*); teacher ed. 9.95 (*0-8134-2875-0*) Interstate.
Boone, Lalia. Idaho Place Names: A Geographical Dictionary. 448p. 1987. pap. 17.95 (*0-89301-119-3*) U of Idaho Pr.
Boone, Laura, jt. auth. see Boone, Don.
Boone, Laurel, ed. see Roberts, G. D.
Boone, Louis. Quotable Business. 2nd ed. LC 98-36528. 1998. pap. 17.95 (*0-375-70308-X*) Random Ref & Info.
Boone, Louis & Kurtz, David. Business 1995. 95th ed. 496p. (C). 1995. text 72.50 (*0-03-010642-7*) Dryden Pr.
— Contemporary Marketing, Vol. 1, Chapters 1-12. 8th ed. 440p. (C). 1994. pap. text, teacher ed. 33.75 (*0-03-003909-6*) Harcourt Coll Pubs.
— Contemporary Marketing, Vol. 2, Chapters 13-20. 8th ed. 319p. (C). 1994. pap. text, teacher ed. 33.75 (*0-03-003912-6*) Harcourt Coll Pubs.
Boone, Louis E. Contemporary Business. 9th ed. (C). 1998. pap. text 44.50 (*0-03-021764-4*); pap. text 44.50 (*0-03-021767-9*) Harcourt Coll Pubs.
— Contemporary Business 9th ed. 1998. 88.50 (*0-03-021324-X*, Pub. by Harcourt Coll Pubs) Harcourt.
— Contemporary Business: 1997 Edition. 1997. pap. 51.00 (*0-03-024248-7*) HarBrace.
— Planning Your Financial Future. 1997. pap. text 60.00 (*0-03-024084-0*, Pub. by Harcourt Coll Pubs) Harcourt.
Boone, Louis E. & Bowen, Donald D. The Great Writings in Management. 2nd ed. 446p. (C). 1987. pap. 40.94 (*0-07-555030-X*) McGraw.
Boone, Louis E. & Hackleman, Edwin C. Marketing Strategy: A Marketing Decision Game. 2nd ed. LC 74-27870. iv, 156 p. 1975. write for info. (*0-675-08713-9*) Mrrill.
Boone, Louis E. & Kurtz, David L. Computer Cases: Contemporary Business. 7th ed. (C). 1993. pap. text 21.00 (*0-03-097687-1*) Dryden Pr.
— Contemporary Business. 7th ed. (C). 1993. teacher ed. 17.50 incl. 5.25 hd (*0-03-097597-2*) Dryden Pr.
— Contemporary Business. 7th ed. (C). 1993. teacher ed. 17.50 incl. 3.5 hd (*0-03-097734-7*) Dryden Pr.
— Contemporary Business. 7th ed. (C). 1993. disk 17.75 (*0-03-074702-3*) Dryden Pr.
— Contemporary Business. 9th ed. LC 98-85111. 864p. (C). 1998. text 88.50 (*0-03-022472-1*) Dryden Pr.
— Contemporary Business: Annotated Instructor's Edition. 7th ed. 965p. (C). 1993. teacher ed. 15.00 (*0-03-097207-8*) Dryden Pr.
— Contemporary Business; 1994 Edition. 7th ed. LC 93-73165. 823p. (C). 1994. pap. text 54.50 (*0-03-098472-6*) Dryden Pr.
— CONTEMPORARY BUSINESS, 1997 AN. 9th ed. LC 97-188793. 714p. (C). 1996. pap. text 53.00 (*0-03-019528-4*) Dryden Pr.
— Contemporary Marketing. 9th ed. LC 97-97635. 864p. (C). 1997. text 99.00 incl. cd-rom (*0-03-018597-1*) Dryden Pr.
— Management. 4th ed. (C). 1992. pap. text, student ed. 22.50 (*0-07-006577-2*) McGraw.
Boone, Louis E., et al. Contemporary Business Communication. LC 93-38478. 784p. (C). 1993. text 88.00 (*0-13-174731-2*, Pub. by P-H) S&S Trade.
— Contemporary Business Communication. 2nd ed. LC 96-41642. 645p. (C). 1996. 89.00 (*0-13-531245-0*) P-H.
***Boone, Louis E., et al.** Contemporary Business Communication, Canadian Edition: Instructor's Resource Manual with Video Guide. LC 98-14035. 424p. 1998. teacher ed. write for info. (*0-13-081517-9*) P-H.
Boone, Louis E., et al. Contemporary Marketing. 8th ed. 336p. (C). 1994. pap. text, teacher ed. 33.75 (*0-03-003973-8*) Harcourt Coll Pubs.
— Management. 2nd ed. Donnelly, Paul S., ed. (C). 1984. text. write for info. (*0-318-57307-5*) Random.
— Planning Your Financial Future. 2nd ed. LC 95-83880. 718p. (C). 1996. pap. text 61.50 incl. disk (*0-03-098844-6*) Dryden Pr.
Boone, Louis E., jt. auth. see Kurtz, David L.
***Boone, M. Broughton.** Not Me! I Scream: Poetry of Despair & Inner Peace. LC 99-90207. 56p. 1999. pap. 7.95 (*0-9671203-1-4*) Cape Winds Pr.
— Office Hours. LC 00-190827. (A Cape Winds Weekend Escape Ser.). 124p. 2000. pap. 10.95 (*0-9671203-4-9*) Cape Winds Pr.
Boone, Margaret S. Capital Crime: Black Infant Mortality in America. (Frontiers of Anthropology Ser.: Vol. 4). 256p. (C). 1989. text 52.00 (*0-8039-3373-8*); pap. text 25.00 (*0-8039-3374-6*) Sage.
— Capital Crime: Black Infant Mortality in America. LC 89-4046. (Frontiers of Anthropology Ser.: Vol. 4). 253p. 1989. reprint ed. pap. 78.50 (*0-608-02983-1*, 205962300006) Bks Demand.
— Capital Cubans: Refugee Adaptation in Washington, D. C. LC 88-35145. (Immigrant Communities & Ethnic Minorities in the U. S. & Canada Ser.: No. 40). 1989. 54.00 (*0-404-19450-8*) AMS Pr.
Boone, Mark A. Reunion. 224p. (Orig.). 1989. mass mkt. 2.95 (*0-87067-331-9*, BH331-9) Holloway.
Boone, Mark A., et al. Guildworks: Writings by the West Side Writers Guild. 160p. 1996. pap. 8.95 (*0-9649551-0-5*) Blacksmith Pr.
***Boone, Mary.** Interactive E-Manager: Smart Communication Strategies in an E-Business Era. 2001. 21.95 (*0-07-135866-8*) McGraw.
Boone, Mary E. Leadership & the Computer: Top Executives Reveal How They Personally Use Computers to Communicate, Coach, Convince & Compete. LC 90-49111. (Illus.). 416p. 1991. 24.95 (*1-55958-080-1*) Prima Pub.
— Leadership & the Computer: Top Executives Reveal How They Personally Use Computers to Communicate, Coach Convince & Compete. 397p. 1993. 14.95 (*1-892606-08-9*) NDMA Pubng.
Boone, Mary E., jt. auth. see Meyer, N. Dean.
Boone, Mary Lou. Terre et Feu: Four Centuries of French Ceramics. (Illus.). 104p. 1998. pap. 24.95 (*0-295-97721-3*) U of Wash Pr.
Boone, Morell D., et al. Training Student Library Assistants. LC 90-27837. 140p. (C). 1991. pap. text 25.00 (*0-8389-0561-7*, 0561-7) ALA.
Boone, Pat. Miracle of Prayer. 1989. 8.95 (*0-310-22131-5*) Zondervan.
Boone, Peter, et al, eds. Emerging from Communism: Lessons from Russia, China & Eastern Europe. LC 98-23560. (Illus.). 232p. 1998. 35.00 (*0-262-02447-0*) MIT Pr.
Boone, Randall, jt. ed. see Higgins, Kyle.
Boone, Rebecca. Essentialism as a Grand Unifying Theory: A Response to Conflicts in Feminism. 120p. (C). 1992. text 18.95 (*1-55643-141-4*) North Atlantic.
— From the Mind of a Mother: Essays for the 20th Century & Beyond. LC 95-44870. 321p. 1996. 39.95 (*1-57309-045-X*); pap. 34.95 (*1-57309-044-1*) Intl Scholars.
Boone, Rhonda J. Pocket Guide for Chiropractic Skeletal Radiography. (Illus.). 320p. (C). 1999. pap. 34.95 (*0-8385-8130-7*) McGraw.

B

An Asterisk (*) at the beginning of an entry indicates that the title is appearing for the first time.

Boone, Richard G. Education in the U. S. Its History from the Earliest Settlements. (Select Bibliographies Reprint Ser.). 1977. reprint ed. 24.95 (*0-8369-5924-8*) Ayer.
— History of Education in Indiana. 454p. 1941. 5.00 (*1-885323-46-8*) IN Hist Bureau.
Boone, Robert S. How to Improve Your Test-Taking Skills. LC 95-44443. 192p. 1995. pap. 12.95 (*0-8442-5893-8*, VGM Career) NTC Contemp Pub Co.
Boone, Robert S. What You Need to Know about Developing Your Test-Taking Skills: Reading Comprehension. LC 95-61813. (Illus.). 64p. 1995. pap. 9.95 (*0-8442-5896-2*, 58962) NTC Contemp Pub Co.
— What You Need to Know about Developing Your Test-Taking Skills: Standard English. LC 95-61815. (Illus.). 64p. 1995. pap. 9.95 (*0-8442-5894-6*, 58946) NTC Contemp Pub Co.
— What You Need to Know about Developing Your Test-Taking Skills: Writing Assessment. LC 95-61814. (Illus.). 64p. 1995. pap. 9.95 (*0-8442-5895-4*, 58954) NTC Contemp Pub Co.
Boone, Robert S., jt. ed. see McGee, Leo.
Boone, Shelby. We the Creators: From Shame to Honor. LC 89-91709. (Illus.). 386p. (Orig.). 1989. pap. 17.95 (*0-9622054-0-0*) Breakthrgh MN.
Boone-Smits, Else, jt. auth. see Smits, Johannes G.
Boone, Sylvia A. Radiance from the Waters: Ideals of Feminine Beauty in Mende Art. LC 85-19077. Vol. 34. 303p. (C). 1990. reprint ed. pap. 20.00 (*0-300-04861-0*) Yale U Pr.
Boone-Thomas, Del. For Kids Who Are Coming of Age: Talking to Teenagers in Language They Understand. LC 84-91735. (Illus.). 57p. (Orig.). 1983. pap. 9.95 (*0-9611780-0-0*) Boone-Thomas.
Boone, Wellington. Your Wife Is Not Your Momma: How You Can Have Heaven in Your Home. LC 98-42310. 304p. 1999. 19.95 (*0-385-49416-5*) Doubleday.
***Boone, Wellington.** Your Wife Is Not Your Momma: How You Can Have Heaven in Your Home. 304p. 2000. pap. 10.95 (*0-385-49417-3*) Doubleday.
Boone, Wellington. Your Wife Is Not Your Momma: How You Can Have Heaven in Your Home. 260p. 1997. pap. 15.00 (*0-9662161-0-5*) ProVision Pubns.
Boone, William B. California Tort Guide. 3rd ed. Peyrat, Paul, ed. LC 96-83278. 584p. 1996. ring bd. 119.00 (*0-88124-955-6*, TO-32540) Cont Ed Bar-CA.
— California Tort Guide. 3rd ed. Peyrat, Paul, ed. LC 96-83278. 476p. 1997. ring bd. 35.00 (*0-7626-0099-3*, TO-32541) Cont Ed Bar-CA.
***Boone, William B. & Peyrat, Paul.** California Tort Guide: April 2000 Update. 3rd ed. LC 96-83278. 500p. 2000. 45.00 (*0-7626-0419-0*) Cont Ed Bar-CA.
— California Tort Guide: 4/98 Update. 3rd ed. LC 96-83278. 504p. 1998. ring bd. 44.00 (*0-7626-0210-4*, TO-32542) Cont Ed Bar-CA.
Boone, William B., jt. auth. see Peyrat, Paul.
Boone, William T. Better Gymnastics: How to Spot the Performer. LC 78-368. (Illus.). 225p. 1979. pap. 10.00 (*0-89037-127-X*) Anderson World.
Boonin, Harry D. The Jewish Quarter of Philadelphia: A History & Guide, 1881-1930, No. 1. LC 99-90015. (Illus.). 275p. 1999. 29.95 (*0-9669884-0-X*) Jewish Walk Tours.
Boonin, Elizabeth. Using Excel Visual Basic for Applications. (Illus.). 432p. 1995. 24.99 (*0-7897-0325-4*) Que.
Boonman, J. G. East Africa's Grasses & Fodders: Ecology & Husbandry. LC 92-23961. (Tasks for Vegetation Science Ser.: Vol. 29). 1993. text 335.00 (*0-7923-1867-6*) Kluwer Academic.
***Boonprasat-Lewis, Nantawan & Fortune, Marie M.** Remembering Conquest: Feminist/Womanist Perspectives on Religion, Colonization & Sexual Violence. LC 99-46046. 91p. 1999. 13.95 (*0-7890-0829-7*, Haworth Pastrl) Haworth Pr.
***Boons, Frank, ed.** The Changing Nature of Business: Institutionalisation of Green Organisational Routines in the Netherlands, 1986-1996. 320p. 2000. pap. 29.95 (*90-5727-036-6*, Pub. by Intl Bks) Paul & Co Pubs.
Boons, Geert-Jan, ed. Carbohydrate Chemistry. LC 97-75080. 528p. 1997. write for info. (*0-7514-0396-2*) Kluwer Academic.
***Boonstra, Harry.** Homelink - Worship: A Closer Look. 72p. 2000. pap. 12.75 (*1-56212-566-4*, 420400) CRC Pubns.
Boonyubol, M. & Pramokchutima, S. Trawl Fisheries in the Gulf of Thailand. Bhukaswan, T., tr. (ICLARM Translations Ser.: No. 4). 12p. 1984. write for info. (*971-10-2213-3*, Pub. by ICLARM) Intl Spec Bk.
Boonzaier, Emile, et al. The Cape Herders: A History of the Khoikoi of Southern Africa. LC 96-32136. (Illus.). 155p. (Orig.). 1997. pap. text 19.95 (*0-8214-1174-8*) Ohio U Pr.
Boor, Carl De, see De Boor, Carl.
Boor, Daniel J., ed. see Bremner, Robert H.
Boor, Helmut De & Wisniewski, Roswitha. Mittelhochdeutsche Grammatik. 9th ed. (Sammlung Goeschen Ser.: Vol. 2209). (C). 1984. pap. text 15.25 (*3-11-010191-2*) De Gruyter.
Booraem, Curtis, jt. auth. see Weber, Joseph A.
Booraem, Hendrik. The Provincial: Calvin Coolidge & His World, 1885-1895. LC 94-20106. 1995. 39.50 (*0-8387-5264-0*) Bucknell U Pr.
Boord, R. L., ed. Structure, Development, & Phykogeny of Cranial Nerves. (Journal: Acta Anatomica: Vol. 148, Nos. 2-3, 1993). (Illus.). 104p. 1993. pap. 214.00 (*3-8055-5909-7*) S Karger.
Boord, W. Arthur, ed. Sun Artists (Original Series), Nos. 1[00ad]8. LC 72-9184. (Literature of Photography Ser.). 1979. reprint ed. 48.95 (*0-405-04895-5*) Ayer.
Boore, D. M., et al. Estimation of Response Spectra & Peak Accelerations from Western North America Earthquakes. (Illus.). 72p. (Orig.). (YA). (gr. 12 up). 1994. pap. text 40.00 (*0-7881-0852-2*) DIANE Pub.
Boorer, Suzanne. The Promise of the Land As Oath: A Key to the Formation of the Pentateuch. (Beiheft zur Zeitschrift fuer die Alttestamentliche Wissenschaft Ser.: No. 205). xvi, 470p. (C). 1992. lib. bdg. 141.55 (*3-11-013505-1*) De Gruyter.
***Boorer, Wendy.** Dogs. (Collins Gem Ser.). (Illus.). 256p. 2000. pap. 7.95 (*0-00-472276-0*, Pub. by HarpC) Trafalgar.
Boorkman, C. J. Chicano Bibliography. 1974. 250.00 (*0-87968-398-8*) Gordon Pr.
Boorkman, Joanne, ed. Introduction to Reference Sources in the Health Sciences. 3rd ed. LC 94-10708. 301p. 1995. 37.00 (*0-8108-2889-8*) Scarecrow.
Boorman, Derek. At the Going down of the Sun: War Memorials of World War One. (C). 1989. 53.00 (*1-85072-041-X*, Pub. by W Sessions) St Mut.
Boorman, Gary A., et al, eds. Pathology of the Fischer Rat: Reference & Atlas. 580p. 1990. text 167.00 (*0-12-115640-0*) Acad Pr.
Boorman, Howard L. & Howard, Richard C., eds. Biographical Dictionary of Republican China, 4 vols. Incl. Vol. 1. Ai-Ch'u. LC 67-12006. 1967. text 110.50 (*0-231-08955-4*); Vol. 3. Mao-Wu. LC 67-12006. 1970. text 110.50 (*0-231-08957-0*); Vol. 4. Yang-Bibliography. LC 67-12006. 1971. text 110.50 (*0-231-08958-9*); LC 67-12006. write for info. (*0-318-51404-4*) Col U Pr.
Boorman, Howard L. & Krompart, Janet, eds. Biographical Dictionary of Republican China: A Personal Name Index, Vol. 5. 1979. text 110.50 (*0-231-04558-1*) Col U Pr.
Boorman, John. The General. (Illus.). 160p. 1998. pap. 14.00 (*0-571-19646-2*) Faber & Faber.
— Hope & Glory. (Illus.). 149p. (Orig.). 1988. pap. 7.95 (*0-571-14983-9*) Faber & Faber.
— Projections 8: Film-Makers on Film-Making. 1998. pap. 19.95 (*0-571-19355-2*) Faber & Faber.
— Projections 5: Film-Makers on Film-Making. Donohue, Walter, ed. LC 96-210403. 304p. 1996. pap. 18.95 (*0-571-17811-1*) Faber & Faber.
Boorman, John, et al, eds. Projections 4: Film-Makers on Film-Making. (Projections Ser.: Vol. 4). (Illus.). 288p. (Orig.). 1995. pap. 18.95 (*0-571-17363-2*) Faber & Faber.
Boorman, John & Donohue, Walter, eds. Projections: Film-Makers on Film-Making, No. 6. (Illus.). 304p. (Orig.). 1996. pap. 16.95 (*0-571-17853-7*) Faber & Faber.
— Projections 4 & 1/2: Film-Makers on Film-Making. (Projections Ser.). 288p. 1995. pap. 16.95 (*0-571-17609-7*) Faber & Faber.
— Projections 9: Film-Makers on Film-Making. (Illus.). 384p. 1999. pap. 21.95 (*0-571-19356-0*) Faber & Faber.
— Projections 7: Film-Makers on Film-Making. (Illus.). 304p. (Orig.). 1997. pap. 16.95 (*0-571-19033-2*) Faber & Faber.
— Projections 3: A Year in Film. (Illus.). 288p. 1994. pap. 19.95 (*0-571-17047-1*) Faber & Faber.
Boorman, John T., jt. auth. see Havrilesky, Thomas M.
Boorman, John T., jt. auth. see Schweitzer, Robert.
Boorman, John T., jt. ed. see Havrilesky, Thomas M.
Boorman, K. N., ed. see International Symposium on Protein Metabolism & Nu.
Boorman, Kathleen E., et al. Blood Group Serology. 6th ed. (Illus.). 448p. 1987. text 95.00 (*0-443-02636-X*) Church.
Boorn, G. P. Van Den, see Van Den Boorn, G. P.
Boorsch, Suzanne, ed. The Illustrated Bartsch Vol. 28: Italian Masters of the Sixteenth Century. 1985. 149.00 (*0-89835-028-X*) Abaris Bks.
— The Illustrated Bartsch Vol. 29: Italian Masters of the Sixteenth Century. 1982. lib. bdg. 149.00 (*0-89835-029-8*) Abaris Bks.
Boorsch, Suzanne & Spike, John T., eds. The Illustrated Bartsch Vol. 31: Italian Masters of the Sixteenth Century. 1986. 149.00 (*0-89835-031-X*) Abaris Bks.
Boorsch, Suzanne, et al. Italian Artists of the Sixteenth Century LC 98-150418. (Illustrated Bartsch Ser.). (Illus.). 445p. 1986. write for info. (*0-89835-130-8*) Abaris Bks.
***Boorsma, P. B., et al.** Privatization & Culture: Experiences in the Arts, Heritage & Cultural Industries in Europe. LC 98-32185. 11p. 1999. write for info. (*0-7923-8409-1*) Kluwer Academic.
Boorsma, P. B., et al. Public Priority Setting: Rules & Costs. LC 97-38233. 350p. 1997. lib. bdg. 164.00 (*0-7923-4823-0*, D Reidel) Kluwer Academic.
Boorsma, Peter B., jt. auth. see Halachmi, Arie.
Boorstein, Edward. Allende's Chile: An Inside View. LC 77-4894. 288p. 1987. pap. 5.95 (*0-7178-0488-7*) Intl Pubs Co.
— The Economic Transformation of Cuba: A First-Hand Account. LC 68-13652. 320p. reprint ed. pap. 99.20 (*0-8357-6100-2*, 203433500089) Bks Demand.
Boorstein, Edward & Boorstein, Regula. Counterrevolution: U. S. Foreign Policy. Smith, Betty, ed. LC 90-40845. 330p. (Orig.). 1990. pap. 8.95 (*0-7178-0684-7*) Intl Pubs Co.
Boorstein, Regula, jt. auth. see Boorstein, Edward.
Boorstein, Seymour. Clinical Studies in Transpersonal Psychotherapy. LC 96-23228. (SUNY Series in the Philosophy of Psychology). 191p. (C). 1997. text 49.50 (*0-7914-3333-1*); pap. text 16.95 (*0-7914-3334-X*) State U NY Pr.
Boorstein, Seymour, ed. Transpersonal Psychotherapy. 2nd ed. LC 95-44527. (SUNY Series in the Philosophy of Psychology). 587p. (C). 1996. pap. text 23.95 (*0-7914-2836-2*) State U NY Pr.
Boorstein, Sylvia. Don't Just Do Something, Sit There: A Mindfulness Retreat with Sylvia Boorstein. LC 95-32865. 160p. 1996. pap. 12.00 (*0-06-061252-5*, Pub. by Harper SF) HarpC.
— It's Easier Than You Think: The Buddhist Way to Happiness. LC 95-8046. 160p. 1997. pap. 12.00 (*0-06-251294-3*, Pub. by Harper SF) HarpC.
Boorstein, Sylvia & Lebell, Sharon. That's Funny, You Don't Look Buddhist: Why Jews Are Attracted to Buddhism & How Both Traditions Can Enrich Our Lives. LC 96-16447. 192p. 1998. pap. 13.00 (*0-06-060958-3*, Pub. by Harper SF) HarpC.
***Boorstin.** History USA. annot. ed. (Boorstin-K United States History). 1999. text, teacher ed. write for info. (*0-13-388844-4*, Prentice Hall) P-H.
Boorstin, Daniel J. American National Experience. 1967. pap. 16.00 (*0-394-70358-8*) Knopf.
— The Americans Vol. 1: The Colonial Experience. (YA). (gr. 7-12). 1964. pap. text 9.95 (*0-07-553700-1*) McGraw.
— Americans Vol. 1: The Colonial Experience. LC 75-330427. Vol. 1. 434p. 1964. pap. 13.00 (*0-394-70513-0*) Vin Bks.
— Americans Vol. 2: The National Experience. 1965. pap. 8.95 (*0-685-29461-7*) Vin Bks.
— The Americans Three: The Democratic Experience. LC 74-3298. 1974. pap. 17.00 (*0-394-71011-8*, V-11) Vin Bks.
— Cleopatra's Nose: Essays on the Unexpected. 224p. 1995. pap. 12.00 (*0-679-75518-7*) Vin Bks.
— The Creators: A History of Heroes of the Imagination. LC 93-15502. 832p. 1993. reprint ed. pap. 18.00 (*0-679-74375-8*) Vin Bks.
— The Daniel J. Boorstin Reader. 679p. 1995. 23.00 (*0-679-60165-1*) Random.
— The Discoverers. 1983. 45.00 (*0-394-40229-4*) Random.
— The Discoverers. 1993. pap. 16.00 (*0-394-25633-6*) Vin Bks.
— The Discoverers: A History of Man's Search to Know His World & Himself. 768p. 1985. pap. 16.00 (*0-394-72625-1*) Vin Bks.
Boorstin, Daniel J. Genius of American Politics. LC 53-9434. (Walgreen Foundation Lectures). 208p. 1958. pap. text 11.95 (*0-226-06491-3*, P27) U Ch Pr.
Boorstin, Daniel J. Hidden History. 1992. 25.50 (*0-8446-6614-9*) Peter Smith.
— Hidden History. LC 88-40529. 332p. 1989. pap. 14.00 (*0-679-72223-8*) Vin Bks.
— The Image: A Guide to Pseudo-Events in America. LC 92-50080. 1992. pap. 13.00 (*0-679-74180-1*) Vin Bks.
— The Lost World of Thomas Jefferson. LC 80-26835. 320p. 1981. pap. 12.95 (*0-226-06496-4*) U Ch Pr.
— The Lost World of Thomas Jefferson. LC 93-17196. xiv, 320p. 1993. pap. 14.95 (*0-226-06497-2*) U Ch Pr.
— The Mysterious Science of the Law. (Illus.). 288p. 1996. pap. text 14.95 (*0-226-06498-0*) U Ch Pr.
Boorstin, Daniel J. The Seekers. ed. 25.95 (*0-679-46270-8*) Random.
Boorstin, Daniel J. The Seekers: The Story of Man's Continuing Quest to Understand His World. 352p. 1999. pap. 14.00 (*0-375-70475-2*) Knopf.
— The Seekers: The Story of Man's Continuing Quest to Understand His World. LC 98-15430. 298p. 1998. 25.95 (*0-679-43445-3*) Random.
Boorstin, Daniel J., ed. America in Two Centuries: An Inventory. 1976. 3571.50 (*0-405-07666-5*) Ayer.
— An American Primer. 1968. pap. 19.95 (*0-452-00922-7*, Mer) NAL.
— An American Primer, 2 vols. LC 76-361751. 1012p. reprint ed. pap. 200.00 (*0-608-09391-2*, 205413600004); reprint ed. pap. 200.00 (*0-608-20595-8*, 205456000001) Bks Demand.
— Technology & Society, 53 bks. 1972. reprint ed. 1502.50 (*0-405-04680-4*) Ayer.
Boorstin, Daniel J., ed. An American Primer: 1890-1900: A Citizen's History. abr. ed. (Illus.). 128p. (C). 1996. pap. text 2.25 (*1-877891-30-4*) Paperbook Pr Inc.
Boorstin, Daniel J., ed. see Ellis, John T.
Boorstin, Daniel J., ed. see Glazer, Nathan.
Boorstin, Daniel J., ed. see Hays, Samuel P.
Boorstin, Jon. Making Movies Work: Thinking Like a Filmmaker. (Illus.). 228p. (Orig.). 1995. pap. 19.95 (*1-879505-27-4*) Silman James Pr.
— Pay or Play. LC 99-89202. 278p. 2000. pap. 12.95 (*1-890085-04-9*, Pub. by Siles Pr) SCB Distributors.
Boorstin, Ruth F. Love Is Not . . . Because. LC 98-84271. 192p. 1998. lib. bdg. 14.95 (*1-883477-24-7*) Lone Oak MN.
Boorstin, Sharon, jt. ed. see Gayot, Alain.
Boorstin, Sharon, ed. see Gayot, Andre.
Boorstyn, Neil. Boorstyn on Copyright Law, 2 vols. 2nd ed. LC 94-27684. (IP Ser.). 1994. ring bd. 225.00 (*0-87632-152-X*) West Group.
Boortz, Charles C. Cyclicality in a Commercial Real Estate Market: A View from Dallas in the 1980s. LC 96-85501. (Bruton Center for Development Studies). 232p. 1996. text 72.95 (*1-85972-433-7*, Pub. by Avebry) Ashgate Pub Co.
Boortz, Neal. The Commencement Speech You Need to Hear. 96p. 1997. 12.95 (*1-56352-434-1*) Longstreet.
— The Terrible Truth about Liberals. LC 97-76254. 128p. 1998. 12.95 (*1-56352-487-2*) Longstreet.
Boos, Eric J. Perspectives in Jurisprudence: An Analysis of H. L. A. Hart's Legal Theory, Vol. 184. LC 97-26603. (American University Studies V). 212p. (C). 1998. pap. text 25.95 (*0-8204-3902-9*) P Lang Pubng.
Boos, Florence & Miller, Lynn F., eds. Bibliography of Women & Literature, 2 Vols., Set. LC 81-6989. 808p. 1989. 145.00 (*0-8419-0693-9*) Holmes & Meier.
Boos, Florence S. The Design of William Morris' "The Earthly Paradise" LC 89-12180. (Studies in British Literature: Vol. 6). 592p. 1991. lib. bdg. 119.95 (*0-88946-933-4*) E Mellen.
— The Poetry of Dante G. Rossetti: A Critical Reading & Source Study. (Studies in English Literature: No. 104). 1976. text 61.55 (*90-279-3471-1*) Mouton.
Boos, Florence S., ed. History & Community: Essays in Victorian Medievalism. LC 92-3196. (Illus.). 308p. 1992. text 20.00 (*0-8153-0792-6*, H1563) Garland.
Boos, Florence S., ed. see Morris, William.
Boos-Hamburger, H. Creative Power of Colour. 1973. lib. bdg. 250.00 (*0-87968-488-7*) Krishna Pr.
***Boos, Johann.** Classical & Modern Methods in Summability. (Oxford Mathematical Monographs). 416p. 2001. text 130.00 (*0-19-850165-X*) OUP.
Boos, Kevin. Alpha. (Illus.). 1997. pap. 5.95 (*1-885101-69-4*) Writers Pr ID.
— The Canyon Door. (Illus.). 148p. (Orig.). (J). (gr. 4-6). 1993. pap. 5.95 (*1-885101-00-7*) Writers Pr ID.
— Catch a Poetic Hodgepodge. LC 95-197412. (Illus.). 40p. (Orig.). (J). 1998. pap. 4.95 (*1-885101-15-5*) Writers Pr ID.
Boos, Kevin, et al. Canyon Door Resource Guide. (Illus.). 40p. (Orig.). (J). (gr. 4-8). 1994. pap. 7.99 (*1-885101-03-1*) Writers Pr ID.
Boosalis, Harry M. The Joy of the Holy: Saint Seraphim of Sarov & Orthodox Spiritual Life. LC 93-12991. 1993. write for info. (*1-878997-39-4*) St Tikhons Pr.
***Boosalis, Harry M.** Orthodox Spiritual Life According to Saint Silouan of Mount Athos. LC 00-22089. 2000. pap. write for info. (*1-878997-60-2*) St Tikhons Pr.
Boose, Donald W., Jr., jt. auth. see Gabriel, Richard A.
Boose, John H. & Gaines, Brian R., eds. The Foundations of Knowledge Acquisition. (Knowledge Based Systems Ser.: Vol. 4). 385p. 1990. text 73.00 (*0-12-115922-1*) Acad Pr.
Boose, John H., jt. ed. see Gaines, Brian R.
Boose, Lynda E., jt. auth. see Burt, Richard.
Booser, E. R. The Handbook of Lubrication, Vol. III: Theory - Practice of Tribology. 640p. 1993. boxed set 177.95 (*0-8493-3903-0*) CRC Pr.
Booser, E. R., ed. Handbook of Lubrication (Theory & Practice of Tribology) Applications & Maintenance, Vol. 1. 624p. 1983. boxed set 236.95 (*0-8493-3901-4*, TJ1075) CRC Pr.
— Handbook of Lubrication (Theory & Practice of Tribology) Theory & Design, Vol. 2. 704p. 1988. boxed set 240.95 (*0-8493-3902-2*, TJ1075) CRC Pr.
Booser, E. Richard, ed. Tribology Data Handbook. LC 97-6215. 1120p. 1997. boxed set 159.95 (*0-8493-3904-9*, 3904) CRC Pr.
Booser, Petrie R. T'was a Twig. (Illus.). 80p. 1990. lib. bdg. 19.00 (*0-685-35753-8*) Inniea Pub Co.
Booss, B. & Bleecker, D. D. Topology & Analysis. Mader, A., tr. from GER. (Universitext Ser.). (Illus.). xvi, 451p. 1989. 69.95 (*0-387-96112-7*) Spr-Verlag.
Booss-Bavnbek, Bernhelm & Wojciechowski, Krzysztof P. Elliptic Boundary Problems for Dirac Operators. LC 93-22006. (Mathematics Ser.). (Illus.). 300p. 1993. 54.50 (*0-8176-3681-1*) Birkhauser.
Boostrom, Robert. Developing Creative & Critical Thinking: An Integrated Approach. (Illus.). 320p. 1994. pap. 22.95 (*0-8442-5680-3*, 56803, Natl Textbk Co) NTC Contemp Pub Co.
Boostrom, Ron, ed. Enduring Issues in Criminology. (Enduring Issues Ser.). 310p. (C). 1995. pap. text 17.45 (*1-56510-255-X*, 255X); lib. bdg. 27.45 (*1-56510-256-8*, 2568) Greenhaven.
***Boot.** Savage Wars of Peace. 2000. 30.00 (*0-465-00720-1*, Pub. by Basic) HarpC.
Boot, ed. Statistics. (C). 2000. text. write for info. (*0-321-01613-0*) Addson-Wesley Educ.
Boot, Adrian & Salewicz, Chris. Bob Marley: Songs of Freedom. (Illus.). 288p. 1995. 34.95 (*0-670-85784-X*, Viking Studio) Studio Bks.
Boot, Andrew. Psychic Murder Hunters: Real-Life Stories of Paranormal Detection. (Illus.). 384p. 1995. mass mkt. 11.95 (*0-7472-4302-6*, Pub. by Headline Bk Pub) Trafalgar.
Boot, Andy. ESP: Are You a Mind Reader? (Elements of the Extraordinary Ser.). (Illus.). 128p. (YA). (gr. 5-9). 1998. pap. 5.95 (*1-901881-25-3*, Pub. by Element MA) Penguin Putnam.
***Boot, Andy.** Fragments of Fear: An Illustrated History of British Horror Films. (Cinema Collection : No. 3). (Illus.). 288p. 2000. pap. 19.95 (*1-84068-055-5*, Pub. by Creation Books) Subterranean Co.
Boot, Andy. Fragments of Fear: An Illustrated History of British Horror Movies. (Illus.). 288p. (Orig.). 1996. pap. 17.95 (*1-871592-35-6*) Creation Books.
Boot, John C. Common Globe or Global Commons: Population Regulation & Income Distribution. LC 74-79919. (Business Economics & Finance Ser.: No. 1). 155p. reprint ed. pap. 48.10 (*0-7837-0857-2*, 204116500019) Bks Demand.
Boot, Max. Out of Order: Arrogance, Corruption & Incompetence on the Bench. LC 97-52791. 272p. 1998. 25.00 (*0-465-05432-3*, Pub. by Basic) HarpC.
— Out of Order: Arrogance, Corruption & Incompetence on the Bench. 272p. 1999. pap. 12.00 (*0-465-05375-0*, Pub. by Basic) HarpC.
Boot, Richard, et al, eds. Managing the Unknown: By Creating New Futures. LC 94-15999. 1994. 27.95 (*0-07-707626-5*) McGraw.
Boot, William. Carrot Cake Cookbook: Forty-Five Varieties. 24p. 1986. pap. 3.00 (*0-938592-01-7*) Harriets Kitchen.
— Harriet's Sugar-Free Cookbook 170 recipes. 48p. 1986. pap. 5.95 (*0-938592-00-9*) Harriets Kitchen.
— Harriet's Zucchini Lovers' Cookbook. (Illus.). 260p. 1986. reprint ed. pap. 7.95 (*0-938592-03-3*) Harriets Kitchen.
Boote, Anthony R., et al. Official Financing for Developing Countries. LC 96-135458. 120 p. 1995. write for info. (*1-55775-527-2*) Intl Monetary.

An Asterisk (*) at the beginning of an entry indicates that the title is appearing for the first time.

Boote, K. J. Modeling Crop Photosynthesis - From Biochemistry to Canopy. (Special Publication Ser.: Vol. 19). 140p. 1991. 25.00 (*0-89118-533-X*) Crop Sci Soc Am.

Boote, K. J., et al, eds. Physiology & Determination of Crop Yield. LC 94-12436. 601p. 1994. 66.00 (*0-89118-122-9*) Am Soc Agron.

Boote, Rene, jt. auth. see Reason, Rea.

Bootel, Jaclyn A. & Council for Exceptional Children Staff. CEC Handbook for Strengthening Grassroots Advocacy. LC 99-18238. 1999. write for info. (*0-86586-341-5*) Coun Exc Child.

Bootel, Jaclyn A. & Warger, Cynthia L. Political Advocacy Handbook. 193p. 1997. pap. 85.70 (*0-86586-291-5*) Coun Exc Child.

Booth. Communications Audit. 131p. 1988. 65.95 (*0-566-02725-9*) Ashgate Pub Co.

Booth. Controlling Development: Certainty, Discretion & Accountability. LC 96-219353. 224p. 1996. pap. 24.95 (*1-85728-585-9*, Pub. by UCL Pr Ltd) Taylor & Francis.

— Criticism in the Performing Arts. 1994. 19.18 (*0-02-903870-7*) S&S Trade.

Booth. European Monetary Unions. pap. text. write for info. (*0-471-49109-8*) Wiley.

Booth. Rocks, Minerals, Gems, Fossils, & Crystals. 1995. 15.98 (*0-7858-0242-8*) Bk Sales Inc.

— Small Mammals of West Africa. Date not set. pap. text. write for info. (*0-582-60848-1*, Pub. by Addison-Wesley) Longman.

— Test Assessment & Impressions: Grade 1. 1991. pap. text, teacher ed. 12.50 (*0-03-927238-9*) Harcourt Schl Pubs.

— Test Assessment & Impressions: Grade 2. 1991. pap. text, teacher ed. 12.50 (*0-03-927239-7*) Harcourt Schl Pubs.

— Test Assessment & Impressions: Grade 3. 1991. pap. text, teacher ed. 12.50 (*0-03-927240-0*) Harcourt Schl Pubs.

— Test Assessment & Impressions: Grade 4. 1991. pap. text, teacher ed. 12.50 (*0-03-927241-9*) Harcourt Schl Pubs.

— Test Assessment & Impressions: Grade 5. 1991. pap. text, teacher ed. 12.50 (*0-03-927242-7*) Harcourt Schl Pubs.

— Test Assessment & Impressions: Grade 6. 1991. pap. text, teacher ed. 12.50 (*0-03-927243-5*) Harcourt Schl Pubs.

Booth, A. Roads to Sata. 1996. pap. 15.95 (*0-8348-0246-5*) Weatherhill.

Booth, A. E. Ministry of Peter, John & Paul. 1982. pap. 1.95 (*0-88172-004-6*) Believers Bkshelf.

Booth, Alan. Japan: Land of Myth & Legend. 2nd ed. (Illus.). 256p. 1994. pap. 15.95 (*0-8442-9684-8*, 96848, Passprt Bks) NTC Contemp Pub Co.

— Looking for the Lost: Journeys Through a Vanishing Japan. Urda, John, ed. (Illus.). 416p. 1995. 25.00 (*1-56836-065-7*) Kodansha.

— Looking for the Lost: Journeys Through a Vanishing Japan. Sitzer, Joshua, ed. (Illus.). 416p. 1996. pap. 15.00 (*1-56836-148-3*, Kodansha Globe) Kodansha.

***Booth, Alan.** Practice of University History. 2000. pap. 27.95 (*0-7190-5492-3*, Pub. by Manchester Univ Pr); text 79.95 (*0-7190-5491-5*, Pub. by Manchester Univ Pr) St Martin.

Booth, Alan. The Roads to Sata. large type ed. (Non-Fiction Ser.). 608p. 1992. 27.99 (*0-7089-2654-1*) Ulverscroft.

— The Roads to Sata: A 2000-Mile Walk Through Japan. 304p. 1997. pap. 16.00 (*1-56836-187-4*, Kodansha Globe) Kodansha.

Booth, Alan, ed. Child Care in the 1990s: Trends & Consequences. 264p. 1992. text 69.95 (*0-8058-1060-9*) L Erlbaum Assocs.

— Child Care in the 1990s: Trends & Consequences. 264p. 1992. pap. 29.95 (*0-8058-1061-7*) L Erlbaum Assocs.

— Contemporary Families: Looking Forward, Looking Back. (Illus.). 481p. (Orig.). (C). 1991. pap. text 26.95 (*0-916174-29-8*) Natl Coun Family.

Booth, Alan, et al, eds. Immigration & the Family: Research & Policy on U. S. Immigrants. LC 96-8752. 275p. 1996. 59.95 (*0-8058-2153-8*) L Erlbaum Assocs.

***Booth, Alan & Crouter, Ann C., eds.** Does It Take a Village? Community Effects on Children, Adolescents & Families. LC 99-38654. 304p. 1999. write for info. (*0-8058-3242-4*); pap. write for info. (*0-8058-3243-2*) L Erlbaum Assocs.

Booth, Alan & Crouter, Ann C., eds. Men in Families: When Do They Get Involved? What Difference Does It Make? LC 97-12617. 275p. 1998. 89.95 (*0-8058-2539-8*) L Erlbaum Assocs.

Booth, Alan & Dunn, Judith, eds. Stepfamilies: Who Benefits? Who Does Not? 256p. 1994. text 49.95 (*0-8058-1544-9*) L Erlbaum Assocs.

Booth, Alan & Dunn, Judith F., eds. Family-School Links: How Do They Affect Educational Outcomes? 312p. 1996. text 69.95 (*0-8058-1840-5*) L Erlbaum Assocs.

Booth, Alan, jt. auth. see Amato, Paul R.

Booth, Alan, jt. auth. see Glynn, Sean.

Booth, Alan, jt. ed. see Edwards, John.

Booth, Alan, jt. ed. see Holmes, Colin.

Booth, Alan C., ed. see Shanahan, Michael.

***Booth, Alan R.** Historical Dictionary of Swaziland. 2nd ed. LC 99-53345. (African Historical Dictionaries Ser.: No. 80). 456p. 2000. 75.00 (*0-8108-3749-8*) Scarecrow.

Booth, Alison. Greatness Engendered: George Eliot & Virginia Woolf. LC 91-28120. (Reading Women Writing Ser.). 336p. 1992. text 49.95 (*0-8014-2628-6*); pap. text 17.95 (*0-8014-9930-5*) Cornell U Pr.

Booth, Alison, ed. Famous Last Words: Changes in Gender & Narrative Closure. LC 93-7084. (Feminist Issues Ser.). (Illus.). 400p. 1993. pap. text 19.50 (*0-8139-1437-X*) U Pr of Va.

Booth, Alison & Snower, Dennis J., eds. Acquiring Skills: Market Failures, Their Symptoms & Policy Responses. (Illus.). 371p. (C). 1996. text 69.95 (*0-521-47205-9*) Cambridge U Pr.

Booth, Alison L. The Economics of the Trade Union. (Illus.). 311p. (C). 1995. text 69.95 (*0-521-46467-6*); pap. text 23.95 (*0-521-46839-6*) Cambridge U Pr.

Booth, Alison L. & Snower, Dennis J., eds. Acquiring Skills: Market Failures, Their Smptoms & Policy Responses. 372p. 1996. pap. text 26.95 (*0-521-47957-6*) Cambridge U Pr.

Booth, Allyson. Postcards from the Trenches: Negotiating the Space Between Modernism & the First World War. (Illus.). 200p. 1996. text 42.00 (*0-19-510211-8*) OUP.

***Booth, Alvin.** Alvin Booth Corpus: Beyond the Body. 1999. 65.00 (*3-908161-94-0*) Abbeville Pr.

Booth, Angela. Home Sweet Office: Your Home Office. 136p. (C). 1998. pap. text 19.95 (*0-13-894957-3*) P-H.

— Lifetime: Better Time Management in 21 Days. 152p. (C). 1998. pap. text 19.95 (*0-13-894973-5*) P-H.

Booth, Anne, ed. Sterilization of Medical Devices. LC 98-46879. (Illus.). 424p. 1998. 179.00 (*1-57491-087-6*) Interpharm.

Booth, Anne, et al, eds. Indonesian Economic History of the Dutch Colonial Era. LC 89-51449. (Monographs: No. 35). 367p. 1990. 30.00 (*0-938692-42-9*); pap. 17.00 (*0-685-45589-0*) Yale U SE Asia.

Booth, Annice. Path to Your Ascension: Rediscovering Life's Ultimate Purpose. LC 98-88846. 1999. pap. text 12.95 (*0-922729-47-6*) Summit Univ.

Booth Associates Staff, ed. see Del Giacco, Maureen.

Booth, Barbara, ed. Thesaurus of Sociological Indexing Terms. 4th ed. 350p. (C). 1996. 70.00 (*0-930710-13-4*) Soc Abstracts.

Booth, Barbara D. Mandy. LC 90-19989. (Illus.). 32p. (J). (gr. 1 up). 1991. 16.00 (*0-688-10338-3*) Lothrop.

— Mandy. large type ed. (Illus.). 1993. 9.50 (*0-614-09841-6*, L-34096-00) Am Printing Hse.

Booth, Basil. Earthquakes & Volcanoes. LC 91-44878. (Repairing the Damage Ser.). (Illus.). 48p. (J). (gr. 4-6). 1992. lib. bdg. 13.95 (*0-02-711735-9*, Mac Bks Young Read) S&S Childrens.

— Rocks & Minerals. 80p. 1993. 6.98 (*1-55521-838-5*) Bk Sales Inc.

— Temperate Forests. Furstinger, Nancy, ed. (Our World Ser.). (Illus.). 48p. (J). (gr. 5-8). 1989. lib. bdg. 16.95 (*0-382-09791-2*) Silver Burdett Pr.

— Volcanoes & Earthquakes. (Our World Ser.). (Illus.). 48p. (J). (gr. 5-8). 1991. lib. bdg. 12.95 (*0-382-24227-0*) Silver Burdett Pr.

Booth, Ben, ed. see Boothe, Paulette H.

Booth, Bernard F. The Mill Hill Fathers in West Cameroon: Education, Health & Development, 1884-1970. LC 93-45913. 284p. 1995. 64.95 (*1-883255-41-4*, U Pr W Africa); pap. 44.95 (*1-883255-40-6*, U Pr W Africa) Intl Scholars.

Booth, Bibi, jt. ed. see Mongillo, John.

***Booth, Bob.** Getting Started with Arcinfo 8. 230p. 1999. pap. text 29.95 (*1-879102-61-7*) ESR Inst.

Booth, Bradford A. & Mehew, Ernest, eds. The Letters of Robert Louis Stevenson Vol. 1: 1854-July 1874, 2 vols., Set. abr. ed. LC 93-45419. 640p. 1994. 50.00 (*0-300-05183-2*) Yale U Pr.

— The Letters of Robert Louis Stevenson Vol. 3: August 1879-September 1882, Vol. III. LC 93-45419. Vol. III. 352p. 1994. 50.00 (*0-300-06187-0*) Yale U Pr.

— The Letters of Robert Louis Stevenson Vol. 4: October 1882-June 1884, Vol. IV. LC 93-45419. Vol. IV. 352p. 1994. 50.00 (*0-300-06188-9*) Yale U Pr.

— The Letters of Robert Louis Stevenson Vol. 6: October 1882-June 1884, Vol. VI. LC 93-45419. Vol. VI. 544p. 1994. 50.00 (*0-300-06191-9*) Yale U Pr.

Booth, Bradford A., jt. auth. see Galt, John M.

Booth, Bradford A., ed. see Stevenson, Robert Louis.

Booth, Bradford A., ed. see Trollope, Anthony.

Booth, Bradford E. & Mehew, Ernest, eds. The Letters of Robert Louis Stevenson Vol. 5: October 1882-June 1884, Vol. V. LC 93-45419. Vol. V. 544p. 1994. 50.00 (*0-300-06190-0*) Yale U Pr.

***Booth, Bramwell.** Bible Battleaxes. 2nd rev. ed. 100p. 1998. pap. 6.99 (*0-88019-377-8*) Schmul Pub Co.

Booth-Butterfield, Melanie, ed. Communication, Cognition, & Anxiety. (Illus.). 232p. 1991. 46.00 (*0-8039-4087-4*); pap. 22.95 (*0-8039-4088-2*) Sage.

Booth, C., jt. ed. see Johnston, A.

Booth, C. E. VanDerlip: Vanderlip, Van Derlip, Vander Lippe Family in America, Also Including Some Account of the Von der Liipe Family of Lippe, Germany, from Which the Norwegian, Dutch & American Lines Have Their Descent. (Illus.). 188p. 1993. reprint ed. pap. 29.00 (*0-8328-3425-4*); reprint ed. lib. bdg. 39.00 (*0-8328-3424-6*) Higginson Bk Co.

Booth, Carolyn & Henderson, Mindy B. Grandmother by Another Name. LC 97-5760. (Illus.). 144p. 1997. 12.95 (*1-55853-481-4*) Rutledge Hill Pr.

Booth, Carolyn J. & Henderson, Mindy B. Grandfather by Another Name: Endearing Stories about What We Call Our Grandfathers. LC 98-11052. 144p. 1998. 12.95 (*1-55853-593-4*) Rutledge Hill Pr.

***Booth-Cartwright, Karan.** A Grandma's Love. (Illus.). 30p. (J). (ps-6). 1999. 22.95 (*1-929819-00-5*) At Book.

Booth, Catherine. For God Alone. 189p. 1990. pap. 6.99 (*0-907927-56-4*) Emerald House Group Inc.

— Writings of Catherine Booth, 6 vols. 1101p. 1986. 25.95 (*0-685-17948-6*) Salv Army Suppl South.

Booth, Catherine, jt. auth. see Wilson, James W.

***Booth, Chad.** Utah Boating Guide: Maps, Descriptions & Photographs of over 100 Waters. (Illus.). 2000. pap. 24.95 (*0-9671738-3-3*) Utah Outdoors.

Booth, Charles. Charles Booth on the City: Physical Pattern & Social Structure: Selected Writings. Pfautz, Harold W., ed. LC 67-28466. (Heritage of Sociology Ser.). 320p. reprint ed. pap. 99.20 (*0-608-16527-1*, 202676600052) Bks Demand.

Booth, Charles, et al. Life & Labour of the People in London, 1890-1900, 17 vols. LC 76-113561. reprint ed. write for info. (*0-404-00940-9*) AMS Pr.

Booth, Charles D., ed. Hong Kong Commercial Law: Current Issues & Developments. 224p. 1996. pap. 37.50 (*962-209-426-0*, Pub. by HK Univ Pr) Coronet Bks.

Booth, Cheri. Idioms, Lexikon der Englisch Redewendungen: English-German. 3rd ed. (ENG & GER.). 511p. 1993. 29.95 (*0-7859-8561-1*, 3927 17064) Fr & Eur.

— Lexikon der Englischen Umgangssprache (Idioms) English-German. (ENG & GER.). 508p. 1989. 29.95 (*0-7859-8562-X*, 3927117323) Fr & Eur.

Booth, Christopher. Moscow & St. Petersburg. (Passport's Illustrated Travel Guides Ser.). (Illus.). 192p. 1996. pap. 14.95 (*0-8442-4826-6*, 48266, Passprt Bks) NTC Contemp Pub Co.

Booth, Christopher C., ed. see Fothergill, John.

Booth, Clark. Boston Bruins: Celebrating 75 Years. Babineau, Steve, ed. LC 98-24815. (Illus.). 180p. 1998. lthr. 195.00 (*1-887656-11-1*) Tehabi Bks.

Booth-Clibbon, Edward, ed. see Matveyev, Vladimir.

Booth-Clibborn Editions Staff. Eurobest 4, No. 4. (Illus.). 274p. 1996. 55.00 (*1-873968-96-5*) Watsn-Guptill.

Booth Clibborn Editions Staff. Wear Me - Fashion Graphics Interaction: A View from London. (Illus.). 240p. 1996. 49.95 (*0-8230-6527-8*) Watsn-Guptill.

***Booth-Clibborn Editions Staff, ed.** Native Nations: Journeys in American Photography. (Illus.). 2000. 39.95 (*1-86154-073-6*) Booth-Clibborn.

— We Love You. 2000. pap. 39.95 (*1-86154-088-4*) Booth-Clibborn.

Booth-Clibborn, Edward. American Photography, No. 4. (Illus.). 176p. 1989. 40.00 (*0-89659-948-5*) Abbeville Pr.

Booth-Clibborn, Edward, jt. auth. see Poynor, Rick.

Booth-Clibborn, Edward, ed. see Blackshaw, Ric & Farrely, Liz.

Booth-Clibborn, Stanley. Taxes - Burden or Blessing? (C). 1990. pap. 24.00 (*0-85305-298-0*, Pub. by Arthur James) St Mut.

Booth, Coleen E. Getting Connected: Robin. (Loop Ser.). 1995. per. 3.50 (*0-373-20211-3*, 1-20211-8) Harlequin Bks.

— Going Live. 192p. 1994. pap. 3.50 (*0-380-72039-6*, Avon Bks) Morrow Avon.

Booth, Connie, jt. auth. see Cleese, John.

Booth, Cuthbert & Booth, Reynolds. The Birds of Orkney. (C). 1986. 80.00 (*0-907618-07-3*, Pub. by Orkney Pr) St Mut.

Booth, D. & Ziegler, R., eds. Finsler Set Theory: Platonism & Circularity. 288p. 1996. 74.50 (*3-7643-5400-3*) Spr-Verlag.

Booth, D. A., ed. Neurophysiology of Ingestion. LC 93-34148. (Studies in Neuroscience). 186p. 1993. 171.50 (*0-08-041988-7*, Pergamon Pr) Elsevier.

Booth, D. A., jt. ed. see Ramsay, D. J.

Booth, D. Earl. When Love Comes. 113p. mass mkt. 5.99 (*1-55197-498-3*) Picasso Publ.

Booth, Daryl S. Clinician's Handbook of Exercise Programs & Patient Instructions. Booth, Luz M., ed. 1998. pap. text 49.95 (*0-9664087-0-5*) D S Booth.

Booth, David. The Dust Bowl. (Illus.). 32p. (J). 1996. pap. 5.95 (*1-55074-746-0*) Kids Can Pr.

Booth, David. The Dust Bowl. unabridged ed. (Illus.). 32p. (J). (gr. k-4). 1997. 16.95 (*1-55074-295-7*, Pub. by Kids Can Pr) Genl Dist Srvs.

***Booth, David.** Guiding the Reading Process: Techniques & Strategies for Successful Instruction in K-8 Classrooms. LC 99-33650. 1999. pap. 18.95 (*1-57110-318-X*) Stenhse Pubs.

— Images of Nature: Canadian Poets & the Group of Seven. (Illus.). 32p. (J). 1995. 18.95 (*1-55074-272-8*) Kids Can Pr.

Booth, David. Psychology of Nutrition. LC 93-45603. 264p. 1994. pap. 27.50 (*0-7484-0159-8*, Pub. by Tay Francis Ltd) Taylor & Francis.

— Psychology of Nutrition. LC 93-45603. 264p. 1994. 85.00 (*0-7484-0158-X*) Taylor & Francis.

— Rethinking Social Development: Theory, Research & Practice. (C). 1997. pap. (*0-582-23497-2*) Addison-Wesley.

— Til All the Stars Have Fallen: A Collection of Poems for Children. (Puffin Poetry Bks.). (J). 1994. 12.19 (*0-606-06061-8*, Pub. by Turtleback) Demco.

Booth, David, ed. Doctor Knickerbocker & Other Rhymes: A Canadian Collection. (Illus.). 80p. (J). 1993. 16.95 (*1-55074-079-2*); pap. 8.95 (*1-55074-253-1*) Kids Can Pr.

Booth, David & Thornley-Hall, Carol, eds. The Talk Curriculum. 160p. (C). 1991. pap. text 20.00 (*0-435-08597-2*, 08597) Heinemann.

Booth, David, jt. auth. see Barton, Bob.

Booth, David, jt. auth. see Carnois, Bernard.

Booth, David, jt. auth. see Thornley-Hall, Carol.

Booth, David, ed. see Baravalle, Hermann V.

Booth, David, ed. see Unger, Georg.

Booth, David, ed. see Von Baravalle, Herman.

Booth, David A., jt. ed. see Legg, Charles R.

Booth Davies, John. Drugspeak: The Analysis of Drug Discourse. 220p. 1997. text 42.00 (*90-5702-191-9*, Harwood Acad Pubs); pap. text 20.00 (*90-5702-192-7*, Harwood Acad Pubs) Gordon & Breach.

— The Myth of Addiction. 2nd ed. 192p. 1997. text 40.00 (*90-5702-246-X*, Harwood Acad Pubs); pap. text 20.00 (*90-5702-237-0*, Harwood Acad Pubs) Gordon & Breach.

Booth, Dawn Merton. Small Animal Clinical Pharmacology & Therapeutics. LC 99-87178. 700p. 1997. text. write for info. (*0-7216-4364-7*, W B Saunders Co) Harcrt Hlth Sci Grp.

Booth, Derek. Railways of Southern Quebec. (Illus.). 92p. 1982. 12.00 (*0-919130-37-2*, Pub. by Boston Mills) Genl Dist Srvs.

— Railways of Southern Quebec, Vol. 2. (Illus.). 168p. 18.00 (*1-919130-39-X*, Pub. by Boston Mills) Genl Dist Srvs.

— Railways of Southern Quebec, Vol. II. (Illus.). 168p. 14.00 (*0-919130-39-9*, Pub. by Boston Mills) Genl Dist Srvs.

Booth, Dexter & Turner, John. Business Mathematics. 352p. (Orig.). 1996. pap. 47.50 (*0-7121-0868-8*, Pub. by Pitman Pub) Trans-Atl Phila.

Booth, Dexter J. Maths Made Easy. 280p. 1995. ring bd. 32.95 (*0-412-71870-7*) CRC Pr.

Booth D.J. Foundation Discrete. 1994. pap. write for info. (*0-412-56280-4*) Thomson Learn.

Booth, Don, et al. Sun-Earth Buffering & Superinsulation. LC 83-72283. (Illus.). 1983. 18.95 (*0-9604422-4-3*); pap. 14.95 (*0-9604422-3-5*) Comm Builders.

***Booth, Donna.** Alabama Cemeteries: A Guide to Their Stories in Stone. LC 99-42031. 144p. 1999. pap. 14.95 (*1-57587-105-X*) Crane Hill AL.

Booth, Dorothy. Echoes from the Border Hills. 192p. (C). 1989. text 60.00 (*1-872795-93-5*, Pub. by Pentland Pr) St Mut.

Booth, Dottie. Nature Calls: The History, Lore & Charm of Outhouses. LC 97-50323. (Illus.). 86p. 1998. pap. 12.95 (*0-89815-990-3*) Ten Speed Pr.

***Booth, Dottie.** Nature Calls Calendar 2000. (Illus.). 24p. 1999. pap. 9.95 (*1-58008-083-9*) Ten Speed Pr.

Booth, Douglas. The Race Game: Sport & Politics in South Africa. LC 97-35127. (Sport in the Global Society Ser.). (Illus.). 280p. 1998. 59.50 (*0-7146-4799-3*, Pub. by F Cass Pubs); pap. 26.50 (*0-7146-4354-8*, Pub. by F Cass Pubs) Intl Spec Bk.

— Valuing Nature: The Decline & Preservation of Old Growth Forests. 302p. (Orig.). (C). 1993. pap. text 27.95 (*0-8476-7860-1*); lib. bdg. 66.00 (*0-8476-7859-8*) Rowman.

***Booth, Douglas & Tatz, Colin.** One-Eyed: A View of Australian Sport. (Illus.). 280p. 2000. pap. 24.95 (*1-86508-055-1*, Pub. by Allen & Unwin Pty) Paul & Co Pubs.

Booth, Douglas E. The Environmental Consequences of Growth: Steady-State Economics As an Alternative to Ecological Decline. LC 97-13793. (Advances in Social Economics Ser.). 240p. (C). 1998. pap. 24.99 (*0-415-16991-7*) Routledge.

— The Environmental Consequences of Growth: Steady-State Economics As an Alternative to Ecological Decline. LC 97-13793. (Advances in Social Economics Ser.). (Illus.). 240p. (C). 1998. 75.00 (*0-415-16990-9*) Routledge.

— Regional Long Waves, Uneven Growth & the Cooperative Alternative. LC 87-2348. 126p. 1987. 49.95 (*0-275-92567-6*, C2567, Praeger Pubs) Greenwood.

Booth, E. Concrete Structure Earth. (C). 1994. 89.95 (*0-582-05288-2*, Pub. by Addison-Wesley) Longman.

Booth, E. Donald, jt. ed. see Locke, William N.

Booth, Edmund, ed. Seismic Design Practice into the Next Century: Proceedings of the 6th SECED Conference, Oxford, 26-27 March, 1998. LC 99-496409. (Illus.). 535p. (C). 1998. text 111.00 (*90-5410-934-3*, Pub. by A A Balkema) Ashgate Pub Co.

Booth, Edward C. Miss Parkworth, & 3 Short Stories. LC 72-125204. (Short Story Index Reprint Ser.). 1977. 19.95 (*0-8369-3571-3*) Ayer.

Booth, Edward T. God Made the Country. LC 77-134055. (Essay Index Reprint Ser.). 1977. reprint ed. 25.95 (*0-8369-2486-X*) Ayer.

Booth, Edwin. Between Actor & Critic: Selected Letters of Edwin Booth & William Winter. Watermeier, Daniel J., ed. & intro. by. LC 72-113012. 351p. reprint ed. pap. 108.90 (*0-7837-9472-X*, 206021400004) Bks Demand.

Booth, Edwin & Grossman, Edwina B. Edwin Booth: Recollections by His Daughter Edwina Booth Grossman & Letters to Her & to His Friends. 1972. 26.95 (*0-405-08584-2*, 1594) Ayer.

Booth, Edwin P. Martin Luther: The Great Reformer. LC 98-24325. (Heroes of the Faith Ser.). 208p. (YA). (gr. 5 up). 1999. lib. bdg. 17.95 (*0-7910-5037-8*) Chelsea Hse.

Booth, Eric. The Everyday Work of Art: Awakening the Extraordinary in Your Daily Life. 304p. 1999. pap. 14.95 (*1-57071-438-X*) Sourcebks.

— The Everyday Work of Art: The Ultimate Use of Ordinary Genius. LC 97-22796. 304p. 1997. 18.95 (*1-57071-192-5*) Sourcebks.

Booth, Ernest, et al. Mammals. 4th ed. (Pictured Key Nature Ser.). 208p. (C). 1982. text. write for info. (*0-697-04781-4*, WCB McGr Hill) McGrw-H Hghr Educ.

Booth, Ernest, jt. auth. see Chiasson, Robert B.

Booth, Frank. The Independent Walker's Guide to France. (Independent Walker Ser.). (Illus.). 216p. (Orig.). 1996. pap. 14.95 (*1-56656-184-1*) Interlink Pub.

— The Independent Walker's Guide to Great Britain. 2nd ed. (Independent Walker Ser.). (Illus.). 192p. (Orig.). 1998. pap. 14.95 (*1-56656-295-3*) Interlink Pub.

— The Independent Walker's Guide to Ireland: 35 Memorable Walks in Ireland's Green Countryside. LC 99-18564. (Illus.). 224p. 1999. pap. 14.95 (*1-56656-288-0*) Interlink Pub.

— The Independent Walker's Guide to Italy. LC 96-38970. (Independent Walker Ser.). (Illus.). 224p. (Orig.). 1998. pap. 14.95 (*1-56656-210-4*) Interlink Pub.

— It's Easy to Play Ballet Music. 1983. pap. 12.95 (*0-7119-0287-9*, AM32939) Music Sales.

— It's Easy to Play Opera. pap. 12.95 (*0-7119-0212-7*, AM32152) Music Sales.

— It's Easy to Play Ragtime. 1981. pap. 12.95 (*0-86001-044-9*, AM14143) Music Sales.

***Booth, Frank.** It's Easy to Play Richard Clayderman. (It's Easy to Play Ser.). 2000. pap. text 12.95 (*0-7119-0795-1*) Music Sales.

B

Booth, Frank. Songs of England, Scotland, & Ireland. LC 48-. (Illus.). 48p. 1982. pap. 12.95 (*0-7119-0178-3*, AM31857) Music Sales.

Booth, Frank, ed. The Essential Duke Ellington. 64p. (Orig.). 1995. pap. 14.95 (*0-8256-1476-7*, AM928961, Amsco Music) Music Sales.

Booth, Frank, selected by. How to Play Boogie Woogie. (Illus.). 48p. 1983. pap. 13.95 (*0-7119-0326-3*, AM33317) Music Sales.

— It's Easy to Play: Richard Clayerman. (Illus.). 48p. 1987. pap. 12.95 (*0-8256-1175-X*, AM61599) Music Sales.

— It's Easy to Play Bob Dylan. (Illus.). 48p. 1990. pap. 12.95 (*0-8256-1277-2*, AM78890) Music Sales.

— It's Easy to Play Clayderman, No. 2. (Illus.). 48p. 1987. pap. 12.95 (*0-7119-1139-8*, AM65921) Music Sales.

— The Pavarotti Collection. rev. ed. (Illus.). 80p. 1998. pap. text 21.95 (*0-7119-2465-1*, AM 944603) Music Sales.

Booth, Frederick. The Story of My Life: The Autobiography of a Working Man. 120p. (C). 1988. 29.95 (*0-7212-0724-3*, Pub. by Regency Pr GBR) St Mut.

Booth, George. The Essential George Booth. (Essential Cartoonists Library Ser.). (Illus.). 165p. 1999. pap. 10.95 (*0-7611-1251-0*) Workman Pub.

Booth, George C. The Food & Drink of Mexico. LC 75-39349. (Cookbook Ser.). (Illus.). 380p. 1976. reprint ed. pap. 5.95 (*0-486-23314-6*) Dover.

Booth, George W. Personal Reminiscenses, 1861-1865. 25.50 (*0-8488-0920-3*) Amereon Ltd.

— Pianos, Piano-Tuners & Their Problems. 320p. 1996. 39.95 (*1-85756-215-1*, Pub. by Janus Pubng) Paul & Co Pubs.

***Booth, George Wilson.** A Maryland Boy in Lee's Army: Personal Reminiscences of a Maryland Soldier in the War Between the States, 1861-1865. 177p. 2000. pap. 12.00 (*0-8032-6175-6*, Bison Books) U of Nebr Pr.

Booth, Gotthard. The Cancer Epidemic: Shadow of the Conquest of Nature. LC 59-7362. (Illus.). 277p. 1980. 89.95 (*0-88946-625-4*) E Mellen.

Booth, Harold S. Inorganic Syntheses, 1. 212p. 1978. 35.00 (*0-88275-630-3*) Krieger.

Booth, Heather. The Migration Process in Britain & West Germany: Two Demographic Studies of Migrant Populations. 100p. 1992. 67.95 (*1-85628-058-6*, Pub. by Avebry) Ashgate Pub Co.

Booth, Helen E. The Shareholder Proposal Rule: SEC Interpretations & Lawsuits. Mathiasen, Carolyn, ed. 114p. (Orig.). 1987. pap. 25.00 (*0-931035-14-7*) IRRC Inc DC.

Booth, Henry. Account of the Liverpool & Manchester Railway. (Illus.). 104p. 1969. reprint ed. 30.00 (*0-7146-1433-5*, Pub. by F Cass Pubs) Intl Spec Bk.

— Henry Booth. 231p. (C). 1988. 72.00 (*0-7855-3786-4*, Pub. by A H S Ltd) St Mut.

Booth, Herb. In the Sporting Tradition: The Art of Herb Booth. LC 93-4144. (Joe & Betty Moore Texas Art Ser.: No. 8). (Illus.). 176p. (C). 1993. 49.50 (*0-89096-571-4*) Tex A&M Univ Pr.

Booth, Howard. Healing Through Caring. (C). 1990. pap. text 24.00 (*0-85305-293-X*, Pub. by Arthur James) St Mut.

***Booth, Howard.** Health, Healing & Wholeness. 128p. 1999. pap. 28.00 (*0-85305-475-4*, Pub. by Arthur James) St Mut.

— Seven Whole Days. 200p. 1999. pap. 22.00 (*0-85305-325-1*, Pub. by Arthur James) St Mut.

Booth, Howard, ed. Stepping-Stones. (C). 1990. pap. 24.00 (*0-85305-297-2*, Pub. by Arthur James) St Mut.

***Booth, Howard J.** Modernism & Empire 1890-1940. 2000. pap. 29.95 (*0-7190-5307-2*, Pub. by Manchester Univ Pr) St Martin.

— Modernism & Empire 1890-1940. (Illus.). 256p. 2000. text 69.95 (*0-7190-5306-4*) Manchester Univ Pr.

Booth, J. Literary Lovers: The Private & Public Passions of Famous Writers. (Illus.). 180p. 1999. text 19.95 (*0-233-99436-X*, Pub. by Andre Deutsch) Trafalgar.

Booth, J. C., jt. auth. see Grose, Edward F.

Booth, J. E. Textile Mathematics, Vol. 1. 162p. 1975. 70.00 (*0-7855-7231-7*) St Mut.

— Textile Mathematics, Vol. 3. 144p. 1977. 70.00 (*0-7855-7232-5*) St Mut.

Booth, James. Interpreting the World: Kant's Philosophy of History & Politics. 224p. 1987. text 30.00 (*0-8020-2577-3*) U of Toronto Pr.

— Sylloge of Coins of the British Isles Northern Museums: Ancient British, Anglo-Saxon, Norman & Plantagenet Coins to 1279. (Sylloge of Coins of the British Isles: Vol. 48). (Illus.). 298p. (C). 1997. text 150.00 (*0-19-726166-3*) OUP.

— Writers & Politics in Nigeria. LC 80-17670. (Writers & Politics Ser.). 128p. (C). 1981. pap. text 16.50 (*0-8419-0651-3*, Africana) Holmes & Meier.

Booth, James, ed. New Larkins for Old: Critical Essays. LC 99-16693. 247p. 1999. text 59.95 (*0-312-22669-1*) St Martin.

Booth, Jay, ed. see Byron, William J., et al.

Booth, Jerry. You Animal! LC 95-8457. (Illus.). 48p. (J). (gr. 3-7). 1996. pap. 15.00 (*0-15-200696-6*, Gulliver Bks) Harcourt.

Booth, Jerry, jt. ed. see Lewis, Peter.

Booth, Jim & Sawyer, Steve. Effective Techniques for Application Development with Visual FoxPro 6.0. Dingle, Steven P., ed. 500p. 1998. pap. 49.95 (*0-9655093-7-0*) Hentzenwerke.

***Booth, Joan & Lee, Guy.** Catullus to Ovid: Reading Latin Love Elegy. rev. ed. (Classical Studies Ser.). (LAT., Illus.). 160p. (C). 1999. pap. text 25.95 (*1-85399-606-8*, Pub. by Brist Class Pr) Focus Pub-R Pullins.

Booth, Joan Booth, ed. see Ovid.

Booth, Joe & Lief, Greg. Network Programming in CA-Clipper 5.2. (Programming Ser.). (Illus.). 464p. 1993. pap. 29.95 incl. disk (*1-56276-119-6*, Ziff-Davis Pr) Que.

— Network Programming in Fox Pro. (Programming Ser.). (Illus.). 304p. 1993. pap. 29.95 incl. disk (*1-56276-167-6*, Ziff-Davis Pr) Que.

Booth, John. The Day War Broke Out: Stories of Life in a Village at War. 112p. (C). 1984. pap. text 40.00 (*0-906853-04-4*, Pub. by Cambdge Hse Bks) St Mut.

— The Fine Art of Hocus Pocus. (Illus.). 304p. 1995. write for info. (*0-9645559-0-5*) R Goulet.

— Keys to Magic's Inner World: Create or Own a Piece of Its History. LC 99-70229. (Illus.). 190p. 1999. 39.95 (*0-9645559-1-3*) R Goulet.

— Looking at Old Prints. 195p. (C). 1989. pap. text 65.00 (*0-906853-06-0*, Pub. by Cambdge Hse Bks) St Mut.

— Our Forgotten History: The Early Map Makers. (C). 1986. pap. text 60.00 (*0-906853-05-2*, Pub. by Cambdge Hse Bks) St Mut.

— Psychic Paradoxes. LC 84-60005. (Illus.). 258p. (C). 1986. pap. 22.95 (*0-87975-358-7*) Prometheus Bks.

— That Time o' Day. 1993. pap. 12.00 (*0-86025-404-6*, Pub. by I Henry Pubns) Empire Pub Srvs.

— A Toast to Ireland: A Celebration of Irish Traditional Drinks. LC 95-204027. (Illus.). 128p. 1995. pap. text 19.95 (*0-85640-536-1*, Pub. by Blackstaff Pr) Dufour.

— Vivaldi. (Illustrated Lives of the Great Composers Ser.). (Illus.). 128p. 1996. 17.95 (*0-7119-1727-2*, OP 45202) Omnibus NY.

Booth, John & Henning, Doug. Wonders of Magic. LC 86-60002. (Illus.). xiv, 301p. 1986. text 39.50 (*0-943230-03-9*) Ridgeway Pr.

Booth, John A. Costa Rica: Quest for Democracy. LC 98-9707. (Nations of the Modern World Ser.). 256p. (C). 1998. text 69.00 (*0-8133-7631-9*, Pub. by Westview) HarpC.

***Booth, John A.** Costa Rica: Quest for Democracy. 256p. 1999. pap. 25.00 (*0-8133-3714-3*) Westview.

Booth, John A. The End & the Beginning: The Nicaraguan Revolution. 2nd ed. LC 82-2690. (Latin America & the Caribbean Special Studies). 363p. 1982. text 36.00 (*0-89158-939-2*) Westview.

Booth, John A. & Seligson, Mitchell A., eds. Political Participation in Latin America Vol. 2: Politics & the Poor. 1979. 34.50 (*0-8419-0405-7*); pap. 15.95 (*0-8419-0406-5*) Holmes & Meier.

Booth, John A. & Walker, Thomas W. Understanding Central America. 3rd ed. LC 99-15267. 288p. (C). 1999. pap. text 24.00 (*0-8133-3070-X*, Pub. by Westview) HarpC.

Booth, John A., jt. ed. see Seligson, Mitchell A.

Booth, John N. Booths in History: Their Roots & Lives, Encounters & Achievements. LC 82-5421. (Illus.). 243p. 1982. pap. text 16.95 (*0-943230-01-2*) Ridgeway Pr.

— Conjurians' Discoveries. LC 92-60082. (Illus.). 287p. 1992. 38.00 (*0-943230-06-3*) Ridgeway Pr.

— Creative World of Conjuring. (Illus.). 284p. 1990. text 38.00 (*0-943230-05-5*) Ridgeway Pr.

— Dramatic Magic. (Illus.). 257p. 1988. 35.00 (*0-943230-04-7*) Ridgeway Pr.

Booth, John W., et al. "Right or Wrong, God Judge Me" Writings of John Wilkes Booth. LC 96-51249. 200p. 1997. 24.95 (*0-252-02347-1*) U of Ill Pr.

Booth, Joseph. Essential Windows APIS for Visual Developers. (Illus.). 512p. 1997. pap. 44.95 (*0-07-913649-4*) McGraw.

Booth, Joseph D. From Xbase to Windows. 256p. 1996. pap. 27.95 (*1-55851-480-5*, M&T Bks) IDG Bks.

— Visual Objects: A Developer's Guide. 1995. pap. 39.95 incl. disk (*1-55851-410-4*, M&T Bks) IDG Bks.

Booth, Julianne. Parables of Jesus. (Arch Bks.). (Illus.). 24p. (J). (gr. k-4). 1982. pap. 1.99 (*0-570-06163-6*, 59-1309) Concordia.

Booth, Kathryn M. & Hill, Steven L. The Essence of Optoelectronics. LC 97-34155. (Essence of Engineering Ser.). 240p. (C). 1997. pap. text 19.95 (*0-13-533654-6*) P-H.

Booth, Kathy. Culture Builds Communities: A Guide to Partnership Building & Putting Culture to Work on Social Issues. McNulty, Robert, ed. LC 96-131912. (Illus.). 86p. 1995. pap. 14.95 (*0-941182-21-5*) Partners Livable.

— Institutions As Fulcrums of Change: A Creative Reimagination of Every Community's Assets. 83p. 1996. pap. text 14.95 (*0-941182-22-3*) Partners Livable.

Booth, Katie. Working with Children & Their Parents. LC 99-34209. 1998. pap. text 29.95 (*0-632-04246-X*) Blackwell Sci.

***Booth, Kellogg S. & Fournier, Alain.** 1998 Graphics Interface Proceedings. Davis, Wayne, ed. 246p. 1998. pap. 50.00 (*2-558-60550-X*) Morgan Kaufmann.

Booth, Ken. International Relations Theory Today. 380p. 1992. pap. text 19.50 (*0-271-01462-8*) Pa St U Pr.

— Law, Force & Diplomacy at Sea. 250p. (C). 1985. 39.95 (*0-04-341027-8*); pap. text 18.95 (*0-04-341028-6*) Routledge.

— Navies & Foreign Policy. LC 79-2254. 1979. 39.95 (*0-8419-0518-5*) Holmes & Meier.

— Strategic Cultures In The Asia-pacific Region. LC 98-40517. 1999. text 69.95 (*0-312-21797-8*) St Martin.

Booth, Ken, ed. Industrial Packaging Adhesives. 1990. 111.00 (*0-8493-7143-0*, TP968) CRC Pr.

— Statecraft & Security: The Cold War & Beyond. LC 97-40985. 374p. (C). 1998. text 59.95 (*0-521-47453-1*); pap. text 19.95 (*0-521-47977-0*) Cambridge U Pr.

Booth, Ken & Smith, Steve, eds. International Relations Theory Today. 380p. 1995. 70.00 (*0-271-01461-X*) Pa St U Pr.

Booth, Leo. The Angel & the Frog: A Spiritual Fable. (Illus.). 300p. (Orig.). 1997. pap. 12.95 (*0-9623282-5-1*) SCP Ltd.

— The God Game: It's Your Move. 208p. 1998. reprint ed. pap. 15.00 (*0-9623282-8-6*) SCP Ltd.

— Healing Thoughts: Reflections. 124p. (Orig.). Date not set. pap. 10.00 (*0-9623282-1-9*) SCP Ltd.

— Heilsame Gedanken: Widerspiegelungen. Waller, Hans G., tr.Tr. of Healing Thoughts-Reflections. (GER.). 1998. pap. write for info. (*0-9623282-6-X*) SCP Ltd.

— Heilung Von Religioesem Missbrauch und Religioeser Abhaengigkeit: Ein Weg in die Spirituelle Freiheit. Engel, Herbert, tr.Tr. of When God Becomes a Drug/Breaking the Chains of Religious Addiction & Abuse. (GER.). 1998. pap. write for info. (*0-9623282-7-8*) SCP Ltd.

— Meditations for Compulsive People: Creating Healthy Spirituality. rev. ed. (Illus.). 136p. 1995. pap. 10.00 (*0-9623282-2-7*) SCP Ltd.

— Say Yes to Life: Daily Meditations for Recovery. 2nd rev. ed. 380p. 1997. pap. 10.00 (*0-9623282-3-5*) SCP Ltd.

— Spirituality & Recovery: A Guide to Positive Living. (Illus.). 135p. (Orig.). 1997. pap. 10.00 (*0-9623282-4-3*) SCP Ltd.

— When God Becomes a Drug: Breaking the Chains of Religious Addiction & Abuse. 273p. 1998. reprint ed. pap. 15.00 (*0-9623282-9-4*) SCP Ltd.

— When God Becomes a Drug: Breaking the Chains of Religious Addiction & Abuse - Attaining Healthy Spirituality. LC 92-18430. 288p. 1992. pap. 13.95 (*0-87477-703-8*, Tarcher Putnam) Putnam Pub Group.

***Booth, Leo.** Wisdom of Letting Go: The Path of the Wounded Soul. 1999. pap. 15.00 (*1-892841-01-0*) SCP Ltd.

Booth, Letha & Dutton, Joan P. The Williamsburg Cookbook. enl. rev. ed. LC 75-2328. (Illus.). 174p. 1975. 16.95 (*0-910412-91-X*) Colonial Williamsburg.

***Booth, Liz.** Florida. 2nd ed. (Globetrotter Travel Guides Ser.). (Illus.). 128p. 2000. pap. 10.95 (*1-85974-353-6*) New5 Holland.

Booth, Luz M., ed. see Booth, Daryl S.

Booth, Lynn. Cooking with Colorado's Greatest Chefs. (Illus.). 160p. 1995. 14.98 (*1-56579-127-4*) Westcliffe Pubs.

Booth, M., & Associates Staff. Promoting Issues & Ideas: A Guide to Public Relations for Nonprofit Organizations. rev. ed. LC 94-45862. 188p. 1995. 29.95 (*0-87954-594-1*) Foundation Ctr.

Booth, M. L., tr. Marble Workers' Manual. (Illus.). 295p. 1985. reprint ed. pap. text 25.00 (*0-87556-352-X*) Saifer.

Booth, Marcella, ed. A Catalogue of the Louis Zukofsky Manuscript Collection. LC 70-38572. (Tower Bibliographical Ser.: No. 11). (Illus.). 1975. 22.50 (*0-87959-038-6*) U of Tex H Ransom Ctr.

Booth, Margaret. Rayden & Jackson on Divorce & Family Matters, 2 vols. 16th ed. 4600p. 1991. boxed set 889.00 (*0-406-35130-9*, U.K., MICHIE) LEXIS Pub.

Booth, Marilyn, tr. from ARA. My Grandmother's Cactus: Stories by Egyptian Women. 208p. 1991. 19.95 (*0-7043-2649-3*, Pub. by Quartet) Interlink Pub.

— Stories by Egyptian Women: My Grandmother's Cactus. LC 92-43065. 175p. (C). 1993. pap. 10.95 (*0-292-70803-3*) U of Tex Pr.

Booth, Marilyn, tr. see El-Saadawi, Nawal.

Booth, Marilyn, tr. & intro. see Tawfiq, Sahar.

Booth, Mark W. American Popular Music: A Reference Guide. LC 82-21062. (American Popular Culture Ser.). 212p. 1983. lib. bdg. 55.00 (*0-313-21305-4*, BPM/, Greenwood Pr) Greenwood.

Booth, Martin. British Poetry Nineteen Sixty-Four to Nineteen Eighty-Four: Driving Through the Barricades. 288p. 1985. 35.00 (*0-7100-9606-2*, Routledge Thoemms) Routledge.

— Devils' Wine. 112p. 1980. 21.00 (*0-86140-039-9*) Dufour.

— Devils' Wine. 112p. 1980. 17.95 (*0-685-17705-X*, Pub. by Smyth) Dufour.

— Devils' Wine. 112p. 1980. pap. 9.95 (*0-86140-044-5*, Pub. by Smyth) Dufour.

***Booth, Martin.** The Doctor & the Detective: A Biography of Sir Arthur Conan Doyle. (Illus.). 384p. 2000. text 27.95 (*0-312-24251-4*) St Martin.

— The Dragon Syndicates: The Global Phenomenon on the Triads. (Illus.). 368p. 2000. 25.00 (*0-7867-0735-6*, Pub. by Carroll & Graf) Publishers Group.

— Industry of Souls. 256p. 2000. pap. 13.00 (*0-312-26753-3*, Picador USA) St Martin.

Booth, Martin. The Industry of Souls. 2nd ed. LC 99-38419. 256p. 1999. text 22.95 (*0-312-24203-4*) St Martin.

— Missile Summer. (C). 1988. 30.00 (*0-904524-36-1*, Pub. by Rivelin Grapheme Pr) St Mut.

— Opium: A History. LC 98-14951. 381p. 1998. text 24.95 (*0-312-18643-6*) St Martin.

— Opium: A History. 1999. pap. 14.95 (*0-312-20667-4*, St Martins Paperbacks) St Martin.

***Booth, Martin.** Panther. LC 00-28358. (Illus.). (J). 2001. write for info. (*0-689-82976-0*) McElderry Bks.

Booth, Martin. War Dog: A Novel. LC 96-52570. 144p. (J). (gr. 7-12). 1997. per. 15.00 (*0-689-81380-5*) Aladdin.

Booth, Martin, et al. Bismarck. Yapp, Martin et al, eds. (World History Program Ser.). (Illus.). 32p. (J). (gr. 6-11). 1980. reprint ed. pap. text 5.90 (*0-89908-023-5*) Greenhaven.

— Partnership in Initial Teacher Training. 192p. 1990. pap. text 45.00 (*0-304-31984-8*) Continuum.

Booth, Martin, jt. ed. see MacBeth, George.

Booth, Mary H. How to Read Character in Handwriting. 72p. 1993. pap. 6.50 (*0-89540-220-3*, SB-220) Sun Pub.

Booth, Mary L., tr. see Cochin, Augustin.

Booth, Mary L., tr. see De Gasparin, Agenor.

Booth, Mary L., tr. see Mace, Jean.

***Booth, Matthew.** Sherlock Holmes & the Giant's Hand & Other Stories: A Sherlock Holmes Mystery. 176p. 2000. pap. 14.95 (*0-947533-14-1*, Pub. by Breese Bks) Midpt Trade.

Booth, Maud B. A Rector's Daughter in Victorian England: Memories of Childhood & Girlhood. Welty, Susan F., ed. & intro. by. LC 94-62068. (Illus.). 85p. 1994. 7.00 (*1-885287-01-1*) Volunteers Amer.

Booth, Maycock & Poulson Staff. Bird Family History. 171p. 1994. reprint ed. pap. 26.50 (*0-8328-4117-X*); reprint ed. lib. bdg. 36.50 (*0-8328-4116-1*) Higginson Bk Co.

Booth, Michael G. Cayuse Indians, the Art of Michael G. Booth. 130p. 1995. pap. 25.00 (*1-888236-01-9*) Art Wise.

— Paintings of Michael Booth, the Reservation. 1996. pap. text 25.00 (*1-888236-13-2*) Art Wise.

— A Sketch of Pendleton. (Illus.). 134p. 1993. pap. write for info. (*1-888236-12-4*) Art Wise.

— Watercolor Strategy. 150p. 1996. pap. text 25.00 (*1-888236-00-0*) Art Wise.

Booth, Michael R. Hiss the Villain: Six English & American Melodramas. 1972. 26.95 (*0-405-09121-4*, 1701) Ayer.

Booth, Michael R., ed. English Plays of the Nineteenth Century, 5 vols. Incl. Vol. 3. Comedies. (Illus.). 484p. (C). 1973. text 85.00 (*0-19-812465-1*); Vol. 4. Farces, 1973. (Illus.). 392p. (C). 1973. text 79.00 (*0-19-812466-X*); (Illus.). 1969. write for info. (*0-318-54822-4*) OUP.

Booth, Michael R. & Kaplan, Joel H., eds. The Edwardian Theatre: Essays on Performance & the Stage. LC 97-6260. (Illus.). 255p. (C). 1996. text 54.95 (*0-521-45375-5*) Cambridge U Pr.

Booth, Michael R., et al. Three Tragic Actresses: Siddons, Rachel, Ristori. LC 96-36762. (Illus.). 210p. (C). 1996. text 52.95 (*0-521-41115-7*) Cambridge U Pr.

Booth, Michelle. Gold in the Ashes. LC 93-16926. (Tapestry Collection). 96p. (Orig.). 1993. pap. 6.50 (*1-56476-050-2*, 6-3050, Victor Bks) Chariot Victor.

— Steadfast Faith in Times of Turmoil. (Tapestry Collection). 108p. (Orig.). 1995. pap. 6.50 (*1-56476-326-9*, 6-3326, Victor Bks) Chariot Victor.

Booth, Mike, jt. auth. see Dalichow, Irene.

Booth, Nan. Meeting Room Games: Getting Things Done in Committees. LC 95-44837. (Illus.). 128p. (Orig.). 1996. pap. 14.95 (*0-918420-25-3*) Brighton Pubns.

Booth, Nan & Fischler, Gary. Romantic at-Home Dinners: Sneaky Strategies for Couples with Kids. LC 93-33634. 160p. (Orig.). 1994. pap. 9.95 (*0-918420-19-9*) Brighton Pubns.

Booth, Nancy M., jt. auth. see Makela, Casey.

Booth, Nate. Strategies for Fast-Changing Times: The Art of Using Change to Your Advantage. LC 97-27421. 336p. 1997. per. 16.00 (*0-7615-1134-2*) Prima Pub.

— Thriving on Change: The Art of Using Change to Your Advantage. (Illus.). 300p. 1996. 24.95 (*0-9649500-0-6*) Harrison Acorn.

Booth, Neil. Tolley's National Insurance Contributions, 1993-94. 500p. 1993. 96.00 (*0-85459-775-1*, Pub. by Tolley Pubng) St Mut.

Booth, Neil D. Tolley's National Insurance Contributions, 1995. 500p. 1994. pap. 150.00 (*0-85459-894-4*, Pub. by Tolley Pubng) St Mut.

— Tolley's National Insurance Contributions, 1995-96. Golding, Jon, ed. 510p. 1995. 195.00 (*1-86012-013-X*, Pub. by Tolley Pubng) St Mut.

Booth, Newell S. African Religions: A Symposium. LC 73-88062. 390p. 1977. text 21.50 (*0-88357-012-2*) NOK Pubs.

Booth, Nicholas. Exploring the Solar System. (Illus.). 176p. (C). 1996. 24.95 (*0-521-58005-6*) Cambridge U Pr.

— How Soon Is Now? The Truth about the Ozone Layer. (Illus.). 419p. 1999. reprint ed. text 30.00 (*0-7881-6127-X*) DIANE Pub.

Booth, Norman K. Basic Elements of Landscape Architectural Design. (Illus.). 315p. (C). 1990. reprint ed. text 50.95 (*0-88133-478-2*) Waveland Pr.

Booth, Norman K. & Hiss, James E. Residential Landscape Architecture: Design Process for the Private Residence. 2nd ed. LC 98-11189. 448p. (C). 1998. 97.00 (*0-13-632019-8*) P-H.

Booth, P. H., et al, eds. Modern Actuarial Theory & Practice. LC 98-46642. 716p. 1999. 79.95 (*0-8493-0388-5*) CRC Pr.

***Booth, Pat.** American Icon. 432p. 2000. mass mkt. 6.50 (*1-57566-564-6*) Kensgtn Pub Corp.

Booth, Pat. American Icon: A Novel. LC 98-13367. 384p. (gr. 8). 1999. 23.00 (*0-316-10212-1*) Little.

Booth, Pat. Deadline: My Story LC 98-140443. 232p. 1997. write for info. (*0-670-87929-0*, Viking) Viking Penguin.

Booth, Pat. Marry Me. 384p. 1997. mass mkt. 5.99 (*1-57566-191-8*, Knsington) Kensgtn Pub Corp.

— Marry Me. large type ed. 528p. 1996. lib. bdg. 25.95 (*0-7838-1865-3*, G K Hall Lrg Type) Mac Lib Ref.

— Palm Beach. 1986. mass mkt. 5.99 (*0-345-33357-8*) Ballantine Pub Grp.

***Booth, Pat F.** Indexing: The Manual of Good Practice. 500p. 2000. 100.00 (*1-85739-287-6*) Bowker-Saur.

Booth, Patricia. Accurate Coding for Critical Care Services & Pulmonary Medicine. O'Donohue, Walter J., Jr. et al, eds. 75p. 1996. write for info. (*0-916609-08-1*) Am Chest Phys.

Booth, Patsy R. Canticle of Love: Directed Journaling for Life's Singers. 170p. 1993. pap. 12.95 (*0-614-04903-2*) Cedar Tree.

— Celebrate Me: Directed Discovery Journal. 102p. (J). (gr. 4 up). 1994. pap. 10.95 (*1-884393-26-8*) Cedar Tree.

— Footprints in My Story: Journaling for Recovery. 170p. 1994. pap. 12.95 (*1-884393-10-1*) Cedar Tree.

— How Far Is It to Babylon? A Directed Travel Journal. 90p. 1994. pap. 10.95 (*1-884393-07-1*) Cedar Tree.

An Asterisk (*) at the beginning of an entry indicates that the title is appearing for the first time.

— If I Could Talk to God, I'd Say: Directed Discovery Journal. 102p. (J). (gr. 4 up). 1994. 10.95 (*1-884393-24-1*) Cedar Tree.
— Tapestry: Directed Journaling for Life Weavers. 172p. 1994. pap. 12.95 (*1-884393-02-0*) Cedar Tree.
— What's It Like to Be Me? Directed Discovery Journal. 100p. (YA). (gr. 4 up). 1994. pap. 10.95 (*1-884393-25-X*) Cedar Tree.
Booth, Paulette, ed. see Boothe, Ben B.
Booth, Penny. Booth: GCSE Law. 1997. pap. write for info. (*0-406-04465-1*, GBL, MICHIE) LEXIS Pub.
Booth, Penny, et al. A Level Law. Shears, Peter & Cappi, Paul, eds. (Questions & Answers Ser.). 376p. 1995. 18.00 (*1-874241-32-5*, Pub. by Cavendish Pubng) Gaunt.
***Booth, Percy T.** Alaska Diary. Booth, Richard, ed. (Illus.). 73p. 1999. pap. 9.50 (*1-885813-08-2*, Pub. by B & B Pubng) Partners-West.
Booth, Percy T. Grants Pass the Golden Years: Memories in the Dustprints of Time. 2nd ed. (Illus.). 114p. (C). 1996. reprint ed. pap. 9.95 (*1-885813-02-3*) B & B Pubng.
— Grants Pass, the Golden Years: Memories in the Dustprints of Time. 2nd rev. ed. (Illus.). 108p. 1996. 19.95 (*1-885813-05-8*) B & B Pubng.
— The Legend of Indian Mary & Umpqua Joe. 70p. 1994. pap. 7.95 (*1-885813-01-5*) B & B Pubng.
— Until the Last Arrow. 1997. pap. text 19.95 (*1-885813-06-6*) B & B Pubng.
— Valley of the Rogues. 71p. 1993. pap. 6.95 (*1-885813-00-7*) B & B Pubng.
— Valley of the Rogues. (Illus.). 71p. 1995. 14.50 (*1-885813-04-X*) B & B Pubng.
Booth, Peter. Management Control in a Voluntary Organization: Accounting & Accountants in Organization Context. LC 95-22958. (New Works in Accounting History). 304p. 1995. text 66.00 (*0-8153-2239-9*) Garland.
Booth, Philip. Controlling Development: Certainty, Discretion & Accountability. LC 96-219353. 224p. 1996. 75.00 (*1-85728-584-0*, Pub. by UCL Pr Ltd) Taylor & Francis.
***Booth, Philip.** Lifelines: Selected Poems, 1950-1999. 2000. pap. 18.00 (*0-14-058926-0*) Penguin Putnam.
Booth, Philip. Selves. 96p. 1991. pap. 9.95 (*0-14-058646-6*) Viking Penguin.
— Social Security in America. LC 73-620091. (Policy Papers in Human Resources & Industrial Relations Ser.: No. 19). 180p. 1973. 10.00 (*0-87736-119-3*); pap. 5.00 (*0-87736-120-7*) U of Mich Inst Labor.
Booth, Philip, ed. see Social Security Conference Staff.
Booth, Phillip. Pairs: New Poems. LC 94-3899. (Poets Ser.). 96p. 1994. pap. 12.95 (*0-14-058724-1*, Penguin Classics) Viking Penguin.
— Trying to Say It: Outlook & Insights on How Poems Happen. LC 96-11039. 168p. 1996. pap. 13.95 (*0-472-06586-6*, 06586); text 39.50 (*0-472-09586-2*, 09586) U of Mich Pr.
Booth, Phyllis B., jt. auth. see Jernberg, Ann M.
Booth, Reynolds, jt. auth. see Booth, Cuthbert.
Booth, Richard. Bats in the Basement. LC 91-51223. (Orig.). 1992. pap. 6.00 (*0-88734-249-3*) Players Pr.
***Booth, Richard.** My Kingdom of Books. 318p. 1999. 24.95 (*0-86243-495-5*, Pub. by Y Lolfa) Intl Spec Bk.
Booth, Richard. Parallel Lines Never Meet. LC 90-53077. (Orig.). 1990. pap. 6.00 (*0-88734-226-4*) Players Pr.
— Return to the Valley. 1998. pap. 7.95 (*1-57532-046-0*) Press-Tige Pub.
— Where Did You Spend the Night? LC 93-4583. 1993. pap. 6.00 (*0-88734-273-6*) Players Pr.
Booth, Richard & Jung, Marshal. Romancing the Net: A "Tell All" Guide to Love Online. 256p. 1996. 19.95 (*0-7615-0322-6*) Prima Pub.
Booth, Richard, ed. see Booth, Percy T.
Booth, Richard A. Bones in the Attic. LC 88-93067. (Illus.). 41p. 1989. pap. 6.00 (*0-88734-220-5*) Players Pr.
— Grampa, Who Made God?... And Other Good Questions. (Illus.). (Orig.). (C). 1998. pap. 11.95 (*1-885813-07-4*) B & B Pubng.
— Looking Back a Moment . . . And Other Poems. (Illus.). 84p. 1995. pap., per. 9.95 (*1-885813-03-1*) B & B Pubng.
— Room 23: Playscript. LC 88-93073. (Illus.). 41p. (Orig.). 1989. pap. 6.00 (*0-88734-218-3*) Players Pr.
— The Valley of No Return. abr. ed. (Valley Stories Ser.: Vol. 1). 151p. (Orig.). 1996. pap. 7.95 (*1-56901-435-3*) B & B Pubng.
Booth, Rick. Inner Loops: A Sourcebook for High Performance 32 Bit Software Design. LC 96-36332. 384p. (C). 1996. pap. text 39.95 (*0-201-47960-5*) Addison-Wesley.
Booth, Robert. Boston's Freedom Trail: A Souvenir Guide. 4th rev. ed. Moskow, Shirley, ed. LC 97-50504. (Illus.). 96p. 1998. pap. 5.95 (*0-7627-0167-6*) Globe Pequot.
Booth, Robert A., jt. auth. see Schwartz, William.
Booth, Robert C. Airline Pasionado: Before, Braniff & After. (Illus.). 256p. 1998. 30.00 (*1-888962-06-2*) Paladwr Pr.
***Booth, Robert E.** Official Book of the Basset Hound. 1999. 79.95 (*0-7938-0508-2*) TFH Pubns.
Booth, Robert E., et al. Culturally Disadvantaged: A Bibliography & Keyword out-of-Context (KWOC) Index. LC 66-27901. 813p. reprint ed. pap. 200.00 (*0-608-16562-X*, 202766600055) Bks Demand.
— Total Hip Arthroplasty. (Illus.). 336p. 1988. text 135.00 (*0-03-013328-9*, W B Saunders Co) Harcrt Hlth Sci Grp.
Booth, Robert R. Children of the Promise: The Biblical Case for Infant Baptism. 206p. (Orig.). 1995. pap. 9.99 (*0-87552-165-7*) P & R Pubng.
***Booth, Roger.** Bruno: The Bruno Lawrence Story. (Illus.). 260p. (Orig.). 1999. pap. 29.95 (*0-908812-83-3*, Pub. by Canterbury Univ) Accents Pubns.
Booth, Roger P. Jesus & the Laws of Purity: Tradition History & Legal History in Mark 7. (JSNT Supplement Ser.: No. 13). 278p. 1987. pap. 28.50 (*1-85075-022-X*, Pub. by Sheffield Acad) CUP Services.
Booth, Ronald R. Collective Bargaining & the Illinois School Board Member. Glaub, Gerald R., ed. 112p. (Orig.). 1995. pap. 6.00 (*1-880331-06-3*) IL Assn Sch Bds.
— Collective Bargaining & the School Board Member. 96p. 1993. pap. 6.00 (*1-880331-04-7*) IL Assn Sch Bds.
Booth, Roy, ed. Elizabethan Sonnets. 240p. 1994. 7.50 (*0-460-87363-6*, Everyman's Classic Lib) Tuttle Pubng.
— The Love Poetry of Shakespeare. 162p. 1995. 14.95 (*1-85626-138-7*, Pub. by Cathie Kyle) Trafalgar.
Booth, Rupert. Conquer the Cost - Service Compromise: A Five-Step Program to Improve Performance & Reduce Costs. 200p. 1994. text 50.00 (*0-7863-0210-0*, Irwn Prfssnl) McGraw-Hill Prof.
— Control Your Overheads: A Practical Programme to Improve Performance & Reduce Costs. (Financial Times Management Ser.). 272p. 1994. 72.50 (*0-273-03859-1*, Pub. by Pitman Pub) Trans-Atl Phila.
Booth, Russell H., Jr. A Brief History of Guernsey County, Ohio: Celebrating 200 Years of Settlement. (Illus.). 96p. 1998. pap. 10.00 (*0-9640634-0-9*) Gomber Hse.
— Holiday Whimsies: Three-Minute Plays Suitable Only for Persons Who Have a Sense of Humor & Don't Take Themselves, & These Plays, Too Seriously. 86p. (Orig.). 1996. pap. 8.00 (*0-9640634-5-X*) Gomber Hse.
— The Tuscarawas Valley in Indian Days, 1750-1797: Original Journals & Old Maps. LC 94-75795. (Illus.). 424p. 1994. 27.50 (*0-9640634-6-8*) Gomber Hse.
Booth, S. James. Essential Microbiology Review. 200p. 1996. pap. 21.95 (*0-86542-486-1*) Blackwell Sci.
Booth, Sara, jt. auth. see Stannard, Catherine F.
Booth, Shirley. Learning to Program: A Phenomenographic Perspective. (Coteborg Studies in Educational Sciences: 89). 308p. (Orig.). 1992. pap. 42.50 (*91-7346-256-X*) Coronet Bks.
Booth, Shirley, jt. auth. see Marton, Ference.
Booth, Simon A. Crisis Management Strategy: Competition & Change in Modern Enterprises. LC 92-42828. 320p. 1993. pap. 28.95 (*0-415-06231-4*) Thomson Learn.
— Crisis Management Strategy: Competition & Change in Modern Industries. LC 92-42828. 320p. (C). (gr. 13). 1993. pap. 65.95 (*0-415-06230-6*) Thomson Learn.
Booth, Simon A., jt. auth. see Moore, Chris.
Booth, Stanley. A. J. Munnings. (Illus.). 66p. 1995. pap. 25.00 (*0-85667-325-0*) Sothebys Pubns.
Booth, Stanley. Elvis Presley's Graceland. (Illus.). 1988. 27.78 (*0-89381-190-4*) Aperture.
Booth, Stanley. Keith: Standing in the Shadows. 224p. 1996. pap. 12.95 (*0-312-14116-5*) St Martin.
***Booth, Stanley.** Rhythm Oil: A Journey Through the Music of the American South. 2000. pap. 16.00 (*0-306-80979-6*, Pub. by Da Capo) HarpC.
— The True Adventures of the Rolling Stones. LC 99-48688. 2000. 16.95 (*1-55652-400-5*) A Cappella Bks.
***Booth, Stephen.** Black Dog: A Crime Novel. LC 00-37154. 2000. pap. write for info. (*0-684-87301-X*) Atheneum Yung Read.
Booth, Stephen. Precious Nonsense: The Gettysburg Address, Ben Jonson's Epitaphs on His Children, & Twelfth Night. LC 97-27979. 216p. 1998. 35.00 (*0-520-21288-6*, Pub. by U CA Pr) Cal Prin Full Svc.
***Booth, Stephen, ed.** Shakespeare's Sonnets. 616p. 2000. pap. 19.95 (*0-300-08506-0*) Yale U Pr.
Booth, Sterling H. & Vance, Robert W., eds. Applications of Cryogenic Technology, Vol. 8. LC 68-57815. (Cryogenic Society of America Applications of Cryogenic Technology Ser.). (Illus.). 1976. text 30.00 (*0-87936-010-0*) Scholium Intl.
Booth, Sterling H., ed. see Conference of the Cryogenic Society of America, 5t.
Booth, Sterling R., Jr. Allergy Cures Your Allergist Never Mentioned. LC 80-20698. 1989. 22.95 (*0-87949-191-4*) Ashley Bks.
Booth, Steve. Selected Peak Marking Features in the Gospel of John. LC 95-26223. (American University Studies: Series 7, Vol. 178). XIII, 183p. 1996. 39.95 (*0-8204-2474-9*) P Lang Pubng.
Booth, Steven C. Selected Peak Marking Features in the Gospel of John, Vol. 178. LC 94-47007. (American University Studies: Ser. VII). XIX, 212p. (C). 1995. text 39.95 (*0-8204-2749-7*) P Lang Pubng.
Booth, Stuart, et al, eds. Pen & Brush Lettering: A Book of Alphabets. (Illus.). 112p. 1994. pap. 12.95 (*0-289-80099-4*) Sterling.
Booth, T. Michael, et al. Paratrooper: The Life of General James M. Gavin. (Illus.). 494p. 1994. 27.50 (*0-671-73226-9*) S&S Trade.
Booth, T. William & Wilson, William H. Carl F. Gould: A Life in Architecture & the Arts. LC 94-28501. (Illus.). 288p. 1995. 40.00 (*0-295-97360-9*) U of Wash Pr.
***Booth, Tanis.** For the Love of Football. Craats, Rennay, ed. (For the Love of Sports Ser.). (Illus.). 24p. (J). (gr. k-3). 2000. write for info. (*1-930954-25-5*) Weigl Pubs.
Booth, Taylor L. Introduction to Computer Engineering: Hardware & Software Design. 3rd ed. LC 84-2252. 682p. (C). 1984. text 68.50 (*0-471-87321-7*) Krieger.
— Sequential Machines & Automata Theory. LC 67-25924. (Illus.). 608p. 1967. reprint ed. pap. 188.50 (*0-7837-3431-X*, 205775200008) Bks Demand.
Booth, Ted. High Water over the Road: Seven Generations of an American Family. LC 68-56355. (Illus.). 236p. reprint ed. pap. 73.20 (*0-608-10222-9*, 201291000083) Bks Demand.
Booth, Tim. Developing Policy Research. 225p. 1988. text 82.95 (*0-566-05216-4*, Pub. by Avebry) Ashgate Pub Co.
Booth, Tim & Booth, Wendy. Growing up with Parents Who Have Learning Difficulties. LC 97-41065. 272p. (C). 1998. pap. 24.99 (*0-415-16656-X*) Routledge.
— Growing up with Parents with Learning Difficulties. 232p. (C). 1998. 75.00 (*0-415-16655-1*) Routledge.
— Parenting under Pressure: Mothers & Fathers with Learning Difficulties. LC 94-230. 1994. pap. 31.95 (*0-335-19194-0*) OpUniv Pr.
Booth, Tim, et al. Outward Bound: Relocation & Community Care for People with Learning Difficulties. 192p. 1990. 113.00 (*0-335-15431-X*); pap. 40.95 (*0-335-15430-1*) OpUniv Pr.
***Booth, Tom.** Cry the Gospel. 136p. 1999. pap. 8.95 (*1-57992-066-7*) OR Catholic.
Booth, Tom. Find Us Ready Songbook. 112p. 1997. pap. 8.95 (*0-915531-64-X*) OR Catholic.
Booth, Tony. Labour of Love. (Illus.). 320p. (Orig.). 1997. pap. 9.95 (*1-85782-181-5*, Pub. by Blake Publng) Seven Hills Bk.
Booth, Tony & Ainscow, Mel, eds. From Them to Us: An International Study of Inclusion in Education. LC 97-43154. 523p. (C). 1998. pap. 25.99 (*0-415-13979-1*, D5697) Routledge.
— From Them to Us: An International Study of Inclusion in Education. LC 97-43154. 280p. (C). (gr. 13). 1998. 80.00 (*0-415-18739-7*, D5693) Routledge.
Booth, Tony & Coulby, David, eds. Producing & Reducing Disaffection. (Curricula All Ser.). 288p. 1987. 113.00 (*0-335-15976-1*); pap. 33.95 (*0-335-15975-3*) OpUniv Pr.
Booth, Tony & Swann, Will, eds. Including Pupils with Disabilities. 288p. 1987. pap. 33.95 (*0-335-15977-X*) OpUniv Pr.
Booth, Trish. Before You Get Pregnant. 31p. 1987. 1.50 (*0-317-56637-7*) Intl Childbirth.
***Booth, Trudie M.** French Phonetics: A Guide to Correct Pronunciation of French And Cahier D'Exercises. LC 00-44327. (ENG.). 2000. pap. write for info. (*0-7618-1778-6*) U Pr of Amer.
Booth-Tucker, Frederick. The Salvation Army in America: Selected Reports, 1899-1903. LC 79-38439. (Religion in America, Ser. 2). 212p. 1976. reprint ed. 21.95 (*0-405-04060-1*) Ayer.
Booth, Turdie M. French Phonetics: A Guide to Correct Pronunciation of French & Cahier d'Exercices. LC 97-41772. (FRE.). 152p. (C). 2000. pap. 24.50 (*0-7618-0967-8*) U Pr of Amer.
Booth, V. Hartley. British Extradition Law & Procedure, Vol. II. 604p. 1980. lib. bdg. 80.00 (*90-286-0079-5*) Kluwer Academic.
Booth, Vernon. Communicating in Science: Writing a Scientific Paper & Speaking at Scientific Meetings. 2nd ed. 94p. (C). 1993. pap. text 15.95 (*0-521-42915-3*) Cambridge U Pr.
***Booth, Virginia Saffold.** Six Plays by Virginia Saffold Booth. LC 99-98150. 2000. 22.95 (*0-533-13443-9*) Vantage.
***Booth, W.** Modern Ventilation Techniques. 1998. pap. 100.00 (*0-86022-493-7*, Pub. by Build Servs Info Assn) St Mut.
Booth, W. B. & Potter, I. N. Carbon Dioxide-Controlled Mechanical Ventilation Systems. 1994. pap. 60.00 (*0-86022-389-2*, Pub. by Build Servs Info Assn) St Mut.
Booth, W. D. Marketing Strategies for Design-Build Contracting. (Illus.). 183p. (gr. 13). 1995. text 44.95 (*0-412-99591-3*) Chapman & Hall.
— Upgrading & Refurbishing the Older Fiberglass Sailboat. LC 84-46109. (Illus.). 292p. reprint ed. pap. 90.60 (*0-608-20038-7*, 207131000010) Bks Demand.
Booth, Waldon L. Manager's Guide to Alternative Work Schedules. 267p. (C). 1982. pap. text 23.95 (*1-884566-00-6*) Inst Police Tech.
Booth, Wayne. The Art of Deliberalizing: A Handbook for True Professionals. 13p. 1990. 2.00 (*0-911696-48-2*) Assn Am Coll.
Booth, Wayne. The Art of Deliberalizing: A Handbook for True Professionals, the 76th Annual Meeting, January 1990. LC LB2326.B66. 15p. reprint ed. pap. 30.00 (*0-608-01792-2*, 206244500003) Bks Demand.
— The Company We Keep: An Ethics of Fiction. 580p. 1988. pap. 19.95 (*0-520-06210-8*, Pub. by U CA Pr) Cal Prin Full Svc.
— Critical Understanding: The Powers & Limits of Pluralism. LC 78-15107. 422p. 1982. pap. text 10.95 (*0-226-06555-3*) U Ch Pr.
— Critical Understanding: The Powers & Limits of Pluralism. LC 78-15107. 1995. 27.00 (*0-226-06554-5*) U Ch Pr.
— Critical Understanding: The Powers & Limits of Pluralism. LC 78-15107. 422p. reprint ed. pap. 130.90 (*0-608-08820-X*, 206945900004); reprint ed. pap. 130.60 (*0-608-20596-6*, 205456100003) Bks Demand.
— For the Love of It: Amateuring & It's Rivals. LC 98-42920. 217p. 1999. 22.00 (*0-226-06585-5*) U Ch Pr.
— Modern Dogma & the Rhetoric of Assent. LC 73-89786. xviii, 254p. 1974. reprint ed. pap. text 19.00 (*0-226-06572-3*, P595) U Ch Pr.
— Now Don't Try to Reason with Me: Essays & Ironies for a Credulous Age. LC 73-12359. 1970. lib. bdg. 9.50 (*0-226-06579-0*) U Ch Pr.
— Now Don't Try to Reason with Me: Essays & Ironies for a Credulous Age. LC 73-12359. 1972. pap. text 2.95 (*0-226-06580-4*, P461) U Ch Pr.
— Now Don't Try to Reason with Me: Essays & Ironies for a Credulous Age. LC 73-12359. 397p. Date not set. reprint ed. pap. 123.10 (*0-608-20598-2*, 205456300003) Bks Demand.
— Rhetoric of Fiction. 2nd ed. LC 82-13592. 576p. 1983. pap. text 18.00 (*0-226-06558-8*) U Ch Pr.
— A Rhetoric of Irony. LC 73-87298. xviii, 312p. 1975. reprint ed. pap. text 15.95 (*0-226-06553-7*, P641) U Ch Pr.
— The Vocation of a Teacher: Rhetorical Occasions, 1967-1988. LC 88-14297. 372p. 1989. 29.95 (*0-226-06581-2*) U Ch Pr.
— The Vocation of a Teacher: Rhetorical Occasions, 1967-1988. LC 88-14297. 384p. 1990. pap. 17.95 (*0-226-06582-0*) U Ch Pr.
Booth, Wayne, ed. The Art of Growing Older: Writers on Living & Aging. LC 96-28550. (Illus.). 328p. 1996. pap. 14.95 (*0-226-06549-9*) U Ch Pr.
— The Knowledge Most Worth Having. LC 66-23684. 223p. Date not set. reprint ed. pap. 69.20 (*0-608-20597-4*, 205456200003) Bks Demand.
Booth, Wayne, selected by. The Art of Growing Older: Writers on Living & Aging. LC 92-22720. (Illus.). 320p. 1992. 22.00 (*0-671-78192-8*) S&S Trade.
Booth, Wayne & Gregory, Marshall. The Harper & Row Rhetoric: Thinking As Writing-Writing As Thinking. 478p. (C). 1987. pap. 23.00 (*0-06-040837-5*) Addson-Wesley Educ.
***Booth, Wayne & Gregory, Marshall.** The Harper & Row Rhetoric: Writing As Thinking, Thinking As Writing. 1998. pap. text 36.56 (*0-201-45669-9*) Addison-Wesley.
Booth, Wayne, et al. The Craft of Research. LC 95-2295. 306p. 1995. pap. 13.00 (*0-226-06584-7*) U Ch Pr.
Booth, Wayne, jt. auth. see Gregory, Paul R.
Booth, Wendy, jt. auth. see Booth, Tim.
Booth, William. How to Preach. 84p. (Orig.). 1979. pap. 3.95 (*0-89216-026-8*) Salv Army Suppl South.
— In Darkest England & the Way Out. 296p. 1984. reprint ed. 9.95 (*0-86544-024-7*) Salv Army Suppl South.
— In Darkest England & the Way Out: With Intros. & Index Added. LC 76-108240. (Criminology, Law Enforcement, & Social Problems Ser.: No. 142). 1975. reprint ed. 30.00 (*0-87585-142-8*) Patterson Smith.
Booth, William, ed. see Hauck, Phillip E.
Booth, William C., et al. The Craft of Research. 296p. (C). 1995. 25.00 (*0-226-06583-9*) U Ch Pr.
Booth, William C., ed. see Bly, Robert.
Booth, William D. Design-Build Marketing: Strategies & Procedures for the Small & Mid-Size Contractor. (Competitive Contractor Ser.). (Illus.). 200p. 1992. text 39.95 (*0-442-01086-9*) Chapman & Hall.
— Metal Building Contracting & Construction. LC 98-43601. (Illus.). 255p. 1999. 64.95 (*0-07-006964-6*, 639785308799) McGraw.
Booth, William J. Households: The Moral Architecture of the Economy. LC 92-25141. 320p. 1993. text 42.50 (*0-8014-2791-6*) Cornell U Pr.
Booth, William J., et al, eds. Politics & Rationality: Rational Choice in Application. (Illus.). 319p. (C). 1994. text 59.95 (*0-521-43409-2*); pap. text 20.95 (*0-521-43568-4*) Cambridge U Pr.
Booth, William J., jt. ed. see Beiner, Ronald S.
Booth, Zilpha M. Finding a Friend. 2nd ed. LC 96-60479. (Illus.). 40p. (J). 1996. pap. 8.95 (*1-883650-32-1*) Windswept Hse.
— Mommy, Don't Cry. (Orig.). 1982. pap. 9.00 (*0-914562-11-8*) Merriam-Eddy.
— Mommy Don't Cry. Weinberger, Jane, ed. LC 89-85362. (Illus.). 96p. 1989. reprint ed. pap. 5.95 (*0-932433-63-4*) Windswept Hse.
Boothby, Guy. A Bid for Fortune, or Dr. Nikola's Vendetta. (Oxford Popular Fiction Ser.). 236p. 1996. pap. 9.95 (*0-19-283240-9*) OUP.
— Dr. Nikola. 272p. 1999. pap. text 7.95 (*1-902058-17-8*, Pub. by Pulp Fictions) Seven Hills Bk.
— Dr. Nikola Returns. LC 80-22358. (Dr. Nikola, Master of Occult Mystery Ser.: No. 2). 256p. 1976. pap. 5.95 (*0-87877-034-8*, X-34) Newcastle Pub.
— Pharos the Egyptian. 390p. 1999. pap. text 7.95 (*1-902058-19-4*, Pub. by Pulp Fictions) Seven Hills Bk.
— Pharos, the Egyptian. Reginald, R. & Menville, Douglas A., eds. LC 75-46256. (Supernatural & Occult Fiction Ser.). (Illus.). 1976. reprint ed. lib. bdg. 33.95 (*0-405-08115-4*) Ayer.
Boothby, J. Lee. Mind-Power: The Ultimate 15-Second Formula to Transform Your Life Forever. 322p. (Orig.). 1997. pap. 23.95 (*0-9652926-0-6*) Mind-Power.
Boothby, William M. An Introduction to Differentiable Manifolds & Riemannian Geometry. 2nd ed. LC 85-13327. (Pure & Applied Mathematics Ser.). 1986. pap. text 68.00 (*0-12-116053-X*) Acad Pr.
Boothby, William M. & Weiss, Guido L., eds. Symmetric Spaces: Short Courses Presented at Washington University. LC 74-182213. (Pure & Applied Mathematics Ser.: No. 8). (Illus.). 502p. reprint ed. pap. 155.70 (*0-608-30568-5*, 202150600022) Bks Demand.
Boothe, B., et al, eds. Perception - Evaluation - Interpretation. rev. ed. LC 95-76265. (Swiss Monographs in Psychology: Vol. 3). (Illus.). 188p. 1995. pap. 37.00 (*0-88937-140-7*) Hogrefe & Huber Pubs.
Boothe, Ben B. A Banker Tells You How to Borrow All the Money You'll Ever Need. Booth, Paulette, ed. LC 92-11227. 304p. 1992. 21.95 (*0-8092-3920-5*) Unicorn Pr USA.
— A Banker Tells You How to Borrow All the Money You'll Ever Need. Booth, Paulette, ed. 304p. 1993. pap. 12.95 (*0-8092-3719-9*) Unicorn Pr USA.
— Confessions of a Banker. 2nd ed. Boothe, Paulette, ed. 270p. 1991. reprint ed. 16.95 (*0-89015-767-7*) Unicorn Pr USA.
— Grandpa's Hat: A Common Sense Guide to Life. Boothe, Paulette H., ed. LC 90-90192. (Common Sense Guide to Life Ser.). (Illus.). 120p. (Orig.). 1990. pap. 8.00 (*1-878162-00-4*) Unicorn Pr USA.
— How to Bullet-Proof Your Real Estate Portfolio from Charge Offs. Boothe, Paulette H., ed. 290p. 1992. 89.95 (*1-878162-04-7*) Unicorn Pr USA.
— To Be or Not to Be an SOB: A Reaffirmation of Business Ethics. 2nd ed. Boothe, Paulette H., ed. 81p. 1991. reprint ed. 10.00 (*0-89015-737-5*) Unicorn Pr USA.

B

Boothe, Brigitte & Wyl, Agnes von. Erzahlen Als Konfliktdarstellung. 180p. 1999. 31.95 (*3-906762-24-6*) P Lang.

Boothe, Brigitte, ed. see Neukom, Marius.

Boothe, Jeffrey & Gayken, Julie. The CLMA Guide to Medicare Compliance for the Laboratory. 332p. 1997. ring bd. 399.00 (*0-9625414-8-6*) Clinical Lab Mgmnt Assn.

***Boothe, Lou & Tolman, Marvin N.** Super Simple Science for Preschoolers. 2000. pap. 18.95 (*0-89334-331-5*, Humanics Pub) Humanics Ltd.

Boothe, Paulette, ed. see Boothe, Ben B.

Boothe, Paulette H. A Quiet Place: A Collection of Poems. Booth, Ben, ed. (Illus.). 110p. (Orig.). 1992. pap. 10.00 (*1-878162-02-0*) Unicorn Pr USA.

Boothe, Paulette H., ed. see Boothe, Ben B.

Boothe, Viva B. The Political Party As a Social Process. LC 73-19131. (Politics & People Ser.). (Illus.). 130p. 1974. reprint ed. 13.95 (*0-405-05856-X*) Ayer.

Boothe, Viva B., ed. Women in the Modern World: (the Annals of the American Academy of Political & Social Science, Vol. 143, May, 1929) LC 74-3929. (Women in America Ser.). (Illus.). 404p. 1974. reprint ed. 31.95 (*0-405-06078-5*) Ayer.

Boothman, Derek, ed. & tr. see Gramsci, Antonio.

***Boothman, Nicholas.** How to Make People Like You in 90 Seconds or Less. (Illus.). 160p. 2000. 14.95 (*0-7611-1940-X*) Workman Pub.

***Boothman, Nick.** How to Make People Like You in 90 Seconds or Less. 96p. 1999. pap. 9.95 (*0-9684543-0-5*) Fleetwood Pr.

Boothroyd, Catherine & Emmett, Jeremy. Risk Management: A Practical Guide for Construction Professionals. 1996. pap. 100.00 (*1-85609-120-1*, Pub. by Witherby & Co) St Mut.

Boothroyd, Geoffrey. Assembly Automation & Product Design. (Manufacturing Engineering & Materials Processing Ser.: Vol. 37). (Illus.). 432p. 1991. text 110.00 (*0-8247-8547-9*) Dekker.

— Gun Collecting. (Illus.). 208p. 1989. 29.95 (*0-948253-10-X*, Pub. by Sportsmans Pr) Trafalgar.

— The Handgun. (Illus.). 570p. 1990. 65.00 (*0-948253-27-4*, Pub. by Sportsmans Pr) Trafalgar.

— The Shotgun. (Illus.). 240p. 1993. 35.00 (*0-940143-92-5*) Safari Pr.

— Shotguns & Gunsmiths. (Illus.). 240p. 1993. 35.00 (*0-940143-91-7*) Safari Pr.

— Sidelocks & Boxlocks: The Classic British Shotguns. 271p. 1999. 35.00 (*1-57157-118-3*, Pub. by Safari Pr) Natl Bk Netwk.

Boothroyd, Geoffrey & Poli, A. Applied Engineering Mechanics: Statics & Dynamics. (Manufacturing Engineering Ser.: No. 5). (Illus.). 368p. 1980. text 75.00 (*0-8247-6945-7*) Dekker.

Boothroyd, Geoffrey, et al. Product Design for Manufacture & Assembly. LC 93-43398. (Illus.). 552p. 1994. text 165.00 (*0-8247-9176-2*) Dekker.

Boothroyd, Gregory. Going Home: A Therapeutic & Spiritual Guide Toward Eliminating Self-Defeating Behaviors. (Illus.). 112p. (C). 1995. reprint ed. pap. write for info. (*0-9671416-0-5*) Greenwood Assocs.

Boothroyd, John C. & Komuniecki, Richard, eds. Molecular Approaches to Parasitology. (MBL Lectures in Biology: Vol. 12). 560p. 1995. 235.00 (*0-471-10342-X*); pap. 109.95 (*0-471-10341-1*) Wiley.

Boothroyd, Jon, et al. The Geological Characteristics of the Coast of Ecuador: Information & Recommendations for Managing the Development of the Coastline. 143p. 1994. write for info. (*1-885454-00-7*) Coastal Res.

***Boothroyd, Peter & Pham Xuam Nam, eds.** Socioeconomic Renovation in Viet Nam: The Origin, Evolution & Impact of Doi Moi. 200p. 2000. pap. 20.00 (*0-88936-904-6*, Pub. by IDRC Bks) Stylus Pub VA.

Boothroyd, Stephen & Barney, Peter. Railroads in Early Postcards: Northern New England, Vol. 2. LC 89-70721. (Illus.). 112p. (Orig.). 1992. pap. 11.95 (*1-879511-04-5*, Vestal Pr) Madison Bks UPA.

Bootle, Roger. The Death of Inflation: Surviving & Thriving in the Zero Era. LC 96-7874. (Illus.). 272p. 1997. pap. 15.95 (*1-85788-148-6*) Nicholas Brealey.

Bootman, J. Lyle, et al. Principles of Pharmacoeconomics. 2nd ed. 312p. 1996. pap. 54.75 (*0-929375-17-3*) H W Bks.

Bootman, Tyler. Myself in the Street: Poems. (Orig.). 1966. 4.50 (*0-8079-0087-7*); pap. 1.95 (*0-8079-0088-5*) October.

Booton, Richard C. Computational Methods for Electromagnetics & Microwaves. LC 91-34450. (Series in Microwave & Optical Engineering). 192p. 1992. 94.95 (*0-471-52804-8*) Wiley.

Booton, Terry L. Cracking New Accounts: Quick Tips & Inside Techniques to Help You Gain Market Share & Close the Sale in Half the Time. 235p. 1991. 25.00 (*0-9633282-0-4*) Advan Mktg Instruct.

— Cracking New Accounts: Tips & Techniques for Opening & Closing the Sale in Half the Time. 225p. 1994. text 24.95 (*1-55738-817-2*, Irwn Prfssnl) McGraw-Hill Prof.

Boots, B. N. & Getis, Arthur. Point Pattern Analysis. LC 88-60304. (Scientific Geography Ser.: No. 8). 93p. 1988. reprint ed. pap. 30.00 (*0-608-01449-4*, 205949300001) Bks Demand.

Boots, Gypsy, et al. The Gypsy in Me. 102p. 1993. pap. 9.95 (*0-9640640-0-6*) Gypsy Boots.

Boots, Sharon, jt. auth. see Bisio, Attilio.

Boots, Sharon, jt. ed. see Bisio, Attilio.

***Boots, Tiffany.** Five Men. 144p. 2000. mass mkt. 7.95 (*1-56201-180-4*, Pub. by Blue Moon Bks) Publishers Group.

Booty, Bruce. Guide to Nuclear Physics. LC 73-330797. (Illus.). 174p. reprint ed. pap. 54.00 (*0-8357-8896-2*, 203345500086) Bks Demand.

Booty, John. An American Apostle: The Life of Stephen Fielding Bayne, Jr. LC 97-7837. (Illus.). 256p. 1997. 20.00 (*1-56338-208-3*) TPI PA.

***Booty, John.** Reflections on the Theology of Richard Hooker: An Elizabaethan Addresses Modern Aglicanism. LC 98-61674. 229p. 1998. pap. 20.00 (*0-918769-45-0*) Univ South Pr.

Booty, John & Sykes, Stephen, eds. The Study of Anglicanism. enl. rev. ed. 464p. 1998. pap. 36.00 (*0-8006-3151-X*, 1-3151) Augsburg Fortress.

Booty, John E. The Church in History. (Church's Teaching Ser.: Vol. 3). 320p. 1984. 5.95 (*0-8164-0420-8*) Harper SF.

— John Donne: Selections from Divine Poems, Sermons, Devotions & Prayers. (Classics of Western Spirituality Ser.). 1990. 26.95 (*0-8091-0435-0*); pap. 19.95 (*0-8091-3160-9*) Paulist Pr.

— Mission & Ministry: A History of Virginia Theological Seminary. LC 95-7419. (Illus.). 416p. 1995. 34.95 (*0-9644169-1-3*) Morehouse Pub.

— The Servant Church: Diaconal Ministry & the Episcopal Church. LC 82-81429. 112p. 1982. pap. 7.95 (*0-8192-1316-0*) Morehouse Pub.

— What Makes Us Episcopalians? LC 82-80468. 44p. (Orig.). 1990. pap. 4.95 (*0-8192-1302-0*) Morehouse Pub.

Booty, John E., ed. The Divine Drama in History & Liturgy: Essays Presented to Horton Davies on His Retirement from Princeton University. LC 84-4629. (Pittsburgh Theological Monographs, New Ser.: No. 10). 1984. pap. 10.00 (*0-915138-67-0*) Pickwick.

Booty, John E. & Thomas, Owen C. The Spirit of Anglicanism: Hooker - Maurice - Temple. Wolf, William J. et al, eds. LC 79-122562. (Anglican Studies Ser.). 224p. 1986. pap. 11.95 (*0-8192-1263-6*) Morehouse Pub.

Booty, John E., ed. see Hooker, Richard.

Bootz, Friedrich & Muller, Gottfried H. Microvascular Tissue Transplant in the Head & Neck. LC 93-8837.Tr. of Mikrovaskul are Gewebetransplantation im Kopt-Hals-Bereich. (GER.). 101p. 1993. 105.00 (*0-86577-503-6*) Thieme Med Pubs.

Bootzin, Richard R., et al. Abnormal Psychology: Current Perspectives. rev. ed. (C). 1994. text 57.74 incl. audio (*0-07-911953-0*) McGraw.

— Abnormal Psychology: Current Perspectives. 6th ed. LC 92-49206. 1993. write for info. (*0-07-006536-5*) McGraw.

— Psychology Today. 7th ed. 728p. (C). 1991. 79.06 (*0-07-006539-X*); pap., student ed. 23.75 (*0-07-006541-1*) McGraw.

Boovier, Leon, jt. auth. see Garling, Scipio.

Booy, Anna & Horton, Audrey, eds. Sweet & Maxwell's EC Intellectual Property Materials. 1994. pap. 52.00 (*0-421-51200-8*) Sweet & Maxwell.

Booy, Derrick M. Rock of Exile: Tristan da Cunha. 10.00 (*0-8159-6711-X*) Devin.

Booy, Geert & Van Marle, Jaap, eds. Yearbook of Morphology. viii, 328p. (Orig.). (C). 1988. 98.50 (*90-6765-375-6*) Mouton.

Booy, Theodoor N. De, see De Booy, Theodoor N.

Booyens, S. W. Dimension of Nursing Management. 2nd ed. 719p. 1998. pap. 75.00 (*0-7021-4211-5*, Pub. by Juta & Co) Intl Spec Bk.

— Dimensions of Nursing Management. 1993. pap. 64.75 (*0-7021-2988-7*, Pub. by Juta & Co) Gaunt.

Booysen, H. Volkereg - en Sy Verhouding Tot die Suid-Africaanse Reg. 612p. 1989. pap. write for info. (*0-7021-1057-4*, Pub. by Juta & Co) Gaunt.

Booysen, P. De V., see De V. Booysen, P., ed.

Booz-Allen & Hamilton, Inc. Staff. Zero-Emission Vehicle Technology Assessment (Aug. 1995) (Electric Vehicle Information Ser.: Vol. 19). (Illus.). 105p. 1996. pap. 85.00 (*0-89934-277-9*, BT046); lib. bdg. 135.00 (*0-89934-278-7*, BT946) Bus Tech Bks.

Booz, Allen & Hamilton Staff. An Economic Analysis of Imported LNG in Selected End-Use Markets. 65p. 1978. pap. 3.00 (*0-318-12601-X*, F00685) Am Gas Assn.

Booz, Elisabeth B. New Zealand. 3rd ed. LC 98-32374. (Odyssey Passport Ser.). (Illus.). 301p. 1999. pap. 19.95 (*962-217-533-3*) Norton.

Booz, Elizabeth. New Zealand. 2nd ed. LC 90-63333. (Asian Guides Ser.). (Illus.). 232p. 1993. reprint ed. pap. 12.95 (*0-8442-9724-0*, Passprt Bks) NTC Contemp Pub Co.

— New Zealand: Picturesque Land. 3rd ed. (Illus.). 232p. 1996. pap. 15.95 (*0-8442-9886-7*, Passprt Bks) NTC Contemp Pub Co.

— Tibet. (Illus.). 228p. 1992. pap. 12.95 (*0-8442-9806-9*, Passprt Bks) NTC Contemp Pub Co.

Booz, J. & Ebert, H. G., eds. Sixth Symposium, Microdosimetry, 2 vols., Vol. 1. (Commission of the European Communities Ser.). xiv, 688p. 1978. text 332.00 (*0-906346-02-9*) Gordon & Breach.

— Sixth Symposium, Microdosimetry, 2 vols., Vol. 2. (Commission of the European Communities Ser.). xiv, 572p. 1978. text 332.00 (*0-906346-03-7*) Gordon & Breach.

Booz, J., jt. ed. see Ebert, H. G.

Booz, Noel. Biological Anthropology. 1995. pap. text 39.95 (*0-9644248-0-0*) Intl Inst Human Evol.

Booz, Paddy. Yunnan. (Illus.). 208p. 1987. pap. 9.95 (*0-8442-9822-0*, Passprt Bks) NTC Contemp Pub Co.

Booz, Patrick R. Bali. large type ed. (Guidebook Ser.). (Illus.). 1991. pap. 9.95 (*962-217-111-7*) L A Michaux.

— Bali: A Travel Portrait. 1996. pap. text 9.95 (*962-593-082-5*) Periplus.

Boozer, William. William Faulkner's First Book: The Marble Faun Fifty Years Later. LC 75-6916. (Illus.). 1975. 7.50 (*0-686-12125-2*) Pigeon Roost Pr.

Boozer, William & Wells, Dean F., eds. The Faulkner Newsletter Collected Issues. LC 94-60634. (Illus.). 270p. 1994. lib. bdg. 75.00 (*0-916242-66-8*) Yoknapatawpha.

Bope, Edward T. & Verhoff, William A. The Family Practice Office Manual. (Office Manual Ser.). 246p. 1994. 115.00 (*1-890018-05-8*) Anadem Pubng.

Bope, Edward T., et al. Saunders Review of Family Practice. 2nd ed. Kersey, Ray, ed. LC 96-16715. (Illus.). 416p. 1996. pap. text 52.00 (*0-7216-5817-2*, W B Saunders Co) Harcrt Hlth Sci Grp.

Bope, Edward T., jt. auth. see Rakel, Robert E.

Bopp, Andrew, ed. SGCD TechNoteBook: Glass & Ceramic Decorating Manual, Vols. 1-3. 2nd rev. ed. (Illus.). 864p. 1997. ring bd. 495.00 (*0-9656502-0-0*) Soc of Glass.

Bopp, Emily, jt. auth. see Hoshizaki, Jon.

Bopp, Franz. A Comparative Grammar of the Sanscrit, Zend, Greek, Latin, Lithuanian, Gothic, German, & Slavonic Languages, 3 vols. in 2, Set. Wilson, Horace H., ed. (Documenta Semiotica Ser.). xv, 1462p. 1985. reprint ed. lib. bdg. 320.00 incl. 3.5 hd (*3-487-07489-3*) G Olms Pubs.

— Uber das Conjugationssystem der Sanskritsprache. (Documenta Semiotica, Ser. 1). xlvi, 312p. 1975. reprint ed. 80.00 (*3-487-05354-3*) G Olms Pubs.

Bopp, Franz & Koerner, E. F. Analytical Comparison of the Sanskrit, Greek, Latin, & Teutonic Languages, Shewing the Original Identity of Their Grammatical Structure. 2nd rev. ed. LC 74-84628. (Amsterdam Classics in Linguistics Ser.: No. 3). xxxviii, 68p. 1989. 33.00 (*90-272-0874-3*) J Benjamins Pubng Co.

Bopp, Gordon R., ed. Federal Lab Technology Transfer: Issues & Policies. LC 88-1605. (Illus.). 228p. 1988. 59.95 (*0-275-92956-6*, C2956, Praeger Pubs) Greenwood.

Bopp, James, Jr., ed. Human Life & Health Care Ethics. LC 84-29133. 320p. 1985. lib. bdg. 55.00 (*0-313-27064-3*, U7064, Greenwood Pr) Greenwood.

Bopp, Judie, et al. The Sacred Tree: Reflections on Native American Spirituality. LC 89-63193. (Illus.). 87p. 1990. pap. 10.95 (*0-941524-58-2*) Lotus Pr.

Bopp, Lawrence J., jt. auth. see Bockmiller, Stephen R.

Bopp, M. J., jt. ed. see Kramer, D. A.

Bopp, Mary S. Research in Dance: A Guide to Resources. LC 92-42508. (Reference Ser.). 304p. 1993. 55.00 (*0-8161-9065-8*, Hall Reference) Macmillan.

Bopp, Richard E. & Smith, Linda C., eds. Reference & Information Services: An Introduction. rev. ed. (Library Science Text Ser.). xxiv, 626p. 1995. pap. text 45.00 (*1-56308-129-6*) Libs Unl.

— Reference & Information Services: An Introduction. 2nd rev. ed. (Library Science Text Ser.). xxiv, 626p. 1995. lib. bdg. 55.00 (*1-56308-130-X*) Libs Unl.

Bopp, Stephan. Computerimplementation der Italienischen Flexions - & Wortbilungsmorphologie. (Informatik und Sprache Ser.: Bd. 2). (GER.). 1993. write for info. (*3-487-09810-5*) G Olms Pubs.

Bopp, Stephen, jt. auth. see Zaccaria, Joseph.

Boppana, Ravi B., ed. see NSF Science & Technology Center in Discrete Mathem & DIMACS Staff.

***Boquist, John A., et al.** The Value Sphere: Secrets of Creating & Retaining Shareholder Wealth. LC 99-9114. (Illus.). 256p. 1999. pap. 39.95 (*0-9675564-0-6*) Value Integr.

Bor-Komorowski, Tadeusz. The Secret Army. (Allied Forces Ser.: No. 2). (Illus.). 408p. 1984. reprint ed. 32.50 (*0-89839-082-6*) Battery Pr.

Bor, N. L. The Grasses of Burma, Ceylon, India & Pakistan. (C). 1988. 170.00 (*0-7855-3232-3*, Pub. by Scientific) St Mut.

— Grasses of Burma, Ceylon, India & Pakistan (Excluding Bambuseae) (C). 1979. text 510.00 (*0-89771-562-4*, Pub. by Intl Bk Distr) St Mut.

— The Grasses of Burma, Ceylon, India & Pakistan (Excluding Bambuseae) 767p. 1979. reprint ed. 500.00 (*0-7855-6633-3*, Pub. by Intl Bk Distr) St Mut.

— Manual of Indian Forestry Botany. 441p. 1953. 200.00 (*0-7855-6634-1*, Pub. by Intl Bk Distr) St Mut.

Bor, Robert. The Family & HIV. (Sexual Politics Ser.). 208p. 1994. pap. 37.95 (*0-304-32985-1*, Pub. by Cassell) LPC InBook.

***Bor, Robert.** The Trainee Handbook: A Guide for Counseling & Psychotherapy Trainees. LC 98-61584. 290 p. 1999. write for info. (*0-7619-5852-5*) Sage.

Bor, Robert & Elford, Jonathan. The Family & HIV Today. 300p. 1998. 75.00 (*0-304-70405-9*); pap. 24.95 (*0-304-70188-2*) Continuum.

Bor, Robert & Miller, Riva. Internal Consultation in Health Care Settings. 102p. 1992. pap. 22.00 (*1-85575-020-1*, Pub. by H Karnac Bks Ltd) Other Pr LLC.

Bor, Robert, et al. Counselling in Health Care Settings. LC 98-220788. 224p. 1998. 69.95 (*0-304-33985-7*); pap. 24.95 (*0-304-33986-5*) Continuum.

— Theory & Practice of HIV Counselling: A Systemic Approach. LC 92-48338. 208p. 1993. pap. text 23.95 (*0-87630-717-9*) Brunner-Mazel.

Bor, Wout Van den, see Van den Bor, Wout.

***Bora, Bijit.** Human Capital, Foreign Ownership & Wages. LC 99-181301. (Working Paper Ser.). 45 p. 1998. write for info. (*0-07-258769-5*) McGraw-Hill Prof.

Bora, Bijit & Findlay, Christopher, eds. Regional Integration & the Asia-Pacific. (Illus.). 272p. 1998. reprint ed. pap. text 32.00 (*0-19-550753-3*) OUP.

Bora, Bijit & Pangestu, Mari. Priority Issues in Trade & Investment Liberalization: Implications for the Asia Pacific Region. LC 98-474063. ix, 215p. 1996. write for info. (*981-00-7785-8*, Pub. by AgBe Pub) Balogh.

Bora, F. William. The Pediatric Upper Extremity: Diagnosis & Management. (Illus.). 429p. 1986. text 155.00 (*0-7216-1872-3*, W B Saunders Co) Harcrt Hlth Sci Grp.

Bora, Gy, jt. auth. see Bencze, I.

Bora, R. S. Himalayan Migration: A Study of the Hill Region of Uttar Pradesh. LC 96-6135. 196p. 1996. 39.95 (*0-8039-9310-2*) Sage.

Bora, S. Student Revolution in Asaam. (C). 1992. 28.00 (*81-7099-332-6*, Pub. by Mittal Pubs Dist) S Asia.

Boraas, Alan, ed. see Kalifornsky, Peter.

Boraas, Roger S. & Geraty, Lawrence T. Heshbon 1974: The Fourth Campaign at Tell Hesban: A Preliminary Report. (Andrews University Monographs). (Illus.). 258p. (C). 1976. 15.99 (*0-943872-09-X*) Andrews Univ Pr.

— Heshbon 1976: The Fifth Campaign at Tell Hesban: A Preliminary Report. LC 89-80164. (Andrews University Monographs). (Illus.). 366p. (C). 1978. 15.99 (*0-943872-10-3*) Andrews Univ Pr.

Boraas, Roger S. & Horn, Siegfried H. Heshbon 1971: The Second Campaign at Tell Hesban: A Preliminary Report. (Andrews University Monographs). (Illus.). 188p. (C). 1973. 15.99 (*0-943872-06-5*) Andrews Univ Pr.

— Heshbon 1973: The Third Campaign at Tell Hesban: A Preliminary Report. (Andrews University Monographs). (Illus.). 207p. (C). 1975. 15.99 (*0-943872-08-1*) Andrews Univ Pr.

***Boraas, Tracey.** Animal Caretaker. LC 00-24692. (Career Explorations Ser.). (Illus.). 48p. (YA). (gr. 5 up). 2000. lib. bdg. 21.26 (*0-7368-0590-7*, Capstone Bks) Capstone Pr.

Boraas, Tracey. Auto Mechanics. LC 98-17961. (Community Helpers Ser.). (J). 1998. 14.00 (*0-7368-0072-7*, Bridgestone Bks) Capstone Pr.

***Boraas, Tracey.** Automotive Master Mechanic. LC 99-53970. (Career Exploration Ser.). 48p. (YA). (gr. 5 up). 2000. lib. bdg. 21.26 (*0-7368-0486-2*, Capstone Bks) Capstone Pr.

— Cosmetologist. LC 00-22447. (Career Explorations Ser.). (Illus.). 48p. (YA). (gr. 5 up). 2000. lib. bdg. 21.26 (*0-7368-0592-3*, Capstone Bks) Capstone Pr.

— Machinist. LC 99-54148. (Career Exploration Ser.). 48p. (YA). (gr. 5 up). 2000. lib. bdg. 21.26 (*0-7368-0491-9*, Capstone Bks) Capstone Pr.

Boraas, Tracey. Plumbers. LC 98-16855. (Community Helpers Ser.). (J). 1998. 14.00 (*0-7368-0073-5*, Bridgestone Bks) Capstone Pr.

***Boraas, Tracey.** Police Detective. (Career Explorations Ser.). 48p. (YA). (gr. 5 up). 2000. lib. bdg. 21.26 (*0-7368-0597-4*) Capstone Pr.

Boraas, Tracey. School Principals. LC 98-18471. (Community Helpers Ser.). (J). 1998. 14.00 (*0-7368-0074-3*, Bridgestone Bks) Capstone Pr.

— TV Reporters. LC 98-16804. (Community Helpers Ser.). (J). 1998. 14.00 (*0-7368-0075-1*, Hilltop Bks) Capstone Pr.

***Boraas, Tracey.** U.S. Air Force Special Forces: Special Operations Wings. LC 99-25470. 1999. 19.93 (*0-7368-0336-X*) Capstone Pr.

Borah, Jogeswar. Folk Elements in Ramaswarasvati: A Mdajor Neo-Vaisnavite Poet of North East India. (C). 1996. 30.00 (*81-86791-03-5*, Pub. by Punthi Pus) S Asia.

Borah, William E. American Problems: A Selection of Speeches & Prophecies. Green, Horace, ed. LC 77-111472. (BCL Ser.: I). reprint ed. 49.50 (*0-404-00624-8*) AMS Pr.

— American Problems: A Selection of Speeches & Prophecies. (History - United States Ser.). 329p. 1992. reprint ed. lib. bdg. 89.00 (*0-7812-6214-3*) Rprt Serv.

— American Problems: A Selection of Speeches & Prophecies. 1971. reprint ed. 13.00 (*0-403-00874-3*) Scholarly.

Borah, Woodrow. Price Trends of Royal Tribute Commodities in Nueva Galicia. 1992. pap. 42.50 (*0-520-09769-6*, Pub. by U CA Pr) Cal Prin Full Svc.

Borah, Woodrow, jt. auth. see Cook, Sherburne F.

Borak, Jonathan, et al. Hazardous Materials Exposure: Emergency Response & Patient Care. 304p. 1990. pap. text 53.00 (*0-89303-722-2*) P-H.

— Managing Hazardous Materials Incidents Vol. III: Medical Management Guidelines for Acute Chemical Exposures. 495p. 1996. reprint ed. pap. text 50.00 (*0-7881-3256-3*) DIANE Pub.

Boraks, Lucius. Religions of the East. 106p. 1988. pap. 7.95 (*1-55612-140-7*) Sheed & Ward WI.

— Religions of the East-West. LC 86-63499. (Illus.). 92p. (Orig.). 1988. pap., teacher ed. 9.95 (*1-55612-155-5*) Sheed & Ward WI.

— Religions of the West. LC 87-63499. 116p. (Orig.). (YA). 1988. pap. 7.95 (*1-55612-141-5*) Sheed & Ward WI.

Boraks-Nemetz, Lillian. The Old Brown Suitcase: A Teenager's Story of War & Peace. LC 94-76876. 148p. (Orig.). (YA). (gr. 8-12). 1994. pap. 9.50 (*0-914539-10-8*) Ben-Simon.

***Boraks-Nemetz, Lillian.** The Sunflower Diary. (On Time's Wing Ser.). 216p. (YA). (gr. 7). 1999. pap. 5.95 (*1-896184-58-8*) Roussan Pubs.

Boral, H. & Faudemay, P., eds. Database Machines. (Lecture Notes in Computer Science Ser.: Vol. 368). vi, 387p. 1989. 43.00 (*0-387-51324-8*, 3164) Spr-Verlag.

Boral, H., jt. ed. see DeWitt, D. J.

Boralevi, Lea C., jt. ed. see Cranston, Maurice.

***BorAm, A.** Guide to the Golan Heights: Israeli Landscapes. 2000. 25.00 (*965-90048-0-X*, Pub. by Israel Shalem) Shalom.

Boram, Clifford. How to Get Parts Cast for Your Antique Stove: Dealing with a Foundry Is Easier Than You May Think. (Illus.). 52p. 1982. pap. 5.00 (*0-9612204-0-6*) Autonomy Hse.

— What Is My Antique Stove Worth? 9p. 1987. reprint ed. pap. 2.00 (*0-9612204-3-0*) Autonomy Hse.

Boran, George. Youth Ministry That Works: Practical Ideas for Working with Young People. 160p. 1996. pap. 11.95 (*0-8091-3666-X*) Paulist Pr.

An Asterisk (*) at the beginning of an entry indicates that the title is appearing for the first time.

Boran, Pat. Familiar Things. 84p. 1993. pap. 10.95 (1-873790-32-5) Dufour.

*Boran, Pat. The Portable Creative Writing Workshop. LC 99-191098. 204 p. 1999. 16.95 (1-897648-51-0) Dufour.

Boran, Pat. The Shape of Water. LC 96-156174. 1996. 18.95 (1-873790-86-4) Dufour.

— The Shape of Water. LC 96-156174. 80p. 1997. pap. 11.95 (1-873790-85-6) Dufour.

— Strange Bedfellows. 116p. 1991. pap. 13.95 (0-948339-65-9, Pub. by Poolbeg Pr) Dufour.

Borang, Kasja K. Principles of Reiki. 1998. pap. 11.00 (0-7225-3406-X) Genl Dist Srvs.

Borangiu, Theodore, et al. Intelligent Manufacturing Systems 1995: IMS '95: A Proceedings Volume from the 3rd IFAC, IFIP, IFORS Workshop, Bucharest, Romania, 24-26 October 1995. LC 97-16395. 1997. write for info. (0-08-042595-X, Pergamon Pr) Elsevier.

Borasi, Rafaella. Reconceiving Mathematics Instruction: A Focus on Errors. (Issues in Curriculum Theory, Policy, & Research Ser.). (Illus.). 321p. 1996. pap. 39.50 (1-56750-168-0); text 73.25 (1-56750-167-2) Ablx Pub.

Borasi, Raffaella. Learning Mathematics Through Inquiry. LC 91-25704. 234p. (C). (gr. 9). 1991. pap. text 29.50 (0-435-08324-4, 08324) Heinemann.

*Borasi, Raffaella & Siegel, Marjorie Gail. Reading Counts: Expanding the Role of Reading in Mathematics Classrooms. LC 99-57206. (Ways of Knowing in Science Ser.). 240p. 2000. write for info. (0-8077-3921-9) Tchrs Coll.

— Reading Counts: Expanding the Role of Reading in Mathematics Classrooms. LC 99-57206. 240p. (YA). 2000. pap. text 23.95 (0-8077-3920-0) Tchrs Coll.

Borasky, Leslie W., ed. see Morledge, Richard A.

Boratav, Olus, et al, eds. Turbulence Modeling & Vortex Dynamics: Proceedings of a Workshop Held at Istanbul, Turkey, 2-6 September 1996. LC 97-20900. (Lecture Notes in Physics Ser.: No. 491). xii, 245p. 1997. 68.00 (3-540-63051-1) Spr-Verlag.

Boravia, Judy. Silk Road: From Xian to Kashgar. 2nd ed. (Illus.). 320p. 1994. pap. 16.95 (0-8442-9951-0, Passprt Bks) NTC Contemp Pub Co.

Borawski, Walta. Sexually Dangerous Poet. 1984. pap. 5.00 (0-915480-16-6) Good Gay.

Boraz, Edward S. Understanding the Talmud: A Modern Reader's Guide for Study. LC 96-5142. 232p. 1996. 40.00 (1-56821-616-5) Aronson.

Boraz, Ellen, jt. auth. see Kohlhagen, Gale G.

Borba, Craig & Borba, Michele. The Good Apple Guide to Learning Centers. (Illus.). 208p. 1978. 15.99 (0-916456-33-1, GA86) Good Apple.

Borba, Michele. The Building Blocks of Self-Esteem. 72p. 1994. 89.95 incl. audio (1-880396-22-X, JP9622-X) Jalmar Pr.

Borba, Michele. Caring: A Program to Develop the Skills of Caring in Students. Conte, Marie, ed. (Character Builders Ser.: No. 5). (Illus.). 144p. Date not set. pap. 19.95 (1-880396-58-0, JP9658-0) Jalmar Pr.

— Esteem Builder Resources: A Compendium of Self-Esteem Resources. 160p. 1994. pap. 34.95 (1-880396-25-4, JP9625-4) Jalmar Pr.

— Esteem Builders: A Self-Esteem Curriculum for Improving Student Achievement, Behavior & School-Home Climate. Taylor-McMillan, Birah, ed. LC 88-80769. (Creative Teaching & Parenting Ser.). (Illus.). 444p. 1989. spiral bd. 49.95 (0-915190-88-5, JP9088-5) Jalmar Pr.

— Esteem Builders: A Self-Esteem Curriculum for Improving Student Achievement, Behavior & School-Home Climate. Taylor-McMillan, Birah, ed. LC 88-80769. (Creative Teaching & Parenting Ser.). (Illus.). 444p. (J). (gr. k-8). 1989. pap. 39.95 (0-915190-53-2, JP9053-2R) Jalmar Pr.

— Fairness & Cooperation: A K-8 Program to Develop the Skills of Fairness & Cooperation in Students. Conte, Marie, ed. (Character Builders Ser.: No. 3). (Illus.). 144p. Date not set. pap. 19.95 (1-880396-56-4, JP9656-4) Jalmar Pr.

— Home Esteem Builders: Activities to Strengthen the Partnership Between Home & School. LC 93-27066. 304p. 1994. 34.95 (0-915190-65-6, JP9065-6) Jalmar Pr.

— Overview of the Esteem Builders' Complete Program. 1994. pap. 44.95 (1-880396-00-9, JP9600-9) Jalmar Pr.

— Parents Do Make a Difference: How to Raise Kids with Solid Character, Strong Minds, & Caring Hearts. LC 98-58112. 272p. 1999. pap. text 18.00 (0-7879-4605-2) Jossey-Bass.

— Positive Attitudes & Peacemaking for Younger Children: A Program to Enhance Positive Attitudes & Peacemaking Skills for Pre-School Through Third Grade. Conte, Marie, ed. (Character Builders Ser.: No. 5). (Illus.). 144p. 2000. pap. 19.95 (1-880396-59-9, JP9659-9) Jalmar Pr.

— Respect for Self & Others: A K-8 Program to Develop the Skills of Respect in Students. Conte, Marie, ed. (Character Builders Ser.: No. 2). (Illus.). 144p. 2000. pap. 19.95 (1-880396-55-6, JP9655-6) Jalmar Pr.

— Responsibility & Trustworthiness: A K-8 Program to Develop the Skills of Responsibility in Students. Conte, Marie, ed. (Character Builders Ser.: No. 1). (Illus.). 144p. 2000. pap. 19.95 (1-880396-54-8, JP9654-8) Jalmar Pr.

— Staff Esteem Builders: The Administrator's Bible for Enhancing Self-Esteem. 336p. 1993. pap. 44.95 (1-880396-04-1, JP 9604-1) Jalmar Pr.

— Trainer's Manual for Training the Staff in Esteem-Building Development. 408p. 1994. ring bd. 129.95 (1-880396-03-3, JP9078-8) Jalmar Pr.

Borba, Michele & Ungaro, Dan. Bookends. 128p. (J). (gr. 1-4). 1982. 12.99 (0-86653-065-7, GA 432) Good Apple.

— The Complete Letter Book. 112p. (J). (ps-3). 1980. 12.99 (0-916456-80-3, GA 182) Good Apple.

Borba, Michele, jt. auth. see Borba, Craig.

Borba, Philip S. & Appel, David, eds. Benefits, Costs & Cycles in Workers Compensation. (S. S. Huebner International Ser.). (C). 1990. lib. bdg. 55.50 (0-7923-9037-7) Huebner Foun Insur.

Borba, Philip S., jt. ed. see Durbin, David.

Borbas, Margit, tr. see McCullough, Colleen.

Borbe, Tasso, ed. Semiotics Unfolding, 3 vols., Set. LC 83-13439. (Approaches to Semiotics Ser.: No. 68). 1983. 323.10 (3-11-009779-6) Mouton.

Borbein, A. H. Le Francais Actif Cassette, No. 2A. 160p. text 11.95 (0-88729-810-9) Langenscheidt.

Borbein, Adolf, jt. ed. see Kaestner, Ursula.

Borbein, Volker. Menschen in Deutschland. (GER., Illus.). 136p. 1995. 17.50 (3-468-49475-0) Langenscheidt.

Borbely, A. A., jt. ed. see Inoue, Shojiro.

Borbely, Alexander. Secrets of Sleep. LC 85-83887. (Illus.). 240p. 1988. pap. 18.00 (0-465-07593-2, Pub. by Basic) HarpC.

Borbely, James A., jt. auth. see Schemel, George J.

Borbidge, Raymond A. How to Conduct a Human Resources Effectiveness Audit: A Systematic Approach for Creating Value-Added Human Resources Services. 152p. 1996. ring bd. 79.95 (0-9639557-3-X, Jacob-Cameron) A R K Co.

Borbone, P. G., jt. auth. see Jenner, K. D.

*Borbowko, Magorzata, ed. Computational Methods in Surface & Colloid Science. LC 99-89301. (Surfactant Science Ser). 941p. 2000. 225.00 (0-8247-0323-5) Dekker.

Borceux, F., ed. Categorical Algebra & Its Applications. (Lecture Notes in Mathematics Ser.: Vol. 1348). viii, 375p. 1988. 52.95 (0-387-50362-5) Spr-Verlag.

Borceux, F. & Van Den Bossche, G. Algebra in a Localic Topos with Applications to Ring Theory. (Lecture Notes in Mathematics Ser.: Vol. 1038). 240p. 1983. 35.95 (0-387-12711-9) Spr-Verlag.

Borceux, Francis. A Handbook of Categorical Algebra: Basic Category Theory. LC 93-3225. (Encyclopedia of Mathematics & Its Applications Ser.: No. 50). 361p. (C). 1994. text 85.00 (0-521-44178-1) Cambridge U Pr.

— Handbook of Categorical Algebra, Vol. 2: Categories & Structures. (Encyclopedia of Mathematics & Its Applications Ser.: No. 51). 461p. (C). 1995. text 95.00 (0-521-44179-X) Cambridge U Pr.

— Handbook of Categorical Algebra, Vol. 3: Sheaf Theory. (Encyclopedia of Mathematics & Its Applications Ser.: No. 52). 540p. (C). 1995. text 105.00 (0-521-44180-3) Cambridge U Pr.

Borch-Jacobsen, Mikkel. The Emotional Tie: Psychoanalysis, Mimesis, & Affect. LC 92-20356. 216p. 1993. 39.50 (0-8047-2035-5); pap. 13.95 (0-8047-2037-1) Stanford U Pr.

— The Freudian Subject. Porter, Catherine, tr. from FRE. LC 87-30548.Tr. of Sujet Freudien. 288p. 1988. 45.00 (0-8047-1440-1) Stanford U Pr.

— Lacan: The Absolute Master. Brick, Douglas, tr. from FRE. LC 90-43813. 320p. 1991. 42.50 (0-8047-1556-4); pap. 16.95 (0-8047-1728-1) Stanford U Pr.

— Remembering Anna O. 144p. (C). 1996. 55.00 (0-415-91776-X); pap. 16.99 (0-415-91777-8) Routledge.

Borch, K., et al. Economics of Insurance. (Advanced Textbooks in Economics Ser.: No. 29). xiv,402p. 1989. 93.75 (0-444-87344-9, North Holland) Elsevier.

*Borch, Marianne, ed. Narratives of Remembrance. 136p. 2000. pap. 18.00 (87-7838-497-4, Pub. by Odense Univ) Intl Spec Bk.

Borchard. Progress Analytical. 1996. 73.00 (3-7985-0910-7) Spr-Verlag.

Borchard, Therese & Leach, Michael, eds. I Like Being Catholic. 1999. pap. 14.95 (0-8245-1786-5) Crossroad NY.

Borchard-Berendsohn, Ruth. Light of Qabalah on the Unknown Secret of the Bible. LC 96-71338. 1997. pap. 20.00 (0-88400-197-0, Shengold Bks) Schreiber Pub.

*Borchard, Edwin M. Declaratory Judgments. 2nd ed. LC 00-39620. 2000. write for info. (1-57588-638-3) W S Hein.

Borchard, Edwin M. Guide to the Law & Legal Literature of Argentina, Brazil, & Chile. (Latin America Ser.). 1979. lib. bdg. 250.00 (0-8490-2931-7) Gordon Pr.

Borchard, Maria. Riga. (GER & ENG., Illus.). 114p. 1999. 62.00 (3-930698-61-7, Pub. by Edition A Menges) Natl Bk Netwk.

Borchard, R. E., et al. Drug Dosage in Laboratory Animals. 1989. lib. bdg. 125.00 (0-936923-19-9) Telford Pr.

Borchard, Therese J. Everyone's Problem: Addiction & Recovery, Director's Manual. Sawyer, Kieran, ed. LC 97-221568. (Developing Faith Ser.). (Illus.). 160p. 1997. pap. text, teacher ed. 16.95 (0-87793-623-4) Ave Maria.

— Everyone's Problem: Addiction & Recovery: Participant Book. Sawyer, Kieran, ed. (Developing Faith Ser.). 80p. (YA). (gr. 9-12). 1997. pap. text 5.95 (0-87793-622-6) Ave Maria.

— Our Catholic Devotions: A Popular Guidebook. LC 97-43776. 144p. 1998. pap. 9.95 (0-8245-1739-3) Crossroad NY.

— Our Catholic Prayer: A Popular Guidebook. LC 98-46462. 144p. 1999. pap. 9.95 (0-8245-1606-0) Crossroad NY.

— Whitney Rides the Whale with Jonah: And Learns She Can't Run Away. LC 99-21276. 80p. 1999. pap. 7.95 (0-8091-6663-1) Paulist Pr.

— Whitney Sews Joseph's Many-Colored Coat: And Learns a Lesson about Jealousy. LC 99-14351. 80p. 1999. pap. 7.95 (0-8091-6664-X) Paulist Pr.

— Woman, Why Are You Weeping? A Lenten Companion for Women. LC 97-69606. 112p. 1997. pap. 9.95 (0-8245-1721-0) Crossroad NY.

Borchard, Therese Johnson. Our Blessed Mother. LC 99-16159. 1999. pap. 9.95 (0-8245-1819-5) Crossroad NY.

*Borchard, Therese Johnson. Taste & See the Goodness of the Lord. LC 99-52516. (Illus.). 32p. (J). (ps-1). 2000. 7.95 (0-8091-6665-8) Paulist Pr.

Borchard, Therese Johnson. Whitney Coaches David on Fighting Goliath: And Learns to Stand up for Herself. LC 99-42615. 80p. 2000. pap. 5.95 (0-8091-6669-0) Paulist Pr.

— Whitney Solves a Dilemma with Solomon: And Learns the Importance of Honesty. LC 99-42582. 80p. 2000. pap. 5.95 (0-8091-6668-2) Paulist Pr.

*Borchard, Therese Johnson. Whitney Stows Away on Noah's Ark: And Learns How to Deal with Peer Pressure. LC 99-55102. (Emerald Bible Collection). (Illus.). 80p. (J). (gr. 4-7). 2000. pap. 5.95 (0-8091-6674-7) Paulist Pr.

Borchard, Therese Johnson, see Johnson Borchard, Therese.

Borchard, Therese Johnson, jt. auth. see Leach, Michael.

Borchard, W., et al, eds. Progress in Analytical Ultracentrifugation. (Progress in Colloid & Polymer Science Ser.: Vol. 86). 200p. 1992. 69.95 (0-387-91407-2) Spr-Verlag.

Borchard, William M. Trademarks & the Arts. 100p. (C). 1988. pap. text. write for info. (0-318-64034-1) CUSLCLA.

— Trademarks & the Arts. 86p. 1989. pap. 12.00 (0-929912-00-4, 7780) CUSLCLA.

— Trademarks & the Arts. 1990. pap. text 12.50 (0-685-59975-2) Col U Pr.

Borchardt, Alice. Devoted. 1996. mass mkt. 6.99 (0-451-40396-7, Onyx) NAL.

— Night of the Wolf. LC 99-31102. 464p. 1999. 24.50 (0-345-42362-3) Ballantine Pub Grp.

*Borchardt, Alice. Night of the Wolf. 480p. 2000. mass mkt. 6.99 (0-345-42363-1) Ballantine Pub Grp.

Borchardt, Alice. The Silver Wolf. LC 98-4802. 464p. 1998. 24.95 (0-345-42360-7, Del Rey) Ballantine Pub Grp.

— The Silver Wolf. 1999. mass mkt. 6.99 (0-345-42361-5, Del Rey) Ballantine Pub Grp.

Borchardt, Audrey F., jt. auth. see Pollack-Johnson, Bruce.

Borchardt, D. H. & Francis, R. D. How to Find Out in Psychology: A Guide to the Literature & Methods of Research. LC 84-2827. (How to Find Out Ser.). 155p. 1984. 95.00 (0-08-031280-2, Pub. by Pergamon Repr) Franklin.

Borchardt, D. H. & Horacek, John. Librarianship in Australia, New Zealand & Oceania. pap. write for info. (0-08-019752-3, Pergamon Pr) Elsevier.

— Librarianship in Australia, New Zealand & Oceania. 1976. 24.00 (0-08-019920-8, Pergamon Pr) Elsevier.

Borchardt, Danuta, tr. see Gombrowicz, Witold.

Borchardt, Frank L. Doomsday Speculation As a Strategy of Persuasion: A Study of Apocalypticism As Rhetoric. LC 90-44688. (Studies in Comparative Religion: Vol. 4). 264p. 1990. lib. bdg. 89.95 (0-88946-506-1) E Mellen.

— German Antiquity in Renaissance Myth. LC 75-166484. 368p. reprint ed. pap. 114.10 (0-608-11995-4, 202299900031) Bks Demand.

Borchardt, Gary C. Thinking Between the Lines: Computers & the Comprehension of Casual Descriptions. LC 93-36770. (Artificial Intelligence Ser.). (Illus.). 320p. 1994. 40.00 (0-262-02374-1) MIT Pr.

Borchardt, Glenn. The Scientific Worldview. (Illus.). xiii, 343p. (Orig.). (C). 1984. 49.95 (0-917929-01-2); pap. 29.95 (0-917929-00-4) Progressive Sci Inst.

Borchardt, John K. Career Management for Scientists & Engineers. LC 99-27070. (An American Chemical Society Publication). 288p. 2000. text. write for info. (0-8412-3525-2, Pub. by Am Chemical) OUP.

Borchardt, John K. & Teh Fu Yen, eds. Oil-Field Chemistry: Enhanced Recovery & Production Stimulation. LC 89-6829. (Symposium Ser.: No. 396). (Illus.). xi, 616p. 1989. 129.95 (0-8412-1630-4) Am Chemical.

— Oil Field Chemistry: Enhanced Recovery & Production Stimulation. LC 89-6829. (ACS Symposium Ser.: No. 396). (Illus.). 714p. 1989. reprint ed. pap. 200.00 (0-608-03206-9, 206372500007) Bks Demand.

Borchardt, Kenneth A. & Noble, Michael A. Sexually Transmitted Diseases: Epidemiology, Pathology, Diagnosis, & Treatment. LC 96-39561. 368p. 1997. boxed set 94.95 (0-8493-9476-7) CRC Pr.

Borchardt, Klaus-Dieter. European Integration: The Origins & Growth of the European Union. 4th ed. (Illus.). 30p. (C). 1998. pap. text 25.00 (0-7881-7142-9) DIANE Pub.

Borchardt, Knut. Perspectives on Modern German Economic History & Policy. 295p. (C). 1991. text 59.95 (0-521-36310-1); pap. text 24.95 (0-521-36858-8) Cambridge U Pr.

Borchardt, Marylan. Designers Digest, Vol. 1. unabridged ed. (Illus.). 180p. 1999. pap. 25.00 (0-9661792-1-8) MFay Patterns.

— Designer's Digest & Workroom Manual. (Illus.). 375p. 1998. ring bd. 55.00 (0-9661792-0-X) MFay Patterns.

Borchardt-Ott, W. Crystallography: An Introduction. Gould, R., tr. from GER. (Illus.). xiii, 290p. 1993. pap. write for info. (3-540-56679-1) Spr-Verlag.

— Crystallography: An Introduction. Gould, R., tr. from GER. (Illus.). xiii, 290p. 1993. pap. 29.95 (0-387-56679-1) Spr-Verlag.

— Crystallography: An Introduction. 2nd ed. 307p. 1995. pap. text 32.95 (3-540-59478-7) Spr-Verlag.

Borchardt, R. T., et al. Integration of Pharmaceutical Discovery & Development: Case Histories. LC 98-27185. (Pharmaceutical Biotechnology Ser.: Vol. 11). (Illus.). 384p. (C). 1998. text 125.00 (0-306-45743-1, Kluwer Plenum) Kluwer Academic.

Borchardt, Ronald T., et al, eds. Biological Methylation & Drug Design: Experimental & Clinical Roles of S-Adenosylmethionine. LC 86-7212. (Experimental Biology & Medicine Ser.: Vol. 12). (Illus.). 480p. 1986. 119.50 (0-89603-102-0) Humana.

— Directed Drug Delivery: A Multidisciplinary Approach. LC 85-2291. (Experimental Biology & Medicine Ser.: Vol. 7). (Illus.). 384p. 1985. 125.00 (0-89603-089-X) Humana.

— Models for Assessing Drug Absorption & Metabolism. (Pharmaceutical Biotechnology Ser.: Vol. 8). (Illus.). 436p. (C). 1996. text 95.00 (0-306-45243-X, Kluwer Plenum) Kluwer Academic.

Borchardt, Sandra, ed. see Ernst & Young LLP Staff, et al.

Borchegrevink, Carl. Perspectives on the Hospitality Industry. 480p. 1999. per. 39.95 (0-7872-4864-9, 41486401) Kendall-Hunt.

Borchelt, J., ed. Masonry: Materials, Properties & Performance - STP 778. 277p. 1982. 39.00 (0-8031-0610-6, STP778) ASTM.

Borchelt, Peter L., jt. auth. see Favre, David.

Borcherding, David, ed. Mystery Writer's Sourcebook: Where to Sell Your Manuscripts. 2nd ed. 475p. 1995. 19.99 (0-89879-724-1, Wrtrs Digest Bks) F & W Pubns Inc.

Borcherding, David H., ed. Science Fiction & Fantasy Writer's Sourcebook: Where to Sell Your Manuscripts. 2nd ed. 480p. 1996. 19.99 (0-89879-762-4, Wrtrs Digest Bks) F & W Pubns Inc.

*Borcherding, Sherry. Documentation Manual for Writing SOAP Notes in Occupational Therapy. (Illus.). 256p. 2000. pap. text 24.00 (1-55642-441-8) SLACK Inc.

Borcherds, Petrus B. Autobiographical Memory of Petrus Borchardus Borcherds. LC 72-5526. (Black Heritage Library Collection). 1977. reprint ed. 40.95 (0-8369-9135-4) Ayer.

Borcherdt, Bill. Feeling Right When Things Go Wrong. LC 98-35775. 272p. 1998. pap. 21.95 (1-56887-036-1, FRBP) Pro Resource.

— Fundamentals of Cognitive-Behavior Therapy: From Both Sides of the Desk. LC 96-5122. 249p. (C). 1996. 49.95 (0-7890-6030-2) Haworth Pr.

— Head over Heart in Love: 25 Guides to Rational Passion. LC 95-53944. 190p. 1996. pap. 20.95 (1-56887-017-5, HHLBP, Prof Resc Pr) Pro Resource.

— Making Families Work & What to Do When They Don't: Thirty Guides for Imperfect Parents of Imperfect Children. LC 96-14633. 1996. pap. 19.95 (0-7890-0127-6) Haworth Pr.

— Making Families Work & What to Do When They Don't: Thirty Guides for Imperfect Parents of Imperfect Children. 232p. 1996. lib. bdg. 39.95 (0-7890-0073-3) Haworth Pr.

— Think Straight! Feel Great! Twenty-One Guides to Emotional Self-Control. LC 88-43055. 184p. (Orig.). 1989. pap. 20.95 (0-943158-53-2, TSFGBP) Pro Resource.

*Borcherdt, Bill. You Can Control Anger! 21 Ways to Do It. LC 00-28078. 272p. 2000. pap. 17.95 (1-56887-061-2, YCABP, Prof Resc Pr) Pro Resource.

Borcherdt, Bill. You Can Control Your Feelings! Twenty-Four Guides to Emotional Well-Being. LC 92-46866. 270p. (Orig.). 1993. pap. 21.95 (0-943158-73-7, YCCBP, Prof Resc Pr) Pro Resource.

Borcherdt, R. D., et al. National Planning Considerations for the Acquisition of Strong Ground-Motion Data. 55p. 1984. pap. 10.00 (0-685-14409-7) Earthquake Eng.

Borchers, jt. auth. see Minuck.

Borchers, Dagmar. Der Grobe Graben - Heidegger und Die Analytische Philosophie. (Philosophie und Geschichte der Wissenschaften, Studien und Quellen: No. 34). (GER., Illus.). 161p. 1997. 35.95 (3-631-31869-3) P Lang Pubng.

Borchers, E., jt. auth. see Charpentreau, Jacque.

Borchers, Elisabeth & Wagner, Anneliese. Fish Magic: Selected Poems. 108p. 1989. pap. 14.95 (0-85646-192-X, Pub. by Anvil Press) Dufour.

Borchers, Elizabeth S. Family Law Forms, 1982-1992. (Nebraska Legal Forms Ser.). 310p. 1991. suppl. ed. 35.00 (0-685-49529-9, MICHIE); ring bd. 85.00 incl. disk (0-685-49528-0, MICHIE); ring bd. 50.00 (0-685-70857-8, MICHIE) LEXIS Pub.

— Nebraska Legal Forms: Family Law. 1982. ring bd. 69.95 (0-327-01009-6, 81998, MICHIE) LEXIS Pub.

— Nebraska Legal Forms: Family Law. 310p. 1993. ring bd. 69.95 incl. disk (0-614-05913-5, MICHIE) LEXIS Pub.

Borchers, Hans-Jurgen. Translation Group & Particle Representations in Quantum Field Theory. LC 96-16949. (Lecture Notes in Physics Ser.: Vol. 40). 131p. 1996. 43.00 (3-540-61140-1) Spr-Verlag.

*Borchers, Heidi & Jackson, Aleene. Aleene's Handmade Gifts. LC 98-68395. 144p. 1999. pap. 14.95 (0-8487-1878-X) Oxmoor Hse.

Borchers, Heidi, ed. see Hall, Starr.

Borchers, James, ed. Land Subsidence Case Studies & Current Research. LC 98-3871. (AEG Special Publication: No. 8). (Illus.). 576p. 1997. lib. bdg. 69.95 (0-89863-197-1, 197-1) Star Pub CA.
Environmental & engineering geologists, hydrologists & other experts on land subsidence from around the world were invited to contribute papers for this comprehensive volume. Their articles describe current & historical research, innovative theory & monitoring equipment, case histories including site exploration & evaluation, predictive modeling, damage to infrastructure, engineering of remedial

B

construction, & discussion of political & legal issues related to land subsidence. Contributors are from the U.S.A. & ten other countries, including practitioners, researchers, planners, & attorneys with experience with the study, mitigation & societal impact of land subsidence. Topics include subsidence associated with: Migration or removal of subsurface fluids such as brine, ground water, hydrocarbons; Hydrocompaction of moisture deficient sediments: debris flow deposits; Artificial fill; Oxidation of peat deposits; Collapse of underground & solution mine voids; Tunneling: karst terrain; Tectonics. A 576 page hardcover, large format, 8 1/2 X 11 inches, enhanced by hundreds of maps, photographs & other illustrations. Star Publishing Company, P. O. Box 68, Belmont, CA 94002-0068. FAX: 650-591-3898, Phone: 650-591-3505, e-mail: mail@starpublishing.com.
Publisher Paid Annotation.

Borchers, Jeffrey G. & Maser, Chris. Understanding Constraints & Monitoring. (Sustainable Community Development Ser.). 2000. write for info. (*1-57444-186-8*) St Lucie Pr.

***Borchers, Patrick J. & Zekoll, Joachim, eds.** International Conflict of Laws for the Third Millennium - Essays in Honor of Friedrich K. Juenger. 250p. 2000. 125.00 (*1-57105-128-7*) Transnatl Pubs.

Borchers, W., et al, eds. Visualization Methods in High Performance Computing & Flow Simulation: Proceedings of the International Workshop on Visualization, Paderborn. (Illus.). 190p. 1996. 155.00 (*90-6764-214-2*, Pub. by VSP) Coronet Bks.

Borchert. Draussen vor der Tur. (GER.). (C). 1989. 9.95 (*0-8442-2827-3*, X2827-3) NTC Contemp Pub Co.
— Encyclopedia of Philosophy Blue Supplement. 1996. 95.00 (*0-02-513630-5*, Hall Reference) Macmillan.
— Die Traurigen Geranien. (GER.). (C). 1962. 9.95 (*0-8442-2755-2*, X2755-2) NTC Contemp Pub Co.

Borchert, Bruno. Mysticism: Its History & Challenge. LC 93-17157. (Illus.). 464p. (Orig.). 1994. pap. 19.95 (*0-87728-772-4*) Weiser.

Borchert, Christian. Zeitreise: Dresden, 1954-1995. (GER., Illus.). 196p. 1996. text 47.00 (*90-5705-023-4*) Gordon & Breach.

***Borchert, Donald M.** Philosophy & Ethics. LC 99-25219. (Macmillan Compendium Ser.). 1999. 173.75 (*0-02-865366-1*) Mac Bks.

Borchert, Donald M., jt. auth. see Castell, Alburey.

Borchert, Festschrift H. Beitraege Zur Lagerstaettenkunde - Contributions to Ore Geology. (Monograph Series on Mineral Deposits: No. 22). (GER.). v, 178p. 1983. 70.00 (*3-443-12022-9*, Pub. by Gebruder Borntraeger) Balogh.

Borchert, Gerald L. John 1-11. LC 96-26847. (New American Commentary Ser.). 400p. 1996. 29.99 (*0-8054-0125-3*, 4201-25) Broadman.

Borchert, James. Alley Life in Washington: Family, Community, Religion, & Folklife in the City, 1850-1970. LC 80-12375. (Blacks in the New World Ser.). (Illus.). 352p. 1982. pap. text 19.95 (*0-252-01003-5*) U of Ill Pr.

Borchert, James R., jt. auth. see Lundrigan, Robert F.

Borchert, John R. Megalopolis: Washington D. C. to Boston. LC 92-9986. (Touring North America Ser.). (Illus.). 188p. 1992. 25.00 (*0-8135-1876-8*); pap. 9.95 (*0-8135-1877-6*) Rutgers U Pr.

***Borchert, Peter.** This Is South Africa. 2000. 39.95 (*1-85974-265-3*, Pub. by New5 Holland) BHB Intl.

Borchert, Wolfgang. The Man Outside. rev. ed. Porter, A. D., tr. from GER. LC 76-145929. 1971. pap. 11.95 (*0-8112-0011-6*, NDP319, Pub. by New Directions) Norton.

Borchet, Carol E., et al. The Installation of Historic Architecture at Winterthur. LC 98-10593. 96 p. 1998. 20.00 (*0-912724-47-1*) Winterthur.

***Borchet, Wolfgang.** Allein Mit Meinem Schatten und Dem Mond: Briefe, Gedichte und Dokumente. LC 97-117215. 1999. 17.95 (*3-499-13983-9*) Midwest European Pubns.

Borchgrevink & Holte Staff. Labour of Love. 160p. 1995. 63.95 (*1-85972-043-9*) Ashgate Pub Co.

Borchgrevink, Carsten E. First on the Antarctic Continent: Being an Account of the British Antarctic Expedition, 1898-1900. LC 81-141386. 373p. reprint ed. pap. 115.70 (*0-7837-1034-8*, 204134500020) Bks Demand.

Borchmeyer, Dieter. Richard Wagner: Theory & Theatre. Spencer, Stewart, tr. 444p. 1991. text 98.00 (*0-19-315322-X*) OUP.

Borchsenius, F., jt. ed. see Laegaard, S.

Borchsenius, Finn, et al. Flora Neotropica No. 70-73: Aiphanes (Palmae) - Roystonea (Arecaceae: Arecoieae) - Euterpe, Prestoea, & Neonicholsonia (Palmae) - Allagoptera (Palmae) 1996. text 50.00 (*0-89327-410-0*) NY Botanical.

***Borchsenius, Finn, et al.** Manual to the Palms of Ecuador. (AAU Reports: Vol. 37). (Illus.). 217p. 1998. pap. 12.95 (*87-87600-53-6*, Pub. by Aarhus Univ Pr) David Brown.

Borchsensius. Two Ways to God. Date not set. 18.00 (*0-85303-011-1*, Pub. by M Vallentine & Co) Intl Spec Bk.

Borchserius, jt. ed. see Henderson.

Borcht, Pieter Van Der, see Bochius, Johannes & Van Der Borcht, Pieter.

Borchus, Heidi. Aleene's Christmas Craft Quickies. LC 96-68031. 144p. 1996. pap. 14.95 (*0-8487-1511-X*) Oxmoor Hse.

Borcia, Yvette, jt. auth. see Stern, Gerry.

***Borck, Jim S.** The Eighteenth Century: A Current Bibliography. 502p. 1999. 159.50 (*0-404-62223-2*) AMS Pr.

Borck, Jim S., ed. The Eighteenth Century: A Current Bibilography, N. S. 15 for 1989. 489p. 1997. 112.50 (*0-404-62220-8*) AMS Pr.
— The Eighteenth Century: A Current Bibliography, 13 vols. 533p. write for info. (*0-404-62200-3*) AMS Pr.
— The Eighteenth Century: A Current Bibliography. 500p. 1998. 139.50 (*0-404-62222-4*) AMS Pr.
— The Eighteenth Century, No. 3 Vol. 50: A Current Bibliography, Old Series. 1970. 92.50 (*0-404-62201-1*) AMS Pr.
— The Eighteenth Century, No. 3 Vol. No. 51: A Current Bibliography, Old Series. 1971. 92.50 (*0-404-62202-X*) AMS Pr.
— The Eighteenth Century, No. 3 Vol. No. 51: A Current Bibliography, Old Series. 1972. 92.50 (*0-404-62203-8*) AMS Pr.
— The Eighteenth Century, No. 4 Vol. No. 53: A Current Bibliography, Old Series. 1973. 92.50 (*0-404-62204-6*) AMS Pr.
— The Eighteenth Century, No. 4 Vol. No. 54: A Current Bibliography, Old Series. 1974. 92.50 (*0-404-62205-4*) AMS Pr.

Borck, Jim S., jt. ed. see Becker, Robert A.

Borck, Jim S., ed. see Defoe, Daniel, et al.

Borck, Leslie E. & Fawcett, Stephen B. Learning Counseling & Problem-Solving Skills. LC 82-2916. 160p. (Orig.). (C). 1982. text 44.95 (*0-917724-30-5*); pap. text 19.95 (*0-917724-35-6*) Haworth Pr.

Borcoman, James. Yousuf Karsh: The Art of the Portrait. (Illus.). 176p. 1994. 29.95 (*0-88884-591-X*, Pub. by Natl Gallery) U Ch Pr.

Borcoman, James, ed. Magicians of Light: Photographs from the Collection of the National Gallery of Canada. (Illus.). 316p. 1996. pap. 24.95 (*0-88884-627-4*, Pub. by Natl Gallery) U Ch Pr.

***Borcz, Geri.** Loving Glory. (Splendor Historical Romances Ser.). 320p. 2000. mass mkt. 4.99 (*0-8217-6469-1*, Zebra Kensgtn) Kensgtn Pub Corp.

Borczon, Ronald. Music Therapy: Group Vignettes. LC 99-163039. 200p. (C). 1997. pap. text 24.00 (*0-9624080-9-3*) Barcelona Pubs.

Bord, Colin, jt. auth. see Bord, Janet.

Bord, Donald J. & Ostdiek, Vernon J. Inquiry into Physics. 2nd ed. Westby, ed. 572p. (C). 1991. text 59.75 (*0-314-79885-4*) West Pub.
— Inquiry into Physics. 3rd ed. LC 94-33566. 608p. (C). 1995. mass mkt. 58.25 (*0-314-04354-3*) West Pub.

Bord, Donald J., jt. auth. see Ostdiek, Vernon J.

Bord, Janet. Fairies: Real Encounters with Little People. 256p. 1998. mass mkt. 5.99 (*0-440-22612-0*) Dell.

Bord, Janet & Bord, Colin. Atlas of Magical Britain. 1993. 10.98 (*1-55521-945-4*) Bk Sales Inc.
— Prehistoric Britain from the Air. (Illus.). 160p. 1998. 29.95 (*1-57076-102-7*) Trafalgar.
— Unexplained Mysteries of the 20th Century. (Illus.). 432p. 1990. pap. 16.95 (*0-8092-4113-7*, 411370, Contemporary Bks) NTC Contemp Pub Co.
— The World of the Unexplained: An Illustrated Guide to the Paranormal. (Illus.). 176p. 1999. 29.95 (*0-7137-2746-2*) Blandford Pr.

Bord, Lucien-Jean & Gaudart de Soulages, Michel. Dictionnaire Genealogique des Familles de l'Inde Francais. (FRE.). 1984. 195.00 (*0-7859-8256-6*, 2-9500353-0-2) Fr & Eur.

Bord, Nancy A., et al. Measuring Employment Effects in the Regulatory Process: Recommendations & Background Study. (Illus.). 78p. (Orig.). (C). 1994. pap. text 25.00 (*0-7881-0694-5*) DIANE Pub.

Borda, Ivan & Koff, Raymond, eds. NSAIDs: A Profile of Adverse Effects. (Illus.). 240p. 1992. text 39.00 (*1-56053-018-9*) Hanley & Belfus.

***Bordag, Michael.** Casimir Effect 50 Years Later: Proceedings of the Fourth Workshop on Quantum Field Theory Under. 400p. 1999. 78.00 (*981-02-3820-7*) World Scientific Pub.

Bordahl, Vibeke. Along the Broad Road of Realism: Qin Zhaoyang's World of Fiction. (SIAS Monographs: No. 59). (Illus.). 260p. (C). 1996. pap. text 21.00 (*0-7007-0221-0*, Pub. by Curzon Pr Ltd) UH Pr.
— The Eternal Storyteller: Oral Literature in Modern China. (Nordic Institute of Asian Studies, Studies in Asian Topics: Vol. 24). 368p. 1998. text 55.00 (*0-7007-0982-7*, Pub. by Curzon Pr Ltd) UH Pr.
— The Oral Tradition of Yangzhou Storytelling. (NIAS Monographs in Asian Studies: No. 73). 495p. (C). 1996. text 65.00 (*0-7007-0436-1*, Pub. by Curzon Pr Ltd) UH Pr.

Bordalo, O., ed. European Pancreatic Club, (EPC), 16th Meeting, Cascais, Sept. 1984. (Journal: Digestion: Vol. 30, No. 2). (Illus.). 66p. 1984. pap. 50.50 (*3-8055-3956-8*) S Karger.

Bordao, Rafael. Escurriduras de la Soledad. LC 96-61894. (SPA.). 52p. 1995. pap. 5.95 (*1-881531-00-7*, Palmar Pr) Ed Arcas.
— Libro de las Inteferencia (The Book of Interferences) Bourne, Louis, tr. LC 94-61894. (SPA.). 53p. (Orig.). (C). 1995. pap. text 5.95 (*0-9623552-7-5*, Palmar Pr) Ed Arcas.

***Bordao, Rafael.** Los Descosidos Labios del Silencio. (SPA.). 51p. 2000. pap. 8.95 (*1-881531-02-3*, Palmar Pr) Ed Arcas.

Bordao, Rafael. La Revolucion de Castro: Un Aborto Perfumado. (SPA.). 44p. 1999. pap. 8.00 (*1-881531-01-5*, Palmar Pr) Ed Arcas.

Bordas. Dictionnaire Francais-Italien, Italien-Francais. (FRE & ITA.). 1990. write for info. (*0-7859-7708-2*, 2040192441); write for info. (*0-7859-8613-8*, 204019228X) Fr & Eur.
— Dictionnaire Garzanti Bordas. (FRE.). 1988. write for info. (*0-7859-7705-8*, 2040182330) Fr & Eur.

Bordas, P. English-French, French-English Dictionary. 1992. write for info. (*0-7859-8130-6*, 2-86311-173-6) Fr & Eur.

Bordas, Philippe, jt. auth. see Dib, Mohammed.

Bordas Staff. Aerospace Dictionary. (ENG, FRE, GER & SPA.). 851p. 1991. 295.00 (*0-8288-0020-0*, F24740); 295.00 (*0-8288-0021-9*, M4636); 295.00 (*0-8288-0018-9*, F23060); 325.00 (*0-8288-0019-7*, F25001) Fr & Eur.
— Dictionary of Economic Spanish: Dictionnaire de l'Espagnol Economique. (ENG, FRE & SPA.). 1985. 65.00 (*0-8288-0828-7*, F49990) Fr & Eur.

Borde, Andrew. The Breuiary of Helthe, for All Maner of Syckenesses & Diseases, the Whiche May Be in Man, or Woman Deth Folowe, 2 pts., Set. LC 71-38106. (English Experience Ser.: No. 362). 356p. 1971. reprint ed. 50.00 (*90-221-0362-5*) Walter J Johnson.

Borde, Simon M., et al. Doing Business in France, 2 vols. 1983. ring bd. 650.00 (*0-8205-1445-4*) Bender.

Bordeau, Elvi L. Then the Foreigners Will See: A Collection of Short Stories. 192p. 1998. 17.00 (*0-8059-4318-8*) Dorrance.

Bordeaux, Darlene B. Twelve Steps to Personal & Professional Development. Morgan, Beth, ed. (Illus.). 243p. 1993. 21.95 (*0-9637703-0-6*) Wld Flower Pr.

Bordeaux, Henry. Georges Guynemer, Knight of the Air. LC 73-169405. (Literature & History of Aviation Ser.). 1972. reprint ed. 20.95 (*0-405-03751-1*) Ayer.

Bordeaux, Jean-Luc & Pacquement, Alfred, texts. Unstretched Surfaces: Los Angeles-Paris. (ENG & FRE., Illus.). 47p. 1977. pap. 20.00 (*0-911291-02-4*, Pub. by Fellows Cont Art) RAM Publications.

Bordeaux, Jean-Luc & Wortz, Melinda. Hans Burkhardt Pastels: Fifty Years of Figurative Expressionism. (Illus.). 32p. 1984. pap. 30.00 (*1-880566-02-8*) J Rutberg Fine Arts.

Bordeaux, Norma N. Dewdrops on a Lotus Leaf: Haikus in Mexico. (Illus.). 28p. 1974. pap. 2.95 (*0-89564-076-7*) IBS Intl.

Bordeaux, Norma N., jt. auth. see Szekely, Edmond B.

Bordeianu, Sever, jt. auth. see Benaud, Claire-Lise.

Bordeje Morencos, Fernando De. Diccionario Militar Estrategico & Politico. (SPA.). 199p. 1981. pap. 24.95 (*0-8288-1913-0*, S60466) Fr & Eur.

Bordeleau, Leo P. Action & Vie Sociale dans l'Oeuvre de Maurice Blondel. LC 79-398407. (Collection Philosophica: Vol. 12). (FRE.). 208p. 1978. reprint ed. pap. 64.50 (*0-608-02195-4*, 206286500003) Bks Demand.

Bordell, Sally, jt. auth. see Sussman, Lesley.

Bordelon, Carolyn. Octopus Goes to School. (Illus.). 8p. (J). (gr. k-1). 1995. pap. 3.75 (*1-880612-36-4*) Seedling Pubns.

Bordelon, Jane A. Cooking & Chatting with Sadie. Berumen, Paula, ed. LC 92-97229. (Illus.). 200p. 1993. pap. 12.95 (*0-9638092-0-2*) J A Bordelon.

Bordelon, Pamela, ed. see Hurston, Zora Neale.

Borden. Arab Horse. 1949. 16.00 (*0-87505-112-X*) Borden.
— Sports Activity Book: Bowling. 2nd ed. 2001. pap. text 9.26 (*0-07-235381-3*) McGraw.

Borden, Allison M., jt. auth. see McGinn, Noel F.

Borden, Arthur M. Going Private. 1000p. 1982. ring bd. 95.00 (*0-318-20274-3*, 00574) NY Law Pub.

Borden, Arthur R., Jr., tr. see Moerenhout, J. A.

Borden, Bill. The Big Book of Big Little Books. LC 97-1004. 120p. 1997. 16.95 (*0-8118-1741-5*) Chronicle Bks.

Borden, Brett. Radar Imaging of Airborne Targets: A Primer for Applied Mathematicians & Physicists. LC 99-19620. (Illus.). 25p. 1999. 85.00 (*0-7503-0617-3*) IOP Pub.

Borden, D. L. & Wellauer, E. J. Analysis of Factors Used for Strength Rating of Worm Wheel Gear Teeth. (Technical Papers: Vol. P229.18). (Illus.). 14p. 1974. pap. text 30.00 (*1-55589-285-X*) AGMA.

Borden, Diane L. & Harvey, Kerric, eds. The Electronic Grapevine: Rumor, Reputation, & Reporting in the New Online Environment. LC 97-27985. (Telecommunications Ser.). 350p. 1997. 49.95 (*0-8058-2171-6*); pap. write for info. (*0-8058-2172-4*) L Erlbaum Assocs.

Borden, Diane L., jt. auth. see Bowles, Dorothy A.

Borden, Donald L., jt. auth. see Wellauer, E. J.

Borden, Eli. The Death of the Beast. 2nd ed. 362p. (Orig.). 1996. pap. 15.95 (*1-56794-118-4*, C-2144) Star Bible.
— You Can Count on It: God's Design Through Numbers. (Orig.). 1988. pap. 8.95 (*0-940999-32-3*, C-2145) Star Bible.

Borden, Fred & Elias, Jay. Bowling: Knowledge Is the Key. 2nd ed. (Illus.). 138p. (Orig.). (C). 1986. pap. 19.95 (*0-9619177-0-9*) Bowling Concepts.
— Bowling: Ten Keys to Success. (Illus.). 114p. (Orig.). 1991. pap. 19.95 (*0-9619177-1-7*) Bowling Concepts.

Borden, G. F. Easter Day Nineteen Forty-One. 265p. 1988. mass mkt. 3.95 (*0-446-34992-5*) Warner Bks.
— When the Poor Boys Dance. 272p. 1997. mass mkt. 6.50 (*0-446-60407-0*, Pub. by Warner Bks) Little.

Borden, Gale, jt. auth. see Benjamin, Ben E.

Borden, George A. Human Communication Systems. 2nd ed. (Illus.). 340p. (Orig.). 1989. pap. text 27.95 (*0-89641-182-6*) American Pr.

Borden, Gloria J., et al. Speech Science Primer: Physiology, Acoustics, & Perception of Speech. 3rd ed. LC 93-7592. (Illus.). 319p. 1994. 43.00 (*0-683-00944-3*) Lppncott W & W.

Borden, Guy. Control Valves. LC 98-14192. (Practical Guide Ser.). 739p. 1998. 145.00 (*1-55617-565-5*) ISA.

***Borden, Iain.** Dissertation - An Architectural Student's Handbook. (Illus.). 288p. 2000. pap. 29.95 (*0-7506-4769-8*, Architectural Pr) Buttrwrth-Heinemann.

Borden, Iain, et al, eds. Strangely Familiar: Narratives of Architecture in the City. LC 95-50629. (Illus.). 96p. (C). 1996. pap. 22.99 (*0-415-14418-3*) Routledge.

***Borden, Ian, et al, eds.** The Unknown City: Contesting Architecture & Social Space. LC 00-20375. (Illus.). 600p. 2000. 50.00 (*0-262-02471-3*) MIT Pr.

***Borden, James D. & Brucker, Roger W.** Beyond Mammoth Cave: A Tale of Obesession in the World's Largest Cave. LC 00-21610. 2000. pap. 26.95 (*0-8093-2346-X*) S Ill U Pr.

Borden, Jamie W., jt. auth. see Hamm, Brian.

Borden, Kay. Bulletproof News Releases: Help at Last for the Publicity Deficient. LC 93-72466. (Illus.). 176p. (Orig.). 1994. pap. 18.95 (*0-9637477-0-3*) Franklin-Sarrett Pubs.

Borden, Kay, ed. Welcome to Georgia, Kids! A Collection of Stories & Art by Georgia's Children. (Illus.). 48p. (Orig.). (J). (gr. 1-6). 1996. pap. 10.00 (*0-9637477-4-6*) Franklin-Sarrett Pubs.

Borden, Kay, jt. auth. see Katz, Ed.

Borden, Leon M., ed. see Holmes, Susan.

Borden, Louise. A. Lincoln & Me. LC 98-51921. (Illus.). 32p. (J). (ps-3). 1999. 15.95 (*0-590-45714-4*, Pub. by Scholastic Inc) Penguin Putnam.
— Albie the Lifeguard. LC 91-11327. (Illus.). 32p. (J). (ps-3). 1993. 14.95 (*0-590-44585-5*) Scholastic Inc.
— Albie the Lifeguard. (Illus.). 32p. (J). (ps-3). 1999. pap. 5.99 (*0-590-44586-3*) Scholastic Inc.

***Borden, Louise.** America. LC 00-28372. (Illus.). 2002. write for info. (*0-689-83900-6*) McElderry Bks.
— Caps, Hats, Socks & Mittens. (Illus.). (J). 1989. 13.50 (*0-8335-8854-0*) Econo-Clad Bks.

Borden, Louise. Caps, Hats, Socks, & Mittens: A Book about the Four Seasons. (Illus.). 32p. (J). (ps-1). 1992. pap. 4.99 (*0-590-44872-2*, Blue Ribbon Bks) Scholastic Inc.

***Borden, Louise.** Day Eddie Met the Author. LC 99-46922. (gr. k-3). 2001. per. 15.00 (*0-689-83405-5*) S&S Childrens.

Borden, Louise. General Gage & the Sleds on Boston Common: A Story from 1774. LC 99-18080. (J). 2000. 13.01 (*0-689-82812-8*, Rabbit Ears) Little Simon.
— Good Luck, Mrs. K.! LC 97-50553. (Illus.). 32p. (J). (gr. 1-5). 1999. 15.00 (*0-689-82147-6*) S&S Childrens.

***Borden, Louise.** Goodbye, Charles Lindbergh. LC 97-11542. (Illus.). 40p. (J). (gr. k-4). 1998. pap. 16.00 (*0-689-81536-0*) McElderry Bks.

Borden, Louise. Just in Time for Christmas. LC 93-40082. (Illus.). 32p. (J). (ps-3). 1994. 14.95 (*0-590-45355-6*) Scholastic Inc.
— The Little Ships: The Heroic Rescue at Dunkirk in World War II. LC 95-52557. (Illus.). 32p. (J). (gr. 4-7). 1997. 15.00 (*0-689-80827-5*) S&S Childrens.
— Neighborhood Trucker. (J). 1997. pap. 3.95 (*0-590-46037-4*) Scholastic Inc.
— Thanksgiving Is . . . LC 97-8767. (Hello Reader! Ser.). (Illus.). (J). (gr. 1-3). 1997. 3.50 (*0-590-33128-0*) Scholastic Inc.

Borden, Louise. Thanksgiving Is..., Level 3. (Hello, Reader! Ser.). (J). 1997. 8.70 (*0-606-11975-2*, Pub. by Turtleback) Demco.

Borden, Louise, et al. Fly High! The Story of Bessie Coleman. LC 99-17398. 2000. 20.01 (*0-689-82457-2*) S&S Childrens.

Borden, Louise, jt. auth. see Kroeger, Mary K.

Borden, Marian E. Smart Start: The Parents' Complete Guide to Preschool Education. LC 97-11599. 224p. 1997. 24.95 (*0-8160-3604-7*); pap. 14.95 (*0-8160-3677-2*) Facts on File.
— Winning Soccer for Girls. 160p. 1997. pap. text 12.95 (*0-8160-3272-6*) Facts on File.

Borden, Marian E., et al. In Addition to Tuition: The Parents' Survival Guide to Freshman Year of College. LC 94-41725. 224p. 1995. 24.95 (*0-8160-3099-5*) Facts on File.
— In Addition to Tuition: The Parents' Survival Guide to Freshman Year of College. LC 94-41725. 224p. 1996. pap. 10.95 (*0-8160-3341-2*) Facts on File.

Borden, Marian E., jt. auth. see Poretta, Vicki.

Borden, Morton. Federalism of James A. Bayard. LC 68-59262. (Columbia University. Studies in the Social Sciences: No. 584). reprint ed. 32.50 (*0-404-51584-3*) AMS Pr.
— Jews, Turks, & Infidels. fac. ed. LC 83-19863. 173p. 1984. reprint ed. pap. 53.70 (*0-7837-8060-5*, 204781300008) Bks Demand.
— Parties & Politics in the Early Republic, 1789-1815. Eisenstadt, A. S. & Franklin, John H., eds. LC 67-14298. (American History Ser.). 128p. (C). 1967. pap. text 11.95 (*0-88295-704-X*) Harlan Davidson.

Borden, Neil H. Advertising in Our Economy. Assael, Henry, ed. LC 78-239. (Century of Marketing Ser.). 1979. reprint ed. lib. bdg. 26.95 (*0-405-11172-X*) Ayer.
— The Economic Effects of Advertising. LC 75-39233. (Getting & Spending: The Consumer's Dilemma Ser.). 1976. reprint ed. 84.95 (*0-405-08010-7*) Ayer.

Borden, Penn. Civilian Indoctrination of the Military: World War I & Future Implications for the Military-Industrial Complex, 80. LC 88-7700. (Contributions in Military Studies Ser.). 177p. 1989. 49.95 (*0-313-26381-7*, BCZ, Greenwood Pr) Greenwood.

Borden, R. J., et al, eds. Human Ecology - Coming of Age: An International Overview. (Illus.). 256p. 1994. pap. 24.95 (*90-70289-81-4*) Paul & Co Pubs.

***Borden, Richard C.** Art of Writing Badly: Valentin Kataev's Mauvism & the Rebirth of Russian Modernism. LC 99-32585. 1999. 69.95 (*0-8101-1691-X*) Northwestern U Pr.

Borden, Richard C., tr. see Dobychin, Leonid.

An Asterisk (*) at the beginning of an entry indicates that the title is appearing for the first time.

***Borden, Richard Carl.** Section Eight. unabridged limited ed. (Illus.). 274p. 1999. per. 20.00 (*0-9675456-0-9*) Arm Press.

Borden, Richard J., et al, eds. Human Ecology: A Gathering of Perspectives. (C). 1986. pap. text 10.00 (*0-940051-00-1*) Soc Human Ecology.

Borden, Richard J. & Jacobs, Jamien, eds. International Directory of Human Ecologists. 2nd ed. 212p. 1989. pap. text 10.00 (*0-940051-02-8*) Soc Human Ecology.

Borden, Robert C., ed. see National Symposium on the Future Availability of G.

Borden, Robert S. A Course in Advanced Calculus. unabridged ed. LC 97-43366. (Illus.). 402p. 1998. reprint ed. pap. 11.95 (*0-486-67290-5*) Dover.

Borden, Roy H., jt. ed. see Byle, Michael J.

Borden, Victor M. & Banta, Trudy W., eds. Using Performance Indicators to Guide Strategic Decision Making. LC 85-645339. (New Directions for Institutional Research Ser.: No. IR 82). 124p. (Orig.). 1994. pap. 22.00 (*0-7879-9964-4*) Jossey-Bass.

Borden, Weston T., ed. Diradicals. LC 82-8604. (Illus.). 357p. reprint ed. pap. 110.70 (*0-608-18199-4*, 205660300078) Bks Demand.

***Borden, William.** Eurydice's Song. (Illus.). 61p. 1999. 16.95 (*1-879934-58-2*) St Andrews NC.

Borden, William. Superstoe. large type ed. LC 96-2293. 1996. 23.95 (*1-56895-309-7*) Wheeler Pub.

— Superstoe. LC 95-70750. 304p. 1996. reprint ed. 22.00 (*0-9642949-5-8*) Orloff Pr.

***Borden, William, ed.** Comparative Approaches in Brief Dynamic Psychotherapy. LC 99-43056. (Psychoanalytic Social Work Monograph Ser.: Vol. 6, Nos. 3-4). 245p. (C). 1999. pap. text 24.95 (*0-7890-0844-0*) Haworth Pr.

— Comparative Approaches in Brief Dynamic Psychotherapy. LC 99-43056. (Psychoanalytic Social Work Monograph Ser.: Vol. 6, Nos. 3-4). 245p. (C). 1999. 49.95 (*0-7890-0833-5*) Haworth Pr.

Borden, William S. The Pacific Alliance: United States Foreign Economic Policy & Japanese Trade Recovery, 1947-1955. LC 83-14541. 336p. 1984. text 28.95 (*0-299-09550-9*) U of Wis Pr.

Bordenave, Ed, et al. Surplus Lines Insurance Practices. Feldhaus, William R., ed. LC 96-79435. 219p. (C). 1996. pap. text 41.00 (*0-89462-110-6*, 16202) IIA.

Bordenave, Eileen. Hoofin' It in the Bay Area: With Eileen & Fran. Orput, Fran, ed. (Illus.). 113p. 1992. 11.00 (*0-9638415-0-5*) E & F Creat.

Bordenave, M. L., ed. Applied Petroleum Geochemistry. 516p. (C). 1993. 785.00 (*2-7108-0629-0*, Pub. by Edits Technip) Enfield Pubs NH.

Bordenkercher, S. A. How to Win Your Crown: A Teen's Guide to Pageant Competition. LC 88-90918. (Illus.). 88p. (YA). 1998. pap. 12.95 (*0-9661771-0-X*, 07508) Abby Publ.

Bordenkircher, D. E. Tiger Cage: An Untold Story. LC 97-93396. (Illus.). 244p. 1998. pap. 14.95 (*0-9661771-4-2*, 07324) Abby Publ.

Bordens, Kenneth S. & Abbott, Bruce B. Research Design & Methods: A Process Approach. 4th ed. LC 98-4480. xix, 583p. 1998. text 66.95 (*0-7674-0507-2*, 0507-2) Mayfield Pub.

— Research Design & Methods: A Process Approach. 4th ed. LC 95-24591. iv, 107p. (C). 1998. pap. text, teacher ed. write for info. (*0-7674-0696-6*, 0696-8) Mayfield Pub.

— Research Design & Methods: Study Guide. 4th ed. LC 95-24591. v, 190p. (C). 1998. pap. text, student ed. 19.95 (*0-7674-0508-0*, 0508-0) Mayfield Pub.

— Research Design & Methods Test Bank. 4th rev. ed. 150p. (C). 1998. pap. text. write for info. (*0-7674-0694-X*, 0694-X) Mayfield Pub.

***Bordens, Kenneth S. & Horowitz, Irwin A.** Social Psychology. 400p. 2000. pap. write for info. (*0-8058-3520-2*) L Erlbaum Assocs.

Bordens, Kenneth S., jt. auth. see Horowitz, Irwin A.

Border, Barbara. Food Safety & Sanitation. (Careers in Home Economics Ser.). (Illus.). 1979. text 17.80 (*0-07-006511-X*) McGraw.

Border, Denny L. Wire 'Em & Win: Turning Thoroughbred Selections into Race Betting Profits, Handicapping Edition. rev. ed. LC 95-90734. 1995. pap. 12.95 (*0-9642669-1-1*) Winrose Pubng.

Border, John R., et al. Blunt Multiple Trauma: Pathophysiology & Comprehensive Therapy. (Illus.). 1024p. 1990. text 295.00 (*0-8247-8172-4*) Dekker.

Border, K., jt. auth. see Aliprantis, C. D.

Border, Kim C. Fixed Point Theorems with Applications to Economics & Game Theory. (Illus.). 144p. 1990. pap. text 22.95 (*0-521-38808-2*) Cambridge U Pr.

Border, Kim C., jt. auth. see Aliprantis, Charalambos D.

Border, Laura L. & Chism, Nancy V., eds. Teaching for Diversity. LC 85-644763. (New Directions for Teaching & Learning Ser.: No. TL 49). 100p. 1992. 22.00 (*1-55542-763-4*) Jossey-Bass.

Border, Laura L., et al. Collage: An Intermediate French Program. 2nd ed. Incl. Reader 2. Literary Reader. 1985. pap. text Reader 3. Cultural Reader. 1985. pap. text 9.00 (C). 1985. pap. text. write for info. (*0-318-57753-4*) Random.

Border, Peter, et al. Gulf War Illnesses: Dealing with the Uncertainties. LC 98-131886. 55p. 1997. write for info. (*1-897941-66-8*) Parl Ofc Sci.

***Border, Rosemary.** Pollution. (Illus.). 24p. 1999. pap. 6.95 (*0-19-422868-1*) OUP.

Border, Rosemary. Recycling. (Illus.). 32p. 1996. pap. text 6.95 (*0-19-422806-1*) OUP.

— Under the Ground. (Illus.). 22p. 1996. pap. text 6.95 (*0-19-422807-X*) OUP.

Borders, Bruce E., jt. auth. see Shiver, Barry D.

***Borders, Christine Kareem.** Gram Makes a House Call. LC 99-62955. (Illus.). 77p. (J). (gr. 2-4). 1999. pap. 5.95 (*0-9671160-0-7*) Greenhills Pr.

Borders, Denise G., jt. auth. see Lucas, Ceil.

Borders, Denise G., jt. ed. see Lucas, Ceil.

***Borders, Deryl & Poling, Doug.** Not My Heart, But Yours: Story of a Transplant. deluxe ed. 196p. 1999. pap. 12.95 (*0-9673558-0-X*) D Borders.

Borders, Donald B. & Doyle, Terrence W., eds. Enediyne Antibiotics as Antitumor Agents. LC 94-37776. (Illus.). 478p. 1994. text 185.00 (*0-8247-8938-5*) Dekker.

Borders, Earl, Jr. The Bus Trip Handbook. LC 84-60654. (Illus.). 112p. (Orig.). 1985. pap. 8.95 (*0-917125-00-2*) Home Run Pr.

Borders, James, ed. Early Medieval Chants from Nonantola Pt. I: Ordinary Chants & Tropes. (Recent Researches in Music of the Middle Ages & Early Renaissance Ser.: Vol. RRM30). (Illus.). lxxxiii, 84p. 1996. pap. 50.00 (*0-89579-328-8*) A-R Eds.

— Early Medieval Chants from Nonantola Pt. II: Proper Chants & Tropes. (Recent Researches in Music of the Middle Ages & Early Renaissance Ser.: Vol. RRM31). (Illus.). lxxi, 83p. 1996. pap. 50.00 (*0-89579-329-6*) A-R Eds.

— Early Medieval Chants from Nonantola Pt. III: Processional Antiphons. (Recent Researches in Music of the Middle Ages & Early Renaissance Ser.: Vol. RRM32). (Illus.). lxxii, 152p. 1996. pap. 70.00 (*0-89579-338-5*) A-R Eds.

Borders, Karl. Village Life Under the Soviets. LC 72-12699. (Select Bibliographies Reprint Ser.). 1977. reprint ed. 18.95 (*0-8369-7131-0*) Ayer.

— Village Life Under the Soviets. 200p. reprint ed. lib. bdg. 18.00 (*0-8290-0812-8*) Irvington.

Borders-Killian, Linda, ed. see Gouveia, Leann.

Borders, L. D. & Leddick, George R. Handbook of Counseling Supervision. 87p. 1987. pap. text 11.95 (*1-55620-037-4*, 72184) Am Coun Assn.

Borders, L. DiAnne & Drury, Sandra M. Counseling Programs: A Guide to Evaluation. (Essential Tools for Educators Ser.). 112p. 1992. pap. 24.95 (*0-8039-6036-0*) Corwin Pr.

Borders, Merwyn. The Circle Comes Full: New England Southern Baptists, 1958-1998. (Illus.). 400p. 1998. pap. 19.95 (*1-57736-087-7*) Providence Hse.

Borders, Randy. Stay Focused: A Practical Message for Leaders & Laymen. 100p. (Orig.). 1997. pap. 9.95 (*1-57502-433-0*, PO1321) Morris Pubng.

Borders, Raymond. The Winds of September. (Illus.). 405p. 1994. pap. 5.95 (*0-9648528-0-2*) Bastion Bks.

Borders, Rebecca & Dockery, C. C. Beyond the Hill: A Directory of Congress from 1984 to 1993 Where Have All the Members Gone? 240p. (Orig.). (C). 1995. pap. text 19.50 (*0-8191-9820-X*); lib. bdg. 48.00 (*0-8191-9819-6*) U Pr of Amer.

Borders, Rex J. The Dictionary of Health Physics & Nuclear Sciences Terms. Steinmeyer, K. Paul, ed. 440p. 1991. 95.00 (*0-9630191-0-4*) RSA Pubns.

Borders, William D. Spiritual Living in Secular Society: The Teachings of Archbishop William D. Borders. 160p. 1996. 24.00 (*1-885938-04-7*); pap. 16.00 (*1-885938-06-3*) Cathdrl Fndtn Pr.

Borders, William H., jt. ed. see Young, Henry J.

Bordes, Charles, ed. Anthologie Des Maitres Religieux Primitifs des 15th, 16th & 17th Siecles, 6 vols., Set. (Music Ser.). 1981. reprint ed. lib. bdg. 250.00 (*0-306-76089-4*) Da Capo.

— Anthologie Des Maitres Religieux Primitifs des 15th, 16th & 17th Siecles, 6 vols., Vol. 1; IV. (Music Ser.). 184p. 1981. reprint ed. lib. bdg. 47.50 (*0-306-76114-9*) Da Capo.

— Anthologie Des Maitres Religieux Primitifs des 15th, 16th & 17th Siecles, 6 vols., Vol. 2; VIII. (Music Ser.). 194p. 1981. reprint ed. lib. bdg. 47.50 (*0-306-76115-7*) Da Capo.

— Anthologie Des Maitres Religieux Primitifs des 15th, 16th & 17th Siecles, 6 vols., Vol. 3; IV. (Music Ser.). 184p. 1981. reprint ed. lib. bdg. 47.50 (*0-306-76116-5*) Da Capo.

— Anthologie Des Maitres Religieux Primitifs des 15th, 16th & 17th Siecles, 6 vols., Vol. 4; IV. (Music Ser.). 190p. 1981. reprint ed. lib. bdg. 47.50 (*0-306-76117-3*) Da Capo.

— Anthologie Des Maitres Religieux Primitifs des 15th, 16th & 17th Siecles, 6 vols., Vol. 5; II. (Music Ser.). 190p. 1981. reprint ed. lib. bdg. 47.50 (*0-306-76118-1*) Da Capo.

— Anthologie Des Maitres Religieux Primitifs des 15th, 16th & 17th Siecles, 6 vols., Vol. 6; II. (Music Ser.). 202p. 1981. reprint ed. lib. bdg. 47.50 (*0-306-76119-X*) Da Capo.

Bordes, Christian, et al, eds. European Currency Crises & After. 1995. text 79.95 (*0-7190-4707-2*, Pub. by Manchester Univ Pr) St Martin.

Bordes, Gerard. La Grande Encyclopedie Alpha des Sciences et des Techniques, 20 vols., Set. (FRE.). 1976. 1495.00 (*0-8288-5700-8*, M6290) Fr & Eur.

— Grande Encyclopedie Atlas de la Medecine, 9 vols., Set. (FRE.). 320p. 1976. 995.00 (*0-8288-5701-6*, M6291) Fr & Eur.

***Bordessoule, Nadine.** De Proies et d'Ombres: Escritures de la Chasse dans la Litterature Francaise due XIV Siecle. (Studies in the Humanities: 31). (FRE.). 160p. 2000. 47.95 (*0-8204-3473-6*) P Lang Pubng.

Bordeux, Jeanne. Eleonore Duse: The Story of Her Life. LC 79-91896. 308p. 1971. 26.95 (*0-8369-9693-3*) Ayer.

Bordewich, Fergus M. Killing the White Man's Indian: Reinventing Native Americans at the End of the Century. 400p. 1997. pap. 14.00 (*0-385-42036-6*) Doubleday.

— My Mother's Ghost. 2000. 23.95 (*0-385-49129-8*) Bantam.

Bordewijk, Ferdinand. Character. Prince, E. M., tr. from DUT. 286p. (C). 1990. 17.95 (*0-941533-96-4*, NAB) I R Dee.

— Character: A Novel of Father & Son. Prince, E. M., tr. from DUT. LC 98-45232. 288p. 1999. pap. 14.95 (*1-56663-227-7*, Elephant Paperbacks) I R Dee.

Bordewijk, P., jt. auth. see Bottcher, C. J.

Bordewijk, P., ed. see Bottcher, C. J., et al.

Bordewyk, H. W., et al. Netherlands & the World War Vol. 4: Studies in the War History of a Neutral: Effect of the War upon Banking & Currency-War Finances in the Netherlands, 1918-1922-Costs of the War. (Economic & Social History of the World War Ser.). 1928. 85.00 (*0-686-83642-1*) Elliots Bks.

Bordignon, Carla. Perfume Bottles: Profumi Mignon LC 94-45122. (Bella Cosa Ser.).Tr. of Profumi Mignon. (ENG & ITA., Illus.). 144p. 1995. pap. 12.95 (*0-8118-1061-5*) Chronicle Bks.

Bordillon, Henri, ed. see Jarry, Alfred.

Bordin, Edward S. Research Strategies in Psychotherapy. LC 74-11272. (Wiley Series on Personality Processes). 284p. reprint ed. pap. 88.10 (*0-608-30390-9*, 205156900089) Bks Demand.

Bordin, Ruth. Women at Michigan: "The Dangerous Experiment," 1870s to the Present. LC 98-40109. (Illus.). 200p. 1999. text 29.95 (*0-472-10871-9*, 10871) U of Mich Pr.

Bordin, Ruth B. Alice Freeman Palmer: The Evolution of a New Woman. 328p. (C). 1993. text 57.50 (*0-472-10392-X*, 10392) U of Mich Pr.

Bording, Ralph Phillip & Lines, Larry R. Seismic Modeling & Imaging with the Complete Wave Equation. Young, Roger A., ed. (Course Notes Ser.: No. 8). (Illus.). 100p. 1997. pap. text 16.00 (*1-56080-047-X*) Soc Expl Geophys.

Bordley, John B. A Summary View of the Courses of Crops in the Husbandry of England & Maryland. LC 72-89075. (Rural America Ser.). 1973. reprint ed. 8.00 (*0-8420-1477-2*) Scholarly Res Inc.

Bordley, John E. The History of the American Council of Otolaryngology, 1968-1981. (Illus.). 89p. (Orig.). 1993. pap. text 30.00 (*1-56772-000-5*, 4763015) AAO-HNS.

***Bordman, Gerald.** American Musical Theater: A Chronicle. 3rd ed. 840p. 2000. 75.00 (*0-19-513074-X*) OUP.

Bordman, Gerald. American Musical Theatre: A Chronicle. 2nd ed. 832p. 1992. text 75.00 (*0-19-507242-1*) OUP.

— American Theater: A Chronicle of Comedy & Drama, 1914-1930. 464p. 1995. 60.00 (*0-19-509078-0*) OUP.

— The American Theatre: A Chronicle of Comedy & Drama, 1869-1914. LC 92-16066. 808p. 1994. text 95.00 (*0-19-503764-2*) OUP.

— The Oxford Companion to the American Theater. 2nd ed. 752p. 1992. 65.00 (*0-19-507246-4*, 11857) OUP.

Bordman, Gerald M. American Theatre: A Chronicle of Comedy & Drama, 1930-1969. LC 96-17572. 480p. 1996. 60.00 (*0-19-509079-9*) OUP.

Bordne, Erich F. Water Resources of a Western New York Region: A Case Study of Water Resources & Use in the Genesee Valley & Western Lake Ontario Basin. LC 60-9945. (Illus.). 149p. (Orig.). 1960. pap. 35.00 (*0-89366-007-8*) Ultramarine Pub.

Bordner, Diane C. & Petersen, David M. Campus Policing: The Nature of University Police Work. 274p. (Orig.). (C). 1983. pap. text 24.00 (*0-8191-3362-0*); lib. bdg. 53.00 (*0-8191-3361-2*) U Pr of Amer.

Bordner, Marie S. Marvels & Mysteries. 96p. (Orig.). 1986. pap. 4.95 (*0-912661-09-7*) Woodsong Graph.

Bordo, Michael, ed. Financial Crises, 2 vols., Set. (International Library of Macroeconomic & Financial History: No. 5). 788p. 1992. 290.00 (*1-85278-432-6*) E Elgar.

Bordo, Michael D. Essays on the Gold Standard & Related Regimes: Collected Essays. LC 98-39626. (Studies in Macroeconomic History). (Illus.). 536p. (C). 1999. text 69.95 (*0-521-55006-8*) Cambridge U Pr.

Bordo, Michael D., ed. Money, History, & International Finance: Essays in Honor of Anna J. Schwartz. LC 88-39779. (National Bureau of Economic Research Conference Report Ser.). (Illus.). xii, 288p. 1989. lib. bdg. 42.00 (*0-226-06593-6*) U Ch Pr.

Bordo, Michael D. & Capie, Forrest. Monetary Regimes in Transition. LC 92-43109. (Studies in Monetary & Financial History). (Illus.). 408p. (C). 1993. text 69.95 (*0-521-41906-9*) Cambridge U Pr.

Bordo, Michael D. & Schwartz, Anna J., eds. A Retrospective on the Classical Gold Standard, 1821-1931: 1821-1931. LC 84-2440. (National Bureau of Economic Research Conference Report Ser.). 634p. 1984. lib. bdg. 83.00 (*0-226-06590-1*) U Ch Pr.

Bordo, Michael D. & Sylla, Richard, eds. Anglo-American Financial Systems: Institutions & Markets in the Twentieth Century. LC 95-36199. (Illus.). 496p. 1995. text 60.00 (*0-7863-0826-5*, Irwn Prfssnl) McGraw-Hill Prof.

Bordo, Michael D., et al. The Defining Moment: The Great Depression & the American Economy in the Twentieth Century. LC 97-29751. (National Bureau of Economic Research Project Report Ser.). 491p. 1997. 60.00 (*0-226-06589-8*) U Ch Pr.

Bordo, Michael D., jt. ed. see Eichengreen, Barry J.

***Bordo, Susan.** The Male Body: A New Look at Men in Public & in Private. LC 99-25386. (Illus.). 368p. 1999. text 25.00 (*0-374-28065-7*) FS&G.

— The Male Body: A New Look at Men in Public & in Private. (Illus.). 368p. 2000. pap. 14.00 (*0-374-52732-6*) FS&G.

Bordo, Susan. Twilight Zones: The Hidden Life of Cultural Images from Plato to O. J. LC 97-2223. 252p. 1997. 35.00 (*0-520-21101-4*, Pub. by U CA Pr) Cal Prin Full Svc.

— Twilight Zones: The Hidden Life of Cultural Images from Plato to O.J. 252p. 1999. pap. 17.95 (*0-520-21102-2*, Pub. by U CA Pr) Cal Prin Full Svc.

— Unbearable Weight: Feminism, Western Culture, & the Body. LC 92-41582. 362p. 1993. 45.00 (*0-520-07979-5*, Pub. by U CA Pr) Cal Prin Full Svc.

— Unbearable Weight: Feminism, Western Culture, & the Body. 1995. pap. 17.95 (*0-520-08883-2*, Pub. by U CA Pr) Cal Prin Full Svc.

Bordo, Susan R. The Flight to Objectivity: Essays in Cartesianism & Culture. LC 87-10066. (SUNY Series in Philosophy). 145p. (C). 1987. pap. text 19.95 (*0-88706-411-6*) State U NY Pr.

Bordo, Susan R., jt. ed. see Jaggar, Alison M.

Bordon, David E. & American Bar Association Staff. Directors & Officers Liability Insurance: Deskbook. LC 96-85116. xix, 257 p. 1998. pap. write for info. (*1-57073-340-6*) ABA Prof Educ Pubns.

Bordon, Louise. Caps, Hats, Socks, & Mittens. (Big Bks.). (J). (ps-3). 1992. 19.95 (*0-590-72429-0*) Scholastic Inc.

Bordonaro, Charles T. Free to Be Me: A Practical Guide to Biblical Security. Keena, Lynda K., ed. & photos by by. LC 98-93501. (Illus.). 184p. 1998. pap. 9.95 (*1-892810-11-5*) Beacon Light.

Bordons, C., jt. auth. see Camacho, E. F.

Bordow, Joan W. The Ultimate Loss: Coping with the Death of a Child. LC 81-18182. 192p. 1982. 12.95 (*0-8253-0091-6*) Beaufort Bks NY.

Bordow, Richard A. Manual of Clinical Problems in Pulmonary Medicine. 1991. 10.95 (*0-316-10271-7*, Little Brwn Med Div) Lppncott W & W.

Bordow, Richard A., et al, eds. Manual of Clinical Problems in Pulmonary Medicine. 2nd ed. (Spiral Manual Ser.). 1985. 24.50 (*0-316-10265-2*, Little Brwn Med Div) Lppncott W & W.

Bordow, Richard A. & Moser, Kenneth M., eds. Manual of Clinical Problems in Pulmonary Medicine: With Annotated Key References. 4th ed. 576p. 1995. spiral bd. 37.95 (*0-316-10270-9*) Lppncott W & W.

Bordow, Sita, compiled by. The Master's Touch: Disciples' Stories. LC 84-28857. 1984. pap. 8.95 (*0-932040-26-8*) Integral Yoga Pubns.

Bordow, Sita, et al. Sri Swami Satchidananda: Apostle of Peace. LC 86-10533. (Illus.). 454p. (Orig.). 1986. pap. 14.95 (*0-932040-31-4*) Integral Yoga Pubns.

Bordt, Rebecca L. The Structure of Women's Nonprofit Organizations. LC 97-5225. (IU Center on Philanthropy Series in Governance). 1997. 24.95 (*0-253-33347-4*) Ind U Pr.

Bordugh, Rex D. Tracking Your Life & Times Vol. 1: A New Concept for Writing Your Life Story with Historical Sketches for Each Year of the Twentieth Century. Herbison, Kathleen, ed. LC 95-77805. (Illus.). 220p. 1995. ring bd. 23.95 (*1-880988-03-8*) Amer W Bks.

Bordwell. Film Art. 6th ed. 2000. pap. 31.00 (*0-07-231725-6*) McGraw.

Bordwell, David. The Cinema of Eisenstein. LC 92-45678. (Illus.). 336p. (C). 1993. 68.50 (*0-674-13137-1*); pap. 36.50 (*0-674-13138-X*) HUP.

— French Impressionist Cinema. Jowett, Garth S., ed. LC 79-6668. (Dissertations on Film, 1980 Ser.). 1980. lib. bdg. 27.95 (*0-405-12902-5*) Ayer.

— Making Meaning: Inference & Rhetoric in the Interpretation of Cinema. LC 89-30324. (Harvard Film Studies). (Illus.). 348p. 1989. 40.00 (*0-674-54335-1*) HUP.

— Making Meaning: Inference & Rhetoric in the Interpretation of Cinema. (Harvard Film Studies). 352p. (C). 1991. pap. 21.50 (*0-674-54336-X*) HUP.

— Narration in the Fiction Film. LC 84-40491. (Illus.). 370p. (C). 1985. reprint ed. pap. 24.95 (*0-299-10174-6*) U of Wis Pr.

— On the History of Film Style. LC 97-4016. (Illus.). 352p. 1998. 60.00 (*0-674-63428-4*); pap. 24.95 (*0-674-63429-2*) HUP.

— Ozu & the Poetics of Cinema. (Illus.). 384p. 1988. pap. text 39.50 (*0-691-00822-1*, Pub. by Princeton U Pr) Cal Prin Full Svc.

***Bordwell, David.** Planet Hong Kong: Popular Cinema & the Art of Entertainment. LC PN1993.5.H6B63 2000. 384p. 2000. pap. 29.95 (*0-674-00214-8*) HUP.

— Planet Hong Kong: Popular Cinema & the Art of Entertainment. LC PN1993.5.H6B63 2000. (Illus.). 384p. 2000. 65.00 (*0-674-00213-X*) HUP.

Bordwell, David & Carroll, Noel, eds. Post-Theory: Reconstructing Film Studies. LC 95-37052. (Wisconsin Studies in Film). (Illus.). 582p. 1996. pap. 24.95 (*0-299-14944-7*) U of Wis Pr.

— Post-Theory: Reconstructing Film Studies. LC 95-37052. (Wisconsin Studies in Film). (Illus.). 582p. (C). 1996. 45.00 (*0-299-14940-4*) U of Wis Pr.

Bordwell, David & Thompson, Kristin. Film Art: An Introduction. 5th ed. (Illus.). 528p. (C). 1996. pap. 42.50 (*0-07-006634-5*) McGraw.

Bordwell, David, et al. The Classical Hollywood Cinema: Film Style & Mode of Production in 1960. LC 85-372. (King's Crown Paperback Ser.). (Illus.). 506p. 1987. pap. text 36.50 (*0-231-06055-6*, King's Crown Paperbacks) Col U Pr.

Bordwell, David, jt. auth. see Thompson, Kristin.

Bordwell, Percy. Law of War Between Belligerents: A History & Commentary. xxiv, 374p. 1994. reprint ed. 45.00 (*0-8377-1975-5*, Rothman) W S Hein.

Bordwell, Sally. The Aaha Encyclopedia of Dog Health & Care. LC 96-21453. 292p. 1996. pap. 14.00 (*0-688-14771-2*, Quil) HarperTrade.

— The American Animal Hospital Association Encyclopedia of Dog Health & Care. 1996. pap. 14.00 (*0-614-97735-5*, Quil) HarperTrade.

— Baby Names for the New Century. 512p. 1994. mass mkt. 6.50 (*0-06-100753-6*, Harp PBks) HarpC.

Bordwine, James E. The Pauline Doctrine of Male Headship: The Apostle vs. Biblical Feminists. 334p. 1996. text 29.95 (*1-884416-17-9*) A Press.

Borecki, M. & Kwasniewski, M., eds. Application of Analytical Methods to Mining Geomechanics: Proceedings of the 7th Plenary Scientific Session of the International Bureau of Rock Mechanics, World Mining Congress, Katowice, 24-26 June 1981. 168p. (C). 1982. 207.00 (90-6191-260-1, Pub. by A A Balkema) Ashgate Pub Co.

Borecky, L. & Lackovic, V., eds. Physiology & Pathology of Interferon System. (Beitraege Zur Onkologie, Contributions to Oncology Ser.: Vol. 20). (Illus.). x, 390p. 1984. 68.75 (3-8055-3839-1) S Karger.

***Boreen, Jean, et al.** Mentoring Beginning Teachers: Guiding, Reflecting, Coaching. Stratton, Philippa, ed. LC 99-51645. 144p. 2000. pap. text 17.50 (1-57110-309-0) Stenhse Pubs.

Boreham. A Guide to Windows 95. (NETWORKING). (C). 1998. pap. 43.00 (0-7600-1105-2) Course Tech.

Boreham, F. W. Pathway of Roses. 1997. pap. 8.99 (1-898787-10-7) Emerald House Group Inc.

Boreham, Frank. When Scripture Changes Lives. 155p. 1995. 7.99 (1-884543-03-0) O M Lit.

Boreham, Frank W. A Bunch of Everlastings, Vol. 1. LC 93-37844. (Life Verses Ser.: No. 1). (Illus.). 256p. 1993. pap. 12.99 (0-8254-2167-5) Kregel.

— A Bundle of Torches. LC 93-37844. (Life Verses Ser.: No. 4). 274p. 1994. pap. 12.99 (0-8254-2165-9) Kregel.

— A Casket of Cameos, Vol. 3. LC 93-37844. (Life Verses Ser.: No. 3). (Illus.). 274p. 1994. pap. 12.99 (0-8254-2168-3) Kregel.

— A Handful of Stars. LC 93-37844. (Life Verses Ser.: No. 2). 264p. 1994. pap. 12.99 (0-8254-2169-1) Kregel.

— The Luggage of Life. 256p. 1985. pap. 12.99 (0-8254-2164-0, 95-007) Kregel.

— Mountains in the Mist. (Illus.). 288p. 1995. pap. 12.99 (0-8254-2163-2, 95-008) Kregel.

— A Temple of Topaz, Vol. 5. LC 93-37844. (Life Verses Ser.: No. 5). 274p. 1994. pap. 12.99 (0-8254-2166-7) Kregel.

Boreham, Peter L. & Atwell, Richard B., eds. Dirofilariasis. (Parasitologists & Veterinarians Ser.). 272p. 1988. 148.00 (0-8493-6488-4, SF992, CRC Reprint) Franklin.

***Boreham, Richard & Prescott-Clarke, Patricia, eds.** Health Survey for England '97: The Health of Young People '95-97, Vols. 1 & 2. (On Spines Series HS: No. 7). 596p. 1998. 165.00 (0-11-322266-1, Pub. by Statnry Office) Balogh.

Boreham, Roland S., Jr. The Three-Legged Stool: Relationships First - Success Follows. (Illus.). 164p. 1999. 21.95 (1-58244-016-6) Rutledge Bks.

Borek, Ernest. The Atoms Within Us. rev. ed. LC 80-19010. 272p. 1980. text 60.00 (0-231-04386-4); pap. text 21.00 (0-231-04387-2) Col U Pr.

— Code of Life. LC 65-10944. 1965. text 57.50 (0-231-02634-X) Col U Pr.

— The Sculpture of Life. LC 73-6831. (Illus.). 203p. reprint ed. pap. 63.00 (0-8357-4589-9, 203752000008) Bks Demand.

Borel, Armand. Algebraic D-Modules. (Perspectives in Mathematics Ser.). 368p. 1987. text 78.00 (0-12-117740-8) Acad Pr.

— Automorphic Forms on SL2. (Tracts in Mathematics Ser.: Vol. 130). 202p. (C). 1997. text 47.95 (0-521-58049-8) Cambridge U Pr.

— Linear Algebraic Groups. 2nd enl. ed. Ewing, J. H. et al, eds. (Graduate Texts in Mathematics Ser.: Vol. 126). 304p. 1997. reprint ed. text 49.95 (0-387-97370-2) Spr-Verlag.

— Oeuvres - Collected Papers, 3 vols. 2240p. 1983. 350.00 (0-387-12126-9) Spr-Verlag.

— Topics in the Homology Theory of Fibre Bundles. (Lecture Notes in Mathematics Ser.: Vol. 36). 1967. pap. 19.90 (0-387-03907-4) Spr-Verlag.

Borel, Armand & Casselman, W., eds. Automorphic Forms, Representations & L-Functions, 2 pts., Pt. 1. LC 78-21184. (Proceedings of Symposia in Pure Mathematics Ser., Humboldt State University, Arcata, CA, July 29-August 16, 1974: Vol. 33). 322p. 1979. pap. 36.00 (0-8218-1435-4, PSPUM/33.1) Am Math.

— Automorphic Forms, Representations & L-Functions, 2 pts., Pt. 2. LC 78-21184. (Proceedings of Symposia in Pure Mathematics Ser., Humboldt State University, Arcata, CA, July 29-August 16, 1974: Vol. 33). 382p. 1979. pap. 36.00 (0-8218-1437-0, PSPUM/33.2) Am Math.

— Automorphic Forms, Representations & L-Functions, 2 pts., Set. LC 78-21184. (Proceedings of Symposia in Pure Mathematics Ser., Humboldt State University, Arcata, CA, July 29-August 16, 1974: Vol.33). 704p. 1979. pap. 60.00 (0-8218-1474-5, PSPUM/33) Am Math.

Borel, Armand & Wallach, Nolan R. Continuous Cohomology, Discrete Subgroups, & Representations of Reductive Groups. 2nd ed. LC 98-44527. (Mathematical Surveys & Monographs Ser.). 1999. 59.00 (0-8218-0851-6) Am Math.

Borel, Armand, et al. Intersection Cohomology. (Progress in Mathematics Ser.: No. 50). 235p. 1984. 45.00 (0-8176-3274-3) Birkhauser.

— Lie Algebras & Lie Groups. LC 52-42839. (Memoirs Ser.: No. 1/14). 54p. 1972. reprint ed. pap. 17.00 (0-8218-1214-9, MEMO/1/14) Am Math.

Borel, Armand, ed. see Pure Mathematics Symposium Staff.

Borel, Armand, ed. see Seminar on Algebraic Groups & Related Finite Group.

Borel, B., jt. auth. see De Valuy, A.

Borel, Beryl A., jt. ed. see Clarke, Margaret A.

Borel, Beryl T., jt. ed. see Clarke, Margaret A.

Borel, Corinne, tr. see Deonna, Laurence.

Borel, France. Bacon: Portraits & Self-Portraits. LC 96-61099.Tr. of: Bacon: Portraits et Autoportraits. (Illus.). 216p. 1997. 60.00 (0-500-09266-4, Pub. by Thames Hudson) Norton.

Borel, J. F., ed. Ciclosporin. (Progress in Allergy Ser.: Vol. 38). (Illus.). vi, 474p. 1986. 169.75 (3-8055-4221-6) S Karger.

Borel, Jacques, jt. auth. see Verlaine, Paul M.

Borel, Jacques, ed. see Verlaine, Paul M.

Borel, Marie-Jeanne, et al. Essai de Logique Naturelle. (Sciences pour la Communication Ser.: Vol. 4). (FRE.). X, 241p. 1992. 31.55 (3-261-05073-X) P Lang Pubng.

Borel, P. Champavert. 260p. 1997. 15.99 (0-947757-98-8, Pub. by Atlas Pr) Serpents Tail.

Borell, Brigitte & Rittig, Dessa. Orientalische und Griechische Bronzereliefs aus Olympia. 368p. 1998. text 200.00 (3-11-015091-3) De Gruyter.

Borell, Merriley. Album of Science: 20th Century-Biological Sciences. Cohen, I. Bernard, ed. LC 88-14715. 320p. 1988. 95.00 (0-684-16483-3, Scribners Ref) Mac Lib Ref.

Borella, Andrea, et al. WDMA Optical Networks. LC 98-2922. 322p. 1998. 93.00 (0-89006-657-4) Artech Hse.

***Borella, Jean.** The Sense of the Supernatural. Champoux, John, tr. 128p. 1999. 35.95 (0-567-08643-7, Pub. by T & T Clark) Bks Intl VA.

Borella, Poul & Borella, Sigrid, eds. Danish Zoological Bibliography, 1907-1945, 2 vols., Set. (Acta Historica Scientarium Ser.: No. 36-37). (Orig.). 1986. pap. 143.00 (87-7421-518-3) Coronet Bks.

Borella, Sigrid, jt. ed. see Borella, Poul.

Borelli, Alessando, jt. auth. see Cippriani, Curzio.

Borelli, Andrew. All Fall Down. (Cyberpunk Ser.). 32p. 1992. pap. 8.00 (1-887801-39-1, Atlas Games) Trident MN.

Borelli, Andrew, et al. Streetfighting: An Official Cyberpunk 2020 Adventure Anthology. (Cyberpunk Ser.). 64p. 1993. pap. 10.00 (1-887801-36-7, Atlas Games) Trident MN.

Borelli, Antonio A., et al. Our Lady at Fatima: Prophecies of Tragedy or Hope? 3rd ed. Parrot, Edward, ed. (Illus.). 104p. (C). 1994. pap. 7.95 (1-877905-28-3) Am Soc Defense TFP.

Borelli, Deborah. Redy-Refs for Critical Care Nurses. (Illus.). 50p. 1996. text 12.95 (0-943202-57-4) H & H Pub.

— Redy-Refs for Medical - Surgical Nurses. (Illus.). 40p. 1996. text 12.95 (0-943202-56-6) H & H Pub.

Borelli, G. A. On the Movement of Animals. (Illus.). 480p. 1989. 216.00 (0-387-19419-3) Spr-Verlag.

Borelli, George. A Collection of Pop Psychology Articles. 1994. pap. text 12.95 (1-885792-07-7) Gemini Pubng.

— The Great Wizard of Imp. 28p. (J). (gr. 4). 1994. pap. text 7.95 (1-885792-01-8) Gemini Pubng.

— The Great Wizard of Imp & the Boogaloo Pirates. 28p. (J). (gr. k-4). 1995. pap. text 7.95 (1-885792-02-6) Gemini Pubng.

— The Great Wizard of Imp & the Day Santa Claus Got Lost. (J). 1997. pap. text 7.95 (1-885792-03-4) Gemini Pubng.

— Role Simulation Manual: A Technique for Resolving Human Conflict. 115p. (C). 1994. pap. text 9.95 (1-885792-00-X) Gemini Pubng.

Borelli, John, et al, eds. Advances in Irrigation & Drainage: Surviving External Pressures. LC 83-71586. 568p. 1983. pap. 7.00 (0-87262-370-X) Am Soc Civil Eng.

Borelli, John & Erickson, John H. The Quest for Unity: Orthodox & Catholics in Dialogue - Documents of the Joint International Commission & Official Dialogues in the United States, 1965-1995. LC 96-23082. 1996. 11.95 (0-88141-113-2) St Vladimirs.

Borelli, John, et al. The Living Light Vol. 32, No. 2: Special Feature - Interreligious Dialogue. Marthaler, Berard L., ed. (Quarterly Journal). 96p. (Orig.). (C). 1995. pap. 8.95 (1-55586-064-8) US Catholic.

Borelli, Luigi & Borelli, Mary. Leggende e Racconti Italiani: An Easy Reader for Beginners. (C). 1989. 10.95 (0-913298-03-4) S F Vanni.

Borelli, Mary, jt. auth. see Borelli, Luigi.

Borellius, Petrus. Bibliotheca Chimica, Sue Catalogus Librorum Philosophicorum Hermeticorum, in Quo 4000 Circiter Authorum Chimicorum, ... Usque Annum 1653 Continentur. 254p. 1969. reprint ed. 80.00 (0-318-71746-8) G Olms Pubs.

Borello, Pierre. L' Improvisation a la Guitare/le Blues. Lefferts, Michael, ed. (FRE.). 48p. (Orig.). (C). 1997. pap. text 16.95 (0-7692-1318-9, 01010345) Wrner Bros.

Borelo, Osvaldo R. For a Select Few. Jacobs, Linda, ed. (Illus.). 150p. (Orig.). 1992. pap. text 9.95 (0-9634786-3-X) Mass Media Dist.

Boreman, G. D. Basic Optics for Electrical Engineers. LC 97-52690. (Tutorial Texts in Optical Engineering Ser.). 97p. 1998. pap. 42.00 (0-8194-2806-X) SPIE.

Boreman, G. D., jt. auth. see Dereniak, Eustace L.

***Boreman, Glenn D.** Fundamentos De Electro-Optica para Ingenieros. 112p. 1999. 42.00 (0-8194-3323-3) SPIE.

Boreman, J. S., et al, eds. Northwest Atlantic Groundfish: Perspectives on a Fishery Collapse. LC 97-77481. 242p. 1997. pap. text 56.00 (1-888569-06-9, 550.23P) Am Fisheries Soc.

Boremanse, Didier. Hach Winik: The Lacandon Maya of Chiapas, Southern Mexico. LC 98-75561. (Institute for Mesoamerican Studies Monograph: Vol. 11). (Illus.). xxii, 178p. (C). 1999. pap. 27.00 (0-942041-16-X) Univ Albany IFMS.

Boren, Blanche. Thorns to Velvet: Devotionals from a Life Time of Christian Experience. Cowden, Frances, ed. (Illus.). 172p. 1998. 17.95 (1-884289-23-1) Grandmother Erth.

Boren, Colonel Van, see Van Boren, Colonel.

***Boren, David L.** Preparing America's Foreign Policy for the Twenty-First Century. LC 98-43713. 1999. 24.95 (0-8061-3123-3) U of Okla Pr.

***Boren, David L. & Perkins, Edward J., eds.** Preparing America's Foreign Policy for the Twenty-First Century. 448p. 2000. pap. 19.95 (0-8061-3271-X) U of Okla Pr.

Boren, Gary & Stein, Norman P. Qualified Deferred Compensation Plans: Treatise, 2 vols., Set. LC 83-23912. 1446p. 1990. 240.00 (0-317-11357-7) West Group.

Boren, Henry C. Roman Society: A Social, Economic, & Cultural History. 2nd ed. (Civilization & Society Ser.). 338p. (C). 1992. pap. text 27.16 (0-669-17801-2) HM Trade Div.

Boren, Jim & Rechin, Bill. Twiggle: A Lexicon of New Words for Everyone Condemned to Spend Part of His or Her Life in an Office. 1989. mass mkt. 5.95 (0-446-38085-7, Pub. by Warner Bks) Little.

***Boren, Kerry R. & Boren, Lisa L.** The Gold of Carre-Shinob. 1999. pap. 19.95 (1-55517-411-6) CFI Dist.

Boren, Lisa L., jt. auth. see Boren, Kerry R.

Boren, Lynda S. Eurydice Reclaimed: Language, Gender, & Voice in Henry James. Litz, A. Walton, ed. LC 89-20190. (Studies in Modern Literature: No. 107). 157p. 1989. reprint ed. pap. 48.70 (0-8357-2026-8, 207069600004) Bks Demand.

Boren, Lynda S. & Davis, Sara D., eds. Kate Chopin Reconsidered: Beyond the Bayou. LC 91-29368. (Southern Literary Studies). 256p. (C). 1992. text 35.00 (0-8071-1721-8) La State U Pr.

— Kate Chopin Reconsidered: Beyond the Bayou. LC 91-29368. (Southern Literary Studies). 264p. 1999. pap. 14.95 (0-8071-2435-4) La State U Pr.

***Boren, Minx.** Soul Notes. 2000. pap. 13.00 (0-9702550-0-4) Fourfold Path.

Borene, Jan. Serenity: An Inspirational Journal. (Illus.). 144p. 1998. pap. text 19.95 (1-55670-807-6) Stewart Tabori & Chang.

— Woman's Journal of Hopes, Dreams & Desires. 144p. 1998. text 15.95 (1-55670-725-8) Stewart Tabori & Chang.

Borene, Scott, et al, eds. INS Forms for Applications & Petitions. 3rd ed. 672p. 1995. 90.00 (1-878677-88-8, 54.10) Amer Immi Law Assn.

Borengasse. English Writing & Skills. 1988. text, wbk. ed. 16.00 (0-03-014672-0) Holt R&W.

— English Writing & Skills, 1988. 1988. wbk. ed. 20.00 (0-03-014673-9) Holt R&W.

Borenson, Henry. Class Set of Hands-On Equations for Teacher & Forty (40) Students. (Illus.). 66p. 1988. pap. 345.00 (0-9618105-7-2) Borenson & Assocs.

— Class Set of Hands-On Equations for Teacher & Ten (10) Students. rev. ed. (Illus.). 66p. 1994. pap., teacher ed. 195.00 (0-9618105-4-8) Borenson & Assocs.

— Class Set of Hands-On Equations for Teacher & Thirty (30) Students. rev. ed. (Illus.). 66p. 1988. pap., teacher ed. 295.00 (0-9618105-6-4) Borenson & Assocs.

— Class Set of Hands-On Equations for Teacher & Twenty (20) Students. rev. ed. (Illus.). 66p. 1994. pap., teacher ed. 245.00 (0-9618105-5-6) Borenson & Assocs.

— The Hands-On Equations Learning System. rev. ed. (Illus.). 66p. 1994. pap. 34.95 (0-9618105-2-1) Borenson & Assocs.

— The Hands-on Equations Learning System. 2nd ed. (Illus.). 66p. (J). (gr. 3-8). 1988. reprint ed. 34.95 (0-9618105-0-5) Borenson & Assocs.

Borenstein, Audrey. Chimes of Change & Hours: Views of Older Women in Twentieth-Century America. LC 82-48159. 520p. 1983. 65.00 (0-8386-3170-3) Fairleigh Dickinson.

Borenstein, David G., et al. Low Back Pain: Medical Diagnosis & Comprehensive Management. 2nd ed. LC 93-41601. 1994. text. write for info. (0-7216-5411-8, W B Saunders Co) Harcrt Hlth Sci Grp.

— Neck Pain: Medical Diagnosis & Comprehensive Management. Lampert, Richard, ed. 512p. 1996. text 89.00 (0-7216-5412-6, W B Saunders Co) Harcrt Hlth Sci Grp.

***Borenstein, Eliot.** Men Without Women: Masculinity & Revolution in Russian Fiction, 1917-1929. 336p. 2000. lib. bdg. 59.95 (0-8223-2578-0) Duke.

— Men Without Women: Masculinity & Revolution in Russian Fiction, 1917-1929. LC 00-30309. 336p. 2001. pap. 19.95 (0-8223-2592-6) Duke.

Borenstein, Eliot, ed. see Lipovetsky, Mark.

Borenstein, Israel. Capital & Output Trends in Mining Industries, 1870-1948. (Occasional Papers: No. 45). 96p. 1954. reprint ed. 25.00 (0-87014-359-X) Natl Bur Econ Res.

Borenstein, Michael, et al, eds. Power & Precision. 1997. 495.00 incl. disk (1-56321-198-X) LEA S&AM.

Borenstein, Michael & Cohen, Jacob. Statistical Power Analysis: A Computer Program. 2nd ed. 1989. disk 10.00 (1-56321-006-1); disk 125.00 (1-56321-008-8); disk 10.00 (1-56321-010-X) L Erlbaum Assocs.

— Statistical Power Analysis: A Computer Program. 2nd ed. 567p. 1989. student ed. 140.00 incl. disk (1-56321-009-6) L Erlbaum Assocs.

Borenstein, Nathaniel, ed. see IFIP TC6-WG6.5 International Working Conference St.

Borenstein, Nathaniel S. Programming As If People Mattered: Friendly Programs, Software Engineering, & Other Noble. 200p. 1992. pap. text 16.95 (0-691-03763-9, Pub. by Princeton U Pr) Cal Prin Full Svc.

Borenstein, Ruth. Little Gorilla. (Carry-Along Book & Cassette Favorites Ser.). (Illus.). (J). (ps-1). 1995. pap. 9.95 incl. audio (0-395-72091-5, 111771, Clarion Bks) Ticknor & Flds Bks Yng Read.

Borenstein, Susan W. Microbiologically Influenced Corrosion Handbook. 310p. 1994. 79.95 (0-8311-3056-3) Indus Pr.

Borenstein, Susan Watkins. Microbiologically Influenced Corrosion Handbook. 304p. 1994. boxed set 153.00 (1-85573-127-4, Pub. by Woodhead Pubng) Am Educ Systs.

***Borenstein, Walter, tr. from SPA.** Journeys in Time & Place: Two Works of Azorin, Confessions of a Little Philosopher & the Route of Don Quixote. LC 99-75870. 220p. 2000. 30.00 (0-938972-31-6) Spanish Lit Pubns.

Borenstein, Walter, tr. see Bazan, Emilia P.

Borensztein, Eduardo, et al. The Behavior of Non-Oil Commodity Prices. LC 94-33965. (Occassional Papers: 112). 1994. 15.00 (1-55775-412-8) Intl Monetary.

Borer, Alain. The Essential Joseph Beuys. LC 97-5927. (Illus.). 239p. 1997. 65.00 (0-262-02431-4) MIT Pr.

Borer, Brooke M., ed. see Carpenter, William S.

***Borer, Douglas.** Superpowers Defeated: A Comparison of Vietnam & Afghanistan. LC 98-31628. 288p. 1999. pap. 17.50 (0-7146-4409-9, Pub. by F Cass Pubs) Intl Spec Bk.

Borer, Douglas. Superpowers Defeated: A Comparison of Vietnam & Afghanistan: A Comparison of Vietnam & Afghanistan. LC 98-31628. 288p. 1999. 52.50 (0-7146-4851-5, Pub. by F Cass Pubs) Intl Spec Bk.

Borer, Douglas A., jt. auth. see Berger, Mark T.

Borer, H. Parametric Syntax: Case Studies in Semitic & Romance Languages. Koster, Jan & Riemsdyk, H. V., eds. (Studies in Generative Grammar: No. 13). ix, 260p. 1984. pap. 57.70 (90-6765-025-0) Mouton.

Borer, Hagit. Syntax & Semantics Vol. 19: The Syntax of Pronominal Cities, Vol 19. 365p. 1986. text 125.00 (0-12-613519-3) Acad Pr.

Borer, J. S., ed. Non-Invasive Techniques in Cardiology Journal: Cardiology, Vol. 71, No. 2-3, 1984. (Illus.). 112p. 1984. pap. 69.75 (3-8055-3886-3) S Karger.

***Borer, J. S. & Somberg, John C.** Cardiovascular Drug Development: Protocol Design & Methodology. LC 98-44759. (Fundamental & Clinical Cardiology Ser.). (Illus.). 248p. 1998. text 130.00 (0-8247-1927-1) Dekker.

***Borer, Jeffrey S.** Contemporary Diagnosis & Management of Valvular Heart Disease. (Illus.). 190p. 2000. pap. 29.95 (1-884065-58-9, Hndbks Hlth Care) Assocs in Med.

Borer, Katarina T. Frontiers of Exercise Biology. Edington, D. W. & White, Timothy P., eds. LC 83-81601. (Big Ten Body of Knowledge Symposium Ser.: No. 13). (Illus.). 303p. 1983. reprint ed. pap. 94.00 (0-608-06459-9, 206729700009) Bks Demand.

Borer, Mary C. Story of Covent Garden. (Illus.). 191p. 1984. 29.95 (0-7090-1481-3) Trans-Atl Phila.

— Two Villages: Story of Chelsea & Kensington. (Illus.). 288p. 1974. 18.00 (0-491-01061-3) Transatl Arts.

Borer, Tristan A. Challenging the State: Churches As Political Actors in South Africa, 1980-1994. LC 98-18608. (Helen Kellogg Institute for International Studies Ser.). 289p. 1998. pap. 16.95 (0-268-00829-9) U of Notre Dame Pr.

Borer, William Z., ed. see Conn, Rex B., et al.

Bores, Jaime G. Construya en Ingles. (SPA., Illus.). 190p. 1997. pap. text 12.98 (968-13-2520-6, Pub. by Edit Diana) Libros Fronteras.

Bores, Jaime G. Construya en Ingles. (BBC Phrase Books for Teenagers). (SPA., Illus.). 192p. 1994. pap. 7.95 (0-8442-7123-3, Passprt Bks) NTC Contemp Pub Co.

— Conversando en Ingles: English Conversational Grammar for Spanish Speakers. (ENG & SPA., Illus.). 208p. 1995. pap. 7.95 (0-8442-7101-2, Natl Textbk Co) NTC Contemp Pub Co.

Bores, Jaime G. Diviertase Aprendiendo Ingles. (SPA.). 1997. pap. text 12.98 (968-13-2497-8) Libros Fronteras.

— Ingles Extractado. (SPA.). 1997. pap. text 12.98 (968-13-2517-6, Pub. by Edit Diana) Libros Fronteras.

Bores, Jaime G. Manual Completo de los Verbos en Ingles: Complete Handbook of English Verbs. (ENG & SPA., Illus.). 208p. 1994. pap. 8.95 (0-8442-7102-0, Natl Textbk Co) NTC Contemp Pub Co.

Bores, Jaime G. Verbos Irregulares En Ingles. (SPA.). 1997. pap. text 5.98 (968-13-1037-3) Diana-Etna Inc.

Bores, Leo D. Atlas of Refractive Eye Surgery. LC 92-21895. (Illus.). 624p. 1992. 250.00 (0-86542-152-8) Blackwell Sci.

***Bores, Leo S.** Refractive Eye Surgery. 2nd ed. (Illus.). 592p. 2000. 250.00 (0-632-04364-4) Blackwell Sci.

Boresch, A., et al. Applications of Noncovariant Gauges in the Algebraic Renormalization Procedure. LC 98-16441. 150p. 1998. 28.00 (981-02-3456-2) World Scientific Pub.

***Boresi.** Elasticity in Engineering Mechanics. 2nd ed. 1999. pap. text. write for info. (0-471-38100-4, Wiley Heyden) Wiley.

Boresi. Engineering Mechanics: Dynamic. LC 99-87175. (General Engineering Ser.). (C). 2000. pap. 74.95 (0-534-95162-7) PWS Pubs.

— Engineering Mechanics: Statics. LC 99-87176. (General Engineering Ser.). (C). 2000. pap. 74.95 (0-534-95152-X) PWS Pubs.

Boresi, Arthur P. & Chong. Approximate Solutions Methods in Solid Mechanics. 1991. mass mkt. 99.95 (1-85166-572-2) Elsevier.

Boresi, Arthur P. & Chong, K. P. Elasticity in Engineering Mechanics. 635p. 1987. 56.25 (0-444-01177-3) P-H.

Boresi, Arthur P., et al. Advanced Mechanics of Materials. 5th ed. LC 92-30349. 832p. 1993. text 106.95 (0-471-55157-0) Wiley.

— Advanced Mechanics of Materials. 5th ed. 480p. 1993. pap. text 39.95 (0-471-58302-2) Wiley.

Boreson, Lynn. A Programming Guide for Emotional Disturbance. 168p. (C). 1994. pap. text 27.00 (1-57337-018-5) WI Dept Pub Instruct.

An Asterisk (*) at the beginning of an entry indicates that the title is appearing for the first time.

Boress. Building Entrepreneurial People. 95th ed. 1995. 39.00 (*0-15-601712-1*) Harcourt Legal.
Boress. Expreselo Todo En Ingles. (SPA.). 1997. pap. text 12.98 (*968-13-2498-6*) Libros Fronteras.
Boress, Allan S. The I Hate Selling Book: Business-Building Advice for Consultants, Attorneys, Accountants, Engineers, Architects & Other Professionals. LC 94-33738. 224p. 1994. 24.95 (*0-8144-0245-3*) AMACOM.
Borestone Mountain Poetry Awards Staff, ed. Best Poems of 1958: Borestone Mountain Poetry Awards 1959, Vol. 11. LC 49-49262. xiv, 110p. 1959. 15.95 (*0-87015-095-2*) Pacific Bks.
— Best Poems of 1960: Borestone Mountain Poetry Awards 1961, Vol. 13. LC 49-49262. xii, 124p. 1961. 15.95 (*0-87015-105-3*); pap. 8.95 (*0-87015-106-1*) Pacific Bks.
— Best Poems of 1963: Borestone Mountain Poetry Awards 1964, Vol. 16. LC 49-49262. xiv, 150p. 1964. 15.95 (*0-87015-126-6*); pap. 8.95 (*0-87015-127-4*) Pacific Bks.
— Best Poems of 1964: Borestone Mountain Poetry Awards 1965, Vol. 17. LC 49-49262. xvi, 141p. 1965. 15.95 (*0-87015-142-8*) Pacific Bks.
— Best Poems of 1966: Borestone Mountain Poetry Awards 1967, Vol. 19. LC 49-49262. xvi, 145p. 1967. 15.95 (*0-87015-157-6*) Pacific Bks.
— Best Poems of 1967: Borestone Mountain Poetry Awards, 1968, Vol. 20. LC 49-49262. xx, 142p. 1968. 15.95 (*0-87015-171-1*) Pacific Bks.
— Best Poems of 1968: Borestone Mountain Poetry Awards 1969, Vol. 21. LC 49-49262. xviii, 149p. 1969. 15.95 (*0-87015-179-7*) Pacific Bks.
— Best Poems of 1969: Borestone Mountain Poetry Awards 1970, Vol. 22. LC 49-49262. xx, 159p. 1970. 15.95 (*0-87015-186-X*) Pacific Bks.
— Best Poems of 1970: Borestone Mountain Poetry Awards 1971, Vol. 23. LC 49-49262. xviii, 126p. 1971. 15.95 (*0-87015-195-9*) Pacific Bks.
— Best Poems of 1971: Borestone Mountain Poetry Awards 1972, Vol 24. LC 49-49262. xvi, 127p. 1972. 15.95 (*0-87015-200-9*) Pacific Bks.
— Best Poems of 1972: Borestone Mountain Poetry Awards 1973, Vol. 25. LC 49-49262. xviii, 134p. 1973. 15.95 (*0-87015-208-4*) Pacific Bks.
— Best Poems of 1973: Borestone Mountain Poetry Awards 1974, Vol. 26. LC 49-49262. xx, 138p. 1974. 15.95 (*0-87015-217-3*) Pacific Bks.
— Best Poems of 1974: Borestone Mountain Poetry Awards 1975, Vol. 27. LC 49-49262. xvi, 124p. 1975. 15.95 (*0-87015-219-X*) Pacific Bks.
— Best Poems of 1975: Borestone Mountain Poetry Awards 1976, Vol. 28. LC 49-49262. xvi, 119p. 1976. 15.95 (*0-87015-223-8*) Pacific Bks.
— Best Poems of 1976: Borestone Mountain Poetry Awards 1977, Vol.29. LC 49-49262. xvi, 119p. 1977. 15.95 (*0-87015-227-0*) Pacific Bks.
Boreth, Craig. The Hemingway Cookbook. LC 98-20246. (Illus.). 214p. 1998. 24.00 (*1-55652-297-5*) Chicago Review.
Boretz, Alan. Room Service. 1944. pap. 5.25 (*0-8222-0962-4*) Dramatists Play.
Boretz, Alvin. I Remember You: A Romantic Play. (Illus.). 28p. 1993. pap. 4.00 (*0-88680-383-7*) I E Clark.
Boretz, Benjamin. If I Am a Musical Thinker: Talk. 56p. 1985. pap. 9.95 (*0-88268-002-1*) Station Hill Pr.
— Language, As a Music: Six Marginal Pretexts for Composition. LC 80-80807. (Illus.). 88p. 1980. lib. bdg. 13.95 (*0-939044-20-X*) Lingua Pr.
— Music Columns from the Nation, 1962-68. LC 91-90386. 168p. 1991. write for info. (*0-9629865-0-X*) Open Space NY.
Boretz, Benjamin & Randall, J. K. Being about Music: The Collected Writings of Benjamin Boretz & J. K. Randall. LC 91-90391. 350p. 1994. write for info. (*0-9629865-3-4*) Open Space NY.
— Meta-Variations: Studies in the Foundations of Musical Thought - Compose Yourself: A Manual for the Young. LC 91-90388. 500p. 1994. write for info. (*0-9629865-1-8*) Open Space NY.
Boretz, Elizabeth. Mysterious Realms: Functions of Imagery in Traditional Spanish Lyric & Balladry. viii, 178p. 1998. pap. 14.00 (*0-936388-25-0*) Juan de la Cuesta.
***Boretzky, Norbert.** Die Verwandtschaftsbeziehungen Zwischen Den Sudbalkanischen Romani-Dialekten: Mit einem Kartenanhang. (Studien Zur Tsiganologie und Folkloristik Ser.). 294p. 1999. 45.95 (*3-631-35070-8*) P Lang Pubng.
Boreus, Lars O., ed. see Symposium on Fetal Pharmacology Staff.
***Boreyko, Jason.** Making the Impossible Possible: Think It! Act It! Become It! LC 99-60931. 256p. 1999. 22.95 (*0-9670400-0-0*, Pub. by J Boreyko) BookWorld.
Borg, A. The Cultural History of Russia. (Great Civilizations Ser.). 90p. 1988. 60.00 (*0-7855-0840-6*) St Mut.
Borg, Albert & Azzopardi-Alexander, Marie. Maltese. LC 96-13272. (Descriptive Grammars Ser.). 416p. (C). 1996. 180.00 (*0-415-02243-6*) Routledge.
Borg, Axel E., jt. auth. see Amerine, M. A.
Borg, Barbara & Bruce, Mary A. The Group System: The Therapeutic Activity Group in Occupational Therapy. LC 89-43517. 275p. 1990. pap. 29.00 (*1-55642-065-X*) SLACK Inc.
— Occupational Therapy Stories: Psychosocial Interaction in Practice. LC 96-53891. 192p. (C). 1997. pap. 29.00 (*1-55642-313-6*, 33136) SLACK Inc.
Borg, Barbara, jt. auth. see Bruce, Mary A.
Borg, Barbara, jt. auth. see Bruce, Mary Ann.
Borg, Daniel R. The Old Prussian Church & the Weimar Republic: A Study in Political Adjustment, 1917-1927. LC 83-40559. 387p. reprint ed. pap. 120.00 (*0-8357-6508-3*, 203587900097) Bks Demand.
Borg, Dorothy. The United States & the Far Eastern Crisis of 1933-1938: From the Manchurian Incident Through the Initial Stage of the Undeclared Sino-Japanese War. LC 64-13421. (Harvard East Asian Ser.: No. 14). 684p. 1964. pap. 200.00 (*0-7837-4100-6*, 205792300011) Bks Demand.
Borg, Dorothy & Heinrichs, Waldo H., eds. Uncertain Years: Chinese-American Relations, 1947-1950. LC 79-28297. (Studies of the East Asian Institute). 1980. text 61.00 (*0-231-04738-X*) Col U Pr.
Borg, G. An Introduction to Borg's RPE-Scale. (Illus.). 26p. 1985. pap. 4.95 (*0-317-59363-3*) Mouvement Pubns.
Borg, Gunnar. Borg's Perceived Exertion & Pain Scales. LC 97-46439. (Illus.). 120p. 1998. pap. text 24.00 (*0-88011-623-4*, BBOR0623) Human Kinetics.
Borg, I. & Lingoes, J. Multidimensional Similarity Structure Analysis. (Illus.). xiv, 390p. 1987. 54.00 (*0-387-96525-4*) Spr-Verlag.
Borg, I. H. Van Der, see Van Der Borg, I. H.
Borg, I. Y. & Smith, D. K. Calculated X-Ray Powder Patterns for Silicate Minerals. LC 72-110814. (Geological Society of America, Memoir Ser.: No. 122). 908p. reprint ed. pap. 200.00 (*0-8357-7964-5*, 202373000033) Bks Demand.
Borg, Ingwer & Groenen, Patrick J. Modern Multidimensional Scaling Theory & Applications. LC 96-30269. (Statistics Ser.). 471p. 1997. 54.95 (*0-387-94845-7*) Spr-Verlag.
Borg, Ingwer & Mohler, Peter, eds. Trends & Perspectives in Empirical Social Research. LC 94-26590. 375p. 1994. lib. bdg. 98.95 (*3-11-014311-9*) De Gruyter.
— Trends & Perspectives in Empirical Social Research. LC 94-26590. 375p. (C). 1994. pap. text 49.95 (*3-11-014312-7*) De Gruyter.
Borg, Ingwer, et al. Facet Theory: Form & Content. (Advanced Quantitative Techniques Ser.: Vol. 5). (Illus.). 216p. 1995. 44.00 (*0-8039-4756-9*) Sage.
Borg, Jim. Tigers of the Sea: Hawaii's Deadly Sharks. 88p. 1993. pap. 12.95 (*1-56647-048-X*) Mutual Pub HI.
Borg, John. Descriptive Flora of the Maltese Islands Including the Ferns & Flowering Plants: Flora of the World II. (Illus.). 846p. 1976. reprint ed. 115.00 (*3-87429-104-9*, 001705, Pub. by Koeltz Sci Bks) Lubrecht & Cramer.
Borg, Kirsten E. The Place I Call Home: What's Wrong with U. S. & What We Can Do about It. (Illus.). 209p. 1987. 9.00 (*0-9617604-0-0*) Dragon Tree IA.
Borg, Malcolm. International Transfers of Managers in Multinational Corporations. (Acta Upsaliensis Oecon. Negotorum Ser.: No. 27). 141p. (Orig.). 1988. pap. 35.50 (*91-554-2136-9*, Pub. by Uppsala Univ Acta Univ Uppsaliensis) Coronet Bks.
Borg, Marcus, et al, eds. The Lost Gospel Q: The Original Sayings of Jesus. 2nd ed. (Illus.). 128p. 1999. pap. 11.95 (*1-56975-189-7*) Ulysses Pr.
Borg, Marcus & Powelson, Mark, eds. The Lost Gospel Q: The Original Sayings of Jesus. Riegert, Ray, tr. 128p. 1996. 15.00 (*1-56975-100-5*) Ulysses Pr.
Borg, Marcus & Riegert, Ray, eds. Jesus & Buddha: The Parallel Sayings. LC 97-9423. 272p. 1997. 19.95 (*1-56975-121-8*) Ulysses Pr.
— Jesus & Buddha: The Parallel Sayings. LC 98-52095. 272p. 1999. reprint ed. pap. 14.00 (*1-56975-169-2*) Ulysses Pr.
Borg, Marcus J. Conflict, Holiness & Politics in the Teachings of Jesus. LC 84-9029. (Studies in the Bible & Early Christianity: Vol. 5). 397p. 1984. lib. bdg. 99.95 (*0-88946-603-3*) E Mellen.
— Conflict, Holiness, & Politics in the Teachings of Jesus. LC 98-22816. 304p. 1998. pap. 23.00 (*1-56338-227-X*) TPI PA.
— The God We Never Knew: Beyond Dogmatic Religion to a More Authentic Contemporary Faith. LC 96-52871. 192p. 1998. pap. 12.00 (*0-06-061035-2*, Pub. by Harper SF) HarpC.
— The God We Never Knew: Beyond Dogmatic Religion to a More Authentic Faith. 1997. 18.00 (*0-614-27507-5*) Harper SF.
— Jesus: A New Vision: Spirit, Culture, & the Life of Discipleship. LC 91-55090. 224p. 1991. reprint ed. pap. 15.00 (*0-06-060814-5*, Pub. by Harper SF) HarpC.
— Jesus in Contemporary Scholarship. LC 94-18255. 224p. (C). 1994. pap. 18.00 (*1-56338-094-3*) TPI PA.
— Meeting Jesus Again for the First Time: The Historical Jesus & the Heart of Contemporary Faith. LC 93-25390. 160p. 1995. pap. 12.00 (*0-06-060917-6*, Pub. by Harper SF) HarpC.
Borg, Marcus J., ed. Jesus at 2000. 192p. (C). 1998. pap. text 16.00 (*0-8133-3253-2*, Pub. by Westview) HarpC.
***Borg, Marcus J. & Mackenzie, Ross, eds.** God at 2000. 160p. 2000. 20.00 (*0-8192-1858-8*) Morehouse Pub.
Borg, Marcus J. & Wright, N. T. The Meaning of Jesus: Two Visions. LC 98-30672. 304p. 1999. 24.00 (*0-06-060875-7*, Pub. by Harper SF) HarpC.
— Meaning of Jesus: Two Visions. LC 98-30672. 304p. 2000. pap. 15.00 (*0-06-060876-5*, Pub. by Harper SF) HarpC.
Borg-Marks, Clifford, jt. auth. see Khoon, Tan L.
Borg, Mary. Writing Your Life: An Easy-to-Follow Guide to Writing an Autobiography. 3rd rev. ed. LC 98-193324. (Illus.). 160p. 1998. pap. text 18.95 (*1-877673-07-2*, WLA) Cottonwood Pr.
— Writing Your Life: Autobiographical Writing Activities for Young People. rev. ed. 60p. (YA). (gr. 5-12). 1998. pap. text 14.95 (*1-877673-09-9*, WLT) Cottonwood Pr.
***Borg, Mary G. & Virden, William.** Go to the Source: Discovering 20th Century U. S. History Through Colorado Documents. (Illus.). 144p. 2000. pap. 29.95 (*1-877673-44-7*) Cottonwood Pr.
Borg, Mary O., et al. The Economic Consequences of State Lotteries. LC 90-27434. 160p. 1991. 47.95 (*0-275-93570-1*, C3570, Praeger Pubs) Greenwood.
Borg, Nicholas & David, Leonard. Arson: A Multi-Dimensional Problem. 1976. 2.50 (*0-686-17606-5*, TR 76-4) Society Fire Protect.
Borg, Quentin & McNally, JoLouise. When Life Went Hectic: The Incredible Journey of Quentin Borg a True Story. (Illus.). 208p. (Orig.). 1996. pap. 10.00 (*0-9652309-0-2*) Crex Land.
Borg, R. Sun Wars. 1992. 15.00 (*1-56076-394-9*) Random.
Borg, Richard J. & Dienes, G. J. An Introduction to Solid State Diffusion. 360p. 1988. text 81.00 (*0-12-118425-0*) Acad Pr.
— The Physical Chemistry of Solids. (Illus.). 584p. (C). 1991. text 59.00 (*0-12-118420-X*) Acad Pr.
Borg, Robert, ed. Together We Pray: General Intercessions for Sundays, Solemnities, Feasts, & Other Celebrations. 260p. (Orig.). 1993. pap. text 39.95 (*0-8146-2266-6*) Liturgical Pr.
Borg, S. F. Fundamentals of Engineering: Elasticity. 308p. 1990. text 55.00 (*981-02-0164-8*); pap. text 32.00 (*981-02-0165-6*) World Scientific Pub.
— Matrix-Tensor Methods in Continuum Mechanics. rev. ed. 356p. (C). 1990. text 71.00 (*981-02-0166-4*); pap. text 37.00 (*981-02-0167-2*) World Scientific Pub.
Borg, S. F., ed. Earthquake Engineering: Mechanisms, Damage Assessment & Structural Design. 348p. (C). 1988. text 81.00 (*9971-5-0435-9*) World Scientific Pub.
Borg, Sidney F. Earthquake Engineering: Damage Assessment & Structural Design. LC 83-1304. (Wiley Series in Methods & Applications in Civil Engineering). 124p. reprint ed. pap. 38.50 (*0-608-15890-9*, 203078400074) Bks Demand.
Borg, Sonia, jt. auth. see Maris, Hyllus.
Borg, Susan, jt. auth. see Lasker, Judith.
Borg, Susan O., jt. auth. see Lasker, Judith N.
Borg, Tom. Service Factor: Leveraging Customer Satisfaction in Small Business. 1991. pap. 7.50 (*0-9631663-0-1*) W & A Pub.
Borg, Veronique. The Next Balcony Down. (Child's World Library). (Illus.). 32p. (J). (gr. k-5). 1992. lib. bdg. 18.50 (*0-89565-757-0*) Childs World.
Borg, Walter R. & Gall, Meredith D. Educational Research. 5th ed. 944p. (C). 1989. text 53.95 (*0-8013-0334-5*, 78109) Longman.
Borg, Walter R., et al. Applying Educational Research: A Practical Guide for Teachers. 3rd ed. LC 92-20899. 464p. (C). 1993. text 66.56 (*0-8013-0486-5*, 78319) Longman.
Borgaonkar, Digamber S. Chromosomal Variation in Man: A Catalog of Chromosomal Variants & Anomalies. 8th ed. LC 97-37684. 1175p. 1997. 200.00 (*0-471-24232-9*, Wiley-Liss) Wiley.
Borgard, Conard M. From COOS to Korea. Borgard, Douglas, ed. LC 98-90009. (Illus.). vi, 137p. 1998. pap. 12.95 (*0-9662537-0-1*) White Cedar.
Borgard, Douglas, ed. see Borgard, Conard M.
***Borgardt, Marianne.** My Funny Faces. (Illus.). 12p. (J). 1999. 5.95 (*1-892374-17-X*) Weldon Owen.
— Peekaboo You! (Illus.). 12p. (J). 1999. reprint ed. 5.95 (*1-892374-15-3*) Weldon Owen.
Borgardt, Marianne. What Do You Do with a Potty? An Important Pop-Up Book. (Illus.). 10p. (J). 1994. 7.95 (*0-307-17610-X*, 17610) Gldn Bks Pub Co.
***Borgardt, Marianne.** Yellow at Home: A Counting Book of Yellow. (Gymboree Colorblock Ser.). (Illus.). 20p. (J). 1999. reprint ed. 4.95 (*1-892374-11-0*) Weldon Owen.
Borgatta, Edgar F., ed. Encyclopedia of Sociology, Vol. 1. 1991. 100.00 (*0-02-897052-7*) Mac Lib Ref.
— Encyclopedia of Sociology, Vol. 2. 1991. 100.00 (*0-02-897053-5*) Mac Lib Ref.
— Encyclopedia of Sociology, Vol. 3. 1991. 100.00 (*0-02-897055-1*) Mac Lib Ref.
— Encyclopedia of Sociology, Vol. 4. 1991. 100.00 (*0-02-897056-X*) Mac Lib Ref.
— Sociological Methodology, 1970. LC 68-54940. (Jossey-Bass Behavioral Science Ser.). 352p. reprint ed. pap. 109.20 (*0-8357-4969-X*, 203790200009) Bks Demand.
Borgatta, Edgar F. & Cook, Karen S., eds. The Future of Sociology. 480p. (C). 1988. text 45.00 (*0-8039-3024-0*) Sage.
— The Future of Sociology. LC 88-10898. 424p. 1988. reprint ed. pap. 131.50 (*0-608-02794-4*, 206386100007) Bks Demand.
Borgatta, Edgar F., et al. Social Workers' Perceptions of Clients: A Study of the Caseload of a Social Agency. LC 80-27204. 92p. 1981. reprint ed. lib. bdg. 59.75 (*0-313-22812-4*, BOSW, Greenwood Pr) Greenwood.
Borgatta, Edgar J. & Montgomery. Encyclopedia of Sociology, 1. 2nd ed. 1999. 110.00 (*0-02-864849-8*) S&S Trade.
— Encyclopedia of Sociology, 2. 2nd ed. 1999. 110.00 (*0-02-864850-1*) S&S Trade.
— Encyclopedia of Sociology, 3. 2nd ed. 1999. 110.00 (*0-02-864851-X*) S&S Trade.
— Encyclopedia of Sociology, 4. 2nd ed. 1999. 110.00 (*0-02-864852-8*) S&S Trade.
Borgatta, Montgomery. Encyclopedia of Sociology. 2nd ed. 1999. 375.00 (*0-02-864853-6*) Macmillan.
Borgatti, Jean M. & Brilliant, Richard. Likeness & Beyond: Portraits from Africa & the World. LC 90-1354. (Illus.). 1990. 53.50 (*0-945802-05-6*); pap. 27.50 (*0-945802-06-4*) Museum African.
***Borge, Brenton P.** A Chorus of Magical Litabies. 96p. 2000. pap. 8.95 (*1-56167-530-X*) Am Literary Pr.
***Borge, Dan.** The Book of Risk. (Wiley Investment Classics Ser.: Vol. 67). 224p. 2001. 27.95 (*0-471-32378-0*) Wiley.
Borge, Tomas. Carlos, the Dawn Is No Longer Beyond Our Reach. Randall, Margaret, tr. from SPA. (Illus.). 96p. (C). 1984. pap. 2.00 (*0-919573-25-8*) Left Bank.
— Christianity & Revolution: Tomas Borge's Theology of Life. Reding, Andrew, ed. LC 86-23788. 176p. reprint ed. pap. 54.60 (*0-8357-2688-6*, 204022400015) Bks Demand.
— Un Grano de Maiz (A Grain of Corn) Conversacion Con Fidel Castro (Conversation with Fidel Castro) (SPA.). 275p. 1992. pap. 13.99 (*968-16-3918-9*, Pub. by Fondo) Continental Bk.
— Have You Seen a Red Curtain in My Weary Chamber? Bartley, Russell et al, trs. LC 88-43573. 160p. (Orig.). 1989. pap. 9.95 (*0-915306-81-6*) Curbstone.
— The Patient Impatience. Bartley, Russell et al, trs. LC 91-55410. 452p. (Orig.). 1992. 24.95 (*0-915306-97-2*) Curbstone.
— Women & the Nicaraguan Revolution. 30p. 1982. pap. 2.50 (*0-87348-475-4*) Pathfinder NY.
Borge, Tomas, et al. Nicaragua: The Sandinista People's Revolution. LC 85-61096. (Illus.). 412p. (C). 1985. pap. 21.95 (*0-87348-653-6*); lib. bdg. 60.00 (*0-87348-652-8*) Pathfinder NY.
— Sandinistas Speak: Speeches & Writings of Nicaragua's Leaders. LC 82-82051. 160p. 1986. reprint ed. pap. 13.95 (*0-87348-619-6*) Pathfinder NY.
Borge, Tomas, jt. auth. see Castro, Fidel.
***Borgeas, Ted.** Love Virus: Why We Jump from Youthful Purpose to Mature Confusion. 100p. 2000. spiral bd. 9.95 (*0-9666110-3-9*) Age-Trott.
Borgeas, Ted. Outrageous... At Any Age: Personal Coaching Yourself! 105p. 1999. 15.95 (*0-9666110-4-7*) Age-Trott.
— Real People Ain't Sweatin' Anti-Aging & Longevity. large type ed. LC 98-93810. (Real People Ain't Ser.). 1998. spiral bd. 15.95 (*0-9666110-6-3*) Age-Trott.
— Real People Ain't Sweatin' Creative Cooking. large type ed. (Real People Ain't Sweatin' Ser.). 85p. 1998. spiral bd. 15.95 (*0-9666110-5-5*) Age-Trott.
Borgeaud, Charles. Adoption & Amendment of Constitutions in Europe & America. Hazen, Charles D., tr. from SPA. xxi, 353p. 1989. reprint ed. 47.50 (*0-8377-1950-X*, Rothman) W S Hein.
Borgeaud, Philippe. The Cult of Pan in Ancient Greece. Atlass, Kathleen & Redfield, James, trs. (Illus.). 312p. 1994. pap. text 16.95 (*0-226-06596-0*) U Ch Pr.
— The Cult of Pan in Ancient Greece. Atlass, Kathleen & Redfield, James, trs. (Illus.). 296p. 1999. lib. bdg. 51.00 (*0-226-06595-2*) U Ch Pr.
Borgefors, G., ed. Theory & Applications of Image Analysis II: Selected Papers from the 9th Scandinavian Conference on Image Analysis. 400p. 1995. text 72.00 (*981-02-2448-6*, REe-BR2920) World Scientific Pub.
Borgehammar, Stephan. How the Holy Cross Was Found: From Event to Medieval Legend (With an Appendix of Texts) (Bibliotheca Theologiae Practicae Kyrkov Studier Ser.: No. 47). 326p. (Orig.). 1991. pap. 59.50 (*91-22-01432-2*) Coronet Bks.
Borgen, Johan. Lillelord. Moen, Elizabeth B. & Peterson, Ronald E., trs. from NOR. LC 81-14216. 384p. 1982. 16.00 (*0-8112-0826-5*, Pub. by New Directions); pap. 7.95 (*0-8112-0827-3*, NDP531, Pub. by New Directions) Norton.
— Lillelord. 1994. pap. 11.95 (*0-7145-3879-5*) Riverrun NY.
— The Scapegoat. Rokkan, Elizabeth, tr. from NOR. 187p. 1994. pap. 23.00 (*1-870041-21-6*, Pub. by Norvik Pr) Dufour.
Borgen, Ole E. John Wesley on the Sacraments. 312p. 1986. pap. 15.95 (*0-310-75191-8*, 17085P) Zondervan.
Borgen, Patrick I. & Hill, Arnold. Breast Cancer. 2000. spiral bd. 45.00 (*1-57059-578-X*) Landes Bioscience.
Borgen, Peder. Early Christianity & Hellenistic Judaism. 416p. 1996. text 54.95 (*0-567-08501-5*, Pub. by T & T Clark) Bks Intl VA.
— Early Christianity & Hellenistic Judaism. 388p. 1998. pap. 34.95 (*0-567-08626-7*, Pub. by T & T Clark) Bks Intl VA.
— Philo of Alexandria: An Exegete for His Time. LC 97-29997. (Novum Testamentum, Supplements Ser.: No. 86). x, 322p. 1997. 112.50 (*90-04-10388-0*) Brill Academic Pubs.
Borgen, Peder & Giversen, Soren, eds. The New Testament & Hellenistic Judaism. 300p. (Orig.). (C). 1995. 39.00 (*87-7288-458-4*, Pub. by Aarhus Univ Pr) David Brown.
— The New Testament & Hellenistic Judaism. LC 96-52508. 294p. (Orig.). 1997. pap. 24.95 (*1-56563-261-3*) Hendrickson MA.
***Borgen, Peder, et al.** The Philo Index. LC 99-46459. (GRE & ENG.). 1999. pap. write for info. (*0-8028-4681-5*) Eerdmans.
— The Philo Index: A Complete Greek Word Index to the Writings of Philo of Alexandria. 384p. 1999. 55.00 (*90-04-11477-7*) Brill Academic Pubs.
— The Philo Index: A Complete Greek Word Index to the Writings of Philo of Alexandria. LC 99-58967. 383p. 2000. 55.00 (*0-8028-3883-9*) Eerdmans.
Borgen, Robert. Sugawara No Michizane & the Early Heian Court. LC 93-36993. (Illus.). 456p. (C). 1994. reprint ed. pap. text 20.00 (*0-8248-1590-4*) UH Pr.
Borgen, William A., jt. ed. see Young, Richard A.
***Borgenicht, David.** The Jewish Mother Goose. (Illus.). 96p. (J). 2000. 12.95 (*0-7624-0675-5*) Running Pr.
Borgenicht, David. The Little Book of Stupid Questions: 300 Hilarious, Bold, Embarrassing, Personal & Basically Pointless Queries. 1999. pap. 7.95 (*1-887166-50-5*, Hysteria Pubns) Sourcebks.
***Borgenicht, David.** Sesame Street Unpaved: Scripts, Stories, Secrets, & Songs. LC 98-6391. (Illus.). 193p. (YA). (gr. 5 up). 1998. 24.95 (*0-7868-6460-5*, Pub. by Hyperion) Time Warner.
Borgenicht, Miriam. Booked for Death. 1989. mass mkt. 3.50 (*0-373-26038-5*) Harlequin Bks.
— No Bail for Dalton. LC 73-10705. (Black Bat Mystery Ser). 192p. 1974. 5.95 (*0-672-51881-3*, Bobbs) Macmillan.

B

— No Duress. (Worldwide Library Mysteries). 1992. per. 3.99 (*0-373-26105-5*, 1-26105-6) Harlequin Bks.
— Undue Influence. 1990. per. 3.50 (*0-373-26062-8*) Harlequin Bks.
Borger, E., ed. Computability, Complexity, Logic. (Studies in Logic & the Foundations of Mathematics: No. 128). xx,592p. 1989. 173.00 (*0-444-87406-2*, North Holland) Elsevier.
— Computation Theory & Logic. (Lecture Notes in Computer Science Ser.: Vol. 270). ix, 442p. 1987. 49.00 (*0-387-18170-9*) Spr-Verlag.
Borger, E., et al, eds. Computer Science Logic: Fifth Workshop, CSL '91, Berne, Switzerland, October 1991: Proceedings. LC 92-23683. (Lecture Notes in Computer Science Ser.: Vol. 626). viii, 428p. 1992. 63.95 (*0-387-55789-X*) Spr-Verlag.
— Computer Science Logic: Fourth Workshop, CSL '90 Heidelberg, Germany, October 1-5, 1990 Proceedings. (Lecture Notes in Computer Science Ser.: Vol. 533). viii, 399p. 1991. 44.95 (*0-387-54487-9*) Spr-Verlag.
— Computer Science Logic: Selected Papers of the 6th Workshop, CSL 92, San Miniato, Italy, September 28-October 2, 1992. (Lecture Notes in Computer Science Ser.: Vol. 702). viii, 439p. 1993. 61.95 (*0-387-56992-8*) Spr-Verlag.
— CSL 'Eighty-Eight. (Lecture Notes in Computer Science Ser.: Vol. 385). vi, 399p. 1989. 47.00 (*0-387-51659-X*, 3505) Spr-Verlag.
— CSL 'Eighty-Nine: Third Workshop on Computer Science Logic Kaiserslautern, FRG, October 2-6, 1989 Proceedings. (Lecture Notes in Computer Science Ser.: Vol. 440). vi, 437p. 1990. 43.00 (*0-387-52753-2*) Spr-Verlag.
— CSL 1987. (Lecture Notes in Computer Science Ser.: Vol. 329). vi, 346p. 1988. 39.00 (*0-387-50241-6*) Spr-Verlag.
— Logic & Machines-Decision Problems & Complexity: Proceedings of the Symposium "Rekursive Kombinatorik" Held from May 23-28, 1983 at the Institut fur Mathematische Logik und Grundlagenfroschung der Universitat Munster-Westfalen. (Lecture Notes in Computer Science Ser.: Vol. 171). vi, 456p. 1984. pap. 27.50 (*0-685-08952-5*, 13331-3) Spr-Verlag.
Borger, Egon. Architecture Design & Validation Methods. 1998. 59.95 (*3-540-64976-X*) Spr-Verlag.
Borger, Egon, ed. Specification & Validation Methods. (International Schools for Computer Scientists Ser.). (Illus.). 470p. 1995. text 115.00 (*0-19-853854-5*) OUP.
Borger, Egon, et al, eds. Computer Science Logic: Seventh Workshop, CSL '93, Swansea, United Kingdom, September 13-17, 1993, Selected Papers. LC 94-28234. (Lecture Notes in Computer Science Ser.: Vol. 832). 1994. 50.95 (*0-387-58277-0*) Spr-Verlag.
Borger, Gary A. Designing Trout Flies. LC 90-71770. (Illus.). 224p. 1991. 16.95 (*0-9628392-1-3*) Tomorrow Riv Pr.
— Designing Trout Flies. limited ed. LC 90-71770. (Illus.). 224p. 1991. 125.00 (*0-9628392-2-1*) Tomorrow Riv Pr.
— Naturals: A Guide to Food Organisms of the Trout. LC 79-23099. 224p. 1980. 19.95 (*0-8117-1006-8*) Stackpole.
— Nymphing: A Basic Book. LC 78-11358. (Illus.). 192p. 1979. 18.95 (*0-8117-1010-6*) Stackpole.
— Presentation. (Illus.). 320p. 1995. 34.95 (*0-9628392-5-6*) Tomorrow Riv Pr.
— Presentation. deluxe limited ed. (Illus.). 320p. 1995. 250.00 (*0-9628392-6-4*) Tomorrow Riv Pr.
Borger, Irene, ed. From a Burning House: The AIDS Project Los Angeles Writers Workshop Collection. 1996. pap. 14.00 (*0-614-97818-1*, WSP) PB.
— From a Burning House: The AIDS Project Los Angeles Writers Workshop Collection. 224p. 1996. pap. 14.00 (*0-671-53517-X*) S&S Trade.
Borger, Judy. Cat. LC 96-67591. (Illus.). 28p. (Orig.). (J). (gr. k-4). 1996. pap. 4.95 (*0-9642086-8-7*) Popular Press.
— Go, Vol. 25. LC 97-75430. (Illus.). 32p. (J). (gr. k-4). 1998. pap. 4.95 (*0-9642086-7-9*) Popular Press.
— Pop. LC 94-74040. (Illus.). 32p. (Orig.). (J). (gr. k-3). 1995. pap. 4.95 (*0-9642086-9-5*) Popular Press.
Borger, Mona M. Chinas, Dolls for Study & Admiration. LC 83-91074. (Illus.). 160p. 1983. 21.95 (*0-9611838-0-2*) Borger Pubns.
Borger, Rykle. Handbuch der Keilschriftliteratur, Vol. 1: Repertorium. (C). 1977. 86.95 (*3-11-000125-X*) De Gruyter.
— Handbuch der Keilschriftliteratur, Vol. 2: Anhang-Zur Kuyunjick-Sammlung. (GER.). xxxii, 395p. (C). 1975. 76.15 (*3-11-005960-6*) De Gruyter.
— Handbuch der Keilschriftliteratur, Vol. 3: Inhaltliche Ordnung der sumerischen und akkadischen Texte. (GER.). viii, 168p. (C). 1975. 46.95 (*3-11-002487-X*) De Gruyter.
Borgerhoff, Cornelia N., tr. see Maritain, Jacques.
Borgers, Bill & Thompson, Tommy A. Implementing Continuous Improvement Management (CIM) in the Schools. LC 93-31779. 1995. 29.95 (*0-590-49502-X*, 2805b66 1994) Scholastic Inc.
Borgers, M., et al, eds. Current Topics in Medical Mycology, Vol. 4. (Illus.). xi, 274p. 1991. 190.00 (*0-387-97504-7*) Spr-Verlag.
Borgers, M., jt. ed. see McGinnis, Michael R.
Borges, Albert F. Elective Incisions & Scar Revision. 1973. 55.00 (*0-316-10269-5*, Little Brwn Med Div) Lppncott W & W.
***Borges, Carlos R.** Elementary Topology & Applications. LC 00-24152. 2000. write for info. (*981-02-4240-9*) World Scientific Pub.
Borges, Carole. Disciplining the Devil's Country. LC 87-72607. 72p. (Orig.). 1988. 6.95 (*0-914086-76-6*); pap. 9.95 (*0-914086-77-4*) Alice James Bks.
Borges, Charles J., ed. Goa & Portugal: Their Cultural Links. LC 98-903084. (XCHR Studies: No. 7). (C). 1997. 36.00 (*81-7022-659-7*, Pub. by Concept) S Asia.
Borges, Dain. The Family in Bahia, Brazil, 1870-1945. 440p. (C). 1992. 55.00 (*0-8047-1921-7*) Stanford U Pr.
Borges, Dain, ed. see Machado de Assis, Joaquim Maria.
Borges, Dibio L. & Kaestner, Celso A. Advances in Artificial Intelligence: 13th Brazilian Symposium on Artificial Intelligence, SBIA '96, Curitiba, Brazil, October 23-25, 1996 Proceedings. LC 96-41957. (Lecture Notes in Artificial Intelligence Ser.: Vol. 1159). 243p. 1996. text 49.00 (*3-540-94900-3*) Spr-Verlag.
Borges, Jorge Luis. El Aleph. (SPA.). pap. 15.95 (*84-206-1309-6*, Pub. by Alianza Editorial) Continental Bk.
— El Aleph. (SPA.). 10.95 (*0-8288-2555-6*, S662) Fr & Eur.
— El Aleph. (SPA.). 184p. 1991. pap. 9.95 (*0-7859-4971-2*) Fr & Eur.
***Borges, Jorge Luis.** El Aleph. 17th ed. (SPA.). 1998. pap. 11.95 (*84-206-3311-9*) Alianza Editorial.
Borges, Jorge Luis. Antiguas Literaturas Germanicas. (Breviarios Ser.). (SPA.). pap. 7.99 (*968-16-1092-X*, Pub. by Fondo) Continental Bk.
— Antologia Poetica. (SPA.). pap. 16.95 (*84-206-1805-5*, Pub. by Alianza Editorial) Continental Bk.
***Borges, Jorge Luis.** Antologia Poetica, 1923-1977. 10th ed. (SPA.). 1999. pap. 11.95 (*84-206-3318-6*) Alianza Editorial.
Borges, Jorge Luis. Borges el Memorioso (Borges, Remembrance) (SPA.). 313p. 1997. reprint ed. pap. 14.99 (*968-16-2524-2*, Pub. by Fondo) Continental Bk.
— Borges On Writing. Di Giovanni, Norman T. et al, eds. 1994. pap. 12.00 (*0-88001-368-0*) HarpC.
***Borges, Jorge Luis.** Borges Poems, Vol. 2. 2000. pap. 17.95 (*0-14-058721-7*, Penguin Bks) Viking Penguin.
— Collected Fictions Bk. 3. Hurley, Andrew, tr. 576p. 1999. pap. 16.95 (*0-14-028680-2*, Penguin Bks) Viking Penguin.
Borges, Jorge Luis. Collected Fictions Bk. 3, 3. Hurley, Andrew, tr. from SPA. LC 98-21217. 565p. 1998. 40.00 (*0-670-84970-7*, Viking) Viking Penguin.
— A Concordance to the Works of Jorge Luis Borges, Argentine Author, 1899-1986. Standish, Peter, ed. LC 91-45038. 452p. 1992. lib. bdg. 109.95 (*0-7734-9628-9*) E Mellen.
***Borges, Jorge Luis.** Cuentos Latinoamericanos: Antologia. (SPA.). 134p. 1999. pap. 11.50 (*958-24-0061-7*) Santillana.
Borges, Jorge Luis. Dreamtigers. Boyer, Mildred & Morland, Harold, trs. from SPA. LC 63-17614. (Texas Pan American Ser.). Orig. Title: El hacedor. (Illus.). 96p. 1985. pap. 9.95 (*0-292-71549-8*) U of Tex Pr.
— Espejo de Escritores. Roffe, Reina, ed. (SPA.). 222p. 1985. pap. 12.50 (*0-910061-23-8*, 1504) Ediciones Norte.
— Everything & Nothing. Yates, Donald A. et al, trs. from SPA. LC 98-54217. (New Directions Bibelot Ser.). 108p. 1999. pap. 7.50 (*0-8112-1400-1*, NDP872, Pub. by New Directions) Norton.
— Ficcionario (Fictionary) Antologia de Sus Textos (Anthology of His Texts) (SPA.). 483p. 1985. pap. 21.99 (*968-16-2028-3*, Pub. by Fondo) Continental Bk.
— Ficciones. (SPA.). pap. 15.95 (*84-206-3312-7*, Pub. by Alianza Editorial); pap. 15.95 (*84-206-1320-7*, Pub. by Alianza Editorial) Continental Bk.
— Ficciones. (SPA.). 9.95 (*0-8288-2556-4*, S4) Fr & Eur.
— Ficciones. 208p. 1991. pap. 10.95 (*0-7859-5175-X*) Fr & Eur.
— Fictions. LC 92-55353.Tr. of Ficciones. 1993. 15.00 (*0-679-42299-4*) Everymns Lib.
— Fictions.Tr. of Ficciones. (FRE.). 192p. 1974. pap. 10.95 (*0-7859-1791-8*, 2070366146) Fr & Eur.
— Fictions. Kerrigan, Anthony, ed. & intro. by.Tr. of Ficciones. 1991. pap. 8.95 (*0-7145-4083-8*) Riverrun NY.
— Hacedor. (SPA.). 158p. 1981. 10.00 (*0-8288-8559-1*) Fr & Eur.
***Borges, Jorge Luis.** Historia de la Eternidad. 15th ed. (SPA.). 1999. pap. 12.95 (*84-206-1338-X*) Alianza Editorial.
— Historia Universal de la Infamia. 14th ed. (SPA.). 1999. pap. 12.75 (*84-206-3314-3*) Alianza Editorial.
Borges, Jorge Luis. El Informe de Brodie. (SPA.). pap. 12.95 (*84-206-1499-8*, Pub. by Alianza Editorial) Continental Bk.
***Borges, Jorge Luis.** El Informe de Brodie. 12th ed. (SPA.). 1999. pap. 10.95 (*84-206-3332-1*) Alianza Editorial.
— An Introduction to American Literature. Keating, Louis Clark et al, eds. LC 73-147854. 107p. reprint ed. pap. 33.20 (*0-608-17705-9*, 203004900067) Bks Demand.
Borges, Jorge Luis. Jorge Luis Borges: Conversations. Burgin, Richard, ed. LC 98-36711. (Literary Conversations Ser.). 256p. 1998. text 45.00 (*1-57806-075-3*) U Pr of Miss.
***Borges, Jorge Luis.** Jorge Luis Borges: Ficciones. Botherston, G. & Hulme, P., eds. (Modern Language Ser.). (SPA.). 324p. 1999. pap. text 20.95 (*1-85399-590-8*, Pub. by Brist Class Pr) Focus Pub-R Pullins.
Borges, Jorge Luis. Labyrinths, Selected Stories & Other Writings. Yates, Donald A. & Irby, James E., eds. LC 64-25440. 1964. reprint ed. pap. 11.95 (*0-8112-0012-4*, NDP186, Pub. by New Directions) Norton.
***Borges, Jorge Luis.** The Library of Babel. Hurley, Andrew, tr. from SPA. (Pocket Paragon Ser.). (Illus.). 36p. 2000. 20.00 (*1-56792-123-X*) Godine.
Borges, Jorge Luis. Libro de Arena. (SPA.). pap. 15.95 (*84-206-3313-5*, Pub. by Alianza Editorial) Continental Bk.
— El Libro de Arena. 2nd ed. (SPA.). 128p. 1991. pap. 6.95 (*0-7859-4974-7*) Fr & Eur.
— El Libro de la Arena. (SPA.). pap. 15.95 (*84-206-1662-1*, Pub. by Alianza Editorial) Continental Bk.
— Livre de Prefaces Suivi d'Essai d'Autobiographique. (FRE.). 337p. 1987. pap. 11.95 (*0-7859-2057-9*, 2070377946) Fr & Eur.
— Le Livre de Sable. (FRE.). 1983. pap. 10.95 (*0-7859-1973-2*, 2070374610) Fr & Eur.
— Luis Tlon, Uqbar, Orbis Tertius. 78p. 1983. pap. write for info. (*0-88984-072-5*) Porcup Quill.
— Narraciones. Barnatan, Marcos Ricardo, ed. (SPA.). pap. 13.95 (*84-376-0235-1*, Pub. by Ediciones Catedra) Continental Bk.
— Narraciones. 6th ed. (SPA.). 256p. 1988. pap. write for info. (*0-7859-4973-9*) Fr & Eur.
— Obra Poetica. (SPA.). pap. 17.50 (*84-206-3048-9*, Pub. by Alianza Editorial) Continental Bk.
— Obra Poetica, 1923-1967. 6th ed. (SPA.). 560p. 1990. pap. 49.95 (*0-7859-4972-0*) Fr & Eur.
— Other Inquisitions, 1937-1952. Simms, Ruth L., tr. from SPA. (Texas Pan American Ser.). 223p. 1964. pap. 14.95 (*0-292-76002-7*) U of Tex Pr.
— Otras Inquisiciones. (SPA.). pap. 13.95 (*84-206-1604-4*, Pub. by Alianza Editorial) Continental Bk.
Borges, Jorge Luis. A Personal Anthology. LC 67-29764. 224p. 1968. pap. 12.00 (*0-8021-3077-1*, Grove) Grove-Atltic.
Borges, Jorge Luis. Qu'Est-Ce Que le Bouddhisme. (FRE.). 122p. 1979. pap. 10.95 (*0-7859-1682-2*, 2070354040) Fr & Eur.
— Le Rapport de Brodie. (FRE.). 160p. 1984. pap. 10.95 (*0-7859-1999-6*, 2070375889) Fr & Eur.
***Borges, Jorge Luis.** Secret Books. 1999. pap. 35.00 (*0-918172-21-7*) Leetes Isl.
— Selected Non-Fictions. 576p. 2000. pap. 17.00 (*0-14-029011-7*) Penguin Putnam.
Borges, Jorge Luis. Selected Non-Fictions. Weinberger, Eliot, ed. Allen, Esther et al, trs. from SPA. LC 99-12386. 516p. 1999. 40.00 (*0-670-84947-2*, Viking) Viking Penguin.
— Selected Poems Bk. 2. Coleman, Andrew, ed. LC 99-10318. 480p. 1999. 40.00 (*0-670-84941-3*, Viking) Viking Penguin.
— Seven Nights. Weinberger, Eliot, tr. from SPA. LC 84-1018. Orig. Title: Siete Noches. 128p. 1984. pap. 8.95 (*0-8112-0905-9*, NDP576, Pub. by New Directions) Norton.
— Siete Noches (Seven Nights) (SPA.). 173p. 1980. pap. 9.99 (*968-16-0607-8*, Pub. by Fondo) Continental Bk.
***Borges, Jorge Luis.** This Craft of Verse. 160p. 2000. 22.95 (*0-674-00290-3*) HUP.
Borges, Jorge Luis. Tiempo Falto. 44p. 1989. pap. 7.95 (*0-912159-02-2*) Center Pr CA.
Borges, Jorge Luis, et al. Dante Studies Vol. I: Dante in the Twentieth Century. deluxe limited ed. Caso, A., ed. 1982. 50.00 (*0-937832-17-0*) Dante U Am.
— Dante Studies Vol. I: Dante in the Twentieth Century, Vol. I. Caso, A., ed. 1982. 25.95 (*0-937832-16-2*) Dante U Am.
— Quarterly Review of Literature: The 1960s, Prose, Vol. XV, Nos. 3-4. 1960. pap. 10.00 (*1-888545-33-X*) Quarterly Rev.
***Borges, Luz.** Debt of Love. (Encanto Ser.). 384p. 2000. mass mkt. 5.99 (*0-7860-1119-X*, Pinncle Kensgtn) Kensgtn Pub Corp.
Borges, Phil, photos by. Enduring Spirit. LC 98-7764. (Illus.). 128p. 1998. 30.00 (*0-8478-2142-0*, Pub. by Rizzoli Intl) St Martin.
— Tibetan Portrait: The Power of Compassion. LC 95-49939. (Illus.). 96p. 1996. 27.50 (*0-8478-1957-4*, Pub. by Rizzoli Intl) St Martin.
Borges, Renato, ed. see Maciel, Jairo.
Borges, Sharon E. Poems to Ease the Spirit. 195p. pap. 15.00 (*0-9648658-0-7*) S Borges.
Borgese, Elisabeth. The Oceanic Circle. LC 98-40090. 1998. write for info. (*92-808-1013-8*); pap. 19.95 (*92-808-1028-6*) Brookings.
***Borgese, Elisabeth M.** Ocean Yearbook, Vol. 15. (Illus.). 1999. lib. bdg. 77.00 (*0-226-06618-5*) U Ch Pr.
Borgese, Elisabeth M., et al, eds. Ocean Yearbook, 11. 692p. 1995. lib. bdg. 77.00 (*0-226-06614-2*) U Ch Pr.
— Ocean Yearbook, No. 8. LC 79-642855. 702p. 1990. lib. bdg. 78.00 (*0-226-06611-8*) U Ch Pr.
— Ocean Yearbook, No. 9. 544p. 1992. lib. bdg. 78.00 (*0-226-06612-6*) U Ch Pr.
— Ocean Yearbook, Vol. 10. 568p. (C). 1993. lib. bdg. 64.95 (*0-226-06613-4*) U Ch Pr.
Borgese, Elisabeth M. & Ginsburg, Norton S. Ocean Yearbook, No. 3. LC 79-642855. 598p. 1982. lib. bdg. 59.00 (*0-226-06604-5*) U Ch Pr.
Borgese, Elisabeth M. & Ginsburg, Norton S., eds. Ocean Yearbook, No. 2. LC 79-642855. 724p. 1981. lib. bdg. 48.00 (*0-226-06603-7*) U Ch Pr.
— Ocean Yearbook, No. 4. LC 79-642855. 640p. 1984. lib. bdg. 59.00 (*0-226-06605-3*) U Ch Pr.
— Ocean Yearbook, No. 5. LC 79-642855. 570p. 1985. lib. bdg. 59.00 (*0-226-06606-1*) U Ch Pr.
— Ocean Yearbook, No. 6. LC 79-642855. Vol. 6. 696p. 1987. lib. bdg. 66.00 (*0-226-06608-8*) U Ch Pr.
— Ocean Yearbook 1, No. 1. 908p. 1979. lib. bdg. 36.00 (*0-226-06602-9*) U Ch Pr.
Borgese, Elisabeth M., et al. Ocean Yearbook, 12. 650p. 1996. lib. bdg. 77.00 (*0-226-06615-0*) U Ch Pr.
— Ocean Yearbook, No. 7. 634p. 1989. lib. bdg. 71.00 (*0-226-06609-6*) U Ch Pr.
Borgese, Elisabeth M., tr. see Schenker, Heinrich.
Borgese, Elisabeth Mann, see Mann Borgese, Elisabeth.
Borgese, Paul. Hunting for the Whipperwoo. LC 95-82032. (Illus.). 48p. (J). (ps-4). 1996. 11.95 (*1-886489-06-8*) Laugh & Learn.
— If Fish Went Peopling. (J). (gr. k up). 1989. pap. 11.95 (*1-878347-05-5*) NL Assocs.
— On the Other Side. (J). (gr. k up). 1986. pap. 6.95 (*1-878347-06-3*) NL Assocs.
— A Sunday Stroll. LC 95-82029. (Illus.). 32p. (J). (ps-4). 1996. 15.95 (*1-886489-08-4*) Laugh & Learn.
— When Fish Go Peopling. LC 95-82030. (Illus.). 48p. (J). (ps-4). 1996. 11.95 (*1-886489-07-6*) Laugh & Learn.
Borgesen, P., et al, eds. Thin Films: Stresses & Mechanical Properties IV. (Symposium Proceedings Ser.: Vol. 308). 775p. 1993. text 30.00 (*1-55899-204-9*) Materials Res.
Borgesen, Peter, et al, eds. Materials Reliability in Microelectronics IV Vol. 338: Materials Research Society Symposium Proceedings. 629p. 1994. text 30.00 (*1-55899-238-3*) Materials Res.
Borgeson, Bet. Basic Colored Pencil Techniques. LC 96-32634. (Basic Techniques Ser.). (Illus.). 128p. 1997. pap. 17.99 (*0-89134-736-4*, North Lght Bks) F & W Pubns Inc.
— The Colored Pencil: Key Concepts For Handling the Medium. rev. ed. (Illus.). 144p. 1995. pap. 22.50 (*0-8230-0749-9*) Watsn-Guptill.
— Colored Pencil for the Serious Beginner: Basic Lessons in Becoming a Good Artist. LC 98-28204. 144p. 1998. pap. 19.95 (*0-8230-0761-8*) Watsn-Guptill.
***Borgeson, Griff.** The Last Great Miller: The Four Wheel Drive Indy Car. LC 00-36542. (Illus.). 344p. 2000. 39.00 (*0-7680-0500-0*, R-244) Soc Auto Engineers.
Borgeson, Griffith. The Golden Age of the American Racing Car. 2nd ed. LC 97-27778. 300p. 1997. 39.00 (*0-7680-0023-8*, R-196) Soc Auto Engineers.
Borgeson, Jess, et al. The Complete Works of William Shakespeare. abr. ed. LC 93-38692. (Illus.). 144p. 1993. pap. 8.95 (*1-55783-157-2*) Applause Theatre Bk Pubs.
Borgeson, Josephine & Wilson, Lynne, eds. Reshaping Ministry: Essays in Memory of Wesley Frensdorff. 286p. 1990. pap. 16.00 (*1-879145-00-6*) Jethro Pubns.
Borgeson, Paul W., Jr. Hacia el Hombre Nuevo: Poesia Y Pensamiento de Ernesto Cardenal. (Monagrafias A Ser.: Vol. CIV). 200p. (C). 1984. 58.00 (*0-7293-0172-9*, Pub. by Tamesis Bks Ltd) Boydell & Brewer.
Borgford, Christie L. & Summerlin, Lee R. Chemical Activities. LC 86-20673. (Illus.). xii, 244p. 1988. pap. text, teacher ed. 27.00 (*0-8412-1416-6*, Pub. by Am Chemical); student ed., spiral bd. 22.00 (*0-8412-1417-4*, Pub. by Am Chemical) OUP.
Borggaard, Jeffrey. Computational Methods in Optimal Design & Control. LC 98-16280. 1998. 79.95 (*3-7643-4064-9*) Birkhauser.
Borggaard, Jeffrey, ed. see Workshop on Optimal Design & Control Staff.
Borggaard, Jeffrey T., et al, eds. Computational Methods in Optimal Design & Control. LC 98-16280. (Progress in Systems & Control Theory Ser.). 400p. 1998. 79.95 (*0-8176-4064-9*) Birkhauser.
***Borghans, Lex & De Grip, Andries, eds.** The Overeducated Worker? The Economics of Skill Utilization. LC 99-87189. 288p. 2000. 90.00 (*1-84064-155-X*) E Elgar.
Borghans, Lex, jt. ed. see Heijke, Hans.
Borghesani, Craig. Controls Tutor Using MATLAB: Mac Version. 44p. 1995. pap. 34.95 incl. disk (*0-534-94998-3*) PWS Pubs.
— Linear Algebra. (Mathematics Ser.). 1998. student ed., suppl. ed. 28.95 (*0-534-95249-6*) PWS Pubs.
— Mastering Digital Signal Processing Using Matlab. LC 97-28987. 72p. 1997. pap. 30.80 (*0-13-534976-1*) P-H.
Borghesani, W. H., Jr. The Law & Inter-Corporate Trucking by Conglomerates. 1.00 (*0-686-31449-2*) Private Carrier.
Borghese, J. Valerio. Sea Devils: Italian Navy Commandos in World War II. Sweetman, Jack, ed. LC 95-32082. (Classics of Naval Literature Ser.). (Illus.). 264p. 1995. 32.95 (*1-55750-072-X*) Naval Inst Pr.
Borghesi, A., et al, eds. C, H, N & O in Si & Characterization & Simulation of Materials & Processes: Proceedings of Symposium G on Atomic Scale Characterization & Stimulation of Materials & Processes, & Symp N on Carbon, Hydrogen, Nitrogen & Oxygen in Silicon & Other Elemental Semiconductors of the 1995 E-MRS Spring Conference. LC 96-229399. (European Materials Research Society Symposia Proceedings Ser.: Vol. 56). 570p. 1996. text 273.00 (*0-444-82413-8*, North Holland) Elsevier.
Borghetti, A., jt. ed. see Bruschi, G.
Borghgraef, R. & Schotsmans, R., eds. The Technological Advances in Health Sciences & the Moral & Theological Implications. 90p. (Orig.). 1993. pap. 27.50 (*90-6186-579-4*, Pub. by Leuven Univ) Coronet Bks.
Borghi, Armando. Mussolini: Red & Black. LC 73-20389. (Studies in Political Science: No. 94). 1974. lib. bdg. 75.00 (*0-8383-1765-0*) M S G Haskell Hse.
***Borghi, R. P. & Destriau, M.** Combustion & Flames: Chemical & Physical Principles. LC 99-208655. 371p. 1998. 98.00 (*2-7108-0740-8*) Edits Technip.
Borghi, R. P. & Murthy, S. N., eds. Turbulent Reactive Flows. (Lecture Notes in Engineering Ser.: Vol. 40). (Illus.). 940p. 1989. 193.95 (*0-387-96887-3*) Spr-Verlag.
Borghini, Raffaelo. Il Riposo. (Illus.). 648p. 1969. reprint ed. 160.00 (*0-318-71582-1*) G Olms Pubs.
Borghoff, Kent, jt. auth. see Baumheckel, Ralph.
Borghoff, U. M. Catalogue of Distributed File-Operating Systems. xi, 214p. 1991. 49.95 (*0-387-54450-X*) Spr-Verlag.
***Borghoff, U. M. & Schlichter, J. H.** Computer-Supported Cooperative Work. xvii, 527p. 2000. 49.95 (*3-540-66984-1*) Spr-Verlag.
Borghoff, Uwe & Pareschi, R., eds. Information Technology for Knowledge Mamagement. LC 98-5676. (Illus.). xi, 232p. 1998. 44.95 (*3-540-63764-8*) Spr-Verlag.
Borghuis, Marthyn, et al. Tulip: Final Report. LC 97-163463. 368p. 1996. write for info. (*0-444-82540-1*) Elsevier.
Borgia, Anthony. Here & Hereafter. Rigby, Mike, ed. 138p. 1993. pap. 10.00 (*0-9636435-3-3*) M A P.

— Life in the World Unseen. 202p. 1993. pap. 12.00 (*0-9636435-0-9*) M A P.

— Ma Vie au Paradis. 286p. 1989. 19.95 (*2-920083-39-2*) Edns Roseau.

— More about Life in the World Unseen. Rigby, Mike, ed. 168p. 1993. pap. 10.00 (*0-9636435-2-5*) M A P.

— Le Paradis Retrouve. 180p. 1992. 19.95 (*2-920083-61-9*) Edns Roseau.

Borgia, Brian T. Northern California's Guide for Fun, Excitement & Romance. 163p. (Orig.). 1995. pap. 10.95 (*0-9645476-1-9*) Valntne Pr.

Borgia, Rubi, jt. auth. see Wilkes, Angela.

Borgias, Alaine, ed. see Dunn, Ray.

Borgiasz, William S. The Strategic Air Command: Evolution & Consolidation of Nuclear Forces, 1945-1955. LC 95-22014. 176p. 1996. 57.95 (*0-275-94861-7*, Praeger Pubs) Greenwood.

Borglin, A. Optimality in Infinite Horizon Economies. Vol. 269. 188p. 1986. 25.95 (*0-387-16475-8*) Spr-Verlag.

Borglum Carter, Robin. Gutzon Borglum: His Life & Work. (Illus.). 96p. (Orig.). 1998. pap. 21.95 (*1-57168-247-3*, Eakin Pr) Sunbelt Media.

***Borglum, Keith C.** Medical Practice Forms: Every Form You Need to Succeed. 300p. (Orig.). 1998. pap. text 44.95 (*1-57066-083-2*) Practice Mgmt Info.

Borglum, Lincoln. Mount Rushmore: The Story Behind the Scenery. Morales, Brigitte, tr. (GER., Illus.). 48p. 1994. pap. 8.95 (*0-88714-782-8*) KC Pubns.

— Mount Rushmore: The Story Behind the Scenery. Petzinger, Saori, tr. (JPN., Illus.). 48p. 1994. pap. 8.95 (*0-88714-783-6*) KC Pubns.

— Mount Rushmore: The Story Behind the Scenery. Le Bras, Yvon, tr. (FRE., Illus.). 48p. 1997. pap. 8.95 (*0-88714-817-4*) KC Pubns.

— Mount Rushmore: The Story Behind the Scenery. rev. ed. LC 93-77025. (Illus.). 48p. 1993. pap. 7.95 (*0-88714-074-2*) KC Pubns.

— My Father's Mountain: Mt. Rushmore National Memorial & How It Was Carved. rev. ed. 16p. 1997. pap. text. write for info. (*0-913062-02-2*) Fenwyn Pr.

Borgman, Albert S. Thomas Shadwell: His Life & Comedies. LC 68-56540. 1972. reprint ed. 24.95 (*0-405-08289-4*, Pub. by Blom Pubns) Ayer.

***Borgman, Christine L.** From Gutenberg to the Global Information Infrastructure: Access to Information in the Networked World. LC 99-39906. (Digital Libraries & Electronic Publishing Ser.). (Illus.). 340p. 2000. 42.00 (*0-262-02473-X*) MIT Pr.

Borgman, Christine L., ed. Scholarly Communication & Bibliometrics. (Illus.). 336p. (C). 1990. 55.00 (*0-8039-3879-9*) Sage.

Borgman, Christine L. & Moghdam, Dineh. Effective Online Searching: A Basic Text. (Books in Library & Information Sciences: Vol. 45). (Illus.). 224p. 1984. text 85.00 (*0-8247-7142-7*) Dekker.

Borgman, Danelle, jt. auth. see Borgman, Richard.

Borgman, Dean. When Kumbaya Is Not Enough: A Practical Theology for Youth Ministry. LC 97-20785. 240p. 1997. pap. 16.95 (*1-56563-247-8*) Hendrickson MA.

Borgman, Dean & Cook, Christine, eds. Agenda for Youth Ministry. 176p. 1998. pap. 21.95 (*0-281-05152-6*) Intl Pubs Mktg.

Borgman, Jim, jt. auth. see Scott, Jerry.

***Borgman, Leon E.** Statistical Analysis of Ocean Waves & Other Environmental Data. (Advanced Series on Ocean Engineering). 2000. pap. text 55.00 (*981-02-4202-6*) World Scientific Pub.

Borgman, Lori. I Was a Better Mother Before I Had Kids. LC 98-53404. 196p. 1999. 21.00 (*0-671-02722-0*) S&S Trade.

***Borgman, Lori.** I Was a Better Mother Before I Had Kids. 208p. 2000. reprint ed. per. 12.95 (*0-671-02723-9*) PB.

***Borgman, Peggy Wynne.** Four Seasons of Inner & Outer Beauty: At-Home Rituals & Recipes for Well-Being Throughout the Year. LC 99-88222. 272p. 2000. pap. 17.95 (*0-7679-0375-7*) Broadway BDD.

Borgman, Richard & Borgman, Danelle. Enlarge My Heart. 150p. 1996. pap. write for info. (*1-888563-01-X*) Lion & Lamb Outrch.

— The God of the Flat Tire. 100p. 1996. pap. write for info. (*1-888563-00-1*) Lion & Lamb Outrch.

Borgmann. Philosophy of Language: Historical Foundations & Contemporary Issues. 182p. 1974. pap. text 88.00 (*90-247-1589-X*, Pub. by M Nijhoff) Kluwer Academic.

Borgmann, Albert. Crossing the Postmodern Divide. LC 91-31971. 182p. (C). 1993. pap. 10.00 (*0-226-06627-4*) U Ch Pr.

— Crossing the Postmodern Divide. LC 91-31971. 182p. 1997. 19.95 (*0-226-06626-6*) U Ch Pr.

— Holding on to Reality: The Nature of Information at the Turn of the Millennium. LC 98-38578. 1999. 22.00 (*0-226-06625-8*) U Ch Pr.

— Technology & the Character of Contemporary Life: A Philosophical Inquiry. LC 84-8639. viii, 312p. 1987. pap. text 17.95 (*0-226-06629-0*) U Ch Pr.

Borgnakke, Claus, jt. auth. see Sonntag, Richard E.

Borgnes, Philip A. Evaluating OS-2 with PageMaker. Kotick, Margy, ed. (Illus.). 30p. 1989. write for info. (*1-56026-001-7*) Aldus.

Borgnine, Ernest & Ten Boom, Corrie. Snowflakes in September: Stories about God's Mysterious Ways. LC 91-42389. 96p. (Orig.). 1992. pap. 8.00 (*0-687-38782-5*) Dimen for Liv.

Borgnine, Tova. Being Married Happily Forever. 304p. 1998. pap. 12.95 (*0-425-16502-7*) Berkley Pub.

***Borgohain, Bani.** Human Rights: Social Justice & Political Challenge. 1999. 38.50 (*81-7391-284-X*, Pub. by Kaniska Pubs Dist) S Asia.

Borgos, Seth, jt. auth. see Adamson, Madeleine.

Borgsdorf, Charles W. Michigan Corporate Forms, 2 vols. 1989. disk 75.00 (*0-685-74621-6*, MICHIE) LEXIS Pub.

— Michigan Corporate Forms, 2 vols. 1994. suppl. ed. 79.00 (*0-685-74620-8*, MICHIE) LEXIS Pub.

— Michigan Corporate Forms, Issue 10. 160p. 1999. ring bd. write for info. (*0-327-01262-5*, 8170515) LEXIS Pub.

— Michigan Corporate Forms, 2 vols., Set. 1520p. 1994. spiral bd. 259.00 (*0-8342-0074-0*, 81701-10, MICHIE) LEXIS Pub.

Borgstadt. Understanding & Caring for Human Diseases. 2nd ed. (Health Occupations Ser.). 56p. 1996. pap. text, teacher ed. 12.50 (*0-8273-7431-3*) Delmar.

Borgstadt, Chip. Growing Spiritually. (YouthSearch: Small-Group Resources Ser.: Vol. 12). 64p. 1996. pap. 5.95 (*0-687-05542-3*) Abingdon.

Borgstadt, Chip, et al. Lifegivers: A Practical Guide to Reaching Youth in a Challenging World. 160p. 1996. ring bd. 24.95 (*0-687-05575-X*) Abingdon.

Borgstadt, Marcia. Understanding & Caring for Human Diseases. rev. ed. LC 95-13518. 464p. (C). 1995. 36.95 (*0-8273-6605-1*) Delmar.

Borgstadt, Nancy, ed. see Rosenstrach, Jerry, et al.

Borgstedt, H. U. Liquid Metal Systems: Material Behavior & Physical Chemistry in Liquid Metal Systems, Vol. 2. (Illus.). 432p. (C). 1995. text 130.00 (*0-306-45069-0*, Kluwer Plenum) Kluwer Academic.

Borgstedt, H. U. & Mathews, C. K. Applied Chemistry of the Alkali Metals. LC 87-2466. (Illus.). 292p. (C). 1987. text 89.50 (*0-306-42326-X*, Kluwer Plenum) Kluwer Academic.

Borgstrom, B. & Brockman, H. L. Lipases. 500p. 1984. 318.75 (*0-444-80526-5*, I-208-84) Elsevier.

Borgstrom, Bengt-Erik. Cherished Moments: Engaging with the Past in a Swedish Parish. (Stockholm Studies in Social Anthropology: No. 40). 153p. 1997. pap. 49.50 (*91-7153-514-4*, Pub. by Almqvist Wiksell) Coronet Bks.

Borgstrom, Wendy. Rapture & the Second Coming. 200p. (Orig.). 1990. pap. 7.95 (*1-55583-166-4*) Alyson Pubns.

Borgwardt, K. H. The Simplex Method. (Algorithms & Combinatorics Ser.: Vol. 1). (Illus.). xi, 268p. 1986. 71.95 (*0-387-17096-0*) Spr-Verlag.

Borhamaie, H. L. Rabino di, see Rabino di Borhamaie, H. L.

Borhan, Pierre, ed. Andre Kertesz: His Life & Work. (Illus.). 368p. 1994. 75.00 (*0-8212-2140-X*, Pub. by Bulfinch Pr) Little.

***Borhan, Pierre, ed.** Andre Kertsz: His Life & Work. (Illus.). 368p. 2000. pap. 29.95 (*0-8212-2648-7*, Pub. by Bulfinch Pr) Little.

Borhegyi, Stephen F. De, see De Borhegyi, Stephen F.

Borhek, Mary V. Coming Out to Parents: A Two-Way Survival Guide for Lesbians & Gay Men & Their Parents. 2nd rev. ed. LC 83-3971. 320p. 1993. pap. 15.95 (*0-8298-0957-0*) Pilgrim OH.

— My Son Eric. LC 79-16161. 168p. (Orig.). 1984. pap. 11.95 (*0-8298-0729-2*) Pilgrim OH.

Borhidi, A. Phytogeography & Vegetation Ecology of Cuba. 752p. 1995. 550.00 (*963-05-6956-6*, Pub. by Akade Kiado) St Mut.

Borhidi, Attila. Phytogeography & Vegetation Ecology of Cuba. LC 97-200394. 857p. (C). 1991. 222.00 (*963-05-5295-7*, Pub. by Akade Kiado) St Mut.

Borho, W., et al. Lebendige Zahlen - Fuenf Exkhursionen. (Mathematical Miniatures Ser.: Vol. 1). 116p. (C). 1980. 35.50 (*0-8176-1203-3*) Birkhauser.

Boriani, Maria L., jt. auth. see Chiusoli, Alessandro.

Borich. Computer Tutorial Effective Teaching. 3rd ed. 1995. 13.75 (*0-02-312463-6*) P-H.

***Borich.** Effective Teaching Methods. 4th ed. LC 99-34485. 515p. 1999. pap. text 60.00 (*0-13-936130-8*) P-H.

Borich, Barrie J. Restoring the Color of Roses. LC 93-647. 168p. (Orig.). 1993. pap. 9.95 (*1-56341-027-3*); lib. bdg. 20.95 (*1-56341-028-1*) Firebrand Bks.

Borich, Barrie Jean. My Lesbian Husband. 294p. 1999. 24.95 (*1-55597-292-6*, Pub. by Graywolf) SPD-Small Pr Dist.

***Borich, Barrie Jean.** My Lesbian Husband. 294p. 2000. reprint ed. pap. 14.00 (*1-55597-310-8*) Graywolf.

Borich, Gary. Becoming a Teacher. (Falmer Press Teacher's Library: No. 7). 140p. 1995. 79.95 (*0-7507-0264-8*, Falmer Pr); pap. 24.95 (*0-7507-0265-6*, Falmer Pr) Taylor & Francis.

Borich, Gary, ed. S/G Educational Psychology. 2nd ed. (C). 1997. pap. text, student ed. 23.00 (*0-673-98534-2*) Addison-Wesley.

Borich, Gary D., ed. Evaluating Educational Programs & Products. LC 74-1298. 520p. 1974. 44.95 (*0-87778-070-6*) Educ Tech Pubns.

Borich, Gary D. & Bayles, Deborah L. Observation Skills for Effective Teaching. 3rd ed. LC 98-22994. 302p. 1998. pap. text 36.00 (*0-13-860396-0*, Merrill Coll) P-H.

Borich, Gary D., et al. Educational Psychology. LC 94-18670. 576p. (C). 1997. pap. text 85.00 (*0-673-46915-8*) Addson-Wesley Educ.

Borich, Gary D., jt. auth. see Tombari, Martin L.

Borich, Judy G. Touch & Go - The Nature of Intimacy: Relating in the Coming Times. (Illus.). 250p. (Orig.). 1998. write for info. (*0-614-07555-6*) Borich.

Borich, Michael. The Black Hawk Songs. Poems. LC 74-23379. 86p. 1975. 9.95 (*0-252-00528-7*) U of Ill Pr.

Borich, Timothy O. & Ayres, Janet. Transportation Action: A Local Input Model to Engage Community Transportation Planning. Stewart, Julie, ed. 148p. 1996. pap. text 15.00 (*0-936913-11-8*, RRD 174) NCRCRD.

Borichevsky, Vladimir S. St. Herman of Alaska. (Illus.). 80p. (Orig.). 1970. pap. 4.50 (*1-878997-06-8*) St Tikhons Pr.

Borichevsky, Vladimir S., tr. from RUS. The Rite of Betrothal & Crowning. 32p. (Orig.). 1992. pap. 0.75 (*1-878997-27-0*) St Tikhons Pr.

Borie, E. & Hochschild, G., eds. Gyrotrons Five, Vol. 64, No. 1. (International Journal of Electronics Ser.). 1988. 60.00 (*0-85066-896-4*) Taylor & Francis.

Borie, E., tr. see Straumann, N.

Borie, Lou. Bugby Hole, St. Croix, U. S. Virgin Islands: A Land Use Plan. 41p. 1979. 7.50 (*0-318-14611-8*) Isl Resources.

Borie, Lysbeth B. Poems for Peter. rev. ed. Lewis, I. Murphy, ed. LC 96-67927. (Illus.). 112p. (J). (ps-5). 1996. 14.95 (*1-888959-25-8*) Shank Painter Pub.

Borie, Marcia & Wilkerson, Tichi. Hollywood Legends: The Golden Years of the Hollywood Reporter. 2nd ed. (Illus.). 350p. (YA). (gr. 7 up). 1988. reprint ed. pap. 14.95 (*0-942139-03-8*) Tale Weaver.

Boriharnwanaket, Sujin. Metta: Loving Kindness in Buddhism. 128p. 1995. pap. 11.95 (*1-897633-14-9*, Pub. by Triple Gem) Assoc Pubs Grp.

Borik, Otto. Kasparows Schacheroffnungen. (GER., Illus.). 136p. 1992. 20.00 (*3-283-00319-X*) G Olms Pubs.

Borin, Fabrizio, jt. auth. see Funch, Bjarne S.

Borin, Jeffrey N. The Turover Aid Society of Detroit. 144p. per. write for info. (*0-318-68936-7*) Harlo Pr.

Borin, Lydia F. Beadwrangler's Hand on Crochet with Beads & Fiber. (Beadwrangler's Hands on Ser.). 68p. 1997. pap. 14.95 (*1-891302-01-9*) Hooty Owl.

— Beadwrangler's Hands on Bead Stringing. (Beadwrangler's Hands on Ser.). 44p. 1997. pap. 9.95 (*1-891302-00-0*) Hooty Owl.

Boring, Edwin G. & Lindzey, Gardner, eds. History of Psychology in Autobiography, Vol. 5. LC 30-20129. (Century Psychology Ser.). (Illus.). 1967. 34.50 (*0-89197-216-1*) Irvington.

Boring, Edwin G., jt. ed. see Herrnstein, Richard J.

Boring, Holland, ed. Songs of Hope. 1979. pap. 2.75 (*0-88027-059-4*) Firm Foun Pub.

Boring, John. Gilbert Said: An Oldtimer's Tales of the Haida-Tlingit Waterways of Alaska. LC 92-72443. 118p. (Orig.). 1993. reprint ed. pap. 14.50 (*0-9625429-4-6*) Hardscratch Pr.

Boring, John & Kreins, David. Special Edition Using Oracle. (Illus.). 1024p. (Orig.). 1996. 49.99 (*0-7897-0101-4*) Que.

Boring, M. Eugene. Disciples & the Bible: A History of Disciples Biblical Interpretation in North America. LC 97-15912. 440p. (Orig.). 1997. 54.99 (*0-8272-0623-2*); pap. 39.99 (*0-8272-0622-4*) Chalice Pr.

— 1 Peter. LC 99-11067. (Abingdon New Testament Commentaries Ser.). 176p. 1999. pap. 19.95 (*0-687-05854-6*) Abingdon.

— Revelation. (Interpretation: a Bible Commentary for Preaching & Teaching Ser.). 240p. 1989. 25.00 (*0-8042-3150-8*) Westminster John Knox.

Boring, M. Eugene, et al, eds. Hellenistic Commentary to the New Testament. 768p. 1995. 69.95 (*0-687-00916-2*) Abingdon.

Boring, M. Eugene, tr. see Conzelman, Hans.

Boring, M. Eugene, tr. see Schnelle, Udo.

Boring, Mel. Birds, Nests, & Eggs. LC 95-31570. (Take-Along Guide Ser.). (Illus.). 48p. (J). (gr. 3-7). 1998. pap. 6.95 (*1-55971-624-X*, NorthWord Pr) Creat Pub Intl.

— Caterpillars, Bugs & Butterflies. (Take-Along Guide Ser.). (Illus.). 48p. (J). 1999. pap. 6.95 (*1-55971-674-6*, NorthWord Pr) Creat Pub Intl.

***Boring, Mel.** Caterpillars, Bugs & Butterflies. (Illus.). (J). 1999. 12.40 (*0-606-18075-3*) Turtleback.

Boring, Mel. Incredible Constructions & the People Who Built Them. LC 84-19522. 96p. (J). (gr. 4 up). 1985. lib. bdg. 13.85 (*0-8027-6560-2*) Walker & Co.

— Rabbits, Squirrels, & Chipmunks. LC 96-11582. (Take-Along Guide Ser.). (Illus.). 48p. (J). (gr. 3-7). 1996. pap. 6.95 (*1-55971-579-0*, NorthWord Pr) Creat Pub Intl.

Boring, Mel, et al. Fun with Nature. LC 98-31913. (Take-Along Guide Ser.). (Illus.). (J). (gr. 1-5). 1998. pap. 22.95 (*1-55971-684-3*, NorthWord Pr); pap. text 14.95 (*1-55971-702-5*, NorthWord Pr) Creat Pub Intl.

Boring, Phyllis Z. Elena Quiroga. LC 77-5953. (Twayne's World Authors Ser.). 151p. (C). 1977. text 20.95 (*0-8057-6296-5*) Irvington.

Boring, Ronald. Illusions of Truth: A Collection of Intriguing Poems Based on Truth & Deceit. (Illus.). 90p. (Orig.). 1997. pap. 10.95 (*1-57502-438-1*, PO1327) Morris Pubng.

Borins, ed. Massachusetts Appellate Tax Board Reporter. 75p. 1998. ring bd. 85.00 (*0-327-00311-1*, 8142426) LEXIS Pub.

— Massachusetts Appellate Tax Board Reporter 21:3. 75p. 1998. ring bd. 85.00 (*0-327-00310-3*, 8142425) LEXIS Pub.

Borins, Jennifer, ed. Connecticut Family Law Journal. 1216p. 1993. ring bd. 120.00 (*0-88063-010-8*, 80353-10, MICHIE) LEXIS Pub.

— Massachusetts Appellate Tax Board Reporter. 1981. ring bd. 85.00 (*0-614-05894-5*, MICHIE) LEXIS Pub.

Borins, Sandford. Innovating with Integrity: How Local Heroes Are Transforming American Government. LC 98-12628. 336p. 1998. 55.00 (*0-87840-687-5*); pap. 23.95 (*0-87840-688-3*) Georgetown U Pr.

Borins, Sandford F. The Language of the Skies: The Bilingual Air Traffic Control Conflict in Canada. (Canadian Public Administration Ser.). 303p. 1983. 49.95 (*0-7735-0402-8*, Pub. by McG-Queens Univ Pr); pap. 27.95 (*0-7735-0403-6*, Pub. by McG-Queens Univ Pr) CUP Services.

— The Language of the Skies: The Bilingual Air Traffic Control Conflict in Canada. LC 83-214911. (Canadian Public Administration Ser.). (Illus.). 303p. reprint ed. pap. 94.00 (*0-7837-6905-9*, 204673500003) Bks Demand.

Borins, Sanford, jt. auth. see Blakeney, Allan.

Borinsky, Alicia. Dreams of the Abandoned Seducer: Vaudeville Novel. Franzen, Cola, tr. LC 97-35668. (Latin American Women Writers Ser.). (ENG & SPA.). 212p. 1998. pap. 15.00 (*0-8032-6144-6*, Bison Books); text 45.00 (*0-8032-1286-0*, Bison Books) U of Nebr Pr.

— Mean Woman (Mina Cruel) Franzen, Cola, tr. & intro. by. LC 92-37129. (Latin American Women Writers Ser.: Vol. 2). xiv, 179p. (C). 1993. pap. 10.95 (*0-8032-6112-8*, Bison Books); text 42.00 (*0-8032-1234-8*) U of Nebr Pr.

— Theoretical Fables: The Pedagogical Dream in Contemporary Latin-American Literature. LC 93-26561. (Pennsylvania Studies in Contemporary American Fiction). 176p. (C). 1993. text 32.50 (*0-8122-3234-8*) U of Pa Pr.

Boris, Constance M. & Krutilla, John V. Water Rights & Energy Development in the Yellowstone River. LC 79-3741. (Resources for the Future Ser.). 1980. text 25.00 (*0-8018-2368-4*) Johns Hopkins.

— Water Rights & Energy Development in the Yellowstone River Basin: An Integrated Analysis. LC 79-3741. (Illus.). 294p. reprint ed. pap. 91.20 (*0-608-18083-1*, 203214400078) Bks Demand.

***Boris, Cynthia.** Buffy the Vampire Slayer Pop Quiz. (Illus.). 100p. (J). (gr. 7-12). 1999. per. 4.99 (*0-671-04258-0*) S&S Trade.

Boris, Edna Z. Shakespeare's English Kings, the People & the Law: A Study in the Relationship Between the Tudor Constitution & the English History Plays. LC 76-19838. 261p. 1978. 35.00 (*0-8386-1990-8*) Fairleigh Dickinson.

Boris, Eileen. Home to Work: Motherhood & the Politics of Industrial Homework in the United States. (Illus.). 403p. (C). 1994. text 74.95 (*0-521-44370-9*); pap. text 19.95 (*0-521-45548-0*) Cambridge U Pr.

Boris, Eileen & Chaudhuri, Nupur, eds. Voices of Women Historians: The Personal, the Political, the Professional. LC 98-51191. (Illus.). 272p. 1999. pap. 19.95 (*0-253-21275-8*); text 39.95 (*0-253-33494-2*) Ind U Pr.

Boris, Eileen & Daniels, Cynthia R., eds. Homework: Historical & Contemporary Perspectives on Paid Labor at Home. LC 88-23232. (Illus.). 288p. 1989. pap. text 14.95 (*0-252-06054-7*) U of Ill Pr.

***Boris, Eileen & Janssens, Angelique, eds.** Complicating Categories: Gender, Class, Race & Ethnicity. LC 99-55823. (International Review of Social History Supplements Ser.: No. 7). 176p. 2000. pap. 19.95 (*0-521-78641-X*) Cambridge U Pr.

Boris, Eileen & Lichtenstein, Nelson, eds. Major Problems in the History of American Workers: Documents & Essays. LC 90-82495. (Major Problems in American History Ser.). 681p. (C). 1991. pap. text 29.16 (*0-669-19925-7*) HM Trade Div.

Boris, Eileen & Prugl, Elisabeth, eds. Homeworkers in Global Perspective: Invisible No More. (Illus.). 320p. (C). 1995. pap. 20.99 (*0-415-91007-2*, B3873) Routledge.

Boris, Elizabeth T. & Steverle, C. Eugene, eds. Nonprofits & Government: Collaboration & Conflict. LC 98-47103. 1999. pap. 29.50 (*0-87766-687-3*); lib. bdg. 57.50 (*0-87766-686-5*) Urban Inst.

Boris, Harold N. Envy. LC 93-24377. 224p. 1994. 40.00 (*1-56821-083-3*) Aronson.

— Passions of the Mind: Unheard Melodies: A 3rd Principle of Mental Functioning. LC 93-15084. 288p. (C). 1993. text 55.00 (*0-8147-1204-5*) NYU Pr.

— Sleights of Mind: One & Multiples of One. LC 93-3833. 400p. 1994. 60.00 (*1-56821-082-5*) Aronson.

Boris, J. P., jt. auth. see Oran, Elaine S.

Boris, Jamie. Conversando En Ingles. (SPA.). 1997. pap. text 12.98 (*968-13-2530-3*) Libros Fronteras.

Boris, Jay P., jt. ed. see Oran, Elaine S.

Borisenko, A. I. High Temperature Protective Coatings. (C). 1987. 28.00 (*0-8364-2120-5*, Pub. by Oxford IBH) S Asia.

Borisenko, A. I. & Tarapov, I. E. Vector & Tensor Analysis with Applications. LC 79-87809. 257p. (C). 1979. reprint ed. pap. 8.95 (*0-486-63833-2*) Dover.

Borisenko, Leonid F. Scandium: Its Geochemistry & Mineralogy. LC 62-15551. 82p. reprint ed. pap. 30.00 (*0-608-11381-6*, 200335800021) Bks Demand.

Borisenko, S. Neuropharmacology Reviews Vol. 2, Pt. 3: Blood-Brain Barrier, Vol. 2. 78p. 1992. pap. text 80.00 (*3-7186-5285-4*, Harwood Acad Pubs) Gordon & Breach.

***Borisenko, V E.** Physics, Chemistry & Application of Nanostructures: Reviews & Short Notes to Nanomeeting 99. 1999. 122.00 (*981-02-3889-4*) WSC Inst MA Studies.

***Borisenko, V. E., ed.** Semiconducting Silicides: Basics, Formation, Properties. LC 99-88577. (Illus.). 345p. 2000. 99.00 (*3-540-66111-5*) Spr-Verlag.

Borisenko, V. E. & Hesketh, P. J. Rapid Thermal Processing of Semiconductors. LC 97-3783. (Microdevices Ser.). (Illus.). 380p. (C). 1997. 95.00 (*0-306-45054-2*, Plenum Trade) Perseus Pubng.

Borish, Elaine. A Legacy of Names: British Places in the New World. (Illus.). 260p. 1996. pap. 15.95 (*0-9524881-2-4*, Pub. by Fidelio Pr) IPG Chicago.

— Literary Lodgings: Historic Hotels in Britain Where Famous Writers Lived. 1996. pap. 17.95 (*0-9524881-0-8*, Pub. by Fidelio Pr) IPG Chicago.

— Novel Cuisine: Recipes That Recreate the Culinary Highlights of Famous Novels. 1999. pap. 16.95 (*0-9524881-3-2*) FID1 UK.

— Unpublishable! Rejected Writers from Jane Austen to Zane Grey. 1997. pap. 12.95 (*0-9524881-1-6*, Pub. by Fidelio Pr) IPG Chicago.

Borish, Ilona, ed. see Hicks, Larry K. & Lorren, McGee.

Borish, Irving M., jt. auth. see Brooks, Clifford W.

Borish, Michael S. & Noel, Michel. Private Sector Development During Transition: The Visegrad Countries. LC 96-10. (World Bank Discussion Papers: No. 318). 188p. 1996. pap. 22.00 (*0-8213-3569-3*) World Bank.

Borish, Michael S., et al. On the Road to EU Accession: Financial Sector Development in Central Europe. (Discussion Paper Ser.: No. 345). 176p. 1996. pap. 22.00 (*0-8213-3800-5*, 13800) World Bank.

— Restructuring Banks & Enterprises: Recent Lessons from Transition Countries. LC 94-49594. (World Bank Discussion Papers: No. 279). 84p. 1995. pap. 22.00 (*0-8213-3193-0*, 13193) World Bank.

Borish, Steven M. The Land of the Living: The Danish Folk High Schools & Denmark's Non-Violent Path to Modernization. LC 91-12365. (Illus.). 512p. (C). 1991. 27.95 (*0-931892-62-7*) B Dolphin Pub.

Borishade, Adetokunbo F. Classical African Values & Yoruba Philosophy: For African American Intervention & Personality Development. 46p. 1999. pap. 7.50 (*0-9654009-1-3*) Sankofa Pr.

— Re-Aligning African Heads: Yoruba Curatives for Maafa-Related Ailments. (Illus.). xxi, 101p. (Orig.). 1996. pap. text 10.00 (*0-9654009-0-5*) Sankofa Pr.

Borishanskii, V. M., jt. auth. see Kutateladze, S. S.

Boriskovsky, V. G., jt. auth. see Parton, V. Z.

Borisoff, Alexander. How to Write a Melody. 119p. 1981. pap. 14.95 (*0-938170-01-5*) Wimbledon Music.

Borisoff, Deborah. Conflict Management. 2nd ed. LC 97-22524. 247p. 1997. pap. text 50.00 (*0-205-27294-0*) P-H.

Borisoff, Deborah & Merrill, Lisa. The Power to Communicate: Gender Differences As Barriers. 3rd rev. ed. LC 99-195446. 151p. 1998. pap. text 12.50 (*0-88133-989-X*) Waveland Pr.

Borisoff, Deborah & Purdy, Michael, eds. Listening in Everyday Life: A Personal & Professional Approach. 338p. (C). 1991. pap. text 24.50 (*0-8191-8212-5*) U Pr of Amer.

Borisoff, Deborah, jt. auth. see Arliss, Laurie P.

Borisoff, Deborah, jt. ed. see Purdy, Michael.

Borisov, A. A., ed. Dynamic Structure of Detonation in Gaseous & Dispersed Media. (C). 1991. text 204.50 (*0-7923-1340-2*) Kluwer Academic.

Borisov, Oleg B. & Koloskov, B. T. Soviet-Chinese Relations, Nineteen Forty-Five to Nineteen Hundred Seventy. Petrov, Vladimir, ed. LC 74-31443. 382p. reprint ed. pap. 118.50 (*0-608-17131-X*, 205621900056) Bks Demand.

Borisov, Sergei N., et al. Organosilicon Heteropolymers & Hetercompounds. Turton, Nigel & Turton, Tatiani I., trs. from RUS. LC 68-13393. (Monographs in Inorganic Chemistry). 655p. 1970. reprint ed. pap. 200.00 (*0-608-05410-0*, 206587900006) Bks Demand.

Borisov, V. F. & Zelikin, M. I. Theory of Chattering Control with Applications to Astronautics, Robotics, Economics, & Engineering. LC 93-51121. (Systems & Control: Foundations & Applications Ser.). (Illus.). 312p. 1994. 86.50 (*0-8176-3618-8*) Birkhauser.

Borisova, A. A., et al. Immunology Reviews: Immunodeficiency in Patients with Chronic Lung Diseases: Approaches to Immunomodulation, Vol. 3. Petrov, R. V., ed. (Soviet Medical Reviews Ser.: Vol. 3, Pt. 1). vi, 134p. 1989. pap. text 161.00 (*3-7186-4937-3*) Gordon & Breach.

Borisova, B. Russian Art Nouveau. (C). 1990. 650.00 (*0-7855-4485-2*, Pub. by Collets) St Mut.

Borisova, Z. U. Glassy Semiconductors. Adashko, J. George, tr. from RUS. LC 81-17734. 514p. 1981. 125.00 (*0-306-40609-8*, Plenum Trade) Perseus Pubng.

Borisovich, Y. G., et al, eds. Global Analysis - Studies & Applications V. (Lecture Notes in Mathematics Ser.: Vol. 1520). vii, 284p. 1992. 53.95 (*0-387-55583-8*) Spr-Verlag.

Borisovich, Y. G. & Gliklikh, Y. E., eds. Global Analysis: Studies & Applications, No. IV. (Lecture Notes in Mathematics Ser.: Vol. 1453). vi, 320p. 1991. 52.95 (*0-387-53407-5*) Spr-Verlag.

— Global Analysis - Studies & Applications I, Vol. 1108. v, 301p. 1985. 46.95 (*0-387-13910-9*) Spr-Verlag.

— Global Analysis - Studies & Applications II. (Lecture Notes in Mathematics Ser.: Vol. 1214). v, 275p. 1986. 38.95 (*0-387-16821-4*) Spr-Verlag.

Borisovich, Yuri G., et al. Introduction to Differential & Algebraic Topology. LC 95-12568. (Texts in the Mathematical Sciences Ser.: Vol. 9). 504p. (C). 1995. text 268.50 (*0-7923-3499-X*) Kluwer Academic.

Boriss-Krimsky, Carolyn. The Creativity Handbook: A Visual Arts Guide for Parents & Teachers. LC 99-18109. (Illus.). 186p. 1999. pap. 26.95 (*0-398-06962-X*) C C Thomas.

***Boriss-Krimsky, Carolyn.** The Creativity Handbook: A Visual Arts Guide for Parents & Teachers. LC 99-18109. (Illus.). 181p. 1999. 38.95 (*0-398-06961-1*) C C Thomas.

Borissov, M. Disordered Systems & New Materials. 944p. (C). 1989. text 141.00 (*9971-5-0790-0*) World Scientific Pub.

Borissov, M., ed. Molecular Electronics: Proceedings of the 4th International School on Condensed Matter Physics. 748p. 1987. text 164.00 (*9971-5-0201-1*) World Scientific Pub.

— Nonlinear Phenomena in Solids, Modern Topics: Proceedings of the 3rd International School on Condensed Matter Physics, Yarna, Bulgaria, Sept. 21-29, 1984. 484p. 1985. 100.00 (*9971-966-72-7*) World Scientific Pub.

— Optical & Acoustic Waves in Solids - Modern Topics: Proceedings of the International School on Condensed Matter Physics, 2nd, Varna, Bulgaria Sept. 23-30, 1982. 490p. 1983. 108.00 (*9971-950-61-8*) World Scientific Pub.

Borissov, M. & Kirov, N. Electronic & Optoelectronic Materials for the Twenty-First Century. 660p. 1993. text 121.00 (*981-02-1431-6*) World Scientific Pub.

Borissov, M., et al. New Physical Problems in Electronic Materials: Proceedings of the 6th ISCMP. 572p. 1991. text 151.00 (*981-02-0474-4*) World Scientific Pub.

— Surface Waves in Solids & Layered Structures, Acoustoelectronics '89: 2nd-4th International Symposium-Conference. 480p. 1990. text 151.00 (*981-02-0091-9*) World Scientific Pub.

Borisute, Moshe, jt. tr. see Arno, Sholomo.

Borisy, Gary G., et al, eds. Molecular Biology of the Cytoskeleton. LC 84-17566. 512p. 1984. 62.00 (*0-87969-174-3*) Cold Spring Harbor.

Boritt, Gabor S. Historian's Lincoln: Pseudohistory, Psychohistory, & History. LC 96-216294. 456p. 1996. 16.95 (*0-252-06544-1*) U of Ill Pr.

— Jefferson Davis's Generals. LC 98-49045. (Gettysburg Civil War Institute Bks.). (Illus.). 256p. 1999. 27.50 (*0-19-512062-0*) OUP.

— Lincoln & the Economics of the American Dream. LC 94-21005. 416p. 1994. reprint ed. 16.95 (*0-252-06445-3*) U of Ill Pr.

— Why the Confederacy Lost. 224p. 1992. text 30.00 (*0-19-507405-X*) OUP.

Boritt, Gabor S., ed. The Gettysburg Nobody Knows. LC 96-52524. (Gettysburg Lectures). (Illus.). 288p. 1997. 27.50 (*0-19-510223-1*) OUP.

— The Gettysburg Nobody Knows. (Gettysburg Lectures). (Illus.). 288p. 1999. pap. 13.95 (*0-19-512906-7*) OUP.

***Boritt, Gabor S., ed.** Jefferson Davis's Generals. (Gettysburg Civil War Institute Books Ser.). (Illus.). 256p. 2000. pap. 13.95 (*0-19-513921-6*) OUP.

Boritt, Gabor S., ed. Of the People, by the People, for the People & Other Quotations from Abraham Lincoln. 224p. 1996. 21.00 (*0-231-10326-3*) Col U Pr.

— Why the Civil War Came. 272p. 1996. text 30.00 (*0-19-507941-8*) OUP.

— Why the Civil War Came. 272p. 1997. reprint ed. pap. 13.95 (*0-19-511376-4*) OUP.

— Why the Confederacy Lost. 224p. (C). 1993. reprint ed. pap. text 13.95 (*0-19-508549-3*, 11094) OUP.

Boritt, Gabor S. & Forness, Norman O., eds. The Historian's Lincoln: Pseudohistory, Psychohistory, & History. (Illus.). 456p. 1988. 29.95 (*0-252-01527-4*) U of Ill Pr.

Boritt, Gabor S., ed. see Fellman, Michael, et al.

Boritz, J. Efrim & Wensley, Antony K. Capex: A Knowledge-Based Expert System for Substantive Audit Planning. (Rutgers Series on Accounting Research). 314p. (C). 1996. text 49.95 (*1-55876-056-3*) Wiener Pubs Inc.

Boritzer, Etan. What Is Death? LC 98-75397. (What Is? Ser.). (Illus.). 32p. (J). (gr. k-5). 1999. 14.95 (*0-9637597-4-4*) V Lane Bks.

— What Is Death? LC 98-75397. (What Is? Ser.). (Illus.). 32p. (J). (gr. k-5). 1999. pap. 6.95 (*0-9637597-5-2*) V Lane Bks.

— What Is God? (Illus.). 32p. (Orig.). (J). (gr. 4-7). 1990. 14.95 (*0-920668-89-5*); pap. 6.95 (*0-920668-88-7*) Firefly Bks Ltd.

— What Is Love? LC 93-94066. (Illus.). 32p. (J). (gr. 1-4). 1996. 14.95 (*0-9637597-2-8*) V Lane Bks.

Borja. Derecho Politico y Constitucional. (SPA.). pap. 15.99 (*968-16-3437-3*, Pub. by Fondo) Continental Bk.

Borja, Arthur, jt. auth. see Moch, Joseph W.

Borja, Corinne, jt. auth. see Borja, Robert.

***Borja, Erik.** Zen Gardens. (Illus.). 2000. 29.95 (*0-7063-7855-5*) Ward Lock Ltd UK.

Borja, Jordi & Castells, Manuel. The Local & the Global: Management of Cities in the Information Age. LC 97-222100. 320p. 1997. pap. 40.00 (*1-85383-441-6*, Pub. by Escan Pubns) Island Pr.

Borja, Lalo, tr. see Molina, Armando.

Borja, Manola. Antoni Tapies: New Paintings. (Illus.). 54p. (Orig.). 1995. pap. 15.00 (*1-878283-58-8*) PaceWildenstein.

***Borja, Paul & Kraus, Krandall.** It's Never about What It's About: What We Learned about Living While Waiting to Die. 2000. pap. 12.95 (*1-55583-571-6*, Pub. by Alyson Pubns) Consort Bk Sales.

***Borja, Paul A. & Kraus, Krandall A.** It's Never about What It's about: What We Learned about Living While We Were Waiting to Die. viii,200p. 1999. pap. 15.95 (*0-9671867-0-6*) Commun Life Pr.

Borja, Phillip C. Chamorros According to Einstein, Mendel, Fuller, & Christ. LC 96-86362. (Illus.). vi, 116p. (Orig.). 1997. pap. 9.95 (*0-9654039-0-4*) Chamorro Nation.

Borja, Robert & Borja, Corinne. Making Chinese Papercuts. Tucker, Kathleen, ed. LC 79-18358. 40p. (J). (gr. 3-8). 1980. lib. bdg. 14.95 (*0-8075-4948-7*) A Whitman.

Borja, Rodrigo. Enciclopedia de la Politica (Encyclopedia of Politics) (SPA.). 1015p. 1997. 105.99 (*968-16-5217-7*, Pub. by Fondo) Continental Bk.

Borjars, Kersti, ed. Feature Distribution in Swedish Noun Phrases. LC 99-22552. (Publications of the Philological Society: Vol. 32). xiv, 290p. 1998. pap. 29.95 (*0-631-20871-2*) Blackwell Pubs.

Borjas. Labor Economics. 2nd ed. LC 99-52902. 544p. 1999. 78.75 (*0-07-231198-3*) McGraw.

— Labor Economics. 2nd ed. 2000. student ed. 19.25 (*0-07-231193-2*) McGraw.

***Borjas, George J.** Heaven's Door: Immigration Policy & the American Economy. LC 99-12997. 1999. 27.95 (*0-691-05966-7*, Pub. by Princeton U Pr) Cal Prin Full Svc.

Borjas, George J. International Differences in the Labor Market Performance of Immigrants. LC 88-28017. 106p. 1988. text 19.00 (*0-88099-065-1*); pap. text 9.00 (*0-88099-064-3*) W E Upjohn.

***Borjas, George J.** Issues in the Economics of Immigration LC 99-39690. (National Bureau of Economic Research Conference Report Ser.). 2000. 55.00 (*0-226-06631-2*) U Ch Pr.

Borjas, George J. Labor Economics. LC 95-21464. 656p. (C). 1995. 78.75 (*0-07-006597-7*) McGraw.

— Labor Economics. (C). 1995. pap., student ed. 24.69 (*0-07-006599-3*) McGraw.

— Union Control of Pension Funds: Will the North Rise Again? LC 79-66581. 41p. 1979. pap. 9.95 (*0-917616-36-7*) ICS Pr.

Borjas, George J. & Freeman, Richard B., eds. Immigration & the Work Force: Economic Consequences for the United States & Source Areas. LC 92-15620. (National Bureau of Economic Research Project Report Ser.). (Illus.). 291p. 1992. 49.50 (*0-226-06633-9*) U Ch Pr.

Borjesson, Gunnar. Methane Oxidation in Landfill Cover Soils. (Acta Uiversitatis Agriculturae Seuciae, Agraia: No. 44). (Illus.). 110p. 1997. pap. 34.00 (*91-576-5298-8*) Coronet Bks.

Bork. Diseases of Oral Mucosa & the Mouth. 1996. text 99.00 (*0-7216-4039-7*, W B Saunders Co) Harcrt Hlth Sci Grp.

— The Tempting of America. 448p. 1997. per. 14.00 (*0-684-84337-4*, Touchstone) S&S Trade Pap.

— The War in the Culture. 1994. 24.95 (*0-02-903763-8*) S&S Trade.

Bork, Albert G., tr. see Florescano, Enrique.

Bork, B. A., ed. Researchers in Powder Metallurgy, Vol. 1. Michalewicz, Zbigniew, tr. from RUS. LC 66-15306. 156p. reprint ed. pap. 48.40 (*0-608-11242-9*, 202067500018) Bks Demand.

Bork, Christopher E., ed. Research in Physical Therapy. (Illus.). 384p. 1993. text 38.00 (*0-397-54803-6*) Lppncott W & W.

Bork, David. Family Business, Risky Business: How to Make It Work. LC 86-47594. 186p. 1993. reprint ed. pap. 13.00 (*0-9637028-0-7*) BorkInst Fmly.

Bork, David, et al. Working with Family Businesses: A Guide for Professionals. LC 95-36409. (The Jossey-Bass Management Ser.). 252p. 1995. 32.95 (*0-7879-0172-5*) Jossey-Bass.

Bork, Dieter, jt. auth. see Mayland, Hans J.

Bork, Egon & Kaper, E. Danish-German Dictionary: Dansk-Tysk Ordbog. (DAN & GER.). 626p. 1981. 45.00 (*0-7859-0909-5*, M1283) Fr & Eur.

— Tysk-Dansk Rode Ordboger. 12th ed. 604p. 1986. 49.95 (*0-7859-3724-2*) Fr & Eur.

Bork, K. R. The Rotary Rig & Its Components. 4th ed. LC 93-49573. (Rotary Drilling Ser.: Unit 1, Lesson 1). (Illus.). 128p. 1995. pap. text 16.00 (*0-88698-166-2*, 2.10140) PETEX.

Bork, K. R., ed. see Davis, L. D.

Bork, Kathryn R., tr. see Florescano, Enrique.

Bork, Kathy, intro. The Bit. 4th ed. (Unit I, Lesson 2: Unit I). (Illus.). 152p. 1995. pap. text 16.00 (*0-88698-167-0*, 2.10240) PETEX.

Bork, Kathy, ed. see Baker, Ron.

Bork, Kathy, ed. see Gregston, Terry G.

Bork, Kathy, ed. see Horton, S. T.

Bork, Kathy, ed. see Van Dyke, Kate.

Bork, Kathy, ed. & intro. see Davis, Laurel D.

Bork, Kennard B. Kirtley Fletcher Mather: Scientist, Teacher, Social Activist, 1888-1978. LC 94-6486. 1994. 31.95 (*0-934394-09-1*) AAASPD.

***Bork, Peer.** Analysis of Amino Acid Sequences. Vol. 54. (Illus.). 514p. 2000. 110.00 (*0-12-034254-5*) Acad Pr.

Bork, Robert. Slouching Towards Gomorrah. 1997. pap. 13.00 (*0-614-28103-2*, ReganBks) HarperTrade.

Bork, Robert H. American Constitutional Tradition. Date not set. pap. write for info. (*0-06-098861-4*, ReganBks) HarperTrade.

— American Constitutional Tradition. 2002. write for info. (*0-06-039377-7*, ReganBks) HarperTrade.

Bork, Robert H. The Antitrust Paradox: A Policy at War with Itself. LC 92-39587. 1993. pap. 19.95 (*0-02-904456-1*) Free Pr.

— Litigating Against the Government: Leveling the Playing Field LC 99-165558. 22p. 1996. pap. write for info. (*0-937299-51-0*) Natl Legal Ctr Pub Interest.

— Slouching Towards Gomorrah: Modern Liberalism & American Decline. 400p. 1997. pap. 14.00 (*0-06-098719-7*) HarpC.

Borka, H., jt. ed. see Slamecka, V.

Borkakoti, Jitendralal, et al. International Trade & Labour Markets. LC 97-22991. 1997. text 65.00 (*0-312-17733-X*) St Martin.

***Borkan, Jeffrey M., et al, eds.** Patients & Doctors: Life-Changing Stories from Primary Care. LC 99-19758. 240p. 1999. text 24.95 (*0-299-16340-7*) U of Wis Pr.

Borkar, V. S. Probability Theory: An Advanced Course. (Universitext Ser.). 160p. 1995. 36.95 (*0-387-94558-X*) Spr-Verlag.

Borkar, V. V. & Ambewadikar, R. M. Co-Operative Movement & the Weaker Sections. 1989. 14.00 (*81-202-0238-4*, Pub. by Ajanta) S Asia.

Borkar, Vivek S. Topics in Controlled Markov Chains. LC 90-42154. (Pitman Research Notes in Mathematics Ser.: Vol. 240). 191p. 1991. reprint ed. pap. 59.30 (*0-608-03595-5*, 206441800009) Bks Demand.

Borkenau, Franz. European Communism. (WV Encore Edition Ser.). (C). 1996. pap. text 45.00 (*0-8133-7103-1*) Westview.

— The Totalitarian Enemy. LC 78-63654. (Studies in Fascism: Ideology & Practice). reprint ed. 42.50 (*0-404-16914-7*) AMS Pr.

— Der Ubergang Vom Feudalen Zum Burgerlichen Weltbild. LC 74-25740. (European Sociology Ser.). 574p. 1975. reprint ed. 47.95 (*0-405-06496-9*) Ayer.

Borkenhagen, Lea M. & Abramovitz, Janet N. Proceedings of the International Conference on Women & Biodiversity. 104p. (Orig.). 1993. pap. write for info. (*1-883242-00-2*) Comm Women & Biodiv.

Borkenstein, H. M., jt. ed. see Roth, Roswitha.

Borkent, A. Biting Midges in the Cretaceous Amber of North America (Diptera - Ceratopogonidae) (Illus.). 237p. 1995. 71.00 (*90-73348-40-4*, Pub. by Backhuys Pubs) Balogh.

Borkent, Hans. Linguistic Bibliography for the Year, 1983. Janse, Mark, ed. 1985. text 477.00 (*90-247-3241-7*) Kluwer Academic.

Borker, Christoph & Burow, Johannes. Die Hellenistischen Amphorenstempel aus Pergamon. 142p. 1997. text 99.00 (*3-11-015621-0*) De Gruyter.

Borker, Susan R., jt. auth. see Rudolph, Claire S.

***Borkhuis, Charles.** Alpha Ruins. 112p. 2000. 19.95 (*0-8387-5442-2*) Bucknell U Pr.

Borkhuis, Charles. Dinner with Franz. (Poetry New York Pamphlet Ser.: Vol. 9). 20p. 1998. pap. 5.00 (*0-923389-19-9*) Meet Eyes Bind.

— Hypnogogic Sonnets. 16p. 1992. pap. 3.00 (*0-87376-073-5*) Red Dust.

— Mouth of Shadows: Hamlet's Ghosts Perform Hamlet & Sunspots. LC 99-40608. (Illus.). 120p. 2000. pap. 12.00 (*1-881471-32-2*) S Duyvil.

— Proximity (Stolen Arrows) 1994. pap. 9.95 (*0-9623806-3-6*) SINK Pr.

Borkin, Ann. Problems in Form & Function. Ross, John R. & Lakoff, George, eds. LC 82-11417. (Language & Being Ser.). 160p. 1985. text 73.25 (*0-89391-116-X*) Ablx Pub.

Borkin, Joseph, jt. auth. see Waldrop, Frank.

Borklund, C. W. Military Leaders since World War II, 1945-1990. (American Profiles Ser.). (Illus.). 144p. 1992. lib. bdg. 17.95 (*0-8160-2606-8*) Facts on File.

— U. S. Defense & Military Fact Book. LC 90-23756. x, 293 p. 1991. lib. bdg. 55.00 (*0-87436-593-7*) ABC-CLIO.

Borklund, Carl W., jt. auth. see Hayward, John T.

Borklund, Elmer, ed. Contemporary Literary Critics. 2nd ed. 600p. 1982. 140.00 (*0-912289-33-3*, 200059) St James Pr.

Borkman, Thomasina J. Understanding Self-Help/Mutual-Aid: Experiential Learning in the Commons. LC 98-50649. 260p. (C). 1999. pap. 23.00 (*0-8135-2630-2*); text 50.00 (*0-8135-2629-9*) Rutgers U Pr.

Borko, Harold, ed. Targets for Research in Library Education. LC 72-9923. 253p. reprint ed. pap. 78.50 (*0-608-12479-6*, 202422300035) Bks Demand.

Borkoff, Steve, jt. auth. see Baylin, Frank.

Borkovec, A. B. & Gelman, Dale B., eds. Insect Neurochemistry & Neurophysiology - 1986. LC 86-27753. (Experimental & Clinical Neuroscience Ser.). 504p. 1987. 119.50 (*0-89603-119-5*) Humana.

Borkovec, A. B. & Masler, Edward P., eds. Insect Neurochemistry & Neurophysiology 1989. LC 90-4001. (Experimental & Clinical Neuroscience Ser.). (Illus.). 482p. 1990. 119.50 (*0-89603-168-3*) Humana.

Borkovec, Alexei B. Insect Neurochemistry & Neurophysiology. 416p. 1994. 180.95 (*0-8493-4591-X*) CRC Pr.

Borkovskii, A. B. English-Russian Dictionary of Computers & Programming. (ENG & RUS.). 334p. (C). 1992. text 110.00 (*0-569-24321-1*, Pub. by Collets) St Mut.

***Borkowska, Grazyna.** Alienated Women: A Study on Polish Women's Writing, 1845-1918. 200p. (C). 2000. 47.95 (*963-9241-03-2*) Ctrl Europ Univ.

***Borkowski, Andrew.** Deathbed Gifts. 300p. 1999. 41.50 (*1-85431-938-8*, Pub. by Blackstone Pr) Gaunt.

Borkowski, Andrew. Textbook of Succession. 371p. 1997. pap. 42.00 (*1-85431-627-3*, Pub. by Blackstone Pr) Gaunt.

Borkowski, Cezar. The Complete Idiot's Guide to Martial Arts. LC 98-87606. 352p. 1998. 16.95 (*0-02-862947-7*) Macmillan Gen Ref.

Borkowski, Gary L. & Allen, Matthew. The Laboratory Small Ruminant. (Laboratory Animal Pocket Reference Ser.). 176p. 1999. spiral bd. 44.95 (*0-8493-2568-4*) CRC Pr.

Borkowski, John D. & Day, Jeanne D., eds. Cognition in Special Children: Comparative Approaches to Retardation, Learning Disabilities, & Giftedness. LC 87-11421. 256p. (C). 1987. text 73.25 (*0-89391-296-4*) Ablx Pub.

Borkowski, John G., jt. ed. see Day, Jeanne D.

Borkowski, P. An English-Polish Dictionary of Idioms & Phrases. (ENG & POL.). 203p. 1982. pap. 9.95 (*0-8288-1630-1*, M8165) Fr & Eur.

Borkowski, Richard P. School Sports Safety Handbook. LC 97-51723. 1998. 54.00 (*1-57834-006-3*) LRP Pubns.

Borkowski, Tadeusz, tr. & contrib. by see Perdue, William D.

Borland. Pediatric Airway. 1992. 39.00 (*0-316-10276-8*, Little Brwn Med Div) Lppncott W & W.

Borland, Carroll. Countess Dracula: A Novel. 144p. 1995. pap. 19.95 (*1-882127-32-3*) Magicimage Filmbooks.

Borland, Deedee & McCormack, Barbara. Angiporto, Inc. Story & Cookbook. rev. ed. 193p. 1991. pap. text 10.80 (*0-9630876-0-6*) Angiporto.

Borland, Douglas. Homeopathy in Practice. LC 82-84366. 176p. 1983. reprint ed. pap. 9.95 (*0-87983-326-2*, 33262K, Keats Publng) NTC Contemp Pub Co.

Borland, Hal. How to Write & Sell Non-Fiction. LC 72-7972. 223p. 1973. reprint ed. lib. bdg. 45.00 (*0-8371-6558-X*, BONF, Greenwood Pr) Greenwood.

— Sundial of the Seasons. 1994. reprint ed. lib. bdg. 32.95 (*1-56849-256-1*) Buccaneer Bks.

— This Hill, This Valley. 1990. pap. 16.95 (*0-8018-4020-1*) Johns Hopkins.

— When the Legends Die. 304p. (YA). (gr. 6-12). 1984. mass mkt. 5.99 (*0-553-25738-2*) Bantam.

An Asterisk (*) at the beginning of an entry indicates that the title is appearing for the first time.

— When the Legends Die. (YA). (gr. 6-12). 1964. 10.60 (*0-606-01571-X*, Pub. by Turtleback) Demco.

Borland, Harriet. Soviet Literary Theory & Practice During the First Five-Year Plan, 1928-1932. LC 69-13833. 256p. 1969. reprint ed. lib. bdg. 65.00 (*0-8371-1075-0*, BOSL, Greenwood Pr) Greenwood.

Borland, Isabel A. Cuban-American Literature of Exile: From Person to Persona. (New World Studies). 190p. 1998. pap. 19.50 (*0-8139-1813-8*) U Pr of Va.

Borland, James A. Christ In The Old Testament; Old Testament Appearances Of Christ In Human Form. 1999. pap. text 15.99 (*1-85792-448-7*) Christian Focus.

— A General Introduction to the New Testament. rev. ed. (Illus.). 216p. (C). 1995. pap. 17.95 (*0-936461-04-7*) Univ Book Hse.

— Lectures on Bible Prophecy. 123p. (Orig.). (C). 1991. pap. text 9.95 (*0-936461-03-9*) Univ Book Hse.

— Old Testament Life & Literature. (Illus.). 194p. (C). 1989. pap. text 15.95 (*0-936461-02-0*) Univ Book Hse.

Borland, James H. Planning & Implementing Programs for the Gifted. (Education & Psychology of the Gifted Ser.). 272p. 1989. pap. text 20.95 (*0-8077-2966-3*) Tchrs Coll.

Borland, Kathryn K. & Speicher, Helen R. Harry Houdini: Young Magician. LC 90-23321. (Childhood of Famous Americans Ser.). (Illus.). 192p. (J). (gr. 3-7). 1991. reprint ed. mass mkt. 4.95 (*0-689-71476-9*) Aladdin.

Borland, Kathryn Kilby. Harry Houdini: Young Magician. 1991. 10.05 (*0-606-07625-5*, Pub. by Turtleback) Demco.

Borland, Lee. Double Your Recurring Revenue! How to Sell Service Agreements. 2nd rev. ed. (Illus.). 124p. 1992. ring bd. 125.00 (*1-892594-01-3*) Security Pr Inc.

— How to Sell Service Agreements: A Comprehensive Program. (Illus.). iii, 75p. 1991. ring bd. 125.00 (*1-892594-00-5*) Security Pr Inc.

Borland, Lee & Driscoll, Edward B., Jr. How to Become a Master of Marketing: 101 Secrets to a Six Figure Income for Alarm Dealers. (Illus.). 412p. 1997. ring bd. 195.00 (*1-892594-07-2*) Security Pr Inc.

Borland, Lee & Security Press, Inc. Staff. The Excitement of Home Entertainment! How to Start Your Business. 314p. 1995. ring bd. 145.00 (*1-892594-06-4*) Security Pr Inc.

— Get Paid! Effective Accounts Receivable Management for Alarm Companies. (Illus.). 390p. 1993. ring bd. 169.00 (*1-892594-04-8*) Security Pr Inc.

— Get Paid! Effective Accounts Receivable Management for Small Business. (Illus.). 350p. 1995. ring bd. 95.00 (*1-892594-05-6*) Security Pr Inc.

Borland, Lee, jt. auth. see Chamberlain, Jeffrey.

Borland, Lorelie J. Basics of Environmental Law. (Real Estate Law & Practice Ser.). 584p. 1991. pap. text 70.00 (*0-685-56944-6*, N4-4556) PLI.

***Borland, Polly, photos by.** The Babies. (Illus.). 2000. 50.00 (*1-57687-083-9*, pwerHse Bks) pwerHse Cultrl.

Borland, Russell. Microsoft Exchange 5.0 in Business: Project Management, Scheduling, E-Mail, Forms, Public Folders. LC 95-44648. 512p. 24.95 (*1-57231-218-1*) Microsoft.

— Running Microsoft Outlook 97. LC 97-14337. 416p. 1997. 29.99 incl. cd-rom (*1-57231-608-X*) Microsoft.

— Running Microsoft Word for Windows 95: In-Depth Reference & Inside Tips from THE Software Experts. (Running Ser.). 1056p. 1995. pap. 29.95 (*1-55615-848-3*) Microsoft.

— Running Microsoft Windows NT Workstation, Version 4.0. LC 96-40186. 1104p. 39.95 incl. cd-rom (*1-57231-320-X*) Microsoft.

Borland, Russell & Ross, John. Introducing Microsoft Windows 98. 2nd ed. LC 98-6572. (Introducing Ser.). 432p. 24.99 (*1-57231-920-8*) Microsoft.

Borland, Vance, ed. see Crowley, Aleister, et al.

Borlander, Donald O. New Webster Spelling Dictionary. 1990. mass mkt. 5.99 (*0-425-12474-6*) Berkley Pub.

Borlase, Tim. Songs of Labrador. 232p. 1993. pap. 14.95 (*0-86492-156-X*, Pub. by Goose Ln Edits) Genl Dist Srvs.

Borlase, W. C. Borlase: The Descent, Name & Arms of Borlase in the County of Cornwall. 205p. 1992. reprint ed. pap. 33.00 (*0-8328-2642-1*); reprint ed. lib. bdg. 43.00 (*0-8328-2641-3*) Higginson Bk Co.

Borlenghi, Patricia. Angel Activity Book. (Illus.). 12p. (J). 1995. pap. write for info. (*1-85479-675-5*, Pub. by M OMara) Trafalgar.

Borley, H. V. & Kidner, R. W. West London Railway & the W. L. E. R. (C). 1985. 39.00 (*0-85361-174-2*) St Mut.

Borley, N. R., jt. auth. see Grace, P. A.

Borley, Neil R. Concise Guide to Clinical Surface Anatomy. (Medical Ser.). 1997. pap. 25.00 (*0-7637-0594-2*) Jones & Bartlett.

***Borley, Neil R. & Achan, Vinod.** Instant Physiology. LC 99-29385. (Illus.). 224p. (C). 2000. pap. 25.95 (*0-632-05004-7*) Blackwell Sci.

Borley, Neil R., jt. auth. see Whitaker, Robert H.

Borloo, E., et al, eds. Qualification of Inspection Procedures: Proceedings of an Advanced Seminar on Non-Destructive Testing Techniques for the Inspection of Industrial Structural Components, Joint Research Centre, Ispra, Italy, 25-29 October 1993. LC 94-39302. (Eurocourses: Mechanical & Materials Science Ser.: Vol. 2). 1995. text 272.50 (*0-7923-3257-1*) Kluwer Academic.

Borman, Gary L. & Ragland, Kenneth W. Combustion Engineering. LC 97-34198. 640p. 1998. 102.81 (*0-07-006567-5*) McGraw.

***Borman, Geoffrey D., et al, eds.** Title I: Compensatory Education at the Crossroads. (A Volume in the Sociocultural, Political & Historical Studies in Education Series). 208p. 2001. write for info. (*0-8058-3549-0*); pap. write for info. (*0-8058-3550-4*) L Erlbaum Assocs.

Borman, Gilbert & Thompson, Frank H., Jr. 1984 Notes. (Cliffs Notes Ser.). 56p. 1967. pap. 4.95 (*0-8220-0899-8*, Cliff) IDG Bks.

Borman, John & Tangborn, Inger. Tunisia: Human Rights Report of 1989. Frey, Barbara, ed. 74p. (Orig.). (C). 1990. pap. 7.00 (*0-929293-09-6*) MN Advocates.

Borman, K. M. The Social Life of Children in a Changing Society. (Illus.). 320p. (C). 1982. text 69.95 (*0-89859-187-2*) L Erlbaum Assocs.

Borman, Kathryn & Baber, M. Yvette. Ethnic Diversity in Communities & Schools: Recognizing & Building Strengths. LC 98-5761. (David C. Anchin Ser.). 1998. 73.25 (*1-56750-386-1*) Ablx Pub.

Borman, Kathryn & Schneider, Barbara, eds. The Adolescent Years: Social Influences & Educational Challenges. 240p. 1998. 27.00 (*0-226-06636-3*) U Ch Pr.

Borman, Kathryn M. The First "Real" Job: A Study of Young Workers. LC 90-9910. (SUNY Series, the New Inequalities). 153p. (C). 1991. pap. text 21.95 (*0-7914-0599-0*) State U NY Pr.

Borman, Kathryn M., ed. The Social Life of Children in a Changing Society. LC 82-11557. 296p. (C). 1982. text 73.25 (*0-89391-165-8*) Ablx Pub.

Borman, Kathryn M., et al, eds. Implementing Educational Reform: Sociological Perspectives on Educational Policy. LC 96-13154. (Social & Policy Issues in Education Ser.). 496p. 1996. pap. 24.95 (*1-56750-267-9*); text 73.25 (*1-56750-266-0*) Ablx Pub.

— Women in the Workplace: Effects of Families. LC 84-2941. (Modern Sociology Ser.). 280p. 1984. text 73.25 (*0-89391-166-6*) Ablx Pub.

Borman, Kathryn M. & Baber, M. Yvette. Ethnic Diversity in Communities & Schools: Recognizing & Building Strengths. LC 98-5761. (David C. Anchin Ser.). 1998. pap. 24.95 (*1-56750-387-X*) Ablx Pub.

Borman, Kathryn M. & Greenman, Nancy P., eds. Changing American Education: Recapturing the Past or Inventing the Future? LC 92-42842. (SUNY Series, Teacher Preparation & Development). 416p. (C). 1994. text 74.50 (*0-7914-1659-3*); pap. text 24.95 (*0-7914-1660-7*) State U NY Pr.

Borman, Kathryn M. & Obermiller, Phillip J., eds. From Mountain to Metropolis: Appalachian Migrants in American Cities. 1993. text. write for info. (*0-89189-367-9*, Bergin & Garvey) Greenwood.

— From Mountain to Metropolis: Appalachian Migrants in American Cities. LC 93-11855. 248p. 1994. 55.00 (*0-89789-367-0*, Bergin & Garvey) Greenwood.

Borman, Kathryn M & Reisman, Jane, eds. Becoming a Worker. LC 86-1083. 296p. 1986. text 73.25 (*0-89391-314-6*) Ablx Pub.

Borman, Kathryn M., jt. auth. see Yinger, Robert J.

Borman, Kathryn M., jt. ed. see Dubeck, Paula J.

Borman, Kathryn M., jt. ed. see Johnston, J. Howard.

Borman, Kathryn M., jt. ed. see Jones, Bruce A.

Borman, Kathryn M., jt. ed. see Stegelin, Dolores A.

Borman, Laurie D. The Smart Woman's Guide to Business Travel. LC 98-49899. (Smart Woman's Guides Ser.). 192p. 1999. pap. 14.99 (*1-56414-372-4*) Career Pr Inc.

Borman, Leonard D., et al, eds. Helping People to Help Themselves: Self-Help & Prevention. LC 82-924. (Prevention in Human Services Ser.: Vol. 1, No. 3). 129p. 1982. text 39.95 (*0-917724-67-4*) Haworth Pr.

— Helping People to Help Themselves: Self-Help & Prevention. 129p. 1991. pap. 19.95 (*1-56024-173-X*) Haworth Pr.

Borman, Mark, jt. auth. see Williams, Howard.

Borman, Stuart A., ed. Instrumentation in Analytical Chemistry, Vol. 2. LC 72-95641. (Other Technical Bks.). 1982. pap. 27.95 (*0-8412-0738-0*) Am Chemical.

— Instrumentation in Analytical Chemistry, Vol. 2. LC 72-95641. (Other Technical Bks.). 414p. 1982. text 48.00 (*0-8412-0726-7*, Pub. by Am Chemical) OUP.

— Instrumentation in Analytical Chemistry, Vol. 2. LC 72-95641. (ACS Reprint Collection). (Illus.). 427p. 1982. reprint ed. pap. 132.40 (*0-608-04352-4*, 206513300002) Bks Demand.

— Instrumentation in Analytical Chemistry, 1982-86. LC 86-3453. (An American Chemical Society Publication). (Illus.). 336p. 1986. text 50.00 (*0-8412-0969-3*, Pub. by Am Chemical) OUP.

— Instrumentation in Analytical Chemistry, 1982-86. LC 86-3453. (Illus.). 333p. 1986. reprint ed. pap. 103.30 (*0-608-04350-8*, 206513100001) Bks Demand.

Borman, Susan, et al. Through the Looking Glass: A Field Guide to Aquatic Plants. (Illus.). 256p. 1998. pap. 24.95 (*0-932310-32-X*) U of Wis-Stevens Point.

Borman, Suzanne & Levine, Joel M. A Practical Guide to Elementary Instruction: From Plan to Delivery. LC 96-38717. 396p. 1997. pap. text 57.00 (*0-205-14188-9*) Allyn.

Borman, Suzanne & Levine, Joel M. A Practical Guide to Elementary Instruction: From Plan to Delivery. (C). 1997. pap., teacher ed. write for info. (*0-205-26516-2*, T6516-3) Allyn.

Borman, Walter C., ed. Performance Evaluation. (International Library of Management). 500p. 1994. 265.95 (*1-85521-402-4*, Pub. by Dartmth Pub) Ashgate Pub Co.

Borman, Walter C. & Motowidlo, Stephan J., eds. Organizational Citizenship Behavior & Contextual Performance: A Special Issue of "Human Performance" 120p. 1997. pap. 20.00 (*0-8058-9875-1*) L Erlbaum Assocs.

Borman, William. Gandhi & Non-Violence. LC 86-1889. (SUNY Series in Philosophy). 287p. (C). 1986. pap. text 18.95 (*0-88706-331-4*) State U NY Pr.

Bormanis, Andre. Star Trek Science Logs. 1998. per. 16.00 (*0-671-00997-4*, PB Trade Paper) PB.

Bormann, Ernest G. & Bormann, Nancy C. Effective Small Group Communication. 6th ed. 1996. pap. write for info. (*0-8087-8495-1*) Pearson Custom.

Bormann, Ernest G., jt. auth. see Howell, William S.

Bormann, F. H. & Likens, Gene E. Pattern & Process in a Forested Ecosystem: Disturbance, Development & the State Based on the Hubbard Brook Ecosystem Study. LC 94-211107. 264p. 1996. 43.95 (*0-387-94344-7*) Spr-Verlag.

— Pattern & Process in a Forested Ecosystem: Disturbance, Development & the Steady State Based on the Hubbard Brook Ecosystem Study. LC 78-6015. (Illus.). 1991. 44.00 (*0-387-90321-6*) Spr-Verlag.

Bormann, F. H., jt. auth. see Likens, Gene E.

Bormann, F. Herbert & Kellert, Stephen R., eds. Ecology, Economics, Ethics: The Broken Circle. LC 91-15191. (Illus.). 224p. (C). 1992. 35.00 (*0-300-04976-5*) Yale U Pr.

— Ecology, Economics, Ethics: The Broken Circle. (Illus.). 224p. (C). 1993. pap. 17.00 (*0-300-05751-2*) Yale U Pr.

Bormann, F. Herbert, et al. Redesigning the American Lawn: A Search for Environmental Harmony. (Illus.). 1995. pap. 15.00 (*0-300-06197-8*) Yale U Pr.

Bormann, F. Herbert, jt. auth. see Likens, Gene E.

Bormann, Lukas, et al, eds. Religious Propaganda & Missionary Competition in the New Testament World: Essays in Honor of Dieter Georgi. LC 94-9716. (Supplements to Novem Testamentum Ser.: Vol. 74). xiii, 570p. 1994. 168.00 (*90-04-10049-0*) Brill Academic Pubs.

Bormann, Martin. The Bormann Letters. Trevor-Roper, Hugh R., ed. Stevens, R. H., tr. LC 78-63655. (Studies in Fascism: Ideology & Practice). (Illus.). reprint ed. 47.50 (*0-404-16908-2*) AMS Pr.

Bormann, Nancy C., jt. auth. see Bormann, Ernest G.

Bormann, Rudiger, et al, eds. Metastable Phases & Microstructures: Materials Research Society Symposium Proceedings. (MRS Symposium Proceedings Ser.: Vol. 400). 368p. 1996. 73.00 (*1-55899-303-7*, 400) Materials Res.

Bormans, Maurice, jt. auth. see Pontifical Council for Interreligious Dialogue Sta.

Bormaster, Jeffrey S. & Treat, Carol L. Building Interpersonal Relationships Through Talking, Listening, Communicating. 2nd ed. 139p. (C). 1994. spiral bd. 29.00 (*0-89079-592-4*, 6690) PRO-ED.

— Talking, Listening, Communicating: Building Interpersonal Relationships. LC 82-3702. 120p. (Orig.). (C). 1982. pap. text 24.00 (*0-936104-26-0*, 0072) PRO-ED.

Bormbai, H. & Flien, Michael S. Medieval Russian Culture. 395p. 1985. 140.00 (*0-7855-0890-2*) St Mut.

Borms, J., et al, eds. The Female Athlete. (Medicine & Sport Science Ser.: Vol. 15). (Illus.). xiv, 218p. 1982. 108.00 (*3-8055-2739-X*) S Karger.

Bormuth, John R. On the Theory of Achievement Test Items. LC 70-102071. 1970. lib. bdg. 10.50 (*0-226-06630-4*) U Ch Pr.

— On the Theory of Achievement Test Items With an Appendix by Peter Menzel: On the Linguistic Bases of the Theory of Writing Items. LC 70-102071. 173p. Date not set. reprint ed. pap. 53.70 (*0-608-20599-0*, 205456400003) Bks Demand.

Born. Handbook of Experimental Pharmacology. 1993. 380.00 (*0-387-56937-5*) Spr-Verlag.

Born, A. J., ed. Tears & Laughter. 192p. 1990. 10.00 (*0-945242-13-1*) Shri Ram Chandra.

***Born, Anne.** Planting Light. 77p. 2000. pap. 11.95 (*1-902096-58-4*, Pub. by Headland Pubns) Intl Spec Bk.

Born, Anne & Smith, Alex. Histories. 1999. 10.95 (*3-7052-0159-X*, Pub. by Poetry Salzburg) Intl Spec Bk.

Born, Anne, tr. see Dinesen, Isak.

Born, Anne, tr. see Gaarder, Jostein.

Born, Anne, tr. see Hauger, Torill Thorstad.

Born, Anne, tr. see Heinesen, William.

Born, Anne, tr. see Holmas, Stig.

Born, Anne, tr. see Naess, Atle.

Born, Anne, tr. see Petterson, Per.

Born, Anne, tr. see Pleijel, Agneta.

Born, Anne, tr. see Schmidt, Ane.

Born, Anne, tr. see Schoultz, Solveig Von.

Born, Anne, tr. see Stangerup, Henrik.

Born, Anne, tr. see Tafdrup, Pia.

Born, Anne, tr. & intro. see Carpelan, Bo.

Born, Daniel. The Birth of Liberal Guilt: English Novels from Dickens to Wells. LC 95-11705. 240p. (C). 1996. pap. text 18.95 (*0-8078-4544-2*); lib. bdg. 49.95 (*0-8078-2241-8*) U of NC Pr.

Born, Donna K., ed. see Kleinberg, Howard.

Born, Donna K., ed. see Kleinberg, Howard & Reardon, L. F.

Born, Dorothy. Diabetes in the Family. LC 81-18024. (Illus.). 1982. pap. 9.95 (*0-13-208463-5*) P-H.

Born, Erhard. Lexikon Fuer Eisenbahnfreunde. (GER.). 1977. pap. 59.95 (*0-8288-5494-7*, M7200) Fr & Eur.

Born, Ernst. Lexikon Fuer die Graphische Industrie. (GER.). 135.00 (*0-8288-7621-5*, M7201) Fr & Eur.

— Lexikon Fuer die Graphische Industrie. 2nd ed. (GER.). 125.00 (*3-87641-184-X*, M7201) Fr & Eur.

Born, Franz. Hengst der Sonne. (Illus.). 210p. 1997. reprint ed. 60.00 (*3-487-08389-2*) G Olms Pubs.

Born, G. V., et al, eds. Opioids 2. (Handbook of Experimental Pharmacology Ser.: Vol. 104/II). (Illus.). 880p. 1993. 510.00 (*0-387-55517-X*) Spr-Verlag.

Born, G. V., jt. auth. see Bagge, U.

Born, Gary. Process Management to Quality Improvement: The Way to Design, Document & Reengineer Business Systems. 304p. 1994. 95.00 (*0-471-94283-9*) Wiley.

Born, Gary, jt. auth. see Lange, Dieter.

Born, Gary B. International Arbitration & Forum Selection Agreements: Planning, Drafting & Enforcing. LC 99-28352. 1999. 60.00 (*90-411-9342-1*) Kluwer Law Intl.

— International Commercial Arbitration in United States Courts. LC 94-17187. 1994. pap. text 86.50 (*90-6544-853-5*); lib. bdg. 125.00 (*90-6544-855-1*) Kluwer Academic.

Born, Gary B. & Westin, David. International Civil Litigation in United States Courts: Commentary & Materials. 2nd ed. LC 92-31471. 1992. 85.00 (*90-6544-645-1*); pap. 60.00 (*90-6544-647-8*) Kluwer Law Intl.

Born, Georgina. Rationalizing Culture: IRCAM, Boulez, & the Institutionalisation of the Avant-Garde. LC 93-39386. 392p. 1995. pap. 22.50 (*0-520-20216-3*, Pub. by U CA Pr) Cal Prin Full Svc.

***Born, Georgina & Hesmondhalgh, David, eds.** Western Music & Its Others: Difference, Representation, & Appropriation in Music. LC 00-29871. (Illus.). 409p. 2000. 60.00 (*0-520-22083-8*); pap. 24.95 (*0-520-22084-6*, Pub. by U CA Pr) Cal Prin Full Svc.

Born, Gregory. A Two-Phased Approach to Model Validation for the Susceptibility Model Assessment & Range Test (SMART) Project. LC 94-19233. 1994. pap. text 9.00 (*0-8330-1554-0*, MR-399-AF) Rand Corp.

***Born, Gunter.** Advanced Development with Microsoft Windows Script Host. 450p. 2000. 49.99 (*0-7356-1137-8*) Microsoft.

Born, Gunter. The File Formats Handbook. (Illus.). 1216p. 1995. mass mkt. 81.95 (*1-85032-117-5*) ITCP.

— Inside the Microsoft Windows 98 Registry. LC 98-25678. 495p. 39.99 incl. cd-rom (*1-57231-824-4*) Microsoft.

— Inside the Registry for Microsoft Windows 95. LC 96-37067. 320p. 1997. pap. text 24.99 (*1-57231-424-9*) Microsoft.

***Born, Gunter.** Learn Microsoft Windows Script Host 2.0 Now. (DV-DLT Learn Now Ser.). (Illus.). 2000. pap. text 49.99 (*0-7356-0931-4*) Microsoft.

Born, Joachin & Stickel, Gerhard, eds. Deutscsh als Verkehrssprache in Europa. (Institut fuer Deutsche Sprache - Jahrbuch, 1991 Ser.). (GER.). vi, 342p. (Orig.). (C). 1993. pap. text 98.50 (*3-11-014006-3*) De Gruyter.

Born, Jurgen, ed. Deutschsprachige Literatur Prags und Bohmischen Landern, 1900-1925. (GER.). 326p. 1993. lib. bdg. 38.00 (*3-598-11091-X*) K G Saur Verlag.

Born, Karl E. International Banking in the 19th & 20th Centuries. Berghahn, Volker R., tr. 353p. 1983. 39.50 (*0-907582-03-6*) Berg Pubs.

Born-Lechleitner, Ilse. The Motif of Adultery in Elizabethan, Jacobean & Caroline Tragedy. LC 95-5397. (Salzburger Studien Ser.). 428p. 1995. text 109.95 (*0-7734-1284-0*) E Mellen.

Born, M. Physics in My Generation. 2nd rev. ed. LC 68-59281. (Heidelberg Science Library: Vol. 7). (Illus.). 1989. 29.95 (*0-387-90008-X*) Spr-Verlag.

***Born, Mark A.** Tidelog 2000 Graphic Almanac: Chesapeake. (Illus.). 144p. 1999. pap. 14.95 (*0-936521-85-6*) Pac Pubs.

— Tidelog 2000 Graphic Almanac: Long Island Sound. (Illus.). 144p. 1999. pap. 14.95 (*0-936521-86-4*) Pac Pubs.

— Tidelog 2000 Graphic Almanac: Mid-Atlantic. (Illus.). 144p. 1999. pap. 14.95 (*0-936521-87-2*) Pac Pubs.

— Tidelog 2000 Graphic Almanac: Northern California. (Illus.). 144p. 1999. pap. 14.95 (*0-936521-80-5*) Pac Pubs.

— Tidelog 2000 Graphic Almanac: Northern New England. (Illus.). 144p. 1999. pap. 14.95 (*0-936521-83-X*) Pac Pubs.

— Tidelog 2000 Graphic Almanac: Puget Sound. (Illus.). 144p. 1999. pap. 14.95 (*0-936521-82-1*) Pac Pubs.

— Tidelog 2000 Graphic Almanac: Southeastern. (Illus.). 144p. 1999. pap. 14.95 (*0-936521-88-0*) Pac Pubs.

— Tidelog 2000 Graphic Almanac: Southern California. (Illus.). 144p. 1999. pap. 14.95 (*0-936521-81-3*) Pac Pubs.

— Tidelog 2000 Graphic Almanac: Southern New England. (Illus.). 144p. 1999. pap. 14.95 (*0-936521-84-8*) Pac Pubs.

Born, Max. Atomic Physics. 8th ed. 495p. 1989. pap. 13.95 (*0-486-65984-4*) Dover.

— Einstein's Theory of Relativity. rev. ed. (Illus.). 376p. (C). 1962. pap. 9.95 (*0-486-60769-0*) Dover.

Born, Max & Huang, Kun. Dynamical Theory of Crystal Lattices. LC 99-192617. (Oxford Classic Texts in the Physical Sciences Ser.). (Illus.). 432p. 1998. pap. text 29.95 (*0-19-850369-5*) OUP.

Born, Max & Wolf, E. Principles of Optics: Electromagnetic Theory of Propagation, Interference & Diffraction of Light. 6th ed. (Illus.). 808p. 1980. pap. 65.00 (*0-08-026481-6*, Pergamon Pr) Elsevier.

Born, Max & Wolf, Emil. Principles of Optics: Electromagnetic Theory of Propagation, Interference & Diffraction of Light. 7th ed. (Illus.). 900p. (C). 1999. 59.95 (*0-521-64222-1*) Cambridge U Pr.

Born, Renate. Michigan German in Frankenmuth: Variation & Change in an East Franconian Dialect. LC 93-9927. (GERM Ser.). xvi, 137p. 1994. 60.00 (*1-879751-59-3*) Camden Hse.

Born, Richard & Hartley, Keith. From Blast to Pop: Aspects of Modern British Art, 1915-1965. LC 97-65940. (Illus.). 136p. (Orig.). 1997. pap. text 29.95 (*0-935573-18-6*) D & A Smart Museum.

Born, Richard, jt. auth. see Adrian, Dennis.

Born, Richard A. & Taylor, Sue, eds. The David & Alfred Smart Museum of Art: A Guide to the Collection. (Illus.). 216p. 1990. 45.00 (*1-55595-061-2*) D & A Smart Museum.

Born, Richard A., jt. ed. see Taylor, Sue.

Born, Richard A., tr. see David & Alfred Smart Museum of Art Staff.

Born, Roscoe C. The Suspended Sentence: A Guide for Writers. LC 93-24797. 224p. (C). 1993. 19.95 (*0-8138-2401-X*) Iowa St U Pr.

Born, Siegfried. In Nazi Uniform. LC 96-69832. (Illus.). 297p. (Orig.). 1997. pap. 21.95 (1-57197-041-X) Pentland Pr.

Born, Stephen M., ed. Redefining National Water Policy: New Roles & Directions. fac. ed. LC HD1694.A5R43. (AWRA Special Publication: No. 89-1). 99p. (Orig.). 1989. reprint ed. pap. 30.70 (0-608-00999-7, 206185700012) Bks Demand.

Born, Stephen M., et al. Exploring Wisconsin Trout Streams: The Angler's Guide. LC 97-9446. (North Coast Bks.). (Illus.). 320p. 1997. 35.00 (0-299-15550-1); pap. 19.95 (0-299-15554-4) U of Wis Pr.

Born, Vibeke. Silk Painting. Bowler, Tim, tr. (Illus.). 76p. 1997. pap. 18.95 (0-86417-731-3, Pub. by Kangaroo Pr) Seven Hills Bk.

— Silk Painting. (Illus.). 1996. 18.95 (1-870586-25-5, D Porteous-Parkwest) Parkwest Pubns.

Born, Warren C., ed. The Foreign Language Teacher in Today's Classroom Environment. 1979. pap. 10.95 (0-915432-79-X) NE Conf Teach Foreign.

— Goals Clarification: Curriculum, Teaching, Evaluation. 1975. pap. 10.95 (0-915432-75-7) NE Conf Teach Foreign.

— Language: Acquisition, Application, Appreciation. 1997. pap. 10.95 (0-915432-77-3) NE Conf Teach Foreign.

— Language Application. 1976. pap. 10.95 (0-915432-76-5) NE Conf Teach Foreign.

— Toward Student-Centered Foreign-Language Programs. (Reports of the Northeast Conference on the Teaching of Foreign Languages). 180p. 1974. pap. 10.95 (0-87352-122-6) NE Conf Teach Foreign.

Born, Warren C. & Geno, Thomas H., eds. New Contents, New Teachers, New Publics. 1978. pap. 10.95 (0-915432-78-1) NE Conf Teach Foreign.

Bornakke, Claus & Sonntag, Richard E. Thermodynamic & Transport Properties. LC 97-154330. 241p. 1997. pap. text 24.95 incl. disk (0-471-12170-3) Wiley.

Bornand, Odette, ed. see Rossetti, William M.

***Bornat, Joanna.** Oral History Health & Welfare LC 99-20476. 1999. text. write for info. (0-415-19156-4) Routledge.

Bornat, Joanna, ed. Reminiscence Reviewed: Perspectives, Evaluations, Achievements. LC 93-22968. (Rethinking Aging Ser.). 160p. 1993. pap. 33.95 (0-335-19041-3) OpUniv Pr.

Bornath, T., et al. Physics of Strongly Coupled Plasma: Proceedings of International Conference. 550p. 1996. text 128.00 (981-02-2348-X) World Scientific Pub.

Borne. Society. 3rd ed. 272p. 1996. pap. text, student ed. 15.20 (0-13-457078-2) P-H.

— Sociology. 5th ed. 1994. pap. text, student ed. 24.00 (0-13-118522-5) P-H.

Borne, Barbara W. 100 Research Topic Guides for Students. LC 95-42446. (Greenwood Professional Guides in School Librarianship Ser.). 256p. 1996. 39.95 (0-313-29552-2, Greenwood Pr) Greenwood.

Borne, P. Systems Control Dictionary, French-English/ English-French. (ENG & FRE.). 1998. 395.00 (0-7859-9708-3) Fr & Eur.

Borne, Pierre, jt. ed. see Atherton, Derek P.

Bornecque, Henri. Les Declamations et les Declamateurs d'Apres Seneque le Pere. 214p. 1967. reprint ed. 35.00 incl. 3.5 hd (0-318-71080-3) G Olms Pubs.

Bornecque, Henri & Cauet, Fernand. Dictionnaire Latin-Francais.Tr. of Latin-French Dictionary. (FRE & LAT.). 560p. 1953. 75.00 (0-8288-6878-6, M6044) Fr & Eur.

Bornecque, Henri, ed. see Dumas, Alexandre.

Bornecque, Jacques-Henry. Les Annees d'Apprentissage d'Alphonse Daudet. (FRE.). 538p. 1951. pap. 29.95 (0-7859-5306-X) Fr & Eur.

Bornedal, Peter. The Interpretations of Art. LC 95-45504. 378p. (C). 1996. pap. text 39.00 (0-7618-0178-2); lib. bdg. 58.00 (0-7618-0177-4) U Pr of Amer.

— Speech & System. 533p. 1996. 92.00 (87-7289-352-4, Pub. by Mus Tusculanum) Paul & Co Pubs.

Bornell, Donald G., jt. auth. see Anderson, Bob.

Borneman, Diane, ed. see Daily, Kathleen K. & Guenin, Gaylord T.

Borneman, Dianne, ed. see Hood, Mary H.

Borneman, Eric, jt. auth. see Puterbaugh, Ed.

Borneman, Eric H. Aquarium Corals: Husbandry, Selection & Natural History. LC 99-58676. (Illus.). 432p. 2000. 49.95 (1-890087-47-5) Microcosm Ltd.

***Borneman, Eric H.** Aquarium Corals: Husbandry, Selection & Natural History. LC 99-58676. (Illus.). 432p. 2000. pap. 39.95 (1-890087-48-3) Microcosm Ltd.

Borneman, Ernest. Childhood Phases of Maturity: Sexual Developmental Psychology. Lombardi-Nash, Michael A., tr. from GER. LC 94-18036. 325p. (C). 1994. 59.95 (0-87975-895-3) Prometheus Bks.

Borneman, J. H. The History of the Borneman Family in America, since the First Settlers, 1721-1878. 114p. 1988. reprint ed. pap. 22.50 (0-8328-0285-9); reprint ed. lib. bdg. 30.50 (0-8328-0284-0) Higginson Bk Co.

Borneman, John. Settling Accounts: Violence, Justice, & Accountability in Postsocialist Europe. LC 97-12041. (Studies in Culture - Power - History). 216p. 1997. text 49.50 (0-691-01682-8, Pub. by Princeton U Pr); pap. text 14.95 (0-691-01681-X, Pub. by Princeton U Pr) Cal Prin Full Svc.

— Subversions of International Order: Studies in the Political Anthropology of Culture. LC 97-23444. (SUNY Series in National Identities). 341p. (C). 1997. pap. text 19.95 (0-7914-3584-9) State U NY Pr.

— Subversions of International Order: Studies in the Political Anthropology of Culture. LC 97-23444. (SUNY Series in National Identities). 341p. (C). 1997. text 59.50 (0-7914-3583-0) State U NY Pr.

Borneman, John & Peck, Jeffrey M. Sojourners: The Return of German Jews & the Question of Identity. LC 95-3125. (Texts & Contexts Ser.: Vol. 16). xi, 309p. 1995. text 50.00 (0-8032-1255-0) U of Nebr Pr.

Borneman, John, ed. see Lemke, Jurgen.

Borneman, John, ed. see National Audubon Society Staff.

Borneman, Walter R. & Lampert, Lyndon J. A Climbing Guide to Colorado's Fourteeners: 20th Anniversary Edition. 3rd anniversary ed. LC 98-7604. 255p. 1998. pap. 16.95 (0-87108-850-9) Pruett.

Bornemann, Alfred. Stendhal As Economist, Vol. 7. LC 93-37343. (American University Studies: No. XVI). IX, 156p. (C). 1994. text 36.95 (0-8204-1546-4) P Lang Pubng.

Bornemann, F. Homogenization in Time of Singularly Perturbed Mechanical Systems. LC 98-20309. (Lecture Notes in Mathematics Ser.: Vol. 1687). xii, 156p. 1998. pap. 33.00 (3-540-64447-4) Spr-Verlag.

***Bornemann, Robert.** A Grammar of Biblical Hebrew Pts. 1 & 2: An Introduction to Biblical Hebrew; Continuing Biblical Hebrew. LC 98-20786. 296p. (C). 1998. pap. 32.50 (0-7618-1185-0) U Pr of Amer.

Bornemann Spies, Karen. Franklin D. Roosevelt. LC 98-19645. (United States Presidents Ser.). 128p. (YA). (gr. 5 up). 1999. lib. bdg. 20.95 (0-7660-1038-4) Enslow Pubs.

— John F. Kennedy. LC 98-29553. (United States Presidents Ser.). (Illus.). 160p. (YA). (gr. 5 up). 1999. lib. bdg. 20.95 (0-7660-1039-2) Enslow Pubs.

Bornemann, Thomas H., jt. ed. see Holtzman, Wayne H.

Bornemeier, Pam, ed. see Manton, Charlotte.

Bornemisza, Elmer & Alvarado, Alfredo. Soil Management in Tropical America, 2 Vols., Set. 1978. lib. bdg. 600.00 (0-8490-2622-9) Gordon Pr.

Borner, G. & Gottlober, S. The Evolution of the Universe. LC 97-24718. (Dahlem Workshop Reports). 328p. 1997. 185.00 (0-471-96524-3) Wiley.

Borner, Gerhard. The Early Universe: Facts & Fiction. 2nd enl. ed. (Texts & Monographs in Physics). (Illus.). xvi, 462p. 1992. pap. 59.00 (0-387-54656-1) Spr-Verlag.

— The Early Universe: Facts & Fiction. 3rd ed. LC 93-13622. (Texts & Monographs in Physics). (Illus.). 466p. 1995. 69.95 (0-387-56729-1) Spr-Verlag.

— The Early Universe: Facts & Fiction. 3rd enl. ed. (Texts & Monographs in Physics). (Illus.). xvi, 466p. 1993. pap. write for info. (3-540-56729-1) Spr-Verlag.

— The Early Universe: Facts & Fictions. (Texts & Monographs in Physics). (Illus.). xiv, 439p. 1988. 79.50 (0-387-16187-2) Spr-Verlag.

Borner, Gerhard, ed. see Lipunov, M.

Borner, H., et al, eds. Analysis of Pesticides in Ground & Surface Water II. (Chemistry of Plant Protection Ser.: Vol. 12). 221p. 1995. 180.95 (3-540-59053-6) Spr-Verlag.

— Chemistry of Plant Protection: Pesticides in Ground & Surface Water, Vol. 9. 312p. 1994. 174.95 (0-387-58180-4) Spr-Verlag.

Borner, J. & Houser, D. Dynamic Distribution of Load & Stress on External Involute Gearings. (Technical Papers: Vol. 96FTM7). (Illus.). 12p. 1996. pap. text 30.00 (1-55589-674-X) AGMA.

Borner, J., jt. auth. see Linke, H.

Borner-Klein, Dagmar. Midrasch Sifre Numeri: Voruntersuchungen zur Redaktionsgeschichte. (Judentum und Umwelt Ser.: Bd. 39). (GER.). 104p. 1993. 31.80 (3-631-45670-0) P Lang Pubng.

Borner, Peter, ed. see Von Wolzogen, Caroline.

Borner, Silvio. Internationalization of Industry. 175p. 1986. 95.95 (0-387-16872-9) Spr-Verlag.

Borner, Silvio, et al. Institutional Obstacles to Latin American Growth. 25p. 1992. pap. 9.95 (1-55815-172-9) ICS Pr.

— The Political Dimension of Economic Growth: Proceedings of the IEA Conference, held in San Jose, Costa Rica. LC 97-22800. (IEA Conference Ser.). 352p. 1998. text 79.95 (0-312-21008-6) St Martin.

Bornet, E. & Flahault, C. Revision des Noostocacees Heterocystees: Contocacees Dans les Principaux Herbiers De France, Vol. 1. 1969. 48.00 (3-7682-0002-7) Lubrecht & Cramer.

Bornet, E. & Thuret, G. Notes Algologiques: Recueil d'Observation sur les Algues, 2 parts in 1 vol. (Bibliotheca Phycologica Ser.: Vol. 9). (Illus.). 1969. 150.00 (3-7682-0601-7) Lubrecht & Cramer.

Bornet, Vaughn D. An Independent Scholar in Twentieth Century America: The Autobiography of Vaughn Davis Bornet. (Illus.). 383p. (Orig.). 1995. pap. 18.00 (0-9632366-0-1) Bornet Bks.

— It's a Dog's Life & I Like It! LC 91-78055. 40p. (Orig.). (J). (gr. 1-9). 1991. pap. 8.95 (0-9632366-2-8) Bornet Bks.

— Labor Politics in a Democratic Republic: Moderation, Division, & Disruption in the Presidential Election of 1928. (Illus.). xviii, 376p. 1996. reprint ed. 15.00 (0-9632366-3-6) Bornet Bks.

— The Presidency of Lyndon B. Johnson. LC 83-12560. (American Presidency Ser.). xvi, 416p. 1984. 29.95 (0-7006-0237-2); pap. 17.95 (0-7006-0242-9) U Pr of KS.

— Welfare in America. (Illus.). 319p. 1997. 20.00 (0-9632366-4-4) Bornet Bks.

Bornet, Vaughn D., jt. auth. see Robinson, Edgar E.

***Bornewasser, Manfred & Wakenhut, Roland.** Ethnisches und Nationales Bewuatsein - Zwischen Globalisierung und Regionalisierung. (GER.). 257p. 1999. 45.95 (3-631-34587-9) P Lang Pubng.

Bornfeld, N., et al, eds. Tumors of the Eye. LC 91-35368. (Illus.). 700p. 1991. lib. bdg. 200.00 (90-6299-082-7, Pub. by Kugler) Kugler Pubns.

Bornfield, Gail. Attention Deficit Hyperactivity Disorder: A Practical Guide for Teachers. 40p. 1995. pap. text 8.95 (1-886979-03-0) Practicl Pr.

***Bornfield, Gail.** Practical Strategies for Mathematics Instruction. (Illus.). 120p. (C). 1999. pap. 15.95 (1-886979-13-8) Practicl Pr.

Bornfield, Gail. Practical Strategies for Reading Instruction. (Illus.). 88p. (Orig.). 1997. pap. text 13.95 (1-886979-11-1) Practicl Pr.

— Practical Strategies for Written Language Instruction. (Illus.). 40p. (Orig.). 1996. pap. 8.95 (1-886979-08-1) Practicl Pr.

Bornhoft, Simon. High-Speed Boats. LC 98-43753. (Need for Speed Ser.). 32p. (J). (gr. 3-9). 1999. 23.93 (0-8225-2488-0, LernerSports) Lerner Pub.

***Bornhoft, Simon.** High-Speed Boats. 32p. (YA). (gr. 5-8). 1999. pap. 7.95 (0-8225-9856-6, LernerSports) Lerner Pub.

***Bornholdt, Jeanette, ed.** The Heritage of Baldwin County, Alabama. (Heritage of Alabama Ser.: Vol. 2). 320p. 2001. 50.00 (1-891647-35-0) Herit Pub Consult.

Bornholdt, Jenny. Miss New Zealand: Selected Poems LC 98-144030. 127 p. 1997. write for info. (0-86473-323-2) Victoria Univ Pr.

***Bornholdt, Jenny.** These Days. 72p. 2000. 14.95 (0-86473-385-2, Pub. by Victoria Univ Pr) Paul & Co Pubs.

Bornholdt, Jenny, et al, eds. An Anthology of New Zealand Poetry in English. 582p. 1998. pap. text 26.00 (0-19-558355-8) OUP.

***Bornhop, Darryl J., et al, eds.** Biomedical Imaging. 272p. 1999. pap. text 103.00 (0-8194-3070-6) SPIE.

Bornhorst, Heidi L. Growing Native Hawaiian Plants: A How-To Guide for the Gardener. (Illus.). 80p. (Orig.). 1996. pap. 14.95 (1-57306-009-7) Bess Pr.

Borning, A., ed. Principles & Practice of Constraint Programming. (Lecture Notes in Computer Science Ser.: Vol. 874). 361p. 1994. 55.95 (3-540-58601-6) Spr-Verlag.

Borning, Alan, ed. see Workshop on the Principles of Constraint Programmi.

Bornkamm. Hawaii Criminal & Traffic Law Manual, 1993 Edition. 1993. 30.00 (0-614-05832-5, MICHIE) LEXIS Pub.

Bornkamm, Gunther. Jesus of Nazareth. McLuskey, Irene & McLuskey, Fraser, trs. 256p. 1995. pap. 21.00 (0-8006-2887-X, Fortress Pr) Augsburg Fortress.

— The New Testament: A Guide to Its Writings. LC 73-79009. 174p. (Orig.). reprint ed. pap. 54.00 (0-608-15538-1, 202977100064) Bks Demand.

— Paul. LC 95-2159. 288p. 1995. pap. 22.00 (0-8006-2898-5, 1-2898, Fortress Pr) Augsburg Fortress.

Bornkamm, Heinrich. Luther & the Old Testament. Gruhn, Victor I., ed. Gritsch, Eric W. & Gritsch, Ruth C., trs. from GEH. 320p. 1997. reprint ed. pap. 22.00 (0-9623642-8-2) Sigler Pr.

Bornman, Chris H., et al. Research, Breeding & Production of Crop Plants: Proceedings of the First Nordic Cell & Tissue Culture Symposium. (Illus.). 170p. (Orig.). 1985. pap. text 83.00 (0-685-17226-0) Coronet Bks.

Bornmann, Fritz, ed. Nietzsche Werke: Kritische Gesamtausgabe: II. Abteilung: Philologica Band 5: Vorlesungsaufzeichnungen (WS 1874/75-WS1878/79) (GER.). vi, 527p. (C). 1995. lib. bdg. 180.75 (3-11-013913-8) De Gruyter.

— Nietzsche Werke Abteilung II, Bd. 4: Kritische Gesamtausgabe: Vorlesungsaufzeichnungen (WS 1871-72 - WS 1874-75) 643p. (C). 1995. lib. bdg. 207.70 (3-11-013912-X) De Gruyter.

***Bornoff, Nicholas.** Japan. (National Geographic Traveler Ser.). 400p. 2000. per. 27.95 (0-7922-7563-2) Natl Geog.

Bornoff, Nicholas. Pink Samurai. Grose, Bill, ed. 1992. pap. 12.00 (0-671-74266-3) PB.

— Pink Samurai: Love, Marriage, & Sex in Contemporary Japan LC 91-177895. xvi, 492p. 1991. write for info. (0-246-13453-4) Grfton HrprCllns.

Bornoff, Nick. Japan. LC 96-27537. (Country Insights Ser.). (J). 1997. lib. bdg. 25.69 (0-8172-4786-6) Raintree Steck-V.

Bornokai, I. Lexicon Latinitatis Medii Aevi Hungariae Vol. 1-1: A, Ab, Abs-Aeternaliter. 102p. (C). 1987. pap. 60.00 (963-05-4251-X, Pub. by Akade Kiado) St Mut.

— Lexicon Latinitatis Medii Aevi Hungariae Vol. 11-2: Cliciarius-Conor. 160p. (C). 1991. pap. 86.00 (963-05-5780-0, Pub. by Akade Kiado) St Mut.

Bornokai, I., ed. Lexicon Latinitatis Medii Aevi Hungariae Vol. 11-1: Cabalia-Cliciarius. 152p. (C). 1991. pap. 75.00 (963-05-5394-5, Pub. by Akade Kiado) St Mut.

Bornong, Wallace L. A Brief Introduction to the Evidence: Jesus As Christ & God. LC 91-90120. 60p. (Orig.). 1991. pap. 5.00 (0-9629121-3-1) W Bornong.

Borns, Harold W., Jr., et al, eds. Late Pleistocene History of Northeastern New England & Adjacent Quebec. LC 84-25965. (Geological Society of America Ser.: Vol. 197). (Illus.). 170p. 1985. reprint ed. pap. 52.70 (0-608-07726-7, 206781400010) Bks Demand.

Borns, Harold W., jt. auth. see Andersen, Bjorn G.

Borns, Nicholas F., jt. auth. see Davis, Reginald F.

Borns, Robert J., jt. auth. see Garrod, Susan A.

Bornscheuer, Uwe & Kazlauskas, Romas. Hydrolases In Organic Synthesis: Regio or Stereoselective Biotransformations. 352p. 1999. 159.95 (3-527-30104-6) Wiley.

***Bornschier, Volker.** State-building in Europe: The Revitalization of European Integration. (Illus.). 314p. 2000. pap. write for info. (0-521-78619-3) Cambridge U Pr.

Bornschier, Volker. Western Society in Transition. LC 96-389. 453p. 1996. text 49.95 (1-56000-227-1) Transaction Pubs.

***Bornschier, Volker, ed.** State-building in Europe: The Revitalization of European Integration. LC 99-85966. (Illus.). 314p. 2000. write for info. (0-521-78103-5) Cambridge U Pr.

Bornschier, Volker & Chase-Dunn, Christopher K. Multinational Corporations & Underdevelopment. 192p. 1985. 49.95 (0-275-90063-0, 0063, Praeger Pubs) Greenwood.

Bornschier, Volker & Lengyel, Peter, eds. Conflicts & New Departures in World Society. (World Society Studies: Vol. 3). 409p. (C). 1994. text 54.95 (1-56000-129-1) Transaction Pubs.

— Waves, Formations & Values in the World System Vol. 2: World Society Studies. 311p. (C). 1992. 49.95 (1-56000-056-2) Transaction Pubs.

Bornstein. Freud's Legacy. (Psychoanalytic Inquiry Ser.: Vol. 5, No. 3). 1985. 20.00 (0-88163-973-7) Analytic Pr.

— Gorilita.Tr. of Little Gorilla. (SPA.). 32p. (J). (ps-2). 1993. pap. 2.50 (0-590-12086-7) Scholastic Inc.

— Interaction: Reflections on One- or Two-Person Psychology. (Psychoanalytic Inquiry Ser.: Vol. 16, No. 1). 1996. 20.00 (0-88163-940-0) Analytic Pr.

— Methodology in Psychoanalytic Research. (Psychoanalytic Inquiry Ser.: Vol. 9, No. 2). 1989. 20.00 (0-88163-958-3) Analytic Pr.

— On Power. (Psychoanalytic Inquiry Book Ser.: Vol. 6, No. 1). 1995. 20.00 (0-88163-971-0) Analytic Pr.

— Principles of Child Development. 2001. write for info. (0-07-006550-0); teacher ed. write for info. (0-07-006555-1) McGraw.

— Values & Neutrality in Psychoanalysis. (Psychoanalytic Inquiry Ser.: Vol. 3, No. 4). 1994. 20.00 (0-88163-980-X) Analytic Pr.

Bornstein, ed. Aggression: An Interdisciplinary Approach. (Psychoanalytic Inquiry Ser.: Vol. 2, No. 1). 1994. 20.00 (0-88163-987-7) Analytic Pr.

— Commentaries on Abend, Porder & Willicks "Borderline Patients - Psychoanalytic Perspectives" (Psychoanalytic Inquiry Ser.: Vol. 8, No. 3). 1988. 20.00 (0-88163-961-3) Analytic Pr.

— Commentaries on Lawrence Friedman's "The Anatomy of Psychotherapy" (Psychoanalytic Inquiry Ser.: Vol. 16, No. 4). 1996. pap. 20.00 (0-88163-937-0) Analytic Pr.

— Commentaries on Merton Gill's "Analysis of Transference" (Psychoanalytic Inquiry Ser.: Vol. 4, No. 3). 1984. 20.00 (0-88163-977-X) Analytic Pr.

— Construction & Reconstruction in Psychoanalysis. (Psychoanalytic Inquiry Ser.: Vol. 3, No. 2). 1983. 20.00 (0-88163-982-6) Analytic Pr.

— Essays Inspired by Theodore Jacobs's "The Use of the Self" (Psychoanalytic Inquiry Ser.: Vol. 17, No. 1). 1997. pap. 20.00 (0-88163-936-2) Analytic Pr.

— The Mirror: Psychoanalytic Perspectives. (Psychoanalytic Inquiry Ser.: Vol. 5, No. 2). 1995. 20.00 (0-88163-974-5) Analytic Pr.

— Object Relations Theory in Perspective. (Psychoanalytic Inquiry Ser.: Vol. 10, No. 2). 1990. 20.00 (0-88163-954-0) Analytic Pr.

— A Reappraisal of Heinz Hartmann's Contributions. (Psychoanalytic Inquiry Ser.: Vol. 6, No. 4). 1995. 20.00 (0-88163-968-0) Analytic Pr.

— Regression. (Psychoanalytic Inquiry Ser.: Vol. 1, No. 1). 1994. 20.00 (0-88163-991-5) Analytic Pr.

— Ten Years of Inquiry by Psychoanalyts: A Special Issue - The Decade of the Eighties. (Psychoanalytic Inquiry Ser.: Vol. 11, Nos. 1 & 2). 1991. 40.00 (0-88163-951-6) Analytic Pr.

— Termination. (Psychoanalytic Inquiry Ser.: Vol. 2, No. 3). 1982. 20.00 (0-88163-985-0) Analytic Pr.

Bornstein & Gonzales, eds. Commentaries on Ping-Nie Pao's "Schizophrenic Disorders" (Psychoanalytic Inquiry Ser.: Vol. 3, NO. 1). 1983. 20.00 (0-88163-983-4) Analytic Pr.

Bornstein & Gosline. Labor & Employment Arbitration, 3 vols. 2nd ed. 1988. ring bd. 465.00 (0-8205-1443-8, 443) Bender.

Bornstein & Silver. On Empathy. (Psychoanalytic Inquiry Book Ser.: Vol. 1, No. 3). 1994. 20.00 (0-88163-989-3) Analytic Pr.

Bornstein & Wolf, eds. Commentaries on Heinz Kohut's "How Does Analysis Cure?" (Psychoanalytic Inquiry Ser.: Vol. 6, No. 3). 1986. 20.00 (0-88163-969-9) Analytic Pr.

Bornstein, Arthur. Memory: Arthur Bornstein's Memory Training Course. Orig. Title: Bornstein's Miracle Memory Course. (Illus.). 1979. reprint ed. 22.50 (0-686-26172-0) Bornstein Schl Mem.

Bornstein, Christine, et al. The Meeting of Two Worlds: The Crusades & the Mediterranean Context. (Illus.). 103p. 1981. pap. 15.00 (0-912303-24-7) Michigan Mus.

Bornstein, Christine V., jt. ed. see Goss, Vladimir P.

Bornstein, Daniel & Rusconi, Roberto, eds. Women & Religion in Medieval & Renaissance Italy. LC 95-44343. 320p. 1996. pap. text 16.95 (0-226-06639-8) U Ch Pr.

— Women & Religion in Medieval & Renaissance Italy. Schneider, Margery J., tr. from ITA. LC 95-44343. 1996. lib. bdg. 50.00 (0-226-06637-1) U Ch Pr.

Bornstein, Daniel E. The Bianchi of Thirteen Hundred Ninety-Nine: Popular Devotion in Late Medieval Italy. (Illus.). 248p. 1994. text 37.50 (0-8014-2910-2) Cornell U Pr.

— Dino Compagni's Chronicle of Florence. LC 85-29512. (Middle Ages Ser.). (Illus.). 140p. (Orig.). (C). 1986. pap. text 17.95 (0-8122-1221-5) U of Pa Pr.

Bornstein, Daniel E., ed. see Vauchez, Andre.

Bornstein, Daniel Ethan, ed. & tr. see Riccoboni, Bartolomea.

Bornstein, David. The Price of a Dream: The Story of the Grameen Bank & the Idea That Is Helping the Poor to Change Their Lives. LC 97-22604. 370p. (gr. 2). 1997. pap. 15.95 (0-226-06644-4) U Ch Pr.

Bornstein, Diane, ed. Ideals for Women in the Works of Christine de Pizan. LC 81-51033. (Medieval & Renaissance Monograph: Vol. 1). 147p. reprint ed. pap. 45.60 (*0-608-18709-7*, 202702400053) Bks Demand.

Bornstein, Diane, jt. auth. see Fisher, John H.

Bornstein, Diane D. An Introduction to Transformational Grammar. LC 84-5125. 272p. (C). 1984. reprint ed. pap. text 22.00 (*0-8191-3905-X*) U Pr of Amer.

Bornstein, George. Poetic Remaking: The Art of Browning, Yeats, & Pound. LC 87-25789. 176p. 1988. lib. bdg. 35.00 (*0-271-00620-X*) Pa St U Pr.

— Tranformations of Romanticism in Yeats, Eliot & Stevens. LC 75-43241. 1976. 25.00 (*0-226-06643-6*) U Ch Pr.

— Transformations of Romanticism in Yeats, Eliot, & Stevens. LC 75-43241. 276p. Date not set. reprint ed. pap. 85.60 (*0-608-20600-8*, 205456500003) Bks Demand.

— Yeats & Shelley. LC 73-92050. 1970. lib. bdg. 20.00 (*0-226-06645-2*) U Ch Pr.

— Yeats & Shelley. LC 73-92050. 255p. Date not set. reprint ed. pap. 79.10 (*0-608-20668-7*, 207210500003) Bks Demand.

Bornstein, George, ed. Ezra Pound among the Poets. LC 85-1076. (Illus.). xiv, 256p. 1988. pap. text 12.00 (*0-226-06642-8*) U Ch Pr.

— Representing Modernist Texts. 304p. (C). 1991. text 49.50 (*0-472-09439-4*, 09439) U of Mich Pr.

Bornstein, George, ed. Representing Modernist Texts. 304p. (C). 1991. pap. text 20.95 (*0-472-06439-8*, 06439) U of Mich Pr.

Bornstein, George & Tinkle, Theresa L., eds. The Iconic Page in Manuscript, Print, & Digital Culture. LC 97-33788. (Editorial Theory & Literary Criticism Ser.). (Illus.). 304p. (C). 1998. text 49.50 (*0-472-10865-4*, 10865) U of Mich Pr.

Bornstein, George & Williams, Ralph G., eds. Palimpsest: Editorial Theory in the Humanities. LC 92-41139. (Editorial Theory & Literary Criticism Ser.). (Illus.). 328p. 1993. text 54.50 (*0-472-10371-7*, 10371) U of Mich Pr.

Bornstein, George, jt. ed. see Finneran, Richard J.

Bornstein, George, ed. see Yeats, William Butler.

Bornstein, Harry. Fire Fighter Brown. (Signed English Ser.). (Illus.). 16p. (J). (ps). 1976. pap. 3.50 (*0-913580-50-3*, Pub. by K Green Pubns) Gallaudet Univ Pr.

— Good Manners: Level 3. 1976. pap. 4.00 (*0-913580-58-9*) Gallaudet Univ Pr.

— Signed English for the Classroom. LC 75-2974. (Signed English Ser.). 73p. (J). (ps-6). 1975. pap. 6.50 (*0-913580-37-6*, Pub. by K Green Pubns) Gallaudet Univ Pr.

— The Three Little Pigs. (Signed English Ser.). (Illus.). 44p. (J). (ps-3). 1972. pap. 6.50 (*0-913580-09-0*, Pub. by K Green Pubns) Gallaudet Univ Pr.

— We're Going to the Doctor. (Signed English Ser.). (Illus.). 28p. (J). (ps-3). 1974. pap. 5.50 (*0-913580-26-0*, Pub. by K Green Pubns) Gallaudet Univ Pr.

— With My Legs. (Signed English Ser.). (Illus.). 16p. (J). (ps). 1975. pap. 3.50 (*0-913580-42-2*, Pub. by K Green Pubns) Gallaudet Univ Pr.

Bornstein, Harry, ed. Manual Communication: Implications for Education. LC 90-40934. (Illus.). 208p. 1990. text 34.95 (*0-930323-57-2*) Gallaudet Univ Pr.

Bornstein, Harry, et al, eds. The Comprehensive Signed English Dictionary. LC 82-82830. (Illus.). 464p. (J). 1983. 35.00 (*0-913580-81-3*, Clerc Bks) Gallaudet Univ Pr.

Bornstein, Harry & Hamilton, Lillian B. The Clock Book. (Signed English Ser.). (Illus.). 36p. (J). (ps-2). 1975. pap. 5.95 (*0-913580-48-1*, Pub. by K Green Pubns) Gallaudet Univ Pr.

— Mouse's Christmas Eve. (Signed English Ser.). (Illus.). 44p. (J). (ps-3). 1974. pap. 5.95 (*0-913580-28-7*, Pub. by K Green Pubns) Gallaudet Univ Pr.

— Oliver in the City. (Signed English Ser.). (Illus.). 56p. (J). (ps-3). 1975. pap. 6.50 (*0-913580-49-X*, Pub. by K Green Pubns) Gallaudet Univ Pr.

— The Pet Shop. (Signed English Ser.). (Illus.). 16p. (J). (ps). 1976. pap. 3.50 (*0-913580-54-6*, Pub. by K Green Pubns) Gallaudet Univ Pr.

— Police Officer Jones. (Signed English Ser.). (Illus.). 16p. (J). (ps). 1976. pap. 3.50 (*0-913580-53-8*, Pub. by K Green Pubns) Gallaudet Univ Pr.

Bornstein, Harry & Jordan, I. King. Functional Signs: A New Approach from Simple to Complex. LC 83-16825. (Illus.). 392p. 1984. text 49.00 (*0-8391-1839-2*, 1260) PRO-ED.

Bornstein, Harry & Saulnier, Karen L. Goldilocks & The Three Bears Told in Signed English. LC 96-20023. (Illus.). 54p. (J). 1996. 15.95 (*1-56368-057-2*, Pub. by K Green Pubns) Gallaudet Univ Pr.

— Little Red Riding Hood: Told in Signed English. (Awareness & Caring Ser.). (Illus.). 48p. (J). (ps-3). 1990. lib. bdg. 16.95 (*1-878363-26-3*) Forest Hse.

— Little Red Riding Hood: Told in Signed English. LC 90-3477. (Signed English Ser.). (Illus.). 48p. (J). (ps-2). 1990. 14.95 (*0-930323-63-7*, Pub. by K Green Pubns) Gallaudet Univ Pr.

— Nursery Rhymes from Mother Goose: Told in Signed English. (Awareness & Caring Ser.). (Illus.). 48p. (J). (gr. k-3). 1992. lib. bdg. 17.95 (*1-56674-034-7*) Forest Hse.

— Nursery Rhymes from Mother Goose: Told in Signed English. LC 91-42409. (Signed English Ser.). (Illus.). 48p. (J). (ps-2). 1992. 14.95 (*0-930323-99-8*, Pub. by K Green Pubns) Gallaudet Univ Pr.

— The Signed English Starter, Pt. I. LC 84-4042. (Signed English Ser.). (Illus.). 230p. (J). (ps-6). 1984. pap., teacher ed. 13.95 (*0-913580-82-1*, Clerc Bks) Gallaudet Univ Pr.

— The Signed English Starter Book & Videotape Set. LC 84-4042. 388p. 1995. teacher ed. 75.00 incl. VHS (*1-56368-041-6*, Clerc Bks) Gallaudet Univ Pr.

— Signing: Signed English - A Basic Guide. (Illus.). 240p. 1988. pap. 12.00 (*0-517-56132-8*, Crown) Crown Pub Group.

Bornstein, Harry, et al. Be Careful. (Signed English Ser.). (Illus.). 32p. (J). (ps-3). 1976. pap. 5.50 (*0-913580-55-4*, Pub. by K Green Pubns) Gallaudet Univ Pr.

— A Book about Me. (Signed English Ser.). (Illus.). 16p. (J). (ps). 1974. pap. 3.50 (*0-913580-19-8*, Pub. by K Green Pubns) Gallaudet Univ Pr.

— Circus Time. (Signed English Ser.). (Illus.). 16p. (J). (ps). 1976. pap. 3.50 (*0-913580-51-1*, Pub. by K Green Pubns) Gallaudet Univ Pr.

— Count & Color. (Signed English Ser.). (Illus.). 16p. (J). (ps). 1973. pap. 3.50 (*0-913580-20-1*, Pub. by K Green Pubns) Gallaudet Univ Pr.

— Don't Be a Grumpy Bear: A Coloring Book about Manners in Signed English. (Signed English Ser.). (Illus.). 32p. (J). (ps-2). 1986. pap. 7.95 (*0-930323-26-2*, Pub. by K Green Pubns) Gallaudet Univ Pr.

Bornstein, Harry, et al. A Guide to the Selection & Use of the Teaching Aids of the Signed English System LC 76-378133. (Signed English Ser.). 20 p. 1976. write for info. (*0-913580-59-7*) Gallaudet Univ Pr.

Bornstein, Harry, et al. The Holiday Book. (Signed English Ser.). (Illus.). 48p. (J). (ps-2). 1974. pap. 5.95 (*0-913580-30-9*, Pub. by K Green Pubns) Gallaudet Univ Pr.

— I Want to Be a Farmer. LC 72-84675. (Signed English Ser.). (Illus.). 48p. (J). (ps-2). 1972. pap. 6.50 (*0-913580-14-7*, Pub. by K Green Pubns) Gallaudet Univ Pr.

— Jack & the Beanstalk. (Signed English Ser.). (Illus.). 64p. (J). (ps-3). 1975. pap. 6.50 (*0-913580-47-3*, Pub. by K Green Pubns) Gallaudet Univ Pr.

— Little Poems for Little People. (Signed English Ser.). (Illus.). 56p. (J). (ps-3). 1974. pap. 6.50 (*0-913580-31-7*, Pub. by K Green Pubns) Gallaudet Univ Pr.

— My Animal Book. (Signed English Ser.). (Illus.). 16p. (J). (ps). 1973. pap. 3.50 (*0-930323-38-6*, Pub. by K Green Pubns) Gallaudet Univ Pr.

— My Toy Book. (Signed English Ser.). (Illus.). 16p. (J). (ps). 1973. pap. 3.50 (*0-913580-22-8*, Pub. by K Green Pubns) Gallaudet Univ Pr.

— Songs in Signed English. (Signed English Ser.). (Illus.). 44p. (J). (ps-2). 1984. pap. 9.00 (*0-913580-12-0*, Pub. by K Green Pubns) Gallaudet Univ Pr.

— The Ugly Duckling. (Signed English Ser.). (Illus.). 48p. (J). (ps-2). 1974. pap. 6.50 (*0-913580-29-5*, Pub. by K Green Pubns) Gallaudet Univ Pr.

Bornstein, Howard. Falcon 3: Official Combat Strategy Book. rev. ed. LC 94-66178. (Illus.). 384p. 1994. pap. 19.95 (*1-55958-643-5*) Prima Pub.

Bornstein, Howard. Falcon 3: The Official Combat Strategy Book: The Ultimate Book-&-Disk Combo, Including Exclusive Missions Based on Actual Pilot Experience. (Illus.). 384p. (Orig.). 1992. per. 27.95 (*1-55958-160-3*) Prima Pub.

***Bornstein, Jerry.** An American Chronology. LC 99-56396. 350p. 2000. pap. 59.95 (*1-55570-369-0*) Neal-Schuman.

Bornstein, Kate. Gender Outlaw: On Men, Women & the Rest of Us. LC 93-46979. 224p. (C). (gr. 13). 1994. 30.00 (*0-415-90897-3*) Routledge.

— Gender Outlaw: On Men, Women & the Rest of Us. LC 94-23477. 1995. pap. 13.00 (*0-679-75701-5*) Vin Bks.

— My Gender Workbook: How to Become a Real Man, a Real Woman, the Real You or Something Else Entirely. LC 98-134184. (Illus.). 272p. 1997. pap. 17.99 (*0-415-91673-9*) Routledge.

— My Gender Workbook: How to Become a Real Man, a Real Woman, the Real You or Something Else Entirely. LC 98-134184. (Illus.). 272p. (C). 1998. 75.00 (*0-415-91672-0*) Routledge.

Bornstein, M. H. & Bruner, Jerome S., eds. Interaction in Human Development. (Crosscurrents in Contemporary Psychology Ser.). 320p. (C). 1989. text 69.95 (*0-8058-0035-2*) L Erlbaum Assocs.

Bornstein, M. H., jt. ed. see Krasnegor, Norman A.

Bornstein, Marc, ed. Sensitive Periods in Development: Interdisciplinary Perspectives. (Crosscurrents in Contemporary Psychology Ser.). 304p. 1987. text 59.95 (*0-89859-696-3*) L Erlbaum Assocs.

Bornstein, Marc H., ed. Comparative Methods in Psychology. LC 79-27558. (Crosscurrents in Contemporary Psychology Ser.). (Illus.). 320p. 1980. text 69.95 (*0-89859-037-X*) L Erlbaum Assocs.

— Cultural Approaches to Parenting. 232p. (C). 1991. text 36.00 (*0-8058-1002-1*) L Erlbaum Assocs.

— Handbook of Parenting Vol. 1: Children & Parenting. 456p. 1995. text 99.95 (*0-8058-1892-8*) L Erlbaum Assocs.

— Handbook of Parenting Vol. 2: Biology & Ecology of Parenting. 464p. 1995. text 99.95 (*0-8058-1893-6*) L Erlbaum Assocs.

— Handbook of Parenting Vol. 3: Status & Social Conditions of Parenting. 616p. 1995. text 125.00 (*0-8058-1894-4*) L Erlbaum Assocs.

— Handbook of Parenting Vol. 4: Applied & Practical Parenting. 616p. 1995. text 135.00 (*0-8058-1895-2*) L Erlbaum Assocs.

— Psychology & Its Allied Disciplines. (Cross Currents in Contemporary Psychology Bornstein Ser.). 992p. (C). 1984. lib. bdg. 145.00 (*0-89859-318-2*) L Erlbaum Assocs.

— Psychology & Its Allied Disciplines, 3 vols., Set. (Crosscurrents in Contemporary Psychology Ser.). 1984. pap. 79.95 (*0-89859-319-0*) L Erlbaum Assocs.

— Psychology & Its Allied Disciplines Vol. 1: Psychology & the Humanities. 352p. 1984. 34.50 (*0-89859-320-4*) L Erlbaum Assocs.

— Psychology & Its Allied Disciplines Vol. 2: Psychology & the Social Sciences. 304p. 1984. pap. 32.50 (*0-89859-321-2*) L Erlbaum Assocs.

Bornstein, Marc H. & Genevro, Janice L., eds. Child Development & Behavioral Pediatrics: Toward Understanding Children & Health. (Crosscurrents in Contemporary Psychology Ser.). 200p. 1996. text 39.95 (*0-8058-2364-6*) L Erlbaum Assocs.

Bornstein, Marc H. & Lamb, Michael E. Development in Infancy: An Introduction. 3rd ed. 704p. (C). 1992. 66.56 (*0-07-006552-7*) McGraw.

Bornstein, Marc H. & Lamb, Michael E., eds. Developmental Psychology: An Advanced Textbook. 3rd rev. ed. 856p. 1992. text 45.00 (*0-8058-1007-2*) L Erlbaum Assocs.

Bornstein, Marc H. & Pierson, Herbert, eds. Developmental Psychology: An Advanced Textbook. 4th ed. LC 98-44280. 664p. 1999. 49.95 (*0-8058-3072-3*) L Erlbaum Assocs.

Bornstein, Marc H., jt. auth. see Hammeal, Robin J.

Bornstein, Morris, ed. Comparative Economic Systems: Models & Cases. 7th ed. LC 93-2552. 656p. (C). 1993. text 69.75 (*0-256-09593-0*, Irwn McGrw-H) McGrw-H Hghr Educ.

— The Soviet Economy: Continuity & Change. LC 80-21159. 381p. (Orig.). (C). 1981. pap. text 23.90 (*0-89158-959-7*) Westview.

— The Soviet Economy: Continuity & Change. LC 80-21159. 381p. (Orig.). (C). 1981. text 56.00 (*0-89158-958-9*) Westview.

Bornstein, Morris, intro. Plan & Market: Economic Reform in Eastern Europe. LC 72-91289. (Yale Russian & East European Studies: No. 12). (Illus.). 424p. reprint ed. pap. 131.50 (*0-608-10716-6*, 202198200024) Bks Demand.

Bornstein, N. M. & Turpie, A. G., eds. New Concepts in Stroke Pathophysiology & Prevention. (Journal: Cerebrovascular Diseases Ser.: Vol. 4, Suppl. 1, 1994). (Illus.). iv, 48p. 1994. pap. 22.75 (*3-8055-5966-6*) S Karger.

Bornstein, Robert A. & Brown, Gregory G., eds. Neurobehavioral Aspects of Cerebrovascular Disease. (Illus.). 384p. 1991. text 68.00 (*0-19-505431-8*) OUP.

Bornstein, Robert F. The Dependent Personality. LC 92-49466. 241p. 1993. lib. bdg. 35.00 (*0-89862-991-8*) Guilford Pubns.

Bornstein, Robert F. & Masling, Joseph M., eds. Empirical Perspectives on the Psychoanalytic Unconscious. LC 97-37667. 291p. 1997. 49.95 (*1-55798-463-8*, 431-6970) Am Psychol.

— Empirical Studies of the Therapeutic Hour. LC 98-36423. 321p. 1998. 49.95 (*1-55798-526-X*, 431-607A) Am Psychol.

Bornstein, Robert F., jt. ed. see Masling, Joseph M.

Bornstein, Ruth. Little Gorilla, 001. LC 75-25508. (Illus.). 32p. (J). (ps-2). 1979. 15.00 (*0-395-28773-1*, Clarion Bks) HM.

***Bornstein, Ruth.** Little Gorilla. (Illus.). 28p. (J). (ps-k). 2000. 4.95 (*0-618-05158-9*, Clarion Bks) HM.

Bornstein, Ruth. Little Gorilla. (Carry Along Book & Cassette Favorites Ser.). (J). 1986. 11.15 (*0-606-12398-9*, Pub. by Turtleback) Demco.

— Rabbit's Good News. (Illus.). 32p. 1997. pap. 4.95 (*0-395-84514-9*, Clarion Bks) HM.

Bornstein, Ruth L. Dancing Man. rev. ed. (Illus.). 32p. (gr. 1-3). 1977. 15.00 (*0-395-83429-5*, Pub. by Ticknor & Fields) HM.

— Little Gorilla. LC 75-25508. (Illus.). 32p. (J). (ps-2). 1986. pap. 5.95 (*0-89919-421-4*, Clarion Bks) HM.

— Rabbit's Good News. LC 93-30719. (Illus.). 32p. (J). (ps-2). 1995. 13.95 (*0-395-68700-4*, Clarion Bks) HM.

— The Seedling Child. LC 86-19581. (Illus.). 28p. (J). (ps-2). 1987. 12.95 (*0-15-272459-1*) Harcourt.

— That's How It Is When We Draw. LC 96-49646. (Illus.). 32p. (J). (ps-2). 1997. 14.00 (*0-395-82509-1*) HM.

Bornstein, Sandy. What Makes You What You Are? A First Look at Genetics. Steltenpohl, Jane, ed. (Illus.). 128p. (J). (gr. 7 up). 1989. pap. 6.95 (*0-671-68650-X*, Julian Messner) Silver Burdett Pr.

Bornstein, Scott. Vocabulary Mastery. (Illus.). 272p. (YA). (gr. 9-12). 1982. 22.50 (*0-9602610-1-X*); pap. 14.95 (*0-9602610-2-8*) Bornstein Schl Mem.

— Y2K Vital Functions. 2nd rev. ed. Ericson, Jim, ed. LC 98-96909. 106p. 1998. mass mkt. 8.99 (*0-9668053-1-3*) USABC.

Bornstein, Stephen, et al, eds. The State in Capitalist Europe: A Casebook. (Casebook Series on European Politics & Society: No. 3). 1987. pap. text 24.95 (*0-04-350059-5*) Routledge.

Bornstien, ed. Introduction to Psychology. (C). 1920. pap. text, student ed. write for info. (*0-321-01384-0*) Addison-Wesley Educ.

Borntrager, Mary C. Andy. LC 93-20059. (Ellie's People Ser.: Vol. 6). 144p. (Orig.). (J). 1993. pap. 7.99 (*0-8361-3633-0*) Herald Pr.

Borntrager, Mary C. Andy. large type ed. LC 93-20059. (Ellie's People Ser.: Vol. 6). 144p. (Orig.). (J). (gr. 5-7). 1993. pap. 8.99 (*0-8361-3641-1*) Herald Pr.

— Annie. LC 96-50126. (Ellie's People Ser.: Vol. 10). 144p. (Orig.). (J). 1997. pap. 7.99 (*0-8361-9070-X*) Herald Pr.

— Annie. large type ed. (Ellie's People Ser.: Vol. 10). 144p. (Orig.). (J). 1997. pap. 8.99 (*0-8361-9071-8*) Herald Pr.

— Daniel. LC 90-24955. (Ellie's People Ser.: Vol. 4). 160p. (J). 1991. pap. 7.99 (*0-8361-3548-2*) Herald Pr.

— Daniel. large type ed. (Ellie's People Ser.: Vol. 4). 160p. (J). 1993. pap. 8.99 (*0-8361-3639-X*) Herald Pr.

Borntrager, Mary C. Ellie. LC 88-2779. (Ellie's People Ser.: Vol. 1). 168p. (J). 1988. pap. 7.99 (*0-8361-3468-0*) Herald Pr.

Borntrager, Mary C. Ellie. large type ed. (Ellie's People Ser.: Vol. 1). 168p. (J). 1993. pap. 8.99 (*0-8361-3636-5*) Herald Pr.

— Ellie's People Series, 9 bks. (J). 1995. pap. 79.90 (*0-8361-9003-3*) Herald Pr.

— Ellie's People Series, 9 bks. large type ed. (J). 1993. pap. 89.90 (*0-8361-9004-1*) Herald Pr.

— Mandy. LC 96-2461. (Ellie's People Ser.: Vol. 9). 144p. (Orig.). (J). (gr. 4 up). 1996. pap. 7.99 (*0-8361-9046-7*) Herald Pr.

— Mandy. large type ed. (Ellie's People Ser.: Vol. 9). 144p. (Orig.). (J). 1996. pap. 8.99 (*0-8361-9048-3*) Herald Pr.

— Polly. LC 94-5645. (Ellie's People Ser.: Vol. 7). 144p. (Orig.). (J). 1994. pap. 7.99 (*0-8361-3670-5*) Herald Pr.

— Polly. large type ed. (Ellie's People Ser.: Vol. 7). 144p. (Orig.). (J). 1994. pap. 8.99 (*0-8361-9008-4*) Herald Pr.

— Rachel. LC 90-45033. (Ellie's People Ser.: Vol. 3). 160p. (Orig.). (J). 1990. pap. 7.99 (*0-8361-3539-3*) Herald Pr.

— Rachel. large type ed. (Ellie's People Ser.: Vol. 3). 160p. (Orig.). (J). 1993. pap. 8.99 (*0-8361-3638-1*) Herald Pr.

Borntrager, Mary C. Rebecca. LC 89-32328. (Ellie's People Ser.: Vol. 2). 176p. (Orig.). (J). 1989. pap. 7.99 (*0-8361-3500-8*) Herald Pr.

Borntrager, Mary C. Rebecca. large type ed. (Ellie's People Ser.: Vol. 2). 176p. (Orig.). (J). 1993. pap. 8.99 (*0-8361-3637-3*) Herald Pr.

— Reuben. LC 92-5432. (Ellie's People Ser.: Vol. 5). 160p. (Orig.). (J). 1992. pap. 7.99 (*0-8361-3593-8*) Herald Pr.

— Reuben. large type ed. (Ellie's People Ser.: Vol. 5). 160p. (Orig.). (J). 1993. pap. 8.99 (*0-8361-3640-3*) Herald Pr.

— Sarah. LC 95-7716. (Ellie's People Ser.: Vol. 8). 144p. (J). 1995. pap. 7.99 (*0-8361-9019-X*) Herald Pr.

— Sarah. large type ed. LC 95-7716. (Ellie's People Ser.: Vol. 8). 144p. (J). 1995. pap. 8.99 (*0-8361-9020-3*) Herald Pr.

***Borntrager, Mary Christner.** Annie. large type ed. LC 99-58079. (Christian Fiction Ser.). 2000. 23.95 (*0-7862-2379-0*) Thorndike Pr.

Boro, Len. Cowboy Jeans & Chili Beans. (Illus.). 24p. (J). (ps-3). 1986. pap. 2.00 (*0-935810-28-5*) R H Pub.

Borochov, Ber. Class Struggle & the Jewish Nation: Selected Essays in Marxist Zionism. Cohen, Mitchell, ed. LC 83-4695. 358p. 1983. 44.95 (*0-87855-479-3*) Transaction Pubs.

Borocz, Jozsef. Leisure Migration: A Sociological Study on Tourism. (Tourism Social Science Ser.). 230p. 1996. text 69.00 (*0-08-042560-7*, Pergamon Pr) Elsevier.

— Modern Hungary. 112p. 2000. pap. 13.44 (*0-07-034429-9*) McGraw.

Borocz, Jozsef & Smith, David A., eds. A New World Order? Global Transformations in the Late Twentieth Century. LC 94-47418. 272p. 1995. pap. 21.95 (*0-275-95122-7*, Praeger Pubs) Greenwood.

— A New World Order? Global Transformations in the Late Twentieth Century, 164. LC 94-47418. (Contributions in Economics & Economic History Ser.: No. 164). 272p. 1995. 65.00 (*0-313-29573-5*, Greenwood Pr) Greenwood.

Boroczky, K. & Toth, G. Fejes, eds. Intuitive Geometry. (Colloquia Mathematica Societatis Janos Bolyai Ser.: Vol. 63). 520p. 1994. 222.00 (*0-444-81906-1*, North Holland) Elsevier.

Borod, Joan C. The Neuropsychology of Emotion. (Series in Affective Science). (Illus.). 520p. 2000. text 69.50 (*0-19-511464-7*) OUP.

Borod, Ronald S. Securitization: Asset-Backed & Mortgaged-Backed Securities. 590p. 1994. spiral bd. 125.00 (*0-88063-281-X*, MICHIE) LEXIS Pub.

Borodic, Gary E. & Townsend, Daniel J. Atlas of Eyelid Surgery. (Illus.). 160p. 1993. text 115.00 (*0-7216-3640-3*, W B Saunders Co) Harcrt Hlth Sci Grp.

Borodich, Y., et al. The Revolutionary Guide to Turbo Pascal. 350p. 1993. pap. 34.95 incl. disk (*1-874416-11-7*) Wrox Pr Inc.

Borodin. "Polovtsian Dances" & "In the Steppes of Central Asia" in Full Score. 1998. pap. 9.95 (*0-486-29556-7*) Dover.

Borodin, A. N. & Ibragimov, I. A. Limit Theorems for Functionals of Random Walks. (Proceedings of the Steklov Institute of Mathematics Ser.: Vol. 195). 259p. 1994. 221.00 (*0-8218-0438-3*, STEKLO/195C) Am Math.

Borodin, A. N. & Salminen, Paavo. Handbook of Brownian Motion: Facts & Formulae. LC 96-35951. (Probability & Its Applications Ser.). 1996. 129.00 (*0-8176-5463-1*); 129.00 (*3-7643-5463-1*) Birkhauser.

Borodin, Alexander, jt. auth. see Tchaikovsky, Peter Ilich.

Borodin, Allan & El-Yaniv, Ran. Online Computation & Competitive Analysis. LC 97-38652. (Illus.). 448p. (C). 1998. text 54.95 (*0-521-56392-5*) Cambridge U Pr.

Borodin, Allan & Munro, I. C. The Computational Complexity of Algebraic & Numeric Problems. LC 74-21786. (Elsevier Computer Science Library, Theory of Computation Ser.: No. 1). 184p. reprint ed. pap. 57.10 (*0-608-16374-0*, 202627300049) Bks Demand.

Borodin, Leonid. Partings. 1987. 15.95 (*0-15-170978-5*) Harcourt.

Borodina, I. Central Asia: Architectural Monuments of the Ninth to Nineteenth Centuries. 216p. 1987. text 350.00 (*0-569-09067-9*) St Mut.

Borodkin. Cloze Look at English. 1992. teacher ed. 5.00 (*0-8384-3011-2*) Heinle & Heinle.

— Cloze Look at English. pap. text, teacher ed. 7.25 (*0-8384-3900-4*) Thomson Learn.

Borodkin, Thelma L. Cloze Look at English. (J). 1991. mass mkt. 27.95 (*0-8384-3010-4*) Heinle & Heinle.

Borodovsky, jt. auth. see Lore.

B

An Asterisk (*) at the beginning of an entry indicates that the title is appearing for the first time.

***Borodovsky, Lev & Lore, Marc, eds.** The Professional's Handbook of Financial Risk Management. LC 99-88517. 832p. 2000. 299.00 (*0-7506-4111-8*) Buttrwrth-Heinemann.

Boroff, Edith. American Operas: A Checklist. LC 92-35617. (Detroit Studies in Music Bibliography: No. 69). xx, 325p. 1992. 40.00 (*0-89990-063-1*) Harmonie Park Pr.

— An Introduction to Elisabeth Claude Jacquet de la Guerre. (Wissenschaftliche Abhandlungen-Musicological Studies: Vol. 12). 140p. 1969. lib. bdg. 32.00 (*0-912024-82-8*) Inst Mediaeval Mus.

Borofka, David. Hints of His Mortality. (Iowa Short Fiction Award Ser.). 240p. 1996. 22.95 (*0-87745-557-0*) U of Iowa Pr.

— The Island. LC 97-20583. 218p. 1997. 19.50 (*1-878448-78-1*) MacMurray & Beck.

Borofka, Michael. Emergency Survival Guide: You Can Survive Anything. LC 94-60498. (Illus.). 135p. (Orig.). 1994. pap. 11.95 (*0-9640856-0-7*) M Borofka.

Borofsky, Robert, ed. Assessing Cultural Anthropology. LC 93-5323. 566p. (C). 1993. pap. 44.69 (*0-07-006578-0*) McGraw.

***Borofsky, Robert, ed.** Remembrance of Pacific Pasts: An Invitation to Remake History. LC 99-54778. 530p. 2000. text 56.00 (*0-8248-2189-0*); pap. text 24.95 (*0-8248-2301-X*) UH Pr.

Borofsky, Robert, jt. ed. see Howard, Alan.

Boroian, Donald, jt. auth. see Mancuso, Joseph R.

Borojevic, S. Principles & Methods of Plant Breeding. (Developments in Crop Science Ser.: Vol. 17). 364p. 1990. 154.50 (*0-444-98832-7*, DIC 17) Elsevier.

Borok, V. M., et al. Eight Papers on Functional Analysis & Partial Differential Equations. (Translations Ser.: Series 2, Vol. 5). 333p. 1957. 41.00 (*0-8218-1705-1*, TRANS2/5) Am Math.

Borokov, A. A. Mathematical Statistics. Moullagaliev, A., tr. from RUS. 592p. 1998. text 140.00 (*90-5699-018-7*) Gordon & Breach.

Borokov, K. A. Russian-English - English-Russian Dictionary on Probability, Statistics, & Combinatorics. LC 93-47250. (Miscellaneous Bks.: Vol. 40). (ENG & RUS.). viii, 154p. 1994. pap. 54.00 (*0-89871-316-1*) Soc Indus-Appl Math.

Boron, Atilio A. State, Capitalism, & Democracy in Latin America. 220p. 1995. lib. bdg. 23.50 (*1-55587-508-4*) L Rienner.

Boron, L. L., tr. see Zeidler, Eberhard.

Boron, Leo F., tr. see Aigner, M., et al.

Boron, Leo F., tr. see Bonnesen, T. & Fenchel, W.

Boron, Leo F., tr. see Gramain, Andre.

Boron, Leo F., tr. see Reidemeister, Kurt.

Boron, Leo F., tr. see Zykov, A. A.

Boron, Leon F., tr. see Gnedenko, Boris V. & Khinchin, Alexander Y.

Boron, Robert De, see De Boron, Robert.

***Boronico, Jess S.** Studies in the Strategy & Tactics of Competitive Advantage: Management in the New Millennium. LC 99-57759. (Studies in Business: Vol. 12). 316p. 2000. text 99.95 (*0-7734-7849-3*) E Mellen.

Boronina, E. Siberian Forest Adventure. Birkett, G. A., ed. LC 66-25018. (RUS.). (C). 1966. pap. text 5.75 (*0-89197-485-7*) Irvington.

Boronkai, I., ed. Lexicon Latinitatis Medii Aevi Hungariae Vol. 1-3: Assignatio-Byzantius. 101p. (C). 1989. pap. 60.00 (*963-05-4858-5*, Pub. by Akade Kiado) St Mut.

Boronkai, I., tr. Lexicon Latinitatis Medii Aevi Hungariae Vol. 1-2: Aeternaliter-Assignatio. 160p. (C). 1988. pap. 60.00 (*963-05-4252-8*, Pub. by Akade Kiado) St Mut.

Boronow, Eugene L. Fundamentals of Engineering (F. E.) Examination. pap. 12.95 (*0-317-52079-2*) P-H.

Borooah, A. M. English-Sanskrit Dictionary. 783p. 1981. 49.95 (*0-8288-1780-4*, F128968) Fr & Eur.

Borooah, Romy, et al. Capturing Complexity: An Interdisciplinary Look at Women, Households, & Development. LC 93-34794. 300p. (C). 1994. text 38.00 (*0-8039-9145-2*) Sage.

Borooah, Vani K. Growth, Unemployment, Distribution, & Government: Essays on Current Economic Issues. LC 96-10819. 192p. 1996. text 75.00 (*0-312-16158-1*) St Martin.

— The Structure of Consumption Decisions: A Disaggregated Analysis. (Illus.). 128p. 1989. text 82.95 (*0-566-05772-7*, Pub. by Avebry) Ashgate Pub Co.

Borooah, Vani K., et al. Regional Income Inequality & Poverty in the U. K. An Analysis Based on the 1985 Family Expenditure Survey. 208p. 1991. text 72.95 (*1-85521-075-4*, Pub. by Dartmth Pub) Ashgate Pub Co.

Boroos, C. Essentials of Business Writing. 138p. 1998. pap. text 5.95 (*0-87891-060-3*) Res & Educ.

Boros, A. & Jarai-Komlodi, M., eds. An Atlas of Recent European Moss Spores. 466p. (C). 1975. 90.00 (*963-05-0212-7*, Pub. by Akade Kiado) St Mut.

Boros, E. Erato: The Drawings of Mihaly Zichy. (Illus.). 72p. (C). 1989. 200.00 (*0-7855-4531-X*, Pub. by Collets) St Mut.

Boros, Elizabeth J. Minority Shareholders' Remedies. (Illus.). 386p. 1996. text 89.00 (*0-19-825975-1*) OUP.

Boros, James. Brian Ferneyhough: Collected Writings. Toop, Richard, ed. 368p. 1995. pap. text 22.00 (*3-7186-5577-2*, Harwood Acad Pubs) Gordon & Breach.

Boros, Janos, et al. Psychology & Criminal Justice: International Review of Theory & Practice. LC 98-36246. (Publications of the European Association of Psychology & Law). 1998. 127.25 (*3-11-016329-2*) De Gruyter.

Boros, Julius. Swing Easy, Hit Hard. LC 95-11835. (Illus.). 160p. 1995. pap. 14.95 (*1-55821-416-X*) Burford Bks.

Boros, Katalin. Beginner's Hungarian. 101p. (Orig.). 1993. pap. 7.95 (*0-7818-0209-1*) Hippocrene Bks.

Boros, Ladislaus. Angels & Men. 128p. 1990. pap. text 30.00 (*0-85532-375-2*, Pub. by Srch Pr) St Mut.

— God's Image & Faith. Cunningham, Robert, tr. 67p. 1983. pap. 1.00 (*0-8199-0858-4*, Frncscn Herld) Franciscan Pr.

— Meditations. 110p. 1990. pap. 24.00 (*0-85532-316-7*, Pub. by Srch Pr) St Mut.

Boros, Steven. Hepatocyte Growth Factor: The Basic Principles. LC 99-11153. 200p. 1999. pap. 89.95 (*1-57059-535-6*) Landes Bioscience.

***Boroson, Martin.** Becoming Me: A Story of Creation. 32p. 2000. 16.95 (*1-893361-11-X*) SkyLight Paths.

Boroson, Todd, et al, eds. New Observing Modes for the Next Century. (ASP Conference Series Proceedings: Vol. 87). 262p. 1996. 34.00 (*1-886733-08-2*) Astron Soc Pacific.

Boroson, Warren. Keys to Investing for Your Child's Future. Shenkman, Martin M., ed. LC 92-14790. (Parenting Keys Ser.). 1992. pap. 6.95 (*0-8120-4961-6*) Barron.

— Keys to Investing in Mutual Funds. 3rd ed. LC 96-33503. (Barron's Business Keys Ser.). 1997. pap. 4.95 (*0-8120-9644-4*) Barron.

***Boroson, Warren.** Keys to Investing in Your 401"k" 2nd ed. 2000. pap. text. write for info. (*0-7641-1298-8*, Pub. by Barron) Prodn Assocs.

Boroson, Warren. Keys to Retirement Planning. 2nd ed. LC 94-44567. (Barron's Business Keys Ser.). 1995. pap. 4.95 (*0-8120-9013-6*) Barron.

— Keys to Saving Money on Income Taxes. 2nd ed. LC 94-35581. (Barron's Business Keys Ser.). 1995. pap. 4.95 (*0-8120-9012-8*) Barron.

— Mutual Fund Switch Strategies & Timing Tactics. (Investor's Self-Teaching Seminar Ser.). 225p. 1991. per. 24.95 (*1-55738-184-4*, Irwn Prfssnl) McGraw-Hill Prof.

— The Ultimate Mutual Fund Guide: Seventeen Experts Pick the 46 Top Funds You Should Own. 250p. 1993. per. 18.95 (*1-55738-425-8*, Irwn Prfssnl) McGraw-Hill Prof.

— Ultimate Mutual Fund Guide: 17 Experts Pick the 46 Top Funds You Should Own. rev. ed. 250p. 1995. 16.95 (*1-55738-864-4*, Irwn Prfssnl) McGraw-Hill Prof.

— The Ultimate Mutual Fund Guide: 20 Experts Pick the 46 Top Funds You Should Own. 2nd rev. ed. 288p. 1996. per. 18.95 (*0-7863-1130-4*, Irwn Prfssnl) McGraw-Hill Prof.

Boroson, Warren & Austin, Ken. Home Buyer's Inspection Guide: Everything You Need to Know to Save Money & Get a Better House. 240p. 1993. pap. 19.95 (*0-471-57450-3*) Wiley.

Boroson, Warren & Solorzano, Lucia. Keys to Investing in Your 401(k) 3rd ed. (Barron's Business Keys Ser.). 140p. (Orig.). 1994. pap. 4.95 (*0-8120-1873-7*) Barron.

Boroson, Warren, jt. auth. see Shenkman, Martin M.

Borota, J. Tropical Forests. (Developments in Agricultural & Managed Forest Ecology Ser.: Vol. 22). xii,274p. 1991. 154.50 (*0-444-98768-1*) Elsevier.

Borough, John. Notes of the Treaty Carried on at Ripon Between King Charles First & the Covenanters of Scotland, A. D. 1640. Bruce, John, ed. (Camden Society, London. Publications, First Ser.: No. 100). reprint ed. 30.00 (*0-404-50200-8*) AMS Pr.

Borough, Rex D. A Woman's Place. Herbison, Kathleen, ed. (Illus.). 374p. 1992. text 16.95 (*1-880988-00-3*) Amer W Bks.

Borough, Rube, jt. auth. see Lindsey, Ben B.

Boroujerdi, Mehrzad. Iranian Intellectuals & the West: The Tormented Triumph of Nativism. LC 96-27371. 320p. 1996. text 49.95 (*0-8156-2726-2*, BOTT); pap. text 19.95 (*0-8156-0433-5*, BOTTP) Syracuse U Pr.

Borovcnik, Manfred, jt. ed. see Kapadia, Ramesh.

Borover, Bill & Langley, Tammy. Office & Career Management for the Eyecare Paraprofessional. LC 96-51005. (Basic Bookshelf for Eyecare Professionals Ser.). 144p. 1997. pap. text 30.00 (*1-55642-331-4*, 63314) SLACK Inc.

Borover, William A. Opticianry: The Practice & the Art, 4 vols., Set. Incl. Vol. I. Introduction to Dispensing. (Illus.). 259p. 1981. per. 48.00 (*0-9606398-0-2*); Vol. II. Science of Opticianry. (Illus.). 300p. 1982. per. 48.00 (*0-9606398-2-9*); Vol. III. Dynamics of Dispensing. (Illus.). 1983. per. 48.00 (*0-9606398-3-7*); Vol. IV. Business of Opticianry. 1984. per. 48.00 (*0-9606398-4-5*); (Illus.). Set pap. 192.00 (*0-9606398-1-0*) Gracie Ent.

Borovetz, Fran. Ha Motzi Bracha Kit. (Illus.). 32p. (Orig.). (J). (gr. 3-4). 1985. pap. text 4.95 (*0-933873-03-4*) Torah Aura.

Borovik, Alexandre & Nesin, Ali. Groups of Finite Morley Rank. (Logic Guides Ser.: Vol. 26). 426p. 1995. text 75.00 (*0-19-853445-0*) OUP.

Borovik, Artyom. Hidden War: A Russian Journalist's Account of the Soviet War in Afghanistan. 252p. 1992. pap. 10.95 (*0-87113-521-3*, Atlntc Mnthly) Grove-Atltic.

Borovik-Romanov, A. S. Physics Reviews Vol. 15, Pt. 3: Spin Super-Current & Magnetic Relaxation in Helium-3, Vol. 15. (Soviet Scientific Reviews Ser.: Section A). 57p. 1990. text 69.00 (*3-7186-5050-9*, Harwood Acad Pubs) Gordon & Breach.

Borovik-Romanov, A. S. & Sinha, S. K., eds. Spin Waves & Magnetic Excitations, Pt. 1. (Modern Problems in Condensed Matter Sciences Ser.: Vol. 22). xii,502p. 1988. 204.00 (*0-444-87068-7*) Elsevier.

— Spin Waves & Magnetic Excitations, Pt. 2. (Modern Problems in Condensed Matter Sciences Ser.: Vol. 22). 502p. 1988. 204.00 (*0-444-87078-4*) Elsevier.

Borovikov, V. A. Modelling the Effects of Blasting on Rock Breakage. Vanyagin, I. F., tr. from RUS. LC 99-226794. (Russian Translation Ser.: No. 114). (Illus.). 250p. (C). 1995. text 104.00 (*90-5410-222-5*, Pub. by A A Balkema) Ashgate Pub Co.

— Uniform Stationary Phase Method. (IEE Electromagnetic Waves Ser.: No. 40). 240p. 1994. boxed set 95.00 (*0-85296-812-4*) INSPEC Inc.

Borovikov, V. A. & Ye Kinber, B. Geometrical Theory of Diffraction. (Electromagnetic Waves Ser.: No. 37). 350p. 1993. boxed set 99.00 (*0-85296-830-2*, EW037) INSPEC Inc.

Borovits, Israel. Management of Computer Operations. (Illus.). 288p. (C). 1984. text 49.00 (*0-13-549493-1*) P-H.

***Borovkov, A.** Ergodicity & Stability of Stochastic Processes. Yurinsky, V., tr. LC 98-7736. 618p. 1998. 189.95 (*0-471-97913-9*) Wiley.

Borovkov, A. A. Probability Theory. 488p. 1999. text 81.00 (*90-5699-046-2*, ECU104, Harwood Acad Pubs) Gordon & Breach.

Borovkov, A. A., ed. Advances in Probability: Limit Theorems & Related Problems. 500p. 1984. 101.95 (*0-387-90945-1*) Spr-Verlag.

Borovkov, A. A., et al. Nineteen Papers on Statistics & Probability. LC 61-9803. (Selected Translations on Mathematical Statistics & Probability Ser.: Vol. 2). 251p. 1962. 34.00 (*0-8218-1452-4*, STAPRO/2) Am Math.

Borovkov, A. A., jt. ed. see Balakrishnan, A. V.

Borovksky, Yosef Y. Lamah U'Maduan Heichan U'Kaman (Who What When Where) (HEB.). 218p. 1996. 12.00 (*0-8266-1302-0*) Kehot Pubn Soc.

Borovoi, Mikhail. Abelian Galois Cohomology of Reductive Groups. LC 97-47116. (Memoirs of the American Mathematical Society Ser.). 50p. 1998. pap. 35.00 (*0-8218-0650-5*) Am Math.

Borovskikh, Y. V. & Korolyuk, Vladimir S. Random Permanents. 202p. 1994. 145.00 (*90-6764-184-7*, Pub. by VSP) Coronet Bks.

Borovskikh, Y. V., jt. ed. see Skorokhod, A. V.

Borovskikh, Yu V. U-Statistics in Banach Spaces. 432p. 1996. 225.00 (*90-6764-200-2*, Pub. by VSP) Coronet Bks.

Borovskikh, Yu V. & Korolyuk, Vladimir S., eds. Martingale Approximations. LC 99-496394. (Illus.). 334p. 1997. 187.50 (*90-6764-271-1*, Pub. by VSP) Coronet Bks.

Borovsky, Alexander, jt. auth. see Gelburd, Gail.

Borovsky, D. & Speilman, A. Host Regulated Developmental Mechanisms in Vector Arthropods, 1989. 324p. 1989. 22.50 (*0-9615224-4-5*, ESAVA9) Entomol Soc.

— Host Regulated Developmental Mechanisms in Vector Arthropods, 1993. 328p. 1993. 26.25 (*0-9615224-2-9*, ESAVA3) Entomol Soc.

Borovsky, Joseph E., ed. see Pfaff, Robert F., et al.

Borovsky, Natasha. Lost Heritage. 686p. (Orig.). 1995. pap. 18.40 (*0-9647178-0-8*) Sila-Nova Pr.

Borovsky, Victor, jt. ed. see Leach, Robert.

***Boroweic, Andrew.** Along the Ohio. LC 99-53363. (Illus.). 152p. 2000. 55.00 (*0-8018-6381-3*); pap. 24.95 (*0-8018-6382-1*) Johns Hopkins.

Borowiak. Model Discrimination for Nonlinear Regression Models. (Statistics: Textbooks & Monographs: Vol. 101). (Illus.). 200p. 1989. text 135.00 (*0-8247-8053-1*) Dekker.

Borowiak, Kenneth, ed. see Brady, Michael K.

***Borowick, Jerome N.** How to Write a Lab Report LC 99-35922. 2000. write for info. (*0-13-013562-3*) P-H.

— Technical Communication & Its Application. 2nd ed. LC 99-19977. 436p. (C). 1999. text 64.00 incl. disk (*0-13-020996-1*) P-H.

***Borowiec, Andrew.** Cyprus: A Troubled Island. LC 99-37528. 216p. 2000. write for info. (*0-275-96533-3*, Praeger Pubs) Greenwood.

Borowiec, Andrew. The Mediterranean Feud. LC 82-16624. 190p. 1983. 55.00 (*0-275-90950-6*, C0950, Praeger Pubs) Greenwood.

— Modern Tunisia: A Democratic Apprenticeship. LC 97-32948. 176p. 1998. 55.00 (*0-275-96136-2*, Praeger Pubs) Greenwood.

— Yugoslavia after Tito. LC 77-83466. (Praeger Special Studies). 122p. 1977. 55.00 (*0-275-90255-2*, C0255, Praeger Pubs) Greenwood.

Borowiec, Andrzej, ed. Spinors, Twistors & Clifford Algebras: Proceedings of the Second Max Born Syposium Held Near Wroclaw, Poland, September, 1992. (Fundamental Theories of Physics Ser.). 472p. (C). 1993. lib. bdg. 218.50 (*0-7923-2251-7*) Kluwer Academic.

Borowiec, Andrzej, ed. see Max Born Symposium Staff.

Borowiec, Piotr. Animated Short Films: A Critical Index to Theatrical Cartoons. LC 98-23687. 240p. 1998. 45.00 (*0-8108-3503-7*) Scarecrow.

Borowiec, Steven, jt. auth. see Sharpe, Kevin.

Borowiecki, Barbara, ed. Encyclopedia of Wisconsin: A Reference Guide to the Badger State. (Encyclopedia of the United States Ser.). (Illus.). vi, 518p. 1991. lib. bdg. 79.00 (*0-403-09907-2*) Somerset Pub.

Borowiecki, M., et al, eds. Graph Theory. (Lecture Notes in Mathematics Ser.: Vol. 1018). 289p. 1983. 42.95 (*0-387-12687-2*) Spr-Verlag.

Borowik, P., jt. auth. see Bolc, L.

Borowik, P., jt. auth. see Bolc, Leonard.

Borowitz, Albert, jt. auth. see Borowitz, Helen.

***Borowitz, Andy.** The Trillionaire Next Door: The Greedy Investor's Guide to Day Trading. 112p. 2000. 20.00 (*0-06-662076-7*, HarpBusn) HarpInfo.

Borowitz, Eugene B. Choices in Modern Jewish Thought: A Partisan Guide. 2nd rev. ed. Behrman, David, ed. LC 95-2583. (Illus.). 1995. pap. 16.95 (*0-87441-581-0*) Behrman.

— Choosing a Sex Ethic: A Jewish Inquiry. LC 73-79123. (gr. 10-12). 1987. pap. 6.95 (*0-8052-0276-5*) Schocken.

— Exploring Jewish Ethics: Papers on Covenant Responsibility. LC 89-29202. (Illus.). 500p. (C). 1990. text 49.95 (*0-8143-2199-2*) Wayne St U Pr.

— Exploring Jewish Ethics: Papers on Covenant Responsibility. LC 89-29202. 499p. reprint ed. pap. 154.70 (*0-608-10552-X*, 2071172) Bks Demand.

— Judaism after Modernity: Papers from a Decade of Fruition. LC 98-52554. 432p. 1999. pap. 34.50 (*0-7618-1330-6*) U Pr of Amer.

***Borowitz, Eugene B.** Judaism after Modernity: Papers from a Decade of Fruition. LC 98-52554. 432p. 1999. 57.00 (*0-7618-1329-2*) U Pr of Amer.

Borowitz, Eugene B. Liberal Judaism. LC 83-17997. 468p. (Orig.). 1984. pap. 12.00 (*0-8074-0264-8*, 386050) UAHC.

— Reform Judaism Today. 800p. 1983. pap. text 15.95 (*0-87441-315-X*) Behrman.

— Renewing the Covenant: A Theology for the Postmodern Jew. 320p. 1996. pap. 19.95 (*0-8276-0627-3*) JPS Phila.

Borowitz, Eugene B., ed. Reform Jewish Ethics & the Halakhah: An Experiment in Decision Making. 1995. 29.95 (*0-87441-571-3*) Behrman.

Borowitz, Eugene B. & Patz, Naomi. Explaining Reform Judaism. 90p. (J). (gr. 6-8). 1985. pap., wbk. ed. 4.95 (*0-317-60043-5*); pap. text 8.95 (*0-87441-394-X*) Behrman.

Borowitz, Eugene B. & Schwartz, Francine. The Jewish Moral Virtues. LC 98-43921. 384p. 1999. 24.95 (*0-8276-0664-8*) JPS Phila.

Borowitz, Eugene B., et al. Explaining Reform Judaism. 96p. 1985. pap., teacher ed. 14.95 (*0-87441-436-9*) Behrman.

Borowitz, Eugene B., jt. auth. see Ingall, Carol K.

Borowitz, Helen & Borowitz, Albert. Pawnshop & Palaces: The Fall & Rise of the Campana Art Museum. LC 90-10228. (Illus.). 322p. (C). 1991. text 32.00 (*1-56098-010-9*) Smithsonian.

Borowitz, Helen O. The Impact of Art on French Literature: From Scudery to Proust. LC 83-40317. (Illus.). 248p. 1985. 45.00 (*0-87413-249-5*) U Delaware Pr.

Borowitz, Jeri B. Roscoe I. 159p. 1995. 7.50 (*0-9645624-0-5*) Clinton Pub.

Borowitz, Michael, contrib. by. Clinical Applications of Flow Cytometry: Immunophenotyping of Leukemic Cells; Proposed Guideline (1993) 1993. 85.00 (*1-56238-219-5*, H43-P) NCCLS.

***Borowitz, Mike.** Cases in Flow Cytometry: Interactive CD-Rom for Specialists. (Illus.). 1999. audio compact disk 100.00 (*1-891524-07-0*) Carden Jennings.

Borowitz, Sidney. Essentials of Physics: A Text for Students of Science & Engineering. LC 70-131201. (Series in Physics). 576p. reprint ed. pap. 178.60 (*0-608-30556-1*, 205204400029) Bks Demand.

— Farewell Fossil Fuels: Renewing America's Energy Policy. LC 98-5671. (Illus.). 178p. (C). 1999. 34.95 (*0-306-45780-6*, Pub. by Perseus Pubng); pap. 19.95 (*0-306-45781-4*, Pub. by Perseus Pubng) HarpC.

Borowski, Allan, et al, eds. Ageing & Social Policy in Australia. LC 97-19608. (Illus.). 360p. (C). 1998. text 59.95 (*0-521-49661-6*); pap. text 22.95 (*0-521-49820-1*) Cambridge U Pr.

Borowski, E. Dictionary of Mathematics. 1989. pap. 19.95 (*0-00-434347-6*, Pub. by HarpC) Trafalgar.

Borowski, E. J. & Borwein, J. J. The HarperCollins Dictionary of Mathematics. LC 90-56001. (Illus.). 672p. 1991. pap. 20.00 (*0-06-461019-5*, Harper Ref) HarpC.

Borowski, Harry R. A Hollow Threat: Strategic Air Power & Containment Before Korea, 25. LC 81-4228. (Contributions in Military History Ser.: No. 25). 242p. 1982. 55.00 (*0-313-22235-5*, BHT/, Greenwood Pr) Greenwood.

Borowski, Oded. Every Living Thing: Daily Use of Animals in Ancient Israel. LC 97-21228. 296p. 1997. 65.00 (*0-7619-8918-8*); pap. 22.95 (*0-7619-8919-6*) AltaMira Pr.

Borowski, Tadeusz. This Way for the Gas, Ladies & Gentlemen. Vedder, Barbara, tr. 192p. 1992. pap. 12.95 (*0-14-018624-7*, Penguin Classics) Viking Penguin.

Borowsky, Irvin. Opportunities in Printing Careers. LC 97-38631. (Opportunities in...Ser.). (Illus.). 160p. 1998. 14.95 (*0-8442-2306-9*, 23069, VGM Career); pap. 11.95 (*0-8442-2307-7*, 23077, VGM Career) NTC Contemp Pub Co.

Borowsky, Irvin J. Artists Confronting the Inconceivable. (Illus.). 136p. (YA). 1992. 100.00 (*1-881060-00-4*) Am Interfaith.

— Opportunities in Printing Careers. (Opportunities In . . . Ser.). (Illus.). 160p. pap. 12.95 (*0-8442-8178-6*, 297OIPRIN, VGM Career) NTC Contemp Pub Co.

— Opportunities in Printing Careers. (Opportunities in...Ser.). (Illus.). 160p. 1994. 14.95 (*0-8442-8177-8*, VGM Career) NTC Contemp Pub Co.

Borowsky, Irving J. Opportunities in Printing Careers. (Illus.). 160p. 1987. 13.95 (*0-8442-6189-0*, VGM Career) NTC Contemp Pub Co.

— Opportunities in Printing Careers. (Illus.). 160p. 1993. pap. 10.95 (*0-8442-6190-4*, VGM Career) NTC Contemp Pub Co.

Borowsky, Irwin J., jt. ed. see Kee, Howard C.

Borowsky, Kay. Kunst und Leben. (Germanistische Texte und Studien: Bd. 2). (GER.). xii, 131p. 1976. write for info. (*3-487-06007-8*) G Olms Pubs.

Borowsky, Larry, jt. auth. see Burger, Harry.

Borowsky, Philip, jt. auth. see Larson, Lex K.

Borozne, Joseph, et al, eds. Administration & Supervision for Safety in Sports. LC 78-107560. (Sports Safety Monographs: No. 1). 67p. reprint ed. pap. 30.00 (*0-8357-5105-8*, 202660700050) Bks Demand.

— Safety in Outdoor Recreational Activities. LC GV0344.S2. (Sports Safety Monographs: No. 6). 76p. reprint ed. pap. 30.00 (*0-608-16579-4*, 202661200050) Bks Demand.

Borqe, P. Cosmetic Analysis: Selective Methods & Techniques. (Cosmetic Science & Technology Ser.: Vol. 4). (Illus.). 552p. 1985. text 250.00 (*0-8247-7113-3*) Dekker.

An Asterisk (*) at the beginning of an entry indicates that the title is appearing for the first time.

Borque, Blair B., et al. Boot Camps for Juvenile Offenders: An Implementation Evaluation of Three Demonstration Programs. (Illus.). 116p. (Orig.). 1997. pap. text 40.00 (*0-7881-3795-6*) DIANE Pub.

Borque, Jose M., ed. Actor y Tecnica De la Representacion Del Teatro Clasico: Madrid, 17-19 de mayo de 1988) (Series A; Monagrafias, CXL). (SPA.). 224p. (Orig.). (C). 1990. 35.00 (*0-7293-0307-1*, Pub. by Tamesis Bks Ltd) Boydell & Brewer.

Borquez de la Fuente, Rufina, tr. see Holmes, William H.

Borradaile, G. J., et al, eds. Atlas of Deformational & Metamorphic Rock Fabrics. (Illus.). 530p. 1982. 215.95 (*0-387-11278-2*) Spr-Verlag.

Borradori, Giovanna. The American Philosopher: Conversations with Quine, Davidson, Putnam, Nozick, Danto, Rorty, Cavell, MacIntyre, & Kuhn. Crocitto, Rosanna, tr. LC 93-5294. 192p. 1993. pap. 13.95 (*0-226-06648-7*) U Ch Pr.

— The American Philosopher: Conversations with Quine, Davidson, Putnam, Nozick, Danto, Rorty, Cavell, MacIntyre, & Kuhn. Crocitto, Rosanna, tr. LC 93-5294. 168p. 1995. lib. bdg. 34.95 (*0-226-06647-9*) U Ch Pr.

Borras, F. M. & Christian, Reginald F. Russian Prose Composition: Annotated Passages for Translation into Russian. 1964. 4.50 (*0-19-815618-9*) OUP.

Borras, G. M., jt. auth. see Fatas Cabeza, Guillermo.

Borras, M., et al. Homenatge A Joan Prats. (Ediciones Especiales y de Bibliofilo Ser.). (CAT, ENG, FRE & SPA., Illus.). 1993. 750.00 (*84-600-1894-6*) Elliots Bks.

Borras, Maria L. Arte del Objeto Japones. (ENG, FRE, GER & SPA., Illus.). 244p. 1993. 100.00 (*84-343-0049-4*) Elliots Bks.

— Picabia. (Grandes Monografias). (SPA., Illus.). 552p. 1993. 350.00 (*84-343-0414-7*) Elliots Bks.

Borras, Tracey. School Principals. (Community Helpers Ser.). (J). 1998. 14.00 (*0-516-21348-2*) Childrens.

— TV Reporters. (Community Helpers Ser.). (J). 1998. 14.00 (*0-516-21349-0*) Childrens.

Borre & Pandey. Nepalese Political Behaviour. 1994. pap. 48.00 (*0-7855-0466-4*, Pub. by Ratna Pustak Bhandar) St Mut.

Borre, K., jt. auth. see Strang, Gilbert.

Borre, Ole & Andersen, Jorgen G. Voting & Political Attitudes in Denmark: A Study of the 1994 Election. 352p. (C). 1997. 33.00 (*87-7288-542-4*, Pub. by Aarhus Univ Pr) David Brown.

Borre, Ole & Scarbrough, Elinor, eds. The Scope of Government. (Beliefs in Government Ser.: Vol. 3). (Illus.). 460p. 1996. text 65.00 (*0-19-827954-X*) OUP.

— The Scope of Government, Vol. 3. (Beliefs in Government Ser.). (Illus.). 450p. 1998. reprint ed. pap. text 35.00 (*0-19-829474-3*) OUP.

Borre, Ole, et al. Nepalese Political Behaviour: Comprehensive Study of Nepalese Voters. (Illus.). 240p. (Orig.). (C). 1994. pap. 19.95 (*87-7288-483-5*, Pub. by Aarhus Univ Pr) David Brown.

Borrebaeck, Carl A., ed. Antibody Engineering. 2nd ed. (Breakthroughs in Molecular Biology Ser.). (Illus.). 416p. 1995. pap. text 60.00 (*0-19-509150-7*) OUP.

Borrego, C., et al, eds. Urban Transport & the Environment for the 21st Century IV. LC 99-208778. (Advances in Transport Ser.: Vol. 1). 636p. 1998. 295.00 (*1-85312-597-0*, 5970, Pub. by WIT Pr) Computational Mech MA.

Borrego, Jose M., jt. auth. see Mortenson, Kenneth E.

Borrel, Eugene. L' Interpretation de la Musique Francaise: De Lully a la revolution. LC 76-43908. (Music & Theatre in France in the 17th & 18th Centuries Ser.). reprint ed. 48.50 (*0-404-60151-0*) AMS Pr.

Borrell, Jerry. Macworld Read Me First Book. LC 91-75702. 298p. 1991. pap. 22.95 (*1-878058-19-3*) IDG Bks.

Borrell, Martin T. By the Far Collins. (C). 1989. text 50.00 (*1-85821-012-7*, Pub. by Pentland Pr) St Mut.

***Borrell, P. & Borrell, P. M., eds.** Transport & Chemical Transformation of Pollutants in the Troposphere: An Overview of the Work of EUROTRAC. (Transport & Chemical Transformation of Pollutants in the Troposphere Ser.). (Illus.). xxii, 496p. 2000. 159.00 (*3-540-66775-X*) Spr-Verlag.

Borrell, P. M., et al, eds. Eurotrac Symposium 96: Transport & Transformation of Pollutants in the Troposphere, 2 vols. LC 96-72111. 1948p. 1997. 495.00 (*1-85312-495-8*, 4958, Pub. by WIT Pr) Computational Mech MA.

— Eurotrac Symposium '90: Transport & Transformation of Pollutants in the Troposphere. (Illus.). xxiii, 586p. 1991. 163.00 (*90-5103-058-4*, Pub. by SPB Acad Pub) Balogh.

— Eurotrac Symposium '92: Photo-Oxidants: Precursors & Products. xxxi, 830p. 1993. 188.00 (*90-5103-082-7*, Pub. by SPB Acad Pub) Balogh.

— Eurotrac Symposium '94: Transport & Transformation of Pollutants in the Troposphere. xxxiii, 1283p. 1994. 312.50 (*90-5103-095-9*, Pub. by SPB Acad Pub) Balogh.

Borrell, P. M., jt. ed. see Borrell, P.

Borrell, Peter & Builtjes, P. Photo-Oxidants, Acidification & Tools: Policy Applications of Eurotrac Result: The Report of the Eurotrac Application Project. LC 96-45984. (Transport & Chemical Transformation of Pollutants in the Troposphere Ser.: Vol. 10). (Illus.). 209p. 1997. 99.95 (*3-540-61783-3*) Spr-Verlag.

Borrelli. Differential Equations: A Modeling Perspective. 219p. 1997. pap. text, student ed. 34.95 (*0-471-24589-5*) Wiley.

***Borrelli, Laird.** Stylishly Drawn: Contemporary Fashion Illustration. (Illus.). 176p. 2000. 39.95 (*0-8109-4122-8*, Pub. by Abrams) Time Warner.

Borrelli, Laird, jt. auth. see Steele, Valerie.

Borrelli, Maryanne & Martin, Janet M. The Other Elites: Women, Politics, & Power in the Executive Branch. LC 96-43234. 1997. 55.00 (*1-55587-658-7*) L Rienner.

Borrelli, Nicholas F. Microoptics Technology: Fabrication & Applications of Lens Arrays & Devices. LC 98-56646. (Optical Engineering Ser.: Vol. 36). (Illus.). 360p. 1999. text 175.00 (*0-8247-1348-6*) Dekker.

Borrelli, Peter, ed. Crossroads: Environmental Priorities for the Future. LC 88-22338. 334p. 1988. pap. text 22.00 (*0-933280-67-X*) Island Pr.

— Crossroads: Environmental Priorities for the Future. LC 88-22338. 334p. 1989. text 40.00 (*0-933280-68-8*) Island Pr.

Borrelli, R. L. Differential Equations: A Collection of Experiments, Explorations, & Modeling Projects for the Computer. 368p. 1992. pap., lab manual ed. 40.95 (*0-471-55142-2*) Wiley.

Borrelli, Robert L. & Coleman, Courtney S. Differential Equations: A Modeling Perspective. LC 97-28427. 720p. 1997. text 96.95 (*0-471-04230-7*) Wiley.

Borrello, Alfred. Gabriel Fielding. LC 73-16101. (Twayne's English Authors Ser.). 155p. (C). 1974. text 20.95 (*0-8057-1194-5*) Irvington.

Borrello, Helen A. Kareem Abdul-Jabbar. LC 94-5774. (Basketball Legends Ser.). (Illus.). 64p. (J). (gr. 3 up). 1994. lib. bdg. 15.95 (*0-7910-2426-1*) Chelsea Hse.

Borrello, Joe. Recipes from the Wineries of the Great Lakes. Moen, Ruth, ed. 200p. (Orig.). 1997. pap. 17.00 (*1-881892-04-2*) Spradlin & Assocs.

Borremans. Golf. 1998. 29.95 (*0-7893-0139-3*, Pub. by Universe) St Martin.

Borremans, Gary & Taylor, Chuck. The Hevil in Del City & Plant Your Head in an Iron Glee. 24p. 1982. pap. 2.50 (*0-941720-06-3*) Slough Pr TX.

Borremans, Nina, et al. Discovering Florida after the Ice Age. 2nd ed. (Series of Lesson Plans: Ser. 1, No. 11). (Illus.). 12p. (J). (gr. k-12). 1997. write for info. (*1-889030-01-5*) FL Div Hist Res.

— Fort Mose: A Free Black Community. 2nd ed. (Series of Lesson Plans: Series 1, No. 9). (Illus.). 12p. 1996. write for info. (*0-9642289-9-8*) FL Div Hist Res.

— Hurricanes & Florida's Heritage. 2nd ed. (Series of Lesson Plans: Series 1, No. 8). (Illus.). 16p. 1996. write for info. (*0-9642289-8-X*) FL Div Hist Res.

— Should We Preserve? 2nd ed. (Series of Lesson Plans: Ser. 1, No. 10). (Illus.). 8p. (J). (gr. k-12). 1997. write for info. (*1-889030-00-7*) FL Div Hist Res.

Borren, Charles V. Sources of Keyboard Music in England. Matthew, James E., tr. LC 78-106714. 378p. 1970. reprint ed. lib. bdg. 69.50 (*0-8371-3444-7*, BOKM, Greenwood Pr) Greenwood.

Borrer, Shellie E., tr. see Riehl, Rudiger & Baensch, Hans A.

Borrero, Beatriz Botero De, see Botero de Borrero, Beatriz.

Borrero, Juan M. La Luna Blanca de Chesed. (Nueva Austral Ser.: No. 91). (SPA.). 1991. pap. text 24.95 (*84-239-1891-2*) Elliots Bks.

Borrero, Martha O. Botero De, see Botero de Borrero, Beatriz & Botero de Borrero, Martha O.

Borresen, Kari E. Image of God: Gender Models in the Judaeo-Christian Tradition. 320p. 1995. pap. 26.00 (*0-8006-2951-5*, 1-2951) Augsburg Fortress.

— Women's Studies of the Christian & Islamic Traditions: Ancient, Medieval & Renaissance Foremothers. (Diverse Ser.). 368p. (C). 1993. lib. bdg. 164.50 (*0-7923-2206-1*, Pub. by Kluwer Academic) Kluwer Academic.

Borreson, Glenn L. A Case for Excellence: Case Studies in Congregational Ministry. LC 97-26638. 173p. 1998. pap. 15.95 (*0-7880-1182-0*) CSS OH.

Borri, Christoforo. Cochin-China: Containing Many Admirable Rarities of That Countrey. LC 71-25710. (English Experience Ser.: No. 223). 1970. reprint ed. 20.00 (*90-221-0223-8*) Walter J Johnson.

Borri, Dino, ed. see Khakee, Abdul & Lacirignola, Cosimo.

Borrie, Gordon J. Commercial Law. 6th ed. 392p. 1988. pap. text 38.00 (*0-406-55846-9*, UK, MICHIE) LEXIS Pub.

Borrie, M. S., jt. auth. see Burghes, D. N.

Borrie, W. D. The Growth & Control of World Population. LC 70-541673. x, 340 p. 1970. write for info. (*0-297-00137-X*) Weidenfeld & Nicolson.

Borrie, W. D., ed. see International Union for the Scientific Study of Po.

Borriello, Gaetano & Ebeling, Carl. Research on Integrated Systems: Proceedings of the 93 Symposium. (Illus.). 355p. 1993. 65.00 (*0-262-02357-1*) MIT Pr.

Borriello, Luigi. Spiritual Doctrine of Blessed Elizabeth of the Trinity: Apostolic Contemplative. Aumann, Jordan, tr. from SPA. LC 86-3446. 154p. (Orig.). 1986. pap. 7.95 (*0-8189-0500-X*) Alba.

Borriello, S. P., ed. Antibiotic Associated Diarrhoea & Colitis. (Developments in Gastroenterology Ser.). 188p. 1984. text 122.00 (*0-89838-623-3*) Kluwer Academic.

Borriello, S. P. & Hardie, J. M., eds. Recent Advances in Anaerobic Bacteriology. (New Perspectives in Clinical Microbiology Ser.). 1986. text 206.50 (*0-89838-847-3*) Kluwer Academic.

Borriello, S. Peter, ed. Clostridia in Gastrointestinal Disease. 248p. 1985. 143.00 (*0-8493-5656-3*, RC862, CRC Reprint) Franklin.

Borries, Philip Von, see Von Borries, Philip.

Borrill. Backplane Business Design. 2001. text 49.68 (*0-13-065772-7*) P-H.

Borrione, Dominique & Ernst, Rolf, eds. Design, Automation & Test in Europe: Proceedings. Conference & Exhibition, 1999. LC 99-60127. 798p. 1999. pap. 160.00 (*0-7695-0078-1*) IEEE Comp Soc.

***Borris, John P.** Electric Circuits Using Electronics Workbench: Hardware & Simulation Exercises. 2nd ed. 206p. 1999. pap. 39.00 (*0-13-016618-9*, Prentice Hall) P-H.

Borris, John P. Linear Integrated Circuit Applications: Hardware & Software Exercises Using Electronics Workbench. LC 99-20176. 195p. 1999. pap. text 41.00 (*0-13-280835-8*) P-H.

***Borris, John P.** Semiconductor Devices Using Electronics Workbench. 2nd ed. (Illus.). 320p. 1999. pap. 41.00 (*0-13-026083-5*) P-H.

***Borris, Kenneth.** Allegory & Epic in English Renaissance Literature: Heroic Form in Sidney, Spenser & Milton. LC 99-87474. (Illus.). 344p. (C). 2000. Price not set. (*0-521-78129-9*) Cambridge U Pr.

Borris, Stephen W., jt. auth. see Borris, William M.

Borris, William M. & Borris, Stephen W. Deer Guts on a Doorknob: A Handbook of Useful & Tasteless Expressions. (Illus.). 120p. (Orig.). 1987. pap. 4.95 (*0-9618428-0-6*) Great Expressions.

Borrmann, Axel, et al. The EC's Generalized System of Preferences. 276p. 1981. 56.00 (*90-286-2111-3*) Kluwer Academic.

— The European Community's Generalized System of Preferences. 276p. 1981. lib. bdg. 147.00 (*90-247-2547-X*) Kluwer Academic.

Borrmans, M. Statut Personal et Famille au Maghreb de 1940 a Nos Jours. 107.70 (*90-279-7713-5*) Mouton.

Borrmans, Maurice. Guidelines for Dialogue Between Christians & Muslims. Speight, R. Marston, tr. 132p. 1996. pap. 12.95 (*0-614-21666-4*, 362) Kazi Pubns.

Borroel, Roger. The Concordance of Lieutenant Colonel Jose Enrique de la Pena's Diary & Appendixes: A Comparative Critical Analysis. LC 97-61791. (Illus.). 61p. 1997. pap. 9.00 (*0-9624727-3-5*) LaVillita Pubns.

***Borroel, Roger.** The Itineraries of the Zapadores & San Luis Baitalions During the Texas War of 1836: Mexican Baitalion Series of the Alamo. LC 99-94298. (Illus.). 80p. 1999. pap. 12.99 (*1-928792-03-0*) LaVillita Pubns.

Borroel, Roger. Mexican Accounts of the Battle of the Alamo: A Collection & Critical Analysis. LC 98-60887. (Illus.). 143p. 1998. pap. 12.99 (*1-928792-00-6*) LaVillita Pubns.

— Mexican Documents of the Texan Revolt, 1836. (Illus.). 30p. 1998. pap. 5.99 (*1-928792-02-2*) LaVillita Pubns.

— The Papers of Lieutenant Colonel Jose Enrique de la Pena: Selected Appendixes from His Diary, 1836-1839. (Illus.). 65p. (Orig.). 1997. pap. 11.99 (*0-9624727-2-7*) LaVillita Pubns.

— The Papers of Lieutenant Colonel Jose Enrique de la Pena Vol. II: The Last of the Appendixes from His Diary, 1836-1837. LC 97-60773. (Illus.). 109p. 1997. pap. 10.99 (*0-9624727-5-1*) LaVillita Pubns.

— A Small Affair: The Fall of the Alamo As Seen Through the Eyes of a Survivor: Enrique Esparza. (Illus.). 153p. 1998. pap. 11.99 (*0-9624727-4-3*) LaVillita Pubns.

— The Teenager & the War: Vietnam War Stories of a Screaming Eagle. (Illus.). 78p. (Orig.). 1997. pap. 4.99 (*0-9624727-8-6*) LaVillita Pubns.

— The Texan Revolution of 1836: A Concise Historical Perspective, Based on Original Sources. LC 89-90463. (Illus.). 160p. (J). (ps-12). 1990. pap. 14.99 (*0-9624727-6-X*) LaVillita Pubns.

— With the Screaming Eagles in Vietnam: A Personal Narrative of a Soldier in the 101st Airborne Division, 1968-1969. LC 95-94850. (Illus.). 116p. 1995. reprint ed. pap. text 13.00 (*0-9624727-0-0*) LaVillita Pubns.

— A Young Soldier's Adventure in Vietnam with the 101st Airborne Division, 1968-1969: A Brief Scrapbook. LC 96-90309. (Illus.). 100p. (Orig.). (J). (ps-12). 1996. pap. 6.98 (*0-9624727-1-9*) LaVillita Pubns.

Borroel, Roger, ed. see De La Pena, Jose E.

Borroel, Roger, ed. see De La Portilla, Nicolas.

Borroel, Roger, ed. & tr. see Garza, J. Sanchez.

Borroff, Edith. Keep Trying: My Life. 500p. 1998. pap. write for info. (*1-888701-13-7*) Jarrett Pr.

— Listen to the World: A Book of Sounds. (Illus.). 62p. (J). (gr. 4-5). 1998. pap. write for info. (*1-888701-14-5*) Jarrett Pr.

— Music in Europe & the United States: A History. 2nd ed. 60p. 1990. pap. text, teacher ed. write for info. (*0-912675-46-2*) Ardsley.

— Music in Europe & the United States: A History. 2nd ed. (Illus.). 794p. 1990. text 44.95 (*0-912675-44-6*) Ardsley.

— Music Melting Round: A History of Music in the United States. (Illus.). 387p. (C). 1995. text 39.95 (*1-880157-17-9*) Ardsley.

— Music Melting Round: A History of Music in the United States. (Illus.). 387p. (C). 1995. pap. text. write for info. (*1-880157-18-7*) Ardsley.

— Notations & Editions. LC 76-58563. (Music Reprint Ser.). 1977. reprint ed. lib. bdg. 32.50 (*0-306-70867-1*) Da Capo.

— Three American Composers. (Illus.). 310p. (Orig.). 1986. lib. bdg. 48.50 (*0-8191-5371-0*) U Pr of Amer.

Borroff, Marie. Language & the Poet: Verbal Artistry in Frost, Stevens, & Moore. LC 78-14567. (Illus.). 1979. 18.00 (*0-226-06651-7*) U Ch Pr.

— Pearl: A New Verse Translation. 40p. (C). 1977. pap. text 11.25 (*0-393-09144-9*) Norton.

Borroff, Marie, tr. Sir Gawain & the Green Knight: A Stylistic & Metrical Study. (Orig.). (C). 1967. pap. text 11.25 (*0-393-09754-4*) Norton.

***Borromeo-Buehler, Soledad.** The Cry of Balintawak: A Contrived Controversy. LC 98-947858. (Illus.). 238p. 1999. pap. text 18.00 (*971-550-278-4*, Pub. by Ateneo de Manila Univ Pr) UH Pr.

Borromeo, Georgina, ed. see Friedman, Florence Dunn, et al.

Borror, D. Bird Song & Bird Behavior. (Donald J. Borror Bird Song Library). 32p. 1989. pap. 8.95 incl. audio (*0-486-99924-6*) Dover.

Borror, Donald J. Common Bird Songs, Vol. 181. (Donald J. Borror Bird Song Library). 64p. (Orig.). 1984. pap., student ed. 8.95 incl. audio (*0-486-99911-4*, 99911-4) Dover.

— Dictionary of Word Roots & Combining Forms. LC 60-15564. 134p. (C). 1960. pap. text 9.95 (*0-87484-053-8*, 053) Mayfield Pub.

— Songs of Eastern Birds. 81st ed. (Donald J. Borror Bird Song Library). 64p. 1984. pap. 9.95 incl. audio (*0-486-99912-2*, 99912-2) Dover.

— Songs of Western Birds. 81st ed. 64p. 1984. pap. 8.95 incl. audio (*0-486-99913-0*) Dover.

Borror, Donald J. & Giltz, Maurice L. Florida Bird Songs. (Donald J. Borror Bird Song Library). 32p. 1989. pap. 9.95 incl. audio (*0-486-99926-2*) Dover.

Borror, Donald J., et al. An Introduction to the Study of Insects. 6th ed. (Illus.). 800p. (C). 1989. text 87.50 (*0-03-025397-7*, Pub. by SCP) Harcourt.

Borror, James. WordPerfect 5.1 for DOS Beginners. (QuickSteps to Learning Ser.). (Illus.). 163p. 1993. spiral bd. 22.95 (*1-56951-001-6*) Sftware Trng.

Borror, Jeffrey A. Java Principles of Object-Oriented Programming. 500p. 1999. pap. 49.95 (*0-87930-583-5*) Miller Freeman.

Borroughs, Joseph N. Journey with the Wagon Master. Greenlee, Carolyn W., ed. LC 98-24324. (Illus.). 78p. 1998. pap. 12.50 (*1-887400-16-8*) Earthen Vessel Prodns.

Borrow, George. Wild Wales: It's People, Language & Scenery. 544p. pap. 19.95 (*1-871083-26-5*, Pub. by J Jones Pub) Dufour.

Borrow, George (Henry). Lavengro: The Classic Account of Gypsy Life in Nineteenth-Century England. (Illus.). 608p. 1991. reprint ed. pap. 12.95 (*0-486-26915-9*) Dover.

— Welsh Poems & Ballads. LC 78-72620. (Celtic Language & Literature Ser.: Goidelic & Brythonic). reprint ed. 37.50 (*0-404-17537-6*) AMS Pr.

— Wild Wales. 577p. 1995. 60.00 (*0-8464-4647-2*) Beekman Pubs.

— Wild Wales. 544p. 1998. pap. 29.95 (*0-8464-4886-6*) Beekman Pubs.

— Works, 16 vols., Set. Shorter, Clement K., ed. LC 24-5080. reprint ed. 1224.00 (*0-404-00970-0*) AMS Pr.

Borrow, Hugh. A Long Time Ago & Half a World Away. unabridged ed. 169p. 1998. pap., per. 12.95 (*0-938911-14-7*) Indiv Ed - Poppy Ln.

Borrowdale, Andrew & Rowe, David, eds. Essays in Commercial Law. xix, 271p. 1991. pap. 50.00 (*0-9598001-0-7*) Gaunt.

Borrowman, Jerry, jt. auth. see Wobbe, Rudi.

Borrowman, Merle L., ed. Teacher Education in America: A Documentary History. LC 65-17004. 264p. reprint ed. 81.90 (*0-8357-9609-4*, 201692500005) Bks Demand.

Borrows, F. The Dancer's Guide to the Nineteen Eighties. (Ballroom Dance Ser.). 1986. lib. bdg. 250.00 (*0-8490-3300-4*) Gordon Pr.

— History of Ballroom Dancing: The Dancing Master. (Ballroom Dance Ser.). 1986. lib. bdg. 250.00 (*0-8490-3335-7*) Gordon Pr.

Borrows, Toby. British University Libraries. 171p. 1989. 49.95 (*0-86656-917-0*) Haworth Pr.

Borrud, Robert. Like a Bulging Wall. LC 91-65104. 192p. 1991. pap. 8.95 (*0-914984-28-4*) Starburst.

Borrup, Roger. Hartford & Wethersfield Horse Railway Co. (Transportation Bulletin Ser.: No. 77). (Illus.). 1970. 7.50 (*0-910506-02-7*) De Vito.

— Plattsburgh (N.Y.) Traction Co. (Illus.). 51p. 1971. 7.50 (*0-910506-14-0*) De Vito.

Borrup, Roger & Smith, Carl L. Hyde Park Division. (Transportation Bulletin Ser.: No. 82). (Illus.). 1977. 7.50 (*0-910506-18-3*) De Vito.

Borrus, Beth. Fast Divorce Bankruptcy. LC 97-129855. 142p. (Orig.). 1995. pap. 12.00 (*1-884615-08-2*) Incommodo San Diego.

Borrus, Kathy. The Fearless Shopper: How to Get the Best Deals on the Planet. LC 99-34442. 278p. 1999. pap. 14.95 (*1-885211-39-2*, 39-2, Pub. by Trvlers Tale) OReilly & Assocs.

Borrus, Kathy, jt. auth. see Merriam, Caroline R.

***Borrus, Michael, et al.** International Production Networks in Asia: Rivalry or Riches. LC 99-87582. (Advances in Asia-Pacific Business Ser.). (Illus.). 2000. write for info. (*0-415-22170-6*) Routledge.

Borrus, Michael G. Competing for Control: America's Stake in Microelectronics. 288p. 1988. text 34.95 (*0-88730-306-4*, HarpBusn) HarpInfo.

Bors, Wolf, et al, eds. Oxygen Radicals in Chemistry & Biology: Proceedings - Third International Conference. LC 84-1691. xix, 1029p. 1984. 192.35 (*3-11-009704-4*) De Gruyter.

Borsa, F. & Tognetti, V., eds. Magnetic Properties of Matter: Proceedings of the Italian National School on Condensed Matter. 556p. (C). 1988. pap. 54.00 (*9971-5-0371-9*); text 138.00 (*9971-5-0368-9*) World Scientific Pub.

Borsa, Gorgio, ed. Trade & Politics in the Indian Ocean: Historical & Contemporary Perspectives. (C). 1991. 25.00 (*81-85425-11-6*, Pub. by Manohar) S Asia.

Borsa, John, jt. auth. see Weishaar, Mary E.

Borsani, Nancy. Getting Organized. 1997. pap. write for info. (*0-7880-0940-0*) CSS OH.

Borsanyi, Gyorgy. The Life of a Communist Revolutionary: Bela Kun. (Atlantic Studies on Society & Change: No. 75). 320p. (C). 1993. text 50.00 (*0-88033-260-3*, 363, Pub. by East Eur Monographs) Col U Pr.

***Borsarello, J.** Camouflage Uniforms of European & Nato Armies: 1945 to the Present. (Illus.). 120p. 2000. pap. 29.95 (*0-7643-1018-6*) Schiffer.

Borsarello, J. F., jt. auth. see Beaver, Michael D.

B

An Asterisk (*) at the beginning of an entry indicates that the title is appearing for the first time.

Borsarello, Jean-Francois. Dictionnaire de Medicine Chinoise Traditionelle. (FRE.). 248p. 1984. 225.00 (*0-7859-7826-7*, 2225800855) Fr & Eur.

***Borsay, Anne.** Medicine & Charity in Georgian Bath: A Social History of the General Infirmary, 1739-1830. LC 99-63692. (History of Medicine in Context Ser.). (Illus.). 496p. 1999. text 96.95 (*0-7546-0060-2*, Pub. by Ashgate Pub) Ashgate Pub Co.

Borsay, Peter. 18th Century Town. 1990. text 45.25 (*0-582-05135-5*, Pub. by Addison-Wesley) Longman.

— 18th Century Town. (C). 1991. pap. text 28.50 (*0-582-05134-7*, Pub. by Addison-Wesley) Longman.

— The English Urban Renaissance: Culture & Society in the Provincial Town 1660-1770. (Oxford Studies in Social History). (Illus.). 440p. 1991. reprint ed. pap. text 32.00 (*0-19-820255-5*) OUP.

***Borsay, Peter.** The Image of Georgian Bath, 1700-2000: Towns, Heritage & History. LC 99-88933. (Illus.). 400p. 2000. text 95.00 (*0-19-820265-2*) OUP.

Borsay, Peter, ed. The Eighteenth Century Town: A Reader in English Urban History, 1688-1820. (Readers in Urban History Ser.). (Illus.). 352p. (C). 1991. pap. text 23.75 (*0-685-72458-1*, 78599) Longman.

Borsboom, Ad, jt. ed. see Otto, Ton.

Borsboom, P. P. Field Analysis of Integrated-Optical Gratings. 160p. 1994. pap. 57.50 (*90-407-1025-2*, Pub. by Delft U Pr) Coronet Bks.

Borsch, Frederick H. Outrage & Hope: A Bishop's Reflections in Times of Change & Challenge. LC 96-10961. 280p. (Orig.). 1996. pap. 15.00 (*1-56338-170-2*) TPI PA.

Borsch, Frederick H. & Ritley, M. R. Christian Discipleship & Sexuality. 80p. (Orig.). 1993. pap., student ed. 3.95 (*0-88028-141-3*, 1210) Forward Movement.

Borsch, Frederick Houk, ed. The Bible's Authority in Today's Church. LC 93-6017. 224p. (C). 1999. pap. 15.00 (*1-56338-084-6*) TPI PA.

Borsch, Supan A. Econometric Analysis of Discrete Choice. (Lecture Notes in Economics & Mathematical Systems Ser.: Vol. 296). viii, 211p. 1987. 38.70 (*0-387-18534-8*) Spr-Verlag.

Borsch-Supan, Helmut. Karl Friedrich Schinkel 2 vols. Buhnenentwurfe/Stage Designs. (GER & ENG., Illus.). 110, 136p. 240.00 (*3-932565-19-3*) Edition A Menges.

Borschberg, Peter. Hugo Grotius "Commentarius in Theses XI" An Early Treatise on Sovereignty, the Just War, & the Legitimacy of the Dutch Revolt. 308p. 1998. pap. 46.95 (*3-906752-83-6*) P Lang Pubng.

Borsche, Tilman, et al, eds. Centauren-Geburten: Wissenschaft, Kunst und Philosophie Beim Jungen Nietzsche. (Monographien und Texte Zur Nietzsche-Forschung Ser.: Bd. 27). (GER.). 558p. (C). 1994. lib. bdg. 215.40 (*3-11-013796-8*) De Gruyter.

Borsche, Tilman & Stegmaier, Werner, eds. Zur Philosophie des Zeichens. (GER.). xiii, 231p. (C). 1992. lib. bdg. 75.40 (*3-11-013638-4*) De Gruyter.

Borsdorf, A., jt. auth. see Wilhelmy, H.

Borsdorf, Wolfgang, jt. auth. see Gross, H. W.

Borse, Garold G. Numerical Methods for Scientists & Engineers Using Metlab. LC 96-39300. 656p. 1996. mass mkt. 94.95 (*0-534-93822-1*) PWS Pubs.

Borsellino, A., et al, eds. Sensory Transduction. LC 90-42555. (NATO ASI Ser.: Vol. 194). (Illus.). 290p. 1990. 114.00 (*0-306-43677-9*, Kluwer Plenum) Kluwer Academic.

***Borsellino, Lewis J. & Commins, Patricia.** The Day Trader: From the Pit to the PC. LC 99-10019. 256p. 1999. 29.95 (*0-471-33265-8*) Wiley.

Borsenberger & Weiss, David S., eds. Organic Photoreceptors for Imaging Systems. (Optical Engineering Ser.: Vol. 39). (Illus.). 472p. 1993. text 185.00 (*0-8247-8926-1*) Dekker.

Borsenberger, Paul M. & Weiss, David S. Organic Photoreceptors for Xerography. LC 98-2799. (Optical Engineering Ser.). (Illus.). 792p. 1998. text 195.00 (*0-8247-0173-9*) Dekker.

Borsenik, Frank D. & Stutts, Alan T. The Management of Maintenance & Engineering Systems in the Hospitality Industry. 4th ed. LC 96-39997. 680p. 1997. 69.95 (*0-471-14105-4*) Wiley.

— The Management of Maintenance & Engineering Systems in the Hospitality Industry. 4th ed. 228p. 1997. pap., teacher ed. write for info. (*0-471-17217-0*) Wiley.

Borshch, A. A., et al. Refractive Nonlinearity of Wide Band Semiconductors & Applications. Letokhov, V. S., ed. (Laser Science & Technology Ser.: Vol. 9). xiv, 142p. 1990. pap. text 189.00 (*3-7186-4971-3*) Gordon & Breach.

Borsi, Emilia, jt. auth. see Rogg, Fay F.

Borsi, Franco. Architecture & Utopia. (Illus.). 200p. 1997. pap. 12.95 (*2-85025-540-8*) Dist Art Pubs.

Borsi, Franco & Borsi, Stefano. Paolo Uccello. LC 93-39788. (Illus.). 376p. 1994. 95.00 (*0-8109-3919-3*, Pub. by Abrams) Time Warner.

Borsi, Gabriele M., jt. ed. see Klein, Ricarda.

Borsi-Kalman, Bela. Hungarian Exiles & the Romanian National Movement, 1849-1867. 333p. 1992. text 69.50 (*0-88033-228-X*, 331, Pub. by East Eur Monographs) Col U Pr.

Borsi, Stefano, jt. auth. see Borsi, Franco.

Borska, Zdenka. Dictionary of Building & Civil Engineering. (CZE & ENG.). 1996. 150.00 (*0-7859-9709-1*) Fr & Eur.

Borsky, Mary. Influence of the Moon. 136p. 1995. pap. write for info. (*0-88984-163-2*) Porcup Quill.

Borsley, Robert. Syntactic Theory: A Unified Approach. 2nd ed. LC 98-47418. (An Arnold Publication). 288p. 1999. pap. text 24.95 (*0-340-70610-4*) OUP.

Borsley, Robert & Przepiorkowski, Adam, eds. Slavic in Head-Driven Phrase Structure Grammar. LC 99-19822. (Studies in Constraint-Based Lexicalism (SCBL)). 350p. (C). 1999. pap. text 24.95 (*1-57586-174-7*) CSLI.

— Slavic in Head-Driven Phrase Structure Grammer. LC 99-19822. (Studies in Constraint-Based Lexicalism (SCBL)). 350p. (C). 1999. text 64.95 (*1-57586-175-5*) CSLI.

Borsley, Robert D. Modern Phrase Structure Grammar. (Textbooks in Linguistics Ser.). 300p. (C). 1996. pap. 33.95 (*0-631-18407-4*) Blackwell Pubs.

— Syntactic Theory: A Unified Approach. (Illus.). 256p. 1995. pap. text 22.50 (*0-7131-6543-X*, A6314, Pub. by E A) St Martin.

***Borsley, Robert D., ed.** The Nature & Function of Syntactic Categories. (Syntax & Semantics Ser.: Vol. 32). 318p. 1999. 99.00 (*0-12-613532-0*) Acad Pr.

Borsley, Robert D., jt. ed. see Roberts, Ian G.

Borsodi, Ralph. The Distribution Age: A Study of the Economy of Modern Distribution. LC 75-39235. (Getting & Spending: The Consumer's Dilemma Ser.). (Illus.). 1976. reprint ed. 29.95 (*0-405-08011-5*) Ayer.

— This Ugly Civilization. LC 74-2668. (American Utopian Adventure Ser.). (Illus.). viii, 468p. 1972. reprint ed. lib. bdg. 49.50 (*0-87991-025-9*) Porcupine Pr.

Borsody, Stephen. The New Central Europe: Triumphs & Tragedies. 321p. 1993. 58.50 (*0-88033-263-8*, 366, Pub. by East Eur Monographs) Col U Pr.

— The New Central Europe: Triumphs & Tragedies. rev. ed. (Illus.). 322p. (C). pap. 20.00 (*1-882785-03-7*) Matthias Corvinus.

— The Tragedy of Central Europe. rev. ed. LC 80-51032. (Yale Russian & East European Publications: No. 2). (Illus.). xviii, 274p. 1980. 18.50 (*0-936586-01-X*, Pub. by Yale Russian) Slavica.

— The Tragedy of Central Europe: Nazi & Soviet Conquest & Aftermath. LC 80-51032. (Russian & East European Publications: No. 2). 274p. 1980. 18.50 (*0-685-09610-6*) Yale Russian.

Borsody, Stephen, tr. & intro. see Janics, Kalman.

Borsoi, Edward, tr. see Gala, Antonio.

Borson, Roo. Night Walk: Selected Poems. 92p. (C). 1994. pap. (*0-19-541082-3*) OUP.

— Water Memory. 112p. 1996. pap. 12.99 (*0-7710-1589-5*) McCland & Stewart.

Borson, Roo & Maltman, Kim. The Transparence of November Snow. 68p. 1985. pap. 12.95 (*0-919627-30-7*, Pub. by Quarry Pr) LPC InBook.

Borsook, David, ed. Molecular Neurobiology of Pain. LC 97-36742. (Progress in Pain Research & Management Ser.: Vol. 9). (Illus.). 384p. 1997. 76.00 (*0-931092-19-1*) Intl Assn Study Pain.

Borsook, David, et al, eds. The Massachusetts General Hopsital Handbook of Pain Management. 400p. 1996. pap. text 35.95 (*0-316-54946-0*, Little Brwn Med Div) Lppncott W & W.

Borsook, Eve. The Companion Guide to Florence. LC 97-4309. (Illus.). 424p. 1999. pap. 24.95 (*1-900639-19-X*) Boydell & Brewer.

— The Companion Guide to Florence. (Companion Guide Ser.). (Illus.). 448p. 1991. pap. 18.95 (*0-685-48921-3*, Harper Ref) HarpC.

— Messages in Mosaic: The Royal Programmes of Norman Sicily, 1130-1187. 256p. 1998. reprint ed. pap. 55.00 (*0-85115-591-X*, Boydell Pr) Boydell & Brewer.

Borsook, Eve & Gioffredi, Fiorella Superbi, eds. Italian Altarpieces, 1250-1550: Function & Design. (Illus.). 306p. 1994. text 75.00 (*0-19-817223-0*) OUP.

***Borsook, Paulina.** Cyberselfish: A Critical Romp Through the Terribly Libertarian Culture of High Tech. 256p. 2000. 24.00 (*1-891620-78-9*, Pub. by PublicAffairs NY) HarpC.

Borsos, John D. Double-Force Tennis Strokes. LC 93-61856. (Illus.). 350p. 1994. 21.00 (*0-9624182-4-2*) Third Level Bks.

Borssen, Jonas. Eat the Heat. LC 97-22894. (Illus.). 160p. 1998. pap. 16.95 (*0-89815-949-0*) Ten Speed Pr.

Borssuck, B. The Star of David Needlepoint Book. LC 78-32036. 128 p. 1979. write for info. (*0-668-04659-7*, ARCO) Macmillan.

Borst, Arno. Medieval Worlds: Barbarians, Heretics, & Artists in the Middle Ages. Hansen, Eric, tr. LC 91-36241. 288p. 1992. 45.00 (*0-226-06656-8*) U Ch Pr.

— Medieval Worlds: Barbarians, Heretics, & Artists in the Middle Ages. (Illus.). 274p. (C). 1996. reprint ed. pap. text 17.95 (*0-226-06657-6*) U Ch Pr.

— The Ordering of Time: From the Ancient Computus to the Modern Computer. Winnard, Andrew, tr. from GER. LC 93-27993.Tr. of Computus. 178p. 1993. lib. bdg. 39.95 (*0-226-06658-4*) U Ch Pr.

— Ordering Time: From the Ancient Computus to the Modern Computer. Winnard, Andrew, tr. x, 178p. 1993. pap. text 17.95 (*0-226-06659-2*) U Ch Pr.

Borst, B. Environmental Dictionary: German/English/German. (ENG & GER.). 1996. 59.95 (*0-320-00518-6*) Fr & Eur.

Borst, Bill. The Best of Seasons: The 1944 St. Louis Cardinals & St. Louis Browns. LC 94-35084. (Illus.). 331p. 1994. pap. 22.95 (*0-89950-974-6*) McFarland & Co.

— The Brooklyn Dodgers: A Fan's Memoir, 1953-1957. (Illus.). 106p. (Orig.). 1982. pap. 5.95 (*0-686-46429-X*) Krank Pr.

— The October Classic. 124p. 1989. pap. 7.95 (*0-9612260-7-2*) Krank Pr.

— Ohio State Football Trivia. 1988. 7.95 (*0-685-44817-7*) Krank Pr.

— The Pride of St. Louis: A Cooperstown Gallery. (Illus.). 96p. (Orig.). 1984. pap. 6.95 (*0-9612260-0-5*) Krank Pr.

— We Could Have Finished Last Without You. 48p. (Orig.). 1986. pap. 3.95 (*0-9612260-3-X*) Krank Pr.

Borst, Bill, ed. Ables to Zoldak, Vol. II. 96p. 1990. pap. 6.95 (*0-9612260-5-6*) Krank Pr.

— Ables to Zoldak, Vol. III. 108p. 1991. pap. 7.95 (*0-9612260-6-4*) Krank Pr.

Borst, Bill & Fischer, Erv. A Jockstrap Full of Nails. 1992. pap. 9.95 (*1-880629-01-1*) Krank Pr.

Borst, Bill & Riley, Pat. World Series Trivia. 1982. 2nd ed. (Suds Ser.). (Illus.). 48p. 1982. pap. text 3.95 (*0-686-47437-6*) Krank Pr.

Borst, Bill & Scott, Jim. The Browns Through the Years. 20p. 1987. pap. 7.95 (*0-9612260-2-1*) Krank Pr.

Borst, Bill, ed. see St. Louis Browns Fan Club Staff.

Borst, Charlotte G. Catching Babies: The Professionalization of Childbirth, 1870-1920. LC 95-5261. (Illus.). 288p. (C). 1995. 44.50 (*0-674-10262-2*) HUP.

Borst, Donna & Mitchell, Judy, eds. The Best of Holidays & Seasonal Celebrations, Issues 5-8. (Illus.). 320p. (J). (ps-3). 1997. pap. 24.95 (*1-57310-100-1*) Teachng & Lrning Co.

***Borst, Donna & Mitchell, Judy, eds.** The Best of Holidays & Seasonal Celebrations: Issues 1-4. (Illus.). 320p. (J). (ps-k). 1999. 24.95 (*1-57310-197-4*) Teachng & Lrning Co.

— The Best of Holidays & Seasonal Celebrations: Issues 13-17. (Illus.). 320p. (J). (gr. 1-3). 1999. pap. 24.95 (*1-57310-198-2*) Teachng & Lrning Co.

Borst, Donna & Mitchell, Judy, eds. Celebrate the Seasons Issues 9-12: The Best of Holidays & Seasonal Celebrations. (Illus.). 320p. (Orig.). (J). (ps-3). 1998. pap., teacher ed. 24.95 (*1-57310-110-9*) Teachng & Lrning Co.

— Classroom Celebrations: The Best of Holidays & Seasonal Celebrations, Issues 1-4. (Illus.). 320p. (J). (ps-3). 1996. pap. 24.95 (*1-57310-047-1*) Teachng & Lrning Co.

Borst, Donna, jt. ed. see Mitchell, Judy.

Borst, Hans G., et al. Surgical Treatment of Aortic Dissection. LC 95-37913. 357p. 1995. text 144.00 (*0-443-07531-X*) Church.

Borst, James. Coming to God in Stillness. 80p. 1996. pap. 6.99 (*0-86347-051-3*, Pub. by Eagle Bks) Shaw Pubs.

Borst, R. De, see De Borst, R.

Borst, Raymond R. Henry David Thoreau: A Descriptive Bibliography. LC 81-50638. (Series in Bibliography). (Illus.). 256p. 1981. 100.00 (*0-8229-3445-0*) U of Pittsburgh Pr.

— Henry David Thoreau: A Reference Guide, 1835-1899. (G. K. Hall Reference Ser.). 300p. (C). 1987. 45.00 (*0-8161-8822-X*, Hall Reference) Macmillan.

— The Thoreau Log: A Documentary Life of Henry David Thoreau, 1817-1862. 1995. 24.95 (*0-7838-1399-6*) Macmillan.

Borst, Raymond R., ed. see Thoreau, Henry David.

Borst, Renede & Giessen, E. Material Instabilities in Solids. LC 98-8796. 576p. 1998. 140.00 (*0-471-97460-9*) Wiley.

Borst, Sophie, jt. ed. see Noam, Gil G.

Borst, Steve. Forward in Faith: Church, Family, Work, Sexuality, Relationships. (Twenty-Something Bible Study Ser.: Bk. 1). 48p. 1997. pap. 12.99 (*0-570-09691-X*, 20-3060) Concordia.

— Forward in Faith: Church, Family, Work, Sexuality, Relationships. (Twenty-Something Bible Study Ser.: Bk. 2). 48p. 1997. pap. 12.99 (*0-570-09692-8*, 20-3061) Concordia.

Borst, Steven B. Men & Relationships. LC 97-154628. (Godly Man Ser.). 96p. 1996. per. 5.50 (*0-570-09671-5*, 20-3025) Concordia.

Borst, W. A. Liberalism: Fatal Consequences. LC 98-75318. 304p. 1998. pap. 14.99 (*1-56384-153-3*) Huntington Hse.

Borst, William A. Baseball Through a Knothole. (Illus.). 120p. (Orig.). 1981. pap. 4.95 (*0-940056-05-4*) Krank Pr.

***Borstad, Karen A.** The Madaba Plains Project Database Entry & Information Retrieval System Manual. (Illus.). 93p. 1999. pap. 10.00 (*0-9642060-3-X*) Inst of Archaeol.

Borsteen, D. M. Larger Firmer Breasts Through Self-Hypnosis. 101p. 1991. pap. 16.95 (*0-9630685-0-4*) Piedras Pr.

Borstein, ed. Introduction to Psychology. (C). 1999. text. write for info. (*0-321-01383-2*) Addson-Wesley Educ.

***Borstel, Gunnar, et al.** Defects & Surface-Induced Effects in Advanced Perovskites. 508p. 2000. pap. 85.00 (*0-7923-6217-9*) Kluwer Academic.

Borsten, Rick. The Great Equalizer. 334p. 1986. 22.00 (*0-932966-69-1*) Permanent Pr.

— Rainbow Rhapsody. LC 88-22294. 224p. 1989. 17.95 (*0-932576-68-0*) Breitenbush Bks.

Borsting, Elizabeth. Celebrity Weddings & Honeymoon Getaways. LC 68-585. 256p. 1997. pap. 16.95 (*1-883323-62-2*) Open Rd Pub.

***Borsting, Elizabeth.** Southern California Guide. 768p. 1999. 18.95 (*1-892975-19-X*) Open Rd Pub.

Borsy, Z., jt. ed. see Kadar, L.

Bort, Eberhard & Evans, Neil, eds. Networking Europe: Essays on Regionalism & Social Democracy. 400p. 1998. pap. 23.95 (*0-85323-941-X*, Pub. by Liverpool Univ Pr) Intl Spec Bk.

Bort, Eberhard, jt. ed. see Anderson, Malcolm.

Bort, John & Helms, Mary. Panama in Transition: Local Reactions to Development Policies. (Monographs in Anthropology: No. 6). (Illus.). v, 195p. 1983. pap. 9.50 (*0-913134-75-9*) Mus Anthro MO.

Bort, Julie & Felix, Bradley. Building an Extranet: Connect Your Intranet with Vendors & Customers. LC 97-7641. 326p. 1997. pap. 29.99 (*0-471-17910-8*) Wiley.

***Bort, Mary H. & Page, Margot.** Art & Soul: The History of the Southern Vermont Artists & the Southern Vermont Art Center. LC 00-34768. (Illus.). 2000. pap. write for info. (*0-9669382-4-0*) Gallery Press.

Bort, Richard. Corporate Cash Management Handbook. 560p. 1989. 135.00 (*0-7913-0239-3*) Warren Gorham & Lamont.

— Corporate Cash Management Handbook, No. 1. 560p. 1991. suppl. ed. 49.75 (*0-7913-1015-9*) Warren Gorham & Lamont.

— Corporate Cash Mgmt. Handbook. LC 93-60954. 1994. 135.00 (*0-7913-1751-X*) Warren Gorham & Lamont.

Borteck, jt. auth. see Martin.

Borteck, Benjamin. Having Accomplished So Little. 40p. (Orig.). 1997. pap. 5.00 (*1-890887-00-5*) Mille Grazie.

Borteck, Robert D., jt. auth. see Martin, Alvin C.

Borten, Helen. Halloween. 48p. (J). (gr. 2-5). 1998. 15.00 (*0-06-023582-9*) HarpC Child Bks.

— Halloween. 48p. (J). (gr. 2-5). 1999. lib. bdg. 14.89 (*0-06-023583-7*) HarpC Child Bks.

***Bortenschlager, S., et al, eds.** The Iceman & his Natural Environmnet: Palaeobotanical Results. (Man in the Ice Ser.: 4). 200p. 2000. (*3-211-82660-2*) Spr-Verlag.

Bortfeld, R. K., jt. ed. see Meissner, R.

Bortfeld, T., jt. ed. see Schlegel, W.

Borth, Frank. Borthicons. Symbols of Our Times. 22.95 (*0-8488-1554-8*) Amereon Ltd.

Borth, Martha. Sitting at His Feet. (Illus.). 85p. (Orig.). 1985. pap. 5.95 (*0-935993-00-2*) Clar Call Bks.

Borthwick, Donald. Donald Borthwick: Selected Paintings & Drawings 1958-1988. (Illus.). 20p. (Orig.). 1988. pap. text 25.00 (*0-317-91181-3*) D Borthwick.

Borthwick-Duffy, Sharon, et al. Foster Family Care for Persons with Mental Retardation. (AAMD Monographs). 200p. (Orig.). (C). 1992. pap. 22.95 (*0-940898-27-6*) Am Assn Mental.

Borthwick, E. Mark, ed. see Pacific Economic Cooperation Council Staff.

Borthwick, Evelyn. For My Daughter. (Illus.). 48p. 1994. 8.95 (*0-8378-6988-9*) Gibson.

***Borthwick, Evelyn.** For My Daughter. (Illus.). 2000. 9.99 (*0-7667-6661-6*) Gibson.

— For My Son. (Illus.). 2000. 9.99 (*0-7667-6660-8*) Gibson.

Borthwick, H. M. Borthwick Family: History & Genealogy of the Family of Borthwick, Chiefly in Scotland & America. (Illus.). 127p. 1993. reprint ed. pap. 19.50 (*0-8328-3646-X*); reprint ed. lib. bdg. 29.50 (*0-8328-3645-1*) Higginson Bk Co.

Borthwick, J. S. Bodies of Water. 304p. 1991. mass mkt. 4.50 (*0-312-92603-0*) St Martin.

— The Bridled Groom: A Dead Letter Mystery. 1995. mass mkt. 4.99 (*0-312-95505-7*) St Martin.

***Borthwick, J. S.** Coup de Grace. LC 99-56354. (Illus.). 352p. 2000. text 24.95 (*0-312-25313-3*) St Martin.

Borthwick, J. S. Dolly Is Dead. 1996. mass mkt. 5.50 (*0-312-95675-4*) St Martin.

— The Down-East Murders. 304p. 1991. mass mkt. 5.99 (*0-312-92606-5*) St Martin.

— Dude on Arrival: A Christmas Mystery. 1992. mass mkt. 4.50 (*0-312-92955-2*) St Martin.

— The Garden Plot, Vol. 1. 336p. 1998. pap. 5.99 (*0-312-96291-6*, Pub. by Tor Bks) St Martin.

— My Body Lies over the Ocean. LC 98-41754. 304p. 1998. text 22.95 (*0-312-19991-0*) St Martin.

***Borthwick, J. S.** My Body Lies over the Ocean. 304p. 1999. mass mkt. 5.99 (*0-312-97040-4*, St Martins Paperbacks) St Martin.

Borthwick, J. S. The Student Body. 304p. 1991. mass mkt. 4.50 (*0-312-92605-7*) St Martin.

Borthwick, John. The Circumference of the Knowable World: Travel Stories. 1994. pap. 16.95 (*0-7022-2655-6*, Pub. by Univ Queensland Pr) Intl Spec Bk.

— Essential Australia. (Essential Travel Guides Ser.). (Illus.). 128p. (Orig.). 1995. pap. 7.95 (*0-8442-8943-4*, Passprt Bks) NTC Contemp Pub Co.

***Borthwick, Mark.** Mark Borthwick: 2000-1 Maison Martin Margiela Autumn/winter 1998-99. 1999. pap. text 30.00 (*2-9512460-0-5*) MIAS.

Borthwick, Mark. Pacific Century: The Emergence of Modern Pacific Asia. 2nd ed. LC 97-42756. 600p. (C). 1998. pap. text 40.00 (*0-8133-3471-3*, Pub. by Westview) HarpC.

— Synthetic Voices. 1998. pap. text 35.00 (*4-915877-63-9*) Synergy Inc.

Borthwick, Meredith. The Changing Role of Women in Bengal, 1849-1905. LC 83-43061. 421p. 1984. reprint ed. pap. 130.60 (*0-608-03329-4*, 206404100008) Bks Demand.

Borthwick, Meredith, tr. see Pramoj, M. R. Kukrit.

Borthwick, Paul. How to Be a World Class Christian. 1999. reprint ed. pap. 9.99 (*1-884543-22-7*) O M Lit.

— A Mind for Missions. LC 87-62360. 168p. (Orig.). 1987. pap. 9.00 (*0-89109-191-2*) NavPress.

***Borthwick, Paul.** Missions. (LifeGuide Bible Studies). 2000. pap. 4.99 (*0-8308-3090-1*) InterVarsity.

Borthwick, Paul. One Hundred One Ways to Simplify Your Life. 144p. (Orig.). 1992. pap. 1.80 (*0-89693-058-0*, 6-1058, Victor Bks) Chariot Victor.

— Six Dangerous Questions: To Transform Your View of the World. LC 96-33500. 144p. (Orig.). 1997. pap. 8.99 (*0-8308-1685-2*, 1685) InterVarsity.

Bortignon, P. F. Giant Resonances: Nuclear Structure at Finite Temperature. (Contemporary Concepts in Physics Ser.: Vol. 10). 296p. 1998. text 60.00 (*90-5702-570-1*, ECU74); pap. text 30.00 (*90-5702-571-X*, ECU41) Gordon & Breach.

Bortin, Virginia. Elinor Remick Warren: A Bio-Bibliography, 46. LC 93-20008. (Bio-Bibliographies in Music Ser.: No. 46). 320p. 1993. lib. bdg. 75.00 (*0-313-25879-1*, BWE, Greenwood Pr) Greenwood.

— Publicity for Volunteers: A Handbook. LC 81-50233. 128p. 1981. 10.95 (*0-8027-0685-1*); pap. 6.95 (*0-8027-7176-9*) Walker & Co.

An Asterisk (*) at the beginning of an entry indicates that the title is appearing for the first time.

Bortis, Heinrich. Institutions, Behaviour & Economic Theory: A Contribution to Classical-Keynesian Political Economy. 462p. (C). 1996. text 69.95 (*0-521-57055-7*) Cambridge U Pr.

Bortitz, S., jt. ed. see Dassler, H. G.

Bortman, Henry. Guide to the BeOS. 300p. 1997. 29.99 (*1-56276-551-5*, Ziff-Davis Pr) Que.

Bortman, Marci, et al. Testing the Waters VII: How Does Your Vacation Beach Rate. 145p. 1997. pap. 10.50 (*1-893340-02-3*) Natl Resources Defense Coun.

***Bortnam, Patricia L.** Bleacher Buddies. (Illus.). 2000. write for info. (*0-9679079-0-X*) P L Bortnem.

Bortner, Doyle M. Public Relations for Public Schools. LC 79-183947. 425p. 1983. pap. 18.95 (*0-87073-509-8*) Schenkman Bks Inc.

Bortner, M. A. & Williams, Linda M. Youth in Prison: We the People of Unit Four. LC 97-17823. 256p. (C). 1997. 85.00 (*0-415-91438-8*) Routledge.

Bortner, M. A., et al. Black Adolescents & Juvenile Justice: Background Report to the 1990 Arizona Black Town Hall. 122p. (C). 1990. pap. write for info. (*1-879286-00-9*) AZ Bd Regents.

Bortner, Margaret & Williams, Linda. Youth in Prison: We the People of Unit Four. LC 97-17823. 256p. (C). 1997. pap. 20.99 (*0-415-91439-6*) Routledge.

Bortnick, Barry. Deadly Urges. LC 97-138557. 256p. 1997. mass mkt. 5.99 (*0-7860-0370-7*, Pinncle Kensgtn) Kensgtn Pub Corp.

— Polly Klaas. 1996. mass mkt. 5.99 (*0-7860-0408-8*) Kensgtn Pub Corp.

— Polly Klaas: Murder of America's Child. 1995. mass mkt. 4.99 (*0-7860-0195-X*) Kensgtn Pub Corp.

Bortoft, Henri. Goethe's Scientific Consciousness. 86p. 1986. pap. 10.00 (*0-904674-10-X*, Pub. by Octagon Pr) ISHK.

— The Wholeness of Nature: Goethe's Way Toward a Science of Conscious Participation in Nature. (Goethean Science Ser.). (Illus.). 212p. (Orig.). 1996. pap. 24.95 (*0-940262-79-7*, Lindisfarne) Anthroposophic.

Bortolani, V., et al. Interaction of Atoms & Molecules with Solid Surfaces. (Physics of Solids & Liquids Ser.). (Illus.). 700p. (C). 1990. text 145.00 (*0-306-43424-5*, Kluwer Plenum) Kluwer Academic.

***Bortolazzo, Paul.** Still Here: The Sequence of Events That Precede the Rapture. Odle, Susan & Lee, Elizabeth, eds. 420p. 1999. pap. 14.99 (*0-9675683-0-7*) Seven Seals.

Bortolotti, Bernardo & Fiorentini, Gianluca, eds. Organized Interests & Self-Regulation: An Economic Approach. 288p. 2000. text 68.00 (*0-19-829652-5*) OUP.

Bortolotti, Fabio, et al, eds. ICC Model Commercial Agency Contract: A Commentary. 125p. (C). 1994. pap. 149.95 (*92-842-1146-8*, 512) ICC Pub.

Bortolotti, Fabio, et al. The ICC Agency Model Contract: A Commentary. LC 93-35597. 1993. 109.00 (*90-6544-780-6*) Kluwer Law Intl.

Bortolotti, Gary R., jt. auth. see Gerrard, Jon M.

Bortolozzi, Flavio, jt. ed. see Murshed, Nabeel A.

Borton, Brett, jt. auth. see Links Magazine Editors.

Borton, Christopher C. The Challenge to Change - Mirrors. 97p. (Orig.). 1996. pap. write for info. (*0-9634873-1-0*); pap. 3.00 (*0-9634873-0-2*) C C Borton.

Borton, D. B. Five Alarm Fire. 240p. 1996. mass mkt. 5.99 (*0-425-15338-X*, Prime Crime) Berkley Pub.

— Four Elements of Murder. 256p. (Orig.). 1995. mass mkt. 5.99 (*0-425-14722-3*, Prime Crime) Berkley Pub.

— One for the Money. 208p. 1993. pap. 4.99 (*0-425-15328-2*) Berkley Pub.

— Six Feet Under. 240p. 1997. mass mkt. 5.99 (*0-425-15700-8*, Prime Crime) Berkley Pub.

— Two Points for Murder. 1993. mass mkt. 4.99 (*0-425-13947-6*) Berkley Pub.

Borton de Trevino, Elizabeth. Leona, a Love Story. LC 93-38751. 176p. (J). 1994. 15.00 (*0-374-34382-9*) FS&G.

Borton, Della. Fade to Black. 320p. 1999. mass mkt. 5.99 (*0-449-00407-4*) Fawcett.

— Freeze Frame: A Movie Lover's Mystery. 2000. mass mkt. 6.50 (*0-449-00408-2*) Fawcett.

Borton, Enrique R. Trevino, tr. see De Trevino, Elizabeth B.

Borton, Enrique T., tr. see De Trevino, Elizabeth B.

Borton, Hugh. Japan's Modern Century: From Perry to 1970. 2nd ed. LC 70-110544. 620p. reprint ed. pap. 192.20 (*0-608-13289-6*, 205575800037) Bks Demand.

Borton, Hugh, ed. A Selected List of Books & Articles on Japan in English, French & German. enl. rev. ed. LC 53-5055. (Harvard-Yenching Institute Publications). 286p. 1954. 18.50 (*0-674-79800-7*) HUP.

Borton, Hugh, et al. Japan Between East & West. LC 76-40008. 327p. 1976. reprint ed. lib. bdg. 38.50 (*0-8371-9102-5*, BOJE, Greenwood Pr) Greenwood.

Borton, Lady. After Sorrow: An American among the Vietnamese. 1999. pap. 9.95 (*0-14-016716-1*, Viking) Viking Penguin.

— After Sorrow: An American among the Vietnamese. LC 96-16431. (Illus.). 320p. 1996. reprint ed. pap. 14.00 (*1-56836-161-0*, Kodansha Globe) Kodansha.

— Boat People & Vietnamese Refugees in the United States. rev. ed. Starr, Jerold M., ed. (Lessons of the Vietnam War Ser.). (Illus.). 32p. (C). 1991. pap. text 5.00 (*0-945919-11-5*) Ctr Social Studies.

— Junk Pile. LC 94-6735. (Illus.). 32p. (J). (ps-3). 1997. 15.95 (*0-399-22728-8*, Philomel) Peng Put Young Read.

Borton, Mark, jt. ed. see Quarrier, Ian.

Borton, Mark C., et al, eds. Complete Boating Guide to the Connecticut River. 2nd ed. (Illus.). 240p. (Orig.). 1990. pap. 11.95 (*0-9616371-1-0*) CT River Watershed.

Borton, P. & Cave, V. Batteries & Magnets. (How to Make Ser.). (Illus.). 32p. (J). (gr. 3-7). 1995. pap. 6.95 (*0-7460-2083-X*, Usborne); lib. bdg. 14.95 (*0-88110-757-3*, Usborne) EDC.

Borton, P., jt. auth. see Gee, R.

Borton, P., jt. auth. see Gibson, R.

Borton, Paula. Big Book of Papercraft. (Big Bks.). (Illus.). 96p. (J). (gr. 2-5). 1996. pap. 14.95 (*0-7460-2286-7*, Usborne) EDC.

Borton, Paula & Cave, Vicky. The Usborne Book of Batteries & Magnets. (Usborne Kid Kits Ser.). (Illus.). 32p. (J). (gr. 3-7). 1996. 18.95 (*0-88110-872-3*, Usborne) EDC.

Borton, Samuel L., tr. see Steiner, Rudolf.

***Bortone, Stephen A.** Seagrasses: Monitoring, Ecology, Physiology & Management. LC 99-39826. (Marine Science Ser.). 336p. 1999. boxed set 89.95 (*0-8493-2045-3*) CRC Pr.

Bortovski, R. S. Air-Sea Exchange of Heat & Moisture During Storms. (C). 1987. text 206.50 (*90-277-2346-X*) Kluwer Academic.

Borts, George H. Regional Cycles of Manufacturing Employment in the United States, 1914-1953. (Occasional Papers: No. 73). 57p. 1960. reprint ed. 20.00 (*0-87014-387-5*) Natl Bur Econ Res.

Borts, Ian & Webb, Kenneth. Healer: The Remarkable Story of Ian Borts, the Edgar Cayce of Our Time. 1989. 17.45 (*0-671-65867-0*) S&S Trade.

Borts, Lawrence. Missions & Medals - The Medals & Ribbons of the United Nations: United Nations Service Medals & Decorations. LC 96-76063. (Illus.). 96p. 1997. 24.95 (*1-884452-31-0*); pap. 19.95 (*1-884452-30-2*) MOA Press.

Borts, Lawrence, jt. auth. see Foster, Frank.

***Bortz, Alfred B.** Techno-Matter: The Materials Behind the Marvels. LC 00-34390. 2001. lib. bdg. write for info. (*0-7613-1469-5*) TFC Bks NY.

Bortz, Alfred B. To the Young Scientist: Reflections on Doing & Living Science. LC 96-25864. (Venture Bks.). (J). 1997. lib. bdg. 24.00 (*0-531-11325-6*) Watts.

Bortz, Bruce, ed. see Cowherd, Kevin.

Bortz, Bruce, ed. see Steinbach, Alice.

Bortz, E. B. Voices of a Wanderer. LC 93-93717. 61p. (Orig.). 1993. pap. 7.00 (*0-9639226-0-2*) Out There Pubs.

Bortz, Fred. Catastrophe! Great Engineering Failure - And Success. (Illus.). 80p. (J). (gr. 4-8). 1998. 19.95 (*0-9663334-0-3*) Dr Freds Cert Bks.

— Catastrophe! Great Engineering Failure - And Success. (Illus.). 80p. (YA). (gr. 4-8). 1998. pap. 13.95 (*0-9663334-1-1*) Dr Freds Cert Bks.

— Dr. Fred's Weather Watch: Create & Run Your Own Weather Station. LC 00-23730. (Illus.). 98p. (gr. 7 up). 2000. pap. 11.95 (*0-07-134799-2*) McGraw.

— Martian Fossils on Earth: The Story of Meteorite ALH 84001. LC 97-6190. (Illus.). 64p. (J). (gr. 5 up). 1997. lib. bdg. 21.40 (*0-7613-0270-0*) Millbrook Pr.

— Mind Tools: The Science of Artificial Intelligence. LC 92-16653. (Venture Bks.). (Illus.). 144p. (YA). (gr. 7-12). 1992. lib. bdg. 24.00 (*0-531-12515-7*) Watts.

Bortz, Lauri. "Tonight at 8:00" Two Great Plays. (Illus.). 104p. (C). 1997. pap. 15.00 (*0-9677326-0-3*) Abaton Bk.

***Bortz, Lauri, ed.** 5 & 10: Five & Dime. limited ed. (Illus.). 300p. (C). 2000. boxed set 200.00 (*0-9677326-2-X*) Abaton Bk.

Bortz, Sheri L. Mandala Journey. (Illus.). 28p. (Orig.). 1997. pap. 16.95 (*0-9658154-0-4*) Wise Snail.

Bortz, W. M., jt. ed. see Holmes, W. L.

Bortz, Walter. Dare to Be 100: 99 Steps to a Long, Healthy Life. 288p. 1996. pap. 12.00 (*0-684-80021-7*, Fireside) S&S Trade Pap.

Boruah, Bijoy H. Fiction & Emotion: A Study in Aesthetics & the Philosophy of Mind. 144p. 1989. text 55.00 (*0-19-562093-3*) OUP.

Boruch, Behn. The Patriarchs. 28p. 1959. 3.95 (*0-88482-729-1*) Hebrew Pub.

Boruch, Frank, ed. Behavioral Health Services Delivery: Models & Methods. LC 97-78158. 400p. 1998. 60.00 (*0-924674-59-8*) Am Coll Phys Execs.

Boruch, Marianne. Moss Burning: Poems. LC 93-85658. (Field Poetry Ser.: No. 2). 90p. 1993. 22.95 (*0-932440-64-9*); pap. 12.95 (*0-932440-63-0*) Oberlin Coll Pr.

— Poetry's Old Air. LC 94-44312. (Poets on Poetry Ser.). 160p. 1995. pap. 13.95 (*0-472-06584-X*, 06584); text 39.50 (*0-472-09584-6*, 09584) U of Mich Pr.

— A Stick That Breaks & Breaks. LC 97-66614. (Field Poetry Ser.: Vol. 5). 80p. 1997. 22.95 (*0-932440-79-7*); pap. 12.95 (*0-932440-80-0*) Oberlin Coll Pr.

Boruch, R. F., jt. ed. see Pearson, R. W.

Boruch, Robert F. Randomized Experiments for Planning & Evaluation: A Practical Guide. LC 96-25315. (Applied Social Research Methods Ser.: Vol. 44). 248p. 1996. 46.00 (*0-8039-3509-9*); pap. 21.95 (*0-8039-3510-2*) Sage.

Boruch, Robert F., et al, eds. Reanalyzing Program Evaluations. LC 81-2841. (Jossey-Bass Social & Behavioral Science Ser.). 423p. reprint ed. pap. 131.20 (*0-608-17774-1*, 205655900072) Bks Demand.

***Boruchoff, S. Arthur.** Cornea - A Diagnostic Atlas. (Illus.). 304p. 2000. 155.00 (*0-7506-7181-5*) Buttrwrth-Heinemann.

Boruchowitz, David. African Cichlids of Lake Tanganyika. (Illus.). 64p. 1996. 12.95 (*0-7938-0119-2*, WW016) TFH Pubns.

***Boruchowitz, David.** African Cichlids of Lake Tanganyika. 64p. 2000. 12.95 (*0-7938-3026-5*) TFH Pubns.

Boruchowitz, David. Dwarf Cichlids: Keeping & Breeding Them in Captivity. (Illus.). 64p. 1998. pap. 6.95 (*0-7938-0356-X*, RE-607) TFH Pubns.

— Malawi Cichlids: Keeping & Breeding Them in Captivity. (Illus.). 64p. 1997. pap. 6.95 (*0-7938-0359-4*, RE-610) TFH Pubns.

Boruchowitz, David E. Guide to Marine Aquariums. LC 99-210403. (Illus.). 64p. 1997. pap. 6.95 (*0-7938-0360-8*, RE-611) TFH Pubns.

***Borulia, E.** Mastering the Bishop Pair. (Illus.). 200p. 1999. pap. 19.95 (*1-879479-78-8*) ICE WA.

***Borum, Finn.** Organization, Power & Change. LC 95-211656. 1999. 29.00 (*87-16-13248-3*) Mksgaard.

Borum, Finn, et al. Social Dynamics of the IT Field: The Case of Denmark. LC 92-19766. (Studies in Organization: No. 39). xvi, 328p. 1992. lib. bdg. 64.95 (*3-11-012981-7*) De Gruyter.

Borum, Maggie M. The Truth about Rome. (Illus.). 54p. 1999. pap. 12.50 (*0-9672538-0-2*) T-Minus Pr.

***Borum, Maggie McKinney.** Red Flag. (Illus.). 52p. 2001. pap. 10.00 (*0-9672538-1-0*) T-Minus Pr.

Borun, Minda, et al. Women's Liberation: An Anthropological View. 1971. pap. 2.00 (*0-912786-19-1*) Know Inc.

Borunda, Alfredo, tr. see Harshberger, Claudette.

***Borunda, Michael, ed.** Search for Solutions: Child Abuse & Domestic Violence Nexus: Findings from the Office of Criminal Justice Planning Public Policy Forums Report. 92p. (C). 2000. reprint ed. pap. text 20.00 (*0-7881-8838-0*) DIANE Pub.

Borunova, S. N., et al. Orthoepic Dictionary of the Russian Language. 4th ed. Avanesova, R. I., ed. (RUS.). 704p. 1988. reprint ed. 21.95 (*0-8285-5375-0*) Firebird NY.

***Borup, D. T.** Inverse Scattering for Wave & Diffusion Equations. (Advanced Series in Mathematical Physics). 2000. pap. 41.00 (*981-02-4173-9*) World Scientific Pub.

Borup-Nielsen, Gra. A Study of the Two Experimental Schools of C. N. Starcke & John Dewey. LC 94-37028. 224p. 1995. text 89.95 (*0-7734-2281-1*) E Mellen.

***Borup-Nielsen, Grja.** Collected Essays. LC 99-86406. 96p. 2000. 32.50 (*0-7618-1635-6*) U Pr of Amer.

Borus, Daniel H. Writing Realism: Howells, James, & Norris in the Mass Market. LC 89-31157. xii, 260p. (C). 1989. 55.00 (*0-8078-1869-0*) U of NC Pr.

Borus, Daniel H., ed. These United States: Portraits of America from the 1920s. LC 91-39031. (Illus.). 432p. 1992. text 37.50 (*0-8014-2747-9*) Cornell U Pr.

Borus, Daniel H., ed. see Bellamy, Edward.

Borus, Michael E., ed. Youth & the Labor Market: Analyses from the National Longitudinal Survey. LC 84-2367. 295p. 1984. text 24.00 (*0-88099-015-5*) W E Upjohn.

Borus, Michael E., ed. Youth & the Labor Market: Analyses from the National Longitudinal Survey. LC 84-2367. 295p. 1984. pap. text 14.00 (*0-88099-016-3*) W E Upjohn.

Borus, Michael E. & Tash, William R. Measuring the Impact of Manpower Programs: A Primer. LC 73-633548. (Policy Papers in Human Resources & Industrial Relations Ser.: No. 17). (Orig.). 1970. pap. 5.00 (*0-87736-117-7*) U of Mich Inst Labor.

***Borushek, Allan.** Doctor's Pocket Calorie & Fat Counter. (Illus.). 272p. 1999. pap. 6.99 (*0-9587991-6-4*) A Borushek.

— The Doctor's Pocket Calorie, Fat & Carbohydrate Counter: Plus 70 Fast-Food Chains & Restaurants. (Illus.). 1998. pap. write for info. (*0-9587991-5-9*) A Borushek.

Borushek, Allan. The Pocket Food & Exercise Diary. 3rd rev. ed. (Illus.). 96p. 1996. pap. 3.95 (*0-9587991-3-X*) A Borushek.

Borwanker, Prabha. Practical Approach to Acupuncture. (C). 1988. 34.00 (*0-8364-2396-8*, Pub. by Popular Prakashan) S Asia.

***Borwein, J. J. & Lewis, A. S.** Convex Analysis & Nonlinear Optimization. LC 00-20826. (CMS Advanced Book in Mathematics Ser.: Vol. 3). 320p. 2000. 69.95 (*0-387-98940-4*) Spr-Verlag.

Borwein, J. J., jt. auth. see Borowski, E. J.

Borwein, J. J., ed. see Arnold, D.

Borwein, Jonathan M. Organic Mathematics: Proceedings of the Organic Mathematics Workshop, December 12-14, 1995, Simon Fraser University. LC 97-179. (Conference Proceedings, Canadian Mathematical Society Ser.: Vol. 20). 412p. 1997. pap. 79.00 (*0-8218-0668-8*, CMSAMS/20) Am Math.

***Borwein, Jonathan M. & Borwein, Peter B.** PI & the AGM: A Study in Analytic Number Theory & Computational Complexity, Vol. 1. (Canadian Mathematical Society Series & Advanced Texts). 432p. 1998. pap. 64.95 (*0-471-31515-X*) Wiley.

Borwein, P., ed. see Arnold, D.

Borwein, Peter & Erdelyi, Tamas. Polynomials & Polynomial Inequalities. LC 95-8374. (Graduate Texts in Mathematics Ser.: Vol. 160). 482p. 1995. 64.95 (*0-387-94509-1*) Spr-Verlag.

Borwein, Peter B., jt. auth. see Borwein, Jonathan M.

Borwick, Jim & Dulfur, Brett. Forgotten Missourians Who Made History. (Show Me Missouri Ser.). (Illus.). 144p. (Orig.). 1996. pap. 14.95 (*0-9646625-8-2*, MG3440) Pebble Pub.

Borwick, John. Loudspeaker & Headphone Handbook. 2nd rev. ed. LC 94-22160. (Illus.). 608p. 1994. pap. text 95.00 (*0-240-51371-1*, Focal) Buttrwrth-Heinemann.

— Microphones: Technology & Technique. LC 89-71327. (Illus.). 253p. reprint ed. pap. 78.50 (*0-608-20294-0*, 207155300001) Bks Demand.

— Sound Recording Practice. 4th ed. (Illus.). 624p. 1996. pap. text 45.00 (*0-19-816608-7*) OUP.

***Borwick, John, ed.** Loudspeaker & Headphone Handbook. 3rd ed. (Illus.). 608p. 2000. pap. 120.00 (*0-240-51578-1*, Focal) Buttrwrth-Heinemann.

Bory, Jean-Louis. La Peau des Zebres. (FRE.). 1981. pap. 14.95 (*0-7859-1931-7*, 2070372650) Fr & Eur.

— Un Prix d'Excellence. (FRE.). 219p. 1988. pap. 10.95 (*0-7859-2095-1*, 2070380602) Fr & Eur.

Boryczka, Raymond & Cary, Lorin L. No Strength Without Union: An Illustrated History of Ohio Workers, 1803-1980. (Illus.). 328p. 19.95 (*0-318-00987-0*) Ohio Hist Soc.

Borys, Andrzej. Nonlinear Aspects of Telecommunication. (Electronic Engineering Systems Ser.). 1999. write for info. (*0-8493-2571-4*) CRC Pr.

Borys, Jurij. The Sovietization of Ukraine, 1917-1923: The Communist Doctrine & Practice of Self-Determination. LC 80-91020. xxii, 488p. 19.95 (*0-920862-01-2*); pap. 12.95 (*0-920862-03-9*) Ukrainian Acad.

Borysenko, Joan. Fire in the Soul. 256p. 1999. reprint ed. 29.95 (*0-7351-0055-1*) Replica Bks.

Borysenko, Joan. Fire in the Soul: A New Psychology of Spiritual Optimism. 256p. 1994. mass mkt. 13.99 (*0-446-67015-4*, Pub. by Warner Bks) Little.

Borysenko, Joan. Guilt Is the Teacher, Love Is the Lesson: A Book to Heal You, Heart & Soul. 1991. mass mkt. 13.95 (*0-446-39224-3*, Pub. by Warner Bks) Little.

— Minding the Body, Mending the Mind. 256p. 1988. pap. 15.95 (*0-553-34556-7*) Bantam.

— Minding the Body, Mending the Mind. 1988. 11.00 incl. audio (*0-671-66778-5*, Sound Ideas) S&S Trade.

Borysenko, Joan. Pocketful of Miracles. 432p. (Orig.). 1994. mass mkt. 12.95 (*0-446-39536-6*, Pub. by Warner Bks) -Little.

— 7 Paths to God: The Ways of the Mystic. Orig. Title: Ways of the Mystic. 140p. 1999. pap. 8.95 (*1-56170-610-8*) Hay House.

Borysenko, Joan. The Ways of the Mystic: 7 Paths to God. LC 97-37757. 128p. 1997. 12.95 (*1-56170-392-3*, 898) Hay House.

— A Woman's Book of Life: Biology, Psychology, & Spirituality of the Feminine Life Cycle. 320p. 1998. pap. 14.00 (*1-57322-651-3*, Riverhd Trade) Berkley Pub.

— A Woman's Journey to God: Finding the Feminine Path. LC 99-40416. 336p. 1999. 23.95 (*1-57322-144-9*, Riverhead Books) Putnam Pub Group.

Borysenko, Joan & Borysenko, Miroslav. The Power of the Mind to Heal: Renewing Body, Mind & Spirit. LC 94-31668. 272p. 1994. 19.95 (*1-56170-093-2*, 157) Hay House.

— The Power of the Mind to Heal: Renewing Body, Mind & Spirit. LC 94-31668. 240p. 1995. pap. 12.00 (*1-56170-144-0*, 157T) Hay House.

Borysenko, Miroslav, jt. auth. see Borysenko, Joan.

Borysenko, Myrin & Beringer, Theodore. Functional Histology. 2nd ed. 400p. 1984. pap. text 23.00 (*0-316-10304-7*) Lppncott W & W.

Borysewicz, Alfonse. Alfonse Borysewicz: Exhibition Catalogue of Artwork. (Illus.). 20p. 1993. 10.00 (*0-9626731-2-9*) Yoshii Gallery.

Borysewicz, Edward, et al. Bicycle Road Racing: The Complete Program for Training & Competition. LC 84-52282. (Illus.). 288p. (Orig.). 1985. pap. 24.95 (*0-941950-07-7*) Vitesse Pr.

***Borz, Walter.** Healthy Aging for Dummies. (For Dummies Ser.). 384p. 2000. pap. 19.99 (*0-7645-5233-3*) IDG Bks.

***Borza, Eugene N.** Before Alexander: Constructing Early Macedonia. LC 99-57520. (Publications of the Association of Ancient Historians: Vol. 6). (Illus.). 96p. 1999. pap. 12.95 (*0-941690-96-2*) Regina Bks.

Borza, Eugene N. In the Shadow of Olympus: The Emergence of Macedon. (Illus.). 352p. 1990. pap. text 18.95 (*0-691-00880-9*, Pub. by Princeton U Pr) Cal Prin Full Svc.

— Makedonika. Thomas, Carol G., ed. LC 95-8423. 270p. 1995. 37.95 (*0-941690-64-4*); pap. 18.95 (*0-941690-65-2*) Regina Bks.

Borza, Eugene N., ed. see National Gallery of Art Staff.

Borzellino, Joe, jt. auth. see Reichman, Louis.

Borzello, Frances. Civilising Caliban: The Misuse of Art 1875-1975. (Illus.). 192p. 1987. lib. bdg. 45.00 (*0-7102-0675-5*, Routledge Thoemms) Routledge.

— Seeing Ourselves: Women's Self-Portraits. LC 97-41441. (Illus.). 224p. 1998. 55.00 (*0-8109-4188-0*, Pub. by Abrams) Time Warner.

***Borzello, Frances.** A World of Our Own: Women As Artists since the Renaissance. (Illus.). 224p. 2000. 50.00 (*0-8230-5874-3*) Watsn-Guptill.

Borzello, Frances, jt. ed. see Rees, A. L.

Borzeszkowski, H. H. Von, see Von Borzeszkowski, H. H.

***Borzillo, Carrie.** Nirvana: A Day-by-Day Eyewitness Chronicle. (Illus.). 2000. pap. 19.95 (*1-56025-274-X*, Thunders Mouth) Avalon NY.

Borzillo, Michelle. Stock Market Secrets: How Even a Rookie Can Make Big Money in the Market! 133p. (Orig.). 1995. pap. 12.95 (*0-9648582-0-7*) Old Twn Pr.

Borzova, L. V. Extracorporeal Reconstruction of Blood in Clinical Practice, Vol. 6. (Soviet Medical Reviews Series, Section C: Hematology Reviews: Vol. 6, Pt. 1). 114p. 1993. pap. text 161.00 (*3-7186-5395-8*) Gordon & Breach.

Borzsak, ed. Taciti, P. Corneli Tom. I, Fascicule 1: Ab Excessu Divi Augusti. (Annales Ser.: Libri I-VI). (LAT.). 1992. 43.50 (*3-8154-1835-6*, T1835, Pub. by B G Teubner) U of Mich Pr.

***Borzsak, Istvan.** Eine Handvoll: Ausgewahlte Kleine Schriften. xii, 786p. 1999. 90.00 (*963-05-7623-6*) Intl Spec Bk.

Borzyskowski, M. & Mundy, A. R. Neuropathic Bladder in Childhood. (Clinics in Developmental Medicine Ser.: No. 111). (Illus.). 120p. (C). 1991. text 44.95 (*0-521-41194-7*, Pub. by Mc Keith Pr) Cambridge U Pr.

Borzyszkowski, Andrzej M. & Sokolowski, Stefan, eds. Mathematical Foundations of Computer Science, 1993: 18th International Symposium, MFCS '93, Gdansk, Poland, August 30-September 3, 1993: Proceedings. LC 93-11820. (Lecture Notes in Computer Science Ser.: Vol. 711). 1993. pap. 107.00 (*0-387-57182-5*) Spr-Verlag.

B

Bos. Introduction to Business Forecasting. (SWC-Economics Ser.). 1989. mass mkt., teacher ed. 33.75 (*0-538-80248-0*) S-W Pub.

Bos, A. P. Cosmic & Meta-Cosmic Theology in Aristotle's Lost Dialogues. LC 89-9855. (Brill's Studies in Intellectual History: Vol. 16). 242p. 1989. text 89.50 (*90-04-09155-6*) Brill Academic Pubs.

Bos, Adriaan & Siblesz, Hugo, eds. Realism in Law-Making. 1986. lib. bdg. 130.50 (*90-247-3399-5*) Kluwer Academic.

Bos, Bert, jt. auth. see Lie, Hakon Wiun.

Bos, Bev. Together We're Better: Establishing a Coactive Learning Environment. Glowes, Kay, ed. LC 90-71653. (Illus.). 175p. (C). 1990. pap. 17.95 (*0-931793-01-7*) Turn-the-Page.

Bos, Beverley J. Before the Basics: Creating Conversations with Children. LC 82-74059. (Illus.). 1983. pap. 12.50 (*0-931540-01-1*) Turn-the-Page.

— Don't Move the Muffin Tins: A Hands-off Guide to Art for the Young Child. LC 78-53276. (Illus.). 1978. pap. 7.50 (*0-931540-00-3*) Turn-the-Page.

***Bos, Burny.** Alexander the Great. (Illus.). 32p. (gr. k-3). 2000. 15.95 (*0-7358-1343-4*); lib. bdg. 15.88 (*0-7358-1344-2*) North-South Bks NYC.

— Fun with the Molesons. (Illus.). 48p. (gr. 1-4). 2000. 13.95 (*0-7358-1353-1*); lib. bdg. 13.88 (*0-7358-1354-X*) North-South Bks NYC.

Bos, Burny. Leave It to the Molesons! James, J. Alison, tr. LC 95-12311. (Illus.), 48p. (J). (gr. 2-4). 1995. lib. bdg. 13.88 (*1-55858-432-3*, Pub. by North-South Bks NYC) Chronicle Bks.

— Leave It to the Molesons! LC 95-12311. (Illus.). 48p. (J). (gr. 1-4). 1998. pap. 5.95 (*1-55858-993-7*, Pub. by North-South Bks NYC) Chronicle Bks.

— Meet the Molesons. James, J. Alison, tr. LC 93-49587. (Illus.). 48p. (J). (ps-3). 1995. pap. 4.95 (*1-55858-409-9*, Pub. by North-South Bks NYC) Chronicle Bks.

Bos, Burny. Meet the Molesons. 1995. 10.15 (*0-606-08820-2*, Pub. by Turtleback) Demco.

Bos, Burny. More from the Molesons. LC 94-40892. (Illus.). 48p. (J). (gr. 1-4). 1997. pap. 5.95 (*1-55858-778-0*, Pub. by North-South Bks NYC) Chronicle Bks.

— Ollie the Elephant. LC 89-42608. (Illus.). 32p. (J). (gr. k-3). 1995. pap. 6.95 (*1-55858-485-4*, Pub. by North-South Bks NYC) Chronicle Bks.

— Ollie the Elephant. 1995. 12.15 (*0-606-08837-7*, Pub. by Turtleback) Demco.

— Ollie the Elephant: A Pop-Up Book. (Illus.). 12p. (J). (ps-2). 1997. bds. 15.95 (*1-55858-709-8*, Pub. by North-South Bks NYC) Chronicle Bks.

Bos, Candace, jt. ed. see Chard, David.

Bos, Candace S. & Vaughn, Sharon. Strategies for Teaching Students with Learning & Behavior Problems. 4th ed. LC 97-10906. 556p. 1997. pap. text 65.00 (*0-205-27228-2*) Allyn.

— Strategies for Teaching Students with Learning & Behavior Problems: Examination Copy. 4th ed. 576p. (C). 1997. pap. text. write for info. (*0-205-27687-3*, T7687-1) Allyn.

Bos, Candace S., jt. auth. see Fletcher, Todd V.

Bos, Carole D., jt. auth. see Buchanan, John C.

Bos, Cees J. Fungal Genetics, Vol. 13. (Mycology Ser.). (Illus.). 456p. 1996. text 185.00 (*0-8247-9544-X*) Dekker.

Bos, Charles Du, see Du Bos, Charles.

Bos, Claire, jt. auth. see Bos, Maarten.

Bos, Coenraad V. The Well-Tempered Accompanist: Music Book Index. 162p. 1993. reprint ed. lib. bdg. 69.00 (*0-7812-9658-7*) Rprt Serv.

Bos, D. Public Enterprise Economics. 1996. write for info. (*0-614-17901-7*, North Holland) Elsevier.

Bos, D., jt. auth. see Wurzel, E.

Bos, D., ed. see Maier, G.

Bos, Dieter. Pricing & Price Regulation: An Economic Theory for Public Enterprises & Public Utilities. 3rd ed. LC 94-36208. (Advanced Textbooks in Economics Ser.: Vol. 34). 470p. 1994. 76.50 (*0-444-88478-5*, North Holland) Elsevier.

— Privatization: A Theoretical Treatment. (Illus.). 328p. 1993. text 65.00 (*0-19-828369-5*) OUP.

— Public Enterprise Economics: Theory & Applications. (Advanced Textbooks in Economics Ser.: Vol. 23). vi,472p. 1989. 88.00 (*0-444-87899-8*, North Holland) Elsevier.

Bos, Dieter & Felderer, Bernhard, eds. The Political Economy of Progressive Taxation. (Illus.). ix, 220p. 1989. 74.95 (*0-387-51554-2*) Spr-Verlag.

Bos, Dieter & Seidl, C., eds. Welfare Economics of the Second Best. (Journal of Economics: Suppl. 5). (Illus.). viii, 280p. 1986. 94.95 (*0-387-81942-8*) Spr-Verlag.

Bos, Dieter, et al. Fiscal Implications of an Aging Population. Cnossen, S. et al, eds. (Population Economics Ser.). (Illus.). xi, 191p. 1992. 82.95 (*0-387-55072-0*) Spr-Verlag.

Bos, Dieter, ed. see Carlberg, M.

Bos, Dieter, ed. see Czerkawski, C. J.

Bos, Dieter, ed. see Savioz, M.

Bos, Dieter, ed. see Woittiez, I.

Bos, Dolores. Out of the Dark. LC 97-221992. (Illus.). 152p. (Orig.). (J). (gr. 6-11). 1997. mass mkt. 5.99 (*0-87508-720-5*, 720) Chr Lit.

Bos, E. P. & Meijer, P. A., eds. On Proclus & His Influence in Medieval Philosophy. (Philosophia Antiqua Ser.: No. 53). viii, 206p. 1991. 74.50 (*90-04-09429-6*) Brill Academic Pubs.

Bos, E. P., ed. see De Rijk, Lambertus M.

Bos, E. P., ed. see Nuchelmans, Gabriel.

Bos, Eduard, et al. Health, Nutrition & Population Indicators: A Statistical Handbook. LC 98-30586. (Health, Nutrition, & Population Ser.). (Illus.). 88p. 1998. pap. 22.00 (*0-8213-4184-7*, 14184) World Bank.

Bos, Egbert P. Marsilius of Inghen. 1983. lib. bdg. 162.50 (*90-277-1343-X*) Kluwer Academic.

Bos, Gerrit, ed. Qusta Ibn Luqa's Medical Regime for the Pilgrims to Mecca: The Risala Fi Tadbir Safar Al-Hajj. LC 91-29098. (Islamic Philosophy, Theology & Science, Studies & Texts Ser.: Vol. 11). vi, 186p. 1992. 70.50 (*90-04-09541-1*) Brill Academic Pubs.

Bos, Gerrit, ed. see Maimonides, Moses.

Bos, Gerritt. Ibn Al-Jazzar on Fevers: A Critical Edition. 220p. 1997. 127.50 (*0-7103-0570-2*, Pub. by Kegan Paul Intl) Col U Pr.

Bos, H. J., ed. see Life & Work of Christiaan Huygens Symposium Staff.

Bos, Heleen & Schermer, Trude, eds. Sign Language Research, 1994. (International Studies on Sign Language & the Communication of the Deaf: Vol. 29). 360p. 1995. text 45.00 (*3-927731-57-9*, Pub. by Signum-Verlag) Gallaudet Univ Pr.

Bos, Henk J. Lectures in the History of Mathematics. LC 93-28299. (History of Mathematics Ser.: No. 7). 197p. 1993. pap. 39.00 (*0-8218-0920-2*) Am Math.

— Lectures in the History of Mathematics. LC 93-28299. (History of Mathematics Ser.: No. 7). 197p. 1993. 86.00 (*0-8218-9001-8*, HMATH/7) Am Math.

***Bos, J.** Design & Testing of a Marine Gearbox. (Technical Papers: Vol. 99FTM10). 13p. 1999. pap. 30.00 (*1-55589-748-7*) AGMA.

***Bos, J. L., ed.** Molecular Mechanisms of Signal Transduction. (NATO Science Ser.: Vol. 316). 294p. 2000. 117.00 (*1-58603-016-7*) IOS Press.

Bos, Jan D., ed. Skin Immune System: Cutaneous Immunology & Clinical Immunodermatology. 2nd ed. LC 96-41754. 752p. 1997. boxed set 179.95 (*0-8493-4016-0*) CRC Pr.

— Skin Immune System (SIS) 520p. 1990. lib. bdg. 239.00 (*0-8493-4945-1*, RL97) CRC Pr.

Bos, Klaus. Walking. LC 97-35493. (Illus.). 112p. 1997. 12.95 (*0-8069-9814-8*) Sterling.

Bos, L. Introduction to Plant Virology. 160p. 1992. pap. 275.00 (*81-7089-185-X*, Pub. by Intl Bk Distr) St Mut.

***Bos, L.** Plant Viruses, Unique & Intriguing Pathogens: A Textbook of Plant Virology. (Illus.). 358p. 1999. 85.00 (*90-5782-012-9*, Pub. by Backhuys Pubs) Balogh.

Bos, Lambert Van Den. Position of the "Roode En Witte Roos" in the Saga of "King Richard Third" Campbell, Oscar J., ed. LC 72-131494. reprint ed. 37.50 (*0-404-01375-9*) AMS Pr.

Bos, M. G., ed. Long-Throated Flumes & Broad-Crested Weirs. 1984. text 136.00 (*90-247-3113-5*) Kluwer Academic.

Bos, Maarten. Webster's Wardrobe. LC 97-76057. (Illus.). 20p. (J). (ps-k). 1998. 8.95 (*0-531-30097-8*) Orchard Bks Watts.

Bos, Maarten & Bos, Claire. Maurice the Hippo. LC 97-76056. (Illus.). 20p. (J). (ps-k). 1998. 8.95 (*0-531-30098-6*) Orchard Bks Watts.

Bos, Maarten & Brownlie, Ian, eds. Liber Amicorum for Lord Wilberforce. 264p. 1987. text 69.00 (*0-19-825595-0*) OUP.

Bos, Marilyn. Beginning Country Fiddle. (Illus.). 96p. pap. 17.95 (*0-8256-0294-7*, OK64725, Oak) Music Sales.

— Country Fiddle. 68p. 1988. pap. text 7.95 (*0-931759-21-8*) Centerstream Pub.

Bos, Marinuys G., ed. The Inter-Relationship Between Irrigation, Drainage & the Environment in the Aral Sea Basin: Proceedings of the NATO Advanced Research Workshop on Drainage & Development in Arid Zones, Wageningen, the Netherlands, 4-8 January 1995. LC 96-38431. (NATO Advanced Science Institutes Ser.). 256p. (C). 1996. text 144.00 (*0-7923-4258-5*) Kluwer Academic.

Bos, Marylin. Advanced Country Fiddle. 38p. (Orig.). 1989. pap. text 8.95 (*0-931759-38-2*) Centerstream Pub.

Bos, P. V., et al, eds. Concentration Control in the European Economic Community. 304p. 1992. lib. bdg. 146.00 (*1-85333-570-3*, Pub. by Graham & Trotman) Kluwer Academic.

Bos, Theodore & Fetherston, Thomas A., eds. Advances in Pacicic Basin Financial Markets, Vol. 2, Pt. A & B. 414p. 1996. 157.00 (*0-7623-0093-0*) Jai Pr.

— Advances in Pacific Basin Financial Markets, Vol. 1. 407p. 1995. 78.50 (*1-55938-861-7*) Jai Pr.

— Advances in Pacific Basin Financial Markets, Vol. 3. 1997. 78.50 (*0-7623-0196-1*) Jai Pr.

— Advances in Pacific Basin Financial Markets: In Preparation, Spring, 1998, Vol. 4. 344p. 1998. 78.50 (*0-7623-0319-0*) Jai Pr.

Bos, Theodore, jt. auth. see Newbold, Paul.

Bosac, Sue & Hother, Pauline, eds. The Art of Walking on Water - The Water Shoe: An Introduction to the Stand-Up Paddle Boat - Leonardo da Vinci Water Shoes. (Illus.). 197p. (YA). (gr. 8-9). 1995. pap. text 20.00 (*0-9670508-0-4*) Robinson Water.

***Bosacchi, Bruno, et al, eds.** Applications & Science of Neural Networks, Fuzzy Systems & Evolutionary Computation II. 1999. pap. text 72.00 (*0-8194-3298-9*) SPIE.

Bosacchi, Bruno, et al, eds. Applications of Soft Computing, Vol. 3165. LC 98-122047. 340p. 1997. 80.00 (*0-8194-2587-7*) SPIE.

Bosak, Juraj. Decompositions of Graphs. (C). 1990. text 201.00 (*0-7923-0747-X*) Kluwer Academic.

Bosak, P., et al, eds. Paleokarst: A Systematic & Regional Review. (Developments in Earth Surface Processes Ser.: No. 1). 726p. 1990. 295.00 (*0-444-98874-2*) Elsevier.

Bosak, Steve, ed. South Side Stories: A Multicultural Anthology of Contemporary Short Stories. (Orig.). 1993. pap. 9.95 (*0-9627425-2-X*) City Stoop Pr.

***Bosak, Susan V.** How to Build the Grandma Connection. (Complete Pocket Guides Ser.). 2000. pap. 8.95 (*1-896232-03-5*) Commun Proj.

Bosak, Susan V. Science Is... A Source Book of Fascinating Facts, Projects & Activities. 2nd ed. (Illus.). 515p. (J). (gr. 3-7). 1992. otabind 29.95 (*0-590-74070-9*, Pub. by Scholastic) Firefly Bks Ltd.

Bosak, Susan V. Something to Remember Me By: An Illustrated Story for Young & Old. (Illus.). 32p. (J). (gr. 1-6). 1997. 15.95 (*1-896232-01-9*) Commun Proj.

***Bosak, Susan V.** Something to Remember Me By: An Illustrated Story for Young & Old. LC 97-930692. (Illus.). 32p. 2000. pap. text 5.95 (*1-896232-02-7*) Commun Proj.

Bosakowski, Phil. Chopin in Space. 1986. pap. 5.25 (*0-8222-0209-3*) Dramatists Play.

— Crossin' the Line. 1988. pap. 3.25 (*0-8222-0254-9*) Dramatists Play.

Bosakowski, Thomas. Northern Goshank. Miller, Nancy, ed. (Illus.). 80p. 1999. pap. 35.00 (*0-88839-454-3*) Hancock House.

Bosanac, S. D., jt. auth. see Murrell, J. N.

Bosanac, S. Danko. Long-Lived States in Collisions. 208p. 1988. 108.00 (*0-8493-6871-5*, QC794, CRC Reprint) Franklin.

Bosanquet. After the New Right. 1989. pap. 32.95 (*1-85521-079-7*) Ashgate Pub Co.

Bosanquet, Bernard. The Collected Works of Bernard Bosanquet, 20 Vol. 7000p. 1999. 1850.00 (*1-85506-600-9*) Thoemmes Pr.

— Essays & Addresses. 1977. 15.95 (*0-8369-7211-2*, 8010) Ayer.

— History of Aesthetic. 1986. reprint ed. pap. 32.95 (*0-935005-18-8*); reprint ed. lib. bdg. 49.95 (*0-935005-17-X*) Lincoln-Rembrandt.

— Logic: The Morphology of Knowledge, 2 vols. in 1. 663p. 1994. reprint ed. pap. 36.95 (*1-57171-003-5*) Lincoln-Rembrandt.

— Logic: or The Morphology of Knowledge. 1986. reprint ed. lib. bdg. 53.95 (*0-935005-21-8*) Lincoln-Rembrandt.

— The Philosophical Theory of the State. (Modern Revivals in Philosophy Ser.). 328p. 1993. 74.95 (*0-7512-0204-5*, Pub. by Gregg Revivals) Ashgate Pub Co.

— Philosophical Theory of the State. 2nd ed. 1986. reprint ed. pap. 28.95 (*0-935005-20-X*); reprint ed. lib. bdg. 45.95 (*0-935005-19-6*) Lincoln-Rembrandt.

— The Philosophical Theory of the State & Related Essays. Gaus, Gerald F. & Sweet, William, eds. (Key Texts Ser.). 360p. 1999. pap. 22.95 (*1-85506-584-3*) Thoemmes Pr.

— Science & Philosophy, & Other Essays. LC 67-23180. (Essay Index Reprint Ser.). 1977. 20.95 (*0-8369-0224-6*) Ayer.

— Social & International Ideals: Being Studies in Patriotism. LC 67-23181. (Essay Index Reprint Ser.). 1977. reprint ed. 23.95 (*0-8369-0225-4*) Ayer.

— Three Lectures on Aesthetic. Ross, Ralph G., ed. LC 63-22370. (Orig.). 1963. pap. 1.70 (*0-672-60376-4*, LLA154, Bobbs) Macmillan.

— What Religion Is: 1920 Edition. 96p. 1996. reprint ed. 34.00 (*1-85506-183-X*) Bks Intl VA.

***Bosanquet, Bernard, et al.** The Philosophical Theory of the State & Related Essays. LC 99-45575. 2000. pap. text 25.00 (*1-890318-65-5*) St Augustines Pr.

Bosanquet, Bernard, tr. see Hegel, Georg Wilhelm Friedrich.

Bosanquet, Bernard, tr. see Wilhelm, Georg & Hegel, Friedrich.

Bosanquet, Eustace F. English Printed Almanacks & Prognostications: A Bibliographical History to the Year 1600. LC 18-6815. (Bibliographical Society, London, Illustrated Monographs: No. 17). 264p. reprint ed. pap. 81.90 (*0-608-14349-9*, 205192000014) Bks Demand.

Bosanquet, Nick. After the New Right. 1983. text 54.95 (*0-435-84078-9*) Ashgate Pub Co.

Bosanquet, Nick & Leese, Brenda. Family Doctors & Economic Incentives. 150p. 1989. text 72.95 (*1-85521-009-6*, Pub. by Dartmth Pub) Ashgate Pub Co.

Bosanquet, Nick & Salisbury, Chris. Providing Palliative Care Services: Towards an Evidence Base. LC 98-40982. 286p. 1999. pap. text 49.95 (*0-19-262991-3*) OUP.

Bosanquet, Nick, jt. ed. see Huttin, Christine.

Bosanquet, T. Henry James at Work. (Studies in Henry James: No. 17). 1970. reprint ed. pap. 19.95 (*0-8383-0009-X*) M S G Haskell Hse.

— Paul Valery. LC 74-6412. (Studies in French Literature: No. 45). 1974. lib. bdg. 75.00 (*0-8383-1969-6*) M S G Haskell Hse.

Bosanquet, Theodora. Harriet Martineau: An Essay in Comprehension. (BCL1-PR English Literature Ser.). 255p. 1992. reprint ed. lib. bdg. 79.00 (*0-7812-7592-X*) Rprt Serv.

— Henry James at Work. (BCL1-PS American Literature Ser.). 33p. 1992. reprint ed. lib. bdg. 59.00 (*0-7812-6769-2*) Rprt Serv.

Bosar, Gary J., ed. see Technical Association of the Pulp & Paper Industry.

Bosarge, Charlotte, ed. see Andrus, Carol.

Bosarge, Charlotte, ed. see Braham, Barbara & Wahl, Chris.

Bosarge, Charlotte, ed. see Finch, Lloyd.

Bosarge, Charlotte, ed. see McDowell, Joyce.

Bosatta, Ernesto, jt. auth. see Agren, Goran I.

Bosatta, Ernesto, jt. auth. see Ogren, Goran I.

Bosbach, Franz & Pohl, Hans, eds. Prince Albert Studies (Prinz-Albert-Studien) Vol. 14: Banking Systems in Modern History (Das Kreditwesen in der Neuzeit) 160p. 1997. write for info. (*3-598-21414-6*) K G Saur Verlag.

Bosc, Jacques Du, see Du Bosc, Jacques.

Bosc, P. & Kaeprzyk, J., eds. Fuzziness in Database Management Systems. (Studies in Fuzziness: Vol. 5). (Illus.). viii, 433p. 1996. 135.00 (*3-7908-0858-X*) Spr-Verlag.

Boscaljon, Karen. Mental Pull-Ups: For Shaping up Your Health. Acheson, Alice B., ed. 160p. (Orig.). 1995. pap. 5.95 (*1-882835-33-6*) STA-Kris.

***Boscardin, Marco D.** Jacked Tunnel Design & Construction: Proceedings of Session on Tunnel Jacking at Geo-Congress '98 Sponsored by the Geo-Institute of the American Society of Civil Engineers, Boston, Massachusetts, October 18-21, 1998. LC 98-48487. (Geotechnical Special Publication Ser.). 293p. 1998. 25.00 (*0-7844-0406-2*) Am Soc Civil Eng.

***Boscaro, Adriana.** Tanizaki in Western Languages: A Bibliography of Translations & Studies. LC 99-49891. (Illus.). xiii, 82p. (C). 2000. text 19.95 (*0-939512-99-8*) U MI Japan.

Boscaro, Adriana, et al, eds. Rethinking Japan Vol. I: Literature, Visual Arts & Linguistics. (Illus.). 354p. (C). 1996. text 59.00 (*0-904404-78-1*, Pub. by Curzon Pr Ltd) UH Pr.

— Rethinking Japan Vol. II: Social Sciences, Ideology & Thought. 416p. (C). 1996. text 59.00 (*0-904404-79-X*, Pub. by Curzon Pr Ltd) UH Pr.

Boscaro, Adriana & Chambers, Anthony H., eds. A Tanizaki Feast. LC 98-39890. (Michigan Monograph Series in Japanese Studies: No. 24). xi, 191p. 1999. 42.95 (*0-939512-90-4*) U MI Japan.

Boscarol, M., et al, eds. Foundations of Logic & Functional Programming. (Lecture Notes in Computer Science Ser.: Vol. 306). v, 218p. 1988. 33.00 (*0-387-19129-1*) Spr-Verlag.

Bosch. Fachwoerterbuch Kraftfahrtechnik, 2 vols., Vol. 1. (ENG & GER.). 354p. 1976. 125.00 (*0-8288-5695-8*, M7638) Fr & Eur.

— Fachwoerterbuch Kraftfahrtechnik, 2 vols., Vol. 2. (ENG & GER.). 369p. 1977. 125.00 (*0-8288-5435-1*, M7639) Fr & Eur.

Bosch, Adriana. Reagan: An American Story. LC 98-172610. (Illus.). 352p. 1998. 24.95 (*1-57500-065-2*, Pub. by TV Bks) HarpC.

***Bosch, Adriana.** Reagan: An American Story. LC 00-37704. (Illus.). 352p. 2000. pap. 14.95 (*1-57500-140-3*, Pub. by TV Bks) HarpC.

Bosch, Anna. A Handbook of Creek (Muscogee) Grammar. (MUS.). 35p. 1984. reprint ed. pap. 5.00 (*0-940392-15-1*) Indian U Pr OK.

Bosch, Anna R., tr. see Vandeloise, Claude.

Bosch, B. E. Van den, see Van den Bosch, B. E.

Bosch, Brian J. The Salvadoran Officer Corps & the Final Offensive of 1981. LC 99-26678. (Illus.). 165p. 1999. lib. bdg. 35.00 (*0-7864-0612-7*) McFarland & Co.

Bosch, C. Making the Grade. LC 90-62674. (Decision Is Yours Ser.). (Illus.). 64p. (Orig.). (J). (gr. 3-6). 1991. pap. 5.95 (*0-943990-48-3*) Parenting Pr.

Bosch, Carl. Bully on the Bus. LC 88-42650. (Decision Is Yours Ser.: No. 2). (Illus.). 64p. (Orig.). (J). (gr. 2-5). 1988. pap. 5.95 (*0-943990-42-4*); lib. bdg. 16.95 (*0-943990-43-2*) Parenting Pr.

Bosch, Carl W. Making the Grade. LC 90-62674. (Decision Is Yours Ser.). (Illus.). 64p. (J). (gr. 3-6). 1991. lib. bdg. 16.95 (*0-943990-49-1*) Parenting Pr.

— Schools under Siege: Guns, Gangs, & Hidden Dangers. LC 96-36363. (Issues in Focus Ser.). (Illus.). 112p. (YA). (gr. 6 up). 1997. lib. bdg. 20.95 (*0-89490-908-8*) Enslow Pubs.

Bosch, D. A. Stereotactic Techniques in Clinical Neurosurgery. (Illus.). 288p. 1986. 112.00 (*0-387-81878-2*) Spr-Verlag.

Bosch, David J. Believing in the Future: Toward a Missiology of Western Culture. Neely, Alan et al, eds. LC 95-16093. (Christian Mission & Modern Culture Ser.). 80p. (Orig.). 1995. pap. 7.00 (*1-56338-117-6*) TPI PA.

— Transforming Mission: Paradigm Shifts in Theology of Mission. LC 90-21619. (American Society of Missiology Ser.). 1991. pap. 27.00 (*0-88344-719-3*) Orbis Bks.

Bosch, Donald & Bosch, Eloise. Seashells of Oman. LC 81-14236. (Illus.). 1982. text 35.00 (*0-582-78309-7*) Longman.

Bosch, Eloise, jt. auth. see Bosch, Donald.

Bosch, Eric, tr. see Dore, Gustave.

Bosch, F. A. Van Den, see Van Den Bosch, F. A.

Bosch, F. K. Golden Germ: An Introduction to Indian Symbolism. (C). 1994. 38.00 (*81-215-0633-6*, Pub. by M Manoharial) Coronet Bks.

Bosch, Guillermo. Rain. 1995. pap. 12.95 (*1-56333-232-9*, R Kasak Bks) Masquerade.

Bosch, H. G., jt. auth. see DeHaan, Martin R.

Bosch, Henry G., jt. auth. see DeHaan, Martin Ralph.

Bosch, Henry G., jt. ed. see DeHaan, Richard W.

Bosch, Hubert & Werning, Heiko. Green Iguanas & Other Iguanids. (Illus.). 224p. 1997. 22.95 (*0-7938-0127-3*, LR-102) TFH Pubns.

Bosch, Jaime & Groszmann, Roberto J., eds. Portal Hypertension: Pathophysiology & Treatment. LC 94-5895. (Illus.). 190p. 1994. 70.00 (*0-86542-846-8*) Blackwell Sci.

***Bosch, Jan.** Design & Use of Software: Adopting & Evolving a Product Line. 400p. 2000. pap. text 49.95 (*0-201-67494-7*) Addison-Wesley.

Bosch, Jan, et al, eds. Object-Oriented Technology: ECOOP'97 Workshops, Jyvsskyls, Finland, June 9-13, 1997, Proceedings, Vol. 135. LC 98-2587. (Lecture Notes in Computer Science Ser.: Vol. 1361). xiv, 555p. 1998. pap. 79.00 (*3-540-64039-8*) Spr-Verlag.

Bosch, Jan & Demeyer, Serge, eds. Object-Oriented Technology: Proceedings of the Ecoop '98 Workshop Reader: Ecoop '98 Workshops, Demos & Posters: Brussels, Belgium, July 20-24, 1998. LC 98-53820. xxi, 568p. 1999. pap. 79.00 (*3-540-65460-7*) Spr-Verlag.

An Asterisk (*) at the beginning of an entry indicates that the title is appearing for the first time.

Bosch, John A., ed. Coordinate Measuring Machines & Systems. LC 95-3641. (Manufacturing Engineering & Materials Processing Ser.: Vol. 42). (Illus.). 496p. 1995. text 155.00 (*0-8247-9581-4*) Dekker.

Bosch, Juan & Stanley, Avelino R. Antologia Personal. LC 98-26250. 1998. pap. 5.95 (*0-8477-0350-9*) U of PR Pr.

Bosch, Juan P., ed. Hemodialysis: High Efficiency Treatments. (Illus.). 360p. 1993. text 99.00 (*0-443-08848-9*) Church.

***Bosch, Karen A. & Kersey, Katharine C.** The First Year Teacher: Teaching with Confidence (K-8) LC 00-41890. 2000. write for info. (*0-8106-2014-6*) NEA.

Bosch, Karen A. & Kersey, Katherine C. The First Year Teacher: Teaching with Confidence. 1994. pap. 18.95 (*0-8106-1862-1*) NEA.

Bosch, L., et al, eds. The Guanine - Nucleotide Binding Proteins: Common Structural & Functional Properties. (NATO ASI Series A, Life Sciences: Vol. 165). (Illus.). 420p. 1989. 115.00 (*0-306-43154-8*, Plenum Trade) Perseus Pubng.

Bosch, L. Van den, see Van den Bosch, L.

Bosch, Linda. A Hard Choice. LC 95-31721. (Open Door Bks.). 1995. pap. 3.95 (*1-56212-129-4*) CRC Pubns.

— Leaving Home. (Open Door Bks.). (Illus.). 70p. (Orig.). 1992. pap. text 3.95 (*1-56212-015-8*, 1740-2110) CRC Pubns.

— Life in a New Land. (Open Door Bks.). (Illus.). 69p. (Orig.). 1992. pap. text 3.95 (*1-56212-016-6*, 1740-2160) CRC Pubns.

Bosch, Lynette M. F. Devotion & Fantasy in Renaissance Spain: Art, Culture & History in Castilla, 1446-1492. LC 99-20429. 2000. write for info. (*0-271-01968-9*) Pa St U Pr.

Bosch, Lynette M. F., jt. auth. see Sobre, Judith B.

Bosch, M. Protein Phosphatase Type-2A in Xenopus Laevis. No. 90. 164p. (Orig.). 1994. pap. 47.50 (*90-6186-630-8*, Pub. by Leuven Univ) Coronet Bks.

Bosch, M., jt. auth. see Klingelnberg, D.

Bosch, P. & Van der Sandt, R., eds. Focus: Linguistic, Cognitive, & Computational Perspectives. LC 98-17211. (Studies in Natural Language Processing). 384p. (C). 1998. text 69.95 (*0-521-58305-5*) Cambridge U Pr.

Bosch, P., jt. auth. see Schlag, Gunther O.

Bosch, P. P. Van den, see Van den Bosch, P. P.

Bosch, Pedro. El Carbono: Cuentos Orientales. (Ciencia Para Todos Ser.). (SPA.). pap. 6.99 (*968-16-4733-5*, Pub. by Fondo) Continental Bk.

— Pioneros de las Ciencias Nucleares. (Ciencia para Todos Ser.). (SPA.). pap. 6.99 (*968-16-4213-9*, Pub. by Fondo) Continental Bk.

— La Zeolita. (Ciencia para Todos Ser.). (SPA.). pap. 6.99 (*968-16-2858-6*, Pub. by Fondo) Continental Bk.

Bosch, Robert. Automotive Brake Systems. (Illus.). 192p. 1996. pap. text 29.95 (*0-8376-0331-5*) Bentley Pubs.

— Automotive Handbook. 4th ed. 852p. 1997. 34.95 (*0-8376-0333-1*) Bentley Pubs.

— Bosch Automotive Electric-Electronic Systems Handbook. (Illus.). 347p. pap. 38.95 (*0-8376-0467-2*) Bentley Pubs.

— Bosch Technical Instruction: Alternators. (Illus.). pap. 14.95 (*0-8376-0479-6*) Bentley Pubs.

— Bosch Technical Instruction: Automotive Electronics for Safety, Comfort & Reliability. (Illus.). pap. 14.95 (*0-8376-0473-7*) Bentley Pubs.

— Bosch Technical Instruction: Battery Ignition. (Illus.). pap. 14.95 (*0-8376-0477-X*) Bentley Pubs.

— Bosch Technical Instruction: Braking Systems for Passenger Cars. (Illus.). pap. 14.95 (*0-8376-0472-9*) Bentley Pubs.

— Bosch Technical Instruction: Components for Compressed-Air Brake Systems. (Illus.). pap. 14.95 (*0-8376-0499-0*) Bentley Pubs.

— Bosch Technical Instruction: Compressed-Air Brake Systems. (Illus.). pap. 14.95 (*0-8376-0498-2*) Bentley Pubs.

— Bosch Technical Instruction: Diesel Fuel-Injection--An Overview. (Illus.). pap. 14.95 (*0-8376-0494-X*) Bentley Pubs.

— Bosch Technical Instruction: Diesel Fuel-Injection Pumps Types PE-PF. (Illus.). pap. 14.95 (*0-8376-0496-6*) Bentley Pubs.

— Bosch Technical Instruction: Distributor Fuel-Injection Pump Type VE. (Illus.). pap. 14.95 (*0-8376-0495-8*) Bentley Pubs.

— Bosch Technical Instruction: Electronics & Microcomputers. (Illus.). pap. 14.95 (*0-8376-0481-8*) Bentley Pubs.

— Bosch Technical Instruction: Emission Control for Spark-Ignition Engines. (Illus.). pap. 14.95 (*0-8376-0474-5*) Bentley Pubs.

— Bosch Technical Instruction: Engine Electronics. (Illus.). pap. 14.95 (*0-8376-0475-3*) Bentley Pubs.

— Bosch Technical Instruction: Governors for In-Line Pumps. (Illus.). pap. 14.95 (*0-8376-0497-4*) Bentley Pubs.

— Bosch Technical Instruction: Graphical Symbols & Circuit Diagrams for Automotive Electrics. (Illus.). pap. 14.95 (*0-8376-0493-1*) Bentley Pubs.

— Bosch Technical Instruction: Interference Suppression. (Illus.). pap. 14.95 (*0-8376-0476-1*) Bentley Pubs.

— Bosch Technical Instruction: K-Jetronic Fuel-Injection System. (Illus.). pap. 14.95 (*0-8376-0468-0*) Bentley Pubs.

— Bosch Technical Instruction: KE-Jetronic Fuel-Injection System. (Illus.). pap. 14.95 (*0-8376-0469-9*) Bentley Pubs.

— Bosch Technical Instruction: L-Jetronic Fuel-Injection System. (Illus.). pap. 14.95 (*0-8376-0470-2*) Bentley Pubs.

— Bosch Technical Instruction: Mono-Jetronic. (Illus.). pap. 14.95 (*0-8376-0492-3*) Bentley Pubs.

— Bosch Technical Instruction: Motronic Combined Ignition & Fuel-Injection System. (Illus.). pap. 14.95 (*0-8376-0471-0*) Bentley Pubs.

— Bosch Technical Instruction: Spark Plugs. (Illus.). pap. 14.95 (*0-8376-0478-8*) Bentley Pubs.

— Bosch Technical Instruction: Starting Systems. (Illus.). pap. 14.95 (*0-8376-0480-X*) Bentley Pubs.

— Bosch Technical Instruction: Symbols for Compressed-Air Brake Systems. (Illus.). pap. 14.95 (*0-8376-0597-0*) Bentley Pubs.

— Diesel Fuel Injection. (Illus.). 199p. 1995. pap. text 29.95 (*0-8376-0603-9*) Bentley Pubs.

Bosch, Robert Van Den, see Van Den Bosch, Robert.

Bosch, S., et al. Neron Models. (Ergebnisse der Mathematik und Ihrer Grenzgebiete Ser.: Vol. 21). (Illus.). 340p. 1990. 164.95 (*0-387-50587-3*) Spr-Verlag.

Bosch, Siegfried. Algebra. 1995. pap. text 35.00 (*3-540-60410-3*) Spr-Verlag.

Bosch, Stephen, et al. Guide to Selecting & Acquiring CD-ROMS, Software, & Other Electronic Publications. LC 93-43298. (Acquisitions Guidelines Ser.: No. 9). 48p. (Orig.). 1994. pap. 15.00 (*0-8389-0629-X*) ALA.

Bosch, Susanna A. Sturdy Black Bridges on the American Stage: The Portrayal of Black Motherhood in Selected Plays by Contemporary African American Women Playwrights. Martin, Richard & Schreyer, Rudiger, eds. LC 97-141986. (Aachen British & American Studies: Vol. 8). (Illus.). 318p. 1996. 63.95 (*3-631-30136-7*) P Lang Pubng.

— Sturdy Black Bridges on the American Stage: The Portrayal of Black Motherhood in Selected Plays by Contemporary African American Women Playwrights. Martin, Richard & Schreyer, Rudiger, eds. LC 97-141986. (Aachen British & American Studies: Vol. 8). (Illus.). 318p. 1996. 63.95 (*0-8204-3179-6*) P Lang Pubng.

Bosch, Thierry & Lescure, Marc, eds. Selected Papers on Laser Distance Measurements. (SPIE Milestone Ser.: Vol. MS 115). 1995. 118.00 (*0-8194-2010-7*) SPIE.

Boschan, Charlotte, jt. auth. see Bry, Gerhard.

Bosche. Jenny Lives with Eric & Martin. 1995. per. 7.95 (*0-907040-22-5*, Pub. by Gay Mens Pr) LPC InBook.

Boschee, Floyd. Grouping Equals Growth. 112p. 1989. 19.95 (*0-8403-5518-1*) Kendall-Hunt.

Boschee, Floyd & Baron, Mark A. Outcome-Based Education: Developing Programs Through Strategic Planning. LC 93-61024. 150p. 1996. pap. text 24.95 (*1-56676-083-6*) Scarecrow.

Boschee, Floyd, et al. Effective Reading Programs: The Administrator's Role. LC 92-83977. 240p. 1993. pap. text 19.95 (*0-87762-988-9*) Scarecrow.

— School Bond Success: A Strategy for Building America's Schools. LC 98-87282. 171 p. 1998. pap. 29.95 (*1-56676-705-9*) Scarecrow.

— Special & Compensatory Programs: The Administrator's Role. LC 97-60882. 285p. 1997. text 39.95 (*1-56676-537-4*) Scarecrow.

Boschee, Floyd, jt. auth. see Baron, Mark A.

***Boschee, Jerr.** Merging Mission & Money: A Board Member's Guide to Social Entrepreneurship. 22p. 1998. pap. text 16.00 (*0-925299-81-2*) Natl Ctr Nonprofit.

***Boscheinen-Morrin, Judith, et al.** The Hand: Fundamentals of Therapy. LC 99-30121. (Illus.). 224p. 2000. pap. text 49.50 (*0-7506-4577-6*) Buttrwrth-Heinemann.

Boscheinen-Morrin, Judith, et al. The Hand: Fundamentals of Therapy. 2nd ed. rev. ed. (Illus.). 276p. 1992. pap. text 40.00 (*0-7506-0570-7*) Buttrwrth-Heinemann.

Boschen, Lothar & Barth, Jurgen. The Porsche Book: A Definitive Illustrated History. LC 78-695. 472 p. 1978. 29.95 (*0-668-04576-0*, Arco) Macmillan Gen Ref.

— The Porsche Book: A Definitive Illustrated History. LC 78-394959. 472p. 1978. write for info. (*0-85059-301-8*) P Stephenson.

Boscher, Winfried. Vietnamese-German Dictionary: Woerterbuch Vietnamesisch-Deutsch. 5th ed. (GER & VIE.). 738p. 1989. 135.00 (*0-8288-1086-9*, F65620) Fr & Eur.

Boscherini, E. G. Lexicon Spinozanum, Set. (International Archives of the History of Ideas Ser.: No. 28). 1411p. 1987. lib. bdg. 574.00 (*90-247-0205-4*) Kluwer Academic.

Boschert, Kenneth R. & James, Henry. Netvet: Mosby's Veterinary Guide to the Internet, Vol. 1. (Illus.). 275p. (gr. 13). 1997. pap. text 24.95 incl. 3.5 hd (*0-8151-2935-1*, 31825) Mosby Inc.

Boschetti, F. Dictionary Francais-Hindi. (FRE & HIN.). 382p. 1994. 150.00 (*0-320-00939-4*) Fr & Eur.

Boschetti, Federica. Dictionnaire Hindi-Francais. (FRE & HIN.). 1991. write for info. (*0-7859-8260-4*, 2-9506068-0-6) Fr & Eur.

Boschetti, Norma, tr. see Smelser, G. K., et al.

Boschetto-Sandoval, Sandra M., jt. ed. see Sandoval, Ciro A.

Boschetto, Sandra M. & McGowan, Marcia P., eds. Claribel Alegria & Central American Literature: Critical Essays. (Monographs in International Studies, Latin America Ser.: No. 21). 233p. (Orig.). (C). 1993. pap. text 20.00 (*0-89680-179-9*) Ohio U Pr.

Boschi, E., et al, eds. Recent Evolution & Seismicity of the Mediterranean Region: Proceedings of the NATO Advanced Research Workshop, Erice, Italy, September 17-18, 1992. LC 93-19532. (NATO Advanced Science Institutes Series C: Mathematical & Physical Sciences). 436p. (C). 1993. text 264.50 (*0-7923-2325-4*) Kluwer Academic.

***Boschi, Nadia.** Education & Training in Indoor Air Science LC 99-40943. (NATO Science Series 2, Environmental Security). 1999. write for info. (*0-7923-5910-0*) Kluwer Academic.

Boschiere, R. Dictionnaire des Pierres Utilisees en Lithotheraphies. (FRE.). 1998. 24.95 (*0-320-00262-2*) Fr & Eur.

Boschini, Henny & Boschini, Luciano. Chasing Whales off Norway. LC 72-90690. (Illus.). 32p. (J). (gr. k-4). 1973. 11.95 (*0-87592-010-1*) Scroll Pr.

Boschini, Luciano, jt. auth. see Boschini, Henny.

Boschke, F. L. Chemistry & Physics with Related Applications: Chemie und Physik mit Anwendungsgebieten. 2nd ed. (ENG & GER.). 200p. 1981. 49.95 (*0-8288-0860-0*, M15298) Fr & Eur.

Boschke, F. L., ed. Large Amplitude Motion in Molecules II. (Topics in Current Chemistry Ser.: Vol. 82). (Illus.). 1979. 74.95 (*0-387-09311-7*) Spr-Verlag.

Boschloo, Anton W. The Prints of the Remondinis: An Attempt to Reconstruct an Eighteenth-Century World of Pictures. LC 98-161396. (Illus.). 450p. 1998. 75.00 (*90-5356-273-7*, Pub. by Amsterdam U Pr) U of Mich Pr.

Boschma, et al. Lesen, na Und? 104p. 1987. 13.00 (*3-468-49466-1*) Langenscheidt.

***Boschma, Symon.** The Coming Days of Thunder: Discovering the End from Beginnings. LC 99-63450. 176p. 2000. pap. 11.95 (*1-57921-226-3*, Pub. by WinePress Pub) BookWorld.

***Boschman, LaMar.** Future Worship. LC 99-13638. 1999. 10.99 (*0-8307-2421-4*) Gospel Lght.

Boschman, LaMar. A Heart of Worship. 180p. 1994. pap. 10.99 (*0-88419-359-4*) Creation House.

Boschman, LaMar. A Passion for His Presence. 170p. (Orig.). 1992. pap. 9.99 (*1-56043-704-9*) Destiny Image.

Boschman, LaMar. The Prophetic Song. 115p. 1999. write for info. (*1-883092-01-9*) L Boschman Minist.

— The Rebirth of Music: English Version. 112p. (Orig.). 1988. pap. 8.99 (*0-914903-80-2*) Destiny Image.

Boschmann. Chemistry in Action. 4th ed. 1991. student ed. 26.87 (*0-07-006534-9*) McGraw.

Boschmann & Wells. Chemistry in Action: A Laboratory Manual. 4th ed. 438p. (C). 1990. lab manual ed. 53.94 (*0-07-006531-4*) McGraw.

Boschmann, Erwin, ed. The Electronic Classroom. 240p. 1995. 42.50 (*0-938734-89-X*) Info Today Inc.

Boschot, ed. see Gautier, Theophile.

Boscia Mule, Patricia. Authentic Ethnicities: The Interaction of Ideology, Gender Power & Class in the Italian-American Experience, 124. LC 98-45031. (Contributions in Sociology Ser.: Vol. 124). 192p. 1999. 55.00 (*0-313-30946-9*) Greenwood.

Bosco, Anthony. The Beginning of Christmas. (Illus.). 24p. (J). (gr. 1-2). 1997. pap. 7.00 (*0-8059-4227-0*) Dorrance.

Bosco, Antoinette. Coincidences: Touched by a Miracle. LC 97-61921. 208p. 1998. pap. 12.95 (*0-89622-749-9*) Twenty-Third.

— Finding Peace through Pain. LC 95-94227. 160p. 1995. pap. 9.00 (*0-345-39646-4*) Ballantine Pub Grp.

— The Pummeled Heart: Finding Peace Through Pain. LC 93-61500. 140p. 1994. pap. 9.95 (*0-89622-584-4*) Twenty-Third.

Bosco, Carl S. Against the Tide: A Novel of Southern California, 1968. 227p. (Orig.). 1996. pap. 10.00 (*0-9648697-2-1*) Orlando Bks.

Bosco, Clyde. Pipe Down. Ashby, Ruth, ed. (Nintendo Adventure Bks.: No. 5). 128p. (J). 1991. mass mkt. 3.50 (*0-671-74203-5*, Archway) PB.

Bosco, Dominick. Bedlam: A Year in the Life of a Mental Hospital. 288p. 1992. 19.95 (*1-55972-113-8*, Birch Ln Pr) Carol Pub Group.

Bosco, Dominick, jt. auth. see Rosenbaum, Michael E.

Bosco, Francesca C. Lorenzo Lotto: The Frescoes in the Oratorio Suardi at Trescore. (Illus.). 190p. 1999. boxed set 65.00 (*88-8118-319-6*, Pub. by Skira IT) Abbeville Pr.

Bosco, Frederick J., jt. auth. see Glassman, Nina D.

Bosco, Henri. L' Ane Culotte. (FRE.). 1973. pap. 10.95 (*0-7859-1735-7*, 2070363376) Fr & Eur.

— L' Antiquaire. (FRE.). 538p. 1979. pap. 14.95 (*0-7859-1884-1*, 2070370828) Fr & Eur.

— L' Enfant et la Riviere. (FRE.). 160p. 1975. pap. 10.95 (*0-7859-1801-9*, 2070366790) Fr & Eur.

— Hyacinthe. (FRE.). 241p. 1977. pap. 10.95 (*0-7859-1858-2*, 2070369668) Fr & Eur.

— Le Jardin d'Hyacinthe. (FRE.). 1983. pap. 11.95 (*0-7859-1967-8*, 2070374343) Fr & Eur.

— Malicroix. (FRE.). 1973. pap. 11.95 (*0-7859-2202-4*, 207036397X) Fr & Eur.

— Le Mas Theotime. (FRE.). 448p. 1972. pap. 11.95 (*0-7859-1706-3*, 2070361683) Fr & Eur.

— El Nino y el Rio (The Child & the River) Rivas, Jose L., tr. (SPA., Illus.). 120p. (J). (gr. 5-6). 1992. pap. 5.99 (*968-16-4706-8*, Pub. by Fondo) Continental Bk.

— Tante Martine. (FRE.). 318p. 1990. pap. 11.95 (*0-7859-2239-3*, 207038229X) Fr & Eur.

— Le Trestoulas. (FRE.). 320p. 1979. pap. 11.95 (*0-7859-1903-1*, 2070371468) Fr & Eur.

Bosco, J. Mahatma Gandhi: Prophet of Freedom. 1989. pap. 15.00 (*0-86217-266-7*, Pub. by Veritas Pubns) St Mut.

Bosco, James. The Misadventures of Wags & Freckles Kid-Pak: A Lesson in the Dangers of Alcohol. rev. ed. Lupo, Ann, ed. (Life-Skill Builder Educational Ser.). (Illus.). 28p. (J). (ps-3). 1991. pap. text 3.95 (*1-56230-136-5*); pap. text 4.95 incl. audio (*1-56230-126-8*) Syndistar.

Bosco, James J. & Robin, Stanley S., eds. The Hyperactive Child & Stimulant Drugs. LC 76-57934. 199p. 1977. reprint ed. pap. 61.70 (*0-608-18214-1*, 205661800078) Bks Demand.

Bosco, John. Memoirs of the Oratory of Saint Francis de Sales from 1815 to 1855: The Autobiography of Saint John Bosco. Lyons, Daniel, tr. from ITA. LC 89-36115. (Illus.). lxvi, 478p. 1990. 29.95 (*0-89944-139-4*); per. 24.95 (*0-89944-135-1*, 135-1) Salesiana Pubs.

Bosco, Joseph. Temples of the Empress of Heaven. LC 98-31735. (Images of Asia Ser.). (Illus.). 96p. 1999. text 12.95 (*0-19-590355-2*) OUP.

Bosco, Peter. World War I. (America at War Ser.). (Illus.). 144p. (J). (gr. 5-12). 1991. 19.95 (*0-8160-2460-X*) Facts on File.

Bosco, Rocco Lo, see Lo Bosco, Rocco.

Bosco, Ronald A., ed. Lessons for the Children of Godly Ancestors. LC 82-5844. (Sermon in America Ser.). 416p. 1982. 75.00 (*0-8201-1381-6*) Schol Facsimiles.

— The Poems of Michael Wigglesworth. LC 88-34214. 374p. (C). 1989. lib. bdg. 48.00 (*0-8191-7345-2*) U Pr of Amer.

— Puritan Sermon in America, 1630-1750, 4 vols. LC 78-114749. (Sermon in America Ser.). 1840p. 1978. reprint ed. 200.00 (*0-8201-1320-4*) Schol Facsimiles.

Bosco, Ronald A., ed. see Emerson, Ralph Waldo.

Bosco, Ronald A., ed. see Mather, Cotton.

Boscolo, Bertrando, jt. auth. see Boscolo, Luigi.

Boscolo, Luigi & Boscolo, Bertrando. Systemic Therapy with Individuals. 320p. 1996. pap. 33.00 (*1-85575-094-5*, Pub. by H Karnac Bks Ltd) Other Pr LLC.

Boscolo, Luigi, et al. Milan Systemic Family Therapy: Conversations in Theory & Practice. LC 87-71985. 352p. 1987. 42.00 (*0-465-04596-0*, Pub. by Basic) HarpC.

***Boscorelli, Nicholas.** The Stomp Box Cookbook: Build Advanced Effects for Electric Guitar & Bass. 2nd ed. (Illus.). 259p. 1999. pap. 29.95 (*0-9663824-1-2*) Guitar Project.

***Boscowan, Robert.** Armoured Guardsman. 2000. 36.95 (*0-85052-748-1*, Pub. by Pen & Sword Bks Ltd) Combined Pub.

Bosdeed, Ashish. Demography of Tribal Development. (C). 1991. 32.00 (*81-7018-601-3*) S Asia.

Bosdogianni, Panagiota, jt. auth. see Petrou, Maria.

Bose. Neural Networks. 2nd ed. 2001. 59.50 (*0-07-232080-X*) McGraw.

Bose, A. & Hamza, M. H., eds. High Technology in the Power Industry: Power High Tech '88: Proceedings of IASTED Symposium, Scottsdale, U. S. A., March 1-4, 1988. 350p. 1988. 103.00 (*0-88986-099-8*, 119) Acta Pr.

Bose, A. N. Coastal Aquaculture Engineering. 1991. 64.00 (*81-204-0500-5*, Pub. by Oxford IBH) S Asia.

Bose, Ajay K., jt. auth. see Manhas, Maghar S.

Bose, Ajoy, jt. auth. see Dayal, John.

Bose, Amitava, et al, eds. Issues in Economic Theory & Public Policy: Essays in Honour of Professor Tapas Majumdar. LC 97-903274. (Illus.). 336p. (C). 1997. text 35.00 (*0-19-563949-9*) OUP.

Bose, Anima. Dimensions of Peace & Nonviolence: The Gandhian Perspective. 176p. 1987. 17.50 (*81-212-0076-8*, Pub. by Gian Publng Hse) S Asia.

Bose, Animesh. Advances in Particulate Materials. LC 94-44281. 422p. 1995. text 160.00 (*0-7506-9156-5*) Buttrwrth-Heinemann.

Bose, Animesh, et al, eds. Reviews in Particulate Materials, Vol. 4. (Illus.). 300p. 1996. pap. 95.00 (*0-614-14709-3*) Metal Powder.

Bose, Animesh & Dowding, Robert J., eds. Tungsten & Refractory Metals 3. LC 97-113095. (Illus.). 250p. (Orig.). 1995. pap. 150.00 (*1-878954-58-X*) Metal Powder.

— Tungsten & Tungsten Alloys 2, 1994: Proceedings of the 1994 Second International Conference. (Illus.). 750p. 1995. pap. 170.00 (*1-878954-53-9*) Metal Powder.

Bose, Animesh, jt. auth. see German, Randall M.

Bose, Animesh, jt. ed. see Dowding, Robert J.

Bose, Animesh, ed. see International Conference on Tungsten & Refractory.

Bose, Animesh, ed. see International Conference on Tungsten & Tungsten Al.

Bose, Arabinda, ed. see International Conference on International Strategi.

Bose, Arabinda, ed. see Intl. Conf. on Intl. Strategies for the Eradicatio.

Bose, Arindam, jt. ed. see Ladisch, Michael R.

Bose, Ashish. India & the Asian Population Perspective. (C). 1993. 19.50 (*81-7018-765-6*, Pub. by BR Pub) S Asia.

— India's Basic Demographic Statistics: 177 Key Tables with Graphics. 1996. 39.00 (*81-7018-915-2*, Pub. by BR Pub) S Asia.

— Population of India: Census Results & Methodology, 1991. (C). 1991. 9.50 (*81-7018-667-6*, Pub. by BR Pub) S Asia.

— Population Profile of Religion in India: Districtwise Data from 1991 Census. LC 97-914471. (C). 1997. 48.50 (*81-7018-937-3*, Pub. by BR Pub) S Asia.

Bose, Ashish, ed. Population Transition in South Asia. (C). 1992. 24.00 (*81-7018-623-4*, Pub. by BR Pub) S Asia.

Bose, Ashish & Desai, P. B., eds. Population Planning in India: Policy Issues & Research Priorities. 1990. 27.50 (*81-7018-575-0*, Pub. by BR Pub) S Asia.

Bose, Ashish, et al. Demographic Zones in India. (C). 1994. 32.00 (*81-7018-867-9*, Pub. by BR Pub) S Asia.

Bose, Aurobindo, tr. see Tagore, Rabindranath.

Bose, B. K., ed. Modern Power Electronics: Evolution, Technology, & Applications. LC 91-39029. (Illus.). 608p. (C). 1991. text 79.95 (*0-87942-282-3*, PC0276-6) Inst Electrical.

Bose, Bimal K., ed. Power Electronics & Variable Frequency Drives: Technology & Applications. LC 96-6092. 664p. 1996. 94.95 (*0-7803-1084-5*, PC4382) Inst Electrical.

Bose, Christine & Spitze, Glenna D., eds. Ingredients for Women's Employment Policy. LC 86-14550. (SUNY Series on Women & Work). 296p. (C). 1987. text 69.50 (*0-88706-420-5*); pap. text 24.95 (*0-88706-421-3*) State U NY Pr.

B

Bose, Christine E. Jobs & Gender: Sex & Occupation. LC 85-6305. 222p. 1985. 57.95 (*0-275-90064-9*, C0064, Praeger Pubs) Greenwood.

***Bose, Christine E.** Women in 1900: Gateway to the Political Economy of the 20th Century. (Women in the Political Economy Ser.). 256p. 2001. 69.50 (*1-56639-837-1*); pap. 22.95 (*1-56639-838-X*) Temple U Pr.

Bose, Christine E., et al, eds. Hidden Aspects of Women's Work. LC 87-2449. 390p. 1987. 62.95 (*0-275-92415-7*, C2415, Praeger Pubs) Greenwood.

Bose, Christine E. & Acosta-Belen, Edna, eds. Women in the Latin American Development Process. LC 94-27400. 296p. (Orig.). (C). 1995. pap. text 22.95 (*1-56639-293-4*) Temple U Pr.

— Women in the Latin American Development Process. LC 94-27400. 296p. (Orig.). (C). 1995. lib. bdg. 69.95 (*1-56639-292-6*) Temple U Pr.

Bose, D. N. Tantras: Their Philosophy & Occult Secrets with Critical Intro & Index. 1992. 14.00 (*0-8364-2868-4*, Pub. by Eastern Bk Linkers) S Asia.

Bose, D. N., ed. Tantras: Their Philosophy & Occult Secrets. (C). 1997. 17.50 (*81-215-0652-2*, Pub. by Vikas) S Asia.

Bose, Frank. Rock Solid. 320p. 1993. mass mkt. 5.99 (*0-515-11076-0*, Jove) Berkley Pub.

***Bose, Indranil.** Database Management: The First Step. 136p. (C). 1998. per. 30.95 (*0-7872-4707-3*) Kendall-Hunt.

Bose, J. C. Life Movement in Plants, 2 vols. 650p. 1993. pap. 160.00 (*81-7041-172-6*, Pub. by Print Hse) St Mut.

— Plant Response, 2 vols. 1991. 400.00 (*81-7158-248-6*, Pub. by Scientific Pubs) St Mut.

Bose, J. P. Concept of Business Organisation. 1985. 75.00 (*0-7855-0724-8*, Pub. by Current Dist) St Mut.

— An Outline of Business Management. (C). 1989. 35.00 (*0-89771-435-0*, Pub. by Current Dist) St Mut.

Bose, James. Geothermal Heat Pumps: Introductory Guide. Fischer, Irene, ed. LC 97-10105. (Illus.). 99p. (Orig.). 1997. pap. 20.00 (*0-929974-05-0*) GSHP Pubns.

Bose, James, et al. Closed-Loop - Ground-Source Heat Pump System Installation Guide. Fisher, Irene, ed. (Orig.). 1988. pap. text 75.00 (*0-929974-01-8*) GSHP Pubns.

Bose, James E., ed. see Salomone, L. H. & Marlowe, J. I.

Bose, Johanne C. Farewell to Durango: A German Lady's Diary in Mexico, 1910-1911. Blew, Robert W., ed. Bose, John C., tr. from GER. LC 78-50471. (Western Americana Bks.). (Illus.). (Orig.). 1978. pap. 10.00 (*0-913626-41-4*) S S S Pub Co.

Bose, John C., tr. see Bose, Johanne C.

Bose, Jonaki. Characteristics of the 100 Largest Public Elementary & Secondary School Districts in the United States, 1993-94. 54p. 1996. pap. 3.75 (*0-16-048674-2*) USGPO.

Bose, K. C. Pharmacopoeit India. 300p. (C). 1984. 65.00 (*0-7855-3301-X*, Pub. by Scientific) St Mut.

Bose, Keith W. Aviation Electronics. 4th ed. LC 92-44735. (Illus.). 384p. 1990. pap. text 25.95 (*0-89100-352-5*, JS312662) Jeppesen Sanderson.

Bose, M. Classical Indian Dancing. 216p. 1970. 15.95 (*0-318-36309-7*) Asia Bk Corp.

Bose, M. L. Social & Cultural History of Ancient India. 1990. 24.00 (*81-7022-287-7*, Pub. by Concept) S Asia.

— Social History of Assam. (C). 1989. 17.00 (*81-7022-224-9*, Pub. by Concept) S Asia.

Bose, Mandakranta. Dance Vocabulary of Classical India. (C). 1995. 40.00 (*81-7030-439-3*, Pub. by Sri Satguru Pubns) S Asia.

— Movements & Mimesis: The Idea of Dance in the Sanskritic Tradition. (Studies of Classical India). 352p. (C). 1991. lib. bdg. 180.50 (*0-7923-1325-9*, Pub. by Kluwer Academic) Kluwer Academic.

Bose, Mandakranta, ed. Women in Indian Society: Faces of the Feminine in Ancient, Medieval & Modern Times. LC 98-8137. (Illus.). 368p. 2000. text 39.95 (*0-19-512229-1*) OUP.

Bose, Manjula. Economic Studies, Nineteen Eighty-Four India. 1986. pap. 8.50 (*0-8364-1479-9*, Pub. by KP Bagchi) S Asia.

Bose McKinney & Evans Attorneys at Law Staff. Model Employee Policies for Indiana Employees. 3rd ed. LC 99-193986. 149p. 1998. pap. 89.00 (*1-883698-21-9*) IN Chamber Comm.

— Model Employee Policies for Indiana Employers: With Legal Commentary. 132p. 1995. pap., per. 36.00 (*1-883698-07-3*) IN Chamber Comm.

— Model Employee Policies for Indiana Employers: With Legal Commentary. 2nd ed. 116p. 1996. per. 48.00 (*1-883698-11-1*) IN Chamber Comm.

Bose, Meena. Shaping & Signaling Presidential Policy: The National Security Decision Making of Eisenhower & Kennedy. LC 98-21374. (Joseph V. Hughes, Jr. & Holly O. Hughes Series in the Presidency & Leadership Studies: Vol. 2). 224p. 1998. 29.95 (*0-89096-833-0*) Tex A&M Univ Pr.

Bose, Mihir. False Messiah. 356p. 1996. 40.00 (*0-233-98998-6*, Pub. by Andre Deutsch) Trafalgar.

***Bose, Mihir.** Manchester Unlimited: The Money, Egos & Infighting Behind the World's Richest Soccer Club. (Illus.). 2000. 27.95 (*1-58799-008-3*) Texere.

Bose, Mihir. The Sporting Alien: English Sport's Lost Camelot. (Illus.). 224p. 1996. 29.95 (*1-85158-745-4*, Pub. by Mainstream Pubng) Trafalgar.

Bose, N. K. Cultural Anthropology. (C). 1988. 21.00 (*0-8364-2340-2*, Pub. by Mittal Pubs Dist) S Asia.

— Digital Filters: Theory & Applications. rev. ed. LC 92-27996. 524p. (C). 1993. reprint ed. 66.50 (*0-89464-792-X*) Krieger.

Bose, N. K., ed. see Rao, C. R.

Bose, Nirmal K. & Liang, Ping. Neural Network Fundamentals with Graphs, Algorithms & Applications. LC 95-16922. (Electrical & Computer Engineering Ser.: Communications & Signal Processing). 512p. (C). 1995. 77.50 (*0-07-006618-3*) McGraw.

Bose, P. K. Higher Education at Cross Road. 111p. 1977. 8.95 (*0-318-36816-1*) Asia Bk Corp.

Bose, Prabodh C. Introduction to Juristic Psychology. (Historical Foundations of Forensic Psychiatry & Psychology Ser.). 426p. 1980. reprint ed. lib. bdg. 42.50 (*0-306-76062-2*) Da Capo.

Bose, Pradip, ed. Programming Languages & Data Structures (BASIC, Cobol, Pascal, FORTRAN, ADA, Lisp) (C). 1989. 100.00 (*0-89771-388-5*, Pub. by Current Dist) St Mut.

Bose, Pramatha N. History of Hindu Civilisation During British Rule. (C). 1993. 22.00 (*81-85557-49-7*, Pub. by Low Price) S Asia.

— Swaraj: Cultural & Political. 1986. reprint ed. 32.50 (*0-8364-1950-2*, Pub. by Usha) S Asia.

Bose, Ram C. Hindu Philosophy. 420p. 1986. reprint ed. 28.00 (*0-8364-1757-7*, Pub. by Manohar) S Asia.

Bose, S. & Tyagi, S., eds. High Temperature Superconductivity: Proceedings of the Drexel International Conference, Philadelphia, Pa., 29-30 July 1987. (Progress in High Temperature Superconductivity Ser.: Vol. 3). 300p. (C). 1988. pap. 49.00 (*9971-5-0411-1*); text 125.00 (*9971-5-0410-3*) World Scientific Pub.

Bose, S. K., jt. auth. see Chatterjee, U. K.

Bose, Sarmila. Money, Energy & Welfare: The State & the Household in India's Rural Electrification Policy. 2nd ed. 138p. (C). 1994. text 13.95 (*0-19-563143-9*) OUP.

Bose, Shankar, jt. auth. see Singh, V. B.

Bose, Sisir K. & Bose, Sugata, eds. The Essential Writings of Netaji Subhas Chandra Bose. LC 97-165261. (Illus.). 356p. (C). 1997. text 35.00 (*0-19-563982-0*) OUP.

***Bose, Sisir K. & Bose, Sugata, eds.** Essential Writings of Netaji Subhas Chandra Bose. (Illus.). 348p. 1999. pap. text 14.95 (*0-19-564854-4*) OUP.

Bose, Sisir K., ed. see Bose, Subhas C.

Bose, Sisir Kumar, ed. see Bose, Subhas Chandra.

Bose Staff. Multidimensional Systems. (Mathematics & Its Applications Ser.). 1985. text 184.00 (*90-277-1764-8*) Kluwer Academic.

Bose, Subash Ch., jt. auth. see F. R. C. S. Staff.

***Bose, Subhas C.** The Indian Struggle, 1920-1942. Bose, Sisir K., ed. (Illus.). 430p. (Orig.). 1998. pap. text 18.95 (*0-19-564149-3*) OUP.

Bose, Subhas C. Netaji: Collected Works: The Alternative Leadership, Vol. 10. Kumar, Sisir & Bose, Sugata, eds. LC 99-165331. (Illus.). 262p. 1998. text 19.95 (*0-19-564153-1*) OUP.

— Netaji Vol. 7: Collected Works: Letters to Emilie Schenkl 1934-1942. Bose, Sisir K. & Bose, Sugata, eds. LC 95-128175. (Illus.), 266p. 1995. 32.00 (*0-19-563409-8*) OUP.

— Netaji Vol. 8: Collected Works: Letters, Articles, Speeches & Statements 1933-1937. Bose, Sisir K. & Bose, Sugata, eds. LC 95-182048. (Illus.). 472p. 1995. 32.00 (*0-19-563560-4*) OUP.

— Netaji: Collected Works Vol. 1: An Indian Pilgrim : An Unfinished Autobiography. Bose, Sisir K. & Bose, Sugata, eds. (Oxford India Paperbacks Ser.). (Illus.). 296p. (Orig.). 1998. pap. text 15.95 (*0-19-564148-5*) OUP.

Bose, Subhas Chandra. Netaji Vol. 9: Collected Works: Congress President: Speeches, Articles, & Letters, January 1938-May 1939. Bose, Sisir Kumar & Bose, Sugata, eds. (Illus.). 332p. 1996. text 15.95 (*0-19-563706-2*) OUP.

Bose, Sudha, ed. Rupa-Ikshana: Development of Indian Art & Culture. (C). 1991. 59.50 (*81-85067-74-0*, Pub. by Sundeep Prak) S Asia.

Bose, Sudhindra. Fifteen Years in America. LC 73-13121. (Foreign Travelers in America, 1810-1935 Ser.). (Illus.). 528p. 1974. reprint ed. 41.95 (*0-405-05444-0*) Ayer.

Bose, Sugata. Peasant Labour & Colonial Capital: Rural Bengal since 1770. LC 92-12666. (New Cambridge History of India Ser.: III: 2). (Illus.). 248p. (C). 1993. 47.95 (*0-521-26694-7*) Cambridge U Pr.

Bose, Sugata, ed. Credit, Markets, & the Agrarian Economy of Colonial India. (India Readings: Themes in Indian History Ser.). 344p. 1994. 21.00 (*0-19-563308-3*) OUP.

— South Asia & World Capitalism. (Illus.). 418p. 1991. text 39.95 (*0-19-562544-7*) OUP.

Bose, Sugata & Jalal, Ayesha. Modern South Asia: History, Culture & Political Economy. LC 97-14688. 320p. (C). 1998. 75.00 (*0-415-16951-8*) Routledge.

— Modern South Asia: History, Culture & Political Economy. LC 97-14688. (Illus.). 320p. (C). 1998. pap. 22.99 (*0-415-16952-6*) Routledge.

Bose, Sugata, jt. ed. see Bose, Sisir K.

Bose, Sugata, ed. see Bose, Subhas C.

Bose, Sugata, ed. see Bose, Subhas Chandra.

Bose, Sumantra. The Challenge in Kashmir: Democracy, Self-Determination & a Just Peace. LC 96-36651. 180p. (C). 1997. 19.95 (*0-8039-9350-1*, 93501) Sage.

— States, Nations, Sovereignty: Sri Lanka, India, & the Tamil Eelam Movement. LC 93-49452. 1994. 33.50 (*0-8039-9170-3*) Sage.

Bose, Sunil. Indian Classical Music. (Orig.). (C). 1993. 9.00 (*0-7069-7263-5*, Pub. by Vikas) S Asia.

Bose, Sunil. Indian Classical Music. (Orig.). 1995. pap. 11.00 (*0-7069-9950-9*, Pub. by Vikas) S Asia.

Bose, T. K. Orchids of India. (C). 1988. 200.00 (*0-7855-3280-3*, Pub. by Scientific) St Mut.

Bose, T. K., ed. Fruits of India: Tropical & Subtropical. (Illus.). 658p. (C). 1987. 82.50 (*81-85109-39-7*, Pub. by Naya Prokash) S Asia.

Bose, T. K. & Mitra, S. K. Mineral Nutrition of Fruit Crops. 850p. (C). 1986. 118.00 (*81-85109-44-3*, Pub. by Naya Prokash) S Asia.

— Propagation of Tropical & Subtropical Horticultural Crops. 580p. (C). 1986. 82.50 (*81-85109-40-0*, Pub. by Naya Prokash) S Asia.

Bose, T. K. & Som, M. G. Vegetable Crops in India. (Illus.). 770p. (C). 1986. 115.00 (*81-85109-41-9*, Pub. by Naya Prokash) S Asia.

Bose, T. K. & Yadav, L. P. Commercial Flowers in India. 850p. (C). 1986. 37.50 (*81-85109-48-6*, Pub. by Naya Prokash) S Asia.

Bose, Tarun C., ed. Indian Federalism: Problems & Issues. 239p. (C). 1987. 22.00 (*81-7074-005-3*) S Asia.

Bose, Walter B. Los Origenes del Correo Terrestre en Guatemala. (Guatemala Postal History Pamphlet Ser.: No. 1). 1984. reprint ed. pap. 4.25 (*0-913129-03-8*) La Tienda.

Bosek, Jeff S. Desert Scopes. 122p. (Orig.). 1995. pap. 5.95 (*0-9648145-0-1*, PA703-745) Northstr Bks.

Bosek, Rita. Area Labor - Management Committees. Linger, Juyne, ed. 8p. (Orig.). 1977. pap. 8.00 (*0-317-04918-6*) Natl Coun Econ Dev.

Bosela, Theodore R. Introduction to Electrical Power System Technology. LC 96-33742. 510p. 1996. 113.00 (*0-13-186537-4*) P-H.

Boselly, S. Edward, III, et al. Road Weather Information Systems Vol. 2: Implementation Guide. 82p. (C). 1993. pap. text 10.00 (*0-309-05274-2*, SHRP-H-351) SHRP.

Boselovic, Len, ed. see Benedict, John T.

Boseman, Glenn & Powell, Kay, eds. Managing Sales Professionals. 2nd ed. LC 92-71834. 400p. 1993. text 40.00 (*0-943590-38-8*) Amer College.

Bosen, Victor, jt. auth. see Pringsheim, Klaus H.

Bosenberg, Walter R. & Fejer, Martin M., eds. Advanced Solid State Lasers. LC 97-81323. (Trends in Optics & Photonics Ser.: Vol. 19). (Illus.). 612p. 1998. pap. 55.00 (*1-55752-523-4*) Optical Soc.

Bosence, D. W. & Allison, P. A., eds. Marine Palaeoenvironmental Analysis from Fossils. (Special Publication Ser.: No. 83). (Illus.). 272p. 1995. pap. 64.00 (*1-897799-31-4*, 221, Pub. by Geol Soc Pub Hse) AAPG.

Boserup, A., et al, eds. The Challenge of Nuclear Armaments: Essays Dedicated to Niels Bohr & His Appeal for an Open World. (Illus.). 346p. (Orig.). 1986. pap. 78.00 (*87-7245-142-4*) Coronet Bks.

Boserup, Dan & Gouge, Gerald. The Case Management Model: Concept, Implementation & Training. rev. ed. 178p. 1980. 6.00 (*0-318-16342-X*, B2) Regional Inst Social Welfare.

Boserup, Ester. The Conditions of Agricultural Growth: The Economics of Agrarian Change under Population Pressure. 128p. 1992. 22.00 (*1-85383-159-X*, Pub. by Escan Pubns) Island Pr.

— Economic & Demographic Relationships in Development. LC 89-35239. (Studies in Development). 320p. 1990. pap. text 22.50 (*0-8018-3930-0*) Johns Hopkins.

***Boserup, Ester.** My Professional Life, 1929-98: With a Selected Bibliography. 69p. 1999. (*87-7289-520-9*, Pub. by Mus Tusculanum) Paul & Co Pubs.

Boserup, Ester. Population & Technological Change: A Study of Long-Term Trends. LC 80-21116. (Illus.). 268p. 1983. pap. text 12.95 (*0-226-06674-6*) U Ch Pr.

— Woman's Role Economic Development. 288p. 1988. 20.00 (*1-85383-040-2*, Pub. by Escan Pubns) Island Pr.

Boserup, Ester & Sachs, Ignacy, eds. Foreign Aid to Newly Independent Countries. LC 70-129142. (European Coordination Centre for Research & Documentation in the Social Sciences Publications). (ENG & FRE.). 184p. 1971. text 21.55 (*90-279-6907-8*) Mouton.

Bosetti, Elena. Yahweh: Shepherd of the People: Pastoral Symbolism in the Old Testament. 174p. 1993. 40.00 (*0-85439-441-9*, Pub. by St Paul Pubns) St Mut.

Bosgra, T. J. Abortion: The Bible & the Church. 2nd rev. ed. 241p. 1987. pap. 12.95 (*0-919225-30-6*) Life Cycle Bks.

Bosh, Nancy L., et al. Michigan Appellate Handbook. 2nd ed. LC 91-78185. 786p. 1992. ring bd. 110.00 (*0-685-65988-7*, 85-009) U MI Law CLE.

Bosha, Francis J. Faulkner's "Soldier's Pay" A Bibliographical Study. LC 80-54205. x, 531p. 1982. 62.50 (*0-87875-211-0*) Whitston Pub.

Bosha, Francis J., ed. The Critical Response to John Cheever. 6. LC 93-8974. (Critical Responses in Arts & Letters Ser.: No. 6). 352p. 1993. lib. bdg. 65.00 (*0-313-28355-9*, Greenwood Pr) Greenwood.

***Boshara, Ray, et al.** Building Assets for Stronger Families, Better Neighborhoods & Realizing the American Dream. 64p. 1998. pap. 12.00 (*1-883187-24-9*) Corp Ent Dev.

Boshardy, Louisa M. Simple Selling: Common Sense That Guarantees Your Success. LC 99-60332. 178p. 1999. reprint ed. 19.95 (*0-9669917-1-0*) Success Press.

***Boshart, Char.** Oral-Motor Analysis & Remediation Techniques. 2nd rev. ed. (Illus.). 156p. 1998. pap. 37.00 (*0-9666844-4-3*) Speech Dyn Inc.

Boshart, Char. Thumbsucking: Guidelines & Activities. Moramarco, Cindy, ed. (Little Books with Great Expectations: Vol. 2). (Illus.). 47p. 1997. pap. 25.00 (*0-9666844-1-9*) Speech Dyn Inc.

Boshart, Char, ed. see Marshalla, Pamela.

Bosher, J. F. French Revolution. (Revolutions in the Modern World Ser.). (Illus.). (C). 1989. pap. text 14.75 (*0-393-95997-X*) Norton.

— The Gaullist Attack on Canada, 1967-1997. 331p. 1998. 34.95 (*0-7735-1808-8*) McG-Queens Univ Pr.

***Bosher, J.F.** The Gaullist Attack on Canada, 1967-1997. 344p. 2000. pap. 24.95 (*0-7735-2025-2*, Pub. by McG-Queens Univ Pr) CUP Services.

***Boshers, Bo.** Doing Life with God. 2000. pap. 6.99 (*0-7644-2227-8*) Group Pub.

Boshers, Bo. Small Group Resources: Twelve Lessons That Will Impact the World, Vol. 4. (Student Impact Ser.). (Illus.). 112p. (Orig.). 1997. pap. 14.99 (*0-310-20128-4*) Zondervan.

— Small Group Resources/Learning: Twelve Lessons That Will Change Your Friends' Lives, Vol. 2. (Student Impact Ser.). (Illus.). 112p. (Orig.). 1997. pap. 14.99 (*0-310-20126-8*) Zondervan.

— Small Group Resources/Walking with Christ Vol. 1: Twelve Lessons That Will Change Your Life. (Student Impact Ser.). (Illus.). 112p. (Orig.). 1997. pap. 14.99 (*0-310-20124-1*) Zondervan.

Boshers, Bo & Anderson, Kim. Student Ministry for the 21st Century: Transforming Your Youth Group into a Vital Student Ministry. LC 97-4240. (Student Impact Ser.). (Illus.). 256p. 1997. 19.99 (*0-310-20122-5*) Zondervan.

***Boshers, Bo, et al.** Reaching Kids Most Youth Ministries Miss. LC 99-54693. 2000. text 14.99 (*0-7644-2148-4*) Group Pub.

Boshers, Bo, jt. auth. see Student Impact Team Staff.

Boshers, Martha, jt. auth. see Dixon, Louisa.

Boshkoff, Douglass. Bankruptcy & Creditor's Rights. 5th ed. (Sum & Substance Ser.). 1989. 17.95 (*0-940366-42-8*) Sum & Substance.

Boshner, J. F. The Canada Merchants 1713-1763. (Illus.). 248p. 1987. text 65.00 (*0-19-821134-1*) OUP.

***Boshoff, Eben & Morkel, Pieter, compiled by.** Juta's Education Law & Policy Handbook. 400p. 1999. pap. 65.00 (*0-7021-4815-6*, Pub. by Juta & Co) Gaunt.

Boshtchanovsky, Basil. Uroki Po Pastirskomu Bogosloviju.Tr. of Studies in Pastoral Theology. 100p. 1961. pap. text 5.00 (*0-317-30267-1*) Holy Trinity.

***Boshyk, Yuri.** Business-Driven Action Learning: Global Best Practices. LC 99-50208. (Illus.). 2000. text 59.95 (*0-312-23094-X*) St Martin.

Boshyk, Yury, et al, eds. Ukraine During World War II: History & Its Aftermath. LC 85-98965. (Illus.). xix, 291p. 1986. 19.95 (*0-920862-37-3*); pap. 9.95 (*0-920862-36-5*) Ukrainian Acad.

Bosi, Roberto. The Lapps, Vol. 17--17. Cadell, James, tr. LC 75-32455. 220p. 1977. reprint ed. lib. bdg. 38.50 (*0-8371-8545-9*, BOTL, Greenwood Pr) Greenwood.

Bosik, J. J. Common Names of Insects & Related Organisms. 232p. 1997. pap., spiral bd. 45.00 (*0-938522-64-7*, ESACNI) Entomol Soc.

Bosiljevac, T. L. SEALs: UDT - SEAL Operations in Vietnam. (Library of Vietnam Literature). 755p. 1991. mass mkt. 5.95 (*0-8041-0722-X*) Ivy Books.

Bosiljevac, Tim L. & Demarest, J. Seal Team: Rollback. 320p. 1999. mass mkt. 5.99 (*0-380-78714-8*, Avon Bks) Morrow Avon.

Bosinelli, R. M., et al, eds. Myriadminded Man: Jottings on Joyce. 296p. 1995. pap. 22.95 (*88-8091-438-3*) Paul & Co Pubs.

Bosinelli, Rosa M. & Mosher, Harold F., eds. ReJoycing: New Readings of Dubliners. LC 97-47260. (Irish Literature, History & Culture Ser.). (Illus.). 256p. (C). 1998. pap. 19.00 (*0-8131-0949-3*) U Pr of Ky.

Bosinelli, Rosa Maria, et al, eds. The Languages of Joyce: Selected Papers from the 11th International James Joyce Symposium, Venice, 12-18 June 1988. LC 92-31117. xx, 277p. 1992. pap. 27.95 (*1-55619-474-9*) J Benjamins Pubng Co.

— The Languages of Joyce: Selected Papers from the 11th International James Joyce Symposium, Venice, 1988. LC 92-31117. xx, 277p. 1992. 74.00 (*1-55619-473-0*) J Benjamins Pubng Co.

Bosing, Walter. Bosch. (Illus.). 1994. pap. 9.99 (*3-8228-0563-7*) Taschen Amer.

— El Bosch. (SPA.). 1996. pap. 9.99 (*3-8228-0214-X*) Taschen Amer.

Bosisio, E., jt. ed. see Galli, G.

Bositis, David A. Black Elected Officials: A Statistical Summary, 1993-1997. 20p. 1998. pap. 10.00 (*0-7618-1319-5*) U Pr of Amer.

— Research Designs for Political Science: Contrivance & Demonstration in Theory & Practice. LC 89-38397. 184p. (C). 1990. text 31.95 (*0-8093-1600-5*) S Ill U Pr.

Bositis, David A., ed. Redistricting & Minority Representation: Learning from the Past, Preparing for the Future. LC 98-209636. (Joint Center for Political & Economic Studies). 224p. 1998. 45.00 (*0-7618-1194-X*); pap. 24.95 (*0-7618-1195-8*) U Pr of Amer.

Bositis, David A., jt. auth. see Baer, Denise L.

***Bosk, Beth.** The New Settler Interviews: Boogie on the Brink. LC 00-26896. (Illus.). 320p. 2000. pap. 22.95 (*1-890132-39-X*) Chelsea Green Pub.

Bosk, Beth & Thompson, Gary, eds. Mendocino Rust. (Illus.). 88p. (Orig.). 1981. pap. 9.99 (*0-9604100-0-7*) Albion Albums.

Bosk, Charles L. All God's Mistakes: Genetic Counseling in a Pediatric Hospital. LC 91-36938. 222p. 1992. 27.50 (*0-226-06681-9*) U Ch Pr.

— All God's Mistakes: Genetic Counseling in a Pediatric Hospital. 222p. 1995. pap. text 12.95 (*0-226-06682-7*) U Ch Pr.

— Forgive & Remember: Managing Medical Failure. LC 78-16596. 248p. 1981. pap. text 11.00 (*0-226-06680-0*) U Ch Pr.

Boske, Leigh. Economic Regulation of Western Coal Transportation: An Unnecessary Conflict Between National Energy & Transportation Policies. LC 80-82502. (Policy Research Project Report Ser.: No. 38). (Illus.). xiii, 405p. 1980. pap. 5.00 (*0-89940-638-6*) LBJ Sch Pub Aff.

Boske, Leigh & Hadden, Susan. Hazardous Materials Transportation in Texas. (Policy Research Project Report Ser.: No. 82). 176p. 1987. pap. 12.00 (*0-89940-686-6*) LBJ Sch Pub Aff.

An Asterisk (*) at the beginning of an entry indicates that the title is appearing for the first time.

B

An Asterisk (*) at the beginning of an entry indicates that the title is appearing for the first time.

Bosman, William. New & Accurate Description of the Coast of Guinea, 1705. 4th rev. ed. (Illus.). 577p. 1967. 65.00 (*0-7146-1793-8*, Pub. by F Cass Pubs) Intl Spec Bk.

Bosmans, Phil. Whispering Hope. 128p. (C). 1990. text 39.00 (*0-85439-328-5*, Pub. by St Paul Pubns) St Mut.

Bosnak, Robert. A Little Course in Dreams. 1998. pap. 10.00 (*1-57062-386-4*, Pub. by Shambhala Pubns) Random.

Bosnia, Nella. The Five Wives of Silverbeard: Adda, Francesca & Nella. 32p. 6.95 (*0-904613-60-7*) Writers & Readers.

Bosnia, Nella, jt. auth. see Turin, Adela.

Bosniak, Stephen. Principles & Practice of Ophthalmic Plastic & Reconstructive Surgery, 2 vols., Set. LC 95-12616. (Illus.). 1152p. 1995. text 375.00 (*0-7216-3559-8*, W B Saunders Co) Harcrt Hlth Sci Grp.

Bosniak, Stephen L. Cosmetic Blepharoplasty. 128p. 1990. text 125.00 (*0-88167-643-8*) Lppncott W & W.

Bosniak, Stephen L. & Smith, Byron C. Complex Socket Deformities. (Advances in Ophthalmic Plastic & Reconstructive Surgery Ser.: No. 9). (Illus.). 272p. 1991. 82.50 (*0-08-040293-3*, Pub. by PPI) McGraw.

Bosniak, Stephen L. & Zilkha, Marian. Cosmetic Blepharoplasty. 2nd ed. LC 98-7633. 189p. 1998. text 145.00 (*0-397-58469-5*) Lppncott W & W.

Bosnich, B., ed. Asymmetric Catalysis. 1985. text 140.50 (*90-247-3259-X*) Kluwer Academic.

Bosnich, Victor W. Congressional Voting Guide: A Ten Year Compilation. LC 94-94050. 621p. (Orig.). 1994. 39.95 (*0-9618958-5-3*) CVG Pr.

— Congressional Voting Guide: A Ten Year Compilation. 3rd ed. LC 87-91609. 624p. (Orig.). 1991. pap. 27.00 (*0-9618958-3-7*) CVG Pr.

Bosnick, Anthony J., ed. see Bevan, Carol S.

Bosnjak, Zeljko J., et al, eds. Advances in Pharmacology Vol. 31: Anesthesia & Cardiovascular Disease. (Illus.). 666p. 1994. text 104.00 (*0-12-032932-8*); pap. text 63.00 (*0-12-118860-4*) Acad Pr.

Bosoi, E. S., et al. Theory, Construction & Calculations of Agricultural Machines, Vol. 1. (Russian Translation Ser.: No. 66). 325p. (C). 1988. text 95.00 (*90-6191-914-2*, Pub. by A A Balkema) Ashgate Pub Co.

— Theory, Construction & Calculations of Agricultural Machines, Vol. I. (C). 1987. 36.00 (*81-7087-021-6*, Pub. by Oxford IBH) S Asia.

— Theory, Construction & Calculations of Agricultural Machines, Vol. 2. (Russian Translation Ser.: No. 83). (Illus.). 510p. (C). 1990. text 168.00 (*90-6191-999-1*, Pub. by A A Balkema) Ashgate Pub Co.

Bosolet, George. Executive Workout Travel Handbook. 2nd rev. ed. (Illus.). 30p. 1991. spiral bd. 12.98 (*0-9664359-0-7*) G Bosolet Ent.

Bosom, Monica, ed. The Ugly Duckling. (Illus.). 32p. (J). (ps-3). 1999. 8.95 (*0-7641-5149-5*) Barron.

Bosompem, Kwasi. Confessions of a Neglected African Daughter. 92p. 1996. pap. 8.00 (*0-9649351-0-4*) PRDC Pubng.

— Confessions of a Neglected African Daughter. rev. ed. (Illus.). 93p. 1997. mass mkt. 9.60 (*0-9649351-1-2*) PRDC Pubng.

— How to Write, Publish & Market Your Book While You Work from 9 to 5. 50p. 1998. pap. 5.60 (*0-9649351-2-0*) PRDC Pubng.

***Bosompem, Kwasi.** Let's Go Ghana: A Visitor's Guide to Business Opportunities, Networking & Tourism in Ghana. (Illus.). 96p. 2000. pap. 10.00 (*0-9649351-3-9*) PRDC Pubng.

Bosonetto, Gillian. Danger Island: A Story Tellers Collection. (Illus.). 42p. (J). (gr. 2-5). 1999. pap. 11.95 (*1-929078-15-3*) Gods Kids.

Bosoni, Giampiero, ed. see Nouvel, Jean.

Bosoni, Anthony J. Post-Release Assistance Programs for Prisoners: A National Directory. 2nd ed. LC 94-46308. 189p. 1995. pap. 34.50 (*0-7864-0025-0*) McFarland & Co.

Bosonnet, Margot, et al. Skyscraper Ted: And Other Zany Verse. (Illus.). 96p. (J). (gr. 3-6). 1995. pap. 6.95 (*0-86327-406-4*) Dufour.

Bosoppi, Ivana, jt. auth. see Mussato, Albertino.

***Bosq, D.** Linear Processes in Function Spaces: Theory & Applications. (Lecture Notes in Statistics Ser.: Vol. 149). 296p. 2000. pap. 59.95 (*0-387-95052-4*) Spr-Verlag.

Bosq, D. Nonparametric Statistics for Stochastic Processes: Estimation & Prediction. LC 96-13588. (Lecture Notes in Statistics Ser.: Vol. 110). 169p. 1996. pap. 43.95 (*0-387-94713-2*) Spr-Verlag.

Bosq, Denis. Nonparametric Statistics for Stochastic Processes: Estimation & Prediction. 2nd ed. Bickel, P. et al, eds. LC 98-28496. (Lecture Notes in Statistics Ser.: Vol. 110). 214p. 1998. pap. 34.95 (*0-387-98590-5*) Spr-Verlag.

Bosq, Denis & Nguyen, Hung T. A Course in Stochastic Processes: Stochastic Models & Statistical Inference. LC 96-18940. (Theory & Decision Library). 1996. text 175.00 (*0-7923-4087-6*, Kluwer Acad) Kluwer Academic.

Bosque, Elena & Watson, Sheila. Safe & Sound. rev. ed. LC 96-34318. (Illus.). 160p. 1997. pap. 10.95 (*0-312-15204-3*) St Martin.

Bosque, Gloria. Strange Meat: Poems, 1968-1974. LC 74-23345. 1974. 2.00 (*0-914134-03-5*) Konocti Bks.

Bosque, I. & Perez Fernandez, M. Diccionario Inverso de la Lengua Espanola. (SPA.). 716p. 1993. 125.00 (*84-249-1080-X*) Elliots Bks.

Bosquet, Alain. God's Torment: Poems by Alain Bosquet. Roditi, Edouard, tr. from FRE. LC 94-11452. 78p. 1994. text 22.00 (*0-8214-1091-1*) Ohio U Pr.

— Un Homme Pour un Autre. (FRE.). 306p. 1989. pap. 12.95 (*0-7859-2113-3*, 2070381188) Fr & Eur.

— Un Jour Apres la Vie, Maitre Objet. (FRE.). 1988. pap. 16.95 (*0-7859-2810-3*) Fr & Eur.

— Lettre a Mon Pere Qui Aurait Eu Cent Ans. (FRE.). 283p. 1990. pap. 11.95 (*0-7859-2154-0*, 2070383210) Fr & Eur.

— No Matter No Fact. Beckett, Samuel et al, trs. from FRE. LC 87-7910. 128p. 1988. 21.95 (*0-8112-1039-1*, Pub. by New Directions); pap. 9.95 (*0-8112-1040-5*, NDP646, Pub. by New Directions) Norton.

— Poemes I, 1945-1967: Les Testaments. (FRE.). 1985. pap. 16.95 (*0-7859-2796-4*) Fr & Eur.

— A Russian Mother. Bray, Barbara, tr. from FRE. (French Expressions Ser.). 284p. 1996. 26.00 (*0-8419-1329-3*) Holmes & Meier.

— Sonnets pour une Fin de Siecle. (FRE.). 1982. pap. 11.95 (*0-7859-2785-9*) Fr & Eur.

***Bosquet, Alain.** Stances Perdues/Lost Quatrains. 54p. 2000. pap. 13.95 (*1-901233-41-3*, Pub. by Dedalus) Dufour.

Bosquet, Alain & Little, Roger. No More Me & Other Poems. LC 96-102164. 160p. 1995. pap. 15.95 (*1-873790-80-5*) Dufour.

Bosquet, Michel. Capitalism in Crisis & Everyday Life. LC 76-41383. 199 P. ;p. 1977. write for info. (*0-391-00670-3*) Humanities.

Bosredon de Ransijat, Chevalier. The Seven Year Balance Sheet of the Sovereign, Military & Hospitaller Order of St. John of Jerusalem, of Rhodes & of Malta: From May 1st, 1778 to End of April 1785. Dingli-Attard-Inguanez, Marcel V., ed. (Illus.). 79p. (Orig.). 1984. pap. 10.00 (*0-9610740-2-7*) U Intel Data Bank.

Bosrock, Mary M. Put Your Best Foot Forward - Asia: A Fearless Guide to International Communication & Behavior. Wolkerstorfer, Terry, ed. LC 93-79394. (Put Your Best Foot Forward Ser.). (Illus.). 552p. (C). 1994. pap. 19.95 (*0-9637530-4-5*) Int Educ Systs.

— Put Your Best Foot Forward - Asia: A Fearless Guide to International Communication & Behavior. 2nd ed. LC 93-79394. (Put Your Best Foot Forward Ser.: Vol. 2). (Illus.). 572p. 1997. reprint ed. pap. 22.95 (*0-9637530-7-X*) Int Educ Systs.

— Put Your Best Foot Forward - Europe: A Fearless Guide to International Communication & Behavior. (Put Your Best Foot Forward Ser.). (Illus.). 504p. 1995. pap. 22.95 (*0-9637530-3-7*) Int Educ Systs.

— Put Your Best Foot Forward - Mexico-Canada: A Fearless Guide to Communication & Behavior - NAFTA. (Put Your Best Foot Forward Ser.: Bk. 3). (Illus.). (Orig.). 1995. pap. 14.95 (*0-9637530-5-3*) Int Educ Systs.

— Put Your Best Foot Forward - Russia: A Fearless Guide to International Communication & Behavior. (Put Your Best Foot Forward Ser.: Bk. 4). (Illus.). (Orig.). 1995. pap. 11.95 (*0-9637530-6-1*) Int Educ Systs.

— Put Your Best Foot Forward - South America: A Fearless Guide to International Communication & Behavior. LC 97-71673. (Put Your Best Foot Forward Ser.: Vol. 5). (Illus.). 400p. (Orig.). 1997. pap. 22.95 (*0-9637530-8-8*) Int Educ Systs.

Boss. Medizinisches Woerterbuch. 36th ed. (GER.). 864p. 1994. 49.95 (*0-7859-7443-1*, 3541159464) Fr & Eur.

Boss, Alan. Looking for Earths: The Race to Find New Solar Systems. LC 97-49033. 256p. 1998. 27.95 (*0-471-18421-7*) Wiley.

***Boss, Alan.** Looking for Earths: The Race to Find New Solar Systems. 256p. 2000. pap. 16.95 (*0-471-37911-5*) Wiley.

***Boss, Angela, et al.** Living with P. C. O. S. Polycystic Ovarian Syndrome. 165p. 2000. pap. 14.95 (*1-886039-49-6*, Pub. by Addicus Bks) LPC Group.

Boss, Florence H. & Kendrick, Ruth A. Vacation Cooking: Good Food! Good Fun! 80p. 1991. pap. 6.98 (*0-88290-349-7*) Horizon Utah.

Boss, Gary. Department of Energy: Uncertain Progress in Implementing National Laboratory Reforms. (Illus.). 65p. (C). 1999. text 20.00 (*0-7881-7916-0*) DIANE Pub.

— Nuclear Regulation: Preventing Problem Plants Requires More Effective NRC Action. (Illus.). 77p. (C). 1998. pap. text 20.00 (*0-7881-4131-7*) DIANE Pub.

Boss, Helen. Theories of Surplus & Transfer: Parasites & Producers in Economic Thought. 300p. 1989. 55.00 (*0-04-330371-4*) Routledge.

— Theories of Surplus & Transfer: Parasites & Producers in Economic Thought. LC 89-9122. 300p. (C). 1989. pap. 29.95 (*0-04-330372-2*) Routledge.

BOSS Inc. Staff. Using Oracle Applications. LC 99-63998. (Special Edition Using... Que Ser.). 944p. 2000. 75.00 (*0-7897-1280-6*) Que.

Boss, Jake & Ziesman, Kevin. Dare to Hit .400. LC 98-88848. (Art & Science of Coaching Ser.). 95p. 1999. 14.95 (*1-57167-362-8*) Sagamore Pub.

***Boss, Judith A.** Analyzing Moral Issues. LC 98-39192. 752p. 1998. pap. text 44.95 (*0-7674-0161-1*) Mayfield Pub.

Boss, Judith A. Ethics for Life: An Interdisciplinary & Multicultural Introduction. LC 97-25256. x, 454p. 1997. pap. text 33.95 (*1-55934-575-6*, 1575) Mayfield Pub.

— Ethics for Life: Perspectives on Ethics. 2001. pap. text. write for info. (*0-7674-0100-X*) Mayfield Pub.

— Perspectives on Ethics. LC 97-41495. xxiv, 504p. 1997. pap. text 38.00 (*1-55934-970-0*, 1970) Mayfield Pub.

Boss, Ken, jt. auth. see Wiseman, Nigel A.

Boss, Kittie. Cat Tails. (Books for Young Learners). (Illus.). 8p. (J). (gr. k-2). 1999. pap. text 5.00 (*1-57274-139-2*) R Owen Pubs.

***Boss, Kittie.** Rabos de Gato. Romo, Alberto, tr. (Books for Young Learners).Tr. of Cat Tails. (SPA., Illus.). 8p. (J). (gr. k-2). 1999. pap. text 5.00 (*1-57274-345-X*, A2893) R Owen Pubs.

***Boss, Laura.** Arms: New & Selected Poems. (Essential Poets Ser.: Vol. 96). 84p. 1999. pap. 10.00 (*1-55071-095-8*, Pub. by Guernica Editions) Paul & Co Pubs.

Boss, Laura. On the Edge of the Hudson. Esapova, Ana, tr.Tr. of Na Bregovite na Xadson. (ENG & MAC.). 96p. 1989. 15.00 (*0-89304-064-9*); pap. 7.50 (*86-373-0302-1*) Cross-Cultrl NY.

— On the Edge of the Hudson. Barkan, Stanley H., ed. (Review Women Writers Chapbook Ser.: No. 4).Tr. of Na Bregovite na Xadson. 48p. 1989. reprint ed. audio 10.00 (*0-89304-419-9*) Cross-Cultrl NY.

— On the Edge of the Hudson. Barkan, Stanley H., ed. (Review Women Writers Chapbook Ser.: No. 4).Tr. of Na Bregovite na Xadson. 48p. 1989. reprint ed. 15.00 (*0-89304-417-2*); reprint ed. 15.00 (*0-89304-415-6*, CCC163); reprint ed. pap. 5.00 (*0-89304-416-4*); reprint ed. pap. 5.00 (*0-89304-418-0*); reprint ed. boxed set 50.00 (*0-89304-909-3*); reprint ed. boxed set 25.00 (*0-89304-908-5*) Cross-Cultrl NY.

— Stripping. LC 82-4192. (Illus.). 52p. (Orig.). 1982. pap. 5.00 (*0-941608-01-8*) Chantry Pr.

— Stripping Sulla Sponda dell'Hudson: English & Italian Poetry. Scammacca, Nina & Scammacca, Nat, trs.Tr. of Stripping on the Edge of the Hudson. (ITA.). 1988. 15.00 (*0-89304-523-3*); pap. 7.50 (*0-89304-522-5*) Cross-Cultrl NY.

Boss, Laura & Gillan, Maria, eds. The New Jersey Poetry Resource Book. 3rd ed. 1996. pap. text 5.00 (*0-9621495-0-0*) Poetry Ctr PCCC.

Boss, Laura & Gillan, Maria M., eds. Media Directory for Metropolitan North Jersey. 1996. pap. text 5.00 (*0-9621495-3-5*) Poetry Ctr PCCC.

— Passaic County Arts Guide. 1994. pap. text 5.00 (*0-9621465-4-4*) Poetry Ctr PCCC.

Boss, Laura, jt. ed. see Barkan, Stanley H.

Boss, Laura, ed. see Gillan, Maria M.

Boss, Michael, jt. ed. see Westarp, Karl-Heinz.

Boss, P., et al, eds. Sourcebook of Family Theories & Methods: A Contextual Approach. (Illus.). 772p. (C). 1993. 114.00 (*0-306-44264-7*, Plenum Trade) Perseus Pubng.

Boss, Pauline. Ambiguous Loss: Learning to Live with Unresolved Grief. LC 98-50585. 192p. 1999. 22.00 (*0-674-01738-2*) HUP.

***Boss, Pauline.** Ambiguous Loss: Learning to Live with Unresolved Grief. 176p. 2000. pap. 14.00 (*0-674-00381-0*) HUP.

Boss, Pauline. Family Stress Management. (Family Studies Text Ser.: Vol. 8). 150p. (C). 1988. text 42.00 (*0-8039-2380-5*); pap. text 18.95 (*0-8039-2381-3*) Sage.

Boss, Peter, et al, eds. Profile of Young Australians: Facts, Figures & Issues. LC 94-49559. 1995. text 55.00 (*0-443-05257-3*) Church.

Boss, R. Wayne. Organizational Development in Health Care. (Organization Development Ser.). (Illus.). 150p. (C). 1989. pap. text 26.95 (*0-201-18364-1*) Addison-Wesley.

Boss, R. Wayne, ed. Organization Development in Health Care Settings: A Special Issue of Consultation: An International Journal. 76p. 1988. pap. 12.95 (*0-89885-425-3*, Kluwer Acad Hman Sci) Kluwer Academic.

Boss, Richard W. Information Technologies & Space Planning for Libraries & Information Centers. (Professional Librarian Ser.). 120p. 1987. 40.00 (*0-8161-1859-0*, Hall Reference); 30.00 (*0-8161-1870-1*) Macmillan.

— The Library Administrator's Automation Handbook. LC 96-52791. 226p. 1997. 39.50 (*1-57387-038-2*) Info Today Inc.

— The Library Manager's Guide to Automation. 3rd ed. (Professional Librarian Ser.). 1990. 45.00 (*0-8161-1942-2*, Hall Reference) Macmillan.

— Telecommunications for Library Management. LC 84-26140. (Professional Librarian Ser.). 184p. 1985. 45.00 (*0-86729-126-5*, Hall Reference) Macmillan.

***Boss, Sarah.** Empress & Handmaid: Nature & Gender in the Cult of the Virgin Mary. 2000. 57.95 (*0-304-33926-1*) Continuum.

— Empress & Handmaid: Nature & Gender in the Cult of the Virgin Mary. (Illus.). 253p. 2000. pap. 24.95 (*0-304-70781-3*) Continuum.

— Mary's Story. (Illus.). 48p. (J). (ps up). 1999. 16.95 (*1-901223-44-2*) Barefoot Bks NY.

Boss, Shirley, ed. see Pagano, Carmen F. P.

***Boss, Thomas G., et al.** New Perspectives on F. Holland Day. (Illus.). 1998. 20.00 (*0-9660964-1-X*) Stonehill Coll.

Boss, Valentin. Milton & the Rise of Russian Satanism. 254p. 1991. text 60.00 (*0-8020-5795-0*) U of Toronto Pr.

— Newton & Russia: The Early Influence, 1698-1796. LC 73-188352. (Russian Research Center Studies: No. 69). 367p. reprint ed. pap. 113.80 (*0-7837-2225-7*, 205731500004) Bks Demand.

Boss, W. Gary. The Secrets of Sex Appeal from Head to Heel. (Illus.). 68p. (Orig.). 1989. pap. 18.00 (*0-9623763-0-2*) Boss Enterprises.

— Successful Man-Hunting: How to Find Him, Attract Him, Hold Him. (Illus.). 52p. (Orig.). 1991. pap. 18.00 (*0-9623763-1-0*) Boss Enterprises.

Bossa, Barry. Brown Scapular of Mt. Carmel. 50p. 1987. 2.50 (*0-911988-67-X*, 51313) AMI Pr.

Bossaert, Leo & European Resuscitation Council Staff. European Resuscitation Council Guidelines for Resuscitation. LC 98-22179. 1998. 72.00 (*0-444-82957-1*) Elsevier.

Bossard, Andre. Law Enforcement in Europe: Building Effective Cooperation. LC 93-6574. 100p. 1993. pap. 7.95 (*0-942511-63-8*) OICJ.

Bossard, Andre. Transnational Crime & Criminal Law. 100p. 1990. pap. 7.95 (*0-942511-33-6*) OICJ.

***Bossard, Carla C., et al, eds.** Invasive Plants of California's Wildlands. (Illus.). 360p. 2000. 60.00 (*0-520-22546-5*, Pub. by U CA Pr); pap. 29.95 (*0-520-22547-3*, Pub. by U CA Pr) Cal Prin Full Svc.

Bossard, James H. Children in a Depression Decade. LC 74-1667. (Children & Youth Ser.). 302p. 1974. reprint ed. 26.95 (*0-405-05948-5*) Ayer.

Bossard, James H. & Boll, Eleanor S. The Large Family System. LC 74-25536. 325p. 1975. reprint ed. lib. bdg. 38.50 (*0-8371-7871-1*, BOLF, Greenwood Pr) Greenwood.

— Ritual in Family Living. LC 75-45454. 228p. 1976. reprint ed. lib. bdg. 35.00 (*0-8371-8678-1*, BORF, Greenwood Pr) Greenwood.

Bossard, James H. & Boll, Eleanor S., eds. Adolescents in Wartime. LC 74-1668. (Children & Youth Ser.). 180p. 1974. reprint ed. 20.95 (*0-405-05947-7*) Ayer.

Bossard, James H. & Dewhurst, J. Frederic. University Education for Business. LC 73-1993. (Big Business; Economic Power in a Free Society Ser.). 1973. reprint ed. 40.95 (*0-405-05076-3*) Ayer.

Bossard, Marcus. Eighty-One Years of Living. (American Autobiography Ser.). 77p. 1995. reprint ed. lib. bdg. 69.00 (*0-7812-8461-9*) Rprt Serv.

Bossart, H. & Perret, C., eds. Lactate in Acute Conditions: Proceedings of the International Symposium, Basel, March, 1978. (Illus.). 1979. 77.50 (*3-8055-2968-6*) S Karger.

Bossart, Johann J. Christian Georg Andreas Oldendorp, 2 vols. (GER.). 1130p. 1995. reprint ed. write for info. (*3-487-10009-6*) G Olms Pubs.

Bossavit, Alain. Computational Electromagnetism. LC 97-41012. (Electromagnetism Ser.). (Illus.). 352p. 1997. text 99.00 (*0-12-118710-1*) Morgan Kaufmann.

Bossche, G. Van Den, see Borceux, F. & Van Den Bossche, G.

Bossche, H. Vanden, et al, eds. Aspergillus & Aspergillosis. LC 88-4132. (Illus.). 342p. 1988. 85.00 (*0-306-42828-8*, Plenum Trade) Perseus Pubng.

Bossche, Hugo V., et al, eds. Host-Fungus Interplay: Proceedings of the 5th Symposium on Topics in Mycology. LC 97-65223. (Illus.). 331p. 1997. text 40.00 (*0-9614520-2-1*) NFID.

Bossche, J. P. & Bernacsek, G. M. Source Book for the Inland Fishery Resources of Africa, No. 18. (Commission for Inland Fisheries of Africa Technical Papers: No. 3). 252p. 1991. pap. 30.00 (*92-5-103073-1*, F0731, Pub. by FAO) Bernan Associates.

Bosscher, Brian. Face It! In-Your-Face Devotions for Teens. LC 98-21257. 85p. 1998. pap. 7.95 (*1-56212-353-X*) CRC Pubns.

Bosscher, D., et al, eds. American Mass Culture in the Netherlands. LC 97-102952. (European Contributions to American Studies: Vol. 30). 250p. 1995. pap. 30.00 (*90-5383-305-6*, Pub. by VU Univ Pr) Paul & Co Pubs.

— Cultural Transmissions & Receptions: American Culture in Europe. (European Contributions to American Studies: No. 25). 350p. (Orig.). 1993. pap. 42.50 (*90-5383-207-6*, Pub. by VU Univ Pr) Paul & Co Pubs.

Bosschere, Jean de & Morris, M. C. Christmas Tales of Flanders. (Illus.). (J). (gr. 4-8). 1990. 12.50 (*0-8446-4516-8*) Peter Smith.

Bosse, Abraham. Maniere Universelle de Monsieur Desargues. (FRE., Illus.). 520p. (C). 1998. reprint ed. pap. 240.00 (*1-85297-027-8*, Pub. by Archival Facs) St Mut.

— Sentimen's Svr la Distinction des Diverses Manieres de Peinture . . . fac. ed. (Documents of Art & Architectural History Ser.: Series II, Vol. 5). (FRE., Illus.). 142p. 1981. lib. bdg. 30.00 (*0-89371-205-1*) Broude Intl Edns.

Bosse, David. Civil War Newspaper Maps: A Historical Atlas. LC 92-33942. (Illus.). 160p. (C). 1993. 36.00 (*0-8018-4553-X*) Johns Hopkins.

Bosse, David, compiled by. Civil War Newspaper Maps: A Cartobibliography of the Northern Daily Press, 5. LC 92-43100. (Bibliographies & Indexes in Military Studies: No. 5). 288p. 1993. lib. bdg. 82.95 (*0-313-28705-8*, GR8705, Greenwood Pr) Greenwood.

Bosse, Hennig Von, see Von Bosse, Hennig.

Bosse, John G. van, see Van Bosse, John G.

Bosse, Malcolm. Deep Dream of the Rain Forest. LC 92-55095. 192p. (J). 1993. 15.00 (*0-374-31757-7*) FS&G.

— Deep Dream of the Rain Forest. 192p. (YA). (gr. 4-7). 1994. pap. text 5.95 (*0-374-41702-4*) FS&G.

— Deep Dream of the Rain Forest. large type ed. LC 93-42093. (J). 1994. pap. 15.95 (*0-7862-0145-2*) Thorndike Pr.

— The Examination. LC 94-50955. 320p. (J). (gr. 7 up). 1994. 17.00 (*0-374-32234-1*) FS&G.

— The Examination. LC 93-50955. 304p. (YA). (gr. 7 up). 1996. pap. 7.95 (*0-374-42223-0*) FS&G.

— Ordinary Magic. LC 93-7956. Orig. Title: Ganesh. 192p. (J). 1993. pap. 5.95 (*0-374-42517-5*) FS&G.

— Ordinary Magic. Orig. Title: Ganesh. 1994. 17.75 (*0-8446-6774-9*) Peter Smith.

— Tusk & Stone. LC 95-23448. 244p. (YA). (gr. 5 up). 1995. 15.95 (*1-886910-01-4*) Front Str.

Bosse, Malcolm. Tusk & Stone. (J). 1996. 10.09 (*0-606-12017-3*, Pub. by Turtleback) Demco.

Bosse, Malcolm J. Examination. 1996. 13.05 (*0-606-10804-1*, Pub. by Turtleback) Demco.

— Ganesh. LC 80-2453. 192p. (YA). (gr. 7 up). 1981. lib. bdg. 11.89 (*0-690-04103-9*) HarpC Child Bks.

— The Seventy-Nine Squares. LC 79-7591. (YA). (gr. 7 up). 1979. lib. bdg. 11.89 (*0-690-04000-8*) HarpC Child Bks.

Bossel, Hartmut. Earth at a Crossroads: Paths to a Sustainable Future. LC 97-41738. (Illus.). 352p. (C). 1998. pap. 19.95 (*0-521-63995-6*); text 59.95 (*0-521-63005-3*) Cambridge U Pr.

— Low-Cost Windmill for Developing Nations. 45p. 1970. pap. 9.50 (*0-86619-035-X*) Vols Tech Asst.

— Modeling & Simulation. LC 94-1847. (Illus.). 504p. (C). 1994. text 65.00 incl. disk (*1-56881-033-4*) AK Peters.

Bosselaar, Laure-Anne. The Hour Between Dog & Wolf. LC 96-86385. (New Poets of America Ser.: Vol. 18). 80p. 1997. 12.50 (*1-880238-47-0*) BOA Edns.

Bosselaar, Laure-Anne, ed. Outsiders: Poems about Rebels, Exiles, & Renegades. LC 98-32217. 282p. 1999. pap. 16.95 (*1-57131-409-1*) Milkweed Ed.

***Bosselaar, Laure-Anne, ed.** Urban Nature: Poems about Wildlife in the City. LC 99-49399. 272p. 2000. pap. 16.95 (*1-57131-410-5*) Milkweed Ed.

Bosselaar, Laure-Anne, jt. ed. see Brown, Kurt.

Bosselaers, Antoon & Preneel, Bart, eds. Integrity Primitives for Secure Information Systems: Final RIPE Report of RACE Integrity Primitives Evaluation. LC 95-47443. (Lecture Notes in Computer Science Ser.: No. 1007). 239p. 1995. 43.00 (*3-540-60640-8*) Spr-Verlag.

Bosselman, Fred P., et al. Managing Tourism Growth: Issues & Applications. LC 99-10999. (Illus.). 420p. 1999. pap. 40.00 (*1-55963-605-X*) Island Pr.

— The Permit Explosion: Coordination of the Proliferation. LC 76-55844. (Management & Control of Growth Ser.). 96p. reprint ed. pap. 30.00 (*0-8357-8266-2*, 203394700087) Bks Demand.

Bosselman, Robert H., jt. auth. see Barrows, Clayton W.

***Bosselmann, Klaus.** When Two Worlds Collide: Society & Ecology. 363p. 1999. pap. 22.00 (*0-9597948-3-2*, Pub. by RSVP Pub Co) Intl Spec Bk.

***Bosselmann, Klaus & Richardson, Benjamin J., eds.** Environmental Justice & Market Mechanisms: Key Challenges for Environmental Laws & Policy. (International Environmental Law & Policy Ser.: Vol. 54). 320p. 1999. 120.00 (*90-411-9727-3*) Kluwer Law Intl.

Bosselmann, Peter. Representation of Places: Reality & Realism in City Design. LC 97-81. 232p. 1997. 35.00 (*0-520-20658-4*, Pub. by U CA Pr) Cal Prin Full Svc.

Bossen, Howard. Henry Holmes Smith, Man of Light. LC 83-9208. (Studies in Photography: No. 1). 203p. reprint ed. pap. 63.00 (*0-8357-1459-4*, 207043100089) Bks Demand.

Bossen, Laurel H. The Redivision of Labor: Women & Economic Choice in Four Guatemalan Communities. LC 83-426. (SUNY Series in the Anthropology of Work). (Illus.). 396p. (C). 1984. text 59.50 (*0-87395-740-7*); pap. text 19.95 (*0-87395-741-5*) State U NY Pr.

Bossenbrook, William J., ed. Mid-Twentieth Century Nationalism. LC 65-11610. (Franklin Memorial Lectures Ser.: No. 13). 125p. reprint ed. pap. 38.80 (*0-7837-3806-4*, 204362600010) Bks Demand.

Bossenga, Gail. The Politics of Privilege: Old Regime & Revolution in Lille. 285p. (C). 1991. text 59.95 (*0-521-39282-9*) Cambridge U Pr.

Bosser, Philippe. Misericordes. 1984. 29.95 (*0-7859-8157-8*, 2-86853-000-1) Fr & Eur.

Bosser, Thomas. Learning in Man-Computer Interaction. (Research Reports ESPRIT, Project 385, HUFIT: Vol. 1). xi, 218p. 1987. 29.00 (*0-387-18391-4*) Spr-Verlag.

Bosser, Thomas, jt. auth. see McFarland, David J.

Bosserman, Phillip, tr. see Gurvitch, Georges.

Bosserman, Tony. LovaBULL Stories & Adventures, Vol. 1. LC 96-97175. (Illus.). 92p. (Orig.). (J). (gr. 4-6). 1997. 18.95 (*0-9654673-0-9*) Cncord Pr.

***Bossert.** Channel Coding for Telecommunications. LC 99-32323. 512p. 1999. 130.00 (*0-471-98277-6*) Wiley.

Bossert. Quality Function Deployment: The Practitioner's Approach. (Quality & Reliability Ser.: Vol. 21). (Illus.). 152p. 1990. text 45.00 (*0-8247-8378-6*) Dekker.

Bossert, Helmuth, ed. Treasury of Historic Folk Ornament in Full Color. LC 96-4257. (Illus.). 64p. 1996. pap. 16.95 (*0-486-29094-8*) Dover.

Bossert, James L. Quality Function Deployment: A Practitioner's Approach. 127p. 1990. 34.00 (*0-87389-089-2*, H0607) ASQ Qual Pr.

Bossert, James L., ed. Supplier Management Handbook. LC 93-41960. 364p. 1994. 50.00 (*0-87389-284-4*, H0840) ASQ Qual Pr.

Bossert, Jill. Illustration Techniques. (Illus.). 160p. 1996. pap. text 35.00 (*0-8230-6549-9*) Watsn-Guptill.

— Kid's Books: A Guide to Professional Techniques. (Pro-Illustration Ser.). (Illus.). 160p. 1998. pap. 37.50 (*2-88046-335-1*, Rotovision) Watsn-Guptill.

Bossert, Jill, ed. see Klein, Larry.

Bossert, Karen W., jt. auth. see Demchak, MaryAnn.

Bossert, P. J., ed. Phenomenological Perspectives: Historical & Systematic Essays in Honor of Herbert Spiegelberg. (Phaenomenologica Ser.: No. 62). 290p. 1975. lib. bdg. 126.50 (*90-247-1701-9*, Pub. by M Nijhoff) Kluwer Academic.

Bossert, P. J., tr. see Husserl, Edmund.

Bossert, William H., jt. auth. see Wilson, Edward O.

Bosseur, Jean-Yves. Sound in the Visual Arts. (Illus.). 160p. (Orig.). 1992. pap. 24.95 (*2-906571-26-1*, Pub. by Editions Dis Voir) Dist Art Pubs.

Bossewell, John. Workes of Armorie, 3 bks. LC 72-173. (English Experience Ser.: No. 145). 1969. reprint ed. 50.00 (*90-221-0145-2*) Walter J Johnson.

Bosshard, Andreas, contrib. by. Renaturierung Artenreicher Wiesen Auf Naehrstoffreichen Boeden Ein Beitrag zur Optimierung der Oekologischen Aufwertung der Kulturlandschaft und Zum Verstaendnis Mesischer Wiesenoekosysteme. (Dissertationes Botanicae Ser.: Band 303). (GER., Illus.). 202p. 1999. pap. 55.00 (*3-443-64215-2*) E Schweizerbartsche.

Bosshard, B. Holzkunde: Mikroskopie und Makroskopie des Holzes, Vol. 1. 225p. 1980. 74.00 (*0-8176-1328-5*) Birkhauser.

Bosshard-Nepustil, Erich. Rezeptionen von Jesaia 1-39 Im Zwolfprophetenbuch: Untersuchungen Zur Literarischen Verbindung Von Prophetenbuchern in Babylonischer und Persischer Zeit. (Orbis Biblicus et Orientalis Ser.: No. 154). (GER.). 533p. 1997. text 98.00 (*3-7278-1123-4*, 154, Pub. by Presses Univ Fribourg) Eisenbrauns.

Bosshardt, Alexa, jt. auth. see Rovenger, Holli.

Bosshardt, Christoph. Beitrage zu Transformationsprozessen und Strukturanpassungsprogrammen. 1997. 34.95 (*3-906764-16-8*, Pub. by P Lang) P Lang Pubng.

— Problembereiche interdisziplinarer Forschung, 29. 1999. 46.95 (*3-906763-29-3*, Pub. by P Lang) P Lang Pubng.

***Bossi, Annalisa.** Logic-Based Program Synthesis & Transformation: Selected Papers of the 9th International Workshop, LOPSTR '99, Venice, Italy, September 1999. International Workshop on Logic Program Synthesis & Transformation Staff, ed. LC 00-41921. (Lecture Notes in Computer Science). 2000. pap. write for info. (*3-540-67628-7*) Spr-Verlag.

Bossi, E., ed. Praktische Neonatologie. (Paediatrische Fortbildungskurse fuer die Praxis Ser.: Vol. 57). (Illus.). xii, 208p. 1983. pap. 85.25 (*3-8055-3657-7*) S Karger.

Bossi, Lisa Burnett, jt. auth. see Goshine, Andrea Alban.

Bossi, Richard & Cintron, Gilberto. Manglares del Gran Caribe: Hacia un Manejo Sostenible. Gonzalez, Jose, tr. from ENG. (SPA., Illus.). 48p. (Orig.). 1991. pap. write for info. (*1-879358-02-6*) Panos Inst.

— Les Mangroves de la Caraibe: Pour une Gestion Durable. Kamara, Fota, tr. from ENG. (FRE., Illus.). 48p. (Orig.). 1991. pap. write for info. (*1-879358-03-4*) Panos Inst.

— Mangroves of the Wider Caribbean: Toward Sustainable Management. (Illus.). 52p. (Orig.). 1990. pap. write for info. (*1-879358-00-X*) Panos Inst.

Bossi, Richard H. & Moran, Tom, eds. Nondestructive Evaluation for Process Control in Manufacturing, Vol. 2948. 310p. 1996. 85.00 (*0-8194-2352-1*) SPIE.

Bossi, Richard H. & Pepper, David M., eds. Process Control & Sensors for Manufacturing, Vol. 3399. 258p. 1998. 69.00 (*0-8194-2848-5*) SPIE.

***Bossie, David N. & Brown, Floyd G.** Prince Albert: The Life & Lies of Al Gore. 192p. 2000. 9.95 (*0-936783-28-1*, Pub. by Merril Pr) Midpt Trade.

Bossiere, Olivier. New Museums. (Illus.). 160p. 24.95 (*2-7450-0036-5*) Telleri Edit.

Bossis, Gabrielle. He & I. 392p. 1988. pap. 9.00 (*2-89039-807-2*, SP0270) Pauline Bks.

Bossler, Beverly J. Powerful Relations: Kinship, Status, & the State in Sung China (960-1279) LC 97-27130. (Harvard-Yenching Institute Monograph Ser.). 370p. 1998. 45.00 (*0-674-69592-5*) HUP.

Bossler, C. T. B&O Color Guide to Freight & Passenger Equipment. (Illus.). 1996. 49.95 (*1-878887-58-0*) Morning NJ.

— CNJ-LV Color Guide to Freight & Passenger Equipment. (Illus.). 128p. 1995. 49.95 (*1-878887-38-6*) Morning NJ.

— RDG Color Guide to Freight & Passenger Equipment. (Illus.). 128p. 1994. 49.95 (*1-878887-29-7*) Morning NJ.

Bossler, John D., jt. auth. see Moffitt, Francis H.

Bossler, R. B., jt. auth. see Hardersen, C. P.

Bossley, Michele M. Breathing Not Required. 84p. (J). (gr. 3-8). 1995. bds. 16.95 (*1-55028-475-4*) Formac Dist Ltd.

Bossley, Michele Martin, see Martin Bossley, Michele.

Bosso, Christopher J. American Government. (C). Date not set. pap. text. write for info. (*0-395-65949-3*); pap. text, teacher ed. 11.96 (*0-395-65950-7*) HM.

— Pesticides & Politics: The Life Cycle of a Public Issue. LC 86-19245. (Series in Policy & Institutional Studies). (Illus.). 312p. 1987. reprint ed. text 49.95 (*0-8229-3547-3*) U of Pittsburgh Pr.

— Pesticides & Politics: The Life Cycle of a Public Issue. LC 86-19245. (Series in Policy & Institutional Studies). (Illus.). 312p. 1988. reprint ed. pap. 16.95 (*0-8229-5418-4*) U of Pittsburgh Pr.

Bosso, Christopher J., et al. American Government. LC 99-54177. 464p. 1999. pap. 29.95 (*0-8133-6871-5*) Westview.

Bossom, Diane. Serge Art: Wearable Art for the Creative Serger. LC 98-86783. (Illus.). 144p. 1999. pap. 21.95 (*0-87341-705-4*, SAWA) Krause Pubns.

Bossom, Michael. Encaustic Art: How to Paint with Wax. 1997. pap. 16.95 (*0-85532-826-6*, Pub. by Srch Pr) A Schwartz & Co.

Bossomaier, T., et al, eds. The Transputer in Australasia: Proceedings of the Third Australian Transputer & Occam User Group Conference, Sydney, Australia, June 28-29, 1990. (Transputer & Occam Engineering Ser.). 170p. (YA). (gr. 12). 1990. pap. 60.00 (*90-5199-034-0*, Pub. by IOS Pr) IOS Press.

Bossomaier, T., jt. ed. see Green, D.

***Bossomaier, Terry & Green, David.** Patterns in the Sand: Computers, Complexity & Everyday Life. 224p. 1999. pap. text 13.00 (*0-7382-0172-3*, Pub. by Perseus Pubng) HarpC.

Bossomaier, Terry R., jt. ed. see Green, David G.

Bosson, James E. Treasury of Aphoristic Jewels: The Subhasitaratnanidhi of Sa Skya Pandita in Tibetan & Mongolian. (Uralic & Altaic Ser.: Vol. 92). 1969. pap. text. write for info. (*0-87750-080-0*) Mongolia.

Bosson, Jo-Ellen. Wild & Free: The Story of a Black-Footed Ferret. (Smithsonian Wild Heritage Collection). 1992. 10.15 (*0-606-08383-9*, Pub. by Turtleback) Demco.

Bossonnault, William G., jt. auth. see Goodman, Catherine C.

Bossu, Jean-Bernard. New Travels in North America, 1770-1772. Dickinson, Samuel D., ed. LC 82-81335. 163p. 1982. 17.50 (*0-917898-07-9*) NSU Pr LA.

***Bossuet, Jacques.** Bossuet: "Politics Drawn from the Very Words of Holy Scripture" Riley, Patrick, ed. (Cambridge Texts in the History of Political Thought Ser.). 495p. (C). 1999. pap. text 27.95 (*0-521-36807-3*) Cambridge U Pr.

Bossuet, Jacques B. Discourse on Universal History. Ranum, Orest, ed. Forster, Elborg, tr. LC 75-9062. (Classic European Historians Ser.). 422p. Date not set. reprint ed. pap. 130.90 (*0-608-20601-6*, 205456600003) Bks Demand.

— History of the Variations of the Protestant Churches, 2 vols., Set. LC 83-45603. reprint ed. 75.00 (*0-404-19872-4*) AMS Pr.

Bossuet, Jacques-Benigne. Oeuvres. deluxe ed. Velat & Champaailler, eds. (FRE.). 1612p. 1971. 110.00 (*0-7859-4643-8*) Fr & Eur.

— Oraison Funebres. (Class. Hatier Ser.). pap. 6.95 (*0-685-34206-9*, F35542) Fr & Eur.

— Oraisons Funebres. 461p. 1961. 19.95 (*0-8288-7470-0*) Fr & Eur.

Bossuet, Jacques-Benigne, et al, eds. Relations sur le Quietisme. (Pleiade Ser.). 1936. write for info. Schoenhof.

— Sermons. 1936. write for info. Fr & Eur.

— Sermons. (Pleiade Ser.). 1936. write for info. Schoenhof.

Bossuyt, X. Regulation of Hepatic Microsomal UDP-Glucuronosyltransferases & Nucleotide Sugar. No. 78. 161p. (Orig.). 1994. pap. 39.50 (*90-6186-601-4*, Pub. by Leuven Univ) Coronet Bks.

Bossuyt, A. & Deconinck, F. Amplitude-Phase Patterns in Dynamic Scintigraphic Imaging. (Developments in Nuclear Medicine Ser.). 1984. text 141.50 (*0-89838-641-1*) Kluwer Academic.

Bossuyt, Ignace, ed. Jean de Castro Vol. 3: Opera Omnia - Madrigals, Chansons & Motets. (Illus.). 188p. (Orig.). 1995. pap. 87.50 (*90-6186-695-2*, Pub. by Leuven Univ) Coronet Bks.

Bossuyt, Marc & Griffiths, J. Human Rights in Surinam: Report of a Mission (Feb.-March, 1983) LC JC0599.S75. 16p. reprint ed. pap. 30.00 (*0-608-16890-4*, 202777400056) Bks Demand.

Bossuyt, Marc J. Guide to the "Travaux Preparatoires" of the International Covenant on Civil & Political Rights. LC 86-27604. 1987. lib. bdg. 376.50 (*90-247-3467-3*) Kluwer Academic.

Bossuyt, P. A Comparison of Probabilistic Unfolding Theories for Paired Comparisons Data. (Recent Research in Psychology Ser.). xi, 186p. 1990. pap. 28.00 (*0-387-52491-6*) Spr-Verlag.

Bossy, John. Christianity in the West, 400-1700. (Opus Ser.). 200p. 1985. pap. text 17.95 (*0-19-289162-6*) OUP.

Bossy, John. Giordano Bruno & the Embassy Affair. (Illus.). 352p. (C). 1992. 42.00 (*0-300-04993-5*) Yale U Pr.

— Peace in the Post-Reformation: The Birkbeck Lectures, 1995. LC 98-24990. 120p. (C). 1998. text 49.95 (*0-521-64061-X*); pap. text 14.95 (*0-521-64605-7*) Cambridge U Pr.

Bossy, Michel-Andre, et al, eds. Artists, Writers & Musicians. (Lives & Legacies Ser.: Vol. 4). (Illus.). 256p. 2000. boxed set 69.95 (*1-57356-154-1*) Oryx Pr.

***Bost, J. B., et al, eds.** Courbes Semi-Stables et Groupe Fondamental en Geometrie Algebrique. (Progress In Mathematics Ser.: Vol. 187). (Illus.). 304p. 2000. 69.95 (*3-7643-6308-8*, Pub. by Birkhauser) Spr-Verlag.

Bost, Jacques-Laurent. Le Dernier Des Metiers. (FRE.). 247p. 1977. pap. 10.95 (*0-7859-1850-7*, 2070369242) Fr & Eur.

***Bost, John.** Estate Planning & Taxation: 2000 Annual Edition. 11th ed. 1096p. (C). 1999. per. 63.95 (*0-7872-6377-X*) Kendall-Hunt.

Bost, John. Experiencing Biology: A Laboratory Manual. 4th ed. 266p. (C). 1998. spiral bd., lab manual ed. 29.95 (*0-7872-5362-6*, 41536201) Kendall-Hunt.

Bost, John. Instructor's Manual to Accompany Estate Planning & Taxation: 2000 Annual Edition. 11th ed. 312p. (C). pap. text. write for info. (*0-7872-6501-2*) Kendall-Hunt.

Bost, M. With Passport. 160p. 1998. 12.95 (*1-57641-021-8*) Hudson Pk.

Bost, Rosann, ed. see Friday, Paul J.

***Bost, Toby.** My North Carolina Garden: A Gardener's Journal. (Illus.). 2000. spiral bd. 19.95 (*1-930604-04-1*) Cool Springs Pr.

Bost, Toby. North Carolina Gardener's Guide: The What, Where, When, How & Why of Gardening in North Carolina. LC 97-181166. (Illus.). 400p. (Orig.). 1997. pap. 19.95 (*1-888608-09-9*) Cool Springs Pr.

Bosta, Diana, jt. auth. see Allen, Bud.

Bostanbakhsh, Shapur, jt. auth. see Windfuhr, Gernot L.

Bostaph, Charles, jt. auth. see Moore, Marti.

***Bostaph, Charles P. & Vendeland, Roland B.** The Employment Portfolio: Identifying Skills, Training, Accomplishments & References for the Job. LC 99-19736. (Illus.). 200p. 1999. pap. text 31.60 (*0-13-956699-6*) P-H.

Bostdorff, Denise M. The Presidency & the Rhetoric of Foreign Crisis. LC 93-21561. 315p. 1993. text 34.95 (*0-87249-968-5*) U of SC Pr.

Boster, Frank, ed. Progress in Communication Sciences Vol. 13: Advances in Persuasion. 262p. 1997. pap. 39.50 (*1-56750-360-8*) Ablx Pub.

Boster, Franklin J., jt. ed. see Barnett, George.

Boster, Gregory, ed. see Padgett, James E.

Bostert, Russell H. Newhall & Williams College: Selected Papers of a History Teacher at New England College, 1917-1973. XIII, 403p. 1989. text 25.00 (*0-8204-0542-6*) P Lang Pubng.

Bostetter, Edward E. Romantic Ventriloquists: Wordsworth, Coleridge, Keats, Shelley, Byron. rev. ed. LC 63-10795. 372p. 1975. reprint ed. pap. 10.00 (*0-295-95318-7*) U of Wash Pr.

Bosticco, Isabel L. Personal Letters for Business People. 290p. 1986. text 61.95 (*0-566-02593-0*) Ashgate Pub Co.

Bosticco, Mary. Instant Business Letters. 2nd ed. 184p. 1986. text 61.95 (*0-566-02592-2*, Pub. by Gower) Ashgate Pub Co.

Bostick, Curtis V. The Antichrist & the Lollards: Apocalypticism in Late Medieval & Reformation England. LC 98-18999. (Studies in Medieval & Reformation Thought: Vol. 70). 228p. 1998. 76.50 (*90-04-11088-7*) Brill Academic Pubs.

Bostick, Emily, et al. The Wireless Primer: A Basic Description of MMDS Television Systems. (Illus.). 76p. (Orig.). 1995. pap. 29.95 (*1-888552-02-6*) Elect Pr.

Bostick, Glyn, et al. CATV 'Trapping' Security Filtering for Pay Television. LC 97-60597. (Illus.). 186p. 1997. pap. 39.95 (*1-888552-07-7*, B-020) Elect Pr.

Bostick, William A. Back to the Second Basic R--'Ritin' A Manual for Adults & Children to Learn the Beautiful & Legible Handwriting of the Italian Renaissance. 2nd rev. ed. (Illus.). 24p. 1998. pap. 10.95 (*0-9606630-3-7*) La Stampa Calligrafica.

Bostitis, David A. The Congressional Black Caucus in the One Hundred Third Congress. 180p. (C). 1994. pap. text 25.00 (*0-8191-9561-8*); lib. bdg. 57.50 (*0-8191-9560-X*) U Pr of Amer.

Bostle, Eileen, jt. ed. see Clarke, Jean M.

Bostley, Edward. Musical Development for the Classroom Teacher. 4th ed. 246p. (C). spiral bd. 47.95 (*0-7872-6683-3*) Kendall-Hunt.

Bostley, Edward. Teaching the Recorder in the Elementary Classroom. 2nd ed. LC 98-147450. 162p. (C). 1997. spiral bd. 33.95 (*0-7872-4181-4*) Kendall-Hunt.

Bostley, Edward. Teaching the Recorder in the Elementary Classroom. 3rd ed. 170p. (C). spiral bd. write for info. (*0-7872-6765-1*) Kendall-Hunt.

Bostley, Edward J. Musical Development for the Classroom Teacher. 368p. (C). 1994. pap. text, spiral bd. 37.95 (*0-8403-9522-1*) Kendall-Hunt.

— Musical Development for the Classroom Teacher. 3rd ed. 240p. (C). 1997. spiral bd. 38.95 (*0-7872-4386-8*) Kendall-Hunt.

— A Recorder Method Textbook. 260p. (C). 1994. pap. text, spiral bd. 32.95 (*0-8403-9685-6*) Kendall-Hunt.

Bostock, jt. auth. see Wallace.

Bostock, Anna, tr. see Lukacs, Georg.

Bostock, David. Intermediate Logic. LC 97-11503. (Illus.). 402p. 1997. pap. text 24.00 (*0-19-875142-7*) OUP.

— Intermediate Logic. LC 97-11503. (Illus.). 402p. (C). 1997. text 75.00 (*0-19-875141-9*) OUP.

— Plato's Phaedo. 236p. (C). 1986. pap. text 32.00 (*0-19-824918-7*) OUP.

Bostock, David, tr. & comment see Aristotle.

Bostock, E. H. Menageries, Circuses & Theatres. LC 72-80140. (Illus.). 315p. 1972. reprint ed. 24.95 (*0-405-08290-8*, Pub. by Blom Pubns) Ayer.

Bostock, Frances & Jones, Geoffrey. Planning & Power in Iran: Ebtehaj & Economic Development under the Shah. (Illus.). 238p. 1989. text 47.50 (*0-7146-3338-0*, Pub. by F Cass Pubs) Intl Spec Bk.

Bostock, Geoff. FPGAs & Programmable LSI: A Designer's Handbook. (Illus.). 240p. 1996. pap. text 56.95 (*0-7506-2883-9*) Buttrwrth-Heinemann.

— Programmable Logic Handbook. 2nd ed. LC 92-27737. (EDN Ser.). (Illus.). 256p. 1993. pap. text 66.95 (*0-7506-0808-0*) Buttrwrth-Heinemann.

Bostock, H., et al, eds. The Neurobiology of Disease: Contributions from Neuroscience to Clinical Neurology. LC 95-33564. (Illus.). 462p. (C). 1996. text 125.00 (*0-521-45132-9*) Cambridge U Pr.

Bostock, J. Knight. A Handbook on Old High German Literature. 2nd ed. King, K. C. & McLintock, D. R., eds. (Illus.). 360p. 1976. text 69.00 (*0-19-815392-9*) OUP.

Bostock, L. & Chandler, S. Applied Mathematics 1. 576p. 1994. pap. 37.50 (*0-85950-019-5*, Pub. by S Thornes Pubs) Trans-Atl Phila.

— Core Maths for A-Level. 2nd ed. 880p. 1994. pap. 47.50 (*0-7487-1779-X*, Pub. by S Thornes Pubs) Trans-Atl Phila.

***Bostock, L. & Chandler, S.** Core Maths for Advanced Level. 3rd ed. (Illus.). 720p. (YA). 2000. pap. 49.50 (*0-7487-5509-8*, Pub. by S Thornes Pubs) Trans-Atl Phila.

Bostock, L. & Chandler, S. Further Mechanics & Probability. 480p. (C). 1994. pap. 32.50 (*0-85950-142-6*, Pub. by S Thornes Pubs) Trans-Atl Phila.

— Mathematics - Mechanics & Probability. 672p. (C). 1994. pap. 39.00 (*0-85950-141-8*, Pub. by S Thornes Pubs) Trans-Atl Phila.

— Modular Mathematics, Module C, Statistics 1. 352p. 1994. pap. 39.00 (*0-7855-2690-0*) St Mut.

— Modular Mathematics: Module A, Pure Maths 1, Module A, Pure Maths! 2nd ed. 448p. 1994. pap. 39.00 (*0-7487-1777-3*, Pub. by S Thornes Pubs) Trans-Atl Phila.

— Modular Mathematics: Module B, Pure Maths 2, Module B, Pure Maths 2. 2nd ed. 480p. 1994. pap. 32.50 (*0-7487-1775-7*, Pub. by S Thornes Pubs) Trans-Atl Phila.

— Modular Mathematics: Module D, Statistics 2, Module D, Statistics 2. 1995. pap. 32.50 (*0-7487-1773-0*, Pub. by S Thornes Pubs) Trans-Atl Phila.

— Modular Mathematics: Module E, Mechabics 1, Module E, Mechanics 1. (Module E, Mechanics 1 ser.). 352p. 1994. pap. 32.50 (*0-7487-1502-9*, Pub. by S Thornes Pubs) Trans-Atl Phila.

— Modular Mathematics: Module F, Mechanics 2, Module F, Mechanics 2. 1995. pap. 32.50 (*0-7487-1774-9*, Pub. by S Thornes Pubs) Trans-Atl Phila.

Bostock, L. & Chandler, S. Pure Mathematics 1. 768p. 1994. pap. 38.50 (*0-85950-092-6*, Pub. by S Thornes Pubs) Trans-Atl Phila.

Bostock, L. & Chandler, S. Pure Mathematics 2. 656p. 1994. pap. 39.00 (*0-85950-097-7*) St Mut.

B

Bostock, L. & Chandler, S., eds. Applied Mathematics 2. 392p. 1994. pap. 37.50 (*0-85950-024-1*, Pub. by S Thornes Pubs) Trans-Atl Phila.

Bostock, L., et al. Further Pure Mathematics. 752p. (C). 1994. pap. 47.50 (*0-85950-103-5*, Pub. by S Thornes Pubs) Trans-Atl Phila.

— STP National Curriculum: Mathematics 11A. 464p. 1998. pap. 36.00 (*0-7487-3192-X*) St Mut.

Bostock, Louise. Speaking in Public. 1994. pap. 10.00 (*0-00-470264-6*) Collins.

***Bostock, Paddy.** The Cricket. 333p. 1999. pap. 19.95 (*0-7541-0571-7*, Pub. by Minerva Pr) Unity Dist.

Bostock, Simant, jt. auth. see James, David.

Bostock, Stephen J. & Seifert, Roger V., eds. Microcomputers in Adult Education. 176p. 1986. 37.50 (*0-7099-3944-2*, Pub. by C Helm) Routldge.

Bostock-Wood, C. Trees in Society in Rural Karnataka, India. (Illus.). 223p. 1993. pap. 60.00 (*0-902500-47-3*, Pub. by Nat Res Inst) St Mut.

Boston. C'Est a Vous. 1988. pap. text 12.13 (*0-582-35526-5*, 78047); audio 23.00 (*0-582-35570-2*, 78046) Longman.

Boston Area Music Libraries Staff. The Boston Composers Project: A Bibliography of Contemporary Music. 795p. 1983. 70.00 (*0-262-02198-6*) MIT Pr.

Boston Athenaeum Staff. Catalog of the Library of the Boston Athenaeum. 1994. 210.00 (*0-7838-2231-6*, G K Hall & Co) Mac Lib Ref.

B

***Boston Based Adaptation Research in Nursing Society Staff.** Roy Adaptation Model-Based Research: 25 Years of Contributions to Nursing Science. (Monographs). (Illus.). 371p. 1999. pap. text 39.95 (*0-9656391-8-5*, 1086) Sigma Theta Tau.

Boston, Bernard. History of the Three Hundred Ninety-Eighth Infantry Regiment in World War II. (Combat Arms Ser.: No. 7). (Illus.). 208p. 1982. reprint ed. 34.95 (*0-89839-063-X*) Battery Pr.

Boston, Bruce. Accursed Wives. (Illus.). 28p. (Orig.). 1994. pap. 3.50 (*0-9626708-7-1*) Talisman IN.

— Cold Tomorrows, No. 4. (Gothic Chapbook Ser.). (Illus.). 50p. 1998. pap. 6.00 (*0-913045-07-1*) Gothic Pr.

— Conditions of Sentient Life. (Gothic Chapbook Ser.: No. 2). (Illus.). 48p. 1996. pap. 6.00 (*0-913045-05-5*) Gothic Pr.

— Confessions of a Body Thief. 8p. 1998. pap. 5.00 (*0-938075-75-6*) Ocean View Bks.

— Dark Tales & Light. 68p. 1998. pap. 6.95 (*1-888993-15-4*) Dark Regions.

— Hypertales & Metafictions. (Booklet Ser.: No. 34). (Illus.). 64p. (Orig.). 1990. pap. 4.00 (*0-936055-45-6*) C Drumm Bks.

— Hypertales & Metafictions. deluxe ed. (Booklet Ser.: No. 34). (Illus.). 64p. (Orig.). 1990. pap. 7.00 (*0-936055-46-4*) C Drumm Bks.

***Boston, Bruce.** In the Darkened Hours: Eleven Award Winning Poems of Science Fiction, Fantasy. limited ed. 2000. write for info. (*0-9676666-1-9*) Miniature Sun Pr.

Boston, Bruce. Jackbird. 88p. (Orig.). 1976. pap. 9.95 (*0-917658-05-1*) BPW & P.

***Boston, Bruce.** The Lesions of Genetic Sin. limited ed. (Illus.). 1999. 4.00 (*0-9676666-0-0*) Miniature Sun Pr.

Boston, Bruce. The New Bruce Boston Omnibus, 5 bks., Set. 210p. 1991. boxed set 39.95 (*0-938075-20-9*) Ocean View Bks.

— Sensuous Debris: Selected Poems, 1970-1995. deluxe limited ed. (Illus.). 96p. 1996. 59.95 (*0-938075-63-2*) Ocean View Bks.

— Sensuous Debris: Selected Poems, 1979-1995. (Illus.). 96p. 1995. 40.00 (*0-9626708-8-X*) Talisman IN.

— She Comes When You're Leaving. 64p. (Orig.). 1982. pap. 9.95 (*0-917658-14-0*) BPW & P.

— Short Circuits. (Illus.). 88p. 1990. 39.95 (*0-938075-15-2*); pap. 11.95 (*0-938075-16-0*) Ocean View Bks.

— Skin Trades. (Booklet Ser.: No. 31). 64p. 1988. pap. text 3.50 (*0-936055-39-1*) C Drumm Bks.

— Specula: Selected Uncollected Poems, 1968-1993. 64p. (Orig.). 1993. pap. 6.95 (*0-9626708-5-5*) Talisman IN.

— Stained Glass Rain: A Novel of the Sixties. LC 93-5326. 460p. 1993. pap. 16.95 (*0-938075-30-6*) Ocean View Bks.

— Stained Glass Rain: A Novel of the Sixties. deluxe limited ed. LC 93-5326. 460p. 1993. 59.95 (*0-938075-29-2*) Ocean View Bks.

Boston, Bruce, ed. see Crawford, Gary W.

Boston, Bruce O. The American High School: Time for Reform. 33p. (C). 1982. pap. 3.00 (*0-317-20289-8*) Coun Basic Educ.

— Education Policy & the Education for all Handicapped Children Act (P.L. 94-142) (Policy Paper: No. 3). 88p. 1977. 4.00 (*0-318-03025-X*) Inst Educ Lead.

Boston, Bruce O., jt. auth. see Mahlmann, John J.

Boston, Bruce O., ed. see Music Educators National Conference Staff.

Boston, Carol A. The Pennypincher's Guide to Landscaping. LC 84-17775. 192p. 1984. 17.95 (*0-13-655937-9*, Busn); pap. 7.95 (*0-13-655929-8*, Busn) P-H.

Boston Children Museum Staff. Great Explorations. LC 97-27502. 1997. per. 12.00 (*0-671-52857-2*, PB Trade Paper) PB.

Boston Childrens' Hospital Staff. The New Child Health. 768p. 1987. pap. 23.95 (*0-440-50646-8*, Dell Trade Pbks) Dell.

Boston Children's Museum Staff. Antique Fashion Paper Dolls of the 1890s in Full Color. 81st ed. (Paper Dolls Ser.). 32p. 1984. pap. 4.95 (*0-486-24622-1*) Dover.

Boston City Council Staff. Memorial of Crispus Attucks, Samuel Maverick, James Caldwell, Samuel Gray & Patrick Carr, from the City of Boston. LC 71-79022. (Black Heritage Library Collection). 1977. 13.95 (*0-8369-8515-X*) Ayer.

Boston College Museum of Art Staff. America's Eye: Irish Paintings from the Collection of Brian P. Burns. Dalsimer, Adele & Kreilkamp, Vera, eds. (Illus.). 144p. (Orig.). (C). 1996. pap. text 29.95 (*0-9640153-4-X*) McMullen Mus Art.

— Memory & the Middle Ages. Netzer, Nancy & Reinburg, Virginia, eds. LC 94-74254. (Illus.). 106p. (Orig.). (C). 1995. pap. text 19.95 (*0-9640153-2-3*) McMullen Mus Art.

— Protection, Power & Display: Shields of Island Southeast Asia & Melanesia. Tavarelli, Andrew, ed. & intro. by. LC 95-79803. (Illus.). 108p. (Orig.). (C). 1995. pap. text 12.95 (*0-9640153-3-1*) McMullen Mus Art.

Boston Committee to Consider the Police Situation, jt. auth. see Boston Police Department Annual Report Staff.

Boston Computer Society Staff, compiled by. Things the Manual Never Told You: Tips, Techniques, & Shortcuts from the Nation's Largest User Group. write for info. (*0-318-59575-3*) Addison-Wesley.

***Boston Consulting Group Staff.** Breaking Compromises: Opportunities for Action in Consumer Markets from the Boston Consulting Group. 176p. 2000. text 29.95 (*0-471-38433-X*) Wiley.

Boston Consulting Group Staff. Perspectives on Experience. LC 72-180882. 109p. reprint ed. pap. 33.80 (*0-7837-0000-8*, AU0003900059) Bks Demand.

Boston, David. Wonder Tales from Around the World. (American Storytelling Ser.). 160p. (J). 1995. pap. 16.95 (*0-87483-422-8*) August Hse.

Boston, Gerald W. Environmental & Toxic Torts Cases, Materials & Problems, Teacher's Manual to Accompany Law Of. Madden, M. Stuart, ed. (American Casebook Ser.). 710p. 1994. pap. text, teacher ed. write for info. (*0-314-04087-0*) West Pub.

— Punitive Damages in Tort Law, 1 vol. LC 92-76065. 1993. ring bd. 135.00 (*0-685-68854-2*) West Group.

Boston, Gerald W. & Madden, M. Stuart. Law of Environmental & Toxic Torts: Cases, Materials & Problems. LC 93-42310. (American Casebook Ser.). 681p. (C). 1994. 57.50 (*0-314-03354-8*) West Pub.

***Boston, Graham.** Astrology: A Beginner's Guide. (Headway Guides for Beginners Ser.). (Illus.). 96p. 2000. pap. 11.95 (*0-340-77485-1*, Pub. by Headway) Trafalgar.

Boston, Graham. Astrology: A Beginner's Guide. (Beginner's Guide Ser.). (Illus.). 96p. 1998. pap. 11.95 (*0-340-72080-8*, Pub. by Hodder & Stought Ltd) Trafalgar.

Boston, Gypsy D. Hurry Before the Magic Ends. LC 89-83523. (Illus.). 115p. 1989. pap. 8.95 (*0-944419-21-6*) Everett Inc.

— The Rainbow Fairies. (Illus.). (J). 1991. pap. 4.95 (*0-9631503-1-6*) Gypsy Damaris.

Boston, Henry. Forsaken Fountain: The Need to Review International Drug Laws in the Light of the Christian Faith. 52p. (Orig.). 1998. pap. 7.00 (*0-9627423-9-2*, FF) Candlestick.

***Boston, James.** DTV Survival Guide. (Engineering Handbook Ser.). 480p. 2000. 65.00 (*0-07-135061-6*) McGraw.

Boston, Jane. Breaking the Silence Vol. 1: The Art of Hearing God's Voice. 180p. 1997. pap. 19.95 (*0-9659870-0-0*) Motivations.

Boston, Jenny. A Touch of Love. large type ed. 1995. 27.99 (*0-7089-3401-3*) Ulverscroft.

Boston, John. Wish Coupons for Kids: The Book of Yes. (Illus.). 128p. 1994. mass mkt. 3.50 (*0-380-77294-9*, Avon Bks) Morrow Avon.

Boston, John & Manville, Daniel E. Prisoners' Self-Help Litigation Manual. 3rd ed. LC 95-17299. 1088p. 1995. pap. text 32.95 (*0-379-21212-9*) Oceana.

Boston, Jonathan & Holland, Martin, eds. The Fourth Labour Government: Politics & Policy in New Zealand. 2nd ed. (Illus.). 304p. 1990. pap. text 32.50 (*0-19-558213-6*) OUP.

***Boston, Jonathan & Victoria University of Wellington. Institute of Policy Studies.** Governing under Proportional Representation: Lessons from Europe. LC 99-229683. 1998. 29.00 (*0-908935-34-X*) Vict U Well IPS.

Boston, Jonathan, et al. A New Politics? Continuity & Change under MMP. LC 96-173925. 200p. 1996. pap. 24.95 (*1-86940-138-7*, Pub. by Auckland Univ) Paul & Co Pubs.

— Public Management: The New Zealand Model. LC 97-189281. 416p. 1996. pap. text 65.00 (*0-19-558325-6*) OUP.

— Redesigning the Welfare State in New Zealand: Problems, Policies, Prospects. LC 99-220443. (Illus.). 336p. 1999. pap. text 39.95 (*0-19-558373-6*) OUP.

***Boston, Jordanna.** Autumn's Eve. large type ed. LC 00-28621. 312p. 2000. write for info. (*0-7862-2582-3*) Thorndike Pr.

Boston, Kelvin & Kimbro, Dennis. Smart Money Moves for African-Americans. 336p. 1997. pap. 12.00 (*0-399-52262-X*, Perigee Bks) Berkley Pub.

Boston, L. M. Children of Green Knowe. (Voyager/HBJ Bks.). (J). 1977. 11.10 (*0-606-01092-0*, Pub. by Turtleback) Demco.

— The Enemy at Green Knowe. (Voyager/HBJ Bks.). 1979. 9.05 (*0-606-01590-6*, Pub. by Turtleback) Demco.

— River at Green Knowe. 1959. 9.05 (*0-606-02244-9*, Pub. by Turtleback) Demco.

Boston Language Institute Staff, tr. see Tracqui, Valerie.

Boston, Les, ed. see Wei, Wu.

Boston Lesbian Psychologies Collective, ed. Lesbian Psychologies: Explorations & Challenges. LC 86-30736. 384p. (C). 1987. 16.95 (*0-252-01404-9*); text 34.95 (*0-252-01403-0*) U of Ill Pr.

Boston, Linda M. Huff & Puff & Me. 2nd ed. (J). 1988. 15.00 (*0-941549-09-7*) Creative Hlth.

***Boston, Lloyd.** Men of Color: Fashion, History, & Fundamentals. (Illus.). 256p. 2000. pap. 25.00 (*1-57965-167-4*, 85167) Artisan.

Boston, Lloyd. Men of Color: Fashion, History, Fundamentals. LC 98-22189. (Illus.). 256p. 1998. 35.00 (*1-57965-112-7*, 85112) Artisan.

Boston, Lucy. The Children of Green Knowe. LC 77-4506. (Illus.). 157p. (J). (gr. 4-7). 1989. pap. 3.95 (*0-15-217151-7*, Odyssey) Harcourt.

— The Treasure of Green Knowe. LC 89-2074. (Illus.). 224p. (J). (gr. 4-7). 1989. pap. 3.95 (*0-15-289982-0*, Odyssey) Harcourt.

Boston, Lucy M. The Chimneys of Green Knowe. large type ed. (Illus.). 272p. (J). (gr. 3 up). 1990. 18.95 (*0-7451-1175-0*, G K Hall Lrg Type) Mac Lib Ref.

— River at Green Knowe. LC 89-2071. 176p. (J). (gr. 4-7). 1989. pap. 3.95 (*0-15-267450-0*, Odyssey) Harcourt.

— Sea Egg. LC 67-10200. (Illus.). (J). (gr. 2-6). 1967. 8.95 (*0-15-271050-7*, Harcourt Child Bks) Harcourt.

— A Stranger at Green Knowe. LC 78-71150. (Illus.). 208p. (J). (gr. 5-9). 1989. pap. 6.00 (*0-15-281755-7*, Odyssey) Harcourt.

— A Stranger at Green Knowe. (Voyager/HBJ Bks.). 1979. 11.10 (*0-606-01621-X*, Pub. by Turtleback) Demco.

Boston, Mary & Szur, Rolene, eds. Psychotherapy with Severely Deprived Children. 176p. 1983. pap. 11.95 (*0-7100-9536-8*, Routledge Thoemms) Routledge.

Boston, Mary & Szur, Rolene, eds. Psychotherapy with Severely Deprived Children. 168p. 1990. reprint ed. pap. text 26.50 (*0-946439-97-4*, Pub. by H Karnac Bks Ltd) Other Pr LLC.

Boston, Mary, jt. ed. see Daws, Dilys.

Boston Media, Inc. Staff. The Smart Business Guide for African-Americans. 1998. pap. write for info. (*0-399-52380-4*, Perigee Bks) Berkley Pub.

Boston Medical Commission. The Sanitary Condition of Boston: The Report of a Medical Commission. Rosenkrantz, Barbara G., ed. LC 76-25655. (Public Health in America Ser.). 1977. reprint ed. lib. bdg. 19.95 (*0-405-09808-1*) Ayer.

Boston Mills Press Staff. Oak Ridges Moraine. LC 98-111728. 1997. 28.00 (*1-55046-191-5*, Pub. by Boston Mills) Genl Dist Srvs.

Boston Museum of Fine Arts Staff. Bulletin of the Boston Museum of Fine Arts 1903-1942, 8 Vols. LC 71-119596. (Illus.). 1971. reprint ed. 44.00 (*0-685-73166-9*); reprint ed. 49.50 (*0-685-03214-0*) Ayer.

— Bulletin of the Boston Museum of Fine Arts 1903-1942, 8 vols., Set. LC 71-119596. (Illus.). 1971. reprint ed. 441.00 (*0-405-01242-X*) Ayer.

— Leslie Lindsey Mason Collection. (Music Book Index Ser.). 503p. 1992. reprint ed. lib. bdg. 99.00 (*0-685-59992-2*) Rprt Serv.

Boston Museum of Fine Arts Staff, ed. Albrecht Durer: Master Printmaker. LC 87-80023. 1988. reprint ed. lib. bdg. 75.00 (*0-87817-316-1*) Hacker.

Boston, P. & Thompson. Impossible Life. pap. 23.95 (*1-58542-008-5*, Tarcher Putnam) Putnam Pub Group.

Boston Parents' Paper Staff. The Boston Children's Yellow Pages: A Resource Book for Parents & Children. 1988. pap. 8.95 (*0-201-11534-4*) Addison-Wesley.

Boston Parents' Paper Staff, compiled by. Children's Yellow Pages: A Resource Book for Parents & Children, 1987 Boston Edition. pap. 7.95 (*0-201-11165-9*) Addison-Wesley.

***Boston, Penelope J., ed.** The Case for Mars V. (Science & Technology Ser.: Vol. 97). 564p. 2000. 80.00 (*0-87703-459-1*, Am Astronaut Soc); pap. 55.00 (*0-87703-460-5*, Am Astronaut Soc) Univelt Inc.

Boston Police Department Annual Report Staff & Boston Committee to Consider the Police Situation. The Boston Police Strike: Two Reports. 1975. 19.95 (*0-405-03362-1*, 16924) Ayer.

Boston Public Library Staff. Canadian Manuscripts in the Boston Public Library: A Descriptive Catalog. 1971. 80.00 (*0-8161-0930-3*, G K Hall & Co) Mac Lib Ref.

— Catalog of the Defoe Collection in the Boston Public Library. 1994. 175.00 (*0-7838-2317-7*, G K Hall & Co) Mac Lib Ref.

— Dictionary Catalog of the Music Collection. 1975. 2265.00 (*0-8161-1514-1*, G K Hall & Co) Mac Lib Ref.

— Young Adult Catalog of the Boston Public Library. 1994. 255.00 (*0-7838-2283-9*, G K Hall & Co) Mac Lib Ref.

Boston Public Schools Staff. New Directions at Madison Park Technical-Vocational High School. 492p. 1993. 30.00 (*0-614-22227-3*) Ctr Law & Ed.

Boston Publishing Company Editors & Doleman, E., eds. Tools of War: Technology in Vietnam, 1965-1973. (Illus.). 192p. 1985. 16.30 (*0-201-11269-8*) Addison-Wesley.

Boston Publishing Company Editors, et al. A Contagion of War the Way the War Was Fought, 1965-1967. (Vietnam Experience Ser.). 192p. 1983. 16.30 (*0-201-15858-2*) Addison-Wesley.

— Pawns of War. (Vietnam Experience Ser.). (Illus.). 192p. 1987. 16.30 (*0-201-11678-2*) Addison-Wesley.

Boston Publishing Company Editors, ed. see Casey, Michael, et al.

Boston Publishing Company Editors, ed. see Dougan, Clark.

Boston Publishing Company Editors, ed. see Dougan, Clark, et al.

Boston Publishing Company Editors, ed. see Doyle, Edward G. & Lipsman, Samuel L.

Boston Publishing Company Editors, ed. see Morrocco, John.

Boston Publishing Company Editors, ed. see Weiss, Stephen & Doyle, Edward G.

Boston, Ray, jt. auth. see Linton, David.

Boston Reed Co. Staff. Clinical Medical Asst Training Prog Wrkbk. (MEDICAL ASSISTING). (C). 1998. pap., wbk. ed. 16.00 (*0-7668-0933-1*) Delmar.

Boston Registry Department Staff. Records Relating to the Early History of Boston, 39 vols. LC 74-19611. reprint ed. write for info. (*0-404-12343-0*) AMS Pr.

Boston, Richard. Boudu Saved from Drowning. LC 95-166788. (BFI Film Classics Ser.). 83 p. 1994. pap. 10.95 (*0-85170-467-0*, Pub. by Ind U Pr) Ind U Pr.

***Boston, Robert.** Close Encounters with the Religious Right: Journeys into the Twilight Zone of Religion & Politics. LC 99-58537. 280p. 2000. pap. 19.95 (*1-57392-797-X*) Prometheus Bks.

Boston, Robert. The Most Dangerous Man in America? Pat Robertson & the Rise of the Christian Coalition. LC 96-4169. 248p. 1996. pap. text 17.95 (*1-57392-053-3*) Prometheus Bks.

— Why the Religious Right Is Wrong: About the Separation of Church & State. LC 93-31403. 257p. (C). 1993. pap. 17.95 (*0-87975-834-1*) Prometheus Bks.

Boston, Robert E. How to Write & Use Performance Objectives to Individualize Instruction, 4 vols. 376p. 1972. pap. 49.95 (*0-87778-040-4*) Educ Tech Pubns.

Boston, Sarah. Too Deep for Tears. 1994. pap. 13.00 (*0-04-440891-9*, Pub. by Rivers Oram) NYU Pr.

Boston Staff. Short Narrative of the Horrid Massacre in Boston: Perpetrated in the Evening of the Fifth Day of March, Seventeen Seventy, by Soldiers of the Twenty Ninth Regiment. LC 71-150170. (Select Bibliographies Reprint Ser.). 1977. reprint ed. 23.95 (*0-8369-5683-4*) Ayer.

***Boston Symphony Orchestra Staff.** Cooking with Music: Celebrating the Tastes & Traditions of the Boston Symphony Orchestra. (Illus.). 332p. 1999. 29.95 (*0-9671148-0-2*, Pub. by Boston Symphony) Wimmer Bks.

Boston Systems Group, Inc. Staff, et al. The dBASE Systems Development Handbook. 900p. 1988. pap. 39.95 (*0-685-25567-0*) P-H.

Boston, Thomas. The Art of Man Fishing. 128p. Date not set. 4.99 (*1-85792-106-2*) Christian Focus.

— How to Profit from Our Afflictions. Crenshaw, Curtis I., tr. 1992. pap. 9.95 (*1-877818-07-0*) Footstool Pubns.

— John Calvin's Sermons on Galations. 671p. 1997. reprint ed. 46.99 (*0-85151-699-8*) Banner of Truth.

— Memoirs of Thomas Boston. 576p. 1988. reprint ed. 27.99 (*0-85151-528-2*) Banner of Truth.

Boston, Thomas D. Affirmative Action & Black Entrepreneurship. LC 99-183108. 128p. 1998. 25.00 (*0-415-09594-8*) Routledge.

— Affirmative Action & Black Entrepreneurship. 224p. (C). 1998. pap. 24.99 (*0-415-12713-0*) Routledge.

— Race, Class & Conservatism. LC 88-982. (Illus.). 192p. (C). 1988. pap. 24.99 (*0-04-330369-2*) Routledge.

— Race, Class & Conservatism. 1988. 34.95 (*0-04-330368-4*) Routledge.

Boston, Thomas D., ed. A Different Vision: Africa American Economic Thought. LC 96-6999. 336p. (C). 1996. 100.00 (*0-415-09590-5*); pap. 29.99 (*0-415-12715-7*) Routledge.

— Different Vision: Race & Public Policy, Vol. 2. 464p. (C). 1996. 100.00 (*0-415-09591-3*); pap. 29.99 (*0-415-12716-5*) Routledge.

Boston, Thomas D. & Ross, Catherine L. The Inner City: Urban Poverty & Economic Development in the Next Century. LC 96-50096. 357p. 1997. pap. text 24.95 (*1-56000-980-2*) Transaction Pubs.

Boston University Institute for Employment Policy., jt. auth. see Marine Law Institute, Staff.

Boston University, Institute of Jewish Law Staff. The Jewish Law Annual, Vol. 8. viii, 300p. 1989. text 102.00 (*3-7186-0504-X*) Gordon & Breach.

Boston University Libraries Staff. Index to the Classed Catalog of the Boston University Libraries, 2 vols, Set. 3rd rev. ed. 1187p. 1972. 230.00 (*0-8161-1029-8*, G K Hall & Co) Mac Lib Ref.

Boston University Staff. Microcosmos: A Curriculum Guide to Exploring Microbial Space. 480p. 1995. boxed set 36.95 (*0-8403-8386-X*) Kendall-Hunt.

Boston Women's Health Book Collective Staff. Our Bodies, Ourselves for the New Century: A Book for & by Women. rev. ed. LC 98-12725. (Illus.). 784p. 1998. per. 24.00 (*0-684-84231-9*, Touchstone) S&S Trade Pap.

***Boston Women's Health Collective Staff.** Nuestros Cuerpos, Nuestras Vidas: Our Bodies, Ourselves.Tr. of Our Bodies, Ourselves. (SPA.). 704p. 2000. pap. 24.00 (*1-58322-024-0*) Seven Stories.

Boston Women's Health Staff. Our Bodies, Ourselves. 1998. 34.00 (*0-8446-6981-4*) Peter Smith.

Boston's Children's Hospital Staff, et al. Parent's Guide to Nutrition. 1987. pap. write for info. (*0-318-61793-5*) Addison-Wesley.

Bostridge, Ian. Witchcraft & Its Transformations, c. 1650-c. 1750. LC 97-164756. (Oxford Historical Monographs). (Illus.). 288p. (C). 1997. text 75.00 (*0-19-820653-4*) OUP.

Bostridge, Mark, jt. auth. see Berry, Paul.

Bostrom, Carl O., frwd. The First Forty Years: A Pictorial Account of the Johns Hopkins Applied Physics Laboratory since Its Founding in 1942. (Illus.). 191p. 1993. 10.00 (*0-912025-00-X*); pap. 5.00 (*0-912025-01-8*) JHU Applied Physics.

Bostrom, Christopher J. Philosophy of Religion. 1962. 69.50 (*0-685-69791-6*) Elliots Bks.

***Bostrom, Chuck.** An Educator's Investing Guide: What School Didn't Teach You about Investing & Should Have. 1999. pap. 19.95 (*0-9668881-1-1*) Mt Top Consultants.

An Asterisk (*) at the beginning of an entry indicates that the title is appearing for the first time.

Bostrom, Chuck. Inve$ting for Educators (And Others) A Manual Written in Plain English by an Educator for Those Who Know Little about the Stock Market or Investing & Wish to Learn. 217p. 1998. pap. 24.95 (*0-9668881-0-3*) Mt Top Consultants.

Bostrom, Francisco. The Magic of the Crystals. 126p. 1998. pap. 14.95 (*1-886708-00-2*) Merrill-West Pub.

Bostrom, H. & Ljungstedt, N., eds. Detection & Prevention of Adverse Drug Reactions. 294p. (Orig.). 1984. pap. text 60.00 (*91-22-00680-X*) Coronet Bks.

— Medical Aspects of Mortality Statistics. (Illus.). 388p. (Orig.). 1981. pap. text 58.00 (*91-22-00440-8*) Coronet Bks.

— Theoretical & Clinical Aspects of Allergic Diseases. (Illus.). 302p. 1983. text 75.00 (*91-22-00595-1*) Coronet Bks.

— Trace Elements in Health & Disease. (Illus.). 285p. 1985. text 78.00 (*91-22-00733-4*) Coronet Bks.

Bostrom, Kathleen. The World That God Made. LC 97-217911. (J). 1997. 10.99 (*0-8423-8294-1*) Tyndale Hse.

Bostrom, Kathleen Long. Value-Able Child: Teaching Values at Home & School. 1999. pap. text 13.95 (*0-673-58639-1*) Addison-Wesley.

***Bostrom, Kathleen Long.** Who Is Jesus? LC 98-48044. 75p. 1999. 9.99 (*0-8423-5144-2*) Tyndale Hse.

Bostrom, Lennart. The God of the Sages: The Portrayal of God in the Book of Proverbs. (Coniectanea Biblica. Old Testament Ser.: No. 29). 260p. (Orig.). 1990. pap. 48.50 (*91-22-01340-7*) Coronet Bks.

Bostrom, Otto H. Alternative Readings in the Hebrew of the Books of Samuel. LC 18-8964. (Augustana College Library Publications: No. 8). 60p. 1918. pap. 1.00 (*0-910182-05-1*) Augustana Coll.

Bostrom, Robert C. Tectonic Consequences of the Earth's Rotation. (Illus.). 272p. 2000. text 80.00 (*0-19-509028-4*) OUP.

Bostrom, Robert N. Communicating: Speaking & Listening. (Illus.). 400p. (C). 1988. pap. text 27.20 (*0-8087-4981-1*) Pearson Custom.

— Communication Research. (Illus.). 314p. (C). 1998. pap. text 19.95 (*1-57766-014-5*) Waveland Pr.

Bostrom, Robert N., ed. Competence in Communication: A Multidisciplinary Approach. LC 83-24617. (Sage Focus Editions Ser.: No. 66). (Illus.). 271p. 1984. reprint ed. pap. 84.10 (*0-608-01115-0*, 205941900001) Bks Demand.

Bostrom, Robert N., et al. Getting There: Functional Public Speaking. rev. ed. (Illus.). 223p. (C). 1997. pap. 20.95 (*0-88133-971-7*) Waveland Pr.

Bostrum, Hank. Ocean Black. 1995. mass mkt. 5.50 (*0-7860-0196-8*, Pinncle Kensgtn) Kensgtn Pub Corp.

Bostwick, Arthur E. Earmarks of Literature. LC 67-22074. (Essay Index Reprint Ser.). 1977. 19.95 (*0-8369-1319-1*) Ayer.

— Librarian's Open Shelf: Essays on Various Subjects. LC 67-23182. (Essay Index Reprint Ser.). 1977. 23.95 (*0-8369-0226-2*) Ayer.

— Library Essays. LC 71-84299. (Essay Index Reprint Ser.). 1977. 24.95 (*0-8369-1076-1*) Ayer.

Bostwick, Arthur E., ed. Library & Society. LC 68-54330. (Essay Index Reprint Ser.). 1977. 23.95 (*0-8369-0227-0*) Ayer.

Bostwick, Burdette E. Resume Writing: A Comprehensive How-to-Do-It Guide. 4th ed. LC 89-37360. 352p. 1990. pap. 14.95 (*0-471-51416-0*) Wiley.

Bostwick, David G. & Dundore, P. Biopsy Pathology of the Prostate. LC 96-86621. (Biopsy Pathology Ser.). (Illus.). 272p. 1996. text 110.00 (*0-412-75510-6*, Pub. by E A) OUP.

Bostwick, David G., jt. auth. see Foster, Christopher S.

Bostwick, David G., ed. see Young.

Bostwick, Frank. Upcountry Odyssey. (Illus.). 150p. 1998. pap. 10.95 (*1-891118-29-3*, Wind Canyon Bks) Wind Canyon.

Bostwick-Harkenrider, Sandra. 15 Minute Magic: Spontaneous Learning Activities for Young Children. (Illus.). 64p. (J). (ps-k). 1992. pap. text 8.95 (*0-86530-194-8*, 195-4) Incentive Pubns.

Bostwick, Jeri. Hawaii 1985. Fisher, Robert C., ed. (Fisher Annotated Travel Guides Ser.). 258p. 1984. 12.95 (*0-8116-0024-6*) NAL.

— Pua Nani: Hawaii Is a Garden. (Illus.). 136p. 1987. boxed set 19.95 (*0-935180-60-5*) Mutual Pub HI.

Bostwick, John, III. Aesthetic & Reconstructive Breast Surgery. LC 82-8306. (Illus.). 748p. (C). (gr. 13). 1983. text 180.00 (*0-8016-0731-0*, 00731) Mosby Inc.

***Bostwick, John, 3rd.** Plastic & Reconstructive Breast Surgery. 2nd ed. LC 99-46503. (Illus.). 1606p. 1999. text 420.00 (*1-57626-104-2*) Quality Med Pub.

Bostwick, John, III, et al. Endoscopic Plastic Surgery. LC 94-40344. (Illus.). 584p. 1994. 325.00 (*0-942219-65-1*) Quality Med Pub.

Bostwick, John, 3rd, et al. Endoscopic Plastic Surgery. 2nd ed. (Illus.). 350p. 2000. 275.00 (*1-57626-005-4*) Quality Med Pub.

Bostwick, John, III, jt. auth. see Berger, Karen.

Bostwick, Kathryn B., jt. auth. see Gidel, Robert D.

Bostwick, Kathy, jt. auth. see Gidel, Bob.

Bostwick, Mark. Four-Wheeling in the B. C. Interior: The Kootenays to Bella Coola. (Illus.). 200p. 1997. pap. 17.95 (*1-55017-156-9*) Harbour Pub Co.

***Bostwick, Miriam.** The Conquering Soul: The Key to Understanding Spiritual Psychology. LC 00-100661. 250p. 2000. pap. 14.95 (*1-885003-42-0*, Pub. by R D Reed Pubs) Midpt Trade.

Bostwick, Roberta L. New York State, History of Smithboro, along the Susquehanna River in Tioga County, 1787-1997. LC 98-111366. (Illus.). xviii, 524p. (Orig.). 1997. 37.95 (*0-9661819-1-3*); ring bd. 27.95 (*0-9661819-0-5*) Oakwood Est.

Bosua, W. & Schutte, M. Basic Financial Accounting. 101p. (C). 1993. pap. text 19.60 (*0-7021-2923-2*, Pub. by Juta & Co) Intl Spec Bk.

Bosum, Wilhelm, jt. auth. see Hahn, Albrecht.

Bosveld, Jane. While a Tree Was Growing. LC 96-46862. (Illus.). 48p. (J). (gr. 1 up). 1997. 13.95 (*0-7611-0540-9*, 10540) Workman Pub.

Bosveld, Jennifer. Contrary to Popular Opinion. 50p. Date not set. pap. 12.95 (*0-944754-58-9*) Pudding Hse Pubns.

— Jazz Kills the Paperboy. 39p. 1994. pap. 7.95 (*0-944754-22-8*) Pudding Hse Pubns.

— Maggie Lynn & Her Perpetual State of Fulfillment in Johnstown, Ohio: A Novella by Brad James. (Illus.). 60p. 1996. pap. 7.95 (*0-944754-37-6*) Pudding Hse Pubns.

— Topics for Getting in Touch: A Poetry Therapy Sourcebook. (Illus.). 150p. 1997. pap. 25.00 (*0-944754-38-4*) Pudding Hse Pubns.

Bosveld, Jennifer, ed. The Pocket Poetry Parenting Guide. 1999. pap. 12.95 (*0-944754-59-7*) Pudding Hse Pubns.

— Prayers to Protest: Poems That Center & Bless Us. xii, 227p. 1998. pap. 19.95 (*0-944754-46-5*) Pudding Hse Pubns.

— The Unitarian Universalist Poets: A Contemporary American Survey. 208p. 1996. pap., per. 18.95 (*0-944754-33-3*) Pudding Hse Pubns.

Bosveld, Jennifer & DeRhodes, David. The Gargantuan Pudding House Word Jar of Best Words for Writing Work - & Playshops. 30p. 1998. pap. 14.00 (*0-944754-61-9*) Pudding Hse Pubns.

Bosveld, Jennifer & Welch, Jennifer G. Free with the Purchase of a Spaghetti Fork: The Flea Market Poems. 1981. pap. 7.95 (*0-944754-63-5*) Pudding Hse Pubns.

Bosveld, Jennifer W., ed. Zoo Poems (Preservation Copy) limited ed. 122p. 1988. pap. 50.00 (*0-944754-15-5*) Pudding Hse Pubns.

Boswell. The Kindness of Strangers. LC 98-19356. (Illus.). 488p. 1998. pap. text 18.00 (*0-226-06712-2*) U Ch Pr.

Boswell, Barbara. Another Whirlwind Courtship. (Bestselling Authors Ser.). 1998. mass mkt. 1.99 (*0-373-48374-0*, 1-48374-2) Harlequin Bks.

— The Baby Track. (Desire Ser.: No. 651). 1991. per. 2.75 (*0-373-05651-6*) Harlequin Bks.

— The Baby Track. (Born in the U. S. A. Ser.). 1997. per. 4.50 (*0-373-47198-X*, 1-47198-6) Harlequin Bks.

***Boswell, Barbara.** Bachelor Doctor. (Desire Ser.: Bk. 1303). 2000. mass mkt. 3.99 (*0-373-76303-4*, 1-76303-6) Silhouette.

Boswell, Barbara. The Best Revenge. (Desire Ser.). 1993. per. 2.99 (*0-373-05821-7*, 5-05821-9) Silhouette.

— The Brennan Baby: Man of the Month. (Desire Ser.: No. 1123). 1998. per. 3.75 (*0-373-76123-6*, 1-76123-8) Silhouette.

— The Bridal Price. (Here Come the Grooms Ser.: No. 7). 1996. per. 3.99 (*0-373-30107-3*, 1-30107-6) Harlequin Bks.

— The Engagement Party. (Desire Ser.). 1995. per. 3.25 (*0-373-05932-9*, 1-05932-8) Silhouette.

— Family Feud. (Desire Ser.). 1994. per. 2.99 (*0-373-05877-2*, 1-05877-5) Silhouette.

— Forever Flint: Man of the Month Anniversary. (Desire Ser.: No. 1243). 1999. per. 3.75 (*0-373-76243-7*, 1-76243-4) Silhouette.

— A Fortune's Children Wedding: The Hoodwinked Bride. (Silhouette Promo Ser.). 1999. pap. 5.99 (*0-373-48378-3*, 1-48378-3) Silhouette.

***Boswell, Barbara.** Irresistible You. 2001. mass mkt. 3.99 (*0-373-76333-6*, 1-76333-3) Silhouette.

Boswell, Barbara. License to Love. (Desire Ser.: No. 685). 1992. per. 2.79 (*0-373-05685-0*) Harlequin Bks.

— Quien Es el Jefe.Tr. of Who's the Boss?. (SPA.). 1998. per. 3.50 (*0-373-35219-0*) Harlequin Bks.

— Red Velvet. 400p. (Orig.). 1995. mass mkt. 5.99 (*0-515-11743-9*, Jove) Berkley Pub.

— Se Necesita Esposa (The Wilde Bunch) 1996. per. 3.50 (*0-373-35136-4*) Harlequin Bks.

***Boswell, Barbara.** Siempre Tu. (Deseo Ser.: Bk. 205).Tr. of Forever You. (SPA.). 156p. 2000. per. 3.50 (*0-373-35335-9*, 1-35335-8) Harlequin Bks.

Boswell, Barbara. Solo Vecinos (Only Neighbors) (SPA.). 1999. mass mkt. 3.50 (*0-373-35273-5*, 1-35273-1) Harlequin Bks.

— Stand-In Bride. (Fortune's Children Ser.). 1996. per. 4.50 (*0-373-50180-3*, 1-50180-8) Harlequin Bks.

— That Marriageable Man! 1998. per. 3.75 (*0-373-76147-3*, 1-76147-7) Silhouette.

— Triple Trato. (SPA.). 1997. per. 3.50 (*0-373-35187-9*, 1-35187-3) Harlequin Bks.

— Triple Treat. (Desire Ser.). 1993. per. 2.99 (*0-373-05787-3*, 5-05787-2) Silhouette.

— The Valentine Street Hustle. (Desire Ser.: No. 609). 1990. per. 2.50 (*0-373-05609-5*) Silhouette.

— When Lightning Strikes Twice. 384p. 1997. mass mkt. 5.99 (*0-380-72744-7*, Avon Bks) Morrow Avon.

— Who's the Boss? (Man of the Month Ser.). 1997. per. 3.50 (*0-373-76069-8*, 1-76069-3) Silhouette.

— Wicked Games. 384p. (Orig.). 1994. mass mkt. 5.99 (*0-515-11487-1*, Jove) Berkley Pub.

— The Wilde Bunch. (Desire Ser.). 1995. per. 3.25 (*0-373-05943-4*, 1-05943-5) Silhouette.

— Winning Ways. 384p. 1996. mass mkt. 5.99 (*0-380-72743-9*, Avon Bks) Morrow Avon.

Boswell, Barbara, et al. Magic Slippers. 1996. mass mkt. 5.99 (*0-380-78370-3*, Avon Bks) Morrow Avon.

Boswell, Bethanie L. Hablamos Dos Idiomas. (Vida Latina Ser.). (SPA.). 48p. (J). (gr. 4-8). 1995. lib. bdg. 23.93 (*0-86625-562-1*) Rourke Pubns.

— Los Seminola. (Pueblos Americanos Nativos Ser.). (SPA.). 32p. (J). (gr. 5-8). 1990. lib. bdg. 21.27 (*0-86625-451-X*) Rourke Pubns.

— Speaking Two Languages. LC 95-2016. (Latino Life Ser.). (Illus.). 48p. (J). (gr. 4-8). 1995. lib. bdg. 23.93 (*0-86625-543-5*) Rourke Pubns.

Boswell, Bethanie L. & Jensen, Jeffry. Sports. LC 95-2029. (Latino Life Ser.). 48p. (J). (gr. 4-8). 1995. lib. bdg. 23.93 (*0-86625-544-3*) Rourke Pubns.

Boswell, Carol. How to Dad. 80p. 1990. 11.95 (*0-440-50302-7*) Dell.

Boswell, Charles S. An Irish Precursor of Dante. (Grimm Library: No. 18). reprint ed. 45.00 (*0-404-53561-5*) AMS Pr.

Boswell, Charley. Now I See. deluxe limited ed. 212p. 1991. reprint ed. 39.95 (*0-9630273-1-X*) Highland AL.

— Now I See. 212p. 1991. reprint ed. 18.50 (*0-9630273-0-1*) Highland AL.

Boswell, David. Embedded Java Programming. 600p. Date not set. pap. text 59.99 (*0-672-31705-2*) Macmillan.

— Setting up In-House Surface Mount Technology: Practical Management & Technical Guidelines. 324p. 1997. pap. 252.00 (*0-901150-28-2*) St Mut.

— Surface Mount Guidelines for Process Control, Quality, & Reliability. 160p. 1992. 30.00 (*0-07-707571-4*) McGraw.

Boswell, David, jt. ed. see Evans, Jessica.

Boswell, David M. & Beeley, Brian W. Malta. 2nd rev. ed. 304p. 1998. lib. bdg. 79.00 (*1-85109-269-2*) ABC-CLIO.

***Boswell, Delphine.** Playtime Art for Preschoolers. LC 98-34859. 96p. 1998. pap. 14.99 (*0-7644-2111-5*) Group Pub.

Boswell, Eleonore. Restoration Court Stage, 1660-1702. LC 65-16227. (Illus.). 400p. 1972. 23.95 (*0-405-18138-8*) Ayer.

***Boswell, Evault.** Texas Boys in Gray: Confederate War Letters. LC 00-38704. (Illus.). 275p. 2000. pap. 17.95 (*1-55622-777-9*, Rep of TX Pr) Wordware Pub.

Boswell, F. E., jt. auth. see Mather, J. E.

Boswell, F. E., jt. auth. see Mather, R. E.

Boswell, F. E., jt. auth. see Mather, Ruth E.

Boswell, Frank W. & Bennett, J. Craig. Advances in the Cyrstallographic & Microstructural Analysis of Charge Density Wave Modulated Crystals. LC 99-11485. (Physics & Chemistry of Materials with Low-dimensional Structures Ser.). 1999. write for info. (*0-7923-5604-7*) Kluwer Academic.

Boswell, Fred & Boswell, Jeanetta. What Men or Gods Are These? A Genealogical Approach to Classical Mythology. LC 80-13780. 324p. 1980. 41.50 (*0-8108-1314-9*) Scarecrow.

Boswell, Fred E., jt. auth. see Mather, Ruth E.

Boswell, George C., ed. Litchfield, Connecticut, Book of Days: A Collation of the Historical, Biographical & Literary Reminiscences of the Town of Litchfield, Connecticut. (Illus.). 221p. 1992. reprint ed. lib. bdg. 27.50 (*0-8328-2354-6*) Higginson Bk Co.

Boswell, Gwyneth. Young & Dangerous. 184p. 1996. 66.95 (*1-85972-191-5*, Pub. by Avebury) Ashgate Pub Co.

Boswell, Gwyneth, et al. Contemporary Probation Practice. 224p. 1993. 66.95 (*1-85628-451-4*, Pub. by Avebry) Ashgate Pub Co.

Boswell, Hazel. Town House, Country House: Recollections of a Quebec Childhood. (Illus.). 152p. (C). 1990. 39.95 (*0-7735-0721-3*, Pub. by McG-Queens Univ Pr) CUP Services.

Boswell, Holly. Christmas Crafts Year-Round: 60 Great Gifts You Can Make from January to December. LC 97-10660. (Illus.). 128p. (Orig.). 1997. pap. 14.95 (*1-57990-001-1*, Pub. by Lark Books) Random.

— The Decoupage Book: More Than Sixty Decorative Projects Using Simple Techniques. LC 93-36461. (Illus.). 128p. 1994. 27.95 (*0-8069-0610-3*) Sterling.

— The Decoupage Book: More Than 60 Decorative Projects Using Simple Techniques. (Illus.). 128p. 1995. pap. 14.95 (*0-8069-0611-1*) Sterling.

Boswell, Holly, ed. see Casagranda, Brigitte.

Boswell, J., jt. auth. see Beard, Henry.

Boswell, Jackson C. Dante's Fame in England: References in Printed British Books, 1477-1640. LC 98-21559. 232p. 1999. 36.00 (*0-87413-605-9*) U Delaware Pr.

Boswell, Jacquelyn, ed. see Music in Early Childhood Conference Staff.

Boswell, James. Boswell: The Applause of the Jury: 1782-1785: The Yale Editions of the Private Papers of James Boswell. 1981. write for info. (*0-318-66903-X*) McGraw.

— Boswell: The Ominous Years: 1774-1776: The Yale Editions of the Private Papers of James Boswell. 1963. write for info. (*0-318-66900-5*) McGraw.

— Boswell for the Defence, 1769-1774: The Yale Editions of the Private Papers of James Boswell. 1962. write for info. (*0-318-66898-X*) McGraw.

— Boswell in Holland, Seventeen Sixty-Two to Seventeen Sixty-Four: The Yale Editions of the Private Papers of James Boswell. 1952. write for info. (*0-318-66859-9*) McGraw.

— Boswell in Search of a Wife, 1766-1769: The Yale Editions of the Private Papers of James Boswell. 1956. write for info. (*0-318-66897-1*) McGraw.

— Boswell, Laird of Auchinleck: 1778-1782: The Yale Editions of the Private Papers of James Boswell. 1977. write for info. (*0-318-66902-1*) McGraw.

— Boswell on the Grand Tour: Germany & Switzerland, 1764-1953: The Yale Editions of the Private Papers of James Boswell. 1953. write for info. (*0-318-66895-5*) McGraw.

— Boswell on the Grand Tour: Italy, Corsica & France, 1765-1766: The Yale Editions of the Private Papers of James Boswell. 1955. write for info. (*0-318-66896-3*) McGraw.

Boswell, James. Boswell's Journal of a Tour to the Hebrides with Samuel Johnson. (Oxford Standard Authors Ser.). 1930. 25.00 (*0-19-254131-5*) OUP.

Boswell, James. Boswell's Journal of a Tour to the Hebrides with Samuel Johnson, LL.D., 1773: The Yales Editions of the Private Papers of James Boswell. 1962. write for info. (*0-318-66899-8*) McGraw.

— Boswell's London Journal, 1762-1763. Pottle, Frederick A., ed. 408p. (Orig.). (C). 1992. pap. 19.00 (*0-300-05735-0*) Yale U Pr.

— Dorando: A Spanish Tale. Hunting, Robert S., ed. LC 73-78276. 1973. 3.50 (*0-913006-05-X*) Puckerbrush.

— Hypochondriack, 2 vols. Bailey, Margery, ed. LC 78-39512. reprint ed. 85.00 (*0-404-07654-8*) AMS Pr.

— The Journal of a Tour to the Hebrides. (Illus.). 2000. pap. text 7.95 (*3-8290-3002-9*) Konemann.

— The Journals of James Boswell, 1762-1795. LC 92-60414. 448p. (C). 1992. 40.00 (*0-300-05652-4*) Yale U Pr.

— Letters, 2 vols. reprint ed. 59.00 (*0-403-04137-6*) Somerset Pub.

— Letters, 2 vols., Set. 1988. reprint ed. lib. bdg. 99.00 (*0-7812-0083-0*) Rprt Serv.

— The Life of Johnson. LC 92-52915. 1328p. 1992. 25.00 (*0-679-41717-6*) Everymns Lib.

— The Life of Johnson. 2000. 22.00 (*0-679-60204-6*) Modern Lib NY.

— Life of Johnson. (English Library). 384p. 1979. pap. 11.95 (*0-14-043116-0*, Penguin Classics) Viking Penguin.

***Boswell, James.** Life of Johnson: Unabridged. Chapman, R. W. & Fleeman, J. D., eds. (Oxford World's Classics Ser.). 1536p. 1998. pap. 17.95 (*0-19-283531-9*) OUP.

Boswell, James. Life of Samuel Johnson. (Modern Library College Editions). 559p. (C). 1964. pap. 8.44 (*0-07-553645-5*, T62) McGraw.

— A View of the Edinburgh Theatre During the Summer Season, 1759. LC 92-543. (Augustan Reprints Ser.: No. 179). 1992. reprint ed. 14.50 (*0-404-70179-5*, PN2605) AMS Pr.

Boswell, James, et al. Boswell, Laird of Auchinleck: 1778-1782: The Yale Editions of the Private Papers of James Boswell. LC 94-209865. xxxiv, 570 p. 1993. 80.00 (*0-7486-0392-1*, Pub. by Edinburgh U Pr) Col U Pr.

— Boswell, Laird of Auchinleck: 1778-1782: The Yale Editions of the Private Papers of James Boswell. LC 76-44502. (The Yale Editions of the Private Papers of James Boswell Ser.). xxxiv, 570p. 1977. write for info. (*0-07-051520-4*) McGraw.

Boswell, James, et al. The Correspondence of James Boswell with James Bruce & Andrew Gibb: Overseers of the Auchinleck Estate. LC 97-135371. (Yale Editions of the Private Papers of James Bowell.). lvi, 276 p. 1998. 87.00 (*0-7486-0624-6*) Edinburgh U Pr.

Boswell, James, jt. auth. see Johnson, Samuel.

Boswell, James, jt. auth. see Thrale, Hester L.

Boswell, James, ed. see Barrett, John P.

Boswell, James, ed. see Shakespeare, William.

Boswell, Jeanetta. The American Renaissance & the Critics. LC 90-5996. 526p. 1990. 55.00 (*0-89341-599-5*, Longwood Academic) Hollowbrook.

— Herman Melville & the Critics: A Checklist of Criticism, 1900-1978. LC 80-25959. (Author Bibliographies Ser.: No. 53). 259p. 1981. 29.00 (*0-8108-1385-8*) Scarecrow.

— Nathaniel Hawthorne & the Critics: A Checklist of Criticism, 1900-1978. LC 81-9398. (Author Bibliographies Ser.: No. 57). 283p. 1982. 29.00 (*0-8108-1471-4*) Scarecrow.

— Ralph Waldo Emerson & the Critics: A Checklist of Criticism, 1900-1977. LC 79-4670. (Author Bibliographies Ser.: No. 39). 1979. 26.50 (*0-8108-1211-8*) Scarecrow.

— The Schoolroom Poets: A Bibliography of Bryant, Holmes, Longfellow, Lowell & Whittier with Selective Annotation. LC 83-19276. 311p. 1983. 31.00 (*0-8108-1659-8*) Scarecrow.

— Spokesman for the Minority: A Bibliography of Sidney Lanier, William Vaughn Moody, Henry Timrod, Frederick Goddard Tuckerman, & Jones Very, with Selective Annotations. LC 86-24828. x, 296p. 1987. 34.50 (*0-8108-1944-9*) Scarecrow.

— Theodore Dreiser & the Critics, 1911-1982: A Bibliography with Selective Annotations. LC 85-14405. (Author Bibliographies Ser.: No. 73). 319p. 1986. 34.50 (*0-8108-1837-X*) Scarecrow.

— Walt Whitman & the Critics: A Checklist of Criticism, 1900-1978. LC 80-20528. (Author Bibliographies Ser.: No. 51). 270p. 1980. 26.50 (*0-8108-1355-6*) Scarecrow.

Boswell, Jeanetta, jt. auth. see Boswell, Fred.

Boswell, John. The Best Fryer Cookbook Ever. LC 97-7174. 224p. 1998. 16.95 (*0-06-018764-6*) HarpC.

— The Best Ice Cream Maker Cookbook Ever. LC TX795.F35 1998. 224p. 1998. 16.95 (*0-06-018765-4*) HarpC.

— Christianity, Social Tolerance, & Homosexuality: Gay People in Western Europe from the Beginning of the Christian Era to the Fourteenth Century. LC 79-11171. (Illus.). xviii, 424p. 1981. pap. 19.95 (*0-226-06711-4*) U Ch Pr.

— The Insider's Guide to Getting Published: Why They Always Reject Your Manuscript & What You Can Do about It. LC 96-29034. 176p. 1996. pap. 12.00 (*0-385-47936-0*, Main St Bks) Doubleday.

— A Man & His Pan: If You Can't Cook It in a Non-Stick Skillet, It's Not Worth Cooking! LC 99-24099. 251p. 1999. pap. 16.95 (*0-8362-7854-2*) Andrews & McMeel.

— The Royal Treasure: Muslim Communities under the Crown of Aragon in the Fourteenth Century. LC 77-76303. 542p. reprint ed. pap. 168.10 (*0-8357-8762-1*, 203367600087) Bks Demand.

— Same-Sex Unions in Premodern Europe. 1995. pap. 13.00 (*0-679-75164-5*) Vin Bks.

— Everyday Cooking for the Jewish Home: More Than 350 Delectable Recipes. LC 97-30089. 384p. 1997. 27.50 (*0-06-017295-9*) HarpC.

Boswell, John & Fisher, David. Fenway Park: Legendary Home of the Boston Red Sox. LC 92-22579. 16p. 1992. pap. 19.95 (*0-316-10337-3*); pap. 99.75 (*0-316-10351-9*) Little.

Boswell, John & Starer, Dan. Five Rings, Six Crises, Seven Dwarfs & 38 Ways to Win an Argument. (Illus.). 256p. 1997. 7.99 (*1-57866-008-4*) Galahad Bks.

Boswell, John, et al. Chuck & Di Have a Baby. 1982. write for info. (*0-318-57011-4*) PB.

Boswell, John, jt. auth. see Beard, Henry.

Boswell, Jonathan. Community & the Economy: The Theory of Public Co-Operation. 256p. (C). 1994. pap. 27.99 (*0-415-11607-4*, B4191) Routledge.

Boswell, Jonathan & Peters, James. Capitalism in Contention: Business Leaders & Political Economy in Modern Britain. LC 97-8959. 265p. (C). 1998. text 59.95 (*0-521-58225-3*); pap. text 22.95 (*0-521-58804-9*) Cambridge U Pr.

Boswell, Kathryn & O'Connor, Francine M. ABCs of the Ten Commandments. (Illus.). 32p. (J). (gr. 1-4). 1980. pap. 4.95 (*0-89243-125-3*) Liguori Pubns.

Boswell, Kathryn, jt. auth. see O'Connor, Francine M.

Boswell, L. F., ed. The Jack-Up Drilling Platform: Design & Operation. LC 85-82049. (Illus.). 373p. 1986. reprint ed. pap. 115.70 (*0-608-04549-7*, 206529100001) Bks Demand.

Boswell, L. F. & D'Mello, C., eds. Recent Developments in Jack-Up Platforms: Design, Construction, & Operation. LC 92-10000. (Illus.). 1992. 165.00 (*0-632-03281-2*) Blackwell Sci.

Boswell, L. F., jt. ed. see Noor, F. A.

Boswell, Laird. Rural Communism in France, 1920-1939. LC 97-44193. (Illus.). 304p. 1998. 47.50 (*0-8014-3421-1*) Cornell U Pr.

Boswell, Laurence. Beauty & the Beast. (Nick Hern Bks.). 96p. 1997. pap. 14.95 (*1-85459-307-2*, Pub. by N Hern Bks) Theatre Comm.

Boswell, Laurence, tr. see Calderon de la Barca, Pedro.

Boswell, Lawrence, tr. see De Molina, Tirso.

***Boswell, Marshall.** John Updike's Rabbit Tetralogy: Mastered Irony in Motion. 312p. 2000. 34.95 (*0-8262-1310-3*) U of Mo Pr.

Boswell, Mary C. Elvis & Us in the 60s. 2nd ed. 25p. 1997. pap. 14.95 (*1-881242-03-X*) Pyramid Educ Inc.

Boswell, Mary R., ed. see Lindsay, Eldress B.

Boswell, Mary Rose, jt. auth. see Beale, Galen.

***Boswell, Michael, et al.** Florida's Future: A Guide to Revising Florida's State Comprehensive Plan. De Haven-Smith, Lance et al, eds. (Illus.). 200p. (C). 1999. pap. text. write for info. (*0-9649227-3-8*) Fla Inst Gov.

Boswell, P., ed. Storm: Der Schimmelreiter. (Bristol German Texts Ser.). (GER.). 165p. 1994. pap. 18.95 (*1-85399-290-9*, Pub. by Brist Class Pr) Focus Pub-R Pullins.

Boswell, Parley A. & Loukides, Paul. Reel Rituals: Ritual Occasions from Baptisms to Funerals in Hollywood Films, 1945-1995. LC 99-11699. 135p. 1999. pap. 40.95 (*0-87972-791-8*) Bowling Green Univ Popular Press.

Boswell, Patricia M., ed. Storm: Aquis Submersus. (Bristol German Texts Ser.). (GER.). 160p. 1992. pap. 15.95 (*1-85399-289-5*, Pub. by Brist Class Pr) Focus Pub-R Pullins.

Boswell, Paul. No Anchovies on the Moon: Three Score & Ten Washington Pictures & Poems. LC 93-44800. (Illus.). 192p. 1994. 29.95 (*0-929765-33-8*) Seven Locks Pr.

Boswell, Peter & Scott, Deborah E. Joel Shapiro: Outdoors. (Illus.). 1995. pap. 16.95 (*0-935640-48-7*) Walker Art Ctr.

Boswell, Peter, et al. The Photomontages of Hannah Hoch. (Illus.). 224p. 1996. pap. 35.00 (*0-935640-53-3*) Walker Art Ctr.

***Boswell, Peter, et al.** 2000 B. C. Pt. II: The Bruce Conner Story. LC 99-33602. (Illus.). 280p. 1999. 59.95 (*0-935640-61-4*, Pub. by Walker Art Ctr) Dist Art Pubs.

Boswell, Richard. Immigration Law. 3rd ed. 1997. text. write for info. (*0-89089-671-2*) Carolina Acad Pr.

Boswell, Richard A. Attorney's Desk Library. 1994. write for info. (*0-318-72688-2*) West Group.

— Immigration & Nationality Law, Supplement. 134p. 1997. pap., suppl. ed. 15.00 (*0-89089-024-2*) Carolina Acad Pr.

Boswell, Richard A. & Carrasco, Gilbert P. Immigration & Nationality Law. 2nd ed. LC 91-78016. 750p. (C). 1992. lib. bdg. 65.00 (*0-89089-490-6*) Carolina Acad Pr.

— Immigration & Nationality Law: Selected Statutory Provisions. 2nd ed. 168p. (C). 1997. suppl. ed. 15.00 (*0-89089-003-X*) Carolina Acad Pr.

Boswell, Robert. American Owned Love. 323p. 1997. 24.00 (*0-679-43251-5*) Knopf.

— Dancing in the Movies. LC 85-13966. (Iowa Short Fiction Award Ser.). 153p. 1986. 10.00 (*0-87745-134-6*) U of Iowa Pr.

— Mystery Ride. large type ed. LC 93-10508. 665p. 1993. lib. bdg. 23.95 (*1-56054-750-2*) Thorndike Pr.

— Mystery Ride. LC 93-27188. 352p. 1994. reprint ed. pap. 13.00 (*0-06-097585-7*, Perennial) HarperTrade.

— Mystery Ride: A Novel. 1993. 22.00 (*0-679-41292-1*) Knopf.

Boswell, Robert & Voigt, Ellen B., eds. Ploughshares Winter, 1996-97. 247p. (Orig.). 1996. pap. 8.95 (*0-933277-18-0*) Ploughshares.

Boswell, Robert B., tr. see Racine, Jean.

Boswell, Sharon. Hank-Willy. (Illus.). x, 155p. (J). (ps-6). 1999. pap. 12.99 (*0-9668894-0-1*) Lorgnette Bks.

Boswell, Sharon, contrib. by. Elmer C. Huntley: An Oral History. (Illus.). xii, 130p. (Orig.). 1996. pap. write for info. (*1-889320-04-8*) WA St Oral Hist.

— William A. Gissberg: An Oral History. (Illus.). xii, 130p. (Orig.). 1996. pap. write for info. (*1-889320-03-X*) WA St Oral Hist.

Boswell, Sharon, ed. see Goldsworthy, Robert F.

Boswell-Stone, W. G. Shakespeare's Holinshed. LC 66-29420. 1972. reprint ed. 33.95 (*0-405-08291-6*, Pub. by Blom Pubns) Ayer.

Boswell, Suzanne. Menswear: Suiting the Customer. LC 92-22908. 208p. (C). 1993. pap. text 29.20 (*0-13-571423-0*) P-H.

— The Mystery Patient's Guide to Gaining & Retaining Patients. LC 96-50954. 1997. 49.95 (*0-87814-654-7*) PennWell Bks.

Boswell, Terry, ed. Revolution in the World-System, 94. LC 88-37518. (Contributions in Economics & Economic History Ser.: No. 94). 253p. 1989. 65.00 (*0-313-26726-X*, BRX/, Greenwood Pr) Greenwood.

Boswell, Terry & Bergesen, Albert, eds. America's Changing Role in the World System. LC 86-25245. 320p. 1987. 69.50 (*0-275-92417-3*, C2417, Praeger Pubs) Greenwood.

Boswell, Terry & Chase-Dunn, Christopher. The Spiral of Capitalism & Socialism: Toward Global Democracy. LC 99-16269. (Political Sociology Ser.). 281p. 2000. pap. 23.50 (*1-55587-849-0*) L Rienner.

— The Spiral of Capitalism & Socialism: Toward Global Democracy. LC 99-16269. (Political Sociology Ser.). 281p. 2000. lib. bdg. 55.00 (*1-55587-824-5*) L Rienner.

Boswell, Thom. The Bird Feeder Book: How to Build Unique Bird Feeders from the Purely Practical to the Simply Outrageous. LC 92-40584. (Illus.). 144p. 1993. 24.95 (*0-8069-0295-7*) Sterling.

— The Bird Feeder Book: How to Build Unique Bird Feeders from the Purely Practical to the Simply Outrageous. (Illus.). 144p. 1995. pap. 14.95 (*0-8069-0296-5*) Sterling.

Boswell, Thom, ed. The Rug Hook Book: Techniques, Projects & Patterns for This Easy. (Illus.). 144p. 1994. pap. 16.95 (*0-8069-8359-0*) Sterling.

Boswell, Thomas D. & Conway, Dennis. The Caribbean Islands. LC 92-11579. (Touring North America Ser.). (Illus.). 220p. (C). 1992. pap. 9.95 (*0-8135-1895-4*) Rutgers U Pr.

Boswell, Thomas D. & Curtis, James R. The Cuban-American Experience: Culture, Images & Perspectives. LC 83-16042. 214p. 1984. text 57.00 (*0-86598-116-7*, R3912) Rowman.

Boswell, William. Life on the Road: A Beginner's Guide to the Stage Production Industry. 704p. (C). 1989. pap. text 51.00 (*0-536-57489-8*) Pearson Custom.

Boswell, William R., ed. Life on the Road: A Beginner's Guide to the Stage Production Touring Industry. 3rd rev. ed. LC 97-140967. 646p. (C). 1996. pap. text 56.00 (*0-536-59800-2*) Pearson Custom.

Boswick, John, Jr. Complications in Hand Surgery. (Illus.). 401p. 1986. text 155.00 (*0-7216-1877-4*, W B Saunders Co) Harcrt Hlth Sci Grp.

Boswick, John A., Jr., ed. The Art & Science of Burn Care. fac. ed. LC 86-25923. (Illus.). 413p. pap. 128.10 (*0-7837-7441-9*, 204723500006) Bks Demand.

Boswick, John A., ed. Current Concepts in Hand Surgery. LC 82-24897. (Illus.). 298p. reprint ed. pap. 92.40 (*0-8357-7640-9*, 205696400096) Bks Demand.

Boswick, Steve. Wheels on the Bus: And Other Songs that Go. LC 98-234953. 1997. write for info. (*0-7853-2641-3*) Pubns Intl Ltd.

Boswick, Storm. Guide to the Universities of Europe. 304p. 1991. 35.00 (*0-8160-2359-X*) Facts on File.

Boswinkel, A., et al. Berichtungsliste der Griechischen Papyruskunden aus Agypten, Band 7. (GER.). x, 364p. 1986. 128.00 (*90-04-07102-4*) Brill Academic Pubs.

Boswinkel, E., et al, eds. Berichtigungsliste der Griechischen Papyrusurkunden Aus Agypten, Vol. 8. LC 20-22953. (GER.). x, 626p. 1992. 261.50 (*90-04-09621-3*) Brill Academic Pubs.

Boswood, Tim, ed. New Ways of Using Computers in Language Teaching. 309p. 1997. pap. 27.95 (*0-939791-69-2*) Tchrs Eng Spkrs.

Bosworth. The Economics of Labour Market. 1992. pap. text. write for info. (*0-582-44377-6*, Pub. by Addison-Wesley) Longman.

Bosworth, ed. Hudud Al-Alam-The Regions of the World: A Persian Geography. (Gibb Memorial New Ser.: Vol. 11). 1937. 72.00 (*0-906094-03-8*, Pub. by Aris & Phillips) David Brown.

Bosworth, et al. AIDS. (Body Awareness Resource Network Ser.). (YA). (gr. 7-12). 120.00 incl. disk (*0-912899-53-0*) Lrning Multi-Systs.

— Alcohol & Other Drugs. (Body Awareness Resource Network Ser.). (YA). (gr. 7-12). 120.00 incl. disk (*0-912899-59-X*) Lrning Multi-Systs.

— Body Management. (Body Awareness Resource Network Ser.). (YA). (gr. 7-12). 120.00 incl. disk (*0-912899-58-1*) Lrning Multi-Systs.

— Human Sexuality. (Body Awareness Resource Network Ser.). (YA). (gr. 7-12). 120.00 incl. disk (*0-912899-55-7*) Lrning Multi-Systs.

— Implementing BARN. (Body Awareness Resource Network Ser.). (YA). (gr. 7-12). write for info. incl. disk (*0-912899-54-9*) Lrning Multi-Systs.

— Smoking. (Body Awareness Resource Network Ser.). (YA). (gr. 7-12). 120.00 incl. disk (*0-912899-56-5*) Lrning Multi-Systs.

— Stress Management. (Body Awareness Resource Network Ser.). (YA). (gr. 7-12). 120.00 incl. disk (*0-912899-57-3*) Lrning Multi-Systs.

Bosworth, A. B. Alejandro Magno: Conquest & Empire: The Reign of Alexander the Great. (Illus.). 504p. (C). 1996. pap. 19.95 (*0-521-55567-1*) Cambridge U Pr.

— Conquest & Empire: The Reign of Alexander the Great. (Canto Book Ser.). (Illus.). 346p. (C). 1993. pap. 12.95 (*0-521-40679-X*) Cambridge U Pr.

— A Historical Commentary on Arrian's History of Alexander, Vol. I: Bks. I-III. (Illus.). 412p. 1980. text 125.00 (*0-19-814828-3*) OUP.

— A Historical Commentary on Arrian's History of Alexander Vol. 2: Books IV-V, Bks. IV & V. (Illus.). 400p. 1995. text 75.00 (*0-19-814829-1*) OUP.

Bosworth, A. B., ed. From Arrian to Alexander: Studies in Historical Interpretation. (Illus.). 236p. 1988. text 65.00 (*0-19-814863-1*) OUP.

***Bosworth, A. B. & Baynham, Elizabeth.** Alexander the Great in Fact & Fiction. LC 99-57300. 400p. 2000. text 60.00 (*0-19-815287-6*) OUP.

Bosworth, A. S. A History of Randolph County, West Virginia: From Its Earliest Exploration & Settlement to the Present Time. 448p. 1997. reprint ed. pap. 35.00 (*0-8063-4700-7*) Clearfield Co.

Bosworth, Albert B. Alexander & the East: The Tragedy of Triumph. (Illus.). 240p. 1998. reprint ed. pap. text 24.95 (*0-19-815262-0*) OUP.

Bosworth, Barry & Burtless, Gary, eds. Aging Societies: The Global Dimension. LC 98-8944. 323p. 1998. pap. 18.95 (*0-8157-1025-9*); text 44.95 (*0-8157-1026-7*) Brookings.

Bosworth, Barry, et al. Capital Needs in the Seventies. LC 75-5157. 97p. reprint ed. pap. 30.10 (*0-608-14529-7*, 202536400043) Bks Demand.

— Macroeconomic Policy. (Seminar Ser.). 59p. 1990. 12.00 (*0-944826-20-2*) Economic Policy Inst.

Bosworth, Barry P. Saving & Investment in a Global Economy. 188p. (C). 1993. 34.95 (*0-8157-1044-5*); pap. 14.95 (*0-8157-1043-7*) Brookings.

— Tax Incentives & Economic Growth. LC 84-9625. 208p. 1984. 34.95 (*0-8157-1036-4*); pap. 14.95 (*0-8157-1035-6*) Brookings.

Bosworth, Barry P., et al, eds. Coming Together? Mexico-U. S. Relations. LC 97-4738. 191p. 1997. text 38.95 (*0-8157-1028-3*); pap. text 16.95 (*0-8157-1027-5*) Brookings.

Bosworth, Barry P. & Lawrence, Robert Z. Commodity Prices & the New Inflation. LC 81-70467. 215p. 1982. 31.95 (*0-8157-1034-8*); pap. 12.95 (*0-8157-1033-X*) Brookings.

Bosworth, Barry P. & Ofer, Gur, eds. Reforming Planned Economies in an Integrating World Economy. (Integrating National Economies Ser.). 186p. (C). 1995. 34.95 (*0-8157-1048-8*); pap. 14.95 (*0-8157-1047-X*) Brookings.

Bosworth, Barry P. & Rivlin, Alice M., eds. The Swedish Economy. LC 86-29920. 338p. 1987. 18.95 (*0-8157-1042-9*) Brookings.

Bosworth, Barry P., et al. The Chilean Economy: Policy Lessons & Challenges. LC 93-43252. 441p. (C). 1994. 52.95 (*0-8157-1046-1*); pap. 24.95 (*0-8157-1045-3*) Brookings.

— Critical Choices. 228p. 1989. pap. 6.95 (*0-8157-1273-1*) Brookings.

— The Economics of Federal Credit Programs. LC 85-48205. 214p. 1987. 34.95 (*0-8157-1038-0*); pap. 14.95 (*0-8157-1037-2*) Brookings.

Bosworth, Barry P., jt. ed. see Collins, Susan M.

Bosworth, Beth. A Burden of Earth & Other Stories. LC 95-9871. 168p. 1995. 20.00 (*1-882413-19-9*); pap. 12.00 (*1-882413-18-0*) Hanging Loose.

Bosworth, Brian & Brown, Daniel, eds. The Network Toolkit Vol. I: Manufacturing Networks & Competitive Manufacturing. (Illus.). 267p. (Orig.). (C). 1997. pap. 60.00 (*0-9636927-7-1*) Reg Tech Strat.

Bosworth, Brian & Rosenfeld, Stuart. Significant Others: Exploring the Potential of Manufacturing Networks. 52p. (Orig.). 1993. pap. 7.00 (*0-9636927-0-4*) Reg Tech Strat.

Bosworth, Bruce & Nagel, Harry L. Programming in BASIC for Microcomputers. 1992. teacher ed. write for info. (*0-02-800294-6*) Glencoe.

Bosworth, C. E. The Arabs, Byzantium & Iran: Studies in Early Islamic History & Culture. LC 96-4771. (Collected Studies: No. CS529). 330p. 1996. 101.95 (*0-86078-583-1*, Pub. by Variorum) Ashgate Pub Co.

— The Encyclopaedia of Islam Vol. X: Fascicule 165-166. Bianquis, T. H., ed. 112p. 1998. pap. 56.00 (*90-04-11066-6*) Brill Academic Pubs.

— The Later Ghaznavids: Slendour & Decay: The Dynasty in Afghanistan & Northern India, 1040-1186. LC 77-7879. (Persian Studies Ser.: Vol. 7). vi, 196p. 1977. text 22.00 (*0-231-04428-3*) Bibliotheca Persica.

Bosworth, C. E., ed. The History of al-Tabari Vol. 30: The 'Abbasid Caliphate in Equilibrium: The Caliphates of Musa al-Hadi & Harun al-Rashid, A. D. 785-809 - A. H. 169-193. LC 87-7124. (SUNY Series in Near Eastern Studies). 365p. (C). 1989. pap. text 26.95 (*0-88706-566-X*) State U NY Pr.

— The History of al-Tabari Vol. 30: The 'Abbasid Caliphate in Equilibrium: The Caliphates of Musa al-Hadi & Harun al-Rashid, A. D. 785-809 - A. H. 169-193. LC 87-7124. (SUNY Series in Near Eastern Studies). 365p. (C). 1989. text 59.50 (*0-88706-564-3*) State U NY Pr.

Bosworth, C. E., et al, eds. The Encyclopaedia of Islam: Volume X Fascicule 163-164. 112p. 1998. pap. 49.00 (*90-04-11056-9*) Brill Academic Pubs.

— The Encyclopaedia of Islam Vol. VIII: New Edition. (Illus.). 1995. 526.50 (*90-04-09834-8*) Brill Academic Pubs.

— The Encyclopaedia of Islam Vol. 9: San-Sze. (Illus.). 1000p. 1997. 526.50 (*90-04-10422-4*) Brill Academic Pubs.

Bosworth, C. E., tr. The History of al-Tabari: Storm & Stress along the Northern Frontiers of the 'Abbasid Caliphate - The Caliphate of al-Mu'tasim A. D., Vol. 33. LC 90-33516. (SUNY Series in Near Eastern Studies). 261p. (C). 1991. pap. text 22.95 (*0-7914-0494-3*) State U NY Pr.

— The History of al-Tabari: Storm & Stress along the Northern Frontiers of the 'Abbasid Caliphate - The Caliphate of al-Mu'tasim A. D., Vol. 33. LC 90-33516. (SUNY Series in Near Eastern Studies). 261p. (C). 1991. text 59.50 (*0-7914-0493-5*) State U NY Pr.

— The History of Al-Tabari Vol. V: The Sasanids, the Lakhmids & Yemen. LC 99-38279. (SUNY Series in Near Eastern Studies). (Illus.). 528p. (C). 1999. text 64.50 (*0-7914-4355-8*); pap. text 21.95 (*0-7914-4356-6*) State U NY Pr.

— The History of al-Tabari Vol. 32: The Reunification of the Abbasid Caliphate, A. D. 812-833, A. H. 198-213. LC 84-16311. (SUNY Series in Near Eastern Studies). 281p. (C). 1987. text 57.50 (*0-88706-058-7*); pap. text 23.95 (*0-88706-057-9*) State U NY Pr.

Bosworth, C. E. & Hillenbrand, Carole, eds. Qajar Iran: Political, Social & Cultural Changes, 1800-1925. (Illus.). 462p. (C). 1992. reprint ed. pap. text 25.00 (*0-939214-98-9*) Mazda Pubs.

Bosworth, C. E. & Lewis, B., eds. L' Encyclopedie de L'Islam Tome IX: Livraison 165-166. 1998. pap. 69.00 (*90-04-11068-2*) Brill Academic Pubs.

Bosworth, C. E., jt. ed. see Schacht, Joseph.

Bosworth, C. E., tr. see Al-Tabari.

Bosworth, Charles. Killer among Us: A True Story of a Family's Triumph over Tragedy. LC 98-213306. 1998. mass mkt. 6.99 (*0-451-40854-3*, Onyx) NAL.

Bosworth, Charles, Jr., jt. auth. see Weber, Don W.

Bosworth, Charles, Jr., jt. auth. see Wecht, Cyril.

Bosworth, Clifford. The Ghaznavids. (Arab Background Ser.). 1973. 20.00 (*0-86685-005-8*) Intl Bk Ctr.

Bosworth, Clifford E. Ghaznavids: Their Empire in Afghanistan & Eastern Iran, 994-1040. (C). 1992. reprint ed. 34.00 (*81-215-0573-9*, Pub. by M Manoharial) Coronet Bks.

— The History of the Saffarids of Sistan & the Maliks of Nimruz, No. 247/861 to 949/1542-3. LC 93-38220. (Columbia Lecture Ser.: Vol. 8). vii, 525p. 1994. text 30.00 (*1-56859-015-6*) Bibliotheca Persica.

— The Later Ghaznavids: Splendour & Decay: The Dynasty in Afghanistan & Northern India 1040-1186. (C). 1992. reprint ed. text 20.00 (*81-215-0577-1*, Pub. by M Manoharial) Coronet Bks.

— The New Islamic Dynasties: A Chronological & Genealogical Manual. rev. ed. LC 96-28471. 320p. 1996. 47.50 (*0-231-10714-5*) Col U Pr.

Bosworth, Clifford E., jt. auth. see Netton, Ian R.

Bosworth, D. L., jt. auth. see Wilson, R. A.

Bosworth, David. The Death of Descartes. LC 81-50637. (Drue Heinz Literature Prize Ser.). 92p. 1981. text 22.50 (*0-8229-3448-5*) U of Pittsburgh Pr.

— From My Father, Singing. 1986. 13.95 (*0-916366-36-7*, Pub. by Pushcart Pr) Norton.

— From My Father, Singing. 1989. pap. 8.95 (*0-916366-50-2*, Pub. by Pushcart Pr) Norton.

— Open Learning. Hills, Philip, ed. (Issues in Education Ser.). 140p. 1991. text 90.00 (*0-304-32389-6*); pap. text 31.95 (*0-304-32388-8*) Continuum.

Bosworth-Davies, R. & Saltmarsh, G. Money Laundering: A Practical Guide to the New Legislation. 320p. 1994. mass mkt. 89.95 (*0-412-57530-2*) Chapman & Hall.

Bosworth, Derek, et al. Skill Shortages: Causes & Consequences. 218p. 1992. 82.95 (*1-85628-320-8*, Pub. by Avebry) Ashgate Pub Co.

— Technological Change: The Role of Scientists & Engineers. 149p. 1992. 77.95 (*1-85628-322-4*, Pub. by Avebry) Ashgate Pub Co.

Bosworth, F. F. Christ the Healer. LC 73-17492. 244p. (gr. 11). 1991. pap. 9.99 (*0-8007-5124-8*) Revell.

***Bosworth, F. F.** Christ the Healer. LC 00-9171. 2000. pap. write for info. (*0-88368-591-4*) Whitaker Hse.

Bosworth, Frank. The Oxyoke. large type ed. (Lythway Ser.). 160p. 1991. 19.95 (*0-7451-1250-1*, G K Hall Lrg Type) Mac Lib Ref.

Bosworth-Gerome, Sally, et al. Comprendre l'Anglais Scientifique et Technique. (ENG & FRE.). 381p. 1992. 79.95 (*0-7859-1007-7*, 2729892206) Fr & Eur.

Bosworth, Kenneth L. Edward Colborne of Ipswich, MA 1618-1712 & Five Generations of His Descendants. (Illus.). 286p. (Orig.). 1994. pap. text 39.00 (*1-55613-992-6*) Heritage Bk.

— William Adams of Ipswich, Massachusetts & Some of His Descendants, 1594-1661. (Illus.). 179p. 1992. pap. 27.50 (*1-55613-650-1*) Heritage Bk.

— William Adams of Ipswich, Massachusetts & Some of His Descendants, 1594-1661. rev. ed. (Illus.). 208p. 1996. pap. 33.50 (*0-7884-0528-4*) Heritage Bk.

Bosworth, Kris & Hamilton, Sharon J., eds. Collaborative Learning: Underlying Processes & Effective Techniques. LC 85-644763. (New Directions for Teaching & Learning Ser.: No. TL 59). 106p. (Orig.). 1994. pap. 22.00 (*0-7879-9998-9*) Jossey-Bass.

Bosworth, Louise M. The Living Wage of Women Workers: Study of Incomes & Expenditures of 450 Women in the City of Boston. LC 75-16459. (Social Problems & Social Policy Ser.). 1976. reprint ed. 13.95 (*0-405-07477-8*) Ayer.

Bosworth, Martha, et al. Landscapes with Women: Four American Poets. 136p. 1999. pap. 12.00 (*1-880286-37-8*) Singular Speech Pr.

Bosworth, Mary. Resisting Identities: Agency & Power in Women's Prisons. LC 98-52034. (Advances in Criminology Ser.). 232p. 1999. text 86.95 (*1-84014-739-3*) Ashgate Pub Co.

Bosworth, Michael. My Own Place. LC 93-27058. (Voyages Ser.). (Illus.). (J). 1994. 4.25 (*0-383-03766-2*) SRA McGraw.

Bosworth, Michael T. Solution Selling: Creating Buyers in Difficult Selling Markets. 91st ed. 270p. 1994. text 27.50 (*0-7863-0315-8*, Irwn Prfssnl) McGraw-Hill Prof.

Bosworth, Michal, jt. auth. see Ciccotosto, Emma.

An Asterisk (*) at the beginning of an entry indicates that the title is appearing for the first time.

Bosworth, Patricia. Anything Your Little Heart Desires: An American Family Story. (Illus.). 416p. 1998. pap. 15.00 (*0-684-83848-6*, Touchstone) S&S Trade Pap.
— Diane Arbus. 464p. 1985. pap. 10.95 (*0-380-69927-3*, Avon Bks) Morrow Avon.
— Diane Arbus. 400p. 1995. pap. 15.95 (*0-393-31207-0*) Norton.
— Montgomery Clift: A Biography. LC 89-49725. (Illus.). 438p. 1990. reprint ed. pap. 18.00 (*0-87910-135-0*) Limelight Edns.
***Bosworth, Patricia.** Ruth Orkin. (Illus.). 48p. 2000. 18.00 (*1-893920-00-3*, Pub. by H Greenberg) Dist Art Pubs.
— St. Mary's Cathedral Basilica: Texas's Oldest Cathedral. 40p. 1999. pap. 9.00 (*0-8059-4518-0*) Dorrance.
Bosworth, R. J. The Italian Dictatorship: Problems & Perspectives in the Interpretation of Mussolini & Fascism. (An Arnold Publication). 288p. 1998. text 75.00 (*0-340-67728-7*, Pub. by E A); pap. text 19.95 (*0-340-67727-9*, Pub. by E A) OUP.
— Italy & the Wider World, 1860-1960. LC 95-17352. 264p. (C). 1996. 80.00 (*0-415-13477-3*) Routledge.
***Bosworth, Richard.** The Box Seat Dream. (Illus.). 126p. (YA). (gr. 3-9). 2000. pap. 6.95 (*0-9679395-0-X*, 33) Boz Imagine.
Bosworth, Richard. A Practical Course in Functional Programming Using ML. LC 95-51. 1995. 19.95 (*0-07-707625-7*) McGraw.
Bosworth, Richard & Melia, Margot, eds. Aspects of Ethnicity in Western Australia. (Studies in Western Australian History: Vol. XII). pap. 19.95 (*0-86422-115-0*, Pub. by Univ of West Aust Pr) Intl Spec Bk.
Bosworth, Sheila. Almost Innocent. LC 84-14164. (Voices of the South Ser.). 268p. (C). 1996. pap. 14.95 (*0-8071-2066-9*) La State U Pr.
— Slow Poison. LC 97-43646. (Voices of the South Ser.). 336p. 1998. pap. 16.95 (*0-8071-2278-5*) La State U Pr.
Bosworth Smith, R. Mohammed & Mohammedanism. 344p. 1986. 220.00 (*1-85077-081-6*, Pub. by Darf Pubs Ltd) St Mut.
***Bosworth, Stefan.** MCAT Complete Review. 960p. 1999. pap. text 54.95 (*0-02-863562-0*, Arco) Macmillan Gen Ref.
Bosworth, Stefan. MCAT Sample Exams. 3rd ed. 240p. 1998. pap. text 13.95 (*0-02-862501-3*, Arc) IDG Bks.
***Bosworth, Stefan.** MCAT Subject Review with Tests. (Illus.). 464p. 1999. pap. text 39.95 incl. audio compact disk (*0-02-863255-9*, Arco) Macmillan Gen Ref.
— MCAT Verbal Reasoning Review. 256p. 2000. pap. text 14.95 (*0-02-863561-2*, Arco) Macmillan Gen Ref.
Bosworth, Stefan & Brisk, Marion. Learning Skills for the Science Student. Savige, Katherine, ed. (Illus.). 75p. 1986. pap. text 5.95 (*0-943202-21-3*) H & H Pubs.
Bosworth, Stefan, et al. MCAT Sample Exams. 2nd ed. LC 96-209878. 240p. 1996. pap. 13.95 (*0-02-861312-0*, Arco) Macmillan Gen Ref.
— MCAT Sample Tests with CD. (Illus.). 256p. 1999. pap. 34.95 incl. cd-rom (*0-02-863253-2*, Arco) Macmillan Gen Ref.
— MCAT SuperCourse. 4th ed. 720p. 1997. 39.95 (*0-02-861711-8*, Arc) IDG Bks.
— MCAT Supercourse. 22nd ed. 720p. 1996. 35.00 (*0-02-861083-0*) Macmillan.
Bosworth, Stefan, ed. see Martinson, Thomas H. & Fazzone, Juliana.
Bosworth, Timothy W. Community Health Need Assessment. LC 95-36932. 256p. (C). 1995. text 45.00 (*1-55738-647-1*, Irwn Prfssnl) McGraw-Hill Prof.
Boswoth, C. E., et al. Encyclopedie de L'Islam, Vol. 7. LC 92-45167. 1993. 596.00 (*90-04-09420-2*) Brill Academic Pubs.
Boszormeny. Parallel Computation: Third International ACPC Conference with Special Emphasis on Parallel Databases & Parallel IO, Klagenfurt, Austria, September 1996: Proceedings. LC 96-38442. (Lecture Notes in Computer Science Ser.: Vol. 1127). 235p. 1996. 43.00 (*3-540-61695-0*) Spr-Verlag.
Boszormenyi, L. Programming in Style: An Introduction to Programming with Modula-3. (Illus.). 592p. 1996. 39.00 (*0-387-57912-5*) Spr-Verlag.
Boszormenyi, Laszlo & Weich, Carsten. Programming in Modula-3: An Introduction in Programming with Style. LC 96-38492. 1996. 39.00 (*3-540-57912-5*) Spr-Verlag.
Boszormenyi-Nagy, Ivan. Foundations of Contextual Therapy: Collected Papers of Ivan Boszormenyi-Nagy. LC 86-26846. 360p. 1987. text 45.95 (*0-87630-449-8*) Brunner-Mazel.
Boszormenyi-Nagy, Ivan & Framo, James L., eds. Intensive Family Therapy: Theoretical & Practical Aspects. 2nd ed. LC 85-13270. 528p. 1985. text 59.95 (*0-87630-412-9*) Brunner-Mazel.
Boszormenyi-Nagy, Ivan & Krasner, Barbara R. Between Give & Take: A Clinical Guide to Contextual Therapy. LC 86-2219. 450p. 1986. text 48.95 (*0-87630-418-8*) Brunner-Mazel.
Boszormenyi-Nagy, Ivan & Spark, Geraldine M. Invisible Loyalties. 5th ed. LC 83-26300. 408p. 1986. reprint ed. text 48.95 (*0-87630-359-9*) Brunner-Mazel.
Boszormnyi, Ivan, jt. auth. see Zuk, Gerald H.
Bot, Kees De, see De Bot, Kees.
Bot, Kees De, see Bongaerts, Theo & De Bot, Kees, eds.
Bot, Yvon Le, see Le Bot, Yvon.
Botafogo, Dolores. The Art of Brazilian Cookery. (International Cookbook Classics Ser.). 240p. 1993. pap. 12.95 (*0-7818-0130-3*) Hippocrene Bks.
Botana, Natalio R. Domingo Faustino Sarmiento. (SPA.). 111p. 1996. pap. 19.99 (*950-557-222-0*, Pub. by Fondo) Continental Bk.
Botanica Editors, jt. auth. see Advantage Publishing Staff.
Botanical Society of America, Inc., ed. Directory. 85p. 1982. 12.00 (*0-317-46938-X*, NO.161) Botanical Soc.
Botar, Oliver, et al. Laszlo Moholy-Nagy: From Budapest to Berlin, 1914-1923. Chapp, Belena S., ed. LC 95-61286. 200p. 1995. pap. 30.00 (*1-887421-00-9*) Univ Gall U of DE.
***Botash, Ann S.** Evaluating Child Sexual Abuse: Education Manual for Medical Professionals. LC 00-30925. (Illus.). 256p. 2000. spiral bd. 27.50 (*0-8018-6550-6*) Johns Hopkins.
Botbol, J. M. Composite & Disaggregated Maps As Preliminary Aids to Analysis of Manganese Nodule Geochemistry. (Illus.). 52p. (Orig.). (C). 1993. pap. text 25.00 (*1-56806-358-X*) DIANE Pub.
Botchan, Michael, et al, eds. DNA Tumor Viruses: Control of Gene Expression & Replication. LC 86-50649. (Cancer Cells Ser.). 620p. (Orig.). 1986. pap. 75.00 (*0-87969-192-1*) Cold Spring Harbor.
— DNA Tumor Viruses: Control of Gene Expression & Replication. LC 86-50649. (Cancer Cells Ser.: No. 4). 640p. (Orig.). reprint ed. pap. 198.40 (*0-7837-2005-X*, 204227900002) Bks Demand.
Botchie, G. Employment & Multinational Enterprises in Export Processing Zones: The Cases of Liberia & Ghana. (Multinational Enterprises Programme Working Papers: No. 30). iv, 74p. (Orig.). 1984. pap. 13.50 (*92-2-103770-3*) Intl Labour Office.
Botchis, Lilli. Plants in the Light of Healing. (Illus.). 30p. (Orig.). 1995. pap. text 3.95 (*0-9643535-1-2*) Time Portal.
Bote, Eduardo V. Derecho Privado de Puerto Rico. (SPA.). 1993. 800.00 (*0-88063-607-6*, 82880-10, MICHIE) LEXIS Pub.
— Tratado TeUrico, Practico y Critico De Derecho Privado De PuertoriqueOo. 1992. 800.00 (*0-614-05985-2*, MICHIE) LEXIS Pub.
Boteach, Shmuel. Dreams. 180p. 1991. 14.95 (*0-932351-28-X*) B P Marketing.
— Wisdom, Understanding, & Knowledge: Basic Concepts of Hasidic Thought. LC 95-6052. 296p. 1996. pap. 30.00 (*0-87668-557-2*) Aronson.
— Wrestling with the Divine: A Jewish Response to Suffering. LC 94-1288. 312p. 1995. 40.00 (*1-56821-176-7*) Aronson.
***Boteach, Shmuley.** Dating Secrets of the Ten Commandments. LC 99-37912. 288p. 2000. 21.00 (*0-385-49620-6*) Doubleday.
Boteach, Shmuley. Kosher Sex. LC 98-39540. 304p. 1999. 19.95 (*0-385-49465-3*) Doubleday.
***Boteach, Shmuley.** Kosher Sex: A Recipe for Passion & Intimacy. LC 99-54936. 304p. 2000. pap. 11.95 (*0-385-49466-1*, Main St Bks) Doubleday.
Boteach, Shmuley, jt. auth. see Geller, Uri.
Botein, Bernard. Trial Judge: The Candid, Behind the Bench Story of Justice Bernard Botein. (American Constitutional & Legal History Ser). 337p. 1974. reprint ed. lib. bdg. 39.50 (*0-306-70630-X*) Da Capo.
Botein, Michael. Regulation of the Electronic Mass Media: Law & Policy for Radio, Television, Cable & the New Video Technologies. LC 97-47668. (American Casebook Ser.). 650p. 1998. 57.50 (*0-314-21122-5*) West Pub.
— Statutory Supplement to Regulation of the Electronic Mass Media: Law & Policy for Radio, Television, Cable & the New Video Technologies. 3rd ed. (American Casebook Ser.). 216p. 1998. pap., suppl. ed. 20.00 (*0-314-23404-7*) West Pub.
Botein, Stephen. Early American Law & Society. LC 82-17158. (Borozi Books in Law & American Society). (C). 1983. pap. text 6.00 (*0-685-07492-7*, KnopfC) Knopf.
— Mr. Zenger's Malice & Falshood: Six Issues of the New York Weekly Journal, 1733-34. (AAS Facsimiles Ser.: No. 3). 48p. 1985. pap. 10.00 (*0-912296-73-9*, 42175) Oak Knoll.
Botel, A. Morton. Spelling - Writing for Young Authors: Level D. (Illus.). 144p. (J). (gr. 4-6). 1998. pap. 55.00 (*1-891564-08-0*) M Botel Assocs.
Botel, Morton. Botel Reading Milestone Tests: Advanced, Vol. A. 3rd rev. ed. 8p. (J). (gr. 1-12). 1996. pap. 21.00 (*1-891564-05-6*) M Botel Assocs.
— Botel Reading Milestone Tests: Advanced, Vol. B. 3rd rev. ed. 8p. (J). (gr. 1-12). 1996. pap. 21.00 (*1-891564-06-4*) M Botel Assocs.
— Botel Reading Milestone Tests: Foundations, Vol. A. 3rd rev. ed. 8p. (J). (gr. 1-12). 1996. pap. 21.00 (*1-891564-03-X*) M Botel Assocs.
— Botel Reading Milestone Tests: Foundations, Vol. B. 3rd rev. ed. 8p. (J). (gr. 1-12). 1996. pap. 21.00 (*1-891564-04-8*) M Botel Assocs.
— Spelling - Writing for Young Authors, Vol. C. 96p. (J). (gr. 1-3). 1997. pap. 45.00 (*1-891564-02-1*) M Botel Assocs.
— Spelling - Writing for Young Authors, Vol. A. (Illus.). 56p. (J). (gr. 1-3). 1997. pap. 40.00 (*1-891564-00-5*) M Botel Assocs.
— Spelling - Writing for Young Authors, Vol. B. (Illus.). 96p. (J). (gr. 1-3). 1997. pap. 45.00 (*1-891564-01-3*) M Botel Assocs.
Botel, Morton & Seaver, Joann T. Reading - Writing - Talking Across the Curriculum: A Resource Book for Primary & Middle Grade Teachers. (Illus.). 228p. 1991. pap. text 20.00 (*1-891564-07-2*) M Botel Assocs.
Botel, Morton, jt. auth. see Bartoli, Jill.
Botel, Morton, ed. see Granowsky, Alvin.
Boteler, Alexander R., et al. John Brown's Raid at Harpers Ferry, West Virginia, 1859. (Illus.). 1980. pap. 4.95 (*0-89646-055-X*) Vistabooks.
Boteler, Alison. Children's Party Handbook. 160p. 1991. pap. 16.95 (*0-8120-4747-8*) Barron.
— Country Fair Cookbook. LC 94-42420. (Illus.). 176p. 1995. 12.95 (*0-8120-6522-0*) Barron.
— Country Fair Craft Book. (Illus.). 176p. 1995. 12.95 (*0-8120-6439-9*) Barron.
***Boteler, Alison.** Creative Children's Parties. (Illus.). 192p. 2000. pap. 14.95 (*0-7641-0881-6*) Barron.
Boteler, Alison. Disney Party Handbook. LC 91-58610. (Illus.). 176p. (J). 1992. pap. 8.05 (*1-56282-173-3*, Pub. by Disney Pr) Little.
— The Disney Party Handbook: 14 Fun-Filled Parties! LC 97-26148. (Illus.). 224p. (J). 1998. pap. 15.95 (*0-7868-4105-2*, Pub. by Disney Pr) Time Warner.
— The Great American Bake Sale. 1991. pap., spiral bd. 14.95 (*0-8120-4314-6*) Barron.
— What Should I Bring? Great Gifts for Every Occasion. (Illus.). 250p. 1992. spiral bd. 13.95 (*0-8120-4941-1*) Barron.
Boteler, Alison M. Party Handbook. LC 97-26148. 224p. (J). 1998. lib. bdg. 19.49 (*0-7868-5049-3*, Pub. by Disney Pr) Little.
Botelho, Joyce M. Right & Might: The Dorr Rebellion & the Struggle for Equal Rights, 4 bks. (Illus.). 103p. (Orig.). 1992. pap. 9.95 (*0-932840-10-8*) RI Hist Soc.
***Botelho, L. A., ed.** Churchwardens' Accounts for Cratfield, 1640-1660. 160p. 1999. 54.00 (*0-85115-759-9*, Suffolk Records Soc) Boydell & Brewer.
Botelho, Richard. The New Individualism: Personal Change to Transform Society. 176p. 1995. 19.95 (*0-9643926-1-5*); pap. 12.95 (*0-9643926-2-3*) Windstream Pubng.
***Botella, J., et al, eds.** Chronic Inflammation in Hemodialysis. (Blood Purification Ser.: Vol. 18, No. 3). (Illus.). vi, 78p. 2000. 98.00 (*3-8055-7083-X*) S Karger.
Botello. California Real Estate Law Cases & Materials. (C). 1994. pap. text 23.00 (*0-07-006624-8*) McGraw.
Botello, Judy G. The Other Side: Journeys in Baja, California. LC 98-22892. (Illus.). 178p. 1997. pap. 12.95 (*0-932653-25-1*) Sunbelt Pubns.
Boter, G. J. The Textual Tradition of Plato's Republic. 1989. pap. 87.00 (*90-04-08787-7*, MNS, 107) Brill Academic Pubs.
Boter, Gerard, jt. auth. see Epictetus.
Boterbloem, Kees. Life & Death under Stalin: Kalinin Province 1945-1953. 49.95 (*0-7735-1811-8*) McG-Queens Univ Pr.
Botermans, Jack. Paper Capers: An Amazing Array of Games, Puzzles, & Tricks. LC 86-7596. (Illus.). 120p. 1995. pap. 16.95 (*0-8050-0139-5*, Owl) H Holt & Co.
— Paper Flight: 48 Models Ready for Take-Off. Ogle, Deborah, tr. from DUT. LC 83-49043. 120p. 1995. pap. 16.95 (*0-8050-0500-5*, Owl) H Holt & Co.
Botermans, Jack & Weve, Alice. Kite Flight: 40 Models Ready for Takeoff. LC 85-17641. (Illus.). 120p. 1995. pap. 9.95 (*0-03-008518-7*, Owl) H Holt & Co.
Botero de Borrero, Beatriz & Botero de Borrero, Martha O. Bonsai Ways. (Illus.). 308p. 1993. 35.00 (*958-33-0058-6*, Pub. by Borrero & Gomez) MBIPubg.
Botero de Borrero, Martha O., jt. auth. see Botero de Borrero, Beatriz.
Botero, Giovanni. The Traveller's Breviant, or an Historical Description of the Most Famous Kingdomes. LC 72-175. (English Experience Ser.: No. 143). 180p. 1969. reprint ed. 35.00 (*90-221-0143-6*) Walter J Johnson.
— A Treatise, Concerning the Causes of the Magnificence & Greatness of Cities. LC 79-84090. (English Experience Ser.: No. 910). 128p. 1979. reprint ed. lib. bdg. 25.00 (*90-221-0910-0*) Walter J Johnson.
***Botero, Rodrigo.** Ambivalent Embrace: America's Relations with Spain from the Revolutionary War to the Cold War, 78. LC 00-35356. (Contributions to the Study of World History Ser.: Vol. 78). 200p. 2000. 64.00 (*0-313-31570-1*) Greenwood.
Botero, Rodrigo. Reflections on the Modernization of Spain. LC 92-8644. 32p. 1992. 9.95 (*1-55815-199-0*) ICS Pr.
Botet, R., jt. auth. see Jullien, R.
Botet, Serge. Langue, Langage et Strategies Linguistiques Chez Heidegger. (Contacts Ser.: Series III, Vol. 36). (FRE.). xii, 552p. 1997. 63.95 (*3-906754-63-4*, Pub. by P Lang) P Lang Pubng.
Botev, N., ed. The Game & the Man: Proceedings of the XXII Congress of the International Congress of Game Biology, Sofia, September, 1995. (Illus.). 532p. 1996. pap. 89.95 (*954-642-013-1*) Intl Scholars.
Botey, Joseph M. Oscar Niemeyer. (Illus.). 240p. 1996. pap. text 19.95 (*84-252-1576-5*) Watsn-Guptill.
Botez, Dan & Scifres, Don R., eds. Diode Laser Arrays. (Cambridge Studies in Modern Optics: No. 14). (Illus.). 464p. (C). 1994. text 110.00 (*0-521-41975-1*) Cambridge U Pr.
Both, Bibi, jt. ed. see Tisdale, Mary E.
Both, Ernst E. The Boletes of North America: A Compendium. 431p. 1993. pap. 10.00 (*0-944032-54-0*) Buffalo SNS.
Both, Ernst E., ed. see Clark, Arthur R., et al.
Both, Norbert. From Indifference to Entrapment: The Netherlands & the Yugoslav Crisis, 1990-1995. (Illus.). 216p. (C). pap. text 31.00 (*90-5356-453-5*, Pub. by Amsterdam U Pr) U of Mich Pr.
Both, Norbert & Honig, Jan W. Srebrenica: Record of a War Crime. LC 97-195172. 224p. 1997. pap. 11.95 (*0-14-026632-1*) Viking Penguin.
Both, Zilpha. Stories on Rocks. Weinberger, Jane, ed. LC 93-61627. (Illus.). 80p. (J). (gr. 4-8). 1994. pap. 8.00 (*1-883650-08-9*) Windswept Hse.
Botha, A. Association of Law Societies Practice Manual, 10 pts., Ser. ring bd. 176.00 (*0-409-00644-0*, SA, MICHIE) LEXIS Pub.
Botha, C. Statutory Interpretation: An Introduction for Students. 3rd ed. 1998. 28.00 (*0-7021-4533-5*, Pub. by Juta & Co) Gaunt.
Botha, C. R. Statutory Interpretation: An Introduction for Students. 132p. 1991. pap. write for info. (*0-7021-2676-4*, Pub. by Juta & Co) Gaunt.
— Statutory Interpretation: An Introduction for Students. 2nd ed. 191p. (C). 1996. pap. 27.50 (*0-7021-3623-9*, Pub. by Juta & Co) Gaunt.
— Wetsuitleg - 'N Inleiding vir Studente. 132p. 1991. pap. write for info. (*0-7021-2604-7*, Pub. by Juta & Co) Gaunt.
Botha, Eugene J., jt. auth. see Vorster, W. S.
Botha, J. Eugene. Jesus & the Samaritan Woman: A Speech Act Reading of John 4: 1-42. LC 91-31184. (Novum Testamentum, Supplements Ser.: No. 65). xii, 220p. 1991. 91.00 (*90-04-09505-5*) Brill Academic Pubs.
Botha, J. F., jt. auth. see Cakmak, A. S.
Botha, Rudolf B. Methodological Status of Grammatical Argumentation. LC 79-126050. (Janua Linguarum, Series Major: No. 105). (Orig.). 1970. pap. text 35.40 (*90-279-0714-5*) Mouton.
Botha, Rudolf P. The Conduct of Linguistic Inquiry: A Systematic Introduction to the Methodology of Generative Grammar. 462p. 1981. text 61.55 (*90-279-3299-9*) Mouton.
— Form & Meaning in Word Formation: A Study of Afrikaans Reduplication. (Cambridge Studies in Linguistics: Supplementary Volumes). 200p. 1988. text 49.95 (*0-521-35260-6*) Cambridge U Pr.
— The Justification of Linguistic Hypotheses. (Janua Linguarum, Series Major: No. 84). 1973. text 75.40 (*90-279-2542-9*) Mouton.
Botha, Rudolph P. Methodological Aspects of Transformational Generative Phonology. (Janua Linguarum, Ser. Minor: No. 112). 266p. 1971. pap. text 38.50 (*90-279-1761-2*) Mouton.
Botha, Thozamile, jt. ed. see Wolpe, Harold.
Botha, W. A Duty of Memory. (African Writers Ser.). 1993. pap. 13.95 (*0-435-91007-8*) Heinemann.
Botha, W. P. Wantok. (African Writers Ser.). 182p. 1995. pap. 10.95 (*0-435-90969-X*, 90969) Heinemann.
Botha, W.P.B. The Reluctant Playwright. (African Writers Ser.). 232p. (C). 1993. pap. 10.95 (*0-435-90589-9*, 90589) Heinemann.
Bothamley, Jennifer, ed. Dictionary of Theories. 637p. 1993. 85.00 (*1-873477-05-8*, 101460) Gale.
Bothe. Fuzzy Logic. 1993. 31.95 (*0-387-56166-8*) Spr-Verlag.
Bothe, Davis R. Measuring Process Capability: Techniques & Calculations for Quality & Manufacturing Engineers. LC 96-30087. (Illus.). 897p. 1997. 99.95 (*0-07-006652-3*) McGraw.
Bothe, E. Marie. Be Right or Go Wrong: A Fundamentally Different Way of Life. large type ed. 79p. 1996. pap. 8.00 (*1-881074-05-6*) Alpha Pub Hse.
Bothe, Hans-Werner & Trebst, A., eds. Biology of Inorganic Nitrogen & Sulfur Metabolism. (Proceedings in Life Sciences Ser.). (Illus.). 370p. 1981. 86.95 (*0-387-10486-0*) Spr-Verlag.
Bothe, M., et al. New Rules for Victims of Armed Conflict. 1982. lib. bdg. 342.50 (*90-247-2537-2*) Kluwer Academic.
Bothe, Michael, ed. Amazonia & Siberia: Legal Aspects of the Preservation of the Environment & Development in the Last Open Spaces. (International Environmental Law & Policy Ser.). 376p. (C). 1993. lib. bdg. 104.50 (*1-85333-903-2*, Pub. by Graham & Trotman) Kluwer Academic.
Bothe, Michael, et al, eds. The OSCE in the Maintenance of Peace & Security: Conflict Prevention, Crisis Management & Peaceful Settlement of Disputes. LC 97-44704. 580p. 1997. 182.00 (*90-411-0446-1*) Kluwer Academic.
***Bothe, Michael, et al.** Basic Materials on UN Peacekeeping. LC 99-47159. 344p. 1999. pap. 117.00 (*90-411-9774-5*) Kluwer Law Intl.
Bothe, Michael, et al. The New Chemical Weapons Convention--Implementation & Prospectus. LC 98-42960. 1998. 189.00 (*90-411-1099-2*) Kluwer Academic.
Bothe, Michael, jt. ed. see Fleck, Dieter.
Botheroyd, Paul F. Ich und Er: First & Third-Person Self-Reference & Problems of Identity in Three Contemporary German-Language Novels. (De Proprietatibus Litterarum, Ser. Practica: No.67). 143p. (Orig.). 1976. pap. text 36.95 (*90-279-3214-X*) Mouton.
Botheroyd, Sylvia. Lexikon der Keltischen Mythologie. (GER.). 378p. 1992. 105.00 (*0-7859-8356-2*, 3424010774) Fr & Eur.
Botherston, G., ed. see Borges, Jorge Luis.
***Bothma, J. P.** Larger Carnivores of the African Savannas. 2000. 52.00 (*0-627-02411-4*, Pub. by J L Van Schaik) BBN Intl.
Bothma, Jacobus du P. Carnivore Ecology in Arid Lands. Cloudsley-Thompson, J. L., ed. LC 97-37163. (Adaptations of Desert Organisms Ser.). (Illus.). 200p. 1998. 130.00 (*3-540-59265-2*) Spr-Verlag.
Bothma, Jacobus du P. & Walker, Clive. Larger Carnivores of the African Savannas. LC 99-21370. 1999. write for info. (*3-540-65660-X*) Spr-Verlag.
Bothmer, A. James, jt. auth. see Walsh, Jim.
Bothmer, Dietrich Von, see Von Bothmer, Dietrich, ed.
Bothmer, Gerry, tr. see Lindgren, Astrid.
Bothmer, R. Von, see Von Bothmer, R.
Bothmer, Richard, jt. auth. see Mullen, Gail S.
Bothner-By, Aksel A., et al, eds. Biochemical Structure Determination by NMR. LC 81-22055. (Illus.). 246p. reprint ed. pap. 76.30 (*0-7837-4738-1*, 204454600004) Bks Demand.
Bothorel, J. & Dufoure, J., eds. Trends in Colloid & Interface Science III. (Progress in Colloid & Polymer Science Ser.: Vol. 79). 356p. 1989. 158.00 (*0-387-91364-5*) Spr-Verlag.
Bothorel, Pierre, jt. auth. see Friberg, Stig E.

B

Bothun, Gregory. Modern Cosmological Observations & Problems. 300p. 1997. 95.00 (*0-7484-0332-9*, Pub. by Tay Francis Ltd); pap. 34.95 (*0-7484-0645-X*, Pub. by Tay Francis Ltd) Taylor & Francis.

Bothun, Linda. Dialogues about Adoption: Conversations Between Parents & Their Children. LC 94-69688. 216p. (Orig.). 1994. pap. 12.95 (*0-9619559-1-0*) Swan Pubns.

— When Friends Ask about Adoption: A Question & Answer Guide for Non-Adoptive Parents & Other Caring Adults. rev. ed. 96p. (Orig.). 1996. pap. 5.95 (*0-9619559-0-2*) Swan Pubns.

Bothwell, Al, et al. Methods for Cloning & Analysis of Eukaryotic Genes. 336p. (Orig.). 1990. spiral bd. 75.00 (*0-86720-103-7*) Jones & Bartlett.

***Bothwell, Bruce.** At the Beep. (Illus.). iii, 57p. 1998. pap. 10.00 (*1-929764-00-6*) Bothwell Bks.

— 1,000 Words Is Worth a Picture. iii, 147p. 1999. pap. 10.00 (*1-929764-03-0*) Bothwell Bks.

— Private Lives. 89p. 2000. pap. 10.00 (*1-929764-05-7*) Bothwell Bks.

— Simple Simon. ii, 103p. 1999. pap. 10.00 (*1-929764-01-4*) Bothwell Bks.

— Thanksgiving. ii, 130p. 1999. pap. 10.00 (*1-929764-02-2*) Bothwell Bks.

— Toynbee & Son. 150p. 2000. pap. 10.00 (*1-929764-06-5*) Bothwell Bks.

— You Teach Good for an Injun. 337p. 2000. spiral bd. 15.00 (*1-929764-04-9*) Bothwell Bks.

***Bothwell, Cecil L. & Gregutt, Peter.** Gorillas in the Myth: A Duck Soup Reader. 2000. pap. 8.00 (*0-9700125-0-0*) Brave Ulysses.

Bothwell, Dick. Alligators. LC 62-52731. 88p. (Orig.). 1962. pap. 3.95 (*0-8200-0302-6*) Great Outdoors.

Bothwell, Dorr & Mayfield, Marlys. Notan: The Dark-Light Principle of Design. (Illus.). 80p. 1991. reprint ed. pap. 5.95 (*0-486-26856-X*) Dover.

Bothwell, Etta K. Alienation in the Jewish American Novel of the Sixties. LC 78-3559. 227p. 1979. pap. 8.00 (*0-8477-3191-X*) U of PR Pr.

Bothwell, James H. Affaires du conte de Boduel. LC 71-39513. (Bannatyne Club, Edinburgh. Publications: No. 29). (FRE.). reprint ed. 42.50 (*0-404-52735-3*) AMS Pr.

Bothwell, James L. Financial Derivatives: Actions Needed to Protect the Financial System. (Illus.). 210p. (Orig.). (C). 1994. pap. text 45.00 (*0-7881-1606-1*) DIANE Pub.

Bothwell, Reece B. La Ciudadania en Puerto Rico. 2nd ed. LC 78-24031. (SPA., Illus.). 1980. pap. 2.00 (*0-8477-2451-4*) U of PR Pr.

— Manual de Procedimiento Parlamentario. 7th rev. ed. 225p. (C). 1990. 7.00 (*0-8477-3028-X*) U of PR Pr.

— Puerto Rico: Cien Anos de Lucha Politica, 5 vols. LC 77-10904. 1980. 100.00 (*0-8477-2444-1*) U of PR Pr.

— Trasfondo Constitucional de Puerto Rico: Primera Parte, 1887-1914. 3rd ed. 65p. (C). 1971. pap. 2.00 (*0-8477-0821-7*) U of PR Pr.

Bothwell, Reece B. & Cruz Monclava, Lidio. Los Documentos "Que Dicen" 602p. (C). 1975. pap. 5.50 (*0-8477-0820-9*) U of PR Pr.

Bothwell, Robert. Canada & Quebec: One Country, Two Histories. (Illus.). 288p. 1995. 34.95 (*0-7748-0524-2*) U of Wash Pr.

— Canada & Quebec: One Country, Two Histories. rev. ed. 288p. 1995. pap. 24.95 (*0-7748-0542-0*) U of Wash Pr.

***Bothwell, Robert.** Canada & Quebec: One Country, Two Histories. rev. ed. LC 98-174674. 296p. 1999. pap. 25.95 (*0-7748-0653-2*, Pub. by UBC Pr) U of Wash Pr.

Bothwell, Robert. Canada & the United States: The Politics of Partnership. (Twayne's International History Ser.: No. 10). 200p. (C). 1992. 27.95 (*0-8057-7914-0*, Twyne); pap. 20.00 (*0-8057-9213-9*, Twyne) Mac Lib Ref.

— Canada & the United States: The Politics of Partnership. 1992. pap. text 18.95 (*0-8020-7383-2*) U of Toronto Pr.

— Eldorado: Canada's National Uranium Company. (Illus.). 512p. 1984. text 35.00 (*0-8020-3414-4*) U of Toronto Pr.

— History of Canada since 1867. rev. ed. LC 97-127555. (ACSUS Papers Ser.). 50p. 1996. pap. 7.50 (*0-87013-399-3*) Mich St U Pr.

— Nucleus: A History of Atomic Energy of Canada Limited. (Illus.). 576p. 1988. 34.95 (*0-8020-2670-2*) U of Toronto Pr.

Bothwell, Robert, et al. Canada Nineteen Hundred to Nineteen Forty-Five. 1987. pap. text 21.95 (*0-8020-6801-4*) U of Toronto Pr.

— Canada since Nineteen Forty-Five. 2nd ed. (Illus.). 512p. 1989. text 45.00 (*0-8020-2647-8*); pap. text 24.95 (*0-8020-6672-0*) U of Toronto Pr.

— Canada since Nineteen Forty-Five: Power, Politics, & Provincialism. LC 81-152041. (Illus.). 515p. reprint ed. pap. 159.70 (*0-7837-0537-9*, 204086500019) Bks Demand.

Bothwell, Robert, jt. auth. see Granatstein, Jack L.

Bothwell, Robert O. Workplace Fundraising a Primer. 18p. 1997. pap. 5.00 (*1-891465-01-5*) Natl Comm Philan.

Bothwell, Robert O. & Paprocki, Steve. Corporate Grantmaking: Racial/Ethnic Populations. 465p. 1993. pap. 25.00 (*1-891465-00-7*) Natl Comm Philan.

Bothwell, Robert O., jt. auth. see Paprocki, Steve L.

Bothwell, Robert O., jt. auth. see Paprocki, Steven L.

Bothwell, Roberta, jt. auth. see Robinson, Zan Dale.

Bothwell, Thomas H. & Carlton, Robert W. Carence En Fer Chez la Femme. Cook, James D. et al, eds. Vicent, Marc, tr. (FRE., Illus.). 136p. (Orig.). 1983. pap. text 3.50 (*0-935368-37-X*) ILSI.

— Deficiencia De Hierro en la Mujer. Cook, James D. et al, eds. Arroyave, Guillermo, tr. (SPA., Illus.). 139p. (Orig.). 1985. pap. text 3.50 (*0-318-35289-3*) ILSI.

Bothwell, Thomas H. & Charlton, Robert W. Iron Deficiency in Women. Cook, James D. et al, eds. (Illus.). 68p. (Orig.). 1981. pap. text 3.50 (*0-935368-25-6*) ILSI.

Bothwell, Thomas H., et al. The Effects of Cereals & Legumes on Iron Availability. (Illus.). 44p. (Orig.). 1982. pap. text 3.50 (*0-935368-28-0*) ILSI.

— Measurements of Iron Status. DeMaeyer, Edouard M. & Kahn, Samuel G., eds. (Illus.). 78p. (Orig.). 1985. pap., student ed. 18.00 (*0-935368-47-7*) ILSI.

Bothwell, Thomas H., ed. see Dallman, Peter R., et al.

***Botique-Sha Staff.** 3D Origami. (Illus.). 90p. 2000. pap. 17.00 (*4-88996-057-0*) Japan Pubn Trad.

Botjer, George F. Sideshow War: The Italian Campaign, 1943-1945. LC 96-14400. (Texas A&M University Military History Ser.: No. 49). (Illus.). 232p. 1996. 29.95 (*0-89096-718-0*) Tex A&M Univ Pr.

Botkin. Delete. 7th ed. pap. text. write for info. (*0-471-37118-1*) Wiley.

— Environmental Science. 3rd ed. 736p. 1999. text 92.95 (*0-471-32173-7*) Wiley.

***Botkin.** Environmental Science Survey, Set. 3rd ed. 1999. text 43.00 (*0-471-35988-2*) Wiley.

Botkin. Science Lab Manual: Take Note Set 3rd ed. 1999. text 73.00 (*0-471-37714-7*) Wiley.

— The Study Guide to Environmental Science. 3rd ed. 1999. pap. text. write for info. (*0-471-36273-5*) Wiley.

Botkin, ed. Principles of Ecology. (C). Date not set. text. write for info. (*0-321-01478-2*) Addson-Wesley Educ.

Botkin, B. A. Civil War Treasury of Tales, Legends & Folklore. 648p. 1981. 10.98 (*0-88394-049-3*) Promntory Pr.

— Treasury of American Anecdotes. 1989. 7.98 (*0-88365-616-7*) Galahad Bks.

Botkin, B. A., ed. A Civil War Treasury of Tales. 36.95 (*0-88411-860-6*) Amereon Ltd.

***Botkin, B. A., ed.** A Civil War Treasury of Tales, Legends, & Folklore. (Illus.). 645p. 2000. reprint ed. pap. 24.95 (*0-8032-6172-1*, Bison Books) U of Nebr Pr.

Botkin, Benjamin A. The American People: Stories, Legends, Tales, Traditions & Songs. LC 97-27086. 356p. 1997. pap. 22.95 (*1-56000-984-5*) Transaction Pubs.

— The American People: Stories, Legends, Tales, Traditions, & Songs. 500p. 1998. text 27.95 (*1-56000-509-2*) Transaction Pubs.

— Sidewalks of America: Folklore, Legends, Sagas, Traditions, Customs, Songs, Stories, & Sayings of City Folk. LC 76-44361. (Illus.). 605p. 1977. reprint ed. lib. bdg. 85.00 (*0-8371-9312-5*, BOSA, Greenwood Pr) Greenwood.

Botkin, Daniel B. Discordant Harmonies: A New Ecology for the Twenty-First Century. (Illus.). 256p. 1992. pap. 13.95 (*0-19-507469-6*) OUP.

***Botkin, Daniel B.** Environment 3e Take Note Set, Set. 3rd ed. 1999. text 63.00 (*0-471-36362-6*) Wiley.

Botkin, Daniel B. Forest Dynamics: An Ecological Model. (Illus.). 328p. (C). 1993. text 70.00 (*0-19-506555-7*) OUP.

— JABOWA-II: The Forest Growth Model. (Illus.). 1993. 275.00 incl. disk (*0-19-507683-4*) OUP.

***Botkin, Daniel B.** No Man's Garden: Thoreau & a New Vision for Civilization & Nature. (Illus.). 288p. 2000. 24.95 (*1-55963-465-0*, Shearwater Bks) Island Pr.

Botkin, Daniel B. Our Natural History: The Lessons of Lewis & Clark. 320p. 1996. reprint ed. pap. 14.00 (*0-399-52242-5*, Perigee Bks) Berkley Pub.

***Botkin, Daniel B.** Passage of Discovery: American Rivers Guidebook to the Missouri River of Lewis & Clark. LC 98-56643. 272p. 1999. pap. 15.95 (*0-399-52510-6*, Perigee Bks) Berkley Pub.

Botkin, Daniel B., et al, eds. Changing the Global Environment: Perspectives on Human Involvement. 459p. 1989. pap. text 53.00 (*0-12-118731-4*) Acad Pr.

Botkin, Daniel B. & Keller, Edward A. Environmental Science: Earth as a Living Planet. 75p. 1995. pap. text 250.95 (*0-471-59777-5*) Wiley.

— Environmental Science: Earth as a Living Planet. 2nd ed. 1108p. 1997. text 114.95 (*0-471-25315-4*) Wiley.

Botkin, James, et al. The Innovators: Rediscovering America's Creative Energy. LC 85-24659. 320p. (C). 1986. reprint ed. pap. 18.95 (*0-8122-1224-X*) U of Pa Pr.

Botkin, James W., et al. No Limits to Learning: Bridging the Human Gap: The Club of Rome Report. LC 79-40911. (Pergamon International Library Science Technology Engineering & Social Studies). 1979. 82.00 (*0-08-024705-9*, Pub. by Pergamon Repr) Franklin.

Botkin, Jana & Coughran, Jane. The Cabins of Mineral King. LC 98-87741. 127 p. 1998. write for info. (*0-9666968-0-8*) Cabinart Bks.

Botkin, Jeffrey R., et al, eds. Genetics & Criminality: The Potential Misuse of Scientific Information in Court. LC 99-20607. 277p. 1999. 39.95 (*1-55798-580-4*, 431-728A) Am Psychol.

Botkin, Jeffrey R., jt. auth. see Mehlman, Maxwell J.

Botkin, Jim. Smart Business: How Knowledge Communities Can Revolutionize Your Company. LC 99-17727. (Illus.). 304p. 1999. 24.50 (*0-684-85024-9*) Free Pr.

Botkin, M. P., et al. Sheep & Wool: Science, Production & Management. (Illus.). 512p. 1988. text 50.80 (*0-13-808494-7*) P-H.

Botkin, Mark E., jt. ed. see Bennett, James A.

Botkin, Nancy. Signs of Life. 24p. 1999. pap. 4.00 (*1-929123-05-1*, NB0699P) No Exit Press.

***Botley, Simon & McEnery, Anthony Mark, eds.** Corpus-Based & Computational Approaches to Discourse Anaphora. LC 99-43484. (Studies in Corpus Linguistics: Vol. 3). vi, 255p. 2000. 79.00 (*1-55619-397-1*) J Benjamins Pubng.

***Botman, Selma.** Engendering Citizenship in Egypt. LC 98-36348. (History & Society of the Middle East Ser.). 256p. 1998. pap. 17.50 (*0-231-11299-8*); lib. bdg. 45.00 (*0-231-11298-X*) Col U Pr.

Botman, Selma. The Rise of Egyptian Communism, 1939-1970. LC 88-4916. (Contemporary Issues in the Middle East Ser.). 168p. 1988. text 42.50 (*0-8156-2443-3*) Syracuse U Pr.

***Botman, Steven & National Center for Health Statistics Staff.** Design & Estimation for the National Health Interview Survey, 1995-2004. LC 00-37092. (Vital & Health Statistics Ser.). 2000. write for info. (*0-8406-0562-5*) Natl Ctr Health Stats.

Botnarescue, Helen M., jt. auth. see Machado, Jeanne M.

Botnick, David I. Probate Forms: Ontario. rev. ed. (Legal Ser.). 96p. (C). 1995. 17.95 (*1-55180-103-5*) Self-Counsel Pr.

***Botnick, Michael R., ed.** Gay Community Survival in the New Millennium. LC 99-58929. (Journal of Homosexuality Monograph Ser.: Vol. 38, No. 4). 168p. 2000. 49.95 (*0-7890-0791-6*, Harrington Park); pap. text 19.95 (*1-56023-131-9*, Harrington Park) Haworth Pr.

Botoman, Rodica. Discover Romanian: An Introduction to the Language & Culture. LC 93-21808. (Illus.). 425p. (C). 1995. pap. text 50.00 (*0-8142-0536-4*) Ohio St U Pr.

Botoman, Rodica C., et al. Imi Place Limba Romana: A Romanian Reader. (Illus.). iii, 199p. 1982. pap. text 17.95 (*0-89357-087-7*) Slavica.

Botos, E. P. Vine & Wine Economy: Proceedings of the International Symposium, Kecskemet, Hungary, June 25-29, 1990. 333p. 1991. 160.00 (*963-05-6039-9*, Pub. by Akade Kiado) St Mut.

Botos, Leslie & Mihalko, Carolyn, eds. Donor Recruitment: Strategies for Success. LC 96-21201. (Illus.). 233p. (Orig.). 1996. spiral bd. 69.00 (*1-56395-059-6*, PC97-PR9606) Am Assn Blood.

Botosaneanu, L., ed. Studies in Crenobiology: The Biology of Springs & Springbrooks. (Illus.). 262p. 1998. 89.00 (*90-73348-04-8*, Pub. by Backhuys Pubs) Balogh.

Botoseanu, Lazare, jt. auth. see Illies, Joachim.

Botre, Robert D., jt. auth. see Newman, Paul.

Bots, H. Correspondance de Jacques Dupuy & de Nicolas Heinsius (1646-1656) (International Archives of the History of Ideas Ser.: No. 40). 288p. 1971. lib. bdg. 99.50 (*90-247-5092-X*) Kluwer Academic.

Botsai, Elmer, jt. auth. see Dost, William.

Botsai, L. R. Electric Motors for Gearmotor Applications. (Technical Papers: Vol. P160). (Illus.). 27p. 1937. pap. text 30.00 (*1-55589-430-5*) AGMA.

Botsaris & Glazman. Interfacial Phenomena in Coal Technology. 2nd rev. ed. (Surfactant Science Ser.: Vol. 32). (Illus.). 464p. 1988. text 215.00 (*0-8247-7853-7*) Dekker.

Botsaris, Gregory D. & Toyokura, Ken, eds. Separation & Purification by Crystallization, Vol. 667. LC 97-11250. (ACS Symposium Ser.: No. 667). (Illus.). 312p. 1997. text 105.00 (*0-8412-3513-9*, Pub. by Am Chemical) OUP.

Botsch, Robert E. Organizing the Breathless: Cotton Dust, Southern Politics, & the Brown Lung Association. (Illus.). 240p. 1993. text 32.50 (*0-8131-1818-2*) U Pr of Ky.

— We Shall Not Overcome: Populism & Southern Blue-Collar Workers. fac. ed. LC 80-11567. 253p. 1980. reprint ed. pap. 78.50 (*0-7837-8054-0*, 204780700008) Bks Demand.

Botschantzeva, Z. Tulips: Taxonomy, Morphology, Cytology, Phytogeography & Physiology. Varekamp, H., ed. 282p. (C). 1982. text 135.00 (*90-6191-029-3*, Pub. by A A Balkema) Ashgate Pub Co.

Botsford, Clarissa, tr. see Pera, Marcello.

Botsford, Elizabeth. Fall Girl. unabridged ed. LC 97-94159. vii, 279p. 1998. pap. 12.99 (*0-9659210-4-2*) Blaze Pub.

Botsford, James. Biology 190 Lab Manual. 160p. (C). 1994. pap. text, spiral bd., lab manual ed. 12.95 (*0-7872-0105-7*) Kendall-Hunt.

***Botsford, Keith.** Out of Nowhere. 2000. write for info. (*1-902881-24-9*, Pub. by Toby Pr Ltd); pap. 15.95 (*1-902881-25-7*, Pub. by Toby Pr Ltd) Toby Pr.

Botsford, Keith, tr. see D'Arzo, Silvio.

Botsford, Keith, tr. see Gentile, Emilio.

Botsford, L. W., jt. ed. see Jain, Subodh K.

Botsford, Margot & Matz, Ruth G. Handbook of Legal Research in Massachusetts. LC 87-62742. 1988. ring bd. 75.00 (*0-944490-04-2*) Mass CLE.

Botsford, Margot, et al. Chapter 93A Rights & Remedies, 1997 Supplement. LC 89-62762. 186p. 1997. ring bd., suppl. ed. 39.50 (*1-57589-070-4*, 97-05.59-SP) Mass CLE.

— Chapter 93A Rights & Remedies, 1996 Supplement: Replacement Contents. LC 89-62762. 578p. 1996. ring bd., suppl. ed. 95.00 (*1-57589-031-3*, 96-05.49-SP) Mass CLE.

— Handbook of Legal Research in Massachusetts, 1997 Supplement. LC 87-62742. 134p. 1997. ring bd., suppl. ed. 39.50 (*0-944490-85-9*, 97-11.04-SP) Mass CLE.

Botsford, Shirley. Daddy's Ties. LC 94-21722. (Illus.). 96p. 1994. pap. 16.95 (*0-8019-8521-8*) Krause Pubns.

— Shirley Botsford's Decorating with Fabric Crafts: Elegant Home Accessory Designs Ispired by Architectural Elements. LC 98-84109. (Illus.). 128p. 1999. pap. 21.95 (*0-87341-677-5*, SBDEC) Krause Pubns.

***Botsiou, Konstantina.** Griechenlands Weg nach Europa. 1999. 68.95 (*3-631-34725-1*, Pub. by P Lang) P Lang Pubng.

Botsis, Alexander, et al. Suicide: Biopsychosocial Approaches. LC 97-46414. (International Congress Series.: Vol. 484 & Advances in Tumor Prevention & Detective: 1145). (Illus.). 284p. 1997. 175.50 (*0-444-82755-2*) Elsevier.

Botsko, Michael W. An Invitation to Real Analysis. LC 96-31164. 1996. write for info. (*0-929914-20-1*) Eadmer Pr.

— An Invitation to Real Analysis. 2nd ed. LC 98-29347. 1998. 50.00 (*0-929914-22-8*) Eadmer Pr.

***Botstein.** History of Listening. 2000. 27.50 (*0-465-00730-9*, Pub. by Basic); pap. 15.00 (*0-465-00731-7*, Pub. by Basic) HarpC.

Botstein. Music & Its Public. (C). 1990. lib. bdg. 34.95 (*0-226-06724-6*) U Ch Pr.

Botstein, David, jt. ed. see Fedoroff, Nina.

Botstein, Leon. Jefferson's Children: Education & the Promise of American Culture. 240p. 1997. 22.95 (*0-385-47555-1*) Doubleday.

Botstein, Leon, ed. The Compleat Brahms: A Guide to the Musical Works of Johannes Brahms. LC 98-43968. 350p. 1999. 35.00 (*0-393-04708-3*) Norton.

Botswana Wetlands Coordinating Committee., et al. Wetlands Management in Botswana: Proceedings of a Conference Held at Kasane, 14-16 November, 1994. Masundire, H. M. et al, eds. LC 98-985349. 160 p. 1995. write for info. (*99912-900-0-1*) Walker & Co.

Bott. Professional Issue Software Engineering. 2nd ed. 256p. 1995. pap. 29.95 (*1-85728-450-X*, Pub. by UCL Pr Ltd) Taylor & Francis.

Bott, Alan & Clephane, Irene. Our Fathers: Manners & Customs of the Ancient Victorians. LC 75-160614. (Illus.). 1972. 30.95 (*0-405-08292-4*, Pub. by Blom Pubns) Ayer.

— Our Mothers. LC 73-81813. (Illus.). 1972. 27.95 (*0-405-08293-2*, Pub. by Blom Pubns) Ayer.

Bott, Alan J., see Contact, pseud.

Bott, Alexander J. Handbook of United States Election Laws & Practices: Political Rights. LC 90-32460. 560p. 1990. lib. bdg. 89.50 (*0-313-25935-6*, BHE, Greenwood Pr) Greenwood.

Bott, Anita F. A Cookie for the President. LC 95-78157. (Illus.). 36p. (J). (gr. k-4). 1995. 14.95 (*1-880851-20-2*) Greene Bark Pr.

Bott, Daniel R. & Chambers, Larry. The Wrap Account Investment Advisor: How to Profit from Wall Street's Hottest New Product. 325p. 1993. text 32.50 (*1-55738-497-5*, Irwn Prfssnl) McGraw-Hill Prof.

Bott, Diane, jt. auth. see Provo, Diane.

***Bott, Ed.** Practical Windows 2000 Professional. 600p. 2000. pap. text 24.99 (*0-7897-2124-4*) Que.

— Special Edition Using Microsoft Windows: Millennium Edition. 950p. 2000. pap. 39.99 (*0-7897-2446-4*) Que.

— Special Edition Using Windows 98. 2nd ed. 1000p. 1999. pap. 39.99 (*0-7897-2203-8*) Que.

Bott, Ed. Using Microsoft Office. LC 94-69628. (Illus.). 412p. (Orig.). 1994. 19.99 (*0-7897-0091-3*) Que.

— Using Microsoft Office for Windows 95. (Illus.). 508p. (Orig.). 1995. 19.99 (*0-7897-0176-6*) Que.

***Bott, Ed.** Using Microsoft Office 2000, Small Business Edition. 1999. pap. text 34.99 (*0-7897-1969-X*) Que.

Bott, Ed. Using Microsoft Office 97. 3rd ed. LC 98-84389. (Using... Ser.). 640p. 1998. pap. text 29.99 (*0-7897-1567-8*) Que.

— Using Windows 95. (Illus.). 486p. 1995. pap. 19.99 (*0-7897-0092-1*) Que.

— Windows NT 4.O at Work. 700p. 1998. 29.99 (*0-7897-1512-0*) Que.

Bott, Ed & Leonhard, Woody. Using Microsoft Office 2000 With CDROM: Special Edition. LC 98-86859. (Special Edition Using... Que Ser.). (Illus.). 1473p. 1999. pap. 39.99 (*0-7897-1842-1*) Que.

Bott, Elizabeth. Urban Families: Conjugal Roles & Social Networks. (Reprint Series in Social Sciences). (C). 1993. reprint ed. pap. text 2.90 (*0-8290-2679-7*, S-554) Irvington.

Bott, F., jt. ed. see Gross, Rolf W.

***Bott, Frank.** Professional Issues in Software Engineering. 3rd ed. LC 00-37780. 2000. pap. write for info. (*0-7484-0951-3*) Taylor & Francis.

Bott-Geanangel. General Chemistry Laboratory. 224p. (C). 1998. per. 12.95 (*0-7872-5088-0*) Kendall-Hunt.

Bott, Gerhard. Jens-Rudiger Lorenzen: Jewelry Sculptures. 1997. 59.00 (*3-925369-67-8*, Pub. by Arnoldsche Art Pubs) Antique Collect.

Bott, Jenny. Rhythmic Gymnastics: The Skills of the Game. (Illus.). 128p. 1995. pap. 19.95 (*1-85223-918-2*, Pub. by Crolwood) Trafalgar.

Bott, Keith, jt. auth. see Stevens, Scott.

Bott, Margaret D., ed. see Sheehan, Jack.

Bott, Martin H., et al, eds. Structure & Development of the Greenland-Scotland Ridge: New Methods & Concepts. (NATO Conference Series IV, Marine Sciences: Vol. 8). 696p. 1982. 135.00 (*0-306-41019-2*, Plenum Trade) Perseus Pubng.

Bott, Paul. A Roomful of Flowers. (Illus.). 144p. 1992. 34.95 (*0-8109-3763-8*, Pub. by Abrams) Time Warner.

Bott, Paul A. Teaching Your Occupation to Others: A Guide to Surviving the First Year. 1986. pap. text 9.95 (*0-935920-40-4*, Ntl Pubs Blck) P-H.

— Teaching Your Occupation to Others: A Guide to Surviving the First Year. 2nd ed. LC 97-1295. 177p. 1997. pap. text 43.00 (*0-205-27101-4*) Allyn.

— Testing & Assessment in Occupational & Technical Education. LC 95-1709. 224p. 1995. pap. text 46.00 (*0-205-16878-7*) Allyn.

Bott, R. Fouling of Heat Exchange Surfaces. write for info. (*0-318-58444-1*) Elsevier.

Bott, R. & Tu, L. W. Differential Forms in Algebraic Topology. (Graduate Texts in Mathematics Ser.: Vol. 82). (Illus.). 288p. 1997. text 59.95 (*0-387-90613-4*) Spr-Verlag.

Bott, Randy L. Home with Honor: A Guide for Returned Missionaries. LC 95-33309. (Orig.). 1995. pap. 10.95 (*0-87579-956-6*) Deseret Bk.

— Prepare with Honor: A Guide for Future Missionaries. LC 95-35451. (Orig.). (YA). (gr. 7-12). 1995. pap. 10.95 (*0-87579-954-X*) Deseret Bk.

— Serve with Honor: A Guide for Missionaries. LC 95-35438. 1995. pap. 10.95 (*0-87579-955-8*) Deseret Bk.

An Asterisk (*) at the beginning of an entry indicates that the title is appearing for the first time.

Bott, Raoul, ed. Current Developments in Mathematics, 1996, Vol. 2. (Illus.). 282p. (C). 1998. 15.00 (*1-57146-035-7*) Intl Pr Boston.

Bott, Raoul, et al, eds. Current Developments in Mathematics, 1995. LC 95-82048. 1994. 42.00 (*1-57146-029-2*, INPR/20C) Intl Pr Boston.

Bott, Raoul & Jaffe, Arthur, eds. Current Developments in Mathematics, 1997, Vol. 3. (Illus.). 368p. (C). 1999. 15.00 (*1-57146-075-6*) Intl Pr Boston.

Bott, Richard & Betzel, Christian, eds. Subtilisin Enzymes: Practical Protein Engineering. LC 95-35808. (Advances in Experimental Medicine & Biology Ser.: Vol. 379). 259p. (C). 1995. text 89.50 (*0-306-45108-5*, Kluwer Plenum) Kluwer Academic.

***Bott, Sebastian.** Friends & Lovers of Virtue: Tugendethische Handlungsorientierungen Im Kontext der Schottischen Aufklarung 1750-1800. VI, 267p. 1999. 45.95 (*3-631-34272-1*) P Lang Pubng.

Bott, Simon. Lab Book for "The Context of Chemistry" (C). 1996. pap. text 18.31 (*1-56870-259-0*) RonJon Pub.

Bott, T. R. Fouling of Heat Exchangers. LC 95-11933. (Chemical Engineering Monographs: Vol. 26). (Illus.). 546p. 1995. 265.50 (*0-444-82186-4*) Elsevier.

Bott, T. R., et al. Fouling Mitigation of Industrial Heat Exchangers. LC 96-37802. 500p. 1996. 117.50 (*1-56700-056-8*) Begell Hse.

Bott, T. R., jt. auth. see International Conference on Understanding Heat Exchanger Fouling & Its Mitigation Staff.

Bott, Victor. Spiritual Science & the Art of Healing: Rudolf Steiner's Anthroposophical Medicine. LC 96-4207. (Illus.). 208p. (Orig.). 1996. reprint ed. pap. 12.95 (*0-89281-636-8*, Heal Arts VT) Inner Tradit.

Botta, Anne C. Memoirs of Anne C. L. Botta, Written by Her Friends. (American Biography Ser.). 459p. 1991. reprint ed. lib. bdg. 89.00 (*0-7812-8030-3*) Rprt Serv.

Botta, David A., tr. see Lozano, Leopoldo.

Botta, J. R. Evaluation of Seafood Freshness Quality. 180p. 1995. 124.00 (*0-471-18580-9*) Wiley.

Botta, J. Richard. Evaluation of Seafood Freshness Quality. LC 94-40213. (Food Science & Technology Ser.). (Illus.). viii, 184p. 1995. 85.00 (*1-56081-612-0*, Wiley-VCH) Wiley.

Botta, J. Richard, jt. ed. see Voigt, Michael N.

***Botta, Kathleen & Mendonca, Claire.** More... Than a Cookbook. 3rd rev. ed. 328p. 1998. 24.95 (*0-9701111-0-X*) More Than A Cookbk.

Botta, Mario. The Ethics of Building. (Illus.). 176p. 1997. pap. 29.95 (*3-7643-5742-8*, Pub. by Birkhauser) Princeton Arch.

Botta, Mario, jt. auth. see Cucchi, Enzo.

Botta, Mario, jt. auth. see Musi, Pino.

Bottaci, Leonardo & Jones, John. Formal Specification Using Z: A Modelling Approach. 300p. 1996. mass mkt. 36.25 (*1-85032-109-4*) ITCP.

Bottagaro, Anthony G. Revolution: A Challenge of Love. 272p. (Orig.). (C). 1988. write for info. (*0-9621433-1-6*); pap. write for info. (*0-9621433-0-8*) Interloc Pub.

Bottani, C. E., jt. ed. see Balakrishnan, V.

***Bottari, George.** To Love & Be Loved. 176p. 1999. write for info. (*1-57579-168-4*, Pub. by Pine Hill Pr) Penmarch Pub.

Bottari, Giovanni G. & Ticozzi, Stefano. Raccolta Di Lettre Sulla Pittura, Scultura Ed Architettura, 8 vols. (Bibliotheca Scelta Di Opere Italiane Antiche E Moderne Ser.: Vol. VI, 1). xvi, 4282p. 1976. reprint ed. 785.00 (*3-487-06013-2*) G Olms Pubs.

***Bottari, Paolo.** Free in Christ: Your Complete Handbook on the Ministry of Deliverance, Vol. 1. 1999. pap. 12.99 (*0-88419-657-7*) Creation House.

— Libres en Cristo. (SPA.). 1999. pap. 8.99 (*0-88419-605-4*) Casa Creacion.

Bottazini, U. The Higher Calculus: A History of Real & Complex Analysis from Euler to Weierstrass. (Illus.). 335p. 1986. 59.95 (*0-387-96302-2*) Spr-Verlag.

Bottcher, A. & Gohberg, I., eds. Singular Integral Operators & Related Topics: Joint German-Israeli Workshop, Tel Aviv, March 1-10, 1995, Vol. 90. LC 96-36429. (Operator Theory & Its Application Ser.). 324p. 1996. 122.95 (*3-7643-5466-6*) Birkhauser.

Bottcher, A. & Silbermann, B. Analysis of Toeplitz Operators. 496p. 1990. 118.95 (*0-387-52147-X*) Spr-Verlag.

Bottcher, A., tr. see Maz'ya, V. G. & Nikol'skij, S. M.

Bottcher, A., tr. see Michlin, S. G. & Prossdorf, S.

Bottcher, A. B. & Izuno, F. T., eds. Everglades Agricultural Area: Water, Soil, Crop, & Environmental Management. LC 94-3871. (Illus.). 322p. 1994. 49.95 (*0-8130-1294-5*) U Press Fla.

Bottcher, Albrecht & Gohberg, I. Singular Integral Operators & Related Topics: Joint German-Israeli Workshop, Tel Aviv, March 1-10, 1995. LC 96-36429. (Operator Theory, Advances & Applications Ser.). 1996. 122.95 (*0-8176-5466-6*) Birkhauser.

***Bottcher, Albrecht & Grudsky, Sergei M.** Toeplitz Matrices, Asymptotic Linear Algebra & Functional Analysis. LC 00-23663. (Illus.). 2000. write for info. (*0-8176-6290-1*) Birkhauser.

— Toeplitz Matrices, Asymptotic Linear Algebra & Functional Analysis. 104p. 2000. pap. 34.95 (*3-7643-6290-1*, Pub. by Birkhauser) Spr-Verlag.

Bottcher, Albrecht & Karlovich, Y. I. Carleson Curves, Muckenhoupt Weights, & Toeplitz Operators. LC 97-38051. (Progress in Mathematics Ser.: Vol. 154). xv, 397p. 1997. text 75.00 (*3-7643-5796-7*) Birkhauser.

Bottcher, Albrecht & Karlovich, Yuri I. Carleson Curves, Muckenhoupt Weights, & Toeplitz Operators. LC 97-38051. (Progress in Mathematics Ser.). 1997. pap. write for info. (*0-8176-5796-7*) Birkhauser.

Bottcher, Albrecht & Silbermann, B. Introduction to Large Truncated Toeplitz Matrices. LC 98-9923. (Universitext Ser.). (Illus.). 269p. 1998. 49.95 (*0-387-98570-0*) Spr-Verlag.

Bottcher, Albrecht, et al. Lectures on Operator Theory & Its Applications. Lancaster, Peter, ed. LC 95-43465. (Fields Institute Monographs: No. 3). 339p. 1995. 99.00 (*0-8218-0457-X*, FIM/3) Am Math.

Bottcher, C., et al, eds. Nuclear & Atomic Physics at One Gigaflop, Vol. 16. (Nuclear Science Research Conference Ser.: Vol. 6). xiv, 326p. 1989. pap. text 107.00 (*3-7186-0492-2*) Gordon & Breach.

Bottcher, C., et al. Computational Atomic & Nuclear Physics. 424p. (C). 1990. text 92.00 (*981-02-0125-7*) World Scientific Pub.

Bottcher, C. J. & Bordewijk, P. Theory of Electric Polarization Vol. 2: Dielectrics in Time Dependent Fields. 2nd ed. 562p. 1980. 334.00 (*0-444-41579-3*) Elsevier.

Bottcher, C. J., et al. Theory of Electric Polarization Vol. 1: Dielectrics in Static Fields. 2nd ed. Bordewijk, P. & Rip, A., eds. LC 72-83198. xx,378p. 1973. 326.50 (*0-444-41019-8*) Elsevier.

Bottcher, Gunter M. Die Umweltvertraglichkeitsprufung in Deutschland und der Schweiz: Verfassungsrechtliche Herleitung und Rechtsvergleich. (Europaische Hochschulschriften Ser.: Reihe 2, Bd. 2178). (GER.). 354p. 1997. 63.95 (*3-631-32228-3*) P Lang Pubng.

Bottcher, Reinhard, et al. Festschrift Fur Walter Odersky: Zum 65. Geburtstag am 17. Juli 1996. xviii, 1101p. 1996. write for info. (*3-11-014365-8*) De Gruyter.

Bottcher, Robert W. & Hoff, Steven J., eds. Livestock Environment: Proceedings of the 5th International Symposium. LC 97-71782. 1116p. 1997. pap. 79.00 (*0-929355-84-9*, P0197) Am Soc Ag Eng.

Bottcher, Winfried. Soziales Europa, 1993: Noch eine Illusion. (GER.). 234p. 1990. pap. 44.00 (*3-7890-1971-2*, Pub. by Nomos Verlags) Intl Bk Import.

***Bottcher, Wolfgang Michael.** Auftritt der Tod im Wirbel der Konfetti: Erzahlen zwischen Erfinden und Verschwinden in Gerhard Kopfs Fruhwerk. 2000. 45.95 (*3-631-35737-0*) P Lang Pubng.

Botte, Bernard. From Silence to Participation. Sullivan, John, tr. 1988. pap. 14.95 (*0-912405-54-6*, Pastoral Press) OR Catholic.

Botte, Deborah, ed. see Sheets, Loris Hanson.

Botte, Michael J., jt. ed. see Nickel, Vernon L.

Botte, Xavier, tr. see Van der Laan, Hans.

Bottema, O. & Roth, B. Theoretical Kinematics. 558p. 1990. pap. 12.95 (*0-486-66346-9*) Dover.

Bottema, S., et al, eds. Man's Role in the Shaping of the Eastern Mediterranean Landscape: Proceedings of the Symposium on the Impact of Ancient Man on the Landscape of the Eastern Mediterranean Region & the Near East, Groningen, 6-9 March 1989. (Illus.). 352p. (C). 1990. text 123.00 (*90-6191-138-9*, Pub. by A A Balkema) Ashgate Pub Co.

Bottemiller, Cliff, jt. auth. see Kelly, Clint.

Botten, Neil & McManus, John. Competitive Strategies for Service Organizations. LC 99-28619. 1999. 62.95 (*1-55753-174-9*, Ichor Busn Bks) Purdue U Pr.

***Botten, Neil & McManus, John.** Competitive Strategies for Service Organizations. 1999. pap. 32.95 (*1-55753-196-X*, Ichor Busn Bks) Purdue U Pr.

Bottenberg, Joanna. Shared Creation: Words & Music in the Hofmannsthal-Strauss Operas. LC 95-52949. (German Studies in Canada: Bd. 6). 368p. 1996. pap. 61.95 (*0-8204-2974-0*, ML410) P Lang Pubng.

Bottenbruch, Ludwig, ed. Engineering Thermoplastics: Polycarbonates, Polyacetals, Polyesters, Cellulose Esters. LC 96-31005. 497p. 1996. 198.00 (*1-56990-183-X*) Hanser-Gardner.

Bottenstein, Jane E. & Sato, Gordon H., eds. Cell Culture in the Neurosciences. LC 85-3435. (Current Topics in Neurobiology Ser.). 402p. 1985. 99.50 (*0-306-41942-4*, Plenum Trade) Perseus Pubng.

Botterbusch, Karl F., jt. auth. see Lytel, Robert B.

Botterill, Carl, jt. auth. see Orlick, Terry.

Botterill, G. S., ed. British Chess. (Chess Ser.). (Illus.). 300p. 1983. 105.00 (*0-08-024134-4*, Pergamon Pr) Elsevier.

Botterill, George & Carruthers, Peter. The Philosophy of Psychology. LC 98-33301. (Illus.). 312p. (C). 1999. pap. 21.95 (*0-521-55915-4*) Cambridge U Pr.

Botterill, George, jt. auth. see Carruthers, Peter.

Botterill, Ruth D. The New Book of Patience Games. 64p. 1995. pap. 6.95 (*0-572-01169-5*, Pub. by Foulsham UK) Assoc Pubs Grp.

Botterill, Steven. Dante & the Mystical Tradition: Bernard of Clairvaux in the "Commedia" (Cambridge Studies in Medieval Literature: No. 22). 281p. (C). 1994. text 80.00 (*0-521-43454-8*) Cambridge U Pr.

Botterill, Steven, ed. & tr. see Dante Alighieri.

***Bottero, Jean.** The Birth of God: The Bible & the Historian. LC 00-21352. (Hermeneutics, Studies in the History of Religions). 2000. pap. write for info. (*0-271-02061-X*) Pa St U Pr.

Bottero, Jean. Mesopotamia: Writing, Reasoning, & the Gods. Bahrani, Zainab & Van de Mieroop, Marc, trs. (Illus.). 312p. 1995. pap. text 17.00 (*0-226-06727-0*) U Ch Pr.

— Mesopotamia: Writing, Reasoning, & the Gods. Bahrani, Zainab & Van de Mieroop, Marc, trs. LC 91-25917. (Illus.). 326p. 1997. 43.95 (*0-226-06726-2*) U Ch Pr.

***Bottero, Jean.** Oldest Religion in Mesopotamia. 1998. 25.00 (*0-226-06717-3*) U Ch Pr.

Bottero, Jean. Textes Culinaires Mesopotamien: Mesopotamian Culinary Texts. LC 94-23705. (Mesopotamian Civilizations Ser.: Vol. 6). (Illus.). x, 252p. 1995. text 45.00 (*0-931464-92-7*) Eisenbrauns.

Bottero, Jean, et al. Ancestor of the West: Writing, Reasoning & Religion in Mesopotamia, Elam & Greece. LC 99-23113. 2000. write for info. (*0-226-06716-5*) U Ch Pr.

Botterweck. Issues: Exercises in Political & Social Decision Making. 4th ed. Botterweck, Phyllis, ed. 212p. 2000. pap. 13.00 (*0-911541-45-4*) Gregory Pub.

Botterweck, G. Johannes. Diccionario Teologico del Antiguo Testamento, 4 vols., Set.Tr. of Theological Dictionary of the Old Testament. (SPA.). 1116p. 1978. 450.00 (*0-8288-5161-1*, S50106) Fr & Eur.

Botterweck, G. Johannes, et al, eds. Theological Dictionary of the Old Testament, Vol. III. 584p. 1996. 48.00 (*0-8028-2332-7*) Eerdmans.

— Theological Dictionary of the Old Testament, 7 vols., Vol. 7. 600p. 1995. text 48.00 (*0-8028-2331-9*) Eerdmans.

— Theological Dictionary of the Old Testament, Vol. IX. 592p. 1998. 48.00 (*0-8028-2333-5*) Eerdmans.

Botterweck, G. Johannes & Ringgren, Helmer, eds. Theological Dictionary of the Old Testament, 8 vols. 560p. 1996. 375.00 (*0-8028-2338-6*) Eerdmans.

— Theological Dictionary of the Old Testament, 7 vols., Vol. 1. 560p. 1974. 48.00 (*0-8028-2325-4*) Eerdmans.

— Theological Dictionary of the Old Testament, 7 vols., Vol. 2. 560p. 1975. 48.00 (*0-8028-2326-2*) Eerdmans.

— Theological Dictionary of the Old Testament, 7 vols., Vol. 3. 560p. 1979. 48.00 (*0-8028-2327-0*) Eerdmans.

— Theological Dictionary of the Old Testament, 7 vols., Vol. 4. 560p. 1981. 48.00 (*0-8028-2328-9*) Eerdmans.

— Theological Dictionary of the Old Testament, 7 vols., Vol. 5. 560p. 1986. 48.00 (*0-8028-2329-7*) Eerdmans.

— Theological Dictionary of the Old Testament, 7 vols., Vol. 6. 560p. 1990. 48.00 (*0-8028-2330-0*) Eerdmans.

Botterweck, G. Johannes. Theological Dictionary of the Old Testament, Vol. X. 656p. 1999. 48.00 (*0-8028-2334-3*) Eerdmans.

Botterweck, Michael, et al. People & Politics (1999) 3th ed. (Illus.). 501p. 1999. pap. 30.00 (*0-911541-59-4*) Gregory Pub.

Botterweck, Michael C. Crossroads of Existence: Ethical, Moral & Religious Dilemmas. 282p. pap. 9.95 (*0-911541-05-5*) Gregory Pub.

Botterweck, Phyllis, ed. see Botterweck.

Bottery, Mike. Competition & Efficiency in Education & Health: The Professional's Response. LC 99-231554. 1998. 89.50 (*0-304-70156-4*); pap. 32.50 (*0-304-70157-2*) Continuum.

— The Ethics of Educational Management. Sayer, John, ed. (Education Management Ser.). 224p. 1992. pap. text 39.95 (*0-304-32429-9*) Continuum.

— The Morality of the School: The Theory & Practice of Values in Education. 192p. 1989. pap. text 37.95 (*0-304-31830-2*) Continuum.

***Bottery, Mike & Wright, Nigel.** Teachers & the State: International Perspectives. LC 99-53301. 2000. 90.00 (*0-415-21347-9*) Routledge.

Bottger, Friedrich. Die "Comedie-Ballet" von Moliere-Lully. 269p. 1979. reprint ed. write for info. (*3-487-06689-0*) G Olms Pubs.

Bottger, Tete. Robert Lebeck Vis-a-vis. 1999. 44.95 (*3-88243-649-2*) Steidl.

Botti. Ohio Creditors' Rights. pap. 62.00 (*0-87084-102-5*) Anderson Pub Co.

Botti, Timothy J. Ace in the Hole: Why the United States Did Not Use Nuclear Weapons in the Cold War, 1945 to 1965, 165. LC 95-50451. (Contributions in Military Studies Ser.: Vol. 165). 328p. 1996. 59.95 (*0-313-29976-5*, Greenwood Pr) Greenwood.

— The Long Wait: The Forging of the Anglo-American Nuclear Alliance 1945-58, 64. LC 87-7530. (Contributions in Military Studies Ser.: No. 64). 282p. 1987. 65.00 (*0-313-25902-X*, BLW/, Greenwood Pr) Greenwood.

Botticelli. Spring, Detail. 1983. 6.95 (*0-394-52602-3*) Random.

Botticelli, Sandro, jt. auth. see Zollner, Frank.

Bottieri, Bob. Kid Made: Easily Made Sets for Action Toys. unabridged ed. LC 99-177292. (Illus.). 48p. (J). (gr. 5-7). 1993. pap. 4.95 (*0-19-540898-5*) STDK.

Bottigheimer, Karl S. Ireland & the Irish. LC 82-4160 (Illus.). 301p. 1984. pap. text 23.00 (*0-231-04611-1*) Col U Pr.

Bottigheimer, Ruth B. The Bible for Children: From the Age of Gutenberg to the Present. LC 95-38965. (Illus.). 338p. 1996. 40.00 (*0-300-06488-8*) Yale U Pr.

Bottigheimer, Ruth B., et al. Grimms' Bad Girls & Bold Boys. LC 87-2219. 224p. (C). 1989. reprint ed. pap. 17.00 (*0-300-04389-9*) Yale U Pr.

Bottiglia, William F., ed. Current Issues in Language Teaching. 1962. 10.95 (*0-915432-62-5*) NE Conf Teach Foreign.

— The Language Classroom. 84p. 1957. pap. 10.95 (*0-915432-57-9*) NE Conf Teach Foreign.

— Language Learning: The Intermediate Phase. 85p. 1963. pap. 10.95 (*0-915432-63-3*) NE Conf Teach Foreign.

Bottignolo, Bruno. Celebrations with the Sun: An Overview of Religious Phenomena among the Badjaos. LC 95-947427. 288p. 1997. pap. text 26.00 (*971-550-149-4*, Pub. by Ateneo de Manila Univ Pr) UH Pr.

Bottinelli, L., jt. ed. see Corwin, H. G.

Botting, C. G., jt. auth. see Hillard, A. E.

***Botting, Douglas.** Dr. Eckener's Dream Machine. 2001. text 26.00 (*0-8050-6458-3*) H Holt & Co.

— Dr. Eckener's Dream Machine. 2002. pap. 13.00 (*0-8050-6459-1*) H Holt & Co.

Botting, Douglas. Gerald Durrell. 656p. 1999. 29.95 (*0-7867-0655-4*) Carroll & Graf.

***Botting, Douglas.** Gerald Durrell: The Authorized Biography. (Illus.). 672p. 2000. reprint ed. pap. 16.95 (*0-7867-0796-8*, Pub. by Carroll & Graf) Publishers Group.

— The Saga of Ring of Bright Water: The Enigma of Gavin Maxwell. (Illus.). 2000. pap. 17.95 (*1-897784-85-6*, Pub. by N Wilson Pubng) Interlink Pub.

Botting, Douglas. Wild Britain: A Traveller's Guide. LC 99-27825. 224p. 2000. pap. 19.95 (*1-56656-321-6*) Interlink Pub.

— Wild France: A Traveller's Guide. LC 99-39121. (Wild Guides Ser.). (Illus.). 224p. 2000. pap. 19.95 (*1-56656-333-X*) Interlink Pub.

Botting, Douglas, ed. Wild France. LC 93-28771. (Sierra Club Adventure Travel Guides Ser.). (Illus.). 224p. (Orig.). 1994. reprint ed. pap. 16.00 (*0-87156-476-9*, Pub. by Sierra) Random.

Botting, Douglas, jt. auth. see Botting, Kate.

Botting, Fred. The Gothic. LC 95-7521. (New Critical Idiom Ser.). 208p. (C). (gr. 13). 1995. pap. 12.99 (*0-415-09219-1*) Routledge.

— Sex, Machines & Navels: Fiction, Fantasy & History in the Future Present. 256p. 1999. 69.95 (*0-7190-5536-9*, Pub. by Manchester Univ Pr) St Martin.

— Sex, Machines & Navels: Fiction, Fantasy & History in the Future Present. 256p. 1999. pap. 24.95 (*0-7190-5625-X*) Manchester Univ Pr.

Botting, Fred & Wilson, Scott, eds. Bataille: A Critical Reader. LC 97-10147. (Critical Readers Ser.). 272p. (C). 1997. text 62.95 (*0-631-19956-X*); pap. text 26.95 (*0-631-19957-8*) Blackwell Pubs.

— The Bataille Reader. (Readers Ser.). 224p. (C). 1997. text 62.95 (*0-631-19958-6*); pap. text 26.95 (*0-631-19959-4*) Blackwell Pubs.

Botting, Gary, jt. auth. see Botting, Heather.

Botting, Heather & Botting, Gary. The Orwellian World of Jehovah's Witnesses. (Illus.). 224p. 1984. pap. 16.95 (*0-8020-6545-7*) U of Toronto Pr.

Botting, Heather D. The Orwellian World of Jehovah's Witnesses. LC 84-196541. (Illus.). 247p. reprint ed. pap. 76.60 (*0-8357-8257-3*, 203397600088) Bks Demand.

Botting, J., ed. Animal Experimentation & the Future of Medical Research. (Portland Press Proceedings Ser.: Vol. 3). (Illus.). 107p. (Orig.). (C). 1993. 34.00 (*1-85578-038-0*) Portland Pr Ltd.

Botting, Jack H., jt. ed. see Vane, John R.

Botting, Kate & Botting, Douglas. Sex Appeal: The Art & Science of Sexual Attraction. (Illus.). 192p. 1998. text 25.00 (*0-7881-5604-7*) DIANE Pub.

Botting, Michelle, jt. auth. see Strauss, D. F. M.

Bottino, Joseph C., et al, eds. Liver Cancer. (Developments in Oncology Ser.). 1985. text 219.00 (*0-89838-713-2*) Kluwer Academic.

Bottino, P. J. Methods in Plant Tissue Culture. (Illus.). 74p. 1981. student ed. 13.40 (*1-877960-00-4*, 2-503) Kemtec Educ.

Bottino, Patti, jt. auth. see Santana, Altagracia.

Bottino, Patti, jt. auth. see Santana, Altagracia A.

Bottino, Paul J., jt. auth. see Burns, George W.

Bottiroli, Giovanni F., et al, eds. Effects of Low-Power Light on Biological Systems III. LC 98-164535. (Europto Ser.: Vol. 3198). 132p. 1997. 69.00 (*0-8194-2630-X*) SPIE.

— Effects of Low-Power Light on Biological Systems IV. (Europto Ser.: Vol. 3569). 1998. 59.00 (*0-8194-3031-5*) SPIE.

Bottjer, David J., et al, eds. Late Cretaceous Depositional Environments & Paleogeography, Santa Ana Mountains, Southern California. (Illus.). 121p. 1982. pap. 5.00 (*1-878861-48-4*) Pac Section SEPM.

Bottjer, David J., jt. ed. see Allmon, Warren.

Bottjer, David J., ed. see Erwin, Douglas H.

Bottke, Karl G., ed. see Bernard, Jean-Jacques.

Bottle, R. T. & Rowland, J. F., eds. Information Sources in Chemistry. 4th ed. LC 92-17946. (Guides to Information Sources Ser.). 350p. 1993. lib. bdg. 75.00 (*1-85739-016-4*) Bowker-Saur.

Bottles, Scott L. Los Angeles & the Automobile: The Making of the Modern City. (Illus.). 315p. 1991. pap. 17.95 (*0-520-07395-9*, Pub. by U CA Pr) Cal Prin Full Svc.

Bottligieri, Matt, et al. Hopefully Soon. (Illus.). 1999. pap. 10.00 (*0-9671946-0-1*) Blue Moon NY.

***Bottner.** Marsha Is Only a Flower. (Illus.). 48p. (J). 2000. write for info. (*0-307-46330-3*) Gldn Bks Pub Co.

Bottner, Barbara. Bootsie Barker Ballerina. LC 96-27259. (I Can Read Bks.). (Illus.). 48p. (J). (ps-3). 1997. lib. bdg. 14.89 (*0-06-027101-9*) HarpC Child Bks.

— Bootsie Barker Ballerina. (I Can Read Bks.). (Illus.). 48p. (J). (gr. 2-4). 1998. pap. 3.95 (*0-06-444241-1*) HarpC Child Bks.

— Bootsie Barker Bites. (Illus.). 32p. (J). (ps-3). 1992. 15.95 (*0-399-22125-5*, G P Putnam) Peng Put Young Read.

— Bootsie Barker Bites. (Illus.). 32p. (J). (ps-3). 1997. pap. 5.99 (*0-698-11427-2*, PapStar) Peng Put Young Read.

Bottner, Barbara. Bootsie Barker Bites. LC 91-12182. 1997. 11.15 (*0-606-11157-3*, Pub. by Turtleback) Demco.

Bottner, Barbara. Dumb Old Casey Is a Fat Tree. LC 78-19474. (Trophy Bk.). (Illus.). 64p. (J). (gr. 1-4). 1991. pap. 3.50 (*0-06-440346-7*, HarpTrophy) HarpC Child Bks.

— Let Me Tell You Everything: Memoirs of a Lovesick Intellectual. LC 88-22066. 160p. (YA). (gr. 7 up). 1989. 12.95 (*0-06-020596-2*) HarpC Child Bks.

— Marsha Makes Me Sick. LC 98-5800. (Road to Reading Ser.). (Illus.). 32p. (J). 1998. pap. 3.99 (*0-307-26302-9*, 26302) Gldn Bks Pub Co.

***Bottner, Barbara.** Marsha Makes Me Sick. (J). 1999. 9.44 (*0-606-16139-2*) Turtleback.

Bottner, Barbara. Nana Hannah's Piano. LC 94-39159. (Illus.). 32p. (J). (ps-3). 1996. 15.95 (*0-399-22656-7*, G P Putnam) Peng Put Young Read.

— Nothing in Common. LC 85-45834. 176p. (YA). (gr. 7 up). 1986. 12.95 (*0-06-020604-7*) HarpC Child Bks.

B

— Two Messy Friends. LC 98-21323. (Hello Reader! Ser.). (Illus.). 32p. (gr. k-2). 1999. 3.99 (*0-590-63285-X*) Scholastic Inc.

***Bottner, Barbara & Brunkus, Denise.** Marsha Is Only a Flower. LC 99-24650. (Road to Reading Ser.). 48p. (J). 2000. pap. text 3.99 (*0-307-26330-4*, Whitman Coin) St Martin.

***Bottner, Keith.** Professional Com Patterns. 400p. 1998. pap. 49.99 (*1-86100-137-1*) Wrox Press.

***Botto.** Dictionary of E-Commerce. LC 99-89915. 2000. pap. write for info. (*0-471-88145-7*) Wiley.

Botto, Francis. Dictionary of Multimedia & Internet Applications: A Guide for Developers & Users. LC 98-29155. 372p. 1999. 69.95 (*0-471-98624-0*) Wiley.

Botto, Robert E. & Sanada, Yuzo, eds. Magnetic Resonance of Carbonaceous Solids: Developed by a Symposium Sponsored by the 1989 International Chemical Congress of Pacific Basin Societies, Honolulu, Hawaii, December 17-22, 1989. LC 92-36495. (Advances in Chemistry Ser.: No. 229). (Illus.). 678p. 1993. 165.00 (*0-8412-1866-8*, Pub. by Am Chemical) OUP.

— Magnetic Resonance of Carbonaceous Solids: Developed from a Symposium Sponsored by the International Chemical Congress of the Pacific Basin Societies. LC 92-36495. (Advances in Chemistry Ser.: No. 229). (Illus.). 680p. 1993. reprint ed. pap. 200.00 (*0-608-06801-2*, 206699800009) Bks Demand.

Bottom, Angela D. & Stowers, Mary M. Love Notes: Nurture Activities for Families. 54p. (Orig.). 1996. pap. text, spiral bd. 10.00 (*1-888406-01-1*) Phoenix Access.

— Quest: Activities for the Pursuit of Empowerment. 112p. (Orig.). 1996. pap. text, spiral bd. 15.00 (*1-888406-02-X*) Phoenix Access.

Bottom, Daniel L., et al, eds. Sustainability Issues for Resource Managers. (Illus.). 64p. 1997. reprint ed. 12.50 (*0-89904-578-2*, Bear Meadows Resrch Grp); reprint ed. pap. 7.50 (*0-89904-579-0*, Bear Meadows Resrch Grp) Crumb Elbow Pub.

Bottom, Daniel L., et al. Sustainability Issues for Resource Managers. (Illus.). 64p. 1997. 12.50 (*0-89904-504-9*, Bear Meadows Resrch Grp); spiral bd. 7.50 (*0-89904-505-7*, Bear Meadows Resrch Grp) Crumb Elbow Pub.

— Sustainability Issues for Resource Managers. (Illus.). 54p. 1997. pap. text 25.00 (*0-7881-4699-8*) DIANE Pub.

Bottom, Gloria T. A Thankful & Joyful Heart. 32p. (Orig.). 1997. pap. 2.50 (*0-88028-196-0*, 1453) Forward Movement.

Bottom Line Books (Firm). Bottom Line Secrets of Success. LC 97-177198. 1997. write for info. (*0-88723-138-1*) Boardroom.

Bottom-Line Communication Staff, tr. see Stockdale, Linda.

Bottom Line Communications Staff, tr. see Stockdale, Linda.

Bottom-Line Communications Staff, tr. see Stockdale, Linda & Simmons, Harvey.

Bottom Line Personal, Experts Staff, ed. The Book of Inside Information. LC 86-30972. 512p. 1995. 59.00 (*0-88723-113-6*) Boardroom.

Bottom Line Staff. The Bottom Line Personal Book of Bests. Edelston, Martin, ed. LC 96-29543. (Illus.). 352p. 1997. pap. 14.95 (*0-312-15069-5*) St Martin.

Bottom, Lori & Chaney, Ronda. Make it Your Own: Personalizing Patterns for Creative Design. LC 94-1491. (Illus.). 160p. 1994. pap. 18.95 (*0-8019-8380-0*) Krause Pubns.

— Make it Your Own: Personalizing Patterns for Creative Design. (Illus.). 168p. 1999. reprint ed. pap. text 19.00 (*0-7881-6018-4*) DIANE Pub.

Bottom, Lori, jt. auth. see Young, Tammy.

Bottome. Handbook of Abestos Management. 400p. 69.95 (*0-471-15734-1*) Wiley.

Bottome, Edgar M. The Balance of Terror: Nuclear Weapons & the Illusion of Security, 1945-1985. rev. ed. LC 85-47948. 315p. reprint ed. pap. 97.70 (*0-8357-3061-1*, 203931700012) Bks Demand.

— Missile Gap: A Study of the Formulation of Military & Political Policy. LC 77-129964. 265p. 1975. 29.50 (*0-8386-7734-7*) Fairleigh Dickinson.

Bottome, Paula. Completing the Circle: Taking Gestalt to Asia. 305p. (Orig.). 1997. pap. text 25.00 (*0-931425-24-7*) Clear Glass.

Bottome, Phyllis. From the Life. LC 70-134056. (Essay Index Reprint Ser.). 1977. reprint ed. 16.95 (*0-8369-2215-8*) Ayer.

— Man & Beast. LC 79-122689. (Short Story Index Reprint Ser.). (Illus.). 1977. 15.95 (*0-8369-3523-3*) Ayer.

***Bottome, Phyllis.** The Mortal Storm: A Novel. LC 98-24701. xxv, 357p. 1998. pap. text 18.95 (*0-8101-1471-2*) Northwestern U Pr.

Bottome, Phyllis. Old Wine. LC 98-227923. 360p. 1998. pap. text 18.95 (*0-8101-1472-0*) Northwestern U Pr.

Bottome, Robert, et al. In the Shadow of the Debt: Emerging Issues in Latin America. LC 92-5469. 1992. 10.95 (*0-87078-339-4*) Century Foundation.

Bottomer, Paul. Let's Dance: Learn to Salsa, Fox-Trot, Rumba, Tango, Line Dance, Lambada, Cha-Cha, Waltz, Two-Step. 256p. 1998. 19.98 (*1-57912-046-6*) Blck Dog & Leventhal.

— Line Dancing. (Dance Crazy Ser.). (Illus.). 64p. 1996. 12.95 (*1-85967-231-0*, Lorenz Bks) Anness Pub.

— Tango Argentino. (Dance Crazy Ser.). (Illus.). 64p. 1996. 12.95 (*1-85967-216-7*, Lorenz Bks) Anness Pub.

Bottomley. Geriatric Rehabilitation: A Textbook for the Therapist Assistant. (C). 2002. pap. 40.00 (*0-8385-2284-X*) Appleton & Lange.

Bottomley, et al. Intersexions: Gender - Class - Culture - Ethnicity. 208p. pap. 19.95 (*0-04-442325-X*, Pub. by Allen & Unwin Pty) Paul & Co Pubs.

Bottomley, A. Keith & Pease, Kenneth. Crime & Punishment: Interpreting the Data. LC 86-819. 224p. 1986. pap. 34.95 (*0-335-15389-5*) OpUniv Pr.

Bottomley, Anne, ed. Feminist Perspectives on the Foundational Subjects of Law. LC 96-161380. 300p. 1996. pap. 28.00 (*1-85941-194-0*, Pub. by Cavendish Pubng) Gaunt.

Bottomley, Arthur. Commonwealth, Comrades & Friends. 216p. 1986. 32.00 (*0-8364-1835-2*, Pub. by Somaiya) S Asia.

Bottomley, D., et al. Unemployment & Jobseeking. (DSS Research Report Ser.). 1997. write for info. (*0-11-762452-7*, Pub. by Statnry Office) Bernan Associates.

Bottomley, Gordon. Gruach & Britain's Daughter: Two Plays. LC 79-50018. (One-Act Plays in Reprint Ser.). 1980. reprint ed. 20.00 (*0-8486-2042-9*) Roth Pub Inc.

Bottomley, I. Arms & Armor of the Samurai. (Illus.). 192p. 1993. 17.99 (*0-517-10318-4*) Random Hse Value.

***Bottomley, Jennifer M.** Quick Reference Dictionary for Physical Therapy. 592p. 2000. pap. text 24.00 (*1-55642-426-4*) SLACK Inc.

***Bottomley, K. M., et al, eds.** Metalloproteinases as Targets for Anti-Inflammatory Drugs. LC 99-32920. (Progress in Inflammation Research Ser.). 230p. 1999. 139.00 (*3-7643-5856-4*, Pub. by Birkhauser) Spr-Verlag.

Bottomley, Keith A. Decisions in the Penal Process. (Law in Society Ser.). 270p. 1973. reprint ed. text 11.75 (*0-8377-1935-6*, Rothman) W S Hein.

Bottomley, Ruth. Rocking Horses. (Illus.). 32p. 1989. pap. 4.75 (*0-7478-0138-X*, Pub. by Shire Pubns) Parkwest Pubns.

Bottomley, Stephen & Parker, Stephen. Law in Context. 2nd ed. 391p. 1997. pap. 54.00 (*1-86287-233-3*, Pub. by Federation Pr) Gaunt.

Bottomley, Stephen, jt. auth. see Tomasic, Roman.

Bottomley, Tom. Boatman's Handbook. 2nd rev. ed. LC 87-23647. (Illus.). 320p. (Orig.). 1988. pap. 12.95 (*0-688-07754-4*, Wm Morrow) Morrow Avon.

Bottomore. Political Sociology. 2nd ed. (C). 1996. 53.95 (*0-7453-0651-9*) Westview.

Bottomore, Mary, tr. see Aron, Raymond.

Bottomore, Stephen. I Want to See This Annie Mattygraph: A Cartoon History of the Coming of the Movies. (Distributed for the British Film Institute Ser.). (Illus.). 250p. 1996. text 95.00 (*88-86155-04-2*, Pub. by British Film Inst) Ind U Pr.

Bottomore, Thomas B. Between Marginalism & Marxism: The Economic Sociology of J. A. Schumpeter. LC 92-32885. 160p. 1993. text 39.95 (*0-312-09105-2*) St Martin.

— Critics of Society: Radical Thought in North America. 2nd ed. LC 86-29451. 162p. 1987. lib. bdg. 59.50 (*0-313-25695-0*, BOCS, Greenwood Pr) Greenwood.

— Elites & Society. 2nd ed. LC 92-38181. 160p. (C). 1993. pap. 16.99 (*0-415-08271-4*) Routledge.

— The Frankfurt School & Critical Theory. 1984. pap. 10.95 (*0-85312-468-X*, NO. 3752, Pub. by Tavistock-E Horwood) Routldge.

— Sociology: A Guide to Problems & Literature. 3rd ed. 368p. (C). 1986. text 39.95 (*0-04-300108-4*); pap. text 17.95 (*0-04-300109-2*) Routledge.

Bottomore, Thomas B., ed. A Dictionary of Marxist Thought. 544p. 1983. 56.00 (*0-674-20525-1*) HUP.

Bottomore, Thomas B., ed. see Larrain, Jorge A.

Bottomore, Thomas B., tr. see Aron, Raymond.

Bottomore, Thomas B., tr. see Simmel, Georg.

Bottomore, Tom. A Dictionary of Marxist Thought. 2nd ed. Harris, Lawrence et al, eds. 672p. 1992. pap. 35.95 (*0-631-18082-6*) Blackwell Pubs.

— Marxist Sociology. LC 75-5986. 66p. (C). 1975. 12.00 (*0-8419-0201-1*) Holmes & Meier.

Bottomore, Tom, jt. ed. see Outhwaite, William.

Bottomore, Tom B. The Socialist Economy: Theory & Practice. LC 90-36084. 160p. 1990. pap. text 18.95 (*0-89862-453-3*) Guilford Pubns.

Bottoms, Anthony & Stelmar, Andrew. Social Inquiry Reports: A Framework for Practice Development. (Community Care Practice Handbook Ser.: No. 29). 1988. text 18.95 (*0-7045-0579-7*, Pub. by Gower) Ashgate Pub Co.

Bottoms, Anthony E. & Light, Roy. Problems of Long-Term Imprisonment. (Cambridge Criminology Ser.: No. 58). 250p. 1987. text 72.95 (*0-566-05427-2*, Pub. by Avebry) Ashgate Pub Co.

Bottoms, Bette L. & Goodman, Gail S., eds. International Perspectives on Child Abuse & Children's Testimony: Psychological Research & Law. LC 96-9953. 312p. 1996. 49.95 (*0-8039-5627-4*); pap. 23.50 (*0-8039-5628-2*) Sage.

Bottoms, Bette L., jt. ed. see Goodman, Gail S.

Bottoms, David. Armored Hearts: New & Selected Poems. LC 95-6256. 150p. (Orig.). 1995. 25.00 (*1-55659-073-3*) Copper Canyon.

— Armored Hearts: Selected & New Poems. LC 95-6256. 150p. 1995. pap. 14.00 (*1-55659-072-5*) Copper Canyon.

— Easter Weekend. LC 97-43696. (Voices of the South Ser.). 216p. 1998. pap. 12.95 (*0-8071-2277-7*) La State U Pr.

— Vagrant Grace. LC 99-6389. 96p. 1999. 22.00 (*1-55659-130-6*, Pub. by Copper Canyon); pap. 14.00 (*1-55659-129-2*, Pub. by Copper Canyon) Consort Bk Sales.

Bottoms, David, intro. Georgia on My Mind. LC 90-55232. (America on My Mind Ser.). (Illus.). 120p. 1990. 29.95 (*1-56044-027-9*) Falcon Pub Inc.

Bottoms, David, jt. ed. see Smith, Dave.

***Bottoms, Greg.** Angelhead: My Brother's Descent into Madness. 208p. 2000. 22.00 (*0-609-60626-3*) Crown Pub Group.

***Bottoms, Jesse Voyd, Jr.** The Medicine Man. 138p. 1999. pap. 12.00 (*0-9669962-0-8*, Pub. by Jubi Christ) Spring Arbor Dist.

***Bottoms, Stephen J.** Albee: Who's Afraid of Virginia Woolf? LC 99-56106. (Illus.). 224p. 2000. write for info. (*0-521-63209-9*) Cambridge U Pr.

— Albee: Who's Afraid of Virginia Woolf? LC 99-56106. (Plays in Production Ser.). (Illus.). 224p. (C). 2000. pap. write for info. (*0-521-63560-8*) Cambridge U Pr.

Bottoms, Stephen J. The Theatre of Sam Shepard: States of Crisis. LC 97-11991. (Studies in American Theatre & Drama: Vol. 9). (Illus.). 314p. (C). 1998. text 59.95 (*0-521-58242-3*) Cambridge U Pr.

Botton, Alain De, see De Botton, Alain.

Bottone, Edward J., ed. Unusual Microorganisms: Gram-Negative Fastidious Species. LC 83-1933. (Microbiology Ser.: No. 10). 136p. reprint ed. pap. 42.20 (*0-7837-3361-5*, 204331900008) Bks Demand.

— Yersinia Enterocolitica. 240p. 1981. 135.00 (*0-8493-5545-1*, QK201, CRC Reprint) Franklin.

Bottone, Gail. Florida Beachfront Lodgings: The West Coast. LC 97-48385. (Illus.). 236p. 1998. pap. 12.95 (*1-56164-145-6*) Pineapple Pr.

— Florida on the Beach: A Guide to Gulf Front Accommodations. LC 95-92662. (West Central Edition Ser.). (Illus.). 103p. (Orig.). 1996. pap. 9.95 (*0-9646290-0-3*) Coast Intl Enter.

Bottone, Norma L., jt. ed. see Worthington, Mary A.

Bottoni, Lois. Numbers 10 to 100. (Step Ahead Workbooks Ser.). (Illus.). 32p. (J). (ps-3). 1985. pap. 2.09 (*0-307-03586-7*, 03586, Goldn Books) Gldn Bks Pub Co.

Bottoni, Lois & Reynolds, Patti, eds. Getting Ready for Math & Reading. (Golden Step Ahead Workbooks Ser.). (Illus.). 32p. (J). (ps-3). 1985. 2.09 (*0-307-23538-6*, 03538, Goldn Books) Gldn Bks Pub Co.

— Letters & Sounds. (Golden Step Ahead Workbooks Ser.). (Illus.). 36p. 1985. 2.09 (*0-307-23536-X*, 03536) Gldn Bks Pub Co.

— Numbers 1 to 10. (Golden Step Ahead Workbooks Ser.). (Illus.). 36p. (ps-3). 1985. 2.09 (*0-307-23537-8*, 03537, Goldn Books) Gldn Bks Pub Co.

Bottorff, J. Douglas. A Practical Guide to Prosperous Living. LC 97-52696. 172p. 1998. pap. 11.95 (*0-87159-220-7*) Unity Bks.

Bottorff, William K. James Lane Allen. LC 63-20615. (Twayne's United States Authors Ser.). 1964. pap. text 6.95 (*0-89197-987-5*); lib. bdg. 20.95 (*0-89197-806-2*) Irvington.

Bottorff, William K., jt. auth. see Kaplan, Lloyd S.

Bottorff, William K., ed. see Allen, James L.

Bottrall, Margaret. The Divine Image: A Study of Blake's Interpretation of Christianity. 119p. (C). 1950. reprint ed. pap. 75.00 (*0-8383-0005-7*) M S G Haskell Hse.

Bottrall, Margaret S. Every Man a Phoenix: Studies in Seventeenth-Century Autobiography. LC 72-3301. (Essay Index Reprint Ser.). 1977. reprint ed. 18.95 (*0-8369-2894-6*) Ayer.

Bottrall, Margaret S. & Bottrall, Ronald, eds. Collected English Verse. LC 68-59366. (Granger Index Reprint Ser.). 1977. 18.95 (*0-8369-6050-5*) Ayer.

Bottrall, Ronald, jt. ed. see Bottrall, Margaret S.

Bottrell, David & Jones, Jessie. Dearly Departed. 1992. pap. 5.25 (*0-8222-1303-6*) Dramatists Play.

Bottrell, Donna, ed. see Wine Advisory Board Staff.

Bottrell, Melissa M., et al. Geriatric Nursing Protocols for Best Practice. Abraham, Ivo, ed. LC 98-52113. (Series on Geriatric Nursing). 1999. 33.95 (*0-8261-1251-X*) Springer Pub.

Bottrich, Christfried. Adam Als Mikrokosmos: Eine Untersuchung zum Slavischen Henochbuch. (Judentum und Umwelt Ser.: Bd. 59). (GER., Illus.). 95p. 1995. 26.95 (*3-631-48270-1*) P Lang Pubng.

Botts, Betty, jt. auth. see Lowery, Linda.

Botts, Gene. The Border Game: Enforcing America's Immigration Laws. x, 357p. 1997. pap. 14.95 (*1-890183-01-6*) Compass Rose.

Botts, Jack. A Pocketful of Plums: Jim River Days. (Illus.). 1995. pap. 9.95 (*0-911007-42-3*) Twin Pines Pub.

— Straight & Level: Growing up in the '40s. (Illus.). 1996. pap. 14.95 (*0-9654527-0-0*) Twin Pines Pub.

Botts, Mary L. Taylor's Halloween. large type ed. LC 98-90471. 16p. (J). (gr. k-6). 1999. pap. 3.99 (*0-9668891-1-8*) Teach Child.

Botts, Rian D. Alone with My Thoughts. 55p. 1997. 15.95 (*1-887750-57-6*) Rutledge Bks.

Botts, Ricky J. A Complete Identification Guide to the Wurlitzer Jukebook. LC 83-82604. (Illus.). 114p. (Orig.). 1987. pap. 20.00 (*0-912789-01-8*) Jukebox Coll New.

— Jukebox Restoration: Restoration Articles - Tips & Techniques Taken from Jukebox Collector Newsletter & Victory Glass Newsletter. LC 83-80797. (Illus.). 88p. (Orig.). 1983. pap. 15.00 (*0-912789-00-X*) Jukebox Coll New.

Botts, Ricky J., ed. see Wurlitzer, Rudolph, Co. Staff.

Botts, Timothy. Birthdays & Special Dates. 1990. 16.00 (*0-8378-1468-5*) Gibson.

Botts, Timothy R. The Book of Psalms. LC 97-10899. 1997. 25.00 (*0-8423-4955-3*) Tyndale Hse.

— Doorposts. 128p. 1986. 19.99 (*0-8423-0595-5*) Tyndale Hse.

— Messiah. 112p. 1991. 14.99 (*0-8423-4235-4*) Tyndale Hse.

— Psalms. 1998. pap. 9.99 (*0-8423-8817-6*) Tyndale Hse.

— Sunday Doorposts, No. II. 64p. (Orig.). 1991. pap. 12.95 (*1-55612-462-7*, LL1462) Sheed & Ward WI.

— Sunday Doorposts, Vol. 2. (Illus.). 64p. (Orig.). 1987. pap. 12.95 (*1-55612-078-8*) Sheed & Ward WI.

Botts, Timothy R., ed. Proverbs: Seventy-Five Proverbs from the Living Bible. LC 94-12127. (Illus.). 160p. 1994. 16.99 (*0-8423-5034-9*) Tyndale Hse.

Botula, et al. Jakandor: Isle of Destiny. 1998. 21.95 (*0-7869-1245-6*, Pub. by TSR Inc) Random.

Botula, Kirk. Knorrman Steel. 144p. 1998. 21.95 (*0-7869-0371-6*, Pub. by TSR Inc) Random.

Botula,Donovan,Strohm, et al. Jakandor: Land of Legend. 1998. 21.95 (*0-7869-1246-4*, Pub. by TSR Inc) Random.

Botume, Elizabeth H. First Days Amongst the Contrabands. LC 68-28986. (American Negro: His History & Literature, Ser. 1). 1976. reprint ed. 25.95 (*0-405-01805-3*) Ayer.

Botvin, Gilbert J. Life Skills Training: Promoting Health & Personal Development. (Illus.). 48p. (J). (gr. 6-9). 1998. pap. text, student ed., wbk. ed. 4.00 (*0-933665-05-9*) Princeton Hlth.

— Life Skills Training: Promoting Health & Personal Development, 3 vols., Set. (Illus.). 198p. (YA). 1996. pap., teacher ed., ring bd. 85.00 (*0-933665-00-8*); pap., student ed., wbk. ed. 6.00 (*0-933665-01-6*) Princeton Hlth.

— Life Skills Training: Promoting Health & Personal Development - Teacher's Manual, Level 2. (Illus.). 155p. 1997. teacher ed., ring bd. 65.00 (*0-933665-02-4*) Princeton Hlth.

— Life Skills Training: Promoting Health & Personal Development, Level 2. (Illus.). 60p. (Orig.). (J). (gr. 6-9). 1997. pap., student ed. 5.00 (*0-933665-03-2*) Princeton Hlth.

— Life Skills Training Level 3: Promoting Health & Personal Development/Teacher Manual. (Illus.). 112p. 1998. teacher ed., ring bd. 55.00 (*0-933665-04-0*) Princeton Hlth.

Botvin, Gilbert J., et al, eds. Drug Abuse Prevention with Multiethnic Youth. LC 95-13489. 368p. (C). 1995. 56.00 (*0-8039-5711-4*); pap. 26.50 (*0-8039-5712-2*) Sage.

Botvin, Gilbert J. & Schinke, Steven P., eds. The Etiology & Prevention of Drug Abuse among Minority Youth. LC 97-161106. 117p. 1997. 29.95 (*0-7890-0330-9*) Haworth Pr.

Botvinick, Elias H. Pharmacological Stress. LC 98-26415. (Nuclear Medicine Self-Study Program III Ser.: Vol. 2). 195p. 1998. pap. text 45.00 (*0-932004-60-1*) Soc Nuclear Med.

Botvinick, Elias H., et al. Nuclear Medicine Self-Study Program, Cardiology Vol. III, Unit 1: Physical & Technical Aspects of Nuclear Cardiology. LC 97-25005. (Nuclear Medicine Self-Study Program III). (Illus.). 96p. 1997. pap. 35.00 (*0-932004-52-0*) Soc Nuclear Med.

Botvinnik, B., tr. see Novikov, S. P., ed.

Botvinnik, Boris I. Manifolds with Singularities & the Adams-Novikov Spectral Sequence. (London Mathematical Society Lecture Note Ser.: No. 170). (Illus.). 197p. (C). 1992. pap. text 44.95 (*0-521-42608-1*) Cambridge U Pr.

Botvinnik, M. M. Achieving the Aim LC 80-40437. (Pergamon Russian Chess Ser.). 226p. 1981. write for info. (*0-08-024119-0*, Pergamon Pr) Elsevier.

Botvinnik, Mikhael M. Achieving the Aim. LC 80-40437. (Russian Chess Ser.). (Illus.). 226p. 1981. 21.95 (*0-08-024120-4*, Pergamon Pr) Elsevier.

— Anatoly Karpov: His Road to the World Championship. Neat, Kenneth P., tr. LC 77-30655. 182p. 1978. text 19.95 (*0-08-021139-9*, Pergamon Pr); pap. text 11.95 (*0-08-021138-0*, Pergamon Pr) Elsevier.

— Half a Century of Chess. (Russian Chess Ser.). (Illus.). 300p. 1984. 33.95 (*0-08-026919-2*, Pergamon Pr); pap. 19.95 (*0-08-029739-0*, Pergamon Pr) Elsevier.

— Selected Games Nineteen Sixty-Seven to Nineteen Seventy. Neat, Kenneth P., tr. (Russian Chess Ser.). (Illus.). 318p. 1981. 29.95 (*0-08-024124-7*, Pergamon Pr); pap. 17.95 (*0-08-024123-9*, Pergamon Pr) Elsevier.

— Solving Inexact Search Problems. Brown, A. A., tr. (Symbolic Computation Ser.). (Illus.). 255p. 1983. 72.95 (*0-387-90869-2*) Spr-Verlag.

Botvinnik, Mikhail. Botvinnik on the Endgame. Marfia, Jim, tr. 81p. (Orig.). 1985. pap. 6.00 (*0-931462-43-6*) Chess Ent.

Botvinnik, Mikhail M. Fifteen Games & Their Stories. Marfia, Jim, tr. from RUS. (Illus.). 76p. (Orig.). 1982. pap. 5.00 (*0-931462-15-0*) Chess Ent.

— One Hundred Selected Games. (Illus.). 272p. 1960. pap. 8.95 (*0-486-20620-3*) Dover.

Botwin, Carol. Men Who Can't Be Faithful: Build a Better, More Intimate Relationship-Based on New Trust, Honesty, & Love. 304p. 1989. mass mkt. 6.50 (*0-446-35623-9*, Pub. by Warner Bks) Little.

Botwinick, Aryeh. Postmodernism & Democratic Theory. LC 92-15679. 288p. 1993. 59.95 (*0-87722-997-X*) Temple U Pr.

— Skepticism & Political Participation. 256p. (C). 1990. 37.95 (*0-87722-657-1*) Temple U Pr.

— Skepticism, Belief, & the Modern: Maimonides to Nietzsche. LC 97-19770. 264p. 1997. 39.95 (*0-8014-3208-1*) Cornell U Pr.

Botwinick, Aryeh, jt. auth. see Bachrach, Peter.

Botwinick, Rita S. A History of the Holocaust. 234p. 1996. pap. text 34.40 (*0-13-099292-5*) P-H.

— A History of the Holocaust: From Ideology to Annihilations. 2nd ed. LC 99-48801. 288p. 2000. pap. 29.33 (*0-13-011285-2*) P-H.

Botwinick, Rita S. Holocaust Reader. LC 97-39843. 207p. 1997. pap. 30.67 (*0-13-842238-9*) P-H.

Botwinick, Rita S. Winzig, Germany, 1933-1946: The History of a Town under the Third Reich. LC 91-35255. 176p. 1992. 52.95 (*0-275-94185-X*, C4185, Praeger Pubs) Greenwood.

Botz, Dan La, see La Botz, Dan.

Botzler, Richard G. & Armstrong, Susan J. Environmental Ethics: Divergence & Convergence. 2nd ed. LC 97-5654. 696p. 1997. pap. 44.06 (*0-07-006180-7*) McGraw.

An Asterisk (*) at the beginning of an entry indicates that the title is appearing for the first time.

Botzman, Harvey. Erie Canal Bicyclist & Hiker Route Guide. (Illus.). 200p. (Orig.). 1996. pap. 21.95 (*1-889602-09-4*); spiral bd. 21.95 (*1-889602-10-8*) Cyclotour Guide.
— Erie Canal Bicyclist & Hiker Tour Guide. 2nd rev. ed. Orig. Title: Erie Canal Bicyclist & Hiker Route Guide. (Illus.). 220p. 1999. pap. 21.95 (*1-889602-20-5*) Cyclotour Guide.
— Finger Lakes Bicyclist's Tour Guide. (Illus.). 284p. 1998. pap. 24.95 (*1-889602-15-9*); spiral bd. 24.95 (*1-889602-16-7*) Cyclotour Guide.
— Long Distance Bicycle Touring Primer. (Illus.). 72p. 1995. pap. 10.95 (*1-889602-01-9*) Cyclotour Guide.
— 'Round Lake Erie: A Bicyclist's Tour Guide. (Great Lakes Bicycle Touring Ser.). 156p. 1996. spiral bd. 21.95 (*1-889602-07-8*) Cyclotour Guide.
— 'Round Lake Erie: A Bicyclist's Tour Guide. (Great Lakes Bicycle Touring Ser.). (Illus.). 156p. 1996. pap. 21.95 (*1-889602-06-X*) Cyclotour Guide.
— Round Lake Huron: A Bicyclist's Tour Guide. (Great Lakes Bicycle Touring Ser.). (Illus.). 200p. (Orig.). 1999. pap. 24.95 (*1-889602-11-6*); spiral bd. 24.95 (*1-889602-12-4*) Cyclotour Guide.
— Round Lake Michigan: A Bicyclist's Tour Guide. (Great Lakes Bicycle Touring Ser.). (Illus.). 200p. (Orig.). 1997. pap. 21.95 (*1-889602-13-2*); spiral bd. 21.95 (*1-889602-14-0*) Cyclotour Guide.
— 'Round Lake Ontario: A Bicyclist's Tour Guide. 2nd rev. ed. LC 99-90013. (Great Lakes Bicycle Touring Ser.). (Illus.). 236p. 1999. pap. 24.95 (*1-889602-18-3*); spiral bd. 24.95 (*1-889602-19-1*) Cyclotour Guide.
— Round Lake Superior: A Bicyclist's Tour Guide. (Great Lakes Bicycle Touring Ser.: Vol. 5). (Illus.). 288p. 2001. pap. 24.95 (*1-889602-24-8*); spiral bd. 24.95 (*1-889602-25-6*) Cyclotour Guide.
Botzman, Thomas J. Technology & Competitiveness in Mexico: An Industrial Perspective. LC 99-18473. 176p. 1999. 49.00 (*0-7618-1371-3*); pap. 27.50 (*0-7618-1372-1*) U Pr of Amer.
Botzow, Hermann S. Auto Fleet Management. LC 67-30632. 211p. reprint ed. pap. 65.50 (*0-8357-9842-9*, 201235400081) Bks Demand.
Bouafoux, Pascal. Sophia Vari-Papers on Canvas, 1992-1995. (Illus.). 88p. 1995. 20.00 (*1-886125-02-3*) N Haime Gallery.
Bouakel, Hacene, tr. see Jimenez, Ignacio.
Bouamama, B. Ould, jt. auth. see Thoma, Jean U.
Bouandel, Youcef. Human Rights & Comparative Politics. LC 96-39519. (Illus.). 256p. 1997. text 72.95 (*1-85521-874-7*, Pub. by Dartmth Pub) Ashgate Pub Co.
Bouarouy, William K. The Roots of the Conflicts in Indochina: With Chronology of Laos History, & Major Successive Political Events in Laos from 1316 Through 1975. (Illus.). 201p. 1992. text 35.00 (*0-9646220-0-9*) Asian-Am Res Ctr.
Bouatouch, K., et al, eds. Photorealism in Computer Graphics: Eurographic Seminars. (Illus.). 256p. 1992. 111.95 (*0-387-54265-5*) Spr-Verlag.
Bouazza, A., et al, eds. Environmental Geotechnics: Proceedings of the 1st Australian - New Zealand Conference Geoenvironment 97, Melbourne, 26-28 November 1997. (Illus.). 580p. (C). 1997. text 123.00 (*90-5410-903-3*, Pub. by A A Balkema) Ashgate Pub Co.
Boubat, Edouard. It's a Wonderful Life. 1997. text 22.95 (*2-84323-012-8*) St Martin.
Boubein, et al. Le Francais Actif Cassette, No. 1A. (Textbook Ser.). 180p. 21.00 incl. audio (*0-88729-800-1*) Langenscheidt.
Boubel, Richard W., et al. Fundamentals of Air Pollution. 3rd ed. Turner, D. Bruce & Stern, Arthur C., eds. (Illus.). 574p. 1994. text 78.00 (*0-12-118930-9*) Acad Pr.
Boublik, V. Art of Make up for Stage, Television & Film. LC 68-18519. 1968. 91.00 (*0-08-012651-0*, Pub. by Pergamon Repr) Franklin.
Bouc, Serge. Green Functors & G-Sets, Vol. 167. Dold, A. & Takens, F., eds. LC 97-37135. (Lecture Notes in Mathematics Ser.: Vol. 1671). vii, 342p. 1997. pap. text 57.00 (*3-540-63550-5*) Spr-Verlag.
Boucart, Muriel. Neuroscience of Perceptual Integration: A Special Issue of the Journal Visual Cognition. 224p. 1999. 49.95 (*0-86377-604-3*) L Erlbaum Assocs.
Boucaut, T. P. The Arab, the Horse of the Future. (Illus.). xx, 249p. reprint ed. write for info. (*0-318-71575-9*) G Olms Pubs.
Bouccara, Lucien. Medical Dictionary of Women: Dictionnaire Medical de la Femme. 500p. 1981. 29.95 (*0-8288-1792-8*, M15419) Fr & Eur.
Bouce, Paul-Gabriel. The Novels of Tobias Smollett. White, Antonia, tr. LC 75-31687. ix, 405p. 1976. write for info. (*0-582-50023-0*) Addison-Wesley.
Boucek, Mark Jr., jt. auth. see Purdy, Ralph E.
Boucek, Z. Australasian Chalcidoidea (Hymenoptera) 832p. 1988. text 205.00 (*0-85198-607-2*) OUP.
Boucek, Z., jt. auth. see Delvare, G.
Bouchard, A., tr. see Garrigou-Lagrange, Reginald.
Bouchard, Angeline, tr. see Galot, Jean.
Bouchard, C. & Bray, G. A., eds. Regulation of Body Weight: Biological & Behavioral Mechanisms. LC 96-177566. (Dahlem Workshop Reports Life Science). 342p. 1996. 199.95 (*0-471-96373-9*) Wiley.
Bouchard, Cathy. Your Perfect Wedding Planner. LC 97-6194. 264p. 1997. 24.95 (*1-57071-168-2*, Casablanca) Sourcebks.
Bouchard, Charles E. Whatever Happened to Sin? The Truth about Catholic Morality. LC 95-80151. 144p. (Orig.). 1995. pap. 5.95 (*0-89243-849-5*) Liguori Pubns.
Bouchard, Claude. The Genetics of Obesity. 256p. 1994. lib. bdg. 179.00 (*0-8493-4880-3*, RC628) CRC Pr.
***Bouchard, Claude, ed.** Physical Activity & Obesity. LC 99-88071. (Illus.). 408p. 2000. 48.00 (*0-88011-909-8*) Human Kinetics.
Bouchard, Claude, et al, eds. Physical Activity, Fitness, & Health: International Proceedings & Consensus Statement. LC 93-38996. (Illus.). 1080p. 1994. text 79.00 (*0-87322-522-8*, BBOU0522) Human Kinetics.
— Physical Activity Sciences. LC 91-2011. (Illus.). 280p. (Orig.). (C). 1991. text 24.00 (*0-87322-334-9*, BBOU0334) Human Kinetics.
Bouchard, Claude & Johnston, Francis E. Fat Distribution during Growth & Later Health Outcomes: A Symposium Held at Manoir St. Castin, Lac Beauport, Quebec, June 9-11, 1987. LC 87-32504. (Current Topics in Nutrition & Disease Ser.). 1988. write for info. (*0-8451-1616-9*) A R Liss.
Bouchard, Claude, et al. Genetics of Fitness & Physical Performance. LC 97-9083. (Illus.). 408p. (C). 1997. text 45.00 (*0-87322-951-7*, BBOU0951) Human Kinetics.
Bouchard, Claude, jt. auth. see Malina, Robert M.
Bouchard, Claude, ed. see International Conference on Exercise, Fitness, & H.
Bouchard, Claude, ed. see Olympic Scientific Congress (1984, Eugene, OR) Staff.
Bouchard, Claude, ed. see Olympic Scientific Congress (1984: Eugene, OR) Sta.
Bouchard, Constance B. Cartulary of Flavigny. LC 90-62436. (Medieval Academy Bks.: No. 99). (Illus.). ix, 166p. 1992. 24.00 (*0-915651-05-X*) Medieval Acad.
— Holy Entrepreneurs: Cistercians, Knights & Economic Exchange in Twelfth-Century Burgundy. LC 91-8929. 256p. 1991. text 39.95 (*0-8014-2527-1*) Cornell U Pr.
— Spirituality & Administration: The Role of the Bishop in Twelfth-Century Auxerre. LC 78-55889. 1979. 20.00 (*0-910956-79-0*, SAM5); pap. 12.00 (*0-910956-67-7*) Medieval Acad.
— Strong of Body, Brave & Noble: Chivalry & Society in Medieval France. LC 97-38906. (Illus.). 232p. 1998. pap. 14.95 (*0-8014-8548-7*); text 39.95 (*0-8014-3097-6*) Cornell U Pr.
— Sword, Miter, & Cloister: Nobility & the Church in Burgundy, 980-1198. LC 86-29158. (Illus.). 416p. 1987. text 57.50 (*0-8014-1974-3*) Cornell U Pr.
Bouchard, Constance B. & Stearns, Peter N. Life & Society in the West. (Orig.). (C). 1988. pap. text, teacher ed. 2.50 (*0-15-550728-1*) Harcourt Coll Pubs.
— Life & Society in the West. 512p. (Orig.). (C). 1988. pap. text 33.50 (*0-15-550726-5*, Pub. by Harcourt Coll Pubs) Harcourt.
— Life & Society in the West. 512p. (Orig.). (C). 1988. pap. text 35.50 (*0-15-550727-3*, Pub. by Harcourt Coll Pubs) Harcourt.
***Bouchard, Daniel.** Diminutive Revolutions. 79p. (C). 1999. pap. 10.00 (*0-9666303-9-4*, Subpress Bks) A A Arts.
Bouchard, Dave. If Sarah Will Take Me. LC 96-72451. (Illus.). 32p. (J). 1997. 16.95 (*1-55143-081-9*) Orca Bk Pubs.
— If You're Not from the Prairie. (Illus.). 32p. 1998. 14.95 (*1-895714-66-4*) Raincoast Bk.
— Prairie Born. (Illus.). 32p. (ps-3). 1999. pap. 6.95 (*1-55143-152-1*) Orca Bk Pubs.
***Bouchard, David.** A Barnyard Bestiary. LC 98-83004. (Illus.). 32p. (J). (gr. 4-7). 1999. 14.95 (*1-55143-131-9*) Orca Bk Pubs.
Bouchard, David. The Dragon New Year: A Chinese Legend. LC 99-46292. (Illus.). 31p. (J). (gr. 1-5). 1999. 16.95 (*1-56145-210-6*) Peachtree Pubs.
— Elders Are Watching. 3rd ed. 1998. 15.95 (*1-55192-110-3*) Raincoast Bk.
— The Great Race. LC 97-2217. (Illus.). 32p. (J). (gr. 3-6). 1997. lib. bdg. 21.40 (*0-7613-0305-7*) Millbrook Pr.
— If You're Not from the Prairie. (Illus.). 32p. (J). (gr. 1-5). 1995. 16.00 (*0-689-80103-3*) Atheneum Yung Read.
— If You're Not from the Prairie. (Illus.). 32p. 1998. per. 5.99 (*0-689-82035-6*) S&S Childrens.
— The Journal of Etienne Mercier. LC 97-81098. (Illus.). 40p. 1998. 22.95 incl. cd-rom (*1-55143-128-9*) Orca Bk Pubs.
***Bouchard, David.** The Mermaid's Muse. 223p. 2000. 15.95 (*1-55192-248-7*) Raincoast Bk.
Bouchard, Denis. The Semantics of Syntax: A Minimalist Approach to Grammar. LC 95-8405. 540p. 1995. pap. text 35.95 (*0-226-06733-5*) U Ch Pr.
— The Semantics of Syntax: A Minimalist Approach to Grammar. LC 95-8405. 540p. 1998. lib. bdg. 95.00 (*0-226-06732-7*) U Ch Pr.
Bouchard, Denis, jt. auth. see Leffel, Katherine.
***Bouchard, Diane.** Desserticide II: AKA Just Desserts & Deathly Advice. 164p. 2000. pap. 12.99 (*0-9679037-0-X*, Pub. by Sis in Crime) Midpt Trade.
Bouchard, Donald F., ed. see Foucault, Michel.
Bouchard, Ed & Wright, Ben. Kinesthetic Ventures: Informed by the Work of F. M. Alexander, Stanislavski, Peirce & Freud. (Illus.). 225p. (Orig.). 1997. pap. text 24.00 (*0-941938-12-3*) Mesa Pr.
Bouchard, Elizabeth. Everything You Need to Know about Sexual Harassment. 3rd rev. ed. (Need to Know Library). (Illus.). 64p. (YA). (gr. 7-12). 1997. lib. bdg. 17.95 (*0-8239-2610-9*) Rosen Group.
Bouchard, Eric. Radiology Management: A Guide for Administrators, Supervisors, & Students, 2 vols. LC 94-21553. (Orig.). (C). 1993. pap. text 49.95 (*1-881795-06-3*) Bellwether-Cross.
— Radiology Management: A Guide for Administrators, Supervisors, & Students, 2 vols., Vol. 1. 269p. (Orig.). (C). 1993. pap. text 27.95 (*1-881795-04-7*) Bellwether-Cross.
***Bouchard, Gary M.** Colin's Campus: Cambridge Life & the English Ecologue. LC 00-27731. 160p. 2000. 33.50 (*1-57591-044-6*) Susquehanna U Pr.
Bouchard, Jean J. Radiation Therapy of Tumors & Diseases of the Nervous System. LC 66-23233. (Illus.). 244p. reprint ed. pap. 75.70 (*0-608-30257-0*, 201452700093) Bks Demand.
Bouchard, Jerry. Graduating to the Nine-Five World. 204p. 1991. pap. 11.95 (*0-942710-50-9*) Impact VA.
Bouchard, Kenneth R., jt. ed. see Kartush, Jack M.
Bouchard, Larry D. Tragic Method & Tragic Theology: Evil in Contemporary Drama & Religious Thought. LC 88-21827. 240p. 1989. lib. bdg. 37.50 (*0-271-00655-2*) Pa St U Pr.
Bouchard, Larry D., jt. ed. see Richesin, L. Dale.
Bouchard, M. Angeline, tr. see Galot.
Bouchard, Michael Marc. Lilies. (FRE.). 1998. pap. 9.95 (*0-88754-545-9*) Theatre Comm.
***Bouchard, Michel Marc.** The Tale of Teeka. Gaboriau, Linda, tr. from FRE.Tr. of L'Histoire de l'Oie. 64p. 1999. pap. 9.95 (*0-88922-410-2*) Talonbks.
***Bouchard, Michel Marc & Gaboriau, Linda.** The Corontion Voyage.Tr. of Le Voyage du Couronnement. 128p. 2000. pap. 11.95 (*0-88922-422-6*) Talonbks.
Bouchard, Norma & Pravadelli, Veronica, eds. Umberto Eco's Alternative: The Politics of Culture & the Ambiguities of Interpretation. LC 97-12505. VI, 317p. (C). 1999. pap. text 32.95 (*0-8204-3789-1*) P Lang Pubng.
Bouchard, P., et al, eds. GnRH, GnRH Analogs, Gonadotropins & Gonadal Peptides. LC 93-23508. (Illus.). 598p. 1994. 98.00 (*1-85070-471-6*) Prthnon Pub.
***Bouchard, P. J. & Pellet, Lizz.** Getting Your Shift Together: Making Sense of Organizational Culture & Change. Caputo, Sal, ed. 265p. 2000. pap. 29.95 (*0-9673248-0-7*) CCI Press.
Bouchard, Paul. There's a Gun in the House! What Do We Do? LC 98-60245. (Illus.). 12p. (J). (gr. k-8). 1998. pap. text 9.95 (*0-9663220-0-2*) Zack Pub.
Bouchard, Philip. Dawn in the Desert: Sketchbook Diary of a Journey with Archaeologists in Saudi Arabia. (Illus.). 160p. 1995. 115.00 (*1-898162-25-5*, Pub. by IMMEL Pubng) St Mut.
— Dawn in the Desert: Sketchbook Diary of a Journey with Archaeologists in Saudi Arabia. (Illus.). 74p. (C). 1995. 80.00 (*0-907151-15-9*, Pub. by IMMEL Pubng) St Mut.
— From Surrealism to Orientalism. 74p. (C). 1990. 150.00 (*0-7855-7018-7*, Pub. by IMMEL Pubng) St Mut.
Bouchard, R., et al. Childhood Epilepsy: A Pediatric-Psychiatric Approach. LC 76-46814. 136p. 1977. 27.50 (*0-8236-0774-7*) Intl Univs Pr.
Bouchard, Randy, jt. auth. see Kennedy, Dorothy.
Bouchard, Rene, ed. Culture Populaire et Litteratures au Quebec. (Stanford French & Italian Studies: Vol. 19). (FRE.). vi, 310p. 1980. pap. 56.50 (*0-915838-20-6*) Anma Libri.
Bouchard, Robert. Let's Play the Recorder. (J). (gr. 6 up). 9.95 (*0-8283-1471-3*) Branden Bks.
Bouchard, Robert, jt. auth. see Brittain, C. Dale.
Bouchard, Robert F., jt. auth. see Franklin, Justin D.
Bouchard, Ronald, et al. Cost-Effective Strategies for Managing the Human Resources Function. 79p. 1992. 15.00 (*1-878240-12-9*) Coll & U Personnel.
Bouchard, Ronald A. Human Resource Practices for Small Colleges. Reeder, Jefferson, ed. 196p. 1992. 44.95 (*0-685-62919-8*) NACUBO.
Bouchard, Sharon, jt. auth. see Fruehling, Rosemary T.
Bouchard, Thomas J., Jr. & Propping, Peter, eds. Twins As a Tool of Behavior Genetics: Report of the Dahlem Worshop on What Are the Mechanisms Mediating the Genetic & Environmental Determinants of Behavior? LC 93-8773. (Dahlem Workshop Reports, Life Sciences Research Report: Vol. 53). 326p. 1993. 245.95 (*0-471-94174-3*) Wiley.
Bouchardon, Patrice. The Healing Energies of Trees. (Illus.). 1999. pap. 17.95 (*1-885203-71-3*) Tuttle Pubng.
***Bouchaud, Jean-Philippe & Potters, Marc.** Theory of Financial Risks: From Statistical Physics to Risk Management. (Illus.). 250p. 2000. write for info. (*0-521-78232-5*) Cambridge U Pr.
Bouche, Brieuc. A Master Carver's Legacy: Essentials of Wood Carving Techniques. (Illus.). 160p. 1986. 24.95 (*0-8306-0329-8*, 2629) McGraw-Hill Prof.
Bouche, Daniel & Molinet, F. Asymptotic Methods in Electromagnetics. LC 96-39966. (Illus.). 510p. 1997. 99.00 (*3-540-61574-1*) Spr-Verlag.
Bouche, Henri, jt. auth. see Dollfus, Charles.
Bouche-Leclercq, Auguste. Histoire de la Divination dans l'Antiquite, 4 vols. LC 75-7305. (Roman History Ser.). (FRE.). 1975. reprint ed. 134.95 (*0-405-07182-3*) Ayer.
— Histoire de la Divination dans l'Antiquite, 4 vols., Vol. 1. LC 75-7305. (Roman History Ser.). (FRE.). 1975. reprint ed. 66.95 (*0-405-07183-3*) Ayer.
— Histoire de la Divination dans l'Antiquite, 4 vols., Vol. 3. LC 75-7305. (Roman History Ser.). (FRE.). 1975. reprint ed. 60.50 (*0-405-07184-1*) Ayer.
— Les Pontifes de L'Ancienne Rome: Etudes Historique sur les Institutions Religieuses de Rome. LC 75-10630. (Ancient Religion & Mythology Ser.). (FRE.). 1976. reprint ed. 36.95 (*0-405-07006-3*) Ayer.
Bouche, Nicole. Digitization for Scholarly Use: The Boswell Papers Project at the Beinecke Rare Book & Manuscript Library. 19p. 1999. pap. 15.00 (*1-887334-66-1*) Coun Lib & Info.
***Boucher.** Diabetes Recipes. LC 99-219957. 173p. 1999. pap. 15.95 (*0-471-34794-9*) Wiley.
Boucher & Zarb, George A. Prosthodontic Treatment for Edentulous Patients. 11th ed. LC 96-51006. (Illus.). 576p. (C). (gr. 13). 1997. text 76.00 (*0-8151-9899-X*, 24125) Mosby Inc.
Boucher, Alan, tr. see Friis, Erik J., ed.
Boucher, Anthony. The Case of the Baker Street Irregulars. 256p. 1995. mass mkt. 4.95 (*0-7867-0221-4*) Carroll & Graf.
***Boucher, Anthony.** The Compleat Boucher: SF & Fantasy Stories. Mann, James A., ed. (NESFA's Choice Ser.). 532p. 1999. 25.00 (*1-886778-02-7*, NESFA Pr) New Eng SF Assoc.
Boucher, Anthony. Nine Times Nine. 254p. 1986. pap. 4.95 (*0-930330-37-4*) Intl Polygonics.
— Rocket to the Morgue. 176p. 1988. pap. 4.95 (*0-930330-82-X*) Intl Polygonics.
Boucher, Anthony & Green, Denis. The New Adventures of Sherlock Holmes: The Strange Case of the Demom Barber & the Mystery of the Headless Monk, Vol. 4. abr. ed. 1989. 9.95 incl. audio (*0-671-68088-9*, Audioworks) PB.
— The New Adventures of Sherlock Holmes Gift Set, Vol. 4. abr. ed. 1993. audio 25.00 (*0-671-87587-6*) S&S Audio.
— The New Adventures of Sherlock Holmes, Vol. 1: The Unfortunate Tobacconist & The Paradol Chamber, Vol. 1. abr. ed. 1988. 9.95 incl. audio (*0-671-66076-4*, Audioworks) PB.
— The New Adventures of Sherlock Holmes, Vol. 3: The Aprl Fool's Day Adventure & The Strange Adventure of the Uneasy Easy Chair, Vol. 3. abr. ed. 1989. 9.95 incl. audio (*0-671-67785-3*, Audioworks) PB.
Boucher, Anthony, et al. The Haunting of Sherlock Holmes & Baconian Cipher. 26th abr. ed. (New Adventures of Sherlock Holmes Ser.: Vol. 26). 1994. 12.00 incl. audio (*0-671-79417-5*) S&S Trade.
Boucher, Anthony, jt. auth. see Green, Denis.
Boucher, Avery. Meade County, Kentucky, 1860 Census. 118p. 1981. pap. 16.00 (*1-889221-29-5*) Ancestral Trails.
Boucher, B. The Parables. 1989. pap. 21.00 (*0-86217-029-X*, Pub. by Veritas Pubns) St Mut.
Boucher, B. J. Walking in Wildness: A Guide to the Weminuche Wilderness. Sumner, Judith, ed. (Illus.). 200p. Date not set. pap. 17.95 (*1-887805-03-6*, Herald Pr CO) Durango Herald.
Boucher, Brian, et al. Handbook & Catalog for Instructional Media Selection. LC 72-11983. 214p. 1973. pap. 33.95 (*0-87778-045-5*) Educ Tech Pubns.
Boucher, Britt, jt. auth. see Oderwald, Richard.
Boucher, Bruce. Andrea Palladio: The Architect in His Time. LC 93-3120. (Illus.). 336p. 1993. 95.00 (*1-55859-381-0*) Abbeville Pr.
— Andrea Palladio: The Architect in His Time. (Illus.). 320p. 1998. 49.95 (*0-7892-0416-9*); pap. 39.95 (*0-7892-0300-6*) Abbeville Pr.
— Italian Baroque Sculpture. LC 97-60251. (World of Art Ser.). (Illus.). 216p. (Orig.). 1998. pap. 14.95 (*0-500-20307-5*, Pub. by Thames Hudson) Norton.
— The Sculpture of Jacopo Sansovino, 2 vols., Set. (Illus.). 652p. (C). 1991. 170.00 (*0-300-04759-2*) Yale U Pr.
Boucher, C., et al, eds. Earth Rotation & Coordinate Reference Frames. (International Association of Geodesy Symposia Ser.: Vol. 105). x, 166p. 1990. 79.95 (*0-387-97269-2*) Spr-Verlag.
Boucher, C. Robin. Students in Discord: Adolescents with Emotional & Behavioral Disorders. LC 98-30492. (Greenwood Educators' Reference Collection). 416p. 1999. lib. bdg. 75.00 (*0-313-30799-7*, Greenwood Pr) Greenwood.
Boucher, Carter. Tiger Dave. (Books for Young Learners). (Illus.). 8p. (J). (gr. k-2). 1999. pap. text 5.00 (*1-57274-151-1*) R Owen Pubs.
***Boucher, Charles, Jr.** From My Treasures. 1999. pap. write for info. (*1-58235-303-4*) Watermrk Pr.
Boucher, Chris. Corpse Marker. 1999. mass mkt. 6.95 (*0-563-55575-0*) BBC Worldwide.
— Last Man Running. 1998. pap. 5.95 (*0-563-40594-5*) BBC.
Boucher, David. Devil Wind Fire Wagons: Los Angeles County Fire Department Apparatus, 1920-1995. Magee, R. Dale, ed. (Illus.). 170p. 1996. 39.50 (*0-9625946-5-2*) Carter-Grove Pub.
— Political Theories of International Relations: From Thucydides to the Present. LC 99-179454. 456p. 1998. pap. text 24.95 (*0-19-878054-0*) OUP.
Boucher, DAvid. Political Theories of International Relations: From Thucydides to the Present. LC 99-179454. 456p. 1998. 110.00 (*0-19-878053-2*) OUP.
Boucher, David. Ride the Devil Wind: A History of the Los Angeles County Forester & Fire Warden Department & Fire Protection Districts. Magee, R. Dale et al, eds. 254p. 1991. lib. bdg. 55.00 (*0-941943-03-8*) Fire Pubns.
— Texts in Context: Revisionist Methods for Studying the History of Ideas. (Martinus Nijhoff Philosophy Library: No. 12). 290p. 1985. lib. bdg. 129.50 (*90-247-3121-6*, Pub. by M Nijhoff) Kluwer Academic.
Boucher, David, ed. The British Idealists. LC 96-36914. (Cambridge Texts in the History of Political Thought Ser.). 354p. (C). 1997. text 69.95 (*0-521-45336-4*); pap. text 24.95 (*0-521-45951-6*) Cambridge U Pr.
Boucher, David, et al, eds. Philosophy, Politics & Civilization: Essays on R. G. Collingwood. 352p. 1996. 65.00 (*0-7083-1308-6*, Pub. by Univ Wales Pr) Paul & Co Pubs.
Boucher, David & Kelly, Paul, eds. The Social Contract from Hobbes to Rawls. LC 94-4918. (Illus.). 336p. (C). 1994. pap. 27.99 (*0-415-10846-2*, B4681) Routledge.
— Social Justice: From Hume to Walzer. LC 98-6009. 304p. (C). 1998. 85.00 (*0-415-14997-5*); pap. 27.99 (*0-415-14998-3*) Routledge.
Boucher, David & Vincent, Andrew. A Radical Hegelian: The Political & Social Philosophy of Henry Jones. LC 93-39173. 1994. text 49.95 (*0-312-12079-6*) St Martin.
Boucher, David & Vincent, Andrew, eds. A Radical Hegelian: The Political & Social Philosophy of Henry Jones. x, 267p. 1993. write for info. (*0-7083-1207-1*, Pub. by Univ Wales Pr) Paul & Co Pubs.
Boucher, David, ed. see Collingwood, R. G.
Boucher, David, ed. & intro. see Collingwood, R. G.
Boucher, Denise & Brown, Alan, trs. The Fairies Are Thirsty. 64p. 1993. pap. 9.95 (*0-88922-200-2*) Genl Dist Srvs.
Boucher, Diane, jt. auth. see Boucher, Mike.

B

Boucher, Douglas H. The Biology of Mutualism-Ecology & Evolution. 368p. 1985. pap. 175.00 (*0-7855-0344-7*, Pub. by Intl Bks & Periodicals) St Mut.

***Boucher, Douglas H.** Paradox of Plenty: Hunger in a Bountiful World. LC 99-18244. 368p. 1999. pap. text 18.95 (*0-935028-71-4*) Inst Food & Develop.

Boucher, Douglas H., ed. The Biology of Mutualism: Ecology & Evolution. (Illus.). 400p. 1988. pap. text 40.00 (*0-19-505392-3*) OUP.

Boucher, E. A., jt. auth. see Murrell, John N.

Boucher, Eric & Corns, David. GCSE Law Casebook. 2nd ed. 130p. 1992. pap. 24.00 (*1-85431-207-3*, Pub. by Blackstone Pr) Gaunt.

— GCSE Law Casebook. 3rd ed. 224p. 1995. pap. 22.00 (*1-85431-464-5*, Pub. by Blackstone Pr) Gaunt.

Boucher, Francine & Binette, Andre. Living Well with Stress: Self-Management Guide. Hodder, Blanche, tr. (Illus.). 189p. 1999. reprint ed. pap. text 15.00 (*0-7881-6212-8*) DIANE Pub.

Boucher, Francois. Twenty Thousand Years of Fashion: The History of Costume & Personal Adornment. expanded ed. (Illus.). 356p. 1987. 49.50 (*0-8109-1693-2*, Pub. by Abrams) Time Warner.

Boucher, Geoff, jt. auth. see Ruiz, Mona.

Boucher, Harold. California Living Trust & Wills: What You Must Know Before You Make a Will. LC 94-155269. 1999. pap. 19.95 (*0-9638626-0-X*) Pennoyer Pr.

Boucher, Harold I. California Living Trusts & Wills: What You Should Know Before You See a Lawyer. 2nd rev. ed. 160p. Date not set. pap. 19.95 (*0-9638626-1-8*) Pennoyer Pr.

Boucher, Herbert. Miracle of Survival: A Holocaust Memoir. (Illus.). 196p. 1997. pap. 12.95 (*0-943376-64-5*) Magnes Mus.

Boucher, I. A., ed. see Advanced Medicine Symposia Staff.

Boucher, Jackie. No-Fuss Diabetes Recipes for 1 or 2: 125 Healthy & Delicious Meals & Desserts. 192p. 1999. pap. text 15.95 (*1-56561-178-0*) Wiley.

Boucher, Jackie, jt. auth. see Maggi, Annette.

Boucher, James R. Traffic System Design Handbook: Timesaving Telecommunication Traffic Tables & Programs. LC 92-30770. (Illus.). 200p. (C). 1992. pap. 49.95 (*0-7803-0428-4*, PP0325-1) Inst Electrical.

— Voice Teletraffic Systems Engineering. LC 88-24226. (Artech House Telecommunications Library). 179p. 1988. reprint ed. pap. 55.50 (*0-608-02366-3*, 206300800004) Bks Demand.

Boucher, Jeff W. Baluchi Woven Treasures. (Illus.). 152p. 1996. 50.00 (*1-85669-079-2*, Pub. by L King Pubng) Antique Collect.

Boucher, Jerry. Fire Truck Nuts & Bolts. LC 92-37476. (J). (ps-5). 1993. lib. bdg. 22.60 (*0-87614-783-X*, Carolrhoda) Lerner Pub.

— Fire Truck Nuts & Bolts. (Illus.). 48p. (J). (gr. k-4). 1993. pap. 5.95 (*0-87614-619-1*, First Ave Edns) Lerner Pub.

Boucher, Jerry, et al, eds. Ethnic Conflict: International Perspectives. LC 86-17885. (Sage Focus Editions Ser.: No. 84). 331p. 1987. reprint ed. pap. 102.70 (*0-608-01129-0*, 205943300001) Bks Demand.

Boucher, Jill, jt. ed. see Carruthers, Peter.

Boucher, John & Boucher, Therese. Christian Marriage: Sacrament of Abiding Friendship. (Spirit Life Ser.). 64p. 1995. pap. 4.95 (*1-878718-25-8*, Resurrection Pr) Catholic Bk Pub.

— An Introduction to the Catholic Charismatic Renewal. 16p. pap. 0.99 (*0-89283-848-5*) Servant.

Boucher, John N. Old & New Westmoreland (County), 4 vols. Hedley, Fenwick Y., ed. (Illus.). 2617p. 1997. reprint ed. lib. bdg. 236.00 (*0-8328-6461-7*) Higginson Bk Co.

Boucher, John N., ed. A Century & a Half of Pittsburg & Her People, 3 vols. (Illus.). 1558p. 1997. reprint ed. lib. bdg. 157.50 (*0-8328-6440-4*) Higginson Bk Co.

***Boucher, Joseph W., et al.** LLCS & LLPS: A Wisconsin Handbook. rev. ed. LC 99-19741. 1999. ring bd. 165.00 incl. disk (*1-57862-026-0*) State Bar WI.

Boucher, Joseph W., et al. Organizing a Wisconsin Business Corporation: Articles, Bylaws, & Other Forms. 2nd ed. LC 98-15027. 1998. ring bd. 165.00 incl. disk (*1-57862-011-2*) State Bar WI.

— Wisconsin Condominium Law Handbook. 2nd ed. LC 93-48243. 1994. ring bd. 90.00 (*0-945574-59-2*) State Bar WI.

Boucher, Karen & Katz, Fima. Essential Guide to Object Monitors. LC 98-53559. 272p. 1999. pap. 34.99 (*0-471-31971-6*) Wiley.

Boucher, Karen J., et al. Multistate S Corporation Tax Guide: Annual. Kaiser, Laura B., ed. 600p. 1991. pap. text 96.00 (*1-878375-60-1*) Panel Pubs.

Boucher, Karen J., jt. auth. see Raabe, William A.

Boucher, Keith & Harris, Nicola. Environmental Research Register. LC 77-369863. (African Environment: Special Reports: Vol. 4). 146p. 1977. reprint ed. pap. 45.30 (*0-8357-3213-4*, 205708400010) Bks Demand.

Boucher, Louis J., jt. auth. see Renner, Robert P.

Boucher, Madeleine. The Mysterious Parable: A Literary Study. Vawter, Bruce, ed. LC 76-51260. (Catholic Biblical Quarterly Monographs: No. 6). ix, 101p. 1977. pap. 2.50 (*0-915170-05-1*) Catholic Bibl Assn.

Boucher, Mark. The Hedge Fund Edge - Maximum Profit-Minimum Risk: Global Trend Trading Strategies. LC 98-18230. (Trading Advantage Ser.). 374p. 1998. 59.95 (*0-471-18538-8*) Wiley.

Boucher, Mark, et al. The TRADEHARD.COM Guide to Conquering the Trading Markets. Etzkorn, Mark, ed. (Illus.). 166p. 1999. 29.95 (*1-893756-02-5*) M Gordon Pubng.

Boucher, Michelle. Bon Voyage: Leaving the Kids Home, the Complete Guide to Overnight Childcare. (Illus.). 110p. (Orig.). Date not set. pap. 10.00 (*0-9658110-1-8*) Hands of the Sun.

***Boucher, Mike & Boucher, Diane.** High Performance Programming. (C). 2000. pap. 48.00 (*0-13-016671-5*) P-H.

Boucher, Neil. Celluar Radio Handbook: A Reference for Cellular System Operation. 800p. 1998. 215.00 (*0-471-29776-3*) Wiley.

***Boucher, Neil.** Paging Technology Handbook. 327p. 1998. 104.95 (*0-471-29775-5*) Wiley.

***Boucher, Neil J.** The Cellular Radio Handbook: A Reference for Cellular System Operation. 4th ed. 1000p. 2000. 225.00 (*0-471-38725-8*) Wiley.

Boucher, Neil J. The Trunked Radio & Enhanced PMR Radio Handbook. LC 99-34062. 448p. 1999. 94.95 (*0-471-35289-6*) Wiley.

Boucher, Nellie A. Breckinridge County, Kentucky 1860 Census. 226p. 1993. pap. 21.00 (*1-889221-01-5*) Ancestral Trails.

Boucher, Philip, ed. Proceedings of the Eleventh Meeting of the French Colonial Historical Society, Quebec, May, 1985. (Illus.). 338p. (Orig.). (C). 1987. pap. 56.00 (*0-8191-5658-2*) U Pr of Amer.

Boucher, Philip, jt. ed. see Galloway, Patricia.

Boucher, Philip P. Les Nouvelles Frances (France in America) 1500-1815: An Imperial Perspective. (Illus.). 143p. (Orig.). 1989. pap. 25.00 (*0-916617-32-7*, Pub. by J C Brown) Oak Knoll.

Boucher, Philip P., ed. Proceedings of the Tenth Meeting of the French Colonial Historical Society, April 12-14, 1984. LC 76-644752. (Illus.). 290p. (Orig.). 1986. pap. 59.00 (*0-8191-4916-0*); pap. text 27.00 (*0-8191-4917-9*) U Pr of Amer.

— Proceedings of the Thirteenth & Fourteenth Meetings of the French Colonial Historical Society. (Illus.). 248p. (C). 1990. lib. bdg. 49.00 (*0-8191-7637-0*) U Pr of Amer.

Boucher, Philip P. & Courville, Serge, eds. The Twelfth Meeting of the French Colonial Historical Society Ste. Genevieve, May 1986: Proceedings. (Illus.). 168p. (Orig.). (C). 1989. lib. bdg. 40.50 (*0-8191-7205-7*) U Pr of Amer.

Boucher, Rita. A Misbegotten Match. 192p. 1994. mass mkt. 3.99 (*0-380-77714-2*, Avon Bks) Morrow Avon.

— Miss Gabriel's Gambit. 224p. (Orig.). 1993. mass mkt. 3.99 (*0-380-77090-3*, Avon Bks) Morrow Avon.

— Poet & the Paragon. 224p. 1999. mass mkt. 4.99 (*0-451-19578-7*, Sig) NAL.

— The Scandalous Schoolmistress. 256p. (Orig.). 1992. mass mkt. 3.99 (*0-380-76529-2*, Avon Bks) Morrow Avon.

Boucher, Robert. The Understanding & Management of Conflict in Sport Organizations. Zeigler, Earle F., ed. (Monograph Series on Sport & Physical Education Management). 33p. (C). 1995. pap. text 4.40 (*0-87563-566-0*) Stipes.

Boucher, Robert, jt. auth. see Nakayama, Yasuki.

Boucher, Ronald. Picture Compression with JPEG. (C). 1995. text. write for info. (*0-201-52885-1*) Addison-Wesley.

Boucher, Sandy. Discovering Kwan Yin: Buddhist Goddess of Compassion. LC 98-41118. (Illus.). 128p. 1999. 20.00 (*0-8070-1340-4*) Beacon Pr.

***Boucher, Sandy.** Discovering Kwan Yin, Buddhist Goddess of Compassione: A Path Toward Clarity & Peace. 2000. pap. 12.00 (*0-8070-1341-2*) Beacon Pr.

— Hidden Spring: A Buddhist Woman Confronts Cancer. 224p. 2000. pap. 16.95 (*0-86171-171-8*) Wisdom MA.

Boucher, Sandy. Opening the Lotus: A Woman's Guide to Buddhism. 208p. 1998. pap. 12.00 (*0-8070-7309-1*) Beacon Pr.

— Turning the Wheel: American Women Creating the New Buddhism. rev. ed. LC 93-16630. (Illus.). 400p. 1993. pap. 16.00 (*0-8070-7305-9*) Beacon Pr.

Boucher Stetson, Debi & Peters, Jo. The Insiders' Guide to Cape Cod, Nantucket & Martha's Vineyard. 4th ed. (Insiders' Guide Travel Ser.). 1999. pap. 16.95 (*1-57380-110-0*, The Insiders' Guide) Falcon Pub Inc.

Boucher, Steve, et al. Legal Uncertainty & Land Disputes in Peri-Urban Areas of Mozambique: Land Markets in Transition. (Research Paper Ser.: Vol. 121). (Illus.). xxvi, 111p. (C). 1995. pap. 7.00 (*0-934519-33-1*, RP121) U of Wis Land.

***Boucher, Theresa.** Evangelizing Unchurched Children. 80p. 2000. pap. 9.95 (*0-89390-496-1*) Resource Pubns.

Boucher, Therese, jt. auth. see Boucher, John.

Boucher, Tracy, tr. see De La Gueriniere, Francois R.

Boucher, Virginia. Interlibrary Loan Practices Handbook. 2nd ed. LC 96-18419. 250p. 1996. pap. 45.00 (*0-8389-0667-2*, 0667-2-2045) ALA.

Boucher, W. I., jt. ed. see Quade, Edward S.

Boucher, Wayne I. Spinoza: 18th & 19th-Century Discussions, 6 Vol. 2100p. 1999. 595.00 (*1-85506-579-7*) Thoemmes Pr.

— Spinoza in English: A Bibliography from the Seventeenth Century to the Present. LC 91-24542. (BSIH Ser.: No. 28). ix, 226p. 1991. 94.50 (*90-04-09499-7*) Brill Academic Pubs.

— Spinoza in English: A Bibliography from the 17th Century to the Present, 1 Vol. 300p. 1999. 120.00 (*1-85506-612-2*) Thoemmes Pr.

Boucherle, Gary, jt. auth. see Burge, David L.

***Boucheron, Rose.** The Butterfly Field. large type ed. 400p. 1999. 31.99 (*0-7505-1359-4*, Pub. by Mgna Lrg Print) Ulverscroft.

Boucheron, Rose. The End of a Long Summer. large type ed. 1995. 11.50 (*0-7505-0783-7*, Pub. by Mgna Lrg Print) Ulverscroft.

***Boucheron, Rose.** Farewells. 320p. 2000. 31.99 (*0-7505-1497-3*) Ulverscroft.

Boucheron, Rose. Secrets of the Past. large type ed. (Magna Large Print Ser.). 463p. 1996. 27.99 (*0-7505-0875-2*, Pub. by Mgna Lrg Print) Ulverscroft.

— Victoria's Emeralds. large type ed. (Magna Large Print Ser.). 362p. 1997. 27.99 (*0-7505-1070-6*) Ulverscroft.

***Bouchery, Jean.** 1944-45 British Soldier: Headress, Uniforms & Equipment, 2. 1998. 34.95 (*2-908182-74-2*, 182742) Histoire.

Bouchet, Andre du, see Du Bouchet, Andre.

Bouchet, Lionel G., et al. MIRD Head & Brain Dosimetry: Absorbed Fractions of Energy & Absorbed Dose Per Unit Cumulated Activity Within Pediatric & Adult Head & Brain Models for Use in Nuclear Medicine Internal Dosimetry. (Illus.). 206p. 1999. pap. 70.00 (*0-932004-70-9*, Pub. by Soc Nuclear Med) Matthews Medical Bk Co.

Bouchet, Michael H. The Political Economy of International Debt: What, Who, How Much, & Why? LC 87-2474. 238p. 1987. 67.95 (*0-89930-185-1*, BTP/, Quorum Bks) Greenwood.

Bouchet, Paule du, see Bernadac, Marie-Laure & Du Bouchet, Paule.

Bouchet-Saulnier, F. Dictionnaire Pratique du Droit Humanitaire. (FRE.). 1998. 99.00 (*0-320-00189-X*) Fr & Eur.

Bouchette, Ed. The Pittsburgh Steelers. LC 94-16792. 1994. pap. 9.99 (*0-312-11325-0*) St Martin.

Bouchette, Joseph. British Dominions in North America, 2 vols., Set. LC 68-56073. reprint ed. 295.00 (*0-404-00936-0*) AMS Pr.

Bouchey, Stuart, ed. see Rae, John B.

Bouchey, Stuart, ed. see U. S. House of Representatives Staff.

Bouchez, Colette, jt. auth. see Lauersen, Niels H.

Bouchez, Colette, jt. auth. see Laurensen, Niels H.

Bouchez, J. L., et al, eds. Granite: From Segregation of Melt to Emplacement Fabrics. LC 97-3668. (Petrology & Structural Geology Ser.). 368p. (C). 1997. text 174.00 (*0-7923-4460-X*) Kluwer Academic.

***Bouchez, L. J., et al.** Reflections on Principles & Practice of International Law: Essays in Honour of Leo J. Bouchez. Gill, Terry D. & Heere, Wybo P., eds. LC 99-86509. 300p. 2000. 119.00 (*90-411-1343-6*) Kluwer Law Intl.

Bouchier, Chili. Shooting Star. large type ed. (Ulverscroft Large Print Ser.). (Illus.). 528p. 1997. 27.99 (*0-7089-3860-4*) Ulverscroft.

Bouchier, David. The Accidental Immigrant: My Life in America. unabridged ed. 325p. (Orig.). 1996. pap. 12.95 (*0-9652475-0-3*) Mid Atlntic.

— Composers. (Illus.). 1999. pap. 9.95 (*0-7611-1206-5*) Workman Pub.

— Only in America: Essays from Public Radio & the New York Times. 321p. (Orig.). 1999. pap. 14.95 (*0-9652475-1-1*, Pub. by Mid Atlntic) LPC InBook.

Bouchier, E. S., ed. see Arnold, William T.

Bouchier, Ian A., jt. auth. see Bateson, Malcolm C.

Bouchier, Ian A. D., et al. French's Index of Differential Diagnosis. 13th ed. LC 97-189034. (Illus.). 812p. 1996. pap. text 67.50 (*0-7506-1434-X*) Buttrwrth-Heinemann.

Bouchitte, G., et al. Calculus of Variations, Homogenizations & Continuum Mechanics. (Series on Advances in Mathematics). 312p. 1994. text 86.00 (*981-02-1783-8*) World Scientific Pub.

Bouchitte, Vincent & Morvan, Michael, eds. Orders, Algorithms, & Applications: International Workshop ORDAL '94. LC 94-3555. (Lecture Notes in Computer Science Ser.: Vol. 831). 1994. 39.95 (*0-387-58274-6*) Spr-Verlag.

Bouchon-Meunier, Bernadette, et al. Uncertainty in Knowledge Bases: Third International Conference on Information Processing & Management of Uncertainty in Knowledge-Based Systems, IPMU '90, Paris, France, July, 1990 Proceedings. Goos, G. et al, eds. (Lecture Notes in Computer Science Ser.: Vol. 521). x, 609p. 1991. 63.95 (*0-387-54346-5*) Spr-Verlag.

Bouchon, Genevieve. L' Asie du Sud a l'Epoque des Grandes Decouvertes. (Collected Studies: No. CS260). (FRE.). 342p. (C). 1987. reprint ed. lib. bdg. 124.95 (*0-86078-208-5*, Pub. by Variorum) Ashgate Pub Co.

Bouchon-Meunier, B. & Kacprzyk, J., eds. Aggregation & Fusion of Imperfect Information. LC 97-38732. (Studies in Fuzziness & Soft Computing: Vol. 12). (Illus.). viii, 278p. 1997. 76.00 (*3-7908-1048-7*) Spr-Verlag.

***Bouchon-Meunier, B., et al.** Information, Uncertainty & Fusion LC 99-37150. (International Series In Engineering & Computer Science). 1999. write for info. (*0-7923-8590-X*) Kluwer Academic.

Bouchon-Meunier, Bernadette, et al, eds. Fuzzy Logic & Soft Computing. LC 95-22063. (Advances in Fuzzy Systems Ser.: Vol. 4). 470p. 1995. 118.00 (*981-02-2345-5*) World Scientific Pub.

Bouchon-Meunier, Bernadette & Yager, Ronald R. Uncertainty in Knowledge-Based Systems. (Lecture Notes in Computer Science Ser.: Vol. 286). vii, 405p. 1987. 45.00 (*0-387-18579-8*) Spr-Verlag.

***Bouchoule, Andre.** Dusty Plasmas: Physics, Chemistry & Technological Impacts in Plasma Processing. LC 98-50683. 418p. 1999. 170.00 (*0-471-97386-6*) Wiley.

Bouchoux, Deborah E. Business Organizations for Paralegals, Incl. instr's. manual. LC 96-79006. 700p. 1997. teacher ed., boxed set 54.00 (*1-56706-484-1*, 64841) Panel Pubs.

***Bouchoux, Deborah E.** Cite-Checker. (Paralegal Ser.). (C). 2000. pap. 14.95 (*0-7668-1893-4*) Delmar.

Bouchoux, Deborah E. Cite Mate. 1997. 59.50 (*1-56706-533-3*, 65333) Panel Pubs.

— Legal Research & Writing for Paralegals. LC 93-80970. 656p. 1994. pap. 34.00 (*0-316-10366-7*, Aspen Law & Bus) Aspen Pub.

— Legal Research & Writing for Paralegals. 2nd ed. LC 97-39358. 1998. pap. text 40.95 (*1-56706-639-9*) Aspen Law.

— Write Mate. 1995. 59.50 (*0-316-10323-3*, 03233) Panel Pubs.

Boucias, D., jt. ed. see Latge, J. P.

Boucias, Drion G. & Pendland, Jacquelyn C. Principles of Insect Pathology. LC 98-45713. 568p. 1998. 250.00 (*0-412-03591-X*) Kluwer Academic.

***Boucicault, Dion.** Belle Lamar: An Episode of the Civil War. (Americana Series). 2000. reprint ed. pap. 4.95 (*0-937657-57-3*) Feedbk Theabks & Prospero.

Boucicault, Dion. London Assurance. Smith, James L., ed. (New Mermaid Ser.). 137p. (C). 1984. pap. text 9.75 (*0-393-90050-9*) Norton.

— Octoroon: or Life in Louisiana: A Play in Five Acts. LC 77-93418. (Black Heritage Library Collection). 1977. 13.95 (*0-8369-8521-4*) Ayer.

— Selected Plays. Parkin, Andrew, ed. LC 85-31345. (Irish Drama Selections Ser.: No. 4). 407p. 1987. 16.95 (*0-8132-0616-2*); pap. 16.95 (*0-8132-0617-0*) Cath U Pr.

Bouck, James R. The Church of Modesto: A City's Journey Towards Christ Centered Unity. LC 98-75647. (Illus.). 344p. 1999. pap. 9.95 (*0-9637265-9-5*, 9901) Glenhaven Pr.

Bouck, William, jt. auth. see Broderick, Warren F.

Bouckaert, Boudewijn, ed. Bibliography of Law & Economics. 684p. (C). 1992. lib. bdg. 284.50 (*0-7923-1645-2*) Kluwer Academic.

Bouckaert, Boudewijn & De Geest, Gerrit, eds. Encyclopedia of Law & Economics, Vols. I-V. LC 99-38062. 4400p. 1999. 1390.00 (*1-85898-565-X*) E Elgar.

— Encyclopedia of Law & Economics: Civil Law & Economics. 600p. 1999. write for info. (*1-85898-985-X*) E Elgar.

— Encyclopedia of Law & Economics: The Economics of Public Law & Tax. 600p. 1999. write for info. (*1-85898-987-6*) E Elgar.

— Encyclopedia of Law & Economics: The History & Methodology of Law & Economics. LC 99-38062. 600p. 2000. write for info. (*1-85898-984-1*) E Elgar.

— Encyclopedia of Law & Economics: The Law & Economics of Crime & Criminal Procedure. 600p. 1999. write for info. (*1-85898-988-4*) E Elgar.

— Encyclopedia of Law & Economics: The Regulation of Contracts. 600p. 1999. write for info. (*1-85898-986-8*) E Elgar.

— Essays in Law & Economics No. II: Contract Law, Regulation, & Reflections on Law & Economics. LC 98-187113. 306p. 1996. pap. 80.00 (*90-6215-427-1*, Pub. by Maklu Uitgev) Gaunt.

***Bouckaert, Boudewijn & Godart-Van der Kroon, Annette, eds.** Hayek Revisited. LC 99-55084. 176p. 2000. 80.00 (*1-85898-449-1*) E Elgar.

Bouckaert, G. & Halachini, Arie, eds. Public Productivity Through Quality & Strategic Management. LC 94-7847. (YA). (gr. 12). 1995. 120.00 (*90-5199-189-4*) IOS Press.

Bouckaert, Geert & Helgason, Sigurdur. In Search of Results: Performance Management Practices. LC 98-196450. 136p. 1997. pap. 33.00 (*92-64-15574-0*, 42-97-02-1, Pub. by Org for Econ) OECD.

Bouckaert, Geert, jt. auth. see Halachmi, Arie.

Bouckaert, Geert, jt. auth. see Pollitt, Christopher.

Bouckaert, Geert, jt. ed. see Halachmi, Arie.

Boucke, Laurie. Brief Encounters: A Dictionary of Briefs & Phrases for Court Reporters. 2nd ed. LC 97-14159. 650p. (C). 1997. pap. 50.00 (*1-888580-07-0*) White-Boucke.

— Categorically Speaking: A Reference Work & Study Guide for Court Reporting. LC 96-204456. 462p. 1996. pap. 37.50 (*1-888580-01-1*) White-Boucke.

***Boucke, Laurie.** Infant Potty Training: A Gentle & Primeval Method Adapted to Modern Living. LC 00-21543. (Illus.). 520p. 2000. pap. 19.50 (*1-888580-10-0*) White-Boucke.

Boucke, Laurie. Medical Briefs: A Dictionary of Realtime Briefs for Court Reporters, 2 vols. LC 98-8417. 1380p. 1998. pap. 75.00 (*1-888580-02-X*) White-Boucke.

— Trickle Treat: Diaperless Infant Toilet Training. White, Colin, ed. LC RJ476.E6B68 1991. (Illus.). 85p. (Orig.). 1991. pap. 7.50 (*0-9625006-2-3*) White-Boucke.

Boucke, Laurie, jt. auth. see White, Colin.

Boucke, Laurie, ed. see Carlson, Linda F.

Boucke, Laurie, ed. see Diamond, Dickson.

Boucke, Laurie, ed. see Doucette, Eugene F.

Boucke, Laurie, ed. see Kaufman, Phil & White, Colin.

Boucke, Laurie, ed. see Palumbo, Anne V.

Boucke, Laurie, ed. see Smith, Donald G.

Boucke, Laurie, ed. see Stewart, David.

Boucke, Rick, ed. see Archer, Jeff.

Boucklund McLean, Terri. New Harmonies: Choosing Contemporary Music for Worship. 17.95 (*1-56699-206-0*) Alban Inst.

Boucot, A. J. & Lawson, J. D., eds. Paleocommunities: A Case Study from the Silurian & Lower Devonian. (World & Regional Geology Ser.: No. 6). (Illus.). 600p. (C). 1999. text 300.00 (*0-521-36398-5*) Cambridge U Pr.

Boucot, Arthur J. Principles of Benthic Marine Paleo-Ecology. LC 79-8535. 1981. text 107.00 (*0-12-118980-5*) Acad Pr.

Boucot, Arthur J., ed. Evolutionary Paleobiology of Behavior & Coevolution. 750p. 1990. 243.25 (*0-444-88034-8*) Elsevier.

Boucot, Arthur J., jt. ed. see Gray, Jane.

Boucourechliev, Andre. Stravinsky. Cooper, Martin, tr. from FRE. LC 86-33488. 336p. 1987. 45.00 (*0-8419-1058-8*); pap. 24.50 (*0-8419-1162-2*) Holmes & Meier.

Boucquey, Thierry. Mirages de la Farce: Fete des Fous, Bruegel et Moliere. LC 90-28663. (Purdue University Monographs in Romance Languages: Vol. 33). (FRE., Illus.). xviii, 158p. 1991. 53.00 (*1-55619-085-9*); pap. 22.95 (*1-55619-086-7*) J Benjamins Pubng Co.

— Six Medieval French French Farces. LC 99-14293. (Medieval Studies: Vol. 11). 248p. 1999. text 89.95 (*0-7734-8038-2*) E Mellen.

Boucsein, W. Electrodermal Activity. (Behavioral Psychophysiology Ser.). (Illus.). 456p. (C). 1992. text 89.50 (*0-306-44214-0*, Kluwer Plenum) Kluwer Academic.

Boucsein, Wolf, jt. ed. see Backs, Richard W.

Boud, David. Enhancing Learning Through Self-Assessment. 256p. 1995. pap. 29.95 (*0-7494-1368-9*, Kogan Pg Educ) Stylus Pub VA.

— Understanding Learning at Work. LC 98-45949. 1999. pap. 32.99 (*0-415-18229-8*) Routledge.

***Boud, David.** Understanding Learning at Work. LC 98-45949. 1999. 100.00 (*0-415-18228-X*) Routledge.

Boud, David & Feletti, Grahame. The Challenge of Problem-Based Learning. 2nd ed. 336p. 1997. 59.95 (*0-7494-2291-2*, Kogan Pg Educ) Stylus Pub VA.

Boud, David & Feletti, Grahame. The Challenge of Problem-Based Learning. 2nd ed. 336p. 1998. pap. 32.50 (*0-7494-2560-1*, Kogan Pg Educ) Stylus Pub VA.

Boud, David & Miller, Nod. Working with Experience: Animating Learning. LC 96-2155. (Illus.). 232p. (C). 1996. pap. 22.99 (*0-415-14246-6*) Routledge.

***Boud, David & Solomon, Nicky.** Work-Based Learning: A New Higher Education? LC 00-44122. (C). 2001. pap. write for info. (*0-335-20580-1*, Pub. by OpUniv Pr) Taylor & Francis.

Boud, David & Walker, David. Experience & Learning: Reflection at Work. 115p. (C). 1991. 48.00 (*0-7300-1248-4*, Pub. by Deakin Univ) St Mut.

Boud, David, et al. Teaching in Laboratories. 208p. 1986. pap. 47.95 (*0-335-15609-6*) OpUniv Pr.

Boud, George, ed. see Ayodo, Awor & Odhiambo, Atieno.

Boudaille, Georges, jt. auth. see Daix, Pierre.

Boudard, Alain & Chamouard, P. A., eds. The 20 Years of Saturne-2: Paris, France 4-5 May 1998. 350p. 1999. 82.00 (*981-02-3679-4*) World Scientific Pub.

Boudard, Alphonse. Le Banquet des Leopards. (FRE.). 288p. 1982. pap. 10.95 (*0-7859-2223-7*, 207037419X) Fr & Eur.

— Bleubite. (FRE.). 1976. pap. 10.95 (*0-7859-1829-9*, 2070367991) Fr & Eur.

— La Cerise. (FRE.). 1973. pap. 10.95 (*0-7859-1748-9*, 2070364038) Fr & Eur.

— Cinoche. (FRE.). 288p. 1975. pap. 10.95 (*0-7859-1805-1*, 2070366847) Fr & Eur.

— Les Combattants Du Petit Bonheur. (FRE.). 379p. 1990. pap. 11.95 (*0-7859-2191-5*, 2253052183) Fr & Eur.

— Le Corbillard De Jules. (FRE.). 1981. pap. 10.95 (*0-7859-1935-X*, 2070372820) Fr & Eur.

— Dictionnaire de l'Argot. (ENG & FRE.). 700p. 1995. 75.00 (*0-7859-9936-1*) Fr & Eur.

— L' Hopital. (FRE.). 384p. 1974. pap. 11.95 (*0-7859-1783-7*, 2070365727) Fr & Eur.

— La Metamorphose des Cloportes. (FRE.). 246p. 1987. pap. 10.95 (*0-7859-2189-3*, 2253041904) Fr & Eur.

Boudart, Jennifer & Fletcher, Rusty. Johnny Appleseed: A Tale of Love. LC 97-220723. (Illus.). 1997. write for info. (*0-7853-2135-7*) Pubns Intl Ltd.

Boudart, M., jt. ed. see Anderson, J. R.

Boudart, Marina, et al, eds. Modern Belgium. LC 90-61813. 592p. 1990. 45.00 (*0-930664-10-8*) SPOSS.

Boudart, Michel, tr. see Semenov, Nikolai N.

Boudean, T. Bubba. Country Proverbs, Don't Cackle 'til the Egg Is Laid. (Illus.). 64p. 1993. 9.95 (*1-56245-071-9*) Great Quotations.

Boudeaux, Michael. Risen Indeed: Lessons of Faith from the U. S. S. R. 113p. (Orig.). 1983. pap. text 8.95 (*0-88141-021-7*) St Vladimirs.

Boudebaba, Rabah. Urban Growth & Housing Policy in Algeria: A Case Study of a Migrant Community in the City of Cons. 300p. 1991. 79.95 (*1-85628-247-3*, Pub. by Avebry) Ashgate Pub Co.

Boudemagh, M. E. Dictionary of Investment. (FRE & GER.). 566p. 1995. pap. 145.00 (*2-910956-00-8*) IBD Ltd.

— English-French Dictionary of Financial Market Terms. (ENG & FRE.). 1989. pap. 42.50 (*0-7859-8971-4*) Fr & Eur.

Boudemagh, Mohamed. Investor's Dictionary in Six Languages: English, French, German, Italian, Portuguese, Spanish. (ENG, FRE, GER, ITA & POR.). 566p. 1995. 175.00 (*0-7859-9935-3*) Fr & Eur.

Boudet, A. M., jt. ed. see Ranjeva, R.

Boudet De Puymaigre, T. J. Romanceiro: Choix de Vieux Chants Portugais. LC 78-20109. (Collection de contes et de chansons populaires: No. 2). reprint ed. 21.50 (*0-404-60352-1*) AMS Pr.

Boudet, Jacques. Les Mots de l'Histoire: Dictionnaire Historique Universel des Mots, des Moeurs et des Mentalites. (FRE.). 1374p. 1990. pap. 155.00 (*0-7859-7801-1*, 2221052528) Fr & Eur.

Boudeville, J. R. Le Complexe Agricole. (Economies et Societes Series L: No. 12). 1963. pap. 11.00 (*0-8115-0737-8*) Periodicals Srv.

Boudewijnse, Barbara, et al, eds. More Than Opium: An Anthropological Approach to Latin American & Caribbean Pentecostal Praxis. LC 97-30704. (Studies in Evangelicalism: No. 14). 336p. 1998. 55.00 (*0-8108-3390-5*) Scarecrow.

Boudewyns, Patrick A. & Shipley, Robert H., eds. Flooding & Implosive Therapy: Direct Therapeutic Exposure in Clinical Practice. LC 83-2380. 248p. 1983. 49.50 (*0-306-41155-5*, Plenum Trade) Perseus Pubng.

Boudhe. Income Tax Guide: For 1998 Returns, 1999 Edition. 112p. 1998. pap. 13.00 (*0-687-08430-X*) Abingdon.

Boudier, E. Histoire et Classification des Discomycetes d'Europe: Description des Genres avec Indication des Especes, Historique, Localites et Epoques de Recolte, Organographie, Partie Chimique, Usages, etc. (FRE.). 252p. 1968. reprint ed. lib. bdg. 25.00 (*90-6123-024-1*) Lubrecht & Cramer.

Boudier, J. Dictionary of Dairy Products French-English/ English-French. 2nd ed. Orig. Title: Dictionnaire Laitier. 220p. 1981. 62.00 (*2-85206-092-2*, Pub. by Technique et Documentation) IBD Ltd.

Boudier, J. F. & Luquet, F. M. French-English, English-French Dairy Dictionary: Dictionnaire Laitier. deluxe ed. (ENG & FRE.). 220p. 1981. 89.95 (*0-8288-4446-1*, M9627) Fr & Eur.

Boudin, H. L., ed. see De Crevecoeur, St. John.

Boudin, Louis B. Government by Judiciary, 2 vols., Set. LC 92-75949. 1188p. 1993. reprint ed. 250.00 (*1-56169-027-9*) Gaunt.

Boudinot, Elias. Journal of Historical Recollections of American Events During the Revolutionary War. LC 67-29029. (Eyewitness Accounts of the American Revolution Ser.). 1975. reprint ed. 22.95 (*0-405-01106-7*) Ayer.

— Star in the West: A Humble Attempt to Discover the Long Lost Ten Tribes of Israel. LC 79-121499. (Select Bibliographies Reprint Ser.). 1977. 19.95 (*0-8369-5457-2*) Ayer.

***Boudinot, Elias.** A Star in the West: or A Humble Attempt to Discover the Long Lost Ten Tribes of Israel, Preparatory to Their Return to Their Beloved City, Jerusalem. (LC History-America-E). 312p. 1999. reprint ed. lib. bdg. 99.00 (*0-7812-4310-6*) Rprt Serv.

Boudjedra, Rachid. L' Escargot Entete. (FRE.). 149p. 1985. pap. 10.95 (*0-7859-2020-X*, 2070376869) Fr & Eur.

— Insolation. (Folio Ser.: No. 1871). (FRE.). 252p. 1987. pap. 9.95 (*2-07-037871-3*) Schoenhof.

— L' Insolation. (FRE.). 252p. 1987. pap. 11.95 (*0-7859-2072-2*, 2070378713) Fr & Eur.

— Mille et Une Annees de la Nostalgie. (Folio Ser.: No. 1998). (FRE.). 1988. pap. 14.95 (*2-07-038087-4*) Schoenhof.

— Les One Thousand One Annees de la Nostalgie. (FRE.). 435p. 1988. pap. 16.95 (*0-7859-2104-4*, 2070380874) Fr & Eur.

— La Repudation. (FRE.). 1981. pap. 10.95 (*0-7859-2898-7*) Fr & Eur.

— The Repudiation. Lambrova, Golda, tr. from FRE. 195p. 1995. 28.00 (*0-89410-729-1*, Three Contnts); pap. 14.00 (*0-89410-730-5*, Three Contnts) L Rienner.

— Repudiation. (Folio Ser.: No. 1326). (FRE.). 251p. 1986. pap. 8.95 (*2-07-037326-6*) Schoenhof.

— Topographie Ideale pour une Agression Caracterisee. (FRE.). 250p. 1986. pap. 11.95 (*0-7859-2046-3*, 2070377660) Fr & Eur.

— Le Vainqueur de Coupe. (FRE.). 246p. 1989. pap. 11.95 (*0-7859-2116-8*, 2070381374) Fr & Eur.

Boudjema, F., jt. ed. see Dombey, N.

Boudman, Clifton. Belief & Desire: In My Mind's Eye. (Illus.). 80p. (Orig.). 1996. pap., pap. text 42.50 (*0-9651348-1-4*) Rum Rapids.

Boudon, Philippe. Lived-in Architecture: Le Corbusier's Pessac Revisited. LC 72-169842. (ENG.). 200p. 1972. write for info. (*0-85331-313-X*) Lund Humphries.

— Lived-in Architecture: Le Corbusier's Pessac Revisited. LC 70-155321. (ENG.). 200p. 1972. write for info. (*0-262-02083-1*) MIT Pr.

***Boudon, Pierre.** Le Reseau du Sens: Une Approche Monadologique pour la Comprehension du Discours. (Illus.). xxii, 258 p. 1999. 40.95 (*3-906761-95-9*, Pub. by P Lang Pubng) P Lang Pubng.

Boudon, Raymond. The Analysis of Ideology. Slater, Malcolm, tr. LC 89-4930. 250p. 1989. 47.95 (*0-226-06730-0*) U Ch Pr.

— The Art of Self-Persuasion: The Social Explanation of False Beliefs. Slater, Malcolm, tr. from FRE. 320p. (C). 1997. pap. text 28.95 (*0-7456-1913-4*) Blackwell Pubs.

— Larousse Dictionnaire de la Sociologie. (FRE.). 1993. pap. 29.95 (*0-7859-8611-1*, 203720227x) Fr & Eur.

***Boudon, Raymond.** The Origin of Values: Essays in the Sociology & Philosophy of Beliefs. 248p. 2000. 39.95 (*0-7658-0043-8*) Transaction Pubs.

Boudon, Raymond, et al, eds. The Classical Tradition in Sociology: The European Tradition. 1664p. 1997. 750.00 (*0-7619-5324-8*) Sage.

Boudon, Raymond & Bourricaud, Francois. A Critical Dictionary of Sociology. Hamilton, Peter, tr. & selected by by. LC 89-4868. 452p. 1989. 60.00 (*0-226-06728-9*) U Ch Pr.

Boudon, Raymond & Bourricaud, R. Critical Dictionary of Sociology: Dictionnaire Critique De la Sociologie. 4th rev. ed. (FRE.). 736p. 1994. 175.00 (*0-8288-2357-X*, M14125) Fr & Eur.

Boudot-Lamotte, E., ed. see Stendhal, pseud.

Boudou, Alain & Ribeyre, Francis, eds. Aquatic Ecotoxicology: Fundamental Concepts & Methodologies, 2 Vols., Vol. I. 320p. 1989. 228.00 (*0-8493-4828-5*, QH541) CRC Pr.

— Aquatic Ecotoxicology: Fundamental Concepts & Methodologies, 2 Vols., Vol. II. 272p. 1989. 178.00 (*0-8493-4829-3*, QH541, CRC Reprint) Franklin.

Boudoulas, Harisios, et al, eds. Functional Abnormalities of the Aorta. (Illus.). 416p. 1996. 85.00 (*0-87993-619-3*) Futura Pub.

***Boudoulas, Harisios & Wooley, Charles F., eds.** Mitral Valve: Floppy Mitral Valve, Mitral Valve Prolapse, Mitral Valvular Regurgitation. 2nd rev. ed. (Illus.). 780p. 2000. 145.00 (*0-87993-448-4*) Futura Pub.

Boudouris, James. Parents in Prison: Addressing the Needs of Families. LC 96-25772. 120p. 1996. pap. 22.95 (*1-56991-050-2*) Am Correctional.

Boudout, ed. see Hugo, Victor.

Boudreau. First Course in Statistics. 6th ed. 1997. pap. text, student ed. 29.33 (*0-13-595539-4*) P-H.

— Statistics by Example. 5th ed. (C). 1993. pap. text, student ed. 26.40 (*0-02-312716-3*, Macmillan Coll) P-H.

— Statistics for Business & Economics. 7th ed. 1997. pap. text, student ed. 26.67 (*0-13-625260-5*) P-H.

— Understanding Social Life. Date not set. pap. text, teacher ed. write for info. (*0-314-01714-3*) West Pub.

Boudreau & Mendenhall. Statistical Engineering & Science. 4th ed. 1995. pap. text, student ed. 29.33 (*0-02-312718-X*) P-H.

Boudreau, Amy. Mighty Miss & Other Poems. 1974. 4.95 (*0-614-30803-8*, BMIGHT) Claitors.

— Mighty Mississippi. 1967. pap. 3.00 (*0-685-08193-1*) Claitors.

— Story of the Acadians. (Illus.). 32p. 1971. pap. 3.25 (*0-911116-30-3*) Pelican.

— Story of the Christian Year. 1971. 6.50 (*0-685-27196-X*) Claitors.

Boudreau, Armand, jt. ed. see Godon, Bernard.

Boudreau, Bernard P. Diagenetic Models & Their Implementation: Modelling Transport & Reaction in Aquatic Sediments. LC 96-31565. (Illus.). 430p. 1996. 78.00 (*3-540-61125-8*) Spr-Verlag.

— Diagenetic Models & Their Solution: Modelling Transport & Reaction in Aquatic Sediments. LC 96-31565. (Illus.). xvi, 414p. 1996. write for info. (*0-387-61125-8*) Spr-Verlag.

***Boudreau, Bernard P. & Jrgensen, Bo Barker.** The Benthic Boundary Layer: Transport Processes & Biogeochemistry. LC 99-46200. 400p. 2000. text 79.95 (*0-19-511881-2*) OUP.

Boudreau, Dawn, tr. see Dailey, D. C.

Boudreau, Dennis. Beginning Franco-American Genealogy. iv, 75p. 1986. spiral bd. 7.00 (*1-929920-50-4*) American French.

— Les Mariages des Iles-de-la-Madeleine, PQ, 1794-1900. xliv, 325p. 1984. per. 21.00 (*1-929920-25-3*) American French.

Boudreau, Eugene H. Move over, Don Porfiro: Tales from the Sierra Madre. LC 75-35308. (Illus.). 96p. 1975. pap. 10.00 (*0-686-10963-5*) Redbud Press.

— Ways of the Sierra Madre: Crafts of the Sierra Madre. LC 74-22999. (Illus.). 96p. 1974. 12.00 (*0-686-10332-7*) Redbud Press.

Boudreau, Eugene H., ed. see Grisby, Robert F.

Boudreau, Frances A., et al, eds. Sex Roles & Social Patterns. LC 85-12247. 335p. 1985. 69.50 (*0-275-90196-3*, C0196, Praeger Pubs) Greenwood.

Boudreau, Gerald J. The Promotion. LC 97-90905. 245p. 1998. pap. 12.95 (*0-533-12508-1*) Vantage.

Boudreau, H. L. Intertextual Persuits: Literary Mediations in Modern Spanish Narrative. Brownlow, Jeanne P. & Kronik, John W., eds. LC 97-19958. 272p. 1998. 42.50 (*0-8387-5370-1*) Bucknell U Pr.

Boudreau, H. L. & Gonzalez-del-Valle, Luis T., eds. Studies in Honor of Sumner M. Greenfield. LC 83-51006. (ENG & SPA.). 236p. 1985. pap. 25.00 (*0-89295-030-7*) Society Sp & Sp-Am.

Boudreau, J. The Happiness of Heaven. LC 83-51548. 258p. 1984. reprint ed. pap. 8.00 (*0-89555-232-9*) TAN Bks Pubs.

Boudreau, James C., ed. Food Taste Chemistry. LC 79-26461. (ACS Symposium Ser.: No. 115). 1979. 38.95 (*0-8412-0526-4*); pap. 24.95 (*0-8412-0645-7*) Am Chemical.

— Food Taste Chemistry. LC 79-26461. (ACS Symposium Ser.: Vol. 115). 271p. 1979. reprint ed. pap. 84.10 (*0-608-03054-6*, 206350700007) Bks Demand.

Boudreau, John, jt. auth. see Milkovich, George.

Boudreau, John W., jt. auth. see Milkovich, George T.

Boudreau, Joseph A. Alberta, Aberhart, & Social Credit. LC 75-1630. v, 122p. 1975. write for info. (*0-03-925860-2*) Dryden Pr.

***Boudreau, Julie-Anne.** The Megacity Saga: Democracy & Citezenship in This Global Age. 252p. 2000. 19.99 (*1-55164-164-X*) Black Rose.

— Megacity Saga: Democracy & Citizenship in This Global Age. 2000. 48.99 (*1-55164-165-8*) Black Rose.

Boudreau, Lou & Schneider, Russell. Lou Boudreau: Covering All of the Bases April, 1997. LC 93-84610. (Illus.). 203p. 1997. 24.95 (*0-915611-72-4*) Sports Pub.

Boudreau, Martina, ed. Apple Magic, Vol. 4. LC 84-50105. 64p. (Orig.). 1984. pap., per. 3.95 (*0-942320-09-3*) Am Cooking.

Boudreau, Martina, ed. see Kaufman, Sheilah.

Boudreau, Michael, jt. auth. see Bonadies, John.

Boudreau, Michael, jt. auth. see Bonadles, John.

***Boudreau, Nancy S., ed.** Statistics: Student's Solutions Manual. 8th ed. 344p. 2000. student ed. 28.00 (*0-13-022560-6*, Prentice Hall) P-H.

Boudreau, Nancy S. & McClave. Statistics. 7th ed. 1996. pap. text, student ed. 29.33 (*0-13-471666-3*) P-H.

Boudreau, Richard, ed. The Literary Heritage of Wisconsin, Vol. II, Pt. A. 360p. 1995. 35.00 (*1-55780-142-8*); pap. 25.00 (*1-55780-141-X*) Juniper Pr ME.

Boudreau, Richard, intro. The Literary Heritage of Wisconsin Vol. 1: An Anthology of Wisconsin Literature from Beginnings to 1925. (Inland Seas Ser.: No. 4). 440p. (Orig.). 1986. 35.00 (*1-55780-079-0*) Juniper Pr ME.

— The Literary Heritage of Wisconsin Vol. 1: An Anthology of Wisconsin Literature from Beginnings to 1925. deluxe ed. (Inland Seas Ser.: No. 4). 440p. (Orig.). 1986. 50.00 (*1-55780-090-1*) Juniper Pr ME.

Boudreau, Thomas E. Protecting the Innocent: Enhancing the Humanitarian Role of the United Nations in Natural Disasters & Other Disaster Situations. 1983. pap. write for info. (*0-87641-310-6*) Carnegie Ethics & Intl Affairs.

— The Secretary - General & Satellite Diplomacy. 1984. pap. write for info. (*0-87641-311-4*) Carnegie Ethics & Intl Affairs.

— Sheathing the Sword: The U. N. Secretary-General & the Prevention of Internation Conflict, 273. LC 90-47520. (Contributions in Political Science Ser.: No. 273). 208p. 1991. 55.00 (*0-313-26109-1*, BDK/, Greenwood Pr) Greenwood.

— Universitas: The Social Restructuring of American Undergraduate Education. LC 97-23660. 232p. 1998. 55.00 (*0-275-95584-2*, Praeger Pubs) Greenwood.

Boudreault, Jody, ed. United Nations Resolutions on Palestine & the Arab-Israeli Conflict Vol. 4: 1987-1991. (U. N. Resolutions on Palestine & the Arab-Israeli Conflict Ser.: Vol. 4). (C). 1993. text 29.95 (*0-88728-240-7*); pap. text 19.95 (*0-88728-241-5*) Inst Palestine.

Boudreaux, Aleta. Song of the White Swan. LC 97-73404. 420p. 1997. pap. 10.00 (*0-9659701-6-7*) Laughing Owl.

Boudreaux, Curt. The ABC's of Self-Esteem: A Practical Approach. unabridged ed. (Illus.). 196p. 1996. pap. 20.00 (*1-889968-50-1*, Pub. by Gestalt Inst Pr) C Boudreaux.

— Never Kiss an Alligator on the Lips! Vol. I: The Life & Trying Times of Boudreaux the Cajun. unabridged ed. LC 99-160042. (Illus.). 171p. 1998. pap. 20.00 (*1-889968-55-2*, Pub. by Gestalt Inst Pr) C Boudreaux.

***Boudreaux, Curt.** Never Kiss an Alligator on the Lips! Vol. II: The Life & Trying Times of Boudreaux the Cajun. (Illus.). 236p. 1999. pap. 20.00 (*1-889968-56-0*, Pub. by Gestalt Inst Pr) C Boudreaux.

Boudreaux, Donald J. & Pritchard, Adam C. Civil Forfeiture As a "Sin Tax" (Independent Policy Reports). 32p. (Orig.). 1996. pap. 5.95 (*0-945999-50-X*) Independent Inst.

Boudreaux, Edmond. Pre-Exam for Nursing Home Administrator Examinees Preparing for the Licensure Examination. 4th ed. 44p. (C). 1991. pap. text 10.00 (*1-878199-01-3*) Pro Exam Review.

— Pre-Exam for Nursing Home Administrator Examinees Preparing for the Licensure Examination. 4th ed. 40p. (C). 1995. pap. text 10.00 (*1-878199-08-0*) Pro Exam Review.

— A Programmed Manual for Nursing Home Administrator Examinees. 11th ed. 172p. (Orig.). (C). 1991. pap. text 35.00 (*1-878199-02-1*) Pro Exam Review.

— A Programmed Manual for Nursing Home Administrator Examinees. 12th ed. 160p. (Orig.). (C). 1995. pap. text 35.00 (*1-878199-07-2*) Pro Exam Review.

— Supplement to a Programmed Manual for Nursing Home Administrator Examinees. 11th ed. 20p. (C). 1995. pap. text 5.00 (*1-878199-06-4*) Pro Exam Review.

Boudreaux, Edward A. Elementary Aspects of Chemical Periodicity. 1976. spiral bd. 9.35 (*0-88252-061-X*) Paladin Hse.

Boudreaux, F. J., jt. auth. see Schawlow, A. L.

Boudreaux, Florentin. God Our Father. LC 65-36485. 220p. reprint ed. pap. 68.20 (*0-608-10958-4*, 200166400003) Bks Demand.

Boudreaux, Gwendolyn Duhon, jt. auth. see Harris, Whitney G.

Boudreaux, Gwendolyn M. Duhon, see Duhon Boudreaux, Gwendolyn M.

Boudreaux, H. Bruce. Arthropod Phylogeny. LC 84-3960. 328p. (C). 1987. reprint ed. lib. bdg. 39.00 (*0-89874-746-5*) Krieger.

***Boudreaux, Helen.** Cajun Survivor: Lady Trucker's Trail of Tears. (Illus.). 200p. 1999. pap. write for info. (*0-9676607-0-X*) B Charpentier.

Boudreaux, J. C., jt. ed. see Gruver, W. A.

***Boudreaux, Keith.** Getting to the Root: Confronting Issues of the Heart. 142p. 1999. pap. 11.95 (*0-7392-0346-0*, PO3524) Morris Pubng.

***Boudreaux, Larry.** Dat Boudreaux Ain't Me, It's Ma Cousin. 1999. pap. 12.00 (*0-9676002-0-0*) Boudreaux Cajun Gnl.

Boudreaux Montgomery, Linda. A Colorful Tour of Louisiana's Cajun Country. (Illus.). 20p. (J). (gr. 1-6). 1995. pap. text 4.95 (*1-890113-12-3*) LB Collection.

***Boudreaux Montgomery, Linda.** A Visit to the California Capitol - Sacramento, California. (Illus.). 20p. (J). (gr. 3-6). 2000. pap. text 4.95 (*1-890113-15-8*) LB Collection.

Boudreaux, Warren L. Memoirs of a Cajun Bishop. Aguirre, Louis G. & Michel, Irene C., eds. 400p. 1995. 14.95 (*0-9649183-0-7*) H-T Pubng.

Boue, Andre, ed. Fetal Medicine: Prenatal Diagnosis & Management. Vekemans, Michel & Cartier, Lola, trs. LC 93-39528. (Oxford Monographs on Medical Genetics). (Illus.). 304p. (C). 1995. text 98.50 (*0-19-261904-7*) OUP.

Boue, Juan Carlos. Venezuela: The Political Economy of Oil. (Institute for Energy Studies). (Illus.). 248p. 1994. text 80.00 (*0-19-730012-X*) OUP.

Bouet, P., et al, eds. Cyprianus - Cyprien, Traites, Concordance, 2 vols., Set. (Alpha-Omega, Reihe A Ser.: Vol. LXVII). (GER.). xlvi, 1399p. 1986. 400.00 incl. 3.5 hd (*3-487-07698-5*) G Olms Pubs.

***Bouet, Thierry.** Hotel People. LC 99-24730. (Motta Photography Ser.). (Illus.). 60p. 1999. 24.95 (*1-56098-855-X*) Smithsonian.

Bouey, Gerald K. Monetary Policy: Finding a Place to Stand. LC 86-2991. (Per Jacobsson Lecture Ser.: Vol. 1982). 36p. reprint ed. pap. 30.00 (*0-608-08757-2*, 206939600004) Bks Demand.

— Politica Monetaria: En Busca de Asidero. LC HG0655.B68. (Conferencia Per Jacobsson de 1982 Ser.). (SPA.). 37p. reprint ed. pap. 30.00 (*0-608-08759-9*, 206939800004) Bks Demand.

— Politique Monetaire: A la Recherche d'un Point Dancrage. LC 91-10906. (Fondation Per Jacobsson Ser.). (FRE.). 39p. reprint ed. pap. 30.00 (*0-608-08758-0*, 206939700004) Bks Demand.

Bouey, P. D. & Basgall, M. E. Archaeological Patterns along the South Central Coast, Point Piedras Blancas, San Luis Obispo County, California. (Illus.). 424p. 1991. reprint ed. pap. text 44.38 (*1-55567-435-6*) Coyote Press.

Bouffler, Christine, jt. auth. see Bean, Wendy.

Bouffler, Chrystine, ed. Literacy Evaluation: Issues & Practicalities. LC 92-40331. 120p. (C). 1993. pap. text 16.50 (*0-435-08791-6*, 08791) Heinemann.

Bouffler, Chrystine, jt. auth. see Bean, Wendy.

Boufford. Dosage Calculations for Veterinary Programs. (C). 2000. pap. text 29.95 (*0-7668-0756-8*) Delmar.

Boufford, Bob. The Gardener's Computer Companion: Hundreds of Easy Ways to Use Your Computer for Gardening. LC 97-41637. (Illus.). 302p. 1998. pap. 39.95 incl. cd-rom (*1-886411-18-2*) No Starch Pr.

Boufford, Jo I. & Shonubi, Pat A. Community Oriented Primary Care: Training for Urban Practice. LC 85-6495. 187p. 1985. 45.00 (*0-275-91307-4*, C1307, Praeger Pubs) Greenwood.

Boufis, Christina & Olsen, Victoria C., eds. On the Market: Surviving the Academic Job Search. LC 97-8549. 368p. 1997. pap. 12.95 (*1-57322-626-2*, Riverhd Trade) Berkley Pub.

Bougai, Nikloai. The Deportation of Peoples in the Soviet Union. 217p. 1996. 85.00 (*1-56072-371-8*) Nova Sci Pubs.

Bougainville, Louis A. Adventure in the Wilderness: The American Journals of Louis Antoine de Bougainville, 1756-1760. Hamilton, Edward P., ed. & tr. by. LC 64-11318. (American Exploration & Travel Ser.: Vol. 42). (Illus.). 384p. 1990. pap. 17.95 (*0-8061-2248-X*) U of Okla Pr.

B

Bougainville, Louis-Antoine De, see De Bougainville, Louis-Antoine.

***Bougard, Marie-Therese, ed.** Take off in French: A Complete Language Learning Pack. 256p. 2000. 24.95 incl. audio (*0-19-860274-X*); audio compact disk 32.50 (*0-19-860298-7*) OUP.

Bougard, Marie-Therese & Bourdais, Daniele. The French Experience Level 1: A Multimedia Course for Beginners Learning French, Level 1. (ENG & FRE.). 160p. (C). teacher ed., spiral bd. 31.79 (*0-8442-1656-9*, VF1656-9) NTC Contemp Pub Co.

— The French Experience Level 1: A Multimedia Course for Beginners Learning French, 4 cass., Level 1. (ENG & FRE., Illus.). 288p. (C). pap., student ed. 55.95 incl. audio (*0-8442-1663-1*, VF1663-1); pap., student ed. 34.95 (*0-8442-1655-0*, VF1655-0); pap., wbk. ed. 11.60 (*0-8442-1657-7*, VF1657-7) NTC Contemp Pub Co.

— The French Experience 1: A Multimedia Course for Beginners Learning French. (ENG & FRE., Illus.). 288p. (C). 1995. pap. 105.90 incl. audio compact disk (*0-8442-1745-X*) NTC Contemp Pub Co.

Bougard, Marie-Therese, et al. The French Experience Kit: A Self-Guided Course of Beginners Learning. (Self-Guided Language...Ser.). (FRE.). 288p. 1996. pap. 49.95 incl. audio (*0-8442-1759-X*, 1759X) NTC Contemp Pub Co.

Bougard, Marie-Therese, tr. see Morton, Lone.

Bougaud, Emile. The Life of St. Margaret Mary Alacoque, 1647-1690. LC 86-80329. (Illus.). 388p. 1994. reprint ed. pap. 13.50 (*0-89555-297-3*) TAN Bks Pubs.

Bouge, L. Euro-Par'96: Parallel Processing: Second International Euro-Par Conference, Lyon, France, August 1996: Proceedings. LC 96-3338. (Lecture Notes in Computer Science Ser.: Vol. 1124). 926p. 1996. 129.50 (*3-540-61627-6*) Spr-Verlag.

Bougen, Philip D. Accounting & Industrial Relations: Some Historical Evidence on Their Interaction. (Foundations of Accounting Ser.: No. 3). 333p. 1988. text 15.00 (*0-8240-6115-2*) Garland.

***Bougeois, Paulette & Clark, Brenda.** Franklin's Secret Club. (Franklin Ser.). (Illus.). 32p. (J). (ps-3). 1999. pap. 9.95 incl. audio (*1-55074-672-3*) Kids Can Pr.

Bougerol, Guy J. Introduction to the Works of St. Bonaventure. 240p. 1964. 6.00 (*0-8199-0525-9*, Frncscn Herld) Franciscan Pr.

Bougerol, Jacques G. Saint Bonaventure: Etudes sur les Sources de Sa Pensee. (Collected Studies: No. CS306). (FRE.). 310p. (C). 1989. reprint ed. text 117.95 (*0-86078-254-9*, Pub. by Variorum) Ashgate Pub Co.

Bough, Bennie, jt. auth. see Condrill, Jo.

Bough, G. Gordon & Agrelius, M. It Takes a Village Idiot: Lessons We've Learned from the Clinton Administration - A Handbook for the New "Nationwide Intern Program" 32p. 1998. pap. 4.98 (*1-886472-33-5*) Sounds of Zion.

Bougher, H. U., et al. Venus II: Geology, Geophysics, Atmosphere, & Solar Wind Environment. LC 97-28602. (Space Science Ser.). 1376p. 1998. 100.00 (*0-8165-1830-0*) U of Ariz Pr.

Bougher, Neale & Syme, Katrina. Fungi of Southern Australia. LC 98-141861. (Illus.). 400p. 1997. 75.00 (*1-875560-80-7*, Pub. by Univ of West Aust Pr) Intl Spec Bk.

Boughey, Howard N. Ordinary Social Occasions Sandcastles & Structural Reproduction: A Sociology of Everybody's Social Life. LC 95-6676. 200p. (C). 1995. text 39.95 (*0-391-03938-5*) Humanities.

Boughey, Joseph, rev. Hadfield's British Canals: The Inland Waterways of Britain & Ireland. 8th rev. ed. (Illus.). 352p. 1998. pap. 36.95 (*0-7509-1840-3*, Pub. by Sutton Pub Ltd) Intl Pubs Mktg.

Boughey, Joseph & Hadfield, Charles. Charles Hadfield: Canal Man & More. LC 99-179865. (Illus.). xv, 223p. 1998. 39.95 (*0-7509-1052-6*, Pub. by Sutton Pub Ltd) Intl Pubs Mktg.

Boughn, Michael. Michael Jordan: Airborne. (Champion Sports Biography Ser.). (Illus.). 91p. (J). (gr. 7-12). 1999. pap. 8.95 (*1-894020-51-0*) Warwick Publ.

Boughn, Mike. Stone Work. (Local Habitations Ser.). 32p. 1991. 15.00 (*0-9628035-8-8*); pap. 6.00 (*0-9628035-9-6*) Shuffaloff Bks.

Boughn, Stephen, ed. Proceedings of the 1992 Undergraduate Symposium on Research in Astronomy. 120p. (C). 1993. pap. text write for info. (*1-882334-02-7*) Keck NE Astron.

Boughn, Susan, jt. auth. see Rathus, Spencer A.

Boughner, Eloise, ed. see Perry, Larry D.

Boughner, Fred. Airmail Antics. (Illus.). 186p. 1988. pap. 9.95 (*0-940403-08-0*) Linns Stamp News.

— Linn's U. S. Stamp Yearbook, 1987. (Illus.). 240p. (Orig.). 1988. pap. 22.00 (*0-940403-07-2*) Linns Stamp News.

— Linn's U. S. Stamp Yearbook, 1983. (Illus.). 240p. (Orig.). 1984. pap. 22.00 (*0-940403-31-5*) Linns Stamp News.

— Linn's U. S. Stamp Yearbook, 1985. 304p. (Orig.). 1985. pap. 22.00 (*0-940403-33-1*) Linns Stamp News.

— Linn's U. S. Stamp Yearbook, 1986. (Illus.). 240p. 1987. reprint ed. pap. 25.00 (*0-940403-01-3*) Linns Stamp News.

— Linn's U. S. Stamp Yearbook, 1984. 288p. 1985. reprint ed. pap. 25.00 (*0-940403-32-3*) Linns Stamp News.

Boughner, Robert, jt. auth. see Aronson, Andrew C.

Boughter, Judith A. Betraying the Omaha Nation, 1790-1916. LC 98-4456. (Illus.). 304p. 1998. 27.95 (*0-8061-3091-1*) U of Okla Pr.

Boughton, Brian. Reinforced Concrete Detailer's Manual. 2nd ed. (Illus.). 136p. 1971. pap. 27.95 (*0-8464-0788-4*) Beekman Pubs.

***Boughton, C.** Killers by Choice. LC 99-91855. 2000. 25.00 (*0-7388-1328-1*); pap. 18.00 (*0-7388-1329-X*) Xlibris Corp.

Boughton, Dimon. Treasury of 20th Century Child. 1998. lib. bdg. 41.99 (*0-679-98647-2*, Pub. by Knopf Bks Yng Read) Random.

Boughton, Doug, ed. Evaluation & Assessment in Visual Arts Education. 1995. pap. 24.00 (*0-7300-1797-4*, Pub. by Deakin Univ) St Mut.

Boughton, Doug, et al, eds. Evaluating & Assessing the Visual Arts in Education: International Perspectives. 352p. (C). 1996. text 49.00 (*0-8077-3511-6*) Tchrs Coll.

Boughton, J. Bouton Boughton Family. (Illus.). 684p. 1988. reprint ed. pap. 90.00 (*0-8328-0287-5*); reprint ed. lib. bdg. 100.00 (*0-8328-0286-7*) Higginson Bk Co.

Boughton, James M. The Monetary Approach to Exchange Rates: What Now Remains? LC 88-27496. (Essays in International Finance Ser.: No. 171). 28p. 1988. pap. text 10.00 (*0-88165-078-1*) Princeton U Int Finan Econ.

Boughton, James M. & Lateef, K. Sarwar, eds. Fifty Years After Bretton Woods: The Future of IMF & the World Bank. LC 95-16779. 1995. pap. write for info. (*1-55775-487-X*) Intl Monetary.

Boughton, Jill A. You & Your Aging Parent: The Practical Side of Love. 140p. (Orig.). 1994. pap. 7.95 (*0-937779-28-8*) Greenlawn Pr.

Boughton, Nathaniel W., jt. auth. see Gilley, Jerry W.

Boughton, Pat, jt. auth. see Meagher, Jack.

Boughton, Richard. Rent-a-Puppy, Inc. (J). 1995. 9.05 (*0-606-08071-6*) Turtleback.

Boughton, Rutland. The Reality of Music. LC 72-80495. 260p. 1977. reprint ed. 17.95 (*0-405-08294-0*, Pub. by Blom Pubns) Ayer.

Boughton, Simon, jt. ed. see Schulman, Janet.

Boughton, Willis A. Bouton, Boughton & Farnam Families. 214p. 1996. reprint ed. pap. 34.00 (*0-8328-5230-9*); reprint ed. lib. bdg. 44.00 (*0-8328-5229-5*) Higginson Bk Co.

Bougie & Morgenthal. Aging Body. 1999. pap. text 80.00 (*0-8385-0331-4*) Appleton & Lange.

Bougle, Celestin C. Bilan De la Sociologie Francaise Contemporaine: Balance Sheet of Contemporary French Sociology. LC 74-25741. (European Sociology Ser.). 184p. 1975. reprint ed. 17.95 (*0-405-06497-7*) Ayer.

— Essays on the Caste System. LC 79-154506. (European Understanding of India Ser.). 244p. reprint ed. pap. 69.60 (*0-608-13037-0*, 2024508) Bks Demand.

— The Evolution of Values: Studies in Sociology with Special Application to Teaching. LC 78-97976. xxxvii, 277p. 1970. reprint ed. 45.00 (*0-678-00542-7*) Kelley.

— La Sociologie de Proudhon. Mayer, J. P., ed. LC 78-67336. (European Political Thought Ser.). (FRE.). 1980. reprint ed. lib. bdg. 28.95 (*0-405-11681-0*) Ayer.

Bougouint, jt. auth. see Bessieres.

***Bougrine, Hassan.** The Economics of Public Spending: Debts, Deficits & Economic Performance. LC 00-26458. 2000. write for info. (*1-84064-397-8*) E Elgar.

Bouguer, Pierre. Pierre Bouguer's Optical Treatise on the Gradation of Light. Middleton, W. E., tr. LC 61-19105. 264p. reprint ed. pap. 81.90 (*0-608-10077-3*, 201414000090) Bks Demand.

Bouguettaya, Athman. Ontologies & Databases. LC 98-49398. 1999. write for info. (*0-7923-8412-1*) Kluwer Academic.

Bouguettaya, Athman, et al. Interconnecting Heterogeneous Information Systems. LC 98-8682. 1998. 110.00 (*0-7923-8216-1*) Kluwer Academic.

Bouhabib, Abdallah R. The Long-Run of New Reserves of Crude Oil in the U. S., 1966-1973. Bruchey, Stuart, ed. LC 78-22665. (Energy in the American Economy Ser.). (Illus.). 1979. lib. bdg. 19.95 (*0-405-11968-2*) Ayer.

Bouhana, James. TEC Course - Software Design Methods, Tools & Techniques. 1991. ring bd. write for info. (*0-201-41874-6*) Addison-Wesley.

Bouhanna, F. & Dardour, J. C. Hair Replacement Surgery: Textbook & Atlas, Vol. VIII. (Illus.). 350p. 1996. 150.00 (*3-540-59030-7*) Spr-Verlag.

Bouhdiba, Abdelwahab. Sexuality in Islam. 290p. 1998. pap. 29.95 (*0-86356-086-5*, Pub. by Saqi) Intl Spec Bk.

Bouhours, Dominique. Art of Criticism. LC 81-8900. 336p. 1981. reprint ed. 50.00 (*0-8201-1364-6*) Schol Facsimiles.

— Les Entretiens d'Ariste et d'Eugene. (FRE.). xi, 478p. reprint ed. write for info. (*0-318-71325-X*) G Olms Pubs.

Bouhring-Uhle, Christian. Arbitration & Mediation in International Business Vol. 4: Designing Procedures for Effective Conflict Management. LC 96-23684. (International Arbitration Law Library). 546p. 1996. 250.00 (*90-411-0242-6*) Kluwer Law Intl.

Bouie, Patrick J., jt. auth. see Vanderhaeghe, Lorna R.

Bouilhet. Le Coeur a Droite. Unwin, ed. (Exeter French Texts Ser.: No. 85). (FRE.). 85p. Date not set. pap. text 19.95 (*0-85989-395-2*, Pub. by Univ Exeter Pr) Northwestern U Pr.

Bouillane De Lacoste, Henry D. Rimbaud et le probleme des Illuminations. LC 77-10253. reprint ed. 23.50 (*0-404-16308-4*) AMS Pr.

***Bouille, Belen.** La Guerra de la Cocaina. (SPA.). 2000. pap. 15.95 (*0-553-06114-3*) Bantam.

Bouillier, Francisque. Histoire de la Philosophie Cartesienne, 2 vols., Set. viii, 1278p. 1972. reprint ed. lib. bdg. 225.00 (*3-487-04496-X*) G Olms Pubs.

Bouillon, H. Lexicon of Economic & Commercial Terms: Lexique de Termes Economiques et Commerciaux. (FRE & GER.). 196p. 1988. pap. 45.00 (*0-7859-4736-1*) Fr & Eur.

Bouillon, Hardy, ed. Libertarians & Liberalism: Essays in Honour of Gerard Radnitzky. (Avebury Series in Philosophy). 360p. 1997. text 87.95 (*1-85972-460-4*, Pub. by Avebury) Ashgate Pub Co.

Bouillon, Hardy, jt. auth. see Radnitzky, Gerard.

Bouillon, Jean, et al, eds. Modern Trends in the Systematics, Ecology, & Evolution of Hydroids & Hydromedusae. (Illus.). 354p. 1987. text 85.00 (*0-19-857190-9*) OUP.

Bouillon, Jean-Paul. Braquemond: The Graphic Work, 1849-1859. (FRE.). 232p. 1987. 125.00 (*1-55660-151-4*) A Wofsy Fine Arts.

Bouillon, Jo, jt. auth. see Baker, Josephine.

Bouillon, Joan, jt. auth. see Hardwick, E. Russell.

Bouin, Olivier, et al. Different Paths to a Market Economy: China & European Economies in Transition. (Development Centre Seminars Ser.). 204p. 1998. pap. 33.00 (*92-64-16088-4*, 41 98 06 1 P, Pub. by Org for Econ) OECD.

Bouis, Antonina W., tr. see Krasilshchik, S., ed.

Bouis, Antonina W., tr. see Rasputin, Valentin.

Bouis, Antonina W., tr. see Sakharov, Andrei D.

Bouis, Antonina W., tr. see Sevela, Ephraim.

Bouis, Antonina W., tr. see Volkov, Solomon.

Bouis, Antonina W., tr. see Volkov, Solomon, ed.

Bouis, Antonina W., tr. see Yevtushenko, Yevgeny.

Bouis, Antonina W., tr. see Zheleznikov, Vladimir.

Bouis, Howarth, jt. auth. see Kennedy, Eileen.

Bouis, Howarth E. Gender Equality & Investments in Adolescents in the Rural Philippines. LC 98-53452. (Research Reports). 1998. write for info. (*0-89629-111-1*) Intl Food Policy.

Bouis, Howarth E. & Haddad, Lawrence J. Agricultural Commercialization, Nutrition, & the Rural Poor: A Study of Philippine Farm Households. LC 90-8074. 190p. 1990. lib. bdg. 32.00 (*1-55587-206-9*) L Rienner.

Bouis, Nina, ed. see Herz, Stanley.

Bouis, Nina, tr. see Gaevsky, Vadim.

Bouis, Paul. Optical Spectroscopy. (C). 2001. pap. text 14.95 (*0-13-123225-8*) P-H.

Bouissac, Paul. La Mesure des Gestes: Prolegomenes a la Semiotique Gestuelle. (Approaches to Semiotics Ser.: No. 3). 1973. pap. 55.40 (*90-279-2377-9*) Mouton.

Bouissac, Paul, ed. Encyclopedia of Semiotics. LC 98-23092. (Illus.). 720p. 1998. text 125.00 (*0-19-512090-6*) OUP.

Bouisson, Maurice. Magic: Its Rites & History. Almayrac, G., tr. from FRE. LC 79-8094. (Satanism Ser.). (Illus.). 1985. reprint ed. 36.00 (*0-404-18405-7*) AMS Pr.

Bouissou, Jean-Christophe. Christ & Community. Edwards, Paul M., ed. LC 96-47155. (Faith Exploration Ser.). 152p. 1996. pap. text 12.00 (*0-8309-0753-X*) Herald Pub Hse.

Bouissy, Andre, ed. see Pirandello, Luigi.

Boujut, Michel. Louis Armstrong. LC 98-65883. (Illus.). 144p. 1998. 40.00 (*0-8478-2131-5*, Pub. by Rizzoli Intl) St Martin.

Boukerche, Azzedine, et al, eds. Distributed Interactive Simulation & Real-Time Applications, 1st International Workshop. LC 96-79896. 100p. 1997. pap. 50.00 (*0-8186-7773-2*) IEEE Comp Soc.

Bouklas, George. Psychotherapy with the Elderly: Becoming Methuselah's Echo. LC 96-46668. 392p. 1997. 60.00 (*0-7657-0051-4*) Aronson.

Bouknight, Joanne Kellar. The Kitchen Idea Book. LC 98-41873. (Illus.). 201p. 1999. 29.95 (*1-56158-161-5*, 070291) Taunton.

Boukreev, Anatoli & DeWalt, G. Weston. The Climb: Tragic Ambitions on Everest. LC 97-23194. (Illus.). 288p. 1997. text 24.95 (*0-312-16814-4*) St Martin.

— The Climb: Tragic Ambitions on Everest, Vol. 1. (Illus.). 255p. 1998. pap. 6.99 (*0-312-96533-8*, Pub. by Tor Bks) St Martin.

Boukreev, Anatoli & DeWalt, Weston. The Climb: Tragic Ambitions on Everest. 272p. 1999. pap. 13.95 (*0-312-20637-2*) St Martin.

Boukydis, C. F. Research on Support for Parents & Infants in the Postnatal Period. LC 87-1349. 288p. 1987. text 73.25 (*0-89391-333-2*) Ablx Pub.

Boukydis, C. F., ed. Support for Parents & Infants: A Manual for Parent Organization & Professionals. 256p. 1986. 29.95 (*0-7102-0038-2*, 0038W, Routledge Thoemms) Routledge.

Boukydis, C. F., jt. ed. see Lester, Barry M.

***Boulagouaz, Mahammed & Tignol, Jean-Pierre.** Algebra & Number Theory: Proceedings of a Conference Held in Fez, Morocco. LC 99-51463. (Lecture Notes in Pure & Applied Mathematics Ser.). 286p. 1999. write for info. (*0-8247-0341-3*) Dekker.

Boulahbal, Djamil, et al. Detection of Fatigue Cracks in Gears with the Continuous Wavelet Transform. (Technical Papers: Vol. 97FTM3). (Illus.). 6p. 1997. pap. text 30.00 (*1-55589-697-9*) AGMA.

Boulainvilliers, H. De, see De Boulainvilliers, H.

Boulais, Katina. Simple Circuits. (Illus.). 74p. 1994. ring bd. write for info. (*0-614-00951-0*) E&L Instru.

Boulais, Katina, ed. see Petrillo, Maureen L.

Boulais, Sue. Andres Galarraga. LC 97-43511. (Real-Life Reader Biographies Ser.). (Illus.). 32p. (J). (gr. 3-8). 1998. lib. bdg. 15.95 (*1-883845-61-0*) M Lane Pubs.

— Famous People. 1995. 6.95 (*1-55708-455-6*, MCC938) McDonald Pub Co.

— Gloria Estefan. LC 97-42783. (Real-Life Reader Biographies Ser.). (Illus.). 32p. (J). (gr. 3-8). 1999. lib. bdg. 15.95 (*1-883845-62-9*) M Lane Pubs.

***Boulais, Sue.** Katie Holmes. (Real-Life Reader Biography Ser.). (Illus.). 32p. (J). (gr. 3-8). 2000. lib. bdg. 15.95 (*1-58415-038-6*) M Lane Pubs.

Boulais, Sue. Learning How: BMX Riding. James, Jody, ed. (Learning How Sports Ser.). (Illus.). 48p. (J). (gr. 4-7). 1992. pap. 5.95 (*0-944280-41-2*); lib. bdg. 14.95 (*0-944280-36-6*) Bancroft-Sage.

— Learning How: Football. James, Jody, ed. (Learning How Sports Ser.). (Illus.). 48p. (J). (gr. 4-7). 1992. pap. 5.95 (*0-944280-43-9*); lib. bdg. 14.95 (*0-944280-37-4*) Bancroft-Sage.

***Boulais, Sue.** Liv Tyler. (Real-Life Reader Biography Ser.). (Illus.). 32p. (J). (gr. 3-8). 2000. lib. bdg. 15.95 (*1-58415-041-6*) M Lane Pubs.

Boulais, Sue. Math. 1994. 6.95 (*1-55708-418-1*, MCC900) McDonald Pub Co.

— Multicultural. 1993. 6.95 (*1-55708-388-6*, MCC919) McDonald Pub Co.

— Plants. 1995. 3.95 (*1-55708-475-0*, MCT1006) McDonald Pub Co.

— Shape Up. 1994. 6.95 (*1-55708-425-4*, C898) McDonald Pub Co.

— Transportation. 1995. 3.95 (*1-55708-479-3*, T1010) McDonald Pub Co.

— Trivia. 1994. 6.95 (*1-55708-424-6*, C924) McDonald Pub Co.

— Vanessa Williams. (Real-Life Reader Biographies Ser.). (Illus.). 32p. (YA). (gr. 3-8). 1998. lib. bdg. 15.95 (*1-883845-75-0*) M Lane Pubs.

— Water. 1995. 3.95 (*1-55708-480-7*, T1011) McDonald Pub Co.

— Weather. 1995. 3.95 (*1-55708-471-8*, T1002) McDonald Pub Co.

— Writing-Everyday Res. 1993. 5.95 (*1-55708-409-2*, S950) McDonald Pub Co.

Boulais, Sue, jt. auth. see Marvis, Barbara.

Bouland, Heber. Barns Across America. LC 98-73792. (Illus.). 152p. 1998. pap. 15.95 (*0-929355-96-2*, H1398) Am Soc Ag Eng.

Boulanger, Ari A. How to Entertain People You Hate: Tips on How to Have a Good Time with Bad Company. Carle, Cliff, ed. 1993. pap. 5.95 (*0-918259-43-6*) CCC Pubns.

Boulanger, Chantal. The Goddess' Justice. (Illus.). 154p. 1997. 10.50 (*0-9661496-0-2*) Shakti Press.

— Saris, an Illustrated Guide to the Indian Art of Draping. LC 97-97143. (Illus.). 144p. 1997. 19.50 (*0-9661496-1-0*) Shakti Press.

Boulanger, Daniel. Le Chemin De Caracoles. (FRE.). 214p. 1988. pap. 10.95 (*0-7859-2096-X*, 2070380610) Fr & Eur.

— Connaissez-Vous Maronne? (FRE.). 115p. 1986. pap. 10.95 (*0-7859-2041-2*, 2070377539) Fr & Eur.

— La Dame De Coeur. (FRE.). 160p. 1989. pap. 10.95 (*0-7859-2129-X*, 2070381986) Fr & Eur.

— L' Enfant de Boheme. (FRE.). 1990. pap. 12.95 (*0-7859-2150-8*, 2070382958) Fr & Eur.

— Fouette, Cocher! (FRE.). 296p. 1980. pap. 11.95 (*0-7859-1904-X*, 2070371603) Fr & Eur.

— La Porte Noir. (FRE.). 160p. 1981. pap. 10.95 (*0-7859-2220-2*, 207037324X) Fr & Eur.

— Table d'Hote. (FRE.). 273p. 1985. pap. 11.95 (*0-7859-2023-4*, 2070376974) Fr & Eur.

— Le Temeraire. (FRE.). 1984. pap. 10.95 (*0-7859-1985-6*, 2070375250) Fr & Eur.

— Vessies et Lanternes. (FRE.). 339p. 1987. pap. 11.95 (*0-7859-2076-5*, 2070378918) Fr & Eur.

Boulanger, Ghislaine & Kadushin, Charles, eds. The Vietnam Veteran Redefined: Fact & Fiction. 200p. (C). 1986. text 39.95 (*0-89859-761-7*) L Erlbaum Assocs.

Boulanger, Graciela R. Graciela Rodo Boulanger. Cassanetti, Michelle L., ed. LC 86-83286. (Illus.). 200p. 1987. 150.00 (*0-941393-13-5*) Lublin Graph.

Boulanger, Henry. How to Interpret Your Dreams: From A to Z. 268p. 1995. pap. 9.95 (*0-8065-0991-0*, Citadel Pr) Carol Pub Group.

Boulanger, Jacques, ed. see Rabelais, Francois.

Boulanger, L. Deux Morceaux Pour Violon et Piano Nocturne & Cortege. 12p. 1986. pap. 7.95 (*0-7935-3773-8*, 50335330) H Leonard.

Boulanger, Norman C. Theatre Lighting A to Z. LC 92-14620. (Illus.). 206p. 1992. pap. 24.95 (*0-295-97214-9*) U of Wash Pr.

Boulanger, Norman C., jt. auth. see Lounsbury, Warren C.

Boulanger, Philippe & Hayes, Michael A. Bivectors & Waves in Mechanics & Optics. LC 93-17173. 288p. (gr. 13). 1993. ring bd. 78.95 (*0-412-46460-8*, Chap & Hall CRC) CRC Pr.

Boulanger, Pierre, ed. Rapid Product Development Technologies, Vol. 2910. LC 96-69762. 234p. 1997. 66.00 (*0-8194-2312-2*) SPIE.

Boulanger, Richard. The CSound Book: Perspectives in Software Synthesis, Sound Design, Signal Processing & Programming. LC 99-14922. (Illus.). 782p. 2000. pap. 55.00 incl. cd-rom (*0-262-52261-6*) MIT Pr.

Boulanger, Robert. American Recycling Market Directory/Reference Manual. 14th ed. 1200p. (Orig.). 1998. spiral bd. 305.00 (*1-880978-00-8*) RDMC.

Boulanger, Ross W., jt. ed. see Seed, Raymond B.

Boulard, Bernard. Dictionnaire de Botanique. (FRE.). 1988. lib. bdg. 49.95 (*0-8288-2598-X*) Fr & Eur.

An Asterisk (*) at the beginning of an entry indicates that the title is appearing for the first time.

Boulard, Chantal & Thornberry, H., eds. Warble Fly Control in Europe: A Symposium in the EC Programme of Coordination of Research on Animal Pathology, Brussels, 16-17 September 1982. 168p. (C). 1984. text 91.00 (*90-6191-529-5*, Pub. by A A Balkema) Ashgate Pub Co.

Boulard, Garry. Huey Long Invades New Orleans: The Siege of a City, 1934-36. LC 98-29376. (Illus.). 256p. 1998. pap. text 14.95 (*1-56554-303-3*) Pelican.

— Just a Gigolo: The Life & Times of Louis Prima. 212p. 1989. 20.00 (*0-940984-49-0*) Univ LA Lafayette.

Boulares, Habib. Islam: The Fear & the Hope. LC 90-46693. 192p. (C). 1990. pap. 19.95 (*0-86232-945-0*, Pub. by St Martin) St Martin.

BouLay, Benedict Du, see Thornton, Chris & Du Boulay, Benedict.

BouLay, Benedict Du, see Thornton, Christopher & Du Boulay, Benedict.

Boulay, Cathy J., illus. see Ratliff, Randy L.

Boulay, Cathy J., tr. see Brooks, Charles J.

Boulay, Du, ed. Artificial Intelligence in Education. (Frontiers in Artificial Intelligence Applications Ser.: Vol. 39). 1997. 108.00 (*90-5199-353-6*) IOS Press.

Boulay, F. R. Du, see Du Boulay, F. R.

Boulay, G. H. Du, see Du Boulay, G. H.

Boulay, Jacques, jt. auth. see Desrosier, Georges.

Boulay, Jacques, jt. auth. see Desrosiers, G.

Boulaye, G. & Lewin, Douglas, eds. Computer Architecture. (NATO Advanced Study Institutes Series C, Mathematical & Physical Sciences: No. 32). (Illus.). 1977. text 121.50 (*90-277-0803-7*) Kluwer Academic.

Boulby, Mark. Karl Philipp Moritz: At the Fringe of Genius. LC 78-13651. 320p. reprint ed. pap. 99.20 (*0-608-17010-0*, 202642500049) Bks Demand.

Boulden, Jim. All Together: Blended Family Activity Book. (Illus.). 32p. (J). (gr. 1-7). 1991. pap. 5.95 (*1-878076-10-8*) Boulden Pub.

— Alone Together: Single Parent Activity Book. (Illus.). 32p. (J). (gr. 1-7). 1991. pap. 5.95 (*1-878076-09-4*) Boulden Pub.

— Feeling Good: Self Esteem Activity Book. (Illus.). 32p. (J). (gr. 1-7). 1991. pap. 5.95 (*1-878076-11-6*) Boulden Pub.

— Feelings & Faces: Feelings Activity Book. (Illus.). 32p. (Orig.). (J). (gr. 1-7). 1993. pap. 5.95 (*1-878076-20-5*) Boulden Pub.

— Glad to Be Me: Self Esteem Activity Book. (Illus.). 32p. (J). (gr. 3-6). 1993. pap. 5.95 (*1-878076-26-4*) Boulden Pub.

***Boulden, Jim.** A Guide for Caregivers: When Death Threatens. Boulden, Joan & Howard, Janet, eds. (Illus.). 16p. 1999. pap. 1.95 (*1-892421-15-1*, 15-1) Boulden Pub.

— A Guide for Living: When Death Threatens. Boulden, Joan & Howard, Janet, eds. (Illus.). 16p. 1999. pap. 1.95 (*1-892421-13-5*) Boulden Pub.

— Honoring the Memory: When Death Happens. Boulden, Joan & Howard, Janet, eds. (Illus.). 16p. 1999. pap. 1.95 (*1-892421-14-3*, 14-3) Boulden Pub.

Boulden, Jim. How I Feel: Feelings Activity Book. (Illus.). 32p. (Orig.). (J). (gr. 1-7). 1993. pap. 5.95 (*1-878076-21-3*) Boulden Pub.

— My Secret: Parental Substance Abuse Activity Book. (Illus.). 32p. (J). (gr. 1-7). 1991. pap. 5.95 (*1-878076-13-2*) Boulden Pub.

— Saying Goodbye. rev. ed. (Illus.). 32p. (Orig.). (J). (gr. 1-7). 1991. reprint ed. pap. 3.95 (*1-878076-12-4*) Boulden Pub.

— Saying Goodbye. 2nd ed. (SPA., Illus.). (Orig.). (J). (gr. 1-7). 1991. pap. 3.95 (*1-878076-02-7*) Boulden Pub.

— Uncle Jerry Has AIDS: Attitudes & Emotions Activity Book. (Illus.). 32p. (J). (gr. 3-7). 1992. pap. 3.95 (*1-878076-18-3*) Boulden Pub.

Boulden, Jim & Boulden, Joan. Bulldog vs. Monstros. Tate, Susan, ed. (Illus.). 24p. (J). (gr. 4-6). 1999. pap. 5.95 (*1-892421-10-0*, 10-0AB) Boulden Pub.

— A Deadly Secret. Kennedy, Kari, ed. (Illus.). 32p. (YA). (gr. 7-11). 1999. pap. 5.95 (*1-892421-11-9*, 11-9AB) Boulden Pub.

— Divorce Happens: Divorce Activity Book. Ward, Evelyn M., ed. (Illus.). 16p. (Orig.). (J). (gr. k-2). 1994. pap. 5.95 (*1-878076-34-5*) Boulden Pub.

— Double Trouble: Misbehavior Activity Book. Farness, JoAnn, ed. (Illus.). 16p. (Orig.). (J). (gr. 3-4). 1996. pap. 5.95 (*1-878076-79-5*) Boulden Pub.

— From Mad to Worse: Anger Control Activity Book. Farness, JoAnn, ed. (Illus.). 32p. (J). (gr. 3-5). 1995. pap. 5.95 (*1-878076-45-0*) Boulden Pub.

— Fun to Share: Conflict Resolution Activity Book. Farness, JoAnn, ed. (Illus.). 16p. (J). (gr. k-2). 1995. pap. 5.95 (*1-878076-42-6*) Boulden Pub.

— Fun with Friends: Friendship Activity Book. Farness, JoAnn, ed. (Illus.). 16p. (J). (gr. k-2). 1996. pap. 5.95 (*1-878076-78-7*) Boulden Pub.

— Getting Along: Communication Skills Activity Book. Farness, Joann, ed. (Illus.). 16p. (Orig.). (J). (gr. 3-5). 1996. pap. 5.95 (*1-878076-65-5*) Boulden Pub.

— Give & Take: Conflict Resolution Activity Book. Farness, JoAnn, ed. (Illus.). 32p. (J). (gr. 3-5). 1995. pap. 5.95 (*1-878076-41-8*) Boulden Pub.

— Goodbye Forever: Bereavement Activity Book. Ward, Evelyn M., ed. (Illus.). 16p. (Orig.). (J). (gr. k-2). 1994. pap. 3.95 (*1-878076-31-0*) Boulden Pub.

— Happy to Be Me: Self Esteem Activity Book. Ward, Evelyn M., ed. (Illus.). 16p. (Orig.). (J). (gr. k-2). 1994. pap. 5.95 (*1-878076-38-8*) Boulden Pub.

— Hard Choices. Farness, JoAnn, ed. (Illus.). 32p. (Orig.). (J). (gr. 5-8). 1996. pap. 5.95 (*1-878076-80-9*) Boulden Pub.

— The Last Goodbye II: Bereavement Guide. Ward, Evelyn M., ed. (Illus.). 32p. (Orig.). (YA). (gr. 10-12). 1994. pap. 5.95 (*1-878076-33-7*) Boulden Pub.

— Let's Talk: Early Separation & Divorce Activity Book. (Illus.). (J). (gr. 3-5). 1991. pap., student ed. 5.95 (*1-878076-05-1*) Boulden Pub.

— Life with One Parent: Single Parent Activity Book. Ward, Evelyn M., ed. (Illus.). 16p. (Orig.). (J). (gr. k-2). 1994. pap. 5.95 (*1-878076-35-3*) Boulden Pub.

— The Lion Roars. Kennedy, Kari, ed. (Illus.). 24p. (J). (gr. 4-7). 1999. pap. 5.95 (*1-892421-09-7*, 09-7AB) Boulden Pub.

— Mad Me: Anger Control Activity Book. Farness, JoAnn, ed. (Illus.). 16p. (J). (gr. k-2). 1995. pap. 5.95 (*1-878076-46-9*) Boulden Pub.

— Mom & Me: Single Parent Activity Book. (Illus.). 32p. (J). (gr. 3-6). 1993. pap. 5.95 (*1-878076-25-6*) Boulden Pub.

— My New Family: Foster Family Activity Book. Farness, JoAnn, ed. (Illus.). 16p. (J). (gr. k-2). 1996. pap. 5.95 (*1-878076-75-2*) Boulden Pub.

— My Story: Divorce & Remarriage Activity Book. (J). (gr. 1-7). 1991. pap., student ed. 5.95 (*1-878076-06-X*) Boulden Pub.

— A New Beginning: Foster Family Activity Book. Farness, JoAnn, ed. (Illus.). 32p. (Orig.). (J). (gr. 3-4). 1996. pap. 5.95 (*1-878076-76-0*) Boulden Pub.

— Playground Push-Around: Bully & Victim Activity Book. Ward, Evelyn M., ed. (Illus.). 16p. (Orig.). (J). (gr. k-2). 1994. pap. 5.95 (*1-878076-36-1*) Boulden Pub.

— Rumor & Revenge. Farness, Joann, ed. (Illus.). 24p. (Orig.). (J). (gr. 5-8). 1996. pap. 5.95 (*1-878076-81-7*) Boulden Pub.

— Secrets That Hurt: Sexual Abuse Activity Book. (Illus.). 32p. (J). (gr. 1-6). 1993. pap. 5.95 (*1-878076-28-0*) Boulden Pub.

— The Silver Dollar Mystery. Tate, Susan, ed. (Illus.). 24p. (J). (gr. 4-6). 1999. pap. 5.95 (*1-892421-08-9*, 08-9AB) Boulden Pub.

— Someone Special Is Very Sick: Serious Illness Activity Book. Farness, JoAnn, ed. (Illus.). 16p. (J). (gr. k-2). 1996. pap. 5.95 (*1-878076-44-2*) Boulden Pub.

— Tall Paul. Tate, Susan, ed. (Illus.). 24p. (YA). (gr. 6-9). 1999. pap. 5.95 (*1-892421-12-7*, 12-7ab) Boulden Pub.

— Three Friends: Friendship Activity Book. Farness, JoAnn, ed. (Illus.). 32p. (J). (gr. 3-4). 1996. pap. 5.95 (*1-878076-77-9*) Boulden Pub.

— Tough Times: Verbal & Physical Abuse Activity Book. (Illus.). 32p. (J). (gr. 1-6). 1993. pap. 5.95 (*1-878076-29-9*) Boulden Pub.

— A Trip to the Zoo: Feelings Coloring Book. Ward, Evelyn M., ed. (Illus.). 16p. (Orig.). (J). (gr. k-2). 1994. pap. 5.95 (*1-878076-39-6*) Boulden Pub.

— When Someone Is Very Sick: Serious Illness Activity Book. Farness, JoAnn, ed. (Illus.). 32p. (J). (gr. 3-5). 1995. pap. 5.95 (*1-878076-43-4*) Boulden Pub.

Boulden, Jim, et al. The Last Goodbye I: Bereavement Guide I. Ward, Evelyn M., ed. (Illus.). 32p. (Orig.). (J). (gr. 6-9). 1994. pap. 5.95 (*1-878076-32-9*) Boulden Pub.

— Push & Shove: Bully & Victim Activity Book. Ward, Evelyn M., ed. (Illus.). 32p. (Orig.). (J). (gr. 2-6). 1994. pap. 5.95 (*1-878076-37-X*) Boulden Pub.

Boulden, Joan, jt. auth. see Boulden, Jim.

Boulden, Joan, ed. see Boulden, Jim.

Boulden, William. GE & Me. LC 93-206539. 300p. 1992. pap. write for info. (*0-9634814-0-1*) Hopewell Pr.

Bouldin, Barbara M. Agents of Change: Managing the Introduction of Automated Tools. 224p. (C). 1988. text 47.20 (*0-13-018508-6*) P-H.

***Bouldin, Carol Walker.** Four Angels at Your Bed: An Inspirational Memoir of Three Generations of Women. Robbins, Lynn, ed. 224p. 2000. pap. 13.95 (*0-9677569-0-1*) SunRise Ohio.

Bouldin, D. R., jt. ed. see Barber, S. A.

Bouldin, Debby, ed. see Nemeth, Bonnie.

Boulding, Elise. Born Remembering. LC 74-30805. 32p. (Orig.). 1975. pap. 4.00 (*0-87574-200-9*) Pendle Hill.

— Building a Global Civic Culture: Education for an Independent World. (Syracuse Studies on Peace & Conflict Resolution). 192p. 1990. pap. text 17.95 (*0-8156-2487-5*) Syracuse U Pr.

— Children & Solitude. LC 62-22235. (C). 1962. pap. 4.00 (*0-87574-125-8*) Pendle Hill.

— Children's Rights & the Wheel of Life. LC 78-62890. 179p. 1979. 34.95 (*0-87855-295-2*) Transaction Pubs.

***Boulding, Elise.** Culture of Peace: The Hidden Side of History. LC 99-87443. (Illus.). 280p. 2000. text 49.95 (*0-8156-2831-5*) Syracuse U Pr.

— Cultures of Peace: The Hidden Side of History. LC 99-87443. (Illus.). 280p. 2000. pap. 24.95 (*0-8156-2832-3*) Syracuse U Pr.

Boulding, Elise. The Family As a Way into the Future. LC 78-70884. (C). 1978. pap. 4.00 (*0-87574-222-X*) Pendle Hill.

— New Agendas for Peace Research: Conflict & Security Reexamined. LC 91-31610. 199p. 1992. lib. bdg. 38.00 (*1-55587-290-5*) L Rienner.

— One Small Plot of Heaven: Reflections on Family Life by a Quaker Sociologist. LC 89-16082. 231p. 1993. pap. 13.00 (*0-87574-912-7*, 1063) Pendle Hill.

— Sonnets from Later Life, 1981-1993. LC 94-30016. 180p. 1995. pap. 12.00 (*0-87574-920-8*, 1069) Pendle Hill.

— The Underside of History: A View of Women Through Time. LC 75-30558. 750p. 1977. pap. text 28.90 (*0-89158-056-5*) Westview.

— The Underside of History: A View of Women Through Time, Vol. 1. 392p. (C). 1992. 55.00 (*0-8039-4768-2*); pap. 26.00 (*0-8039-4769-0*) Sage.

— The Underside of History: A View of Women Through Time, Vol. 2. (Illus.). 372p. 1992. 55.00 (*0-8039-4816-6*); pap. 26.00 (*0-8039-4817-4*) Sage.

— Women: The Fifth World. LC 80-65602. (Headline Ser.: No. 248). (Illus.). 64p. (Orig.). 1980. pap. 5.95 (*0-87124-059-9*) Foreign Policy.

Boulding, Elise, ed. Building Peace in the Middle East: Challenges for States & Civil Society. LC 93-28581. 348p. 1993. lib. bdg. 55.00 (*1-55587-436-3*) L Rienner.

Boulding, Elise & Boulding, Kenneth E. The Future: Images & Process. 1994. pap. 22.95 (*0-8039-5790-4*) Sage.

— The Future: Images & Prophecies. 245p. 1994. 48.00 (*0-8039-5789-0*) Sage.

Boulding, J. Russell. Description & Sampling of Contaminated Soils: A Field Guide. 2nd ed. LC 93-47072. 240p. 1994. lib. bdg. 65.00 (*1-56670-050-7*, L1050) Lewis Pubs.

— Ground Water & Wellhead Protection Handbook. (Illus.). 269p. (Orig.). (C). 1994. pap. text 50.00 (*0-7881-1471-9*) DIANE Pub.

— Practical Handbook of Soil, Vadose Zone, & Ground Water Contamination: Assessment, Prevention, & Remediation. 960p. 1995. lib. bdg. 99.95 (*1-56670-051-5*, L1051) Lewis Pubs.

— Subsurface Characterization & Monitoring Techniques: A Desk Reference Guide, Vol. 1: Solids & Ground Water. (Illus.). 363p. 1996. reprint ed. pap. text 50.00 (*0-7881-3204-0*) DIANE Pub.

— Use of Airborne, Surface, & Borehole Geophysical Techniques at Contaminated Site: A Reference Guide. (Illus.). 380p. (C). 1998. pap. text 50.00 (*0-7881-4757-9*) DIANE Pub.

Boulding, J. Russell, ed. EPA Environmental Assessment Sourcebook. 400p. (C). 1996. ring bd. 74.95 (*1-57504-009-3*) CRC Pr.

— EPA Environmental Engineering Sourcebook. 400p. (C). 1996. ring bd. 74.95 (*1-57504-002-6*) CRC Pr.

Boulding, K. E. National Images & International Systems. (Reprint Series in Social Sciences). (C). 1993. reprint ed. pap. text 5.00 (*0-8290-3216-9*, PS-30) Irvington.

Boulding, Kenneth E. Collected Papers of Kenneth E. Boulding, 2. LC 77-135288. (Illus.). 518p. pap. 160.60 (*0-8357-5525-8*, 203514200002) Bks Demand.

— Collected Papers of Kenneth E. Boulding, 3. LC 77-135288. (Illus.). 624p. pap. 193.50 (*0-8357-5526-6*, 203514200003) Bks Demand.

— Collected Papers of Kenneth E. Boulding, 4. LC 77-135288. (Illus.). 631p. pap. 195.70 (*0-8357-5527-4*, 203514200004) Bks Demand.

— Collected Papers of Kenneth E. Boulding, 5. LC 77-135288. (Illus.). 438p. pap. 135.80 (*0-8357-5528-2*, 203514200005) Bks Demand.

— Collected Papers of Kenneth E. Boulding, 6. LC 77-135288. (Illus.). 703p. pap. 200.00 (*0-8357-5529-0*, 203514200006) Bks Demand.

— Ecodynamics: A New Theory of Societal Evolution. LC 77-27282. (Illus.). 384p. (C). 1978. 35.00 (*0-8039-0945-4*); pap. 21.95 (*0-8039-1683-3*) Sage.

— Ecodynamics: A New Theory of Societal Evolution. LC 77-27282. (Sageview Edition Ser.). 368p. 1978. reprint ed. pap. 114.10 (*0-608-02771-5*, 206383700007) Bks Demand.

— Economics As a Science. (Illus.). 170p. (C). 1988. reprint ed. pap. text 20.00 (*0-8191-7100-X*) U Pr of Amer.

— The Economics of Human Betterment. LC 84-3575. 220p. (C). 1985. text 17.50 (*0-87395-925-6*) State U NY Pr.

— The Economics of Peace. LC 72-5620. (Essay Index Reprint Ser.). 1977. reprint ed. 20.95 (*0-8369-2982-9*) Ayer.

— Evolutionary Economics. LC 81-8953. (Illus.). 192p. (C). 1981. 32.00 (*0-8039-1648-5*) Sage.

— Evolutionary Economics. LC 81-8953. (Illus.). 200p. 1981. reprint ed. pap. 62.00 (*0-608-01135-5*, 205943600001) Bks Demand.

— The Evolutionary Potential of Quakerism. LC 64-22764. (C). 1964. pap. 4.00 (*0-87574-136-3*) Pendle Hill.

— Human Betterment. LC 84-24938. 224p. 1985. reprint ed. pap. 69.50 (*0-608-02789-8*, 206385600007) Bks Demand.

— The Image: Knowledge in Life & Society. 184p. 1956. pap. text 16.95 (*0-472-06047-3*, 06047, Ann Arbor Bks) U of Mich Pr.

— Mending the World: Quaker Insights on the Social Order. LC 86-60283. 1986. pap. 4.00 (*0-87574-266-1*) Pendle Hill.

— New Nations for Old. (C). 1942. pap. 4.00 (*0-87574-017-0*) Pendle Hill.

— There Is a Spirit: The Nayles Sonnets. 1998. pap. 4.00 (*0-87574-337-4*) Pendle Hill.

— Three Faces of Power. 264p. (C). 1989. pap. 25.00 (*0-8039-3862-4*); text 52.00 (*0-8039-3554-4*) Sage.

— Towards a New Economics: Critical Essays on Ecology, Distribution & Other Themes. (Economists of the Twentieth Century Ser.). 368p. 1992. text 100.00 (*1-85278-568-3*) E Elgar.

— The World As a Total System. 1985. 35.00 (*0-8039-2443-7*) Sage.

Boulding, Kenneth E., ed. Peace & the War Industry. rev. ed. LC 72-87664. 159p. 1975. reprint ed. pap. text 18.95 (*0-87855-545-5*) Transaction Pubs.

— Peace & the War Industry. 2nd rev. ed. LC 72-87654. 159p. 1975. reprint ed. 29.95 (*0-87855-052-6*) Transaction Pubs.

Boulding, Kenneth E. & Chi, Meng. The Structure of a Modern Economy: The United States, 1929-89. As a Case Study. LC 92-29613. 215p. (C). 1993. text 65.00 (*0-8147-1203-7*) NYU Pr.

Boulding, Kenneth E. & Mayer, Milton. Mayer Boulding Dialogue on Peace Research. Murphy, Carol R., ed. LC 67-23313. (Orig.). 1967. pap. 1.00 (*0-87574-153-3*) Pendle Hill.

Boulding, Kenneth E., jt. auth. see Boulding, Elise

Boulding, Maria. Gateway to Hope: An Exploration of Failure. LC 87-4339. 158p. 1987. reprint ed. pap. 7.95 (*0-932506-53-4*) St Bedes Pubns.

— Marked for Life: Prayer in the Easter Christ. 128p. 1995. pap. 11.95 (*0-687-06628-X*) Abingdon.

Boulding, Maria, tr. see Augustine, Saint.

Boulding, Maria, tr. see Thomas of Villanova.

Boulding, Russell. The Lost Harvest: A Study of the Surface Mining Act's Failure to Reclaim Prime Farmland in the Midwest- Executive Summary. Mavrolas, Pamela & Sheketoff, Chuck, eds. (Illus.). (Orig.). 1984. pap. 5.00 (*0-943724-04-X*) Illinois South.

— The Lost Harvest: A Study of the Surface Mining Act's Failure to Reclaim Prime Farmland in the Midwest- Executive Summary. (Illus.). (Orig.). 1984. pap. 15.00 (*0-943724-05-8*) Illinois South.

— Prime Farmland Restoration. Mavrolas, Pamela & Sheketoff, Chuck, eds. (Your Rights in the Coalfields Ser.). 1984. pap. 3.00 (*0-943724-06-6*) Illinois South.

— A Technical Guide for Reviewing Prime Farmland Restoration Plans in the Midwest. (Illus.). 1984. pap. 5.00 (*0-943724-07-4*) Illinois South.

***Bouldrey, Brian.** Best American Gay Fiction. 1998. mass mkt. 15.00 (*0-316-19077-2*) Little.

— The Best American Gay Fiction, 2 vols. (J). 1998. mass mkt. 14.95 (*0-316-19078-0*) Little.

— Love, the Magician. LC 00-28183. 179p. (C). 2000. 49.95 (*1-56023-993-X*, Harrington Park) Haworth Pr.

— Love, the Magician. LC 00-28183. 179p. 2000. pap. text 19.95 (*1-56023-994-8*) Haworth Pr.

Bouldrey, Brian. Wrestling with the Angels: An Anthology of Essays about Homosexuality & Religion. 1995. pap. write for info. (*0-316-10367-5*) Little.

Bouldrey, Brian, ed. Best American Gay Fiction, Vol. 2. 320p. 1997. pap. 14.95 (*0-316-10299-7*) Little.

— Best American Gay Fiction 3, 3. 304p. 1998. pap. 15.00 (*0-316-10236-9*) Little.

***Bouldrey, Brian, ed.** Traveling Souls: Contemporary Pilgrimage Stories. 224p. 1999. pap. 14.95 (*1-883513-08-1*, Pub. by Whereabouts) SPD-Small Pr Dist.

Bouldrey, Brian, ed. Writing Home: Award-Winning Literature from the New West. LC 99-40589. 270p. 2000. pap. 14.95 (*1-890771-22-8*, Pub. by Heyday Bks) SPD-Small Pr Dist.

***Boule, Jean-Pierre.** Guibert: A l'Ami Qui Ne Ma Pas Sauve la Vie, etc. 64p. 1999. pap. 35.00 (*0-85261-463-2*, Pub. by U of Glasgow) St Mut.

Boule, Jean Pierre. Herve Guibert: Voices of the Self. (Modern French Writers: 4). 320p. 1999. pap. 24.95 (*0-85323-871-5*, Pub. by Liverpool Univ Pr) U of Pa Pr.

— Herve Guibert: Voices of the Self. (Modern French Writers: Vol. 4). 320p. 1999. 53.95 (*0-85323-861-8*, Pub. by Liverpool Univ Pr) U of Pa Pr.

Boule, Marcellin. Fossil Men: Elements of Human Paleontology. LC 78-72691. reprint ed. 69.50 (*0-404-18262-3*) AMS Pr.

— California's Native American Tribes, No. 1: Achumawi Tride. (Illus.). 44p. (Orig.). (J). (gr. 2-3). 1992. pap. 7.95 (*1-877599-25-5*) Merryant Pubs.

— California's Native American Tribes, No. 10: Maidu-KonKow Tribe. (Illus.). 56p. (Orig.). (J). (gr. 4-5). 1992. pap. 7.95 (*1-877599-34-4*) Merryant Pubs.

— California's Native American Tribes, No. 11: Coast Miwok. (Illus.). 52p. (Orig.). (J). (gr. 2-4). 1992. pap. 7.95 (*1-877599-35-2*) Merryant Pubs.

— California's Native American Tribes, No. 12: Eastern Miwok Tribe. (Illus.). 52p. (Orig.). (J). (gr. 3-5). 1992. pap. 7.95 (*1-877599-36-0*) Merryant Pubs.

— California's Native American Tribes, No. 13: Lake Miwok Tribe. (Illus.). 52p. (Orig.). (J). (gr. 3-5). 1992. pap. 7.95 (*1-877599-37-9*) Merryant Pubs.

— California's Native American Tribes, No. 14: Ohlone Tribe. (Illus.). 56p. (Orig.). (J). (gr. 4-5). 1992. pap. 7.95 (*1-877599-38-7*) Merryant Pubs.

B

— California's Native American Tribes, No. 15: Patwin Tribe. (Illus.). 52p. (Orig.). (J). (gr. 3-5). 1992. pap. text 7.95 (*1-877599-49-2*) Merryant Pubs.

— California's Native American Tribes, No. 16: Western & N. E. Pomo Tribe. (Illus.). 52p. (Orig.). (J). (gr. 2-3). 1992. pap. 7.95 (*1-877599-39-5*) Merryant Pubs.

— California's Native American Tribes, No. 17: East & S. E. Pomo Tribe. (Illus.). 52p. (Orig.). (J). (gr. 3-4). 1992. pap. 7.95 (*1-877599-40-9*) Merryant Pubs.

— California's Native American Tribes, No. 18: Salinan Tribe. (Illus.). 56p. (Orig.). (J). (gr. 4-5). 1992. pap. 7.95 (*1-877599-41-7*) Merryant Pubs.

— California's Native American Tribes, No. 19: Shasta Tribe. (Illus.). 52p. (Orig.). (J). (gr. 2-4). 1992. pap. 7.95 (*1-877599-42-5*) Merryant Pubs.

— California's Native American Tribes, No. 2: Atsugewi Tribe. (Illus.). 48p. (Orig.). (J). (gr. 2-3). 1992. pap. 7.95 (*1-877599-26-3*) Merryant Pubs.

— California's Native American Tribes, No. 20: Tolowa Tribe. (Illus.). 44p. (Orig.). (J). (gr. 2-3). 1992. pap. 7.95 (*1-877599-43-3*) Merryant Pubs.

— California's Native American Tribes, No. 21: Tubatulabal Tribe. (Illus.). 52p. (J). (gr. 2-4). 1992. pap. 7.95 (*1-877599-24-7*) Merryant Pubs.

— California's Native American Tribes, No. 22: Wintu Tribe. (Illus.). 60p. (Orig.). (J). (gr. 4-5). 1992. pap. 7.95 (*1-877599-44-1*) Merryant Pubs.

— California's Native American Tribes, No. 23: Valley Yokuts Tribe. (Illus.). 56p. (Orig.). (J). (gr. 4-5). 1992. pap. 7.95 (*1-877599-45-X*) Merryant Pubs.

— California's Native American Tribes, No. 24: Foothill Yokuts Tribe. (Illus.). 52p. (Orig.). (J). (gr. 3-5). 1992. pap. 7.95 (*1-877599-46-8*) Merryant Pubs.

— California's Native American Tribes, No. 25: Yuki Tribe. (Illus.). 48p. (Orig.). (J). (gr. 2-3). 1992. pap. 7.95 (*1-877599-47-6*) Merryant Pubs.

— California's Native American Tribes, No. 26: Yurok Tribe. (Illus.). 48p. (Orig.). (J). (gr. 2-4). 1992. pap. 7.95 (*1-877599-48-4*) Merryant Pubs.

— California's Native American Tribes, No. 3: Cahuilla Tribe. (Illus.). 52p. (Orig.). (J). (gr. 2-4). 1992. pap. 7.95 (*1-877599-27-1*) Merryant Pubs.

— California's Native American Tribes, No. 4: Chumash Tribe. (Illus.). 52p. (Orig.). (J). (gr. 3-5). 1992. pap. 7.95 (*1-877599-28-X*) Merryant Pubs.

— California's Native American Tribes, No. 5: Diegueno (Ipai-Tipai) (Illus.). 48p. (Orig.). (J). (gr. 2-4). 1992. pap. 7.95 (*1-877599-29-8*) Merryant Pubs.

— California's Native American Tribes, No. 6: Gabrielino Tribe. (Illus.). 56p. (Orig.). (J). (gr. 4-5). 1992. pap. 7.95 (*1-877599-30-1*) Merryant Pubs.

— California's Native American Tribes, No. 7: Hupa Tribe. (Illus.). 52p. (Orig.). (J). (gr. 2-4). 1992. pap. 7.95 (*1-877599-31-X*) Merryant Pubs.

— California's Native American Tribes, No. 8: Karok Tribe. (Illus.). 48p. (Orig.). (J). (gr. 2-3). 1992. pap. 7.95 (*1-877599-32-8*) Merryant Pubs.

— California's Native American Tribes, No. 9: Luiseno Tribe. (Illus.). 52p. (Orig.). (J). (gr. 4-5). 1992. pap. 7.95 (*1-877599-33-6*) Merryant Pubs.

— The Missions - California's Heritage, 21 bks. Kenyon, Nancy N., ed. (Illus.). 1988. pap. 79.00 (*1-877599-21-2*) Merryant Pubs.

— The Missions - California's Heritage No. 1: Mission San Diego de Alcala. (Illus.). 24p. (Orig.). (J). (gr. 4-6). 1988. pap. 6.95 (*1-877599-00-X*) Merryant Pubs.

— The Missions - California's Heritage No. 2: Mission San Carlos Borromeo de Carmelo. (Illus.). 24p. (Orig.). (J). (gr. 4-6). 1988. pap. 6.95 (*1-877599-01-8*) Merryant Pubs.

— The Missions - California's Heritage No. 3: Mission San Antonio de Padua. (Illus.). 24p. (Orig.). (J). (gr. 4-6). 1988. pap. 6.95 (*1-877599-02-6*) Merryant Pubs.

— The Missions - California's Heritage No. 4: Mission San Gabriel Arcangel. (Illus.). 24p. (Orig.). (J). (gr. 4-6). 1988. pap. 6.95 (*1-877599-03-4*) Merryant Pubs.

— The Missions - California's Heritage No. 5: Mission San Luis Obispo de Tolosa. (Illus.). 24p. (Orig.). (J). (gr. 4-6). 1988. pap. 6.95 (*1-877599-04-2*) Merryant Pubs.

— The Missions - California's Heritage No. 6: Mission San Francisco de Asis. (Illus.). 24p. (Orig.). (J). (gr. 4-6). 1988. pap. 6.95 (*1-877599-05-0*) Merryant Pubs.

— The Missions - California's Heritage No. 7: Mission San Juan Capistrano. (Illus.). 24p. (Orig.). (J). (gr. 4-6). 1988. pap. 6.95 (*1-877599-06-9*) Merryant Pubs.

— The Missions - California's Heritage No. 8: Mission Santa Clara de Asis. (Illus.). 24p. (Orig.). (J). (gr. 4-6). 1988. pap. 6.95 (*1-877599-07-7*) Merryant Pubs.

— The Missions - California's Heritage No. 9: Mission San Buenaventura. (Illus.). 24p. (Orig.). (J). (gr. 4-6). 1988. pap. 6.95 (*1-877599-08-5*) Merryant Pubs.

— The Missions - California's Heritage No. 10: Mission Santa Barbara. (Illus.). 24p. (Orig.). (J). (gr. 4-6). 1988. pap. 6.95 (*1-877599-09-3*) Merryant Pubs.

— The Missions - California's Heritage No. 11: Mission la Purisima Concepcion. (Illus.). 24p. (Orig.). (J). (gr. 4-6). 1988. pap. 6.95 (*1-877599-10-7*) Merryant Pubs.

— The Missions - California's Heritage No. 12: Mission Santa Cruz. (Illus.). 24p. (Orig.). (J). (gr. 4-6). 1988. pap. 6.95 (*1-877599-11-5*) Merryant Pubs.

— The Missions - California's Heritage No. 13: Mission Nuestra Senora de la Soledad. (Illus.). 20p. (Orig.). (J). (gr. 4-6). 1988. pap. 6.95 (*1-877599-12-3*) Merryant Pubs.

— The Missions - California's Heritage No. 14: Mission San Jose. (Illus.). 28p. (Orig.). (J). (gr. 4-6). 1988. pap. 6.95 (*1-877599-13-1*) Merryant Pubs.

— The Missions - California's Heritage No. 15: Mission San Juan Bautista. (Illus.). 24p. (Orig.). (J). (gr. 4-6). 1988. pap. 6.95 (*1-877599-14-X*) Merryant Pubs.

— The Missions - California's Heritage No. 16: Mission San Miguel Arcangel. (Illus.). 24p. (Orig.). (J). (gr. 4-6). 1988. pap. 6.95 (*1-877599-15-8*) Merryant Pubs.

— The Missions - California's Heritage No. 17: Mission San Fernando Rey de Espana. (Illus.). 24p. (Orig.). (J). (gr. 4-6). 1988. pap. 6.95 (*1-877599-16-6*) Merryant Pubs.

— The Missions - California's Heritage No. 18: Mission San Luis Rey de Francia, 21 Bks. (Illus.). 24p. (Orig.). (J). (gr. 4). 1988. pap. 6.95 (*1-877599-17-4*) Merryant Pubs.

— The Missions - California's Heritage No. 19: Mission Santa Ines. (Illus.). 24p. (Orig.). (J). (gr. 4-6). 1988. pap. 6.95 (*1-877599-18-2*) Merryant Pubs.

— The Missions - California's Heritage No. 20: Mission San Rafael Arcangel. (Illus.). 24p. (Orig.). (J). (gr. 4-6). 1988. pap. 6.95 (*1-877599-19-0*) Merryant Pubs.

— The Missions - California's Heritage No. 21: Mission San Francisco Solano. (Illus.). 24p. (Orig.). (J). (gr. 4-6). 1988. pap. 6.95 (*1-877599-20-4*) Merryant Pubs.

— Native Americans of North America: Basin Region: Northern Paiute. Harding, Virginia, ed. (Illus.). 64p. (gr. 3-6). 1999. text 7.95 (*1-877599-55-7*) Merryant Pubs.

— Native Americans of North America: Plateau Tribes: Cayuse, Walla Walla & Umatilla People. Harding, Virginia, ed. (Illus.). 64p. (J). (gr. 3-6). 1999. pap. text 7.95 (*1-877599-54-9*) Merryant Pubs.

*__Boule, Mary N.__ Washoe People. Harding, Virginia, ed. (Illus.). 64p. 2000. 7.95 (*1-877599-56-5*) Merryant Pubs.

Boule, Mary Null. Native Americans of North America: Northwest Coastal Tribes: Tlingit. LC 98-125191. (Illus.). 68p. (J). (gr. 3-5). 1996. pap. 7.95 (*1-877599-50-6*) Merryant Pubs.

— Native Americans of North America: NW Coastal Tribes: Salish. LC 98-125194. (Illus.). 68p. (J). (gr. 3-5). 1996. pap. text 7.95 (*1-877599-51-4*) Merryant Pubs.

— Native Americans of North America: Plateau Tribes: Nez Perce People. (Illus.). 64p. (J). (gr. 3-6). 1999. pap. text 7.95 (*1-877599-53-0*) Merryant Pubs.

— Native Americans of North America: Plateau Tribes: Yakama Nation. LC 98-125193. (Illus.). 64p. (J). (gr. 3-5). 1996. pap. 7.95 (*1-877599-52-2*) Merryant Pubs.

*__Boule, P., ed.__ Environmental Photochemistry. (Handbook of Environmental Chemistry Ser.: Vol. 2, Pt. L). (Illus.). 310p. 1998. 199.00 (*3-540-62913-0*) Spr-Verlag.

*__Boule, Phillippe.__ Aberrant: Teragen. 2000. pap. text 17.95 (*1-56504-683-8*) White Wolf.

Bouleau, Nicolas & Hirsch, Francis. Dirichlet Forms & Analysis on Wiener Space. (Studies in Mathematics: Vol. 14). x, 325p. (C). 1991. lib. bdg. 79.95 (*3-11-012919-1*) De Gruyter.

Bouleau, Nicolas & Lepingle, Dominique. Numerical Methods for Stochastic Processes. LC 93-10302. (Series in Probability & Mathematical Statistics). 384p. 1993. 115.00 (*0-471-54641-0*) Wiley.

Boulenger, ed. see Rabelais, Francois.

Boulenger, G. A. Catalogue of the Batrachia Gradienta S. Caudata & Batrachia Apoda: Collection of the British Museum. 2nd ed. (Illus.). 1966. 40.00 (*3-7682-0289-5*) Lubrecht & Cramer.

— Catalogue of the Batrachia Salienta S. Ecaudata: Collection of the British Museum. (Illus.). 1966. 112.00 (*3-7682-0291-7*) Lubrecht & Cramer.

— Catalogue of the Chelonians, Rhynchocephalians, & Crocodiles in the British Museum. (Illus.). 1966. 60.00 (*3-7682-0443-X*) Lubrecht & Cramer.

— Catalogue of the Lizards in the British Museum, 3 vols. in 2. (Illus.). 1964. 432.00 (*3-7682-0239-9*) Lubrecht & Cramer.

— Fishes of the Nile. 1964. reprint ed. 260.00 (*0-685-03113-6*) Lubrecht & Cramer.

Boulenger, George A. The Tailless Batrachians of Europe, 2 pts., 1 bk. Sterling, Keir B., ed. LC 77-81096. (Biologists & Their World Ser.). (Illus.). 1978. reprint ed. lib. bdg. 42.95 (*0-405-10679-3*) Ayer.

Boulenger, Jacques R. Seventeenth Century. LC 70-181913. (National History of France Ser.: No. 4). reprint ed. 45.00 (*0-404-50794-8*) AMS Pr.

*__Boulerice Lyons, Dianne J.__ Your Career in Alternative Medicine: A Guide to Degree & CertificatePrograms in Alternative Healthcare. 2nd ed. LC 00-27084. 444p. 2000. pap. 21.95 (*1-58333-042-9*, Avery) Penguin Putnam.

*__Boulesbaa, Ahcene.__ The U. N. Convention on Torture & the Prospects for Enforcement. LC 99-18785. (International Studies in Human Rights). xviii, 366p. 1999. 135.00 (*90-411-0457-7*) Kluwer Law Intl.

Boulesteix, C. Diffusionless Phase Transitions & Related Structures in Oxides. (Key Engineering Materials Ser.: Vol. 68). 348p. 1992. text 116.00 (*0-87849-629-7*, Pub. by Trans T Pub) Enfield Pubs NH.

Boulesteix, C., ed. Oxides: Phase Transitions, Non Stoichiometry, Superconductors. (Key Engineering Materials Ser.: Vols. 155-156). (Illus.). 476p. (C). 1998. text 172.00 (*0-87849-798-6*, Pub. by Trans T Pub) Enfield Pubs NH.

Boulesteix, C. & Gavarri, J. R. Phase Transitions in Materials: A Special Issue of the Journal Phase Transitions. Glazer, A. M., ed. 328p. 1989. pap. text 663.00 (*0-677-25780-5*) Gordon & Breach.

Boulesteix, Ed C. Diffusionless Phase Transitions in Oxides: And Some Reconstructive & Martensitic Phase Transitions. (Key Engineering Materials Ser.: Vol. 101-102). (Illus.). 442p. (C). 1995. text 200.00 (*0-87849-691-2*, Pub. by Trans T Pub) Enfield Pubs NH.

Boulestin, X. Marcel. Boulestin's Round-the-Year Cookbook. 256p. 1975. reprint ed. pap. 4.95 (*0-486-23214-X*) Dover.

Boulet. Methods of Orbit Determination for the Micro Computer. 1991. 24.95 (*0-943396-34-4*) Willmann-Bell.

Boulet, Ann, ed. see Bayou Civic Club, Inc. Staff.

Boulet, J. Dictionnaire de L'Homeopathie. (FRE.). 1998. 69.95 (*0-320-00227-6*) Fr & Eur.

Boulet, Louis-Philippe. Asthma: Theory, Treatment & Education. (Illus.). 400p. 1998. text 75.00 (*0-7735-1609-3*, Pub. by McG-Queens Univ Pr) CUP Services.

Boulet, Louis-Philippe, jt. auth. see Boutin, Helene.

Boulet, M., jt. ed. see Burger, H.

Boulet, Susan. A Susan Seddon Boulet Bestiary: A Book of Postcards. (Illus.). pap. 9.95 (*0-87654-812-5*, A581) Pomegranate Calif.

Boulet, Susan S. Shaman: The Paintings of Susan Seddon Boulet. LC 88-64077. (Illus.). 128p. (Orig.). 1989. pap. 26.95 (*0-87654-433-2*) Pomegranate Calif.

Boulet, Susan S. Susan Seddon Boulet: The Goddess Paintings. LC 93-87362. 128p. 1994. pap. 29.95 (*1-56640-957-8*) Pomegranate Calif.

Boulette, Jack, jt. auth. see Warns, E. Fredy.

Bouleur, Joseph, ed. see Levi, Eliphas.

Bouleur, Joseph, ed. & tr. see Levi, Eliphas.

Bouleur, Joseph, ed. & tr. see Mesmer, Franz A.

Boulevard Books Staff. Bundyisms: The Wit & Wisdom of America's Last Family. LC 97-185250. 144p. 1997. pap. 9.95 (*1-57297-251-3*) Blvd Books.

Boulevard Books Staff. Young Jedi Knights Boxed Set, 3 vols. (Star Wars). (J). (gr. 3-5). 1997. boxed set 17.97 (*1-57297-344-7*) Blvd Books.

*__Boulevard, Roscoe.__ Things You Will Never Hear Them Say... Carle, Cliff, ed. 96p. 1999. pap. 6.95 (*1-57644-091-5*) CCC Pubns.

Bouley, Allan. The Catholic Rites Today: Abridged Texts for Students. 608p. (Orig.). 1992. pap. text 34.95 (*0-8146-2032-9*) Liturgical Pr.

— From Freedom to Formula: The Evolution of the Eucharistic Prayer from Oral Improvisation to Written Texts. LC 80-19716. (Catholic University of America Studies in Christian Antiquity: No. 21). 320p. reprint ed. pap. 99.20 (*0-608-18729-1*, 202951200061) Bks Demand.

Bouley, Charles H. Harrington. Narrative History of the Harrington Family in Worcester, Massachusetts. 77p. 1997. reprint ed. pap. 14.50 (*0-8328-8992-X*); reprint ed. lib. bdg. 24.50 (*0-8328-8991-1*) Higginson Bk Co.

Boulez, Pierre. Orientations. Nattiez, Jean-Jacques, ed. Cooper, Martin, tr. 544p. 1986. 39.95 (*0-674-64375-5*) HUP.

— Orientations: Collected Writings. Nattiez, Jean-Jacques, ed. Cooper, Martin, tr. 544p. 1990. pap. 20.50 (*0-674-64376-3*) HUP.

— Stocktakings from an Apprenticeship. Walsh, Stephen, tr. (Illus.). 348p. 1991. text 90.00 (*0-19-311210-8*, 7416) OUP.

Boulger, Demetrius C. The History of China, 2 vols. 1972. lib. bdg. 600.00 (*0-87968-489-5*) Krishna Pr.

— History of China, 2 Vols. LC 77-39406. (Select Bibliographies Reprint Ser.). 1977. reprint ed. 64.95 (*0-8369-9902-9*) Ayer.

Boulger, George S., jt. auth. see Hawks, Ellison.

Boulger, James D. The Calvinistic Temper in English Poetry. (De Proprietatibus Litterarum, Ser. Major: No. 21). 1980. text 103.85 (*90-279-7575-2*) Mouton.

Boulhosa, Stephen R. You Only Get What You Settle For: A Collection of Poems. LC 92-44219. 64p. 1993. pap. 14.95 (*0-7734-2760-0*, Mellen Poetry Pr) E Mellen.

Boulic, R., et al, eds. Computer Animation & Simulation '96: Proceedings of the Eurographics Workshop in Poitiers, France, August 31-September 1, 1996. (Illus.). x, 225p. 1996. pap. 69.50 (*3-211-82885-0*) Spr-Verlag.

Boulikas, Teni. Chromatin Structure - DNA Replication - Repair - Gene Ex - Carcino. 320p. 2000. write for info. (*0-8493-4450-6*) CRC Pr.

— Gene Therapy & Molecular Biology Vol. 1: From Basic Mechanisms to Clinical Applications. (Illus.). 832p. 1998. 127.00 (*1-892245-00-0*) Gene Therapy.

Boulikas, Teni, ed. Gene Therapy & Molecular Biology, Vols. 2 & 3. (Illus.). 536p. 1999. 127.00 (*1-892245-01-9*) Gene Therapy.

Boulima, Jamila. Negotiated Interaction in Target Language Classroom Discourse. LC 99-27156. (Pragmatics & Beyond New Ser.: Vol. 51). xiv, 338p. 1999. lib. bdg. 79.00 (*1-55619-813-2*) J Benjamins Pubng Co.

Boulind, Richard, tr. see Didier, Charles.

Boulineau, Fred. Jesus' Precious Powerful Blood. 208p. (Orig.). 1993. write for info. (*0-9638934-1-6*); pap. write for info. (*0-9638934-0-8*) Jesus Blood.

Bouliou, Noelle. Behind the Bars, Behind the Words. 1992. pap. 21.00 (*1-85635-002-9*) Dufour.

Boullart & Carlo-Stella. Modular Automation in the Batch Plant Environment. 1997. text. write for info. (*0-08-042021-4*, Pergamon Pr) Elsevier.

Boullart, L., et al, eds. Application of Artificial Intelligence in Process Control: Lecture Notes Erasmus Intensive Course. LC 92-26606. 531p. 1993. 151.00 (*0-08-042016-8*, Pergamon Pr); pap. 61.00 (*0-08-042017-6*, Pergamon Pr) Elsevier.

— Industrial Process Control Systems: Reliability, Availability & Maintainability. (IFAC Publication: No. 86). 194p. 1989. 100.00 (*0-08-036238-9*, Pergamon Pr) Elsevier.

Boullart, L. & De La Puente, J. A., eds. Real-Time Programming (WRTP '92) Preprints of the IFAC Workshop, Bruges, Belgium, 23-26 June 1992. LC 92-40442. 290p. 1992. pap. 109.00 (*0-08-041894-5*, Pergamon Pr) Elsevier.

Boullart, L., et al. Computer Aided Control Systems Design. LC 97-27758. (IPV IFAC Proceedings Ser.). (Illus.). 386p. 1997. pap. 76.50 (*0-08-042383-3*, Pergamon Pr) Elsevier.

Boullart, L., jt. ed. see Fleming, P. J.

Boullata, Issa, tr. see Berrada, Mohamet.

Boullata, Issa, tr. see Nasrallah, Emily.

Boullata, Issa J. Trends & Issues in Contemporary Arab Thought. LC 89-31277. (SUNY Series in Middle Eastern Studies). 219p. (C). 1990. text 24.50 (*0-7914-0194-4*) State U NY Pr.

Boullata, Issa J., ed. Critical Perspectives on Modern Arabic Literature. LC 78-13850. 384p. (Orig.). 1980. reprint ed. 35.00 (*0-89410-007-6*, Three Contnts) L Rienner.

*__Boullata, Issa J., ed.__ Religious Meaning in the Qur'an: Aspects of Literature Structure. 320p. 2000. 89.50 (*0-7007-1256-9*, Pub. by Curzon Pr Ltd) Paul & Co Pubs.

Boullata, Issa J. & DeYoung, Terri, eds. Tradition & Modernity in Arabic Literature. LC 97-6667. 1997. 34.00 (*1-55728-447-4*) U of Ark Pr.

Boullata, Issa J., tr. see Jabra, Jabra I.

Boullata, Issa J., tr. see Samman, Ghada.

Boullata, Kamal, ed. Women of the Fertile Crescent: Modern Poetry by Arab Women. 2nd rev. ed. LC 77-3834. (Illus.). 251p. 1994. reprint ed. pap. 16.00 (*0-914478-42-7*, Three Contnts) L Rienner.

Boullata, Kamal & Ghossein, Mirene, eds. The World of Rashid Hussein: A Palestinian Poet in Exile. LC 78-62611. (Monographs: No. 12). (Illus.). 208p. (Orig.). (C). 1979. pap. 6.50 (*0-937694-07-X*) Assn Arab-Amer U Grads.

Boulle, L. Employees & the Law. 192p. 1992. pap. 35.00 (*0-614-05471-0*, Austral, MICHIE) LEXIS Pub.

— Mediation: Principles, Process, Practice. 275p. 1996. pap. write for info. (*0-409-30975-3*, MICHIE) LEXIS Pub.

*__Boulle, L.__ Planet of the Apes. LC 00-24533. (Cinema Classics Ser.). 192p. 2000. 7.99 (*0-517-20948-9*) Random Hse Value.

Boulle, L. J., et al. Constitutional & Administrative Law. 403p. 1989. pap. 40.00 (*0-7021-2316-1*, Pub. by Juta & Co) Gaunt.

Boulle, Philippe. Constantinople by Night. (Vampire Ser.). 1996. pap. text 15.00 (*1-56504-278-6*) White Wolf.

*__Boulle, Philippe.__ Innocents. (Hunter Ser.). 2000. pap. 14.95 (*1-56504-742-7*) White Wolf.

Boulle, Pierre. Aux Sources de la Riviere Kwai. (FRE.). 215p. 1985. 11.95 (*0-7859-1184-7*, 2266015915) Fr & Eur.

— Le Boulevard des Illusions. (FRE.). 214p. 1981. 11.95 (*0-7859-1183-9*, 2266009680) Fr & Eur.

— The Bridge on the River Kwai. 21.95 (*0-89190-571-5*) Amereon Ltd.

*__Boulle, Pierre.__ The Bridge on the River Kwai. (Cinema Classics Ser.). 224p. 2000. pap. text 7.99 (*0-517-20741-9*) Random Hse Value.

Boulle, Pierre. L' Etrange Croisade de Frederic II. (FRE.). 244p. 1968. 16.95 (*0-7859-1162-6*, 2080603612) Fr & Eur.

— Histoires Charitables. (FRE.). 296p. 1965. pap. 9.95 (*0-7859-5346-9*) Fr & Eur.

— Histoires Perfides: Six Nouvelles. (FRE.). 232p. 1976. 27.95 (*0-7859-1167-7*, 2080609092) Fr & Eur.

— Les Oreilles de Jungle. (FRE.). 240p. 1972. 24.95 (*0-7859-1163-4*, 2080605739) Fr & Eur.

— Le Photographe. 188p. 1974. pap. 3.95 (*0-686-54109-X*) Fr & Eur.

— Planet of the Apes. 1993. reprint ed. lib. bdg. 25.95 (*0-89968-331-2*, Lghtyr Pr) Buccaneer Bks.

— La Planete des Singes. 9.95 (*0-686-54110-3*, M4878) Fr & Eur.

— Le Pont de la Riviere Kwai. 9.95 (*0-686-54111-1*, M11077); pap. 11.95 (*0-8288-7623-1*, 2266023055) Fr & Eur.

— Les Vertus de l'Enfer. (FRE.). 272p. 1976. pap. 29.95 (*0-7859-1165-0*, 2080606921) Fr & Eur.

— William Conrad. 284p. 1972. pap. 3.95 (*0-686-54119-7*) Fr & Eur.

Boullet, Cityoen, jt. auth. see Fabris, Jacopo.

Boullier, Dianna. Exploring Irish Music & Dance. LC 99-175481. (Illus.). 160p. (YA). (gr. 5 up). 1998. 12.95 (*0-86278-558-8*, Pub. by OBrien Pr) Irish Amer Bk.

Boullin, David J. Cerebral Vasospasm. LC 79-40735. (Wiley-Interscience Publications). 347p. 1980. reprint ed. pap. 107.60 (*0-608-12373-0*, 205206800033) Bks Demand.

Boullin, David J., ed. Serotonin in Mental Abnormalities. LC 77-1828. 328p. reprint ed. pap. 101.70 (*0-608-30214-7*, 201920700010) Bks Demand.

Boullosa. La Salvaja. (SPA.). pap. 8.99 (*968-16-3236-2*, Pub. by Fondo) Continental Bk.

Boullosa, Carmen. Duerme (Sleep) 160p. 1995. pap. 12.50 (*0-679-76323-6*) Vin Bks.

— Solo para Muchachos. 1998. pap. text 9.95 (*968-19-0325-0*) Libros Fronteras.

Boullosa, Carmen. They're Cows, We're Pigs. Chambers, Leland H., tr. from SPA. LC 96-40086. 192p. 1997. 23.00 (*0-8021-1610-8*, Grove) Grove-Atltic.

Boullosa, Carmen. Todo los Amores. 1998. pap. text 11.95 (*968-19-0362-5*) Aguilar.

*__Boullosa, Carmen.__ Treinta Anos. (SPA.). 2000. pap. 15.95 (*968-19-0566-0*) Aguilar.

Boulmetis, John. The ABCs of Evaluation: Timeless Techniques for Program & Project Managers. LC 99-6597. 224p. 1999. text 29.95 (*0-7879-4432-7*) Jossey-Bass.

Boulnois, Helen. Law of Being (1920) 112p. 1998. reprint ed. pap. 12.95 (*0-7661-0556-3*) Kessinger Pub.

Boulnois, Helen M. Sorcery in France & Africa. Abel, R. Christopher, ed. 1999. pap. 7.95 (*1-55818-395-7*) Holmes Pub.

Boulogne, Duchenne De, see De Boulogne, Duchenne.

Boulogne, Jean, et al. The Making of a Gymnast. LC 77-95185. 96 p. 1978. 8.95 (*0-8015-4803-9*) NAL.

Boulon, M. J., jt. ed. see Selvadurai, A. P.

Boulos, Alfred J. Opportunities for Energy Investment in Russia & the Republics in the 1990s. 24p. 1992. pap. 10.00 (*0-918714-33-8*) Intl Res Ctr Energy.

An Asterisk (*) at the beginning of an entry indicates that the title is appearing for the first time.

Boulos, Jawad. Les Peuples et les Civilisations du Proche-Orient: Essai d'une Histoire Comparee, des Origines a nos Jours, Tomes II-V. Incl. Proche-Orient Ottoman (1517-1918) et Postottoman (1918-1930) 300p. 1968. pap. text 28.00 Tome II. De 1600 a 64 Avant J.-C. 430p. 1962. pap. text 36.00 (*3-11-000018-0*); Tome III. De la Conquete Romaine a l'Expansion Arabo-Islamique (64 av. J.-C. to 640 ap. J.-C.) 400p. 1964. pap. text 21.60 Tome IV. De l'Expansion Arabo-Islamique a la Conquete Turco-Ottomane (640-1517) 550p. 1964. pap. text 45.35 Set pap. 32.75 (*0-685-03445-3*) Mouton.

Boulos, Loufty, et al. The Street Trees of Egypt. rev. ed. (Illus.). 138p. 1989. pap. 15.00 (*977-424-173-8*, Pub. by Am Univ Cairo Pr) Col U Pr.

Boulos, Loutfy. Medicinal Plants of North Africa. Ayensu, Edward S., ed. LC 82-20412. (Medicinal Plants of the World Ser.: No. 3). (Illus.). 300p. 1983. 45.00 (*0-917256-16-6*) Ref Pubns.

Boulos, Loutfy & El-Hadidi, M. Nabil. The Weed Flora of Egypt. (Illus.). 370p. 1995. 40.00 (*977-424-323-4*, Pub. by Am Univ Cairo Pr) Col U Pr.

— The Weed Flora of Egypt: A Practical Guide. 1985. pap. 20.00 (*977-424-038-3*, Pub. by Am Univ Cairo Pr) Col U Pr.

Boulos, M. I., et al. Thermal Plasmas: Fundamentals & Applications, Vol. 1. (Illus.). 468p. (C). 1994. text 110.00 (*0-306-44607-3*, Kluwer Plenum) Kluwer Academic.

Boulougouris, John C., ed. Learning Theory Approaches to Psychiatry. LC 81-16514. 284p. reprint ed. pap. 88.10 (*0-608-18414-4*, 203044300069) Bks Demand.

Bouloukos, Theodore, jt. auth. see Lady Chablis.

Boulous, Edward N. & Platts, Dennis R., eds. Glass & Optical Materials No. I: Fracture & Strength, Glass Structure & Processing, Modeling & Computer Simulation. (Illus.). 442p. 1994. 90.00 (*0-944904-83-1*, GL01) Am Ceramic.

— Glass & Optical Materials No. II: Optoelectronics, Thin Film Coating, Sol-Gel Processing. (Illus.). 346p. 1994. 90.00 (*0-944904-84-X*, GL02) Am Ceramic.

Bouloux. Sapt Medicine, '97. 1996. mass mkt. 15.95 (*0-7234-2464-0*); mass mkt. 15.95 (*0-7234-2465-9*); mass mkt. 15.95 (*0-7234-2466-7*); mass mkt. 15.95 (*0-7234-2467-5*) Wolfe Pubng AZ.

Bouloux, P. M., jt. auth. see Lumley, J. S.

Bouloux, Pierre M. & Rees, Lesley H., eds. Diagnostic Tests in Endocrinology & Diabetes. LC 93-20474. (Diagnostic Tests Ser.). 328p. 1993. pap. text 45.00 (*0-412-35200-1*, Pub. by E A) OUP.

Bouloux, Pierre-Marc G. Sapt Clinical Medicine. (C). (gr. 13). 1993. 35.00 (*0-8151-0436-7*, 23140) Mosby Inc.

Bouloux, Pierre-Mare G. Clinical Medicine: Self-Assessment Questions in Colour. 1993. pap. 29.95 (*1-56375-613-7*, Pub. by Wolfe Pub) Mosby Inc.

Boulpaep. Medical Physiology. (C). 1995. text. write for info. (*0-7216-3256-4*, W B Saunders Co) Harcrt Hlth Sci Grp.

Boult, Adrian C. Handbook on the Technique of Conducting. 1988. reprint ed. lib. bdg. 59.00 (*0-7812-0381-3*) Rprt Serv.

— A Handbook on the Technique of Conducting. 7th rev. ed. LC 75-181113. 1951. reprint ed. 29.00 (*0-403-01512-X*) Scholarly.

***Boult, Betty.** 176 Ways to Involve Parents. LC 98-61832. 117 p. 1999. write for info. (*1-57517-153-8*) SkyLght.

Boult, Katharine F., tr. see Berlioz, Hector.

Boult, Pamela, ed. see Newhouse, Flower A.

Boultbee, Paul G. The Bahamas. LC 90-157525. (World Bibliographical Ser.). 488p. 1990. lib. bdg. 57.00 (*1-85109-102-5*) ABC-CLIO.

Boultenhouse, Charles, ed. see Tyler, Parker.

Boulter, Carmen. Angels & Archetypes: An Evolutionary Map of Feminine Consciousness. LC 96-36167. (Illus.). 312p. 1997. per. 22.00 (*0-926524-38-0*) Blue Wtr Pubng.

Boulter, Carmen. Angels & Archetypes: An Evolutionary Map of Feminine Consciousness. pap. 15.00 (*1-893183-09-2*) Granite Pub.

Boulter, D., ed. Nucleic Acids & Proteins in Plants I: Structure, Biochemistry & Physiology of Proteins. (Encyclopedia of Plant Physiology Ser.: Vol. 14A). (Illus.). 760p. 1982. 336.95 (*0-387-11008-9*) Spr-Verlag.

Boulter, D., jt. ed. see Parthier, B.

Boulter, David & Darr, David. North American Timber Trends Study. LC 96-220706. (UN ECE/FAO Timber & Forest Studies: No. 9). 48p. 25.00 (*92-1-116637-3*, 68691) UN.

Boulter, Eric, jt. auth. see Dobree, John H.

Boulter, Louise, jt. auth. see Bendell, Tony.

Boulter, Michael. The Art of Utopia: A New Direction in Contemporary Aboriginal Art. (Illus.). 180p. 1991. text 30.00 (*976-8097-15-9*) Gordon & Breach.

Boulter, Michael C. & Fisher, Helen C. Cenozoic Plants & Climates of the Arctic. (NATO ASI Ser.: Vol. 27). 1994. 227.95 (*3-540-58616-4*) Spr-Verlag.

Boulthee, Paul G. & Raine, David F. Bermuda. LC 99-494727. (World Bibliographical Ser.). 186p. 1998. lib. bdg. 74.50 (*1-85109-170-X*) ABC-CLIO.

Boulting, William. Four Pilgrims. (C). 1992. reprint ed. 27.00 (*81-206-0805-4*, Pub. by Asian Educ Servs) S Asia.

— Giordano Bruno: His Life, Thought & Martyrdom. LC 72-5438. (Select Bibliographies Reprint Ser.). 1977. reprint ed. 23.95 (*0-8369-6898-0*) Ayer.

— Tasso & His Times. LC 68-24953. (World History Ser.: No. 48). 1969. reprint ed. lib. bdg. 75.00 (*0-8383-0915-1*) M S G Haskell Hse.

***Boultinghouse, Dennis.** The Shoe Box Stories. (Illus.). 69p. 2000. 24.95 (*0-9676856-0-5*) Boults Bks.

***Boultinghouse, Philis, ed.** A Little Book of Hugs for Friends: Inspiration for the Heart. (Little Book of Hugs Ser.). (Illus.). 80p. 2000. 4.99 (*1-58229-118-7*) Howard Pub LA.

— A Little Book of Hugs for Mom: Inspiration for the Heart. (Little Book of Hugs Ser.). (Illus.). 80p. 2000. 4.99 (*1-58229-119-5*) Howard Pub LA.

— A Little Book of Hugs for Sisters: Inspiration for the Heart. (Little Book of Hugs Ser.). (Illus.). 80p. 2000. 4.99 (*1-58229-123-3*) Howard Pub LA.

— A Little Book of Hugs for Teachers: Inspiration for the Heart. (Little Book of Hugs Ser.). (Illus.). 80p. 2000. 4.99 (*1-58229-122-5*) Howard Pub LA.

— A Little Book of Hugs for Women: Inspiration for the Heart. (Little Book of Hugs Ser.). (Illus.). 80p. 2000. 4.99 (*1-58229-121-7*) Howard Pub LA.

— A Little Book of Hugs to Encourage & Inspire: Inspiration for the Heart. (Little Book of Hugs Ser.). (Illus.). 80p. 2000. 4.99 (*1-58229-120-9*) Howard Pub LA.

***Boultinghouse, Philis & Weiss, LeAnn.** Hugs for Sisters: Stories, Sayings, & Scriptures to Encourage & Inspire. LC 99-59673. (Hugs Ser.). 128p. 2000. 10.99 (*1-58229-095-4*) Howard Pub LA.

Boulton. The Foot in Diabetes. text. write for info. (*0-471-48974-3*) Wiley.

Boulton & Paul Limited Staff. Boulton & Paul, Ltd. - 1898 Catalogue. 2nd ed. (Classic Reprint Ser.). 415p. 1998. reprint ed. 14.95 (*0-921335-21-0*, Pub. by LVTL) Veritas Tools.

Boulton, Alan A., et al, eds. Amines & Their Metabolites. LC 85-24868. (Neuromethods Ser.: Vol. 2). (Illus.). 543p. 1985. 119.50 (*0-89603-076-8*) Humana.

— Amino Acids. LC 85-24862. (Neuromethods Ser.: Vol. 3). (Illus.). 281p. 1985. 119.50 (*0-89603-077-6*) Humana.

— Analysis of Psychiatric Drugs. LC 88-13342. (Neuromethods Ser.: Vol. 10). (Illus.). 564p. 1988. 139.50 (*0-89603-121-7*) Humana.

— Animal Models in Psychiatry, No. I. LC 91-7076. (Neuromethods Ser.: Vol. 18). (Illus.). 430p. 1991. 125.00 (*0-89603-198-5*) Humana.

— Animal Models in Psychiatry, No. II. LC 91-7076. (Neuromethods Ser.: Vol. 19). (Illus.). 406p. 1991. 119.50 (*0-89603-177-2*) Humana.

— Animal Models of Drug Addiction. LC 92-49180. (Neuromethods Ser.: Vol. 24). (Illus.). 460p. 1992. 119.50 (*0-89603-217-5*) Humana.

— Animal Models of Neurological Disease Vol. I: Neurodegenerative Diseases. LC 91-35401. (Neuromethods Ser.: Vol. 21). (Illus.). 388p. 1992. 120.00 (*0-89603-208-6*) Humana.

— Animal Models of Neurological Disease Vol. II: Metabolic Encephalopathies & the Epilepsies. LC 91-35401. (Neuromethods Ser.: Vol. 22). (Illus.). 380p. 1992. 125.00 (*0-89603-211-6*) Humana.

— Carbohydrates & Energy Metabolism. LC 88-26609. (Neuromethods Ser.: Vol. 11). (Illus.). 403p. 1989. 139.50 (*0-89603-143-8*) Humana.

— Drugs As Tools in Neurotransmitter Research. LC 88-32044. (Neuromethods Ser.: Vol. 12). (Illus.). 532p. 1989. 125.00 (*0-89603-122-5*) Humana.

— Imaging & Correlative Physiochemical Techniques. LC 88-9191. (Neuromethods Ser.: Vol. 8). 442p. (C). 1988. 139.50 (*0-89603-116-0*) Humana.

— In Vivo Neuromethods. (Neuromethods Ser.: Vol. 32). (Illus.). 408p. 1997. 99.50 (*0-89603-511-5*) Humana.

— Intracellular Messengers. LC 91-20801. (Neuromethods Ser.: Vol. 20). (Illus.). 580p. 1992. 125.00 (*0-89603-207-8*) Humana.

— Lipids & Related Compounds. LC 88-8909. (Neuromethods Ser.: Vol. 7). (Illus.). 360p. 1989. 99.50 (*0-89603-124-1*) Humana.

— Molecular Neurobiological Techniques. LC 89-2053. (Neuromethods Ser.: Vol. 16). (Illus.). 310p. 1989. 84.50 (*0-89603-140-3*) Humana.

— Neurobiology of the Trace Amines. LC 84-626. (Illus.). 597p. 1984. 119.50 (*0-89603-063-6*) Humana.

— The Neuronal Microenvironment. LC 87-3668. (Neuromethods Ser.: Vol. 9). (Illus.). 752p. 1988. 139.50 (*0-89603-115-2*) Humana.

— Neurophysiological Techniques I: Basic Methods & Concepts. LC 89-26855. (Neuromethods Ser.: Vol. 14). (Illus.). 408p. 1990. 89.50 (*0-89603-160-8*) Humana.

— Neurophysiological Techniques II: Applications to Neural Systems. LC 90-44264. (Neuromethods Ser.: Vol. 15). (Illus.). 391p. 1990. 89.50 (*0-89603-185-3*) Humana.

— Neuropsychology. LC 89-26859. (Neuromethods Ser.: Vol. 17). (Illus.). 381p. 1990. 119.50 (*0-89603-133-0*) Humana.

— Neuropsychopharmacology of the Trace Amines: Experimental & Clinical Aspects. LC 85-24904. 510p. 1986. 125.00 (*0-89603-099-7*) Humana.

— Neurotransmitter Enzymes. LC 86-10309. (Neuromethods Ser.: Vol. 5). (Illus.). 619p. 1986. 125.00 (*0-89603-079-2*) Humana.

— Neurotrophic Factors. (Neuromethods Ser.: Vol. 25). (Illus.). 440p. 1993. 120.00 (*0-89603-249-3*) Humana.

— Patch-Clamp Applications & Protocols. (Neuromethods Ser.: Vol. 26). (Illus.). 336p. 1995. 115.00 (*0-89603-311-2*) Humana.

— Peptides. LC 87-4064. (Neuromethods Ser.: Vol. 6). (Illus.). 509p. 1987. 125.00 (*0-89603-105-5*) Humana.

— Practical Cell Culture Techniques. LC 92-1518. (Neuromethods Ser.: Vol. 23). 380p. 1992. 69.50 (*0-89603-214-0*); pap. 79.50 (*0-89603-348-1*) Humana.

— Psychopharmacology. LC 88-32813. (Neuromethods Ser.: Vol. 13). (Illus.). 836p. 1989. 129.50 (*0-89603-129-2*) Humana.

— Receptor Binding. LC 86-7142. (Neuromethods Ser.: Vol. 4). (Illus.). 584p. 1986. 125.00 (*0-89603-078-4*) Humana.

— Trace Amines: Comparative & Clinical Neurobiology. LC 88-6847. (Experimental & Clinical Neuroscience Ser.). (Illus.). 496p. 1988. 125.00 (*0-89603-144-6*) Humana.

— Voltammetric Methods in Brain Systems. (Neuromethods Ser.: Vol. 27). (Illus.). 365p. 1995. 125.00 (*0-89603-312-0*) Humana.

Boulton, Alan A. & Baker, Glen B., eds. General Neurochemical Techniques. LC 85-30503. (Neuromethods Ser.: Vol. 1). 555p. 1986. 89.50 (*0-89603-075-X*) Humana.

Boulton, Alan A., et al. Cell Neurobiology Techniques. (Neuromethods Ser.: Vol. 33). (Illus.). 320p. 1998. 99.50 (*0-89603-510-7*) Humana.

— In Vitro Neurochemical Techniques. (Neuromethods Ser.: Vol. 34). (Illus.). 416p. 1998. 99.50 (*0-89603-509-3*) Humana.

Boulton, Alexander O. Frank Lloyd Wright, Architect: A Picture Biography. LC 93-12188. (Illus.). 128p. (J). 1993. 24.95 (*0-8478-1683-4*, Pub. by Rizzoli Intl) St Martin.

Boulton, Andrew J., et al, eds. The Foot in Diabetes: Aetiology & Clinical Management. 2nd ed. 268p. 1994. 120.00 (*0-471-94259-6*) Wiley.

Boulton, Clair C. The Meaning of Symbolism. Wilcox, Paul L., ed. 192p. (C). 1989. write for info. (*0-318-65066-5*) Placer Acad Pr.

Boulton, Connie, jt. auth. see McKay, Michael J.

***Boulton, D'A. J. D.** Knights of the Crown: The Monarchical Orders of Knighthood in Later Medieval Europe, 1325-1520. (Illus.). 566p. 2000. pap. 45.00 (*0-85115-795-5*) Boydell & Brewer.

Boulton, David, ed. Voices from the Crowd. LC 65-25493. 1964. 19.95 (*0-8023-1012-5*) Dufour.

Boulton, James T. The Language of Politics in the Age of Wilkes & Burke. LC 64-55133. (Studies in Political History). 296p. reprint ed. pap. 91.80 (*0-608-16231-0*, 202651100050) Bks Demand.

Boulton, James T., ed. Johnson: The Critical Heritage. 1978. 69.50 (*0-7100-7030-6*, Routledge Thoemms) Routledge.

Boulton, James T., ed. see Burke, Edmund.

Boulton, James T., ed. see Lawrence, D. H.

Boulton, Jane & Boulton, Peter. Psychic Beam to Beyond. LC 82-74522. 144p. 1983. pap. 6.95 (*0-87516-514-1*) DeVorss.

Boulton, Jane, jt. auth. see Whiteley, Opal.

Boulton, John, et al, eds. Long Term Consequences of Early Feeding. LC 95-23864. (Nestle Nutrition Workshop Ser.: Vol. 36). 256p. 1995. text 69.00 (*0-397-51728-5*) Lppncott W & W.

Boulton-Lewis, Gillian & Catherwood, Di, eds. The Early Years. LC 94-146313. 316p. 1994. pap. 22.50 (*0-86431-139-7*, Pub. by Aust Council Educ Res) Stylus Pub VA.

Boulton-Lewis, Gillian & Catherwood, Di, eds. The Early Years: Development, Learning & Teaching. 320p. 1995. pap. 52.50 (*0-273-61886-5*, Pub. by F T P-H) Trans-Atl Phila.

***Boulton, Marsha.** Scared Silly! A Halloween Book for the Brave. 64p. (J). 2000. pap. 7.95 (*0-316-10372-1*) Little.

Boulton, Marureen B. The Old French Evangile de L'Enfance: An Edition with Introduction & Notes. (ENG & FRO.). x, 117p. pap. text 18.29 (*0-88844-070-7*) Brill Academic Pubs.

Boulton, Mary, ed. Challenge & Innovation: Methodological Advances in Social Research on HIV-AIDS. LC 94-4131. (Social Aspects of AIDS Ser.). 240p. 1994. 75.00 (*0-7484-0197-0*, Pub. by Tay Francis Ltd) Taylor & Francis.

— Challenge & Innovation: Methodological Advances in Social Research on HIV-AIDS. LC 94-4131. (Social Aspects of AIDS Ser.). 240p. 1994. pap. 29.95 (*0-7484-0198-9*) Taylor & Francis.

Boulton, Maureen. The Song in the Story: Lyric Insertions in French Narrative Fiction, 1200-1400. LC 93-22097. (Middle Ages Ser.). 352p. (C). 1993. text 42.50 (*0-8122-3199-6*) U of Pa Pr.

***Boulton Paul Association Staff.** Boulton Paul Aircraft. (Transport Ser.). 1999. pap. 18.99 (*0-7524-0625-6*) Arcadia Publng.

Boulton, Peter, jt. auth. see Boulton, Jane.

***Boulton, Richard, et al.** Cracking the Value Code: How Successful Businesses Are Creating Wealth in the New Economy. LC 99-59633. 288p. 2000. 27.00 (*0-06-662063-5*, HarpBusn) HarpInfo.

Boulton, Roger B., jt. auth. see Singleton, Vernon L.

Boulton, Susie. Malta. (Illustrated Travel Guides from Thomas Cook Ser.). (Illus.). 192p. 1994. pap. 12.95 (*0-8442-9069-6*, Passprt Bks) NTC Contemp Pub Co.

— Malta. 2nd ed. (Passport's Illustrated Travel Guides Ser.). (Illus.). 192p. 1998. pap. 14.95 (*0-8442-4824-X*, 4824X, Passprt Bks) NTC Contemp Pub Co.

***Boulton, Susie.** Malta & Gozo. 3rd ed. (Illustrated Travel Guides Ser.). (Illus.). 2000. pap. 14.95 (*0-658-00507-3*, Passprt Bks) NTC Contemp Pub Co.

Boulton, Susie. Venice. 2nd ed. (Passport's Illustrated Travel Guides Ser.). (Illus.). 192p. 1998. pap. 14.95 (*0-8442-4819-3*, 48193, Passprt Bks) NTC Contemp Pub Co.

Boulton, T. B., jt. ed. see Atkinson, R. S.

Boulton, Thomas B. & Blogg, Colin E. Ostlere & Bryce-Smith's Anaesthetics for Medical Students. 10th ed. (Illus.). 276p. 1989. pap. text. write for info (*0-443-02821-4*) Church.

Boulton, W. H. The Pageant of Transport Through the Ages. 1976. lib. bdg. 344.95 (*0-8490-2398-X*) Gordon Pr.

Boulton, Wayne G. Out of Step: The Family, American Society, & the Christian Gospel. 106p. (Orig.). (C). 1992. pap. 16.00 (*0-8191-8502-7*); lib. bdg. 34.00 (*0-8191-8501-9*) U Pr of Amer.

Boulton, Wayne G., et al, eds. From Christ to the World: Introductory Readings in Christian Ethics. LC 94-21944. 551p. (Orig.). 1994. pap. text 30.00 (*0-8028-0640-6*) Eerdmans.

Boulton, William B. Amusements of Old London, 2 vols., 1 bk. LC 75-82820. (Illus.). 1972. 46.95 (*0-405-08295-9*, Pub. by Blom Pubns) Ayer.

— Amusements of Old London, Vol. 1. 1977. 23.95 (*0-405-30182-0*) Ayer.

— Amusements of Old London, Vol. 2. 1977. 23.95 (*0-405-30183-9*) Ayer.

Boulton, William H. The Pageant of Transport Through the Ages. LC 77-81514. (Illus.). 245p. 1972. 24.95 (*0-405-08296-7*, Pub. by Blom Pubns) Ayer.

Boultwood, Jackie, ed. Gene Isolation & Mapping Protocols. LC 96-43729. (Methods in Molecular Biology Ser.: Vol. 68). (Illus.). 328p. 1996. pap. 79.50 (*0-89603-382-1*) Humana.

Boultwood, Jacqueline, ed. Gene Isolation & Mapping Protocols. LC 96-43729. (Methods in Molecular Biology Ser.: Vol. 68). 328p. 1996. 99.50 (*0-89603-482-8*) Humana.

***Boultwood, Jacqueline & Fidler, Carrie, eds.** Molecular Analysis of Cancer. 380p. 2000. 89.50 (*0-89603-622-7*) Humana.

Boulud, Daniel. Cooking with Daniel Boulud. 1993. 50.00 (*0-679-40409-0*) Random.

Boulud, Daniel & Greenspan, Dorie. Daniel Boulud's Cafe Boulud Cookbook. LC 99-26665. 384p. 1999. 35.00 (*0-684-86343-X*) Scribner.

Boulvert, Y. Documents Phytogeographiques sur les Savanes Centrafricaines (Phytogeographic Literature on the Central African Savannas)Tr. of Phytogeographic Literature on the Central African Savannas. (FRE., Illus.). 142p. 1986. pap. 60.00 (*2-7099-1246-5*, Pub. by LInstitut Francais) Balogh.

Boulware, Chris, ed. see Noble, Alfredo D.

Boulware, Chris, ed. see Patterson, Victoria.

Boulware, Jack. San Francisco Bizarro. (Illus.). 192p. 2000. pap. 16.95 (*0-312-20671-2*) St Martin.

— Sex, American Style: An Illustrated Romp Through the Golden Age of Heterosexuality. LC 98-169951. 1997. pap. 16.95 (*0-922915-46-6*) Feral Hse.

Boulware, Lemuel R. The Truth about Boulwarism: Trying to Do Right Voluntarily. LC 77-91413. 192p. reprint ed. pap. 59.60 (*0-608-14108-9*, 202430500037) Bks Demand.

Boulware, Marcus. Snoring. LC 73-94369. 1974. 6.95 (*0-912834-02-1*) Am Faculty Pr.

Boulware, Marcus H. Oratory of Negro Leaders, 1900-1968, 1. LC 72-90794. 312p. 1970. 65.00 (*0-8371-1849-2*, BOO&, Greenwood Pr) Greenwood.

— The Riddle of Snoring. 50p. 1996. reprint ed. spiral bd. 11.00 (*0-7873-1223-1*) Hlth Research.

***Boulyjenkov, V., et al, eds.** Genes & Resistance to Diseases. (Illus.). x, 174p. 2000. 95.00 (*3-540-66724-5*) Spr-Verlag.

Bouma, A. H. & Carter, R. M., eds. Facies Models in Exploration & Development of Hydrocarbon & Ore Deposits: Proceedings of the 28th International Geological Congress. 272p. 1991. 115.00 (*90-6764-134-0*, Pub. by VSP) Coronet Bks.

Bouma, A. H., ed. see Rhodes, E. G. & Moslow, T. F.

Bouma, Anke. Lateral Asymmetries & Hemispheric Specialization: Theoretical Models & Research. xiii, 164p. 1990. 38.00 (*90-265-1079-9*) Swets.

Bouma, Arnold H. Offshore Geologic Hazards: A Short Course Presented at Rice University, May 2-3, 1981 for the Offshore Technology Conference. LC QE0026.2.A43. (Education Course Note Ser.: Vol. 18). 469p. reprint ed. pap. 145.40 (*0-608-08730-0*, 206936900004) Bks Demand.

Bouma, Arnold H., ed. Shell Dredging & Its Influence on Gulf Coast Environments. LC 75-39416. (Illus.). 464p. reprint ed. pap. 143.90 (*0-608-18476-4*, 203286100082) Bks Demand.

Bouma, Arnold H., et al, eds. Framework, Facies, & Oil-Trapping Characteristics of the Upper Continental Margin: Based on Papers Presented at the 1976 AAPG Short Course, Beyond the Shelf Break, Conducted at the New Orleans National Meeting. LC 78-64610. (Studies in Geology: No. 7). (Illus.). 344p. reprint ed. pap. 106.70 (*0-7837-5229-6*, 204496200005) Bks Demand.

***Bouma, Arnold H. & Stone, Charles G., eds.** Fine-Grained Turbidite Systems. LC 00-22368. (Memoir Ser.: No. 72). (Illus.). 352p. 2000. 103.00 (*0-89181-353-5*, 583) AAPG.

Bouma, Donald H. The Dynamics of School Integration: Problems & Approaches in a Northern City. LC 68-20582. 158p. reprint ed. pap. 49.00 (*0-608-30283-X*, 201295900083) Bks Demand.

Bouma, Erin L., ed. see World Media Association Staff.

***Bouma, Gary.** The Research Process. 248p. 2000. pap. 29.95 (*0-19-551224-3*) OUP.

Bouma, Gary D. The Research Process. 3rd ed. (Illus.). 252p. 1997. 38.00 (*0-19-553938-9*) OUP.

Bouma, Gary D. & Atkinson, G. B. A Handbook of Social Science Research: A Comprehensive & Practical Guide for Students. 2nd ed. (Illus.). 260p. (C). 1996. pap. text 21.00 (*0-19-828001-7*) OUP.

Bouma, Gosse, et al, eds. Constraints & Resources in Natural Language Syntax & Semantics. LC 99-34322. (Studies in Constraint-Based Lexicalism (SCBL)). 400p. 1999. 69.95 (*1-57586-221-2*, Pub. by CSLI); pap. 27.95 (*1-57586-222-0*, Pub. by CSLI) Cambridge U Pr.

Bouma, H. & Graafmans, J., eds. Gerontechnology: Proceedings of the First International Conference on Technology & Aging, Eindhoven, Aug. 26-29, 1991. LC 92-53266. (Studies in Health Technology & Informatics: Vol. 3). 462p. (gr. 12). 1992. 95.00 (*90-5199-072-3*, Pub. by IOS Pr) IOS Press.

Bouma, Hans. An Eye on Israel. LC 77-10641. 144p. reprint ed. pap. 44.70 (*0-8357-9128-9*, 201272800083) Bks Demand.

Bouma, Hendrik. Secession. Doleantie, & Union, 1834-1892. Plantinga, Theodore, tr. from DUT. LC 95-31943. 302p. (Orig.). 1995. pap. 13.90 (*0-921100-36-1*) Inhtce Pubns.

Bouma, Herman, jt. ed. see Elsendoorn, Ben A.

Bouma, J., et al, eds. Eco-Regional Approaches for Sustainable Land Use & Food Production: Proceedings of a Symposium on Eco-Regional Approaches in Agricultural Research, 12-16 December 1994, ISNAR, The Hague. LC 95-21138. (System Approaches for Sustainable Agricultural Development Ser.: Vol. 4). 520p. (C). 1995. text 232.00 (*0-7923-3608-9*) Kluwer Academic.

Bouma, Jelle. Marcus Iunius Nypsus: Introduction, Text, Translation, & Commentary. LC 93-309. (Studien zur Klassischen Philologie).Tr. of Fluminis varatio, Limitis Repositio. (ENG & LAT., Illus.). 196p. 1993. 37.00 (*3-631-45588-7*) P Lang Pubng.

Bouma, L. G., jt. auth. see Velthuijsen, H.

Bouma, Lowell. The Semantics of the Modal Auxiliaries in Contemporary German. (Janua Linguarum, Series Practica: No. 146). 1973. pap. text 40.80 (*90-279-2390-6*) Mouton.

B

Bouma, Paddy, jt. auth. see Carrick, Carol.

Bouma-Prediger, Steven. The Greening of Theology: The Ecological Models of Rosemary Radford Ruether, Joseph Sittler, & Jurgen Moltmann. LC 95-33570. (American Academy of Religion Academy Ser.: No. 91). 338p. (C). 1995. 35.95 (*0-7885-0163-1*, 010191) OUP.

Bouma-Prediger, Steven, ed. see Sittler, Joseph.

Bouma, Ralph. Believe & Receive Christ. unabridged ed. 95p. 1993. pap. 4.98 (*1-58339-004-9*, A4) Triangle Press.

— Born of the Spirit. unabridged ed. 82p. 1996. pap. 4.95 (*1-58339-007-3*, A7) Triangle Press.

***Bouma, Ralph.** Christus und die Familie. Kaluza, Hans, tr. (GER.). 143p. 1999. 5.50 (*1-58339-022-7*) Triangle Press.

Bouma, Ralph. The Circumcision Covenant: Or the Roman Yoke. unabridged ed. 92p. 1996. pap. 8.50 (*1-58339-015-4*, A15) Triangle Press.

— The Complete Works of Ralph Bouma, Vol. 1. unabridged ed. 183p. 1989. pap. 6.95 (*1-58339-018-9*, A18) Triangle Press.

— The Complete Works of Ralph Bouma, Vol. 2. unabridged ed. 203p. 1990. pap. 6.95 (*1-58339-019-7*, A19) Triangle Press.

— Family Focus on Christ. unabridged ed. 137p. 1989. pap. 5.50 (*1-58339-001-4*, A1) Triangle Press.

— For God So Loved the World. unabridged ed. 83p. 1995. pap. 4.98 (*1-58339-006-5*, A6) Triangle Press.

— The Friends of Jesus. unabridged ed. 146p. 1996. pap. 5.95 (*1-58339-008-1*, A8) Triangle Press.

— The Hour Is Come. unabridged ed. 21p. 1990. pap. 1.50 (*1-58339-020-0*, A20) Triangle Press.

***Bouma, Ralph.** Judicial Conspiracy to Keep the Change. 1998. pap. 15.00 (*1-58339-162-2*) Triangle Press.

Bouma, Ralph. The Law of Reward or Consequences & Christ Our Surety. unabridged ed. 142p. 1997. pap. 5.95 (*1-58339-005-7*, A5) Triangle Press.

— Sermon on the Mount, Vol. 1. unabridged ed. 217p. 1991. pap. 8.60 (*1-58339-009-X*, A9) Triangle Press.

— Sermon on the Mount, Vol. 2. unabridged ed. 254p. 1993. pap. 8.60 (*1-58339-010-3*, A10) Triangle Press.

— The Sermon on the Mount, Vol. 3. unabridged ed. 248p. 1993. pap. 8.60 (*1-58339-011-1*, A11) Triangle Press.

— The Sermon on the Mount, Vol. 4. unabridged ed. 302p. 1994. pap. 8.60 (*1-58339-012-X*, A12) Triangle Press.

— The Sermon on the Mount, Vol. 5. unabridged ed. 250p. 1995. pap. 8.60 (*1-58339-013-8*, A13) Triangle Press.

— The Sermon on the Mount, Vol. 6. unabridged ed. 322p. 1995. pap. 8.60 (*1-58339-014-6*, A14) Triangle Press.

— Short Devotions. unabridged ed. 206p. 1990. pap. 6.95 (*1-58339-016-2*, A16) Triangle Press.

— Spiritual Wrestling. unabridged ed. 170p. 1989. pap. 6.95 (*1-58339-017-0*, A17) Triangle Press.

— Training & Nurturing Children. iv, 60p. 1995. pap. text 4.25 (*1-58339-002-2*) Triangle Press.

— When God's Plan in Marriage Is Broken. unabridged ed. 17p. 1990. pap. 1.50 (*1-58339-021-9*, A21) Triangle Press.

— Why Confusion Reigns. unabridged ed. (Illus.). 48p. 1996. pap. 4.00 (*1-58339-003-0*, A3) Triangle Press.

Bouman, F. Development of Ovule & Seed Coat Structure in Angiosperms. (International Bioscience Monographs: No. 6). 80p. 1978. 7.50 (*0-88065-067-2*) Scholarly Pubns.

Bouman, F. J. Small, Short & Unsecured: Informal Rural Finance in India. 160p. 1990. 14.95 (*0-19-562454-8*) OUP.

Bouman, H. J., tr. see Luther, Martin.

Bouman, Herbert, tr. see Schlink, Edmund.

Bouman, Herbert J., tr. see Luther, Martin.

Bouman, John. Essential Principles Of Macroeconomics. 136p. (C). 1994. text 23.80 (*0-536-58663-2*) Pearson Custom.

— Essential Principles of Microeconomics. 140p. (C). 1994. text 23.80 (*0-536-58664-0*) Pearson Custom.

Bouman, L. N. & Jongsma, H. J. Cardiac Rate & Rhythm. 1982. text 268.50 (*90-247-2626-3*) Kluwer Academic.

Bouman, Lane J., jt. auth. see Robillard, Walter G.

Bouman, Mark H. And There Was No One Left to Bury Them. 1999p. 1999. pap. 10.95 (*0-7392-0172-7*, PO3133) Morris Pubng.

Bouman, O. Thomas & Brand, David G., eds. Sustainable Forests: Global Challenges & Local Solutions. LC 95-52446. (Journal of Sustainable Forestry Ser.: Vols. 4 & 5). 392p. (C). 1996. 69.95 (*1-56022-055-4*); pap. text 29.95 (*1-56022-058-9*) Haworth Jrnl Co-Edits.

Bouman, Ole. Realspace in Quicktimes: Architecture & Digitization. 1996. pap. text 24.95 incl. cd-rom (*90-5662-017-7*, Pub. by NAi Uitgevers) Dist Art Pubs.

Bouman, Stephen P., et al. Re-Rooting in Our Communities: The Area Mission Strategy Process. 124p. 1998. spiral bd. 24.95 (*0-9661326-0-2*) Metrop NY Mission.

Bouman, Sylvia E., ed. see Hagopian, John V.

Bouman, Walter R. & Setzer, Sue M. What Shall I Say? Discerning God's Call to Ministry. 1998. pap. 6.95 (*0-9636630-1-1*) Evang Luth Church.

Boumans, P. W. Atomic Absorption Spectroscopy - Past, Present & Future: To Commemorate the 25th Anniversary of Alan Walsh's Landmark Paper in Spectrochimica Acta. 248p. 1981. pap. 39.00 (*0-08-026267-8*, Pergamon Pr) Elsevier.

— Inductively Coupled Plasma Emission Spectroscopy Part 1: Methodology Instrumentation & Performance. LC 86-18984. (Chemical Analysis Ser.). 608p. 1987. 210.00 (*0-471-09686-5*) Wiley.

— Inductively Coupled Plasma Emission Spectroscopy Part 2: Applications & Fundamentals, Vol. 2. (Chemical Analysis Ser.). 504p. 1987. 210.00 (*0-471-85378-X*) Wiley.

Boumans, P. W., ed. Analytical Spectroscopy: A Polychrome Branch of Science: Proceedings of the 23rd Colloquium International, including the 10th International Conference on Atomic Spectroscopy, Amsterdam, 26 June-1 July 1983. 1984th ed. 224p. 1984. pap. 61.00 (*0-08-031403-1*, Pergamon Pr) Elsevier.

— Atomic Absorption Spectroscopy Pt. 2: Past - Present & Future: To Commemorate the 25th Anniversary of Alan Walsh's Landmark Paper in Spectrochimica Acta. (Spectrochimica Acta B Ser.: Vol. 36, No. 5). iv, 92p. 1981. pap. 19.25 (*0-08-026287-2*, Pergamon Pr) Elsevier.

— Plasma Spectrochemistry: Proceedings of the 1985 European Winter Conference on Plasma Spectrochemistry, 7-11 January 1985, Leysin, Switzerland. 1986. pap. 64.00 (*0-08-033925-5*, Pub. by PPL) Elsevier.

Boumans, P. W., et al, eds. A Profile of Current Developments in Atomic Spectroscopy: Dedicated to Kurt Laqua on the Occasion of His 65th Birthday. 400p. 1985. pap. 91.00 (*0-08-031447-3*, Pergamon Pr) Elsevier.

Boumans, Paul W. Theory of Spectrochemical Excitation. LC 66-27686. 394p. reprint ed. pap. 122.20 (*0-608-13246-2*, 205579100038) Bks Demand.

***Boumbouras, Mary.** A Second Chance. deluxe large type ed. (Illus.). 112p. 1999. 31.00 (*1-887774-06-8*) Canmore Pr.

Boumelha, Penny. Charlotte Bronte. (Key Women Writers Ser.). 166p. 1990. pap. 5.25 (*0-253-25455-8*) Ind U Pr.

Boumelha, Penny & Hardy, Thomas. Jude the Obscure: Thomas Hardy. LC 99-15876. 2000. text 49.95 (*0-312-22701-9*) St Martin.

Boumil, Marcia M. Law, Ethics & Reproductive Choice. LC 94-15353. xii, 137p. 1994. pap. 35.00 (*0-8377-0365-4*, Rothman) W S Hein.

— Law, Ethics & Reproductive Choice: An Anthology of Modern American Legal Humor. xix, 165p. 1989. pap. text 27.50 (*0-8377-0356-5*, Rothman) W S Hein.

Boumil, Marcia M. & Elias, Clifford E. The Law of Medical Liability in a Nutshell. LC 95-35002. (Nutshell Ser.). 266p. (C). 1995. pap. 21.00 (*0-314-06660-8*) West Pub.

Boumil, Marcia M. & Friedman, Joel. Dead-Beat Dads: A National Child Support Scandal. LC 95-34410. 168p. 1996. 35.00 (*0-275-95125-1*, Praeger Pubs) Greenwood.

Boumil, Marcia M. & Hicks, Stephen C. Women & the Law. LC 92-9675. xv, 642p. 1992. 65.00 (*0-8377-0360-3*, Rothman) W S Hein.

Boumil, Marcia M., et al. Law & the Gender Bias. LC 93-27891. xii, 248p. 1995. pap. 37.50 (*0-8377-0363-8*, Rothman) W S Hein.

Boumil, Marcia M., jt. auth. see Friedman, Joel.

Boumphrey, Frank. Professional Style Sheets with HTML & XML. 500p. 1998. pap. 39.99 (*1-86100-165-7*, Pub. by Wrox Press) Wrox Pr Inc.

Boumphrey, Frank, jt. auth. see Wrox Press Inc., Staff.

Bound. Lost Ships. 192p. 1998. 30.00 (*0-684-85077-X*) S&S Trade.

Bound, David, et al. Teaching in Laboratories. LC 86-1443. 208p. 1986. pap. 29.95 (*0-85059-109-0*) OpUniv Pr.

Bound, Mensun. Lost Ships: The Discovery & Exploration of the Ocean's Sunken Treasures. LC 98-36551. (Illus.). 192p. 1998. 35.00 (*0-684-85251-9*, S&S Edns) Simon & Schuster.

Boundas, Constantin V. & Olkowski, Dorothea, eds. Gilles Deleuze & the Theater of Philosophy: Critical Essays. 352p. (C). 1994. pap. 20.99 (*0-415-90505-2*, A6457) Routledge.

Boundas, Constantin V., ed. see Deleuze, Gilles.

Bounds. Introduction to Business. (GB - Basic Business Ser.). 1998. text, student ed. 18.95 (*0-538-86176-2*) S-W Pub.

— Introduction to Business. LC 97-16792. (GB - Basic Business Ser.). 1998. pap. 69.95 (*0-538-86174-6*) S-W Pub.

— Module 4: Money & Banking - Introduction to Business. (Gb - Basic Business Ser.). 1997. pap. 2.95 (*0-538-86183-5*) S-W Pub.

— Module 2: Small Business - Introduction to Business. (GB - Basic Business Ser.). 1997. pap. 2.95 (*0-538-86181-9*) S-W Pub.

***Bounds & Woods.** Supervision. 1999. pap. 62.95 (*968-7529-45-8*) Thomson Learn.

Bounds, jt. auth. see Hecht.

Bounds, Clyde H. Black River Bolly. LC 89-91943. (Illus.). 150p. 1990. 14.95 (*0-9624389-0-1*) C H Bounds.

Bounds, E. M. The Best of E. M. Bounds on Prayer. (Best Ser.). 234p. (YA). (gr. 10). 1986. pap. 10.99 (*0-8010-0935-9*) Baker Bks.

— The Complete Works of E. M. Bounds on Prayer. 576p. (gr. 10). 1990. pap. 12.99 (*0-8010-0985-5*) Baker Bks.

— E. M. Bounds on Prayer. LC 97-3207. 622p. (Orig.). 1997. pap. 17.99 (*0-88368-416-0*) Whitaker Hse.

— The Essentials of Prayer. 165p. 1994. mass mkt. 5.99 (*0-88368-309-1*) Whitaker Hse.

— Inside Heaven's Gates. LC 99-24258. Orig. Title: Catching a Glimpse of Heaven. 140p. 1999. pap. 6.99 (*0-88368-569-8*) Whitaker Hse.

— The Necessity of Prayer. 143p. 1984. mass mkt. 5.99 (*0-88368-139-0*) Whitaker Hse.

— Obtaining Answers to Prayer. 140p. 1984. mass mkt. 5.99 (*0-88368-142-0*) Whitaker Hse.

— Possibilities of Prayer. 175p. 1994. mass mkt. 5.99 (*0-88368-315-6*) Whitaker Hse.

— Power Through Prayer. (E. M. Bounds Classics on Prayer Ser.). 96p. (gr. 10). 1992. pap. 6.99 (*0-8010-1013-6*) Baker Bks.

— Power Through Prayer. (Classics Ser.). mass mkt. 4.99 (*0-8024-6729-6*, 393) Moody.

— Power Through Prayer. 105p. 1983. mass mkt. 5.99 (*0-88368-117-X*) Whitaker Hse.

— Prayer & Praying Men. (E. M. Bounds Classics on Prayer Ser.). 160p. (gr. 10). 1992. pap. 6.99 (*0-8010-1006-3*) Baker Bks.

***Bounds, E. M.** Praying That Receives Answers. Orig. Title: Obtaining Answers to Prayer. 140p. 1999. mass mkt. 6.99 (*0-88368-594-9*) Whitaker Hse.

Bounds, E. M. Purpose in Prayer. 189p. 1997. mass mkt. 5.99 (*0-88368-438-1*) Whitaker Hse.

— The Reality of Prayer. (E. M. Bounds Classics on Prayer Ser.). 120p. (gr. 10). 1992. pap. 6.99 (*0-8010-1012-8*, Hour Glass) Baker Bks.

— The Resurrection: The Ineffable Glory. LC 96-79956. 142p. 1997. reprint ed. 12.95 (*1-886787-03-4*) Messengers Hope.

— A Treasury of Prayer. LC 53-9865. 192p. 1961. pap. 8.99 (*0-87123-543-9*) Bethany Hse.

— The Weapon of Prayer. 190p. 1996. mass mkt. 5.99 (*0-88368-457-8*) Whitaker Hse.

— The Weapon of Prayer. rev. ed. (E. M. Bounds Classics on Prayer Ser.). 120p. (gr. 10). 1991. pap. 6.99 (*0-8010-1004-7*) Baker Bks.

— Winning the Invisible War. 153p. 1984. mass mkt. 5.99 (*0-88368-145-5*) Whitaker Hse.

Bounds, Edward M. Heaven: A Place, a City, a Home. LC 91-61488. 151p. 1991. reprint ed. 10.95 (*0-9605642-3-3*) Messengers Hope.

***Bounds, Edward M.** Thy Will Be Done. LC 00-8799. 2000. pap. write for info. (*0-88368-449-7*) Whitaker Hse.

Bounds, Elizabeth. Coming Together/Coming Apart: Religion, Community, & Modernity. LC 95-26368. 200p. (C). 1997. 75.00 (*0-415-91261-X*); pap. 23.99 (*0-415-91262-8*) Routledge.

Bounds, Elizabeth M., et al, eds. Welfare Policy: Feminist Critiques. LC 98-53434. (Pilgrim Library of Ethics). 224p. 1999. pap. 21.95 (*0-8298-1305-5*) Pilgrim OH.

Bounds, Greg. Beyond Total Quality Management: Toward the Emerging Paradigm. LC 93-38388. 832p. (C). 1994. 80.31 (*0-07-006678-7*) McGraw.

Bounds, Greg & Woods, John. Supervision: Improving Processes for Customer Value. LC 97-27951. (GZ - Supervision Ser.). 448p. 1997. pap. 67.95 (*0-538-85942-3*) Thomson Learn.

Bounds, Gregory M. Cases in Quality. LC 94-49390. 672p. (C). 1995. text 32.75 (*0-256-18227-2*, Irwn McGrw-H) McGrw-H Hghr Educ.

Bounds, Gregory M., et al. Management: A Total Quality Perspective. LC 94-33898. (C). 1994. mass mkt. 87.95 (*0-538-84344-6*) S-W Pub.

Bounds, Gregory M., jt. ed. see Stahl, Michael J.

Bounds, J. Dennis. Perry Mason: The Authorship & Reproduction of a Popular Hero. LC 96-5458. (Contributions to the Study of Popular Culture Ser.: Vol. 56). 240p. 1996. 59.95 (*0-313-29809-2*, Greenwood Pr) Greenwood.

***Bounds, Laura, et al.** Health & Fitness: A Guide to a Healthy Lifestyle. 192p. (C). 1999. pap. text 19.95 (*0-7872-6221-8*) Kendall-Hunt.

Bounds, Marjorie, jt. auth. see Aylin, Elizabeth.

Bounds, Wayne. Good News for Mankind. (Orig.). 1996. pap. 6.95 (*1-56794-107-9*, C-2423) Star Bible.

Boundy, Charles. A Concise Business Guide to Contract Law. LC 97-6794. 250p. 1998. pap. 34.95 (*0-566-07921-6*, Pub. by Gower) Ashgate Pub Co.

Boundy, Donna, jt. auth. see Washton, Arnold M.

Boundy, Kathleen B., jt. auth. see Ordover, Eileen L.

Boundy, Ray H. & Lawrence, J., eds. A History of the Dow Chemical Physics Lab: The Freedom to Be Creative. 264p. 1990. text 150.00 (*0-8247-8097-3*) Dekker.

Bounegru, Octavian & Zahariade, Mihail. Les Forces Navales du Bas Danube et de la Mer Noire aux 1er-6eme Siecles. (Colloquia Pontica Ser.: No. 2). (FRE., Illus.). 135p. 1996. pap. 33.00 (*1-900188-17-1*, Pub. by Oxbow Bks) David Brown.

Bounel. Welfare Economics & The Theory of State. 224p. 1993. 61.95 (*0-7512-0107-3*) Ashgate Pub Co.

Bounford, Trevor. Diagrams & Charts. (On the Spot Guides Ser.). (Illus.). 96p. 1994. 7.95 (*1-56970-502-X*) Bks Nippan.

***Bounford, Trevor.** Digital Diagrams: How to Design & Present Statistical Information Effectively. (Illus.). 192p. 2000. pap. 29.95 (*0-8230-1572-6*) Watsn-Guptill.

Bounhoure, J. P. & Magrassi, P., eds. Ibopamine in the Management of Congestive Heart Failure: Journal: Cardiology, Vol. 77, Suppl. 5, 1990. (Illus.). vi, 96p. 1990. pap. 30.50 (*3-8055-5309-9*) S Karger.

Bounia, jt. auth. see Pearce.

Bounin. La Soltane. Heath, ed. (Exeter French Texts Ser.: Vol. 27). (FRE.). 115p. Date not set. pap. text 19.95 (*0-85989-097-X*, Pub. by Univ Exeter Pr) Northwestern U Pr.

Bounking, Vikham, tr. see Burns Knight, Margy.

Bounoua, Lahouari, jt. auth. see Krishnamurti, T. N.

Bounous, Denise I., jt. auth. see Eades, Susan C.

Bounous, Gustavo, ed. Uses of Elemental Diets in Clinical Situations. LC 87-24283. 352p. 1992. 235.00 (*0-8493-6680-1*, RM229, CRC Reprint) Franklin.

***Bounous, Gustavo & Somersall, Allan.** Breakthrough in Cell-Defense: How to Benefit from the Real Glutathione Revolution. 260p. 1999. pap. 14.95 (*1-890412-86-4*) Glden Eight Intl.

Bountis, T. Chaotic Dynamics: Theory & Practice. LC 92-21986. (NATO ASI Series B, Physics: Vol. 298). (Illus.). 430p. (C). 1992. 129.50 (*0-306-44247-7*, Plenum Trade) Perseus Pubng.

— Proton Transfer in Hydrogen-Bonded Systems. (NATO ASI Ser.: Vol. 291). (Illus.). 379p. (C). 1992. text 120.00 (*0-306-44216-7*, Kluwer Plenum) Kluwer Academic.

Bounty, Blanca A. La, see Rice, Dona & La Bounty, Blanca A.

Bounyavong, Othine, et al. Mother's Beloved: Stories from Laos. LC 98-17631. 198p. 1998. pap. 14.95 (*0-295-97736-1*) U of Wash Pr.

Bouquard, Thomas J. Arson Investigation: The Step-by-Step Procedure. 132p. 1983. 30.95 (*0-398-04839-8*); pap. 20.95 (*0-398-06025-8*) C C Thomas.

Bouquerel, Catherine. Laine & Lin. (FRE., Illus.). 104p. 1998. 36.00 (*2-84229-048-8*, DE17, Pub. by C Armand) Lacis Pubns.

Bouquet, Alan C. Religious Experience: Its Nature, Types, & Validity. LC 75-40997. 140p. 1976. reprint ed. lib. bdg. 59.50 (*0-8371-8714-1*, BORL, Greenwood Pr) Greenwood.

Bouquet, Betty J. B. J.'s Joke Book. (Illus.). 74p. (Orig.). 1989. pap. 9.95 (*0-937041-81-5*) Systems Co.

— Fine Chefs of the Southwest Cookbook. (Illus.). 95p. (Orig.). 1989. 25.00 (*0-937041-68-8*); pap. 18.00 (*0-937041-69-6*) Systems Co.

Bouquet-Boyer, Marie-Therese & Bonniffet, Pierre, eds. Claude Le Jeune et Son Temps en France et dans les Etats de Savoie (1530-1600) Musique et Litterature Actes du Colloque International de Chambery (4-7.11.1991) Organise par l'Universite de Savoie, le Centre d'Etudes Franco-Italiennes des Universites de Savoie et de Turin et l'Institut de Recherches et d'Histoire Musicale des Etats de Savoie. (FRE.). 500p. 1996. 60.95 (*3-906754-42-1*, Pub. by P Lang) P Lang Pubng.

Bouquet, F. L. Engineering Properties of Teflon (FEP & PFA), Vol. 2. (Illus.). 150p. 1989. 79.00 (*0-937041-66-1*); pap. 49.00 (*0-937041-67-X*) Systems Co.

— Lake Havasu Cookbook. (Illus.). 120p. (Orig.). 1990. 25.00 (*0-937041-78-5*); pap. 18.00 (*0-937041-79-3*) Systems Co.

— Radiation Damage in Materials. 3rd ed. (Illus.). 170p. 1990. 70.00 (*0-937041-74-2*); pap. 40.00 (*0-937041-75-0*) Systems Co.

— Radiation Effects on Electronics. 3rd ed. (Illus.). 70p. 1989. 55.00 (*0-937041-76-9*); pap. 35.00 (*0-937041-77-7*) Systems Co.

Bouquet, Frank L. Chefs of the Southwest Cookbook. rev. ed. (Illus.). 115p. 1989. 25.00 (*0-937041-64-5*); pap. 18.00 (*0-937041-65-3*) Systems Co.

— Do-It-Yourself Mutual Funds, 1994. 6th ed. (Illus.). 100p. 1994. 59.00 (*1-56216-114-8*); pap. 29.00 (*1-56216-115-6*) Systems Co.

— Do-It-Yourself-Stocks. (Illus.). 101p. (Orig.). 1989. 50.00 (*0-937041-42-4*); pap. 20.00 (*0-937041-43-2*) Systems Co.

— Do-It-Yourself Stocks. 4th ed. (Illus.). 120p. 1994. 59.00 (*1-56216-207-1*); pap. 29.00 (*1-56216-208-X*) Systems Co.

— Engineering Properties of Kapton. 2nd ed. (Illus.). 160p. 1993. 110.00 (*1-56216-164-4*); pap. 80.00 (*1-56216-165-2*) Systems Co.

— Engineering Properties of Teflon, Vol. I (PTFE) (Illus.). 175p. (Orig.). (C). 1989. 79.00 (*0-937041-57-2*) Systems Co.

— Engineering Properties of Teflon Vol. 1: Teflon PTFE. 2nd ed. (Illus.). 160p. 1993. 100.00 (*1-56216-166-0*); pap. 70.00 (*1-56216-167-9*) Systems Co.

— Engineering Properties of Teflon Vol. 2: Teflon PFA & FEP. 2nd ed. (Illus.). 180p. 1993. 100.00 (*1-56216-168-7*); pap. 70.00 (*1-56216-169-5*) Systems Co.

— Engineering Properties of Teflon (TFE, Vol. I (PTFE), Vol. I (TFE) (Illus.). 175p. (Orig.). (C). 1989. pap. 49.00 (*0-937041-58-0*) Systems Co.

— Engineer's Guide to Autos. (Illus.). 100p. (Orig.). 1994. 59.00 (*1-56216-170-9*); pap. 29.00 (*1-56216-171-7*) Systems Co.

— Exoatmospheric & Space Travel. (Illus.). 140p. (Orig.). 1994. 100.00 (*1-56216-172-5*); pap. 70.00 (*1-56216-200-4*) Systems Co.

— Introduction to Electronic Radiation Effects. (Illus.). 76p. (Orig.). 1994. 75.00 (*1-56216-203-9*); pap. 45.00 (*1-56216-204-7*) Systems Co.

— Introduction to Materials Engineering. 3rd ed. (Illus.). 125p. (Orig.). 1990. 70.00 (*0-937041-72-6*); pap. 40.00 (*0-937041-73-4*) Systems Co.

— Introduction to Materials Engineering. 4th ed. LC 94-25491. (Illus.). 150p. (Orig.). 1994. 99.00 (*1-56216-118-0*); pap. 69.00 (*1-56216-119-9*) Systems Co.

— Introduction to Seals & Gaskets Engineering. (Illus.). 116p. 1988. 70.00 (*0-937041-30-0*); pap. 40.00 (*0-937041-31-9*) Systems Co.

— Introduction to Seals & Gaskets Engineering. 2nd ed. (Illus.). 130p. 1993. 99.00 (*1-56216-106-7*); pap. 69.00 (*1-56216-107-5*) Systems Co.

— Nuclear Energy Simplified. 2nd ed. (Illus.). 137p. 1994. 75.00 (*1-56216-219-5*); pap. 45.00 (*1-56216-220-9*) Systems Co.

— Nuclear Energy Simplified: An Overview of the Nuclear Technology of Reactors, Space & Medicine. (Illus.). 130p. (Orig.). 1992. pap. 40.00 (*1-56216-074-5*); text 70.00 (*1-56216-073-7*) Systems Co.

— Paints & Coatings for Space. (Illus.). 150p. (Orig.). 1993. 100.00 (*1-56216-173-3*); pap. 70.00 (*1-56216-174-1*) Systems Co.

— Paints & Coatings for Space. 2nd ed. (Illus.). 160p. (Orig.). 1994. 110.00 (*1-56216-217-9*); pap. 80.00 (*1-56216-218-7*) Systems Co.

— Practical Guide to Autos: Operation, Safety & Maintenance. (Illus.). 100p. (C). 1991. 45.00 (*1-56216-050-8*); pap. 25.00 (*1-56216-051-6*) Systems Co.

— Practical Guide to Autos - 1992. 2nd ed. (Illus.). 150p. (Orig.). 1992. pap. 30.00 (*1-56216-103-2*); text 50.00 (*1-56216-102-4*) Systems Co.

— Radiation Damage in Materials. 4th ed. (Illus.). 180p. 1994. 99.00 (*1-56216-155-5*); pap. 69.00 (*1-56216-156-3*) Systems Co.

— Radiation Effects on Electronics. 4th ed. (Illus.). 85p. 1994. text 75.00 (*1-56216-055-9*); pap. text 45.00 (*1-56216-056-7*) Systems Co.

— Radiation Effects on Kapton. 2nd ed. (Illus.). 100p. 1993. 90.00 (*1-56216-162-8*); pap. 60.00 (*1-56216-163-6*) Systems Co.

— Radiation Effects on KaptonR. (Illus.). 90p. (Orig.). (C). 1990. text 75.00 (*0-937041-86-6*); pap. text 45.00 (*0-937041-87-4*) Systems Co.

— Radiation Effects on Nonelectronic Materials. (Illus.). 361p. (Orig.). 1994. 110.00 (*1-56216-201-2*); pap. 80.00 (*1-56216-202-0*) Systems Co.

— Radiation Effects on Teflon. (Illus.). 190p. (Orig.). 1989. text 79.00 (*0-937041-60-2*); pap. text 49.00 (*0-937041-61-0*) Systems Co.

— Radiation Effects on Teflon. 2nd ed. (Illus.). 180p. (Orig.). 1993. 89.00 (*1-56216-151-2*); pap. 59.00 (*1-56216-152-0*) Systems Co.

— Solar Energy-Simplified. 3rd ed. (Illus.). 125p. 1989. 49.00 (*0-937041-54-8*); text 30.00 (*0-937041-55-6*) Systems Co.

— Solar Energy Simplified. 4th ed. (Illus.). 130p. 1991. text 52.00 (*1-56216-053-2*); pap. text 32.00 (*1-56216-054-0*) Systems Co.

— Solar Energy Simplified. 5th ed. (Illus.). 155p. 1994. 70.00 (*1-56216-122-9*); pap. 40.00 (*1-56216-123-7*) Systems Co.

— Solar Energy Technology 1991. (Illus.). 125p. (Orig.). (C). 1991. text 59.00 (*1-56216-023-0*); pap. text 29.00 (*1-56216-024-9*) Systems Co.

— Solar Energy Technology, 1992. 2nd ed. (Illus.). 150p. 1992. pap. 32.00 (*1-56216-105-9*); text 62.00 (*1-56216-104-0*) Systems Co.

— Spacecraft Design - Thermal & Radiation. (Illus.). 225p. (Orig.). (C). 1991. 89.00 (*1-56216-011-7*); pap. 60.00 (*1-56216-012-5*) Systems Co.

— Spacecraft Design - Thermal & Radiation. 2nd ed. (Illus.). 230p. (Orig.). 1993. 95.00 (*1-56216-124-5*); pap. 65.00 (*1-56216-150-4*) Systems Co.

— Starting Your Business, Vol. 1: Planning & Organization, Vol. 1. (Illus.). 125p. 1992. 35.00 (*1-56216-008-7*); pap. 25.00 (*1-56216-064-8*) Systems Co.

— Starting Your Business, Vol. 2: Operating Techniques & Pitfalls Procedures, Vol. 2. (Illus.). 125p. (C). 1992. 35.00 (*1-56216-052-4*); pap. 25.00 (*1-56216-065-6*) Systems Co.

— Strengthened Glass Technology. (Illus.). 60p. (Orig.). 1991. 79.00 (*1-56216-009-5*) Systems Co.

— Strengthened Glass Technology. abr. ed. (Illus.). 60p. (Orig.). 1991. pap. 49.00 (*1-56216-010-9*) Systems Co.

— Strengthened Glass Technology for Solar Applications. (Illus.). 65p. (C). 1991. 69.00 (*1-56216-021-4*); pap. 39.00 (*1-56216-022-2*) Systems Co.

— Successful Decision-Making. LC 94-10608. (Illus.). 50p. (Orig.). 1994. 29.00 (*1-56216-112-1*); pap. 17.00 (*1-56216-113-X*) Systems Co.

Bouquet, Frank L., ed. & illus. see Stocker, Hugh G.

Bouquet, Jeff S. Young Man's Guide to Autos. 2nd ed. 100p. (Orig.). 1992. pap. 29.00 (*1-56216-111-3*); text 59.00 (*1-56216-110-5*) Systems Co.

— Young Man's Guide to Autos: Basics, Operation, Safety & Maintenance. (Illus.). 80p. (YA). 1991. 55.00 (*1-56216-017-6*); pap. 25.00 (*1-56216-018-4*) Systems Co.

***Bouquet, P., et al, eds.** Modeling & Using Context: Proceedings, 2nd International & Interdisciplinary Conference, CONTEXT'99, Trento, Italy, September 9-11, 1999. LC 99-44750. (Lecture Notes in Artificial Intelligence Ser.: Vol. 1688). xii, 528p. 1999. pap. 79.00 (*3-540-66432-7*) Spr-Verlag.

Bouquet, Simon. Simon Bouquet's Imitations et Traduction de Cent Dix-Huit Emblemes d'Alciat. LC 89-45848. (Studies in the Emblem: No. 5). 1993. 63.00 (*0-404-63705-1*) AMS Pr.

Bouquet, Tim A. Bicycling with Safety. (Illus.). 100p. 1992. pap. 23.00 (*1-56216-067-2*); text 40.00 (*1-56216-066-4*) Systems Co.

— Worldwide Bicycling with Safety. (Illus.). 80p. (Orig.). 1991. pap. 30.00 (*1-56216-007-9*); text 50.00 (*1-56216-006-0*) Systems Co.

Bouquiaux, Luc & Thomas, Jacqueline M. Studying & Describing Unwritten Languages. Roberts, James, tr. LC 92-80686. xii, 728p. 1992. pap. 50.00 (*0-88312-814-4*) S I L Intl.

Bouquiaux, Luc, et al. Dictionnaire Sango. (FRE.). 1978. 125.00 (*0-7859-8076-8*, 2-85297-016-3) Fr & Eur.

Bouquillon, A. Ceramic Heritage. (Illus.). 82p. (C). 1997. text 48.00 (*0-87849-765-X*, Pub. by Trans T Pub) Enfield Pubs NH.

Bour-Chollet, Celine, jt. auth. see Verdet, Andre.

Bour, Daniele. The House from Morning to Night (La Maison du Matin au Soir) (Illus.). 14p. (J). (ps-k). 1998. pap. 7.95 (*0-916291-85-5*) Kane-Miller Bk.

Bour, Laura. Bears. (First Discovery Book). (Illus.). 24p. (J). (ps-3). 1992. 10.95 (*0-590-45270-3*, 038, Cartwheel) Scholastic Inc.

— Whales. LC 92-41413. (First Discovery Book). (Illus.). 24p. (J). (ps-3). 1993. 11.95 (*0-590-47130-9*, Cartwheel) Scholastic Inc.

Bour, Laura, ed. The River. LC 92-41415. (First Discovery Book). (J). 1993. 11.95 (*0-590-47128-7*) Scholastic Inc.

Bourachot, Henri. Dictionnaire des Sciences Economiques et Sociales. (FRE.). 192p. 1992. pap. 24.95 (*0-7859-7710-4*, 2040193030) Fr & Eur.

Bourantonis, Dimitris. The United Nations & the Quest for Nuclear Disarmament. 218p. 1993. 72.95 (*1-85521-344-3*, Pub. by Dartmth Pub) Ashgate Pub Co.

Bourantonis, Dimitris & Evriviades, Marios L. A United Nations for the Twenty-First Century: Peace, Security & Development. LC 96-48835. 1997. 235.00 (*90-411-0312-0*) Kluwer Law Intl.

Bourantonis, Dimitris & Wiener, Jarrod, eds. United Nations in New World Order: The World Organization at Fifty. 230p. 1996. pap. 21.95 (*0-312-16118-2*) St Martin.

Bouraoui, Nina. Forbidden Vision. 1998. pap. 9.95 (*1-886449-69-4*, Pub. by Barrytown Ltd) Consort Bk Sales.

***Bouras, Gillian.** Saving Christmas. 2000. pap. 13.95 (*0-7022-3135-5*, Pub. by Univ Queensland Pr) Intl Spec Bk.

Bouras, Harry, intro. Nathan Lerner: 50 Years of Photographic Inquiry. (Illus.). 48p. 1984. 15.00 (*0-932026-14-1*) Columbia College Chi.

Bouras, Nick, ed. Psychiatric & Behavioural Disorders in Developmental Disabilities & Mental Retardation. LC 98-38465. (Illus.). 480p. (C). 1999. pap. text 59.95 (*0-521-64395-3*) Cambridge U Pr.

Bourassa, Andre G. Surrealism & Quebec Literature: History of a Cultural Revolution. Czarnecki, Mark, tr. LC 84-238283. (University of Toronto Romance Ser.: No. 50). 409p. reprint ed. pap. 126.80 (*0-7837-1229-4*, 204136600020) Bks Demand.

Bourassa, Arthur W. The Mafia Puppets. 1994. 16.95 (*0-533-10720-2*) Vantage.

Bourassa, Hester, ed. see Partridge, Penny M.

Bourassa, Robert. James Bay. LC 74-169569. (Regional Canadian Ser.). 124p. reprint ed. pap. 38.50 (*0-608-13492-9*, 202228600026) Bks Demand.

Bourassa, Steven C. The Aesthetics of Landscape. (Illus.). 186p. 1992. text 55.00 (*1-85293-071-3*) St Martin.

Bourbaki, N. Algebra II: Chapters Four-Seven. 460p. 1990. 149.95 (*0-387-19375-8*) Spr-Verlag.

— Algebra One: Chapters 1-3. 736p. 1989. 79.00 (*0-387-19373-1*) Spr-Verlag.

— Commutative Algebra: Chapters 1-7. 655p. 1989. 79.00 (*0-387-19371-5*) Spr-Verlag.

— Elements of Mathematics: Algebra 1. xxiv, 710p. 1998. pap. 49.95 (*3-540-64243-9*) Spr-Verlag.

— Elements of Mathematics: Topological Vector Spaces. vii, 365p. 1987. 153.95 (*0-387-13627-4*) Spr-Verlag.

— Elements of Mathematics Chapters 1-3: Lie Groups & Lie Algebras. (Illus.). xviii, 462p. 1998. pap. 49.95 (*3-540-64242-0*) Spr-Verlag.

— Elements of Mathematics Chapters 1-4: General Topology. viii, 438p. 1998. pap. 49.95 (*3-540-64241-2*) Spr-Verlag.

— Elements of Mathematics Chapters 1-7: Commutative Algebra. xxiv, 626p. 1998. pap. 49.95 (*3-540-64239-0*) Spr-Verlag.

— Elements of Mathematics Chapters 5-10: General Topology. iv, 363p. 1998. pap. 49.95 (*3-540-64563-2*) Spr-Verlag.

— Elements of the History of Mathematics. (Illus.). 305p. 1994. 62.95 (*0-387-19376-6*) Spr-Verlag.

— Functions of a Real Variable. 1982. text. write for info. (*0-201-00640-5*) Addison-Wesley.

— General Topology Chapt. 1-4. 450p. 1989. 79.00 (*0-387-19374-X*) Spr-Verlag.

— General Topology Chapt. 5-10. 368p. 1989. 102.95 (*0-387-19372-3*) Spr-Verlag.

— Lie Groups & Lie Algebras, Chapters 1-3. 470p. 1989. 111.95 (*0-387-50218-1*) Spr-Verlag.

Bourbaki, Nicolas. Elements of the History of Mathematics. LC 98-39221. viii, 301p. 1994. write for info. (*3-540-19376-6*) Spr-Verlag.

— Elements of the History of Mathematics. LC 98-39221. 309p. 1999. pap. 54.95 (*3-540-64767-8*) Spr-Verlag.

Bourbakis, N. G. Artificial Intelligence Methods & Applications. (Advanced Series on Artificial Intelligence). 732p. 1992. text 116.00 (*981-02-1057-4*) World Scientific Pub.

— Knowledge-Engineering Shells: Systems & Techniques. (Advanced Series on Artificial Intelligence). 500p. 1993. text 109.00 (*981-02-1056-6*) World Scientific Pub.

Bourbakis, N. G., ed. Applications of Learning & Planning Methods. (Series in Computer Science: Vol. 26). 392p. (C). 1991. text 101.00 (*981-02-0546-5*) World Scientific Pub.

Bourbakis, Nikolaos G., ed. Artificial Intelligence & Automation. LC 98-199776. 550p. 1997. lib. bdg. 59.00 (*981-02-2637-3*) World Scientific Pub.

***Bourbeau, Lise.** Listen to Your Body: Your Best Friend on Earth, 1. 3rd ed. 1999. pap. text 16.95 (*2-920932-02-0*) E T C.

Bourbeau, Philippe. Lexique des Sciences Biologiques. (ENG & FRE.). 650p. 1996. 110.00 (*0-320-00028-1*) Fr & Eur.

Bourbie, Thierry, et al. Acoustics of Porous Media. (Illus.). 352p. (C). 1987. 162.00 (*2-7108-0516-2*, Pub. by Ashgate Pub Co) Enfield Pubs NH.

Bourbon. Tresor's Literaries. 160p. 1999. pap. 22.19 (*0-07-290415-1*) McGraw.

Bourbon, Anne-Marie, tr. see Labe, Louise.

Bourbon, Fabio. Egypt: Yesterday & Today. LC 96-69814. (Illus.). 272p. 1996. 60.00 (*1-55670-518-2*) Stewart Tabori & Chang.

***Bourbon, Fabio.** The Lost Cities of the Mayas: The Life, Art & Discoveries of Frederick Catherwood. LC 99-38982. (Illus.). 200p. (J). 2000. 35.00 (*0-7892-0623-4*, Abbeville Kids) Abbeville Pr.

Bourbon, Jacques R. Pulmonary Surfactant: Biochemical, Functional, Regulatory, & Clinical Concepts. (Illus.). 448p. 1991. boxed set 271.95 (*0-8493-6924-X*, QP752) CRC Pr.

Bourbon, Wendy. Teach Yourself Beginner's French. (Teach Yourself Beginner's Grammar Ser.). 224p. 1999. pap. 10.95 (*0-8442-2688-2*, Teach Yrslf) NTC Contemp Pub Co.

Bourchier, David. Dynamics of Dissent in Indonesia: Sawito & the Phantom Coup. LC 84-227917. (Interim Reports Ser.). 140p. reprint ed. pap. 43.40 (*0-7837-2427-6*, 204257400005) Bks Demand.

Bourchier, J., tr. see Froissart, Jean.

Bourchier, John, tr. see Froissart, Jean.

Bourchier, John, tr. see Lee, S. L., ed.

Bourcier, Georges. An Introduction to the History of the English Language. 230p. 1981. pap. 30.00 (*0-85950-482-4*) Dufour.

Bourcier, Paul, ed. Dance & Society in France, Vol. 2, Part 1. 150p. 1992. pap. text 15.00 (*3-7186-5257-9*, Harwood Acad Pubs) Gordon & Breach.

Bourcier, Paul G. History in the Mapping: Four Centuries of Adirondack Cartography. (Illus.). (Orig.). 1986. pap. 6.95 (*0-910020-37-X*) Adirondack Mus.

***Bourdain, Anthony.** Bone in the Throat. 304p. 2000. pap. 13.95 (*1-58234-102-8*) Bloomsbury Pubg.

— Gone Bamboo. 304p. 2000. pap. 13.95 (*1-58234-103-6*) Bloomsbury Pubg.

— Kitchen Confidential: Adventures in the Culinary Underbelly. 282p. 2000. pap. 24.95 (*1-58234-082-X*) Bloomsbury Pubg.

Bourdain, G. S., tr. see Crespin, Regine.

Bourdais, Daniele, jt. auth. see Bougard, Marie-Therese.

Bourdarot, E., et al, eds. Dam Fracture & Damage: Proceedings of the International Workshop, Chambery, France, March 1994. (Illus.). 260p. (C). 1994. text 128.00 (*90-5410-369-8*, Pub. by A A Balkema) Ashgate Pub Co.

***Bourdarot, Gilles.** Well Testing: Interpretation Methods. 350p. 1999. 59.00 (*2-7108-0738-6*) PennWell Bks.

Bourdeau, John & Larsen, Sonja. Legal Research for Beginners. LC 96-39398. 272p. 1997. pap. 12.95 (*0-8120-9768-8*) Barron.

Bourdeau, Larry F. The Historic Archaeology of Cabo's Tavern (CA-BUT-712) xv, 395p. (C). 1986. reprint ed. pap. text 42.50 (*1-55567-018-0*) Coyote Press.

Bourdeau, Philippe. Methods for Assessing & Reducing Injury from Chemical Accidents. Green, Gareth M., ed. LC 89-30661. 330p. 1989. 450.00 (*0-471-92278-1*) Wiley.

Bourdeau, Philippe, et al, eds. Ecotoxicology & Climate: With Special Reference to Hot & Cold Climates (SCOPE 38) 412p. 1989. 450.00 (*0-471-91831-8*) Wiley.

— Short-Term Toxicity Tests for Non-Genotoxic Effects. LC 89-22693. (Scientific Committee on Problems of the Environment Ser.: No. 41). 386p. 1990. 475.00 (*0-471-92506-3*) Wiley.

Bourdeau, Philippe, jt. auth. see Stanners, David.

Bourdeau, Pierre-Yves & Roy, Claudine. Unemployment Insurance Act & Regulations. annot. ed. 700p. 1993. pap. 55.00 (*0-409-91938-1*, CN, MICHIE) LEXIS Pub.

Bourdeaux, Michael. Gorbachev, Glasnost & the Gospel. (Illus.). 226p. 1990. pap. 25.00 (*0-340-54193-8*, Pub. by Hodder & Stought Ltd) Lubrecht & Cramer.

Bourdeaux, Michael, ed. The Politics of Religion in Russia & the New States of Eurasia. 352p. 1995. pap. text 19.95 (*0-563-24357-0*) M E Sharpe.

Bourdelet, P. English for Diving: French/English/French. (ENG & FRE.). 1998. 39.95 (*0-320-00145-8*) Fr & Eur.

***Bourdet, Yves.** The Economics of Transition in Laos: From Socialism to ASEAN Integration. LC 99-87645. 192p. 2000. 75.00 (*1-85898-747-4*) E Elgar.

Bourdet, Yves. International Integration, Market Structure & Prices. 368p. 1988. lib. bdg. 57.50 (*0-415-00395-8*) Routledge.

Bourdier, Jean-Paul & Alsayyad, Nezar, eds. Dwellings, Settlements & Tradition: Cross-Cultural Perspectives. LC 89-34496. 548p. 1989. pap. 53.50 (*0-8191-7524-2*) U Pr of Amer.

Bourdier, Jean-Paul & Minh-ha, Trinh T. African Spaces: Designs for Living in Upper Volta. (Illus.). 275p. (C). 1985. 69.50 (*0-8419-0890-7*, Africana) Holmes & Meier.

— Drawn from African Dwellings. LC 95-35891. (Illus.). 320p. 1997. 59.95 (*0-253-33043-2*) Ind U Pr.

Bourdieu. Sociology in Question. 272p. 1993. pap. 22.95 (*0-8039-8338-7*) Sage.

Bourdieu, Pierre. Academic Discourse: Linguistic Misunderstanding & Professorial Power. LC 93-86459. viii, 136p. 1994. 45.00 (*0-8047-2333-8*) Stanford U Pr.

***Bourdieu, Pierre.** Acts of Resistance: Against the Tyranny of the Market. Nice, Richard, tr. from FRE. 108p. 1999. pap. 12.95 (*1-56584-523-4*, 800.233.4830, Pub. by New Press NY) Norton.

Bourdieu, Pierre. Distinction: A Social Critique of the Judgement of Taste. Nice, Richard, tr. from FRE. LC 84-491. (Illus.). 640p. 1987. pap. text 22.95 (*0-674-21277-0*) HUP.

— The Field of Cultural Production: Essays on Art & Literature. Johnson, Randal et al, eds. LC 92-33843. (European Perspectives Ser.). 322p. (C). 1994. pap. 19.00 (*0-231-08287-8*) Col U Pr.

— Free Exchange. Haacke, Hans & Johnson, Randal, trs. (Illus.). 150p. 1995. 35.00 (*0-8047-2495-4*); pap. 14.95 (*0-8047-2496-2*) Stanford U Pr.

— Homo Academicus. Collier, Peter, tr. from FRE. 370p. 1988. 47.50 (*0-8047-1466-5*); pap. 17.95 (*0-8047-1798-2*) Stanford U Pr.

— In Other Words: Essays Toward a Reflexive Sociology. Adamson, Matthew, tr. 230p. 1990. 37.50 (*0-8047-1557-2*); pap. 13.95 (*0-8047-1725-7*) Stanford U Pr.

— Language & Symbolic Power. Thompson, John B., ed. Raymond, Gino & Adamson, Mathew, trs. 302p. (C). 1991. 39.95 (*0-674-51040-2*) HUP.

— Language & Symbolic Power. Thompson, John B., ed. Adamson, Mathew, tr. 302p. (C). 1993. pap. 25.50 (*0-674-51041-0*) HUP.

— The Logic of Practice. Nice, Richard, tr. from FRE. LC 88-63435. 337p. 1990. 47.50 (*0-8047-1727-3*); pap. 16.95 (*0-8047-2011-8*) Stanford U Pr.

— On Television. Ferguson, Priscilla P., tr. from FRE. LC 97-40535. 112p. 1998. 18.95 (*1-56584-407-6*, Pub. by New Press NY) Norton.

***Bourdieu, Pierre.** On Television. Ferguson, Priscilla Parkhurst, tr. from FRE. 104p. 1999. pap. 12.95 (*1-56584-512-9*, Pub. by New Press NY) Norton.

Bourdieu, Pierre. Outline of a Theory of Practice. LC 76-11073. (Cambridge Studies in Social & Cultural Anthropology: No. 16). (Illus.). 224p. 1977. pap. text 21.95 (*0-521-29164-X*) Cambridge U Pr.

***Bourdieu, Pierre.** Pascalian Meditations. 2000. 49.50 (*0-8047-3331-7*); pap. 18.95 (*0-8047-3332-5*) Stanford U Pr.

Bourdieu, Pierre. Photography: A Middle-Brow Art. Whiteside, Shaun, tr. LC 89-62321. 230p. (Orig.). 1996. pap. 14.95 (*0-8047-2689-2*) Stanford U Pr.

— The Political Ontology of Martin Heidegger. Collier, Peter, tr. from FRE. LC 90-70309. 146p. 1991. 37.50 (*0-8047-1698-6*) Stanford U Pr.

— The Political Ontology of Martin Heidegger. 1996. pap. text 12.95 (*0-8047-2960-3*) Stanford U Pr.

— Practical Reason: On the Theory of Action. Johnson, Randal et al, trs. 162p. 1998. 14.95 (*0-8047-3363-5*); pap. 39.50 (*0-8047-3362-7*) Stanford U Pr.

— Reproduction in Education, Society & Culture. 2nd ed. (Theory, Culture & Society Ser.: Vol. 4). 256p. (C). 1990. text 49.95 (*0-8039-8319-0*); pap. text 22.00 (*0-8039-8320-4*) Sage.

— The Rules of Art: Genesis & Structure of the Literary Field. Emanuel, Susan, tr. from FRE. LC 94-74140. (Meridian: Crossing Aesthetics Ser.). 288p. 1995. 49.50 (*0-8047-2568-3*) Stanford U Pr.

— The Rules of Art: Genesis & Structure of the Literary Field. Emanuel, Susan, tr. LC 94-74140. (Meridian Ser.: Crossing Aesthetics). 288p. 1995. pap. 15.95 (*0-8047-2627-2*) Stanford Univ Committee on Linguistics.

— State Nobility: Elite Schools in the Field of Power. LC 89-51756. 1996. 55.00 (*0-8047-1778-8*) Stanford U Pr.

— State Nobility: Elite Schools in the Field of Power. 1998. pap. 24.95 (*0-8047-3346-5*) Stanford U Pr.

***Bourdieu, Pierre.** Weight of The World: Social Suffering in Contemporary Societies. 1999. pap. text 29.95 (*0-8047-3845-9*) Stanford U Pr.

— The Weight of the World: Social Suffering in Contemporary Society. 2000. 85.00 (*0-8047-3844-0*) Stanford U Pr.

Bourdieu, Pierre & Darbel, Alain. The Love of Art: European Art Museums & Their Public. Beattie, Caroline & Merriman, Nick, trs. from FRE. LC 90-70310. 190p. 1991. 35.00 (*0-8047-1558-0*) Stanford U Pr.

Bourdieu, Pierre & Passeron, Jean-Claude. The Inheritors: French Students & Their Relation to Culture with a New Epilogue, 1979. Nice, Richard, tr. from FRE. LC 78-31532. (Illus.). 1979. 18.00 (*0-226-06739-4*) U Ch Pr.

Bourdieu, Pierre & Wacquant, Loic. An Invitation to Reflexive Sociology. 348p. 1992. pap. 17.00 (*0-226-06741-6*) U Ch Pr.

— An Invitation to Reflexive Sociology. 348p. 1992. lib. bdg. 45.00 (*0-226-06740-8*) U Ch Pr.

Bourdieu, Pierre, et al. The Craft of Sociology: Epistemological Preliminaries. xvi, 271p. (C). 1991. pap. 27.95 (*3-11-011940-4*); lib. bdg. 62.90 (*3-11-013004-1*) De Gruyter.

— Photography: A Middle-Brow Art. Whiteside, Shaun, tr. from FRE. LC 89-62321. 288p. (Orig.). 1990. 35.00 (*0-8047-1760-5*) Stanford U Pr.

Bourdieu, Pierre J., et al, eds. Le Metier de Sociologue: Prealables Epistemologiques. 4th ed. (Textes de Sciences Sociales Ser.: No. 1). 1983. pap. 44.65 (*90-279-6964-7*) Mouton.

Bourdillon, T. F. Forest Trees of Travancore. (C). 1976. text 350.00 (*0-89771-563-2*, Pub. by Intl Bk Distr) St Mut.

Bourdillon, A. & Tan-Bourdillon, N. X. High Temperature Superconductors: Processing & Science. (Illus.). 288p. 1993. text 82.00 (*0-12-117680-0*) Acad Pr.

Bourdillon, F. W., ed. Cest Oaucasi & de Nicolete. LC 80-2241. (Illus.). reprint ed. 45.00 (*0-404-19036-7*) AMS Pr.

B

Bourdillon, Hilary. Women As Healers: The History of Women & Medicine. (Women in History Ser.). (Illus.). 48p. (C). 1989. pap. 13.95 (*0-521-31090-3*) Cambridge U Pr.

Bourdillon, Hilary, ed. History & Social Studies: Methodologies of Textbook Analysis. (European Meetings on Educational Research Ser.: Vol. 27). 208p. 1992. 70.00 (*90-265-1230-9*) Swets.

Bourdillon, J. F., et al. Spinal Manipulation. 5th ed. (Illus.). 381p. 1992. text 65.00 (*0-7506-0576-6*) Buttrwrth-Heinemann.

Bourdillon, T. F. Forest Trees of Travancore. 456p. 1995. pap. 1000.00 (*81-7089-237-6*, Pub. by Intl Bk Distr) St Mut.

— Forest Trees of Travancore. 456p. 1976. reprint ed. 180.00 (*0-7855-6632-5*, Pub. by Intl Bk Distr) St Mut.

Bourdin, Francoise. Juillet en Hiver. large type ed. 1996. pap. 25.99 (*2-84011-143-8*) Ulverscroft.

Bourdin, Henri L., ed. see Crevacoeur, Michel G.

***Bourdon.** Understanding Animal Breeding. 2nd ed. LC 99-34849. 538p. (C). 1999. 94.00 (*0-13-096449-2*, Prentice Hall) P-H.

Bourdon, Anne. Revision with White Tulip. 50p. (Orig.). 1991. pap. 6.00 (*0-9629364-0-5*) Bourdon Pub.

Bourdon, Anne L., ed. Ruah, 1994, Vol. 4. 48p. 1994. 5.00 (*1-883734-05-3*) Power of Poetry.

Bourdon, David. Warhol. (Illus.). 1989. 49.50 (*0-8109-1761-0*) Abrams.

— Warhol. (Illus.). 432p. 1995. pap. 24.95 (*0-8109-2634-2*, Pub. by Abrams) Time Warner.

Bourdon, David, ed. Nancy Graves. LC 91-60299. (Illus.). 32p. (Orig.). 1991. pap. 20.00 (*1-879173-00-X*) Locks Gallery.

Bourdon, David, et al. Jackie Ferrara Sculpture: A Retrospective. Eickel, Nancy & Chilson, Kathleen, eds. (Illus.). 108p. (Orig.). 1992. pap. 24.95 (*0-916758-33-8*) Ringling Mus Art.

Bourdon, Jean-Louis. Jock. Johns, Timothy, tr. from FRE. 100p. (Orig.). 1992. pap. 7.95 (*0-913745-37-5*) Ubu Repertory.

Bourdon, Jean-Paul, et al. Dictionnaire Normand-Francais. (FRE.). 1993. write for info. (*0-7859-8085-7*, 2-85319-250-4) Fr & Eur.

Bourdon, Paul & Shapiro, Joel H. Cyclic Phenomena for Composition Operators. LC 96-44756. (Memoirs of the American Mathematical Society Ser.: Vol. 125/596). 105p. 1997. pap. 38.00 (*0-8218-0630-0*, MEMO/125/596) Am Math.

Bourdon, Roger J. Bourdon Advanced Pick: Database & Operating System 2E. 2nd ed. 864p. (C). 1996. pap. 54.95 (*0-201-87696-5*) Addison-Wesley.

Bourdot, H. & Galzin, A. Hymenomycetes De France: Heterobasidies-Homobasidies Gymnocarpes. (Bibliotheca Mycologica Ser.: No.23). 1969. reprint ed. 130.00 (*3-7682-0655-6*) Lubrecht & Cramer.

Bourdouxhe, Madeleine. La Femme de Gilles. Evans, Faith, tr. from FRE. (European Classics Ser.). 122p. 1994. reprint ed. pap. 11.95 (*0-8101-1197-7*) Northwestern U Pr.

Boureau. Lords First Night. Cochrane, Lydia G., tr. LC 97-36598. 1998. pap. text 19.00 (*0-226-06743-2*); lib. bdg. 55.00 (*0-226-06742-4*) U Ch Pr.

Boureau. La Papesse Jean: (Pope Joan) (Illus.). (C). text. write for info. (*0-472-09668-0*); pap. text. write for info. (*0-472-06668-4*) U of Mich Pr.

***Boureau, Alain.** Pope Joan. 1999. pap. text 19.00 (*0-226-06745-9*); lib. bdg. 58.00 (*0-226-06744-0*) U Ch Pr.

Boureau, Alain, et al. The Culture of Print: Power & the Uses of Print in Early Modern Europe. Chartier, Roger, ed. Cochrane, Lydia G., tr. LC 89-4043. (Illus.). 375p. reprint ed. pap. 116.30 (*0-608-09107-3*, 206973900005) Bks Demand.

Bouree, Patrice. Dictionnaire de Parasitologie. (FRE.). 126p. 1989. pap. 29.95 (*0-7859-7979-4*, 2729889248) Fr & Eur.

Boureqeade, Pierre. L' Empire Des Livres. (FRE.). 250p. 1991. pap. 10.95 (*0-7859-2179-6*, 2070384314) Fr & Eur.

Bouregois, C. M., et al, eds. Microbiological Control for Foods & Agricultural Products. LC 95-7026. (Analysis & Control Methods for Foods & Agricultural Products Ser.). Orig. Title: Techniques d'Analyse et de Controle Dans les Industries Agro-Alimentaires. (Illus.). x, 548p. 1995. 145.00 (*1-56081-673-2*, Wiley-VCH) Wiley.

Bourell, David L., ed. see Minerals, Metals & Materials Society Staff.

Bourelly, Pierre. Les Algues d'Eau douce. Initiation a la Systematique. Vol. 3: Algues Bleues et Rouges. Pyrrophytes-Algues rouges ou Rhodophytes-Algues bleues on Cyanophycees-Systematics des Algues d'Eau douce. rev. ed. (Fannes et Flores Actuelles Ser.). (FRE., Illus.). 544p. 1983. lib. bdg. 130.00 (*2-85004-040-1*) Lubrecht & Cramer.

Bouret, Claude & Sauvage, Anne-Marie. Toulouse-Lautrec: Prints & Posters from the Bibliotheque Nationale. (ENG & FRE., Illus.). 224p. 1991. pap. 50.00 (*0-7242-4478-6*, Pub. by Queensland Gov) Wittenborn Art.

Bouret, Jean. Bonnard: The Magic Ring. (Rhythem & Color Two Ser.). 1970. 9.95 (*0-8288-9514-7*) Fr & Eur.

— Henri Rousseau: The Paintings. (FRE., Illus.). 268p. 1961. 150.00 (*1-55660-086-0*) A Wofsy Fine Arts.

— Henri Rousseau: With a Catalogue of the Paintings. (FRE., Illus.). 268p. 1961. 150.00 (*0-8150-0011-1*) Wittenborn Art.

— Pablo Picasso Dessins. (FRE., Illus.). 1950. lib. bdg. 95.00 (*0-8288-3976-X*) Fr & Eur.

Bourexis, Patricia & Norman, Michael. Including Students with Disabilities in School-to-Work Opportunities. 30p. 1995. pap. write for info. (*1-884037-06-2*) Coun Chief St Schl Offs.

Bourg, Wendy. A Child Interviewer's Guidebook. LC 98-40282. (Interpersonal Violence Ser.). 256p. 1999. 14.99 (*0-7619-1763-2*) Sage.

***Bourg, Wendy.** A Child Interviewer's Guidebook. LC 98-40282. (Interpersonal Violence Ser.: Vol. 23). 256p. 1999. 34.00 (*0-7619-1762-4*) Sage.

Bourgain, J., et al. Banach Spaces with a Unique Unconditional Basis, up to Permutation. LC 84-28116. (Memoirs Ser.: No. 54/322). 111p. 1990. reprint ed. pap. 21.00 (*0-8218-2323-X*, MEMO/54/322) Am Math.

Bourgain, Jean. Global Solutions of Nonlinear Schrhodinger Equations LC 99-13066. (Colloquium Publications). 1999. write for info. (*0-8218-1919-4*) Am Math.

Bourgain, Jean, et al. Banach Spaces with a Unique Unconditional Basis, up to Permutation. LC 84-28116. (American Mathematical Society Ser.: No. 322). 117p. reprint ed. pap. 36.30 (*0-608-09182-0*, 205268600002) Bks Demand.

Bourgaize, David B. Introduction to Biotechnology: Demystifying the Concepts. LC 99-36737. 416p. (C). 1999. pap. text 63.00 (*0-8053-4602-3*) Addison-Wesley.

Bourgault, Louise M. Mass Media in Sub-Saharan Africa. LC 94-27829. 320p. 1995. 35.00 (*0-253-31250-7*); pap. 14.95 (*0-253-20938-2*) Ind U Pr.

Bourgault, Luc. The American Indian Secrets of Crystal Healing. 128p. 1996. pap. 19.95 (*0-572-02263-8*, Pub. by W Foulsham) Trans-Atl Phila.

Bourgeacq, Jacques. A la Rencontre des Mots: Methode d'Analyse et d'Acquisition du Vocabulaire. 274p. (Orig.). (C). 1994. pap. text 28.50 (*0-8191-9116-7*) U Pr of Amer.

Bourgeacq, Jacques A., jt. auth. see Limouzy, Pierre.

Bourgeade, Pierre. Les Immortelles. (FRE.). 160p. 1980. pap. 10.95 (*0-7859-1907-4*, 2070371689) Fr & Eur.

— The Passport & the Door: A Book of 2 Plays. Zeig, Sande, tr. from FRE. 120p. (Orig.). 1984. pap. text 8.95 (*0-913745-06-5*) Ubu Repertory.

— Les Serpents. (FRE.). 271p. 1986. pap. 11.95 (*0-7859-2025-0*, 2070377040) Fr & Eur.

Bourgeau, Art. The Seduction. 288p. 1989. mass mkt. 4.95 (*0-446-35551-8*, Pub. by Warner Bks) Little.

***Bourgeault, Cynthia.** Love Is Stronger Than Death: The Mystical Union of Two Souls. LC 98-56526. 224p. 1999. 21.00 (*0-609-60473-2*, CPG Pr) IDG Bks.

Bourgeault, Cynthia, et al, eds. Island Journal Vol. VIII: An Annual Publication of the Island Institute. (Illus.). 92p. (Orig.). 1991. pap. 7.95 (*0-942719-10-7*) Island Inst.

Bourgeault, Cynthia & Conkling, Philip, eds. Island Journal Vol. X: An Annual Publication of the Island Institute. (Illus.). 92p. 1993. pap. 7.95 (*0-942719-12-3*) Island Inst.

Bourgeault, Cynthia & Conkling, Philip W., eds. Island Journal Vol. XI: An Annual Publication of the Island Institute. (Illus.). 96p. 1994. pap. 7.95 (*0-942719-13-1*) Island Inst.

Bourgeault, Cynthia, jt. ed. see Conkling, Philip W.

Bourgeo. Strategic Management. 2nd ed. 1996. 99.00 (*0-03-019093-2*) Harcourt Coll Pubs.

— Strategic Management & Cases. 1996. teacher ed. 69.50 (*0-03-018332-4*) Harcourt Coll Pubs.

Bourgeois. Strategic Management. (C). 1996. pap. text, teacher ed. 28.00 (*0-03-072254-3*) Harcourt.

— Strategic Management. (C). 1995. text 90.00 (*0-03-055789-5*) Harcourt Coll Pubs.

***Bourgeois.** Strategic Management. 2nd ed. (C). 1998. text 65.50 (*0-03-022613-9*) Harcourt.

Bourgeois. Strategic Management. 2nd ed. LC 98-73693. (C). 1998. text 97.50 (*0-03-022373-3*, Pub. by Harcourt Coll Pubs) Harcourt.

— Strategic Management: Test Bank. (C). 1996. pap. text, suppl. ed. 31.00 (*0-03-072257-8*, Pub. by Harcourt Coll Pubs) Harcourt.

Bourgeois, Anna S. Blueswomen: Profiles of 37 Early Performers, with an Anthology of Lyrics, 1920-1945. LC 96-1158. 184p. 1996. lib. bdg. 36.50 (*0-89950-963-0*) McFarland & Co.

***Bourgeois, Anna S.** Fair Isle Sweaters Simplified. (Illus.). 144p. 2000. pap. write for info. (*1-56477-311-6*, B428, Pub. by Martingale & Co) F & W Pubns Inc.

Bourgeois, Arthur P., ed. Ojibwa Narratives of Charles & Charlotte Kawbawgam & Jacques LePique, 1893-1895. LC 93-32783. (Illus.). 168p. 1994. text 29.95 (*0-8143-2514-9*, Great Lks Bks); pap. text 17.95 (*0-8143-2515-7*, Great Lks Bks) Wayne St U Pr.

Bourgeois, Bernard, ed. see Hegel, Georg Wilhelm Friedrich.

Bourgeois, C. Food Microbiology, 2 vols. 334p. 1993. 45.00 (*0-13-327891-3*) P-H.

***Bourgeois, Etienne.** The Adult University. LC 98-44936. 194p. 1999. 36.95 (*0-335-19907-0*) OpUniv Pr.

— The Adult University. LC 98-44936. 1999. 105.00 (*0-335-19908-9*) Taylor & Francis.

Bourgeois, F. John, et al. Obstetrics & Gynecology Recall. LC 97-10753. (Recall Ser.). (Illus.). 256p. 1997. pap. 27.00 (*0-683-18214-5*) Lppncott W & W.

Bourgeois, Helen Le, see Ward, Ola M.

Bourgeois, Helen Le, see Ward, Ola M. & Le Bourgeois, Helen.

Bourgeois, Henri. On Becoming Christian. (C). 1988. 45.00 (*0-85439-230-0*, Pub. by St Paul Pubns) St Mut.

Bourgeois, Ivan M., jt. auth. see Sutton, Richard.

Bourgeois, J. H., ed. Subsidies & International Trade. 240p. 1991. pap. 72.00 (*90-6544-529-3*) Kluwer Law Intl.

Bourgeois, Jean-Francois. Los Ninos de la Biblia. Maecha, Alberto, ed. Orig. Title: Les Enfants de la Bible. (SPA., Illus.). 40p. (J). (gr. 3-5). 1984. pap. write for info. (*0-942504-11-9*) Overcomer Pr.

Bourgeois, Jean-Louis & Davidson, Basil Risbridger. Spectacular Vernacular: The Adobe Tradition. (Illus.). 192p. 1996. pap. 60.00 (*0-89381-672-8*) Aperture.

Bourgeois, Joanne, jt. auth. see McCann, Anna M.

***Bourgeois, K. M.** Requiem. 2000. pap. 18.00 (*0-7388-2229-9*) Xlibris Corp.

Bourgeois, Louise. Album. (Illus.). 123p. 1994. text 150.00 (*0-935875-13-1*) P Blum Edit.

— Destruction of the Father: Writings & Interviews, 1923-1997. Bernadac, Marie-Laure & Obrist, Hans-Ulrich, eds. LC 97-43132. (Illus.). 384p. 1998. pap. text 30.00 (*0-262-52246-2*) MIT Pr.

Bourgeois, Louise & Rinder, Lawrence. Louise Bourgeois: Drawings & Observations. LC 95-80663. 192p. 1996. 27.50 (*0-8212-2299-6*, Pub. by Bulfinch Pr) Little.

Bourgeois, Louise, jt. auth. see Gorovoy, Jerry.

Bourgeois, Maurice. John Millington Synge & the Irish Theatre. LC 65-16228. (Illus.). 353p. 1972. 24.95 (*0-405-08297-5*, Pub. by Blom Pubns) Ayer.

— John Millington Synge & the Irish Theatre. LC 68-906. (Studies in Irish Literature: No. 16). 1969. reprint ed. lib. bdg. 75.00 (*0-8383-0511-3*) M S G Haskell Hse.

— John Millington Synge & the Irish Theatre. (BCL1-PR English Literature Ser.). 337p. 1992. reprint ed. lib. bdg. 89.00 (*0-7812-7686-1*) Rprt Serv.

***Bourgeois Molzahn, Arlene.** The Green Bay Packers Football Team. LC 98-35038. (Great Sports Teams Ser.). 48p. (J). (gr. 4-10). 1999. lib. bdg. 18.95 (*0-7660-1100-3*) Enslow Pubs.

***Bourgeois, Pamela.** New Voices. 5th ed. 122p. (C). 1999. per. 19.95 (*0-7872-6424-5*, 41642401) Kendall-Hunt.

***Bourgeois, Patrick L.** Philosophy at the Boundary of Reason: Ethics & Postmodernity. LC 00-26525. (C). 2000. pap. text 24.95 (*0-7914-4822-3*) State U NY Pr.

— Philosophy at the Boundary of Reason: Ethics & Postmodernity. LC 00-26525. (C). 2001. text 73.50 (*0-7914-4821-5*) State U NY Pr.

Bourgeois, Patrick L. The Religious Within Experience & Existence: A Phenomenological Investigation. LC 89-38120. 170p. 1989. text 23.95 (*0-8207-0214-5*) Duquesne.

Bourgeois, Patrick L. & Rosenthal, Sandra B. Thematic Studies in Phenomenology & Pragmatism. viii, 147p. (Orig.). 1983. pap. 22.00 (*90-6032-238-X*) J Benjamins Pubng Co.

Bourgeois, Patrick L., jt. auth. see Rosenthal, Sandra B.

Bourgeois, Paulette. Amazing Dirt Book. (J). 1990. pap. 8.95 (*0-201-55096-2*) Addison-Wesley.

Bourgeois, Paulette. Big Sarah's Little Boots. (Illus.). 32p. (J). 1987. pap. 5.95 (*0-921103-70-0*) Kids Can Pr.

Bourgeois, Paulette. Big Sarah's Little Boots. (Illus.). 32p. (J). (ps-1). 1992. pap. 4.95 (*0-590-42623-0*, Blue Ribbon Bks) Scholastic Inc.

— Big Sarah's Little Boots. (Blue Ribbon Bks.). (J). 1987. 10.15 (*0-606-01788-7*, Pub. by Turtleback) Demco.

Bourgeois, Paulette. Canadian Fire Fighters. (Illus.). 32p. (J). 1991. pap. 4.95 (*1-55074-137-3*); text 15.95 (*1-55074-042-3*) Kids Can Pr.

— Canadian Garbage Collectors. (Illus.). 32p. (J). 1991. 15.95 (*1-55074-040-7*); pap. 4.95 (*1-55074-138-1*) Kids Can Pr.

— Canadian Police Officers. (Illus.). (J). 1991. 15.95 (*1-55074-060-1*); pap. 4.95 (*1-55074-133-0*) Kids Can Pr.

— Canadian Postal Workers. (Illus.). 32p. (J). 1991. 15.95 (*1-55074-058-X*); pap. 4.95 (*1-55074-135-7*) Kids Can Pr.

Bourgeois, Paulette. El Club Secreto de Franklin. Varela, Alejandra L., tr. from ENG. (Franklin Ser.). Orig. Title: Franklin's Secret Club. (SPA., Illus.). 32p. (J). (ps-3). 1998. pap. 4.95 (*1-880507-50-1*) Lectorum Pubns.

Bourgeois, Paulette. Finders Keepers for Franklin. (Franklin Ser.). (Illus.). 32p. (J). (ps-3). 1997. pap. 5.95 (*1-55074-370-8*) Kids Can Pr.

Bourgeois, Paulette. Finders Keepers for Franklin. (Franklin Ser.). (Illus.). (J). (ps-3). 1998. 12.95 (*1-55074-368-6*, Pub. by Kids Can Pr) Genl Dist Srvs.

— Finders Keepers for Franklin. LC 98-165427. (Franklin Ser.). (Illus.). 32p. (J). (ps-3). 1998. pap. 3.99 (*0-590-02633-X*) Scholastic Inc.

— Finders Keepers for Franklin. (Franklin Ser.). (J). (ps-3). 1998. 9.19 (*0-606-12932-4*, Pub. by Turtleback) Demco.

***Bourgeois, Paulette.** Fire Fighter. (In My Neighborhood Ser.). (Illus.). 32p. (J). (gr. k-3). 2000. pap. 5.95 (*1-55074-783-5*, Pub. by Kids Can Pr) Genl Dist Srvs.

— Fire Fighters. (Illus.). (J). 2000. 11.40 (*0-606-18224-1*) Turtleback.

Bourgeois, Paulette. Fire Fighters. unabridged ed. (In My Neighborhood Ser.). (Illus.). 32p. (J). (ps-3). 1998. 12.95 (*1-55074-438-0*, Pub. by Kids Can Pr) Genl Dist Srvs.

— Franklin & Me. LC 95-14128. (Franklin Ser.). (Illus.). 40p. (J). (ps-3). 1995. pap. 3.95 (*0-590-25488-X*) Scholastic Inc.

Bourgeois, Paulette. Franklin & Me: My First Record of Favourite Things, Personal Facts & Special Memories. LC 96-932406. (Franklin Ser.). (Illus.). (J). (ps-3). 1997. pap. 5.95 (*1-55074-335-X*) Kids Can Pr.

Bourgeois, Paulette. Franklin & Me: My First Record of Favourite Things, Personal Facts & Special Memories. unabridged ed. (Franklin Ser.). (Illus.). 32p. (J). (ps-2). 1998. 9.95 (*1-55074-442-9*, Pub. by Kids Can Pr) Genl Dist Srvs.

***Bourgeois, Paulette.** Franklin & the Thunderstorm. (Franklin Ser.). 32p. (J). (ps-3). 1998. pap. 5.95 (*1-55074-405-4*) Kids Can Pr.

Bourgeois, Paulette. Franklin & the Thunderstorm. (Franklin Ser.). (Illus.). 32p. (J). (ps-3). 1998. 10.95 (*1-55074-403-8*, Pub. by Kids Can Pr) Genl Dist Srvs.

— Franklin & the Thunderstorm. LC 98-164528. (Franklin Ser.). (Illus.). 32p. (J). (ps-2). 1998. pap. 3.99 (*0-590-02635-6*, Cartwheel) Scholastic Inc.

***Bourgeois, Paulette.** Franklin & the Thunderstorm. (J). 1998. 9.19 (*0-606-13403-4*, Pub. by Turtleback) Demco.

— Franklin & the Tooth Fairy. (Franklin Ser.). (Illus.). 32p. (J). (ps-3). 1995. pap. 5.95 (*1-55074-280-9*) Kids Can Pr.

Bourgeois, Paulette. Franklin & the Tooth Fairy. (Franklin Ser.). (Illus.). 32p. (J). (ps-3). 1997. 12.95 (*1-55074-270-1*, Pub. by Kids Can Pr) Genl Dist Srvs.

***Bourgeois, Paulette.** Franklin & the Tooth Fairy. (Franklin Ser.). (Illus.). 32p. (J). (ps-3). 1999. pap. 9.95 incl. audio (*1-55074-793-2*) Kids Can Pr.

Bourgeois, Paulette. Franklin & the Tooth Fairy. LC 96-7322. (Franklin Ser.). (Illus.). 32p. (J). (ps-3). 1996. pap. 3.95 (*0-590-25469-3*) Scholastic Inc.

Bourgeois, Paulette. Franklin & the Tooth Fairy. (Franklin Ser.). (J). (ps-3). 1996. 9.15 (*0-606-08745-1*, Pub. by Turtleback) Demco.

Bourgeois, Paulette. Franklin Assortment. (Franklin Ser.). (J). (ps-3). 1999. pap. 10.95 (*1-55074-758-4*) Genl Dist Srvs.

***Bourgeois, Paulette.** Franklin en el Museo. LC 99-34650. (Franklin Ser.). Orig. Title: Franklin's Class Trip. (SPA., Illus.). (J). (ps-3). 1999. pap. 5.95 (*1-880507-57-9*) Lectorum Pubns.

Bourgeois, Paulette. Franklin es un Mandon. Lopez Varela, Alejandra, tr. from ENG. (Franklin Ser.).Tr. of Franklin is Bossy. (SPA., Illus.). 32p. (J). (ps-3). 1998. pap. 4.95 (*1-880507-42-0*) Lectorum Pubns.

Bourgeois, Paulette. Franklin es un Mandon. (Franklin Ser.).Tr. of Franklin is Bossy. (SPA.). (J). (ps-3). 1993. 9.15 (*0-606-06390-0*, Pub. by Turtleback) Demco.

Bourgeois, Paulette. Franklin Fibs. (Franklin Ser.). (Illus.). 32p. (J). (ps-3). 1991. 12.95 (*1-55074-038-5*, Pub. by Kids Can Pr) Genl Dist Srvs.

Bourgeois, Paulette. Franklin Fibs. (Franklin Ser.). (Illus.). 32p. (J). (ps-3). 1992. pap. 5.95 (*1-55074-077-6*) Kids Can Pr.

Bourgeois, Paulette. Franklin Fibs. (Franklin Ser.). (Illus.). 30p. (J). (ps-3). 1992. pap. 3.95 (*0-590-44647-9*) Scholastic Inc.

Bourgeois, Paulette. Franklin Fibs. (Franklin Ser.). (J). (ps-3). 1991. 9.15 (*0-606-01840-9*, Pub. by Turtleback) Demco.

— Franklin Forgets. (Franklin TV Storybook Ser.: Vol. 4). (Illus.). 32p. (J). (ps-3). 2000. pap. 4.50 (*0-439-08368-0*) Scholastic Inc.

— Franklin Goes to Day Camp: A Story & Activity Book. (Franklin Ser.). (Illus.). 32p. (J). (ps-3). pap. 4.95 (*1-55074-372-4*) Kids Can Pr.

Bourgeois, Paulette. Franklin Goes to Day Camp: A Story & Activity Book. (Franklin Ser.). (Illus.). (J). (ps-3). 1998. pap. text 3.99 (*0-590-06828-8*, Cartwheel) Scholastic Inc.

— Franklin Goes to School. (Franklin Ser.). (Illus.). 32p. (J). (ps-3). 1995. 12.95 (*1-55074-268-X*, Pub. by Kids Can Pr); 10.95 (*1-55074-424-0*, Pub. by Kids Can Pr) Genl Dist Srvs.

Bourgeois, Paulette. Franklin Goes to School. (Franklin Ser.). (Illus.). 32p. (J). (ps-3). 1995. pap. 5.95 (*1-55074-276-0*) Kids Can Pr.

Bourgeois, Paulette. Franklin Goes to School. LC 95-212406. (Franklin Ser.). (Illus.). 32p. (J). (ps-2). 1995. pap. 3.95 (*0-590-25467-7*) Scholastic Inc.

— Franklin Goes to School. (Franklin Ser.). (J). (ps-3). 1995. 9.15 (*0-606-07537-2*, Pub. by Turtleback) Demco.

***Bourgeois, Paulette.** Franklin Goes to the Hospital. (Franklin Ser.). 32p. (J). (ps-3). 2000. pap. 5.95 (*1-55074-734-7*) Kids Can Pr.

— Franklin Goes to the Hospital. (Franklin Ser.). (Illus.). 32p. (J). (ps-2). 2000. pap. 4.50 (*0-439-08370-2*) Scholastic Inc.

— Franklin Goes to the Hospital. (Illus.). (J). 2000. 9.95 (*0-606-18547-X*) Turtleback.

— Franklin Goes to the Hospital. unabridged ed. (Franklin Ser.). (Illus.). 32p. (J). (ps-3). 2000. text 12.95 (*1-55074-732-0*, Pub. by Kids Can Pr) Genl Dist Srvs.

— Franklin Has a Sleepover. (Franklin Ser.). (Illus.). 32p. (J). (ps-3). 1996. pap. 5.95 (*1-55074-302-3*) Kids Can Pr.

Bourgeois, Paulette. Franklin Has a Sleepover. (Franklin Ser.). (Illus.). 32p. (J). (ps-3). 1997. 12.95 (*1-55074-300-7*, Pub. by Kids Can Pr) Genl Dist Srvs.

— Franklin Has a Sleepover. LC 96-140882. (Franklin Ser.). (Illus.). 30p. (J). (ps-3). 1996. pap. 3.95 (*0-590-61759-1*) Scholastic Inc.

Bourgeois, Paulette. Franklin Has a Sleepover. LC 96-140882. (Franklin Ser.). (J). (ps-3). 1996. 9.15 (*0-606-09295-1*, Pub. by Turtleback) Demco.

Bourgeois, Paulette. Franklin in the Dark. (Franklin Ser.). (Illus.). 32p. (J). (ps-3). 1986. 12.95 (*0-919964-93-1*, Pub. by Kids Can Pr) Genl Dist Srvs.

Bourgeois, Paulette. Franklin in the Dark. (Franklin Ser.). (Illus.). 32p. (J). (ps-3). 1992. pap. 5.95 (*0-921103-31-X*) Kids Can Pr.

Bourgeois, Paulette. Franklin in the Dark. (Franklin Ser.). (J). (ps-3). 1992. 19.95 (*0-590-72701-X*) Scholastic Inc.

***Bourgeois, Paulette.** Franklin in the Dark. (Franklin Ser.: Vol. 2). (Illus.). 12p. (J). (ps-k). 2000. 5.99 (*0-439-19425-3*) Scholastic Inc.

— Franklin in the Dark. (Franklin Ser.). (J). (ps-3). 1987. 9.15 (*0-606-03218-5*, Pub. by Turtleback) Demco.

Bourgeois, Paulette. Franklin in the Dark. LC 87-181130. (Franklin Ser.). (Illus.). 30p. (J). (ps-3). 1987. reprint ed. pap. 4.95 (*0-590-44506-5*) Scholastic Inc.

— Franklin Is Bossy. (Franklin Ser.). (Illus.). 32p. (J). (ps-3). 1993. 12.95 (*1-55074-119-5*, Pub. by Kids Can Pr) Genl Dist Srvs.

Bourgeois, Paulette. Franklin Is Bossy. (Franklin Ser.). (Illus.). 32p. (J). (ps-3). 1995. pap. 5.95 (*1-55074-257-4*) Kids Can Pr.

Bourgeois, Paulette. Franklin Is Bossy. LC 96-139874. (Franklin Ser.). (Illus.). 30p. (J). (ps-3). 1994. pap. 3.95 (*0-590-47757-9*) Scholastic Inc.

An Asterisk (*) at the beginning of an entry indicates that the title is appearing for the first time.

*Bourgeois, Paulette.** Franklin Is Lost. (Franklin Ser.). (Illus.). (J). (ps-3). 1999. pap. 11.70 (*0-7857-0678-X*) Econo-Clad Bks.

Bourgeois, Paulette. Franklin Is Lost. (Franklin Ser.). (Illus.). 32p. (J). (ps-3). 1992. 12.95 (*1-55074-053-9*, Pub. by Kids Can Pr) Genl Dist Srvs.

Bourgeois, Paulette. Franklin Is Lost. (Franklin Ser.). (Illus.). 32p. (J). (ps-3). 1992. pap. 5.95 (*1-55074-105-5*) Kids Can Pr.

Bourgeois, Paulette. Franklin Is Lost. LC 96-139876. (Franklin Ser.). (Illus.). 32p. (J). (ps-2). 1993. pap. 3.95 (*0-590-46255-5*) Scholastic Inc.

— Franklin Is Lost. (Franklin Ser.). (J). (ps-3). 1992. 9.15 (*0-606-05299-2*, Pub. by Turtleback) Demco.

— Franklin is Messy. (Franklin Ser.). (Illus.). 32p. (J). (ps-3). 1994. 12.95 (*1-55074-243-4*, Pub. by Kids Can Pr) Genl Dist Srvs.

Bourgeois, Paulette. Franklin is Messy. (Franklin Ser.). (Illus.). 32p. (J). (ps-3). 1994. pap. 12.95 (*1-55074-245-0*) Kids Can Pr.

Bourgeois, Paulette. Franklin is Messy. LC 96-139875. (Franklin Ser.). (Illus.). 30p. (J). (ps-3). 1995. pap. 3.95 (*0-590-48686-1*) Scholastic Inc.

— Franklin is Messy. (Franklin Ser.). (J). (ps-3). 1994. 9.15 (*0-606-07538-0*, Pub. by Turtleback) Demco.

— Franklin is Messy. unabridged ed. (Franklin Ser.). (Illus.). 32p. (J). (ps-3). 1994. 10.95 (*1-55074-426-7*, Pub. by Kids Can Pr) Genl Dist Srvs.

— Franklin Juega al Futbol. Lopez-Varela, Alejandra, tr. (Franklin Ser.).Tr. of Franklin Plays the Game. (SPA., Illus.). 32p. (J). (ps-3). 1998. pap. 4.95 (*1-880507-44-7*) Lectorum Pubns.

*Bourgeois, Paulette.** Franklin Miente. LC 99-40295. (Franklin Ser.).Tr. of Franklin Fibs. (SPA., Illus.). (J). (gr. k-2). 2000. pap. 5.95 (*1-880507-69-2*) Lectorum Pubns.

— Franklin Miente.Tr. of Franklin Fibs. (Illus.). (J). 2000. 11.40 (*0-606-18243-8*) Turtleback.

— Franklin Plays the Game. (Franklin Ser.). (Illus.). 32p. (J). (ps-3). 1995. pap. 5.95 (*1-55074-255-8*) Kids Can Pr.

Bourgeois, Paulette. Franklin Plays the Game. LC 95-212405. (Franklin Ser.). (Illus.). 32p. (J). (ps-2). 1995. pap. 4.95 (*0-590-22631-2*) Scholastic Inc.

Bourgeois, Paulette. Franklin Plays the Game. (Franklin Ser.). (J). (ps-3). 1995. 9.15 (*0-606-08519-X*, Pub. by Turtleback) Demco.

Bourgeois, Paulette. Franklin Plays the Game. unabridged ed. (Franklin Ser.). (Illus.). 32p. (J). (ps-3). 1997. 12.95 (*1-55074-254-X*, Pub. by Kids Can Pr) Genl Dist Srvs.

— Franklin Quiere una Mascota. Varela, Alejandra L., tr. (Franklin Ser.). Orig. Title: Franklin Wants a Pet. (ENG & SPA., Illus.). 32p. (J). (ps-3). 1998. pap. 4.95 (*1-880507-49-8*) Lectorum Pubns.

— Franklin Rides a Bike. (Franklin Ser.). (Illus.). 32p. (J). (ps-3). 1997. 10.95 (*1-55074-414-3*, Pub. by Kids Can Pr) Genl Dist Srvs.

Bourgeois, Paulette. Franklin Rides a Bike. (Franklin Ser.). (Illus.). 32p. (J). (ps-3). 1997. pap. 5.95 (*1-55074-354-6*) Kids Can Pr.

Bourgeois, Paulette. Franklin Rides a Bike. LC 97-154340. (Franklin Ser.). (Illus.). 32p. (J). (ps-3). 1997. pap. 3.99 (*0-590-69333-6*) Scholastic Inc.

— Franklin Rides a Bike. (Franklin Ser.). (J). (ps-3). 1997. 9.19 (*0-606-11351-7*, Pub. by Turtleback) Demco.

*Bourgeois, Paulette.** Franklin Se Pierde. LC 99-40296. (Franklin Ser.).Tr. of Franklin is Lost. (SPA., Illus.). (J). (gr. k-2). 2000. pap. 5.95 (*1-880507-70-6*) Lectorum Pubns.

— Franklin Se Pierde.Tr. of Franklin is Lost. (SPA., Illus.). (J). 2000. 11.40 (*0-606-18244-6*) Turtleback.

Bourgeois, Paulette. Franklin Tiene un Mal Dia. Varela, Alejandra Lopez, tr. from ENG. (Franklin Ser.).Tr. of Franklin's Bad Day. (SPA.). (J). (ps-3). pap. 4.95 (*1-880507-52-8*) Lectorum Pubns.

*Bourgeois, Paulette.** Franklin Treasury. (Illus.). (J). 2000. 15.95 (*1-55337-018-X*) Kids Can Press.

Bourgeois, Paulette. Franklin Va a la Escuela. Lopez Varela, Alejandra, tr. from ENG. (Franklin Ser.).Tr. of Franklin Goes to School. (SPA., Illus.). 32p. (J). (ps-3). 1998. pap. 4.95 (*1-880507-41-2*) Lectorum Pubns.

— Franklin Wants a Pet. (Franklin Ser.). (Illus.). 32p. (J). (ps-2). 1994. 12.95 (*1-55074-247-7*, Pub. by Kids Can Pr) Genl Dist Srvs.

Bourgeois, Paulette. Franklin Wants a Pet. (Franklin Ser.). (Illus.). 32p. (J). (ps-3). 1995. pap. 5.95 (*1-55074-249-3*) Kids Can Pr.

— Franklin Wants a Pet. (Franklin Ser.). (Illus.). 32p. (J). (ps-3). 2000. pap. 9.95 incl. audio (*1-55074-795-9*) Kids Can Pr.

Bourgeois, Paulette. Franklin Wants a Pet. LC 95-212404. (Franklin Ser.). (Illus.). 32p. (J). (gr. 1-4). 1995. pap. 4.95 (*0-590-48915-1*) Scholastic Inc.

— Franklin Wants a Pet. (Franklin Ser.). (J). (ps-3). 1995. 9.15 (*0-606-07539-9*, Pub. by Turtleback) Demco.

*Bourgeois, Paulette.** Franklin y el Regalo de Navidad. LC 99-31981. (Franklin Ser.).Tr. of Franklin's Christmas Gift. (SPA., Illus.). (J). (ps-3). 1999. pap. 5.95 (*1-880507-56-0*) Lectorum Pubns.

— Franklin's Baby Sister. (Franklin Ser.). (Illus.). 32p. (J). (ps-3). pap. 5.95 (*1-55074-858-0*) Kids Can Pr.

— Franklin's Baby Sister. (Franklin Ser.). (Illus.). 32p. (J). (ps-3). 2000. 12.95 (*1-55074-794-0*, Pub. by Kids Can Press) Genl Dist Srvs.

— Franklin's Baby Sister. (Franklin Ser.). (Illus.). 32p. (J). (ps-2). 2000. pap. text 4.50 (*0-439-20378-3*) Scholastic Inc.

— Franklin's Bad Day. (Franklin Ser.). 32p. (J). (ps-3). 1996. pap. 5.95 (*1-55074-293-0*) Kids Can Pr.

Bourgeois, Paulette. Franklin's Bad Day. (Franklin Ser.). (Illus.). 32p. (J). (ps-3). 1997. 12.95 (*1-55074-291-4*, Pub. by Kids Can Pr) Genl Dist Srvs.

— Franklin's Bad Day. LC 97-135097. (Franklin Ser.). (Illus.). 32p. (J). (ps-2). 1997. pap. 3.95 (*0-590-69332-8*) Scholastic Inc.

— Franklin's Bad Day. (Franklin Ser.). (J). (ps-3). 1997. 9.15 (*0-606-10813-0*, Pub. by Turtleback) Demco.

Bourgeois, Paulette. Franklin's Blanket. (Franklin Ser.). (Illus.). 32p. (J). (ps-3). 1995. pap. 5.95 (*1-55074-278-7*) Kids Can Pr.

Bourgeois, Paulette. Franklin's Blanket. (Franklin Ser.). (Illus.). 32p. (J). (ps-3). 1997. 12.95 (*1-55074-154-3*, Pub. by Kids Can Pr) Genl Dist Srvs.

*Bourgeois, Paulette.** Franklin's Blanket. (Franklin Ser.). 32p. (J). (ps-3). 2000. pap. 9.95 incl. audio (*1-55074-686-3*) Kids Can Pr.

Bourgeois, Paulette. Franklin's Blanket. LC 96-21361. (Franklin Ser.). (Illus.). 32p. (J). (ps-2). 1996. pap. 3.95 (*0-590-25468-5*) Scholastic Inc.

— Franklin's Blanket. (Franklin Ser.). (J). (ps-3). 1995. 9.15 (*0-606-08520-3*, Pub. by Turtleback) Demco.

*Bourgeois, Paulette.** Franklin's Christmas Gift. (Franklin Ser.). (Illus.). 32p. (J). (ps-3). 1998. pap. 5.95 (*1-55074-468-2*) Kids Can Pr.

Bourgeois, Paulette. Franklin's Christmas Gift. (Franklin Ser.). (Illus.). 32p. (J). (ps-3). 1998. 12.95 (*1-55074-466-6*, Pub. by Kids Can Pr) Genl Dist Srvs.

— Franklin's Christmas Gift. (Franklin Ser.). (J). (ps-3). 1998. pap. 4.50 (*0-590-02611-9*, Cartwheel); pap. 54.00 (*0-590-95169-6*, Cartwheel) Scholastic Inc.

*Bourgeois, Paulette.** Franklin's Class Trip. (Franklin Ser.). (Illus.). 32p. (J). (ps-3). 1999. pap. 5.95 (*1-55074-472-0*) Kids Can Pr.

Bourgeois, Paulette. Franklin's Class Trip. LC 99-199266. (Franklin Fibs. (Franklin Ser.). (Illus.). 32p. (J). (ps-2). 1999. pap. 4.50 (*0-590-13002-1*) Scholastic Inc.

*Bourgeois, Paulette.** Franklin's Class Trip. (Illus.). (J). 1999. 11.40 (*0-606-18548-8*) Turtleback.

Bourgeois, Paulette. Franklin's Class Trip. unabridged ed. (Franklin Ser.). (Illus.). 32p. (J). (ps-3). 1999. 12.95 (*1-55074-470-4*, Pub. by Kids Can Pr) Genl Dist Srvs.

— Franklin's Class Trip Display. (Franklin Ser.). (J). (ps-3). 1999. pap. 54.00 (*0-439-05975-5*) Scholastic Inc.

*Bourgeois, Paulette.** Franklin's Classic Treasury. (Franklin Ser.). (Illus.). 128p. (J). (ps-3). 1999. 15.95 (*1-55074-742-8*) Kids Can Pr.

— Franklin's Classic Treasury, Vol. 2. unabridged ed. (Franklin Ser.: Vol. 2). (Illus.). 128p. (J). (ps-3). 2000. 15.95 (*1-55074-813-0*, Pub. by Kids Can Pr) Genl Dist Srvs.

— Franklin's Friendship Treasury: Franklin Has a Sleepover; Franklin's Bad Day; Franklin's New Friend. (Franklin Ser.). (Illus.). 120p. (J). (ps-3). 2000. 15.95 (*1-55074-872-6*, Pub. by Kids Can Press) Genl Dist Srvs.

— Franklin's Halloween. (Franklin Ser.). 32p. (J). (ps-3). 1996. pap. 5.95 (*1-55074-285-X*) Kids Can Pr.

Bourgeois, Paulette. Franklin's Halloween. (Franklin Ser.). (Illus.). 32p. (J). (ps-3). 1997. 12.95 (*1-55074-283-3*, Pub. by Kids Can Pr) Genl Dist Srvs.

— Franklin's Halloween. LC 96-216394. 32p. (J). (ps-3). 1996. pap. text 3.95 (*0-590-69330-1*) Scholastic Inc.

Bourgeois, Paulette. Franklin's Halloween. (Franklin Ser.). (J). (ps-3). 1996. 9.15 (*0-606-09296-X*, Pub. by Turtleback) Demco.

— Franklin's Neighborhood. (Franklin Ser.). 32p. (J). (ps-3). 1999. text 12.95 (*1-55074-702-9*) Kids Can Pr.

— Franklin's Neighborhood. (Franklin Ser.). 32p. (J). (ps-3). 1999. pap. 5.95 (*1-55074-704-5*) Kids Can Pr.

— Franklin's Neighborhood. (Franklin Ser.). (Illus.). 32p. (J). (ps-2). 1999. pap. text 4.50 (*0-439-08369-2*) Scholastic Inc.

— Franklin's New Friend. (Franklin Ser.). 32p. (J). (ps-3). pap. 5.95 (*1-55074-363-5*) Kids Can Pr.

Bourgeois, Paulette. Franklin's New Friend. (Franklin Ser.). (Illus.). 32p. (J). (ps-3). 1997. 12.95 (*1-55074-352-X*, Pub. by Kids Can Pr); 10.95 (*1-55074-361-9*, Pub. by Kids Can Pr) Genl Dist Srvs.

— Franklin's New Friend. LC 98-1975. (Franklin Ser.). (Illus.). 32p. (J). (ps-2). 1997. pap. 3.99 (*0-590-02592-9*) Scholastic Inc.

— Franklin's New Friend. (Franklin Ser.). (J). (ps-3). 1997. 9.19 (*0-606-11352-5*, Pub. by Turtleback) Demco.

*Bourgeois, Paulette.** Franklin's Pet Problem. (Franklin Ser.: Vol. 1). (Illus.). 22p. (J). (ps-k). 2000. 4.99 (*0-439-19424-5*) Scholastic Inc.

— Franklin's School Play. (Franklin Ser.). (Illus.). 28p. (J). (ps-3). 1996. pap. 5.95 (*1-55074-289-2*) Kids Can Pr.

Bourgeois, Paulette. Franklin's School Play. (Franklin Ser.). (Illus.). 32p. (J). (ps-3). 1997. 12.95 (*1-55074-287-6*, Pub. by Kids Can Pr) Genl Dist Srvs.

— Franklin's School Play. (Franklin Ser.). (FRE., Illus.). 32p. (J). (ps-3). 1996. pap. 6.99 (*0-590-16032-X*) Scholastic Inc.

— Franklin's School Play. LC 97-135098. (Franklin Ser.). (Illus.). 30p. (J). (ps-2). 1996. pap. 3.95 (*0-590-69331-X*) Scholastic Inc.

— Franklin's School Play. (Franklin Ser.). (J). (ps-3). 1996. 9.15 (*0-606-10188-8*, Pub. by Turtleback) Demco.

*Bourgeois, Paulette.** Franklin's Secret Club. (Illus.). (J). 1999. pap. 11.70 (*0-613-11556-2*) Econo-Clad Bks.

— Franklin's Secret Club. (Franklin Ser.). (Illus.). 32p. (J). (ps-3). 1998. pap. 5.95 (*1-55074-476-3*) Kids Can Pr.

Bourgeois, Paulette. Franklin's Secret Club. (Franklin Ser.). (Illus.). 32p. (J). (ps-3). 1998. 12.95 (*1-55074-474-7*, Pub. by Kids Can Pr) Genl Dist Srvs.

— Franklin's Secret Club. LC 98-214528. (Franklin Ser.). (Illus.). 32p. (J). (ps-3). 1998. pap. 3.99 (*0-590-13000-5*, Little Apple) Scholastic Inc.

*Bourgeois, Paulette.** Franklin's Secret Club. (Franklin Ser.). (J). (ps-3). 1998. 9.19 (*0-606-13406-9*, Pub. by Turtleback) Demco.

— Franklin's Valentine Cards. (Franklin Ser.). (Illus.). 16p. (J). (ps-3). 1998. pap. 2.99 (*1-55074-625-1*) Kids Can Pr.

— Franklin's Valentine Cards. Burak, Hally, ed. (Franklin Ser.). (Illus.). 16p. (J). (ps-3). 1999. pap. 2.99 (*0-439-05123-1*) Scholastic Inc.

— Franklin's Valentines. (Franklin Ser.). (Illus.). 32p. (J). (ps-3). 1998. pap. 5.95 (*1-55074-482-8*) Kids Can Pr.

Bourgeois, Paulette. Franklin's Valentines. (Franklin Ser.). (Illus.). 32p. (J). (ps-3). 1998. 12.95 (*1-55074-480-1*, Pub. by Kids Can Pr) Genl Dist Srvs.

*Bourgeois, Paulette.** Franklin's Valentines. (Franklin Ser.). (J). (ps-3). 1999. pap. 54.00 (*0-439-04355-7*) Scholastic Inc.

Bourgeois, Paulette. Franklin's Valentines. (Franklin Ser.). (Illus.). 32p. (J). (ps-2). 1999. pap. 4.50 (*0-590-13001-3*) Scholastic Inc.

Bourgeois, Paulette. Fun with Franklin: A Learning to Read Book. (Franklin Ser.). (Illus.). (J). (ps-3). 9.75 (*1-55074-646-4*) Kids Can Pr.

— Fun with Franklin: A Learning to Read Book. (Franklin Ser.). (Illus.). 32p. (J). (ps-3). 1997. pap. 1.95 (*1-55074-391-0*) Kids Can Pr.

— Fun with Franklin: Activity Book. (Franklin Ser.) (Illus.). 32p. (J). (ps-3). 1997. pap. 1.95 (*1-55074-392-9*) Kids Can Pr.

— Fun with Franklin: Math Activity Book. (Franklin Ser.). (Illus.). 32p. (J). (ps-3). 1998. pap. 1.95 (*1-55074-452-6*) Kids Can Pr.

— Fun with Franklin: Puzzle Book. (Franklin Ser.). (Illus.). 32p. (J). (ps-3). 1997. pap. 1.95 (*1-55074-394-5*) Kids Can Pr.

— Fun with Franklin: Trace & Colour Book. (Franklin Ser.). (Illus.). 16p. (J). (ps-3). 1997. pap. 1.95 (*1-55074-396-1*) Kids Can Pr.

— Garbage Collectors. (Illus.). (J). 2000. 11.40 (*0-606-18225-X*) Turtleback.

Bourgeois, Paulette. Garbage Collectors. unabridged ed. (In My Neighborhood Ser.). (Illus.). 32p. (J). (ps-3). 1998. 12.95 (*1-55074-440-2*, Pub. by Kids Can Pr) Genl Dist Srvs.

*Bourgeois, Paulette.** Garbage Collectors. unabridged ed. (In My Neighborhood Ser.). (Illus.). 32p. (J). (gr. k-3). 2000. pap. 5.95 (*1-55074-826-2*, Pub. by Kids Can Pr) Genl Dist Srvs.

Bourgeois, Paulette. El Hallazgo de Franklin. Varela, Alejandra Lopez, tr. from ENG. (Franklin Ser.).Tr. of Finders Keepers for Franklin. (SPA.). (J). (ps-3). pap. 4.95 (*1-880507-51-X*) Lectorum Pubns.

*Bourgeois, Paulette.** La Hermanita de Franklin.Tr. of Franklin's Little Sister. (SPA., Illus.). (ps-3). 2000. 10.95 (*1-880507-84-6*) Lectorum Pubns.

— La Hermanita de Franklin. (Franklin Ser.).Tr. of Franklin's Little Sister. (SPA., Illus.). (J). (ps-3). 2000. pap. 5.95 (*1-880507-83-8*) Lectorum Pubns.

— Hurry up, Franklin. (Franklin Ser.). (Illus.). 32p. (J). (ps-3). 1992. pap. 5.95 (*1-55074-016-4*) Kids Can Pr.

Bourgeois, Paulette. Hurry up, Franklin. (Franklin Ser.). (Illus.). 32p. (J). (ps-3). 1997. 12.95 (*0-921103-68-9*, Pub. by Kids Can Pr) Genl Dist Srvs.

— Hurry up, Franklin. LC 89-10246. (Franklin Ser.). (Illus.). 31p. (J). (ps-2). 1991. pap. 3.95 (*0-590-42621-4*) Scholastic Inc.

— The Many Hats of Mr. Minches. unabridged ed. (Illus.). 32p. (J). (ps up). 1994. 12.95 (*0-7737-2839-2*) STDK.

— The Many Hats of Mr. Minches. unabridged ed. (Illus.). 32p. (J). (ps up). 1996. pap. 7.95 (*0-7737-5793-1*) STDK.

— The Moon. unabridged ed. (Starting with Space Ser.). (Illus.). 40p. (J). (gr. 2-6). 1997. 14.95 (*1-55074-157-8*, Pub. by Kids Can Pr) Genl Dist Srvs.

— The Moon. unabridged ed. (Starting with Space Ser.). (Illus.). 40p. (J). (gr. 2-6). 1999. pap. 6.95 (*1-55074-332-5*, Pub. by Kids Can Pr) Genl Dist Srvs.

*Bourgeois, Paulette.** Police Officers. (Illus.). (J). 2000. 11.40 (*0-606-18226-8*) Turtleback.

— Police Officers. unabridged ed. (In My Neighborhood Ser.). (Illus.). 32p. (J). (gr. k-3). 2000. pap. 5.95 (*1-55074-787-8*, Pub. by Kids Can Pr) Genl Dist Srvs.

— Postal Workers. (Illus.). (J). 2000. 11.40 (*0-606-18227-6*) Turtleback.

— Postal Workers. unabridged ed. (In My Neighborhood Ser.). (Illus.). 32p. (J). (gr. k-3). 2000. pap. 5.95 (*1-55074-785-1*, Pub. by Kids Can Pr) Genl Dist Srvs.

Bourgeois, Paulette. Strategic Management. (C). 1994. write for info. (*0-201-10717-1*) Addison-Wesley.

— The Sun. unabridged ed. (Starting with Space Ser.). (Illus.). 40p. (J). (gr. 2-6). 1997. 14.95 (*1-55074-158-6*, Pub. by Kids Can Pr) Genl Dist Srvs.

— The Sun. unabridged ed. (Starting with Space Ser.). (Illus.). 40p. (J). (gr. 2-6). 1999. pap. 6.95 (*1-55074-330-9*, Pub. by Kids Can Pr) Genl Dist Srvs.

— Too Many Chickens! (Illus.). 32p. (J). (ps-2). 1990. pap. 5.95 (*1-55074-067-9*, Pub. by Kids Can Pr) Genl Dist Srvs.

*Bourgeois, Paulette, reader.** Hurry up, Franklin. (Franklin Ser.). 32p. (J). (ps-3). 2000. pap. 9.95 incl. audio (*1-55074-682-0*) Kids Can Pr.

*Bourgeois, Paulette & Clark, Brenda.** Franklin Fibs. (Franklin Ser.). (Illus.). 32p. (J). (ps-3). 1999. pap. 9.95 incl. audio (*1-55074-668-5*) Kids Can Pr.

— Franklin Forgets. (Franklin TV Storybook Ser.). 32p. (J). (ps-3). 2000. pap. 4.95 (*1-55074-726-6*) Kids Can Pr.

— Franklin Forgets. (Franklin TV Storybook Ser.). (Illus.). 32p. (J). (ps-3). 2000. text 10.95 (*1-55074-722-3*) Kids Can Pr.

— Franklin Has a Sleepover. (Franklin Ser.). (Illus.). 32p. (J). (ps-3). 1999. pap. 9.95 incl. audio (*1-55074-664-2*) Kids Can Pr.

— Franklin Helps Out. (Franklin Ser.). (Illus.) (J). (ps-3). 2000. pap. 4.50 (*0-439-20379-1*) Scholastic Inc.

— Franklin Is Lost. (Franklin Ser.). (Illus.). 32p. (J). (ps-3). 1999. pap. 9.95 incl. audio (*1-55074-670-7*) Kids Can Pr.

— Franklin is Messy. (Franklin Ser.). 18p. (J). (ps-3). 1999. pap. 9.95 incl. audio (*1-55074-678-2*) Kids Can Pr.

— Franklin Says Sorry. (Franklin TV Storybook Ser.). (J). (ps-3). 1999. 4.95 (*1-55074-714-2*) Kids Can Pr.

— Franklin Says Sorry. (Franklin TV Storybook Ser.). (Illus.). 32p. (J). (ps-3). 1999. 10.95 (*1-55074-712-6*) Kids Can Pr.

— Franklin Says Sorry. (Franklin TV Storybook Ser.). (Illus.). 32p. (J). (ps-2). 2000. pap. 4.50 (*0-439-08366-4*) Scholastic.

— Franklin's Bicycle Helmet. (Franklin TV Storybook Ser.). 32p. (J). (ps-3). 2000. pap. 4.95 (*1-55074-728-2*) Kids Can Pr.

— Franklin's Bicycle Helmet. (Franklin TV Storybook Ser.). (Illus.). 32p. (J). (ps-3). 2000. text 10.95 (*1-55074-730-4*) Kids Can Pr.

— Franklin's Bicycle Helmet. (Franklin TV Storybook Ser.: Vol. 3). (Illus.). 32p. (J). (ps-3). 2000. pap. 4.50 (*0-439-08367-2*) Scholastic Inc.

— Franklin's Neighborhood. (Franklin Ser.). (Illus.). 32p. (J). (ps-3). 1999. pap. 9.95 incl. audio (*1-55074-752-5*) Kids Can Pr.

— Franklin's New Friend. (Franklin Ser.). (Illus.). 180p. (J). (ps-3). 1999. pap. 9.95 (*1-55074-797-5*) Kids Can Pr.

Bourgeois, Paulette & LaFave, Kim. Postal Workers. unabridged ed. LC 98-93196. (In My Neighborhood Ser.). (Illus.). 32p. (J). (ps-2). 1998. 12.95 (*1-55074-504-2*, Pub. by Kids Can Pr) Genl Dist Srvs.

Bourgeois, Paulette & Slavin, Bill. Starting with Space: The Moon.Tr. of Destination Univers: La Lune. (FRE., Illus.). 40p. (J). mass mkt. 8.99 (*0-590-16020-6*) Scholastic Inc.

— Starting with Space: The Sun.Tr. of Destination Univers: Le Soleil. (FRE., Illus.). 40p. (J). pap. 8.99 (*0-590-16019-2*) Scholastic Inc.

Bourgeois, Paulette & Wolfish, Martin. Changes in You & Me: A Book about Puberty, Mostly for Boys. LC 94-1162. (Illus.). 96p. (YA). (gr. 7-12). 1994. spiral bd. 14.95 (*0-8362-2814-6*) Andrews & McMeel.

— Changes in You & Me: A Book about Puberty, Mostly for Girls. LC 94-1161. (Illus.). 96p. (YA). (gr. 7-12). 1994. spiral bd. 14.95 (*0-8362-2815-4*) Andrews & McMeel.

Bourgeois, Paulette, et al. The Amazing Milk Book. unabridged ed. (Illus.). 80p. (J). 1991. pap. 6.95 (*1-55074-020-2*, Pub. by Kids Can Pr) Genl Dist Srvs.

— The Amazing Paper Book. unabridged ed. (Illus.). 80p. (J). (gr. 3-7). 1997. pap. 6.95 (*0-921103-82-4*, Pub. by Kids Can Pr) Genl Dist Srvs.

— Franklin en la Oscuridad. Lopez-Varela, Alejandra, tr. from ENG. (Franklin Ser.).Tr. of Franklin in the Dark. (SPA., Illus.). 32p. (J). (ps-3). 1998. pap. 4.95 (*1-880507-43-9*) Lectorum Pubns.

Bourgeois, Peter & LaFave, Kim. Police Officers. unabridged ed. LC 98-93196. (In My Neighborhood Ser.). (Illus.). 32p. (J). (ps-2). 1998. 14.95 (*1-55074-502-6*, Pub. by Kids Can Pr) Genl Dist Srvs.

Bourgeois, Robert. Building Strategic Relationships for Managed Care: Positioning Your Organization for Competitive Advantage. (Illus.). 300p. 1998. 60.00 (*0-07-006954-9*) McGraw.

Bourgeois, Tamyra. How to Raise Happy, Loving, Emotionally Intelligent Kids. 1998. pap. 14.95 (*0-9666393-0-8*) Enlightened Parents.

*Bourgeois, Tamyra.** How to Raise Happy, Loving, Emotionally Intelligent Kids. 310p. 2000. 19.95 (*0-9678023-3-4*) Smart Family Pub.

Bourgeois, Warren. Persons: What Philosophers Say about You. LC 96-135942. viii, 340p. (C). 1995. pap. 29.95 (*0-88920-251-6*) W Laurier U Pr.

Bourgeon, A., jt. ed. see Champault, G.

*Bourgeouis, Paulette & Wolfish, Martin.** Changes in You & Me: A Book about Puberty Mostly for Boys. (Illus.). 64p. (J). (gr. 5-8). 1998. pap. 14.95 (*0-921051-93-X*) Somerville Hse.

— Changes in You & Me: A Book about Puberty Mostly for Girls. (Illus.). 64p. (J). (gr. 4-7). 1998. pap. 14.95 (*0-921051-95-6*) Somerville Hse.

Bourgeron, P. S., et al, eds. An Integrated Ecological Assessment Protocols Guidebook. (Illus.). 464p. 1998. 119.00 (*0-387-98582-4*); pap. 59.95 (*0-387-98583-2*) Spr-Verlag.

Bourges, Bernard. European Simplified Methods for Active Solar System Design. (C). 1991. text 194.00 (*0-7923-1230-9*) Kluwer Academic.

Bourges, Bernard, ed. Climatic Data Handbook for Europe: Climatic Data for the Design of Solar Energy Buildings. 300p. (C). 1992. text 141.50 (*0-7923-1716-5*) Kluwer Academic.

Bourges, Elemir. Le Crepuscule Des Dieux. (FRE., Illus.). 266p. 1995. pap. 64.95 (*0-614-14016-1*) Intl Scholars.

Bourges, Jean. Color Bytes: Artists' Colors for Technology. Ghent, Janet S., ed. LC 97-212582. (Illus.). 160p. (Orig.). 1997. pap. 34.95 (*1-888551-00-3*) Chromatics Pr.

Bourget-Besnier, Elizabeth, jt. auth. see Huysmans, Joris-Karl.

Bourget, Genevieve, jt. auth. see Anderson, Mel.

Bourget, Geri S. Addy's Craft Book & Kit. (American Girls Collection). 44p. (YA). (gr. 2 up). 1996. 19.95 (*1-56247-144-9*) Pleasant Co.

— Felicity's Craft Book & Kit. (American Girls Collection). 44p. (YA). (gr. 2 up). 1996. 19.95 (*1-56247-142-2*) Pleasant Co.

— Kirsten's Craft Book & Kit. (American Girls Collection). 44p. (YA). (gr. 2 up). 1996. 19.95 (*1-56247-143-0*) Pleasant Co.

B

— Molly's Craft Book & Kit. (American Girls Collection). 44p. (YA). (gr. 2 up). 1996. text 19.95 (*1-56247-146-5*) Pleasant Co.

— Samantha's Craft Book & Kit. (American Girls Collection). 44p. (YA). (gr. 2 up). 1996. text 19.95 (*1-56247-145-7*) Pleasant Co.

— Tiny Treasures: Amazing Miniatures You Can Make! LC 98-16438. (J). (gr. 3 up). 1998. pap. text 9.95 (*1-56247-667-X*) Pleasant Co.

Bourget, Paul C. Antigone: And Other Portraits of Women. Marchant, William, tr. LC 71-150469. (Short Story Index Reprint Ser.). 1977. reprint ed. 20.95 (*0-8369-3809-7*) Ayer.

— Domestic Dramas: (Drames De Famille) Marchant, William, tr. LC 76-37259. (Short Story Index Reprint Ser.). 1977. reprint ed. 23.95 (*0-8369-4070-9*) Ayer.

— Monica & Other Stories. Marchant, William, tr. LC 77-106249. (Short Story Index Reprint Ser.). 1977. 20.95 (*0-8369-3286-2*) Ayer.

Bourget, Paul G., jt. auth. see Riordan, Pauline.

Bourghei, S. R., et al. Piety. Tavakoli, Amir, tr. from PER. 1980. pap. 2.00 (*0-318-03827-7*) Book Dist Ctr.

***Bourgholtzer, Frank.** Aleksandr Chayanov & Russian Berlin. LC 99-34317. (Library of Peasant Studies). (Illus.). 176p. 1999. 52.50 (*0-7146-5024-2*, Pub. by F Cass Pubs); pap. 24.50 (*0-7146-8080-X*, Pub. by F Cass Pubs) Intl Spec Bk.

Bourgin. Contemporary Musicians. (Contemporary Musicians Ser.: Vol. 15). 313p. 1995. text 81.00 (*0-8103-9316-6*) Gale.

Bourgin, Georges. Histoire de la Commune. 1907. 49.50 (*0-404-07549-5*) AMS Pr.

Bourgin, Hubert. L' Ecole Normale at la Politique: De Jaures a Leon Blum. (FRE.). 526p. 1971. pap. text 63.00 (*0-677-50375-X*) Gordon & Breach.

Bourgine & Walliser. Economics & Cognitive Science. 232p. 1992. 129.50 (*0-08-041050-2*, Pergamon Pr) Elsevier.

Bourgine, Paul, jt. ed. see Varela, Francisco J.

Bourgoignie, Thierry & Trubek, David M., eds. Integration Through Law - Europe & the American Federal Experience Vol. 3: Consumer Law, Common Markets & Federalism in Europe & the United States. (European University Institute, Series A (Law): Nos. 2 & 3). xxiv, 271p. 1986. lib. bdg. 86.95 (*3-11-010741-4*) De Gruyter.

Bourgoin. Contemporary Musicians, Vol. 14. 340p. 1995. text 81.00 (*0-8103-5738-0*) Gale.

Bourgoin. Islamic Patterns. (Illus.). 48p. 1977. pap. 4.95 (*0-486-23537-8*) Dover.

Bourgoin, Edward. Foreign Languages & Your Career. 4th rev. ed. 120p. 1993. 9.95 (*0-88432-698-5*) Audio-Forum.

Bourgoin, J. Arabic Allover Patterns. (Illus.). 48p. 1976. pap. 4.95 (*0-486-23390-1*) Dover.

— Arabic Geometrical Pattern & Design. (Illus.). 224p. 1973. reprint ed. pap. 9.95 (*0-486-22924-6*) Dover.

Bourgoin, J. & Lannoo, M. Point Defects in Semiconductors II: Experimental Aspects. (Solid-State Sciences Ser.: Vol. 35). (Illus.). 295p. 1983. 60.95 (*0-387-11515-3*) Spr-Verlag.

Bourgoin, J., jt. auth. see Lannoo, M.

Bourgoin, J. C. Physics of DX Centers in GaAs Alloys. 310p. 1990. 116.00 (*3-908044-05-7*, Pub. by Trans T Pub) Enfield Pubs NH.

Bourgoin, J. C., jt. ed. see Stievenard, D.

Bourgoin, Suzanne M. Small Business Profiles Vol. 1: A Guide to Today's Top Opportunities for Entrepreneurs. 277p. 1994. 105.00 (*0-8103-9178-3*) Gale.

Bourgoin, Suzanne M., ed. Contemporary Musicians: Profiles of the People in Music, Vol. 13. 322p. 1994. text 81.00 (*0-8103-5737-2*) Gale.

Bourgoin, Suzanne M. & Byers, Paula K. Encyclopedia of World Biography, 17 vols. 2nd ed. LC 97-42327. 9443p. (YA). (gr. 9 up). 1997. 975.00 (*0-7876-2221-4*) Gale.

Bourgoing, Pascale De, see De Bourgoing, Pascale.

Bourgois, Jacques, jt. ed. see Aubouin, Jean.

Bourgois, Louis G., jt. auth. see Berrett, Joshua.

Bourgois, Philippe I. In Search of Respect: Selling Crack in El Barrio. (Structural Analysis in the Social Sciences Ser.: No. 10). (Illus.). 406p. (C). 1996. text 26.95 (*0-521-43518-8*) Cambridge U Pr.

— In Search of Respect: Selling Crack in El Barrio. rev. ed. (Structural Analysis in the Social Sciences Ser.: No. 10). (Illus.). 392p. 1996. pap. text 16.95 (*0-521-57460-9*) Cambridge U Pr.

Bourgouin, P., jt. auth. see Duvernoy, Henri M.

Bourgoyne, A. T., Jr., et al. Applied Drilling Engineering. 510p. 1986. 58.00 (*1-55563-001-4*, DRILTEXT002) Soc Petrol Engineers.

Bourguet, M. N. Dechiffrer la France: LaStatistique Departementale a l'Epoque Napoleonienne. (FRE.). 480p. 1988. pap. text 73.00 (*2-88124-225-1*) Gordon & Breach.

Bourguet, M. N., et al, eds. Between History & Memory. 196p. 1990. text 83.00 (*3-7186-5067-3*) Gordon & Breach.

Bourgui, Erika. Psychological Anthropology. (C). 1979. write for info. (*0-03-034921-4*) Harcourt Coll Pubs.

Bourguignon, Erika & Greenbaum, Lenora. Diversity & Homogeneity in World Societies. LC 73-86218. (Comparative Studies). (Illus.). 208p. 1973. 15.00 (*0-87536-329-6*); pap. 10.00 (*0-87536-330-X*) HRAFP.

Bourguignon, Erika, ed. see Schneider, Bronka.

Bourguignon, F., jt. ed. see Atkinson, A. B.

Bourguignon, Francois, jt. auth. see Berthelemy, Jean-Claude.

Bourguignon, Jean P., et al, eds. Geometric Theory of Singular Phenomena in Partial Differential Equations. (Symposia Mathematica Ser.: No. 38). (Illus.). 196p. (C). 1998. text 69.95 (*0-521-63246-3*) Cambridge U Pr.

Bourguignon, Lawrence. A Friend for Tiger. LC 95-20410. (Illus.). 32p. (J). (gr. k-2). 1997. 14.95 (*0-8167-3907-2*) BrdgeWater.

Bourguignon, Paul. The Greener Grass. 210p. (Orig.). 1993. pap. 13.95 (*0-918056-05-5*) Ariadne Pr.

Bourguignon, Stephane. Sandman Blues. LC 96-153662. 240p. (Orig.). 1996. pap. 14.95 (*0-7737-5783-X*) Stoddart Publ.

Bourguina, Anna M. & Jakobson, Michael, compiled by. Guide to the Boris I. Nicolaevsky Collection in the Hoover Institution Archives. (Bibliographical Ser.: No. 74). 800p. 1989. pap. 15.98 (*0-8179-2742-5*) Hoover Inst Pr.

Bourhill, E. J. & Drake, J. B. Fairy Tales from South Africa. LC 78-67690. (Folktale Ser.). (Illus.). reprint ed. 39.50 (*0-404-16058-1*) AMS Pr.

Bourhis, Richard Y., ed. Conflict & Language Planning in Quebec. 304p. 1984. 99.00 (*0-905028-16-3*); pap. 39.95 (*0-905028-25-2*) Taylor & Francis.

Bouriant, M. U. Memoires: Publies par les Membres de la Mission Archeologique Francaise au Caire, 2 Vols., Set. (ARA & FRE.). 1979. 40.00 (*0-86685-333-2*) Intl Bk Ctr.

Bouriaux, Sylvie, jt. ed. see Himick, Michael.

Bourie, Ric & Turner, Erin, eds. Exploring Mount Helena. LC 97-20017. (Illus.). 96p. (Orig.). 1996. pap. 9.95 (*1-56044-524-6*) Falcon Pub Inc.

Bourie, Steve. American Casino Guide, 1999. (Illus.). 450p. 1998. pap. 14.95 (*1-883768-08-X*) Casino Vac.

***Bourie, Steve.** American Casino Guide, 2000. 520p. 1999. pap. 14.95 (*1-883768-09-8*, Pub. by Casino Vac) Login Pubs Consort.

Bourie, Steve. American Casino Guide, 1998. (Illus.). 336p. (Orig.). 1997. pap. 14.95 (*1-883768-07-1*) Casino Vac.

***Bourie, Steve.** American Casino Guide 2001. 2000. pap. 14.95 (*1-883768-10-1*) Casino Vac.

Bourin, Jeanne. Amours Blessees. (Folio Ser.: No. 2031). (FRE.). 1989. pap. 10.95 (*2-07-038119-6*) Schoenhof.

— Les Amours Blessees. (FRE.). 415p. 1989. pap. 11.95 (*0-7859-2114-1*, 2070381196) Fr & Eur.

— Le Grand Feu. (FRE.). 608p. 1988. pap. 11.95 (*0-7859-2086-2*, 2070379256) Fr & Eur.

Bourin, Philippe. European Investment Bank: Its Structure & Functions in Financing Community & Non-Community Projects. (European Community Law Ser.: Vol. 5). 240p. (C). 1996. text 85.00 (*0-485-70001-8*, Pub. by Athlone Pr) Humanities.

Bouris, Karen. The First Time: What Parents & Teenage Girls Should Know about "Losing Your Virginity" 2nd ed. 208p. (YA). 1995. pap. 9.95 (*0-943233-93-3*) Conari Press.

Bourisaw, Diana, jt. auth. see Sweeney, Jim.

Bourjaily, Philip. The Field & Stream Turkey Hunting Handbook. LC 99-10279. (Field & Stream Fishing And Hunting Library). (Illus.). 1999. pap. 9.95 (*1-55821-913-7*) Lyons Pr.

Bourjaily, Vance N. The Unnatural Enemy: Essays on Hunting. LC 84-8640. (Illus.). 195p. 1984. reprint ed. pap. 55.60 (*0-608-00728-5*, 2061504) Bks Demand.

Bourjat, P. Radiology of the Hand. (Exercises in Radiological Diagnosis Ser.). (Illus.). 230p. 1987. 35.00 (*0-387-16537-1*) Spr-Verlag.

Bourke, Andrew F. & Franks, Nigel R. Social Evolution in Ants. LC 95-5959. 550p. 1995. text 85.00 (*0-691-04427-9*, Pub. by Princeton U Pr); pap. text 32.50 (*0-691-04426-0*, Pub. by Princeton U Pr) Cal Prin Full Svc.

***Bourke, Angela.** Burning of Bridget Cleary: A True Story. LC 00-26891. (Illus.). 304p. 2000. 24.95 (*0-670-89270-X*, Viking) Viking Penguin.

Bourke, Angela. By Salt Water: Stories by Angela Bourke. LC 97-101138. 168p. (Orig.). 1996. pap. 11.95 (*1-874597-39-1*, Pub. by New Island Books) Irish Bks Media.

Bourke, Bob, jt. auth. see Markrich, Mike.

Bourke, Colin, et al, eds. Aboriginal Australia: An Introductory Reader in Australia Studies. rev. ed. LC 98-216749. 1998. pap. 19.95 (*0-7022-3051-0*, Pub. by Univ Queensland Pr) Intl Spec Bk.

Bourke, Cormac, ed. Northern Flame: Studies on the Legacy of Columba. 256p. 1996. 45.00 (*1-85182-268-2*, Pub. by Four Cts Pr) Intl Spec Bk.

Bourke, Dale H. Everyday Miracles: Glimpses of Grace in a Mother's Day. LC 98-50390. 176p. 1999. pap. 13.99 (*0-8054-2030-4*) Broadman.

— The Sleep Management Plan: A Six-Step Plan to Add Hours to Your Week & Increase Your Energy. 160p. 1998. mass mkt. 5.50 (*0-06-104214-5*, Pub. by Harper SF) HarpC.

Bourke, Desmond O. French-English Agricultural Dictionary, with English-French Index: With English-French Index. (ENG & FRE.). 304p. 1992. text 105.00 (*0-85198-767-2*) OUP.

— Horticultural Dictionary: French-English. (ENG & FRE.). 1974. 125.00 (*0-8288-6052-1*, M9713) Fr & Eur.

— Spanish-English Horticultural Dictionary. 148p. 1987. pap. text 35.00 (*0-85198-572-6*) C A B Intl.

Bourke, Desmond O., compiled by. French-English Horticultural Dictionary. 2nd ed. LC 97-4393. 248p. (C). 1989. text 75.00 (*0-85198-626-9*) OUP.

Bourke, Desmond O., et al. Spanish-English Horticultural Dictionary. 148p. 1987. pap. 95.00 (*0-8288-0064-2*, F46900) C A B Intl.

Bourke, E., et al, eds. Moving Points in Nephrology: Festschrift in Honor of Professor Geoffrey M. Berlyne. (Contributions to Nephrology Ser.: Vol. 102). (Illus.). xvi, 254p. 1992. 49.75 (*3-8055-5642-X*) S Karger.

Bourke, Eva. Spring in Henry Street. LC 96-140219. 1996. 18.95 (*1-873790-91-0*) Dufour.

— Spring in Henry Street. LC 96-140219. 88p. 1997. pap. 11.95 (*1-873790-90-2*) Dufour.

Bourke, Fergus. Kindred. LC 98-105983. (Illus.). 312p. 1997. 34.95 (*1-86059-047-0*, Pub. by Town Hse) Roberts Rinehart.

Bourke, Geoffrey J., ed. The Epidemiology of Cancer. LC 84-70185. 374p. 1983. text 29.95 (*0-914783-03-3*) Charles.

Bourke, Geoffrey J., jt. auth. see Daly, Leslie E.

Bourke, Glenn & Rutherford, Mark. Championship Laser Racing. (Illus.). 95p. (C). pap. 16.95 (*0-906754-85-2*, 128332AE, Pub. by Fernhurst Bks) St Mut.

Bourke, Joanna. Dismembering the Male: Men's Bodies, Britain, & the Great War. LC 95-44964. (Illus.). 320p. (C). 1996. 32.50 (*0-226-06746-7*) U Ch Pr.

***Bourke, Joanna.** An Intimate History of Killing. (Illus.). 512p. 2000. pap. 15.00 (*0-465-00738-4*, Pub. by Basic) HarpC.

Bourke, Joanna. An Intimate History of Killing: Face-to-Face Killing in 20th Century Warfare. 544p. 1999. text 30.00 (*0-465-00737-6*, Pub. by Basic) HarpC.

— Working Class Cultures in Britain, 1890-1960: Gender, Class, & Ethnicity. LC 93-18891. (Illus.). 272p. (C). 1993. pap. 24.99 (*0-415-09898-X*) Routledge.

— Working Class Cultures in Britain, 1890-1960: Gender, Class, & Ethnicity. LC 93-18891. (Illus.). 272p. (C). (gr. 13). 1994. 80.00 (*0-415-09897-1*) Routledge.

***Bourke, Joanna, ed.** The Misfit Soldier: A War Story, 1914-1932. LC 99-197993. 96p. 1999. pap. 12.95 (*1-85918-188-0*, Pub. by Cork Univ) Intl Spec Bk.

Bourke, John, et al, eds. Pesticide Waste Management: Technology & Regulation. LC 92-32304. (ACS Symposium Ser.: No. 510). (Illus.). 273p. 1992. text 70.00 (*0-8412-2480-3*, Pub. by Am Chemical) OUP.

Bourke, John G. Apache Medicine-Men. LC 93-36083. (Illus.). 176p. 1994. reprint ed. pap. text 8.95 (*0-486-27842-5*) Dover.

— The Medicine Men of the Apache: A Paper from the Ninth Annual Report of the Bureau of American Ethnology 1887-1888. LC 77-135517. (Beautiful Rio Grande Classics Ser.). (Illus.). 187p. 1983. reprint ed. lib. bdg. 22.50 (*0-87380-050-8*) Popular E Commerce.

— On the Border with Crook. (American Biography Ser.). 491p. 1991. reprint ed. lib. bdg. 89.00 (*0-7812-8031-1*) Rprt Serv.

— On the Border with Crook. LC 74-155699. vii, 491p. 1971. reprint ed. pap. 17.95 (*0-8032-5741-4*, Bison Books) U of Nebr Pr.

— The Snake-Dance of the Moquis of Arizona. LC 84-16379. (Illus.). 371p. 1984. reprint ed. pap. 19.95 (*0-8165-0872-0*) U of Ariz Pr.

Bourke, John G. & Remington, Frederic. General Crook in the Indian Country: A Scout with the Buffalo Soldiers. 2nd ed. (Illus.). 40p. (Orig.). 1997. reprint ed. pap. 4.95 (*0-86541-037-2*) Filter.

Bourke, John G., et al. Bourke's Diary: From Journals of First Lieutenant John Gregory Bourke, from June 27-September 15, during Indian War of Eighteen Seventy-Six. Willert, James, ed. & intro. by. (Illus.). 270p. 1986. 40.00 (*0-930798-09-0*); pap. text 25.00 (*0-930798-10-4*) J Willert.

Bourke, John P., et al, eds. Ventricular Tachyarrhythmias in the Normal Heart. LC 98-4645. (Clinical Approaches to Tachyarrhythmias Ser.: Vol. 8). (Illus.). 107p. 1998. 19.00 (*0-87993-400-X*) Futura Pub.

Bourke, John P., et al. Bourke's Police & Summary Offences, Victoria: Comprising of the Police Offences Act 1958, Summary Offences Act 1966, Protection of Animals Act 1966, Vagrancy Act 1966, Lotteries Gaming & Betting Act 1966, Being the Second Edition of Bourke's Police Offences. 2nd ed. LC 71-580843. 468p. 1970. write for info. (*0-409-35402-3*) Buttrwrth-Heinemann.

Bourke, Lawrence. A Vivid Steady State: Les Murray & Australian Poetry. 174p. 1992. pap. 22.95 (*0-86840-045-9*, Pub. by New South Wales Univ Pr) Intl Spec Bk.

Bourke, Linda. Eye Spy. (Illus.). 64p. (J). (ps up). 1991. 15.95 (*0-87701-805-7*) Chronicle Bks.

— Eye Spy. (Illus.). 64p. (J). (ps-3). 1995. pap. 6.95 (*0-8118-1076-3*) Chronicle Bks.

Bourke, Linda. Eye Spy: A Book of Alphabet Puzzles. 1991. 12.15 (*0-606-08920-9*, Pub. by Turtleback) Demco.

Bourke, Linda. Signs of a Friend. LC 84-40790. (Illus.). (J). 1982. pap. 2.95 (*0-201-10094-0*) HarpC Child Bks.

Bourke, Linda, jt. auth. see Sullivan, Mary B.

Bourke, Michael K. Strategy & Architecture of Health Care Information Systems. LC 93-27727. (Illus.). 356p. 1994. 54.00 (*0-387-97982-4*) Spr-Verlag.

Bourke, Paul & DeBats, Donald. Washington County: Politics & Community in Antebellum America. LC 94-34055. (Reconfiguring American Political History). (Illus.). 312p. 1995. text 45.00 (*0-8018-4950-0*) Johns Hopkins.

Bourke, Richard S. St. Petersburg & Moscow: A Visit to the Court of the Czar. LC 70-115508. (Russia Observed, Series I). 1970. reprint ed. 31.95 (*0-405-03005-3*) Ayer.

Bourke, S. J. & Brewis, R. A. L. Lecture Notes on Respiratory Disease. 5th ed. LC 98-3473. (Lecture Notes Ser.). (Illus.). 1998. pap. 34.95 (*0-632-04968-5*) Blackwell Sci.

Bourke, Thomas. Japan & the Globilisation of European Integration. 236p. 1996. text 77.95 (*1-85521-834-8*, Pub. by Dartmth Pub) Ashgate Pub Co.

Bourke, Tim, jt. auth. see Bird, David.

Bourke, Tim, jt. auth. see Kelsey, Hugh.

Bourke, Vernon, ed. The Pocket Aquinas. 372p. 1991. per. 5.99 (*0-671-73991-3*, WSP) PB.

Bourke, Vernon J. Augustine's Love of Wisdom: An Introspective Philosophy. LC 91-46448. (Series in the History of Philosophy). 240p. (C). 1992. 36.95 (*1-55753-025-4*); pap. 17.95 (*1-55753-026-2*) Purdue U Pr.

— St. Thomas & the Greek Moralists. (Aquinas Lectures). 1947. 15.00 (*0-87462-111-9*) Marquette.

Bourke, Vernon J., jt. compiled by see Miethe, Terry L.

Bourke, Vernon J., tr. see Augustine, Saint.

Bourke-White, Margaret. Eyes on Russia. LC 79-39515. 1968. reprint ed. 49.50 (*0-404-00939-5*) AMS Pr.

Bourke-White, Margaret, photos by. Margaret Bourke-White, Photographer. LC 98-71654. (Illus.). 160p. (gr. 8). 1998. 65.00 (*0-8212-2490-5*) Little.

Bourke-White, Margaret & Caldwell, E. Say, Is This the U. S. A. LC 77-9598. (Photography Ser.). (Illus.). 1977. reprint ed. pap. 8.95 (*0-306-80071-3*); reprint ed. lib. bdg. 35.00 (*0-306-77434-8*) Da Capo.

Bourke-White, Margaret, jt. auth. see Caldwell, Erskine.

Bourkoff, Etan. Toolkit: Maple V for Engineers. 128p. 1997. pap. text 19.00 (*0-8053-6444-7*) Addison-Wesley.

Bourkoff, Etan, jt. auth. see Meade, Douglas.

Bourlakis, C. A. Applied Industrial Economics & Business Strategy. 512p. (gr. 13). 1996. pap. text 31.00 (*0-412-62130-4*) Chapman & Hall.

Bourland, D. David, Jr. & Bourland, Elizabeth J. A Course in Advanced Squirrelly Semantics: A Coloring Book for Some Adults. (Illus.). (Orig.). 1993. pap. 19.95 (*0-918970-39-3*) Intl Gen Semantics.

Bourland, D. David & Johnston, Paul D. E-Prime III! A Third Anthology. LC 97-49160. 562p. 1997. 29.95 (*0-918970-46-6*) Intl Gen Semantics.

Bourland, Elizabeth J., jt. auth. see Bourland, D. David, Jr.

***Bourland, Julia.** The Go-Girl Guide: Surviving Your 20s with Savvy, Soul & Style. LC 99-59379. (Illus.). 256p. 2000. pap. 14.95 (*0-8092-2476-3*, 247630, Contemporary Bks) NTC Contemp Pub Co.

Bourland, W. George. Who Gets the Antelope's Liver? 12.95 (*0-686-37633-1*) Harp & Thistle.

Bourlard, Herve A. Connectionist Speech Recognition: A Hybrid Approach. LC 93-30148. (International Series in Engineering & Computer Science, VLSI, Computer Architecture, & Digital Screen Processing). 352p. (C). 1993. text 157.50 (*0-7923-9396-1*) Kluwer Academic.

Bourles, Jean-Claude. Louis Guilloux. (FRE., Illus.). 1997. pap. write for info. (*2-86808-110-X*) Intl Scholars.

Bourlet, Alan. Police Intervention in Marital Violence. 160p. 1990. 113.00 (*0-335-09293-4*); pap. 36.95 (*0-335-09292-6*) OpUniv Pr.

Bourl'Honne, P. George Eliot: Essai de Biographie Intellectuelle et Morale, 1819-1854. LC 76-148754. reprint ed. 39.50 (*0-404-08727-2*) AMS Pr.

Bourlier, Karen. The Hitchhiker's Guide to Point-of-Care Testing. 88p. 1998. pap. 15.00 (*1-890883-06-9*, 202026) Am Assn Clinical Chem.

Bourliere, F. Tropical Savannas. (Ecosystems of the World Ser.: Vol. 13). 730p. 1983. 405.75 (*0-444-42035-5*) Elsevier.

Bourliere, F., jt. ed. see Harmelin-Viven, M.

Bourman, Anatole. Tragedy of Nijinsky. LC 70-98822. 291p. 1970. reprint ed. lib. bdg. 35.00 (*0-8371-2965-6*, BOTN, Greenwood Pr) Greenwood.

Bourman, John. Reflections on Man & the Human Condition. abr. ed. Kollas, Philip, ed. 200p. 1995. 19.95 (*0-9650797-0-8*) J L Bowman.

Bourmaut, Richard, jt. auth. see Thiltges, Alex.

Bourn & Winter. Destiny of Kings. (Adventure Ser.). 1998. 8.95 (*0-7869-1377-0*, Pub. by TSR Inc) Random.

Bourn, jt. auth. see Cigno.

***Bourn, Colin, ed.** The Transfer of Undertakings in the Public Sector. (Employment & European Union Law Ser.). 277p. 2000. text 78.95 (*1-84014-772-5*, Pub. by Ashgate Pub) Ashgate Pub Co.

Bourn, Diana, jt. ed. see Cigno, Katy.

Bourn, Grant L. Advertiser's Copy Prompter. 28p. 1985. reprint ed. pap. 5.00 (*0-931061-07-5*) Mail Trade.

Bourn, John, ed. Public Sector Management, 2 vols., Set. LC 95-7413. (International Library of Management). 784p. 1995. 346.95 (*1-85521-517-9*, Pub. by Dartmth Pub) Ashgate Pub Co.

Bourn, Michael. Funding & Financial Management in Higher Education. 2nd ed. 256p. 1996. 55.00 (*0-412-57390-3*) Chapman & Hall.

Bournas, Helen, tr. see Vassilakis, Nico.

Bournas, Mary, tr. see Vassilakis, Nico.

Bournaud, M. & Tachet, H., eds. Fifth International Symposium on Trichoptera, Lyon (France) 21-26 July 1986: Proceedings. (Entomologica Ser.). 1987. lib. bdg. 230.50 (*90-6193-620-9*) Kluwer Academic.

Bournazel, Eric, jt. auth. see Poly, Jean-Pierre.

Bourne. Fish for Data Using Net. 1996. 12.74 (*0-07-006687-6*) McGraw.

***Bourne.** Healing Fear. 416p. 2000. 9.98 (*1-56731-382-5*, MJF Bks) Fine Comms.

Bourne. Lighting in the Domestic Interior, Renaissance to Art Nouveau. 1991. 95.00 (*0-85667-397-8*) Sothebys Pubns.

— Turbulent Mixing & Chemical Reactions. LC 98-30337. 890p. (C). 1999. 415.00 (*0-471-98171-0*) Wiley.

Bourne, A. J., jt. auth. see Green, Albert E.

Bourne, Amanda & Bourne, Troy. A Taste of Utah County: A Guide to the Area's Best Restaurants. (Illus.). x, 102p. 1998. pap. 7.95 (*0-9665623-0-5*) Dalton Grp.

Bourne, Barbara. Exploring Space: Using Seymour Simon's Astronomy Books in the Classroom. LC 93-51249. 1994. 16.00 (*0-688-13643-5*, Wm Morrow) Morrow Avon.

***Bourne, Barbara.** Taking Inquiry Outdoors: Reading, Writing & Science Beyond the Classroom Walls. Stratton, Philippa, ed. LC 99-33923. 152p. (C). 1999. pap. 17.00 (*1-57110-302-3*) Stenhse Pubs.

Bourne, Barbara & Saul, Wendy. Exploring Space: Using Seymour Simon's Astronomy Books in the Classroom. (Illus.). 96p. 1994. pap. 9.95 (*0-614-03064-1*, Wm Morrow) Morrow Avon.

An Asterisk (*) at the beginning of an entry indicates that the title is appearing for the first time.

Bourne, Barbara, jt. auth. see Rowan, Thomas E.

Bourne, Bill, et al, eds. Modernity & Its Discontents: Voices from the Channel 4 Television Series. 119p. 1987. 42.50 (*0-85124-472-6*, Pub. by Spkesman); pap. 24.50 (*0-85124-482-3*, Pub. by Spkesman) Coronet Bks.

— Writers & Politics. 96p. 1987. 30.00 (*0-85124-483-1*) Dufour.

Bourne, Caroline. On Rapture's Wing. 1988. mass mkt. 3.75 (*0-8217-1352-3*, Zebra Kensgtn) Kensgtn Pub Corp.

— Wild Southern Rose. 1985. mass mkt. 3.75 (*0-8217-1603-4*, Zebra Kensgtn) Kensgtn Pub Corp.

Bourne, Charles, et al. Civil Advocacy: A Practical Guide. 230p. 1997. pap. 40.00 (*1-874241-12-0*, Pub. by Cavendish Pubng) Gaunt.

***Bourne, Colin.** The Discrimination Acts, Explained. (Point of Law Ser.). 300p. 2000. pap. 50.00 (*0-11-702382-5*, Pub. by Statnry Office) Balogh.

Bourne, Compton, jt. ed. see Worrell, DeLisle.

Bourne, Daniel. The Household Gods. (CSU Poetry Ser.: No. XLV). 88p. 1995. pap. 10.00 (*1-880834-13-8*) Cleveland St Univ Poetry Ctr.

Bourne, Daniel & Jastrun, Tomasz. On the Crossroads of Asia & Europe. 104p. 1998. pap. 10.00 (*1-887573-05-4*) Salmon Run.

Bourne, Dave, jt. auth. see Adolph, Harold P.

Bourne, David. Back to the Cutting Edge. 1999. write for info. (*0-201-55066-0*) Addison-Wesley.

Bourne, David, jt. auth. see Adolph, Harold P.

Bourne, David, jt. auth. see Medoza, Staci.

Bourne, David, jt. auth. see Wint, William.

Bourne, David A., jt. auth. see Wright, Paul K.

Bourne, David W. Mathematical Modeling of Pharmacokinetic Data. LC 94-61269. 142p. 1995. text 104.95 (*1-56676-204-9*) Technomic.

Bourne, David W., et al. Pharmacokinetics for the Non-Mathematical. 1986. text 119.00 (*0-85200-712-4*) Kluwer Academic.

Bourne, Douglas J. New Uses of Sulfur II: A Symposium. LC 78-1004. (Advances in Chemistry Ser.: No. 165). (Illus.). 293p. 1978. reprint ed. pap. 90.90 (*0-608-04357-5*, 206513800001) Bks Demand.

Bourne, Douglas J., ed. New Uses of Sulfur II. LC 78-1004. (Advances in Chemistry Ser.: No. 165). 1978. 32.95 (*0-8412-0391-1*) Am Chemical.

Bourne, Edmund. Healing Fear: New Approaches to Overcoming Anxiety. LC 98-66698. 320p. 1998. pap. 16.95 (*1-57224-116-0*) New Harbinger.

Bourne, Edmund J. The Anxiety & Phobia Workbook. 368p. 1995. reprint ed. 12.98 (*1-56731-074-5*, MJF Bks) Fine Comms.

— Anxiety & Phobia Workbook. 2nd ed. 448p. 1994. pap. 19.95 (*1-57224-003-2*) New Harbinger.

— Overcoming Specific Phobia - Therapist Protocol: A Hierarchy & Exposure-Based Protocol for the Treatment of All Specific Phobias. LC 98-66708. (Best Practices Ser.). 90p. 1998. pap. 19.95 (*1-57224-114-4*) New Harbinger.

— Overcoming Specific Phobias - Client Manual: A Hierarchy & Exposure-Based Protocol for the Treatment of All Specific Phobias. (Best Practices Ser.). 60p. 1998. pap. 9.95 (*1-57224-115-2*) New Harbinger.

Bourne, Edward E. History of Wells & Kennebunk, from the Earliest Settlement to the Year 1820, at Which Time Kennebunk Was Set off & Incorporated, with Biographical Sketches. (Illus.). 797p. 1997. reprint ed. lib. bdg. 79.50 (*0-8328-5925-7*) Higginson Bk Co.

— The History of Wells, & Kennebunk, Maine. 832p. 1984. 55.00 (*0-917890-43-4*) Heritage Bk.

***Bourne, Edward G.** Columbus, Ramon Pane, & the Beginnings of American Anthropology. (LC History-America-E). 41p. 1999. reprint ed. lib. bdg. 69.00 (*0-7812-4294-0*) Rprt Serv.

Bourne, Edward G. Discovery Conquest, & Early History of the Philippine Islands. (Works of Edward Gaylord Bourne). 1989. reprint ed. lib. bdg. 79.00 (*0-7812-2013-0*) Rprt Serv.

— Essays in Historical Criticism. LC 67-23183. (Essay Index Reprint Ser.). 1977. 23.95 (*0-8369-0228-9*) Ayer.

— Essays in Historical Criticism. (Works of Edward Gaylord Bourne). 1989. reprint ed. lib. bdg. 79.00 (*0-7812-2010-6*) Rprt Serv.

— Essays in Historical Criticism. (BCL1 - U. S. History Ser.). 304p. 1991. reprint ed. lib. bdg. 79.00 (*0-7812-6020-5*) Rprt Serv.

— Historical Introduction to the Philippine Islands. (Works of Edward Gaylord Bourne). 1989. reprint ed. lib. bdg. 79.00 (*0-7812-2011-4*) Rprt Serv.

— Prince Henry: The Navigator. (Works of Edward Gaylord Bourne). 1989. reprint ed. lib. bdg. 79.00 (*0-7812-2008-4*) Rprt Serv.

— The Proposed Absorbtion of Mexico in 1847-48. (Works of Edward Gaylord Bourne). 1989. reprint ed. lib. bdg. 79.00 (*0-7812-2009-2*) Rprt Serv.

— Spain in America. (Works of Edward Gaylord Bourne). 1989. reprint ed. lib. bdg. 79.00 (*0-7812-2012-2*) Rprt Serv.

— Surplus Revenue of 1837. (Works of Edward Gaylord Bourne). 1989. reprint ed. lib. bdg. 79.00 (*0-7812-2007-6*) Rprt Serv.

— The Works of Edward Gaylord Bourne. 1989. reprint ed. lib. bdg. 79.00 (*0-685-27338-5*) Rprt Serv.

Bourne, Edward G., ed. Narratives of the Career of Hernando De Soto in the Conquest of Florida As Told by a Knight of Elvas, 2 Vols, Set. Smith, Buckingham, tr. LC 72-2823. (American Explorers Ser.). (Illus.). reprint ed. 87.00 (*0-404-54901-2*) AMS Pr.

Bourne, Eulalia. Nine Months Is a Year at Baboquivari School. fac. ed. LC 68-57760. (Southwest Chronicle Ser.). (Illus.). 282p. 1969. reprint ed. pap. 87.50 (*0-7837-8020-6*, 204777600008) Bks Demand.

***Bourne, F. W., ed.** Billy Bray the King's Son. 4th rev. ed. 104p. 1998. pap. 5.99 (*0-88019-381-6*) Schmul Pub Co.

Bourne, Geoffrey H., ed. Applied Nutritional Principles in Health & Disease. (World Review of Nutrition & Dietetics Ser.: Vol. 53). (Illus.). x, 302p. 1987. 237.50 (*3-8055-4681-5*) S Karger.

— Aspects of Childhood Nutrition. (World Review of Nutrition & Dietetics Ser.: Vol. 58). (Illus.). x, 166p. 1989. 128.75 (*3-8055-4918-0*) S Karger.

— Aspects of Food Production, Consumption & Energy Values. (World Review of Nutrition & Dietetics Ser.: Vol. 61). (Illus.). 212p. 1989. 172.25 (*3-8055-4993-8*) S Karger.

— Aspects of Human & National Nutrition. (World Review of Nutrition & Dietetics Ser.: Vol. 41). (Illus.). xii, 260p. 1983. 204.50 (*3-8055-3591-0*) S Karger.

— Aspects of Human Nutrition. (World Review of Nutrition & Dietetics Ser.: Vol. 57). (Illus.). x, 334p. 1988. 258.50 (*3-8055-4810-9*) S Karger.

— Aspects of Human Nutrition & Food Contaminants. (World Review of Nutrition & Dietetics Ser.: Vol. 34). (Illus.). 1979. 144.50 (*3-8055-3069-2*) S Karger.

— Aspects of Nutritional Physiology. (World Review of Nutrition & Dietetics Ser.: Vol. 56). (Illus.). x, 262p. 1988. 195.00 (*3-8055-4785-4*) S Karger.

— Aspects of Some Vitamins, Minerals & Enzymes in Health & Disease. (World Review of Nutrition & Dietetics Ser.: Vol. 62). (Illus.). 216p. 1990. 188.00 (*3-8055-4994-6*) S Karger.

— Dietary Research & Guidance in Health & Disease. (World Review of Nutrition & Dietetics Ser.: Vol. 48). (Illus.). viii, 270p. 1986. 202.75 (*3-8055-4341-7*) S Karger.

— Energy: Nutrition of Women. (World Review of Nutrition & Dietetics Ser.: Vol. 52). (Illus.). x, 266p. 1987. 211.50 (*3-8055-4664-5*) S Karger.

— Human & Animal Nutrition. (World Review of Nutrition & Dietetics Ser.: Vol. 32). (Illus.). 1978. 128.75 (*3-8055-2855-8*) S Karger.

— Human & Veterinary Nutrition. (World Review of Nutrition & Dietetics Ser.: Vol. 26). (Illus.). 1977. 144.50 (*3-8055-2392-0*) S Karger.

— Human & Veterinary Nutrition, Biochemical Aspects of Nutrients. (World Review of Nutrition & Dietetics Ser.: Vol. 30). (Illus.). 1978. 128.75 (*3-8055-2789-6*) S Karger.

— Human Nutrition & Animal Feeding. (World Review of Nutrition & Dietetics Ser.: Vol. 37). (Illus.). xii, 292p. 1981. 215.00 (*3-8055-2143-X*) S Karger.

— Human Nutrition & Diet. (World Review of Nutrition & Dietetics Ser.: Vol. 36). (Illus.). x, 226p. 1981. 167.00 (*3-8055-1347-X*) S Karger.

— Human Nutrition & Nutrition & Pesticides in Cattle. (World Review of Nutrition & Dietetics Ser.: Vol. 35). (Illus.). 238p. 1980. 167.00 (*3-8055-0442-X*) S Karger.

— Impact of Nutrition on Health & Disease. (World Review of Nutrition & Dietetics Ser.: Vol. 59). (Illus.). 220p. 1989. 179.25 (*3-8055-4919-9*) S Karger.

— International Nutrition in Health & Disease. (World Review of Nutrition & Dietetics Ser.: Vol. 51). (Illus.). x, 240p. 1987. 182.75 (*3-8055-4581-9*) S Karger.

— International Review of Cytology, Vol. 96. (Serial Publication Ser.). 1985. text 129.00 (*0-12-364496-8*) Acad Pr.

— Minerals in Food & Nutritional Topics. (World Review of Nutrition & Dietetics Ser.: Vol. 46). (Illus.). xii, 260p. 1985. 191.50 (*3-8055-4058-2*) S Karger.

— Nutrients & Energy. (World Review of Nutrition & Dietetics Ser.: Vol. 42). (Illus.). xii, 228p. 1983. 172.25 (*3-8055-3710-7*) S Karger.

— Nutrition & the Quality of Life. (World Review of Nutrition & Dietetics Ser.: Vol. 49). (Illus.). x, 218p. 1987. 168.75 (*3-8055-4450-2*) S Karger.

— Nutrition Education & Modern Concepts of Food Assimilation. (World Review of Nutrition & Dietetics Ser.: Vol. 40). (Illus.). xii, 192p. 1982. 141.75 (*3-8055-3519-8*) S Karger.

— Nutrition in Arabian Gulf Countries: Malnutrition & Minerals. (World Review of Nutrition & Dietetics Ser.: Vol. 54). (Illus.). xii, 292p. 1987. 226.75 (*3-8055-4682-3*) S Karger.

— Nutrition in Disease & Development. (World Review of Nutrition & Dietetics Ser.: Vol. 39). (Illus.). x, 194p. 1982. 139.25 (*3-8055-3459-0*) S Karger.

— Nutritional Considerations in a Changing World. (World Review of Nutrition & Dietetics Ser.: Vol. 44). (Illus.). x, 218p. 1984. 143.50 (*3-8055-3837-5*) S Karger.

— Nutritional Disorders & Requirements. (World Review of Nutrition & Dietetics Ser.: Vol. 50). (Illus.). xii, 272p. 1987. 208.75 (*3-8055-4506-1*) S Karger.

— Nutritional Problems & Education: Selected Topics. (World Review of Nutrition & Dietetics Ser.: Vol. 47). (Illus.). xii, 208p. 1986. 161.00 (*3-8055-4214-3*) S Karger.

— Nutritional Value of Cereal Products, Beans & Starches. (World Review of Nutrition & Dietetics Ser.: Vol. 60). (Illus.). viii, 260p. 1989. 200.00 (*3-8055-4992-X*) S Karger.

— Physiology & Social Nutrition & Nutritional Education. (World Review of Nutrition & Dietetics Ser.: Vol. 38). (Illus.). x, 230p. 1982. 141.75 (*3-8055-3048-X*) S Karger.

— Sociological & Medical Aspects of Nutrition. (World Review of Nutrition & Dietetics Ser.: Vol. 55). (Illus.). xii, 252p. 1988. 201.00 (*3-8055-4703-X*) S Karger.

— Some Aspects of Human & Veterinary Nutrition. (World Review of Nutrition & Dietetics Ser.: Vol. 28). 1978. 140.00 (*3-8055-2672-5*) S Karger.

— Some Special Aspects of Nutrition. (World Review of Nutrition & Dietetics Ser.: Vol. 33). (Illus.). 1979. 137.50 (*3-8055-2942-2*) S Karger.

— The Structure & Function of Nervous Tissue. Incl. Vol. 1. 1968. 95.00 (*0-12-119281-4*); Vol. 2. 1969. 95.00 (*0-12-119282-2*); Vol. 3. 1969. 95.00 (*0-12-119283-0*); Vol. 4. 1972. 95.00 (*0-12-119284-9*); Vol. 5. 1972. 95.00 (*0-12-119285-7*); Vol. 6. 1972. 95.00 (*0-12-119286-5*); write for info. (*0-318-50366-2*) Acad Pr.

— World Nutritional Determinants. (World Review of Nutrition & Dietetics Ser.: Vol. 45). (Illus.). x, 226p. 1984. 172.25 (*3-8055-3948-7*) S Karger.

— World Review of Nutrition & Dietetics, Vol. 12. 1970. 167.00 (*3-8055-0663-5*) S Karger.

— World Review of Nutrition & Dietetics, Vol. 13. 1971. 85.25 (*3-8055-1180-9*) S Karger.

— World Review of Nutrition & Dietetics, Vol. 14. 1972. 116.75 (*3-8055-1282-1*) S Karger.

— World Review of Nutrition & Dietetics, Vol. 15. (Illus.). 300p. 1972. 99.25 (*3-8055-1397-6*) S Karger.

— World Review of Nutrition & Dietetics, Vol. 17. (Illus.). 300p. 1973. 125.25 (*3-8055-1336-4*) S Karger.

— World Review of Nutrition & Dietetics, Vol. 18. 1973. 143.50 (*3-8055-1458-1*) S Karger.

— World Review of Nutrition & Dietetics, Vol. 19. (Illus.). 319p. 1974. 143.50 (*3-8055-1589-8*) S Karger.

— World Review of Nutrition & Dietetics, Vol. 20. (Illus.). 350p. 1975. 151.25 (*3-8055-1841-2*) S Karger.

— World Review of Nutrition & Dietetics, Vol. 21. (Illus.). x, 327p. 1975. 164.50 (*3-8055-2133-2*) S Karger.

— World Review of Nutrition & Dietetics, Vol. 22. (Illus.). 1975. 172.25 (*3-8055-2135-9*) S Karger.

— World Review of Nutrition & Dietetics, Vol. 23. (Illus.). xii, 315p. 1975. 155.00 (*3-8055-2243-6*) S Karger.

— World Review of Nutrition & Dietetics, Vol. 24. (Illus.). 250p. 1976. 132.25 (*3-8055-2344-0*) S Karger.

— World Review of Nutrition & Dietetics, Vol. 25. (Illus.). 300p. 1976. 149.75 (*3-8055-2363-7*) S Karger.

Bourne, Geoffrey H., et al, eds. International Review of Cytology, Vol. 100. (Serial Publication Ser.). 1987. text 119.00 (*0-12-364500-X*) Acad Pr.

— International Review of Cytology, Vol. 102. (Serial Publication Ser.). 324p. 1986. text 119.00 (*0-12-364502-6*) Acad Pr.

— International Review of Cytology, Vol. 103. (Serial Publication Ser.). 408p. 1986. text 129.00 (*0-12-364503-4*) Acad Pr.

— International Review of Cytology, Vol. 104. (Serial Publication Ser.). 384p. 1986. text 129.00 (*0-12-364504-2*) Acad Pr.

— International Review of Cytology, Vol. 105. (Serial Publication Ser.). 332p. 1986. text 119.00 (*0-12-364505-0*) Acad Pr.

— International Review of Cytology, Vol. 106. (Serial Publication Ser.). 286p. 1987. text 119.00 (*0-12-364506-9*) Acad Pr.

— International Review of Cytology, Vol. 107. (Serial Publication Ser.). 455p. 1987. text 129.00 (*0-12-364507-7*) Acad Pr.

— International Review of Cytology, Vol. 109. (Serial Publication Ser.). 348p. 1987. text 109.00 (*0-12-364509-3*) Acad Pr.

— International Review of Cytology, Vol. 112. (Serial Publication Ser.). 260p. 1988. text 109.00 (*0-12-364512-3*) Acad Pr.

— International Review of Cytology, Vol. 113. (Serial Publication Ser.). 352p. 1988. text 109.00 (*0-12-364513-1*) Acad Pr.

— International Review of Cytology, Vol. 116. (Survey of Cell Biology Ser.). 348p. 1989. text 109.00 (*0-12-364516-6*) Acad Pr.

— International Review of Cytology, Supplement 17. 4th ed. 864p. 1987. text 167.00 (*0-12-364378-3*) Acad Pr.

Bourne, Geoffrey H. & Cama, H. R., eds. Vitamin & Carrier Functions of Polyprenoids. (World Review of Nutrition & Dietetics Ser.: Vol. 31). (Illus.). 1978. 120.00 (*3-8055-2801-9*) S Karger.

Bourne, Geoffrey H. & Danielli, James F. International Review of Cytology, Vol. 69. (Serial Publication Ser.). 1981. text 137.00 (*0-12-364469-0*) Acad Pr.

— International Review of Cytology, Vol. 86. (Serial Publication Ser.). 1984. text 121.00 (*0-12-364486-0*) Acad Pr.

— International Review of Cytology, Vol. 87. (Serial Publication Ser.). 1984. text 121.00 (*0-12-364487-9*) Acad Pr.

— International Review of Cytology, Vol. 88. (Serial Publication Ser.). 1984. text 129.00 (*0-12-364488-7*) Acad Pr.

— International Review of Cytology, Vol. 89. (Serial Publication Ser.). 1984. text 121.00 (*0-7506-1558-3*); text 129.00 (*0-12-364489-5*) Acad Pr.

Bourne, Geoffrey H. & Danielli, James F., eds. International Review of Cytology, 74. LC 52-5203. (Serial Publication Ser.). 1982. text 121.00 (*0-12-364474-7*) Acad Pr.

— International Review of Cytology, 75. LC 52-5203. (Serial Publication Ser.). 1982. text 121.00 (*0-12-364475-5*) Acad Pr.

— International Review of Cytology, Vol. 58. (Serial Publication Ser.). 1979. text 150.00 (*0-12-364358-9*) Acad Pr.

— International Review of Cytology, Vol. 59. LC 52-5203. (Serial Publication Ser.). 1979. text 150.00 (*0-12-364359-7*) Acad Pr.

— International Review of Cytology, Vol. 60. (Serial Publication Ser.). 1979. text 150.00 (*0-12-364360-0*) Acad Pr.

— International Review of Cytology, Vol. 61. LC 52-5203. (Serial Publication Ser.). 1979. text 158.00 (*0-12-364461-5*) Acad Pr.

— International Review of Cytology, Vol. 62. LC 52-5203. (Serial Publication Ser.). 1980. text 158.00 (*0-12-364462-3*) Acad Pr.

— International Review of Cytology, Vol. 63. LC 52-5203. (Serial Publication Ser.). 1980. text 158.00 (*0-12-364463-1*) Acad Pr.

— International Review of Cytology, Vol. 64. LC 52-5203. (Serial Publication Ser.). 1980. text 158.00 (*0-12-364464-X*) Acad Pr.

— International Review of Cytology, Vol. 65. (Serial Publication Ser.). 1980. text 137.00 (*0-12-364465-8*) Acad Pr.

— International Review of Cytology, Vol. 66. (Serial Publication Ser.). 1980. text 137.00 (*0-12-364466-6*) Acad Pr.

— International Review of Cytology, Vol. 67. (Serial Publication Ser.). 1980. text 137.00 (*0-12-364467-4*) Acad Pr.

— International Review of Cytology, Vol. 68. (Serial Publication Ser.). 1980. text 137.00 (*0-12-364468-2*) Acad Pr.

— International Review of Cytology, Vol. 70. (Serial Publication Ser.). 1981. text 137.00 (*0-12-364470-4*) Acad Pr.

— International Review of Cytology, Vol. 71. (Serial Publication Ser.). 1981. text 137.00 (*0-12-364471-2*) Acad Pr.

— International Review of Cytology, Vol. 72. (Serial Publication Ser.). 1981. text 137.00 (*0-12-364472-0*) Acad Pr.

— International Review of Cytology, Vol. 77. (Serial Publication Ser.). 284p. 1982. text 121.00 (*0-12-364477-1*) Acad Pr.

— International Review of Cytology, Vol. 78. (Serial Publication Ser.). 360p. 1982. text 121.00 (*0-12-364478-X*) Acad Pr.

— International Review of Cytology, Vol. 79. (Serial Publication Ser.). 315p. 1982. text 121.00 (*0-12-364479-8*) Acad Pr.

— International Review of Cytology, Vol. 80. (Serial Publication Ser.). 322p. 1982. text 121.00 (*0-12-364480-1*) Acad Pr.

— International Review of Cytology, Vol. 81. 1983. text 121.00 (*0-12-364481-X*) Acad Pr.

— International Review of Cytology, Vol. 83. (Serial Publication Ser.). 1983. text 121.00 (*0-12-364483-6*) Acad Pr.

— International Review of Cytology, Vol. 84. (Serial Publication Ser.). 1983. text 121.00 (*0-12-364484-4*) Acad Pr.

— International Review of Cytology, Vol. 85. (Serial Publication Ser.). 1983. text 121.00 (*0-12-364485-2*) Acad Pr.

— International Review of Cytology, Vol. 90. (Serial Publication Ser.). 1984. text 129.00 (*0-12-364490-9*) Acad Pr.

— International Review of Cytology, Vol. 92. (Serial Publication Ser.). 1984. text 129.00 (*0-12-364492-5*) Acad Pr.

— International Review of Cytology, Vol. 97. (Serial Publication Ser.). 1985. text 129.00 (*0-12-364497-6*) Acad Pr.

— International Review of Cytology, Vol. 98. (Serial Publication Ser.). 1986. text 129.00 (*0-12-364498-4*) Acad Pr.

— International Review of Cytology, Vol. 101. (Serial Publication Ser.). 1986. text 119.00 (*0-12-364501-8*) Acad Pr.

— International Review of Cytology, Vols. 74-75. 1982. write for info. (*0-318-56778-4*) Acad Pr.

Bourne, Geoffrey H., et al. International Review of Cytology, Vol. 82. (Serial Publication Ser.). 1983. text 121.00 (*0-12-364482-8*) Acad Pr.

Bourne, George. Book & Slavery Irreconcilable. LC 76-82176. (Anti-Slavery Crusade in America Ser.). 1977. reprint ed. 17.95 (*0-405-00615-2*) Ayer.

— Picture of Slavery in the United States. LC 74-92420. (Illus.). 228p. 1972. reprint ed. 29.00 (*0-403-00179-X*) Scholarly.

— Slavery Illustrated in Its Effects upon Woman & Domestic Society. LC 72-6480. (Black Heritage Library Collection). 1977. reprint ed. 16.95 (*0-8369-9174-5*) Ayer.

Bourne, George, ed. Spirit of the Public Journals: or Beauties of the American Newspapers. LC 74-125679. (American Journalists Ser.). 1977. reprint ed. 20.95 (*0-405-01654-9*) Ayer.

Bourne, Gloria, jt. auth. see Bailey, Katharine R.

Bourne, Gordon. Pregnancy. rev. ed. (Illus.). 575p. (Orig.). 1996. pap. 24.00 (*0-330-33912-5*, Pub. by Pan) Trans-Atl Phila.

***Bourne, H.** Florist Manual. (Illus.). 288p. 2000. pap. 17.95 (*1-55709-386-5*) Applewood.

Bourne, H. The Florist's Manual. LC 87-31443. (Illus.). 288p. 1988. reprint ed. 49.95 (*0-940983-19-2*) OPUS Pubns.

Bourne, H. C., ed. Some Aspects of Human Nutrition. (World Review of Nutrition & Dietetics Ser.: Vol. 27). 1977. 99.25 (*3-8055-2393-9*) S Karger.

Bourne, H. R. English Merchants. xvi, 492p. 1994. reprint ed. 99.00 (*0-7812-0685-5*) Rprt Serv.

Bourne, Heidi L. A Great Deal! Compensation Negotiation for Nurse Practitioners & Physician Assistants. 2nd rev. ed. 56p. 1996. pap. 24.00 (*0-9654977-0-4*) Western Practnr Res.

— A Great Deal! . . . Compensation Negotiation for Nurse Practitioners & Physician Assistants. 3rd rev. ed. Sweig, Carol & Banducci, Don, eds. 72p. 1998. pap. 29.95 (*0-9654977-1-2*) Western Practnr Res.

Bourne, Henry. Antiquitates Vulgaries: Or, the Antiquities of the Common People. 1977. 24.95 (*0-405-10081-7*, 14706) Ayer.

Bourne, Iain, jt. auth. see Brown, Allan.

Bourne, J., et al, eds. The Influence of Technology on Engineering Education. 348p. 1995. per. 84.95 (*0-8493-2639-7*) CRC Pr.

Bourne, J. M. Patronage & Society in Nineteenth-Century England. LC 86-213668. ix, 198 p. 1986. 30.00 (*0-7131-6484-0*) E Arnld Pubs.

Bourne, John. Britain & the Great War: 1914-1918. (Illus.). 256p. 1989. pap. 14.95 (*0-7131-6592-8*, Pub. by E A) Routldge.

Bourne, Joi, ed. see Bourne, Ronald S.

Bourne, Joyce. Who's Who in Opera: A Guide to Opera Characters. Kennedy, Michael, ed. LC 98-7977. (Illus.). 476p. 1998. 35.00 (*0-19-210023-8*) OUP.

— Who's Who in Opera: A Guide to Opera Characters. Kennedy, Michael, ed. (Oxford Paperback Reference Ser.). (Illus.). 480p. 2000. pap. 16.95 (*0-19-280054-X*) OUP.

Bourne, Joyce, ed. see Kennedy, Michael.

Bourne, K. The Letters of Third Viscount Palmerston to Laurence & Elizabeth Sullivan 1804-1863. (Camden Fourth Ser.: Vol. 23). 362p. 27.00 (*0-901050-55-5*) David Brown.

Bourne, K. C. Year 2000 Solutions for Dummies. 2nd ed. LC QA76.76.S64B68 1998. (For Dummies Ser.). 408p. 1998. pap. 29.99 incl. cd-rom (*0-7645-0465-7*) IDG Bks.

Bourne, Kelly C. Testing Client Server Systems. LC 97-22888. (Illus.). 572p. 1997. pap. 49.95 (*0-07-006688-4*) McGraw.

Bourne, Kenneth. Palmerston. (Illus.). 750p. 1982. write for info. (*0-318-54242-0*) Macmillan.

Bourne, Kenneth & Taylor, William B., eds. The Horner Papers: Selections from the Correspondence & Miscellaneous Writings of Francis Horner, M. P., 3 vols. 1994. text 125.00 (*0-7486-0398-0*, Pub. by Edinburgh U Pr) Col U Pr.

Bourne, Kenneth, et al. British Documents on Foreign Affairs: Series K: Economic Affairs, Cultural Propaganda & the Reform of the Foreign Office, 4 vols. LC 96-47611. (British Documents on Foreign Ser.). Date not set. lib. bdg. 610.00 (*0-89093-618-8*) U Pubns Amer.

Bourne, Larry S. Private Redevelopment of the Central City: Spatial Processes of Structural Change in the City of Toronto. LC 66-30638. (University of Chicago, Department of Geography, Research Paper Ser.: No. 112). 215p. reprint ed. pap. 66.70 (*0-7837-0392-9*, 204071300018) Bks Demand.

— Urban Systems - Strategies for Regulation. (Illus.). (C). 1976. pap. 15.95 (*0-19-874055-7*) OUP.

Bourne, Larry S., et al, eds. The Form of Cities in Central Canada: Selected Papers. LC 73-84353. (University of Toronto, Department of Geography Research Publications: No. 11). 258p. reprint ed. pap. 80.00 (*0-608-16559-X*, 202635900049) Bks Demand.

— Urban Futures for Central Canada: Perspectives on Forecasting Urban Growth & Form. LC 73-92297. 376p. reprint ed. pap. 116.60 (*0-608-12828-7*, 202359500033) Bks Demand.

Bourne, Larry S. & Hitchcock, John R., eds. Urban Housing Markets: Recent Directions in Research & Policy: Proceedings of a Conference Held at the University of Toronto, October 27-29, 1977. LC 79-310508. 342p. reprint ed. pap. 106.10 (*0-8357-8362-6*, 203405300088) Bks Demand.

Bourne, Larry S. & Ley, David F., eds. The Changing Social Geography of Canadian Cities. (Canadian Association of Geographers Series in Canadian Geography). 496p. 1993. 75.00 (*0-7735-0926-7*, Pub. by McG-Queens Univ Pr); pap. 32.95 (*0-7735-0972-0*, Pub. by McG-Queens Univ Pr) CUP Services.

Bourne, Lesley-Anne. The Story of Pears. (Poetry Ser.: No. 23). 72p. 1990. pap. 9.95 (*0-921254-21-0*, Pub. by Penumbra Pr) U of Toronto Pr.

Bourne, Louis, tr. see Bordao, Rafael.

Bourne, Louis, tr. see De la Nuez Caballero, Sebastian, ed.

Bourne, Louis, tr. & intro. see Padron, Justo J.

***Bourne, Lyle E., Jr.** Psychology with the Instant Psychology. 1998. text 60.50 (*0-393-97389-1*) Norton.

***Bourne, Lyle E., Jr. & Russo.** Psychology with Study Guide. 1998. pap. text 56.50 (*0-393-97309-3*) Norton.

Bourne, Lyle E. & Russo, Nancy F. Psychology: Behavior in Context. LC 97-43774. 1998. text 78.50 (*0-393-97209-7*) Norton.

Bourne, Lyle E., Jr., jt. ed. see Healy, Alice F.

***Bourne, Malcolm.** Food Texture & Viscosity. 2nd ed. 400p. 1999. 89.95 (*0-12-119062-5*) Morgan Kaufmann.

Bourne, Malcolm. Food Texture Seven Viscosity: Concepts & Measurement. (Food Science & Technology Ser.). 312p. 1982. text 94.00 (*0-12-119060-9*) Acad Pr.

— Gustav, P. I. The Case of the Bloodless Politician. LC 98-212815. (Illus.). 48p. 1998. pap. 2.99 (*1-56163-205-8*) NBM.

Bourne, Marlene Avis. E-050R Uninterruptible Power Supply Systems: Continuous Service & Network Systems. LC 99-175695. 154p. 1998. 3150.00 (*1-56965-168-X*) BCC.

Bourne, Michael. Inventory of Historic Sites in Caroline County. (Illus.). 80p. 1980. pap. 5.00 (*1-878399-14-4*) Div Hist Cult Progs.

Bourne, Michael O., et al. Architecture & Change in the Chesapeake: A Field Tour on the Eastern & Western Shores. 155p. 1998. pap. 15.00 (*1-878399-76-4*) Div Hist Cult Progs.

Bourne, Nicholas. Business Law & Practice. 435p. 1994. pap. write for info. (*1-874241-77-5*, Pub. by Cavendish Pubng) Gaunt.

— Business Law & Practice. 2nd ed. 450p. 1996. pap. 32.00 (*1-85941-196-7*, Pub. by Cavendish Pubng) Gaunt.

— Company Law. 2nd ed. (Lecture Notes...Ser.). 289p. 1995. pap. 32.00 (*1-85941-164-9*) Gaunt.

— Essential Company Law. (Essential Law Ser.). 140p. 1995. pap. write for info. (*1-85941-126-6*, Pub. by Cavendish Pubng) Gaunt.

Bourne, Nicholas & Pillans, Brian. Scottish Company Law. 338p. 1996. pap. 36.00 (*1-85941-204-1*, Pub. by Cavendish Pubng) Gaunt.

Bourne, Nicholas, ed. see Aquino, Tracey.

Bourne, Nicholas, ed. see Beale, Andrew.

Bourne, Nicholas, ed. see Chinhengo, Austin M.

Bourne, Nicholas, ed. see Geary, Roger.

Bourne, Nicholas, ed. see Iwobi, Andrew.

Bourne, Nicholas, ed. see McCormick-Watson, Jan.

Bourne, Nicholas, ed. see Morgan, Keith.

Bourne, Nicholas, ed. see Owen, Richard.

Bourne, Nicholas, ed. see Suff, Marnah.

Bourne, Nicholas, ed. see Williams, Iris.

Bourne, Peter. The Church in Crisis. LC 97-30638. 78p. 1997. pap. 4.50 (*0-930887-30-1*) Wenzel Pr.

— Homilies for Living the Faith. LC 95-11861. 286p. (C). 1995. 24.95 (*0-930887-27-1*) Wenzel Pr.

***Bourne, Peter.** The Last Things: Heaven, Hell & Judgement. LC 99-52433. 64p. 2000. pap. 4.50 (*0-930887-36-0*) Wenzel Pr.

Bourne, Peter. Mary in Today's World. LC 97-17413. (Illus.). 90p. 1997. pap. 4.50 (*0-930887-29-8*) Wenzel Pr.

— Oh Happy Venture: A Treatise on Carmelite Prayer. 55p. 1992. pap. 2.95 (*0-930887-14-X*) Wenzel Pr.

— St. John of the Cross & the Dark Night: Understanding His Ascent & Dark Night in Easy Stages. LC 93-60166. (Illus.). 216p. (C). 1995. 19.95 (*0-930887-15-8*) Wenzel Pr.

— St. Teresa's Castle of the Soul: A Study of the Interior Castle. LC 94-31700. 150p. (C). 1995. 19.95 (*0-930887-19-0*) Wenzel Pr.

***Bourne, Peter.** St. Teresa's Way: The Real Story Behind Her "Way of Perfection" LC 99-51413. 80p. 2000. pap. 4.95 (*0-930887-35-2*) Wenzel Pr.

Bourne, Philip. Windows NT Web Server Cookbook. 400p. (C). 2001. pap. text 49.95 (*0-13-520008-3*) P-H.

Bourne, Philip E. UNIX for OpenVMS Users. 2nd ed. LC 98-35518. 448p. 1998. pap. text 42.95 (*1-55558-155-2*, Digital DEC) Buttrwrth-Heinemann.

***Bourne, Philip E. & Watenpaugh, Keith D., eds.** Crystallographic Computing 7: Macromolecular Crystallographic Data. (Illus.). 352p. 2000. text 130.00 (*0-19-850334-2*) OUP.

Bourne, Philip E., jt. auth. see Hart, David L.

Bourne, Phyllis M. Las Cosas Cambian: Big Book. (Que Maravilla! Ser.). (SPA., Illus.). 24p. (Orig.). (J). (gr. 1-3). 1992. pap. text 29.95 (*1-56334-028-3*) Hampton-Brown.

— Las Cosas Cambian Small: Level 2. (Que Maravilla! Ser.). (SPA.). 24p. (Orig.). 1992. pap. 36.00 (*1-56334-219-7*) Hampton-Brown.

— Things Change, Big bk. (Wonders! Ser.). (Illus.). 24p. (Orig.). (J). (gr. 1-3). 1992. pap. text 29.95 (*1-56334-067-4*) Hampton-Brown.

— Things Change, Small bk. (Wonders! Ser.). (Illus.). 24p. (Orig.). (J). (gr. 1-3). 1992. pap. text 6.00 (*1-56334-073-9*) Hampton-Brown.

Bourne, Randolph. History of a Literary Radical & Other Essays. LC 69-17713. 1969. reprint ed. 28.00 (*0-8196-0225-6*) Biblo.

— Randolph Bourne: The Radical Will: Selected Writings 1911-1918. (C). 1992. pap. 18.95 (*0-520-07715-6*, Pub. by U CA Pr) Cal Prin Full Svc.

— War Is the Health of the State. 1991. lib. bdg. 75.00 (*0-8490-4141-4*) Gordon Pr.

— Youth & Life. 1972. 59.95 (*0-8490-1346-1*) Gordon Pr.

***Bourne, Randolph S.** War & the Intellectuals: Collected Essays, 1915-1919. Resek, Carl, ed. LC 99-16787. (C). 1999. pap. text 9.95 (*0-87220-500-2*); lib. bdg. 29.95 (*0-87220-501-0*) Hackett Pub.

Bourne, Randolph S. Youth & Life. LC 67-23184. (Essay Index Reprint Ser.). 1977. 23.95 (*0-8369-0229-7*) Ayer.

Bourne, Richard. Lords of Fleet Street: The Harmsworth Dynasty LC 90-227554. 1990. write for info. (*0-04-440450-6*, Pub. by Allen & Unwin Pty) Paul & Co Pubs.

Bourne, Richard. News on a Knife Edge. LC 96-196350. 1997. 26.00 (*1-86020-524-0*, Pub. by U of Luton Pr) Bks Intl VA.

Bourne, Richard & Levin, Jack. Social Problems: Causes, Consequences, Interventions. (Illus.). 422p. (C). 1983. pap. text 45.25 (*0-314-69661-X*); pap. text, teacher ed. write for info. (*0-314-71081-7*) West Pub.

Bourne, Richard B., et al. Artificial Insemination. LC 72-13433. (Illus.). 220p. (C). 1972. text 21.50 (*0-8422-7077-9*) Irvington.

Bourne, Richard W., jt. auth. see Lynch, John A., Jr.

Bourne, Rodger & Burrell, Joan. San Antonio Self-Guiding Auto Tour. (Illus.). 40p. 1990. pap. 5.00 (*0-915266-21-0*) Awani Pr.

Bourne, Ronald S. The Story Behind Medjugorje. Bourne, Joi, ed. 52p. (Orig.). 1992. pap. 2.50 (*0-9630569-1-3*) Follow Me Comm.

— When I Was in Prison You Visited Me. 42p. (Orig.). 1991. pap. 2.00 (*0-9630569-2-1*) Follow Me Comm.

Bourne, Ross, ed. Serials Librarianship. LC 81-129419. (Handbooks on Library Practice). 269p. 1980. reprint ed. pap. 83.40 (*0-7837-9275-1*, 206001300004) Bks Demand.

Bourne, Russell. Americans on the Move: The History of Waterways, Railways & Highways. (Illus.). 144p. 1995. 39.95 (*1-55591-183-8*) Fulcrum Pub.

— Invention in America: With Images from the Library of Congress. LC 95-35784. (Library of Congress Ser.). (Illus.). 152p. 1995. 32.95 (*1-55591-231-1*) Fulcrum Pub.

— The Red King's Rebellion: Racial Politics in New England 1675-1678. (Illus.). 304p. 1991. pap. 12.95 (*0-19-506976-5*, 12173) OUP.

— Rivers of America: Birthplaces of Culture, Commerce & Community. LC 98-19089. (Illus.). 288p. 1998. 29.95 (*1-55591-305-9*) Fulcrum Pub.

Bourne, Sarah, jt. auth. see Mason, Rita A.

Bourne, Stephen. Black in the British Frame: Black People in British Film & Television, 1896-1996. LC 97-18002. 276p. 1998. 75.00 (*0-304-33374-3*); pap. 24.95 (*0-304-33375-1*) Continuum.

— Brief Encounters: Lesbians & Gays in British Cinema 1930-1971. (Film Studies). (Illus.). 268p. 1996. 69.95 (*0-304-33283-6*); pap. 21.95 (*0-304-33286-0*) Continuum.

***Bourne, Stephen.** Financial Due Diligence: A Guide to Ensuring Successful Acquisitions. (Management Briefings Ser.). (Illus.). 1999. pap. 187.50 (*0-273-64224-3*, Pub. by F T P-H) Trans-Atl Phila.

Bourne, Terry & Marcombe, David. The Burton Lazars Cartulary: A Medieval Leicestershire Estate. (C). 1987. text 30.00 (*0-7855-3217-X*, Pub. by Univ Nottingham) St Mut.

Bourne, Tom & George, Jeannette Clift. Ligature: That Which Binds or Ties Together. Dillard, Peggy N. & Eckols, Deborah, eds. (Illus.). 80p. 1991. pap., student ed. 6.95 (*0-9616513-9-3*) Manor of Grace.

Bourne, Tom H., et al, eds. Transvaginal Colour Doppler: The Scientific Basis & Practical Application of Colour Doppler in Gynaecology. LC 95-2189. (Illus.). 208p. 1995. 140.00 (*3-540-58432-3*) Spr-Verlag.

Bourne, Troy, jt. auth. see Bourne, Amanda.

Bourne, Ursula. East Anglian Village & Town Signs. 1989. pap. 25.00 (*0-85263-786-1*, Pub. by Shire Pubns) St Mut.

— Snuff. (Album Ser.: No. 258). (Illus.). 32p. 1999. pap. 6.25 (*0-7478-0089-8*, Pub. by Shire Pubns) Parkwest Pubns.

Bourne, Val, ed. The Second Leicester International Dance Festival, Vol. 3, Part 1. 110p. 1992. pap. text 15.00 (*3-7186-5320-6*, Harwood Acad Pubs) Gordon & Breach.

***Bourne, Wade.** Decoys: And Proven Methods for Using Them. (Illus.). 192p. 2000. 24.50 (*1-57223-392-3*) Willow Creek Pr.

Bourne, Wade. Fishing Fundamentals. 1989. pap. 11.95 (*0-929384-03-2*) In-Fisherman.

Bourne, Wade L. Ultimate Turkey Hunting. LC 94-70372. (Illus.). 182p. 1993. pap. text 11.95 (*1-887180-00-1*) Knight & Hale.

Bourne, William. A Booke Called the Treasure for Travellers. LC 77-25950. (English Experience Ser.: No. 911). 276p. 1979. reprint ed. lib. bdg. 30.00 (*0-902210-91-2*) Walter J Johnson.

Bourne, William O. History of the Public School Society of the City of New York. LC 79-165733. (American Education Ser., No. 2). 1972. reprint ed. 39.95 (*0-405-03601-9*) Ayer.

***Bournea, R. C.** Chloe. LC 99-93405. 752p. 1999. text 24.95 (*0-9673723-0-5*) Mousetrap Bks.

***Bourner, Tom.** New Directions in Professional Higher Education. 2000. pap. text 39.95 (*0-335-20614-X*) OpUniv Pr.

Bourneuf, Jacques. Petit Larousse de la Medecine. Domart, Andre, ed. (FRE.). 852p. 1976. 85.00 (*0-8288-5750-4*, F12060) Fr & Eur.

Bourneuf, Jacques, jt. auth. see Domart, Andre.

Bourneuf, Jacques, jt. ed. see Domart, Andre.

Bournois, F. Glossary of Human Resources Management German-English-French. (FRE & GER.). 222p. 1993. pap. 51.00 (*2-212-03573-X*, Pub. by Eyrolles) IBD Ltd.

Bournonville, August & Jurgensen, Knud Arne. Letters on Dance & Choreography. (Illus.). 77p. 19.95 (*1-85273-073-0*) Princeton Bk Co.

Bournoutian, George A. Abraham of Erevan: History of the Wars, 1721-1736. LC 99-20719. (Armenian Studies Ser.: No. 3). 240p. 1999. text 26.95 (*1-56859-085-7*) Mazda Pubs.

— A History of the Armenian People, Vol. 1: Pre-History to 1500 A. D. LC 92-39705. (Illus.). 176p. (Orig.). (C). 1993. pap. text 14.95 (*0-939214-96-2*) Mazda Pubs.

— Russia & the Armenians of Transcaucasia, 1797-1889: A Documentary Record. LC 98-9892. 423p. 1998. text 49.95 (*1-56859-068-7*) Mazda Pubs.

Bournoutian, George A., ed. The Chronicle of Abraham of Crete. LC 98-32126. (Armenian Studies Ser.: No. 1). 202p. 1998. lib. bdg. 24.95 (*1-56859-082-2*) Mazda Pubs.

Bournoutian, George A., ed. & tr. see Qarabaghi, Mirza J.

Bouroncle, Victoria. The Circle & the Line. 64p. 1994. pap. 8.00 (*0-944550-34-7*) Pygmy Forest Pr.

Bourqia, Rahma. In the Shadow of the Sultan: Culture, Power & Politics in Morocco, Vol. 31. (Middle Eastern Monographs). 352p. 1999. pap. 19.95 (*0-932885-20-9*) Harvard CMES.

Bourquard, Jo A., jt. auth. see Thergesen, Steve.

Bourque. Practice Tests for Nursing Students. 160p. (C). (gr. 13). 1990. pap. text 15.95 (*0-8016-0737-X*, 00737) Mosby Inc.

Bourque, jt. auth. see Conway.

Bourque, B. J. Diversity & Complexity in Prehistoric Maritime Societies: A Gulf of Maine Perspective. LC 95-1085. (Interdisciplinary Contributions to Archaeology Ser.). (Illus.). 430p. (C). 1995. 62.50 (*0-306-44874-2*, Plenum Trade) Perseus Pubng.

Bourque, Bruce J. Prehistory of the Central Maine Coast. LC 90-24498. (Evolution of North American Indians Ser.). (Illus.). 328p. 1992. text 10.00 (*0-8240-2049-9*) Garland.

Bourque, Daniel P., et al, eds. 1999 Environmental Assessment: Rising to the Challenge of a New Century. (Illus.). 114p. 1999. pap. 9.00 (*0-9667828-1-X*) VHA Inc.

Bourque, Joan. Dreams of Dolphins Dancing. LC 96-97020. (Kids for Conservation Ser.: Vol. 1). (Illus.). 32p. (J). (gr. 1). 1996. 15.95 (*0-9654327-0-X*) Curtis AZ.

Bourque, Linda B. Defining Rape. LC 88-30764. (Illus.). xix, 428p. 1989. text 64.95 (*0-8223-0901-7*) Duke.

Bourque, Linda B. & Clark, Virginia A. Processing Data: The Survey Example. LC 92-9653. (Quantitative Applications in the Social Sciences Ser.: Vol. 85). 96p. (C). 1992. pap. text 10.95 (*0-8039-4741-0*) Sage.

Bourque, Linda B. & Fielder, Eve P. How to Conduct Self-Administered & Mail Surveys. (Survey Kit Ser.: Vol. 3). 240p. 1995. pap. 20.95 (*0-8039-7168-0*) Sage.

***Bourque, Martin.** Transforming the Cuban Countryside: Advances in Sustainable Agriculture. 2000. pap. 14.95 (*0-935028-78-1*) Inst Food & Develop.

Bourque, Michael H., ed. IBD Network Profile, 1987-1989: The Official Directory of the Institute of Business Designers. (Illus.). 132p. 1987. pap. text 75.00 (*0-317-59041-3*) Inst Busn Desn.

Bourque, Monique & Anderson, R. Joseph. The Balch Institute: A Guide to Manuscript & Microfilm Collections. (Illus.). 129p. 1992. 15.00 (*0-937437-11-5*) Balch IES Pr.

Bourque, Monique & Anderson, R. Joseph, eds. A Guide to the Manuscript & Microfilm Collections of the Research Library of the Balch Institute for Ethnic Studies. 1992. 15.00 (*0-614-14830-8*) Balch Inst Ethnic Studies.

***Bourque, Pierre.** Car Buying Online for Dummies. (For Dummies Ser.). (Illus.). 384p. 2000. pap. text 24.99 incl. cd-rom (*0-7645-0697-8*) IDG Bks.

Bourque, Pierre. Government Online in Canada. LC 98-225616. 256p. (Orig.). 1996. pap. 28.95 (*0-7737-5819-4*) Stoddart Publ.

Bourque, Susan C. & Warren, Kay B. Women of the Andes. (Women & Culture Ser.; Patriarchy & Social Change in Two Peruvian Towns). 272p. 1981. pap. text 17.95 (*0-472-06330-8*, 06330) U of Mich Pr.

Bourque, Warrick. Compelling Alliance: Trek Adventure & Romance. LC 94-70205. 265p. 1997. per. write for info. (*0-9640237-0-9*) Also Bks.

Bourquin, David R. First Century Palestinian Judaism: An Annotated Guide to Works in English. 2nd expanded rev. ed. Burgess, Michael, ed. LC 95-5121. (Studies in Judaica & the Holocaust: No. 6). Date not set. pap. write for info. (*0-8095-1401-X*) Millefleurs.

— The Work of Bruce McAllister: An Annotated Bibliography & Guide. rev. ed. Clarke, Boden, ed. LC 85-22400. (Bibliographies of Modern Authors Ser.: No. 10). 32p. 1986. pap. 13.00 (*0-89370-489-X*) Millefleurs.

Bourquin, S., ed. Paulina Dlamini: Servant of Two Kings. (Killie Campbell Africana Library Publication: No. 1). (Illus.). 146p. 1986. pap. 14.95 (*0-86980-523-1*, Pub. by Univ Natal Pr) Intl Spec Bk.

Bourrel, Maurice & Schechter, Robert S. Microemulsions & Related Systems: Formulation, Solvency, & Physical Properties. (Surfactant Science Ser.: Vol. 30). (Illus.). 504p. 1988. text 250.00 (*0-8247-7951-7*) Dekker.

Bourrelly, Louis, et al, contrib. by. Data Bank Applications in Archaeology. LC 81-901. (Illus.). 162p. 1981. pap. 50.30 (*0-608-05647-2*, 206610100006) Bks Demand.

Bourrelly, Pierre. Les Algues D'Eau Douce: Complements Au Tome 1. (FRE., Illus.). 182p. 1988. text 75.00 (*0-685-32242-4*, Pub. by Editions Boubees) Lubrecht & Cramer.

— Algues d'Eau Douce des Mares d'Alpage de la Region de Lunz am See, Autriche. (Bibliotheca Phycologica Ser.: Vol. 76). (FRE., Illus.). 182p. 1987. 89.00 (*3-443-60003-4*, Pub. by Gebruder Borntraeger) Balogh.

— Les Algues d'Eau douce. Initiation a la Systematique Vol. 2: Algues Jaunes et Brunes. Generalities sur les Chromophytes-Crysophysees-Pheophycees-Zantophycees-Diamophycees. rev. ed. (Faunes et Flores Actuelles Ser.). (FRE., Illus.). 440p. 1981. lib. bdg. 130.00 (*2-85004-029-0*) Lubrecht & Cramer.

— Les Algues d'Eau douce. Initiation a la Systematique Volume 1. rev. ed. (Faunes et Flores Actuelles Ser.). (FRE., Illus.). 511p. 1988. lib. bdg. 130.00 (*0-685-43966-6*) Lubrecht & Cramer.

— Recherches sur les Chrysophycees: Morphologie, Phylogenie, Systematique. (Illus.). 1971. reprint ed. 70.00 (*3-7682-0703-X*) Lubrecht & Cramer.

Bourrelly, Pierre & Coute, A. Desmidiees de Madagascar (Chlorophyta, Zygophyceae) (Bibliotheca Phycologica Ser.: Vol. 86). (FRE., Illus.). 350p. 1991. 77.00 (*3-443-60013-1*, Pub. by Gebruder Borntraeger) Balogh.

Bourrely, C., et al, eds. Electromagnetic & Acoustics Scattering: Detection & Inverse Problems. 372p. (C). 1989. text 93.00 (*9971-5-0748-X*) World Scientific Pub.

Bourret, Jeffrey A., jt. auth. see Burg, Fredric D.

Bourret, Joan L., compiled by. Life in Amana, 1867-1935: Reporters' Views. 204p. 1998. pap. 14.95 (*1-57216-050-0*) Penfield.

Bourret, Joan L., photos by. Joyful Nordic Humor: A Family Album. LC 95-69797. (Illus.). 144p. 1997. pap. 9.95 (*1-57216-051-9*) Penfield.

***Bourret, Joan Liffring-Zug.** The Amanas: A Photographic Journey, 1959-1999. Crum, Dorothy & Bradnan, Melinda, eds. (Illus.). 112p. 2000. pap. 16.95 (*1-57216-086-1*) Penfield.

Bourret, Joan Liffring-Zug, jt. auth. see McDonald, Julie Jensen.

Bourriau, Janine, ed. Understanding Catastrophe. (Darwin College Lectures). (Illus.). 219p. (C). 1992. 36.95 (*0-521-41324-9*) Cambridge U Pr.

Bourriau, Janine, ed. see Lamb, Trevor.

Bourricaud, Francois. The Sociology of Talcott Parsons. Goldhammer, Arthur, tr. LC 81-1348. xvi, 340p. 1984. pap. text 14.95 (*0-226-06756-4*) U Ch Pr.

Bourricaud, Francois, jt. auth. see Boudon, Raymond.

Bourricaud, R., jt. auth. see Boudon, Raymond.

An Asterisk (*) at the beginning of an entry indicates that the title is appearing for the first time.

Bourrinet, Jacques, ed. Wildland Fires & the Law: Legal Aspects of Forest Fires Worldwide. LC 92-31200. 1992. lib. bdg. 87.50 (0-7923-1974-5) Kluwer Academic.

Bourriot, Felix. Kalos Kagathos, Kalokagathia. (Spudasmata Ser.: Vol. 58). (GER.). xvi, 1280p. 1995. write for info. (3-487-10000-2) G Olms Pubs.

Bourrut. COBOL Microcomputer. 1985. 23.95 (0-13-139758-3) P-H.

Boursault. Les Fables D'Esope. Allott, ed. (Exeter French Texts Ser.: Vol. 67). (FRE.). 184p. Date not set. pap. text 19.95 (0-85989-249-2, Pub. by Univ Exeter Pr) Northwestern U Pr.

Boursicaud, Henri Le, see Le Boursicaud, Henri.

Boursier, Helen T. Black & White Portrait Photography. LC 97-77174. (Illus.). 128p. 1998. pap. 29.95 (0-936262-61-3) Amherst Media.

— Family Portrait Photography. LC 98-72909. (Illus.). 120p. 1999. pap. 29.95 (0-936262-75-3) Amherst Media.

*Boursier, Helen T. Marketing & Selling Black & White Portrait Photography. (Illus.). 128p. 2000. pap. 29.95 (1-58428-015-8) Amherst Media.

Boursier, Helen T. Marketing Madness: (Power Marketing for Portrait Wedding Photographers) 2nd ed. (Illus.). 205p. 1992. reprint ed. pap. 39.50 (0-934420-13-0) Studio Pr NE.

— Modern B-W Portrait (Selectively Tinted) (How to Triple Your Sales Without Raising Prices) 3rd ed. (Illus.). 87p. 1991. reprint ed. pap. 29.50 (0-934420-11-4, 1409) Studio Pr NE.

*Boursier, Helen T. Photographing Children in Black & White. (Illus.). 128p. 2000. pap. 29.95 (1-58428-014-X) Amherst Media.

— Watercolor Portrait Photography: The Art of Manipulating Polaroid SX-70 Images. (Illus.). 120p. 2000. pap. 29.95 (1-58428-032-8, Pub. by Amherst Media) IPG Chicago.

*Boursin, Didier. Advanced Origami: More Than 60 Fascinating & Challenging Projects for the Serious Folder. (Illus.). 144p. 2000. pap. 19.95 (1-55209-527-4) Firefly Bks Ltd.

Boursin, Jean-Louis. DEMO: Dictionnaire Elementaire de Mathematiques Modernes: Elementary Dictionary of Modern Math. (FRE.). 181p. 1987. pap. write for info. (0-7859-4809-0) Fr & Eur.

Bourso-Leiand, Natalia, tr. see Flint, V. E., et al.

Boury-Esnault, Nicole & Rutzler, Klaus. Thesaurus of Sponge Morphology. LC 97-20213. (Smithsonian Contributions to Zoology Ser.: No. 596). (Illus.). 59p. 1997. reprint ed. pap. 30.00 (0-608-07974-X, 206794600012) Bks Demand.

Bousard, Lorraine, jt. auth. see Wardell, Sandra.

Bouscaren, Anthony T. Imperial Communism. LC 75-1341. 256p. 1975. reprint ed. lib. bdg. 65.00 (0-8371-8009-0, BOIC, Greenwood Pr) Greenwood.

Bouscaren, Anthony T., ed. All Quiet on the Eastern Front: The Death of South Vietnam. LC 76-18443. 1976. 12.00 (0-8159-5018-7); pap. 7.95 (0-8159-5019-5) Devin.

Bouscaren, Elisabeth. Model Theory & Algebraic Geometry: An Introduction to E. Hrushovski's Proof of the Geometric Mordell-Lang Conjecture, Vol. 169. LC 98-38720. (Lecture Notes in Mathematics Ser.). 211p. 1999. pap. 41.00 (3-540-64863-1) Spr-Verlag.

*Bouse, Derek. Wildlife Films. 2000. 55.00 (0-8122-3555-X); pap. text. write for info. (0-8122-1728-4) U of Pa Pr.

Bousfield, A. K. Homological Localization Towers for Groups & Pi-Modules. LC 77-3716. (Memoirs Ser.: No. 10/186). 68p. 1977. pap. 21.00 (0-8218-2186-5, MEMO/10/186) Am Math.

— Homotopy Limits, Completions & Localizations. (Lecture Notes in Mathematics Ser.: Vol. 304). v, 349p. 1987. 51.95 (0-387-06105-3) Spr-Verlag.

Bousfield, A. K. & Gugenheim, V. M. On PL DeRham Theory & Rational Homotopy Type. LC 76-44398. 94p. 1976. pap. 21.00 (0-8218-2179-2, MEMO/8/179) Am Math.

*Bousfield, Ann. The Relationship Between Liberalism & Conservatism: Parasitic, Competitive or Symbiotic? LC 99-72662. 1999. write for info. (0-7546-1046-2, Pub. by Ashgate Pub) Ashgate Pub Co.

Bousfield, Douglas W., ed. see Technical Association of the Pulp & Paper Industry.

Bousfield, Jonathan & Richardson, Dan. Austria. (Rough Guide Ser.). (Illus.). 464p. (Orig.). 1998. pap. 17.95 (1-85828-325-6) Rough Guides.

Bousfield, Shirley, jt. auth. see Wallace, Arthur.

Bousfield, Trevor. A Practical Guide To Autocad Autolisp. 200p. (C). 1999. pap. text 57.95 (0-582-32673-7) Addison-Wesley.

— A Practical Guide to Autocad 3-D Design. 400p. (C). 1999. pap. 44.00 (0-582-36935-5) Addison-Wesley.

Bosh, Karen, ed. see Brod, Charles.

Boushahla, Jo J. & Reidel-Geubtner, Virginia. The Dream Dictionary: One Thousand Dream Symbols from A to Z. 1992. pap. 11.95 (0-425-13190-4) Berkley Pub.

*Boushel, Margaret, et al. Early Childhood: Theories, Rights & Circumstances. LC 00-27797. (Working Together for Children, Young People & Their Familes Ser.). 2000. write for info. (0-632-05157-4) Blackwell Sci.

Boushka, Bill. Do Ask, Do Tell: A Gay Conservative Lashes Back: Individualism, Identity, Personal Rights, Responsibility & Community in a Libertarian Third Millennium. LC 97-93949. 350p. (Orig.). 1997. pap. 11.95 (0-9656744-0-1) High Productivity.

— Our Fundamental Rights & How We Can Reclaim Them: A Psychological Approach. LC 98-96799. 91p. 1998. pap. 9.95 (0-9656744-2-8) High Productivity.

Bousingen, Denis Durand de, see Rogers, Arthur.

Bousingen, Denis Durand de, see Rogers, Arthur & Durand de Bousingen, Denis.

Bousky, Samuel. A Likely Story. LC 93-24001. (Illus.). 80p. (Orig.). 1993. 13.95 (0-9634250-7-2) J & L Pubns.

— The Wizard of Oz - Revealed. 64p. pap. 10.00 (0-9641660-3-8) Writers Consort.

Bousman, Kelly. L. C. Armstrong: Making & Unmaking. (Illus.). 28p. (Orig.). 1995. pap. 5.00 (1-879293-08-0) Contemp Art Mus.

Bouson, J. Brooks. Brutal Choreographies: Oppositional Strategies & Narrative Design in the Novels of Margaret Atwood. LC 93-2964. 216p. (C). 1993. 27.50 (0-87023-845-0) U of Mass Pr.

— The Empathic Reader: A Study of the Narcissistic Character & the Drama of the Self. LC 89-4695. 216p. (C). 1989. lib. bdg. 30.00 (0-87023-678-4) U of Mass Pr.

*Bouson, J. Brooks. Quiet As It's Kept: Shame, Trauma, & Race in the Novels of Toni Morrison. LC 99-16422. (C). 1999. text 65.50 (0-7914-4423-6); pap. text 21.95 (0-7914-4424-4) State U NY Pr.

*Bousquet. Harnessing 3D Studio Max Release 3. LC 99-89118. 352p. 2000. pap. 59.95 (0-7668-0576-X) Delmar.

Bousquet. West Indian Women at War. (C). 1991. pap. 19.50 (0-85315-743-X, Pub. by Lawrence & Wishart) NYU Pr.

Bousquet, Antoine. Providing a Secure Environment for Learning. 84p. 1998. pap. 19.00 (92-64-05756-0, 95 98 01 3 P, Pub. by Org for Econ) OECD.

Bousquet, Catherine. Incredibly Hidden. LC 93-9459. (Frontiers of the Invisible Ser.). (Illus.). 48p. (YA). (gr. 6 up). 1993. lib. bdg. 14.95 (0-02-711737-5, New Dscvry Bks) Silver Burdett Pr.

Bousquet Chop, Carol. Decorating Secrets Revealed! 2nd rev. ed. (Illus.). 500p. 1978. pap. text, ring bd., wbk. ed. 45.00 (1-893419-01-0, 1661WB) Designers Lib.

— The Designers' Library: Trade Secrets Revealed. 2nd rev. ed. (Illus.). 900p. 1986. pap. text, ring bd. 95.00 (1-893419-00-2, 1661WB) Designers Lib.

Bousquet, Don. Don Bousquet's Next Book. (Illus.). 128p. 1997. pap. 9.95 (0-924771-99-2) Douglas Charles Ltd.

— The Quahog State of Mind. (Illus.). 128p. (Orig.). 1996. pap. 10.95 (0-924771-62-3, Covered Brdge Pr) Douglas Charles Ltd.

— The Quahog Stops Here. (Illus.). 128p. 1992. pap. 8.95 (0-924771-38-0, Covered Brdge Pr) Douglas Charles Ltd.

— Quahogs Are a Girl's Best Friend. (Illus.). 128p. 1994. pap. 9.95 (0-924771-50-X, Covered Brdge Pr) Douglas Charles Ltd.

— Revenge of the Quahog. (Illus.). 128p. 1998. pap. 9.95 (1-58066-020-7, Covered Brdge Pr) Douglas Charles Ltd.

— A Rhode Island Album. (Illus.). 160p. 1996. 24.95 (0-924771-78-X, Covered Brdge Pr) Douglas Charles Ltd.

Bousquet, Georges H. A French View of the Netherlands Indies. Lilienthal, Philip E., tr. from FRE. LC 75-30048. (Institute of Pacific Relations Ser.). reprint ed. 42.50 (0-404-59510-3) AMS Pr.

*Bousquet, Gilles & Irving, Andrew. Mosaiques Cahier Dintroduction a l'Analuse Culturelle. 2nd ed. 100p. 1999. per. 20.95 (0-7872-6264-1, 41626401) Kendall-Hunt.

Bousquet, Gisele L. Behind the Bamboo Hedge: The Impact of Homeland Politics in the Parisian Vietnamese Community. 208p. 1991. text 42.50 (0-472-10174-9, 10174) U of Mich Pr.

Bousquet, Jean & Yssel, Hans, eds. Immunotherapy of Asthma. LC 99-37341. (Lung Biology in Health & Disease Ser.). (Illus.). 669p. 1999. text 225.00 (0-8247-0176-3) Dekker.

Bousquet, Michel, jt. auth. see Maral, Gerard.

Bousquet, Michele. Animals & People: 3D Studio Tips & Tricks. 240p. 1994. mass mkt. 15.75 (0-8273-7016-4) Delmar.

Bousquet, Michele. Concepts in Computer Animation. (CAD/CAM Ser.). 1997. 31.50 (0-8273-7460-7, VNR) Wiley.

— Materials & Lighting: 3D Studio Tips & Tricks. (3D Studio Tips & Tricks Ser.). (Illus.). 160p. 1994. pap. 14.95 (0-8273-7012-1) Delmar.

— Shaping & Lofting: 3D Studio Tips & Tricks. 144p. 1995. mass mkt. 15.75 (0-8273-7015-6) Delmar.

Bousquet, Michele. 3-D Studio Max: Tutorials from the Masters. LC 97-4062. 512p. 1996. pap. 49.95 (0-8273-8391-6) Delmar.

Bousquet, Michele. The 3-D Studio Max 2.0 Quick Reference. LC 97-43425. 704p. 1998. mass mkt. 36.95 (0-7668-0152-7) Delmar.

Bousquet, Michele, et al. Linking AutoCAD to 3D Studio V2 for Architecture. LC 96-2519. 224p. (C). 1996. pap. 55.95 (0-8273-8081-X) Delmar.

*Bousquet, Paula. Stars in a Midnight Sky. 2000. pap. write for info. (1-58235-372-7) Watermrk Pr.

Bousquet, Paula, jt. auth. see Fitzsimmons, Judith.

Bousquet, Richard & Bousquet, Suzanne. Scotch Plains & Fanwood. (Images of America Ser.). 1995. pap. 16.99 (0-7524-0235-8) Arcadia Publng.

Bousquet, Suzanne, jt. auth. see Bousquet, Richard.

Bousquets, Jorge L. La Busqueda del Metodo Natural. (Ciencia para Todos Ser.). (SPA.). pap. 6.99 (968-16-3420-9, Pub. by Fondo) Continental Bk.

Boussac, Marie-Francoise & Salles, Jean-Francois, eds. Athens, Aden, Arikamedu: Essays on the Interrelations Between India, Arabia, & the Eastern Mediterranean. (C). 1995. 33.00 (81-7304-079-6, Pub. by Abhinav) S Asia.

Bousse, Luc, ed. Technical Digest of Solid State Sensor & Actuator Workshop, 1998, Vol. 3. (Illus.). 1998. pap. 75.00 (0-9640024-2-6) Transducer Res.

Bousser. Cerebral Venous Thrombosis. 1997. text 94.50 (0-7020-1937-2) Bailliere Tindall.

Bousser, Marie-Germaine, jt. auth. see Olesen, Jes.

Bousset, Wilhelm. Der Antichrist in der Uberlieferung Des Judentums, Des Neuen Testaments und der Alten Kirche. (GER.). vi, 186p. 1983. reprint ed. 40.00 (3-487-07335-8) G Olms Pubs.

— The Antichrist Legend: A Chapter in Christian & Jewish Folklore. 1977. lib. bdg. 59.95 (0-8490-1439-5) Gordon Pr.

— The Antichrist Legend: A Chapter in Christian & Jewish Folklore. LC 79-8095. (Satanism Ser.). 344p. reprint ed. 47.50 (0-404-18406-5) AMS Pr.

— Judisch-Christlicher Schulbetrieb in Alexandria und Rom. (Forschungen Zur Religion und Literatur Des Alten und Neuen Testaments Ser.: No. 232, N. F. 6). (GER.). viii, 319p. 1975. reprint ed. 80.00 (3-487-05611-9) G Olms Pubs.

Boussinot, R. Dictionary of Synonyms, Analogies & Antonyms: Dictionnaire des Synonymes, Analogies et Antonymes. (ENG & FRE.). 1031p. 1981. 59.55 (0-8288-1930-0, M4559) Fr & Eur.

Boustani, Rafic & Fargues, Philippe. The Atlas of the Arab World: Geopolitics & Society. Rudy-Gervais, Darla, tr. from FRE. (Illus.). 144p. 1991. 50.00 (0-8160-2346-8) Facts on File.

Boustany, Rose-Mary, jt. auth. see Hannun, Yusuf A.

Boustead, C. M., jt. ed. see Kenny, J.

Bousted, Mary, ed. see Eliot, George, pseud.

Bout, David, et al, eds. Using Experience for Learning. LC 92-47423. 1993. pap. 42.95 (0-335-19095-2) OpUniv Pr.

Bout, David E. Van Den, see Van Den Bout, David E.

Boutan, Mila. Cezanne. (Art Activity Packs Ser.). (Illus.). 13p. (J). (ps-5). 1996. pap. 9.95 (0-8118-1333-9) Chronicle Bks.

— Degas Art Activity Pack. (Art Activity Packs Ser.). (Illus.). 13p. (J). (ps-3). 1997. pap. 9.95 (0-8118-1688-5, 703941T) Chronicle Bks.

— Gauguin Art Activity Pack. (Art Activity Packs Ser.). (Illus.). 13p. (J). (ps-3). 1997. pap. 9.95 (0-8118-1689-3, 703954T) Chronicle Bks.

— Matisse. (Art Activity Packs Ser.). (Illus.). 13p. (J). (ps-5). 1996. pap. 9.95 (0-8118-1310-X) Chronicle Bks.

— Monet. (Art Activity Packs Ser.). (Illus.). 13p. (J). (ps-5). 1996. pap. 9.95 (0-8118-1335-5) Chronicle Bks.

*Boutan, Mila. Picasso. (Art Activity Ser.). (Illus.). (J). (gr. k-7). 1998. pap. 9.95 (0-8118-2029-7) Chronicle Bks.

Boutan, Mila. Renoir Art Activity Pack. (Art Activity Packs Ser.). (Illus.). 13p. (J). (ps-3). 1997. pap. 9.95 (0-8118-1690-7, 706764T) Chronicle Bks.

— Rousseau Art Activity Pack. (Art Activity Packs Ser.). (Illus.). 13p. (J). (ps-3). 1997. pap. 9.95 (0-8118-1691-5, 706777T) Chronicle Bks.

— Van Gogh. (Art Activity Packs Ser.). (Illus.). 13p. (J). (ps-5). 1996. pap. 9.95 (0-8118-1312-6) Chronicle Bks.

Boutaric, Edgard. Actes du Parlement de Paris, Ser. (Inventaires et Documents Publies Par Ordre De l'Empereur Sous la Direction De M. le Comte (Marquis) De Laborde Ser.). cccxxx, 1261p. 1975. reprint ed. 440.00 (3-487-05863-4) G Olms Pubs.

Boutegege, Regine, jt. auth. see Longo, Susanna.

Boutel, Rachel M. 50 College Lessons from Outside the Classroom. 64p. 1999. pap. 5.95 (0-9671170-9-7) Arch Pubg Co.

Boutell, Charles. Arms & Armour in Antiquity & the Middle Ages. (Medieval Military Library). (Illus.). 352p. 1995. pap. 14.95 (0-938289-62-4, 289624) Combined Pub.

Boutell, Thomas. CGI Programming in C & Perl. 416p. (C). 1996. pap. 37.95 incl. audio compact disk (0-201-42219-0) Addison-Wesley.

Boutelle, Ann E. Thistle & Rose: A Study of Hugh MacDiamid's Poetry. LC 81-65859. 259p. 1981. 35.00 (0-8387-5023-0) Bucknell U Pr.

Boutelle, Clarence M. Man of Mt. Moriah (1898) 386p. 1999. reprint ed. pap. 19.95 (0-7661-0815-5) Kessinger Pub.

Boutelle, J. A. The Burke & Alvord Memorial: A Genealogical Account of the Descendants of Richard Burke of Sudbury, Mass. 239p. 1989. reprint ed. pap. 35.50 (0-8328-0347-2); reprint ed. lib. bdg. 45.50 (0-8328-0346-4) Higginson Bk Co.

Boutelle, Sara H. Julia Morgan, Architect. expanded rev. ed. LC 87-29008. (Illus.). 272p. 1995. pap. 39.95 (0-7892-0019-8) Abbeville Pr.

Boutellier, Roman, et al. Managing Global Innovation: Uncovering the Secrets of Future Competitiveness. LC 98-55583. (Illus.). viii, 627p. 1999. 109.00 (3-540-65256-6) Spr-Verlag.

*Boutellier, Roman, et al. Managing Global Innovation: Uncovering the Secrets of Future Competitiveness. 2nd rev. ed. viii, 627p. 2000. 109.00 (3-540-66832-2) Spr-Verlag.

Bouteneff, Michael C. The Bouteneff Family Chronicle. (Illus.). 300p. (Orig.). 1989. pap. write for info. (0-318-65398-2) M C Bouteneff.

— The Bouteneff Family Chronicle LC 90-130558. xii, 295 p. 1989. write for info. (0-9623655-0-5) M C Bouteneff.

Bouteneff, Peter, ed. Daily Readings in Orthodox Spirituality. LC 95-62274. 96p. 1996. pap. text 4.95 (0-87243-218-1) Templegate.

Bouteneff, Vera, tr. Father Arseny, 1893-1973: Prisoner, Priest & Spiritual Father. LC 98-4429. viii, 277p. 1998. pap. text 12.95 (0-88141-180-9) St Vladimirs.

Boutenko, Irene A. & Razlogov, Kyrill E., eds. Recent Social Trends in Russia 1960-1995. LC 98-234797. (Comparative Charting of Social Change Ser.). 400p. 1997. 75.00 (0-7735-1610-7, Pub. by McG-Queens Univ Pr) CUP Services.

Bouterin, Antoine & Schwartz, Joan. Cooking Provence: Four Generations of Traditions & Recipes. LC 94-7743. 1994. pap. 25.00 (0-02-513955-X) Macmillan.

Bouterse, Wesley. Scriptural Light on Speaking in Tongues. 1980. pap. 2.95 (0-86544-010-7) Salv Army Suppl South.

Bouterwek, Friedrich. Asthetik: Leipzig, 1806. 1976. write for info. (3-487-05989-4) G Olms Pubs.

— Geschichte der Spanischen und Portugiesishen Poesie und Beredsamkeit. (Textos y Estudios Clasicos De las Literaturas Hispanicas Ser.). xx, 618p. 1975. reprint ed. 110.00 (3-487-05633-X) G Olms Pubs.

— Historia de la Literatura Espanola. (Illus.). xi, 276p. 1971. reprint ed. 65.00 (0-318-71614-3) G Olms Pubs.

— Kleine Schriften Philosophischen, Asthetischen und Litterarischen Inhalts. 1975. write for info. (3-487-05491-4) G Olms Pubs.

Bouterwek, Friedrich, ed. Neues Museum der Philosophie und Literatur, 3 Bande in 1. (GER.). v, 935p. 1979. write for info. (3-487-06679-3) G Olms Pubs.

Bouterwek, Friedrich, jt. ed. see Gottlieb, Johann.

Boutet De Monvel, L. & Guillemin, V. The Spectral Theory of Toeplitz Operators. LC 80-8538. (Annals of Mathematics Studies: No. 99). 167p. reprint ed. pap. 51.80 (0-608-06623-0, 206682000009) Bks Demand.

Boutet de Monvel, Louis. D-Modules, Representation Theory & Quantum Groups: Lectures Given at the 2nd Session of the Centro Internazionale Matematico Estivo (C.I.M.E.) Held in Venezia, Italy, June 12-20, 1992. LC 93-41202. (Lecture Notes in Mathematics Ser.: Vol. 1565). 1994. 41.95 (0-387-57498-0) Spr-Verlag.

Boutet, Frederic. Dictionnaire des Sciences Occultes. (FRE.). 412p. 1993. pap. 45.00 (0-7859-8109-8, 2857043899) Fr & Eur.

Boutet, Josaine. Construire le Sens. 2nd ed. (Sciences pour la Communication Ser.: Vol. 42). (FRE.). x, 236p. 1997. 39.95 (3-906758-00-1, Pub. by P Lang) P Lang Pubng.

Boutflower, Charles. The Journal of an Army Surgeon During the Peninsular War. 192p. 1997. 80.00 (1-873376-85-5, Pub. by Spellmnt Pubs) St Mut.

Boutflower, Charles. Journal of an Army Surgeon in Peninsula War. 1997. 29.95 (1-885119-49-6) Sarpedon.

Bouth, Anita J. Focus on Integrating Art into the Classroom. Romano, Louis G., ed. (Illus.). 14p. 1987. pap. text 3.00 (0-918449-09-X) MI Middle Educ.

Boutier, A., ed. New Trends in Instrumentation for Hypersonic Research. LC 92-33756. (NATO Advanced Study Institutes Series E, Applied Sciences: Vol. 224). (C). 1993. text 340.50 (0-7923-2024-7) Kluwer Academic.

Boutiere, Jean, ed. see Albertet de Sestero.

Boutilier, Craig & Goldszmidt, Moises, eds. Extending Theories of Action: Formal Theory & Practical Applications: Papers from the 1995 Spring Symposium. (Technical Reports). (Illus.). 205p. 1995. spiral bd. 30.00 (0-929280-90-3) AAAI Pr.

Boutilier, James A., et al, eds. Mission, Church, & Sect in Oceania. (ASAO Monographs: No. 6). (Illus.). 514p. 1984. reprint ed. pap. text 40.50 (0-8191-3838-X); reprint ed. lib. bdg. 68.00 (0-8191-3837-1) U Pr of Amer.

Boutilier, Mary A. & SanGiovanni, Lucinda. The Sporting Woman. LC 82-83147. (Illus.). 307p. reprint ed. pap. 95.20 (0-608-06450-5, 206728800009) Bks Demand.

Boutilier, Nancy. According to Her Contours. LC 92-27428. 233p. (Orig.). (C). 1992. pap. 12.50 (0-87685-884-1) Black Sparrow.

— According to Her Contours, signed ed. deluxe ed. LC 92-27428. 233p. (Orig.). (C). 1992. 30.00 (0-87685-886-8) Black Sparrow.

*Boutilier, Nancy. On the Eighth Day Adam Slept Alone: New Poems. LC 00-29742. 200p. 2000. 30.00 (1-57423-133-2); pap. 16.00 (1-57423-132-4) Black Sparrow.

— On the Eighth Day Adam Slept Alone: New Poems. aut. ed. LC 00-29742. 200p. 2000. 40.00 (1-57423-134-0) Black Sparrow.

Boutilier, Robert. Targeting Families: Marketing to & Through the New Family Structures. LC 93-71268. 160p. 1993. pap. 29.95 (0-936889-23-3) American Demo.

Boutillette, Linda K. & Burdett, Marilyn. Deliver Us from Evil: "Spencer Hidden Secret" Sweeney, William, ed. (Illus.). ix, 250p. 1997. 19.95 (0-9659272-1-0) Philip Roy Publ.

Boutillette, Linda K. & Burdett, Marilyn J. Deliver Us from Evil: Spencers' Hidden Secret. 4th ed. Sweeney, William, ed. LC 97-92293. (Illus.). ix, 256p. (Orig.). 1997. reprint ed. pap. 11.95 (0-9659272-0-2) Philip Roy Publ.

Boutillier, Michel & Cordier, J. Economic Modelling at the Bank of France. (International Studies in Economic Modelling). 250p. 1997. mass mkt. 95.00 (0-412-57120-X, Chap & Hall NY) Chapman & Hall.

Boutillier, Michel & Cordier, Jean, eds. Economic Modelling at the Bank of France: Financial Deregulation & Economic Development in France. (Illus.). 272p. (C). 1996. 110.00 (0-415-13645-8) Routledge.

Boutin, C., et al, eds. Practical Thoracoscopy. (Illus.). 112p. 1992. 163.00 (0-387-52369-3) Spr-Verlag.

Boutin, Gerard E. Emotional Muscle. 62p. (Orig.). (C). 1989. pap. 5.00 (0-317-93673-5) G E Boutin.

— How to Be Your Own Child Psychologist Sometimes. (C). 1989. pap. 7.00 (0-317-93675-1) G E Boutin.

— How to Be Your Own Psychologist - Sometimes. 260p. (Orig.). (C). 1989. pap. 10.00 (0-317-93674-3) G E Boutin.

Boutin, Helene & Boulet, Louis-Philippe. Understand & Control Your Asthma. (Illus.). 120p. 1995. 49.95 (0-7735-1210-1, Pub. by McG-Queens Univ Pr); pap. 19.95 (0-7735-1263-2, Pub. by McG-Queens Univ Pr) CUP Services.

*Boutin-Lawlor, Dorothy. Roses & Thorns. 2000. 15.95 (0-533-13557-5) Vantage.

B

An Asterisk (*) at the beginning of an entry indicates that the title is appearing for the first time.

Boutin, Otto J. A Catfish in the Bodoni: The Golden Age of Tramp Printers. LC 70-141186. (Illus.). 1971. 9.95 (*0-87839-004-9*) North Star.

Boutin-Quesnel, Rachel, et al. Systematic Vocabulary of Terminology. (FRE.). 38p. 1985. pap. 29.95 (*0-8288-9391-8*) Fr & Eur.

Boutlebee, Paul G. Turks & the Caicos Islands. LC 92-146816. (World Bibliographical Ser.). 118p. 1992. lib. bdg. 59.00 (*1-85109-162-9*) ABC-CLIO.

Boutman, Herbert J., tr. see Stiller, Gunther.

Boutmy, Emile. Studies in Constitutional Law: France - England - United States. 2nd ed. Dicey, E. M., tr. from FRE. xiv, 183p. 1982. reprint ed. 35.00 (*0-8377-0332-8*, Rothman) W S Hein.

Bouton, Barbara, jt. auth. see Bouton, Gary D.

Bouton, C. P. Neurolinguistics: Historical & Theoretical Perspectives. LC 90-7853. (Applied Psycholinguistics & Communication Disorders Ser.). (Illus.). 286p. (C). 1990. 65.00 (*0-306-43691-4*, Plenum Trade) Perseus Pubng.

Bouton, Cynthia A. The Flour War: Gender, Class, & Community in Late Ancien Regime French Society. LC 93-20349. 312p. 1993. 50.00 (*0-271-01053-3*); pap. 19.95 (*0-271-01055-X*) Pa St U Pr.

Bouton, David W. Echoes in an Empty Hallway: Adult Singleness in an Apparently Doubles World. (Illus.). 126p. (Orig.). 1993. pap. 16.95 (*1-881494-04-7*, EP93G); pap., spiral bd. 14.95 (*1-881494-03-9*, EP93C) Continuum Pubs.

— Me 'n God 'n Maybe You. 3rd ed. 112p. 1993. pap., spiral bd. 14.95 (*1-881494-08-X*, MP393C) Continuum Pubs.

— The Monarch Butterfly: A Fragile Tissue in the Wind. 2nd ed. (Illus.). 94p. 1995. pap. 16.95 (*1-881494-06-3*, MB95P) Continuum Pubs.

— The Monarch Butterfly: A Fragile Tissue in the Wind. 3rd ed. (Illus.). 112p. 1999. pap. 26.75 (*1-881494-15-2*) ADP-Hollander.

— On Being Butterfly Friendly: The Step Beyond Butterfly Gardening. 3rd ed. (Illus.). 62p. 1999. pap. 18.95 (*1-881494-14-4*) Continuum Pubs.

Bouton, E. Lyn, jt. auth. see Bouton, Kenneth A.

***Bouton, Eldonna.** Journaling from the Heart: A Writing Workshop in Three Parts. 128p. 2000. 14.95 (*0-9670384-1-3*) Whole Hrt.

Bouton, Eldonna. Loose Ends: A Journaling Tool for Tying up the Incomplete Details of Your Life & Heart. (Illus.). 172p. 1999. pap. 13.95 (*0-9670384-0-5*) Whole Hrt.

***Bouton, Eldonna.** Write Away: A Journal Writing Tool Kit. 32p. 2000. pap. 5.95 (*0-9670384-2-1*) Whole Hrt.

Bouton, Gary D. Inside Adobe Photoshop 4. LC 96-30069. 896p. 1997. pap. 44.99 (*1-56205-681-6*) New Riders Pub.

— Inside Extreme 3-D. LC 96-38751. 608p. 1997. 44.99 (*1-56205-662-X*) New Riders Pub.

Bouton, Gary D. & Bouton, Barbara. Inside Adobe Photoshop. LC 98-138136. 1134p. 1997. 59.99 (*1-56205-800-2*) New Riders Pub.

Bouton, Gary D., et al. CorelDRAW! Expert's Edition: Expert's Edition. (Illus.). 704p. (Orig.). 1995. pap. 45.00 (*1-56205-469-4*) New Riders Pub.

— Inside Adobe Photoshop 5. LC 98-84024. (Illus.). 742p. 1998. pap. text 44.99 (*1-56205-884-3*) New Riders Pub.

***Bouton, Gary David.** Adobe Photoshop 5.5 Fundamentals with ImageReady 2, Vol. 2. LC 99-66562. 550p. 1999. pap. 39.99 incl. disk (*0-7357-0928-9*) New Riders Pub.

— Inside Adobe Photoshop 5.5. (Illus.). 900p. 2000. pap. text 44.99 (*0-7357-1000-7*) New Riders Pub.

Bouton, Gary David. Inside Adobe Photoshop 5, Limited Edition. LC 98-86040. 1998. 55.00 (*1-56205-951-3*) New Riders Pub.

Bouton, Jim. Ball Four: Twentieth-Anniversary Edition. rev. ed. 465p. 1990. reprint ed. pap. 15.00 (*0-02-030665-2*) Macmillan.

Bouton, Kenneth A. & Bouton, E. Lyn. Nevada Trivia. LC 99-18326. 192p. 1999. pap. 6.95 (*1-55853-730-9*) Rutledge Hill Pr.

Bouton, Lawrence & Sumlinski, Mariusz. Trends in Private Investment in Developing Countries: Statistics for 1970-95. (IFC Discussion Papers: No. 31). 52p. 1997. pap. 22.00 (*0-8213-3874-9*, 13874) World Bank.

Bouton, Mark E. & Fanselow, Michael S., eds. Learning, Motivation, & Cognition: The Functional Behaviorism of Robert C. Bolles. LC 97-25299. (Illus.). 451p. 1997. text 49.95 (*1-55798-436-0*, 431-6910) Am Psychol.

Bouton, Marshall M. Agrarian Radicalism in South India. LC 85-3411. 348p. 1985. reprint ed. pap. 107.90 (*0-7837-9302-2*, 206004200004) Bks Demand.

Bouton, Marshall M. & Oldenburg, Philip, eds. India Briefing: A Transformative 50 Years. (Asia Society Briefings Ser.). 320p. 1999. text 66.95 (*0-7656-0338-1*); pap. text 25.95 (*0-7656-0339-X*) M E Sharpe.

Bouton, Nathaniel. History of Concord, New Hampshire, from its First Grant in 1725 to 1853: With a History of the Ancient Penacooks. (Illus.). 786p. 1988. reprint ed. lib. bdg. 79.50 (*0-8328-0048-1*, NH0009) Higginson Bk Co.

Bouton, Nathaniel, ed. see New Hampshire State Legislature Staff.

***Bouton, Warren Hussey.** Sea Chest in the Attic: A Spooky Tale from Nantucket. (Illus.). 86p. (J). (gr. 2-6). 2000. pap. 5.95 (*0-9700555-0-1*) Hither Creek.

Boutos, Pericles. Venice Carnival Unmasked. (Illus.). 108p. 1999. 39.95 (*88-8158-176-0*) Charta.

***Boutquin, Pierre.** Beginning VB Application Development. 800p. 2000. pap. 39.99 (*1-86100-109-6*) Wrox Pr Inc.

Boutquin, Pierre, et al. Professional Visual Basic 6 Web Programming. 1081p. 1999. pap. text 49.99 (*1-86100-222-X*) Wrox Pr Inc.

Boutros-Ghali, Boutros. Agenda for Development. LC 98-107605. 1998. pap. text 7.50 (*92-1-100644-9*) UN.

— An Agenda for Peace. 2nd ed. LC 95-211367. 159p. pap. 7.50 (*92-1-100555-8*, E.95.I.15) UN.

— Confronting New Challenges: Report of the Work of the Organization from the 49th Session to the 50th Session of the General Assembly. (United Nations Blue Bks.). 388p. pap. 14.95 (*92-1-100595-7*, E.95.I.47) UN.

— 50th Anniversary Annual Report on the Work of the Organization. 376p. pap. 14.95 (*92-1-100615-5*, JX1977) UN.

— United Nations & Apartheid. 236p. pap. 4.95 (*92-1-100614-7*, 71474) UN.

— Unvanquished: A U. S. - U. N. Saga. 384p. 1999. 29.95 (*0-375-50050-2*) Random House.

Boutros-Ghali, Boutros, ed. The United Nations & Rwanda, 1993-1996. LC 96-181845. (Blue Bks.: Vol. X). 750p. 29.95 (*92-1-100561-2*, E.96.I.20) UN.

Boutros-Ghali, Boutros, frwd. Voice of Indigenous Peoples: A Plea to the World: Native People Address the United Nations. LC 93-36081. (Illus.). 120p. 1993. pap. 12.95 (*0-940666-31-6*) Clear Light.

Boutros-Ghali, Boutros, intro. The United Nations & Mozambique, 1992-1995. LC 95-192058. (Blue Bks.: Vol. V). 321p. 29.95 (*92-1-100559-0*, E.95.I.20) UN.

— The United Nations & the Advancement of Women, 1945-1996. (Blue Bks.: Vol. VI). 852p. 49.95 (*92-1-100603-1*, E.96.I.9) UN.

— Visions: 50 Years of United Nations, 1945-1995. LC 95-7891. (Illus.). 1995. 50.00 (*0-688-14313-X*, Hearst) Hearst Commns.

Boutros-Ghali, Boutros, jt. ed. see Carter, Jimmy.

Boutros, Nashaat N., jt. auth. see Clark, David L.

Buttaz, Jean-Louis. Dictionnaire Phonologique et Orthographique du Francais Fond. (FRE.). 1979. 19.95 (*0-7859-7941-7*, 2-7135-0277-2) Fr & Eur.

Boutte, Gloria. Multicultural Education: Raising Consciousness. LC 97-36020. 352p. (C). 1998. text 51.95 (*0-8273-8159-X*) Delmar.

Bouttiaux-Ndiaye, Anne-Marie. Senegal Behind Glass: Images of Religious & Daily Life. LC 95-224540. (Illus.). 168p. 1994. 60.00 (*3-7913-1424-6*, Pub. by Prestel) te Neues.

Bouttier, Michel. Prayers for My Village. 1994. pap. 7.95 (*0-687-60887-2*) Abingdon.

— Prayers for My Village. Williamson, Lamar, tr. from FRE. 96p. 1994. pap. 8.00 (*0-8358-0711-8*) Upper Room Bks.

Boutton, Thomas W. & Yamasaki, Shin-ichi, eds. Mass Spectrometry of Soils. (Books in Soils, Plants & the Environment: Vol. 49). (Illus.). 520p. 1996. text 199.00 (*0-8247-9699-3*) Dekker.

***Boutwell.** Quick Reference to Voluntary Compliance. 548p. 1999. pap. text 125.00 (*0-7355-1176-4*) Panel Pubs.

Boutwell, Clinton E. Shell Game: Corporate America's Agenda for Schools. LC 97-67352. 367p. 1997. 35.00 (*0-87367-499-5*, SG) Phi Delta Kappa.

Boutwell, Elaine, ed. see Stanley, Charles A.

***Boutwell, Florence.** Love According to Teresa. LC 99-89760. (Illus.). (YA). 2000. write for info. (*0-87062-298-6*, Millwood Pub) A H Clark.

Boutwell, Florence. The Spokane Valley Vol. III: Out in the Gravel - a Supplement. (Illus.). 112p. 1996. 25.00 (*0-87062-269-2*); pap. 15.00 (*0-87062-268-4*) A H Clark.

— Teresa & the Coeur D'alene Indians: An Historical Adventure Story for Young & Old. LC 98-44015. (Illus.). 175 p. (J). 1998. write for info. (*0-87062-288-9*) A H Clark.

— Teresa of Northwood Prairie: An Historical Adventure Story for Young & Old. LC 98-14835. (Illus.). 175p. (J). 1998. 17.95 (*0-87062-284-6*) A H Clark.

Boutwell, George S. Constitution of the United States at the End of the First Century. xviii, 412p. 1987. reprint ed. 52.50 (*0-8377-1943-7*, Rothman) W S Hein.

Boutwell, Jeffrey. The German Nuclear Dilemma. LC 89-46168. (Cornell Studies in Security Affairs). (Illus.). 288p. 1990. text 42.50 (*0-8014-2402-X*) Cornell U Pr.

Boutwell, Jeffrey, et al, eds. The Nuclear Confrontation in Europe. LC 85-14062. 247p. 1985. 59.95 (*0-86569-128-2*, Auburn Hse) Greenwood.

Boutwell, Jeffrey & Klare, Michael T., eds. Light Weapons & Civil Conflict: Controlling the Tools of Violence. LC 98-55389. 256p. 1999. 65.00 (*0-8476-9484-4*) Rowman.

— Light Weapons & Civil Conflict: Controlling the Tools of Violence. LC 98-55389. (Carnegie Commission on Preventing Deadly Conflict Ser.). 256p. 1999. pap. 22.95 (*0-8476-9485-2*) Rowman.

Boutwell, Jeffrey & Mendelsohn, Everett. Israeli-Palestinian Security: Issues in the Permanent Status Negotiations. 124p. (C). 1995. pap. text 10.00 (*0-87724-003-5*, Cmtte Intl Sec Stud) Am Acd Arts Sciences.

Bouty, Michel. DIMACO, Dictionnaire des Mathematiques au College. rev. ed. (FRE.). 447p. 1991. 29.95 (*0-7859-4846-5*) Fr & Eur.

Boutzarelos, Irene, jt. auth. see Pappas, Barbara.

Bouvard, Marguerite. The Body's Burning Fields: Poems of Illness & Healing. (Illus.). 33p. 1997. pap. 6.95 (*0-9636545-7-8*) Wind Pubns.

Bouvard, Marguerite & Gladu, Evelyn. The Path Through Grief: A Compassionate Guide. LC 97-44051. 331p. 1998. pap. text 17.95 (*1-57392-189-0*) Prometheus Bks.

Bouvard, Marguerite G. Grandmothers: Granddaughters Remember. LC 98-24246. 1998. 29.95 (*0-8156-0534-X*) Syracuse U Pr.

— Journeys over Water. (QRL Poetry Bks.: Vol. XXIII). 1982. 20.00 (*0-614-06398-1*) Quarterly Rev.

— Of Light & Silence. LC 90-70708. 80p. 1990. pap. 8.95 (*0-944072-12-7*) Zoland Bks.

— Revolutionizing Motherhood: The Mothers of the Plaza De Mayo. LC 93-41428. (Latin American Silhouettes Ser.). (Illus.). 261p. 1994. 45.00 (*0-8420-2486-7*); pap. 17.95 (*0-8420-2487-5*) Scholarly Res Inc.

— Voices from an Island. LC 85-3831. 70p. 1985. 14.95 (*0-932576-25-7*); pap. 6.95 (*0-932576-26-5*) Breitenbush Bks.

— Women Reshaping Human Rights: How Extraordinary Activists Are Changing the World. LC 96-5126. (Illus.). 319p. 1996. 50.00 (*0-8420-2562-6*); pap. 18.95 (*0-8420-2563-4*) Scholarly Res Inc.

Bouvard, Maurice. Mobile Barrages & Intakes on Sediment Transporting Rivers. 320p. 1991. 136.00 (*90-6191-150-8*, Pub. by A A Balkema) Ashgate Pub Co.

Bouvard, Pierre, jt. auth. see Marx, Steve.

Bouve, Pauline C. Their Shadows Before: A Story of the Southampton Insurrection. LC 72-39078. (Black Heritage Library Collection). 1977. reprint ed. 25.95 (*0-8369-9016-1*) Ayer.

Bouveresse, Jacques. La Philosophie d'un Anti-Philosophe: Paul Valery. 32p. 1994. pap. text 8.95 (*0-19-815196-9*) OUP.

Bouveresse, Jacques. Wittgenstein Reads Freud: The Myth of the Unconscious. 168p. 1995. pap. text 12.95 (*0-691-02904-0*, Pub. by Princeton U Pr) Cal Prin Full Svc.

— Wittgenstein Reads Freud: The Myth of the Unconscious. Cosman, Carol, tr. from FRE. LC 94-40607. (New French Thought Ser.). (ENG & FRE.). 176p. 1995. text 29.50 (*0-691-03425-7*, Pub. by Princeton U Pr) Cal Prin Full Svc.

Bouveresse, Jacques & Parret, Herman H., eds. Meaning & Understanding. 442p. (C). 1981. 106.15 (*3-11-008116-4*) De Gruyter.

Bouvet, Charles. Une Dynastie des Musiciens Francais: Les Couperins, Organistes de l'Eglise Saint-Gervais. (Illus.). xiv, 304p. 1977. reprint ed. 65.00 (*3-487-06294-1*) G Olms Pubs.

Bouvet, Danielle. Path to Language: Toward Bilingual Education for Deaf Children. 300p. 1990. 99.00 (*1-85359-079-7*, Pub. by Multilingual Matters); pap. 39.95 (*1-85359-078-9*, Pub. by Multilingual Matters) Taylor & Francis.

Bouvet, Francis. Bonnard: The Complete Graphic Work. (Illus.). 352p. 1981. 125.00 (*0-915346-74-5*) A Wofsy Fine Arts.

Bouvet, M. & Bienvenu, G., eds. High-Resolution Methods in Underwater Acoustics. (Lecture Notes in Control & Information Sciences: Vol. 155). (Illus.). xi, 240p. 1991. 47.95 (*0-387-53716-3*) Spr-Verlag.

Bouvette, Marguerite A. Communicable Diseases: Policies & Procedures. 3rd ed. 238p. (C). 1996. ring bd. 28.50 (*1-877735-23-X*, 2139PP) Prof Prnting & Pub.

— Communicable Diseases 1998 Edition: Policies & Procedures. 1998. 52.00 (*0-929442-34-2*, 2143PP) Prof Prnting & Pub.

— Infection Control in Long Term Care Facilities. 2nd ed. 91p. (C). 1987. 14.00 (*1-877735-15-9*, 2128PP) Prof Prnting & Pub.

— Quality Assessment, Assurance, Forms & Worksheets: Forms & Worksheets. 94p. 1995. 23.50 (*1-877735-39-6*, 2223PP) Prof Prnting & Pub.

— Rehabilitative & Restorative Nursing in LTC. (Illus.). 122p. (C). 1988. 16.50 (*1-877735-24-8*, 2141PP) Prof Prnting & Pub.

Bouvier, Alain. Diccionario de Matematicas. (SPA.). 896p. 1984. 175.00 (*0-7859-9794-6*) Fr & Eur.

— Dictionnaire des Mathematiques. 4th ed. (FRE.). 968p. 1993. 235.00 (*0-7859-7750-3*, 2130454917) Fr & Eur.

Bouvier de la Mothe-Guion, see Guion, Jeanne M., pseud.

Bouvier, Edouard S., jt. ed. see McDonald, Patrick D.

***Bouvier, Geoff, et al.** Noon. (Illus.). 2000. pap. 9.00 (*0-9676211-0-0*) Noon Inc.

***Bou'vier, Hugh Mitchell.** Dubious & Darling. 105p. 2000. pap. 13.95 (*1-881524-68-X*) Milligan Bks.

Bouvier, Jacques, jt. auth. see Francis, Jack.

Bouvier, John. Bouvier's Law Dictionary, 2 vols., Set. 1991. lib. bdg. 475.95 (*0-8490-5111-8*) Gordon Pr.

— Bouvier's Law Dictionary & Concise Encyclopedia, 2 vols. in 3. 8th ed. 3532p. 1984. reprint ed. lib. bdg. 195.00 (*0-89941-335-8*, 303280) W S Hein.

— Bouvier's Law Dictionary & Concise Encyclopedia: 1914 Version. unabridged ed. Baldwin, W. E., ed. 1360p. 1992. reprint ed. ring bd. 120.00 (*1-877767-62-X*) Univ Publng Hse.

— L' Historien sur Son Metier: Etudes Economiques XIXe-XXe Siecles. 518p. 1989. pap. text 94.00 (*2-88124-194-8*) Gordon & Breach.

— Institutes of American Law: New Edition, 1880. LC 98-54288. 1999. reprint ed. 250.00 (*1-886363-80-3*) Lawbk Exchange.

— A Law Dictionary: Adapted to the Constitution & Laws of the United States & the Several States of the American Union; With References to the Civil & Other Systems of Foreign Law, 1839 First Edition, 2 vols. LC 99-47231. 1187p. 1993. reprint ed. 130.00 (*0-9630106-7-0*) Lawbk Exchange.

Bouvier, Kathleen. Black Jack Bouvier. 288p. 1999. mass mkt. 5.99 (*0-7860-0650-1*) Pinnacle Books.

Bouvier, Leon F. Fifty Million Californians? 93p. 1991. pap. 9.95 (*1-881290-24-7*) Ctr Immigrat.

— Fifty Million Californians? abr. ed. (Illus.). 115p. 1992. reprint ed. pap. 5.00 (*0-935776-10-9*) F A I R.

— Immigration. (Think Ser.). 160p. (YA). (gr. 7 up). 1988. pap. 5.95 (*0-8027-6756-7*); lib. bdg. 14.85 (*0-8027-6755-9*) Walker & Co.

— Peaceful Invasions: Immigration & Changing America. 244p. (C). 1991. pap. text 24.50 (*0-8191-8403-9*); lib. bdg. 51.00 (*0-8191-8402-0*) U Pr of Amer.

— Think about Immigration: Social Diversity in the U. S. LC 91-16888. (Think Ser.). 1992. write for info. (*0-8027-8115-2*); pap. write for info. (*0-8027-7367-2*) Walker & Co.

Bouvier, Leon F. & Jenks, Rosemary E. Shaping Illinois: The Effects of Immigration - 1970-2020. (Illus.). 16p. (Orig.). 1996. pap. 6.00 (*1-881290-13-1*) Ctr Immigrat.

Bouvier, Leon F. & Martin, John L. Foreign-Born Scientists, Engineers & Mathematicians in the United States. (Illus.). 91p. (Orig.). 1995. pap. 12.00 (*1-881290-15-8*) Ctr Immigrat.

Bouvier, Leon F. & Poston, Dudley L. Thirty Million Texans? LC 92-75793. (Illus.). 113p. (Orig.). 1993. pap. 9.95 (*1-881290-20-4*) Ctr Immigrat.

Bouvier, Leon F. & Rao, Sethu. Socioreligious Factors in Fertility Decline. LC 75-26602. 224p. 1975. text 25.00 (*0-88410-352-8*, HarpBusn) HarpInfo.

Bouvier, Leon F. & Simcox, David. Foreign Born Professionals in the United States. 68p. (Orig.). 1994. pap. 12.00 (*1-881290-19-0*) Ctr Immigrat.

Bouvier, Leon F., et al. Shaping Florida: The Effects of Immigration - 1970-2020. (Illus.). 16p. (Orig.). 1995. pap. 6.00 (*1-881290-14-X*) Ctr Immigrat.

Bouvier, Leon F., jt. auth. see Martin, John L.

Bouvier, Nicolas. The Japanese Chronicles. Dickerson, Anne, tr. from FRE. LC 91-12014. 240p. 1992. pap. 11.95 (*1-56279-046-3*) Mercury Hse Inc.

— The Japanese Chronicles. Dickerson, Anne, tr. from FRE. LC 91-12014. (Illus.). 240p. 1992. 19.95 (*1-56279-008-0*) Mercury Hse Inc.

— The Japanese Chronicles. 1995. 18.00 (*0-7486-6192-1*, Pub. by Polygon) Subterranean Co.

— The Way of the World. Marsack, Robyn, tr. from FRE. LC 92-60851. 220p. 1992. 29.95 (*0-910395-86-1*); pap. 14.95 (*0-910395-87-X*) Marlboro Pr.

Bouvier, Robert. Le Parler Marseillais Dictionnaire Argotique. (FRE.). 182p. 1987. pap. 30.95 (*0-7859-8127-6*, 2862760900) Fr & Eur.

Bouvier, Virginia M. Alliance or Compliance: Implications of the Chilean Experience for the Catholic Church in Latin America. LC 83-960. (Foreign & Comparative Studies Program, Latin American Ser.: No. 3). (Orig.). 1983. pap. text 7.00 (*0-915984-94-6*) Syracuse U Foreign Comp.

Bouvy, Eugene. Daumier: The Complete Engravings. (FRE., Illus.). 640p. 1995. reprint ed. 175.00 (*1-55660-224-3*) A Wofsy Fine Arts.

Bouw, R. De, see De Bouw, R.

Bouwens, Luc, ed. NK Cells in the Liver. LC 95-1069. (Medical Intelligence Unit Ser.). 136p. 1995. text 79.00 (*1-57059-249-7*) Landes Bioscience.

Bouwer. Groundwater Hydrology. 1978. student ed. 27.50 (*0-07-006716-3*) McGraw.

Bouwer, Herman. Groundwater Hydrology. (Environment Water & Resources Ser). (Illus.). (C). 1978. text 82.50 (*0-07-006715-5*) McGraw.

— Groundwater Recharge: Natural & Artificial Technologies & Water Reuse Management. 1999. 69.95 (*1-56670-287-9*, L1287) Lewis Pubs.

Bouwhuis, D. G., jt. ed. see Taylor, Martin M.

Bouwkamp, Burton, ed. United States - Japan Trade: White Paper. 59p. (C). 1998. reprint ed. pap. text 20.00 (*0-7881-7225-5*) DIANE Pub.

Bouwkamp, John C., ed. Sweet Potato Products: A Natural Resource for the Tropics. 280p. 1985. 160.00 (*0-8493-5428-5*, TP444, CRC Reprint) Franklin.

Bouwknegt, P. W Symmetry. (Advanced Series in Mathematical Physics). 904p. 1995. text 109.00 (*981-02-1762-5*) World Scientific Pub.

Bouwknegt, P., et al. Recent Progress in Statistical Mechanics & Quantum Field Theory. 600p. 1995. text 150.00 (*981-02-2065-0*) World Scientific Pub.

— The W B3 S Algebra: Modules, Semi-Infinite Cohomology & BV Algebras. LC 96-29230. (Lectures Notes in Physics Ser.). 204p. 1996. 49.00 (*3-540-61528-8*) Spr-Verlag.

Bouwman, A. F. Approaches to Scaling of Trace Gas Fluxes in Ecosystems. LC 99-17159. (Developments in Atmospheric Science Ser.). 372p. 1999. 149.50 (*0-444-82934-2*) Elsevier.

— Long-Term Scenarios of Livestock-Crop-Land Use Interactions in Developing Country Land & Water. LC 98-126631. (Land & Water Bulletin Ser.: No. 6). 144p. 1997. pap. 19.00 (*92-5-103985-2*, F39852, Pub. by FAO) Bernan Associates.

Bouwman, Constance, et al. Beginning Spanish Bk. 1: A Teacher's Manual: Comprehension Based Activities for the Learnables. (Illus.). 163p. (YA). (gr. 7 up). 1989. pap. text, teacher ed. 40.00 (*0-939990-78-4*) Intl Linguistics.

Bouwman, Dorothy L., jt. auth. see Grin, Oliver D.

Bouwman, Dorothy L., jt. auth. see Robson, Larry J.

Bouwman, Dorothy L., ed. see Brintnall, Bruce B. & Brintnall, Ruth A.

Bouwman, Dorothy L., ed. see Davidson, Robert C. & Busman, Denise.

Bouwman, Dorothy L., ed. see Herz, David A. & Looman, Janice E.

Bouwman, Dorothy L., ed. see Lojek, Michael A. & Bement, Patricia.

Bouwman, Dorothy L., ed. see MacKeigan, John M. & Hillary, Kathleen M.

Bouwman, Dorothy L., ed. see Patzelt, Lawrence H. & Berends, Nancy L.

Bouwman, Dorothy L., ed. see Wiley, D. Eugene & Roberts, Carol E.

Bouwman, Elisabeth, jt. auth. see Reedijk, Jan.

Bouwman, Fred. The Practical Camp Cook. 218p. 1988. 17.98 (*0-88290-328-4*) Horizon Utah.

Bouwman, Harry, ed. Relaunching Videotex. (Diverse Ser.). 188p. (C). 1992. text 152.50 (*0-7923-1711-4*) Kluwer Academic.

An Asterisk (*) at the beginning of an entry indicates that the title is appearing for the first time.

***Bouwmeester, Dik, et al, eds.** The Physics of Quantum Information: Quantum Cryptography, Quantum Teleportation, Quantum Computation. (Illus.). xvi, 316p. 2000. 54.00 (*3-540-66778-4*) Spr-Verlag.

Bouwmeester, H. J., jt. auth. see Gellings, P. J.

Bouwsma, O. K. Bouwsma's Notes on Wittgenstein's Philosophy, 1965-1975. Craft, J. L. & Hustwit, Ronald, eds. LC 95-9292. (Studies in the History of Philosophy: Vol. 37). 460p. 1995. text 109.95 (*0-7734-8885-5*) E Mellen.

— Toward a New Sensibility: Essays of O. K. Bouwsma. Craft, J. L. & Hustwit, Ronald E., eds. LC 81-16117. 299p. reprint ed. pap. 92.70 (*0-7837-4664-4*, 204439100002) Bks Demand.

— Without Proof or Evidence: Essays of O. K. Bouwsma. Hustwit, Ronald E., ed. LC 83-10269. 177p. reprint ed. pap. 54.90 (*0-7837-4665-2*, 204439200002) Bks Demand.

— Wittgenstein: Conversations, 1949-1951. Craft, J. L. & Hustwit, Ronald E., eds. LC 85-27222. 112p. (C). 1986. pap. 9.95 (*0-87220-008-6*); lib. bdg. 29.95 (*0-87220-009-4*) Hackett Pub.

Bouwsma, Ward D. & Corle, Clyde G. Basic Mathematics for Elementary Teachers. LC 67-11887. 352p. reprint ed. pap. 109.20 (*0-8357-5981-4*, 20124480008l) Bks Demand.

Bouwsma, William J. John Calvin: A Sixteenth-Century Portrait. (Illus.). 320p. 1989. reprint ed. pap. text 16.95 (*0-19-505951-4*) OUP.

— A Usable Past: Essays in European Cultural History. 1990. 55.00 (*0-520-06438-0*, Pub. by U CA Pr); pap. 19.95 (*0-520-06990-0*, Pub. by U CA Pr) Cal Prin Full Svc.

— Venice & the Defense of Republican Liberty: Renaissance Values in the Age of the Counter Reformation. LC 68-14642. (Illus.). 1968. pap. 17.95 (*0-520-05221-8*, Pub. by U CA Pr) Cal Prin Full Svc.

***Bouwsma, William J.** Waning of the Renaissance, 1550-1640. (Intellectual History of the West Ser.). (Illus.). 352p. 2000. 29.95 (*0-300-08537-0*) Yale U Pr.

Bouyer, Chriatian. Dictionnaire des Reines. (FRE.). 260p. 1992. 85.00 (*0-7859-7868-2*, 2262007896) Fr & Eur.

Bouyer, Louis. The Christian Mystery: From Pagan Myth to Christian Mysticism. Trethowan, Illtyd, tr. 312p. 1990. 49.95 (*0-567-09514-2*, Pub. by T & T Clark) Bks Intl VA.

— The Christian Mystery: From Pagan Myth to Christian Mysticism. Trethowan, Illtyd, tr. from FRE. LC 94-17518. 303p. 1995. reprint ed. pap. 29.95 (*1-879007-07-X*) St Bedes Pubns.

— The Church of God. Quinn, Charles U., tr. 567p. 1983. 25.00 (*0-8199-0777-4*, Frncscn Herld) Franciscan Pr.

— Cosmos. DeFontnouvelle, Pierre, tr. from FRE. LC 88-18592. 274p. (Orig.). 1988. pap. 24.95 (*0-932506-66-6*) St Bedes Pubns.

— Diccionario de Teologia. 6th ed.Tr. of Dictionary of Theology. (SPA.). 672p. 1990. write for info. (*0-7859-5061-3*) Fr & Eur.

— Eucharist: Theology & Spirituality of the Eucharist Prayer. Quinn, Charles U., tr. LC 68-17064. 1968. pap. 19.50 (*0-268-00498-6*) U of Notre Dame Pr.

— A History of Christian Spirituality Vol. 3: Orthodox Spirituality & Protestant & Anglican Spirituality. 230p. 1994. pap. 30.00 (*0-86012-115-1*, Pub. by Srch Pr) St Mut.

— The Invisible Father: Approaches to the Mystery of the Divinity. Gilbert, Hugh, tr. from FRE. LC 98-42504. 319p. 1999. pap. 24.95 (*1-879007-29-5*) St Bedes Pubns.

— St. Philip Neri: A Portrait. 94p. 1995. pap. 7.95 (*0-85244-299-8*, 968, Pub. by Gracewing) Morehouse Pub.

— The Spirituality of the New Testament & the Fathers. (History of Christian Spirituality Ser.: Vol. 1). 560p. 1982. reprint ed. 18.95 (*0-8164-2372-5*) Harper SF.

— Women Mystics. Nash, Ann E., tr. from FRE. LC 92-75067. 200p. (Orig.). 1993. pap. 13.95 (*0-89870-434-0*) Ignatius Pr.

Bouyer, Louis, et al. Word & Spirit No. 10: Mary & Monasticism: Our Lady's Place in Monastic Life. LC 81-644362. (Word & Spirit Ser.: No. 10). 151p. 1988. pap. 8.00 (*0-932506-63-1*) St Bedes Pubns.

Bouyet, Barbara. The Akita: An Owner's Guide to a Happy, Healthy Pet. 1996. 12.95 (*0-87605-491-2*) Howell Bks.

***Bouyoucas, Pan.** A Father's Vengeance: A Novel. Tombs, George, tr. 250p. 2000. pap. 15.00 (*1-55071-116-4*, Pub. by Guernica Editions) Paul & Co Pubs.

Bouysset, M. & Cedex, Pierre B. Bone & Joint Disorders of the Foot & Ankle. (Illus.). xviii, 357p. 1998. 185.00 (*3-540-63992-6*) Spr-Verlag.

Bouysset, Maurice & Bardot, Andre. Bone & Joint Disorders of the Foot & Ankle. LC 97-42750. 1997. 144.00 (*3-540-59593-7*) Spr-Verlag.

Bouza, Anthony V. A Carpet of Blue: An Ex-Cop Takes a Tough Look at America's Drug Problem. LC 91-72993. 176p. 1992. 19.95 (*0-925190-20-9*); pap. 12.95 (*0-925190-21-7*) Fairview Press.

— Police Intelligence: The Operations of an Investigative Unit. LC 75-8667. (Studies in Criminal Justice: No. 2). 1976. 32.50 (*0-404-13138-7*) AMS Pr.

— The Police Mystique: An Insider's Look at Cops, Crime & the Criminal Justice System. LC 89-29450. (Illus.). 312p. (C). 1990. 23.50 (*0-306-43464-4*, Plenum Trade) Perseus Pubng.

Bouza, Tony. Bronx Beat: Reflections of a Police Commander. 164p. 1990. pap. 9.95 (*0-942511-27-1*) OICJ.

— Bronx Beat: Reflections of a Police Commander. 1990. 19.95 (*0-942511-29-8*) OICJ.

Bouza, Tony. The Decline & Fall of the American Empire: Corruption, Decadence, & the American Dream. (Illus.). 320p. (C). 1996. 27.95 (*0-306-45407-6*, Plenum Trade) Perseus Pubng.

Bouzaher, Aziz, jt. ed. see Johnson, S. R.

***Bouzane, Lillian.** In the Hands of the Living God. 360p. 1999. pap. 14.95 (*0-88801-233-0*, Pub. by Turnstone Pr) Genl Dist Srvs.

Bouzas, Roberto & Ros, Jaime, eds. Economic Integration in the Western Hemisphere. LC 94-15937. (C). 1994. text 34.50 (*0-268-00930-9*); pap. text 17.50 (*0-268-00931-7*) U of Notre Dame Pr.

Bouzeghoub, Mokrane, et al. Object Technology: Concepts & Methods. (ITCP-UK Computer Science Ser.). (C). 1997. pap. 39.99 (*1-85032-301-1*) Thomson Learn.

Bouzek, Jan. Greece, Anatolia & Europe: Cultural Interrelations During the Early Iron Age. (Studies in Mediterranean Archaeology: Vol. CXXII). (Illus.). 495p. 1997. pap. 142.50 (*91-7081-168-7*, Pub. by P Astroms) Coronet Bks.

Bouzereau, Laurent. The Cutting Room Floor: Movie Scenes Which Never Made It to the Movies. LC 93-45401. 1994. pap. 12.95 (*0-8065-1491-4*, Citadel Pr) Carol Pub Group.

— Star Wars: The Annotated Screenplays. LC 97-93469. (Star Wars Ser.). 352p. 1997. pap. 12.95 (*0-345-40981-7*, Del Rey) Ballantine Pub Grp.

— Ultraviolent Movies: From Sam Peckinpah to Quentin Tarantino. (Illus.). 256p. 1996. pap. 17.95 (*0-8065-1787-5*, Citadel Pr) Carol Pub Group.

— Ultraviolent Movies: From Sam Peckinpah to Quentin Tarantino. rev. ed. LC 98-39469. (Illus.). 272p. 1998. pap. 19.95 (*0-8065-2045-0*, Citadel Pr) Carol Pub Group.

Bouzereau, Laurent & Duncan, Jody. The Making of Star Wars: Episode I: The Phantom Menace. LC 99-90347. 1999. 39.95 (*0-345-43111-1*, Del Rey) Ballantine Pub Grp.

— Star Wars: The Making of Episode I. (Star Wars Ser.). (Illus.). 161p. 1999. pap. 19.95 (*0-345-43119-7*, Del Rey) Ballantine Pub Grp.

Bouzidi, Med, ed. see Miller, Janice.

Bouzon, J., jt. auth. see Vergnaud, J. M.

***Bova, Ben.** Are We Alone in the Cosmos? The Search for Alien Contact in the New Millennium. 1999. per. 16.00 (*0-671-03892-3*) Aladdin.

Bova, Ben. As on a Darkling Plain. 1991. mass mkt. 3.99 (*0-8125-1546-3*, Pub. by Tor Bks) St Martin.

— The Astral Mirror. 288p. (Orig.). 1985. pap. 2.95 (*0-8125-3217-1*, Pub. by Tor Bks) St Martin.

— Battle Station. 1990. pap. 3.95 (*0-8125-1300-2*, Pub. by Tor Bks) St Martin.

— Challenges. 352p. 1994. mass mkt. 4.99 (*0-8125-1408-4*, Pub. by Tor Bks) St Martin.

— Colony. 512p. 1999. mass mkt. 6.99 (*0-380-79315-6*, Eos) Morrow Avon.

— The Craft of Writing Science Fiction That Sells. LC 93-38613. 224p. 1994. 16.99 (*0-89879-600-8*, Wrtrs Digest Bks) F & W Pubns Inc.

— Cyberbooks. 1990. mass mkt. 4.50 (*0-8125-0319-8*, Pub. by Tor Bks) St Martin.

— Empire Builders. 384p. 1995. 5.99 (*0-8125-1165-4*, Pub. by Tor Bks) St Martin.

— Escape Plus. 288p. (Orig.). 1984. pap. 2.95 (*0-8125-3212-0*, Pub. by Tor Bks) St Martin.

— The Exiles Trilogy. 496p. 1994. reprint ed. mass mkt. 6.99 (*0-671-87631-7*) Baen Bks.

— Future Crime. 1990. mass mkt. 4.95 (*0-8125-3241-4*) Tor Bks.

— Immortality: How Science is Extending Your Life Span--& Changing the World. LC 98-3950. 288p. 1998. 24.00 (*0-380-97518-1*, Avon Bks) Morrow Avon.

***Bova, Ben.** Immortality: How Science is Extending Your Life Span & Changing the World, Vol. 1. 304p. 2000. pap. 13.50 (*0-380-79318-0*, Avon Bks) Morrow Avon.

— Jupiter. 2001. text 22.95 (*0-312-87217-8*) St Martin.

— The Kinsman Saga. 544p. 2000. mass mkt. 6.99 (*0-380-79317-2*, Avon Bks) Morrow Avon.

Bova, Ben. Mars. 560p. 1993. mass mkt. 6.99 (*0-553-56241-X*) Bantam.

— Moonrise. 592p. 1998. mass mkt. 6.99 (*0-380-78697-4*, Avon Bks) Morrow Avon.

***Bova, Ben.** Moonwar. LC 97-18177. 400p. 1998. mass mkt. 23.00 (*0-380-97303-0*, Avon Bks) Morrow Avon.

Bova, Ben. Moonwar. 512p. 1998. mass mkt. 6.99 (*0-380-78698-2*, Eos) Morrow Avon.

— Orion. 432p. 1992. reprint ed. mass mkt. 4.99 (*0-8125-3247-3*, Pub. by Tor Bks) St Martin.

— Orion among the Stars. 320p. 1995. 22.95 (*0-312-85637-7*) Tor Bks.

— Orion among the Stars. 1996. mass mkt. 5.99 (*0-8125-3511-1*, Pub. by Tor Bks) St Martin.

— Orion & the Conqueror. 352p. 1995. 5.99 (*0-8125-2376-8*, Pub. by Tor Bks) St Martin.

— Orion in the Dying Time. 1991. mass mkt. 4.99 (*0-8125-1429-7*, Pub. by Tor Bks) St Martin.

— The Peacekeepers. 384p. 1989. mass mkt. 4.95 (*0-8125-0238-8*, Pub. by Tor Bks) St Martin.

— Prometheans. (Illus.). 288p. (Orig.). 1986. pap. 2.95 (*0-8125-3219-8*, Pub. by Tor Bks) St Martin.

***Bova, Ben.** Return to Mars. LC 99-21635. 416p. 1999. 25.00 (*0-380-97640-4*, Eos) Morrow Avon.

— Return to Mars. 560p. 2000. mass mkt. 6.99 (*0-380-79725-9*) Morrow Avon.

Bova, Ben. Sam Gunn Forever. 288p. 1998. mass mkt. 5.99 (*0-380-79726-7*, Eos) Morrow Avon.

— The Starcrossed. 224p. 1988. pap. 2.95 (*0-8125-3231-7*, Pub. by Tor Bks) St Martin.

— Test of Fire. 320p. 1985. pap. 2.95 (*0-8125-3208-2*, Pub. by Tor Bks) St Martin.

— Triumph. 256p. 1994. mass mkt. 4.99 (*0-8125-2063-7*, Pub. by Tor Bks) St Martin.

— Twice Seven. LC 97-94887. 320p. 1998. mass mkt. 6.50 (*0-380-79741-0*, Eos) Morrow Avon.

— Vengeance of Orion. 352p. 1989. pap. 3.95 (*0-8125-3161-2*, Pub. by Tor Bks) St Martin.

***Bova, Ben.** Venus. (Illus.). 384p. 2000. 24.95 (*0-312-87216-X*, Pub. by Tor Bks) St Martin.

Bova, Ben. Viewpoint. (Boskone Bks.). (Illus.). 1977. 8.00 (*0-915368-14-5*) New Eng SF Assoc.

— Voyagers. 1989. mass mkt. 4.95 (*0-8125-0076-8*, Pub. by Tor Bks) St Martin.

— Voyagers III: Star Brothers. 1991. mass mkt. 4.95 (*0-8125-3236-8*, Pub. by Tor Bks) St Martin.

— Voyagers, II: The Alien Within. 1991. mass mkt. 4.95 (*0-8125-1337-1*, Pub. by Tor Bks) St Martin.

— The Watchmen. 432p. 1994. mass mkt. 5.99 (*0-671-87598-1*) Baen Bks.

— The Winds of Altair. 1988. pap. 3.95 (*0-8125-3227-9*, Pub. by Tor Bks) St Martin.

Bova, Ben & Austin, A. J. To Fear the Light. 1996. pap. write for info. (*0-614-05521-0*); mass mkt. 6.99 (*0-8125-2382-2*, Pub. by Tor Bks) St Martin.

— To Save the Sun. 384p. 1993. mass mkt. 4.99 (*0-8125-1448-3*, Pub. by Tor Bks) St Martin.

Bova, Ben & Lewis, Anthony R. Space Travel. LC 96-36003. (Science Fiction Writing Ser.). (Illus.). 288p. 1997. pap. 16.99 (*0-89879-747-0*, Wrtrs Digest Bks) F & W Pubns Inc.

Bova, Ben & Pogue, Bill. The Trikon Deception. 480p. 1993. mass mkt. 5.99 (*0-8125-0735-5*, Pub. by Tor Bks) St Martin.

Bova, Ben, et al. Future Quartet. 304p. 1995. mass mkt. 5.50 (*0-380-71886-3*, Avon Bks) Morrow Avon.

— Lamps on the Brow: (Science Fiction Stories in the Future) Cahill, James, ed. 200p. 1998. 125.00 (*0-9640454-7-8*) J Cahill Pubng.

Bova, Ben, jt. auth. see Glashow, Sheldon L.

Bova, Ben, ed. see Gillett, Stephen L.

***Bova, Benjamin W.** Privateers. 400p. 2000. mass mkt. 6.99 (*0-380-79316-4*, Avon Bks) Morrow Avon.

Bova, Joyce. Don't Ask Forever: My Love Affair with Elvis Presley. 1994. 20.00 (*0-8217-4616-2*, Zebra Kensgtn) Kensgtn Pub Corp.

Bova, Joyce & Nowels, William C. Don't Ask Forever. 448p. 1995. mass mkt. 4.99 (*0-7860-0157-7*, Pinncle Kensgtn) Kensgtn Pub Corp.

Bova, Joyce & Nowles, William. Don't Ask Forever. 448p. 1995. mass mkt. 4.99 (*0-8217-0157-6*, Zebra Kensgtn) Kensgtn Pub Corp.

Bova, Patrick & Worley, Michael P. NORC Bibliography of Publications, 1941-1991: A Fifty Year Cumulation. x, 452p. 1991. pap. 15.00 (*0-932132-46-4*) Natl Opinion Res.

***Bova, Regina M., ed.** Desktop Guide to Basic Contracting Terms. 5th ed. 264p. 1999. pap. 39.95 (*0-940343-97-5*) Natl Contract Mgmt.

Bova, Regina M., ed. see Bruggeman, Linda S., et al.

Bova, Rodolfo, jt. auth. see Micheli, Maria R.

Bovair, Keith, et al, eds. Special Curricula Needs. 160p. 1992. pap. 32.50 (*1-85346-216-0*, Pub. by David Fulton) Taylor & Francis.

Bovair, Keith & McLaughlin, Colleen, eds. Counselling in Schools - A Reader. 144p. 1993. pap. 27.50 (*1-85346-224-1*, Pub. by David Fulton) Taylor & Francis.

Bovair, Keith, jt. auth. see Baker, Derek.

Bovair, Keith, jt. ed. see Baker, Derek.

Bovaird, Anne. Goodbye U. S. A. - Bonjour France: A Language Learning Adventure. (FRE & ENG., Illus.). 48p. (J). (gr. 3-7). 1993. 12.95 (*0-8120-6406-2*); pap. 5.95 (*0-8120-4960-8*) Barron.

— Goodbye U. S. A. - Bonjour la France: A Language Learning Adventure, Vol. II. (FRE & ENG., Illus.). 48p. (J). (gr. 3-8). 1994. 12.95 (*0-8120-6384-8*); pap. 5.95 (*0-8120-1390-5*) Barron.

— Goodbye U. S. A. - Ola Mexico! (SPA & ENG., Illus.). 48p. (J). (gr. 3-7). 1994. 12.95 (*0-8120-6374-0*); pap. 5.95 (*0-8120-1388-3*) Barron.

Bovaird, Chris, jt. auth. see Harris, Simon.

Bovaird, Tony, et al, eds. Recreation Management & Pricing: The Effects of Charging Policy on Demand at Countryside Recreation Sites. LC 84-10151. 182p. 1984. text 91.95 (*0-566-00671-5*) Ashgate Pub Co.

Bovard, James. America's Unfairest Taxes: Tariffs & Quotas. (C). 1992. pap. 10.00 (*0-943802-74-1*, 171) Natl Ctr Pol.

— The Fair Trade Fraud: How Congress Pillages the Consumer & Decimates America's Competitiveness. 288p. 1992. pap. 13.95 (*0-312-08344-0*) St Martin.

***Bovard, James.** Feeling Your Pain: The Explosion & Abuse of Power During the Clinton-Gore Years. 352p. 2000. 26.95 (*0-312-23082-6*) St Martin.

Bovard, James. Freedom in Chains: The Rise of the State & the Demise of the Citizen. LC 98-38006. 352p. 1999. text 26.95 (*0-312-21441-3*) St Martin.

***Bovard, James.** Freedom in Chains: The Rise of the State & the Demise of the Citizen. (Illus.). 2000. pap. 16.95 (*0-312-22967-4*) St Martin.

Bovard, James. Lost Rights: The Destruction of American Liberty. LC 95-20797. 416p. 1995. pap. 14.95 (*0-312-12333-7*, St Martin Griffin) St Martin.

— Two Cheers for GATT. 21p. 1994. pap. 5.00 (*1-56808-052-2*, BG135) Natl Ctr Pol.

Bovard, Victoria & Barrett, Elizabeth. And His Love Shown Down. LC 98-160679. 266p. 1997. pap. 9.95 (*0-9654962-0-1*) Lynsa Pub.

Bovarsky, Abraham & Sarna, Lazar, eds. Canadian Yiddish Writings. LC 77-362060. 150p. reprint ed. pap. 46.50 (*0-608-11579-7*, 202228700026) Bks Demand.

Bovary, Flaubert & Madame, jt. auth. see Vargas Llosa, Mario.

Bovati, Pietro. Re-Establishing Justice: Legal Terms, Concepts & Procedures in the Hebrew Bible. LC 94-212518. (Journal for the Study of the Old Testament Supplement Ser.: Vol. 105). 478p. 1994. 85.00 (*1-85075-290-7*, Pub. by Sheffield Acad) CUP Services.

***Bovberg, Jason & Whitham, Kirk, eds.** Skull Full of Spurs: A Roundup of Weird Westerns. (Illus.). 265p. 2000. 29.95 (*0-9662629-1-3*) Dark Hwy.

***Bovbjerg, Barbara D.** Social Security Reform: Implementation Issues for Individual Accounts. 56p. (C). 2000. pap. text 20.00 (*0-7881-8821-6*) DIANE Pub.

Bovbjerg, Dana & Iggers, Jeremy. The Joy of Cheesecake. 208p. 1989. pap. 15.95 (*0-8120-4278-6*) Barron.

Bovbjerg, Richard. Steaming as Before. LC 94-18875. 259p. 1996. 59.95 (*1-883255-12-0*); pap. 39.95 (*1-883255-05-8*) Intl Scholars.

***Bove & Rhodes Staff.** Only Living Trust Book You'll Ever Need. 1999. text 24.95 (*0-8050-3931-7*) St Martin.

Bove, Alexander A. The Complete Book of Wills & Estates. LC 88-31380. 1995. pap. 10.95 (*0-8050-1464-0*, Owl) H Holt & Co.

— The Complete Book of Wills, Estates & Trusts. rev. ed. LC 99-20542. 272p. 2000. pap. 15.00 (*0-8050-6298-X*) H Holt & Co.

— The Medicaid Planning Handbook: A Guide to Protecting Your Family's Assets from Nursing Home Costs. 2nd rev. ed. LC 95-30835. 208p. 1996. pap. 13.95 (*0-316-10374-8*) Little.

Bove, Alfred A. Diving Medicine. 3rd ed. LC 96-16714. 1997. text 69.00 (*0-7216-6056-8*, W B Saunders Co) Harcrt Hlth Sci Grp.

B

Bove, Anthony & Rhodes, Cheryl. Pocket Guide: WordStar. (Micro Computer Ser.). 1983. pap. 7.25 (*0-201-07754-X*) Addison-Wesley.

Bove, Bob. Accordion Man: The Legendary Dick Contino. 176p. 1994. 14.95 (*0-942407-29-6*) Father & Son.

Bove, Carol M., tr. see Doubrovsky, Serge.

Bove, Cheryl, jt. auth. see Fletcher, John.

Bove, Cheryl K. Understanding Iris Murdoch. LC 92-35180. (Understanding Contemporary British Literature Ser.). 225p. (C). 1993. text 29.95 (*0-87249-876-X*) U of SC Pr.

***Bove, Emmanuel.** Armand. Louth, Janet, tr. LC 99-52866. 112p. 1999. pap. 14.95 (*0-8101-6056-0*, Marlboro) Northwestern U Pr.

Bove, Emmanuel. A Man Who Knows. Louth, Janet, tr. from FRE. LC 99-14136. 136p. 1999. pap. 15.95 (*0-8101-6057-9*, Marlboro) Northwestern U Pr.

— My Friends. Louth, Janet, tr. 152p. 2000. pap. 15.95 (*0-8101-6058-7*) Northwestern U Pr.

— Night Departure & No Place (Case Dismissed) Volk, Carol, tr. from FRE. LC 92-43032. 468p. 1995. 25.00 (*0-941423-91-3*); pap. 14.95 (*0-941423-98-0*) FWEW.

— Quicksand. Di Bernado, Dominic, tr. from FRE. LC 91-61534. 192p. 1991. 29.95 (*0-910395-69-1*) Marlboro Pr.

— Quicksand. Di Bernardi, Dominic, tr. from FRE. LC 91-61534. 192p. 1993. pap. 11.95 (*0-910395-70-5*) Marlboro Pr.

— A Singular Man. Di Bernardi, Dominic, tr. from FRE. LC 92-62875. 200p. 1993. 29.95 (*0-910395-94-2*) Marlboro Pr.

— A Singular Man. Di Bernardi, Dominic, tr. LC 95-37381. 200p. (C). 1995. pap. 12.95 (*0-8101-6002-1*, Marlboro) Northwestern U Pr.

— The Stepson. LC 93-80765. 1994. 22.95 (*1-56897-004-8*) Marlboro Pr.

— The Stepson. Favre-Gilly, Nathalie, tr. from FRE. LC 93-80765. 330p. 1994. 22.95 (*1-56897-029-3*) Marlboro Pr.

— A Winter's Journal. Favre-Gilly, Nathalie, tr. from FRE. LC 97-43700. 270p. 1997. 59.95 (*0-8101-6046-3*, Marlboro); pap. 15.95 (*0-8101-6047-1*, Marlboro) Northwestern U Pr.

Bove, Eugene. Uncle Gene's Breadbook for Kids! (Illus.). 64p. (J). (gr. 5-12). 1986. pap. 11.95 (*0-937395-00-5*) Happibook Pr.

Bove, Frederick J, et al, eds. The Balberta Project: The Terminal Formative-Early Classic Transition on the Pacific Coast of Guatemala. Blick, Jeffrey P. et al, trs. LC 93-2044. (University of Pittsburgh Memoirs in Latin American Archaeology Ser.: No. 6). (ENG & SPA., Illus.). xviii, 202p. 1993. pap. 19.00 (*1-877812-08-0*, M006) UPLAAP.

Bove, Frederick J. & Heller, Lynette, eds. New Frontiers in the Archaeology of the Pacific Coast of Southern Mesoamerica. LC 88-84021. (Anthropological Research Papers: No. 39). (Illus.). xvii, 292p. (Orig.). 1989. pap. 30.00 (*0-936249-02-1*) AZ Univ ARP.

Bove, Joseph M. Virus & Virus-Like Diseases of Citrus in the Near East. 538p. 1996. 135.00 (*92-5-103827-9*, F38279, Pub. by FAO) Bernan Associates.

Bove, Linda. Sesame Street Sign Language ABC with Linda Bove. LC 85-1845. (Pictureback Ser.). (Illus.). 32p. (J). (gr. 3-8). 1985. pap. 3.25 (*0-394-87516-8*, Pub. by Random Bks Yng Read) Random.

Bove, Mary. An Encyclopedia of Natural Healing for Children & Infants. 352p. (Orig.). 1996. pap. 14.95 (*0-87983-692-X*, Keats Publng) NTC Contemp Pub Co.

Bove, Mary & Costarella, Linda. Herbs for Women's Health. LC 96-52332. (Good Herb Guide Ser.). 96p. (Orig.). 1997. mass mkt. 4.95 (*0-87983-759-4*, Keats Publng) NTC Contemp Pub Co.

***Bove, Paul A.** Edward Said & the Work of the Critic: Speaking Truth to Power. LC 99-49997. (A Boundary Book Ser.). 352p. 2000. pap. 21.95 (*0-8223-2522-5*) Duke.

Bove, Paul A. Edward W. Said. 1998. pap. 12.00 (*0-8223-6459-X*) Duke.

Bove, Paul A. In the Wake of Theory. LC 91-50366. 203p. 1992. pap. 18.95 (*0-8195-6254-8*, Wesleyan Univ Pr) U Pr of New Eng.

Bove, Paul A. Mastering Discourse: The Politics of Intellectual Culture. LC 91-41256. 269p. 1992. text 54.95 (*0-8223-1232-8*); pap. text 19.95 (*0-8223-1245-X*) Duke.

Bove, Paul A., ed. Early Postmodernism: Foundational Essays. LC 95-6211. (Boundary Two Book Ser.: No. 2). 336p. 1995. text 54.95 (*0-8223-1635-8*); pap. text 17.95 (*0-8223-1649-8*) Duke.

Bove, Paul A., jt. auth. see Mariniello, Silvestra.

Bove, Paul A., jt. ed. see Mariniello, Silvestra.

Bove, Paul A., tr. see Doubrovsky, Serge.

Bove, Robert. Nectar. Mycue, Edward, ed. (Took Modern Poetry in English Ser.: No. 26). (Illus.). 28p. (Orig.). 1991. pap. 3.00 (*1-879457-27-X*) Norton Coker Pr.

Bove, Tony. Inside the Web TV. 300p. Date not set. pap. text 35.00 (*1-57521-296-X*) Sams.

Bove, Tony & Rhodes, Cheryl. The Well-Connected Macintosh. 1987. 19.95 (*0-15-195610-3*, Harvest Bks) Harcourt.

Bove, V. Michael, et al, eds. Multimedia Networks Vol. 3228: Security, Displays, Terminals & Gateways. LC 98-145678. 440p. 1998. 89.00 (*0-8194-2661-X*) SPIE.

Bove, Valeria. Veneto Villas. 191p. 1999. pap. 9.95 (*88-7743-203-9*) Arsenale Editrice.

Bovee & Thill. Business Communication Today. 6th ed. 1999. pap. text 12.00 (*0-13-030043-8*) P-H.

Bovee & Thill, John. Business Communcation Today. 5th ed. LC 97-45879. 816p. (C). 1997. text 69.33 (*0-13-783002-5*) P-H.

Bovee, Courtland L. Contemporary Advertising. 5th ed. 1996. 61.00 (*0-256-18414-3*) McGraw-Hill Prof.

— Techniques of Writing Business Letters, Memos, & Reports. 2nd rev. ed. LC 77-92913. 96p. (C). 1989. reprint ed. pap. text. write for info. (*0-935732-15-2*) Roxbury Pub Co.

Bovee, Courtland L. & Arens, William F. Contemporary Advertising International. 4th ed. (C). 1992. student ed., per. 32.95 incl. 5.25 hd (*0-256-12821-9*, Irwn McGrw-H) McGrw-H Hghr Educ.

Bovee, Courtland L. & Thill, John V. Business Communication Today. 4th ed. LC 94-4095. 1994. text. write for info. (*0-07-006876-3*) McGraw.

— Business Communications Today. 4th ed. (C). 1994. pap. text, student ed. write for info. (*0-07-006910-7*) McGraw.

Bovee, Courtland L., et al. Advertising. LC 94-12495. (Series in Marketing). (C). 1994. text 67.50 (*0-07-006847-X*) McGraw.

— Marketing. 2nd ed. LC 94-12132. (Series in Marketing). (C). 1994. text 65.25 (*0-07-006879-8*) McGraw.

— Marketing. 2nd ed. (C). 1994. pap. text, student ed. 23.75 (*0-07-006911-5*) McGraw.

Bovee, Courtland L., jt. auth. see Morreale, Sherwyn P.

Bovee, Marvin H. Christ & the Gallows: Or, Reasons for the Abolition of Capital Punishment. LC 82-45656. (Capital Punishment Ser.). 1983. reprint ed. 40.00 (*0-404-62403-0*) AMS Pr.

***Bovee, Warren G.** Discovering Journalism, 56. LC 98-37717. Vol. 56. 232p. 1999. 59.95 (*0-313-30947-7*) Greenwood.

Bovee, Warren G., ed. The By-Line Awards: Talks Presented at the Ceremonies Honoring Marquette University Journalism Alumni. LC 95-8837. 1995. 30.00 (*0-87462-004-X*) Marquette.

Bovell. Physiology: Scientific Basis Physics. 1995. pap. text 41.50 (*0-7020-1936-4*, W B Saunders Co) Harcrt Hlth Sci Grp.

— Transform Methods. 2001. 45.00 (*0-02-312911-5*) P-H.

Bovell, Andrew. After Dinner. 1997. pap. 16.95 (*0-86819-518-9*, Pub. by Currency Pr) Accents Pubns.

Bovell, Andrew. Speaking in Tongues. (Orig.). pap. 14.95 (*0-86819-419-0*, Pub. by Currency Pr) Accents Pubns.

Boven, Epie & Winograd, Benjamin. Nude Mouse in Oncology Research. (Illus.). 352p. 1991. lib. bdg. 229.00 (*0-8493-6531-7*, RC267) CRC Pr.

Bovenberg, Lans & Cnossen, Sijbren, eds. Public Economics & the Environment in an Imperfect World. (Natural Resource Management & Policy Ser.). 388p. (C). 1995. lib. bdg. 163.50 (*0-7923-9618-9*) Kluwer Academic.

Bovenmars, Jan G. A Biblical Spirituality of the Heart. LC 91-7738. 230p. (Orig.). 1991. pap. 12.95 (*0-8189-0584-0*) Alba.

Bovens. Understanding Policy Fiascoes. 173p. 1998. pap. text 21.95 (*0-7658-0451-4*) Transaction Pubs.

Bovens, Mark. The Quest for Responsibility: Accountability & Citizenship in Complex Organisations. LC 97-10236. (Theories of Institutional Design Ser.). (Illus.). 264p. (C). 1998. text 59.95 (*0-521-48163-5*); pap. text 22.95 (*0-521-62898-9*) Cambridge U Pr.

Bovens, Mark & Hart, Paul T. Understanding Policy Fiascoes. LC 95-9318. 184p. 1995. 34.95 (*1-56000-214-X*) Transaction Pubs.

Bovensiepen, Gustav, jt. ed. see Sidoli, Mara.

Boventer, Hermann & Baumann, Uwe, eds. Europa: Wiege des Humanismus und der Reformation. (GER., Illus.). 436p. 1997. 63.95 (*3-631-32109-0*) P Lang Pubng.

Bover, David. Introduction to Ada. (C). 1991. pap. text 29.66 (*0-201-50992-X*) Addison-Wesley.

Bover, Eduard A. Vocabulari Castella-Catala. (CAT & SPA.). 465p. 1961. pap. 9.95 (*0-7859-5128-8*, S50355) Fr & Eur.

Boverie, Bill. From Burden to Joy. 1988. pap. 7.45 (*0-89137-572-4*) Quality Pubns.

— From Caves to Cathedrals. 1988. pap. 7.75 (*0-89137-573-2*) Quality Pubns.

Boverie, S., jt. ed. see Bidan, P.

Boves, L. The Phonetic Basis of Perceptual Ratings of Running Speech. (Netherlands Phonetic Archives Ser.). xii, 188p. 1984. pap. 42.35 (*90-6765-035-8*) Mouton.

Bovet, D. Only Living Trust Book You'll Ever Need. 1996. pap. 12.95 (*0-8050-3932-5*) St Martin.

Bovet, D. & Vurgen, A. Muscarinic & Nicotinic Stimulant Actions Autonomic Ganglia, Vol. 1. LC 66-22361. (International Encyclopedia of Pharmacology & Therapeutics Ser.: Sec. 12). 1966. 60.00 (*0-08-012062-8*, Pub. by Pergamon Repr) Franklin.

Bovet, D. P. & Petreschi, R. Algorithms & Complexity: Proceedings of the 1st Italian Conference. Ausiello, G. et al, eds. 228p. 1990. pap. 28.00 (*981-02-0399-3*); text 84.00 (*981-02-0398-5*) World Scientific Pub.

***Bovet, Daniel P.** Understanding the Linux Kernel. 2000. pap. 34.95 (*0-596-00002-2*) OReilly & Assocs.

***Bovet, David, et al.** Value Nets: Breaking the Supply Chain to Unlock Hidden Profits. LC 99-88480. 304p. 2000. text 29.95 (*0-471-36009-0*) Wiley.

Bovet, J., jt. ed. see Leresche, G.

Bovet, L. Psychiatric Aspects of Juvenile Delinquency. (WHO Monograph Ser.: No. 1). 90p. 1951. 5.00 (*92-4-140001-3*) World Health.

Bovet, Lucien. Psychiatric Aspects of Juvenile Delinquency. LC 74-98747. 90p. 1970. reprint ed. lib. bdg. 55.00 (*0-8371-3019-0*, BOPA, Greenwood Pr) Greenwood.

Bovey, Frank A. NMR Data Tables for Organic Compounds, Vol. 1. LC 67-20258. 619p. reprint ed. pap. 191.90 (*0-8357-9943-3*, 201647400004) Bks Demand.

Bovey, Frank A. & Mirau, Peter. NMR of Polymers. LC 96-28240. (Illus.). 459p. 1996. text 95.00 (*0-12-119765-4*) Acad Pr.

Bovey, Frank A., jt. ed. see Woodward, Arthur E.

Bovey, Robin. Birds of Calgary. (Illus.). 1990. pap. 9.95 (*0-919433-82-0*) Lone Pine.

— Birds of Edmonton. (Illus.). 1990. pap. 9.95 (*0-919433-80-4*) Lone Pine.

Bovey, Robin & Campbell, Wayne. Birds of Vancouver. (Illus.). 1989. pap. 9.95 (*0-919433-73-1*) Lone Pine.

Bovey, Robin, et al. Birds of Victoria. (Illus.). 1989. pap. 9.95 (*0-919433-75-8*) Lone Pine.

Bovey, Shelley. The Empty Nest: When Children Leave Home. 1995. pap. 16.50 (*0-04-440898-6*, Pub. by Rivers Oram) NYU Pr.

— The Forbidden Body: Why Being Fat Is Not a Sin. 198p. 1994. pap. text 12.00 (*0-04-440871-4*) NYU Pr.

Bovey, Shirley E., ed. see Etter, Wayne E.

Bovia. Saunders First Responder. 1999. pap. text. write for info. (*0-7216-8660-5*, W B Saunders Co) Harcrt Hlth Sci Grp.

Bovia, Anna L. Camp Perry Revisited, 1905-1996. (Illus.). 400p. 1997. 20.00 (*0-9639976-2-9*); pap. 15.00 (*0-9639976-3-7*) A L Bovia.

Bovia, Anna L. & Wirzylo, Gary L. Camp Perry, 1906-1991. (Illus.). 205p. 1992. 20.00 (*0-9639976-0-2*); pap. 15.00 (*0-9639976-1-0*) A L Bovia.

Bovich, Edward H., et al. The Art of Fund-Raising: What Every Health Care Trustee Needs to Know. LC 94-24891. 199p. 1994. pap. 35.00 (*1-55648-123-3*, 196128) AHPI.

***Bovie, Palmer, ed.** Euripides 4: Ion, Children of Heracles, the Madness of Heracles, Iphigenia in Tauris, Orestes by Euripides. Roberts, Deborah H. et al, trs. LC 97-28892. 1999. pap. 19.95 (*0-8122-1697-0*) U of Pa Pr.

Bovie, Palmer & Slavitt, David R., eds. Plautus: The Comedies, Vol. 2. (Complete Roman Drama in Translation Ser.). 384p. 1995. pap. 15.95 (*0-8018-5057-6*) Johns Hopkins.

— Plautus: The Comedies, Vol. 3. (Complete Roman Drama in Translation Ser.). 392p. 1995. pap. 15.95 (*0-8018-5068-1*) Johns Hopkins.

— Plautus: The Comedies, Vol. 4. (Complete Roman Drama in Translation Ser.). 360p. 1995. pap. 15.95 (*0-8018-5073-8*) Johns Hopkins.

Bovie, Palmer, et al. Terence: The Comedies. LC 91-33984. (Roman Drama in Translation Ser.). 424p. 1992. reprint ed. pap. 18.95 (*0-8018-4354-5*) Johns Hopkins.

Bovie, Palmer, jt. ed. see Slavitt, David R.

Bovie, Palmer, ed. see Sophocles.

Bovie, Palmer, ed. see Sophocles, et al.

Bovie, Palmer, ed. see Terence.

Bovie, Palmer, tr. see Euripides.

Bovie, Palmer, tr. see Terence.

Bovie, Smith P. Georgics. LC 56-11264. 142p. 1997. pap. text 8.00 (*0-226-85740-9*) U Ch Pr.

Bovie, Smith P., tr. Satires & Epistles. LC 59-16413. 1959. pap. text 15.95 (*0-226-06777-7*, P39) U Ch Pr.

Bovie, Smith P., tr. see Horace.

Bovie, Smith P., tr. see Virgil.

Bovier, Anton, et al, eds. Mathematical Aspects of Spin Glasses & Neural Networks. LC 97-20693. (Progress in Probability Ser.: No. 41). 400p. 1997. 98.50 (*0-8176-3863-6*) Birkhauser.

Bovier, Anton & Picco, Pierre. Mathematical Aspects of Spin Glasses & Neural Networks. LC 97-20693. (Progress in Probability Ser.). 1997. write for info. (*3-7643-3863-6*) Birkhauser.

Bovier, Lionel. John M Armleder: At Any Speed. 1999. pap. text 49.95 (*3-89322-970-1*) Dr Cantz sche Druckerei GmbH.

***Bovik, Alan C.** Handbook of Image & Video Processing. LC 99-69120. (Communications, Networking, & Multimedia Ser.). (Illus.). 912p. 2000. 99.95 (*0-12-119790-5*) Acad Pr.

Bovill, Bruce, jt. auth. see Baeseler, Frank.

Bovill, Carl. Fractal Geometry in Architecture & Design. LC 95-35170. 1995. write for info. (*3-7643-3795-8*) Birkhauser.

— Fractal Geometry in Architecture & Design. LC 95-35170. (Illus.). 195p. 1995. 43.50 (*0-8176-3795-8*) Birkhauser.

Bovill, Edward W. The Golden Trade of the Moors: West African Kingdoms in the Fourteenth Century. 2nd ed. 269p. 1995. pap. 18.95 (*1-55876-091-1*) Wiener Pubs Inc.

Bovin, Mette & Manger, Leif, eds. Adaptive Strategies in African Arid Lands. 181p. 1990. 23.95 (*91-7106-311-0*, Pub. by Nordic Africa) Transaction Pubs.

Bovin, Murray. Centrifugal or Lost Wax Jewelry Casting for Schools, Tradesmen, Craftsmen. rev. ed. LC 71-135667. (Illus.). 143p. (C). 1977. 22.95 (*0-910280-06-1*); pap. 16.95 (*0-910280-05-3*) Bovin.

— Jewelry Making for Schools, Tradesmen, Craftsmen. rev. ed. LC 67-20040. (Illus.). 288p. (C). 1979. reprint ed. 29.95 (*0-910280-02-9*); reprint ed. pap. 22.95 (*0-910280-01-0*) Bovin.

— Silversmithing & Art Metal for Schools, Tradesmen, Craftsmen. rev. ed. LC 64-2766. (Illus.). 176p. (C). 1977. 22.95 (*0-910280-04-5*); pap. 17.95 (*0-910280-03-7*) Bovin.

Bovinet, James W. Decision Time. (Illus.). 125p. (Orig.). (C). 1995. pap. text 16.00 (*0-9650629-1-0*) Coulee Region.

— Vision. (Illus.). 75p. (Orig.). (C). 1995. pap. text 14.00 (*0-9650629-0-2*) Coulee Region.

Boving, Knud G., ed. NDE Handbook: Non-Destructive Examination Methods for Condition Monitoring. 432p. 1989. 180.00 (*0-408-04392-X*, Pub. by Woodhead Pubng) Am Educ Systs.

Bovino, Jerald A. Macular Surgery. (Illus.). 184p. (C). 1994. pap. text 135.00 (*0-8385-6082-2*, A6082-0, Apple Lange Med) McGraw.

Bovis, Christopher. The Liberalisation of Public Procurement & Its Effects on the Common Market. LC 98-20665. 229p. 1998. pap. 72.95 (*1-84014-440-8*, KJE5632.B678, Pub. by Ashgate Pub) Ashgate Pub Co.

— Public Procurement Law in the EC. LC 96-47753. (European Law Ser.). x, 133p. 1997. pap. 28.00 (*0-582-29439-8*, 15714) Gaunt.

Bovo, F., et al. Libro Degli Esercizi 2. (GER.). 128p. 1997. pap. write for info. (*3-468-96774-8*) Langenscheidt.

Bovo, M. J. On the Road to Motherhood. 1997. pap. text 19.95 (*1-889972-33-9*) Newpt Media.

Bovo, Mary J. Breaking the Chains That Bind Vol. 1: Empower Yourself & Stop Being a Victim. unabridged ed. 250p. 1997. 19.95 (*1-889972-57-6*) Newpt Media.

— Do You Have Any Questions? Vol. 1: A Woman Doctor Answers the 100 Most Asked Questions in Pregnancy. unabridged ed. O'Brien, Christine, ed. (Illus.). 108p. (Orig.). 1997. pap. 6.95 (*1-889972-73-8*) Newpt Media.

Bovon, Francois. Luke the Theologian: Thirty-Three Years of Research (1950-1983) McKinney, Ken, tr. from FRE. LC 87-7969. (Princeton Theological Monographs: No. 12).Tr. of Luc le theologien: Vingt-cinq ans de recherches (1950-1975). (Orig.). 1987. pap. 25.00 (*0-915138-93-X*) Pickwick.

— New Testament Traditions & Apocryphal Narratives. (Princeton Theological Monographs: No. 36). 253p. (Orig.). 1995. pap. 25.00 (*1-55635-024-4*) Pickwick.

Bovon, Francois, et al, eds. The Apocryphal Acts of the Apostles: Harvard Divinity School Studies. (Religions of the World Ser.). 365p. 1998. 34.95 (*0-945454-17-1*); pap. 24.95 (*0-945454-18-X*) Harvard U Wrld Relig.

Bovon, Francois & Rouiller, Gregoire, eds. Exegesis: Problems of Method & Exercises in Reading (Genesis 22 & Luke 15) Miller, Donald G., tr. from FRE. LC 78-27622. (Pittsburgh Theological Monographs: No. 21). Orig. Title: Exegesis; Problemes de Methode et Exercices de Lecture. 1978. pap. 15.00 (*0-915138-25-5*) Pickwick.

Bovy, Edward, ed. The Spirit of Denali. (Mini-Bks.). 24p. (Orig.). 1994. pap. text 4.95 (*0-936425-22-9*) Greatland Graphics.

— The Spirit of Southeast Alaska Vol. 1. (Mini-Bks.). (Illus.). 24p. (Orig.). 1994. pap. text 5.95 (*0-936425-23-7*) Greatland Graphics.

Bovy, Edward, ed. see Crandall, Alissa.

Bovy, Edward, ed. see Langdon, Steve J.

Bovy, Edward, ed. see Woolcock, Iris.

Bovy, Piet H. Motorway Traffic Analysis: New Methodologies & Recent Empirical Findings. (Illus.). 326p. 1998. pap. 57.50 (*90-407-1651-X*, Pub. by Delft U Pr) Coronet Bks.

Bovy, Piet H., ed. Transportation Modelling for Tomorrow: Rudi-Mental Contributions. xviii, 284p. (Orig.). 1996. pap. 67.50 (*90-407-1317-0*, Pub. by Delft U Pr) Coronet Bks.

Bovy, Piet H. & Stern, Eliahu. Route Choice: Wayfinding in Transport Networks. (C). 1990. lib. bdg. 171.00 (*0-7923-0812-3*) Kluwer Academic.

***Bow, Beverly, et al, eds.** For a Later Generation: The Transformation of Tradition in Israel, Early Judaism & Early Christianity. 336p. 2000. 40.00 (*1-56338-325-X*) TPI PA.

Bow, Jane. Dead & Living. 250p. 15.95 (*0-920544-96-7*, Pub. by Mercury Bk) LPC InBook.

Bow, Jean. A Tale of Two Sisters. 1991. 12.50 (*0-533-09395-3*) Vantage.

Bow, Sandra. Globetrotter Cruise Guide. (Illus.). 176p. 1998. pap. 14.95 (*1-85368-880-0*, Pub. by New5 Holland) Sterling.

— Working on Cruise Ships. 1997. pap. 15.95 (*1-85458-150-3*, Pub. by Vac Wrk Pubns) Petersons.

— Working on Cruise Ships. 2nd ed. 208p. 1999. pap. 16.95 (*1-85458-215-1*, Pub. by Vac Wrk Pubns) Seven Hills Bk.

Bow, Sing-Tzo. Pattern Recognition: Applications to Large Data-Set Problems. (Electrical Engineering & Electronics Ser.: Vol. 23). (Illus.). 336p. 1984. text 125.00 (*0-8247-7176-1*) Dekker.

Bow, Sing-Tzo, ed. Pattern Recognition & Image Processing. (Electrical Engineering & Electronics Ser.: Vol. 77). (Illus.). 580p. 1991. text 215.00 (*0-8247-8583-5*) Dekker.

Bowan, Julie, ed. see Gray, Margie.

Bowan, Linda K. Family Support & Socially Vulnerable Communities: Three Case Studies & Lessons Learned. 70p. 1994. pap. 12.00 (*1-885429-07-X*) Family Resource.

Bowater, Margaret. Dreams & Visions: Language of the Spirit. LC 98-55279. 1999. pap. 14.95 (*0-89594-966-0*) Crossing Pr.

Bowbeer, Anne A., jt. auth. see Schwartz, Donald R.

Bowbrick, Peter. The Economics of Quality, Grades & Brands. (Illus.). 352p. (C). 1992. pap. text 17.95 (*0-415-07848-2*) Routledge.

— The Economics of Quality, Grades & Brands. LC 91-41640. (Illus.). 256p. (C). (gr. 13). 1992. text 74.95 (*0-415-07847-4*, A7334) Routledge.

— Effective Communication for Professionals & Executives. (C). 1988. lib. bdg. 112.00 (*1-85333-081-7*, Pub. by Graham & Trotman) Kluwer Academic.

— Practical Economics for the Real Economist. (C). 1988. lib. bdg. 96.50 (*1-85333-076-0*, Pub. by Graham & Trotman) Kluwer Academic.

Bowbrow, Leonard S. Elementary Linear Circuit Analysis. 2nd ed. LC 96-30994. (Oxford Series in Electrical & Computer Engineering). (Illus.). 736p. 1995. text 92.00 (*0-19-511372-1*) OUP.

***Bowbrowski, Cox.** Gateway To Management. 1999. 39.75 (*0-07-238305-4*) McGraw.

Bowcock, Anne M. Breast Cancer: Molecular Genetics, Pathogenesis & Therapeutics. LC 98-21525. (Contemporary Cancer Research Ser.). 608p. 1999. 145.00 (*0-89603-560-3*) Humana.

Bowd, Gavin. Guillevic, Sauvage de la Modernite. 116p. 1993. 49.00 (*0-85261-346-6*, Pub. by Univ of Glasgow) St Mut.

Bowdean, T. Bubba. Country Proverbs. 366p. (Orig.). 1993. pap., spiral bd. 8.95 (*1-56245-100-6*) Great Quotations.

***Bowden.** Clinical Manual of Pediatric Nursing Procedure. 2001. pap. text. write for info. (*0-7216-5178-X*, W B Saunders Co) Harcrt Hlth Sci Grp.

Bowden. Economics. 7th ed. (SWC-Economics Ser.). 1992. mass mkt., student ed. 21.75 (*0-538-81227-3*) S-W Pub.

— Economics: The Science of Common Sense. 6th ed. (SWC-Economics Ser.). 1988. mass mkt., student ed. 14.50 (*0-538-80107-7*) S-W Pub.

— Economics: The Scinece of Common Sense. 6th abr. ed. (SWC-Economics Ser.). 1989. mass mkt., student ed. 12.50 (*0-538-80108-5*) S-W Pub.

— Economics Study Guide. 7th abr. ed. (SWC-Economics Ser.). 1992. mass mkt., student ed. 17.25 (*0-538-81228-1*) S-W Pub.

***Bowden.** Managing to Make a Difference. 398p. 2000. 84.95 (*1-84014-859-4*) Ashgate Pub Co.

Bowden & Raleigh. Transplant Infections. LC 98-17228. 592p. 1998. text 145.00 (*0-397-58776-7*) Lppncott W & W.

Bowden, A. Ministry in the Countryside. LC 75-153122. pap. 21.95 (*0-264-67321-2*) Continuum.

***Bowden, Aberdeen O.** The Day Before Yesterday in America. (LC History-America-E). 283p. 1999. reprint ed. lib. bdg. 79.00 (*0-7812-4238-X*) Rprt Serv.

Bowden, Adele L., ed. see Eikelberner, George & Agadjanian, Serge.

***Bowden, Andrew.** Local Ministry Today. 2000. pap. 21.95 (*0-304-70625-6*) Continuum.

Bowden, Ann, jt. auth. see Todd, William B.

Bowden, Betsy. Listeners' Guide to Medieval English: A Discography. LC 88-24325. 164p. 1989. text 10.00 (*0-8240-6347-3*, 912) Garland.

Bowden, Betsy, ed. Eighteenth-Century Modernizations from the "Canterbury Tales" (Chaucer Studies: No. 16). 283p. 1991. 90.00 (*0-85991-309-0*) Boydell & Brewer.

Bowden, Calvin. Whistling at a Deaf Horse. 1990. 16.95 (*1-878096-04-4*) Best E TX Pubs.

Bowden, Charles. Blue Desert. LC 86-11413. 179p. 1986. pap. 15.95 (*0-8165-1081-4*) U of Ariz Pr.

— Desierto: Memories of the Future. 240p. 1993. pap. 8.95 (*0-393-31009-4*) Norton.

— Frog Mountain Blues. LC 87-5028. (Illus.). 165p. 1986. 26.95 (*0-8165-0929-8*) U of Ariz Pr.

— Frog Mountain Blues. LC 87-5028. (Illus.). 165p. 1994. reprint ed. pap. 15.95 (*0-8165-1501-8*) U of Ariz Pr.

— Juarez: The Laboratory of Our Future. (Illus.). 131p. 1998. 53.00 (*0-89381-776-7*) Aperture.

— Killing the Hidden Waters. (Illus.). 206p. 1985. reprint ed. pap. 12.95 (*0-292-74306-8*) U of Tex Pr.

— Paul Dickerson. LC 99-70530. (Illus.). 1999. pap. 25.00 (*0-9671443-0-2*) P Dickerson Estate.

Bowden, Charmel, jt. auth. see Miller, Steve.

Bowden, D. M., jt. ed. see Srivatsan, T. S.

Bowden, Dan. Flatpicking Masters: 11 Legendary Flatpicking Solos. 68p. 1997. pap. 19.95 incl. audio compact disk (*0-7866-3084-1*, 96778BCD) Mel Bay.

— Mance Lipscomb/Texas Blues Guitar Solos. 80p. 1994. pap. 25.95 incl. audio compact disk (*0-7866-1237-1*, 95239CDP) Mel Bay.

— Wes Montgomery - The Early Years. 68p. 1997. pap. 22.95 incl. audio compact disk (*0-7866-2954-1*, 95315BCD) Mel Bay.

Bowden, Dan, tr. Fred McDowell/The Voice of Mississippi Delta Blues. (Illus.). 68p. 1996. pap. 12.95 (*0-7866-0571-5*, 95501) Mel Bay.

— Lightnin' Hopkins Blues Guitar Legend. 96p. 1995. pap. 12.95 (*0-7866-0238-4*, 95344) Mel Bay.

— Lightnin' Hopkins/The Gold Star Years: Intermediate Level. 120p. 1998. spiral bd. 17.95 (*0-7866-3050-7*, 96594) Mel Bay.

Bowden, Dan, tr. see Fite, Buddy.

Bowden, Dan, tr. see Lipscomb, Mance.

***Bowden, Darsie.** Mythology of Voice LC 99-34080. (Crosscurrents Ser.). 1999. 21.00 (*0-86709-481-8*, Pub. by Boynton Cook Pubs) Heinemann.

An Asterisk (*) at the beginning of an entry indicates that the title is appearing for the first time.

Bowden, David. Cambodia. 2nd ed. (Illus.). 176p. 1999. pap. 14.95 (*1-86315-132-X*) Little Hills.
— Commercial Software Development: Tips, Tricks & Techniques. 1998. pap. text 42.95 (*1-55622-593-8*) Wordware Pub.
***Bowden, David.** Learn Advanced JavaScript. (Illus.). 2000. pap. text 59.95 (*1-55622-728-0*) Wordware Pub.
Bowden, David. Poetry to Devour. (Illus.). 47p. (Orig.). (YA). (gr. 6-12). 1995. pap. text 7.95 (*1-887172-08-4*) G Bowden.
***Bowden, David.** Taman Negara: Malaysia's Premier National Park. (Globetrotter Visitor's Guides Ser.). 2000. pap. 14.95 (*1-85974-259-9*) New5 Holland.
Bowden, David, et al. Delphi Developer's Guide to Microsoft Windows API. LC 97-35969. (Illus.). 500p. 1997. pap. 59.95 (*1-55622-556-3*) Wordware Pub.
— Microsoft DirectX 2 Games Programming with Delphi. (Illus.). 500p. Date not set. pap. 49.95 (*1-55622-557-1*) Wordware Pub.
— Software & Interface Design Guide for Delphi. (Illus.). 600p. Date not set. pap. 49.95 (*1-55622-555-5*) Wordware Pub.
Bowden, Douglas M., tr. see Luria, A. R.
Bowden, Edwin T., compiled by. Peter De Vries: A Bibliography, 1934-1977. LC 76-620049. (Tower Bibliographical Ser.: No. 14). 1978. 15.00 (*0-87959-079-3*) U of Tex H Ransom Ctr.
Bowden, Edwin T. & Farmer, David, eds. The Holy Bible at the University of Texas. rev. ed. Orig. Title: The Holy Bible, an Exhibit. (Illus.). 1967. 12.00 (*0-87959-027-0*) U of Tex H Ransom Ctr.
Bowden, Edwin T., ed. see Irving, Washington.
Bowden, Edwin T., ed. see Trumbull, John.
Bowden, Elbert & Bowden, Judith. Instuctor's Manual: Economics in Perspective: Economics In Perspective Changing Times Evolving Principles-current Issues & Problems. 6th ed. 110p. (C). 1996. pap. text. write for info. (*0-7872-3021-9*) Kendall-Hunt.
Bowden, Elbert V. Economics: The Science of Common Sense. 5th ed. (C). 1985. text 31.00 (*0-538-08980-6*, H98) S-W Pub.
— Economics: The Science of Common Sense. 6th ed. 896p. (C). 1989. text 30.25 (*0-538-80106-9*, HB98FA2) S-W Pub.
— Economics: The Science of Common Sense. 7th ed. 900p. (C). 1991. text 37.50 (*0-538-81226-5*); mass mkt. 54.25 (*0-538-81225-7*, HB98GA1) S-W Pub.
— Economics: The Science of Common Sense. 8th abr. ed. (HB - Economics Ser.). (C). 1994. mass mkt. 68.95 (*0-538-84368-3*) S-W Pub.
— Economics: The Science of Common Sense, Abridged. 5th ed. 458p. (C). 1986. text 29.00 (*0-538-08990-3*, H99) S-W Pub.
— Money & Banking. Date not set. text 65.75 (*0-314-72626-8*) West Pub.
Bowden, Elbert V. & Bowden, Judith. Economics in Perspective. LC 96-77490. 368p. (C). 1996. pap. text, per. 26.95 (*0-7872-2630-0*) Kendall-Hunt.
Bowden, Elizabeth. We Can All Be Doctors of Commonsense. 156p. (C). 1990. 60.00 (*0-9589059-3-2*, Pub. by Pascoe Pub) St Mut.
***Bowden, Ellen P.** An Investigation of Faunal Material from Four Virginiatown Loci: Areas D, B, Bl, C. (Illus.). 116p. (C). 1999. pap. text 13.13 (*1-55567-833-5*) Coyote Press.
Bowden, Ernest M., compiled by. The Imitation of Buddha: Quotations from Buddhist Literature for Each Day of the Year. 146p. 1993. pap. 10.00 (*0-89540-291-2*, SB-291) Sun Pub.
Bowden, Francis, et al. HIV Medicine Handbook: A Manual for Clinicians Working with HIV Infection. 264p. 1996. pap. 34.95 (*0-522-84613-0*, Pub. by Melbourne Univ Pr) Paul & Co Pubs.
Bowden, Frank P. & Yoffa, A. D. Fast Reactions in Solids. LC QC0176.B64. 176p. reprint ed. pap. 54.60 (*0-608-10146-X*, 205133800095) Bks Demand.
***Bowden, G. T. & Fischer, S. M.** Chemical Carcinogens & Anticarcinogens, 13 vols. (Comprehensive Toxicology Ser.: Vol. 12), 498p. 1999. 165.00 (*0-08-042977-7*) Elsevier.
Bowden, Henry L. Boards of Trustees: Their Organization & Operation at Private Colleges & Universities. LC 82-7991. 58p. 1982. text 8.95 (*0-86554-040-3*, MUP-H035) Mercer Univ Pr.
Bowden, Henry S., ed. see Simpson, Richard.
Bowden, Henry W. American Indians & Christian Missions: Studies in Cultural Conflict. LC 80-27840. (Chicago History of American Religion Ser.). 276p. (C). 1985. pap. text 17.95 (*0-226-06812-9*) U Ch Pr.
— American Indians & Christian Missions: Studies in Cultural Conflict. LC 80-27840. (Chicago History of American Religion Ser.). (C). 1992. lib. bdg. 18.00 (*0-226-06811-0*) U Ch Pr.
— Church History in an Age of Uncertainty: Historiographical Patterns in the United States, 1906-1990. 296p. (C). 1991. 31.95 (*0-8093-1621-8*) S Ill U Pr.
— Church History in the Age of Science: Historiographical Patterns in the United States, 1876-1918. LC 90-32749. 287p. (C). 1991. 31.95 (*0-8093-1620-X*) S Ill U Pr.
— Dictionary of American Religious Biography. 2nd enl. rev. ed. LC 92-35524. 720p. (Orig.). 1993. lib. bdg. 85.00 (*0-313-27825-3*, BDO, Greenwood Pr) Greenwood.
Bowden, Henry W., ed. A Century of Church History: The Legacy of Philip Schaff. LC 87-15630. 398p. 1988. text 41.95 (*0-8093-1439-8*) S Ill U Pr.
Bowden, Henry W., ed. see Eliot, John.
Bowden, Henry W., ed. see Kemeny, P. C.
Bowden, Ilona, ed. see Farkas, Gyorgy.
Bowden, J. J. The Exodus of Federal Forces from Texas, 1861. (Illus.). 140p. 1985. 14.95 (*0-89015-522-4*) Sunbelt Media.
Bowden, Jack, jt. auth. see White-Bowden, Susan.
Bowden, James. The History of the Society of Friends in America, 2 vols. LC 73-38440. (Religion in America, Ser. 2). 870p. 1977. reprint ed. 64.95 (*0-405-04061-X*) Ayer.
Bowden, Jean K. John Lightfoot: His Work & Travels. (Illus.). 255p. 1989. 32.00 (*0-913196-51-7*, Pub. by Royal Botnic Grdns) Balogh.
Bowden, Jesse E. The Write Way: Editor's Guidebook for Students of Writing. (Illus.). 166p. (Orig.). (YA). (gr. 7 up). 1990. pap. text 12.95 (*0-9626673-0-7*) JEA FL.
Bowden, Jesse E., frwd. Emerald Coast Review Vol. V: West Florida Authors & Artists. (Illus.). 186p. 1993. pap. 9.95 (*0-614-20061-X*) W FL Lit Fed.
— Emerald Coast Review Vol. VI: West Florida Authors & Artists. (Illus.). 193p. 1995. pap. 9.95 (*0-614-20062-8*) W FL Lit Fed.
Bowden, Jesse E., et al. Pensacola Florida's First Place City. (Illus.). 207p. 1989. 29.95 (*0-89865-777-6*) Pensacola Hist.
***Bowden, Jesse Earle.** Look & Tremble: A Novel of West Florida. 304p. 2000. 21.95 (*0-942407-53-9*) Father & Son.
Bowden, Jim. Cap. large type ed. (Linford Western Library). 1991. pap. 16.99 (*0-7089-7089-3*) Ulverscroft.
— Hired Gun. large type ed. (Linford Western Library). 224p. 1994. pap. 16.99 (*0-7089-7501-1*, Linford) Ulverscroft.
— Incident at Bison Creek. large type ed. (Linford Western Library). 272p. 1994. pap. 16.99 (*0-7089-7493-7*, Linford) Ulverscroft.
— A Man Called Abe. large type ed. (Linford Western Library). 224p. 1994. pap. 16.99 (*0-7089-7580-1*, Linford) Ulverscroft.
— Showdown in Salt Fork. large type ed. (Linford Western Library). 1991. pap. 16.99 (*0-7089-7034-6*) Ulverscroft.
— Thunder in Montana. large type ed. (Linford Western Library). 288p. 1993. pap. 16.99 (*0-7089-7369-8*, Linford) Ulverscroft.
***Bowden, Joan.** The Bouncy Baby Bunny. LC 98-85511. (Family Storytime Ser.: No. 5). (Illus.). 32p. (J). (ps-k). 1998. 9.95 (*0-307-10217-3*, 10217, Goldn Books) Gldn Bks Pub Co.
Bowden, Joan. Pop up Just Ben. (J). 1989. 4.95 (*0-671-67555-9*) S&S Trade.
— Why the Tides Ebb & Flow. (Illus.). 48p. (J). (gr. k-3). 1990. pap. 7.95 (*0-395-54952-3*) HM.
Bowden, Joan C. Why the Tides Ebb & Flow. (J). 1979. 11.15 (*0-606-04587-2*, Pub. by Turtleback) Demco.
***Bowden, John.** After Dinner Speaking. (Essentials Ser.). 64p. 2000. pap. 9.95 (*1-85703-522-4*, Pub. by How To Bks) Midpt Trade.
Bowden, John. Herbert W. Armstrong & His Worldwide Church of God: An Exposure & an Indictment. (Illus.). 43p. 1987. reprint ed. 4.00 (*0-910309-31-0*) Am Atheist.
***Bowden, John.** Making an after Dinner Speech: How to Make a Speech That Has Them Rolling in the Aisles. (Illus.). 144p. 1999. pap. 19.95 (*1-85703-478-3*, Pub. by How To Bks) Trans-Atl Phila.
Bowden, John. Making Effective Speeches. 144p. 1998. pap. 19.95 (*1-85703-291-8*, Pub. by How To Bks) Trans-Atl Phila.
***Bowden, John.** Making the Best Man's Speech. (Essentials Ser.). 77p. 2000. pap. 9.95 (*1-85703-527-5*, Pub. by How To Bks) Midpt Trade.
— Making the Bridegroom's Speech. (Essentials Ser.). (Illus.). 64p. 2000. pap. 9.95 (*1-85703-567-4*, Pub. by How To Bks) Midpt Trade.
— Making the Father of the Bride's Speech. (Essentials Ser.). (Illus.). 64p. 2000. pap. 9.95 (*1-85703-568-2*, Pub. by How To Bks) Midpt Trade.
— Speaking in Public. (Essentials Ser.). 64p. 2000. pap. 9.95 (*1-85703-511-9*, Pub. by How To Bks) Midpt Trade.
— Toasts & Short Speeches. (Essentials Ser.). 64p. 2000. pap. 9.95 (*1-85703-589-5*, Pub. by How To Bks) Midpt Trade.
— Writing Good Reports. (Essentials Ser.). 77p. 2000. pap. 9.95 (*1-85703-510-0*, Pub. by How To Bks) Midpt Trade.
Bowden, John, jt. auth. see Marton, Ference.
Bowden, John, jt. ed. see Richardson, Alan.
Bowden, John, tr. see Albertz, Rainer.
Bowden, John, tr. see Cullman, Oscar.
Bowden, John, tr. see De Boer, Esther.
Bowden, John, tr. see Ellinger, Herbert.
Bowden, John, tr. see Gibellini, Rosino.
Bowden, John, tr. see Hamman, Adalbert.
Bowden, John, tr. see Hengel, Martin.
Bowden, John, tr. see Hengel, Martin & Schwemer, Anna M.
Bowden, John, tr. see Kuitert, H. M.
Bowden, John, tr. see Kung, Hans.
Bowden, John, tr. see Ludemann, Gerd & Ozen, Alf.
Bowden, John, tr. see Luedemann, Gerd.
Bowden, John, tr. see Machatschke, Roland.
Bowden, John, tr. see Moltmann, Jurgen.
Bowden, John, tr. see Moltmann-Wendel, Elisabeth.
Bowden, John, tr. see Pawlowsky, Peter.
Bowden, John, tr. see Rendtorff, Rolf.
Bowden, John, tr. see Schillebeeckx, Edward.
Bowden, John, tr. see Schillebeeckx, Edward & Halkes, Catharina.
Bowden, John, tr. see Six, Jean-Francois.
Bowden, John, tr. see Soggin, J. Alberto.
Bowden, John, tr. see Solle, Dorothee.
Bowden, John, tr. see Theissen, Gerd.
Bowden, John, tr. see Wind, Renate.
Bowden, John, tr. see Witvliet, Theo.
Bowden, John C. An Investigator's Guide to Interviews & Interrogations. 218p. (Orig.). (C). 1995. pap. text 25.50 (*1-887172-07-6*) G Bowden.
— Investigator's Guide to Interviews & Interrogations Instructor Guide. (Illus.). (C). 1998. teacher ed. 56.50 (*1-887172-11-4*) G Bowden.
— Report Writing for Law Enforcement & Corrections. (Illus.). 116p. (Orig.). 1993. pap. 26.50 (*1-887172-00-9*) G Bowden.
— Report Writing for Law Enforcement & Corrections, No. 1. 218p. (Orig.). (C). 1995. teacher ed. 56.50 (*1-887172-04-1*) G Bowden.
— Report Writing for Law Enforcement & Corrections, No. 2. 218p. (Orig.). (C). 1995. teacher ed. 159.50 (*1-887172-05-X*) G Bowden.
— Report Writing for Law Enforcement & Corrections No. 3: Power Point Presentation. (Illus.). 510p. (Orig.). (C). 1995. teacher ed. 128.50 (*1-887172-06-8*) G Bowden.
Bowden, John C., ed. see Hernandez, David E.
Bowden, John S., tr. see Grillmeier, Aloys.
Bowden, Judith, jt. auth. see Bowden, Elbert.
Bowden, Judith, jt. auth. see Bowden, Elbert V.
Bowden, Julia D., jt. auth. see Gravitz, Herbert L.
Bowden, K. F. The Physical Oceanography of Coastal Waters. 302p. 1984. text 94.95 (*0-470-27505-7*) P-H.
Bowden, Kathi, jt. ed. see Branzinsky, Terri C.
Bowden, Kathi, jt. ed. see Brazinsky, Terri C.
***Bowden, Ken.** Methods of Golf's Masters: How They Played & What You Can Learn from Them. 2000. pap. 19.95 (*1-58574-048-9*) Lyons Pr.
Bowden, Ken, jt. auth. see Aultman, Dick.
Bowden, Ken, jt. auth. see Jacobs, John.
Bowden, Ken, jt. auth. see Nichlaus, Jack.
Bowden, Ken, jt. auth. see Nicklaus, Jack.
Bowden, Leon, jt. auth. see Shiffer, M. M.
Bowden, Leon, ed. see Polya, George.
Bowden, Marcia. Nature for the Very Young: A Handbook of Indoor & Outdoor Activities. LC 88-33747. (Illus.). 240p. 1989. pap. 14.95 (*0-471-62084-X*) Wiley.
***Bowden, Mark.** Black Hawk Down: A Story of Modern War. LC 98-46688. (Illus.). 400p. 1999. 24.00 (*0-87113-738-0*, Atlntc Mnthly) Grove-Atltic.
— Black Hawk Down: A Story of Modern War. 400p. 2000. pap. 13.95 (*0-14-028850-3*, Penguin Bks) Viking Penguin.
— Black Hawk Down: A Story of Modern War. large type ed. LC 99-86852. (G. K. Hall American History Ser.). 583p. 2000. 28.95 (*0-7838-8983-6*, G K Hall Lrg Type) Mac Lib Ref.
— Bringing the Heat. LC 99-46323. (Illus.). 512p. 2000. pap. 15.00 (*0-87113-772-0*, Pub. by Grove-Atltic) Publishers Group.
Bowden, Mark. Doctor Dealer. 352p. 1989. mass mkt. 4.95 (*0-446-35669-7*, Pub. by Warner Bks) Little.
***Bowden, Mark.** Doctor Dealer: The Rise & Fall of an All-American Boy & His Multimillion-Dollar Cocaine Empire. 2000. pap. text 14.00 (*0-8021-3757-1*, Grove) Grove-Atltic.
— Unraveling the Landscape. LC 99-494725. (Illus.). 1999. 32.50 (*0-7524-1447-X*, Pub. by Tempus Pubng) Arcadia Publng.
Bowden, Martha F., ed. see Davys, Mary.
Bowden, Mary E. Chemical Achievers. (Illus.). 100p. (Orig.). 1997. pap. 20.00 (*0-941901-12-2*) Chem Heritage Fnd.
— Chemistry Is Electric! (Illus.). 50p. 1997. pap. 12.00 (*0-941901-17-3*) Chem Heritage Fnd.
Bowden, Mary E. & Benfey, Otto Theodor. Robert Burns Woodward & the Art of Organic Synthesis: To Accompany an Exhibit by the Beckman Center for the History of Chemistry. (BCHOC Publication: No. 9). (Illus.). 48p. (Orig.). 1992. pap. 8.00 (*0-941901-08-4*) Chem Heritage Fnd.
Bowden, Mary E. & Smith, John K. American Chemical Enterprise. LC 97-5508. (Chemical Societies Ser.). (Illus.). 96p. 1994. pap. 18.00 (*0-941901-13-0*) Chem Heritage Fnd.
Bowden, Mary E., jt. auth. see Achilladelis, Basil.
Bowden, Murrae J. & Turner, Richard S., eds. Polymers For High Technology: Electronics & Photonics. LC 87-14573. (ACS Symposium Ser.: No. 346). x, 631p. 1987. 104.95 (*0-8412-1406-9*, Pub. by Am Chemical) OUP.
Bowden, Murrae J. & Turner, S. Richard, eds. Electronic & Photonic Applications of Polymers: Developed from a Symposium Sponsored by the Division of Polymeric Materials: Science & Engineering at the 192nd Meeting of the American Chemical Society, Anaheim, CA, September 7-12, 1986. LC 88-21099. (Advances in Chemistry Ser.: No. 218). (Illus.). 392p. 1988. reprint ed. pap. 121.60 (*0-608-06780-6*, 206697700009) Bks Demand.
— Polymers for High Technology: Electronics & Photonics. LC 87-14573. (ACS Symposium Ser.: Vol. 346). 640p. 1987. reprint ed. pap. 198.40 (*0-608-03539-4*, 206425800008) Bks Demand.
Bowden, P. & Kinnaird, J., eds. African Geology Reviews. LC QE0320.A69. (Geological Journals: Vol. 22, Winter Thematic Issue 1987). 592p. reprint ed. pap. 183.60 (*0-7837-3223-6*, 204324000007) Bks Demand.
Bowden, Peta. Caring: An Investigation in Gender-Sensitive Ethics. LC 96-5488. 240p. (C). 1996. pap. 24.99 (*0-415-13384-X*) Routledge.
Bowden, Peter J. Wool Trade in Tudor & Stuart England. 242p. 1971. 37.50 (*0-7146-1275-8*, Pub. by F Cass Pubs) Intl Spec Bk.
Bowden, Rob, jt. auth. see Binns, Tony.
Bowden, Robert, jt. auth. see Levine, Shar.
Bowden, Robert D. Boies Penrose: Symbol of an Era. LC 75-175690. (Select Bibliographies Reprint Ser.). 1977. reprint ed. 23.95 (*0-8369-6605-8*) Ayer.
— In Defense of Tomorrow. LC 77-121450. (Essay Index Reprint Ser.). 1977. 20.95 (*0-8369-1697-2*) Ayer.
Bowden, Roger J. Statistical Games & Human Affairs: The View from Within. (Illus.). 336p. 1989. text 64.95 (*0-521-36178-8*) Cambridge U Pr.
Bowden, Russell & Wijasuriya, Donald, eds. Art Architecture & Design Libraries: Current Trends. (IFLA Publications: Vol. 74). 441p. 1995. 125.00 (*3-598-21801-X*) K G Saur Verlag.
— The Image of the Library & Information Profession: How We See Ourselves - An Investigation. LC 96-119950. (IFLA: vol. 71). 86p. 1995. 55.00 (*3-598-21798-6*) K G Saur Verlag.
— The Status, Reputation & Image of the Library & Information Profession: Proceedings of the IFLA Pre-Session Seminar, Delhi, 24-28 August 1992. LC 94-238679. (IFLA Publications: Vol. 68). 228p. 1994. 60.00 (*3-598-21795-1*) K G Saur Verlag.
Bowden, Scott. Armies at First Manassas. (Armies of the American Civil War Ser.). 40p. 1988. pap. 9.95 (*0-913037-07-9*) Empire Games Pr.
— Armies at Gettysburg: Armies of the American Civil War. (Illus.). 64p. 1988. pap. 9.95 (*0-913037-06-0*) Empire Games Pr.
— Armies at Waterloo. LC 83-80946. (Armies of the Napoleonic Wars Research Ser.). (Illus.). 356p. 1983. 34.95 (*0-913037-02-8*) Empire Games Pr.
— Napoleon & Austerlitz. (Illus.). 560p. 1997. 49.95 (*0-9626655-7-6*, Pub. by Emperors Pr) Combined Pub.
— Napoleon's Grande Armee' of 1813. (Armies of the Napoleonic Wars Research Ser.). (Illus.). 376p. 1990. 34.95 (*0-9626655-1-7*, Pub. by Emperors Pr); lib. bdg. 34.95 (*0-318-50061-2*) Emperors Pr.
Bowden, Scott & Tarbox, Charles. Armies on the Danube, Eighteen Hundred Nine. LC 80-65117. (Armies of the Napoleonic Wars Research Ser.). (Illus.). 198p. 1980. 19.95 (*0-913037-00-1*) Empire Games Pr.
— Armies on the Danube, Eighteen Hundred Nine. exp. rev. ed. LC 80-65117. (Armies of the Napoleonic Wars Research Ser.). (Illus.). 256p. 1989. 26.95 (*0-913037-08-7*) Empire Games Pr.
Bowden, Scott, jt. auth. see Kopp, Joan A.
Bowden-Smith, Rosemary. The Chinese Pavilion: Boughton House, Northamptonshire. LC 90-111555. (English Garden Features, 1600-1900). 67p. 1988. write for info. (*0-9512398-1-3*) Avenue Bks.
***Bowden, Susan.** Forget Me Not. 384p. 1999. mass mkt. 6.99 (*0-451-19934-0*, Sig) NAL.
— Forget Me Not. large type ed. LC 00-24537. 2000. 25.95 (*1-57490-267-9*, Beeler LP Bks) T T Beeler.
Bowden, Susan. Say Goodbye to Daddy. 1998. mass mkt. 5.99 (*0-451-19221-4*, Sig) NAL.
***Bowden, Tim.** Antarctic Eyewitness: South with Mawson & Shackleton's Argonauts. (Illus.). 336p. 2000. 17.95 (*0-207-19617-6*) HarpC.
— Antartica & Back in Sixty Days. (Illus.). 224p. 2000. 19.95 (*1-86508-099-3*, Pub. by Allen & Unwin Pty) Paul & Co Pubs.
Bowden, Tim. The Silence Calling: Australians in Antarctica, 1947-97. LC 97-184410. (Illus.). 624p. 1997. 59.95 (*1-86448-311-3*, Pub. by Allen & Unwin Pty) Paul & Co Pubs.
Bowden, Tom. Army in the Service of the State. 168p. 1976. 39.95 (*0-87855-219-7*) Transaction Pubs.
— The Breakdown of Public Security: The Case of Ireland, 1916-1921 & Palestine, 1936-1939. LC 76-56682. (Sage Studies in 20th Century History: Vol. 8). 356p. reprint ed. pap. 110.40 (*0-8357-7394-9*, 202187200026) Bks Demand.
Bowden, Vicky R., et al. Children & Their Families: The Continuum of Care. Law, Kevin, ed. LC 97-11069. (Illus.). 1824p. 1998. text 69.95 (*0-7216-5179-8*, W B Saunders Co) Harcrt Hlth Sci Grp.
Bowden, William, jt. ed. see Hodges, Richard.
Bowden, Witt. The Industrial History of the United States. LC 67-19583. (Library of Early American Business & Industry: No. 16). x, 511p. 1967. reprint ed. 57.50 (*0-678-00238-X*) Kelley.
Bowden, Witt, et al. Economic History of Europe since 1750. LC 75-111686. (BCL Ser. I). 1970. reprint ed. 34.50 (*0-404-00962-X*) AMS Pr.
Bowder, Diana, ed. Who Was Who in the Greek World. 240p. 1982. text 47.50 (*0-8014-1538-1*) Cornell U Pr.
Bowders, John J., et al. Geosynthetics in Foundation Reinforcemnt & Erosion Control Systems: Proceedings of the Sessions of the Geo-Congress Sponsored by the Geosynthetics Committee of the Geo-Institute of the American Society of Civil Engineers, Boston, Massachusetts, October 18-21, 1998. LC 98-38065. (Geotechnical Special Publication Ser.). 160p. 1998. 30.00 (*0-7844-0383-X*) Am Soc Civil Eng.
Bowdich, Thomas E. An Account of the Discoveries of the Portuguese in the Interior of Angola & Mozambique. LC 74-15013. reprint ed. 52.50 (*0-404-12008-3*) AMS Pr.
Bowdich, Thomas E., ed. see Mollien, G.
Bowdin, Ruth. Your Baby Talks to You. 2nd ed. (Illus.). 57p. 1993. pap., teacher ed. write for info. (*1-55997-168-1*) Websters Intl.
Bowdish, Lynea. The Carousel Ride. LC 97-43649. (Rookie Readers Ser.). (Illus.). (J). 1998. lib. bdg. 17.00 (*0-516-20967-1*) Childrens.
— The Carousel Ride. (Rookie Readers Ser.). (Illus.). 32p. (YA). (gr. k-3). 1999. pap. text 4.95 (*0-516-26410-9*) Childrens.
— Living with My Stepfather Is Like Living with a Moose. LC 96-21313. (Illus.). 64p. (J). (gr. 2-4). 1997. 14.00 (*0-374-34630-5*) FS&G.

B

— One Glad Man. LC 98-53086. (Rookie Readers Ser.). 32p. (J). (gr. 1-2). 1999. write for info. (*0-516-21595-7*) Childrens.

***Bowdish, Lynea.** One Glad Man. (Rookie Readers Ser.). (J). 2000. pap. text 4.95 (*0-516-26545-8*) Childrens.

Bowdish, Lynea. This Is Me, Laughing. LC 95-13860. (Illus.). 32p. (J). (gr. k-3). 1996. 16.00 (*0-374-37489-9*) FS&G.

***Bowdish, Lynea & Carpenter, Nancy.** Brooklyn, Bugsy & Me. LC 99-36267. 96p. (J). (gr. 4-7). 2000. 15.00 (*0-374-30993-0*) FS&G.

Bowditch, B. H. Treelike Structures Arising from Continua & Convergence Groups. LC 99-19220. (Memoirs of the Society Ser.). 1999. write for info. (*0-8218-1003-0*) Am Math.

Bowditch, Charles. Mexican & Central American Antiquities, Calendar Systems & History. (Bureau of American Ethnology Bulletins Ser.). 682p. 1995. lib. bdg. 149.00 (*0-7812-4028-X*) Rprt Serv.

Bowditch, Charles P., tr. see Cano, Fray A.

Bowditch, Charles P., tr. see De Avendano y Loyola, Fray A.

Bowditch, Henry I. Consumption in New England: Locality, One of Its Chief Causes & Is Consumption Contagious, or Communicated by One Person to Another in Any Manner?, 2 vols. Rosenkrantz, Barbara G., ed. LC 76-25653. (Public Health in America Ser.). (Illus.). 1977. reprint ed. lib. bdg. 17.95 (*0-405-09806-5*) Ayer.

— Public Hygiene in America. LC 70-180557. (Medicine & Society in America Ser.). (Illus.). 415p. 1972. reprint ed. 29.95 (*0-405-03937-9*) Ayer.

Bowditch, Henry P. The Life & Writings of Henry Pickering Bowditch, Vol. 2. 1980. 44.95 (*0-405-12536-4*) Ayer.

— The Life & Writings of Henry Pickering Bowditch: An Original Anthology, 2 vols., Set. Cohen, I. Bernard, ed. LC 79-7950. (Three Centuries of Science in America Ser.). (Illus.). 1980. lib. bdg. 88.95 (*0-405-12531-3*) Ayer.

Bowditch, James L. & Buono, Anthony F. A Primer on Organizational Behavior. 4th ed. LC 96-26881. (Wiley Series in Management). 416p. 1996. pap. 48.95 (*0-471-16006-7*) Wiley.

— Quality of Work Life Assessment: A Survey-Based Approach. LC 82-3945. 188p. 1982. 49.95 (*0-86569-067-7*, Auburn Hse) Greenwood.

Bowditch, James L. & Lewicki, Roy J. A Primer in Organizational Behavior: With Lewicki Experience in Management of Organizational Behavior. 3rd ed. 912p. 1993. text 39.50 (*0-471-04296-X*) Wiley.

Bowditch, John & Ramsland, Clement, eds. Voices of the Industrial Revolution: Selected Readings from the Liberal Economists & Their Critics. 208p. 1961. pap. text 16.95 (*0-472-06053-8*, 06053, Ann Arbor Bks) U of Mich Pr.

Bowditch, Kevin E. & Bowditch, Mark A. Oxyfuel Gas Welding. LC 98-44626. (Illus.). 130p. (YA). (gr. 9-12). 1999. text 17.20 (*1-56637-508-8*) Goodheart.

Bowditch, Kevin E., jt. auth. see Bowditch, William A.

Bowditch, Kevin E. & Rockwood Hudson, Joyce. Welding Projects. LC 98-44480. (Illus.). 96p. (YA). (gr. 9-12). 1999. text 13.28 (*1-56637-502-9*) Goodheart.

Bowditch, Mark A., jt. auth. see Bowditch, Kevin E.

Bowditch, Nancy. George de Forest Brush: A Joyous Painter (1855-1941) LC 72-88207. (Illus.). 1970. 25.00 (*0-87233-008-7*) Bauhan.

***Bowditch, Nathaniel.** American Practical Navigator. (Notable American Authors Ser.: Pt. I). 2000. reprint ed. lib. bdg. 120.00 (*0-7812-2024-6*) Rprt Serv.

Bowditch, Nathaniel. The American Practical Navigator: Being an Epitome of Navigation. 1995. reprint ed. 95.00 (*0-403-09895-5*, Regency) Scholarly.

— Bowditch for Yachtsmen: Piloting. 1980. pap. 9.95 (*0-679-50930-5*) McKay.

— A History of the Massachusetts General Hospital to August 5, 1851. 2nd ed. LC 74-180558. (Medicine & Society in America Ser.). (Illus.). 768p. 1972. reprint ed. 50.95 (*0-405-03938-7*) Ayer.

— The Last Emerging Market: From Asian Tigers to African Lions? The Ghana File. LC 99-18011. 224p. 1999. 55.00 (*0-275-96588-0*) Greenwood.

— Leplace's Mecanique Celeste. (Works of Nathaniel Bowditch). 1989. reprint ed. lib. bdg. 79.00 (*0-7812-2022-X*) Rprt Serv.

— New American Practical Navigator. (Works of Nathaniel Bowditch). 1989. reprint ed. lib. bdg. 79.00 (*0-7812-2021-1*) Rprt Serv.

— Useful Tables. (Works of Nathaniel Bowditch). 1989. reprint ed. lib. bdg. 79.00 (*0-7812-2023-8*) Rprt Serv.

— The Works of Nathaniel Bowditch. 1989. reprint ed. lib. bdg. 63.00 (*0-685-27332-6*) Rprt Serv.

Bowditch, Vincent Y. Life & Correspondence of Henry Ingersoll Bowditch, 2 vols, Set. LC 72-121501. (Select Bibliographies Reprint Ser.). 1977. reprint ed. 44.95 (*0-8369-5459-9*) Ayer.

Bowditch, William A. & Bowditch, Kevin E. Welding Technology Fundamentals. LC 96-3968. (Illus.). 368p. 1997. 38.60 (*1-56637-314-X*) Goodheart.

***Bowdle, Donald N., et al.** The Spirit & the Mind: Essays in Informed Pentecostalism. LC 99-86326. 336p. 2000. pap. 37.50 (*0-7618-1628-3*) U Pr of Amer.

Bowdle, Donald W. Redemption Accomplished & Applied. 1981. pap. 9.99 (*0-87148-727-6*) Pathway Pr.

Bowdle, T. Andrew. Pharmacological Basis of Anesthesiology: Basic Science & Practical Applications. 1994. text 120.00 (*0-443-08878-0*) Church.

Bowdle, T. Andrew, et al. Cardiac Output: Biophysical Measurements. 65p. (C). 1990. 28.00 (*0-9627449-2-1*) SpaceLabs.

Bowdler, A. J., ed. The Spleen. (Illus.). 536p. 1990. 159.95 (*0-442-31209-1*) Chapman & Hall.

Bowdler, Anthony J. Handbook of the Spleen: Structure, Function & Clinical Disorders. 2nd ed. 600p. 1999. 125.00 (*0-89603-555-7*) Humana.

Bowdler, Roger. Queen's Bedfellow. 1975. 19.95 (*0-8464-0775-2*) Beekman Pubs.

***Bowdoin College Staff.** Memorable Histories & Historic Memories. LC 99-195086. 64p. 1998. write for info. (*0-916606-29-5*) Bowdoin Coll.

Bowdoin, Gabrielle D., jt. auth. see Collins, Joseph.

Bowdoin, Ruth. Ayude a Que Su Hijo Lea Mejor. 2nd ed. (Bowdoin Method I Ser.). Orig. Title: Help Your Child Read Better. (SPA., Illus.). 28p. 1991. reprint ed. pap. write for info. (*1-55997-068-5*) Websters Intl.

— Bowdoin Book Set, 10 vols., Set. Wier, Ana, tr. from ENG. (Metodo Bowdoin Ser.). (SPA., Illus.). (Orig.). 1989. pap. text. write for info. (*1-55997-058-8*) Websters Intl.

— The Bowdoin Method Manual. 2nd ed. (Illus.). 110p. 1978. pap. text. write for info. (*1-55997-002-2*) Websters Intl.

— The Bowdoin Method Manual, No. II. (Illus.). 98p. 1991. reprint ed. teacher ed. write for info. (*1-55997-123-1*) Websters Intl.

— Como Aprende el Nino. 2nd ed. (Bowdoin Method I Ser.). Orig. Title: How Your Child Learns. (SPA., Illus.). 24p. 1991. reprint ed. pap. write for info. (*1-55997-062-6*) Websters Intl.

— Como Se Ven las Cosas, 10 vols. Wier, Ana, tr. from ENG. (Metodo Bowdoin Ser.: Vol. VII). (SPA., Illus.). 48p. (Orig.). 1978. pap. text. write for info. (*1-55997-066-9*) Websters Intl.

— En Equipo con su Hijo. Sanz, Maria T., tr. (Metodo Bowdoin Ser.). (SPA., Illus.). 302p. 1997. 27.50 (*1-58087-014-7*) C D Stampley Ent.

— Expanding Your Child's Math Ability. (Bowdoin Method II Ser.). (Illus.). 24p. (Orig.). 1990. pap. write for info. (*1-55997-112-6*) Websters Intl.

— Expanding Your Child's Reading Ability. (Bowdoin Method II Ser.). (Illus.). 24p. (Orig.). 1993. pap. write for info. (*1-55997-111-8*) Websters Intl.

— Harmony at Home. (Bowdoin Method II Ser.). (Illus.). 24p. (Orig.). 1993. pap. write for info. (*1-55997-109-6*) Websters Intl.

— Healthy Minds, Healthy Feelings. (Bowdoin Method II Ser.). (Illus.). 24p. (Orig.). 1991. pap. write for info. (*1-55997-110-X*) Websters Intl.

— Help Your Child Say NO to Alcohol, Tobacco & Drugs. (Bowdoin Method II Ser.). (Illus.). 32p. (Orig.). 1991. pap. write for info. (*1-55997-133-9*) Websters Intl.

— How to Control Your Child with Good Words: Words That Win Children. 2nd ed. (Bowdoin Method I Ser.). (Illus.). 40p. 1986. reprint ed. pap. write for info. (*1-55997-007-3*) Websters Intl.

— How to Develop Values for Responsible Living. (Bowdoin Method II Ser.). (Illus.). 24p. (Orig.). 1993. pap. write for info. (*1-55997-108-8*) Websters Intl.

— How to Develop Your Child's Self-Esteem: The Importance of Good Feelings. 2nd ed. (Bowdoin Method I Ser.). (Illus.). 28p. 1986. reprint ed. pap. write for info. (*1-55997-009-X*) Websters Intl.

— How to Help Your Child Develop Emotionally: My Mommy Likes Me. 2nd ed. (Bowdoin Method I Ser.). (Illus.). 24p. 1986. reprint ed. pap. write for info. (*1-55997-013-8*) Websters Intl.

— How to Help Your Child Develop Pre-Reading Skills: Getting Ready for Reading. 2nd ed. (Bowdoin Method I Ser.). (Illus.). 40p. 1986. reprint ed. pap. write for info. (*1-55997-011-1*) Websters Intl.

— How to Help Your Child Learn: How Your Child Learns. 2nd ed. (Bowdoin Method I Ser.). (Illus.). 24p. 1986. reprint ed. pap. write for info. (*1-55997-006-5*) Websters Intl.

— How to Help Your Child Learn by Looking & Listening: How Things Look, 10 vols. (Bowdoin Method Ser.: Vol. VII). (Illus.). 48p. (Orig.). 1986. pap. text. write for info. (*1-55997-010-3*) Websters Intl.

— How to Help Your Child with Reading: Help Your Child Read Better. 2nd ed. (Bowdoin Method I Ser.). (Illus.). 28p. 1986. reprint ed. pap. write for info. (*1-55997-012-X*) Websters Intl.

— How to Manage Your Child for Good Behavior: Instead of Nagging. 2nd ed. (Bowdoin Method I Ser.). (Illus.). 28p. 1986. reprint ed. pap. write for info. (*1-55997-008-1*) Websters Intl.

— How to Teach Your Child at Home: Parents Are Teachers, 10 vols. (Bowdoin Method Ser.: Vol. 1). (Illus.). 48p. (Orig.). 1986. pap. text. write for info. (*1-55997-004-9*) Websters Intl.

— How to Teach Your Child Word Meanings: Thousands & Thousands of Words. 2nd ed. (Bowdoin Method I Ser.). (Illus.). 28p. 1986. reprint ed. pap. write for info. (*1-55997-005-7*) Websters Intl.

— El Metodo Bowdoin Manual. 2nd ed. Garay, Rene, tr. from ENG. (SPA., Illus.). 88p. 1978. pap. text. write for info. (*1-55997-059-6*) Websters Intl.

— Mi Mama' Me Ama. rev. ed. (Bowdoin Method I Ser.). Orig. Title: My Mommy Likes Me. (SPA., Illus.). 23p. (Orig.). 1991. pap. write for info. (*1-55997-069-3*) Websters Intl.

— Miles & Miles de Palabras. 3rd ed. (Bowdoin Method I Ser.). Orig. Title: Thousands & Thousands of Words. (SPA., Illus.). 30p. 1991. reprint ed. pap. write for info. (*1-55997-061-8*) Websters Intl.

— No Sea Reganon. 2nd ed. (Bowdoin Method I Ser.). Orig. Title: Instead of Nagging. (SPA., Illus.). 28p. (Orig.). 1991. reprint ed. pap. write for info. (*1-55997-064-2*) Websters Intl.

— Los Padres Son Maestros. Diaz Zayas, Carmen E., tr. (Metodo Bowdoin Ser.). (Illus.). 320p. 1992. 30.00 (*0-915741-32-6*) C D Stampley Ent.

— Los Padres Son Maestros, 10 vols. Wier, Ana, tr. from ENG. (Metodo Bowdoin Ser.: Vol. I). (SPA., Illus.). 48p. 1978. pap. text. write for info. (*1-55997-060-X*) Websters Intl.

— Palabras Que Se Ganan a los Ninos. 2nd ed. (Bowdoin Method I Ser.). Orig. Title: Words That Win Children. (SPA., Illus.). 36p. 1991. reprint ed. pap. write for info. (*1-55997-063-4*) Websters Intl.

— Preparandose Para la Lectura. 2nd ed. (Bowdoin Method I Ser.). Orig. Title: Getting Ready for Reading. (Illus.). 36p. 1991. reprint ed. pap. write for info. (*1-55997-067-7*) Websters Intl.

Bowdoin, Ruth. "Secretis" Oue Cada Padre Debe Saber, Pero Muchas Veces Ignora. Gleaves, Gretchen L., ed. (Bowdoin Method of Parent Education Ser.). (SPA.). 130p. 1992. pap. text 6.95 (*1-55997-170-3*) Websters Intl.

— "Secrets" Every Parent Ought to Know But... Often Doesn't. Gleaves, Gretchen L., ed. (Bowdoin Method of Parent Education Ser.). 128p. 1990. pap. text 6.95 (*1-55997-166-5*) Websters Intl.

— "Secrets" for Parenting a School-Age Child. 2nd ed. Gleaves, Gretchen L., ed. (Bowdoin Method of Parent Education Ser.). 155p. 1994. reprint ed. pap. text 6.95 (*1-55997-200-9*) Websters Intl.

— The Secrets of Parenting Your New Baby. Gleaves, Gretchen L., ed. (Bowdoin Method of Parent Education Ser.). 104p. 1994. pap. text 6.95 (*1-55997-201-7*) Websters Intl.

Bowdoin, Ruth. The Single Parent. (Bowdoin Method II Ser.). (Illus.). 24p. (Orig.). 1991. pap. write for info. (*1-55997-107-X*) Websters Intl.

— Su Bebe les Habla. Sanz, Maria T., tr. (Metodo Bowdoin Ser.). (SPA., Illus.). 96p. 1993. 12.50 (*0-915741-49-0*) C D Stampley Ent.

— Your Baby Talks to You. 2nd rev. ed. (Illus.). 63p. 1993. pap. write for info. (*1-55997-167-3*) Websters Intl.

Bowdoin, Sally, jt. auth. see Higginbotham, Barbara B.

Bowdon, Boyce A. The Child Friendly Church: 150 Models of Ministry with Children. LC 99-17228. 136p. 1999. pap. 10.00 (*0-687-07574-2*) Abingdon.

— Selling Your Church in the '90s: A Public Relations Guide for Clergy & Laity. 112p. (Orig.). 1992. pap. 8.95 (*0-9632495-0-9*) Koinonia Pr.

Bowdon, Susan J., jt. auth. see Munger, Evelyn M.

Bowdre, Becky, et al. Table Talk: From Bridge to Brunches. (Illus.). 202p. (Orig.). 1986. spiral bd. 8.00 (*0-9616705-0-9*) Table Talk Bridge.

Bowdren, Kelly A., ed. Employment Practices Liability Insurance. 2nd ed. 388p. 1999. 79.00 (*0-923240-28-4*) Stndrd Publishing.

Bowdring, Paul. The Night Season. LC 98-152315. 256p. 1997. pap. 12.95 (*1-895387-89-2*) Creative Bk Pub.

Bowe. Early Childhood Special Education. 2nd ed. LC 98-36544. (Early Childhood Education Ser.). 544p. (C). 1999. pap. 63.95 (*0-7668-0236-1*) Delmar.

Bowe, Frank G. Approaching Equality. 1991. pap. 12.95 (*0-932666-39-6*) T J Pubs.

— Birth to Five. (Special Education Ser.). 72p. 1995. teacher ed. 18.95 (*0-8273-6472-5*) Delmar.

— Birth to Five: Early Childhood Special Education. LC 94-11494. (Illus.). 600p. (C). 1995. mass mkt. 60.95 (*0-8273-6471-7*) Delmar.

— Changing the Rules. 1986. 8.95 (*0-932666-31-0*) T J Pubs.

***Bowe, Frank G.** Teaching Students with Physical & Health Impariments. LC 99-28064. (Illus.). 368p. (C). 1999. pap. text 46.00 (*0-13-660903-1*) P-H.

— Universal Design in Education: Teaching Nontraditional Students. LC 00-31200. 132p. 2000. 49.00 (*0-89789-688-2*, Bergin & Garvey) Greenwood.

Bowe, John. With the 13th Minnesota Unit in the Philippines, from the Diary of John Bowe. Richardson, Antona H., ed. (Spanish-American War Centennial Edition Ser.). 210p. 1998. reprint ed. spiral bd. 12.95 (*0-9659271-4-8*, 983) Paduan Pr.

Bowe, Kate. Love's Glittering Web. large type ed. 512p. 1984. 27.99 (*0-7089-1096-3*) Ulverscroft.

***Bowe, Marisa, et al, eds.** Gig: Americans Talk About Their Jobs at the Turn of the Millennium. LC 99-58544. 542p. 2000. 25.00 (*0-609-60588-7*, SOC026000, Crown) Crown Pub Group.

Bowe, Michael & Dean, James W. Has the Market Solved the Sovereign-Debt Crisis? LC 97-25689. (Studies in International Finance: Vol. 83). 1997. pap. 13.50 (*0-88165-255-5*) Princeton U Int Finan Econ.

Bowe, N. Gordon, ed. Art & the National Dream. (Illus.). 256p. 1993. 16.95 (*0-7165-2491-0*, Pub. by Irish Acad Pr) Intl Spec Bk.

Bowe, N. Gordon, et al, eds. Gazatteer of Irish Stained Glass: The Works of Harry Clarks & the Artists of An Tur Gloine. 116p. 1988. 14.95 (*0-7165-2413-9*, Pub. by Irish Acad Pr) Intl Spec Bk.

Bowe, Nicola G. The Life & Works of Harry Clarke. (Illus.). 301p. 1989. reprint ed. 49.50 (*0-7165-2452-X*, Pub. by Irish Acad Pr); reprint ed. pap. 29.50 (*0-7165-2534-8*, Pub. by Irish Acad Pr) Intl Spec Bk.

Bowe, Nicola G. & Cumming, Elizabeth. Arts & Crafts in Dublin & Edinburgh. LC 96-152373. (Illus.). 160p. 1997. 39.95 (*0-7165-2579-8*, Pub. by Irish Acad Pr) Intl Spec Bk.

Bowe, Patrick. Gardens of Central Europe. (Illus.). 116p. 1991. 55.00 (*0-85667-399-4*) M T Train.

— The Gardens of Ireland. 1986. 39.95 (*0-317-60018-4*) Little.

Bowe, William J. Estate Planning & Taxation, 2 vols., Set. LC 57-13191. 1958. 75.00 (*0-89941-591-1*, 500250) W S Hein.

Bowe, William J., et al. Page on Wills: Bowe-Parker Revision, 8 vols. 7732p. 1983. text. write for info. (*0-87084-682-5*) Anderson Pub Co.

Bowei, Qin. Qin Bowei Anthology. Felt, Robert L., Jr., ed. Chace, Charles, tr. LC 97-4783. 220p. (Orig.). (C). 1997. pap. text 35.00 (*0-912111-41-0*) Paradigm Publns.

Bowell, E. B., tr. Harsa-Carita of Bana. (C). 1993. reprint ed. 22.00 (*81-208-0791-X*, Pub. by Motilal Bnarsidass) S Asia.

Bowell, Gary. Stones with Fair Colors. pap. 7.99 (*0-88019-111-2*) Schmul Pub Co.

Bowen. Casino Marketing. 400p. 54.95 (*0-471-16020-2*) Wiley.

— Investor's Equation. 1998. pap. 20.50 (*0-07-134375-X*) McGraw.

— Maren's Nest. 48p. (J). Date not set. pap. 6.95 (*0-06-440790-X*) HarpC Child Bks.

— Neurochemistry of Alzheimer's Disease. 300p. 1999. write for info. (*0-12-120540-1*) Acad Pr.

— Occult Way. 1978. pap. 14.95 (*0-7229-5071-3*) Theos Pub Hse.

Bowen. Occult Way. 1978. 14.95 (*0-7229-5096-9*) Theos Pub Hse.

— Politics of Ballistic Missile. LC 99-16201. 1999. text 65.00 (*0-312-22618-7*) St Martin.

— Religion in Culture & Society. LC 97-43077. 248p. (C). 1997. pap. text, suppl. ed. 29.00 (*0-205-20010-9*) Allyn.

— Religion in Practice. LC 97-33578. 271p. 1997. pap. text 38.00 (*0-205-20011-7*) P-H.

Bowen. Religion in Practice & Religion, 2 bks. 1999. text 54.00 (*0-205-28814-6*) Allyn.

***Bowen & Rhodes.** Chemical Engineering. 2000. pap. text 49.95 (*0-7506-4526-1*) Buttrwrth-Heinemann.

Bowen & Simon & Schuster Children's. Dancing Baby Flip Book. (Illus.). 80p. (J). (gr. 3-7). 1998. pap. 2.99 (*0-689-82452-1*) S&S Childrens.

Bowen, et al. Inside Teaching. 176p. 1994. pap. text 20.00 (*0-435-24088-9*) Heinemann.

— Mastering Spanish, 11 CDs. (Mastering Ser.). (ENG & SPA.). 1992. pap. 100.00 incl. audio compact disk (*0-8120-7871-3*) Barron.

Bowen, jt. auth. see Crowe.

Bowen & Bowen Type Setters Staff, ed. see Potter, Jerold C.

***Bowen, A. J., ed.** Xenophon: Symposium. 145p. 1998. 59.95 (*0-85668-681-6*, Pub. by Aris & Phillips); pap. 22.00 (*0-85668-682-4*, Pub. by Aris & Phillips) David Brown.

Bowen, Alexandria. A World of Knowing: A Story about Thomas Hopkins Gallaudet. LC 95-1900. (Creative Minds Bks.). (Illus.). 64p. (J). (gr. 3-6). 1995. pap. 5.95 (*0-87614-954-9*, Carolrhoda); lib. bdg. 14.95 (*0-87614-871-2*, Carolrhoda) Lerner Pub.

Bowen, Alice. Return to Laughter. 320p. 1964. pap. 13.00 (*0-385-05312-6*, Anchor NY) Doubleday.

Bowen, Amy M. Conard. Descendants of John Conrad of Loudoun Colorado, Virginia. (Illus.). 91p. 1997. reprint ed. pap. 18.00 (*0-8328-8026-4*); reprint ed. lib. bdg. 28.00 (*0-8328-8025-6*) Higginson Bk Co.

Bowen, Andy R. Back of Beyond: A Story about Lewis & Clark. (Creative Minds Ser.). (Illus.). 64p. 1998. pap. text 5.95 (*1-57505-224-5*, Carolrhoda) Lerner Pub.

— The Back of the Beyond: A Story about Lewis & Clark. LC 95-51267. (Carolrhoda Creative Minds Bks.). (Illus.). (J). 1996. lib. bdg. 19.93 (*1-57505-010-2*, Carolrhoda) Lerner Pub.

— Flying Against the Wind: A Story about Beryl Markham. LC 97-13649. (Carolrhoda Creative Minds Bks.). (Illus.). 64p. (J). (gr. 3-6). 1997. lib. bdg. 19.93 (*1-57505-081-1*, Carolrhoda) Lerner Pub.

— A Head Full of Notions: A Story about Robert Fulton. LC 96-5752. (Illus.). (J). 1996. lib. bdg. 19.95 (*0-87614-876-3*, Carolrhoda) Lerner Pub.

— Head Full of Notions: A Story about Robert Fulton. (Illus.). 64p. 1996. pap. text 5.95 (*1-57505-026-9*, Carolrhoda) Lerner Pub.

Bowen, Ann Herd. First Baptist Church of Greenwood, South Carolina, 1870-1999. LC 99-66972. 29.95 (*1-57736-156-3*) Providence Hse.

***Bowen, Anne M.** I Loved You Even Befor You Were Born. LC 99-47325. 32p. (ps-3). 2001. lib. bdg. 15.89 (*0-06-028721-7*) HarpC Child Bks.

— I Loved You Even Before You Were Born. LC 99-47325. (Illus.). 32p. (ps-3). 5.95 (*0-06-443631-4*) HarpC.

— I Loved You Even Before You Were Born. LC 99-47325. 32p. (J). (ps-3). 2001. 15.95 (*0-06-028720-9*) HarpC Child Bks.

Bowen, Anne M. The Sources & Text of Richard Wagner's Opera "Die Meistersinger Von Nuernberg" LC 74-24047. reprint ed. 29.50 (*0-404-12870-X*) AMS Pr.

Bowen, Annette P. Get a Life, Jennifer Parker. LC 93-24538. vi, 201p. (Orig.). (YA). (gr. 8-12). 1993. pap. 8.95 (*0-87579-756-3*) Deseret Bk.

— Live & Learn, Jennifer Parker. LC 95-5208. 180p. (Orig.). (YA). (gr. 9-12). 1995. pap. 9.95 (*0-87579-879-9*) Deseret Bk.

Bowen, Anthony, ed. see Cook & Marchant.

Bowen, Anthony A., ed. Aeschylus: Choephori. (Bristol Greek Texts Ser.). (GRE.). 196p. 1986. pap. 22.95 (*0-86292-070-1*, Pub. by Brist Class Pr) Focus Pub-R Pullins.

Bowen, Asta. The Huckleberry Book. LC 88-16798. (Illus.). 96p. (Orig.). 1988. pap. 9.95 (*0-938314-46-7*) Am Wrld Geog.

Bowen, Asta & Meyer, Jane. Hungry for Home. LC 96-28362. 1997. 21.50 (*0-684-82361-6*) S&S Trade.

Bowen, B. A. & Behr. The Logical Design of Multiple Microprocessor Systems. (Illus.). 272p. 1980. text 48.00 (*0-13-539908-4*) P-H.

Bowen, B. A. & Brown, William R. Systems Design: VLSI for Digital Signal Processing, Vol. II. (Illus.). 432p. 1985. text 40.00 (*0-317-20146-8*) P-H.

Bowen, Barbara, ed. see Linkon, Sherry L.

An Asterisk (*) at the beginning of an entry indicates that the title is appearing for the first time.

Bowen, Barbara C. The Age of Bluff: Paradox & Ambiguity in Rabelais & Montaigne. LC 71-165041. (Illinois Studies in Language & Literature: No. 62). 180p. reprint ed. pap. 55.80 (*0-8357-6008-1*, 203442700090) Bks Demand.
— Enter Rabelais, Laughing. LC 98-8865. 216p. (C). 1998. 27.95 (*0-8265-1306-9*) Vanderbilt U Pr.
— One Hundred Renaissance Jokes: A Critical Anthology. LC 88-61672. 128p. 1988. lib. bdg. 21.95 (*0-917786-65-3*) Summa Pubns.
— Words & the Man in French Renaissance Literature. LC 83-80027. (French Forum Monographs: No. 45). 163p. (Orig.). 1983. pap. 12.95 (*0-917058-45-3*) French Forum.
Bowen, Barbara C., ed. Rabelais in Context: Proceedings of the 1991 Vanderbilt Conference. LC 93-85166. (Illus.). 210p. 1994. lib. bdg. 39.95 (*0-917786-95-5*) Summa Pubns.
Bowen, Barbara C. & Nash, Jerry C., eds. Lapidary Inscriptions: Renaissance Essays for Donald A. Stone, Jr. LC 91-73323. (French Forum Monographs: No. 74). 205p. (Orig.). 1991. pap. 17.95 (*0-917058-78-X*) French Forum.
Bowen, Barbara C. & Reid, Tom. Selecting Contract Types. rev. ed. Gibbs, Anne M. & Rumbaugh, Margaret G., eds. 128p. 1990. pap. 37.45 (*0-940343-01-0*, TYPE) Natl Contract Mgmt.
Bowen, Barbara C., ed. see Daymond, Margaret.
Bowen, Barbara E. Gender in the Theater of War: Shakespeare's Troilus & Cressida. LC 92-29131. (Gender & Genre in Literature Ser.: Vol. 4). 256p. 1993. text 15.00 (*0-8153-0042-5*, H1415) Garland.
Bowen, Barbara M. Strange Scriptures That Perplex the Western Mind. 1953. pap. 8.00 (*0-8028-1511-1*) Eerdmans.
Bowen, Betsy. Antler, Bear, Canoe: A Northwoods Alphabet Year. (Illus.). 32p. (J). (gr. k-3). 1995. pap. 5.95 (*0-316-10315-2*) Little.
***Bowen, Betsy.** Gathering: A Northwoods Counting Book. LC 99-17223. (Illus.). 32p. (J). (gr. k-3). 1999. 16.00 (*0-395-98133-6*) HM.
— Gathering: A Northwoods Counting Book. LC 99-17223. (Illus.). 32p. (J). (ps-3). 1999. pap. 5.95 (*0-395-98134-4*) HM.
Bowen, Betsy. Tracks in the Wild. 32p. 1998. pap. 5.95 (*0-395-88400-4*) HM.
— Tracks in the Wild. 32p. (J). (gr. k-3). 1998. 16.00 (*0-395-92067-1*) HM.
***Bowen, Betsy.** The Troll with No Heart in His Body. LC 98-43244. 92p. (J). (gr. k-7). 1999. 18.00 (*0-395-91371-3*) HM.
Bowen, Bobby, Sr. The Community's Force: A History of the Melbourne & Eau Gallie Police. LC 95-94630. 80p. (Orig.). 1995. pap. write for info. (*1-57502-011-4*, P00418) Morris Pubng.
Bowen, Brian C. Spine Imaging: Case Review. (Illus.). 224p. (C). 1999. text. write for info. (*0-323-00507-1*) Mosby Inc.
***Bowen, Carl.** Aberrant: The Directive. (Aberrant Ser.). 2000. pap. 14.95 (*1-56504-685-4*) White Wolf.
— Predator & Prey: Vampire. 2000. pap. 6.50 (*1-56504-969-1*) White Wolf.
***Bowen, Carl, et al.** Project Utopia. (Aberrant Ser.). (Illus.). 144p. 1999. pap. 19.95 (*1-56504-631-5*, 8504) White Wolf.
Bowen, Carol. Combination Oven Cookery. ring bd. 12.95 (*0-948817-37-2*, Pub. by Grub St) Seven Hills Bk.
Bowen, Carol. Goldilocks & the Three Bears, Includes Bowl, Spoon & Wig. (Illus.). 24p. (J). (ps-2). 1995. pap. 12.95 (*1-882651-05-7*) Come Alive Pubns.
***Bowen, Carol.** The Microwave Kitchen Bible. 256p. 2000. pap. 19.95 (*1-84215-109-6*) Anness Pub.
— Microwave Magic: Step-by-Step from Family Suppers to Gourmet Entertaining. (Illus.). 2000. pap. 14.95 (*0-7548-0511-5*, Lorenz Bks) Anness Pub.
***Bowen, Carol, contrib. by.** Mind's Eye Theatre Journal. (Mind's Eye Theatre Ser.: Vol. 4). (Illus.). 80p. 1999. pap. 7.95 (*1-56504-780-X*, 5404) White Wolf.
Bowen, Carol, jt. auth. see Stashko, Ilona K.
Bowen, Carol W. Fairy Princess & the Dragon. (Illus.). 24p. (J). (ps-4). 1995. pap. 4.95 (*1-882651-01-4*) Come Alive Pubns.
— Fairy Princess & the Dragon, Includes Crown, Wand & Wings. (Illus.). 24p. (J). (ps-4). 1995. pap. 12.95 (*1-882651-04-9*) Come Alive Pubns.
***Bowen, Caroline.** Developmental Phonological Disorders. 48p. 1998. pap. 18.95 (*0-86431-256-3*, Pub. by Aust Council Educ Res) Stylus Pub VA.
Bowen, Carolyn C. Angling for Words. 1972. student ed. 20.00 (*0-87879-047-0*); student ed. 12.00 (*0-87879-048-9*) Acad Therapy.
Bowen, Carolyn M. & Perkins, George R. Energizing Employees. 112p. 1998. pap. 17.95 (*0-9659452-1-9*, 9701EE) Davis Debo Pub.
Bowen, Catherine D. Francis Bacon: The Temper of a Man. xxv, 245p. 1993. reprint ed. 30.00 (*0-8232-1537-7*) Fordham.
— Francis Bacon: The Temper of a Man. 2nd ed. LC 93-32785. xxv, 245p. 1993. reprint ed. pap. 20.00 (*0-8232-1538-5*) Fordham.
— Friends & Fiddlers. 261p. 1990. reprint ed. lib. bdg. 69.00 (*0-7812-9249-2*) Rprt Serv.
— Friends & Fiddlers. (American Autobiography Ser.). 261p. 1995. reprint ed. lib. bdg. 79.00 (*0-7812-8462-7*) Rprt Serv.
— The Lion & the Throne: The Life & Times of Sir Edward Coke (1552-1634) 1990. pap. 12.95 (*0-685-45399-5*) Little.
— Miracle at Philadelphia. 368p. Date not set. 26.95 (*0-8488-2565-9*) Amereon Ltd.
— Miracle at Philadelphia: The Story of the Constitutional Convention, May to September 1787. 346p. 1986. reprint ed. pap. 16.95 (*0-316-10398-5*) Little.
Bowen, Charlene. The Knight Next Door. 192p. 1997. lib. bdg. 18.95 (*0-8034-9244-8*, Avalon Bks) Bouregy.
— Montana Sunrise. LC 96-95279. 192p. 1997. 17.95 (*0-8034-9189-1*, Avalon Bks) Bouregy.
— Rancher's Lady. LC 98-96616. 192p. 1998. 18.95 (*0-8034-9327-4*, Avalon Bks) Bouregy.
***Bowen, Charles.** Going Online with CompuServe 2000. (Illus.). 128p. 2000. pap. 8.99 (*0-7645-8625-4*, CPG Pr) IDG Bks.
Bowen, Charles. Hitchhikers Guide to America Online. 1994. pap. 21.95 (*1-55828-396-X*, MIS Pr) IDG Bks.
***Bowen, Charles.** The Official Compuserve 2000 Tour Guide LC 99-38590. 1999. write for info. (*1-891556-55-X*) Amer Online.
— Official CompuServe 2000 Tour Guide. (Illus.). 576p. 2000. pap. 24.99 (*0-7645-3492-0*) IDG Bks.
Bowen, Clarence W. Boundary Disputes of Connecticut. (Illus.). 90p. 1997. reprint ed. pap. 16.00 (*0-8328-5620-7*) Higginson Bk Co.
Bowen, Clarence W., et al. History of Woodstock & Genealogies of Woodstock Families, 8 vols., Vols. II-VIII. (Illus.). 1997. reprint ed. lib. bdg. 499.00 (*0-8328-5704-1*) Higginson Bk Co.
***Bowen, Clarence W., et al.** History of Woodstock (CT) With Genealogies of Woodstock Families, 7 vols. 5363p. 2000. 499.00 (*0-7404-0030-4*) Higginson Bk Co.
Bowen, Connie. I Believe in Me: A Book of Affirmations. (Illus.). 64p. (J). (ps up). 1995. pap. 12.95 (*0-87159-072-7*, 126) Unity Bks.
— I Turn to the Light. LC 97-32788. (Illus.). 64p. 1998. pap. 12.95 (*0-87159-216-9*) Unity Bks.
— I Turn to the Light. LC 97-32788. (Illus.). 64p. 1998. lib. bdg. 16.95 (*0-87159-229-0*, 172) Unity Bks.
— Yo Creo En Mi. LC 99-10252.Tr. of I Believe in Me. (SPA.). 64p. (J). (ps up). 1999. pap. 12.95 (*0-87159-226-6*, 296) Unity Bks.
Bowen Cooke, C. J. British Locomotives, 1894. 396p. 1980. 65.00 (*0-905418-72-7*, Pub. by Gresham Bks) St Mut.
Bowen, D. The Family of Griffith Bowen, Welsh Puritan Immigrant, Boston, 1638-1639. 278p. 1988. reprint ed. pap. 44.00 (*0-8328-0289-1*); reprint ed. lib. bdg. 54.00 (*0-8328-0288-3*) Higginson Bk Co.
Bowen, D. M. Air Pollution. 1991p. (C). 1991. text 350.00 (*0-89771-564-0*, Pub. by Intl Bk Distr) St Mut.
Bowen, D. Q., ed. Quaternary Science Reviews, Vol. 3. (Illus.). 328p. 1985. pap. 105.00 (*0-08-032760-5*, Pub. by PPL) Elsevier.
— Quaternary Science Reviews, Vol. 1. (Illus.). 340p. 1984. 92.00 (*0-08-031491-0*, Pergamon Pr) Elsevier.
— Quaternary Science Reviews, Vol. 2. (Illus.). 328p. 1984. 105.00 (*0-08-031736-7*, Pergamon Pr) Elsevier.
— A Revised Correlation of Quaternary Deposits in the British Isles. (Geological Society Special Report Ser.: No. 23). 174p. 1999. 65.00 (*1-86239-042-8*, Pub. by Geol Soc Pub Hse) AAPG.
Bowen, Dana T. Lore of the Lakes. 1940. pap. 13.75 (*0-912514-12-4*) Freshwater.
— Memories of the Lakes. 1946. pap. 13.75 (*0-912514-14-0*) Freshwater.
— Shipwrecks of the Lakes. 1952. pap. 13.75 (*0-912514-21-3*) Freshwater.
Bowen, David. Multimedia. 1994. pap. 12.95 (*0-906097-14-2*) LPC InBook.
Bowen, David. Picture Book of San Antonio. (Illus.). 32p. (J). 1978. pap. 6.95 (*0-931722-02-0*) Corona Pub.
Bowen, David, ed. Columbus & the Crowns: Edited from William H. Prescott's History of the Reign of Ferdinand & Isabella. LC 90-80855. (Illus.). 110p. 1991. 15.95 (*0-931722-82-9*) Corona Pub.
Bowen, David & Ascencio, Juan A., eds. Pyramids of Glass: Short Fiction from Modern Mexico. Grossman, E. et al, trs. from SPA. LC 94-71404. xxii, 244p. (C). 1994. 22.95 (*0-931722-99-3*); pap. 12.95 (*0-931722-83-7*) Corona Pub.
Bowen, David E., jt. auth. see Schneider, Benjamin.
Bowen, David H. Software Success Reference Book, 1992. 547p. (Orig.). 1992. pap. 9.95 (*0-9625967-1-X*) Software Success.
Bowen, David W. Andrew Johnson & the Negro. LC 88-9668. 256p. 1989. text 31.00 (*0-87049-584-4*) U of Tenn Pr.
Bowen, Debbie, ed. see Dannhauss, Dianne.
Bowen, Debbie, ed. see Sargent, Dave.
Bowen, Debbie, ed. see Sargent, Dave & Tirella, Laura.
Bowen, Debbie, ed. see Sargent, Pat L.
Bowen, Debbie, ed. see Wilson, Jane L.
Bowen, Debbie, ed. see Wise, Charles.
Bowen, Desmond. History & the Shaping of Irish Protestantism, Vol. 4. (Irish Studies). XXI, 718p. (C). 1995. pap. text 39.95 (*0-8204-2750-0*) P Lang Pubng.
— The Idea of the Victorian Church: A Study of the Church of England, 1833-1889. LC 67-30137. 435p. reprint ed. pap. 134.90 (*0-7837-6928-8*, 204675700003) Bks Demand.
— The Protestant Crusade in Ireland, 1800-70: A Study of Protestant-Catholic Relations Between the Act of Union & Disestablishment. 1978. 39.95 (*0-7735-0295-5*, Pub. by McG-Queens Univ Pr) CUP Services.
***Bowen, Diane.** Butterflies of Texas. (Illus.). 2p. 1999. pap. 10.95 (*0-9672990-2-0*, L-5308) Texas Agr Extnsn.
***Bowen, Diane, ed.** Butterflies of Texas. rev. ed. (Illus.). 2p. 2000. 10.95 (*0-9672990-3-9*, L-5308) Texas Agr Extnsn.
Bowen, Diane, ed. see Mathews, Christopher K. & Van Holde, Kensal E.
Bowen, Donald D., et al. Experiences in Management & Organizational Behavior. 4th ed. LC 96-29422. 432p. 1996. pap. 49.95 (*0-471-30826-9*) Wiley.
Bowen, Donald D., jt. auth. see Boone, Louis E.
Bowen, Donald H. Passing the Torch. (When the Time Comes to Let Go Ser.). 100p. 1998. pap. 8.00 (*0-9663658-0-1*) Sonrise Minist.
Bowen, Donna L. & Early, Evelyn A., eds. Everyday Life in the Muslim Middle East. LC 92-40710. (Indiana Series in Arab & Islamic). 352p. (C). 1993. pap. text 19.95 (*0-253-20779-7*) Ind U Pr.
***Bowen, Dore & Grady, Pam, texts.** Scott MacLeod: 2000 Adaline Kent Award Exhibition. (Illus.). 28p. 2000. pap. 5.00 (*0-930495-35-7*) San Fran Art Inst.
Bowen, Douglas J., jt. ed. see Kaylin, Arleen.
Bowen, Douglas J., jt. ed. see Keylin, Arleen.
Bowen, E. G. Radar Days. (Illus.). 248p. 1987. 39.00 (*0-85274-590-7*) IOP Pub.
Bowen, Edward. Where Have All Children Gone? 1996. pap. 4.99 (*0-9645307-1-6*) Via Verde Pub.
Bowen, Edward A. Lineage of the Bowens of Woodstock, Conn. (Illus.). 251p. 1988. reprint ed. pap. 37.50 (*0-8328-0291-3*); reprint ed. lib. bdg. 45.50 (*0-8328-0290-5*) Higginson Bk Co.
***Bowen, Edward L.** Dynasties: Great Thoroughbred Stallions. 256p. 2000. 34.95 (*1-58150-054-8*, Pub. by Blood-Horse) IPG Chicago.
— Man O' War: Thoroughbred Legends. 2000. 24.95 (*1-58150-040-8*) Blood-Horse.
Bowen, Edward L. Matriarchs: Great Mares of the 20th Century. 1999. 35.00 (*1-58150-022-X*, Pub. by Blood-Horse) IPG Chicago.
***Bowen, Edward L.** Matriarchs: Great Mares of the 20th Century. limited ed. (Illus.). 224p. 1999. 195.00 (*1-58150-036-X*) Blood-Horse.
Bowen, Edward L., jt. auth. see Wharton, Mary E.
Bowen, Elbert R., et al. Communicative Reading. 4th ed. 452p. (C). 1990. reprint ed. pap. text 28.50 (*0-88133-557-6*) Sheffield WI.
Bowen, Eli. The United States Post-Office Guide. LC 75-22802. (America in Two Centuries Ser.). 1976. reprint ed. 30.95 (*0-405-07674-6*) Ayer.
Bowen, Eliza A. The Story of Wilkes County, Georgia. 192p. 1997. reprint ed. pap. 22.50 (*0-8063-4731-7*) Clearfield Co.
Bowen, Elizabeth. Ann Lee's & Other Stories. LC 70-103497. (Short Story Index Reprint Ser.). 1977. 18.95 (*0-8369-3239-0*) Ayer.
— Coll Stories Bowen. 784p. 1998. reprint ed. pap. 17.00 (*0-88001-493-8*) HarpC.
— The Collected Stories of Elizabeth Bowen. 784p. 1989. reprint ed. pap. 13.95 (*0-88001-224-2*) HarpC.
***Bowen, Elizabeth.** The Death of the Heart. 336p. 2000. pap. 13.00 (*0-385-72017-3*, Anchor NY) Doubleday.
Bowen, Elizabeth. Eva Trout. 1993. 22.00 (*0-8446-6709-9*) Peter Smith.
Bowen, Elizabeth. Friends & Relations. 192p. (YA). (gr. 7 up). 1980. pap. 2.25 (*0-380-49601-1*, 49601-1, Avon Bks) Morrow Avon.
Bowen, Elizabeth. Heat of the Day. 258p. 1981. reprint ed. lib. bdg. 25.95 (*0-89966-259-5*) Buccaneer Bks.
— Irish Stories. 135p. 1996. pap. 12.95 (*0-905169-81-6*, Pub. by Poolbeg Pr) Dufour.
***Bowen, Elizabeth.** The Last September. 224p. 2000. pap. 12.00 (*0-385-72014-9*, Anchor NY) Doubleday.
Bowen, Elizabeth. The Mulberry Tree: Writings of Elizabeth Bowen. Lee, Hermione, ed. LC 86-29446. (Illus.). 1987. 19.95 (*0-15-163240-5*) Harcourt.
— Selected Stories. LC 83-45415. reprint ed. 20.00 (*0-404-20037-0*) AMS Pr.
Bowen, Elizabeth, et al. Why Do I Write? LC 75-22190. (English Literature Ser.: No. 33). 1975. lib. bdg. 75.00 (*0-8383-2094-5*) M S G Haskell Hse.
Bowen, Elizabeth C. & Schneller, Beverly E. Writing about Science. 2nd ed. (Illus.). 400p. (C). 1991. pap. text 26.95 (*0-19-506274-4*) OUP.
***Bowen, Eric J.** An American View of Wales. LC 98-90989. 64 p. 1999. write for info. (*0-9668689-0-0*) Tillicum Bks.
Bowen, Ezra. Hypothesis of Population Growth. LC 68-58550. (Columbia University, Studies in the Social Sciences: No. 343). reprint ed. 32.50 (*0-404-51343-3*) AMS Pr.
***Bowen, Ezra.** This Fabulous Century: 1930-1940. (Illus.). 288p. 2000. reprint ed. 20.00 (*0-7881-9442-9*) DIANE Pub.
Bowen, F. C. Wooden Walls in Action: The History of Ships from 1340 to 1866. 1977. lib. bdg. 69.95 (*0-8490-2841-8*) Gordon Pr.
Bowen, Francis, ed. Documents of the Constitution of England & America: From Magna Charta to the Federal Constitution of 1789. vii, 142p. 1993. reprint ed. 35.00 (*0-8377-1954-2*, Rothman) W S Hein.
Bowen-Franz, Jennifer. Southern Schuylkill County. (Images of America Ser.). 128p. 1998. pap. 16.99 (*0-7524-0886-0*) Arcadia Publng.
Bowen, Fred. The Final Cut. LC 98-37337. (Allstar SportStory Ser.). (Illus.). 112p. (J). (gr. 3-7). 1999. pap. 4.95 (*1-56145-192-4*, 51924) Peachtree Pubs.
— Full Court Fever. LC 97-35294. (Allstar SportStory Ser.). (Illus.). (J). 1998. pap. 4.95 (*1-56145-160-6*) Peachtree Pubs.
— The Golden Glove. LC 96-14694. (Allstar SportStory Ser.: Vol. 2). (Illus.). 112p. (Orig.). (J). (gr. 3-7). 1996. pap. 4.95 (*1-56145-133-9*, Peachtree) Peachtree Pubs.
— Kid Coach. LC 96-45923. (Allstar Sports Ser.). (Illus.). 112p. (Orig.). (J). 1997. pap. 4.95 (*1-56145-140-1*) Peachtree Pubs.
— Off the Rim. LC 98-20967. (Allstar SportStory Ser.). (Illus.). 112p. (J). (gr. 3-7). 1998. pap. 4.95 (*1-56145-161-4*, Peachtree) Peachtree Pubs.
— On the Line. LC 99-22977. (Allstar SportStory Ser.). (Illus.). 112p. (J). (gr. 3-7). 1999. pap. 4.95 (*1-56145-199-1*) Peachtree Pubs.
— Playoff Dreams. LC 97-10447. (AllStar Sport Story Ser.). (Illus.). 112p. (Orig.). (J). (gr. 3-7). 1997. pap. 4.95 (*1-56145-155-X*) Peachtree Pubs.
— T. J. 's Secret Pitch. LC 95-44474. (Allstar SportStory Ser.). (Illus.). 112p. (J). (gr. 3-7). 1996. pap. 4.95 (*1-56145-119-3*) Peachtree Pubs.
***Bowen, Fred.** Winners Take All. LC 00-8580. (Allstar Sportstory Ser.). (Illus.). 112p. (J). (gr. 3-7). 2000. pap. 4.95 (*1-56145-229-7*) Peachtree Pubs.
Bowen, G. R., ed. Cyber Magick: Lesbian SF. 32p. 1995. pap. 5.00 (*1-887666-07-9*) Obelesk Bks.
Bowen, G. Stephen, ed. HIV-AIDS Work Group on Health Care Access Issues for African Americans. (Illus.). 46p. (C). 1998. reprint ed. pap. text 20.00 (*0-7881-7054-6*) DIANE Pub.
Bowen, Gail. Colder Kind of Death: A Joanne Kilbourn Mystery. LC 94-229488. 240p. 1995. 19.95 (*0-7710-1482-1*) McCland & Stewart.
— Colder Kind of Death: A Joanne Kilbourn Mystery. 232p. 1996. pap. text 7.99 (*0-7710-1483-X*) McCland & Stewart.
***Bowen, Gail.** Deadly Appearances. 280p. 2000. pap. 7.99 (*0-7710-1491-0*) McCland & Stewart.
— Deadly Appearances: A Joanne Kilbourn Mystery. write for info. (*0-88894-703-8*) DGL.
Bowen, Gail. Deadly Appearances: A Joanne Kilbourn Mystery. 256p. 1997. mass mkt. 7.99 (*0-7710-1485-6*) McCland & Stewart.
— A Killing Spring: A Joanne Kilburn Mystery. LC 97-122935. 264p. 1997. 22.95 (*0-7710-1484-8*) McCland & Stewart.
— A Killing Spring: A Joanne Kilburn Mystery. (Joanne Kilbourn Mystery Ser.). 1998. pap. text 5.95 (*0-7710-1486-4*) McCland & Stewart.
***Bowen, Gail.** Murder at the Mendel. 216p. 2000. mass mkt. 7.99 (*0-7710-1492-9*) McCland & Stewart.
Bowen, Gail. Murder at the Mendel: A Joanne Kilbourn Mystery. 1992. pap. 7.99 (*0-7710-1480-5*) McCland & Stewart.
— Striking Out. 280p. 1997. mass mkt. 5.99 (*0-7710-3415-6*) McCland & Stewart.
— Verdict in Blood: A Joanne Kilbourn Mystery. LC 98-931135. (Joanne Kilbourn Mystery Ser.: Bk. 6). 256p. 1998. text 20.95 (*0-7710-1487-2*) McCland & Stewart.
— Verdict in Blood: A Joanne Kilbourn Mystery. 264p. 1999. pap. 7.95 (*0-7710-1489-9*) McCland & Stewart.
Bowen, Gail. The Wandering Soul Murders: A Joanne Kilbourn Mystery. 1993. pap. 7.99 (*0-7710-1481-3*) McCland & Stewart.
Bowen, Gary. Diary of a Vampire. (Orig.). 1995. mass mkt. 6.95 (*1-56333-331-7*, Rhinoceros) Masquerade.
— Man Hungry. (Orig.). 1996. mass mkt. 5.95 (*1-56333-374-0*, Badboy) Masquerade.
***Bowen, Gary.** The Mare's Nest. (Illus.). 48p. (J). (gr. 1-5). 2000. 17.95 (*0-06-028408-0*); lib. bdg. 17.89 (*0-06-028407-2*) HarpC Child Bks.
Bowen, Gary. Queer Destinies: Erotic Science Fiction. LC 94-219733. (Illus.). 64p. (Orig.). 1994. pap. 5.95 (*0-9633970-7-9*) Circlet Pr.
***Bowen, Gary.** Stranded at Plimoth Plantation 1626. LC 93-31016. (Trophy Chapter Book Ser.). (Illus.). 88p. (J). (gr. 3-7). 1998. pap. 10.95 (*0-06-440719-5*) HarpC.
— Stranded at Plimoth Plantation 1626. LC 93-31016. (Illus.). 88p. (J). (gr. 3-7). 1994. 19.95 (*0-06-022541-6*) HarpC Child Bks.
Bowen, Gary. Winter of the Soul: Gay Vampire Fiction. 32p. 1995. pap. 5.00 (*1-887666-06-0*) Obelesk Bks.
Bowen, Gary, ed. Floating Worlds: Oriental Fantasies. 48p. (Orig.). 1996. pap. 6.00 (*1-888667-15-X*) Obelesk Bks.
— Green Echo: Ecological SF. 40p. 1995. pap. 5.00 (*1-887666-05-2*) Obelesk Bks.
— Icarus & Angels: Flights of Fantasy Gaysf. 48p. 1996. pap. 6.00 (*1-887666-13-3*, Triangle Titles) Obelesk Bks.
— Western Trails. (Orig.). 1996. mass mkt. 6.50 (*1-56333-477-1*, Badboy) Masquerade.
Bowen, Gary, ed. see Buis, Lela E., et al.
Bowen, Gary L. Navigating the Marital Journey: MAP: A Corporate Support Program for Couples. LC 91-3553. 208p. 1991. 55.00 (*0-275-93423-3*, C3423, Praeger Pubs) Greenwood.
Bowen, Gary L. & Orthner, Dennis K., eds. The Organization Family: Work & Family Linkages in the U. S. Military. LC 88-32440. 218p. 1989. 55.00 (*0-275-92813-6*, C2813, Praeger Pubs) Greenwood.
***Bowen, Geraint.** Welsh Recusant Writing. 120p. 1999. pap. (*0-7083-1515-1*, Pub. by Univ Wales Pr) Paul & Co Pubs.
Bowen, Gilbert, tr. see Eluard, Paul.
Bowen, Glen. Pen Aficionado (Pen Speak) (Illus.). 130p. 1996. 12.95 (*0-614-13017-4*) Wrld Pubns.
Bowen, Glenn. Collectible Fountain Pens: Parker, Sheaffer, Wahl-Eversharp, Waterman & Many More. 11th rev. ed. LC 82-90494. (Illus.). 346p. (Orig.). 1996. reprint ed. pap. 21.95 (*0-910173-00-1*) L-W Inc.
Bowen, Glyn D. & Nambiar, E. K. Nutrition in Forest Trees in Plantations. 1985. text 184.00 (*0-12-120980-6*) Acad Pr.
Bowen, H. Kent, et al. The Perpetual Enterprise Machine: Seven Keys to Corporate Renewal Through Successful Product Development. LC 93-43172. (Illus.). 464p. (C). 1994. 30.00 (*0-19-508052-1*) OUP.
Bowen, H. V. Revenue & Reform: The Indian Problem in British Politics, 1757-1773. 216p. (C). 1991. text 54.95 (*0-521-40316-2*) Cambridge U Pr.
— War & British Society, 1688-1815. LC 97-42249. (New Studies in Economic & Social History: No. 35). 112p. (C). 1998. text 39.95 (*0-521-57226-6*); pap. text 11.95 (*0-521-57645-8*) Cambridge U Pr.
Bowen, H. V., jt. ed. see Barlow, R. A.

B

An Asterisk (*) at the beginning of an entry indicates that the title is appearing for the first time.

Bowen, Harold. The Life & Times of Ali Ibn Isa: The Good Vizier. LC 77-180320. (Mid-East Studies). reprint ed. 42.50 (*0-404-56215-9*) AMS Pr.

Bowen, Harry P., et al. Applied International Trade Analysis. LC 97-26326. (Studies in International Trade Policy). (Illus.). 678p. (C). 1998. text 90.00 (*0-472-09670-2*, 09670); pap. text 32.50 (*0-472-06670-6*, 06670) U of Mich Pr.

Bowen, Hilary. Decorative Techniques for Woodturners. (Illus.). 176p. 1997. pap. 20.95 (*1-86108-015-8*, Pub. by Guild Master) Sterling.

— Woodturning Jewellery. (Illus.). 160p. 1995. pap. 15.95 (*0-946819-83-1*, Pub. by Guild Master) Sterling.

Bowen, Howard. Investment in Learning: The Individual & Social Value of American Higher Education. 533p. 1996. pap. text 29.95 (*1-56000-888-1*) Transaction Pubs.

Bowen, Howard R. The Costs of Higher Education: How Much Do Colleges & Universities Spend Per Student & How Much Should They Spend? LC 80-8321. (Carnegie Council Ser.). 313p. reprint ed. pap. 97.10 (*0-7837-0163-2*, 204046000017) Bks Demand.

— Investment in Learning: The Individual & Social Value of American Higher Education. LC 96-45438. 536p. 1996. reprint ed. pap. text 22.95 (*0-8018-5530-6*) Johns Hopkins.

— The State of the Nation & the Agenda for Higher Education. LC 81-20746. (Jossey-Bass Series in Higher Education). 232p. reprint ed. pap. 72.00 (*0-8357-4860-X*, 203779200009) Bks Demand.

Bowen, Howard R., et al. Investment in Learning: The Individual & Social Value of American Higher Education. LC 77-82069. (Carnegie Council Ser.). 529p. reprint ed. pap. 164.00 (*0-7837-2535-3*, 204269400006) Bks Demand.

Bowen, I. D. & Lockshin, R. Cell Death in Biology & Pathology. (Illus.). 450p. 1981. 85.00 (*0-412-16010-2*, NO.6491) Chapman & Hall.

Bowen, Ian. Economics & Demography. LC 76-373793. (Studies in Economics: 10). 168p. reprint ed. pap. 52.10 (*0-608-15060-6*, 202327200032) Bks Demand.

Bowen, J. & Mazzaferri, E. L. Contemporary Internal Medicine: Clinical Case Studies, Vol. 1. LC 88-22379. (Illus.). 336p. (C). 1988. text 95.00 (*0-306-43000-2*, Kluwer Plenum) Kluwer Academic.

— Contemporary Internal Medicine: Clinical Case Studies, Vol. 2. (Illus.). 296p. (C). 1989. text 95.00 (*0-306-43329-X*, Kluwer Plenum) Kluwer Academic.

— Contemporary Internal Medicine: Clinical Case Studies, Vol. 3. (Illus.). 304p. (C). 1991. text 95.00 (*0-306-43684-1*, Kluwer Plenum) Kluwer Academic.

Bowen, J., jt. auth. see Bowen, Rhys.

Bowen, J., jt. auth. see Gorman, Jack M.

Bowen, J. Donald. Spoken Tagalog. LC 65-25321. (Spoken Language Ser.). 551p. (Orig.). (C). 1982. pap. text 40.00 (*0-87950-465-X*) Spoken Lang Serv.

— Spoken Tagalog, Bk. 1: Dialogues. LC 65-25321. (Spoken Language Ser.). 551p. (C). pap. 135.00 incl. audio (*0-87950-407-2*) Spoken Lang Serv.

Bowen, J. Donald. Spoken Tagalog, Bk. 1: Dialogues, No. I, Units 1-12. LC 65-25321. (Spoken Language Ser.). 551p. (C). audio 95.00 (*0-87950-466-8*) Spoken Lang Serv.

Bowen, J. Donald. Spoken Tagalog, Bk. 2: Notes, Exercises, Drills, Bks. I & II. LC 65-25321. (Spoken Language Ser.). 551p. (C). pap. 245.00 incl. audio (*0-87950-469-2*) Spoken Lang Serv.

Bowen, J. Donald. Spoken Tagalog, Bk. 2: Notes, Exercises, Drills, No. II, Exercise Tests. LC 65-25321. (Spoken Language Ser.). 551p. (C). audio 110.00 (*0-87950-468-4*) Spoken Lang Serv.

Bowen, J. Donald, ed. Beginning Tagalog: A Course for Speakers of English. LC 65-25321. (Orig.). 1965. pap. 39.95 (*0-520-00156-7*, Pub. by U CA Pr) Cal Prin Full Svc.

Bowen, J. Donald & Stockwell, Robert P. Patterns of Spanish Pronunciation: A Drillbook. LC 60-16841. (Orig.). 1960. pap. text 4.50 (*0-226-06831-5*) U Ch Pr.

Bowen, J. Donald, jt. auth. see Stockwell, Robert P.

Bowen, J. Donald, tr. see Cabrera, Neonetta C., et al.

Bowen, J. K., jt. auth. see Phillips, J. H.

Bowen, J. P., et al, eds. ZUM '97 - The Z Formal Specification Notation: 10th International Conference of Z Users, Reading, UK, April 3-4, 1997, Proceedings. (Lecture Notes in Computer Science Ser.: Vol. 1212). x, 435p. 1997. pap. 67.00 (*3-540-62717-0*) Spr-Verlag.

Bowen, J. P. & Edward, J. E., eds. Z User Workshop: Proceedings of the Seventh Annual Z user Meeting, London, 14-15 December 1992. 7th ed. LC 93-3819. 1993. 85.95 (*0-387-19818-0*) Spr-Verlag.

***Bowen, J. P. & Fettweis, A.** Zum'98: The Z Formel Specification Notation. Hinchey, M. G., ed. 417p. 1998. pap. 67.00 (*3-540-65070-9*) Spr-Verlag.

Bowen, J. P. & Hall, J. A., eds. Z User Workshop, Cambridge, 1994: Proceedings of the 8th Z User Meeting, Cambridge, 29-30 June 1994. LC 94-15509. (Workshops in Computing Ser.). 1994. 78.95 (*0-387-19884-9*) Spr-Verlag.

Bowen, J. P., jt. auth. see Hinchey, Michael G.

Bowen, J. R., et al, eds. Dynamics of Explosions. LC 86-22170. (PAAS Ser.: Vol. 106). (Illus.). 664p. 1986. 47.00 (*0-930403-15-0*, V-106) AIAA.

— Dynamics of Flames & Reactive Systems. LC 84-21560. (PAAS Ser.). (Illus.). 766p. 1985. 92.95 (*0-915928-92-2*, V-95) AIAA.

— Dynamics of Reactive Systems. (PAAS Ser.: Vol. 113). 1988. 68.00 (*0-614-16781-7*, V-113) AIAA.

— Dynamics of Reactive Systems, Pt. I. LC 86-22171. (PAAS Ser.: Vol. 105). (Illus.). 1986. 68.00 (*0-930403-14-2*, V105) AIAA.

— Dynamics of Shock Waves, Explosions, & Detonations. LC 84-21564. (PAAS Ser.: Vol. 94). (Illus.). 595p. 1984. 86.95 (*0-915928-91-4*, V-94) AIAA.

— Flames, Lasers & Reactive Systems. LC 83-15463. (PAAS Ser.: Vol. 88). (Illus.). 436p. 65.95 (*0-915928-77-9*, V-88) AIAA.

Bowen, J. Ray, ed. Dynamics of Exothermicity: In Honor of Antoni Kazimierz Oppenheim. (Combustion Science & Technology Ser). 432p. 1996. text 66.00 (*2-88449-170-8*) Gordon & Breach.

Bowen, J. Richard, jt. ed. see Epps, Charles H., Jr.

Bowen, J. W., ed. see Congress On Africa.

***Bowen, Jack.** A Bit of Yesterday. 1999. pap. write for info. (*1-58235-086-8*) Watermrk Pr.

Bowen, James. Soviet Education: Anton Makarenko & the Years of Experiment. LC 62-15991. 244p. 1962. reprint ed. pap. 75.70 (*0-608-01941-0*, 206259600003) Bks Demand.

Bowen, James, jt. auth. see Purkis, Jon.

Bowen, James, jt. ed. see Fernig, Leo.

Bowen, James, jt. ed. see Purkis, Jon.

Bowen, Jan. Child Support: A Practitioner's Guide. 293p. 1994. pap. 45.00 (*0-455-21273-2*, Pub. by LawBk Co) Gaunt.

Bowen, Janine L. Foreign Aid & Economic Growth: A Theoretical & Empirical Investigation. LC 97-78315. (Illus.). 112p. 1998. text 61.95 (*1-85972-590-2*, Pub. by Ashgate Pub) Ashgate Pub Co.

Bowen, Jean, et al. Square Pegs: Building Success in School & Life. LC 97-24342. xi, 178p. 1997. 36.00 (*1-56976-075-6*) Zephyr Pr AZ.

Bowen, Jean D. & Stockwell, Robert P. Patterns of Spanish Pronunciation: A Drillbook. LC 60-16841. 137p. reprint ed. pap. 42.50 (*0-608-09392-0*, 205413700004) Bks Demand.

— Patterns of Spanish Pronunciation, a Drillbook. LC 60-16841. 147p. Date not set. reprint ed. pap. 45.60 (*0-608-20602-4*, 205456700003) Bks Demand.

Bowen, Jerry, ed. see Davis, Duane.

Bowen, John. Adventuring along the Southeast Coast: The Sierra Club Travel Guide to the Low Country, Beaches, & Barrier Islands of North Carolina, South Carolina & Georgia. LC 92-25831. (Adventure Travel Guide Ser.). (Illus.). 480p. (Orig.). 1993. pap. 15.00 (*0-87156-553-6*, Pub. by Sierra) Random.

— Adventuring in the Chesapeake Bay Area. LC 89-10551. (Adventure Travel Guide Ser.). (Illus.). 400p. 1990. pap. 14.00 (*0-87156-680-X*, Pub. by Sierra) Random.

— Adventuring in the Chesapeake Bay Area: The Tidewater Country of Maryland, Virginia & Washington D. C., from Baltimore to the Virginia Cape. 2nd ed. LC 99-19996. (Illus.). 464p. 1999. pap. 16.00 (*1-57805-036-7*, Pub. by Sierra) Random.

— After the Rain: A Play in Three Acts. 93p. 1967. 14.95 (*0-910278-90-3*) Boulevard.

— Bowen: Plays One. 256p. 1998. pap. 18.95 (*1-84002-035-0*, Pub. by Oberon Bks Ltd) Consort Bk Sales.

— A Canadian Guide to International Adoptions: How to Find, Adopt, & Bring Home Your Child. (Reference Ser.). 160p. (Orig.). 1992. pap. 11.95 (*0-88908-538-2*) Self-Counsel Pr.

— History & Battlefields of the Civil War. 351p. 1996. 22.98 (*1-55521-750-8*) Bk Sales Inc.

— Hospitality Marketing Today. 124p. (C). 1994. 18.95 (*0-8403-9242-7*) Kendall-Hunt.

— Miniature Merchant Ships: A Guide to Waterline Ship Modelling in 1/1200 Scale. LC 97-132234. (Illus.). 240p. 1997. 38.95 (*0-85177-659-0*, Pub. by Brasseys) Brasseys.

— Model Shipwright: An Anthology 1972-1997. (Conway Classics Ser.). 1998. 32.95 (*0-85177-729-5*) Brasseys.

***Bowen, John.** Other Dickens: Pickwick to Chuzzlewit. LC 99-16104. 240p. 2000. text 70.00 (*0-19-818506-5*) OUP.

***Bowen, John & Chambers, Larry.** Institutional Asset Class Investing for Private Clients: A Handbook for Financial Advisers. 275p. 1999. 55.00 (*1-57958-189-7*) Fitzroy Dearborn.

Bowen, John, Jr. & Horan, Jo. Alpha Transition: Special Report. LC 95-37680. 1995. write for info. (*1-880935-37-6*) Pinnacle WA.

Bowen, John & Petersen, Roger, eds. Critical Comparisons in Politics & Culture. (Illus.). 240p. (C). 1999. 64.95 (*0-521-65301-0*); pap. 23.95 (*0-521-65379-7*) Cambridge U Pr.

Bowen, John E. Mark-to-Market: Managing the Bank Portfolio under FASB No. 115. 125p. (C). 1993. text 60.00 (*1-55738-701-X*, Irwn Prfssnl) McGraw-Hill Prof.

Bowen, John J. The Prudent Investor's Guide to Beating the Market. 2nd ed. LC 98-6270. (Illus.). 200p. 1998. 24.95 (*0-07-052760-1*) McGraw.

Bowen, John R. Muslims Through Discourse: Religion & Ritual in Gayo Society. LC 92-34217. (Illus.). 370p. (C). 1993. text 57.50 (*0-691-09475-6*, Pub. by Princeton U Pr); pap. text 21.95 (*0-691-02870-2*, Pub. by Princeton U Pr) Cal Prin Full Svc.

Bowen, Jonathan. Formal Specification & Documentation. (C). 1995. mass mkt. 44.95 (*1-85032-230-9*, VNR) Wiley.

Bowen, Jonathan, ed. Towards Verified Systems. LC 94-30630. (Real-Time Safety Critical Systems Ser.: Vol. 2). 322p. 1994. 165.00 (*0-444-89901-4*) Elsevier.

Bowen, Jonathan P., et al, eds. ZUM '95: The Z Formal Specification Notation: 9th International Conference of Z Users, Limerick, Ireland, September 7-9, 1995, Proceedings. Vol. XI. LC 95-38127. (Lecture Notes in Computer Science Ser.: Vol. 967). 571p. 1995. 87.00 (*3-540-60271-2*) Spr-Verlag.

Bowen, Jonathan P. & Hinchey, Michael G., eds. Applications of Formal Methods. 442p. 1995. 71.00 (*0-13-366949-1*) P-H.

Bowen, Joseph. For Healing & Wholeness. 1993. pap. write for info. (*1-55673-595-2*, Fairway Pr) CSS OH.

Bowen, Judith. The Doctor's Daughter: Men of Glory. (Superromance Ser.). (Orig.). 1999. per. 4.25 (*0-373-70835-1*, 1-70835-3) Harlequin Bks.

— Heart of the North. (Romance Ser.: No. 860). 1992. per. 2.69 (*0-373-08860-4*, 5-08860-4) Silhouette.

— His Brother's Bride: Men of Glory. (Superromance Ser.: No. 872). 1999. per. 4.25 (*0-373-70872-6*, 1-70872-6) Harlequin Bks.

— Like Father, Like Daughter: Men of Glory. (Superromance Ser.: No. 791). 1998. per. 4.25 (*0-373-70791-6*, 1-70791-8) Harlequin Bks.

— The Man from Blue River (Home on the Ranch) (Superromance Ser.). 1996. per. 3.99 (*0-373-70689-8*, 1-70689-4) Harlequin Bks.

— O Little Town of Glory. 1998. per. 4.25 (*0-373-70814-9*) Silhouette.

***Bowen, Judith.** Rancher Takes a Wife. (Superromance Ser.: Vol. 900). 2000. per. 4.50 (*0-373-70900-5*) Harlequin Bks.

Bowen, Judith. The Rancher's Runaway Bride. (Men of Glory Ser.). 1997. per. 3.99 (*0-373-70739-8*, 1-70739-7) Harlequin Bks.

Bowen, Judith C., et al. The College Admissions Game...How to Play & Win. (Illus.). 112p. (YA). (gr. 9-12). 1992. pap. 19.95 (*1-882707-02-8*) Coll Info Srv.

Bowen, Julie, et al. Study Buddies: Parent Tutoring Tactics. (Homework Partners Ser.). (Illus.). 124p. 1996. pap. 16.50 (*1-57035-014-0*, 44STUDY) Sopris.

Bowen, K. A. Model Theory for Modal Logic: Kripke Models for Modal Predicate Calculi. (Synthese Library: Vol. 127). 137p. 1978. text 85.50 (*90-277-0929-7*, D Reidel) Kluwer Academic.

Bowen, K. C. Research Games. 126p. 1978. 31.00 (*0-85066-169-2*) Taylor & Francis.

Bowen, K. C., ed. Management Science in Defence. 105p. 1985. pap. 39.00 (*0-08-032658-7*, Pergamon Pr) Elsevier.

Bowen, Karen A. Meeting Your Match: A Practical Guide for Finding Your Perfect Mate. rev. ed. 180p. 1995. pap. 13.00 (*0-9649343-0-2*) Ariadne Pubs.

Bowen, Keith. Snowdon Shepherd. 1997. pap. 29.95 (*0-8464-4801-7*) Beekman Pubs.

Bowen, Keith. Among the Amish. 144p. 1998. 17.98 (*0-7624-0385-3*, Courage) Running Pr.

***Bowen, Keith & Gutman, Dan.** Katy's Gift: An Amish Story. LC 96-71603. (Illus.). 32p. (J). (ps-7). 1998. 6.98 (*0-7624-0169-9*, Courage) Running Pr.

Bowen, Kenneth. Prolog & Expert Systems. 448p. (C). 1991. pap. 54.69 (*0-07-006731-7*) McGraw.

***Bowen, Kevin.** Forms of Prayer at the Hotel Edison: Poems by Kevin Bowen. LC 98-26218. 76p. 1998. pap. 12.95 (*1-880684-55-1*) Curbstone.

Bowen, Kevin. Playing Basketball with the Viet Cong. LC 94-30715. 63p. (Orig.). 1983. pap. 10.95 (*1-880684-20-9*) Curbstone.

***Bowen, Kevin.** Wil's Bones. 240p. 2000. pap. write for info. (*1-930892-12-8*) Engage Pub.

Bowen, Kevin, et al, eds. Mountain River: Vietnamese Poetry from the Wars, 1948-1993. Ba Chung, Nguyen et al, trs. LC 98-12598. (ENG & VIE). 296p. (Orig.). 1998. 40.00 (*1-55849-140-6*); pap. 17.95 (*1-55849-141-4*) U of Mass Pr.

Bowen, Kevin & Weigl, Bruce. Not on the Map. LC 97-132788. 32p. 1996. pap. 10.95 (*1-873790-95-3*, Pub. by Dedalus) Dufour.

Bowen, Kevin & Weigl, Bruce, eds. Writing Between the Lines: An Anthology on War & Its Social Consequences. LC 96-9591. 336p. (C). 1997. pap. 19.95 (*1-55849-054-X*); text 55.00 (*1-55849-053-1*) U of Mass Pr.

Bowen, Kevin, tr. see Duy, Nguyen.

Bowen, Kurt. Evangelism & Apostasy: The Evolution & Impact of Evangelicals in Modern Mexico. LC 97-117926. 288p. 1996. 49.95 (*0-7735-1379-5*, Pub. by McG-Queens Univ Pr) CUP Services.

— Protestants in a Catholic State: Ireland's Privileged Minority. 240p. 1983. 55.00 (*0-7735-0412-5*, Pub. by McG-Queens Univ Pr) CUP Services.

Bowen, Larry S. The Wizards of Odds: Leadership Journeys of Education Deans. 1995. 18.00 (*0-89333-133-3*) AACTE.

Bowen, Larry S. & Gittler, Joseph B., eds. The Annual Review of Conflict Knowledge & Conflict Resolution, Vol. 3: The Role of Formal Education in Conflict Resolution. LC 10-478671. 256p. 1993. text 20.00 (*0-8153-1306-3*, SS902) Garland.

Bowen, Laurie. Food for the Family Spirit: A Sourcebook for Religious Education. LC 98-104771. 176p. 1997. pap. 19.95 (*1-55612-945-9*, LL1945) Sheed & Ward WI.

***Bowen, Linda C.** Graphic Design Creative Market. LC 98-35011. 192p. 1999. pap. 34.95 (*0-471-29314-8*) Wiley.

Bowen, Lindsey M. Cicada Grove. 96p. (Orig.). 1992. pap. 7.50 (*1-881048-01-2*) Paladin Contemp.

— Second Touch. 32p. (Orig.). 1990. pap. 3.00 (*1-881048-00-4*) Paladin Contemp.

Bowen, Lynne. Three Dollar Dreams. (Illus.). 408p. 1987. text 19.95 (*0-88982-065-1*, Pub. by Oolichan Bks) Genl Dist Srvs.

Bowen, M. This Shining Woman: Mary Wollstonecraft. 1972. lib. bdg. 59.95 (*0-8490-1196-5*) Gordon Pr.

Bowen, Marjorie. Defender of the Faith. LC 94-38674. (William & Mary Trilogy Ser.: Vol. 2). (Illus.). 282p. (Orig.). 1994. pap. 13.90 (*0-921100-43-4*) Inhtce Pubns.

— For God & the King. LC 95-21737. (William & Mary Trilogy Ser.: Vol. 3). (Illus.). 351p. (Orig.). 1995. pap. 15.90 (*0-921100-44-2*) Inhtce Pubns.

— I Will Maintain. LC 93-38791. (William & Mary Trilogy Ser.: Vol. 1). 383p. 1993. pap. 15.90 (*0-921100-42-6*) Inhtce Pubns.

— Kecksies & Other Twilight Tales. LC 76-17992. 1976. 12.95 (*0-87054-077-7*) Arkham.

— The Soldier of Virginia: A Novel on George Washington. LC 97-32035. 1997. pap. 12.90 (*0-921100-99-X*) Inhtce Pubns.

— Sundry Great Gentlemen: Some Essays in Historical Biography. LC 68-29192. (Essay Index Reprint Ser.). 1977. reprint ed. 23.95 (*0-8369-0230-0*) Ayer.

— Viper of Milan. LC 65-25494. (J). (gr. 4-8). 1965. 14.95 (*0-8023-1014-1*) Dufour.

— William III & the Revolution of 1688 & Gustavus Adolphus II Elected King of Sweden of the Goths & Vandals. 143p. 1988. pap. 7.95 (*0-921100-06-X*) Inhtce Pubns.

***Bowen, Mark.** Untitled Nonfiction On Dr. Lonnie Thompson's Ice Core Research. 2001. text 27.50 (*0-8050-6443-5*) H Holt & Co.

— Untitled Nonfiction on Dr. Lonnie Thompson's Ice Core Research. 2002. pap. 13.50 (*0-8050-6444-3*) H Holt & Co.

Bowen, Marshall E. Utah People in the Nevada Desert: Homestead & Community on a Twentieth Century Farmer's Frontier. (Illus.). 134p. (C). 1994. 10.00 (*0-87421-168-9*) Utah St U Pr.

***Bowen, Mary & Ruth, Monty.** To Be Safe During an Earthquake & Other Emergencies. (Illus.). 96p. (J). (ps-6). 2000. wbk. ed. 28.95 (*0-9702765-0-8*) Global Vision.

Bowen, Meirion, ed. see Gerhard, Roberto.

Bowen, Meirion, ed. see Tippett, Michael.

Bowen, Meiron. Michael Tippett. (Contemporary Composers Ser.). (Illus.). 318p. 1998. pap. 19.95 (*1-86105-099-2*, Pub. by Robson Bks) Parkwest Pubns.

***Bowen, Merle L.** The State Against the Peasantry: Rural Struggles in Colonial & Postcolonial Mozambique. (Illus.). 320p. 2000. 65.00 (*0-8139-1910-X*); pap. 19.50 (*0-8139-1917-7*) U Pr of Va.

Bowen, Michael. Collateral Damage. LC 99-21331. 1999. text 22.95 (*0-312-20289-X*) St Martin.

— The Fourth Glorious Mystery. LC 99-18278. 208p. 1999. pap. 14.95 (*0-8283-2037-3*) Branden Bks.

Bowen, Michael A. & Butler, Brian E. The Wisconsin Fair Dealership Law. 2nd ed. LC 95-136. 400p. 1995. ring bd. 125.00 (*0-945574-73-8*) State Bar WI.

Bowen, Mike. Straight from the Heart. (C). 1990. 30.00 (*0-7316-7410-3*, Pub. by Pascoe Pub) St Mut.

— Window to My Soul. (C). 1990. 40.00 (*0-7316-0491-1*, Pub. by Pascoe Pub) St Mut.

Bowen, Murray. Family Therapy in Clinical Practice. LC 84-45863. 584p. 1978. 65.00 (*0-87668-761-3*) Aronson.

Bowen, Murray, jt. auth. see Kerr, Michael E.

Bowen, Nicholas. Tolley's Tax Legislation, 1993-1994: Inheritance Tax. 320p. 1993. 75.00 (*0-85459-777-8*, Pub. by Tolley Pubng) St Mut.

Bowen, Nicholas & Dolton, Alan. Tolley's Tax Data, 1993-1994. 80p. 1993. 69.00 (*0-85459-699-2*, Pub. by Tolley Pubng) St Mut.

Bowen, Nicholas & Wareham, Robert. Tolley's Tax Legislation, 1993-1994: Income Tax, Corporation Tax & Capital Gains Tax. 4000p. 1993. 96.00 (*0-85459-776-X*, Pub. by Tolley Pubng) St Mut.

Bowen, Nicholas, jt. auth. see Wareham, Robert.

Bowen, Norman R., ed. see Kane, Elizabeth.

***Bowen, Otis R. & Du Bois, William P.** Doc: Memories from a Life in Public Service. LC 00-24321. 2000. write for info. (*0-253-33767-4*) Ind U Pr.

Bowen, P. A Communications Based Analysis of the Theory of Price Planning & Price Control. 1995. pap. 30.00 (*0-85406-675-6*, Pub. by R-I-C-S Bks) St Mut.

Bowen, Pat, ed. see Danna, Minta.

Bowen, Patrick G. The Sayings of the Ancient One. 1972. lib. bdg. 250.00 (*0-87968-490-9*) Krishna Pr.

Bowen, Paul. Air to Air: Photography LC 98-93073. 224 p. 1998. 70.00 (*0-9665095-0-1*) P Bowen Photo.

Bowen, Paul, ed. Themes & Issues in Hinduism. LC 97-15235. (World Religions). 224p. 1998. 75.00 (*0-304-33850-8*, Pub. by Cassell); pap. 26.95 (*0-304-33851-6*, Pub. by Cassell) Cassell.

Bowen, Paul N. A Longing for Land: Tradition & Change in a Swazi Agricultural Community. 256p. 1993. 72.95 (*1-85628-398-4*, Pub. by Avebry) Ashgate Pub Co.

***Bowen, Peter.** Coyote Wind & Specimen Song: Two Montana Mysteries Featuring Gabriel du Pre. 368p. 2000. pap. 14.95 (*0-312-26514-X*) St Martin.

Bowen, Peter. Long Son. LC 98-48954. 272p. 1999. text 22.95 (*0-312-19917-1*) St Martin.

***Bowen, Peter.** Long Son: A Montana Mystery Featuring. 272p. 2000. pap. 13.95 (*0-312-25398-2*) St Martin.

Bowen, Peter. Notches: A Gabriel Du Pre Mystery. (Dead Letter Mysteries Ser.). 1998. mass mkt. 5.50 (*0-312-96492-7*) St Martin.

— Specimen Song. 1996. mass mkt. 5.50 (*0-312-95763-7*, Pub. by Tor Bks) St Martin.

***Bowen, Peter.** Stick Game: A Montana Mystery Featuring Gabriel Du Pre. LC 99-86349. 288p. 2000. text 23.95 (*0-312-20297-0*, Minotaur) St Martin.

Bowen, Peter. Thunder Horse. LC 97-49628. (Montana Mystery Ser.). 304p. 1998. text 22.95 (*0-312-18303-8*) St Martin.

— Thunder Horse. (Montana Mystery Ser.). 256p. 1999. mass mkt. 5.99 (*0-312-96887-6*) St Martin.

— Wolf, No Wolf. 1997. mass mkt. write for info. (*0-614-20527-1*) St Martin.

— Wolf, No Wolf. large type ed. LC 97-13071. (Core Ser.). 286p. 1997. lib. bdg. 25.95 (*0-7838-8215-7*, G K Hall Lrg Type) Mac Lib Ref.

— Wolf, No Wolf: A Dead Letter Mystery. large type ed. LC 95-44420. 226p. 1997. mass mkt. 5.99 (*0-312-96103-0*) St Martin.

An Asterisk (*) at the beginning of an entry indicates that the title is appearing for the first time.

— Yellowstone Kelly. LC 86-27193. (Frontier Library). 260p. 1988. 27.50 (*0-915463-40-7*, Frontier Libr) Jameson Bks.

***Bowen, Phil.** A Gallery to Play To. 176p. 1999. pap. 18.95 (*1-900152-63-0*, Pub. by Stride Pubns) SPD-Small Pr Dist.

Bowen, R. On Axiom A Diffeomorphisms. LC 78-6745. (CBMS Regional Conference Series in Mathematics: Vol. 35). 45p. 1978. reprint ed. pap. 19.00 (*0-8218-1685-3*, CBMS/35C) Am Math.

Bowen, R., ed. Isotopes in the Earth Sciences. 632p. 1988. pap. 224.95 (*1-85166-145-X*) Thomson Learn.

Bowen, R. L. The Early Arabian Necropolis of Ain Jawan: A Pre-Islamic & Early Islamic Site on the Persian Gulf. (American Schools of Oriental Research, Supplement Ser.: Vols. 7-9). 70p. 1950. pap. text 10.00 (*0-89757-309-9*) Am Sch Orient Res.

— Obsolete Banknotes & Scrip of Michigan, 2 bks. LC 84-70009. (Illus.). 1984. reprint ed. lib. bdg. 50.00 (*0-942666-37-2*) S J Durst.

Bowen, R. M. Introduction to Continuum Mechanics for Engineers. (Mathematical Concepts & Methods in Science & Engineering Ser.: Vol. 39). (Illus.). 256p. (C). 1989. 75.00 (*0-306-43050-9*, Plenum Trade) Perseus Pubng.

Bowen, R. M. & Wang, C. C. Introduction to Vectors & Tensors, 2 vols. Incl. Introduction to Vectors & Tensors Vol. 2: Vector & Tensor Analysis. LC 75-28115. (Illus.). 192p. (C). 1976. 66.00 (*0-306-37509-5*, Plenum Trade); No. 2. Linear & Multilinear Algebra. LC 75-28115. (Illus.). 242p. (C). 1976. 55.00 (*0-306-37508-7*, Plenum Trade); LC 75-28115. (Mathematical Concepts & Methods in Science & Engineering Ser.: Vols. 1 & 2). 1976. write for info. (*0-318-55326-0*, Plenum Trade) Perseus Pubng.

***Bowen, Rachel.** The Way It Was. 55p. 1999. 14.95 (*0-9661949-2-6*) Harrah Hse.

Bowen, Rhoda A. Georgia Confederate Soldier Obituaries: Henry, Newton & Rockdale Counties 1879-1943. Turner, Freda R., ed. 454p. 1992. 40.00 (*0-9628557-1-5*) Genlgcl Socs Henry & Clayton.

— Henry County, Georgia Obituaries 1879-1899. 380p. 1993. 40.00 (*0-9628557-5-8*) Genlgcl Socs Henry & Clayton.

***Bowen, Rhys.** Evan & Elle: A Constable Evans Mystery. LC 99-54824. (Constable Evans Mysteries Ser.). 288p. 2000. text 22.95 (*0-312-25244-7*) St Martin.

Bowen, Rhys. Evan Help Us. LC 98-22796. 224p. 1998. text 21.95 (*0-312-19411-0*) St Martin.

***Bowen, Rhys.** Evan Help Us. large type ed. LC 99-33388. (Mystery Ser.). 1999. write for info. (*1-57490-213-X*, Beeler LP Bks) T T Beeler.

— Evan Help Us. 224p. 1999. reprint ed. mass mkt. 5.99 (*0-425-17261-9*, Prime Crime) Berkley Pub.

— Evanly Choirs. (Constable Evans Mysteries Ser.). 256p. 2000. mass mkt. 5.99 (*0-425-17613-4*) Berkley Pub.

Bowen, Rhys. Evanly Choirs. LC 99-19879. 192p. 1999. text 22.95 (*0-312-20539-2*) St Martin.

***Bowen, Rhys.** Evanly Choirs. large type ed. LC 99-51850. (Beeler Large Print Mystery Ser.). 1999. 25.95 (*1-57490-241-5*) T T Beeler.

— Evans Above. large type ed. LC 99-25073. (Mystery Ser.). 1999. 24.95 (*1-57490-208-3*, Beeler LP Bks) T T Beeler.

Bowen, Rhys. Evans Above. 224p. 1998. reprint ed. pap. 5.99 (*0-425-16642-2*, Prime Crime) Berkley Pub.

Bowen, Rhys & Bowen, J. Evans Above. LC 97-24776. (Evan Evans Ser.). 236p. 1997. text 21.95 (*0-312-16828-4*) St Martin.

Bowen, Rich, et al. Apache Server Unleashed. pap. 49.99 (*0-672-31808-3*) Sams.

Bowen, Richard A. The Art of Hearing: Seven Practical Methods for Improving Your Hearing. (Illus.). 1996. pap. 6.95 (*0-9649343-3-7*) Ariadne Pubns.

— Spirit & Nature. (Illus.). 78p. (Orig.). 1995. pap. 9.95 (*0-9649343-1-0*) Ariadne Pubns.

Bowen, Richard L. Early Rehoboth Vols. I-IV: Documented Historical Studies of Families & Events in This Plymouth Colony Township. (Illus.). 716p. 1997. reprint ed. lib. bdg. 59.50 (*0-8328-5962-1*) Higginson Bk Co.

— Some Factors Affecting Employee Motivation at the University of South Dakota. 1982. 1.00 (*1-55614-115-7*) U of SD Gov Res Bur.

Bowen, Richard L. & Albright, Frank. Archaeological Discoveries in South Arabia. LC 57-12447. (American Foundation for the Study of Man Ser.: Vol. 2). 342p. reprint ed. pap. 106.10 (*0-8357-5710-2*, 200186300008) Bks Demand.

Bowen, Robert. Universal Ice: Science & Ideology in the Nazi State. LC 92-43689. 195p. 1993. text 59.00 (*1-85293-190-6*) St Martin.

Bowen, Robert A. Call of the Sea & Other Verse. (Illus.). 1969. pap. 2.00 (*0-912462-01-9*) Foun Hist Rest.

— Footfalls & Echoes: Verses About Old Pendelton. (Illus.). 1964. pap. 2.00 (*0-912462-02-7*) Foun Hist Rest.

— When Sweet Birds Sing. (Illus.). 1967. pap. 2.00 (*0-912462-03-5*) Foun Hist Rest.

Bowen, Robert D. Excellence in Staffing Using ISO 9000 for Success. (Illus.). (Orig.). 1996. pap. write for info. (*0-9654748-0-1*) R Bowen Intl.

Bowen, Robert E. Negotiating an International Regime to Mine the Deep Seabed. (Pew Case Studies in International Affairs). 50p. (C). 1992. pap. 3.50 (*1-56927-423-1*) Geo U Inst Dplmcy.

Bowen, Robert G., Jr. My Philosophy: Why My Paintings are Signed "A Friend of Civilization" LC 81-69045. (Orig.). 1982. 30.00 (*0-9607512-1-1*); 30.00 (*0-9607512-3-8*); pap. 4.00 (*0-9607512-0-3*); pap. 6.00 (*0-9607512-2-X*) R G Bowen.

Bowen, Robert M. Introduction to Financial Accounting. (C). 1995. pap. text. write for info. (*0-03-013364-5*); pap. text, teacher ed. write for info. (*0-03-014177-X*); pap. text, student ed. write for info. (*0-03-014179-6*) Harcourt Coll Pubs.

— Introduction to Financial Accounting: Test Bank. (C). 1995. pap. text, suppl. ed. write for info. (*0-03-014184-2*) Harcourt Coll Pubs.

Bowen, Robert S. Dusty Ayres & His Battle Birds - Black Lightning. Gunnison, John P., ed. & intro. by. (High Adventure Ser.: 44). (Illus.). 96p. (C). 1999. pap. 6.00 (*1-886937-31-1*) Adventure Hse.

Bowen, Roger. Inga. LC 79-52903. 1979. 9.95 (*0-9602986-1-4*) Normandie.

— Just Like a Movie. 201p. (Orig.). 1996. pap. 10.00 (*0-9602986-3-0*) Normandie.

— "Many Histories Deep" The Personal Landscape Poets in Egypt, 1940-45. rev. ed. LC 94-34717. (Illus.). 248p. 1995. 39.50 (*0-8386-3567-9*) Fairleigh Dickinson.

— The Silent '50s. LC 94-69199. (Orig.). 1994. pap. write for info. (*0-9602986-2-2*) Normandie.

Bowen, Roger W. Innocence Is Not Enough: The Life & Death of Herbert Norman. LC 88-3055. (Illus.). 409p. 1988. reprint ed. pap. 126.80 (*0-7837-9966-7*, 206069300006) Bks Demand.

Bowen, Roy & Spear, Robert K. U. S. Army Soldiers' Promotion Board Study Guide. 150p. (Orig.). 1990. pap. 8.95 (*0-9622627-3-0*) U Force Dynamics.

***Bowen, Russ.** Raiders of Spanish Flat. large type ed. 288p. 1999. pap. 20.99 (*1-85389-900-3*, Dales) Ulverscroft.

Bowen, Russell S. The Immaculate Deception: The Bush Crime Family Exposed. 210p. (Orig.). (C). 1991. pap. text 12.95 (*0-922356-80-7*) Amer West Pubs.

Bowen, Ruth M. Yea! I'm an Orphan. 1986. write for info. (*0-935087-12-5*) Wright Pub Co.

Bowen, Sally. Down by the Christmas Stream. (Illus.). 38p. (J). 1992. pap. 10.95 (*0-9633546-0-4*) Bowen & Assocs.

— Down by the Enchanted Stream. (Illus.). 38p. (J). 1992. pap. 10.95 (*0-9633546-1-2*) Bowen & Assocs.

Bowen, Shelly, ed. see Chambers, Veronica.

***Bowen, Sherry H.** Pigeon Feathers. (Books for Young Learners). (Illus.). 16p. (J). (gr. k-2). 1999. pap. text 5.00 (*1-57274-279-8*, A2761) R Owen Pubs.

Bowen, Sheryl P. & Wyatt, Nancy. Transforming Visions: Feminist Critiques in Communication Studies. Rakow, Lana, ed. LC 92-38173. (Communication Series: Feminist Perspectives). 288p. (C). 1993. text 62.50 (*1-881303-06-3*); pap. text 27.50 (*1-881303-07-1*) Hampton Pr NJ.

Bowen, Sidney. Dearest Isabel: Letters from an Enlisted Man in World War II. (Illus.). 232p. 1992. pap. 18.95 (*0-89745-150-3*) Sunflower U Pr.

Bowen-Simpkins, Peter & Pugh, David. Pocket Examiner in Obstetrics & Gynaecology. 2nd ed. 260p. 1993. pap. text 19.95 (*0-443-03929-1*) Church.

Bowen, Stella & Ford, Ford Madox. The Correspondence of Ford Madox Ford & Stella Bowen. Stang, Sondra J. & Cochran, Karen, eds. LC 91-45613. (Illus.). 500p. (C). 1994. 65.00 (*0-253-35494-3*) Ind U Pr.

Bowen, Stephen, ed. Human Rights, Self-Determination & Political Change in the Occupied Palestinian Territories. LC 97-229079. (International Studies in Human Rights Ser.: No. 52). 324p. 1997. 109.00 (*90-411-0502-6*) Kluwer Academic.

Bowen, T. & Marles, J. The Pronunciation Book: Student Centered Activities for Pronunciation Work. (Pilgrims Longman Resource Bks.). 85p. 1995. pap. text 22.39 (*0-582-06491-0*, 79849) Addison-Wesley.

Bowen, T. J. Adventures & Missionary Labours in Several Countries in the Interior of Africa from 1849-1856. 2nd rev. ed. 359p. 1968. reprint ed. 45.00 (*0-7146-1863-2*, Pub. by F Cass Pubs) Intl Spec Bk.

Bowen, Thomas E. & Bellamy, Ronald F., eds. Emergency War Surgery. rev. ed. (Illus.). 446p. (C). 1994. text 60.00 (*0-7881-0291-5*) DIANE Pub.

Bowen, Thomas G. Seri Prehistory: The Archaeology of the Central Coast of Sonora, Mexico. LC 74-29360. (Anthropological Papers of the University of Arizona: No. 27). 120p. reprint ed. pap. 37.20 (*0-8357-7790-1*, 203615100002) Bks Demand.

***Bowen, Tim.** The Silence Calling: Australians in Antarctica, 1947-1997. (Illus.). 624p. 2000. 45.00 (*1-86448-859-X*, Pub. by Allen & Unwin Pty) Paul & Co Pubs.

Bowen, Toni. Filing Fundamentals: A Step-by-Step Approach to Setting Up & Using a Basic Filing System. (Illus.). 50p. (Orig.). (YA). (gr. 10-12). 1993. pap. text 14.95 (*0-9633167-0-2*) Positive Results.

Bowen, W. G. Ever the Teacher. 624p. 1988. text 49.50 (*0-691-09692-9*, Pub. by Princeton U Pr) Cal Prin Full Svc.

***Bowen, Wayne H.** Spaniards & Nazi Germany: Collaboration in the New Order. 280p. 2000. 34.95 (*0-8262-1300-6*) U of Mo Pr.

Bowen, William & Rudenstine, Neil. In Pursuit of the Ph.D. 352p. 1992. text 55.00 (*0-691-04294-2*, Pub. by Princeton U Pr) Cal Prin Full Svc.

Bowen, William G. Ever the Teacher: William G. Bowen's Writings As President of Princeton. LC 87-32690. (Illus.). 636p. 1988. reprint ed. pap. 197.20 (*0-608-07132-3*, 206735800009) Bks Demand.

— Inside the Boardroom: Governance by Directors & Trustees. 208p. 1994. 45.00 (*0-471-02501-1*) Wiley.

***Bowen, William G.** Shape of the River: Long-Term Consequences of Considering Race in College & University Admission. 2000. pap. text 16.95 (*0-691-05019-8*, Pub. by Princeton U Pr) Cal Prin Full Svc.

Bowen, William G. Wage Behavior in the Postwar Period, No. 100--100. LC 73-10582. (Princeton University Industrial Relations Ser.). (Illus.). 137p. 1973. reprint ed. lib. bdg. 57.50 (*0-8371-7013-3*, BOWB, Greenwood Pr) Greenwood.

— Wage-Price Issue: A Theoretical Analysis. LC 72-90471. 447p. 1969. reprint ed. lib. bdg. 79.50 (*0-8371-2286-4*, BOWP, Greenwood Pr) Greenwood.

Bowen, William G. & Ashenfelter, Orley C., eds. Labor & the National Economy. rev. ed. (Problems of Modern Economy Ser.). (C). 1975. write for info. (*0-393-05456-X*) Norton.

Bowen, William G. & Bok, Derek C. The Shape of the River: Long-Term Consequences of Considering Race in College & University Admissions. LC 98-19900. (Illus.). 472p. 1998. 24.95 (*0-691-00274-6*, Pub. by Princeton U Pr) Cal Prin Full Svc.

Bowen, William G. & Finegan, T. Aldrich. The Economics of Labor Force Participation. LC 69-17396. (Illus.). 923p. reprint ed. pap. 200.00 (*0-7837-6496-0*, 204658600003) Bks Demand.

Bowen, William G. & Shapiro, Harold T. Universities & Their Leadership. LC 97-41085. 256p. 1998. text 29.95 (*0-691-05921-7*, Pub. by Princeton U Pr) Cal Prin Full Svc.

Bowen, William G., et al. The Charitable Non-Profits: An Analysis of Institutional Dynamics & Characteristics. LC 94-21301. (Nonprofit Sector Ser.). 326p. 1994. text 43.95 (*0-7879-0024-9*) Jossey-Bass.

Bowen, William G., jt. auth. see Baumol, William J.

Bowen, William G., jt. auth. see Shulman, James Lawrence.

Bowen, William H. & Tabak, Lawrence A., eds. Cariology for the Nineties. LC 92-48515. (Illus.). 475p. (C). 1993. 90.00 (*1-878822-17-9*) Univ Rochester Pr.

Bowen, Wyn Q. & Dunn, David H., eds. American Security Policy: Beyond Containment. (Issues in International Security Ser.). (Illus.). 224p. 1996. 82.95 (*1-85521-610-8*, Pub. by Dartmth Pub); pap. 31.95 (*1-85521-615-9*, Pub. by Dartmth Pub) Ashgate Pub Co.

Bowen, York. Pedalling the Modern Pianoforte. 1936. pap. 13.95 (*0-19-322105-5*) OUP.

Bowen, Zack. Bloom's Old Sweet Song: Essays on Joyce & Music. LC 94-27517. (Florida James Joyce Ser.). (Illus.). 162p. (C). 1995. 39.95 (*0-8130-1327-5*) U Press Fla.

— A Reader's Guide to John Barth. LC 93-10378. 176p. 1993. lib. bdg. 57.95 (*0-313-27978-0*, BJR/, Greenwood Pr) Greenwood.

Bowen, Zack, ed. & frwd. see Nadel, Ira B.

Bowen, Zack R. Irish Renaissance Annual IV. LC 80-644275. (Illus.). 176p. 1983. 25.00 (*0-87413-236-3*) U Delaware Pr.

— Mary Lavin. LC 73-126002. (Irish Writers Ser.). 77p. 1975. 8.50 (*0-8387-7762-7*); pap. 1.95 (*0-8387-7701-5*) Bucknell U Pr.

— Musical Allusions in the Works of James Joyce: Early Poetry Through "Ulysses" LC 74-13314. 372p. (C). 1974. text 24.50 (*0-87395-248-0*) State U NY Pr.

— Ulysses As a Comic Novel. LC 89-32238. (Irish Studies). 167p. 1989. reprint ed. pap. 51.80 (*0-608-07594-9*, 205990900010) Bks Demand.

Bowen, Zack R., ed. Irish Renaissance Annual I. (Irish Renaissance Annual Ser.). 192p. 1980. 25.00 (*0-87413-168-5*) U Delaware Pr.

— Irish Renaissance Annual II. 192p. 1981. 25.00 (*0-87413-185-5*) U Delaware Pr.

Bowen, Zack R. & Carens, James F., eds. A Companion to Joyce Studies. LC 83-1479. (Illus.). 818p. 1984. lib. bdg. 115.00 (*0-313-22832-9*, BJS/, Greenwood Pr) Greenwood.

Bowen, Zack R., ed. see Cotsell, Michael.

Bowens, Kenneth. Lil' Black Girl Eyes 'n Frozen & Dirtied Brown Leaves. James, Carolyn, ed. 187p. 1996. pap. 21.95 (*0-9653447-0-3*) Lil Black Girl.

Bower. Adventure Play. 200p. 1998. pap. text 5.45 (*0-536-01760-3*) Pearson Custom.

— Business Policy. 8th ed. 1995. 38.74 (*0-256-11593-1*) McGraw.

— The Craft of General Management. 400p. 1992. pap. 23.96 (*0-07-103364-5*) McGraw.

— Leica M. Photography. (Illus.). 160p. 1998. pap. 24.95 (*0-7153-0842-4*, Pub. by D & C Pub) Sterling.

— When Markets Quake. 240p. 1986. 22.36 (*0-07-103213-4*) McGraw.

Bower & Langenderfer. Income Tax Procedure Text. 87th ed. (Thomson Executive Press Ser.). 1988. 2.00 (*0-538-80155-7*) S-W Pub.

Bower, Alan. Scandinavian Texts for Handel's Messiah: A Study of Translation Technique Applied to a Libretto. x, 194p. (Orig.). 1996. pap. 24.00 (*0-9643394-3-9*) Stonehill MI.

— A Synopsis of Old Icelandic Grammar. 80p. (C). 1994. pap. 24.00 (*0-9643394-1-2*) Stonehill MI.

Bower, Alan, tr. see Bach, Johann Sebastian.

Bower, Alan, tr. see Jacobsen, Jorgen-Frantz.

Bower, Alan, tr. see Jensen, Johannes V.

Bower, Alan W., ed. see Arbuthmot, John.

Bower, Alex, jt. auth. see Burch, Preston M.

Bower, Anne L. Epistolary Responses: The Letter in 20th-Century American Fiction & Criticism. LC 96-3595. 208p. 1997. text 34.95 (*0-8173-0836-9*) U of Ala Pr.

Bower, Anne L., ed. Recipes for Reading: Community Cookbooks, Stories, Histories. LC 97-9292. (Illus.). 271p. 1997. pap. 18.95 (*1-55849-089-2*); text 45.00 (*1-55849-088-4*) U of Mass Pr.

Bower, Anthony, tr. see Camus, Albert.

***Bower, B. M.** Chip, of the Flying U. 1999. 19.00 (*0-7540-8066-8*, Gunsmoke) Chivers N Amer.

Bower, B. M. Chip, of the Flying U. LC 95-4570. (Illus.). vii, 264p. 1995. pap. 8.95 (*0-8032-6121-7*, Bison Books) U of Nebr Pr.

— Flying U Ranch. LC 96-14954. (Illus.). 253p. Date not set. pap. 10.00 (*0-8032-6129-2*, Bison Books) U of Nebr Pr.

— Happy Family of the Flying U. LC 96-8041. (Illus.). xix, 323p. 1996. pap. 12.00 (*0-8032-6130-6*, Bison Books) U of Nebr Pr.

— The Haunted Hills. large type ed. LC 96-42233. (Sagebrush Large Print Westerns Ser.). 1996. lib. bdg. 17.95 (*1-57490-045-5*) T T Beeler.

— Lonesome Land. LC 96-49022. (Illus.). xiii, 326p. 1997. pap. 13.95 (*0-8032-6134-9*, Bison Books) U of Nebr Pr.

***Bower, B. M.** Open Land. large type ed. LC 00-40275. 2000. write for info. (*1-57490-288-1*, Sagebrush LP West) T T Beeler.

Bower, B. M. Pirates of the Range. large type ed. 1998. 18.95 (*1-57490-156-7*, Sagebrush LP West) T T Beeler.

***Bower, Bert, et al.** History Alive! Engaging All Learners in the Diverse Classroom. 2nd rev. ed. (Illus.). 224p. 1999. pap. 28.00 (*1-58371-007-8*, TCI-007, History Alive) Teachers Curriculum Inst.

Bower, Bill & Werner, David B. Aprendiendo a Promover la Salud: Un Libro de Metodos, Materiales e Ideas para Instructores que Trabajan en la Comunidad. Gordon, Lynn & Briggs, Anna M., eds. LC 81-85010.Tr. of Helping Health Workers Learn: A Book of Methods, Aids & ideas for instructors at the Village Level. (SPA., Illus.). 640p. (C). 1985. pap. 20.00 (*0-942364-14-7*) Hesperian Found.

— Helping Health Workers Learn: A Book of Methods, Aids, & Ideas for Instructors at the Village Level. LC 81-85010. (Illus.). 640p. (C). 1982. pap. 20.00 (*0-942364-10-4*) Hesperian Found.

Bower, Blair T., ed. Regional Residuals Environmental Quality Management Modeling. LC 77-92413. (Resources for the Future, RFF Research Paper Ser.: NO. R-7). 244p. reprint ed. pap. 75.70 (*0-608-12264-5*, 202378600034) Bks Demand.

Bower, Blair T. & Katsuki, Takao, eds. Who Speaks for Tokyo Bay? (IFIAS Coastal Waters Ser.: No. 3). (Illus.). 156p. (C). 1993. text 91.00 (*90-5410-130-X*, Pub. by A A Balkema) Ashgate Pub Co.

Bower, Blair T., et al. Incentives in Water Quality Management: France & the Ruhr Area. LC 81-47032. 302p. 1981. pap. 18.95 (*0-8018-2661-6*) Resources Future.

Bower, Blair T., jt. auth. see Kneese, Allen V.

Bower, Blair T., jt. auth. see Waddell, Thomas E.

Bower, Blair T., jt. ed. see Basta, Daniel J.

Bower, Blair T., jt. ed. see Kneese, Allen V.

Bower, Bobbie, jt. auth. see Johnson, Evelyn M.

Bower, Brian. The Leica Lens Book. LC 99-209695. (Illus.). 1999. 45.00 (*0-7153-0817-3*, Pub. by D & C Pub) Sterling.

— Leica M Photography. (Illus.). 160p. 1996. 39.95 (*0-7153-0318-X*, Pub. by D & C Pub) Sterling.

— Leica Reflex Photography: New Edition Featuring the Leica R8. LC 97-183392. (Illus.). 152p. 1997. pap. 24.95 (*0-7153-0627-8*) Sterling.

— Lens, Light & Landscape: The Art & Technique of Scenic Photography. (Illus.). 192p. 1996. pap. 19.95 (*0-7153-0463-1*, Pub. by D & C Pub) Sterling.

Bower, C. M., ed. Composites Materials Glossary. 68p. 1991. reprint ed. pap. 18.00 (*0-938648-22-5*) T-C Pr CA.

Bower, Carol. Karina Has Down Syndrome: One Family's Account of the Early Years with a Child Who Has Special Need. 1999. pap. 17.95 (*1-85302-820-7*) Jessica Kingsley.

Bower, Carol E. The Basic Marine Aquarium: A Simplified, Modern Approach to the Care of Saltwater Fishes. (Illus.). 290p. 1983. pap. 41.95 (*0-398-04736-7*) C C Thomas.

Bower, Cecil E. The Almighty One Guide Catalogue. (Illus.). 256p. (Orig.). 1989. write for info. (*0-9623894-0-4*) C E Bower.

Bower, D. I. & Maddams, W. F. The Vibrational Spectroscopy of Polymers. (Cambridge Solid State Science Ser.). (Illus.). 342p. (C). 1992. pap. text 44.95 (*0-521-42195-0*) Cambridge U Pr.

Bower, D. Jane. Company & Campus Partnership: Strategies for Risk Reduction. LC 91-48102. 208p. (C). 1992. pap. 77.95 (*0-415-07080-5*, A6951) Thomson Learn.

Bower, David. The Effects of Original Sin & the Availability of Sovereign Grace. 72p. 1996. 7.00 (*0-8059-3871-0*) Dorrance.

Bower, Dee S. & Wells, Mary E. Homemade to Go: The Complete Guide to Co-op Cooking. LC 97-91843. (Illus.). 128p. 1997. pap. 14.95 (*0-9657913-9-4*) Purrfect Pub.

Bower, Donna L. & Early, Evelyn A., eds. Everyday Life in the Muslim Middle East. LC 92-40710. (Indiana Series in Arab & Islamic). 352p. 1993. 42.00 (*0-253-31253-1*) Ind U Pr.

Bower, Fay L. Nurses Taking the Lead: Personal Qualities of Effective Leadership. LC 99-31083. (Illus.). 315p. (C). 2000. pap. text. write for info. (*0-7216-8169-7*, W B Saunders Co) Harcrt Hlth Sci Grp.

Bower, Frank A. & Ward, Richard B., eds. Stratospheric Ozone & Man Vol. I: Stratospheric Ozone. 232p. 1982. 131.00 (*0-8493-5753-5*, QC879, CRC Reprint) Franklin.

— Stratospheric Ozone & Man Vol. II: Man's Interactions & Concerns. 280p. 1981. 129.95 (*0-8493-5755-1*, QC879) CRC Pr.

Bower, Frederick O. Plants & Man. (C). 1980. text 235.00 (*0-89771-565-9*, Pub. by Intl Bk Distr) St Mut.

— Plants & Man. 365p. 1980. reprint ed. 500.00 (*0-7855-3073-8*, Pub. by Intl Bk Distr) St Mut.

— Thex Ferns, 3 vols. (C). 1988. 80.00 (*0-7855-3258-7*) St Mut.

Bower, Gordon H., ed. The Psychology of Learning & Motivation Vol. 27: Advances in Research & Theory. (Illus.). 349p. (C). 1991. text 99.95 (*0-12-543327-1*) Acad Pr.

Bower, Gordon H. & Bower, Sharon A. Asserting Yourself: A Practical Guide for Positive Change. LC 76-5077. (Illus.). 244p. 1976. pap. 9.57 (*0-201-00838-6*) Addison-Wesley.

B

Bower, Gordon H. & Hilgard, Ernest J. Theories of Learning. 5th ed. (Illus.). 640p. (C). 1980. text 54.80 (*0-13-914432-3*) P-H.

Bower, Gordon H. & Kihlstrom, John F. Basic Behavioral Science Research for Mental Health: A National Investment. 137p. (C). 1998. reprint ed. pap. text 40.00 (*0-7881-3301-2*) DIANE Pub.

Bower, Gordon H., jt. auth. see Anderson, John R.

Bower, H. A. Grow Hair Now! Ask Me How! (Illus.). 32p. 1989. pap. 3.50 (*0-9616735-2-4*) Warrior Pub WI.

Bower, Hamilton. Diary of a Journey Across Tibet. (C). 1994. reprint ed. 27.00 (*81-206-0901-8*, Pub. by Asian Educ Servs) S Asia.

— Diary of a Journey Across Tibet. 310p. (C). 1976. reprint ed. 125.00 (*0-89771-101-7*, Pub. by Ratna Pustak Bhandar) St Mut.

Bower, Herbert M. The Elevation & Procession of the Ceri at Gubbio. (Folk-Lore Society, London Monographs: Vol. 39). 1972. reprint ed. pap. 25.00 (*0-8115-0517-0*) Periodicals Srv.

Bower, Hilary. Natural Way: Psoriasis. LC 96-2737. (Natural Way Ser.). 128p. 1996. pap. 5.95 (*1-85230-832-X*, Pub. by Element MA) Penguin Putnam.

Bower, Humphrey. Natural Life. (Orig.). pap. 14.95 (*0-86819-555-3*, Pub. by Currency Pr) Accents Pubns.

Bower, J. & Beeman, D. The Book of GENESIS. 1997. pap. 54.95 incl. cd-rom (*0-614-28530-5*) Spr-Verlag.

***Bower, J. M., ed.** Computational Neuroscience. 1110p. 1999. 177.50 (*0-444-50307-2*) Elsevier.

Bower, J. M., ed. Computational Neuroscience: Trends in Research, 1998. LC 98-25793. (Illus.). 658p. (C). 1998. text 175.00 (*0-306-45919-1*, Kluwer Plenum) Kluwer Academic.

Bower, James E., et al. Field & Laboratory Methods for General Ecology. 4th ed. LC 97-15263. 240p. (C). 1997. spiral bd. write for info. (*0-697-24358-3*, WCB McGr Hill) McGrw-H Hghr Educ.

Bower, James M. Book of GENESIS: Exploring Realistic Neural Models with the GEneral NEural SImulation System. (Illus.). 432p. 1994. 67.95 (*0-387-94019-7*) Spr-Verlag.

— Book of Genesis: Exploring Realistic Neural Models With The General Neural Simulation System. 2nd ed. LC 97-33270. 436p. 1997. 59.95 (*0-387-94938-0*) Spr-Verlag.

Bower, James M., ed. Computational Neuroscience: Trends in Research. LC 96-207956. (International Review of Neurobiology Supplement Ser.: No. 1). (Illus.). 489p. 1996. text, suppl. ed. 99.00 (*0-12-121040-5*); pap. text, suppl. ed. 59.95 (*0-12-121041-3*) Acad Pr.

— Computational Neuroscience: Trends in Research, 1997: Proceedings of the Annual Computational Neuroscience Conference Held in Boston, Massachusetts, July 14-17, 1996. LC 97-23178. 982p. 1997. 195.00 (*0-306-45699-0*, Kluwer Plenum) Kluwer Academic.

***Bower, James M. & Bolouri, Hamid.** Computational Modeling of Genetic & Biochemical Networks. LC 00-24605. (Computational Molecular Biology Ser.). (Illus.). 390p. 2000. 59.95 (*0-262-02481-0*, Bradford Bks) MIT Pr.

Bower, James M. & Getty, Murtha B., eds. Union List of Artist Names Vol. 1: Aa-Dzw, Set. LC 93-46729. 2912p. 1994. 495.00 (*0-8161-0725-4*, G K Hall Lrg Type) Mac Lib Ref.

Bower, James M., jt. auth. see Eeckman, Frank H.

Bower, James M., ed. see Conference on Computation & Neural Systems Staff.

Bower, Jane. Painting. LC 98-122237. (Arts & Crafts Skills Ser.). 32p. (J). 1998. 20.00 (*0-516-20457-2*) Childrens.

Bower, John. The Cat Owner's Problem Solver: Practical & Expert Advice on Caring for Cats. (Owner's Problem Solvers Ser.). 208p. 1998. pap. 22.95 (*0-7621-0056-7*, Pub. by RD Assn) Penguin Putnam.

— The Dog Owner's Problem Solver: Practical & Expert Advice on Caring for Dogs. (Owner's Problem Solvers Ser.). 208p. 1998. pap. 22.95 (*0-7621-0058-3*, Pub. by RD Assn) Penguin Putnam.

— The Health of Your Dog. LC 89-6845. (Illus.). 240p. 1989. 14.95 (*0-931866-45-6*) Alpine Pubns.

— Healthy House. 1991. pap. 16.95 (*0-8184-0550-3*) Carol Pub Group.

— The Healthy House: How to Buy One, How to Build One, How to Cure a "Sick" One. 1989. 17.95 (*0-8184-0494-9*) Carol Pub Group.

— Healthy House: How to Buy One, How to Cure a Sick One & How to Build One. rev. ed. 416p. 1997. pap. text 18.95 (*0-8065-1937-1*, Citadel Pr) Carol Pub Group.

***Bower, John.** Healthy House Building for the New Millennium: A Design & Construction Guide. LC 99-95477. 416p. 2000. pap. 21.95 (*0-9637156-8-2*) Hlthy Hse.

Bower, John. Understanding Ventilation: How to Design, Select & Install Residential Ventilation Systems. LC 94-96635. (Illus.). 432p. 1995. 31.95 (*0-9637156-5-8*) Hlthy Hse.

Bower, John & Bower, Lynn M. The Healthy House Answer Book: Answers to the 133 Most Commonly Asked Questions. LC 97-94365. 192p. 1998. pap. 8.95 (*0-9637156-4-X*) Hlthy Hse.

Bower, John & Society of Practicing Veterinary Surgeons Staff. Veterinary Practice Management. 2nd ed. LC 96-48694. 1997. 42.95 (*0-632-04129-3*) Blackwell Sci.

Bower, Joseph L. Craft of General Management. 1992. pap. 30.94 (*0-07-006762-7*) McGraw.

Bower, Joseph L., selected by. Craft of General Management. (Practice of Management Ser.). 320p. 1992. pap. 29.95 (*0-87584-313-1*) Harvard Busn.

Bower, Joseph L., et al. Business Policy: Managing Strategic Processes. 8th ed. LC 95-2575. 912p. (C). 1995. text 72.75 (*0-256-11591-5*, Irwn McGrw-H) McGrw-H Hghr Educ.

Bower, Kathleen A. Case Management by Nurses. 80p. 1992. pap. 17.95 (*1-55810-073-3*, NS-32) Am Nurses Pub.

Bower, Kathrin M. Ethics & Remembrance in the Poetry of Nelly Sachs & Rose Auslander. (Studies in German Literature, Linguistics & Culture). 220p. 2000. 55.00 (*1-57113-191-4*, Pub. by Camden Hse) Boydell & Brewer.

Bower, Lael, jt. auth. see Forstner, Penny.

Bower, Lynn M. The Healthy Household: A Complete Guide for Creating a Healthy Indoor Environment. LC 94-96634. 480p. 1995. pap. 17.95 (*0-9637156-3-1*) Hlthy Hse.

Bower, Lynn M., jt. auth. see Bower, John.

***Bower, Lynn Marie.** Creating a Healthy Household: The Ultimate Guide for Healthier, Safer, Less-Toxic Living. LC 99-96306. 701p. 2000. pap. 23.95 (*0-9637156-7-4*) Hlthy Hse.

Bower, Marion & Trowell, Judith, eds. The Emotional Needs of Young Children & Their Families: Using Psychoanalytic Ideas in the Community. LC 95-16139. 320p. (C). 1996. pap. 25.99 (*0-415-11613-9*) Routledge.

— The Emotional Needs of Young Children & Their Families: Using Psychoanalytic Ideas in the Community. LC 95-16139. (Illus.). 320p. (C). (gr. 13). 1996. 85.00 (*0-415-11612-0*) Routledge.

Bower, Martha G. Eugene O'Neill's Unfinished Threnody & Process of Invention in Four Cycle Plays. LC 92-40839. (Illus.). 196p. 1993. text 79.95 (*0-7734-9199-6*) E Mellen.

Bower, Marvin. The Will to Lead: Running a Business with a Network of Leaders. LC 96-45357. 208p. 1997. 27.95 (*0-87584-758-7*) Harvard Busn.

Bower, Michael. Newcomer's Handbook for San Francisco. (Newcomer's Handbook Ser.). (Illus.). 168p. 1997. 13.95 (*0-912301-34-1*) First Bks.

***Bower, Miranda.** Weather. (Interfact Ser.). (Illus.). (J). (gr. 2-7). 2000. spiral bd. 14.95 (*1-58728-470-7*) Two Can Pub.

Bower, Miranda. Weather. LC 98-4282. (Interfact Ser.). (Illus.). 48p. (J). (gr. 2-8). 1998. spiral bd. write for info. incl. cd-rom (*0-7166-7236-7*) World Bk.

Bower, Muriel. Foil Fencing. 8th ed. LC 95-83965. 128p. (C). 1996. text. write for info. (*0-697-25874-2*) Brown & Benchmark.

Bower, Paula R. Apartheid Is Wrong: A Curriculum for Young People. (Illus.). 280p. (J). (gr. 1-12). 1989. ring bd. 15.00 (*1-878537-00-8*) Educ Racism & Apart.

— Apartheid Is Wrong: A Curriculum for Young People. 2nd ed. 1990. write for info. (*1-878537-03-2*) Educ Racism & Apart.

Bower, Peter. The Oxford Papers, Studies in British Paper History. (Studies in British Paper History: Vol. 1). (Illus.). 108p. 1996. pap. 29.95 (*0-9525757-0-1*) Oak Knoll.

Bower, Peter & Tate Gallery. Turner's Later Papers: A Study of the Manufacture, Selection & Use of His Drawing Papers 1820-1851. LC 99-21460. (Illus.). 144p. 1999. 39.95 (*1-884718-97-3*) Oak Knoll.

Bower, Peter C., ed. Handbook for the Revised Common Lectionary. 296p. 1996. pap. 19.95 (*0-664-25657-0*) Westminster John Knox.

***Bower, Reuben E.** The Unreached Indian: A Treatise on Indian Life & Indian Missions. (LC History-America-E). 124p. 1999. reprint ed. lib. bdg. 69.00 (*0-7812-4239-8*) Rprt Serv.

Bower, Richard A. Cuentos Panamenos: Stories of Struggle & Hope in Rural Panama. LC 92-20850. 1993. pap. 11.95 (*0-377-00249-6*) Friendship Pr.

Bower, Robert K. Administering Christian Education. LC 64-22018. 1964. pap. 12.00 (*0-8028-1559-6*) Eerdmans.

Bower, Robert T. & Jux, Ulrick. Afro-Arabian Geology: A Kinematic View. 300p. (C). (gr. 13). 1987. text 82.00 (*0-412-29700-0*) Chapman & Hall.

Bower, Sharon. Painless Public Speaking. 4th ed. (Illus.). 227p. 1990. reprint ed. pap. 20.00 (*0-9665262-0-1*) Confi Train.

***Bower, Sharon, et al.** Czechoslovakian Pottery: Czeching Out America. (Illus.). 224p. 1999. 44.95 (*1-57080-062-6*); pap. 34.95 (*1-57080-061-8*) Antique Pubns.

Bower, Sharon A. Asserting Yourself. 1976. 8.95 (*0-201-00837-8*) Addison-Wesley.

— Asserting Yourself: A Practical Guide for Positive Change. 2nd rev. ed. 244p. 1991. pap. 15.00 (*0-201-57088-2*) Addison-Wesley.

Bower, Sharon A., jt. auth. see Bower, Gordon H.

Bower, Tom. A Blind Eye to Murder: Britain, America & the Purging of Nazi Germany - A Pledge Betrayed. (Illus.). 544p. 1983. pap. 11.00 (*0-586-08422-3*) Academy Chi Pubs.

— The Paperclip Conspiracy: The Hunt for Nazi Scientists. 288p. 1988. 17.95 (*0-316-10399-3*) Little.

— Spy Wars. 1999. pap. write for info. (*0-670-84886-7*) Viking Penguin.

Bower, Virgina, et al. Decorative Arts Pt. II: Far Eastern Ceramics & Paintings; Persian & Indian Rugs & Carpets. (A National Gallery of Art USA Publication). 360p. 1998. 120.00 (*0-89468-252-0*) OUP.

Bower, Walter. Scotichronicon, Bks. XV & XVI. Watt, D. R., ed. 440p. 1987. text 70.00 (*0-08-034527-1*, Pub. by Aberdeen U Pr) Macmillan.

— Scotichronicon, Vol. 6, Bks. 11-12. Watt, D. E., ed. 570p. 1991. text 68.00 (*0-08-041222-X*, Pergamon Pr) Elsevier.

Bower, Walter & Watt, Der. Scotichronicon Vol. 3: 1058-1153. 568p. 1997. 140.00 (*1-873644-49-3*, Pub. by Mercat Pr Bks) St Mut.

— Scotichronicon Vol. 4: 1153-1214. 704p. 1997. 140.00 (*1-873644-35-3*, Pub. by Mercat Pr Bks) St Mut.

— Scotichronicon Vol. 7: 1320-1390. 580p. 1997. 140.00 (*1-873644-55-8*, Pub. by Mercat Pr Bks) St Mut.

Bower, Water & Watt, Der. Scotichronicon Vol. 1: Mythical Beginnings, C 400. 450p. 1997. 140.00 (*1-873644-21-3*, Pub. by Mercat Pr Bks) St Mut.

Bower, William C. The Living Bible. 229p. 1977. 22.95 (*0-8369-1394-9*) Ayer.

Bower, William C., ed. Church at Work in the Modern World. LC 67-26717. (Essay Index Reprint Ser.). 1977. 20.95 (*0-8369-0231-9*) Ayer.

Bower, Wilma & Willard, Hildegard. Growing & Thinking Slim. 2nd rev. ed. (Illus.). 156p. (Orig.). 1978. pap. text 20.00 (*0-9606810-0-0*) Willard-Bower.

Bower, Wilma, et al. Infectious Diseases Update. rev. ed. (Illus.). pap. text 4.95 (*0-9616270-2-6*) Alliance Schl Health.

Bowerbank, Sylvia L., ed. see Newcastle, Margaret C.

Bowering, George. Blonds on Bikes. LC 98-143709. 128p. 1997. pap. 11.95 (*0-88922-381-5*, Pub. by Talonbks) Genl Dist Srvs.

— Diamondback Dog. LC 99-182194. 207p. (J). (gr. 7-9). 1998. pap. 9.95 (*1-896184-48-0*) Roussan Pubs.

***Bowering, George.** His Life: A Poem. 140p. 2000. pap. 14.95 (*1-55022-408-5*, Pub. by ECW) LPC InBook.

Bowering, George. Moustache: Memories of Greg Curnoe. 1993. pap. (*0-88910-457-3*) Talonbks.

— Parents from Space. 200p. (YA). (gr. 6 up). 1994. pap. 5.95 (*1-896184-00-6*) Roussan Pubs.

— The Rain Barrel & Other Stories. LC 94-197223. 272p. 1994. pap. 16.95 (*0-88922-345-9*, Pub. by Talonbks) Genl Dist Srvs.

— Sticks & Stones. LC 89-216998. (NFS Canada Ser.). 64p. 1989. pap. 9.95 (*0-88922-268-1*, Pub. by Talonbks) Genl Dist Srvs.

— Urban Snow. 112p. (Orig.). 1992. pap. 11.95 (*0-88922-305-X*, Pub. by Talonbks) Genl Dist Srvs.

Bowering, George, ed. Imago 20. 104p. 1974. pap. 12.95 (*0-88922-068-9*, Pub. by Talonbks) Genl Dist Srvs.

Bowering, George, ed. see Nichol, B. P.

Bowering, George, ed. & intro. see McFadden, David.

Bowering, Ian. Bowering's Guide to Eastern Ontario. LC 92-90451. (Illus.). 224p. 1992. pap. 14.95 (*1-55082-051-6*, Pub. by Quarry Pr) LPC InBook.

Bowering, Marilyn. Anyone Can See I Love You. 80p. 1987. pap. write for info. (*0-88984-104-7*) Porcup Quill.

— To All Appearances. 1999. pap. 8.95 (*0-14-013313-5*) Viking Penguin.

— Visible Worlds. LC 97-53054. 304p. 1998. 24.00 (*0-06-019148-1*, HarperFlamingo) HarpC.

— Visible Worlds: A Novel. 304p. 1999. pap. 13.00 (*0-06-092926-X*) HarpC.

Bowerman. Applied Statistics. 1997. pap., student ed. 28.75 (*0-256-24725-0*) McGraw.

— Business Statistics Practice. 2nd ed. 2000. 68.00 (*0-07-232058-3*) McGraw.

— Forecasting & Time. (Business Statistics Ser.). 1979. teacher ed. 7.50 (*0-87150-661-0*) PWS Pubs.

Bowerman, B. L. & O'Connell, R. T. Computer Modeling for Business & Industry. (Statistics Ser.: Vol. 59). (Illus.). 232p. 1984. text 65.00 (*0-8247-7296-2*) Dekker.

Bowerman, Bruce L. & O'Connell, Richard. Linear Statistical Models: An Applied Approach. 614p. (C). 1986. pap. 39.00 (*0-87150-904-0*, 36G8200) PWS Pubs.

Bowerman, Bruce L. & O'Connell, Richard T. Applied Statistics: Improving Business Processes. LC 96-38966. 896p. (C). 1996. text 71.25 (*0-256-19386-X*, Irwn McGrw-H) McGrw-H Hghr Educ.

— Forecasting & Time Series: An Applied Approach. 3rd ed. LC 92-23049. 726p. 1993. pap. 80.95 (*0-534-93251-7*) Wadsworth Pub.

— Linear Statistical Models - Cloth. 2nd ed. (Business Statistics). 1024p. (C). 1990. pap. 54.50 (*0-534-92177-9*) Wadsworth Pub.

— Time Series Forecasting: Unified Concepts & Computer Implementation. 2nd ed. (C). 1987. pap. 44.75 (*0-87150-070-1*) Wadsworth Pub.

Bowerman, George F. Censorship & the Public Library, with Other Papers. LC 67-30199. (Essay Index Reprint Ser.). 1977. 20.95 (*0-8369-0232-7*) Ayer.

Bowerman, L. D. & Monsees, J. E., eds. Proceedings of the Rapid Excavation & Tunneling Conference, 1993. LC 93-83948. (Illus.). 1308p. 1993. 82.00 (*0-87335-127-4*, 127-4) SMM&E Inc.

Bowerman, Melissa. Early Syntactic Development: A Cross-linguistic Study with Special Reference to Finnish. LC 72-83596. (Cambridge Studies in Linguistics: 11). 314p. reprint ed. pap. 89.50 (*0-608-12278-5*, 2024424) Bks Demand.

***Bowerman, Melissa & Levinson, Stephen C., eds.** Language Acquisition & Conceptual Development. (Language, Culture & Cognition Ser.: No. 3). (Illus.). 420p. (C). 2000. pap. 27.95 (*0-521-59659-9*); text 74.95 (*0-521-59358-1*) Cambridge U Pr.

Bowerman, Melissa & Slobin, Dan I., eds. Crosslinguistics Evidence for the Language-Making Capacity: What Shapes Children's Grammars. (Crosslinguistic Study of Language Acquisition Ser.). 80p. 1986. pap. 14.95 (*0-89859-851-6*) L Erlbaum Assocs.

***Bowerman, Peter.** The Well-Fed Writer: Financial Self-Sufficiency as a Freelance Writer in Six Months or Less. 304p. 2000. pap. 19.95 (*0-9670598-4-4*) Fanove Pub.

Bowerman, William, jt. auth. see Fox, Glen.

Bowerman, William J. & Freeman, William H. High-Performance Training for Track & Field. 2nd ed. LC 90-36286. (Illus.). 264p. 1990. pap. 25.00 (*0-88011-390-1*, PBOW0390) Human Kinetics.

***Bowermaster, John.** Birthplace of the Winds: Storming Alaska's Islands of Fire & Ice. 2001. 26.00 (*0-7922-7506-3*) Natl Geog.

Bowermaster, Jon. Governor: An Oral Biography of Robert D. Ray. LC 87-11223. 380p. 1987. reprint ed. pap. 117.80 (*0-608-00093-0*, 206085800006) Bks Demand.

Bowermaster, Jon, jt. auth. see Steger, Will.

Bowers. Dune County: A Naturalist's Look at the Plant Life of Southwestern Sand Dunes. LC 98-2957. (Illus.). 156p. 1998. pap. 15.95 (*0-8165-1890-4*) U of Ariz Pr.

— Fear Falls Away: And Other Essays from Hard & Rocky Places. LC 97-4659. 175p. 1997. pap. 16.95 (*0-8165-1718-5*) U of Ariz Pr.

— The Legend of Jonah. 1971. lib. bdg. 57.00 (*90-247-5132-2*, Pub. by M Nijhoff) Kluwer Academic.

***Bowers.** Soil Mechanics. 1999. write for info. (*0-07-006737-6*) McGraw.

— Understanding Papers in Clinic. pap. text. write for info. (*0-471-48976-X*) Wiley.

Bowers & Collete. Shaping College Pathways. 1998. pap. text 18.00 (*0-536-01700-X*) Pearson Custom.

***Bowers & Donahue.** Science Academic Achievment. 2nd ed. 256p. 1998. pap. text 26.95 (*0-536-01491-4*) Pearson Custom.

Bowers & Godfrey. What in the World? Exploring Global Issues. (Illus.). 108p. (C). 1994. text 18.00 (*0-13-180613-0*) P-H.

***Bowers, A. Anne.** When We Become They: Basic Communication Skills. (Illus.). 121p. 1999. pap. 25.95 (*0-9671766-0-3*) Huron Valley.

— When We Become They: Communication for Professionals. (Illus.). 110p. (C). 1999. pap. 24.95 (*0-9671766-1-1*) Huron Valley.

Bowers, A. R., ed. see Eckenfelder, W. W.

Bowers, Al. Naked in a Pinstriped Suit. LC 97-66959. 234p. 1997. 21.95 (*1-889274-02-X*) Posterity Press.

Bowers, Alan, ed. see Eckenfelder, W. W.

Bowers, Alan R., ed. see Eckenfelder, W. W.

Bowers, Alan W. On Duty Vol. 2: Interviews with Military Veterans from North of Quabbin. LC 94-78652. (Illus.). 120p. (Orig.). 1995. pap. 9.95 (*1-884540-10-4*) Haleys.

— On Duty Vol. 3: Interviews with Military Veterans from North of Quabbin. LC 95-78652. (Illus.). 220p. (Orig.). 1995. pap. 19.95 (*1-884540-14-7*) Haleys.

— On Duty, Multi-Volume: Interviews with Military Veterans from North of Quabbin. LC 94-78649. (Illus.). 112p. (Orig.). 1994. pap. 9.95 (*1-884540-08-2*) Haleys.

Bowers, Alfred W. Hidatsa Social & Ceremonial Organization. LC 92-15146. (Illus.). xiv, 528p. 1992. reprint ed. pap. 15.95 (*0-8032-6098-9*, Bison Books) U of Nebr Pr.

Bowers, Arden C. Clinical Manual of Health Assessment. 4th ed. (Illus.). 657p. (C). (gr. 13). 1991. pap. text 47.95 (*0-8016-0826-0*, 00826) Mosby Inc.

Bowers, B. & Symons, L., eds. Curiosity Prefectly Satisfyed: Faraday's Travels in Europe, 1813-1815. (History of Technology Ser.: No. 16). 170p. 1991. 42.00 (*0-86341-234-3*, HT016) INSPEC Inc.

Bowers, B., ed. see Poulter, J. D.

Bowers, Barbara. 1000 Years, 1000 People: The Men & Women Who Charted the Course of History for the Last Millennium. 1998. 25.00 (*1-56836-273-0*) Kodansha.

— What Color Is Your Aura? 1989. per. 14.00 (*0-671-70763-9*) PB.

Bowers, Barbara, et al. 1,000 Years, 1,000 People: Ranking the Men & Women Who Shaped the Millennium. LC 98-40381. 331p. 1998. pap. 17.00 (*1-56836-253-6*) Kodansha.

Bowers, Bob, jt. auth. see Moyer, Chris.

Bowers, Brent, jt. auth. see Geneen, Harold.

Bowers, Brian. Lengthening the Day: A History of Lighting Technology. (Illus.). 238p. 1998. 45.00 (*0-19-856548-8*) OUP.

***Bowers, Bryan G.** A Color Atlas of Plant Structure. (Illus.). 192p. 2000. pap. 49.95 (*0-8138-2693-4*) Iowa St U Pr.

Bowers, C. A. Critical Essays on Education, Modernity, & the Recovery of the Ecological Imperative. LC 93-18527. 240p. (C). 1993. text 45.00 (*0-8077-3245-1*); pap. text 18.95 (*0-8077-3244-3*) Tchrs Coll.

— The Culture of Denial: Why the Environmental Movement Needs a Strategy for Reforming Universities & Public Schools. LC 96-43769. (SUNY Series in Environmental Public Policy). 277p. (C). 1997. text 54.50 (*0-7914-3463-X*); pap. text 19.95 (*0-7914-3464-8*) State U NY Pr.

— Educating for an Ecologically Sustainable Culture: Rethinking Moral Education, Creativity, Intelligence, & Other Modern Orthodoxies. LC 94-22747. (SUNY Series in Environmental Public Policy). 233p. (C). 1995. pap. text 19.95 (*0-7914-2498-7*) State U NY Pr.

— Education, Cultural Myths, & the Ecological Crisis: Toward Deep Changes. LC 92-13356. 232p. 1992. pap. text 18.95 (*0-7914-1256-3*) State U NY Pr.

— Education, Cultural Myths, & the Ecological Crisis: Toward Deep Changes. LC 92-13356. (SUNY Series, The Philosophy of Education). 232p. (C). 1992. text 49.50 (*0-7914-1255-5*) State U NY Pr.

***Bowers, C. A.** Let Them Eat Data: How Computers Affect Education, Cultural Diversity & the Prospects of Ecological Sustainability. LC 00-26718. 2000. write for info. (*0-8203-2230-X*) U of Ga Pr.

Bowers, C. A. The Promise of Theory: Education & the Politics of Cultural Change. LC 86-23056. (John Dewey Lecture Ser.: No. 19). 128p. 1987. reprint ed. pap. 39.70 (*0-608-04167-X*, 206490100011) Bks Demand.

— The Promise of Theory: Education & the Politics of Cultural Change. 128p. (C). 1986. reprint ed. text 21.00 (*0-8077-2840-3*) Tchrs Coll.

Bowers, C. A. & Flinders, David J. Culturally Responsive Teaching & Supervision: A Handbook for Staff Development. 64p. (C). 1991. pap. text 9.95 (*0-8077-3078-5*) Tchrs Coll.

— Responsive Teaching: An Ecological Approach to Classroom Patterns of Language, Culture, & Thought. (Advances in Contemporary Educational Thought Ser.). 288p. (C). 1990. text 40.00 (*0-8077-2998-1*); pap. text 19.95 (*0-8077-2997-3*) Tchrs Coll.

An Asterisk (*) at the beginning of an entry indicates that the title is appearing for the first time.

Bowers, C. Michael. Forensic Digital Photography. (Illus.). Date not set. write for info. (*0-9677866-1-4*) Forensic Imaging Inst.

***Bowers, C. Michael & Johansen, Raymond.** Digital Analysis of Bitemark Evidence. (Illus.). vi, 110p. 2000. pap. 29.95 (*0-9677866-0-6*) Forensic Imaging Inst.

Bowers, Carla, jt. auth. see Grass, James.

Bowers, Carol, ed. see Brown, John F.

Bowers, Carol, ed. see Estes, Donald H.

Bowers, Carol, ed. see Rojas, John, Jr.

Bowers, Carolyn J., jt. auth. see Walle, Dennis F.

Bowers, Cathy S. The Love That Ended Yesterday in Texas. x, 86p. 1992. 16.50 (*0-89672-301-1*) Tex Tech Univ Pr.

Bowers, Charlotte, jt. auth. see Johnson, Connie.

Bowers, Claude G. Chile Through Embassy Windows, Nineteen Thirty-Nine to Nineteen Fifty-Three. LC 76-56739. 375p. 1977. reprint ed. lib. bdg. 69.50 (*0-8371-9435-0*, BOCH, Greenwood Pr) Greenwood.

— Jefferson & Hamilton. 1988. reprint ed. lib. bdg. 79.00 (*0-7812-0374-0*) Rprt Serv.

— Jefferson & Hamilton. LC 75-144890. (Illus.). 542p. 1972. reprint ed. 79.00 (*0-403-14489-2*) Scholarly.

— The Tragic Era: The Revolution after Lincoln. (History - United States Ser.). 567p. 1992. reprint ed. lib. bdg. 99.00 (*0-7812-6201-1*) Rprt Serv.

Bowers, Claude G. & Browder, Earl. The Heritage of Jefferson. Franklin, Francis, ed. LC 82-24251. 48p. 1983. reprint ed. lib. bdg. 55.00 (*0-313-23839-1*, BOHE, Greenwood Pr) Greenwood.

Bowers, Curt & Van Dyne, Glen. Forward Edge of the Battle Area: A Chaplain's Story. 2nd ed. (Illus.). 108p. 1987. pap. 7.99 (*0-8341-1220-5*) Beacon Hill.

Bowers, D. & Ruddy, J. United States Half Cents. LC 83-51003. (Illus.). 1984. pap. 10.00 (*0-317-27384-1*) S J Durst.

Bowers, D. F. Foreign Influences in American Life. (Illus.). 1990. 16.50 (*0-8446-1084-4*) Peter Smith.

Bowers, Dan M. Access Control & Personal Identification Systems. 2nd ed. 240p. 1999. 39.95 (*0-7506-9732-6*) Buttrwrth-Heinemann.

— Make Your Home into Your Castle: The Complete Do-It-Yourself Book of Home Security. LC 94-96523. 264p. 1994. 15.00 (*0-9643804-0-4*) D M Bowers.

Bowers, David. Coins & Collectors. (Illus.). 216p. 1988. reprint ed. pap. 10.00 (*0-943161-11-8*) S J Durst.

— Statistics from Scratch: An Introduction for Health Care Professionals. LC 95-49518. 192p. 1996. pap. 44.95 (*0-471-96325-9*) Wiley.

Bowers, David, jt. auth. see Bowers, Sharon.

Bowers, David A. Forecasting for Control & Profit: For Control & Profit. Christopher, Bill, ed. LC 97-65797. (Management Library). (Illus.). 90p. (Orig.). 1997. pap. 12.95 (*1-56052-433-2*) Crisp Pubns.

— An Introduction to Business Cycles & Forecasting. LC 84-16786. 432p. 1985. text 32.75 (*0-201-10163-7*) Addison-Wesley.

Bowers, David F., ed. Foreign Influences in American Life: Essays & Critical Bibliographies. LC 44-4627. 280p. reprint ed. pap. 86.80 (*0-8357-4672-0*, 203761800008) Bks Demand.

Bowers, David Q., jt. auth. see Leach, Frank A.

Bowers, David S. From Data to Database. 1969. pap. text. write for info. (*0-471-85294-5*) Wiley.

— From Data to Database. 2nd ed. LC 92-31148. (Aspects of Information Technology Ser.). 1992. write for info. (*0-442-31671-2*) Chapman & Hall.

Bowers, David S., ed. see British National Conference on Databases.

Bowers, Dawn, jt. ed. see Harrower, Molly.

Bowers, Deborah, jt. auth. see Daniels, Tom.

Bowers, Detine L. Theory & Practice Estranged. Hodges, Graham, ed. (Studies in African American History & Culture). 250p. 1996. text 50.00 (*0-8153-2002-7*) Garland.

Bowers, Detine L., ed. see Bowers, Mary L.

Bowers, Don. Back of the Pack: An Iditarod Musher's Alaska Pilgrimage to Nome. LC 98-65166. (Illus.). 396p. 1998. pap. text 17.95 (*1-888125-24-1*) Publ Consult.

Bowers, Don, ed. see Alaska Airmen's Assoc. Staff.

Bowers, Dorothy W. The Irwins & the Harrisons. 1973. 10.00 (*0-686-05443-1*, 73-88914) Irwinton.

Bowers, Dwight B., jt. auth. see Henderson, Amy.

Bowers, Edgar. Chaco Canyon. deluxe limited ed. 4p. (Orig.). 1988. pap. 15.00 (*0-936576-14-6*) Symposium Pr.

— Collected Poems. LC 96-38580. 192p. 1997. 25.00 (*0-679-45456-X*) Knopf.

— Collected Poems. 192p. 1999. pap. 15.00 (*0-679-76607-3*) Knopf.

— Living Together. 84p. 1988. 15.00 (*0-936576-12-X*); pap. 5.00 (*0-936576-13-8*) Symposium Pr.

— Witnesses. 22p. (Orig.). 1981. 20.00 (*0-936576-05-7*) Symposium Pr.

Bowers, Elisabeth. Ladies' Night. LC 88-19897. (International Women's Crime Ser.). 238p. (Orig.). 1988. pap. 8.95 (*0-931188-65-2*) Seal Pr WA.

Bowers, Elizabeth. The Inner Garden: Affirmative Haiku for Each Day of the Year. (Illus.). 60p. (Orig.). 1997. pap. 10.95 (*0-9644473-4-7*) Adept Pubng.

— Poetry Can Be Fun: A Child's Guide to Poetry Writing. (Illus.). 60p. (Orig.). (J). (gr. 3-6). 1997. pap. write for info. (*0-9644473-1-2*) Adept Pubng.

Bowers, Elizabeth, et al. Pieces of the Tapestry. LC 94-74245. 336p. 1994. pap. 21.95 (*0-9644473-0-4*) Adept Pubng.

Bowers, Faubion. Dance in India. LC 78-181075. (BCL Ser. I). reprint ed. 32.50 (*0-404-00963-8*) AMS Pr.

— Scriabin, a Biography. 2nd rev. ed. (Illus.). 656p. 1996. pap. text 16.95 (*0-486-28897-8*) Dover.

— Theatre in the East. LC 79-7753. (Dance Ser.). (Illus.). 1980. reprint ed. lib. bdg. 67.95 (*0-8369-9278-4*) Ayer.

Bowers, Faubion, ed. The Classic Tradition of Haiku: An Anthology. LC 96-13877. (Thrift Editions Ser.). 96p. (Orig.). 1996. pap. 1.50 (*0-486-29274-6*) Dover.

Bowers, Fergal. Hep C Niamh's Story LC 97-161153. 224p. 1997. write for info. (*1-86023-053-9*) Martello Bks.

— The Work: An Investigation into the History of Opus Dei. LC 89-50988. 176p. (Orig.). 1989. pap. 9.95 (*1-85371-037-7*, Pub. by Poolbeg Pr) Dufour.

Bowers-Fox. Sports Physiology. 4th ed. 2000. 42.40 (*0-697-23331-6*, WCB McGr Hill) McGrw-H Hghr Educ.

Bowers, Fredson. Essays in Bibliography, Text, & Editing. LC 74-18055. 558p. reprint ed. pap. 173.00 (*0-8357-7900-9*, 203632800002) Bks Demand.

— Principles of Bibliographical Description. LC 94-4383. 536p. 1995. pap. 29.95 (*1-884718-00-0*) Oak Knoll.

— Textual & Literary Criticism. (Sanders Lectures in Bibliography: 1957-58). 196p. reprint ed. pap. 55.90 (*0-608-12277-7*, 2024423) Bks Demand.

Bowers, Fredson, ed. Elizabethan Dramatists. (Dictionary of Literary Biography Ser.: Vol. 62). 336p. 1987. text 155.00 (*0-8103-1740-0*) Gale.

— Jacobean & Caroline Dramatists. (Dictionary of Literary Biography Ser.: Vol. 58). 400p. 1987. text 155.00 (*0-8103-1736-2*) Gale.

Bowers, Fredson, ed. The Red Badge of Courage: A Facsimile of the Manuscript. limited ed. 1972. boxed set 200.00 (*0-910971-28-5*) Bruccoli.

Bowers, Fredson, ed. see Crane, Stephen.

Bowers, Fredson, ed. see Dryden, John.

Bowers, Fredson, ed. see Fielding, Henry.

Bowers, Fredson, ed. see James, William.

Bowers, Fredson, ed. see Kroll, Leon.

Bowers, Fredson, ed. see Nabokov, Vladimir.

Bowers, Fredson, ed. see Studies in Bibliography Staff.

Bowers, Fredson, ed. see Turner, Robert K.

Bowers, Fredson, ed. see Whitman, Walt.

Bowers, G. M. The Faith & Doctrines of the Early Church. LC 78-60521. 1978. pap. 4.95 (*0-917182-09-X*) Triumph Pub.

***Bowers, George K.** Aside Lines to Keep You on Line. 484p. 2000. 29.95 (*0-7880-1473-0*, Fairway Pr) CSS OH.

Bowers, George K. Soren Kierkegaard: The Mystique of Prayer & Prayer. LC 94-29859. 144p. (Orig.). 1995. pap. 13.75 (*0-7880-0301-1*) CSS OH.

— Soren Kierkegaard; The Mystique of Prayer & Pray-er. 1997. pap. text 13.75 (*0-7880-0302-X*) CSS OH.

Bowers, Heidi H., ed. see Dunlop, James J.

Bowers, Irene & Weller, Linda. Bonjour, Mes Amis - Hello, My Friends, 2 cass., Set. (FRE & ENG., Illus.). 32p. (J). (ps-3). 1994. pap. 16.95 incl. audio (*0-8120-8150-1*) Barron.

Bowers, J. & Benford, S., eds. Studies in Computer Supported Cooperative Work: Theory, Practice & Design. (Human Factors in Information Technology Ser.: No. 8). 356p. 1991. 173.50 (*0-444-88811-X*, North Holland) Elsevier.

Bowers, J. K. & Cheshire, Paul C. Agriculture, the Countryside & Land Use: An Economic Critique. LC 83-13069. 192p. (C). 1983. pap. 25.99 (*0-416-31830-4*, NO. 3925) Routledge.

Bowers, J. Z., jt. ed. see Warren, K. S.

Bowers, Jack. Successful Investing with Fidelity Funds. 2nd rev. ed. LC 96-47767. 304p. 1996. per. 18.00 (*0-7615-0842-2*) Prima Pub.

***Bowers, Jack.** Successful Investing with Fidelity Funds. 3rd ed. LC 99-27983. 1999. pap. 18.00 (*0-7615-2100-3*) Prima Pub.

Bowers, Jack, ed. Successful Investing with Fidelity Funds. LC 94-34101. 1995. 22.95 (*1-55958-647-8*) Prima Pub.

Bowers, Jackie, jt. auth. see Haugen, Janie.

Bowers, Jacqueline H., tr. see Nahon, Marco.

Bowers, James. Reading Cormac McCarthy's Blood Meridian. (Western Writers Ser: Vol. 139). (C). pap. 5.95 (*0-88430-138-9*) Boise St U W Writ Ser.

Bowers, James A. A God Who Hates & Other Sermons. 114p. (Orig.). 1994. pap. 9.95 (*0-87921-086-9*) Attic Pr.

Bowers, James R. American Stories: Case Studies in Politics & Government. LC 92-17211. 343p. (C). 1992. pap. text 37.00 (*0-534-14502-7*) Harcourt.

— Pro-Choice & Anti-Abortion: Constitutional Theory & Public Policy. LC 93-14739. 152p. 1994. 57.95 (*0-275-94964-8*, Praeger Pubs) Greenwood.

— Pro-Choice & Anti-Abortion: Constitutional Theory & Public Policy. LC 93-14739. 160p. 1997. pap. 19.95 (*0-275-95964-3*, Praeger Pubs) Greenwood.

— Regulating the Regulators: An Introduction of the Legislative Oversight. LC 89-36697. 156p. 1990. 47.95 (*0-275-93354-7*, C3354, Praeger Pubs) Greenwood.

***Bowers, James R. & Rich, Wilbur C., eds.** Governing Middle-Sized Cities: Studies in Mayoral Leadership. LC 99-56088. 252p. 2000. 55.00 (*1-55587-895-4*); pap. 19.95 (*1-55587-870-9*) L Rienner.

Bowers, Jan. Flowers & Shrubs of the Mojave Desert. LC 98-46900. (Illus.). 192p. 1998. pap. 9.95 (*1-877856-79-7*) SW Pks Mnmts.

Bowers, Jane & Tick, Judith, eds. Women Making Music: The Western Art Tradition, 1150-1950. LC 85-8642. (Illus.). 424p. 1987. pap. text 16.95 (*0-252-01470-7*) U of Ill Pr.

Bowers, Jane, tr. see Devienne, Francois.

Bowers, Jane P. Gertrude Stein. LC 92-46267. (Women Writers Ser.). 144p. 1993. text 24.95 (*0-312-09533-3*) St Martin.

— They Watch Me As They Watch This: Gertrude Stein's Metadrama. LC 91-9165. 160p. (C). 1991. text 27.50 (*0-8122-3057-4*) U of Pa Pr.

Bowers, Janice E. Chiricahua National Monument. Priehs, T. J. & Dodson, Carolyn, eds. LC 88-62022. (Illus.). 64p. (Orig.). 1988. pap. 6.95 (*0-911408-79-7*) SW Pks Mnmts.

— Fear Falls Away: And Other Essays from Hard & Rocky Places. LC 97-4659. 175p. 1997. 35.00 (*0-8165-1717-7*) U of Ariz Pr.

— A Full Life in a Small Place: And Other Essays from a Desert Garden. LC 92-30727. 168p. (Orig.). 1993. pap. 15.95 (*0-8165-1357-0*) U of Ariz Pr.

— The Mountains Next Door. LC 91-11824. (Illus.). 147p. 1991. 15.95 (*0-8165-1243-4*) U of Ariz Pr.

— One Hundred Desert Wildflowers of the Southwest. Priehs, T. J., ed. LC 88-63877. (Illus.). 64p. (Orig.). 1987. pap. 7.95 (*0-911408-72-X*) SW Pks Mnmts.

— One Hundred Roadside Wildflowers of the Southwest Woodlands. Priehs, T. J., ed. LC 87-60531. (Illus.). 64p. (Orig.). 1989. pap. 7.95 (*0-911408-73-8*) SW Pks Mnmts.

— A Sense of Place: The Life & Work of Forrest Shreve. LC 88-14014. 195p. 1988. 23.50 (*0-8165-1072-5*) U of Ariz Pr.

— Shrubs & Trees of the Southwest Deserts. Foreman, Ronald J. & Priehs, T. J., eds. LC 93-84560. (Illus.). 120p. (Orig.). 1993. pap. 9.95 (*1-877856-34-7*) SW Pks Mnmts.

***Bowers, Jean M. & Perl, Raphael.** Terrorism: A Bibliography & Federal Policies & Practices. (Illus.). 44p. (C). 1999. reprint ed. pap. text 20.00 (*0-7881-8174-2*) DIANE Pub.

Bowers, John. Bowers on Employment Law. 3rd ed. 440p. 1990. pap. 58.00 (*1-85431-043-7*, Pub. by Blackstone Pr) Gaunt.

— Bowers on Employment Law. 4th ed. 533p. 1997. pap. 64.00 (*1-85431-289-8*, Pub. by Blackstone Pr) Gaunt.

***Bowers, John.** Bowers on Employment Law. 5th ed. 565p. 2000. pap. 63.00 (*1-85431-945-0*, Pub. by Blackstone Pr) Gaunt.

Bowers, John. Chickamauga & Chattanooga: The Battles That Doomed the Confederacy. (Illus.). 288p. 2000. reprint ed. pap. 13.00 (*0-380-72509-6*) Morrow Avon.

— In the Land of Nyx. 180p. 1985. pap. 7.95 (*0-88184-163-3*) Carroll & Graf.

— Introduction to Two-Dimensional Design: Understanding Form & Function. LC 98-29590. (Illus.). 128p. 1999. pap. 34.95 (*0-471-29224-9*) Wiley.

***Bowers, John.** Matrices & Quadratic Forms. (Modular Mathematics Series). 280p. 2000. pap. text 19.95 (*0-340-69138-7*) E A.

Bowers, John. Stonewall Jackson: Portrait of a Soldier. 368p. 1990. reprint ed. pap. 12.00 (*0-380-71164-8*, Avon Bks) Morrow Avon.

— Sustainabil & Enviro Econ. (C). 1998. pap. text 65.63 (*0-582-27656-X*, Pub. by Addison-Wesley) Longman.

***Bowers, John.** Tennessee River Country: A Glovebox Guide to TVA Places for Family Fun. unabridged ed. LC 99-71429. (Illus.). 120p. 1999. pap. 10.00 (*0-87077-008-X*) TVA.

Bowers, John. Termination of Employment. 3rd ed. (Practice Notes Ser.). 99p. 1995. pap. 32.00 (*0-7520-0080-2*, Pub. by Cavendish Pubng) Gaunt.

Bowers, John & Auerbach, Simon. The Employment Act, 1988. 188p. (C). 1988. 130.00 (*1-85431-024-0*, Pub. by Blackstone Pr) St Mut.

Bowers, John & Gatt, Ian. Procedure in Courts & Tribunals. (Practice Notes Ser.). 105p. 1990. pap. write for info. (*0-85121-526-2*, Pub. by Cavendish Pubng) Gaunt.

Bowers, John & Honeyball, Simon. Labour Law. 4th ed. 442p. 1996. pap. 42.00 (*1-85431-446-7*, Pub. by Blackstone Pr) Gaunt.

— Textbook on Labour Law. 3rd ed. 476p. 1993. pap. 40.00 (*1-85431-302-9*, Pub. by Blackstone Pr) Gaunt.

— Textbook on Labour Law. 5th ed. 450p. 1998. pap. 42.00 (*1-85431-753-9*) Gaunt.

Bowers, John & Woodward, V. The Anatomy of Regional Activity Rates, No. 1. (Economic & Social Research Ser.). 1971. pap. 15.95 (*0-521-07719-2*) Cambridge U Pr.

Bowers, John, et al. The Rhetoric of Agitation & Control. 2nd ed. (Illus.). 159p. (C). 1993. pap. text 14.95 (*0-88133-712-9*) Waveland Pr.

Bowers, John, jt. ed. see Nuss, Martin.

Bowers, John D. Save Thousands When You Buy or Sell Your Home. 132p. (Orig.). (C). 1974. pap. 8.95 (*0-685-02679-5*) J D Bowers.

Bowers, John M. The Crisis of Will in Piers Plowman. LC 85-25498. 265p. reprint ed. pap. 82.20 (*0-7837-4632-6*, 204435600002) Bks Demand.

***Bowers, John M.** The Politics of Pearl: Court Poetry in the Age of Richard II. LC 00-39842. 2001. write for info. (*0-85991-599-9*, DS Brewer) Boydell & Brewer.

Bowers, John M., ed. see Chaucer, Geoffrey.

Bowers, John S. The Theory of Grammatical Relations. LC 80-21018. (Illus.). 288p. reprint ed. pap. 89.30 (*0-608-08082-9*, 206904100002) Bks Demand.

Bowers, John Z. Western Medical Pioneers in Feudal Japan. LC 73-86098. (Josiah Macy Foundation Ser.). 256p. 1970. 45.00 (*0-8018-1081-7*) Johns Hopkins.

— When the Twain Meet: The Rise of Western Medicine in Japan. LC 80-22356. (Henry E. Sigerist Supplements to the Bulletin of the History of Medicine Ser.: No. 5). 187p. 1980. reprint ed. pap. 58.00 (*0-608-03642-0*, 206446800009) Bks Demand.

Bowers, John Z., et al, eds. Science & Medicine in Twentieth-Century China: Research & Education. LC 88-36952. (Science, Medicine, & Technology in East Asia Ser.: No. 3). 283p. 1989. text 50.00 (*0-89264-077-4*); pap. text 25.00 (*0-89264-076-2*) Ctr Chinese Studies.

Bowers, John Z. & Purcell, Elizabeth F., eds. Advances in American Medicine: Essays at the Bicentennial, Vol. 1. LC 76-3162. 467p. 1976. reprint ed. 144.80 (*0-8357-5138-4*, 202669200001) Bks Demand.

— Advances in American Medicine: Essays at the Bicentennial, Vols. 1 & 2. LC 76-3162. 467p. reprint ed. pap. 144.80 (*0-608-18519-1*, 202669200002) Bks Demand.

Bowers, Joyce, ed. see Paradis, Noni.

Bowers, Judy K., jt. ed. see Small, Ann R.

Bowers, K. L. & Lund, J., eds. Computation & Control IV: Proceedings of the Fourth Bozeman Conference, Bozeman, Montana, August 3-9, 1994. (Progress in Systems & Control Theory Ser.: Vol. 20). (Illus.). 356p. 1995. 108.00 (*0-8176-3774-5*) Birkhauser.

Bowers, Kenneth. Hypnosis for the Seriously Curious. (C). 1983. pap. text 21.95 (*0-393-95339-4*) Norton.

Bowers, Kenneth, jt. auth. see Lund, John.

Bowers, Kenneth L. & Lund, John. Computation & Control: Proceedings of a Conference Held in Bozeman, Montana, Aug. 1988. (Progress in Systems & Control Theory Ser.: No. 1). 400p. 1989. 84.00 (*0-8176-3438-X*) Birkhauser.

— Computation & Control III: Proceedings of the Third Bozeman Conference, Bozeman, Montana, August 5-11, 1992. LC 93-14021. (Progress in Systems & Control Theory Ser.: Vol. 15). (Illus.). 407p. 1993. 115.00 (*0-8176-3656-0*) Birkhauser.

Bowers, Kenneth L. & Lund, John, eds. Computation & Control II: Proceedings of the Conference at Bozeman, Montana, 2nd, Summer, 1990. (Progress in Systems & Control Theory Ser.: Vol. 11). xi, 369p. 1991. 100.50 (*0-8176-3611-0*) Birkhauser.

Bowers, Keri. Single Pregnancy - Single Parenting: Creating a Positive, Fulfilling Experience. LC 96-92334. (Illus.). 310p. (Orig.). 1996. pap. 12.95 (*0-9652441-0-5*) Park Alxndr.

Bowers, Len. The Social Nature of Mental Illness. LC 97-42740. 232p. (C). 1998. 85.00 (*0-415-17002-8*) Routledge.

***Bowers, Linda J., et al.** Cognitive Retraining for Everyday Problem Solving. 180p. 1999. spiral bd. 37.95 (*0-7606-0309-X*) LinguiSystems.

Bowers, Linda J., et al. The Listening Test: Complete Set. (J). 1992. spiral bd. 89.95 (*1-55999-240-9*) LinguiSystems.

— The Listening Test: Examiner's Manual. 1992. spiral bd. 66.00 (*1-55999-241-7*) LinguiSystems.

— The TOPS - Adolescent (Tasks of Problem Solving) A Real-Life Approach to Thinking & Reasoning. 192p. 1992. spiral bd. 39.95 (*1-55999-234-4*) LinguiSystems.

— The TOPS - Elementary (Tasks of Problem Solving) A Program to Build Thinking & Reasoning Skills. 209p. (J). (gr. k-6). 1990. spiral bd. 44.95 (*1-55999-117-8*) LinguiSystems.

Bowers, Linda J., jt. auth. see Mootz, Robert D.

Bowers, Louis, jt. ed. see Thompson, Donna.

Bowers, Malcolm B., Jr. A Psychiatrist Recollects: Stories from the Lives of Psychiatric Patients. LC 88-2791. (Insight Book Ser.). 150p. 1989. 21.95 (*0-89885-433-4*, Kluwer Acad Hman Sci) Kluwer Academic.

Bowers, Marcia & Williams, Karen. The JCAHO Home Health Mock Survey Made Simple. LC 99-203976. (Illus.). 150p. 1998. pap. text 67.00 (*1-57839-026-5*) Opus Communs.

Bowers, Maria, jt. auth. see Brofka, Maria A.

Bowers, Marissa, ed. see Frye, Joyce C.

***Bowers, Marjorie Foster.** Waiting for Daddy, 1943-1945. (Illus.). 123p. 1999. pap. 16.50 (*0-9643859-1-0*) True Story.

Bowers, Mary B. & Thompson, William H., III, eds. Enjoying Hummingbirds More: A Special Publication from Bird Watcher's Digest. (Illus.). 32p. (Orig.). 1995. pap. write for info. (*1-880241-01-3*) Bird Watchers.

Bowers, Mary B., ed. see Blom, Eirik A. T.

Bowers, Mary B., ed. see Glassberg, Jeffrey.

Bowers, Mary B., ed. see Shalaway, Scott & Thompson, William, III.

Bowers, Mary B., ed. see Thompson, Bill.

Bowers, Mary B., ed. see Wolinski, Richard A. & Thompson, William H., III.

Bowers, Mary B., ed. see Zickefoose, Julie.

Bowers, Mary L. A Farm Melody: The Wisdom of Mumma. large type ed. Bowers, Detine L., ed. (Illus.). vii, 19p. (Orig.). 1910. pap. 7.95 (*1-889551-00-7*) Harmony Blssngs.

Bowers, Melvyn K. Easy Bulletin Boards, Vol. 2. LC 73-21798. 209p. reprint ed. pap. 64.80 (*0-608-15225-0*, 202749000055) Bks Demand.

Bowers, Michael, ed. Painting in Oils. (Illus.). 128p. pap. 22.50 (*0-85532-703-0*, 703-0, Pub. by Srch Pr) A Schwartz & Co.

Bowers, Michael W. The Nevada State Constitution: A Reference Guide, 18. LC 93-20347. (Reference Guides to the State Constitutions of the United States Ser.: No. 18). 216p. 1993. lib. bdg. 75.00 (*0-313-27977-2*, BNV) Greenwood.

— The Sagebrush State: Nevada's History, Government, & Politics. LC 96-15678. (Wilbur S. Shepperson Series in History & Humanities: No. 38). 1996. pap. text 14.95 (*0-87417-249-7*) U of Nev Pr.

***Bowers, Michelle & Steinfeld Galett, Melissa.** How We Met: Real-Life Tales of How Happily Married Couples Found Each Other. LC 99-58573. (Illus.). 128p. 2000. pap. 11.95 (*0-312-24303-0*) St Martin.

Bowers, Mildred. Twist O' Smoke. LC 77-144731. (Yale Series of Younger Poets: No. 24). reprint ed. 37.50 (*0-404-53824-X*) AMS Pr.

Bowers, Mollie H. & DeCenzo, David A. Essentials of Labor Relations. 192p. (C). 1992. pap. text 22.80 (*0-13-282690-9*, 140702) P-H.

B

Bowers Museum of Cultural Art Staff. African Icons of Power: An Illustrated Curriculum Guide. Walsh, Daniella B., ed. 84p. 1994. pap. text. write for info. (*0-9633959-2-0*) Bowers Mus.

Bowers, Nancy B. Brown Munro, Sr. (1829-1909) A Life in Time. (Illus.). 368p. 1994. pap. text. write for info. (*0-9635812-3-6*) Sigler Print.

Bowers, Neal. James Dickey: The Poet as Pitchman. LC 84-21956. (Literary Frontiers Ser.). 96p. 1985. pap. 9.95 (*0-8262-0459-7*) U of Mo Pr.

***Bowers, Neal.** Loose Ends: A Novel. LC 00-34166. 2001. write for info. (*0-375-50499-0*) Random.

Bowers, Neal. Night Vision. LC 92-6036. 1993. pap. 8.00 (*0-933532-94-6*) BkMk.

— Theodore Roethke: The Journey from I to Otherwise. LC 81-10410. 240p. 1982. text 29.95 (*0-8262-0347-7*) U of Mo Pr.

Bowers, Norman A. Hidatsa Suprasegmentals: A Phonological Study of Hidatsa, an American Indian Language. 288p. 1996. text 99.95 (*0-89301-191-6*) U of Idaho Pr.

Bowers, P. Managerial Economics for the Service Industries. 336p. 1994. mass mkt. 34.95 (*0-412-57790-9*) Chapman & Hall.

Bowers, Patricia, jt. ed. see Rhoton, Jack.

Bowers, Peter. Boeing B-29 Superfortress, Vol. 14. (Warbird Tech Ser.). 1999. pap. text 16.95 (*0-933424-79-5*) Specialty Pr.

Bowers, Peter M. Boeing Aircraft since Nineteen Sixteen. 2nd ed. (Putnam Aviation Ser.). (Illus.). 560p. 1989. 55.00 (*0-87021-037-8*) Naval Inst Pr.

— A Complete Guide to Aviation Photography. 2nd ed. (Illus.). 240p. 1988. pap. 16.95 (*0-8306-0924-5*, 2424) McGraw-Hill Prof.

— Curtiss Navy Hawks in Action. LC 96-111051. (Aircraft in Action Ser.). (Illus.). 50p. 1995. pap. 9.95 (*0-89747-342-6*) Squad Sig Pubns.

— Guide to Homebuilts. 8th ed. (Illus.). 208p. 1982. pap. 7.95 (*0-8306-2314-0*, 2314) McGraw-Hill Prof.

— Scale Aircraft Drawings Vol. 2: World War II, Vol. II. (Illus.). 151p. 1991. 17.95 (*0-911295-14-3*, Pub. by Air Age) Motorbooks Intl.

— Unconventional Aircraft. (Illus.). 288p. (Orig.). 1984. pap. 17.95 (*0-8306-2384-1*, 2384) McGraw-Hill Prof.

— Wings of Stearman: The Story of Lloyd Stearman & the Classic Stearman Biplanes. LC 98-40944. 1998. 39.95 (*0-911139-28-1*) Flying Bks.

Bowers, Peter M., jt. auth. see Stringfellow, Curtis K.

Bowers, Peter M., jt. auth. see Swanborough, Gordon.

Bowers, Q. David. American Coin Treasures & Hoards. Hodder, Michael, ed. (Illus.). 456p. 1997. 59.95 (*0-943161-69-X*) Bowers & Merena.

— The American Numismatic Association Centennial History, 2 vols., Vols. I-II. (Illus.). 1991. text 159.00 (*0-943161-29-0*); write for info. (*0-943161-30-4*); write for info. (*0-943161-31-2*) Bowers & Merena.

— American Numismatics Before the Civil War, 1760-1860: Emphasizing the Story of Augustus B. Sage. (Illus.). 432p. 1998. 89.95 (*0-943161-75-4*) Bowers & Merena.

— A Buyer's & Enthusiast's Guide to Flying Eagle & Indian Cents. (Illus.). 544p. (Orig.). 1996. pap. 45.00 (*0-943161-68-1*) Bowers & Merena.

— A Buyers' Guide to Silver Dollars & Trade Dollars of the United States. (Illus.). 312p. 1996. pap. 19.95 (*0-943161-66-5*) Bowers & Merena.

— A Buyer's Guide to Silver Dollars & Trade Dollars of the United States. 2nd rev. ed. (Illus.). 304p. 1997. pap. 19.95 (*0-943161-70-3*) Bowers & Merena.

— A Buyer's Guide to the Rare Coin Market. 372p. (Orig.). 1990. pap. text 14.95 (*0-943161-26-6*) Bowers & Merena.

— A Buyer's Guide to the Rare Coin Market. 2nd ed. (Illus.). 372p. (Orig.). 1992. pap. text 19.95 (*0-943161-47-9*) Bowers & Merena.

— Buyer's Guide to United States Gold Coins. (Illus.). 122p. (Orig.). 1989. text 19.95 (*0-943161-22-3*); pap. text 12.95 (*0-943161-17-7*) Bowers & Merena.

— Commemorative Coins of the United States: A Complete Encyclopedia. (Illus.). 768p. 1991. 75.00 (*0-943161-36-3*); text 49.95 (*0-943161-35-5*); pap. text 39.95 (*0-943161-34-7*) Bowers & Merena.

— Encyclopedia of Automatic Musical Instruments. LC 78-187497. (Illus.). 1008p. 1972. 89.95 (*0-911572-08-2*, Vestal Pr) Madison Bks UPA.

— High Profits from Rare Coin Investment. 13th ed. (Illus.). 440p. 1991. pap. text 19.95 (*0-943161-38-X*) Bowers & Merena.

— History of Wolfeboro, NH 1770-1994, 3 vols., Set. (Illus.). 1996. text 125.00 (*0-614-14034-X*) Bowers & Merena.

— History of Wolfeboro, NH 1770-1994, Vol. I. (Illus.). 628p. 1996. text. write for info. (*0-943161-61-4*) Bowers & Merena.

— History of Wolfeboro, NH 1770-1994, Vol. II. (Illus.). 600p. 1996. text. write for info. (*0-943161-62-2*) Bowers & Merena.

— History of Wolfeboro, NH 1770-1994, Vol. III. (Illus.). 592p. 1996. text. write for info. (*0-943161-63-0*) Bowers & Merena.

— How to Be a Successful Coin Dealer. (Illus.). 184p. (Orig.). 1988. pap. text 14.95 (*0-943161-05-3*) Bowers & Merena.

— Louis E. Eliasberg Sr., King of Coins. (Illus.). 176p. 1996. text 62.50 (*0-943161-64-9*) Bowers & Merena.

— The Moxie Encyclopedia, Vol. 1. LC 85-5325. (Illus.). 760p. 1999. pap. 19.95 (*0-911572-43-0*, Vestal Pr) Madison Bks UPA.

— Muriel Ostriche: Princess of Silent Films. LC 87-1981. (Illus.). 240p. 1987. 24.95 (*0-911572-63-5*, Vestal Pr); pap. 19.95 (*0-911572-64-3*, Vestal Pr) Madison Bks UPA.

— Nickelodeon Theatres & Their Music. LC 86-5594. (Illus.). 212p. 1986. 24.95 (*0-911572-49-X*, Vestal Pr); pap. 14.95 (*0-911572-50-3*, Vestal Pr) Madison Bks UPA.

***Bowers, Q. David.** The Rare Silver Dollars Dated 1804: And the Exciting Adventures of Edmund Roberts. LC 99-85876. (Illus.). 492p. 2000. 69.95 (*0-943161-82-7*, BBM-407) Bowers & Merena.

Bowers, Q. David. A Review of the Commemorative Coin Market. (Bowers & Merena Galleries' Little Editions Ser.). (Illus.). 32p. 1997. pap. 5.95 (*0-943161-74-6*) Bowers & Merena.

— Silver Dollars & Trade Dollars of the United States, Vols. 1-2: A Complete Encyclopedia. (Illus.). 2192p. 1993. 195.00 (*0-943161-50-9*) Bowers & Merena.

— Silver Dollars & Trade Dollars of the United States, Vols. 1-2: A Complete Encyclopedia, Set. (Illus.). 2192p. 1993. text 149.00 (*0-943161-48-7*); pap. text 99.00 (*0-943161-49-5*) Bowers & Merena.

***Bowers, Q. David.** Thanhouser Films: An Encyclopedia & History. 1998. 139.95 (*0-8108-3455-3*) Scarecrow.

Bowers, Q. David. Thanhouser Films, 1909-1917: An Illustrated History. (Illus.). 288p. 1999. 49.95 (*1-887322-01-9*) Emprise NY.

— The Treasure Ship S. S. Brother Jonathan: Her Life & Loss, 1850-1865. (Illus.). 416p. 1999. 69.95 (*0-943161-81-9*) Bowers & Merena.

— United States Coins by Design Types: An Action Guide for the Collector & Investor. rev. ed. (Illus.). 248p. 1988. reprint ed. pap. 9.95 (*0-943161-13-4*) Bowers & Merena.

— The Waterford Water Cure: A Numismatic Inquiry. (Illus.). 224p. 1992. text 49.95 (*0-943161-45-2*) Bowers & Merena.

— Woodward's Sale of the John F. McCoy Collection. (Bowers & Merena Galleries' Little Editions Ser.). (Illus.). 32p. 1997. pap. 5.95 (*0-943161-71-1*) Bowers & Merena.

Bowers, Q. David, ed. The Coin Dealer Newsletter: A Study in Rare Coin Price Performance, 1963-1988. 528p. (Orig.). 1988. pap. 34.95 (*0-943161-15-0*) Bowers & Merena.

— The Numismatist's Countryside Companion, Vol. V. 192p. 1994. pap. text 12.95 (*0-943161-51-7*) Bowers & Merena.

— The Numismatist's Downtown Companion, Vol. VII. 192p. 1994. pap. text 12.95 (*0-943161-53-3*) Bowers & Merena.

— The Numismatist's Fireside Companion, Vol. 2. 224p. (Orig.). 1988. pap. text 9.95 (*0-943161-10-X*) Bowers & Merena.

— The Numismatist's Lakeside Companion. 224p. (Orig.). 1990. pap. text 9.95 (*0-943161-25-8*) Bowers & Merena.

— The Numismatist's Topside Companion, Vol. VIII. 192p. 1994. pap. text 12.95 (*0-943161-54-1*) Bowers & Merena.

— The Numismatist's Traveling Companion, Vol. 6. 192p. 1994. pap. text 12.95 (*0-943161-52-5*) Bowers & Merena.

— The Numismatist's Weekend Companion, Vol. IV. 224p. (Orig.). 1992. pap. text 9.95 (*0-943161-41-X*) Bowers & Merena.

Bowers, Q. David, intro. Collecting Coins & Making Money: A Peek into the 19th Century. (Illus.). 192p. 1996. pap. 29.95 (*0-943161-65-7*) Bowers & Merena.

— United States Three-Cent & Five-Cent Pieces: An Action Guide for the Collector & Investor. (Illus.). 168p. 1988. reprint ed. pap. text 9.95 (*0-943161-06-1*, BBM-303) Bowers & Merena.

Bowers, Q. David, et al. The Numismatist's Bedside Companion, Vol. I. (Illus.). 224p. (Orig.). 1988. pap. 9.95 (*0-943161-02-9*) Bowers & Merena.

Bowers, Q. David, jt. auth. see Hodder, Michael.

Bowers, Q. David, jt. auth. see Hodder, Michael J.

Bowers, Q. David, ed. see Drummond, A. L.

Bowers, Q. David, ed. see Orosz, Joel J.

Bowers, R. G., et al. Talking About Grammar. (YA). (gr. 9-12). 1987. pap. text 13.95 (*0-582-55899-9*, 78323) Longman.

Bowers, Raymond. Communications for Mobile Society: An Assessment of New Technology. Lee, Alfred M., ed. LC 77-28119. 432p. reprint ed. pap. 134.00 (*0-608-10802-2*, 202187300026) Bks Demand.

Bowers, Richard & Deeming, Terry. Astrophysics, Vol. 1: Stars. (Illus.). 343p. (C). 1984. pap. 50.00 (*0-86720-018-9*) Jones & Bartlett.

— Astrophysics, Vol. 2: Interstellar Matter & Galaxies. (Illus.). 288p. (C). 1984. pap. 50.00 (*0-86720-047-2*) Jones & Bartlett.

Bowers, Richard & Fox, Edward L. Sports Physiology. 3rd ed. 464p. (C). 1992. text. write for info. (*0-697-13008-8*) Brown & Benchmark.

— Sports Physiology. 3rd ed. 464p. (C). 1992. text. write for info. (*0-697-20864-8*) Brown & Benchmark.

Bowers, Richard A. Optical-Electronic Publishing Directory. 110p. 1986. pap. 30.00 (*0-937665-00-2*) Info Arts.

Bowers, Richard L. Numerical Modeling in Applied Physics & Astrophysics. 512p. 1991. 75.00 (*0-86720-123-1*) Jones & Bartlett.

Bowers, Richard W. & Fox, Edward L. Sports Physiology. 5th ed. 2002. pap. text 33.00 (*0-697-29501-X*) McGraw.

Bowers, Rick, ed. Thomas Phaer & the Boke of Chyldren, 1544. LC 98-53175. (Medieval & Renaissance Texts & Studies: Vol. 201). 112p. 1999. 22.00 (*0-86698-243-4*, MR201) MRTS.

Bowers, Robert G. & Brewer, James F. Cabooses of the Norfolk & Western. Hughes, Laura S., ed. LC 94-65928. (Illus.). 248p. 1994. text 49.95 (*0-9633254-1-8*) Norfolk & Wstrn HS.

Bowers, Robert G. & Withers, Paul K. Norfolk Southern, 1982-1994, Motive Power Review. LC 94-62162. 1995. 38.95 (*1-881411-04-4*) Withers Pub.

Bowers, Robert G., jt. auth. see Withers, Paul K.

Bowers, Robert H., ed. Three Middle English Religious Poems. LC 63-63267. (University of Florida Humanities Monographs: No. 12). 72p. reprint ed. pap. 30.00 (*0-7837-5017-X*, 204468400004) Bks Demand.

Bowers, Roger. English Church Polyphony: Singers & Sources from the 14th to the 17th Century. LC 98-52422. (Variorum Collected Studies Ser.). 9p. 1999. text 97.95 (*0-86078-778-8*) Ashgate Pub Co.

Bowers, Roy A., jt. auth. see Cowen, David L.

Bowers, Russell H. Someone or Nothing? Vol. 27: Nishitani's Religion & Nothingness As a Foundation for Christian-Buddhist Dialogue. (Asian Thought & Culture Ser.). 264p. (C). 1995. text 49.95 (*0-8204-2832-9*) P Lang Pubng.

Bowers, Ruth, jt. auth. see Short, Anita.

Bowers, S., ed. see Swords, S. S.

***Bowers, Sharon.** Lucifer Rising. 352p. 2000. pap. 16.99 (*0-9677687-2-1*, Pub. by Justice Hse) BkMstrs TX.

Bowers, Sharon & Bowers, David. Bake It Like a Man: Playing with Fire, Bottling Your Own Brew, Cooking for a Crowd, Fueling Chile Fever, & Deep-Frying Your Way to Culinary Prowess. LC 98-49127. (Illus.). 304p. 1999. pap. 16.00 (*0-688-15580-4*, Wm Morrow) Morrow Avon.

Bowers, Stephen R. & Neterowicz, Eva M. Tibet: Endurance of the National Ideal. (Journal of Social, Political & Economic Studies: No. 23). 1995. pap. text 15.00 (*0-930690-52-4*) Coun Soc Econ.

Bowers, Susan R., jt. auth. see Dotterer, Ronald.

Bowers, Susan R., jt. ed. see Dotterer, Ronald.

Bowers, T. S., et al. Equilibrium Activity Diagrams. xli, 398p. 1987. 135.95 (*0-387-13796-3*) Spr-Verlag.

Bowers, Terrell L. Crossfire at Broken Spoke. LC 98-96075. (Broken Spoke Western Ser.: Bk. 3). 192p. 1998. 18.95 (*0-8034-9301-0*, Avalon Bks) Bouregy.

— Destiny at Broken Spoke. LC 98-96340. 192p. 1998. lib. bdg. 18.95 (*0-8034-9321-5*, Avalon Bks) Bouregy.

— Feud at Broken Spoke. LC 97-94022. (Broken Spoke Western Ser.: Bk. 1). 192p. 1997. 18.95 (*0-8034-9260-X*, Avalon Bks) Bouregy.

— Gun Law at Broken Spoke. LC 97-97119. (Broken Spoke Western Ser.: Bk. 2). 192p. 1998. lib. bdg. 18.95 (*0-8034-9280-4*, Avalon Bks) Bouregy.

— Noose at Sundown. LC 96-95480. 192p. 1997. 18.95 (*0-8034-9231-6*, Avalon Bks) Bouregy.

— Ride Against the Wind. LC 96-18656. 200p. 1996. 21.95 (*0-8027-4156-8*) Walker & Co.

— Ride Against the Wind. large type ed. Date not set. 30.00 (*0-7838-0433-4*, G K Hall Lrg Type) Mac Lib Ref.

— Ride Against the Wind. large type ed. LC 97-332. (Western Ser.). 288p. 1997. 20.95 (*0-7862-1076-1*) Thorndike Pr.

Bowers, Terrell L. The Secret of Snake Canyon. LC 93-9756. 168p. 1993. 19.95 (*0-8027-1264-9*) Walker & Co.

Bowers, Thomas, et al. Law of Commercial Transactions & Business Associations: Concepts & Cases. LC 94-38814. (Legal Studies in Business). 976p. (C). 1994. text 64.50 (*0-256-17864-X*, Irwn McGrw-H) McGrw-H Hghr Educ.

Bowers, Thomas A., jt. auth. see Fletcher, Alan D.

Bowers, Tim. Drawing: Face to Face with Tim Bowers. (Illus.). 24p. (J). (gr. 1-6). 1994. pap. write for info. (*0-9641192-0-X*) Bowers Studio.

Bowers, Tim, jt. illus. see Rylant, Cynthia.

Bowers, Toni. The Politics of Motherhood: British Writing & Culture, 1680-1760. LC 96-227991. (Illus.). 278p. (C). 1996. text 59.95 (*0-521-55174-9*) Cambridge U Pr.

Bowers, Tony. Managing Special Needs. 192p. 1990. 113.00 (*0-335-09257-8*) OpUniv Pr.

Bowers, Tony, ed. Special Educational Needs & Human Resource Management. 192p. 1987. pap. text 19.95 (*0-7099-5014-4*, Pub. by C Helm) Routldge.

Bowers, Tressa. Alandra's Lilacs: The Story of a Mother & Her Deaf Daughter. LC 99-23063. (Illus.). 132p. 1999. pap. 13.95 (*1-56368-082-3*) Gallaudet Univ Pr.

***Bowers, V.** British Columbia. (Hello Canada Ser.). 1999. pap. 7.95 (*1-55041-274-4*) Fitzhenry & W Ltd.

Bowers, Vivien. British Columbia. LC 94-25539. (Hello Canada Ser.). (Illus.). 76p. (J). (gr. 4-7). 1995. lib. bdg. 19.93 (*0-8225-2755-3*, Lerner Publctns) Lerner Pub.

— Crime Science: How Investigators Use Science to Track down the Bad Guys. LC 96-932529. (Illus.). 64p. (YA). (gr. 4 up). 1997. 19.95 (*1-895688-68-X*, Pub. by Owl Bks); pap. 10.95 (*1-895688-69-8*, Pub. by Owl Bks) Firefly Bks Ltd.

— Crime Science: How Investigators Use Science to Track down the Bad Guys. (J). 1997. 16.15 (*0-606-12665-1*, Pub. by Turtleback) Demco.

— Wow, Canada! Exploring This Land from Coast to Coast to Coast. (Illus.). 160p. (J). (gr. 4-7). 1999. 29.95 (*1-895688-93-0*, Pub. by Owl Bks) Firefly Bks Ltd.

Bowers, Vivien & Hobbs, Daniel C. Wow, Canada! Exploring the Land from Coast to Coast to Coast. (Illus.). 160p. (J). (gr. 3-7). 1999. pap. 19.95 (*1-895688-94-9*, Pub. by Owl Bks) Firefly Bks Ltd.

Bowers, W., et al. Engineering Applications in Agriculture. 1986. spiral bd. 19.80 (*0-87563-281-5*) Stipes.

Bowers, W. S., ed. see Naumann, K.

Bowers, Wendell. Machinery Replacement Strategies. Reynolds, Ralph & Holmes, Robert G., eds. (Farm Business Management Ser.). (Illus.). 104p. (C). 1994. pap. text 39.95 incl. disk (*0-86691-233-9*, FBM13101NC) Deere & Co.

— Machinery Replacement Strategies. Reynolds, Ralph & Holmes, Robert G., eds. (Farm Business Management Ser.). 90p. (C). 1994. teacher ed. 33.95 incl. trans. (*0-86691-213-4*, FBM13501T) Deere & Co.

— Machinery Replacement Strategies. Reynolds, Ralph & Holmes, Robert G., eds. (Farm Business Management Ser.). (Illus.). 42p. 1994. student ed. 21.95 (*0-86691-214-2*, FBM13601W) Deere & Co.

Bowers, William H., ed. The Interphalangeal Joints. (Hand & Upper Limb Ser.: Vol. 1). (Illus.). 320p. 1987. text 129.75 (*0-443-03216-5*) Church.

Bowers, William J. Legal Homicide: Death As Punishment in America, 1864-1982. LC 81-11309. 648p. 1984. text 65.00 (*0-930350-25-1*) NE U Pr.

Bowers, William P. & Kinkaid, Philip M. Texas Limited Liability Company Forms & Practice Manual, 2 vols. 2nd ed. LC 94-46843. 772p. 1996. ring bd. 239.90 (*1-57400-008-X*) Data Trace Pubng.

Bowers, William S. Craftsmen of Franklin County Pennsylvania, 1784-1884. 232p. 1985. 35.00 (*0-318-04635-0*) Irwinton.

— Gunsmiths of Pen-Mar-Va., 1790-1840. (Illus.). 209p. 1979. 49.50 (*0-318-04634-2*) Irwinton.

Bowers, William T. Black Soldier-White Army (Paperbound) Edition) The 24th Infantry Regiment in Korea 312p. 1997. per. 26.00 (*0-16-048804-4*) USGPO.

— Black Soldier/White Army (Clothbound) Edition: The 24th Infantry Regiment in Korea. 312p. 1997. boxed set 32.00 (*0-16-048803-6*) USGPO.

Bowers, William T., et al. Black Soldier, White Army: The 24th Infantry Regiment in Korea. (Illus.). 294p. (Orig.). 1997. pap. text 50.00 (*0-7881-3990-8*) DIANE Pub.

Bowersj. Introduction to Two-Dimensional Design. (Design & Graphic Design Ser.). 1998. pap. 34.95 (*0-442-02488-6*, VNR) Wiley.

Bowersock, G. W. Fiction As History: Nero to Julian. LC 93-49581. (Sather Classical Lectures: No. 58). 1995. 45.00 (*0-520-08824-7*, Pub. by U CA Pr) Cal Prin Full Svc.

— Fiction As History: Nero to Julian. LC 93-49581. (Sather Classical Lectures: Vol. 58). 1997. pap. 16.95 (*0-520-20881-1*, Pub. by U CA Pr) Cal Prin Full Svc.

— Hellenism in Late Angiquity. 132p. (C). 1996. pap. 21.95 (*0-472-06418-5*, 06418) U of Mich Pr.

— Martyrdom & Rome. 118p. (C). 1995. text 34.95 (*0-521-46539-7*) Cambridge U Pr.

— Roman Arabia. (Illus.). 256p. 1994. pap. 17.95 (*0-674-77756-5*, BOWROX) HUP.

***Bowersock, G. W., et al, eds.** Late Antiquity: A Guide to the Post-Classical World. LC 99-25639. (Reference Library). (Illus.). 757p. 1999. 49.95 (*0-674-51173-5*) HUP.

Bowersock, G. W., ed. see Momigliano, Arnaldo D.

Bowersock, Glen W. Augustus & the Greek World. LC 81-13432. 176p. 1982. reprint ed. lib. bdg. 49.75 (*0-313-23298-9*, BOAG, Greenwood Pr) Greenwood.

— Julian the Apostate. 152p. 1978. 26.95 (*0-674-48881-4*) HUP.

— Roman Arabia. (Illus.). 256p. (C). 1983. 33.50 (*0-674-77755-7*) HUP.

Bowersock, Glen W., et al, eds. Arktouros: Hellenic Studies Presented to Bernard M. W. Knox on the Occasion of His 65th Birthday. 471p. 1979. 150.00 (*3-11-007798-1*) De Gruyter.

— Edward Gibbon & the Decline & Fall of the Roman Empire. LC 76-48192. (Illus.). 271p. 1977. reprint ed. pap. 84.10 (*0-7837-1674-5*, 205720600024) Bks Demand.

Bowersock, Glen W., tr. Scripta Minora, Vol. VII. (Loeb Classical Library: No. 183). 564p. 1925. 18.95 (*0-674-99202-4*) HUP.

Bowersock, Glen W., ed. see Branham, R. Bracht.

***Bowersock, Terri.** Success, It Can Be Yours! How to Be a Millionaire by Using Your Determination. LC 99-97050. 192p. 2000. pap. 12.00 (*0-9676174-0-5*) Terris Pub & Speak.

Bowersock, William L. The Christmas Card. Miller, Tanya A., ed. LC 97-133604. 131p. 1996. pap. 12.95 (*1-57248-030-0*) Galt Pr.

***Bowersox, Bob.** In the Kitchen with Bob: Christmas Collection. (Illus.). 2000. 24.00 (*1-928998-03-8*) Q V C Pubg.

— Light & Easy. (In the Kitchen with Bob Ser.: Vol. 2). (Illus.). 128p. 2000. 24.00 (*1-928998-01-1*) Q V C Pubg.

— My Family's Best. (In the Kitchen with Bob Ser.: Vol. 1). (Illus.). 128p. 1999. 24.00 (*1-928998-00-3*) Q V C Pubg.

— Picnics & Barbecues: In the Kitchen with Bob. (Illus.). 2000. 24.00 (*1-928998-02-X*) Q V C Pubg.

Bowersox, Donald J. & Closs, David J. Logistical Management: The Integrated Supply Chain Process. LC 95-42252. (Series in Marketing). (Illus.). xix, 730 p. (C). 1996. text 65.74 (*0-07-006883-6*) McGraw.

— Logistical Managements: The Integrated Supply Chain Process, Loga: Simulation Software. 1996. pap. text. write for info. (*0-07-841322-2*) McGraw.

Bowersox, Gary W., jt. auth. see Chamberlin, Bonita E.

Bowerstock, G. W. & Cornell, T. J. A. D. Momigliano: Studies on Modern Scholarship. 1994. pap. 17.95 (*0-520-08545-0*, Pub. by U CA Pr) Cal Prin Full Svc.

Bowery, N. G., ed. Actions & Interactions of GABA & Benzodiazepines: A Biological Council Symposium. LC 83-42617. (Illus.). 312p. 1984. reprint ed. pap. 96.80 (*0-7837-9573-4*, 206032200005) Bks Demand.

Bowery, N. G., jt. ed. see Tanaka, C.

Bowery, Norman. 2nd International GABAg Symposium, Vol. 2, No. 1 & 2. x, 180p. 1992. pap. text 182.00 (*3-7186-5352-4*, Harwood Acad Pubs) Gordon & Breach.

Bowery, Norman, jt. ed. see Enna, Sam J.

Bowery, Norman G., jt. ed. see Erdo, Sandor L.

Bowes. No One Need Apply. 1987. 27.95 (*0-07-103214-2*) McGraw.

— Verses I Like. 1977. 18.95 (*0-8369-6324-5*) Ayer.

Bowes, Alison & Sim, Duncan. Perspectives on Welfare: The Experience of Minority Ethnic Groups in Scotland. LC 97-71720. (Research in Ethnic Relations Ser.). (Illus.). 256p. 1997. text 64.95 (*1-85972-415-9*, Pub. by Ashgate Pub) Ashgate Pub Co.

Bowes, Alison M. Kibbutz Goshen: An Israeli Commune. (Illus.). 165p. (C). 1989. pap. text 11.50 (*0-88133-395-6*) Waveland Pr.

Bowes, Andrea, ed. see Bowes, Peter.

Bowes, Betty. Life of the Party: A Guide to Building Your Party Plan Business. 1998. pap. text 10.95 (*1-56052-471-5*) Crisp Pubns.

Bowes-Brooks, Yvonne. 100 Ways to Become a Successful Student: Motivational Book for Students. large type ed. 90p. (YA). (gr. 5-12). Date not set. pap. 10.98 (*0-9682530-1-6*) Brooks & Brooks.

Bowes, Bryon G. A Color Atlas of Plant Propagation & Conservation. 1998. pap. 55.00 (*0-89327-423-2*, 423-2) NY Botanical.

Bowes, Clare. The Hippo Bus. LC 92-34264. (Voyages Ser.). (Illus.). (J). 1993. 14.00 (*0-383-03629-1*) SRA McGraw.

Bowes, D. R. Encyclopedia of Igneous & Metamorphic Patrology. 666p. (C). (gr. 13). 1989. mass mkt. 389.95 (*0-442-20623-2*) Chapman & Hall.

Bowes, David B. Creating the Globally Competitive Community: A Local Leadership Guide to Economic Growth & Quality of Life with Smaller Manufacturers Poised to Grow. LC 98-191030. 80p. 1997. pap. text 14.95 (*0-941182-20-7*) Partners Livable.

Bowes, Deborah. The Ballet Book: The Young Performer's Guide to Classical Dance. (Illus.). 144p. (YA). (gr. 4 up). 1999. pap. 12.95 (*1-55209-353-0*) Firefly Bks Ltd.

Bowes, Eric. The New Gospel: Good News for Christians. 88p. 1958. reprint ed. 14.95 (*0-933770-67-7*) Kalimat.

Bowes, Frederick P. The Culture of Early Charleston. LC 78-897. (Illus.). 156p. 1978. reprint ed. lib. bdg. 49.75 (*0-313-20278-8*, BOCE, Greenwood Pr) Greenwood.

Bowes, Henry N., jt. ed. see Straight, William G.

Bowes, James L. Japanese Enamels: Including Chinese & European. LC 76-28880. (Cloisonne Enamels Ser.: Vol. 1). (Illus.). 1976. 37.95 (*0-89344-007-8*) Ars Ceramica.

— Japanese Marks & Seals. (Illus.). 1976. reprint ed. 39.95 (*0-89344-002-7*) Ars Ceramica.

Bowes, Jennifer, jt. auth. see Goodnow, Jacqueline.

Bowes, John E., jt. auth. see Stamm, Keith R.

Bowes, Michael D. & Krutilla, John V. Multiple-Use Management: The Economics of Public Forestlands. LC 89-4018. 357p. 1989. 48.95 (*0-915707-41-1*) Resources Future.

Bowes, P. The Hindu Religious Traditions. 322p. 1978. 16.95 (*0-318-37169-3*) Asia Bk Corp.

Bowes, Paula. First & Second Samuel. (Collegeville Bible Commentary - Old Testament Ser.). 128p. 1985. pap. 4.95 (*0-8146-1415-9*) Liturgical Pr.

Bowes, Peter. The Word Within. Bowes, Andrea, ed. 184p. (Orig.). 1991. pap. text 9.95 (*0-9628517-0-1*, 399-008) Chariot Pub.

Bowes, Pratima. Hindu Intellectual Tradition. 218p. 1977. 13.95 (*0-318-37156-1*) Asia Bk Corp.

Bowes, Richard. Feral Cell. 208p. (Orig.). 1987. mass mkt. 2.95 (*0-445-20352-8*, Pub. by Warner Bks) Little.

— Goblin Market. 256p. 1988. mass mkt. 3.50 (*0-445-20354-4*, Pub. by Warner Bks) Little.

Bowes, Richard. Minions of the Moon. LC 98-43981. (Illus.). 320p. 1999. 23.95 (*0-312-86566-X*, Pub. by Tor Bks) St Martin.

***Bowes, Richard.** Minions of the Moon. 320p. 2000. pap. text 13.95 (*0-312-87228-3*, Pub. by Tor Bks) St Martin.

Bowes, Sue. Love Spells & Rituals Gift Set. (Illus.). 64p. 1998. 19.95 (*0-8069-2439-X*) Sterling.

Bowes, Susan. Life Magic: The Power of Positive Witchcraft. LC 98-41095. (Illus.). 176p. 1999. 20.50 (*0-684-85354-X*) S&S Trade.

— Notions & Potions: A Safe, Pracctical Guide to Creating Magic & Miracles. LC 96-40136. (Illus.). 112p. 1997. pap. 14.95 (*0-8069-9602-1*) Sterling.

Bowes, William H., et al. Mechanics of Engineering Materials. LC 83-12341. 1456p. (C). 1984. pap. text 65.00 (*0-471-87374-8*) Wiley.

Bowet, Derek W., jt. ed. see Brownlie, Ian.

Bowett, B., et al. The International Court of Justice: Process, Practice & Procedure. 130p. 1997. 105.00 (*0-903067-60-9*, Pub. by Brit Inst ICL) St Mut.

Bowett, Derek, jt. ed. see Brownlie, Ian.

Bowett, Derek W. The British Year Book of International Law 1988, Vol. 59. 2nd ed. Brownlie, Ian, ed. 616p. 1990. text 145.00 (*0-19-825408-3*) OUP.

Bowett, Derek W., jt. auth. see Brownlie, Ian.

Bowett, Derek W., ed. see Brownlie, Ian.

Bowett, Derek W., jt. ed. see Brownlie, Ian.

Bowey, Angela M. Managing Salary & Wage Systems. 2nd ed. (Illus.). 448p. 1989. text 96.95 (*0-566-02732-1*, Pub. by Gower) Ashgate Pub Co.

Bowey, Angela M., ed. Handbook of Salary & Wage Systems. 2nd ed. 472p. 1982. text 79.95 (*0-566-02261-3*) Ashgate Pub Co.

Bowey, Judith A. Metalinguistic Functioning in Children. 81p. (C). 1988. 51.00 (*0-7300-0551-8*, Pub. by Deakin Univ) St Mut.

Bowhay, Robert W., jt. auth. see Russell, Charles W.

Bowhill, S. A., ed. Review Papers: International Solar-Terrestrial Physics Symposium, Sao-Paolo, June, 1974. 212p. 1976. pap. 50.00 (*0-08-019959-3*, Pergamon Pr) Elsevier.

Bowhill, S. A., et al, eds. COSPAR Space Research XIV: Proceedings of the Fourteenth Plenary Meeting of COSPAR, Washington, U. S. A. & Selected Symposia. (Space Research Ser.). (Illus.). 1815p. 1977. 140.00 (*0-08-021786-9*, Pergamon Pr) Elsevier.

Bowhser, Alice M., ed. see Burkhardt, Ann M.

Bowick, Chris. RF Circuit Design. LC 96-51612. (Illus.). 176p. 1997. pap. text 26.95 (*0-7506-9946-9*) Buttrwrth-Heinemann.

Bowick, M., jt. ed. see Gursey, F.

Bowie. Twenty Questions. 3rd ed. LC 95-79694. (C). 1995. pap. text 59.00 (*0-15-502660-7*, Pub. by Harcourt Coll Pubs) Harcourt.

— Twenty Questions. 4th ed. (C). 1999. text 47.50 (*0-15-507854-2*, Pub. by Harcourt Coll Pubs) Harcourt.

Bowie, A. M. Aristophanes: Myth, Ritual & Comedy. 344p. 1996. pap. text 22.95 (*0-521-57575-3*) Cambridge U Pr.

Bowie, Alasdair & Unger, Danny. The Politics of Open Economies: Indonesia, Malaysia, the Philippines & Thailand. LC 96-49358. (Asia-Pacific Studies: Vol. 4). (Illus.). 258p. (C). 1997. text 59.95 (*0-521-58343-8*); pap. text 19.95 (*0-521-58683-6*) Cambridge U Pr.

Bowie, Alisdair. Crossing the Industrial Divide. 222p. 1991. text 34.50 (*0-231-07212-0*) Col U Pr.

Bowie, Andrew. Aesthetics & Subjectivity from Kant to Neitzsche. (Theory & History of Literature Ser.). 304p. 1993. text 29.95 (*0-7190-4011-6*) Manchester Univ Pr.

— From Romanticism to Critical Theory: The Philosophy of German Literary Theory. 368p. (C). 1996. 85.00 (*0-415-12762-9*); pap. 25.99 (*0-415-12763-7*) Routledge.

— Schelling & Modern European Philosophy: An Introduction. LC 93-13079. 192p. (C). 1994. pap. 22.99 (*0-415-10347-9*) Routledge.

Bowie, Andrew, ed. see Frank, Manfred.

Bowie, Andrew, ed. & tr. see Schelling, Friedrich Wilhelm Joseph.

Bowie, Andrew, ed. & tr. see Schleiermacher, Friedrich Daniel Ernst.

Bowie, Angela & Carr, Patrick. Backstage Passes: Life on the Wild Side with David Bowie. 320p. 1994. mass mkt. 5.99 (*0-515-11352-2*, Jove) Berkley Pub.

Bowie, Angus M. Aristophanes: Myth, Ritual, & Comedy. LC 92-39415. 344p. (C). 1993. text 69.95 (*0-521-44012-2*) Cambridge U Pr.

— The Poetic Dialect of Sappho & Alcaeus. rev. ed. Connor, W. R., ed. LC 80-2641. (Monographs in Classical Studies). 1981. lib. bdg. 22.00 (*0-405-14029-0*) Ayer.

Bowie, Anne & Bowie, P. S. Understanding the Emotionally Depleted Woman. LC 95-77815. 221p. 1996. pap. 12.95 (*0-9646913-0-2*) Gldn Quill NV.

Bowie, Anne, jt. auth. see Bowie, Peter S.

Bowie, Anus M. The Poetic Dialect of Sappho & Alcaeus. 1981. 24.95 (*0-88143-020-X*) Ayer.

Bowie, Bonnie M., jt. auth. see Bowie, Granville H.

Bowie, C. W. Busy Toes. LC 96-30588. (Illus.). 32p. (J). (ps-2). 1998. 15.95 (*1-879085-72-0*, Whispering Coyote) Charlesbridge Pub.

***Bowie, C. W.** Busy Toes. (Illus.). 28p. (J). (ps-1). 2000. bds. 6.95 (*1-58089-056-3*, Whispering Coyote) Charlesbridge Pub.

Bowie, Christopher J. & Platt, Alan. British Nuclear Policymaking. LC 83-22953. 1984. pap. text 7.50 (*0-8330-0534-0*, R-3085-AF) Rand Corp.

Bowie, Christopher J., et al. The New Calculus: Analyzing Airpower's Changing Role in Joint Theater Campaigns. LC 93-16125. 1993. pap. 15.00 (*0-8330-1322-X*, MR-149-AF) Rand Corp.

— Trends in the Global Balance of Airpower. LC 94-42440. xxv, 111p. 1995. pap. 15.00 (*0-8330-1601-6*, MR-478-1-AF) Rand Corp.

— Trends in the Global Balance of Airpower: Supporting Data. LC 94-42441. v, 115p. 1995. pap. text 13.00 (*0-8330-1602-4*, MR-478/2-AF) Rand Corp.

Bowie, David. David Bowie Anthology. (Piano-Vocal-Guitar Personality Folio Ser.). 216p. 1985. per. 24.95 (*0-88188-360-3*, HL 00356339) H Leonard.

— 21 Talk. 1998. pap. text 29.95 (*1-901785-02-5*, Pub. by Twenty-One) Dist Art Pubs.

Bowie, Donald. Cable Harbor. 336p. 1982. pap. 3.50 (*0-380-59493-5*, 59493-5, Avon Bks) Morrow Avon.

Bowie, Douglas & Shoebridge, Tom, eds. Best Canadian Screenplays. LC 92-253193. 440p. 1992. pap. 23.95 (*1-55082-045-1*, Pub. by Quarry Pr) LPC InBook.

Bowie, Effie G. Across the Years in Prince George's County (Maryland) LC 74-18310. (Illus.). 904p. 1997. reprint ed. pap. 60.00 (*0-8063-0643-2*) Clearfield Co.

***Bowie, Fiona.** The Anthropology of Religion: An Introduction. 224p. 1999. pap. text 26.95 (*0-631-20848-8*) Blackwell Pubs.

— The Anthropology of Religion: An Introduction. (Illus.). 224p. 1999. 59.95 (*0-631-20847-X*) Blackwell Pubs.

Bowie, Fiona, ed. Hildegard of Bingen: Mystical Writings. (Spiritual Classics Ser.). (Illus.). 144p. (Orig.). 1990. pap. 11.95 (*0-8245-1027-5*) Crossroad NY.

Bowie, Fiona, et al, eds. Women & Missions: Past & Present: Anthropological & Historical Perceptions. LC 92-15997. (Cross-Cultural Perspectives on Women Ser.). 279p. 1994. 49.50 (*0-85496-738-9*, Pub. by Berg Pubs); pap. 19.50 (*0-85496-872-5*, Pub. by Berg Pubs) NYU Pr.

Bowie, Fiona & Deacy, Christopher, eds. The Coming Deliverer: Millennial Themes in World Religions. 260p. 1997. pap. 18.95 (*0-7083-1338-8*, Pub. by Univ Wales Pr) Paul & Co Pubs.

Bowie, Fiona, jt. ed. see Davies, Oliver.

Bowie, G. Lee, et al. Thirteen Questions in Ethics & Social Philosophy. 2nd ed. LC 97-74862. 688p. (C). 1997. pap. text 47.50 (*0-15-503684-X*, Pub. by Harcourt Coll Pubs) Harcourt.

Bowie, Gary, et al. Competency Development in Sport & Physical Education Management. (Monograph Series on Sport & Physical Education Management). 64p. 1988. pap. 4.00 (*0-87563-316-1*) Stipes.

Bowie, Gary W., jt. auth. see Zeigler, Earle F.

Bowie, Granville H. & Bowie, Bonnie M. Kodiak - A Love Story: The Biography of an Alaskan Malamute & His Human Family. LC 97-94346. (Illus.). 613p. 1998. 125.00 (*0-9660837-1-7*) Kodiak Pub.

— Kodiak - A Love Story: The Biography of an Alaskan Malamute & His Human Family. limited ed. LC 97-94346. (Illus.). 613p. 1998. lthr. write for info. (*0-9660837-0-9*) Kodiak Pub.

Bowie, Herb. Why Die? A Beginner's Guide to Living Forever. LC 97-66499. xiii, 301p. (Orig.). 1998. pap. 12.95 (*1-890457-07-8*, B02) PowerSurge.

Bowie, Jack. Insight & Innovation in Data Visualization, Vol. 2. (C). 1996. text. write for info. (*0-201-58158-2*) Addison-Wesley.

Bowie, Jennifer W. A Captain's Lady. large type ed. 544p. 1996. 27.99 (*0-7089-3443-9*) Ulverscroft.

Bowie, Katherine A. Rituals of National Loyalty: An Anthropology of the State & the Village Scout Movement in Thailand. LC 96-38184. 1997. 52.00 (*0-231-10390-5*); pap. 19.50 (*0-231-10391-3*) Col U Pr.

Bowie, Katherine A. & Singh, Samruam. Voices from the Thai Countryside: The Short Stories of Samruam Singh. LC 90-71960. (Monographs: No. 6). (Illus.). 130p. (Orig.). (C). pap. 11.95 (*1-881261-01-8*) U Wisc Ctr SE Asian.

Bowie, Katherine A., ed. & tr. see Singh, Samruam.

Bowie, Leland. The Impact of the Protege System in Morocco, 1880-1912. LC 72-13634. (Papers in International Studies: Africa Ser.: No. 11). 28p. reprint ed. pap. 30.00 (*0-608-11819-2*, 200741900063) Bks Demand.

Bowie, Lemuel J. Automated Instrumentation for Radioimmunoassay. 224p. 1980. 119.00 (*0-8493-5747-0*, QP519, CRC Reprint) Franklin.

Bowie, Malcolm. Lacan. 224p. 1991. 26.95 (*0-674-50852-1*, BOWLAC) HUP.

— Lacan. 256p. (C). 1993. pap. 16.00 (*0-674-50853-X*) HUP.

Bowie, Malcolm. The Morality of Proust. 28p. 1994. pap. text 8.95 (*0-19-952265-0*) OUP.

— Proust among the Stars. LC 98-8064. 348p. 1999. 28.50 (*0-231-11490-7*) Col U Pr.

— Proust among the Stars. 352p. 2000. pap. text 16.95 (*0-231-11491-5*) Col U Pr.

Bowie, Malcolm. Psychoanalysis & the Future of Theory. (Bucknell Lectures in Literary Theory). (Illus.). 192p. 1993. pap. text 18.95 (*0-631-18926-2*) Blackwell Pubs.

Bowie, Melvin M., jt. auth. see McDougald, Dana.

Bowie, Norman E. Business Ethics: A Kantian Perspective. LC 98-28676. 300p. 1998. 64.95 (*0-631-21173-X*); pap. 24.95 (*0-631-21174-8*) Blackwell Pubs.

— Towards a New Theory of Distributive Justice. LC 72-150315. 160p. 1971. reprint ed. pap. 49.60 (*0-608-04439-3*, 206497100012) Bks Demand.

— University-Business Partnership: An Assessment. 300p. (C). 1994. pap. text 26.95 (*0-8476-7897-0*); lib. bdg. 68.00 (*0-8476-7896-2*) Rowman.

Bowie, Norman E., ed. Ethical Issues in Government. 251p. 1981. 29.95 (*0-87722-165-0*) Temple U Pr.

— Ethical Theory in the Last Quarter of the Twentieth Century. LC 82-1006. 155p. (C). 1983. lib. bdg. 24.00 (*0-915145-34-0*) Ridgeview.

Bowie, Norman E. & Duska, Ronald. Business Ethics. 2nd ed. LC 89-38973. 160p. 1989. pap. text 38.40 (*0-13-095910-3*) P-H.

Bowie, Norman E. & Simon, Robert L. The Individual & the Political Order: An Introduction to Social & Political Philosophy. 3rd ed. LC 98-4965. 282p. 1998. pap. 24.95 (*0-8476-8780-5*) Rowman.

Bowie, Norman E., jt. auth. see Beauchamp, Thomas L.

Bowie, Norman E., jt. ed. see Beauchamp, Thomas L.

Bowie, P. S., jt. auth. see Bowie, Anne.

Bowie, Paddy, jt. auth. see Hills, Peter.

Bowie, Peter S. Football for Women: A Reference Guide for Understanding American Football. LC 95-195743. 125p. 1996. pap. 7.95 (*0-9646913-2-9*) Gldn Quill NV.

Bowie, Peter S. & Bowie, Anne. How to Appraise Your Own Home. LC 95-77814. 61p. 1996. pap. 19.95 (*0-9646913-1-0*) Gldn Quill NV.

Bowie, Robert. A Roast for Coach Dan Spear: Small Town Football Dreams from the Florida Fifties. LC 97-91972. 256p. 1997. pap. 12.95 (*0-9658258-7-6*) O Zakamora Pubns.

Bowie, Robert, tr. & pref. see Bunin, Ivan A.

***Bowie, Robert R. & Immerman, Richard H.** Waging Peace. 336p. 2000. pap. 19.95 (*0-19-514048-6*) OUP.

Bowie, Robert R. & Immerman, Richard H. Waging Peace: Eisenhower's Strategy for National Security. LC 97-8447. 336p. (C). 1998. text 49.95 (*0-19-506264-7*) OUP.

Bowie, S H. & Thornton, Iain, eds. Environmental Geochemistry & Health. 1985. lib. bdg. 76.50 (*90-277-1879-2*) Kluwer Academic.

Bowie, Silyl K., ed. see Weems, I. U.

Bowie, Theodore, ed. Langdon Warner Through His Letters. LC 66-63378. 237p. reprint ed. pap. 73.50 (*0-608-11075-2*, 200573500059) Bks Demand.

Bowie, Theodore, et al, eds. The Sculpture of Thailand. LC 74-27410. (Asia Society Ser.). (Illus.). 1976. reprint ed. 36.95 (*0-405-06559-0*) Ayer.

Bowie, Theodore, et al. Art of the Surimono. LC 81-126210. (Illus.). 192p. 1981. 45.00 (*0-253-30474-1*) Ind U Pr.

Bowie, Theodore, ed. see De Honnecourt, Villard.

Bowie, Theodore R. East-West in Art: Patterns of Cultural & Aesthetic Relationships. LC 66-12723. (Indiana University International Studies). (Illus.). 191p. reprint ed. pap. 59.30 (*0-608-11251-8*, 205186200012) Bks Demand.

Bowie, Tom. Three Last Plays for Reading. 367p. 1991 29.95 (*0-932508-09-X*) Seven Oaks.

— Three More Plays for Reading. 1988. 29.95 (*0-932508-08-1*) Seven Oaks.

— Three Plays for Reading. LC 79-64092. 1979. 29.95 (*0-932508-04-9*) Seven Oaks.

— Three Screenplays for Reading. 1992. 29.95 (*0-932508-10-3*) Seven Oaks.

Bowie, Vaughan. Coping with Violence: A Guide for Human Service Workers. (Illus.). xviii, 188 p. 1996. pap. 25.00 (*1-871177-46-4*, Pub. by Whiting & Birch) Paul & Co Pubs.

Bowie, W. W. The Bowies of Their Kindred: A Genealogical & Biographical History. (Illus.). 523p. 1991. reprint ed. pap. 78.50 (*0-8328-1964-6*); reprint ed. lib. bdg. 88.50 (*0-8328-1963-8*) Higginson Bk Co.

Bowie, William C. The Conservator's Song. LC 92-29036. 88p. 1993. 20.00 (*1-55728-275-7*); pap. 12.00 (*1-55728-276-5*) U of Ark Pr.

Bowin, jt. auth. see Hinds.

Bowin, Carl. Caribbean Gravity Field & Plate Tectonics. LC 76-16261. (Geological Society of America, Special Paper: No. 169). 135p. reprint ed. pap. 41.90 (*0-608-13933-5*, 202373800033) Bks Demand.

***Bowin, R. B. & Harvey, Donald F.** Human Resource Management: An Experiential Approach. 2nd ed. 600p. 2000. pap. 56.00 (*0-13-017788-1*, Prentice Hall) P-H.

Bowin, Robert B. Behavioral Human Resource Management. 110p. (C). 1992. pap. text 20.00 (*0-9628796-0-6*) Bjorklund Pub.

Bowin, Robert B., jt. auth. see Harvey, Donald F.

Bowing, Stella. Everyday Cooking for Diabetics. LC 96-47314. (Illus.). 204p. (Orig.). 1997. pap. 15.95 (*1-55561-118-4*) Fisher Bks.

Bowker, Alfred, ed. see Harrison, Frederic.

Bowker, David. The Butcher of Glastonbury. 224p. 1998. pap. 10.95 (*0-575-60203-1*, Pub. by V Gollancz) Trafalgar.

— Death Prayer. 1996. pap. 11.99 (*1-56504-846-6*, Borealis) White Wolf.

— The Secret Sexist. 192p. 1998. pap. 10.95 (*0-575-40054-4*, Pub. by V Gollancz) Trafalgar.

Bowker, David, et al. Building Bridges. (Patchwork Ser.: No. 5). (Illus.). 12p. 1993. pap. 18.00 (*1-873791-60-7*) Taylor & Francis.

— Developing Relationships. (Patchwork Ser.: No. 4). (Illus.). 12p. 1993. pap. 18.00 (*1-873791-55-0*) Taylor & Francis.

— A Fresh Start. (Patchwork Ser.: No. 1). (Illus.). 12p. 1993. pap. 18.00 (*1-873791-35-6*) Taylor & Francis.

— Getting On. (Patchwork Ser.: No. 2). (Illus.). 12p. 1993. pap. 18.00 (*1-873791-40-2*) Taylor & Francis.

— Patchwork Accessor's Manual. (Illus.). 1993. 116.00 (*1-873791-75-5*) Taylor & Francis.

— Planning Together. (Patchwork Ser.: No. 6). (Illus.). 12p. 1993. pap. 18.00 (*1-873791-65-8*) Taylor & Francis.

— Risks & Responsibilities. (Patchwork Ser.: No. 3). (Illus.). 12p. 1993. pap. 18.00 (*1-873791-45-3*) Taylor & Francis.

Bowker, Francis E. Atlantic Four-Master: The Story of the Schooner Herbert L. Rawding, 1919-1947. x, 96p. 1986. pap. 13.95 (*0-913372-42-0*) Mystic Seaport.

Bowker, Geoffrey, et al, eds. Social Science, Technical Systems & Cooperative Work: The Great Divide. LC 96-40366. (Computers, Cognition, & Work Ser.). 412p. 1997. write for info. (*0-8058-2402-2*); pap. write for info. (*0-8058-2403-0*) L Erlbaum Assocs.

Bowker, Geoffrey C. Science on the Run: Information Management & Industrial Geophysics at Schlumberger, 1920-1940. LC 93-29647. (Inside Technology Ser.). 200p. 1994. 30.00 (*0-262-02367-9*) MIT Pr.

Bowker, Geoffrey C. & Star, Susan L. Sorting Things Out: Classification & Its Consequences. LC 99-26894. (Inside Technology Ser.). (Illus.). 368p. 1999. 35.00 (*0-262-02461-6*) MIT Pr.

***Bowker, Geoffrey C. & Star, Susan Leigh.** Sorting Things Out: Classification & Its Consequences. (Illus.). 389p. (C). 2000. reprint ed. pap. 17.95 (*0-262-52295-0*) MIT Pr.

Bowker, Gordon. Pursued by Furies. 1997. pap. 19.95 (*0-312-16356-8*) St Martin.

Bowker, John. The Complete Bible Handbook: An Illustrated Companion. LC 98-4478. (Illus.). Date not set. 39.95 (*0-7894-3568-3*) DK Pub Inc.

— The Meanings of Death. (Canto Book Ser.). 257p. (C). 1993. pap. 11.95 (*0-521-44773-9*) Cambridge U Pr.

Bowker, John. The Oxford Dictionary of World Religions. 1,135p. pap. write for info. (*0-19-866242-4*) OUP.

Bowker, John. Problems of Suffering in the Religions of the World. LC 77-93706. 330p. 1975. pap. text 22.95 (*0-521-09903-X*) Cambridge U Pr.

— The Religious Imagination & the Sense of God. 1978. text 46.00 (*0-19-826646-4*) OUP.

— Sense of God: Sociological, Anthropological & Psychological Approaches to the Origin of the Sense of God. LC 95-221113. 237p. 1995. pap. 14.95 (*1-85168-093-4*, Pub. by Onewrld Pubns) Penguin Putnam.

— Los Significados de la Muerte.Tr. of Meanings of Death. (SPA.). 362p. (C). 1996. pap. 17.95 (*0-521-47832-4*) Cambridge U Pr.

— Voices of Islam. 220p. 1996. pap. 14.95 (*0-614-21453-X*, 1290) Kazi Pubns.

— Voices of Islam. 220p. 1995. pap. 14.95 (*1-85168-095-0*, Pub. by Onewrld Pubns) Penguin Putnam.

— What Muslims Believe. 224p. 1999. pap. 14.95 (*1-85168-169-8*, Pub. by Onewrld Pubns) Penguin Putnam.

— World Religions. LC 96-38277. 192p. 1997. 34.95 (*0-7894-1439-2*) DK Pub Inc.

— Year to Live. 1992. pap. text 15.95 (*0-687-86700-2*) Abingdon.

***Bowker, John, ed.** The Concise Oxford Dictionary of World Religions. (Oxford Paperback Reference Ser.). 700p. 2000. pap. 15.95 (*0-19-280094-9*) OUP.

Bowker, John, ed. The Oxford Dictionary of World Religions. LC 97-166787. 1,124p. 1997. 60.00 (*0-19-213965-7*) OUP.

Bowker, John, jt. ed. see Holm, Jean.

B

Bowker, John H. & Pfeifer, Michael A. Levin & O'Neal's the Diabetic Foot. 6th ed. (Illus.). 600p. (C). 2001. text. write for info. (*1-55664-471-X*) Mosby Inc.

Bowker, John W., jt. ed. see Holm, Jean.

Bowker, Judy, jt. auth. see Bate, Barbara.

Bowker, Lee, jt. auth. see Zastrow, Charles H.

Bowker, Lee H. Beating Wife-Beating. LC 82-48603. 176p. 1983. text 35.00 (*0-669-06345-2*) Free Pr.

— Ending the Violence: A Guidebook Based on the Experiences of One Thousand Battered Wives. rev. ed. LC 85-45000. 128p. (Orig.). 1998. pap. 13.95 (*1-55691-153-X*, 53X) Learning Pubns.

— Masculinities & Violence. LC 97-33904. (Research on Men & Masculinities Ser.). 1997. 58.00 (*0-7619-0451-4*); pap. 26.00 (*0-7619-0452-2*) Sage.

Bowker, Michael. The Basis & Applications of Heterogeneous Catalysis. (Oxford Chemistry Primers Ser.: No. 53). (Illus.). 96p. (C). 1998. pap. text 12.95 (*0-19-855958-5*) OUP.

Bowker, Michael, jt. auth. see Crawford, Roger.

Bowker, Mike. Russian Foreign Policy & the End of the Cold War. LC 96-39521. 320p. 1997. text 83.95 (*1-85521-461-X*, Pub. by Dartmth Pub) Ashgate Pub Co.

***Bowker, Mike & Ross, Cameron.** Russia after the Cold War. LC 99-10634. 300p. 1999. pap. 28.60 (*0-582-36815-4*) Longman.

Bowker, Mike & Williams, Phil. Superpower Detente: A Reappraisal. (Royal Institute of International Affairs Ser.: Vol. 2). 288p. (C). 1988. text 39.95 (*0-8039-8041-8*); pap. text 19.95 (*0-8039-8042-6*) Sage.

Bowker, Nancy. John Rarey: Horse Tamer. 1996. pap. 50.00 (*0-85131-663-8*, Pub. by J A Allen) Trafalgar.

Bowker, P. G., et al. Odor & Corrosion Control in Sanitary Sewerage Systems & Treatment Plants. 132p. 1989. 49.95 (*0-89116-067-1*) Hemisp Pub.

Bowker, Richard. Senator. 432p. 1995. mass mkt. 5.99 (*0-380-72056-6*, Avon Bks) Morrow Avon.

Bowker, Robert. Beyond Peace: The Search for Security in the Middle East. LC 96-15504. (Canberra Studies on Peace). 212p. 1996. 49.95 (*1-55587-663-3*, 876633) L Rienner.

Bowker, Robert P. Guide to Septage Treatment & Disposal. (Illus.). 67p. (C). 1998. pap. text 25.00 (*0-7881-7222-0*) DIANE Pub.

Bowker, Robert P., et al. Odor & Corrosion Control in Sanitary Sewerage Systems & Treatment Plants. LC 88-38435. (Pollution Technology Review Ser.: No. 165). (Illus.). 130p. 1989. 39.00 (*0-8155-1192-2*) Noyes.

Bowker Staff. American Art Directory 1997-98. 56th ed. 916p. 1997. 209.95 (*0-8352-3819-9*) Bowker.

— American Book Publishing Record Cumulative 1997, 2 vols. 2458p. 1998. 290.00 (*0-8352-3977-2*) Bowker.

— American Library Directory: 1999-2000 Edition. 52nd ed. (American Library Directory Ser.). 1999. 259.95 (*0-8352-4118-1*) Bowker.

— Annual Register of Grant Support: A Directory of Funding Sources, 1999. 32nd ed. 1400p. 1998. 199.95 (*0-8352-4180-7*) Bowker.

— Broadcasting & Cable Yearbook 1998, 2 vols. 1998. write for info. (*0-8352-4003-7*) Bowker.

***Bowker Staff.** Broadcasting & Cable Yearbook 1999. (Illus.). 1999. 212.50 (*0-8352-4112-2*) Bowker.

Bowker Staff. Copyright: Its Law & Its Literature - Being a Summary of the Principles & Law of Copyright, with Special Reference to Books. 55, 60p. 1986. reprint ed. 30.00 (*0-8377-1942-9*, Rothman) W S Hein.

— Medical & Health Care Books & Serials in Print 1998, Set, 2 vols., Vols. 1 & 2. 1998. 249.95 (*0-8352-3992-6*) Bowker.

— Music Publisher's International ISMN Directory, 1998/99. 2nd ed. 1999. 210.00 (*3-598-22248-3*) K G Saur Verlag.

***Bowker Staff.** New Zealand Books in Print: 2000. 28th ed. 2000. 60.00 (*1-86452-036-1*) D W Thorpe.

— The Software Encyclopedia 1998: A Guide for Personal, Professional & Business Users Including Application Software, 2 vol., 1. 1748p. 1998. pap. 0.00 (*0-8352-4020-7*) Bowker.

— The Software Encyclopedia 1998: A Guide for Personal, Professional & Business Users Including Application Software on CD-ROM, 2 vol., 2. 1998. pap. write for info. (*0-8352-4021-5*) Bowker.

— The Software Encyclopedia 1999: A Guide for Personal, Professional & Business Users Including Application Software on CD-ROM, 2 vols., Set. 1999. pap. 265.00 (*0-8352-4223-4*) Bowker.

— The Software Encyclopedia 2000: A Guide for Personal, Professional & Business Users Including Application Software on CD-ROM, 2 vol., 1. 1798p. 2000. pap. 265.00 (*0-8352-4314-1*) Bowker.

— The Software Encyclopedia 2000: A Guide for Personal, Professional & Business Users Including Application Software on CD-ROM, 2 vol., 2. 1678p. 2000. pap. 265.00 (*0-8352-4315-X*) Bowker.

— The Software Encyclopedia 2000: A Guide for Personal, Professional & Business Users Including Application Software on CD-ROM, 2 vols., Set. 2,700p. 2000. pap. 265.00 (*0-8352-4313-3*) Bowker.

–Subject Guide to Books in Print 2000-2001, 7 vols., Set. annuals 15000p. 2000. 399.00 (*0-8352-4327-3*) Bowker.

"...as basic to libraries as shelves."--AMERICAN REFERENCE BOOKS ANNUAL. "There is no excuse for any library lacking this one."--RUSQ. For the questions that begin," Are there any books on...," here's the authorative source with *all* the answers! Indexing the more than 2.5 million nonfiction titles from Books In Print 2000-2001 under more than 84,000 Library of Congress subject headings, this indispensable tool helps you & your patrons find the latest books on every conceivable subject or topic. The 2000-2001 edition brings you: *3,000 new headings - reflecting the latest trends in more that 200,000 new titles - & thousands of entry revisions *A stand-alone Subject Thesaurus - listing & cross-referencing all headings from the Subject Guide for easier more thorough researching *The same authorative bibliographic, ordering, & publisher information found in Books In Print. *Thousands of publisher-provided annotations that provide capsule summaries of books. When you need the most trusted subject research & collection development aid in the book industry, turn to Subject Guide to Books In Print 2000-2001. *Publisher Paid Annotation.*

— Whitaker's Books in Print: British 2000, 5 Vols. 2000. 897.25 (*0-85021-280-4*) Whitaker.

Bowker Staff, ed. American Book Publishing Record Cumulative 1998, 2 vols., Set 2800p. 1999. 342.50 (*0-8352-4085-1*) Bowker.

***Bowker Staff, ed. American Book Publishing Record Cumulative 1999, 2 vols., set. 2500p. 2000. 299.00 (*0-8352-4335-4*) Bowker.**

"An essential tool for library cataloging & order departments." --American Reference Books Annual(s). Comprehensive & convenient, ABPR 1999 brings you catalog records for the entire year of book publishing in one cost-effective volume. More than 68,000 cataloged entries for books publish or distributed in the United States are arranged in Dewey sequence, with separate sections for Adult & Juvenile Fiction. Author, Title & Subject indexes conveniently refer you to main section entries. *Publisher Paid Annotation.*

— American Book Trade Directory. 47th ed. 1827p. 2001. 255.00 (*0-8352-4362-1*) Bowker.

Bowker Staff, ed. American Book Trade Directory, 1996-97. 1997. 240.00 (*3-598-07660-6*) K G Saur Verlag.

***Bowker Staff, ed.** American Book Trade Directory 1999-2000. 45th ed. 1999. 249.95 (*0-8352-4221-8*) Bowker.

Bowker Staff, ed. American Book Trade Directory 2000-2001. 46th ed. 1800p. 2000. 255.49 (*0-8352-4273-0*) Bowker.

"No public or academic library should be without this thorough & well-organized volume."--American Reference Books Annual. Finding your way through the huge U.S. book trade community has never been easier! This comprehensive volume profiles more than 30,000 retail & antiquarian book dealers, plus 1,200 book & magazine wholesalers, distributors, & jobbers - in all 50 states & territories, too. This useful tool will help you: * Keep tabs on the entire bookselling industry - from the smallest specialty bookstore to the largest chains, distributors, & jobbers. * Locate wholesalers & jobbers for hard-to-find books, software & audiocassettes. * Track down foreign book dealers, importers, exporters, library collection appraisers, & specialty sidelines. * Provide valuable directory assistance for patrons in the business of selling books, software, magazines, or audiocassettes. Organized by state & city, entries include store or company size, specialties, years in business, owner & key personnel, contact information (including e-mail addresses) & notations for those businesses that also handle audiocassettes, software & other sidelines. For added time-saving usefulness, you'll also find: * An Index to Dealers in Foreign Language Books, arranged by language. * A Types of Source Index, listing stores under bookselling categories. * An Index to Wholesale Remainder Dealers, Paperback Distributors, Exporters, & Importers. * An Index to Retailers & Wholesalers. *Publisher Paid Annotation.*

***Bowker Staff, ed.** American Library Directory, 2000-2001, 2 vols., Set. 53rd ed. 2000. 269.95 (*0-8352-4280-3*) Bowker.

— American Men & Women of Science: A Biographical Directory of Today's Leaders in Physical, Biological & Related Sciences, 2000-2001, 8 vols., Set 21st ed. 8,500p. 1999. 975.00 (*0-8352-4344-3*) Bowker.

Bowker Staff, ed. American Men & Women of Science, 1998-99: A Biographical Directory of Today's Leaders in Physical, Biological & Related Sciences, 8 vol. set. 20th ed. 8500p. 1998. 900.00 (*0-8352-3748-6*) Bowker.

***Bowker Staff, ed.** Annual Register of Grant Support 2001: A Directory of Funding Sources. 34th ed. 1,400p. 2000. 210.00 (*0-8352-4325-7*) Bowker.

— Annual Register of Grant Support 2000: A Directory of Funding Sources. 33rd ed. 1999. 210.00 (*0-8352-4237-4*) Bowker.

Bowker Staff, ed. AV Market Place 1999. 1999. pap. 165.00 (*0-8352-4098-3*) Bowker.

— AV Market Place 2000: The Complete Business Directory of Products & Services for the Audio Video Industry. 28th ed. 2000. 206.75 (*0-8352-4268-4*) Bowker.

***Bowker Staff, ed.** AV Market Place 2001: The Complete Business Directory of Products & Services for the Audio Video Industry. 29th ed. 1600p. 2001. pap. write for info. (*0-8352-4363-X*) Bowker.

— Books in Print Supplement 1998-1999, 3 vols., Set. 1999. 270.00 (*0-8352-4063-0*) Bowker.

— Books in Print Supplement 2000-2001, 3 vols. set. 7000p. 2001. 279.00 (*0-8352-4364-8*) Bowker.

–Books in Print Supplement 1999-2000, 3 vols, Set. 7000p. 2000. 279.00 (*0-8352-4275-7*) Bowker.

Here's the sure way to keep your Books In Print fresh & current. This essential mid-year supplement brings you up to date with six full months of book publishing changes, to ensure top performance & service in your library or bookstore throughout the year. The Supplement features separate Title, Author, Subject & Publisher indexes so you'll handle the latest reference & ordering questions just as easily as with Books In Print. You'll find: Complete bibliographic & ordering information for more than 115,000 new & forthcoming titles. More than 500,000 entries with major revisions & more than 120,000 flagged out-of-print or out-of-stock. Another 4,500 new publishers - plus hundreds of publisher address changes & new toll-free numbers. Use this information to answer patron queries...keep your collection current...verify prices...confirm availability & keep the latest book world information in your sights all year long. *Publisher Paid Annotation.*

–Books in Print 2000-2001, 9 vols., Set. annuals 53rd ed. 2500p. 2000. 595.00 (*0-8352-4291-9*) Bowker.

"Books In Print has continued to expand & enhance the variety of information & accessibility to it."--REFERENCE & RESEARCH BOOK NEWS. "There is simply no other work that can replace it." --AMERICAN REFERENCE BOOKS ANNUAL(s). Here's the indispensable print complement to your Books In Print on DISC & online capabilities. With almost two million up-to-date entries, the new Books In Print 2000-2001 is the definitive information source in print format on books published & distributed in the United States. In nine volumes of author, title & publisher indexes, this core reference guide delivers: Entries for over 1.8 million active citations of all kinds - adult, juvenile, popular, cholarly & reprints - with more than 200,000 new titles added annually. The most complete & current bibliographic & ordering information for every title - updated by the publishers themselves - from pages, price & publisher to edition, binding & ISBN. Some one million price & entry revisions, reflecting the rapid changes taking place in the publishing world today. A Stand-alone Publishers Index to more than 63,000 firms. In the fast-changing world of book publishing, nothing you can put on your shelf keeps your reference, acquisitions & collection development activities as organized & up to date as Books In Print 2000-2001. It's the one unfailing resource you can count on to stay on top of all book changes. *Publisher Paid Annotation.*

Bowker Staff, ed. Books in Print, 1997-1998, 9 vols. 50th anniversary ed. Incl. Vol. 2. 50th anniversary ed. 1997. Not sold separately (*0-8352-3937-3*); Vol. 3. 50th anniversary ed. 1997. Not sold separately (*0-8352-3938-1*); Vol. 4. 50th anniversary ed. 1997. Not sold separately (*0-8352-3940-3*); Vol. 5. 50th anniversary ed. 1997. Not sold separately (*0-8352-3941-1*); Vol. 6. 50th anniversary ed. 1997. Not sold separately (*0-8352-3943-8*); Vol. 7. 50th anniversary ed. 1997. Not sold separately (*0-8352-3944-6*); Vol. 8. 50th anniversary ed. 1997. Not sold separately (*0-8352-3945-4*); 525.00 (*0-8352-3935-7*) Bowker.

***Bowker Staff, ed.** Books in Print 1999-2000, 9 vols. 52nd ed. 25,000p. 1999. 550.00 (*0-8352-4250-1*) Bowker.

— The Bowker Annual Library & Book Trade Almanac 1999. 1999. 185.00 (*0-8352-4222-6*) Bowker.

— The Bowker Annual Library & Book Trade Almanac 2000: Facts, Figures & Reports. 45th ed. 900p. 2000. 185.00 (*0-8352-4324-9*) Bowker.

Bowker Staff, ed. Bowker's Complete Video Directory 1999, 4 vols. 1999. pap. 259.95 (*0-8352-4202-1*) Bowker.

***Bowker Staff, ed.** Bowker's Complete Video Directory 2000, Set, 4 vols. 6,100p. 2000. 275.00 (*0-8352-4305-2*) Bowker.

Bowker Staff, ed. Bowker's Complete Video Directory 1998: Entertainment, Set, 2 vols., Vols. 1 & 2. 1998. 124.95 (*0-8352-4016-9*) Bowker.

— Bowker's Complete Video Directory 1998: Entertainment & Special Interest, Set, 4 vols., Vol. 1-4. 4600p. 1998. 249.95 (*0-8352-4014-2*) Bowker.

— Bowker's Complete Video Directory 1998: Special Interest, Set, 2 vols., Vols. 3 & 4. 1998. 161.95 (*0-8352-4015-0*) Bowker.

— Bowker's Directory of Audiocassettes for Children 1998. 340p. (Orig.). 1998. pap. 49.95 (*0-8352-4060-6*) Bowker.

— Bowker's Directory of Audiocassettes for Children 1999. 350p. 1999. pap. 55.00 (*0-8352-4200-5*) Bowker.

— Bowker's Directory of Videocassettes for Children 1999. 750p. 1999. pap. 65.00 (*0-8352-4201-3*) Bowker.

***Bowker Staff, ed.** Bowker's Directory of Videocassettes for Children 2000. 750p. 2000. 69.95 (*0-8352-4323-0*) Bowker.

Bowker Staff, ed. Bowker's Law Books Supplement 1998. 1998. suppl. ed. write for info. (*0-8352-4108-4*) Bowker.

***Bowker Staff, ed. Broadcasting & Cable Yearbook 2000. 2300p. 2000. pap. 179.95 (*0-8352-4285-4*) Bowker.**

"A Comprehensive directory." --Association Trends For the latest & most comprehensive information on the radio, TV cable industries, the best place to turn is the Broadcasting & Cable Yearbook 2000. This exhaustive resource provides: Up-to-date listings for all radio & TV stations in the United States & Canada, providing addresses, telephone & fax numbers, frequencies, ownerhsip, programming & more. Comprehensive cable coverage of multiple systems operators (MSOs) & independent owners with 1,000 subscribers or more. Suppliers of key industry services -networks ...producers, distributors & production services...brokers...law firms...consultants...satellites...equipment manufacturers ...programming services ...& others.. .Station ownership & cross-ownership listings & an index of radio & TV station call letters ...Information on satellite owners & operators, low power TV stations, regional cable TV news program networks, wireless cable companies & teleports. Current market statistics, plus information about trade associations...trade shows...broadcasting education...awards...government agencies of interest to broadcasters & cable...& more *Publisher Paid Annotation.*

Bowker Staff, ed. Broadcasting & Cable Yearbook 1999, 2 vols., set. 1999. 179.95 (*0-8352-4110-6*) Bowker.

***Bowker Staff, ed.** Children's Books in Print 1999, 2 vols., Set. 1999. 169.00 (*0-8352-4077-0*) Bowker.

–Children's Books In Print 2001, 2 vols., Set. annuals 2500p. 2000. 175.95 (*0-8352-4320-6*) Bowker.

"...the most complete list of currently available children's books published in the U.S." --Booklist. No children's collection is complete without this practical resource standing front & center on the reference shelf. The 2001 edition of Children's Books In Print puts the entire world of children's books at your fingertips, arranging more than 151,000 in print titles by title, author & illustrator for fast, convenient access. Updated with 12,000 new entries & thousands of entry revisions, this comprehensive work helps you: *Track down any children's books - even hard-to-find titles from small presses. Locate all works by favorite authors or illustrators * Cut ordering time & effort with current prices, ISBNs, publishers' telephone numbers & addresses, Offer patrons a definitive, easy-access guide to all available titles geared for young readers. *Publisher Paid Annotation.*

— Children's Books in Print 2000, 2 vols., Set. 1999. 169.95 (*0-8352-4239-0*) Bowker.

Bowker Staff, ed. The Complete Directory of Large Print Books & Serials, 1999. large type ed. 450p. 1999. pap. 189.95 (*0-8352-4067-3*) Bowker.

***Bowker Staff, ed. Complete Directory of Large Print Books & Serials 2000. 20th large type ed. 1,100p. 2000. pap. 189.95 (*0-8352-4312-5*) Bowker.**

"...fills an important niche...will prove indispensable to all libraries having visually handicapped patrons." --ACADEMIC LIBRARY BOOK REVIEW. If you're building or managing a large-print collection, this proven guide helps you keep tabs on the fast growing large-print field like no other resource available - & the entire volume is printed in 14-point type to facilitate use by sight-impaired readers! You'll discover current, accurate bookfinding & ordering information on more than 15,000 titles - including scores of forthcoming works - with full entries for each in separate Subject (General, Children's & Textbook), Author & Title indexes. Books from British publishers are also listed. Up-to-date subject

An Asterisk (*) at the beginning of an entry indicates that the title is appearing for the first time.

Bowleg, Lisa & Stoll, Kathleen D. More Harm Than Help: The Ramifications for Rape Survivors of Mandatory HIV Testing of Rapists. (Violence Against Women Ser.). (Orig.). (C). 1991. pap. 10.00 (1-877966-08-8) Ctr Women Policy.

***Bowleg, Lisa, et al.** Inaccessible Miracles? Women's Access to HIV-AIDS Medications. 1999. pap. 8.00 (1-877966-60-6) Ctr Women Policy.

Bowlen, Bruce. The Orvis Wing-Shooting Handbook: Proven Techniques for Better Shotgunning. LC 85-17084. (Illus.). 96p. (Orig.). 1985. pap. 10.95 (0-941130-05-3) Lyons Pr.

Bowler, jt. auth. see Snider.

Bowler, Dave. Biography of Sir Alf Ramsey. (Illus.). 256p. 1998. 40.00 (0-575-06601-6, Pub. by V Gollancz) Trafalgar.

Bowler, Dave & Dray, Bryan. Aerosmith: What It Takes. (Illus.). 137p. 1997. pap. 17.95 (0-7522-2243-0, Pub. by Boxtree) Trafalgar.

— R. E. M. From Chronic Town to Monster. LC 95-22310. (Illus.). 216p. 1995. pap. 12.95 (0-8065-1724-7, Citadel Pr) Carol Pub Group.

Bowler, David. Danny Blanchflower. (Illus.). 256p. 1998. 40.00 (0-575-06504-4, Pub. by V Gollancz) Trafalgar.

***Bowler, Gerald.** The World Encyclopedia of Christmas. (Illus.). 336p. 2000. 39.95 (0-7710-1531-3) McClelland & Stewart.

Bowler, I. R. Government & Agriculture: A Spatial Perspective. LC 79-40129. (Topics in Applied Geography Ser.). 121p. reprint ed. pap. 37.60 (0-608-14477-0, 202527100043) Bks Demand.

Bowler, I. R., et al, eds. Contemporary Rural Systems in Transition Vol. 2: Economy & Society. (Illus.). 336p. 1992. text 90.00 (0-85198-812-1) OUP.

— Contemporary Rural Systems in Transition, Vol. 1 Vol. 1: Agriculture & Environment. (Illus.). 296p. 1992. text 90.00 (0-85198-811-3) OUP.

— Contemporary Rural Systems in Transition, Vol. 2: Ecology & Society, 2 vols., Set. 250p. 1992. 133.00 (0-85198-813-X) C A B Intl.

Bowler, Ian, jt. auth. see Atkins, Peter.

Bowler, Ian R. Agriculture under the Common Agriculture Policy: A Geography. LC 84-25041. 255p. 1985. pap. 15.00 (0-685-09209-7, Pub. by Manchester Univ Pr) St Martin.

— The Geography of Agriculture in Developed Market Economies. 1992. pap. 49.95 (0-582-30161-0, Pub. by Addison-Wesley) Longman.

Bowler, Ian R., ed. The Geography of Agriculture in Developed Market Economies. 1993. write for info. (0-318-69325-9) Longman.

Bowler, Jill, et al. Living Together Precedents. (Waterlow Publications). 80p. 1989. pap. 99.00 (0-08-040119-8, Pergamon Pr) Elsevier.

Bowler, Joseph D., ed. see De Sales, Francis.

Bowler, K., jt. auth. see Cossins, A. R.

Bowler, K. Christie, jt. auth. see Osborne, Rick.

Bowler, M. G. Nuclear Physics. 444p. (C). 1973. 191.00 (0-08-018990-3, Pub. by Pergamon Repr) Franklin.

Bowler, Marion. The Odd One. LC 77-86486. 1979. pap. 19.95 (0-87949-092-6, 77-86486) Ashley Bks.

Bowler, Michael. Destiny of Dreams. 200p. (Orig.). 1990. pap. 14.95 (1-85371-065-2, Pub. by Poolbeg Pr) Dufour.

Bowler, N. P. & Malone, C. B. Record of the Descendants of Charles Bowler. (Illus.). 298p. 1988. reprint ed. pap. 44.50 (0-8328-0293-X); reprint ed. lib. bdg. 52.50 (0-8328-0292-1) Higginson Bk Co.

Bowler, Osborne. Who is Sam Harrington? 12.99 (0-310-23203-1) HarpC.

Bowler, Peter. Earth Encompassed. pap. 18.95 (0-393-32080-4) Norton.

Bowler, Peter. Superior Person's Book of Weird & Wondrous Words. LC 84-48326. (Illus.). 128p. 1985. 15.95 (0-87923-556-X) Godine.

***Bowler, Peter.** The Superior Person's Third Book of Well-Bred Words. (Illus.). 2000. 16.95 (1-56792-161-2) Godine.

Bowler, Peter. Your Child from One to Ten. (C). 1990. 65.00 (0-86431-034-X, Pub. by Aust Council Educ Res) St Mut.

Bowler, Peter & Linke, Pam, eds. Your Child from One to Ten. 2nd ed. xi, 124p. 1996. pap. 55.00 (0-86431-196-6, Pub. by Aust Council Educ Res) St Mut.

Bowler, Peter, jt. auth. see Hughes, Denis.

Bowler, Peter J. Biology & Social Thought 1850-1914. Heilbron, John L., ed. LC 92-64057. (Berkeley Papers in History of Science: No. 15). 95p. (Orig.). 1993. pap. text 18.00 (0-918102-19-7) U Cal Hist Sci Tech.

— Charles Darwin: The Man & His Influence. LC 96-176241. (Science Biographies Ser.). (Illus.). 262p. (C). 1996. pap. 17.95 (0-521-56668-1); text 54.95 (0-521-56222-8) Cambridge U Pr.

— Darwinism. LC 93-431. (Twayne's Studies in Intellectual & Cultural History). 155p. 1993. 33.00 (0-8057-8613-9, Twyne); per. 14.95 (0-8057-8638-4, Twyne) Mac Lib Ref.

— The Eclipse of Darwinism: Anti-Darwinian Evolution Theories in the Decades Around 1900. 312p. 1992. reprint ed. pap. text 16.95 (0-8018-4391-X) Johns Hopkins.

— Evolution: The History of an Idea. rev. ed. 432p. (C). 1989. pap. 19.95 (0-520-06386-4, Pub. by U CA Pr) Cal Prin Full Svc.

— Lifes Splendid Drama. 526p. 1998. pap. text 22.00 (0-226-06922-2) U Ch Pr.

— Life's Splendid Drama: Evolutionary Biology & the Reconstruction of Life's Ancestry, 1860-1940. LC 95-25394. (Science & its Conceptual Foundations Ser.). (Illus.). 552p. 1996. 37.95 (0-226-06921-4) U Ch Pr.

— The Mendelian Revolution: The Emergence of Hereditarian Concepts in Modern Science & Society. LC 89-30914. 248p. 1989. text 38.50 (0-8018-3888-6) Johns Hopkins.

— Norton History of Environmental Sciences. Porter, Roy, ed. (History of Science Ser.). (Illus.). 652p. 1993. 35.00 (0-393-03535-2); pap. 17.95 (0-393-31042-6) Norton.

— Theories of Human Evolution: A Century of Debate, 1844-1944. LC 86-3029. (Illus.). 360p. 1986. text 42.00 (0-8018-3258-6) Johns Hopkins.

Bowler, R. Arthur, ed. see Rundell, Maria E.

Bowler, Rosemarie, jt. ed. see Cone, James.

Bowler, Rosemary, jt. auth. see Olivier, Carolyn.

Bowler, Shaun, et al, eds. Citizens As Legislators: Direct Democracy in the United States. LC 98-13863. (Parliaments & Legislatures Ser.). 328p. 1998. text 50.00 (0-8142-0777-4, BOWCIT); pap. text 19.95 (0-8142-0778-2, BOWCIX) Ohio St U Pr.

— Party Discipline & Parliamentary Government. LC 98-11722. (Parliaments & Legislatures Ser.). (Illus.). 313p. 1999. text 59.95 (0-8142-0796-0, BOWPAR); pap. text 22.50 (0-8142-5000-9, BOWPAX) Ohio St U Pr.

Bowler, Shaun & Donovan, Todd. Demanding Choices: Opinion, Voting, & Direct Democracy. (Illus.). 216p. (C). pap. text 21.95 (0-472-08715-0, 08715) U of Mich Pr.

Bowler, Shaun & Donovan, Todd. Demanding Choices: Opinion, Voting, & Direct Democracy. LC 98-19714. (Illus.). 216p. 1998. text 42.50 (0-472-10942-1, 10942) U of Mich Pr.

Bowler, Shaun & Grofman, Bernard, eds. Elections in Australia, Ireland & Malta under the Single Transferable Vote: Reflections on an Embedded Institution. (Illus.). 280p. (C). text 57.50 (0-472-11159-0, 11159) U of Mich Pr.

Bowler, Tim. Dragon's Rock. 154p. Date not set. pap. write for info. (0-19-271693-X) OUP.

***Bowler, Tim.** Midget. (Illus.). 160p. (YA). (gr. 7). 2000. 8.00 (0-689-82909-4) Aladdin.

— Midget. LC 94-46963. 160p. (YA). (gr. 7 up). 1995. pap. 15.00 (0-689-80115-7) McElderry Bks.

— River Boy. LC 99-20418. 160p. (gr. 7-12). 2000. 16.00 (0-689-82908-6) McElderry Bks.

Bowler, Tim, tr. see Born, Vibeke.

Bowles. Creative Editing for the Print Media. 3rd ed. LC 99-33126. (Mass Communication). 1999. pap. 65.95 (0-534-56178-0) Wadsworth Pub.

Bowles & Carver. Catchpenny Prints: One Hundred Sixty-Three Popular Engravings from the 18th Century. LC 79-103068. (Pictorial Archive Ser.). (Illus.). 163p. (Orig.). 1970. pap. 9.95 (0-486-22569-0) Dover.

Bowles & Willi. Blue Mountain Ballads Voice & Piano. 16p. 1986. pap. 7.95 (0-7935-5104-8, 50334790) H Leonard.

Bowles, jt. ed. see Gidley.

Bowles, Brad. Grandma's Band. (Illus.). 48p. (J). (gr. k-4). 1989. lib. bdg. 14.95 (0-88045-112-2) Stemmer Hse.

Bowles, C. R., Jr., et al. Consumer Bankruptcy Practice in Kentucky: Chapter 13 Practice. (Illus.). xiv, 253p. 1996. pap. 45.00 (1-58757-015-7, UM027) Univ of KY.

— Consumer Bankruptcy Practice in Kentucky: Chapter 7 Practice. (Illus.). xx, 359p. 1996. pap. 45.00 (1-58757-014-9, UM026) Univ of KY.

Bowles, Chester. Africa's Challenge to America. LC 78-100280. (Illus.). 134p. 1970. reprint ed. lib. bdg. 55.00 (0-8371-2918-4, BOCA) Greenwood.

— The Conscience of a Liberal. LC 74-15558. 351p. 1975. reprint ed. lib. bdg. 65.00 (0-8371-7826-6, BOCO, Greenwood Pr) Greenwood.

Bowles, D. & Metcalf, P. GCSE Maths: The Modular Course. 464p. 1998. pap. 32.50 (0-7487-2430-3, Pub. by S Thornes Pubs) Trans-Atl Phila.

Bowles, D. J., ed. Essays in Biochemistry Vol. 32: Cell Signalling. (Illus.). 176p. (C). 1997. pap. text 30.50 (1-85578-071-2, Pub. by Portland Pr Ltd) Ashgate Pub Co.

Bowles, D. J., et al, eds. Molecular Botany: Signals & the Environment. LC 95-182887. (Biochemical Society Symposium Ser.: Vol. 60). (Illus.). 290p. (C). 1994. text 110.50 (1-85578-050-X, Pub. by Portland Pr Ltd) Ashgate Pub Co.

Bowles, D. J., jt. ed. see Gurr, S. J.

***Bowles, David & Metcalf, Paul.** GCSE Maths: The Modular Course. rev. ed. (Illus.). 480p. (YA). (gr. 9-11). 2000. pap. 39.50 (0-7487-5510-1, Pub. by S Thornes Pubs) Trans-Atl Phila.

Bowles, David S. & Hon-Yim Ko, eds. Probabilistic Characterization of Soil Properties: Bridge Between Theory & Practice. 189p. 1984. 24.00 (0-87262-398-X) Am Soc Civil Eng.

Bowles, David S. & O'Connell, P. Edna, eds. Recent Advances in the Modeling of Hydrologic Systems. 684p. (C). 1991. text 301.50 (0-7923-1398-4) Kluwer Academic.

Bowles, Dorcas D., jt. ed. see Jacobs, Carolyn.

***Bowles, Dorothy A.** Media Law in Tennessee. 2nd rev. ed. 214p. (C). 1999. pap. text 18.95 (1-58107-022-5, Pub. by New Forums) Booksource.

Bowles, Dorothy A. & Borden, Diane L. Creative Editing for Print Media. 2nd ed. LC 96-28004. (Wadsworth Series in Mass Communication & Journalism). (Illus.). 389p. (C). 1996. pap. 42.75 (0-534-50893-6) Wadsworth Pub.

Bowles, Dorothy A., et al. Creative Editing for Print Media. 310p. (C). 1992. mass mkt. 30.00 (0-534-19098-7) Wadsworth Pub.

Bowles, Doug. Over in the Meadow: A Book of Colors & Counting. 8p. (J). 1999. 9.99 (1-58476-001-X) Innovative Kids.

Bowles, E. A. My Garden in Autumn & Winter. LC 98-17491. (Illus.). 348p. 1998. 24.95 (0-88192-459-8) Timber.

— My Garden in Spring. LC 96-38286. 308p. 1997. 24.95 (0-88192-375-3) Timber.

— My Garden in Summer. LC 97-41260. (Illus.). 393p. 1998. reprint ed. 24.95 (0-88192-413-X) Timber.

Bowles, Edmund. Timpani: A History in Pictures. 2000. 54.00 (0-945193-85-8) Pendragon NY.

Bowles, Edward A. My Garden in Spring. LC 78-178004. (Illus.). 1971. reprint ed. 12.50 (0-685-61145-0) Theophrastus.

Bowles, Ella S. Homespun Handicrafts. LC 75-183343. (Illus.). 251p. 1972. reprint ed. 23.95 (0-405-08298-3, Pub. by Blom Pubns) Ayer.

***Bowles, Ella Shannon & Towle, Dorothy S.** Secrets of New England Cooking. 2000. pap. 7.95 (0-486-41367-5) Dover.

Bowles, G. Strategies for Women's Studies in the Eighties. 100p. 1984. pap. 19.25 (0-08-031320-5, Pergamon Pr) Elsevier.

Bowles, Garrett H., compiled by. Ernst Krenek: A Bio-Bibliography, 22. LC 89-1883. (Bio-Bibliographies in Music Ser.: No. 22). 442p. 1989. lib. bdg. 75.00 (0-313-25250-5, BEK, Greenwood Pr) Greenwood.

Bowles, Gay. Beaded Cross-Stitch Treasures: Designs from Mill Hill. LC 99-35626. (Illus.). 128p. 1999. 27.95 (0-8069-5527-9) Sterling.

Bowles, Gloria. Louise Bogan's Aesthetic of Limitation. LC 86-45954. 166p. 1987. reprint ed. pap. 51.50 (0-608-01048-0, 205935600001) Bks Demand.

— Theories of Women's Studies. (Orig.). 1983. pap. 15.95 (0-7100-9488-4) Routledge.

Bowles, Gloria & Duelli-Klein, Renate, eds. Theories of Women's Studies. 270p. (Orig.). 1983. pap. 13.95 (0-415-04289-5) Routledge.

Bowles, Gordon T., jt. ed. see Count, Earl W.

Bowles, Helen M. Simply Good Low Fat-Low Cal Cookbook. 115p. (Orig.). 1995. pap. 11.95 (0-9647254-0-1) H Bowles.

***Bowles, James.** The Gods, Gemini & the Great Pyramid. LC 99-179928. (Illus.). 270p. 1998. pap. 16.00 (0-9666371-1-9, Pub. by Gemini) Adventures Unltd.

Bowles, Jane. My Sister's Hand in Mine: The Collected Works of Jane Bowles. rev. ed. 476p. 1966. pap. 17.00 (0-374-50652-3) FS&G.

— Out in the World: Selected Letters of Jane Bowles, 1935-1970. Dillon, Millicent, ed. LC 84-24470. (Illus.). 321p. 1990. reprint ed. 25.00 (0-87685-626-1); reprint ed. pap. 15.00 (0-87685-625-3) Black Sparrow.

— Two Serious Ladies. 200p. 1996. pap. 18.95 (0-7206-1006-0, Pub. by P Owen Ltd) Dufour.

Bowles, Jane, jt. auth. see Bates, Graham.

Bowles, Jennifer, jt. auth. see Lindenberger, Jan.

Bowles, Jerry & Hammond, Joshua. Beyond Quality. 256p. 1992. pap. 12.00 (0-425-13408-3) Berkley Pub.

Bowles, John B. Distribution & Biogeography of Mammals of Iowa. (Special Publications: No. 9). (Illus.). 184p. (Orig.). 1975. pap. 12.00 (0-89672-034-9) Tex Tech Univ Pr.

Bowles, John B., jt. auth. see Vichnevetsky, Robert.

Bowles, John P., ed. Soils. (Plants & Gardens Ser.). (Illus.). 240p. 1990. pap. 7.95 (0-945352-43-3) Bklyn Botanic.

Bowles, Joseph E. Engineering Properties of Soils & Their Measurement. 4th ed. 1992. text. write for info. (0-07-006778-3) McGraw.

— Foundation Analysis & Design. 2nd ed. (Illus.). 1977. text. write for info. (0-07-006750-3) McGraw.

— Foundation Analysis & Design. 3rd ed. 1982. text 64.08 (0-07-006770-8) McGraw.

— Foundation Analysis & Design. 4th ed. 1024p. 1988. text. write for info. (0-07-006776-7) McGraw.

— Foundation Analysis & Design. 5th ed. Incl. 5th ed. 1996. text (0-07-006873-9); LC 95-37880. 1024p. (C). 1995. 98.13 (0-07-912247-7) McGraw.

— Foundation Analysis & Design. 5th ed. 1995. 71.95 (0-07-006872-0) McGraw.

Bowles, K. L., et al. Problem Solving Using UCSD Pascal. 2nd ed. (Illus.). 350p. 1984. 58.95 (0-387-90822-6) Spr-Verlag.

***Bowles, Kate.** Tomorrow Never Knows: Soap on Australian Television. (Moving Image Ser.). 1998. pap. 12.00 (0-646-19209-4) Damned Pubng.

Bowles, Lan A. & Prickett, Glenn T., eds. Footprints in the Jungle: Natural Resource Industries, Infrastructure & Biodiversity Conservation. LC 99-18433. (Illus.). 352p. 2000. 45.00 (0-19-512578-9) OUP.

Bowles, Lenora. Jessie's Rebirth. 88p. 1998. pap. 10.00 (0-8059-4135-5) Dorrance.

Bowles, Marilyn L. & Whelan, Christopher J., eds. Restoration of Endangered Species: Conceptual Issues, Planning & Implementation. 416p. 1996. pap. text 31.95 (0-521-57422-6) Cambridge U Pr.

Bowles, Mark H. Did Someone Say Tomorrow? (Illus.). 450p. (Orig.). 1995. pap. 20.00 (0-9647024-0-1) Purpose Intl.

Bowles, Marlin L. & Whelan, Christopher J., eds. Restoration of Endangered Species: Conceptual Issues, Planning, & Implementation. LC 93-43593. (Illus.). 408p. (C). 1995. text 74.95 (0-521-41863-1) Cambridge U Pr.

Bowles, Michael. The Art of Conducting. LC 74-23419. (Music Ser.). 210p. 1975. reprint ed. lib. bdg. 29.50 (0-306-70718-7) Da Capo.

Bowles, Nigel. The Government & Politics of the United States. LC 93-2280. 1993. pap. 18.95 (0-312-10206-2) St Martin.

— The White House & Capitol Hill. 300p. 1987. 59.00 (0-19-827478-5) OUP.

Bowles, Norma, ed. Friendly Fire: An Anthology of 3 Plays by Queer Street Youth. (Illus.). 234p. 1997. pap. write for info. (0-9658335-0-X) A S K Theatre.

***Bowles, Norma & Rosenthal, Mark, eds.** Cootie Shots: Theatrical Inoculations Against Bigotry for Kids, Parents & Teachers. (Illus.). 160p. 2000. pap. 15.95 (1-55936-184-0, Pub. by Theatre Comm) Theatre Comm.

Bowles, Patrick, tr. see Beckett, Samuel.

Bowles, Patrick, tr. see Castelain, Daniel.

Bowles, Patrick, tr. see Durrenmatt, Friedrich.

Bowles, Paul. Collected Stories of Paul Bowles, 1939-1976. LC 79-4569. 420p. 1994. reprint ed. 25.00 (0-87685-397-1); reprint ed. pap. 17.50 (0-87685-396-3) Black Sparrow.

— The Delicate Prey. (Neglected Books of the 20th Century Ser.). 307p. 1990. reprint ed. pap. 12.00 (0-88001-263-3) HarpC.

— Distant Episode. 300p. (C). 1996. pap. 17.00 (0-88001-501-2) HarpC.

— A Hundred Camels in the Courtyard. 2nd ed. 96p. 1986. pap. 6.95 (0-87286-002-7) City Lights.

— In Touch. limited ed. 1994. 100.00 (0-374-18511-5) FS&G.

— In Touch: The Letters of Paul Bowles. Miller, Jeffrey, ed. LC 92-36994. 1994. 30.00 (0-374-18510-7) FS&G.

— In Touch: The Letters of Paul Bowles. Miller, Jeffery, ed. 606p. 1995. pap. 16.00 (0-374-52459-9) FS&G.

— James Brown: The Moroccan. 1994. pap. 29.95 (1-881616-30-4) Dist Art Pubs.

— Let It Come Down. LC 80-24825. 296p. 1994. reprint ed. 20.00 (0-87685-480-3); reprint ed. pap. 15.00 (0-87685-479-X) Black Sparrow.

— Midnight Mass. LC 81-4803. 176p. 1991. reprint ed. 17.50 (0-87685-477-3); reprint ed. pap. 12.50 (0-87685-476-5) Black Sparrow.

— Paul Bowles Photographs: How Could I Send a Picture into the Desert. 1993. 39.95 (1-881616-07-X, Pub. by Scalo Pubs) Dist Art Pubs.

— Points in Time. LC 83-16571. 96p. (C). 1999. pap. 9.95 (0-88001-117-3) HarpC.

— Port Bowles. 1999. pap. 22.00 (0-670-84461-6) Viking Penguin.

***Bowles, Paul.** The Sheltering Sky. 320p. 2000. 25.00 (0-06-019916-4, Ecco Press) HarperTrade.

Bowles, Paul. The Sheltering Sky. 1991. pap. 9.95 (0-685-48186-7) Vin Bks.

— The Sheltering Sky. 2nd ed. LC 77-22233. 320p. 1998. reprint ed. pap. 14.00 (0-88001-582-9) HarpC.

— The Spider's House. rev. ed. LC 82-4195. 410p. (C). 1994. reprint ed. 25.00 (0-87685-546-X); reprint ed. pap. 17.50 (0-87685-545-1) Black Sparrow.

Bowles, Paul. Their Heads Are Green. LC 83-16577. 1984. pap. 8.50 (0-88001-043-6) HarpC.

Bowles, Paul. Their Heads Are Green, Their Hands Are Blue. 2nd ed. 188p. 1994. pap. 13.00 (0-88001-301-X) HarpC.

— Too Far From Home. 1995. pap. 17.00 (0-88001-391-5) HarpC.

— Too Far from Home: The Selected Writings of Paul Bowles. 1999. 29.95 (0-88001-295-1) HarpC.

— Unwelcome Words. 100p. (Orig.). 1987. pap. 8.00 (0-939180-44-8) Tombouctou.

— Up Above The World. 223p. 1996. pap. 15.00 (0-88001-500-4) HarpC.

— Up above the World. rev. ed. 223p. 1991. pap. 15.00 (0-88001-302-8) HarpC.

— Without Stopping: An Autobiography. 1999. pap. 16.00 (0-88001-675-2) HarpC.

Bowles, Paul & Rorem, Ned. Dear Paul Dear Ned. (Illus.). 141p. 1997. 150.00 (0-9640399-7-4) Elysium Pr.

Bowles, Paul & Santoro, Vittorio. The Time of Friendship. (Illus.). 68p. 1996. 40.00 (3-9520497-2-7, 610201, Pub. by Memory-Cage) Dist Art Pubs.

Bowles, Paul & Vargas Llosa, Mario. Claudio Bravo: Paintings & Drawings. LC 97-169342. (Illus.). 273p. 1997. 95.00 (0-7892-0207-7) Abbeville Pr.

***Bowles, Paul, et al.** Japan after the Economic Miracle: In Search of New Directions. LC 99-52367. 1999. write for info. (0-7923-6031-1) Kluwer Academic.

Bowles, Paul, jt. auth. see Logan, Owen.

Bowles, Paul, tr. see Choukri, Mohamed.

Bowles, Paul, tr. see Eberhardt, Isabelle.

Bowles, Paul, tr. see Mrabet, Mohammed.

Bowles, Paul, tr. see Rey-Rosa, Rodrigo.

Bowles, Paul, tr. see Rosa, Rodrigo R.

Bowles, Rachel & Evans, Peter. Factfinders: Maps. (Fact Finders Ser.). (Illus.). (J). pap. 8.95 (0-563-37274-5, BBC-Parkwest) Parkwest Pubns.

Bowles, Robert N. How to Buy Gold for Thirty Percent Below Market: And to Avoid Confiscation by the Government. 1981. 67.50 (0-940372-00-2) Berot Bk.

Bowles, Roger & Jones, Philip. Professional Liability: An Economic Analysis. (David Hume Papers: No. 11). 92p. 1989. pap. text 14.00 (0-08-037962-1, Pub. by Aberdeen U Pr) Macmillan.

Bowles, Samuel. Across the Continent: A Summer's Journey to the Rocky Mountains, the Mormons, & the Pacific States with Speaker Colfax. (American Biography Ser.). 438p. 1991. reprint ed. lib. bdg. 89.00 (0-7812-8032-X) Rprt Serv.

— Life & Times of Samuel Bowles, 2 vols. Merriam, George S., ed. LC 75-87417. (American Scene Ser.). 1970. reprint ed. lib. bdg. 95.00 (0-306-71562-7) Da Capo.

— Our New West: Records of Travel Between the Mississippi & the Pacific Ocean. LC 72-9429. (Far Western Frontier Ser.). (Illus.). 528p. 1973. reprint ed. 35.95 (0-405-04960-9) Ayer.

— Our New West: Records of Travel Between the Mississippi River & the Pacific Ocean. (Illus.). 526p. 1990. reprint ed. pap. 31.50 (1-55613-354-5) Heritage Bk.

— The Parks & Mountains of Colorado: A Summer Vacation in the Switzerland of America, 1868. LC 92-28589. (Illus.). 256p. 1994. pap. 12.95 (*0-8061-2625-6*) U of Okla Pr.

— Recasting Egalitarianism: New Rules for Communities, States & Markets. LC 98-35498. 352p. 2000. 60.00 (*1-85984-863-X*, Pub. by Verso) Norton.

Bowles, Samuel, et al, eds. Markets & Democracy: Participation, Accountability, & Efficiency. LC 92-30242. (Illus.). 358p. (C). 1993. text 69.95 (*0-521-43223-5*) Cambridge U Pr.

— The Politics & Economics of Power. LC 98-35367. (The Siena Summer School Ser.). 320p. (C). (gr. 13). 1999. 75.00 (*0-415-18542-4*, D6266) Routledge.

Bowles, Samuel & Edwards, Richard, eds. Radical Political Economy, 2 vols. (Schools of Thought in Economics Ser.: No. 8). (Illus.). 848p. 1990. text 360.00 (*1-85278-122-X*) E Elgar.

Bowles, Samuel & Gintis, Herbert M. Recasting Egalitarianism: New Rules for Communities, States & Markets. LC 98-35498. (Real Utopias Project Ser.). (Illus.). 397p. 1999. pap. 15.00 (*1-85984-255-0*, Pub. by Verso) Norton.

— Schooling in Capitalist America: Educational Reform & the Contradictions of Economic Life. LC 75-7267. 352p. 1977. pap. 20.00 (*0-465-09718-9*, Pub. by Basic) HarpC.

Bowles, Samuel, et al. After the Waste Land: A Democratic Economics for the Year 2000. LC 90-9078. 288p. (gr. 13). 1991. text 69.95 (*0-87332-644-X*) M E Sharpe.

Bowles, Samuel, et al. After the Waste Land: A Democratic Economics for the Year 2000. LC 90-9078. 288p. (gr. 13). 1991. pap. text 32.95 (*0-87332-645-8*) M E Sharpe.

Bowles, Samuel, ed. see Gordon, David M.

Bowles, Sharon, jt. ed. see Walker, Maxine.

Bowles, Sheldon, jt. auth. see Blanchard, Ken.

Bowles, Sheldon, jt. auth. see Blanchard, Kenneth.

Bowles, Stephen E. An Approach to Film Study: A Selected Booklist & Bibliography. (Cinema Ser.). 1974. 250.00 (*0-87700-206-1*) Revisionist Pr.

— The Film Anthologies Index. LC 94-13541. 1994. 60.00 (*0-8108-2896-0*) Scarecrow.

Bowles, Victoria. Teach Yourself Beginner's Italian, Set. (Teach Yourself Ser.). (ITA.). 224p. 1996. pap. 17.95 incl. audio (*0-8442-3881-3*, Teach Yrslf) NTC Contemp Pub Co.

— Teach Yourself Italian: Beginner's Book. (Teach Yourself Ser.). 1992. 13.95 (*0-8288-8362-9*); 33.95 incl. audio (*0-8288-8363-7*) Fr & Eur.

Bowles, Vittoria. Teach Yourself Beginner's Italian. (ENG & ITA., Illus.). 224p. 1995. pap. 9.95 (*0-8442-3801-5*, Teach Yrslf) NTC Contemp Pub Co.

— Teach Yourself Beginner's Italian. (Teach Yourself Beginner's Grammar Ser.). 224p. 1999. pap. 10.95 (*0-8442-2689-0*, Teach Yrslf) NTC Contemp Pub Co.

Bowles, Wendy, jt. auth. see Alston, Margaret.

Bowles, Willa V. & Wirth, Carl G. Insomnia Plus... The Answer to Sleeplessness. 141p. 1990. pap. 7.95 (*0-9625716-0-1*) Temple Treasures Pubns.

Bowles, William A. Authentic Memoirs of William Augustus Bowles, Esquire, Ambassador from the United Nations of Creeks & Cherokees, to the Court of London. LC 73-146376. (First American Frontier Ser.). 1976. reprint ed. 22.95 (*0-405-02827-X*) Ayer.

Bowles, William L. Fourteen Sonnets. LC 91-8630. 30p. 1991. reprint ed. 43.00 (*1-85477-059-4*) Continuum.

Bowley, Al & Stamp, Josiah. Three Studies of National Income: London School of Economics. (LSE Scarce Tracts in Economics Ser.). 145p. (C). 1997. 60.00 (*0-415-14392-6*) Routledge.

Bowley, Arthur L. F. Y. Edgeworth's Contributions to Mathematical Statistics. LC 68-24161. (Reprints of Economic Classics Ser.). vii, 139p. 1972. reprint ed. 29.50 (*0-678-00889-2*) Kelley.

Bowley, C. C., et al, eds. Blood Transfusion & Addendum 1978: A Guide to the Formation & Operation of a Transfusion Service. 147p. 1978. pap. text 14.00 (*92-4-154013-3*, 1150016) World Health.

Bowley, David W. The Wreck of the General Arnold: The Mystery of a Revolutionary Privateer in Plymouth Harbor. Johnson, Doris M., ed. LC 92-70659. (Illus.). 196p. (Orig.). 1992. pap. 15.00 (*0-9628738-3-7*) Jones Riv Pr.

Bowley, Freeman S., jt. auth. see Seagrave, Ronald R.

Bowley, James E., ed. Living Traditions of the Bible: Scripture in Jewish, Christian & Muslim Practice. LC 99-29735. 224p. 1999. pap. 19.99 (*0-8272-2127-4*, 985685, Pub. by Chalice Pr) Abingdon.

Bowley, Marian. The British Building Industry: Four Studies in Response & Resistance to Change. LC 65-14856. 502p. reprint ed. pap. 143.10 (*0-8357-3608-3*, 2027276) Bks Demand.

***Bowley, Mary F.** Taking Baby Steps: Toward Walking with God. 100p. 1999. pap. 5.00 (*0-7392-0314-2*, PO3455) Morris Pubng.

Bowley, R. L. Teaching Without Tears. 204p. 1973. pap. 17.95 (*0-8464-0909-7*) Beekman Pubs.

Bowley, Roger & Sanchez, Mariana. Introductory Statistical Mechanics. 2nd ed. LC 99-25577. (Illus.). 360p. 2000. pap. text 37.50 (*0-19-850576-0*) OUP.

Bowlin. Financial Analysis. 2nd ed. 1990. teacher ed. 22.18 (*0-07-006806-2*) McGraw.

Bowlin, John R. Contingency & Fortune in Aquinas's Ethics. LC 98-35103. (Cambridge Studies in Religion & Critical Thought: No. 6). 272p. (C). 1999. text 59.95 (*0-521-62019-8*) Cambridge U Pr.

Bowlin, Oswald D., et al. Guide to Financial Analysis. 2nd ed. (C). 1990. text 48.50 (*0-07-006805-4*) McGraw.

Bowlin, William R. A Book of Fireside Poems. 157p. 1977. 20.95 (*0-8369-8232-0*) Ayer.

Bowlin, William R., ed. A Book of Living Poems. LC 72-3088. (Granger Index Reprint Ser.). 1977. reprint ed. 20.95 (*0-8369-8233-9*) Ayer.

— A Book of Treasured Poems. LC 72-3090. (Granger Index Reprint Ser.). 1977. reprint ed. 22.95 (*0-8369-8234-7*) Ayer.

Bowling, ed. see Woods, B. J.

Bowling, Ann. Measuring Disease. LC 94-28081. 17.99p. 1994. pap. text 36.95 (*0-335-19225-4*) OpUniv Pr.

Bowling, Ann & Cartwright, Ann. Life after a Death: A Study of the Elderly Widowed. 239p. 1982. 29.95 (*0-422-78230-0*, NO. 3712, Pub. by Tavistock) Routldge.

Bowling, Ann T. Horse Genetics. (A CAB International Publication). 224p. 1996. pap. text 37.50 (*0-85199-101-7*) OUP.

***Bowling, Ann T. & Ruvinsky, Anatoly.** The Genetics of the Horse. LC 99-57248. (CABI Publishing Ser.). 576p. 2000. 160.00 (*0-85199-429-6*) C A B Intl.

***Bowling, Barbara L.** The Berry Grower's Companion. LC 00-26907. (Illus.). 350p. 2000. 29.95 (*0-88192-489-X*) Timber.

Bowling, Benjamin. Violent Racism: Victimization, Policing & Social Context. LC 97-47464. (Clarendon Studies in Criminology). (Illus.). 402p. 1998. text 75.00 (*0-19-826252-3*) OUP.

Bowling, Charles M. Principles & Elements of Thought Construction, Artificial Intelligence & Cognitive Robotics. LC 87-73448. (Illus.). 152p. (C). 1987. 29.95 (*0-945541-00-7*) CSY Pub Inc.

Bowling, D. Measuring Health: A Review of Quality of Life Measurement Scales. 2nd ed. LC 96-50373. 1997. pap. 30.95 (*0-335-19754-X*) OpUniv Pr.

— Research Methods in Health: Investigating Health & Health Services. LC 97-7997. 1997. pap. 31.95 (*0-335-19885-6*) OpUniv Pr.

Bowling, David L. & Bowling, Patricia H. Clean up Your Act, Dirty Dinjy Daryl. (Dirty Dingy Daryl Ser.). (Illus.). 32p. (Orig.). (J). (ps-4). 1994. pap., per. 4.95 (*0-939700-04-2*) I D I C P.

— Dirty Dingy Daryl. LC 81-83120. (Dirty Dingy Daryl Ser.). (Illus.). 24p. (J). (ps-4). 1981. pap. 4.95 (*0-939700-01-8*) I D I C P.

— Dirty Dingy Daryl for President. LC 83-82273. (Dirty Dingy Daryl Ser.). (Illus.). 40p. (J). (gr. 1-4). 1983. pap. 4.95 (*0-939700-03-4*) I D I C P.

Bowling, Evelyn. After Your First Six Words ... I Know You: A Guide to Tooling, up the Great You. Brown, Jack, ed. 232p. (Orig.). 1988. pap. 15.00 (*0-923834-06-0*) Shenandoah Val Bk.

— Voice Power. (Illus.). 219p. (Orig.). 1988. pap. 15.00 (*0-923834-04-4*) Shenandoah Val Bk.

***Bowling, H.** As Time Goes By. 1998. text 27.00 (*0-7472-2090-5*, Pub. by Headline Bk Pub) Trafalgar.

— Down Milldyke Way. 1999. pap. 11.00 (*0-7472-5543-1*, Pub. by Headline Bk Pub) Trafalgar.

— Farrans of Fellmonger Street. 1999. pap. 11.00 (*0-7472-4795-1*, Pub. by Headline Bk Pub) Trafalgar.

— Gaslight in Page Street. 1999. pap. 13.00 (*0-7472-3690-9*, Pub. by Headline Bk Pub) Trafalgar.

— Girl from Cotton Lane. 1999. pap. 11.00 (*0-7472-3869-3*, Pub. by Headline Bk Pub) Trafalgar.

***Bowling, Harry.** As Time Goes By. large type ed. 448p. 2000. write for info. (*0-7505-1435-3*, Pub. by Mgna Lrg Print) Ulverscroft.

Bowling, Harry. Down Milldyke Way. large type ed. (Magna Large Print Ser.). 524p. 1998. 29.99 (*0-7505-1229-6*, Pub. by Mgna Lrg Print) Ulverscroft.

— That Summer in Eagle Street. large type ed. (Magna Large Print Ser.). 616p. 1997. 27.99 (*0-7505-1063-3*) Ulverscroft.

— Waggoner's Way. large type ed. (Magna Large Print Ser.). 656p. 1996. 27.99 (*0-7505-0984-8*, Pub. by Mgna Lrg Print) Ulverscroft.

***Bowling, Jimmy.** Vietnam Poetry from a Blacklion Grunt. 48p. (YA). (gr. 6 up). 2000. pap. 7.00 (*0-923242-74-0*) Sparrowgrass Poetry.

Bowling, John C. Grace-Full Leadership: Understanding the Heart of a Christian Leader. Date not set. pap. 15.99 (*0-8341-1775-4*) Beacon Hill.

Bowling, John C. Way with Words: The Power & Presence of Our Language. LC 99-13413. 160p. 1999. pap. text 12.99 (*0-8341-1802-5*) Beacon Hill.

Bowling, Kenneth R. The Creation of Washington D. C. The Idea & Location of the American Capital. LC 90-39255. (Illus.). 310p. (Orig.). (C). 1993. 24.95 (*0-913969-29-X*); pap. 16.95 (*0-913969-59-1*) Univ Pub Assocs.

Bowling, Kenneth R. & Kennon, Donald R., eds. Inventing Congress: Origins & Establishment of the First Federal Congress. LC 98-46969. 304p. 1999. 44.95 (*0-8214-1271-X*) Ohio U Pr.

***Bowling, Kenneth R. & Kennon, Donald R., eds.** Neither Separate nor Equal: Congress in the 1790s. (Perspectives on the History of Congress Ser.: No. 2). (Illus.). 368p. 2000. 44.95 (*0-8214-1327-9*, Ohio U Ctr Intl) Ohio U Pr.

Bowling, Kenneth R. & Veit, Helen E., eds. Documentary History of the First Federal Congress of the United States of America, March 4, 1789-March 3, 1791 Vol. 9: The Diary of William Maclay & Other Notes on Senate Debates. LC 87-22793. 576p. 1988. pap. 15.95 (*0-8018-3683-2*); text 75.00 (*0-8018-3535-6*) Johns Hopkins.

Bowling, Kenneth R., et al. Petition Histories: Revolutionary War Related Claims. LC 97-7834. (Documentary History of the First Federal Congress of the United States of America Ser.: Vol. 7). 636p. 1998. 75.00 (*0-8018-5565-9*) Johns Hopkins.

— Petition Histories & Nonlegislative Official Documents. LC 97-4994. (Documentary History of the First Federal Congress of the United States of America Ser.: Vol. 8). 912p. 1997. 75.00 (*0-8018-5566-7*) Johns Hopkins.

Bowling, Kenneth R., jt. auth. see Bickford, Charlene B.

***Bowling, Les.** Leave the Crowd Behind. 2000. pap. 9.99 (*1-930027-00-1*) Insght Pub.

Bowling, P. J. The Depression Coloring Book. (Illus.). 50p. (Orig.). 1995. pap. 13.95 (*0-9653013-0-3*, 1010) Silent Storm.

Bowling, Patricia H., jt. auth. see Bowling, David L.

Bowling, Ray. California Criminal Procedure Workbook. 4th ed. (Illus.). 143p. (C). 1996. pap. 14.95 (*1-9289?6-05-8*) Copperhouse.

Bowling, Sarah. Exploring the Word: Discovering Rich Treasure in God's Word. 1998. pap. 6.95 (*1-56441-034-X*) M Hickey Min.

— Face to Face with the Father. 1998. pap. 1.00 (*1-56441-174-5*) M Hickey Min.

— Jump Start Your Heart: Breathing New Life into Your Walk with God. 1997. pap. 6.95 (*1-56441-032-3*) M Hickey Min.

— Prevailing Through Prayer. 1998. pap. 1.00 (*1-56441-177-X*) M Hickey Min.

Bowling, Sue A., jt. auth. see Weller, Gunter.

***Bowling, Tim.** The Downriver Drift. 250p. 2000. pap. 18.95 (*1-55017-220-4*) Harbour Pub Co.

— The Thin Smoke of the Heart. (Hugh MacLennan Poetry Ser.). 90p. 2000. pap. 12.95 (*0-7735-1905-X*, Pub. by McG-Queens Univ Pr) CUP Services.

Bowlt & Misler. The Russian Narrative of Art, 1901-2000: Towards Historiography of Modern Art Russia. 1998. 85.00 (*0-7838-2034-8*) Mac Lib Ref.

Bowlt, John. The Silver Age: Russian Art in the Early Twentieth Century & the World Art Group. 2nd ed. (Illus.). 456p. 1982. 38.00 (*0-89250-063-8*) Orient Res Partners.

***Bowlt, John.** Painting Revolution: Kandinsky, Malevich & the Russian Avant Garde. 212p. 2000. pap. write for info. (*0-9678451-0-6*) Fndt for Intl Arts.

Bowlt, John E. Laboratory of Dreams: The Russian Avant-Garde & Cultural Experiment. 1999. pap. text 19.95 (*0-8047-3652-9*) Stanford U Pr.

— Ten Plus Ten: Contemporary Soviet & American Painters. (Illus.). 170p. 1989. 39.95 (*0-8109-1668-1*, Pub. by Abrams) Time Warner.

Bowlt, John E., ed. Russian Stage Design: Scenic Innovation, 1900-1930: from the Collection of Mr. & Mrs. Nikita D. Lobanov-Rostovsky. viii, 344p. 1982. pap. 15.95 (*1-884445-12-8*) C Schlacks Pub.

***Bowlt, John E. & Drutt, Matthew, eds.** Amazons of the Avant-Garde. (Illus.). 352p. 2000. 39.95 (*0-8109-6924-6*, Pub. by Abrams) Time Warner.

Bowlt, John E. & Kasak, Nikolai. From Action to Dynamic Silence: The Art of Nikolai Kasak. LC 91-60961. 179p. 1991. 39.50 (*1-884445-11-X*) C Schlacks Pub.

Bowlt, John E., jt. auth. see Balakina, Natalia M.

Bowlt, John E., ed. see Livshits, Benedikt.

Bowlt, L. Russian Art of the Avant Garde: Theory & Criticism, 1902-1934. (C). 1990. pap. 160.00 (*0-7855-4453-4*, Pub. by Collets) St Mut.

Bowlus, Charles R. Franks, Moravians, & Magyars: The Struggle for the Middle Danube, 788-907. (Middle Ages Ser.). (Illus.). 384p. (C). 1995. text 49.95 (*0-8122-3276-3*) U of Pa Pr.

Bowlus, Charley D. Chambers: Evolution of the Chambers, Bowlus & Remsburg Families. (Illus.). 108p. 1997. reprint ed. pap. 17.00 (*0-8328-7904-5*); reprint ed. lib. bdg. 27.00 (*0-8328-7903-7*) Higginson Bk Co.

Bowlware, Chris, ed. see Nogle, Alfredo D.

Bowly, Devereux, Jr. The Poorhouse: Subsidized Housing in Chicago, 1895-1976. LC 77-28271. (Illus.). 267p. 1978. 26.95 (*0-8093-0831-2*) S Ill U Pr.

Bowman. Business Communication Strategies. (General Business & Business Education Ser.). 1997. pap., suppl. ed. 62.95 (*0-8273-6876-3*) Delmar.

— Business Communication Strategies. (General Business & Business Education Ser.). (C). 1997. suppl. ed. 76.95 (*0-8273-6880-1*) Delmar.

— Business Communication Strategies. annot. ed. (General Business & Business Education Ser.). 1997. 76.95 (*0-8273-6878-X*) Delmar.

— Hawaii Rules of Evidence Manual. 2nd ed. LC 98-87062. 701p. 1998. 99.00 (*0-327-00854-7*, 6062611) LEXIS Pub.

— Issues. Date not set. pap. text. write for info. (*0-17-555727-6*) Addison-Wesley.

— The 1993-1994 Debate on Health Care: Did the Polls Mislead the Policy Makers? 50p. (Orig.). 1995. pap. 9.95 (*0-8447-7031-0*) Am Enterprise.

— State & Local Government, 3 vols. (C). 1995. pap., teacher ed., suppl. ed. 11.96 (*0-395-73042-2*) HM.

— State & Local Government, 3 vols. 3rd ed. LC 95-75927. (C). 1995. text 56.76 (*0-395-73041-4*) HM.

— Strategy in Practice 2nd ed. 1998. pap. 41.00 (*0-13-356486-X*) P-H.

Bowman, ed. Thomas Jefferson & the Republican Vision. (L.A.B. Ser.). (C). 1999. text. write for info. (*0-673-99830-4*) Addison-Wesley.

Bowman & Campbell. Our National Heritage Vol. 1: Essays in American History Before 1865. 2nd ed. 352p. 1993. per. 19.95 (*0-8403-8221-9*) Kendall-Hunt.

Bowman & Hampton. Local Democracies: A Study. Date not set. pap. text. write for info. (*0-582-71220-3*, Pub. by Addison-Wesley) Longman.

***Bowman & Milligan.** Real Estate Law in California. 10th ed. LC 99-12024. (Illus.). 482p. 1999. 66.00 (*0-13-022035-3*) P-H.

***Bowman, A. & McColl, J., eds.** Statistical Problem Solving Through Steps: Computer Based Modules for Practical Work. (Arnold Publications). 260p. 1999. text 200.00 (*0-340-73180-X*) OUP.

Bowman, A. W. & Robinson, D. R. Introduction to Probability. (Illus.). 100p. 1986. disk 270.00 (*0-7503-0087-6*) IOP Pub.

— An Introduction to Regression & Analysis of Variance. (Illus.). 228p. (C). 1990. pap. 39.00 (*0-85274-332-7*); disk 170.00 (*0-7503-0091-4*) IOP Pub.

— Introduction to Statistics. (Illus.). 216p. 1987. pap. 39.00 (*0-85274-408-0*); disk 270.00 (*0-7503-0094-9*) IOP Pub.

Bowman, Addison. Hawaii Rules of Evidence Manual: 1992 Supplement. 52p. 1992. write for info. (*0-87473-769-9*, 60627-10, MICHIE) LEXIS Pub.

Bowman, Addison M. Hawaii Rules of Evidence Manual. 1994. suppl. ed. write for info. (*0-614-05835-X*, MICHIE) LEXIS Pub.

— Hawaii Rules of Evidence Manual: With 1992 Supplement. 557p. 1990. 99.00 (*0-87473-639-0*, 60626-10, MICHIE) LEXIS Pub.

Bowman, Adrian W. & Azzalini, Adelchi. Applied Smoothing Techniques for Data Analysis: The Kernel Approach with S-Plus Illustrations. LC 98-100617. (Oxford Statistical Science Ser.: No. 18). (Illus.). 204p. 1997. text 50.00 (*0-19-852396-3*) OUP.

***Bowman, Alan, et al, eds.** The Cambridge Ancient History: The High Empire, AD 70-192, Vol. 11. (Illus.). 1200p. (C). 2001. Price not set. (*0-521-26335-2*) Cambridge U Pr.

Bowman, Alan K. Egypt after the Pharaohs, 332 BC-AD 642. rev. ed. (Illus.). 272p. (C). 1996. pap. 17.95 (*0-520-20531-6*, Pub. by U CA Pr) Cal Prin Full Svc.

— Egypt after the Pharaohs, 332 BC-AD 642: From Alexander to the Arab Conquest. LC 86-11355. (Illus.). 264p. reprint ed. pap. 81.90 (*0-7837-4835-3*, 204448200003) Bks Demand.

— Life & Letters on the Roman Frontier: Vindolanda & Its People. LC 97-52950. 160p. (C). 1998. 75.00 (*0-415-92024-8*); pap. 20.99 (*0-415-92025-6*) Routledge.

Bowman, Alan K., et al, eds. The Cambridge Ancient History Vol. 10: The Augustan Empire, 43 B.C.-A.D. 69. 2nd ed. 1215p. (C). 1996. text 160.00 (*0-521-26430-8*) Cambridge U Pr.

Bowman, Alan K. & Rogan, Eugene, eds. Agriculture in Egypt from Pharaonic to Modern Times, Vol. 96. (Proceedings of the British Academy Ser.). (Illus.). 456p. 1999. text 72.00 (*0-19-726183-3*) OUP.

Bowman, Alan K. & Woolf, Greg, eds. Literacy & Power in the Ancient World. (Illus.). 259p. 1997. pap. text 19.95 (*0-521-58736-0*) Cambridge U Pr.

Bowman, Alan P. Index to the 1850 Census of the State of California. LC 70-148609. 605p. 1997. pap. 45.00 (*0-8063-0484-7*) Clearfield Co.

Bowman, Albert H. The Struggle for Neutrality: Franco-American Diplomacy. LC 73-21917. 480p. reprint ed. pap. 148.80 (*0-8357-6912-7*, 203797000009) Bks Demand.

Bowman, Alice W. Twinkle-Dust. rev. ed. LC 95-78256. 24p. (J). (gr. k-6). 1998. pap. 7.95 (*0-9645870-6-8*) Big Ft Pub.

— Twinkle-Dust: A Cool Adventure. LC 97-94160. (Illus.). 24p. (J). (gr. k-5). 1997. pap. 6.95 (*0-9645870-5-X*) Big Ft Pub.

— Twinkle-Dust: A Dazzling Adventure. LC 96-83952. (Illus.). 32p. (J). (gr. k-6). 1996. pap. 6.95 (*0-9645870-3-3*) Big Ft Pub.

— Twinkle Dust - His Awesome Adventure. LC 95-78257. (Twinkle Dust Ser.: No. 2). (Illus.). 24p. (Orig.). (J). (ps-6). 1998. pap. 6.95 (*0-9645870-2-5*) Big Ft Pub.

Bowman, Allen. Morale of the American Revolutionary Army. (History - United States Ser.). 160p. 1993. reprint ed. lib. bdg. 69.00 (*0-7812-4874-4*) Rprt Serv.

Bowman, Andrew L. Being Human. (Orig.). 1970. pap. 3.45 (*0-930254-01-5*) Alethes.

Bowman, Angie. Hitchcock County, NE. (Illus.). 555p. 1990. 60.00 (*0-88107-157-9*) Curtis Media.

Bowman, Ann, jt. ed. see Lester, James P.

Bowman, Ann G. & Allen, Diane M. California Water Code, 1995. 1995. 65.00 (*0-07-172716-7*) Shepards.

Bowman, Ann O., jt. auth. see Pagano, Michael A.

***Bowman, Ann O'M. & Kearney, Richard C.** State & Local Government. 4th ed. LC 98-71990. 12 p. 1999. text 45.57 (*0-395-90617-2*) HM.

Bowman, Barbara. Master Space: Film Images of Capra, Lubitsch, Sternberg, & Wyler, 31. LC 91-33480. (Contributions to the Study of Popular Culture Ser.: No. 31). 192p. 1992. 49.95 (*0-313-28026-6*, BWQ, Greenwood Pr) Greenwood.

Bowman, Barbara T., jt. ed. see Kagan, Sharon L.

Bowman, Betty A., jt. auth. see Hale, George.

Bowman, Betty B., jt. auth. see Haleem, Muzaffar.

Bowman, Billye G. Had I Known You Better, Lord I'd a Come Runnin' with a Bucket. Goodman, James, ed. 240p. (Orig.). 1996. pap. 9.95 (*0-89896-140-8*, Linolean Pr) Larksdale.

Bowman, Bob. Best of East Texas, 1. 1991. 12.95 (*1-878096-13-3*) Best E TX Pubs.

— Best of East Texas, 2. 1991. 13.95 (*1-878096-14-1*) Best E TX Pubs.

— Best of East Texas, 3. 1991. 14.95 (*1-878096-15-X*) Best E TX Pubs.

***Bowman, Bob.** East Texas Calling: The Centennial History of the Lufkin-Conroe Telephone Exchange. 160p. 1998. write for info. (*1-878096-49-4*, Epigram Pr) Best E TX Pubs.

Bowman, Bob. East Texas Sunday Drive. 1990. 16.95 (*1-878096-00-1*) Best E TX Pubs.

***Bowman, Bob.** The Gift of Las Sabinas: The History of the Sabine River Authority of Texas. 280p. 1999. write for info. (*1-878096-45-1*, Epigram Pr) Best E TX Pubs.

— He's Wetting on My Leg, It's Warm but it Feels Good. 180p. 1998. 24.95 (*1-878096-41-9*, Epigram Pr) Best E TX Pubs.

Bowman, Bob. I Would've Been a Lumberjack. 1991. 16.95 (*1-878096-21-4*) Best E TX Pubs.

— I'm Meeting Myself Coming Back from Where I've Been. 140p. 17.95 (*1-878096-30-3*) Best E TX Pubs.

— Plant Watermelons on My Grave. 1991. 16.95 (*1-878096-20-6*) Best E TX Pubs.

*Bowman, Bob. Rub Onions & Skunk Oil on My Chest & Call Me Well. 160p. 1998. 19.95 (*1-878096-44-3*, Epigram Pr) Best E TX Pubs.

Bowman, Bob. Say . . . Do You Know a Good Place to Eat? 133p. 12.95 (*1-878096-16-8*) Best E TX Pubs.

— They Left No Monuments. 1991. 9.95 (*1-878096-18-4*) Best E TX Pubs.

— Thirty-Five Best Ghost Towns. 1991. 16.95 (*1-878096-12-5*) Best E TX Pubs.

Bowman, Bob. Wag: The Story of Texas Coaching Legend Floyd Wagstaff. 108p. 24.95 (*1-878096-33-8*, Epigram Pr) Best E TX Pubs.

***Bowman, Bob & Bowman, Doris.** The Search for an Alamo Soldier. 168p. 1998. 20.00 (*1-878096-47-8*, Epigram Pr) Best E TX Pubs.

Bowman, Bruce. Waikiki. 245p. (Orig.). 1988. pap. text 3.95 (*0-9620175-0-7*) Makai Pub.

Bowman, C. E., jt. auth. see Griffiths, D. A.

Bowman, Carl, jt. auth. see Bowman, Lori.

Bowman, Carl F. Brethren Society: The Cultural Transformation of a "Peculiar People" LC 94-19329. (Illus.). 512p. 1995. text 65.00 (*0-8018-4904-7*); pap. text 19.95 (*0-8018-4905-5*) Johns Hopkins.

Bowman, Carol. Children's Past Lives: How Past Life Memories Affect Your Child. 368p. 1998. reprint ed. mass mkt. 6.99 (*0-553-57485-X*) Bantam.

Bowman, Carol, ed. see Wade, Charles R.

Bowman, Catherine. Crystal Ascension: Spiritual Growth & Planetary Healing. LC 96-36246. (Illus.). 192p. (Orig.). 1996. pap. 6.95 (*1-56718-075-2*, K-075-2) Llewellyn Pubns.

— Crystal Awareness. LC 87-46112. (New Age Ser.). (Illus.). 224p. (Orig.). 1999. mass mkt. 3.95 (*0-87542-058-3*) Llewellyn Pubns.

— Rock Farm. LC 96-17261. (Illus.). 64p. (Orig.). 1996. pap. 12.95 (*0-87905-745-9*) Gibbs Smith Pub.

Bowman, Charles. The White Plume. (Illus.). 160p. 10.00 (*0-8092-7911-8*, Pub. by Boston Mills) Genl Dist Srvs.

Bowman, Charles, ed. Wisdom of the Gurus: A Vision for Object Technology. (SIGS Referency Library: No. 8). 465p. (Orig.). (C). 1998. pap. 29.95 (*0-13-499849-9*) Cambridge U Pr.

Bowman, Charles F. Algorithms & Data Structures: An Approach in C. (Illus.). 352p. 1994. text 69.95 (*0-19-511443-4*) OUP.

— The New X Window System: An Internet Architecture for Clustered. LC 99-57912. 153p. (C). 2000. pap. text 32.95 (*0-201-18463-X*) Addison-Wesley.

— Objectifying Motif. (Advances in Object Technology Ser.: No. 10). 516p. (Orig.). 1995. pap. 39.95 (*0-13-234436-X*) Cambridge U Pr.

Bowman, Christopher. How Do You Know? Wisdom in the Bible. (Generation Why: Vol. 2:2). 36p. (YA). (gr. 9-12). 1996. pap. 12.95 (*0-87303-266-7*) Faith & Life.

— Wisdom. LC 95-18011. 88p. 1995. pap. 4.95 (*0-87178-944-2*) Brethren.

Bowman, Claude C. The College Professor in America: An Analysis of Articles Published in the General Magazines, 1890-1938. Metzger, Walter P., ed. LC 76-55170. (Academic Profession Ser.). 1977. reprint ed. lib. bdg. 18.95 (*0-405-10001-9*) Ayer.

Bowman, Claude C., ed. Humanistic Sociology: Readings. LC 72-13116. 1973. pap. text 12.95 (*0-89197-221-8*) Irvington.

Bowman, Cliff. Essence of Strategic Management. (C). 1991. pap. 19.95 (*0-13-284738-8*) P-H.

Bowman, Cliff, jt. auth. see Faulkner, David.

***Bowman, Constance.** Slacks & Calluses: Our Summer in a Bomber Factory. LC 99-31365. (Illus.). 192p. 1999. pap. 14.95 (*1-56098-368-X*) Smithsonian.

Bowman County Historical Society Staff. Prairie Tales II: A History of Bowman County, N. D. (Illus.). 652p. 1989. 42.50 (*0-317-93516-X*) Bowman County.

Bowman, Craig T. & Birkeland, Jorgen, eds. Alternative Hydrocarbon Fuels: Combustion & Chemical Kinetics. LC 78-7278. (PAAS Ser.: Vol. 62). (Illus.). 463p. 1978. 65.95 (*0-915928-25-6*, 4-62) AIAA.

Bowman, Crystal. Cracks in the Sidewalk: Children's Daily Adventures. Hartman, Alan G., ed. (Illus.). 128p. (J). (gr. k-8). 1993. 12.00 (*0-9636050-1-1*); pap. 6.00 (*0-9636050-0-3*) Cygnet Pub.

— If Peas Could Taste Like Candy: And Other Funny Poems for Kids. LC 97-40082. (Illus.). 128p. (J). 1998. 12.99 (*0-310-21950-7*) Zondervan.

— Ivan & the Dynamos. LC 96-51150. 148p. (J). (gr. 5-9). 1997. 15.00 (*0-8028-5087-1*, Eerdmans Bks) Eerdmans.

— Ivan & the Dynamos. LC 96-51150. 148p. (YA). (gr. 5-9). 1997. pap. 5.00 (*0-8028-5090-1*, Eerdmans Bks) Eerdmans.

— Jonathan James Says, "Happy Birthday to Me!" LC 97-1201. (Jonathan James Ser.). (Illus.). 48p. (J). 1997. pap. 4.99 (*0-310-21208-1*) Zondervan.

— Jonathan James Says, "I Can Be Brave!" LC 95-2127. (Jonathan James Ser.: Bk. 1). (Illus.). 48p. (J). (ps-3). 1995. pap. 4.99 (*0-310-49591-1*) Zondervan.

— Jonathan James Says, "I Can Hardly Wait!" LC 96-42264. (Jonathan James Ser.). (Illus.). 48p. (Orig.). (J). (ps-3). 1997. pap. 4.99 (*0-310-21207-3*) Zondervan.

— Jonathan James Says, "I Can Help" LC 95-6662. (Jonathan James Ser.: Bk. 3). (Illus.). 48p. (J). (ps-3). 1995. pap. 4.99 (*0-310-49611-X*) Zondervan.

— Jonathan James Says, "Let's Be Friends" LC 95-8053. (Jonathan James Ser.: Bk. 2). (Illus.). 48p. (J). (ps-3). 1995. pap. 4.99 (*0-310-49601-2*) Zondervan.

— Jonathan James Says, "Let's Play Ball" LC 95-6661. (Jonathan James Ser.: Bk. 4). (Illus.). 48p. (J). (ps-3). 1995. pap. 4.99 (*0-310-49621-7*) Zondervan.

— Jonathan James Says, "School's Out!" LC 96-29652. (Jonathan James Ser.). (Illus.). 48p. (Orig.). (J). (ps-3). 1997. pap. 4.99 (*0-310-21209-X*) Zondervan.

— Mommy, May I Hug Fishes? 2000. 6.99 (*0-310-23209-0*) HarpC.

***Bowman, Crystal.** See the Country See the City. (J). 2000. 6.99 (*0-310-23210-4*, Zondervan Childrens Bks) Zondervan.

— Windmills & Woodenshoes. (Illus.). 40p. (gr. 2-6). 1999. 15.00 (*0-9636050-2-X*) Cygnet Pub.

***Bowman, Cynthia Ann, ed.** Using Literature to Help Troubled Teenagers Cope with Health Issues. LC 99-36669. (Using Literature to Help Troubled Teenagers Ser.). 336p. 2000. 39.95 (*0-313-30531-5*) Greenwood.

***Bowman, D. M. J. S.** Australian Rainforests: Islands of Green in a Land of Fire. LC 99-24978. (Illus.). 344p. (C). 2000. 85.00 (*0-521-46568-0*) Cambridge U Pr.

Bowman, Daria P. Adams Presentations. LC 97-30456. xiv, 210 p. 1998. pap. 9.95 (*1-55850-798-1*) Adams Media.

— Paths & Walkways. LC 97-13134. (For Your Garden Ser.). (Illus.). 72p. 1997. 12.95 (*1-56799-482-2*, Friedman-Fairfax) M Friedman Pub Grp Inc.

— Writing Notes with a Personal Touch. 72p. 1998. 12.50 (*1-56799-662-0*, Friedman-Fairfax) M Friedman Pub Grp Inc.

Bowman, Daria P. & Lamarca, Maureen. Pleasures of Porch. LC 96-70340. 144p. 1997. 35.00 (*0-8478-2005-X*, Pub. by Rizzoli Intl) St Martin.

Bowman, Daria Price. Hot Color Gardens. LC 99-17312. (For Your Garden Ser.). 1999. pap. text 12.95 (*1-56799-746-5*) M Friedman Pub Grp Inc.

— Hydrangeas: All about a Favorite Garden Flower. LC 99-17300. 1999. text 22.50 (*1-56799-737-6*, Friedman-Fairfax) M Friedman Pub Grp Inc.

— Thoughtful Gestures: Word & Gifts That Say You Care. LC 99-189120. 1998. 12.50 (*1-56799-682-5*, Friedman-Fairfax) M Friedman Pub Grp Inc.

***Bowman, David.** Bunny Modern. 1998. pap. 13.00 (*0-316-19084-5*, Back Bay) Little.

Bowman, David. Bunny Modern. LC 97-25429. 224p. (J). 1999. pap. 13.00 (*0-316-10202-4*) Little.

***Bowman, David.** Fa Fa Fa Fa Fa Fa: A History of the Talking Heads. 2001. write for info. (*0-380-97846-6*, HarpEntertain) Morrow Avon.

Bowman, David. Let the Dog Drive. LC 92-31757. (C). 1993. 19.95 (*0-8147-1205-3*) NYU Pr.

— Let the Dog Drive. 320p. 1994. reprint ed. pap. 10.95 (*0-14-023724-0*, Penguin Bks) Viking Penguin.

— Thomas Jefferson & the Republican Vision. (C). 2000. pap. text. write for info. (*0-321-04854-7*) Addison-Wesley Educ.

Bowman, Dean R. 20 Plays for U. S. History Classes. LC 99-185751. 168 p. 1998. write for info. (*0-8251-3826-4*) J W Walch.

Bowman, Diana L. The Pennsylvania Herald & York General Advertiser, 1794-1798, Bk. 2. 132p. 1993. per. 12.95 (*1-55856-134-X*, 034) Closson Pr.

Bowman, Diana L, compiled by. Armstrong County, PA WB Index, 1805-1900. 53p. 1988. pap. text 10.00 (*0-933227-91-4*, 487) Closson Pr.

Bowman, Diana L., compiled by. The Pennsylvania Herald & York General Advertiser, 1789-1793, Bk. 1. 214p. 1996. per. 19.95 (*1-55856-225-7*, 033) Closson Pr.

Bowman, Dicy V., ed. A Guide to Genealogical Resources in Escambia County. (Illus.). 32p. (Orig.). 1983. pap. 2.85 (*0-939566-03-6*) Pensacola Hist.

Bowman, Don. The Battle of Jefferson Canyon: And Other Skirmishes in the War on the West. LC 96-92273. vii, 165p. (Orig.). 1996. pap. 9.95 (*0-9652738-0-5*) Spur Inc.

— Go Seek the Pow Wow on the Mountain: And Other Indian Stories of the Sacandaga Valley. LC 93-78205. (Illus.). 116p. (Orig.). 1993. pap. 12.95 (*0-912678-87-9*) Greenfld Rev Lit.

Bowman, Donald L. Organization for Manufacturing. Vernon, Ivan R., ed. LC 79-110568. (Manufacturing Management Ser.: No. 2). (Illus.). 262p. reprint ed. pap. 81.30 (*0-8357-6482-6*, 203585300097) Bks Demand.

Bowman, Doris, jt. auth. see Bowman, Bob.

***Bowman, Doug.** Copelands. LC 99-26718. 288p. 1999. 23.95 (*0-312-86547-3*, Pub. by Forge NYC) St Martin.

— Copelands. 288p. 2000. mass mkt. 6.99 (*0-8125-4048-4*) Tor Bks.

— The Guns of Billy Free. 288p. 2000. mass mkt. 5.99 (*0-8125-9028-7*) Forge NYC.

Bowman, Doug. The Guns of Billy Free. LC 98-8267. 320p. 1998. text 23.95 (*0-312-86573-2*) St Martin.

— H & R Cattle Company. 1997. mass mkt. 5.99 (*0-8125-6757-9*, Pub. by Forge NYC) St Martin.

— Houston. 1999. mass mkt. 5.99 (*0-8125-9029-5*, Pub. by Tor Bks) St Martin.

— The Quest of Jubal Kane. LC 99-21178. 304p. 1999. 22.95 (*0-312-86546-5*, Pub. by Forge NYC) St Martin.

***Bowman, Doug.** Quest of Jubal Kane. 2000. mass mkt. 5.99 (*0-8125-4047-6*, Pub. by Tor Bks) St Martin.

Bowman, Doug. Sam Curtin. 320p. (Orig.). 1994. pap. 4.99 (*0-8125-3453-0*, Pub. by Forge NYC) St Martin.

— Three Lives of Littleton Blue, Vol. 1. 1996. mass mkt. 4.99 (*0-8125-3454-9*, Pub. by Forge NYC) St Martin.

***Bowman, Doug.** West of Comanche County. 304p. 2000. 23.95 (*0-312-86545-7*) Forge NYC.

Bowman, Duwayne Leslie. One More Story: Contemporary Seneca Tales of the Supernatural. 1989. pap. 9.95 (*0-912678-78-X*) Greenfld Rev Lit.

Bowman, Dwight D. Georgi's Parasitology for Veterinarians. 6th ed. (Illus.). 432p. (C). 1994. text 62.00 (*0-7216-5589-0*, W B Saunders Co) Harcrt Hlth Sci Grp.

— Georgis' Parasitology for Veterinarians. 7th ed. Kersey, Ray, ed. LC 98-17175. (Illus.). 415p. (C). 1998. text. write for info. (*0-7216-7097-0*, W B Saunders Co) Harcrt Hlth Sci Grp.

Bowman, Eddie. The Dust of Butterfly Wings. LC 96-54229. (Illus.). (J). 1997. write for info. (*1-56763-328-5*); pap. write for info. (*1-56763-329-3*) Ozark Pub.

— Gilbert the Goose. LC 98-37900. (Illus.). (J). 1998. write for info. (*1-56763-427-3*); pap. write for info. (*1-56763-428-1*) Ozark Pub.

— Gravy on a Bucket Lid. LC 98-37899. (Illus.). (J). 1998. write for info. (*1-56763-429-X*); pap. write for info. (*1-56763-430-3*) Ozark Pub.

— Roddy the Rooster. LC 96-54301. (Illus.). (J). 1997. write for info. (*1-56763-326-9*); pap. write for info. (*1-56763-327-7*) Ozark Pub.

— Silly Dog. LC 96-54014. (Illus.). (J). 1997. write for info. (*1-56763-324-2*); pap. write for info. (*1-56763-325-0*) Ozark Pub.

— Sonny the Trick Horse. LC 96-54011. (Illus.). (J). 1997. write for info. (*1-56763-322-6*); pap. write for info. (*1-56763-323-4*) Ozark Pub.

— Sophie the Snowflake. LC 96-54300. (Illus.). (J). 1997. write for info. (*1-56763-320-X*); pap. write for info. (*1-56763-321-8*) Ozark Pub.

***Bowman, Elena.** Sarah's Landing. 1999. write for info. (*1-928781-46-2*) Hollis Bks.

Bowman, Elizabeth. Minor & Fragmentary Sentences of a Corpus of Spoken English. LC 66-63898. (General Publications: Vol. 42). (Orig.). 1966. pap. text 16.00 (*0-87750-130-0*) Res Inst Inner Asian Studies.

Bowman, Elizabeth A. White Chocolate. 384p. 1999. mass mkt. 6.99 (*0-8125-7181-9*, Pub. by Forge NYC) St Martin.

— White Chocolate. LC 98-5522. 352p. 1998. text 23.95 (*0-312-86306-3*) St Martin.

***Bowman, Elizabeth Atkins.** Dark Secret. 416p. 2000. 25.95 (*0-312-86806-5*) Forge NYC.

— Sean "Puffy" Combs. LC 00-23221. 2000. pap. 9.95 (*0-7910-6017-9*) Chelsea Hse.

— Sean "Puffy" Combs. (Black Americans of Achievement Ser.). (Illus.). (J). 2001. 19.95 (*0-7910-6016-0*) Chelsea Hse.

Bowman, Eric. Before I Wake. 326p. 1998. reprint ed. mass mkt. 6.99 (*0-515-12353-6*, Jove) Berkley Pub.

***Bowman, Eva Jean.** Chief Ninham: Forgotten Hero. (Illus.). 43p. (YA). (gr. 2 up). 1999. pap. 14.00 (*0-935790-04-7*) Muh-He-Con-Neew.

Bowman, Frank. Introduction to Bessel Functions. (Illus.). 135p. (C). 1958. pap. 5.95 (*0-486-60462-4*) Dover.

Bowman, Frank O. & Haines, Roger W. Federal Forfeiture Guide. 1999. 225.00 (*0-938065-94-7*) James Pub Santa Ana.

Bowman, Frank P. French Romanticism: Intertextual & Interdisciplinary Readings. LC 89-15422. (Parallax: Re-Visions of Culture & Society Ser.). 256p. 1990. text 42.00 (*0-8018-3884-3*) Johns Hopkins.

Bowman, Fred Q. Eight Thousand More Vital Records of Eastern New York State, 1804-1850. LC 92-150586. 296p. 1991. lib. bdg. 24.00 (*1-56012-114-9*, 107) Kinship Rhinebeck.

— Landholders of Northeastern New York, 1739-1802. LC 83-80308. 228p. 1987. reprint ed. 20.00 (*0-8063-1026-X*) Genealog Pub.

— New York's Detailed Census of 1855 Greene County, Extracted & Systematized. Kelly, Arthur C., ed. LC F127.G7B69 1986. 277p. 1988. lib. bdg. 21.95 (*1-56012-090-8*, 90) Kinship Rhinebeck.

— 10,000 Vital Records of Central New York, 1813-1850, Vol. 2. 338p. 1999. reprint ed. 25.00 (*0-8063-1149-5*, 641) Genealog Pub.

— 10,000 Vital Records of Eastern New York, 1777-1834, Vol. III. 356p. 1999. reprint ed. 25.00 (*0-8063-1165-7*, 642) Genealog Pub.

— 10,000 Vital Records of Western New York, 1809-1850. LC 84-81870. 318p. 1999. reprint ed. 25.00 (*0-8063-1099-5*) Genealog Pub.

Bowman, Fred Q. & Lynch, Thomas J. 7,000 Hudson-Mohawk Valley (NY) Vital Records, 1808-1850. LC 97-73581. 368p. 1997. 30.00 (*0-8063-1530-X*) Genealog Pub.

Bowman, Fred Q. & Lynch, Tom. Directory to Collections of New York Vital Records 1726-1989. 91p. 1995. 29.00 (*0-7884-0275-7*) Heritage Bk.

Bowman, Gail B. Raising Meat Goats for Profit. (Illus.). viii, 256p. 1999. pap. 19.95 (*0-9670381-0-3*) Bowman Commns.

***Bowman, Gail E.** Praying the Sacred in Secular Settings. 2000. pap. text. write for info. (*0-8272-2962-3*) Chalice Pr.

Bowman, Gary L., et al, eds. The Work & Family Interface: Toward a Contextual Effects Perspective. (Families in Focus Ser.: Vol. 1). 533p. (Orig.). (C). 1995. pap. 36.95 (*0-916174-45-X*, OP9412) Natl Coun Family.

Bowman, Gary M. Highway Politics in Virginia. 200p. (C). 1992. 48.00 (*0-913969-45-1*) Univ Pub Assocs.

Bowman, Gary W., et al, eds. The Changing Structure of Corrections: Emerging Private Supply. 225p. (C). 1991. pap. text. write for info. (*0-8133-0573-X*) Westview.

Bowman, Gary W. & Seidenstat, Paul. Privatizing Correctional Institutions. Hakim, Simon W. et al, eds. 292p. (C). 1992. 34.95 (*1-56000-055-4*) Transaction Pubs.

Bowman, Gary W., ed. see Hakim, Simon W. & Seidenstat, Paul.

Bowman, George C. Our Greatest Hope. (Illus.). 120p. (Orig.). 1987. pap. 3.95 (*0-932807-24-0*) Overmountain Pr.

Bowman, George E. The Mayflower Reader: A Selection of Articles from the Mayflower Descendant. LC 77-99092. (Illus.). 537p. 1996. reprint ed. pap. 39.95 (*0-8063-0797-8*) Clearfield Co.

Bowman, George E., ed. The Mayflower Descendant, Vol. 7, 1905. (Illus.). 301p. 1995. reprint ed. text 25.00 (*0-7884-0178-5*) Heritage Bk.

— The Mayflower Descendant, Vol. 8, 1906. (Illus.). 300p. 1995. reprint ed. text 25.00 (*0-7884-0179-3*) Heritage Bk.

— The Mayflower Descendant, Vol. 13. (Illus.). 327p. 1995. reprint ed. text 25.00 (*0-7884-0317-6*) Heritage Bk.

— The Mayflower Descendant, Vol. 14. (Illus.). 328p. 1995. reprint ed. text 25.00 (*0-7884-0318-4*) Heritage Bk.

— The Mayflower Descendant: 1907, Vol. 9. (Illus.). 302p. 1995. 25.00 (*0-7884-0201-3*) Heritage Bk.

— The Mayflower Descendant Vol. 1: 1899. (Illus.). 281p. 1994. reprint ed. text 25.00 (*0-7884-0053-3*) Heritage Bk.

— The Mayflower Descendant Vol. 2: 1900. (Illus.). 283p. 1994. reprint ed. text 25.00 (*0-7884-0054-1*) Heritage Bk.

— The Mayflower Descendant Vol. 3: 1901. (Illus.). 286p. 1995. text 25.00 (*0-7884-0092-4*) Heritage Bk.

— The Mayflower Descendant Vol. 4: 1902. 284p. 1995. text 25.00 (*0-7884-0093-2*) Heritage Bk.

— The Mayflower Descendant Vol. 5: 1903. (Illus.). 292p. 1995. reprint ed. text 25.00 (*0-7884-0131-9*) Heritage Bk.

— The Mayflower Descendant Vol. 6: 1904. (Illus.). 287p. 1994. reprint ed. text 25.00 (*0-7884-0132-7*) Heritage Bk.

— The Mayflower Descendant Vol. 10: 1908. (Illus.). 305p. 1995. reprint ed. text 25.00 (*0-7884-0202-1*) Heritage Bk.

Bowman, George E., ed. see Massachusetts Society of Mayflower Descendants Sta.

Bowman, George W., III. Dying, Grieving, Faith, & Family: A Pastoral Care Approach. LC 97-14091. 150p. (C). 1997. 39.95 (*0-7890-0262-0*, Haworth Pastrl) Haworth Pr.

— Dying, Grieving, Faith, & Family: A Pastoral Care Approach. LC 97-14091. 150p. (C). 1997. pap. 19.95 (*0-7890-0263-9*, Haworth Pastrl) Haworth Pr.

Bowman, Glinda. Miniature Perfume Bottles. LC 94-65619. (Illus.). 160p. (Orig.). 1994. pap. text 29.95 (*0-88740-628-9*) Schiffer.

— More Miniature Perfume Bottles. (Illus.). 176p. 1996. pap. 29.95 (*0-88740-999-7*) Schiffer.

Bowman, Greg & Shirley, Christopher. Steel in the Field: A Farmer's Guide to Weed-Management Tools. LC 97-8406. (Sustainable Agriculture Network Handbook Ser.: Vol. 2). (Illus.). 112p. 1997. pap. write for info. (*1-888626-02-X*) Sustnble Agri.

Bowman, Greg, ed. see New Farm Staff, et al.

Bowman, Hamilton B. Handbook of Precision Sheet, Strip & Foil. LC 80-12092. (Illus.). 312p. reprint ed. pap. 96.80 (*0-608-15947-6*, 203306200083) Bks Demand.

Bowman, Harold M. Administration of Iowa: A Study in Centralization. LC 70-82248. (Columbia University. Studies in the Social Sciences: No. 46). reprint ed. 20.00 (*0-404-51046-9*) AMS Pr.

Bowman, Helena, ed. see Sutton, Elly.

Bowman, Herbert J., tr. see Luther, Martin.

***Bowman, Howard & Derrick, John, eds.** Formal Methods for Distributed Processing: A Survey of Object-Oriented Approaches. 500p. (C). 2000. 54.95 (*0-521-77184-6*) Cambridge U Pr.

Bowman-Howard, Michelle. Anesthesia Review. LC 99-24538. 384p. 1999. pap. text 39.95 (*0-683-30671-5*) Lppncott W & W.

Bowman, Isaiah. The Andes of Southern Peru. LC 68-23277. (Illus.). 336p. 1968. reprint ed. lib. bdg. 35.00 (*0-8371-0025-9*, B0AP, Greenwood Pr) Greenwood.

— Desert Trails of Atacama. LC 76-111776. (BCL Ser. I). reprint ed. 20.00 (*0-404-00964-6*) AMS Pr.

— Design for Scholarship. LC 71-152159. (Essay Index Reprint Ser.). 1977. 18.95 (*0-8369-2181-X*) Ayer.

— Forest Physiography: Physiography of the United States & Principles of Soils in Relation to Forestry. LC 78-125732. (American Environmental Studies). 1975. reprint ed. 57.95 (*0-405-02659-5*) Ayer.

— The Pioneer Fringe. LC 71-160960. (Select Bibliographies Reprint Ser.). 1977. reprint ed. 42.95 (*0-8369-5828-4*) Ayer.

Bowman, Isaiah, ed. Limits of Land Settlement: A Report on Present-Day Possiblities. LC 67-30200. (Essay Index Reprint Ser.). 1977. 26.95 (*0-8369-0233-5*) Ayer.

Bowman, J. & Measher, R. Frommer's Greece. 448p. 1996. 19.95 (*0-02-860902-6*, Pub. by Macmillan) S&S Trade.

Bowman, J. A. Third Reich Daggers, 1933-45: A Guide to Identification, Reproduction Recognition & Values. (Illus.). 496p. 1994. 65.00 (*1-884849-00-8*) R&R Bks.

Bowman, J. C. & Susmel, P., eds. The Future of Beef Production in the European Community. (Current Topics in Veterinary Medicine & Animal Science Ser.: No. 5). 1979. text 234.00 (*90-247-2234-9*) Kluwer Academic.

Bowman, J. J., et al, eds. Electromagnetic & Acoustic Scattering by Simple Shapes. 728p. 1987. 215.00 (*0-89116-672-6*) Hemisp Pub.

— Electromagnetic & Acoustic Scattering by Simple Shapes. 728p. 1988. pap. 69.95 (*0-89116-885-0*) Hemisp Pub.

Bowman, J. M., ed. Molecular Collision Dynamics. (Topics in Current Physics Ser.: Vol. 33). (Illus.). 158p. 1983. 40.95 (*0-387-12014-9*) Spr-Verlag.

Bowman, J. N. & Heizer, Robert F. Anza & the Northwest Frontier of New Spain. 182p. 1967. 12.50 (*0-916561-04-6*) Southwest Mus.

Bowman, J. Wilson. America's Black & Tribal Colleges: The Comprehensive Guide to Historically & Predominantly Black & American Indian Colleges & Universities. 3rd rev. ed. LC 98-67139. (Illus.). 328p. 1998. pap. 21.95 (*0-9663562-0-9*) R J Enterprises.

Bowman, James. The Hollywood Cartoon Parade. (Illus.). 1985. pap. 4.00 (*0-934969-00-0*) Bowman Pub Inc.

— Public Integrity, Vol. 1, No. 2. 1999. pap. text. write for info. (*0-8133-6833-2*) Westview.

B

An Asterisk (*) at the beginning of an entry indicates that the title is appearing for the first time.

Bowman, James, ed. Ghosts. (Pocket Classics Ser.: No. 1). 52p. 1986. pap. 2.95 (*0-934969-02-7*) Bowman Pub Inc.
— A Little Address Book of 1000 Stars. 1986. pap. 7.50 (*0-934969-01-9*) Bowman Pub Inc.
Bowman, James, jt. auth. see Rabin, Jack.
Bowman, James, jt. ed. see Lord Hailsham of St. Marylebone.
Bowman, James E. Genetic Variation & Disorders in Peoples of African Origin. 488p. 1998. pap. text 35.00 (*0-8018-5884-4*) Johns Hopkins.
Bowman, James E. & Murray, Robert F. Genetic Variation & Disorders in Peoples of African Origin. LC 90-4014. (Series in Contemporary Medicine & Public Health). 480p. 1990. text 80.00 (*0-8018-3962-9*) Johns Hopkins.
Bowman, James P. Functional Neuroanatomy. (Illus.). 280p. (Orig.). (C). 1996. pap. 40.00 (*0-9615226-8-2*) Giddings Studio Pub.
Bowman, James S. & Elliston, Frederick A., eds. Ethics, Government, & Public Policy: A Reference Guide. LC 88-3110. 349p. 1988. lib. bdg. 85.00 (*0-313-25192-4*, BGT/, Greenwood Pr) Greenwood.
Bowman, James S. & Menzel, Donald C., eds. Teaching Ethics & Values in Public Administration Programs: Innovations, Strategies, & Issues. LC 97-30642. (SUNY Series in Public Administration). 352p. (C). 1997. text 65.50 (*0-7914-3509-1*); pap. text 21.95 (*0-7914-3510-5*) State U NY Pr.
Bowman, James T. & Graves, W. H. Placement Services & Techniques. 1976. pap. 11.80 (*0-87563-124-X*) Stipes.
Bowman, Janie, jt. ed. see Hartmann, Thom.
Bowman, Jayne, ed. The Gift of Christmas. (Illus.). 96p. 1987. 8.95 (*0-8378-1822-2*) Gibson.
Bowman, Jeanne. City Hospital Nurse. large type ed. (Linford Romance Library). 272p. 1995. pap. 16.99 (*0-7089-7742-1*, Linford) Ulverscroft.
— Girl Executive. large type ed. (Romance Ser.). 240p. 1993. 27.99 (*0-7089-2982-6*) Ulverscroft.
— Girl in the Mirror. large type ed. (Linford Romance Library). 272p. 1993. pap. 16.99 (*0-7089-7405-8*) Ulverscroft.
— Lakeville Lady. large type ed. 1990. pap. 16.99 (*0-7089-6871-6*) Ulverscroft.
— Lovelorn Lady. large type ed. 272p. 1992. pap. 16.99 (*0-7089-7133-4*, Linford) Ulverscroft.
— A Measure of Love. large type ed. (Linford Romance Library). 272p. 1993. pap. 16.99 (*0-7089-7449-X*, Linford) Ulverscroft.
— Nurse Betrayed. large type ed. (Linford RomanceLarge Print Ser.). 256p. 1995. pap. 16.99 (*0-7089-7678-6*, Linford) Ulverscroft.
— Nurse Elsa. large type ed. (Ulverscroft). 224p. 1994. 27.99 (*0-7089-3054-9*) Ulverscroft.
— Nurse of Polka Dot Island. large type ed. (Linford Romance Library). 1991. pap. 16.99 (*0-7089-7104-0*) Ulverscroft.
— A Penny for Love. large type ed. (Linford Romance Library). 240p. 1992. pap. 16.99 (*0-7089-7209-8*, Linford) Ulverscroft.
— Shoreline Nurse. large type ed. (Romance Ser.). 1994. pap. 16.99 (*0-7089-7614-X*, Linford) Ulverscroft.
— Small Town Nurse. large type ed. (Romance Ser.). 1994. pap. 16.99 (*0-7089-7602-6*, Linford) Ulverscroft.
— Trust in Love. large type ed. (Linford Romance Library). 1991. pap. 16.99 (*0-7089-6969-0*) Ulverscroft.
Bowman, Jeffrey H., jt. auth. see Miller, Arthur S.
Bowman, Jerome K., jt. auth. see Chadd, Charles M.
Bowman, Jim. Novell's CIP Internet Business Strategist. LC HD30.37.B69 1998. 456p. 1996. pap. 39.99 (*0-7645-4549-3*) IDG Bks.
***Bowman, Jim.** Novell's CIP Web Authoring & Design Study. LC 98-70589. 752p. 1998. pap. 49.99 (*0-7645-4548-5*) IDG Bks.
Bowman, Jim & West, Jonathan. Public Integrity: Inaugural Issue. 118p. 1998. pap. text. write for info. (*0-8133-6678-X*) Westview.
Bowman, Jim & Zoss, Joel. Diamonds in the Rough. LC 89-8131. 480p. 1989. text 29.95 (*0-02-633590-5*) Macmillan.
Bowman, Joel. Advances in Molecular Vibrations & Collision Dynamics, Vol. 3. 1998. 109.50 (*1-55938-790-4*) Jai Pr.
Bowman, Joel M., ed. Advances in Molecular Vibrations & Collision Dynamics, 2 vols., Vol. 1. 1991. 219.00 (*1-55938-293-7*) Jai Pr.
— Advances in Molecular Vibrations & Collision Dynamics, Vol. 1, Pt. A. 360p. 1991. 109.50 (*1-55938-294-5*) Jai Pr.
— Advances in Molecular Vibrations & Collision Dynamics, Vol. 1, Pt. B. 327p. 1991. 109.50 (*1-55938-295-3*) Jai Pr.
— Advances in Molecular Vibrations & Collision Dynamics, Vol. 2, Pt. A. 293p. 1994. 109.50 (*1-55938-705-X*) Jai Pr.
— Advances in Molecular Vibrations & Collision Dynamics, Vol. 2, Pt. B. 236p. 1994. 109.50 (*1-55938-706-8*) Jai Pr.
— Advances in Molecular Vibrations & Collision Dynamics: Quantum Reactive Scattering, 2 vols., Vol. 2. 1994. 219.00 (*1-55938-547-2*) Jai Pr.
— Advances in Vibrational Spectrocopy & Dynamics, Vol. 1. Date not set. 109.50 (*0-89232-870-3*) Jai Pr.
Bowman, Joel P. & Branchaw, Bernadine P. BUSINESS REPORT WRITING 2/E. 2nd rev. ed. (Illus.). 599p. (C). 1988. text 79.00 (*0-03-013244-4*) Dryden Pr.
— How to Write Proposals that Produce. LC 92-16994. 248p. 1992. pap. 23.50 (*0-89774-656-2*) Oryx Pr.
Bowman, Joel P., jt. auth. see Branchaw, Bernadine P.
Bowman, John. America at War, Set. 1997. 155.60 (*0-8160-3803-1*) Facts on File.
Bowman, John. The Fourth Gospel & the Jews: A Study of R. Akiba, Esther, & the Gospel of John. LC 75-40461. (Pittsburgh Theological Monographs: No. 8). 1975. pap. 12.00 (*0-915138-10-7*) Pickwick.
— The History of the American Presidency. 1998. 17.99 (*0-7858-0936-8*) Bk Sales Inc.
— Nobody's Perfect. 150p. 1998. pap. 9.95 (*0-9650797-3-2*) J L Bowman.
— The Samaritan Problem: Studies in the Relationship of Samaritanism, Judaism, & Early Christianity. Johnson, Alfred M., Jr., tr. from GER. LC 75-20042. (Pittsburgh Theological Monographs: No. 4). 1975. pap. 20.00 (*0-915138-04-2*) Pickwick.
— The Traveller's Guide to Crete. rev. ed. 320p. 1985. pap. 14.95 (*0-224-02285-7*, Pub. by Jonathan Cape) Macmillan.
Bowman, John, ed. The Facts on File Scientific Yearbook, 1987. LC 85-642413. 223p. reprint ed. pap. 69.20 (*0-7837-1221-9*, 204175200023) Bks Demand.
Bowman, John, ed. Samaritan Documents Relating to Their History, Religion & Life. LC 77-4949. (Pittsburgh Original Texts & Translations Ser.: No. 2). 1977. pap. 15.00 (*0-915138-27-1*) Pickwick.
Bowman, John, jt. auth. see Zoss, Joel.
Bowman, John, ed. see Golay, Michael.
Bowman, John, ed. see Greenblatt, Miriam.
Bowman, John, ed. see Isserman, Maurice.
Bowman, John, ed. see Marker, Sherry.
Bowman, John, ed. see Mills, Bronwyn.
Bowman, John, ed. see Minks, Louise & Minks, Benton.
Bowman, John D. Psalms. (Covenant Bible Studies). 48p. (Orig.). 1989. pap. 4.95 (*0-87178-723-7*, 8237) Brethren.
Bowman, John G. The World That Was. (American Biography Ser.). 83p. 1991. reprint ed. lib. bdg. 59.00 (*0-7812-8033-8*) Rprt Serv.
Bowman, John H., ed. Taxation of Business Property: Is Uniformity Still a Valid Norm? LC 94-2983. 224p. 1995. 59.95 (*0-275-94310-0*, Praeger Pubs) Greenwood.
Bowman, John J. What You Should Know about Sports & Drugs. (Family Forum Library). 16p. 1992. 1.95 (*1-56688-020-3*) Bur For At-Risk.
Bowman, John J., jt. auth. see Hardy, R. Allen.
Bowman, John L. Arabidopsis: An Atlas of Morphology & Development. LC 93-5262. (Illus.). 466p. 1997. 84.95 (*0-387-94089-8*) Spr-Verlag.
— Selected Topics in Philosophy. LC 97-93391. 200p. (Orig.). 1997. pap. 19.95 (*0-9650797-1-6*) J L Bowman.
Bowman, John R. Capitalist & Collective Action: Conflict & Cooperation in the Coal Industry. (Studies in Marxism & Social Theory). 272p. (C). 1989. text 80.00 (*0-521-36265-2*) Cambridge U Pr.
***Bowman, John S.** Columbia Chronologies of Asian History & Culture. LC 99-47017. 2000. 89.00 (*0-231-11005-7*) Col U Pr.
— Columbia Chronologies of Asian History & Culture. 2000. 85.00 (*0-231-11004-9*) Col U Pr.
Bowman, John S. Sportsmanship. (Values Library). (Illus.). (YA). (gr. 7-12). 1990. lib. bdg. 15.95 (*0-8239-1110-1*) Rosen Group.
Bowman, John S., ed. The Cambridge Dictionary of American Biography. 941p. 1995. 49.95 (*0-521-40258-1*) Cambridge U Pr.
— The Civil War Almanac. 400p. 1986. pap. 14.95 (*0-345-35434-6*, World Almanac) Newspaper Ent.
— Facts about the American Wars. LC 97-40298. 750p. 1998. 70.00 (*0-8242-0929-X*) Wilson.
Bowman, John S., et al. Frommer's Greece. 2nd ed. (Illus.). 610p. 1999. pap. 19.95 (*0-02-862608-7*, Pub. by Macmillan) S&S Trade.
— Frommer's Greek Islands. (Illus.). 404p. 1999. pap. 16.95 (*0-02-862609-5*, Pub. by Macmillan) S&S Trade.
Bowman, Jon, ed. see New Mexico Magazine Staff.
Bowman, Joye. Ominous Transition: Commerce & Colonial Expansion in the Senegambia & Guinea, 1857-1919. LC 96-86716. (Making of Modern Africa Ser.). (Illus.). 224p. 1997. text 69.95 (*1-85972-154-0*, Pub. by Avebry) Ashgate Pub Co.
***Bowman, Judith.** Dream House: Eight Steps to the Peace & Joy You Deserve. 136p. 2000. pap. 15.00 (*0-9677019-1-0*) LoveLight Intl Pr.
— Showers of Bliss: Your Portable Paradise of Inspiration & Hope. 72p. 2000. pap. 15.00 (*0-9677019-0-2*) LoveLight Intl Pr.
Bowman, Judith, jt. auth. see Bertz, William L.
Bowman, Judith S., et al. The Practical SQL Handbook: Using Structured Query Language. 3rd ed. LC 96-20301. 496p. (C). 1996. pap. text 39.95 incl. cd-rom (*0-201-44787-8*) Addison-Wesley.
Bowman, K. O. & Shenton, L. R. Properties of Estimators for the Gamma Distribution. (Statistics: Textbooks & Monographs: Vol. 89). (Illus.). 288p. 1987. text 127.50 (*0-8247-7556-2*) Dekker.
Bowman, K. O., jt. auth. see Shenton, Leonard R.
Bowman, Karl. Sexual Being vs. Governments That Promote Homosexuality. LC 93-83108. 64p. (Orig.). 1993. pap. 6.00 (*0-914752-32-4*) Sovereign Pr.
Bowman, Karlyn H., jt. auth. see Ladd, Everett C.
Bowman, Karlyn H., jt. auth. see Ladd, Everett Carll.
Bowman, Keith J., et al, eds. Handbook on Discontinuously Reinforced Ceramic Matrix Composites. LC 95-48924. 1995. write for info. (*0-931682-42-8*) Purdue U Pubns.
Bowman, Kelly A., ed. see Cogdill, John L., Jr. & Cogdill, J. J.
Bowman, Ken, jt. auth. see Lovie-Kitchin, Jan E.
Bowman, Kenneth M., jt. auth. see Tracey, Melissa.
Bowman, Kent A. Voices of Combat: A Century of Liberty & War Songs, 1765-1865, 10. LC 86-25724. (Contributions to the Study of Music & Dance Ser.: No. 10). 181p. 1987. 49.95 (*0-313-25408-7*, BVC/, Greenwood Pr) Greenwood.
***Bowman-Kruhm, Mary.** Careers in Child Care. LC 00-28005. (Careers Ser.). (Illus.). (YA). 2000. lib. bdg. 18.95 (*0-8239-2891-8*) Rosen Group.
Bowman-Kruhm, Mary. A Day in the Life of a Teacher. LC 98-5093. (Kids' Career Library). 24p. (J). (gr. k-4). 1999. 17.26 (*0-8239-5295-9*, PowerKids) Rosen Group.
— A Day in the Life of a Veterinarian. LC 98-15980. (Kids' Career Library). (J). (gr. k-4). 1999. 17.26 (*0-8239-5296-7*, PowerKids) Rosen Group.
— A Day in the Life of an Architect. (Kids' Career Library: No. 1). (Illus.). 24p. (J). (gr. k-4). 1999. 17.26 (*0-8239-5297-5*, PowerKids) Rosen Group.
***Bowman-Kruhm, Mary.** Money: Save It, Manage It, Spend It. (Teen Issues Ser.). (Illus.). 64p. (YA). (gr. 6 up). 2000. lib. bdg. 17.95 (*0-7660-1363-4*) Enslow Pubs.
— N Is for New York. (Alpha Flight Bks.). (Illus.). 60p. (ps-3). 2000. 17.95 (*1-892920-44-1*) G H B Pubs.
— New York. (Illus.). 64p. (gr. 1-5). 2000. pap. 5.95 (*1-892920-49-2*) G H B Pubs.
Bowman-Kruhm, Mary & Wirths, Claudine G. A Day in the Life of a Coach. LC 96-48943. (Kids' Career Library). (J). (gr. k-4), 1997. lib. bdg. 15.93 (*0-8239-5097-2*, PowerKids) Rosen Group.
— A Day in the Life of a Doctor. LC 96-53130. (Kids' Career Library). (J). (gr. k-4). 1997. lib. bdg. 15.93 (*0-8239-5096-4*, PowerKids) Rosen Group.
— A Day in the Life of a Firefighter. LC 96-53129. (Kids' Career Library). (J). (gr. k-4). 1997. lib. bdg. 15.93 (*0-8239-5094-8*, PowerKids) Rosen Group.
— A Day in the Life of a Newspaper Reporter. LC 98-17483. (Kids' Career Library). 24p. (J). (gr. k-4). 1999. 17.26 (*0-8239-5306-8*) Rosen Group.
— A Day in the Life of a Police Officer. LC 96-54021. (Kids' Career Library). (J). (gr. k-4). 1997. lib. bdg. 15.93 (*0-8239-5095-6*, PowerKids) Rosen Group.
— A Day in the Life of an EMT. LC 96-53132. (Kids' Career Library). (Illus.). 24p. (J). (gr. k-4). 1997. lib. bdg. 15.93 (*0-8239-5099-9*, PowerKids) Rosen Group.
Bowman-Kruhm, Mary, jt. auth. see Wirths, Claudine G.
Bowman, Larry W. Politics in Rhodesia: White Power in an African State. LC 73-75057. 224p. 1973. 34.95 (*0-674-68786-8*) HUP.
— South Africa's Outward Strategy: A Foreign Policy Dilemma for the United States. LC 72-183388. (Papers in International Studies: Africa Ser.: No. 13). 39p. reprint ed. pap. 30.00 (*0-608-18612-0*, 200742100062) Bks Demand.
Bowman, Laura L., jt. auth. see Merriman, William E.
Bowman, Laura Y. Mirrors: Reflections of a Woman's Soul. LC 89-80576. (Orig.). 1989. pap. 9.95 (*0-9622434-0-0*) Lu-Bow Pub.
Bowman, Lee, ed. see Wade, Charles R.
Bowman, LeRoy. The American Funeral: A Study in Guilt, Extravagance & Sublimity. viii, 181p. 1990. reprint ed. lib. bdg. 30.00 (*1-55888-884-5*) Omnigraphics Inc.
Bowman, Leslie G. American Arts & Crafts: Virtue in Design. (Illus.). 256p. 1992. pap. 40.00 (*0-8212-1920-0*, Pub. by Bulfinch Pr) Little.
***Bowman, Leslie Greene.** National Museum of Wildlife Art: Highlights from the Collection. Sackrey, Ponteir & Kerr, William, eds. (Illus.). 60p. 1999. pap. write for info. (*0-9674644-0-4*) Museum of Wildlif.
Bowman, Lewis, jt. ed. see Hadley, Charles D.
Bowman, Lewis S. Happy Days at Teetor Town: Or, Growing Up in Hagerstown, Indiana, in the 1880s. Teetor, Charles, ed. (Illus.). 128p. (Orig.). 1991. pap. 6.00 (*0-9628651-0-9*) Teetor Twn Pr.
Bowman, Linda. Free Food...& More. (More-for-Your-Money Guide Ser.). 150p. 1991. per. 9.95 (*1-55738-220-4*, Irwn Prfssnl) McGraw-Hill Prof.
— Free Stuff for Your Pet. (More-for-Your-Money Guide Ser.). 150p. 1991. per. 9.95 (*1-55738-271-9*, Irwn Prfssnl) McGraw-Hill Prof.
— Freebies (& More) for Folks over 50. (More-for-Your-Money Guide Ser.). 150p. 1991. pap. 9.95 (*1-55738-218-2*, Irwn Prfssnl) McGraw-Hill Prof.
— Freebies for Kids & Parents Too! (More-for-Your-Money Guide Ser.). 150p. 1991. per. 9.95 (*1-55738-272-7*, Irwn Prfssnl) McGraw-Hill Prof.
— How to Fly for Free. (More-for-Your-Money Guide Ser.). 150p. 1991. pap. 9.95 (*1-55738-217-4*, Irwn Prfssnl) McGraw-Hill Prof.
— How to Go to College for Free. (More-for-Your-Money Guide Ser.). 150p. 1991. pap. 9.95 (*1-55738-219-0*, Irwn Prfssnl) McGraw-Hill Prof.
— Pay Attention! Stop, Think & Listen: A Self-Monitoring Program for Classroom & Home Behavior Management. 16p. (Orig.). 1995. pap. 19.00 (*1-886941-04-1*, 0980) Spec Pr FL.
Bowman, Lois B. & Smith, George M., trs. from GER. Solomon Church Baptisms, Seventeen Ninety-Three to Eighteen Fifty, Forestville, Virginia. (Genealogical Source Bk.: No. 11). (Illus.). 58p. 1989. pap. 10.00 (*0-917968-15-8*) Shenandoah Hist.
Bowman, Lori & Bowman, Carl. In Pictures Petrified Forest: The Continuing Story. LC 91-60041. 48p. (Orig.). 1991. pap. 7.95 (*0-88714-056-4*) KC Pubns.
— In Pictures Petrified Forest: The Continuing Story. Morales, Brigitte, tr. LC 91-60041. (GER., Illus.). 48p. (Orig.). 1991. pap. 8.95 (*0-88714-750-X*) KC Pubns.
— In Pictures Petrified Forest: The Continuing Story. Le Bras, Yvon, tr. (FRE., Illus.). 48p. (Orig.). 1991. pap. 8.95 (*0-88714-751-8*) KC Pubns.
— In Pictures Petrified Forest: The Continuing Story. Petzinger, Saori, tr. (JPN., Illus.). 48p. (Orig.). 1991. pap. 8.95 (*0-88714-752-6*) KC Pubns.
Bowman, M. Professional Nurse: Coping with Change, Now & the Future. (Illus.). 272p. 1994. pap. text 44.95 (*1-56593-297-8*, 0621) Singular Publishing.
Bowman, M. J., et al, eds. Tidal Mixing & Plankton Dynamics. (Lecture Notes on Coastal & Estuarine Studies: Vol. 17). (Illus.). x, 502p. 1986. 128.95 (*0-387-96346-4*) Spr-Verlag.
Bowman, Malcolm C. Carcinogens & Related Substances: Analytical Chemistry for Toxicological Research. LC 79-20476. (Illus.). 328p. reprint ed. pap. 101.70 (*0-7837-0861-0*, 204116900019) Bks Demand.
— Handbook of Carcinogens & Hazardous Substances: Chemical & Trace Analysis. 768p. 1982. text 235.00 (*0-8247-1683-3*) Dekker.
***Bowman, Marcus, et al.** The Book of Charts: Micro Trend Chart Analysis. (Illus.). 65p. 1999. ring bd. 150.00 (*0-9662601-3-9*) Microtrade.
— The Microtrading Manual. (Illus.). 120p. 1999. pap. 80.00 (*0-9662601-1-2*) Microtrade.
Bowman, Margaret K., et al. Leighton. Ancestors & Descendants of George Leighton & Jean Guthrie Who Lived in West Ogil, Tannadice Parish, Angus Shire (Forfarshire) Scotland in the 18th Century, with Related Families. (Illus.). 718p. 1997. pap. 105.00 (*0-8328-7006-4*); lib. bdg. 115.00 (*0-8328-7005-6*) Higginson Bk Co.
Bowman, Marilyn L. Individual Differences in Posttraumatic Response: Problems with the Adversity-Distress Connection. LC 97-1892. 175p. 1997. text. write for info. (*0-8058-2713-7*) L Erlbaum Assocs.
Bowman, Marion, ed. Healing & Religion. 1996. pap. 18.95 (*1-874312-29-X*, Pub. by Hisarlik Pr) Intl Spec Bk.
Bowman, Marion, jt. auth. see Sutcliffe, Steven J.
Bowman, Marjorie A. Ambulatory Care. (Clerkship Ser.). 1998. pap. 24.95 (*1-889325-06-6*) Fence Crk Pubng.
Bowman, Marjorie A., ed. 2003 Year Book of Family Practice. 550p. Date not set. write for info. (*0-323-01524-7*) Mosby Inc.
Bowman, Marjorie A. & Allen, Deborah I. Stress & Women Physicians. (Illus.). 160p. 1988. 30.00 (*0-387-96117-8*) Spr-Verlag.
— Stress & Women Physicians. 2nd ed. (Illus.). xi, 216p. 1990. pap. 19.50 (*0-387-97319-2*) Spr-Verlag.
Bowman, Martin. B-17 Flying Fortress. 192p. 1998. 44.95 (*1-86126-170-5*, Pub. by Crolwood) Motorbooks Intl.
***Bowman, Martin.** B-17 Flying Fortress Units of the Eighth Air Force. (Combat Aircraft Ser.: Vol. 18). (Illus.). 96p. 2000. pap. 17.95 (*1-84176-021-8*, 130035AE, Pub. by Ospry) Motorbooks Intl.
Bowman, Martin. B-24 Liberator. 192p. 1998. 44.95 (*1-86126-143-8*, Pub. by Crolwood) Motorbooks Intl.
— The Bedford Triangle: U. S. Undercover Operations from England in World War II. (Illus.). 240p. 1990. 24.95 (*0-85059-934-2*, Pub. by P Stephens) Haynes Manuals.
***Bowman, Martin.** Boeing 747. (Illus.). 200p. 2000. 52.95 (*1-86126-242-6*, 130054AE, Pub. by Crolwood) Motorbooks Intl.
Bowman, Martin. De Havilland Mosquito. (Illus.). 192p. 1997. 44.95 (*1-86126-075-X*, Pub. by Crolwood) Motorbooks Intl.
— Four Miles High. (Illus.). 248p. 1992. 39.95 (*1-85260-406-9*) Haynes Manuals.
— Lockheed C-130 Hercules. LC 99-488320. (Illus.). 200p. 1999. 52.95 (*1-86126-205-1*, 128161AE) Motorbooks Intl.
— Mosquito Bomber Units. LC 98-181178. (Combat Ser.). (Illus.). 96p. 1997. pap. 17.95 (*1-85532-690-6*, Pub. by Ospry) Stackpole.
— Mosquito Fighter Squadrons of World War II. (Combat Aircraft Ser.: No. 9). (Illus.). 96p. 1998. pap. 16.95 (*1-85532-731-7*, Pub. by Ospry) Motorbooks Intl.
— RAF Bomber Stories, Dramatic First-Hand Accounts of British & Commonwealth Airmen in WW 2. LC 97-76834. (Illus.). 192p. 1998. 34.95 (*1-85260-567-7*) Haynes Manuals.
— The Reich Intruders: Dramatic Accounts of RAF Medium Bomber Raids over Europe in World War II. (Illus.). 182p. 1997. 39.95 (*1-85260-539-1*) Haynes Manuals.
— The Royal Air Force at War: Memories & Personal Experiences: 1039 to the Present Day. LC 96-78557. (Illus.). 192p. 1997. 42.95 (*1-85260-540-5*) Haynes Manuals.
— Spirits in the Sky: Classic Aircraft of World War II. 1999. 17.99 (*0-7858-1063-3*) Bk Sales Inc.
— Thunder in the Heavens: Classic American Aircraft of World War II. 1999. 17.99 (*0-7858-1061-7*) Bk Sales Inc.
***Bowman, Martin.** The USAF, 1947-1999. 192p. 2000. 34.95 (*0-7509-2172-2*) Sutton Publng.
Bowman, Martin. World's Fastest Aircraft. 1990. 19.95 (*1-85260-093-4*, Pub. by P Stephens) Haynes Manuals.
Bowman, Martin & Cushing, Tom. Confounding the Reich: The Operational History of 100 Group, Bomber Support, RAF. (Illus.). 232p. 1996. 24.98 (*1-85260-507-3*, Pub. by J H Haynes & Co) Motorbooks Intl.
Bowman, Martin, et al. Raiders of the Reich: Air Battle Western Europe 42-45. LC 97-3953. (Illus.). 224p. 1996. 19.98 (*0-7603-0391-6*) Motorbooks Intl.
Bowman, Martin W. The Bedford Triangle: U. S. Undercover Operations from England in World War 2. (Illus.). 256p. 1996. pap. 22.95 (*0-7509-1229-4*, Pub. by Sutton Pub Ltd) Intl Pubs Mktg.
— Boeing. (Transport Ser.). 128p. 1998. pap. 16.99 (*0-7524-1537-9*) Arcadia Publng.
***Bowman, Martin W.** Castles in the Air: The Story of the B-17 Flying Fortress Crews of the U. S. 8th Air Force. 2000. pap. 27.95 (*1-57488-320-8*) Brasseys.
— Consolidated - Convair. (Images of Aviation Ser.). (Illus.). 128p. 1999. pap. 18.99 (*0-7524-1703-7*, Tempus Publng) Arcadia Publng.
— Douglas. (Images of Aviation Ser.). (Illus.). 128p. 1999. pap. 18.99 (*0-7524-1615-4*, Tempus Publng) Arcadia Publng.
Bowman, Martin W. English Electric Lightning. (Illus.). 192p. 1998. 54.95 (*1-86126-099-7*, Pub. by Crolwood) Motorbooks Intl.

B

*Bowman, Martin W. Grumman. (Images of Aviation Ser.). (Illus.). 128p. 1999. pap. 18.99 (0-7524-1616-2, Tempus Publng) Arcadia Publng.

Bowman, Martin W. Helton's Hellcats: A Pictorial History of the 493rd Bomb Group. LC 98-60437. 152p. 1998. write for info. (1-56311-418-6) Turner Pub KY.

— Lockheed. (Transport Ser.). 128p. 1999. pap. 16.99 (0-7524-1536-0) Arcadia Publng.

— Mediterranean MTBS at War: U.S. Naval Aviation in Camera, 1946-1999. 224p. 2000. 36.00 (0-7509-2274-5) Sutton Publng.

— The Men Who Flew the Mosquito: Compelling Accounts of the Wooden Wonder's Triumphant WWII Career. (Illus.). 192p. 1995. 44.95 (1-85260-488-3, Pub. by J H Haynes & Co) Motorbooks Intl.

— Mosquito Photo-Reconnaissance Units of World War II, Vol.13. 1999. pap. text 17.95 (1-85532-891-7) Osprey.

*Bowman, Martin W. Shades of Blue: U. S. Naval Air Power Since 1947. (Illus.). 144p. 1999. 29.95 (0-7603-0844-6, 129700AP, Pub. by MBI Pubg) Motorbooks Intl.

— Stearman. (Transport Ser.). (Illus.). 128p. (C). 1999. pap. 18.99 (0-7524-1685-5) Arcadia Publng.

Bowman, Martin W. Stearman: A Pictorial History. LC 97-40628. 150p. 1997. 39.95 (0-7603-0479-3) MBI Pubg.

*Bowman, Martin W. U. S. Naval Aviation, 1946-1999. (Illus.). 2000. 34.95 (0-7509-2175-7) Sutton Publng.

Bowman, Martin W. USAAF Handbook, 1939-45. LC 96-48473. (Illus.). 288p. 1997. 29.95 (0-8117-1822-0) Stackpole.

*Bowman, Martin W. USAAF, 1926-45. (Illus.). 2000. 34.95 (0-7509-2467-5, Pub. by Sutton Publng) Intl Pubs Mktg.

Bowman, Mary. Abstracts & Extracts of Legislative Acts & Resolutions of the State of Ohio: Volumes 20 to 29:1821:1831. 442p. 39.95 (0-935057-90-0) OH Genealogical.

— Abstracts & Extracts of the Legislative Acts & Resolutions of the State of Ohio: 1803-1821. 1994. 34.95 (0-935057-77-3) OH Genealogical.

Bowman, Mary, ed. Some Civil War Manuscripts: A Finding Tool. 1997. per. 13.00 (0-935057-89-7) OH Genealogical.

Bowman, Mary A. Western Mysticism: A Guide to the Basic Works. fac. ed. LC 78-18311. 121p. 1978. pap. 37.60 (0-7837-7318-8, 204724500007) Bks Demand.

Bowman, Mary A., compiled by. Library & Information Science Journals & Serials: An Analytical Guide, 1. LC 84-15787. (Annotated Bibliographies of Serials: A Subject Approach Ser.: No. 1). 140p. 1985. lib. bdg. 55.00 (0-313-23807-3, BLF/, Greenwood Pr) Greenwood.

Bowman, Mary Ann & Stamas, Joan D. Written Communication in Business: A Selective Bibliography. 104p. (Orig.). 1980. pap. 6.90 (0-931874-09-2) Assn Busn Comm.

Bowman, Mary J. Collective Choice in Education. (Studies in Public Choice). 1982. lib. bdg. 126.00 (0-89838-091-X) Kluwer Academic.

— Educational Choice & Labor Markets in Japan. LC 80-25557. 320p. (C). 1981. lib. bdg. 30.00 (0-226-06923-0) U Ch Pr.

— Educational Choice & Labor Markets in Japan. LC 80-25557. (Illus.). 385p. reprint ed. pap. 119.40 (0-608-09393-9, 2054138); reprint ed. pap. 119.10 (0-608-20603-2, 205456800003) Bks Demand.

Bowman, Mary J. & Haynes, W. Warren. Resources & People in East Kentucky: Problems & Potentials of a Lagging Economy. LC 83-11766. (Resources for the Future, Inc. Publications). 480p. reprint ed. 78.50 (0-404-60328-9) AMS Pr.

— Resources & People in East Kentucky: Problems & Potentials of a Lagging Economy. LC 63-17668. 477p. reprint ed. pap. 147.90 (0-7837-3145-0, 204284100006) Bks Demand.

*Bowman, Max. Gay Star Signs: How to Meet & Keep the Man of Your Dreams. 2000. 24.95 (1-56924-605-X) Marlowe & Co.

Bowman, Meg. Dramatic Readings on Feminist Issues, Vol. I. 279p. 1988. pap. 10.95 (0-940483-02-5) Hot Flash Pr.

— Fun Flyers. Unger, Joanna, ed. (Illus.). 67p. (Orig.). 1991. pap. 6.95 (0-940483-06-8) Hot Flash Pr.

— Goddesses, Witches & the Paradigm Shift: Dramatic Readings on Feminist Issues. LC 96-171467. (Illus.). 240p. (Orig.). 1994. pap. 14.95 (0-940483-03-3) Hot Flash Pr.

— Gross Flyers. Hager, Peter, ed. (Illus.). 73p. (Orig.). 1992. pap. 6.95 (0-940483-07-6) Hot Flash Pr.

— Lilith - Adam's First Wife: And Other Dramatic Readings. (Dramatic Readings on Feminist Issues Ser.: Vol. IV). (Illus.). 265p. (Orig.). 1996. pap. 14.95 (0-940483-13-0) Hot Flash Pr.

— Memorial Services for Women. 156p. 1986. pap. 8.95 (0-940483-01-7) Hot Flash Pr.

— Women's History Vol. 3: Dramatic Readings on Feminist Issues. (Illus.). 210p. (Orig.). (C). 1994. pap. 12.95 (0-940483-08-4) Hot Flash Pr.

Bowman, Meg, ed. Nice Flyers. (Illus.). 155p. 1996. spiral bd. 8.95 (0-940483-14-9) Hot Flash Pr.

— Office Tales: Don't Push It. (Illus.). 154p. 1996. spiral bd. 9.95 (0-940483-12-2) Hot Flash Pr.

— Silly Flyers. (Illus.). 112p. 1995. spiral bd. 8.95 (0-940483-11-4) Hot Flash Pr.

Bowman, Meg & Haywood, Diane, eds. Readings for Older Women. 2nd ed. 1997. 11.95 (0-940483-04-1) Hot Flash Pr.

Bowman, Meg & Heath, Mary, eds. Telling Our Stories: Celebrating Ourselves - History of Women & Religion Task Force, PCD-UUA. (Illus.). 150p. 1998. pap. 12.00 (0-940483-15-7) Hot Flash Pr.

Bowman, Meg & Springer, Connie, eds. Readings for Women's Programs. expanded rev. ed. 125p. (Orig.). 1996. pap. 8.95 (0-940483-00-9) Hot Flash Pr.

Bowman, Michael. The Professional Nurse: Coping with Change, Now & the Future. LC 94-72657. 246p. 1995. pap. 41.50 (0-412-47100-0) Chapman & Hall.

Bowman, Michael, jt. ed. see Redgwell, Catherine.

Bowman, Michael K., jt. ed. see Kevan, Larry.

Bowman, Michael S. Applied Economic Analysis for Technologists, Engineers & Managers. LC 98-35687. 561p. (C). 1998. 81.00 (0-13-375932-6) P-H.

Bowman, Myron. Santa Carving with Myron Bowman. (Illus.). 50p. 1985. pap. 12.95 (1-56523-076-0) Fox Chapel Pub.

Bowman, Nettie Ann. Through the Storm. 63p. 1999. pap. 5.99 (0-89114-300-9) Baptist Pub Hse.

Bowman, Nicole, ed. see Doherty, Craig A. & Doherty, Katherine M.

Bowman, Nicole, ed. see Pascoe, Elaine.

Bowman, Norman M. Seed Thoughts in Prose & Verse. LC 92-22155. 100p. (Orig.). 1992. pap. 9.95 (0-926487-12-4) Rowan Mtn Pr.

Bowman, Owen. Carroll County, Virginia: The Early Days to 1920. LC 92-41168. 1993. write for info. (0-89865-855-1) Donning Co.

Bowman, Pat. Feelings from Within. (Illus.). iii, 82p. (Orig.). 1996. pap. 9.95 (0-9655814-0-3) Silent Voices.

Bowman, Patricia A. & Teeter, James W. The Distribution of Living & Fossil Foraminifera & Their Use in the Interpretation of the Post-Pleistocene History of Little Lake, San Salvador Island, Bahamas. (Occasional Papers - 1982: No. 2). 27p. 1982. pap. text 2.25 (0-935909-05-2) Bahamian.

Bowman, Peg. At Home with Sacraments: Confirmation. 48p. 1991. pap. text 3.95 (0-89622-477-5) Twenty-Third.

Bowman, Pete. A Surprise for Easter: A Revolving Picture Book. (Illus.). 12p. (Orig.). (J). (ps-2). 1992. pap. 11.95 (0-689-71552-8) Aladdin.

— Teddy's Christmas: A Pop-Up Book with Christmas Cards. LC 96-49485. (Illus.). 24p. (J). (ps-k). 1997. 14.95 (0-7868-0345-2, Pub. by Hyprn Child) Time Warner.

Bowman, Peter. I Wish I Were Big. (Illus.). 32p. (J). (gr. 1-3). 1998. 15.95 (0-09-176588-9, Pub. by Hutchnson) Trafalgar.

Bowman, R. Lewis. Bumfuzzled. Kuykendall, B. J., ed. & illus. by. Smith, Tammy et al, illus. 150p. 1995. 25.95 (0-9646758-2-X); pap. 15.95 (0-9646758-1-1) R L Bowman.

Bowman, Ray & Hall, Eddy. When Not to Borrow: Unconventional Financial Wisdom to Set Your Church Free. LC 96-33859. (Illus.). 144p. (C). 1996. pap. 9.99 (0-8010-9021-0) Baker Bks.

— When Not to Build: An Architect's Unconventional Wisdom for the Growing Church. 160p. 1992. pap. 9.99 (0-8010-1031-4) Baker Bks.

*Bowman, Ray & Hall, Eddy. When Not to Build: An Architect's Unconventional Wisdom for the Growing Church. 2nd rev. ed. 176p. (gr. 13 up). 2000. pap. 11.99 (0-8010-9106-3) Baker Bks.

Bowman, Raymond A. Aramaic Ritual Texts from Persepolis. LC 65-55148. (Oriental Institute Publications: No. 91). 194p. 1970. lib. bdg. 42.00 (0-226-62194-4) U Ch Pr.

Bowman, Richard G. Walking with Beauty: The Art & Life of Gerard Curtis Delano. (Illus.). 174p. 1990. 67.50 (0-9625410-0-1) R G Bowman.

Bowman, Robert, ed. see Bligh, William.

Bowman, Robert C. The Sermon on the Mount. (Covenant Bible Studies). 48p. (Orig.). 1988. pap. 4.95 (0-87178-777-6, 8776) Brethren.

Bowman, Robert H. Mechanic's Lien in New York. LC 93-73624. 1992. 110.00 (0-317-05376-0) West Group.

Bowman, Robert I., et al, eds. Patterns of Evolution in Galapagos Organisms. LC 83-62392. 568p. (Orig.). 1983. 32.50 (0-934394-05-9) AAASPD.

Bowman, Robert M., Jr. Jehovah's Witnesses. (Guide to Cults & Religious Movements Ser.). 96p. 1995. pap. 5.99 (0-310-70411-1) Zondervan.

— Understanding Jehovah's Witnesses: Why They Read the Bible the Way They Do. LC 91-3034. (Christian Research Institute Ser.). 168p. (YA). (gr. 10). 1991. pap. 7.99 (0-8010-0995-2) Baker Bks.

— Why You Should Believe in the Trinity: An Answer to Jehovah's Witnesses. LC 89-39309. (Christian Research Institute Ser.). 160p. (Orig.). (gr. 10). 1989. pap. 9.99 (0-8010-0981-2) Baker Bks.

Bowman, Robert M., Jr., jt. auth. see Boa, Kenneth D.

Bowman, Robert P. Test Buster Pep Rally. Sorenson, Don L., ed. Merle, tr. (Illus.). 180p. 1987. ring bd. 79.95 (0-932796-21-4) Ed Media Corp.

Bowman, Robert P. & Bowman, Susan C. Becoming a Co-Pilot Mentor Handbook. VanGilder, Rebecca, ed. (Illus.). 150p. (J). (gr. k-5). 1997. pap. 14.95 (1-889636-04-5) Youtlight.

— Becoming a Co-Pilot Mentor Handbook. VanGilder, Rebecca, ed. (Illus.). 150p. (YA). (gr. 6-12). 1997. pap. 14.95 (1-889636-05-3) Youtlight.

— Becoming a Co-Pilot Reader's Guide. VanGilder, Rebecca, ed. (Illus.). 150p. 1997. pap. 69.95 (1-889636-03-7) Youtlight.

Bowman, Robert P., jt. auth. see Myrick, Robert D.

Bowman, Robin. Escaping the Venus Trap: For the Woman Who Says I Don't Want It All, But I Want More Than This! LC 95-80641. 212p. (Orig.). 1996. pap. 14.95 (1-885221-30-4) BookPartners.

Bowman, Ron. Basic Integrated Circuit Technology Reference Manual. McClean, William J. & Griffin, Jim, eds. (Illus.). 208p. 335.00 (1-877750-24-7) Integrated Circuit.

Bowman, Russell. Making Marks: Drawing in the 20th Century from Picasso to Kiefer. 72p. 1998. pap. 19.95 (0-944110-59-2) Milwauk Art Mus.

Bowman, Russell & Cardinal, Roger. Driven to Create: The Anthony Petullo Collection of Self-Taught & Outsider Art. LC 93-33028. (Illus.). 112p. (Orig.). 1993. pap. 24.95 (0-944110-36-3) Milwauk Art Mus.

Bowman, Russell, et al. Common Ground - Uncommon Vision: The Michael & Julie Hall Collection of American Folk Art. LC 93-95442. (Illus.). 335p. 1993. 65.00 (0-944110-43-6); pap. 39.95 (0-944110-33-9) Milwauk Art Mus.

— Jim Nutt. (Illus.). 180p. (Orig.). 1995. pap. 28.95 (0-944110-47-9) Milwauk Art Mus.

Bowman, Ruth. Murals Without Walls: Arshile Gorky's Aviation Murals Rediscovered. LC 78-13898. 1978. pap. 7.95 (0-932828-01-9) Newark Mus.

Bowman, S. D. Modern Methods of Pipe Fabrication. 8th rev. ed. 1982. pap. 6.25 (0-87511-008-X) Claitors.

— Selected Piping Problems. 1980. pap. 7.00 (0-87511-009-6) Claitors.

Bowman, S. Loren. Power & Polity among the Brethren: A Study of Church Governance. LC 87-6345. 169p. 1987. reprint ed. pap. 52.40 (0-608-02154-7, 206282300004) Bks Demand.

Bowman, Sally. An Old-Fashioned Christmas: A One-Act Comedy. (Illus.). 12p. 1996. pap. 3.25 (0-88680-424-8) I E Clark.

— Will Santa Ever Ride Again? A Christmas Play for Grown-Ups. (Illus.). 7p. 1997. pap. 2.50 (0-88680-440-X) I E Clark.

*Bowman, Scott. Decision Making & Judgement for Healthcare Professionals. (Illus.). 224p. 2000. pap. text 32.50 (0-7506-3841-9) Buttrwrth-Heinemann.

Bowman, Scott. The Turning Point: A Personal Account of the Montana "Freemen" Standoff. unabridged ed. LC 99-217283. (Illus.). 200p. 1998. pap. 12.99 (0-9663789-0-3) S Bowman.

Bowman, Scott R. The Modern Corporation & American Political Thought. LC 94-45439. 424p. 1996. 60.00 (0-271-01472-5); pap. 19.95 (0-271-01473-3) Pa St U Pr.

*Bowman, Sharon. How to Give It So They Get It! A Flight Plan for Teaching Anyone Anything & Making It Stick. (Illus.). 225p. (Orig.). 1998. pap. 17.95 (0-9656851-2-8) Bowperson Pub.

— Shake, Rattle & Roll! Using the Ordinary to Make Your Training Extraordinary. (Illus.). 176p. (Orig.). 1999. pap. 17.95 (0-9656851-3-6) Bowperson Pub.

Bowman, Sharon L. Presenting with Pizzazz! Terrific Tips for Topnotch Trainers! LC 97-92966. (Illus.). 107p. (Orig.). 1997. pap. 14.95 (0-9656851-0-1) Bowperson Pub.

Bowman, Sheridan. Radiocarbon Dating. 1990. pap. 13.95 (0-520-07037-2, Pub. by U CA Pr) Cal Prin Full Svc.

Bowman, Sheridan, ed. Science & the Past. (Illus.). 192p. 1991. text 40.00 (0-8020-5997-X) U of Toronto Pr.

Bowman, Sheritha. Soul Inspiration: For Women Married to Unbelievers. 1998. pap. 10.95 (0-9662389-0-7) Scribes-Vibes Bk.

Bowman, Stephen. When the Eagle Screams: America's Vulnerability to Terrorism. LC 93-47233. 1994. 21.95 (1-55972-228-2, Birch Ln Pr) Carol Pub Group.

Bowman, Steve & Wright, Steve. Arkansas Duck Hunter's Almanac. (Illus.). 256p. 1997. pap. 29.95 (0-9638832-2-4, Ozark Delta Pr) White Riv Chronicle.

*Bowman, Steve & Wright, Steve. Arkansas Duck Hunter's Almanac. (Illus.). 272p. 1999. 55.00 (0-9638832-0-8) White Riv Chronicle.

Bowman, Steven. The Jews of Byzantium, 1204-1453. LC 83-17230. (Judaic Studies). 398p. 1985. reprint ed. pap. 113.50 (0-608-01661-6, 2062316) Bks Demand.

Bowman, Steven, ed. see Nahon, Marco.

Bowman, Susan C., jt. auth. see Bowman, Robert P.

Bowman, Suzanne, ed. see Nimmons, Carol A.

Bowman, Sylvia, ed. see Gimmestad, Victor E.

Bowman, Sylvia, ed. see Stephens, Edna B.

Bowman, Sylvia E., jt. auth. see Anderson, David D.

Bowman, Sylvia E., jt. auth. see Winston, George P.

Bowman, Sylvia E., ed. see Anderson, David D.

Bowman, Sylvia E., ed. see Bernhardt-Kabisch, Ernest.

Bowman, Sylvia E., ed. see Brittain, Joan T.

Bowman, Sylvia E., ed. see Brown, Arthur W.

Bowman, Sylvia E., ed. see Bryan, Mary.

Bowman, Sylvia E., ed. see Bucco, Martin.

Bowman, Sylvia E., ed. see Currie, Harold W.

Bowman, Sylvia E., ed. see Duran, James C.

Bowman, Sylvia E., ed. see Fairbanks, Henry C.

Bowman, Sylvia E., ed. see Foster, Edward H.

Bowman, Sylvia E., ed. see Harrison, Stanley R.

Bowman, Sylvia E., ed. see Hatvary, George E.

Bowman, Sylvia E., ed. see Howe, Edgar W.

Bowman, Sylvia E., ed. see Lee, L. L.

Bowman, Sylvia E., ed. see Moore, Rayburn S.

Bowman, Sylvia E., ed. see Moorman, Charles.

Bowman, Sylvia E., ed. see Munro, John M.

Bowman, Sylvia E., ed. see Rueckert, William H.

Bowman, Sylvia E., ed. see Stein, Allen F.

Bowman, Sylvia E., ed. see Taylor, Lloyd C.

Bowman, Sylvia E., ed. see Wermuth, Paul C.

Bowman, Sylvia E., ed. see Whisnant, David E.

Bowman, Sylvia E., ed. see White, Sydney H.

Bowman, Sylvia E., ed. see Young, T. D.

Bowman, Sylvia E., ed. see Zegger, Hrisey D.

Bowman, Thea. Round the Glory Manger: Christmas Spirituals. 72p. pap. 7.95 (0-8198-6428-5) Pauline Bks.

Bowman, Thea, Sr., ed. Families: Black & Catholic, Catholic & Black, Readings, Resources & Family Activities. 180p. 1985. pap. 15.95 (1-55586-890-8) US Catholic.

Bowman, Thomas. Bonding - The Universal Glue. Dennison, T. E., ed. (Illus.). 45p. 1996. 5.00 (0-923231-20-X) Mohican Pub.

— Understanding Solar Cookers & Ovens. Crouch, Margaret, ed. (Technical Papers: No. 36). 26p. (Orig.). 1987. 9.95 (0-86619-247-6) Vols Tech Asst.

Bowman, Thomas E. & Tareen, Inam U. Cymothoidae from Fishes of Kuwait, Arabian Gulf: Crustacea: Isopoda. LC 83-600096. (Smithsonian Contributions to Zoology Ser.: No. 382). 34p. reprint ed. pap. 30.00 (0-608-14205-0, 202186500023) Bks Demand.

Bowman, Thomas F., et al. Finding Your Best Place to Live in America. LC 81-51506. (Illus.). 352p. (Orig.). 1981. pap. 9.95 (0-940162-00-8) Red Lion.

— Finding Your Best Place to Live in America. 416p. (Orig.). 1982. pap. 9.95 (0-940162-02-4) Red Lion.

*Bowman, Thomas L. General Chemistry. 2nd ed. 132p. (C). 2000. lab manual ed. 20.00 (0-923231-36-6) Mohican Pub.

Bowman, Thomas L. General Chemistry for the Agri-Sciences. 2nd ed. Dennison, Scott, ed. (Illus.). 96p. (Orig.). (C). 2001. pap. text 10.00 (0-923231-02-1) Mohican Pub.

Bowman, Valcar A., Jr. Effective Environmental Management Systems (EMS), Vol. 1. 92p. 1997. pap. text 34.95 (1-57450-076-7) Cahners Busn Des Plaines.

— Environmental Emergency Prevention, Control & Countermeasure Plans Vol. 1: A Plan for Sara. 60p. 1997. pap. text 34.95 (1-57450-075-9) Cahners Busn Des Plaines.

Bowman, W. C. Diccionario de Farmacologia. (SPA.). 250p. 1989. pap. 125.00 (0-7859-6394-4, 8486193206) Fr & Eur.

Bowman, W. C., ed. Pharmacology & Therapeutics, Vol. 12, No. 1. LC 77-25743. (Illus.). 283p. 1981. pap. 73.00 (0-08-026854-4, Pergamon Pr) Elsevier.

— Pharmacology & Therapeutics, Vol. 12, No. 2. (Illus.). 190p. 1981. pap. 73.00 (0-08-026855-2, Pergamon Pr) Elsevier.

Bowman, W. Dodgson. Charlie Chaplin: His Life & Art. LC 74-1090. (American Biography Ser.: No. 32). 1974. lib. bdg. 75.00 (0-8383-1841-X) M S G Haskell Hse.

Bowman, W. E. The Ascent of Rum Doodle & the Cruise of the Talking Fish. 256p. 1993. pap. 19.95 (0-7126-5479-8, Pub. by Pimlico) Trafalgar.

Bowman, Walter P. & Ball, Robert H. Theatre Language, a Dictionary. LC 60-10495. 1976. pap. 8.95 (0-87830-551-3, Thtre Arts Bks) Routledge.

Bowman, Ward S., Jr. Patent & Antitrust Law: A Legal & Economic Appraisal. 1973. lib. bdg. 25.00 (0-226-06925-7) U Ch Pr.

Bowman, Warren D. Outdoor Emergency Care: Comprehensive First Aid for Nonurban Settings. 2nd ed. Ayers, Rebecca W., ed. LC 93-84167. (Illus.). 546p. 1993. pap. 30.00 (0-929752-01-5) Natl Ski Patrol.

Bowman, Wayne D. Philosophical Perspectives on Music. 496p. (C). 1998. text 47.95 (0-19-511296-2) OUP.

Bowman, William D. Priest & Parish in Vienna, 1780 to 1880. LC 99-22629. (Studies in Central European Histories). 1999. write for info. (0-391-04094-4) Humanities.

Bowman, William J. Graphic Communication. LC 67-29931. (Wiley Series on Human Communication). (Illus.). 222p. reprint ed. pap. 68.90 (0-608-11223-2, 205123800090) Bks Demand.

Bowmann, Sylvia E., jt. auth. see Day, A. Grove.

Bowmann, R. C., Jr., jt. ed. see Bambakidis, Gust.

Bowmar, Robert H. Lien Priorities in New York. LC 86-83245. 1991. 115.00 (0-317-04606-3) West Group.

— Lien Priorities in New York. LC 86-83245. 1993. suppl. ed. 50.00 (0-317-04750-7) West Group.

— Mortgage Liens in New York. LC 89-63829. 1989. 115.00 (0-317-03792-7) West Group.

— Mortgage Liens in New York. LC 89-63829. 1993. suppl. ed. 65.00 (0-317-03793-5) West Group.

Bowmen, M. R. & Whitmore, T. C. A Second Look at Agathis. 1980. 40.00 (0-85074-053-3) St Mut.

*Bowmer, Jan. Staying off the Beaten Track. 1998. pap. 15.95 (0-09-979651-1, Pub. by Random) Trafalgar.

*Bowmer, Jan, ed. Staying Off the Beaten Track in England & Wales 2000. (Illus.). 368p. 1999. pap. 15.95 (0-09-979661-9, Pub. by Arrow Bks) Trafalgar.

Bown. Radiographer's Pocket Companion. (C). 1998. pap. text 29.00 (0-7020-2166-0) Bailliere Tindall.

Bown, Deni. Action Pack: Castle. 16p. (J). (gr. 3). 1996. boxed set 19.95 (0-7894-0456-7) DK Pub Inc.

— Action Pack: Puzzle. 16p. (J). (gr. 3). 1996. boxed set 19.95 (0-7894-0457-5) DK Pub Inc.

— Airplanes. (Mighty Machines Ser.: No. 3). (Illus.). 24p. (J). 1995. pap. 9.95 (0-7894-0211-4, 5-70624) DK Pub Inc.

— Amsterdam. LC 95-7625. (Eyewitness Travel Guides Ser.). (Illus.). 312p. 1995. pap. 22.95 (0-7894-0186-X, 6-70500) DK Pub Inc.

— Ancient Egypt. (Ultimate Sticker Books Ser.). (Illus.). 20p. (J). (gr. 2 up). 1994. pap. 6.95 (1-56458-560-3) DK Pub Inc.

— Ancient Egypt. LC 95-146. (DK Pockets Ser.). (Illus.). 128p. (YA). (gr. 7 up). 1995. pap. 6.95 (0-7894-0216-5, 5-70629) DK Pub Inc.

— Ancient Greece & Rome. (Ultimate Sticker Books Ser.). (Illus.). 20p. (J). (ps-3). 1994. pap. 6.95 (1-56458-716-9) DK Pub Inc.

— Animal. (Ultimate Sticker Books Ser.). (Illus.). 20p. (J). (ps-3). 1994. pap. 6.95 (1-56458-481-X) DK Pub Inc.

— Animal Families. LC 97-32189. (Henry Silhouettes Ser.). (Illus.). 12p. (J). (ps). 1998. bds. 4.95 (0-7894-3029-0) DK Pub Inc.

— Aquarium Fish. (101 Essential Tips Ser.). (Illus.). 72p. 1997. pap. 4.95 (0-7894-1074-5) DK Pub Inc.

An Asterisk (*) at the beginning of an entry indicates that the title is appearing for the first time.

— Arms & Armor. (Ultimate Sticker Books Ser.). (Illus.). 20p. (J). (ps-3). 1995. pap. 6.95 (*0-7894-0008-1*) DK Pub Inc.

***Bown, Deni.** Aroids: Plants of the Arum Family. 2nd rev. ed. LC 00-25541. (Illus.). 464p. 2000. 34.95 (*0-88192-485-7*) Timber.

Bown, Deni. Around the House. (What Can You Find? Ser.). 10p. (J). (ps). 1993. 4.95 (*1-56458-268-X*) DK Pub Inc.

— At Home. (Treasure Hunt Board Bks.). 10p. (J). 1996. 4.95 (*0-7894-0629-2*) DK Pub Inc.

— Baby Animals. LC 91-27723. (Eye Openers Ser.). (Illus.). 24p. (J). (ps-k). 1992. pap. 7.95 (*0-689-71563-3*) Aladdin.

— Balloons. (Funpax Ser.). (Illus.). (J). (gr. 4-8). 1998. pap. 4.95 (*0-7894-3008-8*) DK Pub Inc.

— Barbecuing. LC 97-45838. (One Hundred One Essential Tips Ser.). (Illus.). 72p. 1998. pap. 4.95 (*0-7894-2780-X*) DK Pub Inc.

— Basic Gardening. LC 97-43130. (One Hundred One Essential Tips Ser.). (Illus.). 72p. 1998. pap. 4.95 (*0-7894-2777-X*) DK Pub Inc.

— Basic Meditation. LC 97-15844. (One Hundred One Essential Tips Ser.). (Illus.). 72p. 1997. pap. 3.95 (*0-7894-2187-9*) DK Pub Inc.

— Basic Sewing. LC 97-24329. (One Hundred One Essential Tips Ser.). (Illus.). 72p. 1997. pap. 3.95 (*0-7894-1977-7*) DK Pub Inc.

— Bendy Beasts. (Funpax Ser.). (Illus.). (J). (gr. 4-8). 1998. pap. 4.95 (*0-7894-3000-2*) DK Pub Inc.

— Bible Companion. LC 96-36696. (Pockets Ser.). (Illus.). 128p. (YA). (gr. 6 up). 1997. pap. 6.95 (*0-7894-1495-3*) DK Pub Inc.

— The Big Book of Things That Go. LC 94-643. (Illus.). 32p. (J). (ps). 1994. 14.95 (*1-56458-462-3*) DK Pub Inc.

— Big Rig. (Mighty Machines Ser.). 24p. (J). 1996. 9.95 (*0-7894-0575-X*) DK Pub Inc.

— Birds. (J). 1998. 6.95 (*0-7894-2973-X*) DK Pub Inc.

— Bonsai. (101 Essential Tips Ser.). 72p. 1996. pap. 4.95 (*0-7894-1075-3*) DK Pub Inc.

— Breast Care. LC 97-17384. (One Hundred One Essential Tips Ser.). (Illus.). 72p. 1997. pap. 3.95 (*0-7894-1975-0*) DK Pub Inc.

— Bug. (Ultimate Sticker Books Ser.). (Illus.). 20p. (J). (ps-3). 1994. pap. 6.95 (*1-56458-480-1*) DK Pub Inc.

— Bulbs. LC 96-47960. (Eyewitness Garden Handbks.). 192p. 1997. 18.95 (*0-7894-1454-6*) DK Pub Inc.

— Bulldozers. LC 94-41309. (Look Inside Cross-Sections Ser.). (Illus.). 32p. (J). (gr. 1-4). 1995. 5.95 (*0-7894-0012-X*) DK Pub Inc.

— Bunny. LC 97-131151. (Shaped Board Bks.). (Illus.). 12p. (J). 1997. bds. 3.95 (*0-7894-1544-5*) DK Pub Inc.

— Cacti & Succulents. (101 Essential Tips Ser.). (Illus.). 72p. 1997. pap. 4.95 (*0-7894-1076-1*) DK Pub Inc.

— Cakes. LC 96-51846. (101 Essential Tips Ser.: Vol. 27). 72p. 1997. pap. 4.95 (*0-7894-1461-9*) DK Pub Inc.

— California. LC 96-44378. (Eyewitness Travel Guides Ser.). (Illus.). 630p. 1997. pap. 29.95 (*0-7894-1451-1*) DK Pub Inc.

— Car. (Ultimate Sticker Books Ser.). (Illus.). 20p. (J). (ps-3). 1993. pap. 6.95 (*1-56458-399-6*) DK Pub Inc.

— Card Games. (Funpax Ser.). (Illus.). (J). (gr. 4-8). 1998. 4.95 (*0-7894-3007-X*) DK Pub Inc.

— The Caregiver's Handbook: A Complete Guide to Home Health Care. LC 97-35911. 192p. 1998. pap. 14.95 (*0-7894-1969-6*) DK Pub Inc.

— Cars. LC 95-145. (DK Pockets Ser.). (Illus.). 128p. (YA). (gr. 7 up). 1995. pap. 6.95 (*0-7894-0217-3*, 5-70630) DK Pub Inc.

— Castle & Knight. (Ultimate Sticker Books Ser.). (Illus.). 20p. (J). (gr. k-7). 1997. pap. 6.95 (*0-7894-1528-3*) DK Pub Inc.

— Cat. (Ultimate Sticker Books Ser.). 20p. (J). (ps-3). 1993. 6.95 (*1-56458-241-8*) DK Pub Inc.

— Cat Care. (101 Essential Tips Ser.). (Illus.). 72p. 1997. 4.95 (*1-56458-986-2*) DK Pub Inc.

— Cats & Kittens: Animal-Shaped Book. 10p. (J). 1996. 3.95 (*0-7894-0620-9*) DK Pub Inc.

— Cat's Cradle. (Funpax Ser.). (Illus.). (J). (gr. 4-8). 1998. pap. 4.95 (*0-7894-3001-0*) DK Pub Inc.

— Chick. LC 97-131149. (Shaped Board Bks.). (Illus.). 10p. (J). 1997. bds. 3.95 (*0-7894-1543-7*) DK Pub Inc.

— Childbirth. (101 Essential Tips Ser.). (Illus.). 72p. 1997. pap. 4.95 (*0-7894-1079-6*) DK Pub Inc.

— Chinese Jump Rope. (Funpax Ser.). (Illus.). (J). (gr. 4-8). 1998. pap. 4.95 (*0-7894-3019-3*) DK Pub Inc.

— Chronicle of the Cinema. rev. ed. (Illus.). 944p. 1997. 59.95 (*0-7894-2249-2*) DK Pub Inc.

— Clothes. LC 97-35224. (Touch & Feel Ser.). (Illus.). 12p. (J). (ps-1). 1998. 6.95 (*0-7894-2919-5*) DK Pub Inc.

— Color Fun. (Tab Board Bks.). 8p. (J). 1995. 3.95 (*0-7894-0230-0*, 5-70642) DK Pub Inc.

— Color Puzzles: A First Book & Puzzle. (Jigsaw Puzzles Ser.). 8p. (J). (gr. 4-7). 1996. 4.95 (*0-7894-0615-2*) DK Pub Inc.

— The Complete Book of Sewing: A Practical Step-by-Step Guide to Sewing Techniques. LC 96-10834. 320p. 1996. 39.95 (*0-7894-0419-2*) DK Pub Inc.

— Cooking with Spices. LC 97-46922. (One Hundred One Essential Tips Ser.). (Illus.). 72p. 1998. pap. 4.95 (*0-7894-2778-8*) DK Pub Inc.

— Cooking with Vegetables. LC 97-24330. (One Hundred One Essential Tips Ser.). (Illus.). 72p. 1997. pap. 4.95 (*0-7894-1976-9*) DK Pub Inc.

— Costume. (Ultimate Sticker Books Ser.). (Illus.). 20p. (J). (ps-3). 1993. pap. 6.95 (*1-56458-400-3*) DK Pub Inc.

— Counting. (Sticker Activity Ser.). (Illus.). 16p. (J). (gr. 3 up). 1993. pap. 6.95 (*1-56458-395-3*) DK Pub Inc.

— The DK Encyclopedia of Fishing: The Complete Guide to the Fish, Tackle & Techniques of Fresh & Saltwater Angling. LC 93-28861. (Illus.). 288p. 1994. 39.95 (*1-56458-492-5*) DK Pub Inc.

— The DK World Atlas. LC 97-12426. 338p. 1997. 50.00 (*0-7894-1974-2*) DK Pub Inc.

— Dog. (Ultimate Sticker Books Ser.). (J). (ps-3). 1993. 6.95 (*1-56458-242-6*) DK Pub Inc.

— Dog Care. (101 Essential Tips Ser.). (Illus.). 72p. 1997. 6.95 (*1-56458-989-7*) DK Pub Inc.

— Dogs & Puppies: Animal-Shaped Book. 10p. (J). 1996. 3.95 (*0-7894-0621-7*) DK Pub Inc.

— Doll. (Ultimate Sticker Books Ser.). (Illus.). 20p. (J). (ps-3). 1994. pap. 6.95 (*1-56458-482-8*) DK Pub Inc.

Bown, Deni. Encyclopedia. LC 96-34446. (Pockets Ser.). (Illus.). 512p. (YA). 1997. pap. 14.95 (*0-7894-1498-8*) DK Pub Inc.

Bown, Deni. Encyclopedia of Herbs & Their Uses: The Definitive Guide to the Identification, Cultivation & Uses of 1,000 Herbs. LC 95-8171. (Illus.). 424p. 1995. 39.95 (*0-7894-0184-3*, 6-70498) DK Pub Inc.

— Essential Facts. (Pocket Guides Ser.: No. 23). (Illus.). 128p. (J). 1996. pap. 6.95 (*0-7894-1020-6*) DK Pub Inc.

— Everyday Things. LC 91-60898. (Eyewitness Visual Dictionaries Ser.). (Illus.). 64p. (J). (gr. 4 up). 1991. 16.99 (*1-879431-17-3*) DK Pub Inc.

— Exotic Bird. LC 97-35383. (Shaped Board Bks.). (Illus.). 12p. (J). (ps). 1998. bds. 3.95 (*0-7894-2931-4*) DK Pub Inc.

— Exploring Multimedia. LC 97-24328. (One Hundred One Essential Tips Ser.). (Illus.). 72p. 1997. pap. 3.95 (*0-7894-1979-3*) DK Pub Inc.

— Eyewitness Atlas, 1996. 160p. (J). 1996. 24.95 (*0-7894-0841-4*) DK Pub Inc.

— Eyewitness Garden Handbook: Annuals & Biennials. LC 97-19526. 192p. 1997. 18.95 (*0-7894-1983-1*) DK Pub Inc.

— Family History Detective, 6 vols. (First Activity Packs Ser.). (Orig.). (J). (gr. k-3). 1996. pap. 16.95 (*0-7894-0572-5*) DK Pub Inc.

— Farm Animals: Animal-Shaped Book. 10p. (J). 1996. 3.95 (*0-7894-0618-7*) DK Pub Inc.

— Finger Puppets: Make Your Own. (Fun Pax Activity Ser.). (Illus.). (J). (gr. 4-8). 1998. pap. 4.95 (*0-7894-3002-9*) DK Pub Inc.

— Fire Truck: Other Building Machines. LC 95-12442. (Mighty Machines Ser.: No. 4). (Illus.). 24p. (J). 1995. pap. 9.95 (*0-7894-0212-2*, 5-70625) DK Pub Inc.

— First Word Puzzles. (First Book & Puzzle Ser.). 8p. (J). 1996. 4.95 (*0-7894-0617-9*) DK Pub Inc.

— Flag. (Ultimate Sticker Books Ser.). (Illus.). 20p. (J). (gr. 1-6). 1993. pap. 6.95 (*1-56458-401-1*) DK Pub Inc.

— Flight: An Interactive Guide to Aviation & Flying Things. (Illus.). (YA). (gr. 3 up). 1996. pap. 17.95 (*0-7894-1006-0*) DK Pub Inc.

— Florida. LC 97-12453. (Eyewitness Travel Guides Ser.). 384p. 1997. vinyl bd. 24.95 (*0-7894-1946-7*) DK Pub Inc.

— France. LC 94-15654. (Eyewitness Travel Guides Ser.). (Illus.). 672p. 1994. pap. 29.95 (*1-56458-646-4*) DK Pub Inc.

— Garden Herbs. LC 97-32178. (Eyewitness Garden Handbks.). 176p. 1998. pap. 18.95 (*0-7894-2397-9*) DK Pub Inc.

— Garden Trees. LC 95-43913. (Eyewitness Handbooks Ser.). 200p. 1996. pap. 17.95 (*0-7894-0428-1*) DK Pub Inc.

— Golf. (101 Essential Tips Ser.). (Illus.). 72p. 1995. pap. 4.95 (*0-7894-0172-X*, 6-70493) DK Pub Inc.

— Great Britain. LC 95-7620. (Illus.). 672p. 1995. pap. 29.95 (*0-7894-0187-8*, 6-70501) DK Pub Inc.

— Greece. LC 96-44381. (Eyewitness Travel Guides Ser.). 368p. 1997. 24.95 (*0-7894-1452-X*) DK Pub Inc.

— Greek Islands: The Islands. LC 96-44380. (Eyewitness Travel Guides Ser.). 400p. 1997. 24.95 (*0-7894-1453-8*) DK Pub Inc.

— Growing Herbs. LC 95-19034. (Illus.). 78p. 1995. 19.95 (*0-7894-0191-6*, 6-70505) DK Pub Inc.

— Happy Times. (Tab Board Bks.). 8p. (J). 1995. 3.95 (*0-7894-0229-7*, 5-70641) DK Pub Inc.

— Hawaii. LC 97-35006. (Eyewitness Travel Guides Ser.). 208p. 1998. pap. 22.95 (*0-7894-2750-8*) DK Pub Inc.

— Healthy Pregnancy. (101 Essential Tips Ser.). (Illus.). 72p. 1997. pap. 4.95 (*0-7894-1078-8*) DK Pub Inc.

— Hiking. LC 97-41745. (One Hundred One Essential Tips Ser.). (Illus.). 72p. 1998. pap. 4.95 (*0-7894-2776-1*) DK Pub Inc.

— Home. (Sticker Activity Ser.). (Illus.). 16p. (J). (ps-1). 1994. pap. 6.95 (*1-56458-525-5*) DK Pub Inc.

— Home. LC 97-42331. (Touch & Feel Ser.). (Illus.). 12p. (J). (ps-2). 1998. 6.95 (*0-7894-2917-9*) DK Pub Inc.

— Home Decorating. (101 Essential Tips Ser.). (Illus.). 72p. 1995. pap. 4.95 (*0-7894-0173-8*, 6-70494) DK Pub Inc.

— Horse. (Ultimate Sticker Books Ser.). 20p. (J). (ps-3). 1993. 6.95 (*1-56458-243-4*) DK Pub Inc.

— Human Body. LC 98-31076. (Eyewitness Explorers Ser.). (Illus.). 64p. (J). (gr. 4-7). 1998. pap. 5.95 (*0-7894-2982-9*) DK Pub Inc.

— The Human Body. (Eyewitness Visual Dictionaries Ser.). (Illus.). 64p. (J). (gr. 4 up). 1991. 16.95 (*1-879431-18-1*) DK Pub Inc.

— In the Yard. (What Can You Find? Ser.). 10p. (J). (ps). 1993. 4.95 (*1-56458-267-1*) DK Pub Inc.

— The Internet: How to Get Connected & Explore the World Wide Web, Exchange News & E-Mail, Download Software, & Communicate On-Line. 176p. 1997. 16.95 (*0-7894-1288-8*) DK Pub Inc.

— Ireland. LC 95-7605. (Eyewitness Travel Guides Ser.). (Illus.). 384p. 1995. pap. 24.95 (*0-7894-0188-6*, 6-70502) DK Pub Inc.

— Istanbul. LC 97-35005. (Eyewitness Travel Guides Ser.). 288p. 1998. pap. 24.95 (*0-7894-2751-6*) DK Pub Inc.

Bown, Deni. Italy. LC 95-4502. (Eyewitness Travel Guides Ser.). (Illus.). 672p. 1996. pap. 29.95 (*0-7894-0425-7*) DK Pub Inc.

Bown, Deni. The Jungle. (Ultimate Sticker Books Ser.). (Illus.). 20p. (J). (ps-3). 1996. pap. 6.95 (*0-7894-1102-4*) DK Pub Inc.

— Koala. LC 97-35384. (Shaped Board Bks.). (Illus.). 12p. (J). (ps). 1998. bds. 3.95 (*0-7894-2928-4*) DK Pub Inc.

— Lamb. LC 97-131148. (Shaped Board Bks.). (Illus.). 10p. (J). 1997. bds. 3.95 (*0-7894-1545-3*) DK Pub Inc.

— Let's Count. (Tab Board Bks.). 8p. (J). 1995. 3.95 (*0-7894-0232-7*, 5-70644) DK Pub Inc.

— Lisbon. LC 97-16878. (Eyewitness Travel Guides Ser.). 192p. 1997. 22.95 (*0-7894-2253-0*) DK Pub Inc.

— The Loire Valley. LC 95-4501. (Eyewitness Travel Guides Ser.). 264p. 1996. pap. 22.95 (*0-7894-0426-5*) DK Pub Inc.

— Look Inside Cross-Sections: Tanks. (Look Inside Cross-Sections Ser.). (Illus.). 32p. (J). 1996. pap. 6.95 (*0-7894-0768-X*) DK Pub Inc.

— Mammals. LC 92-54312. (Eyewitness Explorers Ser.). (Illus.). 64p. (J). (gr. 4-7). 1998. pap. 5.95 (*0-7894-2983-7*) DK Pub Inc.

— Microwave Cooking. (101 Essential Tips Ser.). (Illus.). 72p. 1997. 4.95 (*1-56458-987-0*) DK Pub Inc.

— Millennium Baby's First Year. (Illus.). 56p. 1999. 17.95 (*1-56458-851-3*) DK Pub Inc.

— Motorcycle. (Ultimate Sticker Books Ser.). (Illus.). 20p. (J). (ps-3). 1995. pap. 6.95 (*0-7894-0010-3*) DK Pub Inc.

— Multimedia: The Complete Guide. 192p. 1996. 24.95 (*0-7894-0422-2*) DK Pub Inc.

— My First ABC Board Book. LC 97-36186. (Illus.). 32p. (J). (ps). 1998. bds. 6.95 (*0-7894-2781-8*) DK Pub Inc.

— My First Animal Board Book. LC 97-32131. (Illus.). 32p. (J). (ps). 1998. bds. 6.95 (*0-7894-2783-4*) DK Pub Inc.

— My Sticker Book Atlas. (Illus.). 20p. (J). (ps-2). 1994. pap. 6.95 (*1-56458-714-2*) DK Pub Inc.

— My Sticker Book of the Body. (Illus.). 20p. (J). (ps-2). 1996. pap. 6.95 (*0-7894-1196-2*) DK Pub Inc.

— My Sticker Book of Time. (Illus.). 20p. (J). (ps-2). 1996. pap. 6.95 (*0-7894-1197-0*) DK Pub Inc.

— My Sticker Book of Words. (Illus.). 20p. (J). (ps-2). 1994. pap. 6.95 (*1-56458-715-0*) DK Pub Inc.

— Naples. LC 97-32279. (Eyewitness Travel Guides Ser.). 192p. 1998. pap. 22.95 (*0-7894-2752-4*) DK Pub Inc.

— Nature Explorer. (First Activity Packs Ser.). 24p. (J). (ps-3). 1995. pap. 16.95 (*1-56458-950-1*) DK Pub Inc.

— Number Puzzles. (Jigsaw Puzzles Ser.). 8p. 1996. 4.95 (*0-7894-0616-0*) DK Pub Inc.

— On the Beach. (What Can You Find? Ser.). 10p. (J). (ps). 1993. 4.95 (*1-56458-270-1*) DK Pub Inc.

— On the Farm. (What Can You Find? Ser.). 12p. (J). (ps). 1993. 4.95 (*1-56458-269-8*) DK Pub Inc.

— Photography. (101 Essential Tips Ser.). (Illus.). 72p. 1995. pap. 4.95 (*0-7894-0174-6*, 6-70495) DK Pub Inc.

— Tennis. (101 Essential Tips Ser.). (Illus.). 72p. 1995. pap. 4.95 (*0-7894-0182-7*, 6-70496) DK Pub Inc.

— Planning a Small Yard. (101 Essential Tips Ser.). 72p. 1996. pap. 4.95 (*0-7894-0564-4*) DK Pub Inc.

— Baby Care: Baby Care. (101 Essential Tips Ser.). 72p. 1996. pap. 4.95 (*0-7894-0567-9*) DK Pub Inc.

— Cooking with Children: Cooking with Chicken. (101 Essential Tips Ser.). 72p. 1996. pap. 4.95 (*0-7894-0562-8*) DK Pub Inc.

— Decorating with Fabric: Decorating with Fabric. (101 Essential Tips Ser.). (Illus.). 72p. 1995. pap. 4.95 (*0-7894-0171-1*) DK Pub Inc.

— Healthy Living: Healthy Living. (101 Essential Tips Ser.). 72p. 1996. pap. 4.95 (*0-7894-0566-0*) DK Pub Inc.

— Houseplants: House Plants. (101 Essential Tips Ser.). 72p. 1996. pap. 4.95 (*0-7894-0565-2*) DK Pub Inc.

— Making Salads: Making Salads. (101 Essential Tips Ser.). 72p. 1996. pap. 4.95 (*0-7894-0563-6*) DK Pub Inc.

— Video: Video. (101 Essential Tips Ser.). (Illus.). 72p. 1995. pap. 4.95 (*0-7894-0183-5*, 6-70497) DK Pub Inc.

— Organizing Hints & Tips. LC 97-14618. 144p. 1997. 19.95 (*0-7894-1998-X*) DK Pub Inc.

— Our Family Tree Record Book. 64p. 1997. 17.95 (*0-7894-2076-7*) DK Pub Inc.

— Pasta. (101 Essential Tips Ser.). (Illus.). 72p. 1997. 4.95 (*1-56458-988-9*) DK Pub Inc.

— Perennials. LC 95-43903. (Eyewitness Handbooks Ser.). 352p. 1996. pap. 19.95 (*0-7894-0430-3*) DK Pub Inc.

— The Pirate. (Ultimate Sticker Books Ser.). (Illus.) 20p. (J). (gr. k-7). 1997. pap. 6.95 (*0-7894-1527-5*) DK Pub Inc.

— Playtime. (Treasure Hunt Board Bks.). 10p. (J). 1996. 4.95 (*0-7894-0627-6*) DK Pub Inc.

— Pocket Science Encyclopedia. LC 97-80368. (Pocket Guides Ser.). (Illus.). 512p. (YA). (gr. 5 up). 1998. pap. 9.95 (*0-7894-2871-7*) DK Pub Inc.

— Pond Life. (Look Closer Ser.). 32p. (J). (gr. 3-6). 1998. pap. 4.95 (*0-7894-2970-5*) DK Pub Inc.

— Pony. (Ultimate Sticker Books Ser.). (Illus.). 20p. (J). (ps-3). 1996. pap. 6.95 (*0-7894-1101-6*) DK Pub Inc.

— Portugal. LC 97-12455. (Eyewitness Travel Guides Ser.). 480p. 1997. 24.95 (*0-7894-1948-3*) DK Pub Inc.

— Prehistoric Sticker Book. (Ultimate Sticker Books Ser.). (Illus.). 20p. (J). (gr. 2 up). 1994. pap. 6.95 (*1-56458-561-1*) DK Pub Inc.

— Preserving Fruits. LC 97-46921. (One Hundred One Essential Tips Ser.). (Illus.). 72p. 1998. pap. 4.95 (*0-7894-2779-6*) DK Pub Inc.

— Provence & The Cote D'Azur. LC 94-44323. (Eyewitness Travel Guides Ser.). (Illus.). 264p. 1995. pap. 22.95 (*1-56458-860-2*) DK Pub Inc.

— Race Car. (Mighty Machines Ser.). 24p. (J). (gr. k-3). 1996. 9.95 (*0-7894-0574-1*) DK Pub Inc.

— Rain Forest. (Look Closer Ser.). 32p. (J). (gr. 3-6). 1998. pap. 4.95 (*0-7894-2971-3*) DK Pub Inc.

— Record Breakers. LC 95-12485. (Look Inside Cross-Sections Ser.). (Illus.). 32p. (YA). (gr. 5 up). 1995. pap. 5.95 (*0-7894-0320-X*, 5-70670) DK Pub Inc.

— Relaxation. LC 97-32818. (One Hundred One Essential Tips Ser.). 72p. 1998. pap. 4.95 (*0-7894-2775-3*) DK Pub Inc.

— Rescue Vehicles. LC 94-23756. (Look Inside Cross-Sections Ser.). (Illus.). (J). (gr. 1-4). 1995. 5.95 (*1-56458-879-3*) DK Pub Inc.

— Rocks & Minerals. (Ultimate Sticker Books Ser.). (Illus.). 20p. (J). (ps-3). 1995. pap. 6.95 (*0-7894-0007-3*) DK Pub Inc.

— Roses. LC 95-43904. (Eyewitness Garden Handbks.). (Illus.). 160p. 1996. pap. 18.95 (*0-7894-0607-1*) DK Pub Inc.

— San Francisco & Northern California. LC 94-3379. (Eyewitness Travel Guides Ser.). (Illus.). 312p. 1994. pap. 22.95 (*1-56458-645-6*) DK Pub Inc.

— Seville & Andalusia. LC 95-4500. (Eyewitness Travel Guides Ser.). 272p. 1996. pap. 22.95 (*0-7894-0427-3*) DK Pub Inc.

— Shape Puzzles. (Jigsaw Puzzles Ser.). 8p. 1996. 4.95 (*0-7894-0614-4*) DK Pub Inc.

— Shapes Galore. (Tab Board Bks.). 8p. (J). 1995. 3.95 (*0-7894-0231-9*, 5-70643) DK Pub Inc.

— Shark. (Eyewitness Activity Files Ser.). (J). 1998. pap. 9.95 (*0-7894-2793-1*) DK Pub Inc.

— Shark & Whale. (Ultimate Sticker Books Ser.). (Illus.). 20p. (J). (ps-3). 1994. pap. 6.95 (*1-56458-717-7*) DK Pub Inc.

— Shells. LC 92-54311. (Eyewitness Explorers Ser.). (Illus.). 64p. (J). (gr. 4-7). 1998. pap. 5.95 (*0-7894-2984-5*) DK Pub Inc.

— Ships. LC 93-46382. (Look Inside Cross-Sections Ser.). (Illus.). 32p. (J). (gr. 1-4). 1994. pap. 5.95 (*1-56458-521-2*) DK Pub Inc.

— Shopping. (Sticker Activity Ser.). (Illus.). 16p. (J). (ps-1). 1993. pap. 6.95 (*1-56458-396-1*) DK Pub Inc.

— Shrubs & Climbers. LC 95-43914. (Eyewitness Garden Handbks.). 336p. 1996. pap. 19.95 (*0-7894-0429-X*) DK Pub Inc.

— Sorting. (Sticker Activity Ser.). 16p. (J). (ps-1). 1993. pap. 6.95 (*1-56458-246-9*) DK Pub Inc.

— Soups. LC 97-14911. (One Hundred One Essential Tips Ser.). (Illus.). 72p. 1997. pap. 3.95 (*0-7894-1980-7*) DK Pub Inc.

— Space. (Ultimate Sticker Books Ser.). (Illus.). 20p. (J). (ps-3). 1993. pap. 6.95 (*1-56458-402-X*) DK Pub Inc.

— Space, Stars, Planets & Spacecraft. LC 91-60144. (See & Explore Library). 64p. (J). 1998. pap. 7.95 (*0-7894-2966-7*) DK Pub Inc.

Bown, Deni. Spain. LC 96-14182. (Eyewitness Travel Guides Ser.). (Illus.). 672p. 1996. pap. 29.95 (*0-7894-1068-0*) DK Pub Inc.

Bown, Deni. Sydney. LC 96-14187. (Eyewitness Travel Guides Ser.). 264p. 1996. pap. 22.95 (*0-7894-1069-9*) DK Pub Inc.

— Thailand. LC 97-5191. (Eyewitness Travel Guides Ser.). 504p. 1997. 24.95 (*0-7894-1949-1*) DK Pub Inc.

— Things That Go. (Sticker Activity Ser.). (Illus.). 16p. (J). (ps-1). 1994. pap. 6.95 (*1-56458-523-9*) DK Pub Inc.

— Things to Eat. (Treasure Hunt Board Bks.). 10p. (J). 1996. 4.95 (*0-7894-0628-4*) DK Pub Inc.

— Tide Pool. (Look Closer Ser.). 32p. (J). (gr. 3-6). 1998. pap. 4.95 (*0-7894-2972-1*) DK Pub Inc.

— Tiger. LC 98-134176. (Shaped Board Bks.). (Illus.). 12p. (J). (ps). 1998. bds. 3.95 (*0-7894-2930-6*) DK Pub Inc.

— Time. (Sticker Activity Ser.). (Illus.). 16p. (J). (ps-1). 1993. pap. 6.95 (*1-56458-398-8*) DK Pub Inc.

— Transportation. (Ultimate Sticker Books Ser.). (Illus.). 20p. (J). (gr. 2 up). 1994. pap. 6.95 (*1-56458-479-8*) DK Pub Inc.

— Travel Fun, 6 Vols. (J). (gr. 4-7). 1996. pap. 15.95 (*0-7894-0571-7*) DK Pub Inc.

— Travel Games. (Activity Fun Packs Ser.). (Illus.). (J). (gr. 4-8). 1998. pap. 4.95 (*0-7894-3004-5*) DK Pub Inc.

— Trees & Flowers. (Ultimate Sticker Books Ser.). (Illus.). 20p. (J). (ps-3). 1995. pap. 6.95 (*0-7894-0009-X*) DK Pub Inc.

— The Ultimate Dinosaur Sticker Book: Create Your Own Picture Book. (Ultimate Sticker Books Ser.). (Illus.). 8p. (J). (ps-3). 1993. pap. 6.95 (*1-56458-247-7*) DK Pub Inc.

— The Ultimate Kitten Sticker Book. (Illus.). (J). (ps-7). 1996. 6.95 (*0-7894-1347-7*) DK Pub Inc.

— Ultimate Pocket Flags of the World. LC 97-13688. 240p. 1997. pap. 12.95 (*0-7894-2085-6*) DK Pub Inc.

— Ultimate Pocket World Factfile. 240p. 1996. pap. 12.95 (*0-7894-0439-7*) DK Pub Inc.

— The Ultimate Puppy Sticker Book. (Illus.). 16p. (J). (ps-7). 1996. 6.95 (*0-7894-1348-5*) DK Pub Inc.

— Ultimate Sticker Books. (J). 1998. 6.95 (*0-7894-2817-2*) DK Pub Inc.

— Venice & the Veneto. LC 94-44310. (Eyewitness Travel Guides Ser.). (Illus.). 312p. 1995. pap. 22.95 (*1-56458-861-0*) DK Pub Inc.

— Vienna. LC 94-18210. (Eyewitness Travel Guides Ser.). (Illus.). 288p. 1994. pap. 22.95 (*1-56458-647-2*) DK Pub Inc.

— The Visual Dictionary of Ancient Civilizations. LC 94-8395. (Eyewitness Visual Dictionaries Ser.). (Illus.). 64p. (J). (gr. 4 up). 1994. 18.95 (*1-56458-701-0*) DK Pub Inc.

— The Visual Dictionary of Animals. LC 91-60901. (Eyewitness Visual Dictionaries Ser.). (Illus.). 64p. (J). (gr. 4 up). 1991. 18.95 (*1-879431-19-X*) DK Pub Inc.

— The Visual Dictionary of Cars. LC 91-58205. (Eyewitness Visual Dictionaries Ser.). (Illus.). 64p. (J). (gr. 4 up). 1992. 16.95 (*1-56458-007-5*) DK Pub Inc.

B

— The Visual Dictionary of Dinosaurs. LC 72-91418. (Eyewitness Visual Dictionaries Ser.). (Illus.). 64p. (J). (gr. 4 up). 1993. 16.95 (1-56458-188-8) DK Pub Inc.

— The Visual Dictionary of Everyday Things. LC 92-52830. (Eyewitness Visual Dictionaries Ser.). (Illus.). 64p. (J). (gr. 4 up). 1991. 15.99 (1-879431-32-7) DK Pub Inc.

— The Visual Dictionary of Military Uniforms. LC 91-58206. (Eyewitness Visual Dictionaries Ser.). (Illus.). 64p. (J). (gr. 4 up). 1992. 18.95 (1-56458-010-5); 15.99 (1-56458-011-3) DK Pub Inc.

— The Visual Dictionary of Plants. LC 91-58208. (Eyewitness Visual Dictionaries Ser.). (Illus.). 64p. (YA). (gr. 4 up). 1992. 15.95 (1-56458-016-4) DK Pub Inc.

— The Visual Dictionary of Special Military Forces. LC 92-53448. (Eyewitness Visual Dictionaries Ser.). (Illus.). 64p. (J). (gr. 4 up). 1993. 18.95 (1-56458-189-6) DK Pub Inc.

— The Visual Dictionary of the Horse. LC 93-20819. (Eyewitness Visual Dictionaries Ser.). (Illus.). 64p. (J). (gr. 4 up). 1993. 18.95 (1-56458-504-2) DK Pub Inc.

— Warsaw. LC 97-15211. (Eyewitness Travel Guides Ser.). 288p. 1997. 22.95 (0-7894-1614-X) DK Pub Inc.

— Weather. LC 95-147. (DK Pockets Ser.). (Illus.). 128p. (YA). (gr. 7 up). 1995. pap. 6.95 (0-7894-0218-1, 5-70631) DK Pub Inc.

— Weather Station. (Henderson Activity Packs Ser.). (Illus.). (J). (gr. 4-8). 1998. pap. 4.95 (0-7894-3006-1) DK Pub Inc.

— The Wedding Planner & Record Book: Wedding Planning Made Simple & Memorable. 80p. 1996. 17.95 (0-7894-0446-X) DK Pub Inc.

— Wild Animals. LC 97-38701. (Touch & Feel Ser.). (Illus.). 12p. (J). (ps-2). 1998. 6.95 (0-7894-2918-7) DK Pub Inc.

— Wild Animals: Animal-Shaped Book. 10p. (J). 1996. 3.95 (0-7894-0619-5) DK Pub Inc.

— Wine. LC 96-6591. (101 Essential Tips Ser.: Vol. 30). 72p. 1997. pap. 4.95 (0-7894-1464-3) DK Pub Inc.

— World Atlas. LC 95-148. (DK Pockets Ser.). (Illus.). 160p. (YA). (gr. 7 up). 1995. pap. 5.95 (0-7894-0215-7, 5-70628) DK Pub Inc.

— World Explorer. (First Activity Packs Ser.). 24p. (J). (ps-3). 1995. pap. 16.95 (1-56458-898-X) DK Pub Inc.

— World Reference Atlas. LC 94-19376. (Illus.). 732p. 1996. 49.95 (0-7894-1085-0) DK Pub Inc.

Bown, Deni. Yoga. (101 Essential Tips Ser.). (Illus.). 72p. 1997. pap. 4.95 (1-56458-991-9) DK Pub Inc.

Bown, Deni. Young Detective. (First Activity Packs Ser.). 24p. (J). (ps-3). 1995. pap. 16.95 (1-56458-899-8) DK Pub Inc.

— Young Scientist, 6 vols. (J). (ps-7). 1996. pap. 16.95 (0-7894-0573-3) DK Pub Inc.

Bown, Deni & Claiborne, Michele. Human Body. (DK Action Packs Ser.). (Illus.). 16p. (J). (gr. 3 up). 1995. pap. 19.95 (1-56458-894-7, 5-70550) DK Pub Inc.

— Tutankhamun & Ancient Egypt: An Interactive Guide to the Mystery of Tutankhamun. (Illus.). (YA). (gr. 3 up). 1996. pap. 19.95 (0-7894-1005-2) DK Pub Inc.

***Bown, Deni & Ferry-Swainson, Kate.** Ginger. LC 99-42974. (Herb Library). (Illus.). 80p. 2000. pap. 12.95 (1-58290-015-9, Pub. by Jrny Editions) Tuttle Pubng.

— Mint. LC 99-42983. (Herb Library). 2000. pap. 12.95 (1-58290-016-7) Jrny Editions.

Bown, Fred, jt. auth. see Chase, Warren.

Bown, Jane, photos by. Jane Bown, Observer. LC 96-60010. (Illus.). 128p. (Orig.). 1996. pap. 19.95 (0-500-27891-1, Pub. by Thames Hudson) Norton.

Bown, Matthew C. Art under Stalin. LC 91-11281. (Illus.). 256p. 1991. 40.00 (0-8419-1299-8) Holmes & Meier.

— Socialist Realist Painting. LC 97-28079. (Illus.). 528p. 1998. 75.00 (0-300-06844-1) Yale U Pr.

Bown, S. Cullerne. Contemporary Russian Art. (C). 1990. 250.00 (0-7855-4470-4, Pub. by Collets) St Mut.

Bown, Stephen G., et al, eds. Thermal Therapy, Laser Welding & Tissue Interaction. LC 99-192234. (Europto Ser.: Vol. 3565). 1998. 69.00 (0-8194-3027-7) SPIE.

Bown, T. M. & Rose, K. D., eds. Dawn of the Age of Mammals in the Northern Part of the Rocky Mountain Interior. (Special Papers: No. 243). (Illus.). 260p. 1990. pap. 20.00 (0-8137-2243-8) Geol Soc.

Bown, Virginia. The Veiled Vixen. 224p. 1992. 19.95 (0-8027-1189-8) Walker & Co.

***Bownas, David A.** Building Services Design Methodology: A Practical Guide. LC 00-30902. (Illus.). 2000. pap. write for info. (0-419-25280-0, E & FN Spon) Routledge.

Bownas, Geoffrey, jt. auth. see Norbury, Paul.

Bownas, Geoffrey, jt. ed. see Mishima, Yukio, pseud.

Bownas, Geoffrey, tr. see Akutagawa, Ryunosuke.

Bownas, Geoffrey, tr. see Watsuji, Tetsuro.

Bownas, Samuel. A Description of the Qualifications Necessary to a Gospel Minister. LC 89-2948. 1993. reprint ed. 10.00 (0-87574-911-9) Pendle Hill.

Bownds, Deric. The Biology of Mind: Origins & Structures of Mind, Brain & Consciousness. LC 99-26155. (Illus.). 330p. 1999. pap. 29.95 (1-891786-07-5) Fitzgerald Sci.

Bowne, jt. auth. see Alley, Joseph W.

Bowne, Borden P. The Essence of Religion. LC 75-3070. reprint ed. 34.50 (0-404-59069-1) AMS Pr.

— The Immanence of God. LC 75-3071. reprint ed. 37.50 (0-404-59070-5) AMS Pr.

— Introduction to Psychological Theory. LC 75-3072. (Philosophy in America Ser.). reprint ed. 34.50 (0-404-59071-3) AMS Pr.

— Metaphysics . . . rev. ed. LC 75-948. (Philosophy in America Ser.). reprint ed. 47.50 (0-404-59072-1) AMS Pr.

— Personalism. LC 75-949. reprint ed. 34.50 (0-404-59073-X) AMS Pr.

— The Principles of Ethics. LC 75-3073. (Philosophy in America Ser.). reprint ed. 49.50 (0-404-59074-8) AMS Pr.

— Studies in Christianity. LC 75-3074. reprint ed. 28.50 (0-404-59075-6) AMS Pr.

— Theism . . . Comprising the Deems Lectures for 1902. LC 75-3075. (Philosophy in America Ser.). reprint ed. 37.50 (0-404-59076-4) AMS Pr.

Bowne, Dale R. Paradigms & Principal Parts for the Greek New Testament. LC 86-33989. 60p. (Orig.). (C). 1987. pap. text 14.00 (0-8191-6099-7) U Pr of Amer.

Bowne, Eliza S. A Girl's Life Eighty Years Ago: Selection from the Letters of Eliza Southgate Bowne. LC 74-3933. (Women in America Ser.). (Illus.). 280p. 1974. reprint ed. 23.95 (0-405-06079-3) Ayer.

— A Girl's Life Eighty Years Ago: Selections from the Letters of Eliza Southgate Bowne. 239p. 1980. reprint ed. 24.95 (0-87928-105-7) Corner Hse.

Bowne, Elizabeth. Louisa . . . A Southern Girls' Escape in 1864. LC 96-166529. 1995. pap. 12.00 (0-9634826-5-3) New Hope AL.

Bowne Publishing Division Staff & Hood, Susan, eds. Rules & Regulations of the Securities & Exchange Commission: Red Box Service. 2500p. 1997. 250.00 (1-885100-04-3, R-1) Bowne Pubng.

Bowne Publishing Division Staff & Sanders-Harris, Barbara E., eds. Securities Act Handbook. 2300p. 1997. ring bd. 250.00 (1-886100-02-0, A-1) Bowne Pubng.

Bowness, Alan. Bernard Meadows: Sculpture & Drawings. (British Sculptors & Sculpture Ser.: Vol. 4). (Illus.). 160p. (C). 1994. 75.00 (0-85331-644-9, Pub. by Lund Humphries) Antique Collect.

— The Conditions of Success: How the Modern Artist Rises to Fame. (Illus.). 1990. 12.95 (0-500-55021-2, Pub. by Thames Hudson) Norton.

— Gauguin. (Color Library). (Illus.). 128p. (C). 1994. reprint ed. pap. 14.95 (0-7148-2683-9, Pub. by Phaidon Press) Phaidon Pr.

— Henry Moore: Complete Sculpture, 1981-86, 1, 6. 1999. 90.00 (0-85331-767-4) Lund Humphries.

— Modern European Art: Impressionism to Abstract Art. LC 95-60189. (World of Art Ser.). (Illus.). 224p. 1995. pap. 14.95 (0-500-20205-2, Pub. by Thames Hudson) Norton.

Bowness, Alan, ed. Henry Moore, Complete Sculpture Vol. 2: (1949-54), Vol. 2. 3rd rev. ed. (Illus.). 208p. (C). 1986. 80.00 (0-85331-494-2, Pub. by Lund Humphries) Antique Collect.

— Henry Moore, Complete Sculpture Vol. 3: 1955-64, Vol. 3. 2nd rev. ed. (Illus.). 212p. (C). 1986. 80.00 (0-85331-495-0, Pub. by Lund Humphries) Antique Collect.

— Henry Moore, Complete Sculpture Vol. 4: 1964-73, Vol. 4. (Illus.). 280p. (C). 1991. 80.00 (0-85331-392-X, Pub. by Lund Humphries) Antique Collect.

— Henry Moore, Complete Sculpture Vol. 5: 1974-80. 2nd rev. ed. (Illus.). 240p. (C). 1994. 80.00 (0-85331-660-0, Pub. by Lund Humphries) Antique Collect.

— Henry Moore, Complete Sculpture Vol. 6: 1980-86, Vol. 6. (Illus.). 240p. (C). 1988. 80.00 (0-85331-524-8, Pub. by Lund Humphries) Antique Collect.

Bowness, Nicholas & Zyszkowski, Alina, eds. Small Islands Big Issues: Sustainable Development of Islands. (Illus.). 141p. 1997. per. 20.00 (0-9659002-0-7) Counterpt Intl.

Bowra, C. M. The Romantic Imagination. (Oxford Paperbacks Ser.). 318p. 1976. pap. 17.95 (0-19-281006-5) OUP.

Bowra, C. M., tr. & intro. see Pindar, Peter.

Bowra, C. Maurice, ed. see Pindar, Peter.

Bowra, Cecil M. The Background of Modern Poetry. LC 75-22207. (Studies in Poetry: No. 38). (C). 1975. lib. bdg. 75.00 (0-8383-2075-9) M S G Haskell Hse.

— Edith Sitwell. LC 75-38540. (Studies in Poetry: No. 38). 1976. lib. bdg. 49.00 (0-8383-2114-3) M S G Haskell Hse.

— In General & Particular. LC 72-156615. (Essay Index Reprint Ser.). 1977. reprint ed. 21.95 (0-8369-2752-4) Ayer.

— Inspiration & Poetry. LC 77-106407. (Essay Index Reprint Ser.). 1977. 21.95 (0-8369-1452-X) Ayer.

— The Lyrical Poetry of Thomas Hardy. LC 75-22227. (Studies in Thomas Hardy: No. 14). 1975. lib. bdg. 75.00 (0-8383-2098-8) M S G Haskell Hse.

— Tradition & Design in the Iliad. LC 77-3065. 278p. 1977. reprint ed. lib. bdg. 38.50 (0-8371-9561-6, BOTD, Greenwood Pr) Greenwood.

Bowra, Cecil M., ed. A Second Book of Russian Verse. LC 73-114472. 153p. 1971. reprint ed. lib. bdg. 55.00 (0-8371-4814-6, BORW, Greenwood Pr) Greenwood.

Bowra, Cecile. Historia de la Literatura Griega (History of Greek Literature) (Breviarios Ser.). (SPA.). 216p. 1948. pap. 7.99 (968-16-0396-6, Pub. by Fondo) Continental Bk.

Bowra, K., jt. auth. see Conboy, K.

Bowrey, Thomas. Geographical Account of Countries Around the Bay of Bengal, 1669 to 1679. Temple, R. C., ed. (C). 1993. reprint ed. text 44.00 (81-206-0848-8, Pub. by Asian Educ Servs) S Asia.

— Geographical Account of Countries Round the Bay of Bengal, 1669-1679. 1998. 44.00 (81-215-0791-X) M Manoharial.

***Bowring, Bill & Fottrell, Deidre.** Minority & Group Rights in the New Millennium. LC 99-48138. 1999. 111.00 (90-411-1013-5) Kluwer Law Intl.

Bowring-Carr, Christopher & West-Burnham, John. Effective Learning in Schools: How to Integrate Learning & Leadership for a Successful School. 208p. 1996. pap. 52.50 (0-273-62413-X, Pub. by F T P-H) Trans-Atl Phila.

Bowring, Dave. Bowhunting for Whitetails: Your Best Methods for Taking North America's Favorite Deer. LC 84-16187. (Illus.). 304p. 1985. pap. 19.95 (0-8117-3076-X) Stackpole.

***Bowring, Finn.** Andre Gorz & the Sartrean Legacy: Arguments for a Person-Centered Social Theory. LC 99-53012. (Illus.). 2000. text 59.95 (0-312-23103-2) St Martin.

Bowring, Ian. Exploding Egg. (J). (gr. 4-7). 1994. pap. 3.95 (0-207-17392-3) HarpC.

Bowring, Isabel, jt. auth. see Hoy, Ken.

Bowring, Jane. Sam's Surprise. 1998. pap. 6.95 (0-207-18771-1) HarpC.

Bowring, John. The Kingdom & People of Siam, 2 vols. LC 70-179172. (South & Southeast Asia Studies). (Illus.). reprint ed. 145.00 (0-404-54802-4) AMS Pr.

— Report on the Commercial Statistics of Syria. LC 73-6271. (Middle East Ser.). 1973. reprint ed. 18.95 (0-405-05326-6) Ayer.

Bowring, John, tr. see Chamisso, Adelbert Von.

Bowring, Joseph. Competition in a Dual Economy. LC 85-43271. 217p. 1986. reprint ed. pap. 67.30 (0-608-04627-2, 206531400003) Bks Demand.

Bowring, Larry A. StationMasters: Pocket Guide to Metrorail Station Neighborhoods. 4th rev. ed. LC 96-86611. (Illus.). 84p. 1997. pap. 4.95 (0-9618322-3-1) Bowring Cartograph.

Bowring, Lewin B. Haidar Ali & Tipu Sultan & the Struggle with the Musalman Powers of the South. LC 98-904937. 233 p. 1997. 24.00 (81-206-1299-X, Pub. by Asian Educ Servs) S Asia.

Bowring, Maggie. Working with Texts: A Core Book for Language Analysis. LC 96-43097. (Intertext Ser.). 352p. (C). 1997. pap. 20.99 (0-415-14597-X) Routledge.

— Working with Texts: A Core Book for Language Analysis. LC 96-43097. (Intertext Ser.). 352p. (C). 1997. 75.00 (0-415-14596-1) Routledge.

Bowring, Mary. Vet in Charge. large type ed. 1993. 17.95 (0-7505-0473-0, Pub. by Mgna Lrg Print) Ulverscroft.

— Vets at Variance. large type ed. 269p. 1994. 27.99 (0-7505-0663-6) Ulverscroft.

— Vets in Love. large type ed. (Magna Romance Ser.). 284p. 1992. 27.99 (0-7505-0393-9) Ulverscroft.

Bowring, Nona, jt. auth. see Chester, D. N.

Bowring, Richard. Diary of Lady Murasaki. Date not set. lib. bdg. 16.95 (0-8488-1957-8) Amereon Ltd.

Bowring, Richard & Laurie, Haruko Urya. An Introduction to Modern Japanese Bk. 1: Grammar Lessons. 503p. (C). 1992. text 69.95 (0-521-43839-X) Cambridge U Pr.

— An Introduction to Modern Japanese Bk. 2: Exercises & Word Lists. 387p. (C). 1992. text 69.95 (0-521-43840-3) Cambridge U Pr.

Bowring, Richard J. & Kornicki, Peter F., eds. Cambridge Encyclopedia of Japan. (Illus.). 410p. (C). 1993. 64.95 (0-521-40352-9) Cambridge U Pr.

Bowron, Bernard R., Jr. Henry B. Fuller of Chicago, 11. LC 70-140915. (Contributions in American Studies: No. 11). (Illus.). 278p. 1974. 59.95 (0-8371-5820-6, BHF/, Greenwood Pr) Greenwood.

Bowron, Edgar P. European Paintings Before 1900 in the Fogg Art Museum. (Illus.). 392p. 1990. 35.00 (0-916724-76-X, 476-X) Harvard Art Mus.

***Bowron, Edgar Peters & Morton, Mary G.** Masterworks of European Painting in the Museum of Fine Arts, Houston. (Illus.). 2000. 60.00 (0-691-00460-9) Princeton U Pr.

***Bowron, Edgar Peters, et al.** Art in Rome in the 18th Century. LC 00-24655. (Illus.). 2000. write for info. (0-87633-136-3) Phila Mus Art.

Bowron, Edgar Peters, et al. Italian Paintings of the Seventeenth & Eighteenth Centuries. LC 95-32927. (National Gallery of Art USA Publication). (Illus.). 412p. 1996. 105.00 (0-89468-216-4) OUP.

***Bowron, Peter.** Art in Rome in the Eighteenth Century. 2000. 95.00 (1-85894-098-2) Merrell Holberton.

Bows, Ray. Vietnam Military Lore: Legends, Shadows & Heroes. LC 96-72069. (Illus.). 1208p. 1998. 50.00 (0-929973-01-1) Bows & Sons.

— Vietnam Military Lore: Legends, Shadows & Heroes. LC 96-72069. (Illus.). 1208p. 1998. 50.00 (0-8158-0527-6) Chris Mass.

— Vietnam Military Lore, 1959-1973: Another Way to Remember. (Illus.). 720p. (Orig.). (C). 1988. pap. 29.95 (0-929973-00-3) Bows & Sons.

Bowser, et al. Performing Arts Resources, Vol. 2. Perry, Ted, ed. LC 75-646287. 132p. 1976. 25.00 (0-910482-73-X) Theatre Lib.

Bowser, A. B. Bowser Family History. (Illus.). 310p. 1992. reprint ed. pap. 47.00 (0-8328-2469-0); reprint ed. lib. bdg. 57.00 (0-8328-2468-2) Higginson Bk Co.

Bowser, Benjamin P. Black Male Adolescents: Parenting & Education in Community Context. 352p. (C). 1994. pap. text 29.50 (0-8191-9115-9) U Pr of Amer.

Bowser, Benjamin P., ed. Black Male Adolescents: Parenting & Education in Community Context. 352p. (C). 1990. lib. bdg. 58.00 (0-8191-7975-2) U Pr of Amer.

— Racism & Anti-Racism in World Perspective. LC 95-16620. (Race & Ethnic Relations Ser.: Vol. 13). 304p. 1995. 52.00 (0-8039-4953-7); pap. 24.00 (0-8039-4954-5) Sage.

Bowser, Benjamin P., et al, eds. Census Data with Maps for Small Areas of New York City 1910-1960: A Guide to the Microfilm Collection. 35p. 1981. 30.00 (0-89235-028-8) Primary Srce Media.

Bowser, Benjamin P. & Hunt, Raymond G. Impacts of Racism on White Americans. 2nd ed. LC 95-41797. 320p. 1996. 58.00 (0-8039-4993-6); pap. 26.00 (0-8039-4994-4) Sage.

Bowser, Benjamin P. & Hunt, Raymond G., eds. Impacts of Racism on White Americans. LC 81-9111. (Sage Focus Editions Ser.: Vol. 36). 288p. 1981. pap. 89.30 (0-7837-8960-2, 204974100003) Bks Demand.

Bowser, Benjamin P., et al. Confronting Diversity Issues on Campus. (Survival Skills for Scholars Ser.: Vol. 6). (Illus.). 128p. (C). 1993. text 37.00 (0-8039-5215-5); pap. text 16.50 (0-8039-5216-3) Sage.

Bowser, Benjamin P., ed. see Young, Gale A.

Bowser, Charles W. Let the Bunker Burn: The Final Battle with MOVE. LC 89-505. 192p. 1989. 17.50 (0-940159-08-2) Camino Bks.

Bowser, Eileen. History of the American Cinema, Vol. 2: The Transformation of Cinema, 1907-1915, Vol. 2. Harpole, Charles H. et al, eds. LC 90-48306. (Illus.). 337p. 1990. 85.00 (0-684-18414-1, Scribners Ref) Mac Lib Ref.

— The Transformation of Cinema, 1907-1915. LC 93-41317. 1994. 19.95 (0-520-08534-5, Pub. by U CA Pr) Cal Prin Full Svc.

Bowser, Eileen & Kuiper, John, eds. A Handbook for Film Archives, Two IFFA: International Federation of Film Archives. LC 91-13493. 248p. 1991. text 35.00 (0-8240-3533-X) Garland.

Bowser, Eileen & University Publications of America Inc. The Merritt Crawford Papers. LC 88-890243. (Cinema History Microfilm Ser.). 5 p. 1986. write for info. (0-89093-947-0) U Pubns Amer.

Bowser, James. Inorganic Chemistry. 736p. (C). 1992. 66.00 (0-534-17532-5) Brooks-Cole.

— Twenty Voices: A Pentecost Celebration. 20p. 1991. pap. 5.95 (1-877871-13-3, 3520) Ed Ministries.

Bowser, James R. Inorganic Chemistry. 1992. mass mkt., teacher ed. write for info. (0-534-17533-3) Brooks-Cole.

Bowser, John D. & Sherman, Ross. The Principal's Companion: A Workbook for Future School Leaders. 2nd ed. LC 96-14343. 174p. 1996. pap. text 26.50 (0-7618-0339-4); lib. bdg. 49.50 (0-7618-0338-6) U Pr of Amer.

Bowser, Kathryn. The AIVF Guide to Film & Video Distributors. 3rd rev. ed. 172p. (Orig.). 1996. pap. 12.00 (0-9622448-3-X) FIVF.

— The AIVF Guide to International Film & Video Festivals. 4th rev. ed. LC 96-216507. 223p. 1996. pap. 17.00 (0-9622448-2-1) FIVF.

Bowser, Lennie. The Plymouth Heritage Cookbook. LC 97-67590. (Illus.). 104p. (Orig.). 1997. spiral bd. 19.95 (1-882792-45-9) Proctor Pubns.

Bowser, M. & MacLean, Alistair. Tobias: Follow Me to Yesterday. (Yesterday & Tomorrow Bible Cartoon Ser.: Vol. 1, Bk. 1). (SPA., Illus.). 75p. 1994. lib. bdg. 10.00 (0-940178-30-3) Sitare.

Bowser, Maria S., ed. Urban Commentaries: Selected Speeches, Articles & Poetry of Charles W. Bowser from 1960 - 1997. LC 99-17263. 424p. 1999. 25.00 (0-940159-50-3) Camino Bks.

***Bowser, Mark.** Power Nuggets: 101 Reflections for Empowered Living. 1999. pap. 11.95 (0-7880-1424-2, Fairway Pr) CSS OH.

Bowser, Milton. Safe Chemical Hair Straightening. (SPA., Illus.). 100p. 1999. spiral bd. 10.00 (0-940178-97-4) Sitare.

Bowser, Paula. Jonah: God's Global Reach. (Covenant Bible Studies). 48p. 1992. pap. 4.95 (0-87178-474-2, 8726) Brethren.

***Bowser, Pearl & Spencer, Louise.** Writing Himself into History: Oscar Micheaux, His Silent Films, & His Audiences. LC 99-55380. (Illus.). 280p. 2000. text 52.00 (0-8135-2802-X); pap. text 20.00 (0-8135-2803-8) Rutgers U Pr.

Bowser, R. Max. Making Dollars with Pennies: How the Small Investor Can Beat the Wizards on Wall Street. LC 97-74045. (Illus.). 200p. 1998. pap. 19.95 (0-915216-98-1) Marathon Intl Bk.

***Bowser, R. Max.** Penny Stock Winners: True Stories of Successful Investors. (Illus.). 220p. 2000. pap. 19.95 (1-928877-00-1) Marathon Intl Bk.

Bowsher, Alice M., ed. see Burkhardt, Ann M.

Bowsher, J. M., ed. see Wood, Alexander.

Bowsher, Jack E. Educating America: Lessons Learned in the Nation's Corporations. LC 88-39747. 245p. 1989. 24.95 (0-471-60066-0) Wiley.

— Revolutionizing Workforce Performance: A Systems Approach. LC 97-21087. 224p. 1997. 39.95 (0-7879-0798-7, Pfffr & Co) Jossey-Bass.

Bowsher, John, tr. see Meyer, Jurgen.

Bowsher, Joseph C. Lima, Ohio Police Department: A Century of Service. LC 94-37248. 1994. write for info. (0-89865-922-1) Donning Co.

Bowsher, Julian. Biblical Sites. (Digging up the Past Ser.). (Illus.). 48p. (J). (gr. 5-6). 1996. lib. bdg. 24.26 (0-8172-4522-7) Raintree Steck-V.

Bowskill, Derek. The East Coast: A Pilot-Guide from Ramsgate to the Wash. 176p. (C). 1987. text 91.00 (0-85288-106-1, Pub. by Laurie Norie & Wilson Ltd) St Mut.

— The East Coast: A Pilot Guide from the Wash to Ramsgage. 230p. 1998. pap. 125.00 (0-85288-369-2, Pub. by Laurie Norie & Wilson Ltd) St Mut.

— The East Coast - A Pilot-Guide from Ramsgate to the Wash. 176p. 1984. 75.00 (0-85288-092-8, Pub. by Laurie Norie & Wilson Ltd) St Mut.

— Irish Waterways. (Illus.). 1997. pap. 125.00 (2-910185-04-4, Pub. by Laurie Norie & Wilson Ltd) St Mut.

— Map of the Rivers Cam & Lower Great Ouse: Cambridge to Denver. (Illus.). 1996. spiral bd. 125.00 (0-85288-374-9, Pub. by Laurie Norie & Wilson Ltd) St Mut.

— Map of the Upper Ouse Bedford to Pope's Corner. (Illus.). 1996. spiral bd. 125.00 (0-85288-364-1, Pub. by Laurie Norie & Wilson Ltd) St Mut.

— The Middle Level Map (Fenland) (Illus.). 1997. 125.00 (*0-85288-367-6*, Pub. by Laurie Norie & Wilson Ltd) St Mut.

— Northeast Waterways: A Guide to the Trent, Witham, Ouse & Associated Waterways. (Illus.). 200p. (C). 1986. pap. 125.00 (*0-85288-099-5*, Pub. by Laurie Norie & Wilson Ltd) St Mut.

— The River Medway: Gillingham to Tonbridge. (Illus.). 1998. spiral bd. 125.00 (*0-85288-391-9*, Pub. by Laurie Norie & Wilson Ltd) St Mut.

— River Nene. (Illus.). 1996. 125.00 (*0-85288-390-0*, Pub. by Laurie Norie & Wilson Ltd) St Mut.

— The River Seine Cruising Guide. (Illus.). 85p. (C). 1996. 125.00 (*0-85288-289-0*, Pub. by Laurie Norie & Wilson Ltd) St Mut.

— River Wey Navigation. (Illus.). 1979. 125.00 (*0-85288-116-9*, Pub. by Laurie Norie & Wilson Ltd) St Mut.

— The Solent: A Cruising Guide from Selsey Bill to the Needles. (Illus.). 200p. (C). 1990. 125.00 (*0-85288-140-1*, Pub. by Laurie Norie & Wilson Ltd) St Mut.

Bowskill, Derek, ed. The East Coast: A Pilot Guide from the Wash to Ramsga. 196p. (C). 1992. 110.00 (*0-85288-158-4*, Pub. by Laurie Norie & Wilson Ltd) St Mut.

Bowskill, Derek & Linacre, Anthea. Men: The Sensitive Sex. 1977. 45.00 (*0-584-10252-6*) St Mut.

Bowsky, Samuel. The Wizard of Oz - Revealed. 64p. 1995. 20.00 (*0-9641660-1-1*) Writers Consort.

Bowtell, H. D. Reservoir Railways of the Yorkshire Pennines. 128p. (C). 1985. 39.00 (*0-85361-242-0*) St Mut.

Bowyer. Houses & Homes. (World Geography Ser.). 32p. (J). (gr. 3-6). 1999. lib. bdg. 14.95 (*0-88110-117-6*, Usborne) EDC.

Bowyer, Adrian, ed. Computer-Aided Surface Geometry & Design. (Institute of Mathematics & Its Applications Conference Series, New Ser.: No. 48). (Illus.). 488p. 1994. text 110.00 (*0-19-853648-8*) OUP.

Bowyer, Anthony C., et al. Technical Assessment: Presidential Election Kyrgyzstan, December 24, 1995. ii, 50p. 1996. pap. 7.00 (*1-879720-59-0*) Intl Fndt Elect.

Bowyer-Bell, J. IRA Tactics & Targets: An Analysis of Tactical Aspects of the Armed Struggle, 1969-1989. 122p. 1997. pap. 13.95 (*1-85371-603-0*) Dufour.

Bowyer, Carol. Houses & Homes. (World Geography Ser.). (Illus.). 96p. (J). (gr. 3-6). 1978. pap. 6.95 (*0-86020-191-0*, Usborne) EDC.

Bowyer, Chaz. For Valour: The Air V.C.s. (Grub Street Aviation Classics Ser.). (Illus.). 548p. 1993. 55.00 (*0-948817-57-7*, Pub. by Grub St) Seven Hills Bk.

Bowyer, Chaz, ed. RFC Communiques, 1917-1918. (Illus.). 240p. 1998. 34.95 (*1-898697-79-5*, Pub. by Grub St) Seven Hills Bk.

Bowyer, Edith M. Gabriel the Acadian. Date not set. lib. bdg. 18.95 (*0-8488-0168-7*) Amereon Ltd.

Bowyer, Edwin J. The Conglomerate. LC 97-91260. 1998. pap. 13.95 (*0-533-12610-X*) Vantage.

Bowyer, George. Commentaries on Universal Public Law. 338p. 1985. reprint ed. 42.50 (*0-8377-0343-3*, Rothman) W S Hein.

Bowyer, J. R., jt. ed. see Baker, N. R.

Bowyer, J. R., jt. ed. see Harwood, J. L.

Bowyer, Jan. Journeys into the Toilet Zone: A Reservoir of Life Essays. LC 83-51362. (Illus.). 60p. 1984. 4.95 (*0-915621-01-0*) Sunland Pub.

Bowyer, Jim L., jt. auth. see Haygreen, John G.

Bowyer, K., jt. auth. see Stark, L.

Bowyer, K. W. & Astley, S. State of the Art in Digital Mammographic Image Analysis. (Series in Machine Perception & Artificial Intelligence: Vol. 9). 308p. 1994. text 109.00 (*981-02-1509-6*) World Scientific Pub.

***Bowyer, Kevin.** Ethics & Computing: Living Responsibly in a Computerized World. 2nd ed. LC 00-33594. 2000. write for info. (*0-7803-6019-2*) IEEE Standards.

Bowyer, Kevin & Ahuja, Narendra, eds. Advances in Image Understanding: A Festschrift for Azriel Rosenfeld. 360p. 1996. pap. 45.00 (*0-8186-7644-2*) IEEE Comp Soc.

Bowyer, Kevin & Hall, Lawrence, eds. Machine Learning in Computer Vision - What, Why, & How? Papers from the 1993 Fall Symposium. (Technical Reports). (Illus.). 166p. (Orig.). 1994. spiral bd. 25.00 (*0-929280-53-9*) AAAI Pr.

Bowyer, Kevin & Phillips, P.J. Empirical Evaluation Techniques in Computer Vision. LC 98-18854. 1998. 45.00 (*0-8186-8401-1*) IEEE Comp Soc.

Bowyer, Kevin W., ed. Ethics & Computing. LC 95-21582. 472p. 1995. pap. 45.00 (*0-8186-7130-0*, BP07130) IEEE Comp Soc.

Bowyer, Kevin W. & Tomboulian, Sherryl J. Pascal for the IBM-PC: Turbo Pascal, PC-DOS Pascal, & UCSD System Pascal. 5th rev. ed. (Illus.). 438p. 1995. pap., wbk. ed. 25.67 (*0-89303-766-4*) Brady Pub.

***Bowyer, Mathew J.** General George Washington's Great Secret: The Man Who Twizzled America. 260p. 2000. pap. 15.95 (*0-87714-528-8*) Denlingers.

— The Post Office Delivers: Humor - The Left-Footed Postman. (Illus.). 121p. 1999. pap. 12.95 (*0-7414-0169-X*) Buy Books.

Bowyer, Michael J. Fighting Colours: RAF Fighter Camouflage & Markings, 1937-1969. LC 75-467385. 192p. 1969. write for info. (*0-85059-041-8*, Pub. by P Stephens) Haynes Manuals.

Bowyer, Michael J. Force for Freedom: USAF in the UK, 1948-1993. (Illus.). 232p. 1994. 41.95 (*1-85260-415-8*, Pub. by J H Haynes & Co) Motorbooks Intl.

Bowyer, Peter. Diesel Boat Engines. (Illus.). 144p. 1989. 29.95 (*0-85429-696-4*, F696, Pub. by GT Foulis) Haynes Manuals.

Bowyer, Richard. Dictionary of Military Terms. 1999. pap. text 15.95 (*1-901659-24-0*) IPG Chicago.

***Bowyer, Richard, ed.** Dictionary of Military Terms. 240p. 1999. lib. bdg. 45.00 (*1-57958-156-0*) Fitzroy Dearborn.

Bowyer, Steven, ed. see Fritz, Ron.

Bowyer, Stuart & Leinert, Christoph, eds. The Galactic & Extragalactic Background Radiation. (C). 1990. pap. text 82.00 (*0-7923-0842-5*); lib. bdg. 180.50 (*0-7923-0841-7*) Kluwer Academic.

Bowyer, Stuart & Malina, Roger F., eds. Astrophysics in the Extreme Ultraviolet: Proceedings of Colloquium No. 152 of the International Astronomical Union, Held in Berkeley, California, March 27-30, 1995. LC 95-52284. 620p. (C). 1996. text 154.50 (*0-7923-3908-8*) Kluwer Academic.

Bowyer, William, tr. see Trapp, Joseph.

***Box.** Ready Steady Christmas. 1999. pap. 5.95 (*0-7459-4079-X*, Pub. by Lion Pubng) Trafalgar.

***Box & Sage.** My First Christmas Fun Book. (J). 1998. pap. 6.95 (*0-7459-3691-1*, Pub. by Lion Pubng) Trafalgar.

Box, Barbara. Storytelling Wedding Photography: Techniques & Images in Black & White. 128p. 1999. pap. text 29.95 (*0-936262-93-1*, Pub. by Amherst Media) IPG Chicago.

***Box, Ben.** Footprint Brazil Handbook. 2nd ed. (Footprint Handbooks Ser.). 780p. 2000. pap. 19.95 (*0-658-00653-3*, 006533) NTC Contemp Pub Co.

— Mexico & Central America Handbook 2000. 10th ed. (Footprints Bks.). 1344p. 1999. pap. 25.95 (*0-8442-4838-X*, 4838X, Natl Textbk Co) NTC Contemp Pub Co.

Box, Ben. Mexico & Central American Handbook, 1994. 4th ed. 800p. 1994. pap. 21.95 (*0-8442-9977-4*, Passprt Bks) NTC Contemp Pub Co.

— South American: 1999 Footprint Handbooks. (Footprints Ser.). 39.95 (*0-8442-4886-X*) NTC Contemp Pub Co.

— South American Handbook, 1994. 70th ed. 1424p. 1994. pap. 39.95 (*0-8442-9979-0*, Passprt Bks) NTC Contemp Pub Co.

— South American Handbook, 1998. 74th ed. (Footprint Handbks.). (Illus.). 1680p. 1997. 39.95 (*0-8442-4783-9*, Passprt Bks) NTC Contemp Pub Co.

***Box, Ben.** South American Handbook 2000. 76th ed. (Footprints Bks.). 1696p. 1999. pap. 39.95 (*0-8442-4984-X*, 4984X, Natl Textbk Co) NTC Contemp Pub Co.

Box, Ben, ed. Mexico & Central American Handbook. (Handbooks of the World Ser.). 1995. pap. 21.95 (*0-614-15526-6*) NTC Contemp Pub Co.

— Mexico & Central American Handbook. 6th ed. (Illus.). 928p. 1995. 21.95 (*0-8442-8882-9*, Passprt Bks) NTC Contemp Pub Co.

— 1997 Mexico & Central America Handbook. 7th rev. ed. (Footprint Handbks.). (Illus.). 928p. 1996. 21.95 (*0-8442-4906-8*, Passprt Bks) NTC Contemp Pub Co.

— 1997 South American Handbook. 73rd rev. ed. (Footprint Handbks.). (Illus.). 1552p. 1996. 39.95 (*0-8442-4904-1*, Passprt Bks) NTC Contemp Pub Co.

— South American Handbook. 72nd ed. (Illus.). 1552p. 1995. 39.95 (*0-8442-8881-0*, Passprt Bks) NTC Contemp Pub Co.

Box, Ben & Cameron, Sarah, eds. Caribbean Islands Handbook: With The Bahamas. 7th ed. (Illus.). 1024p. 1995. 21.95 (*0-8442-8883-7*, Passprt Bks) NTC Contemp Pub Co.

Box, Ben, jt. ed. see Cameron, Sarah.

***Box, Betty.** Lifting the Lid: The Life of a Pioneering British Filmmaker. (Illus.). 288p. 2000. 30.00 (*1-85776-489-7*, Pub. by Book Guild Ltd) Trans-Atl Phila.

***Box, C. J.** Travel Smart: Montana, Wyoming, Idaho. (Illus.). 304p. 2000. pap. 17.95 (*1-56261-508-4*, Travel Smart) Avalon Travel.

Box, Don. Creating Components with DCOM & C++ 1997. pap. 39.76 (*0-614-28442-2*) Addison-Wesley.

— Effective COM. LC 98-46027. 240p. (C). 1998. pap. text 44.95 (*0-201-37968-6*) Addison-Wesley.

— Essential Com. LC 97-45836. (Object Technology Ser.). 464p. (C). 1997. pap. text 39.95 (*0-201-63446-5*) Addison-Wesley.

***Box, Don.** Essential XML: Beyond Markup. 256p. 2000. pap. 34.95 (*0-201-70914-7*) Addison-Wesley.

Box, Douglas A. Professional Secrets for Photographing Children. LC 98-72978. (Illus.). 128p. 1999. pap. 29.95 (*0-936262-76-1*) Amherst Media.

***Box, Douglas Allen.** Professional Secrets of Natural Light Portrait Photography: Techniques & Images. (Illus.). 128p. 2000. pap. 29.95 (*1-58428-045-X*, Pub. by Amherst Media) IPG Chicago.

Box, Douglas Allen. Professional Secrets of Wedding Photography. 128p. 1999. pap. text 29.95 (*0-936262-92-3*, Pub. by Amherst Media) IPG Chicago.

Box, E. O. Macroclimate & Plant Forms: An Introduction to Predictive Modeling in Phytogeography. (Tasks for Vegetation Science Ser.: No. 1). 272p. 1981. text 234.00 (*90-6193-941-0*) Kluwer Academic.

Box, E. O., et al, eds. Vegetation Science in Forestry: Global Perspective Based on Forest Ecosystems of East & Southeast Asia. LC 94-683. (Handbook of Vegetation Science Ser.: Pt. 12). 640p. (C). 1995. text 331.50 (*0-7923-2679-2*) Kluwer Academic.

Box, George E. The Collected Works of George E. P. Box, Vol. I. Tiao, George C., ed. 688p. (C). (gr. 13). 1984. text 72.95 (*0-534-03307-5*, Chap & Hall CRC) CRC Pr.

— The Collected Works of George E. P. Box, Vol. II. Tiao, George C., ed. 736p. (C). (gr. 13). 1984. ring bd. 83.95 (*0-534-03308-3*, Chap & Hall CRC) CRC Pr.

***Box, George E.** Evolutionary Operation: A Statistical Method for Process Improvement. LC 98-165320. (Wiley Classics Library). 237p. 1998. pap. 54.95 (*0-471-25551-3*) Wiley.

Box, George E. & Jenkins, Gwilym. Time Series Analysis, Forecasting & Control. rev. ed. LC 76-8713. 500p. 1976. text 59.95 (*0-8162-1104-3*) Holden-Day.

Box, George E. & Luceno, Alberto. Statistical Control by Monitoring & Feedback Adjustment. LC 97-459. (Series in Probability & Statistics). (Illus.). 327p. 1997. 89.95 (*0-471-19046-2*) Wiley.

Box, George E. & Tiao, George C. Bayesian Inference in Statistical Analysis. LC 92-3745. (Classics Library). 608p. 1992. pap. 84.95 (*0-471-57428-7*) Wiley.

Box, George E., et al. Empirical Model-Building & Response Surfaces. LC 86-4064. (Probability & Mathematical Statistics Ser.). 688p. 1987. 119.95 (*0-471-81033-9*) Wiley.

— Statistics for Experimenters: An Introduction to Design, Data Analysis & Model Building. (Probability & Mathematical Statistics Ser.). 672p. 1978. text 84.95 (*0-471-09315-7*) Wiley.

— Time Series Analysis: Forecasting & Control. 3rd ed. LC 93-34620. 592p. 1994. 90.00 (*0-13-060774-6*) P-H.

Box, Harry C. Set Lighting Technician's Handbook: Film Lighting Equipment, Practice, & Electrical Distribution. 2nd ed. LC 96-24075. (Illus.). 416p. 1996. pap. 39.95 (*0-240-80257-8*, Focal) Buttrwrth-Heinemann.

Box, Harry C. & Fitt, Brian. The Gaffer's Handbook: Film Lighting Equipment, Practice, & Electrical Distribution. LC 98-35044. 1998. write for info. (*0-240-51523-4*, Focal) Buttrwrth-Heinemann.

***Box, Hilary & Gibson, Kathleen, eds.** Mammalian Social Learning: Comparative & Ecological Perspectives. LC 98-41965. (Symposia of the Zoological Society of London Ser.: No. 72). (Illus.). 432p. (C). 1999. 95.00 (*0-521-63263-3*) Cambridge U Pr.

Box, Hilary O. & Buchanan-Smith, Hannah M., eds. Biology & Conservation of New World Primates. (Folia Primatologica Ser.: Vol. 68, No. 3-5, 1997). (Illus.). 208p. 1997. pap. 101.75 (*3-8055-6512-7*) S Karger.

Box, Hubert S. The Principles of Canon Law. LC 86-3163. 82p. 1986. reprint ed. lib. bdg. 35.00 (*0-313-25204-1*, BPRC, Greenwood Pr) Greenwood.

Box, Ian C. The Social Thought of Francis Bacon. (Studies in History of Philosophy: Vol. 10). 250p. 1989. write for info. (*0-88946-313-1*) E Mellen.

Box, James E., jt. auth. see International Society of Root Research Staff.

Box, Pelham H. Three Master Builders, & Another: Studies in Modern Revolutionary & Liberal Statesmanship. LC 68-22904. (Essay Index Reprint Ser.). 1977. 23.95 (*0-8369-0234-3*) Ayer.

***Box, Richard.** Basic Drawing Techniques, Vol. 10 (Step-by-Step Leisure Arts Ser.). (Illus.). 2000. pap. 10.95 (*0-85532-842-8*) Srch Pr.

— Color & Design for Embroidery. (Illus.). 144p. 2000. pap. 24.00 (*1-57488-272-4*) Brasseys.

— Cross Stitch Cats. 2000. pap. 22.95 (*0-312-25380-X*) St Martin.

Box, Richard. Drawing for the Terrified: A Complete Course for Beginners. LC 97-192056. (Illus.). 128p. 1997. 24.95 (*0-7153-0351-1*) Sterling.

***Box, Richard.** Drawing for the Terrified! A Complete Course for Beginners. 128p. 1999. pap. text 17.95 (*0-7153-0860-2*) Strlng Pub CA.

Box, Richard C. Citizen Governance: American Communities in the 21st Century. LC 97-33722. 1998. write for info. (*0-7619-1257-6*); pap. write for info. (*0-7619-1258-4*) Sage.

Box, Sally, et al, eds. Crisis at Adolescence: Object Relations Therapy with the Family. LC 93-9010. 296p. 1994. 50.00 (*1-56821-094-9*) Aronson.

Box-Steffensmeier, Janet M., jt. ed. see Weisberg, Herbert F.

Box, Steven. Power Crime & Mystification. 300p. (Orig.). (C). 1984. pap. 20.99 (*0-415-04572-X*) Routledge.

— Recession, Crime, & Punishment. LC 87-1825. 240p. 1987. 56.50 (*0-389-20724-1*, 08282) B&N Imports.

Box, Su. You Are Very Special: With a Suprise to Show How Special God Made You. LC 96-226284. (Illus.). 32p. (J). 1996. 13.95 (*0-7459-3638-5*) Lion USA.

Box, Willie E., Jr. African-American Hidden Treasure Resources. 73p. (Orig.). 1993. lib. bdg. write for info. (*1-882901-37-1*) W Box & Assocs.

— The Official African-American Museum & Cultural Galleries Directory. 276p. (Orig.). 1993. lib. bdg. write for info. (*1-882901-38-X*) W Box & Assocs.

Boxall, Larry G., ed. see Metallurgical Society of AIME Staff.

Boxall, Marjorie, jt. auth. see Bennathan, Marion.

Boxall, R. Construction Drawing for Technicians, Level 1. LC TH0431.. (Longman Technician Series, Construction & Civil Engineering). (Illus.). 208p. reprint ed. pap. 64.50 (*0-8357-2980-X*, 203924200011) Bks Demand.

Boxberger, Daniel L. To Fish in Common: The Ethnohistory of Lummi Indian Salmon Fishing. LC 99-51725. (Illus.). 237p. 1999. pap. 17.95 (*0-295-97848-1*) U of Wash Pr.

— To Fish in Common: The Ethnohistory of Lummi Indian Salmon Fishing. LC 88-20705. 227p. 1989. reprint ed. pap. 64.70 (*0-608-02681-6*, 2063334) Bks Demand.

Boxberger, Daniel L., jt. ed. see Mignon, Molly R.

Boxberger, Linda, tr. from ARA. Visits & Customs: The Visit to the Tomb of Propher Hud.Tr. of Shakyn 'Abdalqadir Muhammad Al-Sabban. Date not set. write for info. (*1-882557-06-9*) Am Inst Yemeni.

Boxel, Piet Van, see Musacchio, Jacqueline & Van Boxel, Piet.

***Boxell, Geoff.** Wolden's Wolf. Finton, Kenneth H. ed. LC 98-87886. 1999. pap. 24.95 (*1-892977-00-1*, 00-1) H T Commun.

Boxell, Tim, ed. Commies from Mars: The Red Planet. 160p. 1997. pap. 9.95 (*0-86719-343-3*) Last Gasp.

Boxer. Organic Chemistry: Short. 396p. 1997. pap., student ed. 24.69 (*0-697-14062-8*) McGraw.

Boxer, Adam J., ed. The New Bauhaus - School of Design in Chicago: Photographs, 1937-1944. (Illus.). 56p. (Orig.). 1993. pap. 20.00 (*0-9638522-0-5*) Banning & Assoc.

Boxer, Andrew. The Conservative Government, 1951-1964. LC 96-9287. (Seminar Studies in History). 152p. (C). 1996. pap. 15.93 (*0-582-20913-7*) Addison-Wesley.

Boxer, Andrew, jt. auth. see Herdt, Gilbert.

Boxer, Arabella. Herb & Spice Handbook. LC 99-24591. (Illus.). 208p. 1999. pap. 22.00 (*1-57959-047-0*, SOMA) BB&T Inc.

***Boxer, Arabella.** The Spice Book: The Complete Guide to Culinary Spices. (Illus.). 255p. 2000. reprint ed. 30.00 (*0-7881-9284-1*) DIANE Pub.

***Boxer, Barbara & Women of the Senate Members.** Nine & Counting: American Politics as Seen by the Most Influential Women Who Make & Shape It. 288p. 2000. 25.00 (*0-06-019767-6*) HarpC.

Boxer, Barbara, et al. California Women Speak: Speeches of California Women in Public Office. Earnshow, Doris, ed. LC 94-221744. (Illus.). 122p. 1994. pap. 12.50 (*0-9640574-0-9*) Alta Vista Pr.

Boxer, Baruch. Israeli Shipping & Foreign Trade. LC 57-13901. 176p. reprint ed. pap. 54.60 (*0-8357-3715-2*, 203643700003) Bks Demand.

— Ocean Shipping in the Evolution of Hong Kong. LC 61-16294. (University of Chicago, Department of Geography, Research Paper Ser.: No. 72). 111p. reprint ed. pap. 34.50 (*0-7837-0386-4*, 204070700018) Bks Demand.

Boxer, C. R. Dutch Merchants & Mariners in Asia, 1602-1795. (Collected Studies: No. CS284). (Illus.). 352p. (C). 1988. reprint ed. lib. bdg. 122.95 (*0-86078-232-8*, Pub. by Variorum) Ashgate Pub Co.

— From Lisbon to Goa, 1500-1750: Studies in Portuguese Maritime Enterprise. (Collected Studies: No. CS194). 320p. 1984. reprint ed. text 109.95 (*0-86078-142-9*, Pub. by Variorum) Ashgate Pub Co.

— Portuguese Conquest & Commerce in Southern Asia, 1500-1750. (Collected Studies: No. CS208). (Illus.). 312p. (C). 1985. reprint ed. lib. bdg. 109.95 (*0-86078-156-9*, Pub. by Variorum) Ashgate Pub Co.

— Portuguese Merchants & Missionaries in Feudal Japan, 1543-1640. (Collected Studies: No. CS232). 338p. 1986. reprint ed. text 109.95 (*0-86078-180-1*, Pub. by Variorum) Ashgate Pub Co.

Boxer, Charles R. The Church Militant & Iberian Expansion, 1440-1770. LC 77-18386. (Johns Hopkins Symposia in Comparative History Ser.: No. 10). 160p. reprint ed. pap. 49.60 (*0-8357-8074-0*, 203413500088) Bks Demand.

— Portuguese Emigration to the U. S., 1820-1930. LC 79-65354. (Studies in Japanese History & Civilization). 172p. 1979. lib. bdg. 62.50 (*0-313-26982-3*, U6982) Greenwood.

— Race Relations in the Portuguese Colonial Empire, 1415-1825. LC 85-740. 136p. 1985. reprint ed. lib. bdg. 49.75 (*0-313-24733-1*, BORR, Greenwood Pr) Greenwood.

Boxer, Daniel, jt. auth. see Ahrens, Chip.

Boxer, Diana. Complaining & Commiserating: A Speech Act View of Solidarity in Spoken American English. LC 92-35429. (History & Language Ser.: Vol. 2). 224p. (C). 1993. text 49.95 (*0-8204-2021-2*) P Lang Pubng.

Boxer, G. Mecanica de Fluidos. (SPA.). 208p. (C). 1994. pap. text 13.66 (*0-201-62550-4*) Addison-Wesley.

— Thermodinamica Para Ingenieria. (SPA.). 208p. (C). 1993. pap. text 13.33 (*0-201-60147-8*) Addison-Wesley.

Boxer, Joe. A Brief History of Shorts: The Ultimate Guide to Understanding Your Underwear. (Illus.). 92p. 1998. pap. text 15.00 (*0-7881-5975-5*) DIANE Pub.

Boxer, Judy, jt. auth. see McCulloch, Gary F.

Boxer, Keith, jt. auth. see Scheuermann, Rudi.

Boxer, Marilyn J. When Women Ask the Questions: Creating Women's Studies in America. LC 97-48491. 344p. 1998. 29.95 (*0-8018-5834-8*) Johns Hopkins.

***Boxer, Marilyn J. & Quataert, Jean H.** Connecting Spheres: European Women in a Globalizing World, 1500 to the Present. 2nd ed. LC 99-19863. (Illus.). 352p. (C). 1999. text 49.95 (*0-19-510950-3*); pap. text 24.95 (*0-19-510951-1*) OUP.

Boxer, Marilyn J. & Quataert, Jean H., eds. Socialist Women: European Socialist Feminism in the Nineteenth & Early Twentieth-Centuries. LC 77-16618. 260p. 1981. lib. bdg. 29.95 (*0-444-99042-9*, BSW/) Greenwood.

Boxer, Martin. Landlord & Tenant: The New Regime & Its Pitfalls. 1996. pap. 40.00 (*1-85941-283-1*, Pub. by Cavendish Pubng) Gaunt.

Boxer, Robert J. Essentials of Organic Chemistry. 688p. (C). 1997. text. write for info. (*0-07-114034-4*, WCB McGr Hill) McGrw-H Hghr Educ.

— Organic Chemistry. 1997. pap., student ed. 81.56 (*0-07-290404-6*) McGraw.

Boxer, Robert J., ed. Organic Chemistry Exam File. (Exam File Ser.). 534p. 1988. pap. 24.50 (*0-910554-66-8*) Engineering.

Boxer, Robert W. Boxer's Shorts: (More Than Just a Brief Attempt at Humor) - Round 2. LC 94-92101. (Illus.). 144p. (Orig.). 1994. pap. 9.95 (*0-9620687-1-3*) Punchline Pr.

— Boxer's Shorts (More Than Just a Brief Attempt at Humor) LC 88-90962. (Illus.). 144p. (Orig.). 1988. pap. 7.95 (*0-9620687-0-5*) Punchline Pr.

Boxer, Stanley. Stanley Boxer: Forty Years of Drawing. (Illus.). (Orig.). 1991. write for info. (*0-925941-03-4*) Dorsky Gallery.

Boxer, Tim. Tim Boxer's Jewish Celebrity Anecdotes. LC 96-17366. 276p. 1996. pap. 19.95 (*0-8246-0391-5*) Jonathan David.

— Tim Boxer's Jewish Celebrity Anecdotes. 1998. pap. text 16.95 (*0-8246-0411-3*) Jonathan David.

Boxerman, Stuart B., jt. auth. see Austin, Charles J.

B

Boxill, Edith H. The Miracle of Music Therapy. LC 99-164236. (Illus.). 212p. 1997. pap. text 22.00 (0-9624080-8-5) Barcelona Pubs.

— Music Therapy for Living: The Principle of Normalization Embodied in Music Therapy. (Horizon Ser.: Vol. 6). 100p. (Orig.). 1989. pap. 10.50 (0-918812-54-2, ST 179) MMB Music.

— Music Therapy for the Developmentally Disabled. LC 84-15752. (Illus.). 270p. 1985. text 36.00 (0-89079-190-2, 2054) PRO-ED.

*Boxill, Holger H. Ian, ed. The End of the Asian "Model?" LC 99-13731. 272p. 1999. pap. 31.00 (3-11-016487-6) De Gruyter.

Boxill, Ian, jt. auth. see Henke, Holger.

Boxill, Ian, jt. ed. see Henke, Holger.

Boxill, Nancy A., ed. Homeless Children: The Watchers & the Waiters. LC 90-30434. (Child & Youth Services Ser.: Vol. 14, No. 1). 156p. 1990. text 39.95 (0-86656-789-5) Haworth Pr.

Boxleitner, Bruce. Frontier Earth. LC 99-31097. 1999. 21.95 (0-441-00589-6) Ace Bks.

*Boxleitner, Bruce. Searcher. LC 00-40174. (Frontier Earth Ser.: No. 2). 2000. write for info. (0-441-00799-6) Ace Bks.

Boxleitner, W. Electrostatic Discharge & Electronic Equipment: A Practical Guide for Designing to Prevent ESD Problems. LC 88-21852. (Illus.). 128p. 1988. text 39.95 (0-87942-244-0, PC02352) Inst Electrical.

Boxman, Raymond L., et al, eds. Handbook of Vacuum ARC Science & Technology: Fundamentals & Applications. LC 95-22677. (Illus.). 710p. 1996. 145.00 (0-8155-1375-5) Noyes.

Boxshall, G. A. & Schminke, H. K., eds. Biology of Copepods. (Developments in Hydrobiology Ser.). (C). 1988. text 461.50 (90-6193-654-3) Kluwer Academic.

Boxshall, G. A., jt. auth. see Lincoln, R. J.

Boxt, Mathew A., jt. ed. see Dillon, Brian D.

Boxtel, C. J. Van, see Van Boxtel, C. J., ed.

Boxtel, C. J. Van, see Aronson, J. K. & Van Boxtel, C. J., eds.

Boxton, Edward F. & Fulton, Susan. New Business for Ad Agencies. LC 87-81308. 252p. 1989. pap. 35.00 (0-917168-11-9) Executive Comm.

Boxtree Ltd. Staff. The Best of Treasure Hunt. 128p. (C). 1990. 60.00 (1-85283-240-1, Pub. by Boxtree) St Mut.

Boxtree Ltd. Staff, ed. The Photographs of Herbie Knott: One Hundred Photographs Reproduced in Superb Duotone. 128p. (C). 1990. 100.00 (1-85283-283-5, Pub. by Boxtree) St Mut.

Boxwell, R. J. Benchmarking for Competitive Advantage. 224p. 1993. 34.95 (0-07-006899-2) McGraw.

Boxx, Buzz, ed. Pick-Up Lines: The Best & Worst on Planet Earth. LC 96-84514. 144p. (Orig.). 1996. pap. 7.95 (1-885174-02-0) Andrews & McMeel.

*Boxx, T. William & Qinlivan, Gary M., eds. Public Morality, Civic Virtue & the Problem of Modern Liberalism. LC 99-88895. 231p. 2000. pap. 18.00 (0-8028-4754-4) Eerdmans.

Boxx, T. William & Quinlivan, Gary M. The Cultural Context of Economics & Politics. 103p. (C). 1994. pap. text 18.50 (0-8191-9680-0); lib. bdg. 38.50 (0-8191-9679-7) U Pr of Amer.

Boxx, T. William & Quinlivan, Gary M., eds. Culture in Crisis & the Renewal of Civil Life. 152p. 1996. pap. text 20.95 (0-8476-8288-9); lib. bdg. 52.50 (0-8476-8287-0) Rowman.

*Boxx, T. William & Quinlivan, Gary M., eds. Foundations of American Civilization. v, 104p. (C). 1999. pap. text 5.00 (0-9673717-0-8) Cntr Econo & Policy.

Boxx, T. William & Quinlivan, Gary M., eds. Toward the Renewal of Civilization: The Political Order & Culture. LC 98-4448. 222p. 1998. pap. 16.00 (0-8028-4534-7) Eerdmans.

Boy, Angelo V. & Pine, Gerald J. Child-Centered Counseling & Psychotherapy. LC 95-13348. 262p. (C). 1995. text 62.95 (0-398-06521-7); pap. text 36.95 (0-398-06522-5) C C Thomas.

— A Person-Centered Foundation for Counseling & Psychotherapy. 2nd ed. LC 99-20307. 274p. 1999. text 54.95 (0-398-06964-6); pap. text 39.95 (0-398-06966-2) C C Thomas.

Boy, Daniel & Mayer, Nonna, eds. The French Voter Decides. Schloch, Cynthia, tr. from FRE. 240p. (C). 1993. reprint ed. text 52.50 (0-472-10438-1, 10438) U of Mich Pr.

Boy, Guy A. Cognitive Function Analysis. LC 98-16378. (Contemporary Studies in Cognitive Science & Technology). 1998. 73.25 (1-56750-376-4) Ablx Pub.

— Cognitive Function Analysis. Lesgold, Alan & Patel, Vimla, eds. LC 98-16378. (Contemporary Studies in Cognitive Science & Technology: Vol. 2). 250p. 1998. pap. 39.50 (1-56750-377-2) Ablx Pub.

Boy Scouts of America. American Business. (Illus.). 48p. (YA). (gr. 6-12). 1975. pap. 2.90 (0-8395-3325-X, 33325) BSA.

Boy Scouts of America. American Cultures. (Illus.). 56p. (YA). (gr. 6-12). 1980. pap. 2.90 (0-8395-3399-3) BSA.

Boy Scouts of America. American Heritage. (Illus.). 48p. (YA). (gr. 6-12). 1976. pap. 2.90 (0-8395-3398-5, 33398) BSA.

— American Labor. (Illus.). 48p. (YA). (gr. 6-12). 1987. pap. 2.90 (0-8395-3326-8, 33326) BSA.

— Animal Science. (Illus.). 96p. (YA). (gr. 6-12). 1984. pap. 2.90 (0-8395-3395-0, 33395) BSA.

Boy Scouts of America. Archery. (Illus.). 56p. (YA). (gr. 6-12). 1986. pap. 2.90 (0-8395-3259-8) BSA.

Boy Scouts of America. Art. (Illus.). 48p. (J). (gr. 6-12). 1968. pap. 2.90 (0-8395-3320-9, 33320) BSA.

— Astronomy. (Illus.). 80p. (YA). (gr. 6-12). 1983. pap. 2.90 (0-8395-3303-9, 33303) BSA.

— Athletics. (Illus.). 22p. (YA). (gr. 6-12). 1964. pap. 2.90 (0-8395-3324-1, 33324) BSA.

— Atomic Energy. (Illus.). 78p. (YA). (gr. 6-12). 1983. pap. 2.90 (0-8395-3275-X, 33275) BSA.

— Aviation. (Illus.). 72p. (YA). (gr. 6-12). 1968. pap. 2.90 (0-8395-3293-8, 33293) BSA.

— Backpacking. 80p. (YA). (gr. 6-12). 1995. pap. 2.90 (0-8395-3232-6, 33232) BSA.

— Basketry. (Illus.). 32p. (YA). (gr. 6-12). 1986. pap. 2.90 (0-8395-3313-6, 33313) BSA.

Boy Scouts of America. Bear Cub Scout Book. rev. ed. 264p. (J). (gr. 3). 1984. 4.95 (0-8395-3107-9) BSA.

Boy Scouts of America. Camping. (Illus.). 72p. (YA). (gr. 6-12). 1984. pap. 2.90 (0-8395-3256-3, 33256) BSA.

Boy Scouts of America. Citizenship in the Community. (Illus.). 36p. (YA). (gr. 6-12). 1984. pap. 2.90 (0-8395-3249-0) BSA.

— Citizenship in the Nation. (Illus.). 40p. (YA). (gr. 6-12). 1984. pap. 2.90 (0-8395-3248-2) BSA.

Boy Scouts of America. Citizenship in the World. (Illus.). 96p. (YA). (gr. 6-12). 1995. pap. 2.90 (0-8395-3260-1, 33260) BSA.

— Coin Collecting. (Illus.). 32p. (YA). (gr. 6-12). 1975. pap. 2.90 (0-8395-3390-X, 33390) BSA.

— Communications. (Illus.). 72p. (YA). (gr. 6-12). 1972. pap. 2.90 (0-8395-3258-X, 33258) BSA.

Boy Scouts of America. Cub Scout Academics & Sports: Program Guide. (Illus.). 96p. 1996. pap. 5.95 (0-8395-4299-2) BSA.

— Cub Scout Leader Book. (Illus.). 260p. (YA). (gr. 9). 1982. pap. 7.65 (0-8395-3221-0) BSA.

— Cub Scout Leader How-To Book. rev. ed. 472p. 1988. pap. 9.30 (0-8395-3832-4) BSA.

Boy Scouts of America. Cycling. (Illus.). 96p. (YA). (gr. 6-12). 1996. pap. 2.90 (0-8395-3226-1, 33226) BSA.

— Dentistry. (Illus.). 40p. (YA). (gr. 6-12). 1975. pap. 2.90 (0-8395-3394-2, 33394) BSA.

— Disabilities Awareness. (Illus.). 48p. (YA). (gr. 6-12). 1981. pap. 2.90 (0-8395-3370-5, 33370) BSA.

— Dog Care. (Illus.). 48p. (YA). (gr. 6-12). 1984. pap. 2.90 (0-8395-3289-X, 33289) BSA.

Boy Scouts of America. Drafting. (Illus.). 32p. (YA). (gr. 6-12). 1965. pap. 2.90 (0-8395-3262-8) BSA.

Boy Scouts of America. Energy. (Illus.). 64p. (YA). (gr. 6-12). 1978. pap. 2.90 (0-8395-3335-7, 33335) BSA.

— Engineering. (Illus.). 48p. (YA). (gr. 6-12). 1978. pap. 2.90 (0-8395-3376-4, 33376) BSA.

— Environmental Science. (Illus.). 96p. (YA). (gr. 6-12). 1983. pap. 2.90 (0-8395-3363-2, 33363) BSA.

— Farm Mechanics. (Illus.). 104p. (YA). (gr. 6-12). 1984. pap. 2.90 (0-8395-3346-2, 33346) BSA.

— Fingerprinting. (Illus.). 32p. (YA). (gr. 6-12). 1983. pap. 2.90 (0-8395-3287-3, 33287) BSA.

— Fire Safety. (Illus.). 72p. (YA). (gr. 6-12). 1995. pap. 2.90 (0-8395-3318-7, 33318) BSA.

— Fish & Wildlife Management. 40p. (YA). (gr. 6-12). 1990. pap. 2.90 (0-8395-3307-1, 33307) BSA.

— Fishing. rev. ed. (Illus.). 80p. (YA). (gr. 6-12). 1967. pap. 2.90 (0-8395-3231-8, 33231) BSA.

— Forestry. (Illus.). 80p. (YA). (gr. 6-12). 1984. pap. 2.90 (0-8395-3302-0, 33302) BSA.

— Gardening. (Illus.). 64p. (YA). (gr. 6-12). 1982. pap. 2.90 (0-8395-3240-7, 33240) BSA.

— Genealogy. (Illus.). 72p. (YA). (gr. 6-12). 1988. pap. 2.90 (0-8395-3383-7, 33383) BSA.

— Geology. (Illus.). 96p. (YA). (gr. 6-12). 1985. pap. 2.90 (0-8395-3284-9, 33284) BSA.

— Golf. (Illus.). 80p. (YA). (gr. 6-12). 1977. pap. 2.90 (0-8395-3397-7, 33397) BSA.

— Graphic Arts. (Illus.). 96p. (YA). (gr. 6-12). 1988. pap. 2.90 (0-8395-3374-8, 33374) BSA.

Boy Scouts of America. Home Repairs. (Illus.). 64p. (YA). (gr. 6-12). 1961. pap. 2.90 (0-8395-3247-4) BSA.

Boy Scouts of America. Horsemanship. (Illus.). 64p. (YA). (gr. 6-12). 1986. pap. 2.90 (0-8395-3298-9, 33298) BSA.

— Indian Lore. (Illus.). 104p. (YA). (gr. 6-12). 1996. pap. 2.90 (0-8395-3360-8, 33360) BSA.

— Insect Study. (Illus.). 72p. (YA). (gr. 6-12). 1985. pap. 2.90 (0-8395-3353-5, 33353) BSA.

— Journalism. (Illus.). 80p. (YA). (gr. 6-12). 1983. pap. 2.90 (0-8395-3350-0, 33350) BSA.

Boy Scouts of America. Junior Leader Training Conference Staff Guide. (Illus.). 346p. 1992. pap. 16.00 (0-8395-4533-9) BSA.

Boy Scouts of America. Landscape Architecture. (Illus.). 48p. (YA). (gr. 6-12). 1969. pap. 2.90 (0-8395-3355-1, 33355) BSA.

— Law. (Illus.). 64p. (YA). (gr. 6-12). 1975. pap. 2.90 (0-8395-3389-6, 33389) BSA.

— Leatherwork. (Illus.). 56p. (YA). (gr. 6-12). 1983. pap. 2.90 (0-8395-3310-1, 33310) BSA.

Boy Scouts of America. Lifesaving. (Illus.). 80p. (YA). (gr. 6-12). 1980. pap. 2.90 (0-8395-3297-0) BSA.

Boy Scouts of America. Mammal Study. (Illus.). 48p. (YA). (gr. 6-12). 1972. pap. 2.90 (0-8395-3271-7, 33271) BSA.

— Metalwork. (Illus.). 36p. (YA). (gr. 6-12). 1969. pap. 2.90 (0-8395-3312-8, 33312) BSA.

— Model Design & Building. (Illus.). 56p. (YA). (gr. 6-12). 1964. pap. 2.90 (0-8395-3280-6, 33280) BSA.

— Motorboating. (Illus.). 64p. (YA). (gr. 6-12). 1996. pap. 2.90 (0-8395-3345-4, 33345) BSA.

Boy Scouts of America. Music & Bugling. (Illus.). 80p. (YA). (gr. 6-12). 1990. pap. 2.90 (0-8395-3341-1) BSA.

Boy Scouts of America. Nature. (Illus.). 64p. (YA). (gr. 6-12). 1973. pap. 2.90 (0-8395-3285-7, 33285) BSA.

— Oceanography. (Illus.). 72p. (YA). (gr. 6-12). 1983. pap. 2.90 (0-8395-3306-3, 33306) BSA.

— Orienteering. (Illus.). 40p. (YA). (gr. 6-12). 1992. pap. 2.90 (0-8395-3385-3, 33385) BSA.

— Painting. (Illus.). 32p. (YA). (gr. 6-12). 1983. pap. 2.90 (0-8395-3372-1, 33372) BSA.

— Personal Fitness. (Illus.). 92p. (YA). (gr. 6-12). 1990. pap. 2.90 (0-8395-3286-5, 33286) BSA.

— Personal Management. (Illus.). 80p. (YA). (gr. 6-12). 1996. pap. 2.90 (0-8395-5002-2, 35002) BSA.

— Pets. (Illus.). 64p. (YA). (gr. 6-12). 1984. pap. 2.90 (0-8395-3281-4, 33281) BSA.

Boy Scouts of America. Photography. (Illus.). 56p. (YA). (gr. 6-12). 1983. pap. 2.90 (0-8395-3340-3) BSA.

— Pioneering. (Illus.). 104p. (YA). (gr. 6-12). 1974. pap. 2.90 (0-8395-3377-2) BSA.

Boy Scouts of America. Plant Science. (Illus.). 48p. (YA). (gr. 6-12). 1983. pap. 2.90 (0-8395-3396-9, 33396) BSA.

— Plumbing. (Illus.). 48p. (YA). (gr. 6-12). 1989. pap. 2.90 (0-8395-3386-1, 33386) BSA.

— Pottery. (Illus.). 64p. (YA). (gr. 6-12). 1969. pap. 2.90 (0-8395-3314-4, 33314) BSA.

— Public Speaking. (Illus.). 44p. (YA). (gr. 6-12). 1969. pap. 2.90 (0-8395-3373-X, 33373) BSA.

— Pulp & Paper. (Illus.). 48p. (YA). (gr. 6-12). 1974. pap. 2.90 (0-8395-3343-8, 33343) BSA.

— Radio. (Illus.). 80p. (YA). (gr. 6-12). 1996. pap. 2.90 (0-8395-3361-6, 33361) BSA.

— Railroading. (Illus.). 48p. (YA). (gr. 6-12). 1978. pap. 2.90 (0-8395-3292-X, 33292) BSA.

Boy Scouts of America. Reading. (Illus.). 48p. (YA). (gr. 6-12). 1983. pap. 2.90 (0-8395-3378-0) BSA.

Boy Scouts of America. Reptile & Amphibian Study. (Illus.). 80p. (YA). (gr. 6-12). 1993. pap. 2.90 (0-8395-3288-1, 33288) BSA.

— Rowing. (Illus.). 88p. (YA). (gr. 6-12). 1993. pap. 2.90 (0-8395-3404-3, 33404) BSA.

Boy Scouts of America. Rural/Low-Income Urban Venturing Action Ideas. 82p. 1990. 5.00 (0-8395-3628-3) BSA.

Boy Scouts of America. Safety. (Illus.). 80p. (YA). (gr. 6-12). 1986. pap. 2.90 (0-8395-3347-0, 33347) BSA.

— Salesmanship. LC 19-600. (Illus.). 40p. (YA). (gr. 6-12). 1987. pap. 2.90 (0-8395-3351-9, 33351) BSA.

— Scholarship. (Illus.). 72p. (YA). (gr. 6-12). 1988. pap. 2.90 (0-8395-3384-5, 33384) BSA.

— Sculpture. (Illus.). 24p. (YA). (gr. 6-12). 1969. pap. 2.90 (0-8395-3322-5, 33322) BSA.

— Skating. (Illus.). 96p. (YA). (gr. 6-12). 1996. pap. 2.90 (0-8395-5006-5, 35006) BSA.

— Small-Boat Sailing. (Illus.). 80p. (YA). (gr. 6-12). 1995. pap. 2.90 (0-8395-3356-X, 33356) BSA.

*Boy Scouts of America. Snow Sports. (Illus.). 96p. (YA). (gr. 6-12). 1999. pap. 2.90 (0-8395-3365-9) BSA.

Boy Scouts of America. Soil & Water Conservation. (Illus.). 88p. (YA). (gr. 6-12). 1983. pap. 2.90 (0-8395-3291-1, 33291) BSA.

— Space Exploration. (Illus.). 64p. (YA). (gr. 6-12). 1983. pap. 2.90 (0-8395-3354-3, 33354) BSA.

— Sports. (Illus.). 80p. (YA). (gr. 6-12). 1996. pap. 2.90 (0-8395-5007-3, 35007) BSA.

— Surveying. (Illus.). 48p. (YA). (gr. 6-12). 1984. pap. 2.90 (0-8395-3327-6, 33327) BSA.

— Textile. 64p. (YA). (gr. 6-12). 1972. pap. 2.90 (0-8395-3344-6, 33344) BSA.

— Theater. 88p. (YA). (gr. 6-12). 1968. pap. 2.90 (0-8395-3328-4, 33328) BSA.

Boy Scouts of America. Tours & Expeditions. 49p. 1971. pap. 6.70 (0-8395-3737-9) BSA.

Boy Scouts of America. Traffic Safety. (Illus.). 64p. (YA). (gr. 6-12). 1975. pap. 2.90 (0-8395-3391-8, 33391) BSA.

— Truck Transportation. (Illus.). 32p. (YA). (gr. 6-12). 1973. pap. 2.90 (0-8395-3371-3, 33371) BSA.

— Veterinary Medicine. (Illus.). 48p. (YA). (gr. 6-12). 1996. pap. 2.90 (0-8395-5004-9, 35004) BSA.

— Waterskiing. (Illus.). 48p. (YA). (gr. 6-12). 1996. pap. 2.90 (0-8395-3348-9, 33348) BSA.

— Weather. 80p. (YA). (gr. 6-12). 1963. pap. 2.90 (0-8395-3274-1, 33274) BSA.

Boy Scouts of America. Webelos Scout Book. rev. ed. (Illus.). 472p. (J). (gr. 4-6). 1987. pap. 5.50 (0-8395-3108-7) BSA.

Boy Scouts of America. Wilderness Survival. (Illus.). 48p. (YA). (gr. 6-12). 1984. pap. 2.90 (0-8395-3265-2, 33265) BSA.

Boy Scouts of America. Wolf Cub Scout Book. rev. ed. (Illus.). 232p. (J). (gr. 2). 1986. pap. 4.95 (0-8395-3106-0) BSA.

— Wood Carving. (Illus.). 40p. (YA). (gr. 6-12). 1966. pap. 2.90 (0-8395-3309-8) BSA.

Boy Scouts of America. Woodwork. (Illus.). 48p. (YA). (gr. 6-12). 1970. pap. 2.90 (0-8395-3316-0, 33316) BSA.

*Boy Scouts of America & Birkby, Robert C. Boy Scout Handbook. 11th ed. LC 98-40936. (Illus.). 472p. (YA). (gr. 6-12). 1998. 7.95 (0-8395-3105-2) BSA.

Boy Scouts of America Staff. Archaeology. (Merit Badge Ser.). 96p. (YA). (gr. 6-12). 1997. pap. 2.90 (0-8395-5000-6) BSA.

Boy Scouts of America Staff. Architecture. (Illus.). 48p. (YA). (gr. 6-12). 1995. pap. 2.90 (0-8395-3304-7, 33304) BSA.

Boy Scouts of America Staff. Auto Mechanics. (Merit Badge Ser.). (Illus.). 80p. (YA). (gr. 6-12). 1992. pap. 2.90 (0-8395-3241-5) BSA.

Boy Scouts of America Staff. Bird Study. (Illus.). 104p. (YA). (gr. 6-12). 1996. pap. 2.90 (0-8395-3300-4, 33300) BSA.

— Canoeing. (Illus.). 88p. (YA). (gr. 6-12). 1996. pap. 2.90 (0-8395-3305-5, 33305) BSA.

Boy Scouts of America Staff. Cinematography. (Merit Badge Ser.). (Illus.). 48p. (YA). (gr. 6-12). 1990. pap. 2.90 (0-8395-3238-5) BSA.

— Climbing. (Merit Badge Ser.). (Illus.). 96p. (YA). (gr. 6-12). 1999. pap. 2.90 (0-8395-5001-4) BSA.

Boy Scouts of America Staff. Collections. (Illus.). 48p. (YA). (gr. 6-12). 1991. pap. 2.90 (0-8395-3242-3, 33242) BSA.

Boy Scouts of America Staff. Computers. (Merit Badge Ser.). (Illus.). 48p. (YA). (gr. 6-12). 1993. pap. 2.90 (0-8395-3246-6) BSA.

Boy Scouts of America Staff. Cooking. (Illus.). 80p. (YA). (gr. 6-12). 1996. pap. 2.90 (0-8395-3349-7) BSA.

Boy Scouts of America Staff. Crime Prevention. (Merit Badge Ser.). (Illus.). 56p. (YA). (gr. 6-12). 1996. pap. 2.90 (0-8395-3400-0) BSA.

Boy Scouts of America Staff. Cub Scout Sports: Fishing. 40p. (J). (gr. 2-5). 1988. pap. 1.49 (0-8395-4086-8, 34086) BSA.

— Electricity. (Illus.). 80p. (YA). (gr. 6-12). 1996. reprint ed. pap. 2.90 (0-8395-3408-6, 33408) BSA.

— Electronics. (Illus.). 88p. (YA). (gr. 6-12). 1996. pap. 2.90 (0-8395-5003-0, 35003) BSA.

— Emergency Preparedness. (Illus.). 80p. (YA). (gr. 6-12). 1995. pap. 2.90 (0-8395-3368-3, 33368) BSA.

Boy Scouts of America Staff. Entrepreneurship. (Merit Badge Ser.). (Illus.). 96p. (YA). (gr. 6-12). 1997. pap. 2.90 (0-8395-5008-1) BSA.

Boy Scouts of America Staff. Family Life. (Illus.). 40p. (YA). (gr. 6-12). 1991. pap. 2.90 (0-8395-3243-1, 33243) BSA.

— First Aid. (Illus.). 92p. (YA). (gr. 6-12). 1995. pap. 2.90 (0-8395-3301-2, 33301) BSA.

— Hiking. (Illus.). 56p. (YA). (gr. 6-12). 1996. pap. 2.90 (0-8395-3407-8, 33407) BSA.

— Learning for Life: Fifth Grade. (Illus.). 265p. (J). (gr. 5). 1996. pap. 5.00 (0-8395-2110-3, 32110) BSA.

— Medicine. (Illus.). 70p. (YA). (gr. 6-12). 1991. pap. 2.90 (0-8395-3244-X, 33244) BSA.

— The Official Handbook for Boys. (Illus.). 416p. (J). (gr. 3 up). 1996. reprint ed. pap. 14.95 (1-55709-441-1) Applewood.

*Boy Scouts of America Staff. Project COPE. (Illus.). 152p. 1999. pap. 25.95 (0-8395-4371-9) BSA.

— Ranger Guidebook. (Illus.). 84p. (YA). (gr. 8 up). 1998. pap. 5.95 (0-8395-3128-1) BSA.

Boy Scouts of America Staff. Rifle Shooting. (Illus.). 96p. (YA). (gr. 6-12). 1990. pap. 2.90 (0-8395-3330-6, 33330) BSA.

— Shotgun Shooting. (Illus.). 64p. (YA). (gr. 6-12). 1989. pap. 2.90 (0-8395-3331-4, 33331) BSA.

— Stamp Collecting. (Illus.). 40p. (YA). (gr. 6-12). 1993. pap. 2.90 (0-8395-3296-2, 33296) BSA.

Boy Scouts of America Staff. Swimming. (Merit Badge Ser.). (Illus.). 56p. (YA). (gr. 6-12). 1993. pap. 2.90 (0-8395-3352-7) BSA.

— Topping Out: A BSA Climbing - Rappelling Manual. (Illus.). 160p. 1999. pap. 14.95 (0-8395-3207-5) BSA.

— Venturer Handbook. (Illus.). 88p. (YA). (gr. 8 up). 1999. pap. 5.95 (0-8395-3493-0) BSA.

— Whitewater. (Merit Badge Ser.). (Illus.). 72p. (YA). (gr. 6-12). 1989. pap. 2.90 (0-8395-3405-1) BSA.

Boyack, Kenneth, ed. The New Catholic Evangelization. LC 91-47721. 256p. 1992. pap. 12.95 (0-8091-3310-5) Paulist Pr.

Boyack, Kenneth, et al. Catholic Faith Inventory. 1986. pap. 9.95 (0-8091-5196-0); pap. 4.95 (0-8091-2866-7); pap. 24.95 (0-8091-5197-9) Paulist Pr.

Boyack, Kenneth, jt. auth. see DeSiano, Frank.

*Boyadjian, Berge. Create Fun @ Work: Improve Your Productivity, Quality of Life & the Morale. Persson, Alison Noel, ed. (Illus.). 250p. 1999. pap. 15.00 (0-9676648-0-2) Knowledge.

Boyajian, Ann, jt. auth. see Morrison, Lillian.

Boyajian, James C. Portuguese Trade in Asia under the Habsburgs, 1580-1640. LC 92-12042. 384p. 1993. text 50.00 (0-8018-4405-3) Johns Hopkins.

Boyan, A. C., ed. Trail Master Flashbacks 2. (Illus.). 119p. 1997. pap. 15.95 (0-9671795-0-5) Trail Master.

*Boyan, A. Stephen, Jr. Ecology & Politics. 3rd ed. 2000. pap. 29.00 (0-8133-6814-6, Pub. by Westview) HarpC.

Boyan, Lee. Successful Cold Call Selling. 2nd ed. LC 88-48041. 288p. 1989. pap. 16.95 (0-8144-7718-6) AMACOM.

Boyan, Norman. Handbook of Research in Educational Administration. 864p. (C). 1988. text 84.95 (0-582-28517-8, 71545) Longman.

Boyang, Zuo, tr. see Hua, Li.

Boyar, Burt, jt. auth. see Davis, Sammy, Jr.

Boyarin, Daniel. Carnal Israel: Reading Sex in Talmudic Culture. LC 92-9507. 1993. 45.00 (0-520-08012-2, Pub. by U CA Pr); pap. 16.95 (0-520-20336-4, Pub. by U CA Pr) Cal Prin Full Svc.

*Boyarin, Daniel. Dying for God. LC 99-40509. (Figure Ser.). 1999. write for info. (0-8047-3617-0) Stanford U Pr.

— Dying for God: Martyrdom & The Making of Christianity & Judaism. 1999. pap. text 16.95 (0-8047-3704-5) Stanford U Pr.

Boyarin, Daniel. A Radical Jew: Paul & the Politics of Identity. LC 93-36269. (Contraversions Ser.: No. 1). (C). 1994. 45.00 (0-520-08592-2, Pub. by U CA Pr) Cal Prin Full Svc.

— A Radical Jew: Paul & the Politics of Identity. 1997. pap. text 18.95 (0-520-21214-2, Pub. by U CA Pr) Cal Prin Full Svc.

— Unheroic Conduct: The Rise of Heterosexuality & the Invention of the Jewish Man. LC 96-46047. (Contraversions Ser.: Vol. 8). (Illus.). 433p. 1997. 55.00 (0-520-20033-0, Pub. by U CA Pr); pap. 19.95 (0-520-21050-6, Pub. by U CA Pr) Cal Prin Full Svc.

Boyarin, Daniel, ed. see Boyarin, Jonathan.

Boyarin, Jonathan. Jews & Other Differences: The New Jewish Cultural Studies. Boyarin, Daniel, ed. LC 96-14966. 392p. (C). 1997. pap. 22.95 (0-8166-2751-7); text 57.95 (0-8166-2750-9) U of Minn Pr.

An Asterisk (*) at the beginning of an entry indicates that the title is appearing for the first time.

B

***Boyarin, Jonathan.** Jews Indians Europe. 1998. pap. text 15.00 (*0-226-06920-6*); lib. bdg. 40.00 (*0-226-06919-2*) U Ch Pr.

Boyarin, Jonathan. Palestine & Jewish History: Criticism at the Borders of Ethnography. LC 95-39566. 1996. pap. 19.95 (*0-8166-2765-7*); text 49.95 (*0-8166-2764-9*) U of Minn Pr.

— Storm from Paradise: The Politics of Jewish Memory. 192p. (C). 1992. pap. 14.95 (*0-8166-2095-4*); text 39.95 (*0-8166-2094-6*) U of Minn Pr.

— A Storyteller's Worlds: Education of Shlomo Noble in Europe & America. (New Perspectives: Jewish Life & Thought Ser.). 240p. 1994. text 34.95 (*0-8419-1343-9*) Holmes & Meier.

— Thinking in Jewish. 200p. 1996. pap. text 14.95 (*0-226-06927-3*); lib. bdg. 39.95 (*0-226-06926-5*) U Ch Pr.

Boyarin, Jonathan, ed. The Ethnography of Reading. LC 92-34690. 1993. 48.00 (*0-520-07955-8*, Pub. by U CA Pr); pap. 17.95 (*0-520-08133-1*, Pub. by U CA Pr) Cal Prin Full Svc.

— Remapping Memory: Space, Time, & the Politics of Memory. LC 94-9358. 1994. pap. 19.95 (*0-8166-2453-4*); text 49.95 (*0-8166-2452-6*) U of Minn Pr.

Boyarin, Jonathan, jt. ed. see Kugelmass, Jack.

Boyars, Arthur, tr. see Yevtushenko, Yevgeny.

Boyars, Carl. Propellants Manufacture, Hazards, & Testing: A Symposium. LC 75-87208. (Advances in Chemistry Ser.: No. 88). 405p. reprint ed. pap. 125.60 (*0-608-17750-4*, 205225100074) Bks Demand.

Boyars, Marion, ed. see Schmidt, Arno B.

Boyarski, Jennie & Hickey, Kate, eds. Collection Management in the Electronic Age: A Manual for Creating Community College Collection Development Policy Statements. 197p. (C). 1994. pap. 43.00 (*0-8389-7737-5*) Assn Coll & Res Libs.

Boyarsky, Abraham & Gora, Pawel. Laws of Chaos: Invariant Measures & Dynamical Systems in One Dimension. LC 97-22134. (Probability & Its Applications). (Illus.). xv, 399p. 1997. write for info. (*3-7643-4003-7*) Birkhauser.

— Laws of Chaos: Invariant Measures & Dynamical Systems in One Dimension. LC 97-22134. (Probability & Its Applications Ser.). (Illus.). 416p. 1997. 59.95 (*0-8176-4003-7*) Birkhauser.

Boyarsky, Bill & Lavin, Enrique. Los Angeles: City of Dreams. LC 98-56459. (Urban Tapestry Ser.). (Illus.). 1998. 44.95 (*1-881096-63-7*) Towery Pub.

***Boyarsky, Nicholas & Murphy, Nicola.** Action Research: Architecture & Urbanism 1. 64p. 1998. pap. 15.95 (*1-901033-45-7*, Pub. by Black Dog Pubg) RAM Publications.

Boyatis & Dunn. Child Growth & Development 1996/97. 3rd annot. ed. 1995. teacher ed. (*0-697-32794-9*, WCB McGr Hill) McGrw-H Hghr Educ.

Boyatzis, Chris & Junn, Ellen N. Annual Editions: Child Growth & Development, 97-98. 4th ed. 256p. (C). 1997. text 12.25 (*0-697-37221-9*) Brown & Benchmark.

Boyatzis, Chris J., jt. auth. see Junn, Ellen N.

Boyatzis-Junn. Child Growth & Development. 2nd ed. 1995. 12.74 (*1-56134-337-4*) McGraw.

— Child Growth & Development: 1999-2000 Edition. 6th ed. 1999. pap., student ed. 16.56 (*0-07-040122-5*) McGraw.

Boyatzis, Richard E. The Competent Manager: A Model for Effective Performance. LC 81-13113. 328p. 1982. 89.95 (*0-471-09031-X*) Wiley.

— Thematic Analysis: Coding As a Process for Transforming Qualitative Information. LC 97-45405. 184p. 1998. 51.00 (*0-7619-0960-5*); pap. 24.50 (*0-7619-0961-3*) Sage.

Boyatzis, Richard E., et al. Innovating in Management Education: A Journey from Teaching to Learning. (Management Ser.). 304p. 1994. 37.95 (*0-7879-0032-X*) Jossey-Bass.

Boybeyi, Z., ed. Mesoscale Atmospheric Dispersion. (Advances in Air Pollution Ser.). 500p. 2000. 262.00 (*1-85312-732-9*, 7329, Pub. by WIT Pr) Computational Mech MA.

Boyce. Dictionary of Shakespeare. (Wordsworth Collection). 1998. pap. text 6.95 (*1-85326-372-9*, Pub. by Wrdsworth Edits) NTC Contemp Pub Co.

Boyce. Elementary Differential Equations. pap. text 44.00 (*0-471-37367-2*) Wiley.

Boyce. Elementary Differential Equations & Elementary Differential Equations & Boundary Value Problems by Haines, 2 vols., Set. 6th ed. 1996. pap. text, student ed. 25.00 (*0-471-13582-8*) Wiley.

— Environmental Technology. 1998. pap. text, teacher ed. write for info. (*0-471-32358-6*) Wiley.

— Mathematics for Technical & Vocational Students. 1997. pap. text, student ed. 25.00 (*0-13-253915-2*) P-H.

— Sails for Rent. (DF - Computer Applications Ser.). 1989. mass mkt. 20.95 (*0-538-60300-3*) S-W Pub.

— Wheels for Sale: A Computer Application. 2nd ed. (DF - Computer Applications Ser.). 1991. mass mkt. 20.95 (*0-538-60845-5*) S-W Pub.

Boyce & Auvil. Omega Desktop, Inc. - A Desktop Publishing. (DF - Computer Applications Ser.). 1990. mass mkt. 18.95 (*0-538-60535-9*) S-W Pub.

Boyce, et al. Metropolitan Plan Making. (Monographs: No. 4). 1970. 25.00 (*1-55869-075-1*) Regional Sci Res Inst.

Boyce, jt. auth. see McCaig, Barbara.

Boyce, A. J. & Mascie-Taylor, C. G., eds. Molecular Biology & Human Diversity. (Society for the Study of Human Biology Symposium Ser.: No. 38). (Illus.). 318p. (C). 1996. text 69.95 (*0-521-56086-1*) Cambridge U Pr.

Boyce, A. J., jt. ed. see Harrison, G. Ainsworth.

Boyce, A. J., jt. ed. see Reynolds, V.

Boyce, Ann. Applique: The Ann Boyce Way. (Illus.). 182p. 1999. reprint ed. pap. text 19.00 (*0-7881-6323-X*) DIANE Pub.

Boyce, Ann. Introduction to Environmental Technology. 478p. 1996. pap. 49.95 (*0-471-28733-4*, VNR) Wiley.

Boyce, Ann. Introduction to Environmental Technology. LC 96-47635. (Environmental Engineering Ser.). (Illus.). 496p. 1996. text 39.95 (*0-442-02142-9*, VNR) Wiley.

— A New Serge in Wearable Art. LC 95-23435. (Illus.). 128p. 1995. pap. 18.95 (*0-8019-8396-7*) Krause Pubns.

Boyce, B. L. Mercury Systems. 2nd ed. 176p. 1986. pap. text 9.96 (*0-07-006903-4*) McGraw.

— Mercury Systems Inc. Practice Set in Word-Information Processing for Conventional & Text-Editing Typewriters. 1981. 12.56 (*0-07-006901-8*) McGraw.

Boyce, B. L. & Popyk, Marilyn K. The Electronic Office & You: Word Processing Concepts. 192p. 1985. text 11.96 (*0-07-006921-2*) McGraw.

Boyce-Ballweber, Hettie. The First People of Maryland. LC 87-61066. 110p. (J). (gr. 1-6). 1987. 15.75 (*0-917882-24-5*) MD Hist Pr.

Boyce, Barry. A Traveller's Guide to the Galapagos Islands. 3rd rev. ed. (Illus.). 300p. (Orig.). 1998. pap. 16.95 (*1-55650-850-6*) Hunter NJ.

The Galapagos Islands, a remote paradise, are mysterious as ever. But the details of travel to the Galapagos are no longer a mystery. The essentials of a how-to travel adventure to the Land of Darwin are now available in the comprehensive TRAVELLER'S GUIDE TO THE GALAPAGOS ISLANDS. From which airlines to choose & why to a detailed analysis of the Tour Operator network, Barry Boyce describes the rules & tells the reader how to play the Galapagos adventure travel game. Entire chapters are devoted to topics such as choosing a tour (with descriptions, analyses, & price structures of all the yachts & cruise ships), what to pack & what not to pack, photographic opportunities & equipment on land & underwater, Galapagos history, wildlife, & a detailed tour of the islands. First Edition reviews - "BOYCE'S EXCITEMENT & KNOWLEDGE MIX TO PRODUCE A COMPREHENSIVE & RESPONSIBLE GUIDE TO TOURING THE GALAPAGOS."--BRAD HOOPER, BOOKLIST. "JUST ON THE MARKET & BADLY NEEDED...BOYCE'S EFFORT IS LIKELY TO BE DEFINITIVE WORK."--ZEKE WIGGLESWORTH, SAN JOSE MERCURY NEWS. To order, call or write Hunter Publishing, 130 Campus Drive, Edison, NJ 08818, (800) 255-0343. *Publisher Paid Annotation.*

Boyce, Benjamin. The Benevolent Man: A Life of Ralph Allen of Bath. LC 67-11667. (Illus.). 318p. reprint ed. pap. 98.60 (*0-7837-1675-3*, 205720700024) Bks Demand.

— The Character Sketches in Pope's Poems. LC 62-10050. 153p. reprint ed. pap. 47.50 (*0-608-15098-3*, 202619000048) Bks Demand.

Boyce, Bert R., et al. Measurement in Information Science. (Illus.). 283p. 1994. text 64.95 (*0-12-121450-8*) Acad Pr.

Boyce, Bert R., jt. auth. see Kraft, Donald H.

Boyce, Betsy D. The Rebels of Hastings. (Illus.). 232p. 1992. text 45.00 (*0-8020-5986-4*); pap. text 16.95 (*0-8020-6920-7*) U of Toronto Pr.

Boyce, Bret. The Language of the Freedmen in Petronius' Cena Trimalchionis. LC 91-18778. (Mnemosyne Ser.: Supplement 117). vi, 113p. 1991. 53.50 (*90-04-09431-8*) Brill Academic Pubs.

Boyce, Byrl N., ed. Real Estate Appraisal Terminology. rev. ed. LC 80-23713. 384p. 1981. text 34.95 (*0-88410-597-0*, HarpBusn) HarpInfo.

Boyce, Charles. Dictionary of Furniture. 331p. 1995. pap. 19.95 (*0-8050-0752-0*, Owl) H Holt & Co.

***Boyce, Charles.** Dictionary of Furniture. 2nd ed. (Illus.). 384p. 2000. 50.00 (*0-8160-4229-2*); pap. 19.95 (*0-8160-4158-X*, Checkmark) Facts on File.

Boyce, Charles. Shakespeare A to Z: The Essential Reference to His Plays, His Poems, His Life & Times. (Illus.). 752p. 1990. 55.00 (*0-8160-1805-7*) Facts on File.

— Shakespeare A to Z: The Essential Reference to His Plays, His Poems, His Life & Times, & More. 752p. 1991. pap. 20.95 (*0-385-31361-6*, Delta Trade) Dell.

Boyce, Chris. Antiques: Guide to Wisconsin Antique Stores. McCaig, Barbara, ed. (Illus.). 100p. (Orig.). 1990. pap. 4.95 (*0-935201-20-3*) Affordable Adven.

— Florida Parks Guide. McCaig, Barbara, ed. 100p. (Orig.). 1988. pap. text 5.95 (*0-935201-35-1*) Affordable Adven.

— New York Parks Guide. McCaig, Barbara, ed. 150p. (Orig.). 1988. pap. text 5.95 (*0-935201-39-4*) Affordable Adven.

— North Carolina Biking Guide. McCaig, Barbara, ed. 100p. (Orig.). 1989. pap. text 5.95 (*0-935201-79-3*) Affordable Adven.

— Pennsylvania Parks Guide. McCaig, Barbara, ed. 100p. (Orig.). 1988. pap. text 5.95 (*0-935201-37-8*) Affordable Adven.

— Washington Parks Guide. McCaig, Barbara, ed. 100p. (Orig.). 1988. pap. text 5.95 (*0-317-67996-1*) Affordable Adven.

Boyce, Chris & McCaig, Margie. Indiana Parks Guide. McCaig, Barbara, ed. (Illus.). 100p. (Orig.). 1988. pap. text 5.95 (*0-935201-52-1*) Affordable Adven.

Boyce, Chris, jt. auth. see McCaig, Barbara.

Boyce, Chris, ed. see Keadle, Chris & Dorn, Rich.

Boyce, Chris, ed. see McCaig, Barbara.

***Boyce, Christopher.** Little Ha-Ha. (J). (gr. 2-5). 2000. pap. 5.95 (*0-533-13264-9*) Vantage.

Boyce, D. E., et al, eds. Regional Science: Retrospect & Prospect. (Illus.). viii, 505p. 1991. 123.95 (*0-387-53493-8*) Spr-Verlag.

Boyce, D. George. Englishmen & Irish Troubles: British Public Opinion & the Making of Irish Policy 1918-22. (Modern Revivals in History Ser.). 264p. 1994. 61.95 (*0-7512-0239-8*, Pub. by Gregg Revivals) Ashgate Pub Co.

— The Irish Question & British Politics, 1868-1996. 2nd ed. LC 96-11513. (British Industries in the Twentieth Century Ser.). 192p. 1996. text 49.95 (*0-312-16106-9*) St Martin.

— The Making of Modern Irish History. 272p. (C). 1996. pap. 22.99 (*0-415-12171-X*) Routledge.

— Nationalism in Ireland. 3rd ed. LC 94-48350. 512p. (C). 1995. pap. 25.99 (*0-415-12776-9*) Routledge.

— Nineteenth Century Ireland: The Search for Stability. 256p. (C). 1990. text 69.00 (*0-389-20934-1*) B&N Imports.

Boyce, D. George, ed. see O'Day, Alan.

Boyce, David E. Equilibrium Solutions to Combined Urban Residential Location, Modal Choice, & Trip Assignment Models. (Discussion Papers: No. 98). 1977. pap. 10.00 (*1-55869-041-7*) Regional Sci Res Inst.

Boyce, David E., et al. A Computer Program for Optimal Regression Analysis. (Discussion Papers: No. 28). 1969. pap. 10.00 (*1-55869-015-8*) Regional Sci Res Inst.

— The Development of a Planning Oriented Method for Estimating the Value of Development Easements on Agricultural Land. (Discussion Papers: No. 105). 1978. pap. 10.00 (*1-55869-024-7*) Regional Sci Res Inst.

Boyce, David E., jt. auth. see Ran, Bin.

***Boyce, David George.** Decolonization &The British Empire, 1775-1997. LC 99-12192. 1999. text 59.95 (*0-312-22325-0*) St Martin.

***Boyce, David George & O'Day, Alan.** Defenders of the Union: A Survey of British & Irish Unionism since 1801. LC 00-32168. (Illus.). 2000. pap. write for info. (*0-415-17422-8*) Routledge.

Boyce-Davies, Carole. Moving Beyond Boundaries, Vol. 1. (C). 1996. 66.50 (*0-7453-0758-2*); pap. 19.95 (*0-7453-0759-0*) Westview.

— Moving Beyond Boundaries, Vol. 2. (C). 1996. pap. 19.95 (*0-7453-0881-3*) Westview.

Boyce-Davies, Carole, ed. Moving Beyond All Boundaries. (C). 1996. pap. text 38.95 (*0-7453-0883-X*) Westview.

Boyce, Eugene M. The Coming Revolution in Education: Basic Education & the New Theory of Schooling. 98p. (Orig.). (C). 1983. pap. text 14.00 (*0-8191-3407-4*) U Pr of Amer.

Boyce, Everett R., ed. The Challenge: Victory - A Survival Manual for Christians Living Under Pressure. 2nd rev. ed. 120p. 1997. pap. text 5.95 (*0-910796-17-3*) Intl Students Inc.

Boyce, Everett R., ed. see Hooper, Ben W.

Boyce, Frank C. Welcome to Sarajevo. 1997. pap. 13.95 (*0-571-19385-4*) Faber & Faber.

Boyce, Fred J. The Other Nevada, As Painted by Fred Boyce: Nevada Paintings. (Illus.). 97p. Date not set. write for info. (*0-9630399-0-3*) Boyce Art.

Boyce, George A. Neither Red nor White: And Other Indian Stories. Muth, Marcia, ed. LC 95-2900. 128p. (Orig.). 1996. pap. 12.95 (*0-86534-237-7*) Sunstone Pr.

***Boyce, Geraldine.** Homefront: A Story of Love & War. 160p. 2000. pap. 12.95 (*1-56474-341-1*) Fithian Pr.

***Boyce, Gordon.** Co-Operative Structures in Global Business: A New Approach to Networks, Technology Transfer Agreements, Strategic Alliances & Agency Relationships. LC 00-35383. 2000. write for info. (*0-415-21644-3*) Routledge.

Boyce, J. R., et al, eds. Soil Mechanics & Foundation Engineering: Proceedings of the 8th Regional Conference for Africa, Harare, 4-7 June 1984, 2 vols., Set. 1000p. (C). 1987. text 407.00 (*90-6191-531-7*, Pub. by A A Balkema) Ashgate Pub Co.

Boyce, J. S. Host Relationships & Distribution of Conifer Rusts in the U. S. & Canada. (Connecticut Academy of Arts & Sciences Ser., Trans.: Vol. 35). 1943. pap. 49.50 (*0-685-22906-8*) Elliots Bks.

***Boyce, James John.** Praising God in Carmel: Studies in Carmelite Liturgy LC 99-21601. 1999. write for info. (*0-9656910-1-2*) Carmelite Inst.

Boyce, James K. The Philippines: The Political Economy of Growth & Impoverishment in the Marcos Era. LC 92-26934. 400p. 1993. text 28.00 (*0-8248-1521-1*); pap. text 15.75 (*0-8248-1522-X*) UH Pr.

Boyce, James K., ed. Economic Policy for Building Peace: The Lessons of El Salvador. 359p. 1996. lib. bdg. 55.00 (*1-55587-526-2*, 87-526-2) L Rienner.

Boyce, James K., jt. auth. see Hartman, Betsy.

Boyce, James K., jt. auth. see Hartmann, Betsy.

Boyce, James P. Abstract of Systematic Theology. 556p. 1996. 19.99 (*0-87552-872-4*) P & R Pubng.

Boyce, Japheth B. & Haag, Terri. Japh's Pretty Good Fossil Book of the Dakota Territories. (Illus.). 60p. (Orig.). 1991. pap. 9.95 (*0-9635445-2-7*) Sahuarita Pr.

Boyce, Jean B. Just Ask Mom. LC 96-96166. (Illus.). 64p. 1996. 9.95 (*1-56684-190-9*) Evans Bk Dist.

Boyce, Jefferson C. Modern Electronics: A Survey of the New Technology. Zuredjian, George Z., ed. (Illus.). 256p. (C). 1982. text 66.50 (*0-07-006915-8*) McGraw.

— Understanding Microcomputer Concepts: A Guide for Beginners & Hobbyists. LC 83-62030. (Illus.). 336p. 1984. 18.95 (*0-13-936956-2*) P-H.

Boyce, Jim. Inside Windows 3.1 Platinum Ed. LC 94-25472. 1029p. 1994. 39.99 incl. cd-rom (*1-56205-328-0*) New Riders Pub.

— Inside Windows 95 Certified Administrator's Resource Edition. 1997. 69.99 (*1-56205-803-7*) New Riders Pub.

— Inside Windows 98. LC 98-85098. 1998. 39.99 (*1-56205-788-X*) New Riders Pub.

***Boyce, Jim.** Microsoft Windows 2000 Installation & Configuration Handbook with CD-ROM. LC 99-65437. (Illus.). 598p. 2000. pap. 39.99 (*0-7897-2133-3*) Que.

Boyce, Jim. Upgrading PC's Illustrated. LC 96-72221. 744p. 1997. 34.99 (*0-7897-0986-4*) Que.

— Using Microsoft Office 97 Professional: Special Edition, Best Seller Edition. 2nd ed. LC 97-68761. 1320p. 1997. 39.99 (*0-7897-1396-9*) Que.

— Using PC's. 1997. pap. text 19.99 (*0-7897-1451-5*) Que.

— Windows 98 User Manual. LC 98-84523. 1998. pap. 19.99 (*0-7897-1657-7*) Que.

***Boyce, Jim, et al.** Inside Windows 95. 1120p. 1999. pap. text 53.00 (*0-536-02409-X*) Pearson Custom.

Boyce, Jim, et al. Inside Windows 95. deluxe ed. LC 97-104684. 1264p. 1996. 59.99 (*1-56205-695-6*) New Riders Pub.

— Windows NT Workstation 4.O Advanced Technical Reference. LC 96-70612. 888p. 1996. 59.99 (*0-7897-0863-9*) Que.

Boyce, John G., et al. Mathematics for Technical & Vocational Students. 10th ed. LC 99-22852. (Illus.). 644p. (C). 1999. 83.00 (*0-13-010432-9*) P-H.

Boyce, Julia G. Not Very Messy, Unless . . . (Illus.). 8p. (J). (gr. k-2). 1998. pap. 3.75 (*1-880612-79-8*) Seedling Pubns.

Boyce, Kim. Beauty to Last a Lifetime. rev. ed. LC 92-12611. (Illus.). 191p. (J). (gr. 8-12). 1997. pap. 15.99 (*0-7814-3034-8*) Chariot Victor.

Boyce, Kim & Abraham, Ken. Beauty to Last a Lifetime: A Step by Step Guide to Inner & Outer Beauty for Teenage Girls. LC 92-12611. 208p. 1992. pap. 15.99 (*0-7814-0988-8*, Chariot Bks) Chariot Victor.

— In Focus: Devotions to Help You Make Sense Out of a Senseless World. LC 92-31299. (Illus.). 160p. (J). 1993. pap. 7.99 (*0-7814-0814-8*, Chariot Bks) Chariot Victor.

— In Process: Devotions to Help You Develop Your Faith. Reck, Sue, ed. LC 93-32713. 160p. (YA). (gr. 7-12). 1994. pap. 7.99 (*0-7814-0822-9*) Chariot Victor.

***Boyce, Kim & Saxton, Heidi Hess.** Touched by Kindness. 2001. pap. 10.99 (*1-56955-180-4*) Servant.

Boyce, Laurie A., jt. auth. see Steinhauser, William P.

Boyce, M., ed. Mechanics of Plastics & Plastic Composites - 1995 Vol. 68-215: Proceedings of the ASME International Mechanical Engineering Congress & Exposition, 1995, San Francisco, CA. LC 95-81264. (1995 ASME International Mechanical Engineering Congress & Exposition Ser.: MD-Vol. 68/AMD-Vol. 215). 444p. 1995. 110.00 (*0-7918-1750-4*, H01031) ASME.

Boyce, Margaurite P. I Heard the Donkey's Bray: Thirty Years in the Mission Field. (Illus.). 192p. 1992. pap. 12.95 (*1-881576-02-7*) Providence Hse.

Boyce, Marguerite P. Captain Brenton's Heritage: The Gospel Message for Southwest Mexico. (Illus.). 96p. (Orig.). 1994. pap. 10.95 (*1-881576-34-5*) Providence Hse.

Boyce, Mark S. Ecosystem Management: Applications for Sustainable Forest & Wildlife Resources. (Illus.). 392p. 1999. pap. text 18.00 (*0-300-07858-7*) Yale U Pr.

— Evolution of Life Histories of Mammals Theory & Pattern. LC 87-29480. 373p. (C). 1988. 65.00 (*0-300-04084-9*) Yale U Pr.

Boyce, Mark S. & Haney, Alan W. Ecosystem Management: Applications for Sustainable Forest & Wildlife Resources. LC 96-3407. (Illus.). 361p. 1997. 40.00 (*0-300-06902-2*) Yale U Pr.

Boyce, Mark S., jt. ed. see Keiter, Robert B.

Boyce, Mary. A History of Zoroastrianism: The Early Period, Vol. 1. 3rd ed. LC 95-46928. (Handbuch Der Orientalistik. Erste Abteilung, Der Nahe Und Der Mittlere Osten: Vol. 8). xvi, 350p. 1996. 129.50 (*90-04-10474-7*) Brill Academic Pubs.

— A Persian Stronghold of Zoroastrianism: Based on the Ratanbai Katrak Lectures, 1975. LC 89-35817. (Persian Studies: No. 12). (Illus.). 308p. (C). 1989. reprint ed. lib. bdg. 43.00 (*0-8191-7529-3*) U Pr of Amer.

— Zoroastrianism: Its Antiquity & Constant Vigour. (Columbia Lecture Ser.: Vol. 7). xiv, 204p. 1992. text 28.00 (*0-939214-89-X*) Bibliotheca Persica.

— Zoroastrians. Hinnells, John, ed. (Library of Religious Beliefs & Practices). 260p. (C). 1986. pap. text 17.95 (*0-7102-0156-7*, Routledge Thoemms) Routledge.

Boyce, Mary, ed. History of Zoroastrianism, Vol. 2: Under the Achaemenians. LC 88-19450. (Handbuch der Orientalistik Ser.: Vol. 1-2-2). xvi, 306p. 1982. pap. 101.50 (*90-04-06506-7*) Brill Academic Pubs.

Boyce, Mary, ed. Textual Sources for the Study of Zoroastrianism. (Textual Sources for the Study of Religion Ser.). (Illus.). x, 176p. 1990. pap. text 16.00 (*0-226-06930-3*) U Ch Pr.

Boyce, Mary & Grenet, Frantz. A History of Zoroastrianism: Zoroastrianism under Macedonian & Roman Rule, Vol. 3. LC 88-19450. (Handbuch der Orientalistik, 1 Abt., 8. Bd., 1. Abschn., 2. Lief). (Illus.). xx, 596p. 1991. 235.50 (*90-04-09271-4*) Brill Academic Pubs.

Boyce, Mary A. Murrieta - Old Town, New Town: A Community History. (Illus.). 208p. (Orig.). 1995. pap. 14.95 (*0-9648634-0-5*) Rosemar Pubng.

Boyce, Meherwan P. Gas Turbine Engineering Handbook. LC 82-6158. 604p. 1987. 95.00 (*0-87201-878-4*) Gulf Pub.

B

Boyce, N. B. Real Estate Appraisal Terminology. 367p. 59.95 (*0-318-42554-8*, M8555); 59.95 (*0-8288-7624-X*, M8555) Fr & Eur.

Boyce, Nani. A Working Glossary of English-Russian Housing Terms. LC 97-70897. 112p. 1997. text 59.95 (*1-85972-490-6*, Pub. by Ashgate Pub) Ashgate Pub Co.

Boyce, Neith. Folly of Others. LC 73-122690. (Short Story Index Reprint Ser.). 1977. 17.95 (*0-8369-3511-X*) Ayer.

***Boyce, Oren B.** The Power of Indirect Suggestion: Hypnosis, Genetics & Depression. LC 99-93695. 2000. pap. 12.50 (*0-533-13104-9*) Vantage.

Boyce, Peter. The Genus Arum: A Kew Magazine Monograph. (Illus.). 192p. 1993. 55.00 (*0-11-250085-4*, HM00854, Pub. by Statnry Office) Bernan Associates.

Boyce, Pieuke, tr. see Achterberg, Gerrit.

Boyce, R. M., jt. auth. see Masterman, A. H.

Boyce, Robert P. Keck & Keck. LC 92-26846. (Illus.). 176p. 1993. 34.95 (*1-878271-18-0*); pap. 24.95 (*1-878271-17-2*) Princeton Arch.

Boyce, Robert W. French Foreign & Defence Policy, 1918-1940: The Decline & Fall of a Great Power. LC 97-32013. 304p. (C). 1998. 90.00 (*0-415-15039-6*) Routledge.

***Boyce, Roland G.** 90 Seconds with God. LC 00-102740. 203p. 2000. pap. 9.95 (*0-9678882-3-9*) MBrio Bks.

Boyce, Ronald N. Criminal Law & Procedure, Manual for Teachers to Accompany Cases & Materials. 7th ed. (University Casebook Ser.). 483p. 1989. pap. text. write for info. (*0-88277-762-9*) Foundation Pr.

Boyce, Ronald N. & Perkins, Rollin M. Criminal Law & Procedure: Cases & Materials. 7th ed. (University Casebook Ser.). 1263p. 1991. reprint ed. text 43.75 (*0-88277-706-8*) Foundation Pr.

Boyce, Ronald N., jt. auth. see Perkins, Rollin M.

Boyce, Stephen G. Landscape Forestry. 239p. 1995. 110.00 (*0-471-00784-6*) Wiley.

Boyce, Susan M., et al. Writing Travel Books & Articles. 224p. (Orig.). 1997. pap. 15.95 (*1-55180-104-3*) Self-Counsel Pr.

Boyce, Terry. Car Interior Restoration. 3rd ed. LC 81-9175. (Illus.). 144p. 1983. pap. 9.95 (*0-8306-2102-4*, 2102) McGraw-Hill Prof.

Boyce Thompson Institute for Plant Research Confer. Linking Research to Crop Production. Staples, Richard C. & Kuhr, Ronald J., eds. LC 79-25737. (Illus.). 249p. 1980. reprint ed. pap. 77.20 (*0-608-05442-9*, 206591100006) Bks Demand.

Boyce, Timothy J. & Turner, Ronald. Fair Representation, the NLRB & the Courts. rev. ed. LC 84-48291. (Labor Relations & Public Policy Ser.: No. 18). 208p. reprint ed. pap. 64.50 (*0-8357-3152-9*, 203941500012) Bks Demand.

Boyce, Tommy. How to Write a Hit Song & Sell It. 1974. pap. 10.00 (*0-87980-291-X*) Wilshire.

Boyce, W. Illustrated South America, 2 vols. 1976. lib. bdg. 450.00 (*0-8490-2037-9*) Gordon Pr.

Boyce, W. Scott. Economic & Social History of Chowan County, N.C. 1880-1915. LC 73-76716. (Columbia University. Studies in the Social Sciences: No. 179). reprint ed. 20.00 (*0-404-51179-1*) AMS Pr.

Boyce, William. William Boyce: Two Anthems for the Georgian Court I. Van Nice, John R., ed. (Recent Researches in Music of the Baroque Era Ser.: Vol. RRB7). (Illus.). 97p. 1970. pap. 35.00 (*0-89579-026-2*) A-R Eds.

— William Boyce: Two Anthems for the Georgian Court II. Van Nice, John R., ed. (Recent Researches in Music of the Baroque Era Ser.: Vol. RRB8). (Illus.). 98p. 1970. pap. 35.00 (*0-89579-027-0*) A-R Eds.

Boyce, William & DiPrima, Richard C. Introduction to Differential Equation. 326p. 1988. reprint ed. text 41.00 (*0-471-09338-6*) Krieger.

Boyce, William D. & Jensen, Larry C. Moral Reasoning: A Psychological-Philosophical Integration. fac. ed. LC 78-5935. 303p. 1978. reprint ed. pap. 94.00 (*0-7837-8102-4*, 204790600008) Bks Demand.

Boyce, William E. & DiPrima, Richard C. Element Differential Equations & Boundary Valve Problems. 6th ed. LC 96-19864. 768p. 1996. text 103.95 (*0-471-08955-9*) Wiley.

Boyce, William E. & DiPrima, Richard C. Elementary Differential Equations. 6th ed. LC 96-23075. 608p. 1996. text 99.95 (*0-471-08953-2*) Wiley.

***Boyce, William E. & DiPrima, Richard C.** Elementary Differential Equations. 7th ed. 608p. (C). 2000. text. write for info. (*0-471-31998-8*) Wiley.

— Elementary Differential Equations & Boundary Value Problems. 7th ed. 768p. 2001. write for info. (*0-471-31999-6*) Wiley.

Boyce, William E., et al. Elementary Differential Equations & Boundary Value Problems Sixth Edition & Differential Equations with Mathematica, Second Edition & Student Solutions Manual to Accompany Elementary Differential Equations & Boundary Value Problems Sixth Edition. 1256p. 1997. text 167.85 (*0-471-28292-8*) Wiley.

Boyce, william G., jt. auth. see Sweeney, J. Gray.

Boych, Vladimir, et al. A Thousand Years of Czech Culture: Riches from the National Museum in Prague. LC 96-8564. (Illus.). 180p. (Orig.). 1996. pap. 39.95 (*1-879704-02-1*) Old Salem NC.

Boychuk, Bohdan, ed. & tr. see Pasternak, Boris.

Boychuk, Gerard W. Patchworks of Purpose: The Development of Provincial Social Assistance Regimes in Canada. pap. 22.95 (*0-7735-1739-1*) McG-Queens Univ Pr.

— Patchworks of Purpose: The Development of Provincial Social Assistance Regimes in Canada. 184p. 1998. text 60.00 (*0-7735-1699-9*, Pub. by McG-Queens Univ Pr) CUP Services.

Boychuk, Terry. The Making & Meaning of Hospital Policy in the United States & Canada. LC 98-58120. 200p. (C). 1999. text 42.50 (*0-472-10928-6*, 10928) U of Mich Pr.

Boycko, Maxim, et al. Privatizing Russia. LC 94-25308. 175p. 1995. 25.00 (*0-262-02389-X*) MIT Pr.

— Privatizing Russia. (Illus.). 175p. 1997. reprint ed. pap. text 12.50 (*0-262-52228-4*) MIT Pr.

Boyd. Bach. 2nd ed. (Dent Master Musicians Ser.). (Illus.). 304p. (C). 1994. pap. (*0-19-816466-1*) OUP.

***Boyd.** Baroness Cox: Voice for the Voiceless. 1999. pap. 14.95 (*0-7459-3735-7*, Pub. by Lion Pubng) Trafalgar.

— Broadcast Journalism. 5th ed. 400p. 2000. pap. text 44.95 (*0-240-51571-4*) Buttrwrth-Heinemann.

Boyd. Flannery O'Connor Short Stories. 1995. 50.00 (*0-8161-8971-4*, Twyne) Mac Lib Ref.

— In Their Own Words. 1992. pap. text, student ed. write for info. (*0-17-555692-X*) Addison-Wesley.

— Listening & Speaking for Beginning Students of the English Language, Bk. 1. 112p. 1996. pap. text 15.73 (*0-13-299785-1*) P-H.

— Marketing Management. 4th ed. 2001. 54.00 (*0-07-231523-7*) McGraw.

— Prev. Alcohol. (JRA Ser.: Vol. 4, No. 2). 1994. 20.00 (*0-8058-9972-3*) L Erlbaum Assocs.

— Sapt Veterinary Medicine in Clinical Anatomy. 1995. mass mkt. 32.95 (*0-7234-2142-0*) Mosby Inc.

— Writing with Logic in Mind. (C). 1994. pap. text 13.50 (*0-15-501909-0*, Pub. by Harcourt Coll Pubs) Harcourt.

Boyd & Brown. Cpse Rdgs African Americ Histo. 1996. pap. text 22.50 (*0-07-006983-2*) McGraw.

Boyd & Gottschalk. Parrish. The Parrish Family, Including the Allied Families of Belt, Boyd, Cole-Malone, Clokey, Garrett, Merryman, Parsons, Price & Tipton. 413p. 1991. reprint ed. pap. 63.00 (*0-8328-1980-8*); reprint ed. lib. bdg. 73.00 (*0-8328-1979-4*) Higginson Bk Co.

Boyd, et al. How Humans Evolved. 2nd ed. pap. text. write for info. (*0-393-97576-2*) Norton.

Boyd, jt. auth. see Lipkowitz, Kenny B.

Boyd, jt. auth. see Tower.

Boyd, jt. auth. see Twiname.

Boyd, ed. see Aden, et al.

Boyd & Fraser Staff. CorelDRAW! 6.0 for Windows: Star Series. (DF - Computer Applications Ser.). 1996. pap. 12.95 (*0-7895-0346-8*) Course Tech.

— Freelance Graphics 3.0 for Windows: Star Series. (DF - Computer Applications Ser.). 1995. pap. 12.95 (*0-7895-0173-2*) Course Tech.

— Microsoft Excel 5.0 for Windows. (Acumen Ser.). (C). 1995. mass mkt. 20.95 (*0-87709-980-4*) Course Tech.

— PageMaker 6.0 for Windows. (STAR Ser.). 1996. pap. 12.95 (*0-7895-0348-4*) Course Tech.

— Windows 95. (STAR Ser.). 1996. pap. 12.95 (*0-7895-0180-5*) Course Tech.

Boyd & Fraser Staff & Reilly, Micheal. Microsoft Access 2.0 for Windows: Acumen Series. (DF - Computer Applications Ser.). 272p. (C). 1995. mass mkt. 20.95 (*0-87709-983-9*) Course Tech.

Boyd, A. W., ed. Radiation Chemistry in Nuclear Reactor Technology. 70p. 1983. pap. 25.00 (*0-08-029156-2*, Pergamon Pr) Elsevier.

Boyd, A. W., jt. auth. see Hood, R. Maurice.

Boyd, A. W., jt. auth. see Morrison, Robert T.

Boyd, Aaron. First Lady: The Story of Hillary Rodham Clinton. LC 93-21195. (Notable Americans Ser.). (Illus.). 112p. (YA). (gr. 5 up). 1994. lib. bdg. 17.95 (*1-883846-02-1*) M Reynolds.

***Boyd, Aaron.** John Coltrane: Jazz Revolutionary. (Masters of Music Ser.). (Illus.). 112p. (YA). (gr. 5 up). 2001. lib. bdg. 19.95 (*1-883846-57-9*) M Reynolds.

Boyd, Aaron. Smart Money: The Story of Bill Gates. LC 94-48273. (Notable Americans Ser.). (Illus.). 112p. (YA). (gr. 5 up). 1995. lib. bdg. 17.95 (*1-883846-09-9*) M Reynolds.

— Tiger Woods. LC 97-2980. (Great Athletes Ser.). (Illus.). 64p. (J). (gr. 3 up). 1997. lib. bdg. 17.95 (*1-883846-19-6*) M Reynolds.

Boyd, Alan & Fraser. dBASE IV 2.0. (C). text. write for info. (*0-318-70350-5*, BF4179) S-W Pub.

— WordPerfect 6.0. (C). 1994. text. write for info. (*0-318-70351-3*, BF4152) S-W Pub.

Boyd, Alan S. The Skin Sourcebook. LC 98-51989. (Illus.). 416p. 1998. pap. 22.95 (*0-7373-0003-5*, 00035W) NTC Contemp Pub Co.

Boyd, Alex, ed. Guide to Multicultural Resources, 1997-1998. (Illus.). 584p. 1997. pap. 25.00 (*0-917846-83-4*) Highsmith Pr.

Boyd, Andrew. The Activist Cookbook: Creative Actions for a Fair Economy. (Illus.). 102p. 1997. 15.00 (*0-9659249-0-4*) United Fair Econo.

— An Atlas of World Affairs. 8th ed. (Illus.). 216p. 1987. 45.00 (*0-416-01172-1*, A0632); pap. 13.95 (*0-416-01182-9*, A0636) Routledge.

— Atlas of World Affairs. 10th ed. (Illus.). 256p. (C). 1998. 75.00 (*0-415-10670-2*); pap. 24.99 (*0-415-10671-0*) Routledge.

— Broadcast Journalism: Techniques of Radio & TV News. 4th ed. LC 97-7642. 400p. 1997. pap. 44.95 (*0-240-51465-3*, Focal) Buttrwrth-Heinemann.

— Life's Little Deconstruction Book: Self-Help for the Post-Hip. LC 98-34020. 160p. 1998. pap. 7.95 (*0-393-31870-2*, Norton Paperbks) Norton.

Boyd, Ann. The Devil with James Bond. LC 73-15312. 123p. 1975. reprint ed. lib. bdg. 38.50 (*0-8371-7182-2*, BOJB, Greenwood Pr) Greenwood.

Boyd, Anne. Ancient Egyptians. 16p. (YA). 1981. pap. 10.95 (*0-521-28233-0*) Cambridge U Pr.

— Life in a Medieval Monastery. 2nd ed. (Cambridge Introduction to World History Topic Bks.). (Illus.). 48p. (YA). (gr. 7 up). 1988. pap. 12.95 (*0-521-33724-0*) Cambridge U Pr.

***Boyd, Anne, ed.** NY 411 2000: A Reference Guide for Film & Television Production. 450p. 2000. pap. 49.00 (*1-879930-15-3*, Pub. by Media Pub Intl) SCB Distributors.

— TE 411: International Reference Guide for Themed Entertainment. 500p. 2000. pap. 49.00 (*1-879930-16-1*, Pub. by LA Four-Eleven) SCB Distributors.

***Boyd, Anne A.** Help Me Decide! (Illus.). (YA). 1999. pap. 13.95 (*0-673-58663-4*, GoodYrBooks) Addson-Wesley Educ.

Boyd, Anthony, ed. see Wright, Jill.

Boyd, Arrie F., jt. auth. see McClure, Peggy J.

Boyd, Arthur & Porter, Peter. Mars. (Illus.). 112p. 1989. 34.95 (*0-233-98006-7*, Pub. by Andre Deutsch) Trafalgar.

Boyd, Ashley, jt. auth. see Piprell, Collin.

Boyd, Aubrey E., 3rd, ed. The Endocrine Society Forty-Fourth Postgraduate Assembly Syllabus, 1992. (Illus.). 617p. (C). 1992. pap. text 15.00 (*1-879225-06-9*) Endocrine Soc.

Boyd, B. Exploring Jazz Scales for Keyboard. 80p. 1992. pap. 12.95 (*0-7935-1544-0*, 00221015) H Leonard.

— Intermediate Jazz Chord Voicing for Keyboard. 64p. 1991. pap. 12.95 (*0-7935-0056-7*, 00290204) H Leonard.

— Jazz Delights: Lower Intermediate Level. 32p. 1988. pap. 6.95 (*0-7935-2621-3*, 00240435) H Leonard.

— Jazz Fest: Upper Intermediate Level. 40p. 1988. pap. 6.95 (*0-7935-1996-9*, 00240436) H Leonard.

— Jazz Preliminaries: Five Finger Piano Solos. 24p. 1995. pap. 4.95 (*0-7935-4522-6*, 00290032) H Leonard.

— Jazz Starters II: Early Elementary Piano Solos. 24p. 1993. pap. 6.95 (*0-7935-2537-3*, 00290434) H Leonard.

— Jazz Starters III: Late Elementary Piano Solos. 24p. 1994. pap. 6.95 (*0-7935-3464-X*, 00290465) H Leonard.

— Jazz Starters Piano Solos: Early Elementary. 24p. 1993. pap. 6.95 (*0-7935-2359-1*, 00290425) H Leonard.

— Think Jazz, Bk. 1. 88p. 1994. pap. 10.95 (*0-7935-2318-4*, 00290417) H Leonard.

Boyd, B. & Montanari, R. The Passion. LC 97-32291. 416p. 1999. mass mkt. 6.99 (*0-380-79094-7*, Avon Bks) Morrow Avon.

Boyd, B. R. The New Abolitionists: Animal Rights & Human Liberation. rev. ed. (Illus.). 24p. 1987. 1.75 (*0-9616792-1-2*) Taterhill.

Boyd, Barbara W. Ovid's Literary Loves: Influence & Innovation in the "Amores" LC 97-24003. 264p. (C). 1997. text 42.50 (*0-472-10759-3*, 10759) U of Mich Pr.

— Vergil's Aeneid, 10 & 12: Pallas & Turnus (Teacher Edition) 1998. pap., teacher ed. 3.00 (*0-86516-428-2*) Bolchazy-Carducci.

Boyd, Barbara W., ed. see Virgil.

Boyd-Barrett, Oliver. Computers & Learning. 353p. (C). 1991. pap. 46.00 (*0-201-54411-3*) Addison-Wesley.

Boyd-Barrett, Oliver. The International News Agencies. LC 80-51779. (Communication & Society Ser.: Vol. 13). 284p. 1980. reprint ed. pap. 88.10 (*0-608-02795-2*, 206386200007) Bks Demand.

Boyd-Barrett, Oliver & Newbold, Chris, eds. Approaches to Media: A Reader. LC 95-11093. (Foundations in Media Ser.). 576p. 1995. pap. text 19.95 (*0-340-65229-2*, Pub. by E A) OUP.

— Approaches to Media: A Reader. LC 95-11093. 1995. text 69.95 (*0-340-65230-6*, Pub. by E A) St Martin.

Boyd-Barrett, Oliver & O'Malley, Pam, eds. Education Reform in Contemporary Spain. LC 94-34163. (International Developments in School Reform Ser.). 256p. (C). (gr. 13). 1995. 100.00 (*0-415-09148-9*, C0260) Routledge.

***Boyd-Barrett, Oliver & Rantanen, Tehri, eds.** The Globalization of News. LC 98-61246. 256p. 1998. pap. 27.95 (*0-7619-5387-6*) Sage.

Boyd-Barrett, Oliver & Rantanen, Terhi, eds. The Globalization of News. LC 98-61246. 230 p. 1998. write for info. (*0-7619-5386-8*) Sage.

Boyd-Barrett, Oliver, jt. auth. see Alvarado, Manuel.

Boyd-Barrett, Oliver, jt. ed. see Graddol, David.

Boyd, Belle. Belle Boyd in Camp & Prison. LC 97-43697. (Illus.). 200p. 1997. pap. 16.95 (*0-8071-2214-9*) La State U Pr.

— Belle Boyd in Camp & Prison. (American Biography Ser.). 448p. 1991. reprint ed. lib. bdg. 89.00 (*0-7812-8034-6*) Rprt Serv.

Boyd, Benjamin F. Highlights, 4 vols. (ENG & SPA.). (C). 1993. text. write for info. (*958-95544-1-5*, Pub. by Highlights Opthal) SLACK Inc.

Boyd, Bernadine. Puppets & Puppets. (Illus.). 72p. (J). 1998. pap. 14.00 (*0-8059-4394-3*) Dorrance.

Boyd, Beverly. Chaucer & the Medieval Book. LC 73-77021. (Illus.). 177p. 1973. reprint ed. pap. 54.90 (*0-7837-6675-0*, 204629100011) Bks Demand.

Boyd, Beverly, ed. see Chaucer, Geoffrey.

***Boyd, Bill.** Blind Obedience: A True Story of Family Loyalty & Murder in South Georgia. 2000. 24.95 (*0-86554-707-6*, H525) Mercer Univ Pr.

— Bolivar: Liberator of a Continent. 1999. pap. 16.95 (*1-892123-16-9*) Capital VA.

— Fat, Dumb & Happy down in Georgia. LC 99-43942. 192p. 1999. 19.95 (*0-86554-675-4*) Mercer Univ Pr.

— For Love & Glory: A Novel. 2000. 21.95 (*1-892123-17-7*) Capital VA.

— Gentle Infantryman. 2000. 22.95 (*1-892123-18-5*) Capital VA.

Boyd, Bill. Jazz Chord Progressions - Piano Method. 96p. 1997. pap. 12.95 (*0-7935-7038-7*) H Leonard.

— Jazz Keyboard Basics - Piano. 96p. 1996. pap. 12.95 (*0-7935-6670-3*) H Leonard.

— Jazz Sketches. 24p. 1996. pap. 6.95 (*0-7935-6959-1*) H Leonard.

Boyd, Billy R. Circumcision Exposed: Rethinking a Medical Cultural Tradition. rev. ed. LC 97-52376. (Illus.). 128p. 1998. pap. 14.95 (*0-89594-939-3*) Crossing Pr.

— For the Vegetarian in You. LC 87-50062. 256p. (Orig.). 1995. pap. text 12.95 (*0-7615-0123-1*) Prima Pub.

— Noise & Your Health. 32p. 1996. pap. 3.50 (*0-9616792-6-3*) Taterhill.

Boyd, Blanche. Terminal Velocity. LC 97-5825. 1997. 3.99 (*0-679-43008-3*) Knopf.

— Terminal Velocity. 272p. 1998. pap. 12.00 (*0-679-75032-0*) Vin Bks.

Boyd, Blanche M. The Redneck Way of Knowledge. 1995. pap. 10.00 (*0-679-75767-8*) Vin Bks.

— The Revolution of Little Girls. 1992. pap. 12.00 (*0-679-73812-6*) Vin Bks.

Boyd-Bowman, Peter. From Latin to Romance in Sound Charts. LC 80-11645. 134p. 1980. pap. text 12.95 (*0-87840-077-X*) Georgetown U Pr.

— Indice y Extractos del Archivo de Protocolos de Puebla de los Angeles, Mexico (1538-1556) (Colonial Spanish American Ser.: No. 1). 52p. 1988. 10.00 incl. fiche (*0-940639-26-2*) Hispanic Seminary.

— Lexico Hispanoamericano del Siglo XVI. (Monagrafias A Ser.: Vol. XVI). (SPA.). 1004p. (C). 1971. 81.00 (*0-900411-28-7*, Pub. by Tamesis Bks Ltd) Boydell & Brewer.

Boyd, Bradford B., compiled by. Supervisory Training Approaches & Methods. 162p. 8.25 (*0-318-13287-7*, BOSTP) Am Soc Train & Devel.

Boyd, Brendan. Racing Days. 88p. 1995. pap. 22.50 (*0-8050-4293-8*) H Holt & Co.

— Racing Days. 3rd ed. (Illus.). 1999. reprint ed. 35.00 (*0-9666776-1-7*, Pub. by Pond Press) Consort Bk Sales.

Boyd, Brent D., jt. auth. see Boyd, Patricia M.

***Boyd, Brian.** The Helen-Dahlonega Pocket COmpanion: Great Days Trips Within 30 Minutes of Northeast GA's Helen & Dahlonega. (Southern Appalachian Guidebook Ser.). 80p. 2000. pap. 4.95 (*1-893651-05-3*) Fern Creek Pr.

Boyd, Brian. Nabokov's Ada: The Place of Consciousness. 255p. 1985. 22.95 (*0-88233-906-0*) Ardis Pubs.

***Boyd, Brian.** Nabokov's "Pale Fire" The Magic of Artistic Discovery. LC 99-30682. 303p. 2000. 29.95 (*0-691-00959-7*, Pub. by Princeton U Pr) Cal Prin Full Svc.

Boyd, Brian. Vladimir Nabokov: The American Years. (Illus.). 783p. 1991. text 75.00 (*0-691-06797-X*, Pub. by Princeton U Pr); pap. text 19.95 (*0-691-02471-5*, Pub. by Princeton U Pr) Cal Prin Full Svc.

— Vladimir Nabokov: The Russian Years. (Illus.). 619p. 1990. pap. text 19.95 (*0-691-02470-7*, Pub. by Princeton U Pr) Cal Prin Full Svc.

— Vladimir Nabokov: The Russian Years. (Illus.). 598p. (C). 1990. text 65.00 (*0-691-06794-5*, Pub. by Princeton U Pr) Cal Prin Full Svc.

Boyd, Brian, ed. see Nabokov, Vladimir.

Boyd, Brian, ed. & illus. see Wheeler, Tony.

Boyd, Brian A. Chattooga Wild & Scenic River. 3rd rev. ed. (Illus.). 132p. 1998. pap. 9.95 (*0-9625737-9-5*) Fern Creek Pr.

— The Highlands - Cashiers Outdoors Companion. rev. ed. (Southern Appalachian Guidebooks Ser.). (Illus.). 88p. (Orig.). 1998. pap. 7.95 (*0-9625737-6-0*) Fern Creek Pr.

— The Rabun County Outdoors Companion. 2nd ed. (Illus.). 112p. 1996. pap. 7.95 (*0-9625737-7-9*) Fern Creek Pr.

— Summits of the South: A Visitor's Guide to Twenty-Five Southern Appalachian Peaks. (Illus.). 112p. (Orig.). 1993. pap. text 8.95 (*0-9625737-5-2*) Fern Creek Pr.

— The Tallulah Falls Railroad: A Photographic Remembrance. (Illus.). 64p. 1998. pap. 11.95 (*1-893651-00-2*) Fern Creek Pr.

— Waterfalls of the Southern Appalachians. 3rd rev. ed. (Illus.). 162p. 1998. pap. 9.95 (*0-9625737-8-7*) Fern Creek Pr.

— Yesterday's Rabun: A Collection of Historic Images from Rabun County, GA. (Illus.). 116p. 1998. pap. 11.95 (*1-893651-01-0*) Fern Creek Pr.

Boyd, Brian A., ed. see Howell, Don.

Boyd, Brian E. When You Were Born in Korea: A Memory Book for Children Adopted from Korea. 44p. 1993. 16.00 (*0-9638472-0-1*) Yeong & Yeong.

Boyd, Bruce, ed. Long-Term Care: Knowing the Risk, Paying the Price. LC 97-176580. 248p. 1997. pap. text 30.00 (*1-879143-34-8*) Health Ins Assn Am.

Boyd, Bruce, et al. Iron Ore 2000: Poised for the Next Century. LC 98-180163. ix, 128p. 1997. write for info. (*0-662-25626-3*, Pub. by Minerva Pr) Unity Dist.

Boyd-Buggs, Debra & Scott, Joyce Hope. Camel Tracks: Critical Perspectives on Sahelian Literatures LC 99-15524. 1999. write for info. (*0-86543-757-2*) Africa World.

Boyd, Byron A. Rudolf Virchow: The Scientist As Citizen. LC 91-12024. (Modern European History Outstanding Studies & Dissertations). 286p. 1991. text 20.00 (*0-8153-0412-9*) Garland.

Boyd, C. E. Water Quality Management for Pond Fish Culture. (Developments in Aquaculture & Fisheries Science Ser.: Vol. 9). xii,318p. 1982. 162.00 (*0-444-42054-1*) Elsevier.

Boyd, Candy D. Charlie Pippin. 192p. (J). (gr. 3-7). 1988. pap. 4.99 (*0-14-032587-5*, PuffinBks) Peng Put Young Read.

Boyd, Candy D. Charlie Pippin. (J). 1987. 10.09 (*0-606-03752-7*, Pub. by Turtleback) Demco.

Boyd, Candy D. Circle of Gold. LC 85-101897. 128p. (Orig.). (J). (gr. 4-7). 1996. pap. 3.99 (*0-590-43266-4*, Apple Paperbacks) Scholastic Inc.

— A Different Beat. (J). (gr. 3-7). 1996. pap. 3.99 (*0-614-15701-3*, PuffinBks) Peng Put Young Read.

— Forever Friends. (Novels Ser.). 192p. (J). (gr. 5-9). 1986. pap. 4.99 (*0-14-032077-6*, PuffinBks) Peng Put Young Read.

— Kwaanza Storybook. (Orig.). (J). 1999. pap. 12.99 (*0-670-86160-X*) Viking Penguin.

An Asterisk (*) at the beginning of an entry indicates that the title is appearing for the first time.

Boyd, Candy Dawson. Chevrolet Saturdays. LC 94-30185. 192p. (J). (gr. 3-7). 1995. pap. 4.99 (*0-14-036859-0*, Puffin Bks) Peng Put Young Read.

— Chevrolet Saturdays. LC 92-32119. 192p. (J). (gr. 3-7). 1993. lib. bdg. 16.00 (*0-02-711765-0*, Mac Bks Young Read) S&S Childrens.

— Chevrolet Saturdays. (J). 1995. 9.09 (*0-606-07361-2*, Pub. by Turtleback) Demco.

Boyd, Candy Dawson. Circle of Gold. 1984. 9.09 (*0-606-05061-2*, Pub. by Turtleback) Demco.

Boyd, Candy Dawson. Different Beat. LC 95-49569. 1996. 10.09 (*0-606-09190-4*, Pub. by Turtleback) Demco.

Boyd, Carl. American Command of the Sea Through Carriers, Codes, & the Silent Service: World War II & Beyond. (Illus.). 80p. 1995. pap. 13.95 (*0-917376-43-9*) Mariners Mus.

— Hitler's Japanese Confidant: General Oshima Hiroshi & Magic Intelligence, 1941-1945. LC 92-28142. (Modern War Studies). (Illus.). xxii, 272p. 1993. 29.95 (*0-7006-0569-X*) U Pr of KS.

Boyd, Carol, ed. see Martin-McRae, Bettye.

Boyd, Carole & Good, James, readers. Sleepy Songs & Stories. abr. ed. (J). mass mkt. incl. audio (*1-84032-046-X*) HOD2.

Boyd, Carolyn O., jt. ed. see Munhall, Patricia L.

Boyd, Carolyn P. Historia Patria: Politics, History, & National Identity in Spain, 1875-1975. LC 96-45261. 384p. 1997. text 49.50 (*0-691-02656-4*, Pub. by Princeton U Pr) Cal Prin Full Svc.

Boyd, Celia, ed. Blueprints Organizer. rev. ed. (Illus.). 39p. 1991. 9.95 (*1-57896-014-2*, 1011) Hewitt Res Fnd.

Boyd, Charles D. Individual Commitment & Organizational Change: A Guide for Human Resource & Organization Development Specialists. LC 91-31556. 240p. 1992. 55.00 (*0-89930-641-1*, BIO/, Quorum Bks) Greenwood.

Boyd, Charles D., jt. auth. see Denton, D. Keith.

Boyd, Charles D., jt. auth. see Tilson, M. David.

Boyd, Charles E. At Liberty on Bear Creek, 1835-1985. 1984. 14.95 (*0-685-09685-8*); pap. 9.95 (*0-685-09686-6*) Banner Pr AL.

— Devil's Den, at Gettysburg: Forty-Fourth Alabama Regiment (Confederate), Its Action, Roster, & Family Connections. 1987. pap. 19.95 (*0-685-10283-1*); text 26.95 (*0-87121-445-8*) Banner Pr AL.

Boyd, Charles F. Different Children, Different Needs: The Art of Adjustable Parenting. LC 94-21370. 219p. 1994. pap. 12.99 (*0-88070-685-6*) Multnomah Pubs.

***Boyd, Charles F., et al.** Different Children, Different Needs. (Illus.). 219p. 2000. pap. 10.99 (*1-57673-750-0*) Multnomah Pubs.

Boyd, Charles W. Your Legacy from Thaddeus Stevens Republican of the First Time. 206p. 1987. pap. 15.00 (*0-318-23880-2*) Bomax Pubs.

***Boyd, Claude E.** Water Quality: An Introduction. LC 00-31337. 2000. write for info. (*0-7923-7853-9*) Kluwer Academic.

Boyd, Claude E. & Tucker, C. S. Pond Aquaculture Water Quality Management. LC 97-48251. 720p. 1998. write for info. (*0-412-07181-9*) Kluwer Academic.

Boyd, Claude E., jt. auth. see Egna, Hillary S.

Boyd, Colin. Information Security & Privacy: 3rd Australasian Conference, ACISP '98, Brisbane, Australia, July 13-15, 1998, Proceedings. Lotasch, H. K. et al, eds. LC 98-35424. (Lecture Notes in Computer Science Ser.: Vol. 1438). xi, 423p. 1998. pap. 67.00 (*3-540-64732-5*) Spr-Verlag.

***Boyd, Colin, et al.** Information Security & Privacy: 5th Australasian Conference, Acisp '2000, Brisbane, Australia, July 10-12, 2000 Proceedings. LC 00-55630. (Lectures Notes in Computer Science). 2000. pap. write for info. (*3-540-67742-9*) Spr-Verlag.

Boyd, D. H. Leith Hospital. 180p. 1989. 40.00 (*0-7073-0584-5*, Pub. by Mercat Pr Bks) St Mut.

Boyd, Daniel R. & Lewis, Stephen D. Secretarial Administration & Management. (Illus.). 550p. (C). 1985. student ed. 8.95 (*0-13-798315-8*) P-H.

Boyd, Daniel R., et al. Federal Taxation of Partners & Partnerships. (Illus.). 384p. (C). 1986. text 51.95 (*0-13-313479-2*) P-H.

Boyd, David. Film & the Interpretive Process: A Study of Blow-up, Rashomon, 8 1 2, Vertigo, & Persona. (Ars Medica Ser.). 246p. (C). 1989. text 41.95 (*0-8204-0987-1*) P Lang Pubng.

— Silent Songs. (Illus.). 112p. 1998. pap. 14.00 (*0-8059-4257-2*) Dorrance.

Boyd, David, ed. Perspectives on Alfred Hitchcock. LC 94-35398. (Perspectives on Film Ser.). 200p. 1995. 55.00 (*0-8161-1603-2*, G K Hall & Co) Mac Lib Ref.

— Rereading Frye: The Published & the Unpublished Works. (Illus.). 163p. 1999. pap. text 26.95 (*0-8020-8094-4*) U of Toronto Pr.

Boyd, David. Moby Dick: or The Catfish. LC 98-66373. (Trailer Park Classics Ser.: Vol. 1). 80p. 1998. pap. 8.95 (*1-56352-530-5*) Longstreet.

Boyd, David & Salusinszky, Imre, eds. Rereading Frye: The Published & the Unpublished Works. 352p. 1999. text 65.00 (*0-8020-4252-X*) U of Toronto Pr.

Boyd, David, jt. auth. see Katz, Michael.

Boyd, David C. & MacDowell, John F., eds. Commercial Glasses. LC 86-10723. (Advances in Ceramics Ser.: No. 18). (Illus.). 238p. reprint ed. pap. 73.80 (*0-7837-4335-1*, 204404600012) Bks Demand.

Boyd, David R., jt. ed. see Wren, Daniel A.

Boyd-Davis, Edna, jt. auth. see Johnson, Joyce Young.

Boyd, Dawn, jt. auth. see Barros-Bailey, Mary.

Boyd, Deidre. Element Guide: Addictions: Your Questions Answered. LC 97-45122. 1998. pap. 9.95 (*1-86204-180-6*, Pub. by Element MA) Penguin Putnam.

Boyd, Derick A. Economic Management, Income Distribution, & Poverty in Jamaica. LC 87-36140. 172p. 1988. 47.95 (*0-275-92651-6*, C2651, Praeger Pubs) Greenwood.

***Boyd, Donald B.** Reviews in Computational Chemistry, Vol. 12. Lipkowitz, Kenny B., ed. (Reviews in Computational Chemistry Ser.). 432p. 1998. 139.00 (*0-471-24671-9*) Wiley.

Boyd, Donald B. & Lipkowitz, Kenneth B. Reviews in Computational Chemistry, Vol. 4. 280p. 1993. 110.00 (*1-56081-620-1*, Wiley-VCH) Wiley.

— Reviews in Computational Chemistry, Vol. 5. 458p. 1994. 110.00 (*1-56081-658-9*, Wiley-VCH) Wiley.

Boyd, Donald B. & Lipkowitz, Kenneth B., eds. Reviews in Computational Chemistry, Vol. 3. LC 92-30192. 272p. 1993. 110.00 (*1-56081-619-8*, Wiley-VCH) Wiley.

— Reviews in Computational Chemistry, Vol. 7. 7th ed. (Illus.). 585p. 1995. 110.00 (*1-56081-915-4*, Wiley-VCH) Wiley.

— Reviews in Computational Chemistry, Vol. 8. (Illus.). 350p. 1996. 110.00 (*1-56081-929-4*, Wiley-VCH) Wiley.

— Reviews in Computational Chemistry, Vol. 9. (Illus.). 300p. 1996. 110.00 (*1-56081-930-8*, Wiley-VCH) Wiley.

Boyd, Donald B., jt. auth. see Lipkowitz, Kenny B.

Boyd, Donald B., jt. ed. see Lipkowitz, Kenneth B.

Boyd, Donald B., jt. ed. see Lipkowitz, Kenny B.

Boyd, Donald B., jt. ed. see Lipowitz, K. B.

***Boyd, Donald W.** Systems Analysis & Modeling: A Macro-To-Micro Approach with Multidisciplinary Applications. 400p. 2000. 79.95 (*0-12-121851-1*) Acad Pr.

Boyd, Donna. The Passion. LC 97-32291. 400p. 1998. mass mkt. 15.95 (*0-380-97449-5*, Avon Bks) Morrow Avon.

***Boyd, Donna.** Promise. 2000. mass mkt. 6.99 (*0-380-79096-3*) Morrow Avon.

— The Promise, Vol. 1. LC 99-20949. 352p. 1999. 23.00 (*0-380-97450-9*, Avon Bks) Morrow Avon.

Boyd, Donna, ed. see Morrison, Susan, et al.

Boyd, Doug. Mad Bear. 368p. 1994. pap. 12.00 (*0-671-75945-0*, Touchstone) S&S Trade Pap.

— Mystics, Magicians & Medicine People: Tales of a Wanderer. 173p. (C). 1995. pap. 11.95 (*1-56924-880-X*) Marlowe & Co.

— Swami: Encounters with Modern Mystics. LC 95-121381. 330p. 1995. pap. 17.95 (*0-89389-142-8*) Himalayan Inst.

Boyd, Douglas, jt. auth. see Ben-Tovim, Atarah.

***Boyd, Douglas R.** Broadcasting in the Arab World: A Survey of the Electronic Media in the Middle East. 3rd ed. LC 99-37250. (Illus.). 412p. 1999. 59.95 (*0-8138-0467-1*) Iowa St U Pr.

Boyd, E. H. L. Mencken. LC 74-1446. (American Literature Ser.: No. 49). 1974. lib. bdg. 55.00 (*0-8383-2038-4*) M S G Haskell Hse.

— New Mexico Santos: Religious Images in the Spanish New World. (Illus.). 64p. 1995. pap. 12.95 (*0-89013-284-4*) Museum NM Pr.

— Saints & Saintmakers of New Mexico. (Illus.). 124p. 1997. pap. text 24.95 (*1-889921-02-5*) Western Edge Pr.

Boyd, E., jt. auth. see De Borhegyi, Stephen F.

Boyd, E. W. English Cathedrals: Their Architecture, Symbolism & History (1883) 68p. 1996. reprint ed. pap. 12.00 (*1-56459-546-3*) Kessinger Pub.

Boyd, Eddie L., et al. Home Remedies & the Black Elderly: A Reference Manual for Health Care Providers. 26p. (C). 1991. reprint ed. pap. 9.95 (*0-9631310-0-1*) Pharm Info.

Boyd, Edith. The Growth of the Surface Area of the Human Body, Vol. 10. LC 75-14249. (University of Minnesota Institute of Child Welfare Monographs: No. 10). (Illus.). 145p. 1970. reprint ed. lib. bdg. 45.00 (*0-8371-8069-4*, CWBS, Greenwood Pr) Greenwood.

Boyd, Edward K., jt. auth. see Boyd, Gregory A.

Boyd, Edward M. Alaska Broker. LC 88-72058. (Illus.). 364p. (Orig.). 1988. pap. 13.95 (*0-8323-0464-6*) Binford Mort.

Boyd, Eric. Mike & Me. 2nd ed. 1996. mass mkt. 5.95 (*1-56333-419-4*, Badboy) Masquerade.

— Mike & the Marines. 2nd ed. 1997. reprint ed. mass mkt. 6.50 (*1-56333-497-6*, Badboy) Masquerade.

Boyd, Eric L. Demihuman Deities. 192p. 1998. 24.95 (*0-7869-1239-1*, Pub. by TSR Inc) Random.

— Powers & Pantheons Lorebook. (Forgotten Realms Game World Ser.). 1997. 21.95 (*0-7869-0657-X*, Pub. by TSR Inc) Random.

Boyd, Ernest, tr. see D'Aurevilly, Barbey.

Boyd, Ernest A. Appreciations & Depreciations: Irish Literary Studies. LC 68-16913. (Essay Index Reprint Ser.). 1977. 18.95 (*0-8369-0235-1*) Ayer.

— Literary Blasphemies. LC 76-90472. 265p. 1970. reprint ed. lib. bdg. 65.00 (*0-8371-2516-2*, BOLB, Greenwood Pr) Greenwood.

— Literary Blasphemies. (BCL1-PR English Literature Ser.). 265p. 1992. reprint ed. lib. bdg. 79.00 (*0-7812-7008-1*) Rprt Serv.

— Portraits. LC 79-93318. (Essay Index Reprint Ser.). 1977. 21.95 (*0-8369-1274-8*) Ayer.

— Portraits: Real & Imaginary. LC 77-126702. (BCL Ser. I). reprint ed. 31.50 (*0-404-00965-4*) AMS Pr.

— Portraits: Real & Imaginary. LC 71-131641. 1970. reprint ed. 8.00 (*0-403-00528-0*) Scholarly.

— Studies from Ten Literatures. LC 68-20287. (Essay Index Reprint Ser.). 1977. 23.95 (*0-8369-0236-X*) Ayer.

Boyd, Ernest A., ed. see Maupassant, Guy de.

Boyd, Ernest A., tr. see Maupassant, Guy de.

Boyd, Eva J. Noble Brutes: Camels on the American Frontier. LC 94-12228. 278p. 1994. pap. 12.95 (*1-55622-379-X*, Rep of TX Pr) Wordware Pub.

— That Old Overland Stagecoaching. (Illus.). 224p. (Orig.). 1992. pap. 12.95 (*1-55622-250-5*, Rep of TX Pr) Wordware Pub.

— Wagon Tongues & the North Star: Tales of the Cattle Trails. 1997. pap. 14.95 (*1-55622-535-0*, Rep of TX Pr) Wordware Pub.

***Boyd, Eva Jolene.** Native Dancer. (Thoroughbred Legends Ser.: Vol. 6). 144p. 2000. 24.95 (*1-58150-048-3*, Pub. by Blood-Horse) IPG Chicago.

Boyd, F. R. & Meyer, H. O., eds. Mantle Sample: Inclusions in Kimberlites & Other Volcanics: Proceedings of the Second International Kimberline Conference, Vol. 2. (Illus.). 424p. 1979. 25.00 (*0-87590-213-8*) Am Geophysical.

Boyd, Frances. Making Business Decisions: Real Cases from Real Companies. 176p. (C). 1994. pap. text 25.65 (*0-201-59281-9*) Addison-Wesley.

— Making Business Decisions: Real Cases from Real Companies. LC 93-34169. 1994. pap. text. write for info. (*0-8013-0821-6*) Longman.

Boyd, Frances & Quinn, David. Stories from Lake Wobegon: Advanced Listening & Conversation Skills. (Illus.). 184p. (YA). 1990. pap. text 23.45 (*0-8013-0312-5*, 78017) Longman.

Boyd, Frank M. Baptized in the Spirit. (Spiritual Discovery Ser.). (Illus.). 128p. 1996. pap., teacher ed. 9.95 (*0-88243-211-7*, 02-0211) Gospel Pub.

— Baptized in the Spirit. (Spiritual Discovery Ser.). (Illus.). 96p. 1996. pap. 4.95 (*0-88243-111-0*, 02-0111) Gospel Pub.

Boyd-Franklin, Nancy. Black Families in Therapy: A Multisystems Approach. LC 88-24416. 274p. 1989. lib. bdg. 34.00 (*0-89862-735-4*) Guilford Pubns.

Boyd-Franklin, Nancy, et al, eds. Children, Families & HIV/AIDS: Psychosocial & Therapeutic Issues. LC 93-34761. 334p. 1995. pap. text 24.00 (*0-89862-502-5*) Guilford Pubns.

***Boyd-Franklin, Nancy & Bry, Brenna Hafer.** Reaching Out in Family Therapy: Home-Based, School & Community Interventions. LC 99-49066. 220p. 1999. lib. bdg. 30.00 (*1-57230-519-3*, CO519) Guilford Pubns.

***Boyd-Franklin, Nancy, et al.** Boys into Men: Raising Our African American Teenage Sons. LC 99-57187. 272p. 2000. text 23.95 (*0-525-94496-6*, Dutt) Dutton Plume.

Boyd, Gary. Coping with Surgery: A Guide to Self Help. 56p. (Orig.). 1990. pap. 6.95 (*0-910467-09-9*) Heritage Assocs.

Boyd, Gary W., et al. Sustaining the Wings: A Fifty-Year History of Sheppard Air Force Base: 1941-1991. (Illus.). 160p. 1991. 20.00 (*0-915323-04-4*) Midwestern St U Pr.

Boyd, Gavin. Region Building in the Pacific. (Policy Studies on International Politics). 280p. 1982. 74.00 (*0-08-025985-5*, Pergamon Pr) Elsevier.

— Structuring International Economic Cooperation. LC 90-19782. 250p. 1991. text 49.95 (*0-312-05802-0*) St Martin.

Boyd, Gavin, ed. Competitive & Cooperative Macromanagement: The Challenges of Structural Interdependence. LC 95-6827. (New Horizons in International Business Ser.). (Illus.). 288p. 1995. 95.00 (*1-85898-144-1*) E Elgar.

— Structural Competitiveness in the Pacific: Corporate & State Rivalries. LC 95-49729. (New Horizons in International Business Ser.). (Illus.). 328p. 1996. 95.00 (*1-85898-233-2*) E Elgar.

— The Struggle for World Markets: Competition & Cooperation Between NAFTA & the European Union. LC 97-18422. (New Horizons in International Business Ser.). 264p. 1998. 90.00 (*1-85898-549-8*) E Elgar.

Boyd, Gavin & Dunning, John H., eds. Structural Change & Cooperation in the Global Economy. LC 98-27889. (New Horizons in International Business Ser.). 320p. 1999. 85.00 (*1-85898-754-7*) E Elgar.

Boyd, Gavin & Rugman, Alan M., eds. Euro-Pacific Investment & Trade: Strategies & Structural Interdependencies. LC 96-23172. (New Horizons in International Business Ser.). (Illus.). 320p. (C). 1997. 95.00 (*1-85898-368-1*) E Elgar.

Boyd, Gavin, jt. auth. see Cohen, Stephen S.

Boyd, Gavin, jt. ed. see Brewer, Thomas L.

Boyd, Gavin, jt. ed. see Rugman, Alan M.

Boyd, Gayle M., et al, eds. Alcohol Problems among Adolescents: Current Directions in Prevention Research. 264p. 1995. text 39.95 (*0-8058-1915-0*) L Erlbaum Assocs.

***Boyd, George E.** Consecrated Ground. 72p. 2000. pap. 10.95 (*0-921368-91-7*) Blizzard Publ.

Boyd, Gerald Lee, jt. auth. see Shiraev, Eric.

Boyd, Ginger. When Mommy Gets Sick. (Illus.). 32p. (J). (gr. 3-5). 1998. pap. 11.99 (*1-57532-180-7*) Press-Tige Pub.

Boyd, Glenn. The A. R. T. of Agape-Listening: The Miracle of Mutuality. LC 97-153684. 110p. (Orig.). 1996. pap. 9.95 (*0-9652743-0-6*) Agape Hse Pr.

Boyd, Greg. Carnival Aptitude: Being an Exuberance in Short Prose & Photomautage. LC 93-70302. (Illus.). 120p. 1993. pap. 9.95 (*1-878580-47-7*) Asylum Arts.

***Boyd, Greg.** Modern Love: And Other Tall Tales. 112p. (Orig.). 2000. pap. 11.95 (*1-888996-22-6*, Red Hen Press) Valentine CA.

Boyd, Greg. Sacred Hearts. LC 96-76622. 128p. 1996. pap. 13.00 (*1-57650-049-7*) Hi Jinx Pr.

— Water & Power: And Other Stories. LC 90-83543. 128p. 1999. reprint ed. pap. 12.00 (*1-878580-33-7*) Asylum Arts.

Boyd, Greg, ed. Asylum Annual, 1993. (Illus.). 160p. (Orig.). 1993. pap. 12.95 (*1-878580-17-5*) Asylum Arts.

— Asylum Annual, 1994. (Illus.). 160p. (Orig.). 1994. pap. 12.95 (*1-878580-51-5*) Asylum Arts.

— Asylum Annual 1995. (Illus.). 160p. (Orig.). 1995. pap. 12.95 (*1-878580-95-7*) Asylum Arts.

— Unscheduled Departures: The Asylum Anthology of Short Fiction. LC 90-86266. 112p. (Orig.). 1991. pap. 7.95 (*1-878580-11-6*) Asylum Arts.

Boyd, Gregory A. Cynic Sage or Son of God? LC 95-8773. 416p. (C). 1996. pap. text 17.99 (*0-8010-2118-9*, Bridgept Bks) Baker Bks.

— God at War: The Bible & Spiritual Conflict. LC 96-29821. 412p. (Orig.). 1997. pap. 19.99 (*0-8308-1885-5*, 1885) InterVarsity.

***Boyd, Gregory A.** God of the Possible: A Biblical Introduction to the Open View of God. 176p. 2000. pap. 12.99 (*0-8010-6290-X*) Baker Bks.

Boyd, Gregory A. Jesus under Siege. 144p. 1995. pap. 5.99 (*1-56476-533-4*, 6-3533, Victor Bks) Chariot Victor.

— Oneness Pentecostals & the Trinity. LC 91-48111. (Christian Research Institute Ser.). 240p. 1992. pap. 16.99 (*0-8010-1019-5*) Baker Bks.

— Trinity & Process: A Critical Examination & Reconstruction of Hartshorne's Di-Polar Theism Towards a Trinitarian Metaphysics. LC 91-37789. (American University Studies: Theology & Religion: Ser. VII, Vol. 119). 424p. (C). 1992. text 60.95 (*0-8204-1660-6*) P Lang Pubng.

Boyd, Gregory A. & Boyd, Edward K. Letters from a Skeptic. LC 93-33314. 180p. 1993. 10.99 (*1-56476-244-0*, 6-3244, Victor Bks) Chariot Victor.

Boyd, Gwen. Nashville after Sunset: Nashville Nightlife & Southern Bartending. LC 97-163309. (Illus.). 260p. 1997. pap. 9.95 (*0-9657643-0-3*) After Sunset.

Boyd, Harper W. & Walker, Orville C. Marketing Management. 3rd ed. LC 97-22528. 608p. (C). 1997. text 58.95 (*0-256-22632-6*, Irwn McGrw-H) McGrw-H Hghr Educ.

Boyd, Harper W., Jr., et al. CPS Marketing Essentials for the University of Tennessee MBA Core. 2nd ed. 704p. (C). 1995. text 65.95 (*0-256-21128-0*, Irwn McGrw-H) McGrw-H Hghr Educ.

Boyd, Harper W., et al. Marketing Management: A Strategic Approach with a Global Orientation. 2nd ed. LC 94-20955. (Marketing Ser.). 576p. (C). 1994. text 58.95 (*0-256-12576-7*, Irwn Prfssnl) McGraw-Hill Prof.

— Marketing Management: A Strategic Approach with a Global Orientation. 3rd ed. LC 97-22528. 1997. write for info. (*0-07-115429-9*) McGraw.

Boyd, Harper W., Jr., et al. Marketing Strategy, International: Planning & Implementation. (C). 1991. text, student ed. 32.50 (*0-256-11271-1*, Irwn McGrw-H) McGrw-H Hghr Educ.

Boyd, Helen M. The True Horoscope of the U. S. LC 75-7188. 1975. 14.95 (*0-88231-007-0*) ASI Pubs Inc.

Boyd, Helen S. Washington Inscription on All Stones Still Standing in Cemeteries in the Town of Washington, Connecticut. 105p. 1997. reprint ed. pap. 15.00 (*0-8328-5691-6*) Higginson Bk Co.

Boyd, Herb. African History for Beginners Part 1: African Dawn - A Diasporan View. (Writers & Readers Documentary Comic Bks.). (Illus.). 192p. (Orig.). 1991. pap. 9.95 (*0-86316-144-8*) Writers & Readers.

***Boyd, Herb.** Autobiography of a People. 2001. reprint ed. pap. 15.00 (*0-385-49279-0*, Anchor NY) Doubleday.

Boyd, Herb. Black Panthers for Beginners. (Illus.). 192p. 1995. pap. 11.00 (*0-86316-196-0*) Writers & Readers.

— Brotherman: The Odyssey of Black Men in America-An Anthology. 1999. pap. text 19.95 (*0-345-91505-4*) Ballantine Pub Grp.

— Down the Glory Road. LC 94-32027. 320p. (Orig.). 1995. pap. 12.50 (*0-380-77523-9*, Avon Bks) Morrow Avon.

***Boyd, Herb, ed.** Autobiography of a People: Three Centuries of African-American History Told by Those Who Lived It. LC 99-16576. 576p. 2000. 27.50 (*0-385-49278-2*) Doubleday.

Boyd, Herb & Allen, Robert. Brotherman: The Odyssey of Black Men in America - Anthology. 960p. 1996. pap. 19.95 (*0-345-38317-6*) Ballantine Pub Grp.

Boyd, Hilary. The Step-Parent's Survival Guide. LC 98-177848. 160p. 1998. pap. 14.95 (*0-7063-7732-X*) Sterling.

Boyd, Howard P. A Field Guide to the Pine Barrens of New Jersey: Its Flora, Ecology & Historical Sites. (Illus.). 423p. 1991. 32.95 (*0-937548-18-9*); pap. 22.95 (*0-937548-19-7*) Plexus Pub.

— A Pine Barrens Odyssey: A Naturalist's Year in the Pine Barrens of New Jersey. LC 97-22070. (Illus.). 275p. 1997. pap. 19.95 (*0-937548-34-0*) Plexus Pub.

***Boyd, Howard P.** Wildflowers of the Pine Barrens of New Jersey. (Illus.). 2000. pap. 19.95 (*0-937548-45-6*) Plexus Pub.

Boyd, I. L., jt. auth. see Boyd, J. M.

Boyd, I. W. Laser Processing of Thin Films & Microstructures. (Materials Science Ser.: Vol. 3). 310p. 1987. 75.95 (*0-387-17951-8*) Spr-Verlag.

***Boyd, I. W.** Surface Processing: Laser, Lamp, Plasma: Proceedings of Symposium G on Surface Processing: Laser, Lamp, Plasma of the E-MRS Spring Conference, Strasbourg, France, 16-19 June 1998. LC 99-209826. (European Materials Research Society Symposia Proceedings Ser.). 672p. 1999. 190.50 (*0-08-043610-2*) Elsevier.

Boyd, I. W. & Jackman, R. B., eds. Photochemical Processing of Electronic Materials. (Illus.). 531p. 1991. text 205.00 (*0-12-121740-X*) Acad Pr.

Boyd, Ian. Calculator Games. 1997. pap. 7.95 (*0-8167-4224-3*) Troll Communs.

— Lots of Knots. (Illus.). 24p. (Orig.). (J). (gr. 3-7). 1996. pap. 5.95 (*0-8167-4066-6*) Troll Communs.

— Outrageous 3-D Big Bugs. LC 98-125650. (Illus.). 24p. (J). (ps-3). 1998. pap. 4.95 (*0-8167-4354-1*) Troll Communs.

— Outrageous 3-D Deadly Hunters. (Illus.). 24p. (J). (ps-3). 1999. pap. 4.95 (*0-8167-4960-4*) Troll Communs.

— Outrageous 3-D Outer Space. (Illus.). 24p. (J). (ps-3). 1998. pap. 4.95 (*0-8167-4959-0*) Troll Communs.

***Boyd, Ian.** Slime Lab Science. (Illus.). 16p. 2000. pap. 8.95 (*0-8167-6606-1*) Troll Communs.

An Asterisk (*) at the beginning of an entry indicates that the title is appearing for the first time.

Boyd, Ian. Super Stunts: World's Best Paper Airplanes. (Illus.). 32p. (J). (gr. 3-7). 1998. pap. 4.95 (*0-8167-4549-8*) Troll Communs.

— 3-D Outrageous Reptiles. (Illus.). 24p. (Orig.). (J). (ps-3). 1996. pap. 4.95 (*0-8167-4142-5*) Troll Communs.

— When Pigs Fly. (J). 1997. pap. 5.95 (*0-8167-4212-X*) Troll Communs.

***Boyd, Ian.** World-Record Super Stunts: Make 10 Fantastic Flyers. 32p. (J). (gr. 3-7). 1999. pap. 4.95 (*0-8167-6345-3*) Troll Communs.

Boyd, Imagene G. The Guthery Family of Cullman County, Alabama. 3rd rev. ed. 441p. 1990. pap. 25.00 (*0-9600502-1-3*) Ima Boyd.

Boyd, Imagene G., ed. see Guthery, Ernest M.

Boyd, J. Caleb, ed. see Griffith, Benjamin, et al.

Boyd, J. D. Biophysical Control of Microfibril Orientation in Plant Cell Walls. (Forestry Sciences Ser.). 1985. text 147.00 (*90-247-3101-1*) Kluwer Academic.

Boyd, J. D., jt. auth. see Garvin, J. W.

Boyd, J. I. Narrow Gauge Railways in Mid-Wales (1850-1970) 304p. (C). 1985. 50.00 (*0-85361-024-X*) St Mut.

— Narrow Gauge Railways in North Caernarvonshire Vol. 1: West. 282p. (C). 1985. 50.00 (*0-85361-273-0*) St Mut.

— Narrow Gauge Railways in North Caernarvonshire Vol. 2: Penrhyn Quarry Railways. 176p. (C). 1985. 50.00 (*0-85361-312-5*) St Mut.

— Narrow Gauge Railways in North Caernarvonshire Vol. 3: Dinorwic Quarries & Others. 240p. (C). 1985. 39.00 (*0-85361-328-1*) St Mut.

Boyd, J. M. & Boyd, I. L. The Hebrides: A Habitable Land. (Hebrides Ser.). (Illus.). 136p. pap. 16.95 (*1-874744-55-6*, Pub. by Birlinn Ltd) Dufour.

— The Hebrides: A Mosaic of Islands. (Hebrides Ser.). (Illus.). 148p. pap. 16.95 (*1-874744-57-2*, Pub. by Birlinn Ltd) Dufour.

— The Hebrides: A Natural Tapestry. (Hebrides Ser.). (Illus.). 220p. pap. 18.95 (*1-874744-56-4*, Pub. by Birlinn Ltd) Dufour.

Boyd, J. Morton. Fraser Darling's Islands. 208p. 1986. 25.00 (*0-85224-514-9*, Pub. by Edinburgh U Pr) Col U Pr.

Boyd, Jack. Encore: A Guide to Enjoying Music. 1991. 22.95 incl. audio (*1-55934-062-2*, 1062); 37.95 incl. audio compact disk (*1-55934-101-7*, 1101) Mayfield Pub.

Boyd, Jack. Rehearsal Guide for the Choral Director. LC 77-2051. (C). 1977. reprint ed. pap. text 16.95 (*0-916656-03-9*, MFBK 03) Mark Foster Mus.

— Teaching Choral Sight Reading. LC 75-12658. 209p. 1981. reprint ed. pap. text 16.95 (*0-916656-17-9*, MFBK 17) Mark Foster Mus.

Boyd, James. Drums. LC 95-14812. (Illus.). 432p. (YA). (gr. 7 up). 1995. mass mkt. 25.00 (*0-689-80176-9*) Atheneum Yung Read.

— Elements of English Composition, 1700-1900: Grammatical, Rhetorical, Logical, & Practical. LC 98-41370. (American Linguistics Ser.). 1998. write for info. (*0-8201-1517-7*) Schol Facsimiles.

— The Era of Goethe: Essays Presented to James Boyd. 1977. 20.95 (*0-8369-0418-4*) Ayer.

— Goethe's Knowledge of English Literature. LC 72-6894. (Studies in German Literature: No. 13). 320p. 1972. reprint ed. lib. bdg. 75.00 (*0-8383-1637-9*) M S G Haskell Hse.

— Onion Chronicles, Pt. 1. 1988. pap. 10.00 (*0-938645-10-2*) In His Steps.

— Roll River. 1993. reprint ed. lib. bdg. 89.00 (*0-7812-5431-0*) Rprt Serv.

Boyd, James C., jt. auth. see Harris, Eugene K.

Boyd, James E. Faith Is Sort of Like This. (Illus.). 64p. (Orig.). 1986. pap. 9.95 (*1-55630-012-3*) Brentwood Comm.

Boyd, James H., et al. Carcinoma of the Supraglottic Larynx. (Self-Instructional Package Ser.). (Illus.). 77p. 1993. pap. text 25.00 (*1-56772-008-0*) AAO-HNS.

Boyd, James P. Boyd's Bible Dictionary. Orig. Title: Vest Pocket Bible Dictionary. 1979. pap. 5.99 (*0-87981-087-4*) Broadman.

Boyd, James R. The Bible Method of Daily Living: On the Basis of Discourses by Matthew Henry, V. D. M., the Celebrated English Commentator. LC 97-39104. 1998. 10.00 (*1-57683-088-8*) NavPress.

Boyd, James S. Buildings for Small Acreages: Farm, Ranch, & Recreation. 2nd ed. (Illus.). 287p. 1996. pap. text 36.25 (*0-8134-2973-0*) Interstate.

— Practical Farm Buildings: A Text & Handbook. 3rd ed. LC 78-179872. 1993. teacher ed. 9.95 (*0-8134-2964-1*); pap. 43.75 (*0-8134-2940-4*, 2054) Interstate.

Boyd, James W. & Kotwal, Firoze M. A Guide to the Zoroastrian Religion: A Nineteenth-Century Catechism with Modern Commentary. LC 82-3236. (Studies in World Religions). 270p. (C). 1982. pap. 13.50 (*0-89130-574-2*, 03 00 03) Harvard U Wrld Relig.

Boyd, James W., jt. ed. see Kotwal, Firoze M.

Boyd, Jan. Outrageous 3-D Dangerous Creatures. LC 98-120099. (Illus.). (J). (ps-3). 1997. pap. 4.95 (*0-8167-4355-X*) Troll Communs.

— Volcanoes. (Illus.). (J). (gr. 3-7). 1997. pap. 7.95 (*0-8167-4443-2*) Troll Communs.

Boyd, Jean. The Caliph's Sister: Nana Asma'u (1793-1865) Teacher, Poet & Islamic Leader. (Illus.). 184p. 1988. text 49.50 (*0-7146-3319-4*, Pub. by F Cass Pubs) Intl Spec Bk.

— The Caliph's Sister: Nana Asma'u (1793-1865) Teacher, Poet & Islamic Leader. (Illus.). 284p. 1995. pap. 24.50 (*0-7146-4067-0*, Pub. by F Cass Pubs) Intl Spec Bk.

Boyd, Jean, jt. auth. see Mack, Beverly B.

Boyd, Jean A. The Jazz of the Southwest: An Oral History of Western Swing. LC 97-33740. (Illus.). 296p. 1998. 37.50 (*0-292-70859-9*, BOYJAZ); pap. 17.95 (*0-292-70860-2*, BOYJAP) U of Tex Pr.

Boyd, Jeanne F. & Stricker, Gregory L. Why 2000? A Year 2000 Personal Preparedness Guide: Because What You Don't Know about the Year 2000 Computer Crisis Could Hurt You & Your Loved Ones. Roberts, Carol, ed. LC 99-90049. (Illus.). 368p. 1999. pap. 23.95 (*0-9670185-0-1*) Para Path.

Boyd, Jeffrey H. Affirming the Soul: Remarkable Conversations Between Mental Health Professionals & an Ordained Minister. LC 93-93584. 275p. (Orig.). 1994. pap. 14.95 (*0-9636990-3-2*) Soul Res Inst.

— Reclaiming the Soul: The Search for Meaning in a Self-Centered Culture. LC 95-51177. 192p. (Orig.). 1996. pap. 15.95 (*0-8298-1080-3*) Pilgrim OH.

— Soul Psychology: How to Understand Your Soul in Light of the Mental Health Movement. LC 93-92740. 464p. 1994. pap. 14.95 (*0-9636990-6-7*) Soul Res Inst.

Boyd, Jennifer. Frank Norris: Spatial Form & Narrative Time. LC 92-39421. (American University Studies: American Literature: Ser. XXIV, Vol. 43). (Illus.). 160p. (C). 1993. text 39.95 (*0-8204-1940-0*) P Lang Pubng.

Boyd, Jerry D. Prisoner of the Fifth Moon: Doyan 1. 176p. 1994. pap. text. write for info. (*0-9641152-0-4*) East KY Pubng.

Boyd, Jim. Fairbanks-Morse Locomotives in Color. (Illus.). 1996. 49.95 (*1-878887-63-7*) Morning NJ.

— Illinois Central: Monday Mornin' Rails. (Illus.). 128p. 1993. text 49.95 (*0-944119-13-1*) Andover Junction.

Boyd, Joe. Build It Twice: The Path to a Successful Building Project. LC 98-35010. (Illus.). 415p. 1999. pap. 30.00 (*0-9663620-0-4*) Split Rock.

Boyd, John. Annals & Family Records of Winchester, Connecticut. (Illus.). 632p. 1988. reprint ed. lib. bdg. 65.00 (*0-8328-0019-8*, CT0028) Higginson Bk Co.

— Out of My Class. LC 85-20016. 192 p. 1985. write for info. (*0-85640-337-7*) Blckstaff Pr.

— Sir George Etienne Cartier, Bart: His Life & Times: A Political History of Canada from 1814 until 1873. (BCL1 - History - Canada Ser.). 1991. reprint ed. text 99.00 (*0-7812-6361-1*) Rprt Serv.

— Tenko! Rangoon Jail. 168p. Date not set. 29.95 (*1-56311-286-8*) Turner Pub KY.

Boyd, John D. A College Poetics. 348p. (Orig.). (C). 1983. lib. bdg. 58.50 (*0-8191-3380-9*) U Pr of Amer.

— The Function of Mimesis & Its Decline. LC 68-28691. 335p. 1980. reprint ed. pap. 103.90 (*0-7837-5594-5*, 204550000005) Bks Demand.

Boyd, John E., jt. auth. see Sworder, David D.

Boyd, John H., III, jt. auth. see Becker, Robert A.

Boyd, John M., ed. Fraser Darling in Africa: A Rhino in the Thorns. (Illus.). 256p. 1993. text 60.00 (*0-7486-0368-9*, Pub. by Edinburgh U Pr) Col U Pr.

***Boyd, John P.** Chebyshev & Fourier Spectral Methods. 2nd rev. ed. 2000. pap. 26.95 (*0-486-41183-4*) Dover.

Boyd, John P. Social Semigroups: A Unified Theory of Scaling & Blockmodeling. 280p. (C). 1991. lib. bdg. 49.50 (*0-913969-34-6*) Univ Pub Assocs.

— Weakly Nonlocal Solitary Waves & Beyond-All-Orders Asymptotics: Generalized Solitons & Hyperasymptotic Perturbation Theory. LC 98-23067. (Mathematics & Its Applications Ser.). 1998. 198.00 (*0-7923-5072-3*) Kluwer Academic.

Boyd, John R. The Middle of My Journey. 240p. (Orig.). 1990. pap. 14.95 (*0-85640-438-1*, Pub. by Blackstaff Pr) Dufour.

— Sir George Etienne Cartier, Bart: His Life & Times. LC 74-164590. (Select Bibliographies Reprint Ser.). 1977. reprint ed. 48.95 (*0-8369-5874-8*) Ayer.

Boyd, John R. & Boyd, Mary A. Before: Listening Activities for Prebeginning Students of English, Bk. 1. 2nd ed. 112p. (C). 1991. pap. text 15.13 (*0-13-068289-6*, 640104) P-H.

— Before Book One: Teacher's Manual. (Illus.). 30p. (gr. 9-12). 1987. pap. text 5.75 (*0-13-072554-4*, 20660) Prentice ESL.

— Begin at the Beginning. 80p. (Orig.). 1988. teacher ed. 2.95 (*0-933759-12-6*); pap. text 3.95 (*0-933759-11-8*); audio 29.95 (*0-933759-13-4*) Abaca Bks.

— Beginning Listening Cycles. 112p. (Orig.). 1986. student ed. 4.50 (*0-933759-06-1*); pap. 6.95 (*0-933759-05-3*); audio 39.95 (*0-933759-07-X*) Abaca Bks.

— Input - Output. (Illus.). 272p. (Orig.). (YA). (gr. 7-12). 1989. pap. 8.95 (*0-933759-14-2*); 4.95 (*0-933759-15-0*); audio 29.95 (*0-933759-16-9*) Abaca Bks.

— Listening Cycles. 112p. (Orig.). 1985. teacher ed. 1.95 (*0-933759-01-0*); student ed. 4.50 (*0-933759-02-9*); pap. text 8.95 (*0-933759-00-2*); audio 19.95 (*0-933759-03-7*) Abaca Bks.

Boyd, John R. & Boyd, Mary Ann. Before Book One. 2nd ed. 140p. 1991. text, teacher ed. 18.40 (*0-13-068321-3*, Macmillan Coll) P-H.

***Boyd, John Wright.** A Family History, Lt. Thomas Fortson, 1742-1824 & Some of His Descendants. (Illus.). 1020p. 1999. 60.00 (*1-890307-20-3*) Boyd Pub Co.

Boyd, Jolene, contrib. by. Double Blessings. 63p. 1988. 10.99 (*0-8341-9096-6*, MB-601) Lillenas.

— Little Fingers Go to Church, Bk. 1. 40p. 1989. 7.99 (*0-8341-9630-1*, MB-605) Lillenas.

Boyd, Jon M. & Scheffler, Michael J. Water Problems in Building Exterior Walls: Evaluation, Prevention & Repair. LC 99-30845. (STP Ser.). (Illus.). 330p. 1999. text 95.00 (*0-8031-2607-7*, STP1352) ASTM.

Boyd, Joseph A., Jr. Animal Friends. unabridged ed. (Illus.). 126p. (Orig.). (J). (gr. 2-6). 1997. pap. text. write for info. (*1-888781-05-X*) J A Boyd.

— Haunted Hills. unabridged ed. 401p. (Orig.). 1995. pap. write for info. (*1-888781-00-9*) J A Boyd.

— Researching Ancestors. unabridged ed. 60p. (Orig.). (J). 1996. pap. text. write for info. (*1-888781-04-1*) J A Boyd.

— Roads to Success. unabridged ed. 299p. (Orig.). 1995. pap. write for info. (*1-888781-02-5*) J A Boyd.

— Rufus & Rachel. unabridged ed. (Illus.). 156p. (Orig.). (J). (gr. k-6). 1991. pap. write for info. (*1-888781-03-3*) J A Boyd.

— Verses of Life. unabridged ed. 275p. (Orig.). 1995. pap. write for info. (*1-888781-01-7*) J A Boyd.

Boyd, Josh, jt. auth. see Boyd, Steve.

Boyd, Julia. Hannah Riddell: An Englishwoman in Japan. 216p. (Orig.). 1996. pap. 16.95 (*0-8048-2050-3*) Tuttle Pubng.

***Boyd, Julia A.** Can I Get a Witness? Black Women & Depression. 176p. 1999. pap. 11.95 (*0-452-28022-2*, Plume) Dutton Plume.

Boyd, Julia A. Embracing Fire. 1999. pap. 10.95 (*0-452-27393-5*, Plume) Dutton Plume.

— Embracing the Fire: Sisters Talk about Sex. 1997. 19.95 (*0-614-20426-7*, Dutt) Dutton Plume.

— Girlfriend to Girlfriend: Everyday Wisdom & Affirmations from the Sister Circle. LC 97-49894. 160p. 1999. pap. 10.95 (*0-452-27392-7*, Plume) Dutton Plume.

— In the Company of My Sisters. 1997. pap. 9.95 (*0-452-27246-7*, Plume) Dutton Plume.

Boyd, Julia W. Uncommon Ground: Virginia Artists, 1996. LC 95-42164. (Illus.). 64p. 1996. pap. 9.95 (*0-917046-42-0*) Va Mus Arts.

Boyd, Julian P. The Declaration of Independence: The Evolution of a Text. rev. ed. Gewalt, Gerard W., ed. LC 98-54837. (Illus.). 102p. 1999. 29.95 (*0-8444-0980-4*, Pub. by Lib Congress) U Pr of New Eng.

— Number Seven: Alexander Hamilton's Secret Attempts to Control American Foreign Policy, with Supporting Documents. LC 64-8515. 184p. 1964. reprint ed. pap. 57.10 (*0-7837-9303-0*, 206004300004) Bks Demand.

Boyd, Julie, jt. auth. see Dalton, Joan.

Boyd, K. T. ATP-FAR 135, Airline Transport Pilot. 3rd ed. LC 94-20778. (Illus.). 202p. 1994. pap. 29.95 (*0-8138-0508-2*) Iowa St U Pr.

Boyd, Keith & Osborn, Kevin. Complete Idiot's Guide to Parenting a Preschooler. 100th ed. LC 97-70663. (Complete Idiot's Guide Ser.). (Illus.). 368p. 1997. 16.95 (*0-02-861733-9*) Macmillan Gen Ref.

Boyd, Kelly, ed. Encyclopedia of Historians & Historical Writing, 2 vols. LC 98-193149. 2000p. 1999. lib. bdg. 275.00 (*1-884964-33-8*) Fitzroy Dearborn.

Boyd, Kenneth M., ed. The New Dictionary of Medical Ethics. 285p. 1997. pap. 37.00 (*0-7279-1001-9*, Pub. by BMJ Pub) Login Brothers Bk Co.

Boyd, Kenneth W. The Historical Markers of Metropolitan Atlanta. LC 90-25003. (Illus.). 288p. (Orig.). 1995. pap. 18.95 (*0-87797-216-8*) Cherokee.

— The Historical Markers of North Georgia. LC 91-27463. (Illus.). 288p. (Orig.). 1991. pap. 16.95 (*0-87797-234-6*) Cherokee.

— Vermont Historical Markers, Covered Bridges, Historic Sites & Museums. Selph, Alexa M., ed. (Illus.). 128p. (Orig.). 1994. pap. 14.95 (*0-87797-132-3*) Cherokee.

Boyd, Kenneth W., compiled by. The Historical Markers of Coastal Georgia: Coastal Counties - Bryan, Camden, Chatham, Glynn, Liberty & McIntosh Counties. LC 90-25003. (Illus.). 184p. 1996. reprint ed. pap. 14.95 (*0-87797-271-0*) Cherokee.

Boyd, Kevin W. Complete Aquarium Logbook. 1993. pap. 7.95 (*1-56465-112-6*, 16007) Tetra Pr.

— The Complete Aquarium Problem Solver. (Illus.). 32p. (YA). (gr. 10). 1989. pap. write for info. (*0-318-65747-3*) Boylen.

— The Complete Aquarium Problem Solver: A Total Trouble - Shooting Guide for Freshwater & Marine Aquariums. 1990. 19.95 (*1-56465-142-8*, 16099) Tetra Pr.

Boyd, L. Chronicles of Cynthiana: And Other Chronicles. (Illus.). 259p. 1997. reprint ed. lib. bdg. 32.00 (*0-8328-6731-4*) Higginson Bk Co.

— Irvine, the Irvines & Their Kin: History of the Irvine Family & Their Descendants. (Illus.). 115p. 1991. reprint ed. pap. 18.00 (*0-8328-1742-2*) Higginson Bk Co.

— Irvine, the Irvines & Their Kin: History of the Irvine Family & Their Descendants; Also, Sketches of Their Kindred. rev. ed. (Illus.). 432p. 1991. reprint ed. pap. 67.50 (*0-8328-1784-8*); reprint ed. lib. bdg. 77.50 (*0-8328-1783-X*) Higginson Bk Co.

Boyd, L. Miniatures for Guitar. 56p. 1994. pap. 14.95 (*0-7935-2339-7*, 00699385); pap. 17.95 (*0-7935-2340-0*, 00699386) H Leonard.

Boyd, L. M. Clancy's Treasure Book for Children. (Illus.). 166p. (Orig.). (J). (gr. k-5). 1981. pap. 5.95 (*0-941620-34-4*) Carson Ent.

Boyd, L. M. & Carson, H. G. Colorado Ghost Town Atlas I. (Illus.). 134p. (Orig.). 1984. pap. text 14.95 (*0-941620-19-0*) Carson Ent.

— Colorado Ghost Town Atlas II. (Illus.). 185p. (Orig.). (C). 1985. pap. text 16.95 (*0-941620-35-2*) Carson Ent.

Boyd, Larry. Resources Handbook: A Guide to Legal Studies for New South Wales. (Illus.). 168p. 1989. pap. 44.00 (*0-409-30134-5*, Austral, MICHIE) LEXIS Pub.

Boyd, Lee & Houpt, Katherine A., eds. Przewalski's Horse: The History & Biology of an Endangered Species. LC 93-2363. (SUNY Series in Endangered Species). (Illus.). 313p. (C). 1994. pap. text 21.95 (*0-7914-1890-1*) State U NY Pr.

— Przewalski's Horse: The History & Biology of an Endangered Species. LC 93-2363. (SUNY Series in Endangered Species). (Illus.). 313p. (C). 1994. text 64.50 (*0-7914-1889-8*) State U NY Pr.

Boyd, Leo R. Reality Religion: A Religion for Americans in the 21st Century. LC 97-92213. (Illus.). vi, 128p. 1997. pap. 9.20 (*0-9660394-0-8*) Reality Hse.

Boyd, Linda, jt. auth. see Ross, Sharon.

Boyd, Liona. In My Own Key: My Life in Love & Art. LC 98-224221. (Illus.). 320p. 1998. 26.95 (*0-7737-3121-0*, Pub. by Stoddart Publ) Genl Dist Srvs.

Boyd, Lizi. Baby's Journal. LC 96-109770. (Illus.). 64p. 1995. 14.95 (*0-8118-0780-0*) Chronicle Bks.

Boyd, Lizi. Forest. LC 98-39612. (Illus.). 12p. (J). 1999. bds. 5.95 (*0-8118-2126-9*) Chronicle Bks.

— Lulu Crow's Garden: A Silly Old Story with Brand-New Pictures. LC 96-49012. (Illus.). 32p. (J). (gr. k-3). 1998. 14.95 (*0-316-10419-1*) Little.

***Boyd, Lizi.** Pond. LC 98-8435. (Illus.). 12p. (J). 1999. 5.95 (*0-8118-2118-8*) Chronicle Bks.

Boyd, Lizi. Willy & the Cardboard Boxes. 1999. pap. 3.95 (*0-14-054342-2*) NAL.

Boyd, Lizzie, ed. British Cookery: A Complete Guide to Culinary Practice in England, Scotland, Ireland & Wales. LC 78-60775. (Illus.). 640p. 1979. 37.95 (*0-87951-087-0*, Pub. by Overlook Pr) Penguin Putnam.

Boyd, Lois A. & Brackenridge, R. Douglas. Presbyterian Women in America: Two Centuries of a Quest for Status, 46. LC 95-50519. (Contributions to the Study of Religion Ser.: Vol. 46). 216p. 1996. 57.95 (*0-313-29841-6*, Greenwood Pr) Greenwood.

Boyd, Loree. Spirit Moves: The Story of Six Generations of Native Women. LC 95-9264. (Illus.). 448p. 1995. pap. 17.95 (*1-880032-59-7*) New Wrld Lib.

Boyd, Lori, ed. Images: A Collection of Poetry by Children. 200p. (J). (gr. 1-6). 1997. pap. 6.95 (*0-9658543-0-2*, 051597) Images Pubns.

Boyd, Luke. Coon Dogs, Outhouses & Other Southern Samplings. 164p. 1998. pap. text 12.95 (*1-888608-58-7*) Cool Springs Pr.

Boyd, Lyle G., jt. auth. see Jones, Bessie Z.

Boyd, M., tr. see Beraud, Henri.

***Boyd, Malcolm.** Bach. 3rd ed. (Master Musicians Ser.). (Illus.). 320p. 2000. 35.00 (*0-19-514222-5*) OUP.

— Bach: Chorale Harmonization & Instrumental Counterpoint. 80p. 2000. pap. 15.95 (*1-871082-72-2*, Pub. by Kahn & Averill) Paul & Co Pubs.

Boyd, Malcolm. Bach: "The Brandenburg Concertos" LC 92-39751. (Cambridge Music Handbooks Ser.). (Illus.). 121p. (C). 1993. pap. text 12.95 (*0-521-38713-2*) Cambridge U Pr.

— Go Gentle into That Good Night. 1998. 12.95 (*1-885478-48-8*, Pub. by Genesis Press) BookWorld.

— Grace Williams. 100p. 1997. pap. 14.95 (*0-7083-1372-8*, Pub. by Univ Wales Pr) Paul & Co Pubs.

— Oxford Composer: J.S. Bach. LC 98-19587. (Oxford Composer Companion Ser.). (Illus.). 656p. 1999. 49.95 (*0-19-866208-4*) OUP.

***Boyd, Malcolm.** Running with Jesus: The Prayers of Malcolm Boyd. LC 00-29294. 2000. 15.99 (*0-8066-4068-5*, Augsburg) Augsburg Fortress.

Boyd, Malcolm & Carreras, Juan J., eds. Music in Spain During the Eighteenth Century. LC 97-41924. (Illus.). 275p. (C). 1998. 69.95 (*0-521-48139-2*) Cambridge U Pr.

Boyd, Malcom. Bach. (Master Musicians Ser.). (Illus.). 304p. 1997. 35.00 (*0-02-864813-7*) S&S Trade.

Boyd, Margaret A. The Crafts Supply Sourcebook: A Comprehensive Shop-by-Mail Guide for Thousands of Craft Materials. 5th ed. LC 98-43318. 288p. 1999. pap. 18.99 (*1-55870-506-6*, Betrwy Bks) F & W Pubns Inc.

Boyd, Marie A. Model: The Complete Guide for Men & Women. (Illus.). Date not set. pap. 25.95 (*0-87314-200-4*) Peter Glenn.

Boyd, Marie A. & Barker, Richard H. Our Legacy... Baldy View Entrepreneurs: Twenty-Five Profiles. (Citrus Roots... Our Legacy Ser.: Vol. III). (Illus.). 1999. pap. 15.00 (*0-9669508-3-6*) Upland Public.

Boyd, Marion. Say It Graciously. iv, 35p. 1992. reprint ed. pap. 4.00 (*0-88053-321-8*, S-296) Macoy Pub.

Boyd, Marion M. Silver Wands. LC 70-144724. (Yale Series of Younger Poets: No. 17). reprint ed. 18.00 (*0-404-53817-7*) AMS Pr.

Boyd, Mark D. The Book of the Revelation of Jesus Christ: A Teachers Guide & Notes. LC 96-96978. 192p. 1996. pap., teacher ed. write for info. (*1-57502-307-5*, P01051) Morris Pubng.

— Where Is That in the Bible? An Index to the New Testament Psalms & Proverbs. 306p. 2000. lib. bdg. 23.95 (*1-56072-476-5*, Nova Troitsa Bks) Nova Sci Pubs.

Boyd, Mark F. Here They Once Stood: The Tragic End of The Apalachee Missions. LC 99-25593. 1999. pap. text 29.95 (*0-8130-1725-4*) U Press Fla.

— Historic Sites in & Around the Jim Woodruff Reservoir Area, Florida - Georgia, Paper No. 13. fac. ed. (Smithsonian Institution, Bureau of American Ethnology Ser.: Bulletin 169). (Illus.). 131p. (C). 1958. reprint ed. pap. text 14.38 (*1-55567-688-X*) Coyote Press.

Boyd, Marlyn. Health Teaching in Nursing Practice: A Professional Model. 3rd ed. LC 96-53077. (C). 1997. pap. text 34.95 (*0-8385-3681-6*, A3681-2) Appleton & Lange.

Boyd, Mary A., jt. auth. see Boyd, John R.

Boyd, Mary Ann & Nihart, Mary Ann. Psychiatric Mental Health Nursing. LC 97-30272. 1212p. 1998. text 52.95 (*0-397-55178-9*) Lppncott W & W.

— Study Guide to Accompany Psychiatric Mental Health Nursing. 200p. 1998. pap. text 18.95 (*0-397-55179-7*) Lppncott W & W.

Boyd, Mary Ann, jt. auth. see Boyd, John R.

Boyd, Maurice. Kiowa Voices Vol. I: Ceremonial Dance, Ritual & Song. LC 81-50977. (Kiowa Voices Ser.). (Illus.). 164p. (J). 1981. 29.95 (*0-912646-67-5*) Tex Christian.

— Kiowa Voices Vol. II: Myths, Legends & Folktales. LC 81-50977. (Kiowa Voices Ser.). (Illus.). 324p. (J). 1983. 39.95 (*0-912646-76-4*) Tex Christian.

An Asterisk (*) at the beginning of an entry indicates that the title is appearing for the first time.

Boyd, Melba J. Discarded Legacy: Politics & Poetics in the Life of Frances E. W. Harper, 1825-1911. LC 93-36922. (African American Life Ser.). (Illus.). 262p. (C). 1994. 39.95 (*0-8143-2488-6*); pap. text 14.95 (*0-8143-2489-4*) Wayne St U Pr.

— The Inventory of Black Roses. 62p. (Orig.). 1989. pap. 6.00 (*0-9622474-1-3*) Past Tents Pr.

— Letters to Che. 36p. 1996. pap. text 8.00 (*1-56439-055-1*) Ridgeway.

Boyd, Michael. The Reflexive Novel: Fiction As Critique. LC 81-72029. 320p. 1983. 39.50 (*0-8387-5029-X*) Bucknell U Pr.

Boyd, Mike. How to Bankroll a Funeral Without Breaking the Bank. (Illus.). 128p. 1995. pap. 22.95 (*0-9648425-0-5*) Boyd & Boyd.

Boyd, Mildred & Tower, Barbara. Medical-Surgical Nursing. 3rd ed. LC 96-29017. (Springhouse Notes Ser.). (Illus.). 416p. 1996. 22.95 incl. disk (*0-87434-861-7*) Springhouse Corp.

Boyd, Minnie C. Alabama in the Fifties: A Social Study. LC 31-33199. (Columbia University. Studies in the Social Sciences: No. 353). reprint ed. 32.50 (*0-404-51353-0*) AMS Pr.

Boyd, Morrison C. Elizabethan Music & Musical Criticism. LC 73-1837. (Illus.). 363p. 1973. reprint ed. lib. bdg. 69.50 (*0-8371-6805-8*, BOEL, Greenwood Pr) Greenwood.

Boyd, Natasha. Ola Anfenson: Pioneer Photographer. Harden, Neva N., ed. LC 97-75055. (Illus.). 84p. 1997. pap. 14.95 (*0-913945-59-5*) Horizon Comms.

***Boyd, Neil.** The Beast Within: Why Men Are Violent. 208p. 2000. 22.95 (*1-55054-766-6*, Pub. by DGL) Sterling.

Boyd, Neva L. Handbook of Recreational Games. LC 75-13385. 128p. 1975. reprint ed. pap. 4.95 (*0-486-23204-2*) Dover.

Boyd, Norah & Mence, Neil. The Royal Road to Abundant Living: Daily Guides to Greater Health, Happiness & Prosperity. LC 98-72255. 144p. 1998. pap. 10.95 (*0-87516-720-9*) DeVorss.

***Boyd, Norman Napier.** Model Ship: It's Purpose & History. 1999. 49.50 (*1-85149-327-1*) Antique Collect.

Boyd, Orsemus B. Cavalry Life in Tent & Field - Mrs. Orsemus Bronson Boyd (Frances Anne Mullen Boyd) LC 81-19772. 386p. reprint ed. pap. 119.70 (*0-7837-4662-8*, 204438800002) Bks Demand.

Boyd, P. D. Joining Nations: A History of the International Institute of Welding 1947-1990. (Illus.). 96p. 1993. 69.95 (*1-85573-126-6*, Pub. by Woodhead Pubng) Am Educ Systs.

Boyd, Pamela. Odd Fish: A Play. LC 94-18974. 96p. 1994. pap. 8.95 (*0-88734-281-7*, Pub. by Red Deer) Empire Pub Srvs.

***Boyd, Patricia & Coffey, Lonny.** How to Buy & Sell Your Home: Without Getting Ripped Off! LC 99-89129. (Illus.). 202p. 2000. pap. 16.95 (*0-7931-3706-3*) Dearborn.

***Boyd, Patricia M. & Boyd, Brent D.** Office Procedures in Managed Health Care with Data Disk for MediSoft for Windows. LC 98-39160. 400p. 1999. text 35.00 incl. disk (*0-02-801222-4*) Glencoe.

Boyd, Patricia M. & Boyd, Brent D. Office Procedures in Managed Health Care with Medisoft for Windows Data Disk. 400p. write for info. (*0-02-801223-2*) McGraw-Hill HPD.

***Boyd, Paula.** Hot Enough to Kill: A Jolene Jackson Mystery. LC 99-91113. (Jolene Jackson Mysteries Ser.). 254p. 1999. pap. 11.95 (*0-9674786-0-X*) Diomo.

Boyd, Pauline, jt. auth. see Boyd, Selma.

Boyd, Primrose, jt. auth. see Gray, Patience.

Boyd Publications Staff. The Holy Bible: Old & New Testament in the King James Version: Words of Christ in Red: Translated Out of the Original Tongues & with Previous Translations Diligently Compared & Revised. LC 99-181283. 1820 p. 1998. write for info. (*1-890436-14-3*) Boyd Pubns TN.

Boyd, R., Jr., jt. auth. see Fleming, Robert.

Boyd, R. D., Sr. & Kandlikar, S. G., eds. Fundamentals of Subcooled Flow Boiling. (HTD Ser.: Vol. 217). 64p. 1992. 27.50 (*0-7918-1058-5*, G00702) ASME.

Boyd, R. D. & Kroeger, P. G., eds. Fundamentals of Natural Convection, 1993. LC 89-71690. 141p. 1993. pap. 45.00 (*0-7918-1010-0*) ASME.

Boyd, R. Maurice. The Fine Art of Being Imperfect: And Other Broadcast Talks. LC 97-49916. 112p. 1998. pap. 10.00 (*0-687-45909-5*) Abingdon.

***Boyd, Randy.** Bridge Across the Ocean. 2000. pap. 12.95 (*0-9665333-5-6*) W Bch Bks.

Boyd, Randy. Uprising: The Suspense Thriller. LC 98-96304. 335p. 1998. pap. 11.95 (*0-9665333-7-2*, 966-001) W Bch Bks.

Boyd, Richard, et al, eds. The Philosophy of Science. (Illus.). 592p. 1991. pap. text 37.50 (*0-262-52156-3*, Bradford Bks) MIT Pr.

Boyd, Richard H. & Phillips, Paul J. The Science of Polymer Molecules. (Solid State Science Ser.). (Illus.). 428p. (C). 1994. text 95.00 (*0-521-32076-3*) Cambridge U Pr.

— The Science of Polymer Molecules. (Cambridge Solid State Science Ser.). 423p. 1996. pap. text 36.95 (*0-521-56508-1*) Cambridge U Pr.

Boyd, Robert. Advanced Circuit Analysis with the HP-42S. (Illus.). (Orig.). (C). 1988. pap. text 9.95 (*0-685-54319-6*, 2063S) Interfab Corp.

— Born to Die: Understanding Christ's Life. LC 96-61529. (Illus.). 224p. 1997. pap. 12.99 (*0-529-10743-0*) World Publng.

— Critical Reasoning: The Fixation of Belief. LC 92-73355. 416p. (C). 1992. pap. text 19.95 (*0-938991-94-9*) Colonial Pr AL.

***Boyd, Robert.** How Humans Evolved. 2nd ed. LC 99-28071. 1999. pap. text 64.00 (*0-393-97477-4*, Norton Paperbks) Norton.

Boyd, Robert. Paul, the Apostle: His Life & Times. LC 95-197275. (Illus.). 479p. (Orig.). 1995. kivar 12.99 (*0-529-10252-8*, PAUL) World Publng.

— People of the Dalles: The Indians of Wascopam Mission. LC 95-38916. (Studies in the Anthropology of North American Indians). (Illus.). xi, 414p. 1996. text 60.00 (*0-8032-1236-4*) U of Nebr Pr.

***Boyd, Robert.** Tolerance Analysis of Electron Circuits Using MATHCAD. 216p. 1999. per. 29.95 (*0-8493-2339-8*) CRC Pr.

Boyd, Robert. Tolerance Analysis of Electronic Circuits Using Matlab LC 99-26898. 160p. 1999. per. 19.95 (*0-8493-2276-6*) CRC Pr.

— What Is the Future for a Primary Care-Led NHS? LC 96-53158. (National Primary Care Research & Development Centre Ser.). 1997. write for info. (*1-85775-265-1*, Radcliffe Med Pr) Scovill Paterson.

Boyd, Robert, ed. Indians, Fire & the Land in the Pacific Northwest. LC 98-54743. (Illus.). 320p. (Orig.). 1999. pap. 34.95 (*0-87071-459-7*) Oreg St U Pr.

Boyd, Robert & Richerson, Peter J. Culture & the Evolutionary Process. LC 84-24125. (Illus.). viii, 332p. 1985. lib. bdg. 29.95 (*0-226-06931-1*) U Ch Pr.

— Culture & the Evolutionary Process. LC 84-24125. (Illus.). viii, 339p. 1996. pap. text 15.95 (*0-226-06933-8*) U Ch Pr.

Boyd, Robert & Silk, Joan B. How Humans Evolved. LC 96-48024. (C). 1997. pap. 61.25 (*0-393-97076-0*) Norton.

Boyd, Robert, ed. see Bode, Vaughn.

Boyd, Robert, ed. see Conner, Jeff.

Boyd, Robert, ed. see Crumb, R.

Boyd, Robert, ed. see Feiffer, Jules.

Boyd, Robert D. Personal Transformations in Small Groups: A Jungian Perspective. (International Library of Group Psychotherapy & Group Process Ser.). 304p. (C). (gr. 13). 1991. text 49.95 (*0-415-04362-X*, A5080) Routledge.

— Personal Transformations in Small Groups: A Jungian Perspective. LC 94-8489. (International Library of Group Psychotherapy & Group Process Ser.). 256p. (C). 1994. pap. 29.99 (*0-415-04363-8*, B4780) Routledge.

Boyd, Robert D. & Apps, Jerold W., eds. Redefining the Discipline of Adult Education. LC 80-8006. (Adult Education Association Handbook Series in Adult Education). 239p. reprint ed. pap. 74.10 (*0-8357-4933-9*, 203786300009) Bks Demand.

Boyd, Robert F. Basic Medical Microbiology. 5th ed. LC 94-24134. 680p. 1995. text 58.00 (*0-316-10445-0*) Lppncott W & W.

Boyd, Robert F. & Hoerl, Bryan G. Basic Medical Microbiology. 3rd ed. 976p. 1985. 42.50 (*0-316-10441-8*, Little Brwn Med Div) Lppncott W & W.

Boyd, Robert F. & Marr, Joseph J. Medical Microbiology. (Illus.). 760p. 1980. 35.00 (*0-316-10432-9*, Little Brwn Med Div) Lppncott W & W.

Boyd, Robert G. Amerikanuak! Basques in the High Desert. Cooper, Jack, ed. (Illus.). 32p. 1998. pap. 12.00 (*0-9663487-1-0*) High Desert Mus.

Boyd, Robert G. & Adams, Vivian. Strong Medicine: A Century of High Desert Remedies. Cooper, Jack, ed. (Western Heritage Ser.: Vol. 2). (Illus.). 40p. 1998. pap. 12.95 (*0-9663487-0-2*) High Desert Mus.

Boyd, Robert K., jt. auth. see Morrison, Robert T.

Boyd, Robert N. Sex Behind Bars: A Novella, Short Stories & True Accounts. 240p. 1995. reprint ed. 14.95 (*0-917342-34-8*) Gay Sunshine.

Boyd, Robert N., ed. The Boys of Vaseline Alley. (Orig.). 1994. pap. 14.95 (*0-943595-47-9*) Leyland Pubns.

Boyd, Robert N., jt. auth. see Morrison, Robert T.

Boyd, Robert T. Boyd's Handbook of Practical Apologetics. LC 95-18159. 256p. 1996. pap. 12.99 (*0-8254-2161-6*) Kregel.

***Boyd, Robert T.** Coming of the Spirit of Pestilence: Introduced Infectious Diseases & Population Decline. LC 99-28736. (Illus.). 428p. 1999. 50.00 (*0-295-97837-6*) U of Wash Pr.

Boyd, Robert T. World's Bible Handbook. LC 92-22091. 1992. 17.99 (*0-529-07311-0*, WBH) World Publng.

Boyd, Robert W., II. His Father's Son. 176p. 1997. 8.00 (*0-8059-4259-9*) Dorrance.

Boyd, Robert W. Nonlinear Optics. (Illus.). 439p. (C). 1991. text 75.00 (*0-12-121680-2*) Acad Pr.

— Radiometry & the Detection of Optical Radiation. LC 82-20222. (Pure & Applied Optics Ser.). 272p. 1983. 129.00 (*0-471-86188-X*) Wiley.

Boyd, Robert W., jt. ed. see Agrawal, Govind P.

Boyd, Roland. The Fisherman & His Wife. rev. ed. Wright, Carol, ed. (Illus.). 20p. (J). (gr. 1-2). pap. 6.95 (*0-9701573-0-4*) Chameleon Desgns.

Boyd, Ron, jt. illus. see Delaney, John.

Boyd, Roy & Hyde, William F. Forestry Sector Intervention: The Impacts of Public Regulation on Social Welfare. LC 88-619. (Illus.). 307p. 1989. reprint ed. pap. 95.20 (*0-608-00057-4*, 206082300006) Bks Demand.

Boyd, Roy G. The Economic Effects of a Flat Tax. 13p. 1996. pap. 10.00 (*1-56808-073-5*, 205) Natl Ctr Pol.

Boyd, Roy G. & Sheldon, Barry J. The Economic Effects of the Dole Tax Plan. 1996. write for info. (*1-56808-025-5*, 207) Natl Ctr Pol.

Boyd-Rush, Dorothy A. Marriage Notices from Extant Issues of the "Rockingham Register," Harrisonburg, Virginia, 1822-1870. viii, 495p. (Orig.). 1993. pap. 33.50 (*1-55613-822-9*) Heritage Bk.

— Register of Free Blacks, Rockingham County, Virginia, 1807-1859. 252p. (Orig.). 1992. pap. 22.00 (*1-55613-658-7*) Heritage Bk.

Boyd, Ruth, jt. auth. see Harman, Tony.

Boyd, Selma & Boyd, Pauline. The How: Making the Best of a Mistake. LC 80-13513. (Illus.). 32p. (J). (ps-3). 1981. 16.95 (*0-87705-176-3*, Kluwer Acad Hman Sci) Kluwer Academic.

Boyd, Sharon. How to Absolutely, Positively Look 5-10 Years Younger. LC 94-62103. 156p. 1995. pap. 12.00 (*0-87554-584-X*, B937) Valley Sun.

Boyd, Sharon. Vistors to New Zealand from the U. S. A. A Compilation of Recent Research. LC 89-184809. (NZTP Overseas Market Research Ser.). 183p. 1988. write for info. (*0-478-02073-2*, Pub. by Manaaki Whenua) Balogh.

Boyd-Smith, Wendy. No Catnapping in the Kitchen. (Illus.). 160p. 1996. 9.95 (*0-87605-695-8*) Howell Bks.

Boyd, Stephen, jt. auth. see Butler, Richard.

Boyd, Stephen, ed. see El Ghaoui, Laurent, et al.

Boyd, Stephen B. The Men We Long to Be: Beyond Lonely Warriors & Desperate Lovers. LC 97-29641. 272p. (Orig.). 1997. pap. 17.95 (*0-8298-1201-6*) Pilgrim OH.

— Pilgram Marpeck: His Life & Social Theology. LC 90-44076. (Duke Monographs in Medieval & Renaissance Studies). 375p. 1992. text 39.95 (*0-8223-1100-3*) Duke.

Boyd, Stephen B., et al, eds. Redeeming Men: Religion & Masculinities. LC 96-21403. 304p. (Orig.). 1996. pap. 32.95 (*0-664-25544-2*) Westminster John Knox.

Boyd, Stephen D. Moments with the Master. 1987. pap. 4.75 (*0-89137-334-9*) Quality Pubns.

Boyd, Steve & Boyd, Josh. From Dull to Dynamic: Transforming Your Presentations. 216p. 1998. 21.00 (*1-57087-391-7*) Prof Pr NC.

Boyd, Steven R. Alternative Constitutions for the United States: A Documentary History, 145. LC 91-38208. (Contributions in American History Ser.: No. 145). 308p. 1992. 65.00 (*0-313-25419-2*, BDE, Greenwood Pr) Greenwood.

Boyd, Steven R., ed. The Whiskey Rebellion: Past & Present Perspectives, 109. LC 84-22437. (Contributions in American History Ser.: No. 109). (Illus.). 212p. 1985. 55.00 (*0-313-24534-7*, BWH/, Greenwood Pr) Greenwood.

Boyd, Stewart C., jt. auth. see Mustill, Lord.

Boyd, Susan, et al, eds. Drinking Water: A Community Action Guide. rev. ed. 30p. (Orig.). 1986. pap. text 4.00 (*0-937345-03-2*) CONCERN.

Boyd, Susan & McGrath, Cynthia, eds. Farmland: A Community Issue. (Community Action Guides). 22p. (Orig.). 1987. pap. text 4.00 (*0-937345-04-0*) CONCERN.

Boyd, Susan, et al. Global Warming & Energy Choices: A Community Action Guide. (Community Action Guides Ser.). (Illus.). 38p. (Orig.). (YA). (gr. 5-12). 1991. 4.00 (*0-937345-07-5*) CONCERN.

— Pesticides in Our Communities: Choices for Change. (Community Action Guides Ser.). (Illus.). 32p. (Orig.). 1992. pap. text 4.00 (*0-937345-08-3*) CONCERN.

Boyd, Susan, ed. see Craig, Dorothy.

Boyd, Susan A. & Mango, Marlia M., eds. Ecclesiastical Silver Plate in Sixth-Century Byzantium. LC 92-9331. (Illus.). 244p. 1993. 120.00 (*0-88402-203-X*, BMES) Dumbarton Oaks.

Boyd, Susan B., ed. Challenging the Public - Private Divide: Feminism, Law, & Public Policy. LC 97-226785. (Illus.). 416p. 1997. pap. text 24.95 (*0-8020-7652-1*) U of Toronto Pr.

Boyd, Susan C. Mothers & Illict Drugs: Transcending the Myths. (Illus.). 272p. 1999. text 50.00 (*0-8020-4331-3*); pap. text 19.95 (*0-8020-8151-7*) U of Toronto Pr.

Boyd, Susan J., ed. see Hurst, Jane.

Boyd-Swan, Francisco R. El Teatro en Alicante, 1901-1910: Cartelera y Estudio. (Fuentes Ser.: Vol. 23). (Illus.). 440p. (C). 1994. pap. 54.00 (*1-85566-036-9*, Pub. by Tamesis Bks Ltd) Boydell & Brewer.

Boyd, T. J. & Mahr, D. FBC & AFBC: Projects & Technology. LC 93-73001. (FACT Ser.: Vol. 16). 136p. 1993. 35.00 (*0-7918-0994-3*, H00826) ASME.

Boyd, T. J., jt. auth. see Coulson, Charles A.

Boyd, Thomas. Shadow of the Long Knives. 25.95 (*0-88411-861-4*) Amereon Ltd.

— Through the Wheat: A Novel of the World War I Marines. 272p. 2000. pap. 13.95 (*0-8032-6168-3*, Bison Books) U of Nebr Pr.

Boyd, Thomas A. Points of Honor. LC 72-5859. (Short Story Index Reprint Ser.). 1977. reprint ed. 24.95 (*0-8369-4192-6*) Ayer.

— Poor John Fitch: Inventor of the Steamboat. LC 75-150171. (Select Bibliographies Reprint Ser.). 1977. reprint ed. 23.95 (*0-8369-5684-2*) Ayer.

— Poor John Fitch, Inventor of the Steamboat. 1992. reprint ed. lib. bdg. 89.00 (*0-7812-5432-9*) Rprt Serv.

— Professional Amateur: The Biography of Charles Franklin Kettering. LC 72-5036. (Technology & Society Ser.). (Illus.). 242p. 1980. reprint ed. 20.95 (*0-405-04689-8*) Ayer.

Boyd, Thomas H. The History of Montgomery County, Maryland. 187p. 1998. reprint ed. pap. 20.00 (*0-8063-7954-5*, 655) Clearfield Co.

Boyd, Thomas H., ed. see Arnold, John P. & Kernkamp, Howard H.

Boyd, Thomas J. & Mahr, Daniel, eds. Fluidized Bed: Projects & Technology. 105p. 1994. pap. 50.00 (*0-7918-1384-3*) ASME.

Boyd, Todd. Am I Black Enough for You? Popular Culture from the 'Hood & Beyond. LC 96-30365. 1997. 35.00 (*0-253-33242-7*); pap. 14.95 (*0-253-21105-0*) Ind U Pr.

***Boyd, Todd & Shropshire, Kenneth L., eds.** Basketball Jones: America, above the Rim. (Fast Track Ser.). 288p. 2000. pap. 18.95 (*0-8147-1316-5*); text 55.00 (*0-8147-1315-7*) NYU Pr.

Boyd, Todd, jt. auth. see Baker, Aaron.

Boyd, Ty. Visions: From the Leaders of Today for the Leaders of Tomorrow. 176p. (C). 1996. pap. 10.00 (*0-937539-16-3*) Executive Bks.

Boyd, W. E., frwd. Well Cleanout & Repair Methods. (Well Servicing & Workover Ser.: Lesson 8). (Illus.). 32p. (Orig.). 1971. pap. text 12.00 (*0-88698-064-X*, 3.70810) PETEX.

— Well Stimulation Treatments. (Well Servicing & Workover Ser.: Lesson 11). (Illus.). 44p. (Orig.). 1971. pap. text 12.00 (*0-88698-067-4*, 3.71110) PETEX.

Boyd, W. Harland. Stagecoach Heyday. (Illus.). 1983. 12.00 (*0-943500-10-9*) Kern Historical.

Boyd, W. Harland, ed. Kern Country Wayfarers. 72p. 1977. pap. 4.00 (*0-943500-03-6*) Kern Historical.

Boyd, W. J. P., ed. Aldred's Marginalia. 62p. 1977. pap. text 19.95 (*0-85989-036-8*, Pub. by Univ Exeter Pr) Northwestern U Pr.

Boyd, W. P. History of the Boyd Family & Descendants. (Illus.). 521p. 1988. reprint ed. pap. 78.00 (*0-8328-0295-6*); reprint ed. lib. bdg. 86.00 (*0-8328-0294-8*) Higginson Bk Co.

Boyd-Whyte. Ove Arup & Partners. text. write for info. (*0-471-48948-4*) Wiley.

Boyd, William. Armadillo. LC 98-14578. 352p. 1998. 24.00 (*0-375-40223-3*) Knopf.

— Armadillo. 2000. pap. 14.00 (*0-375-70216-4*) Knopf.

— Blue Afternoon, Vol. 1. 1997. pap. 13.00 (*0-679-77260-X*) McKay.

— Brazzaville Beach. 336p. 1992. mass mkt. 4.99 (*0-380-71385-3*, Avon Bks) Morrow Avon.

Boyd, William. Brazzaville Beach Co T. 320p. 1995. pap. 12.00 (*0-380-78049-6*, Avon Bks) Morrow Avon.

Boyd, William. The Destiny of Nathalie X & Other Stories. LC 96-17564. 177p. 1997. 22.00 (*0-679-44705-9*) Knopf.

— The Destiny of Nathalie X & Other Stories. 1997. pap. 12.00 (*0-679-76784-3*) Random.

— Emile of Jean Jacques Rousseau. (Classics in Education Ser.). 198p. 1962. pap. text 9.00 (*0-8077-1107-1*) Tchrs Coll.

— A Good Man in Africa. 336p. 1994. mass mkt. 5.99 (*0-380-72341-7*, Avon Bks) Morrow Avon.

— An Ice Cream War. LC 99-18313. 416p. 1999. pap. 14.00 (*0-375-70502-3*) Vin Bks.

— An Ice-Cream War. 384p. 1992. reprint ed. pap. 10.00 (*0-380-71567-8*, Avon Bks) Morrow Avon.

***Boyd, William.** Nat Tate. 69p. 1998. 15.95 (*1-901785-01-7*, Pub. by Twenty-One) Dist Art Pubs.

Boyd, William. The New Confession. 1999. pap. 15.00 (*0-375-70503-1*) Vin Bks.

— On the Yankee Station. 1999. pap. write for info. (*0-375-70511-2*) Vin Bks.

— Stars & Bars. 1999. pap. write for info. (*0-375-70501-5*) Vin Bks.

Boyd, William & King, Edmund. The History of Western Education. 12th ed. 528p. (C). 1994. lib. bdg. 49.50 (*0-389-21008-0*) B&N Imports.

Boyd, William, et al. The Reconstruction of Education. (School Development Ser.). (Illus.). 208p. 1996. 80.00 (*0-304-33176-7*); pap. 31.95 (*0-304-33179-1*) Continuum.

Boyd, William D., tr. see Schottenloher, Karl.

Boyd, William E. A Pollen Flora of the Native Plants of South Australia & Southern Northern Territory. (SA Geographical Papers: No. 3). (Illus.). 212p. (C). 1992. 75.00 (*0-7855-0331-5*, Pub. by Royal Geograp Soc) St Mut.

Boyd, William H. Lower Kern River Country, 1850-1950: Wilderness to Empire. (Illus.). 233p. 1997. 18.95 (*0-943500-15-X*) Kern Historical.

Boyd, William H. The Shasta Route, 1863 to 1887: The Railroad Link Between the Sacremento & the Columbia. Bruchey, Stuart, ed. LC 80-1276. (Railroads Ser.). 1981. lib. bdg. 18.95 (*0-405-13751-6*) Ayer.

Boyd, William H., ed. Kern County Tall Tales: Selected Folk History. (Illus.). 38p. 1980. pap. 5.00 (*0-943500-01-X*) Kern Historical.

Boyd, William J. Bullets Don't Cry. 352p. (Orig.). 1994. mass mkt. 3.99 (*0-8125-2453-5*) Tor Bks.

Boyd, William K. Ecclesiastical Edicts of the Theodosian Code. LC 70-77991. (Columbia University. Studies in the Social Sciences: No. 63). reprint ed. 39.50 (*0-404-51063-9*) AMS Pr.

Boyd, William L. Poetic Penguins. LC 91-66936. 108p. 1992. 14.95 (*0-933598-36-X*) NC Wesleyan Pr.

— Poetic Penguins. deluxe limited ed. LC 91-66936. 108p. 1992. 30.00 (*0-933598-37-8*) NC Wesleyan Pr.

— Political Science & Educational Administration. 134p. (C). 1983. 45.00 (*0-7300-0006-0*, Pub. by Deakin Univ) St Mut.

Boyd, William L. & Walberg, Herbert J., eds. Choice in Education: Potential & Problems. LC 89-63477. 287p. (C). 1990. 35.75 (*0-8211-0138-2*) McCutchan.

Boyd, William L., jt. auth. see Meyer, Heinz-Dieter.

Boyd, William L., jt. ed. see Beare, Hedley.

Boyd, William L., jt. ed. see Hartman, William T.

Boyd, William P. History of the Town of Conesus, Livingston County, from Its First Settlement in 1793 to 1887, with a Brief Genealogical Records of the Conesus Families. 207p. 1995. reprint ed. lib. bdg. 32.50 (*0-8328-4710-0*) Higginson Bk Co.

***Boyd, William Y.** Panama. LC 99-39375. 192p. 1999. 21.95 (*1-892123-15-0*) Capital VA.

Boyd, Willie F. How to Get Rich in Real Estate Without Leaving Your Job. LC 93-72955. (Illus.). 150p. (Orig.). (C). 1993. pap. 19.95 (*0-9637944-1-8*) Eno Pubng.

***Boyde, A.** An Imaging Atlas on Osteoporotic Bone Disease. (Illus.). 2001. write for info. (*1-85070-483-X*) Prthnon Pub.

B

Boyde, Patrick. Dante's Style in His Lyric Poetry. LC 74-130906. 371p. reprint ed. pap. 105.80 (0-608-17086-0, 2027287) Bks Demand.

***Boyde, Patrick.** Human Vices & Human Worth in Dante's Comedy. (Illus.). 300p. (C). 2000. text Price not set. (0-521-66067-X) Cambridge U Pr.

Boyde, Patrick. Perception & Passion in Dante's "Comedy" LC 92-40938. 362p. (C). 1993. text 69.95 (0-521-37009-4) Cambridge U Pr.

Boyde, Patrick, jt. ed. see Baranski, Zygmunt G.

***Boydell & Leary.** Identifying Training Needs. 208p. 2000. pap. 44.95 (0-8464-5071-2) Beekman Pubs.

Boydell, Barra, ed. Music at Christ Church Before 1800: Documents & Selected Anthems. LC 99-191127. (Christ Church Ser.). 220p. 1998. boxed set 45.00 (1-85182-413-8, Pub. by Four Cts Pr) Intl Spec Bk.

Boydell, Brian. A Dublin Musical Calendar, 1700-60. 320p. 1988. 14.95 (0-7165-2430-9, Pub. by Irish Acad Pr) Intl Spec Bk.

— Rotunda Music in Eighteenth-Century Dublin. (Illus.). 224p. 1992. 14.95 (0-7165-2487-2, Pub. by Irish Acad Pr) Intl Spec Bk.

Boydell, Craig L., et al. The Administration of Criminal Justice in Canada. LC 76-367851. vii, 311 p. 1974. write for info. (0-03-928172-8) Holt R&W.

Boydell, John, ed. The Boydell Shakespeare Prints. LC 68-21362. (Illus.). 1972. reprint ed. 48.95 (0-405-08299-1, Pub. by Blom Pubns) Ayer.

Boydell, Tom. A Guide to Job Analysis. (C). 1973. pap. 60.00 (0-85171-013-1, Pub. by IPM Hse) St Mut.

— A Guide to the Identification of Training Needs. (C). 1990. pap. 60.00 (0-85171-059-X, Pub. by IPM Hse) St Mut.

Boydell, Tom & Leary, Malcolm. Identifying Training Needs. 160p. 1996. pap. 36.00 (0-85292-630-8, Pub. by IPM Hse) St Mut.

Boyden, D. D. The Hill Collection of Musical Instruments. (Illus.). 54p. 1995. 19.95 (0-900090-40-5, 0405, Pub. by Ashmolean Mus) A Schwartz & Co.

Boyden, David. Violin Family. rev. ed. (New Grove Ser.). Date not set. pap. write for info. (0-393-30519-8) Norton.

Boyden, David D. The History of Violin Playing from Its Origins to 1761: And Its Relationship to the Violin & Violin Music. (Illus.). 594p. 1990. pap. text 48.00 (0-19-816183-2) OUP.

— Violin Family. 1989. pap. 14.95 (0-393-30517-1) Norton.

Boyden, David D., ed. see Geminiani, Francesco.

***Boyden, Heide P.** The Jelly Boat Book. Guevara, Linda L., ed. (Illus.). 32p. 2000. spiral bd. 12.95 (0-9700863-3-4) All About Kids.

Boyden Howes, Elizabeth. Intersection & Beyond, Vol. II. LC 86-3067. 200p. (Orig.). 1986. pap. 8.50 (0-917479-07-6) Guild Psy.

Boyden, J., jt. auth. see Bequele, A.

Boyden, James M. The Courtier & the King: Ruy Gomez de Silva, Philip II, & the Court of Spain. LC 93-41011. 1995. 45.00 (0-520-08622-8, Pub. by U CA Pr) Cal Prin Full Svc.

Boyden, Jo, jt. auth. see Pratt, Brian.

Boyden, Jo, jt. ed. see Bequele, Assefa.

Boyden, Martha & American Academy in Rome Staff. Nunzio, Martin Puryear: Forma Lignea. LC 98-202561. 119 p. 1997. write for info. (88-435-6285-1) Electa.

Boyden, Matthew. Richard Strauss. LC 99-21100. (Illus.). 431p. 1999. 29.95 (1-55553-418-X) NE U Pr.

Boyden, Stephen. Western Civilization in Biological Perspective: Patterns in Biohistory. (Illus.). 384p. 1990. reprint ed. pap. text 35.00 (0-19-857742-7) OUP.

Boyden, Stephen, ed. Biohistory: The Interplay Between Human Society & the Biosphere. (Man & the Biosphere Ser.: Vol. 8). (Illus.). 265p. (C). 1992. 68.00 (1-85070-371-X) Prthnon Pub.

Boyden, Terry G. Warrior of the Mist: A Title Suggested by Lucullus Virgil McWhorter: a Biography of Qualchan, Chief Owhi's Son. LC 96-8156. 1995. 24.95 (0-87770-586-0) Ye Galleon.

Boyden, Wallace C., et al. Thomas Boyden & His Descendants. (Illus.). 267p. 1988. reprint ed. pap. 40.00 (0-8328-0297-2); reprint ed. lib. bdg. 48.00 (0-8328-0296-4) Higginson Bk Co.

Boyds Mills Press Staff. Merry Things to Make: Christmas Fun & Crafts. (Illus.). 64p. (J). (gr. k-7). 1999. pap. 7.95 (1-56397-838-5) Boyds Mills Pr.

Boydston, Jeanne. Home & Work: Housework, Wages & the Ideology of Labor in the Early Republic. 248p. (C). 1994. reprint ed. pap. text 20.95 (0-19-508561-2) OUP.

Boydston, Jeanne & Lewis, Jan. A History of the United States. 24p. (C). 2001. write for info. (0-02-308659-9, Macmillan Coll) P-H.

Boydston, Jeanne, et al. The Limits of Sisterhood: The Beecher Sisters on Women's Rights & Woman's Sphere. LC 87-19771. (Gender & American Culture Ser.). (Illus.). xxvi, 369p. (C). 1988. pap. 24.95 (0-8078-4207-9) U of NC Pr.

Boydston, Jeanne M., et al, eds. Serials Cataloging at the Turn of the Century. LC 97-33060. (Serials Librarian Ser.: Vol. 32, Nos. 1-2). 209p. 1997. 39.95 (0-7890-0373-2) Haworth Pr.

Boydston, Jo A., ed. The Later Works of John Dewey, 1885-1953 Vol. 17: Miscellaneous Writings. abr. ed. LC 80-27285. (Later Works of John Dewey, 1925-1953). 606p. (C). 1991. pap. 16.95 (0-8093-1683-8) S Ill U Pr.

— The Later Works of John Dewey, 1925-1953: Essays, Reviews, Miscellany, & a Common Faith, 1933-1934, Vol. 9. 472p. (C). 1989. pap. text 16.95 (0-8093-1577-7) S Ill U Pr.

— The Later Works of John Dewey, 1935-1937 Vol. 11: Essays & "Liberalism & Social Action" LC 80-27285. (Later Works of John Dewey, 1925-1953). 634p. (C). 1991. pap. 16.95 (0-8093-1677-3) S Ill U Pr.

— The Later Works of John Dewey, 1938 Vol. 12: Logic: The Theory of Inquiry. abr. ed. LC 80-27285. (Later Works of John Dewey, 1925-1953). 550p. (C). 1991. pap. 16.95 (0-8093-1678-1) S Ill U Pr.

— The Later Works of John Dewey, 1938-1939 Vol. 13: "Experience & Education," "Freedom & Culture," "Theory of Valuation," & Essays. abr. ed. LC 80-27285. (Later Works of John Dewey, 1925-1953). 430p. (C). 1991. pap. 16.95 (0-8093-1679-X) S Ill U Pr.

— The Later Works of John Dewey, 1939-1941 Vol. 14: Essays, Reviews, & Miscellany. abr. ed. LC 80-27285. (Later Works of John Dewey, 1925-1953). 532p. (C). 1991. pap. 16.95 (0-8093-1680-3) S Ill U Pr.

— The Later Works of John Dewey, 1942-1948 Vol. 15: Essays, Reviews, & Miscellany. abr. ed. LC 80-27285. (Later Works of John Dewey, 1925-1953). 538p. (C). 1991. pap. 16.95 (0-8093-1681-1) S Ill U Pr.

— The Later Works of John Dewey, 1949-1952 Vol. 16: Essays, Typescripts, & "Knowing & the Known" abr. ed. LC 80-27285. (Later Works of John Dewey, 1925-1953). 522p. (C). 1991. pap. text 16.95 (0-8093-1682-X) S Ill U Pr.

Boydston, Jo Ann. John Dewey's Personal & Professional Library: A Checklist. LC 81-18393. (Bibliographic Contributions Ser.). 128p. (Orig.). 1982. pap. 10.95 (0-8093-1068-6) S Ill U Pr.

Boydston, Jo Ann, ed. see Dewey, John.

Boydston, Jo Anne, ed. see Dewey, John.

Boydston, Joanne, ed. see Dewey, John.

Boye. Economics, 3 vols. (C). 1996. text, teacher ed., suppl. ed. 76.76 (0-395-74657-4) HM.

Boye, Alan. The Complete Roadside Guide to Nebraska. 2nd ed. (Illus.). 512p. (Orig.). 1993. pap. 18.95 (0-913473-11-1) Saltillo Pr.

— A Guide to the Ghosts of Lincoln. 2nd ed. 145p. (Orig.). 1987. pap. 5.95 (0-913473-08-1) Saltillo Pr.

***Boye, Alan, contrib. by.** Holding Stone Hands: On the Trail of the Cheyenne Exodus. LC 98-49783. (Illus.). 1999. 29.95 (0-8032-1294-1) U of Nebr Pr.

Boye, Alan, ed. Passumpsic River Canoeing & Recreation Guide. (Illus.). 74p. 1997. spiral bd. 2.95 (0-913473-12-X) Saltillo Pr.

Boye, Amelia, ed. & illus. see Collins, Penny.

Boye, Dale E. & Kavanaugh, Edward A. Elementary Algebra. Williams, Larry G., ed. 608p. (C). 1991. text 65.95 (0-534-92319-4) PWS Pubs.

Boye, Karin. Complete Poems. LC 94-183668. 192p. 1995. pap. 18.95 (1-85224-109-8, Pub. by Bloodaxe Bks) Dufour.

— Kallocain. Lannestock, Gustaf, tr. from SWE. LC 66-13798. (Nordic Translation Ser.). 219p. 1966. reprint ed. pap. 67.90 (0-608-01930-5, 206258500003) Bks Demand.

Boye, Robert. Underwater Paradise: The World's Best Diving Sites. (Illus.). 192p. 1989. 39.95 (0-8109-1159-0, Pub. by Abrams) Time Warner.

Boyens, Ingeborg. Unnatural Harvest: How Corporate Science Is Secretly Altering Our Food. 288p. 1999. 23.50 (0-385-25749-X) Bantam.

Boyer. Accident Kids. deluxe ed. LC 73-93019. (Safety Ser.). (Illus.). 32p. (J). (gr. 2-5). 1974. pap. 3.94 (0-87783-120-3) Oddo.

— American Foreign Policy. 2nd ed. 1996. 18.20 (0-697-32683-7, WCB McGr Hill) McGrw-H Hghr Educ.

— The American Nation in the 20th Century. 1996. text, teacher ed. 90.50 (0-03-094973-4); text, student ed. 57.00 (0-03-097683-9) H Holt & Co.

— The American Nation in the 20th Century. 98th ed. 1998. text 65.25 (0-03-050674-3) Holt R&W.

— Bob Rafelson. LC 96-33405. 1996. pap. 20.00 (0-8057-4613-7, Twyne) Mac Lib Ref.

— Boyer Enduring Vision Essen Ct. 1999. pap. text 99.87 (0-395-90123-5) HM.

— Boyer's the American Nation. 98th ed. 1996. text 66.75 (0-03-050673-5) Holt R&W.

— Boyer's the American Nation. 98th ed. LC 97-141366. 1998. text 98.80 (0-03-050789-8) Holt R&W.

— Brunner & Suddarth's Textbook of Medical-Surgical Nursing. 8th ed. 448p. 1996. pap. text, student ed. 16.95 (0-397-55230-0) Lppncott W & W.

— Concepts in Biochemistry with Infotrac. (Chemistry Ser.). 1998. 60.00 (0-534-36401-2) Brooks-Cole.

— Cpsq Exceling in Finance. 3rd ed. 1998. pap. text 22.50 (0-07-230535-5) McGraw.

— Enduring Vision Essen Ct. 1999. pap. text 99.87 (0-395-90122-7) HM.

***Boyer.** Enduring Vision Essentials. 1999. pap. text 22.47 (0-395-98233-2); pap. text 22.47 (0-395-98234-0) HM.

Boyer. Introductory Biochemistry. LC 98-6134. (Chemistry Ser.). 1998. mass mkt. 61.00 (0-534-17208-3) Wadsworth Pub.

Boyer. Mean Jeans Manufacturing Co. A Business Community Simulation. 2nd ed. 1990. text 160.00 (0-538-60282-1) Thomson Learn.

Boyer. Mean Jean's Manufacturing Company, Reference Manual: Business Communication Simulation. 2nd ed. (GB - Basic Business Ser.). 1990. mass mkt. 12.95 (0-538-60283-X) S-W Pub.

— Mean Jean's Manufacturing Company Simulation: A Business. (GB - Basic Business Ser.). 1983. 190.95 (0-538-07100-1) S-W Pub.

— Nitroazoles. LC 86-15667. (Organic Nitro Chemistry Ser.). 368p. 1987. text 120.00 (0-89573-148-7, Wiley-VCH) Wiley.

— Operations Man-Mean Jeans Manufacturing: Business Communication. 2nd ed. (GB - Basic Business Ser.). 1990. mass mkt. 31.95 (0-538-60284-8) S-W Pub.

— Tabla Cronologica del Nuevo Testamento - Chronological Chart of the New Testament. (Tablas Cronologicas - Chronological Chart Ser.). (SPA.). write for info. (1-56063-935-0) Editorial Unilit.

— Tabla Cronologica del Periodo Intertestamentario - Chronological Chart of the Period Between the Testaments. (Tablas Cronologicas Ser.). (SPA.). write for info. (1-56063-934-2) Editorial Unilit.

Boyer, et al, eds. Columbia Poetry Review, No. 5. (Orig.). 1992. pap. 6.00 (0-932026-29-X) Columbia College Chi.

Boyer, et al. The Hiring Handbook. 2nd ed. 775p. 1993. 106.00 (1-878375-94-6, S95) Panel Pubs.

— The Hiring Handbook. 2nd ed. 1994. write for info. (1-56706-075-7, S95) Panel Pubs.

Boyer-Alexander, jt. auth. see Rozmanjzl.

Boyer, Arlynda L. Social Security: Smashing the Tinkering Approach. (Illus.). 114p. 1997. pap. 9.95 (0-9672691-0-5) Third Mill NY.

Boyer, Arthur L., jt. ed. see Wright, Ann E.

Boyer, Barbara A., jt. auth. see Semrau, Penelope.

Boyer, Barbaranne. Muskoka's Grand Hotels. (Illus.). 192p. 1992. pap. 24.95 (1-55046-051-X, Pub. by Boston Mills) Genl Dist Srvs.

Boyer, Bruce, jt. auth. see Goddard, Connie.

Boyer, Bruce A. & Geraghty, Thomas F. Problems & Cases for Training the Child Advocate. 152p. 1994. pap. 21.95 (1-55681-454-2) Natl Inst Trial Ad.

Boyer, Bruce H., jt. auth. see Weingartner, Fannia.

Boyer, Carl, 3rd. Ancestral Lines: 206 Families in England, Wales, The Netherlands, Germany, New England, New York, New Jersey & Pennsylvania. 3rd ed. LC 97-78403. (Illus.). 960p. 1998. 70.00 (0-936124-18-0) C Boyer.

Boyer, Carl, III. How to Publish & Market Your Family History. 4th ed. LC 92-97111. 160p. 1993. 12.50 (0-936124-16-4) C Boyer.

Boyer, Carl, 3rd. Jacobus' Index to Genealogical Periodicals. rev. ed. 373p. 1995. 25.00 (0-89725-238-1, 1627) Picton Pr.

Boyer, Carl, 3rd, et al. Brown Families of Bristol Counties, Massachusetts & Rhode Island & Descendants of Jared Talbot. LC 80-68755. (New England Colonial Families Ser.: Vol. 1). 219p. 1982. 9.00 (0-936124-04-0) C Boyer.

Boyer, Carl B. History of Analytic Geometry: Its Development from the Pyramids to the Heroic Age. (Illus.). 302p. (C). 1988. reprint ed. pap. text 12.95 (0-945726-12-0); reprint ed. lib. bdg. 35.00 (0-945726-11-2) Scholars Bookshelf.

— A History of Mathematics. 2nd ed. 736p. 1991. pap. 34.95 (0-471-54397-7) Wiley.

— History of Mathematics. 2nd ed. LC 89-5325. 762p. 1989. text 95.95 (0-471-09763-2) Wiley.

— History of the Calculus & Its Conceptual Development. Orig. Title: Concepts of Calculus. 346p. (C). 1959. pap. 9.95 (0-486-60509-4) Dover.

— The Rainbow: From Myth to Mathematics. LC 87-2288. (Princeton Paperbacks Ser.). (Illus.). 376p. reprint ed. pap. 116.60 (0-608-06357-6, 206671800008) Bks Demand.

Boyer, Carol M. & Lewis, Darrell R. And on the Seventh Day: Faculty Consulting & Supplemental Income. Fife, Jonathan D., ed. LC 85-72834. (ASHE-ERIC Higher Education Reports: No. 85-3). 89p. (Orig.). (C). 1985. pap. 24.00 (0-913317-22-5) GWU Grad Schl E&HD.

Boyer, Charles C. Boyer: American Boyers. rev. ed. 663p. 1993. reprint ed. pap. 99.50 (0-8328-3271-5); reprint ed. lib. bdg. 109.50 (0-8328-3270-7) Higginson Bk Co.

Boyer, Charles D., et al, eds. Physiology, Biochemistry, & Genetics of Nongreen Plastids: Fourth Annual Penn State Symposium in Plant Physiology. LC 89-80455. 300p. (Orig.). (C). 1989. pap. text 20.00 (0-943088-15-1) Am Soc of Plan.

Boyer, Chris. Louisiana Parks Guide. McCarg, Barbara, ed. 100p. (Orig.). 1988. pap. text 4.95 (0-935201-33-5) Affordable Adven.

— Missouri Parks Guide. McCarg, Barbara, ed. 100p. (Orig.). 1988. pap. text 5.95 (0-935201-32-7) Affordable Adven.

Boyer, Chris, ed. see McCarg, Barbara.

Boyer, Chris, ed. see McCarg, Margie.

Boyer, Clarence V. The Villain As Hero in Elizabethan Tragedy. (BCL1-PR English Literature Ser.). 264p. 1992. reprint ed. lib. bdg. 79.00 (0-7812-7102-9) Rprt Serv.

Boyer, Dale, ed. see Blessing, Richard.

Boyer, Dale, ed. see Crews, Judson.

Boyer, Dale, ed. see Partridge, Dixie.

Boyer, Dale, ed. see Romero, Leo.

Boyer, Dale, ed. see Taggard, Genevieve.

Boyer, Dale, ed. see Witherup, William.

Boyer, Dale K., ed. see Bierds, Linda.

Boyer, Dale K., ed. see Coles, Katharine.

Boyer, Dale K., ed. see Cooper, Wyn.

Boyer, Dale K., ed. see Hales, Corrinne.

Boyer, Dale K., ed. see Hearle, Kevin.

Boyer, Dale K., ed. see McCullough, Ken.

Boyer, Dale K., ed. see Romero, Leo.

Boyer, Dale K., ed. see Smith, D. J.

Boyer, Dale K., ed. see Wright, Carolyne L.

Boyer, Darla. Introduction To Computing. 100p. (C). 1993. text 21.40 (0-536-58344-7) Pearson Custom.

— Introduction to Computing. 2nd ed. 154p. (C). 1995. text 21.40 (0-536-58874-0) Pearson Custom.

Boyer, David L. The Philosopher's Annual, 1979, Vol. 1. Grim, Patrick et al, eds. 231p. 1979. 38.50 (0-8476-6105-9) Rowman.

Boyer, David L., et al, eds. The Philosopher's Annual, 1980, Vol. III. xii, 225p. (Orig.). (C). 1980. lib. bdg. 32.00 (0-917930-38-X) Ridgeview.

— The Philosopher's Annual, 1981, Vol. IV. xii, 250p. (Orig.). (C). 1981. pap. text 10.00 (0-917930-61-4); lib. bdg. 32.00 (0-917930-75-4) Ridgeview.

— The Philosopher's Annual, 1982, Vol. V. xi, 250p. (Orig.). (C). 1982. lib. bdg. 32.00 (0-917930-77-0) Ridgeview.

— The Philosopher's Annual, 1979, Vol. 2. 231p. 1979. 38.50 (0-8476-6202-0) Rowman.

Boyer, David L., ed. see Sanders, John T.

Boyer, Dennis. Driftless Spirits: Ghosts of Southwestern Wisconsin. LC 96-43649. (Illus.). 240p. (Orig.). (YA). 1996. pap. 14.95 (1-879483-35-1) Prairie Oak Pr.

— Giants in the Land: Folk Tales & Legends of Wisconsin. LC 97-35598. (Illus.). 176p. 1997. pap. 12.95 (1-879483-45-9) Prairie Oak Pr.

***Boyer, Dennis.** Great Wisconsin Taverns: 101 Distinctive Badger Bars. Stoga, Stan, ed. LC 99-73862. (Illus.). 152p. 1999. pap. 14.95 (0-915024-76-4) Trails Media.

Boyer, Dennis. Northern Frights: A Supernatural Ecology of the Wisconsin Headwaters. LC 98-8584. (Illus.). 224p. 1998. pap. 14.95 (1-879483-53-X) Prairie Oak Pr.

Boyer, Dennis & Isherwood, Justin, eds. A Place to Which We Belong: Wisconsin Writers on Wisconsin Landscapes. (Illus.). 1998. pap. 16.95 (0-9666359-0-6) One Thous Friends.

Boyer, Don & Garret, Clay. Howell Book of Lizards. 1999. 27.95 (0-87605-370-3) Howell Bks.

Boyer, Don & Garrett, Clay. Howell Book of Snakes. 1999. 27.95 (0-87605-369-X) Howell Bks.

Boyer, Dwight. Ghost Ships of the Great Lakes. (Illus.). 294p. 1968. reprint ed. pap. 13.75 (0-912514-47-7) Freshwater.

— Great Stories of the Great Lakes. (Illus.). 242p. 1960. reprint ed. pap. text 13.75 (0-912514-49-3) Freshwater.

— Ships & Men of the Great Lakes. 208p. 1960. pap. 13.75 (0-912514-51-5) Freshwater.

— Strange Adventures of the Great Lakes. 248p. 1960. pap. 13.75 (0-912514-52-3) Freshwater.

— True Tales of the Great Lakes. (Illus.). 340p. 1960. reprint ed. pap. 13.75 (0-912514-48-5) Freshwater.

Boyer, E. Gil, jt. ed. see Simon, Anita.

Boyer, Elizabeth. A Colony of One. LC 83-50742. (Illus.). 1983. 30.00 (0-915964-05-8) Veritie Pr.

— Marguerite De la Roque: A Story of Survival. LC 75-20805. 1975. 20.00 (0-915964-01-5) Veritie Pr.

Boyer, Ernest. Cornerstones for a New Century. 48p. 1992. pap. 7.95 (0-8106-1846-X) NEA.

Boyer, Ernest, et al. Perspectives on the Freshman Year, Vol. II. (Freshman Year Experience Monograph Ser.: No. 8). (Orig.). 1992. pap. 20.00 (1-889271-06-3) Nat Res Ctr.

Boyer, Ernest L. The Basic School: A Community for Learning. LC 95-11506. 255p. (Orig.). 1995. pap. 15.00 (0-931050-48-0) Carnegie Fnd Advan Teach.

— Ernest L. Boyer, Selected Speeches, 1979-1995. LC 97-24826. 1997. 15.00 (0-931050-60-X) Carnegie Fnd Advan Teach.

— Promises to Keep: The United States since World War II. 2nd ed. LC 98-71991. 1998. pap. text 26.37 (0-395-90386-6) HM.

— Ready to Learn: A Mandate for the Nation. 1994. 14.00 (0-89333-119-8) AACTE.

— Ready to Learn: A Mandate for the Nation. LC 91-46817. (Illus.). 193p. 1991. pap. 12.00 (0-931050-44-8) Carnegie Fnd Advan Teach.

— Scholarship Reconsidered: Priorities of the Professoriate. LC 90-22684. 147p. (Orig.). 1990. pap. 12.00 (0-7879-4069-0) Carnegie Fnd Advan Teach.

Boyer, Ernest L., frwd. Campus Life: In Search of Community. LC 90-32888. 148p. 1990. pap. 12.00 (0-931050-38-3) Carnegie Fnd Advan Teach.

— A Classification of Institutions of Higher Education, 1994. LC 94-36243. (Technical Reports). 1994. 15.00 (0-931050-46-4) Carnegie Fnd Advan Teach.

— School Choice. LC 92-40895. 129p. 1992. 12.00 (0-931050-45-6) Carnegie Fnd Advan Teach.

— Tribal Colleges: Shaping the Future of Native America. LC 89-27994. 103p. 1989. pap. text 8.00 (0-931050-36-7) Carnegie Fnd Advan Teach.

Boyer, Ernest L. & Boyer, Paul. Smart Parents Guide to College: The 10 Most Important Factors for Students & Parents to Know When Choosing a College. LC 96-31264. 256p. (Orig.). 1996. pap. 16.95 (1-56079-591-3) Petersons.

Boyer, Ernest L. & Carnegie Foundation for the Advancement of Teachin. College: The Undergraduate Experience in America. LC 97-33424. 352p. 1997. reprint ed. pap. 12.00 (0-06-091458-0, PL-1458) Carnegie Fnd Advan Teach.

Boyer, Ernest L. & Hechinger, Fred M. Higher Learning in the Nation's Service. LC 81-70738. 69p. 1981. pap. 6.50 (0-931050-20-0) Carnegie Fnd Advan Teach.

Boyer, Ernest L. & Levine, Arthur. A Quest for Common Learning: The Aims of General Education. LC 81-66307. 68p. 1981. pap. 12.00 (0-931050-18-9) Carnegie Fnd Advan Teach.

Boyer, Ernest L. & Mitgang, Lee D. Building Community: A New Future for Architecture Education & Practice: A Special Report. LC 96-13832. 1996. 12.00 (0-931050-59-6) Carnegie Fnd Advan Teach.

Boyer, Francois. Jeux Interdits. (FRE.). 1973. pap. 10.95 (0-7859-1757-8, 2070364534) Fr & Eur.

Boyer, G. Bruce. Elegance: A Guide to Quality in Menswear. LC 84-27271. (Illus.). 1987. pap. 9.95 (0-393-30438-8) Norton.

Boyer, G. G. Dorn. large type ed. LC 91-33087. 292p. 1992. reprint ed. lib. bdg. 16.95 (1-56054-285-3) Thorndike Pr.

— Winchester Affidavit. 1997. 17.95 (0-614-27914-3) Five Star.

— Winchester Affidavit. large type ed. LC 96-53880. (Five-Star Western Ser.). 338p. 1997. 17.95 (0-7862-0739-6) Thorndike Pr.

— Winchester Affidavit. large type ed. LC 98-5430. 1998. 22.95 (0-7862-0762-0) Thorndike Pr.

Boyer, Gerald D. Vehicle Identification, 1992-1993. 144p. (Orig.). 1993. pap. 18.00 (0-939818-23-X) Lee Bks.

— Vehicle Identification, 1994-1995. 1995. pap. 18.00 (0-939818-26-4) Lee Bks.

An Asterisk (*) at the beginning of an entry indicates that the title is appearing for the first time.

— Vehicle Identification, 1996-1997. 144p. 1997. pap. 18.00 (*0-939818-27-2*) Lee Bks.

Boyer, Gerald D. & Cole, Lee S. The Investigation of Vehicle Thefts. 3rd ed. (Illus.). 240p. (Orig.). 1995. pap. 34.95 (*0-939818-24-8*) Lee Bks.

Boyer, Gerald D., jt. auth. see Cole, Lee S.

***Boyer, Glenn G.** The Earp Curse. (Illus.). 219p. 1999. pap. 26.95 (*1-890670-13-8*) Hist Research.

Boyer, Glenn G. Suppressed Murder of Wyatt Earp. rev. ed. (Illus.). 168p. 1997. lib. bdg. 39.95 (*1-890670-07-3*) Hist Research.

— Wyatt Earp Vol. I: Family, Friends & Foes: Who Was Big Nose Kate?, 6 vols. rev. ed. (Illus.). 30p. 1997. reprint ed. pap. 7.95 (*1-890670-06-5*) Hist Research.

— Wyatt Earp Vol. II: Facts, Previously Unpublished Childhood & Youth of Wyatt's Wife, Josephine Sarah Marcus, 6 vols. rev. ed. (Illus.). 34p. 1997. reprint ed. pap. 7.95 (*1-890670-01-4*) Hist Research.

— Wyatt Earp Vol. II: Family, Friends & Foes: Who Was Sheriff Johnny Behan?, 6 vols. rev. ed. (Illus.). 26p. 1997. reprint ed. pap. 7.95 (*1-890670-08-1*) Hist Research.

— Wyatt Earp Vol. III: Facts, Trailing an American Myth & Those Marryin' Earp Men, 6 vols. rev. ed. (Illus.). 48p. 1997. reprint ed. pap. 7.95 (*1-890670-02-2*) Hist Research.

— Wyatt Earp Vol. III: Family, Friends & Foes: Morgan Earp, Brother in the Shadow, 6 vols. rev. ed. (Illus.). 26p. 1997. reprint ed. pap. 7.95 (*1-890670-09-X*) Hist Research.

— Wyatt Earp Vol. IV: Facts, Wyatt Earp's Wild Boyhood & Youth in Pella, Iowa, 6 vols. rev. ed. (Illus.). 38p. 1997. reprint ed. pap. 7.95 (*1-890670-03-0*) Hist Research.

— Wyatt Earp Vol. IV: Family, Friends & Foes: Curly Bill Has Been Killed at Last, 6 vols. rev. ed. (Illus.). 26p. 1997. reprint ed. pap. 7.95 (*1-890670-10-3*) Hist Research.

— Wyatt Earp Vol. V: Facts, by Wagon Train from Iowa to California - 1864, 6 vols. rev. ed. (Illus.). 28p. 1997. reprint ed. pap. 7.95 (*1-890670-04-9*) Hist Research.

— Wyatt Earp Vol. V: Friends, Family & Foes: Who Killed John Ringo, 6 vols. rev. ed. (Illus.). 34p. 1997. reprint ed. pap. 7.95 (*1-890670-11-1*) Hist Research.

— Wyatt Earp Vol. VI: Facts, Wyatt Wears His First Badge - Lamar, MD - 1870, 6 vols. rev. ed. (Illus.). 34p. 1997. reprint ed. pap. 7.95 (*1-890670-05-7*) Hist Research.

— Wyatt Earp Vol. VI: Friends, Family & Foes: Murder at Millville, 6 vols. rev. ed. (Illus.). 18p. 1997. reprint ed. pap. 7.95 (*1-890670-12-X*) Hist Research.

— Wyatt Earp's Tombstone Vendetta. 368p. 1993. 49.95 (*0-9631772-2-2*) Talei Pubs.

Boyer, Glenn G., compiled by. Wyatt Earp's Tombstone Vendetta. large type ed. LC 94-739. 441p. (J). 1994. lib. bdg. 21.95 (*0-8161-5959-9*, G K Hall Lrg Type) Mac Lib Ref.

Boyer, Glenn G., ed. see Earp, Josephine.

Boyer, H. E., ed. Atlas of Creep & Stress-Rupture Curves. 663p. 1988. 204.00 (*0-87170-322-X*) ASM.

Boyer, H. Patsy, tr. see De Zayas, Maria.

Boyer, Harriet, jt. ed. see Cabrera, Vicente.

Boyer, Heidi. Mastering the Secrets of True Love: How to Find True Love, How to Solve Love Problems, How to Keep Your Love Alive. (Illus.). 240p. (Orig.). 1994. pap. write for info. (*0-9638452-0-9*) Lakewood Ent.

***Boyer, Horace C.** The Golden Age of Gospel. LC 99-55024. (Music in American Life Ser.). 2000. pap. 19.95 (*0-252-06877-7*) U of Ill Pr.

Boyer, Horace C. How Sweet the Sound: The Golden Age of Gospel. LC 95-234266. (Illus.). 248p. 1995. 29.95 (*1-880216-19-1*, Elliott Clark) Black Belt Communs.

Boyer, Howard E. Practical Heat Treating. 243p. 1984. 97.00 (*0-87170-178-2*, 6518) ASM.

Boyer, Howard E. & Cary, Philip R., eds. Quenching & Control of Distortion. LC 88-171400. 301p. reprint ed. pap. 93.40 (*0-7837-2769-0*, 204316000006) Bks Demand.

Boyer, Howard E., ed. see American Society for Metals Staff.

Boyer, Irma & Sparkman, LaVonne M. Where the Big Bottom Begins: Randle History. LC 95-67170. (Illus.). 256p. 1995. 24.95 (*0-9645570-0-2*) Sparkman Pub.

Boyer, J. L. & Bianchi, L., eds. Liver Cirrhosis. (Falk Ser.: No. 44). 1987. text 206.50 (*0-85200-993-3*) Kluwer Academic.

Boyer, James B. & Baptiste, H. Prentice. Transforming the Curriculum for Multicultural Understandings: A Practitioner's Handbook. LC 96-30455. 266p. 1996. 19.95 (*1-880192-19-5*) Caddo Gap Pr.

Boyer, James B. & Boyer, Joe L. Curriculum & Instruction after Desegregation. 1975. pap. 5.00 (*0-686-00371-3*) AG Pr.

Boyer, James L. A Manual of Greek Forms. pap. 4.99 (*0-88469-007-5*) BMH Bks.

— Prophecy, Things to Come. pap. 7.99 (*0-88469-006-7*) BMH Bks.

Boyer, Jan. Sidney Lumet. LC 93-28388. (Twayne's Filmmakers Ser.). 240p. 1993. pap. 20.00 (*0-8057-9330-5*); text 26.95 (*0-8057-9329-1*) Macmillan.

Boyer, Jay. As Far Away As China. LC 88-93039. 78p. (C). 1989. pap. 8.95 (*0-923707-02-6*) Pratt CO.

— Bob Rafelson, Film Director. LC 96-33405. 1996. 33.00 (*0-8057-4612-9*, Twyne) Mac Lib Ref.

— Ishmael Reed. LC 93-70138. (Western Writers Ser.: No. 110). (Illus.). 52p. 1993. pap. 4.95 (*0-88430-109-5*) Boise St U W Writ Ser.

***Boyer, Jefferson, ed.** Art Calendar Annual Artists Resource Directory. 174p. 1999. pap. 18.00 (*0-945388-25-X*) Art Calendar.

Boyer, Jill W. Breaking Camp. LC 83-82772. (Illus.). 61p. (YA). (gr. 9-12). 1984. per. 6.00 (*0-916418-52-9*) Lotus.

Boyer, Joe L., jt. auth. see Boyer, James B.

Boyer, John H. Mass Communication Law in West Virginia. (State Law Ser.). 110p. 1992. pap. text 11.95 (*0-913507-36-9*) New Forums.

Boyer, John S. Measuring the Water Status of Plants & Soils. LC 95-10872. (Illus.). 178p. 1995. 32.00 (*0-12-122260-8*) Acad Pr.

Boyer, John S., jt. auth. see Kramer, Paul J.

Boyer, John W. Culture & Crisis in Vienna. LC 94-36240. 718p. 1995. 37.50 (*0-226-06960-5*) U Ch Pr.

— Political Radicalism in Late Imperial Vienna: Origins of the Christian Social Movement, 1848-1897. LC 80-17302. (Illus.). 1981. 40.00 (*0-226-06957-5*) U Ch Pr.

— Political Radicalism in Late Imperial Vienna: Origins of the Christian Social Movement, 1848-1897. 592p. 1995. pap. text 24.95 (*0-226-06956-7*) U Ch Pr.

Boyer, John W., et al, eds. University of Chicago Reading in Western Civilization, Vol. 9: Twentieth Century Europe. LC 85-16328. (Readings in Western Civilization Ser.). 640p. (C). 1987. pap. text 18.00 (*0-226-06954-0*); lib. bdg. 48.00 (*0-226-06953-2*) U Ch Pr.

— University of Chicago Readings in Western Civilization: Medieval Europe, Vol. 4. LC 85-16328. x, 462p. 1986. pap. text 17.00 (*0-226-06943-5*); lib. bdg. 36.00 (*0-226-06942-7*) U Ch Pr.

— University of Chicago Readings in Western Civilization: The Church in the Roman Empire, Vol. 3. LC 85-16328. 256p. 1986. pap. text 14.00 (*0-226-06939-7*); lib. bdg. 24.00 (*0-226-06938-9*) U Ch Pr.

— University of Chicago Readings in Western Civilization: The Greek Polis, Vol. 1. LC 85-16328. (Readings in Western Civilization Ser.). viii, 360p. (C). 1986. pap. text 12.00 (*0-226-06935-4*); lib. bdg. 30.00 (*0-226-06934-6*) U Ch Pr.

— University of Chicago Readings in Western Civilization: The Renaissance, Vol. 5. LC 85-16328. (Readings in Western Civilization Ser.). x, 448p. (C). 1986. pap. text 16.95 (*0-226-06945-1*); lib. bdg. 36.00 (*0-226-06944-3*) U Ch Pr.

— University of Chicago Readings in Western Civilization Vol. 2: Rome: Late Republic & Principate. LC 85-16328. vii, 316p. (C). 1986. pap. text 13.00 (*0-226-06937-0*) U Ch Pr.

— University of Chicago Readings in Western Civilization Vol. 2: Rome: Late Republic & Principate. LC 85-16328. Vol. 2. vii, 320p. (C). 1986. lib. bdg. 30.00 (*0-226-06936-2*) U Ch Pr.

— University of Chicago Readings in Western Civilization, Vol. 6, Early Modern Europe: Crisis of Authority. LC 85-16328. (Readings in Western Civilization Ser.). x, 618p. (C). 1987. pap. text 17.95 (*0-226-06948-6*); lib. bdg. 40.00 (*0-226-06947-8*) U Ch Pr.

— University of Chicago Readings in Western Civilization, Vol. 7: The Old Regime & the French Revolution. LC 85-16328. (Readings in Western Civilization Ser.). x, 480p. (C). 1987. lib. bdg. 40.00 (*0-226-06949-4*) U Ch Pr.

— University of Chicago Readings in Western Civilization, Vol. 7: The Old Regime & the French Revolution. LC 85-16328. (Readings in Western Civilization Ser.: Vol. 7). x, 480p. (C). 1987. pap. text 14.00 (*0-226-06950-8*) U Ch Pr.

— University of Chicago Readings in Western Civilization, Vol. 8, Nineteenth-Century Europe: Liberalism & Its Critics. LC 86-16328. (Readings in Western Civilization Ser.). x, 584p. (C). 1987. pap. text 19.00 (*0-226-06952-4*); lib. bdg. 45.00 (*0-226-06951-6*) U Ch Pr.

Boyer, John W., jt. ed. see Geyer, Michael.

Boyer, Joseph, jt. auth. see Nordhaus, William D.

Boyer, K. L., et al. Applications of AI, Machne Vision & Robotics. (Machine Perception & Artificial Intelligence Ser.: Vol. 17). 268p. 1995. text 61.00 (*981-02-2150-9*) World Scientific Pub.

Boyer, Karl P. Positive & Black: A Resource Directory of Famous Contemporary African Americans & Organizations. 31p. (J). (gr. 8). 1993. pap. text 6.00 (*0-9642154-0-3*) Positive & Black.

Boyer, Kathryn L., et al. Primary Care Oncology. Kuhn, Shirley, ed. LC 98-5822. (Illus.). 416p. (C). 1998. pap. text 45.00 (*0-7216-7316-3*, W B Saunders Co) Harcrt Hlth Sci Grp.

Boyer, Keith, jt. auth. see Kemp, Kathy.

Boyer, Kenneth D. Principles of Transportation Economics. LC 97-24731. 416p. (C). 1997. 93.00 (*0-321-01103-1*) Addson-Wesley Educ.

Boyer, Kenneth D. & Shepherd, William G., eds. Economic Regulation: Essays in Honor of James R. Nelson. LC 81-81384. (MSU Public Utilities Papers: Vol. 1981). 388p. reprint ed. pap. 120.30 (*0-608-20490-0*, 207174200002) Bks Demand.

Boyer, Kenneth R. The Encyclopedia of Crossword Sticklers. 250p. (YA). write for info. (*0-9675357-1-9*) Person Secur.

Boyer, Kent. Chiropractor: The Quest for Professional Respect. LC 93-28885. 188p. 1994. pap. text 24.95 (*1-879904-12-8*) Halo Bks.

Boyer, Kent L. Topographical & Motion Palpation of the Appendicular Skeleton. LC 95-9283. (Illus.). 184p. 1995. pap. text 29.95 (*0-7734-9919-9*) E Mellen.

— Topographical & Motion Palpation of the Axial Skeleton. LC 91-19648. (Illus.). 128p. 1991. pap. 39.95 (*0-7734-9904-0*) E Mellen.

***Boyer, Kim L. & Sarkar, Sudeep.** Perceptual Organization for Artificial Vision Systems. 368p. 2000. 125.00 (*0-7923-7799-0*) Kluwer Academic.

Boyer, Kim L., jt. auth. see Sudeep, Sarkar.

Boyer, L. Bryce. Childhood & Folklore: A Psychoanalytic Study of Apache Personality. (Illus.). 1979. pap. 10.95 (*0-914434-09-8*) Psychohistory Pr.

— Countertransference & Regression. 1998. pap. 40.00 (*1-56821-706-4*) Aronson.

Boyer, L. Bryce, et al, eds. The Psychoanalytic Study of Society: Essays in Honor of George A. De Vos, Vol. 19. 392p. 1994. text 45.00 (*0-88163-183-3*) Analytic Pr.

Boyer, L. Bryce & Boyer, Ruth, eds. The Psychoanalytic Study of Society Vol. 17: Essays in Honor of George D. & Louise A. Spindler. 384p. 1992. text 36.00 (*0-88163-151-5*) Analytic Pr.

Boyer, L. Bryce & Boyer, Ruth M., eds. The Psychoanalytic Study of Society: Essays in Honor of A. Irving Hallowell, Vol. 16. 344p. 1991. 36.00 (*0-88163-140-X*) Analytic Pr.

Boyer, L. Bryce & Giovacchini, Peter L., eds. Master Clinicians on Treating the Regressed Patient, Vol. 1. LC 89-6975. 408p. 1990. 60.00 (*0-87668-834-2*) Aronson.

Boyer, L. Bryce & Grolnick, Simon A., eds. The Psychoanalytic Study of Society: Essays in Honor of George Devereux, Vol. 12. (Muensterberger Ser.). 248p. (C). 1987. text 29.95 (*0-88163-069-1*) Analytic Pr.

— The Psychoanalytic Study of Society: Essays in Honor of Melford E. Spiro, Vol. 15. (Muensterberger Ser.). 416p. 1990. text 39.95 (*0-88163-115-9*) Analytic Pr.

— The Psychoanalytic Study of Society: Essays in Honor of Paul Parin, Vol. 14. (Muensterberger Ser.). 344p 1989. 36.00 (*0-88163-085-3*) Analytic Pr.

— The Psychoanalytic Study of Society: Essays in Honor of Werner Muensterberger, Vol. 11. (Muensterberger Ser.). 264p. (C). 1985. text 29.95 (*0-88163-032-2*) Analytic Pr.

— The Psychoanalytic Study of Society: Essays in Honor of Westo LaBarre, Vol. 13. (Muensterberger Ser.). 200p. 1988. text 29.95 (*0-88163-079-9*) Analytic Pr.

Boyer, L. Bryce, et al. The Psychoanalytic Study of Society Vol. 18: Essays in Honor of Alan Dundes. 522p. 1993. 45.00 (*0-88163-161-2*) Analytic Pr.

Boyer, L. Bryce, jt. auth. see De Vos, George A.

Boyer, L. Bryce, jt. ed. see Giovacchini, Peter.

Boyer, Linda. God Made Me. (Happy Day Bks.). (Illus.). 24p. (Orig.). (J). (ps). 1995. pap. 1.99 (*0-7847-0350-7*, 04230) Standard Pub.

Boyer, Lucretia, ed. see Kider, Mitchel & Noel, Lisa.

Boyer, M. Christine. The City of Collective Memory: Its Historical Imagery & Architectural Entertainments. (Illus.). 572p. 1994. 55.00 (*0-262-02371-7*) MIT Pr.

— The City of Collective Memory: Its Historical Imagery & Architectural Entertainments. (Illus.). 576p. 1996. reprint ed. pap. text 27.50 (*0-262-52211-X*) MIT Pr.

— Dreaming the Rational City: The Myth of American City Planning. 344p. 1986. pap. text 21.00 (*0-262-52111-3*) MIT Pr.

Boyer, Marie-France. Cabin Fever: Sheds & Shelters, Huts & Hideaways. LC 93-60122. (Illus.). 112p. 1993. 19.95 (*0-500-01575-9*, Pub. by Thames Hudson) Norton.

***Boyer, Marie-France.** Cult of the Virgin: Offerings, Ornaments & Festivals. LC 99-66192. (Illus.). 112p. 2000. 24.95 (*0-500-01988-6*, Pub. by Thames Hudson) Norton.

Boyer, Marie-France. The French Cafe. LC 94-60273. (Illus.). 112p. 1994. 19.95 (*0-500-01622-4*, Pub. by Thames Hudson) Norton.

— Private Paris: The 30 Most Beautiful Apartments. (Illus.). 192p. 1988. 50.00 (*0-89659-922-1*) Abbeville Pr.

— The Private Realm of Marie-Antoinette. LC 95-61617. (Illus.). 112p. 1996. 19.95 (*0-500-01690-9*, Pub. by Thames Hudson) Norton.

— Really Rural: Authentic French Country Interiors. Wood, John & Wood, Veronique, trs. from FRE. LC 97-60246. (Illus.). 120p. 1997. 22.50 (*0-500-01799-9*, Pub. by Thames Hudson) Norton.

— Tree-Talk. LC 96-60251. (Illus.). 112p. 1996. 19.95 (*0-500-01729-8*, Pub. by Thames Hudson) Norton.

— Village Voices: French Country Life. LC 99-70949. (Illus.). 112p. 1999. 24.95 (*0-500-01945-2*, Pub. by Thames Hudson) Norton.

Boyer, Marilyn, jt. auth. see Boyer, Rick.

Boyer, Marjorie N. Medieval French Bridges: A History. LC 75-36478. (Medieval Academy Bks.: No. 84). 1976. 25.00 (*0-910956-58-8*) Medieval Acad.

Boyer, Mark. Following the Star: Daily Reflections for Advent & Christmas. LC 89-84465. 128p. 1989. pap. 5.95 (*0-89243-305-1*) Liguori Pubns.

Boyer, Mark A. The G-7 Negotiates Soviet Aid: From Enemies to Benefactors & the 1991 Summit Aid Package. (Pew Case Studies in International Affairs). 50p. (C). 1993. pap. text 3.50 (*1-56927-155-0*) Geo U Inst Dplmcy.

— International Cooperation & Public Goods: Opportunities for the Western Alliance. LC 92-14737. 208p. 1993. text 35.00 (*0-8018-4440-1*) Johns Hopkins.

Boyer, Mark A. & Rourke, John T. International Politics on the World Stage. abr. ed. 448p. (C). 1996. text. write for info. (*0-697-32380-3*) Brown & Benchmark.

Boyer, Mark A., jt. auth. see Rourke, John T.

Boyer, Mark G. Adults: Preparing to Celebrate a Christian Funeral: Adults, Vol. 1. LC 98-51062. Vol. 1. 176p. 1999. pap. 19.95 (*0-8146-2544-4*) Liturgical Pr.

— Baptized into Christ's Death & Resurrection: Preparing to Celebrate a Christian Funeral: Children, Vol. 2 LC 98-51062. 110p. 1999. pap. 14.95 (*0-8146-2545-2*) Liturgical Pr.

— Day by Ordinary Day with Luke, 3 vols. 1997. [illegible]8.95 (*0-8189-0786-X*) Alba.

— Day by Ordinary Day with Luke: Daily Reflections for Ordinary Time: Weeks 22-34. LC 96-44890. (Day by Ordinary Day Ser.: Vol. 3). 350p. (Orig.). 1997. pap. 17.95 (*0-8189-0785-1*) Alba.

— Day by Ordinary Day with Mark: Daily Reflections for Ordinary Time: Weeks 1-9. LC 96-44890. 1997. pap. 12.95 (*0-8189-0783-5*) Alba.

— Day by Ordinary Day with Matthew: Daily Reflections for Ordinary Time: Weeks 10-21. LC 96-44890. (Day by Ordinary Day Ser.: Vol. 2). 350p. (Orig.). 1997. pap. 17.95 (*0-8189-0784-3*) Alba.

***Boyer, Mark G.** Greatest Gift of All: Relections & Prayers for the Christmas Season. LC 99-65632. 96p. (YA). 1999. pap. 8.95 (*0-87946-206-X*) ACTA Pubns.

Boyer, Mark G. Home Is a Holy Place: Reflections, Prayers & Meditations Inspired by the Ordinary. 88p. (Orig.). 1997. pap. 6.95 (*0-87946-155-1*) ACTA Pubns.

— The Liturgical Environment: What the Documents Say. 176p. (Orig.). 1991. pap. 9.95 (*0-8146-1963-0*) Liturgical Pr.

***Boyer, Mark G.** Meditations for Ministers. LC 00-101209. 160p. 2000. pap. 9.95 (*0-87946-213-2*) ACTA Pubns.

Boyer, Mark G. Month by Month Guide to Entertaining Angels: Meeting God's Messengers in Scripture & in Our Lives. LC 95-78803. 192p. 1995. pap. 11.95 (*0-87946-121-7*) ACTA Pubns.

— Return to the Lord: A Lenten Journey of Daily Reflections. LC 90-24013. 183p. 1991. pap. 8.95 (*0-8189-0605-7*) Alba.

— Why Suffer? The Answer of Jesus. 1994. pap. text 11.95 (*1-56929-019-9*, Pastoral Press) OR Catholic.

Boyer, Martha. Mongol Jewelry. LC 95-60286. (Carlsberg Nomad Ser.). (Illus.). 272p. 1995. 50.00 (*0-500-01660-7*, Pub. by Thames Hudson) Norton.

Boyer, Mary. Arizona in Literature. LC 78-129967. (American History & Americana Ser.: No. 47). 1970. reprint ed. lib. bdg. 75.00 (*0-8383-1168-7*) M S G Haskell Hse.

Boyer, Mary J. Lippincott's Need-to-Know ECG Facts. 192p. 1997. pap. text 14.95 (*0-397-55461-3*) Lppncott W & W.

Boyer, Mary Jo. Math for Nurses: A Pocket Guide to Dosage Calculation & Drug Administration. 4th ed. LC 97-42716. 320p. 1998. spiral bd. 15.95 (*0-7817-1021-9*) Lppncott W & W.

Boyer, Mary Jo. Study Guide to Accompany Brunner & Suddarth's Textbook of Medical Surgical Nursing. 9th ed. 400p. pap. text 19.95 (*0-7817-2305-1*) Lppncott W & W.

Boyer, Mary Manning, jt. auth. see Kratt, Mary.

Boyer, Mary Manning, jt. auth. see Kratt, Mary Norton.

Boyer, Michael H. Personal Property Insurance Fraud Checklists, 1991. LC 88-17496. 1991. spiral bd. 68.00 (*0-87632-772-2*) West Group.

Boyer, Mildred, tr. see Borges, Jorge Luis.

Boyer, O. Biog./Grandes Cristianos, Vol. 1.Tr. of Heroes of the Faith. 160p. 1983. pap. 5.99 (*0-8297-1342-5*) Vida Pubs.

— Biog./Grandes Cristianos, Vol. 2.Tr. of Heroes of the Faith. (SPA.). 176p. 1983. pap. 5.99 (*0-8297-1343-3*) Vida Pubs.

Boyer, P. Art of Rene Lalique. 192p. 1996. 24.98 (*0-7858-0645-8*) Bk Sales Inc.

Boyer, Pascal. The Naturalness of Religious Ideas: A Cognitive Theory of Religion. LC 92-37506. 1994. 45.00 (*0-520-07559-5*, Pub. by U CA Pr) Cal Prin Full Svc.

— Tradition As Truth & Communication: A Cognitive Description of Traditional Discourse. (Cambridge Studies in Social & Cultural Anthropology: No. 68). 153p. (C). 1990. text 59.95 (*0-521-37417-0*) Cambridge U Pr.

Boyer, Patricia A. & Jeffrey, Ronnald J. A Guide for the Family Therapist. LC 83-3799. 192p. 1984. 35.00 (*0-87668-637-4*) Aronson.

— A Guide for the Family Therapist. LC 83-3799. 190p. 1994. pap. 35.00 (*1-56821-285-2*) Aronson.

Boyer, Patricia E. & National Gallery of Art (U. S.) Staff. Artists & the Avant-Garde: Theatre in Paris, 1887-1900. LC 97-44775. (Martin & Liane W. Atlas Collection Ser.). (Illus.). 180p. 1999. pap. 40.00 (*0-89468-274-1*) Natl Gallery Art.

Boyer, Patrick. Hands-on Democracy: How You Can Take Part in Canada's Renewal. 120p. 1993. pap. 7.95 (*0-7737-5597-7*) Genl Dist Srvs.

— A Passion for Justice: The Legacy of James Chalmers McRuer. (Osgood Society for Canadian Legal History Ser.). (Illus.). 438p. 1994. text 35.00 (*0-8020-0656-6*) U of Toronto Pr.

Boyer, Paul. Building & Displaying Scale Model Aircraft with Paul Boyer: An Illustrated Guide. LC 97-225322. (Illus.). 88p. (Orig.). 1997. pap. 12.95 (*0-89024-237-2*, 12151, Kalmbach Books) Kalmbach.

— By the Bomb's Early Light: American Thought & Culture at the Dawn of the Atomic Age. LC 94-4241. (Illus.). 470p. 1994. reprint ed. pap. 19.95 (*0-8078-4480-2*) U of NC Pr.

***Boyer, Paul.** The Enduring Vision: A History of the American People. 4th ed. 1999. pap. text, teacher ed. 8.97 (*0-395-96081-9*) HM.

Boyer, Paul. Fallout: A Historian Reflects on America's Half-Century Encounter with Nuclear Weapons. LC 97-47144. 288p. 1998. text 45.00 (*0-8142-0785-5*, BOYFAL); pap. text 18.95 (*0-8142-0786-3*, BOYFAX) Ohio St U Pr.

— Promises to Keep: The United States since World War II. LC 94-70648. 560p. (C). 1995. pap. text 33.16 (*0-669-20350-5*) HM Trade Div.

— Urban Masses & Moral Order in America, 1820-1920. (Illus.). 432p. (C). 1992. pap. 20.50 (*0-674-93110-6*) HUP.

— When Time Shall Be No More: Prophecy Belief in Modern American Culture. (Studies in Cultural History). (Illus.). 512p. 1992. text 35.00 (*0-674-95128-X*) HUP.

— When Time Shall Be No More: Prophecy Belief in Modern American Culture. (Studies in Cultural History). 490p. (C). 1994. pap. text 18.50 (*0-674-95129-8*) HUP.

Boyer, Paul, ed. Reagan As President: Contemporary Views of the Man, His Politics, & His Policies. 288p. 1990. pap. text 8.95 (*0-929587-28-6*, Elephant Paperbacks) I R Dee.

An Asterisk (*) at the beginning of an entry indicates that the title is appearing for the first time.

Boyer, Paul & Nissenbaum, Stephen. Salem Possessed. LC 97-72757. (Illus.). 232p. 1997. pap. 7.98 (*1-56731-226-8*, MJF Bks) Fine Comms.

Boyer, Paul & Nissenbaum, Stephen. Salem Possessed: The Social Origins of Witchcraft. LC 73-84399. 320p. 1976. pap. 15.95 (*0-674-78526-6*) HUP.

Boyer, Paul & Nissenbaum, Stephen, eds. Salem-Village Witchcraft: A Documentary Record of Local Conflict in Colonial New England. rev. ed. 416p. 1993. text 47.50 (*1-55553-164-4*); pap. text 17.95 (*1-55553-165-2*) NE U Pr.

— The Salem Witchcraft Papers: Verbatim Transcripts, 3 vols., Set. (Civil Liberties in American History Ser.). 1977. lib. bdg. 145.00 (*0-306-70655-5*) Da Capo.

Boyer, Paul, et al. The Enduring Vision: A History of the American People. LC 89-83818. 1159p. (C). 1990. text 65.16 (*0-669-09798-5*); pap. text, teacher ed. 2.66 (*0-669-09801-9*) HM Trade Div.

— The Enduring Vision: A History of the American People, 1. LC 89-83818. 1159p. (C). 1990. pap. text 48.76 (*0-669-09799-3*); pap. text, student ed. 22.36 (*0-669-18202-8*) HM Trade Div.

— The Enduring Vision: A History of the American People, 2. LC 89-83818. 1159p. (C). 1990. pap. text 48.76 (*0-669-09800-0*); pap. text, student ed. 22.36 (*0-669-18203-6*) HM Trade Div.

Boyer, Paul, jt. auth. see Boyer, Ernest L.

Boyer, Paul D., ed. The Enzymes, Vol. 14. 3rd ed. LC 75-117107. 1981. text 189.00 (*0-12-122714-6*) Acad Pr.

Boyer, Paul D. & Krebs, Edwin G., eds. The Enzymes, Vol. 18. 3rd ed. 512p. 1987. text 139.00 (*0-12-122718-9*) Acad Pr.

Boyer, Paul D., jt. ed. see Sigman, David S.

Boyer, Paul S. & Clark, Clifford E., Jr. The Enduring Vision To 1877: A History of the American People, Concise Edition, Vol. 1. 2nd ed. 384p. (C). 1995. pap. 27.16 (*0-669-33169-4*) HM Trade Div.

Boyer, Paul S., et al. The Enduring Vision: A History of the American People, 2 vols. 2nd ed. 1114p. (C). 1993. text 65.16 (*0-669-28114-X*); pap. text, student ed. 25.16 (*0-669-29796-8*); teacher ed. 2.66 (*0-669-29799-2*) HM Trade Div.

— The Enduring Vision: A History of the American People, 2 vols., Vol. I: To 1877. 2nd ed. 580p. (C). 1993. pap. text 48.76 (*0-669-29794-1*) HM Trade Div.

— The Enduring Vision: A History of the American People, 2 vols., Vol. I Document Sets: Enduring Voices. 2nd ed. 1114p. (C). 1993. suppl. ed. 13.56 (*0-669-29802-6*) HM Trade Div.

— The Enduring Vision: A History of the American People, 2 vols., Vol. II. 2nd ed. 1114p. (C). 1993. student ed. 22.36 (*0-669-29798-4*) HM Trade Div.

— The Enduring Vision: A History of the American People, 2 vols., Vol. II: Since 1865. 2nd ed. 650p. (C). 1993. pap. text 48.76 (*0-669-29795-X*) HM Trade Div.

— The Enduring Vision: A History of the American People, 2 vols., Vol. II Document Sets: Enduring Voices. 2nd ed. 1114p. (C). 1993. suppl. ed. 13.56 (*0-669-29803-4*) HM Trade Div.

— The Enduring Vision: A History of the American People, Concise. 2nd ed. (C). 1995. text, teacher ed. 2.66 (*0-669-33172-4*) HM Trade Div.

— The Enduring Vision: A History of the American People, Concise Edition. 2nd ed. 688p. (C). 1995. pap. text 36.76 (*0-669-33168-6*) HM Trade Div.

— The Enduring Vision: A History of the American People, 1890s-Present. 3rd ed. 375p. (C). 1996. pap. text 39.56 (*0-669-41590-1*) HM Trade Div.

— The Enduring Vision From 1865: A History of the American People, Vol. 2. 2nd ed. 384p. (C). 1995. pap. text 27.16 (*0-669-33170-8*) HM Trade Div.

— The Enduring Vision Vol. 1: A History of the American People: To 1877. 3rd ed. LC 94-74581. 533p. (C). 1996. pap. text 48.76 (*0-669-39772-5*) HM Trade Div.

— The Enduring Vision Vol. 2: A History of the American People: Since 1865. 3rd ed. LC 94-74581. 588p. (C). 1996. pap. text 48.76 (*0-669-39770-9*) HM Trade Div.

— The Enduring Vision: A History of the American People, Concise: Student Guide with Map Exercises, Vol. I. 2nd ed. (C). 1995. text 13.16 (*0-669-39450-5*) HM Trade Div.

— The Enduring Vision: A History of the American People, Concise: Student Guide with Map Exercises, Vol. II. 2nd ed. (C). 1995. pap. text 13.16 (*0-669-39451-3*) HM Trade Div.

Boyer, Pelham G. & Wood, Robert S., eds. Strategic Transformation & Naval Power in the 21st Century. LC 98-38142. 251p. 1998. pap. write for info. (*1-884733-11-5*) Naval War Coll.

***Boyer, Pelham G. & Wood, Robert S., eds.** Strategic Transformation & Naval Power in the 21st Century. 358p. (C). 2000. reprint ed. pap. text 30.00 (*0-7881-8777-5*) DIANE Pub.

Boyer, Pierre. Enciclopedia del Cine Amateur. 2nd ed. (SPA.). 416p. 1976. 59.95 (*0-8288-5663-X*, S14382) Fr & Eur.

Boyer, R. & Keinath, S., eds. Molecular Motion in Polymers by ESR. (MMI Press Symposium Ser.: Vol. 1). xii, 328p. 1980. text 274.00 (*3-7186-0012-9*) Gordon & Breach.

Boyer, R. E., ed. Atlas of Fatigue Curves. 518p. 1986. 198.00 (*0-87170-214-2*, 6156) ASM.

Boyer, Ralph E. Nonprofit Corporation Statutes: A Critique & Proposal. LC 57-63886. (Michigan Legal Publications). 269p. 1957. 40.00 (*1-57588-343-0*, 300100) W S Hein.

Boyer, Ralph E. & Rayan, William M. Florida Real Estate Transactions, 6 vols. 1975. ring bd. 1010.00 (*0-8205-1150-1*) Bender.

Boyer, Ralph E., et al. The Law of Property, an Introductory Survey. 4th ed. 696p. (C). 1991. 39.50 (*0-314-82936-9*) West Pub.

Boyer, Raymond F., ed. Technological Aspects of the Mechanical Behavior of Polymers. LC 74-181576. (Applied Polymer Symposia Ser.: No. 24). 121p. reprint ed. 37.60 (*0-8357-9378-8*, 200737100065) Bks Demand.

Boyer, Raymond F., ed. see Alfrey, Turner.

Boyer, Reba, jt. auth. see Reksten, Harald.

Boyer, Reba B. McMinn County Tennessee, Marriages, 1820-1870. (Orig.). 1983. reprint ed. pap. 25.00 (*0-89308-330-5*) Southern Hist Pr.

— Monroe County, Tennessee, Records, 1820-1870, Vol. 1. 198p. 1983. reprint ed. pap. 25.00 (*0-89308-329-1*) Southern Hist Pr.

— Monroe County Tennessee, Records, 1820-1870, Vol. 2. 198p. 1983. reprint ed. pap. 25.00 (*0-89308-327-5*) Southern Hist Pr.

— Wills & Estate Records of McMinn Co. Tennessee, 1820-1870. 202p. 1983. reprint ed. pap. 25.00 (*0-89308-328-3*) Southern Hist Pr.

Boyer, Regis, ed. Sagas Islandais. deluxe ed. (FRE.). 2064p. 1987. 155.00 (*0-7859-3877-X*, 2070111172) Fr & Eur.

Boyer, Richard. Lives of the Bigamists: Marriage, Family, & Community in Colonial Mexico. 341p. 1995. 24.95 (*0-8263-1571-2*) U of NM Pr.

Boyer, Richard & Morais, Herbert. Labor's Untold Story. 380p. 1955. 6.95 (*0-916180-01-8*) United Elec R&M.

Boyer, Richard & Spurling, eds. Colonial Lives: Documents on Latin American History, 1550-1850. LC 99-18180. (Illus.). 368p. (C). 1999. text 49.95 (*0-19-512511-8*) OUP.

Boyer, Richard, jt. auth. see Savageau, David.

Boyer, Richard G. Accident Kids. LC 73-93019. (Safety Ser.). (Illus.). 32p. (J). (gr. 2-5). 1974. lib. bdg. 9.95 (*0-87783-119-X*) Oddo.

— Let's Walk Safely. LC 80-82953. (Safety Ser.). (Illus.). 32p. (J). (gr. 1-6). 1981. lib. bdg. 9.95 (*0-87783-159-9*) Oddo.

— Lucky Bus. LC 73-87801. (Safety Ser.). (Illus.). 32p. (J). (gr. k-2). 1974. ring bd. 12.35 (*0-87783-131-9*) Oddo.

— Oddo Safety Series, 4 vols., Set. (Illus.). (J). (ps-6). lib. bdg. 44.60 (*0-87783-170-X*) Oddo.

— Safety on Wheels. LC 73-87802. (Safety Ser.). (Illus.). 32p. (J). (gr. k-5). 1974. ring bd. 12.35 (*0-87783-133-5*); audio 7.94 (*0-87783-199-8*) Oddo.

— Safety on Wheels. deluxe ed. LC 73-87802. (Safety Ser.). (Illus.). 32p. (J). (gr. k-5). 1974. pap. 3.94 (*0-87783-134-3*) Oddo.

***Boyer, Richard G. & Spurling, eds.** Colonial Lives: Documents on Latin American History, 1550-1850. LC 99-18180. (Illus.). 368p. (C). 1999. pap. text 22.95 (*0-19-512512-6*) OUP.

Boyer, Rick. The Man Who Whispered. 266p. 1998. mass mkt. 5.99 (*0-8041-1044-1*) Ivy Books.

— Sherlockian Quartet. 1999. pap. text 16.95 (*1-57090-084-1*) Alexander Dist.

— The Whale's Footprints. large type ed. (General Ser.). 392p. 1989. lib. bdg. 18.95 (*0-8161-4764-7*, G K Hall Lrg Type) Mac Lib Ref.

Boyer, Rick & Boyer, Marilyn. A Boyer's Dozen: 7 of One, Half a Dozen of the Other. 185p. Date not set. lib. bdg. 10.99 (*0-9645396-4-0*, Home School Pr) Holly Hall.

— Fun Projects for Hands on Character Building. 140p. 1996. pap. text 7.99 (*0-9645396-5-9*, Home School Pr) Holly Hall.

— Home Educating with Confidence: How Ordinary Parents Can Produce Extraordinary Children. 260p. 1996. pap. text 9.99 (*0-9645396-3-2*, Home School Pr) Holly Hall.

— What about Socialization: Answering the Questions about Homeschool & Social Interaction. 150p. Date not set. lib. bdg. 10.99 (*0-9645396-2-4*, Home School Pr) Holly Hall.

Boyer, Rita L., et al. A Biblical & Theological Guide to Free the Horses: A Self-Esteem Adventure. 88p. (Orig.). 1994. pap. 7.95 (*1-880283-09-3*) Active Parenting.

Boyer, Robert. Amazing Art of Pyrography. LC 93-70275. (Illus.). 448p. 1993. 49.95 (*1-879260-12-3*) Evanston Pub.

***Boyer, Robert.** Japanese Capitalism in Crisis: A Regulationist Interpretation. 240p. 2000. 90.00 (*0-415-20559-X*) Routledge.

Boyer, Robert. The Regulation School: A Critical Introduction. 152p. 1990. text 61.50 (*0-231-06548-5*) Col U Pr.

Boyer, Robert, ed. States Against Markets. 464p. (C). 1996. 100.00 (*0-415-13725-X*); pap. 32.99 (*0-415-13726-8*) Routledge.

Boyer, Robert, et al, eds. Between Imitation & Innovation: The Transfer & Hybridization of Productive Models in the International Automobile Industry. (Illus.). 408p. 1999. text 90.00 (*0-19-829368-2*) OUP.

Boyer, Robert, jt. ed. see Hollingsworth, J. Rogers.

Boyer, Robert D., compiled by. Realism in European Theater & Drama, 1870-1920: A Bibliography. LC 78-19934. 236p. 1979. lib. bdg. 49.95 (*0-313-20607-4*, BOR/, Greenwood Pr) Greenwood.

Boyer, Robert E. Oceanography. 1984. pap. 9.95 (*0-8331-1707-6*, 6611) Hubbard Sci.

Boyer, Robert E., ed. International Air Transportation: A New International Airport: Proceedings of the 22nd Conference, Denver, Colorado, June 25-28, 1992. LC 92-15380. 272p. 1992. pap. text 31.00 (*0-87262-871-X*) Am Soc Civil Eng.

Boyer, Robert H. Visions & Imaginings. 375p. 1992. pap. 13.95 (*0-89733-361-6*) Academy Chi Pubs.

Boyer, Robert S., ed. Automated Reasoning: Essays in Honor of Woody Bledsoe. 380p. (C). 1991. lib. bdg. 129.50 (*0-7923-1409-3*) Kluwer Academic.

Boyer, Robert S. & Moore, J. Strother. A Computational Logic Handbook. 408p. 1988. text 71.00 (*0-12-122952-1*) Acad Pr.

— A Computational Logic Handbook. 2nd ed. (International Series in Formal Methods). (Illus.). 512p. 1997. text 69.95 (*0-12-122955-6*) Morgan Kaufmann.

— The Correctness Problem in Computer Science. LC 81-67887. (International Lecture Series in Computer Mathematics). 1982. text 108.00 (*0-12-122920-3*) Acad Pr.

Boyer, Rodney F. Modern Experimental Biochemistry. 2nd ed. LC 92-35064. (Series in the Life Sciences & Chemistry). 519p. (C). 1992. 60.00 (*0-8053-0545-9*) Benjamin-Cummings.

— Modern Experimental Biochemistry. 3rd ed. 520p. (C). 2000. pap. 46.67 (*0-8053-3111-5*) Benjamin-Cummings.

***Boyer, Rodney F., et al, eds.** Fatigue Behaviour of Titanium Alloys: Proceedings International Symposium, Chicago, IL, 1998. LC 99-70639. (Illus.). 382p. 1999. 106.00 (*0-87339-434-8*) Minerals Metals.

Boyer, Rodney R., ed. see Symposium on Microstructure Property Relationships.

***Boyer, Ross E.** Boy Howdy!! Was I Lucky!! 340p. 2000. pap. write for info. (*0-7392-0506-4*, PO2953) Morris Pubng.

Boyer, Ruth, jt. ed. see Boyer, L. Bryce.

Boyer, Ruth M. & Gayton, Narcissus D. Apache Mother & Daughters: Four Generations of a Family. LC 92-54149. (Illus.). 416p. 1992. 27.95 (*0-8061-2447-4*) U of Okla Pr.

— Apache Mothers & Daughters: Four Generations of a Family. LC 92-54149. (Illus.). 416p. 1997. pap. 16.95 (*0-8061-2922-0*) U of Okla Pr.

Boyer, Ruth M., jt. ed. see Boyer, L. Bryce.

Boyer, S. & Mari, J. L. Seismic Surveying & Well Logging: Oil & Gas Exploration Techniques. Carpenter, M. S., tr. from FRE. LC 97-194038. 192p. 1997. 350.00 (*2-7108-0712-2*, Pub. by Edits Technip) Enfield Pubs NH.

Boyer, Thomas D., jt. auth. see Zakim, David.

Boyer, Thomas H. Amigados Express. 1986. 29.95 (*0-553-50046-5*) Bantam.

Boyer, Timothy P., jt. auth. see Levitus, Sydney.

Boyer, Trevor, jt. auth. see Gooders, John.

Boyer, W. F., jt. auth. see Feighner, J. P.

Boyer, W. F., jt. ed. see Feighner, J. P.

Boyer-White, Rene, jt. auth. see Rozmajzl, Michon.

Boyer, William. Birdie on the Back Nine: A Play. unabridged ed. 58p. 1997. pap. 7.95 (*1-56439-068-3*) Ridgeway.

— Deer Crossing & Leap Years Away: Two Short American Plays. 110p. (Orig.). (C). 1992. pap. 7.95 (*1-56439-023-3*) Ridgeway.

— Poems by Bill: Also Poems to Live By. 130p. 1997. pap. write for info. (*1-57502-610-4*, PO1752) Morris Pubng.

Boyer, William H. America's Future: Transition to the 21st Century. LC 83-27021. 188p. 1984. 29.95 (*0-275-91734-7*, C1734, Praeger Pubs) Greenwood.

— America's Future: Transition to the 21st Century. 1984. 33.00 (*0-03-071121-5*) New Politics Pub.

— Education for Annihilation. LC 72-88420. 1972. reprint ed. pap. 4.95 (*0-911776-18-4*) New Politics Pub.

— Simply the Best: A Celebration of the First 50 Years in the Life & Times of Best Western International. 120p. 1996. write for info. (*0-929690-28-1*) Herit Pubs AZ.

Boyer, William N., jt. auth. see Clark, Gail I.

Boyer, William P. Thunderbird: An Odyssey in Automotive Design. LC 86-13426. 1987. 25.00 (*0-517-56475-0*) Crown Pub Group.

Boyer, William W. Bureaucracy on Trial: Policy Making by Government Agencies. LC 63-16942. 1964. 22.95 (*0-672-51129-0*) Irvington.

***Boyer, William W.** Governing Delaware: Policy Problems of the First State. LC 99-88319. 344p. 2000. 46.50 (*0-87413-721-7*) U Delaware Pr.

Boyer, William W. & Byong Man Ahn. Rural Development in South Korea: A Sociopolitical Analysis. LC 90-50708. (Illus.). 160p. 1992. 32.50 (*0-87413-431-5*) U Delaware Pr.

Boyer, William W., jt. auth. see Huddleston, Mark W.

Boyer-Xambeu, Marie-Therese, et al. Private Money & Public Currencies: The 16th Century Challenge. Azodi, Azizeh, tr. from FRE. LC 93-45467. 247p. (C). (gr. 13). 1994. pap. text 36.95 (*1-56324-508-6*) M E Sharpe.

Boyers, Peggy, jt. ed. see Boyers, Robert.

Boyers, Robert. After the Avant-Garde. LC 86-43029. 250p. 1988. 30.00 (*0-271-00609-9*) Pa St U Pr.

— Atrocity & Amnesia: The Political Novel since 1945. LC 85-13745. 268p. 1987. pap. text 24.95 (*0-19-505082-7*) OUP.

— R. P. Blackmur, Poet-Critic: Toward a View of Poetic Objects. LC 80-15414. (Literary Frontiers Editions Ser.). 96p. 1980. pap. 9.95 (*0-8262-0315-9*) U of Mo Pr.

Boyers, Robert, ed. The Search for Labour Market Flexibility: The European Economies in Transition. (Illus.). 328p. 1988. 75.00 (*0-19-828560-4*) OUP.

Boyers, Robert & Boyers, Peggy, eds. The New Salmagundi Reader. LC 96-8965. (C). 1996. pap. 24.95 (*0-8156-0384-3*, BOSRP); text 49.00 (*0-8156-2704-1*, BOSR) Syracuse U Pr.

— The Salmagundi Reader. LC 82-49294. 637p. reprint ed. pap. 197.50 (*0-608-18246-X*, 205669400081) Bks Demand.

Boyers, Sara Jane. First-Timer's Guide to Voting. LC 99-52192. 128p. (YA). (gr. 9 up). 1999. 24.90 (*0-7613-1307-9*, Copper Beech Bks) Millbrook Pr.

***Boyers, Sara Jane.** Teen Power Politics. 128p. (YA). (gr. 7). 2000. pap. text 9.95 (*0-7613-1391-5*, Copper Beech Bks) Millbrook Pr.

Boyers, W. Hayden, tr. see Bastiat, Frederic.

Boyertown Area Historical Society Staff. Boyertown Area Cookery or the Boyertown Housewife & Kitchen Efficiency Guide & Companion. 2nd ed. (Illus.). 204p. 1985. pap. text 12.00 (*0-9616068-0-0*) Boyertown Hist.

Boyes. Boyes Fundamentals of Econ Ctb. 1999. pap. text 99.87 (*0-395-90343-2*) HM.

— Complete Economics, 2 vols. 2nd ed. (C). 1993. text 76.76 (*0-395-67541-3*) HM.

— Economic Laserdisc Guide, 3 vols. 3rd ed. (C). 1994. pap. text 11.96 (*0-395-71187-8*) HM.

— Economics, 2 vols. (C). Date not set. text, teacher ed., suppl. ed. 76.76 (*0-395-69063-3*) HM.

— Economics. (C). 1991. pap. text, teacher ed. 5.16 (*0-395-57099-9*) HM.

— Economics, 2 vols. (C). 1993. pap., teacher ed. 7.96 (*0-395-68245-2*); pap., teacher ed., suppl. ed. 8.76 (*0-395-68247-9*) HM.

— Economics, 3 vols. (C). 1996. pap., teacher ed., suppl. ed. 11.96 (*0-395-74437-7*) HM.

— Economics, 3 vols. 3rd ed. (C). Date not set. pap. write for info. (*0-395-78144-2*) HM.

— Economics, 3 vols. 3rd ed. (C). 1995. pap. text 39.56 (*0-395-74432-6*) HM.

— Economics, 3 vols., Vol. 1. (C). 1996. pap., teacher ed., suppl. ed. 11.96 (*0-395-74438-5*) HM.

— Economics, 3 vols., Vol. 2. (C). 1996. pap., teacher ed., suppl. ed. 9.96 (*0-395-74439-3*) HM.

— Macroeconomics, 2 vols. (C). Date not set. text, teacher ed., suppl. ed. 54.76 (*0-395-69064-1*) HM.

— Macroeconomics, 2 vols. 2nd ed. LC 93-78702. (C). 1993. pap. text 54.76 (*0-395-67542-1*) HM.

— Macroeconomics, 2 vols. 2nd ed. (C). 1993. pap. text, student ed. 16.76 (*0-395-67544-8*) HM.

— Macroeconomics, 3 vols. 3rd ed. LC 95-76929. (C). 1995. pap. text 29.16 (*0-395-74433-4*) HM.

— Macroeconomics, 3 vols. 3rd ed. (C). 1995. pap. text, student ed. 16.76 (*0-395-74435-0*) HM.

— Macroeconomics, 3 vols. 3rd ed. (C). 1996. pap. 13.96 (*0-395-78007-1*) HM.

— Macroeconomics Exam, 3 vols. (C). 1996. pap. 54.76 (*0-395-74658-2*) HM.

— Managerial Economics. 2001. text 50.97 (*0-395-82835-X*) HM.

— Microeconomics, 2 vols. (C). Date not set. text, teacher ed., suppl. ed. 54.76 (*0-395-69065-X*) HM.

— Microeconomics, 2 vols. (C). 1993. pap., student ed. 16.76 (*0-395-67545-6*) HM.

— Microeconomics, 3 vols. (C). 1996. pap., teacher ed., suppl. ed. 54.76 (*0-395-74659-0*) HM.

— Microeconomics, 2 vols. 2nd ed. (C). 1993. pap. text 54.76 (*0-395-67543-X*) HM.

— Microeconomics, 3 vols. 3rd ed. (C). Date not set. pap. write for info. (*0-395-78145-0*) HM.

— Microeconomics, 3 vols. 3rd ed. (C). 1995. pap. text 29.16 (*0-395-74434-2*) HM.

— Microeconomics, 3 vols. 3rd ed. (C). 1995. pap. text, student ed. 16.76 (*0-395-74436-9*) HM.

Boyes, Anne J. Golden Gate Associates: A Word-Information Processing Simulation. 125p. (C). 1989. mass mkt. 19.95 (*0-538-80209-X*, WS61AB) S-W Pub.

Boyes, G. T. The Diaries & Letters of G. T. W. B. Boyes: 1820-1832, Vol. 1. Chapman, Peter, ed. (Illus.). 1986. 175.00 (*0-19-554454-4*) OUP.

Boyes, Gayle B., jt. auth. see Beckman, Paula.

Boyes, J. Essential Fashion Design. 1999. pap. text 17.95 (*0-7134-7699-0*) B T Burch.

Boyes, John. The Company of Adventurers. LC 96-31415. (Resnick Library of African Adventures: Vol. 4). 208p. 1997. reprint ed. pap. 16.95 (*1-57090-042-6*) Alexander Dist.

Boyes, Jon L. Macroeconomics. 4th ed. LC 98-71995. 1998. pap. text 44.97 (*0-395-90806-X*) HM.

— Microeconomics. 4th ed. LC 98-71996. 1998. pap. text 44.97 (*0-395-90807-8*) HM.

Boyes, Jon L. & Andriole, Stephen J., eds. Principles of Command & Control. LC 87-3574. (AFCEA Signal Magazine C3I Ser.: Vol. VI). (Illus.). 500p. 1987. 21.95 (*0-916159-12-4*) AFCEA Intl Pr.

Boyes, Michael C., jt. auth. see Lefton, Lester A.

Boyes, Vivien. The Druid's Head. (J). (gr. 4-8). 1998. pap. 13.95 (*0-8464-4596-4*) Beekman Pubs.

— The Druid's Head. (J). 1997. pap. 22.00 (*1-85902-459-9*, Pub. by Gomer Pr) St Mut.

Boyes, W. Killed Twice - Buried Once. LC 86-70755. (Illus.). 265p. 1986. 17.95 (*0-938225-00-6*) Chesapeake Bay Pr.

Boyes, W., ed. Low Cost Jigs, Fixtures & Gages for Limited Production. LC 85-62533. 320p. 1985. 58.00 (*0-87263-207-5*) SME.

Boyes, William & Bakerjian, Ramon, eds. Handbook of Jig & Fixture Design. 2nd ed. LC 89-62218. (Illus.). 1192p. 1989. reprint ed. 126.00 (*0-87263-365-9*) SME.

Boyes, William & Melvin, Michael. Fundamentals of Economics. LC 98-71994. xiii, 336p. 1999. pap. text 44.37 (*0-395-90339-4*) HM.

Boyes, William E. Jigs & Fixtures. LC 79-64915. (Manufacturing Update Ser.). 278p. reprint ed. pap. 86.20 (*0-608-30846-3*, 201911900010) Bks Demand.

— Jigs & Fixtures. 2nd ed. LC 82-80101. (Manufacturing Update Ser.). (Illus.). 456p. reprint ed. pap. 141.40 (*0-608-30847-1*, 204599300010) Bks Demand.

Boyes, William E., ed. Jigs & Fixtures. 2nd ed. LC 82-80101. (Manufacturing Update Ser.). (Illus.). 456p. reprint ed. pap. 130.00 (*0-7837-6278-X*, 2045993) Bks Demand.

Boyes, William J. Macro: Theory/pol. (Thomson Executive Press). 552p. (C). 1984. mass mkt. 34.25 (*0-538-08700-5*, H70) S-W Pub.

***Boyes, William J. & Melvin, Michael.** Economics. 4th ed. LC 98-71993. xxi, 951p. 1999. write for info. (*0-395-90805-1*) HM.

Boyesen, Hjalmar H. Essays on German Literature. LC 74-37509. (Essay Index Reprint Ser.). 1977. reprint ed. 22.95 (*0-8369-2536-X*) Ayer.

An Asterisk (*) at the beginning of an entry indicates that the title is appearing for the first time.

— Essays on Scandinavian Literature. LC 72-80496. 1977. reprint ed. 24.95 (*0-405-08300-9*, Pub. by Blom Pubns) Ayer.

— Ilka on the Hill-Top. LC 78-142259. (Short Story Index Reprint Ser.). 1977. 19.95 (*0-8369-3743-0*) Ayer.

— The Mammon of Unrighteousness. LC 78-104421. 386p. reprint ed. lib. bdg. 29.00 (*0-8290-2395-X*) Irvington.

— The Mammon of Unrighteousness. 386p. (C). 1987. reprint ed. pap. text 8.95 (*0-8290-2378-X*) Irvington.

— The Modern Vikings: Stories of Life & Sport in the Norseland. 1977. 23.95 (*0-8369-4266-3*, 6065) Ayer.

— Queen Titania. LC 77-122691. (Short Story Index Reprint Ser.). 1977. 19.95 (*0-8369-3524-1*) Ayer.

— Tales from Two Hemispheres. LC 78-98563. (Short Story Index Reprint Ser.). 1977. 20.95 (*0-8369-3137-8*) Ayer.

Boyet, Howard. HERO 1: Advanced Programming Experiments. rev. ed. Johnson, Ron, ed. LC 84-10722. (Illus.). 305p. (C). 1984. reprint ed. student ed. 24.95 (*0-87119-036-2*, EB-1802) Heathkit-Zenith Ed.

Boyett, Gene W. Hardscrabble Frontier: Pope County, Arkansas in the 1850's. 266p. (C). 1990. lib. bdg. 46.00 (*0-8191-7708-3*) U Pr of Amer.

Boyett, Jimmie T., jt. auth. see Boyett, Joseph H.

Boyett, Joseph H. & Boyett, Jimmie T. The Guru Guide: The Best Ideas of the Top Management Thinkers. LC 97-41058. 400p. 1998. 24.95 (*0-471-18242-7*) Wiley.

***Boyett, Joseph H. & Boyett, Jimmie T.** The Guru Guide: The Best Ideas of the Top Management Thinkers. 385p. 2000. pap. 16.95 (*0-471-38054-7*) Wiley.

— The Guru Guide to Entrepreneurship: A Concise Guide to the World's Top Entrepreneurs. 400p. 2000. 24.95 (*0-471-39084-4*) Wiley.

Boyett, Joseph H. & Conn, Henry P. Maximum Performance Management: How to Manage & Compensate People to Meet World Competition. 2nd rev. ed. LC 94-73144. (Illus.). 323p. 1994. 24.95 (*0-944435-25-4*) Glenbridge Pub.

— Workplace 2000: The Revolution Reshaping American Business. 384p. 1992. pap. 14.95 (*0-452-26804-4*, Plume) Dutton Plume.

Boyett, Steven R. Treks Not Taken: What If Stephen King, Anne Rice, Bret Easton Ellis, & Other Literary Greats Had Written Episodes of Star Trek, the Next Generation? LC 98-18310. (Illus.). 208p. (Orig.). 1998. pap. write for info. (*0-06-095276-8*, Perennial) HarperTrade.

— Treks Not Taken: What If Stephen King, Anne Rice, Bret Easton Ellis, & Other Literary Greats Had Written Episodes of Star Trek, the Next Generation? 170p. (Orig.). 1996. pap. 12.95 (*1-882813-05-7*) Sneaker Pr.

Boyette, Michael. The Attention Deficit Answer Book: The Best Medications & Parenting Strategies for Your Child. LC 97-13422. 160p. 1998. pap. 10.95 (*0-452-27941-0*, Plume) Dutton Plume.

Boyette, Pat, jt. auth. see Miller, William.

Boyfen, Claudia L. A Friend Indeed. (God's Little Wonders Ser.). 120p. 1998. spiral bd. 4.50 (*1-879127-76-8*) Lighten Up Enter.

— A Mother's Touch. (God's Little Wonders Ser.). 120p. 1998. spiral bd. 4.50 (*1-879127-81-4*) Lighten Up Enter.

— Of Friends & Angels. (God's Little Wonders Ser.). 120p. 1998. spiral bd. 4.50 (*1-879127-80-6*) Lighten Up Enter.

— A Teacher's Keepsake. (God's Little Wonders Ser.). 120p. 1998. spiral bd. 4.50 (*1-879127-79-2*) Lighten Up Enter.

— With Praise & Glory. (God's Little Wonders Ser.). 1998. spiral bd. 4.50 (*1-879127-78-4*) Lighten Up Enter.

Boyington, Benjamin, ed. see De Rueda, Marta F.

Boyington, Evelyn, jt. auth. see Baker, Barbara.

Boyington, Gregory. Baa Baa Black Sheep. 1976. 18.95 (*0-405-03752-X*) Ayer.

Boyington, Pappy. Baa Baa Black Sheep. 368p. 1977. mass mkt. 6.99 (*0-553-26350-1*) Bantam.

— Baa Baa Black Sheep. 1982. 16.00 (*0-933458-00-2*) Wilson Pr.

— Baa Baa Black Sheep. (Military Classics Ser.). 384p. 1989. reprint ed. 22.95 (*0-8306-4008-8*) McGraw-Hill Prof.

— Tonya. 1983. 16.00 (*0-933458-01-0*) Wilson Pr.

Boyington, Robert W. The Power Consumer. 93p. 1992. pap. text. write for info. (*0-9632365-0-4*) Blk Sheep.

Boyink, Betty. Baskets for Quilters. 52p. (Orig.). 1982. pap. 10.50 (*0-9612608-0-7*) B Boyink.

— Child's Play for Quilters. 60p. (Orig.). 1984. pap. 10.50 (*0-9612608-3-1*) B Boyink.

— Christmas for Quilters. 72p. (Orig.). 1993. pap. 14.50 (*0-925623-05-9*) B Boyink.

— Double Wedding Ring Design Variations. 68p. (Orig.). 1988. pap. 13.50 (*0-9612608-9-0*) B Boyink.

— Fans Galore for Modern Quilters. 68p. (Orig.). 1987. pap. 13.50 (*0-9612608-8-2*) B Boyink.

— Flower Gardens & Hexagons for Quilters. 60p. (Orig.). 1984. pap. 10.50 (*0-9612608-4-X*) B Boyink.

— Nautical Voyages for Quilters. 72p. (Orig.). 1990. pap. 14.50 (*0-925623-02-3*) B Boyink.

— Nine Patch Design Variations. 72p. (Orig.). 1991. pap. 14.50 (*0-925623-04-0*) B Boyink.

— One Patch & Beyond: A Study in Quilt Making - Shapes, How-To, Lots of Samples. (Illus.). 72p. 1997. pap. 14.95 (*0-925623-07-5*) B Boyink.

— Quilt Challenges. 72p. (Orig.). 1991. pap. 13.50 (*0-685-72806-4*) B Boyink.

— Quilters Hearts with Flowing Ribbons. 68p. (Orig.). 1989. pap. 13.50 (*0-925623-00-8*) B Boyink.

— Star Quest for Quilters. 80p. (Orig.). 1986. pap. 13.50 (*0-9612608-7-4*) B Boyink.

Boyink, Betty & Splitstone, Milly. Michigan Quilters & Their Designs. 52p. (Orig.). 1983. pap. 10.50 (*0-9612608-2-3*) B Boyink.

Boyk, James. To Hear Ourselves As Others Hear Us: Tape Recording As a Tool in Music Practicing & Teaching. 88p. (Orig.). (C). 1996. pap. text 9.95 (*0-918812-87-9*, SE0205) MMB Music.

Boyken, Hans-Georg. Where Did They Stay? East Frisians in America. LC 98-95030.Tr. of Wo Sind Sie Geblleben? - Ostfriesen in Amerika. (GER & ENG., Illus.). xii, 270p. (C). 1999. pap. 32.00i (*0-9670802-1-5*) Boyken & Boyken.

Boyken, Immo. Otto Ernst Schweizer, 1890-1965: Bauten und Projekte. (Illus.). 304p. 1997. 79.00 (*3-930698-01-3*) Edition A Menges.

Boykin, A. Faye. Been Through the Fire, But Didn't Get Burned 100(Illus.). 75p. (Orig.). 1995. pap. 14.06 (*0-9649172-0-3*) Always Finding.

***Boykin, A. Wade & Slavin, Robert E., eds.** Crespar Findings (1994-1999) In Memory of John H. Hollifield, A Special Double Issue of the Journal of Education for Students Placed at Risk. 208p. 2000. pap. write for info. (*0-8058-9761-5*) L Erlbaum Assocs.

Boykin, A. Wade, ed. see Franklin, Anderson J. & Yates, J. Frank.

Boykin, Anne, ed. Living a Caring-Based Program. LC 94-171951. 188p. 1993. 20.95 (*0-88737-591-X*, 14-2536, NLN Pr) Natl League Nurse.

— Power, Politics, & Public Policy: A Matter of Caring. 260p. 1995. 32.95 (*0-88737-644-4*, 14-2684, NLN Pr) Natl League Nurse.

Boykin, Anne & Schoenhofer, Savina. Nursing As Caring: A Model for Transforming Practice. LC 93-23021. 1993. 26.95 (*0-88737-601-0*) Natl League Nurse.

Boykin, Anne, jt. ed. see Gaut, Delores A.

Boykin, Arletha F. No Testimony Without a Test. 99p. 1997. pap. 12.99 (*0-9649172-1-1*) Always Finding.

Boykin, Calvin G., Jr. Gare la Bete: A History of the 814th Tank Destroyer Battalion, 1942-1945. (Illus.). 300p. 1995. 47.00 (*0-9646161-0-6*) C&R Pubns.

Boykin, David W. Seventeen O NMR Spectroscopy in Organic Chemistry. (Illus.). 248p. 1990. lib. bdg. 225.00 (*0-8493-4867-6*) CRC Pr.

Boykin, Ed. The Principal of the Thing: The Journal of a High School Principal. 435p. (Orig.). (C). 1990. pap. 24.95 (*0-9625988-0-1*) Crooked Hacienda Pr.

Boykin, Edna M. The End of the Pillow Slip: The Story of Emilie Clair Watson on Watson Lane, Mesilla Park. 131p. 1991. pap. 6.00 (*0-614-04675-0*) Crooked Hacienda Pr.

Boykin, Edwina. To the Boy I Shared with the Crabapple Tree. Tinsley, Arnold, ed. 105p. 1999. pap. 7.95i (*0-9669230-0-6*) Ebo Ink.

Boykin, James H. Beta, Bene & the Peripheral Diaspora (Black Hebrews in the Diaspora) LC 90-92967. 96p. (Orig.). (C). 1990. pap. 6.99 (*0-9603342-9-7*) Boykin.

— Black Jews: A Study in Minority Experiences. 2nd rev. ed. LC 96-638. 129p. 1996. pap. 6.99 (*1-880833-02-6*, 1880833) Boykin.

— Essays on AIDS: Introduction to the Influence of a Virus on Politics. LC 93-91068. 90p. (Orig.). 1994. lib. bdg. 6.94 (*1-880833-01-8*) Boykin.

— The Hebrew Israelite Diaspora. LC 91-90620. 100p. (C). 1992. pap. 10.49 (*1-880833-00-X*) Boykin.

— Imperialism Theory & Practice. LC 87-91428. 258p. (Orig.). 1987. pap. 11.99 (*0-9603342-7-0*) Boykin.

— North Carolina in 1861. LC 61-15678. 237p. 1961. pap. 6.99 (*0-9603342-8-9*) Boykin.

— Political Intrigue in the Establishment of the Identity of Jesus & Mary. LC 86-90757. 285p. 1986. pap. 11.99 (*0-9603342-6-2*) Boykin.

— The Quest for Concensus. LC 97-93289. vi, 145p. 1997. pap. 16.99 (*1-880833-03-4*, Archdiocese Miami) Boykin.

— Thank God for Black Power. 2nd ed. LC 83-90000. 172p. 1983. pap. 11.99 (*0-9603342-2-X*) Boykin.

— World Blacks: Self Help & Achievement. LC 79-53631. 193p. 1979. pap. 11.99 (*0-9603342-0-3*) Boykin.

Boykin, James H. & Haney, Richard L., Jr. Financing Real Estate. 2nd ed. 544p. (C). 1993. text 51.80 (*0-13-318551-6*) P-H.

Boykin, James H. & Ring, Alfred A. The Valuation of Real Estate. 4th ed. LC 92-12577. 608p. (C). 1992. text 51.80 (*0-13-948431-0*) P-H.

Boykin, Joel S., Jr. The Georgia Entrepreneur's Success Guide: Where to Go & Who to See. 24p. 1993. pap. text 5.95 (*0-9636081-0-X*) Info Comm Unltd.

Boykin, John. Circumstances & the Role of God. 224p. 1986. text 12.95 (*0-310-39590-9*, 12790) Zondervan.

— The Gospel of Coincidence: Is God in Control? 224p. 1990. pap. 9.99 (*0-310-39591-7*) Zondervan.

Boykin, John, ed. see DeLong, Brad.

Boykin, Joseph, et al. Programming under Mach. (Illus.). 480p. (C). 1993. pap. 58.95 (*0-201-52739-1*) Addison-Wesley.

Boykin, Keith. One More River to Cross: Black & Gay in America. 288p. 1997. pap. 14.00 (*0-385-47983-2*, Anchor NY) Doubleday.

***Boykin, Keith.** Respecting the Soul: Daily Reflections for Black Lesbians & Gays. LC 99-11097. 400p. 1999. pap. 10.00 (*0-380-80021-7*, Avon Bks) Morrow Avon.

Boykin, Lorraine S., ed. see Best, Ethel.

Boykin, Mark. Power House: Creative Youth Programs. LC 86-83180. (Illus.). 336p. 1987. teacher ed., ring bd. 29.95 (*0-88243-852-2*, 02-0852) Gospel Pub.

Boykin, Milton L. Citizen Sailors in Changing Society: Policy Issues for Manning the United States Naval Reserve, 50. Zurcher, Louis A. & Merritt, Hardy L., eds. LC 85-14714. (Contributions in Military Studies Ser.: No. 50). (Illus.). 290p. 1986. 59.95 (*0-313-24476-6*, ZPE/) Greenwood.

Boykin, Milton L., jt. ed. see Nichols, W. Gary.

Boykin, Paula J. Hotel Guestroom Design. 144p. 1991. spiral bd. 22.00 (*0-8403-6517-9*) Kendall-Hunt.

Boykin, Rosemary D. The Italians of Steele's Store, Texas. LC 93-71445. (Illus.). 110p. (C). 1993. pap. 15.00 (*0-911317-53-8*) Ericson Bks.

***Boykins, Emma.** Seeds from the Garden of Life. 1999. pap. write for info. (*1-58235-083-3*) Watermrk Pr.

Boykiw, Russel A., II. Yacht Construction for Beginners: How to Loft & Construct a Carvel Plank Sailing Yacht. rev. ed. LC 93-86260. (Illus.). 176p. (Orig.). 1994. pap. 23.00 (*0-9638646-2-9*) Ligeia Pubns.

Boyko, jt. ed. see U. S. S. R., National Standard Reference Data Serv.

Boyko, Carrie, jt. compiled by see Colen, Kimberly.

***Boyko, Carrie J. & Rodgers, Julie B.** Awards & Rewards for Grades 4-6: Certificates, Badges, Crafts & More. Mitchell, Judy, ed. (Illus.). 128p. 1999. pap., teacher ed. 13.95 (*1-57310-184-2*) Teachng & Lrning Co.

— Awards & Rewards for K-3: Certificates, Badges, Crafts & More. Mitchell, Judy, ed. (Illus.). 128p. 1999. pap., teacher ed. 13.95 (*1-57310-183-4*) Teachng & Lrning Co.

Boyko, V. A. Spectroscopic Constants of Atoms & Ions: Spectra of Atoms with One or Two Electrons. LC 93-39797. 240p. 1993. 180.95 (*0-8493-9938-6*) CRC Pr.

Boyko, V. I., jt. ed. see Lyck, L.

Boyko, Vladimir S., et al. Reversible Crystal Plasticity. LC 93-32750. (Illus.). 294p. 1994. text 94.95 (*0-88318-869-4*, AIP Pr) Spr-Verlag.

Boykoff, Thomas M., jt. auth. see Mennell, Robert L.

***Boylan.** Beloved Stranger. 2000. 25.00 (*1-58243-095-9*, Pub. by Counterpt DC) HarpC.

— Biomedical Ethics. LC 99-46581. 447p. 2000. pap. text 25.20 (*0-13-773847-1*) P-H.

Boylan. Professional Applied Ethics. LC 99-46652. 210p. 1999. pap. text 23.80 (*0-13-674292-0*) P-H.

Boylan, jt. ed. see Swarbrick.

Boylan, Ann M. & Taub, Nadine. Adult Domestic Violence: Constitutional, Legislative & Equitable Issues. (Illus.). 430p. (Orig.). 1981. 5.00 (*0-941077-12-8*, 31,841) NCLS Inc.

Boylan, Anne M. Sunday School: The Formation of an American Institution, 1790-1880. 237p. (C). 1990. reprint ed. pap. 16.00 (*0-300-04814-9*) Yale U Pr.

Boylan, Bernard. Development of the Long-Range Escort Fighter. (USAF Historical Studies: No. 136). 321p. 1955. pap. text 47.00 (*0-89126-141-9*) MA-AH Pub.

***Boylan, Bill.** Network Marketing for Christians: A Journey along the King's High Way. 107p. 1999. 11.95 (*0-7414-0166-5*) Buy Books.

Boylan, Bob. Get Everyone in Your Boat Rowing in the Same Direction: 5 Leadership Principles to Follow So Others Will Follow You. 1995. pap. 9.95 (*1-55850-547-4*) Adams Media.

— What's Your Point? 176p. 1990. mass mkt. 15.99 (*0-446-39102-6*) Warner Bks.

***Boylan, Bob.** What's Your Point? The 3-Step Method for Making Effective Presentations. 192p. 2000. pap. 10.95 (*1-58062-460-X*) Adams Media.

Boylan, Charles J., ed. International HR Journal. 215.00 (*0-685-69673-1*, JICB) Warren Gorham & Lamont.

***Boylan, Dan & Holmes, T. Michael.** John A. Burns: The Man & His Times. LC 99-46543. (Illus.). 328p. 2000. pap. 12.95 (*0-8248-2282-X*); text 25.00 (*0-8248-2277-3*) UH Pr.

Boylan, Delia M., jt. auth. see Feinberg, Richard E.

Boylan, Eleanor. The Christmas Ghost: A Florida Fantasy. 80p. (Orig.). 1996. pap. 8.95 (*0-9653937-0-4*) E Boylan.

— Murder Crossed: A Clara Gamadge Mystery. LC 95-34659. 88p. 1995. 20.00 (*0-8050-3922-8*) H Holt & Co.

— Pushing Murder. large type ed. LC 93-33652. 221p. 1994. lib. bdg. 20.95 (*0-7862-0105-3*) Thorndike Pr.

Boylan, Emily. The Gingerbread Boy. LC 95-19535 (Easy-to-Read Classics Ser.). 32p. (J). (gr. k-3). 1995. 13.99 (*0-670-86052-2*, Viking Child) Peng Put Young Read.

Boylan, Esther R. Women & Disability. LC 91-12443. (Women & World Development Ser.). (Illus.). 111p. (C). 1991. pap. 15.95 (*0-86232-987-6*, Pub. by Zed Books); text 49.95 (*0-86232-986-8*, Pub. by Zed Books) St Martin.

Boylan, Eugene. Difficulties in Mental Prayer. 172p. 1997. reprint ed. pap. 9.95 (*0-933932-90-1*) Scepter Pubs.

Boylan, Henry. A Dictionary of Irish Biography. 3rd ed. LC 98-65825. (Illus.). 462p. 1998. 35.00 (*1-57098-236-8*, R Rinehart Intl) Roberts Rinehart.

Boylan, James. Getting In: A Novel. LC 97-51216. 352p. 1998. mass mkt. 14.00 (*0-446-67417-6*, Pub. by Warner Bks) Little.

— The Planets. 1992. pap. 10.00 (*0-679-73906-8*) Vin Bks.

— Remind Me to Murder You Later: Short Stories. LC 88-45417. 144p. 1988. 19.95 (*0-8018-3728-6*) Johns Hopkins.

— Revolutionary Lives: Anna Strunsky & William English Walling. LC 98-26696. (Illus.). 360p. 1999. 34.95 (*1-55849-164-3*) U of Mass Pr.

Boylan, James C., jt. auth. see Swarbrick, James.

Boylan, James C., jt. ed. see Swarbrick, James.

Boylan, Jeanne. Portraits of Guilt: The Woman Who Profiles the Faces of America's Deadliest Criminals. (Illus.). 336p. 2000. 24.95 (*0-671-03485-5*, PB Hardcover) PB.

***Boylan, John.** Robert C. Jones. (Illus.). 64p. 2000. pap. 20.00 (*0-295-97921-6*) U of Wash Pr.

Boylan, John, ed. see Narrin, JaneAnne.

***Boylan, Kristi Meisenbach.** The Seven Sacred Rites of Menopause: The Spiritual Journey to the Wise-Woman Years. 160p. 2000. pap. 11.95 (*1-891661-13-2*, Pub. by Snta Monica) IPG Chicago.

Boylan, M. Eugene. Difficulties in Mental Prayer. 130p. 1998. reprint ed. 16.95 (*0-912141-62-X*) Roman Cath Bks.

— This Tremendous Lover. rev. ed. 376p. 1964. pap. 10.95 (*0-87061-138-0*, 6981) Chr Classics.

Boylan, Mallory, jt. auth. see Spallholz, Julian F.

Boylan, Michael. Ethical Issues in Business. LC 94-76727. (C). 1995. pap. text 59.00 (*0-15-501442-0*, Pub. by Harcourt Coll Pubs) Harcourt.

— Method & Practice in Aristotle's Biology. LC 82-23708. (Illus.). 300p. (Orig.). 1983. lib. bdg. 53.00 (*0-8191-2952-6*) U Pr of Amer.

— Perspectives in Philosophy. (Illus.). 340p. (C). 1993. text 65.00 (*0-15-500111-6*, Pub. by Harcourt Coll Pubs) Harcourt.

— The Power to Get In: Using the Circle of Leverage System to Get in Anyone's Door Faster, More Effectively & with Less Expense. (Illus.). 296p. 1999. text 25.00 (*0-7881-5683-7*) DIANE Pub.

— The Process of Argument. 122p. (C). 1993. reprint ed. pap. text 18.50 (*0-8191-9065-9*) U Pr of Amer.

Boylan, Michael, ed. Gewirth: Critical Essays on Action, Rationality & Community. 256p. 1998. pap. 19.95 (*0-8476-9259-0*) Rowman.

***Boylan, Michael, ed.** Gewirth: Critical Essays on Action, Rationality & Community. 256p. 1999. 59.95 (*0-8476-9258-2*) Rowman.

Boylan, Michael A. The Power to Get In. 204p. 1998. pap. 14.95 (*0-312-19522-2*) St Martin.

Boylan, P. Thoth: The Hermes of Egypt. 215p. 1979. pap. 20.00 (*0-89005-280-8*) Ares.

Boylan, Patricia. All Cultivated People: A History of the United States Arts Club, Dublin. (Illus.). 27p. 1989. 35.00 (*0-86140-266-9*, Pub. by Smyth) Dufour.

Boylan, Patricia, et al. En Directo! A Beginning Course. 2nd ed. LC 93-20993. 544p. (C). 1994. 80.00 (*0-07-006950-6*) McGraw.

— En Directo! A Beginning Course. 2nd ed. LC 93-20993. (C). 1994. pap., lab manual ed. 28.75 (*0-07-006973-5*) McGraw.

Boylan, Patrick, jt. ed. see International Committee of Museums Staff.

***Boylan, Penny.** Christmas Crafts: Fifty Handmade Decorations, Ornaments, Gift-Wraps & Festive Table Settings. 1998. 11.98 (*1-84038-135-3*) Hermes Hse.

— Inspirations: Claywork. 96p. 2000. pap. 12.95 (*1-84215-146-0*) Anness Pub.

— Loving Memories. 2000. 16.95 (*0-7548-0479-8*, Lorenz Bks) Anness Pub.

— Making Memories. 2000. 16.95 (*0-7548-0486-0*, Lorenz Bks) Anness Pub.

Boylan, Penny. Modeling Clay: 20 Decorative Projects to Create for the Home, 1. (Inspirations Ser.). 1999. 12.95 (*1-85967-887-4*) Anness Pub.

— Salt Dough: 20 Practical Projects for the Home. (Inspirations Ser.). (Illus.). 96p. 1997. 12.95 (*1-85967-537-9*, Lorenz Bks) Anness Pub.

Boylan, Peter, jt. auth. see Creasey, Robert K.

Boylan, Richard. Project Epiphany. 296p. (Orig.). 1996. pap. 12.95 (*1-885395-21-3*) Book Tree.

Boylan, Roger. Killoyle: An Irish Farce. LC 96-51796. 248p. (Orig.). 1997. pap. 13.95 (*1-56478-145-3*) Dalkey Arch.

Boylan, T. Kelley. Mastering Internet Explorer 4.0 for Macintosh. 400p. 1996. pap. text 39.99 incl. cd-rom (*1-56830-322-X*) Hayden.

Boylan, Thomas A. & O'Gorman, Paschal F. Beyond Rhetoric & Realism in Economics: Towards a Reformulation of Methodology. (Economics as Social Theory Ser.). 240p. (C). 1995. pap. 29.99 (*0-415-12513-8*, C0422) Routledge.

— Beyond Rhetoric & Realism in Economics: Towards a Reformulation of Methodology. LC 94-39813. (Economics as Social Theory Ser.). 240p. (C). (gr. 13). 1995. 85.00 (*0-415-08220-X*, C0290) Routledge.

Boylan, Thomas A., jt. ed. see Foley, Tadhg.

Boyland & Kuykendall, eds. Plant-Microbe Interactions & Biological Control. (Illus.). 464p. 1998. text 165.00 (*0-8247-0043-0*) Dekker.

Boyland, Alan R. Urban Freight Transport: Problems & Some Possible Solutions. (C). 1977. 29.00 (*0-7855-3879-8*, Pub. by Oxford Polytechnic) St Mut.

Boyland, Anita W. Closing, Shipping, & Warehousing. Linthicum, Bob, ed. 110p. 1999. pap. 35.00 (*0-945359-05-5*) Mortgage Bankers.

Boyle. Blue Blood in Red Hook. 1995. 20.00 (*1-883402-41-7*) S&S Trade.

— Cases in Special Education. 2nd ed. 2001. pap. 17.00 (*0-07-232271-3*) McGraw.

— Cephalopod Life Cycles, 2 vols. 1987. 420.00 (*0-12-123000-7*) Acad Pr.

***Boyle.** Exploring Contemporary Migration. LC 99-222725. 208p. (C). 1998. pap. 47.00 (*0-582-25161-3*) Longman.

— George Antonius & Palestine. 280p. 2000. 65.00 (*0-8133-3759-3*, Pub. by Westview) HarpC.

— Grand Finales: The Art of the Plated Dessert & a Modernist View of Plated Deserts Set. 636p. 89.90 (*0-471-31562-1*) Wiley.

Boyle. Leadership in Nursing Practice. 1999. pap. text. write for info. (*0-7216-4915-7*) Harcourt.

— Personal Nutrition. 2nd rev. ed. 1994. pap. write for info. (*0-314-04960-6*) West Pub.

— Personal Nutrition. 4th ed. (Health Sciences). 2000. pap. 43.75 (*0-534-54603-X*) Wadsworth Pub.

— Rue Morgue Avenue. 1995. 20.00 (*1-883402-42-5*) S&S Trade.

Boyle. The Sea: Ocean History, Vol. 13. 500p. 79.95 (*0-471-17930-2*) Wiley.

Boyle. Your Geography, Bk. A. (J). Date not set. pap. text. write for info. (*0-582-18799-0*, Pub. by Addison-Wesley) Longman.

— Your Geography, Bk. B. (J). Date not set. pap. text. write for info. (*0-582-18800-8*, Pub. by Addison-Wesley) Longman.

B

Boyle & Morris. Community Nutrition. 2nd ed. LC 98-38212. (Health Sciences Ser.). 1998. pap. 73.95 (*0-534-53829-0*) Wadsworth Pub.

***Boyle & Morris.** Community Nutrition. 3rd ed. (Health Sciences Ser.). 2001. 52.50 (*0-534-55188-2*) Wadsworth Pub.

Boyle & Weishaar. Special Education Law & Cases. 256p. 2000. pap. text 44.00 (*0-205-27468-4*, Longwood Div) Allyn.

Boyle, A. & Norton Rose M5 Group Staff, eds. Environmental Regulation & Economic Growth: The Oxford Law Colloquium. 292p. 1995. text 85.00 (*0-19-825910-7*) OUP.

Boyle, A., et al. Two Oxfordshire Anglo-Saxon Cemeteries: Berinsfield & Didcot. (Thames Valley Ser.: Vol. 8). (Illus.). 274p. 1995. pap. 50.00 (*0-947816-86-0*, Pub. by Oxford Univ Comm Arch) David Brown.

Boyle, A. J. The Chaonian Dove: Studies in the Eclogues, Georgics, & Aeneid of Virgil. (Mnemosyne Ser.: Supplement 94). xi, 196p. 1986. pap. 54.00 (*90-04-07672-7*) Brill Academic Pubs.

— Directors' Fiduciary Duties: The Continuing Problem of Effective Enforcement. (Forum Internationale Ser.: No. 10). 1988. 24.00 (*90-6544-379-7*) Kluwer Law Intl.

— Tragic Seneca: An Essay in the Theatrical Tradition. LC 96-52766. 272p. (C). 1997. 80.00 (*0-415-12495-6*) Routledge.

Boyle, A. M. The Ayrshire Book of Burns-Lore. (C). 1988. pap. 40.00 (*0-907526-18-7*, Pub. by Alloway Pub) St Mut.

— Ayrshire Book of Burns Lore. 1980. 30.00 (*0-907526-71-3*, Pub. by Alloway Publ) St Mut.

Boyle, Alan, et al, contrib. by. The Practice & Procedure of the Companies Court. (Lloyd's Commercial Law Library). 400p. 1995. write for info. (*1-85044-502-8*) LLP.

Boyle, Alan & Birnie, Patricia. Basic Documents on International Environmental Law. 704p. 1996. text 98.00 (*0-19-876320-4*); pap. text 38.00 (*0-19-876321-2*) OUP.

***Boyle, Alan & Freestone, David, eds.** International Law & Sustainable Development: Past Achievements & Future Challenges. LC 99-27434. 408p. 1999. text 105.00 (*0-19-829807-2*) OUP.

Boyle, Alan, jt. auth. see Birnie, Patricia.

Boyle, Alan E. & Anderson, Michael R., eds. Human Rights Approaches to Environmental Protection. 334p. 1998. reprint ed. pap. text 39.95 (*0-19-826789-4*) OUP.

***Boyle, Alison.** 1, 2, 3, 4, 5 Once I Caught a Fish Alive! (Illus.). 16p. (J). (ps-k). 2000. 10.95 (*1-86233-116-2*) Levinson Bks.

Boyle, Alison. Playdays Colours & Shapes. (Illus.). 32p. (J). (ps-2). 1992. pap. 3.95 (*0-563-20887-2*, BBC-Parkwest) Parkwest Pubns.

— Playdays Letters & Words. (Illus.). 32p. (J). (ps-2). 1992. pap. 3.95 (*0-563-20890-2*, BBC-Parkwest) Parkwest Pubns.

— Playdays Numbers. (Illus.). 32p. (J). (ps-2). 1992. pap. 3.95 (*0-563-20889-9*, BBC-Parkwest) Parkwest Pubns.

— Playdays Out & About. (Illus.). 32p. (J). (ps-2). 1992. pap. 3.95 (*0-563-20888-0*, BBC-Parkwest) Parkwest Pubns.

***Boyle, Alison.** Twinkle, Twinkle, Little Star. (Illus.). 16p. (J). (ps-k). 2000. 10.95 (*1-86233-111-1*) Levinson Bks.

Boyle, Alistair. Bluebeard's Last Stand: A Gil Yates Private Investigator Novel. LC 98-13798. 155p. 1998. 20.00 (*1-888310-45-6*) A A Knoll Pubs.

— The Con: A Gil Yates Private Investigator Novel. LC 95-52375. 222p. 1996. 19.95 (*0-9627297-9-5*) A A Knoll Pubs.

— The Missing Link: A Gil Yates Private Investigator Novel. LC 94-78009. 224p. 1995. 19.95 (*0-9627297-3-6*) A A Knoll Pubs.

***Boyle, Alistair.** Ship Shapely: A Gil Yates Private Investigator Novel. LC 99-23574. 212p. 1999. 20.00 (*1-888310-99-5*) A A Knoll Pubs.

Boyle, Alistair. The Unlucky Seven: A Gil Yates Private Investigator Novel. LC 96-51686. 176p. 1997. 20.00 (*1-888310-77-4*) A A Knoll Pubs.

***Boyle, Alistair.** What Now, King Lear? (Gil Yates Private Investigator Ser.: Vol. 6). 2001. 22.00 (*1-888310-85-5*) A A Knoll Pubs.

Boyle, Andrew. Ayrshire Heritage. 1980. pap. 30.00 (*0-907526-49-7*, Pub. by Alloway Publ) St Mut.

— Pictorial History of Arran. 1980. pap. 40.00 (*0-907526-57-8*, Pub. by Alloway Publ) St Mut.

Boyle, Ann. Desert Song. large type ed. (General Ser.). 352p. 1993. 27.99 (*0-7089-2836-6*) Ulverscroft.

Boyle, Ann K., jt. auth. see Goodearl, K. R.

Boyle, Anthony. Clinical Research Opportunities: A Physician's Guide to Participating in Clinical Research Studies. Lynch, Maureen & Swanson, Kathryn, eds. LC 95-14125. 175p. 1996. pap. 49.95 (*1-57066-030-1*, ME072) Practice Mgmt Info.

Boyle, Anthony J. Roman Epic. 352p. (C). 1996. pap. 27.99 (*0-415-14357-8*) Routledge.

Boyle, Antonia B., jt. auth. see McKain, Scott.

Boyle, Arthur L., jt. ed. see Hazlett, John D.

Boyle, Bernard M. Wright in Arizona: The Early Work of Pedro E. Guerrero. LC 95-81608. (Illus.). 48p. 1996. pap. text 19.95 (*1-884320-14-7*) ASU Herberger Ctr.

Boyle, Bill. My First Atlas. LC 94-10467. (Illus.). 40p. (J). (gr. k-4). 1994. 14.95 (*1-56458-624-3*) DK Pub Inc.

Boyle, Bill & Christie, Tom, eds. Issues in Setting Standards: Establishing Comparabilities. 1996. 85.00 (*0-7507-0481-0*, Falmer Pr); pap. 29.95 (*0-7507-0482-9*, Falmer Pr) Taylor & Francis.

Boyle, Bill & Clarke, Paul. The Head Teacher As Effective Leader. LC 97-4411. 144p. 1998. pap. 42.95 (*1-85742-402-6*, Pub. by Ashgate Pub) Ashgate Pub Co.

Boyle, Bill & Hopkins, Dave. My First Atlas. (FRE., Illus.). (J). 21.99 (*0-590-24520-1*); text 18.95 (*0-590-24339-X*) Scholastic Inc.

Boyle, Brian. Alundra: Unauthorized Game Secrets. LC 97-69925. 160p. 1998. per. 14.99 (*0-7615-1320-5*) Prima Pub.

— Dark Earth: Prima's Official Strategy Guide. LC 97-69331. 384p. 1997. per. 19.99 (*0-7615-1255-1*) Prima Pub.

— Guardians: Agents of Justice. 240p. Date not set. pap. 19.99 (*0-7615-0952-6*) Prima Pub.

— WCW vs. NWO: World Tour: The Official Strategy Guide. LC 97-69034. 112p. 1997. per. 12.99 (*0-7615-1239-X*) Prima Pub.

Boyle, Brian, jt. auth. see Knight, Michael.

Boyle, Brian, jt. auth. see Ward, Kip.

Boyle, C. Physics. 290p. 1987. 60.00 (*1-85313-001-X*, Pub. by Checkmate Pubns) St Mut.

***Boyle, Cailin.** Color Harmony for the Web. 2001. 40.00 (*1-56496-603-8*) Rockport Pubs.

Boyle, Carmel O. The Irish Children's Songbook. 132p. (J). pap. 11.95 (*0-85342-787-9*, OS10475, Pub. by Mercier Pr) Music Sales.

Boyle, Carol J. Fix It Up & Sell It: Refurbishing Old Houses for the Best Price at the Lowest Cost. (Illus.). 384p. 1987. pap. 14.95 (*0-13-322330-2*) P-H.

— From Ramshackle to Resale: Fixing up Old Houses for Profit. (Illus.). 288p. (Orig.). 1989. 24.95 (*0-8306-1362-5*); pap. 15.95 (*0-8306-3162-3*) McGraw-Hill Prof.

Boyle, Carol L. & Ely, Dean E. From the Smallest Acorn. 54p. 1992. ring bd. 29.95 (*0-9634743-0-8*) ABC&D Creation.

Boyle, Caroline, tr. Legislative History of the Carriage of Goods by Sea Act: And the Travaux Preparatoires of the Hague Rules, 3 vols. 1991. 225.00 (*0-8377-1166-5*, Rothman) W S Hein.

Boyle, Caroline, tr. see Sturley, Michael F., ed.

Boyle, Catherine M. Chilean Theater, 1973-1985: Marginality, Power, Selfhood. LC 88-46172. 224p. 1992. 36.50 (*0-685-50340-2*) Fairleigh Dickinson.

— Thematic Development in Chilean Theatre since 1973: In Search of the Dramatic Conflict. 1992. 39.50 (*0-8386-3363-3*) Fairleigh Dickinson.

***Boyle, Dan, et al.** The First Padres: San Diego Enters the Pacific Coast League. 250p. 2000. spiral bd. 23.95 (*1-893392-05-8*) Baseball Pr Bks.

Boyle, Daniel C. Secrets of a Successful Employee Recognition System. (Illus.). 147p. 1995. text 25.00 (*1-56327-083-8*) Productivity Inc.

Boyle, Daniel J. Sports Medicine for Parents & Coaches. LC 99-13392. (Illus.). 120p. 1999. 29.95 (*0-87840-732-4*); pap. 12.95 (*0-87840-733-2*) Georgetown U Pr.

Boyle, Darl M. Where Lilith Dances. LC 70-144713. (Yale Series of Younger Poets: No. 6). reprint ed. 18.00 (*0-404-53806-1*) AMS Pr.

***Boyle, David.** World War II: A Photographic History. (Illus.). 600p. 2000. 24.98 (*1-58663-094-6*) M Friedman Pub Grp Inc.

Boyle, David J. & Radocy, Rudolf E. Measurement & Evaluation of Musical Experiences. 332p. 1987. 45.00 (*0-02-870300-6*, Schirmer Books) Mac Lib Ref.

Boyle, Deirdre. Subject to Change: Guerrilla Television Revisited. (Illus.). 304p. 1997. pap. 19.95 (*0-19-511054-4*, 650401Q); text 60.00 (*0-19-504334-0*) OUP.

Boyle-Delp. Take Control of Your Career: A Development Guide. 144p. 1992. spiral bd. 15.95 (*0-8403-7368-6*) Kendall-Hunt.

Boyle, Denis, ed. Stragegic Service Management - Beyond the Moment of Truth. (Best of Long Range Planning Ser.). 144p. 1990. text 86.50 (*0-08-037752-1*, Pergamon Pr); pap. text 92.00 (*0-08-037751-3*, Pergamon Pr) Elsevier.

Boyle, Denis, jt. auth. see Stanic, Vlad.

Boyle, Denis, jt. ed. see Stanic, Vlad.

Boyle, Dierdre, jt. ed. see Roberts, Don.

Boyle, Doe. Coral Reef Hideaway: The Story of a Clown Anemonefish. (Smithsonian Oceanic Collection). (Illus.). 32p. (J). (ps-2). 1995. 15.95 (*1-56899-182-7*) Soundprints.

Boyle, Doe. Coral Reef Hideaway: The Story of a Clown Anemonefish. (Smithsonian Oceanic Collection). (Illus.). 32p. (J). (ps-2). 1995. 19.95 incl. audio (*1-56899-186-X*, BC4008) Soundprints.

Boyle, Doe. Coral Reef Hideaway: The Story of a Clown Anemonefish, Incl. large toy. (Smithsonian Oceanic Collection). (Illus.). 32p. (J). (ps-2). 1995. 29.95 (*1-56899-184-3*) Soundprints.

— Coral Reef Hideaway: The Story of a Clown Anemonefish, Incl. micro bk. & small toy. (Smithsonian Oceanic Collection). (Illus.). 32p. (J). (ps-2). 1995. 9.95 (*1-56899-185-1*) Soundprints.

— Coral Reef Hideaway: The Story of a Clown Anemonefish, Incl. Sm. & Lg. Plush Toy. LC 95-6776. (Smithsonian Oceanic Collection). (Illus.). 32p. (J). (ps-2). 1995. 38.95 incl. audio (*1-56899-655-1*) Soundprints.

— Coral Reef Hideaway: The Story of a Clown Anemonefish, Micro bk. (Smithsonian Oceanic Collection). (Illus.). 32p. (J). (ps-2). 1995. 4.95 (*1-56899-183-5*) Soundprints.

— Fun with the Family in Connecticut: Hundreds of Ideas for Day Trips with the Kids. 2nd rev. ed. LC 97-41844. (Fun with the Family Ser.). (Illus.). 256p. 1998. pap. 12.95 (*0-7627-0103-X*) Globe Pequot.

***Boyle, Doe.** Fun with the Family in Connecticut: Hundreds of Ideas for Day Trips with the Kids. 3rd ed. LC 99-89858. (Fun with the Family Ser.). (Illus.). 288p. 2000. pap. 12.95 (*0-7627-0619-8*) Globe Pequot.

Boyle, Doe. Gray Wolf Pup. (Smithsonian Wild Heritage Collection). (Illus.). 32p. (J). (gr. k-3). 1995. pap. 4.95 (*1-56899-136-3*) Soundprints.

— Gray Wolf Pup. (Smithsonian Wild Heritage Collection). 1993. 10.15 (*0-606-08424-X*, Pub. by Turtleback) Demco.

— Gray Wolf Pup, Incl. small toy. (Smithsonian Wild Heritage Collection). (Illus.). 32p. (J). (gr. k-3). 1995. pap. 15.95 (*1-56899-142-8*) Soundprints.

— Guide to the Connecticut Shore. (Illus.). 273p. 1998. pap. 12.95 (*0-7627-0180-3*) Globe Pequot.

— Otter on His Own: The Story of a Sea Otter. LC 94-28696. (Smithsonian Oceanic Collection). (Illus.). 32p. (J). (ps-2). 1995. 15.95 (*1-56899-129-0*); 19.95 incl. audio (*1-56899-133-9*, BC4005) Soundprints.

— Otter on His Own: The Story of a Sea Otter, Incl. 12" plush toy. LC 94-28696. (Smithsonian Oceanic Collection). (Illus.). 32p. (J). (ps-2). 1995. 32.95 (*1-56899-131-2*) Soundprints.

— Otter on His Own: The Story of a Sea Otter, Micro bk. LC 94-28696. (Smithsonian Oceanic Collection). (Illus.). 32p. (J). (ps-2). 1995. 4.95 (*1-56899-130-4*) Soundprints.

— Otter on His Own: The Story of a Sea Otter, Micro bk., incl. 7" plush toy. LC 94-28696. (Smithsonian Oceanic Collection). (Illus.). 32p. (J). (ps-2). 1995. 12.95 (*1-56899-132-0*) Soundprints.

— Summer Coat, Winter Coat: The Story of a Snowshoe Hare. (Smithsonian Wild Heritage Collection). (Illus.). 32p. (J). (gr. k-3). 1995. pap. 4.95 (*1-56899-198-3*) Soundprints.

— Summer Coat, Winter Coat: The Story of a Snowshoe Hare, Incl. 8" tan toy. (Smithsonian Wild Heritage Collection). (Illus.). 32p. (J). (gr. k-3). 1995. pap. 15.95 (*1-56899-209-2*) Soundprints.

— Summer Coat, Winter Coat: The Story of a Snowshoe Hare, Incl. 8" white toy. (Smithsonian Wild Heritage Collection). (Illus.). 32p. (J). (gr. k-3). 1995. pap. 15.95 (*1-56899-204-1*) Soundprints.

— Summer Coat, Winter Coat, The Story of a Snowshoe Hare. (Smithsonian Wild Heritage Collection). (J). 1993. 10.15 (*0-606-08215-8*, Pub. by Turtleback) Demco.

Boyle, Don. SS Totenkopf H. Himmler Honor Ring, 1933-1945. (Illus.). 73p. 1995. 44.50 (*0-685-72342-9*) Johnson Ref Bks.

Boyle, Edward. Biographical Essays, 1790-1890. LC 68-54331. (Essay Index Reprint Ser.). 1977. 20.95 (*0-8369-0237-8*) Ayer.

Boyle, Edward, ed. see National Cargo Bureau, Inc. Staff.

Boyle, Eileen. Irish Pub Crack. 92p. 1998. pap. 11.95 (*0-85640-607-4*, Pub. by Blackstaff Pr) Dufour.

Boyle, Elisabeth L. & Delbridge, Pauline N. Spoken Cantonese, Bk I. 410p. 1980. pap. 25.00 (*0-87950-675-X*) Spoken Lang Serv.

— Spoken Cantonese, Bk. II. 410p. 1980. pap. 35.00 (*0-87950-676-8*) Spoken Lang Serv.

Boyle, Elisabeth L. & Delbridge, Pauline N. Spoken Cantonese, Bks. I & II. Incl. Bk I. Spoken Cantonese. 410p. audio 105.00 (*0-87950-677-6*); Bk. I. Spoken Cantonese. 410p. pap. 130.00 incl. audio (*0-87950-679-2*); Bk. II. Spoken Cantonese. 410p. audio 105.00 (*0-87950-678-4*); Bk. 2. Spoken Cantonese. 410p. pap. 140.00 incl. audio (*0-87950-680-6*); 410p. 1980. Set pap. 250.00 incl. audio (*0-87950-681-4*) Spoken Lang Serv.

Boyle, Elizabeth. Brazen Angel. 400p. 1997. mass mkt. 5.50 (*0-440-22412-8*) Dell.

— Brazen Heiress. 368p. 1998. mass mkt. 5.99 (*0-440-22638-4*) Dell.

— Brazen Temptress. 368p. 1999. mass mkt. 5.99 (*0-440-22639-2*) Dell.

— Cantonese Basic Course. 392p. 1995. pap. 19.95 (*0-7818-0289-X*) Hippocrene Bks.

— Cantonese Intensive Cassette Course: Learn Cantonese Quickly. 392p. 1997. 184.00 incl. audio (*0-9631518-1-9*) Mltilingl Bks.

***Boyle, Elizabeth.** No Marriage of Convenience. 384p. 2000. mass mkt. 5.99 (*0-380-81534-6*) Morrow Avon.

Boyle, F. About Orchids: A Chat. (C). 1988. 60.00 (*0-7855-3279-X*, Pub. by Scientific) St Mut.

***Boyle, Fiona.** Guardian Careers Guide: Law. 2000. pap. 19.95 (*1-85702-631-4*, Pub. by Fourth Estate) Trafalgar.

Boyle, Fran, et al. The Sex Industry: An Australian Survey. LC 97-70899. (Illus.). 176p. 1997. text 59.95 (*1-85972-625-9*, Pub. by Ashgate Pub) Ashgate Pub Co.

Boyle, Frances M. Mothers Bereaved by Stillbirth, Neonatal Death or Sudden Infant Death Syndrome: Patterns of Distress & Recovery. LC 97-70894. (Illus.). 160p. 1997. text 55.95 (*1-85972-149-4*, Pub. by Ashgate Pub) Ashgate Pub Co.

Boyle, Francis, et al. In Re: More Than Fifty-Thousand Nuclear Weapons: Analyses of the Illegality of Nuclear Weapons under International Law. Friel, Howard, ed. LC 91-2294. (Normative International Relations Ser.). 128p. (Orig.). (C). 1991. pap. 12.00 (*0-9623718-5-8*); lib. bdg. 30.00 (*0-9623718-4-X*) Aletheia Pr.

Boyle, Francis A. The Bosnian People Charge Genocide: Proceedings at the International Court of Justice Concerning Bosnia v. Serbia on the Prevention & Punishment of the Crime of Genocide. LC 94-11826. 1994. lib. bdg. write for info. (*1-880831-09-0*) Aletheia Pr.

— The Bosnian People Charge Genocide: Proceedings of the International Court of Justice Concerning Bosnia vs. Serbia on the Prevention & Punishment of the Crime of Genocide. LC 94-11826. 400p. (Orig.). Date not set. pap. text 20.00 (*1-880831-08-2*) Aletheia Pr.

***Boyle, Francis A.** Foundations of World Order: The Legalist Approach to International Relations 1898-1921. LC 98-32014. 264p. 1999. pap. 18.95 (*0-8223-2364-8*) Duke.

— Foundations of World Order: The Legalist Approach to International Relations, 1898-1921. LC 98-32014. 264p. 1999. 54.95 (*0-8223-2327-3*) Duke.

Boyle, Francis A. The Future of International Law & American Foreign Policy. 507p. (C). 1989. lib. bdg. 65.00 (*0-941320-50-2*) Transnatl Pubs.

— World Politics & International Law. LC 85-4374. (Duke Press Policy Studies). xii, 366p. (C). 1985. pap. text 23.95 (*0-8223-0655-7*) Duke.

Boyle, Frank A. A Party of Mad Fellows: The Story of the Irish Regiments in the Army of the Potomac. 443p. 1996. 29.95 (*0-89029-329-5*) Morningside Bkshop.

***Boyle, Frank T.** Swift as Memesis: Modernity & Its Satirist. 2000. 45.00 (*0-8047-3436-4*) Stanford U Pr.

Boyle, George E. & Blood, Charles L. Cat First Aid: A Guide to Emergency Treatment & General Health Care. Watson, Ben, ed. LC 90-50019. (Illus.). 128p. (Orig.). 1990. pap. 9.95 (*0-88266-626-6*) Storey Bks.

Boyle, Gerry. Bloodline. 1996. mass mkt. 5.99 (*0-425-15182-4*) Berkley Pub.

— Borderline. LC 97-24629. 368p. 1998. pap. 22.95 (*0-425-16147-1*) Berkley Pub.

***Boyle, Gerry.** Borderline. (Jack McMorrow Mystery Ser.: No. 6). 2000. reprint ed. mass mkt. 6.99 (*0-425-16964-2*, Prime Crime) Berkley Pub.

— Cover Story. LC 99-27295. (Jack McMorrow Mystery Ser.: No. 7). 384p. 2000. 22.95 (*0-425-16893-X*, Prime Crime) Berkley Pub.

Boyle, Gerry. Deadline: A Jack McMorrow Mystery. 288p. 1995. mass mkt. 5.99 (*0-425-14637-5*, Prime Crime) Berkley Pub.

— Deadline: A Jack McMorrow Mystery. LC 93-6296. 1993. 17.95 (*0-945980-44-2*) Nrth Country Pr.

— Deadline: A Jack McMorrow Mystery. large type ed. LC 93-45435. 462p. 1994. lib. bdg. 20.95 (*0-7862-0163-0*) Thorndike Pr.

— Lifeline. 368p. 1997. mass mkt. 5.99 (*0-425-15688-5*) Berkley Pub.

— Potshot. (Jack McMorrow Mystery Ser.). 1998. mass mkt. 5.99 (*0-425-16233-8*) Berkley Pub.

Boyle, Godfrey, ed. Renewable Energy: Power for a Sustainable Future. LC 96-215446. (Illus.). 479p. (C). 1996. pap. text 48.00 (*0-19-856451-1*) OUP.

Boyle, Grace. The Cookie Crumbles: A Case of Sensory Sleuthing. (BrainLink Ser.: Vol. 3). (Illus.). iv, 38p. (gr. k-8). 1993. pap. write for info. (*1-888997-03-6*) Baylor Coll Med.

— The Cookie Crumbles: A Case of Sensory Sleuthing. rev. ed. (BrainLink Ser.: Vol. 3). (Illus.). iv, 38p. (gr. k-8). 1997. pap. write for info. (*1-888997-19-2*) Baylor Coll Med.

— Skullduggery: A Case of Cranium Confusion. (BrainLink Ser.: Vol. 1). (Illus.). iv, 38p. (J). (gr. k-8). 1992. pap. write for info. (*1-888997-05-2*) Baylor Coll Med.

— Skullduggery: A Case of Cranium Confusion. rev. ed. (BrainLink Ser.). (Illus.). iv, 38p. (gr. k-8). 1997. pap. write for info. (*1-888997-17-6*) Baylor Coll Med.

— Trouble at Tsavo: The Tale of the Black Rhino. (BrainLink Ser.: Vol. 2). (Illus.). iv, 38p. (gr. k-8). 1992. pap. write for info. (*1-888997-04-4*) Baylor Coll Med.

— Trouble at Tsavo: The Tale of the Black Rhino. rev. ed. (BrainLink Ser.: Vol. 2). (Illus.). iv, 38p. (gr. k-8). 1997. pap. text. write for info. (*1-888997-18-4*) Baylor Coll Med.

Boyle, Gregory J. & Langley, Phillip D. Elementary Statistical Methods: For Students of Psychology, Education & the Social Sciences. (Illus.). 220p. 1989. pap. text 24.00 (*0-08-034426-7*) Elsevier.

Boyle, H. B. Transducer Handbook: User's Directory of Electrical Transducers. (Illus.). 240p. 1999. text 62.95 (*0-7506-1194-4*) Buttrwrth-Heinemann.

Boyle, J. A. & Grossman, Stanley I., eds. Cambridge History of Iran, Vol. 5: The Saljuq & Mongol Periods. LC 67-12845. (Illus.). 778p. 1968. text 145.00 (*0-521-06936-X*) Cambridge U Pr.

Boyle, J. David. Instructional Objectives in Music: Resources for Planning, Instruction, & Evaluating Achievement. LC 74-75320. 275p. 1974. reprint ed. pap. 85.30 (*0-608-04215-3*, 206495600011) Bks Demand.

Boyle, J. David, jt. auth. see Radocy, Rudolf E.

Boyle, James. Critical Legal STudies. (C). 1994. pap. text 25.00 (*0-8147-1222-3*) NYU Pr.

— Shamans, Software & Spleens: Law & the Construction of the Information Society. LC 95-42433. 288p. 1996. 37.95 (*0-674-80522-4*) HUP.

— Shamans, Software, & Spleens: Law & the Construction of the Information Society. (Illus.). 288p. 1997. reprint ed. pap. 16.50 (*0-674-80523-2*) HUP.

Boyle, James, ed. Critical Legal Studies. (International Library of Essays in Law & Legal Theory). 656p. (C). 1993. lib. bdg. 30.00 (*0-8147-1173-1*) NYU Pr.

Boyle, James, jt. auth. see House, Louis.

Boyle, James J. Killer Cults. 1995. mass mkt. 5.50 (*0-312-95285-6*) St Martin.

Boyle, James J. & Pindzola, M. S., eds. Many-Body Atomic Physics. LC 96-14068. (Illus.). 440p. (C). 1998. text 69.95 (*0-521-47006-4*) Cambridge U Pr.

Boyle, James R. Planted Forests: Contributions to the Quest for Sustainable Societies. LC 98-31689. (Forestry Sciences Ser.). 1999. write for info. (*0-7923-5468-0*) Kluwer Academic.

Boyle, Jerome M. Apache Sunrise. (Orig.). 1994. mass mkt. 5.99 (*0-8041-1069-7*) Ivy Books.

***Boyle, Jimmy.** Hero of the Underworld. 220p. 2000. pap. 14.00 (*1-85242-608-X*) Broadway BDD.

Boyle, Joan M. & Morriss, James E. The Mirror of Time: Images of Aging & Dying, 7. LC 86-33631. (Contributions to the Study of Aging Ser.: No. 7). 237p. 1987. 55.00 (*0-313-25597-0*, BYM/, Greenwood Pr) Greenwood.

***Boyle, Joe.** Reflections on the Presence of God. 144p. 2000. pap. 12.00 (*1-930051-06-9*, Pub. by Booklight Inc) Bks Intl VA.

An Asterisk (*) at the beginning of an entry indicates that the title is appearing for the first time.

Boyle, John. Boyle Genealogy: John Boyle of Virginia & Kentucky; Notes on Lines of Descent with Some Collateral References. (Illus.). 174p. 1993. reprint ed. pap. 27.50 (*0-8328-3097-6*); reprint ed. lib. bdg. 37.50 (*0-8328-3096-8*) Higginson Bk Co.

Boyle, John A. Persian-English Dictionary, Romanized. (ENG & PER.). 42.50 (*0-87557-057-7*) Saphrograph.

Boyle, John E. The Atman Discovery - Cracking the Code of the Ultimate Enigma: An Unperceived Revolution. (Primers for the Age of Inner Space Ser.: Vol. VI). 292p. (Orig.). 1997. 25.00 (*0-614-29749-4*); pap. 15.00 (*0-614-29750-8*) Wheat Forders.

— The Way of the Essentialist: Contra Sartres Existentialism. (Primers for the Age of Inner Space Ser.: No. 5). 166p. 1993. pap. 15.00 (*0-917888-08-1*) Wheat Forders.

Boyle, John F., pref. Creative Love: The Ethics of Human Reproduction. 252p. (Orig.). 1989. pap. 11.95 (*0-931888-32-8*) Christendom Pr.

Boyle, John H. Modern Japan: The American Nexus. LC 92-72355. 426p. (C). 1993. pap. text 41.50 (*0-15-500324-0*) Harcourt.

Boyle, John J. Landlord Remedies in Florida. Date not set. ring bd. 80.00 (*0-327-00960-8*, 80871, MICHIE) LEXIS Pub.

— Landlord's Remedies in Florida. 1994. ring bd., suppl. ed. 30.00 (*0-685-25719-3*, MICHIE) LEXIS Pub.

Boyle, John J., jt. auth. see Zeller-James, Trisha.

Boyle, John P. Church Teaching Authority: Historical & Theological Studies. LC 94-15468. (C). 1995. text 45.00 (*0-268-00805-1*) U of Notre Dame Pr.

Boyle, John W. The Irish Labor Movement in the Nineteenth Century. LC 87-27983. 400p. 1988. reprint ed. pap. 124.00 (*0-7837-9103-8*, 204990500004) Bks Demand.

Boyle, Joseph, et al. Cases in Special Education. 152p. (C). 1997. text. write for info. (*0-697-35481-4*, WCB McGr Hill) McGrw-H Hghr Educ.

Boyle, Joseph, jt. ed. see Sumner, L. W.

Boyle, Joseph L. From Redcoat to Rebel: The Thomas Sullivan Journal. LC 98-104319. (Illus.). vi, 244p. (Orig.). (C). 1997. pap. 16.50 (*0-7884-0744-9*, B595) Heritage Bk.

***Boyle, Joseph Lee.** "Fire Cake & Water" The Connecticut Infantry at the Valley Forge Encampment. 232p. 1999. pap. 24.00 (*0-8063-4913-1*, Pub. by Clearfield Co) ACCESS Pubs Network.

Boyle, Josephine. Holy Terror. large type ed. (Magna Large Print Ser.). 501p. 1996. 27.99 (*0-7505-0953-8*, Pub. by Mgna Lrg Print) Ulverscroft.

***Boyle, Josephine.** Spirit of The Family. 1999. 26.00 (*0-7278-5491-7*, Pub. by Severn Hse) Chivers N Amer.

Boyle, Joyceen, jt. auth. see Andrews, Margaret M.

Boyle, Joyceen S., jt. auth. see Andrews, Margaret M.

Boyle, Karl, jt. auth. see Smith, Patrick.

Boyle, Katherine, jt. ed. see Anderson, Sue.

***Boyle, Kathy.** A CPA's Basic Guide to Credit & Collection Techniques. 200p. 2000. pap. 45.00 (*0-87051-299-4*, 091001) Am Inst CPA.

Boyle, Katie, jt. ed. see Renfrew, Colin.

Boyle, Kay. Collected Poems. LC 90-85089. 192p. (Orig.). 1991. pap. 10.00 (*1-55659-039-3*) Copper Canyon.

— The Crazy Hunter. LC 93-8246. (Bibelot Ser.). 144p. 1993. reprint ed. pap. 6.00 (*0-8112-1233-5*, NDP769, Pub. by New Directions) Norton.

— Death of a Man. LC 88-26799. (New Directions Classics Ser.). 336p. 1989. reprint ed. pap. 10.95 (*0-8112-1089-8*, NPD670, Pub. by New Directions) Norton.

— Fifty Stories. LC 91-40229. (New Directions Classics Ser.). 640p. 1992. reprint ed. pap. 15.95 (*0-8112-1206-8*, NDP741, Pub. by New Directions) Norton.

— Life Being the Best & Other Stories. LC 87-32059. (New Directions Classics Ser.). 160p. 1988. pap. 8.95 (*0-8112-1053-7*, NDP654, Pub. by New Directions) Norton.

— Monday Night. 274p. 1977. reprint ed. 15.00 (*0-911858-35-0*) Appel.

— Wedding Day: And Other Stories, Vol. 1. LC 72-4420. (Short Story Index Reprint Ser.). 1977. reprint ed. 18.95 (*0-8369-4171-3*) Ayer.

Boyle, Kay, jt. auth. see McAlmon, Robert.

Boyle, Kay, tr. & afterword by see Crevel, Rene.

Boyle, Ken, jt. auth. see Cullen, Paul.

Boyle, Kevin. Freedom of Religion & Belief: World Report. Sheen, Juliet, ed. LC 97-224015. 512p. (C). 1997. pap. 27.99 (*0-415-15978-4*) Routledge.

— The UAW & the Heyday of American Liberalism, 1945-1968. 360p. 1995. text 42.50 (*0-8014-3064-X*) Cornell U Pr.

— The UAW & the Heyday of American Liberalism, 1945-1968. 360p. 1998. pap. 17.95 (*0-8014-8538-X*) Cornell U Pr.

Boyle, Kevin, ed. Organized Labor & American Politics, 1894-1994: The Labor-Liberal Alliance. LC 97-47472. (Series in American Labor History). 320p. (C). 1998. pap. text 23.95 (*0-7914-3952-6*) State U NY Pr.

— Organized Labor & American Politics, 1894-1994: The Labor-Liberal Alliance. LC 97-47472. (Series in American Labor History). 320p. (C). 1998. text 71.50 (*0-7914-3951-8*) State U NY Pr.

Boyle, Kevin & Getis, Victoria. Muddy Boots & Ragged Aprons: Images of Working-Class Detroit, 1900-1930. LC 96-28256. (Illus.). 208p. 1997. pap. 29.95 (*0-8143-2482-7*) Wayne St U Pr.

Boyle, Kevin & Sheen, Juliet, eds. Freedom of Religion & Belief: World Report. LC 97-224015. 512p. (C). 1997. 90.00 (*0-415-15977-6*) Routledge.

Boyle, Kevin & Sherif, Adel O. Human Rights & Democracy: The Role of the Supreme Constitutional Court of Egypt. LC 96-41626. 1996. 172.00 (*90-411-0288-4*) Kluwer Law Intl.

Boyle, Kevin, et al. Law & State: The Case of Northern Ireland. LC 75-10914. 206p. 1975. lib. bdg. 30.00 (*0-87023-197-9*) U of Mass Pr.

— Ten Years on in Northern Ireland. 1980. 40.00 (*0-900137-16-9*, Pub. by NCCL) St Mut.

Boyle, Kevin, jt. auth. see Beetham, David.

Boyle, Kevin, jt. auth. see Weir, Stuart.

Boyle, Leonard E. Medieval Latin Palaeography: A Bibliographical Introduction. 416p. 1984. pap. text 19.95 (*0-8020-6558-9*) U of Toronto Pr.

— Medieval Latin Palaeography: A Bibliographical Introduction. LC 85-157656. (Toronto Medieval Bibliographies Ser.: No. 8). 416p. reprint ed. pap. 129.00 (*0-8357-3657-1*, 203638400003) Bks Demand.

— Survey of the Vatican Archives. text 20.00 (*0-88844-350-1*) Brill Academic Pubs.

Boyle, Leonard E., ed. see Keaveney, Raymond.

Boyle, M., et al. Resolving Maps & the Dimension Group for Shifts of Finite Type. LC 87-25475. (Memoirs Ser.: Vol. 70/377). 146p. 1987. pap. 25.00 (*0-8218-2440-6*, MEMO/70/377) Am Math.

Boyle, M. Ross. Strategic Planning: Developing Strategies for Economic Stability & Growth. Murphy, Jenny, ed. 62p. (Orig.). 1987. pap. 20.00 (*0-317-04869-4*) Natl Coun Econ Dev.

Boyle, Mari & Morris, Diane H. Community Nutrition in Action: An Entrepreneurial Approach. LC 94-8255. 500p. (C). 1994. 48.50 (*0-314-02819-6*) West Pub.

Boyle, Marie. Community Nutrition. 2nd ed. 1998. text 55.95 (*0-534-53743-X*) Brooks-Cole.

Boyle, Marie & Zyla, Gail. Personal Nutrition. 2nd ed. Marshall, ed. 390p. (C). 1992. pap. 45.25 (*0-314-93333-6*) West Pub.

Boyle, Marie A. & Zyla, Gail. Personal Nutrition. 3rd ed. LC 95-45675. 450p. (C). 1996. 60.95 (*0-314-06380-3*) West Pub.

Boyle, Marjorie O. Christening Pagan Mysteries: Erasmus in Pursuit of Wisdom. LC 81-134156. (Erasmus Studies: No. 5). 189p. reprint ed. pap. 58.60 (*0-8357-4722-0*, 203763700009) Bks Demand.

— Divine Domesticity: Augustine of Thagaste to Teresa of Avila. LC 96-30781. (Studies in the History of Christian Thought). x, 295p. 1996. 109.00 (*90-04-10675-8*) Brill Academic Pubs.

— Erasmus on Language & Method in Theology. LC 77-2606. (Erasmus Studies: No. 2). 281p. reprint ed. pap. 87.20 (*0-608-12849-X*, 202359600033) Bks Demand.

— Petrarch's Genius: Pentimento & Prophecy. LC 90-19877. 224p. 1991. 48.00 (*0-520-07293-6*, Pub. by U CA Pr) Cal Prin Full Svc.

— Senses of Touch: Human Dignity & Deformity from Michelangelo to Calvin. LC 98-20862. (Studies in Medieval & Reformation Thought: Vol. 71). 300p. 1998. 98.00 (*90-04-11175-1*) Brill Academic Pubs.

Boyle, Mary E. Re-Thinking Abortion: Psychology, Gender, Power & the Law. LC 97-14933. (Women & Psychology Ser.). 176p. (C). 1997. 70.00 (*0-415-16364-1*); pap. 22.99 (*0-415-16365-X*) Routledge.

Boyle, Mary E., tr. see Breuil, Henri.

Boyle, Maureen. Antenatal Fetal Assessment. 80p. 1997. text 16.00 (*1-898507-25-2*) Buttrwrth-Heinemann.

— Antenatal Investigations. LC 94-219013. (Midwifery Practice Guides Ser.: No. 2). 61p. 1994. pap. 12.50 (*1-898507-04-X*) Buttrwrth-Heinemann.

***Boyle, Nicholas.** Goethe Vol. II: The Poet & the Age: Revolution & Renunciation, 1790-1803. (Illus.). 926p. 2000. 39.95 (*0-19-815869-6*) OUP.

Boyle, Nicholas. Goethe - The Poet & the Age: The Poetry of Desire, 1749-1790, Vol. 1. (Illus.). 828p. 1992. pap. 22.50 (*0-19-282981-5*) OUP.

— Who Are We Now? Christian Humanism & the Global Market from Hegel to Heaney. 312p. 1999. pap. 25.00 (*0-268-01958-4*, Pub. by U of Notre Dame Pr) Chicago Distribution Ctr.

Boyle, Owen F., jt. auth. see Peregoy, Suzanne F.

Boyle, P., jt. ed. see Alexander, F. E.

Boyle, P. R. The UFAW Handbook on the Care & Management of Cephalopods in the Laboratory. 63p. 1991. pap. 80.00 (*0-900767-72-3*, Pub. by Univs Fed Animal Welfare) St Mut.

Boyle, Patrick. The Port Wine Stain: Partick Boyle's Best Short Stroies. Fallon, Peter, ed. (Classic Irish Fiction Ser.). 236p. 1983. 15.95 (*0-8159-6524-9*) Devin.

— Scout's Honor: Sexual Abuse in Americas Most Trusted Institution. (Illus.). 416p. 1995. pap. 12.95 (*0-7615-0024-3*) Prima Pub.

Boyle, Patrick J., jt. auth. see Smith, Karl J.

Boyle, Patrick M. Class Formation & Civil Society: The Politics of Education in Africa. LC 98-74509. (Making of Modern Africa Ser.). 9p. 1999. text 65.95 (*1-84014-933-7*) Ashgate Pub Co.

Boyle, Patton L. Screaming Hawk Returns: Flying Eagle Teaches the Mystic Warrior. LC 95-19718. 135p. 1995. pap. text 9.95 (*0-88268-192-3*) Station Hill Pr.

Boyle, Patton L. Screaming Hawk: Flying Eagle's Training of a Mystic Warrior, a Narrative. LC 93-48778. 135p. 1994. pap. 9.95 (*0-88268-159-1*) Station Hill Pr.

Boyle, Paul & Halfacree, Keith. Migration into Rural Areas: Theories & Issues. LC 97-50257. 338p. 1998. 140.00 (*0-471-96989-3*) Wiley.

Boyle, Peter. Intranets, Extranets & Strategic Alliances: The Weaving of Cyberteams. LC 98-182791. 256p. 1998. pap. text 26.95 (*0-7506-3866-4*) Buttrwrth-Heinemann.

Boyle, Peter, ed. Cephalopod Life Cycles, Vol. 1. LC 83-70445. 1984. text 272.00 (*0-12-123001-5*) Acad Pr.

— Cephalopod Life Cycles, Vol. 2. 441p. 1987. text 272.00 (*0-12-123002-3*) Acad Pr.

Boyle, Peter, et al, eds. Atlas of Cancer Mortality in Central Europe. (IARC Scientific Publications: No. 134). (Illus.). 240p. 1996. text 89.50 (*92-832-2134-6*) OUP.

Boyle, Peter G., ed. The Churchill-Eisenhower Correspondence, 1953-1955. LC 89-77572. (Illus.). xx, 230p. (C). 1990. 34.95 (*0-8078-1910-7*) U of NC Pr.

Boyle, Phelim. Options & the Management of Financial Risk. 1992. text 25.00 (*0-938959-26-3*) Soc Actuaries.

Boyle, Phelim P., et al. Financial Economics: With Applications to Investments, Insurance & Pensions. Panjer, Harry H., ed. LC 97-27424. 1998. text 95 00 (*0-938959-48-4*) Soc Actuaries.

***Boyle, Philiip J., ed.** Getting Doctors to Listen: Ethics & Outcomes Data in Context. LC 97-9533. (Hastings Center Studies in Ethics). 248p. 2000. reprint ed. pap. text 18.95 (*0-87840-782-0*) Georgetown U Pr.

Boyle, Philip, jt. auth. see O'Rourke, Kevin D.

Boyle, Philip, jt. ed. see O'Rourke, Kevin D.

Boyle, Philip J., ed. Getting Doctors to Listen: Ethics & Outcomes Data in Context. LC 97-9533. (Hastings Center Studies in Ethics). 248p. 1998. 45.00 (*0-87840-654-9*) Georgetown U Pr.

***Boyle, P.J.** Migration & Gender in the Developed World. LC 98-44333. 1999. write for info. (*0-415-17144-X*) Routledge.

Boyle, Randall. Darkman. Ryan, Kevin, ed. 256p. 1994. mass mkt. 4.99 (*0-671-78764-0*) PB.

***Boyle, Raymond & Haynes, Richard.** Power Play: Sport, the Media & Popular Culture. LC 99-38838. 256p. 2000. pap. 23.00 (*0-582-36939-8*) Addison-Wesley.

Boyle, Raymond & Lynch, Peter S. Out of the Ghetto: The Catholic Community in Modern Scotland. 200p. 1998. pap. 45.00 (*0-85976-487-7*, Pub. by J Donald) St Mut.

Boyle, Richard & Lemaire, Donald, eds. Building Effective Evaluation Capacity: Lessons from Practice. LC 98-40492. 202p. 1999. 32.95 (*1-56000-396-0*) Transaction Pubs.

Boyle, Richard J. James M. Preston, Pennsylvania Post-Impressionist. Burke, Russell E., III, ed. (Illus.). 80p. (Orig.). 1990. 15.00 (*0-931241-23-5*) Westmoreland.

***Boyle, Richard J.** Living with Spinal Cord Injury. LC 99-93938. 2000. pap. 7.95 (*0-533-13199-5*) Vantage.

Boyle, Richard J. Willard Leroy Metcalf: An American Impressionist. (Illus.). 5p. 1995. pap. write for info. (*0-945936-11-7*) Spanierman Gallery.

Boyle, Richard J., jt. auth. see Lippincott, Louise W.

Boyle, Robert. Robert Boyle: A Free Enquiry into the Vulgarly Received Notion of Nature. Davis, Edward B. & Hunter, Michael, eds. (Cambridge Texts in the History of Philosophy Ser.). 207p. (C). 1996. text 59.95 (*0-521-56100-0*) Cambridge U Pr.

— Robert Boyle: A Free Enquiry into the Vulgarly Received Notion of Nature. Davis, Edward B. & Hunter, Michael, eds. (Cambridge Texts in the History of Philosophy Ser.). (Illus.). 207p. (C). 1996. pap. text 18.95 (*0-521-56796-3*) Cambridge U Pr.

— Robert Boyle on Natural Philosophy: An Essay with Selections from His Writings by Marie Boas Hall. LC 80-12187. (Illus.). 406p. 1980. reprint ed. lib. bdg. 45.50 (*0-313-22394-7*, BOON, Greenwood Pr) Greenwood.

— The Sceptical Chemist. 442p. 1992. reprint ed. pap. 36.00 (*0-922802-90-4*) Kessinger Pub.

— Selected Philosophical Papers of Robert Boyle. rev. ed. LC 91-25480. (HPC Classics Ser.). (Illus.). 288p. (C). 1991. reprint ed. pap. text 18.95 (*0-87220-122-8*); reprint ed. lib. bdg. 37.95 (*0-87220-123-6*) Hackett Pub.

— Seraphic Love: Some Motives & Incentives to the Love of God. 176p. 1992. reprint ed. pap. 16.95 (*1-56459-008-9*) Kessinger Pub.

— The Works of Robert Boyle, 6 Vol. 5150p. 1999. 1200.00 (*1-85506-604-1*) Thoemmes Pr.

— The Works of Robert Boyle, 6 vols., Set. Birch, Thomas W., ed. 4769p. 1966. lib. bdg. 1585.00 (*0-685-13758-9*, 05101127) G Olms Pubs.

Boyle, Robert, jt. auth. see Principe, Lawrence.

Boyle, Robert E. Lone Wolf. 345p. 1998. pap. 17.95 (*1-892896-96-6*) Buy Books.

***Boyle, Robert H.** Bass Boss. Scott, Susan, ed. (Illus.). 366p. 1999. 24.95 (*0-9673831-0-2*) Whitetail Trail.

— Bass Boss - Bass Pro Shop Edition. Scott, Susan, ed. (Illus.). 366p. 1999. text 24.95 (*0-9673831-4-5*) Whitetail Trail.

— Bass Boss - MotorGuide Edition. Scott, Susan, ed (Illus.). 366p. 1999. text 24.95 (*0-9673831-2-9*) Whitetail Trail.

— Bass Boss - Ray Murski Edition. Scott, Susan, ed. (Illus.). 366p. 1999. text 24.95 (*0-9673831-5-3*) Whitetail Trail.

— Bass Boss - SOSpenders Edition. Scott, Susan, ed (Illus.). 366p. 1999. text 24.95 (*0-9673831-3-7*) Whitetail Trail.

— Bass Boss - Triton Edition. Scott, Susan, ed. (Illus.). 366p. 1999. text 24.95 (*0-9673831-1-0*) Whitetail Trail.

Boyle, Robert H. The Hudson River: A Natural & Unnatural History. LC 68-10877. (Illus.). 1979. pap. 9.95 (*0-393-00844-4*) Norton.

Boyle, Robert W. Gold: History & Genesis of Deposits. LC 86-15675. (Illus.). 656p. (gr. 13). 1987. mass mkt. 97.95 (*0-442-21162-7*) Chapman & Hall.

***Boyle, Roger.** You Might As Well Be Happy. LC 98-91116. 1999. pap. 10.95 (*0-533-13054-9*) Vantage.

Boyle, Roger, jt. ed. see Hogg, David.

Boyle, Rosalie. Silver Swimmer: Poems. LC 74-33990. 1975. pap. 5.00 (*0-914562-01-0*) Merriam-Eddy.

Boyle, Russell, jt. auth. see Kilpatrick, S. J., Jr.

Boyle, Sarah P. The Desegregated Heart. Baxter, Annette K., ed. LC 79-8777. (Signal Lives Ser.). 1980. reprint ed. lib. bdg. 32.95 (*0-405-12826-6*) Ayer.

Boyle, Shanna, et al. Crossroads at the Spring: A Pictorial History of Springfield, Missouri. LC 97-28910. (Illus.). 1997. write for info. (*1-57864-015-6*) Donning Co.

Boyle, Sheila T. & Bunie, Andrew. Paul Robeson: The Years of Promise & Achievement. (Illus.). 544p 2001. 39.95 (*1-55849-149-X*) U of Mass Pr.

Boyle, Stephen M., jt. auth. see Carter, Gordon R.

Boyle, Susan C. Los Capitalistas: Hispano Merchants on the Santa Fe Trail. LC 96-35705. 236p. 1997. 45.00 (*0-8263-1789-8*) U of NM Pr.

— Social Mobility in the United States: Historiography & Methods. (Studies in Historical Demography). 254p. 1990. reprint ed. text 25.00 (*0-8240-4696-X*) Garland.

***Boyle, Susan Calafate.** Los Capitalistas: Hispano Merchants & the Santa Fe Trail. 2000. reprint ed. pap. 14.95 (*0-8263-2235-2*) U of NM Pr.

***Boyle, T. C., et al.** Ghost Writing: Haunted Tales from Contemporary Writers. Weingarten, Roger, ed. 304p. 2000. 24.00 (*0-9679683-0-5*, Pub. by Invisible Cities) IPG Chicago.

Boyle, T. Coraghessan. Budding Prospects. 1990. pap. 12.95 (*0-14-029996-3*) Viking Penguin.

— Descent of Man. 256p. 1990. pap. 12.95 (*0-14-029994-7*, Penguin Bks) Viking Penguin.

— East Is East. (Contemporay American Fiction Ser.). 384p. 1991. pap. 12.95 (*0-14-013167-1*, Penguin Bks) Viking Penguin.

***Boyle, T. Coraghessan.** A Friend of the Earth. LC 99-462217. 288p. 2000. 24.95 (*0-670-89177-0*, Viking) Viking Penguin.

Boyle, T. Coraghessan. Greasy Lake & Other Stories. LC 85-25993. (Fiction Ser.). 240p. 1986. pap. 11.95 (*0-14-007781-2*, Penguin Bks) Viking Penguin.

— If the River Was Whiskey. 240p. 1990. pap. 12.95 (*0-14-011950-7*, Penguin Bks) Viking Penguin.

— Riven Rock. LC 97-34632. 480p. 1999. pap. 13.95 (*0-14-027166-X*) Viking Penguin.

— The Road to Wellville. (Contemporay American Fiction Ser.). 480p. 1994. pap. 13.95 (*0-14-016718-8*, Penguin Bks) Viking Penguin.

— T. C. Boyle Stories. LC 98-39739. 624p. 1998. 35.00 (*0-670-87960-6*) Viking Penguin.

***Boyle, T. Coraghessan.** T. C. Boyle Stories. 704p. 1999. pap. 16.95 (*0-14-028091-X*, Penguin Bks) Viking Penguin.

Boyle, T. Coraghessan. The Tortilla Curtain. LC 95-1970. 355p. 2000. pap. 11.95 (*0-14-023828-X*) Viking Penguin.

— The Tortilla Curtain. large type ed. LC 95-50040. 1996. 24.95 (*1-56895-287-2*) Wheeler Pub.

— Water Music. (Contemporay American Fiction Ser.). 448p. 1983. pap. 13.95 (*0-14-006550-4*, Penguin Bks) Viking Penguin.

— Without a Hero: And Other Stories. 256p. 1995. pap. 12.95 (*0-14-017839-2*, Penguin Bks) Viking Penguin.

— World's End. 480p. 1990. pap. 13.95 (*0-14-029993-9*, Penguin Bks) Viking Penguin.

***Boyle, T. Coraghessan, et al.** It's Only Rock & Roll: An Anthology of Rock & Roll Short Stories. Eidus, Janice & Kastan, John, eds. LC 98-35749. 304p. 1998. pap. 16.95 (*1-56792-089-6*) Godine.

Boyle, Terence P., ed. New Approaches to Monitoring Aquatic Ecosystems. LC 86-28666. (Special Technical Publication Ser.: No. 940). (Illus.). 215p. 1987. text 39.00 (*0-8031-0939-3*, STP940) ASTM.

— Validation & Predictability of Laboratory Methods for Assessing the Fate & Effects of Contaminants in Aquatic Ecosystems - STP 865. LC 85-5985. (Illus.). 242p. 1985. text 34.00 (*0-8031-0433-2*, STP865) ASTM.

Boyle, Thomas. The Cold Stove League. (Academy First Mystery Ser.). 221p. 1987. pap. 5.95 (*0-89733-259-8*) Academy Chi Pubs.

Boyle, Thomas A. Precursory Physical Science: The Science You Need Before Taking Science in School. LC 96-90843. (Illus.). xii, 168p. (Orig.). (C). 1997. pap. 17.95 (*0-9655241-2-4*) Technical Directions.

Boyle, Thomas H. Airmail Operations During World War II. LC 98-72485. 928p. 1998. pap. 35.00 (*0-939429-20-9*) Am Air Mail.

Boyle, Timm. Total Fitness the NBA Way: The Official NBA Workout Guide for Athletes & Weekend Warriors, from the Experts Who Train the Pros. Hubbard, Jan, ed. LC 99-49024. (Illus.). 144p. 2000. pap. 19.95 (*0-06-107303-2*, HarpEntertain) Morrow Avon.

Boyle, Timothy J. B., ed. Biodiversity, Temperate Ecosystems, & Global Change. LC 94-14990. (NATO ASI Ser.: Vol. 20). 1994. 216.95 (*0-387-57950-8*) Spr-Verlag.

***Boyle, Tish & Moriarty, Tim.** Chocolate Passion. LC 98-41505. 328p. 1999. 39.95 (*0-471-29317-2*) Wiley.

Boyle, Tish & Moriarty, Timothy. Grand Finales: A Neoclassic View of Plated Desserts. LC 98-50537. (Illus.). 288p. 2000. 44.95 (*0-471-29313-X*) Wiley.

Boyle, Tish & Moriarty, Timothy. Grand Finales: The Art of the Plated Dessert. 368p. 1996. 49.95 (*0-471-28769-5*, VNR) Wiley.

Boyle, Tish & Moriarty, Timothy. Grand Finales: The Art of the Plated Dessert. LC 96-2852. (Culinary Arts Ser.). (Illus.). 350p. 1997. text 49.95 (*0-442-02287-5*, VNR) Wiley.

Boyle, Tish & Moriarty, Timothy. Modernist Plated Desserts. 288p. 1997. 49.95 (*0-471-29251-6*, VNR) Wiley.

Boyle, Tom. Design for Multimedia Learning. LC 96-41423. 275p. 1997. pap. 61.00 (*0-13-242215-8*) P-H.

Boyle, Trish & Moriarty, Timothy. A Modernist View of Plated Desserts. LC 97-24171. (Culinary Arts Ser.). (Illus.). 304p. 1997. 49.95 (*0-442-02547-5*, VNR) Wiley.

Boyle-Truner, Caroline, jt. auth. see Grivel, Marianne.

Boyle, Veolita P. The Fundamental Principles of Yi-King, Tao: The Cabbalas of Egypt & the Hebrews. 134p. 1997. reprint ed. pap. 17.95 (*0-7661-0082-0*) Kessinger Pub.

Boyle, Veronica M. A Mind of Her Own. LC 98-94029. 1999. 18.95 (*0-533-12959-1*) Vantage.

Boyle, Virginia. Masks of a Professional. 160p. 1992. per. 9.95 (*0-8403-8234-0*, 40823401) Kendall-Hunt.

Boyle, Virginia, ed. Facets Non-Violent Non-Sexist Children's Video Guide. (Illus.). 230p. (Orig.). 1995. pap. 12.95 (*0-89733-420-5*) Academy Chi Pubs.

Boyle, Virginia F. Brokenburne: A Southern Auntie's War Tale. LC 77-38642. (Black Heritage Library Collection). (Illus.). 1977. reprint ed. 18.95 (*0-8369-9000-5*) Ayer.

— Devil Tales. LC 70-38643. (Black Heritage Library Collection). (Illus.). 1977. reprint ed. 23.95 (*0-8369-9001-3*) Ayer.

Boyle, W. H. Gallant Deeds. 70p. (C). 1987. 60.00 (*0-7855-2224-7*, Pub. by Picton) St Mut.

Boyle, Wade. Herb Doctors: Pioneers in Nineteenth-Century American Botanical Medicine. (Illus.). 66p. (Orig.). 1988. pap. 10.00 (*0-9623518-0-6*) Eclectic Med.

— Official Herbs: Botanical Substances in the United States Pharmacopoeias: 1820-1990. (Illus.). 97p. (Orig.). 1991. pap. 12.95 (*0-9623518-3-0*) Eclectic Med.

Boyle, Wade & Saine, Andre. Lectures in Naturopathic Hydrotherapy. (Illus.). 235p. (Orig.). 1988. pap. text 22.50 (*0-9623518-1-4*) Eclectic Med.

Boyle, Wade, jt. auth. see Kirchfeld, Friedhelm.

Boyle, Wade, ed. see Jones, Eli G.

Boyle, Wayne. Eight Ways to Finance Transit: A Policymaker's Guide. LC 97-206898. 40p. 1993. pap. text 15.00 (*1-55516-350-5*, 9362) Natl Conf State Legis.

Boyle, William J. A Guide to Bird Finding in New Jersey. (Illus.). 400p. (C). 1986. 22.00 (*0-8135-1145-3*) Rutgers U Pr.

Boyle, William J., Jr., ed. see American Birding Association Staff & USDA Forest Service Staff.

Boyles. Economics, 2 vols. (C). 1993. pap., teacher ed., suppl. ed. 8.76 (*0-395-68246-0*) HM.

Boyles, C. Allan. The Way. LC 90-83636. 323p. 1990. 20.00 (*0-9627283-0-6*) Theophysics.

Boyles, David T. Bio-Energy: Technology, Thermodynamics & Costs. LC 84-4647. (Energy & Fuel Science Ser.: 1-624). 158p. 1984. text 65.95 (*0-470-20085-5*) P-H.

Boyles, Denis. The Lost Lore of a Man's Life: Lots of Cool Stuff Guys Used to Know But Forgot About the Great Outdoors. LC 97-9595. 224p. 1997. pap. 13.00 (*0-06-095224-5*, Perennial) HarperTrade.

— A Man's Life: The Complete Instructions. LC 96-15766. 480p. 1996. pap. 20.00 (*0-06-095141-9*, Perennial) HarperTrade.

Boyles, Denis, et al, eds. A Boy's Life: The Complete Instructions. 320p. (J). 1997. spiral bd. 10.00 (*0-201-15168-5*) Addison-Wesley.

— A Girl's Life: The Complete Instructions. 320p. (J). 1997. spiral bd. 10.00 (*0-201-15167-7*) Addison-Wesley.

Boyles, Denis, frwd. Farm Conveniences: And How to Make Them. LC 98-8673. (Illus.). 256p. 1998. reprint ed. pap. 12.95 (*1-55821-727-4*, 1727-4) Lyons Pr.

Boyles, Denis, jt. auth. see Kennedy, James.

Boyles, Denis, ed. see Sherman, Steven & Stebben, Gregg.

Boyles, Denis, ed. see Stebben, Gregg.

Boyles, Deron. American Education & Corporations: The Free Market Goes to School. LC 98-4443. (Pedagogy & Popular Culture Ser.: Vol. 1). (Illus.). 240p. 1998. 50.00 (*0-8153-2822-2*, SS1159) Garland.

Boyles, Harlan E. & Heatherly, Charles L. Keeper of the Public Purse. 183p. (Orig.). (C). 1994. pap. text 12.95 (*0-9634559-1-5*) Patriot Pr NC.

***Boyles, Lemuel M.** Leadership: The Minister's Responsibility. 256p. 1999. pap. 10.00 (*1-882449-33-9*, 090112) Messenger Pub.

Boyles, Nancy S. Parenting a Child with Attention Deficit/Hyperactivity Disorder. 2nd ed. LC 99-34870. 304p. 1999. pap. 16.95 (*0-7373-0257-7*, 02577W) NTC Contemp Pub Co.

Boyles, Nancy S. & Contadino, Darlene. The Learning Differences Sourcebook. LC 97-37654. 480p. 1998. reprint ed. 30.00 (*1-56565-795-0*, 07950W, Pub. by Lowell Hse) NTC Contemp Pub Co.

— The Learning Differences Sourcebook. LC 97-37654. 480p. 1998. reprint ed. pap. 19.95 (*0-7373-0024-8*, 00248W) NTC Contemp Pub Co.

— Parenting a Child with AD/HD. 272p. 1996. 26.00 (*1-56565-446-3*) Lowell Hse.

Boyles, Nora. The Garden of Aton. (Phoenix Journals). 255p. 1993. pap. 6.00 (*1-56935-011-6*) Phoenix Source.

Boyles, Tim, jt. auth. see Downes, Kevin.

***Boyles, Tish.** Diner Desserts. LC 99-38295. (Illus.). 176p. 2000. pap. 18.95 (*0-8118-2449-7*) Chronicle Bks.

Boylestad & Kousourou, Gabriel. Introduction to Circuit Analysis. 8th ed. 1996. pap. text, lab manual ed. 40.00 (*0-13-237256-8*) P-H.

Boylestad, Robert & Nashelsky, Louis. Electronics: A Survey of Electrical Engineering Principles. 4th ed. LC 95-42168. 624p. 1995. 105.00 (*0-13-375312-3*) P-H.

Boylestad, Robert L. Dc-Ac: The Basics. 960p. (C). 1990. text 66.80 (*0-675-20918-8*, Merrill Coll) P-H.

— Electronic Devices & Circuit Theory. 7th ed. LC 98-24382. 926p. 1998. 99.00 (*0-13-769282-X*) P-H.

***Boylestad, Robert L.** Introductory Circuit Analysis. 9th ed. LC 99-23645. (Illus.). 1200p. 1999. text 96.00 incl. audio compact disk (*0-13-927187-2*) P-H.

Boylestad, Robert L. & Kousourou, Gabriel. Experiments in DC-AC: The Basics. 352p. (C). 1990. pap. text 34.40 (*0-675-21131-X*, Merrill Coll) P-H.

Boylestad, Robert L., jt. auth. see Nashelsky, Louis.

***Boyling, J. D., ed.** Manual Therapy of Peripheral Joints. (Illus.). 592p. 1998. text. write for info. (*0-443-04349-3*) Church.

Boyling, Jeffrey D. & Palastanga, Nigel, eds. Grieve's Modern Manual Therapy: The Vertebral Column. 2nd ed. (Illus.). 924p. 1994. text 174.00 (*0-443-04348-5*) Church.

Boyll, Dale. Good Health God's Way: Living Healthy in an Unhealthy World. LC 99-93599. viii, 263p. (Orig.). 1999. pap. 16.95 (*0-9669720-0-7*) Scriptural.

Boyll, Randall. The Gods of Hell. Shannon, Scott, ed. (Darkman Ser.: No. 3). 224p. (Orig.). 1994. mass mkt. 5.50 (*0-671-79435-3*) PB.

— In the Face of Death. (Illus.). 1995. mass mkt. 5.50 (*0-671-79436-1*) PB.

— Katastrophe: A Novel. LC 99-55683. 560p. 2000. 25.00 (*0-06-019236-4*) HarpC.

— The Price of Fear. Shannon, Scott, ed. (Darkman Ser.: No. 2). 224p. (Orig.). 1994. mass mkt. 5.50 (*0-671-79434-5*) PB.

Boylston & Associates Staff & Lumsden, Ennis. Electrical Safety-Related Work Practices: OSHA 29 CFR 1910.331-.335, Compliance Program Manual. 316p. 1992. lib. bdg. 385.00 (*0-87371-935-2*, L935) Lewis Pubs.

***Boylston, Eula & O'Day, Carol.** Successful EATing: Dementia Swallowing Assessment. Anderson, Kirsteen, ed. 1999. spiral bd. 39.50 (*1-883315-46-8*) Imaginart Intl.

***Boylston, Raymond P., Jr.** Butler's Brigade: That Fighting Civil War Cavalry Brigade from South Carolina. Carrington, William G. & Odzak, Larry L., eds. 1999. pap. text. write for info. (*1-888701-20-X*) Jarrett Pr.

Boylston, Raymond P. Managing Safety & Health Programs. 272p. 1990. 89.95 (*0-471-28977-9*, VNR); text 60.95 (*0-442-31900-2*, VNR) Wiley.

Boylston, Raymond P., Jr., et al. The Safety Profession: Year 2000. 150p. (Orig.). 1991. pap. 6.95 (*0-939874-87-3*) ASSE.

***Boym.** Nostalgia Book. 2000. 30.00 (*0-465-00707-4*, Pub. by Basic); pap. 16.00 (*0-465-00708-2*, Pub. by Basic) HarpC.

Boym, Svetlana. Common Places: Mythologies of Everyday Life in Russia. LC 94-19893. (Illus.). 384p. 1995. text 56.00 (*0-674-14625-5*, BOYCOM); pap. text 25.95 (*0-674-14626-3*, BOYCOX) HUP.

— Death in Quotation Marks: Cultural Myths of the Modern Poet. LC 90-44306. (Studies in Comparative Literature: No. 41). (Illus.). 304p. 1991. 44.00 (*0-674-19427-6*, BOYDEA) HUP.

Boyman, Anne, tr. see Cache, Bernard.

Boymans-Van Beunungen Museum Staff. Album: Family Portraits. (Illus.). 296p. 1996. 45.00 (*90-6918-151-7*, 610632, Pub. by Boymans Mus) Dist Art Pubs.

Boyne, Daniel J. Essential Sculling. LC 00-27370. (Illus.). 160p. 1999. pap. text. write for info. (*1-55821-709-6*) Lyons Pr.

***Boyne, Daniel J.** The Red Rose Crew: A True Story of Women, Winning & the Water. 304p. 2000. 23.95 (*0-7868-6622-5*, Pub. by Hyperion) Time Warner.

***Boyne, George A., ed.** Managing Local Services: From CCT to Best Value. LC 99-21019. 152p. 1999. 39.50 (*0-7146-5020-X*, Pub. by F Cass Pubs); pap. 19.50 (*0-7146-8075-3*, Pub. by F Cass Pubs) Intl Spec Bk.

Boyne, Gil. Self Hypnosis & Other Mind Expanding Techniques. rev. ed. 160p. 1987. pap. 9.95 (*0-914629-41-7*) Prima Pub.

— Transforming Therapy: A New Approach to Hypnotherapy. 2nd ed. 400p. 1989. 37.50 (*0-930298-13-6*) Westwood Pub Co.

Boyne, Gil, ed. Hypnosis: New Tool in Nursing Practice. 197p. (C). 1982. 25.00 (*0-930298-12-8*) Westwood Pub Co.

Boyne, Gil, ed. see Hunter, Roy.

Boyne, Martin & LePan, Don. Common Errors in English: An ESL Guide. 260p. 1993. pap. 12.95 (*1-55111-008-3*) Broadview Pr.

Boyne, Philip J. & Peetz, Michael. Osseous Reconstruction of the Maxilla & the Mandible: Surgical Techniques Using Titanium Mesh & Bone Mineral. LC 96-26147. (Illus.). 116p. 1996. text 68.00 (*0-86715-319-9*) Quint Pub Co.

Boyne, Roy. Foucault & Derrida. 1990. pap. 16.95 (*0-04-445085-0*) Routledge.

— Foucault & Derrida: The Other Side of Reason. 208p. 1990. 44.95 (*0-685-33059-1*) Routledge.

— Foucault & Derrida: The Other Side of Reason. 208p. (C). 1990. pap. 18.99 (*0-415-11916-2*) Routledge.

Boyne, Roy & Rattansi, Ali, eds. Postmodernism & Society. LC 90-8644. (Illus.). 309p. 1990. pap. 15.95 (*0-312-05223-5*) St Martin.

Boyne, Walter. Boeing B-52: A Documentary History. (Illus.). 160p. 1994. 29.95 (*0-88740-600-9*) Schiffer.

— Phantom in Combat. LC 84-52013. (Illus.). 192p. 1994. 35.00 (*0-88740-599-1*) Schiffer.

Boyne, Walter. Pushing the Limits. 27.50 (*0-06-019455-3*); 15.00 (*0-06-093254-6*) HarpC.

***Boyne, Walter J.** Aces in Command: Fighter Pilots as Combat Leaders. 2001. 26.95 (*1-57488-310-0*) Brasseys.

Boyne, Walter J. Beyond the Horizon: The Lockheed Story. LC 98-19397. (Illus.). 542p. 1998. 29.95 (*0-312-19237-1*) St Martin.

***Boyne, Walter J.** Beyond the Horizons. 576p. 1999. pap. 19.95 (*0-312-24438-X*) St Martin.

Boyne, Walter J. Beyond the Wild Blue. (Illus.). 416p. 1998. pap. 17.95 (*0-312-18705-X*) St Martin.

— Beyond the Wild Blue: A History of the U. S. Air Force, 1947-1997. LC 96-53507. (Illus.). 442p. 1997. text 29.95 (*0-312-15474-7*) St Martin.

***Boyne, Walter J.** Beyond the Wild Blue: A History of the U. S. Air Force, 1947-1997. (Illus.). 442p. 1999. reprint ed. text 30.00 (*0-7881-6490-2*) DIANE Pub.

Boyne, Walter J. Boeing B-52: A Documentary History. (Illus.). 160p. 1982. text 32.50 (*0-87474-246-3*, BOBO) Smithsonian.

— Clash of Titans: World War II at Sea. LC 95-5432. (Illus.). 400p. 1995. 27.50 (*0-684-80196-5*) S&S Trade.

Boyne, Walter J. Clash of Titans: World War II at Sea. 384p. 1997. per. 15.00 (*0-684-83914-8*, Touchstone) S&S Trade Pap.

Boyne, Walter J. Clash of Wings. 416p. 1997. per. 15.00 (*0-684-83915-6*, Touchstone) S&S Trade Pap.

— Messerschmitt ME 262: Arrow to the Future. (Illus.). 192p. (Orig.). 1993. pap. 19.95 (*0-88740-665-3*) Schiffer.

— Power Behind the Wheel: Creativity & the Evolution of the Automobile. (Illus.). 240p. 1991. 19.98 (*0-89660-018-1*, Artabras) Abbeville Pr.

— Silver Wings: A History of the United States Air Force. LC 92-42939. (Illus.). 336p. 1993. 50.00 (*0-671-78537-0*) S&S Trade.

— The Smithsonian Book of Flight. Goodwin, Joseph, ed. (Illus.). 288p. 1987. 35.00 (*0-89599-020-2*) Smithsonian Bks.

Boyne, Walter J. & Handleman, Philip. Brassey's Air Combat Reader. LC 99-13246. 320p. 1999. 24.95 (*1-57488-182-5*) Brasseys.

Boyne, Walter J. & Thompson, Steven L. The Wild Blue. 532p. 1998. reprint ed. pap. 14.95 (*1-891118-27-7*, Wind Canyon Bks) Wind Canyon.

Boyne, Walter J., ed. see Donnelly, Tom & Naylor, Sean.

Boyne, Walter J., ed. see Harris, Brayton.

Boyne, Walter J., ed. see Laur, Timothy M. & Llanso, Steven L.

Boyne, Walter J., ed. see Morelock, J. D.

Boyne, Walter J., jt. ed. see Morelock, J. D.

Boyns, Trevor, ed. The Mining Industry, 4 vols. (Tauris Industrial Histories Ser.). (Illus.). 1650p. 1997. text 625.00 (*1-86064-072-9*, Pub. by I B T) St Martin.

— The Steel Industry, 4 vols. LC 96-61060. (Tauris Industrial Histories Ser.). 1659p. 1997. text 625.00 (*1-86064-071-0*, Pub. by I B T) St Martin.

Boyns, Trevor, et al, eds. British Cost Accounting, 1887-1952: Contemporary Essays from the Accounting Literature. LC 95-37266. (New Works in Accounting History). 504p. 1996. text 109.00 (*0-8153-2240-2*) Garland.

Boyns, Trevor, et al. The Birth of Industrial Accounting in France & Britain. LC 97-25939. (New Works in Accounting History). 248p. 1997. text 57.00 (*0-8153-3038-3*) Garland.

Boynton. Student Study Guide to Accompany Modern Auditing. 6th ed. 368p. 1995. pap. 31.95 (*0-471-59690-6*) Wiley.

— Texas. (Discover America Ser.). 1988. 6.99 (*0-8442-7476-3*) NTC Contemp Pub Co.

Boynton & Cook Publishers Incorporated Staff. Beyond Note Cards: Rethinking the Freshman Research Paper. LC 98-48823. 1999. pap. text 20.00 (*0-86709-479-6*, Pub. by Boynton Cook Pubs) Heinemann.

Boynton, Alice B. Priscilla Alden & the First Thanksgiving. 32p. (J). (ps-3). 1996. pap. text 4.95 (*0-382-39474-7*) Silver Burdett Pr.

— Priscilla Alden & the Story of the First Thanksgiving. Brook, Bonnie, ed. (Let's Celebrate Ser.). (Illus.). 32p. (J). (gr. k-2). 1990. lib. bdg. 6.95 (*0-671-69105-8*) Silver Burdett Pr.

Boynton, Alice Benjamin. Priscilla Alden & the First Thanksgiving. LC 89-49539. (Let's Celebrate Ser.). 1990. 10.15 (*0-606-10288-4*, Pub. by Turtleback) Demco.

Boynton, Andrew, et al. Taxation & Accounting for Financial Instruments. 3rd ed. 408p. 1995. 140.00 (*1-873446-08-X*, Pub. by IFR Pub) Am Educ Systs.

Boynton, Andrew C., jt. auth. see Victor, Bart.

Boynton, Billy, jt. auth. see Grossblatt, Robert.

Boynton, Bruce R., et al, eds. New Therapies for Neonatal Respiratory Failure: A Physiological Approach. (Illus.). 377p. (C). 1994. text 130.00 (*0-521-43161-1*) Cambridge U Pr.

Boynton Cook Publishers Staff. Culture, Literacy & Learning English: Voices from the Chinese Classroom. LC 97-52584. 270p. 1998. pap. 32.00 (*0-86709-448-6*, Pub. by Boynton Cook Pubs) Heinemann.

— Sentence Composing: The Theory Booklet. 1998. pap. 5.00 (*0-86709-450-8*, Pub. by Boynton Cook Pubs) Heinemann.

Boynton, Damon, jt. ed. see Whyte, William F.

Boynton, David, jt. auth. see Cook, Chris.

Boynton, David S., photos by. Capturing Hawai'i Kaua'i. (Capturing Hawai'i Ser.). (Illus.). 32p. 1998. pap. 7.95 (*1-56647-214-8*) Mutual Pub HI.

Boynton, Edward C. History of West Point. LC 71-126233. (Select Bibliographies Reprint Ser.). 1977. 35.95 (*0-8369-5458-0*) Ayer.

Boynton, Elsie H. Maine Spring & Other Poems. 61p. (Orig.). 1993. pap. text 6.95 (*0-9639352-0-8*) E H Boynton.

— Round the Dining Room Table: Stories & Recipes of Life on a Maine Saltwater Farm. (Illus.). iv, 116p. 1998. pap. 12.95 (*0-9664628-0-7*) Passaqass River.

Boynton, G. R., jt. auth. see Nelson, John S.

Boynton, George, Sr., jt. auth. see Quillen, Jacqueline L.

Boynton, Graham, ed. Guide to the Business Cities of the World. 278p. 1988. 39.95 (*0-9513031-0-4*) L Erlbaum Assocs.

Boynton, Henry W. Annals of American Bookselling, 1638-1850. (History of the Book: Vol. 5). 232p. 1991. reprint ed. 35.00 (*0-938768-25-5*) Oak Knoll.

— Bret Harte. LC 70-133513. (Select Bibliographies Reprint Ser.). 1977. reprint ed. 12.95 (*0-8369-5545-5*) Ayer.

— World's Leading Poets. LC 68-8439. (Essay Index Reprint Ser.). 1977. 20.95 (*0-8369-0238-6*) Ayer.

***Boynton, Herb.** Sodium Blues. 2001. pap. 11.95 (*1-58333-085-2*, Avery) Penguin Putnam.

Boynton, James. Fishers of Men: The Jesuit Mission at Mackinac 1670-1765. Porter, Phil, ed. (Illus.). 77p. (Orig.). 1996. pap. 7.95 (*0-9654402-0-6*) Saint Annes Church.

Boynton, John. Aims & Means. LC 64-8214. (Background Ser.). (Illus.). 1964. 18.95 (*0-8023-1015-X*) Dufour.

— Answering Machine Etiquette. (Illus.). 64p. (Orig.). 1987. pap. 4.95 (*0-917814-08-8*) AstroArt Ent.

— Love Is Lasting. 96p. (Orig.). 1971. pap. 3.50 (*0-917814-01-0*) AstroArt Ent.

— Love Is Touching. (Illus.). 48p. 1972. pap. 2.95 (*0-917814-03-7*) AstroArt Ent.

Boynton, John R. PolyForm: WebForms Construction Kit & Booklet. (Illus.). 150p. (Orig.). 1996. pap. 149.95 (*1-56592-182-8*) Thomson Learn.

Boynton, Lindsay, ed. Gillow Furniture Designs, 1760-1800. (Illus.). 240p. 1998. 79.50 (*0-9525115-0-9*) Antique Collect.

Boynton, Marilyn I. & Dell, Mary. Goodbye Mother, Hello Woman: Reweaving the Daughter-Mother Relationship. LC 95-69479. (Illus.). 224p. (Orig.). 1995. pap. 14.95 (*1-57224-024-5*) New Harbinger.

Boynton, Mia & Lowrey, Nathan. Motor Camps & Maine Guides: Two Studies. Ives, Edward D., ed. (Northeast Folklore Ser.: Vol. XXVIII). (Illus.). 110p. (Orig.). 1991. pap. 10.00 (*0-943197-20-1*) ME Folklife Ctr.

Boynton, Nat. Media Rare: Adventures of a Grass-Roots Newsman. (Illus.). 384p. (Orig.). 1988. pap. 12.95 (*0-944593-20-8*) Chandler Pr.

Boynton, Percy H. A History of American Literature. (BCL1-PS American Literature Ser.). 513p. 1992. reprint ed. lib. bdg. 99.00 (*0-7812-6603-3*) Rprt Serv.

— More Contemporary Americans. LC 67-26718. (Essay Index Reprint Ser.). 1977. 20.95 (*0-8369-0239-4*) Ayer.

— More Contemporary Americans. (BCL1-PS American Literature Ser.). 230p. 1992. reprint ed. lib. bdg. 79.00 (*0-7812-6618-1*) Rprt Serv.

— More Contemporary Americans. LC 75-131642. 1970. reprint ed. 16.00 (*0-403-00529-9*) Scholarly.

— Rediscovery of the Frontier. LC 69-13836. (Illus.). 184p. 1969. reprint ed. lib. bdg. 55.00 (*0-8371-0480-7*, BORE, Greenwood Pr) Greenwood.

— Some Contemporary Americans. LC 66-23516. 1924. 30.00 (*0-8196-0181-0*) Biblo.

— Some Contemporary Americans: The Personal Equation in Literature. (BCL1-PS American Literature Ser.). 289p. 1992. reprint ed. lib. bdg. 79.00 (*0-7812-6619-X*) Rprt Serv.

***Boynton, Phil.** Silent Thunder. 183p. 1999. pap. 13.95 (*0-7414-0129-0*) Buy Books.

Boynton, Richard W., tr. see Loisy, Alfred F.

Boynton, Robert M., jt. auth. see Kaiser, Peter K.

Boynton, Robert S. Chemistry & Technology of Lime & Limestone. 2nd ed. LC 79-16140. (Information & Resources Ser.). 592p. 1980. 259.00 (*0-471-02771-5*) Wiley.

Boynton, Robert W. & Mack, Maynard. Introduction to the Poem. 3rd ed. LC 85-13297. 235p. (C). 1985. pap. text 18.00 (*0-86709-143-6*, 0143, Pub. by Boynton Cook Pubs) Heinemann.

— Introduction to the Short Story. 4th ed. LC 91-28910. 292p. (YA). (gr. 11). 1992. pap. text 18.00 (*0-86709-291-2*, 0291, Pub. by Boynton Cook Pubs) Heinemann.

Boynton, Robert W., ed. see Shakespeare, William.

Boynton, Rose W. Manual of Ambulatory Pediatrics. 4th ed. LC 97-35923. 528p. 1998. spiral bd. 38.95 (*0-397-55472-9*) Lppncott W & W.

Boynton, Sandra. A Is for Angry: An Animal & Adjective Alphabet. LC 83-40038. (Illus.). 48p. (J). (ps). 1987. pap. 6.95 (*0-89480-507-X*, 1507) Workman Pub.

— Barnyard Dance! LC 93-11289. (Illus.). 24p. (J). (ps). 1999. bds. 6.95 (*1-56305-442-6*, 3442) Workman Pub.

— Birthday Monsters! LC 93-11282. (Illus.). 48p. (J). (ps). 1993. bds. 6.95 (*1-56305-443-4*, 3443) Workman Pub.

— Blue Hat Green Hat. LC 85-123423. (Boynton Board Bks.). (Illus.). 14p. (J). (ps). 1984. 4.99 (*0-671-49320-5*) Litle Simon.

***Boynton, Sandra.** Bob & 6 More Christmas Stories. (Illus.). 18p. (J). (ps-3). 1999. 7.99 (*0-689-82568-4*) Litle Simon.

— Boynton's Greatest Hits. (Illus.). 16p. (J). (ps). 1999. 19.95 (*0-689-82663-X*) Litle Simon.

Boynton, Sandra. Boynton's Greatest Hits, Vol. 1. (Boynton Board Bks.). (Illus.). 16p. (J). (ps). 1998. 19.95 (*0-689-82322-3*) S&S Childrens.

— But Not the Hippopotamus. Klimo, Kate, ed. LC 95-142211. (Boynton Board Bks.). (Illus.). 14p. (J). (ps). 1982. 4.99 (*0-671-44904-4*) Litle Simon.

— Chocolate: The Consuming Passion. LC 81-43781. (Illus.). 112p. 1982. pap. 7.95 (*0-89480-199-6*, 485) Workman Pub.

Boynton, Sandra. Christmastime. LC 87-6204. (Illus.). 112p. 1987. 12.95 (*0-89480-635-1*, 1635) Workman Pub.

Boynton, Sandra. Doggies. (Illus.). 14p. (J). (gr. k-3). 1984. pap. 4.99 (*0-671-49318-3*) Litle Simon.

— Don't Let the Turkeys Get You Down. LC 85-26308. (Illus.). 112p. 1986. pap. 5.95 (*0-89480-013-2*, 1013) Workman Pub.

— The Going to Bed Book. Klimo, Kate, ed. LC 95-142212. (Boynton Board Bks.). (Illus.). 14p. (J). 1982. 4.99 (*0-671-44902-8*) Litle Simon.

— Grunt: Pigorian Chant from Snouto Domoinko de Silo. (Illus.). 28p. (J). (ps up). 1996. bds. 10.95 (*0-7611-0594-8*, 10594) Workman Pub.

***Boynton, Sandra.** Hey! Wake Up! (Boynton on Board Ser.). (Illus.). 24p. (J). (ps). 2000. 6.95 (*0-7611-1976-0*) Workman Pub.

— Hippos Go Berserk. (Illus.). 32p. (J). (ps-3). 2000. 7.99 (*0-689-83434-9*) Litle Simon.

Boynton, Sandra. Hippos Go Beserk. 32p. (J). 1996. mass mkt. 5.99 (*0-689-80818-6*) S&S Childrens.

— Hippos Go Beserk. LC 96-84706. (Illus.). 32p. (J). 1996. 14.00 (*0-689-80854-2*) S&S Childrens.

Boynton, Sandra. Horns to Toes & in Between. (Boynton Board Bks.). (Illus.). 13p. (J). (gr. k-3). 1984. bds. 4.99 (*0-671-49319-1*) Litle Simon.

An Asterisk (*) at the beginning of an entry indicates that the title is appearing for the first time.

B

An Asterisk (*) at the beginning of an entry indicates that the title is appearing for the first time.

Bozoglu, T. Faruk & Ray, Bibek, eds. Lactic Acid Bacteria: Current Advances in Genetics, Metabolism, & Application of Lactic Acid Bacteria. LC 96-16948. (NATO ASI Ser.: Series H, Vol. 98). 404p. 1996. 190.00 (*3-540-61117-7*) Spr-Verlag.

Bozoki, Andras, ed. Intellectuals & Politics in Central Europe. LC 98-43992. 292p. (C). 1998. 49.95 (*963-9116-22-X*); pap. 21.95 (*963-9116-21-1*) Ctrl Europ Univ.

Bozoki, Andras, et al, eds. Post-Communist Transition: Emerging Pluralism in Hungary. LC 92-6508. 208p. 1992. text 49.95 (*0-312-08092-1*) St Martin.

Bozollo, Angelo, jt. auth. see Tisdale, Caroline.

Bozon, Michel & Leridon, Henri, eds. Sexuality & the Social Sciences: A French Survey on Sexual Behaviour. LC 96-19230. 364p. 1996. text 82.95 (*1-85521-820-8*, Pub. by Dartmth Pub) Ashgate Pub Co.

Bozorg Alavi. Her Eyes. Ehsan Yarshater, ed. O'Kane, John, tr. from PER. LC 89-5569. (Modern Persian Literature Ser.: No. 9). (Illus.). 222p. (C). 1989. lib. bdg. 41.00 (*0-8191-7344-4*) U Pr of Amer.

Bozorgmehr, Mehdi, jt. ed. see Waldinger, Roger.

Bozorgnia, S. M. The Role of Precious Metals in European Economic Development: From the Roman Times to the Eve of the Industrial Revolution, 192. LC 97-16717. (Contributions in Economics & Economic History Ser.: Vol. 192). 224p. 1998. 65.00 (*0-313-29445-3*, Greenwood Pr) Greenwood.

Bozorth, Richard M. Ferromagnetism. 992p. 1993. 89.95 (*0-7803-1032-2*, PC3814) Inst Electrical.

— Ferromagnetism. LC QC0753.B69. (Bell Telephone Laboratories Ser.). (Illus.). 986p. reprint ed. pap. 200.00 (*0-608-17947-7*, 205631900058) Bks Demand.

Bozoukoff, Josephine. Lifetime Poetic Conclusions & Wishes. (Illus.). 40p. 1998. pap. 8.00 (*0-8059-4315-3*) Dorrance.

Bozoukoff, Josephine T. Peace on Earth: Your Dreams, My Dreams of Peace & Love. (Illus.). 72p. 1999. pap. 9.00 (*0-8059-4588-1*) Dorrance.

Bozoukoff, Josephine.V. The Truly Innocent. (Illus.). 40p. 1997. pap. 8.00 (*0-8059-4146-0*) Dorrance.

Bozovic, Ivan, et al, eds. Superconducting Superlattices II Vol. 3476: Native & Artifical. LC 99-200350. 1998. 80.00 (*0-8194-2935-X*) SPIE.

***Bozovic, Miran.** An Utterly Dark Spot: Gaze & Body in Early Modern Philosophy. LC 99-50665. (Body, in Theory Ser.). 160p. 2000. text 34.50 (*0-472-11140-X*, 11140) U of Mich Pr.

***Bozulich, Richard.** Get Strong at Handicap Go. (Beginner & Elementary go Books Ser.). 1998. pap. text. write for info. (*4-906574-59-9*) KISEIDO.

— Get Strong at Invading. (Beginner & Elementary go Books Ser.). 1998. pap. text. write for info. (*4-906574-55-6*) KISEIDO.

— Get Strong at Life & Death. (Beginner & Elementary go Books Ser.). 1998. pap. text. write for info. (*4-906574-58-0*) KISEIDO.

— Get Strong at Tesuji. (Beginner & Elementary go Books Ser.). 1998 pap. text. write for info. (*4-906574-56-4*) KISEIDO.

— Get Strong at the Endgame. (Beginner & Elementary Go Bks.). 1998. pap. text 15.00 (*4-906574-57-2*) KISEIDO.

— Get Strong at the Joseki 1. (Beginner & Elementary Go Bks.). (Illus.). (J). 1998. pap. 15.00 (*4-906574-52-1*) KISEIDO.

— Get Strong at the Opening. (Beginner & Elementary Go Bks.). 1998. pap. text. write for info. (*4-906574-51-3*) KISEIDO.

Bozulich, Richard. The Second Book of Go. 1987. pap. 8.95 (*4-87187-031-6*, G31) Ishi Pr Intl.

Bozulich, Richard, ed. The Go Player's Almanac. (Illus.). 272p. 1992. 39.95 (*4-87187-040-5*, G40) Ishi Pr Intl.

Bozulich, Richard, jt. auth. see Davies, James.

Bozulich, Richard, jt. auth. see Yoshiaki, Nagahara.

Bozulich, Richard, ed. see Haruyama Isamu, Eight-Dan & Nagahara, Yoshiaki S.

Bozulich, Richard, tr. see Miyamoto, Naoki.

Bozung, Dick. A Beginning Guitar Simplified Method for Everyone: The Guitar Barre Method. (Illus.). 38p. (YA). (gr. 3 up). 1998. spiral bd. 10.00 (*0-9622341-2-5*) Seven Arrows.

— The Magical Musical Spiraled Seashell, & Friends. (Illus.). 160p. (Orig.). (YA). 1989. pap. 20.00 (*0-9622341-1-7*); audio. write for info. (*0-9622341-5-X*) Seven Arrows.

Bozza, Antony, jt. ed. see Dahl, Shawn.

Bozza, K., et al. Know Your Body Series: Full Set of Curriculum Grades K-6. text 455.00 (*0-935263-17-9*) Amer Hlth Fndtn.

Bozzetti, F. & Dionigi, R., eds. Nutrition in Cancer & Trauma-Sepsis. (Illus.). viii, 204p. 1985. pap. 64.50 (*3-8055-3959-2*) S Karger.

Bozzetti, Piergiuseppe, tr. see Clair, Rene.

Bozzi, Aldo & Madden, Isabel B. Mezzaluna Cookbook. 176p. 1995. 23.00 (*0-517-70181-2*) Random Hse Value.

Bozzi, Ed, jt. auth. see Technology Marketing Staff Editors.

Bozzi, Julie & Dunn, Julie. Julie Bozzi: American Food. LC 92-60927. 29p. 1992. pap. 10.00 (*0-934418-39-X*) Mus Contemp Art.

Bozzo Daltz, Mary Alice. Word Play. 1997. 6.95 (*1-55708-590-0*, C940) McDonald Pub Co.

Bozzo, Jerry Dal, see Dal Bozzo, Jerry.

Bozzo, Paul. Dermatology & Dermatopathology: A Dynamic Interface. LC 98-55499. 1998. text. write for info. (*0-397-58774-0*) Lppncott W & W.

— Implementing Quality Assurance. LC 90-42512. 180p. 1991. 35.00 (*0-89189-290-7*) Am Soc Clinical.

— Managed Health Care in the Lab: Reengineering, Leadership & Best Value. LC 98-21036. 208p. 1998. text 75.00 (*0-397-58773-2*) Lppncott W & W.

Bozzola, John J. & Russell, Lonnie D. Electron Microscopy. 1992. 65.00 (*0-86720-126-6*) Jones & Bartlett.

— Electron Microscopy: Principles & Techniques for Biologists. 2nd ed. LC 98-40315. 670p. 1998. 58.00 (*0-7637-0192-0*) Jones & Bartlett.

Bozzoli, Belinda & Nkotsoe, Mmantho. Women of Phokeng: Consciousness, Life Strategy, & Migrancy in South Africa, 1900-1983. LC 91-9326. (Social History of Africa Ser.). 292p. (C). 1991. pap. 22.95 (*0-435-08056-3*, 08056) Heinemann.

Bozzone. Journey Begins. 1998. 8.00 (*0-07-427401-5*) McGraw.

Bozzone, Vincent. Speed to Market: How to Cut Lead Time & Increase Profits in Job Shops & Custom Manufacturing Environments. LC 97-164955. (Illus.). 128p. 1998. pap. 44.95 (*0-9663598-0-1*) Delta Dynamics.

BPB Instrument Ltd. Staff & Verdier, M. Wireline Logging Tool Catalog: BPB, Dresser Atlas, Gearhart, Geoservices, Micro Log, Prakla Seismos Schmumberger. (French Oil & Gas Industry Association Publications). (Illus.). 424p. (C). 1986. 575.00 (*2-7108-0503-0*, Pub. by Edits Technip) Enfield Pubs NH.

Bpuet, Jeanie & Bridges, Joyce. 1850 Caddo Parish, Louisiana Census. 70p. 1989. pap. 15.00 (*1-57088-054-9*) J&W Ent.

Bra, Lemuel De, see De Bra, Lemuel.

Braack, L. E. Kroger National Park (South Africa) Globetrotter Staff, ed. (Globe Trotter Travel Guides Ser.). (Illus.). 128p. 1996. pap. 10.95 (*1-85368-570-4*, Pub. by New5 Holland) Globe Pequot.

***Braack, Leo.** Kruger National Park. 2nd ed. (Globetrotter Travel Guides Ser.). 2000. pap. 10.95 (*1-85974-471-0*) New5 Holland.

— Malta. 2nd ed. (Globetrotter Travel Guides Ser.). (Illus.). 2001. pap. 10.95 (*1-85974-594-6*) New5 Holland.

Braae, Christel & Ferdinand, Klaus, eds. Contributions to Islamic Studies: Iran, Afghanistan & Pakistan. (Studies of Contemporary Islam: No. 3). 156p. (C). 1987. pap. text 12.95 (*87-7288-039-2*, Pub. by Aarhus Univ Pr) David Brown.

Braak, C. J. Ter, see Ter Braak, C. J.

Braake, Alex L. Ter. Mining in the Netherlands East Indies. Wilkins, Mira, ed. LC 76-29762. (European Business Ser.). (Illus.). 1977. reprint ed. lib. bdg. 17.95 (*0-405-09777-8*) Ayer.

Braaksma, B. L., et al, eds. Dynamical Systems & Bifurcations. (Lecture Notes in Mathematics Ser.: Vol. 1125). v, 129p. 1985. 29.95 (*0-387-15233-4*) Spr-Verlag.

Braam, Geert P. Influence of Business Firms on Government. (New Babylon Studies in the Social Sciences). 320p. 1981. 44.65 (*90-279-3457-6*) Mouton.

Braarvig, Jens. Aksayamatinirdesasutra: The Tradition of Imperishability in Buddhist Thought, Vol. 1. 290p. 1993. 39.50 (*82-560-0916-0*, Pub. by Solum Verlag) Intl Spec Bk.

— Aksayamatinirdesasutra: The Tradition of Imperishability in Buddhist Thought, Vol. 2. 591p. 1993. 39.50 (*82-560-0917-9*, Pub. by Solum Verlag) Intl Spec Bk.

Braasch, et al. Atlas of Abdominal Surgery. (Illus.). 480p. 1990. text 142.00 (*0-7216-5601-3*, W B Saunders Co) Harcrt Hlth Sci Grp.

Braasch, Barbara. California's Gold Rush Country: A Guide to the Best of the Mother Lode. LC 95-49083. (Illus.). 232p. (Orig.). 1996. pap. 14.95 (*1-881409-14-7*) Jhnstn Assocs.

Braasch, Barbara, ed. see Hays, Thomas J.

Braasch, Barbara J., jt. auth. see Smith, Margaret A.

Braasch, Barbara J., ed. see Nix, Janeth J. & Smith, Margaret A.

Braasch, Gary. Photographing the Patterns of Nature. LC 99-26661. (Illus.). 144p. 1999. pap. text 24.95 (*0-8174-5441-1*) Watsn-Guptill.

Braasch, Marvin E. & Page, Lawrence M. Systematic Studies of Darters of the Subgenus Catonotus (Percidae), with the Description of a New Species from Caney Fork, Tennessee. (Occasional Papers: No. 78). 10p. 1979. 1.00 (*0-317-04822-8*) U KS Nat Hist Mus.

Braasch, Marvin E., jt. auth. see Page, Lawrence M.

Braasch, Theodor. Vollstaendiges Woerterbuch Zur Sogenannten Caedmonschen Genesis. (GER.). 1933. 75.00 (*0-685-57725-2*, M7682) Fr & Eur.

Braat, L. C., jt. ed. see Gilbert, A. J.

Braaten. Georgia Criminal & Traffic Law Manual: 1993 Edition. 25.00 (*0-614-05828-7*, MICHIE) LEXIS Pub.

Braaten, Carl & Jenson, Robert W., eds. A Map of Twentieth Century Theology: Readings from Karl Barth to Radical Pluralism. 400p. 1995. pap. 29.00 (*0-8006-2686-9*, 1-2686) Augsburg Fortress.

Braaten, Carl E. The Flaming Center: A Theology of the Christian Mission. LC 76-62605. 176p. reprint ed. pap. 54.60 (*0-608-16926-9*, 202695800053) Bks Demand.

— Justification: The Article by Which the Church Stands or Falls. LC 89-36044. 192p. (Orig.). 1990. pap. 18.00 (*0-8006-2403-3*, 1-2403) Augsburg Fortress.

— Mother Church: Ecclesiology & Ecumenism. LC 98-11785. 1998. pap. 18.00 (*0-8006-3082-3*, Fortress Pr) Augsburg Fortress.

— Principles of Lutheran Theology. LC 82-16542. 160p. 1983. pap. 16.00 (*0-8006-1689-8*, 1-1689, Fortress Pr) Augsburg Fortress.

— The Whole Counsel of God. LC 73-88345. 176p. reprint ed. pap. 54.60 (*0-608-16831-9*, 202684000052) Bks Demand.

Braaten, Carl E. & Jenson, Robert W., eds. The Catholicity of the Reformation. LC 96-44655. 112p. (Orig.). 1996. pap. 12.00 (*0-8028-4220-8*) Eerdmans.

— Christian Dogmatics, 2 vols., Set. LC 83-48007. 1984. 65.00 (*0-8006-0712-0*, 1-712, Fortress Pr) Augsburg Fortress.

— Christian Dogmatics, 2 vols., Vol. 1. LC 83-48007. 572p. 1984. 35.00 (*0-8006-0703-1*, 1-703, Fortress Pr) Augsburg Fortress.

— Christian Dogmatics, 2 vols., Vol. 2. LC 83-48007. 624p. 1984. 35.00 (*0-8006-0704-X*, 1-704, Fortress Pr) Augsburg Fortress.

— Either/Or: The Gospel or Neopaganism. LC 95-8348. 131p. 1995. pap. 12.00 (*0-8028-0840-9*) Eerdmans.

— Marks of the Body of Christ. LC 98-49966. 184p. 1999. pap. 18.00 (*0-8028-4617-3*) Eerdmans.

***Braaten, Carl E. & Jenson, Robert W., eds.** Sin, Death & the Devil. 136p. 2000. pap. 15.00 (*0-8028-4695-5*) Eerdmans.

Braaten, Carl E. & Jenson, Robert W., eds. The Two Cities of God: The Church's Responsibility for the Earthly City. LC 97-8589. 152p. (Orig.). 1997. pap. 18.00 (*0-8028-4304-2*) Eerdmans.

— Union with Christ: The New Finnish Interpretation of Luther. LC 98-28328. 192p. 1998. pap. 21.00 (*0-8028-4442-1*) Eerdmans.

Braaten, David O. & Moran, Robert T., eds. International Directory of Multicultural Resources. LC 96-11545. (Managing Cultural Differences Ser.). 80p. 1996. pap. 50.00 (*0-88415-103-4*, 5103) Gulf Pub.

Braaten, Glenn, jt. auth. see Lord, John.

Braaten, Jane. Habermas's Critical Theory of Society. LC 90-47708. (SUNY Series in the Philosophy of the Social Sciences). 191p. (C). 1991. pap. text 21.95 (*0-7914-0760-8*) State U NY Pr.

Braaten, John. Together . . . Till Death Us Do Part. Sherer, Michael L., ed. LC 86-28386. (Orig.). 1987. pap. 6.85 (*0-89536-852-8*, 7811) CSS OH.

Braaten, Sheldon. Behavioral Objective Sequence: Assessment Manual. 112p. 1998. pap. text 39.95 (*0-87822-384-3*) Res Press.

Braaten, Sheldon & Merbler, John. Behavioral Objective Sequence Reports (Manual & Software Program/PC Version) 1998. pap. text 150.00 incl. disk (*0-87822-383-5*) Res Press.

— Behavioral Objective Sequence Reports (Manual & Software Program/PC Version) 1999. pap. text 150.00 incl. disk (*0-87822-450-5*) Res Press.

***Braathen, Einar & Sther, Gjermund.** Ethnicity Kills? The Politics of War, Peace & Ethnicity in SubSaharan Africa. LC 99-46784. 2000. text. write for info. (*0-312-22988-7*) St Martin.

Braatz, B. V., ed. see United States Country Studies Program Staff.

Braatz, Geraldine A., jt. auth. see Ameche, Yvonne K.

Braatz, Ruth E. Knitting Again with Leftover Yarn. (Illus.). 45p. (Orig.). 1990. pap. 10.95 (*0-9622959-2-2*) Frugal Knitting.

— Knitting with Leftover Yarn. (Illus.). 105p. (Orig.). 1989. pap. text 14.95 (*0-9622959-0-6*) Frugal Knitting.

— More Knitting with Leftover Yarn. (Illus.). 47p. (Orig.). 1990. pap. 7.95 (*0-9622959-1-4*) Frugal Knitting.

— Scrap Yarn Knitting Vol. 1: Holiday & Seasonal Gifts. (Illus.). 36p. 1997. pap. 9.95 (*0-9622959-3-0*) Frugal Knitting.

— Scrap Yarn Knitting Vol. 2: Home & Gift Ideas. (Illus.). 36p. 1997. pap. 9.95 (*0-9622959-4-9*) Frugal Knitting.

— Scrap Yarn Knitting Vol. 3: Knitting for Babies & Children. (Illus.). 40p. 1997. pap. 9.95 (*0-9622959-5-7*) Frugal Knitting.

Braatz, Susan, et al. Conserving Biological Diversity: A Strategy for Protected Areas in the Asia-Pacific Region. LC 92-41431. (Technical Papers: No. 193). 84p. 1993. pap. 22.00 (*0-8213-2307-5*, 12307) World Bank.

Braatz, Thomas, tr. see Steiner, Rudolf.

Brabander. Religion & Human Auto. 1972. lib. bdg. 78.50 (*90-247-1329-3*) Kluwer Academic.

Brabander, Guido L. De, see De Brabander, Guido L.

Brabant, et al. Sociology: A Text Reader. 2nd ed. 270p. (C). 1991. pap. text 41.00 (*0-536-57997-0*) Pearson Custom.

Brabant, Eva, jt. ed. see Falzeder, Ernst.

Brabant, Jozef M. van, see Van Brabant, Jozef M.

Brabant, Sarah. Mending the Torn Fabric: For Those Who Grieve & Those Who Want to Help Them. LC 96-14887. (Death, Value, & Meaning Ser.). 168p. 1996. 30.95 (*0-89503-141-8*) Baywood Pub.

Brabant, Sarah & Forsyth, Craig J. Sociology: Text Reader. 2nd ed. 270p. (C). 1993. text 41.00 (*0-536-58386-2*) Pearson Custom.

Brabazon, Francis. In Dust I Sing. 150p. 1974. 9.95 (*0-940700-08-5*); pap. 6.95 (*0-940700-07-7*) Meher Baba Info.

— The Word at World's End. 88p. 1971. 8.95 (*0-940700-04-2*); pap. 4.95 (*0-940700-03-4*) Meher Baba Info.

***Brabazon, James.** Albert Schweitzer: A Biography. 2nd ed. 516p. 2000. pap. 24.95 (*0-8156-0675-3*) Syracuse U Pr.

— Albert Schweitzer: A Biography. 2nd ed. (Illus.). 516p. 2000. 45.00 (*0-8156-2875-7*) Syracuse U Pr.

Brabazon, James. Dorothy L. Sayers: A Biography. LC 86-672120. xviii, 308 p. 1981. write for info. (*0-575-02728-2*) V Gollancz.

Brabazon, Kevin & Disch, Robert, eds. Intergenerational Approaches in Aging: Implications for Education, Policy, & Practice. LC 97-39668. 276p. 1997. 49.95 (*0-7890-0356-2*) Haworth Pr.

Brabb, E. Pumpkin Companion. Colby, J., ed. LC 95-80493. (Traditional Country Life Recipe Ser.). (Illus.). 96p. (Orig.). 1996. pap. 9.95 (*1-883283-08-6*) Brick Tower.

Brabb, E., jt. auth. see Baker, James W.

Brabb, E. E. & Harrod, B. L., eds. Landslides: Extent & Economic Significance: Proceedings of the 28th International Geological Congress: Symposium on Landslides, Washington, DC, 17 July 1989. 400p. (C). 1989. text 168.00 (*90-6191-876-6*, Pub. by A A Balkema) Ashgate Pub Co.

Brabb, Elizabeth. American Chef's Companion. Garvin, Laurie et al, eds. LC 93-72648. (Traditional Country Life Recipe Ser.). (Illus.). 96p. 1993. pap. 9.95 (*1-883283-01-9*) Brick Tower.

Brabbs, jt. auth. see Herriot, James.

***Brabbs, Derry.** Abbeys & Monasteries. (Country Ser.). (Illus.). 2000. pap. 16.95 (*1-84188-047-7*) Seven Dials.

Brabbs, Derry. English Country Churches. (Country Ser.). (Illus.). 160p. 1997. pap. 17.95 (*0-297-78911-2*, Pub. by Weidenfeld & Nicolson) Trafalgar.

— English Country Pubs. (Country Ser.). (Illus.). 160p. 1997. pap. (*1-85799-923-1*) Phoenix Hse.

— Landmarks: Cottages, Castles & Curiosities of Britain in the Care of the Landmark Trust. (Illus.). 160p. 1998. 27.50 (*0-297-82299-3*, Pub. by Weidenfeld & Nicolson) Trafalgar.

Brabec. Community Health Nursing. (Nursing Education Ser.). 1997. teacher ed. 12.50 (*0-8273-5692-7*) Delmar.

— Community Health Nursing. 5th ed. (Nursing Education Ser.). 1997. write for info. (*0-8273-5693-5*, VNR) Wiley.

Brabec, Barbara. Creative Cash: How to Profit from Your Special Artistry, Creativity, Hand Skills & Related Know-How. 6th ed. LC 98-26647. 240p. 2000. pap. 16.95 (*0-7615-1425-2*) Prima Pub.

— Handmade for Profit: Hundreds of Secrets to Success in Selling Arts & Crafts. LC 96-22960. (Illus.). 256p. 1996. 21.95 (*0-87131-800-8*); pap. 14.95 (*0-87131-812-1*) M Evans.

— Homemade Money. 5th rev. ed. LC 97-25552. (Illus.). 400p. 1997. pap. 21.99 (*1-55870-466-3*, Betrwy Bks) F & W Pubns Inc.

Brabec, Barbara. The Professional Crafter's Business Management & Marketing Guide. (Illus.). 304p. 2000. pap. 16.95 (*0-87131-903-9*) M Evans.

***Brabec, Barbara.** The Professional Crafter's Business Management & Marketing Guide. LC 99-49966. (Illus.). 304p. 2000. 21.95 (*0-87131-902-0*) M Evans.

Brabec, Paula. Community Health NSG/Public Health. (Nursing Education Ser.). 2001. 44.00 (*0-8273-5691-9*) Delmar.

Brabec, Paula D., jt. auth. see Gettrust, Kathy V.

Brabec, V. & Milazzo, G., eds. Experimental Techniques in Bioelectrochemistry, Vol. 3. LC 96-202092. (Bioelectrochemistry: Principles & Practice Ser.). (Illus.). 576p. 1996. 269.50 (*3-7643-5084-9*) Birkhauser.

***Brabeck, Mary M., ed.** Practicing Feminist Ethics in Psychology. LC 99-41175. 285p. 1999. 39.95 (*1-55798-623-1*, 431-2300); pap. 29.95 (*1-55798-635-5*) Am Psychol.

Brabeck, Mary M., ed. Who Cares? Theory, Research & Educational Implications of the Ethic of Care. LC 89-3911. 268p. 1989. 57.95 (*0-275-93253-2*, C3253, Praeger Pubs) Greenwood.

Brabender, Virginia & Fallon, April. Models of Inpatient Group Psychotherapy. (Illus.). 716p. 1993. text 59.95 (*1-55798-174-4*) Am Psychol.

***Brabham, Joe, ed.** The Heritage of Bullock County, Alabama. (Heritage of Alabama Ser.: Vol. 6). 320p. 2001. 50.00 (*1-891647-37-7*) Herit Pub Consult.

Brablett, Reid. The Complete Idiot's Travel Guide to Planning Your Trip to Europe. (Complete Idiot's Travel Guide Ser.). 464p. 1998. pap. text 16.95 (*0-02-862300-2*, Alpha Ref) Macmillan Gen Ref.

Brabner, J. H., ed. The Complete Gazateer of England & Wales. (Early Sources in Reference Ser.). (Illus.). 2218p. (C). 1997. 815.00 (*0-415-16095-2*) Routledge.

Brabner, Joyce, jt. auth. see Pekar, Harvey.

Brabner-Smith, John W., intro. The Custody Dispute Over Seven Human Embryos: The Testimony of Professor Jerome Lejeune, M. D., Ph. D. 90p. (Orig.). (C). 1990. pap. 2.50 (*0-944561-19-5*) Chr Legal.

Brabson, G. Dana, Jr. Integrated Chemical Experimentation Vol. I: Principles & Practice. 120p. 1996. per. 18.95 (*0-8403-8719-9*) Kendall-Hunt.

— Integrated Chemical Experimentation Vol. 3: Second Semester Experiments, 3. 100p. (C). 1994. spiral bd. 21.95 (*0-8403-9171-4*, 40917101) Kendall-Hunt.

Braby, Wayne, jt. auth. see Windrow, Martin.

Braca, Giuseppe, ed. Oxygenates by Homologation or CO Hydrogenation with Metal Complexes. LC 93-23650. (CMCO - Catalysis by Metal Complexes Ser.). 240p. (C). 1994. text 142.00 (*0-7923-2628-8*) Kluwer Academic.

Bracamonte, Jose A. & Spencer, David E. Strategy & Tactics of the Salvadoran FMLN Guerrillas: Last Battle of the Cold War, Blueprint for Future Conflicts. LC 94-42844. 216p. 1995. 62.95 (*0-275-95018-2*, Praeger Pubs) Greenwood.

Bracanti, Vitaliano. Don Giovanni in Sicilia: C Level. text 8.95 (*0-88436-904-8*) EMC-Paradigm.

Bracedi. Dictionary of Literary Biography Vol. 87: British Mystery & Thriller Writers since 1940, First Series, Vol. 87. 400p. 1989. text 155.00 (*0-8103-4565-X*) Gale.

Braccesi, Alessandro. Exploring the Universe. LC 91-24716. 1992. pap. write for info. (*2-88124-512-9*) Gordon & Breach.

Braccesi, Lorenzo & Casanova, Angelo, eds. Lexis, 1990 No. 5-6: Poetica, Retorica e Communicazione Nella Tradizione Classica. (FRE.). 252p. 1992. pap. 44.00 (*90-256-1018-8*, Pub. by AM Hakkert) BookLink Distributors.

Bracchi, G. & Lockemann, P. C., eds. Information Systems Methodology: Proceedings, 2nd Conference of the European Cooperation in Informatics, Venice, Oct. 10-12, 1978. LC 78-12358. (Lecture Notes in Computer Science Ser.: Vol. 65). 1978. 39.95 (*0-387-08934-9*) Spr-Verlag.

***Bracciale, John.** Don't Be Afraid to Dance: A Shy Man's Guide to Dating & Sex. 56p. 2000. pap. 10.00 (*0-8059-5001-X*) Dorrance.

An Asterisk (*) at the beginning of an entry indicates that the title is appearing for the first time.

Bracciano, Alfred. Physical Agent Modalities: Theory & Application for the Occupational Therapist. 176p. 2000. pap. 35.00 (*1-55642-376-4*, 33764) SLACK Inc.

Braccini, Cario, et al, eds. Image Analysis & Processing: 8th International Conference, ICIAP '95, San Remo, Italy, September 13-15, 1995, Proceedings, Vol. XIX. (Lecture Notes in Computer Science Ser.: Vol. 974). 757p. 1995. 113.00 (*3-540-60298-4*) Spr-Verlag.

Braccini, Roberto. Practical Dictionary of Music: English/French/German/Italian. 2nd ed. (ENG, FRE, GER & ITA.). 1994. 65.00 (*0-320-00566-6*) Fr & Eur.

— Praktisches Woerterbuch der Musik, Italian-English-German-French. (ENG, GER & ITA.). 65.00 (*0-7859-6943-8*) Fr & Eur.

Braccio, John H. Outrageous & Scandalous Satire. (Illus.). 246p. 1993. pap. 10.00 (*0-9637854-0-0*) Reg Psychol.

— Sir Harry: The Number One International Chauvinist of the Year. (Illus.). 112p. 1994. pap. 5.95 (*0-9637854-2-7*) Reg Psychol.

Bracciolini, Francisco, tr. Alceste: The Tragedie of Alceste & Eliza. LC 79-84082. (English Experience Ser.: No. 902). 80p. 1979. reprint ed. lib. bdg. 20.00 (*90-221-0902-X*) Walter J Johnson.

Bracciolini, Poggio, ed. see Hammond, Lincoln D. & De Varthema, Ludovico.

Bracco, Kathy Reeves, see Richardson, Richard C., Jr.

Bracco, Maria. Merchants of Hope: British Middlebrow Writers & the First World War, 1919-1939. LC 92-12330. (Legacy of the Great War Ser.). 208p. 1993. 37.50 (*0-85496-706-0*) Berg Pubs.

Bracco, Roberto. Il Piccolo Santo. Luciani, Vincent, ed. (ITA.). (C). 1961. pap. 7.95 (*0-913298-23-9*) S F Vanni.

Bracco, Umberto, jt. ed. see Horisberger, Marc.

Bracco, Umberto, ed. see Nestle Company Staff.

Brace, Andrew. The Essential Guide to Judging Dogs. (Illus.). 176p. 1994. 24.95 (*0-948955-04-X*) Seven Hills Bk.

— Pet Owner's Guide to the Boxer. (Pet Owner's Guide Ser.). (Illus.). 1996. 8.00 (*1-86054-065-1*, Pub. by Ringpr Bks) Seven Hills Bk.

Brace, Andrew, ed. The Ultimate Rottweiler. LC 95-7586. (Illus.). 288p. 1995. 34.95 (*0-87605-293-6*) Howell Bks.

Brace, Andrew, jt. auth. see Clark, Anne R.

Brace, Arthur William & Allen, F. A. Magnesium Casting Technology. LC 58-821. (Illus.). 174p. reprint ed. pap. 54.00 (*0-608-11701-3*, 205132500095) Bks Demand.

Brace, Betty L. & Croghan, Tonita. Understanding Adolescents & Safety at Home & on the Job. LC 79-21803. (Lifeworks Ser.). (Illus.). 1980. text 13.96 (*0-07-060912-8*) McGraw.

***Brace, C. Loring.** Evolution in an Anthropological View. LC 99-56212. 400p. 2000. 69.00 (*0-7425-0262-7*); pap. text 26.95 (*0-7425-0263-5*) Rowman.

Brace, C. Loring. The Stages of Human Evolution. 5th ed. LC 94-35681. 432p. 1994. pap. text 28.20 (*0-13-125485-5*) P-H.

Brace, C. Loring & Metress, James F., eds. Man in Evolutionary Perspective. LC 72-14184. 486p. (C). reprint ed. 150.70 (*0-8357-9926-3*, 201261800082) Bks Demand.

Brace, Corrinne P., jt. auth. see Brase, Charles H.

Brace, Emma. The Life of Charles Loring Brace: Chiefly Told in His Own Letters. LC 75-17205. (Social Problems & Social Policy Ser.). (Illus.). 1976. reprint ed. 41.95 (*0-405-07478-6*) Ayer.

Brace, Gerald, jt. auth. see Moureau, Magdeleine.

Brace, Gerald W. The Department. LC 83-1197. (Phoenix Fiction Ser.). 290p. 1983. pap. 6.95 (*0-226-06968-0*) U Ch Pr.

— The Stuff of Fiction. LC 71-77391. (C). 1972. pap. 2.25 (*0-393-00648-4*) Norton.

— Wind's Will. 1964. 4.50 (*0-393-08435-3*) Norton.

Brace Harber Publishers. Contempory College Algebra. (C). 1999. write for info. (*0-03-025621-6*) Harcourt Coll Pubs.

Brace, Laura. The Idea of Property in Seventeenth-Century England: Tithes & the Individual. LC 97-47405. 208p. 1998. 79.95 (*0-7190-5179-7*, Pub. by Manchester Univ Pr) St Martin.

Brace, Laura & Hoffman, John. Reclaiming Sovereignty. LC 97-1100. 1997. 85.00 (*1-85567-456-4*) Bks Intl VA.

Brace, Paul. State Government & Economic Performance. LC 92-24177. 192p. 1993. text 35.00 (*0-8018-4494-0*) Johns Hopkins.

— State Government & Economic Performance. 176p. 1994. reprint ed. pap. text 16.95 (*0-8018-4971-3*) Johns Hopkins.

Brace, Paul, jt. auth. see Weber, Ronald.

Brace, Paul K., et al. Reporting of Service Efforts & Accomplishments. LC 80-84887. (Financial Accounting Standards Board Research Report Ser.). (Illus.). 114p. (Orig.). 1980. pap. 6.50 (*0-910065-09-8*) Finan Acct Found.

Brace, Robert, et al, eds. Fetal & Neonatal Body Fluids: The Scientific Basis for Clinical Practice. LC 89-8436. (Reproductive & Perinatal Medicine Ser.: No. XI). (Illus.). 1989. 105.00 (*0-916859-32-0*) Perinatology.

Brace, Robert A., et al, eds. Body Fluids & Kidney Function. LC 97-13540. (Fetus & Neonate Ser.: No. 4). (Illus.). 340p. (C). 1998. text 105.00 (*0-521-59392-1*) Cambridge U Pr.

Brace, Sharron K. Fire on the River. LC 95-80554. (Illus.). 285p. 1995. pap. 29.95 (*0-9649362-0-8*) APS Pubng.

— Fire on the River. LC 95-80554. (Illus.). 288p. 1996. lib. bdg. 41.95 (*0-9649362-1-6*) APS Pubng.

Brace, Steve. Bangladesh. LC 94-27843. (Economically Developing Countries Ser.). (Illus.). 48p. (J). (gr. 5-9). 1995. lib. bdg. 24.26 (*1-56847-243-9*) Raintree Steck-V.

— From Beans to Batteries. LC 98-48915. (One World Ser.). (Illus.). 1998. pap. 6.99 (*0-85953-799-4*) Childs Play.

Brace, Steve. Ghana. LC 94-28710. (Economically Developing Countries Ser.). (Illus.). 48p. (J). (gr. 6-8). 1995. lib. bdg. 24.26 (*1-56847-242-0*) Raintree Steck-V.

***Brace, Steve.** Salamatu & Kandoni Go Missing. 1999. pap. text 4.99 (*0-85953-784-6*) Childs Play.

Brace, Steve. Village Life in India. LC 96-229219. (Cambridge Primary Geography Ser.). 48p. (C). 1996. pap. 9.95 (*0-521-55752-6*) Cambridge U Pr.

Brace, Steven. India. LC 98-52758. (Country Studies Ser.). (Illus.). 64p. (YA). 1999. 24.22 (*1-57572-893-1*) Heinemann Lib.

Brace, Tom, jt. auth. see Moen, Patricia.

Bracebridge, C. Holte. Shakespeare No Deerstealer. LC 76-39517. reprint ed. 34.50 (*0-404-00921-2*) AMS Pr.

Bracegirdle & Miles. Atlas de Estructura Vegetal. (SPA.). 126p. 1975. pap. 29.95 (*0-8288-5788-1*, S37583) Fr & Eur.

Bracegirdle, jt. auth. see Freeman, Daniel B.

Bracegirdle, B. Scientific Photomacrography: Recording Specimens at Magnifications Between x1 & x50. (Royal Microscopial Society Handbook Ser.: No. 31). (Illus.). 160p. 1995. pap. 42.50 (*1-872748-49-X*, Pub. by Bios Sci) Bks Intl VA.

Bracegirdle, B. & Bradbury, S. Modern Photomicrography. (Microscopy Handbooks Ser.: No. 33). 112p. 1995. pap. 42.50 (*1-85996-090-1*, Pub. by Bios Sci) Coronet Bks.

Bracegirdle, Brian. Devils, Drugs & Doctors: A Wellcome History of Medicine. 1991. pap. text 9.95 (*0-642-09877-8*) Seven Hills Bk.

— A History of Microtechnique: The Evolution of the Microtome & the Development of Tissue Preparation. 2nd ed. (History of Microscopy Ser.). (Illus.). 1987. 30.00 (*0-940095-00-9*) Sci Heritage Ltd.

Bracegirdle, Brian & Miles, Patricia H. An Atlas of Plant Structure, 2 vols., Vol. 1. (C). 1971. text 27.95 (*0-435-60312-4*, 60312) Heinemann.

Bracegirdle, Brian, jt. auth. see Bradbury, Savile.

Bracegirdle, Brian, jt. auth. see Freeman, W. H.

Bracegirdle, Brian, jt. auth. see McCormick, James B.

***Bracegirdle, Hilary & Connor, Pat.** The Essential Horse. (Illus.). 176p. 2000. 60.00 (*0-85667-524-5*, Pub. by P Wilson) Antique Collect.

Braceland, Lawrence C., tr. see Gilbert.

Braceland, Lawrence C., tr. see Gilbert of Hoyland.

Bracewell. Fourier Transform Applications. 3rd ed. LC 99-21139. 640p. 1999. 109.06 (*0-07-303938-1*) McGraw.

Bracewell, Mark & Karp, David. O'Reilly Utilities - Quick Solutions for Windows 98 Annoyances. Blaber, Gina, ed. 1998. pap. 39.95 (*1-56592-549-1*) OReilly & Assocs.

Bracewell, Catherine W. The Uskoks of Senj: Piracy, Banditry, & Holy War in the Sixteenth- Century Adriatic. LC 91-55548. (Illus.). 352p. 1992. text 52.50 (*0-8014-2674-X*) Cornell U Pr.

Bracewell, Michael. The Crypto-Amnesia Club. 112p. 1991. pap. 8.50 (*1-85242-115-0*) Serpents Tail.

***Bracewell, Michael.** England Is Mine. 1998. pap. 14.95 (*0-00-655015-0*, Pub. by HarpC) Trafalgar.

Bracewell-Milnes, Barry. The Economics of International Tax Avoidance: Political Power vs. Economic Law. (International Taxation Ser.: No. 2). 120p. 1980. lib. bdg. 29.00 (*90-200-0633-9*) Kluwer Academic.

Bracewell-Milnes, Barry, jt. auth. see Carnaghan, Robert.

Bracewell, R. N. The Fourier Transform & Its Applications. 2nd rev. ed. 486p. (C). 1986. 105.31 (*0-07-007015-6*) McGraw.

Bracewell, Ronald N. Two Dimensional Imaging. 640p. 1994. 99.00 (*0-13-062621-X*) P-H.

Bracewell, Wendy, et al. Pre-Modern & Modern National Identity in Russia & Eastern Europe. 236p. 1993. pap. text 53.00 (*2-88124-625-7*) Gordon & Breach.

Bracey, Dorothy H. Baby-Pros: Preliminary Profiles of Juvenile Prostitutes. (Criminal Justice Center Monographs). 1979. pap. text 5.00 (*0-89444-024-1*) John Jay Pr.

— A Functional Approach to Police Corruption. (Criminal Justice Center Monographs). 1978. pap. text 3.00 (*0-318-37484-6*) John Jay Pr.

Bracey, Earnest N. The Black Samurai: A Novel of Feudal Japan. LC 96-90167. 1996. 15.95 (*0-533-11944-8*) Vantage.

Bracey, Ernest N. Prophetic Insight: The Higher Education & Pedagogy of African Americans. LC 99-22439. 160p. 1999. pap. 26.50 (*0-7618-1384-5*) U Pr of Amer.

***Bracey, Ernest N.** Prophetic Insight: The Higher Education & Pedagogy of African Americans. LC 99-22439. 160p. 1999. 45.00 (*0-7618-1383-7*) U Pr of Amer.

Bracey, Gerald. Transforming America's Schools: An Rx for Getting Past Blame. 127p. 1994. pap. 17.95 (*0-87652-211-8*, 21-00470) Am Assn Sch Admin.

***Bracey, Gerald W.** Bail Me Out! Handling Difficult Data & Tough Questions about Public Schools. LC 99-50781. (Illus.). 208p. 2000. pap. 29.95 (*0-7619-7603-5*); lib. bdg. 65.95 (*0-7619-7602-7*) Corwin Pr.

Bracey, Gerald W. Setting the Record Straight: Responses to Misconceptions about Public Education in the United States. LC 96-51260. 1997. pap. 20.95 (*0-87120-279-4*) ASCD.

***Bracey, Gerald W.** A Short Guide to Standardized Testing. (Fastback Ser.: No. 459). 56p. 2000. pap. 3.00 (*0-87367-659-9*) Phi Delta Kappa.

Bracey, Gerald W. & AIT Staff. Final Exam: A Study of the Perpetual Scrutiny of Amercian Education: Historical Perspectives on Assessment, Standards, Outcomes, & Criticism of U. S. Schools. LC 95-61639. 256p. (C). 1995. text 31.25 (*0-7842-0807-7*) Agency Instr Tech.

Bracey, Gerald W. & Resnick, Michael A. Raising the Bar: A School Board Primer on Student Achievement. (Illus.). 56p. 1998. pap. 20.00 (*0-88364-217-4*, 11-121) Natl Sch Boards.

Bracey, H. E. Neighbours: Subdivision Life in England & the United States. LC 64-15877. 220p. 1964. reprint ed. pap. 68.20 (*0-7837-9880-6*, 206060600006) Bks Demand.

Bracey, Hyler, et al. Managing from the Heart. 242p. 1990. 16.95 (*0-9626198-0-9*, Dell Trade Pbks) Dell.

— Managing from the Heart. 208p. 1993. pap. 12.95 (*0-440-50472-4*, Dell Trade Pbks) Dell.

Bracey, John H., et al. Black Nationalism in America. LC 79-99161. 1970. pap. 12.95 (*0-672-60150-8*, AHS89, Bobbs) Macmillan.

— Papers of the NAACP. LC 97-163130. (Black Studies Research Sources). 6 p. 1995. write for info. (*1-55655-544-X*) U Pubns Amer.

— Papers of the NAACP. LC 97-42605. (Black Studies Research Sources Ser.). 1997. 2205.00 (*1-55655-654-3*) U Pubns Amer.

— Papers of the NAACP. LC 98-13788. 1998. 1930.00 (*1-55655-655-1*) U Pubns Amer.

Bracey, John H., jt. ed. see Adams, Maurianne.

Bracey, John-Paul. A Biography of French Pianist Marcel Ciampi, 1891-1980: Music to Last a Lifetime. LC 95-46933. (Studies in the History & Interpretation of Music: Vol. 50). 1996. write for info. (*0-7734-8794-8*) E Mellen.

Bracey, Naida. Colour of Illusion. (Rainbow Romances Ser.: No. 888). 160p. 1994. 14.95 (*0-7090-4935-8*) Parkwest Pubns.

— Colour of Illusion. large type ed. (Romance Ser.). 304p. 1995. pap. 16.99 (*0-7089-7673-5*, Linford) Ulverscroft.

Bracey, Nathaniel. Black Males & the Psychology of Love: A Visionary & Theoretical Look at a New Breed of Black Men for the 21st Century. 39p. (Orig.). 1992. pap. 3.95 (*1-56411-037-0*) Untd Bros & Sis.

Brach, Paul, et al. Our Land - Ourselves: American Indian Contemporary Artists. Ward, Deborah et al, eds. LC 90-71736. (Illus.). 78p. (Orig.). 1990. pap. 18.00 (*0-910763-05-4*) U Albany Art Mus.

Brache, Alan P., jt. auth. see Rummler, Geary A.

Brachenridge, Henry M. History of the Late War. (Works of Henry Marie Brackenridge). 1989. reprint ed. lib. bdg. 79.00 (*0-7812-2028-9*) Rprt Serv.

— Recollections of Persons & Places in the West. (Works of Henry Marie Brackenridge). 1989. reprint ed. lib. bdg. 79.00 (*0-7812-2030-0*) Rprt Serv.

— South America: A Letter to the Present State of That Country to James Monroe. (Works of Henry Marie Brackenridge). 1989. reprint ed. lib. bdg. 79.00 (*0-7812-2029-7*) Rprt Serv.

— Views of Louisiana. (Works of Henry Marie Brackenridge). 1989. reprint ed. lib. bdg. 79.00 (*0-7812-2027-0*) Rprt Serv.

— The Works of Henry Marie Brackenridge. 1989. reprint ed. lib. bdg. 79.00 (*0-685-27325-3*) Rprt Serv.

Bracher. German Dictatorship. (C). 1970. pap. write for info. (*0-03-037556-8*) Harcourt Coll Pubs.

Bracher, D. A., jt. ed. see Garrett, D. A.

Bracher, Karl D. Turning Points in Modern Times: Essays on German & European History. Dunlap, Thomas, tr. LC 94-34988. 352p. 1995. text 54.00 (*0-674-91353-1*, BRATUX); pap. text 26.00 (*0-674-91354-X*, BRATUX) HUP.

Bracher, Mark. Being Form'd: Thinking Through Blake's "Milton" 288p. (Orig.). 1985. 22.50 (*0-88268-013-7*); pap. 9.95 (*0-88268-012-9*) Station Hill Pr.

— Lacan, Discourse, & Social Change: A Psychoanalytic Cultural Criticism. LC 92-31172. 224p. (C). 1993. text 37.50 (*0-8014-2784-3*); pap. text 14.95 (*0-8014-8063-9*) Cornell U Pr.

— Lacanian Theory of Discourse: Subject, Structure, & Society. 1997. pap. text 20.00 (*0-8147-1299-1*) NYU Pr.

— The Writing Cure: Psychoanalysis, Composition & the Aims of Education. LC 98-25267. 1999. 34.95 (*0-8093-2221-8*) S Ill U Pr.

Bracher, Mark, et al, eds. Lacanian Theory of Discourse: Subject, Structure, & Society. LC 94-14079. 215p. (C). 1994. text 50.00 (*0-8147-1191-X*) NYU Pr.

Bracher, Nathan, tr. see Conan, Eric & Rousso, Henry.

Brachet, J., jt. ed. see Abercrombie, M.

Brachet, J., jt. ed. see Delrio, G.

Brachet, Jean & Alexander, H. Introduction to Molecular Embryology. 2nd rev. ed. (Heidelberg Science Library). (Illus.). 240p. 1986. pap. 39.00 (*0-387-16968-7*) Spr-Verlag.

Brachet-Marquez, Vivian. The Dynamics of Domination: State, Class, & Social Reform in Mexico, 1910-1990. LC 93-30949. (Latin American Ser.). 264p. (C). 1994. text 59.95 (*0-8229-3780-8*) U of Pittsburgh Pr.

Brachlianoff, Dominique. The Real & the Spiritual: Nineteenth-Century French Drawings from the Musee des Beaux-Arts de Lyon. McIntosh, DeCourcy E., ed. Bertrand, Anne, tr. from FRE. LC 92-71570. (Illus.). 188p. (Orig.). (C). 1992. pap. 39.95 (*1-881403-30-9*) Frick Art Mus.

Brachlow, Stephen. The Communion of Saints: Racical Puritan & Separatist Ecclesiology, 1570-1625. (Oxford Theological Monographs). 304p. 1989. text 75.00 (*0-19-826726-6*) OUP.

Brachman, Philip S., jt. auth. see Evans, Alfred S.

Brachman, Philip S., jt. ed. see Bennett, John V.

Brachman, Philip S., jt. ed. see Evans, Alfred S.

Brachman, Ronald J. & Levesque, Hector J., eds. Knowledge Representation. (Illus.). 416p. 1992. 41.50 (*0-262-52168-7*) MIT Pr.

— Readings in Knowledge Representation. LC 85-16400. 571p. (Orig.). (C). 1985. pap. text 44.95 (*0-934613-01-X*) Morgan Kaufmann.

Brachman, Ronald J., ed. see Allen, James, et al.

***Brachman, Wayne.** Retro Desserts: Totally Hip, Updated Classic Desserts from the '40s, '50s, '60s & '70s. LC 99-43578. (Illus.). 224p. 2000. 27.00 (*0-688-16444-7*, Wm Morrow) Morrow Avon.

***Bracho, Chela.** Horoscopo, 1999 Edition. 1999. pap. text 13.95 (*968-406-805-0*) F Planeta.

Bracho, Coral, tr. see McDonnell, Christine.

Bracho, Javier. En Que Espacio Vivimos. (Ciencia para Todos Ser.). (SPA.). pap. 6.99 (*968-16-3039-4*, Pub. by Fondo) Continental Bk.

Bracht, Illya, jt. auth. see Shackell, Charlie.

Bracht, Neil, ed. Health Promotion at the Community Level. (Sourcebooks for the Human Services Ser.: Vol. 15). (Illus.). 320p. (C). 1990. text 56.00 (*0-8039-3858-6*); pap. text 26.00 (*0-8039-3859-4*) Sage.

***Bracht, Neil, ed.** Health Promotion at the Community Level: New Advances. 2nd ed. LC 98-40267. 275p. 1999. 56.00 (*0-7619-1844-2*) Sage.

Bracht, Neil F. Health Promotion At the Community Level: New Advances. 2nd ed. LC 98-40267. 384p. 1999. 27.50 (*0-7619-1304-1*) Sage.

— Social Work in Health Care: A Guide to Professional Practice. LC 78-7881. 346p. 1978. 49.95 (*0-917724-04-6*); pap. 7.95 (*0-917724-05-4*) Haworth Pr.

Bracht, Victor. Texas in 1848. (Illus.). 240p. 1995. 21.00 (*1-57168-242-2*) Sunbelt Media.

Bracht, Viktor. Texas in 1848. 1993. reprint ed. lib. bdg. 75.00 (*0-7812-5919-3*) Rprt Serv.

Brack, A., et al, eds. Life Sciences: Space & Mars Recent Results: Proceedings of the F3.1, F3.4, F2.4 & F3.8 Symposia of COSPAR Scientific Commission F Which Were Held During the Thirtieth COSPAR Scientific Assembly, Hamburg, Germany, 11-21 July 1994. (Advances in Space Research Ser.: Vol. 18). 272p. 1996. pap. 94.50 (*0-08-043082-1*, Pergamon Pr) Elsevier.

Brack, Andre, ed. The Molecular Origins of Life: Assembling the Pieces of the Puzzle. (Illus.). 360p. (C). 1998. text 85.00 (*0-521-56412-3*); pap. text 34.95 (*0-521-56475-1*) Cambridge U Pr.

Brack, Duncan. Climate Change Policies & International Trade. 180p. 1998. pap. 18.95 (*1-86203-052-9*, Pub. by Royal Inst Intl Affairs) Brookings.

— Energy Efficiency & International Trade. 192p. 1997. pap. write for info. (*1-85383-438-6*, Pub. by Escan Pubns) Island Pr.

— Trade & Environment. 1998. pap. text 18.95 (*1-85383-577-3*) Island Pr.

Brack, Duncan, ed. Trade & Environment: Conflict or Compatibility? 200p. 1998. pap. 14.95 (*1-86203-086-3*, Pub. by Royal Inst Intl Affairs) Brookings.

Brack, Duncan, jt. auth. see Krueger, Jonathan.

Brack, Duncan, jt. ed. see Grubb, Michael.

Brack, Gene. The Texas Quest for New Mexico, 1836-1850. (Texas History Ser.). (Illus.). 37p. 1984. pap. text 9.95 (*0-89641-144-3*) American Pr.

Brack, Lisa, jt. auth. see Bray, Joan.

Brack, M. Agents Transmissible from Simians to Man. (Illus.). 450p. 1987. 134.60 (*0-387-17559-8*) Spr-Verlag.

Brack, O. M., Jr., ed. Twilight of Dawn: Studies in English Literature in Transition. LC 86-30787. 259p. 1987. pap. 80.30 (*0-608-05650-2*, 206610400006) Bks Demand.

Brack, O M, Jr., ed. Writers, Books & Trade: An Eighteenth-Century English Miscellany for William B. Todd. LC 91-53014. (Studies in the Eighteenth Century: No. 19). 1993. 57.50 (*0-404-63519-9*) AMS Pr.

Brack, O. M., Jr., jt. auth. see Kelley, Robert E.

Brack, O. M., Jr., ed. see De Fenelon, Marquis.

Brack, O M, Jr., ed. see Johnson, Samuel.

Brack, O. M., ed. see Smollett, Tobias George.

Brack, Pat. Moms Don't Get Sick. LC 90-60228. (Illus.). 124p. (Orig.). 1990. pap. 10.95 (*0-937603-07-4*) Melius Pub.

Brack-Schorner, Robin. Small Quantity Generator Handbook: The Smarter Neighbor Quest. (Illus.). (Orig.). (C). 1989. pap. write for info. (*0-318-65928-X*) Amer Hazmat.

Bracke, John M. Jeremiah 1-29. LC 99-43130. (Westminster Bible Companion Ser.). 270p. 1999. pap. 18.95 (*0-664-25582-5*) Westminster John Knox.

***Bracke, John M.** Jeremiah 30-52 & Lamentations. LC 99-43129. (Westminster Bible Companion Ser.). 270p. 1999. pap. 18.95 (*0-664-25583-3*) Westminster John Knox.

***Bracke, Niels.** Die Regierung Waldemars IV: Eine Untersuchung Zum Wandel Von Herrschaftsstrukturen Im Spatmittelalterlichen Danemark. (GER., Illus.). 249p. 1999. 46.00 (*3-631-32411-1*) P Lang Pubng.

Bracke, P., et al. Inorganic Fibres & Composite Materials: A Survey of Recent Developments. LC 83-25736. (European Patent Office Applied Technology Ser.: Vol. 3). 192p. 1984. 90.00 (*0-08-031145-8*, Pub. by Pergamon Repr) Franklin.

Brackelsberg, Phyllis & Marshall, Ruth. Unit Method of Clothing Construction. 7th ed. 280p. (C). Date not set. 29.95 (*1-57766-054-4*) Waveland Pr.

Brackemyre, Lori, ed. 1999 Indiana Media Directory: The Most Up-to-Date, Detailed Listing of All Indiana Media. (Illus.). 232p. 1998. pap. 49.50 (*0-944369-19-7*) Brackemyre Pub.

***Brackemyre, Lori, ed.** 2001 Indiana Media Directory: The Most Up-to-Date, Detailed Listing of All Indiana Media. (Illus.). 240p. 2000. pap. 63.00 (*0-944369-20-0*) Brackemyre Pub.

Bracken. Christmas Decorations. 1998. pap. 3.95 (*0-486-27151-X*) Dover.

— Foundations of Algebra. (C). 1999. text. write for info. (*0-03-022624-4*) Harcourt Coll Pubs.

***Bracken.** Psychoeducatioanl Assessment. 3rd ed. LC 99-23802. 488p. 1999. 78.00 (*0-205-29021-3*) Allyn.

B

Bracken, Bruce A., ed. Handbook of Self-Concept: Developmental, Social, & Clinical Considerations. LC 95-15681. (Personality Processes Ser.). 539p. 1995. 135.00 (*0-471-59939-5*, Wiley-Interscience) Wiley.

Bracken, Bruce A., jt. auth. see McCallum, R.

Bracken, C. Easy-to-Make Gingerbread House. 1989. pap. text 2.95 (*0-486-26073-9*) Dover.

Bracken, Carmel. The Gift of a Friend & Other Verses. 1993. pap. 12.95 (*0-685-66339-6*) Dufour.

Bracken, Carolyn. Baby's First Rattle. (Tubby Bks.). (Illus.). 8p. (J). (ps up). 1984. pap., vinyl bd. 4.95 (*0-671-47668-8*) Litle Simon.

Bracken, Carolyn. Easter Punch-Out Window Decorations. 1994. pap. text 2.95 (*0-486-27841-7*) Dover.

— Easy-to-Make Haunted House. (Illus.). (J). (gr. 4-7). 1991. pap. 3.50 (*0-486-26803-9*) Dover.

Bracken, Carolyn. Gingerbread Boy-Coloring Book. (J). 1989. pap. 1.00 (*0-486-25912-9*) Dover.

— I Love Bear. (J). 2000. pap. 2.99 (*0-375-80498-6*, Pub. by Random Bks Yng Read) Random.

— Mother Goose Stickers & Seals: 40 Full-Color Pressure-Sensitive Designs. (Illus.). (J). 1992. pap. 3.50 (*0-486-27031-9*) Dover.

Bracken, Carolyn. Mouse Sticker Paper Doll, Vol. 108. (Illus.). (J). (gr. k-3). 1993. pap. 1.00 (*0-486-27436-5*) Dover.

— Scary Masks: 6 Punch-Out Designs. (Illus.). (J). (gr. k-3). 1992. pap. 3.95 (*0-486-27240-0*) Dover.

— Silly Animals Punch-Out Masks. (Illus.). (J). (gr. k-3). 1993. pap. 2.95 (*0-486-27702-X*) Dover.

— Super Stickers: 52 Full Color Pressure Sensitive Designs. (Illus.). (J). (gr. k-3). 1993. pap. 3.50 (*0-486-27894-8*) Dover.

Bracken, Carolyn. Santa's Pockets. (J). (ps). 1983. pap. 3.95 (*0-671-47660-2*) Litle Simon.

Bracken, Carolyn & Beylon, Cathy. Santa's Workshop. (Illus.). (J). (ps-3). 1997. pap., student ed. 2.75 (*0-679-88875-6*, Pub. by Random Bks Yng Read) Random.

Bracken, Charles. Tennis: Play Like a Pro. LC 89-27341. (Be the Best! Ser.). (Illus.). 64p. (J). (gr. 4-8). 1990. lib. bdg. 15.85 (*0-8167-1931-4*) Troll Communs.

— Tennis: Play Like a Pro. LC 89-27341. (Be the Best! Ser.). (Illus.). 64p. (J). (gr. 4-8). 1997. pap. 3.95 (*0-8167-1932-2*) Troll Communs.

— Volleyball: A Step-by-Step Guide. LC 89-27352. (Be the Best! Ser.). (Illus.). 64p. (J). (gr. 4-8). 1990. lib. bdg. 15.85 (*0-8167-1951-9*) Troll Communs.

— Volleyball: A Step-by-Step Guide. LC 89-27352. (Be the Best! Ser.). (Illus.). 64p. (J). (gr. 4-7). 1997. pap. 3.95 (*0-8167-1952-7*) Troll Communs.

Bracken, Christopher. The Potlatch Papers: A Colonial Case History. LC 97-9829. 224p. 1997. pap. text 16.95 (*0-226-06987-7*); lib. bdg. 40.00 (*0-226-06986-9*) U Ch Pr.

Bracken, Cindy. Weight Loss & Fitness Facts: Diet - Exercise - Disease Prevention. (Illus.). 36p. (Orig.). 1993. pap. 10.00 (*0-9638588-1-5*) Weight Loss.

— Weight Loss & Fitness Facts: Diet - Exercise - Disease Prevention. 2 cass.; set. (Illus.). 36p. (Orig.). 1994. pap. 480.00 incl. VHS (*0-9638588-0-7*) Weight Loss.

Bracken, David & Center for Creative Leadership Staff. Should 360-Degree Feedback Be Only for Administrative As Well As Development Purposes? LC 97-28278. 48p. 1997. 15.00 (*1-882197-31-3*) Ctr Creat Leader.

Bracken, H. M. Bracken: Wm. Bracken of New Castle Co., Delaware, & His Descendants. 79p. 1994. reprint ed. pap. 16.00 (*0-8328-4300-8*); reprint ed. lib. bdg. 26.00 (*0-8328-4299-0*) Higginson Bk Co.

— The Early Reception of Berkeley's Immaterialism, 1710-1733. (International Archives of the History of Ideas Ser.: No. 10). 144p. 1965. lib. bdg. 66.50 (*90-247-0186-4*, Pub. by M Nijhoff) Kluwer Academic.

Bracken, Harry M. Freedom of Speech: Words Are Not Deeds. LC 93-5444. 176p. 1994. 55.00 (*0-275-94719-X*, Praeger Pubs) Greenwood.

Bracken, James & Silver, Joel, eds. The British Book Trade, 1475-1700, Vol. 1. 7th ed. (Dictionary of Literary Biography Ser.: Vol. 170). 400p. 1996. text 155.00 (*0-8103-9933-4*) Gale.

***Bracken, James K.** The Undergraduate's Companion to American Writers: And Their Websites. 350p. 2000. 30.00 (*1-56308-859-2*) Libs Unl.

Bracken, James K. & Silver, Joel, eds. DLB 154: The British Literary Book Trade, 1700-1820. LC 95-4825. (Dictionary of Literary Biography Ser.: Vol. 154). 366p. 1995. text 155.00 (*0-8103-5715-1*, 007489) Gale.

Bracken, James K. & Sterling, Christopher H. Telecommunications Research Resources: An Annotated Guide. (LEA's Telecommunications Ser.). 184p. 1995. pap. 22.50 (*0-8058-1887-1*); text 39.95 (*0-8058-1886-3*) L Erlbaum Assocs.

***Bracken, James K. & Sterling, Christopher H.** Telecommunications Research Resources: An Annotated Guide, Set. (LEA's Communication Ser.). 1999. 45.00 (*0-8058-3636-5*) L Erlbaum Assocs.

Bracken, Janice M., et al. Women of the Word: Contemporary Sermons by Women Clergy. LC 84-52656. (Illus.). 144p. (Orig.). 1985. pap. 8.95 (*0-932419-00-3*) Cherokee.

Bracken, Jeanne M. Life in the American Colonies: Daily Lifestyles of the Early Settlers. LC 95-68768. (Perspectives on History Ser.). 60p. (YA). (gr. 5 up). 1995. pap. 6.95 (*1-878668-37-4*) Disc Enter Ltd.

Bracken, Jeanne M., ed. American Waterways: The Role of Canals in America. (Perspectives on History Ser.: Vol. 32). (Illus.). 64p. 1997. pap. 6.95 (*1-878668-75-7*) Disc Enter Ltd.

— Iron Horses Across America: The Transcontinental Railroad. (Perspectives on History Ser.). 68p. (J). (gr. 5-12). 1995. pap. 6.95 (*1-878668-36-6*) Disc Enter Ltd.

— Life in the Southern Colonies: Jamestown, Williamsburg, St. Marty's City & Beyond. (Perspectives on History Ser.: Vol. 31). (Illus.). 64p. 1997. pap. 6.95 (*1-878668-74-9*) Disc Enter Ltd.

— The Shot Heard 'Round the World: The Beginnings of the American Revolution. LC 94-71898. (Perspectives on History Ser.). (Illus.). 64p. (YA). 1995. pap. 6.95 (*1-878668-32-3*) Disc Enter Ltd.

— Women in the American Revolution. (Perspectives on History Ser.: Vol. 30). (Illus.). 64p. 1997. pap. 6.95 (*1-878668-73-0*) Disc Enter Ltd.

Bracken, Jerome & Schliefer, Arthur. Tables for Normal Sampling with Unknown Variances: The Student Distribution & Economically Optimal Sampling Plans. LC 64-13716. 208p. reprint ed. pap. 64.50 (*0-608-30308-9*, 200219600012) Bks Demand.

Bracken, Joseph A. Society & Spirit: A Trinitarian Cosmology. LC 90-50601. 192p. 1991. 32.50 (*0-945636-21-0*) Susquehanna U Pr.

— The Triune Symbol: Persons, Process & Community. (Studies in Religion: No. 1). 216p. (Orig.). 1985. lib. bdg. 47.50 (*0-8191-4440-1*) U Pr of Amer.

Bracken, Joseph A. & Suchocki, Marjorie Hewitt, eds. Trinity in Process: A Relational Theology of God. LC 96-22538. 286p. 1996. 34.95 (*0-8264-0878-8*) Continuum.

***Bracken, Len.** Arch Conspirator: Essays & Actions. 1999. pap. text 14.95 (*0-932813-72-0*) Advent Unltd.

Bracken, Len, tr. see Lafargue, Paul.

Bracken, Len, tr. see Sanguinetti, Gianfranco.

Bracken, Michael B. Perinatal Epidemiology. (Illus.). 550p. 1984. text 69.50 (*0-19-503389-2*) OUP.

Bracken, Patrick J. & Petty, Celia, eds. Rethinking the Trauma of War. 200p. 1998. 50.00 (*1-85343-407-8*, Pub. by Free Assoc Bks); pap. 23.50 (*1-85343-408-6*, Pub. by Free Assoc Bks) NYU Pr.

Bracken, Paul. Fire In The East: The Rise of Asian Military Power & the Second Nuclear Age. LC 99-20103. (Illus.). 224p. 1999. 25.00 (*0-06-019344-1*) HarpC.

***Bracken, Paul.** Fire In The East: The Rise of Asian Military Power & the Second Nuclear Age. 224p. 2000. pap. 13.00 (*0-06-093155-8*) HarpC.

Bracken, Paul, et al. Evaluation Framework for Unified Command Plans: A Documented Briefing. LC 93-26336. 1994. pap. text 6.00 (*0-8330-1439-0*, MR-306-A) Rand Corp.

— Shaping & Integrating the Next Military: Organization Options for Defense Acquisition & Technology. 40p. (Orig.). 1996. pap. text 6.00 (*0-8330-2423-X*, DB-177-OSD) Rand Corp.

Bracken, Pauline. Indian Summer. LC 97-184159. 190p. 1997. pap. 12.95 (*1-898256-22-5*) Dufour.

— Light of Other Days: A Dublin Childhood. (Illus.). 144p. 1998. pap. 10.95 (*1-85635-032-0*, Pub. by Mercier Pr) Irish Amer Bk.

Bracken, Peg. The Compleat I Hate to Cook Book. 288p. 1992. 9.99 (*0-88365-794-5*) Galahad Bks.

— The Compleat I Hate to Cook Book. (Illus.). 288p. 1986. 15.95 (*0-15-120480-2*) Harcourt.

— The Complete I Hate to Cook Book. 384p. 1988. mass mkt. 5.99 (*0-553-27130-X*) Bantam.

— I Hate to Cook Book. LC 60-10919. (Illus.). 176p. 1960. 12.95 (*0-15-139263-3*) Harcourt.

— On Getting Old for the First Time. LC 96-85316. (Illus.). 192p. 1996. 14.95 (*1-885221-53-3*) BookPartners.

Bracken, Robert. Spitfire: The Canadians. LC 96-106315. (Illus.). 156p. 1995. 32.00 (*1-55046-148-6*) Boston Mills.

***Bracken, Robert.** Spitfire II: The Canadians. (Illus.). 137p. 1999. 37.95 (*1-55046-267-9*) Boston Mills.

Bracken, Sarah, jt. auth. see Pulleyn, Micah.

Bracken, Thomas. Abraham Lincoln: U. S. President. LC 97-48305. (Overcoming Adversity Ser.). (Illus.). 128p. (YA). (gr. 4-7). 1999. pap. 8.95 (*0-7910-4705-9*) Chelsea Hse.

— Children of the World. LC 97-31058. (Looking into the Past). (Illus.). 64p. (YA). (gr. 5 up). 1999. lib. bdg. 16.95 (*0-7910-4685-0*) Chelsea Hse.

— Good Luck Symbols & Talismans. LC 97-34377. (Looking into the Past). (Illus.). 64p. (YA). (gr. 5 up). 1999. lib. bdg. 16.95 (*0-7910-4683-4*) Chelsea Hse.

Brackenbridge, Hugh H. Incidents of the Insurrection. Marder, Daniel, ed. (Masterworks of Literature Ser.). 1972. 18.95 (*0-8084-0014-2*); pap. 13.95 (*0-8084-0015-0*) NCUP.

***Brackenbury, Alison.** After Beethoven. 80p. 2000. pap. 14.95 (*1-85754-454-4*, Pub. by Carcanet Pr) Paul & Co Pubs.

Brackenbury, ALison. 1892. 64p. 1995. pap. 14.95 (*1-85754-122-7*, Pub. by Carcanet Pr) Paul & Co Pubs.

Brackenbury, H. Ashanti War, 2 vols., Set. 1968. 95.00 (*0-7146-1795-4*, Pub. by F Cass Pubs) Intl Spec Bk.

Brackenbury, Henry. The River Column. (Victorian War Ser.: No. 2). (Illus.). 291p. reprint ed. 34.95 (*0-89839-184-9*) Battery Pr.

Brackenbury, John. Insects: Life Cycles & the Seasons. (Illus.). 160p. 1996. pap. 19.95 (*0-7137-2598-2*, Pub. by Blandford Pr) Sterling.

Brackenbury, K. F., ed. Brackenbury of Lincolnshire: Wills, Etc., Vol. 1. 83p. 1994. reprint ed. pap. 16.00 (*0-8328-4201-X*); reprint ed. lib. bdg. 26.00 (*0-8328-4200-1*) Higginson Bk Co.

Brackenbury, Linda E. Design of VSLI Systems: A Practical Introduction. (Computer Science Ser.). (Illus.). 164p. (C). 1987. text 90.00 (*0-333-40821-7*); pap. text 30.00 (*0-333-40822-5*) Scholium Intl.

Brackenbury, Mark, jt. auth. see Armitage, John.

Brackenbury, Rosalind. The Beautiful Routes of the West: Poems. 80p. (Orig.). 1996. pap. 9.00 (*1-56474-165-6*) Fithian Pr.

— The Circus at the End of the World: A Novel. LC 97-44995. 160p. 1998. pap. 10.95 (*1-56474-249-0*) Fithian Pr.

***Brackenbury, Rosalind.** Seas Outside the Reef: A Novel. LC 99-50882. 224p. 2000. pap. 14.95 (*1-880284-41-3*, Pub. by J Daniel) SCB Distributors.

***Brackenbury, Rosalind, et al.** Beyond Paradise: More New Fiction from the Florida Keys. 1999. pap. write for info. (*0-7392-0345-2*, PO3519) Morris Pubng.

Brackenbury, Terry. Knitted Clothing Technology. Date not set. pap. 44.95 (*0-8464-4387-2*) Beekman Pubs.

— Knitted Clothing Technology. (Illus.). 208p. 1992. pap. 36.95 (*0-632-02807-6*) Blackwell Sci.

Brackenbury, Wade. Yak Butter & Black Tea: A Journey into Tibet. (Illus.). 252p. 1998. pap. 12.95 (*1-56512-201-1*, 72201) Algonquin Bks.

Brackenreg, John. Albert Namatjira. (C). 1990. 36.00 (*0-9598395-7-7*, Pub. by Boolarong Pubns) St Mut.

***Brackenridge, Betty Page.** Diabetes 101: A Pure & Simple Guide for People Who Use Insulin. 3rd ed. LC 99-158831. (Illus.). 224p. 1998. pap. 12.95 (*1-56561-156-X*) Wiley.

Brackenridge, Betty Page. Diabetes 101: A Pure & Simple Guide for People Who Use Insulin. 3rd ed. 224p. 1998. pap. 12.95 (*0-471-34675-6*) Wiley.

Brackenridge, Betty Page & Rubin, Richard. Sweet Kids. LC 96-20277. 256p. 1996. pap. 14.95 (*0-945448-67-8*, 00678Q, Pub. by Am Diabetes) NTC Contemp Pub Co.

— The Take-Charge Guide to Type I Diabetes. LC 94-17538. (Illus.). 288p. 1996. pap. 16.95 (*0-945448-35-X*, 00359Q, Pub. by Am Diabetes) NTC Contemp Pub Co.

Brackenridge, Douglas. The Presbyterian Church (U. S. A.) Foundation: A Bicentennial History, 1799-1999. LC 98-41835. (Illus.). 200p. 1999. 25.95 (*0-664-50043-9*) Geneva Press.

Brackenridge, Henry M. History of the Western Insurrection in Western Pennsylvania, Commonly Called the Whiskey Insurrection, 1794. LC 72-90167. (Mass Violence in America Ser.). 1978. reprint ed. 22.95 (*0-405-01302-7*) Ayer.

— A Topographical Description of Pensacola & Vicinity in 1821. Rucker, Brian R., ed. (Illus.). 69p. (Orig.). 1991. mass mkt. 7.95 (*1-882695-02-X*) Patagonia Pr.

— Voyage to South America, 2 vols. in 1. LC 70-128425. reprint ed. 62.50 (*0-404-00922-0*) AMS Pr.

Brackenridge, Hugh H. The Battle of Bunker's Hill. (Works of Hugh Henry Brackenridge). 1989. reprint ed. lib. bdg. 79.00 (*0-7812-2044-0*) Rprt Serv.

— The Death of General Montgomery. (Works of Hugh Henry Brackenridge). 1989. reprint ed. lib. bdg. 79.00 (*0-7812-2045-9*) Rprt Serv.

— Law Miscellanies. (Works of Hugh Henry Brackenridge). 1989. reprint ed. lib. bdg. 79.00 (*0-7812-2048-3*) Rprt Serv.

— Law Miscellanies: Containing an Introduction to the Study of the Law. LC 73-37967. (American Law: The Formative Years). 600p. 1972. reprint ed. 39.95 (*0-405-03994-8*) Ayer.

— Modern Chivalry. Leary, Lewis, ed. (Masterworks of Literature Ser.). 1965. pap. 14.95 (*0-8084-0221-8*, M4) NCUP.

— Modern Chivalry. 1988. reprint ed. lib. bdg. 99.00 (*0-317-90870-7*) Rprt Serv.

— Modern Chivalry: Containing the Adventures of Captain John Farrago & Teague O Regan, His Servant. (Works of Hugh Henry Brackenridge). 1989. reprint ed. lib. bdg. 79.00 (*0-7812-2047-5*) Rprt Serv.

— The Rising Glory of America. (Works of Hugh Henry Brackenridge). 1989. reprint ed. lib. bdg. 79.00 (*0-7812-2043-2*) Rprt Serv.

— Six Political Discourses. (Works of Hugh Henry Brackenridge). 1989. reprint ed. lib. bdg. 79.00 (*0-7812-2046-7*) Rprt Serv.

— The Works of Hugh Henry Brackenridge. 1989. reprint ed. lib. bdg. 63.00 (*0-685-27308-3*) Rprt Serv.

Brackenridge, Hugh H. & Freneau, Philip. Father Bombo's Pilgrimage to Mecca, 1770. Bell, Michael D., ed. LC 75-5391. (Illus.). 129p. 1975. 20.00 (*0-87811-020-8*) Princeton Lib.

Brackenridge, J. Bruce. The Key to Newton's Dynamics: The Kepler Problem & the Principia. LC 95-32978. (Illus.). 330p. 1995. 55.00 (*0-520-20065-9*, Pub. by U CA Pr); pap. 22.50 (*0-520-20217-1*, Pub. by U CA Pr) Cal Prin Full Svc.

Brackenridge, R. D. & Elder, W. John, eds. Medical Selection of Life Risks. 4th rev. ed. 922p. 1998. 195.00 (*1-56159-196-3*) Groves Dictionaries.

Brackenridge, R. Douglas. Westminster College of Salt Lake City: From Presbyterian Mission School to Independent College. LC 98-19670. (Illus.). 272p. 1998. 24.95 (*0-87421-250-2*) Utah St U Pr.

Brackenridge, R. Douglas, jt. auth. see Boyd, Lois A.

Brackenridge, Sandra, jt. auth. see Elkins, A. D.

Brackenridge, Sandra S. Because of Flowers & Dancers. (Illus.). 14p. (Orig.). 1994. pap. 5.00 (*0-9603534-7-X*) Vet Practice.

Bracker. Cases in Strategic Management. (C). 1991. pap. text, teacher ed. 6.00 (*0-03-055859-X*) Harcourt Coll Pubs.

Bracker, C., jt. ed. see Bartnicki-Garcia, S.

Bracker, Jeffrey S. Cases in Strategic Management. (C). 1991. text 63.00 (*0-03-055858-1*) Harcourt Coll Pubs.

Bracker, Kai, jt. auth. see Sawodny, Michael.

Brackert, Helmut. Der Fremdgewordene Text. 476p. 1997. 173.35 (*3-11-014940-0*) De Gruyter.

Brackert, Helmut, ed. Minnesang: Mittelhochdeutsche Texte Mit Uebertragung und Anmerkungen. (GEH & GER.). 352p. 1996. pap. 18.00 (*3-596-26485-5*, Pub. by Fischer Tasch) Intl Bk Import.

— Das Nibelungenlied Vol. 1: Mittelhochdeutscher Text mit Uebertragung. 23rd ed. (GEH & GER.). 304p. 1998. pap. 15.25 (*3-596-26038-8*, Pub. by Fischer Tasch) Intl Bk Import.

— Das Nibelungenlied Vol. 2: Mittelhochdeutscher Text mit Uebertragung. 21st ed. (GEH & GER.). 310p. 1997. pap. 15.25 (*3-596-26039-6*, Pub. by Fischer Tasch) Intl Bk Import.

Brackert, Helmut, ed. see Grimm, Jacob W. & Grimm, Wilhelm K.

Brackett, Albert G. History of the United States Cavalry, from the Formation of the Federal Government to the 1st of June 1863. LC 74-133514. (Select Bibliographies Reprint Ser.). 1977. 20.95 (*0-8369-5546-3*) Ayer.

Brackett, Anna C. & Eliot, Ida M. Poetry for Home & School. LC 79-38593. (Granger Index Reprint Ser.). 1977. reprint ed. 21.95 (*0-8369-6325-3*) Ayer.

Brackett, D. W. Holy Terror: Armageddon in Tokyo. (Illus.). 232p. 1996. 24.95 (*0-8348-0353-4*) Weatherhill.

Brackett, David. Interpreting Popular Music. LC 94-43515. 274p. (C). 1996. text 54.95 (*0-521-47337-3*) Cambridge U Pr.

***Brackett, David.** Interpreting Popular Music. 256p. 2000. pap. 18.95 (*0-520-22541-4*) U CA Pr.

Brackett, E. A. Materialized Apparitions. 182p. 1996. reprint ed. spiral bd. 12.00 (*0-7873-0116-7*) Hlth Research.

Brackett, Frederick S., ed. see American Association for the Advancement of Science Staff.

Brackett, Ginger R. Elizabeth Cary: Writer of Conscience. LC 96-21120. (World Writers Ser.). (Illus.). 96p. (YA). (gr. 5 up). 1996. lib. bdg. 18.95 (*1-883846-15-3*) M Reynolds.

Brackett, Hannah J. Poems from Jobe. LC 95-92190. 24p. (J). (gr. 1-3). 1995. pap. write for info. (*0-9646501-0-X*) Paw Pub.

Brackett, Herbert I. Brackett Genealogy: Descendants of Anthony Brackett of Portsmouth & Capt. Richard Brackett of Braintree. (Illus.). 624p. 1988. reprint ed. pap. 93.50 (*0-8328-0303-0*); reprint ed. lib. bdg. 103.50 (*0-8328-0302-2*) Higginson Bk Co.

Brackett, Jeffrey R. The Negro in Maryland. LC 69-18529. (Select Bibliographies Reprint Ser.). 1977. 27.95 (*0-8369-5000-3*) Ayer.

— The Negro in Maryland: A Study of the Institution of Slavery. LC 78-64250. (Johns Hopkins University. Studies in the Social Sciences. Thirtieth Ser. 1912: 6). reprint ed. 27.50 (*0-404-61354-3*) AMS Pr.

— Notes on the Progress of the Colored People of Maryland Since the War. LC 76-170689. (Black Heritage Library Collection). 1977. reprint ed. 20.95 (*0-8369-8879-5*) Ayer.

Brackett, Jim, ed. see Brackett, Neva.

Brackett, John. On the Pilgrim's Way: Christian Stewardship & the Tithe. LC 96-23112. 144p. 1996. pap. 10.95 (*0-8192-1663-1*) Morehouse Pub.

Brackett, John K. Criminal Justice & Crime in Late Renaissance Florence, 1537-1609. (Illus.). 172p. (C). 1992. text 52.95 (*0-521-40405-3*) Cambridge U Pr.

Brackett, John T. The Dominators. (Illus.). 280p. (Orig.). 1992. pap. 14.95 (*0-9633270-3-8*) Marcus Pub.

Brackett, Karen & Manley, Rosie. Beautiful Junk. (J). 1990. pap. 12.99 (*0-8224-0626-8*) Fearon Teacher Aids.

— Beautiful Junk II. 1992. pap. 12.99 (*0-86653-937-9*) Fearon Teacher Aids.

Brackett, Leigh. The Ginger Star. (Orig.). 1984. mass mkt. 2.50 (*0-345-31827-7*, Ballantine) Ballantine Pub Grp.

***Brackett, Leigh.** No Good from a Corpse. (Illus.). 576p. 1999. 35.00 (*0-939767-32-5*) D McMillan.

Brackett, Michael H. Data Sharing Using a Common Data Architecture. 478p. 1994. pap. 39.95 (*0-471-30993-1*) Wiley.

— The Data Warehouse Challenge: Taming Data Chaos. LC 96-14608. 579p. 1996. pap. 59.99 (*0-471-12744-2*) Wiley.

Brackett, Neva. Best Gourmet Recipes: From the Chefs of Five Loaves Deli & Bakery. Brackett, Jim, ed. (Illus.). 180p. 1997. pap. 16.95 (*0-9675957-0-3*) Best Gourmet.

Brackett, Peter, jt. auth. see Sedra, Adel S.

Brackett, Shirley. Become a More Positive Person: Three Practical Skills to Improve Your Self Esteem. (Illus.). 72p. 1991. pap. text 10.00 (*0-9628250-0-X*) Relationship Trg.

Brackett, Virginia R. Classic Love & Romance Literature: An Encyclopedia of Works, Characters, Authors & Themes. LC 99-21350. 406p. (YA). (gr. 9 up). 1999. lib. bdg. 75.00 (*0-87436-955-X*) ABC-CLIO.

— Early Women Writers: Voices from the Margins. (Illus.). 140p. (YA). (gr. 9 up). 2000. lib. bdg. 25.00 (*0-208-02410-7*, Linnet Bks) Shoe String.

***Brackett, Virginia R.** Jeff Bezos. (Latinos in the Limelight Ser.). (Illus.). 2000. 17.95 (*0-7910-6104-3*) Chelsea Hse.

***Brackett, William.** Eight Hundred Years of the History of the Name of Brackett, the Keepers of the Hounds: The Keeper of the Hounds. (Illus.). 240p. 1999. 46.00 (*0-8328-9902-X*) Higginson Bk Co.

***Brackey, Jolene.** Creating Moments of Joy for the Person with Alzheimers or Dementia: A Journal for Caregivers. 2000. pap. 14.95 (*1-55753-212-5*) Purdue U Pr.

Brackin, A. J. Clocks: Chronicling Time. LC 91-16713. (Encyclopedia of Discovery & Invention Ser.). (Illus.). 96p. (J). (gr. 5-8). 1991. lib. bdg. 23.70 (*1-56006-208-8*) Lucent Bks.

Brackin, Ivan L. & Fitzgerald, William. All about Darts. rev. ed. (Illus.). 176p. 1986. pap. 12.95 (*0-8092-4984-7*, 498470, Contemporary Bks) NTC Contemp Pub Co.

***Brackin, Ron.** Sweet Persecution: A 30-Day Devotional with Reflections from the Persecuted Church. LC 99-6559. 108p. (Orig.). 1999. pap. 6.99 (*0-7642-2285-6*) Bethany Hse.

Brackley. Group Work in Professional Nursing. 1998. pap. text. write for info. (*0-7216-4184-9*, W B Saunders Co) Harcrt Hlth Sci Grp.

An Asterisk (*) at the beginning of an entry indicates that the title is appearing for the first time.

Brackley, Dean. People Power: Together We Can Change Things. 1989. pap. 1.50 (*0-8091-5203-7*) Paulist Pr.
Brackman, Arnold C. Communist Collapse in Indonesia. LC 70-77399. 1969. 6.95 (*0-393-05377-6*) Norton.
Brackman, Arnold C. The Dream of Troy. LC 74-7078. xi, 246 p. 1974. write for info. (*0-88405-081-5*) Mason & Lipscomb.
Brackman, Arnold C. Indonesian Communism: A History. LC 75-25486. 326p. 1976. reprint ed. lib. bdg. 69.50 (*0-8371-8419-3*, BRIC, Greenwood Pr) Greenwood.
— The Last Emperor. 384p. 1991. pap. 10.95 (*0-88184-700-3*) Carroll & Graf.
Brackman, Barbara. An Encyclopedia of Applique: An Illustrated, Numerical Index to Traditional & Modern Patterns. LC 93-34626. (Illus.). 256p. 1993. pap. 32.95 (*0-939009-75-7*, EPM) Howell Pr VA.
— Kansas Trivia. LC 97-28165. 192p. 1997. pap. 6.95 (*1-55853-539-X*) Rutledge Hill Pr.
— Patterns of Progress: Quilts in the Machine Age. (Illus.). 128p. 1997. 35.00 (*0-614-28310-8*) Autry Mus Wstrn.
— Quilts from the Civil War: Nine Projects, Historical Notes, Diary Entries. Aneloski, Liz & Roberts, Diana, eds. LC 97-12181. (Illus.). 128p. (Orig.). 1997. pap. 25.95 (*1-57120-033-9*, 10157) C & T Pub.
Brackman, Barbara, compiled by. Encyclopedia of Pieced Quilt Patterns. LC 93-7669. 1993. 34.95 (*0-89145-815-8*, 3468, Am Quilters Soc) Collector Bks.
Brackman, Barbara & Dwigans, Cathy, eds. Backyard Visionaries: Grassroots Art in the Midwest. LC 98-16447. (Illus.). 224p. 1998. 39.95 (*0-7006-0904-0*) U Pr of KS.
Brackman, Barbara & Edmonds, Chris W. Influences: Traditional & Contemporary Quilts. LC 83-51460. (Illus.), 43p. 1983. pap. 12.95 (*0-685-57446-6*) Spencer Muse Art.
Brackman, Barbara & Gene Autry Museum of Western Heritage Staff. Patterns of Progress: Quilts in the Machine Age. LC 97-13375. 1997. pap. write for info. (*1-882880-04-8*) Autry Mus Wstrn.
— Patterns of Progress: Quilts in the Machine Age. LC 97-13375. (Illus.). 128p. 1998. pap. 25.00 (*1-882880-03-X*) Autry Mus Wstrn.
Brackman, Barbara, et al. Kansas Quilts & Quilters. LC 92-43108. (Illus.). 216p. 1993. 40.00 (*0-7006-0584-3*); pap. 22.50 (*0-7006-0585-1*) U Pr of KS.
Brackman, Barbara, jt. auth. see Waldvogel, Merikay.
***Brackman, Barbara Ann.** Civil War Women: Their Quilts, Their Roles & Activities for Re-Enactors. Aneloski, Liz & MacFarland, Sara, eds. LC 00-8239. (Illus.). 128p. 2000. pap. 25.95 (*1-57120-104-1*, Pub. by C & T Pub) Watsn-Guptill.
Brackman, Harold. Ministry of Lies: The Truth Behind the Nation of Islam's "The Secret Relationship Between Blacks & Jews" LC 94-7173. (Illus.). 160p. 1994. pap. 10.00 (*1-56858-016-9*) FWEW.
— Mirror of Conflict: The Black Press & Major Issues of Jewish Concern. (Simon Wiesenthal Center Special Reports). 40p. (Orig.). 1988. pap. 10.00 (*0-943058-07-4*) S Wiesenthal Ctr.
Brackman, Henrietta. The Perfect Portfolio. (Illus.). 144p. 1984. pap. 19.95 (*0-8174-5401-2*, Amphoto) Watsn-Guptill.
***Brackman, Roman.** The Secret File of Joseph Stalin: A Hidden Life. (Illus.). 450p. 2000. 49.50 (*0-7146-5050-1*, Pub. by F Cass Pubs) Intl Spec Bk.
Brackmann, Albertus, contrib. by. Regesta Pontificum Romanorum Ivbente Regai Societate Gottingensi Congessit Pavlvs Fridolinvs Kehr Vol. I: Provincia Salisburgensis. (GER.). 412p. 1960. write for info. (*3-296-20801-1*, Pub. by Weidmann) Lubrecht & Cramer.
— Regesta Pontificum Romanorum Ivbente Regai Societate Gottingensi Congessit Pavlvs Fridolinvs Kehr Vol. II, Pt. I: Provincia Maguntinensis. 260p. 1960. write for info. (*3-296-20802-X*, Pub. by Weidmann) Lubrecht & Cramer.
— Regesta Pontificum Romanorum Ivbente Regai Societate Gottingensi Congessit Pavlvs Fridolinvs Kehr Vol. II, Pt. II: Provincia Maguntinensis. (GER.). 320p. 1960. write for info. (*3-296-20803-8*, Pub. by Weidmann) Lubrecht & Cramer.
— Regesta Pontificum Romanorum Ivbente Regai Societate Gottingensi Congessit Pavlvs Fridolinvs Kehr Vol. III, Pt. III: Provincia Maguntinensis. (GER.). 328p. 1960. write for info. (*3-296-20804-6*, Pub. by Weidmann) Lubrecht & Cramer.
Brackmann, Derald E., ed. Neurological Surgery of the Ear & Skull Base. LC 82-5414. (Illus.). 428p. reprint ed. pap. 132.70 (*0-7837-7121-5*, 204695000004) Bks Demand.
Brackmann, Derald E., et al, eds. Otologic Surgery. LC 93-40738. (Illus.). 1994. text 173.00 (*0-7216-6639-6*, W B Saunders Co) Harcrt Hlth Sci Grp.
Brackmann, Derald E., jt. ed. see Jackler, Robert K.
***Brackmann, H. H. & Mariani, G., eds.** Immune Tolerance in Haemophilia & the Treatment of Haemophiliacs with an Inhibitor: 2nd Workshop on Immune Tolerance, Bonn-Konigswinter, August 1997. (Vox Sanguinis Ser.: Vol. 77, Suppl. 1). (Illus.). iv, 100p. 1999. pap. 34.00 (*3-8055-6995-5*) S Karger.
Brackmann, H. H., jt. ed. see Mariani, G.
***Brackner, Joey.** Tributaries: Journal of the Alabama Folklife Association. 1999. pap. 12.95 (*1-881320-60-X*, Black Belt) Black Belt Communs.
Brackner, Joey, jt. auth. see Willett, E. Henry.
Brackney, Charles P. Calculating Child Support in Colorado. 32p. 1999. pap. 9.95 (*1-883726-43-3*) Bradford Pub.
— Colorado Child Support Handbook: The Parents' Guide to Modification & Collection. LC 99-169168. (Illus.). 220p. 1998. pap. 21.95 (*1-883726-10-7*) Bradford Pub.
— Debt Collection: Using Garnishments & Liens in Colorado. 32p. 1999. pap. 9.95 (*1-883726-44-1*) Bradford Pub.
— Filing for Divorce in Colorado (with Children) 40p. 1999. pap. 12.95 (*1-883726-38-7*) Bradford Pub.
— Filing for Divorce in Colorado (Without Children) 32p. 1999. pap. 9.95 (*1-883726-45-X*) Bradford Pub.
— Winning Big in Colorado Small Claims Court: How to Sue & Collect. LC 96-145747. 190p. 1996. pap. 17.50 (*1-883726-04-2*) Bradford Pub.
Brackney, David J. Baja California. rev. ed. Miller, Kristine, ed. 335p. 1998. pap. 14.95 (*1-56413-446-6*) Auto Club.
***Brackney, Susan M.** The Lost Soul Companion: Comfort & Constructive Advice for Struggling Actors, Musicians, Artists, Writers & Other Free Spirits. LC 99-91690. (Illus.). 160p. 2000. 10.00 (*0-9676323-0-7*) Puckitt Pr.
Brackney, William H. The Baptists. LC 87-15047. 176p. 1994. pap. 19.95 (*0-275-94859-5*, Praeger Pubs) Greenwood.
— Baptists, 2. LC 87-15047. (Denominations in America Ser.: No. 2). 349p. 1988. lib. bdg. 59.95 (*0-313-23822-7*, BBA/, Greenwood Pr) Greenwood.
— Bridging Cultures & Hemispheres: The Legacy of Archibald Reekie & Canadian Baptists in Bolivia. LC 97-11344. 160p. 1997. 20.00 (*1-57312-164-9*) Smyth & Helwys.
— Christian Voluntarism in Britain & North America: A Bibliography & Critical Assessment, 35. LC 94-47140. (Bibliographies & Indexes in Religious Studies: Vol. 35). 328p. 1995. lib. bdg. 89.50 (*0-313-28421-0*, Greenwood Pr) Greenwood.
— Historical Dictionary of the Baptists. LC 99-21023. (Historical Dictionaries of Religions, Philosophies & Movements Ser.: No. 25). 552p. 1999. 69.50 (*0-8108-3652-1*) Scarecrow.
Brackney, William H. & Burke, Ruby J., eds. Faith, Life & Witness: The Papers of the Study & Research Division of the Baptist World Alliance 1986-1990. 452p. (Orig.). 1990. pap. write for info. (*0-9625634-0-4*) Samford U Pr.
Brackney, William H., ed. see White, B. R.
Bracks, Lean'Tin L. Writings on Black Women of the Diaspora: History, Language & Identity. LC 97-25403. (Croscurrents in African American History Ser.). 152p. 1997. text 39.00 (*0-8153-2734-X*) Garland.
Brackstone, Lee, ed. First Pressings: An Annual Faber & Faber Journal. 64p. 1999. pap. 9.00 (*0-571-19517-2*) Faber & Faber.
Brackway, Edith. San Jose Reflections. 1977. 13.00 (*0-912314-18-4*); pap. 4.90 (*0-912314-17-6*) Academy Santa Clara.
Brackx, F., et al, eds. Clifford Algebras & Their Applications in Mathematical Physics: Proceedings of the Third Conference Held at Deinze, Belgium, 1993. LC 93-31536. (Fundamental Theories of Physics Ser.). 424p. (C). 1993. text 264.50 (*0-7923-2347-5*) Kluwer Academic.
Brackx, F. & Constales, D. Computer Algebra with LISP & REDUCE: An Introduction to Computer-Aided Pure Mathematics. 304p. 1991. text 155.50 (*0-7923-1441-7*) Kluwer Academic.
Braconi, Joan M., et al. California Workers Rights: A Manual of Job Rights, Protections & Remedies. 2nd ed. LC 94-49150. 1995. pap. write for info. (*0-937817-08-2*) CLRE UCAL Berk.
Bracton, Henry De. De Legibus et Consuetudinibus Angliae, 4. Woodbine, G. E., ed. 1942. 100.00 (*0-686-51370-3*) Elliots Bks.
Bracy, Acquanet, jt. auth. see Hodge, Evelyn.
Bracy, Ihsan. Ibo Landing: A Offering of Short Stories by Ihsan Bracy. (Illus.). 170p. 1998. pap. 12.95 (*1-887276-10-6*) Cool Grove Pub.
— IBO Landing: An Offering of Short Stories by Ihsan Bracy. (Illus.). 154p. 1998. 22.95 (*1-887276-11-4*) Cool Grove Pub.
Bracy, Isabel. Immigrants in Madison County, New York. LC 90-4019. 120p. (Orig.). 1990. pap. 10.00 (*1-55787-066-7*, NY27030) Hrt of the Lakes.
— One Hundred Fifty-Seventh New York Volunteer (Infantry) Reigment, 1862-1865: Madison & Cortland Counties. LC 91-14111. 126p. (Orig.). 1991. pap. 12.00 (*1-55787-080-2*, NY27032) Hrt of the Lakes.
Bracy, Isabel, ed. Revolutionary War Veterans of Madison County, New York. 130p. (Orig.). 1987. pap. 10.00 (*0-932334-96-2*, NY27028) Hrt of the Lakes.
Bracy, Isabel, ed. see Tuttle, William H.
Bracy, Jane & McClintock, Marian. Read to Succeed. 2nd ed. (C). 1980. pap. text, teacher ed. 21.95 (*0-07-007036-9*) McGraw.
Bracy, John. Ba Gua: Advanced Hidden Knowledge in the Taoist Internal Martial Art. LC 98-7085. (Illus.). 180p. 1998. pap. 14.95 (*1-55643-276-3*) North Atlantic.
Bracy, Norma. Grandmother's Scrapbook: Meet Great Grandmother at 99 Years Old. (Bee Bks.). (Illus.). 20p. (Orig.). (J). (gr. k-12). 1999. pap. write for info. (*0-614-29582-3*) Book Binder.
Bracy, Norma M. Light Bulbs. (Illus.). 22p. (J). (ps-12). 1984. pap. text 2.50 (*0-915783-01-0*) Book Binder.
— Poe & Pog. (Illus.). 22p. (J). (ps-12). 1986. pap. text 2.50 (*0-915783-02-9*) Book Binder.
— Rule of Gold. (Illus.). 20p. (J). (ps-12). 1983. pap. text 2.50 (*0-915783-00-2*) Book Binder.
— Salt. (Illus.). 32p. (J). (ps-12). 1986. pap. text 2.50 (*0-915783-03-7*) Book Binder.
Bracy, Norma N. Ping Pong Balls. (Illus.). (J). (ps-12). 1988. pap. text 2.50 (*0-915783-06-1*) Book Binder.
— The Tool Box. (Illus.). 35p. (J). (ps-12). 1987. pap. text 2.50 (*0-915783-04-5*) Book Binder.
B'Racz, Emoke, tr. see Ladik, Katalin.
***Braczyk, Hans Joachim, et al.** Multimedia & Regional Economic Restructing. LC 98-51215. 448p. 1999. 115.00 (*0-415-19857-7*) Routledge.
Brad, J., jt. auth. see Adamzewski.
Brada, Josef C., ed. Quantitative & Analytical Studies in East-West Economic Relations. LC 76-10986. (Studies in East European & Soviet Planning, Development, & Trade: No. 24). (Illus.). 1976. pap. text 6.00 (*0-89249-015-2*) Intl Development.
Brada, Josef C., et al, eds. Economic Adjustment & Reform in Eastern Europe & the Soviet Union: Essays in Honor of Franklyn D. Holzman. LC 88-21130. (Duke Press Policy Studies). 500p. (C). 1988. text 79.95 (*0-8223-0852-5*) Duke.
Brada, Josef C. & Dobozi, Istvan, eds. The Hungarian Economy in the 1980s. LC 88-2943. (Industrial Development & the Social Fabric Ser.: Vol. 9). 277p. 1988. 73.25 (*0-89232-936-X*) Jai Pr.
— Money, Incentives & Efficiency in the Hungarian Economic Reform. LC 89-24210. 200p. (C). (gr 13). 1990. text 85.95 (*0-87332-566-4*) M E Sharpe.
Brada, Josef C. & Singh, Inderjit, eds. Corporate Governance in Central Eastern Europe: Case Studies of Firms in Transition. LC 98-8545. (Microeconomics of Transition Economies Ser.). 352p. (C). 1998. text 120.95 (*0-7656-0274-1*) M E Sharpe.
Brada, Josef C., et al. From Afloat & Firms Adrift: Hungarian Industry & the Economic Transition. LC 93-48903. (The Microeconomics of Transition Economies Ser.). 128p. (gr. 13). 1994. pap. text 63.95 (*1-56324-320-2*) M E Sharpe.
Brada, Stephen A., jt. auth. see Yamamoto, Joshua S.
Bradac, Fran. Slovene-Latin Dictionary: Slovensko-Latinski Slovar. (LAT & SLV.). 347p. 1986. 65.00 (*0-8288-1138-5*, M2039) Fr & Eur.
Bradac, James J., ed. Message Effects in Communication Science. LC 89-5928. (Sage Annual Reviews of Communication Research Ser.: Vol. 17). 320p. 1989. reprint ed. pap. 99.20 (*0-608-02766-9*, 206383200007) Bks Demand.
— Message Effects in Communication Science: Contemporary Approaches. (Annual Reviews of Communication Research Ser.: Vol. 17). 320p. (C). 1989. text 58.00 (*0-8039-3224-3*); pap. text 26.00 (*0-8039-3225-1*) Sage.
Bradac, James J., jt. auth. see Ng Sik Hung.
Bradach, Jeffrey L. Franchise Organizations. LC 97-28868. 256p. 1998. 29.95 (*0-87584-832-X*) Harvard Busn.
Bradach, Wilfred, jt. auth. see Johnson, Thomas M.
Bradamante, F., et al, eds. Antiproton-Nucleon & Antiproton - Nucleus Interactions. LC 90-6767. (Ettore Majorana International Science Series, Life Sciences: Vol. 47). (Illus.). 340p. 1990. 89.50 (*0-306-43571-2*, Plenum Trade) Perseus Pubng.
***Bradard, Laura, ed.** From Test Tube to Patient: Improving Health Through Human Drugs. (Illus.). 99p. 2000. pap. text 25.00 (*0-7881-8890-9*) DIANE Pub.
Bradbeer, James. The Yin of Teaching. LC 98-19134. xi, 145p. 1998. 44.00 (*0-8077-3760-7*) Tchrs Coll.
***Bradbeer, Wilma.** The Correspondence of William James, Vol. 8. McDermott, John J. et al, eds. Vol. 8. 832p. 2000. 80.00 (*0-8139-1926-6*) U Pr of Va.
Bradberry, James. The Seventh Sacrament, Vol. 1. 1995. mass mkt. 4.99 (*0-312-95636-3*) St Martin.
Bradbery, Angela & Lally, Rosemarie. Investigating Sexual Harassment: A Practical Guide to Resolving Complaints. 236p. 1998. pap. write for info. (*0-9670470-1-3*) Thompson Pub Grp.
Bradbery, Jean & Service, Alastair. Standing Stones of Europe: A Guide to the Great Megalithic Monuments. (Illus.). 288p. 1996. pap. 15.95 (*0-297-83545-9*, Pub. by Weidenfeld & Nicolson) Trafalgar.
Bradbrook, A. J. & Croft, C. E. Commercial Tenancy Law in Australia. 488p. 1990. boxed set 111.00 (*0-409-30061-6*, Austral, MICHIE) LEXIS Pub.
Bradbrook, A. J. & Neave, M. A. Easements & Restrive Covenants in Australia. 1981. 90.00 (*0-409-30048-9*, AT, MICHIE) LEXIS Pub.
Bradbrook, Adrian, et al. Australian Real Property Law. lxx, 800p. 1991. pap. 89.00 (*0-455-20993-6*, Pub. by LawBk Co) Gaunt.
Bradbrook, Adrian J., et al. Australian Property Law: Cases & Materials. 2nd ed. 1400p. 1996. 130.00 (*0-455-21377-1*, Pub. by LawBk Co); pap. 95.00 (*0-455-21378-X*, Pub. by LawBk Co) Gaunt.
— Australian Real Property Law. lxx, 800p. 1991. 125.00 (*0-455-20992-8*, Pub. by LawBk Co) Gaunt.
— Australian Real Property Law. 2nd ed. 1004p. 1997. 124.00 (*0-455-21448-4*, Pub. by LawBk Co); pap. 84.00 (*0-455-21449-2*, Pub. by LawBk Co) Gaunt.
Bradbrook, B. R. Karel Capek: In Pursuit of Truth, Tolerance, & Trust. LC 97-38088. 1997. pap. 35.00 (*1-898723-02-8*, Pub. by Sussex Acad Pr) Intl Spec Bk.
Bradbrook, Frank W. Jane Austen & Her Predecessors. LC 66-10245. 187p. reprint ed. pap. 53.30 (*0-608-13319-1*, 2025577) Bks Demand.
Bradbrook, M. C., jt. auth. see Coghill, Nevill.
Bradbrook, Muriel C. Shakespeare: The Poet in His World. LC 78-7611. 272p. 1980. pap. text 22.00 (*0-231-04649-9*) Col U Pr.
— Shakespeare in His Context: The Constellated Globe: The Collected Papers of Muriel Bradbrook, IV. 207p. (C). 1989. lib. bdg. 54.50 (*0-389-20877-9*) B&N Imports.
— Themes & Conventions of Elizabethan Tragedy. 2nd ed. (History of Elizabethan Drama Ser.). 280p. 1980. pap. text 25.95 (*0-521-29695-1*) Cambridge U Pr.
Bradburd, D. C., ed. The Book of Contemporary Myth. (Illus.). 64p. (Orig.). 1988. pap. 5.50 (*0-317-62280-7*) Caitlin Pr.
Bradburd, Daniel. Being There: The Necessity of Fieldwork. LC 97-38155. (Ethnographic Inquiry Ser.). 224p. 1998. text 35.00 (*1-56098-777-4*); pap. text 15.95 (*1-56098-753-7*) Smithsonian.
Bradburd, Daniel J. Ambiguous Relations: Kin, Class & Conflict among Komachi Pastoralists. LC 89-39784. (Series in Ethnographic Inquiry). (Illus.). 256p. 1990. text 37.00 (*0-87474-306-0*) Smithsonian.
Bradburn, Elizabeth. Margaret McMillan: Portrait of a Pioneer. 272p. 1989. 69.50 (*0-415-01254-6*) Routledge.
Bradburn, Frances B. Output Measures for School Library Media Programs. LC 98-45557. 125p. 1999. pap. 49.95 (*1-55570-326-7*) Neal-Schuman.
Bradburn, Frances B., ed. see American Library Association Staff.
Bradburn, J., tr. see De La Hodde, Lucien.
Bradburn-Langer, Rebecca. Harvest of Righteousness. LC 98-18699. (Illus.). 88p. 1998. pap. 10.95 (*0-664-50028-5*) Geneva Press.
Bradburn, Leslie. Masters of the Nyingma Lineage. unabridged ed. Tulku, Tarthang, ed. LC 95-46695. (Crystal Mirror Ser.: Vol. 11). (Illus.). 500p. (Orig.). 1996. pap. 25.00 (*0-89800-275-3*) Dharma Pub.
Bradburn, Niceta C., jt. ed. see Schreiner, Richard L.
Bradburn, Norman M. Structure of Psychological Well-Being. LC 67-27388. (Monographs in Social Research: No. 15). (Illus.). 1969. 15.00 (*0-202-25029-6*) Natl Opinion Res.
Bradburn, Norman M. & Caplovitz, David. Reports on Happiness: A Pilot Study of Behavior Related to Mental Health. LC 64-15605. (Monographs in Social Research: No. 3). 1965. 15.00 (*0-202-30020-X*) Natl Opinion Res.
Bradburn, Norman M. & Sudman, Seymour. Improving Interview Method & Questionnaire Design. LC 79-83569. (Jossey-Bass Social & Behavioral Science Ser.). 232p. reprint ed. pap. 72.00 (*0-8357-4970-3*, 203790300009) Bks Demand.
— Polls & Surveys: Understanding What They Tell Us. LC 88-42778. (Social & Behavioral Science Ser.). 269p. 1988. 35.95 (*1-55542-098-2*) Jossey-Bass.
Bradburn, Norman M, et al. Racial Integration in American Neighborhoods: A Comparative Study. (Report Ser.: No. IIIB). 1970. 15.00 (*0-932132-08-1*) Natl Opinion Res.
Bradburn, Norman M., jt. auth. see Sudman, Seymour.
Bradburne, Jeremy, et al. Butterworths International Taxation of Financial Instruments & Transactions. 2nd ed. 1994. write for info. (*0-406-00365-3*, BITFISET, MICHIE) LEXIS Pub.
Bradbury. Audiences & Intentions: A Book of Arguments. 3rd ed. 605p. (C). 1997. teacher ed., suppl. ed. write for info. (*0-205-26694-0*) Allyn.
— Santa Claus Has a Busy Night. (Christmas Titles Ser.: No. S808-6). (Illus.). (J). 3.95 (*0-7214-5077-6*, Ladybrd) Penguin Putnam.
Bradbury, jt. auth. see Reeves, Diane L.
***Bradbury, Alex.** Belize: The Bradt Travel Guide. 3rd ed. (Country Guides Ser.). (Illus.). 2000. pap. 18.95 (*1-84162-008-4*, Pub. by Bradt Pubns) Globe Pequot.
Bradbury, Alex. Guide to Belize. 2nd ed. LC 96-18726. (Illus.). 325p. 1996. pap. 15.95 (*0-7627-0014-9*, Pub. by Bradt Pubns) Globe Pequot.
— Guide to Brazil. 2nd rev. ed. LC 97-13873. (Bradt Guides Ser.). (Illus.). 256p. (Orig.). 1997. pap. 17.95 (*1-898323-59-3*, Pub. by Bradt Pubns) Globe Pequot.
Bradbury, Alford G. & Hallock, E. Story. A Chronology of Florida Post Offices. 2nd ed. 100p. 1993. reprint ed. pap. 10.00 (*0-9630788-1-X*) Sewalls Pt.
Bradbury, Andrew. NLP for Business Success. (Better Management Skills Ser.). 1997. pap. 12.95 (*0-7494-2151-7*) Kogan Page Ltd.
Bradbury, Anna R. History of the City of Hudson, with Biographical Sketches of Henry Hudson & Robert Fulton. (Illus.). 223p. 1997. reprint ed. lib. bdg. 29.50 (*0-8328-6155-3*) Higginson Bk Co.
Bradbury, Bettina. Canadian Family History: Selected Readings. (C). 1992. pap. text 29.95 (*0-7730-5194-5*) Addison-Wesley.
Bradbury, Brad. Fanrenheit 451. 1998. pap. 6.50 (*84-01-42282-5*) Lectorum Pubns.
Bradbury, Carl W., jt. auth. see Burke, William J.
Bradbury, Carol. Favorite Recipes of Northwest Single Men. 102p. 1992. pap. text 14.95 (*0-9632822-0-4*) Spectrum WA.
Bradbury, Catherine, jt. auth. see Williams, Octavia.
Bradbury, Cecil E. Ten Years in the High Canadian Arctic. 76p. 1994. pap. 6.95 (*0-920884-34-2*) Creative Bk Pub.
Bradbury, Derek & Office for Official Publications of the European Communities. Cereals in Europe: Statistical Systems for Measuring Area, Production & Yield. LC 97-121023. (Agriculture, Forestry & Fisheries Ser.). v, 54 p. 1995. write for info. (*92-827-4710-7*, Pub. by Comm Europ Commun) Bernan Associates.
Bradbury, Dianne, ed. see Landgraf, Sherry.
Bradbury, Dominic, jt. auth. see Waller, Martin.
Bradbury, E. Morton & Nicolini, Claudio, eds. NMR in the Life Sciences. LC 86-9404. (NATO ASI Series A, Life Sciences: Vol. 107). 246p. 1986. 65.00 (*0-306-42279-4*, Plenum Trade) Perseus Pubng.
***Bradbury, E. Morton & Pongor, Sandor, eds.** Structural Biology & Functional Genomics. LC 99-15351. (NATO ASI Ser.: Vol. 71). 313p. 1999. 149.00 (*0-7923-5781-7*) Kluwer Academic.
Bradbury, Eileen. Counselling People with Disfigurement. (Communication & Counselling in Health Care Ser.). 138p. (Orig.). 1996. pap. text 28.00 (*1-85433-176-0*, 1760) P H Brookes.
Bradbury, Ellen, jt. ed. see Merrill, Christopher.
Bradbury, Frances. American Hooked Rug Patterns. (International Design Library). (Illus.). 48p. (Orig.). 1986. pap. 5.95 (*0-88045-084-3*) Stemmer Hse.

— Antique Lace Patterns. (International Design Library). (Illus.). 48p. 1985. pap. 5.95 (0-88045-070-3) Stemmer Hse.

Bradbury, Frances M. Early American Crewel Design. (International Design Library). (Illus.). 48p. (Orig.). 1987. pap. 5.95 (0-88045-092-4) Stemmer Hse.

— English Crewel Designs: Sixteenth to Eighteenth Centuries. (International Design Library). (Illus.). 56p. (Orig.). 1982. pap. 5.95 (0-88045-015-0) Stemmer Hse.

— Faience Designs. (International Design Library). (Illus.). 48p. (Orig.). 1984. pap. 5.95 (0-88045-056-8) Stemmer Hse.

Bradbury, Frank. Banjo Method. 128p. 1967. spiral bd. 11.95 (0-87166-495-X, 93238) Mel Bay.

Bradbury, H. W., jt. auth. see Bullivant, Roger A.

Bradbury-Haehl, Nora, jt. auth. see Theisen, Michael.

Bradbury, I. The Biosphere. 213p. (C). 1991. pap. 275.00 (81-7089-154-X, Pub. by Intl Bk Distr) St Mut.

Bradbury, Ian. The Biosphere. 224p. 1992. text 72.95 (1-85293-037-3, Pub. by P P Pubs); pap. text 30.95 (1-85293-038-1, Pub. by P P Pubs) CRC Pr.

Bradbury, Ian K. The Biosphere. LC 98-36447. 266p. 1999. pap. 44.95 (0-471-98549-X) Wiley.

Bradbury, J. F. Guide to Plant Pathogenic Bacteria. 332p. (C). 1996. pap. text 40.00 (0-85198-557-2) C A B Intl.

— Guide to Plant Pathogenic Bacteria. 332p. (C). 1996. text 60.00 (0-00-000097-3, Pub. by CAB Intntl) OUP.

B

*__Bradbury, J. F. & Saddler, G. S.__ A Guide to Plant Pathogenic Bacteria. 2nd ed. (CABI Publishing Ser.). 500p. 2000. text 110.00 (0-85199-199-8) OUP.

Bradbury, J. H. & Holloway, W. D. Chemistry of Tropical Root Crops: Significance for Nutrition & Agriculture in the Pacific. 201p. (Orig.). 1988. pap. 137.00 (0-949511-61-7) St Mut.

Bradbury, J. P. & Dean, W. E., eds. Elk Lake, Minnesota: Evidence for Rapid Climate Change in the North Central United States. (Special Papers: No. 276). 1993. pap. 31.00 (0-8137-2276-4) Geol Soc.

Bradbury, J. S., et al, eds. Turbulent Shear Flows 2. (Illus.). 480p. 1980. 94.95 (0-387-10067-9) Spr-Verlag.

Bradbury, Jack W. & Vehrencamp, Sandra L. Principles of Animal Communication. LC 97-44014. (Illus.). 780p. (C). 1998. text 69.95 (0-87893-100-7) Sinauer Assocs.

Bradbury, James Edward. Somerset. (Images of America Ser.). 128p. 1996. pap. 16.99 (0-7524-0277-3) Arcadia Publng.

Bradbury, Jim. The Battle of Hastings. LC 98-159748. (Military History Ser.). (Illus.). 256p. 1998. 39.95 (0-7509-1291-X, Pub. by Sutton Pub Ltd) Intl Pubs Mktg.

— The Medieval Archer. (Illus.). 208p. (Orig.). 1999. reprint ed. pap. 29.95 (0-85115-675-4) Boydell & Brewer.

— The Medieval Siege. (Illus.). 378p. (C). 1997. reprint ed. pap. 29.95 (0-85115-357-7) Boydell & Brewer.

— The Medieval Siege. (Illus.). 378p. (C). 1998. reprint ed. 55.00 (0-85115-312-7) Boydell & Brewer.

— Philip Augustus: King of France, 1180-1223. LC 97-45566. (C). 1998. pap. 73.13 (0-582-06058-3, Pub. by Addison-Wesley) Longman.

— Stephen & Matilda: The Civil War of 1139-53. (Illus.). 218p. 1998. pap. 21.95 (0-7509-1872-1, Pub. by Sutton Pub Ltd) Intl Pubs Mktg.

Bradbury, Jim & Miller, Beverly. Lake Fly Fishing Guide. LC 95-111066. 146p. 1994. pap. 9.95 (1-878175-72-6) F Amato Pubns.

Bradbury, John. Travels in the Interiors of America in the Years 1809, 1810, & 1811. LC 85-24615. 320p. reprint ed. pap. 99.20 (0-7837-4650-4, 204437400002) Bks Demand.

Bradbury, John M. The Fugitives. 1958. pap. 16.95 (0-8084-0139-4) NCUP.

Bradbury, John P. Diatom Stratigraphy & Human Settlement in Minnesota. LC 75-21066. (Geological Society of America, Special Paper: No. 171). 79p. reprint ed. pap. 30.00 (0-608-13938-6, 202373900033) Bks Demand.

Bradbury, Jonathan & Mawson, John, eds. British Regionalism & Devolution: The Challenges of State Reform & Europen Integration. LC 95-41376. (Regional Policy & Development Ser.: Vol. 14). 320p. 1996. 29.95 (1-85302-370-1, Pub. by Jessica Kingsley) Taylor & Francis.

Bradbury, Judy. Doggone Lemonade Stand! LC 98-169365. (Illus.). 48p. (J). (ps-2). 1998. pap. 10.95 (0-07-007042-3) McGraw.

— Double Bubble Trouble! LC 97-42998. (Illus.). 45p. (J). (ps-2). 1998. 10.95 (0-07-007040-7) McGraw.

— One Carton of Oops! LC 96-37547. (Illus.). 46p. (J). (ps-2). 1997. 10.95 (0-07-007039-3) McGraw.

— A Peck of Hecklers! (Illus.). 48p. (J). (ps-2). 1997. text 14.95 (0-07-007043-1) McGraw.

— A Rip-Roaring High-Flying Mother's Day Fair! LC 97-44385. (Illus.). 48p. (J). (gr. k-2). 1997. 10.95 (0-07-007041-5) McGraw.

Bradbury, Katharine L. & Downs, Anthony. Energy Costs, Urban Development, & Housing. LC 83-46033. 296p. 1984. 34.95 (0-8157-1050-X); pap. 14.95 (0-8157-1049-6) Brookings.

Bradbury, Katharine L. & Downs, Anthony, eds. Do Housing Allowances Work? LC 81-6689. (Studies in Social Experimentation). 419p. 1981. 34.95 (0-8157-1052-6); pap. 14.95 (0-8157-1051-8) Brookings.

Bradbury, Katherine J., et al. Urban Decline & the Future of American Cities. LC 82-70888. 309p. 1982. 36.95 (0-8157-1054-2); pap. 16.95 (0-8157-1053-4) Brookings.

Bradbury, Ken. Around the World with Freida Marie Crump. large type ed. Crowe, Robert L., ed. 90p. 1997. pap. 9.95 (0-9644681-2-3) Creative Ideas.

Bradbury, L. J., et al, eds. Turbulent Shear Flows 4. (Illus.). 370p. 1985. 122.00 (0-387-13744-0) Spr-Verlag.

Bradbury, L. J., et al. Turbulent Shear Flows 3: University of California, Selected Papers, 1981. (Illus.). 321p. 1983. 103.95 (0-387-11817-9) Spr-Verlag.

Bradbury, M. J., ed. see Genet, Jean C.

Bradbury, M. L. & Gilbert, James B., eds. Transforming Faith: The Sacred & Secular in Modern American History, 23. LC 89-7478. (Contributions to the Study of Religion Ser.: No. 23). 205p. 1989. 55.00 (0-313-25707-8, BYG, Greenwood Pr) Greenwood.

*__Bradbury, Malcolm.__ The Atlas of Literature. LC 98-87011. (Illus.). 352p. 1998. text 35.00 (1-55670-879-3) Stewart Tabori & Chang.

— E. M. Forster A Passage to India. LC 71-515718. (Casebook Ser.). 252p. 1970. write for info. (0-333-01458-8) Macmillan.

Bradbury, Malcolm. Eating People Is Wrong. 248p. 1986. reprint ed. pap. 6.95 (0-89733-189-3) Academy Chi Pubs.

— The History Man. (Fiction Ser.). 240p. 1985. pap. 10.00 (0-14-007630-1, Penguin Bks) Viking Penguin.

— The Modern British Novel. (Orig.). 1999. pap. 25.00 (0-670-85583-9) Viking Penguin.

— Modernism. 688p. 1978. pap. 17.95 (0-14-013832-3, Viking) Viking Penguin.

— No, Not Bloomsbury. 384p. 1988. text 46.00 (0-231-06726-7) Col U Pr.

Bradbury, Malcolm, ed. The Penguin Book of Modern British Short Stories. 448p. 1989. pap. 14.95 (0-14-006306-4, Penguin Bks) Viking Penguin.

Bradbury, Malcolm & Palmer, David, eds. The Contemporary English Novel. LC 79-20447. (Stratford-upon-Avon Studies: No. 18). 214p. (C). 1979. pap. 19.50 (0-8419-0571-1) Holmes & Meier.

— Shakespearean Tragedy. LC 84-81206. (Stratford-upon-Avon Studies: No. 20). 192p. 1984. pap. text 17.50 (0-8419-0982-2) Holmes & Meier.

— Shakespearean Tragedy. LC 84-81206. (Stratford-upon-Avon Studies: No. 20). 192p. 1986. 39.50 (0-8419-0981-4) Holmes & Meier.

*__Bradbury, Malcolm & Temperley, Howard.__ Introduction to American Studies. 3rd ed. LC 98-13563. 384p. (Orig.). (C). 1998. pap. 33.53 (0-582-30738-4) Addson-Wesley Educ.

Bradbury, Malcolm & Temperly, Howard, eds. Introduction American Studies. 2nd ed. (Illus.). 416p. (C). 1989. pap. text 48.00 (0-582-01526-X, 78021) Addson-Wesley Educ.

Bradbury, Malcolm, jt. auth. see Ruland, Richard.

Bradbury, Malcolm, ed. see Crane, Stephen.

Bradbury, Malcolm, ed. see Hawthorne, Nathaniel.

Bradbury, Malcolm, ed. see Irving, Washington.

Bradbury, Malcolm, ed. see James, Henry.

Bradbury, Malcolm, ed. see Twain, Mark, pseud.

Bradbury, Mark. The Somali Conflict: Prospects for Peace:, Oxfam Research Discussion Papers. LC 95-129507. (Oxfam Research Discussion Papers). 150p. (C). 1994. pap. 15.95 (0-85598-271-3, Pub. by Oxfam Pub) Stylus Pub VA.

Bradbury, Mark, jt. auth. see Adams, Mark.

*__Bradbury, Mary.__ Representations of Death: Social Psychological Perspective. LC 99-31070. 1999. text. write for info. (0-415-15021-3) Routledge.

— Representations of Death: Social Psychological Perspective. (Illus.). 240p. (C). 1999. pap. 25.99 (0-415-15022-1) Routledge.

Bradbury, Michael W. The Concept of a Blood-Brain Barrier. LC 78-16764. (Wiley-Interscience Publicatios). 471p. reprint ed. pap. 146.10 (0-7837-3217-1, 204323500007) Bks Demand.

Bradbury, Nancy M. Audiences & Intentions: A Book of Arguments. 3rd ed. LC 96-48203. 605p. 1997. pap. text 39.00 (0-205-26174-4) Allyn.

Bradbury, Nancy M. Writing Aloud: Storytelling in Late Medieval England. LC 97-33922. 248p. 1998. 34.95 (0-252-02403-6) U of Ill Pr.

*__Bradbury, Nick, et al.__ Homesite 4.5 for Dummies. (For Dummies Ser.). 420p. 2000. pap. 24.99 incl. cd-rom (0-7645-0707-9) IDG Bks.

Bradbury, Nicola, ed. & intro. see Dickens, Charles.

Bradbury, Nicola, ed. & intro. see James, Henry.

Bradbury, Pamela Z. Boola's Secrets. (Illus.). 26p. (J). (ps-1). 1988. pap., student ed. 2.95 (0-671-66867-6) Litle Simon.

Bradbury, Parnell. Adventures in Healing. 1969. 22.50 (0-89979-000-3) British Am Bks.

*__Bradbury Peebles, Anne.__ Peebles, Ante 1600-1962. 191p. 1999. 37.50 (0-8328-9891-0); pap. 27.50 (0-8328-9892-9) Higginson Bk Co.

Bradbury, Phil. Border Clip Art for Libraries. xi, 126p. 1989. pap. text, student ed. 26.00 (0-87287-744-2) Libs Unl.

— Button Art: Reading & Libraries. 120p. 1993. pap. 27.50 (0-87287-974-7) Libs Unl.

— Holiday & Seasonal Border Clip Art. (Illus.). 130p. 1990. pap. text 18.00 (0-87287-781-7) Teacher Ideas Pr.

Bradbury, Phyllis C., jt. ed. see Hausmann, Klaus.

Bradbury, R. Acanthaster & the Coral Reef: A Theoretical Perspective: Proceedings of a Workshop Held at the Australian Institute of Marine Science, Townsville, August 6-7, 1988. (Lecture Notes in Biomathematics Ser.: Vol. 88). vi, 339p. 1991. 54.95 (0-387-53501-2) Spr-Verlag.

Bradbury, R. E. The Benin Kingdom & the Edo-Speaking Peoples of South-Western Nigeria. LC DT0515.B7. (Ethnographic Survey of Africa: Western Africa Ser.: Pt. 13). 215p. reprint ed. pap. 66.70 (0-8357-7130-X, 205538300017) Bks Demand.

— Benin Studies. (International African Institute Ser.). (Illus.). 1976. pap. 19.95 (0-19-724198-0) OUP.

— Benin Studies. Morton-Williams, Peter, ed. LC 77-6401. 321p. reprint ed. pap. 99.60 (0-8357-6947-X, 203900600009) Bks Demand.

Bradbury, R. H., jt. auth. see Antonelli, P. L.

Bradbury, Ray. Ahmed & the Oblivion Machines: A Fable. LC 98-22746. (Illus.). 64p. 1998. 14.00 (0-380-97704-4, Avon Bks) Morrow Avon.

— Christus Apollo. (Illus.). 17p. 1998. 350.00 (0-938237-06-3) Gold Stein Pr.

— Classic Stories 1. (Grand Master Editions Ser.). 1990. 12.09 (0-606-03157-X, Pub. by Turtleback) Demco.

— Dandelion Wine. 256p. (J). (gr. 6 up). 1985. mass mkt. 6.50 (0-553-27753-7) Bantam.

— Dandelion Wine. 1988. 5.50 (0-87129-554-7, D43) Dramatic Pub.

— Dandelion Wine. LC 98-93914. 288p. 1999. 15.00 (0-380-97726-5, Avon Bks) Morrow Avon.

— Dandelion Wine. (Grand Master Editions Ser.). 1976. 11.09 (0-606-00520-X, Pub. by Turtleback) Demco.

*__Bradbury, Ray.__ Dandelion Wine. large type ed. (Science Fiction Ser.). 1999. 30.00 (0-7838-8817-1, G K Hall & Co) Mac Lib Ref.

Bradbury, Ray. Dark Carnival. 1994. reprint ed. lib. bdg. 29.95 (1-56849-257-X) Buccaneer Bks.

— Death Has Lost Its Charm for Me. (Illus.). 40p. 1987. 25.00 (0-935716-41-6) Lord John.

— Death Is a Lonely Business. LC 98-52425. 240p. 1999. pap. 12.00 (0-380-78965-5, Avon Bks) Morrow Avon.

— Driving Blind. LC 97-4378. 261p. 1997. mass mkt. 23.00 (0-380-97381-2, Avon Bks) Morrow Avon.

— Driving Blind. LC 97-4378. 272p. 1998. mass mkt. 6.50 (0-380-78960-4, Avon Bks) Morrow Avon.

— Fahrenheit 451. LC 93-10885. 19.95 (0-8488-0147-4) Amereon Ltd.

— Fahrenheit 451. LC 93-10885. 192p. 1987. mass mkt. 6.99 (0-345-34296-8) Ballantine Pub Grp.

— Fahrenheit 451. LC 96-96738. 179p. 1996. pap. 10.00 (0-345-41001-7, Del Rey) Ballantine Pub Grp.

— Fahrenheit 451. LC 93-10885. 192p. 1993. 20.50 (0-671-87036-X, PPAU0433) S&S Trade.

— Fahrenheit 451. 1953. 11.09 (0-606-00628-1, Pub. by Turtleback) Demco.

— Fahrenheit 451. deluxe limited ed. LC 93-10885. 192p. 1993. 100.00 (0-671-87229-X) S&S Trade.

— Fahrenheit 451. large type ed. LC 97-36289. (Perennial Ser.). 227p. 1997. lib. bdg. 23.95 (0-7838-8313-7, G K Hall Lrg Type) Mac Lib Ref.

— Fahrenheit 451. 1990. reprint ed. lib. bdg. 27.95 (0-89968-484-X) Buccaneer Bks.

— Fahrenheit 451, Playscript. LC 93-10885. 1986. pap. 5.50 (0-87129-310-2, F35) Dramatic Pub.

Bradbury, Ray. Fahrenheit Four Fifty-One, Set. unabridged ed. 1995. 39.95 incl. audio (1-56054-959-9, SAB 013, Sterling Audio) Chivers N Amer.

Bradbury, Ray. From the Dust Returned. 288p. 1997. 23.00 (0-380-97382-0, Avon Bks) Morrow Avon.

— Golden Apples of Sun & O. LC 97-93844. 352p. 1997. pap. 12.00 (0-380-73039-1, Avon Bks) Morrow Avon.

— Golden Apples of the Sun. LC 76-135242. (Illus.). 250p. 1971. reprint ed. lib. bdg. 37.50 (0-8371-5160-0, BRGA, Greenwood Pr) Greenwood.

— The Golden Apples of the Sun - R Is for Rocket. (Classics Ser.: No. 1). 368p. 1990. mass mkt. 6.99 (0-553-28637-4, Spectra) Bantam.

— Green Shadows, White Whale. 1998. pap. 10.00 (0-380-78966-3, Avon Bks) Morrow Avon.

— The Halloween Tree. 20.95 (0-8488-0432-5) Amereon Ltd.

— The Halloween Tree. 1994. lib. bdg. 24.95 (1-56849-450-5) Buccaneer Bks.

*__Bradbury, Ray.__ Halloween Tree. 1999. pap. 4.99 (0-375-80301-7, Pub. by Knopf Bks Yng Read) Random.

Bradbury, Ray. I Sing Body Electric. LC 98-92424. 322p. 1998. pap. 10.00 (0-380-78962-0, Avon Bks) Morrow Avon.

— I Sing the Body Electric. 1994. lib. bdg. 27.95 (1-56849-451-3) Buccaneer Bks.

— The Illustrated Man. (Illus.). 192p. 1983. mass mkt. 6.50 (0-553-27449-X, Bantam Classics) Bantam.

— The Illustrated Man. LC 97-93228. (Illus.). 320p. 1997. 15.00 (0-380-97384-7, Avon Bks) Morrow Avon.

— The Illustrated Man. 1967. 11.09 (0-606-00848-9, Pub. by Turtleback) Demco.

Bradbury, Ray. Illustrated Man. abr. ed. 1976. audio 10.50 (0-89845-212-0, CP 1479) HarperAudio.

Bradbury, Ray. The Illustrated Man. large type ed. LC 98-48528. Date not set. 30.00 (0-7838-8466-4, G K Hall Lrg Type) Mac Lib Ref.

— The Illustrated Man. limited ed. (Classics Revisited Ser.). 1996. boxed set 65.00 (1-887368-06-X) Gauntlet.

— The Illustrated Man. 1991. reprint ed. lib. bdg. 25.95 (1-56849-084-4) Buccaneer Bks.

— Kaleidoscope. 22.95 (0-89190-886-2) Amereon Ltd.

— Kaleidoscope. 1994. lib. bdg. 18.95 (1-56849-455-6) Buccaneer Bks.

— Kaleidoscope. 1975. 3.50 (0-87129-571-7, K20) Dramatic Pub.

— Long after Midnight. 1994. lib. bdg. 24.95 (1-56849-432-7) Buccaneer Bks.

— Magic & Madness in the Library: Protagonists among the Stacks. Graeber, Eric, ed. & intro. by. 160p. 1998. pap. 19.00 (0-913559-36-9) Birch Brook Pr.

— Magic & Madness in the Library: Protagonists among the Stacks. aut. limited num. ed. Graeber, Eric, ed. & intro. by. 160p. 1998. 60.00 (0-913559-37-7) Birch Brook Pr.

— The Martian Chronicles. 22.95 (0-88411-862-2) Amereon Ltd.

— The Martian Chronicles. 192p. 1984. mass mkt. 6.50 (0-553-27822-3, Bantam Classics) Bantam.

— The Martian Chronicles. 1986. pap. 5.50 (0-87129-211-4, M64) Dramatic Pub.

— The Martian Chronicles. LC 99-24658. 1999. 24.95 (0-7838-8635-7) Mac Lib Ref.

— The Martian Chronicles. 288p. 1997. 16.00 (0-380-97383-9, Avon Bks) Morrow Avon.

— The Martian Chronicles. 1950. 11.09 (0-606-01042-4, Pub. by Turtleback) Demco.

— The Martian Chronicles. 1991. reprint ed. lib. bdg. 25.95 (1-56849-085-2) Buccaneer Bks.

— Medicine for Melancholy. LC 97-94680. 320p. 1998. pap. 10.00 (0-380-73086-3, Avon Bks) Morrow Avon.

— Medicine for Melancholy: And Other Stories. 1998. 15.10 (0-606-13602-9, Pub. by Turtleback) Demco.

— The October Country. 1985. mass mkt. 5.99 (0-345-32448-X, Del Rey) Ballantine Pub Grp.

*__Bradbury, Ray.__ The October Country. LC 99-94881. (Illus.). 352p. 1999. 16.00 (0-380-97387-1, Avon Bks) Morrow Avon.

Bradbury, Ray. The October Country. aut. limited ed. (Illus.). 337p. 1997. 65.00 (1-887368-15-9) Gauntlet.

— One Timeless Spring. 24.95 (0-89190-345-3) Amereon Ltd.

— Quicker Than the Eye. 272p. 1996. mass mkt. 22.00 (0-380-97380-4, Avon Bks) Morrow Avon.

— Quicker Than the Eye. LC 96-20481. 304p. 1997. mass mkt. 5.99 (0-380-78959-0, Avon Bks) Morrow Avon.

— Quicker Than the Eye. large type ed. LC 96-39257. (Basic Ser.). 347p. 1997. lib. bdg. 26.95 (0-7862-0945-3) Thorndike Pr.

— Ray Bradbury Chronicles, Vol. 4. 1993. pap. 9.95 (0-685-63494-9, Spectra) Bantam.

— Selected from Dark They Were, & Golden-Eyed. abr. ed. (Writers' Voices Ser.). 64p. (Orig.). 1991. pap. text 3.95 (0-929631-24-2, Signal Hill) New Readers.

— La Solitude Est Cercueil de Verre. (FRE.). 371p. 1991. pap. 12.95 (0-7859-2168-0, 2070383946) Fr & Eur.

— Something Wicked This Way Comes. 224p. 1983. mass mkt. 5.50 (0-553-28032-5, Bantam Classics) Bantam.

*__Bradbury, Ray.__ Something Wicked This Way Comes. 320p. 1999. 15.00 (0-380-97727-3, Avon Bks) Morrow Avon.

— Something Wicked This Way Comes. 1963. 10.60 (0-606-04927-4, Pub. by Turtleback) Demco.

Bradbury, Ray. Something Wicked This Way Comes. aut. limited ed. (Illus.). 230p. 1999. 65.00 (1-887368-23-X) Gauntlet.

*__Bradbury, Ray.__ Something Wicked This Way Comes. large type ed. LC 99-54620. 312p. 2000. lib. bdg. 26.95 (1-58547-020-1) Ctr Point Pubg.

Bradbury, Ray. Something Wicked This Way Comes. 304p. 1998. reprint ed. mass mkt. 6.50 (0-380-72940-7, Avon Bks) Morrow Avon.

— Stories. 1980. pap. 39.50 (0-679-44698-2) Random.

— The Stories of Ray Bradbury. LC 80-7655. 928p. 1980. 40.00 (0-394-51335-5) Knopf.

*__Bradbury, Ray.__ Switch on the Night. (Illus.). 40p. (J). (gr. k-2). 2000. lib. bdg. 16.99 (0-375-90608-8, Pub. by Knopf Bks Yng Read) Random.

— Switch on the Night. (Illus.). 40p. (J). (ps-2). 2000. 14.95 (0-375-80608-3, Pub. by Knopf Bks Yng Read) Random.

Bradbury, Ray. The Toynbee Convector. 1988. 17.95 (0-318-32850-X) NAL.

— Twice Twenty-Two. 1994. lib. bdg. 19.95 (1-56849-430-0) Buccaneer Bks.

Bradbury, Ray. The Veldt. 56p. 1972. pap. 3.50 (1-58342-028-2, V19) Dramatic Pub.

Bradbury, Ray. Vintage Bradbury. 1990. pap. 13.00 (0-679-72946-1) Vin Bks.

— Zen in the Art of Writing. 176p. 1992. mass mkt. 6.50 (0-553-29634-5) Bantam.

— Zen in the Art of Writing: Essays on Creativity. 3rd ed. 176p. 1993. pap. 8.95 (1-877741-09-4) J Odell Editions.

Bradbury, Ray, et al. The Best of Whispers. limited ed. Schiff, Stuart D., ed. (Illus.). 471p. 1994. boxed set 65.00 (0-614-12964-8) Whispers.

— Thirteen for Corwin: Estimates of Radio's Foremost Writer-Director-Producer. LC 92-38802. 112p. 1992. pap. 7.95 (0-942637-89-5) Barricade Bks.

Bradbury, Ray, jt. auth. see Center for Learning Network Staff.

Bradbury, Richard, ed. see Barnes, William & Hardy, Thomas.

*__Bradbury, Robert C.__ Twentieth Century United States Miniature Books. (Illus.). 500p. 1999. 75.00 (0-9675186-0-1) Microbiblio.

Bradbury, S., jt. auth. see Bracegirdle, B.

Bradbury, Samuel, ed. Powder Metallurgy Equipment Manual. 3rd ed. LC 76-52333. 200p. 1986. 10.00 (0-918404-68-1) Metal Powder.

Bradbury, Samuel, ed. see American Society for Metals Staff.

Bradbury, Savile & Bracegirdle, Brian. Introduction to Light Microscopy. 2nd ed. LC 97-22880. (Microscopy Handbooks Ser.). (Illus.). 144p. 1997. pap. 32.95 (0-387-91515-X) Spr-Verlag.

Bradbury, Saville. The Microscope. 1968. 129.00 (0-08-012848-3, Pub. by Pergamon Repr) Franklin.

Bradbury, Scott, tr. see Severus of Minorca Staff.

Bradbury, Ted C. Theoretical Mechanics. LC 80-23957. 656p. 1981. reprint ed. text 58.50 (0-89874-235-8) Krieger.

Bradbury, Thomas E. Scraggly's New Home. Goyette, Ron & Funk, Nancy C., trs. (Scraggly, The Stowaway Cat Ser.). (Illus.). 32p. (Orig.). (J). (gr. k-5). 1987. pap. text. write for info. (0-9618945-0-4) Tern Pubns.

Bradbury, Thomas N., ed. The Developmental Course of Marital Dysfunction. LC 97-29630. (Studies in Social & Emotional Development). (Illus.). 375p. (C). 1998. text 59.95 (0-521-45190-6) Cambridge U Pr.

Bradbury, Thomas N., jt. ed. see Fincham, Frank D.

An Asterisk (*) at the beginning of an entry indicates that the title is appearing for the first time.

Bradbury, Tom. Dilworth: The First 100 Years. (Illus.). 144p. (C). 1992. 25.00 (*0-9633643-0-8*) McMillan & Assocs.

***Bradbury, Tom.** Meteorology & Flight: Pilot's Guide to Weather. 3rd ed. (Illus.). 192p. 2000. pap. 24.95 (*0-7136-4226-2*, Pub. by A & C Blk) Midpt Trade.

Bradbury, William B., jt. auth. see Warner, Anna.

Bradbury, William C. Mass Behaviour in Battle & Captivity: The Communist Soldier in the Korean War. Meyers, Samuel M., ed. LC 68-16705. 407p. reprint ed. pap. 126.20 (*0-608-30735-1*, 202003400016) Bks Demand.

Bradby, D., ed. Vinaver: Theatre de Chambre. (French Texts Ser.). (FRE.). 161p. 1995. pap. 18.95 (*1-85399-433-2*, Pub. by Brist Class Pr) Focus Pub-R Pullins.

Bradby, David. The Theater of Michel Vinaver. (Theater: Theory - Text - Performance Ser.). 184p. 1993. text 42.50 (*0-472-10326-1*, 10326) U of Mich Pr.

— The Theatre of Roger Planchon. (Theatre in Focus Ser.). (Illus.). 120p. 1984. pap. write for info. incl. sl. (*0-85964-153-8*) Chadwyck-Healey.

Bradby, David, jt. auth. see Anderson, Rachel.

Bradby, Edward, ed. University Outside Europe. LC 71-107684. (Essay Index Reprint Ser.). 1977. 23.95 (*0-8369-1548-8*) Ayer.

Bradby, G. About Shakespeare & His Plays. LC 76-51373. (Studies in Shakespeare: No. 24). 1977. lib. bdg. 75.00 (*0-8383-2121-6*) M S G Haskell Hse.

— Short Studies in Shakespeare. LC 76-30728. (Studies in Shakespeare: No. 24). 1977. lib. bdg. 75.00 (*0-8383-2169-0*) M S G Haskell Hse.

Bradby, G. F. Problems of Hamlet. (Studies in Shakespeare: No. 24). (C). 1970. reprint ed. pap. 75.00 (*0-8383-0006-5*) M S G Haskell Hse.

Bradby, Godfrey F. Brontes & Other Essays. LC 67-30176. (Essay Index Reprint Ser.). 1977. 18.95 (*0-8369-0240-8*) Ayer.

Bradby, Hannah, ed. Defining Violence: Understanding the Causes & Effects of Violence. LC 96-83234. 160p. 1996. 63.95 (*1-85972-108-7*, Pub. by Avebry) Ashgate Pub Co.

***Bradby, Marie.** Momma, Where Are You From? LC 99-23068. (Illus.). 32p. (J). (ps-2). 2000. 16.95 (*0-531-30105-2*); 17.99 (*0-531-33105-9*) Orchard Bks Watts.

Bradby, Marie. More Than Anything Else. LC 94-48804. (Illus.). 32p. (J). (gr. k-3). 1996. 15.95 (*0-531-09464-2*); lib. bdg. 16.99 (*0-531-08764-6*) Orchard Bks Watts.

Braddick, Bill, ed. Nature of Management Case Studies. 128p. 1990. pap. 125.00 (*0-85297-147-8*, Pub. by Chartered Bank) St Mut.

Braddick, M. J. Parliamentary Taxation in Seventeenth Century England: Local Administration & Response. (Royal Historical Society Studies in History: Vol. 70). (Illus.). 365p. (C). 1995. 75.00 (*0-86193-278-1*, Royal Historical Soc) Boydell & Brewer.

Braddick, Michael J. The Nerves of State: Taxation & the Financing of the English State, 1558-1714. (New Frontiers in History Ser.). 256p. 1996. text 79.95 (*0-7190-3871-5*); text 27.95 (*0-7190-3872-3*, Pub. by Manchester Univ Pr) St Martin.

***Braddick, Michael J.** State Formation in Early Modern England, c. 1550-1700. 464p. 2001. write for info. (*0-521-78346-1*); pap. write for info. (*0-521-78955-9*) Cambridge U Pr.

Braddick, O. J. & Sleigh, A. C., eds. Physical & Biological Processing of Images: London, England, 1982, Proceedings. (Information Sciences Ser.: Vol. 11). (Illus.). 403p. 1983. 78.95 (*0-387-12108-0*) Spr-Verlag.

Braddick, W. A. Management for Bankers. 2nd ed. 390p. 1991. pap. 32.00 (*0-406-00283-5*, U.K., MICHIE) LEXIS Pub.

Braddock, Betty & Covalt, Jeanie. Dodge City: Cowboy Capital; Beautiful Bibulous Babylon; Queen of the Cowtowns; Wicked Little City; The Delectable Burg. LC 82-82026. (Illus.). 50p. (Orig.). 1988. reprint ed. pap. 5.00 (*1-882404-03-3*) KS Herit Ctr.

Braddock, Bill & Braddock, Marge, eds. 392nd Bomb Group. LC 97-60393. (Illus.). 184p. 1997. 52.50 (*1-56311-369-4*) Turner Pub KY.

Braddock, Carolyn J. Body Voices: Using the Power of Breath, Sound & Movement to Heal & Create New Boundaries. LC 94-67842. (Illus.). 288p. 1995. pap. 19.95 (*1-879290-05-7*) PageMill Pr.

Braddock Communications Staff. The Executive Guide to Washington D. C. Stern, J. L. et al, eds. (Illus.). vi, 120p. 1998. pap. 8.95 (*0-931147-06-9*) Braddock Comns.

***Braddock Communications Staff.** Small Business Financial Resource Guide: Sources of Assistance for Small & Growing Companies. Arnold, Paul A., ed. vi, 151p. 1999. pap. 18.95 (*0-931147-07-7*) Braddock Comns.

Braddock, David & Mitchell, Dale. Residential Services & Developmental Disabilities in the U.S. A National Survey of Staff Compensation, Turnover & Related Issues. (Orig.). (C). 1992. pap. 38.95 (*0-940898-28-4*) Am Assn Mental.

Braddock, David L. The State of the States in Developmental Disabilities. 5th ed. LC 97-47452. 1998. write for info. (*0-940898-50-0*) Am Assn Mental.

Braddock, David L., jt. auth. see Schalock, Robert L.

Braddock, David L., ed. see Blanck, Peter D.

Braddock, Hanovi. Ashes of the Sun. (Magic: The Gathering Ser.). 304p. 1996. mass mkt. 5.50 (*0-06-105649-9*) HarpC.

Braddock, J. G., Sr. Wooden Ships - Iron Men: Four Master Mariners of the Colonial South. LC 96-90295. (Illus.). 304p. 1996. 24.95 (*0-9652705-0-5*) VJB Pr.

Braddock, John C. Derivitives Demystified: Using Structured Financial Products, Vol. 603. LC 96-44904. (Financial Engineering Ser.). 320p. 1997. 60.00 (*0-471-14633-1*) Wiley.

Braddock, Judith, tr. see Quetel, Claude.

Braddock, Kathy Mayer, jt. auth. see Masters, Tory Baker.

Braddock, Marge, jt. ed. see Braddock, Bill.

Braddock, Sarah E. & O'Mahony, Marie. Techno Textiles. LC 97-60247. (Illus.). 192p. 1998. 50.00 (*0-500-23740-9*, Pub. by Thames Hudson) Norton.

***Braddock, Sarah E. & O'Mahony, Marie.** Techno Textiles: Revolutionary Fabrics for Fashion & Design. LC 97-60247. (Illus.). 192p. 1999. reprint ed. pap. 29.95 (*0-500-28096-7*, Pub. by Thames Hudson) Norton.

Braddock, Suzanne, et al. Straight Talk about Breast Cancer: From Diagnosis to Recovery. Clark, Melanie M., ed. LC 94-72529. 144p. (Orig.). 1994. pap. 12.95 (*1-886039-21-6*) Addicus Bks.

Braddock, Theda & Huppman, L. Reed. Wetlands: An Introduction to Ecology, the Law & Permitting. 179p. 1995. pap. text 69.00 (*0-86587-467-0*) Gov Insts.

***Braddok, Robert J.** Handbook of Citrus By-Products Technology. LC 99-10821. 247p. 1999. 89.95 (*0-471-19024-1*) Wiley.

Braddom, Randall L. Physical Medicine & Rehabilitation. LC 95-11493. 1168p. 1995. text 180.00 (*0-7216-5243-3*, W B Saunders Co) Harcrt Hlth Sci Grp.

Braddom, Randall L. Physical Medicine & Rehabilitation. 2nd ed. 1275p. Date not set. text. write for info. (*0-7216-8076-3*, W B Saunders Co) Harcrt Hlth Sci Grp.

Braddom, Randall L., jt. ed. see Buschbacher, Ralph.

Braddon, Derek & Foster, Deborah. Privatization: Social Science Themes & Perspectives. 328p. 1996. text 84.95 (*1-85521-674-4*, Pub. by Dartmth Pub) Ashgate Pub Co.

Braddon, Kathryn L., et al. Math Through Children's Literature: Making the NCTM Standards Come Alive. LC 91-34286. xviii, 218p. 1993. pap. text 23.50 (*0-87287-932-1*) Teacher Ideas Pr.

Braddon, Lawrence. EU/USA Strategic Trade. 59.95 (*1-84014-336-3*) Ashgate Pub Co.

Braddon, M. E. Eleanor's Victory. LC 96-181173. (Pocket Classics Ser.). 416p. 1996. pap. 12.95 (*0-7509-1118-2*, Pub. by Sutton Pub Ltd) Intl Pubs Mktg.

— The Fatal Three. LC 98-152595. (Pocket Classics). xiv, 322p. 1997. pap. 12.95 (*0-7509-1664-8*, Pub. by Sutton Pub Ltd) Intl Pubs Mktg.

Braddon, Mary Elizabeth. Aurora Floyd. Nemesvari, Richard & Surridge, Lisa, eds. (Literary Texts Ser.). 635p. 1998. pap. 15.95 (*1-55111-123-3*) Broadview Pr.

— Aurora Floyd. Edwards, P. D., ed. (World's Classics Ser.). 500p. 1996. pap. 12.95 (*0-19-282402-3*) OUP.

***Braddon, Mary Elizabeth.** Aurora Floyd. (World Classics Ser.). 500p. 1999. pap. 12.95 (*0-19-283727-3*) OUP.

— The Cold Embrace & Other Ghost Stories. Dalby, Richard, ed. xxii, 290p. 2000. 42.50 (*1-55310-004-2*) Ash-Tree.

Braddon, Mary Elizabeth. The Doctor's Wife. Pykett, Lyn, ed. LC 98-6755. (Oxford World's Classics Ser.). 464p. 1999. pap. 10.95 (*0-19-283301-4*) OUP.

— John Marchmont's Legacy. Page, Norman & Sasaki, Toru, eds. (Oxford World's Classics Ser.). 536p. 1999. pap. 12.95 (*0-19-283321-9*) OUP.

— Lady Audley's Secret. 496p. 1998. pap. 9.95 (*0-19-283520-3*) OUP.

— Lady Audley's Secret. 512p. 1998. pap. 10.95 (*0-14-043584-0*) Viking Penguin.

— Lady Audley's Secret. (Illus.). 286p. 1974. reprint ed. pap. 8.95 (*0-486-23011-2*) Dover.

— Vixen. LC 93-33711. (Pocket Classics Ser.). 1993. pap. 12.95 (*0-7509-0445-3*, Pub. by Sutton Pub Ltd) Intl Pubs Mktg.

Braddon-Mitchell, David. The Philosophy of Mind & Cognition. LC 95-53332. (Illus.). 320p. (C). 1996. 60.95 (*0-631-19167-4*); pap. 26.95 (*0-631-19168-2*) Blackwell Pubs.

Braddon, Russell. The Naked Island. large type ed. 455p. 1982. 27.99 (*0-7089-8024-4*, Charnwood) Ulverscroft.

— The Thirteenth Trick. LC 73-665. 168p. 1973. 5.95 (*0-393-08375-6*) Norton.

Braddy, Nella, ed. Standard Book of British & American Verse: Preface by Christopher Morley. LC 72-38594. (Granger Index Reprint Ser.). 1977. reprint ed. 37.95 (*0-8369-6326-1*) Ayer.

Brade, et al, eds. Endotoxin in Health & Disease. LC 99-29165. (Illus.). 968p. 1999. text 225.00 (*0-8247-1944-1*) Dekker.

Brade, W. P., et al, eds. Ifosfamide in Tumor Therapy. (Beitraege Zur Onkologie, Contributions to Oncology Ser.: Vol. 26). (Illus.). x, 462p. 1987. 95.00 (*3-8055-4647-5*) S Karger.

Bradebrook, Bohuslava R. Karel Capek: In Pursuit of Truth, Tolerance & Trust. LC 97-38088. (Illus.). 256p. 1998. 65.00 (*1-898723-85-0*, Pub. by Sussex Acad Pr) Intl Spec Bk.

Bradeen, Donald W. Inscriptions, the Funerary Monuments. LC 74-75953. (Athenian Agora Ser.: Vol. 17). (Illus.). xi, 240p. 1974. 40.00 (*0-87661-217-6*) Am Sch Athens.

Brademas, John, et al. Science, Technology, & Government for a Changing World: The Concluding Reports of the Carnegie Commission on Science, Technology, & Government. (Illus.). 96p. (Orig.). 1993. pap. write for info. (*1-881054-11-X*) Carnegie Comm Sci.

Braden. Beyond Borders. 1999. per. 17.95 (*0-02-079251-4*) Macmillan.

— Calculus with Analytic Geometry, Mathematica Problems Manual. 4th ed. 180p. 1992. pap. 31.95 (*0-471-53969-4*) Wiley.

— Engaging Geopolitics. 159p. (C). 1999. pap. 40.00 (*0-582-03565-1*) Longman.

— Getting the Message Across. LC 96-76869. (C). 1996. pap. text 38.76 (*0-395-71623-3*) HM.

Braden, Anne. The Wall Between. rev. ed. LC 99-6193. (Illus.). 376p. 1999. 40.00 (*1-57233-060-0*, Pub. by U of Tenn Pr) U Ch Pr.

— The Wall Between. 2nd rev. ed. LC 99-6193. (Illus.). 376p. 1999. pap. 19.95 (*1-57233-061-9*) U of Tenn Pr.

Braden, Carrie J., jt. auth. see Sidani, Souraya.

Braden, Charles S. Christian Science Today: Power, Policy, Practice. LC 58-11399. 464p. reprint ed. pap. 143.90 (*0-8357-8846-6*, 203341300086) Bks Demand.

— Religious Aspects of the Conquest of Mexico. LC 74-181914. reprint ed. 54.50 (*0-404-00925-5*) AMS Pr.

— Spirits in Rebellion: The Rise & Development of New Thought. LC 63-13245. 584p. 1987. reprint ed. pap. 16.95 (*0-87074-025-3*) SMU Press.

Braden, Charles S., ed. Varieties of American Religion. LC 76-156616. (Essay Index Reprint Ser.). 1977. reprint ed. 17.95 (*0-8369-2307-3*) Ayer.

Braden, Donna R. & Henry Ford Museum & Greenfield Village Staff. Leisure & Entertainment in America LC 88-80580. 367p. 1988. write for info. (*0-933728-32-8*) Henry Ford Mus.

Braden, George D. The Search for Objectivity in Constitutional Law. (Reprint Series in Social Sciences). (C). 1993. reprint ed. pap. text 5.00 (*0-8290-3147-2*, PS-31) Irvington.

Braden, Gordon. The Classics & English Renaissance Poetry: Three Case Studies. LC 77-10888. (Yale Studies in English: No. 187). 319p. reprint ed. pap. 98.90 (*0-8357-8693-5*, 203367800087) Bks Demand.

— Petrarchan Love & the Continental Renaissance. LC 98-50952. 208p. 1999. 25.00 (*0-300-07621-5*) Yale U Pr.

Braden, Gordon, jt. auth. see Kerrigan, William.

Braden, Gregg. Awakening to Zero Point: The Collective Initiation. 2nd rev. ed. (Illus.). 248p. 1997. pap. 17.95 (*1-889071-09-9*) Radio Bookstore.

***Braden, Gregg.** Isaiah Effect: Decoding Our Future Through the Lost Science of Prophecy, Time & Miracles. LC 99-49249. (Illus.). 288p. 2000. 23.00 (*0-609-60534-8*) Harmony Bks.

Braden, Gregg. Walking Between the Worlds: The Science of Compassion. (Illus.). 248p. 1997. pap. 17.95 (*1-889071-05-6*) Radio Bookstore.

Braden, Gregg S. Awakening to Zero Point: The Collective Initiation. 277p. 1995. pap. 14.95 (*0-9648990-4-3*) Sacred Spaces.

Braden, J. B. & Kolstad, C. D., eds. Measuring the Demand for Environmental Quality. (Contributions to Economic Analysis Ser.: No. 198). xii,370p. 1991. 128.50 (*0-444-88877-2*, North Holland) Elsevier.

Braden, J. P. Deafness, Deprivation, & IQ. (Perspectives on Individual Differences Ser.). (Illus.). 242p. (C). 1994. 39.50 (*0-306-44686-3*, Plenum Trade) Perseus Pubng.

Braden, Jennifer S., jt. auth. see Good, Thomas L.

Braden, John B., et al, eds. Environmental Policy with Political & Economic Integration: The European Union & the United States. LC 94-45014. (New Horizons in Environmental Economics Ser.). 512p. (C). 1996. 100.00 (*1-85898-217-0*) E Elgar.

Braden, John B. & Lovejoy, Stephen B., eds. Agriculture & Water Quality: International Perspectives. LC 89-10811. 224p. 1989. lib. bdg. 38.00 (*1-55587-183-6*) L Rienner.

Braden, John B. & Proost, Stef, eds. The Economic Theory of Environmental Policy in a Federal System. LC 96-50094. (New Horizons in Environmental Economics Ser.). 176p. 1997. 85.00 (*1-85898-363-0*) E Elgar.

Braden, John B., jt. ed. see Proost, Stef.

Braden, John R., et al, eds. The Ernst & Young's Oil & Gas Federal Income Taxation. rev. ed. (Illus.). 700p. 1997. pap. text 89.00 (*0-8080-0193-0*) CCH INC.

Braden, John R. & Penick, S. Barksdale, eds. Ernst & Young's Oil & Gas: Federal Income Taxation. rev. ed. (Illus.). 700p. 1998. pap. text 92.95 (*0-8080-0267-8*) CCH INC.

Braden, Kathleen, et al. Beyond Borders: A New Geography of Russia & the United States. (Illus.). 256p. 1996. 24.95 (*0-02-860448-2*) Macmillan.

Braden, Maria. She Said What? Interviews with Women Columnists. LC 92-36460. (Illus.). 216p. 1993. 25.00 (*0-8131-1819-0*) U Pr of Ky.

— Women Politicians & the Media. (Illus.). 248p. 1996. pap. 17.00 (*0-8131-0869-1*) U Pr of Ky.

Braden, Maria & Roth, Richard L. Getting the Message Across: Writing for the Mass Media. (C). 1995. text, teacher ed. 11.96 (*0-395-83847-9*) HM.

Braden, Michael, et al. Polymeric Dental Materials, Vol. XIV. LC 97-457. (Macromolecular Systems - Materials Approach Ser.). (Illus.). 150p. 1997. 149.00 (*3-540-61646-2*) Spr-Verlag.

Braden, Michele. Fast & Fabulous Hors d'Oeuvres. rev. ed. LC 92-14893. 320p. 1992. reprint ed. pap. 17.95 (*0-02-009185-0*) Macmillan.

Braden, Pat. Alfa Romeo Owner's Bible: A Hands-On Guide to Getting the Most From Your Alfa. (Illus.). 288p. 1993. pap. 29.95 (*0-8376-0707-8*) Bentley Pubs.

— Weber Carburetors: Select, Install & Tune Weber Sidedraft & Downdraft Carburetors for Performance or Economy. LC 87-21266. (Illus.). 160p. 1988. pap. 17.95 (*0-89586-377-4*, HP Books) Berkley Pub.

Braden, R. As I Look Back. (Illus.). 242p. 1999. 30.00 (*1-57157-151-5*) Safari Pr.

— As I Look Back. limited ed. 242p. 1999. 60.00 (*1-57157-088-8*) Safari Pr.

Braden, R., jt. auth. see Adams, C.

Braden, Richard. AppStudio Graphics Editor. (Hands-on Windows Programming Ser.: Bk. 7). 144p. 1995. pap. 15.95 incl. disk (*1-55622-478-8*) Wordware Pub.

— C to C++ Conversion. LC 95-43917. (Hands-on Windows Programming Ser.: Bk. 8). 200p. 1995. pap. 15.95 incl. disk (*1-55622-479-6*) Wordware Pub.

— Special Topics & Master Index for Books 1-9. (Hands-on Windows Programming Ser.: Bk. 9). 160p. 1995. pap. 15.95 (*1-55622-480-X*) Wordware Pub.

Braden, Richard P. Child Windows. LC 94-17676. (Hands-On Windows Programming Ser.: Bk. 2). 160p. 1994. pap. 15.95 incl. disk (*1-55622-433-8*) Wordware Pub.

— Introduction to Windows Programming. LC 94-17674. (Introduction to Window Programmings: Bk. 1). 160p. 1994. pap. 15.95 incl. disk (*1-55622-432-X*) Wordware Pub.

— Mouse, Timer, & Keyboard Inputs. 5th ed. (Hands-on-Windows Programming Ser.: Bk. 5). 176p. 1995. pap. 15.95 incl. disk (*1-55622-452-4*) Wordware Pub.

— Painting the Screen. LC 94-17677. (Hands-on Windows Programming Ser.: Bk. 3). 160p. (Orig.). 1994. pap. 15.95 (*1-55622-434-6*) Wordware Pub.

— Text & Special Fonts, Menus, & Printing. 6th ed. (Hands-on-Windows Programming Ser.: Bk. 6). 168p. (Orig.). 1995. pap. 15.95 incl. disk (*1-55622-453-2*) Wordware Pub.

— Transferring Data to & from Windows. LC 94-17675. (Hands-on Windows Programming Ser.: Bk. 4). 160p. (Orig.). 1994. pap. 15.95 (*1-55622-435-4*) Wordware Pub.

Braden, Roberts A., et al, eds. Art, Science & Visual Literacy. (Illus.). 484p. (Orig.). (C). 1993. pap. text 30.00 (*0-945829-07-8*) Intl Visual.

Braden, Su & Than Thi Thien Huong. Video for Development: Lessons from Vietnam. (Oxfam Development Casebks.). 128p. 1998. pap. 12.95 (*0-85598-370-1*, Pub. by Oxfam Pub) Stylus Pub VA.

Braden, Vic. Tennis 2000: Strokes, Strategy & Psychology for a Lifetime. LC 98-12795. (Illus.). 304p. 1998. pap. 19.00 (*0-316-10503-1*) Little.

— Vic Braden's Mental Tennis: How to Psyche Yourself to a Winning Team. 264p. 1994. pap. 13.95 (*0-316-10517-1*) Little.

Braden, Vic. Vic Braden's Quick Fixes: Expert Cures for Common Tennis Problems. LC 87-26099. 135p. 1990. pap. 15.95 (*0-316-10515-5*) Little.

Braden, Vic & Bruns, Bill. Teaching Children Tennis the Vic Braden Way. (Sports Illustrated Book), (Illus.). 1982. 17.95 (*0-316-10512-0*) Little.

— Vic Braden's Laugh & Win at Doubles. 192p. 1997. pap. 14.95 (*0-316-10505-8*) Little.

— Vic Braden's Quick Fixes: Expert Cures for Common Tennis Problems. LC 87-26099. (Illus.). 224p. 1988. 17.95 (*0-316-10514-7*) Little.

— Vic Braden's Tennis for the Future. 1980. 24.95 (*0-316-10510-4*) Little.

Braden, Vic, et al. Championship Tennis by the Experts: How to Play Championship Tennis - Written by the Experts. Assaiante, Paul, ed. LC 80-83978. (West Point Sports/Fitness Ser.: No. 13). (Illus.). 208p. 1981. reprint ed. pap. 64.50 (*0-608-07062-9*, 206726800009) Bks Demand.

Braden, Waldo W. Abraham Lincoln, Public Speaker. LC 88-6793. viii, 119p. (C). 1993. pap. 8.95 (*0-8071-1852-4*) La State U Pr.

— The Oral Tradition in the South. LC 82-20827. 147p. 1983. reprint ed. pap. 45.60 (*0-608-00863-X*, 206165400010) Bks Demand.

Braden, Waldo W., ed. Building the Myth: Selected Speeches Memorializing Abraham Lincoln. 272p. 1991. text 34.95 (*0-252-01734-X*) U of Ill Pr.

— Oratory in the New South. fac. ed. LC 78-25909. 296p. 1979. reprint ed. pap. 91.80 (*0-7837-7937-2*, 204769300008) Bks Demand.

Braden, Warren R. Homies: Peer Mentoring among African-American Males. LC 95-31911. 200p. 1999. per. 17.95 (*1-879528-14-2*) Ed Studies Pr.

Braden-Whartenby, Geri & Finn Connelly, Joan. One-Day Retreats for Junior High Youth. 124p. (J). 1997. pap. 27.95 (*0-88489-436-3*) St Marys.

— One Day Retreats for Senior High Youth. Stamschror, Robert, ed. 144p. (J). 1997. pap. 27.95 (*0-88489-369-3*) St Marys.

Bradenbaugh, Jerry. JavaScript Cookbook. Koman, Richard, ed. (Illus.). 500p. 1999. pap. 34.95 (*1-56592-577-7*) OReilly & Assocs.

Brader-Araje, Laura, jt. ed. see Malloy, Carol E.

Bradfield, Barbara & Slater, Sara. Guest Afloat: The Essential Guide to Being a Welcome Guest on Board a Boat. LC 97-49924. (Illus.). 112p. 1997. pap. 14.95 (*0-943400-94-5*) Marlor Pr.

Bradfield, Bill & Bradfield, Clare, eds. Texas Towns from A to Z: Pronunciation Guide. 118p. 1996. text 14.00 (*0-9637629-5-8*) Three Forks.

Bradfield, Carl. Getting in Shape with Wendell & Myrtle: The Wendells Family, at It Again. LC 93-74512. (Illus.). 247p. (Orig.). (YA). (gr. 8-12). 1994. pap. 4.99 (*0-9632319-4-4*) ASDA Pub.

— Hawaii Calls Wendell & Myrtle: The Wendells Family Make It to the Big Island. (Illus.). 196p. (Orig.). (YA). (gr. 8-12). pap. write for info. (*0-9632319-5-2*) ASDA Pub.

— The Sullivans of Little Horsepen Creek: A Tale of Colonial North Carolina's Regulator Era, Circa: 1760s. (Illus.). 350p. (YA). (gr. 8-12). write for info. (*0-9632319-2-8*) ASDA Pub.

— Tecumseh's Trail: The Appalachian Trail, Then & Now. (Illus.). 137p. (Orig.). (YA). (gr. 8-12). pap. write for info. (*0-9632319-3-6*) ASDA Pub.

— U-Turn, U. S. A. The Wendells Family. LC 93-72329. (Wendells Family - Fiction Ser.). write for info. (*0-614-04114-7*) ASDA Pub.

— U-Turn, U. S. A. The Wendells Family. (Illus.). 150p. 1992. pap. 6.95 (*0-9632319-1-X*) ASDA Pub.

B

Bradfield, Carl W. The Blue Spaders - Vietnam: A Private's Account, 1-26th Inf., 1965-1966. LC 92-72472. (Illus.). 284p. 1992. boxed set 19.95 (0-9632319-0-1) ASDA Pub.

Bradfield, Clare, jt. ed. see Bradfield, Bill.

Bradfield, Dave, jt. auth. see Underhill, Les.

Bradfield, E. G., ed. Franklin in Numismatics: An Anthology. (Illus.). 1982. reprint ed. pap. 10.00 (0-942666-05-4) S J Durst.

***Bradfield, Graham & Glazewski, Jan, eds.** Environmental Justice & the Legal Process: 1999 Edition to Acta Juridica. 388p. 1999. pap. 70.50 (0-7021-5076-2, Pub. by Juta & Co) Gaunt.

***Bradfield, Graham & van der Merwe, Derek, eds.** Meaning in Legal Interpretation, Vol. 1. 347p. 2000. pap. 55.50 (0-7021-4799-0, Pub. by Juta & Co) Gaunt.

Bradfield, J. B. Green Burial: The 'D-I-Y' Guide to Law & Practice. 1993. pap. 35.00 (0-948826-29-0, Pub. by Inst Social Invent) St Mut.

Bradfield, J. C. Verifying Temporal Properties of Systems. (Progress in Theoretical Computer Science Ser.). viii, 113p. 1991. 60.50 (0-8176-3625-0) Birkhauser.

***Bradfield, John, ed.** 1998 Resin & Blending Seminar Proceedings. 176p. 1999. pap. 45.00 (1-892529-05-X, 7266) Forest Prod.

Bradfield, Keith, tr. see Bergman, Ingmar.

Bradfield, Michael, et al. The Seventh Annual Banking Expansion Institute. 481p. write for info. (0-318-61965-2) Harcourt.

Bradfield, Nancy. Costume in Detail, 1730-1930. 2nd rev. ed. (Illus.). 392p. 1997. pap. 35.00 (0-89676-217-3, Costume & Fashion Pr) QSMG Ltd.

— Historical Costumes of England 1066-1968. 3rd rev. ed. (Illus.). 200p. 1997. pap. 29.95 (0-89676-218-1, Costume & Fashion Pr) QSMG Ltd.

Bradfield, Ray, jt. auth. see Adcock, Dennis.

Bradfield, Richard M. Natural History of Associations: A Study in the Meaning of Community, Vol. 1. LC 73-5577. 428p. 1973. 62.50 (0-8236-3495-7) Intl Univs Pr.

— Natural History of Associations: A Study in the Meaning of Community, Vol. 2. LC 73-5577. 596p. 1973. 87.50 (0-8236-3496-5) Intl Univs Pr.

Bradfield, Scott. Dreaming Revolution: Transgression in the Development of American Romance. LC 92-46717. 141p. 1993. text 24.95 (0-87745-395-0) U of Iowa Pr.

— History of Luminous Motion. 288p. 1996. pap. 13.00 (0-312-14089-4) St Martin.

— The History of Luminous Motion. (Vintage Contemporaries Ser.). 288p. 1990. pap. 11.00 (0-679-72943-7) Vin Bks.

Bradfield, Susi & Burns, John. But Some Became Stars. LC 98-35803. (Illus.). 256p. 1998. 14.95 (965-229-193-5) Gefen Bks.

***Bradfield, Terry.** Physics I & II Laboratory Manual. 2nd ed. 214p. (C). 1999. pap. text, wbk. ed. 36.95 (0-7872-6298-6, 41629801) Kendall-Hunt.

Bradfield, William H. Muleshoe & More. LC 98-27975. 300p. 1998. pap. 15.95 (0-88415-865-9, 5865) Gulf Pub.

Bradford. A Year of Growing. 64p. (gr. 2-7). 1985. 1.25 (0-590-05411-2) Scholastic Inc.

Bradford, jt. auth. see Manchester.

Bradford, Camille Q., et al. Institutional Investors, Social Investing & Corporate Governance. LC 96-68086. xii, 76 p. 1996. write for info. (0-937299-43-X) Natl Legal Ctr Pub Interest.

***Bradford, Alden.** Biographical Notices of Distinguished Men in New England: Statesmen, Patriots, Physicians, Lawyers, Clergymen & Mechanics. 466p. 1999. reprint ed. pap. 33.00 (0-7884-1297-3, B601) Heritage Bk.

***Bradford, Alexander W.** American Antiquities & Researches into the Origin & History of the Red Race. (LC History-America-E). 435p. 1999. reprint ed. lib. bdg. 109.00 (0-7812-4311-4) Rprt Serv.

Bradford, Alfred S. Some Even Volunteered: The Wolfhounds Pacify Vietnam. LC 94-8344. 192p. 1994. 35.00 (0-275-94785-8, Praeger Pubs) Greenwood.

***Bradford, Alfred S.** With Arrow, Sword, & Spear: A History of Warfare in the Ancient World. LC 99-52982. 2000. write for info. (0-275-95259-2, Praeger Pubs) Greenwood.

Bradford, Alfred S., compiled by. Philip the Second of Macedon: A Life from the Ancient Sources. LC 92-235. 224p. 1992. 47.95 (0-275-94250-3, C4250, Praeger Pubs) Greenwood.

Bradford, Anita J., jt. auth. see Love, Anami.

Bradford, Ann. Haunted! Ghost Stories from Round & about Stratford, Redditch, Bromsgrove & Alcester. 114p. 1992. pap. 23.00 (0-9519481-0-5, Pub. by Hunt End Bks) St Mut.

Bradford, Augusta. Fain: Notable Southern Families: Fain of Tennessee, Descendants of Nicholas Fain. (Illus.). 31p. 1997. reprint ed. pap. 6.00 (0-8328-8516-9); reprint ed. lib. bdg. 16.00 (0-8328-8515-0) Higginson Bk Co.

Bradford, Barbara Taylor. Act of Will. 448p. 1994. mass mkt. 6.99 (0-06-100811-7, Harp PBks) HarpC.

— Angel. 1995. reprint ed. mass mkt. 6.99 (0-345-38859-3) Ballantine Pub Grp.

***Bradford, Barbara Taylor.** Animal Encyclopedia. LC 00-23782. (Illus.). 376p. (gr. 4-7). 2000. write for info. (0-7894-6499-3, Pub. by DK Pub Inc) Pub Resources Inc.

Bradford, Barbara Taylor. Barbara Taylor Bradford: Three Complete Novels. LC 92-19641. 1992. 10.99 (0-517-08470-8) Random Hse Value.

— Dangerous to Know. 400p. 1996. mass mkt. 6.99 (0-06-109208-8, Harp PBks) HarpC.

— Dangerous to Know. large type ed. 455p. 1995. 25.95 (0-7838-1363-5, G K Hall Lrg Type) Mac Lib Ref.

— Dangerous to Know. large type ed. LC 95-30941. 1996. 23.95 (0-7838-1364-3, G K Hall Lrg Type) Mac Lib Ref.

— Everything to Gain. LC 94-13795. 416p. 1995. mass mkt. 6.99 (0-06-109207-X, Harp PBks) HarpC.

— Everything to Gain. large type ed. LC 94-35473. 1994. 26.95 (1-56895-152-3) Wheeler Pub.

— Her Own Rules. large type ed. LC 96-8313. Orig. Title: w. 371p. 1996. lib. bdg. 28.95 (0-7838-1785-1, G K Hall Lrg Type) Mac Lib Ref.

— Her Own Rules. large type ed. LC 96-8313. Orig. Title: w. 367p. 1997. pap. 28.95 (0-7838-1786-X, G K Hall Lrg Type) Mac Lib Ref.

— Her Own Rules: Her Own Rules. large type ed. Orig. Title: w. 352p. 1997. mass mkt. 6.99 (0-06-109586-9, Harp PBks) HarpC.

— Hold the Dream. 768p. 1994. mass mkt. 7.50 (0-06-100808-7, Harp PBks) HarpC.

— Love in Another Town. LC 95-36834. 240p. 1996. mass mkt. 5.99 (0-06-109209-6) HarpC.

— Love in Another Town. large type ed. LC 95-42560. 208p. 1996. pap. 22.95 (0-7838-1560-3, G K Hall Lrg Type) Mac Lib Ref.

— Love in Another Town. large type ed. 224p. 1999. 24.95 (0-7838-1559-X, G K Hall Lrg Type) Mac Lib Ref.

Bradford, Barbara Taylor. Love in Another Town: Banes,&Lisa, Set. abr. ed. 1995. audio 17.00 (0-694-51598-1, 393244) HarperAudio.

Bradford, Barbara Taylor. Otro Amor, Otra Cluded. 1999. pap. text 9.95 (84-08-02522-8) Planeta.

— Power of a Woman. 432p. 1998. mass mkt. 7.50 (0-06-109440-4) HarpC.

— Power of a Woman. large type ed. LC 97-28016. 1997. 29.95 (0-7862-1223-3) Thorndike Pr.

***Bradford, Barbara Taylor.** Power of a Woman. large type ed. LC 97-28016. 1999. pap. 27.95 (0-7862-1224-1) Thorndike Pr.

— Power of a Woman: Mcteer,&Janet, Set. abr. ed. 1997. audio 25.00 (0-694-51861-1, 695440) HarperAudio.

Bradford, Barbara Taylor. Remember. LC 91-52706. 1992. mass mkt. 6.99 (0-345-37936-5) Ballantine Pub Grp.

— A Secret Affair. large type ed. 272p. 1997. mass mkt. 5.99 (0-06-101228-9, Harp PBks) HarpC.

— A Secret Affair. large type ed. LC 96-43455. 339p. 1998. pap. 24.95 (0-7862-0927-5) Thorndike Pr.

Bradford, Barbara Taylor. A Secret Affair: Eggar,&Samantha, Set. abr. ed. 1996. audio 18.00 (0-694-51728-3, 394519, Pub. by HarperAudio) Lndmrk Audiobks.

— A Sudden Change of Heart. 400p. 1999. mass mkt. 7.99 (0-440-23514-6) Dell.

Bradford, Barbara Taylor. A Sudden Change of Heart. LC 99-196374. 368p. 1999. 24.00 (0-385-49274-X) Doubleday.

— A Sudden Change of Heart. LC 99-15873. 1999. write for info. (1-56895-735-1) Wheeler Pub.

***Bradford, Barbara Taylor.** A Sudden Change of Heart. large type ed. 440p. 2000. write for info. (0-7089-9134-3) Ulverscroft.

— A Sudden Change of Heart. large type ed. 2000. pap. 11.95 (1-56895-965-6) Wheeler Pub.

— Three Complete Novels. LC 99-52867. (Illus.). 650p. 2000. 12.98 (0-7651-1772-X) Smithmark.

Bradford, Barbara Taylor. To Be the Best. 496p. 1994. mass mkt. 6.50 (0-06-100809-5, Harp PBks) HarpC.

— Voice of the Heart. 912p. 1994. mass mkt. 7.50 (0-06-100810-9, Harp PBks) HarpC.

***Bradford, Barbara Taylor.** Where You Belong. 2000. mass mkt. 7.99 (0-440-23515-4) Dell.

Bradford, Barbara Taylor. Where You Belong. LC 99-88133. 416p. 2000. 24.95 (0-385-49275-8, N A Talese) Doubleday.

***Bradford, Barbara Taylor.** Where You Belong. large type ed. 2000. pap. 13.95 (0-375-72797-3) Random.

— Where You Belong. large type ed. LC 99-87930. 432p. 2000. 24.95 (0-375-40974-2) Random Hse Lrg Prnt.

Bradford, Barbara Taylor. A Woman of Substance. 928p. 1994. mass mkt. 7.50 (0-06-100807-9, Harp PBks) HarpC.

— A Woman of Substance. 832p. 1980. mass mkt. 4.50 (0-380-49163-X, Avon Bks) Morrow Avon.

— The Women in His Life. 1991. mass mkt. 6.99 (0-345-34573-8) Ballantine Pub Grp.

— The Women in His Life. large type ed. (General Ser.). 744p. 1991. 16.95 (0-8161-5244-6, G K Hall Lrg Type) Mac Lib Ref.

Bradford, Benjamin S. Sharecropper: And Others. large type ed. 300p. 1999. pap. 10.00 (0-9666716-0-0) B S Bradford.

— Suspended Sentence: The Lynching. rev. ed. (Illus.). 192p. 1997. pap. 10.00 (0-9666716-1-9) B S Bradford.

Bradford, Betsy A. Princess Patty in Peace on Earth. rev. ed. (Illus.). 56p. (J). (gr. k-4). 1995. 16.95 (0-9633846-3-5) Scope Pub.

Bradford, Billie C. ICD-9-CM Coding for Physicians' Offices. 2nd ed. (Illus.). 250p. 1997. pap. 44.95 (1-57066-068-9, ME118) Practice Mgmt Info.

Bradford, Bonnie & Gwynne, Margaret A., eds. Down to Earth: Community Perspectives on Health, Development, & the Environment. LC 95-17307. (Library of Management for Development). (Illus.). 208p. 1995. pap. 24.95 (1-56549-050-9) Kumarian Pr.

Bradford, Burns E. A History of Brazil. 3rd ed. LC 93-12216. 544p. 1993. 73.50 (0-231-07954-0); pap. 26.50 (0-231-07955-9) Col U Pr.

Bradford, C. Steven & Ames, Gary A. Basic Accounting Principles for Lawyers: With Present Value & Expected Value. LC 97-161408. 152p. 1996. pap. 19.95 (0-87084-104-1) Anderson Pub Co.

***Bradford, Charles.** Sabbath Roots: The African Connections. 234p. 1999. pap. write for info. (1-57847-056-0) Genl Conf Svnth-day.

Bradford, Charles E., et al. The Wit & Wisdom of Charles E. Bradford LC 90-8238. 136 p. 1990. write for info. (0-8280-0585-0) Review & Herald.

Bradford, Charles H. The Battle Road: Expedition to Lexington & Concord. 2nd ed. (Illus.). 89p. 1996. pap. 4.95 (1-888213-01-9) Eastern National.

Bradford, Clare. Birthday Wishes. LC 93-20804. (Illus.). (J). 1994. 4.25 (0-383-03737-9) SRA McGraw.

Bradford, Clare, ed. Writing the Australian Child: Text & Contexts in Fictions for Children. LC 97-114578. 1995. pap. 19.95 (1-875560-75-0, Pub. by Univ of West Aust Pr) Intl Spec Bk.

Bradford, Clinton W. Ministry for Retired Persons: A Simple Narrative of the Evolvement of a Concept. LC 87-50591. 123p. (Orig.). 1987. pap. 2.50 (0-9618924-0-4) Reily Mem Univ.

Bradford, Colin I., Jr. & Branson, William H., eds. Trade & Structural Change in Pacific Asia. LC 86-19293. (National Bureau of Economic Research Conference Report Ser.). 576p. (C). 1987. lib. bdg. 72.00 (0-226-07025-5) U Ch Pr.

Bradford, Cynthia A. Basic Ophthalmology for Medical Students & Primary Care Residents. 7th ed. LC 98-27992. xv, 175 p. 1999. pap. 28.00 (1-56055-098-8) Am Acad Ophthal.

Bradford, Daniel. Solo in the City: A Sourcebook for Singles in Metropolitan Denver. 128p. (Orig.). 1985. pap. 6.95 (0-9608012-3-5) Metrosource Pubns.

Bradford, David & Waldherr, Gerhard. New York: Drive by Shootings. (Illus.). 440p. 1999. pap. 19.95 (3-8290-2891-1, 810155) Konemann.

Bradford, David F. Distributional Analysis of Tax Policy. LC 95-18681. 150p. 1995. pap. 19.95 (0-8447-3891-3, AEI Pr) Am Enterprise.

— Essays in the Economics of Property-Casualty Insurance. LC 97-37801. (National Bureau of Economic Research Project Report Ser.). 216p. 1998. 37.50 (0-226-07026-3) U Ch Pr.

— Fundamental Issues in Consumption Taxation. LC 97-105654. (Studies on Tax Reform). 61p. (Orig.). 1996. pap. 9.95 (0-8447-7068-X, AEI Pr) Am Enterprise.

***Bradford, David F.** Taxation, Wealth & Saving. LC 99-31172. (Illus.). 544p. 1999. 57.00 (0-262-02470-5) MIT Pr.

Bradford, David F. Untangling the Income Tax. 386p. 1986. lib. bdg. 29.95 (0-87186-246-8) Comm Econ Dev.

— Untangling the Income Tax. LC 85-27078. (Illus.). 400p. 1988. reprint ed. pap. 21.50 (0-674-93041-X) HUP.

Bradford, David F., ed. Distributional Analysis of Tax Policy. LC 95-18681. 300p. 1995. 39.95 (0-8447-3890-5, AEI Pr) Am Enterprise.

— Tax Policy & the Economy, Vol. 5. 178p. 1991. 30.00 (0-262-02295-8); pap. text 15.00 (0-262-52158-X) MIT Pr.

Bradford, David F. & Max, Derrick A. Intergenerational Transfers under Community Rating. LC 97-105695. 50p. (Orig.). 1996. pap. 9.95 (0-8447-7033-7) Am Enterprise.

Bradford, David F., jt. auth. see Cohen, Allan R.

Bradford, David F., jt. auth. see U. S. Treasury Tax Policy Staff.

Bradford, David G., jt. auth. see Mendel, William W.

Bradford, David L. & Cohen, Allan R. Managing for Excellence: The Guide to Developing High Performance in Contemporary Organizations. (Management Series on Problem Solving, Decision Making & Strategic Thinking: 1-578). Ep. 1986. cd-rom 32.95 (0-471-84702-X) Wiley.

— Managing for Excellence: The Guide to Developing High Performance in Contemporary Organizations. LC 95-50901. 320p. 1997. pap. 16.95 (0-471-12724-8) Wiley.

— Power Up: Transforming Organizations Through Shared Leadership. LC 97-35610. 364p. 1998. 27.95 (0-471-12122-3) Wiley.

Bradford, David S., ed. Master Techniques in Orthopaedic Surgery - The Spine: Master Techniques in Orthopaedic Surgery. (Master Techniques in Orthopaedic Surgery Ser.: vol. 7). (Illus.). 400p. 1996. text 189.00 (0-7817-0033-7) Lppncott W & W.

Bradford, David S., et al, eds. Moe's Textbook of Scoliosis & Other Spinal Deformities. 3rd ed. LC 94-11860. (Illus.). 672p. 1994. text. write for info. (0-7216-5533-5, W B Saunders Co) Harcrt Hlth Sci Grp.

Bradford, David T. Interpretive Reasoning & the Halstead-Reitan Tests. LC 91-72061. 340p. (Orig.). 1992. pap. text 34.95 (0-88422-113-X) Clinical Psych.

Bradford, Dennis E. The Fundamental Ideas. 196p. 1986. 17.50 (0-87527-364-5) Green.

Bradford, Elizabeth, ed. see Bohlke, Dorothee.

Bradford, Elizabeth, ed. see Mann, Marek.

***Bradford, Emma.** Kat. (Stardust Classics). 1999. boxed set 16.95 (1-889514-23-3) Dolls Corp.

Bradford, Emma. Kat & the Emperor's Gift. LC 98-65894. (Stardust Classics). (Illus.). 117p. (J). (gr. 2-6). 1998. 12.95 (1-889514-19-5); pap. 5.95 (1-889514-20-9) Dolls Corp.

— Kat & the Missing Notebooks. LC 99-71562. (Stardust Classics: No. 4). (Illus.). 127p. (J). (gr. 2-5). 1999. 12.95 (1-889514-27-6); pap. 5.95 (1-889514-28-4) Dolls Corp.

— Kat & the Secrets of the Nile. LC 98-65895. (Stardust Classics). (Illus.). 116p. (J). (gr. 2-6). 1998. 12.95 (1-889514-13-6); pap. 5.95 (1-889514-14-4) Dolls Corp.

— Kat the Time Explorer. LC 98-65896. (Stardust Classics). (Illus.). 117p. (J). (gr. 2-6). 1998. 12.95 (1-889514-11-X); pap. 5.95 (1-889514-12-8) Dolls Corp.

Bradford, Ernie. Great Siege: Malta 1565. 1999. pap. text 12.99 (1-84022-206-9) Wrdsworth Edits.

— The Journeying Moon. large type ed. 1990. 27.99 (0-7089-2132-9) Ulverscroft.

— Nelson: The Essential Hero. 1999. pap. text 12.99 (1-84022-202-6) Wrdsworth Edits.

— The Wind off the Island. large type ed. 400p. 1992. 27.99 (0-7089-2672-X) Ulverscroft.

Bradford, Ernle. The Companion Guide to the Greek Islands. rev. ed. (Illus.). 424p. 1998. pap. 29.95 (1-900639-18-1, Pub. by Companion Guide) Boydell & Brewer.

***Bradford, Ernle.** Hannibal. (Illus.). 2000. pap. 12.99 (1-84022-226-3, Pub. by Wrdsworth Edits) Combined Pub.

Bradford, Ernle. Thermopylae: The Battle for the West. (Illus.). 256p. 1993. reprint ed. pap. 13.95 (0-306-80531-6) Da Capo.

Bradford, Gamaliel. As God Made Them: Portraits of Some Nineteenth-Century Americans. (BCL1 - U. S. History Ser.). 294p. 1991. reprint ed. lib. bdg. 79.00 (0-7812-6028-0) Rprt Serv.

— Biography & the Human Heart. LC 68-58772. (Essay Index Reprint Ser.). 1977. 21.95 (0-8369-1023-0) Ayer.

— Confederate Portraits. LC 68-29193. (Essay Index Reprint Ser.). 1977. 31.95 (0-8369-0241-6) Ayer.

— Confederate Portraits. (History - United States Ser.). 291p. 1992. reprint ed. lib. bdg. 79.00 (0-7812-6173-2) Rprt Serv.

— D. L. Moody: A Worker in Souls. (Illus.). 320p. 1977. 31.95 (0-8369-6821-2) Ayer.

— Damaged Souls. (BCL1 - U. S. History Ser.). 284p. 1991. reprint ed. lib. bdg. 79.00 (0-7812-6029-9) Rprt Serv.

— Elizabethan Women. White, Harold O., ed. LC 75-75505. (Select Bibliographies Reprint Ser.). 1977. 23.95 (0-8369-5001-1) Ayer.

— Lee the American. LC 98-71804. (Illus.). 324p. 1998. pap. 16.95 (1-888295-06-6) Elephant Books.

— The Letters of Gamaliel Bradford, 1918-1931. (American Biography Ser.). 377p. 1991. reprint ed. lib. bdg. 79.00 (0-7812-8035-4) Rprt Serv.

— Life & I: An Autobiography of Humanity. (American Biography Ser.). 307p. 1991. reprint ed. lib. bdg. 79.00 (0-7812-8036-2) Rprt Serv.

— Portraits & Personalities. Bessey, M. A., ed. LC 68-8440. (Essay Index Reprint Ser.). 1977. 21.95 (0-8369-0242-4) Ayer.

— Portraits of American Women. (Illus.). 276p. 1977. 19.95 (0-8369-0004-9) Ayer.

— Portraits of American Women. (BCL1 - U. S. History Ser.). 276p. 1991. reprint ed. lib. bdg. 79.00 (0-7812-6030-2) Rprt Serv.

— Portraits of Women. LC 75-90611. (Essay Index Reprint Ser.). 1977. 20.95 (0-8369-1247-0) Ayer.

— Portraits of Women. LC 75-90611. (Essay Index Reprint Ser.). (Illus.). 202p. reprint ed. lib. bdg. 20.00 (0-8290-0469-6) Irvington.

— A Prophet of Joy. LC 77-179506. (Select Bibliographies Reprint Ser.). 1977. reprint ed. 19.95 (0-8369-6635-X) Ayer.

— Samuel Pepys. LC 75-42291. (English Biography Ser.: No. 31). 1974. lib. bdg. 75.00 (0-8383-2061-9) M S G Haskell Hse.

— Union Portraits. LC 68-29194. (Essay Index Reprint Ser.). 1977. 20.95 (0-8369-0243-2) Ayer.

— Union Portraits. (History - United States Ser.). 330p. 1992. reprint ed. lib. bdg. 89.00 (0-7812-6174-0) Rprt Serv.

— Wives. LC 72-2591. (American Women Ser.: Images & Realities). 328p. 1975. reprint ed. 24.95 (0-405-04448-8) Ayer.

— Wives. (BCL1 - U. S. History Ser.). 298p. 1991. reprint ed. lib. bdg. 79.00 (0-7812-6031-0) Rprt Serv.

***Bradford, Gene.** We Can Do More. 2000. pap. text 12.95 (1-878647-70-9) APU Pub Grp.

Bradford, George. How Deep Is Deep Ecology? With an Essay-Review on Woman's Freedom. LC 89-4640. (Illus.). x, 84p. (Orig.). 1989. pap. 5.50 (0-87810-035-0) Times Change.

Bradford, Gertrude. How to Demonstrate Health, Money, Friends (1924) 98p. 1998. reprint ed. pap. 12.95 (0-7661-0555-5) Kessinger Pub.

Bradford, Gertrude A. The Subconcious Mind: How to Reach & Arouse (1924) 164p. 1998. reprint ed. pap. 17.95 (0-7661-0233-5) Kessinger Pub.

Bradford, Gigi, et al, eds. The Politics of Culture: Essays for a New Field. 288p. 2000. pap. 18.95 (1-56584-572-2) Norton.

Bradford, Gigi & Moos, Michael, eds. Sixteen Toes: Anthology. (Illus.). (J). (gr. 2-7). 1978. pap. 2.50 (0-930970-00-4) O'Neill Pr.

Bradford, Grace. Guide for Class Leaders: A Model for Christian Formation. LC 98-88821. 64p. 1999. pap. 13.95 (0-88177-274-7, DR274) Discipleship Res.

— Scriptures Come Alive: Reading Scriptures Aloud. 48p. (Orig.). 1995. pap. 6.95 (0-687-00560-4) Abingdon.

Bradford, Helen. A Taste of Freedom: The ICU in Rural South Africa 1924-1930. LC 87-10451. 448p. 1988. 50.00 (0-300-03873-9) Yale U Pr.

— A Taste of Freedom: The ICU in Rural South Africa, 1924-1930. LC 87-10451. (Illus.). 382p. 1987. reprint ed. pap. 118.50 (0-608-07880-8, 205998700010) Bks Demand.

Bradford, J. Allyn & Guberman, Reuben. Transactional Awareness: Now I've Got You...In Business. 1978. pap. 7.95 (0-201-00320-1) Addison-Wesley.

Bradford, James C., ed. Admirals of the New Steel Navy. LC 89-13517. (Illus.). 416p. 1990. 45.00 (0-87021-003-3) Naval Inst Pr.

— Captains of the Old Steam Navy: Makers of the American Naval Tradition, 1840-1880. LC 86-16399. (Illus.). 356p. 1986. 35.00 (0-87021-013-0) Naval Inst Pr.

An Asterisk (*) at the beginning of an entry indicates that the title is appearing for the first time.

— Crucible of Empire: The Spanish-American War & Its Aftermath. LC 92-46720. (Illus.). 269p. 1993. 38.95 (*1-55750-079-7*) Naval Inst Pr.

— The Military & Conflict Between Cultures: Soldiers at the Interface. LC 96-43015. (Military History Ser.: Vol. 50). (Illus.). 264p. (C). 1997. text 37.95 (*0-89096-743-1*) Tex A&M Univ Pr.

— Quarterdeck & Bridge: Two Centuries of American Naval Leaders. LC 96-43106. (Illus.). 480p. 1996. 22.95 (*1-55750-073-8*) Naval Inst Pr.

Bradford, James C., ed. Quarterdeck & Bridge: Two Centuries of American Naval Leaders. LC 96-43106. (Illus.). 480p. 1996. pap. 22.95 (*1-55750-096-7*) Naval Inst Pr.

Bradford, James N. Escape Route: Surviving the Earth Changes. 180p. 1982. pap. 12.00 (*0-89540-135-5*, SB-135) Sun Pub.

Bradford, Jean. A Dictionary of South African English. 4th ed. (AFR & ENG.). 361p. 1991. 39.95 (*0-7859-4864-3*, M9418) Fr & Eur.

Bradford, Jeff. Songs of the Master's Love: Artistic Piano - Vocal Arrangements. 36p. (Orig.). 1991. pap. 9.98 (*0-88290-369-1*) Horizon Utah.

— Songs of the Savior: Artistic Piano - Vocal Arrangements. 30p. 1989. pap. 9.98 (*0-88290-341-1*) Horizon Utah.

Bradford, Jenny. Bullion Stitch Embroidery: From Roses to Wildflowers. (Illus.). 1991. pap. 12.95 (*1-86351-040-0*, Pub. by Sally Milner) Sterling.

— Little Book of Wildflowers in Silk Ribbon. 1999. 9.95 (*1-86351-227-6*) Sally Milner.

— Little Book of Wool & Silk Embroidery. 1999. 9.95 (*1-86351-228-4*) Sally Milner.

***Bradford, Jenny.** Original Designs for Silk Ribbon Embroidery. (Illus.). 2000. pap. 12.95 (*1-86351-237-3*) Sally Milner.

Bradford, Jenny. Silk Ribbon Embroidery: For Gifts & Garments. (Illus.). 72p. 1991. pap. 12.95 (*1-86351-009-5*, Pub. by Sally Milner) Sterling.

— Textured Embroidery. (Illus.). 112p. 1994. pap. 12.95 (*1-86351-076-1*, Pub. by Sally Milner) Sterling.

***Bradford, Jim & Wantuchowicz, Ray, eds.** Eventfully Texas. (Illus.). 271p. 1999. 14.95 (*0-9676351-0-1*) Classic Pubng.

Bradford, John. Ancient Landscapes: Studies in Field Archaeology. LC 80-23204. (Illus.). 297p. 1980. reprint ed. lib. bdg. 79.50 (*0-313-22849-3*, BRAL, Greenwood Pr) Greenwood.

— Core Competencies. 1998. pap. 10.95 (*1-56052-499-5*) Crisp Pubns.

— Everything's Coming up Fractions. 1995. pap. 9.50 (*0-201-48030-1*) Addison-Wesley.

— Everything's Coming up Fractions: With Cuisenaire Rods. 64p. 1981. pap. text 9.50 (*0-914040-91-X*) Cuisenaire.

— A Sermon of Repentance. LC 74-28835. (English Experience Ser.: No. 716). 1975. reprint ed. 25.00 (*90-221-0716-7*) Walter J Johnson.

— Writings of Bradford, Vols. 1 & 2. 1979. 57.99 (*0-85151-359-X*) Banner of Truth.

Bradford, John, jt. ed. see Oakes, Elizabeth H.

Bradford, June, jt. auth. see Sadler, Judy A.

Bradford, June, jt. auth. see Sadler, Judy Ann.

Bradford, Karen. Write Now! How to Turn Your Ideas into Great Stories. 2nd rev. ed. 88p. (YA). (gr. 4-9). 1996. pap. 4.50 (*0-590-24931-2*) Scholastic Inc.

Bradford, Karleen. Animal Heroes.Tr. of Animaux Heros. (FRE., Illus.). (J). pap. 6.99 (*0-590-24450-7*) Scholastic Inc.

— There Will Be Wolves. LC 96-1399. 208p. (YA). (gr. 7 up). 1996. 15.99 (*0-525-67539-6*, Dutton Child) Peng Put Young Read.

— There Will Be Wolves. (Puffin Novels Ser.). (Illus.). 208p. (YA). (gr. 7-12). 1998. pap. 4.99 (*0-14-038371-9*) Peng Put Young Read.

Bradford, Katie & Matthews, Paul, eds. Butterworths Business Landlord & Tenant Handbook. 1996. pap. write for info. (*0-406-08131-X*, BBLTHB, MICHIE) LEXIS Pub.

***Bradford Landau, Sarah, et al.** Rise of the New York Skyscraper, 1865-1913. (Illus.). 496p. 1999. pap. text 27.50 (*0-300-07739-4*) Yale U Pr.

Bradford, Laurence B. Historic Duxbury in Plymouth County, Massachusetts. (Illus.). 128p. 1993. reprint ed. lib. bdg. 22.50 (*0-8328-3164-6*) Higginson Bk Co.

Bradford, Lawrence, jt. auth. see Raines, Claire.

Bradford, Leigh, jt. auth. see Fryer, Lee.

Bradford, Leland & Bradford, Martha. Retirement: Coping with Emotional Upheavals. LC 79-4101. 1979. text 29.95 (*0-88229-564-0*) Burnham Inc.

Bradford, Linda. Connecting Academic Content with Writing: A Resource Guide of Prepared Assignments for Teachers in All. 224p. (C). 1999. per. 33.95 (*0-7872-5729-X*, 41572901) Kendall-Hunt.

— Improving Classroom Teaching. 176p. (C). 1999. per. 41.95 (*0-7872-5686-2*, 41568601) Kendall-Hunt.

***Bradford, M. A., et al, eds.** Mechanics of Structures & Materials: Proceedings of the 16th Australiasian Conference, Sydney, NSW, Australia, 8-10 December 1999. (Illus.). 760p. (C). 1999. text 110.00 (*90-5809-107-4*, Pub. by A A Balkema) Ashgate Pub Co.

Bradford, M. A. & Trahair, N. S. The Behavior & Design of Steel Structures. (Illus.). 420p. 1988. pap. text 39.95 (*0-412-29480-X*) Chapman & Hall.

Bradford, M. A., jt. auth. see Oehlers, D. J.

Bradford, M. E. Founding Fathers: Brief Lives of the Framers of the United States Constitution. rev. ed. LC 93-20982. 244p. 1994. pap. 15.95 (*0-7006-0657-2*) U Pr of KS.

— Founding Fathers: Brief Lives of the Framers of the United States Constitution. 2nd rev. ed. LC 93-20982. 244p. 1994. 35.00 (*0-7006-0656-4*) U Pr of KS.

— Generations of the Faithful Heart: On the Literature of the South. 216p. (Orig.). 1983. pap. 8.95 (*0-89385-023-3*) Sugden.

— The Reactionary Imperative: Essays Literary & Political. 236p. 1990. 25.95 (*0-89385-032-2*) Sugden.

— The Reactionary Imperative: Essays Literary & Political. 236p. 1990. pap. 12.95 (*0-89385-031-4*) Sugden.

— Religion & the Framers: The Biographical Evidence. (Illus.). 36p. (Orig.). 1991. pap. 3.95 (*0-942516-09-5*) Plymouth Rock Found.

— Remembering Who We Are: Observations of a Southern Conservative. LC 84-22225. 200p. 1985. 25.00 (*0-8203-0766-1*) U of Ga Pr.

— A Worthy Company: Brief Lives of the Framers of the Constitution. 250p. 1982. 10.95 (*0-942516-00-1*); pap. 7.95 (*0-685-04105-0*) Plymouth Rock Found.

Bradford, M. E., ed. From Eden to Babylon: The Social & Political Essays of Andrew Nelson Lytle. LC 89-38147. 260p. (Orig.). 1989. 18.95 (*0-89526-548-6*) Univ South Pr.

Bradford, M. E. & Kirk, Russel. A Better Guide Than Reason: Federalists & Anti-Federalists. LC 93-44711. 230p. (C). 1994. 34.95 (*1-56000-131-3*) Transaction Pubs.

Bradford, M. G. & Kent, W. A. Human Geography: Theories & Their Applications. (Science in Geography Ser.). (Illus.). 184p. 1977. pap. text 21.95 (*0-19-913227-5*) OUP.

Bradford, Marjorie. Under the Same Heaven. LC 99-42039. 450p. 1999. pap. 17.95 (*1-881320-42-1*, Black Belt) Black Belt Communs.

***Bradford, Mark A. & Oehlers, Deric J.** Elementary Behaviour of Composite Steel & Concrete Structural Members. 280p. 2000. pap. 37.95 (*0-7506-3269-0*, Architectural Pr) Buttrwrth-Heinemann.

Bradford, Martha, jt. auth. see Bradford, Leland.

Bradford, Mary E. & Bradford, Richard H. An American Family on the African Frontier: The Burnham Family Letters, 1893-1896. LC 93-85472. (Illus.). 326p. 1993. 24.95 (*1-879373-66-1*) Roberts Rinehart.

Bradford, Mary L. Lowell L. Bennion: Teacher, Counselor, Humanitarian. LC 95-40866. (Illus.). 410p. 1996. 24.95 (*1-56085-081-7*) Signature Bks.

Bradford, Mary M., jt. auth. see Hoekstra, Elizabeth M.

Bradford, Maureen, jt. ed. see MacCrae, Melissa.

Bradford, Melvin E., ed. The Form Discovered: Essays on the Achievement of Andrew Lytle. LC 73-86315. (Mississippi Quarterly Series in Southern Literature). 124p. reprint ed. pap. 38.50 (*0-8357-4338-1*, 203714000007) Bks Demand.

Bradford, Michael. The Healing Energy of Your Hands. (Illus.). 224p. 1995. pap. 12.95 (*0-89594-781-1*) Crossing Pr.

Bradford, Michael & Heart, Rosalie D. Soul Empowerment: A Guidebook for Healing Yourself & Others. LC 97-71512. 208p. (Orig.). 1997. pap. 15.95 (*0-9651576-1-X*) Heart Link.

Bradford, Miles Gerald & Brigham Young University College of Humanities Staff. Ancient Scrolls from the Dead Sea: Photographs & Commentary on a Unique Collection of Scrolls. LC 97-25769. 47 p. 1997. write for info. (*0-934893-27-6*) Res Press UT.

Bradford, Montse, jt. auth. see Bradford, Peter.

Bradford, Ned, ed. Battles & Leaders of the Civil War. (Illus.). 640p. 1989. pap. 18.95 (*0-452-01004-7*, Mer) NAL.

Bradford, Neil. Commissioning Ideas: Canadian National Policy Innovation in Comparative Perspective. 320p. 1998. pap. text 29.95 (*0-19-541179-X*) OUP.

Bradford, Nikki. The Miraculous World of Your Unborn Baby. LC 97-46417. 160p. 1998. pap. 14.95 (*0-8092-2928-5*, 292850, Contemporary Bks) NTC Contemp Pub Co.

***Bradford, Peter.** The Design Art of Nicos Zographos. LC 00-23794. (Illus.). 208p. 2000. 50.00 (*1-58093-066-2*, Pub. by Monacelli Pr) Penguin Putnam.

Bradford, Peter & Bradford, Montse. Cooking with Sea Vegetables. (Illus.). 128p. (Orig.). 1985. pap. 9.95 (*0-89281-283-4*) Inner Tradit.

Bradford, R. W., ed. The Last Democrat. (Illus.). xvi, 184p. (Orig.). 1996. pap. 14.95 (*0-9638732-1-0*) Liberty Pubng.

Bradford, Ralph B., jt. auth. see Bradford, Russell R.

Bradford, Rex E. Real-Time Animation Toolkit in C++ LC 95-18613. 778p. 1995. pap. 49.95 (*0-471-12147-9*) Wiley.

Bradford, Rich. Red Sky at Morning: A Novel. LC 99-12690. (Perennial Classics Ser.). 256p. 1999. pap. 13.00 (*0-06-093190-6*) HarpC.

Bradford, Richard. Introducing Literary Studies. 688p. 1996. pap. 39.00 (*0-13-355223-3*) P-H.

— Kingsley Amis. 128p. 1989. pap. 9.95 (*0-340-49309-7*, A3858, Pub. by E A) Routldge.

— Kingsley Amis. Armstrong, Isobel & Loughrey, Bryan, eds. (Writers & Their Work Ser.). 1997. pap. 19.00 (*0-7463-0858-2*, Pub. by Northcote House) U Pr of Miss.

— Look of It: A Theory of Visual Form in English Peotry. LC 94-151247. 1993. 44.95 (*1-85918-000-0*) Intl Spec Bk.

— Paradise Lost. (Open Guides to Literature Ser.). 112p. 1992. pap. 27.95 (*0-335-09982-3*) OpUniv Pr.

— Red Sky at Morning. Date not set. write for info. (*0-06-093210-4*) HarpC.

— Silence & Sound: Theories of Poetics from the Eighteenth Century. LC 90-56225. 232p. 1992. 35.00 (*0-8386-3435-4*) Fairleigh Dickinson.

— Stylistics. LC 96-27990. (The New Critical Idiom Ser.). 152p. (C). 1997. 49.95 (*0-415-09768-1*); pap. 12.99 (*0-415-09769-X*) Routledge.

Bradford, Richard, jt. auth. see Center for Learning Network Staff.

Bradford, Richard H. The Virginius Affair. LC 20-520000. (Illus.). 198p. reprint ed. pap. 61.40 (*0-8357-5509-6*, 203512400093) Bks Demand.

Bradford, Richard H., jt. auth. see Bradford, Mary E.

Bradford, Roark. How Come Christmas. LC 93-25022. (Illus.). 1987. reprint ed. 14.95 (*0-87797-208-7*) Cherokee.

— John Henry. LC 77-116941. (Short Story Index Reprint Ser.). 1977. 26.95 (*0-8369-3443-1*) Ayer.

— Let the Band Play Dixie, & Other Stories. LC 70-128721. (Short Story Index Reprint Ser.). 1977. 26.95 (*0-8369-3612-4*) Ayer.

Bradford, Robert. Mathematics for Carpenters. LC 75-19525. (C). 1975. teacher ed. 16.00 (*0-8273-1117-6*); mass mkt. 24.75 (*0-8273-1116-8*) Delmar.

Bradford, Robert, ed. see Hempstone, Smith.

Bradford, Robert W., et al. Simplified Strategic Planning: A No-Nonsense Guide for Busy People Who Want Results Fast! 240p. 1999. pap. text 22.95 (*1-886284-46-5*, Pub. by Chandler Hse) Natl Bk Netwk.

Bradford, Robin. Digging In. 28p. (Orig.). 1989. pap. 4.00 (*0-945926-04-9*) Paradigm RI.

Bradford, Robin, compiled by. Guide to the Harry Ransom Humanities Research Center. (Illus.). 117p. 1990. 5.00 (*0-87959-112-9*) U of Tex H Ransom Ctr.

Bradford, Roger. Children, Families, & Chronic Disease: Psychological Models & Methods of Care. LC 95-50973. 232p. (C). 1996. pap. 25.99 (*0-415-13147-2*) Routledge.

— Children, Families, & Chronic Disease: Psychological Models & Methods of Care. LC 95-50973. (Illus.). 232p. (C). 1996. 80.00 (*0-415-13146-4*) Routledge.

Bradford, Russell R. & Bradford, Ralph B. Introduction to Handwriting Analysis & Identification. 480p. 1992. text 57.95 (*0-8304-1241-7*) Burnham Inc.

Bradford, S. Corrosion Control. 352p. (gr. 13). 1992. mass mkt. 80.50 (*0-442-01088-5*) Chapman & Hall.

***Bradford, Sarah.** America's Queen: A Life of Jacqueline Kennedy Onassis. (Illus.). 448p. 2000. 29.95 (*0-670-89191-6*, Viking) Viking Penguin.

Bradford, Sarah. Elizabeth: A Biography of Britain's Queen. LC 96-42966. 576p. 1997. pap. 16.00 (*1-57322-600-9*, Riverhd Trade) Berkley Pub.

— Princess Grace. (Illus.). 242p. 1998. text 12.00 (*0-7881-5300-5*) DIANE Pub.

Bradford, Sarah H. Elizabeth: A Biography of Britain's Queen. LC 95-47619. (Illus.). 564p. 1996. 30.00 (*0-374-14749-3*) FS&G.

— Harriet Tubman: The Moses of Her People. 1990. 16.50 (*0-8446-1717-2*) Peter Smith.

— Harriet Tubman: The Moses of Her People. LC 93-34223. 160p. (J). 1969. reprint ed. pap. 12.95 (*1-55709-217-6*) Applewood.

— Harriet Tubman: The Moses of Her People. 160p. 1995. reprint ed. pap. 9.95 (*0-8065-0415-3*, Citadel Pr) Carol Pub Group.

— Sarah: The Letters & Diaries of a Courtier's Wife, 1906-1936. Shaugnessy, Alfred, ed. LC 89-81665. (Illus.). 144p. 1990. 30.00 (*0-7206-0757-4*, Pub. by P Owen Ltd) Dufour.

— Scenes in the Life of Harriet Tubman. LC 70-154071. (Black Heritage Library Collection). 1980. 22.95 (*0-8369-8782-9*) Ayer.

— Splendours & Miseries: A Life of Sir Sacheverell Sitwell. 1993. 35.00 (*0-374-26789-8*) FS&G.

Bradford, Sarah H., et al. The Sitwells: And the Art of the 1920s & 1930s. LC 95-62140. (Literary Modernism Ser.). (Illus.). 240p. 1996. pap. 34.95 (*0-292-77711-6*) U of Tex Pr.

Bradford, Syd. Can Opener. rev. ed. (Illus.). 170p. (Orig.). 1999. pap. 6.00 (*1-879663-01-5*) Audacious Bottle Pr.

— Fire in the Hole! A World War II Memoir. (Illus.). 100p. 1998. pap. 4.00 (*1-879663-05-8*) Audacious Bottle Pr.

— "You May Fire When Ready, Gridley" (Illus.). 119p. 1998. pap. 5.50 (*1-879663-06-6*) Audacious Bottle Pr.

Bradford, Syd, jt. auth. see Tazwell, Samsventi.

Bradford, Sydney. Tom Sullivan, Forty-Ninth Regiment of Foot: Redcoat to Yankee, 1775-1778. rev. ed. (Illus.). 168p. 1994. pap. 6.50 (*1-879663-00-7*) Audacious Bottle Pr.

Bradford, T. G., tr. see Chevalier, Michael.

Bradford, Thomas H. Say That Again, Please! Insights in Dealing with a Hearing Loss. LC 91-92991. (Illus.). 382p. (Orig.). 1991. 23.95 (*0-9630738-4-2*); 89.95 (*0-9630738-9-3*); pap. 16.95 (*0-9630738-5-0*) Bradford Pubns.

Bradford, Thomas R. Rollin' with the Seventh Army & the 14th Armored Division: "Some Sagas" - Trials & Triumphs, Winter/Spring, '45. (Illus.). 95p. (YA). 1997. pap. 5.00 (*1-879663-04-X*) Audacious Bottle Fr.

Bradford Town History Committee. Two Hundred Plus: History of Bradford, New Hampshire. LC 76-26494. (Illus.). 1976. 20.00 (*0-914016-31-8*) Phoenix Pub.

Bradford, Vance A. Bradford Descendants. LC 85-73175. (Illus.). 820p. 1985. 52.00 (*0-9615983-0-1*) V A Bradford.

Bradford, Vicky. Total Service Medical Practice: 17 Steps to Satisfying Your Internal & External Customers. LC 96-41980. 336p. (C). 1996. text 45.00 (*1-55738-645-5*, Irwn McGrw-H); text 45.00 (*0-7863-1244-0*, Irwn McGrw-H) McGrw-H Hghr Educ.

Bradford, W. Murray & Davis, Glenn B. Personal & Business Tax & Financial Planning for Psychiatrists. LC 84-6189. (Private Practice Monograph Ser.). 191p. reprint ed. pap. 59.30 (*0-8357-7844-4*, 20362900002) Bks Demand.

Bradford, Wendy, jt. auth. see Noble, Colin.

Bradford, William. Bradford's History "Of Plimoth Plantation" From the Original Manuscript. 567p. 1990. reprint ed. pap. 30.00 (*1-55613-296-4*) Heritage Bk.

— Crime of Ruby McCollum. 1976. 20.95 (*0-8488-1377-4*) Amereon Ltd.

— A Dialogue Between Some Young Men & Sundry Ancient Men. (Works of William Bradford). 1989. reprint ed. lib. bdg. 79.00 (*0-7812-2035-1*) Rprt Serv.

— History of Plimmoth Plantation. (Works of William Bradford). 1989. reprint ed. lib. bdg. 180.00 (*0-7812-2037-8*) Rprt Serv.

— Mourt's Relation. 96p. 1922. pap. 9.95 (*0-918222-84-2*) Applewood.

— Of Plymouth Plantation. 385p. (C). 1981. pap. 7.50 (*0-07-554281-1*) McGraw.

— Of Plymouth Plantation, 1620 to 1647. Morison, Samuel Eliot, ed. (American Past Ser.). (Illus.). 1952. 25.00 (*0-394-43895-7*) Knopf.

— The Plymouth Settlement: Of Plimoth Plantation. (Illus.). 354p. 1998. reprint ed. 18.00 (*1-889128-48-1*) Mantle Ministries.

— The Works of William Bradford. 1989. reprint ed. lib. bdg. 63.00 (*0-685-27322-9*) Rprt Serv.

Bradford, William, ed. Correspondence of the Emperor Charles Fifth. reprint ed. 54.50 (*0-404-00926-3*) AMS Pr.

Bradford, William, jt. auth. see Hill, Sam.

***Bradford, William S.** The Power Within You Pt. 1: Through the MetaSpherian Principal. (Illus.). 90p. 2000. pap. 12.99 (*1-56411-236-5*) Untd Bros & Sis.

Bradgate, Robert. Bradgate: Commercial Law. 2nd ed. 1995. pap. write for info. (*0-406-04840-1*, BCL2A, MICHIE) LEXIS Pub.

Bradgate, Robert & White, Fidelma. Commercial Law. (Legal Practice Course Guides Ser.). 422p. 1997. pap. 36.00 (*1-85431-621-4*, Pub. by Blackstone Pr) Gaunt.

— Commercial Law. 3rd ed. (Legal Practice Course Guides Ser.). 300p. 1996. pap. 34.00 (*1-85431-513-7*, MICHIE) LEXIS Pub.

— Commercial Law, Vol. 1. 4th ed. 428p. 1998. pap. 38.00 (*1-85431-713-X*, Pub. by Blackstone Pr) Gaunt.

***Bradgate, Robert & White, Fidelma.** Commercial Law, Vol. 1. 7th ed. 451p. 2000. pap. 40.00 (*1-84174-070-5*, Pub. by Blackstone Pr) Gaunt.

Bradgate, Robert & White, Fidelma. Commercial Law 1999. 6th ed. 443p. 1999. pap. 42.00 (*1-85431-910-8*, Pub. by Blackstone Pr) Gaunt.

Bradgate, Robert, et al. Commercial Law. 630p. 1991. pap. 48.00 (*0-406-51412-7*, UK, MICHIE) LEXIS Pub.

— Commercial Law. 2nd ed. (Legal Practice Course Guides Ser.). 410p. 1995. pap. 34.00 (*1-85431-394-0*, Pub. by Blackstone Pr) Gaunt.

— Commercial Law, 1993-94. (Legal Practice Course Guides Ser.). 368p. 1994. pap. 34.00 (*1-85431-348-7*, Pub. by Blackstone Pr) Gaunt.

Bradhurst, A. M. Bradhurst, My Forefathers: Bradhurst, Broadhurst, de Bradehurst. (Illus.). 364p. 1993. reprint ed. pap. 56.00 (*0-8328-3597-8*); reprint ed. lib. bdg. 66.00 (*0-8328-3596-X*) Higginson Bk Co.

Bradie, Michael. The Secret Chain: Evolution & Ethics. LC 93-47679. (SUNY Series in Philosophy & Biology). 198p. (C). 1994. text 44.50 (*0-7914-2105-8*); pap. text 14.95 (*0-7914-2106-6*) State U NY Pr.

Bradigan, Pamela S., et al, eds. Writer's Guide to Nursing & Allied Health Journals. 200p. 1998. pap. 48.95 (*1-55810-143-8*) Am Nurses Pub.

Bradin, James W. A Visual Novel of the War of Tomorrow: Helicopter Aces. 224p. (Orig.). 1990. pap. 6.95 (*0-380-75847-4*, Avon Bks) Morrow Avon.

***Brading, Alison S.** The Autonomic Nervous System & Its Effectors. LC 97-22696. (Illus.). viii, 370 p. 1999. 125.00 (*0-632-02624-3*) Blackwell Sci.

Brading, D. A. Church & State in Bourbon Mexico: The Diocese of Michoacan, 1749-1810. LC 93-44303. 314p. (C). 1994. text 59.95 (*0-521-46092-1*) Cambridge U Pr.

— The First America: The Spanish Monarchy, Creole Patriots & the Liberal State, 1492-1866. (Illus.). 779p. (C). 1993. pap. text 39.95 (*0-521-44796-8*) Cambridge U Pr.

***Brading, David A.** Orbe Indiano. 770p. 1999. 21.99 (*968-16-3657-0*) Fondo CA.

Bradis, V. M. Lapses in Mathematical Reasoning. LC 99-45828. 216p. 1999. pap. text 7.95 (*0-486-40918-X*) Dover.

Bradkin, Cheryl G. Basic Seminole Patchwork. Pederson, Joan, ed. LC 95-83392. (Illus.). 112p. 1990. 21.95 (*1-57120-010-X*, 10134) C & T Pub.

— Basic Seminole Patchwork. Pederson, Joan, ed. (Illus.). 112p. 1990. reprint ed. pap. text 16.95 (*0-942786-50-5*) Eddies Q Bee.

Bradlaugh, Charles. Labor & Law. LC 68-55490. lxiii, 217p. 1972. reprint ed. 37.50 (*0-678-00888-4*) Kelley.

— A Selection of the Political Pamphlets of Charles Bradlaugh, 1865-1891. LC 77-104611. 662p. 1970. lib. bdg. 57.50 (*0-678-00604-0*) Kelley.

Bradlee, Benjamin C. Conversations with Kennedy. (Illus.). 256p. 1984. pap. 8.95 (*0-393-30189-3*) Norton.

— A Good Life: Newspapering & Other Adventures. 1999. pap. 12.98 (*0-671-04405-2*) PB.

— A Good Life: Newspapering & Other Adventures. LC 95-11361. (Illus.). 512p. 1995. 27.00 (*0-684-80894-3*) S&S Trade.

— A Good Life: Newspapering & Other Adventures. 512p. 1996. per. 14.00 (*0-684-82523-6*) S&S Trade.

Bradlee, Dick. Instant Tennis. (Illus.). 124p. (J). (gr. 7 up). 1962. 9.95 (*0-8159-5811-0*) Devin.

Bradlee, Francis B. Piracy in the West Indies & Its Suppression. (Illus.). 236p. 1990. reprint ed. pap. 12.00 (*0-87380-170-9*) Popular E Commerce.

Bradley. Calculus. 1995. pap. text. write for info. (*0-13-178898-1*) Allyn.

— Empowering Professionals. 3rd ed. 1998. 12.74 (*0-07-229246-6*) McGraw.
— Future Competition in Telecommunications. 356p. 1989. 39.95 (*0-07-103215-0*) McGraw.
— Gender & Power in the Workplace. LC 98-34806. 250p. 1998. text 55.00 (*0-312-21887-7*) St Martin.
— Microeconomics. (C). 1990. text 48.00 (*0-06-040902-9*) HarperTrade.
— Multivariable Calculus. 2nd ed. 471p. 1998. pap. text 76.00 (*0-13-863945-0*) P-H.
— 1999 Year Book Neurology & Neurosurgery. 2nd ed. (Illus.). 448p. 1999. text 81.00 (*0-8151-9649-0*, 24986) Mosby Inc.
***Bradley.** Pop. LC 99-57794. 40p. (J). (ps-1). 2001. 15.95 (*0-06-028700-4*) HarpC.
— Practical Computer Exercises. 1997. pap. write for info. (*0-7299-0261-7*) Addison-Wesley.
Bradley. Programming in Visual Basic TB. 1995. 11.25 (*0-697-20275-5*, WCB McGr Hill) McGrw-H Hghr Educ.
— Programming Visual Basic 6.0. LC 98-43108. 704p. 1998. pap. 54.38 (*0-07-231190-8*) McGraw.
— A Ruskin Chronology. 256p. 1997. text 49.95 (*0-312-16159-X*) St Martin.
***Bradley.** Tiger Burning Bright. 2000. 23.00 (*0-380-97258-1*) Morrow Avon.
Bradley. Urban Forest Landscapes: Integrating Multidisciplinary Perspectives. LC 94-23781. 240p. 1995. 40.00 (*0-295-97438-9*); pap. 20.00 (*0-295-97439-7*) U of Wash Pr.
— Using Pagemaker 6.0. 1997. pap. 52.50 (*0-07-561589-4*); pap., student ed. 52.50 (*0-07-561588-6*) McGraw.
— Using Pagemaker 6.5 Supplement. 1997. pap., student ed. 9.69 (*0-07-289887-9*); pap., student ed. 9.69 (*0-07-289888-7*) McGraw.
Bradley & Smith. Calculus. 2nd ed. LC 98-18962. 1056p. (C). 1998. 114.67 (*0-13-660135-9*) P-H.
— Single Variable Calculus. 1995. pap. text 80.00 (*0-13-207218-1*) P-H.
— Single Variable Calculus. 2nd ed. 815p. 1998. pap. text 89.33 (*0-13-639279-2*) P-H.
***Bradley, et al.** Neurology Clinical Practice Online Renewals. 2000. 195.00 (*0-7506-9994-9*) Buttrwrth-Heinemann.
Bradley, jt. auth. see Stonick, Virginia.
Bradley, jt. auth. see Wade.
Bradley, jt. ed. see Bell.
Bradley, Phil. Internet Power Searching: The Advanced Manual. LC 98-40957. 200p. 1999. pap. 45.00 (*1-55570-350-X*) Neal-Schuman.
Bradley & O'Donnell Staff. Regional Aid & Convergence: Evaluating the Impact. 320p. 1995. 87.95 (*1-85972-146-X*) Ashgate Pub Co.
Bradley, A. C. Oxford Lectures on Poetry. ix, 395p. 1986. reprint ed. pap. 29.95 (*0-935005-35-8*); reprint ed. lib. bdg. 46.95 (*0-935005-16-1*) Lincoln-Rembrandt.
— Shakespearean Tragedy: Lectures on Hamlet, Othello, King Lear & Macbeth. (New Shakespeare Library). 480p. 1991. pap. 14.95 (*0-14-053019-3*, Penguin Bks) Viking Penguin.
Bradley, A. G. Fight with France for North America. LC 77-146377. (First American Frontier Ser.). (Illus.). 1976. reprint ed. 39.95 (*0-405-02828-8*) Ayer.
— Highways & Byways in the Lake District. (Illus.). 340p. 1985. 25.00 (*0-7855-1041-9*, Pub. by Alloway Pub) St Mut.
Bradley, A. W. & Ewing, K. D. Constitutional & Administrative Law. 12th ed. LC 98-133568. liii, 886p. 1997. pap. 46.00 (*0-582-30817-8*, 15719) Gaunt.
— Constitutional & Administrative Law: (With Appendix on Constitutional Reforms) 12th ed. 900p. 1998. pap. 47.50 (*0-582-41443-1*) Gaunt.
Bradley, Adrienne. How Institutions Voted on Social Policy Shareholder Resolutions in the 1994 Proxy Season. Mathiasen, Carolyn, ed. 115p. 1994. pap. text 35.00 (*1-879775-21-2*) IRRC Inc DC.
Bradley, Alan. Optical Storage for Computers: Technology & Applications. 1989. text 49.95 (*0-470-21488-0*) P-H.
Bradley, Alfred, jt. auth. see Bond, Michael.
Bradley, Andrew C. Commentary on Tennyson's In Memoriam. (BCL1-PR English Literature Ser.). 251p. 1992. reprint ed. lib. bdg. 79.00 (*0-7812-7694-2*) Rprt Serv.
— Ideals of Religion. LC 77-27218. (Gifford Lectures: 1907). reprint ed. 42.50 (*0-404-60463-3*) AMS Pr.
— A Miscellany. LC 72-76894. (Essay Index Reprint Ser.). 1977. 21.95 (*0-8369-0005-7*) Ayer.
— A Miscellany. (BCL1-PR English Literature Ser.). 267p. 1992. reprint ed. lib. bdg. 79.00 (*0-7812-7009-X*) Rprt Serv.
— The Reaction Against Tennyson. 1974. 250.00 (*0-87968-139-X*) Gordon Pr.
— The Reaction Against Tennyson. (BCL1-PR English Literature Ser.). 19p. 1992. reprint ed. lib. bdg. 59.00 (*0-7812-7695-0*) Rprt Serv.
— Shakespearean Tragedy: Lectures on Hamlet, Othello, King Lear, Macbeth. (BCL1-PR English Literature Ser.). 498p. 1992. reprint ed. lib. bdg. 99.00 (*0-7812-7298-X*) Rprt Serv.
Bradley, Andrew V., jt. auth. see Hall, Betty L.
Bradley, Ann. Cows Are Vegetarians! A Book for Vegetarian Kids. 4th ed. (Illus.). 24p. (J). (gr. 2-8). 1998. pap. 11.95 (*0-9630893-0-7*) Healthways.
Bradley, Ann, ed. see Family Circle Editors.
Bradley, Ann K. History of the Irish in America. 192p. 1997. 14.98 (*0-7858-0731-4*) Bk Sales Inc.
Bradley, Annette, ed. see Eberle, Harold R.
Bradley, Anthony, ed. Contemporary Irish Poetry. rev. ed. 420p. 1988. pap. 19.95 (*0-520-05874-7*, Pub. by U CA Pr) Cal Prin Full Svc.
Bradley, Anthony & Valiulis, Maryann G., eds. Gender & Sexuality in Modern Ireland. LC 97-26859. 336p. 1997. 50.00 (*1-55849-130-9*); pap. 18.95 (*1-55849-131-7*) U of Mass Pr.
Bradley, Ardyth, et al. Three Winter Poems. (Illus.). 1985. pap. 20.00 (*0-318-41021-4*) Abattoir.
Bradley, Arthur G. Owen Glyndwr. LC 73-14435. (Heroes of the Nations Ser.). xvii, 357 p. 1978. reprint ed. 47.50 (*0-404-58253-2*) AMS Pr.
— The United Empire Loyalists. LC 75-136413. (BCL Ser. I). reprint ed. 20.00 (*0-404-00927-1*) AMS Pr.
Bradley, Austin, ed. & illus. see Omalia, Michael.
Bradley, B. A., jt. auth. see Gore, S. M.
Bradley, Barbara. Hawaiian Kids Cook & Color Book. pap. 5.95 (*0-930492-43-9*) Hawaiian Serv.
Bradley, Barry W. Costume. (Illus.). 35p. 1986. pap. 16.95 (*0-911704-35-3*) Western Res.
Bradley, Barry W., jt. auth. see WRHS Staff.
***Bradley, Bill.** Campaign Continues! (Illus.). 144p. 2000. 18.00 (*1-57965-165-8*) Artisan.
— Life on the Run. LC 99-36343. 295p. 1999. 29.95 (*1-56000-454-1*) Transaction Pubs.
Bradley, Bill. Life on the Run. 1995. pap. 12.00 (*0-679-76208-6*) Vin Bks.
— Time Present, Time Past. 1996. 27.50 (*0-614-13228-2*) Knopf.
— Time Present, Time Past: A Memoir. 442p. 1998. text 26.00 (*0-7881-5778-7*) DIANE Pub.
— Time Present, Time Past: A Memoir. 400p. 1996. 26.00 (*0-679-44488-2*) Knopf.
— Time Present, Time Past: A Memoir. LC 96-48105. 1997. pap. 13.00 (*0-679-76815-7*) Vin Bks.
— Time Present, Time Past: A Memoir. large type ed. LC 96-14353. 757p. 1996. 25.95 (*0-7862-0726-4*) Thorndike Pr.
Bradley, Bill. Values of the Game. LC 98-7280. (Illus.). 160p. 1998. 30.00 (*1-57965-116-X*, 85116) Artisan.
***Bradley, Bill.** Values of the Game. 96p. 2000. pap. 10.00 (*0-7679-0449-4*) Broadway BDD.
Bradley, Bill, et al. The United States & the Multilateral Development Banks. LC 98-152882. (Panel Reports). 153p. (C). 1998. pap. text 25.00 (*0-89206-326-2*) CSIS.
Bradley, Birt. The Romance of an Eastern Capital. (Illus.). 360p. 1986. reprint ed. 26.00 (*0-8364-1751-8*, Pub. by Chanakya) S Asia.
Bradley-Birt, F. B. Bengal Fairy Tales. 1976. lib. bdg. 59.95 (*0-8490-1487-5*) Gordon Pr.
— Chota Nagpur, a Little-Known Province of the Empire. LC 98-906407. xiv, 310 p. 1998. write for info. (*81-206-1287-6*) Asian Educ Servs.
Bradley, Bob, et al. Clemson: Where the Tigers Play: The History of Clemson University Athletics. 300p. 1999. 29.95 (*1-58382-005-1*) Sports Masters.
Bradley, Brendan P. & Thompson, Chris, eds. Psychological Applications in Psychiatry. LC 85-9383. 259p. reprint ed. pap. 80.30 (*0-7837-4411-0*, 204415400012) Bks Demand.
Bradley, Brian P. & Ferrari, Frank D., eds. Ecology & Morphology of Copepods: Proceedings of the 5th International Conference on Copepoda, Baltimore, U. S. A., June 6-13, 1993. LC 94-40635. (Developments in Hydrobiology Ser.: Vol. 102). 544p. (C). 1995. lib. bdg. 334.50 (*0-7923-3225-3*) Kluwer Academic.
Bradley, Bruce. Hugh Glass. 191p. 1999. pap. 15.95 (*0-9669005-0-2*, Pub. by Monarch Pr) ACCESS Pubs Network.
Bradley, Bruce, jt. auth. see Frison, George.
Bradley, Bruce A., jt. auth. see Frison, George C.
Bradley, Bryant W. Two Oilfield Water Systems. LC 86-3004. 272p. (C). 1987. text 48.50 (*0-89874-918-2*) Krieger.
Bradley, Buff. Endings: A Book about Death. LC 84-40752. (J). 1979. 10.95 (*0-201-00422-4*) HarpC Child Bks.
Bradley, C. The Technology of Diabetes Care: Converging Medical & Psychosocial Perspectives. x, 224p. 1991. text 116.00 (*3-7186-5084-3*, Harwood Acad Pubs) Gordon & Breach.
Bradley, C. Alan & Sarjeant, William S. Ms. Holmes of Baker Street: The Truth about Sherlock. (Illus.). 260p. 1989. 19.95 (*0-938501-09-7*) Wessex.
Bradley, C. Ross & Sabol, George P., eds. Zirconium in the Nuclear Industry: 11th International Symposium, No. 1295. (STP Ser.). (Illus.). 925p. 1996. text 195.00 (*0-8031-2406-6*, STP1295) ASTM.
Bradley, Candice, jt. ed. see Weisner, Tom.
Bradley, Carol A., jt. auth. see Ender, Philip B.
Bradley, Carol J. American Music Librarianship: A Biographical & Historical Survey. LC 89-17103. 248p. 1990. lib. bdg. 55.00 (*0-313-26820-7*, BMB/, Greenwood Pr) Greenwood.
— Music Collections in American Libraries: A Chronology. LC 81-2907. (Detroit Studies in Music Bibliography: No. 46). xi, 249p. 1981. 25.00 (*0-89990-002-X*) Harmonie Park Pr.
— Reader in Music Librarianship. LC 73-82994. 340p. 1983. lib. bdg. 59.95 (*0-313-24044-2*, ZRL/, Greenwood Pr) Greenwood.
Bradley, Catherine. The End of Apartheid. LC 95-17669. (Causes & Consequences Ser.). (Illus.). 80p. (YA). (gr. 7 up). 1995. lib. bdg. 27.11 (*0-8172-4055-1*) Raintree Steck-V.
— Freedom of Movement. LC 96-53581. (What Do We Mean by Human Rights? Ser.). 48p. (J). 1998. 22.00 (*0-531-14447-X*) Watts.
— Life in the Mountains. LC 94-231881. 32p. (J). (gr. 4-7). 1993. pap. 4.99 (*0-590-47608-4*) Scholastic Inc.
Bradley, Charles. How to Manage Your Paperwork: A Simple & Practical No-PC Record Keeping System for Individuals, Homes & Small Businesses. LC 87-35593. (Illus.). 128p. 1988. pap. 11.95 (*0-931856-07-8*) Hill Springs Pubns.
Bradley, Charles, ed. & compiled by see Lewis, William D.
Bradley, Charles C. Aleutian Echoes. LC 94-17938. (LanternLight Library: No. 1). (Illus.). xxvi, 286p. 1994. 35.00 (*0-912006-74-9*); pap. 25.00 (*0-912006-75-7*) U of Alaska Pr.
Bradley, Charles C., Jr. The Handsome People: A History of the Crow Indians & the Whites. 310p. 1991. 20.95 (*0-89992-330-5*); pap. text 14.95 (*0-89992-130-2*) Coun India Ed.
Bradley, Charles C. High Pressure Methods in Solid State Research. LC 68-58922. 183p. reprint ed. pap. 56.80 (*0-608-13326-4*, 205579800038) Bks Demand.
Bradley, Chris. Discovery Guide to Yemen. 192p. (C). 1990. 79.00 (*0-7855-7119-1*, Pub. by IMMEL Pubng) St Mut.
Bradley, Christ. Discovery Guide to Yemen. 388p. 1995. pap. 39.00 (*1-898162-15-8*, Pub. by IMMEL Pubng) St Mut.
Bradley, Christopher. The Certified Network Professional Study Guide. 832p. 1996. student ed. 69.99 incl. cd-rom (*0-7821-1902-6*, Network Pr) Sybex.
— Mrs. Thatcher's Cultural Policy: A Comparative Study of Globalised Cultural Systems. LC 98-60733. 200p. 1998. 28.00 (*0-88033-400-2*, Pub. by East Eur Monographs) Col U Pr.
Bradley, Claire, ed. Handbook of Psychology & Diabetes: A Guide to Psychological Measurement in Diabetes Research & Management. LC 94-4391. 437p. 1994. text 63.00 (*3-7186-5562-4*) Gordon & Breach.
— Handbook of Psychology & Diabetes: A Guide to Psychological Measurement in Diabetes Research & Management. LC 94-4391. 1994. pap. write for info. (*3-7186-5563-2*) Gordon & Breach.
Bradley, Clare, jt. ed. see McGee, Hannah M.
Bradley, Clark, jt. auth. see Mckinney, Heather.
Bradley, Colin P., ed. Prescribing in Primary Care. (Oxford General Practice Ser.: No. 42). (Illus.). 228p. 1998. pap. text 52.95 (*0-19-262687-6*) OUP.
Bradley, Concho. Devil's Den. large type ed. 256p. 1998. pap. 17.99 (*0-7089-5370-0*, Linford) Ulverscroft.
— The Flathead Country. large type ed. (Linford Western Large Print Ser.). 256p. 1997. pap. 16.99 (*0-7089-5144-9*) Ulverscroft.
***Bradley, Concho.** Stone Mountain. large type ed. 256p. 1999. pap. 18.99 (*0-7089-5490-1*, Linford) Ulverscroft.
Bradley, Craig M. The Failure of the Criminal Procedure Revolution. LC 92-42021. 280p. (C). 1993. text 35.00 (*0-8122-3200-3*) U of Pa Pr.
Bradley, Craig M., ed. Comparative Criminal Procedure. LC 99-21670. 472p. 1999. pap. 60.00 (*0-89089-670-4*) Carolina Acad Pr.
Bradley-Cromey, Nancy. Authority & Autonomy in l'Entree d'Espagne. LC 93-20545. (Studies in Medieval Literature: Vol. 9). 328p. 1993. text 15.00 (*0-8153-1332-2*, H1730) Garland.
Bradley, Curtis, jt. auth. see Friedenberg, Joan.
Bradley, Curtis H. & Friedenberg, Joan E. Foundations & Strategies for Bilingual Vocational Education: A Handbook for Vocational-Technical Education Personnel. LC LC1047.85.B7. 127p. reprint ed. pap. 39.40 (*0-8357-3343-2*, 203957200013) Bks Demand.
Bradley, Curtis H., jt. auth. see Friedenberg, Joan E.
Bradley, Cynthia. Whitehall, Cheam: A Brief History & Guide to the 16th Century Timber-Framed House in Cheam. 24p. 1985. pap. 40.00 (*0-9503224-4-X*, Pub. by Sutton Libs & Arts) St Mut.
Bradley, D. A. Power Electronics. 2nd ed. 1994. pap. 34.95 (*0-412-57100-5*, Chap & Hall NY) Chapman & Hall.
Bradley, D. A. & Danckwerts, P. Hydrocyclone. LC 64-22369. (International Series of Monographs in Chemical Engineering: Vol. 4). 1965. 152.00 (*0-08-010399-5*, Pub. by Pergamon Repr) Franklin.
***Bradley, D. A., et al.** Mechatronics: And the Development of Intelligent Machines & Systems. (Illus.). 400p. 2000. 27.50 (*0-7487-5443-1*, Pub. by S Thornes Pubs) Intl Spec Bk.
Bradley, David. Burmese: Language Survival Kit. 2nd ed. LC 97-180220. (BUR., Illus.). 176p. 1997. pap. 5.95 (*0-86442-341-1*) Lonely Planet.
— The Chaneysville Incident. 464p. 1982. mass mkt. 4.95 (*0-380-58586-3*, Avon Bks) Morrow Avon.
— The Chaneysville Incident. LC 80-8225. 448p. 1990. reprint ed. pap. 15.00 (*0-06-091681-8*, Perennial) HarperTrade.
— Dartmouth: A Visual Remembrance. Patrick, James B., ed. 144p. 1982. 35.00 (*0-940078-06-6*) Foremost Pubs.
— Hill Tribes Phrasebook. 2nd ed. (Lonely Planet Phrasebooks). 192p. 1999. pap. text 5.95 (*0-86442-635-6*) Lonely Planet.
— An Introduction to the Urantia Revelation. LC 98-92687. Orig. Title: An Introduction to the Urantia Book Revelation. 1998. write for info. (*0-9663270-0-4*) White Egret.
— No Place to Hide, 1946-1984. rev. ed. LC 83-40013. (Illus.). 241p. 1983. reprint ed. pap. 14.95 (*0-87451-275-1*) U Pr of New Eng.
— Thai Hill Tribes Phrasebook. (THA., Illus.). 184p. (Orig.). 1991. pap. 4.95 (*0-86442-131-1*) Lonely Planet.
Bradley, David, ed. New Virginia Review Anthology, Vol. 5. 300p. (Orig.). 1987. pap. 13.50 (*0-939233-01-0*) New VA.
Bradley, David & Fishkin, Shelley F., eds. The Encyclopedia of Civil Rights in America, 3 vols., Set. LC 97-25376. (Illus.). 1152p. (C). (gr. 13). 1997. text 249.00 (*0-7656-8000-9*, Sharpe Ref) M E Sharpe.
Bradley, David, et al. South East Asia: Phrasebook. (Illus.). 380p. 1997. pap. 6.95 (*0-86442-435-3*) Lonely Planet.
Bradley, David, jt. auth. see Begley, Louis.
Bradley, David A., jt. auth. see Creagh, D. C.
Bradley, David A., jt. auth. see Tsipenluk, Iu M.
Bradley, David J., et al. A Review of Environmental Health Impacts in Developing Country Cities. LC 92-24094. (Urban Management Program Ser.: No. 6). 71p. 1992. pap. 22.00 (*0-8213-2194-3*, 12194) World Bank.
Bradley, Denis J. Aquinas on the Twofold Human Good: Reason & Human Happiness in Aquina's Moral Science. 610p. 1997. pap. 39.95 (*0-8132-0952-8*) Cath U Pr.
Bradley, Denise J. Sweet Recovery: A Young Woman's Emotional Ride with Diabetes, Vision Loss, & an Eating Disorder...to Health & Freedom. LC 91-66399. (Illus.). 175p. (Orig.). 1992. pap. 9.95 (*0-9630526-1-6*); lib. bdg. 24.95 (*0-9630526-2-4*) Upbeat Prods.
Bradley, Dennis, ed. see Eberle, Harold R.
Bradley, Dianne F. & King Sears Staff. Teaching Students in Inclusive Settings. LC 96-29157. 432p. 1996. pap. text 55.00 (*0-205-16703-9*) Allyn.
Bradley, Diarmuid, jt. auth. see Smith, Colin.
Bradley, Dick. Understanding Rock 'N' Roll: Popular Music in Britain, 1955-1964. (Popular Music in Britain Ser.). 192p. 1992. 123.95 (*0-335-09755-3*); pap. 34.95 (*0-335-09754-5*) OpUniv Pr.
Bradley, Don. Angels in a Harsh World. 1997. pap. text 17.95 (*1-888298-02-2*) Native Planet.
— Common Sense & the Ageless Wisdom. (Illus.). 390p. (Orig.). 1997. pap. 14.95 (*1-888298-03-0*) Native Planet.
— Freemasonry in the Twenty-First Century. (Illus.). 344p. (Orig.). 1995. pap. 14.95 (*1-888298-00-6*) Native Planet.
— The Significance of the One. (Illus.). (Orig.). 1996. pap. 14.95 (*1-888298-01-4*) Native Planet.
Bradley, Don & Olsten, Haley. Angels in a Harsh World: A Novel. 320p. 1999. reprint ed. pap. 13.00 (*0-425-16690-2*) Berkley Pub.
Bradley, Don J. Behind the Nuclear Curtain: Radioactive Waste Management in the Former Soviet Union. Payson, David R., ed. LC 96-41744. (Illus.). 726p. 1997. 95.00 (*1-57477-022-5*) Battelle.
Bradley, Donal D., jt. ed. see Kippelen, Bernard.
Bradley, E. B. Molecules & Molecular Lasers for Electrical Engineers. (Series in Electrical Engineering). 200p. 1990. 105.00 (*0-89116-788-9*) Hemisp Pub.
Bradley, E. Ross, jt. ed. see Garde, Anand M.
Bradley, E. Sculley, ed. see Whitman, Walt.
***Bradley, Edward.** Diary of a Poet. 1999. pap. write for info. (*1-58235-109-0*) Watermrk Pr.
Bradley, Edward J. The Child & Family Genealogy Reporting System. 2nd ed. 1981. 9.95 (*0-935202-01-3*) Child & Family Ent.
Bradley, Edward L., III. The Patient's Guide to Surgery. Consumer Reports Books Editors, ed. (Illus.). 256p. (C). 1994. text 26.50 (*0-8122-3280-1*) U of Pa Pr.
Bradley, Edward L., III, ed. Acute Pancreatitis: Principles & Practice. LC 93-24917. 320p. 1993. text 131.50 (*0-7817-0091-4*) Lppncott W & W.
Bradley, Edward S. George Henry Boker. LC 68-57753. (Illus.). 1972. reprint ed. 26.95 (*0-405-08301-7*, Pub. by Blom Pubns) Ayer.
— George Henry Boker, Poet & Patriot. LC 70-94467. (BCL Ser. I). (Illus.). reprint ed. 34.50 (*0-404-00928-X*) AMS Pr.
— George Henry Boker, Poet & Patriot. (BCL1-PS American Literature Ser.). 361p. 1992. reprint ed. lib. bdg. 89.00 (*0-7812-6679-3*) Rprt Serv.
Bradley, Edward S., jt. auth. see Teweles, Richard J.
Bradley, Edwin M. The First Hollywood Musicals: A Critical Filmography of 171 Features, 1927-1932. LC 96-11762. (Illus.). 400p. 1996. lib. bdg. 75.00 (*0-89950-945-2*) McFarland & Co.
Bradley, Elihu F., ed. Superalloys: A Technical Guide. LC 88-70147. (Illus.). 292p. 1988. reprint ed. pap. 90.60 (*0-608-02613-1*, 206327100004) Bks Demand.
Bradley, Eliza. An Authentic Narrative of the Shipwreck & Sufferings of Mrs. Eliza Bradley. 1986. 12.95 (*0-87770-371-X*) Ye Galleon.
***Bradley, Elizabeth.** Decorative Victorian Needlework: Over 25 Charted Designs. (Illus.). 168p. 2000. pap. 19.95 (*0-8069-5583-X*) Sterling.
— Needlework Antique Flowers: With over 25 Charted Designs. (Illus.). 2000. pap. 19.95 (*0-8069-5579-1*) Sterling.
Bradley, Erica. I am Lutheran. LC 98-20145. (Religions of the World Ser.). 24p. (J). (gr. k-4). 1999. 17.26 (*0-8239-5263-0*) Rosen Group.
Bradley, F. H. Collected Works of F. H. Bradley. 1999. 775.00 (*1-85506-577-0*) Thoemmes Pr.
— Ethical Studies. 2nd ed. 368p. 1988. pap. text 26.00 (*0-19-881039-3*) OUP.
***Bradley, F. H.** F. H. Bradley: Miscellaneous Writtings, 5 Vol. Carol A. Keene, ed. & intro. by. 2000p. 1999. 750.00 (*1-85506-592-4*) Thoemmes Pr.
Bradley, F. H. Writings on Logic & Metaphysics. Allard, James W. & Stock, Guy, eds. LC 94-10327. 372p. 1995. text 68.00 (*0-19-824445-2*); pap. text 28.00 (*0-19-824438-X*) OUP.
Bradley, F. W., et al. A Word List from South Carolina, Expressions from Rural Florida, Minorcan Dialect Words in St. Augus-tine, Florida. (Publications of the American Dialect Society: No. 14). 81p. 1950. pap. text 8.50 (*0-8173-0614-5*) U of Ala Pr.
Bradley, F. W., jt. auth. see Reed, David W.
Bradley, Fern, ed. see Organic Gardening Editors.
Bradley, Fern M., ed. The Experts Book of Garden Hints: Over 1500 Tips & Techniques from America's Best Gardeners. LC 93-2767. (Illus.). 352p. 1993. text 27.95 (*0-87596-555-5*) Rodale Pr Inc.
— Rodale's Garden Answers. large type ed. 1996. pap. 25.95 (*0-7838-1608-1*, G K Hall Lrg Type) Mac Lib Ref.
Bradley, Fern M. & Ellis, Barbara W., eds. Rodale's All-New Encyclopedia of Organic Gardening: The Indispensable Resource for Every Gardener. LC 91-32088. (Illus.). 704p. 1992. text 29.95 (*0-87857-999-0*, 01-432-0) Rodale Pr Inc.

— Rodale's All-New Encyclopedia of Organic Gardening: The Indispensable Resource for Every Gardener. 704p. 1993. pap. 19.95 (*0-87596-599-7*) Rodale Pr Inc.

Bradley, Fern M. & Marshall, Fern. Rodale's Chemical-Free Yard & Garden: The Ultimate Authority on Successful Organic Gardening. (Illus.). 464p. 1995. pap. 17.95 (*0-87596-694-2*) Rodale Pr Inc.

Bradley, Fern M., jt. auth. see Ellis, Barbara W.

***Bradley, Fern Marshall.** Gardening with Perennials. LC 95-39854. (Illus.). 320p. 2000. pap. text 19.95 (*0-87596-844-9*) Rodale Pr Inc.

— Rodale's Garden Answers: Vegetables, Fruits & Herbs. (Illus.). 2000. pap. 17.95 (*0-87596-845-7*) Rodale Pr Inc.

Bradley, Fern Marshall, ed. see Ellis, Barbara W. & Kaczorowski, Barbara.

Bradley, Fiona. Surrealism. (Movements in Modern Art Ser.). (Illus.). 80p. (C). 1998. pap. 13.95 (*0-521-62756-7*) Cambridge U Pr.

Bradley, Fiona, ed. Rachel Whiteread. LC 96-61179. (Illus.). 132p. (Orig.). 1997. pap. 24.95 (*0-500-27936-5*, Pub. by Thames Hudson) Norton.

Bradley, Fiona, et al. Paula Rego: Retrospective. LC 96-61422. (Illus.). 148p. (Orig.). 1997. pap. 29.95 (*0-500-27943-8*, Pub. by Thames Hudson) Norton.

Bradley, Fiona, jt. ed. see Ades, Dawn.

Bradley, Floyd N. Ten Years Behind the Sacred Desk. 1988. pap. 9.99 (*0-88019-232-1*) Schmul Pub Co.

Bradley, Francine. An Introduction to Poultry Management. (C). 2001. 53.33 (*0-13-474719-4*, Macmillan Coll) P-H.

Bradley, Francis H. Collected Essays, 2 Vols. LC 68-54333. (Essay Index Reprint Ser.). 1977. reprint ed. 44.95 (*0-8369-0244-0*) Ayer.

— The Presuppositions of Critical History Bound with Aphorisms: 1874/1930 Editions. (Key Texts Ser.). 132p. 1996. reprint ed. pap. 19.95 (*1-85506-214-3*) Bks Intl VA.

Bradley, Francis S., ed. see United States Children's Bureau Staff.

Bradley, Francis W., jt. auth. see Pound, Louise.

Bradley, Frank. International Marketing Strategy. 440p. 1991. boxed set 53.33 (*0-13-317900-1*) P-H.

— International Marketing Strategy. 2nd ed. LC 94-36255. 570p. (C). 1995. pap. 89.00 (*0-13-149527-5*, Macmillan Coll) P-H.

— International Marketing Strategy. 3rd ed. LC 98-33968. 504p. 2000. 56.00 (*0-13-010057-9*) P-H.

— Marketing Management: Providing, Communicating & Delivering Value. 990p. 1995. pap. 84.00 (*0-13-065343-8*) P-H.

Bradley, Fred. Credentialing in Counseling. 110p. 1991. pap. text 14.95 (*1-55620-087-0*, 72297) Am Coun Assn.

Bradley, Fred, jt. auth. see Stone, Lloyd.

Bradley, Fred, tr. see Fleck, Ludwig.

Bradley, G. & Hendrick, H. W., eds. Human Factors in Organizational Design & Management IV: Development, Introduction, & Use of New Technology - Challenges for Human Organization & Human Resource Development in a Changing World; Proceedings of the 4th International Symposium on Human Factors in Organizational Design & Management, Stockholm, Sweden, May 29-June2, 1994. 794p. 1994. 171.50 (*0-444-89952-9*, North Holland) Elsevier.

Bradley, G., ed. see Crivello, J. V. & Dietliker, K. K.

Bradley, G. A. The Bremen Town Musicians: 4 Animals Going to Bremen to Make Music. 30p. (J). (gr. 2-4). 1994. 29.95 (*1-886123-02-0*) Geyers Garten.

— Hansel & Gretel. 2nd rev. ed. (Illus.). 36p. (J). (gr. 2-4). 1998. 29.95 (*1-886123-09-8*) Geyers Garten.

— Hansel & Gretel: German Shepherd Dogs As Hansel & Gretel. 30p. (J). (gr. 3). 1994. 26.95 (*1-886123-00-4*) Geyers Garten.

— Three Little Pigs & the Big Bad Wolf: Three Little Rottweilers & the Big, Bad German Shepherd. (Illus.). 34p. (J). (gr. 2-4). 1995. 29.95 (*1-886123-05-5*) Geyers Garten.

Bradley, G. A., photos by. Mother Goose Revisited: German Shepherd Puppies Reenacting Nursery Rhymes. (Illus.). (J). (gr. 2-4). 1994. 29.95 (*1-886123-04-7*) Geyers Garten.

— Mother Goose Revisited: Rottweiler Puppies Reenacting Nursery Rhymes. (Illus.). 32p. (J). (gr. 2-4). 1994. 29.95 (*1-886123-01-2*) Geyers Garten.

***Bradley, G. R.** Of Heartbeats & Heroes. 58p. 2000. pap. 7.95 (*0-915153-38-6*) Gold Star Pr.

Bradley, Gary M., jt. auth. see Stringham, Rex A.

***Bradley, Gaydell.** Meditations. 1999. pap. write for info. (*1-58235-181-3*) Watermrk Pr.

Bradley, Geoffrey L. Never a Dad Around. (Illus.). 14p. (J). (gr. k-4). 1999. pap. 2.99 (*0-9667940-2-8*) World of WISDOM.

— Visions in Poetry. 60p. 1998. pap. 6.95 (*0-9667940-0-1*) World of WISDOM.

Bradley, Geoffrey L. & White, Ashley N. Zeph - The Lion-Hearted. (Illus.). 32p. (J). (ps-3). 1998. pap. 3.99 (*0-9667940-1-X*) World of WISDOM.

Bradley, George. The Fire Fetched Down. 80p. 1996. 21.00 (*0-679-44620-6*) Knopf.

— The Fire Fetched Down. 80p. 1998. pap. 13.00 (*0-679-76602-2*) Knopf.

— Of the Knowledge of Good & Evil. LC 90-53417. 80p. 1992. pap. 12.00 (*0-679-74273-5*) Knopf.

Bradley, George. Problem Solving with Creative Mathematics. 178p. 1994. pap. 36.95 (*0-534-24360-6*) Brooks-Cole.

Bradley, George. Terms to Be Met. LC 85-22584. (Younger Poets Ser.: No. 18). 96p. 1986. 10.00 (*0-300-03598-5*) Yale U Pr.

Bradley, George, ed. The Yale Younger Poets Anthology. LC 97-35444. (Yale Series of Younger Poets). 384p. 1998. 35.00 (*0-300-07472-7*); pap. 16.00 (*0-300-07473-5*) Yale U Pr.

Bradley, George K. Fort Wayne & Wabash Valley Trolleys: Bulletin No. 122. LC 82-71475. (Illus.). 288p. 1983. 36.00 (*0-915348-22-5*) Central Electric.

— Northern Indiana Railway: Bulletin No. 132. LC 98-73157. (Illus.). 244p. 1999. 55.00 (*0-915348-32-2*, B-132) Central Electric.

Bradley, Gerald, jt. auth. see Hoffmann, Laurence D.

Bradley, Gerald L., jt. auth. see Hoffman, Laurence D.

Bradley, Gerald L., jt. auth. see Hoffmann, Laurence D.

***Bradley, Gerald V. & De Marco, Donald, eds.** Science & Faith: Proceeding from the 21st Convention of the Fellowship at Catholic Scholars , 1998. LC 00-8720. 192p. 2000. pap. 16.00 (*1-890318-80-9*, Pub. by St Augustines Pr) U Ch Pr.

Bradley, Gerard V. Church-State Relationships in America, 37. LC 86-27149. (Contributions in Legal Studies: No. 37). 180p. 1987. 49.95 (*0-313-25494-X*, BYC/, Greenwood Pr) Greenwood.

Bradley, Gerard V., jt. ed. see Barry, Robert L.

Bradley, Gibbs. 2001 Year Book of Neurology & Neurosurgery. (Illus.). 512p. 2001. text 78.00 (*0-8151-0930-X*, 30638) Mosby Inc.

— 2000 Year Book of Neurology & Neurosurgery. (Illus.). 512p. 2000. text 78.00 (*0-8151-0322-0*, 30637) Mosby Inc.

Bradley, Gordon A., ed. Land Use & Forest Resources in a Changing Environment: The Urban-Forest Interface. (George S. Long Publications). 238p. 1984. 40.00 (*0-295-96104-X*); pap. 20.00 (*0-295-96145-7*) U of Wash Pr.

Bradley, Graham W. Disease, Diagnosis, & Decision. 200p. 1993. pap. 108.50 (*0-471-93929-3*) Wiley.

Bradley, Gunilla. Computers & the Psychosocial Work Environment. 270p. 1989. pap. 65.00 (*0-85066-457-8*) Taylor & Francis.

***Bradley, Guy.** Ancient Umbria: State, Culture, & Identity in Central Italy from the Iron Age to the Augustan Era. (Illus.). 300p. 2001. text 74.00 (*0-19-815301-5*) OUP.

Bradley, H., ed. see Caxton, William.

Bradley, H. E. Operational Research '90: Selected Papers from the Twelfth International Conference on Operational Research, June 1990. 848p. 1991. pap. 23.50 (*0-08-040239-9*, Pergamon Pr) Elsevier.

Bradley, H. E. & IFORS - International Fed. Op. Res. Societie Staff. Operational Research '90: Selected Papers from the Twelfth International Conference on Operational Research, June 1990. LC 91-8520. 848p. 1991. 366.00 (*0-08-040240-2*, Pub. by Pergamon Repr) Franklin.

Bradley, H. Woodrow. Phases of Life: Observations on Modern Life. LC 93-73425. 236p. (Orig.). 1993. pap. text 9.95 (*0-9639246-0-5*) Dream Pubng.

Bradley, Harriet. Enclosures in England: An Economic Reconstruction. LC 70-76715. (Columbia University. Studies in the Social Sciences: No. 186). reprint ed. 37.50 (*0-404-51186-4*) AMS Pr.

Bradley, Harriett. Fractured Identities: Changing Patterns of Inequality. LC 95-40291. 240p. (C). 1996. pap. text 27.95 (*0-7456-1084-6*, Pub. by Polity Pr) Blackwell Pubs.

— Fractured Identities: Changing Patterns of Inequality. LC 95-40291. 240p. (C). 1996. text 62.95 (*0-7456-1083-8*, Pub. by Polity Pr) Blackwell Pubs.

Bradley, Hassell, jt. auth. see Houser, Peggy.

Bradley, Helen O. His Mistress - His Worst Half. (Orig.). Date not set. pap. write for info. (*0-9658140-1-7*) Bradleys Pub.

— Soulmate. (Orig.). Date not set. pap. write for info. (*0-9658140-2-5*) Bradleys Pub.

— They Say I Broke the Rule. 128p. (Orig.). Date not set. pap. 25.00 (*0-9658140-0-9*) Bradleys Pub.

Bradley, Henry, ed. see Stratmann, Francis H.

Bradley-Hole, Christopher. The Minimalist Garden. LC 99-32815. (Illus.). 208p. 1999. text 50.00 (*1-58093-055-7*, Pub. by Monacelli Pr) Penguin Putnam.

Bradley, Hope. These Hands. LC 99-19157. 24p. (J). (ps-1). 1999. lib. bdg. 15.49 (*0-7868-2320-8*, Pub. by Hyperion) Time Warner.

Bradley, Howard. Staff Development. (School Development & the Management of Change Ser.). 224p. 1991. 75.00 (*1-85000-827-2*, Falmer Pr); pap. 29.95 (*1-85000-828-0*, Falmer Pr) Taylor & Francis.

Bradley, Howard, et al, eds. Developing Teachers Developing Schools: Making INSET Effective for the School. 208p. 1994. pap. 27.00 (*1-85346-321-3*, Pub. by David Fulton) Taylor & Francis.

Bradley, Howard W. Handbook of Coins of the British Isles. 2nd ed. (Illus.). 212p. 1982. 37.50 (*0-7090-0652-7*) Trans-Atl Phila.

Bradley, Hugh. Such Was Saratoga. LC 75-1832. (Leisure Class in America Ser.). 1975. reprint ed. 28.95 (*0-405-06901-4*) Ayer.

Bradley, Hugh H., jt. auth. see Armbrust, Betty J.

***Bradley, Ian.** Book of Hymns. 480p. 2000. 12.99 (*0-517-16241-5*) Random Hse Value.

Bradley, Ian. Celtic Christianity: Making Myths & Chasing Dreams. LC 98-50807. 288p. 1999. text 45.00 (*0-312-22196-7*) St Martin.

— The Celtic Way. pap. write for info. (*0-232-52001-1*) S Asia.

— Metalwork & Machining Hints & Tips. (Workshop Practice Ser.: No. 20). (Illus.). 96p. (Orig.). 1988. pap. 18.50 (*0-85242-947-9*, Pub. by Nexus Special Interests) Trans-Atl Phila.

***Bradley, Ian.** Penguin Book of Carols. 480p. 2000. pap. 12.95 (*0-14-027526-6*, Penguin Bks) Viking Penguin.

Bradley, Ian. The Power of Sacrifice. pap. write for info. (*0-232-52057-7*) S Asia.

Bradley, Ian, ed. The Book of Hymns. LC 88-31254. 476p. 1989. 24.95 (*0-87951-346-2*, Pub. by Overlook Pr) Penguin Putnam.

— The Book of Hymns. 480p. 1992. reprint ed. pap. 15.95 (*0-87951-460-4*, Pub. by Overlook Pr) Penguin Putnam.

— The Complete Annotated Gilbert & Sullivan. (Illus.). 1,212p. 1996. 45.00 (*0-19-816503-X*) OUP.

Bradley, Ian & Hallows, N. The Amateur's Workshop. 3rd ed. (Illus.). 256p. (Orig.). 1984. pap. 26.50 (*1-85486-130-1*, Pub. by Nexus Special Interests) Trans-Atl Phila.

Bradley, Ian C. Abide with Me: The World of Victorian Hymns. LC 97-36372. 299p. (C). 1997. 24.95 (*1-57999-010-X*) GIA Pubns.

Bradley, J. Diagnostic Tests in Nephrology. (Illus.). 312p. 1999. pap. text 49.50 (*0-340-74085-X*, Pub. by E A) OUP.

***Bradley, J.** Major Companies of Scandinavia 2000. 5th ed. 1999. pap. text 560.00 (*1-86099-171-8*, Pub. by G & W) Am Educ Systs.

***Bradley, J. E., ed.** The Top 5,000 European Companies 1999. 1400p. 1999. 630.00 (*1-86099-158-0*, Pub. by G & W) Gale.

Bradley, J. E., tr. see Chernov, A. A., ed.

Bradley, J. E., tr. see Givargizov, E. I. & Grinberg, S. A., eds.

Bradley, J. E., tr. see Sheftal, N. N. & Givargizov, E. I., eds.

Bradley, J. F. Politics in Czechoslovakia, 1945-1989. 200p. 1991. text 42.00 (*0-88033-212-3*, Pub. by East Eur Monographs) Col U Pr.

Bradley, J. L. Ruskin: The Critical Heritage. LC 83-11102. (Critical Heritage Ser.). 436p. 1984. 69.50 (*0-7100-9286-5*, Routledge Thoemms) Routledge.

Bradley, J. N. & Bradley, J. N. Flame & Combustion. 2nd ed. 344p. (C). 1985. text 65.00 (*0-412-23030-5*, NO. 9254); pap. text 35.00 (*0-412-23040-2*, NO. 9255) Chapman & Hall.

Bradley, J. N, jt. auth. see Bradley, J. N.

Bradley, J. S., et al, eds. Chemical Processes in Inorganic Materials: Metal & Semiconductor Clusters & Colloids. (Materials Research Society Symposium Proceedings Ser.: Vol. 272). 331p. 1992. text 30.00 (*1-55899-167-0*) Materials Res.

Bradley, Jack L., jt. auth. see Klein, Jerry.

Bradley, James. Comprehensive Structured COBOL. (C). 1990. text 65.25 (*0-07-007078-4*); pap. text, teacher ed. 23.12 (*0-07-007079-2*) McGraw.

***Bradley, James.** The Deep Field: A Novel. LC 99-55558. 346p. 2000. 26.00 (*0-8050-6111-8*) H Holt & Co.

Bradley, James. Introduction to Discrete Mathematics. LC 87-27067. (Illus.). 528p. (C). 1988. text 52.75 (*0-201-10628-0*) Addison-Wesley.

Bradley, James. Wrack. LC 98-41603. 340p. 1999. 25.00 (*0-8050-6108-8*) H Holt & Co.

***Bradley, James.** Wrack. 2000. pap. 13.00 (*0-8050-6447-8*) St Martin.

— Wrack. LC 97-134901. (Illus.). 1997. write for info. (*0-09-183494-5*) Trafalgar.

Bradley, James & Johnson, Peter, eds. Philosophy after F. H. Bradley. (Idealism Ser.: No. 3). 390p. 1996. 75.00 (*1-85506-484-7*); pap. 27.00 (*1-85506-485-5*) Bks Intl VA.

***Bradley, James & Powers, Ron.** Flags of Our Fathers. LC 00-25803. (Illus.). 384p. 2000. 24.95 (*0-553-11133-7*, Spectra) Bantam.

Bradley, James & Schaefer, Kurt. The Uses & Misuses of Data & Models: The Mathematization of the Human Sciences. LC 98-9037. 212p. 1998. 48.00 (*0-7619-0921-4*); pap. 21.95 (*0-7619-0922-2*) Sage.

Bradley, James, jt. auth. see Duffield, Ian.

Bradley, James E. & Muller, Richard A. Church History: An Introduction to Research, Reference Works, & Methods. LC 94-40617. 228p. (Orig.). 1995. pap. 19.00 (*0-8028-0826-3*) Eerdmans.

Bradley, James E. & Muller, Richard A., eds. Church, Word, & Spirit: Historical & Theological Essays in Honor of Geoffrey W. Bromiley. LC 87-24447. 335p. reprint ed. pap. 103.90 (*0-8357-8559-9*, 203490800091) Bks Demand.

Bradley, James H. The March of the Montana Column: A Prelude to the Custer Disaster. Stewart, Edgar I., ed. LC 61-6494. (American Exploration & Travel Ser.: Vol. 32). (Illus.). 216p. 1991. pap. 11.95 (*0-8061-2316-8*) U of Okla Pr.

Bradley, James T. North American Locomotive Production, 1968-1989. (Illus.). 192p. 1989. 27.50 (*0-9624633-0-2*) Bradley Enterprises.

— North American Maintenance of Way Equipment. (Illus.). 64p. (C). 1992. pap. 19.95 (*0-9624633-4-5*) Bradley Enterprises.

— North American Non Revenue Freight Cars. (Illus.). 64p. (C). 1993. pap. 19.95 (*0-9624633-5-3*) Bradley Enterprises.

Bradley, James W. Evolution of the Onondaga Iroquois: Accommodating Change, 1500-1655. LC 87-1977. (Iroquois Bks.). (Illus.). 271p. 1987. reprint ed. pap. 84.10 (*0-608-06950-7*, 206715800009) Bks Demand.

Bradley, Jana & Bradley, Larry. Improving Written Communication in Libraries. LC 88-10059. 364p. 1988. text 14.00 (*0-8389-0497-1*) ALA.

Bradley, Jane. Living Doll. LC 94-11244. 202p. 1995. 22.00 (*1-877946-54-0*) Permanent Pr.

Bradley, Jane, jt. auth. see Calhoun, Susan.

Bradley, Jane B. World Alive. 40p. 1997. pap. 6.00 (*1-888219-07-6*) Pearl Edit.

***Bradley, Jean Burr.** Trumpet Call. LC 00-190707. 188p. 2000. 25.00 (*0-7388-1942-5*); pap. 18.00 (*0-7388-1943-3*) Xlibris Corp.

Bradley, Jean C. & Edinberg, Mark A. Communication in the Nursing Context. 3rd ed. (Illus.). 276p. (C). 1990. pap. text 32.95 (*0-8385-1327-1*, A1327-4) Appleton & Lange.

Bradley, Jean W. A Home Across the Water. (Illus.). 224p. (Orig.). 1996. pap. 9.95 (*0-9652061-0-6*) Braeward Pub.

***Bradley, Jean Wardle.** Autumn Leaves: Stories, Poems & Memories. (Illus.). 96p. 1999. pap. 10.00 (*0-9652061-1-4*) Braeward Pub.

Bradley, Jeff. Moon Handbooks: Tennessee: Including Nashville, Memphis, the Great Smoky Mountains & Nutbush. 2nd rev. ed. Vol. 2. (Illus.). 540p. 1999. pap. 17.95 (*1-56691-147-8*, Moon Handbks) Avalon Travel.

— A Young Person's Guide to Military Service. rev. ed. LC 86-33719. (Illus.). 240p. (YA). 1987. pap. 9.95 (*0-916782-83-2*) Harvard Common Pr.

Bradley, Jeff, jt. auth. see Struber, Robert.

Bradley, Jenetta. Taints My Soul. 164p. 1997. pap. write for info. (*1-57579-066-1*) Pine Hill Pr.

Bradley, Jerry. Simple Versions of Disaster. LC 91-8955. (Texas Poets Ser.: Vol. 3). 134p. 1991. pap. 9.95 (*0-929398-25-4*) UNTX Pr.

Bradley, Jerry A. The Movement: British Poets of the 1950's. LC 93-7653. (English Authors Ser.: Vol. 302). 170p. 1993. 28.95 (*0-8057-7040-2*, Twyne) Mac Lib Ref.

Bradley, Jesse F. The Jonson Allusion-Book. (BCL1-PR English Literature Ser.). 466p. 1992. reprint ed. lib. bdg. 99.00 (*0-7812-7257-2*) Rprt Serv.

— The Jonson Allusion-Book: A Collection of Allusions to Ben Jonson from 1597 to 1700. (BCL1-PR English Literature Ser.). 466p. 1992. reprint ed. lib. bdg. 99.00 (*0-7812-7246-7*) Rprt Serv.

Bradley, Jesse F. & Adams, Joseph Q., eds. The Jonson Allusion-Book: A Collection of Allusions to Ben Jonson from 1597 to 1700. LC 76-144893. 1971. reprint ed. 16.00 (*0-403-00813-1*) Scholarly.

Bradley, Jessica. Giuseppe Penone. (National Gallery of Canada Ser.). (Illus.). 72p. (C). 1984. pap. 15.00 (*0-685-08531-7*, 56368-5, Pub. by Natl Mus Sci Tech) U Ch Pr.

***Bradley, Jo & Yates, Chris.** Basic Education at a Distance. LC 00-36782. (World Review of Distance Education & Open Learning Ser.). 2000. write for info. (*0-415-23774-2*) Routledge.

Bradley, John. Cases of Greece Spaine, 1-VVI-2. 1998. 80.00 (*0-7494-2339-0*) Kogan Page Ltd.

***Bradley, John.** Ephrata Cloister: Pennsylvania Trail of History Guide. LC 00-39493. (Illus.). 2000. pap. write for info. (*0-8117-2744-0*) Stackpole.

Bradley, John. Love-In-Idleness: The Poetry of Roberto Zingarello. LC 89-51372. 72p. 1989. 10.00 (*0-915380-24-2*) Word Works.

— Modern Pacing Sire Lines. LC 98-36915. 1998. 39.95 (*0-929346-56-4*) R Meerdink Co Ltd.

— Modern Trotting Sire Lines. LC 97-8948. 1997. 40.00 (*0-929346-47-5*) R Meerdink Co Ltd.

Bradley, John. Post-Communist Czechoslovakia. 250p. Date not set. lib. bdg. 35.00 (*0-88033-386-3*, 489, Pub. by East Eur Monographs) Col U Pr.

Bradley, John. Russia: Building Democracy. LC 95-20811. (Topics in the News Ser.). 32p. (J). (gr. 3-6). 1995. lib. bdg. 22.83 (*0-8172-4177-9*) Raintree Steck-V.

— Walled Towns in Ireland. (Irish Treasures Ser.). (Illus.). 48p. (Orig.). (YA). 1995. pap. 8.95 (*0-946172-46-3*, Pub. by Town Hse) Roberts Rinehart.

Bradley, John, ed. Atomic Ghost: Poets Respond to the Nuclear Age. LC 94-29816. (Illus.). 250p. (Orig.). 1995. pap. 15.95 (*1-56689-027-6*) Coffee Hse.

***Bradley, John, ed.** Learning to Glow: A Nuclear Reader. LC 99-6961. 330p. 2000. pap. 22.95 (*0-8165-1956-0*) U of Ariz Pr.

— Learning to Grow: A Nuclear Reader. LC 99-6961. 332p. 2000. lib. bdg. 45.00 (*0-8165-1955-2*) U of Ariz Pr.

Bradley, John & McCluskoy, Jim. Clinical Immunology. LC 96-30986. (Illus.). 588p. (C). 1997. text 98.50 (*0-19-262518-7*) OUP.

Bradley, John, et al. Discovering Your Natural Talents: How to Love What You Do & Do What You Love at Home, Work, Church, Play. LC 90-63216. 184p. (Orig.). 1991. pap. 12.00 (*0-89109-395-8*) NavPress.

— Molecular Medicine. LC 95-8412. (Lecture Notes Ser.). 1995. 29.95 (*0-632-03851-9*) Blackwell Sci.

— Stabilization & Growth in the EC Periphery. (Study of the Irish Economy Ser.). 210p. 1993. 72.95 (*1-85628-539-1*, Pub. by Avebry) Ashgate Pub Co.

Bradley, John, jt. see Anderson, Ken.

Bradley, John, jt. auth. see Baudin, Jeff.

Bradley, John E. Smoke. LC 93-2574. 1995. 23.00 (*0-8050-2421-2*) H Holt & Co.

***Bradley, John Ed.** My Juliet. LC 99-89051. 288p. 2000. 23.95 (*0-385-49803-9*) Doubleday.

Bradley, John F. Czech Nationalism in the 19th Century. 153p. 1984. text 53.50 (*0-88033-049-X*, Pub. by East Eur Monographs) Col U Pr.

— The Czechoslovak Legion in Russia, 1914-1920. 200p. 1992. text 37.50 (*0-88033-218-2*, Pub. by East Eur Monographs) Col U Pr.

— War & Peace since 1945. 204p. 1989. text 49.00 (*0-88033-964-0*, Pub. by East Eur Monographs) Col U Pr.

Bradley, John F., ed. Soviet Perestroika, 1985-1993: Russia's Road to Democracy. 220p. 1996. 31.00 (*0-88033-332-4*, 435, Pub. by East Eur Monographs) Col U Pr.

***Bradley, John Hodgdon.** Farewell Thou Busy World. LC 00-30852. (Illus.). 112p. 2000. 18.95 (*1-58667-013-1*, Pub. by Derrydale Pr) Natl Bk Netwk.

Bradley, John L., ed. see Ruskin, John.

***Bradley, John R.** Henry James's Permanent Adolescence. LC 00-33338. 2000. write for info. (*0-312-23560-7*) St Martin.

Bradley, John S., jt. auth. see Nelson, John D.

Bradley, John S., ed. see International Bar Association, Section on Business.

B

Bradley, John S., jt. ed. see Makrinenko, Leonid I.

Bradley-Johnson, Sharon. Psychoeducational Assessment of Students Who Are Visually Impaired or Blind: Infancy Through High School. 2nd rev. ed. LC 93-23211. (Illus.). 253p. (C). 1994. pap. 29.00 (*0-89079-599-1*, 6693) PRO-ED.

Bradley-Johnson, Sharon & Evans, Larry D. Psychoeducational Assessment of Hearing-Impaired Students: Infancy Through High School. LC 90-27491. 251p. 1991. pap. text 29.00 (*0-89079-455-3*, 1949) PRO-ED.

Bradley-Johnson, Sharon & Johnson, C. Merle. A Handbook for Writing Effective Psychoeducational Reports. LC 97-38330. 60p. 1998. pap. text 14.00 (*0-89079-747-1*, 8549) PRO-ED.

Bradley-Johnson, Sharon & Lesiak, Judi L. Problems in Written Expression: Assessment & Remediation. LC 88-32830. (School Practitioner Ser.). 178p. 1989. pap. text 22.00 (*0-89862-233-6*); lib. bdg. 49.95 (*0-89862-354-5*) Guilford Pubns.

Bradley-Johnson, Sharon, et al. Baby Power: A New Addition. (Illus.). 32p. (Orig.). (YA). 1981. pap. 3.00 (*1-878526-05-7*) Pineapple MI.

Bradley, Jon. Runaway Youth: Stress, Social Support, & Adjustment. LC 96-37894. (Children of Poverty Ser.). 152p. 1997. text 44.00 (*0-8153-2798-6*) Garland.

Bradley, Jonathan. Understanding Your 10 Year Old. Osborne, Elsie, ed. (Understanding Your Child Ser.: Vol. 11). 96p. 1997. pap. 8.95 (*1-894020-10-3*) Warwick Publ.

Bradley, Jonathan & Dubinsky, Helene. Understanding Your 15-17 Year Olds. Osborne, Elsie, ed. (Understanding Your Child Ser.: Vol. 14). 96p. 1997. pap. 8.95 (*1-894020-13-8*) Warwick Publ.

Bradley, Joseph. Ethnic & Religious Identity in Modern Scotland: Culture, Policies & Football. LC 95-79587. 240p. 1995. 68.95 (*1-85972-005-6*, Pub. by Avebry) Ashgate Pub Co.

— Guns for the Tsar: American Technology & the Small Arms Industry in Nineteenth-Century Russia. (Illus.). 210p. (C). 1990. text 32.00 (*0-87580-154-4*) N Ill U Pr.

Bradley, Joseph M. Sport, Culture, Politics & Scottish Society: Irish Immigrants & the Gaelic Athletic Association. 208p. 1998. pap. 36.00 (*0-85976-481-8*, Pub. by J Donald) St Mut.

Bradley, Josephine. A Small Book of Unicorns. LC 94-49450. (Illus.). 96p. 1995. pap. 12.95 (*0-87654-358-1*) Pomegranate Calif.

Bradley, Joshua. Accounts of Religious Revivals in Many Parts of the United States from 1815 to 1818: Collected from Numerous Publications & Letters from Persons of Piety & Correct Information. (Revival Library). 300p. (C). 1980. reprint ed. lib. bdg. 15.00 (*0-940033-13-5*) R O Roberts.

— Some of the Beauties of Freemasonry (1816) 320p. 1998. reprint ed. pap. 24.95 (*0-7661-0152-5*) Kessinger Pub.

Bradley, Julia C. A Quick Guide to the Internet. 109p. 1995. 17.95 (*0-534-26076-4*) Wadsworth Pub.

— QuickBASIC & QBASIC Using Modular Structure, IBM Version. 2nd ed. 560p. (C). 1993. text 48.95 (*0-697-12897-0*) Bus & Educ Tech.

— QuickBASIC & QBASIC Using Modular Structure with Visual Basic. LC 95-35898. 608p. (C). 1995. text 40.00 (*0-256-20797-6*, Irwn McGrw-H) McGrw-H Hghr Educ.

Bradley, Julia C. & Black, Kelly. QuickBasic Using Independent Subprograms. 528p. (C). 1991. text, pap. text 56.55 incl. disk (*0-697-14580-8*, Irwn McGrw-H) McGrw-H Hghr Educ.

Bradley, Julia C. & Giles, Richard P. CPS Quickbasic Using Modular Structures. (C). 1995. 33.50 (*0-256-21459-X*, Irwn McGrw-H) McGrw-H Hghr Educ.

— QuickBASIC Using Modular Structure: Macintosh Version. 496p. (C). 1991. pap. write for info. (*0-697-12434-7*) Bus & Educ Tech.

Bradley, Julia C. & Millspaugh, A. C. Programming in Visual BASIC Version 5.O. LC 97-21935. 1997. 45.75 (*0-256-25941-0*, Irwn Prfssnl) McGraw-Hill Prof.

Bradley, Julia C. & Millspaugh, Anita. Programming in Visual BASIC, Version 4.O & Microsoft Visual BASIC 4.0. (C). 1996. text, pap. text 53.65 incl. cd-rom (*0-256-24731-5*, Irwn McGrw-H) McGrw-H Hghr Educ.

— Visual Basic Using Modular Structure. 400p. (C). 1996. text 39.95 (*0-697-20273-9*, Irwn McGrw-H) McGrw-H Hghr Educ.

Bradley, Julia C., et al. Desktop Publishing Using PageMaker 4 - Macintosh Version. 496p. (C). 1991. spiral bd. 41.32 (*0-697-14481-X*, Irwn McGrw-H) McGrw-H Hghr Educ.

— Desktop Publishing Using PageMaker 5.0, Macintosh Version. 560p. (C). 1993. text 42.95 (*0-697-21359-5*) Bus & Educ Tech.

— Desktop Publishing Using Pagemaker 6.0 Macintosh. 576p. (C). 1996. text 45.25 (*0-256-23337-3*, Irwn McGrw-H) McGrw-H Hghr Educ.

— Desktop Publishing Using Pagemaker 6.0 Windows. 576p. (C). 1996. text 45.25 (*0-256-23334-9*, Irwn McGrw-H) McGrw-H Hghr Educ.

Bradley, Julia Case. CPS - Desktop Publishing Using Pagemaker 5.0 Macintosh & Windows Versions. (C). 1995. pap., text 26.00 incl. disk (*0-256-20308-3*, Irwn McGrw-H) McGrw-H Hghr Educ.

***Bradley, Julia Case & Millspaugh, A. C.** Advanced Programming Using Visual Basic 6.0. LC 00-20914. (Illus.). 2000. write for info. (*0-07-239815-9*) McGraw.

Bradley, Julie C., et al. Desktop Publishing Using Ventura Publisher 3.2 - Macintosh Version. 480p. 1993. spiral bd. write for info. (*0-697-16627-9*) Bus & Educ Tech.

— Desktop Publishing Using Ventura Publisher 4.0 - IBM Windows Version. 496p. (C). 1992. text 58.00 (*0-697-14485-2*) Bus & Educ Tech.

Bradley, Kate. Almost Innocent. (Romance Ser.). 1993. per. 2.75 (*0-373-08951-1*, 5-08951-1) Silhouette.

Bradley, Kathleen & Maccalous, Sarah, eds. Transportation Acronym Guide. 50p. 1999. reprint ed. pap. text 15.00 (*0-7881-7602-1*) DIANE Pub.

Bradley, Keith. Human Resource Management: People & Performance. 164p. 1992. 61.95 (*1-85521-293-5*, Pub. by Dartmth Pub) Ashgate Pub Co.

— Slavery & Society at Rome. LC 93-42802. (Key Themes in Ancient History Ser.). (Illus.). 216p. (C). 1994. pap. text 19.95 (*0-521-37887-7*) Cambridge U Pr.

Bradley, Keith, jt. auth. see Albert, Steven.

Bradley, Keith R. Discovering the Roman Family: Studies in Roman Social History. 240p. (C). 1991. pap. text 20.95 (*0-19-505858-5*) OUP.

— Slavery & Rebellion in the Roman World, 140 B. C.-70 B. C. LC 98-141372. 202p. 1998. pap. 14.95 (*0-253-21169-7*) Ind U Pr.

— Slavery & Rebellion in the Roman World, 140 B.C.-70 B.C. LC 88-45757. 202p. 1989. 39.95 (*0-253-31259-0*) Ind U Pr.

— Slaves & Masters in the Roman Empire: A Study in Social Control. 164p. 1987. pap. text 20.95 (*0-19-520607-X*) OUP.

Bradley, Keith R. & Taylor, Simon. Business Performance in the Retail Sector: The Experience of the John Lewis Partnership. 208p. 1992. 65.00 (*0-19-825694-9*) OUP.

Bradley, Kenneth. International Brigades in Spain, 1936-39. (Elite Ser.). (Illus.). 64p. 1994. pap. 12.95 (*1-85532-367-2*, 9468, Pub. by Ospry) Stackpole.

Bradley, Kenyotla. Remembrance. LC 98-86801. 64p. 1998. pap. 8.95 (*1-56167-474-5*) Am Literary Pr.

Bradley, Kevin. Wings Life Skills Student Manual. 100p. Date not set. student ed., ring bd. write for info. (*0-9666187-2-6*) Paperclip Pr.

Bradley, Kevin, jt. auth. see Stonick, Virginia.

Bradley, Kim B. Ruthie's Gift. 176p. (J). (gr. 2-7). 1999. pap. 4.50 (*0-440-41405-9*) BDD Bks Young Read.

Bradley, Kim Brubaker. One-of-a-Kind Mallie. LC 98-51131. 160p. (J). (gr. 2-7). 1999. 15.95 (*0-385-32694-7*) BDD Bks Young Read.

Bradley, Kimberly B. Ruthie's Gift. LC 97-19396. (Illus.). 160p. (J). (gr. 2-7). 1998. 14.95 (*0-385-32525-8*, Delacorte Pr Bks) BDD Bks Young Read.

Bradley, Kimberly Brubak. Force Makes Things Move. 40p. (gr. k-4). pap. 4.95 (*0-06-445214-X*) HarpC.

— Force Makes Things Move. (Illus.). 40p. (J). (gr. k-4). 15.89 (*0-06-028907-4*); 15.95 (*0-06-028906-6*) HarpC Child Bks.

Bradley, Kimberly Brubaker. Energy Makes Things Happen. (J). Date not set. pap. write for info. (*0-06-445213-1*, HarpTrophy) HarpC Child Bks.

— Energy Makes Things Happen. (Illus.). 40p. (J). (gr. k-4). Date not set. 15.95 (*0-06-028908-2*); lib. bdg. 15.89 (*0-06-028909-0*) HarpC Child Bks.

— Pop: A Book about Bubbles. LC 99-57794. 2001. write for info. (*0-06-028701-2*); write for info. (*0-06-445208-5*) HarpC Child Bks.

— Weaver's Daughter. LC 00-26193. (Illus.). (J). 2000. 14.95 (*0-385-32769-2*) Delacorte.

Bradley, Larry, jt. auth. see Bradley, Jana.

Bradley, Larry C. Jesse James: The Making of a Legend. LC 80-81622. (Illus.). 228p. (Orig.). 1980. pap. 8.95 (*0-9604370-0-2*) Larren Pubs.

Bradley, Laura. Deadly Allure. (Scarlet Ser.). (Orig.). 1997. mass mkt. 3.99 (*1-85487-723-2*, Pub. by Scarlet Bks) London Brdge.

— Nothing but Trouble. (Scarlet Ser.). 1998. mass mkt. 3.99 (*1-85487-568-X*, Pub. by Scarlet Bks) London Brdge.

— Wicked Liaisons. 1997. mass mkt. 3.99 (*1-85487-711-9*, Pub. by Scarlet Bks) London Brdge.

Bradley, Layne & Kim, Irene, eds. Data Center Operations Management. 1992. ring bd. 464.00 (*0-87769-267-X*) Warren Gorham & Lamont.

Bradley, Layne C., ed. Handbook of Data Center Management. 1990. text 150.00 (*0-685-69691-X*, HDCM) Warren Gorham & Lamont.

— Handbook of Data Center Management. 2nd ed. LC 95-120527. 784p. 1995. 150.00 (*0-7913-2130-4*) Warren Gorham & Lamont.

Bradley, Leo. Total Quality Management for Schools. LC 92-61824. 220p. 1994. text 39.95 (*0-87762-972-2*) Scarecrow.

— Total Quality Management for Schools. LC 92-61824. 1997. 169.95 incl. VHS (*1-56676-149-2*) Scarecrow.

Bradley, Leo H. Complete Guide to Competency-Based Education: Practical Techniques for Planning, Developing, Implementing, Evaluating Your Program. 1987. text 29.95 (*0-13-160078-8*, Busn) P-H.

Bradley Lightbody. The Cold War. LC 98-51997. (Questions & Analysis in History Ser.). 1999. pap. write for info. (*0-415-19526-8*) Routledge.

Bradley, Lloyd. Reggae on CD: The Essential Guide. 224p. 1995. pap. 19.95 (*1-85626-177-8*, Pub. by Cathie Kyle) Trafalgar.

— Soul on CD: The Essential Guide. 352p. 1995. pap. 22.95 (*1-85626-162-X*) Cathie Kyle.

***Bradley, Loretta.** Counselor Supervision: Principles, Process & Practice. 3rd ed. 2000. 42.95 (*1-56032-873-8*) Taylor & Francis.

***Bradley, Loretta J., et al.** All about Sex: The School Counselor's Guide to Handling Tough Adolescent Problems. LC 98-40241. (Practical Skills for Counselors (PSFC) Ser.). 128p. 1999. 41.95 (*0-8039-6692-X*); pap. 17.95 (*0-8039-6693-8*) Corwin Pr.

Bradley, Lorraine. State Secrets: A Report to the Taxpayer. LC 98-96528. 113p. 1998. mass mkt. 9.00 (*0-9666280-0-4*) J&L Bradley Pr.

Bradley, Lynette & Bryant, Peter. Rhyme & Reason in Reading & Spelling. LC 84-24153. (International Academy for Research in Learning Disabilities Monograph Ser.: No. 1). (Illus.). 143p. reprint ed. pap. 44.40 (*0-7837-4713-6*, 205906500003) Bks Demand.

***Bradley, Lynn.** Manic Depression: How to Live While Loving a Manic Depressive. 240p. 1999. pap. 16.95 (*1-885373-28-7*, Pub. by Emerald Ink) ACCESS Pubs Network.

Bradley, Lynn. Marketing Your Novel, Vol. 3. (Your Novel Ser.: No. 3). 24p. 1998. pap., wbk. ed. 9.95 (*0-9637150-6-2*) Talent By Lb.

— Refining Your Novel, Vol. 2. (Your Novel Ser.: No. 3). 24p. 1998. pap., wbk. ed. 9.95 (*0-9637150-4-6*) Talent By Lb.

— Stand-In for Murder. (WWL Mystery Ser.). 1996. per. 4.99 (*0-373-26199-3*, 1-26199-5, Wrldwide Lib) Harlequin Bks.

— Stand-In for Murder: A Cole January Mystery. 214p. 1994. 19.95 (*0-8027-3189-9*) Walker & Co.

— TIPS (The Incidental & Pertinent Stuff) for Beginning Fiction Writers. Fowler, Dot, ed. (Illus.). 72p. (Orig.). 1993. pap. 10.00 (*0-9637150-0-3*, T-93) Talent By Lb.

— Writing Your Novel, Vol. 1. (Your Novel Ser.: No. 3). 24p. 1997. pap., wbk. ed. 9.95 (*0-9637150-2-X*) Talent By Lb.

— The "Your Novel" Series, 3 vols., Sets. Ernstes, Lloyd, ed. 1998. wbk. ed. 149.00 incl. VHS (*0-9637150-8-9*) Talent By Lb.

Bradley, Margaret. A Career Biography of Gaspard Clair Fran Cois Marie Riche De Prony, Bridge-Builder, Educator, & Scientist. LC 98-4659. (Studies in French Civilization). 1998. 109.95 (*0-7734-8485-X*) E Mellen.

Bradley, Margaret, ed. see Rosenthal, Beth E.

Bradley, Marion Zimmer. The Bloody Sun: A Novel of Darkover. 416p. 1994. mass mkt. 4.99 (*0-88677-603-1*, Pub. by DAW Bks) Penguin Putnam.

— The City of Sorcery. (Darkover Ser.). 1984. mass mkt. 5.99 (*0-88677-332-6*, Pub. by DAW Bks) Penguin Putnam.

— Darkover Landfall. (Darkover Ser.). 1972. mass mkt. 5.99 (*0-88677-234-6*, UE2234, Pub. by DAW Bks) Penguin Putnam.

— Darkover Landfall. LC 99-29914. 1999. 24.95 (*0-7838-8672-1*) Macmillan Gen Ref.

— Exile's Song. 448p. 1996. pap. 21.95 (*0-88677-705-4*, Pub. by DAW Bks) Penguin Putnam.

— Exile's Song. 496p. 1997. pap. 6.99 (*0-88677-734-8*, Pub. by DAW Bks) Penguin Putnam.

— Fall of Atlantis. 512p. 1987. per. 6.99 (*0-671-65615-5*) Baen Bks.

— The Firebrand. Rubenstein, Julie, ed. 624p. 1991. mass mkt. 6.99 (*0-671-74406-2*) PB.

— The Forbidden Tower. (Darkover Ser.). 368p. 1977. mass mkt. 5.99 (*0-88677-373-3*, Pub. by DAW Bks) Penguin Putnam.

— The Forest House. 432p. 1995. mass mkt. 15.95 (*0-451-45424-3*, ROC) NAL.

— Ghostlight. 304p. 1995. 22.95 (*0-312-85881-7*) Tor Bks.

— Ghostlight. 4th ed. LC PS3552.R228G48 1996. 304p. 1996. pap. 13.95 (*0-312-86218-0*, Pub. by Tor Bks) St Martin.

— Gravelight. LC 97-11948. 352p. 1997. text 24.95 (*0-312-86503-1*) St Martin.

— Gravelight. 352p. 1998. pap. 14.95 (*0-312-86507-4*) St Martin.

— Guide to Avalon. 1999. mass mkt. 6.99 (*0-451-45557-6*, ROC) NAL.

— Hawkmistress. (Darkover Ser.). 336p. (Orig.). 1982. mass mkt. 5.99 (*0-88677-239-7*, Pub. by DAW Bks) Penguin Putnam.

— Heartlight. LC 98-23557. 416p. 1998. 25.95 (*0-312-86508-2*, Pub. by Tor Bks) St Martin.

***Bradley, Marion Zimmer.** Heartlight. 416p. 1999. pap. 16.95 (*0-312-86509-0*, Pub. by Tor Bks) St Martin.

Bradley, Marion Zimmer. The Inheritor. LC 96-33983. (Orig.). 1997. pap. text 15.95 (*0-312-86293-8*) St Martin.

— The Inheritor. 448p. (Orig.). 1984. pap. 3.50 (*0-8125-1600-1*, Pub. by Tor Bks) St Martin.

— The Inheritor. (Orig.). 1997. pap. 14.95 (*0-614-27317-X*) Tor Bks.

— The Keeper's Price. (Darkover Ser.). 208p. 1980. pap. 3.99 (*0-88677-236-2*, UE2236, Pub. by DAW Bks) Penguin Putnam.

— Lady of Avalon. 457p. 1998. mass mkt. 15.95 (*0-451-45652-1*, ROC) NAL.

— Marion Zimmer Bradley's Darkover. 352p. (Orig.). 1993. mass mkt. 4.99 (*0-88677-593-0*, Pub. by DAW Bks) Penguin Putnam.

— The Mists of Avalon. 896p. 1987. pap. 14.00 (*0-345-35049-9*, Del Rey) Ballantine Pub Grp.

***Bradley, Marion Zimmer.** The Mists of Avalon. 2000. 30.00 (*0-345-44118-4*) Ballantine Pub Grp.

Bradley, Marion Zimmer. The Other Side of the Mirror. (Darkover Ser.). 304p. 1987. pap. 4.50 (*0-88677-185-4*, Pub. by DAW Bks) Penguin Putnam.

— The Planet Savers. 1985. pap. 3.50 (*0-441-67026-1*) Ace Bks.

***Bradley, Marion Zimmer.** The Planet Savers: Also Including the Waterfall. LC 00-33492. (Illus.). 2001. write for info. (*0-7838-9065-6*, G K Hall & Co) Mac Lib Ref.

Bradley, Marion Zimmer. The Planet Savers - Winds of Darkover. 320p. 1995. mass mkt. 4.99 (*0-88677-630-9*, Pub. by DAW Bks) Penguin Putnam.

— The Shadow Matrix. LC 97-229068. 1997. 22.95 (*0-88677-743-7*, Pub. by DAW Bks) Penguin Putnam.

— The Shadow Matrix. (Darkover Ser.). 556p. 1999. mass mkt. 6.99 (*0-88677-812-3*, Pub. by DAW Bks) Penguin Putnam.

— Sharra's Exile. (Darkover Ser.). 368p. 1981. mass mkt. 5.99 (*0-88677-309-1*, Pub. by DAW Bks) Penguin Putnam.

— Sharra's Exile. (Darkover Ser.). 368p. 1996. reprint ed. 24.00 (*0-7278-4799-6*) Severn Hse.

— The Shattered Chain. (Darkover Ser.). 1976. pap. 5.99 (*0-88677-308-3*, Pub. by DAW Bks) Penguin Putnam.

— Spell Sword. (Darkover Ser.). 1974. mass mkt. 3.99 (*0-88677-237-0*, Pub. by DAW Bks) Penguin Putnam.

***Bradley, Marion Zimmer.** The Spell Sword. large type ed. LC 00-36987. 245p. 2000. 25.95 (*0-7838-9066-4*, G K Hall & Co) Mac Lib Ref.

Bradley, Marion Zimmer. Star of Danger. 224p. 1994. mass mkt. 4.99 (*0-88677-607-4*, Pub. by DAW Bks) Penguin Putnam.

***Bradley, Marion Zimmer.** Star of Danger. LC 00-39683. (Illus.). 2000. pap. write for info. (*0-7838-9063-X*, G K Hall & Co) Mac Lib Ref.

Bradley, Marion Zimmer. Star of Danger. 192p. 1993. lib. bdg. 20.00 (*0-7278-4513-6*) Severn Hse.

— Storm Queen. (Darkover Ser.). 368p. 1978. mass mkt. 5.99 (*0-88677-310-5*, Pub. by DAW Bks) Penguin Putnam.

— The Sword & the Sorceress, Vol. 14. 352p. (J). 1997. pap. 5.99 (*0-88677-741-0*, Pub. by DAW Bks) Penguin Putnam.

— Sword of Chaos. (Darkover Ser.). 1982. pap. 3.50 (*0-88677-172-2*, Pub. by DAW Bks) Penguin Putnam.

— Thendara House. (Darkover Ser.). 416p. 1983. mass mkt. 5.99 (*0-88677-240-0*, Pub. by DAW Bks) Penguin Putnam.

— Thendara House. (Darkover Ser.). 416p. 1995. reprint ed. 22.00 (*0-7278-4723-6*) Severn Hse.

— Traitor's Sun. LC 99-215583. 528p. 1999. 24.95 (*0-88677-810-7*, Pub. by DAW Bks) Penguin Putnam.

— Traitor's Sun. 544p. 1999. mass mkt. 6.99 (*0-88677-811-5*, Pub. by DAW Bks) Penguin Putnam.

— Two to Conquer. (Darkover Ser.). (Orig.). 1980. mass mkt. 5.99 (*0-88677-174-9*, Pub. by DAW Bks) Penguin Putnam.

***Bradley, Marion Zimmer.** The Winds of Darkover. LC 00-33493. 2000. write for info. (*0-7838-9067-2*, G K Hall & Co) Mac Lib Ref.

— Witch Hill. LC 00-28653. 192p. 2000. pap. 11.95 (*0-312-87283-6*) St Martin.

Bradley, Marion Zimmer. Witch Hill. 1990. pap. 3.95 (*0-8125-0006-7*, Pub. by Tor Bks) St Martin.

— Witch Hunt. LC 97-11948. 352p. 1996. 20.95 (*0-312-85606-7*, Pub. by Forge NYC) St Martin.

— Witchlight. 3rd ed. LC 20-703 //. 304p. 1997. pap. 14.95 (*0-312-85831-0*) St Martin.

— The World Wreckers. (Against the Terrans Ser.). 288p. 1994. mass mkt. 4.99 (*0-88677-629-5*, Pub. by DAW Bks) Penguin Putnam.

Bradley, Marion Zimmer, ed. The Best of Marion Zimmer Bradley's Fantasy Magazine. 256p. (Orig.). 1994. mass mkt. 4.99 (*0-446-60140-3*, Pub. by Warner Bks) Little.

— Sword & Sorceress XV, Vol. 15. 352p. 1998. mass mkt. 5.99 (*0-88677-768-2*, Pub. by DAW Bks) Penguin Putnam.

— Sword & Sorceress XIV. 1997. mass mkt. 5.99 (*0-614-27731-0*) DAW Bks.

***Bradley, Marion Zimmer, ed.** Sword & Sorceress XVII. 320p. 2000. 6.99 (*0-88677-891-3*, Pub. by DAW Bks) Penguin Putnam.

Bradley, Marion Zimmer, ed. Sword & Sorceress XVI. 320p. 1999. mass mkt. 6.99 (*0-88677-843-3*, Pub. by DAW Bks) Penguin Putnam.

— Sword & Sorceress XIII. 1996. mass mkt. 5.99 (*0-88677-703-8*, Pub. by DAW Bks) Penguin Putnam.

Bradley, Marion Zimmer, ed. Free Amazons of Darkover: An Anthology. (Darkover Ser.). 303p. 1985. pap. 3.95 (*0-88677-430-6*, Pub. by DAW Bks) Penguin Putnam.

Bradley, Marion Zimmer & Lackey, Mercedes. Rediscovery: A Novel of Darkover. 368p. 1994. reprint ed. mass mkt. 4.99 (*0-88677-529-9*, Pub. by DAW Bks) Penguin Putnam.

Bradley, Marion Zimmer & Lisle, Holly. Glenraven. 400p. 1996. 23.00 (*0-671-87738-0*) Baen Bks.

— Glenraven. 416p. 1997. per. 6.99 (*0-671-87799-2*) Baen Bks.

***Bradley, Marion Zimmer & Lisle, Holly.** In the Rift. 1999. mass mkt. 6.99 (*0-671-57791-3*) PB.

Bradley, Marion Zimmer & Lisle, Holly. In the Rift: Glenraven II. LC 97-49668. 288p. 1998. 21.00 (*0-671-87870-0*) S&S Trade.

Bradley, Marion Zimmer, et al. Experiment Perilous & Other Essays. 1976. pap. 3.50 (*0-916186-02-4*) Algol Pr.

— Tiger Burning Bright. LC 95-1763. 1995. 23.00 (*0-688-14360-1*, Avon Bks) Morrow Avon.

— Tiger Burning Bright. 512p. 1996. mass mkt. 6.99 (*0-380-77512-3*, Avon Bks) Morrow Avon.

Bradley, Mark. Out There: A Satiric Anthology on the American Biker. (Illus.). 1996. pap. 19.95 (*0-9650916-0-0*) AG Pubng.

Bradley, Mark J., et al. Eckhardt's Workbook for Wisconsin Estate Planners. 3rd ed. LC 97-17079. 735p. 1997. ring bd., wbk. ed. 185.00 incl. disk (*1-57862-002-3*) State Bar WI.

Bradley, Mark L. Last Stand in the Carolinas: The Battle of Betonville. (Illus.). 608p. 1996. reprint ed. 32.95 (*1-882810-02-3*, 02-3) Savas Pub.

***Bradley, Mark L.** This Astounding Close: The Road to Bennett Place. (Illus.). 432p. 2000. 34.95 (*0-8078-2565-4*) U of NC Pr.

***Bradley, Mark Philip.** Imagining Vietnam & America: The Making of Postcolonial Vietnam, 1919-1950. LC 99-88185. (New Cold War History Ser.). 320p. 2000. pap. 19.95 (*0-8078-4861-1*); lib. bdg. 39.95 (*0-8078-2549-2*) U of NC Pr.

Bradley, Marshell C., jt. ed. see Blosser, Philip.

Bradley, Martha. British Housewife, Vol. I. fac. ed. 108p. 1998. pap. 19.00 (*0-907325-66-1*) Food Words.

— British Housewife, Vol. II. fac. ed. 201p. 1998. pap. 19.00 (*0-907325-67-X*) Food Words.

An Asterisk (*) at the beginning of an entry indicates that the title is appearing for the first time.

— British Housewife, Vol. III. fac. ed. 200p. 1998. pap. 19.00 (*0-907325-68-8*) Food Words.

— British Housewife, Vol. IV. fac. ed. 241p. 1998. pap. 19.00 (*0-907325-69-6*) Food Words.

— British Housewife, Vol. V. fac. ed. 235p. 1998. pap. 19.00 (*0-907325-84-X*) Food Words.

— British Housewife, Vol. VI. fac. ed. 225p. 1998. pap. 19.00 (*0-907325-85-8*) Food Words.

Bradley, Martha S. Kidnapped from That Land: The Government Raids on the Short Creek Polygamists. (Publications in Mormon Studies: Vol. 9). (Illus.). 272p. (Orig.). 1996. pap. 14.95 (*0-87480-528-7*) U of Utah Pr.

***Bradley, Martha Sonntag.** A History of Beaver County. LC 98-61325. (Illus.). 1999. write for info. (*0-913738-17-4*) Utah St Hist Soc.

— A History of Kane County. LC 98-61327. (Illus.). 1999. write for info. (*0-913738-40-9*) Utah St Hist Soc.

***Bradley, Martha Sonntag & Woodward, Mary Brown.** The Four Zinas. LC 99-52648. 2000. write for info. (*1-56085-141-4*, Smith Res) Signature Bks.

Bradley, Martin, et al. Churches & Church Membership in the U. S., 1990. LC 92-70469. 1990. pap. 36.00 (*0-914422-22-7*) Glenmary Res Ctr.

Bradley, Mary, jt. auth. see Papanier Wells, MaryAnn.

Bradley, Mary C. 140 Don'ts to Do Before You Die. 8p. 1999. pap. 2.95 (*0-9663931-1-2*) M C Bradley.

Bradley, Mary E. Douglass Farm. Cousin Alice, ed. LC 74-37584. (Black Heritage Library Collection). 1977. reprint ed. 23.95 (*0-8369-8960-0*) Ayer.

Bradley, Maryjane G. & Thompson, Nancy R. Quality Management Integration in Long-Term Care: Guidelines for Excellence. LC 99-27315. 174p. 1999. 31.95 (*1-878812-61-0*) Hlth Prof Pr.

Bradley, Matt. Arkansas. Wilbourn, Judy & Bradley, Susan, eds. (Illus.). 128p. 1996. 55.00 (*0-940716-02-X*) Bradley Pub.

— Arkansas. limited ed. Wilbourn, Judy & Bradley, Susan, eds. (Illus.). 128p. 1996. 90.00 (*0-940716-03-8*) Bradley Pub.

Bradley, Maureen. My First Book of Prayers: A Collection of Everyday Prayers from a Child's Heart. (Illus.). 96p. (J). 1997. 5.99 (*0-88486-181-3*, Inspirational Pr) Arrowood Pr.

Bradley, Maureen L. The Pilgrim's Progress Study Guide. 128p. (Orig.). 1994. pap. 6.99 (*0-87552-108-8*) P & R Pubng.

***Bradley-McBeth, Anna E. & Bradley-McBeth, Nilaja A.** I Eat at Mommy's. LC 99-94844. (Illus.). v, 41p. (J). 1999. 14.99 (*0-9670636-4-7*) Big Brain Pubg.

Bradley-McBeth, Nilaja A., jt. auth. see Bradley-McBeth, Anna E.

Bradley, Melissa, jt. auth. see Drezner, Jeffrey A.

Bradley, Melvin. The Missouri Mule: His Origin & Times. LC 93-73481. (Illus.). 540p. 1998. pap. 35.00 (*0-933842-26-0*, UED99) Extension Div.

Bradley, Michael. The Columbus Conspiracy: An Investigation into the Secret History of Christopher Columbus. 253p. 1992. pap. text 11.95 (*1-881316-11-4*) A&B Bks.

***Bradley, Michael.** The Columbus Conspiracy: An Investigation into the Secret History of Christopher Columbus. (Illus.). 253p. 1999. reprint ed. pap. text 17.00 (*0-7881-6559-3*) DIANE Pub.

Bradley, Michael. Dawn Voyage: The Black African Discovery of America. 192p. 1992. pap. text 11.95 (*1-881316-12-2*) A&B Bks.

— Football All-Stars. Gramling, Scott, ed. 96p. (J). (gr. 2-8). 1999. pap. 3.99 (*1-886749-64-7*) SI For Kids.

— Iceman Inheritance. 230p. 1990. pap. text 22.00 (*0-916157-30-X*) African Islam Miss Pubns.

Bradley, Michael, et al. Michael Jordan Scrapbook. LC 98-66431. 128 p. 1998. write for info. Pubns Intl Ltd.

Bradley, Michael, jt. auth. see Schwarz, Alan.

Bradley, Michael D. The Scientist & Engineer in Court. LC 83-10582. (Water Resources Monograph Ser.: Vol. 8). (Illus.). 111p. (Orig.). 1983. pap. 14.00 (*0-87590-309-6*) Am Geophysical.

Bradley, Michael R. Early on a Frosty Morn: Stories of the Great Depression. LC 95-48257. 1996. write for info. (*0-916078-41-8*) Iris Pr.

— In the Land of Cotton. 86p. 1998. pap. 10.00 (*1-57502-260-5*, PO2489) Morris Pubng.

— Old Times There Are Not Forgotten, Bk. 1 of 3. 62p. (Orig.). 1992. pap. 8.95 (*0-9624100-7-1*) Bell Buckle.

— On the Job: Safeguarding Workers' Rights. LC 92-9015. (Human Rights Ser.). 112p. (J). 1992. lib. bdg. 18.95 (*0-86593-175-5*) Rourke Corp.

***Bradley, Michael R.** Tullahoma: The 1863 Campaign for the Control of Middle Tennessee. LC 99-54334. (Illus.). 114p. 2000. pap. 9.95 (*1-57249-167-1*) White Mane Pub.

Bradley, Michael R. & Payne, Weldon. Matrix of Change. 162p. (C). 1996. pap. text, per. 24.95 (*0-7872-2756-0*) Kendall-Hunt.

Bradley, Mignon L. Cinco de Mayo: An Historical Play. LC 81-8341. (Bilingual Plays by LUISA Ser.). (ENG & SPA., Illus.). 60p. (Orig.). (J). (gr. 4 up). 1981. pap. 6.95 (*0-939584-00-X*) LUISA Prods.

Bradley, Mildred O. The Exceptional Child in Today's Classroom LC 93-215641. 127p. 1991. write for info. (*0-914607-34-0*) Master Tchr.

Bradley, Myrtle K. Win with Numerology. LC 82-70776. (Illus.). 96p. (Orig.). 1982. pap. 5.95 (*0-87516-482-X*) DeVorss.

Bradley, Nancy. The Incredible World of Gold Rush Ghosts: True Tales of Hauntings in the Mother Lode. Amos, Dan, ed. & photos by by. Reppert, Robert et al, photos by. (Illus.). 218p. 1998. pap. 12.95 (*1-57502-801-8*, PO2214) Morris Pubng.

Bradley, Nancy & Gaddis, Vincent H. Gold Rush Ghosts: Strange & Unexplained Phenomena in the Mother Lode. LC 90-60343. (Illus.). 109p. (Orig.). 1990. pap. 9.95 (*0-945685-06-8*) Borderland Sciences.

Bradley, Neil. Concise SGML Companion. 336p. (C). 1996. pap. text 29.95 (*0-201-41999-8*) Addison-Wesley.

— The Concise XM Companion. LC 98-3927. 464p. (C). 1998. pap. text 31.88 (*0-201-34285-5*) Addison-Wesley.

***Bradley, Neil.** XML Companion. 2nd ed. 464p. (C). 1999. pap. text 39.95 (*0-201-67486-6*) Addison-Wesley.

— XSL Companion. 304p. (C). 2000. pap. 34.95 (*0-201-67487-4*) Addison-Wesley.

Bradley, Omar N. A Soldier's Story. Carr, Caleb, ed. LC 98-46973. (Modern Library War Ser.). 1999. pap. 17.95 (*0-375-75421-0*) Modern Lib NY.

Bradley, Omar N., Jr. & Blair, Clay. A General's Life. (Illus.). 752p. 1989. 19.95 (*0-8306-3312-X*) McGraw-Hill Prof.

Bradley, Omar N. & Blair, Clay. A General's Life. 1993. reprint ed. lib. bdg. 44.95 (*1-56849-245-6*) Buccaneer Bks.

Bradley, Owen, contrib. by. A Modern Maistre: The Social & Political Thought of Joseph de Maistre. LC 98-43636. (European Horizons Ser.). 320p. 1999. text 55.00 (*0-8032-1295-X*) U of Nebr Pr.

Bradley, P. A. & Guzik, J. A., eds. A Half Century of Stellar Pulsation Interpretations: A Tribute to Arthur N. Cox. (ASP Conference Series Proceedings: Vol. 135). 511p. 1998. 52.00 (*1-886733-55-4*) Astron Soc Pacific.

Bradley, P. A., jt. ed. see Rawer, Karl.

Bradley, P. J., jt. auth. see Gibbin, K. P.

Bradley, Pamela. Ancient Greece: Using Evidence. Patterson, David, ed. (Illus.). 356p. (C). 1992. pap. text 50.00 (*0-7131-8327-6*, Pub. by Hodder & Stought Ltd) Lubrecht & Cramer.

— Ancient Rome: Using Evidence. (Illus.). 644p. (C). 1992. pap. text 65.00 (*0-7131-8328-4*, Pub. by Hodder & Stought Ltd) Lubrecht & Cramer.

Bradley, Patricia. Slavery, Propaganda, & the American Revolution. LC 98-12915. 176p. 1998. text 40.00 (*1-57806-052-4*) U Pr of Miss.

— Slavery, Propaganda, & the American Revolution. 184p. 1999. pap. 18.00 (*1-57806-211-X*) U Pr of Miss.

Bradley, Patricia, jt. auth. see Minor, Nancy.

Bradley, Patricia B., ed. Creative Healing: An Introduction to Joseph B. Stephenson's "Hand-On" Healing. LC 89-84796. (Illus.). 106p. (Orig.). 1989. pap. text 10.00 (*0-9623416-0-6*) J B Stephenson.

— Creative Healing: An Introduction to Joseph B. Stephenson's "Hand-On" Healing. rev. ed. LC 94-75748. (Illus.). 104p. (Orig.). 1994. reprint ed. pap. 12.95 (*0-9623416-1-4*) J B Stephenson.

***Bradley, Patricia Blaine, ed.** The Stephenson Method of Natural Health Care: Creative Healing. (Illus.). 350p. 2000. pap. 50.00 (*0-9623416-2-2*) J B Stephenson.

Bradley, Patricia J., jt. ed. see Hamilton, J. S.

Bradley, Patrick & Pence, Heather. A Step-by-Step Book about Gerbils. (Step-by-Step Ser.). (Illus.). 64p. (Orig.). 1987. pap. 5.95 (*0-86622-467-X*, SK-011) TFH Pubns.

Bradley, Patrick E., jt. auth. see Collins, Richard L.

Bradley, Paul F. Cryosurgery of Maxillofacial Region: General Principles & Clinical Applications to Benign Lesions. LC 85-22421. 200p. 1986. 157.00 (*0-8493-5219-3*, CRC Reprint) Franklin.

— Cryosurgery of Maxillofacial Region Vol. 2: Clinical Application Malignant Lesions & Comparison Lasers. LC 85-22421. 1986. 145.00 (*0-8493-5220-7*, CRC Reprint) Franklin.

— Cryosurgery of the Maxillofacial Region, 2 vols., Set, Vols. I-II. 1986. 248.00 (*0-8493-5218-5*, RD523) CRC Pr.

Bradley, Peggy. What Songwriters Need to Know about Getting Their Songs Published. 1993. 9.95 (*0-9639326-0-8*) Music Sq Cnslts.

Bradley, Peter. Full of Carp. LC 97-73780. (Illus.). 96p. 1997. pap. text 9.95 (*1-886913-19-6*) Ruminator Bks.

***Bradley, Peter & Burls, Amanda, eds.** Ethics in Public Health. LC 99-29709. 224p. (C). 2000. pap. 25.99 (*0-415-22055-6*) Routledge.

***Bradley, Peter T.** British Maritime Enterprise in the New World: From the Late 15th to the Mid-18th Century. LC 99-43628. (Studies in British History: Vol. 57). 600p. 1999. text 119.95 (*0-7734-7866-3*) E Mellen.

***Bradley, Peter T. & Cahill, David.** Habsburg Peru: Images, Imagination & Memory. 224p. 1999. pap. 19.95 (*0-85323-914-2*, Pub. by Liverpool Univ Pr) Intl Spec Bk.

Bradley, Philip. An Index to the Waverly Novels. LC 75-6838. 695p. reprint ed. pap. 200.00 (*0-608-17846-2*, 203262600080) Bks Demand.

Bradley, Philip B., ed. Methods in Brain Research. LC 74-404. 567p. reprint ed. pap. 175.80 (*0-608-14531-9*, 202479700038) Bks Demand.

Bradley, Philip B. & Hirsch, S. R., eds. The Psychopharmacology & Drug Treatment of Schizophrenia. (British Association for Psychopharmacology Monographs). (Illus.). 475p. 1986. 95.00 (*0-19-261260-3*) OUP.

Bradley, Philip B., et al. Serotonin, CNS Receptors & Brain Function. (Advances in the Biosciences Ser.: Vol. 85). 430p. 1993. 181.50 (*0-08-042051-6*, Pergamon Pr) Elsevier.

Bradley, Philip D. Constitutional Limits to Union Power. (JSPES Monograph: No. 4). 1976. pap. 15.00 (*0-930690-06-0*) Coun Soc Econ.

— The Public Stake in Union Power. LC 59-11490. 392p. reprint ed. pap. 121.60 (*0-8357-2706-8*, 203981900013) Bks Demand.

Bradley, Phillips, ed. see De Tocqueville, Alexis.

Bradley, Preston. The Final Warning: How the World Will End. 720p. 1999. 25.00 (*0-9669709-0-X*) Vision Pubng AL.

Bradley, R. A. & Jones, P. D., eds. Climate since AD, 1500. (Illus.). 724p. (C). 1995. pap. 45.00 (*0-415-12030-6*, C0551) Routledge.

Bradley, R. C. Teaching for "Self-Directed" Living & Learning in Students - How to Help Students Get in Charge of Their Lives: "Self-Directed" Living & Learning. LC 90-85800. 224p. (YA). 1991. text 19.95 (*0-9628624-0-1*) Bassi Bk.

Bradley, R. J. Radiation Technology Handbook. (Illus.). 352p. 1984. text 150.00 (*0-8247-7217-2*) Dekker.

Bradley, Ray. Cadence Count. 270p. (Orig.). (C). 1995. pap. text 9.95 (*1-884707-13-0*) Lifestyles.

***Bradley, Ray.** The Devil's Crown. 190p. 1999. pap. 12.95 (*1-929416-03-2*) Magner Pubg.

Bradley, Ray. Understanding Computer Science for Advanced Level. 4th ed. (Illus.). 720p. (YA). (gr. 11 up). 1999. pap. 57.50 (*0-7487-4046-5*, Pub. by S Thornes Pubs) Trans-Atl Phila.

Bradley, Raymond. The Nature of All Being: A Study of Wittgenstein's Modal Atomism. (Illus.). 272p. 1992. text 60.00 (*0-19-507111-5*) OUP.

Bradley, Raymond S. Paleoclimatology: Reconstructing Climates of the Quaternary. 2nd ed. (International Geophysics Ser.). 613p. 1999. text 69.95 (*0-12-124010-X*) Harcourt.

***Bradley, Raymond S.** Principles of Ocean Physics. 2nd ed. 1999. 79.00 (*0-12-059795-0*) Morgan Kaufmann.

Bradley, Raymond S. Quaternary Paleoclimatology: Methods of Paleoclimatic Reconstruction. (Illus.). (C). 1985. text 90.00 (*0-04-551067-9*); pap. text 39.95 (*0-04-551068-7*) Routledge.

Bradley, Raymond S., et al, eds. Sub-Acute Spongiform Encephalopathies: Proceedings of a Seminar in the CEC Agricultural Research Programme, Held in Brussels, November 12-14, 1990. (Current Topics in Veterinary Medicine & Animal Science Ser.). 304p. 1991. text 180.50 (*0-7923-1458-1*) Kluwer Academic.

Bradley, Raymond S. & Munro, D. High Pressure Chemistry. LC 65-19842. 1965. 88.00 (*0-08-011032-0*, Pub. by Pergamon Repr) Franklin.

Bradley, Raymond S., jt. ed. see Caldwell, J.

***Bradley, Rebecca.** Lady in Gil. 2000. mass mkt. 5.99 (*0-441-00709-0*) Ace Bks.

***Bradley, Richard.** An Archaeology of Natural Places. LC 99-42197. 160p. 2000. pap. write for info. (*0-415-22150-1*) Routledge.

— Archaeology of Natural Places. LC 99-42197. 192p. (C). 2000. text 75.00 (*0-415-22149-8*) Routledge.

Bradley, Richard. Consumption, Change & the Archaeological Record: The Archaeology of Monuments & Deliberate Deposits. 47p. 1986. pap. 8.00 (*0-614-21830-6*) David Brown.

Bradley, Richard. Familiar Favorites: 45 Timeless Standards. 14.95 (*0-7692-9124-4*) Wrner Bros.

Bradley, Richard. Rock Art & the Prehistory of Atlantic Europe: Signing the Land. LC 96-51119. (Illus.). 296p. (C). 1997. 110.00 (*0-415-16535-0*); pap. 34.99 (*0-415-16536-9*) Routledge.

Bradley, Richard. 75 Great Standards. 18.95 (*0-7692-9059-0*) Wrner Bros.

Bradley, Richard. The Significance of Monuments: On the Shaping of Human Experience in Neolithic & Bronze Age Europe. LC 97-27536. (Illus.). 192p. (C). 1998. pap. 24.99 (*0-415-15204-6*) Routledge.

— Significance of Monuments: On the Shaping of Human Experience in Neolithic & Bronze Age Europe. LC 97-27536. (Illus.). 192p. (C). 1998. 75.00 (*0-415-15203-8*) Routledge.

— U. S. Markets for Incontinence Devices. 420p. 1994. spiral bd. 4200.00 (*0-945510-23-3*) Intl Info Assocs.

— U. S. Markets for Wound Care. 350p. 1994. spiral bd. 3500.00 (*0-945510-24-1*) Intl Info Assocs.

Bradley, Richard, ed. Altering the Earth. (Illus.). 150p. 1993. pap. 27.50 (*0-903903-08-3*, Pub. by Soc Antiquaries) David Brown.

— Bradley's Best of Christmas Music: Big Note Piano Edition. 80p. (J). 1993. pap. 8.95 (*0-7692-0134-2*, BP3194A) Wrner Bros.

— Christmas Songs Simplified for Piano: 28 Favorites. 96p. (YA). 1995. pap. text 12.95 (*0-89724-854-6*, BP3340A) Wrner Bros.

Bradley, Richard, jt. ed. see Esposito, Tony.

***Bradley, Richard A.** Spiders. LC 00-102479. (In Ohio's Backyard Ser.: Vol. 4). (Illus.). 150p. (YA). (gr. 5 up). 2000. 15.00 (*0-86727-140-X*) Ohio Biol Survey.

Bradley, Richard E., ed. see University of Florida Symposium on Canine Heartwor.

Bradley, Ritamary. Praying with Julian of Norwich: Selections from "A Revelation of Love" with Commentary by Ritamary Bradley. LC 94-60353. 192p. (Orig.). 1994. pap. 12.95 (*0-89622-601-8*) Twenty-Third.

Bradley, Robert. Compendium of Professional Basketball. 520p. 1999. pap. write for info. (*0-9644774-3-2* Xaler Pr.

Bradley, Robert A. Husband-Coached Childbirth. 4th ed. LC 95-35806. 288p. 1996. pap. 12.95 (*0-553-37556-3*) Bantam.

Bradley, Robert D., et al. The Florida Policy Management System: Growth & Reform in America's Fourth Largest State. Chackerian, Richard, ed. (C). 1994. pap. text 44.95 (*0-932143-02-4*) FL Ctr Public.

Bradley, Robert F. & Michell, R. B. Eight Centuries of French Literature: Chanson de Roland to Sartre. (FRE.). 1951. 47.95 (*0-89197-134-3*) Irvington.

Bradley, Robert I. Fatima & Modernism. (Queen of Apostles Ser.: Vol. XI). 18p. 1991. pap. 0.65 (*1-56036-023-2*, 49742) AMI Pr.

— Fatima & the AntiChrist. (Queen of Apostles Ser. Vol. XIV). 1993. 0.65 (*1-56036-042-9*, 49745) AMI Pr.

— The Masonic Movement & the Fatima Message. (Queen of Apostles Ser.: Vol. X). 12p. 1990. 0.65 (*1-56036-004-6*, 49741) AMI Pr.

Bradley, Robert L., Jr. The Mirage of Oil Protection. LC 88-25125. 284p. 1989. 41.00 (*0-8191-7202-2*); pap. 22.00 (*0-8191-7203-0*) U Pr of Amer.

— Oil, Gas, & Government: The U. S. Experience, 2 vols., Set, Vols. 1 & 2. 2000p. (C). 1996. lib. bdg. 195.00 (*0-8476-8110-6*) Rowman.

— Oil, Gas, & Government: The U. S. Experience, Vol. I. 1000p. (C). 1996. lib. bdg. 125.00 (*0-8476-8108-4*) Rowman.

— Oil, Gas, & Government: The U. S. Experience, Vol. II. 1000p. (C). 1996. lib. bdg. 125.00 (*0-8476-8109-2*) Rowman.

Bradley, Robert L. & Camp, Helen B. The Forts of Pemaquid Maine: An Archaeological & Historical Study. (Occasional Publications in Maine Archaeology). (Illus.). 286p. (Orig.). 1994. pap. 18.00 (*0-935447-11-3*) ME Hist Preserv.

Bradley, Robert M. Basic Oral Physiology. LC 81-4102. (Illus.). 237p. reprint ed. pap. 73.50 (*0-8357-7589-5*, 205691000096) Bks Demand.

— Essentials of Oral Physiology. 208p. (C). 1994. pap. text 39.00 (*1-55664-088-9*) Mosby Inc.

Bradley, Robin. Wine Vintages of the West Coast. 2nd ed. (Illus.). 114p. 1986. pap. 12.95 (*0-9590183-1-X*) Aris Bks.

B

Bradley, Ronald J., ed. International Review of Neurobiology, Vol. 34. (Illus.). 410p. (C). 1992. text 104.00 (*0-12-366834-4*) Acad Pr.

Bradley, Ronald J., et al, eds. International Review of Neurobiology, Vol. 39. (Illus.). 380p. (C). 1996. text 95.00 (*0-12-366839-5*) Acad Pr.

— International Review of Neurobiology, Vol. 42. (Illus.). 345p. 1998. text 99.95 (*0-12-366842-5*) Morgan Kaufmann.

Bradley, Ronald J., Jr., et al, eds. International Review of Neurobiology Vol. 41: The Cerebellum & Cognition. LC 97-202511. (Illus.). 665p. (C). 1997. text 99.95 (*0-12-366841-7*) Morgan Kaufmann.

— International Review of Neurobiology Vol. 41: The Cerebellum & Cognition, 41. LC 97-202511. (International Review of Neurobiology Ser.: Vol. 41). (Illus.). 665p. 1997. pap. text 69.95 (*0-12-625660-8*) Morgan Kaufmann.

Bradley, Ronald J. & Harris, R. Adron, eds. International Review of Neurobiology, Vol. 36. (Illus.). 444p. (C). 1994. text. write for info. (*0-12-366836-0*) Acad Pr.

Bradley, Ronald J. & Harris, R. Adron, eds. International Review of Neurobiology, Vol. 38. (Illus.). 372p. (C). 1995. text 104.00 (*0-12-366838-7*) Acad Pr.

Bradley, Ronald J. & Harris, Robert A., eds. International Review of Neurobiology, Vol. 35. (Illus.). 442p. (C). 1993. text 110.00 (*0-12-366835-2*) Acad Pr.

Bradley, Ronald J., jt. ed. see Smythies, John R.

Bradley, Ruth, tr. see Arrupe, Pedro.

Bradley, S. A., intro. Anglo-Saxon Poetry. 572p. 1994. 11.50 (*0-460-87507-8*, Everyman's Classic Lib) Tuttle Pubng.

Bradley, S. A., ed. see Mandeville, John.

Bradley, Sam. Manspell-Godspell. 80p. 1975. pap. 13.95 (*0-900977-93-0*, Pub. by Anvil Press) Dufour.

Bradley, Sandy. Let the Mocking Bird Sing Herbal Praise. LC 96-61231. 416p. 1996. otabind 29.95 (*1-57258-123-9*) Teach Servs.

Bradley, Sandy, jt. auth. see Hedtke, John.

***Bradley, Sarah.** Classic Convertibles: 75 of the Greatest Open-Top Cars. 1999. pap. text 9.99 (*1-84100-251-8*) Quadrillion Pub.

Bradley, Scott A. The Black Man: Cursed or Blessed?: A Historic-Biblical & Modern Perspective. 150p. 1993. pap. text 9.95 (*0-9636928-0-1*) Riv Life Min.

— Breaking the Spirit of the American Black Male. Divers, Consuelo, ed. 150p. (Orig.). (C). pap. text 9.95 (*0-9636928-1-X*) Riv Life Min.

— Christianity vs. Islam: An Examination over the Black Religious Debate. Divers, Consuelo, ed. 47p. (Orig.). (C). pap. text 4.95 (*0-9636928-2-8*) Riv Life Min.

— Total Healing for the Whole Man. Divers, Consuelo, ed. 1997. pap. text 6.95 (*0-9636928-3-6*) Riv Life Min.

Bradley, Shawn & Yorgason, Brenton. Standing Tall: The Shawn Bradley Story. 1993. 11.95 (*0-88494-912-5*) Bookcraft Inc.

***Bradley, Shelley.** His Lady Bride. (Brothers in Arms Ser.). 2000. mass mkt. 5.50 (*0-8217-6665-1*) Kensgtn Pub Corp.

— One Wicked Night. (Splendor Historical Romances Ser.). 320p. 2000. mass mkt. 4.99 (*0-8217-6467-5*, Zebra Kensgtn) Kensgtn Pub Corp.

Bradley-Springer, Lucy. HIV - AIDS Nursing Care Plans. 2nd rev. ed. LC 99-235965. (Nursing Care Plans Ser.). 230p. (C). 1998. per. 39.95 (*1-56930-097-6*) Skidmore Roth Pub.

Bradley, Stanley & Purcell, Elizabeth F., eds. The Paracellular Pathway: Report of a Conference. LC 82-81100. 390p. reprint ed. pap. 120.90 (*0-608-16367-8*, 202669500051) Bks Demand.

Bradley, Stephen. Getting Ready for Winter & Other Fall Tasks. (Seasonal Garden Workbooks). (Illus.). 112p. 1997. 22.50 (*1-55670-552-2*) Stewart Tabori & Chang.

***Bradley, Stephen.** Winter Gardening. (Illus.). 200p. 2000. pap. 19.95 (*0-7370-0628-5*) Time-Life Educ.

Bradley, Stephen E., Jr., ed. North Carolina Confederate Militia Officers Roster: As Contained in the Adjutant-General's Officers Roster. (Illus.). 439p. 1992. 35.00 (*1-56837-044-X*) Broadfoot.

Bradley, Stephen P., et al, eds. Globalization, Technology, & Competition: The Fusion of Computers & Telecommunications in the 1990s. LC 92-36104. 400p. 1993. 39.95 (*0-87584-338-7*) Harvard Busn.

An Asterisk (*) at the beginning of an entry indicates that the title is appearing for the first time.

Bradley, Stephen P. & Nolan, Richard L., eds. Sense & Respond: Capturing Value in the Network Era. LC 97-39970. 352p. 1998. 45.00 (0-87584-835-4) Harvard Busn.
Bradley, Steve. Candy Man. (Bestsellers I Ser.). (J). 1979. 13.85 (0-606-02378-X, Pub. by Turtleback) Demco.
— The Pruning Handbook. (Illus.). 160p. 1997. pap. 24.95 (1-85223-981-6, Pub. by Cro1wood) Trafalgar.
Bradley, Steve, jt. auth. see Berry, Susan.
Bradley, Steven. Keeping the Garden in Bloom: Watering, Dead-Heading, & Other Summer Tasks. LC 97-39038. (Seasonal Garden Workbook Ser.). 112p. 1998. 22.50 (1-55670-688-X) Stewart Tabori & Chang.
***Bradley, Steven.** Waking up the Garden: Planting, Clearing, & Other Spring Tasks. LC 97-41164. (Seasonal Garden Workbook Ser.: Vol. 8). (Illus.). 112p. 1998. 22.50 (1-55670-606-5) Stewart Tabori & Chang.
Bradley, Susan. How to Be Even More Irresistible. 1998. pap. text 16.95 (1-888670-26-6) Loving Univ.
— How to Be Irresistible to the Opposite Sex: The Art of Dating, Mating, Long Term Relating. 1996. pap. text 19.95 (1-888670-30-4) Loving Univ.
— Pacific Northwest Palate: Four Seasons of Great Cooking. 1989. 22.07 (0-201-51764-7) Addison-Wesley.
— Sudden Money. Beagle, Abbey, ed. Date not set. mass mkt. write for info. (0-9653318-0-6) High Rd Pub.
***Bradley, Susan & Martin, Mary.** Sudden Money: Managing a Financial Windfall. LC 99-55829. 336p. 2000. 24.95 (0-471-38086-5) Wiley.
Bradley, Susan, ed. see Bradley, Matt.
***Bradley, Susan J.** Affect Regulation & the Development of Psychopathology. 315p. 2000. lib. bdg. 40.00 (1-57230-548-7, CO548) Guilford Pubns.
Bradley, Susan J., jt. auth. see Zucker, Kenneth J.
***Bradley, T. Douglas & Floras, John S.** Sleep Apnea: Implications in Cardiovascular & Cerebrovascular Disease. LC 00-29048. (Lung Biology in Health & Disease Ser.). (Illus.). 2000. write for info. (0-8247-0299-9) Dekker.
Bradley, T. J. & Miller, T. A., eds. Measurement of Ion Transport & Metabolic Rate in Insects. (Experimental Entomology Ser.). (Illus.). 290p. 1983. 145.00 (0-387-90855-2) Spr-Verlag.
Bradley, Teresa & Patton, Paul. Essential Mathematics for Economics & Business. LC 97-39662. 740p. 1999. pap. 40.95 (0-471-97511-7) Wiley.
***Bradley, Terris Wade.** Meadows of Howling: or Abortion, Feminism & the Culture of Death. 180p. 2000. 21.95 (0-7541-1362-0, Pub. by Minerva Pr) Unity Dist.
Bradley, Theresa, ed. Public Finance Restructuring for Sustainable Development in Emerging Market Economies. LC 98-87590. 64p. 1998. pap. 20.00 (1-56973-274-4) World Resources Inst.
Bradley, Timothy. The Care & Feeding of Dinosaurs. 48p. (J). (gr. 2-4). 1999. 23.90 (0-7613-1305-2, Copper Beech Bks) Millbrook Pr.
Bradley, Tom. Acting Alone. LC 94-78404. 274p. 1994. 19.95 (1-56313-444-6); pap. 12.95 (1-56313-723-2) BrownTrout Pubs Inc.
— Black Class Cur. 1999. pap. 17.95 (0-7414-0076-6) Buy Books.
— The Curved Jewels. 189p. 1999. pap. 13.95 (0-7414-0030-8) Buy Books.
***Bradley, Tom.** Hustling the East: A Dai-Nippon Trilogy. LC 99-91596. 1999. 25.00 (0-7388-0926-8); pap. 18.00 (0-7388-0927-6) Xlibris Corp.
Bradley, Tom. Kara-Kun, Flip-Kun. 285p. 1999. pap. 16.95 (0-7414-0044-8) Buy Books.
— Killing Bryce. 677p. 1999. pap. 25.95 (0-7414-0090-1) Buy Books.
Bradley, Val, jt. auth. see Raworth, Jenny.
Bradley, Valerie. Town Gardens: Practical Ideas for Transforming Small Urban Spaces. 96p. 1998. 16.95 (1-85967-586-7, Lorenz Bks) Anness Pub.
Bradley, Valerie J., et al. Emerging Issues in Family Support. (AAMD Monographs). 160p. (Orig.). (C). 1992. pap. text 22.95 (0-940898-29-2) Am Assn Mental.
Bradley, W., jt. auth. see Committee on Clay Minerals Staff.
Bradley, W. F. & Hanson, Harold P., eds. Machine Interpretations of Patterson Functions & Alternative Direct Approaches & the Austin Symposium on Gas Phase Molecular Structure. (Transactions of the American Crystallographic Association Ser.: Vol. 2). 1966. pap. 25.00 (0-686-60373-7) Polycrystal Bk Serv.
Bradley, Walter G. 1998 Year Book Neurology & Neurosurgery. (Illus.). 440p. (C). (gr. 13). 1998. text 78.00 (0-8151-9648-2, 24985) Mosby Inc.
— 1997 Year Book of Neurology & Neurosurgery. (Illus.). 608p. (C). (gr. 13). 1997. text 78.00 (0-8151-1209-2, 23003) Mosby Inc.
Bradley, Walter G., ed. Muscle & Nerve, Vol. 6. 1983. text 72.00 (0-471-88977-6) Wiley.
***Bradley, Walter G., et al.** Neurology in Clinical Practice. 3rd ed. LC 99-31264. 2750p. 1999. text 450.00 (0-7506-9973-6) Buttrwrth-Heinemann.
— Pocket Companion to Neurology in Clinical Practice. 3rd ed. LC 96-28924. 758p. 2000. pap. text 25.00 (0-7506-9787-3) Buttrwrth-Heinemann.
***Bradley, Walter G., et al.** Pocket Companion to Neurology in Clinical Practice. 3rd ed. (Illus.). 768p. 2000. pap. 45.00 (0-7506-7264-1) Buttrwrth-Heinemann.
Bradley, Walter G., jt. auth. see Stark, David D.
Bradley, Walter G., ed. see Year Book of Neurology & Neurosurgery Staff.
Bradley, Wendell G. The New Political Consciousness: A Context for Ecocommunity. 176p. (Orig.). 1992. pap. write for info. (0-9632130-2-4) Lysander.
Bradley-Whitecotton, Judith, jt. auth. see Whitecotton, Joseph W.
Bradley, Will. Will Bradley: His Graphic Art. Hornung, Clarence P. & Wong, Roberta W., eds. (Illus.). 97p. 1974. pap. 10.95 (0-486-20701-3) Dover.
Bradley, William A. Acoustical Report on AGMA Gear Sound Manual. (Technical Papers: Vol. 299.06). (Illus.). 23p. 1975. pap. text 30.00 (1-55589-146-2) AGMA.
Bradley, William A., et al, eds. Plasma Lipoproteins Pt. C: Quantitation. (Methods in Enzymology Ser.: Vol. 263). (Illus.). 373p. 1995. text 80.00 (0-12-182164-1) Acad Pr.
Bradley, William A., tr. see Hemon, Louis.
Bradley, William B., ed. see Energy Technology Conference & Exhibition Staff.
Bradley, William G. & Brant-Zawadzki, Michael. MRI of the Brain I. 2nd ed. 256p. text 89.95 (0-7817-2568-2) Lppncott W & W.
Bradley, William G., Jr. & Brant-Zawadzki, Michael. MRI of the Brain One: Non-Neoplastic Disease. (MRI Teaching File Ser.). 256p. 1990. text 76.00 (0-88167-745-0) Lppncott W & W.
Bradley, William G. & Bydder, Graeme. MRI Atlas of the Brain. LC 89-43377. (Illus.). 353p. 1990. reprint ed. pap. 109.50 (0-608-05838-6, 205980400007) Bks Demand.
Bradley, William G., Jr. & Bydder, Graeme M. Advanced MR Imaging Techniques. 320p. 1997. write for info. (1-85317-024-0) Martin Dunitz.
Bradley, William G., Jr., et al. Magnetic Resonance Test & Syllabus, Vol. 31. (Professional Self-Evaluation & Continuing Education Program Ser.). (Illus.). 800p. 1991. 190.00 (1-55903-031-3) Am Coll Radiology.
Bradley, William G., Jr., jt. auth. see Brant-Zawadzki, Michael.
Bradley, William G., Jr., jt. auth. see Hashemi, Ray H.
Bradley, William G., Jr., jt. auth. see Reeder, Maurice M.
Bradley, William G., Jr., jt. ed. see Brant-Zawadzki, Michael.
Bradley, William L. Siam Then: The Foreign Colony in Bangkok Before & After Anna. LC 81-12196. (Illus.). 207p. (Orig.). 1981. pap. 9.95 (0-87808-185-2) William Carey Lib.
Bradley, William S. Emil Nolde & German Expressionism: A Prophet in His Own Land. 196p. 1986. pap. 59.95 (0-7734-2018-5) E Mellen.
Bradley, William W., jt. auth. see Burns, Robert M.
Bradley, Zorro A. Canyon de Chelly: The Story of its Ruins & People. 60p. 1973. pap. text 123.00 (0-16-003421-3) USGPO.
Bradlow, Daniel D., ed. International Borrowing. 3rd ed. LC 97-161096. (International Development & Negotiation Sourcebooks for Policy & Practice Ser.). 597p. 1994. 49.00 (0-935328-74-2) Intl Law Inst.
— International Borrowing: Negotiating & Structuring International Debt Transactions. (Orig.). (C). 1986. lib. bdg. 232.50 (90-247-3402-9) Kluwer Academic.
— International Borrowing: Negotiating & Structuring International Debt Transactions. 3rd ed. 600p. (Orig.). 1994. pap. 90.00 (90-411-0987-0) Kluwer Law Intl.
Bradlow, Daniel D., jt. auth. see Escher, Alfred.
Bradlow, Daniel D., jt. ed. see Sassoon, David M.
***Bradlow, H. L.** Cancer Prevention: Novel Nutrient & Pharmaceutical Developments. (Annals of the New York Academy of Science Ser.). (Illus.). 2000. pap. 21.50 (0-8018-6544-1) Johns Hopkins.
Bradlow, H. L., ed. Neuroendocrine Immune Basis of the Rheumatic Disease: The First International Conference. LC 99-26842. 520p. 1999. lib. bdg. 140.00 (1-57331-215-0) NY Acad Sci.
Bradlow, H. Leon, et al, eds. Cancer: Genetics & the Environment. LC 97-32681. (Annals of the New York Academy of Sciences Ser.: No. 833). 220p. 1997. 60.00 (1-57331-114-6); pap. 60.00 (1-57331-115-4) NY Acad Sci.
***Bradlow, H. Leon, et al.** Cancer Prevention: Novel Nutrient & Pharmaceutical Developments. LC 99-51355. (Annals of the New York Academy of Sciences Ser.). 1999. pap. write for info. (1-57331-199-5) NY Acad Sci.
***Bradman.** Ghost Teacher. (J). 2000. pap. 6.95 (0-552-52976-1, Pub. by Transworld Publishers Ltd) Trafalgar.
— Good Sports. 2000. pap. 6.95 (0-552-54296-2, Pub. by Transworld Publishers Ltd) Trafalgar.
— Incredibly Creepy Stories. 2000. 16.95 (0-385-40676-2, Pub. by Transworld Publishers Ltd) Trafalgar.
— Sam the Detective. 2000. pap. 4.95 (0-440-86310-4, Pub. by Transworld Publishers Ltd) Trafalgar.
— Sensational Cyber Stories. (J). 2000. 17.95 (0-385-40836-6, Pub. by Transworld Publishers Ltd) Trafalgar.
— Stack of Story Poems. 2000. pap. 6.95 (0-552-52709-2, Pub. by Transworld Publishers Ltd) Trafalgar.
Bradman, Don. Farewell to Cricket. large type ed. (Bolinda Large Print Ser.). 1997. pap. 24.95 (1-86340-672-7) T T Beeler.
Bradman, Leo H. The Bradman Approach: Selected Topics. 150p. 1993. pap. write for info. (1-883945-02-X) UniPsych Pr.
— Managed Mental Health Care: The Bradman Approach. 177p. 1992. pap. write for info. (1-883945-01-1) UniPsych Pr.
— Quest for Destiny. Harshman, Ronald C., ed. 200p. (Orig.). 1994. pap. write for info. (1-883945-03-8) UniPsych Pr.
Bradman, Leo H. & Volz, David T. Minds & Money: The Mental Health Business in America. Harshman, Ronald C., ed. LC 93-60952. 350p. 1994. 38.00 (1-883945-04-6); pap. 24.00 (1-883945-00-3) UniPsych Pr.
Bradman, Tony. Baby's Best Book. LC 87-45275. (Illus.). 48p. (J). (ps). 1987. 11.95 (0-06-020716-7) HarpC Child Bks.
— Dilly & the Goody Goody. (Blue Bananas Ser.). (Illus.). 48p. (J). 1997. pap. 4.99 (0-7497-1863-3) London Brdge.
— Dilly Speaks Up. 1999. pap. write for info. (0-14-050605-5) Viking Penguin.
— A Goodnight Kind of Feeling. LC 97-25625. (Illus.). 32p. (J). (ps-4). 1998. lib. bdg. 15.95 (0-8234-1351-9) Holiday.
***Bradman, Tony.** Has Anyone Seen Jack? 24p. (J). 1999. 7.99 (0-7112-0728-3) F Lincoln.
Bradman, Tony. Magnificent Mummies. (Blue Bananas Ser.). (Illus.). 1997. pap. text 4.99 (0-7497-2767-5) London Brdge.
— Michael. (Illus.). 32p. (J). (ps-1). 1998. pap. 9.95 (0-86264-759-2, Pub. by Andersen Pr) Trafalgar.
***Bradman, Tony.** Nicky & the Twins' Lost Rabbit. (Illus.). (J). 1998. pap. 9.95 (0-00-664511-9, Pub. by HarpC) Trafalgar.
— One Nil. 80p. (YA). (gr. 6-9). 1984. pap. 7.95 (0-14-031983-2, Pub. by Pnguin Bks Ltd) Trafalgar.
— Sam The Girl Detective. (J). 2000. pap. 4.95 (0-440-86212-4, Pub. by Transworld Publishers Ltd) Trafalgar.
— Sam the Girl Detective. 2000. pap. 3.95 (0-440-86241-8, Pub. by Transworld Publishers Ltd) Trafalgar.
Bradman, Tony. The Sandal. 1999. pap. 3.95 (0-14-054173-X) NAL.
Bradman, Tony. Smile Please. (J). 1989. pap. 7.95 (0-14-032286-8, Pub. by Pnguin Bks Ltd) Trafalgar.
— Tommy Niner & the Moon of Doom. (Illus.). 98p. (J). 1998. pap. 7.95 (0-14-037592-9, Pub. by Pnguin Bks Ltd) Trafalgar.
Bradman, Tony. Two Minute Puppy Tales. (Illus.). 32p. (J). 1994. 2.99 (0-317-06156-9, Ladybrd) Penguin Putnam.
***Bradnan, Melinda.** Quality Dumpling Recipes. Crum, Dorothy, ed. 120p. 2000. spiral bd. 6.95 (1-57216-071-3) Penfield.
Bradnan, Melinda, ed. Quality Czech Mushroom Recipes. (Illus.). 160p. 1999. spiral bd. 6.95 (1-57216-070-5) Penfield.
Bradnan, Melinda, ed. see Bourret, Joan Liffring-Zug.
Bradnan, Melinda, ed. see Lagerlof, Selma.
Bradner, J. A. Acquisitions. (Technical Papers: Vol. P990.13). (Illus.). 6p. 1965. pap. text 30.00 (1-55589-462-3) AGMA.
— Search for Silence. (Technical Papers: Vol. P990.12). (Illus.). 29p. (Orig.). 1958. pap. text 30.00 incl. audio compact disk (1-55589-385-6) AGMA.
Bradner, Jeanne H. The Board Member's Guide: A Beneficial Bestiary. LC 95-41371. (Illus.). 128p. (Orig.). 1995. 14.95 (0-9634395-3-7); pap. 9.95 (0-9634395-4-5) Conversation Pr.
***Bradner, Jeanne H.** Leading Volunteers for Results: Building Communities Today. 128p. 1999. pap. 11.95 (0-9634395-5-3) Conversation Pr.
Bradner, Jeanne H. Passionate Volunteerism: The Importance of Volunteerism Today & How Government, Nonprofits & Volunteers Can Make It a More Powerful Force. 82p. (Orig.). 1993. pap. 3.95 (0-9634395-2-9) Conversation Pr.
Bradner, John. Symbols of Church Seasons & Days. LC 77-70805. (Illus.). 80p. (Orig.). 1990. pap. 8.95 (0-8192-1228-8) Morehouse Pub.
Bradner, Lawrence H. The Plum Beach Light: The Birth, Life, & Death of a Lighthouse. (Illus.). 196p. (Orig.). 1989. pap. 19.95 (0-9624248-0-3) L H Bradner.
Bradner, Leicester. The Poems of Queen Elizabeth I. LC 64-17778. (Brown University Bicentennial Publications). 111p. reprint ed. 34.50 (0-608-16491-7, 202750300055) Bks Demand.
Bradner, Scott O. IPNG: Internet Protocol Next Generation. Mankin, Allison, ed. LC 95-20944. 352p. (C). 1995. 39.95 (0-201-63395-7) Addison-Wesley.
Bradner, W. T., jt. auth. see Crooke, Stanley T.
Bradney, Anthony. Religion, Rights & Laws. LC 92-42154. 185p. 1993. 49.00 (0-7185-1366-5) St Martin.
Bradney, Anthony & Cowie, Fiona, eds. Transformative Visions of Legal Education. LC 98-15928. (Journal of Law & Society Ser.). 174p. 1999. pap. 39.95 (0-631-21137-3) Blackwell Pubs.
Bradney, Anthony & Cownie, Fiona. Living Without Law. 69.95 (1-85521-555-1) Ashgate Pub Co.
Bradney, Gail. Best Wines! 1998 Vol. 1: The Gold Medal Winners. 2nd rev. ed. (Best Wines! Ser.). 384p. (Orig.). 1997. pap. 14.95 (0-9651750-1-4) Print Proj.
***Bradney, Gail.** Buy Wholesale By Mail 2001: The Consumer's Bible to Bargain Shopping On-Line, By Mail, & By Phone. 688p. 2000. pap. 20.00 (0-06-273677-9) HarpC.
Bradney, Gail, ed. Best Wines! Gold Medal Winners from the Leading Competitions Worldwide. 300p. 1996. pap. text 16.95 (0-9651750-0-6) Print Proj.
***Bradnock, Robert.** Goa Handbook. 2nd ed. (Footprint Handbooks Ser.). (Illus.). 2000. pap. 15.95 (0-658-00015-2, Passprt Bks) NTC Contemp Pub Co.
— Sri Lanka Handbook. 3rd ed. (Footprint Handbooks Ser.). (Illus.). (J). 2000. pap. 18.95 (0-658-01085-9, Passprt Bks) NTC Contemp Pub Co.
Bradnock, Robert & Bradnock, Roma. Goa Handbook. (Footprint Handbooks Ser.). 288p. 1998. 17.95 (0-8442-4807-X, 4807X, Natl Textbk Co) NTC Contemp Pub Co.
— India Handbook. 1999. 8th ed. (Footprint Handbooks Ser.). (Illus.). 1488p. (Orig.). 1998. 29.95 (0-8442-4885-1) NTC Contemp Pub Co.
***Bradnock, Robert & Bradnock, Roma.** India Handbook 2000. 9th ed. (Footprints Bks.). 1488p. 1999. pap. 27.95 (0-8442-4841-X, 4841X, Natl Textbk Co) NTC Contemp Pub Co.
Bradnock, Robert & Bradnock, Roma. India Handbook, 1998. 7th ed. (Footprint Handbks.). (Illus.). 1472p. 1997. 29.95 (0-8442-4788-X, Passprt Bks) NTC Contemp Pub Co.
— Sri Lanka Handbook. 2nd ed. (Footprint Handbooks Ser.). 288p. 1998. 19.95 (0-8442-4953-X, 4953X, Natl Textbk Co) NTC Contemp Pub Co.
Bradnock, Robert W. South Asian Handbook, 1994. 1456p. 1994. pap. 39.95 (0-8442-9980-4, Passprt Bks) NTC Contemp Pub Co.
— Sri Lanka Handbook with the Maldives. (Handbooks of the World Ser.). (Illus.). 288p. 1996. 19.95 (0-8442-4902-5, Passprt Bks) NTC Contemp Pub Co.
Bradnock, Robert W., ed. India Handbook. 5th ed. (Illus.). 1440p. 1995. 29.95 (0-8442-8887-X, Passprt Bks) NTC Contemp Pub Co.
— 1997 India Handbook. 6th rev. ed. (Footprint Handbks.). (Illus.). 1440p. 1996. 29.95 (0-8442-4908-4, Passprt Bks) NTC Contemp Pub Co.
Bradnock, Roma, jt. auth. see Bradnock, Robert.
Brado, Edward. Brado's Guide to Ottawa. (Illus.). 264p. 1991. pap. 13.95 (1-55082-012-5, Pub. by Quarry Pr) LPC InBook.
***Bradow, Stuart N.** Daytona Dirt. (Illus.). 234p. 1999. per. 6.95 (0-9668159-0-4, Pub. by Red Quill Pubg) Southern Bk Service.
Bradsaw, Bonnie A., ed. & des. see Russell, Barbara C.
Bradsby, H. C. History of Bradford Co., PA. (Illus.). 1320p. 1993. reprint ed. lib. bdg. 129.00 (0-8328-2845-9) Higginson Bk Co.
— History of Vigo County, Indiana with Biographical Selections. (Illus.). 1018p. 1993. reprint ed. lib. bdg. 99.50 (0-8328-2565-4) Higginson Bk Co.
Bradsby, H. C., ed. History of Bureau County, Illinois. (Illus.). 710p. 1993. reprint ed. lib. bdg. 72.00 (0-8328-3120-4) Higginson Bk Co.
Bradsby, Larry & Bradsby, Shirley. Resources for Computation. (Math Rescue Ser.). 622p. (J). (gr. k-6). 1998. teacher ed., ring bd. 75.00 (1-57035-191-0, 106COMP) Sopris.
Bradsby, Shirley, jt. auth. see Bradsby, Larry.
Bradshaw. British Problems 1534 - 1707. LC 96-27993. 346p. 1996. text 49.95 (0-312-16042-9) St Martin.
— Foundations of Physical Geography: With Study Book. 1995. 48.50 (0-697-26310-X, WCB McGr Hill) McGrw-H Hghr Educ.
Bradshaw, et al. Trees in the Urban Landscape: Principles & Practice. (Illus.). 288p. (C). 1995. 75.00 (0-419-20100-9, E & FN Spon) Routledge.
Bradshaw, jt. ed. see Soehnlen.
Bradshaw, Alice B. A Promise of Love. 208p. 1996. pap. 20.00 (1-55630-884-1) Brentwood Comm.
Bradshaw, Ann. The Motherhood Career Connection. 155p. 1993. write for info. (0-9637505-1-8) Anthea Pr.
Bradshaw, Annette & Franson, Gwyn. Elegance: Exquisite Doily Patterns Charted for Cross-Stitch. 1984. 5.98 (0-88290-244-X) Horizon Utah.
— Feathered Philosophies: Wise Sayings "from the Birds" 1983. 5.98 (0-88290-228-8) Horizon Utah.
— Fifteen New Mormon Temples, Bk. C: The Personal Touch. 1984. 8.98 (0-88290-243-1) Horizon Utah.
— Friends Forever: Memorable Moments of Childhood. 16p. (Orig.). 1984. pap. 5.98 (0-88290-214-8, 2798) Horizon Utah.
— Garden Goodies: Cheerful Messages to Brighten the Kitchen. 32p. (Orig.). 1983. pap. 5.98 (0-88290-215-6) Horizon Utah.
— In Tribute to Woman, Bk. A: Monuments to Womanhood. 1983. 6.98 (0-88290-199-0) Horizon Utah.
— Mottos for Many Moods: Humorous Slogans to Brighten Your Day (Cross-Stitch) 1983. 5.98 (0-88290-225-3) Horizon Utah.
— Murphy's Laws: Philosophical Quips in Cross Stitch. 1984. 5.98 (0-88290-255-5) Horizon Utah.
— Paint Your Own Rainbow: Upbeat Mottos for the Young in Heart. 1983. 5.98 (0-88290-237-7) Horizon Utah.
— Teddy Bears & Toys: Playtime Memories in Counted Cross- Stitch. 1984. 5.98 (0-88290-264-4) Horizon Utah.
— The Twelve Days of Christmas: 14 Delightful Ornament Designs. 48p. (Orig.). 1981. pap. 5.98 (0-88290-151-6, 2803) Horizon Utah.
— Twelve More Mormon Temples Bk. B: The Personal Touch. 1980. 8.98 (0-88290-150-8) Horizon Utah.
— Twelve Mormon Temples Bk. A: The Personal Touch. 1980. 8.98 (0-88290-149-4) Horizon Utah.
Bradshaw, Annette, et al. A Woman's Gifts Bk. B: Monuments to Womanhood. (Monuments to Womanhood Ser.). 48p. (Orig.). 1982. pap. 6.98 (0-88290-204-0, 2805) Horizon Utah.
— A Woman's Love Bk. C: Monuments to Womanhood. (Monuments to Womanhood Ser.). 48p. (Orig.). 1982. pap. 6.98 (0-88290-205-9, 2806) Horizon Utah.
***Bradshaw, Bill & Smith, Helen Lawton.** Privatization & Deregulation of Transport. LC 99-88250. 2000. write for info. (0-312-23273-X) St Martin.
Bradshaw, Bob. Sedona: Red Rock Country. LC 94-78579. (Illus.). 64p. pap. text. write for info. (0-9629319-1-8) Bradshaw Color.
— Westerns of the Redrock Country: Forty-Three Movies Filmed in Sedona. 1991. 9.95 (0-9629319-0-X) Bradshaw Color.
Bradshaw, Brendan & Roberts, Peter, eds. British Consciousness & Identity: The Making of Britain, 1533-1707. LC 97-33420. 366p. (C). 1998. text 69.95 (0-521-43383-5) Cambridge U Pr.
Bradshaw, Bruce. Bridging the Gap: Evangelism, Development & Shalom. (Innovations in Mission Ser.). 183p. 1994. pap. 11.95 (0-912552-84-0) MARC.
Bradshaw, Buck. Judge Colt. large type ed. (Linford Western Library). 256p. 1996. pap. 16.99 (0-7089-7954-8, Linford) Ulverscroft.

An Asterisk (*) at the beginning of an entry indicates that the title is appearing for the first time.

Bradshaw, Bud. The Guide to Wagering on Golf. (Illus.). 140p. 1996. pap. 12.95 (*0-9667245-1-8*) BBC Enter.
— Understanding Golf Games, a Guide for All Skill Levels. (Illus.). 195p. 1998. pap. 12.95 (*0-9667245-0-X*) BBC Enter.

Bradshaw, C. M. & Szabadi, E. Time & Behaviour: Psychological & Neurobehavioral Analyses. LC 97-14058. (Advances in Psychology Ser.: Vol. 120). 588p. 1997. 149.50 (*0-444-82449-9*) Elsevier.

Bradshaw, Cara H. Pint-Sized Puppets & Poems. (Illus.). 48p. (J). (ps-2). 1994. 6.99 (*0-86653-785-6*, GA1479) Good Apple.

Bradshaw, Carol, et al, contrib. by. Cataloging Manual: 1992 Edition. rev. ed. 219p. 1992. ring bd. 25.00 (*1-891367-12-9*) North State Coop.

Bradshaw, Charles E. Profiles of Faith. 1984. 9.95 (*0-911866-01-9*) LifeSprings Res.

Bradshaw, Chris M., jt. ed. see Szabadi, E.

Bradshaw, Clair. Get Well Therapy. LC 96-85005. (Illus.). 88p. (Orig.). 1996. pap. 4.95 (*0-87029-297-8*, 20157) Abbey.

***Bradshaw Collection Staff.** A Catalogue of the Bradshaw Collection of Irish Books in the University Library, 3 vols. 1700p. 1999. reprint ed. 225.00 (*1-57898-171-9*) Martino Pubng.

Bradshaw, Dave. The ETI Book of Electronics. (Illus.). 200p. (Orig.). 1992. pap. 27.50 (*0-85242-928-2*) Nexus Special Interests.

Bradshaw, David. Searcher of Longvales. 1997. 14.95 (*0-7188-2647-7*, Lutterworth-Parkwest) Parkwest Pubns.

Bradshaw, David, ed. Britain As a Learning Society. 224p. 1995. 85.00 (*0-7507-0394-6*, Falmer Pr) Taylor & Francis.

Bradshaw, David & Frangicetto, Tom. Joe's Boys. 190p. 1995. 14.95 (*1-880683-07-5*) Exeter Hse.

Bradshaw, David, ed. see Huxley, Aldous.

Bradshaw, David, ed. see Lawrence, D. H.

Bradshaw, David J. & Ozment, Suzanne. The Voice of Toil: Nineteenth-Century British Writing about Work. LC 99-33101. 1999. pap. text 29.95 (*0-8214-1293-0*) Ohio U Pr.

***Bradshaw, David J. & Ozment, Suzanne, eds.** The Voice of Toil: Nineteenth-Century British Writings about Work. LC 99-33101. (Illus.). 880p. (C). 1999. text 60.00 (*0-8214-1292-2*) Ohio U Pr.

Bradshaw, Douglas W., jt. auth. see Wilson, John C.

Bradshaw, Emily, et al. A Country Christmas. 352p. 1993. mass mkt. 4.99 (*0-451-17725-8*, Sig) NAL.

Bradshaw, English. My Father's Business. LC 95-61464. 260p. (Orig.). 1996. pap. 12.95 (*1-887798-03-X*) WriteMore Pubns.

Bradshaw, F. M. The Law of Charitable Trusts. 212p. 1982. boxed set 54.00 (*0-409-49070-9*, AT, MICHIE) LEXIS Pub.

Bradshaw, Georgene, jt. auth. see Wrighton, Charlene.

Bradshaw, Georgene E., et al. Zoo-Phonics en Espanol - Manual de Instruccion para Maestros. 2nd rev. ed. (ENG & SPA., Illus.). 60p. 1994. reprint ed. pap. text, teacher ed. 16.95 (*1-886441-17-0*) Zoo-phonics.

Bradshaw, Gillian. Beacon at Alexandria. LC 86-3017. (Hera Ser.). 376p. 1994. pap. 15.00 (*1-56947-010-3*) Soho Press.
— Island of Ghosts. LC 98-13572. 319p. 1998. text 22.95 (*0-312-86439-6*) St Martin.
— Island of Ghosts. 372p. 1999. mass mkt. 5.99 (*0-8125-4514-1*, Pub. by Tor Bks) St Martin.
— The Land of Gold. LC 91-31810. 160p. (J). (gr. 4-7). 1992. 14.00 (*0-688-10576-9*, Grenwillow Bks) HarpC Child Bks.

***Bradshaw, Gillian.** The Sand-Reckoner. LC 99-89827. 352p. 2000. 23.95 (*0-312-87340-9*, Pub. by Forge NYC) St Martin.

Bradshaw, Glenda C., ed. see Fletcher, Robert H.

Bradshaw, Graham. Misrepresentations: Shakespeare & the Materialists. 322p. 1993. text 45.00 (*0-8014-2890-4*); pap. text 17.95 (*0-8014-8129-5*) Cornell U Pr.
— Shakespeare's Scepticism. LC 87-9479. 283p. 1987. pap. 12.95 (*0-685-43929-1*) St Martin.
— Shakespeare's Skepticism. LC 90-46406. 270p. pap. text 17.95 (*0-8014-9910-0*) Cornell U Pr.

Bradshaw, Graham & Kishi, Tetsuo. Shakespeare in Japan. 200p. (C). 1999. 90.00 (*0-485-11499-2*, Pub. by Athlone Pr) Humanities.

Bradshaw, H. H. 4X4 Leadership & the Purpose of the Firm. LC 97-37012. 225p. 1998. 49.95 (*0-7890-0443-7*); pap. 24.95 (*0-7890-0444-5*) Haworth Pr.

Bradshaw, Harold C. The Indians of Connecticut. 64p. pap. 8.95 (*0-941567-60-5*) J C & A L Fawcett.

Bradshaw, Henry. Bradshaw's Life of St. Werburge of Chester. Horstmann, C., ed. (EETS, OS Ser.: No. 88). 1972. reprint ed. 50.00 (*0-527-00085-X*) Periodicals Srv.
— The Skeleton of Chaucer's Canterbury Tales. LC 70-39518. reprint ed. 32.50 (*0-404-00929-8*) AMS Pr.

Bradshaw, Heydon. The Coffee Industry. (International Trade Ser.). (Illus.). 192p. 2000. 710.00 (*1-85573-070-7*, Pub. by Woodhead Pubng) Am Educ Systs.

Bradshaw, J. E. & Mackay, G. R., eds. Potato Genetics. (Illus.). 576p. 1994. text 170.00 (*0-85198-869-5*) OUP.

Bradshaw, J. S., jt. ed. see Izatt, R. M.

Bradshaw, Jane. Name That Baby: Every Parents Guide to Names. LC 98-16140. 512p. 1998. pap. 10.99 (*0-8054-1271-9*) Broadman.

Bradshaw, Jeffrey M., ed. Software Agents. LC 97-1553. (Illus.). 450p. (Orig.). 1997. pap. text 42.00 (*0-262-52234-9*) MIT Pr.

Bradshaw, Jerald S., et al. Aza-Crown Macrocycles, Vol. 51. LC 92-35450. (Chemistry of Heterocyclic Compounds, a Series of Monographs: vOL. 51). 896p. 1993. 379.00 (*0-471-52485-9*) Wiley.

Bradshaw, John. The Behaviour of the Domestic Cat. (Illus.). 240p. (Orig.). 1992. pap. text 40.00 (*0-85198-715-X*) OUP.
— Bradshaw on the Family: A New Way of Creating Solid Self-Esteem. 2nd rev. ed. (Illus.). 303p. 1996. pap. 10.95 (*1-55874-427-4*, 4274) Health Comm.
— A Concordance to the Poetical Works of John Milton. (BCL1-PR English Literature Ser.). 412p. 1992. reprint ed. lib. bdg. 99.00 (*0-7812-7379-X*) Rprt Serv.
— Creating Love: The Next Great Stage of Growth. 400p. 1994. pap. 12.95 (*0-553-37305-6*) Bantam.
— Creating Love: The Next Great Stage of Growth. large type ed. LC 92-47393. 1993. pap. write for info. (*0-8161-5729-4*, G K Hall Lrg Type) Mac Lib Ref.
— Family Secrets: What You Don't Know Can Hurt You. 320p. 1996. pap. 14.95 (*0-553-37498-2*) Bantam.
— Healing the Shame That Binds You. (Illus.). 245p. 1988. pap. 9.95 (*0-932194-86-9*) Health Comm.
— Homecoming: Reclaiming & Championing Your Inner Child. (Illus.). 304p. 1992. pap. 14.95 (*0-553-35389-6*) Bantam.

Bradshaw, John & Brooks, Mel. Business Accounting & Finance for Managers & Business Students. LC 97-187201. 746p. 1996. pap. 48.00 (*0-7021-2983-6*, Pub. by Juta & Co) Gaunt.

***Bradshaw, John L.** Developmental Disorders of the Frontostriatal System: Neuropsychological, Neuropsychiatric & Evolutionary Perspectives. LC 00-40284. (Brain Damage, Behaviour & Cognition Ser.). 2000. write for info. (*1-84169-226-3*) Psychology Pr.

Bradshaw, John L. Hemispheric Specialization & Psychological Function. fac. ed. LC 89-16611. (Illus.). 230p. 1989. reprint ed. pap. 71.30 (*0-608-00961-X*, 206180900011) Bks Demand.
— Human Evolution: A Neuropsychological Perspective. 1998. pap. text 29.95 (*0-86377-505-5*) Taylor & Francis.

Bradshaw, John L. & Mattingley, Jason B. Clinical Neuropsychology: Behavioral & Brain Science. (Illus.). 458p. 1995. pap. text 39.95 (*0-12-124545-4*) Acad Pr.

Bradshaw, John O. Greenberg's Guide to Kusan Trains. Suehle, MaryAnn, ed. (Illus.). 88p. 1987. 25.00 (*0-89778-073-6*, 10-6381, Greenberg Books) Kalmbach.

***Bradshaw, Jonathan.** Absent Fathers. LC 99-23942. 280p. 1999. pap. 25.99 (*0-415-21593-5*) Routledge.

Bradshaw, Jonathan. Budget Standards for the United Kingdom: Constructing the Budget Standards. (Studies in Cash & Care). 272p. 1993. 72.95 (*1-85628-591-X*, Pub. by Avebry) Ashgate Pub Co.

Bradshaw, Jonathan & Gibbs, Ian. Public Support for Private Residential Care. 187p. 1988. text 72.95 (*0-566-05661-5*, Pub. by Avebry) Ashgate Pub Co.

***Bradshaw, Jonathan, et al.** Absent Fathers. LC 99-23942. 280p. (C). 1999. text. write for info. (*0-415-21592-7*) Routledge.

Bradshaw, Joyce G. Toward a New Babel? 379p. 1997. pap. 15.00 (*1-887567-07-0*) CBCCU Amer.

Bradshaw, Kenneth & Pring, David. Parliament & Congress. 9.95 (*0-7043-3353-8*, Pub. by Quartet) Charles River Bks.

Bradshaw, L. Jack. Laboratory Microbiology. 4th ed. 343p. (C). 1992. pap. text 51.00 (*0-03-047442-6*, Pub. by SCP) Harcourt.

***Bradshaw, Landon, et al.** PHP3 & PHP4 Functions Essential Reference. (Essential Reference Ser.). 2000. 52.95 (*0-7357-0970-X*) New Riders Pub.

Bradshaw, Larry, jt. auth. see Combs, Clint.

Bradshaw, Leah. Acting & Thinking: The Political Thought of Hannah Arendt. 1989. text 45.00 (*0-8020-2625-7*) U of Toronto Pr.

Bradshaw, Linda S., ed. see Association of American Geographers Staff.

Bradshaw, Lindsay J. Lindsay Bradshaw's One Hour Party Cakes. 1994. 19.95 (*1-85391-044-9*) Sterling.

Bradshaw, Lindsay J., et al. The Ultimate Book of Birthday Cakes. (Illus.). 1999. 24.95 (*1-85391-742-7*) Tuttle Pubng.

Bradshaw, Lucinda, jt. auth. see Bradshaw, Scott.

Bradshaw, Marion J. Philosophical Foundations of Faith. LC 78-99248. reprint ed. 20.00 (*0-404-00968-9*) AMS Pr.

Bradshaw, Mary I. Sales Agency - A Comparative Analysis: A Survey of BOC Sales Agency Programs for Network Sales. 94p. 1992. pap. 253.00 (*0-940919-33-8*, 235) MultiMedia Telecomm.

Bradshaw, Michael. The Appalachian Regional Commission: Twenty-Five Years of Government Policy. LC 91-26942. (Illus.). 184p. 1992. text 22.50 (*0-8131-1761-5*) U Pr of Ky.
— The New Global Order: A World Regional Geography. LC 96-84098. 624p. (C). 1996. text. write for info. (*0-697-21692-6*, WCB McGr Hill) McGrw-H Hghr Educ.
— The New Global Order: World Regional Geography. 2nd ed. 148p. 1999. pap. 22.81 (*0-697-38517-5*); pap. text 52.25 (*0-697-38514-0*) McGraw.
— Regions & Regionalism in the United States. LC 87-17917. 186p. 1988. text 35.00 (*0-87805-339-5*); pap. text 15.95 (*0-87805-340-9*) U Pr of Miss.

***Bradshaw, Michael.** Resurrection Songs: The Poetry of Thomas Lovell Beddoes. LC 00-30600. (Nineteenth Century Ser.). 2000. write for info. (*0-7546-0103-X*, Pub. by Ashgate Pub) Ashgate Pub Co.

Bradshaw, Michael & Walasek, Richard A. World Regional Geography. 112p. (C). 1997. text, student ed. 20.00 (*0-697-21694-2*, WCB McGr Hill) McGrw-H Hghr Educ.

Bradshaw, Michael & Weaver, Ruth. Foundations of Physical Geography. LC 94-72286. 136p. (C). 1995. text, student ed. 20.00 (*0-697-24087-8*, WCB McGr Hill); text, student ed. write for info. (*0-697-26309-6*, WCB McGr Hill); student ed., per. write for info. (*0-697-25075-X*, WCB McGr Hill) McGrw-H Hghr Educ.
— Physical Geography. 640p. (C). 1992. text. write for info. (*0-697-24085-1*, WCB McGr Hill) McGrw-H Hghr Educ.

Bradshaw, Michael, et al. Physical Geography. 176p. (C). 1993. text, student ed. 21.87 (*0-697-25081-4*, WCB McGr Hill) McGrw-H Hghr Educ.

Bradshaw, Michael, jt. auth. see Guinness, Paul.

Bradshaw, Michael, jt. ed. see Hanson, Philip.

Bradshaw, Michael J., ed. Geography & Transition. LC 96-49976. 244p. 1997. pap. 60.00 (*0-471-94892-6*) Wiley.

Bradshaw, Murray C., ed. see Severi, Francesco.

Bradshaw, P. An Introduction to Turbulence & Its Measurements. Woods, W. A., ed. 218p. 1971. 104.00 (*0-08-016620-2*, Pub. by Pergamon Repr) Franklin.

Bradshaw, P., jt. auth. see Cebeci, T.

Bradshaw, Paul F. Early Christian Worship: A Basic Introduction. 1998. pap. write for info. (*0-8146-2429-4*) Liturgical Pr.
— Ordination Rites of the Ancient Churches of East & West. 288p. 1992. pap. 19.95 (*0-8146-6000-2*, Pueblo Bks) Liturgical Pr.

***Bradshaw, Paul F.** Passover & Easter Vol. 5: Origin & History to Modern Times. LC 98-41342. (Two Liturgical Traditions Ser.). 264p. 1999. reprint ed. pap. 25.00 (*0-268-03859-7*) U of Notre Dame Pr.
— Passover & Easter Vol. 6: The Symbolic Structuring of Sacred Seasons. LC 98-41341. (Two Liturgical Traditions Ser.). 216p. 2000. reprint ed. pap. 25.00 (*0-268-03860-0*) U of Notre Dame Pr.

Bradshaw, Paul F. The Search for the Origins of Christian Worship: Sources & Methods for the Study of Early Liturgy. 240p. 1993. pap. text 19.95 (*0-19-508051-3*) OUP.

Bradshaw, Paul F., ed. Essays on Early Eastern Eucharistic Prayers. LC 97-14102. 150p. (Orig.). 1997. pap. 29.95 (*0-8146-6153-X*, Pueblo Bks) Liturgical Pr.

Bradshaw, Paul F. & Hoffman, Lawrence A., eds. The Changing Face of Jewish & Christian Worship in North America. LC 90-50967. (Two Liturgical Traditions Ser.: Vol. 2). (C). 1992. pap. text 14.00 (*0-268-00785-3*) U of Notre Dame Pr.
— Life Cycles in Jewish & Christian Worship. LC 95-18807. (Two Liturgical Traditions Ser.: Vol. 4). (C). 1997. text 32.95 (*0-268-01307-1*) U of Notre Dame Pr.
— The Making of Jewish & Christian Worship. LC 90-70856. (Two Liturgical Traditions Ser.: Vol. 1). (C). 1992. pap. text 14.00 (*0-268-01208-3*) U of Notre Dame Pr.
— Passover & Easter: Origin & History to Modern Times. LC 98-41342. (Two Liturgical Traditions Ser.: No. 5). 264p. 1999. 38.00 (*0-268-03857-0*) U of Notre Dame Pr.
— Passover & Easter: The Symbolic Structuring of Sacred Seasons. LC 98-41341. (Two Liturgical Traditions Ser.: No. 6). 216p. 1999. 38.00 (*0-268-03858-9*) U of Notre Dame Pr.

Bradshaw, Paul F., jt. ed. see Spinks, Bryan D.

Bradshaw, Peter. English Eighteenth Century Porcelain Figures. (Illus.). 327p. 1980. reprint ed. 57.00 (*0-902028-83-9*) Antique Collect.

Bradshaw, R., tr. see Schumann, Walter.

Bradshaw, Ralph A. & Schneider, Diana M., eds. Proteins of the Nervous System. 2nd fac. ed. LC 80-21584. (Illus.). 407p. pap. 126.20 (*0-7837-7165-7*, 204713200005) Bks Demand.

Bradshaw, Ray. North Light Book of Creative Paint Finishing Techniques. (Illus.). 144p. 1998. 29.99 (*0-89134-823-9*, North Lght Bks) F & W Pubns Inc.

Bradshaw, Ray. 1,200 Paint Effects for the Home Decorator. (Illus.). 192p. 1997. 29.99 (*0-89134-816-6*, North Lght Bks) F & W Pubns Inc.

***Bradshaw, Ray.** 1,200 Paint Effects for the Home Decorator. (Illus.). 192p. 2000. pap. 24.99 (*1-58180-057-6*, North Lght Bks) F & W Pubns Inc.

***Bradshaw, Rita.** The Twisted Cord. 432p. 1999. 26.00 (*0-7278-2223-3*, Pub. by Severn Hse) Chivers N Amer.

Bradshaw, Robert. Frank Duff. 1984. 6.95 (*0-910984-53-0*); pap. 4.95 (*0-910984-54-9*) Montfort Pubns.

Bradshaw, Robert, jt. auth. see Staszkow, Ronald.

Bradshaw, S. D., ed. see Maina, J. N.

Bradshaw, Sandra M. Cotton Candy Clouds. (Illus.). (YA). (gr. 7-12). 1997. pap. 7.95 (*0-9659150-2-6*) Maygan Pub.
— Forever Mine until Death Do Us Part. 112p. 1999. pap. 10.99 (*0-9659150-3-4*) Maygan Pub.
— The Taffy Pull. large type ed. (Illus.). 40p. 1997. pap. 7.95 (*0-9659150-0-X*) Maygan Pub.
— Teardrops from Heaven. (Illus.). 78p. 1997. pap. 10.95 (*0-9659150-1-8*) Maygan Pub.
— Treasures from the Past. (Illus.). 90p. 1997. pap. 9.95 (*0-9659150-9-3*) Maygan Pub.

Bradshaw, Scott & Bradshaw, Lucinda. Namibia: The Independent Traveler's Guide. (Illus.). 313p. (Orig.). 1994. pap. 16.95 (*0-7818-0254-7*) Hippocrene Bks.

Bradshaw, Spencer D. Folic Acid (Pteroylglutamic Acid) - in Health, Deficiency & Therapy: Index of New Information with Authors, Subjects & References. 150p. 1997. 47.50 (*0-7883-1322-3*) ABBE Pubs Assn.
— Folic Acid (Pteroylglutamic Acid) - In Health, Deficiency & Therapy: Index of New Information with Authors, Subjects & References. 150p. 1996. pap. 44.50 (*0-7883-1323-1*) ABBE Pubs Assn.
— Folic Acid (Pteroylglutamic Acid) - In Health, Deficiency & Therapy: Index of New Information with Authors, Subjects & References. rev. ed. 149p. 1998. 47.50 (*0-7883-2068-8*); pap. 44.50 (*0-7883-2069-6*) ABBE Pubs Assn.

***Bradshaw, Stan.** River Safety: A Floater's Guide. LC 00-22024. (Illus.). 2000. write for info. (*1-890373-08-7*) Greycliff Pub.

Bradshaw, Stan, et al. Pocket Guide to Fly Fishing Knots. (Illus.). 28p. 1997. 12.95 (*1-886127-14-X*) Greycliff Pub.
— Pocket Guide to Outdoor Survival. (Illus.). 28p. 1994. spiral bd. 12.95 (*1-886127-04-2*) Greycliff Pub.

Bradshaw, Steve & Duncan, Joyce. Heirs to Misfortune. (Illus.). 147p. 1987. 14.95 (*0-932807-21-6*) Overmountain Pr.

Bradshaw, Susan, tr. see Jameux, Dominique.

Bradshaw, Sydney D. Ecophysiology of Desert Reptiles. 324p. 1987. text 104.00 (*0-12-124575-6*) Acad Pr.
— Homeostasis in Desert Reptiles. LC 96-43589. (Adaptations of Desert Organisms Ser.). (Illus.). 170p. 1997. 139.00 (*3-540-59264-4*) Spr-Verlag.

Bradshaw, Sydney D., ed. see Kaulenas, M. S.

Bradshaw, Sydney D., ed. see Wiltschko, R., et al.

***Bradshaw, Ted.** A Tutorial Guide to PT/Modeler 2.0: Featuring Render, Library & Help Tutorial Guide. (CAD Ser.). 380p. (C). 1998. pap. write for info. (*0-201-30898-3*) Addison-Wesley.

Bradshaw, Ted K. & Bell, Charles G., eds. The Capacity to Respond: California Political Institutions Face Change. LC 87-26244. 123p. reprint ed. pap. 38.20 (*0-608-20131-6*, 207140300011) Bks Demand.

Bradshaw, Ted K. & Blakely, Edward J. Rural Communities in Advanced Industrial Society: Development & Developers. LC 78-19736. 188p. 1979. 49.95 (*0-275-90333-8*, C0333, Praeger Pubs) Greenwood.

Bradshaw, Terry. Terry Bradshaw Fantasy Football Journal, 1996 Edition. 250p. (Orig.). 1996. pap. 9.95 (*0-9636895-5-X*) Fantasy Spts.

Bradshaw, Terry, jt. auth. see Weisman, Larry.

Bradshaw, Thomas I. & Clark, Marsha. Carrier Down: The Story of the Sinking of the U. S. S. Princeton. Roberts, Melissa, ed. (Illus.). 240p. 1990. 18.95 (*0-89015-773-1*) Sunbelt Media.

Bradshaw, Timothy. The Olive Branch: An Evangelical Anglican Doctrine of the Church. xiv, 306p. (Orig.). 1990. pap. text 25.00 (*0-85364-512-4*) Paternoster Pub.
— Praying As Believing: The Lord's Prayer & the Christian Doctrine of God. LC 98-17455. (Regent's Study Guides). 224p. 1998. pap. 15.00 (*1-57312-198-3*) Smyth & Helwys.
— Trinity & Ontology: A Comparative Study of the Theologies of Karl Barth & Wolfhart Pannenberg. LC 92-5144. (Rutherford Studies in Contemporary Theology). 472p. 1992. reprint ed. 109.95 (*0-7734-1641-2*) E Mellen.

Bradshaw, Timothy, ed. Grace & Truth in the Secular Age. LC 98-13685. 320p. 1998. pap. 28.00 (*0-8028-4343-3*) Eerdmans.
— The Way Forward? Christian Voices on Homosexuality & the Church. 240p. 1998. pap. 14.95 (*0-340-69393-2*, 4909, Pub. by Hodder & Stought Ltd) Morehouse Pub.

Bradshaw, Timothy E., Jr. Battery Wagner: The Siege, the Men Who Fought, & the Casualties. 230p. 1993. 35.00 (*0-9639228-0-7*) Palmetto Hist.

Bradshaw, Todd. Canoe Rig: The Essence & the Art: Sailpower for Antique & Traditional Canoes. LC 99-33078. (Illus.). 256p. 2000. pap. 34.95 (*0-937822-57-4*) WoodenBoat Pubns.

Bradshaw, Tony. The Bloomsbury Artists: Prints & Book Design. Beechey, James, ed. (Illus.). 96p. 1999. text 51.95 (*1-85928-277-6*, Pub. by Ashgate Pub) Ashgate Pub Co.

Bradshaw, Vaughn. Building Control Systems. 2nd ed. LC 93-21609. (Illus.). 624p. 1993. 90.00 (*0-471-57378-7*) Wiley.

Bradshaw, Vittoria. From Pure Silence to Impure Dialogue: A Survey of Post-War Italian Poetry, 1945-1965. 1971. 30.00 (*0-913298-61-1*) S F Vanni.

Bradshaw-Weaver. Foundations of Physics. 1995. 85.62 (*0-697-26634-6*, WCB McGr Hill) McGrw-H Hghr Educ.
— Fundamentals of Physical Geography. 1995. 195.93 (*0-697-26635-4*, WCB McGr Hill) McGrw-H Hghr Educ.
— Testbank Physical Geography. 1993. teacher ed. 13.43 (*0-697-25079-2*, WCB McGr Hill) McGrw-H Hghr Educ.

Bradshaw, William R. The Goddess of Atvatabar. 319p. 1996. reprint ed. spiral bd. 22.50 (*0-7873-0117-5*) Hlth Research.
— The Goddess of Atvatabar: History of the Discovery of the Interior World & Conquest of Atvatabar. LC 74-15954. (Science Fiction Ser.). (Illus.). 318p. 1975. reprint ed. 28.95 (*0-405-06279-6*) Ayer.
— The Goddess of Atvatabar Being the History of the Discovery of the Interior World & Conquest of Atvatabar (1891) 320p. 1996. reprint ed. pap. 21.95 (*1-56459-931-0*) Kessinger Pub.

Bradshaw, York W. Education in Comparative Perspective: New Lessons from Around the World. LC 96-229978. (International Studies in Sociology & Social Anthropology: Vol. 63). vi, 191p. 1996. 81.00 (*90-04-10734-7*) Brill Academic Pubs.

***Bradshaw, York W. & Ndegwa, Stephen N.** The Uncertain Promise of Southern Africa. LC 00-40714. 2000. pap. write for info. (*0-253-21424-6*) Ind U Pr.

Bradshaw, York W. & Wallace, Michael. Global Inequalities. LC 95-49168. (Sociology for a New Century Ser.). 1996. pap. 18.95 (*0-8039-9060-X*) Pine Forge.

B

Bradsher, Earl L. Mathew Carey: Editor, Author & Publisher. LC 78-181915. (BCL Ser. I). reprint ed. 31.50 (*0-404-00969-7*) AMS Pr.

— Mathew Carey, Editor, Author & Publisher: A Study in American Literary Development. (BCL1-PS American Literature Ser.). 144p. 1992. reprint ed. lib. bdg. 69.00 (*0-7812-6659-9*) Rprt Serv.

Bradsher, Greg. Holocaust-Era Assets: A Finding Aid to Records at the National Archives at College Park, Maryland. LC 98-52491. 1166p. 1999. pap. 49.95 (*1-880875-19-5*, 200048) National Archives & Recs.

— Nazi Gold: U. S. & Allied Efforts to Recover & Restore Gold & Other Assets Stolen or Hidden by Germany During World War II Finding Aids to Records at the National Archives. (Illus.). 277p. (Orig.). (C). 1997. pap. text 35.00 (*0-7881-4537-1*) DIANE Pub.

Bradsher, Greg. United States & Allied Efforts to Recover & Restore Gold & Other Assets Stolen or Hidden by Germany During World War 2: Appendix, Finding Aid to Records in the National Archives at College Park. 289p. 1997. per. 25.00 (*0-16-061917-3*) USGPO.

Bradsher, Henry S. Afghan Communism & Soviet Intervention. 462p. 1999. text 24.95 (*0-19-579017-0*) OUP.

Bradsher, James G., ed. Managing Archives & Archival Institutions. 320p. 1991. pap. text 23.00 (*0-226-07055-7*) U Ch Pr.

— Managing Archives & Archival Institutions: A Handbook of Theories & Practices. LC 88-15893. xvi, 304p. 1993. 45.00 (*0-226-07054-9*) U Ch Pr.

***Bradstock, Andrew.** Masculinity & Spirituality in Victorian Culture. LC 00-33339. 2000. write for info. (*0-312-23561-5*) St Martin.

— Winstanley & the Diggers, 1649-1999. LC 00-35875. 2000. pap. write for info. (*0-7146-5105-2*) Intl Spec Bk.

Bradstock, Andrew, jt. auth. see Hogan, Anne.

Bradstock, R. A., et al, eds. Conserving Biodiversity: Threats & Solutions. 420p. 1995. 150.00 (*0-7855-2733-8*, Pub. by Surrey Beatty & Sons) St Mut.

Bradstock, R. A., jt. ed. see Noble, J. C.

Bradstock, Timothy R. & Rabinovitch, Judith N., trs. from JPN. An Anthology of Kanshi (Chinese Verse) by Japanese Poets of the Edo Period (1603-1868) LC 97-25575. (Japanese Studies). 444p. 1997. text 109.95 (*0-7734-8560-0*) E Mellen.

Bradstreet, Anne D. The Poems of Mrs. Anne Bradstreet (1612-1672) 1976. reprint ed. 69.00 (*0-685-71977-4*, Regency) Scholarly.

— Tenth Muse. LC 65-10345. 320p. 1978. reprint ed. 50.00 (*0-8201-1006-X*) Schol Facsimiles.

— The Tenth Muse, Lately Sprung up in America. 1989. reprint ed. lib. bdg. 79.00 (*0-7812-2041-6*) Rprt Serv.

***Bradstreet, Anne D.** To My Husband & Other Poems. 2000. pap. 1.50 (*0-486-41408-6*) Dover.

Bradstreet, Anne D. The Works of Anne Bradstreet in Prose & Verse. 1976. reprint ed. 69.00 (*0-403-08995-6*, Regency) Scholarly.

Bradstreet, Anne D. & Hensley, Jeannie. The Works of Anne Bradstreet. LC 67-17312. (John Harvard Library). 368p. 1981. pap. 17.95 (*0-674-95999-X*) Belknap Pr.

Bradstreet, Anne D. & Taylor, Edward. Early New England Meditative Poetry. Hambrick-Stowe, Charles E., ed. (Sources of American Spirituality Ser.). 1988. 24.95 (*0-8091-0416-4*) Paulist Pr.

Bradstreet, Jeffrey W. Hazardous Air Pollutants: Assessment, Liabilities, & Regulatory Compliance. LC 95-31385. (Illus.). 387p. 1996. 109.00 (*0-8155-1386-0*) Noyes.

Bradstreet, Karen. Herbs for Detoxification. (The Woodland Health Ser.). 1997. pap. text 3.95 (*1-885670-68-0*) Woodland UT.

— Natural Medicine vs. Orthodox Medicine. (The Woodland Health Ser.). 1997. pap. text 3.95 (*1-58054-014-7*) Woodland UT.

— Natural Treatments for Infertility. (The Woodland Health Ser.). 1997. pap. text 3.95 (*1-58054-002-3*) Woodland UT.

— Overcoming Infertility Naturally. 1994. pap. 12.95 (*0-913923-86-9*) Woodland UT.

Bradstreet, Ken. 12th Armored Division, Vol. I. LC 86-51588. (Illus.). 264p. 1987. 49.95 (*0-938021-09-5*) Turner Pub KY.

— 12th Armored Division, Vol. II. LC 86-51588. (Illus.). 248p. 1990. 39.95 (*0-938021-92-3*) Turner Pub KY.

Bradstreet, T. J. Before She Wakes. 144p. (J). (gr. 7). 1997. mass mkt. 3.99 (*0-380-78315-0*, Avon Bks) Morrow Avon.

— Lorna's Wish. (Darkest Wish Ser.: No. 2). (J). (gr. 3-7). 1996. pap. 3.99 (*0-380-77817-3*, Avon Bks) Morrow Avon.

Bradt, G. W. & Harrington, Steve. Wildlife Sketches. 2nd rev. ed. Orig. Title: Michigan Wildlife Sketches. (Illus.). 128p. (Orig.). 1999. pap. 12.95 (*0-9624629-3-4*, Pub. by Maritime Pr) Partners Pubs Grp.

Bradt, H., ed. see International Astronomical Union Staff.

Bradt, Hilary. Madagascar. LC 94-178370. (World Bibliographical Ser.). 138p. 1994. lib. bdg. 46.50 (*1-85109-179-3*) ABC-CLIO.

***Bradt, Hilary.** Madagascar: The Bradt Travel Guide. 6th ed. LC 99-44249. 368p. 2000. pap. 18.95 (*1-898323-97-6*) Bradt Pubns.

Bradt, Hilary. Peru & Bolivia: A Bradt Hiking & Trekking Guide. 7th ed. LC 98-27848. (Illus.). 300p. 1998. pap. text 17.95 (*1-898323-75-5*, Pub. by Bradt Pubns) Globe Pequot.

Bradt, Hilary, et al. Madagascar Wildlife. LC 96-13766. (Bradt Country Guides Ser.). (Illus.). 138p. 1996. pap. 19.95 (*1-56440-947-3*, Pub. by Bradt Pubns) Globe Pequot.

Bradt, Hilary, jt. auth. see Mansfield, Stephen.

Bradt, Kevin. Story As a Way of Knowing. LC 96-53175. 192p. (Orig.). 1997. pap. 15.95 (*1-55612-906-8*, LL1906) Sheed & Ward WI.

Bradt, R. C. & Tressler, R. E. Fractography of Glass. LC 94-39370. (Illus.). 310p. (C). 1995. text 95.00 (*0-306-44880-7*, Kluwer Plenum) Kluwer Academic.

Bradt, R. C., et al. Fracture Mechanics of Ceramics Vol. 9: Composites, R-Curve Behavior, & Fatigue. (Illus.). 614p. (C). 1992. 149.50 (*0-306-44202-7*, Plenum Trade) Perseus Pubng.

— Fracture Mechanics of Ceramics Vol. 10: Fracture Fundamental High-Temperature Deformation, Damage, & Design. (Illus.). 666p. (C). 1992. 149.50 (*0-306-44203-5*, Plenum Trade) Perseus Pubng.

Bradt, R. C., et al. Fracture Mechanics of Ceramics Vol. 11: R-Curve Behavior, Toughness Determination, & Thermal Shock. (Illus.). 600p. (C). 1996. 174.00 (*0-306-45378-9*, Kluwer Plenum) Kluwer Academic.

— Fracture Mechanics of Ceramics Vol. 12: Fatigue, Composites, & High-Temperature Behavior. (Illus.). 602p. (C). 1996. 174.00 (*0-306-45379-7*, Kluwer Plenum) Kluwer Academic.

— Plastic Deformation of Ceramics: Proceedings of an International Engineering Conference Held in Snowbird, Utah, August 7-12, 1994. (Illus.). 684p. (C). 1995. text 155.00 (*0-306-45120-4*, Kluwer Plenum) Kluwer Academic.

Bradt, Richard C., et al, eds. Fracture Mechanics of Ceramics, 4 vols. Incl. Vol. 1. Concepts, Flaws & Fractography. LC 73-20399. 472p. 1974. 110.00 (*0-306-37591-5*, Kluwer Plenum); Vol. 2. Microstructure, Materials & Applications. LC 73-20399. 504p. 1974. 110.00 (*0-306-37592-3*, Kluwer Plenum); LC 73-20399. write for info. (*0-318-55319-8*, Plenum Trade) Perseus Pubng.

— Fracture Mechanics of Ceramics Vol. 5: Surface Flaws, Statistics & Microcracking. LC 73-20391. 706p. 1983. 135.00 (*0-306-41021-4*, Plenum Trade) Perseus Pubng.

— Fracture Mechanics of Ceramics Vol. 5: Surface Flaws, Statistics & Microcracking, Set. LC 73-20391. 706p. 1983. 245.00 (*0-685-05676-7*, Plenum Trade) Perseus Pubng.

— Fracture Mechanics of Ceramics Vol. 6: Measurements, Transformations & High Temperature Fracture. LC 73-20399. 688p. 1983. 135.00 (*0-306-41022-2*, Plenum Trade) Perseus Pubng.

— Fracture Mechanics of Ceramics Vol. 6: Measurements, Transformations & High Temperature Fracture, Set. LC 73-20399. 688p. 1983. 185.00 (*0-685-05677-5*, Plenum Trade) Perseus Pubng.

— Fracture Mechanics of Ceramics Vol. 7: Composites, Impact, Statistics & High-Temperature Phenomena. LC 83-641076. 378p. 1986. 95.00 (*0-306-42272-7*, Plenum Trade) Perseus Pubng.

— Fracture Mechanics of Ceramics Vol. 7: Composites, Impact, Statistics & High-Temperature Phenomena, Set. LC 83-641076. 378p. 1986. 135.00 (*0-685-17356-9*, Plenum Trade) Perseus Pubng.

— Fracture Mechanics of Ceramics Vol. 8: Microstructure, Methods, Design & Fatigue. LC 83-641076. 432p. 1986. 105.00 (*0-306-42273-5*, Plenum Trade) Perseus Pubng.

— Fracture Mechanics of Ceramics Vol. 8: Microstructure, Methods, Design & Fatigue, Set. LC 83-641076. 432p. 1986. 135.00 (*0-685-17352-6*, Plenum Trade) Perseus Pubng.

Bradu, Fabienne. Antonieta. (SPA.). 248p. 1991. pap. 12.99 (*968-16-3593-0*, Pub. by Fondo) Continental Bk.

— Damas de Corazon. (SPA.). 289p. 1994. pap. 9.99 (*968-16-4508-1*) Fondo.

— Senas Particulares: Escritora. (SPA.). pap. 9.99 (*968-16-2689-3*, Pub. by Fondo) Continental Bk.

Bradury, W. B., et al, eds. Physiology & Pharmacology of the Blood-Brain Barrier. LC 92-2227. (Handbook of Experimental Pharmacology Ser.: Vol. 103). (Illus.). 520p. 1992. 345.00 (*3-540-54492-5*) Spr-Verlag.

Bradus, Gary L., et al. Forming & Operating California Limited Liability Companies. Fabian, Jane H., ed. LC 95-69630. 444p. 1997. ring bd. 55.00 (*0-7626-0116-7*, BU-32512) Cont Ed Bar-CA.

— Forming & Operating California Limited Liability Companies: May 2000 Update. Brown, Wendy L. & Kronenberg, Hale, eds. LC 95-69630. 870p. 2000. 96.00 (*0-7626-0429-8*, BU-32515) Cont Ed Bar-CA.

Bradway, B. M., et al. Strategic Marketing: A Handbook for Entrepreneurs & Managers. LC 81-3638. 1982. text. write for info. (*0-201-00079-2*) Addison-Wesley.

Bradway, Christine W. Nursing Care of Geriatric Emergencies. (Springer Series on Geriatric Nursing). (Illus.). 304p. 1996. 44.95 (*0-8261-9010-3*) Springer Pub.

Bradway, John S. Progress in Family Law. Lambert, Richard D., ed. LC 71-81088. (Annals Ser.: No. 383). 1969. 28.00 (*0-87761-116-5*); pap. 18.00 (*0-87761-115-7*) Am Acad Pol Soc Sci.

Bradway, Katherine. Sandplay Bridges & Transcendent Function. 1985. 5.00 (*0-317-47621-1*) C G Jung Frisco.

— Villa of Mysteries: Pompeii Initiation Rites of Women. 1982. pap. 5.00 (*0-317-13541-4*) C G Jung Frisco.

Bradway, Katherine & McCoard, Barbara. Sandplay: Silent Workshop of the Psyche. LC 96-16802. (Illus.). 264p. 1997. pap. 27.99 (*0-415-15075-2*) Routledge.

— Sandplay: Silent Workshop of the Psyche. LC 96-16802. (Illus.). 264p. (C). 1997. 85.00 (*0-415-15074-4*) Routledge.

Bradway, Katherine, et al. Sandplay Studies: Origins, Theory, & Practice. rev. ed. Hill, Gareth, ed. (Illus.). 240p. (C). 1991. reprint ed. pap. 19.95 (*0-938434-40-3*) Sigo Pr.

Bradway, Lauren C. & Block, Lawrence. Children with Special Needs. 2nd ed. 1989. pap. 7.95 (*0-929240-08-1*) EMIS.

Bradway, Lauren C. & Hill, Barbara A. How to Maximize Your Child's Learning Ability: A Complete Guide to Choosing & Using the Best Games, Toys, Activities, Learning Aids & Tactics for Your Child. LC 92-32397. 288p. pap. 9.95 (*0-89529-519-9*, Avery) Penguin Putnam.

Bradwejn, Jacques & Vasar, Eero. Cholecystokinin & Anxiety: From Neuron to Behavior. LC 95-548. (Neuroscience Intelligence Unit Ser.). 173p. 1995. 79.00 (*1-57059-293-4*) Landes Bioscience.

Bradwell, Mike, ed. Bush Theatre Book. LC 98-133590. (Frontline Drama Ser.: Vol. 5). 1997. pap. 16.95 (*0-413-71320-2*) Methn.

Bradwell, Stephen. Physick for the Sickness, Commonly Called the Plague. LC 77-6859. (English Experience Ser.: No. 852). 1977. reprint ed. lib. bdg. 15.00 (*90-221-0852-X*) Walter J Johnson.

Bradwin, Edmund W. Bunkhouse Man: A Study of Work & Play in the Camps of Canada, 1903-1914. LC 68-57564. (Columbia University. Studies in the Social Sciences: No. 296). reprint ed. 20.00 (*0-404-51296-8*) AMS Pr.

Bradwin, John A., tr. see Mason, Tim.

Brady. Automotive Computers. 600p. 2000. 64.00 (*0-13-744327-7*) P-H.

— Blockbuster Secret Codes '98. 624p. 1997. pap. 9.99 (*1-56686-749-5*) Brady Pub.

Brady. Chemistry. 456p. 1996. pap. text 36.95 (*0-471-11839-7*) Wiley.

— Chemistry. 2nd ed. 240p. 1996. pap., teacher ed. 34.95 (*0-471-12076-6*) Wiley.

Brady. Chemistry & Descriptive Chemistry of the Elements: The Study of Matter & Its Changes, Set. 2nd ed. 1093p. 1996. text 80.00 (*0-471-16398-8*) Wiley.

Brady. Chemistry & Solutions Set: The Study of Matter & It's Changes. 2nd ed. 1344p. 1996. text 84.00 (*0-471-17113-1*) Wiley.

— Coping with Violent Behavior. 1993. pap. 26.95 (*0-582-22566-3*) Ashgate Pub Co.

— Descriptive Chemistry of the Elements. 2nd ed. 138p. 1995. pap. 18.95 (*0-471-13557-7*) Wiley.

Brady. Final Fantasy, Vol. 4. 200p. 1997. 9.99 (*1-56686-559-X*) Macmillan.

— L' Oeuvre d'Emil Zola. 29.95 (*0-685-37146-8*, F76750) Fr & Eur.

— What Lawyers Earn . . . What You're Worth & How to Negotiate for More! 224p. 1998. pap. text 17.95 (*0-15-900183-8*) Harcourt Legal.

Brady, et al. Financial Accounting: A Transactions Analysis Approach. 1997. 71.95 (*0-87393-441-5*) Dame Pubns.

— Search Is an Emergency: Text for Managing Search Operations. (Illus.). 480p. 1995. 30.00 (*0-913724-28-9*) Emerg Response Inst.

Brady, jt. auth. see Monk.

***Brady, Adrian.** New Perspectives on Hypertension. (New Perspectives Ser.). 2000. pap. text 24.95 (*1-873413-67-X*) Merit Pub Intl.

Brady, Alexander. William Huskisson & Liberal Reform. 2nd ed. 177p. 1967. 35.00 (*0-7146-1456-4*, Pub. by F Cass Pubs) Intl Spec Bk.

Brady, Alexander & Scott, Francis R., eds. Canada after the War. LC 75-128212. (Essay Index Reprint Ser.). 1977. 23.95 (*0-8369-1867-3*) Ayer.

***Brady, Andrea.** Liberties. 48p. 1999. pap. 7.00 (*1-893541-04-5*, Pub. by Potes Poets) SPD-Small Pr Dist.

Brady, Angela & Mallalieu, Robin. Dublin. (Architecture Guides Ser.). 320p. 1998. pap. 5.95 (*3-89508-636-3*, 520330) Konemann.

Brady, Angela J. Been There, Done That. 2nd ed. 204p. 1997. pap., per. 11.95 (*0-9662743-0-X*) Tysseland Pub.

***Brady, Angie.** Serendipity & Other Surprises. (Illus.). 170p. 2000. pap. 11.95 (*0-9662743-2-6*) Tysseland Pub.

Brady, Ann P. Pompilia: A Feminist Reading of Robert Browning's the Ring & the Book. LC 88-1733. 158p. (C). 1988. text 26.95 (*0-8214-0886-0*) Ohio U Pr.

Brady, Anna, compiled by. Women in Ireland: An Annotated Bibliography, 6. LC 87-25043. (Bibliographies & Indexes in Women's Studies: No. 6). 511p. (C). 1988. lib. bdg. 79.50 (*0-313-24486-3*, BWR/, Greenwood Pr) Greenwood.

Brady, Anna, et al, eds. Union List of Film Periodicals: Holdings of Selected American Collections. LC 83-22585. 316p. 1984. lib. bdg. 47.95 (*0-313-23702-6*, BRL/, Greenwood Pr) Greenwood.

Brady, Anne V. Make Your Own Christm. (J Hook Ser.). 1995. mass mkt. 4.99 (*0-425-15058-5*) Berkley Pub.

— Make Your Own Christmas. 144p. (Orig.). 1996. mass mkt. write for info. (*0-614-17549-6*) Berkley Pub.

Brady, April A. Kwanzaa Karamu: Cooking & Crafts for a Kwanzaa Feast. LC 94-20871. (Illus.). 64p. (J). (gr. 3 up). 1995. pap. 6.95 (*0-87614-633-7*, Carolrhoda); lib. bdg. 21.27 (*0-87614-842-9*, Carolrhoda) Lerner Pub.

Brady, B. H. & Brown, E. T. Rock Mechanics: For Underground Mining. (Illus.). 1987. pap. text 49.95 (*0-04-622005-4*) Routledge.

Brady, Ben. Principles of Adaptation for Film & Television. LC 93-8798. 240p. (Orig.). 1994. pap. 14.95 (*0-292-70807-6*); text 30.00 (*0-292-70804-1*) U of Tex Pr.

Brady, Ben & Lee, Lance. The Understructure of Writing for Film & Television. 282p. (Orig.). (C). 1988. pap. 18.95 (*0-292-78515-1*); text 32.50 (*0-292-78514-3*) U of Tex Pr.

Brady, Bernadette. Brady's Book of Fixed Stars. 474p. 1998. 40.00 (*1-57863-886-0*) Weiser.

***Brady, Bernadette.** Brady's Book of Fixed Stars. LC 97-51492. (Illus.). 480p. 1999. 40.00 (*0-87728-886-0*) Weiser.

— Brady's Book of Fixed Stars. (Illus.). 480p. 1999. pap. 24.95 (*1-57863-105-X*, Pub. by Weiser) ACCESS Pubs Network.

Brady, Bernadette. Predictive Astrology: The Eagle & the Lark. LC 98-42896. Orig. Title: The Eagle & the Lark: A Textbook of Predictive Astrology. (Illus.). 388p. 1999. reprint ed. pap. 19.95 (*1-57863-112-2*) Weiser.

Brady, Bernard V. The Moral Bond of Community: Justice & Discourse in Christian Morality. LC 98-5663. 192p. 1998. 49.95 (*0-87840-690-5*); pap. 16.95 (*0-87840-691-3*) Georgetown U Pr.

Brady, Bruce. Bruce Brady's Game Trails. 1991. 21.95 (*1-879034-03-4*) MS River Pub.

Brady, Carol J., jt. auth. see Brod, Evelyn F.

Brady, Caroline F., et al. J. Ottis Adams: American Impressionist in Leland. (Illus.). 20p. (Orig.). 1993. pap. write for info. (*0-9636721-1-8*) Dennos Mus.

Brady, Casey. Beach Invaders, 5. (J). (gr. 4-7). 1996. pap. 3.99 (*0-679-88232-4*, Pub. by Random Bks Yng Read) Random.

— Crash Landing! Baywatch Junior Lifeguard Book, 6. (YA). 1996. pap. 3.99 (*0-679-88233-2*, Bullseye Bks) Random Bks Yng Read.

Brady, Catherine. The End of the Class War. LC 99-19880. 230p. 1999. 27.95 (*0-934971-67-6*, Pub. by Calyx Bks); pap. 13.95 (*0-934971-66-8*) Calyx Bks.

Brady, Cathleen, ed. see Patilla, Peter & Stone, Bob.

Brady, Cathy. Advanced Multilink: Describing Functions. rev. ed. 1996. wbk. ed. 6.99 (*1-884461-19-0*) NES Arnold.

— Advanced Multilink: Finding Patterns. rev. ed. 1996. wbk. ed. 9.99 (*1-884461-18-2*) NES Arnold.

— Putting Mathematics to Use. (Middle School Ser.). 1996. wbk. ed. 9.99 (*1-884461-20-4*) NES Arnold.

Brady, Charles & Perry, Gillian. Professional Skills. 120p. 1992. pap. 26.50 (*1-85811-000-9*, Pub. by CLT Prof) Gaunt.

Brady, Charles E., III. Esophagus - Stomach - GI Bleeding. (Contemporary Management in Internal Medicine Ser.: Vol. 1, No. 3). (Illus.). 218p. 1991. text 37.00 (*0-443-08824-1*) Church.

Brady, Charles E., III, ed. Esophagus, Stomach, GI Bleeding. LC RC0802.E7. (Contemporary Management in Internal Medicine Ser.: Vol. 1, No. 3). (Illus.). 230p. reprint ed. pap. 71.30 (*0-7837-6235-6*, 204594900010) Bks Demand.

Brady, Ciaran. The Chief Governors: The Rise & Fall of Reform Government in Tudor Ireland, 1536-1588. LC 93-43767. (Cambridge Studies in Early Modern British History). 343p. (C). 1995. text 59.95 (*0-521-46176-6*) Cambridge U Pr.

***Brady, Ciaran, ed.** The Encyclopedia of Ireland. (Illus.). 416p. 2000. 39.95 (*0-19-521685-7*) OUP.

Brady, Ciaran, ed. Interpreting Irish History: The Debate on Historical Revisionism. LC 94-177435. 360p. 1999. reprint ed. 52.50 (*0-7165-2499-6*, Pub. by Irish Acad Pr); reprint ed. pap. 24.50 (*0-7165-2546-1*, Pub. by Irish Acad Pr) Intl Spec Bk.

***Brady, Ciaran, ed.** A Viceroy's Vindication: Sir Henry Sidney's Memoir 1583. 96p. 1999. pap. 12.95 (*1-85918-180-5*) Intl Spec Bk.

Brady, Ciaran & Gillespie, Raymond, eds. Natives & Newcomers: The Making of Irish Colonial Society 1534-1641. 260p. 1986. 35.00 (*0-7165-2378-7*, Pub. by Irish Acad Pr) Intl Spec Bk.

Brady, Clark A. & Burroughs, Edgar Rice. The Burroughs Cyclopaedia: Characters, Places, Fauna, Flora, Technologies, Languages, Ideas & Terminologies Found in the Works of Edgar Rice Burroughs. LC 96-32787. 408p. 1996. lib. bdg. 55.00 (*0-89950-896-0*) McFarland & Co.

Brady Computer Books Staff. Tekken 2. 96p. 1996. 9.99 (*1-56686-539-5*) Brady Pub.

— War Gods. 1996. 9.99 (*1-56686-541-7*) Brady Pub.

— X-Com 3. 1996. 19.99 (*1-56686-535-2*) Brady Pub.

Brady, Constance. Right Where You Live. (Illus.). 188p. (Orig.). 1982. pap. 9.95 (*0-89087-242-2*) Conarc.

Brady, Cyrus T. Indian Fights & Fighters. LC 96-5530. Date not set. 19.95 (*1-879582-17-1*) Platinum Pr.

— Indian Fights & Fighters. LC 74-156373. (Illus.). xx, 475p. 1971. reprint ed. pap. 15.00 (*0-8032-5743-0*, Bison Books) U of Nebr Pr.

— Little Book for Christmas. LC 73-167443. (Short Story Index Reprint Ser.). (Illus.). 1977. reprint ed. 19.95 (*0-8369-3969-7*) Ayer.

— Northwestern Fights & Fighters. LC 79-15171. 431p. 1979. reprint ed. pap. 133.70 (*0-7837-8859-2*, 204956900001) Bks Demand.

***Brady, Cyrus T.** Northwestern Fights & Fighters: The Nez Perce & Modoc Wars. 2nd unabridged ed. (Illus.). 434p. 1999. reprint ed. pap. 18.95 (*0-87928-130-8*) Corner Hse.

Brady, Cyrus T. Sir Henry Morgan, Buccaneer. 445p. reprint ed. lib. bdg. 29.95 (*0-88411-175-X*) Amereon Ltd.

— Woven with the Ship. LC 73-128722. (Short Story Index Reprint Ser.). 1977. 24.95 (*0-8369-3613-2*) Ayer.

Brady, Darlene. Le Corbusier: An Annotated Bibliography. LC 82-49267. 320p. 1985. text 81.00 (*0-8240-9134-5*) Garland.

Brady, David. Congressional Voting in a Partisan Era: A Study of the McKinley Houses & a Comparison to the Modern House of Representatives. LC 72-87822. xii, 276p. 1973. 29.95 (*0-7006-0098-1*) U Pr of KS.

— The Contribution of British Writers Between 1560 & 1830 to the Interpretation of Revelation 13. 16-18. 341p. 1983. lib. bdg. 77.50 (*3-16-144497-3*, Pub. by JCB Mohr) Coronet Bks.

Brady, David, jt. auth. see Huff, Lew.

Brady, David W. Critical Elections & Congressional Policy Making. LC 87-18068. (Studies in the New Political History: Vol. 1). 232p. 1988. 37.50 (*0-8047-1442-8*); pap. 12.95 (*0-8047-1840-7*) Stanford U Pr.

An Asterisk (*) at the beginning of an entry indicates that the title is appearing for the first time.

Brady, David W. & Volden, Craig. Revolving Gridlock: Politics & Policy from Carter to Clinton. LC 97-22279. (Transforming American Politics Ser.). 224p. (C). 1997. pap. text 21.00 (*0-8133-2589-7*, Pub. by Westview) HarpC.

***Brady, David W., et al.** Continuity & Change in House Elections. LC 00-39488. 2000. pap. write for info. (*0-8047-3739-8*) Stanford U Pr.

Brady, David W., et al. How the Republicans Captured the House: An Assessment of the 1994 Midterm Elections. LC 94-48430. (Essays in Public Policy Ser.: No. 57). 22p. 1995. pap. 5.00 (*0-8179-5622-0*) Hoover Inst Pr.

— The 1996 House Elections: Reaffirming the Conservative Trend. LC 97-9037. (Essays in Public Policy Ser.: No. 75). 1997. pap. 5.00 (*0-8179-5802-9*) Hoover Inst Pr.

Brady, Dennis A. Hypnosis & the Power of Positive Thinking: From Rags to Riches. large type ed. LC 97-90388. 195p. (Orig.). 1997. 24.95 (*1-890742-00-7*); pap. 19.95 (*1-890742-01-5*) Tamden.

Brady, Dorothy S., ed. Output, Employment, & Productivity in the United States after 1800. (Studies in Income & Wealth: No. 30). 674p. 1966. reprint ed. 160.00 (*0-87014-186-4*) Natl Bur Econ Res.

Brady, E. Michael. Retirement: The Challenge of Change. (Orig.). 1988. pap. 8.00 (*0-939561-02-6*) Univ South ME.

Brady, E. Michael, ed. Perspectives on Adult Learning. 92p. (Orig.). 1986. pap. text 5.00 (*0-939561-00-X*) Univ South ME.

Brady, Edith B., ed. see Tortora, Gerard J.

Brady, Elijah. The Feast of Pentecost Holy Bible. LC 99-11323. (Illus.). 400p. 1999. 74.95 (*1-57309-376-9*, Christ Univ Pr) Intl Scholars.

Brady, Elijah M. The Feast of Pentecost Holy Bible. LC 99-11323. (Illus.). 408p. 1999. pap. 54.95 (*1-57309-375-0*, Christ Univ Pr) Intl Scholars.

Brady, Elizabeth. Marian Engel & Her Works. (Canadian Author Studies). 69p. (C). 1987. pap. text 9.95 (*0-920763-27-8*, Pub. by ECW) Genl Dist Srvs.

Brady, Erika. A Spiral Way: How the Phonograph Changed Ethnography. LC 99-24533. (Illus.). 147p. 1999. 35.00 (*1-57806-173-3*); pap. 15.00 (*1-57806-174-1*) U Pr of Miss.

Brady, Esther W. Toliver's Secret. LC 76-15997. (Illus.). 176p. (J). (gr. 3-7). 1993. pap. 4.99 (*0-679-84804-5*, Pub. by Random Bks Yng Read) Random.

Brady, Esther Wood. Toliver's Secret. 1993. 10.09 (*0-606-08943-8*, Pub. by Turtleback) Demco.

Brady, F. Neil. Ethical Managing: Rules & Results. 251p. (C). 1989. pap. text 37.80 (*0-02-313341-4*, Macmillan Coll) P-H.

Brady, Frank. Bobby Fischer: Profile of a Prodigy. rev. ed. (Illus.). 435p. 1989. pap. 10.95 (*0-486-25925-0*) Dover.

— Mickle, Boswell, Garrick, & "The Siege of Marseilles" LC 86-26593. (Transactions Ser.: Vol. 46, Pt. 5). 62p. 1987. pap. 17.50 (*0-208-02131-0*) CT Acad Arts & Sciences.

Brady, Frank, ed. An Essay on Man: Pope. 80p. (C). 1965. pap. text 8.20 (*0-02-313460-7*, Macmillan Coll) P-H.

— Twentieth Century Interpretations of Gulliver's Travels. LC 68-23699. 9.95 (*0-13-371575-2*, Spectrum IN); pap. 1.25 (*0-13-371567-1*, Spectrum IN) Macmillan Gen Ref.

Brady, Frank & Wimsatt, William K., Jr., eds. Samuel Johnson: Selected Poetry & Prose. 1978. pap. 22.50 (*0-520-03552-6*, Pub. by U CA Pr) Cal Prin Full Svc.

Brady, Frank, ed. see Pope, Alexander.

Brady, Frank B. A Singular View: The Art of Seeing with One Eye. 5th ed. LC 94-189866. (Illus.). 144p. 1994. reprint ed. pap. 15.00 (*0-9614639-2-9*) Frank B Brady.

Brady, Games. Kingpin Life of Crime Official Strategy Guide. 1999. pap. 19.99 (*1-56686-896-3*) Brady Pub.

***Brady, Games.** Kirby 64 Official Strategy Guide. 128p. 2000. pap. 12.99 (*1-56686-997-8*, BradyGAMES) Brady Pub.

— Legend of Mana Official Strategy Guide. 224p. 2000. pap. 14.99 (*1-56686-986-2*, BradyGAMES) Brady Pub.

***Brady Games Staff.** Alundra 2 Official Strategy Guide. (Illus.). 160p. (J). 2000. pap. 14.99 (*1-56686-977-3*, BradyGAMES) Brady Pub.

Brady Games Staff. Authorized Guide to Quake II. 192p. 1997. 19.99 (*1-56686-731-2*) Brady Pub.

***Brady Games Staff.** Cabela's Big Game Hunter 3 Official Strategy Guide. (Strategy Guides Ser.). (Illus.). 208p. 1999. pap. 14.99 (*1-56686-932-3*, BradyGAMES) Brady Pub.

Brady Games Staff. Castlevania: Symphony of the Night Strategy Guide. LC 97-77130. (Brady Games Strategy Guides Ser.). 112p. 1997. pap. text 11.99 (*1-56686-760-6*) Brady Pub.

***Brady Games Staff.** Chocobo's Dungeon 2: Official Strategy Guide. (Illus.). 112p. (J). 2000. pap. 12.99 (*1-56686-894-7*, BradyGAMES) Brady Pub.

— Chrono Cross Official Strategy Guide. (Illus.). 2000. pap. 14.99 (*0-7440-0000-9*) Brady Pub.

— Delta Force 2 Official Strategy Guide. (Illus.). 216p. (J). 1999. pap. 19.99 (*1-56686-963-3*, BradyGAMES) Brady Pub.

— Final Fantasy VIII PC Official Strategy Guide. (Illus.). 320p. (J). 2000. pap. 19.99 (*1-56686-962-5*, BradyGAMES) Brady Pub.

— Front Mission 3 Official Strategy Guide. (Take Your Game Further Ser.). (Illus.). (J). 2000. pap. 14.99 (*1-56686-978-1*, BradyGAMES) Brady Pub.

Brady Games Staff. Hexen 2: Authorized Guide. 216p. 1997. 19.99 (*1-56686-724-X*) Brady Pub.

***Brady Games Staff.** Medal of Honor: Official Strategy Guide. (Strategy Guides Ser.). 1999. pap. 12.99 (*1-56686-926-9*) Brady Pub.

Brady Games Staff. Mortal Kombat II: Official Fighters Kompanion. (Illus.). 157p. (Orig.). 1994. 9.95 (*1-56686-198-5*) Brady Pub.

— Mortal Kombat Mythologies Official Guide. (Illus.). 112p. (J). 1997. 11.99 (*1-56686-722-3*) Brady Pub.

— N Apocalypse Official Strategy Guide. 112p. 1998. 11.99 (*1-56686-727-4*) Brady Pub.

***Brady Games Staff.** NBA Showtime Official Strategy Guide. (Illus.). 128p. 1999. pap. text 12.99 (*1-56686-941-2*, BradyGAMES) Brady Pub.

— Nintendo Game Boy Official Games Guide. (Illus.). (J). 1999. pap. 7.99 (*1-56686-902-1*, BradyGAMES) Brady Pub.

Brady Games Staff. Official Guide to Blade Runner. 192p. 1997. 19.99 (*1-56686-728-2*) Brady Pub.

— Official Guide to Goosebumps: Attack of the Mutant. (Illus.). 192p. (J). 1997. 14.99 (*1-56686-738-X*) Brady Pub.

— Official Guide to Heavy Gear. 192p. 1997. 19.99 (*1-56686-726-6*) Brady Pub.

— Official Guide to Mace: The Dark Ages. (Illus.). 112p. (J). 1997. pap. 11.99 (*1-56686-739-8*) Brady Pub.

— Official Guide to Skullmonkeys. 112p. 1998. pap. 11.99 (*1-56686-741-X*) Brady Pub.

— Official Riven Player's Guide: The Sequel to Myst. (Brady Games Strategy Guides Ser.). 112p. 1997. pap. text 11.99 (*1-56686-762-2*) Brady Pub.

***Brady Games Staff.** Perfect Dark BradyGAMES Official Strategy Guide. 128p. 2000. pap. 12.99 (*1-56686-908-0*, BradyGAMES) Brady Pub.

Brady Games Staff. Quake 64 Official Strategy Guide. 1998. 11.99 (*1-56686-783-5*) Brady Pub.

— Quake 64, Authorized Strategy Guide. (Illus.). 112p. (J). 1998. 11.99 (*1-56686-729-0*) Brady Pub.

***Brady Games Staff.** Resident Evil 2 Official Strategy Guide. (Illus.). 128p. (J). 1999. pap. 12.99 (*1-56686-958-7*, BradyGAMES) Brady Pub.

Brady Games Staff. Ruins Official Strategy Guide. 1996. 19.99 (*1-56686-496-8*) Brady Pub.

***Brady Games Staff.** Secret Codes for Sega Dreamcast. (Illus.). 144p. (J). 1999. pap. 11.95 (*1-56686-956-0*, BradyGAMES) Brady Pub.

— Secret Codes for Sony Playstation, Vol. 5. LC 00-131738. Vol. 5. (Illus.). 128p. 2000. 7.99 (*1-56686-984-6*) Brady Pub.

— Soldier of Fortune Official Strategy Guide. (Strategy Guide Ser.). (Illus.). 208p. (J). 2000. pap. text 19.99 (*1-56686-942-0*, BradyGAMES) Brady Pub.

— Star Trek Voyager: Elite Force Official Strategy Guide. (Take Your Game Further Ser.). (Illus.). 208p. (J). 2000. pap. 19.99 (*1-56686-979-X*, BradyGAMES) Brady Pub.

— Street Fighter Alpha 3: Official Strategy Guide for Dreamcast. LC 99-75466. (Illus.). 144p. (J). 2000. pap. 12.99 (*1-56686-954-4*, BradyGAMES) Brady Pub.

Brady Games Staff. Syphon Filter: Totally Unauthorized Strategy Guide, 1. LC 99-72493. (Brady Games Strategy Guides Ser.). 111p. 1999. pap. 11.99 (*1-56686-895-5*) Brady Pub.

***Brady Games Staff.** Tenchu II Official Strategy Guide. (Take Your Game Further Ser.). (Illus.). 128p. (J). 2000. pap. 12.99 (*1-56686-983-8*, BradyGAMES) Brady Pub.

— Threads of Fate Official Strategy Guide. (Illus.). 176p. 2000. 14.99 (*1-56686-998-6*) Brady Pub.

Brady Games Staff. Totally Unauthorized Bomberman 64. (Brady Games Strategy Guides Ser.). 112p. 1997. pap. text 11.99 (*1-56686-767-3*) Brady Pub.

— Totally Unauthorized Conker's Quest Strategy Guide. (Brady Games Strategy Guides Ser.). 112p. 1998. pap. text 11.99 (*1-56686-763-0*) Brady Pub.

— Totally Unauthorized Crash Bandicoot 2. (Brady Games Strategy Guides Ser.). 112p. 1997. pap. text 11.99 (*1-56686-761-4*) Brady Pub.

— Totally Unauthorized GoldenEye 007 Strategy Guide. 112p. 1997. pap. 11.99 (*1-56686-735-5*) Brady Pub.

— Totally Unauthorized Guide to Diddy Kong Racing. 112p. 1997. pap. 11.99 (*1-56686-756-8*) Brady Pub.

— Totally Unauthorized Nintendo 64 Games Guide, Vol. 3. 112p. 1998. pap. 11.99 (*1-56686-765-7*) Brady Pub.

— Totally Unauthorized PlayStation Games Guide, Vol. 5. (Brady Games Strategy Guides Ser.). 112p. 1998. pap. text 11.99 (*1-56686-764-9*) Brady Pub.

— Totally Unauthorized Silent Hill Strategy Guide, 1. LC 99-72268. (Brady Games Strategy Guide Ser.). (Illus.). 127p. (YA). (gr. 11 up). 1999. pap. 11.99 (*1-56686-883-1*) Brady Pub.

***Brady Games Staff.** Toy Story 2 Official Strategy Guide. (Strategy Guides Ser.). 128p. 1999. pap. 12.99 (*1-56686-950-1*) Brady Pub.

Brady Games Staff. Trespasser Official Strategy Guide: Jurassic Park Official Guide. 216p. 1998. 19.99 (*1-56686-737-1*) Brady Pub.

— Turok Two: Seeds of Evil; Totally Unauthorized Strategy Guide. (Brady Games Strategy Guides Ser.). 1998. pap. 11.99 (*1-56686-813-0*) Brady Pub.

***Brady Games Staff.** Vampire: The Masquerade Official Strategy Guide. (Take Your Game Further Ser.). (Illus.). 208p. (J). 2000. pap. 19.99 (*1-56686-980-3*, BradyGAMES) Brady Pub.

— Vigilante 8: 2nd Offense Official Strategy Guide. (Illus.). 128p. (J). 1999. pap. 12.99 (*1-56686-953-6*, BradyGAMES) Brady Pub.

Brady Games Staff. Wild Arms: Authorized Guide. 1997. 14.99 (*1-56686-723-1*) Brady Pub.

***Brady Games Staff.** Wu-Tang: Shaolin Style Official Strategy Guide. (Illus.). 128p. (J). 1999. pap. 12.99 (*1-56686-952-8*, BradyGAMES) Brady Pub.

Brady Games Staff & Cain, Christine. The Lost World: Jurassic Park 2 Official Guide. 112p. 1997. 11.99 (*1-56686-711-8*) Brady Pub.

Brady Games Staff & Cassady, David. Bushido Blade Official Guide. 128p. 1997. 11.99 (*1-56686-710-X*) Brady Pub.

Brady, Gene F. Management by Involvement: An Action Guide. LC 87-26052. (Insight Book Ser.). 166p. 1989. 35.95 (*0-89885-409-1*, Kluwer Acad Hman Sci); pap. 20.95 (*0-89885-410-5*, Kluwer Acad Hman Sci) Kluwer Academic.

Brady, George K. Samuel Daniel, A Critical Study. (BCL1-PR English Literature Ser.). 38p. 1992. reprint ed. lib. bdg. 59.00 (*0-7812-7196-7*) Rprt Serv.

Brady, George S., et al. Materials Handbook. 14th ed. (Illus.). 1136p. 1996. 99.00 (*0-07-007084-9*) McGraw.

Brady, Gerald P., jt. auth. see Thompson, George C.

Brady, Gordon L. & Tullock, Gordon, eds. Formal Contributions to the Theory of Public Choice: The Unpublished Works of Duncan Black. 296p. (C). 1996. lib. bdg. 109.00 (*0-7923-9556-5*) Kluwer Academic.

Brady, Gordon L., ed. see Tullock, Gordon.

Brady, Hal. Freed by Grace: Release from Life's Imprisonments. 272p. 1998. pap. 10.00 (*0-687-05715-9*) Dimen for Liv.

Brady, Howard, jt. auth. see Brady, Marion.

Brady, Hugh R. & Wilcox, Christopher S. Therapy in Nephrology & Hypertension: A Companion to Brenner & Rector's the Kidney. Zorab, Richard, ed. LC 98-21787. (Illus.). xxvii, 717p. (C). 1999. text 95.00 (*0-7216-7149-7*, W B Saunders Co) Harcrt Hlth Sci Grp.

Brady, Ignatius C., jt. ed. see Armstrong, Regis J.

Brady, Ignatius C., jt. tr. see Armstrong, Regis J.

Brady, Ignatius C., tr. see Clasen, Sophronius.

Brady, Irene. Beaver Year LC 98-232834. 40p. 1979. write for info. (*0-915965-02-X*) Nature Works.

— The Redrock Canyon Explorer. LC 98-91480. (Explorer Library). (Illus.). 112p. (J). (gr. 3-12). 1999. pap. 15.95 (*0-915965-04-6*, RCE) Nature Works.

***Brady, Irene.** Wild Babies: A Canyon Sketchbook. LC QL763.B6. (Illus.). iix, 53p. 1998. pap. 7.95 (*0-915965-03-8*) Nature Works.

Brady, Ivan A., ed. Anthropological Poetics. 410p. (C). 1990. pap. 33.95 (*0-8476-7672-2*); lib. bdg. 77.00 (*0-8476-7636-6*) Rowman.

— Transactions in Kinship: Adoption & Fosterage in Oceania. LC 76-10342. (ASAO Monographs: No. 4). 322p. reprint ed. pap. 91.80 (*0-7837-1305-3*, 2041453) Bks Demand.

Brady, J. D. & Beyersdorf, Eunice. A Manual of Exorcism. 1974. 5.00 (*0-87535-138-7*) Hispanic Soc.

Brady, J. M. The Theory of Computer Science: A Programming Approach. LC 77-729. xiii, 287 p. 1977. write for info. (*0-470-99103-8*) Halsted Pr.

Brady, James. Further Lane. LC 96-53927. 1997. text 22.95 (*0-312-15533-6*) St Martin.

— Further Lane. 1998. 6.50 (*0-312-96598-2*, Pub. by Tor Bks) St Martin.

— Gin Lane. LC 98-11950. 256p. 1998. text 22.95 (*0-312-18579-0*) St Martin.

— Gin Lane: A Novel of Southampton, Vol. 1. (Gin Lane Ser.). 314p. 1999. mass mkt. 6.99 (*0-312-96706-3*, Pub. by Tor Bks) St Martin.

***Brady, James.** A Hampton's Christmas. LC 00-31737. (Illus.). 224p. 2000. 23.95 (*0-312-26604-9*, Thomas Dunne) St Martin.

Brady, James. The House That Ate the Hamptons. LC 99-21749. 256p. 1999. text 23.95 (*0-312-20558-9*) St Martin.

***Brady, James.** The House That Ate the Hamptons. 320p. 2000. pap. 6.99 (*0-312-97120-6*, St Martins Paperbacks) St Martin.

— The Marines of Autumn: A Novel of the Korean War. LC 00-25472. 288p. 2000. 24.95 (*0-312-26200-0*, Thomas Dunne) St Martin.

Brady, James C. Succession Law in Ireland. 1989. boxed set 106.00 (*1-85475-100-X*, UK, MICHIE) LEXIS Pub.

Brady, James E. General Chemistry: Principles & Structure. 5th ed. 448p. 1990. pap., student ed. 36.95 (*0-471-51799-2*) Wiley.

— General Chemistry: Principles & Structures. 5th ed. LC 89-24866. 944p. (C). 1990. text 114.95 (*0-471-62131-5*) Wiley.

— General Chemistry: Principles & Structures. 5th ed. 375p. (C). 1990. pap. 36.95 (*0-471-51420-9*) Wiley.

— General Chemistry Student Solutions Manual: Principles & Structure. 5th ed. 254p. 1990. pap. 36.95 (*0-471-53316-5*) Wiley.

— General Chemistry Text: Principles & Structure, Set. 5th ed. 1386p. 1990. text, student ed. 74.95 (*0-471-52876-5*) Wiley.

Brady, James E. & Holum, John R. Chemistry: The Study of Matter & Its Changes & Chemresources. 1104p. 1997. student ed. 24.95 incl. cd-rom (*0-471-18215-X*) Wiley.

— Descriptive Chemistry of the Elements. 176p. (C). 2000. pap. 19.95 (*0-471-38643-X*) Wiley.

Brady, James E. & Holum, John R. Fundamentals of Chemistry. 2nd ed. LC 83-21796. (Illus.). 966p. 1984. reprint ed. pap. 200.00 (*0-7837-3490-5*, 205782300008) Bks Demand.

***Brady, James E., et al.** Chemistry: The Study of Matter & Its Changes. 233p. 2000. pap., student ed. 38.95 (*0-471-35858-4*) Wiley.

— Chemistry: The Study of Matter & It's Changes. 3rd ed. LC 99-42979. 1208p. 1999. text 111.95 (*0-471-18476-4*) Wiley.

Brady, James E., et al. Chemistry: The Study of Matter & Its Changes Second Edition & Descriptive Chemistry of the Elements & Appling's Math Survival Guide Set. 2nd ed. 1233p. 1996. text 150.85 (*0-471-16941-2*) Wiley.

Brady, James F., tr. see Erasmus, Desiderius.

***Brady, James P.** Coldest War: A Memoir of Korea. 2000. pap. 14.95 (*0-312-26511-5*) St Martin.

Brady, James P. The Coldest War: A Memoir of Korea. McCarthy, Paul, ed. 312p. 1991. reprint ed. pap. 6.50 (*0-671-72525-4*) PB.

— Hurrah for the Artillery: Knap's Independent Battery & Pennsylvania Light Artillery. (Illus.). 464p. (C). 1992. text 29.95 (*0-939631-44-X*) Thomas Publications.

Brady, James P., jt. auth. see Davis, Arthur K.

Brady, James R. Jesus Christ: Divine Man or Son of God? 152p. (C). 1992. lib. bdg. 39.00 (*0-8191-8481-0*) U Pr of Amer.

Brady, Janeen. I Have a Song for You Vol. 1: About People & Nature. rev. ed. (Illus.). 50p. (J). (ps-4). 1986. pap. text, student ed. 9.95 (*0-944803-02-4*) Brite Music.

— I Have a Song for You Vol. 1: About People & Nature. rev. ed. Brady, Ted, ed. (Illus.). 39p. (J). (ps-4). 1979. 9.95 (*0-944803-00-8*) Brite Music.

— I Have a Song for You Vol. 1: About People & Nature. rev. ed. (Illus.). (J). (ps-4). pap., student ed. 9.95 (*0-944803-01-6*) Brite Music.

— I Have a Song for You Vol. 2: About Seasons & Holidays. (Illus.). 50p. (J). (ps-4). 1987. pap., student ed. 9.95 incl. audio (*0-944803-05-9*) Brite Music.

— I Have a Song for You Vol. 3: About Animals. (Illus.). 50p. (J). (ps-4). 1988. pap. text 9.95 (*0-944803-08-3*); digital audio 9.95 (*0-944803-07-5*) Brite Music.

— I Have a Song for You Vol. 3: About Animals. Brady, Ted, ed. (Illus.). 42p. (J). (ps-4). 1979. 9.95 (*0-944803-06-7*) Brite Music.

— My Body Machine. (Illus.). (J). (ps-6). 1989. 10.95 (*0-944803-71-7*); student ed. 4.95 (*0-944803-65-2*) Brite Music.

— My Body Machine. 29p. (J). (ps-6). 1990. 4.95 (*0-944803-73-3*) Brite Music.

— Safety Kids Vol. 3: Protect Their Minds. 24p. (J). (gr. k-6). pap. text 4.95 (*0-944803-82-2*) Brite Music.

— Safety Kids Personal Safety. Underwood, Oscar, tr. (SPA.). (J). (gr. k-6). 1984. audio 4.95 (*0-944803-18-0*) Brite Music.

— Safety Kids Personal Safety, Vol. 1. (Illus.). 14p. (J). (gr. k-6). 1983. student ed. 15.00 (*0-944803-20-2*) Brite Music.

— Safety Kids Personal Safety, Vol. 1. Underwood, Oscar, tr. (SPA.). (J). (gr. k-6). 1984. 4.95 (*0-944803-16-4*); 12.95 incl. audio (*0-944803-17-2*); pap. text 4.95 (*0-944803-19-9*); 8.95 (*0-944803-15-6*) Brite Music.

— Safety Kids Play It Smart Vol. 2: Stay Safe from Drugs. (Illus.). (J). (gr. k-6). 1985. 4.95 (*0-944803-22-9*); 12.95 incl. audio (*0-944803-23-7*); student ed. 15.00 (*0-944803-25-3*); pap. text 4.95 (*0-944803-24-5*); pap. text 8.95 (*0-944803-21-0*) Brite Music.

— Safety Kids Play It Smart, Vol. 2: Stay Safe from Drugs. (Illus.). (J). (gr. k-6). 1985. VHS 19.95 (*0-944803-72-5*) Brite Music.

— Show a Little Love: Songbook. (Illus.). 48p. (J). (gr. k-6). 1981. 9.95 (*0-944803-26-1*) Brite Music.

— Someone Special - You! (Illus.). 26p. (J). (gr. k-9). 1991. student ed. 4.95 (*0-944803-76-8*) Brite Music.

— Standin' Tall Cleanliness. (Illus.). 22p. (J). (ps-6). 1984. pap. text 12.95 incl. audio (*0-944803-55-5*); pap. text, student ed. 4.95 (*0-944803-54-7*) Brite Music.

— Standin' Tall Courage. (Illus.). 22p. (J). (ps-6). 1982. pap. text 11.95 incl. audio (*0-944803-45-8*); pap. text, student ed. 4.95 (*0-944803-43-1*) Brite Music.

— Standin' Tall Forgiveness. (Illus.). 22p. (J). (ps-6). 1981. pap. text 11.95 incl. audio (*0-944803-40-7*); pap. text, student ed. 4.95 (*0-944803-39-3*) Brite Music.

— Standin' Tall Honesty. (Illus.). 22p. (J). (ps-6). 1981. pap. text 11.95 incl. audio (*0-944803-38-5*); pap. text, student ed. 4.95 (*0-944803-37-7*) Brite Music.

— Standin' Tall Obedience. (Illus.). 22p. (J). (ps-6). 1981. pap. text 11.95 incl. audio (*0-944803-36-9*); pap. text, student ed. 4.95 (*0-944803-35-0*) Brite Music.

— Standin' Tall Songbook, Vol. 1. 52p. (J). (ps-6). 1987. pap. text 9.95 (*0-944803-62-8*) Brite Music.

— Standin' Tall Songbook, Vol. 2. 71p. (J). (ps-6). 1988. pap. text 9.95 (*0-944803-63-6*) Brite Music.

— Standin' Tall Songbook, Vol. 3. 72p. (J). (ps-6). 1989. pap. text 9.95 (*0-944803-64-4*) Brite Music.

— Standin' Tall Work. (Illus.). 22p. (J). (ps-6). 1981. pap. text 11.95 incl. audio (*0-944803-42-3*); pap. text, student ed. 4.95 (*0-944803-41-5*) Brite Music.

— Take Your Hat off When the Flag Goes By. (Illus.). 22p. (J). (gr. k-6). 1987. student ed. 4.95 (*0-944803-31-8*); 4.95 (*0-944803-33-4*) Brite Music.

— Take Your Hat off When the Flag Goes By, 20 vols., Set. (Illus.). 22p. (J). (gr. k-6). 1987. student ed. 17.00 (*0-944803-34-2*) Brite Music.

— Take Your Hat off When the Flag Goes By: Songbook. (Illus.). 22p. (J). (gr. k-6). 1987. 9.95 (*0-944803-29-6*) Brite Music.

— Watch Me Sing: Songbook, Vol. 1. (Illus.). 31p. (J). (ps-2). 1977. pap. text 9.95 (*0-944803-09-1*) Brite Music.

— Watch Me Sing: Songbook, Vol. 2. (Illus.). 30p. (J). (ps-2). 1986. pap. text 9.95 (*0-944803-11-3*) Brite Music.

Brady, Janeen & Woolley, Diane. Brite Dreams. (Illus.). 32p. (J). (ps). 1988. pap. 4.95 (*0-944803-79-2*); pap. 12.95 incl. audio (*0-944803-80-6*) Brite Music.

— Standin' Tall Dependability. (Illus.). 22p. (J). (ps-6). 1984. pap. text 11.95 incl. audio (*0-944803-60-1*); pap. text, student ed. 4.95 (*0-944803-59-8*) Brite Music.

— Standin' Tall Gratitude. (Illus.). 22p. (J). (ps-6). 1982. pap. text 11.95 incl. audio (*0-944803-49-0*); pap. text, student ed. 4.95 (*0-944803-48-2*) Brite Music.

— Standin' Tall Happiness. (Illus.). 22p. (J). (ps-6). 1982. pap. text 11.95 incl. audio (*0-944803-47-4*); pap. text, student ed. 4.95 (*0-944803-46-6*) Brite Music.

— Standin' Tall Love. (Illus.). 22p. (J). (ps-6). 1982. pap. text 11.95 incl. audio (*0-944803-51-2*); pap. text, student ed. 4.95 (*0-944803-50-4*) Brite Music.

— Standin' Tall Self-Esteem. (Illus.). 22p. (J). (ps-6). 1984. pap. text 11.95 incl. audio (*0-944803-57-1*); pap. text, student ed. 4.95 (*0-944803-56-3*) Brite Music.

— Standin' Tall Service. (Illus.). 22p. (J). (ps-6). 1984. pap. text 11.95 incl. audio (*0-944803-53-9*); pap. text, student ed. 4.95 (*0-944803-52-0*) Brite Music.

Brady, Janeen J. Safety Kids Vol. 3: Protect Their Minds. (Illus.). 32p. (J). (gr. k-6). 1992. pap. 4.95 (*0-944803-78-4*); pap. 12.95 incl. audio (*0-944803-77-6*) Brite Music.

***Brady, Jay.** Do You Remember? A Country Boy's Memories of Growing up in Post WWII Nebraska. 240p. 1999. pap. write for info. (*0-7392-0417-3*, PO3677) Morris Pubng.

Brady, Jeanne. Schooling Young Children: A Feminist Pedagogy for Liberatory Learning. LC 94-28901. 108p. (C). 1995. text 39.50 (*0-7914-2501-0*); pap. text 12.95 (*0-7914-2502-9*) State U NY Pr.

Brady, Jeff & Sica, Mike. Best of the Skagway, Alaska Police Blotter: And Other True Tales from Alaska's Fun City. (Illus.). 112p. (Orig.). 1996. pap. 8.95 (*0-945284-05-5*) Lynn Canal Pub.

Brady, Jennifer. Jambi & the Lions. Thatch, Nancy R., ed. LC 92-17593. (Books for Students by Students). (Illus.). 26p. (J). (gr. 3-5). 1992. lib. bdg. 15.95 (*0-933849-41-9*) Landmark Edns.

Brady, Jennifer & Herendeen, W. H., eds. Ben Jonson's Sixteen Sixteen Folio. LC 89-40448. (Illus.). 224p. 1991. 35.00 (*0-87413-384-X*) U Delaware Pr.

Brady, Jennifer, et al. Literary Transmission & Authority: Dryden & Other Writers. Miner, Earl, ed. LC 92-29788. (Cambridge Studies in Eighteenth-Century English Literature & Thought: No. 17). 175p. (C). 1993. text 54.95 (*0-521-44111-0*) Cambridge U Pr.

Brady, Jeremiah D. Sylloge of Coins of the British Isles: American Collections, Vol. 30. (British Academy Ser.). (Illus.). 1982. 65.00 (*0-19-726011-X*) OUP.

Brady, Joan. Band-Aides, Bullets & Booze. Liotta, Mary A., ed. LC 93-94346. 134p. 1994. pap. 14.95 (*1-880254-15-8*) Vista.

— Fluff My Pillow, Bend My Straw: The Evolution & Undoing of a Nurse. Diecker, Mary L., ed. LC 92-61477. (Illus.). 195p. 1992. pap. 14.95 (*1-880254-02-6*) Vista.

— God on a Harley. 160p. (Orig.). 1995. 18.00 (*0-671-53621-4*, PB Hardcover) PB.

— God on a Harley. 160p. (Orig.). 1996. per. 5.50 (*0-671-00278-3*) PB.

— Heaven in High Gear. LC 97-13824. 224p. 1997. 18.00 (*0-671-00772-6*) S&S Trade.

— Heaven in High Gear: A Spiritual Fable. 224p. 1999. pap. 12.00 (*0-671-00773-4*) S&S Trade.

— Theory of War: A Novel. 272p. 1994. reprint ed. pap. 11.00 (*0-449-90913-1*, Columbine) Fawcett.

Brady, Joan B. Another Kind of Time. LC 98-88825. (Illus.). 146p. 1999. 21.00 (*1-889853-55-0*) Aah-ha Bks.

Brady, Joan L. God on a Harley: A Spiritual Fable. 160p. 1997. per. 10.00 (*0-671-53622-2*) PB.

Brady, Jody L., ed. see Watt, David B.

Brady, John. Bad Boy: The Life & Politics of Lee Atwater. Bell, J., ed. (Illus.). 352p. 1997. 24.00 (*0-201-62733-7*) Addison-Wesley.

— The Craft of Interviewing. LC 77-76543. 264p. 1977. pap. 15.00 (*0-394-72469-0*) Knopf.

— Heaven in High Gear. large type ed. LC 97-32901. (Inspirational Ser.). 155p. 1998. 22.95 (*0-7838-8364-1*, G K Hall & Co) Mac Lib Ref.

Brady, John & Smith, Timothy. The Greatest Little Transformation Book You'll Ever Read. 67p. (Orig.). 1995. pap. 19.95 (*0-9649230-5-X*) JBA Pr.

***Brady, John & White, Brian.** 50 Hikes in Massachusetts: A Year-Round Guide to Hikes & Walks from the Top of the Berkshires to the tip of Cape Cod. 3rd ed. LC 99-28302. (Illus.). 240p. 1999. pap. 15.95 (*0-88150-454-8*, Pub. by Countryman) Norton.

Brady, John B., et al, eds. Teaching Mineralogy. LC 97-222158. (Illus.). 406p. (C). 1997. pap., wbk. ed. 28.00 (*0-939950-44-8*) Mineralogical Soc.

Brady, John C., II. Drug Addicts: Are They out of Control? McFall, Nancy, ed. LC 90-71961. 240p. (Orig.). (C). 1991. 14.95 (*0-936029-24-2*); pap. text 10.95 (*0-936029-25-0*) Western Bk Journ.

Brady, John F. The Right to Know Handbook. 480p. 1989. ring bd. 99.95 (*1-55645-327-2*) Busn Legal Reports.

— The Supervisor's Complete Guide to Hazardous Waste & Materials Management. rev. ed. 1985. ring bd. 99.95 (*1-55645-303-5*, 303) Busn Legal Reports.

Brady, John F., ed. The BLR Encyclopedia of Safety & Health Training, 2 vols., Set. rev. ed. 1024p. 1988. 199.95 (*1-55645-591-7*, 591) Busn Legal Reports.

— Community Right to Know Compliance Handbook. 430p. 1988. ring bd. 169.95 (*1-55645-325-6*) Busn Legal Reports.

— The Supervisor's Right to Know Handbook. rev. ed. 72p. 1988. per. 24.95 (*1-55645-305-1*, 305) Busn Legal Reports.

Brady, John H. A Familiar Compendium of the Laws Relating to Bankruptcy & Insolvent Debtors, Vol. 1. 164p. 1999. reprint ed. 50.00 (*1-56169-463-0*) Gaunt.

Brady, John P. Classics of American Psychiatry Eighteen-Ten to Nineteen Thirty-Four. LC 72-85641. (Illus.). 336p. 1975. 17.50 (*0-87527-093-X*) Green.

Brady, John S., et al, eds. The Postwar Transformation of Germany: Democracy, Prosperity & Nationhood. LC 99-6174. 544p. 1999. text 75.00 (*0-472-10993-6*, 10993); pap. text 29.95 (*0-472-08591-3*, 08591) U of Mich Pr.

Brady, John W., jt. ed. see French, Alfred D.

Brady, Joseph V., jt. ed. see Meyer, Eugene.

Brady, Judy, jt. auth. see Anthony, Piers.

Brady, Jules M., ed. see Newman, John Henry.

Brady, Julie, jt. auth. see Anthony, Piers.

Brady, Justin L., et al. The Regulation of Insurance. LC 95-77159. (Illus.). 192p. (C). 1995. pap. text 41.00 (*0-89462-092-4*, 20102) IIA.

Brady, Kathleen. Ida Tarbell: Portrait of a Muckraker. LC 89-40207. (Illus.). 172p. 1989. reprint ed. pap. 12.95 (*0-8229-5807-4*) U of Pittsburgh Pr.

Brady, Kathleen. Oh, A-Hunting We Will Go Big Book: Black & White Nellie Edge I Can Read & Sing Big Book. (J). (ps-2). 1988. pap. text 20.00 (*0-922053-14-6*) N Edge Res.

Brady, Kathleen, jt. auth. see Mantis, Hillary J.

Brady, Kimberley S. Keeper for the Sea. LC 94-18506. (J). (gr. k-3). 1995. 16.00 (*0-02-711851-7*, Mac Bks Young Read) S&S Childrens.

— Keeper for the Sea. (Illus.). 32p. (J). (gr. k-3). 1996. 16.00 (*0-689-80472-5*) S&S Childrens.

Brady, Kristin, ed. & intro. see Hardy, Thomas.

***Brady, Kymberli.** Give Them Wings & Let them Fly. 2000. 14.99 (*1-929125-13-5*, Pub. by Loyal Pubng) BookWorld.

Brady, Larry G. How to Raise Kids Without Climbing the Walls. 224p. 1998. pap. 17.98 (*0-88290-618-6*, 1211) Horizon Utah.

Brady, Laurel. Bronson Row. 144p. (gr. 5 up). mass mkt. 4.95 (*0-06-440949-X*) HarpC.

— Bronson Row. 144p. (YA). (gr. 5 up). 14.95 (*0-06-029234-2*); lib. bdg. 14.89 (*0-06-029235-0*) HarpC Child Bks.

Brady, Laurel. Say You Are My Sister. LC 99-87018. (Illus.). 224p. (J). (gr. 5 up). 2000. 14.95 (*0-06-028307-6*); lib. bdg. 14.89 (*0-06-028308-4*) HarpC Child Bks.

Brady, Laurel. What Carter Fellows Knew. LC 99-87018. 224p. (gr. 5 up). mass mkt. 4.95 (*0-06-440765-9*) HarpC.

Brady, Linda. Discovering Your Soul Mission. 1998. write for info. (*0-609-60207-1*) Harmony Bks.

Brady, Linda & St.Lifer, Evan. Discovering Your Soul Mission: How to Use Karmic Astrology to Create the Life You Want. LC 98-12739. (Illus.). 288p. 1998. pap. 13.00 (*0-609-80360-3*) Crown Pub Group.

Brady, Linda P. The Politics of Negotiation: America's Dealings with Allies, Adversaries, & Friends. LC 91-13. xiv, 269p. (C). 1991. 49.95 (*0-8078-1971-9*); pap. 19.95 (*0-8078-4320-2*) U of NC Pr.

Brady, Linda P. & Kaufman, Joyce P., eds. NATO in the 1980's: Challenges & Responses. LC 85-6474. 286p. 1985. 55.00 (*0-275-90065-7*, C0065, Praeger Pubs) Greenwood.

Brady, Lisamarie. Inside Glance. 1998. pap. write for info. (*1-57553-682-X*) Watermrk Pr.

***Brady, Lois S.** Love Lessons. large type ed. LC 99-38388. 1999. 25.95 (*1-56895-772-6*, Wheeler) Wheeler Pub.

Brady, Lois S. Vows: The New York Times Wedding Column. LC 96-22843. (Illus.). 256p. 1997. 23.00 (*0-688-15052-7*, Wm Morrow) Morrow Avon.

Brady, Loretta. Finding Yourself on the Enneagram. LC 98-177416. 160p. 1997. pap. 12.95 (*0-88347-336-4*) T More.

Brady, Luther, jt. ed. see Perez, Carlos A.

Brady, Luther W. T. P. O'Connor & the Liverpool Irish. (Royal Historical Society: Studies in History: No. 39). (Illus.). 320p. 1983. 75.00 (*0-901050-92-X*) Boydell & Brewer.

Brady, Luther W., et al. Ovarian Tumors. (Oncologic Ser.: Vol. 20). (Illus.). 232p. 1984. pap. 120.00 (*0-08-027472-2*, Pergamon Pr) Elsevier.

Brady, Luther W., jt. auth. see Perez, Carlos A.

Brady, M. Michael & Torgersen, Leif. Waxing & Care of Skis & Snowboards. LC 96-19830. 1996. pap. 9.95 (*0-89997-199-7*) Wilderness Pr.

Brady, M. Rosalie. Thought & Style in the Works of Leon Bloy. LC 70-94176. (Catholic University of America. Studies in Romance Languages & Literatures: No. 30). reprint ed. 37.50 (*0-404-50330-6*) AMS Pr.

***Brady, Marie.** I Beheld His Glory. LC 98-91083. 1999. pap. 7.95 (*0-533-13035-2*) Vantage.

Brady, Marion. Max & Me: The Abuse of Power in Florida Community Colleges. 254p. (Orig.). 1995. pap. 5.00 (*0-614-03904-5*) M Brady.

— A Study of Reality: A Supradisciplinary Approach. (Illus.). 185p. (Orig.). 1994. pap., teacher ed. 21.95 (*0-9624475-4-4*) Bks Educators.

— A Study of Reality: A Supradisciplinary Approach. (Illus.). 134p. (Orig.). (YA). (gr. 7-12). 1994. pap., student ed. 13.95 (*0-9624475-5-2*) Bks Educators.

— What Should We Teach? A Guide for Community Dialog. 1998. pap. 149.95 (*1-878631-37-3*) Bks Educators.

— What's Worth Teaching: Selecting, Organizing, & Integrating Knowledge. 2nd ed. Smith, Philip L., ed. 150p. 1997. reprint ed. pap. text 14.95 (*1-878631-35-7*) Bks Educators.

Brady, Marion & Brady, Howard. Idea & Action in American History. 1977. 23.64 (*0-13-448548-3*) P-H.

— Idea & Action in World Cultures. 1977. text 21.72 (*0-685-03871-8*); 58.08 (*0-685-03872-6*) P-H.

Brady, Mark. Growing a Housebuilder: Nourishing Spirit Through Age-Old Art. Elgin, Duane, ed. (Illus.). 248p. (Orig.). 1990. 17.95 (*0-9624345-3-1*) Dovetail CA.

Brady, Martha. Dancing Hearts: Creative Arts with Books Kids Love. LC 97-6050. (Illus.). 224p. (Orig.). (J). (gr. k-6). 1997. pap. text 17.95 (*1-55591-947-2*) Fulcrum Pub.

Brady, Martha & Gleason, Patsy T. Artstarts: Drama, Music, Movement, Puppetry, & Storytelling Activities. (Illus.). xii, 219p. 1994. pap. text 25.00 (*1-56308-148-2*) Teacher Ideas Pr.

Brady, Martin, tr. see Klemperer, Victor.

Brady, Matthew. The Old Town. 96p. 1992. pap. text 5.95 (*0-9631643-2-5*) SF Ind Newspaper.

— The Old Town II: More Tales of Real Life in Early Frisco. LC 98-61865. 117 p. 1998. write for info. (*0-9665020-3-5*) Pan Asia.

Brady, Matthew B., jt. auth. see Elson, Henry W.

***Brady, Matthew K.** Carrier: Prima's Official Strategy Guide. LC 99-69609. (Illus.). 109p. 2000. pap. 14.99 (*0-7615-2594-7*) Prima Pub.

— Kirby 64 - The Crystal Shards: Prima's Official Strategy Guide. 2000. pap. 12.99 (*0-7615-3015-0*) Prima Pub.

— Rollercoaster Tycoon - Corkscrew Follies: Prima's Official Strategy Guide. (Illus.). 240p. 2000. pap. 19.99 (*0-7615-2668-4*) Prima Pub.

***Brady, Maureen.** Beyond Survival: A Writing Journey for Healing Childhood Sexual Abuse. 176p. 1999. reprint ed. pap. text 16.00 (*0-7881-6728-6*) DIANE Pub.

Brady, Maureen. Daybreak: Meditations for Women Survivors of Sexual Abuse. 400p. (Orig.). pap. 11.00 (*0-89486-759-8*, 5053A) Hazelden.

— Folly. LC 94-5905. 224p. 1994. reprint ed. 35.00 (*1-55861-078-2*); reprint ed. pap. 12.95 (*1-55861-079-0*) Feminist Pr.

— Give Me Your Good Ear. LC 78-66097. 160p. 1994. reprint ed. pap. 9.95 (*0-933216-00-9*) Spinsters Ink.

— Midlife: Meditations for Women. LC 94-24328. 1995. pap. 13.00 (*0-06-251148-3*, Pub. by Harper SF) HarpC.

Brady, Maxine, ed. see Nash, Lee.

Brady, Michael. Machine Vision: Advent. 1986. pap. text 95.95 (*0-201-11616-2*) Addison-Wesley.

— Machine Vision: The Advent of Intelligent Robots. 1986. pap. text 95.95 (*0-201-11629-4*) Addison-Wesley.

— Semper Fi. 1988. pap. 6.95 (*0-88145-062-6*) Broadway Play.

Brady, Michael, ed. Robotics Science. (System Development Foundation, Benchmark Ser.). (Illus.). 632p. 1989. 65.00 (*0-262-02284-2*) MIT Pr.

Brady, Michael & Berwick, Robert C., eds. Computational Models of Discourse. (Artificial Intelligence Ser.). 403p. 1983. 52.50 (*0-262-02183-8*) MIT Pr.

Brady, Michael & Paul, Richard P., eds. Robotics Research: The 1st International Symposium. LC 83-25592. (Artificial Intelligence Ser.). (Illus.). 1015p. 1984. 105.00 (*0-262-02207-9*) MIT Pr.

Brady, Michael, et al. Pocket Guide to Golf. (Illus.). 28p. 1995. spiral bd. 12.95 (*1-886127-13-1*) Greycliff Pub.

— Robot Motion: Planning & Control. (Artificial Intelligence Ser.). (Illus.). 585p. 1983. 52.50 (*0-262-02182-X*) MIT Pr.

Brady, Michael, jt. auth. see Caldwell, John, pseud.

Brady, Michael, jt. auth. see Highnam, Ralph.

Brady, Michael, tr. see Flemmen, Asbjorn & Grosvold, Olav.

Brady, Michael K. The Concepts of Residential Real Estate Appraisal. Capella, B. et al, eds. (Illus.). 190p. (Orig.). 1997. pap. 19.95 (*0-9639868-0-5*) Natl Appraisal & Cnslt.

***Brady, Michael K.** Laws, Regulations & Practices Affecting New York Real Estate. 3rd ed. Borowiak, Kenneth & Park, Mia, eds. (Real Estate Ser.). (Illus.). 300p. 2000. pap. 29.95 (*0-9639868-1-3*) Natl Appraisal & Cnslt.

Brady, Neil F. Ethical Universals in International Business. LC 96-38660. (Studies in Economic Ethics & Philosophy). (Illus.). x, 246p. 1997. 99.50 (*3-540-61588-1*) Spr-Verlag.

***Brady, Nelvia M.** This Mother's Daughter. LC 99-98100. 162p. 2000. 24.99 (*0-9673751-0-X*, Pub. by Mothers Day) LPC Group.

— This Mother's Daughter. LC 99-98100. 176p. 2000. pap. 19.99 (*0-9673751-2-6*, Pub. by Mothers Day) LPC Group.

***Brady, Nyle C.** Elements of the Nature & Properties of Soils. LC 99-25749. (Illus.). 559p. 1999. 89.00 (*0-13-014497-5*) P-H.

Brady, Nyle C., ed. Advances in Agronomy, Vol. 43. (Serial Publication Ser.). 373p. 1990. text 122.00 (*0-12-000743-6*) Acad Pr.

Brady, Nyle C. & Weil, Ray R. The Nature & Properties of Soils. 2nd ed. LC 98-13008. 881p. (C). 1998. 100.00 (*0-13-852444-0*) P-H.

***Brady, Pat.** Irresistible Rose Is Rose. (Illus.). 128p. 2000. pap. 9.95 (*0-7407-0554-7*) Andrews & McMeel.

Brady, Pat. License to Dream: A Rose to Rose Collection. LC 97-71629. (Illus.). 128p. (Orig.). 1997. pap. 9.95 (*0-8362-3664-5*) Andrews & McMeel.

— Peace of Mind Is a Blanket That Purrs: A Rose Is Rose Book. LC 98-12867. (Illus.). 128p. 1998. 9.95 (*1-55853-615-9*) Rutledge Hill Pr.

— Rose is Rose: 15th Anniversary Collection. anniversary ed. LC 98-88671. 1999. pap. text 9.95 (*0-8362-8196-9*) Andrews & McMeel.

***Brady, Pat.** Rose Is Rose in Loving Color. LC 99-15448. 1999. pap. 14.95 (*1-55853-788-0*) Rutledge Hill Pr.

Brady, Pat. She's a Momma, Not a Movie Star: A Rose Is Rose Collection. (Illus.). 128p. (Orig.). 1996. pap. 9.95 (*0-8362-1087-5*) Andrews & McMeel.

Brady, Patricia, ed. George Washington's Beautiful Nelly: The Letters of Eleanor Parke Custis Lewis to Elizabeth Bordley Gibson, 1794-1851. LC 91-4797. (Women's Diaries & Letters of the Nineteenth-Century South). 309p. 1996. pap. 14.95 (*1-57003-124-X*) U of SC Pr.

Brady, Patrick. Daughter of Burgundy: Lucette Devignes & the French Tradition. 124p. (Orig.). 1994. pap. text 14.95 (*1-886935-07-6*) New Prdigm Pr.

— Guruwari: A Dreaming of the Australian Outback. 272p. (Orig.). 1997. pap. 19.95 (*1-886935-30-0*) New Prdigm Pr.

— Interdisciplinary Interpretation of Art & Literature: The Principle of Convergence. 102p. (Orig.). 1995. pap. text 12.95 (*1-886935-13-0*) New Prdigm Pr.

— The Mailman. 164p. (Orig.). 1995. pap. 10.95 (*1-886935-31-9*) New Prdigm Pr.

— Memory & History As Fiction: An Archetypal Approach to the Historical Novel. 168p. 1993. pap. text 16.95 (*1-886935-05-X*) New Prdigm Pr.

Brady, Patrick. Rococo Poetry: An Introduction. 109p. 1992. pap. text 12.95 (*1-886935-00-9*) New Prdigm Pr.

Brady, Patrick. Visual & Transient Love: An Anthology of Rococo Poetry in English, French, German, Italian. (ENG, FRE & GER.). 216p. (Orig.). 1995. pap. text 29.95 (*1-886935-01-7*) New Prdigm Pr.

Brady, Patrick, ed. Chaos in the Humanities. (Synthesis Ser.). 200p. (Orig.). 1995. pap. text 19.95 (*1-886935-06-8*) New Prdigm Pr.

— Feminism: Equality &/or Difference? 200p. (Orig.). 1995. pap. text 19.95 (*1-886935-09-2*) New Prdigm Pr.

Brady, Patrick, ed. see Curtis, Jerry L.

Brady, Patrick, jt. ed. see Garvin, Harry R.

***Brady, Patrick F., et al, eds.** Massachusetts Superior Court Civil Practice Manual. LC 97-70625. 1998. write for info. (*1-57589-061-5*) Mass CLE.

Brady, Patrick G., jt. ed. see Nord, H. Juergen.

Brady, Patrick V., ed. Physics & Chemistry of Mineral Surfaces. LC 95-47556. (Chemistry & Physics of Surfaces & Interfaces Ser.). 384p. 1996. boxed set 139.95 (*0-8493-8351-X*) CRC Pr.

Brady, Patrick V., et al. Natural Attenuation of Hazardous Waste: CERCLA, RBCA's, & the Future of Environmental Remediation. LC 97-19742. 245p. 1997. lib. bdg. 65.00 (*1-56670-302-6*) Lewis Pubs.

Brady, Paul L. A Certain Blindness. (Illus.). 325p. 1990. write for info. (*0-9623720-0-5*) ALP Pub.

Brady, Peggy, jt. auth. see Martin, Paul.

Brady, Peter. Animales de La Granja Complete Series, 4 vols. Schon, Isabel, ed. Ferrer, Martin Luis Guzman, tr. (Illus.). 24p. 1999. pap. text 56.00 (*0-7368-0145-6*) Capstone Pr.

Brady, Peter. Camiones de bomberos. Schon, Isabel, ed. Ferrer, Martin Luis Guzman, tr. 15.93 (*1-56065-791-X*, Bridgestone Bks) Capstone Pr.

— Cerdos. Schon, Isabel, ed. Ferrer, Martin Luis Guzman, tr. (Animales de La Granja Ser.). (Illus.). 24p. 1998. 15.93 (*1-56065-789-8*, Bridgestone Bks) Capstone Pr.

Brady, Peter. Farm Animals Series, 4 bks. Incl. Chickens. 24p. (J). (gr. 1-2). 1996. lib. bdg. 13.75 (*1-56065-347-7*, Bridgestone Bks); Cows. 24p. (J). (ps-4). 1996. lib. bdg. 13.75 (*1-56065-344-2*, Bridgestone Bks); Pigs. 24p. (J). (ps-4). 1996. lib. bdg. 13.75 (*1-56065-345-0*, Bridgestone Bks); Sheep. 24p. (J). (ps-4). 1996. lib. bdg. 13.75 (*1-56065-346-9*, Bridgestone Bks); 55.00 (*1-56065-632-8*, Bridgestone Bks) Capstone Pr.

***Brady, Peter.** Ovejas. Schon, Isabel, ed. Ferrer, Martin Luis Guzman, tr. (Animales de La Granja Ser.). (Illus.). 24p. 1999. 15.93 (*1-56065-790-1*, Bridgestone Bks) Capstone Pr.

— Pollos. Schon, Isabel, ed. Ferrer, Martin Luis Guzman, tr. (Animales de La Granja Ser.). (Illus.). 24p. 1999. 15.93 (*1-56065-787-1*, Bridgestone Bks) Capstone Pr.

Brady, Peter. Pollos. (Animales de la Granja). (SPA.). (J). 1998. 14.00 (*0-516-21374-1*) Childrens.

— Tractors. (Early Reader Science Ser.). (Illus.). 24p. (J). (gr. k-3). 1996. 14.00 (*0-516-20119-0*) Childrens.

***Brady, Peter.** Vacas. Schon, Isabel, ed. Ferrer, Martin Luis Guzman, tr. (Animales de La Granja Ser.). (Illus.). 24p. 1999. 15.93 (*1-56065-788-X*, Bridgestone Bks) Capstone Pr.

Brady, Philip. Forged Correspondences. (Orig.). 1996. pap. 10.00 (*0-938621-03-3*) New Myths.

— Reluctant Hero: A Snowy Road to Salem in 1802. 144p. (YA). (gr. 7 up). 1990. 16.95 (*0-8027-6972-1*); lib. bdg. 17.85 (*0-8027-6974-8*) Walker & Co.

— Using Type Right: One Hundred Twenty-One No-Nonsense Rules for Working with Type. (Illus.). 128p. 1994. 24.95 (*0-8442-3375-7*, NTC Business Bks) NTC Contemp Pub Co.

Brady, Philip, et al, eds. Gunter Grass's Der Butt: Sexual Politics & the Male Myth of History. 244p. 1990. text 59.00 (*0-19-815860-2*) OUP.

Brady Publishing Staff. Official Mortal Kombat 4 Arcade Secrets. 112p. 1997. pap. text 11.99 (*1-56686-690-1*) Brady Pub.

Brady Publishing Staff & Cain, Christine. PlayStation Games Book, Vol. 4. 4th ed. 112p. 1997. 11.99 (*1-56686-704-5*) Brady Pub.

Brady, Regina, et al. Cybermarketing: Your Interactive Marketing Consultant. LC 96-47562. (Illus.). 352p. 1997. pap. 22.95 (*0-8442-3442-7*, NTC Business Bks) NTC Contemp Pub Co.

Brady, Robert P. Fundamental of Law & Regulation, Vol. 1. LC 97-202248. 1997. 139.00 (*1-885259-45-X*) Food & Drug Law.

Brady, Robert. Further on This Floating Bridge of Dreams: Poems from Kyoto. Fitzsimmons, Thomas, ed. & intro. by. LC 88-3027. (American Writers Ser.: No. 5). 64p. (Orig.). 1988. pap. 9.50 (*0-942668-12-X*) Katydid Bks.

Brady, Robert, jt. auth. see Maxfield, Albert.

Brady, Robert, tr. see Chimako, Tada.

Brady, Robert, tr. see Fitzsimmons, Thomas & Gozo, Yoshimazu, eds.

Brady, Robert, tr. see Takashi, Tsujii.

Brady, Robert, tr. see Tsujii, Takashi.

Brady, Robert A. Business as a System of Power. LC 76-167311. (Essay Index Reprint Ser.). 1977. reprint ed. 25.95 (*0-8369-2753-2*) Ayer.

— The Spirit & Structure of German Fascism. LC 68-9629. 1970. reprint ed. 47.50 (*0-86527-189-5*) Fertig.

***Brady, Robert A. & Dowd, Douglas.** Business as a System of Power. LC 99-87783. 367p. 1999. pap. 29.95 (*0-7658-0682-7*) Transaction Pubs.

Brady, Robert I. Law for Personnel Managers: How to Hire the People You Need Without Discriminating. rev. ed. 1980. per. 25.46 (*1-55645-460-0*, 460) Busn Legal Reports.

An Asterisk (*) at the beginning of an entry indicates that the title is appearing for the first time.

Brady, Robert L. Before You Say "You'll Have To Go" A Terminations Decision Tree. rev. ed. 158p. 1985. ring bd. 21.20 (*1-55645-437-6*, 437) Busn Legal Reports.
— Law for Personnel Managers: How to Hire the People You Need Without Discriminating. 1982. pap. 24.95 (*1-55645-110-5*) Busn Legal Reports.
Brady, Robert L. & Persson, Leonard N. Employee Compensation in Your State, 2 vols., Set. rev. ed. 1987. ring bd. 395.00 (*1-55645-000-1*) Busn Legal Reports.
Brady, Robert L., jt. auth. see Hartsfield, William E.
Brady, Robert N. Heavy Duty Truck Diesel Fuel Systems: Operation, Service & Maintenance. 656p. 1990. text 63.80 (*0-13-385675-5*) P-H.
— Heavy-Duty Trucks: Powertrains, System & Service. 950p. 1997. 96.00 (*0-13-181470-2*) P-H.
— Mid/Heavy Duty Truck Electrical. 560p. 1991. 105.00 (*0-13-385659-3*, 410101) P-H.
— Modern Diesel Technology. LC 95-17079. 688p. (C). 1995. 93.33 (*0-13-288382-1*) P-H.
— On-Highway Trucks: Power Trains & Suspension Systems. 1982. text 78.80 (*0-8359-5232-0*) P-H.
Brady, Robert N., jt. auth. see Dagel, John F.
Brady, Robert P. Fundamental of Law & Regulation, Vol. 2. LC 97-202248. 1997. 139.00 (*1-885259-47-6*) Food & Drug Law.
Brady, Roscoe O., jt. ed. see Tower, Donald B.
Brady, Rose. Kapitalizm: Russia's Struggle to Free Its Economy. LC 98-38353. (Illus.). 336p. 1998. 35.00 (*0-300-07793-9*) Yale U Pr.
***Brady, Rose.** Kapitalizm: Russia's Struggle to Free Its Economy. LC 98-38353. (Illus.). 336p. 2000. pap. 16.95 (*0-300-08262-2*) Yale U Pr.
***Brady, Ross.** Universal Logic. (Lecture Notes Ser.: Vol. 109). 280p. (C). 2000. write for info. (*1-57586-255-7*, Pub. by CSLI); pap. write for info. (*1-57586-256-5*, Pub. by CSLI) Cambridge U Pr.
Brady, Rowena F. & Brown, Canter. Things Remembered: An Album of African Americans in Tampa. LC 96-51255. 1997. write for info. (*1-879852-53-5*) Univ Tampa.
***Brady, S. Lee.** Light Words: The Metaphysical & New Age Spirituality Glossary. (Illus.). 139p. 2000. 12.95 (*0-9671158-3-3*); pap. 8.99 (*0-9671158-4-1*) Sananda Fndt.
Brady, Sally R. A Yankee Christmas Featuring Vermont Celebrations: Feasts, Treats, Crafts, & Traditions of Wintertime New England. (Illus.). 160p. 1992. 24.95 (*0-89909-358-2*, 80-152-9) Yankee Bks.
Brady, Sandra. Let's Make Books. 176p. (C). 1992. per. 25.95 (*0-8403-7334-1*, 40733401) Kendall-Hunt.
Brady, Sandra & Sills, Toni M. Whole Language: History, Philosophy, & Practice. 240p. (C). 1993. per. 39.95 (*0-8403-8763-6*) Kendall-Hunt.
***Brady, Sean.** Wallace. unabridged ed. 36p. 2000. pap. 6.00 (*0-88734-841-6*) Players Pr.
Brady, Simon, jt. auth. see Ellerton, Victoria.
Brady, Stephen D. & Hillestad, Richard J. Modeling the External Risks of Airports for Policy Analysis. LC 95-34933. (MR-605-EAC/VW Ser.). 76p. (Orig.). 1995. pap. text 13.00 (*0-8330-2299-7*, MR-605-EAC) Rand Corp.
Brady, Steve & Roderus, Frank. Murder Revisited. 296p. (Orig.). 1996. mass mkt. 5.99 (*0-380-77489-5*, Avon Bks) Morrow Avon.
Brady, Susan. Find My Blanket. LC 87-45310. (Illus.). 32p. (J). (ps-1). 1988. 11.95 (*0-397-32247-X*); lib. bdg. 11.89 (*0-397-32248-8*) HarpC Child Bks.
Brady, Susan & Shankweiler, Donald, eds. Phonological Processes in Literacy: A Tribute to Isabelle Y. Liberman. 296p. 1991. text 59.95 (*0-8058-0501-X*) L Erlbaum Assocs.
Brady, Susan & Willard, Carolyn. Microscopic Explorations: A GEMS Festival Teacher's Guide. Bergman, Lincoln et al, eds. (Great Explorations in Math & Science (GEMS) Ser.). (Illus.). 168p. 1998. pap., teacher ed. 21.00 (*0-924886-00-5*, GEMS) Lawrence Science.
Brady, Susan, ed. see Cohen-Stratyner, Barbara, et al.
Brady, Susanne. Homework: Bridging the Gap. Goodfellow, Pamela R., ed. 1994. pap., student ed. 12.99 (*0-9639882-5-5*) Goodfellow Pr.
Brady, Suzanne & Jacobs, Suzie. Mindful of Others: Teaching Children to Teach. LC 93-48126. 222p. 1994. pap. text 23.00 (*0-435-08356-2*, 08356) Heinemann.
Brady, Suzanne, ed. see Taylor, Eldon.
Brady, Taylor. The Kincaids Bk. 1: Raging Rivers. 336p. (Orig.). 1992. mass mkt. 4.50 (*0-380-76332-X*, Avon Bks) Morrow Avon.
— The Kincaids Bk. 2: Prairie Thunder. 352p. (Orig.). 1993. mass mkt. 4.50 (*0-380-76333-8*, Avon Bks) Morrow Avon.
— The Kincaids Bk. 3: Mountain Fury. 352p. (Orig.). 1993. mass mkt. 4.99 (*0-380-77133-0*, Avon Bks) Morrow Avon.
***Brady, Taylor.** Mountain Fury. LC 99-55333. (Kincaids Ser.). 2000. 26.95 (*0-7862-2336-7*) Five Star.
— Prairie Thunder. LC 99-28411. (Romances Ser.). 1999. pap. 24.95 (*0-7862-2085-6*, Five Star MI) Mac Lib Ref.
Brady, Taylor. Raging Rivers: The Kinkaids. LC 98-51969. (Kincaids Ser.). 1999. 24.95 (*0-7862-1774-X*) Thorndike Pr.
***Brady, Taylor.** Westward Winds. LC 00-34749. (Kincaids Ser.). 2000. write for info. (*0-7862-2727-3*) Five Star.
Brady, Taylor. Westward Winds Bk. 4: The Kincaids. 304p. (Orig.). 1993. mass mkt. 4.99 (*0-380-77134-9*, Avon Bks) Morrow Avon.
Brady, Ted, ed. see Brady, Janeen.
Brady, Thomas. Handbook of European History, 1400-1600 Late Middle Ages, Renaissance, & Reformation Visions, Programs, Outcomes, Vol. 2. Oberman, Heiko A., ed. 748p. 1996. pap. text 30.00 (*0-8028-4195-3*) Eerdmans.
Brady, Thomas A., Jr. Communities, Politics, & Reformation: Collected Papers. (Studies in Medieval & Reformation Thought: Vol. 68). xx, 498p. 1998. 171.50 (*90-04-11001-1*) Brill Academic Pubs.
Brady, Thomas A. Politics of the Reformation in Germany: Jacob Sturm (1489-1553) of Strasbourg. 336p. (C). 1996. pap. 19.95 (*0-391-04004-9*) Humanities.
Brady, Thomas A., Jr. Protestant Politics: Jacob Sturm (1489-1553) & the German Reformation. LC 93-3015. (Studies in Central European Histories). 536p. (C). 1995. text 75.00 (*0-391-03823-0*) Humanities.
Brady, Thomas A. Sarapis & Isis: Collected Essays. Mitchel, Fordyce, ed. 129p. 1978. 25.00 (*0-89005-253-0*) Ares.
Brady, Thomas A., Jr., et al, eds. Handbook of European History, 1400-1600: Late Middle Ages, Renaissance, & Reformation, 2 vols. 1996. pap. 60.00 (*0-8028-4210-0*) Eerdmans.
— Handbook of European History, 1400-1600: Late Middle Ages, Renaissance, & Reformation, Vol. 1. 1994. 57.50 (*90-04-09760-0*) Brill Academic Pubs.
— Handbook of European History, 1400-1600 Late Middle Ages, Renaissance, & Reformation Vol. 1: Structures & Assertions, Vol. 1. 733p. 1996. pap. 30.00 (*0-8028-4194-5*) Eerdmans.
Brady, Thomas A., Jr., ed. see Thiebault, John.
Brady, Thomas A., Jr., ed. see Wallace, Peter G.
Brady, Thomas A., Jr., tr. see Blickle, Peter.
Brady-Thomas, Marilyn. Comprehensive Review Course Workbook: For the Regents College Exam "Health Support I" 3rd rev. ed. (Illus.). 467p. (C). 1999. pap. text 99.00 (*1-884591-35-3*) T H E Educ.
— Comprehensive Review Course Workbook No. 1: For the ACT-PEP Test "Commonalities in Nursing: Area A" 4th ed. (Illus.). 407p. (C). 1997. pap. text, wbk. ed. 90.00 (*1-884591-20-5*) T H E Educ.
— Comprehensive Review Course Workbook No. 2: For the ACT-PEP Test Commonalities in Nursing: Area B. 4th ed. (Illus.). 333p. (C). 1997. pap. text, wbk. ed. 90.00 (*1-884591-21-3*) T H E Educ.
— Comprehensive Review Course Workbook No. 3: For the ACT-PEP Test Differences in Nursing: Area A. 2nd ed. (Illus.). 473p. (C). 1994. pap. text, wbk. ed. 90.00 (*1-884591-01-9*) T H E Educ.
— Comprehensive Review Course Workbook No. 4: For the ACT-PEP Test Differences in Nursing: Area B. 3rd ed. (Illus.). 360p. (C). 1995. pap. text, wbk. ed. 90.00 (*1-884591-07-8*) T H E Educ.
— Comprehensive Review Course Workbook No. 5: For the ACT-PEP Test Differences in Nursing: Area C. 2nd ed. (Illus.). 341p. (C). 1994. pap. text, wbk. ed. 90.00 (*1-884591-04-3*) T H E Educ.
— Comprehensive Review Course Workbook No. 6: For the ACT-PEP Test Differences in Nursing: Area B. 3rd ed. (Illus.). 176p. (C). 1995. pap. text, wbk. ed. 90.00 (*1-884591-08-6*) T H E Educ.
— Comprehensive Review Course Workbook No. 8: For the ACT-PEP Test Health Support II. 2nd ed. (Illus.). 355p. (C). 1996. pap. text, wbk. ed. 90.00 (*1-884591-17-5*) T H E Educ.
— Comprehensive Review Course Workbook No. 9: For the ACT-PEP Test Health Restoration I. 2nd ed. (Illus.). 269p. (C). 1996. pap. text, wbk. ed. 90.00 (*1-884591-18-3*) T H E Educ.
— Comprehensive Review Course Workbook No. 10: For the ACT-PEP Test Health Restoration II. 2nd ed. (Illus.). 483p. (C). 1996. pap. text, wbk. ed. 90.00 (*1-884591-19-1*) T H E Educ.
— Comprehensive Review Course Workbook No. 11: For the ACT-PEP Test Professional Strategies. 2nd ed. (Illus.). 193p. (C). 1996. pap. text, wbk. ed. 90.00 (*1-884591-23-X*) T H E Educ.
— Comprehensive Review Course Workbook No. 12: For the ACT-PEP Test Anatomy & Physiology. 2nd ed. (Illus.). 183p. (C). 1996. pap. text, wbk. ed. 90.00 (*1-884591-26-4*) T H E Educ.
— Comprehensive Review Course Workbook No. 13: For the ACT-PEP Test Microbiology. 2nd ed. (Illus.). 207p. (C). 1996. pap. text, wbk. ed. 90.00 (*1-884591-27-2*) T H E Educ.
— Comprehensive Review Course Workbook No. 14: For the ACT-PEP Test Gerontology. 2nd ed. (Illus.). 138p. (C). 1996. pap. text, wbk. ed. 90.00 (*1-884591-28-0*) T H E Educ.
— CPNE Reference Cards. 40p. (C). 1996. pap. text 19.95 (*1-884591-05-1*) T H E Educ.
— HAPE-TPE Reference Cards. 57p. (C). 1997. pap. 19.95 (*1-884591-24-8*) T H E Educ.
— I Can Write English Compositions: For the Regents College Exam "English Composition" 32p. (C). 1998. pap. text 99.00 (*1-884591-45-0*) T H E Educ.
Brady-Thomas, Marilyn, jt. auth. see Cassidy, Hope.
***Brady, Tim.** The American Aviation Experience: A History. LC 99-88092. (Illus.). 2000. 45.00 (*0-8093-2325-7*) S Ill U Pr.
Brady, U. Eugene, et al. Pheromones: Current Research, 2 vols., Vol. 2. 157p. 1974. text 31.50 (*0-8422-7212-7*) Irvington.
Brady, Upton, ed. see Balling, L. Christian.
Brady, Veronica. Can These Bones Live? LC 97-107796. 150p. 1996. pap. 29.00 (*1-86287-221-X*, Pub. by Federation Pr) Gaunt.
— Playing Catholic. 60p. (C). 1991. pap. 11.95 (*0-86819-256-2*, Pub. by Currency Pr) Accents Pubns.
Brady, Vicki. Quiet Moments for Homeschool Moms & Dads. LC 99-32819. 194p. 1999. pap. 10.99 (*1-56955-166-9*, Vine Bks) Servant.
Brady, Vicki A. The Basic Steps to Successful Home Schooling. LC 95-81583. 208p. 1996. pap. 11.99 (*1-56384-113-4*, Vital Issue Pr) Huntington Hse.
***Brady, William.** The Kedge Anchor: or A Young Sailor's Assistant. (Illus.). 400p. 1999. 45.00 (*0-8328-9897-X*) Higginson Bk Co.
Brady, William, jt. auth. see Young, Jeffrey.
***Brady, William H., ed.** The Prevention & First-Aid Treatment of Childhood Injuries. (Illus.). 228p. 1999. reprint ed. pap. text 20.00 (*0-7881-6421-X*) DIANE Pub.
Brady, William S. Bloodrun. large type ed. 1984. 12.50 (*0-685-29743-8*) Ulverscroft.
— Death & Jack Shade. large type ed. 1984. 12.00 (*0-685-29749-7*) Ulverscroft.
— Hawk: Blood Kin. large type ed. (Linford Western Library). 240p. 1985. pap. 16.99 (*0-7089-6093-6*) Ulverscroft.
— Hawk: Fool's Gold. large type ed. (Linford Western Library). 288p. 1985. pap. 16.99 (*0-7089-6085-5*) Ulverscroft.
— Hawk: Killer's Breed. large type ed. 1985. 15.95 (*0-7089-1263-X*) Ulverscroft.
— Hawk: The Sudden Guns. large type ed. (Linford Western Library). 304p. 1985. pap. 16.99 (*0-7089-6137-1*) Ulverscroft.
— Lynch Law. large type ed. 1984. 12.00 (*0-685-29739-X*) Ulverscroft.
— Peacemaker: Comanche! large type ed. (Linford Western Library). 282p. 1985. pap. 16.99 (*0-7089-6089-8*, Linford) Ulverscroft.
— Peacemaker: The Lost. large type ed. (Linford Western Library). 256p. 1986. pap. 16.99 (*0-7089-6201-7*, Linford) Ulverscroft.
— Peacemaker: War Party. large type ed. (Linford Western Library). 256p. 1986. pap. 16.99 (*0-7089-6193-2*, Linford) Ulverscroft.
— Peacemaker: 1000 Dollar Death. large type ed. (Linford Western Library). 256p. 1985. pap. 16.99 (*0-7089-6133-9*, Linford) Ulverscroft.
Brady, Wm, et al. Diabetes. 40p. 1996. reprint ed. spiral bd. 9.00 (*0-7873-1016-6*) Hlth Research.
Bradygames. Castlevania Totally Unauthorized Strategy Guide. LC 98-74683. 1999. pap. text 11.99 (*1-56686-873-4*) Brady Pub.
— Crash Bandicoot 3 Totally Unauthorized Pocket Guide: Warped Totally Unauthorized Pocket Guide. LC 98-74209. 1998. pap. text 7.99 (*1-56686-849-1*) Brady Pub.
— Darkstalkers III Official Strategy Guide. 1998. pap. text 11.99 (*1-56686-852-1*) Brady Pub.
— LEGO Creator: Official Activity Book. 1999. pap. text 14.99 (*1-56686-835-1*) Brady Pub.
***Bradygames.** Nintendo 64 Secret Codes, 3. LC 99-72443. 1999. pap. text 7.99 (*1-56686-892-0*) Brady Pub.
Bradygames. Official Tenchu Strategy Guide: Stealth Assassins. LC 98-73584. 1998. pap. text 11.99 (*1-56686-821-1*) Brady Pub.
— T'Ai Fu: Wrath of the Tiger. LC 98-73572. (Brady Games Strategy Guides Ser.). (Illus.). 111p. 1999. pap. 11.99 (*1-56686-833-5*) Brady Pub.
— 10 Six: Official Strategy Guide. 1999. pap. 19.99 (*1-56686-875-0*) Brady Pub.
***Bradygames.** WWF Attitude: Totally Unauthorized Strategy Guide. (Illus.). 128p. 1999. pap. write for info. (*1-56686-901-3*) Brady Pub.
BradyGames Inc. Staff. Dino Crisis: Official Strategy Guide. 128p. 1999. pap. text 12.99 (*1-56686-905-4*) Brady Pub.
— Jet Force Gemini: Official Strategy Guide. 128p. 1999. pap. text 12.99 (*1-56686-887-4*) Brady Pub.
***BradyGames Inc. Staff.** NBA 2k Official Strategy Guide. 128p. 1999. pap. 12.99 (*1-56686-967-6*, BradyGAMES) Brady Pub.
— Official Brave Fencer Musashi Strategy Guide. (Bradygames Strategy Guides Ser.). (Illus.). 1998. pap. 14.99 (*1-56686-832-7*, BradyGAMES) Brady Pub.
— Sega Dreamcast Official Preview Guide. 1999. pap. 9.99 (*1-56686-929-3*) Brady Pub.
— Slave Zero Official Strategy Guide. 112p. 1999. pap. 12.99 (*1-56686-965-X*, BradyGAMES) Brady Pub.
***Bradygames Publishing Staff.** Tony Hawk's Pro Skater: Official Strategy Guide. 128p. 1999. pap. 12.99 (*1-56686-945-5*) Brady Pub.
Bradygames Staff. Baldur's Gate Official Strategy Guide. 1998. pap. 19.99 (*1-56686-788-6*) Brady Pub.
— Banjo & Kazooie: Totally Unauthorized Strategy Guide. 128p. 1998. pap. text 9.99 (*1-56686-736-3*) Brady Pub.
— Barbie Cool Looks Fashion Designer Activity Book: A Day in the Life of Barbie & Her Friends. LC 98-73119. 1998. pap. 14.99 (*1-56686-809-2*) Brady Pub.
— Biofreaks Official Strategy Guide. 1998. pap. 11.99 (*1-56686-806-8*) Brady Pub.
***BradyGames Staff.** Blue Stinger: Official Strategy Guide. 128p. 1999. pap. 12.99 (*1-56686-927-7*) Brady Pub.
BradyGames Staff. Diablo II Official Strategy Guide. 208p. 2000. pap. 19.99 (*1-56686-891-2*) Brady Pub.
Bradygames Staff. Earthworm Jim 3D Official Strategy Guide. 128p. 1999. pap. 11.99 (*1-56686-812-2*) Brady Pub.
— F-Zero X: Totally Unauthorized Strategy Guide. 1998. pap. text 11.99 (*1-56686-807-6*) Brady Pub.
— Final Fantasy VII Official Strategy Guide: Now for the PC. 272p. 1998. pap. text 19.99 (*1-56686-782-7*) Brady Pub.
***Bradygames Staff.** House of the Dead 2: Official Strategy Guide. 128p. 1999. pap. 12.99 (*1-56686-946-3*) Brady Pub.
BradyGames Staff. Interstate '82: Official Strategy Guide. 208p. 1999. pap. text 19.99 (*1-56686-879-3*) Brady Pub.
Bradygames Staff. Klingon Honor Guard: Official Strategy Guide. (Star Trek the Next Generation Ser.). 1998. pap. 19.99 (*1-56686-831-9*) Brady Pub.
— Legend of Zelda: Ocarina of Time Strategy Guide. 1998. pap. text 11.99 (*1-56686-808-4*) Brady Pub.
— Magic: The Gathering Adventurers Guide. 167p. 1997. pap. text 19.99 (*1-56686-579-4*) Brady Pub.
***BradyGames Staff.** Mob Rule: Official Strategy Guide. 216p. 1999. pap. 19.99 (*1-56686-911-0*) Brady Pub.
BradyGames Staff. NBA Hangtime Players Guide. 96p. 1996. 9.99 (*1-56686-628-6*) Brady Pub.
Bradygames Staff. NFL Blitz Official Strategy Guide. LC 98-73166. 1998. pap. 11.99 (*1-56686-814-9*) Brady Pub.
***BradyGames Staff.** NFL Blitz 2000: Official Strategy Guide. 1999. pap. 12.99 (*1-56686-912-9*) Brady Pub.
— Nightmare Creatures II Vol. 1: Official Strategy Guide. LC 99-73428. (Illus.). 112p. 2000. pap. 12.99 (*1-56686-915-3*) Brady Pub.
— Nintendo Game Boy: Official Games Guide. 112p. 2000. pap. 12.99 (*1-56686-923-4*) Brady Pub.
Bradygames Staff. Official Battlezone Strategy Guide. 1998. pap. text 19.99 (*1-56686-775-4*) Brady Pub.
— Official Descent: Freespace the Great War Strategy Guide. 1999. pap. 19.99 (*1-56686-787-8*) Brady Pub.
— Official M. A. X. 2 Strategy Guide. 1998. pap. text 19.99 (*1-56686-789-4*) Brady Pub.
— Official Mortal Kombat 4 Fighter's Kompanion Strategy Guide. 1998. pap. text 11.99 (*1-56686-795-9*) Brady Pub.
— Official Mortal Kombat 4 Pocket Strategy Guide. 1998. pap. 7.99 (*1-56686-796-7*) Brady Pub.
— Official Pocket Player's Guide to Star Trek: The Next Generation Customizable Card Game. (Illus.). 265p. (Orig.). 1995. 14.99 (*1-56686-248-5*) Brady Pub.
— Official Sin Strategy Guide. 216p. 1998. pap. text 19.99 (*1-56686-776-2*) Brady Pub.
— Official Star Trek: First Contact Strategy Guide. 1998. pap. text 19.99 (*1-56686-774-6*) Brady Pub.
— Official Star Trek: Birth of the Federation Strategy Guide. LC 98-70847. 1998. pap. 19.99 (*1-56686-794-0*) Brady Pub.
— Official Tekken 3 Totally Unauthorized Fighting Guide. 1998. pap. 9.99 (*1-56686-793-2*) Brady Pub.
— Official Toshinden 2 Fighters Guide. 112p. 1996. 9.99 (*1-56686-557-3*) Brady Pub.
— Official Wild 9 Strategy Guide. 1998. pap. 11.99 (*1-56686-786-X*) Brady Pub.
BradyGAMES Staff. 1001 Secret Codes for the Hottest Video Games. 96p. 1996. 9.99 (*1-56686-571-9*) Brady Pub.
Bradygames Staff. Online Games Kit. 1995. pap. 59.99 (*1-56686-505-0*) Brady Pub.
— Pitfall 3D, Official Guide: Beyond the Jungle Strategy Guide. 112p. 1998. pap. text 11.99 (*1-56686-772-X*) Brady Pub.
— Playstation Bundle Bks. 1 & 2: Official Playstation Games. 1996. pap. text 19.98 (*1-56686-587-5*) Brady Pub.
***Bradygames Staff.** Playstation Secret Codes, 4. LC 99-72444. 1999. pap. text 7.99 (*1-56686-893-9*) Brady Pub.
Bradygames Staff. Quake Authorized Strategy Guide. 162p. 1996. 19.99 (*1-56686-494-1*) Brady Pub.
— Quake Construction Guide, with CD-ROM. 700p. 1997. 13.00 incl. cd-rom (*1-56686-504-2*) Brady Pub.
***BradyGames Staff.** Ready 2 Rumble Boxing Official Strategy Guide: Official Strategy Guide. 1999. pap. 12.99 (*1-56686-913-7*) Brady Pub.
Bradygames Staff. Saga Frontier, Official Study Guide. 224p. 1998. pap. text 14.99 (*1-56686-784-3*) Brady Pub.
— Secret Code Overload. 1998. pap. 11.99 (*1-56686-790-8*) Brady Pub.
— Secret Codes for Nintendo 64, Vol. 2. (Nintendo 64 Games Guide Ser.). 1998. pap. 7.99 (*1-56686-798-3*) Brady Pub.
— Secret Codes for Sony PlayStation. 96p. 1996. 7.99 (*1-56686-598-0*) Brady Pub.
— Secret Codes for Sony Playstation, Vol. 3. 1998. pap. 7.99 (*1-56686-799-1*) Brady Pub.
— Secret of Evermore Strategy Guide. (Illus.). 190p. (Orig.). 1995. 12.99 (*1-56686-328-7*) Brady Pub.
— Shadows of the Empire for Ultra 64. 1996. pap. text 9.99 (*1-56686-549-2*) Brady Pub.
— Small Soldiers: Official Strategy Guide. LC 98-73118. (YA). 1998. pap. 14.99 (*1-56686-817-3*) Brady Pub.
***BradyGames Staff.** Sonic Adventure: Official Strategy Guide. 1999. pap. 12.99 (*1-56686-928-5*) Brady Pub.
BradyGames Staff. Space Bar Official Strategy Guide. 1996. pap. text 19.99 (*1-56686-647-2*) Brady Pub.
Bradygames Staff. Sports Games Play Book. 1996. 9.99 (*1-56686-537-9*) Brady Pub.
— Star Trek Next Generation Card Game Bundle. 1996. pap. text 16.99 (*1-56686-516-6*) Brady Pub.
— Star Wars Customizable Card Game Players Guide. 1995. 14.99 (*1-56686-500-X*) Brady Pub.
***BradyGames Staff.** Super Smash Brothers: Official Strategy Guide. (Illus.). 128p. 1999. pap. 12.99 (*1-56686-900-5*) Brady Pub.
BradyGAMES Staff. Tekken Official Strategy Guide. (Illus.). 153p. (Orig.). 1995. 9.99 (*1-56686-441-0*) Brady Pub.
— Terra Nova Official Strategy Guide. (Illus.). 238p. (Orig.). 1995. 19.99 (*1-56686-349-X*) Brady Pub.
Bradygames Staff. Tomb Raider 3 Totally Unauthorized Pocket Guide. 1998. pap. text 7.99 (*1-56686-848-3*) Brady Pub.
— Totally Unauthorized Guide to Tomb Raider 2. 228p. 1997. pap. text 7.99 (*1-56686-734-7*) Brady Pub.
BradyGames Staff. Totally Unauthorized Nintendo 64 Games Guide, Vol. 1. 112p. 1996. 9.99 (*1-56686-631-6*) Brady Pub.
Bradygames Staff. Totally Unauthorized Secrets to Donkey Kong Country 2. 96p. 1995. pap. 9.99 (*1-56686-318-X*) Brady Pub.
— Ultimate Mortal Kombat 3. 121p. 1996. 9.99 (*1-56686-521-2*) Brady Pub.

B

An Asterisk (*) at the beginning of an entry indicates that the title is appearing for the first time.

— Vigilance Official Strategy Guide. LC 98-72588. 1999. pap. 19.99 (*1-56686-797-5*) Brady Pub.

*__BradyGames Staff.__ Virtua Fighter 3TB: Official Strategy Guide. 128p. 1999. pap. 12.99 (*1-56686-931-5*) Brady Pub.

— Warpath: Jurassic Park Official Fighting Guide. 1999. pap. 12.99 (*1-56686-924-2*) Brady Pub.

BradyGAMES Staff. Wing Commander IV Authorized Strategy & Guide. (Illus.). 300p. 1995. 19.99 (*1-56686-414-3*) Brady Pub.

Bradygames Staff. Witchaven Official Strategy Guide. 348p. 1995. 19.99 (*1-56686-412-7*) Brady Pub.

— WWF War Zone Totally Unauthorized Pocket Guide. 1998. pap. 7.99 (*1-56686-815-7*) Brady Pub.

— Yoshi's Story: Totally Unauthorized Strategy Guide. 64th ed. 128p. 1998. pap. text 11.99 (*1-56686-773-8*) Brady Pub.

*__BradyGAMES Staff, ed.__ Dark Reign 2: Official Strategy Guide. (Bradygames Strategy Guides Ser.). (Illus.). 208p. (J). 2000. pap. 19.99 (*1-56686-970-6*, BradyGAMES) Brady Pub.

Bradygames Staff, ed. Fighter Squadron Official Strategy Guide: The Screamin' Demons over Europe. LC 98-74681. (Brady Games Strategy Guides Ser.). (Illus.). 256p. 1999. pap. 19.99 (*1-56686-860-2*) Brady Pub.

— Heretic II Official Strategy Guide. 1998. pap. 19.99 (*1-56686-847-5*) Brady Pub.

*__BradyGames Staff, ed.__ Mario Party 2 Official Strategy Guide. (Bradygames Strategy Guides Ser.). (Illus.). 112p. (J). 2000. pap. 12.99 (*1-56686-973-0*, BradyGAMES) Brady Pub.

*__BradyGAMES Staff, ed.__ SaGa Frontier 2 Official Strategy Guide. (Bradygames Strategy Guides Ser.). (Illus.). 128p. (J). 2000. pap. 14.99 (*1-56686-972-2*, BradyGAMES) Brady Pub.

Bradygames Staff & Schaefer, Steven M. Totally Unauthorized Combat Guide to Duke Nukem 3D. 238p. 1996. 14.99 (*1-56686-509-3*) Brady Pub.

Bradygames Staff & Watson, Christine. Secrets of Hoshis Island: Unauthorized Pocket Guide to Super Mario World 2 for SNES. 1995. 7.99 (*1-56686-518-2*) Brady Pub.

Bradygames Staff & Wessel, Craig. Doom 64. 112p. 1997. 11.99 (*1-56686-708-8*) Brady Pub.

BradyGAMES Staff, et al. Titanic: Adventure Out of Time Official Hints & Solutions. 192p. 1996. 19.99 (*1-56686-657-X*) Brady Pub.

BradyGAMES Staff, jt. auth. see Matthews, Tristan.

BradyGAMES Staff, jt. auth. see Von, Rhonda.

BradyGAMES Staff, jt. auth. see Wartow, Ronald.

Bradygames Staff, ed. see Wessel, Craig.

Brae, Andrew E. Collier, Coleridge & Shakespeare. LC 70-113562. reprint ed. 45.00 (*0-404-01061-X*) AMS Pr.

Braebec, Barbara. The Craft Business Answer Book. LC 97-35315. 1998. 21.95 (*0-87131-832-6*); pap. 14.95 (*0-87131-833-4*) M Evans.

Braeckman, Antoon, jt. ed. see Lucas, George R., Jr.

Braeckman, Dirk. Dirk Braeckman. (Illus.). 96p. 1999. pap. 30.00 (*90-5544-241-0*, 910762, Pub. by Ludion) Dist Art Pubs.

Braeder, Janice W. Appetizing Dips & Spreads. 36p. (Orig.). 1984. pap. 2.75 (*0-940844-19-2*) Wellspring.

— Soups. 36p. (Orig.). 1983. pap. 3.25 (*0-940844-17-6*) Wellspring.

Braeger, Donn F. Modern Bujutsu & Budo. (Martial Arts & Ways of Japan Ser.: Vol. 3). 1996. pap. text 19.95 (*0-8348-0351-8*) Weatherhill.

Braekken, H., ed. see Kunetz, Geza.

Braekstad, H. L. The Constitution of the Kingdom of Norway: An Historical & Political Survey. xiv, 75p. 1998. reprint ed. 40.00 (*1-56169-436-3*) Gaunt.

Braekstad, H. L., tr. Swedish Folk Tales. (Library of Folklore). (Illus.). 190p. (J). (gr. 3-4). 1998. 12.50 (*0-7818-0717-4*) Hippocrene Bks.

Braem, Thomas. Cardiovascular System. 1993. pap. text 19.95 (*1-878576-25-9*) Flash Anatomy Inc.

— Digestive System. 1994. pap. text 19.95 (*1-878576-27-5*) Flash Anatomy Inc.

— Endocrine System. 1994. pap. text 19.95 (*1-878576-34-8*) Flash Anatomy Inc.

— Integument System. 1994. pap. text 19.95 (*1-878576-30-5*) Flash Anatomy Inc.

— Lymphatic System. 1994. pap. 19.95 (*1-878576-26-7*) Flash Anatomy Inc.

— Nervous System. 1994. pap. text 19.95 (*1-878576-28-3*) Flash Anatomy Inc.

— Reproductive System. 1994. pap. text 19.95 (*1-878576-32-1*) Flash Anatomy Inc.

— Respiratory System. 1994. pap. text 19.95 (*1-878576-31-3*) Flash Anatomy Inc.

— Special Senses. 1994. pap. text 19.95 (*1-878576-29-1*) Flash Anatomy Inc.

— Urogenital System. 1994. pap. text 19.95 (*1-878576-33-X*) Flash Anatomy Inc.

Braeman, John. Before the Civil Rights Revolution: The Old Courts & Individual Rights. 41. LC 87-32291. (Contributions in Legal Studies: No. 41). 225p. 1988. 59.95 (*0-313-26205-5*, BCY/, Greenwood Pr) Greenwood.

Braeman, Kathryn M. & Shellenberger, Fran, eds. From Yellow Pads to Computers: Transforming Your Law Office with a Computer. LC 91-71125. 360p. 1991. pap. 69.95 (*0-89707-676-1*, 541-0289) Amer Bar Assn.

Braen, G. Richard, jt. auth. see Jenkins, Jon L.

Braendle, Bob, jt. auth. see Richards, Carl.

Braendlin, Bonnie, ed. Cultural Power - Cultural Literacy: Selected Papers from the 14th Florida State University Conference on Literature & Film. 200p. (C). 1991. pap. 19.95 (*0-8130-1096-9*) U Press Fla.

Braendlin, Bonnie & Braendlin, Hans, eds. Authority & Transgression in Literature & Film: Selected Papers from the Eighteenth Annual Florida State University Conference on Literature & Film. LC 96-7734. (Selected Papers on Literature & Film). 192p. (C). 1996. pap. 17.95 (*0-8130-1436-0*) U Press Fla.

Braendlin, Hans, ed. Ambiguities in Literature & Film. 140p. (Orig.). 1988. pap. 19.95 (*0-8130-0893-X*) U Press Fla.

Braendlin, Hans, jt. ed. see Braendlin, Bonnie.

Braess, D. Nonlinear Approximation Theory. (Computational Mathematics Ser.: Vol. 7). (Illus.). 305p. 1986. 139.95 (*0-387-13625-8*) Spr-Verlag.

Braess, D. & Schumaker, Larry L., eds. Numerical Methods in Approximation Theory, Vol. 9. LC 92-34850. (International Series of Numerical Mathematics: Vol. 105). xiv, 357p. 1992. 122.00 (*0-8176-2746-4*) Birkhauser.

Braess, Dietrich. Finite Element Methods. Schumaker, Larry L., tr. from GER. LC 97-171698. (Illus.). 339p. (C). 1997. text 74.95 (*0-521-58187-7*) Cambridge U Pr.

— Finite Elements: Theory, Fast Solvers & Applications in Solid Mechanics. Schumaker, Larry L., tr. from GER. LC 97-171698. (Illus.). 339p. (C). 1997. pap. text 28.95 (*0-521-58834-0*) Cambridge U Pr.

Braestrup, Kate. Onion. 1999. pap. write for info. (*0-14-012335-0*, Viking) Viking Penguin.

Braet, H., et al, eds. The Theatre in the Middle Ages. No. 13. 388p. (Orig.). 1985. pap. 67.50 (*90-6186-175-6*, Pub. by Leuven Univ) Coronet Bks.

Braet, H. H. & Verbeke, W., eds. Death in the Middle Ages. No. 9. 300p. (Orig.). 1983. pap. 57.50 (*90-6186-136-5*, Pub. by Leuven Univ) Coronet Bks.

Braetter, P. & Schramel, Peter, eds. Trace Element Analytical Chemistry in Medicine & Biology Vol. 3: Proceedings of the 3rd International Workshop. LC 80-26803. (Illus.). xvi, 763p. 1984. 219.25 (*3-11-009821-0*) De Gruyter.

Braetter, Peter & Schramel, Peter, eds. Trace Element Analytical Chemistry in Medicine & Biology, Vol. 2. 1189p. 1983. 253.85 (*3-11-008681-6*) De Gruyter.

Braeunlich, P., ed. Thermally Stimulated Relaxation in Solids. (Topics in Applied Physics Ser.: Vol. 37). (Illus.). 1979. 93.95 (*0-387-09595-0*) Spr-Verlag.

Braff, Kourtney M. Marks & Remarks on a Year of Traveling. (Illus.). 146p. (Orig.). 1993. 75.00 (*0-9637534-0-1*); pap. 25.00 (*0-9637534-1-X*) Thalagoya Pr.

Braff, Richard E. The Universal Silents: A Filmography of the Universal Motion Picture Manufacturing Company, 1912-1929. LC 98-3272. (Illus.). 683p. 1998. lib. bdg. 135.00 (*0-7864-0287-3*) McFarland & Co.

*__Braffort, A., et al, eds.__ Gesture-Based Communication in Human-Computer Interaction: International Gesture Workshop, GW'99, Gif-Sur-Yvette, France, March 17-19, 1999, Proceedings. (Lecture Notes in Artificial Intelligence Ser.: Vol. 1739). xi, 333p. 2000. pap. 56.00 (*3-540-66935-3*) Spr-Verlag.

Braford, M. R., Jr., ed. Evolution of the Forebrain Vol. 46, Nos. 4-5, 1995: Journal: Brain, Behavior & Evolution, 1995. (Journal Ser.: Vol. 46, No. 4-5, 1995). (Illus.). 158p. 1995. pap. 55.75 (*3-8055-6255-1*) S Karger.

Braga, A. P., compiled by. Policy Insurance. rev. ed. LC 93-90021. (Illus.). 146p. 1993. 14.95 (*0-939205-52-1*) S Station Bks.

Braga, Antone P., compiled by. Compiled by A. P. Braga. LC 81-65344. (Illus.). 146p. 1993. pap. 14.95 (*0-939206-02-1*, Acorn MA) S Station Bks.

*__Braga, Carlos Alberto Primo, et al.__ Intellectual Property Rights & Economic Development. LC 00-23812. (World Bank Discussion Paper Ser.). 2000. write for info. (*0-8213-4708-X*) World Bank.

*__Braga, Dario, et al.__ Crystal Engineering: From Molecules & Crystals to Materials LC 99-26682. (Nato Advanced Study Institutes Ser.). 1999. write for info. (*0-7923-5898-8*, Kluwer Plenum) Kluwer Academic.

*__Braga de Macedo, Jorge & Kabbaj, Omar, eds.__ Reform & Growth in Africa. (Development Centre Seminars Ser.). 204p. 2000. pap. 41.00 (*92-64-17644-6*, 41 2000 04 1 P, Pub. by Org for Econ) OECD.

Braga, James. Como Estudar A Biblia.Tr. of How to Study the Bible. (POR.). 152p. 1990. pap. 7.95 (*0-8297-1707-2*) Vida Pubs.

— Como Preparar Mensajes. Orig. Title: How to Prepare Bible Messages. (POR.). 228p. 1986. pap. 8.95 (*0-8297-1609-2*) Vida Pubs.

— Como Preparar Mensajes Biblicos. Orig. Title: How to Prepare Bible Messages. (SPA.). 320p. 1986. pap. 9.99 (*0-8254-1072-X*, Edit Portavoz) Kregel.

— Descubriendo Memorizacion de las Escrituras. (Serie Discipulado - Discipleship Ser.).Tr. of Discovering Scripture Memory. (SPA.). 1992. pap. 1.99 (*1-56063-360-3*, 498253) Editorial Unilit.

— How to Prepare Bible Messages. rev. ed. LC 81-14132. 257p. (C). 1982. pap. 10.99 (*0-930014-71-5*, Multnomah Bks) Multnomah Pubs.

Braga, Joyce. The Friary. 187p. (YA). (gr. 10 up). 2000. pap. 9.99 (*0-88092-302-4*, 3024) Royal Fireworks.

Braga, Newton. CMOS Projects & Experiments: Fun with the 4093 IC. LC 99-40938. 256p. 1999. pap. 29.95 (*0-7506-7170-X*, Newnes) Buttrwrth-Heinemann.

— Fun Projects for the Experimenter. LC 98-66667. (Illus.). 328p. 1998. pap. 24.95 (*0-7906-1149-X*) Prompt Publns.

*__Braga, Newton.__ Sourcebook for Electronics Calculations, Formulas & Tables. 1999. pap. 34.95 (*0-7906-1193-7*) Prompt Publns.

*__Braga, Newton C.__ Electronic Projects from the Next Dimension: Paranormal Experiments for Hobbyists. (Illus.). 256p. 2000. pap. 29.95 (*0-7506-7305-2*, Newnes) Buttrwrth-Heinemann.

— Pirate Radio & Video. 304p. 2000. pap. 29.95 (*0-7506-7331-1*, Newnes) Buttrwrth-Heinemann.

Braga, P. C., jt. ed. see Guslandi, M.

Braga, Pier C. & Allegra, Luigi, eds. Cough. LC 89-3920. (Illus.). 254p. 1989. reprint ed. pap. 78.80 (*0-608-05839-4*, 205980500007) Bks Demand.

— Drugs in Bronchial Mucology. LC 88-39127. (Bronchial Mucology Ser.). 382p. 1989. reprint ed. pap. 118.50 (*0-608-03389-8*, 206408600008) Bks Demand.

— Lungscapes. LC 92-9560. (Illus.). 112p. 1992. 108.00 (*0-387-55249-9*) Spr-Verlag.

— Methods in Bronchial Mucology. LC 86-42945. 424p. 1988. reprint ed. pap. 131.50 (*0-608-04725-2*, 206544600004) Bks Demand.

Braga, Pier C., jt. ed. see Allegra, Luigi.

Braga, Pier Carlo, ed. Drugs in Gastroenterology. 546p. 1991. text 67.00 (*0-88167-864-3*) Lppncott W & W.

Braga, Roman. Exploring the Inner Universe: Joy - The Mistery of Life. Gabriella & Shelden, Ruxandra, eds. LC 96-77519. 154p. (Orig.). 1996. pap. text 10.95 (*0-9643478-2-2*) HDM Pr.

— On the Way of Faith: Faith, Freedom & Love. Gabriella & Shelden, Ruxandra, eds. Nektaria, Veloff, tr. from RUM. LC 96-77520. (RUM., Illus.). 225p. (Orig.). 1997. pap. text 15.00 (*0-9643478-1-4*) HDM Pr.

Braga, Roman, et al. Pe Drumul Credintei: Arhimandrit Roman Braga. HDM Press, Inc. Staff, ed. & intro. by. (Illus.). 358p. (Orig.). 1995. pap. 17.00 (*0-9643478-0-6*) HDM Pr.

Bragadin, Marc'Antonio. The Italian Navy in World War II. Hoffman, Gale, tr. LC 79-6102. (Navies & Men Ser.). (Illus.). 1980. reprint ed. lib. bdg. 35.95 (*0-405-13031-7*) Ayer.

Bragadir, Sabine, jt. auth. see Dioudonnat, Pierre-Marie.

Bragan, Bobby & Guinn, Jeff. You Can't Hit the Ball with the Bat on Your Shoulder: The Baseball Life & Times of Bobby Bragan. (Illus.). 360p. 1992. 19.95 (*1-56530-015-7*) Summit TX.

Bragan, Bobby, jt. auth. see Guinn, Jeff.

Bragan, Jeris E. Beyond Prison Walls: The Jeris Bragan Story. LC 93-12995. 1993. 16.99 (*0-8280-0716-0*) Review & Herald.

Bragan, Kenneth. The Clinical Relevance of the Self. 136p. (C). 1996. pap. 22.99 (*0-415-12788-2*, C0570) Routledge.

— The Clinical Relevance of the Self. 136p. (C). 1996. 60.00 (*0-415-12787-4*, C0569) Routledge.

Braganti, Nancy L. & Devine, Elizabeth. European Customs & Manners. rev. ed. LC 91-42042. (Illus.). 277p. 1992. pap. 10.00 (*0-88166-190-2*) Meadowbrook.

— European Customs & Manners. rev. ed. LC 91-42042. 320p. 1992. 10.00 (*0-671-76030-0*) S&S Trade.

— The Travelers' Guide to Latin American Customs & Manners. (Illus.). 240p. 1989. pap. 14.95 (*0-312-02303-0*) St Martin.

Braganti, Nancy L., ed. see Devine, Elizabeth.

Braganza, Ashley. Business Process Redesign: A View from the Inside. 256p. 1997. pap. 39.99 (*1-86152-187-1*) Thomson Learn.

Braganza, Ashley & Myers, Andrew. Business Process Redesign: A View from the Inside. 264p. 1997. pap. 60.95 (*0-412-74970-X*, Pub. by ITBP) Thomson Learn.

— Business Process Redesign: Inside the Public Sector. 264p. 1996. 45.00 (*0-412-74980-7*) Chapman & Hall.

Braganza, Joan M., ed. New Developments of the Aetiogenesis of Chronic Pancreatitis - Implications for Treatment & Disease Prophylaxis: Symposium Held During the World Congresses of Gastroenterology, Vienna, September 1998, Vol.59. (Digestion Ser.: Vol. 59, Suppl. 4). (Illus.). iv, 60p. 1998. pap. 48.00 (*3-8055-6804-5*) S Karger.

Bragaw, Don & Thomson, Scott D., eds. Multicultural Education: A Global Approach. 300p. (C). 1992. ring bd. 45.00 (*0-944675-51-4*) Amer Forum.

Bragaw, Donald H., jt. ed. see Wronski, Stanley P.

Bragaw, Louis K. Managing a Federal Agency: The Hidden Stimulus. LC 79-27702. (Illus.). 320p. 1980. reprint ed. pap. 99.20 (*0-608-05929-3*, 206626500008) Bks Demand.

Bragdon, Allen. How Sharp Is Your Pencil? 432p. 1999. pap. 17.95 (*0-916410-64-1*, Pub. by A D Bragdon) IPG Chicago.

Bragdon, Allen & Gamon, David. Building Left-Brain Power: Neuron-Strengthening Exercises & Tips to Improve Mood, Develop Language & Math Facility, & Build Uniquely Human Skills. 320p. 1999. pap. 12.95 (*0-916410-63-3*, Pub. by A D Bragdon) IPG Chicago.

*__Bragdon, Allen D., ed.__ Floral Crafts. (Illus.). 112p. 2000. reprint ed. pap. 20.00 (*0-7881-9449-6*) DIANE Pub.

Bragdon, Allen D. & Fellows, Leonard. Exercises for the Whole Brain: Neuron-Builders to Stimulate & Entertain Your Visual, Math & Executive-Planning Skills. 128p. 1999. pap. 7.95 (*0-916410-65-X*, Pub. by A D Bragdon) IPG Chicago.

*__Bragdon, Allen D. & Gamon, David.__ Brains That Work a Little Bit Differently: Recent Discoveries about 10 Common Mental Diversities. (Illus.). 128p. 2000. pap. 7.95 (*0-916410-67-6*, Pub. by A D Bragdon) IPG Chicago.

— Brains That Work a Little Bit Differently: Recent Discoveries about 10 Common Mental Diversities. LC 00-34265. 2000. write for info. (*0-916410-92-7*) A D Bragdon.

— Learning & Remembering: How New & Old Brains Acquire & Recall Information: Recent Discoveries, Practical Applications, Performance Tests, Skill-Building Exercises from Infancy to Old-Age. (Illus.). 128p. 2000. pap. 7.95 (*0-916410-69-2*, Pub. by A D Bragdon) IPG Chicago.

— Use It Or Lose It! How to Protect Your Most Valuable Possession - Mind Maintenance Techniques, Tests of Mental Acuity, Entertaining Exercises for Specific Mental Tasks. (Illus.). 128p. 2000. pap. 7.95 (*0-916410-68-4*, Pub. by A D Bragdon) IPG Chicago.

Bragdon, Allen D. & Monbleau, Marcia. Right Brain Teasers - A Photo-Quiz for the Mind's Eye: Can You Tell What These 75 Old-Time Utensils Were Used For? 160p. 1999. pap. 9.95 (*0-916410-66-8*, Pub. by A D Bragdon) IPG Chicago.

Bragdon, Allend D., jt. auth. see Gamon, David.

Bragdon, Claude. The Arch Lectures: Eighteen Discourses on a Great Variety of Subjects. LC 77-92505. (Essay Index in Reprint Ser.). (Illus.). 1978. reprint ed. 25.00 (*0-8486-3000-9*) Roth Pub Inc.

— The Beautiful Necessity: Seven Essays on Theosophy & Architecture. (Illus.). 101p. 1995. reprint ed. pap. 15.95 (*1-56459-513-7*) Kessinger Pub.

— Episodes from an Unwritten History. 109p. 1974. spiral bd. 8.00 (*0-7873-0118-3*) Hlth Research.

— Episodes from an Unwritten History. 108p. 1997. pap. 9.00 (*0-89540-322-6*, SB-322) Sun Pub.

— Episodes from an Unwritten History (1910) 108p. 1996. reprint ed. pap. 7.95 (*1-56459-855-1*) Kessinger Pub.

— The Eternal Poles. 110p. 1998. reprint ed. pap. 14.95 (*0-7661-0138-X*) Kessinger Pub.

— Four Dimensional Vistas. 138p. 1995. reprint ed. pap. 16.95 (*1-56459-511-0*) Kessinger Pub.

— An Introduction to Yoga. 106p. 1996. reprint ed. pap. 14.95 (*1-56459-582-X*) Kessinger Pub.

— Merely Players (1905) 220p. 1998. reprint ed. pap. 19.95 (*0-7661-0159-2*) Kessinger Pub.

— More Lives Than One (1917) 374p. 1998. reprint ed. pap. 24.95 (*0-7661-0263-7*) Kessinger Pub.

— New Image. (Illus.). 198p. 1998. reprint ed. pap. 19.95 (*0-7661-0427-3*) Kessinger Pub.

— Old Lamps for the New: The Ancient Wisdom in the Modern World. 201p. 1998. reprint ed. pap. 16.95 (*0-7661-0139-8*) Kessinger Pub.

— Primer of Higher Space (1939) 84p. 1998. reprint ed. pap. 12.95 (*0-7661-0468-0*) Kessinger Pub.

— Projective Ornament. (Illus.). 96p. 1992. reprint ed. pap. 3.95 (*0-486-27117-X*) Dover.

— Projective Ornament (1915) 80p. 1998. reprint ed. pap. 14.95 (*0-7661-0177-0*) Kessinger Pub.

— Yoga for You. 122p. 1997. reprint ed. pap. 16.95 (*0-7661-0028-6*) Kessinger Pub.

Bragdon, Claude F. Architecture & Democracy. (Illus.). 213p. 1977. 17.95 (*0-8369-2386-3*) Ayer.

— Frozen Fountain. LC 75-127589. (Essay Index Reprint Ser.). 1977. 18.95 (*0-8369-1784-7*) Ayer.

— Merely Players. LC 72-5692. (Essay Index Reprint Ser.). 1977. reprint ed. 22.95 (*0-8369-2983-7*) Ayer.

Bragdon, Emma. A Sourcebook for Helping People with Spiritual Problems. 2nd rev. ed. (Illus.). 320p. (C). 1994. reprint ed. pap. 14.95 (*0-9620960-1-6*) Lightening Up Pr.

Bragdon, Helen C., ed. see Jilinsky, Andrius.

Bragdon, Henry W. Woodrow Wilson: The Academic Years. LC 67-27081. (Illus.). 536p. reprint ed. pap. 166.20 (*0-7837-4480-3*, 204418800001) Bks Demand.

Bragdon, Henry W. & Eliot, Thomas H. The Bright Constellation: Documents of American Democracy. rev. ed. (Illus.). 277p. (gr. 10-12). 1980. pap. text 8.95 (*0-88334-129-8*) Longman.

Bragdon, Henry W., et al. History of a Free Nation: Teacher's Wraparound Edition. LC 97-227347. 1998. teacher ed. write for info. (*0-02-821384-X*) Glencoe.

Bragdon, Kathleen, jt. auth. see Goddard, Ives.

Bragdon, Kathleen J. Native People of Southern New England, 1500-1650. LC 95-42067. (Civilization of the American Indian Ser.: Vol. 221). (Illus.). 328p. (C). 1996. 28.95 (*0-8061-2803-8*, 2803) U of Okla Pr.

— Native People of Southern New England, 1500-1650, Vol. 221. 1999. pap. text 16.95 (*0-8061-3126-8*) U of Okla Pr.

Bragdon, Lester M. & Frost, John E. York, Maine, Vital Records of, Prior to 1892. LC 91-60426. 832p. 1992. 59.50 (*0-929539-87-7*, 1187) Picton Pr.

Bragdon, Nancy H., jt. auth. see Katzev, Aphra R.

Brager & Perrin, J.S., eds. Effects of Radiation on Materials: 11th International Symposium - STP 782. 1225p. 1982. 69.50 (*0-8031-0753-6*, STP782) ASTM.

Brager, Bruce L. Adolf Eichmann, the Holocaust on Trial. LC 98-30258. (Famous Trials Ser.). (Illus.). 96-128p. (YA). (gr. 4-12). 1998. lib. bdg. 23.70 (*1-56006-469-2*) Lucent Bks.

*__Brager, Bruce L.__ From Santa Anna to Saddam. LC 99-49866. 2000. write for info. (*1-57168-371-2*, Eakin Pr) Sunbelt Media.

Brager, George A. & Holloway, Stephen M. Changing Human Service Organizations: Politics & Practice. LC 77-87572. 1978. 27.95 (*0-02-904620-3*) Free Pr.

Brager, George A., et al. Community Organizing. 2nd ed. LC 72-8947. 416p. 1987. text 46.00 (*0-231-05462-9*) Col U Pr.

Brager, George A., jt. auth. see Holloway, Stephen M.

Bragg. Introduction to Computers. 1998. 6.50 (*0-07-230629-7*) McGraw.

— On Giant's Shoulders: Great Scientists & Their Discovers--From Architect. LC 99-29005. 368p. 1999. 22.95 (*0-471-35732-4*) Wiley.

Bragg, Alicia, jt. auth. see McLellan, Tom.

Bragg, Alyce F. This Holler Is My Home. 182p. (Orig.). 1993. 12.95 (*0-941092-26-7*) Mtn St Pr.

Bragg, B. J. & Robinson, Dawn. Towne. Maternal Lines of William Towne Descendants. (Illus.). 156p. 1997. pap. 24.50 (*0-8328-9527-X*); lib. bdg. 34.50 (*0-8328-9526-1*) Higginson Bk Co.

Bragg, Bernard & Bergman, Eugene. Lessons in Laughter: The Autobiography of a Deaf Actor. LC 89-1493. (Illus.). 237p. 1989. 19.95 (*0-930323-46-7*) Gallaudet Univ Pr.

An Asterisk (*) at the beginning of an entry indicates that the title is appearing for the first time.

Bragg, Bernard & Olson, Jack. Meeting Halfway in American Sign Language: A Common Ground for Effective Communication among Deaf & Hearing People. 192p. 1994. lib. bdg. 39.95 (*0-9634016-7-X*) MSM Prods.

Bragg, C. Kaye, jt. auth. see Grammy, Abbas P.

Bragg, Cathy A. Word Search: Having Fun with Medical Terminology. Zagury, Carolyn S., ed. LC 96-62089. 280p. 1997. pap. 10.95 (*1-880254-42-5*) Vista.

Bragg, Charles. Charles Bragg on Medicine. (Illus.). 80p. (Orig.). 1984. mass mkt. 7.95 (*0-446-38059-8*, Pub. by Warner Bks) Little.

— Charles Bragg on the Law. (Illus.). 80p. (Orig.). 1984. mass mkt. 7.95 (*0-446-38057-1*, Pub. by Warner Bks) Little.

Bragg, Charles, jt. auth. see Bisbort, Alan.

Bragg, David, et al. Micro File Pro 2.1 for the MAC. 54p. 1998. pap. 4.50 (*0-07-230632-7*) McGraw.

— Microsoft Excel 4.0 for the MAC. 78p. 1998. pap. 5.25 (*0-07-230646-7*) McGraw.

— Microsoft Hypercard 2.1. 90p. 1998. pap. 5.74 (*0-07-230631-9*) McGraw.

— Microsoft Word 98 for the MAC. 65p. 1998. pap. 5.25 (*0-07-230628-9*) McGraw.

Bragg, David F. & Curry, Michael. Texas DTPA Forms & Practice Guide. 500p. 1997. ring bd. 149.00 incl. disk (*1-58012-010-5*) James Pub Santa Ana.

Bragg, David G., jt. auth. see Freundlich, Irwin M.

***Bragg, Desmond & Joslin, Paul.** Science Meets the UFO Enigma. LC 99-48359. 2000. 27.95 (*1-56072-742-X*) Nova Sci Pubs.

***Bragg, Donald & Bragg, Matthew J., eds.** Survival: The Unidentified Stage of Grieving. LC 99-97641. 2000. 10.00 (*0-9668844-5-0*) Cameo Pubg.

Bragg, Emma W. Golden Anniversary Class Reunion. 3rd ed. 230p. 1982. pap. 25.00 (*0-9611930-7-7*) E W Bragg.

— Profile of Work Motivation Attitudes of Apparel Workers. LC 79-17776. 1979. 18.00 (*0-8357-0460-2*) E W Bragg.

— Scrapbook: Some Family Reminiscences of a Native Nashville Septuagenarian. LC 85-73699. (Illus.). 50p. (Orig.). 1985. pap. 25.00 (*0-9611930-2-6*) E W Bragg.

— Susanna McGavock Carter: The Trusted Housekeeper Slave of General William Giles Harding of Nashville's Belle Meade Plantation. LC 93-71143. (Illus.). 30p. (Orig.). 1993. 25.00 (*0-9611930-3-4*) E W Bragg.

— Work Motivation Attitudes of Apparel Workers: Methodology Used in the Study. LC 83-61829. (Illus.). 186p. 1983. pap. 24.75 (*0-9611930-0-X*) E W Bragg.

Bragg, Gail. An Historiography of American Slave Women. LC 84-1811. (CompuBibs Ser.: No. 6). 24p. 1984. pap. 8.50 (*0-914791-00-1*) Vantage Info.

— An Historiography of the American Woman Suffrage Movement. LC 84-1810. (CompuBibs Ser.: No. 5). 26p. 1984. pap. 8.50 (*0-914791-01-X*) Vantage Info.

Bragg, George F., Jr. History of the Afro-American Group of the Episcopal Church. (Illus.). 319p. 1998. reprint ed. pap. 45.00 (*1-58073-011-6*) BCP Bks.

Bragg, Gordon, jt. ed. see Strauss, Werner.

Bragg, Jefferson D. Louisiana in the Confederacy. LC 96-49698. 339p. 1997. pap. 16.95 (*0-8071-2179-7*) La State U Pr.

Bragg, Joseph H., Jr., ed. Moments with Children in Worship. 136p. (Orig.). 1989. pap. 9.99 (*0-8272-2320-X*) Chalice Pr.

Bragg, L. E. More Than Petticoats: Remarkable Washington Women. LC 98-7356. (Illus.). 208p. 1998. pap. 9.95 (*1-56044-667-6*) Falcon Pub Inc.

— Seattle, City by the Sound. LC 97-60333. (Illus.). 32p. 1997. 15.95 (*0-9656755-0-5*) East Seattle Pub.

Bragg, Lawrence. The Development of X-Ray Analysis. rev. unabridged ed. Phillips, D. C. & Lipson, H., eds. LC 92-39217. (Illus.). 270p. 1993. reprint ed. pap. text 8.95 (*0-486-67316-2*) Dover.

Bragg, Linda B. Rainbow Roun' Mah Shoulder. 134p. (Orig.). 1984. pap. 7.00 (*0-932112-20-X*) Carolina Wren.

Bragg, Linda W. Fundamental Gymnastics. LC 94-40770. (Fundamental Sports Ser.). (Illus.). 80p. (J). (gr. 3-6). 1995. lib. bdg. 19.93 (*0-8225-3453-3*) Lerner Pub.

***Bragg, Linda Wallenberg.** Gymnastics. LC 99-56745. (Play-by-Play Ser.). (Illus.). 80p. (YA). (gr. 6). 2000. pap. 7.95 (*0-8225-9877-9*, LernerSports) Lerner Pub.

Bragg, Lisa. Living in Sin. LC 97-76654. 112p. 1997. pap. 9.95 (*0-9612974-1-7*) Patten Pr Inc.

Bragg, Lois. The Lyric Speakers of Old English Poetry. LC 89-46414. 1991. 32.50 (*0-8386-3403-6*) Fairleigh Dickinson.

***Bragg, Lois, ed.** Deaf World: A Historical Reader & Primary Sourcebook. 2001. 70.00 (*0-8147-9852-7*) NYU Pr.

Bragg, Lynn E. A River Lost. LC 97-158586. (Illus.). 32p. (Orig.). (J). (gr. 2-8). 1995. pap. 12.95 (*0-88839-383-0*) Hancock House.

Bragg, M. M., ed. Memorial History of Utica, from Its Settlement to the Present Time. With Biographical Sketches. (Illus.). 736p. 1997. reprint ed. lib. bdg. 75.00 (*0-8328-6266-5*) Higginson Bk Co.

Bragg, Mary. Re-Inventing Influence: How to Get Things Done in a World Without Authority. (Illus.). 225p. (Orig.). 1996. pap. text 17.95 (*0-273-62313-3*) F T P-H.

Bragg, Matthew J., jt. ed. see Bragg, Donald.

Bragg, Melvyn. Great Artist. 1987. 17.98 (*0-671-08650-2*) PB.

— Land of the Lakes. (Illus.). 248p. 1991. pap. 24.95 (*0-340-52372-7*, Pub. by Hodder & Stought Ltd) Trafalgar.

***Bragg, Melvyn.** On Giants' Shoulders: Great Scientists & Their Discoveries -- From Archimedes to DNA. 2000. pap. 16.95 (*0-471-39684-2*) Wiley.

Bragg, Melvyn. Richard Burton: A Life. (Illus.). 1989. 22.95 (*0-316-10595-3*) Little.

— Richard Burton: A Life. 1990. mass mkt. 5.95 (*0-446-35938-6*, Pub. by Warner Bks) Little.

— The Seventh Seal. (Illus.). 72p. (C). 1993. pap. 10.95 (*0-85170-391-7*, Pub. by British Film Inst) Ind U Pr.

Bragg, Patricia. Bragg Healthy Lifestyle Vol. 1: Vital Living to 120! 2000. pap. text 7.95 (*0-87790-002-7*) Hlth Sci.

Bragg, Patricia & Bragg, Paul C. Bragg Fitness Program with Spine Motion: Unique Exercises to Banish Backaches. 13th rev. ed. (Illus.). 80p. 1991. pap. 3.95 (*0-87790-054-X*) Hlth Sci.

— Bragg Gourmet Health Recipes: For Life Extension & Vital, Healthy Living to 120. 18th rev. ed. (Illus.). 448p. 1991. pap. 8.95 (*0-87790-031-0*) Hlth Sci.

— Keep Your Heart & Cardiovascular System Healthy & Fit at Any Age! 15th rev. ed. (Illus.). 160p. 2000. pap. 7.95 (*0-87790-096-5*) Hlth Sci.

— The Miracle of Fasting: Proven Throughout History for Physical, Mental & Spiritual Rejuvenation. (Illus.). 272p. 1999. pap. 8.95 (*0-87790-036-1*, Pub. by Hlth Sci) Natl Bk Netwk.

Bragg, Patricia, jt. auth. see Bragg, Paul C.

Bragg, Paul C. & Bragg, Patricia. Apple Cider Vinegar: Miracle Health System. (Illus.). 128p. 1998. pap. 6.95 (*0-87790-042-6*, Pub. by Hlth Sci) Natl Bk Netwk.

— Bragg Healthy Lifestyle: Vital Living to 120! Body Purification, Toxicless Diet & Healing System. Orig. Title: Bragg Toxicless Diet, Body Purification & Healing System. (Illus.). 160p. 1997. pap. 7.95 (*0-87790-004-3*, Pub. by Hlth Sci) Natl Bk Netwk.

— Super Power Breathing: For Super Energy, High Health & Longevity. 21st rev. ed. Orig. Title: Super Brain Breathing for Super Health & High Energy. (Illus.). 160p. 1999. pap. 7.95 (*0-87790-020-5*, Pub. by Hlth Sci) Natl Bk Netwk.

— Water: The Shocking Truth That Can Save Your Life! Orig. Title: The Shocking Truth about Water. (Illus.). 192p. 1999. pap. 7.95 (*0-87790-063-9*, Pub. by Hlth Sci) Natl Bk Netwk.

Bragg, Paul C., jt. auth. see Bragg, Patricia.

Bragg, Richard J. Trade Descriptions. 336p. 1992. text 85.00 (*0-19-825630-2*) OUP.

Bragg, Rick. All over but the Shoutin' LC 97-9918. 329p. 1997. 26.00 (*0-679-44258-8*) Pantheon.

— All over but the Shoutin' (Illus.). 352p. 1998. pap. 14.00 (*0-679-77402-5*) Vin Bks.

***Bragg, Rick.** Somebody Told Me: The Newspaper Stories of Rick Bragg. LC 99-50494. 344p. 2000. 24.95 (*0-8173-1027-4*) U of Ala Pr.

Bragg, Robert, jt. auth. see Pugh, Harry F.

Bragg, Ruth E. Changes & Choices: Personal Development & Relationships. LC 98-31561. 496p. 2000. 38.64 (*1-56637-514-2*) Goodheart.

***Bragg, Ruth E.** Computer Projects for Family & Consumer Sciences. (Illus.). 180p. 2000. pap. text 25.00 (*1-56637-603-3*) Goodheart.

Bragg, Ruth G. Alphabet Out Loud. LC 91-14546. (Illus.). 32p. (J). (gr. k up). 1991. pap. 14.95 (*0-88708-172-X*, Picture Book Studio) S&S Childrens.

— The Birthday Bears. LC 90-7385. (Illus.). 28p. (J). (gr. k up). 1991. pap. 14.95 (*0-88708-139-8*, Picture Book Studio) S&S Childrens.

— Colors of the Day. LC 92-7790. (Illus.). 40p. (J). 1992. pap. 14.95 (*0-88708-245-9*, Picture Book Studio) S&S Childrens.

— Mrs. Muggle's Sparkle. LC 89-31371. (Illus.). 28p. (J). (ps up). 1991. pap. 15.95 (*0-88708-106-1*, Picture Book Studio) S&S Childrens.

Bragg, Sadie, jt. auth. see George, Melvin D.

Bragg, Sara, et al. Improving Environmental Performance: A Guide to a Proven & Effective Approach. (Keynote Ser.). 96p. 1993. pap. 45.00 (*0-7123-0812-1*, Pub. by SRIS) L Erlbaum Assocs.

Bragg, Steven M. Accounting Best Practices. LC 99-21810. 288p. 1999. 59.95 (*0-471-33366-2*) Wiley.

***Bragg, Steven M.** Financial Analysis: A Controller's Guide. 560p. 2000. text 69.95 (*0-471-37672-8*) Wiley.

Bragg, Steven M. Just in Time Accounting: How to Decrease Costs & Increase Efficiency. LC 96-11201. 416p. 1996. 85.00 (*0-471-13768-5*) Wiley.

— Outsourcing: A Guide to . . . Selecting the Correct Business Unit . . . Negotiating the Contract . . . Maintaining Control of the Business. LC 98-9842. 384p. 1998. pap. 64.95 (*0-471-25268-9*) Wiley.

— Outsourcing: A Guide to . . . Selecting the Correct Business Unit . . . Negotiating the Contract . . . Maintaining Control of the Business, 1. LC 98-9842. 384p. 1998. 115.00 (*0-471-24728-6*) Wiley.

Bragg, Steven M. & Anderson, Janice R. The Controller's Function: The Work of the Managerial Accountant. LC 95-36044. (Illus.). 466p. 1996. 59.95 (*0-471-12529-6*) Wiley.

Bragg, Steven M. & Institute of Internal Auditors. Advanced Accounting Systems. LC 98-102735. (Illus.). 1997. write for info. (*0-89413-383-7*) Inst Inter Aud.

***Bragg, Steven M. & Lego, Paul G.** Managing Explosive Corporate Growth. LC 98-27427. 336p. 1998. 34.95 (*0-471-29689-9*) Wiley.

Bragg, Steven M., jt. auth. see Burton, E. James.

Bragg, Steven M., jt. auth. see Burton, Eric James.

Bragg, Steven M., jt. auth. see Roehl-Anderson, Janice M.

Bragg, Terry. 31 Days to High Self-Esteem: How to Change Your Life So You Have Joy, Bliss, & Abundance. (Illus.). 220p. (Orig.). 1997. pap. 19.95 (*0-9654663-0-2*) Peacemakers Trng.

Bragg, Wayne G., ed. from SPA. Sandino in the Streets. LC 90-25231. (Caribbean & Latin America Studies). (Illus.). 144p. 1991. reprint ed. pap. 44.70 (*0-608-09362-9*, 205410800002) Bks Demand.

Bragg, Wayne G., jt. auth. see Shultz, Eugene B.

Bragg, Wayne G., ed. see Interamerican Forum on Technological Development:.

Bragg, William. Car Buyer's & Leaser's Negotiation Book. LC 98-49712. 1999. pap. 14.95 (*0-375-70466-3*) Random Ref & Info.

Bragg, William H. Creative Knowledge. LC 74-134057. (Essay Index Reprint Ser.). 1977. 24.95 (*0-8369-2104-6*) Ayer.

— De Renne: Three Generations of a Georgia Family. LC 98-51167. (Wormsloe Foundation Publications: Vol. 21). (Illus.). 688p. 1999. text 50.00 (*0-8203-2089-7*) U of Ga Pr.

— Joe Brown's Army: The Georgia State Line, 1862-1865. LC 87-1548. (Illus.). 192p. 1987. pap. 16.95 (*0-86554-262-7*, P119) Mercer Univ Pr.

***Bragg, William Harris.** Griswoldville. LC 99-58824. (Illus.). 224p. 2000. 29.95 (*0-86554-678-9*) Mercer Univ Pr.

Bragger. Allons-Voir. (College French Ser.). (C). 1992. text, teacher ed. 21.95 (*0-8384-2409-0*) Heinle & Heinle.

— Allons-Voir. (College French Ser.). (C). 1992. pap., suppl. ed. 61.25 (*0-8384-2408-2*) Heinle & Heinle.

— Allons-Voir. annot. ed. (College French Ser.). (C). 1992. pap., teacher ed. 30.75 (*0-8384-2415-5*) Heinle & Heinle.

— Allons Voir-grammar Review. (C). 1992. pap. text 12.50 (*0-8384-3897-0*) Heinle & Heinle.

— Allons-Y! 2nd ed. (College French Ser.). (C). Date not set. pap. 45.50 (*0-8384-1556-3*); pap., wbk. ed. write for info. (*0-8384-1558-X*) Heinle & Heinle.

— Allons-Y! 3rd ed. (College French Ser.). (C). 1992. pap., suppl. ed. 27.75 (*0-8384-2431-7*) Heinle & Heinle.

— Allons-Y! 3rd ed. (College French Ser.). (C). 1992. pap., suppl. ed. 15.00 (*0-8384-2634-4*) Heinle & Heinle.

— Allons-Y! 3rd ed. (College French Ser.). (C). 1992. pap., suppl. ed. 187.95 (*0-8384-2424-4*) Heinle & Heinle.

— Allons-Y! 4th ed. (College French Ser.). (FRE.). (C). 1995. mass mkt., teacher ed., suppl. ed. 4.95 (*0-8384-6458-0*) Heinle & Heinle.

— Allons-Y! 4th ed. (College French Ser.). (FRE.). (C). 1996. mass mkt., wbk. ed., lab manual ed. 36.95 (*0-8384-6455-6*) Heinle & Heinle.

— Allons-Y! 4th ed. (College French Ser.). (FRE.). (C). 1996. mass mkt., suppl. ed. 36.95 (*0-8384-6457-2*) Heinle & Heinle.

— Allons-Y! 4th annot. ed. (College French Ser.). (FRE.). (C). 1995. pap., teacher ed. 31.95 (*0-8384-6471-8*); pap., teacher ed. 31.95 (*0-8384-6472-6*) Heinle & Heinle.

— Allons-Y! Initiation a la Langue. 3rd ed. (College French Ser.). (C). 1992. 11.50 (*0-8384-2549-6*) Heinle & Heinle.

— Allons-Y! Tapescript. 3rd ed. (College French Ser.). (C). 1992. pap. 13.50 (*0-8384-2430-9*) Wadsworth Pub.

— Allons-Y! Teacher's Annotated Edition. 3rd ed. (College French Ser.). (C). 1992. pap. 45.50 (*0-8384-2428-7*) Wadsworth Pub.

— Branches Et Au Courant, Level 1. (Miscellaneous/ Catalogs Ser.). (FRE.). 2002. mass mkt., wbk. ed., lab manual ed. 30.95 (*0-8384-7393-8*) Heinle & Heinle.

— Du Tac Au Tac. 2nd ed. (College French Ser.). (FRE.). (C). 1991. mass mkt., teacher ed. 19.95 (*0-8384-2204-7*) Heinle & Heinle.

— Du Tac Au Tac. 2nd ed. (College French Ser.). 1991. pap. 36.95 (*0-8384-1979-8*) Wadsworth Pub.

— La France dans Tous Etats. (College French Ser.). (FRE.). (C). 1995. mass mkt., suppl. ed. 6.95 (*0-8384-5661-8*) Heinle & Heinle.

— La France dans Tous ses Etats. (College French Ser.). (FRE.). (C). 1995. mass mkt. 31.25 (*0-8384-4540-3*) Heinle & Heinle.

— La France dans Tous ses Etats. (College French Ser.). (FRE.). (C). 1995. suppl. ed. 91.95 incl. trans. (*0-8384-4544-6*) Heinle & Heinle.

— La France dans Tous ses Etats. (College French). (FRE.). (C). 1996. mass mkt. 47.95 (*0-8384-6081-X*) Heinle & Heinle.

— J'veux Bien. (College French Ser.). (FRE.). (C). 1994. mass mkt., student ed. 71.95 (*0-8384-4475-X*); teacher ed., suppl. ed. 4.95 incl. audio (*0-8384-4479-2*) Heinle & Heinle.

— J'veux Bien. (College French Ser.). (FRE.). (C). 1994. student ed., suppl. ed. 24.95 incl. audio (*0-8384-4478-4*) Heinle & Heinle.

— J'veux Bien. (College French Ser.). (FRE.). (C). 1995. mass mkt., suppl. ed. 36.95 (*0-8384-4480-6*) Heinle & Heinle.

— J'veux Bien. (College French Ser.). (FRE.). 1995. pap., wbk. ed. 33.95 (*0-8384-4477-6*) Heinle & Heinle.

— J'veux Bien. (College French Ser.). (FRE.). (C). 1995. suppl. ed. 39.95 incl. cd-rom (*0-8384-4485-7*) Heinle & Heinle.

— J'veux Bien. (College French Ser.). (FRE.). (C). 1996. suppl. ed. 91.95 incl. trans. (*0-8384-4484-9*) Heinle & Heinle.

— J'veux Bien! (College French Ser.). (FRE.). (C). 1996. text, suppl. ed. 21.95 (*0-8384-5362-7*) Heinle & Heinle.

— J'veux Bien. annot. ed. (College French Ser.). (FRE.). (C). 1994. mass mkt., teacher ed. 52.95 (*0-8384-4476-8*) Heinle & Heinle.

— New Secondary French, Level 1. (Miscellaneous/Catalogs Ser.). 2000. pap., wbk. ed., lab manual ed. 17.95 (*0-8384-7357-1*) Brooks-Cole.

— New Secondary French, Level 1. (Miscellaneous/Catalogs Ser.). 2000. pap. 47.95 (*0-8384-7339-3*) Heinle & Heinle.

— New Secondary French, Level 2. (Miscellaneous/Catalogs Ser.). 2002. mass mkt., student ed. 48.95 (*0-8384-7338-5*) Heinle & Heinle.

— On Y Va! 2nd ed. (Secondary French Ser.). (FRE.). 1994. mass mkt. 37.95 (*0-8384-5535-2*); mass mkt. 37.95 (*0-8384-5536-0*); mass mkt., wbk. ed. 7.95 (*0-8384-5537-9*); mass mkt., wbk. ed. 7.95 (*0-8384-5538-7*) Heinle & Heinle.

— On Y Va! 2nd ed. (Secondary French Ser.). (FRE.). 1994. mass mkt., teacher ed. 36.95 (*0-8384-5491-7*) Heinle & Heinle.

— On Y Va!, Level 1. 2nd ed. (Secondary French Ser.). (FRE.). 1993. mass mkt. 47.95 (*0-8384-4142-4*) Heinle & Heinle.

— On y Va!, Level 1, 2, 3. 2nd ed. (Secondary French Ser.). (FRE.). 1993. audio 18.95 (*0-8384-4182-3*) Heinle & Heinle.

— On y Va!, Level 3. (Secondary French Ser.). 1990. teacher ed. 18.95 (*0-8384-1936-4*) Heinle & Heinle.

— On Y Va! Level 1, Level 1. 2nd ed. (Secondary French Ser.). 1993. mass mkt., suppl. ed. 182.95 (*0-8384-4153-X*); suppl. ed. 196.95 incl. trans. (*0-8384-4156-4*) Heinle & Heinle.

— On Y Va! Level 1, Level 1. 2nd ed. (Secondary French Ser.). (FRE.). 1993. pap., wbk. ed., lab manual ed. 15.95 (*0-8384-4144-0*) Heinle & Heinle.

— On Y Va! Level 1, Level 1. 2nd ed. (Secondary French Ser.). 1993. mass mkt., teacher ed., wbk. ed. 18.95 (*0-8384-4145-9*); teacher ed., student ed. 19.95 incl. audio (*0-8384-4154-8*) Heinle & Heinle.

— On Y Va! Level 1, Level 1. 2nd ed. (Secondary French Ser.). 1993. suppl. ed. 62.95 incl. audio (*0-8384-4319-2*) Heinle & Heinle.

— On Y Va! Level 1, Level 1. 2nd annot. ed. (Secondary French Ser.). 1993. mass mkt., teacher ed. 56.95 (*0-8384-4143-2*) Heinle & Heinle.

— On Y Va! Level 2, Level 2. 2nd ed. (Secondary French Ser.). 1993. mass mkt., suppl. ed. 21.95 (*0-8384-4163-7*) Heinle & Heinle.

— On Y Va! Level 2, Level 2. 2nd ed. (Secondary French Ser.). (SPA.). 1993. mass mkt., wbk. ed., lab manual ed. 15.95 (*0-8384-4160-2*); suppl. ed. 196.95 incl. trans. (*0-8384-4171-8*) Heinle & Heinle.

— On Y Va! Level 2, Level 2. 2nd ed. (Secondary French Ser.). (FRE.). 1993. mass mkt. 49.95 (*0-8384-4158-0*) Heinle & Heinle.

— On Y Va! Level 2, Level 2. 2nd ed. (Secondary French Ser.). 1993. teacher ed., suppl. ed. 18.95 incl. audio (*0-8384-4170-X*); suppl. ed. 303.95 incl. audio (*0-8384-4162-9*) Heinle & Heinle.

— On Y Va! Level 2, Level 2. 2nd ed. (Secondary French Ser.). 1994. suppl. ed. 60.95 incl. audio (*0-8384-4191-2*) Heinle & Heinle.

— On Y Va! Level 2, Level 2. 2nd annot. ed. (Secondary French Ser.). (FRE.). 1993. mass mkt., teacher ed. 57.95 (*0-8384-4159-9*) Heinle & Heinle.

— On Y Va! Level 3, Level 3. 2nd ed. (Secondary French Ser.). (SPA.). 1993. mass mkt., wbk. ed., lab manual ed. 15.95 (*0-8384-4177-7*) Heinle & Heinle.

— On Y Va! Level 3, Level 3. 2nd ed. (Secondary French Ser.). (FRE.). 1993. mass mkt. 50.95 (*0-8384-4172-6*) Heinle & Heinle.

— On Y Va! Level 3, Level 3. 2nd ed. (Secondary French Ser.). 1993. suppl. ed. 196.95 incl. trans. (*0-8384-4180-7*) Heinle & Heinle.

— On Y Va! Level 3, Level 3. 2nd ed. (Secondary French Ser.). 1993. mass mkt., suppl. ed. 21.95 (*0-8384-4174-2*) Heinle & Heinle.

— On Y Va! Level 3, Level 3. 2nd ed. (Secondary French Ser.). 1993. teacher ed., suppl. ed. 18.95 incl. audio (*0-8384-4181-5*); suppl. ed. 62.95 incl. audio (*0-8384-4192-0*) Heinle & Heinle.

— On Y Va! Level 3, Level 3. 2nd ed. (Secondary French Ser.). 1994. suppl. ed. 303.95 incl. audio (*0-8384-4179-3*) Heinle & Heinle.

— On Y Va! Level 3, Level 3. 2nd annot. ed. (Secondary French Ser.). (FRE.). 1993. mass mkt., teacher ed. 59.95 (*0-8384-4173-4*) Heinle & Heinle.

— Quant a Moi. (College French Ser.). (FRE.). (C). 1996. mass mkt., teacher ed. 41.95 (*0-8384-6346-0*) Heinle & Heinle.

— Quant a Moi. (College French Ser.). (FRE.). (C). 1996. text, suppl. ed. 6.95 (*0-8384-6348-7*) Heinle & Heinle.

— Quant a Moi. (College French Ser.). (FRE.). (C). 1996. mass mkt., suppl. ed. 36.95 (*0-8384-6349-5*) Heinle & Heinle.

— Quant a Moi. 2nd ed. (College French Ser.). (FRE.). (C). 1996. suppl. ed. 14.95 incl. audio (*0-8384-6347-9*) Heinle & Heinle.

— A Split-New Secondary French Text B, Level 1. (Miscellaneous/Catalogs Ser.). 2002. text 34.95 (*0-8384-7384-9*) Heinle & Heinle.

— Teaching French Allons-Y! (College French Ser.). (C). Date not set. pap., teacher ed. 15.75 (*0-8384-1569-5*) Heinle & Heinle.

— Tee-New Secondary French, Level 3. (Miscellaneous/ Catalogs Ser.). 2002. pap. 52.95 (*0-8384-7301-6*) Heinle & Heinle.

— Videodisk Guide with Barcodes - Onyva Videodisk Guide with Barcodes, Level 1. 2nd ed. (Secondary French Ser.). 1994. pap. 13.95 (*0-8384-5439-9*) Heinle & Heinle.

Bragger & Rice. Allons-Y! 4th ed. (FRE.). 1996. text 54.00 incl. cd-rom (*0-8384-6474-2*) Heinle & Heinle.

— Allons-Y!, Bks. 1 & 2. 4th annot. ed. 1995. text, teacher ed. 55.00 (*0-8384-6454-8*) Heinle & Heinle.

***Bragger & Rice.** Allons Y: Instructor's Edition. 5th annot. ed. (C). 1999. pap. 52.00 (*0-8384-0248-8*) Thomson Learn.

Bragger & Rice. Branches Level 1: Teachers Resource Book. 2000. pap. text 45.00 (*0-8384-7419-5*) Thomson Learn.

— Branches Level 2: Teachers Annotated Edition. 2000. pap. text 41.00 (*0-8384-7437-3*) Thomson Learn.

***Bragger & Rice.** Branches Level 2: Teachers Resource Book. 2002. pap. text 45.00 (*0-8384-7400-4*) Thomson Learn.

B

Bragger & Rice. J'Veux Bien! (FRE.). 1995. text, wbk. ed. 43.25 incl. audio, cd-rom (*0-8384-4593-4*) Heinle & Heinle.
— J'Veux Bien! (FRE.). 1996. text, wbk. ed. 35.25 incl. cd-rom (*0-8384-6523-4*) Heinle & Heinle.
Bragger & Rice. J'Veux Bien! (FRE.). (C). 1994. text, wbk. ed. 43.50 incl. audio compact disk (*0-8384-5562-X*) Thomson Learn.
— J'Veux Bien! 2nd ed. (FRE.). text, student ed., wbk. ed. 66.40 (*0-8384-9705-5*) Heinle & Heinle.
Bragger & Rice. On y Va!, Level 2. 2nd ed. (SPA.). 1993. text, teacher ed., wbk. ed. 16.50 (*0-8384-4161-0*) Heinle & Heinle.
— On y Va!, Level 3. 2nd ed. (SPA.). 1993. pap. text, teacher ed., wbk. ed. 16.75 (*0-8384-4178-5*) Heinle & Heinle.
— Quant a Moi. (FRE.). 1996. text, wbk. ed. 33.00 incl. audio (*0-8384-5599-9*) Thomson Learn.
***Bragger & Rice.** Quant a Moi. 2nd ed. (C). 2000. text 46.95 (*0-8384-0585-1*) Heinle & Heinle.
Bragger, jt. auth. see Rice, Donald.
Bragger, J. & Rice, Donald. Allons-Y! Le Francais par Etapes. 2nd ed. (C). 1988. teacher ed. write for info. (*0-8384-1554-7*) Heinle & Heinle.
— Allons-Y! Le Francais par Etapes. 2nd ed. (C). 1988. pap., teacher ed. 45.50 (*0-8384-1557-1*); pap., student ed. 26.25 (*0-8384-1559-8*); audio 188.95 (*0-8384-1563-6*) Heinle & Heinle.
Bragger, Jeanette D. & Rice, Donald. Quant a Moi... Temoignages de France et Du Monde Francophone: Manuel de Classe. LC 95-40418. (FRE.). (C). 1996. mass mkt., student ed. 61.95 (*0-8384-6344-4*) Heinle & Heinle.
Bragger, Jeannette & Rice, Donald. Du Tac Au Tac: Managing Conversations in French. 2nd ed. (C). 1991. pap., teacher ed. write for info. (*0-8384-2119-9*) Heinle & Heinle.
— Du Tac Au Tac: Managing Conversations in French. 2nd ed. (C). 1991. pap. 37.95 incl. audio (*0-8384-2221-7*) Heinle & Heinle.
Bragger, Jeannette D. & Ariew, Robert. Chere Francoise: Revision de la Grammaire Francaise. 2nd ed. LC 83-81324. (FRE.). 368p. (C). 1984. audio 17.50 (*0-685-08250-4*) HM.
Bragger, Jeannette D. & Rice, Donald. Allons-Y! Le Francais Par Etapes. 4th ed. LC 95-42316. (College French Ser.). (FRE.). (C). 1995. mass mkt. 57.95 (*0-8384-6449-1*) Heinle & Heinle.
— Allons-Y! Le Francais par Etapes. 4th ed. LC 95-42316. (FRE.). (C). 1995. 57.95 incl. audio (*0-8384-6473-4*) Heinle & Heinle.
***Bragger, Jeannette D. & Rice, Donald.** Allons-Y! Le Franpcais par Betapes. 5th ed. LC 99-34261. 1999. 64.95 (*0-8384-0244-5*) Heinle & Heinle.
Bragger, Jeanette D. & Rice, Donald. Quant a Moi . . . Manuel de Preparation. 2nd ed. (FRE.). (C). 1996. pap. 36.95 (*0-8384-6345-2*) Heinle & Heinle.
Braggins, D. & Hollinghum, J. The Machine Vision Sourcebook. (Illus.). 250p. 1986. 205.95 (*0-387-16355-7*) Spr-Verlag.
***Braggins, Sheila.** Back Care: A Clinical Approach. LC 99-50230. 2000. write for info. (*0-443-06488-1*) Church.
Braggs, Earl. Walking Back from Woodstock. LC 96-78551. 1997. pap. 10.00 (*0-938078-45-3*) Anhinga Pr.
Braggs, Earl S. Hat Dancer Blue. (Anhinga Prize for Poetry, 1992 Ser.). 72p. (Orig.). (C). 1992. pap. 8.00 (*0-938078-36-4*) Anhinga Pr.
***Braggs, Earl S.** House on Fontanka. LC 00-101314. (Illus.). xii, 124p. 2000. pap. 12.00 (*0-938078-65-8*) Anhinga Pr.
Braghieri, Gianni. Aldo Rossi. 4th ed. (Studio Paperback Ser.). (FRE & GER., Illus.). 288p. 1996. pap. 29.95 (*3-7643-5560-3*, Pub. by Birkhauser) Princeton Arch.
Braghin, Andrea & Caruana, Edmund. The Jubilee Guide to Rome: The Four Basilicas: The Great Pilgrimage. Rouillard, Philippe et al, eds. Merola, Carmela, tr. LC 98-24140. (Illus.). 124p. 1998. pap. 11.95 (*0-8146-2535-5*) Liturgical Pr.
Braghine, Alexander. The Shadow of Atlantis: The Temple Church & the Temple. (Atlantis Reprint Ser.). (Illus.). 288p. 1997. reprint ed. pap. 16.95 (*0-932813-33-X*) Adventures Unltd.
Braght, Thieleman J. Van, see Van Braght, Thieleman J.
Braginski, Leon & Powell, Matthew. Running Microsoft Internet Information Server 3.0. LC 98-22764. 700p. 1997. pap. text 39.99 incl. cd-rom (*1-57231-585-7*) Microsoft.
***Braginsky, Benjamin.** On Being Expendable. 74p. 1998. pap. 8.00 (*0-8059-4258-0*) Dorrance.
Braginsky, Benjamin M. Dynamics of Expendability: A Study of the Abbreviation of Man. 124p. (C). 1995. lib. bdg. 26.50 (*0-8191-9804-8*) U Pr of Amer.
Braginsky, Vladimir B. Measurement of Weak Forces in Physics Experiments. Douglass, David H., ed. LC 76-22953. (Illus.). 166p. Date not set. reprint ed. pap. 51.50 (*0-608-20604-0*, 205456900003) Bks Demand.
Braginsky, Vladimir B. & Khalili, F. Y. Quantum Measurement. (Illus.). 212p. (C). 1992. text 69.95 (*0-521-41928-X*) Cambridge U Pr.
Braginsky, Vladimir B. & Manukin, A. B. Measurement of Weak Forces in Physics Experiments. Douglass, David H., ed. LC 76-22953. (Illus.). 1977. lib. bdg. 11.00 (*0-226-07070-0*) U Ch Pr.
Braginsky, Vladimir B., et al. Systems with Small Dissipation. Gliner, Erast, tr. LC 85-20876. (Illus.). xii, 160p. 1986. pap. text 18.00 (*0-226-07073-5*); lib. bdg. 28.00 (*0-226-07072-7*) U Ch Pr.
Braginsky, Vladimir I. & Dyakonova, Yelena M., eds. Images of Nusantaru in Russian Literature. Covalioff, Anatoly A., tr. 516p. 56.00 (*90-6718-127-7*, Pub. by KITLV Pr) Book Bin.
***Bragonier, Dave.** Wild Journey: On the Trail with a Wyoming Game Warden in Yellowstone Country. (Illus.). 192p. 1999. pap. write for info. (*0-9652942-3-4*) WordsWorth.
Bragonier, Reginald & Fisher, David. Que Es Que Spanish English. 1990. 40.00 (*0-8437-3324-1*) Hammond World.
Bragt, Jan Van, see Mommaers, Paul & Van Bragt, Jan.
Braguet, Anne & Noblet, Martine. India. (Tintin's Travel Diaries). (Illus.). 76p. (J). (gr. 5 up). 1994. 11.95 (*0-8120-6427-5*); pap. 6.95 (*0-8120-1866-4*) Barron.
***Braguinsky, Serguey & Yavlinsky, Grigory.** Incentives & Institutions: The Transition to a Market Economy in Russia. 2000. 39.50 (*0-691-00993-7*, Pub. by Princeton U Pr) Cal Prin Full Svc.
***Brah.** Global Futures: Migration, Environment & Globalization. LC 98-54944. (Explorations in Sociology Ser.). 288p. (C). 1999. text 69.95 (*0-312-22135-5*) St Martin.
— Thinking Identities. LC 99-11251. (C). 1999. text 65.00 (*0-312-22317-X*) St Martin.
***Brah, A. & Coombes, Annie E.** Hybridity & Its Discontents: Politics, Science, Culture. LC 00-20158. (Illus.). 2000. write for info. (*0-415-19403-2*) Routledge.
Brah, Avtar. Cartographies of Diaspora: Contesting Identities. LC 96-2571. (Gender, Racism, Ethnicity Ser.). 288p. (C). 1996. 85.00 (*0-415-12125-6*); pap. 24.99 (*0-415-12126-4*) Routledge.
Braha, Dan & Maimon, Oded Z. A Mathematical Theory of Design: Foundations, Algorithms & Applications. LC 98-7545. (Applied Optimization Ser.). 680p. 1998. write for info. (*0-7923-5079-0*) Kluwer Academic.
Braha, James. How to be a Great Astrologer: The Planetary Aspects Explained. LC 91-65831. (Illus.). 262p. (Orig.). 1992. pap. 19.95 (*0-935895-02-7*) Hermetician Pr.
Braha, James T. Ancient Hindu Astrology for the Modern Western Astrologer. LC 85-81314. (Illus.). 350p. 1993. reprint ed. pap. 21.95 (*0-935895-04-3*) Hermetician Pr.
— Astro-Logos, Revelations of a Hindu Astrologer: New Edition of Astro-Logos, Language of Life. 2nd ed. LC 96-76667. (Illus.). 296p. 1996. pap. 9.95 (*0-935895-08-6*) Hermetician Pr.
— How to Predict Your Future: Secrets of Eastern & Western Astrology. LC 94-79421. Orig. Title: Transits of the West - Dasas of the East. (Illus.). 364p. 1995. pap. 22.00 (*0-935895-07-8*) Hermetician Pr.
Braham, Allan. The Architecture of the French Enlightenment. 1980. pap. 40.00 (*0-520-06739-8*, Pub. by U CA Pr) Cal Prin Full Svc.
Braham, Allan & Hager, Hellmut. Carlo Fontana: The Drawings at Windsor Castle. Harris, John & Laing, Alastair, eds. (Studies in Architecture: No. XVIII). (Illus.). 222p. 1986. 125.00 (*0-302-02780-7*, Pub. by Zwemmer Bks) Intl Spec Bk.
Braham, B. Finding Your Purpose: A Guide to Personal Fulfillment. Brett, Elaine, ed. LC 90-83475. (Fifty-Minute Ser.). (Illus.). 103p. (Orig.). 1991. pap. 10.95 (*1-56052-072-8*) Crisp Pubns.
Braham, Barbara. Managing Stress: International Division. LC 93-8155. (Briefcase Bks.). 204p. 1993. per. 13.95 (*0-7863-0204-6*, Irwn Prfssnl) McGraw-Hill Prof.
***Braham, Barbara & Wahl, Chris.** Be Your Own Coach: Your Pathway to Possibility. Woodbury, Debbie & Bosarge, Charlotte, eds. (Crisp Fifty-Minute Book Ser.). (Illus.). 120p. 2000. pap. 12.95 (*1-56052-581-9*) Crisp Pubns.
Braham, Barbara J. Creating a Learning Organization: Promoting Excellence Through Education. Henry, Carol, ed. LC 95-68290. (50-Minute Ser.). (Illus.). 104p. (Orig.). 1995. pap. 10.95 (*1-56052-351-4*) Crisp Pubns.
— Decision Making-Problem Solving. (YA - Adult Education Ser.). 1993. pap., wbk. ed. 5.95 (*0-538-70783-6*) S-W Pub.
— How to Build Self-Esteem. (YA - Adult Education Ser.). 1993. pap., wbk. ed. 5.95 (*0-538-70846-8*) S-W Pub.
— Managing Stress: Keeping Calm under Fire. LC 93-8155. (Briefcase Bks.). 204p. 1993. 17.00 (*1-55623-855-X*, Irwn Prfssnl) McGraw-Hill Prof.
— Problem Solving & Decision Making. (YA - Adult Education Ser.). 1992. pap. 9.95 (*0-538-70555-8*) S-W Pub.
— Problem Solving/Decision Making. (YA - Adult Education Ser.). 1993. pap., wbk. ed. 5.95 (*0-538-70782-8*) S-W Pub.
— Self-Esteem & Getting Ahead. (Adult Education Ser.). 1992. pap. 9.95 (*0-538-70572-8*) S-W Pub.
— Understanding Self-Esteem. (YA - Adult Education Ser.). 1993. pap. 5.95 (*0-538-70847-6*) S-W Pub.
Braham, Bruce. Hotel Front Office. 2nd ed. 200p. 1999. pap. 36.50 (*0-7487-1632-7*, Pub. by S Thornes Pubs) Trans-Atl Phila.
Braham, Clare B. & Esche, Marie B. Kids Celebrate! Activities for Special Days Throughout the Year. LC 97-31182. 1998. pap. 16.95 (*1-55652-292-4*) Chicago Review.
Braham, David, jt. auth. see Harrigan, Edward.
Braham, Jeanne. Crucial Conversations: Interpreting Contemporary American Literary Autobiographies by Women. (Athene Ser.: Vol. 42). 159p. (C). 1995. 38.00 (*0-8077-6279-2*); pap. text 17.95 (*0-8077-6278-4*) Tchrs Coll.
Braham, Jeanne & Peterson, Pamela. Starry Starry Night: Provincetown's Response to the AIDS Epidemic. LC 98-4155. 220p. (Orig.). 1998. pap. 15.95 (*1-57129-058-3*, Lumen Eds) Brookline Bks.
Braham, Mark, ed. see Dartington Conference (1979) Staff.
Braham, Peter, et al, eds. Racism & Antiracism: Inequalities, Opportunities & Policies. 320p. (C). 1992. 55.00 (*0-8039-8581-9*); pap. 19.95 (*0-8039-8582-7*) Sage.
Braham, Randolph. Destruction of Romanian & Ukrainian Jews During the Antonescu Era. LC 97-61666. 424p. 1997. lib. bdg. 60.00 (*0-88033-380-4*, 483, Pub. by East Eur Monographs) Col U Pr.
— Holocaust in Hungary. LC 97-60360. 800p. 1997. lib. bdg. 112.00 (*0-88033-374-X*, Pub. by East Eur Monographs) Col U Pr.
— The Romanian Nationalists & the Holocaust: The Political Exploitation of Unfounded Rescue Attempts. LC 98-60584. 250p. 1998. text 35.00 (*0-88033-977-2*, Pub. by East Eur Monographs) Col U Pr.
Braham, Randolph L. Genocide & Retribution. 1983. lib. bdg. 97.50 (*0-89838-146-0*) Kluwer Academic.
— The Hungarian Jewish Catastrophe: Selected & Annotated Bibliography. 501p. 1984. text 79.50 (*0-88033-054-6*, Pub. by East Eur Monographs) Col U Pr.
— The Hungarian Labor Service System, 1939-1945. (East European Monographs: No. 31). 159p. 1977. text 58.00 (*0-914710-24-9*, Pub. by East Eur Monographs) Col U Pr.
— Perspectives on the Holocaust. (Holocaust Studies). 1983. lib. bdg. 73.50 (*0-89838-124-X*) Kluwer Academic.
— The Politics of Genocide: The Holocaust in Hungary. LC 99-20739. 368p. 1999. 18.95 (*0-8143-2691-9*) Wayne St U Pr.
— The Politics of Genocide: The Holocaust in Hungary, 2 vols., Set. 2nd ed. (East European Monographs: No. 350). 2200p. 1992. 298.00 (*0-88033-247-6*, Pub. by East Eur Monographs) Col U Pr.
***Braham, Randolph L.** Studies on the Holocaust: Selected Writings. 2000. 27.50 (*0-88033-447-9*, 549, Pub. by East Eur Monographs) Col U Pr.
— Vatican & the Holocaust. 2000. 35.00 (*0-88033-448-7*, 550, Pub. by East Eur Monographs) Col U Pr.
Braham, Randolph L., ed. Anti-Semitism & the Treatment of the Holocaust in Postcommunist Eastern Europe: Tragedy of Romanian Jewry. 388p. 1995. 34.00 (*0-88033-301-4*, 404, Pub. by East Eur Monographs) Col U Pr.
— Contemporary Views on the Holocaust. 1983. lib. bdg. 148.50 (*0-89838-141-X*) Kluwer Academic.
— Human Rights: Contemporary Domestic & International Issues & Conflicts. 170p. (C). 1980. 20.95 (*0-8290-0232-4*) Irvington.
— The Origins of the Holocaust: Christian Anti-Semitism. 85p. 1986. text 40.00 (*0-88033-953-5*, 204, Pub. by East Eur Monographs) Col U Pr.
— The Psychological Perspectives of the Holocaust & of Its Aftermath. (Holocaust Studies Series Social Science Monographs). 225p. 1988. text 69.50 (*0-88033-960-8*, Pub. by East Eur Monographs) Col U Pr.
— Social Justice. 192p. 1981. lib. bdg. 60.50 (*0-89838-063-4*) Kluwer Academic.
— Studies on the Holocaust in Hungary. 1990. text 46.50 (*0-88033-198-4*, Pub. by East Eur Monographs) Col U Pr.
— The Tragedy of the Jews in Hungary: Essays & Documents. (East European Monographs: No. 208). 328p. 1987. text 52.50 (*0-88033-105-4*, Pub. by East Eur Monographs) Col U Pr.
— The Wartime System of Labor Service in Hungary. LC 95-67863. 154p. 1995. 25.50 (*0-88033-317-0*, 420, Pub. by East Eur Monographs) Col U Pr.
Braham, Randolph L. & Miller, Scott, eds. The Nazis' Last Victims: The Holocaust in Hungary. LC 97-47721. (Illus.). 224p. 1998. 34.95 (*0-8143-2737-0*) Wayne St U Pr.
Braham, Randolph L. & Vago, Bela, eds. The Holocaust in Hungary: Forty Years Later. 235p. 1986. 55.50 (*0-88033-083-X*, Pub. by East Eur Monographs) Col U Pr.
Braham, Roscoe R., Jr., ed. Precipitation Enhancement: A Scientific Challenge. (Meteorological Monograph: Vol. 21, No. 43). (Illus.). 171p. 1986. 50.00 (*0-933876-65-3*) Am Meteorological.
Braham, Stephen P., et al, eds. The Sixth Canadian Conference on General Relativity & Relativistic Astrophysics. LC 97-11371. (Fields Institute Communications Ser.: Vol. 15). 373p. 1997. text 99.00 (*0-8218-0523-1*) Am Math.
Brahams, J. Fantasies Capriccios Opus 116: Piano Intermezzi. 32p. 1986. pap. 7.95 (*0-7935-4422-X*, 50259690) H Leonard.
Brahce, Carl I. Preretirement Planning: Individual, Institutional, & Social Perspectives. 49p. 1983. 4.95 (*0-318-17789-7*, IN264) Ctr Educ Trng Employ.
Brahe, C., jt. auth. see Bartley, R.
Brahe, Carl. Healing on the Edge of Now: A Practical Guide for the Use of Psychoneuroimmunology. Hofer, Jack, ed. LC 92-80669. 208p. (Orig.). 1992. pap. 11.95 (*0-9615743-2-1*) SunShine CO.
— Lillian: A Novel. LC 93-84239. 280p. 1994. pap. 9.95 (*0-9615743-4-8*) SunShine CO.
— PNI Healing Stories for Children, Vol. I. Hall, Victoria, ed. 84p. (J). (ps-6). 1999. pap. 11.95 (*1-893351-05-X*) Asclepian Pr.
Braheny, John. The Craft & Business of Songwriting. 322p. 1995. pap. 21.99 (*0-89879-653-9*, Wrtrs Digest Bks) F & W Pubns Inc.
Braheny, Mary & Halperin, Diane. Mind-Body-Spirit: Connecting with Your Creative Self. 64p. 1989. 7.95 (*1-55874-039-2*) Health Comm.
Brahier. Secondary Math Methods. LC 99-32768. 405p. (C). 1999. 62.00 (*0-205-28614-3*, Macmillan Coll) P-H.
Brahimi, Denise. Charmes de Paysage. (FRE., Illus.). 224p. 1995. pap. 59.95 (*2-86808-085-5*) Intl Scholars.
Brahimi, Denise, ed. see Sand, George.
Brahm. Purification of a Yogi: A Complete Panchakarma Program. LC 99-189809. 70p. 1998. pap. 95.00 (*0-9665617-0-8*) Vedic Arts.
Brahm, Lauren. China Inc. LC 96-945638. 105p. 1995. text 34.95 (*981-00-6605-8*) Buttrwrth-Heinemann.
Brahm, Laurence. Business Guide to China. LC 97-131426. 280p. 1996. pap. text 24.95 (*981-00-7079-9*) Buttrwrth-Heinemann.
Brahm, Laurence J. Banking & Finance in China. 1996. write for info. (*0-409-99840-0*, MICHIE) LEXIS Pub.
— China As No. 1: The New Superpower Takes Center Stage. LC 97-193256. 178p. 1997. pap. 19.95 (*981-00-6797-6*, Pub. by Select Bks) Weatherhill.
Brahm, William G. De, see De Brahm, William G.
Brahma Kumaris World Spiritual University Staff, ed. Visions of a Better World. (Illus.). 232p. 1993. 24.95 (*0-9637396-9-7*); pap. 19.95 (*0-9637396-8-9*) Brahma Kumaris.
Brahmachari, Bala, tr. see Parmahans, Yogeshwaranand.
Brahmananda, Swami, ed. see Ramakrishna, Sri.
Brahmaprana, Pravrajika, ed. see Atulananda, Swami.
Brahmavidya, Swami. Transcendent-Science or the Science of Self Knowledge (1922) 106p. 1998. reprint ed. pap. 12.95 (*0-7661-0592-X*) Kessinger Pub.
Brahms. Brahms Masterpieces for Solo Piano. pap. text 8.95 (*0-486-40149-9*) Dover.
— Symphony No. 3 in F Major, Op. 90. pap. text 2.95 (*0-486-40125-1*) Dover.
— Symphony Number 4 in E Minor OP 68. 1998. pap. text 3.95 (*0-486-29891-4*, 741730Q) Dover.
Brahms & Mahler, Gustav. German Lieder. Miller, Phillip L. et al, eds. (German Library: Vol. 42). 1990. pap. 19.95 (*0-8264-0328-X*) Continuum.
Brahms, Ann. Run for Your Life. 352p. 1993. mass mkt. 4.50 (*0-8217-4193-4*, Zebra Kensgtn) Kensgtn Pub Corp.
***Brahms, Ann Allen.** The Key Is under the Flower Pot. iv, 230p. 1999. pap. text 12.95 (*0-9613540-0-3*) Brahms Publishing Co.
Brahms, Caryl & Sherrin, Ned. Too Dirty for the Windmill: A Memoir of Caryl Brahms LC 86-206569. xvii, 286p. 1986. pap. write for info. (*0-09-466380-7*) Constable & Co.
Brahms, Caryl & Simon, S. J. A Bullet in the Ballet. 1996. 19.50 (*0-7451-8686-6*, Black Dagger) Chivers N Amer.
Brahms, J. Concerto in D Minor: Opus 15 2 Pianos 4 Hands. 116p. 1986. per. 13.95 (*0-7935-3910-2*, 50259180) H Leonard.
— Create in Me O God No. 2 Opus 29: First Movement a Capella. 4p. 1986. pap. 1.25 (*0-7935-5511-6*, 50297770) H Leonard.
— How Lovely Is Thy Dwelling Place: From Requiem. 12p. 1986. pap. 1.25 (*0-7935-5472-1*, 50295550) H Leonard.
— Hungarian Dances: Piano for Four Hands. 64p. 1992. pap. 10.95 (*0-7935-1774-5*) H Leonard.
— Hungarian Dances Complete 1-4. 80p. 1994. pap. 9.95 (*0-7935-4108-5*, 50482376) H Leonard.
— Hungarian Dances for Piano: Centennial Edition. 48p. 1992. pap. 6.95 (*0-7935-2049-5*) H Leonard.
— O Schone Nacht,Tr. of O Lovely Night. (ENG & GER.). 12p. 1986. pap. 1.25 (*0-7935-5469-1*, 50316790) H Leonard.
— Piano Works, Vol. 2. 160p. 1986. per. 14.95 (*0-7935-5233-8*, 50261470) H Leonard.
— Symphonies for the Piano: Centennial Edition. 160p. 1994. otabind 12.95 (*0-7935-3232-9*, 50482125) H Leonard.
— Variations on a Theme by Haydn for the Piano. 20p. 1992. pap. 5.95 (*0-7935-2058-4*) H Leonard.
***Brahms, Johannes.** Academic Festival Overture & Tragic Overture. 2000. pap. 3.50 (*0-486-41176-1*) Dover.
Brahms, Johannes. Alto Rhapsody: Opus Fifty-Three for Contralto, Men's Chorus, & Orchestra (Text from Goethe's Harzreise im Winter); a Facsimile Edition from the Composer's Autograph Manuscript. LC 82-25959. (Illus.). 76p. 1983. 50.00 (*0-87104-283-5*) NY Pub Lib.
— Alto Rhapsody, Song of Destiny, Nanie & Song of the Fates in Full Score. 128p. pap. 9.95 (*0-486-28528-6*) Dover.
Brahms, Johannes. Brahms: Piano Solo - Complete Edition, 3 Vols. (Urtext Editions for Piano). 608p. boxed set 49.95 (*963-9059-87-0*) Konemann.
Brahms, Johannes. The Brahms Arrangements for Piano - Four Hands of His String Quartets. (Music Scores to Play & Study Ser.). 160p. 1985. reprint ed. pap. 10.95 (*0-486-24835-6*) Dover.
— Brahms for Viols: Organ Chorale Preludes Arranged for Viol Consorts. Ballinger, Peter, ed. (Contemporary Consort Ser.: Vol. 32). 81p. 1997. pap. 32.00 (*1-56571-151-3*, VC032) PRB Prods.
— Complete Chamber Music for Strings & Clarinet Quintet. Gal, Hans, ed. 262p. 1968. pap. 12.95 (*0-486-21914-3*) Dover.
— Complete Chamber Music for Strings & Clarinet Quintet. Gal, Hans, ed. 1990. 12.50 (*0-8446-1724-5*) Peter Smith.
— Complete Concerti in Full Score. Orig. Title: Johannes Brahms, Samtliche Werke. 352p. 1981. reprint ed. pap. 16.95 (*0-486-24170-X*) Dover.
— The Complete Liebeslieder & Zigeunerlieder. 1997. pap. 9.95 (*0-486-29410-2*) Dover.
— Complete Piano Transcriptions, Cadenzas & Exercises. Mandyczewski, Eusebius, ed. LC 72-116826. 178p. 1970. reprint ed. pap. 10.95 (*0-486-22652-2*) Dover.
— Complete Piano Trios. 288p. pap. 14.95 (*0-486-25769-X*) Dover.
— Complete Piano Works for Four Hands. 6th ed. Mandyczewski, Eusebius, ed. LC 75-27674. 217p. 1976. reprint ed. pap. 12.95 (*0-486-23271-9*) Dover.
— Complete Shorter Works for Piano. Mandyczewski, Eusebius, ed. LC 70-116828. 180p. 1970. reprint ed. pap. 9.95 (*0-486-22651-4*) Dover.
— Complete Sonatas & Variations for Solo Piano. Mandyczewski, Eusebius, ed. LC 68-11096. 178p. 1970. reprint ed. pap. 10.95 (*0-486-22650-6*) Dover.

An Asterisk (*) at the beginning of an entry indicates that the title is appearing for the first time.

— Complete Sonatas for Solo Instrument & Piano. 208p. pap. 12.95 (*0-486-26091-7*) Dover.
— The Complete Sonatas for Violin & Piano: With Separate Violin Part. 96p. pap. 9.95 (*0-486-29312-2*) Dover.
— Complete Songs for Solo Voice & Piano: Series I. Mandyczewski, Eusebius, ed. Appelbaum, Stanley, tr. from GER. LC 79-50615. 1979. reprint ed. pap. 12.95 (*0-486-23820-2*) Dover.
— Complete Songs for Solo Voice & Piano: Series II. Mandyczewski, Eusebius, ed. Appelbaum, Stanley, tr. from GER. LC 79-50615. 1979. reprint ed. pap. 12.95 (*0-486-23821-0*) Dover.
— Complete Songs for Solo Voice & Piano: Series III. Mandyczewski, Eusebius, ed. Appelbaum, Stanley, tr. 224p. 1980. reprint ed. pap. 11.95 (*0-486-23822-9*) Dover.
— Complete Symphonies in Full Orchestral Score. Gal, Hans, ed. LC 73-92635. 344p. 1974. reprint ed. pap. 14.95 (*0-486-23053-8*) Dover.
— Concerto for Violin, Op. 77: A Facsimile of the Holograph Score. 125p. 1979. 50.00 (*0-674-08045-9*) HUP.
— German Requiem in Full Score. 208p. 1987. pap. 11.95 (*0-486-25486-0*) Dover.
— The Herzogenberg Correspondence. Kalbeck, Max, ed. Bryant, Hannah, tr. from GER. (Music Reprint Ser.). xxix, 425p. 1987. reprint ed. lib. bdg. 45.00 (*0-306-76281-1*) Da Capo.
— Johannes Brahms: His Life & Letters. Avins, Styra, ed. & tr. by. Eisinger, Josef, tr. LC 97-5417. (Illus.). 886p. (C). 1998. text 49.95 (*0-19-816234-0*) OUP.
— Johannes Brahms: The Herzogenberg Correspondence. Kalbeck, Max, ed. Bryant, Hannah, tr. LC 72-5395. (Select Bibliographies Reprint Ser.). (Illus.). 1977. reprint ed. 25.95 (*0-8369-6899-9*) Ayer.
— Piano Concerto No. 1 in D Minor: The Composer's Original Arrngement for Piano Four-Hands. 80p. 1996. pap. 8.95 (*0-486-29336-X*) Dover.
Brahms, Johannes. Piano Concertos Nos. 1 & 2: With Orchestral Reduction for Second Piano. 192p. Date not set. pap. 14.95 (*0-486-40625-3*) Dover.
— Piano Pieces II: Intermezzi, Caprici. (Music Scores Series). 1998. pap. text 7.98 (*963-9059-30-7*) Kone Music.
Brahms, Johannes. Quintet & Quartet for Piano & String. 298p. 1985. pap. 14.95 (*0-486-24900-X*) Dover.
***Brahms, Johannes.** Serenades Numbers 1 & 2 in Full Score. 2000. pap. 16.95 (*0-486-40854-X*) Dover.
Brahms, Johannes. Symphony No. 1 in C Minor, Op. 68: The Autograph Score. 104p. 1986. pap. 11.95 (*0-486-24976-X*) Dover.
***Brahms, Johannes.** Symphony No. 2 in D Major, Op. 73. 80p. 1999. pap. 3.95 (*0-486-40637-7*) Dover.
Brahms, Johannes. Symphony Number 1 in C Minor OP 68. 1998. 2.95 (*0-486-29797-7*, 741727Q) Dover.
Brahms, Johannes. Three Orchestral Works in Full Score. 112p. 1984. pap. 8.95 (*0-486-24637-X*) Dover.
Brahms, Johannes. Volksweisen fur Clara Schuhmann zum 8. Juni, 1854. 20p. 1997. reprint ed. 40.00 (*3-487-10262-5*) G Olms Pubs.
Brahms, Johannes, et al. Organ Works. 176p. 1991. pap. 11.95 (*0-486-26828-4*) Dover.
Brahms, Johannes, jt. auth. see Schumann, Clara (Wieck).
Brahms, William, et al. Franklin Township. (Images of America Ser.). 1999. pap. 16.99 (*0-7524-0938-7*) Arcadia Publng.
***Brahms, William B.** Franklin Township, Somerset County, NJ: A History. LC 98-89157. 635p. 1998. write for info. (*0-9668586-0-3*) Franklin Twp Libr.
***Brahmstedt, C. A.** The Emasculator. 2000. pap. 18.00 (*0-7388-2233-7*) Xlibris Corp.
Brahmstedt, W. T. The Courtiers of American Business. 192p. 1987. pap. 14.95 (*0-88280-118-X*) ETC Pubns.
— Memo to the Boss from Mack: A Contemporary Rendering of the Prince by Niccolo Machiavelli. (Illus.). 104p. 1986. pap. 12.95 (*0-88280-111-2*) ETC Pubns.
Braibanti, Antonio. Bioenergetics & Thermodynamics: Model Systems. (NATO Advanced Study Institutes Series C, Mathematical & Physical Sciences: No. 55). 483p. 1980. text 176.50 (*90-277-1115-1*) Kluwer Academic.
Braibanti, Ralph. Chief Justice Cornelius of Pakistan: An Analysis with Letters & Speeches. 420p. 1999. text 24.95 (*0-19-579018-9*) OUP.
— The Nature & Structure of the Islamic World. LC 95-19136. (Position Papers: No. 1). 1995. write for info. (*0-614-32361-4*) ISPI.
— The Nature & Structure of the Islamic World. 108p. 1996. pap. 10.00 (*0-614-21443-2*, 1394) Kazi Pubns.
Braibanti, Ralph & Akhter, Javeed. The Nature & Structure of the Islamic World. LC 95-16136. 60p. 1995. write for info. (*0-9647204-0-X*) ISPI.
Braibanti, Ralph, ed. see Spengler, Joseph J., et al.
Braibanti, Ralph J. Research on the Bureaucracy of Pakistan: A Critique of Sources, Conditions, Issues, with Appended Documents. LC 66-14888. (Duke University, Commonwealth-Studies Center, Publication Ser.: No. 26). 610p. reprint ed. pap. 189.10 (*0-608-11945-8*, 202337100032) Bks Demand.
Braibanti, Ralph J., et al. Administration & Economic Development in India. Spengler, Joseph J., ed. LC 63-9006. (Duke University, Commonwealth-Studies Center, Publication Ser.: No. 18). 320p. reprint ed. pap. 99.20 (*0-8357-5103-1*, 202336900032) Bks Demand.
— Asian Bureaucratic Systems Emergent from the British Imperial Tradition. LC 66-27487. (Duke University, Commonwealth-Studies Center, Publication Ser.: No. 28). 761p. reprint ed. pap. 200.00 (*0-8357-5788-9*, 202337000032) Bks Demand.
***Braico, Jennifer, et al.** Work Safe: Key Safety Topics for Construction Field Managers. (Illus.). 103p. 2000. pap. text 64.95 (*0-9648255-1-1*) FMI Corp.
Braid, Helen, ed. A Stranger at My Table: Women Write about Mothering Adolescents. 217p. 1998. pap. 17.95 (*0-7043-4472-6*, Pub. by Womens Press) Trafalgar.
Braid, James. Neurypnology. LC 75-16688. (Classics in Psychiatry Ser.). 1976. reprint ed. 23.95 (*0-405-07418-2*) Ayer.
Braida, Charlene A. Glorious Garlic: A Cookbook. LC 85-45514. (Illus.). 192p. (Orig.). 1986. pap. 12.95 (*0-88266-413-1*, Garden Way Pub) Storey Bks.
Braida, Dolly. From Sad Beginnings to Happy Endings. Gaitskill, Leigh et al, eds. LC 94-69568. (Illus.). 214p. (Orig.). 1995. pap. 14.95 (*1-56550-028-8*) Jo-Eric.
***Braida, Dolly.** New Beginnings: More Reflections by Dolly. Vaughan, Christina, ed. LC 99-95397. (Illus.). 340p. 1999. pap. 18.95 (*0-9658113-4-4*) Jo-Eric.
— Sleep My Sweet Baby: A Lullaby. 1997. pap. text 10.95 (*0-9658113-2-8*) Jo-Eric.
Braida, Dolly. Sleep My Sweet Baby: A Lullaby. Vaughan, Christine, ed. & contrib. by by. LC 96-61846. (Illus.). 24p. (J). (ps-1). 1997. pap. 7.95 incl. audio (*0-9658113-0-1*) Jo-Eric.
Braiden, C. V. Bryant Family History, Ancestry & Descendants of David Bryant (1756) of Springfield, N. J., Washington Co., & Wolf Lake, Noble Co., Ind. (Illus.). 270p. 1992. reprint ed. pap. 42.50 (*0-8328-2308-2*); reprint ed. lib. bdg. 52.50 (*0-8328-2307-4*) Higginson Bk Co.
Braider, Christopher. Refiguring the Real: Picture & Modernity in Word & Image, 1400-1700. (Illus.). 312p. 1992. text 47.50 (*0-691-06957-3*, Pub. by Princeton U Pr) Cal Prin Full Svc.
Braider, Christopher, tr. see Bairoch, Paul.
Braides, A. Approximation of Free-Discontinuity Problems, Vol. 169. LC 98-33844. (Lecture Notes in Mathematics Ser.: Vol. 1694). xi, 149p. 1998. pap. 33.00 (*3-540-64771-6*) Spr-Verlag.
Braides, Andrea & Defranceschi, Annelisse. Homogenization of Multiple Integrals. LC 98-8283. (Oxford Lecture Series in Mathematics & Its Applications: No. 12). 304p. 1999. text 75.00 (*0-19-850246-X*) OUP.
Braidhill, Kathy. Chop Shop, 1. 1999. mass mkt. 5.99 (*0-7860-0636-6*) Kensgtn Pub Corp.
— Evil Secrets. 384p. 1996. mass mkt. 5.99 (*0-7860-0348-0*, Pinncle Kensgtn) Kensgtn Pub Corp.
***Braidhill, Kathy.** To Die For. (Illus.). 272p. 2000. mass mkt. 6.50 (*0-312-97416-7*) St Martin.
Braidi, Susan. The Acquisition of Second-Language Syntax. LC 98-8220. (Arnold Publications). (Illus.). 232p. 1998. text 80.00 (*0-340-64592-X*) OUP.
Braidi, Susan M. The Acquisitions of Second Language Syntax. LC 98-8220. (Illus.). 232p. (C). 1998. pap. text 19.95 (*0-340-64591-1*, Pub. by E A) OUP.
Braidotti, Rosi. Nomadic Subjects: Embodiment & Sexual Difference in Contemporary Feminist Theory. LC 93-40638. (Gender & Culture Ser.). 326p. 1994. 61.50 (*0-231-08234-7*); pap. 17.50 (*0-231-08235-5*) Col U Pr.
— Patterns of Dissonance: A Study of Women in Contemporary Philosophy. Guild, Elizabeth, tr. 324p. (C). 1991. pap. 20.99 (*0-415-90491-9*, A6368) Routledge.
Braidotti, Rosi, et al. Women, the Environment & Sustainable Development: Towards a Theoretical Synthesis. LC 94-1964. 224p. (C). 1994. text 55.00 (*1-85649-183-8*, Pub. by Zed Books) St Martin.
***Braidwood, Barbara.** Start & Run a Profitable Tour Guiding Business. 2nd ed. 248p. 2000. pap. 18.95 (*1-55180-284-8*) Self-Counsel Pr.
***Braidwood, Barbara & Cropp, Richard.** Romantic Days & Nights in Vancouver: Romantic Diversions in & Around the City. 2nd ed. (Romantic Days & Nights Ser.). (Illus.). 264p. 2000. pap. 15.95 (*0-7627-0654-6*) Globe Pequot.
Braidwood, Barbara, jt. auth. see Cropp, Richard.
Braidwood, Robert J., et al, eds. Prehistoric Archaeology along the Zagros Flanks. LC 81-85896. (Oriental Institute Publications: No. 105). (Illus.). ix, 695p. 1983. 130.00 (*0-918986-36-2*) Orient Inst.
Braidwood, Robert J. & Howe, Bruce. Prehistoric Investigations in Iraqi Kurdistan. LC 60-8969. (Illus.). 1960. pap. text 17.00 (*0-226-62404-8*, SAOC31) U Ch Pr.
Braidwood, Robert J., jt. auth. see Morales, Vivian B.
Braier, L. Diccionario Enciclopedico de Medicina "Jims" 4th ed. (ENG, FRE, GER, ITA & LAT.). 1980. 125.00 (*0-8288-0580-6*, S33099) Fr & Eur.
Braighlinn, G. Ideological Innovation under Monarchy: Aspects of Legitimation Activity in Contemporary Brunei. 96p. (Orig.). 1992. pap. text 14.50 (*90-5383-091-X*, Pub. by VU Univ Pr) Paul & Co Pubs.
***Braiker, Harriet B.** Disease to Please: Curing the People-Pleasing Syndrome. 2001. 21.95 (*0-07-136410-2*) McGraw.
Braiker, Harriet B. Getting up When You're Feeling Down: A Woman's Guide to Overcoming & Preventing Depression. 320p. 1990. mass mkt. 5.99 (*0-671-68327-6*) PB.
— Lethal Lovers & Poisonous People: How to Protect Your Health from Relationships That Make You Sick. Regan, Judith, ed. 272p. 1993. reprint ed. mass mkt. 5.99 (*0-671-72423-1*, Pocket Star Bks) PB.
Brail, Richard K. Microcomputers in Urban Planning & Management. LC 86-31767. 351p. 1987. 1.00 (*0-88285-121-7*) Ctr Urban Pol Res.
Brailey, Jeffrey. The Ghosts of November: Memoirs of an Outsider Who Witnessed the Carnage at Jonestown, Guyana. LC 98-88266. 294p. 1998. pap. 19.95 (*0-9667868-0-7*, 110198) J&J Pubs.
Brailey, Nigel. Two Views of Siam: On the Eve of the Chakri Reformation. (Illus.). 164p. (Orig.). (C). 1995. pap. 27.00 (*1-870838-25-4*, Pub. by Kiscadale) Weatherhill.
***Braillard, Philippe.** Switzerland & the Crisis of Dormant Assets & Nazi Gold. 200p. 2000. text 76.50 (*0-7103-0671-7*) Col U Pr.
Braillard, Philippe. Switzerland As a Financial Center. (C). 1988. lib. bdg. 321.00 (*90-247-3639-0*) Kluwer Academic.
Brailofsky, M. Flying with Daniel: A Novel. 1992. 14.99 (*0-89906-408-6*); 11.99 (*0-89906-409-4*) Mesorah Pubns.
Brailoiu, Constantin. Problems of Ethnomusicology. Lloyd, A. L., ed. LC 83-15224. (Illus.). 320p. 1984. text 85.00 (*0-521-24528-1*) Cambridge U Pr.
Brailowsky, Simon. Las Sustancias de los Suenos. (Ciencia para Todos Ser.). (SPA.). pap. 6.99 (*968-16-4585-5*, Pub. by Fondo) Continental Bk.
Brailowsky, Simon, jt. auth. see Stein, Donald G.
Brailsford, Dennis. British Sport: A Social History. LC 92-32237. (Illus.). 160p. 1992. lib. bdg. 49.50 (*0-389-21002-1*) B&N Imports.
Brailsford, H. N. Macedonia: Its Races & Their Future. LC 78-135796. (Eastern Europe Collection). 1980. reprint ed. 43.95 (*0-405-02738-9*) Ayer.
Brailsford, Henry, ed. see Nevinson, Henry W.
Brailsford, Henry N. Shelley, Godwin, & Their Circle. (BCL1-PR English Literature Ser.). 256p. 1992. reprint ed. lib. bdg. 79.00 (*0-7812-7093-6*) Rprt Serv.
— Voltaire. 1963. pap. 8.95 (*0-19-281021-9*) OUP.
Brailsford, Mabel R. Making of William Penn. LC 77-124227. (Select Bibliographies Reprint Ser.). 1977. 24.95 (*0-8369-5416-5*) Ayer.
— Making of William Penn. 1993. reprint ed. lib. bdg. 89.00 (*0-7812-5433-7*) Rprt Serv.
Brailsford, Mabel R., tr. see Pinnow, Hermann.
Braim, Paul. The Test of Battle: The American Expeditionary Forces in the Meuse-Argonne Campaign. LC 85-40991. (Illus.). 240p. 1988. 40.00 (*0-87413-301-7*) U Delaware Pr.
Braim, Paul F. The Test of Battle: The American Expeditionary Forces in the Meuse Argonne Campaign. LC 97-46690. 247p. 1998. 35.00 (*1-57249-085-2*) White Mane Pub.
Brain. Computers in Business & Home. 1990. pap. text. write for info. (*0-582-87148-4*, Pub. by Addison-Wesley) Longman.
— Decision Making in Hematology. 1991. 89.00 (*1-55664-155-9*) Mosby Inc.
Brain, A. G., tr. see Cerna, Jana.
Brain, A. G., tr. see Klima, Ivan.
Brain, A. G., tr. see Viewegh, Michal.
Brain, C. K. The Hunters or the Hunted? An Introduction to African Cave Taphonomy. LC 79-28104. (C). 1981. lib. bdg. 40.00 (*0-226-07089-1*) U Ch Pr.
— The Hunters or the Hunted? An Introduction to African Cave Taphonomy. LC 79-28104. 376p. (C). 1983. pap. text 21.00 (*0-226-07090-5*) U Ch Pr.
Brain, Charles M. Social Security at the Crossroads: Public Opinion & Public Policy. LC 91-5097. (Studies on the Elderly in America). 320p. 1991. text 35.00 (*0-8153-0511-7*) Garland.
***Brain, Dennis.** Johann Karl Wezel: From Religious Pessimism to Anthropological Skepticism. LC 99-25154. (German Life & Civilization Ser.: Vol. 30). 432p. 1999. 66.95 (*0-8204-4464-2*) P Lang Pubng.
Brain, Elizabeth, ed. see Sweeney, George D.
Brain, Elizabeth A., jt. auth. see Hirsh, Jack.
Brain, Jean, et al. Child Care & Health for Nursery Nurses. 3rd ed. 288p. (C). 1989. pap. 37.50 (*1-871402-13-1*, Pub. by S Thornes Pubs) Trans-Atl Phila.
Brain, Jeffrey P. Tunica Archaeology. (Peabody Museum Papers: Vol. 78). (Illus.). 464p. 1988. pap. 40.00 (*0-87365-204-5*) Peabody Harvard.
— Tunica Treasure. LC 79-57107. (Peabody Museum Papers: Vol. 71). (Illus.). 329p. 1979. pap. 35.00 (*0-87365-196-0*, PEMP157) Peabody Essex Mus.
— Winterville: Late Prehistoric Culture Contact in the Lower Mississippi Valley. (Mississippi Department of Archives & History Archaeological Reports: No. 23). (Illus.). 201p. 1989. pap. 15.00 (*0-938896-58-X*) Mississippi Archives.
Brain, Jeffrey P. & Phillips, Philip. Shell Gorgets: Styles of the Late Prehistoric & Protohistoric Southeast. LC 90-64119. (Museum Press Ser.). (Illus.). 542p. 1996. pap. 79.95 (*0-87365-812-4*) Peabody Harvard.
Brain, Jeffrey P., jt. auth. see Williams, Stephen.
Brain, Joseph D., et al, eds. Variations in Susceptibility to Inhaled Pollutants: Identification, Mechanisms, & Policy Implications. LC 87-45484. (Environmental Toxicology Ser.). 528p. 1988. text 85.00 (*0-8018-3503-8*) Johns Hopkins.
Brain, Marshall. Developing Professional Applications in Windows 95 & NT. 2nd ed. (C). 1996. pap. text 49.95 incl. cd-rom (*0-13-616343-2*) P-H.
***Brain, Marshall.** WIN32 System Services: The Heart of Windows 98 & Windows 2000. 3rd ed. (Microsoft Technology Ser.). 300p. 2000. pap. text 49.99 (*0-13-022557-6*) P-H.
Brain, Marshall. The Teenager's Guide to the Real World. LC 97-93314. (Illus.). 368p. (Orig.). (J). (gr. 8). 1997. pap. 19.95 (*0-9657430-3-9*) BYG Pub.
— WIN 32 System Services: The Heart of Windows 95 & Windows NT. 2nd ed. 896p. (C). 1995. pap. 49.95 incl. disk (*0-13-324732-5*) P-H.
— Windows Applications Design with Ole 2.0: For Windows & Windows NT. 400p. (C). 2001. pap. text 39.95 (*0-13-097817-5*) P-H.
— Windows NT 4.O System Administration: Single Systems to Heterogeneous Networks. 304p. 1994. pap. 40.60 (*0-13-176694-5*) P-H.
Brain, Marshall & Campbell, Kelly. Using Windows NT: The Essentials for Professionals. LC 93-4999. 208p. (C). 1993. pap. text 28.20 (*0-13-091977-2*) P-H.
Brain, Marshall & Lovette, Lance. Developing Professional Applications for Windows 98 & NT Using MFC. 3rd ed. (Prentice Hall Series on Microsoft Technologies). (Illus.). 880p. 1999. pap. 49.99 incl. cd-rom (*0-13-085121-3*, Prentice Hall) P-H.
Brain, Marshall, jt. auth. see Gratten, Nick.
Brain, P. F. & Zichichi, Antonio L., eds. Fear & Defence. (Ettore Majorana International Life Sciences Ser.: Vol. 8). x, 420p. 1990. text 162.00 (*3-7186-5015-0*) Gordon & Breach.
Brain, P. F., et al. House Mouse Aggression: A Model for Understanding the Evolution of Social Behavior, 6. x, 340p. 1989. text 190.00 (*3-7186-4860-1*) Gordon & Breach.
***Brain Quest.** My 1st Brain Quest. (Brain Quest Ser.). 75p. (Orig.). 1999. pap. 10.95 (*0-7611-1517-X*) Workman Pub.
***Brain Quest Editors.** Brain Quest: Grade 1. rev. ed. (Illus.). 1999. 10.95 (*0-7611-1021-6*) Workman Pub.
Brain Quest Editors. Brain Quest: Grade 2. 1999. 10.95 (*0-7611-1022-4*) Workman Pub.
***Brain Quest Editors.** Brain Quest: Grade 3. 1999. pap. 10.95 (*0-7611-1023-2*) Workman Pub.
— Brain Quest: Grade 4. 1999. pap. 10.95 (*0-7611-1024-0*) Workman Pub.
— Brain Quest: Grade 5. 1999. pap. 10.95 (*0-7611-1025-9*) Workman Pub.
— Brain Quest: Grade 6. rev. ed. 1999. pap. 10.95 (*0-7611-1026-7*) Workman Pub.
Brain Quest Editors. Brain Quest: Grade 7. rev. ed. 1999. 10.95 (*0-7611-1027-5*) Workman Pub.
***Brain Quest Editors.** Brain Quest: Kindergarten. rev. ed. (Brain Quest Ser.). 1999. 10.95 (*0-7611-1515-3*) Workman Pub.
Brain Quest Editors. Brain Quest after School, Sports. (Illus.). 136p. (J). (gr. 4-6). 1996. pap. 10.95 (*0-7611-0455-0*, 10455) Workman Pub.
— Brain Quest after School, Weird Stuff. (Illus.). 138p. (J). (gr. 4-6). 1996. pap. 10.95 (*0-7611-0456-9*, 10456) Workman Pub.
— Brain Quest for the Car. 1999. 10.95 (*0-7611-1538-2*) Workman Pub.
— My First Bible Brain Quest. (Brain Quest Ser.). (Illus.). 116p. (J). (ps-k). 1997. pap. 10.95 (*0-7611-0928-5*) Workman Pub.
Brain, Robert, tr. see Mauss, Marcel.
Brain, Robert, tr. see Simenon, Georges.
***Brain, Robert D.** Contracts. 6th ed. (Sum & Substance Quick Review Ser.). 1999. pap. 19.95 (*0-314-24283-X*) West Pub.
Brain, Susan, ed. Immunopharmacology of the Microcirculation. (Handbook of Immunopharmacology Ser.). (Illus.). 256p. 1994. text 79.00 (*0-12-125010-5*) Acad Pr.
Brain, Susan D. & Moore, P. K. Pain & Neurogenic Inflammation. (Progress in Inflammation Research Ser.). 330p. 1999. (*3-7643-5875-0*) Birkhauser.
— Pain & Neurogenic Inflammation. LC 98-54474. (Progress in Inflammation Research Ser.). 1999. write for info. (*0-8176-5875-0*) Birkhauser.
Brain, Walter R. Speech Disorders: Aphasia, Apraxia & Agnosia. LC 63-5076. (Illus.). 200p. reprint ed. pap. 62.00 (*0-608-14734-6*, 202573000046) Bks Demand.
***Brain, Yossi.** Ecuador: A Climbing Guide. LC 00-8962. (Illus.). 176p. 2000. pap. 16.95 (*0-89886-729-0*) Mountaineers.
Brain, Yossi. Trekking in Bolivia: A Traveler's Guide. LC 97-2348. (Trekking in...Ser.). (Illus.). 208p. (Orig.). 1997. pap. 16.95 (*0-89886-501-8*) Mountaineers.
Brainard. Twenty-Nine Mini-Essays. 1990. pap. 5.00 (*0-915990-14-8*) Z Pr.
Brainard, et al. Gilbert Family, Descendants of Thomas Gilbert, 1582(?)-1659, of Mt. Wollaston (Braintree), Windsor & Wethersfield. (Illus.). 508p. 1997. reprint ed. pap. 76.50 (*0-8328-8736-6*); reprint ed. lib. bdg. 86.50 (*0-8328-8735-8*) Higginson Bk Co.
***Brainard, Alan J.** Turtle Collectibles. (Illus.). 144p. 1999. pap. 29.95 (*0-7643-0979-X*) Schiffer.
Brainard, C. A. & Wirth, M. Respiratory Care: National Board Review. (Illus.). 495p. (C). 1984. pap. text 35.00 (*0-89303-816-4*, D8164-8) Appleton & Lange.
Brainard, Cecilia M. Philippine Woman in America. 113p. (Orig.). 1991. pap. 12.50 (*971-10-0424-0*, Pub. by New Day Pub) Cellar.
— Song of Yvonne. 183p. (Orig.). 1991. pap. 12.50 (*971-10-0449-6*, Pub. by New Day Pub) Cellar.
— Woman with Horns & Other Stories. 92p. (Orig.). (C). 1988. pap. 9.50 (*971-10-0323-6*, Pub. by New Day Pub) Cellar.
Brainard, Cecilia M., ed. Fiction by Filipinos in America. (Illus.). 240p. (Orig.). 1993. pap. 15.75 (*970-10-0528-7*, Pub. by New Day Pub) Cellar.
Brainard, CeCilia Manguerra. When the Rainbow Goddess Wept. LC 99-29494. (Ann Arbor Paperbacks Ser.). Orig. Title: Song of Yvonne. 232p. 1999. pap. 16.95 (*0-472-08637-5*, 08637) U of Mich Pr.
Brainard, CeCilia Manguerra & Litton, Edmundo F., eds. Journey of 100 Years: Reflections on the Centennial of Philippine Independence. 270p. 17.95 (*0-9632281-0-2*) PAWWA.
Brainard, Edward A. A Hands-On Guide to School Program Evaluation. LC 96-70381. 80p. 1996. pap. 9.00 (*0-87367-493-6*) Phi Delta Kappa.
Brainard, F. Samuel. Reality & Mystical Experience. LC 98-54922. 1999. 55.00 (*0-271-01937-9*) Pa St U Pr.

B

***Brainard, F. Samuel.** Reality & Mystical Experience. LC 99-20705. 1999. pap. 19.95 (*0-271-01973-5*) Pa St U Pr.

Brainard, H. W. The Ishams in England & America. (Illus.). 672p. 1991. reprint ed. pap. 98.50 (*0-8328-2157-8*); reprint ed. lib. bdg. 108.50 (*0-8328-2156-X*) Higginson Bk Co.

Brainard, H. W., jt. auth. see Holley, J. M.

Brainard, Ingrid. The Art of Courtly Dancing in the Early Renaissance. LC 91-58192. (Studies in the Renaissance: No. 33). 1993. write for info. (*0-404-62333-6*) AMS Pr.

Brainard, Ingrid & Cook, Ray. Three Court Dances of the Early Renaissance. (Illus.). 34p. 1977. reprint ed. pap. text 9.95 (*0-932582-10-9*, Pub. by Dance Notation) Princeton Bk Co.

***Brainard, Jack.** If I Were to Train a Horse. 156p. 2000. write for info. (*0-9639724-1-3*) Print Comm.

Brainard, Jack. Western Training: Theory & Practice. 136p. 1990. pap. 12.95 (*0-911647-16-3*) Western Horseman.

Brainard, Jean M. Health & Development in a Rural Kenyan Community. Ser. XI, Vol. 40. (Illus.). XII, 218p. (C). 1991. text 38.95 (*0-8204-0978-2*) P Lang Pubng.

Brainard, Joe. Selected Writings. pap. 3.50 (*0-686-09752-1*) Kulchur Foun.

Brainard, Joe, jt. auth. see Elmslie, Kenward.

Brainard, Lee, ed. see Neil, Dorothy M.

Brainard, Marcus, ed. & tr. see Boeder, Heribert.

***Brainard, Mary G.** Campaigns of the 146th Regiment New York State Volunteers. rev. unabridged ed. Schroeder, Patrick A., ed. (Illus.). 768p. 2000. reprint ed. 49.95 (*1-889246-08-5*) P A Schroeder.

Brainard, Newton C. The Hartford State House of Seventeen Ninety-Six. (Illus.). 68p. 1964. 4.00 (*0-940748-22-3*); pap. 2.00 (*0-940748-23-1*) Conn Hist Soc.

Brainard, Sandy. Path to the Brightest Star. (Illus.). 104p. (Orig.). 1984. pap. 6.00 (*0-942494-54-7*) Coleman Pub.

Brainard, Scott, jt. auth. see Packer, Arnold.

Brainard, Shirley. A Design Manual. 2nd ed. LC 97-37837. 200p. (C). 1997. pap. text 54.67 (*0-13-759234-5*) P-H.

Brainard, Tony. Advanced Cardiac Life Support Exam Preparation. LC 96-48081. (C). 1997. pap. text 21.95 (*0-8385-0259-8*, A0259-0) Appleton & Lange.

Brainard, Willard T. Medical Psychology of Spouse Abuse: Index of New Information with Authors & Subjects. rev. ed. LC 94-34611. 1994. 47.50 (*0-7883-0424-0*); pap. 44.50 (*0-7883-0425-9*) ABBE Pubs Assn.

— Women & Spouse Abuse: Index of Modern Information. LC 90-32062. 150p. 1990. 47.50 (*1-55914-180-8*); pap. 44.50 (*1-55914-181-6*) ABBE Pubs Assn.

Brainard, William, et al, eds. Money, Macroeconomics, & Economic Policy: Essays in Honor of James Tobin. (Illus.). 372p. 1991. 47.50 (*0-262-02325-3*) MIT Pr.

Brainchild Writers Staff. All the Women Were Heroes. LC 97-69300. (Illus.). 200p. 1997. pap. 10.95 (*0-9646037-6-4*) Rosehill Pr IL.

Braine, David. The Human Person: Animal & Spirit. LC 92-53754. (C). 1994. pap. text 19.50 (*0-268-01106-0*) U of Notre Dame Pr.

— The Reality of Time & the Existence of God: The Project of Proving God's Existence. 400p. 1988. text 95.00 (*0-19-824459-2*) OUP.

Braine, George, ed. Non-Native Educators in English Language Teaching. LC 98-50643. 256p. 1999. 49.95 (*0-8058-3204-1*); pap. 24.50 (*0-8058-3205-X*) L Erlbaum Assocs.

Braine, George & May, Claire A. Writing from Sources: A Guide for ESL Students. LC 95-968. (Illus.). 225p. (Orig.). (C). 1996. pap. text 29.95 (*1-55934-441-5*, 1441) Mayfield Pub.

Braine, George, jt. auth. see Belcher, Diane.

Braine, George S. Technical Writing. 200p. Date not set. pap. text 22.50 (*962-201-789-4*, Pub. by Chinese Univ) U of Mich Pr.

Braine, John. Life at the Top. LC 79-24779. 1980. reprint ed. pap. 3.95 (*0-416-00591-8*, NO. 0185) Routledge.

— Room at the Top. 22.95 (*0-8488-0921-1*) Amereon Ltd.

— Room at the Top. large type ed. 288p. 1996. 24.95 (*1-85695-357-2*, Pub. by ISIS Lrg Prnt) Transaction Pubs.

— Room at the Top. 1993. reprint ed. lib. bdg. 18.95 (*1-56849-187-5*) Buccaneer Bks.

Braine, Martin & O'Brien, David P., eds. Mental Logic. LC 97-24744. 350p. 1997. write for info. (*0-8058-2388-3*); pap. write for info. (*0-8058-2389-1*) L Erlbaum Assocs.

Braine, Susan. Drumbeat -- Heartbeat: A Celebration of the Powwow. (We Are Still Here Ser.). (Illus.). (J). 1995. pap. 6.95 (*0-8225-9711-X*, First Ave Edns) Lerner Pub.

Braine, Susan. Drumbeat--Heartbeat: A Celebration of the Powwow. LC 94-42594. (Illus.). (J). (gr. 3-6). 1995. lib. bdg. 21.27 (*0-8225-2656-5*, Lerner Publctns) Lerner Pub.

Brainerd, Alvah. A Pioneer History of the Township of Grand Blanc. LC 64-1263. (Local History Reprints Ser.). 73p. 1964. reprint ed. pap. 3.25 (*0-916699-00-5*) CMU Clarke Hist Lib.

Brainerd, Andrew W. The Infanta Adventure & the Lost Manet. 1989. 49.95 (*0-9618793-1-9*) Reichl Pr.

Brainerd, Charles J. The Origins of the Number Concept. LC 78-21223. 227p. 1979. 65.00 (*0-275-90334-6*, C0334, Praeger Pubs) Greenwood.

Brainerd, Charles J., ed. Recent Advances in Cognitive-Developmental Theory, Progress in Cognitive Developmental Research. (Cognitive Development Ser.). (Illus.). 270p. 1983. 104.00 (*0-387-90767-X*) Spr-Verlag.

Brainerd, Charles J. & Pressley, M., eds. Basic Processes in Memory Development. (Cognitive Development Ser.). (Illus.). 365p. 1985. 85.95 (*0-387-96064-3*) Spr-Verlag.

— Verbal Processes in Children: Progress in Cognitive Developmental Research. (Cognitive Development Ser.). (Illus.). 289p. 1982. 83.95 (*0-387-90648-7*) Spr-Verlag.

Brainerd, Charles J., et al. The Development of Forgetting & Reminiscence. (Monographs of the Society for Research in Child Development: Vol. 55, Nos. 3-4). 120p. 1990. pap. text 15.00 (*0-226-07095-6*) U Ch Pr.

Brainerd, Charles J., jt. ed. see Dempster, Frank N.

Brainerd, Charles J., jt. ed. see Howe, M. L.

Brainerd, Charles J., jt. ed. see Pressley, M.

Brainerd, David. Life & Diary. (American Autobiography Ser.). 384p. 1995. reprt ed. lib. bdg. 89.00 (*0-7812-8463-5*) Rprt Serv.

— The Life & Diary of David Brainerd. Edwards, Jonathan, ed. & compiled by by. 386p. (YA). (gr. 10). 1989. pap. 13.99 (*0-8010-0976-6*) Baker Bks.

Brainerd, David, ed. Memoirs of the Reverend David Brainerd: Missionary to the Indians on the Border of New York, New Jersey & Pennsylvania. LC 70-108477. (American Indian History Ser.). 1970. reprint ed. 69.00 (*0-403-00233-8*) Scholarly.

Brainerd, Edwin, et al. Would You Believe an Angel? Four Plays for the Christmas Season. Johns, Helen, ed. LC 92-72130. (Illus.). 55p. 1992. pap. 6.95 (*0-916035-50-6*) Evangel Indiana.

Brainerd, Eleanor. Concerning Belinda. LC 78-86138. (Short Story Index Reprint Ser.). (Illus.). 1977. 19.95 (*0-8369-3042-8*) Ayer.

Brainerd, George W. The Maya Civilization. LC 76-43669. reprint ed. 39.50 (*0-404-15503-0*) AMS Pr.

— The Maya Civilization. (Illus.). 93p. 1963. reprint ed. 3.00 (*0-916561-52-6*) Southwest Mus.

Brainerd, George W., jt. auth. see Morley, Sylvanus G.

Brainerd, H. A Survey of the Scofill(s) s in England & America, Seven Hundred Years of History & Genealogy. (Illus.). 586p. 1993. reprint ed. pap. 89.00 (*0-8328-3060-7*); reprint ed. lib. bdg. 99.00 (*0-8328-3059-3*) Higginson Bk Co.

Brainerd, J. Grist, ed. The Ultimate Consumer: A Study in Economic Illiteracy. LC 75-39236. (Getting & Spending: The Consumer's Dilemma Ser.). 1976. reprint ed. 23.95 (*0-405-08012-3*) Ayer.

Brainerd, John. Nature Touring: A Guidebook for Travelers & Naturalists. 224p. 1985. 16.95 (*0-13-610338-3*); pap. 7.95 (*0-13-610320-0*) P-H.

Brainerd, Michael, ed. Spacebridges: Television & U. S. -Soviet Dialogue. LC 89-5528. 120p. (Orig.). (C). 1989. pap. text 18.00 (*0-8191-7433-5*); lib. bdg. 35.00 (*0-8191-7432-7*) U Pr of Amer.

Brainerd, W. S. Programmer's Guide to Fortran 90. 3rd ed. 445p. 1995. 39.95 (*0-387-94570-9*) Spr-Verlag.

Brainerd, Walter S. & Landweber, Lawrence H. Theory of Computation. LC 73-12950. reprint ed. pap. 89.30 (*0-608-15352-4*, 2056337) Bks Demand.

— Theory of Computation. LC 73-12950. 357p. 1974. reprint ed. pap. 110.70 (*0-608-10353-5*, 205629300056) Bks Demand.

Brainerd, Walter S., et al. Programmer's Guide to F. LC 96-60076. 388p. (Orig.). (C). 1996. pap. 30.00 (*0-9640135-1-7*) Unicomp.

Brainin, M. & Foulkes, M. A., eds. Stroke Data Banks: Challenges for Research. (Journal: Neuroepidemiology: Vol. 13, No. 6, 1994). (Illus.). iv, 104p. 1994. pap. 47.00 (*3-8055-6016-8*) S Karger.

Brainin, Max, tr. see Kramer, Theodor.

Brainin, Salomea N., tr. see Bettauer, Hugo.

Brainina, Z. & Neyman, E. Electroanalytical Stripping Methods. LC 93-20423. (Chemical Analysis Ser.: Vol. 126). 198p. 1993. 84.95 (*0-471-59506-3*) Wiley.

BrainStorm Inc., Staff. BrainStorm Corel WordPerfect 8: Training Workbook. 72p. 1997. pap., wbk. ed. 19.95 (*1-57830-055-X*) Brainstrm.

BrainStorm, Inc. Staff. The Brainstorm Guide to Novell Group Wise 5 for 32-Bit. 119p. 1997. pap. 19.95 (*1-57830-100-9*) Brainstrm.

BrainStorm Inc., Staff. The BrainStorm Guide to Novell GroupWise Client Training Course: Client Training Workbook. 100p. 1995. pap., wbk. ed. 19.95 (*1-57830-105-X*) Brainstrm.

— The BrainStorm Guide to Novell GroupWise Client Training Course: Trainer's Guide. 100p. 1995. pap., teacher ed. 19.95 (*1-57830-106-8*) Brainstrm.

— The BrainStorm Guide to Novell GroupWise for GroupWise 4.1. 127p. 1995. pap. 19.95 (*1-57830-104-1*) Brainstrm.

— The BrainStorm Guide to Novell GroupWise for GroupWise 5.1 16 Bit. 129p. 1997. pap. 19.95 (*1-57830-102-5*) Brainstrm.

— The BrainStorm Guide to Novell GroupWise for 16-Bit: Client Training Workbook. 100p. 1997. pap., wbk. ed. 19.95 (*1-57830-103-3*) Brainstrm.

— The BrainStorm Guide to Novell GroupWise for 32-Bit: Client Training Workbook. 124p. 1997. pap., wbk. ed. 19.95 (*1-57830-101-7*) Brainstrm.

— The BrainStorm Guide to WordPerfect 6.1: Reference Manual & Workbook. 152p. 1996. pap., wbk. ed. 19.95 (*1-57830-050-9*) Brainstrm.

— BrainStorming Corel WordPerfect 7: Training Workbook. 78p. 1997. pap. 19.95 (*1-57830-051-7*) Brainstrm.

— BrainStorming Corel WordPerfect 7: Reference. 132p. 1997. pap. 19.95 (*1-57830-052-5*) Brainstrm.

— BrainStorming Windows 95: Training Workbook. 96p. 1997. pap., wbk. ed. 19.95 (*1-57830-076-2*) Brainstrm.

— Storming Microsoft Word for Windows 95 (Version 7) Training Workbook. 168p. 1997. pap., wbk. ed. 19.95 (*1-57830-075-4*) Brainstrm.

— Windows 3.1 Client Training Workbook: Desktop Reference. 92p. 1996. pap., wbk. ed. 19.95 (*1-57830-077-0*) Brainstrm.

Brainstorm Staff. Brainstorm Groundwise 5.5 Web Access Training Workbook. (Illus.). 58p. 1999. spiral bd., wbk. ed. 29.95 (*1-57830-109-2*) Brainstrm.

— Brainstorm Groupwise 5.5 Workflow Professional Training Workbook. (Illus.). 54p. 1999. spiral bd., wbk. ed. 29.95 (*1-57830-110-6*) Brainstrm.

***Brainstorm Staff.** BrainStorm Training Workbook Windows NT 4.0. (Illus.). 150p. 1999. spiral bd. write for info. (*1-57830-111-4*) Brainstrm.

Brainwaves Limited Staff. Forgetful Ted: A Book about Telling Time. LC 97-8288. (Illus.). 16p. (J). 1997. 9.95 (*0-7641-5032-4*) Barron.

Brainwaves, Ltd. Staff, creator. Disney's the Hunchback of Notre Dame: Stained Glass Kit. (Illus.). 24p. (J). (gr. 3-7). 1996. 12.95 (*0-7868-3115-4*, Pub. by Disney Pr) Little.

Brainwaves Studio Staff. Pocahontas Bead Book & Kit. LC 95-67717. 32p. (J). (gr. 3-7). 1995. pap. 12.95 (*0-7868-4035-8*, Pub. by Disney Pr) Little.

Braio, Frank P. Lonergan's Retrieval of the Notion of Human Being: Clarifications of the Reflections on the Argument of Insight, Chapters I-XVIII. LC 87-34585. 460p. (C). 1988. lib. bdg. 54.50 (*0-8191-6851-3*) U Pr of Amer.

***Braiotta, Louis.** The Audit Committee Handbook. 3rd ed. LC 99-22088. 446p. 1999. pap. 60.00 (*0-471-34576-8*) Wiley.

Brairton, Betsey, ed. see Beardsley, John, et al.

Brairton, Betsey, ed. see Benson, Cynda L.

Brairton, Betsey, ed. see Benson, Cynda L. & Sallee, Katherine.

Brais, Elyse. L' Instinct du Stress: Choisir ou Subir. LC 97-941203. (FRE.). 217p. 1997. 22.95 (*2-89466-012-X*) Edns Roseau.

Braisted, William R. Meiroku Zasshi: Journal of the Japanese Enlightenment. 579p. 1976. 55.50 (*0-674-56467-7*) HUP.

— The United States Navy in the Pacific, 1897-1909. LC 57-12530. 292p. reprint ed. pap. 90.60 (*0-608-20115-4*, 207138700011) Bks Demand.

— The United States Navy in the Pacific, 1909-1922. LC 75-131957. 761p. reprint ed. pap. 200.00 (*0-608-20098-0*, 207137000011) Bks Demand.

— United States Navy in the Pacific, 1897-1909. LC 70-90473. (Illus.). 1958. reprint ed. 19.50 (*0-8290-0373-8*); reprint ed. pap. text 12.95 (*0-89197-971-9*) Irvington.

Brait, Susan. Chesapeake Gold: Man & Oyster on the Bay. LC 90-12664. 160p. 1990. 22.50 (*0-8131-1716-X*) U Pr of Ky.

Braitenbach, E. H., tr. from GER. On the Texture of Brains: An Introduction to Neuroanatomy for the Cybernetically Minded. LC 77-21851. (Illus.). 1977. 23.95 (*0-387-08391-X*) Spr-Verlag.

Braitenberg, V. & Schuz, A. Anatomy of the Cortex: Statistics & Geometry. Barlow, H. B. et al, eds. (Studies of Brain Function: Vol. 18). (Illus.). ix, 249p. 1991. 42.95 (*0-387-53233-1*) Spr-Verlag.

— Cortex: Statistics & Geometry of Neuronal Connectivity. 2nd ed. (Studies Brain Function Ser.: Vol. 18). (Illus.). 280p. 1998. 99.00 (*3-540-63816-4*) Spr-Verlag.

Braitenberg, Valentino. Vehicles: Experiments in Synthetic Psychology. 168p. (C). 1986. pap. text 14.50 (*0-262-52112-1*, Bradford Bks) MIT Pr.

Braitenberg, Valentino, jt. auth. see Aertsen, Ad.

Braitenberg, Valentino, jt. ed. see Aertsen, Ad.

Braiterman, Zachary. God after Auschwitz: Tradition & Change in Post-Holocaust Jewish Thought. LC 98-16318. 204p. 1998. text 39.50 (*0-691-05941-1*, Pub. by Princeton U Pr) Cal Prin Full Svc.

Braith, Wayne. Photo Techniques. 2nd ed. 144p. (C). 1995. pap., per. 19.95 (*0-7872-1569-4*) Kendall-Hunt.

Braith, Wayne A., et al. Fundamental Photographic Techniques: A Laboratory Manual. 144p. (C). 1993. 17.95 (*0-8403-6734-1*) Kendall-Hunt.

Braithewaite, William S., ed. The Book of Georgian Verse, Vol. 2. LC 76-98076. (Granger Index Reprint Ser.). 1313p. reprint ed. lib. bdg. 38.00 (*0-8290-0488-2*) Irvington.

Braithwait. Learning to Compute 1. 1991. pap. text, student ed. 15.00 (*0-03-047507-4*) Holt R&W.

— Learning to Compute 1 & 2: Answer Key. 1991. pap. text 6.00 (*0-03-047512-0*) Holt R&W.

— Learning to Compute 2. 1991. pap. text 15.00 (*0-03-047508-2*) Holt R&W.

Braithwait, Richard. The English Gentleman: 1630 Edition. 16th ed. Stern, Jeffrey, ed. & intro. by. (Classics in Education Ser.). 482p. 1996. reprint ed. 105.00 (*1-85506-273-9*) Bks Intl VA.

— The English Gentlewoman Drawne Out to the Full Body, Expressing What Habilliments Do Best Attire Her. LC 70-25509. (English Experience Ser.: No. 215). 222p. 1970. reprint ed. 55.00 (*90-221-0215-7*) Walter J Johnson.

Braithwaite. All the Way Home. 1989. mass mkt. 5.95 (*0-7710-1614-X*) McCland & Stewart.

— IT Management. 256p. (Orig.). 2000. pap. 44.95 (*0-471-37308-7*) Wiley.

Braithwaite, Althea. Exploring Emotions, 6 bks. Incl. Being Friends. LC 98-5587. (Illus.). 32p. (J). (gr. 3 up). 1998. lib. bdg. 21.27 (*0-8368-2115-7*); Feeling Angry. LC 98-10295. (Illus.). 32p. (J). (gr. 3 up). 1998. lib. bdg. 21.27 (*0-8368-2116-5*); Feeling Jealous. LC 98-5584. (Illus.). 32p. (J). (gr. 3 up). 1998. lib. bdg. 21.27 (*0-8368-2117-3*); Feeling Scared. LC 98-5586. (Illus.). 32p. (J). (gr. 3 up). 1998. lib. bdg. 21.27 (*0-8368-2118-1*); Feeling Shy. LC 98-5585. (Illus.). 32p. (J). (gr. 3 up). 1998. lib. bdg. 21.27 (*0-8368-2119-X*); Telling the Truth. LC 98-5583. (Illus.). 32p. (J). (gr. 3 up). 1998. lib. bdg. 21.27 (*0-8368-2120-3*); (Illus.). (J). 1998. Set lib. bdg. 127.60 (*0-8368-2114-9*) Gareth Stevens Inc.

— My Two Families. 1997. 11.95 (*0-7136-4542-3*, Pub. by A & C Blk) Midpt Trade.

Braithwaite, Brian. Women's Magazines: The First 300 Years. LC 95-139782. 192p. 1996. pap. 24.95 (*0-7206-0936-4*, Pub. by P Owen Ltd) Dufour.

Braithwaite, Cherrill, jt. auth. see Stevenson, Richard.

Braithwaite, Constance. Conscientious Objection to Various Compulsions under British Law. LC 95-236422. 436p. 1999. pap. 36.00 (*1-85072-127-0*, Pub. by W Sessions) St Mut.

***Braithwaite, Dawn O. & Thompson, Teresa L., eds.** Handbook of Communication & People with Disabilities: Research & Application. LC 99-29094. 400p. 1999. write for info. (*0-8058-3059-6*) L Erlbaum Assocs.

Braithwaite, Diana. Martha & Elvira: A Play. 96p. 1993. per. 10.95 (*0-920813-64-X*) Sister Vis Pr.

Braithwaite, E. R. To Sir, with Love. (YA). (gr. 9-12). 1990. mass mkt. 4.99 (*0-515-10519-8*, Jove) Berkley Pub.

— To Sir, with Love. 1959. 9.09 (*0-606-01487-X*, Pub. by Turtleback) Demco.

— To Sir, with Love. 1999. lib. bdg. 22.95 (*1-56723-208-6*) Yestermorrow.

Braithwaite, E. R. & Haber, J. Molybdenum: An Outline of Its Chemistry & Uses. LC 94-34256. (Studies in Inorganic Chemistry: Vol. 19). 680p. 1994. 349.00 (*0-444-88198-0*) Elsevier.

Braithwaite, J., jt. ed. see Grabosky, P.

***Braithwaite, Jeanine, et al.** Poverty & Social Assistance in Transition Countries LC 99-37662. 1999. text 45.00 (*0-312-22436-2*) St Martin.

Braithwaite, John. Crime, Shame & Reintegration. (Illus.). 238p. 1989. pap. text 19.95 (*0-521-35668-7*) Cambridge U Pr.

— History of the Revolutions in the Empire of Morocco, upon the Death of the Late Emperor, Muley Ishmael. LC 74-88541. (Black Heritage Library Collection). 1977. 32.95 (*0-8369-8522-2*) Ayer.

***Braithwaite, John.** Regulation, Crime & Freedom. LC 99-39395. (Collected Essays in Law Ser.). 300p. 1999. text 101.95 (*0-7546-2005-0*, Pub. by Ashgate Pub) Ashgate Pub Co.

***Braithwaite, John & Drahos, Peter.** Global Business Regulation. (Illus.). 728p. 2000. 79.95 (*0-521-78033-0*); pap. 29.95 (*0-521-78499-9*) Cambridge U Pr.

Braithwaite, John & Pettit, Philip. Not Just Deserts: A Republican Theory of Criminal Justice. 240p. 1990. 70.00 (*0-19-824233-6*) OUP.

— Not Just Deserts: A Republican Theory of Criminal Justice. 238p. 1993. reprint ed. pap. text 22.00 (*0-19-824056-2*) OUP.

Braithwaite, John, jt. auth. see Ayres, Ian.

Braithwaite, John, jt. auth. see Fisse, Brent.

Braithwaite, John, jt. ed. see Grabosky, Peter N.

Braithwaite, John M. & King, Edward J. Multiple-Class Teaching (UNESCO) (Education Studies & Documents: No. 12). 1974. reprint ed. pap. 25.00 (*0-8115-1336-X*) Periodicals Srv.

Braithwaite, Junior, jt. auth. see Scott, Ricardo A.

Braithwaite, Kent. The Wonderland Murders. 326p. 2000. pap. 14.95 (*1-891929-33-X*) Four Seasons.

Braithwaite, Lawrence. Wigger. 96p. 1995. pap. text 9.95 (*1-55152-020-6*, Pub. by Arsenal Pulp) LPC InBook.

***Braithwaite, Lawrence Ytzhak.** Ratz Are Nice (PSP) A Novel. 210p. 2000. pap. 11.95 (*1-55583-554-6*, Pub. by Alyson Pubns) Consort Bk Sales.

Braithwaite, Lee F. Graptolites from the Lower Ordovician Pogonip Group of Western Utah. LC 75-31373. (Geological Society of America, Special Paper: No. 166). 112p. reprint ed. pap. 34.80 (*0-608-13549-6*, 202545400044) Bks Demand.

Braithwaite, Nicholas, et al. Electronic Materials. 336p. 1990. pap. text 54.95 (*0-408-02840-8*) Buttrwrth-Heinemann.

Braithwaite, Pamela A. Byron's Double Discovery. (Illus.). 120p. (Orig.). (J). (gr. 4-10). 1991. pap. 4.50 (*1-880960-00-1*) Script Memory Fl.

Braithwaite, Paul, jt. auth. see Tierney, Francis.

Braithwaite, R. B. Scientific Explanation: 1953 Edition. 388p. 1996. reprint ed. 64.00 (*1-85506-327-1*) Bks Intl VA.

— Theory of Games As a Tool for the Modern Philosopher Bound with an Empiricist's View of the Nature of Religious Belief: 1955 Edition. (Key Texts Ser.). 116p. 1996. reprint ed. pap. 19.95 (*1-85506-315-8*) Bks Intl VA.

Braithwaite, Rella. Some Black Women: Profiles of Black Women in Canada. (Illus.). 130p. 1993. per. 19.95 (*0-920813-84-4*) Sister Vis Pr.

Braithwaite, Roderick. Palmerston & Africa: The Rio Nunez Affair, Competition, Diplomacy & Justice. LC 96-60448. (Illus.). 256p. 1996. text 65.00 (*1-86064-109-1*) St Martin.

Braithwaite, Ronald L. & Taylor, Sandra E., eds. Health Issues in the Black Community. LC 92-20174. (Health-Management Ser.). 403p. 1992. text 45.95 (*1-55542-477-5*) Jossey-Bass.

Braithwaite, Ronald L., et al. Prisons & Aids: A Public Health Opportunity. LC 96-22690. (Jossey-Bass Health Ser.). 1996. 34.95 (*0-7879-0308-6*) Jossey-Bass.

***Braithwaite, S.** The Power of It. 1998. pap. 88.00 (*81-86982-01-9*, Pub. by Business Pubns) St Mut.

Braithwaite, Timothy. The Power of IT: Maximizing Your Technology Investments. 150p. 1996. pap. 27.00 (*0-87389-349-2*, H0902) ASQ Qual Pr.

Braithwaite, Valerie A. & Levi, Margaret, eds. Trust & Governance. LC 98-2935. (Illus.). 384p. (C). 1998. 45.00 (*0-87154-134-3*) Russell Sage.

Braithwaite, William C. The Beginnings of Quakerism. 1999. pap. 36.00 (*0-900657-25-1*, Pub. by W Sessions) St Mut.

— The Beginnings of Quakerism. 610p. 1998. reprint ed. pap. 41.00 (*0-7884-0955-7*, B603) Heritage Bk.

An Asterisk (*) at the beginning of an entry indicates that the title is appearing for the first time.

Braithwaite, William Charles. The Second Period of Quakerism. 1999. pap. 36.00 (*0-900657-49-9*, Pub. by W Sessions) St Mut.

Braithwaite, William S. Anthology of Magazine Verse & Year Book of American Poetry, 6 Vols. text 140.95 (*0-8369-9358-6*, 19729) Ayer.

— Book of Georgian Verse, 2 Vols., Set. LC 76-98076. (Granger Index Reprint Ser.). 1977. 57.95 (*0-8369-6069-6*) Ayer.

— The Book of Georgian Verse, Vol. 1. LC 76-98076. (Granger Index Reprint Ser.). 661p. reprint ed. lib. bdg. 38.00 (*0-8290-0487-4*) Irvington.

— House of Falling Leaves. LC 77-83937. (Black Heritage Library Collection). 1977. 20.95 (*0-8369-8523-0*) Ayer.

— Lyrics of Life & Love. LC 70-88540. (Black Heritage Library Collection). 1988. 12.95 (*0-88143-081-1*) Ayer.

Braithwaite, William S., ed. Anthology of Magazine Verse for Nineteen Fifteen: And Year Book of American Poetry. LC 72-368. (Granger Index Reprint Ser.). 1977. reprint ed. 23.95 (*0-8369-6358-X*) Ayer.

— Anthology of Magazine Verse for Nineteen Fourteen: And Year Book of American Poetry. LC 78-37116. (Granger Index Reprint Ser.). 1977. reprint ed. 19.95 (*0-8369-6309-1*) Ayer.

— Anthology of Magazine Verse for Nineteen Sixteen. And Year Book of American Poetry; Second Ed. 2nd ed. LC 72-368. (Granger Index Reprint Ser.). 1977. reprint ed. 20.95 (*0-8369-6359-8*) Ayer.

— Anthology of Magazine Verse for Nineteen Thirteen. Including the Magazines & the Poets; a Review. LC 72-3537. (Granger Index Reprint Ser.). 1977. reprint ed. 12.95 (*0-8369-8235-5*) Ayer.

— Anthology of Magazine Verse for Nineteen Twenty-Four. And Yearbook of American Poetry. LC 72-3537. (Granger Index Reprint Ser.). 1977. reprint ed. 22.95 (*0-8369-8236-3*) Ayer.

— Anthology of Magazine Verse for Nineteen Twenty Six. And Yearbook of American Poetry. LC 72-3537. (Granger Index Reprint Ser.). reprint ed. 37.00 (*0-8369-8237-1*) Ayer.

Braithwaite, William T. Who Judges the Judges? A Study of Procedures for Removal & Retirement. LC 72-179947. (American Bar Foundation Publications). xviii, 167p. 1972. pap. 25.00 (*1-57588-379-1*, 305070) W S Hein.

Braitmaier, Friedrich. Geschichte der Poetischen Theorie und Kritik von den Diskursen der Maler bis auf Lessing. (GER.). x, 599p. 1972. reprint ed. write for info. (*3-487-04298-3*) G Olms Pubs.

Braitman, Ellen. Dollars & Sense for College Students: How Not to Run Out of Money by Midterms. LC 98-228475. (Princeton Review Ser.). 186p. 1998. pap. 10.95 (*0-375-75206-4*) Random.

Braizat. The Jordanian-Palestinian Relationship: The Bankruptcy of the Confederal Idea. LC 98-232310. 288p. 2000. text 59.50 (*1-86064-291-8*, Pub. by I B T) St Martin.

Brajendranath, tr. see Prashad, Baini, ed.

Brajovic-Bratanovic, Sonja, jt. auth. see Gruening, Hennie van.

Brakas, George. Aristotle's Concept of the Universal. (Studien und Materialien Zur Geschichte der Philosophie Ser.: Bd. 26). (GER.). vi, 114p. 1988. lib. bdg. 40.00 (*3-487-07996-8*) G Olms Pubs.

Brake. Men of Good Character: A History of the Sheet Metal Workers Union. (C). 1985. text 49.50 (*0-85315-580-1*, Pub. by Lawrence & Wishart) NYU Pr.

Brake, Carol B., et al. Great Lakes Region: Grades 1-3. (Illus.). 64p. 1996. pap. 6.95 (*1-889369-12-8*, TI0040) Teaching Ink.

Brake, Cynthia, jt. auth. see Brake, Dennis.

Brake, Dennis & Brake, Cynthia. The Ketogenic Cookbook. LC 97-22250. (Illus.). 128p. 1997. pap. 14.95 (*1-886559-99-6*) Pennycorner.

Brake, Kimberly A., jt. auth. see McMahon, Ann P.

***Brake, Laurel.** Nineteenth-century Media & the Construction of Identities. 2000. text 59.95 (*0-312-23215-2*) St Martin.

Brake, Laurel. Subjugated Knowledges: Journalism, Gender, & Literature in the Nineteenth Century. LC 93-31425. (C). 1994. text 45.00 (*0-8147-1218-5*); pap. text 18.50 (*0-8147-1219-3*) NYU Pr.

— Walter Pater. (Writers & Their Work Ser.). 95p. 1996. pap. text 15.00 (*0-7463-0716-0*, Pub. by Northcote House) U Pr of Miss.

Brake, Laurel, ed. The Endings of Epochs. (Essays & Studies: No. 48). 160p. (C). 1995. 60.00 (*0-85991-474-7*) Boydell & Brewer.

Brake, Michael. Comparative Youth Culture: The Sociology of Youth Cultures & Youth Subcultures in America, Britain & Canada. 224p. (Orig.). 1985. pap. 14.95 (*0-7100-9898-7*, Routledge Thoemms) Routledge.

Brake, Mike. Comparative Youth Culture: Sociology of Youth Cultures & Youth Subcultures in America Britain & Canada. 224p. (C). 1985. pap. 24.99 (*0-415-05108-8*) Routledge.

Brake, Patricia E. Justice in the Valley: A Bicentennial Perspective of the United States District Court for the Eastern District of Tennessee. LC 98-72700. (Illus.). 256p. 1998. 26.95 (*1-57736-106-7*, Hillsboro Pr) Providence Hse.

Brake, Phylip. Welsh in Three Months. LC 98-48006. (Hugo Ser.). 1999. pap. text 14.95 (*0-7894-4431-3*) DK Pub Inc.

Brake, Phylip & Apmyrddin, Mair. Welsh in Three Months. LC 98-48006. (Hugo Ser.). (WEL & ENG.). 1999. 24.95 incl. audio (*0-7894-4440-2*) DK Pub Inc.

Brake, Terence. Doing Business Internationally: The Guide to Cross Cultural Success. 300p. 1994. text 27.50 (*0-7863-0117-1*, Irwn Prfssnl) McGraw-Hill Prof.

— Global Leader: Management Insights from Around the World. LC 96-34765. 216p. 1996. text 29.95 (*0-7863-0821-4*, Irwn Prfssnl) McGraw-Hill Prof.

Brake, Terence & Walker, Danielle M. Doing Business Internationally: The Workbook to Cross-Cultural Success. rev. ed. Piispanen-Krabbe, Tuula, ed. (Illus.). 285p. 1994. pap. text 49.50 (*1-882390-02-4*) Princeton Trng.

Brake, Terence, et al. Doing Business Internationally: A Guide to Cross-Cultural Success, Princeton Training Press - Training Management Corporation. 1995. text 25.00 (*0-7863-0474-X*, Irwn Prfssnl) McGraw-Hill Prof.

Brake, Wayne. Shaping History: Ordinary People in European Politics, 1500-1700. LC 97-36930. 237p. 1998. 40.00 (*0-520-21170-7*, Pub. by U CA Pr); pap. 15.95 (*0-520-21318-1*, Pub. by U CA Pr) Cal Prin Full Svc.

Brakefield, Jay F., jt. auth. see Govenar, Alan B.

Brakefield, Tom. Big Cats: Kingdom of Might. LC 95-47771. (Illus.). 144p. 1996. pap. 19.95 (*0-89658-329-5*) Voyageur Pr.

Brakel, Aat, ed. People & Organizations Interacting. LC 84-5212. 272p. 1985. 215.00 (*0-471-90476-7*) Wiley.

Brakel, Arthur. Phonological Markedness & Distinctive Features. LC 82-49348. (Illus.). 144p. 1983. 29.95 (*0-253-34450-6*) Ind U Pr.

Brakel, Arthur, tr. see Capistrano de Abreu, Joao.

Brakel, Arthur, tr. see De Abreu, Joao C.

Brakel, Arthur, tr. see DosAnjos, Cyro.

Brakel, Arthur, tr. see Reis, Joao J.

Brakel-Papenhuyzen, Clara. The Bedhaya Court Dances of Central Java: A Mataram Tradition of Ritual Art. LC 91-17941. (Illus.). xvi, 350, 16p. 1992. 112.50 (*90-04-09424-5*) Brill Academic Pubs.

— Classical Javanese Dance: The Surakaarta Tradition & Its Terminology. (KITLV Verhandelingen Ser.: No. 155). (Illus.). 236p. (Orig.). 1996. pap. 44.00 (*90-6718-053-X*, Pub. by KITLV Pr) Cellar.

Brakel, Samuel J. American Indian Tribal Courts: The Costs of Separate Justice. LC 78-67458. 156p. reprint ed. pap. 48.40 (*0-8357-5374-3*, 205220400059) Bks Demand.

— Judicare. Public Funds, Private Lawyers, & Poor People. LC 74-75748. xi, 145p. 1974. pap. 20.00 (*0-910058-60-1*, 304850) W S Hein.

— Wisconsin Judicare: A Preliminary Appraisal. LC 72-95564. 122p. 1986. pap. 25.00 (*0-910058-56-3*, 305080) W S Hein.

Brakel, Samuel J. & Benson, Bruce L. Prisons & Corrections. 64p. 1998. pap. 7.95 (*0-945999-60-7*, 1021) Independent Inst.

Brakel, Samuel J., et al. Mentally Disabled & the Law. 3rd rev. ed. LC 85-71886. xxii, 845p. 1985. 85.00 (*0-910059-05-5*, 306030) W S Hein.

Brakeley, George A. Tested Ways to Successful Fund Raising. LC 79-54828. 185p. reprint ed. pap. 57.40 (*0-608-18619-8*, 202354400033) Bks Demand.

***Brakeman, Lyn.** The God Between Us: Healing the Wounds of Relationships. 192p. 2001. pap. 13.95 (*1-880913-48-8*) Innisfree Pr.

Brakeman, Lyn. Spiritual Lemons: Biblical Women, Irreverent Laughter, & Righteous Rage. LC 96-48354. 128p. (Orig.). 1997. pap. 12.95 (*1-880913-22-4*) Innisfree Pr.

Brakeman, Lynne. Chronology of Women Worldwide: People, Places, & Events That Shaped Women's History. LC 96-23915. 600p. 1996. 65.00 (*0-7876-0154-3*, GML00198-108862) Gale.

Brakenhelm, C. R. Problems of Religious Experience. 158p. 1985. pap. 32.50 (*91-554-1657-8*) Coronet Bks.

Brakenhielm, Carl R. How Philosophy Shapes Theories of Religion: An Analysis of Contemporary Philosophies of Religion, with Special Regard to the Thought of John Wislon, John Hick & D. Z. Phillips. (Studia Philosophiae Religionis: Vol. 2). 1975. pap. 36.00 (*91-40-04044-5*) Coronet Bks.

***Braker, Flo.** Simple Art of Perfect Baking. rev. ed. 1998. pap. 19.95 (*0-395-95011-2*, Chapters Bks) HM.

— Sweet Miniatures: The Art of Making Bite-Size Desserts. 2000. pap. 22.95 (*0-8118-2446-2*) Chronicle Bks.

Braker, Regina. Weapons of Women Writers Vol. 16: Bertha Von Suttner's Die Waffen Nieder! As Political Literature in the Tradition of Harriet Beecher Stowe's Uncle Tom's Cabin. LC 94-3633. (Austrian Culture Ser.: 16). 164p. (C). 1995. text 46.95 (*0-8204-2626-1*) P Lang Pubng.

Brakhage, Axel, et al, eds. Aspergillus Fumigatus: Biology, Clinical Aspects & Molecular Approaches to Pathogenicity. LC 99-24266. (Contributions to Microbiology Ser.: Vol. 2 (1998)). (Illus.). xii, 222p. 1998. 172.25 (*3-8055-6714-6*) S Karger.

Brakhage, Cynthia, ed. see Benner, Ludwig, Jr.

Brakhage, Cynthia, ed. see Brock, Pat D.

Brakhage, Cynthia, jt. ed. see Hall, Richard.

Brakhage, Cynthia, ed. see IFSTA Committee & Prendergast, Edward J.

Brakhage, Cynthia, ed. see Wiseman, John.

Brakhage, Cynthia S., jt. auth. see Benner, Ludwig, Jr.

Brakhage, Pamela. The Theology of "La Lozana Andaluza" 27.50 (*0-916379-34-5*) Scripta.

***Brakhage, Stan.** Essential Brakhage: Selected Writings on Filmmaking. 2000. pap. 18.00 (*0-929701-64-X*) McPherson & Co.

Brakhage, Stan. Film at Wit's End: Eight Avant-Garde Filmmakers. LC 89-32072. (Illus.). 183p. 1991. reprint ed. pap. 12.00 (*0-929701-16-X*) McPherson & Co.

— Metaphors on Vision. 2nd ed. (Illus.). 1976. pap. 12.00 (*0-317-55956-7*) Anthology Film.

Brakhage, Stan, jt. auth. see Taaffe, Philip.

Brakke, David. Athanasius & Asceticism. LC 98-21055. 376p. 1998. pap. 17.95 (*0-8018-6055-5*) Johns Hopkins.

Brakman, P., jt. ed. see Blomback, M.

Brakman, Steven & Van Marrewijk, Charles. The Economics of International Transfers. LC 98-3809. (Illus.). 232p. (C). 1998. text 59.95 (*0-521-57214-2*) Cambridge U Pr.

Brakman, Steven, et al. Market Behaviour & Macroeconomic Modelling LC 98-13604. xvi, 416p. 1998. write for info. (*0-333-71836-4*, Pub. by Macmillan) St Martin.

***Brakney, William H., ed.** The Believers Church: A Voluntary Church, Vol. 1. vii, 237p. 1998. pap. 25.00 (*0-9683462-0-0*) Pandora Pr.

Brako, Lois. Phyllopsora: Bacidiaceae. (Flora Neotropica Monographs: No. 55). (Illus.). 76p. 1991. pap. 16.00 (*0-89327-364-3*) NY Botanical.

Brako, Lois, et al. Scientific & Common Names of 7,000 Vascular Plants in the United States. LC 94-79381. (U. S. National Fungus Collections). 301p. (Orig.). 1995. pap. 34.00 (*0-89054-171-X*) Am Phytopathol Soc.

***Braksick, Leslie Wilk.** Unlock Behavior, Unleash Profits. 291p. 1999. 21.95 (*0-07-135878-1*) McGraw.

Bral, Eddy, jt. auth. see DeOliveira, Betty Pontes.

Braley & Thompson, Inc. Staff. Treatment Team Foster Care. 4th ed. (Illus.). 100p. pap. 6.00 (*1-883239-00-1*) Braley & Thompson.

— Treatment Team Foster Care. 5th ed. (Illus.). 100p. pap. 6.00 (*1-883239-01-X*) Braley & Thompson.

Braley, Alan, tr. see Janicke, Martin.

Braley, Alan, tr. see Kepel, Gilles.

Braley, Alan, tr. see Offe, Claire & Heinze, Rolf G.

Braley, Dean. Shaman's Story: The West Va. Petroglyphs. (Orig.). 1993. pap. 15.00 (*0-9638377-0-2*) D Braley.

— Storm Dreamer: The Making of a Shaman. (Illus.). 171p. (Orig.). 1995. pap., per. 15.00 (*0-9638377-1-0*) D Braley.

Braley, R. D. The Giant Clam: A Hatchery & Nursery Culture Manual. 144p. 1992. pap. 114.00 (*1-86320-072-X*, Pub. by ACIAR) St Mut.

Bralla. Handbook of the Manufacturing Process. 2001. 125.00 (*0-07-134906-5*) McGraw.

Bralla, James G. Design for Excellence. LC 95-21927. 325p. 1995. 49.00 (*0-07-007138-1*) McGraw.

— Design for Manufacturability Handbook. 2nd ed. LC 98-23438. (Illus.). 1368p. 1998. 125.00 (*0-07-007139-X*) McGraw.

***Brallier, Jess.** Magnetic Travel Fun. (Illus.). 48p. (J). 2000. 14.99 (*0-448-44086-5*, Plat & Munk) Peng Put Young Read.

— Web-in-a-Book: Surging the Web Without the Wait. (Illus.). (J). 2000. pap. 5.99 (*0-448-44093-8*, Planet Dexter) Peng Put Young Read.

Brallier, Jess. Y2kids: A Guide to the Millennium. LC 99-41440. 1999. pap. 4.99 (*0-448-42088-0*, G & D) Peng Put Young Read.

Brallier, Jess & Chabert, Sally C. Celebrate America. 128p. (Orig.). 1995. pap. 10.00 (*0-399-51943-2*, Perigee Bks) Berkley Pub.

Brallier, Jess M. Lawyers & Other Reptiles. (...And Other Reptiles Ser.). 128p. 1992. 12.00 (*0-8092-3919-1*, 391910, Contemporary Bks) NTC Contemp Pub Co.

Brallier, Jess M., ed. Medical Wit & Wisdom: The Best Medical Quotations from Hippocrates to Groucho Marx. LC 93-83465. (Illus.). 288p. 1993. 15.95 (*1-56138-289-2*) Running Pr.

***Brallier, Jess M. & Chabert, Sally C.** Coach: A Treasury of Inspiration & Laughter. LC 99-23271. 112p. 2000. 12.95 (*0-8092-2589-1*, 258910, Contemporary Bks) NTC Contemp Pub Co.

Brallier, Jess M. & Chabert, Sally C. Presidential Wit & Wisdom: Maxims, Mottos, Soundbites, Speeches & Asides: Memorable Quotes from America's Presidents. LC 95-23184. 336p. 1996. pap. 12.95 (*0-14-023904-9*, Penguin Bks) Viking Penguin.

Brallier, Jess M. & McDonough, R. P. The Pessimist's Journal of Very, Very Bad Days. 1989. pap. 9.95 (*0-316-10600-3*) Little.

Bralow, Lesteet, ed. see Brower, Anne C.

Bralow, Lisette, ed. see Andreoli, Thomas E., et al.

Bralow, Lisette, ed. see Bassett, Lawrence W., et al.

Bralow, Lisette, ed. see Behrman, Richard E., et al.

Bralow, Lisette, ed. see Berci, George & Cuschieri, Alfred.

Bralow, Lisette, ed. see Braner, Dana, et al.

Bralow, Lisette, ed. see Busutil, Ronald W. & Klintmalm, Goran B.

Bralow, Lisette, ed. see Coel, Marc & Leung, Jimmy.

Bralow, Lisette, ed. see Creasy, Robert K. & Resnick, Robert.

Bralow, Lisette, ed. see Davidson, Alan J., et al.

Bralow, Lisette, ed. see Dockery, Gary L.

Bralow, Lisette, ed. see Economou, Steven G. & Economou, Tasia S.

Bralow, Lisette, ed. see Fraser, Richard S., et al.

Bralow, Lisette, ed. see Friedman-Kien, Alvin E.

Bralow, Lisette, ed. see Gamsu, Gordon K. & Patel, Maitray.

Bralow, Lisette, ed. see Goodman, Lawrence R.

Bralow, Lisette, ed. see Gore, Richard M. & Levine, Marc S.

Bralow, Lisette, ed. see Jenson, Hal B.

Bralow, Lisette, ed. see Kliegman, Robert M., et al.

Bralow, Lisette, ed. see Kransdorf, Mark & Murphey, Mark D.

Bralow, Lisette, ed. see Levien, David H.

Bralow, Lisette, ed. see Mettler, Fred A., Jr.

Bralow, Lisette, ed. see Mettler, Fred A., et al.

Bralow, Lisette, ed. see Moore, Wesley S.

Bralow, Lisette, ed. see Ouriel, Kenneth & Rutherford, Robert B.

Bralow, Lisette, ed. see Resnick, Donald.

Bralow, Lisette, ed. see Robinson, N. Edward.

Bralow, Lisette, ed. see Sabiston, David C.

Bralow, Lisette, ed. see Sabiston, David C. & Lyerly, H. Kim.

Bralow, Lisette, ed. see Sperling, Mark A.

Bralow, Lisette, ed. see Svensson, Lars G. & Crawford, E. Stanley.

Bralow, Lisette, ed. see Valji, Karim.

Bralow, Lisette, ed. see Walsh-Sukys, Michele & Krug, Steven E.

Bralow, Lisette, ed. see Webb, W. Richard, et al.

Bralow, Lisette, ed. see Yen, Samuel S., et al.

Bralow, Lisette, ed. see Zwiebel, William J.

Bralver, Belinda J. The Mommy Book. 1989. pap. 5.95 (*0-8184-0503-1*) Carol Pub Group.

Braly, James. Dr. Braly's Food Allergy & Nutrition Revolution. LC 92-27994. 544p. 1992. pap. 17.95 (*0-87983-590-7*, 35907K, Keats Publng) NTC Contemp Pub Co.

***Braly, James.** Food Allergy Relief. (Good Health Guides Ser.). 48p. 2000. pap. 3.95 (*0-658-00723-8*, 007238, Keats Publng) NTC Contemp Pub Co.

Braly, Ken, jt. ed. see Morgan, Rebecca.

Braly, Scott A. & Kay, Robert S. The Effective Audit Committee: The Keystone of Corporate Governance in the 80's. Cavanaugh, John T., ed. 28p. (Orig.). 1982. pap. 5.95 (*0-942640-02-0*) Touche Co.

Braly, William T., et al. Daily Sensorimotor Training Activities. 1968. teacher ed. 8.95 (*0-914296-02-7*) Ed Activities.

Bram, Christopher. The Father of Frankenstein. 320p. 1996. pap. 12.95 (*0-452-27337-4*, Plume) Dutton Plume.

— Gossip. 352p. 1998. pap. 13.95 (*0-452-27338-2*, Plume) Dutton Plume.

— Hold Tight. 288p. 1989. pap. 12.95 (*0-452-26226-7*, Plume) Dutton Plume.

— In Memory of Angel Clare. 1990. pap. 10.95 (*0-452-26434-0*, Plume) Dutton Plume.

B

***Bram, Christopher.** The Notorious Dr. August: His Real Life & Crimes. LC 99-55805. 512p. 2000. 26.00 (*0-688-17569-4*, Wm Morrow) Morrow Avon.

Bram, Christopher. Surprising Myself. LC 86-82182. 400p. 1987. pap. 17.95 (*1-55611-007-3*, Pub. by D I Fine) Penguin Putnam.

— Surprising Myself. 1995. pap. 12.95 (*0-8050-0669-9*, Owl) H Holt & Co.

***Bram, Elisabeth Van, et al.** In Royal Array. LC 99-176025. 253 p. 1998. write for info. (*90-400-9275-3*) Waandrs.

Bram, Joseph, jt. auth. see Saaty, Thomas L.

***Bramadat, Paul A.** The Church on the World's Turf: An Evangelical Christian Group at a Secular University. LC 99-16827. (Religion in America Ser.). 224p. 2000. text 45.00 (*0-19-513499-0*) OUP.

Bramah, Edward & Bramah, Joan. Coffee Makers: Three Hundred Years of Art & Design. (Illus.). 192p. 1989. 95.00 (*1-870948-33-5*, Pub. by Quiller Pr) St Mut.

Bramah, Ernest. Kai Lung Beneath the Mulberry-Tree. Reginald, R. & Melville, Douglas, eds. LC 77-84202. (Lost Race & Adult Fantasy Ser.). 1978. reprint ed. lib. bdg. 28.95 (*0-405-10959-8*) Ayer.

— The Wallet of Kai Lung. 337p. 1977. lib. bdg. 15.95 (*0-89966-269-2*) Buccaneer Bks.

Bramah, Joan, jt. auth. see Bramah, Edward.

Bramald, Rod, et al. Mathematics Cubed. 64p. (J). (gr. 3-11). pap. 12.50 (*1-871098-08-4*, Pub. by Claire Pubns) Parkwest Pubns.

Bramall, Chris. Legacies of Maoist Economic Development in Sichuan. LC 92-44066. 408p. 1993. 69.00 (*0-19-828790-9*, Clarendon Pr) OUP.

***Bramall, Chris.** Sources of Chinese Economic Growth, 1978-1996. (Studies on Contemporary China). 234p. 2000. text 125.00 (*0-19-829697-5*) OUP.

Bramall, Dwin & Jackson, William. The Chiefs. (Illus.). 517p. 1992. text 25.95 (*0-08-040370-0*, Pub. by Brasseys) Brasseys.

Bramall, Joan, jt. auth. see Towler, Jean.

Braman, Ariette. Kids Around the World Create! The Best Crafts & Activities from Many Lands. LC 99-12225. 128p. (J). (gr. 3-8). 1999. pap. 12.95 (*0-471-29005-X*) Wiley.

***Braman, Arlette N.** Kids Around the World Cook! The Best Foods & Recipes from Many Lands. LC 99-46110. (Kids Around the World Ser.). 192p. (J). (gr. 3-7). 2000. pap. text 12.95 (*0-471-35251-9*) Wiley.

— Traditional Native American Arts & Activities. 128p. (J). (gr. 3-7). 2000. pap. 12.95 (*0-471-35992-0*) Wiley.

Braman, Chuck P. Drumming Patterns: The Components of Rhythm & Technique. (Illus.). 176p. (Orig.). 1988. pap. text 25.00 (*0-9622293-0-X*) Drumstroke Pubns.

— Drumming Patterns: The Components of Rhythm & Technique. (Illus.). 176p. (Orig.). 1995. pap. text 28.00 incl. audio (*0-9622293-1-8*) Drumstroke Pubns.

Braman, James D. Where the Fuzzy Marmots Grow: The Rollicking Adventures of Historic Troop 511. unabridged ed. Campbell, Gloria & Campbell, Larry, eds. LC 98-70073. (Illus.). 213p. 1998. pap. 10.95 (*0-9660826-0-5*) Good Scout.

Braman, Sandra & Mohammdi, Annabelle S., eds. Globalization, Communication & Transnational Civil Society. LC 96-22694. (I. A. M. C. R. Bks.). 320p. (Orig.). (C). 1996. text 65.00 (*1-57273-020-X*); pap. text 26.50 (*1-57273-021-8*) Hampton Pr NJ.

Braman, Sandra, ed. see Woolf, Douglas.

Bramann, Jorn K. Buddhist Lovers & Other Troubles. LC 93-85864. 84p. (Orig.). 1994. pap. 8.00 (*0-945073-17-8*) Nightsun MD.

— Camcorder Art: What to Do with Your Video Camera after You Read the Operating Manual. LC 91-60069. (Illus.). 110p. (Orig.). 1991. pap. text 7.50 (*0-945073-12-7*) Nightsun MD.

— Living in the Present: An Anthology of Philosophy & Poetry. 130p. (Orig.). (C). 1982. per. 7.50 (*0-941452-03-4*) Acheron Pr.

— Phantom Doors: Screenplay. LC 95-70027. (Upper Potomacs Ser.). (Illus.). 120p. (Orig.). 1996. pap. 5.00 (*0-945073-19-4*) Nightsun MD.

— Psychoanalysis of a New Freeway. LC 91-62671. (Illus.). 110p. (Orig.). 1992. pap. 7.00 (*0-945073-14-3*) Nightsun MD.

— Traveling Light: An Introduction to Philosophy. LC 91-62676. (Illus.). 170p. (Orig.). (C). 1992. pap. text 15.00 (*0-945073-13-5*) Nightsun MD.

— Walden Zero: A Novella. LC 87-63331. 140p. (Orig.). 1988. pap. 9.99 (*0-945073-07-0*) Nightsun MD.

Bramann, Jorn K., ed. Higher Ed. LC 88-622681. 95p. (Orig.). 1989. pap. 7.00 (*0-945073-09-7*) Nightsun MD.

— Higher Ed: Essays & Poems. 1988. write for info. (*0-318-65915-8*) Nightsun Frostburg.

Bramann, Jorn K., ed. & intro. see Ralston, Jim.

Bramann, Jorn K., tr. see Fichte, Johann G.

Bramante, Gabriele. Willis Faber & Dumas Building: Ipswich 1974 Foster Associates. (Architecture in Detail Ser.). (Illus.). 60p. (C). 1993. pap. 29.95 (*0-7148-2772-X*, Pub. by Phaidon Press) Phaidon Pr.

Bramat, A. Dictionary of Abbreviations & Acronyms in Aeronautics & Space. (ENG, FRE & RUS.). 1997. 96.50 (*0-7859-9721-0*) Fr & Eur.

— Dictionary of Abbreviations & Acronyms in Aeronautics & Space Russian-French-English. (ENG, FRE & RUS.). 483p. 1997. pap. 96.50 (*2-7204-0326-1*, Pub. by Institut dEtude) IBD Ltd.

B

Brambati, Bruno, et al, eds. Chorionic Villus Sampling: Fetal Diagnosis of Genetic Diseases in the First Trimester. LC 85-27457. (Clinical & Biochemical Analysis Ser.: No. 21). 328p. 1986. reprint ed. pap. 101.70 (*0-608-01277-7*, 206202500001) Bks Demand.

Brambila, Rosa & Monjaras-Ruiz, Jesus, eds. Los Arqueologos Frente a las Fuentes. (SPA., Illus.). 230p. 1996. pap. 16.00 (*968-29-5239-5*, IN75, Pub. by Dir Gen Pubicaiones) UPLAAP.

Brambila, Rosa, jt. ed. see Crespo, Ana M.

Brambilla, F. & Bridges. Perspectives in Endocrine Psychobiology. LC 76-27305. 590p. reprint ed. 182.90 (*0-8357-9953-0*, 201616000098) Bks Demand.

Brambilla, F. G., jt. ed. see Ferrari, E.

Brambilla, Marco. Kinetic Theory of Plasma Waves: Homogeneous Plasmas. LC 98-10215. (The International Series of Monographs on Physics: No. 96). (Illus.). 656p. 1998. text 140.00 (*0-19-855956-9*) OUP.

Brambilla, Massimo & Llobera, Jose. Enciclopedia Practica de la Fotografia, 7 vols., Set. (SPA.). 1512p. 1976. 175.00 (*0-7859-0862-5*, S50555) Fr & Eur.

Brambilla, N., jt. auth. see Prosperi, G. M.

Brambilla, R. & Crotti, A. Avanti! Owen, J., ed. (C). 1988. audio 220.00 (*0-85950-848-X*, Pub. by S Thornes Pubs) St Mut.

Brambilla, R., et al. Learning from Galveston. LC 81-51442. (Illus.). 112p. (Orig.). 1983. pap. 6.95 (*0-685-05566-3*) Urban Initiat.

Brambilla, Roberto & Longo, Cranni. Learning from Baltimore. 147p. (Orig.). 1979. pap. 21.95 (*0-87855-832-2*) Transaction Pubs.

Brambilla, Roberto & Longo, Gianni. Learning from Baltimore. LC 79-90201. (Learning from the U. S. A.: What Makes Cities Livable Ser.). (Illus.). 150p. (Orig.). 1979. pap. 6.95 (*0-936020-02-4*) Urban Initiat.

— Learning from Seattle. (Learning from the U. S. A.: What Makes Cities Livable Ser.). 150p. 1980. reprint ed. pap. 21.95 (*0-87855-833-0*) Transaction Pubs.

Brambl, R. & Marzluf, G. A., eds. Biochemistry & Molecular Biology. (Mycota Ser.: Vol. III). (Illus.). 456p. 1996. 199.00 (*0-387-58004-2*) Spr-Verlag.

Brambl, R. & Marzluf, George A., eds. Biochemistry & Molecular Biology. (Mycota Ser.: Vol. 3). (Illus.). 456p. 1996. 229.00 (*3-540-58004-2*) Spr-Verlag.

Bramble, Simon K., jt. ed. see Rudin, Leonid I.

***Bramble, Barry B. & West, Joseph D.** Design-Build Contracting Claims. LC 99-42620. 528p. 1999. boxed set 160.00 (*0-7355-0690-6*) Panel Pubs.

Bramble, Barry B., jt. auth. see Callahan, Michael T.

Bramble, H. David, ed. Classical Myths & Legends in the Middle Ages & Renaissance. 1998. lib. bdg. 100.00 (*1-57958-020-3*) Fitzroy Dearborn.

Bramble, James H. Multigrid Methods. 1993. pap. 43.00 (*0-582-23435-2*, Pub. by Addison-Wesley) Longman.

Bramble, Linda. Undiscovered Niagara. (Illus.). 96p. (Orig.). 1990. pap. 16.95 (*1-919783-61-X*, Pub. by Boston Mills) Genl Dist Srvs.

Bramble, Linda & Darling, Shari. Discovering Ontario's Wine Country. (Illus.). 96p. (Orig.). 1992. pap. 16.95 (*1-55046-054-4*, Pub. by Boston Mills) Genl Dist Srvs.

Bramble, Peter W. The Overcome: A Black Passover. LC 89-81167. (Illus.). 203p. (Orig.). 1989. pap. 14.95 (*0-935132-17-1*) C H Fairfax.

Bramble, William J., jt. auth. see Mason, Emanuel J.

Bramblett, Annette S. Forsyth County, GA: From the Garland Bagley Collection. (Images of America Ser.). (Illus.). 128p. 1998. pap. 16.99 (*0-7524-0419-9*) Arcadia Publng.

Bramblett, Claud A. Patterns of Primate Behavior. 2nd rev. ed. (Illus.). 292p. (C). 1994. pap. text 23.95 (*0-88133-743-9*) Waveland Pr.

Bramblett, Claud A., jt. auth. see Steele, D. Gentry.

***Bramblett, Reid.** Europe for Dummies. (For Dummies Ser.). 624p. 2000. pap. 19.99 (*0-7645-6190-1*) IDG Bks.

Bramblett, Reid, et al. Frommer's Italy from $70 a Day: The Ultimage Guide to Comfortable Low-Cost Travel. 2nd ed. (Illus.). 755p. 1999. pap. 19.95 (*0-02-862447-5*, Frommer) Macmillan Gen Ref.

Brambring, Michael, et al, eds. Children at Risk: Assessment, Longitudinal Research, & Intervention. (Prevention & Intervention in Childhood & Adolescence Ser.: Vol. 7). xiv, 490p. (C). 1989. lib. bdg. 69.95 (*3-11-012134-4*) De Gruyter.

— Early Childhood Intervention: Theory, Evolution, & Practice. LC 96-30392. (Prevention & Intervention in Childhood & Adolescence Ser.: Vol. 20). xii, 513p. (C). 1996. text 98.95 (*3-11-015410-2*, 130/96) De Gruyter.

***Bramdmer, Garu.** Rot. 1999. 40.00 (*1-881475-66-2*) Cemetery Dance.

Brame & Grasselli. Infrared & Raman Spectroscopy, Pt. B. (Practical Spectroscopy Ser.: Vol. 1). (Illus.). 384p. 1977. text 195.00 (*0-8247-6526-5*) Dekker.

***Brame, Charles L.** Honestly Abe: A Cartoon Biography of Abraham Lincoln. 2nd rev. ed. LC 99-96571. (Illus.). 316p. 2000. reprint ed. 24.95 (*0-9659919-3-8*) ABE Pr.

— Honestly Abe: A Cartoon Biography of Abraham Lincoln. 2nd rev. ed. LC 99-96571. (Illus.). 320p. 2000. reprint ed. pap. 16.95 (*0-9659919-1-1*) ABE Pr.

Brame, Charles L. Honestly Abe: A Cartoon Expose of Abraham Lincoln. Williams, Ruth, ed. LC 97-75119. (Illus.). 304p. 1998. 34.95 (*0-9659919-2-X*) ABE Pr.

Brame, Edward G., ed. Applied Spectroscopy Reviews, Vol. 6. LC 68-23774. (Illus.). 391p. reprint ed. pap. 121.30 (*0-8357-5689-0*, 202798700006) Bks Demand.

— Applied Spectroscopy Reviews, Vol. 7. LC 68-23774. (Illus.). 397p. reprint ed. pap. 123.10 (*0-8357-5690-4*, 202798500007) Bks Demand.

Brame, Edward G., Jr. & Grasselli, Jeanette G., eds. Infrared & Raman Spectroscopy, Pt. C. LC 75-32391. (Practical Spectroscopy Ser.). 334p. 1977. reprint ed. pap. 103.60 (*0-608-04616-7*, 204112500003) Bks Demand.

Brame, Edward G., Jr. & Grasselli, Jeannette G., eds. Infrared & Raman Spectroscopy, Pt. B. LC 75-32391. (Practical Spectroscopy Ser.: No. 1). (Illus.), 382p. reprint ed. pap. 118.50 (*0-7837-0810-6*, 204112500002) Bks Demand.

***Brame, Genevieve.** Chez Vous en France: Living & Working In France. 1999. pap. text 19.95 (*0-7494-2902-X*, Kogan Pg Educ) Stylus Pub VA.

Brame, Gloria. Where the Boys Are: A Step-by-Step Guide to Finding Mr. Right. LC 96-71703. 256p. 1997. mass mkt. 5.99 (*0-380-79179-X*, Avon Bks) Morrow Avon.

Brame, Gloria, et al. Different Loving: A Complete Exploration of the World of Sexual Dominance & Submission. 640p. 1996. pap. 19.95 (*0-679-76956-0*) Random.

Brame, Gloria G. Come Hither: A Commonsense Guide to Kinky Sex. LC 99-49475. 336p. 2000. per. 13.00 (*0-684-85462-7*, Fireside) S&S Trade Pap.

Brame, Grace, ed. see Underhill, Evelyn.

***Brame, Grace A.** Faith, the Yes of the Heart. LC 99-44990. 192p. 1999. pap. 14.99 (*0-8066-3805-2*, Augsburg) Augsburg Fortress.

Brame, Luise. Seattle's Gastronomic Shopper. (Illus.). 179p. (Orig.). 1981. pap. 6.95 (*0-932998-02-X*) Reynard Hse.

Brame, Michael, et al, eds. A Festschrift for Sol Saporta. 351p. 1986. write for info. (*0-932998-06-2*) Noit Amrofer.

Brame, Michael, jt. auth. see Bettembourg, Georges.

Brame, Michael K. Base Generated Syntax. LC 78-70404. (Linguistics Research Monograph Ser.). 1978. text 28.00 (*0-932998-00-3*) Noit Amrofer.

— Essays Toward Realistic Syntax. LC 79-67347. (Linguistics Research Monograph Ser.: Vol. 2). 1979. text 38.00 (*0-932998-01-1*) Noit Amrofer.

Bramel, Julien & Simchi-Levi, David. The Logic of Logistics: Theory, Algorithms, & Applications for Logistics Management. LC 96-37582. (Springer Series in Operations Research). 312p. 1997. 49.95 (*0-387-94921-6*) Spr-Verlag.

***Bramen, Carrie Tirado.** Uses of Variety: Modern Americanism & the Quest for National Distinctiveness. 384p. 2001. 45.00 (*0-674-00308-X*) HUP.

Bramer, Ann M. The Meal Planner. 168p. 1993. spiral bd. 15.95 (*0-9643906-0-4*) Menus & More.

Bramer, Brian & Bramer, Susan. C for Engineers. 2nd ed. LC 97-117933. 406p. 1996. 64.95 incl. disk (*0-470-23721-X*) Wiley.

— C for Engineers. 2nd ed. LC 97-117933. 406p. 1997. pap. 39.95 incl. disk (*0-340-67769-4*) Wiley.

— C++ for Engineers. LC 95-37139. (Illus.). 468p. 1996. pap. text 49.95 incl. disk (*0-470-23578-0*) Halsted Pr.

Bramer, Jennifer. Succeeding in College with Attention Deficit Disorders: Issues & Strategies for Students, Counselors & Educators. LC 96-26196. 189p. (Orig.). 1996. pap. 18.00 (*1-886941-06-8*, 0921) Spec Pr FL.

Bramer, M. A. Computer Game - Playing: Theory & Practice. LC 83-10678. (Artificial Intelligence Ser.). 306p. 1983. text 92.95 (*0-470-27466-2*) P-H.

***Bramer, M. A., ed.** Knowledge Discovery & Data Mining. (Professional Applications of Computing Ser.). 308p. 1999. 84.00 (*0-85296-767-5*) INSPEC Inc.

***Bramer, M. A., et al, eds.** Research & Development in Intelligent Systems Vol. XVI: Proceedings of ES99, the 19th SGES International Conference on Knowledge-Bases Systems & Applied Artificial Intelligence. LC 99-56963. x, 350p. 2000. 119.00 (*1-85233-231-X*, Pub. by Spr-Verlag) Spr-Verlag.

Bramer, M. A., jt. ed. see Milne, R.

Bramer, Max A. Adding Structure to BASIC with Comal 80. 288p. 1987. write for info. (*0-201-14632-0*) Addison-Wesley.

Bramer, Max A., ed. Practical Experience in Building Expert Systems. LC 89-27241. (Illus.). 238p. 1990. reprint ed. pap. 73.80 (*0-608-05297-3*, 206583500001) Bks Demand.

Bramer, Max A. & Milne, R. W. Research & Development in Expert Systmes IX: Proceedings of 12th Annual Technical Conference of the BCS Specialist Group, December 1992. (British Computer Society Workshop Ser.). (Illus.). 357p. (C). 1993. text 90.00 (*0-521-44517-5*) Cambridge U Pr.

Bramer, Susan, jt. auth. see Bramer, Brian.

Bramer, William L., jt. auth. see Winslow, Charles D.

Bramfitt, B. L., et al, eds. MiCon 86: Optimization of Processing, Properties & Service Performance Through Microstructural Control. LC 87-30731. (Special Technical Publication Ser.: No. 979). (Illus.). 310p. 1988. text 61.00 (*0-8031-0985-7*, STP979) ASTM.

Bramfitt, B. L., ed. see Metallurgical Society of AIME Staff.

Bramford, Margaret. From Cottage to Palace. large type unabridged ed. (Reminiscence Ser.). 128p. 1998. 23.95 (*0-7531-5073-5*, 150735) ISIS Pub.

Bramhall, David, jt. ed. see Helbrun, Suzanne.

Bramhall, David F., jt. ed. see Helburn, Suzanne W.

Bramhall, David F., jt. ed. see Karaska, Gerald J.

Bramhall, Elizabeth. Ty Loves Flowers: A Toddlers' Environmental Awareness Book. (Illus.). 16p. (J). (ps). 1993. pap. write for info. (*0-9636038-0-9*) E Bramhall.

Bramhall, John. Works of John Bramhall, 5 vols. LC 73-39519. reprint ed. 265.00 (*0-404-52060-X*) AMS Pr.

Bramhall, John W. I Am My Beloved's. Nicholson, J. Boyd, ed. 128p. 1994. pap. 7.95 (*1-882701-08-9*) Uplook Min.

— My Beloved Is Mine. Nicholson, J. Boyd, ed. 127p. 1994. pap. 5.95 (*1-882701-10-0*) Uplook Min.

Bramhall, Martha, jt. auth. see Chenevert, Melodie.

***Bramham, John.** Benchmarking for People Managers. 248p. 2000. pap. 56.95 (*0-8464-5006-2*) Beekman Pubs.

***Bramham, John.** Human Resource Planning. 224p. 2000. pap. 47.95 (*0-8464-5070-4*) Beekman Pubs.

Bramham, John. Human Resource Planning. 160p. (C). 1989. 85.00 (*0-85292-419-4*, Pub. by IPM Hse) St Mut.

— Human Resource Planning. 216p. (C). 1994. pap. 42.00 (*0-85292-554-9*, Pub. by IPM Hse) St Mut.

Bramham, John & Cox, David. Personnel Administration Made Simple: Forms, Cards & Computers. 340p. (C). 1984. 108.00 (*0-85292-306-6*) St Mut.

Bramham, P., et al, eds. Leisure Policies in Europe. (Illus.). 288p. 1993. text 80.00 (*0-85198-819-9*) OUP.

Brami, Claude. La Danse d'Amour Du Vieux Corbeau. (FRE.). 507p. 1986. pap. 16.95 (*0-7859-2026-9*, 2070377091) Fr & Eur.

— Le Garcon Sur la Colline. (FRE.). 320p. 1982. pap. 11.95 (*0-7859-1960-0*, 2070373975) Fr & Eur.

Brami, Elisabeth. Little Moments of Happiness. 1997. 140.95 (*1-55670-685-5*) Stewart Tabori & Chang.

— Little Moments of Happiness. LC 97-16337. (Illus.). 180p. 1997. 14.95 (*1-55670-649-9*) Stewart Tabori & Chang.

— Little Pleasures. (Illus.). 68p. 1996. 12.95 (*0-7892-0046-5*) Abbeville Pr.

***Brami, Elisabeth.** Sweet Dreams, Scary Monsters. McGowan, Siobhan, tr. from FRE. LC 99-29781. (Illus.). 32p. (J). (ps-3). 1999. 14.95 (*1-55670-945-5*) STC Pubns.

— Sweet Treats, Nasty Eats. McGowan, Siobhan, tr. LC 99-29853. (Illus.). 32p. (J). (ps-3). 1999. 14.95 (*1-55670-946-3*) STC Pubns.

Brami, J., et al, eds. Regards sur la France des Annees, 1980: Le Roman. (Stanford French & Italian Studies: No. 80). (FRE.). 256p. 1995. pap. 56.50 (*0-915838-96-6*) Anma Libri.

Bramiley, Mary. Fit to Ride: Train Your Horse, Train Yourself. 228p. (Orig.). 1997. pap. 26.95 (*0-632-04043-2*) Blackwell Sci.

Bramlett, James. Finding Work: A Handbook. Hazzard, David, ed. 224p. 1986. pap. 7.95 (*0-310-39031-1*, 9592P) Zondervan.

Bramlett, James D. The World's Greatest Truths. LC 88-70056. 197p. 1988. 12.95 (*0-945642-06-7*) Creative FL.

Bramlett, Jim. Ride for the High Points: The Real Story of Will James. LC 92-39477. (Illus.). 272p. 1987. pap. 20.00 (*0-87842-288-9*) Mountain Pr.

Bramlett, Perry C. C. S. Lewis: Life at the Center. LC 96-14322. 96p. 1996. pap. 10.00 (*1-57312-054-5*) Smyth & Helwys.

Bramlett, Perry C. & Higdon, Ronald W. Touring C. S. Lewis's Ireland & England. LC 98-24456. (Illus.). 128p. 1998. pap. 12.00 (*1-57312-191-6*) Smyth & Helwys.

Bramlett, Tim. A Kid's Guide to Crafts: Wood Projects. Yonick, Deborah, ed. LC 97-66162. (Illus.). 32p. (Orig.). (J). (gr. 5-7). 1997. pap. 9.95 (*1-881982-02-5*) Stackpole Mag.

Bramley. Blossoms Journal. 1999. 9.95 (*1-84100-112-0*) Quadrillion Media.

— Celestial Journal. 1999. 9.95 (*1-84100-111-2*) Quadrillion Media.

***Bramley.** Flowers. 1998. 19.95 (*1-85833-989-8*) Quadrillion Media.

Bramley. Garden Days Journal. 1999. 9.95 (*1-84100-110-4*) Quadrillion Media.

— Happy Days. 1998. 19.95 (*1-85833-906-5*) CLib Bks.

— Home Spa Aromatherapy Massage Set. 1997. 14.95 (*1-85833-796-8*) Quadrillion Pubng.

— Memories Photograph Album. 1998. 14.95 (*1-85833-988-X*, Pub. by CLib Bks) Whitecap Bks.

— Perfect Pizza Gift Set. 1997. 12.95 (*1-85833-565-5*, Pub. by CLib Bks) Whitecap Bks.

— Poetic Bouquet Journal. 1999. 9.95 (*1-84100-109-0*) Quadrillion Media.

Bramley, et al. Planning, Market Private House: The Local Supply Response. 192p. 1994. 65.00 (*1-85728-162-4*, Pub. by UCL Pr Ltd); pap. 24.95 (*1-85728-163-2*, Pub. by UCL Pr Ltd) Taylor & Francis.

***Bramley, A. N., ed.** Advances in Manufacturing Technology XIII: Proceedings National Conference on Manufacturing Research Bath, UK 1999. 499p. 1999. 435.00 (*1-86058-227-3*) Prof Eng Pubng.

Bramley, G. Equalization Grants & Local Expenditure Needs. 320p. 1990. text 91.95 (*0-566-07115-0*, Pub. by Avebry) Ashgate Pub Co.

Bramley, Glen, jt. auth. see Hill, Michael.

Bramley, Paul, jt. ed. see De Burgh Norman, John E.

***Bramley, Peter.** Evaluating Training. 160p. 2000. pap. 44.99 (*0-8464-5051-8*) Beekman Pubs.

Bramley, Peter. Evaluating Training. 160p. 1996. pap. 36.00 (*0-85292-636-7*, Pub. by IPM Hse) St Mut.

— Evaluating Training Effectiveness: Benchmarking Your Training Activity Against Best Practice. 2nd ed. LC 95-43784. 186p. 1996. pap. 29.95 (*0-07-709028-4*) McGraw.

— Evaluation of Training. (C). 1986. pap. 24.00 (*0-85171-084-0*, Pub. by IPM Hse) St Mut.

Bramley, Peter. Florida's Vanishing Wildlife. 32p. (Orig.). (J). (gr. k-4). 1992. pap. 2.95 (*0-8200-1101-0*) Great Outdoors.

Bramley, Peter & Pahl, Jan. The Evaluation of Training in the Social Services. 1996. pap. 30.00 (*1-899942-06-8*, Pub. by Natl Inst Soc Work) St Mut.

Bramley, William. Gods of Eden. 520p. 1993. mass mkt. 6.99 (*0-380-71807-3*, Avon Bks) Morrow Avon.

Bramley, Wyn. The Broad Spectrum Psychotherapist. 275p. (C). 1996. 55.00 (*1-85343-328-4*, Pub. by Free Assoc Bks) NYU Pr.

— The Broad Spectrum Psychotherapist. (C). 1996. pap. 24.95 (*1-85343-327-6*, Pub. by Free Assoc Bks) NYU Pr.

— The Supervisory Couple in Broad-Spectrum Psychotherapy. 180p. (C). 1997. 50.00 (*1-85343-353-5*, Pub. by Free Assoc Bks); pap. 20.00 (*1-85343-354-3*, Pub. by Free Assoc Bks) NYU Pr.

Bramly, Marine. Artemisia. 192p. 2000. pap. 12.95 (*1-56649-047-2*) Welcome Rain.

***Bramly, Serge.** Anonym. (Illus.). 140p. 2000. pap. 19.95 (*3-934296-12-2*) G Kehayoff.

— Anonym. (Illus.). 140p. 1998. 45.00 (*3-929078-32-5*, Kehayoff) te Neues.

Bramly, Serge. Leonardo: The Artist & the Man. Reynolds, Sian, tr. (Illus.). 512p. 1995. pap. 21.95 (*0-14-023175-7*, Penguin Bks) Viking Penguin.

— Macumba: The Teachings of Marie-Jose, Mother of the Gods. LC 94-290. (Illus.). 240p. (Orig.). 1994. pap. 14.95 (*0-87286-286-0*) City Lights.

***Bramly, Serge & Rheims, Bettina.** I. N. R. I. LC 99-17089. (Illus.). 218p. 1999. text 65.00 (*1-58093-043-3*, Pub. by Monacelli Pr) Penguin Putnam.

Brammar, William J., jt. auth. see Conley, Edward C.

Brammer, Betty. Links to Logic. (Illus.). 96p. 1997. pap. 10.95 (*1-880505-53-3*, CLC0204) Pieces of Lrning.

Brammer, Billy L. The Gay Place: Being Three Related Novels. LC 94-24649. 264p. (Orig.). 1995. pap. 18.95 (*0-292-70831-9*) U of Tex Pr.

Brammer, Deb. Peanut Butter Friends in a Chop Suey World. LC 94-38216. (Illus.). (J). 1994. pap. 6.49 (*0-89084-751-7*, 082685) Bob Jones Univ.

Brammer, Ethriam C., jt. auth. see Venegas, Daniel.

Brammer, Lawrence M. The Helping Relationship: Process & Skills. 4th ed. (Illus.). 192p. 1988. pap. text 24.00 (*0-13-386525-8*) P-H.

— How to Cope with Life Transition. 1990. 53.95 (*0-89116-962-8*) Hemisp Pub.

Brammer, Lawrence M. & Bingea, Marian L. Caring for Yourself While Caring for Others. LC 98-90666. (Orig.). 1999. pap. 14.95 (*0-533-12876-5*) Vantage.

Brammer, Lawrence M., et al. Therapeutic Counseling & Psychotherapy. 6th ed. LC 92-26700. Orig. Title: Therapeutic Psychology. 416p. 1992. 86.00 (*0-13-912817-4*) P-H.

Brammer, Lawrence W. & MacDonald, Ginger. Helping Relationship: Process & Skills. 7th ed. LC 98-20672. 198p. (C). 1998. pap. text 46.00 (*0-205-29042-6*) Allyn.

Brammer, Lee, ed. Transactions of the American Crystallographic Association: Structural Tools in Organometallic & Coordination Chemistry. (Transactions of the American Crystallographic Association Ser.: Vol. 31). 96p. (C). 1998. pap. text 25.00 (*0-937140-41-4*) Am Crystallographic.

***Brammer, Leila R.** Excluded from Suffrage History: Matilda Joslyn Gage, Nineteenth-Century American Feminist, 182. LC 00-21553. (Contributions in Women's Studies: Vol. 182). 2000. write for info. (*0-313-30467-X*) Greenwood.

***Brammer, Ralph.** Football Skills: One-to-One Teaching for the Young Soccer Player. 128p. 2000. pap. 6.95 (*0-7160-2124-2*, Pub. by Elliot RW Bks) Midpt Trade.

Brammer, William J., jt. ed. see Conley, Edward C.

Bramos, Ann S., jt. auth. see Bramos, Helen.

Bramos, Helen & Bramos, Ann S. My Favorite Bedtime Stories. LC 91-76687. (Illus.). 63p. (J). (gr. k-7). 1992. pap. 7.00 (*1-56002-152-7*) A S Bramos.

— My Little Storybook. (Illus.). 63p. (Orig.). (J). (gr. k-7). 1992. pap. 7.00 (*0-9635333-0-4*) A S Bramos.

— My Red Storybook. (Illus.). 77p. (Orig.). (J). (gr. k-7). 1993. pap. 8.00 (*0-9635333-1-2*) A S Bramos.

— A Small Book of Tales. (Illus.). 77p. (Orig.). (J). (gr. k-7). 1995. pap. 8.00 (*0-9635333-3-9*) A S Bramos.

— Story Time. (Illus.). 77p. (Orig.). (J). (gr. k-7). 1994. pap. 8.00 (*0-9635333-2-0*) A S Bramos.

— A Treasury of Tales. (Illus.). 77p. (J). (gr. k-7). 1997. pap. 8.00 (*0-9635333-5-5*) A S Bramos.

Bramos, Helen, et al. Teeny Tiny Tales. (Illus.). 77p. (Orig.). (J). (gr. k-7). 1996. pap. 8.00 (*0-9635333-4-7*) A S Bramos.

***Brampton, Baron.** The Reminiscences of Sir Henry Hawkins, 2 vols. Harris, Richard, ed. 641p. 1998. reprint ed. 178.00 (*1-56169-371-5*) Gaunt.

Brampton, Bill. Golf: Technique, Tactics, Training. (Crowood Sports Guides Ser.). (Illus.). 128p. 1992. pap. 22.95 (*1-85223-604-3*, Pub. by Cro1wood) Trafalgar.

— Golf Lessons With The Swing Doctor. (Illus.). 94p. 1997. 12.95 (*0-86278-492-1*, Pub. by OBrien Pr) Irish Amer Bk.

An Asterisk (*) at the beginning of an entry indicates that the title is appearing for the first time.

Brams, R. S. Construction Claims Deskbook: Management, Documentation, & Presentation of Claims, 1. LC 96-35435. 624p. 1996. boxed set 150.00 (*0-471-00696-3*) Wiley.

Brams, Steven J. The Presidential Election Game. LC 78-5815. 1978. 17.00 (*0-300-02254-9*); pap. 17.00 (*0-300-02296-4*) Yale U Pr.

— Superior Beings-If They Exist, How Would We Know? Game-Theoretic Implications of Omniscience, Immortality, & Incomprehensibility. (Illus.). 192p. 1983. 60.95 (*0-387-91223-1*); 41.95 (*0-387-90877-3*) Spr-Verlag.

— Theory of Moves. (Illus.). 260p. (C). 1993. pap. text 19.95 (*0-521-45867-6*) Cambridge U Pr.

Brams, Steven J. & Taylor, Alan D. The Win-Win Solution: Guaranteeing Fair Shares to Everybody. LC 98-56036. 177p. 1999. 24.95 (*0-393-04729-6*) Norton.

Bramsback, Birgit, ed. Homage to Ireland: Aspects of Culture, Literature & Language. (Uppsala University Studia Anglistica: No. 71). 112p. (Orig.). 1990. pap. 35.00 (*91-554-2581-X*) Coronet Bks.

Bramsback, Birgit & Corrain, Ailbhe, eds. Societas Celtologica Nordica: Proceedings of the Inaugural Meeting & First Symposium, May 1990. (Studia Anglistica Upsaliensia Ser.: No. 76). (Illus.). 100p. 1991. text 36.00 (*91-554-2783-9*) Coronet Bks.

Bramsback, Birgit & Croghan, Martin, eds. Anglo-Irish & Irish Literature: Aspects of Language & Culture, 2 vols., Set. (Studia Anglistica Upsaliensia Ser.: No. 64). 501p. (Orig.). 1988. pap. 84.00 (*91-554-2248-9*, Pub. by Uppsala Univ Acta Univ Uppsaliensis) Coronet Bks.

***Bramsen, Christopher Bo.** Peace & Friendship: Denmark's Official Relations with China, 1675-2000. (Illus.). 160p. 2000. 39.95 (*87-87062-82-8*, Pub. by NIAS) Paul & Co Pubs.

Bramson, A. E., jt. auth. see Birch, Neville H.

Bramson, Ann. Soap: Making It, Enjoying It. LC 75-7286. (Illus.). 120p. 1975. pap. 6.95 (*0-911104-57-7*, 073) Workman Pub.

Bramson, Ann, ed. The Good Housekeeping Illustrated Cookbook. rev. ed. LC 88-2851. (Illus.). 544p. 1988. 27.00 (*0-688-08074-X*, Hearst) Hearst Commns.

Bramson, Ann, ed. see Goldstein, Joyce.

Bramson, Ann, ed. see Jackson, Albert & Day, David.

Bramson, Ann, ed. see La Place, Viana & Kleiman, Evan.

Bramson, Ann, ed. see Niles, Bo.

Bramson, John. Bristol Bay, Alaska from the Hinterlands to Tidewater: A Grassroots Pictorial, 1885-1965. Clarkin, Jean, ed. LC 99-193776. (Illus.). 150p. 1998. pap. write for info. (*0-941555-04-6*) Natl Pk AK.

Bramson, Leon, ed. see MacIver, Robert.

Bramson, M., jt. ed. see Durrett, R.

Bramson, Maury. Convergence of Solutions of the Kolmogorov Equation of Travelling Waves. LC 83-6437. (Memoirs of the American Mathematical Society Ser.: No. 44/285). 196p. 1983. pap. 24.00 (*0-8218-2285-3*, MEMO 44/285) Am Math.

Bramson, Morris. Arco College Board Achievement Test: Mathematics Level II, Level II. LC 82-8882. 1985. pap. 9.00 (*0-671-79997-5*, Arco) Macmillan Gen Ref.

— How to Prepare for the Miller Analogies Test (MAT) (Test Preparation Ser.). 224p. 1991. pap. 13.00 (*0-15-600040-7*) Harcourt.

— SAT II Math: Level I C & Level II C. 8th ed. 288p. 1998. pap. text 12.95 (*0-02-862473-4*, Arc) IDG Bks.

Bramson, Morris, et al. Test Preparation: How to Prepare for the GMAT. 3rd ed. 416p. 1993. pap. 12.95 (*0-15-600655-3*) Harcourt.

Bramson, Phyllis. Phyllis Bramson, 1973-1986. (Illus.). 28p. 1986. pap. 15.00 (*0-941548-10-4*) Ren Soc U Chi.

Bramson, Robert. Coping with Difficult Bosses: Dealing with Ogres, Wafflers, Know-it-alls, & Paranoids that Run the Office. LC 92-17492. 192p. 1992. 16.95 (*1-55972-139-1*, Birch Ln Pr) Carol Pub Group.

— What Your Boss Doesn't Tell You Until Its Too Late: How to Correct Personal Trait. 176p. 1996. pap. 10.00 (*0-684-81146-4*, Fireside) S&S Trade Pap.

Bramson, Robert M. Coping with Difficult Bosses: Dealing with Ogres, Wafflers, Know-it-alls, & Paranoids that Run the Office. LC 92-17492. 192p. 1994. pap. 11.00 (*0-671-79790-5*) S&S Trade.

— Coping with Difficult People. 240p. 1988. mass mkt. 6.99 (*0-440-20201-9*) Dell.

***Bramson, Robert M. & Bramson, Susan.** First Hired, Last Hired: How to Make Yourself Indispensable in an Age of Downsizing, Mergers & Restructuring. 224p. 2000. pap. 12.95 (*0-8092-9814-7*, Contemporary Bks) NTC Contemp Pub Co.

Bramson, Robert M. & Bramson, Susan J. First Hired, Last Fired. LC 98-45610. 255p. 1999. 19.95 (*0-8092-3130-1*, 313010, Contemporary Bks) NTC Contemp Pub Co.

Bramson, Robert M., jt. auth. see Harrison, Allen F.

***Bramson, Steven.** The Win-Win Solution. 192p. 2000. pap. 13.95 (*0-393-32081-2*) Norton.

Bramson, Susan, jt. auth. see Bramson, Robert M.

Bramson, Susan J., jt. auth. see Bramson, Robert M.

Bramsted, Ernest K. Aristocracy & the Middle-Classes in Germany: Social Types in German Literature, 1830-1900. LC 64-15031. 388p. (Orig.). reprint ed. pap. 120.30 (*0-8357-5731-5*, 202003500016) Bks Demand.

— Aristocracy & the Middle-Classes in Germany: Social Types in German Literature, 1830-1900. rev. ed. LC 64-15031. (Orig.). 1964. pap. text 2.95 (*0-226-07107-3*, P163) U Ch Pr.

Bramstedt, Ernest K. Dictatorship & Political Police: The Technique of Control by Fear. LC 75-41034. reprint ed. 34.50 (*0-404-14510-8*) AMS Pr.

Bramston, James. The Art of Politicks, in Imitation of Horace's Art of Poetry. LC 92-25504. (Augustan Reprints Ser.: No. 177). 1976. reprint ed. 14.50 (*0-404-70177-9*, PR3326) AMS Pr.

— The Man of Taste: Occasion'd by an Epistle of Mr. Pope's on That Subject. (Augustan Reprints Ser.: No. 171). 1975. reprint ed. 14.50 (*0-404-70171-X*) AMS Pr.

Bramston, John. Autobiography of Sir John Bramston. LC 10-2212. (Camden Society, London. Publications, First Ser.: No. 32). reprint ed. 95.00 (*0-404-50132-X*) AMS Pr.

Bramwell, Anna. Atlas of Twentieth-Century World-History. 1991. 29.95 (*0-06-016009-8*) HarperTrade.

— Ecology & History: The Greening of the West since 1880. LC 88-7651. 320p. (C). 1989. pap. 25.00 (*0-300-04521-2*) Yale U Pr.

— Fading of the Greens: The Decline of Environmental Politics in the West. LC 94-21029. 240p. 1994. 32.00 (*0-300-06040-8*) Yale U Pr.

Bramwell, Anna C., ed. Refugees in the Age of Total War. 432p. 1988. text 60.00 (*0-04-445194-6*) Routledge.

Bramwell, B. Fitzgerald. Basic Laboratory Principles in General Chemistry with Quantitative Techniques. 272p. 1995. spiral bd. 27.95 (*0-8403-5654-4*) Kendall-Hunt.

Bramwell, M., jt. auth. see Cork, B.

***Bramwell, Martyn.** Africa. LC 00-8050. (World in Maps Ser.). (Illus.). 56p. (YA). (gr. 5-11). 2000. 23.93 (*0-8225-2914-9*, Lerner Publctns) Lerner Pub.

— Australia. (Illus.). 56p. (YA). (gr. 4-7). 2000. 23.93 (*0-8225-2917-3*, Lerner Publctns) Lerner Pub.

— Central & South America. LC 99-6953. (World in Maps Ser.). (Illus.). 56p. (YA). (gr. 4-7). 2000. 23.93 (*0-8225-2912-2*, Lerner Publctns) Lerner Pub.

— Europe. LC 99-6944. (World in Maps Ser.). (Illus.). 56p. (YA). (gr. 4-7). 2000. 23.93 (*0-8225-2913-0*, Lerner Publctns) Lerner Pub.

Bramwell, Martyn. How Maps Are Made. LC 97-10366. (Maps & Mapmakers Ser.). (Illus.). (YA). (gr. 4-12). 1997. lib. bdg. 22.60 (*0-8225-2920-3*, Lerner Publctns) Lerner Pub.

— Mapping Our World. LC 97-50150. (Maps & Mapmakers Ser.). (YA). (gr. 4-12). 1998. 16.95 (*0-8225-2924-6*) Lerner Pub.

— Mapping the Planets & Space. LC 97-12188. (Maps & Mapmakers Ser.). (J). 1998. lib. bdg. 22.60 (*0-8225-2922-X*, Lerner Publctns) Lerner Pub.

— Mapping the Seas & Airways. LC 97-12190. (Maps & Mapmakers Ser.). (J). 1998. lib. bdg. 22.60 (*0-8225-2921-1*, Lerner Publctns) Lerner Pub.

— Maps in Everyday Life. LC 97-27282. (Maps & Mapmakers Ser.). (J). 1997. lib. bdg. 22.60 (*0-8225-2923-8*) Lerner Pub.

***Bramwell, Martyn.** North America & the Caribbean. LC 98-48812. (The World in Maps Ser.). (Illus.). 56p. (YA). (gr. 4-7). 2000. 23.93 (*0-8225-2911-4*, Lerner Publctns) Lerner Pub.

— Northern & Western Asia. (World in Maps Ser.). (Illus.). 56p. (YA). (gr. 4-7). 2000. 23.93 (*0-8225-2915-7*, Lerner Publctns) Lerner Pub.

Bramwell, Martyn. The Simon & Schuster Young Readers' Book of Planet Earth. LC 91-38216. (Illus.). 192p. (J). (gr. 4 up). 1992. pap. 13.00 (*0-671-77830-7*) S&S Bks Yung.

***Bramwell, Martyn.** Southern & Eastern Asia. (Illus.). 56p. (YA). (gr. 5 up). 2000. 23.93 (*0-8225-2916-5*, Lerner Publctns) Lerner Pub.

Bramwell, Martyn. The Visual Dictionary of the Earth. LC 93-18571. (Eyewitness Visual Dictionaries Ser.). (Illus.). 64p. (J). (gr. 4 up). 1993. 18.95 (*1-56458-335-X*) DK Pub Inc.

Bramwell, Martyn, ed. Mammals. LC 93-4336. (Picturepedia Ser.). 48p. (J). (gr. k-3). 1993. 12.95 (*1-56458-386-4*) DK Pub Inc.

***Bramwell, Martyn J.** Our World: An In-Depth Guide to Countries Around the World. (J). 1999. 16.99 (*1-84100-262-3*) Quadrillion Pubng.

— Planet Earth: The Complete Guide to Our Living World. (J). 1999. 16.99 (*1-84100-264-X*) Quadrillion Pubng.

— World Wildlife: The Complete Guide to the Animals of Our World. (J). 1999. 16.99 (*1-84100-263-1*) Quadrillion Pubng.

Bramwell, Paul, jt. auth. see Cooksey, Robert.

Bramwell, Richard, et al. Taxation of Companies & Company Reconstructions. 6th ed. LC 97-149459. 1994. 240.00 (*0-421-52030-2*, Pub. by Sweet & Maxwll) Gaunt.

***Bran, Zoe.** After Yugoslavia. 2001. pap. text 12.95 (*1-86450-030-1*) Lonely Planet.

Brana-Shute, Gary. On the Corner: Male Social Life in a Paramaribo Creole Neighborhood. (Illus.). 123p. 1989. reprint ed. pap. text 10.50 (*0-88133-468-5*) Waveland Pr.

Brana-Shute, Gary, jt. ed. see Brana-Shute, Rosemary.

Brana-Shute, Rosemary & Brana-Shute, Gary, eds. Crime & Punishment in the Caribbean. LC 80-21078. (Illus.). x, 146p. 1981. pap. 14.95 (*0-8130-0685-6*) U Press Fla.

Branagan, Linda & Sierra, Mike. The Frame Handbook: Building FrameMaker Documents That Work. Dougherty, Dale, ed. (Illus.). 542p. (Orig.). 1994. pap. 24.95 (*1-56592-009-0*) Thomson Learn.

Branagan, Thomas. Preliminary Essay on the Oppression of the Exiled Sons of Africa. LC 70-82177. (Anti-Slavery Crusade in America Ser.). 1970. reprint ed. 15.95 (*0-405-00616-0*) Ayer.

Branagan, Thomas & Ames, Julius R. The Guardian Genius of the Federal Union & the Beauties of Philanthropy. 1977. 21.95 (*0-8369-9159-1*, 9034) Ayer.

Branagh, Kenneth. Beginning. 1991. pap. 10.95 (*0-312-05822-5*) St Martin.

— Beginning LC 90-118725. x, 244p. 1989. write for info. (*0-7011-3388-0*) Chatto & Windus.

— A Midwinter's Tale: The Shooting Script. LC 95-45331. (Shooting Script Ser.). 144p. 1996. pap. 14.95 (*1-55704-274-8*, Pub. by Newmarket) Norton.

— Much Ado about Nothing: The Making of the Movie. LC 93-3330. 1993. pap. 15.00 (*0-393-31111-2*) Norton.

Branagh, Kenneth, et al. Mary Shelley's Frankenstein: A Classic Tale of Terror Reborn on Film. LC 94-22945. (Illus.). 192p. 1995. 29.95 (*1-55704-207-1*, Pub. by Newmarket); pap. 17.95 (*1-55704-208-X*, Pub. by Newmarket) Norton.

Branaman, Ann, jt. ed. see Lemert, Charles.

Branaman, Lucinda E., jt. auth. see Rhodes, Nancy C.

Branan, Carl. The Fractionator Analysis Pocket Handbook. LC 77-84383. 96p. (Orig.). 1978. reprint ed. pap. 30.00 (*0-608-01337-4*, 206208100001) Bks Demand.

***Branan, Carl.** Pocket Guide to Chemical Engineering. LC 99-45424. (Illus.). 160p. 1999. 30.00 (*0-88415-311-8*) Gulf Pub.

Branan, Carl. The Process Engineer's Pocket Handbook, Vol. 1. LC 76-1680. (Illus.). 144p. 1976. reprint ed. pap. 44.70 (*0-608-07937-5*, 206791000001) Bks Demand.

— The Process Engineer's Pocket Handbook, Vol. 3. LC 76-1680. (Illus.). 176p. 1976. reprint ed. pap. 54.50 (*0-608-07562-0*, 206161700003) Bks Demand.

— The Process Engineer's Pocket Handbook Vol. 2: Process Systems Development. LC 76-1680. 109p. 1983. reprint ed. pap. 33.80 (*0-608-00828-1*, 206161700002) Bks Demand.

— Rules of Thumb for Chemical Engineers. 2nd ed. LC 98-26530. 1999. pap. 79.00 (*0-88415-788-1*, 5783) Gulf Pub.

Branan, Carl & Mills, John. Process Evaluation & Economic Analysis. LC 76-1680. (Process Engineer's Pocket Handbook Ser.: Vol. 3). 168p. (Orig.). 1984. pap. 15.00 (*0-87201-715-X*, 1715) Gulf Pub.

Branan, Elisabeth G. La Fontaine: Au dela des "Bagatelles", des "Contes", des "Badineries", et des "Fables" LC 91-73984. (French Forum Monographs: No. 79). 240p. (Orig.). 1993. pap. 17.95 (*0-917058-83-6*) French Forum.

***Branand, Claire D.** Overboard! A Provocative History of the U. S. S. J. P. Kennedy, Jr. (DD850) 184p. 1999. 29.95 (*0-9675160-0-5*) Skye Pubng Co.

Branbsby, Carlos, tr. from ENG. Concordancia Tematica De la Biblia: Topical Concordance of the Bible. 199p. 1972. reprint ed. pap. 8.99 (*0-311-42043-5*) Casa Bautista.

Branca, Andrew F. The Law of Self Defense: A Guide for the Armed Citizen. 238p. 1998. pap. 25.00 (*0-9665119-0-5*) Operon Security.

Branca, Glenn, jt. ed. see Ess, Barbara.

Branca, Nicholas. Rec Tiles: A Geometric Introduction to Algebra. 48p. (J). (gr. 5-9). 1991. pap. text 25.95 (*0-938587-19-6*) Cuisenaire.

Branca, Vittore. Merchant Writers of the Italian Renissance: From Boccacio to Machiavelli. LC 99-39085. 163p. 1999. pap. 16.95 (*1-56886-058-7*, Pub. by Marsilio Pubs) Consort Bk Sales.

***Brancaccio.** On the Road with the Host of Public Radio's "Marketplace" 2000. write for info. (*0-684-86499-1*) S&S Trade.

***Brancaccio, David.** Squandering Aimlessly: My Adventures in the American Marketplace. LC 99-55141. 288p. 2000. 25.00 (*0-684-86498-3*) S&S Trade.

Brancaforte, Benito. Guzman de Alfarache: Conversion o Proceso de Degradacion? vi, 230p. 1980. 11.00 (*0-942260-14-7*) Hispanic Seminary.

Brancaforte, Benito, ed. Las Metamorfosis y las Heroidas de Ovidio en la General Estoria de Alfonso el Sabio. (Spanish Ser.: No. 62). xl, 418p. 1990. 30.00 (*0-940639-55-6*) Hispanic Seminary.

Brancaforte, Charlotte L., ed. Fridericus Berghius' Partial Latin Translation of Lazarillo de Tormes & Its Relationship to the Early Lazarillo Translations in Germany. 112p. 1983. 20.00 (*0-942260-32-5*) Hispanic Seminary.

— The German Forty-Eighters in the United States. LC 89-37654. (German Life & Civilization Ser.: Vol. 1). 319p. 1989. 54.95 (*0-8204-1010-1*) P Lang Pubng.

— The Life & Works of Charles Sealsfield (Karl Postl), 1864-1973. (Max Kade Institute Studies). 302p. 1993. 22.50 (*0-924119-72-1*) German-Am Cult Soc.

Brancaleone, Jim. Man with a Broken Heart. (Orig.). 1977. pap. 5.95 (*0-9601186-1-6*) Brancaleone Educ.

— Success Made Fun. LC 81-90660. (Orig.). 1981. pap. 14.95 (*0-9601186-2-4*) Brancaleone Educ.

Brancatelli, Robert. Pilgrimage As Rite of Passage: A Guidebook for Youth Ministry. LC 98-10840. 80p. 1998. pap. 11.95 (*0-8091-3798-4*, 3798-4) Paulist Pr.

Brancatelli, Robert, tr. see Cervantes, Carmen M.

Brancatelli, Robert, tr. see Cervantes, Carmen Maria, et al, eds.

Brancato, Carolyn K. Getting Listed on Wall Street: The Irwin Guide to Financial Reporting Standards in the U. S. 256p. 1995. pap. 65.00 (*0-7863-0329-8*, Irwn Prfssnl) McGraw-Hill Prof.

— Institutional Investors & Corporate Governance: Best Practices for Increasing Corporate Value. 264p. 1996. 50.00 (*0-7863-0558-4*, Irwn Prfssnl) McGraw-Hill Prof.

— New Corporate Performance Measures. (Report / Conference Board Ser.: No. 1118-95-RR). (Illus.). 66p. (Orig.). 1995. pap. text 100.00 (*0-8237-0563-3*) Conference Bd.

Brancato, Helen D., jt. auth. see Mattern, Evelyn.

Brancato, R., et al, eds. Retinal Diseases 2. LC 87-22626. (Illus.). 392p. 1987. lib. bdg. 125.00 (*90-6299-037-1*, Pub. by Kugler) Kugler Pubns.

Brancato, R., et al. Atlas of Iris Fluorescein Angiography. (Illus.). 455p. 1994. text 191.50 (*90-6299-109-2*) Kugler Pubns.

Brancato, Robin F. Winning. 1984. mass mkt. 2.95 (*0-553-26597-0*) Bantam.

Brancato, Robin F. Winning. (J). 1977. 10.09 (*0-606-04368-3*, Pub. by Turtleback) Demco.

Brancato, Ubaldo, tr. see Absolon, Karel B.

Brancelj, A., et al. Cladocera. LC 98-16093. (Developments in Hydrobiology Ser.: Vol. 126). 303p. 1998. 184.00 (*0-7923-5052-9*) Kluwer Academic.

Branch. Export Practice & Management. 3rd ed. 1993. pap. write for info. (*1-86152-498-6*, Pub. by ITBP) Thomson Learn.

Branch. Export Practice & Management 4th ed. 2000. pap. text 23.99 (*1-86152-473-0*) Thomson Learn.

— Office Practice of Medicine. 4th ed. 1999. text. write for info. (*0-7216-7672-3*, W B Saunders Co) Harcrt Hlth Sci Grp.

— Xmas Joy Ppk6, Ruby PB. 65.70 (*0-316-10581-3*) Little.

Branch, A. Maritime Economics: Management & Marketing. 3rd ed. 496p. 1998. pap. 83.00 (*0-7487-3986-6*) St Mut.

Branch, A. E. Import-Export Documentation. 274p. (C). 1990. 210.00 (*0-7855-5718-0*, Pub. by Inst Pur & Supply) St Mut.

Branch, A. J., jt. auth. see Cabell, Hanna.

Branch, Al. Electronic Media for the School Market: 99-2000 Edition. (Illus.). 170p. 1999. 1395.00 (*0-88709-134-2*) Simba Info Inc.

— Print Publishing for the School Market: 99-2000 Review, Trends & Forecast. (Illus.). 175p. 1999. 1995.00 (*0-88709-096-6*) Simba Info Inc.

Branch, Alan E. Dictionary of Commercial Terms & Abbreviations. 458p. (C). 1984. pap. 150.00 (*0-900886-90-0*, Pub. by Witherby & Co) St Mut.

— Dictionary of Shipping: International Trade Terms & Abbreviations. 279p. 1982. 95.00 (*0-900886-70-6*, Pub. by Witherby & Co) St Mut.

— Dictionary of Shipping: International Trade Terms & Abbreviations. 587p. (C). 1986. pap. 145.00 (*0-948691-20-4*, Pub. by Witherby & Co) St Mut.

— Dictionary of Shipping International Business Trade Terms & Abbreviations. (ENG & FRE.). 1100p. 1995. pap. 95.00 (*1-85609-086-8*, Pub. by Witherby & Co) St Mut.

— Economics of Shipping Practice & Management. 2nd ed. 320p. 1988. pap. 39.50 (*0-685-30074-9*) Chapman & Hall.

— Elements of Export Marketing & Management. 2nd ed. 340p. (gr. 13). 1990. mass mkt. 32.95 (*0-412-35540-X*, A4465) Chapman & Hall.

— Elements of Shipping. 6th ed. 400p. 1989. pap. 29.95 (*0-412-32240-4*, A3479) Chapman & Hall.

— Export Practice & Management. 3rd ed. LC 93-8761. 480p. 1993. mass mkt. 35.15 (*0-412-41530-5*) Chapman & Hall.

— Import-Export Documentation. 274p. (C). 1989. 210.00 (*0-7855-4619-7*, Pub. by Inst Pur & Supply) St Mut.

***Branch, Alan E.** International Purchasing. (ITBP Textbooks Ser.). 2001. pap. 24.99 (*1-86152-511-7*) Thomson Learn.

Branch, Alan E. & Hakmeh, Juma A. Dictionary of English-Arabic Commercial International Trade & Shipping Terms. (ARA & ENG.). 257p. (C). 1988. 210.00 (*0-948691-61-1*, Pub. by Witherby & Co) St Mut.

Branch, Alfred. The College Publishing Market: 98-99 Review, Trends, & Forecast. (Illus.). 155p. 1994. 1795.00 (*0-88709-069-9*) Simba Info Inc.

— Electronic Media for the School Market: 1997-98 Review Trends & Forcast. 6th rev. ed. (Illus.). 170p. 1999. 1395.00 (*0-88709-129-6*) Simba Info Inc.

Branch, Alfred, et al. The College Publishing Market 98-99: Analysis of Print & Electronic Learning Materials. 4th rev. ed. Fagnani, Stephanie, ed. (Illus.). 155p. 1998. 1995.00 (*0-88709-151-2*) Simba Info Inc.

Branch, Allan E., et al. Multilingual Dictionary of Commercial International Trade & Shipping Terms. (ENG, FRE, GER & SPA.). 254p. (C). 1990. 220.00 (*0-948691-90-5*, Pub. by Witherby & Co) St Mut.

Branch, Anna H. Shoes That Danced & Other Poems. LC 77-89722. (One-Act Plays in Reprint Ser.). 1988. reprint ed. 25.00 (*0-8486-2027-5*) Roth Pub Inc.

Branch, Bill. Field Guide to Snakes & Other Reptiles of Southern Africa. 3rd enl. rev. ed. LC 98-70012. (Illus.). 368p. 1998. pap. 32.50 (*0-88359-042-5*, RCB-04251, Pub. by R Curtis Pubng) Chelsea Green Pub.

— Field Guide to the Snakes & Other Reptiles of Southern Africa. (Illus.). 328p. 1988. 29.95 (*0-88359-023-9*) R Curtis Pubng.

— Southern African Snakes & Other Reptiles: A Photographic Guide. (Eco-Travel Guides Ser.). (Illus.). 144p. 1998. pap. 15.95 (*0-88359-027-1*, Pub. by R Curtis Pubng) Chelsea Green Pub.

Branch, Brian, jt. ed. see Westley, Glenn D.

Branch, Bruce Wendell. When God Calls You Better Answer: A Novel Based on Drugs, Sex, Power, Greed, Money & God. 232p. 2000. pap. 15.95 (*1-878898-11-6*, Pub. by CAP Pub) ACCESS Pubs Network.

Branch, Charlotte, ed. St. Stephen Rural Cemetery - St. Stephen N. B. Tombstone Inscriptions of Charlotte County, N. B. Canada. LC 96-69777. 368p. 1996. 39.50 (*0-89725-273-X*, 1754) Picton Pr.

Branch, Christine. Let's Play a Rhyme: Ready-to-Use Rhymes to Promote Early Learning Skills. Keeling, Jan, ed. LC 94-75266. (Illus.). 64p. (Orig.). (J). (ps). 1994. pap. text 8.95 (*0-86530-288-X*, 270-3) Incentive Pubns.

Branch, Curtis W. Adolescent Gangs: Old Issues, New Approaches. LC 98-50826. 1998. 59.95 (*0-87630-923-6*); pap. 24.95 (*0-87630-924-4*) Brunner-Mazel.

— Clinical Interventions with Gangs: Adolescents & Their Families. LC 96-53461. (C). 1997. pap. text 25.00 (*0-8133-2904-3*, Pub. by Westview) HarpC.

B

B

Branch, E. Douglas. The Hunting of the Buffalo. LC 97-14550. (Illus.). xlv, 268p. 1997. pap. 12.95 (*0-8032-6137-3*, Bison Books) U of Nebr Pr.

Branch, Edgar M. A Bibliography of James T. Farrell's Writings, 1921-1957. LC 58-10532. 148p. reprint ed. pap. 45.90 (*0-8357-7194-6*, 205118400083) Bks Demand.

— James T. Farrell. LC 63-64001. (University of Minnesota Pamphlets on American Writers Ser.: No. 29). 48p. (Orig.). reprint ed. pap. 30.00 (*0-7837-2898-0*, 205755700006) Bks Demand.

— Mark Twain & the Starchy Boys. 97p. (Orig.). 1992. pap. 10.00 (*1-880817-04-7*) EC Ctr Mark T Stu.

— Men Call Me Lucky: Mark Twain & the Pennsylvania. (Keepsakes Ser.). (Illus.). 87p. (Orig.). 1985. pap. text 20.00 (*0-918761-01-8*) Miami U Pubns.

— Studs Lonigan's Neighborhood: And the Making of James T. Farrell. LC 95-48322. (Illus.). 104p. (Orig.). 1996. pap. 20.00 (*0-933292-22-8*) Arts End.

Branch, Edgar M., et al. A Paris Year: Dorothy & James T. Farell, 1931-1932. LC 98-21295. 225p. 1998. 24.95 (*0-8214-1236-1*) Ohio U Pr.

Branch, Edgar M., ed. see Twain, Mark, pseud.

Branch, Edward D. The Hunting of the Buffalo. LC 62-8408. (Bison Bk.: No. BB130). 288p. reprint ed. pap. 89.30 (*0-7837-4049-2*, 204387900011) Bks Demand.

Branch, Eleanor. Monarch Notes: Toni Morrison's Beloved, The Bluest Eye & Other Stories. 128p. 1988. pap. 4.50 (*0-671-67129-4*, Arco) Macmillan Gen Ref.

Branch, Eleanor F. & Singleton, Mary, eds. Physical Therapy & the Arthritis Patient: Clinical Aspects & Approaches to Management. LC 88-563. (Physical Therapy in Health Care Ser.: Vol. 2, Nos. 1-2). (Illus.). 78p. 1988. text 39.95 (*0-86656-728-3*) Haworth Pr.

Branch, Eleanor F. & Singleton, Mary C., eds. Physical Therapy & the Stroke Patient: Pathologic Aspects & Clinical Management. LC 87-26668. (Physical Therapy in Health Care Ser.: Vol. 1, No. 4). 73p. 1987. text 39.95 (*0-86656-740-2*) Haworth Pr.

Branch, Eleanor F., jt. auth. see Singleton, Mary C.

Branch, Eleanor F., jt. ed. see Singleton, Mary C.

Branch, Elizabeth & Adkins, Jeanette. Scrambling to Master Basic English Sentence Structure. 158p. (C). 1995. pap. text 28.38 (*1-56226-272-6*) CAT Pub.

Branch, Elizabeth, jt. auth. see Jewett, Ann E.

Branch, Fife & Branch, Kinross. The Nature of Fife: Scottish Wildlife Trust. 260p. 1997. pap. 30.00 (*1-84017-008-5*) St Mut.

Branch, Hazel F. Just for Me. LC 92-62879. (Illus.). 57p. (Orig.). (J). (gr. 4-9). 1992. pap. 3.95 (*0-931563-04-6*) Wishing Rm.

Branch, James H., III. Multicultural Stories. Ward, Dick, ed. LC 92-93449. (Illus.). 29p. (J). 1992. 12.50 (*0-9635840-0-6*) Guttenburg Pub.

Branch, Jayne A., ed. see Snider, Alan J.

Branch, John W., ed. see Dankwa, Nano O., III.

***Branch, John Watusi.** Journey to the Motherland. deluxe ed. 350p. 1999. pap. 24.95 (*0-9626487-2-8*) Power Word NY.

Branch, Kinross, jt. auth. see Branch, Fife.

Branch, Liz, ed. FotoFest 1990. (Illus.). 272p. (Orig.). 1990. pap. 19.95 (*0-9619766-1-6*) Houston FotoFest.

Branch, M. A Student's Glossary of Finnish. (ENG, FRE, GER, HUN & RUS.). 378p. 1980. 59.95 (*0-8288-1449-X*, F47180) Fr & Eur.

Branch, Mark A., jt. auth. see Piedmont-Palladino, Susan.

Branch, Melville C. Atlas of Rare City Maps: Comparative Urban Design, 1830-1842. Dickerman, Leah, ed. 1997. 65.00 (*1-56898-073-6*) Princeton Arch.

— Comparative Urban Design: Rare Engravings 1830-1843. (Illus.). 104p. 1978. 54.95 (*0-405-10524-X*) Arno Press.

— Comparative Urban Design-Rare Engravings: 1830-1843. 108p. 49.50 (*0-686-69145-8*) Ayer.

— Comprehensive City Planning: Introduction & Explanation. LC 85-70970. (Illus.). 238p. (C). 1985. pap. 27.95 (*0-918286-41-7*, Planners Press) Am Plan Assn.

***Branch, Melville C.** Comprehensive Planning for the 21st Century: General Theory & Principles. LC 97-34746. 200p. 1998. 55.00 (*0-275-96090-0*, Praeger Pubs); pap. 19.95 (*0-275-96181-8*, Praeger Pubs) Greenwood.

Branch, Melville C. Planning: Universal Process. LC 89-16025. 247p. 1990. 55.00 (*0-275-93160-9*, C3160, Praeger Pubs) Greenwood.

— Planning & Human Survival. LC 91-44569. 192p. 1992. 52.95 (*0-275-93826-3*, C3826, Praeger Pubs) Greenwood.

— The Planning Imperative & Human Behavior. LC 99-14381. 200p. 1999. 55.00 (*0-275-96534-1*) Greenwood.

— Regional Planning: Introduction & Explanation. LC 87-27314. 222p. 1988. 59.95 (*0-275-92403-3*, C2403, Praeger Pubs); pap. 19.95 (*0-275-92539-0*, B2539, Praeger Pubs) Greenwood.

— Simulation, Planning, & Society. LC 96-26291. 224p. 1997. 59.95 (*0-275-95403-X*) Greenwood.

— Telepower, Planning & Society: Crisis in Communication. LC 94-15882. 216p. 1994. 57.95 (*0-275-94599-5*, Praeger Pubs) Greenwood.

— Urban Air Traffic & City Planning: Case Study of Los Angeles County. LC 73-1090. (Special Studies in U. S. Economic, Social & Political Issues). 1973. 52.50 (*0-275-28701-7*) Irvington.

Branch, Michael, ed. Kalevala: The Land of the Heroes. Kirby, W. F., tr. LC 84-21619. 667p. (C). 1985. text 70.00 (*0-485-11258-2*, Pub. by Athlone Pr) Humanities.

Branch, Michael P., ed. Reading the Earth: New Directions in the Study of Literature & Environment. LC 97-39439. 266p. 1998. pap. 29.95 (*0-89301-220-3*) U of Idaho Pr.

Branch, Michael P., et al, eds. Reading the Earth: New Directions in the Study of Literature & Environment. LC 97-39439. 268p. 1998. 50.00 (*0-89301-213-0*) U of Idaho Pr.

Branch, Michael P. & Philippon, Daniel J. The Height of Our Mountains: Nature Writing from Virginia's Blue Ridge Mountains & Shenandoah Valley. LC 97-27555. (Illus.). 448p. 1998. pap. 18.95 (*0-8018-5691-4*); text 39.95 (*0-8018-5632-9*) Johns Hopkins.

Branch, Muriel M. Juneteenth: Freedom Day. LC 97-9656. (J). (gr. 5-8). 1998. 15.99 (*0-525-65222-1*) NAL.

Branch, Muriel M. & Evans, Earlene G. A Step Beyond: Multi-Media Activities for Learning American History. LC 94-37766. 168p. (Orig.). 1995. pap. 27.50 (*1-55570-195-7*) Neal-Schuman.

Branch, Muriel M. & Rice, Dorothy M. Pennies to Dollars: The Story of Maggie Lena Walker. LC 97-20280. (Illus.). xi, 100p. (J). (gr. 3-7). 1997. lib. bdg. 17.95 (*0-208-02453-0*, Linnet Bks) Shoe String.

— Pennies to Dollars: The Story of Maggie Lena Walker. LC 97-20280. (Illus.). xi, 100p. (J). (gr. 3-7). 1997. pap. 13.95 (*0-208-02455-7*, Linnet Bks) Shoe String.

Branch, Muriel M., jt. auth. see Lyons, Mary E.

Branch, Muriel Miller, jt. auth. see Evans, Earlene Green.

Branch, Newton, ed. This Britain. LC 79-90612. (Essay Index Reprint Ser.). 1977. 39.95 (*0-8369-1549-6*) Ayer.

Branch, Newton, tr. see Defourneaux, Marcelin.

Branch, Paul R., Jr. Fort Macon: A History. LC 97-29772. (Illus.). 292p. 1999. 28.95 (*1-877853-45-3*) Nautical & Aviation.

Branch, Paul R., Jr., ed. The Siege of Fort Macon. (Illus.). 105p. (Orig.). 1982. pap. 5.00 (*0-9614000-0-5*) P Branch.

Branch, Robert C., et al. In Our Hands, Adults. Marshak, David et al, eds. (Peace & Social Justice Program Ser.). 68p. (Orig.). 1990. pap. text 15.00 (*1-55896-161-5*) Unitarian Univ.

Branch, Robert M. & Fitzgerald, Mary A., eds. Educational Media & Technology Yearbook, 1999, No. 24. 410p. 1999. pap. 65.00 (*1-56308-636-0*) Libs Unl.

***Branch, Robert M. & Fitzgerald, Mary Anne, eds.** Educational Media & Technology Yearbook, 2000. 300p. 2000. 70.00 (*1-56308-840-1*) Libs Unl.

Branch, Robert M., jt. auth. see Gustafson, Kent L.

Branch, Shelly. Dollar Pinching: A Consumer's Guide to Smart Spending. LC 96-38402. 208p. (Orig.). 1997. mass mkt. 11.99 (*0-446-67246-7*, Pub. by Warner Bks) Little.

***Branch, Susan.** Baby Blessings. 2000. 15.95 (*0-7683-2196-4*) CEDCO Pub.

Branch, Susan. Baby Love. 96p. (gr. 8). 1992. 18.95 (*0-316-10639-9*) Little.

— Baby Love: A Keepsake Book. 1998. (*0-316-18941-3*) Little.

***Branch, Susan.** Birdies. 2000. pap. 4.95 (*0-7683-2191-3*) CEDCO Pub.

— Celebrations. 2000. 15.95 (*0-7683-2197-2*) CEDCO Pub.

Branch, Susan. Christmas from the Heart of the Home. (Illus.). 128p. (gr. 8). 1990. 21.95 (*0-316-10638-0*) Little.

— Christmas Joy: A Keepsake Book from the Heart of the Home, Vol. 1. 48p. (gr. 8). 1995. 10.95 (*0-316-10682-8*) Little.

— Days: From the Heart of the Home. (Illus.). 128p. (gr. 8). 1996. 17.95 (*0-316-10621-6*) Little.

***Branch, Susan.** Drinks. 2000. pap. 4.95 (*0-7683-2192-1*) CEDCO Pub.

— Flowers. 2000. pap. 4.95 (*0-7683-2186-7*) CEDCO Pub.

— Gardens. 2000. pap. 4.95 (*0-7683-2188-3*) CEDCO Pub.

— Girl Power. 2000. pap. 4.95 (*0-7683-2194-8*) CEDCO Pub.

— Girlfriends Forever. (Illus.). 128p. 2000. 23.95 (*0-316-10623-2*) Little.

— Happy Birthday. 2000. pap. 4.95 (*0-7683-2189-1*) CEDCO Pub.

— Hats. 2000. pap. 4.95 (*0-7683-2190-5*) CEDCO Pub.

Branch, Susan. Heart Home Post. 64p. 1994. 8.95 (*0-316-10661-5*) Little.

***Branch, Susan.** Heart of the Home: Notes From. 1998. text 23.95 (*0-316-18946-4*) Little.

Branch, Susan. Heart of the Home: Notes from a Vineyard Kitchen. 159p. (gr. 8). 1986. 23.95 (*0-316-10631-3*) Little.

— Heart of the Home Address Book. 128p. (gr. 8). 1998. 16.95 (*0-316-10287-3*) Little.

***Branch, Susan.** Joy, 64 vols. 2000. pap. text 13.95 (*0-7683-2183-2*) CEDCO Pub.

— Love. 2000. pap. 4.95 (*0-7683-2184-0*) CEDCO Pub.

— Love from the Heart of the Home. 1998. 11.95 (*0-316-18950-2*) Little.

Branch, Susan. Love from the Heart of the Home: A Keepsake Book. 64p. (gr. 8). 1994. 11.95 (*0-316-10658-5*) Little.

***Branch, Susan.** Love Notes, 64 vols. 2000. pap. text 13.95 (*0-7683-2182-4*) CEDCO Pub.

— Pretty Baby. 2000. pap. 4.95 (*0-7683-2187-5*) CEDCO Pub.

— Spring. 2000. pap. 4.95 (*0-7683-2193-X*) CEDCO Pub.

— Summer. 2000. pap. 4.95 (*0-7683-2195-6*) CEDCO Pub.

— The Summer Book. 1998. 23.95 (*0-316-18951-0*) Little.

Branch, Susan. The Summer Book: From the Heart of the Home. LC 94-23703. 128p. (gr. 8). 1995. 23.95 (*0-316-10666-6*) Little.

— Summer Book Party Package from the Heart of the Home. 128p. (gr. 8). 1997. 23.95 (*0-316-10577-5*) Little.

***Branch, Susan.** Sweets to the Sweet. 1998. 11.95 (*0-316-18953-7*) Little.

Branch, Susan. Sweets to the Sweet: From the Heart of the Heart. LC 98-150603. (Illus.). 64p. (gr. 8). 1998. 11.95 (*0-316-10622-4*) Little.

***Branch, Susan.** Tea. 2000. pap. 4.95 (*0-7683-2185-9*) CEDCO Pub.

Branch, Susan. Vineyard Seasons. (Illus.). 160p. (gr. 8). 1988. 23.95 (*0-316-10632-1*) Little.

***Branch, Susan.** Wedding Blessings. 2000. 15.95 (*0-7683-2198-0*) CEDCO Pub.

Branch, Taylor. Parting the Waters: America in the King Years, 1954-1963. 1038p. 1989. pap. 16.00 (*0-671-68742-5*, Touchstone) S&S Trade Pap.

— Pillar of Fire: America in the King Years, 1963-65. (Illus.). 768p. 1999. pap. 17.00 (*0-684-84809-0*, Touchstone) S&S Trade Pap.

— Pillar of Fire: America in the King Years, 1963-65. LC 97-46076. (Illus.). 746p. 1998. 29.50 (*0-684-80819-6*) Scribner.

Branch, Watson G., ed. Herman Melville. (Critical Heritage Ser.). 464p. (C). 1997. 140.00 (*0-415-15931-8*) Routledge.

Branch, William, et al, eds. Cardiology in Primary Care. (Illus.). 600p. 1999. text 55.00 (*0-07-007162-4*) McGraw-Hill Prof.

Branch, William B., ed. Crosswinds: An Anthology of Black Dramatists in the Diaspora. LC 92-26648. (Blacks in the Diaspora Ser.). 448p. 1993. pap. 18.95 (*0-253-20778-9*, MB 778) Ind U Pr.

Branch, William T., ed. Office Practice of Medicine. 3rd ed. LC 93-20531. (Illus.). 1184p. 1994. text 115.00 (*0-7216-4338-8*, W B Saunders Co) Harcrt Hlth Sci Grp.

BRANCHAW. English Made Easy. 3rd ed. 1992. 18.03 (*0-02-800139-7*) McGraw.

Branchaw, Bernadine P. English Made Easy. (gr. 9-12). 1979. text 12.52 (*0-07-007171-3*) McGraw.

— English Made Easy. 2nd ed. 208p. 1985. text 10.88 (*0-07-007174-8*) McGraw.

Branchaw, Bernadine P. & Bowman, Joel P. Delmar Reference Manual: Essentials for the Electronic Office. 96p. 1994. wbk. ed. 13.25 (*0-8273-6696-5*) Delmar.

— Delmar Reference Manual: Essentials for the Electronic Office. 96p. (C). 1994. teacher ed. 17.25 (*0-8273-6474-1*); mass mkt. 34.95 (*0-8273-6473-3*) Delmar.

Branchaw, Bernadine P., jt. auth. see Bowman, Joel P.

Branchaw, Bernadine P., jt. auth. see Hosler, Mary M.

Branchereau, Alain & Berguer, Ramon, eds. Vascular Surgical Approaches. LC 98-43503. (Illus.). 344p. 1999. 115.00 (*0-87993-664-9*) Futura Pub.

Branchereau, Alain & Jacobs, Michael. Critical Limb Ischemia. LC 99-14083. (Illus.). 282p. 1999. 120.00 (*0-87993-412-3*) Futura Pub.

***Branchereau, Alain & Jacobs, Michael.** Surgical & Endovascular Treatment of Aortic Aneurysms. LC 00-23252. (Illus.). 352p. 2000. 125.00 (*0-87993-454-9*) Futura Pub.

Branchereau, Alain & Jacobs, Michael, eds. Long-Term Results of Arterial Interventions. LC 97-3245. (Illus.). 354p. 1997. 95.00 (*0-87993-679-7*) Futura Pub.

— New Trends & Developments in Carotid Artery Disease. LC 98-6275. (Illus.). 284p. 1998. 110.00 (*0-87993-403-4*) Futura Pub.

Brancifort. Parliamo Italian. (C). 1997. pap. text, wbk. ed. 32.36 (*0-395-75768-1*) HM.

Branciforte, Suzanne & Reintjes, Anna G. Parliamo Italiano! (ITA.). (C). 1997. text, teacher ed. 11.96 (*0-395-83508-9*) HM.

— Parliamo Italiano! annot. ed. (ITA.). (C). 1997. text, teacher ed. 63.16 (*0-395-83506-2*) HM.

Branciforte, Suzanne, tr. & intro. see Vigano, Renata.

Branco, C., et al. Mechanical Behaviour of Materials at High Temperature. LC 96-18755. (ASI NATO Ser.). 1996. text 364.50 (*0-7923-4113-9*) Kluwer Academic.

Branco, C. Moura & Rosa, L. Guerra, eds. Advances in Fatigue Science & Technology. (C). 1989. text 426.00 (*0-7923-0105-6*) Kluwer Academic.

Branco, Gustavo Castelo, et al. CP Violation. LC 99-16186. (The International Series of Monographs on Physics: No. 103). (Illus.). 544p. 1999. text 110.00 (*0-19-850399-7*) OUP.

***Branco, J. M., et al, eds.** The Handbook of Enology. LC 98-53087. 250p. 2000. text 145.00 (*0-471-97362-9*) Wiley.

Branco, Miguel R. Dulce Sudor Amargo (Bittersweet Sweat) (SPA., Illus.). 112p. 1985. pap. 8.99 (*968-16-1969-2*, Pub. by Fondo) Continental Bk.

Brancolini, Kristine & Provine, Rick. Video Collections & Multimedia in ARL Libraries: Changing Technologies. (Occasional Papers: No. 19). 54p. 1997. 25.00 (*0-918006-79-1*) ARL.

Brancusi, Constantin. Aforismoj Kaj Tekstoj. Onet, Ionel, tr. from ROM. (RUM.). 35p. 1994. pap. 5.00 (*1-882251-10-5*) Eldonejo Bero.

Branczyk, Alexander, et al. Emotional Digital: A Sourcebook of Contemporary Typographics. LC 99-70866. (Illus.). 275p. 1999. 50.00 (*0-500-01925-8*, Pub. by Thames Hudson) Norton.

***Brand.** Anatomia de las Estruc Orofaci. 6th ed. (C). 1999. text 46.93 (*84-8174-381-X*) Mosby Inc.

Brand. Earth Magic. (Illus.). 62p. 1993. per. write for info. (*0-920813-07-0*) Sister Vis Pr.

— The Fugitive's Mission: A Western Trio. large type ed. LC 98-30798. 1999. 30.00 (*0-7862-0773-6*) Thorndike Pr.

— The Gauntlet. LC 98-29041. 1998. 18.95 (*0-7862-1164-4*) Thorndike Pr.

— Heiress. 1998. per. 4.50 (*0-373-87037-X*, Harlequin) Harlequin Bks.

— Seven Faces. large type ed. LC 98-33782. 1999. 30.00 (*0-7838-0360-5*, G K Hall Lrg Type) Mac Lib Ref.

— The Sheriff Rides. large type ed. LC 98-31642. 1999. 24.95 (*0-7838-0437-7*, G K Hall Lrg Type) Mac Lib Ref.

***Brand, A.** Herd Health & Production Management in Dairy Practice. 543p. 1998. pap. 83.00 (*90-74134-34-3*) Wageningen Pers.

Brand, A. J. A Guide to Divorce: Answers to Questions You Never Knew to Ask. 52p. 1996. pap. 12.95 (*0-9651734-0-2*) Divorce Reform.

Brand, Alice. As It Happens. 64p. 1983. pap. 5.95 (*0-931694-23-X*) Wampeter Pr.

— Court of Common Pleas: Poems. LC 99-56042. 1996. write for info. (*0-7734-2712-0*) E Mellen.

Brand, Alice & Graves, Richard, eds. Presence of Mind: Writing & the Domain Beyond the Cognitive. LC 93-42727. (Illus.). 246p. (C). 1994. pap. text 25.00 (*0-86709-336-6*, 0336, Pub. by Boynton Cook Pubs) Heinemann.

Brand, Alice G. Court of Common Pleas. LC 96-42393. 84p. 1997. pap. 14.95 (*0-7734-2687-6*, Mellen Poetry Pr) E Mellen.

— The Psychology of Writing: The Affective Experience, 13. LC 88-25090. (Contributions in Psychology Ser.: No. 13). 281p. 1989. 59.95 (*0-313-26382-5*, BPH/, Greenwood Pr) Greenwood.

— Studies on Zone. LC 89-13344. 72p. 1989. 8.95 (*0-933532-71-7*) BkMk.

Brand, Charles M. Byzantium Confronts the West, 1180-1204. (Modern Revivals in History Ser.). 402p. 1992. 63.95 (*0-7512-0053-0*, Pub. by Gregg Revivals) Ashgate Pub Co.

Brand, Charles M., tr. see Kinnamos, John.

Brand, Christianna. Cat & Mouse. 240p. 1984. reprint ed. pap. 5.95 (*0-930330-18-8*) Intl Polygonics.

— Death in High Heels. 224p. 1996. mass mkt. 4.95 (*0-7867-0336-9*) Carroll & Graf.

— Fog of Doubt. 272p. 1995. mass mkt. 4.95 (*0-7867-0219-2*) Carroll & Graf.

— Green for Danger. 256p. 1997. mass mkt. 4.95 (*0-7867-0386-5*) Carroll & Graf.

— Green for Danger. LC 78-69778. (Illus.). 271p. 1978. reprint ed. 18.95 (*0-89163-046-5*) Boulevard.

— Suddenly at His Residence. large type ed. (Linford Mystery Library). 416p. 1997. pap. 16.99 (*0-7089-5107-4*, Linford) Ulverscroft.

— Tour de Force. 272p. 1996. mass mkt. 4.95 (*0-7867-0340-7*) Carroll & Graf.

— Tour de Force. 1997. 19.50 (*0-7540-8502-3*, Black Dagger) Chivers N Amer.

Brand, Clive. Planning Law. (C). 1990. 125.00 (*1-85431-088-7*, Pub. by Blackstone Pr) St Mut.

— Planning Law. (C). 1991. text 22.00 (*1-85431-128-X*, Pub. by Blackstone Pr) Gaunt.

— Planning Law. 2nd ed. (Practice Notes Ser.). 109p. 1994. pap. write for info. (*0-85121-870-9*, Pub. by Cavendish Pubng) Gaunt.

— Planning Law. 3rd ed. (Cavendish Practice Notes Ser.). 1996. pap. 32.00 (*1-85941-294-7*, Pub. by Cavendish Pubng) Gaunt.

Brand, Clive & Rowan-Robinson, Jeremy. Compulsory Purchase & Compensation Vol. 1. 1994. 88.00 (*0-421-46540-9*, Pub. by Sweet & Maxwll) Gaunt.

Brand, Dana. The Spectator & the City in Nineteenth Century American Literature. 252p. (C). 1991. text 54.95 (*0-521-36207-5*) Cambridge U Pr.

Brand, Daniel, compiled by. Urban Transportation Innovation. 445p. 1970. pap. 5.00 (*0-87262-044-1*) Am Soc Civil Eng.

Brand, David. Profile of the Last Puritan: Jonathon Edwards, Self-Love, & the Dawn of the Beatific. 165p. 1991. 24.95 (*1-55540-582-7*, 01 01 73); pap. 14.95 (*1-55540-583-5*, 01 01 73) OUP.

Brand, David G., jt. ed. see Bouman, O. Thomas.

Brand, Dennis J., Jr., tr. from SPA. The Book of Causes. LC 84-61118. (Medieval Philosophical Texts in Translation Ser.).Tr. of Liber de Causis. 56p. 1984. pap. 5.00 (*0-87462-225-5*) Marquette.

Brand, Dionne. At the Full & Change of the Moon. LC 99-18152. 304p. 1999. 24.00 (*0-8021-1649-3*, Grove) Grove-Atltic.

***Brand, Dionne.** At the Full & Change of the Moon. (Illus.). 320p. 2000. reprint ed. pap. 13.50 (*0-8021-3723-7*, Grove) Grove-Atltic.

Brand, Dionne. In Another Place, Not Here. LC 97-11312. 256p. 1997. 24.00 (*0-8021-1622-1*, Grove) Grove-Atltic.

***Brand, Dionne.** In Another Place, Not Here! 256p. 2000. pap. 13.00 (*0-8021-3633-8*, Grove) Grove-Atltic.

Brand, Dionne. Sans Souci. 150p. pap. 10.95 (*0-88961-196-3*, Pub. by Womens Pr) LPC InBook.

— Sans Souci & Other Stories. LC 89-23614. 150p. (Orig.). 1989. pap. 8.95 (*0-932379-70-2*); lib. bdg. 18.95 (*0-932379-71-0*) Firebrand Bks.

Brand, Dionne, et al. No Burden to Carry: Narratives of Black Working Women in Ontario 1920s to 1950s. 288p. pap. 15.95 (*0-88961-163-7*, Pub. by Womens Pr) LPC InBook.

— We're Rooted Here & They Can't Pull Us Up: Essays in African Canadian Women's History. Bristow, Peggy, ed. (Illus.). 192p. (C). 1994. text 45.00 (*0-8020-5943-0*); pap. text 17.95 (*0-8020-6881-2*) U of Toronto Pr.

Brand, Donald, jt. auth. see Sauer, Carl Ortwin.

Brand, Donald D. Quiroga: A Mexican Municipio. LC 76-44693. reprint ed. 22.50 (*0-404-15853-6*) AMS Pr.

Brand, Donald R. Corporatism & the Rule of Law: A Study of the National Recovery Administration. LC 88-7167. 352p. 1988. pap. text 18.95 (*0-8014-9495-8*) Cornell U Pr.

Brand, Eileen, ed. see Lundberg, Ferdinand.

Brand, F. J., tr. see Linnaeus, Carl.

***Brand, Fiona.** Blade's Lady. (Intimate Moments Ser.). 2000. mass mkt. 4.50 (*0-373-27093-3*, 1-27093-3) Silhouette.

Brand, Fiona. Cullen's Bride (March Madness) (Intimate Moments Ser.: No. 914). 1999. per. 4.25 (*0-373-07914-1*, 1-07914-4) Harlequin Bks.
— Heart of Midnight. (Intimate Moments Ser.). 2000. mass mkt. 4.25 (*0-373-07977-X*, 1-07977-1) Silhouette.

Brand, Franklin M. Brand Family of Monongalia Co., Va. (Now W. Va.) 426p. 1996. reprint ed. pap. 64.00 (*0-8328-5228-7*); reprint ed. lib. bdg. 74.00 (*0-8328-5227-9*) Higginson Bk Co.
— Fleming: William Fleming Family, a Genealogy, with a Brief Account of Some Other Flemings of Delaware. (Illus.). 652p. 1997. reprint ed. pap. 98.00 (*0-8328-8578-9*); reprint ed. lib. bdg. 108.00 (*0-8328-8577-0*) Higginson Bk Co.

Brand, George. More to Come: The First 100 Years. (Illus.). 181p. 1989. 39.95 (*0-685-24280-3*) CA News Pubs Assn.

Brand, Gerd. Welt, Geschichte, Mythos, Politik. (C). 1978. 76.95 (*3-11-007505-9*) De Gruyter.

Brand-Gomez, Olga, ed. see Bonilla, Frank & Campos, Ricardo.

Brand, H. W. The Fecundity of Mathematical Methods in Economic Theory. Holmstrom, E., tr. from GER. 56p. 1961. lib. bdg. 57.00 (*90-277-0092-3*) Kluwer Academic.

Brand, Hartwig. SAP R/3 Implementation with ASAP: The Official SAP Guide. LC 98-83182. 624p. 1999. 49.99 (*0-7821-2427-5*) Sybex.

Brand, Helena S. Orchards, Gardens & Pieces of Sky. 60p. (Orig.). 1994. pap. text 10.00 (*0-914435-23-X*) Marylhurst Art.

Brand, Irene. Child of Her Heart. (Love Inspired Ser.). 1998. per. 4.50 (*0-373-87019-1*, 1-87019-5) Harlequin Bks.
— Come Gentle Spring. 224p. 1987. pap. 5.70 (*0-310-47661-5*, 15618P) Zondervan.
— A Groom to Come Home to. 1999. per. 4.50 (*0-373-87070-1*, No. 1-87070-8) Harlequin Bks.
— The Hills Are Calling. 189p. (Orig.). 1990. pap. 4.95 (*0-941092-22-4*) Mtn St Pr.
— In This Sign Conquer: In the Time of Constantine. LC 96-10340. (Legacies of Faith Ser.: No. 1). (Illus.). 304p. 1996. pap. 9.99 (*0-8254-2144-6*) Kregel.
— Like a Burning Fire: In the Time of Charlemagne. LC 96-10341. (Legacies of Faith Ser.). (Illus.). 304p. 1996. pap. 9.99 (*0-8254-2145-4*) Kregel.
— Love Is the Key. 224p. 1988. pap. 5.95 (*0-310-47801-4*, 15657P) Zondervan.

***Brand, Irene.** Tender Love. 2000. per. 4.50 (*0-373-87101-5*) Harlequin Bks.
— The Test of Love. (Love Inspired Ser.: Vol. 114). 256p. 2000. mass mkt. 4.50 (*0-373-87120-1*, 1-87120-1) Harlequin Bks.

Brand, Irene. To Love & Honor. 1999. per. 4.50 (*0-373-87049-3*, 1-87049-2, Mira Bks) Harlequin Bks.
— Where Morning Dawns. (Serenade Saga Ser.: No. 33). 1986. pap. 1.49 (*0-310-47522-8*, 15598P) Zondervan.

Brand, Irene B. Only a Clay Vessel. (Illus.). 120p. (Orig.). 1985. pap. 5.00 (*0-9615285-0-8*) Brand.

Brand, J. C. Lines of Light: The Sources of Dispersive Spectroscopy, 1800-1930. 280p. 1995. text 154.00 (*2-88449-162-7*); pap. text 66.00 (*2-88449-163-5*) Gordon & Breach.

Brand, Jack. Power in Parliament: Back-Bench Parties & Policy. (Illus.). 380p. 1992. text 85.00 (*0-19-827705-9*) OUP.

Brand, Jaya, ed. see Friends of Peter.

Brand, Jeanne L. Doctors & the State: The British Medical Profession & Government Action in Public Health, 1870-1912. LC 65-27326. 339p. reprint ed. pap. 105.10 (*0-608-11891-5*, 202308500032) Bks Demand.

Brand, Joan & Alden, Richard. Fundamentals of Grammar & Writing. 2nd ed. 390p. (C). 1989. pap. text 33.71 (*0-929655-40-0*) CAT Pub.

Brand, Johanna. The Life & Death of Anna Mae Aquash. (Illus.). 172p. 1995. reprint ed. pap. 14.95 (*1-55028-422-3*) Formac Dist Ltd.

***Brand, John.** Comanche Moon. large type ed. 240p. 1999. pap. 20.99 (*1-85389-898-8*) Ulverscroft.

Brand, John. Learning about Mission: Mission Matters! 96p. 1999. pap. text 2.99 (*1-85792-402-9*) Christian Focus.

***Brand, John.** The Legend of Johnny Cloud. large type ed. 224p. 1999. pap. 20.99 (*1-85389-915-1*, Dales) Ulverscroft.

Brand, John. Observations on the Popular Antiquities of Great Britain, 3 vols. 3rd ed. Ellis, Henry, ed. LC 71-136368. (Bohn's Antiquarian Library). reprint ed. 125.00 (*0-404-50005-6*) AMS Pr.

Brand, Joseph G. & Teeter, John H., eds. Receptor Events & Transduction in Taste & Olfaction. (Chemical Senses Ser.: 1). (Illus.). 560p. 1989. text 235.00 (*0-8247-8162-7*) Dekker.

Brand, Joseph G., jt. ed. see Spielman, Andrew I.

Brand, Jude. Tokyo Night City: Where to Drink & Party. 172p. 1993. pap. 9.95 (*0-8048-1896-7*) Tuttle Pubng.

Brand, Juliane & Hailey, Christopher, eds. Constructive Dissonance: Arnold Schoenberg & the Transformations of Twentieth-Century Culture. LC 96-24712. (Illus.). 242p. 1997. 45.00 (*0-520-20314-3*, Pub. by U CA Pr) Cal Prin Full Svc.

***Brand, Kay.** Wilmath: A Woman Who Spent a Lifetime Battling Hardship. 200p. 2000. pap. 14.95 (*1-58597-041-7*) Leathers Pub.

Brand, Ken, jt. auth. see Beckett, J. V.

Brand, L. M., et al. Die Schoene Ist Angekommen: Ein Grammatikkrimi. (GER.). 80p. (C). 1995. pap. text 18.00 (*3-12-675318-3*, Pub. by Klett Edition) Intl Bk Import.

Brand, Laurie, jt. auth. see Tessler, Mark.

Brand, Laurie A. Jordan's Inter-Arab Relations: The Political Economy of Alliance Making. LC 94-22342. 350p. 1995. 52.50 (*0-231-10096-5*); pap. 20.50 (*0-231-10097-3*) Col U Pr.
— Palestinians in the Arab World. 286p. 1991. pap. text 22.00 (*0-231-06723-2*) Col U Pr.
— Palestinians in the Arab World: Institution Building & the Search for State. 286p. 1988. text 61.50 (*0-231-06722-4*) Col U Pr.
— Palestinians in the Arab World: Institution Building & the Search for State. 286p. (C). 1998. pap. text 25.00 (*0-7881-5503-2*) DIANE Pub.
— Women, the State, & Political Liberalization: Middle Eastern & North African Experiences. LC 98-4431. 320p. 1998. pap. 18.50 (*0-231-11267-X*); lib. bdg. 50.00 (*0-231-11266-1*) Col U Pr.

Brand, Leonard. Faith, Reason & Earth History: A Paradigm of Earth & Biological Origins by Intelligent Design. LC 96-40000. (Illus.). (Orig.). (C). 1997. pap. text 34.99 (*1-883925-15-0*) Andrews Univ Pr.

Brand, Loren. Barditch, Texas: The Saga Begins. (Illus.). 136p. (Orig.). 1993. pap. 9.95 (*0-9636248-1-4*) Bedford Hse.

Brand, Ludwig, et al, eds. Fluorescence Spectroscopy. (Methods in Enzymology Ser.: Vol. 278). (Illus.). 628p. 1997. text 110.00 (*0-12-182179-X*) Morgan Kaufmann.

Brand, Max. The Abandoned Outlaw. 240p. 1998. mass mkt. 4.50 (*0-8439-4465-X*, Leisure Bks) Dorchester Pub Co.
— The Abandoned Outlaw: A Circle V Western. large type ed. LC 97-40228. (Sagebrush Large Print Westerns Ser.). 1997. lib. bdg. 19.95 (*1-57490-095-1*) T T Beeler.
— Alcatraz. large type ed. LC 90-26041. 309p. 1991. reprint ed. lib. bdg. 17.95 (*1-56054-139-3*) Thorndike Pr.
— Bandit of the Black Hills. reprint ed. lib. bdg. 20.95 (*0-88411-512-7*) Amereon Ltd.
— Battle's End & The Three Crosses. 1990. pap. 3.50 (*0-8125-0522-0*, Pub. by Tor Bks) St Martin.
— The Bells of San Carlos & Other Stories. Tuska, Jon, ed. & frwd. by. LC 95-32017. 206p. 1996. text 30.00 (*0-8032-1266-6*) U of Nebr Pr.

***Brand, Max.** The Bells of San Carlos & Other Stories. Tuska, Jon, ed. & frwd. by. LC 95-32017. 206p. 2000. pap. 12.95 (*0-8032-6173-X*, Bison Books) U of Nebr Pr.

Brand, Max. The Bells of San Filipo. 240p. 1995. reprint ed. pap. text, mass mkt. 3.99 (*0-8439-3819-6*) Dorchester Pub Co.
— Beyond the Outposts. LC 97-9308. 257p. 1997. lib. bdg. 17.95 (*0-7862-0745-0*) Five Star.
— Beyond the Outposts. large type ed. LC 98-24822. 1999. 21.95 (*0-7862-0768-X*) Thorndike Pr.
— The Big Trail. 1976. reprint ed. lib. bdg. 22.95 (*0-88411-513-5*) Amereon Ltd.
— The Black Rider & Other Stories. Tuska, Jon, ed. & frwd. by. LC 95-35342. ix, 193p. 1996. text 30.00 (*0-8032-1263-1*) U of Nebr Pr.
— The Black Rider & Other Stories. large type ed. LC 96-19216. 327p. 1996. 23.95 (*0-7838-1844-0*, G K Hall Lrg Type) Mac Lib Ref.
— Border Bandit. 245p. 1976. reprint ed. lib. bdg. 20.95 (*0-89190-201-5*, Rivercity Pr) Amereon Ltd.
— Brothers of the Trail. 1976. reprint ed. lib. bdg. 22.95 (*0-88411-514-3*) Amereon Ltd.
— Bull Hunter. large type ed. LC 99-27138. 1999. 19.95 (*1-57490-181-8*, Sagebrush LP West) T T Beeler.
— Calling Dr. Kildare. large type ed. LC 92-41195. (General Ser.). 1993. lib. bdg. 15.95 (*0-8161-5717-0*, G K Hall Lrg Type) Mac Lib Ref.

***Brand, Max.** The Catch Colt. large type ed. LC 99-54896. 2000. 20.95 (*1-57490-249-0*) T T Beeler.

Brand, Max. Chinook. LC 98-22718. 287p. 1998. 18.95 (*0-7862-1155-5*) Thorndike Pr.
— Chinook. large type ed. LC 99-21870. 1999. pap. 30.00 (*0-7862-1167-9*) Mac Lib Ref.

***Brand, Max.** The City in the Sky. large type ed. 1998. 19.95 (*1-57490-157-5*, Sagebrush LP West) T T Beeler.

Brand, Max. The Collected Stories of Max Brand. Easton, Robert & Easton, Jane, eds. LC 93-43938. xx, 346p. (C). 1994. text 40.00 (*0-8032-1244-5*) U of Nebr Pr.
— The Cross Brand. large type ed. LC 94-27105. 170p. 1994. lib. bdg. 19.95 (*0-8161-7494-6*, G K Hall Lrg Type) Mac Lib Ref.
— Crossroads. LC 96-37390. ix, 214p. 1997. text 30.00 (*0-8032-1278-X*) U of Nebr Pr.

***Brand, Max.** Crossroads. large type ed. LC 99-43714. 1999. 20.95 (*1-57490-232-6*) T T Beeler.

Brand, Max. Dan Barry's Daughter. 1976. reprint ed. lib. bdg. 25.95 (*0-88411-516-X*) Amereon Ltd.
— Danger Trail. 1976. reprint ed. lib. bdg. 23.95 (*0-88411-517-8*) Amereon Ltd.
— Dead or Alive. 24.95 (*0-88411-518-6*) Amereon Ltd.
— Destry Rides Again. 208p. 1991. pap. 2.95 (*0-671-73543-8*) PB.
— Destry Rides Again. Date not set. reprint ed. lib. bdg. 23.95 (*0-88411-515-1*, Aeonian Pr) Amereon Ltd.
— Destry Rides Again. 1990. reprint ed. lib. bdg. 19.95 (*0-89968-485-8*) Buccaneer Bks.
— Devil Horse. 202p. reprint ed. lib. bdg. 20.95 (*0-88411-522-4*) Amereon Ltd.
— Dr. Kildare Takes Charge. 160p. reprint ed. lib. bdg. 18.95 (*0-88411-531-3*) Amereon Ltd.
— Dr. Kildare's Trial. 174p. reprint ed. lib. bdg. 19.95 (*0-88411-532-1*) Amereon Ltd.
— Donnegan. 320p. 1996. reprint ed. mass mkt. 4.50 (*0-8439-4086-7*, Leisure Bks) Dorchester Pub Co.
— Dr. Kildare's Crisis. large type ed. LC 93-21148. 210p. 1994. lib. bdg. 16.95 (*0-8161-5873-8*, G K Hall Lrg Type) Mac Lib Ref.
— Dr. Kildare's Search & Dr. Kildare's Hardest Case. large type ed. LC 93-34676. 173p. 1994. lib. bdg. 16.95 (*0-8161-5896-7*, G K Hall Lrg Type) Mac Lib Ref.
— The Dude. 1976. reprint ed. lib. bdg. 23.95 (*0-88411-519-4*) Amereon Ltd.

***Brand, Max.** Dust Across the Range/The Cross Brand, 2 vols. in 1. 320p. 2000. mass mkt. 4.50 (*0-8439-4743-8*, Leisure Bks) Dorchester Pub Co.

Brand, Max. Farewell, Thunder Moon. LC 95-43019. vi, 84p. (C). 1996. text 30.00 (*0-8032-1267-4*) U of Nebr Pr.
— Farewell, Thunder Moon. large type ed. LC 98-15046. (Sagebrush Large Print Westerns Ser.). 1998. 17.95 (*1-57490-123-0*) T T Beeler.
— Fighter Squadron at Guadalcanal. LC 96-2902. (Illus.). 248p. 1996. 26.95 (*1-55750-088-6*) Naval Inst Pr.
— Fighter Squadron at Guadalcanal. 1997. per. 6.50 (*0-671-01431-5*) PB.
— The Fighting Four. 1999. write for info. (*0-7540-8043-9*) Chivers N Amer.
— Free Range Lanning. large type ed. LC 94-32525. 285p. 1995. lib. bdg. 19.95 (*0-7838-1146-2*, G K Hall Lrg Type) Mac Lib Ref.
— Fugitive's Fire. large type ed. LC 96-42231. (Sagebrush Large Print Westerns Ser.). 1996. lib. bdg. 18.95 (*1-57490-042-0*) T T Beeler.
— The Fugitive's Mission: A Western Trio. LC 97-27701. 1997. lib. bdg. 17.95 (*0-7862-0750-7*) Five Star.
— The Galloping Broncos. large type ed. 366p. 1991. reprint ed. lib. bdg. 18.95 (*1-56054-169-5*) Thorndike Pr.
— The Gambler. 1976. reprint ed. lib. bdg. 24.95 (*0-88411-520-8*) Amereon Ltd.

***Brand, Max.** Gauntlet: A Western Trio. large type ed. LC 99-41469. (Thorndike Western Ser.). 1999. 30.00 (*0-7862-1176-8*) Thorndike Pr.

Brand, Max. The Gentle Gunman. 1993. 12.00 (*0-86025-441-0*, Pub. by I Henry Pubns) Empire Pub Srvs.
— The Geraldi Trail. LC 99-19829. 250p. 1999. 30.00 (*0-7862-1576-3*) Mac Lib Ref.
— The Geraldi Trail. large type ed. LC 00-24240. (G. K. Hall Western Ser.). 275p. 2000. 25.95 (*0-7838-0314-1*, G K Hall Lrg Type) Mac Lib Ref.
— Ghost Rider. 212p. reprint ed. lib. bdg. 20.95 (*0-88411-521-6*) Amereon Ltd.
— The Ghost Wagon & Other Great Western Adventures. Tuska, Jon, ed. & frwd. by. LC 95-30631. ix, 246p. (C). 1996. text 30.00 (*0-8032-1265-8*) U of Nebr Pr.
— The Ghost Wagon & Other Great Western Adventures. large type ed. Tuska, John, ed. LC 96-22228. 1996. 22.95 (*0-7838-1862-9*, G K Hall Lrg Type) Mac Lib Ref.
— The Gold Trail. 275p. 2000. 30.00 (*0-7862-1587-9*) Thorndike Pr.
— The Gold Trail: A Western Trio. LC 99-35655. (Westerns Ser.). 250p. 1999. 19.95 (*0-7862-1578-X*) Five Star.
— Gun Gentlemen. 240p. 1996. reprint ed. mass mkt. 4.50 (*0-8439-3937-0*) Dorchester Pub Co.
— Gunman's Goal. LC 99-41700. 1999. 19.95 (*0-7862-1857-6*) Mac Lib Ref.
— Gunman's Legacy. 257p. 1976. reprint ed. lib. bdg. 22.95 (*0-89190-202-3*, Rivercity Pr) Amereon Ltd.
— Hunted Riders. large type ed. (General Ser.). 359p. 1991. lib. bdg. 18.95 (*0-8161-5082-6*, G K Hall Lrg Type) Mac Lib Ref.
— In the Hills of Monterey. LC 97-38421. 1998. 18.95 (*0-7862-0988-7*) Five Star.
— In the Hills of Monterey: A Western Story LC 98-43047. (Thorndike Large Print Western Ser.). 340 p. 1999. write for info. (*0-7540-3668-5*) Chivers N Amer.

***Brand, Max.** In the Hills of Monterey: A Western Story. large type ed. LC 98-43047. 1999. 30.00 (*0-7862-1027-3*) Thorndike Pr.

Brand, Max. The Iron Trail. large type ed. LC 90-21278. 376p. 1991. reprint ed. lib. bdg. 16.95 (*1-56054-105-9*) Thorndike Pr.
— King Charlie. 320p. 1997. reprint ed. mass mkt. 4.50 (*0-8439-4182-0*) Dorchester Pub Co.
— King Charlie's Riders: A Western Story. large type ed. LC 93-19645. 256p. 1993. lib. bdg. 20.95 (*0-8161-5712-X*, G K Hall Lrg Type) Mac Lib Ref.

***Brand, Max.** The Legend of Thunder Moon. 256p. 1999. mass mkt. 4.50 (*0-8439-4583-4*, Pub. by Dorchester Pub Co) CMG.

Brand, Max. The Legend of Thunder Moon. LC 95-26142. xvi, 162p. 1996. text 30.00 (*0-8032-1269-0*) U of Nebr Pr.
— The Legend of Thunder Moon. large type ed. LC 97-17581. (Sagebrush Large Print Westerns Ser.). 1997. lib. bdg. 19.95 (*1-57490-090-0*) T T Beeler.
— The Lightning Warrior. 272p. 1998. mass mkt. 4.50 (*0-8439-4420-X*, Leisure Bks) Dorchester Pub Co.
— The Lightning Warrior. large type ed. Date not set. 20.00 (*0-7838-1667-7*, G K Hall Lrg Type) Mac Lib Ref.
— The Lightning Warrior. 320p. 1998. reprint ed. mass mkt. 4.99 (*0-8439-4355-6*, Leisure Bks) Dorchester Pub Co.
— The Lightning Warrior: A North-Western Story. LC 96-6302. 230p. 1996. 16.95 (*0-7862-0656-X*) Five Star.
— The Lost Valley: A Western Trio. LC 98-2606. 1998 20.00 (*0-7862-0997-6*) Thorndike Pr.
— The Lost Valley: A Western Trio. large type ed. LC 99-11212. (Illus.). 1999. 23.95 (*0-7862-1036-2*) Mac Lib Ref.
— Luck. LC 96-37391. ix, 204p. 1997. text 30.00 (*0-8032-1277-1*) U of Nebr Pr.

***Brand, Max.** Luck. large type ed. LC 99-30781. 1999. 20.95 (*1-57490-196-6*, Sagebrush LP West) T T Beeler.
— The Masterman. 197p. 2000. 30.00 (*0-7862-2099-6*) Mac Lib Ref.

Brand, Max. Max Brand's Best Poems: Verses from a Master of Popular Prose - A Centennial Selection. Greenberg, Martin H., ed. LC 91-16615. (Illus.). 104p. 1992. 14.95 (*0-931832-96-9*) Fithian Pr.
— Men Beyond the Law: A Western Trio. large type ed. LC 96-53882. 250p. 1997. 17.95 (*0-7862-0742-6*) Thorndike Pr.
— Men Beyond the Law: A Western Trio. large type ed. LC 98-5428. 1998. 22.95 (*0-7862-0765-5*) Thorndike Pr.
— Montana Rides. 300p. Date not set. reprint ed. lib. bdg. 20.95 (*0-89190-203-1*, Am Repr) Amereon Ltd.
— Montana Rides Again. 253p. Date not set. reprint ed. lib. bdg. 22.95 (*0-89190-204-X*, Am Repr) Amereon Ltd.

***Brand, Max.** Mountain Riders. 158p. 1999. pap. 19.00 (*0-7540-8062-5*) Chivers N Amer.

Brand, Max. The Night Flower. (Library of Crime Classics). 311p. 1987. pap. 4.95 (*0-930330-48-X*) Intl Polygonics.
— The Night Horseman. large type ed. (Sagebrush Large Print Westerns Ser.). 300p. 1995. lib. bdg. 18.95 (*1-57490-007-2*) T T Beeler.

***Brand, Max.** The Oath of Office. large type ed. 1998. 19.95 (*1-57490-158-3*, Sagebrush LP West) T T Beeler.

Brand, Max. The One-Way Trail. 240p. 1998. reprint ed. mass mkt. 4.50 (*0-8439-4379-3*, Leisure Bks) Dorchester Pub Co.
— The One-Way Trail: A Max Brand Western Trio. large type ed. (Sagebrush Large Print Westerns Ser.). 256p. 1996. lib. bdg. 18.95 (*1-57490-014-5*) T T Beeler.
— The Outlaw of Buffalo Flat. 160p. Date not set. 18.95 (*0-8488-2215-3*) Amereon Ltd.

***Brand, Max.** The Outlaw Redeemer. LC 00-23523. 207p. 2000. 30.00 (*0-7862-2106-2*, Five Star MI) Mac Lib Ref.

Brand, Max. Outlaw Valley. Date not set. reprint ed. lib. bdg. 22.95 (*0-89190-205-8*, Am Repr) Amereon Ltd.
— Outlaws All. 272p. 1998. reprint ed. mass mkt. 4.50 (*0-8439-4398-X*, Leisure Bks) Dorchester Pub Co.
— Outlaws All: A Western Trio. large type ed. LC 95-47325. (West-Hall Ser.). 362p. 1997. lib. bdg. 22.95 (*0-7838-1575-1*, G K Hall Lrg Type) Mac Lib Ref.
— Outlaws All: A Western Trio. large type ed. (Five-Star Western Ser.). 1996. 16.95 (*0-7862-0592-X*) Thorndike Pr.
— Outlaw's Code. 210p. Date not set. reprint ed. lib. bdg. 20.95 (*0-89190-206-6*, Am Repr) Amereon Ltd.

***Brand, Max.** The Overland Kid: A Western Trio. LC 99-55131. 2000. 30.00 (*0-7862-1846-0*) Mac Lib Ref.

Brand, Max. Pride of Tyson. 320p. 1996. reprint ed. mass mkt. 4.50 (*0-8439-4113-8*) Dorchester Pub Co.
— The Quest of Lee Garrison, 1. 240p. 1999. mass mkt. 4.50 (*0-8439-4558-3*) Dorchester Pub Co.
— The Quest of Lee Garrison. large type ed. LC 98-26868. 1998. 19.95 (*1-57490-145-1*, Sagebrush LP West) T T Beeler.
— Red Bandanna & Carcajou's Trail. (Special Double Action Western Ser.: No. 15). 1991. pap. 3.50 (*0-8125-1314-2*, Pub. by Tor Bks) St Martin.

***Brand, Max.** Red Devil of the Range. large type ed. LC 99-58232. (G. K. Hall Western Ser.). 2000. 25.95 (*0-7838-8939-9*, G K Hall Lrg Type) Mac Lib Ref.

Brand, Max. Red Devil of the Range. 320p. 1996. reprint ed. mass mkt. 4.50 (*0-8439-4122-7*) Dorchester Pub Co.

***Brand, Max.** Red Wind & Thunder Moon, Vol. 1. 1999. mass mkt. 4.50 (*0-8439-4630-X*, Leisure Bks) Dorchester Pub Co.

Brand, Max. Red Wind & Thunder Moon. LC 95-43100. vi, 166p. (C). 1996. text 30.00 (*0-8032-1268-2*) U of Nebr Pr.
— Rescue of Broken Arrow. 249p. 1976. reprint ed. lib. bdg. 20.95 (*0-89190-207-4*, Rivercity Pr) Amereon Ltd.
— The Return of Free Range Lanning. 1998. 17.50 (*0-7540-8030-7*) Chivers N Amer.
— The Return of Free Range Lanning. large type ed. LC 95-13853. 313p. 1995. 20.95 (*0-7838-1289-2*, G K Hall Lrg Type) Mac Lib Ref.
— The Return of Free Range Lanning. 240p. 1997. reprint ed. mass mkt. 4.50 (*0-8439-4294-0*, Leisure Bks) Dorchester Pub Co.

Brand, Max. Return of the Rancher, Set. unabridged ed. 1994. pap. 19.95 incl. audio (*1-56100-547-9*, Bkcassette) Brilliance.

Brand, Max. Rippon Rides Double. large type ed. LC 96-22227. (Western Ser.). 256p. 1996. 19.95 (*0-7862-0808-2*) Thorndike Pr.

***Brand, Max.** The Rock of Kiever. 224p. 2000. pap. 4.50 (*0-8439-4719-5*, Leisure Bks) Dorchester Pub Co.

Brand, Max. Rock of Kiever. large type ed. LC 98-15045. (Sagebrush Large Print Westerns Ser.). 246 p. 1998. 19.95 (*1-57490-122-2*) T T Beeler.
— Ronicky Doone. 256p. 1995. pap. text, mass mkt. 3.99 (*0-8439-3738-6*) Dorchester Pub Co.
— Ronicky Doone: A Western Story. large type ed. LC 93-13225. 1993. 19.95 (*0-8161-5713-8*) Thorndike Pr.
— Ronicky Doone's Reward. 224p. 1995. pap. text, mass mkt. 3.99 (*0-8439-3779-3*) Dorchester Pub Co.
— Ronicky Doone's Reward. large type ed. LC 94-15062. 326p. 1995. lib. bdg. 20.95 (*0-8161-5999-8*, G K Hall Lrg Type) Mac Lib Ref.
— Ronicky Doone's Treasure. 256p. 1995. pap. text, mass mkt. 3.99 (*0-8439-3748-3*) Dorchester Pub Co.
— Ronicky Doone's Treasure. large type ed. LC 94-13482. 261p. 1994. lib. bdg. 20.95 (*0-8161-5998-X*, G K Hall Lrg Type) Mac Lib Ref.
— Rustlers of Beacon Creek. large type ed. LC 94-45645. 378p. 1995. lib. bdg. 18.95 (*0-7862-0395-1*) Thorndike Pr.
— The Sacking of El Dorado. 288p. 1997. reprint ed. mass mkt. 4.50 (*0-8439-4335-1*, Leisure Bks) Dorchester Pub Co.
— Safety McTee. 240p. 1999. mass mkt. 4.50 (*0-8439-4528-1*, Leisure Bks) Dorchester Pub Co.
— Safety McTee. large type ed. LC 97-39303. (Sagebrush Large Print Westerns Ser.). 1998. 19.95 (*1-57490-116-8*, Sagebrush LP West) T T Beeler.

B

An Asterisk (*) at the beginning of an entry indicates that the title is appearing for the first time.

— Sawdust & Sixguns. 246p. 1976. reprint ed. lib. bdg. 22.95 (*0-89190-208-2*, Rivercity Pr) Amereon Ltd.
— The Secret of Dr. Kildare. large type ed. LC 96-20903. (Nightingale Ser.). 1996. 17.95 (*0-7838-1846-7*, G K Hall Lrg Type) Mac Lib Ref.
— The Secret of Dr. Kildare. 180p. reprint ed. lib. bdg. 19.95 (*0-88411-530-5*, Rivercity Pr) Amereon Ltd.
— Seven Faces. LC 97-22023. vii, 180p. 1998. text 25.00 (*0-8032-1281-X*) U of Nebr Pr.
— Seven Faces large type ed. LC 98-33782. 271p. 1999. write for info. (*0-7540-3552-2*) Chivers N Amer.
— Seven of Diamonds. large type ed. LC 90-11278. 384p. 1990. reprint ed. lib. bdg. 16.95 (*1-56054-076-1*) Thorndike Pr.
— The Shadow of Silver Tip. large type ed. 425p. 1995. 22.95 (*0-7838-1470-4*, G K Hall Lrg Type) Mac Lib Ref.
— Silvertip's Roundup. large type ed. (General Ser.). 246p. 1990. lib. bdg. 17.95 (*0-8161-4979-8*, G K Hall Lrg Type) Mac Lib Ref.
— Singing Guns. 1991. pap. 2.95 (*0-671-73542-X*) S&S Trade.
— Sixteen in Nome. 240p. 1999. mass mkt. 4.50 (*0-8439-4486-2*, Leisure Bks) Dorchester Pub Co.
— Sixteen in Nome. large type ed. 267p. 1996. lib. bdg. 20.95 (*0-7862-0718-3*) Thorndike Pr.
— Sixteen in Nome: A North-Western Story. LC 95-9438. (Five-Star Western Ser.). 200p. 1995. 16.95 (*0-7862-0509-1*) Thorndike Pr.
— Slumber Mountain. 320p. 1998. reprint ed. mass mkt. 4.99 (*0-8439-4442-0*, Leisure Bks) Dorchester Pub Co.
*****Brand, Max.** Slumber Mountain: A Western Trio. 242p. 2000. 19.00 (*0-7540-8078-1*) Chivers N Amer.
Brand, Max. Slumber Mountain: A Western Trio. large type ed. LC 97-18667. (Sagebrush Large Print Westerns Ser.). 1997. lib. bdg. 18.95 (*1-57490-109-5*, Beeler LP Bks) T T Beeler.
— Smiling Charlie. large type ed. (General Ser.). 364p. 1992. lib. bdg. 20.95 (*0-8161-5086-9*, G K Hall Lrg Type) Mac Lib Ref.
*****Brand, Max.** Soft Metal: A Western Trio. 240p. 2000. pap. 4.50 (*0-8439-4698-9*, Leisure Bks) Dorchester Pub Co.
Brand, Max. Soft Metal: A Western Trio. large type ed. LC 98-27482. (Circle V Western Ser.). 1998. 19.95 (*1-57490-144-3*, Sagebrush LP West) T T Beeler.
— The Song of the Whip. 261p. 1975. reprint ed. lib. bdg. 20.95 (*0-89190-210-4*, Rivercity Pr) Amereon Ltd.
— The Song of the Whip. 1990. reprint ed. lib. bdg. 16.95 (*0-89968-486-6*) Buccaneer Bks.
— South of Rio Grande. 223p. Date not set. 21.95 (*0-8488-2216-1*) Amereon Ltd.
— Speedy. 1993. 15.00 (*0-86025-234-5*, Pub. by I Henry Pubns) Empire Pub Srvs.
— Speedy. large type ed. LC 90-34621. 398p. 1990. lib. bdg. 16.95 (*1-56054-001-X*) Thorndike Pr.
— Speedy. 224p. 1995. reprint ed. pap. text 4.50 (*0-8439-3890-0*) Dorchester Pub Co.
— Speedy. unabridged ed. 1996. pap. 19.95 incl. audio (*1-56100-713-7*, Bkcassette) Brilliance.
— Steve Train's Ordeal. 1999. pap. 199.60 (*0-671-75847-0*, Pocket Books) PB.
— The Stingaree. LC 81-38512. 224p. 1982. reprint ed. 16.00 (*0-8376-0461-3*) Bentley Pubs.
— Stolen Gold: A Western Trio. LC 98-52067. 1999. 20.00 (*0-7862-1333-7*) Five Star.
*****Brand, Max.** Stolen Gold: A Western Trio. large type ed. LC 99-58959. (Thorndike Western Ser.). 2000. 24.95 (*0-7862-1341-8*) Thorndike Pr.
Brand, Max. The Stone That Shines. large type ed. LC 96-36734. (Five-Star Western Ser.). 276p. 1997. 17.95 (*0-7862-0734-5*) Five Star.
— The Stone That Shines. large type ed. LC 97-44870. 1998. 19.95 (*0-7862-0757-4*) Thorndike Pr.
— Strange Courage. 213p. 1975. reprint ed. lib. bdg. 20.95 (*0-89190-211-2*, Rivercity Pr) Amereon Ltd.
— The Survival of Juan Oro. LC 98-42372. 1999. 19.95 (*0-7862-1325-6*) Thorndike Pr.
*****Brand, Max.** Tales of the Wild West. 240p. 2000. pap. 4.50 (*0-8439-4769-1*, Leisure Bks) Dorchester Pub Co.
Brand, Max. Tales of the Wild West: Western Stories. large type ed. LC 96-40347. (Circle V Western Ser.). 1997. lib. bdg. 17.95 (*1-57490-078-1*, Beeler LP Bks) T T Beeler.
— Tamer of the Wild. large type ed. LC 95-30741. (Western Ser.). 381p. 1995. 19.95 (*0-7862-0529-6*) Thorndike Pr.
— Thunder Moon & Red Wind. large type ed. LC 97-40227. (Sagebrush Large Print Westerns Ser.). 1997. lib. bdg. 19.95 (*1-57490-096-X*) T T Beeler.
— Thunder Moon & the Sky People. LC 95-43104. vii, 212p. 1996. text 25.00 (*0-8032-1264-X*) U of Nebr Pr.
— Thunder Moon & the Sky People. large type ed. LC 97-39305. (Sagebrush Large Print Westerns Ser.). 1998. 19.95 (*1-57490-117-6*, Sagebrush LP West) T T Beeler.
*****Brand, Max.** Thunder Moon & the Sky People: Thunder Moon--Squawman - Thunder Moon Goes White. 368p. 2000. pap. 5.50 (*0-8439-4673-3*, Leisure Bks) Dorchester Pub Co.
Brand, Max. Timbal Gulch Trail. 224p. 1995. pap. text, mass mkt. 4.50 (*0-8439-3828-5*) Dorchester Pub Co.
— Timbal Gulch Trail. large type ed. LC 95-13693. 353p. 1995. 20.95 (*0-7862-0480-X*) Thorndike Pr.
*****Brand, Max.** Timber Line: A Western Trio. LC 99-14743. 1999. 19.95 (*0-7862-1893-2*) Thorndike Pr.
— Timber Line: A Western Trio. large type ed. LC 99-30684. 1999. 19.95 (*1-57490-169-9*, Sagebrush LP West) T T Beeler.
Brand, Max. Trailin' LC 94-13998. xv, 375p. 1994. text 30.00 (*0-8032-1247-X*) U of Nebr Pr.
— The Trap at Comanche Bend. large type ed. LC 93-7031. 335p. 1993. lib. bdg. 19.95 (*1-56054-700-6*) Thorndike Pr.
— Trouble in Timberline. 192p. 1995. pap. text, mass mkt. 4.50 (*0-8439-3848-X*) Dorchester Pub Co.
— Trouble Trail. large type ed. LC 90-38612. 373p. 1990. reprint ed. lib. bdg. 16.95 (*1-56054-036-2*) Thorndike Pr.
— Two Sixes. 320p. 1999. mass mkt. 4.99 (*0-8439-4508-7*) Dorchester Pub Co.
— Two Sixes: A Western Trio. large type ed. LC 97-24398. (Sagebrush Large Print Westerns Ser.). 1997. lib. bdg. 19.95 (*1-57490-088-9*) T T Beeler.
— The Untamed. LC 94-13997. xiv, 374p. 1994. text 30.00 (*0-8032-1248-8*) U of Nebr Pr.
— The Untamed. large type ed. (Sagebrush Large Print Westerns Ser.). 320p. 1995. lib. bdg. 18.95 (*1-57490-000-5*) T T Beeler.
*****Brand, Max.** Valley of Jewels. large type ed. LC 00-40272. 2000. write for info. (*1-57490-289-X*, Sagebrush LP West) T T Beeler.
Brand, Max. Valley Vultures. large type ed. 374p. 1991. reprint ed. lib. bdg. 17.95 (*1-56054-170-9*) Thorndike Pr.
— Vengeance Trail. LC 98-56113. 1999. 24.95 (*0-7838-8531-8*) Thorndike Pr.
— War Party. LC 81-38502. 224p. 1982. reprint ed. 16.00 (*0-8376-0460-5*) Bentley Pubs.
— Way of the Lawless. 1985. mass mkt. 2.50 (*0-446-32665-8*, Pub. by Warner Bks) Little.
— The White Wolf. 208p. 1995. pap. text, mass mkt. 4.50 (*0-8439-3870-6*) Dorchester Pub Co.
— Wild Freedom. 240p. 1985. mass mkt. 2.50 (*0-446-32769-7*, Pub. by Warner Bks) Little.
— Wine on the Desert. 1976. reprint ed. lib. bdg. 23.95 (*0-88411-511-9*) Amereon Ltd.
— The Wolf Strain: A Western Trio. LC 96-6299. (Five-Star Western Ser.). 1996. 16.95 (*0-7862-0662-4*) Five Star.
— Young Doctor Kildare. 20.95 (*0-89190-212-0*) Amereon Ltd.
Brand, Max & Tuska, Jon. The Bells of San Carlos & Other Stories. large type ed. LC 98-2816. (Western Ser.). 343p. 1998. 23.95 (*0-7838-0121-1*, G K Hall Lrg Type) Mac Lib Ref.
Brand, Max, see Evans, Evan, pseud.
Brand, Michael. Traditions of Asian Art. LC 95-61181. (Illus.). 96p. (Orig.). 1996. pap. 19.95 (*0-500-97432-2*, Pub. by Thames Hudson) Norton.
— Visions of Kings. LC 95-61906. (Illus.). 192p. 1996. pap. 24.95 (*0-500-97438-1*, Pub. by Thames Hudson) Norton.
*****Brand-Miller, Jennie, et al.** The Glucose Revolution Pocket Guide to Sugar & Energy. (Illus.). 128p. 2000. mass mkt. 4.95 (*1-56924-641-6*, Pub. by Marlowe & Co) Publishers Group.
— Glucose Revolution Pocket Guide to the Top 100 Low Glycemic Foods. LC 99-42190. (Illus.). 120p. 2000. mass mkt. 4.95 (*1-56924-678-5*) Marlowe & Co.
— The Glucose Revolution Pocket Guide to Your Heart. (Illus.). 128p. 2000. mass mkt. 4.95 (*1-56924-640-8*, Pub. by Marlowe & Co) Publishers Group.
*****Brand, Moses.** Joe's Trial. 484p. 2000. 16.95 (*0-942520-12-2*) Distributors.
Brand, Myles & Harnish, Robert M. The Representation of Knowledge & Belief. LC 86-24961. (Arizona Colloquim on Cognition Ser.: No. 1). 368p. 1986. 56.00 (*0-8165-0971-9*) U of Ariz Pr.
Brand, Nancy, ed. see Aghevli, Jim D.
Brand, Nancy, ed. see Chew, Alex L.
Brand, Nancy, ed. see Garant, Carl.
Brand, Nancy, ed. see McGregor, Jim.
Brand, Nancy, ed. see Metz, Pamela K.
Brand, Nancy, ed. see O'Shea, Sean & Walker, Meryl.
Brand, Nancy, ed. see Vollbracht, James.
Brand, Norman & White, John O. Legal Writing: The Strategy of Persuasion. 3rd ed. 224p. 1994. pap. text 25.50 (*0-312-08972-4*) St Martin.
Brand, Oliver, jt. auth. see Hornung, Mark R.
Brand, Oscar. The Ballad Mongers: Rise of the Modern Folk Song. LC 78-60137. 240p. 1979. reprint ed. lib. bdg. 59.50 (*0-313-20555-8*, BRBM, Greenwood Pr) Greenwood.
— Songs of Seventy Six: A Folksinger's History of the Revolution. LC 72-83733. (Illus.). 176p. (YA). 1972. 16.95 (*0-87131-092-9*) M Evans.
— Songs of Seventy Six: A Folksinger's History of the Revolution. LC 72-83733. (Illus.). 176p. (YA). 1975. pap. 8.95 (*0-87131-170-4*) M Evans.
Brand, Oscar, jt. reader see Seeger, Pete.
Brand, Paul. The Making of the Common Law. LC 92-25671. 504p. 1992. 70.00 (*1-85285-070-1*) Hambledon Press.
Brand, Paul, ed. Curia Regis Rolls of the Reign of Henry III Preserved in the Public Record Office: 27-30 Henry III (1243-1245), Vol. 18. 600p. 1999. 216.00 (*0-85115-605-3*) Boydell & Brewer.
Brand, Paul & Yancey, Philip. Fearfully & Wonderfully Made. (Illus.). 224p. 1980. 12.95 (*0-310-35450-1*, 10241) Zondervan.
— Fearfully & Wonderfully Made. (Illus.). 224p. 1987. reprint ed. pap. 12.99 (*0-310-35451-X*, 10241P) Zondervan.
— Fearfully & Wonderfully Made - Chinese Edition. Wu, Timothy, tr. (CHI.). 223p. 1993. pap. 10.00 (*1-56582-028-2*) Christ Renew Min.
— In His Image. 224p. 1984. 14.95 (*0-310-35500-1*, 10242) Zondervan.
— In His Image. 304p. 1987. reprint ed. pap. 12.99 (*0-310-35501-X*, 10242P) Zondervan.
— In His Image - Chinese Edition. Kao, David, tr. (CHI.). 276p. 1999. pap. 10.00 (*1-56582-027-4*) Christ Renew Min.
— Pain: The Gift Nobody Wants. 352p. 1999. reprint ed. text 22.00 (*0-7881-6372-8*) DIANE Pub.
Brand, Paul W. Clinical Mechanics of the Hand. 3rd ed. LC 98-42919. (Illus.). 388p. 1999. text 79.00 (*0-8151-2786-3*, 31248) Mosby Inc.
— God's Forever Feasts: Letting God Satisfy Your Deepest Hunger. LC 98-7251. 272p. 1998. reprint ed. pap. 11.99 (*1-57293-032-2*) Discovery Hse Pubs.
Brand, Paul W. & Hollister, Anne. Clinical Mechanics of the Hand. 2nd ed. (Illus.). 386p. (C). (gr. 13). 1992. text 85.00 (*0-8016-6978-2*, 06978) Mosby Inc.
Brand, Paul W. & Yancey, Philip. The Gift of Pain: The Inspiring Story of a Surgeon Who Discovers Why We Hurt & What We Can Do about It. LC 97-22699. 1997. pap. 12.99 (*0-310-22144-7*) Zondervan.
Brand, Peggy Z. & Korsmeyer, Carolyn, eds. Feminism & Tradition in Aesthetics. LC 94-13667. 496p. 1995. 70.00 (*0-271-01340-0*); pap. 19.95 (*0-271-01341-9*) Pa St U Pr.
*****Brand, Peggy Zeglin, ed.** Beauty Matters. LC 99-56085. (Illus.). 368p. 2000. pap. 19.95 (*0-253-21375-4*); lib. bdg. 45.00 (*0-253-33726-7*) Ind U Pr.
Brand, Peter & Pertile, Lino, eds. The Cambridge History of Italian Literature. 736p. (C). 1997. text 99.95 (*0-521-43492-0*) Cambridge U Pr.
*****Brand, Peter & Pertile, Lino, eds.** The Cambridge History of Italian Literature. rev. ed. 736p. (C). 1999. pap. 29.95 (*0-521-66622-8*) Cambridge U Pr.
Brand, Randall, jt. auth. see Barnes, Jake.
Brand, Rebecca. The Ruby Tear. LC 96-29342. 1997. 22.95 (*0-312-86165-6*) Forge NYC.
— The Ruby Tear. 1998. mass mkt. 5.99 (*0-8125-7132-0*, Pub. by Tor Bks) St Martin.
Brand, Renee. The Experiment. 1981. pap. 4.00 (*0-932630-02-2*) C G Jung Frisco.
Brand, Richard W. & Isselhard, Donald E. Anatomy of Orofacial Structures. 6th ed. LC 99-204440. (Illus.). 576p. (C). (gr. 13). 1997. pap. text 42.00 (*0-8151-1000-6*, 29800) Mosby Inc.
*****Brand, Richard W. & Isselhard, Donald E.** Anatomy of Orofacial Structures. 6th ed. (Illus.). 1998. student ed. write for info. (*0-8151-1219-X*) Mosby Inc.
— Anatomy of Orofacial Structures: Includes Testbank. 6th ed. 1998. teacher ed. write for info. (*1-55664-483-3*) Mosby Inc.
Brand, Robert F. How to Collect North American Indian Artifacts. (Illus.). 151p. (Orig.). 1984. pap. text 13.45 (*0-9615727-0-1*) R F Brand.
Brand, Ronald, jt. auth. see Cohen, Steven.
*****Brand, Ronald A.** Fundamentals of International Business Transactions. LC 00-30204. 2000. write for info. (*90-411-9632-3*) Kluwer Law Intl.
Brand, Ronald A., ed. see American Society of International Law Staff.
Brand, Ruth, jt. auth. see Mills, Charles.
Brand, Ruth R. & Mills, Charles. Adventure Stories from the Bible. LC 95-53955. (Professor Appleby & the Maggie B. Tapes Ser.: Vol. 4). 128p. 1996. pap. 8.99 (*0-8280-0958-9*) Review & Herald.
— Miracle Stories from the Bible. LC 96-52247. (Professor Appleby & the Maggie B. Tapes Ser.: Vol. 5). 128p. (J). 1997. pap. 8.99 (*0-8280-0961-9*) Review & Herald.
*****Brand, Sandra.** Glimpses of West Africa. (Illus.). 81p. 1999. pap. 10.95 (*0-88400-204-7*, Shengold Bks) Schreiber Pub.
— I Dared to Live. 4th rev. ed. LC 99-89438. (Illus.). 210p. 2000. 22.95 (*1-887563-50-4*, Pub. by Schreiber Pub); pap. 14.95 (*1-887563-49-0*, Pub. by Schreiber Pub) Natl Bk Netwk.
Brand, Sarah. The Angel on Old Wire Road. 88p. 1998. pap. 9.95 (*0-9668282-0-8*) S Brand.
Brand, Sheila L., ed. Department of Defense Trusted Computer System Evaluation Criteria. (Illus.). 122p. (C). 1998. pap. text 25.00 (*0-7881-4325-5*) DIANE Pub.
Brand, Stewart. Clock of the Long Now: Time & Responsibility. 208p. 1999. 22.00 (*0-465-04512-X*, Pub. by Basic) HarpC.
*****Brand, Stewart.** Clock of the Long Now: Time & Responsibility: The Ideas Behind the World's Slowest Computer. 1. 2000. pap. text 13.00 (*0-465-00780-5*, Pub. by Basic) HarpC.
Brand, Stewart. How Buildings Learn: What Happens After They're Built. 256p. 1995. pap. 25.95 (*0-14-013996-6*, Penguin Bks) Viking Penguin.
Brand, Vanessa, ed. The Study of the Past in the Victorian Age. (Oxbow Monographs in Archaeology: No. 73). (Illus.). 176p. (Orig.). 1998. pap. 36.00 (*1-900188-28-7*, Pub. by Oxbow Bks) David Brown.
Brand, Walter. Hume's Theory of Moral Judgment: A Study in the Unity of a Treatise of Human Nature. (Archives Internationales d'Histoire des Idees (International Archives of the History of Ideas) Ser.). 184p. (C). 1992. lib. bdg. 119.00 (*0-7923-1415-8*, Pub. by Kluwer Academic) Kluwer Academic.
Brand, William R., tr. see Kapuscinski, Ryszard.
Brand, Wulf-D., ed. from GER. Tigerfibel: The Original Tiger Tank Manual.Tr. of Tiger Tank Primer. (Illus.). 174p. 1998. pap. 29.95 (*0-938242-32-6*, D656/27) Portrayal.
Brand, Yancey. Fearfully Made With His Image. Date not set. 24.99 (*0-310-23048-9*) HarpC.
Brandabur, Edward. A Scrupulous Meanness: A Study of Joyce's Early Work. LC 71-131057. 197p. reprint ed. pap. 61.10 (*0-608-13883-5*, 202024100016) Bks Demand.
Brandal, Willy. Numerical Linear Algebra. Christenson, Charles O. & Smith, Bryan A., eds. LC 91-73640. (Illus.). 210p. (Orig.). (C). 1991. pap. 30.00 (*0-914351-05-2*) BCS Assocs.
Brandal, Willy & Barbut, Erol. Torsion Theories over Commutative Rings. LC 96-86309. (Illus.). vi, 120p. (Orig.). (C). 1996. pap. text 28.00 (*0-914351-06-0*) BCS Assocs.
Brandan, M. E., ed. Nuclear Physics: XIV Symposium. 264p. (C). 1991. text 89.00 (*981-02-0601-1*) World Scientific Pub.
Brandan, Maria E. Armas y Explosiones Nucleares. (Ciencia para Todos Ser.). (SPA.). pap. 6.99 (*968-16-4773-4*, Pub. by Fondo) Continental Bk.
— La Radiacion Al Servicio de la Vida. (Ciencia para Todos Ser.). (SPA.). pap. 6.99 (*968-16-3452-7*, Pub. by Fondo) Continental Bk.
*****Brandan, Marla-Ester, et al, eds.** Medical Physics: Second Mexican Symposium. LC 98-86572. (Conference Proceedings Ser.: Vol. 440). (Illus.). x, 232p. 1998. 85.00 (*1-56396-807-X*) Am Inst Physics.
Brandane, John. The Treasure Ship, Rory Aforesaid, the Happy War: 3 Plays. LC 79-50019. (One-Act Plays in Reprint Ser.). 1980. reprint ed. 25.00 (*0-8486-2043-7*) Roth Pub Inc.
Brandani, Edoardo. Giorgio de Chirico, Catalogue Raisonne of the Graphic Work, 1969-1977. (ITA., Illus.). 248p. 1990. boxed set 250.00 (*1-55660-145-X*) A Wofsy Fine Arts.
Brandao, Fiama H. De, see De Brandao, Fiama H.
Brandao, Jose Antonio. Your Fyre Shall Burn No More: Iroquois Policy Toward New France & Its Native Allies to 1701. LC 97-9846. (Illus.). xviii, 377p. 1997. text 65.00 (*0-8032-1274-7*) U of Nebr Pr.
*****Brandao, Jose Antonio.** Your Fyre Shall Burn No More: Iroquois Policy Toward New France & Its Native Allies to 1701. LC 97-9846. (Illus.). 377p. 2000. pap. 19.95 (*0-8032-6177-2*, Bison Books) U of Nebr Pr.
Brandao, Robert H., tr. see Barnard, Neal D.
Brandas, E. & Elander, N., eds. Resonances. (Lecture Notes in Physics Ser.: Vol. 325). xviii, 564p. 1989. 93.95 (*0-387-50994-1*) Spr-Verlag.
Brandau, Alan. Introduction to Coatings Technology. (Illus.). 46p. 1990. pap. 30.00 (*0-934010-24-2*) Fed Soc Coat Tech.
Brandau, Jack. The Ship Model Basin: Tool of the Naval Architect. 64p. (Orig.). (C). 1986. pap. 10.00 (*0-934114-82-X*, BK-550) Marine Educ.
*****Brandau, Karla.** Dance with the Sunbeams of Life. 1998. 10.00 (*1-892968-00-2*) Life Power Pubs.
— Empowering Thoughts: To Wake up the Winner Inside. 1998. 10.00 (*1-892968-01-0*) Life Power Pubs.
— Wake up the Winner Inside. Scriven, John, ed. (Illus.). 133p. 1999. 18.00 (*1-892968-02-9*) Life Power Pubs.
Brandauer, Aline, et al. Agnes Martin: Works on Paper. (Illus.). 48p. 1998. pap. 20.00 (*0-936050-24-1*, Pub. by Burning Bks) Lumen Inc.
*****Brandauer, Aline Chipman & Carnahan, Sumner.** Gail & Zachariah Rieke: Found Objects in an Open World. 48p. 1999. 25.00 (*0-936050-22-5*, Pub. by Burning Bks) Lumen Inc.
Brandauer, Aline Chipman & Carnahan, Sumner. Gail & Zachariah Rieke: Found Objects in an Open World. (MPA NN Contemporary Art Ser.). (Illus.). 48p. 1999. pap. 50.00 (*0-930829-46-8*, Pub. by Lumen Inc) Consort Bk Sales.
Brandauer, Frederick & Huang Chun-chieh, eds. Imperial Rulership & Cultural Change in Traditional China. 330p. 1994. text 40.00 (*0-295-97374-9*) U of Wash Pr.
Brandberg, Bjorn. Latrine Building: A Handbook for Implementing the Sanplat System. (Illus.). 208p. 1997. pap. 19.50 (*1-85339-306-1*, Pub. by Intermed Tech) Stylus Pub VA.
Brandbyge, J. Flora of Ecuador No. 34: Polygonaceae. (Opera Botanica Series B). 61p. 1989. pap. 27.00 (*87-88702-40-5*, Pub. by Coun Nordic Pubs) Balogh.
Brandbyge, J. & Holm-Nielsen, L. B. Reforestation of the High Andes with Local Species. (Reports from the Botanical Institute, University of Aarhus: No. 13). (Illus.). 114p. (C). 1986. pap. 12.95 (*87-87600-16-1*, Pub. by Aarhus Univ Pr) David Brown.
Brande. Malcolm & the Amazing Technicolor. 1996. pap. 7.50 (*0-7459-3170-7*, Pub. by Lion Pubng) Trafalgar.
Brande, Dorothea. Becoming a Writer. LC 80-53146. 192p. 1981. pap. 9.95 (*0-87477-164-1*, Tarcher Putnam) Putnam Pub Group.
Brande, J. L. Van Den, see Van Den Brande, J. L., ed.
Brande, Lieve Van den, see Van den Brande, Lieve.
Brandeau, Margaret L. Modeling the AIDS Epidemic: Planning, Policy, & Prediction. Kaplan, Edward H., ed. LC 93-23684. 656p. 1994. text 99.00 (*0-7817-0164-3*) Lppncott W & W.
Brandeau, Margaret L., jt. ed. see Kaplan, Edward H.
Brandeis, Arthur, ed. Jacob's Well, an English Treatise on the Cleansing of Man's Conscience, Pt. 1. (EETS, OS Ser.: No. 115). 1969. reprint ed. 55.00 (*0-527-00114-7*) Periodicals Srv.
*****Brandeis, Louis D.** Brandeis on Zionism. LC 98-49331. viii, 156p. 1999. reprint ed. 65.00 (*1-886363-60-9*) Lawbk Exchange.
Brandeis, Louis D. Business: A Profession. LC 96-76637. lxxx, 374p. 1996. reprint ed. 58.00 (*1-57588-110-1*, 310650) W S Hein.
— Letters of Louis D. Brandeis, Vol. 2. Urofsky, Melvin I. & Levy, David W., eds. LC 73-129640. 610p. (C). 1972. text 59.50 (*0-87395-091-7*) State U NY Pr.
— Letters of Louis D. Brandeis, Vol. 3. Urofsky, Melvin I. & Levy, David W., eds. LC 73-129640. 750p. (C). 1973. text 59.50 (*0-87395-231-6*) State U NY Pr.
— Letters of Louis D. Brandeis, Vol. 4. Urofsky, Melvin I. & Levy, David W., eds. LC 73-129640. 587p. (C). 1975. text 59.50 (*0-87395-297-9*) State U NY Pr.
— Letters of Louis D. Brandeis, Vol. 5. Urofsky, Melvin I. & Levy, David W., eds. LC 73-129640. 770p. (C). 1978. text 59.50 (*0-87395-330-4*) State U NY Pr.
— The Louis Dembitz Brandeis Papers. LC 88-890709. (American Legal Manuscripts from the Harvard). 94 p. 1985. write for info. (*0-89093-801-6*) U Pubns Amer.

— Other People's Money & How the Bankers Use It. 2nd ed. LC 86-7463. (Reprints of Economic Classics Ser.). lxii, 223p. 1986. reprint ed. lib. bdg. 35.00 (0-678-00856-6) Kelley.

Brandeis, Louis D. & Goldmark, Josephine. Women in Industry. LC 73-89720. (American Labor, from Conspiracy to Collective Bargaining Ser., No. 1). 121p. 1974. reprint ed. 15.95 (0-405-02106-2) Ayer.

Brandeis, Louis D. & Urofsky, Melvyn I., eds. Other People's Money & How the Bankers Use It. 192p. 1995. pap. text 15.95 (0-312-10314-X) St Martin.

***Brandeis, Margaret.** Women Can Find Shipwrecks Too. 372p. 2000. pap. 14.99 (0-9700767-9-7) Comet Ship.

— Women Can Find Shipwrecks Too. LC 99-65662. 347p. 1999. pap. 12.95 (1-893181-28-6) Le Gesse Stevens.

Brandeis, Renee L. Deep Shadows. LC 88-32280. (Illus.). 80p. 1989. 24.95 (0-8290-2225-2) Irvington.

Brandeis University - Poses Institute of Fine Arts, ed. Art Criticism in the Sixties. 1965. pap. 3.25 (0-8079-0008-7) October.

Brandeis University, Institute for Health Policy S. Substance Abuse: The Nation's Number One Health Problem. (Key Indicators for Policy Ser.). (Illus.). 68p. (Orig.). 1993. pap. write for info. (0-942054-08-3) R W Johnson Found.

Brandejs, J. F., ed. Computer Assisted Physicians Offices: Journal: Health Communications & Informatics, Vol. 5, No. 2, 1979. (Illus.). 1979. pap. 16.75 (3-8055-3063-3) S Karger.

Brandel, Roland E. & Abbott, Barry A. Truth in Lending: A Comprehensive Guide. 2nd ed. 1372p. 1991. ring bd. 126.00 (0-13-109380-0) Aspen Law.

Brandel, Roland E. & Teitelbaum, David E. The Community Reinvestment Act: Policies & Compliance. 2nd ed. LC 94-12533. 606p. 1994. ring bd. 126.00 (0-13-310962-3) Aspen Law.

Brandel, Roland E., et al. Truth in Lending. 1000p. 1985. write for info. (0-318-65469-5, H43724) P-H.

— Truth in Lending: A Comprehensive Guide. LC 84-22423. 850p. 1985. suppl. ed. 85.00 (0-15-004372-4, #H43724) Harcourt.

Brandel, Roland E., jt. auth. see Baker, Donald I.

Brandel, Rose & Leichtman, Ellen C. To the Four Corners: A Festschrift in Honor of Rose Brandel. LC 94-23360. (Detroit Monographs in Musicology: Studies in Music: No. 14). 1995. 45.00 (0-89990-070-4) Harmonie Park Pr.

Brandel-Syrier, Mia. "Coming Through" The Search for a New Cultural Identity. LC 79-320465. 217p. 1978. write for info. (0-07-091362-5) McGraw.

Brandelius, Jerilyn L. Grateful Dead Family Album. 1990. mass mkt. 17.99 (0-446-39167-0, Pub. by Warner Bks) Little.

***Brandell.** Of Mice & Metaphors. 2000. 40.00 (0-465-00712-0, Pub. by Basic) HarpC.

Brandell, Gunnar. Strindberg in Inferno. Jacobs, Barry, tr. LC 73-90851. 358p. reprint ed. pap. 111.00 (0-7837-3831-5, 204365200010) Bks Demand.

Brandell, Jerrold. Theory & Practice in Clinical Social Work. LC 96-41714. 704p. 1997. 49.95 (0-684-82765-4) Free Pr.

Brandell, Jerrold R. Theory & Practice in Clinical Social Work. 1997. 35.00 (0-02-874116-1) Free Pr.

Brandell, Jerrold R., ed. Countertransference in Psychotherapy with Children & Adolescents. 1992. pap. 50.00 (0-7657-0281-9) Aronson.

Brandell, Jerrold R., ed. Countertransference in Psychotherapy with Children & Adolescents. LC 91-32229. 376p. 1992. 60.00 (0-87668-481-9) Aronson.

— Narration & Therapeutic Action: The Construction of Meaning in Psychoanalytic Social Work. LC 96-20074. (Journal of Analytic Social Work: Vol. 3, Nos. 2/3). 202p. 1996. 49.95 (1-56024-827-0) Haworth Pr.

Branden Abner, Monica Van den, see Faragasso, Laura B.

Branden Abner, Monica Vanden, see Faragasso, Laura B. & Vanden Branden Abner, Monica.

Branden, Barbara. The Passion of Ayn Rand. LC 85-20704. 464p. 1987. pap. 16.95 (0-385-24388-X, Anchor NY) Doubleday.

Branden, Carl & Tooze, John. Introduction to Protein Structure. LC 91-11788. 320p. 1991. 49.95 (0-8153-0344-0); pap. text 34.95 (0-8153-0270-3) Garland.

— Introduction to Protein Structure. LC 91-11788. 320p. 1991. 165.00 (0-8153-0486-2) Garland.

Branden, Carl-Ivar & Schneider, Gunter, eds. Carbon Dioxide Fixation & Reduction in Biological & Model Systems. LC 93-45258. (Illus.). 320p. 1994. text 145.00 (0-19-854782-X) OUP.

Branden, Carl-Ivar & Tooze, John. Introduction to Protein Structure. 2nd ed. LC 98-34487. 1998. 59.95 (0-8153-2304-2); pap. 45.95 (0-8153-2305-0) Garland.

Branden, F. Van Den, see Van Den Branden, F.

Branden, James R., ed. The Cambridge Guide to Asian Theatre. (Illus.). 261p. 1997. pap. text 24.95 (0-521-58822-7) Cambridge U Pr.

Branden, Nathaniel. The Art of Living Consciously. LC 96-49721. 1997. 22.50 (0-684-81084-0) S&S Trade.

— Art of Living Consciously: The Power of Awareness to Transform Everyday Life. 256p. 1999. pap. 12.00 (0-684-83849-4) S&S Trade.

— Como Mejorar Su Autoestima. 160p. 1997. pap. 11.00 (0-684-84347-1) S&S Trade.

— Honoring the Self: The Psychology of Confidence & Respect. 288p. 1985. mass mkt. 6.99 (0-553-26814-7) Bantam.

— How to Raise Your Self-Esteem. 176p. 1988. mass mkt. 6.99 (0-553-26646-2) Bantam.

— Judgment Day: My Years with Ayn Rand. 1991. pap. 12.95 (0-380-71127-3, Avon Bks) Morrow Avon.

— My Years with Ayn Rand: The Truth Behind the Myths. LC 98-25440. 480p. 1999. pap. 19.00 (0-7879-4513-7) Jossey-Bass.

— A Nathaniel Branden Anthology. 1980. 17.50 (0-686-65215-0) HM.

— Nathaniel Branden's Self-Esteem Every Day: Reflections on Self-Esteem & Spirituality. LC 97-45895. 1998. per. 10.00 (0-684-83338-7, Fireside) S&S Trade Pap.

— The Power of Self-Esteem: An Inspiring Look at Our Most Important Psychological Resource. 97p. (Orig.). 1992. pap. 7.95 (1-55874-213-1) Health Comm.

— The Psychology of Self-Esteem: How Our Judgments about Ourselves Affect Our Success in Love & Human Relationships. (Orig.). 1999. pap. 17.00 (0-7879-4526-9) Jossey-Bass.

— Self-Esteem at Work: How Confident People Make Power Companies. LC 98-9087. (Business & Management Ser.). 128p. 1998. 20.00 (0-7879-4001-1) Jossey-Bass.

— The Six Pillars of Self-Esteem. 368p. 1995. pap. 14.95 (0-553-37439-7) Bantam.

— Taking Responsibility. 256p. 1997. per. 12.00 (0-684-83248-8) S&S Trade Pap.

— A Woman's Self-Esteem: Struggles & Triumphs in the Search for Identity. LC 98-9010. (Health & Psychology Ser.). 160p. 1998. 20.00 (0-7879-4371-1) Jossey-Bass.

Brandenberg, Alexa. Chop, Simmer, Season: A Day at the Top Notch Restaurant. LC 96-5279. (Illus.). 32p. (J). 1997. 14.00 (0-15-200973-6) Harcourt.

— I Am Me! LC 95-17110. (Illus.). 24p. (J). (ps-1). 1996. 12.00 (0-15-200974-4) Harcourt.

Brandenberg, Aliki. My Five Senses. (Let's-Read-And-Find-Out Book Ser.). (J). 1985. 10.15 (0-606-02342-9, Pub. by Turtleback) Demco.

Brandenberg, Franz. Nice New Neighbors. (Illus.). 32p. (J). (ps-2). 1990. pap. 2.75 (0-590-44117-5) Scholastic Inc.

Brandenberger, Ada. Coopetition Pt. 1: A Win/Win Mindset That Redefines Competition. 304p. 1997. pap. 16.95 (0-385-47950-6) Doubleday.

Brandenberger, E. & Stattmann, F. Nuclear Power Dictionary, Vol. 63. (ENG & GER.). 456p. 1978. pap. 95.00 (0-8288-5259-6, M7572) Fr & Eur.

Brandenberger, Hans & Maes, Robert A., eds. Analytical Toxicology for Clinical, Forensic & Pharmaceutical Chemists: For Clinical, Forensic, & Pharmaceutical Chemists. LC 97-2360. (Clinical Biochemistry Ser.: Vol. 5). (Illus.). 784p. (C). 1997. lib. bdg. 369.00 (3-11-010731-7) De Gruyter.

Brandenberger, R. Lectures on Inflationary Universe Models & Cosmic Strings. 250p. (C). 1992. text 53.00 (9971-5-0266-6); pap. text 30.00 (9971-5-0267-4) World Scientific Pub.

Brandenberger, R., jt. auth. see Davis, A. C.

Brandenberger, Robert H., jt. auth. see Manrseurei, Riszea.

Brandenburg & Villani. Handbook of Turfgrass Insect Pests: A Guide to Successful Insect Pest Management. 1995. pap. 35.00 (0-938522-52-3, ESATURF) Entomol Soc.

Brandenburg, Betty, jt. ed. see Adams, Tom.

Brandenburg, Charles A. Introduction to Television Servicing. Schuler, Charles A., ed. (Basic Skills in Electricity & Electronics Ser.). (Illus.). 1979. text 26.96 (0-07-007176-4) McGraw.

Brandenburg, Erich. From Bismark to the World War: A History of German Foreign Policy 1870-1914. Adams, Annie E., tr. LC 83-45416. reprint ed. 49.50 (0-404-20041-9) AMS Pr.

Brandenburg, Franz J., ed. Graph Drawing: Proceedings, Symposium on Graph Drawing, GD '95, Passau, Germany, September 20-22, 1995. LC 96-1665. (Lecture Notes in Computer Science Ser.: Vol. 1027). 526p. 1996. pap. 81.00 (3-540-60723-4) Spr-Verlag.

Brandenburg, Franz J., jt. auth. see Brookes, Diane.

Brandenburg, Hugo. Die Kirche S. Stefano Rotondo in Rome. 80p. 1997. text 18.00 (3-11-015759-4) De Gruyter.

Brandenburg, James. Brother Wolf: A Forgotten Promise. LC 93-19651. 1993. 40.00 (1-55971-210-4, NorthWord Pr) Creat Pub Intl.

— Brother Wolf: A Forgotten Promise. LC 93-19651. 160p. 1998. pap. 24.95 (1-55971-634-7, NorthWord Pr) Creat Pub Intl.

***Brandenburg, Jason.** Ring of the Islander. LC 99-91816. (Divided Children Chronicles Ser.: Bk. 1). 2000. 25.00 (0-7388-1296-X); pap. 18.00 (0-7388-1297-8) Xlibris Corp.

Brandenburg, Jason. The Third Guardian. 285p. 1999. pap. 16.95 (0-7414-0182-7) Buy Books.

Brandenburg, Jim. An American Safari: Adventures on the North American Prairie. (Illus.). 48p. (J). (gr. 3-12). 1997. pap. 7.95 (0-8027-7502-0) Walker & Co.

— An American Safari: Adventures on the North American Prairie. LC 94-24654. (Illus.). 48p. (J). (gr. 3 up). 1997. 16.95 (0-8027-8319-8) Walker & Co.

— An American Safari: Adventures on the North American Prairie. Guernsey, JoAnn B., ed. LC 94-24654. (Illus.). 48p. (J). (gr. 3 up). 1997. lib. bdg. 17.85 (0-8027-8320-1) Walker & Co.

— Chased by the Light: A 90-Day Journey. LC 99-165394. (Illus.). 128p. 1998. 35.00 (1-55971-671-1) Creat Pub Intl.

— Chased by the Light: A 90-Day Journey. LC 97-53162. 1998. write for info. (1-56846-158-5, Creative Eds) Creative Co.

— Sand & Fog: Adventures in Southern Africa. 1996. 11.15 (0-606-10919-6, Pub. by Turtleback) Demco.

— Sand & Fog: Adventures in Southern Africa. LC 93-30425. (Illus.). 48p. (J). (gr. 3 up). 1994. 16.95 (0-8027-8232-9); lib. bdg. 17.85 (0-8027-8233-7) Walker & Co.

— Sand & Fog: Adventures in Southern Africa. LC 93-30425. (Illus.). 48p. (YA). (gr. 4-7). 1996. pap. 6.95 (0-8027-7476-8) Walker & Co.

— Scruffy: A Wolf Finds His Place in the Pack. Guernsey, JoAnn B., ed. LC 96-5446. (Illus.). (J). 1996. lib. bdg. 16.85 (0-8027-8446-1) Walker & Co.

— Scruffy: A Wolf Finds His Place in the Pack. Guernsey, JoAnn B., ed. LC 96-5446. (Illus.). 32p. (J). (ps-3). 1996. 15.95 (0-8027-8445-3) Walker & Co.

***Brandenburg, Jim.** Scruffy: A Wolf Finds His Place in the Pack. (Illus.). 32p. (J). (gr. 2-5). 2000. reprint ed. pap. write for info. (0-8027-7602-7) Walker & Co.

— To the Top of the World: Adventures with Arctic Wolves. 1995. 12.15 (0-606-08888-1, Pub. by Turtleback) Demco.

Brandenburg, Jim. To the Top of the World: Adventures with Arctic Wolves. Guernsey, JoAnn B., ed. LC 93-12105. (Illus.). 48p. (J). (gr. 4 up). 1993. 16.95 (0-8027-8219-1); lib. bdg. 17.85 (0-8027-8220-5) Walker & Co.

— To the Top of the World: Adventures with Arctic Wolves. (Illus.). 48p. (YA). (gr. 3 up). 1995. pap. 6.95 (0-8027-7462-8) Walker & Co.

— White Wolf: Living with an Arctic Legend. 1991. pap. 19.95 (1-55971-093-4, NorthWord Pr) Creat Pub Intl.

***Brandenburg, John & Paxson, Monica Rix.** Dead Mars, Dying Earth. (Illus.). 384p. 2000. reprint ed. 26.95 (1-58091-066-1, Pub. by Crossing Pr) Publishers Group.

Brandenburg, Judith. Confronting Sexual Harassment: What Schools & Colleges Can Do. LC 96-44488 192p. (C). 1997. text 42.00 (0-8077-3591-4); pap. text 18.95 (0-8077-3590-6) Tchrs Coll.

Brandenburg, Judith B. Sexual Harassment: A Challenge to Schools of Education. 1995. 15.00 (0-89333-127-9) AACTE.

Brandenburg, Karlheinz, jt. ed. see Kahrs, Mark.

Brandenburg, M. M., tr. see Baegert, Johann J.

***Brandenburg, Mark A.** Child Safe: A Practical Guide to Preventing Childhood Accidents. 256p. 2000. pap. 14.00 (0-609-80412-X, Three Riv Pr) Crown Pub Group.

Brandenburg, R. O. Cardiology: Fundamentals & Practice, 1986. 2000p. 1987. 110.00 (0-318-32737-6) Mosby Inc.

Brandenburg, Sieghard, ed. Haydn, Mozart & Beethoven: Studies in the Music of the Classical Period: Essays in Honour of Alan Tyson. (Illus.). 328p. 1999. text 75.00 (0-19-816362-2) OUP.

***Brandenburger, Dietmar.** Expo Architeture Documents 1: Ideas, Locations, Plans, Projects. (Illus.). 2000. pap. 14.95 (3-7757-0859-6) Gerd Hatje.

Brandenburger, W. Parasitische Pilze an Gefaesspflanzen in Europe. (Bibliotheca Mycologica Ser.: No. 37). (Illus.). 1248p. 1985. lib. bdg. 315.00 (3-437-30433-X) Lubrecht & Cramer.

— Vademekum Zum Sammeln Parasitischer Pilze. (GER.). 1963. pap. 29.95 (0-685-57724-4, M7136) Fr & Eur.

Brander. Government Policy Toward Business. 3rd ed. 376p. (C). 1995. pap. write for info. (0-471-64141-3) Wiley.

Brander, B. G. Staring into Chaos: Explorations in the Decline of Western Civilization. LC 97-36927. 436p. 1998. 29.95 (0-9653208-5-5) Spence Pub.

Brander, Diane. Blindwalk to Potter's Farm: An Odyssey of Spirit. 200p. (Orig.). 1996. pap. 14.95 (0-9640177-8-4) Windspirit Pr.

Brander, George C., jt. ed. see Cole, D. J.

Brander, James A. & Thorn, Ian, eds. The Surface Application of Paper Chemicals. (Illus.). 288p. 1997. write for info. (0-7514-0370-9) Kluwer Academic.

Brander, John M. Drawing Dreams. LC 91-65565. 80p. (Orig.). 1991. pap. 7.95 (0-9623751-1-X) Sunlight SF.

— The Trail of the Moon: South African Poems. (Illus.). 105p. (Orig.). 1992. pap. write for info. (0-9624205-3-0) Inevitable Pr.

Brander, M. & Macleod, I. World Directory of Scottish Associations. 242p. (C). 1986. 100.00 (0-7855-2151-8) St Mut.

Brander, Michael. Brander's Guide to Scotch Whisky. LC 96-22292. 184p. 1996. pap. 16.95 (1-55821-480-[illegible]) Lyons Pr.

— The Complete Guide to Horsemanship. 2nd ed. (Illus.). 446p. 1998. 32.50 (0-7136-5571-2, Pub. by Sportmans Pr) Trafalgar.

— The Language of the Field. LC 98-203750. 220p. 1998. pap. 25.00 (1-85754-166-9, Pub. by Carcanet Pr) Paul & Co Pubs.

— The Roughshooter's Dog. (Illus.). 198p. 1991. 29.95 (0-948253-38-X, Pub. by Sportmans Pr) Trafalgar.

— The World Directory of Scottish Associations. 240p. 1997. pap. 22.95 (1-897784-27-9, Pub. by N Wilson Pubng) Interlink Pub.

Brander, Michael, ed. The Sword & the Pen. (Illus.). 173p. 1989. 24.95 (0-85052-110-6, Pub. by Leo Cooper) Trans-Atl Phila.

— The Sword & the Pen: A Selection of Military Diaries. (Illus.). 160p. 1997. reprint ed. text 20.00 (0-7881-5056-1) DIANE Pub.

Brandes, Annette T. Stepfamily Life Can Be Hell but It Doesn't Have to Be! 7 Steps to Recreating Family. LC 99-90414. (Illus.). 296p. 1999. pap. write for info. (0-9671343-3-1) Segue Pubg.

Brandes, Beth H. & Ingold, Judy B. Get Real: A Practical Guide to Leading Adolescent Groups. LC 98-129535. 96p. 1997. pap. 12.95 (0-87304-305-7) Manticore Pubs.

Brandes, Charles H. Value Investing Today. 2nd ed. LC 97-26016. (Illus.). 208p. 1997. 29.95 (0-07-007190-X) McGraw.

Brandes, Charles H. & Carlson, Glenn R. International Value Investing: Making the Right Choice at the Right Price. 200p. 1995. 27.00 (1-55623-897-5, Irwn Prfssnl) McGraw-Hill Prof.

Brandes, Donald H., Jr. & Luzier, J. Michael. Developing Difficult Sites: Solutions for Developers & Builders. LC 90-25274. (Illus.). 92p. (Orig.). 1991. 25.00 (0-86718-352-7) Home Builder.

Brandes, Donna & Norris, John. The Gamester's Handbook 3. (Illus.). 160p. (J). (gr. 6-11). 1998. pap. 27.50 (0-7487-3504-6, Pub. by S Thornes Pubs) Trans-Atl Phila.

Brandes, Donna & Phillips, Howard. Gamesters' Handbook Bk. 1: Hundreds of Games for Teachers & Group Leaders. 140p. 1995. teacher ed. 29.50 (0-7487-0341-1, Pub. by S Thornes Pubs) Trans-Atl Phila.

— Gamesters' Handbooks: Hundreds of Games for Teachers & Group Leaders. 145p. 1995. teacher ed. 29.50 (0-7487-0322-5, Pub. by S Thornes Pubs) Trans-Atl Phila.

Brandes, E. A. & Brook, G. B., eds. Smithells Light Metals Handbook. LC 97-48762. (Illus.). 240p. 1998. text 90.00 (0-7506-3625-4) Buttrwrth-Heinemann.

Brandes, Francesca. Tuscany: Places, History & Art. 191p. 1997. pap. text 19.95 (1-56886-047-1) Marsilio Pubs.

Brandes, Francesca, ed. Jewish Itineraries: Venice & Environs; Places, History & Art. (Jewish Itineraries Ser.). 191p. 1996. pap. 19.95 (1-56886-042-0) Marsilio Pubs.

Brandes, Georg. Soeren Kierkegaard. (GER.). iv, 240p. 1975. reprint ed. write for info. (3-487-05552-X) G Olms Pubs.

Brandes, Georg M. William Shakespeare. (BCL1-PR English Literature Ser.). 721p. 1992. reprint ed. lib. bdg. 169.00 (0-7812-7279-3) Rprt Serv.

Brandes, George. Friedrich Nietzsche. LC 72-2133. (Studies in German Literature: No. 13). 1972. reprint ed. lib. bdg. 75.00 (0-8383-1463-5) M S G Haskell Hse.

— Main Currents in Nineteenth Century Literature, 6 vols., Set. LC 72-3577. (Studies in European Literature: No. 56). 1972. reprint ed. lib. bdg. 375.00 (0-8383-1574-7) M S G Haskell Hse.

Brandes, George M. Creative Spirits of the Nineteenth Century. Anderson, R. B., tr. LC 67-26719. (Essay Index Reprint Ser.). 1977. 30.95 (0-8369-0245-9) Ayer.

— Hellas: Travels in Greece. Hartmann, Jacob W., tr. LC 72-90613. (Essay Index Reprint Ser.). 1977. 24.95 (0-8369-1203-9) Ayer.

— Henrik Ibsen. LC 64-14698. 182p. 1972. 17.95 (0-405-08302-5, Pub. by Blom Pubns) Ayer.

— Reminiscences of My Childhood & Youth. LC 74-27967. (Modern Jewish Experience Ser.). 1975. reprint ed. 37.95 (0-405-06697-X) Ayer.

Brandes, Joel R., et al. Law & the Family New York Forms, 6 vols. 2nd ed. LC 95-80415. 3500p. 1995. text 720.00 (0-7620-0008-2) West Group.

Brandes, K., jt. ed. see Vogel, A.

Brandes, Kathleen M. Moon Handbooks: Maine. (Illus.). 690p. 1998. pap. 18.95 (1-56691-094-3, Moon Handbks) Avalon Travel.

Brandes, Kathy, ed. see Grayson, Stan.

Brandes, Klaus, jt. ed. see Vogel, Andreas.

Brandes, Louis G., jt. auth. see Nicosia, Mary E.

Brandes, Mary J., ed. see Vincent, Richard J.

***Brandes, Michael L.** Jesus Manifesto. LC 98-75195. 128p. 2000. pap. 9.95 (1-57921-161-5, Pub. by WinePress Pub) BookWorld.

***Brandes-Miesner, Marta & Miesner, Joseph M., Sr.** Adult Doctor Visits. 168p. 2000. spiral bd. 12.95 (0-9666367-1-6) Sun Bear.

— Senior Doctor Visits. 168p. 2000. spiral bd. 12.95 (0-9666367-2-4) Sun Bear.

Brandes, Paul D. A History of Aristotle's Rhetoric with a Bibliography of Early Printings. LC 88-33713. (Illus.). 230p. 1989. 47.50 (0-8108-1952-X) Scarecrow.

— John Hancock's Life & Speeches: A Personalized Vision of the American Revolution, 1763-1793. 504p. 1996. 70.00 (0-8108-3076-0) Scarecrow.

Brandes, R., jt. auth. see Durkan, Michael J.

Brandes, Ray. Coronado: We Remember. LC 93-73351. (Illus.). 344p. 1993. 40.00 (0-9678743-0-0); pap. 15.00 (0-9678743-1-9) Coronado Hist.

***Brandes, Ray & Carlin, Katherine E.** Coronado: The Enchanted Island. (Illus.). 349p. 1998. 75.00 (0-9678743-2-7); pap. 35.00 (0-9678743-3-5) Coronado Hist.

Brandes, Raymond V. Big-Bang Cannons: The Carbide Cannon, a Unique American Toy. LC 93-83909. 160p. 1993. pap. 19.95 (0-9636127-7-8) Ray-Vin Pub.

Brandes, Stanley. Metaphors of Masculinity: Sex & Status in Andalusian Folklore. LC 79-5258. (Publications of the American Folklore Society, Bibliographical & Special Ser.). 236p. 1980. pap. text 19.95 (0-8122-1105-7) U of Pa Pr.

— Power & Persuasion: Fiestas & Social Control in Rural Mexico. LC 87-19205. (Illus.). 224p. (C). 1988. text 39.95 (0-8122-8077-6) U of Pa Pr.

Brandes, Stanley, et al. El Arte Popular de Espanol y las Americas: El Alma del Pueblo. Oettinger, Marion, ed. Samuel, Mervyn, tr. LC 97-67579. (SPA., Illus.). 200p. 1997. pap. 30.00 (1-883502-07-1) San Ant Mus Art.

— Folk Art of Spain & the Americas: El Alma del Pueblo. Oettinger, Marion, ed. Samuel, Mervyn, tr. LC 97-67578. (Illus.). 200p. 1997. pap. 30.00 (1-883502-06-3) San Ant Mus Art.

Brandes, Stanley H. Forty: The Age & the Symbol. LC 84-29920. 168p. 1985. 24.00 (0-87049-463-5) U of Tenn Pr.

Brandes, Stuart D. American Welfare Capitalism, 1880-1940. LC 75-20886. x, 210p. 1976. 24.00 (0-226-07121-9) U Ch Pr.

— American Welfare Capitalism, 1880-1940. LC 75-20886. x, 210p. 1984. pap. text 7.95 (0-226-07122-7) U Ch Pr.

B

— American Welfare Capitalism, 1880-1940. LC 75-20886. 219p. Date not set. reprint ed. pap. 67.90 (*0-608-20605-9*, 2054570) Bks Demand.

— Warhogs: A History of War Profits in America. LC 96-53139. (Illus.). 384p. 1997. 39.00 (*0-8131-2020-9*) U Pr of Ky.

***Brandes, T., ed.** Low-Dimensional Systems: Interactions & Transport Properties. (Lecture Notes in Physics Ser.: Vol. 554). (Illus.). vii, 219p. 2000. 72.80 (*3-540-67237-0*) Spr-Verlag.

Brandes, Ute. Zwischen Gestern und Morgen: Schriftstellerinnen der DDR aus Amerikanischer Sicht. (GER.). 1992. 44.80 (*3-86032-013-0*) P Lang Pubng.

Brandes, Wolfram. Die Stadte Kleinasiens im 7. und 8. Jahrhundert. 244p. 1989. pap. 55.00 (*90-5063-012-X*, Pub. by Gieben) J Benjamins Pubng Co.

Brandes, Wolfram, jt. ed. see Winkelmann, Friedhelm.

Brandeth, Gyles. The Emergency Joke Kite. (Illus.). (J). (ps-3). 1988. pap. 3.50 (*0-317-69598-3*, PuffinBks) Peng Put Young Read.

— Great Book of Optical Illusions: Scholastic Edition. (J). 1997. 3.95 (*0-8069-1767-9*) Sterling.

Brandetsas, Jim. Life in Fabulous Florida. (Orig.). 1996. pap. 2.95 (*1-888672-08-0*) J Ciano Pubng.

***Brandewie, Ernest.** In the Light of the Word: Divine Word Missionaries of North America. (American Society of Missiology Ser.: No. 29). (Illus.). 450p. 2000. pap. 40.00 (*1-57075-232-X*) Orbis Bks.

***Brandewyne, Rebecca.** Amores Turbulentos, 1vol. (Coleccion Cisne). 1998. pap. text 8.50 (*84-01-50651-4*) Plaza.

Brandewyne, Rebecca. Desire in Disguise. (Orig.). 1994. reprint ed. lib. bdg. 22.00 (*0-7278-4636-1*) Severn Hse.

***Brandewyne, Rebecca.** Desperado. 384p. 2000. mass mkt. 5.50 (*0-505-52376-0*, Love Spell) Dorchester Pub Co.

Brandewyne, Rebecca. Desperado. 384p. 1996. 24.00 (*0-7278-4846-1*) Severn Hse.

— Desperado. 304p. 1992. mass mkt. 5.99 (*0-446-35584-4*, Pub. by Warner Bks) Little.

— Desperado. large type ed. LC 93-619. 448p. 1993. lib. bdg. 18.95 (*1-56054-721-9*) Thorndike Pr.

***Brandewyne, Rebecca.** Destiny's Daughter. 2001. mass mkt. 6.50 (*1-55166-782-7*, Mira Bks) Harlequin Bks.

Brandewyne, Rebecca. Dust Devil. (Mira Bks.). 480p. 1996. per. 5.99 (*1-55166-063-6*, 1-66063-8, Mira Bks) Harlequin Bks.

— Gata Salvaje - Wildcat. (Silhouette Deseo - Silhouette Desire Ser.: Vol. 142').Tr. of Wildcat. (ENG & SPA.). 1996. per. 3.50 (*0-373-35142-9*) Harlequin Bks.

— Glory Seekers. 1997. per. 5.99 (*1-55166-276-0*, 1-66276-6, Mira Bks) Harlequin Bks.

— Heartland, 1 vol. (Love Spell Ser.). 384p. 1999. mass mkt. 5.50 (*0-505-52327-2*) Dorchester Pub Co.

— Heartland. large type ed. 602p. 1991. reprint ed. lib. bdg. 21.95 (*1-56054-117-2*) Thorndike Pr.

— High Stakes. 1999. per. 5.99 (*1-55166-430-5*, 1-66430-9, Mira Bks) Harlequin Bks.

— Hired Husband. 1996. per. 4.50 (*0-373-50177-3*, 1-50177-4) Harlequin Bks.

— The Jacaranda Tree. 384p. 1995. mass mkt. 5.99 (*0-446-36351-0*, Pub. by Warner Bks) Little.

— The Jacaranda Tree. 384p. 1996. reprint ed. 24.00 (*0-7278-4857-7*) Severn Hse.

— The Lioness Tamer: Man of the Month. (Desire Ser.: No. 1171). 1998. per. 3.75 (*0-373-76171-6*, 1-76171-7) Harlequin Bks.

— Love, Cherish Me. 576p. 1999. mass mkt. 5.99 (*0-505-52302-7*) Dorchester Pub Co.

— No Gentle Love. 592p. 1987. mass mkt. 6.50 (*0-446-34689-6*, Pub. by Warner Bks) Little.

— No Gentle Love. 1994. reprint ed. lib. bdg. 22.00 (*0-7278-4686-8*) Severn Hse.

***Brandewyne, Rebecca.** The Outlaw Hearts. 512p. (Orig.). 2000. pap. 5.99 (*0-505-52360-4*, Love Spell) Dorchester Pub Co.

Brandewyne, Rebecca. Passion Moon Rising. 480p. 1988. mass mkt. 5.50 (*0-671-61774-5*) PB.

— Passion Moon Rising. 448p. 1997. 25.00 (*0-7278-5158-6*) Severn Hse.

— Rainbow's End. 1991. mass mkt. 5.99 (*0-446-35582-8*, Pub. by Warner Bks) Little.

— Swan Road. 384p. 1994. mass mkt. 5.99 (*0-446-32701-8*, Pub. by Warner Bks) Little.

— Swan Road. large type ed. LC 93-47341. 578p. 1994. lib. bdg. 22.95 (*0-7862-0132-0*) Thorndike Pr.

— Swan Road. 384p. 1995. reprint ed. 22.00 (*0-7278-4758-9*) Severn Hse.

***Brandewyne, Rebecca.** Triangulo Pasional. 1998. pap. text 6.95 (*84-01-50652-2*) Plaza.

— Upon a Moon-Dark Moor. 400p. 1999. mass mkt. 5.50 (*0-505-52336-1*, Pub. by Dorchester Pub Co) CMG.

— Una Vida Diferente. (Harlequin Deseo Ser.: Vol. 160).Tr. of Different Life. (SPA.). 136p. 1999. per. 3.50 (*0-373-35290-5*, 1-35290-5) Harlequin Bks.

Brandewyne, Rebecca. Wildcat. 1995. per. 3.25 (*0-373-05955-8*, 1-05955-9) Silhouette.

Brandewyne, Rebecca & Stuart, Anne. New Year's Resolution: Husband. LC 96-3538. 377p. 1996. per. 4.99 (*0-373-83312-1*, 1-83312-8) Harlequin Bks.

Brandewyne, Rebecca, et al. Avon Books Presents: Bewitching Love Stories. 432p. (Orig.). 1992. mass mkt. 4.99 (*0-380-76832-1*, Avon Bks) Morrow Avon.

— Avon Books Presents: Night Magic. 400p. (Orig.). 1993. mass mkt. 4.99 (*0-380-76812-7*, Avon Bks) Morrow Avon.

Brandford, Elisabeth. How to Write the Best Research Paper Ever - Teacher's Edition. (Illus.). 32p. 1998. pap., teacher ed. 5.95 (*1-880505-29-0*, CLC0214) Pieces of Lrning.

Brandford, Richard. Roman Jakobson: Life, Language Art. LC 93-26943. (Critics of the Twentieth Century Ser.). 192p. (C). 1994. pap. 25.99 (*0-415-07732-X*) Routledge.

— Roman Jakobson: Life, Language Art. LC 93-26943. (Critics of the Twentieth Century Ser.). 192p. (C). (gr. 13). 1994. 85.00 (*0-415-07731-1*) Routledge.

Brandham, P. E., ed. Kew Chromosome Conference III. xx, 349p. 1988. pap. 36.00 (*0-11-250036-6*, Pub. by Royal Botnic Grdns) Balogh.

Brandham, P. E. & Bennett, M. D., eds. Kew Chromosome Conference IV. (Illus.). 450p. 1995. pap. 70.00 (*0-947643-95-8*, Pub. by Royal Botnic Grdns) Balogh.

Brandhorst, Beatrice, ed. see Mounts, Willard.

Brandhorst, J. P. J., jt. auth. see van Huisstede, P.

Brandhorst, William S. The Flexible Appliance: A Removable Orthodontic Appliance. Hacke, Gregory, ed. (Illus.). 200p. 1995. text 85.00 (*84-7179-266-4*) Med Dent Media.

Brandi, G., et al. Bifidobacteria: Microbiological Aspects & Probiotic Potentialities. 130p. 1998. pap. 59.95 (*88-470-0017-3*) Spr-Verlag.

Brandi, John. Diary from a Journey to the Middle of the World. 1979. per. 10.00 (*0-935724-82-6*) Figures.

— Diary from Baja California. (Illus.). 1978. 4.00 (*0-87922-103-8*) Christophers Bks.

— Heartbeat Geography: New & Selected Poems. (Illus.). 256p. (Orig.). 1995. pap. 15.00 (*1-877727-40-7*) White Pine.

— Hymn for a Night Feast: Poems 1979-1986. LC 87-81570. 76p. (Orig.). 1988. pap. 6.95 (*0-930100-27-1*) Holy Cow.

— In the Desert We Do Not Count the Days. LC 90-82296. 128p. 1991. pap. 10.95 (*0-930100-40-9*) Holy Cow.

— Poems from 4 Corners. 5.00 (*0-686-15301-4*) Great Raven Pr.

— A Question of Journey. (Light a Dust Bks.). 212p. 1995. pap. 15.00 (*0-87924-067-9*) Membrane Pr.

***Brandi, John.** Reflections in the Lizard's Eye: Notes from the High Desert. (Illus.). 208p. 2000. pap. 14.95 (*1-889921-08-4*, Pub. by Western Edge Pr) Mountain Pr.

Brandi, John. River Flowing. 1997. write for info. (*1-881544-08-7*) Yoo-Hoo Pr.

— Shadow Play: Poems, 1987-1991. (Light & Dust Bks.). (Illus.). 80p. (Orig.). 1992. pap. 8.00 (*0-87924-070-9*) Membrane Pr.

***Brandi, John.** Stone Garland: A Haiku Journey, Northern Viet Nam. limited ed. 28p. 2000. pap. 10.00 (*0-940510-19-7*) Tooth of Time.

Brandi, John. That Crow That Visited Was Flying Backwards. (Illus.). 56p. 1982. pap. 6.00 (*0-940510-05-7*) Tooth of Time.

— Weeding the Cosmos: Selected Haiku. 132p. (Orig.). 1994. pap. 10.00 (*0-9631909-1-1*) La Alameda Pr.

Brandi, John, jt. auth. see Sanfield, Steve.

Brandi, John, ed. see Inmates of the New Mexico State Penitentiary Staff.

Brandi, John, tr. see LaMadrid, Enrique E., et al, eds.

Brandi, M. L. & Momenteau, B. Lesekurs fuer Geisteswissenschaftler: Anfaenger. (GER.). 80p. (C). 1992. pap. text 19.75 (*3-12-675360-4*, Pub. by Klett Edition) Intl Bk Import.

— Lesekurs fuer Geisteswissenschaftler: Anhang Englisch. (GER.). 72p. (C). 1992. pap. text 17.25 (*3-12-675363-9*, Pub. by Klett Edition) Intl Bk Import.

— Lesekurs fuer Geisteswissenschaftler: Fortgeschrittene. (GER.). 209p. (C). 1992. pap. text 33.25 (*3-12-675361-2*, Pub. by Klett Edition) Intl Bk Import.

Brandi, Von M. Video im Deutschunterricht: Text. (Fernstudieneinheit Ser.: No. 13). (GER.). 192p. 1997. pap. 11.25 (*3-468-49664-8*) Langenscheidt.

Brandies, Monica. All about Ground Covers. rev. ed. Arbuckle, Nancy, ed. LC 92-61735. (Illus.). 112p. 1993. pap. 9.95 (*0-89721-254-1*, 05280A, Ortho Bks) Meredith Bks.

— All about Trees. Arbuckle, Nancy & Crocker, Cedric, eds. (Illus.). 112p. 1996. 14.95 Meredith Bks.

— Florida Gardening: The Newcomer's Survival Manual. LC 92-75720. (Illus.). 96p. 1997. reprint ed. pap. 9.95 (*0-9616338-3-2*) B B Mackey Bks.

— Ortho's Guide to Herbs. LC 96-67629. (Illus.). 304p. 1992. 29.95 (*0-89721-316-5*); pap. 24.95 (*0-89721-313-0*) Meredith Bks.

Brandies, Monica M. Bless You for the Gifts. LC 97-93109. 200p. (Orig.). 1997. pap. 10.95 (*0-9616338-7-5*) B B Mackey Bks.

— Herbs & Spices for Florida Gardens: How to Grow & Enjoy Florida Plants with Special Uses. Mackey, Betty B., ed. & illus. by. LC 96-75721. 250p. (Orig.). 1996. pap. 15.50 (*0-9616338-6-7*) B B Mackey Bks.

— Sprouts & Saplings: Gardening with a Difference. LC 86-14341. (Illus.). 208p. (Orig.). 1986. pap. 9.95 (*0-89407-066-5*) Strawberry Hill.

***Brandies, Monica Moran.** Xeriscaping for Florida Homes. 2nd rev. ed. LC 99-6691. (Illus.). 184p. 1999. pap. 17.95 (*0-8200-0418-9*) Great Outdoors.

Brandimarte, Cynthia A. Inside Texas: Culture, Identity, & Houses, 1878-1920. LC 91-10249. (Illus.). 460p. 1991. 60.00 (*0-87565-092-9*) Tex Christian.

Brandimarte, P., ed. Optimization Models & Concepts in Production Management. xiv, 339p. 1995. text 88.00 (*2-88449-020-5*) Gordon & Breach.

Brandimarte, P. & Villa, A., eds. Modeling Manufacturing Systems: From Aggregate Planning to Real-Time Control. LC 99-21014. (Illus.). x, 215p. 1999. 74.95 (*3-540-65500-X*) Spr-Verlag.

Brandimarte, Paolo, jt. auth. see Villa, Agostino.

Brandimonte, Maria, et al, eds. Prospective Memory: Theory & Applications. 432p. 1996. text 79.95 (*0-8058-1536-8*) L Erlbaum Assocs.

Brandin, Louis. Lais et Fabliaux du 13E Siecle. 122p. 1932. 13.95 (*0-8288-7427-1*) Fr & Eur.

Brandin, Louis, tr. see Sighele, Scipio.

***Brandin, Vladimir.** Intellectual Levels. 2000. text. write for info. (*0-9673753-4-7*) Gelany.

Branding, Ronice. Fulfilling the Dream: Confronting the Challenge of Racism. LC 98-37398. 144p. 1998. pap. 14.99 (*0-8272-1021-3*) Chalice Pr.

Brandis, Christian A. Geschichte der Entwicklung der Griechischen Philosophie und Ihrer Nachwirkungen Im Romiscshen Reich, 2 vols. in 1. (GER.). xviii, 1011p. 1981. reprint ed. write for info. (*3-487-07050-2*) G Olms Pubs.

Brandis, D. The Forest Flora of North-West & Central India, Set, Vols. 1-2. 1972. reprint ed. 410.00 (*0-7855-3072-X*, Pub. by Intl Bk Distr) St Mut.

— The Forest Flora of North-West & Central India, Vol. 1. 608p. 1972. reprint ed. write for info. (*0-7855-2571-8*, Pub. by Intl Bk Distr) St Mut.

— Forest Flora of North-West & Central India, Vol. 1-2. (C). 1972. text 750.00 (*0-89771-566-7*, Pub. by Intl Bk Distr) St Mut.

— The Forest Flora of North-West & Central India, Vol. 2. 70p. 1972. reprint ed. write for info. (*0-318-63728-6*, Pub. by Intl Bk Distr) St Mut.

— Indian Trees. 767p. 1990. pap. 750.00 (*81-7089-063-2*, Pub. by Intl Bk Distr) St Mut.

— Indian Trees. 767p. 1984. reprint ed. 250.00 (*0-7855-3071-1*, Pub. by Intl Bk Distr) St Mut.

Brandis, G., et al, eds. Liberals Face the Future. (C). 1985. pap. text 22.50 (*0-19-554505-2*) OUP.

Brandis, G. Brender a, see Brender a Brandis, G.

Brandis, Marianne. Elizabeth, Duchess of Somerset, Vol. I. 376p. 1989. pap. write for info. (*0-88984-093-8*) Porcup Quill.

— Elizabeth, Duchess of Somerset, Vol. II. 376p. 1989. pap. write for info. (*0-88984-095-4*) Porcup Quill.

— Fire Ship. 120p. 1992. pap. write for info. (*0-88984-140-3*) Porcup Quill.

— The Quarter-Pie Window. 204p. 1985. pap. write for info. (*0-88984-085-7*) Porcup Quill.

— Rebellion. (Illus.). 288p. 1996. pap. write for info. (*0-88984-175-6*) Porcup Quill.

— The Sign of the Scales. 224p. 1990. pap. write for info. (*0-88984-103-9*) Porcup Quill.

— The Tinderbox. Orig. Title: Fyrtojet. 160p. 1982. pap. write for info. (*0-88984-064-4*) Porcup Quill.

— The Tinderbox. Orig. Title: Fyrtojet. 224p. 1994. mass mkt. write for info. (*0-88984-153-5*) Porcup Quill.

— The Tinderbox. Orig. Title: Fyrtojet. 224p. 1995. mass mkt. write for info. (*0-88984-154-3*) Porcup Quill.

***Brandis, Paul.** The Aerie of Ravenhurst: A Novel of Horror & Romance. LC 00-190165. 2000. 25.00 (*0-7388-1595-0*); pap. 18.00 (*0-7388-1596-9*) Xlibris Corp.

***Brandist, Craig & Tikhanov, Galin.** Materializing Bakhtin. LC 99-40986. 2000. text 65.00 (*0-312-22860-0*) St Martin.

Brandl, Alois. Samuel Taylor Coleridge & the English Romantic School. LC 68-757. (Studies in Coleridge: No. 7). 1969. reprint ed. lib. bdg. 75.00 (*0-8383-0512-1*) M S G Haskell Hse.

Brandl, Alois & Zippel, O. Middle English Literature. 2nd ed. LC 48-3315. 1980. 14.95 (*0-685-01051-1*) Chelsea Pub.

Brandl, Dave. Bus Stop Baptism. 1997. pap. 2.00 (*1-57514-321-6*, 3112) Encore Perform Pub.

— Fit As a Fiddle. unabridged ed. LC 98-28683. (Illus.). 92p. 1998. pap. 15.00 (*0-88734-795-9*) Players Pr.

— How Can They Call It a Fixed Income When We're Always Broke. (Plays for Senior Actors Ser.). 1998. pap. 3.00 (*1-57514-323-2*) Encore Perform Pub.

— Just Til I'm Back on My Feet. 1998. pap. 3.00 (*1-57514-322-4*) Encore Perform Pub.

— Places, Please! 1997. pap. 2.50 (*1-57514-287-2*, 3078) Encore Perform Pub.

— Smooth Sailing? unabridged ed. Landes, William-Alan, ed. LC 98-26230. 88p. 1998. pap. 15.00 (*0-88734-794-0*) Players Pr.

— Vine & Dandy. LC 93-48188. 52p. (Orig.). 1994. pap. 6.00 (*0-88734-260-4*) Players Pr.

Brandl, Dave, et al. Christmas Lottery. 1998. pap. 4.00 (*1-57514-324-0*) Encore Perform Pub.

Brandl, Edmund. Emanzipation Gegen Anthropomorphismus: Der Literarisch Bedingte Wandel der Goethezeitlichen Bildungsgeschichte. (Europaische Hochschulschriften Ser.: Reihe 1, Bd. 1520). 886p. 1996. 127.95 (*3-631-48636-7*) P Lang Pubng.

Brandl, Gary, tr. see Herbstrith, Waltraud, et al.

Brandl, John E. Money & Good Intentions Are Not Enough: or Why a Liberal Democrat Thinks States Need Both Competition & Community. LC 97-45313. 177p. 1998. pap. 16.95 (*0-8157-1059-3*); text 39.95 (*0-8157-1060-7*) Brookings.

Brandl, Mary & Bendickson, Anita. Scenarios in Self-Defense. (Illus.). 57p. (Orig.). (C). 1990. pap. 9.00 (*1-878479-00-8*) BPS Commns.

***Brandl, Roman.** DB2 Universal DRDA Certification Guide. 500p. (C). 1998. pap. text 54.99 (*0-13-082425-9*) P-H.

Brandl, Selma. Modern Riding Techniques: Harmony in Horsemanship. (Illus.). 168p. (Orig.). (YA). 1997. pap. 32.95 (*1-85310-815-4*, Pub. by Swan Hill Pr) Voyageur Pr.

Brandl, Steven G. & Barlow, David E. Classics in Policing. LC 96-83681. 378p. (C). 1996. pap. 31.95 (*0-87084-234-X*) Anderson Pub Co.

Brandle, Werner, ed. Identitat und Schreiben - Martin Walser zu Ehren. (Hildesheimer Universitatsreden Ser.: Bd. 5). 184p. 1997. 28.00 (*3-487-10322-2*) G Olms Pubs.

Brandle, Werner & Stolina, Ralf, eds. Geist und Kirche: Festschrift Fur Eckhard Lessing. (GER.). X, 366p. 1995. 55.95 (*3-631-47262-5*) P Lang Pubng.

Brandle, Werner, et al. Toleranz und Religion - Perspektiven Zum Interreligiosen Gesprach. 171p. 1996. write for info. (*3-487-10210-2*) G Olms Pubs.

Brandlein, J. Ball & Roller Bearings: Theory, Design, & Application. LC 98-29509. 642p. 1999. 169.00 (*0-471-98452-3*) Wiley.

Brandler, Christopher, tr. see Dormann, Johannes.

Brandler, J. L. Out of Nigeria: Witness to a Giant's Toils. (Illus.). 384p. 1994. text 39.50 (*1-85043-732-7*) St Martin.

Brandler, Richard, et al. Patterns of Hypnotic Techniques of Milton H. Erickson, M. D., Vol. 2. LC 75-24584. 1977. 21.95 (*0-916990-02-8*) META Pubns.

Brandler, Sondra & Roman, Camille P. Group Work: Skills & Strategies for Effective Interventions. 2nd ed. LC 99-13598. (Illus.). 352p. (C). 1999. pap. text 24.95 (*0-7890-0740-1*); lib. bdg. 49.95 (*0-7890-0710-X*) Haworth Pr.

— GroupWork: Skills & Strategies for Effective Interventions. LC 91-6772. (Illus.). 272p. 1991. pap. 24.95 (*1-56024-119-5*); lib. bdg. 49.95 (*0-86656-890-5*) Haworth Pr.

Brandley, C. Randall, jt. auth. see Segler, Franklin M.

Brandly, C. A. & Cornelius, Charles E., eds. Advances in Veterinary Science & Comparative Medicine, Vol. 23. (Serial Publication Ser.). 1979. text 172.00 (*0-12-039223-2*); lib. bdg. 73.50 (*0-12-039282-8*) Acad Pr.

— Advances in Veterinary Science & Comparative Medicine, Vol. 24. (Serial Publication Ser.). 1980. text 172.00 (*0-12-039224-0*); lib. bdg. 73.50 (*0-12-039284-4*) Acad Pr.

Brandman. Chords Made Easy, Bk. 1. (Made Easy Ser.). 1990. 7.95 (*0-685-32063-4*, 8403) Hansen Ed Mus.

Brandner, Gary. The Boiling Pool. 256p. 1995. 20.00 (*0-7278-4749-X*) Severn Hse.

Brando, Pasquala. Dynamic Behaviour of the Mooring System of a Deepwater Turret Floating Production Vessel, Etc. 1989. 165.00 (*90-6314-564-0*, Pub. by Lorne & MacLean Marine) St Mut.

Brandoff-Kerr, Joan E. Prehistoric Land Use in the Santa Lucia Mountains: An Overview of the Esselen & Their Settlement Strategy. (Illus.). xi, 142p. 1982. reprint ed. pap. text 16.88 (*1-55567-036-9*) Coyote Press.

Brandois, Pierre. Microsoft Dictionnaire de l'Informatique. (FRE.). 415p. 1992. 120.00 (*0-7859-7731-7*, 2100013149) Fr & Eur.

Brandolini. Airships, Rassegna 67. (Illus.). 110p. 1996. pap. 35.00 (*88-85322-25-5*, Pub. by Birkhauser) Princeton Arch.

— London Underground, Rassegna 66. 1996. pap. 35.00 (*88-85322-24-7*, Pub. by Birkhauser) Princeton Arch.

Brandolini, A. & Haney, D. D. NMR Spectra of Plastics. (Illus.). 573p. 2000. text. write for info. (*0-8247-8970-9*) Dekker.

Brandolini, Dario, jt. ed. see Bonanno, Giacomo.

***Brandolini, Sebastiano.** Kristian Gullichsen. (Library of Architecture). 212p. 2000. pap. text 19.95 (*88-8118-655-1*, Pub. by Skira IT) Abbeville Pr.

Brandom, Ann-Marie, jt. auth. see Wright, Andrew.

***Brandom, Robert B.** Articulating Reasons: An Introduction to Inferentialism. LC 99-57756. 2000. 35.00 (*0-674-00158-3*) HUP.

Brandom, Robert B. Making It Explicit: Reasoning, Representing & Discursive Commitment. LC 93-50631. 752p. 1994. text 57.50 (*0-674-54319-X*, BRAMAK) HUP.

— Making It Explicit: Reasoning, Representing & Discursive Commitment. 768p. 1998. pap. text 24.95 (*0-674-54330-0*) HUP.

***Brandom, Robert B., ed.** Rorty & His Critics. LC 99-86000. (Philosophers & Their Critics Ser.). 384p. 2000. text 64.95 (*0-631-20981-6*); pap. text 29.95 (*0-631-20982-4*) Blackwell Pubs.

Brandon. At a Glance 1999. pap. text 8.97 (*0-395-94404-X*) HM.

— Brandon at a Glance: Paragraph. LC 98-71998. xv, 152p. 1998. pap. text 11.07 (*0-395-91868-5*) HM.

***Brandon.** MCSE TCP/ IP for Dummies. 2nd ed. LC 99-63114. (For Dummies Ser.). 448p. 1999. pap. 29.99 incl. cd-rom (*0-7645-0613-7*) IDG Bks.

— Microstructural Characterization. LC 98-46589. 424p. 1999. pap. 69.95 (*0-471-98502-3*) Wiley.

Brandon. Paragraphs & Essays, 7 vols. 7th ed. (C). Date not set. 44.76 (*0-395-89801-3*) HM.

— South East from 1000 A. D. 1990. pap. text. write for info. (*0-582-49245-9*, Pub. by Addison-Wesley) Longman.

Brandon, Arthur. Milo & Roger: A Magical Life. 424p. 1999. 37.00 (*0-945296-24-X*) Hermetic Pr.

Brandon, Barbara. Where I'm Coming From. (Illus.). 96p. 1993. pap. 8.95 (*0-8362-8016-4*) Andrews & McMeel.

— Where I'm Still Coming From. (Illus.). 96p. 1994. pap. 8.95 (*0-8362-8051-2*) Andrews & McMeel.

Brandon, Bill, jt. auth. see Perry, Gail.

Brandon, Brandy. Groanerz: The Dictionary Webster Hopes to Suppress. (Illus.). 130p. (Orig.). 1991. pap. 9.95 (*0-9630381-0-9*) New Times.

Brandon, Cameron. MCSE TCP/IP for Dummies. (For Dummies Ser.). 480p. 1998. 29.99 incl. cd-rom (*0-7645-0404-5*) IDG Bks.

Brandon, Carter & Ramankutty, Ramesh. Toward an Environmental Strategy for Asia. LC 93-44599. (Discussion Paper Ser.: No. 224). 223p. 1994. pap. 22.00 (*0-8213-2735-6*, 12735) World Bank.

— Toward an Environmental Strategy for Asia: A Summary of a World Bank Discussion Paper No. 224. 40p. 1993. pap. 22.00 (*0-8213-2737-2*, 12737) World Bank.

Brandon, Charles H. & Drtina, Ralph E. Management Accounting: Strategy & Control. 906p. (C). 1996. 89.69 (*0-07-017853-4*) McGraw.

An Asterisk (*) at the beginning of an entry indicates that the title is appearing for the first time.

***Brandon, Choi & Lee, Jim.** WildC.A.T.S: Compendium (D C Comics Graphic Novel) 1999. mass mkt. 9.95 (*1-56389-587-0*, Pub. by DC Comics) Time Warner.

***Brandon, Craig.** The Electric Chair: An Unnatural American History. LC 99-31128. (Illus.). 285p. 1999. lib. bdg. 39.95 (*0-7864-0686-0*) McFarland & Co.

Brandon, Craig. Murder in the Adirondacks: An American Tradegy Revisited. 2nd rev. ed. LC 86-5328. (Illus.). xii, 380p. 1986. pap. 20.00 (*0-932052-58-4*) North Country.

Brandon, D. G. & Kaplan, Wayne D. Joining Processes: An Introduction. LC 96-43512. 378p. 1997. pap. 77.95 (*0-471-96488-3*) Wiley.

Brandon, David & Kaplan, Wayne D. Microstructural Characterization of Materials. LC 98-46589. 424p. 1999. 190.00 (*0-471-98501-5*) Wiley.

***Brandon, Dolores.** In the Shadow of Madness. Herron, Paul, ed. LC 99-76406. (Illus.). 170p. 2000. pap. 14.95 (*0-9652364-5-5*) Sky Blue Pr.

Brandon, Dorothy & Scheider, Alfred F. Max Schling Book of Indoor Gardening. (Illus.). 1963. 20.00 (*0-8392-1065-5*) Astor-Honor.

Brandon-Falcone & Frucht. American Dreams, American Realities: An Introduction to the Uses of History. LC 99-179904. 224p. (C). 1998. pap. 34.95 (*0-7872-5169-0*) Kendall-Hunt.

Brandon, Garrett. The Unofficial Sensuous Women Sexual Men User's Manual: For Women Only. 62p. 1993. pap. 2.95 (*0-9638612-0-4*) Amer Press.

Brandon, George. Light from the Forest: How Santeria Heals Through Plants. 20p. 1991. pap. text 4.50 (*0-9631900-0-8*) Blue Unity Pr.

— Santeria from Africa to the New World: The Dead Cell Memories. (Blacks in the Diaspora Ser.). 1997. pap. text 11.95 (*0-253-21114-X*) Ind U Pr.

— Santeria from Africa to the New World: The Dead Sell Memories. LC 92-24251. (Blacks in the Diaspora Ser.). (Illus.). 228p. 1993. 35.00 (*0-253-31257-4*) Ind U Pr.

Brandon, Henry, ed. In Search of a New World Order: The Future of U. S. - European Relations. 177p. (C). 1992. 24.95 (*0-8157-1058-5*) Brookings.

Brandon, J., ed. The Records of the Town of Cambridge Massachusetts 1630-1703. 397p. 1985. reprint ed. 30.00 (*0-917890-50-7*) Heritage Bk.

Brandon, Jacqueline. A Business Arrangement. large type ed. (Dales Large Print Ser.). (Illus.). 223p. 1996. pap. 18.99 (*1-85389-614-4*) Ulverscroft.

— Perfect Solution. (Rainbow Romances Ser.). 160p. 1993. 14.95 (*0-7090-4894-7*) Parkwest Pubns.

Brandon, James, ed. World Encyclopedia of Contemporary Theatre Vol. 5: Asia - Oceania. (Illus.). 536p. (C). 1998. 140.00 (*0-415-05933-X*, B0392) Routledge.

Brandon, James R. Brandon's Guide to Theater in Asia. LC 75-37506. 178p. 1976. pap. 4.95 (*0-8248-0369-8*) UH Pr.

— Theater in Southeast Asia. LC 67-14338. (Illus.). 383p. 1974. pap. 18.00 (*0-674-87587-7*) HUP.

Brandon, James R., ed. No & Kyogen in the Contemporary World. LC 96-43429. 1997. text 39.00 (*0-8248-1810-5*) UH Pr.

— On Thrones of Gold: Three Japanese Shadow Plays. LC 73-88802. 429p. reprint ed. pap. 133.00 (*0-7837-2226-5*, 205731600004) Bks Demand.

— On Thrones of Gold: Three Javanese Shadow Plays. LC 93-14879. (Illus.). 426p. (C). 1993. reprint ed. pap. text 28.00 (*0-8248-1425-8*) UH Pr.

Brandon, James R., tr. Kabuki: Five Classic Plays. LC 74-82192. 394p. reprint ed. pap. 122.20 (*0-7837-2227-3*, 205731700004) Bks Demand.

— Kabuki: Five Classic Plays. LC 92-12160. (Illus.). 392p. (C). 1992. reprint ed. pap. text 24.00 (*0-8248-1426-6*) UH Pr.

Brandon, James R., et al. Studies in Kabuki: Its Acting, Music, & Historical Context. LC 77-5336. 202p. 1978. pap. text 16.00 (*0-8248-0452-X*) EW Ctr HI.

Brandon, James R., ed. see Langhans, Edward A.

Brandon, James R., tr. see Ariyoshi, Sawako.

***Brandon, Jay.** Afterimage. LC 99-55215. 352p. 2000. 23.95 (*0-312-86542-2*, Pub. by Forge NYC) St Martin.

— Afterimage. 2000. mass mkt. 6.99 (*0-8125-4044-1*) Tor Bks.

Brandon, Jay. Angel of Death. LC 98-21181. 384p. 1998. 24.95 (*0-312-86541-4*, Pub. by Forge NYC) St Martin.

***Brandon, Jay.** Angel of Death. LC 98-21181. 384p. 1999. mass mkt. 6.99 (*0-8125-4043-3*) Forge NYC.

— Deadbolt. LC 98-56129. 1999. 19.95 (*0-7862-1815-0*) Thorndike Pr.

Brandon, Jay. Deadbolt. Isaacson, Dana, ed. 288p. 1992. reprint ed. mass mkt. 4.99 (*0-671-70887-2*) PB.

— Defiance County. 1997. per. 6.99 (*0-671-53655-9*) PB.

— Fade the Heat. 368p. 1991. mass mkt. 5.99 (*0-671-70261-0*) PB.

— Local Rules. 1996. mass mkt. 5.99 (*0-671-88409-3*, PB Trade Paper) PB.

— Local Rules. large type ed. LC 95-2921. 532p. 1995. 24.95 (*0-7862-0490-7*) Thorndike Pr.

— Loose among the Lambs. large type ed. LC 94-922. 686p. 1994. lib. bdg. 23.95 (*0-7862-0197-5*) Thorndike Pr.

— Loose among the Lambs. Grose, Bill, ed. 1994. reprint ed. pap. 6.50 (*0-671-88315-1*) PB.

— Loose among the Lambs. Grose, Bill, ed. 400p. 1994. reprint ed. mass mkt. 5.99 (*0-671-76033-5*) PB.

— Predator's Waltz. Isaacson, Dana, ed. 304p. 1992. reprint ed. mass mkt. 4.99 (*0-671-70889-9*) PB.

— Tripwire. Isaacson, Dana, ed. 320p. 1992. mass mkt. 4.99 (*0-671-70888-0*) PB.

Brandon, Jay & Grose, Bill. Rules of Evidence. Isaacson, Dana, ed. 352p. 1992. reprint ed. mass mkt. 6.50 (*0-671-79389-6*) PB.

Brandon, Jeffrey L. & Rokop, Frank J. Life Between the Tides: The Natural History of the Common Seashore Life of Southern California. LC 84-73217. (Illus.). 230p. (gr. 9-12). 1985. pap. text 19.95 (*0-933177-00-3*) Am Southwest Pub Co.

Brandon, Joel, jt. auth. see Morris, Daniel C.

Brandon, Joseph D. The Castaways of Society: Rejection, Unacceptance & the Way to Restoration. 264p. 1997. 21.00 (*0-9662404-0-5*) Brandon Pubns.

***Brandon, Joseph D.** The Castaways of Society: Rejection, Unacceptance & the Way to Restoration. 2nd rev. unabridged ed. (Illus.). 271p. 1999. pap. 13.00 (*0-9662404-1-3*) Brandon Pubns.

Brandon, Joyce. Write Fiction to Sell! 2nd ed. 148p. (Orig.). 1997. pap. 16.95 (*0-913611-08-5*) W E C Plant.

Brandon, Katrina, et al. People & Parks: Linking Protected Area Management with Local Communities. 112p. 1992. pap. 22.00 (*0-8213-2053-X*, 12053) World Bank.

Brandon, Kelly, jt. auth. see Brandon, Lee.

Brandon-Kirby, Robert. Fly Fishing in Southern Africa. (Fly Fishing International Ser.). (Illus.). 180p. 1996. 75.00 (*0-8117-0625-7*) Stackpole.

***Brandon, Lee.** At a Glance: Essay. LC 98-71997. 224 p. 1999. pap. text 11.07 (*0-395-91869-3*) HM.

Brandon, Lee. Celebrating Diversity: A Multicultural Reader. 420p. (C). 1995. pap. text 31.56 (*0-669-35081-8*) HM Trade Div.

— Paragraphs & Essays: With Multicultural Readings. 6th ed. 444p. (C). 1994. pap. text 37.96 (*0-669-29790-9*) HM Trade Div.

Brandon, Lee & Brandon, Kelly. Sentences & Paragraphs. 448p. (C). 1993. pap. text 37.16 (*0-669-27634-0*); teacher ed. 38.36 (*0-669-27635-9*) HM Trade Div.

— Sentences, Paragraphs, & Beyond: With Culturally Diverse Readings, 2 Vols. (C). 1997. text, teacher ed. write for info. (*0-669-41846-3*) HM Trade Div.

— Sentences, Paragraphs, & Beyond: With Culturally Diverse Readings. 2nd ed. 480p. (C). 1996. pap. text 37.16 (*0-669-41597-9*) HM Trade Div.

— Sentences, Paragraphs, & Beyond: With Culturally Diverse Readings, 2 Vols. 2nd annot. ed. (C). 1997. text, teacher ed. write for info. (*0-669-41853-6*) HM Trade Div.

***Brandon, Lee E.** At a Glance. LC 98-71999. xiii, 161 p. 1999. write for info. (*0-395-89967-2*) HM.

Brandon, Lewis, ed. see Barnes, Harry E.

Brandon, Linda T. The Little Flower Girl. LC 96-2559. (Picturebacks Ser.). (Illus.). 24p. (J). (ps-1). 1997. pap. 3.25 (*0-679-87695-2*) Random.

Brandon, M., tr. see Monin, J. P., et al.

***Brandon, Marian.** Safeguarding Children with the Children Act 1989. LC 99-495125. (Illus.). 1999. write for info. (*0-11-322174-6*) Statnry Office.

Brandon, Mark E. Free in the World: American Slavery & Constitutional Failure. LC 97-25835. 267p. 1998. text 39.50 (*0-691-01581-3*, Pub. by Princeton U Pr) Cal Prin Full Svc.

Brandon, Mark T., et al. The Late Cretaceous San Juan Thrust System, San Juan Islands, Washington. LC 88-4003. (Geological Society of America Ser.: Vol. 221). (Illus.). 94p. 1988. reprint ed. pap. 30.00 (*0-608-07747-X*, 206783500010) Bks Demand.

***Brandon, Mary.** Sir Wimpy. (J). 2000. 10.95 (*0-533-13355-6*) Vantage.

Brandon-Monye, Deloris, jt. ed. see Oyemade, Ura J.

Brandon, P. S. Investment, Procurement & Performance in Construction: The First National RICS Research Conference. 1991. pap. write for info. (*0-442-31509-0*) Thomson Learn.

Brandon, P. S. Quantity Surveying Techniques: New Directions. (Illus.). 288p. 1992. pap. 49.95 (*0-632-03297-9*) Blackwell Sci.

Brandon, Pam. Walt Disney World Souvenir Book. LC 99-172845. (Illus.). 208p. (J). 1997. 21.45 (*0-7868-6386-2*, Pub. by Hyperion); pap. 7.70 (*0-7868-8306-5*, Pub. by Hyperion) Time Warner.

Brandon, Peter & Betts, Martin. Integrated Construction Information. LC 94-69928. (Illus.). 420p. (C). 1995. 160.00 (*0-419-20370-2*, E & FN Spon) Routledge.

Brandon, Peter S., jt. auth. see Ferry, Douglas J.

Brandon, R. Joe, jt. auth. see Westcott, Konnie.

Brandon, Reiko M. The Hawaiian Quilt. (Orig.). pap. 24.95 (*0-681-02833-5*) Booklines Hawaii.

— The Hawaiian Quilt. 2nd ed. (ENG & JPN., Illus.). 132p. (Orig.). (C). 1990. pap. 24.95 (*0-937426-19-9*) Honolu Arts.

Brandon, Reiko M. & Stephan, Barbara B. Textile Art of Okinawa: Collection of Okinawa Prefectural Museum. (Illus.). 60p. (C). 1990. pap. 14.50 (*0-937426-12-1*) Honolu Arts.

Brandon, Robert. Adaptation & Environment. 232p. 1990. text 45.00 (*0-691-08548-X*, Pub. by Princeton U Pr) Cal Prin Full Svc.

Brandon, Robert M., et al. Tax Politics: How They Make You Pay & What You Can Do About It. 297p. 1976. 6.95 (*0-394-49847-X*) Tax Reform Res.

Brandon, Robert N. Adaptation & Environment. 226p. 1990. pap. text 18.95 (*0-691-00152-9*, Pub. by Princeton U Pr) Cal Prin Full Svc.

— Concepts & Methods in Evolutionary Biology. (Cambridge Studies in Philosophy & Biology). (Illus.). 237p. (C). 1995. pap. text 20.95 (*0-521-49888-0*) Cambridge U Pr.

— Concepts & Methods in Evolutionary Biology. (Cambridge Studies in Philosophy & Biology). (Illus.). 237p. (C). 1996. text 59.95 (*0-521-49545-8*) Cambridge U Pr.

Brandon, Robert N. & Burian, Richard M., eds. Genes, Organisms, Populations: Controversies over the Units of Selection. (Illus.). 300p. (C). 1986. pap. text 13.95 (*0-262-52115-6*, Bradford Bks) MIT Pr.

***Brandon, Robin.** Biscay Spain: La Gironde to La Coruna. 230p. 2000. 125.00 (*0-85288-422-2*, Pub. by Laurie Norie & Wilson Ltd) St Mut.

Brandon, Robin. Coastas del Sol & Blanca. (Illus.). 260p. (C). 1995. 125.00 (*0-85288-281-5*, Pub. by Laurie Norie & Wilson Ltd) St Mut.

— La Corse: Corsica. (Illus.). 379p. (C). 1991. 125.00 (*0-85288-145-2*, Pub. by Laurie Norie & Wilson Ltd) St Mut.

— Costas del Azahar, Dorada & Brava. (Illus.). 316p. (C). 1995. 125.00 (*0-85288-287-4*, Pub. by Laurie Norie & Wilson Ltd) St Mut.

— Cote d'Azur Vol. IV: East Cote d'Azur Cap Sicie to Cap Roux. 1988. pap. 125.00 (*0-85288-122-3*, Pub. by Laurie Norie & Wilson Ltd) St Mut.

— Cote d'Azur Vol. V: The Riviera Cap Roux to Punta della Martola. (Illus.). 130p. 1990. pap. 125.00 (*0-85288-130-4*, Pub. by Laurie Norie & Wilson Ltd) St Mut.

— East Spain Pilot: The Balearics. (Illus.). 245p. 1995. 69.95 (*0-85288-285-8*) Bluewater Bks.

— East Spain Pilot, Chapter I: Introduction & Information. 620p. 1983. 75.00 (*0-85288-056-1*, Pub. by Laurie Norie & Wilson Ltd) St Mut.

— East Spain Pilot, Chapter II: Costa del Sol. 620p. 1982. 50.00 (*0-85288-079-0*, Pub. by Laurie Norie & Wilson Ltd) St Mut.

— East Spain Pilot, Chapter III: Costa Blanca. 620p. 1984. 50.00 (*0-7855-0712-4*, Pub. by Laurie Norie & Wilson Ltd) St Mut.

— East Spain Pilot, Chapter IV: Costa del Azahar. 620p. 1977. 50.00 (*0-85288-059-6*, Pub. by Laurie Norie & Wilson Ltd) St Mut.

— East Spain Pilot, Chapter V: Costa Dorada. 620p. 1977. 65.00 (*0-85288-060-X*, Pub. by Laurie Norie & Wilson Ltd) St Mut.

— East Spain Pilot, Chapter VI: Costa Brava. 620p. 1981. 50.00 (*0-85288-075-8*, Pub. by Laurie Norie & Wilson Ltd) St Mut.

— East Spain Pilot, Chapter VII: Islas Baleares. 620p. 1980. 50.00 (*0-85288-070-7*, Pub. by Laurie Norie & Wilson Ltd) St Mut.

— Golfe du Lion. (Illus.). 300p. 1993. 125.00 (*0-85288-163-0*, Pub. by Laurie Norie & Wilson Ltd) St Mut.

— Isles of Scilly Pilot. (Illus.). 60p. 1994. pap. 125.00 (*0-85288-149-5*, Pub. by Laurie Norie & Wilson Ltd) St Mut.

— Cote d'Azur Vol. 1: Introduction & Information. (Illus.). 1988. pap. 125.00 (*0-85288-136-3*, Pub. by Laurie Norie & Wilson Ltd) St Mut.

— South Biscay Pilot: La Gironde to La Coruna. 4th rev. ed. (Illus.). 293p. 1995. 125.00 (*0-7136-3698-X*, Pub by Laurie Norie & Wilson Ltd) St Mut.

— South Biscay Pilot: The Gironde Estuary to la Coruna. 3rd rev. ed. (Illus.). 388p. (C). 1989. 185.00 (*0-229-11680-9*, Pub. by Laurie Norie & Wilson Ltd) St Mut.

— South England Pilot. (C). 1983. text 135.00 (*0-85288-080-4*, Pub. by Laurie Norie & Wilson Ltd) St Mut.

— South England Pilot Vol. I: North Foreland to Selsey Bill. 1984. 60.00 (*0-7855-0713-2*, Pub. by Laurie Norie & Wilson Ltd) St Mut.

— South England Pilot Vol. II: Selsey Bill to Hengistbury Head & the Isle of Wight. 1984. 60.00 (*0-7855-0714-0*, Pub. by Laurie Norie & Wilson Ltd) St Mut.

— South England Pilot Vol. IV: Start Point to Land's End. 160p. 1979. 60.00 (*0-85288-067-7*, Pub. by Laurie Norie & Wilson Ltd) St Mut.

— South France Pilot Chapter I: Introduction & Information. 640p. 1983. 50.00 (*0-85288-088-X*, Pub. by Laurie Norie & Wilson Ltd) St Mut.

— South France Pilot Chapter II: Languedoc-Roussillon. 640p. 1984. 50.00 (*0-7855-0715-9*, Pub. by Laurie Norie & Wilson Ltd) St Mut.

— South France Pilot Chapter III: West Cote d'Azur. 640p. 1984. 50.00 (*0-7855-0716-7*, Pub. by Laurie Norie & Wilson Ltd) St Mut.

— South France Pilot Chapter V: The Riviera. 640p. 1982. 90.00 (*0-85288-078-2*, Pub. by Laurie Norie & Wilson Ltd) St Mut.

— Yachtsman's Pilots Vol. V: The Scilly Isles. 40p. 1983. 100.00 (*0-85288-090-1*, Pub. by Laurie Norie & Wilson Ltd) St Mut.

***Brandon, Ron, ed.** The Hargadon Guides Spring 2000: Hargadon's Directory of Used Computer Dealers & Repair, Parts & Service. 10th rev. ed. 690p. 1999 pap. 95.00 (*0-9659931-3-2*) Am Teleprocessing.

Brandon, Ruth. The Life & Many Deaths of Harry Houdini. Turner, Philip, ed. (Kodansha Globe Ser.). (Illus.). 400p. 1995. pap. 14.00 (*1-56836-100-9*, Kodansha Globe) Kodansha.

— Singer & the Sewing Machine: A Capitalist Romance. Rao, Maya, ed. (Illus.). 256p. 1996. pap. 14.00 (*1-56836-146-7*, Kodansha Globe) Kodansha.

— Surreal Lives: The Surrealists, 1917-1945. LC 99-25492. 544p. 1999. 27.50 (*0-8021-1653-1*, Grove) Grove-Atltic.

***Brandon, Ruth.** Surreal Lives: The Surrealists, 1917-1945. (Illus.). 554p. 2000. reprint ed. pap. 16.00 (*0-8021-3727-X*, Grove) Grove-Atltic.

Brandon, Ruth. The Uncertainty Principle. 306p. 1997. 26.00 (*0-224-04454-0*, Pub. by Jonathan Cape) Trafalgar.

Brandon, S. G. Diccionario de Religiones Comparadas, Vol. 1. (SPA.). 750p. 1975. 55.00 (*0-7859-6106-2*, 8470571893) Fr & Eur.

— Diccionario de Religiones Comparadas, Vol. 2. (SPA.). 726p. 1975. 55.00 (*0-7859-6107-0*, 8470571907) Fr & Eur.

Brandon, Samuel. The Virtuous Octavia. LC 73-133641. (Tudor Facsimile Texts. Old English Plays Ser.: No. 81). reprint ed. 59.50 (*0-404-53381-7*) AMS Pr.

Brandon, Samuel G. Diccionario de Religiones Comparadas, 2 vols., Set. (SPA.). 1553p. 1975. 125.00 (*0-8288-5816-0*, S50104) Fr & Eur.

— Dictionary of Comparative Religions. LC 76-11390. 712p. 1978. 60.00 (*0-684-15561-3*, Scribners Ref) Mac Lib Ref.

Brandon, Samuel G., ed. The Saviour God: Comparative Studies in the Concept of Salvation Presented to Edwin Oliver James. LC 80-14924. 242p. 1980. reprint ed. lib. bdg. 59.50 (*0-313-22416-1*, BRSG, Greenwood Pr) Greenwood.

Brandon, Sue. Buttonhooks & Shoehorns. (Album Ser.: No. 122). (Illus.). 32p. (C). 1989. pap. 4.75 (*0-85263-696-2*, Pub. by Shire Pubns) Parkwest Pubns.

***Brandon, Taylor.** The Bear Who Couldn't Hibernate! (Sleep) LC 96-94833. (The World's Greatest Children's Bks.). (Illus.). 48p. (J). (gr. k-5). 1999. 14.99 (*1-889945-57-9*) Imperius.

— The Bird Who Didn't Want to Fly South for the Winter! LC 96-94841. (The World's Greatest Children's Bks.). (Illus.). 48p. (J). (gr. k-5). 1999. 14.99 (*1-889945-55-2*) Imperius.

— The Bird Who Was Afraid to Clean the Crocodile's Teeth! LC 96-94842. (The World's Greatest Children's Bks.). (Illus.). 48p. (J). (gr. k-5). 1999. 14.99 (*1-889945-56-0*) Imperius.

— The Elephant Who Couldn't Remeber! LC 96-94839. (The World's Greatest Children's Bks.). (Illus.). 48p. (J). (gr. k-5). 1999. 14.99 (*1-889945-53-6*) Imperius.

— The Hyena Who Wouldn't Laugh. LC 96-94854. (The World's Greatest Children's Bks.). (Illus.). 48p. (J). (gr. k-5). 1999. 14.99 (*1-889945-68-4*) Imperius.

— The Penguin Who Hated the Cold Because he Was All Dressed Up & Had No Place To Go. LC 96-94846. (The World's Greatest Children's Bks.). (Illus.). 48p. (J). (gr. k-5). 1999. 14.99 (*1-889945-61-7*) Imperius.

— The Pig Who Didn't Want to Get Dirty. LC 96-94848. (The World's Greatest Children's Bks.). (Illus.). 48p. (J). (gr. k-5). 1999. 14.99 (*1-889945-63-3*) Imperius.

— The Straw That Didn't Break the Camel's Back! LC 96-94844. (The World's Greatest Children's Bks.). 48p. (J). (gr. k-5). 1999. 14.99 (*1-889945-58-7*) Imperius.

— The Turtle Who Felt Boxed In! LC 96-94840. (The World's Greatest Children's Bks.). (Illus.). 48p. (J). (gr. k-5). 1999. 14.99 (*1-889945-54-4*) Imperius.

Brandon, Thomas R., jt. auth. see Drielak, Steven C.

Brandon, Traci, jt. auth. see Graham, Leland.

Brandon, William. Indians. LC 85-13435. (American Heritage Library). (Illus.). 350p. 1985. pap. 9.95 (*0-685-10832-5*) HM.

— The Magic World: American Indian Songs & Poems. LC 90-47852. 168p. (C). 1992. pap. 12.95 (*0-8214-0991-3*) Ohio U Pr.

— New Worlds for Old: Reports from the New World & Their Effect on the Development of Social Thought in Europe, 1500-1800. LC 85-25818. 226p. 1986. pap. text 14.95 (*0-8214-0819-4*) Ohio U Pr.

— Quivira: Europeans in the Region of the Santa Fe Trail, 1540-1820. LC 90-6907. (Illus.). 352p. 1990. 34.95 (*0-8214-0950-6*) Ohio U Pr.

Brandon, William, intro. The Magic World: American Indian Songs & Poems. LC 90-47852. 168p. (C). 1992. reprint ed. 26.95 (*0-8214-0981-6*) Ohio U Pr.

Brandon, William, tr. see Nyiri, Janos.

Brandow, Gregg. Imperial County, California, Earthquake, October 15, 1979. Leeds, David J., ed. 200p. 1980. pap. 12.00 (*0-318-16320-9*, EP-15) Earthquake Eng.

Brandow, John H. The Story of Old Saratoga & the Burgoyne Campaign. (Illus.). 528p. 1997. reprint ed. lib. bdg. 55.00 (*0-8328-6221-5*) Higginson Bk Co.

***Brandow, John Henry.** The Story of Old Saratoga: The Burgoyne Campaign to Which Is Added New York's Share in the Revolution. (Illus.). 574p. 2000. reprint ed. pap. 34.00 (*0-7884-1510-7*, 1510) Heritage Bk.

Brandow, Karen, jt. auth. see Reed, Thomas F.

Brandow, Peter, jt. auth. see Ambrose, James E.

***Brandow, Ron.** 1998 Interconnect Directory: Service, Installation & Maintenance. rev. ed. 133p. 1998. pap. 79.00 (*0-9659931-1-6*) Am Teleprocessing.

***Brandow, Ron, ed.** The Hargadon Guides: Hargadon's Directory of Used Computer Dealers & Repair , Parts & Service Companies. 5th ed. 740 p. 1999. pap. 95.00 (*0-9659931-2-4*) Am Teleprocessing.

Brandreth, D. A., ed. Advances in Foam Aging: A Topic in Energy Conservation, Vol. 1. (Illus.). 226p. (Orig.). 1986. 38.00 (*0-939433-01-X*) Caissa Edit.

Brandreth, D. A., ed. see Ilyin-Genevsky, A.

Brandreth, Dale, ed. Hastings 1936-37: International Chess Tournament. (Tournament Bk.). (Illus.). 55p. (Orig.). 1992. pap. 9.00 (*0-939433-15-X*) Caissa Edit.

Brandreth, Dale, jt. auth. see Hooper, David.

Brandreth, Dale, ed. see Hoffer, Leopold.

Brandreth, Dale A., jt. auth. see Otterstedt, Jan-Erik.

***Brandreth, Gyles.** Breaking the Code: Westminster Dairies. LC 99-231906. 1999. 45.00 (*0-297-64311-8*, Pub. by Weidenfeld & Nicolson) Trafalgar.

Brandreth, Gyles. Famous Last Words & Tombstone Humor. LC 88-24966. (Illus.). 128p. (Orig.). (J). (gr. 4 up). 1989. pap. 5.95 (*0-8069-6950-4*) Sterling.

— The Great Book of Optical Illusions. LC 85-9898. (Illus.). 96p. (Orig.). (J). (gr. 2 up). 1985. pap. 5.95 (*0-8069-6258-5*) Sterling.

— Great Party Games: Over 200 Games for Adults of All Ages. (Illus.). 152p. 1992. pap. 8.95 (*0-86051-672-5*, Robson-Parkwest) Parkwest Pubns.

— Madcap Bumper Book of Horrors--Things That Go Bump. (Illus.). 288p. (J). (gr. 1-6). 1998. pap. 6.95 (*0-233-99084-4*, Pub. by Andre Deutsch) Trafalgar.

B

— Madcap Bumper Book of Magic. (Illus.). 288p. (J). (gr. 1-6). 1998. pap. 6.95 (*0-233-99296-0*, Pub. by Andre Deutsch) Trafalgar.

— Quick & Easy Magic Tricks. (Illus.). 96p. (Orig.). (J). 1988. pap. 1.95 (*0-942025-33-4*) Kidsbks.

***Brandreth, Gyles.** Slippers That Answered Back. (Illus.). 96p. (J). 1999. pap. 6.95 (*0-14-037833-2*, Pub. by Pnguin Bks Ltd) Trafalgar.

— Slippers That Talked. (Illus.). 96p. (J). 1992. pap. 7.95 (*0-14-032451-8*, Pub. by Pnguin Bks Ltd) Trafalgar.

Brandreth, Gyles. The Super Joke Book. LC 83-397. (Illus.). 128p. (J). (gr. 3 up). 1985. pap. 4.95 (*0-8069-6200-3*) Sterling.

***Brandreth, Gyles.** Venice Midnight. large type ed. 344p. 2000. 31.99 (*0-7089-4179-6*) Ulverscroft.

Brandreth, Gyles. Your Vital Statistics. 128p. 1986. pap. 8.95 (*0-8065-0980-5*) Carol Pub Group.

***Brandreth, Gyles, ed.** The Last Word: A Collection of Insults, Epitaphs & Compliments from the Rich & Famous. 192p. 2000. reprint ed. text 20.00 (*0-7881-6814-2*) DIANE Pub.

Brandreth, Henry R. Episcopi Vagantes & the Anglican Church. LC 87-29809. xix, 79p. 1987. pap. 17.00 (*0-912134-06-2*) Millefleurs.

Brandrup, J. Polymer Handbook Electronic Version. write for info. (*0-471-53205-3*) Wiley.

***Brandrup, J., et al, eds.** Polymer Handbook. 4th ed. 2336p. 1999. 350.00 (*0-471-16628-6*) Wiley.

Brandrup, J. & Immergut, Edmund H., eds. Polymer Handbook, Vol. 1. 3rd ed. LC 88-1258. 1904p. 1989. 295.00 (*0-471-81244-7*) Wiley.

Brandrup, Johannes. Recycling & Recovery of Plastics. LC 96-36331. 893p. 1996. 240.00 (*1-56990-214-3*) Hanser-Gardner.

Brands. The United States in the World. LC 93-78669. (C). 1993. pap. text 27.16 (*0-395-62180-1*) HM.

— The United States in the World. (C). 1993. pap., teacher ed. 5.96 (*0-395-62182-8*) HM.

— The United States in the World, Vol. 2. LC 93-78669. (C). 1993. pap. text 31.96 (*0-395-62181-X*) HM.

Brands, Bill, compiled by. W. Page Keeton No. 36: An Oral History Interview. 79p. 1992. 25.00 (*0-935630-42-2*) U of Tex Tarlton Law Lib.

Brands, H. W. Bound to Empire: The United States & the Philippines. 400p. (C). 1992. 35.00 (*0-19-507104-2*) OUP.

Brands, H. W., Jr. Cold Warriors: Eisenhower's Generation & American Foreign Policy. (Contemporary American History Ser.). (Illus.). 247p. 1988. text 49.50 (*0-231-06526-4*) Col U Pr.

Brands, H. W. The Devil We Knew: Americans & the Cold War. 256p. 1994. reprint ed. pap. 11.95 (*0-19-509377-1*) OUP.

***Brands, H. W.** The First American: The Life & Times of Benjamin Franklin. 648p. 2000. 35.00 (*0-385-49328-2*) Doubleday.

Brands, H. W., Jr. India & the United States: The Cold Peace. (Twayne's International History Ser.: No. 6). (Illus.). 248p. (C). 1990. 26.95 (*0-8057-7915-9*); pap. 15.95 (*0-8057-9207-4*) Macmillan.

— Into the Labyrinth: The United States & the Middle East, 1945-1993. LC 93-28110. 224p. (C). 1993. pap. 24.38 (*0-07-007188-8*) McGraw.

Brands, H. W. Masters of Enterprise: Giants of American Business from John Jacob Astor & J. P. Morgan to Bill Gates & Oprah Winfrey. LC 98-51054. 368p. 1999. 24.50 (*0-684-85473-2*) Free Pr.

— Since Vietnam: The United States in World Affairs, 1973-1994. LC 95-2756. (C). 1995. pap. text 14.50 (*0-07-007196-9*) McGraw.

Brands, H. W., Jr. The Specter of Neutralism: The United States & the Emergence of the Third World. (Columbia Studies in Contemporary American History). 372p. 1990. text 57.50 (*0-231-07168-X*) Col U Pr.

***Brands, H. W.** The Use of Force after the Cold War. LC 99-58775. Vol. 3. (Illus.). 352p. 2000. 44.95 (*0-89096-928-0*) Tex A&M Univ Pr.

Brands, H. W. The Wages of Globalism: Lyndon Johnson & the Limits of American Power. LC 96-52764. 304p. 1997. reprint ed. pap. 22.00 (*0-19-511377-2*) OUP.

— What America Owes the World: The Struggle for the Soul of Foreign Policy. LC 97-38837. 335p. (C). 1998. text 54.95 (*0-521-63031-2*); pap. text 17.95 (*0-521-63968-9*) Cambridge U Pr.

Brands, H. W., ed. Foreign Policies of Lyndon Johnson: Beyond Vietnam. LC 98-46981. (Foreign Relations & the Presidency Ser.: Vol. 1). 224p. 1999. 29.95 (*0-89096-873-X*) Tex A&M Univ Pr.

Brands, H. W., jt. ed. see Medhurst, Martin J.

Brands, Ruth, jt. auth. see Mills, Charles.

***Brands, Stefan A.** Rethinking Public Key Infrastructures & Digital Certificates: Building in Privacy. 305p. (C). 2000. 35.00 (*0-262-02491-8*) MIT Pr.

Brandsma, A. S. Ambition & Risk Aversion in the Design of Economic Policies. 200p. 1997. text 61.00 (*981-02-1266-6*) World Scientific Pub.

Brandsma, F. Dorotheus & His Digest Translation. xiv, 336p. (Orig.). 1996. pap. 62.00 (*90-6980-043-8*, Pub. by Egbert Forsten) Hod1der & Stoughton.

Brandsma, Jeff, jt. auth. see Farrelly, Frank.

Brandsma, L. Preparative Acetylenic Chemistry. 2nd ed. (Studies in Organic Chemistry: No. 34). x,322p. 1988. 210.50 (*0-444-42960-3*) Elsevier.

— Preparative Polar Organometallic Chemistry, Vol. 2. (Illus.). xii, 227p. 1991. 69.95 (*0-387-52749-4*) Spr-Verlag.

Brandsma, L. & Verkruijsse, H. D. Preparative Polar Organometallic Chemistry, Vol. 1. 240p. 1987. 69.95 (*0-387-16916-4*) Spr-Verlag.

Brandsma, L., et al. Application of Transition Metal Catalysts in Organic Synthesis. LC 97-35574. (Laboratory Ser.). (Illus.). 350p. 1997. 128.00 (*3-540-62831-2*) Spr-Verlag.

— Application of Transition Metal Catalysts in Organic Synthesis. LC 99-20237. (Desktop Editions in Chemistry Ser.). 240p. 1999. pap. 54.95 (*3-540-65550-6*) Spr-Verlag.

Brandsma, T. F., jt. auth. see Nijhof, Wim J.

Brandstadt, Andreas, et al. Graph Classes: A Survey. LC 99-11680. (Discrete Mathematics & Application Ser.: Vol. 3). (Illus.). xi, 304p. 1999. pap. text 68.00 (*0-89871-432-X*, BKDT0003) Soc Indus-Appl Math.

Brandstatter, Hermann & Davis, James, eds. Group Decision Making. LC 81-66398. (European Monographs in Social Psychology: No. 25). 1982. text 159.95 (*0-12-125820-3*) Acad Pr.

***Brandstatter, Hermann & Eliasz, Andrzej.** Persons, Situations & Emotions: An Ecological Approach. (Series in Affective Science). (Illus.). 272p. 2000. text 49.95 (*0-19-513517-2*) OUP.

Brandstatter, Hermann & Guths, Werner, eds. Essays on Economic Psychology. LC 94-31029. 1994. 140.00 (*3-540-58283-5*) Spr-Verlag.

— Essays on Economic Psychology. LC 94-31029. 1994. 111.95 (*0-387-58283-5*) Spr-Verlag.

Brandstetter, Alois, et al. The Abbey: A Novel. Firchow, Peter E. & Firchow, Evelyn S., trs. from GER. LC 97-16849. (Studies in Austrian Literature, Culture & Thought). 232p. 1998. pap. 19.95 (*1-57241-045-0*) Ariadne CA.

Brandstetter, Jeffrey D., jt. auth. see Naggar, David.

Brandstock, Margaret, jt. ed. see Wakeling, Louise.

Brandstrom, Anders & Tedebrand, Lars-Goran. Society, Health, & Population During the Demographic Transition. (Illus.). 514p. 1988. lib. bdg. 71.00 (*91-22-01216-8*) Coronet Bks.

Brandstrom, Per, et al. Aspects of Agro-Pastoralism in East Africa. (Research Report Ser.: No. 51). 60p. 1979. write for info. (*91-7106-155-X*, Pub. by Nordic Africa) Transaction Pubs.

Brandt. ATM Signalling. 2000. text. write for info. (*0-471-62382-2*) Wiley.

— Clinical Practice Gastroenterology, 2 vols. LC 98-22058. (C). 1998. text 235.00 (*0-443-06520-9*) Church.

— Don't Stop Now. 1988. per. 4.95 (*0-671-65666-X*) PB.

Brandt. Mediterranean Desertification. text. write for info. (*0-471-49113-6*) Wiley.

Brandt, A., et al, eds. Nonlinear Dynamics of Ocean Waves: Proceedings of the Symposium Held at the Applied Physics Laboratory, Johns Hopkins University, 30-31 May 1991. LC 92-16906. 228p. 1992. text 81.00 (*981-02-1071-X*) World Scientific Pub.

Brandt, A. & Last, G. Marked Point Proceddes on the Real Line: The Dynamical Approach. Gani, J. et al, eds. (Probability & Its Applications Ser.). 494p. 1995. 60.95 (*0-387-94547-4*) Spr-Verlag.

Brandt, A. H., ed. Criteria & Methods of Structural Optimzation. 1986. text 262.00 (*90-247-2515-1*) Kluwer Academic.

Brandt, A. M. Cement-Based Composites: Materials, Mechanical Properties & Performance. (Illus.). 488p. (C). 1994. 190.00 (*0-419-19110-0*, E & FN Spon) Routledge.

— Mechanical Properties of Cement-Based Composites. LC 93-3413. 1993. write for info. (*1-85861-029-X*) Elsevier.

Brandt, A. M., ed. Foundations of Optimum Design in Civil Engineering. (C). 1989. text 440.00 (*90-247-2516-X*) Kluwer Academic.

Brandt, A. M., et al, eds. Brittle Matrix Composites 5. 650p. 1998. 260.00 (*1-85573-358-7*, Pub. by Woodhead Pubng) Am Educ Systs.

Brandt, Aage. Morphologies of Meaning: Dynamic Semiotics & Cognitive Linguistics. LC 96-128784. 272p. (C). 1995. pap. 27.00 (*87-7288-514-9*, Pub. by Aarhus Univ Pr) David Brown.

Brandt, Alan & Fernando, H. J., eds. Double Diffusive Convection. LC 95-26425. (Geophysical Monograph Ser.: No. 94). 1995. 70.00 (*0-87590-076-3*) Am Geophysical.

Brandt, Allan. Rise & Fall of the Cigarette: A Cultural History of Smoking in the U. S. 1998. pap. 18.00 (*0-465-07048-5*, Pub. by Basic) HarpC.

— Rise & Fall of the Cigarette: A Social & Cultural History of Smoking in the U. S. 1997. 25.00 (*0-465-07047-7*, Pub. by Basic) HarpC.

Brandt, Allan M. No Magic Bullet: A Social History of Venereal Disease in the United States Since 1880. (Illus.). 290p. 1987. pap. text 14.95 (*0-19-504237-9*) OUP.

Brandt, Allen. The Last Knight of Flanders: Remy Schrijnen & His SS-Leigon "Flandern"/Sturmbrigade "Langemarck" Comrades on the Eastern Front, 1941-1945. LC 98-84260. 272p. 1998. 29.95 (*0-7643-0588-3*) Schiffer.

Brandt, A.M. Optimization Methods for Material Design of Cement-Based Composites. 1998. pap. 110.00 (*0-419-21790-8*) Thomson Learn.

***Brandt, Amy.** Benjamin Comes Back. De la Vega, Eida, tr. LC 99-55117. (Child Care Bks. for Kids).Tr. of Benjamin Regresa. (ENG & SPA., Illus.). 32p. (J). (ps-2). 2000. pap. 11.95 (*1-884834-79-5*, 709801, Pub. by Redleaf Pr) Gryphon Hse.

— When Katie Was Our Teacher. De la Vega, Eida, tr. LC 99-55118. (Child Care Bks. for Kids).Tr. of Cuando Katie Era Nuestra Maestra. (ENG & SPA., Illus.). 32p. (J). (ps-2). 2000. pap. 11.95 (*1-884834-78-7*, 709901, Pub. by Redleaf Pr) Gryphon Hse.

Brandt, Angelika. Antarctic Serolidae & Cirolandidae (Crustaceae, Isopoda) New Genera, Species & Redescriptions. (Theses Zoologicae Ser.: Vol. 10). (Illus.). iv, 172p. 1988. 70.00 (*3-87429-288-6*, 035340, Pub. by Koeltz Sci Bks) Lubrecht & Cramer.

— Antarctic Valviferans (Crustacea, Isopoda, Valvifera) New Genera, New Species & Redescriptions. LC 89-49705. (Illus.). vi, 176p. 1990. pap. 60.00 (*90-04-09238-2*) Brill Academic Pubs.

Brandt, Ann. Crowfoot Ridge. LC 97-4371. 224p. 1997. 22.95 (*1-57090-053-1*) Alexander Dist.

— Crowfoot Ridge. LC 98-21804. 288p. 1999. 20.00 (*0-06-019215-1*) HarpC.

***Brandt, Ann.** Crowfoot Ridge. 368p. 2000. mass mkt. 6.50 (*0-06-109709-8*) HarpC.

Brandt, Anthony. People along the Sand: Three Stories, Six Poems, a Memoir. 83p. (Orig.). 1992. pap. 9.95 (*0-9630164-1-5*) Canios Edit.

Brandt, Anthony. The Pushcart Book of Essays. 30.00 (*1-888889-24-1*, Pub. by Pushcart Pr) Norton.

Brandt, Avrene L. Caregiver's Reprieve: A Guide to Emotional Survival When You're Caring for Someone You Love. LC 97-78261. (Working Caregiver Ser.). 128p. (Orig.). 1997. pap. 11.95 (*1-886230-06-4*) Impact Pubs CA.

Brandt, Barbara, jt. auth. see Fellman, Gordon.

Brandt, Betty. The Adventures of Nicolet. Brandt, Laura, ed. (Illus.). 160p. (Orig.). (YA). (gr. 6-12). 1991. 12.95 (*0-9622014-2-1*) Beaver Valley.

— At the Other End of the Hunt. (Illus.). 128p. (Orig.). 1989. pap. 8.95 (*0-9622014-0-5*) Beaver Valley.

— History of the Library. Albrecht, Grace, ed. (Illus.). 64p. (J). (gr. 4-6). 1995. 8.95 (*0-9622014-4-8*) Beaver Valley.

— Should I Laugh or Cry? Brandt, Laura, ed. (Illus.). 128p. 1990. 8.95 (*0-9622014-1-3*) Beaver Valley.

— The Story of Nicolet. Nestingen, Jan, ed. (Illus.). 64p. (Orig.). (J). (gr. 3-5). 1991. pap. 6.95 (*0-9622014-3-X*) Beaver Valley.

Brandt, Beverly F. Borders of Consciousness, Bk. 3. LC 99-90565. (Consciousness of Commitment Ser.: Vol. 8, Bk. 3). 525p. pap. write for info. (*1-929064-03-9*, 2003-1, Pub. by Brandt Pubns) First Bks.

— The Consciousness of Being, Bk. 2. LC 99-63623. (Consciousness of Commitment Ser.: Vol. 8, Bk. 2). 630p. pap. write for info. (*1-929064-02-0*, 2002-1, Pub. by Brandt Pubns) First Bks.

— The Consciousness of Commitment Series Vols. 1-8: A Vision of Christian Mysticism. pap. write for info. (*1-929064-08-X*, 2008-1, Pub. by Brandt Pubns) First Bks.

— The Fourth Universe, Bk. 5. LC 99-90567. (Consciousness of Commitment Ser.: Vol. 8, Bk. 5). 540p. pap. write for info. (*1-929064-05-5*, 2005-1, Pub. by Brandt Pubns) First Bks.

— God, the Experience, Bk. 4. LC 99-90566. (Consciousness of Commitment Ser.: Vol. 8, Bk. 4). 525p. pap. write for info. (*1-929064-04-7*, 2004-1, Pub. by Brandt Pubns) First Bks.

— The Meaning of Redemption. LC 99-90569. (Consciousness of Commitment Ser.: Vol. 8, Bk. 7). 600p. pap. write for info. (*1-929064-07-1*, 2007-1, Pub. by Brandt Pubns) First Bks.

— The Mystic Reality of Christ Consciousness: The Series Introduction. Paquette, Mari L., ed. LC 99-94499. (Consciousness of Commitment Ser.: Vol. 8). 525p. 2000. pap. 23.45 (*1-929064-00-4*, 2000-1) Brandt Pubns.

— The Seed of Spiritual Sonship, Bk. 1. Paquette, Mari L., ed. LC 99-90564. (Consciousness of Commitment Ser.: Vol. 8, Bk. 1). 740p. pap. write for info. (*1-929064-01-2*, 2001-1, Pub. by Brandt Pubns) First Bks.

— The Seventh Seal. LC 99-90568. (Consciousness of Commitment Ser.: Vol. 8, Bk. 6). 550p. pap. write for info. (*1-929064-06-3*, 2006-1, Pub. by Brandt Pubns) First Bks.

Brandt, Bruce & Brandt, Edward R. Where to Look for Hard-to-Find German-Speaking Ancestors in Eastern Europe: Index to 19,729 Surnames in 13 Books, with Historical Background on Each Settlement. 2nd ed. 148p. 1998. pap. 18.50 (*0-8063-4530-6*, 9042) Clearfield Co.

Brandt, C. Jane. Mediterranean Desertification. text 149.00 (*0-471-98555-4*) Wiley.

Brandt, C. Jane & Thornes, John B., eds. Mediterranean Desertification & Land Use. LC 95-26001. 572p. 1996. 200.00 (*0-471-94250-2*) Wiley.

Brandt, C. Jane, ed. see Diede, Pauline N.

Brandt, Carol, jt. ed. see Higham, Robin.

Brandt, Catharine. We Light the Candles: Devotions Related to Family Use of the Advent Wreath. 40p. (J). 1991. pap. 5.99 (*0-8066-1544-3*, 10-15443, Augsburg) Augsburg Fortress.

Brandt, Catherine, jt. auth. see Stoll, Irma.

Brandt, Charles. Self & Environment. 1997. pap. 7.95 (*0-85305-427-4*, 1942, Pub. by Arthur James) Morehouse Pub.

Brandt, Conrad R. GLpro for Windows - Foundations. LC 97-92876. (Illus.). 416p. 1998. pap. 39.95 (*0-9661871-6-4*) Pallas FL.

***Brandt, Conrad R.** GLPRO Foundations, 2000. LC 00-190051. (Illus.). 464p. 2000. pap. 39.95 (*0-9661871-7-2*) Pallas FL.

Brandt Corstius, H., ed. Grammars for Number Names. (Foundations of Language Supplementary Ser.: No. 7). 123p. 1968. text 85.50 (*90-277-0023-0*) Kluwer Academic.

Brandt, D. & Martin, T. Automated Systems Based on Human Skill: Joint Design of Technology & Organisation. LC 97-137864. (IFAC Postprint Ser.). 266p. 1996. pap. 73.50 (*0-08-042379-5*, Pergamon Pr) Elsevier.

***Brandt, Daniel A. & Warner, J. C.** Metallurgy Fundamentals. LC 98-48494. (Illus.). 300p. (YA). (gr. 9-12). 1999. text 32.64 (*1-56637-543-6*) Goodheart.

Brandt, David. Is That All There Is? Balancing Expectation & Disappointment in Your Life. LC 98-23198. 224p. 1998. pap. 15.95 (*1-886230-13-7*) Impact Pubs CA.

Brandt, David, jt. auth. see Kriegel, Robert J.

Brandt, David, ed. see Brandt, Kari F.

Brandt, David E. & Zlotnick, S. Jack. The Psychology & Treatment of the Youthful Offender. (Illus.). 262p. 1988. pap. 33.95 (*0-398-06027-4*) C C Thomas.

— The Psychology & Treatment of the Youthful Offender. (Illus.). 262p. (C). 1988. text 45.95 (*0-398-05454-1*) C C Thomas.

Brandt, Deborah. Literacy As Involvement: The Acts of Writers, Readers, & Texts. LC 89-27409. 224p. (C). 1990. text 26.95 (*0-8093-1570-X*) S Ill U Pr.

Brandt, Di. Agnes in the Sky. 1997. pap. 7.95 (*0-88801-150-4*, Pub. by Turnstone Pr) Genl Dist Srvs.

— Dancing Naked. 200p. 1997. pap. 16.50 (*1-55128-034-5*, Pub. by Mercury Bk) LPC InBook.

— Jerusalem, Beloved. 71p. 1997. pap. 9.95 (*0-88801-196-2*, Pub. by Turnstone Pr) Genl Dist Srvs.

— Questions I Asked My Mother. 1997. pap. 7.95 (*0-88801-115-6*, Pub. by Turnstone Pr) Genl Dist Srvs.

Brandt, Dietrich & Cernetic, Janko, eds. Automated Systems Based on Human Skill 1997. LC 98-36224. 225p. 1998. write for info. (*0-08-043024-4*, Pergamon Pr) Elsevier.

Brandt, Douglas, et al. Modern Physics Simulations: The Consortium for Upper Level Physics Software. LC 95-35661. 192p. 1995. pap. text 46.95 incl. disk (*0-471-54882-0*) Wiley.

Brandt, E. N. Growth Company: Dow Chemical's First Century. LC 97-749. 1997. 39.95 (*0-87013-426-4*) Mich St U Pr.

Brandt, Ed. Rafael Palmeiro: At Home with the Baltimore Orioles. LC 97-8668. (Illus.). 128p. (YA). (gr. 4-6). 1997. lib. bdg. 21.95 (*1-883845-37-8*) M Lane Pubs.

Brandt, Edward, tr. see Clarke, Beverly G.

Brandt, Edward N., Jr., et al, eds. Enabling America: Assessing the Role of Rehabilitation Science & Engineering. LC 97-21183. 475p. 1997. 47.95 (*0-309-06374-4*) Natl Acad Pr.

Brandt, Edward R. Contents & Addresses of Hungarian Archives: With Supplementary Information for Research on German-Speaking Ancestors from Hungary. 2nd ed. 85p. 1998. pap. 15.00 (*0-8063-4607-8*, 9041) Clearfield Co.

— Where Once They Toiled: A Visit to the Former Mennonite Homelands in the Vistula River Valley. 28p. 1992. pap. 4.50 (*1-883294-04-5*) Masthof Pr.

Brandt, Edward R., et al. Germanic Genealogy: A Guide to Worldwide Sources & Migration Patterns. 2nd ed. (Illus.). 520p. 1997. pap. 32.00 (*0-9644337-3-7*) Germanic Geneal.

Brandt, Edward R., jt. auth. see Brandt, Bruce.

***Brandt, Elizabeth.** Community Action at Work: TAP's 30-Year War on Poverty. 168p. 2000. pap. write for info. (*0-936015-87-X*) Pocahontas Pr.

Brandt, Eric. Dangerous Liaisons: Blacks, Gays, & the Struggle for Equality. LC 98-56062. 336p. 1999. 22.95 (*1-56584-455-6*, Pub. by New Press NY) Norton.

Brandt-Finell, Dorey, jt. auth. see Simon, Ethelyn.

Brandt, Frans M. Personality & Love: An Illustrated Primer on Understanding Human Relationships. (Illus.). 110p. 1998. pap. 14.95 (*1-57502-858-1*, PO2326) Morris Pubng.

***Brandt, Frans M.** The Renewed Mind. LC 99-60156. 208p. 1998. pap. 14.95 (*1-57921-209-3*, Pub. by WinePress Pub) BookWorld.

***Brandt, Frans M. J.** The Consistent Overcomer: How to Have a Victorious Life. LC 99-67062. 204p. 2000. pap. 14.95 (*1-57921-256-5*, Pub. by WinePress Pub) BookWorld.

Brandt, Frederick B. Shattering the Southern Stereotype: Jack Beal, Nell Blaine, Dorothy Coillespie, Sally Mann, Cy Twombly. (Illus.). 36p. 1998. pap. 10.00 (*1-890327-04-2*) Longwood Ctr.

Brandt, Frederick R. Late Nineteenth Century & Early Twentieth Century Decorative Arts: The Sydney & Frances Lewis Collection in the Virginia Museum of Fine Arts. Hamm, Monica M., ed. LC 85-22499. (Illus.). 285p. 1985. pap. 24.95 (*0-917046-16-1*) Va Mus Arts.

— Late Twentieth Century Art: Selections from the Sydney & Frances Lewis Collection in the Virginia Museum of Fine Arts. Spanel, Donald, ed. LC 85-21708. (Illus.). 216p. 1985. 35.00 (*0-917046-22-6*) Va Mus Arts.

Brandt, Frederick R. & Hight, Eleanor M. German Expressionist Art: The Ludwig & Rosy Fischer Collection. Barriault, Anne B., ed. LC 86-28182. (Illus.). 1987. 24.00 (*0-917046-26-9*); pap. 12.00 (*0-917046-25-0*) Va Mus Arts.

***Brandt, Gareth.** Awesome God. (Fast Lane Bible Studies). 43p. (YA). (gr. 7-9). 1999. pap. 9.95 (*0-87303-335-3*) Faith & Life.

Brandt, Geeraert. History of the Reformation & Other Ecclesiastical Transactions in, & about, the Low Countries, from the Beginning of the Eighth Century down to the End of the Famous Synod of Dort, 4 vols. in 2. LC 70-130625. reprint ed. 365.00 (*0-404-07960-1*) AMS Pr.

Brandt, George W. Modern Theories of Drama: A Selection of Writings on Drama & Theatre. LC 97-27188. 356p. 1999. text 90.00 (*0-19-871140-9*); pap. text 18.95 (*0-19-871139-5*) OUP.

***Brandt, Gloria & Lorenzini, Kathryn.** Learn the Art of Permanent Makeup: A Comprehensive Training Manual. 1999. 74.95 (*0-9672362-1-5*) K&G Perm Makeup.

— Learn the Art of Permanent Makeup: A Comprehensive Training Manual. (SPA., Illus.). 68p. 1999. 74.95 (*0-9672362-0-7*) K&G Perm Makeup.

An Asterisk (*) at the beginning of an entry indicates that the title is appearing for the first time.

Brandt, Gloria, et al. Spring's Promise: Four Inspirational Novellas of Budding Springtime. 341p. 1999. pap. 4.97 (*1-57748-501-7*) Barbour Pub.

Brandt, Godfrey L. The Realization of Anti-Racist Teaching. 220p. 1987. pap. 29.95 (*1-85000-127-8*, Falmer Pr) Taylor & Francis.

Brandt, H. Libre de las Ataduras del Pecado.Tr. of Breaking Free from the Bondage of Sin. (SPA.). 198p. 1996. 8.99 (*1-56063-969-5*, 497388) Editorial Unilit.

Brandt, H. E. Selected Papers on Nonlinear Optics. 1991. pap. 45.00 (*0-8194-0631-7*, VOL. MS32) SPIE.

Brandt, Henny & Skinner, Kenny. The Heart of the Problem. 2nd rev. ed. LC 98-15632. 272p. 1998. pap. 14.99 (*0-8054-1667-6*) Broadman.

Brandt, Henry. I Want to Enjoy My Children. rev. ed. Skinner, Kerry L., ed. 224p. 1995. 15.00 (*0-9648743-1-8*) H Blackaby.

***Brandt, Henry.** The Word for the Wise: Making Scripture the Heart of Your Counseling Ministry. (Illus.). 1999. pap. 11.99 (*0-8054-2073-8*) Broadman.

Brandt, Henry & Skinner, Kerry L. I Want to Enjoy My Children. rev. ed. LC 96-177773. (Illus.). 228p. 1995. student ed. 15.00 (*0-9648743-0-X*) H Blackaby.

— Marriage: God's Way. LC 99-23279. 1999. 18.99 (*0-8054-1971-3*) Broadman.

Brandt, Henry R. The Struggle for Peace - Chinese Edition. Hsu, Molica, tr. (CHI.). 120p. 1993. pap. 5.50 (*1-56582-042-8*) Christ Renew Min.

Brandt, Henry R. & Skinner, Kerry L. The Heart of the Problem: How to Stop Coping & Find the Cure for Your Struggles. LC 96-33389. 240p. 1996. 16.99 (*0-8054-6060-8*, 4260-60) Broadman.

Brandt, Herwig. Die Sklaven in Den Rollen Von Dienern und Vertrauten Bei Euripides. (Altertumswissenschaftliche Texte und Studien: No. 1). iv, 148p. 1973. 30.00 (*3-487-04777-2*) G Olms Pubs.

***Brandt, Hilary H. & Chaplin, Adrienne.** Art & Soul: Signposts for Christians in the Arts. (Illus.). 212p. 1999. reprint ed. pap. 25.00 (*1-900507-82-X*, Pub. by Piquant UK) OM Literature.

Brandt, Hilary H., ed. see Zviglyanich, Vladimir A.

Brandt, Howard E., ed. Intense Microwave Pulses IV, Vol. 2843. 338p. 1996. 94.00 (*0-8194-2231-2*) SPIE.

***Brandt, Howard E., ed.** Intense Microwave Pulses VI. 180p. 1999. pap. text 72.00 (*0-8194-3176-1*) SPIE.

Brandt, Ira K., jt. auth. see Weaver, David D.

Brandt, J. Horned Giants: Hunting Eurasian Wild Cattle. limited ed. 1997. 80.00 (*1-57157-036-5*) Safari Pr.

Brandt, J. D., jt. auth. see Sadun, A. A.

Brandt, J. Donald. A History of Gannett 1906-1993. (Illus.). 550p. 1993. write for info. (*0-944347-01-0*) USA Today Bks.

***Brandt, Jane.** Drinks Without Liquor: Slurpies & Smoothies, Cocktails & Punches, 200 Fresh, Fast & Fruity Little Sips & Great Big Gulps. rev. ed. LC 99-30062. (Illus.). 128p. 1999. pap. 7.95 (*0-7611-1573-0*) Workman Pub.

Brandt, Janet, et al. Quick-Sew Fleece: Fast & Fun Fleece for All Seasons from America's Top Designers. LC 98-28575. (Best-Loved Designers' Collections). (Illus.). 128p. 1998. pap. 27.95 (*1-56477-231-4*, DB351, PasTimes) Martingale & Co.

Brandt, Janet C. Special-Occasion Table Runners. (Illus.). 96p. 1999. pap. 21.95 (*1-56477-239-X*, B369, That Patchwrk Pl) Martingale & Co.

***Brandt, Jennifur.** Life Is a Movie Starring You: Guide to Living Your Dreams. 2000. pap. 12.95 (*0-446-67633-0*) Warner Bks.

Brandt, Joan E. Geopoetics: The Politics of Mimesis in Poststructuralist French Poetry & Theory. LC 96-23400. 1997. write for info. (*0-8047-2760-0*); pap. write for info. (*0-8047-2761-9*) Stanford U Pr.

Brandt, Jobst. Das Fahrrad-Rad. (Illus.). 150p. 1995. 24.99 (*0-9607236-5-X*) Natl Acad Pr.

Brandt, Johanna. Argumentative Struktur in Senecas Tragodien. (Beitrage Zur Altertumswissenschaft Ser.: Band 5). (GER.). x, 346p. 1986. 50.00 (*3-487-07803-1*) G Olms Pubs.

— The Grape Cure. 192p. 1971. pap. 2.95 (*0-87904-002-5*) Lust.

— The Grape Cure. 191p. 1996. reprint ed. pap. 16.50 (*0-7873-0119-1*) Hlth Research.

— How to Conquer Cancer Naturally. 3rd rev. ed. Leonardo, Bianca, ed. LC 89-20208. 96p. 1996. pap. 9.95 (*0-930852-35-4*) Tree Life Pubns.

Brandt, John C. Rendezvous in Space: The Science of Comets. LC 91-41170. 1992. pap. text 23.95 (*0-7167-2175-9*) W H Freeman.

Brandt, John C., et al, eds. The Scientific Impact of the Goddard High Resolution Spectrograph. LC 98-71645. (Conference Series Proceedings: Vol. 143). 445p. 1998. 52.00 (*1-886733-63-5*) Astron Soc Pacific.

Brandt, John C. & Chapman, Robert D. The Comet Book. (Illus.). 176p. 1984. pap. 14.95 (*0-86720-029-4*) Jones & Bartlett.

— Introduction to Comets. LC 76-47207. 254p. 1982. pap. text 29.95 (*0-521-27218-1*) Cambridge U Pr.

Brandt, John C., jt. auth. see Petersen, Carolyn C.

Brandt, John H. Soul of the Hunter: A Half Century of Big Game Hunting. LC 96-80505. (Illus.). 308p. (Orig.). 1997. 50.00 (*0-9621314-0-7*) Jungle Tracks.

Brandt, Joseph. Dismantling Racism: The Continuing Challenge to White America. LC 91-23449. 192p. 1991. pap. 15.99 (*0-8066-2576-7*, 9-2576) Augsburg Fortress.

— Gus Hall Bibliography. 181p. 1981. 9.95 (*0-87898-148-9*); pap. 4.95 (*0-87898-149-7*) New Outlook.

Brandt, K. & Apstein, C., eds. Nordisches Plankton, 1911-42, 7 vols. 1964. 720.00 (*90-6123-110-8*) Lubrecht & Cramer.

Brandt, Karen N. & Niederman, Sharon. Living Treasures: A Celebration of the Human Spirit. (Illus.). 216p. 1997. pap. text 32.50 (*1-889921-00-9*) Western Edge Pr.

Brandt, Kari F. Seasons of a Farm Family: A Time to Celebrate Life on the Farm with Recipes & Stories. Brandt, David, ed. LC 96-76030. (Illus.). 192p. 1996. pap. 15.95 (*0-942495-55-1*) Palmer Pubns Inc.

Brandt, Katherine, ed. see National Hospice Organization Staff.

Brandt, Katherine E., ed. see National Hospice Organization Staff.

Brandt, Kathy. It Happened in Gainsville. 1998. pap. 10.95 (*1-57532-070-3*) Press-Tige Pub.

Brandt, Keith. Abe Lincoln: The Young Years. LC 81-23172. (Illus.). 48p. (J). (gr. 4-6). 1997. lib. bdg. 17.25 (*0-89375-750-0*) Troll Communs.

— Abe Lincoln: The Young Years. LC 81-23172. (Illus.). 48p. (J). (gr. 4-6). 1997. pap. 3.95 (*0-89375-751-9*) Troll Communs.

Brandt, Keith. Abe Lincoln, the Young Years. 1982. 8.70 (*0-606-01469-1*, Pub. by Turtleback) Demco.

Brandt, Keith. Babe Ruth, Home Run Hero. LC 85-1091. (Illus.). 48p. (J). (gr. 4-6). 1996. pap. 3.95 (*0-8167-0554-2*) Troll Communs.

— Babe Ruth, Home Run Hero. LC 85-1091. (Illus.). 48p. (J). (gr. 4-6). 1997. lib. bdg. 17.25 (*0-8167-0553-4*) Troll Communs.

— Cabeza de Vaca: New World Explorer. LC 92-36960. (Illus.). 48p. (J). (gr. 4-6). 1997. pap. 3.95 (*0-8167-2830-5*) Troll Communs.

— Cabeza de Vaca: New World Explorer. LC 92-36960. (Illus.). 48p. (J). (gr. 4-6). 1997. lib. bdg. 17.25 (*0-8167-2829-1*) Troll Communs.

— Daniel Boone: Frontier Adventures. LC 82-15915. (Illus.). 48p. (J). (gr. 4-6). 1996. pap. 3.95 (*0-89375-844-2*) Troll Communs.

— Daniel Boone: Frontier Adventures. LC 82-15915. (Illus.). 48p. (J). (gr. 4-6). 1997. lib. bdg. 17.25 (*0-89375-843-4*) Troll Communs.

— Discovering Trees. LC 81-7522. (Illus.). 32p. (J). (gr. 2-4). 1982. lib. bdg. 17.25 (*0-89375-566-4*) Troll Communs.

— Discovering Trees. LC 81-7522. (Illus.). 32p. (J). (gr. 2-4). 1997. pap. 3.50 (*0-89375-567-2*) Troll Communs.

— Indian Crafts. LC 84-2588. (Illus.). 32p. (J). (gr. 3-6). 1985. pap. text 3.50 (*0-8167-0133-4*); lib. bdg. 14.50 (*0-8167-0132-6*) Troll Communs.

— Indian Festivals. LC 84-2644. (Illus.). 32p. (J). (gr. 3-6). 1985. pap. text 3.50 (*0-8167-0183-0*); lib. bdg. 14.50 (*0-8167-0182-2*) Troll Communs.

— Indian Homes. LC 84-2650. (Illus.). 32p. (J). (gr. 3-6). 1985. pap. text 3.50 (*0-8167-0127-X*); lib. bdg. 14.50 (*0-8167-0126-1*) Troll Communs.

— Jackie Robinson: A Life of Courage. LC 91-17852. (Illus.). 48p. (J). (gr. 4-6). 1996. pap. 3.95 (*0-8167-2506-3*) Troll Communs.

— John Paul Jones: Hero of the Seas. LC 82-16045. (Illus.). 48p. (J). (gr. 4-6). 1997. pap. 3.95 (*0-89375-850-7*) Troll Communs.

— John Paul Jones: Hero of the Seas. LC 82-16045. (Illus.). 48p. (J). (gr. 4-6). 1997. lib. bdg. 17.25 (*0-89375-849-3*) Troll Communs.

— Lafayette, Hero of Two Nations. LC 89-33981. (Illus.). 48p. (J). (gr. 4-6). 1997. pap. 3.95 (*0-8167-1772-9*) Troll Communs.

— Lafayette, Hero of Two Nations. LC 89-33981. (Illus.). 48p. (J). (gr. 4-6). 1997. lib. bdg. 17.25 (*0-8167-1771-0*) Troll Communs.

— Lou Gehrig, Pride of the Yankees. LC 85-1075. (Illus.). 48p. (J). (gr. 4-6). 1997. pap. 3.95 (*0-8167-0550-X*) Troll Communs.

— Lou Gehrig, Pride of the Yankees. LC 85-1075. (Illus.). 48p. (J). (gr. 4-6). 1997. lib. bdg. 17.25 (*0-8167-0549-6*) Troll Communs.

— Lou Gehrig, Pride of the Yankees. 1986. 8.70 (*0-606-01629-5*, Pub. by Turtleback) Demco.

— Marie Curie: Brave Scientist. LC 82-16092. (Illus.). 48p. (J). (gr. 4-6). 1996. pap. 3.95 (*0-89375-856-6*) Troll Communs.

— Marie Curie: Brave Scientist. LC 82-16092. (Illus.). 48p. (J). (gr. 4-6). 1997. lib. bdg. 17.25 (*0-89375-855-8*) Troll Communs.

Brandt, Keith. Marie Curie, Brave Scientist. (J). 1983. 8.70 (*0-606-03118-9*, Pub. by Turtleback) Demco.

Brandt, Keith. Paul Revere: Son of Liberty. LC 81-23147. (Illus.). 48p. (J). (gr. 4-6). 1982. pap. 3.95 (*0-89375-767-5*) Troll Communs.

— Paul Revere: Son of Liberty. LC 81-23147. (Illus.). 48p. (J). (gr. 4-6). 1997. lib. bdg. 17.25 (*0-89375-766-7*) Troll Communs.

— Pearl Bailey: With a Song in Her Heart. LC 92-20190. (Easy Biographies Library). (Illus.). 48p. (J). (gr. 4-6). 1992. lib. bdg. 17.25 (*0-8167-2921-2*, BP275) Troll Communs.

— Pearl Bailey: With a Song in Her Heart. LC 92-20190. (Illus.). 48p. (J). (gr. 4-6). 1996. pap. 4.95 (*0-8167-2922-0*) Troll Communs.

— Pearl Bailey: With a Song in Her Heart. 1993. 8.15 (*0-606-02828-5*, Pub. by Turtleback) Demco.

— Rosa Parks. (History Makers Ser.). (Illus.). 48p. (J). (gr. 4-6). 1998. pap. 3.95 (*0-8167-4558-7*) Troll Communs.

— Rosa Parks: Fight for Freedom. LC 91-34939. (Illus.). 48p. (J). (gr. 4-6). 1993. pap. 3.95 (*0-8167-2832-1*) Troll Communs.

— Rosa Parks: Fight for Freedom. LC 91-34939. (Women in History Ser.). (Illus.). 48p. (J). (gr. 4-6). 1997. lib. bdg. 12.89 (*0-8167-2831-3*, BR501) Troll Communs.

— What Makes It Rain? LC 81-7495. (Illus.). 32p. (J). (gr. 2-4). 1982. lib. bdg. 17.25 (*0-89375-582-6*) Troll Communs.

— What Makes It Rain? LC 81-7495. (Illus.). 32p. (J). (gr. 2-4). 1996. pap. 3.50 (*0-89375-583-4*) Troll Communs.

— Wonders of the Seasons. LC 81-7411. (Illus.). 32p. (J). (gr. 2-4). 1982. lib. bdg. 17.25 (*0-89375-580-X*) Troll Communs.

— Wonders of the Seasons. LC 81-7411. (Illus.). 32p. (J). (gr. 2-4). 1996. pap. 3.50 (*0-89375-581-8*) Troll Communs.

***Brandt, Kenneth D.** An Atlas of Osteoarthritis. (Encyclopedia of Visual Medicine Ser.). (Illus.). 120p. 2000. 85.00 (*1-85070-494-5*) Prthnon Pub.

Brandt, Kenneth D. Diagnosis & Nonsurgical Management of Osteoarthritis. (Illus.). 225p. 1996. pap. text 19.95 (*1-884735-09-6*) Prof Comms.

***Brandt, Kenneth D.** Diagnosis & Nonsurgical Management of Osteoarthritis. 2nd ed. 320p. 2000. pap. text 19.95 (*1-884735-57-6*) Prof Comms.

Brandt, Kenneth D., et al, eds. Osteoarthritis. LC 97-11747. (Illus.). 612p. (C). 1998. text 129.50 (*0-19-262755-X*) OUP.

Brandt, Kevin. Betty Hill Brandt: Favorite Family Recipes. 47p. 1999. pap. write for info. (*1-928813-04-6*) K Brandt.

— Commodities: I Used to Lose, Now I Win, Find Out How. 1999. pap. write for info. (*1-928813-02-X*) K Brandt.

— New Fish Tank Blues: How to Solve That Problem. (Illus.). 1999. pap. write for info. (*1-928813-03-8*) K Brandt.

— Stop Smoking in a Nutshell. 142p. 1999. pap. 19.95 (*1-928813-00-3*) K Brandt.

— Stop Smoking in a Nutshell. deluxe limited ed. 142p. 1999. pap. 29.95 (*1-928813-01-1*) K Brandt.

Brandt, Laura, ed. see Brandt, Betty.

Brandt, Lawrence J. Gastrointestinal Disorders of the Elderly. LC 84-9798. (Illus.). 638p. 1984. reprint ed. pap. 197.80 (*0-608-07256-7*, 206748300009) Bks Demand.

Brandt, Lawrence J. & Daum, Fredric. Clinical Practice of Gastroenterology, 2 vols. LC 98-22058. (Illus.). xxv, 1647, 84 p. 1999. write for info. (*0-443-06522-5*) Church.

Brandt, Lawrence J. & Steiner-Grossman, Penny, eds. Treating IBD: A Patient's Guide to the Medical & Surgical Management of Inflammatory Bowel Disease. (Illus.). 219p. 1989. pap. text 21.00 (*0-88167-532-6*, 1996) Lppncott W & W.

Brandt, Leslie F. Psalms Now. LC 96-14857. 224p. 1996. 12.99 (*0-570-04257-7*) Concordia.

Brandt, Lewis W. Psychologists Caught: A Psycho-Logic of Psychology. 248p. 1982. pap. 15.95 (*0-8020-6508-2*) U of Toronto Pr.

Brandt, Lilian. Five Hundred Seventy-Four Deserters & Their Families: A Descriptive Study of Their Characteristics & Circumstances. LC 72-169374. (Family in America Ser.). 210p. 1979. reprint ed. 23.95 (*0-405-03850-X*) Ayer.

Brandt, Linda, ed. Taste the Seasons. LC 85-51259. (Illus.). 136p. 1985. 18.95 (*0-9615260-0-9*) Woodside-Atherton.

Brandt, Loren. Commercialization & Agricultural Development in Central & Eastern China, 1870-1937. (Illus.). 246p. (C). 1990. text 59.95 (*0-521-37196-1*) Cambridge U Pr.

Brandt, M. E., jt. auth. see Jansen, B. H.

Brandt, Mary D. Faxing Safeguards: Guidelines for Transmitting Patient Health Information. 34p. 1997. pap. text 32.00 (*1-58426-005-X*, AB101097) Am Hlth Info.

— HIV & Confidentiality: Guidelines for Managing Health Information Relating to HIV Infection. 68p. 1997. pap. text 32.00 (*1-58426-004-1*, AB100997) Am Hlth Info.

— Release & Disclosure: Guidelines Regarding Maintenance & Disclosure of Health Information. 116p. 1997. pap. text 35.00 (*1-58426-007-6*, AB101197) Am Hlth Info.

Brandt, Nat. The Congressman Who Got Away with Murder. LC 90-26831. (Illus.). 276p. reprint ed. pap. 85.60 (*0-608-07595-7*, 205991000010) Bks Demand.

— Harlem at War: The Black Experience in WWII. 277p. (C). 1996. text 29.95 (*0-8156-0324-X*, BRHW) Syracuse U Pr.

— Harlem at War: The Black Experience in WWII. (Illus.). 272p. 1997. pap. 19.95 (*0-8156-0462-9*) Syracuse U Pr.

— The Man Who Tried to Burn New York. LC 86-5833. (York State Book Ser.). (Illus.). 308p. 1986. reprint ed. pap. 95.50 (*0-608-07597-3*, 205991200010) Bks Demand.

— Massacre in Shansi. LC 93-41314. (Illus.). 358p. 1994. reprint ed. pap. 111.00 (*0-608-07596-5*, 205991100010) Bks Demand.

— The Town That Started the Civil War. LC 89-26094. (Illus.). 336p. 1990. reprint ed. pap. 104.20 (*0-608-07598-1*, 205991300010) Bks Demand.

Brandt, Nat & Tubbs, Charles. Mr. Tubbs' Civil War. LC 96-21719. (Illus.). 240p. 1996. 34.95 (*0-8156-0391-6*, BRMT) Syracuse U Pr.

Brandt, P. A. & Leue, A. E. German-Afrikaans, Afrikaans-German School Dictionary: Schulwoerterbuch Deutsch-Afrikaans-Deutsch. 5th ed. (AFR & GER.). 401p. 1982. 24.95 (*0-8288-0541-5*, M5577) Fr & Eur.

Brandt, Pamela Robin, jt. auth. see Van Gelder, Lindsy.

Brandt, Patricia S. The Little Pupfish of Salt Creek: Death Valley National Park (Endangered Species) large type ed. LC 96-160951. (Illus.). 38p. (Orig.). (J). (gr. k-5). 1995. pap. 5.95 (*0-9649493-0-X*) P S Brandt.

Brandt, Paul, ed. Amorum Libri Tres. 239p. 1977. reprint ed. write for info. (*3-487-00370-8*) G Olms Pubs.

Brandt, Paul, see Licht, Hans, pseud.

Brandt, Paul, ed. see Ovid.

Brandt, Per A. La Charpente Modale du Sens Pour une Semio-Linguistique Morphogenetique et Dynamique. (Nouveaux Actes Semiotiques Ser.: No. 2). (FRE.). 368p. 1992. pap. 47.00 (*90-272-2268-1*) J Benjamins Pubng Co.

— Dynamiques du Sens: Etudes de Semiotique Modale. (Illus.). 283p. 1994. pap. 27.00 (*87-7288-513-0*, Pub. by Aarhus Univ Pr) David Brown.

Brandt, Per A. & Prassoloff, Annie. Qu-Est-Ce Qu-une Promesse? 148p. 1996. pap. 18.95 (*87-7288-398-7*, Pub. by Aarhus Univ Pr) David Brown.

Brandt, R. L. Gifts for the Marketplace. 224p. 1989. pap. 6.95 (*0-88144-142-2*) Christian Pub.

Brandt-Rauf, Paul W., jt. ed. see McCunney, Robert J.

Brandt, Reinhard. The Table of Judgments: Critique of Pure Reason A67-76; B92-101. Watkins, Eric, tr. (North American Kant Society Studies in Philosophy: Vol. 4). ix, 151p. (Orig.). (C). 1996. pap. text 20.00 (*0-924922-24-9*); lib. bdg. 39.00 (*0-924922-74-5*) Ridgeview.

Brandt, Reinhard, ed. John Locke: Symposium Wolfenbuttel, Nineteen Hundred Seventy-Nine. 288p. (C). 1980. text 54.65 (*3-11-008266-7*) De Gruyter.

Brandt, Rhonda, jt. auth. see Reece, Barry L.

Brandt, Richard B. Facts, Values & Morality. 326p. (C). 1996. text 64.95 (*0-521-57059-X*); pap. text 20.95 (*0-521-57827-2*) Cambridge U Pr.

— Morality, Utilitarianism, & Rights. 403p. (C). 1992. text 74.95 (*0-521-41507-1*); pap. text 24.95 (*0-521-42527-1*) Cambridge U Pr.

— A Theory of the Good & the Right. LC 98-17904. (Illus.). 362p. 1998. reprint ed. pap. 18.95 (*1-57392-220-X*) Prometheus Bks.

Brandt, Richard C. Flip Charts: How to Draw Them & How to Use Them. LC 86-73086. (Illus.). 88p. (Orig.). 1987. pap. 24.95 (*0-88390-031-9*) Brandt Mgmt Grp.

Brandt, Richard M. Incentive Pay & Career Ladders for Today's Teachers: A Study of Current Programs & Practices. LC 89-48220. (SUNY Series in Educational Leadership). 286p. (C). 1990. text 24.50 (*0-7914-0399-8*) State U NY Pr.

— Studying Behavior in Natural Settings. LC 81-40189. (Illus.). 416p. 1981. reprint ed. pap. text 30.00 (*0-8191-1830-3*) U Pr of Amer.

Brandt, Robert. Middle Tennessee on Foot: Hikes in the Woods & Walks on Country Roads. LC 97-52606. (Illus.). 1998. pap. 12.95 (*0-89587-212-9*) Blair.

— Touring the Middle Tennessee Backroads. LC 95-15101. (Touring the Backroads Ser.). (Illus.). 412p. (Orig.). 1995. pap. 16.95 (*0-89587-129-7*) Blair.

Brandt, Robert J. & Bicket, Zenas J. The Spirit Helps Us Pray: A Biblical Theology of Prayer. 464p. 1994. 26.99 (*0-88243-678-3*) Gospel Pub.

Brandt, Robert L. A Heart for the Lost. (Spiritual Discovery Ser.). 96p. 1996. pap., teacher ed. 9.95 (*0-88243-213-3*, 02-0213); pap., student ed. 4.95 (*0-88243-113-7*, 02-0113) Gospel Pub.

— A New Way of Life: A Discipleship Manual for New Christians. Hayes, Clancy P., ed. LC 95-76164. 96p. 1995. pap. text 9.95 (*0-88243-204-4*) Gospel Pub.

— A New Way of Life: A Discipleship Manual for New Christians. Hayes, Clancy P., ed. LC 95-79773. (Spiritual Discovery Ser.). 96p. (YA). (gr. 9 up). 1995. pap. text, student ed. 4.95 (*0-88243-104-8*) Gospel Pub.

Brandt, Robert S., jt. ed. see Sierra Club, Tennessee Chapter Staff.

Brandt, Robin. Big Cats. 1998. 17.99 (*0-7858-0985-6*) Bk Sales Inc.

— Wolves. 1999. pap. text 17.99 (*0-7858-1048-X*) Bk Sales Inc.

Brandt, Robin, jt. auth. see Bandsma, Arend.

Brandt, Roger G. Las Vegas to Death Valley Road Guide: History, Geology, Etc. Seen on Roads Between Las Vegas & Death Valley National Park. LC 96-68899. (Illus.). 80p. (Orig.). 1996. pap. 7.95 (*1-889275-04-2*, 11) Pupfish Publns.

Brandt, Ron. Powerful Learning. LC 98-17715. 94p. 1998. pap. 8.95 (*0-87120-305-7*, 198179) ASCD.

— Survival at Sea. (Illus.). 88p. 1994. pap. 15.95 (*0-87364-770-X*) Paladin Pr.

***Brandt, Ronald S., ed.** Education in a New Era. (Illus.). 246p. 2000. pap. 24.95 (*0-87120-363-4*) ASCD.

Brandt, Ronald S., jt. auth. see McBrien, J. Lynn.

Brandt, Rose, jt. auth. see Loman, Susan.

***Brandt, S.** Entrepreneuring - Building a Growth Company. 1998. pap. 347.50 (*81-86982-60-4*, Pub. by Business Pubns) St Mut.

Brandt, S. Statistical & Computational Methods in Data Analysis. 3rd ed. Cowan, G., tr. from GER. LC 98-11969. (Illus.). 696p. 1998. 69.00 incl. cd-rom (*0-387-98498-4*) Spr-Verlag.

Brandt, S. & Dahmen, H. D. Quantum Mechanics on the Macintosh. (Illus.). x, 306p. 1992. 49.95 incl. disk (*0-387-97627-2*) Spr-Verlag.

— Quantum Mechanics on the PC: Macintosh Supplement. (Illus.). 16p. 1991. pap. 19.95 incl. disk (*0-387-14105-7*) Spr-Verlag.

— Quantum Mechanics on the Personal Computer. (Illus.). x, 267p. 1991. 49.50 (*0-387-51541-0*) Spr-Verlag.

— Quantum Mechanics on the Personal Computer. 2nd ed. LC 92-25960. (Illus.). xxi, 267p. 1992. write for info. (*3-540-55722-9*); 59.00 incl. disk (*0-387-55722-9*) Spr-Verlag.

— Quantum Mechanics on the Personal Computer. 3rd ed. LC 93-49418. (Illus.). 327p. 1995. 59.00 incl. disk (*0-387-57470-0*) Spr-Verlag.

Brandt, Siegmund & Dahmen, Hans D. The Picture Book of Quantum Mechanics. 2nd ed. LC 94-30916. (Illus.). 423p. 1995. 49.95 (*0-387-94380-3*) Spr-Verlag.

— Quantum Mechanics on the Macintosh. 2nd ed. LC 94-19963. (Illus.). x, 305p. 1997. 49.95 (*0-387-94272-6*) Spr-Verlag.

Brandt, Steven A., et al. Introduction to Aeronautics: A Design Perspective. LC 97-15439. (Education Ser.). 350p. 1997. 94.95 (*1-56347-250-3*) AIAA.

B

An Asterisk (*) at the beginning of an entry indicates that the title is appearing for the first time.

Brandt, Steven C. Entrepreneuring: The Ten Commandments for Building a Growth Company. LC 82-1660. 225p. 1982. 12.95 (*0-201-10382-6*) Addison-Wesley.
— Entrepreneuring: The Ten Commandments for Building a Growth Company. 3rd rev. ed. LC 96-85780. (Illus.). 208p. 1997. pap. 14.95 (*1-888925-02-7*) Archiplgo Pub.
— Focus Your Business: Strategic Planning in Emerging Companies. 2nd rev. ed. LC 96-85842. Orig. Title: Strategic Planning in Emerging Companies. (Illus.). 224p. 1997. pap. 14.95 (*1-888925-03-5*) Archiplgo Pub.
***Brandt, Steven C.** Locals Only, A Small County in the Sea. 70p. 2000. pap. write for info. (*1-888925-22-1*) Archiplgo Pub.
Brandt, Steven C. Strategic Planning in Emerging Companies. (Illus.). 192p. 1981. 23.95 (*0-201-00942-0*) Addison-Wesley.
Brandt, Steven C., et al. Stay Out of Court & in Business: Every Manager's Guide to Minimizing Legal Troubles. LC 97-73783. (Illus.). 210p. 1997. pap. 19.95 (*1-888925-10-8*) Archiplgo Pub.
Brandt, Sue R. State Flags: Including the Commonwealth of Puerto Rico. LC 92-8948. (Our State Symbols Ser.). (YA). 1992. lib. bdg. 24.00 (*0-531-20001-9*) Watts.
— State Trees: Including the Commonwealth of Puerto Rico. LC 92-8946. (Our State Symbols Ser.). 64p. (YA). 1992. lib. bdg. 24.00 (*0-531-20000-0*) Watts.
Brandt, Susan E., ed. see League of Women Voters of Pennsylvania Education F.
Brandt, T. Vertigo: Its Multisensory Syndromes. Conomy, John P. & Swash, Michael, eds. (Clinical Medicine & the Nervous System Ser.). (Illus.). 344p. 1992. 125.00 (*0-387-19636-6*) Spr-Verlag.
Brandt, Thomas. Vertigo: Its Multisensory Syndromes. 2nd ed. LC 98-26294. (Clinical Medicine & the Nervous System Ser.). 506p. 1999. 249.00 (*3-540-19934-9*) Spr-Verlag.
Brandt, Thomas, et al, eds. Clinical Disorders of Balance, Posture & Gait. LC 96-4706. (Arnold Publication). 360p. 1996. text 98.50 (*0-340-60145-0*, Pub. by E A) OUP.
— Neurological Disorders: Course & Treatment. (Illus.). 1150p. 1996. text 159.95 (*0-12-125830-0*) Acad Pr.
Brandt, Tom. Reaching Public Goals: Managing Government For Results, A Resource Guide. 84p. 1996. per. 8.00 (*0-16-048875-3*) USGPO.
Brandt, V. Etudes for Trumpet. 64p. 1985. pap. 5.95 (*0-7935-3618-9*, 00120234) H Leonard.
Brandt, Walter I. & Lehmann, Helmut T., eds. Luther's Works: The Christian in Society II, Vol. 45. LC 55-9893. 1962. 30.00 (*0-8006-0345-1*, Fortress Pr) Augsburg Fortress.
***Brandt, William.** Alpha Male. 192p. 2000. pap. 18.95 (*0-86473-378-X*, Pub. by Victoria Univ Pr) Paul & Co Pubs.
Brandt, William. The Spirit Helps Us Pray. Life Publishers International Staff, tr. (RUS.). 475p. (C). 1999. write for info. (*0-7361-0082-2*) Life Pubs Intl.
Brandt, William K. & Sampson, Anthony, eds. North-South: A Program for Survival (The Brandt Report) 304p. (Orig.). 1980. pap. text 13.00 (*0-262-52059-1*) MIT Pr.
Brandt, William K., jt. auth. see Hulbert, James M.
Brandt, William K., jt. frwd. see Henry, Frances.
Brandt, Willy. Arms & Hunger. Victor Gollancz, Ltd. Staff, tr. from GER. 208p. 1987. pap. text 11.50 (*0-262-52127-X*) MIT Pr.
— The Ordeal of Coexistence. LC 63-15113. 120p. reprint ed. pap. 37.20 (*0-7837-2228-1*, 205731800004) Bks Demand.
Brandt, Willy, ed. EEC & the Third World, A Survey: The Atlantic Rift, Vol. 3. 242p. 1983. pap. 27.50 (*0-8419-0870-2*) Holmes & Meier.
— EEC & the Third World, A Survey: The Atlantic Rift, Vol. 3. 242p. 1983. 35.00 (*0-8419-0896-6*) Holmes & Meier.
Brandts, Robert. As We Drifted & Other Poems. LC 72-87039. 1972. pap. 3.00 (*0-87922-013-9*) Christophers Bks.
***Brandtstadter, Jochen & Lerner, Richard M., eds.** Action & Self-Development: Theory & Research Through the Life Span. LC 99-6325. 540p. 1999. 85.00 (*0-7619-1543-5*) Sage.
Brandvik, Mary L. English Teacher's Survival Guide: Ready-to-Use Techniques & Materials. LC 93-43186. 256p. 1994. pap. text 28.95 (*0-87628-298-2*) Ctr Appl Res.
— Writing Process Activities Kit. 288p. (C). 1990. pap. text 29.95 (*0-87628-968-5*) P-H.
Brandvold, D. C. Water Treatment: Industrial, Commercial & Municipal. 2nd ed. (Illus.). 1982. pap. 5.00 (*0-9610178-0-5*) DCB Enter.
— Water Treatment: Industrial, Commercial & Municipal. 3rd ed. LC 93-73324. (Illus.). 164p. (C). 1994. pap. text 15.00 (*0-9610178-1-3*) DCB Enter.
Brandvold, Dan. Wingshooter's Guide to Washington: Upland Birds & Waterfowl. 2000. pap. 26.95 (*1-885106-75-0*) Wild Adven Pr.
***Brandvold, Peter.** Blood Mountain, 1 vol. 258p. 1999. mass mkt. 5.99 (*0-425-16976-6*) Berkley Pub.
— Dakota Kill. LC 99-51785. 288p. 2000. 23.95 (*0-312-87212-7*, Pub. by Forge NYC) St Martin.
— Dakota Kill. 1999. mass mkt. 6.99 (*0-8125-7929-1*) Tor Bks.
Brandvold, Peter. Once a Marshal. 288p. 1998. pap. 5.99 (*0-425-16622-8*) Berkley Pub.
***Brandvold, Peter.** Once More with a .44. 2000. mass mkt. 5.99 (*0-425-17556-1*) Berkley Pub.
***Brandwein, Michael.** Training Terrific Staff! A Handbook of Practical & Creative Tools for Camps. LC 99-94647. x, 407p. 1999. spiral bd. 44.95 (*0-9670321-0-5*) M Brandwein.
Brandwein, Pamela. Reconstructing Reconstruction: The Supreme Court & the Production of Historical Truth. LC 98-35155. 1999. 17.95 (*0-8223-2316-8*); pap. 49.95 (*0-8223-2284-6*) Duke.
Brandwein, Paul F., jt. auth. see Morholt, Evelyn.
Brandwein, Pearl J. Mary Queen of Scots in Nineteenth & Twentieth Century Drama: Poetic License with History. (American University Studies: General Literature: Ser. XIX, Vol. 13). XXII, 268p. (C). 1989. text 42.95 (*0-8204-0628-7*) P Lang Pubng.
Brandwein, Peter, jt. ed. see Danzig, Allison.
Brandwein, Ruth A. Battered Women, Children, & Welfare Reform: The Ties That Bind. LC 98-40067. (Series on Violence Against Women). 192p. 1998. 36.00 (*0-7619-1148-0*); pap. 14.99 (*0-7619-1149-9*) Sage.
Brandwein, Yehuda. Tikune Zohar: Hebrew Text, 3 vols., 2. 850p. 1973. write for info. (*0-943688-28-0*) Res Ctr Kabbalah.
— Tikunei Zohar: Hebrew Text, 3 vols., 1. 850p. 1973. write for info. (*0-943688-27-2*) Res Ctr Kabbalah.
Brandwein, Yehuda, jt. auth. see Berg, Philip S.
Brandy Advisory Board Staff. California Brandy Drinks, Cocktails, Punches, Coffee, & Hot Drinks. Hebert, Malcolm P., ed. (Illus.). 160p. 1981. 6.95 (*0-932664-21-0*) Wine Appreciation.
Brandy, Lois S. I Do. Kennedy, Marla H. & Martin, Susan, eds. (Illus.). 96p. 1998. 14.95 (*1-890576-02-6*, 810071) Picture This.
Brandy, Tim. So What? Teaching Children What Matters in Math. LC 99-35787. 144p. 1999. pap. text 17.00 (*0-325-00176-6*) Heinemann.
Brandyopadhyay, A. K. Coastal Soils & Their Management. 270p. 1997. pap. 250.00 (*81-7089-220-1*, Pub. by Intl Bk Distr) St Mut.
Brandys, Kazimierz. Letters to Mrs. Z. Edelson, Morris, tr. LC 87-70598. 176p. 1987. pap. 15.00 (*0-913204-19-6*) December Pr.
— Letters to Mrs. Z. Edelson, Morris, tr. 1986. pap. 5.00 (*0-317-17750-8*) Quixote.
— A question of reality / LC 80-10793. (ENG.). 180 p. :p. 1980. write for info. (*0-684-16599-6*) Free Pr.
Brandys, Robert C. Hazard Communication - Right-to-Know for Health Care Facilities. LC 90-14463. (Management & Compliance Ser.: Vol. 6). (Illus.). 150p. 1991. ring bd. 110.00 (*0-87258-532-8*, 055205) Am Hospital.
Brandywine Conservancy Staff. Brandywine Critters: Nature Crafts from "A Brandywine Christmas" LC 95-34637. (Illus.). 96p. 1995. 16.95 (*1-56148-178-5*) Good Bks PA.
Brandywine Press Staff. Thinking & Writing: A Guide for College Students. (Illus.). 168p. (C). 1997. pap. text 6.50 (*1-881089-41-X*) Brandywine Press.
Branemark, Ingvar, et al. Osseointegration in Skeletal Reconstruction & Joint Replacement: 2nd International Workshop on Osseointegration in Skeletal Reconstruction & Joint Replacement, Rancho Santa Fe, California, October 27-29, 1994. LC 96-51486. 232p. 1997. pap. text 98.00 (*0-86715-325-3*) Quint Pub Co.
Branemark, P. I., jt. auth. see Worthington, Philip.
Branemark, Per-Ingvar & Oliveira, Marcelo F. Craniofacial Prostheses: Anaplastology & Osseointegration. LC 96-50068. 136p. 1997. text 98.00 (*0-86715-321-0*) Quint Pub Co.
Branemark, Per-Ingvar, et al. Rehabilitation of Complex Craniomaxillofacial Defects: The Challenge of Bauru. LC 98-49081. 1999. 98.00 (*0-86715-356-3*) Quint Pub Co.
— Tissue-Integrated Prostheses. (Illus.). 352p. 1985. text 96.00 (*0-86715-129-3*) Quint Pub Co.
Branemark, Per-Ingvar, ed. see Anemark, B. R.
Branen, et al. Food Additives. (Food Science & Technology Ser.: No. 35). (Illus.). 720p. 1989. text 250.00 (*0-8247-8046-9*) Dekker.
Branen, Alfred L. & Davidson, P. Michael, eds. Antimicrobials in Foods. fac. ed. LC 83-18829. (Food Science Ser.: No. 10). 479p. pap. 148.50 (*0-7837-7397-8*, 204719100006) Bks Demand.
Branen, Alfred Larry, et al. Food Additives. 2nd expanded rev. ed. (Food Science & Technology Ser.). (Illus.). Date not set. text. write for info. (*0-8247-9343-9*, 9343-9) Dekker.
Branen, Alfred Larry, jt. ed. see Davidson, P. Michael.
Braner, Dana, et al. CD-ROM for Pediatrics: An Interactive Program. Bralow, Lisette, ed. (C). 1998. text 95.00 (*0-7216-7612-X*, W B Saunders Co) Harcrt Hlth Sci Grp.
Braner, Julia. Mixing Methods: Qualitative & Quantitative Research. 192p. 1995. pap. 31.95 (*1-85972-116-8*, Pub. by Avebry) Ashgate Pub Co.
Branfield, Edwin. Antique Barometers: An Illustrated Survey. 1997. pap. text 14.95 (*0-948382-04-X*, Pub. by Baros Bks) Antique Collect.
Branfield, John. Lanhydrock Days. (Acorn Modern Classics Ser.). 96p. (YA). (gr. 7-10). 1992. pap. 8.95 (*0-575-05081-0*, Pub. by V Gollancz) Trafalgar.
Branfield, Wilfred. Continuous Creation: A Biological Concept of the Nature of Matter. 2nd rev. ed. Mattingly, John, ed. & intro. by. (Illus.). 128p. (C). 1994. reprint ed. text 14.95 (*0-916508-48-X*) Happiness Pr.
Branfman, Steve. Raku: A Practical Approach. LC 90-55875. (Illus.). 176p. 1991. pap. 26.95 (*0-8019-8023-2*) Krause Pubns.
Branfman, Steven. The Potter's Professional Handbook: A Guide to Defining, Identifying & Establishing Yourself in the Craft Community. LC 98-84101. (Illus.). 240p. 1999. pap. 29.95 (*0-87341-678-3*, POTBUS) Krause Pubns.
Branfman, Yaakov, jt. auth. see Tatz, Akiva.
Branford, H. Chance of Safety. mass mkt. 11.95 (*0-340-69963-9*, Pub. by Hodder & Stought Ltd) Trafalgar.
Branford, Henrietta. The Fated Sky. LC 98-51120. (Illus.). 160p. (YA). (gr. 8 up). 1999. 16.99 (*0-7636-0775-4*) Candlewick Pr.
— Fire, Bed & Bone. LC 97-17491. (Illus.). 128p. (J). 1998. 15.99 (*0-7636-0338-4*) Candlewick Pr.
— The Theft of Thor's Hammer. (Myths & Legends Ser.). (Illus.). (J). 1998. (*1-57572-014-0*) Heinemann Lib.
Branford, Henrietta & Jonke, Tim. White Wolf. LC 98-29209. 96p. (J). (gr. 4-7). 1999. 16.99 (*0-7636-0748-7*, Pub. by Candlewick Pr) Penguin Putnam.
Branford, Jean & Branford, William. A Dictionary of South African English. 4th ed. 444p. 1992. text 45.00 (*0-19-570595-5*) OUP.
Branford, Kester A. A Study of Jean-Jacques Bernard's Theatre de L'Inexprime. LC 76-58424. (Romance Monographs: No. 24). 1977. 30.00 (*84-399-6422-6*) Romance.
Branford, Sue & Kucinski, Bernardo. Brazil - Carnival of the Oppressed: Lula & the Brazilian Workers' Party. (Illus.). 100p. 1995. pap. 12.00 (*0-85345-959-2*, PB9592, Pub. by Monthly Rev) NYU Pr.
— The Debt Squads: The U. S., the Banks & Latin America. LC 88-17215. 192p. (C). 1988. text 19.95 (*0-86232-791-1*, Pub. by St Martin) St Martin.
Branford, William. The South African Pocket Oxford Dictionary. rev. ed. 937p. 1988. 18.95 (*0-19-570503-3*) OUP.
Branford, William, jt. auth. see Branford, Jean.
Brang, Peter, et al, eds. Schweizerische Beitraege zum IX Internationalen Slavistenkongress in Kiev. (Slavica Helvetica Ser.: Vol. 22). (GER.). 245p. 1983. 18.00 (*3-261-03240-5*) P Lang Pubng.
Brang, Peter & Zullig, Monika. Kommentierte Bibliographie zur slavischen Soziolinguistik. (Slavica Helvetica Ser.: Vol. 17). (GER., Illus.). XIX, 1639p. 1982. 45.00 (*3-261-04958-8*) P Lang Pubng.
Brange, J. Galenics of Insulin. (Illus.). 110p. 1987. 30.20 (*0-387-17673-X*) Spr-Verlag.
Brange, Jens. Stability of Insulin. 128p. (C). 1995. text 55.50 (*0-7923-8874-7*) Kluwer Academic.
Branges, L. De, see De Branges, L.
***Branham, F. Leigh.** Keeping the People Who Keep You in Business: 24 Ways to Hang on to Your Most Valuable Talent. 2000. 27.95 (*0-8144-0597-5*) AMACOM.
Branham, Gregg. Windows NT Domain Architecture. LC 98-89281. 298p. 1999. 35.00 (*1-57870-112-0*) Cisco Press.
Branham, H. A. Sampras: A Legend in the Works. (Illus.). 262p. 1996. 24.95 (*1-56625-062-5*) Bonus Books.
Branham, Levi B. My Life & Travels. LC 88-18944. 64p. 1994. reprint ed. pap. 7.95 (*0-87797-107-2*) Cherokee.
Branham, Lynn & Krantz, Sheldon. Sentencing, Corrections & Prisoners' Rights, Teacher's Manual to Accompany Cases & Materials on the Law Of. LC 97-154595. (American Casebook Ser.). 175p. 1997. pap. text. write for info. (*0-314-22431-9*) West Pub.
Branham, Lynn S. Corrections & Prisoners' Rights in a Nutshell. 4th ed. (Nutshell Ser.). 338p. (C). 1995. pap. text 17.00 (*0-314-04514-7*) West Pub.
— Sentencing, Corrections & Prisoners' Rights, the Law Of. 5th ed. LC 97-225470. (Nutshell Ser.). 350p. (C). 1997. pap. 21.00 (*0-314-22867-5*) West Pub.
Branham, Lynn S. & American Bar Association. Limiting the Burdens of Pro Se Inmate Litigation: A Technical-Assistance Manual for Courts, Correctional Officials & Attorneys General LC 97-207654. 240p. 1997. write for info. (*1-57073-512-3*) Amer Bar Assn.
Branham, Lynn S. & Krantz, Sheldon. Sentencing, Corrections & Prisoners' Rights, Cases & Materials on the Law Of. 5th ed. LC 96-36925. (American Casebook Ser.). 657p. (C). 1996. 57.50 (*0-314-20469-5*) West Pub.
Branham, Lynn S., jt. auth. see Krantz, Sheldon.
Branham, Mary. Big Black Dog in Vallarta: A Mystery. LC 98-40412. 94p. 1998. 18.95 (*0-86534-277-6*) Sunstone Pr.
— Little Green Man in Ireland: A Mystery. Smith, James C., ed. LC 96-12084. 160p. 1997. 24.95 (*0-86534-248-2*) Sunstone Pr.
***Branham, Mary.** Three Deadly Days in Spain: A Mystery. 128p. 2000. 26.95 (*0-86534-315-2*) Sunstone Pr.
Branham, Michael. Competitive Advantage: The Handbook of Strategic Marketing & Management Systems for Reprographics, Digital Printing, & Quick Copy Businesses. 123p. 1997. pap. 99.95 (*0-9665176-0-1*) Marion St Pr.
***Branham, R. Bracht.** Cynics: The Cynic Movement in Antiquity & Its Legacy, Vol. 23. (Hellenistic Culture & Society Ser.: Vol. XXIII). 462p. 2000. pap. text 19.95 (*0-520-21645-8*, Pub. by U CA Pr) Cal Prin Full Svc.
Branham, R. Bracht. Unruly Eloquence: Lucian & the Comedy of Traditions. Bowersock, Glen W., ed. LC 88-24297. (Revealing Antiquity Ser.: No. 2). (Illus.). 296p. 1989. 41.50 (*0-674-93035-5*) HUP.
Branham, R. Bracht & Goulet-Caze, Marie-Odile, eds. The Cynics: The Cynic Movement in Antiquity & Its Legacy. LC 96-20375. (Hellenistic Culture & Society Ser.: Vol. 23). (Illus.). 413p. 1997. 60.00 (*0-520-20449-2*, Pub. by U CA Pr) Cal Prin Full Svc.
Branham, R. Bracht, jt. tr. see Kinney, Daniel.
Branham, R. L., Jr. Scientific Data Analysis. (Illus.). 250p. 1990. 69.95 (*0-387-97201-3*) Spr-Verlag.
Branham, Robert J. Debate & Critical Analysis: The Harmony of Conflict. 264p. (C). 1991. text 29.95 (*0-8058-0724-1*) L Erlbaum Assocs.
Branham, Robert J., jt. ed. see Foner, Philip S.
Branham, V. C., ed. see Roheim, Geza.
Branick, Michael L. A Comprehensive Glossary of Weather Terms for Storm Spotters. (Monograph Ser.: No. 1-93). 25p. (C). 1993. pap. text 9.00 (*1-883563-09-7*) Natl Weather.
Branick, Vincent P. Understanding the New Testament & Its Message: An Introduction. LC 97-47026. 384p. 1998. pap. 19.95 (*0-8091-3780-1*) Paulist Pr.
Branicki, Frank J., jt. ed. see Leaper, David J.
Braniff, Beatriz. La Estratigrafia Arqueologica de Villa de Reyes, San Luis Potosi. 182p. 1992. pap. 18.00 (*968-29-4531-3*, IN020) UPLAAP.
Branigan, Cat. Wings over Nam No. 1: Chopper Pilot. 192p. (Orig.). 1989. mass mkt. 3.95 (*0-445-20800-7*, Pub. by Warner Bks) Little.
— Wings over Nam No. 3: Linebacker. 192p. (Orig.). 1989. mass mkt. 3.95 (*0-445-20805-8*, Pub. by Warner Bks) Little.
— Wings over Nam No. 4: Carrier War. 1990. mass mkt. 4.95 (*0-445-20806-6*, Pub. by Warner Bks) Little.
— Wings over Nam No. 5: Bird Dog. 1990. mass mkt. 4.95 (*0-445-20808-2*, Pub. by Warner Bks) Little.
— Wings over Nam No. 6: Eagle Eye. 192p. (Orig.). 1990. mass mkt. 4.95 (*0-445-20810-4*, Pub. by Warner Bks) Little.
Branigan, Cynthia. The Reign of the Greyhound: A Popular History of the First Family of Dogs. LC 97-8131. (Illus.). 193p. 1997. 24.95 (*0-87605-696-6*) Howell Bks.
Branigan, Cynthia A. Adopting the Racing Greyhound. 2nd ed. LC 97-53092. 192p. 1998. 12.95 (*0-87605-193-X*) Howell Bks.
Branigan, Edward. Narrative Comprehension & Film. (Sightlines Ser.). (Illus.). 320p. (C). 1992. pap. 24.99 (*0-415-07512-2*, A7036) Routledge.
— Point of View in the Cinema: A Theory of Narration & Subjectivity in Classical Film. (Approaches to Semiotics Ser.: No. 66). xvi, 246p. 1984. 49.95 (*90-279-3079-1*) Mouton.
Branigan, K. Pre-Palatial: The Foundations of Palatial Crete: A Survey of Crete in the Early Bronze Age. xvi, 232p. (Orig.). 1988. pap. 50.00 (*90-256-0954-6*, Pub. by AM Hakkert) BookLink Distributors.
Branigan, K., et al, eds. Lexicon of the Greek & Roman Cities & Place Names in Antiquity ca 1500 BC-AD 500 Fascicule 3: Alga Minor - Anastasiupolis. 80p. 1995. pap. 45.00 (*90-256-0985-6*, Pub. by AM Hakkert) BookLink Distributors.
Branigan, K. & Dearne, M. J. Romano-British Cavemen. (Oxbow Monographs in Archaeology: No. 19). (Illus.). 120p. 1992. pap. 18.00 (*0-946897-43-3*, Pub. by Oxbow Bks) David Brown.
Branigan, Keith. Dancing with Death: Life & Death in Southern Crete C. 3000-2000 BC. x, 159p. 1993. pap. 50.00 (*90-256-1032-3*, Pub. by AM Hakkert) BookLink Distributors.
Branigan, Keith, ed. Cemetery & Society in the Aegean Bronze Age. (SSAA Ser.: Vol. 1). 150p. 1997. pap. 19.95 (*1-85075-822-0*, Pub. by Sheffield Acad) CUP Services.
Branigan, William R. It Is Written: What You Always Wanted to Know about the Bible . . . The Truth. LC 98-70010. 1998. mass mkt., per. 19.95 (*1-889131-24-5*) CasAnanda.
Branigin, Elba L. History of Johnson County. (Illus.). 863p. 1997. reprint ed. lib. bdg. 88.50 (*0-8328-6654-7*) Higginson Bk Co.
Branin, Joseph J., ed. Managing Change in Academic Libraries. LC 96-10289. (Journal of Library Administration Ser.: Vol. 22, Nos. 2 & 3). 152p. (C). 1996. 29.95 (*1-56024-810-6*) Haworth Pr.
Branin, Larissa. Elizabeth Taylor: A Life in Pictures. LC 99-19974. 1999. write for info. (*1-56799-811-9*) M Friedman Pub Grp Inc.
***Branin, Larissa.** Liz: The Pictorial Biography of Elizabeth Taylor. (Illus.). 2000. 19.98 (*0-7624-0774-3*) Running Pr.
Branin, M. Lelyn. The Early Makers of Handcrafted Earthenware & Stoneware in Central & Southern New Jersey. LC 86-45947. (Illus.). 272p. 1988. 55.00 (*0-8386-3235-1*) Fairleigh Dickinson.
Branine, Mohamed & Glover, Ian, eds. Ageism in Work & Employment. 69.95 (*1-84014-149-2*) Ashgate Pub Co.
Brank, Laura M., ed. The NAFTA Handbook. 160p. 1994. spiral bd. 125.00 (*1-893323-00-5*) WorldTrade Exec.
Branker, H. Earle. Fixing the Fourth "F" (Illus.). 200p. 1990. pap. 25.00 (*0-9625884-0-7*) Advan Con NY.
***Branker, Melvin.** My Fantastic Voyage. 1999. pap. write for info. (*1-58235-102-3*) Watermrk Pr.
Brankney, William H. Baptist Life & Thought: A Source Book. 2nd rev. ed. LC 98-38354. 550 p. 1998. pap. 18.00 (*0-8170-1266-4*) Judson.
Brankov, Jordan G. Introduction to Finite-Size Scaling. (Leuven Notes in Mathematical & Theoretical Physics Ser.: Series A, Vol. 8). 146p. (Orig.). 1996. pap. 44.50 (*90-6186-758-4*, Pub. by Leuven Univ) Coronet Bks.
Brankovic, Avram. Bosnia Revelation. 112p. 1998. pap. 10.95 (*0-85449-266-6*) Gay Mens Pr.
Brankston, A. D. Early Ming Wares of Chingtechen. (Oxford Asia Studies in Ceramics). 104p. (C). 1983. reprint ed. 39.95 (*0-19-581522-X*) OUP.
Branley. Gravity Is A Myst. 2nd rev. ed. (Illus.). 40p. (J). (gr. k-4). 15.95 (*0-06-028532-X*) HarpC.
***Branley.** Gravity Is a Mystery. 2nd rev. ed. 40p. (J). (gr. k-4). 2001. pap. 4.95 (*0-06-445201-8*) HarpC Child Bks.
— Gravity Is Mystery. 2nd rev. ed. 40p. (J). (gr. k-4). lib. bdg. 15.89 (*0-06-028533-8*) HarpC Child Bks.
Branley. Sun. 2nd rev. ed. (Illus.). 40p. (J). (gr. k-4). 15.95 (*0-06-028534-6*) HarpC.
***Branley.** Sun. 2nd rev. ed. 40p. (J). (gr. k-4). 2000. lib. bdg. 15.89 (*0-06-028535-4*) HarpC Child Bks.
Branley. Sun & the Solar System. 1996. write for info. (*0-8050-5272-0*) H Holt & Co.
Branley, Franklin. Age of Aquarius. (J). 1979. 9.95 (*0-690-03987-5*) HarpC Child Bks.
— The Sun. 40p. (J). (gr. k-4). 2002. 4.95 (*0-06-445202-6*) HarpC Child Bks.

An Asterisk (*) at the beginning of an entry indicates that the title is appearing for the first time.

Branley, Franklyn. Hurricane Watch. (J). 1985. 12.95 (*0-690-04470-4*) HarpC Child Bks.
— Journey into a Black Hole. (J). 1986. 12.95 (*0-690-04543-3*) HarpC Child Bks.
— Snow Is Falling. LC 98-23106. (Let's-Read-&-Find-Out Science Bks. 1). (Illus.). 40p. (J). (gr. k-4). 2000. lib. bdg. 15.89 (*0-06-027991-5*) HarpC.
— Snow Is Falling. rev. ed. LC 98-23106. (Let's-Read-&-Find-Out Science Bks. 1). (Illus.). 40p. (J). (ps-1). 2000. 15.95 (*0-06-027990-7*) HarpC.
— Space Telescope. (J). 1985. 12.95 (*0-690-04433-X*) HarpC Child Bks.

Branley, Franklyn & Keller, Holly. Snow Is Falling. LC 98-23106. (Let's-Read-&-Find-Out Science Bks. 1). (Illus.). 40p. (J). (ps-1). 2000. pap. 4.95 (*0-06-445186-0*) HarpC.

Branley, Franklyn M. Air Is All Around You. (Let's-Read-And-Find-Out Book Ser.). (J). 1986. 10.15 (*0-606-01794-1*, Pub. by Turtleback) Demco.

Branley, Franklyn M. Air Is All Around You. rev. ed. LC 85-45405. (Trophy Let's-Read-&-Find-Out Book & Cassette Set). (Illus.). 32p. (J). (ps-3). 1986. pap. 4.95 (*0-06-445048-1*, HarpTrophy) HarpC Child Bks.
— Air Is All Around You Book & Tape. abr. ed. LC 85-45405. (J). (gr. 4-7). 1990. 7.95 incl. audio (*1-55994-242-8*, TBC 2428) HarperAudio.
— Big Dipper. LC 62-10999. (Let's-Read-&-Find-Out Science Bks.). (Illus.). (J). (gr. k-3). 1962. lib. bdg. 12.89 (*0-690-01116-4*) HarpC Child Bks.
— The Big Dipper. rev. ed. LC 90-31199. (Let's-Read-&-Find-Out Science Bks.). (Illus.). 32p. (J). (ps-1). 1991. lib. bdg. 13.89 (*0-06-020512-1*) HarpC Child Bks.
— The Big Dipper. rev. ed. LC 90-33198. (Trophy Let's-Read-&-Find-Out Bk.). (Illus.). 32p. (J). (ps-3). 1991. pap. 4.95 (*0-06-445100-3*, HarpTrophy) HarpC Child Bks.
— The Big Dipper. rev. ed. LC 90-31199. (Let's-Read-&-Find-Out Science Bks.). (Illus.). 32p. (J). (ps-1). 1991. 13.95 (*0-06-020511-3*) HarpC Child Bks.
— Big Tracks, Little Tracks. LC 60-6251. (Let's-Read-&-Find-Out Science Bks.). (Illus.). (J). (gr. k-3). 1960. lib. bdg. 12.89 (*0-690-14371-0*) HarpC Child Bks.
— A Book of Flying Saucers for You. LC 72-78278. (Illus.). (J). (gr. 3-6). 1973. lib. bdg. 12.89 (*0-690-15189-6*) HarpC Child Bks.
— Book of Planets for You. rev. ed. LC 66-16919. (Illus.). (J). (gr. 3-6). 1966. lib. bdg. 10.89 (*0-690-15509-3*) HarpC Child Bks.
— Book of the Milky Way Galaxy for You. LC 65-16183. (Illus.). (J). (gr. 3-6). 1965. lib. bdg. 12.89 (*0-690-15367-8*) HarpC Child Bks.
— The Christmas Sky. rev. ed. LC 89-71210. (Illus.). 48p. (J). (gr. 3-7). 1990. lib. bdg. 14.89 (*0-690-04772-X*) HarpC Child Bks.
— Day Light, Night Light: Where Light Comes From. rev. ed. LC 96-33316. (Let's-Read-&-Find-Out Science Bks.). (Illus.). 32p. (J). (gr. k-4). 1998. 14.95 (*0-06-027294-5*); pap. 4.95 (*0-06-445171-2*); lib. bdg. 15.89 (*0-06-027295-3*) HarpC Child Bks.
— Down Comes the Rain. LC 96-3519. (Let's-Read-&-Find-Out Science Ser.: Stage 2). (Illus.). 32p. (J). (gr. k-4). 1997. 15.95 (*0-06-025334-7*); lib. bdg. 15.89 (*0-06-025338-X*) HarpC.
— Down Comes the Rain. LC 96-3519. (Let's-Read-&-Find-Out Science Bks.: Stage 2). (Illus.). 32p. (J). (gr. k-4). 1997. pap. 4.95 (*0-06-445166-6*, HarpTrophy) HarpC Child Bks.

Branley, Franklyn M. Earthquakes. (J). Date not set. write for info. (*0-06-028008-5*); pap. write for info. (*0-06-445188-7*, HarpTrophy); lib. bdg. write for info. (*0-06-028009-3*) HarpC Child Bks.

Branley, Franklyn M. Earthquakes. LC 87-638. (Let's-Read-&-Find-Out-Science Bks.). (Illus.). 32p. (J). (ps-3). 1994. pap. 4.95 (*0-06-445135-6*, HarpTrophy) HarpC Child Bks.
— Eclipse: Darkness in Daytime. LC 73-3492. (Let's-Read-&-Find-Out Science Bks.). (Illus.). (J). (gr. k-3). 1973. lib. bdg. 12.89 (*0-690-25414-8*) HarpC Child Bks.
— Feast or Famine? The Energy Future. LC 79-7817. (Illus.). 128p. (J). (gr. 5 up). 1980. 12.95 (*0-690-04040-7*); lib. bdg. 12.89 (*0-690-04041-5*) HarpC Child Bks.
— Flash, Crash, Rumble & Roll. (J). 1985. 12.95 (*0-690-04424-0*) HarpC Child Bks.
— Flash, Crash, Rumble & Roll. LC 84-48532. (Trophy Let's-Read-&-Find-Out Book & Cassette Set). (Illus.). 32p. (J). (ps-3). 1985. pap. 4.95 (*0-06-445012-0*, HarpTrophy) HarpC Child Bks.
— Flash, Crash, Rumble & Roll. (Let's Read-&-Find-Out Science Ser.). 1985. 10.15 (*0-606-00801-2*, Pub. by Turtleback) Demco.
— Flash, Crash, Rumble, & Roll. LC 97-43599. (Let's-Read-&-Find-Out-Science Bks.). (Illus.). 32p. (J). (gr. k-4). 1999. 15.95 (*0-06-027858-7*); pap. 4.95 (*0-06-445179-8*); lib. bdg. 15.89 (*0-06-027859-5*) HarpC Child Bks.
— Flash, Crash, Rumble, & Roll. rev. ed. LC 84-45333. (Let's-Read-&-Find-Out Science Bks.). (Illus.). 32p. (J). (ps-3). 1985. lib. bdg. 14.89 (*0-690-04425-9*) HarpC Child Bks.
— Floating in Space. LC 97-13052. (Let's Read-&-Find Out Science Ser.). (Illus.). 32p. (J). (gr. k-4). 1998. 15.95 (*0-06-025432-7*); lib. bdg. 15.89 (*0-06-025433-5*) HarpC.
— Floating in Space. LC 97-13052. (Trophy Let's-Read-&-Find-Out Bk., Stage 2). (Illus.). 32p. (J). (gr. k-4). 1998. pap. 4.95 (*0-06-445142-9*) HarpC Child Bks.
— Floating in Space: Stage 2. (J). 1998. 10.15 (*0-606-12934-0*, Pub. by Turtleback) Demco.
— Gravity Is a Mystery. LC 70-101922. (Let's-Read-&-Find-Out Science Bks.). (Illus.). (J). (ps-3). 1970. 11.95 (*0-690-35071-6*) HarpC Child Bks.
— How Little, & How Much: A Book about Scales. LC 75-43643. (Young Math Ser.). (Illus.). 40p. (J). (gr. k-3). 1976. lib. bdg. 9.89 (*0-690-01058-3*) HarpC Child Bks.

***Branley, Franklyn M.** The International Space Station. LC 99-31897. (Let's-Read-&-Find-Out Science Bks.). (Illus.). 40p. (J). (gr. k-4). 2000. 16.95 (*0-06-028702-0*); pap. 5.95 (*0-06-445209-3*, HarpTrophy) HarpC Child Bks.

Branley, Franklyn M. Is There Life in Outer Space? LC 99-10904. (Let's-Read-&-Find-Out Science Bks. 1). (Illus.). 40p. (J). (ps-1). 1999. lib. bdg. 15.89 (*0-06-028145-6*) HarpC.
— Is There Life in Outer Space? (Let's-Read-And-Find-Out Book Ser.). (J). 1984. 10.15 (*0-606-01875-1*, Pub. by Turtleback) Demco.

***Branley, Franklyn M.** Is There Life in Outer Space. LC 99-10904. (Let's-Read-&-Find-Out Science Bks. 1). (Illus.). 40p. (J). (ps-1). 1999. 15.95 (*0-06-028146-4*) HarpC.

Branley, Franklyn M. Is There Life In Outer Space. LC 85-45057. (Trophy Let's-Read-&-Find-Out Science Bk.). (Illus.). 32p. (J). (gr. k-3). 1986. pap. 4.95 (*0-06-445049-X*, HarpTrophy) HarpC Child Bks.
— Is There Life in Outer Space. rev. ed. LC 99-10904. (LRFO 1 Ser.). (Illus.). 40p. (J). (ps-1). 1999. pap. 4.95 (*0-06-445192-5*) HarpC Child Bks.
— It's Raining Cats & Dogs: All Kinds of Weather & Why We Have It. LC 86-27546. (Illus.). 128p. (J). (gr. 3-8). 1987. 16.00 (*0-395-33070-X*) HM.
— It's Raining Cats & Dogs: All Kinds of Weather & Why We Have It. 128p. (J). 1993. pap. 3.50 (*0-380-71849-9*, Avon Bks) Morrow Avon.
— Keeping Time. LC 92-6783. (Illus.). 112p. (J). 1993. 15.00 (*0-395-47777-8*) HM.
— Measure with Metric. LC 74-4056. (Young Math Ser.). (Illus.). 40p. (J). (gr. k-3). 1975. lib. bdg. 12.89 (*0-690-01117-2*) HarpC Child Bks.
— The Moon Seems to Change. rev. ed. LC 86-27097. (Trophy Let's-Read-&-Find-Out Bk.). (Illus.). 32p. (J). (ps-3). 1987. pap. 4.95 (*0-06-445065-1*, HarpTrophy) HarpC Child Bks.
— Oxygen Keeps You Alive. LC 73-139093. (Let's-Read-&-Find-Out Science Bks.). (Illus.). (J). (gr. k-3). 1971. 11.95 (*0-690-60702-4*) HarpC Child Bks.
— Pieces of Another World: The Story of Moon Rocks. LC 71-158684. (Illus.). (J). (gr. 5-8). 1972. lib. bdg. 11.89 (*0-690-62566-9*) HarpC Child Bks.
— The Planets in Our Solar System. LC 79-7894. (Let's-Read-&-Find-Out Science Bks.). (Illus.). 40p. (J). (gr. k-3). 1981. lib. bdg. 12.89 (*0-690-04026-1*) HarpC Child Bks.
— The Planets in Our Solar System. LC 79-7894. (Trophy Let's Read-&-Find-Out Science Bk.). (Illus.). 40p. (J). (gr. k-3). 1983. pap. 3.95 (*0-06-445001-5*, HarpTrophy) HarpC Child Bks.
— Planets in Our Solar System. (Let's-Read-And-Find-Out Book Ser.). (J). 1987. 10.15 (*0-606-01657-0*, Pub. by Turtleback) Demco.
— Planets in Our Solar System. rev. ed. LC 86-45171. (Trophy Let's-Read-&-Find-Out Bk.). (Illus.). 32p. (J). (ps-3). 1987. reprint ed. pap. 4.95 (*0-06-445064-3*, HarpTrophy) HarpC Child Bks.
— The Planets in Our Solar System, Stage 2. LC 97-1174. (Let's-Read-&-Find-Out Science Ser.). (Illus.). 32p. (J). (gr. k-4). 1998. 15.95 (*0-06-027769-6*); pap. 4.95 (*0-06-445178-X*); lib. bdg. 15.89 (*0-06-027770-X*) HarpC.
— Rain & Hail. LC 83-45058. (Let's-Read-&-Find-Out Science Bks.). (Illus.). 40p. (J). (gr. k-3). 1983. lib. bdg. 15.89 (*0-690-04353-8*) HarpC Child Bks.
— The Sky Is Full of Stars. LC 81-43037. (Trophy Let's Read-&-Find-Out Science Bk.). (Illus.). 40p. (J). (ps-3). 1983. pap. 4.95 (*0-06-445002-3*, HarpTrophy) HarpC Child Bks.

Branley, Franklyn M. Snow Is Falling. (Let's-Read-And-Find-Out Book Ser.). (J). 1986. 9.90 (*0-606-03266-5*, Pub. by Turtleback) Demco.

Branley, Franklyn M. Snow Is Falling. rev. ed. LC 85-48256. (Trophy Let's-Read-&-Find-Out Bk.). (Illus.). 32p. (J). (ps-3). 1986. reprint ed. pap. 4.95 (*0-06-445058-9*, HarpTrophy) HarpC Child Bks.
— The Sun: Our Nearest Star. rev. ed. LC 87-47764. (Let's-Read-&-Find-Out Science Bks.). (Illus.). 32p. (J). (ps-3). 1988. lib. bdg. 14.89 (*0-690-04678-2*) HarpC Child Bks.
— Sun Dogs & Shooting Stars: A Skywatcher's Guide. 128p. (J). 1993. pap. 3.50 (*0-380-71848-0*, Avon Bks) Morrow Avon.
— Sunshine Makes the Seasons. (Let's Read-&-Find-Out Science Ser.). (J). 1986. 10.15 (*0-606-01937-5*, Pub. by Turtleback) Demco.
— Sunshine Makes the Seasons. rev. ed. LC 85-42750. (Trophy Let's-Read-&-Find-Out Book & Cassette Set). (Illus.). 32p. (J). (ps-3). 1986. pap. 4.95 (*0-06-445019-8*) HarpC Child Bks.

Branley, Franklyn M. Sunshine Makes the Seasons Book & Tape. unabridged ed. (J). (gr. 4 up). 1990. 7.95 incl. audio (*1-55994-247-9*, TBC 2487) HarperAudio.

Branley, Franklyn M. Think Metric! LC 72-78279. (Illus.). (J). (gr. 3-6). 1972. lib. bdg. 12.89 (*0-690-81862-9*) HarpC Child Bks.
— Tornado Alert. LC 87-29379. (Let's-Read-&-Find-Out Science Bks.). (Illus.). 32p. (J). (ps-3). 1988. lib. bdg. 15.89 (*0-690-04688-X*) HarpC Child Bks.
— Tornado Alert. (Let's Read-&-Find-Out Science Ser.). (J). 1988. 10.15 (*0-606-04562-7*, Pub. by Turtleback) Demco.
— Tornado Alert. LC 87-29379. (Trophy Let's-Read-&-Find-Out Bk.). (Illus.). 32p. (J). (ps-3). 1990. reprint ed. pap. 4.95 (*0-06-445094-5*, HarpTrophy) HarpC Child Bks.
— Venus: Magellan Explores Our Twin Planet. LC 92-32990. (Voyage into Space Bk.). (Illus.). 64p. (J). (gr. 3-5). 1994. 16.00 (*0-06-020298-X*) HarpC Child Bks.
— Venus: Magellan Explores Our Twin Planet. LC 92-32990. (Voyage into Space Bk.). (Illus.). 64p. (J). (gr. 3-5). 1994. lib. bdg. 15.89 (*0-06-020384-6*) HarpC Child Bks.

Branley, Franklyn M. Volcanoes. (J). Date not set. write for info. (*0-06-028011-5*); pap. write for info. (*0-06-445189-5*, HarpTrophy); lib. bdg. write for info. (*0-06-028012-3*) HarpC Child Bks.

Branley, Franklyn M. Volcanoes. (Let's-Read-And-Find-Out Book Ser.). (J). 1986. 10.15 (*0-606-03277-0*, Pub. by Turtleback) Demco.
— Volcanoes. LC 84-45344. (Trophy Let's-Read-&-Find-Out Bk.). (Illus.). 32p. (J). (ps-3). 1986. reprint ed. pap. 4.95 (*0-06-445059-7*, HarpTrophy) HarpC Child Bks.
— Water for the World. LC 81-43321. (Illus.). 96p. (J). (gr. 5 up). 1982. 12.95 (*0-690-04172-1*); lib. bdg. 12.89 (*0-690-04173-X*) HarpC Child Bks.

Branley, Franklyn M. What Happened to the Dinosaurs. LC 88-37626. (Let's-Read-&-Find-Out Science Bks.). (Illus.). 32p. (J). (gr. 1-4). 1989. lib. bdg. 15.89 (*0-690-04749-5*) HarpC Child Bks.
— What Happened to the Dinosaurs. LC 88-37626. (Trophy Let's-Read-&-Find-Out Bk.). (Illus.). 32p. (J). (gr. k-4). 1991. pap. 4.95 (*0-06-445105-4*, HarpTrophy) HarpC Child Bks.

Branley, Franklyn M. What Makes a Magnet. LC 95-23181. (Let's-Read-&-Find-Out Science Bks.: Stage 2). (Illus.). 32p. (J). (ps-3). 1996. 15.95 (*0-06-026441-1*); pap. 4.95 (*0-06-445148-8*, HarpTrophy) HarpC Child Bks.
— What Makes Day & Night. (Let's-Read-And-Find-Out Book Ser.). (J). 1986. 10.15 (*0-606-01965-0*, Pub. by Turtleback) Demco.
— What Makes Day & Night. rev. ed. LC 85-47903. (Trophy Let's-Read-&-Find-Out Bk.). (Illus.). 32p. (J). (gr. k-4). 1986. pap. 4.95 (*0-06-445050-3*, HarpTrophy) HarpC Child Bks.

Branley, Franklyn M. What Makes Day & Night. rev. ed. LC 85-47903. (Let's-Read-&-Find-Out Science Bks.). (Illus.). 32p. (J). (gr. k-4). 1986. lib. bdg. 15.89 (*0-690-04524-7*) HarpC Child Bks.

Branley, Franklyn M. What the Moon Is Like. (J). 1973. pap. 4.76 (*0-690-00203-3*) HarpC Child Bks.
— What the Moon Is Like. LC 85-45400. (Trophy Let's-Read-&-Find-Out Book & Cassette Set). (Illus.). 32p. (J). (gr. k-3). 1986. pap. 4.95 (*0-06-445052-X*) HarpC Child Bks.
— What the Moon Is Like. LC 98-54072. (Let's-Read-&-Find-Out-Science Bks.). (Illus.). 40p. (J). (gr. k-4). 2000. 15.95 (*0-06-027992-3*); lib. bdg. 15.89 (*0-06-027993-1*) HarpC Child Bks.

***Branley, Franklyn M.** What the Moon Is Like. LC 98-54072. (Let's-Read-&-Find-Out-Science Bks.). (Illus.). 40p. (J). (gr. k-4). 2000. pap. 4.95 (*0-06-445185-2*, HarpTrophy) HarpC Child Bks.

Branley, Franklyn M. What the Moon Is Like. (Let's-Read-And-Find-Out Book Ser.). (J). 1986. 10.15 (*0-606-01964-2*, Pub. by Turtleback) Demco.
— What the Moon Is Like Book & Tape. 1. unabridged ed. (J). (gr. 4 up). 1990. 7.95 incl. audio (*1-55994-249-5*, TBC 2495) HarperAudio.

Branley, Franklyn M. & Dorros, Arthur. What Makes Day & Night. (Illus.). (J). (gr. 1-5). 1986. 12.95 (*0-690-04523-9*, 147013) HarpC Child Bks.

***Branley, Franklyn M. & Kelley, True.** The International Space Station. LC 99-31897. (Let's-Read-&-Find-Out Science Bks.). (Illus.). 40p. (J). (gr. k-4). 2000. lib. bdg. 16.89 (*0-06-028703-9*) HarpC Child Bks.

Branley, Franklyn M. & Kelley, True. What the Moon Is Like. (Illus.). (J). (gr. 1-3). 1986. 12.95 (*0-690-04511-5*, 147023) HarpC Child Bks.

Branley, Franklyn M. & Vaughan, Eleanor K. Rusty Rings a Bell. LC 57-7492. (Illus.). (J). (gr. k-3). 1961. lib. bdg. 10.89 (*0-690-71602-8*) HarpC Child Bks.

Branley, Franklyn Mansfield. Day Light, Night Light: Where Light Comes from, Stage 2. (Let's-Read-And-Find-Out Book Ser.). (J). 1998. 10.15 (*0-606-12909-X*, Pub. by Turtleback) Demco.

Branley, Franklyn Mansfield. Down Comes the Rain, Stage 2. (Let's-Read-And-Find-Out Science. Stage 2 Ser.). 1997. 10.15 (*0-606-11276-6*, Pub. by Turtleback) Demco.

Branley, Franklyn Mansfield. Earthquakes. (Let's Read-&-Find-Out Science Ser.). (J). 1990. 10.15 (*0-606-07461-9*, Pub. by Turtleback) Demco.
— What Happened to the Dinosaurs? (Let's-Read-And-Find-Out Book Ser.). (J). 1989. 10.15 (*0-606-05046-9*, Pub. by Turtleback) Demco.
— What Makes a Magnet? LC 95-32181. (Let's-Read-And-Find-Out Science. Stage 2 Ser.). 1996. 10.15 (*0-606-10053-9*, Pub. by Turtleback) Demco.

Brann, Amy B. The Law Dictionary: Pronouncing Edition. 7th ed. LC 96-45448. 1996. pap. 19.95 (*0-87084-517-9*) Anderson Pub Co.

Brann, Darrell W. & Mahesh, Virendra B., eds. Excitatory Amino Acids: Their Role in Neuroendocrine Function. LC 95-36659. 336p. 1995. boxed set 224.95 (*0-8493-7662-9*, 7662) CRC Pr.

Brann, Eva. What, Then, Is Time? LC 99-19014. 256p. 1999. text 30.00 (*0-8476-9292-2*) Rowman.

Brann, Eva, et al. Plato's Phaedo. (Philosophical Library). (GEC.). 140p. (C). 1998. pap. text 7.95 (*0-941051-69-2*) Focus Pub-R Pullins.
— Plato's Sophist: The Professor of Wisdom. (Philosophical Library). (Illus.). 98p. (C). 1996. pap. text 6.95 (*0-941051-51-X*) Focus Pub-R Pullins.

Brann, Eva, tr. see Klein, Jacob.

Brann, Eva T. Late Geometric & Protoattic Pottery, Mid Eighth to Late Seventh Century B.C. LC 75-322663. (Athenian Agora Ser.: Vol. 8). (Illus.). xiv, 135p. 1971. reprint ed. 30.00 (*0-87661-208-7*) Am Sch Athens.
— Paradoxes of Education in a Republic. LC 78-10228. 1979. 12.95 (*0-226-07135-9*) U Ch Pr.
— Paradoxes of Education in a Republic. LC 78-10228. 178p. 1989. pap. text 13.50 (*0-226-07136-7*) U Ch Pr.

Brann, Eva T. H. The World of the Imagination: Sum & Substance. 824p. (C). 1990. lib. bdg. 88.50 (*0-8476-7650-1*) Rowman.

Brann, Jane T., ed. see Cook, Douglas A.

Brann, M., ed. Molecular Biology of G-Protein-Coupled Receptors: Applications of Molecular Genetics to Pharmacology. xvii, 256p. 1992. 75.50 (*0-8176-3465-7*) Birkhauser.

Brann, M. & Elbogen, Ismar. Festschrift zu Israel Lewy's Siebzigstem Geburtstag. Katz, Steven, ed. LC 79-7157. (Jewish Philosophy, Mysticism & History of Ideas Ser.). (GER & HEB.). 1980. reprint ed. lib. bdg. 56.95 (*0-405-12242-X*) Ayer.

Brann, M. & Rosenthal, F. Gedenkbuch zur Erinnerung an David Kaufmann. Katz, Steven, ed. LC 79-7142. (Jewish Philosophy, Mysticism & History of Ideas Ser.). 1980. reprint ed. lib. bdg. 75.95 (*0-405-12292-6*) Ayer.

Brann, Noel L. Trithemius & Magical Theology: A Chapter in the Controversy over Occult Studies in Early Modern Europe. LC 98-14898. (SUNY Series in Western Esoteric Traditions). (Illus.). 352p. (C). 1998. pap. text 23.95 (*0-7914-3962-3*) State U NY Pr.
— Trithemius & Magical Theology: A Chapter in the Controversy over Occult Studies in Early Modern Europe. LC 98-14898. (SUNY Series in Western Esoteric Traditions). (Illus.). 352p. (C). 1998. text 71.50 (*0-7914-3961-5*) State U NY Pr.

Brann, Ross. The Compunctious Poet: Cultural Ambiguity & Hebrew Poetry in Muslim Spain. LC 90-4788. (Jewish Studies). 220p. 1991. text 42.50 (*0-8018-4073-2*) Johns Hopkins.
— Languages of Power in Islamic Spain. LC 97-3720. (Occasional Publications of the Department of Near Eastern Studies & the Program of Jewish Studies, Cornell University: Vol. 3). (Illus.). xii, 222p. 1997. 35.00 (*1-883053-28-5*) CDL Pr.

Brann, William C. Brann's "Scrap Book" LC 71-104422. (C). 1986. reprint ed. pap. text 4.95 (*0-8290-1895-6*); reprint ed. lib. bdg. 15.50 (*0-8398-0171-8*) Irvington.

Brannam, Odena, jt. auth. see Garrett, Howard.

***Brannan.** A Writers Workshop. 2001. pap. text 23.00 (*0-07-239329-7*) McGraw.

Brannan, Beverly W. & Horvath, David, eds. A Kentucky Album: Farm Security Administration Photographs 1935-1943. LC 85-16434. (Illus.). 160p. 1986. 20.00 (*0-8131-1563-9*) U Pr of Ky.

Brannan, Beverly W., jt. ed. see Fleischhauer, Carl.

Brannan, Dan. Courage to Live: Donna Gustavel's Triumph over Cerebral Palsy & Deafness. 1997. pap. 10.95 (*0-9650228-4-6*) D Brannan.
— Life to the Fullest: Stories of People Coping with Diabetes. Orig. Title: Diabetes Doesn't Have to Be a Death Sentence. (Illus.). 221p. (Orig.). 1996. pap. 15.95 (*0-9650228-1-1*) D Brannan.
— Look, Listen & Learn: Ways for Kids to Cope with Diabetes. 136p. 1996. pap. 22.95 incl. audio (*0-9650228-2-X*) D Brannan.

Brannan, Daniel K. Cosmetic Microbiology: A Practical Handbook. LC 96-40142. 336p. 1997. boxed set 134.95 (*0-8493-3713-5*) CRC Pr.

Brannan, David A., et al. Geometry. LC 97-18015. (Illus.). 480p. (C). 1999. text 69.95 (*0-521-59193-7*); pap. text 24.95 (*0-521-59787-0*) Cambridge U Pr.

Brannan, John, ed. Official Letters of the Military & Naval Officers of the United States, During the War with Great Britain in the Years 1812, 13, 14, & 15: With Some Additional Letters & Documents Elucidating the History of That Period. LC 70-146378. (First American Frontier Ser.). 1971. reprint ed. 29.95 (*0-405-02829-6*) Ayer.

Brannan, Joseph D. & Beutel, Frederick K. Beutel's Brannan Negotiable Instruments Law: The Negotiable Instruments Law Annotated, Together with Discussions of Interpretation, Bills of Exchange Act, Statutory Variations, Comparative Tables, Commissioners' Notes, etc. 7th ed. LC 74-92297. 1628p. 1971. reprint ed. lib. bdg. 195.00 (*0-8371-3076-X*, BRNI) Greenwood.

Brannan, Linda, jt. auth. see McCombs, Barbara L.

Brannan, P. T., tr. & intro. see Festugiere, A. J.

Brannan, Robert L., ed. Under the Management of Mr. Charles Dickens: His Production of "The Frozen Deep" LC 66-22927. (Illus.). 173p. 1966. 18.95 (*0-910278-91-1*) Boulevard.

***Brannan, Steve A.** Uniform Regulations, United States Marine Corps, 1937. 224p. 1999. pap. 16.95 (*0-9672780-0-7*) Amer Militaria.

Brannan, Tom. The Effective Advertiser. LC 93-161563. (Marketing Ser.). (Illus.). 199p. 1993. reprint ed. pap. 61.70 (*0-608-07768-2*, 206785600010) Bks Demand.
— A Practical Guide to Integrated Marketing Communication. 2nd ed. 1998. pap. 30.00 (*0-7494-2703-5*) Kogan Page Ltd.

Brannas, K., et al. Econometrics & Stochastic Control in Macroeconomic Planning. 280p. 1981. text 58.00 (*91-22-00478-5*) Coronet Bks.

Brannen, Anne, ed. see Yeats, William Butler.

Brannen, Brett A., ed. Counsel for Catholic Parents. 23p. 1991. 1.00 (*1-56036-017-8*, 55035) AMI Pr.

Brannen, Carl A. Over There: A Marine in the Great War. LC 95-43731. (C. A. Brannen Ser.: No. 1). (Illus.). 192p. 1996. 24.95 (*0-89096-690-7*) Tex A&M Univ Pr.

Brannen, Carl Andrew. Over There: A Marine in the Great War. (C. A. Brannen Ser.: No. 1). 1997. pap. 15.95 (*0-89096-791-1*) Tex A&M Univ Pr.

Brannen, Christalyn. Going to Japan on Business: Protocol, Strategies, & Language for the Corporate Traveler. expanded ed. LC 96-44866. (Illus.). 176p. (Orig.). 1997. pap. 11.95 (*1-880656-19-1*) Stone Bridge Pr.

Brannen, Christalyn & Wilen, Tracey. Doing Business with Japanese Men: A Woman's Handbook. LC 92-36102. (Illus.). 176p. (Orig.). 1993. pap. 9.95 (*1-880656-04-3*) Stone Bridge Pr.

Brannen, Dorothy. Life in Old Bulloch: The Story of a Wiregrass. 732p. 1992. write for info. (*0-9630924-0-5*) State Reg Lib.

Brannen, Jonathan. Ethernity. 28p. (Orig.). 1989. pap. 3.00 (*0-926935-19-4*) Runaway Spoon.

***Brannen, Jonathan.** No Place to Fall. LC 98-86473. 78p. 1999. pap. 10.00 (*0-9623806-4-4*) SINK Pr.

Brannen, Jonathan. Sunset Beach. (Illus.). 51p. (Orig.). 1991. pap. 5.00 (*0-926935-54-2*) Runaway Spoon.

— Warp & Peace. 18p. (Orig.). 1989. pap. 3.00 (*0-926935-17-8*) Runaway Spoon.

Brannen, Julia. Mixing Methods: Qualitative & Quantitative Research. 192p. 1992. 83.95 (*1-85628-184-1*, Pub. by Avebry) Ashgate Pub Co.

Brannen, Julia & O'Brien, Margaret. Children in Families: Research & Policy. LC 95-47528. 240p. 1996. pap. 27.95 (*0-7507-0476-4*, Falmer Pr); text 79.95 (*0-7507-0475-6*, Falmer Pr) Taylor & Francis.

Brannen, Julia & Wilson, Gail, eds. Give & Take in Families: Studies in Resource Distribution. 192p. 1987. text 49.95 (*0-04-301251-5*); pap. text 19.95 (*0-04-301252-3*) Routledge.

***Brannen, Julia, et al.** Connecting Children: Core & Family Life in Later Childhood. LC 00-36885. 2000. pap. write for info. (*0-415-23095-0*) Routledge.

Brannen, Julia, et al. Young People, Health, & Family Life. LC 93-22709. 229p. 1994. pap. 34.95 (*0-335-19097-9*) OpUniv Pr.

Brannen, Julia, jt. ed. see Bernstein, Basil.

Brannen, Laurie. Prospecting the Client: How to Target & Find the New Financial Services Customer. 200p. 1991. text 24.95 (*1-55738-188-7*, Irwn Prfssnl) McGraw-Hill Prof.

Brannen, Leslie. Healing Gifts. 304p. 1998. mass mkt. 5.99 (*0-515-12288-2*, Jove) Berkley Pub.

— Healing Hearts. 304p. 1997. mass mkt. 5.99 (*0-515-12078-2*, Jove) Berkley Pub.

— Love Heals All. 288p. 1997. mass mkt. 5.99 (*0-515-12188-6*, Jove) Berkley Pub.

Brannen, Noah, jt. auth. see Thorlin, Eldora.

Brannen, Noah S. The Practical English-Japanese Dictionary. (ENG & JPN.). 412p. (Orig.). 1991. pap. 12.95 (*0-8348-0187-6*) Weatherhill.

— The Practical Japanese-English Dictionary. LC 97-9665. (ENG & JPN.). 416p. 1997. pap. text 14.95 (*0-8348-0342-9*) Weatherhill.

Brannen, Noah S., ed. see Fujiwara, Yoichi.

Brannen, Noah S., tr. see Sato, Masaaki.

Brannen, William H. Small Business Marketing: A Selected & Annotated Bibliography. LC 78-15082. (American Marketing Association Bibliography Ser.: No. 31). 87p. reprint ed. pap. 30.00 (*0-608-14611-0*, 202335200032) Bks Demand.

Branner, Bodil & Hjorth, Poul, eds. Real & Complex Dynamical Systems: Proceedings of the NATO ASI, Hillerod, Denmark, June 20 - July 2, 1993. LC 95-17075. (NATO A. S. I. Series C, Mathematical & Physical Sciences: No. 464). 343p. (C). 1995. text 180.50 (*0-7923-3521-X*) Kluwer Academic.

***Branner, David Prager.** Problems in Comparative Chinese Dialectology: The Classification of Miin & Hakka. LC 99-52400. (Trends in Linguistics Ser.). 500p. 1999. write for info. (*3-11-015831-0*) Mouton.

***Branner, Esmie G.** Beyond the Veil of Darkness: Despite Threats of Death & Separation from Her Children, Esmie's Faith Took Her. LC 98-32389. 1999. 9.99 (*0-8163-1713-5*) Pacific Pr Pub Assn.

Branner, Hans Christian. The Story of Borge. Planck, Kristi, tr. from DAN. LC 73-1593. (Library of Scandinavian Literature). 1973. lib. bdg. 32.50 (*0-8057-3359-0*) Irvington.

— Two Minutes of Silence: Selected Short Stories. LC 66-22865. (Nordic Translation Ser.). 243p. reprint ed. pap. 75.40 (*0-8357-6776-0*, 203545200095) Bks Demand.

Branner, John C. Caspar Branner of Virginia & His Descendants. (Illus.). 477p. 1988. reprint ed. lib. bdg. 79.50 (*0-8328-0308-1*) Higginson Bk Co.

Branner, Robert. Burgundian Gothic Architecture. Harris, John & Laing, Alastair, eds. (Studies in Architecture: No. III). (Illus.). 206p. 1986. pap. 39.95 (*0-302-02751-3*, Pub. by Zwemmer Bks) Intl Spec Bk.

— Chartres Cathedral. rev. ed. (Illus.). 304p. 1996. pap. 18.95 (*0-393-31438-3*, Norton Paperbks) Norton.

Branner, Robert. Gothic Architecture. pap. 15.95 (*0-8076-1471-8*, Pub. by Braziller) Norton.

Branner, Robert. St. Louis: And the Court Style in Gothic Architecture. Harris, John & Laing, Alastair, eds. (Studies in Architecture: No. VII). (Illus.). 158p. 1986. pap. 39.95 (*0-302-02753-X*, Pub. by Zwemmer Bks) Intl Spec Bk.

Branner, Toni. The Safe Exercise Handbook. 3rd ed. 100p. (C). 1996. pap. text, per. 20.95 (*0-7872-2695-5*, 41269501) Kendall-Hunt.

***Branner, Toni.** The Safe Exercise Handbook. 3rd ed. 104p. (C). 2000. per. 15.95 (*0-7872-7135-7*) Kendall-Hunt.

Brannick, Joan, jt. auth. see Harris, Jim.

Brannick, Michael T., et al, eds. Team Peformance Assessment & Measurement: Theories, Methods, & Applications. LC 96-46274. (Applied Psychology Ser.). 304p. 1997. 79.95 (*0-8058-1638-0*) L Erlbaum Assocs.

***Brannigan.** Experiencing Psychology: Active Learning Adventures. LC 99-32702. 248p. (C). 1999. pap. text 19.20 (*0-321-03282-9*, Prentice Hall) P-H.

Brannigan. The Pulse of Wisdom: Philosophy of India,China & Japan. 2nd ed. LC 99-54805. (Philosophy). 1999. mass mkt. 43.95 (*0-534-55127-0*) Wadsworth Pub.

Brannigan, Augustine & Goldenberg, Sheldon, eds. Social Responses to Technological Change, 56. LC 84-27934. (Contributions in Sociology Ser.: No. 56). (Illus.). 292p. 1985. 69.50 (*0-313-24727-7*, BNT/, Greenwood Pr) Greenwood.

Brannigan, Francis L. Building Construction for the Fire Service. 3rd ed. Linville, Jim L., ed. LC 91-68102. (Illus.). 667p. 1997. 67.00 (*0-87765-381-X*) Natl Fire Prot.

***Brannigan, Gary.** The Sport Scientists: Research Adventures. 200p. (C). 1998. pap. text 34.40 (*0-321-01345-X*, Prentice Hall) P-H.

Brannigan, Gary G. The Sport Scientists: Research Adventures. LC 98-20915. 1998. 25.31 (*0-673-98454-0*) Addison-Wesley.

Brannigan, Gary G., ed. The Enlightened Educator: Research Adventures in the Schools. LC 95-1204. 320p. (C). 1995. pap. 18.75 (*0-07-007260-4*) McGraw.

— The Sex Scientists. LC 97-15833. (C). 1998. text 28.13 (*0-321-01139-2*) Addson-Wesley Educ.

Brannigan, Gary G. & Merrens, Matthew R., eds. The Undaunted Psychologist: Adventures in Research. LC 92-16328. (C). 1992. pap. text 20.00 (*0-07-041531-5*) McGraw.

— The Undaunted Psychologist: Adventures in Research. LC 92-16793. 320p. (C). 1992. 59.95 (*1-56639-015-X*) Temple U Pr.

Brannigan, Gary G. & Merrins, Matther R., eds. The Social Psychologists: Research Adventures. LC 94-16599. (Social Psychology Ser.). 320p. (C). 1994. 23.13 (*0-07-007234-5*) McGraw.

Brannigan, Gary G., jt. auth. see Merrens, Matthew R.

Brannigan, Gary G., jt. ed. see Merrens, Matthew R.

Brannigan, John. New Historicism & Cultural Materialism. LC 97-52610. (Transitions Ser.). 272p. 1998. pap. 19.95 (*0-312-21389-1*) St Martin.

Brannigan, John, et al, eds. Re: Joyce: Test, Culture, Politics. LC 97-34966. 304p. 1998. text 49.95 (*0-312-21181-3*) St Martin.

Brannigan, Michael C. Dialogue: First Step in Philosophy. 206p. (C). 1990. 41.00 (*0-536-57838-9*) Pearson Custom.

— Ethical Issues in Human Cloning. 304p. (C). 2000. pap. 19.95 (*1-889119-11-3*, Pub. by Seven Bridges) Stylus Pub VA.

Brannigan, Michael C. The Pulse of Wisdom: The Philosophies of India, China & Japan. LC 94-28443. 399p. 1994. 24.50 (*0-534-24384-3*) Wadsworth Pub.

Brannigan, Michael C. Striking a Balance: A Primer in Traditional Asian Values. LC 99-11846. (Illus.). 208p. (C). 1999. pap. text 23.95 (*1-889119-05-9*) Seven Bridges.

Branning, C., et al. Good Computer Validation Practices: Common Sense Implementation. Stokes, Teri, ed. (Illus.). 324p. 1994. 249.00 (*0-935184-55-4*) Interpharm.

Branning, D. J. Experiments in Gallium Arsenide Technology. (Advanced Technology Ser.). (Illus.). 256p. 1988. 24.95 (*0-8306-9052-2*, 3052); pap. 16.95 (*0-8306-9352-1*, 3052) McGraw-Hill Prof.

Branningan. Applying to Derrida. LC 96-30918. 267p. 1996. text 49.95 (*0-312-16562-5*) St Martin.

Brannlund, Runar & Gren, Ing-Marie, eds. Green Taxes: Economic Theory & Empirical Evidence. LC 98-46609. (New Horizons in Environmental Economics Ser.). 176p. 1999. 65.00 (*1-85898-859-4*) E Elgar.

Brannock, Martha Lee. Teddy Bear Too-Too. (Illus.). 25p. (J). (ps up). 1995. pap. write for info. (*1-85863-352-4*) M Sanders Ent.

Brannolte, Ulrich, ed. Highway Capacity & Level of Service: Proceedings of the International Symposium on Highway Capacity, Karlsruhe, 24-27 July 1991. (Illus.). 500p. (C). 1991. text 155.00 (*90-5410-011-7*, Pub. by A A Balkema) Ashgate Pub Co.

Brannon, Brian, jt. auth. see Puhallo, Mike.

Brannon, Clift, notes. Keystone Soul Winners' New Testament. 2000. im. lthr. 3.75 (*0-8340-0338-4*, Pub. by Natl Pub) OUP.

— Keystone Soul Winners' New Testament. gif. ed. 2000. im. lthr. 8.75 (*0-8340-0340-6*, Pub. by Natl Pub) OUP.

Brannon, D. Edgar. Fokker Eindecker in Action. LC 96-133528. (Aircraft in Action Ser.). (Illus.). 50p. 1996. pap. 9.95 (*0-89747-351-5*) Squad Sig Pubns.

Brannon, Dave & Brannon, Nancy. Feasting in the Forest: The Recipes & the Love Story of Brannon's Wilderness Lodge...A Gourmet Italian Feasting Place in the Rocky Mountains. LC 89-91608. (Illus.). 165p. (Orig.). 1990. reprint ed. pap. 10.95 (*0-9623036-0-7*) ConAmore Pub.

Brannon, Dave, jt. auth. see Hennings, Chad.

Brannon, Donald R. Toward Excellence in Secondary Vocational Education: Using Evaluation Results. 38p. 1985. 4.75 (*0-318-22222-1*, IN294) Ctr Educ Trng Employ.

Brannon, Edgar. Fokker D VII. (Aircraft in Action Ser.: No. 166). (Illus.). 50p. 1997. pap. 9.95 (*0-89747-371-X*, 1166) Squad Sig Pubns.

***Brannon, Feist.** Health Psychology: An Introduction to Behavior & Health. 4th ed. (Psychology Ser.). 1999. pap., student ed. 17.25 (*0-534-36852-2*) Wadsworth Pub.

Brannon, Frances J. Cardiopulmonary Rehabilitation: Basic Theory & Application. 3rd ed. LC 97-24298. (Contemporary Perspectives in Rehabilitation Ser.). 486p. 1997. 52.95 (*0-8036-0318-5*) Davis Co.

Brannon, Gayle. Fitness for Two: Guidelines for Exercise During Pregnancy. 144p. 1990. pap. 12.95 (*0-929838-06-8*) Blue Zoo.

Brannon, George F. Backbone. 1995. pap. text 10.95 (*0-9645309-0-2*) Brannon Enter.

Brannon, Jack G. Vigil. unabridged ed. 92p. 1997. pap. 12.00 (*0-9660365-0-6*) Abby Pr.

Brannon, Jeffrey T. & Joseph, Gilbert M., eds. Land, Labor & Capital in Modern Yucatan: Essays in Regional History & Political Economy. LC 90-46746. (Illus.). 336p. 1991. pap. 104.20 (*0-608-05126-8*, 206568500005) Bks Demand.

Brannon, Joan G. Trying Summary Ejectment & Other Landlord-Tenant Actions. LC 96-179573. (Special Ser.: Vol. 14). 31p. (Orig.). 1996. pap. text 15.00 (*1-56011-291-3*) Institute Government.

Brannon, Joan G., compiled by. Selected North Carolina Statutes Relating to Civil Duties of Sheriffs. 66p. (Orig.). 1997. pap. 12.00 (*1-56011-310-3*, 97.07) Institute Government.

Brannon, Joan G., jt. auth. see Dellinger, Anne M.

Brannon, Katie G. Sailing into Divine Presence. (Orig.). 1997. write for info. (*1-57553-451-7*) Watermrk Pr.

Brannon, Lil, et al. Writers Writing. LC 82-14587. 179p. (Orig.). (C). 1982. pap. text 19.50 (*0-86709-045-6*, 0045, Pub. by Boynton Cook Pubs) Heinemann.

Brannon, Lil, jt. auth. see Knoblauch, Cyril H.

***Brannon, Linda.** Gender: Psychological Perspectives. 2nd ed. LC 98-3200. 528p. 1998. pap. text 52.00 (*0-205-27589-3*) Allyn.

Brannon, Linda & Feist, Jess. Health Psychology. 2nd ed. (Psychology Ser.). 1992. pap., student ed. 14.50 (*0-534-16538-9*) Brooks-Cole.

— Health Psychology: An Intro to Behavior & Health. 4th ed. LC 99-25890. 608p. 1999. 81.95 (*0-534-36850-6*) Thomson Learn.

— Health Psychology: An Introduction to Behavior & Health. 2nd ed. 544p. (C). 1992. text 43.25 (*0-534-16536-2*) Brooks-Cole.

— Health Psychology: An Introduction to Behavior & Health. 3rd ed. (Psychology Ser.). 560p. (C). 1996. mass mkt. 49.75 (*0-534-34306-6*) Brooks-Cole.

— Health Psychology: An Introduction to Behavior & Health. 3rd ed. (C). 1996. mass mkt., teacher ed. write for info. (*0-534-34308-2*) Brooks-Cole.

— Health Psychology: An Introduction to Behavior & Health Study Guide. 3rd ed. (Psychology Ser.). (C). 1996. mass mkt., student ed. 14.75 (*0-534-34307-4*) Brooks-Cole.

Brannon, Linda, jt. auth. see Feist, Jess.

Brannon, Nancy. Glorious Soups & Breads. LC 94-94231. (Illus.). 156p. (Orig.). 1994. pap. 12.95 (*0-9623036-4-X*) ConAmore Pub.

— The Lighter Side of Italy: A Collection of Authentic Italian Recipes That Happen to Be Low in Fat & Cholesterol. LC 91-90752. 272p. 1992. 17.95 (*0-9623036-2-3*) ConAmore Pub.

Brannon, Nancy, jt. auth. see Brannon, Dave.

Brannon, Nancy M. Levels. LC 96-84254. (Illus.). 80p. 1996. pap. 12.95 (*1-888341-00-9*) Enspirit Pr.

Brannon-Peppas, L. & Harland, R. S., eds. Absorbent Polymer Technology. (Studies in Polymer Science: No. 8). x,278p. 1990. 167.00 (*0-444-88654-0*) Elsevier.

Brannon, Robert L. Intensifying Care: The Hospital Industry, Professionalization & the Reorganization of the Nursing Labor Process. LC 94-11059. (Critical Approaches in the Health Social Sciences Ser.). 180p. 1994. 31.00 (*0-89503-161-2*); pap. 23.26 (*0-89503-162-0*) Baywood Pub.

Brannon, Ronald R., jt. auth. see Metz, Alberta.

Brannon, Scot, et al, eds. Through the Gap: An Anthology of Contemporary Kentucky Poetry. 118p. (Orig.). 1991. pap. 9.00 (*0-9628089-0-3*) Free Pr.

Brannon, Tami, jt. auth. see Licavoli, Lisa.

Brannon, Tom, et al. Open Sesame Multilevel Book. (Open Sesame Ser.). 96p. (J). 1988. pap. text, student ed. 8.50 (*0-19-434261-1*) OUP.

Brannon, Tom & Cardillo, Brent. Bedtime Rhymes. LC 98-234844. 1998. write for info. (*0-7853-2732-0*) Pubns Intl Ltd.

Brannon, Wayne A. & Leonard, Joseph M. Pocket Power No. 4: Dental. 48p. (Orig.). 1988. pap. 2.95 (*0-945893-03-5*) Pocket Power.

Brannon, Wilbur. It's Altar Time. (Christian Living Ser.). 48p. 1988. pap. 3.50 (*0-8341-1231-0*) Beacon Hill.

Branon, Bill. Let Us Prey. large type ed. LC 94-9239. 466p. 1994. reprint ed. lib. bdg. 24.95 (*0-8161-7432-6*, G K Hall Lrg Type) Mac Lib Ref.

— Spider Snatch. 330p. 1999. 24.95 (*0-929712-44-7*) Huntington Pr.

— Timesong. (Illus.). 100p. 1998. 14.95 (*0-929712-54-4*) Huntington Pr.

Branon, Dave. Competitor's Edge: Women Athletes Talk About Sports & Their Faith. LC 99-177814. 1998. pap. 11.99 (*0-8024-7819-0*) Moody.

— First & Goal: NFL Players Talk about Football & Faith. LC 97-147224. pap. 11.99 (*0-8024-7745-3*, 144) Moody.

***Branon, Dave.** Heads Up! Sports Devotions for All Star Kids. (Illus.). (J). 2000. pap. 9.99 (*0-310-70013-2*, Zonderkidz) Zondervan.

— Safe at Home 2: More Winning Players Talk about Baseball & Their Faith, Vol. 2. LC 97-201506. Vol. 2. 352p. 1997. pap. 11.99 (*0-8024-7904-9*, 275) Moody.

Branon, Dave. Slam Dunk: Winning Players Talk about Basketball, Family, & Faith. 250p. (YA). pap. 11.99 (*0-8024-7894-8*, 286) Moody.

— Slam Dunk 2: Winning Players Talk about Basketball, Family & Faith. 1999. pap. 12.99 (*0-8024-7929-4*) Moody.

***Branon, Dave.** A Sports Fan's Guide to Christian Athletes & Sports Trivia. LC 00-23494. 304p. 2000. pap. 14.99 (*0-8024-3084-8*) Moody.

Branon, Dave. Where Do I Go from Here? Understanding & Living Your Christian Faith. LC 93-41779. 224p. 1993. pap. 11.99 (*0-929239-80-6*) Discovery Hse Pubs.

Branon, R. Frost, Jr. A Kenning of Roses. LC 93-38336. 64p. 1993. pap. 14.95 (*0-7734-2714-7*, Mellen Poetry Pr) E Mellen.

Branover, H., et al, eds. Advances in Turbulence Studies. (PAAS Ser.: Vol. 149). 350p. 1993. 89.95 (*1-56347-018-7*) AIAA.

Branover, Herman. The Encyclopedia of Russian Jewry, Vol. II. Date not set. write for info. (*0-7657-6170-X*) Aronson.

Branover, Herman. Return: The Spiritual Odyssey of a Soviet Scientist. LC 95-23256. 264p. 1996. pap. 30.00 (*1-56821-529-0*) Aronson.

Branover, Herman, ed. The Encyclopedia of Russian Jewry, Vol. I. LC 98-9341. 583p. 1998. 100.00 (*0-7657-9981-2*) Aronson.

Branover, Herman, et al, eds. Single & Multiphase Flows in an Electromagnetic Field: Energy, Metallurgical, & Solar Applications. LC 85-19979. (PAAS Ser.). (Illus.). 762p. 1985. 97.95 (*0-930403-04-5*, VOL. 100) AIAA.

Branover, Herman & Unger, Yeshajahu. Progress in Fluid Flow Research: Turbulence & Applied MHD. (Progress in Astronautics & Aeronautics Ser.: Vol. 182). 942p. 1998. 109.95 (*1-56347-284-8*) AIAA.

Branover, Herman & Unger, Yeshajahu, eds. Metallurgical Technologies, Energy Conversion, & Magnetohydrodynamic Flows. (PAAS Ser.: Vol. 148). 730p. 1993. 99.95 (*1-56347-019-5*, V-148) AIAA.

Branquart, P., et al. An Analytical Description of CHILL, the CCITT High Level Language. (Lecture Notes in Computer Science Ser.: Vol. 128). 277p. 1982. 28.00 (*0-387-11196-4*) Spr-Verlag.

Brans, Edward H., et al, eds. The Scarcity of Water, Emerging Legal & Policy Responses. LC 97-9640. (International Environmental Law & Policy Ser.: No. 40). 328p. 1997. 124.00 (*90-411-0657-X*) Kluwer Law Intl.

Brans, Jo. Listen to the Voices: Conversations with Contemporary Writers. LC 87-42939. (Illus.). 284p. 1988. 24.95 (*0-87074-265-5*); pap. 12.95 (*0-87074-266-3*) SMU Press.

Brans, Yves W. & Hay, William W., Jr., eds. Physiological Monitoring & Instrument Diagnosis in Perinatal & Neonatal Medicine. (Illus.). 407p. (C). 1995. text 145.00 (*0-521-41951-4*) Cambridge U Pr.

Brans, Yves W. & Kuehl, Thomas J., eds. Nonhuman Primates in Perinatal Research. LC 87-29578. 500p. (C). 1988. text 85.00 (*0-471-84916-2*) Krieger.

Bransby, Guy. Her Majesty's Interrogator: Falklands. (Illus.). 155p. 1996. 31.95 (*0-85052-471-7*, Pub. by Leo Cooper) Trans-Atl Phila.

— Her Majesty's Vietnam Soldier. 286p. 1992. 24.95 (*1-85421-167-6*, Pub. by Leo Cooper) Trans-Atl Phila.

Bransby, L. Impending Hour, Vol 2. 1993. pap. text 12.50 (*0-00-544585-X*) Lord Byron Found.

Branscomb, Anne W. Cybercommunities & Cybercommerce: Can We Learn to Cope? unabridged ed. 17p. (Orig.). 1996. pap. text. write for info. (*1-879716-28-3*, I-96-1) Ctr Info Policy.

— Mastering the Changing Information World. Ernst, Martin L. & Oettinger, Anthony, eds. LC 92-21400. (Communication & Information Science Ser.). 352p. 1993. pap. 39.50 (*0-89391-989-6*) Ablx Pub.

Branscomb, Anne W. Who Owns Information? From Privacy to Public Access. 256p. 1995. pap. 15.00 (*0-465-09144-X*, Pub. by Basic) HarpC.

Branscomb, Anne W., ed. Emerging Law on the Electronic Frontier. (Communication Ser.). 256p. (C). 1999. 65.00 (*1-57273-193-1*); pap. 26.50 (*1-57273-194-X*) Hampton Pr NJ.

Branscomb, H. Eric. Casting Your Net: A Student's Guide to Research on the Internet. LC 96-38054. 175p. 1997. pap. text, student ed. 21.00 (*0-205-26692-4*) Allyn.

***Branscomb, H. Eric.** Casting Your Net: A Student's Guide to Research on the Internet. 2nd ed. 175p. 2000. pap. 20.00 (*0-205-32272-7*) Allyn.

Branscomb, Lewis. Confessions of a Technophile. LC 94-5330. (AIP Masters of Modern Physics Ser.). 250p. (C). 1994. 34.95 (*1-56396-118-0*, AIP Pr) Spr-Verlag.

Branscomb, Lewis C. Ernest Cushing Richardson: Research Librarian, Scholar, Theologian, 1860-1939. LC 93-29915. 160p. 1993. 24.00 (*0-8108-2672-0*) Scarecrow.

Branscomb, Lewis M. Industrializing Knowledge: University-Industry Linkages in Japan & the United States. LC 99-15447. 1999. 45.00 (*0-262-02465-9*) MIT Pr.

Branscomb, Lewis M., ed. Empowering Technology: Implementing a U. S. Policy. LC 93-23975. 1993. 40.00 (*0-262-02366-0*); pap. text 20.00 (*0-262-52185-7*) MIT Pr.

***Branscomb, Lewis M. & Auerswald, Philip E.** Taking Technical Risks: How Innovators, Managers & Investors Manage Risk. (Illus.). 200p. 2000. 34.95 (*0-262-02490-X*) MIT Pr.

Branscomb, Lewis M. & Keller, James, eds. Converging Infrastructures: Intelligent Transportation & the National Information Infrastructure. LC 96-15787. (Illus.). 406p. 1996. pap. text 27.00 (*0-262-52215-2*) MIT Pr.

Branscomb, Lewis M. & Keller, James H., eds. Investing in Innovation: Creating a Research & Innovation Policy That Works. LC 97-36969. (Illus.). 536p. 1999. pap. 20.00 (*0-262-52267-5*) MIT Pr.

Branscomb, Lewis M. & Kodama, Fumio. Japanese Innovation Strategies: Technical Support for Business Visions. LC 93-8471. (Occasional Papers: Vol. 10). 110p. (Orig.). (C). 1993. pap. text 21.00 (*0-8191-9201-5*); lib. bdg. 44.00 (*0-8191-9200-7*) U Pr of Amer.

Branscomb, Lewis M. & Young-Hwan Choi, eds. Korea at the Turning Point: Innovation-Based Strategies for Development. LC 96-24360. 304p. 1996. 65.00 (*0-275-95147-2*, Praeger Pubs) Greenwood.

Branscomb, Lewis M., jt. auth. see Carnegie Commission on Science, Technology, & Gove.

An Asterisk (*) at the beginning of an entry indicates that the title is appearing for the first time.

Branscombe, N. Amanda. Early Childhood Education. Date not set. pap. text 42.87 (*0-395-73299-9*) HM.

Branscombe, N. Amanda, et al, eds. Students Teaching, Teachers Learning. 343p. (YA). 1992. pap. text 27.50 (*0-86709-299-8*, 0299, Pub. by Boynton Cook Pubs) Heinemann.

Branscombe, Peter. W. A. Mozart: "Die Zauberflote" (Cambridge Opera Handbooks Ser.). 263p. (C). 1991. pap. text 19.95 (*0-521-31916-1*) Cambridge U Pr.

Branscum, Robbie. Cameo Rose. LC 88-21546. 96p. (J). (gr. 6-9). 1989. 11.95 (*0-06-020558-X*) HarpC Child Bks.

— Johnny May Grows Up. LC 86-45780. (Illus.). 128p. (J). (gr. 4-8). 1987. 11.95 (*0-06-020606-3*) HarpC Child Bks.

— The Murder of Hound Dog Bates: A Novel. 1995. 9.09 (*0-606-07900-9*, Pub. by Turtleback) Demco.

Bransden, A. The Physics of Atoms & Molecules, 1. 1996. 84.33 (*0-582-44401-2*) Addison-Wesley.

Bransden, B. H. Introduction to Quantum Mechanics. (C). 1996. pap. text 56.25 (*0-582-44498-5*) Addison-Wesley.

***Bransden, B. H. & Joachain, C. J.** Quantum Mechanics. 2nd ed. LC 99-55742. 2000. write for info. (*0-582-35691-1*) Addison-Wesley.

Bransden, B. H. & Moorhouse, R. Gordon. The Pion-Nucleon System. LC 73-39795. 548p. 1973. reprint ed. pap. 169.90 (*0-7837-9304-9*, 20600440004) Bks Demand.

Bransden, Brian H. & McDowell, Martin R. Charge Exchange & the Theory of Ion-Atom Collisions. (International Series of Monographs on Physics: No. 82). (Illus.). 488p. 1992. text 130.00 (*0-19-852020-4*) OUP.

Bransen, Jan. The Anatomy of Thought: Maimomian Skepticism & the Relation Between Thoughts & Objects. (Nijhoff International Philosophy Ser.). 216p. 1991. lib. bdg. 131.50 (*0-7923-1383-6*, Pub. by Kluwer Academic) Kluwer Academic.

Bransen, Jan & Cuypers, Stefaan E. Human Action, Deliberation, & Causation. LC 98-29680. (Philosophical Studies). 1998. 130.00 (*0-7923-5204-1*) Kluwer Academic.

Bransford, Helen. Welcome to Your Facelift: What to Expect Before, During & After Cosmetic Surgery. (Illus.). 192p. 1998. pap. 11.95 (*0-385-48550-6*, Main St Bks) Doubleday.

Bransford, John B., ed. see National Research Council Staff.

Bransford, John D. Ideal Problem Solver: A Guide to Improving Thinking, Learning, & Creativity. 3rd ed. (C). 1993. 160.00 (*0-7167-2484-7*) W H Freeman.

***Bransford, John D., et al, eds.** How People Learn: Brain, Mind, Experience, & School. 2000. 19.95 (*0-309-07036-8*) Natl Acad Pr.

Bransford, John D. & Stein, Barry S. The Ideal Problem Solver: A Guide for Improving Thinking, Learning, & Creativity. 2nd ed. LC 92-36163. 208p. (C). 1993. pap. text 18.95 (*0-7167-2205-4*) W H Freeman.

Bransford, Stephen. Gay Politics vs. Colorado: The Inside Story of Amendment 2. LC 93-87440. (Illus.). 300p. 1994. 22.00 (*0-9639465-0-1*) Sardis Pr.

Bransford, William L., jt. auth. see Shaw, G. Jerry.

Bransicme, Anna, jt. ed. see Wieck, Stewart.

***Bransilver, Connie, et al.** Florida's Unsung Wilderness: The Swamps. (Illus.). 96p. 2000. pap. 24.95 (*1-56579-386-2*) Westcliffe Pubs.

Branski, D., et al, eds. Gluten-Sensitive Enteropathy. (Frontiers of Gastrointestinal Research Ser.: Vol. 19). (Illus.). viii, 218p. 1991. 205.25 (*3-8055-5331-5*) S Karger.

— Pediatric Gastroenterology. (Frontiers of Gastrointestinal Research Ser.: Vol. 13). (Illus.). viii, 416p. 1986. 292.25 (*3-8055-4331-X*) S Karger.

Bransom, Charles. Ordinations of U. S. Catholic Bishops, 1790-1989: A Chronological List. 288p. 1990. boxed set 59.95 (*1-55586-323-X*) US Catholic.

Bransom, Christine, ed. see Cameron, Craig & Fair, Terry.

Branson, Billy J. Mining the Silver Lining: Taking Triumph from Tragedy. 224p. (Orig.). 1988. pap. 9.95 (*0-925048-00-3*) Sun-Coyote Pr.

Branson, Branley A. & Batch, Donald L. Fishes of the Dix River, Kentucky. unabridged ed. (Kentucky Nature Preserves Commission Scientific & Technical Ser.: Vol. 2). (Illus.). 26p. 1981. pap. 3.36 (*0-9673646-1-2*) KY State Nature.

Branson Cagle, Mary. Moments with Mary. 1998. pap. write for info. (*1-57553-858-X*) Watermrk Pr.

Branson, Clark. Howard Hawks: A Jungian Study. (Illus.). 332p. 1987. 20.00 (*0-88496-261-X*); pap. 11.00 (*0-88496-263-6*) Players Pr.

Branson, D. R. & Dickson, K. L., eds. Aquatic Toxicology & Hazard Assessment (Fourth Conference)- STP 737. 466p. 1981. 43.00 (*0-8031-0799-4*, STP737) ASTM.

Branson, Dave. The Monster Encyclopedia. LC 98-71906. (Illus.). 40p. (J). (gr. k-3). 1998. 16.95 (*1-880851-35-0*) Greene Bark Pr.

Branson, Douglas M. Corporate Governance. 900p. 125.00 (*0-327-01944-1*) LEXIS Pub.

Branson, Douglas M. Corporate Governance. 900p. 1993. 125.00 (*1-55834-072-6*, 60680-10, MICHIE) LEXIS Pub.

— Problems in Corporate Governance. 90p. 1997. pap., wbk. ed. 19.95 (*1-887969-05-5*) Cathedral PA.

Branson, Douglas M., jt. auth. see Barker, Robert L.

Branson, Douglas M., jt. auth. see Pinto, Arthur R.

Branson, Douglas M., jt. ed. see Barker, Robert L.

Branson, Dougls M., jt. auth. see Barker, Robert L.

Branson, Gary D. The Complete Guide to Log & Cedar Homes: All about Buying, Building, Decorating, & Furnishing Log, Cedar, & Post & Beam Homes. (Illus.). 168p. 1993. pap. 17.99 (*1-55870-276-8*, Betrwy Bks) F & W Pubns Inc.

Branson, Helen K. Just People: An Autobiography of a Blind Couple from Idaho. LC 97-29502. 358p. (Orig.). 1997. pap. 16.95 (*0-936015-50-0*) Pocahontas Pr.

Branson, J., et al, eds. Global Continental Changes: The Context of Palaeohydrology. (Geological Society Special Publication Ser.: No. 115). (Illus.). 280p. 1996. 98.00 (*1-897799-69-1*, 356, Pub. by Geol Soc Pub Hse) AAPG.

Branson, Johanna, et al. Ellen Rothenberg. LC 94-11124. (Orig.). (C). 1999. pap. 17.50 (*1-880593-02-5*) Tufts Univ Gallery.

Branson, John J., III. How to Start a Word Processing Business at Home. write for info. (*0-318-59696-2*) S&S Trade.

Branson, Kellie & Babcock, Dale A. I Don't Know Who You Are Anymore: A Family's Struggle with Depression. Terra, Jean, ed. LC 91-76568. 192p. (Orig.). 1992. pap. 12.95 (*0-9625040-3-3*, 297-231-X) Legendary Pub.

Branson, Ken. Happy Together: 500 Things to Do for & with Your Sweet Heart. LC 94-66198. 1994. pap. 7.95 (*0-9641361-0-4*) Shafer Pr.

Branson, Louise, jt. auth. see Doder, Dusko.

Branson, Margaret & Coombs, Fred. Civics for Today, 001. (Illus.). (J). (gr. 7-9). 1980. pap., student ed. 17.84 (*0-395-26203-8*); text 57.92 (*0-395-26201-1*) HM.

Branson, Marla M. The Next Power Frontier! 337p. (Orig.). 1996. per. 19.95 (*0-9651317-0-X*) Unvrsal Spirit.

Branson, Mary. Fun Around the World: Games, Crafts, Food, & Dress Ideas You Can Use! Gross, Karen, ed. (Illus.). 64p. (J). (gr. 1-6). 1992. pap. text 4.95 (*1-56309-052-X*, N927103, New Hope) Womans Mission Union.

Branson, Noreen. History of the Communist Party, 1941-51. LC 97-217247. 1997. pap. 22.50 (*0-85315-862-2*, Pub. by Lawrence & Wishart) NYU Pr.

Branson, O. T. Apache Indian Coloring Book. (Illus.). 32p. (Orig.). (J). (gr. 1-6). 1983. pap. 3.50 (*0-918080-13-4*) Treas Chest Bks.

— Indian Dancer Coloring Book. 32p. (J). (gr. 1-6). 1982. pap. 3.50 (*0-918080-03-7*) Treas Chest Bks.

— Indian Pueblo Coloring Book. 32p. 1984. pap. 3.50 (*0-918080-10-X*) Treas Chest Bks.

— Kachina Coloring Book. 32p. 1982. pap. 3.50 (*0-918080-02-9*) Treas Chest Bks.

— Navajo Indian Coloring Book. 32p. 1983. pap. 3.50 (*0-918080-06-1*) Treas Chest Bks.

Branson, Oscar T. Indian Jewelry Making, Vol. I. LC 76-56058. (Illus.). 64p. 1977. reprint ed. ring bd. 14.95 (*0-918080-15-0*, 20965) Treas Chest Bks.

— Indian Jewelry Making, Vol. II. (Illus.). 64p. 1979. ring bd. 14.95 (*0-918080-17-7*, 20966) Treas Chest Bks.

Branson, Richard. Losing My Virginity: How I've Survived, Had Fun & Made a Fortune Doing Business My Way. LC 98-18979. (Illus.). 370p. 1998. 27.50 (*0-8129-3101-7*, Times Bks) Crown Pub Group.

***Branson, Richard.** Losing My Virginity: How I've Survived, Had Fun & Made a Fortune Doing Business My Way. (Illus.). 384p. 1999. pap. 15.00 (*0-8129-3229-3*, Times Bks) Crown Pub Group.

Branson, Richard, jt. auth. see Conkey, Chip.

Branson, Richard D., et al, eds. Respiratory Care Equipment. LC 94-22641. 592p. 1995. text 54.95 (*0-397-54995-4*) Lppncott W & W.

Branson, Richard D. & Hess, Dean R. Respiratory Care Equipment. 2nd ed. LC 98-21793. 754p. 1998. text 59.95 (*0-7817-1200-9*) Lppncott W & W.

Branson, Richard D., et al. Respiratory Care Equipment. (Illus.). 750p. 1993. text. write for info. (*0-397-50856-5*) Lppncott W & W.

Branson, Richard D., jt. auth. see MacIntyre, Neil R.

Branson, Robert. Beacon Small-Group Bible Studies, Isaiah: Preparing the Way of the Lord. Wolf, Earl C., ed. 96p. (Orig.). 1985. pap. 4.99 (*0-8341-0961-1*) Beacon Hill.

Branson, Robert E. & Norvell, Douglas G. Introduction to Agricultural Marketing. (Illus.). 544p. (C). 1983. text 43.74 (*0-07-007241-8*) McGraw.

Branson, Thomas, et al, eds. Quantization, Nonlinear Partial Differential Equations, & Operator Algebra: 1994 John von Neumann Symposium on Quantization & Nonlinear Wave Equations June 7-11, 1994, Massachusetts Institute of Technology, Cambridge, Massachusetts. LC 96-5187. (Proceedings of Symposia in Pure Mathematics Ser.: Vol. 59). 224p. 1996. text 54.00 (*0-8218-0381-6*, PSPUM/59) Am Math.

Branson, Thomas, jt. auth. see NSF-CBMS Conference on Spectral Problems in Geometry & Arithmetic Staff.

Branson, Thomas P., tr. see Boltyanskii, Vladimir G. & Gokhberg, Izrail T.

Branson, Thomas P., tr. see Fomin, S. V.

Branson, Thomas P., tr. see Solodovnikov, A. S.

Branson-Trent, Gregory. Olivia, More Than Physical: A Collector's Guide. LC 97-5238. (Illus.). 149p. 1995. 12.95 (*0-9695736-6-9*) CN06.

Branson, William H. Headache: Hope Through Research. 36p. 1997. pap. 2.50 (*0-16-048856-7*) USGPO.

Branson, William H. Macroeconomics: Theory & Policy. 3rd ed. 656p. (C). 1997. 121.00 (*0-06-040932-0*) Addison-Wesley Educ.

Branson, William H., et al, eds. International Policy Coordination & Exchange Rate Fluctuations. (National Bureau of Economic Research Conference Report Ser.). (Illus.). 39*2p. 1990. 54.00 (*0-226-07141-3*) U Ch Pr.

Branson, William H., jt. ed. see Bradford, Colin I., Jr.

Branstad, Barbara, jt. auth. see Beam, Joan.

Branstad, Dennis K., ed. Report of the NIST Workshop on Digital Signature Certificate Management. (Illus.). 177p. (C). 1996. reprint ed. pap. text 35.00 (*0-7881-3409-4*) DIANE Pub.

Branster, Mark, jt. auth. see Prahl, Earl J.

Branstetter, Kacy, jt. auth. see American.

Branstner, Evie. Life's Rugged Beauty. Herringshaw, Mark & Herringshaw, Jill, eds. (Illus.). 320p. (Orig.). 1995. pap. write for info. (*0-9649290-0-7*) A & V Miller.

Branston, Barry. Elements of Graphology. LC 95-10692. (Elements of...Ser.). (Illus.). 144p. 1995. pap. 9.95 (*1-85230-646-7*, Pub. by Element MA) Penguin Putnam.

— Graphology Explained: A Workbook. LC 91-23387. (Illus.). 240p. (Orig.). 1991. reprint ed. pap., wbk. ed. 14.95 (*0-87728-735-X*) Weiser.

Branston, Brian. The Lost Gods of England. (Illus.). 194p. 1998. pap. 13.95 (*0-09-473340-6*, Pub. by Constable & Co) Trafalgar.

Branston, Brian. The Lost Gods of England. LC 83-72977. 1984. reprint ed. 10.95 (*0-500-27321-9*, Pub. by Thames Hudson) Norton.

***Branston, Gill.** Cinema & Cultural Modernity. LC 00-34712. (Issues in Cultural & Media Studies). 2000. pap. write for info. (*0-335-20076-1*, Pub. by OpUniv Pr) Taylor & Francis.

Branston, Gill. Media Student's Book. 2nd ed. LC 98-42027. 1999. 85.00 (*0-415-17307-8*) Routledge.

***Branston, Gill & Stafford, Roy.** The Media Student's Book 2nd ed. LC 98-42027. 1999. pap. write for info. (*0-415-17308-6*) Routledge.

Branston, John & Neill, Kenneth. The Making of Modern Memphis. (Illus.). 196p. 1996. reprint ed. pap. 7.50 (*0-9649821-1-0*) Contemp Media.

Branston, Peter. Children & Parents Enjoying Reading: Parents & the Literacy Hour--A Teacher's Guide. 1999. pap. text 24.95 (*1-85346-557-7*) Taylor & Francis.

Branstrom, Marvin. Interactive Physics. (C). 1997. cd-rom 33.95 (*0-8053-2113-6*) Addison-Wesley.

Brant. Rethinking Sexual Harassment. LC 94-25614. (C). 59.95 (*0-7453-0837-6*, Pub. by Pluto GBR); pap. 18.95 (*0-7453-0838-4*, Pub. by Pluto GBR) Stylus Pub VA.

Brant, ed. Algebra for College Students. (C). 1998. text. write for info. (*0-321-01608-4*) Addison-Wesley.

— Beginning Algebra. (C). 1998. text. write for info. (*0-321-01609-2*) Addison-Wesley.

Brant & Zeidman, Edward A. Intermediate Algebra: A Functional Approach. 1996. 12.50 (*0-673-98129-C*) Addson-Wesley Educ.

Brant, Beth. Food & Spirits. LC 91-10343. 128p. 1991. pap. 8.95 (*0-932379-92-3*); lib. bdg. 18.95 (*0-932379-93-1*) Firebrand Bks.

— Food & Spirits. 128p. 1997. pap. write for info. (*0-88974-032-1*, Pub. by Press Gang Pubs) LPC InBook.

Brant, Beth. I'll Sing 'til the Day I Die: Conversations with Tyendinaga Elders. 1996. pap. 11.95 (*0-9698064-2-6*) McGillig Bks.

Brant, Beth. Mohawk Trail. LC 85-3265. 100p. (Orig.). 1985. pap. 9.95 (*0-932379-02-8*); lib. bdg. 16.95 (*0-932379-03-6*) Firebrand Bks.

— Mohawk Trail. 94p. (Orig.). pap. write for info. (*0-88961-151-3*, Pub. by Womens Pr) LPC InBook.

— Writing as Witness: Essay & Talk. 126p. pap. 12.95 (*0-88961-200-5*, Pub. by Womens Pr) LPC InBook.

Brant, Beth, ed. A Gathering of Spirit. (Illus.). 284p. reprint ed. pap. write for info. (*0-88961-135-1*, Pub. by Womens Pr) LPC InBook.

— A Gathering of Spirit: A Collection by North American Indian Women. LC 84-51751. 248p. 1988. pap. 12.95 (*0-932379-55-9*); lib. bdg. 26.95 (*0-932379-56-7*) Firebrand Bks.

Brant, Bob. Build Your Own Electric Car. (Illus.). 288p. 1993. 26.95 (*0-8306-4232-3*, 4283) McGraw-Hill Prof.

— Build Your Own Electric Vehicle. (Illus.). 310p. 1993. pap. 19.95 (*0-07-007256-6*) McGraw-Hill Prof.

— Build Your Own Macintosh: The CAT Mac. (Illus.). 100p. 1990. spiral bd. 24.95 (*0-9624249-0-0*) Brants Bks.

— Build Your Own Macintosh & Save a Bundle. 2nd ed. 1992. 19.95 (*0-07-007233-7*) McGraw-Hill Prof.

— Build Your Own Macintosh & Save a Bundle. 2nd ed. 376p. 1992. pap. 19.95 (*0-8306-3974-8*, 4156, Windcrest) TAB Bks.

Brant, Charles S., ed. The Autobiography of a Kiowa Apache Indian. Orig. Title: Jim Whitewolf: The Life of a Kiowa Apache Indian. (Illus.). 160p. 1991. reprint ed. pap. 5.95 (*0-486-26862-4*) Dover.

Brant, Clare & Purkiss, Dianne, eds. Women, Texts & Histories 1575-1760. LC 91-32120. 304p. (C). (gr. 13). 1992. pap. 27.99 (*0-415-05370-6*, A7145) Routledge.

Brant, David A., ed. Solution Properties of Polysaccharides. LC 81-236. (ACS Symposium Ser.: No. 150). 1981. 63.95 (*0-8412-0609-0*) Am Chemical.

— Solution Properties of Polysaccharides: Based on a Symposium. LC 81-236. (ACS Symposium Ser.: Vol. 150). 592p. 1981. reprint ed. pap. 183.60 (*0-608-03036-8*, 206348900007) Bks Demand.

***Brant, Donald R. & Stewart, Daniel B.** 13 Skulls. (Illus.). 168p. 1999. pap. 7.95 (*0-9666411-1-6*) Mendocino Pub.

Brant, George. Introductory Animal Science. 1994. 20.00 (*0-88252-171-3*) Paladin Hse.

Brant, Herbert A. Childbirth for Men. (Illus.). 200p. 1985. pap. 12.95 (*0-19-261450-9*) OUP.

***Brant, Jonathan.** Downloading the Bible: A Rough Guide to the New Testament. LC 99-55174. 2000. pap. 6.99 (*0-310-23426-3*) Zondervan.

— Downloading the Bible: A Rough Guide to the Old Testament. LC 99-55173. 2000. pap. 6.99 (*0-310-23425-5*) Zondervan.

— Downloading the Bible Pack: A Quick Stroll Through Both Testaments. (Youth Specialities Ser.). 2000. pap. text 12.99 (*0-310-23424-7*) Zondervan.

Brant, Jonathan. Law & Mental Health Professionals: Massachusetts. 2nd ed. Sales, Bruce D. & Miller, Michael O., eds. LC 97-19091. (Law & Mental Health Professionals Ser.). (Illus.). 285p. 1997. 59.95 (*1-55798-446-8*) Am Psychol.

Brant, Kylie. Bringing Benjy Home. (Intimate Moments Ser.). 1996. per. 3.99 (*0-373-07735-1*, 1-07735-3) Silhouette.

— Falling Hard & Fast: Sullivan Brothers. (Intimate Moments Ser.: No. 959). 1999. per. 4.25 (*0-373-07959-1*, 1-07959-9) Silhouette.

— Friday's Child. (Intimate Moments Ser.). 1998. per. 4.25 (*0-373-07862-5*, 1-07862-5) Silhouette.

— Guarding Raine. (Intimate Moments Ser.). 1996. per. 3.99 (*0-373-07693-2*, 1-07693-4) Silhouette.

— Heartbreak Ranch: The Sullivan Brothers. 1999. per. 4.25 (*0-373-07910-9*, Harlequin) Harlequin Bks.

— An Irresistible Man. (Intimate Moments Ser.). 1995. per. 3.75 (*0-373-07622-3*, 1-07622-3) Silhouette.

***Brant, Kylie.** McLain's Law. 2000. mass mkt. 4.50 (*0-373-82236-7*, 1-82236-0) Harlequin Bks.

Brant, Kylie. McLain's Law: Premiere. (Intimate Moments Ser.). 1993. per. 3.50 (*0-373-07528-6*, 5-07528-8) Silhouette.

— Rancher's Choice. (Intimate Moments Ser.). 1994. per. 3.50 (*0-373-07552-9*, 5-07552-8) Silhouette.

***Brant, Kylie.** Undercover Bride. (Intimate Moments Ser.). 2000. mass mkt. 4.50 (*0-373-27092-5*, 1-27092-5) Silhouette.

Brant, Kylie. Undercover Lover. (Intimate Moments Ser.). 1998. per. 4.25 (*0-373-07882-X*, 1-07882-3) Silhouette.

Brant-Love, Joan, jt. auth. see Love, Neil A.

Brant, Lyle A. MCSD Fast Track: Visual Basic 6, Exam 70-175. LC 98-89052. 300p. 1999. pap. 19.99 (*0-7357-0018-4*) New Riders Pub.

Brant, Marley. Jesse James: The Man & the Myth. LC 98-147766. 312p. 1998. pap. 15.00 (*0-425-16005-X*) Berkley Pub.

— Outlaws: The Illustrated History of the James-Younger Gang. LC 95-46715. (Illus.). 220p. 1997. 29.95 (*1-880216-36-1*, Elliott Clark) Black Belt Communs.

— Southern Rockers: The Roots & Legacy of Southern Rock. 288p. 1999. pap. text 18.95 (*0-8230-8420-5*) Watsn-Guptill.

Brant, Michelle. Timeless Walks in San Francisco: A Historical Walking Guide to the City. 2nd ed. 104p. (Orig.). 1996. pap. 8.95 (*0-9611346-1-5*) Brant.

***Brant, Roxanne.** Ministering to the Lord: The Power of His Presence. 96p. 2000. pap. 7.99 (*0-88368-611-2*) Whitaker Hse.

Brant, Sebastian. Narrenschiff. Von Goedeke, Karl, ed. LC 71-181916. (BCL Ser. II). reprint ed. 39.50 (*0-404-01064-4*) AMS Pr.

— Ship of Fools. vii, 399p. 1988. pap. 12.95 (*0-486-25791-6*) Dover.

— The Ship of Fools. 1990. 25.50 (*0-8446-6403-0*) Peter Smith.

— Ship of Fools, 2 vols. Jamieson, T. H., ed. Barclay, Alexander, tr. LC 14-11937. reprint ed. 95.00 (*0-404-01065-2*) AMS Pr.

— Shyp of Folys of the Worlde. Barcley, Alexander, tr. LC 74-25743. (English Experience Ser.: No. 229). 1970. reprint ed. 85.00 (*90-221-0229-7*) Walter J Johnson.

— Tugen Spyl: Nach der Ausgabe des Magister Johann Winckel von Strassburg. Roloff, Hans-Gert, ed. (Ausgaben Deutscher Literatur des XV bis XVIII Jahrhunderts Ser.). (C). 1968. 113.85 (*3-11-000350-3*) De Gruyter.

Brant, Shoko A. & Zeidman, Edward A. Interm Algebra. (C). 1996. text 68.44 (*0-673-46963-8*) Addson-Wesley Educ.

— Intermediate Algebra: Student's Solutions Manual. (C). 1997. pap. text, student ed. 25.00 (*0-673-99537-2*) Addson-Wesley Educ.

Brant, William E. The Core Curriculum: Ultrasound. 416p. text 89.00 (*0-683-30733-9*) Lppncott W & W.

Brant, William E. & Helms, Clyde A., eds. Fundamentals of Diagnostic Radiology. LC 93-34269. (Illus.). 1312p. 1994. 139.00 (*0-683-01011-5*) Lppncott W & W.

— Fundamentals of Diagnostic Radiology. 2nd ed. LC 97-51178. 1460p. 1998. 149.00 (*0-683-30093-8*) Lppncott W & W.

Brant-Zawadzki, Michael. MR Angiography: A Teaching File. LC 93-12956. 256p. 1993. text 79.00 (*0-7817-0093-0*) Lppncott W & W.

Brant-Zawadzki, Michael & Bradley, William G. MRI of the Brain II. 2nd ed. 224p. text 89.95 (*0-7817-2569-0*) Lppncott W & W.

Brant-Zawadzki, Michael & Bradley, William G., Jr., eds. MRI of the Brain Two: Non-Neoplastic Disease. (MRI Teaching File Ser.). 224p. 1990. text 76.00 (*0-88167-696-9*) Lppncott W & W.

Brant-Zawadzki, Michael & Norman, David, eds. Magnetic Resonance Imaging of the Central Nervous System. LC 86-15476. (Illus.). 416p. 1987. reprint ed. pap. 129.00 (*0-608-05840-8*, 205980600007) Bks Demand.

Brant-Zawadzki, Michael, jt. auth. see Bradley, William G.

Brant-Zawadzki, Michael, jt. auth. see Bradley, William G., Jr.

Branta, et al. Physical Activity & Youth Sports: Social & Moral Issues. (Peace & Conflict Ser.: Vol. 2, No. 4). 1997. pap. 20.00 (*0-8058-9879-4*) L Erlbaum Assocs.

Brante, Thomas, et al, eds. Controversial Science: From Content to Contention. LC 92-22543. (SUNY Series in Science, Technology, & Society). 326p. (C). 1993. text 59.50 (*0-7914-1473-6*); pap. text 19.95 (*0-7914-1474-4*) State U NY Pr.

Brantenberg, Gerd. Egalia's Daughters: A Satire of the Sexes. Mackay, Louis, tr. from NOR. 272p. (Orig.). 1995. pap. 12.95 (*1-878067-58-3*) Seal Pr WA.

— The Four Winds. O'Leary, Margaret, tr. 360p. 1996. pap. 12.95 (*1-879679-05-1*) Women Translation.

B

Branthaver, J. F., et al. Binder Characterization & Evaluation Vol. 2: Chemistry. 479p. (Orig.). (C). 1993. pap. text 15.00 (*0-309-05620-9*, SHRP-A-368) SHRP.

Branthaver, Jan F., jt. ed. see Filby, Royston H.

Branthover, Jeanne E. Jobfinder's Guide - What to Do to Get the Job You Want. (BLR Career Development & Outplacement Workshop Ser.). 1986. pap. 21.95 (*1-55645-539-9*) Busn Legal Reports.

Branthwaite, Alan & Rogers, Don, eds. Children Growing up. LC 85-4838. 270p. 1985. pap. 42.95 (*0-335-15067-5*) OpUniv Pr.

Branthwaite, Alan, jt. auth. see Hartley, James.

***Branting, Karl.** Reasoning with Rules & Precedents: A Computational Model of Legal Analysis. LC 99-57391. 236p. 1999. 104.00 (*0-7923-6105-9*) Kluwer Academic.

Branting, Karl, jt. auth. see Sartor, Giovanni.

Brantingham, Barney. The Pro Football Hall of Fame: The Story Behind the Dream. (Illus.). 64p. 1989. pap. 8.95 (*0-917859-27-8*) Sunrise SBCA.

Brantingham, Patricia L., jt. auth. see Brantingham, Paul.

Brantingham, Paul & Brantingham, Patricia L. Environmental Criminology. rev. ed. 282p. (C). 1991. reprint ed. pap. text 17.95 (*0-88133-539-8*) Waveland Pr.

***Brantley.** Basics of English. 2nd ed. (Communication-English Ser.). (C). 1999. 25.95 (*0-538-72299-1*) S-W Pub.

B

Brantley, C. L. Word Smart, Jr. II. (Princeton Review Ser.). 240p. (J). (gr. 6-8). 1997. pap. 12.00 (*0-375-75030-4*) Random.

— Word Smart Junior: How to Build a Straight "A" Vocabulary. (Princeton Review Ser.). (J). (gr. 6-8). 1995. pap. 12.00 (*0-679-75936-0*) Villard Books.

— Writing Smart Junior: An Introduction to the Art of Writing. (J). (gr. 6-8). 1995. pap. 12.00 (*0-679-76131-4*) Villard Books.

Brantley, Clarice P. & Davis, Bobbye J., eds. The Changing Dimensions of Business Education: 1997 NBEA Yearbook. (Yearbook Ser.). 195p. 1997. pap. 15.00 (*0-933964-50-1*) Natl Busn Ed Assoc.

Brantley, Clarice P. & Miller, Michele G. Effective Communication for Colleges. 6th ed. 368p. (C). 1988. mass mkt. 44.00 (*0-538-05340-2*, E34) S-W Pub.

— Effective Communication for Colleges. 7th ed. LC 92-33419. (C). 1993. pap. 52.95 (*0-538-70913-8*) S-W Pub.

Brantley, Clarice Penebaker. Effective Communication for Colleges: Workbook. 8th ed. (PS - Communication/English Ser.). (C). 1997. mass mkt., wbk. ed. 40.50 (*0-538-71751-3*) S-W Pub.

Brantley, Cynthia. The Giriama & Colonial Resistance in Kenya, 1800-1920. LC 81-524. 212p. reprint ed. pap. 65.80 (*0-7837-4758-6*, 204450500003) Bks Demand.

Brantley, Dave, ed. see Terence.

Brantley, Eric L. A Meeting of the Souls. LC 97-140098. 176p. (Orig.). 1996. pap. 12.00 (*0-9653518-0-7*) Sho U Write.

Brantley, Garry K. Digging for Answers: Has Archaeology Disproved the Bible? (Illus.). 178p. (Orig.). 1995. pap. 6.95 (*0-932859-24-0*) Apologetic Pr.

Brantley, Ina C. & Gandy, Mildred C. Home in Texas Vol. 3: The Journey. (Illus.). 285p. (Orig.). (J). 1996. pap. 6.00 (*0-9642549-2-1*, 7566-3) Childbrant.

Brantley, Ina C., jt. auth. see Gandy, Mildred C.

Brantley, Ina Childers, ed. see Scheer, Freda Roberts.

***Brantley, Judi & Brantley, Steven.** The Perfect Christmas Tree. Franklin, Pringle, ed. LC 00-90588. (Illus.). 48p. (J). (ps-6). 2000. 16.95 (*1-892570-05-X*) Spng Hse Bks.

Brantley, Judi S. Camille's Crossroad. LC 98-90766. (Illus.). 48p. (J). (gr. 4-8). 1999. 16.95 (*1-892570-02-5*) Spng Hse Bks.

Brantley, Judi S., jt. auth. see Brantley, Steven.

***Brantley, Karen.** Untold until Now: World War II Stories: Daddy & Other Heroes. LC 99-42769. 1999. 23.95 (*1-56072-715-2*, Nova Kroshka Bks) Nova Sci Pubs.

***Brantley, Mary E.** Winning the Technology Talent War: Recruiting & Retaining Tech Workers in a Dot-Com World. 2001. 24.95 (*0-07-136474-9*) McGraw.

Brantley, Paige. Lady of Gold. 352p. 1997. mass mkt. 4.99 (*0-8217-5684-2*, Zebra Kensgtn) Kensgtn Pub Corp.

Brantley, Renae. The Ultimate Guide to Chicago-Area Private Schools. LC 98-72181. (Illus.). 464p. 1998. pap. 24.95 (*0-9662748-0-6*) Aubergine Communs.

Brantley, Richard E. Anglo-American Antiphony: The Late Romanticism of Tennyson & Emerson. LC 93-30648. 360p. (C). 1994. 49.95 (*0-8130-1247-3*) U Press Fla.

— Coordinates of Anglo-American Romanticism: Wesley, Edwards, Carlyle, & Emerson. LC 92-22954. 219p. 1993. 49.95 (*0-8130-1169-8*) U Press Fla.

— Locke, Wesley & the Method of English Romanticism. LC 83-26026. 311p. 1984. 49.95 (*0-8130-0783-6*) U Press Fla.

— Wordsworth's "Natural Methodism" LC 74-20078. 221p. reprint ed. pap. 68.60 (*0-8357-8774-5*, 203367900087) Bks Demand.

Brantley, S. L., jt. ed. see White, A. F.

Brantley, Sherry. Choices: The Power Is Within You. (Illus.). 170p. 1997. reprint ed. pap. 12.00 (*0-9661996-0-X*) STEPP.

Brantley, Steven & Brantley, Judi S. The Throwaway Cat. LC 98-90767. (Illus.). 48p. (J). (ps-3). 1998. 16.95 (*1-892570-00-9*) Spng Hse Bks.

Brantley, Steven, jt. auth. see Brantley, Judi.

Brantley, Steven R., ed. Klamath Falls, Oregon, Earthquakes on September 20, 1993. (Illus.). 42p. (Orig.). (C). 1994. pap. text 20.00 (*0-7881-1572-3*) DIANE Pub.

Brantley, W. H., Jr. Battle of Horseshoe Bend. (Illus.). 1955. pap. 3.75 (*0-87651-205-8*) Southern U Pr.

Brantley, Whitt. Men of Mt. Rushmore. (Illus.). 36p. 1997. pap. text 4.75 (*1-893916-10-3*, 2004) Project Pr.

Brantley, Will. Feminine Sense in Southern Memoir: Smith, Glasgow, Welty, Hellman, Porter & Hurston. LC 92-39650. 300p. 1995. pap. text 16.95 (*0-87805-802-8*) U Pr of Miss.

Brantley, Will, ed. Conversations with Pauline Kael. LC 96-7200. (Literary Conversations Ser.). 216p. 1996. pap. 17.00 (*0-87805-899-0*) U Pr of Miss.

***Brantley, William A. & Eliades, Theodore.** Orthodontic Materials: Scientific & Clinical Aspects. (Illus.). 256p. 2000. 79.00 (*0-86577-929-5*) Thieme Med Pubs.

Brantley, William H., ed. see Soldano, B. A.

Brantlinger, Ellen. Fighting for Darla: Challenges for Family Care & Professional Responsibility: the Case Study of a Pregnant Adolescent with Autism. 176p. (C). 1994. text 37.00 (*0-8077-3357-1*); pap. text 18.95 (*0-8077-3356-3*) Tchrs Coll.

Brantlinger, Ellen A. The Politics of Social Class in Secondary School: Views of Affluent & Impoverished Youth. LC 93-10134. 256p. 1993. text 44.00 (*0-8077-3270-2*); pap. text 19.95 (*0-8077-3269-9*) Tchrs Coll.

Brantlinger, Patrick. Bread & Circuses: Theories of Mass Culture As Social Decay. LC 83-45134. 312p. (Orig.). (C). 1983. pap. text 17.95 (*0-8014-9338-2*) Cornell U Pr.

— Crusoe's Footprints: Cultural Studies in Britain & America. 224p. (C). 1990. pap. 21.99 (*0-415-90284-3*, A1568) Routledge.

— Fictions of State: Culture & Credit in Britain, 1694-1994. (Illus.). 312p. 1996. text 45.00 (*0-8014-3190-5*) Cornell U Pr.

Brantlinger, Patrick. Fictions of State: Culture & Credit in Britain, 1694-1994. (Illus.). 312p. 1996. pap. text 17.95 (*0-8014-8287-9*) Cornell U Pr.

Brantlinger, Patrick. The Reading Lesson: The Threat of Mass Literacy in Nineteenth-Century British Fiction. LC 98-19906. 320p. 1998. 39.95 (*0-253-33454-3*); pap. 19.95 (*0-253-21249-9*) Ind U Pr.

— Rule of Darkness: British Literature & Imperialism, 1830-1914. LC 87-47823. 328p. 1990. reprint ed. pap. text 17.95 (*0-8014-9767-1*) Cornell U Pr.

— The Spirit of Reform: British Literature & Politics, 1832-1867. LC 76-30537. (Illus.). 303p. 1977. reprint ed. pap. 94.00 (*0-7837-4450-1*, 205798000012) Bks Demand.

Brantlinger, Patrick, ed. Energy & Entropy: Science & Culture in Victorian Britain. LC 87-46250. (Illus.). 376p. 1989. 32.00 (*0-253-31928-5*) Ind U Pr.

— Energy & Entropy: Science & Culture in Victorian Britain. LC 87-46250. (Essays from Victorian Studies). (Illus.). 374p. Date not set. reprint ed. pap. 116.00 (*0-608-20533-8*, 205444700002) Bks Demand.

Brantlinger, Patrick, jt. ed. see Naremore, James.

Brantlinger, Patrick, ed. & intro. see Taylor, Philip M.

Brantly, John E. History of Oil Well Drilling. LC 78-149757. 1552p. reprint ed. pap. 200.00 (*0-8357-2650-9*, 204017500015) Bks Demand.

Brantner, Christina E. Robert Schumann und das Tonkunstler-Bild der Romantiker. (Studies in Modern German Literature: Vol. 32). IX, 196p. 1991. text 43.95 (*0-8204-0973-1*) P Lang Pubng.

Brantome, Pierre De, see De Brantome, Pierre.

***Branton.** The Dulce Wars: Underground Alien Bases & the Battle for Planet Earth. (Illus.). 150p. 2000. pap. 14.95 (*1-892062-12-7*) Inner Light.

***Branton, ed.** Omega Files: Secret Nazi UFO Bases Revealed! (Illus.). 140p. 2000. pap. 25.00 (*1-892062-09-7*) Inner Light.

— The Secrets of the Mojave: Or, the Conspiracy Against Reality. LC 99-75200. (Illus.). 300p. 1999. 29.95 (*1-881808-44-0*, SOM-AW) Creat Arts & Sci.

Branton, James L. & Lovett, Jim D. Automobiles. (Trial Lawyer's Ser.: Vol. 2). (Illus.). 378p. 1985. ring bd. 135.00 (*1-878337-01-7*) Knowles Pub Inc.

— California Depositions. (Trial Lawyer's Ser.: Vols. 1 & 1A). (Illus.). 1984. ring bd. 185.00 (*1-878337-06-8*) Knowles Pub Inc.

— Damages. (Trial Lawyer's Ser.: Vol. 4). (Illus.). 475p. 1987. ring bd. 135.00 (*1-878337-03-3*) Knowles Pub Inc.

— Depositions. (Trial Lawyer's Ser.: Vols. 1 & 1A). (Illus.). 1982. ring bd. 185.00 (*1-878337-05-X*) Knowles Pub Inc.

— Discovery. (Trial Lawyer's Ser.: Vol. 6). (Illus.). 319p. 1988. ring bd. 135.00 (*1-878337-09-2*) Knowles Pub Inc.

— Evidence - National: A User's Guide to Civil Evidence. annuals (Trial Lawyer's Ser.: Vol. 8). 375p. 1991. ring bd., suppl. ed. 135.00 (*1-878337-27-0*) Knowles Pub Inc.

— Family Law. Webb, Brian L., ed. (Trial Lawyer's Ser.: Vol. 7). (Illus.). 350p. 1990. ring bd. 135.00 (*1-878337-22-X*) Knowles Pub Inc.

— Premises Liability. (Trial Lawyer's Ser.: Vols. 3 & 3A). (Illus.). 1986. ring bd. 185.00 (*1-878337-11-4*) Knowles Pub Inc.

— Professional Liability. (Trial Lawyer's Ser.: Vol. 5). (Illus.). 349p. 1988. ring bd. 135.00 (*1-878337-13-0*) Knowles Pub Inc.

— Texas Alternative Dispute Resolution. (Trial Lawyer's Ser.: Vol. 10). 1992. ring bd. 135.00 (*1-878337-33-5*) Knowles Pub Inc.

— Texas Automobiles. (Trial Lawyer's Ser.: Vol. 2). (Illus.). 385p. 1984. ring bd. 135.00 (*1-878337-02-5*) Knowles Pub Inc.

— Texas Damages. (Trial Lawyer's Ser.: Vol. 4). (Illus.). 520p. 1987. ring bd. 135.00 (*1-878337-04-1*) Knowles Pub Inc.

— Texas Depositions. (Trial Lawyer's Ser.: Vols. 1 & 1A). (Illus.). 1982. ring bd. 185.00 (*1-878337-08-4*) Knowles Pub Inc.

— Texas Discovery. (Trial Lawyer's Ser.: Vol. 6). (Illus.). 319p. 1988. ring bd. 135.00 (*1-878337-10-6*) Knowles Pub Inc.

— Texas Evidence: A User's Guide to Texas Civil Evidence. annuals (Trial Lawyer's Ser.: Vol. 8). 375p. 1991. ring bd., suppl. ed. 135.00 (*1-878337-28-9*) Knowles Pub Inc.

— Texas Family Law. Webb, Brian L., ed. (Trial Lawyer's Ser.: Vol. 7). (Illus.). 350p. 1990. ring bd. 135.00 (*1-878337-23-8*) Knowles Pub Inc.

— Texas Premises Liability. (Trial Lawyer's Ser.: Vols. 3 & 3A). (Illus.). 1986. ring bd. 185.00 (*1-878337-12-2*) Knowles Pub Inc.

— Texas Professional Liability. (Trial Lawyer's Ser.: Vol. 5). (Illus.). 349p. 1988. ring bd. 135.00 (*1-878337-14-9*) Knowles Pub Inc.

Branton, James L. & Lovett, Jim D., eds. Alternative Dispute Resolution. (Trial Lawyer's Ser.: Vol. 10). 1992. ring bd. 135.00 (*1-878337-32-7*) Knowles Pub Inc.

Branton, James L., et al. Products Liability. (Trial Lawyer's Ser.: Vol. 9). 510p. 1992. ring bd. 135.00 (*1-878337-29-7*) Knowles Pub Inc.

— Texas Products Liability. (Trial Lawyer's Ser.: Vol. 9). 560p. 1992. ring bd. 135.00 (*1-878337-30-0*) Knowles Pub Inc.

Branton, Lawrence S. Attorney's Guide to California Professional Corporations: June 1992 Update. 4th ed. Dworin, Christopher D., ed. LC 87-71434. 220p. 1992. ring bd. 42.00 (*0-88124-512-7*, TX-30934) Cont Ed Bar-CA.

— Attorney's Guide to California Professional Corporations: June 1993 Update. 4th ed. Dworin, Christopher D., ed. LC 87-71434. 212p. 1993. 40.00 (*0-88124-641-7*, TX-30935) Cont Ed Bar-CA.

— Attorney's Guide to California Professional Corporations: June 1994 Update. 4th ed. Dworin, Christopher D., ed. LC 87-71434. 230p. 1994. 44.00 (*0-88124-767-7*, TX-30936) Cont Ed Bar-CA.

Branton, Matthew. The House of Whacks. 256p. 1999. pap. 13.95 (*1-58234-024-2*) Bloomsbury Pubg.

Branton, N. & Livingstone, J. M. Managerial Economics in Practice. (C). 1989. 75.00 (*0-7855-4096-2*, Pub. by Witherby & Co) St Mut.

Brants, Kees, et al. The Media in Question: Popular Cultures & Public Interests. LC 97-61883. vi, 184p. 1998. write for info. (*0-7619-5723-5*) Sage.

Branum. Critical Care Nursing Review: Questions, Answers. 400p. pap. 23.95 (*0-8016-0789-2*) Mosby Inc.

Branum, Nell. Missions on the Go for Preschoolers. (Illus.). 16p. (J). (ps-k). 1997. pap. text 18.95 (*1-56309-223-9*, N978101, New Hope) Womans Mission Union.

***Branum, Nell, ed.** Together with God: A Year of Missions Resources for Laotian Congregations. (Illus.). 33p. 1999. pap. 9.99 (*1-56309-305-7*) Womans Mission Union.

Branum, Nell, ed. see Foster, Mary.

***Branwhite, Tony.** Helping Adolescents in School. LC 99-86104. 200p. 2000. 65.00 (*0-275-96898-7*, Praeger Pubs) Greenwood.

Branwyn, Gareth. Jamming the Media: A Citizen's Guide; Reclaiming the Tools of Communication. 1997. pap. 18.95 (*0-8118-1795-4*) Chronicle Bks.

— Jargonwatch: A Pocket Dictionary for the Jiterati. 1997. pap. 71.50 (*1-888869-10-0*) Wired Bks.

Branwyn, Gareth, ed. Jargon Watch: A Pocket Dictionary for the Jitterati. LC 97-174475. 168p. 1997. 8.95 (*1-888869-06-2*) Wired Bks.

Branwyn, Garth. Jamming the Media. 1996. pap. 22.00 (*0-8129-6381-4*) Random.

Branyon, Beth. Miss Alma: Friend of Missions. LC 96-68864. (Little MISSionary Bks.). (Illus.). 32p. (Orig.). (J). (gr. 5-8). 1996. pap. 8.95 (*1-57736-012-5*) Providence Hse.

— Miss Eloise: First Lady of Foreign Missions. LC 96-68862. (Little MISSionary Bks.: Vol. 1). (Illus.). 32p. (Orig.). (J). (gr. 3-4). 1996. pap. 8.95 (*1-881576-78-7*) Providence Hse.

— Miss Fannie: Leader for WMU. LC 98-65214. (Little MISSionary Bks.). 32p. (J). (gr. 3-5). 1998. pap. 8.95 (*1-57736-094-X*) Providence Hse.

— Miss Henrietta: Lady of Many Firsts. LC 96-68865. (Little MISSionary Bks.). (Illus.). 32p. (Orig.). (J). (gr. 3-5). 1996. pap. 8.95 (*1-57736-013-3*) Providence Hse.

— Miss Jessie: Missionary Nurse in China. LC 96-68863. (Little MISSionary Bks.: Vol. 2). (Illus.). 32p. (Orig.). (J). (gr. 3-4). 1996. pap. 8.95 (*1-881576-77-9*) Providence Hse.

— Miss Mary Ellen: Watching God Work. LC 98-65215. (Little MISSionary Bks.). 32p. (J). (gr. 3-5). 1998. pap. 8.95 (*1-57736-093-1*) Providence Hse.

Branyon, Bill. The Blue Ridge Blues. 221p. 1995. 10.00 (*0-9648305-0-7*) Urthona Pr.

Branyon, Ricahrd A., tr. see Branyon, Richard A., ed.

Branyon, Richard. Latin Phrases & Quotations. LC 96-38585. 180p. 1997. reprint ed. pap. 14.95 (*0-7818-0260-1*) Hippocrene Bks.

Branyon, Richard, ed. Treasury of French Love Poems, Quotations & Proverbs. 128p. 1994. 11.95 (*0-7818-0307-1*) Hippocrene Bks.

— Treasury of Roman Love Poems, Quotations & Proverbs. 128p. 1994. 11.95 (*0-7818-0309-8*) Hippocrene Bks.

Branyon, Richard A., ed. Treasury of Italian Love Poems, Quotations & Proverbs. Branyon, Ricahrd A., tr. (Bilingual Love Poetry Ser.). 12.95 incl. audio (*0-7818-0366-7*, 581) Hippocrene Bks.

— Treasury of Italian Love Poems, Quotations & Proverbs. (Hippocrene Treasury of Love Poems Ser.). (ITA.). 128p. 1995. 11.95 (*0-7818-0352-7*) Hippocrene Bks.

Branz, Charles G. Beyond the Horizon: Overcoming the Fear of Death. 64p. 1991. 4.95 (*0-9629500-0-9*) C G Branz Min.

Branz, H. M., et al, eds. Amorphous & Heterogeneous Silicon Thin Films Fundamentals to Devices, 1999 Vol. 557: Materials Research Society Symposium Proceedings. 588p. 1999. text 77.00 (*1-55899-464-5*) Materials Res.

Branz, Nedra, jt. ed. see Lawrence, Barbara.

Branzei, D. & Miron, Radu. Backgrounds of Arithmetic & Geometry - An Introduction. LC 96-116257. (Series in Pure Mathematics: Vol. 23). 300p. 1995. text 62.00 (*981-02-2210-6*) World Scientific Pub.

Branzei, Sylvia. Animal Grossology: The Science of Creatures Gross & Disgusting. LC 97-120351. (Illus.). 80p. (J). (gr. 4-8). 1996. pap. 12.99 (*0-201-95994-1*) Addison-Wesley.

— Grossology: The Science of Really Gross Things! LC 96-168347. 64p. (J). 1995. pap. 14.99 (*0-201-40964-X*) Addison-Wesley.

— Grossology Begins at Home. (Illus.). 80p. (J). (gr. 4 up). 1997. pap. 12.99 (*0-201-95993-3*) Addison-Wesley.

***Branzei, Sylvia.** Hands-On Grossology: The Science of Really Gross Experiments. LC 99-42380. 80p. 1999. pap. 5.99 (*0-448-44083-0*) Gd Canyon Railway.

Branzei, Sylvia. Virtual Grossology. (Illus.). 80p. (J). (gr. 4 up). 1997. spiral bd. 19.95 (*0-201-15417-X*) Addison-Wesley.

Branzei-Velasquez, Sylvia. How to Write Your Own Mystery. 1997. spiral bd. write for info. (*0-201-15166-9*) Addison-Wesley.

Branzi, Andrea & Morozzi, Christina. Andrea Branzi. (Illus.). 128p. 1997. pap. 23.50 (*2-906571-61-X*) Dist Art Pubs.

***Branzi, Muschamp A. & Radice, B.** Ettore Sottsass: The Architecture & Design of Sottsass Associates. LC 99-24964. (Illus.). 280p. 1999. pap. 25.00 (*0-7893-0358-2*, Pub. by Universe) St Martin.

Branzinsky, Terri C. & Bowden, Kathi, eds. Santa Catalina Cookbook, Vol. I. 2nd rev. ed. O'Donnell, Carlotta & Santa Catalina Students & Faculty Staff, trs. (Illus.). 293p. 1983. 15.50 (*0-9612300-0-2*) Santa Catalina.

Braquet, P., ed. Platelet-Activating Factor & Cell Immunology. (New Trends in Lipid Mediators Research Ser.: Vol. 1). viii, 180p. 1988. 146.25 (*3-8055-4684-X*) S Karger.

— The Role of Platelet-Activating Factor in Immune Disorders, Part 2. (New Trends in Lipid Mediators Research Ser.: Vol. 2). (Illus.). viii, 214p. 1988. 172.25 (*3-8055-4744-7*) S Karger.

Braquet, P., et al, eds. Biologically Active Ether Lipids. (Progress in Biochemical Pharmacology Ser.: Vol. 22). (Illus.). vi, 198p. 1988. 143.50 (*3-8055-4669-6*) S Karger.

Braquet, Pierre, ed. Handbook of PAF - PAF Antagonists. 296p. 1991. lib. bdg. 219.00 (*0-8493-3524-8*, QP752) CRC Pr.

Braquet, Pierre, et al, eds. Prostaglandins & Membrane Ion Transport. LC 84-24949. (Advances in Ion Transport Regulation Ser.: No. 1). (Illus.). 430p. 1985. reprint ed. pap. 133.30 (*0-608-00658-0*, 206124600007) Bks Demand.

Brar, A. S. & Narayan, P. B. Materials & Processing Failures in the Electronics & Computer Industries. 330p. 1993. 135.00 (*0-87170-468-4*) ASM.

***Brar, K. S.** Operation Blue Star: The True Story. 1998. reprint ed. pap. 11.50 (*81-7476-068-7*, Pub. by UBS Pubs) S Asia.

Brara, N. Vijaylakshmi. Politics, Society, & Cosmology in India's North East. LC 98-902935. (Illus.). 272p. 1998. text 24.95 (*0-19-564331-3*) OUP.

Braren, Ken, jt. auth. see Griffith, Roger.

Bras, Georges le, see Le Bras, Georges.

Bras, Juan M. Hostos, Periodista. 12p. 1988. pap. 3.00 (*0-685-51572-9*) U of PR Pr.

Bras, Karin, jt. ed. see Dalles, Heidi.

Bras, R. L. & Prinn, R. G. The World at Risk: Natural Hazards & Climate Change. (Conference Proceeding Ser.). 1992. 120.00 (*1-56396-066-4*) Am Inst Physics.

Bras, Rafael L. & Rodriguez-Iturbe, Ignacio. Random Functions & Hydrology. LC 93-29005. (Illus.). xv, 559p. 1993. reprint ed. pap. 14.95 (*0-486-67626-9*) Dover.

Bras, Yvon Le, see Dengler, William & Le Bras, Yvon.

Bras, Yvon Le, see Quiring, James P. & Le Bras, Yvon.

Bras, Yvon Le, see Scharf, Janet & Le Bras, Yvon.

Brasavolus, Antonius M. Index Refertissimus in Omnes Galeni Libros Qui Ex Nona Junctarum Editone Extant. 1096p. 1975. reprint ed. 400.00 (*3-487-05838-3*) G Olms Pubs.

Brasch. Reminiscences of a Roving Rabbit. 1999. 20.00 (*0-207-18979-X*, Pub. by Ang Robertson) Consort Bk Sales.

Brasch, R. The Book of Anniversaries. (Illus.). 64p. 1998. 9.00 (*0-207-18509-3*) HarpC.

— Cat's Pyjamas. 1998. pap. 12.95 (*0-207-18970-6*) HarpC.

Brasch, Robert C., et al, eds. MRI Contrast Enhancement in the Central Nervous System: A Case Study Approach. LC 93-25655. (Illus.). 348p. 1993. reprint ed. pap. 107.90 (*0-608-05841-6*, 205980700007) Bks Demand.

Brasch, Walt. Enquiring Minds & Space Aliens: Wandering Through the Mass Media & Popular Culture. 224p. (Orig.). 1995. pap. 14.95 (*0-9624613-4-2*) Mayfly Prodns.

— Sex & One Single Beer Can: Probing the Mass Media & American Culture. 256p. 1997. pap. 19.95 (*0-9624613-6-9*) Mayfly Prodns.

Brasch, Walter M. Betrayed: The Death of an American Newspaper, the Globe Times of Bethlehem, Pennsylvania. LC 95-32888. (C). 1996. write for info. (*0-934223-38-6*) Lehigh Univ Pr.

— Black English & the Mass Media. LC 81-2762. 376p. 1981. lib. bdg. 40.00 (*0-87023-335-1*) U of Mass Pr.

— Brer Rabbit, Uncle Remus & the 'Cornfield Journalist' The Tale of Joel Chandler Harris. 1999. write for info. (*0-89089-690-9*) Carolina Acad Pr.

***Brasch, Walter M.** Brer Rabbit, Uncle Remus & the 'Cornfield Journalist' The Tale of Joel Chandler Harris. (Illus.). 448p. 2000. 29.95 (*0-86554-696-7*) Mercer Univ Pr.

Brasch, Walter M. Columbia County Place-Name. rev. ed. (Illus.). 254p. 1997. 29.95 (*0-9624613-5-0*) Mayfly Prodns.

— Forerunners of Revolution: Muckrakers & the American Social Conscience. 208p. (Orig.). (C). 1990. pap. text 21.50 (*0-8191-7968-X*); lib. bdg. 42.00 (*0-8191-7967-1*) U Pr of Amer.

— With Just Cause: Unionization of the American Journalist. 511p. (Orig.). (C). 1991. pap. text 34.50 (*0-8191-8361-X*); lib. bdg. 57.50 (*0-8191-8360-1*) U Pr of Amer.

Brasch, Walter M. & Ulloth, Dana R. The Press & the State: Sociohistorical & Contemporary Interpretations. LC 86-15855. 826p. (Orig.). (C). 1987. lib. bdg. 84.00 (*0-8191-5502-0*) U Pr of Amer.

Brasch, Walter S., ed. see Zimmerman, Eugene.

***Brasche, Mark.** Child Safety-Nets: How to Protect Your Children from Harm Online. (Illus.). 204p. 1999. 19.95 (*0-9677041-0-3*) New England Web.

Braschi, Giannina. Empire of Dreams. LC 94-648. 232p. 1994. 25.00 (*0-300-05795-4*) Yale U Pr.

— El Imperio de los Suednos. LC 99-43272. 1999. pap. write for info. (*0-8477-0393-2*) U of PR Pr.

— Yo-Yo Boing! LC 98-27655. (ENG & SPA.). 192p. 1998. pap. 15.95 (*0-935480-97-8*, Pub. by Lat Am Lit Rev Pr) Consort Bk Sales.

Braschler, Mathias. Madison Avenue. 1999. 45.00 (*3-905328-16-X*) Scalo Pubs.

Brascome, Anna, jt. ed. see Wieck, Stewart.

Brase. Understanding Basis Statistics. 1999. text 46.77 (*0-618-00460-2*) HM.

***Brase.** Understanding Statistics Excel Guide. 6th ed. 1999. pap. text 5.07 (*0-618-01568-X*) HM.

Brase, ed. see Vance, Timothy J. & Chino, Naoko.

Brase, Charles & Brase, Corrinne. Understanding Basic Statistics. 608p. (C). 1996. pap. text 53.56 (*0-669-39812-8*) HM Trade Div.

— Understanding Basic Statistics. (C). 1996. pap. text, student ed. 19.16 (*0-669-39814-4*) HM Trade Div.

Brase, Charles H. & Brace, Corrinne P. Understandable Statistics: Concepts & Methods. 3rd ed. LC 86-81382. 544p. (C). 1987. text 72.76 (*0-669-12181-9*) HM Trade Div.

Brase, Charles H. & Brase, Corrinne P. Understandable Statistics: Concepts & Methods, 4 Vols. 4th ed. LC 90-83093. 616p. (C). 1991. text 71.16 (*0-669-24477-5*); pap. text, student ed. 22.36 (*0-669-24479-1*); teacher ed. 2.66 (*0-669-24478-3*); 2.66 (*0-669-27152-7*) HM Trade Div.

Brase, Charles H. & Brase, Corrinne P. Understandable Statistics: Concepts & Methods, 5 Vols. (C). 1995. text, teacher ed. 2.66 (*0-669-39478-5*) HM Trade Div.

— Understandable Statistics: Concepts & Methods, 5 Vols. 5th ed. 832p. (C). 1995. text 72.76 (*0-669-35513-5*) HM Trade Div.

— Understandable Statistics: Concepts & Methods, 5 Vols. 5th annot. ed. (C). 1995. text, teacher ed. 64.76 (*0-669-35514-3*) HM Trade Div.

— Understandable Statistics: Concepts & Methods: Study & Solutions Guide, 5 Vols. 5th ed. (C). 1995. pap. text 22.76 (*0-669-39479-3*) HM Trade Div.

***Brase, Charles Henry & Brase, Corrinne Pellillo.** Understandable Statistics: Concepts & Methods. 6th ed. LC 98-72000. xxiv, 775 p. 1999. write for info. (*0-395-90769-1*) HM.

Brase, Corinne P., jt. auth. see Brase, Charles H.

Brase, Corrinne, jt. auth. see Brase, Charles.

Brase, Corrinne P., jt. auth. see Brase, Charles H.

Brase, Corrinne Pellillo, jt. auth. see Brase, Charles Henry.

Brase, Kristin. My Funny Therapist. Dageforde, Linda J., ed. 32p. 1998. pap. 6.95 (*1-886225-32-X*, 1000) Dageforde Pub.

Brase, Lee. Praying from God's Heart: Experiencing the Power of God-Focused Prayer. 96p. (Orig.). 1994. pap. 6.00 (*0-89109-792-9*) NavPress.

Brase, Michael, ed. see Japan Council of International Schools Staff.

Brase, Michael, ed. see Kominz, Laurence R.

***Brasel, Jean.** Forever Friends: The Interactive Guide to Lasting Agreements & Loving Relationships. Sweet, Kate, ed. (Illus.). 76p. 1999. pap. 39.95 incl. VHS (*0-9677651-2-9*) BE Corp.

***Brasel, Jean & Sweet, Kate.** Forever Friends: The Interactive Guide to Lasting Agreements & Loving Relationships. (Illus.). 76p. 1999. pap. 24.95 (*0-9677651-0-2*) BE Corp.

Braselmane & Miller, James Russell. The Wedded Life. 84p. 1979. pap. 3.90 (*0-7399-0211-3*, 2465) Rod & Staff.

Braselton, James, jt. auth. see Abell, Martha.

Braselton, James P., jt. auth. see Abell, Martha L.

Braselton, Susan C., jt. auth. see Civil War Trust Staff.

Brasfield, Barry, jt. auth. see Berry, Arnold.

Brasfield, Curtis G. The Ancestry of Mayor Harold Washington. (Illus.). xii, 113p. (Orig.). 1993. pap. text 20.00 (*1-55613-750-8*) Heritage Bk.

Brasfield, James, tr. see Lysheha, Oleh.

Brasfield, Philip & Elliot, Jeffrey M. Deathman Pass Me By: Two Years on Death Row. LC 82-4126. (Borgo Bioviews Ser.). (Illus.). 96p. 1983. pap. 15.00 (*0-89370-264-1*) Millefleurs.

Brash, Donald T. American Investment in Australian Industry. LC 66-31366. 381p. 1966. 40.00 (*0-674-02500-8*) HUP.

— New Zealand's Remarkable Reforms: Fifth IEA Annual Hayek Memorial Lecture. (Occasional Paper Ser.: No. 100). 56p. 1996. pap. 13.95 (*0-255-36400-8*, Pub. by Inst Economic Affairs) Coronet Bks.

Brash, Gary, photos by. Willamette University - Then & Now: 150th Anniversary. (First Edition Ser.). (Illus.). 112p. 1992. 39.95 (*0-916509-95-8*) Harmony Hse Pub.

Brash, John L. & Horbett, Thomas A., eds. Proteins at Interfaces: Physicochemical & Biochemical Studies. LC 87-14394. (Symposium Ser.: No. 343). x, 715p. 1987. 99.95 (*0-8412-1403-4*) Am Chemical.

— Proteins at Interfaces: Physicochemical & Biochemical Studies. LC 87-14394. (ACS Symposium Ser.: Vol. 343). 716p. 1987. reprint ed. pap. 200.00 (*0-608-03536-X*, 206425500008) Bks Demand.

Brash, John L. & Wojciechowski, eds. Interfacial Phenomena & Bioproducts. (Bioprocess Technology Ser.: Vol. 23). (Illus.). 528p. 1996. text 189.00 (*0-8247-9651-9*) Dekker.

Brash, John L., jt. ed. see Horbett, Thomas A.

Brash, Sarah, ed. see Time-Life Books Editors.

Brashear, Aleeta, et al. Thirteen Tales of the Fae. (Illus.). 131p. 1998. spiral bd. 7.95 (*0-9663820-0-5*) Gerl Publishing.

***Brashear, Charles.** Comeuppance at Kicking Horse Casino. LC 00-101309. (Native American Literature Ser.: 10). 200p. (C). 2000. pap. 15.00 (*0-935626-51-4*) U Cal AISC.

Brashear, Charles. Killing Cynthia Ann. LC 99-27674. 216p. 1999. 21.50 (*0-87565-209-3*, Pub. by Tex Christian) Tex A&M Univ Pr.

— A Writer's Toolkit: Essays, Poems, Stories. 288p. (Orig.). 1991. pap. 14.95 (*0-933362-13-7*) Assoc Creative Writers.

Brashear, H. Robert, Jr. & Raney, Richard B. Handbook of Orthopaedic Surgery. 10th ed. (Illus.). 560p. (C). (gr. 13). 1986. text 57.95 (*0-8016-4080-6*, 04080) Mosby Inc.

Brashear, Jean. The Bodyguard's Bride: Women to Watch. (Special Edition Ser.: No. 1206). 1998. per. 4.25 (*0-373-24206-9*, 1-24206-4) Harlequin Bks.

— A Family Secret. (Special Edition Ser.: No. 1266). 1999. per. 4.25 (*0-373-24266-2*, 1-24266-8) Silhouette.

***Brashear, Jean.** Lonesome No More. (Special Edition Ser.: No. 1302). 2000. per. 4.50 (*0-373-24302-2*, 1-24302-1) Harlequin Bks.

— Texas Royalty. (Special Edition Ser.). 2000. mass mkt. 4.50 (*0-373-24343-X*, 1-24343-5) Silhouette.

Brashear, John A. A Man Who Loved the Stars: The Autobiography of John A. Brashear. LC 87-25190. (Illus.). 224p. 1988. reprint ed. pap. 69.50 (*0-608-00899-0*, 206169300010) Bks Demand.

Brashear, Sally S. & Herman, Eric. W. Quality Initiative Law Offices. 192p. 1995. pap. text, per. 59.95 (*0-7872-0061-1*) Kendall-Hunt.

Brashear, William. A Northwood Lad. Costa, Gwen, ed. LC 90-1137. (YA). (gr. 6 up). 1992. pap. 14.95 (*0-87949-333-X*) Ashley Bks.

Brashear, William R. The Desolation of Reality, Vol. 174. LC 94-40614. (American University Studies: Series V). 106p. (C). 1995. text 37.95 (*0-8204-2735-7*) P Lang Pubng.

— Living Will: A Study of Tennyson & 19th Century Subjectivism. (Studies in English Literature: No. 52). (Orig.). 1969. text 23.10 (*3-11-000275-2*) Mouton.

Brashears & Kinley. Challenging Biases... Facing Our Fears. 272p. (C). 1998. per. 54.95 (*0-7872-5592-0*, 41559201) Kendall-Hunt.

Brashears, Deya. Dribble Drabble: Art Experiences for Young Children. rev. ed. (Illus.). 120p. 1985. reprint ed. pap. 11.95 (*0-9614717-0-0*) Deya Brashears.

Brashears, Deya & Brashears, Lea. More Dribble Drabble: Process-Oriented Art. (Illus.). 120p. (Orig.). 1992. pap. text 14.95 (*0-9614717-2-7*) Deya Brashears.

Brashears, Deya & Krull, Sharron W., eds. Circle Time Activities for Young Children. (Illus.). 139p. (Orig.). 1981. pap. 16.95 (*0-9614717-1-9*) Deya Brashears.

Brashears, Lea, jt. auth. see Brashears, Deya.

***Brasher, Bart.** Implosion: Downsizing the U.S. Military, 1987-2015, 196. LC 99-55182. (Contributions in Military Studies Ser.). 280p. 2000. 62.50 (*0-313-31467-5*, Greenwood Pr) Greenwood.

Brasher, Brenda E. Godly Women: Fundamentalism & Female Power. LC 97-17790. 216p. 1998. pap. 19.00 (*0-8135-2468-7*) Rutgers U Pr.

— Godly Women: Fundamentalism & Female Power. LC 97-17790. 224p. 1998. 48.00 (*0-8135-2467-9*) Rutgers U Pr.

***Brasher, Brenda E., ed.** Encyclopedia of Fundamentalism. (Encyclopedias of Religion & Society Ser.). 512p. 2001. 125.00 (*0-415-92244-5*) Routledge.

Brasher, J. Lawrence. The Sanctified South: John Lakin Brasher & the Holiness Movement. LC 93-13604. (Illus.). 296p. 1994. 39.95 incl. audio, digital audio (*0-252-02116-9*); text 29.95 (*0-252-02050-2*); audio 13.95 (*0-252-02114-2*) U of Ill Pr.

Brasher, Nell. The Weaning: And Other Stories. 192p. 1993. 9.95 (*1-881548-01-5*) Crane Hill AL.

Brasher, Pep. How-To Start a Successful Home-Based Business: An In-Home Business Guide. (Moonlighting Momentarily Ser.). 90p. 1990. pap. 29.95 (*1-57555-002-4*) Cedar Bay Pr.

Brasher, Thomas L. Whitman As Editor of the Brooklyn Daily Eagle. LC 70-91872. 264p. reprint ed. 81.90 (*0-608-16969-2*, 202759500055) Bks Demand.

Brashers, Charles. A Snug Little Purchase: How Richard Henderson Bought Kaintuckee from the Cherokees in 1775. LC 78-74150. (Illus.). 1979. 7.95 (*0-933362-01-3*) Assoc Creative Writers.

Brashers, Dale E., jt. auth. see Jackson, Sally E.

***Brashers, Valentina L.** Clinical Applications of Pathophysiology. (Illus.). 432p. (C). 1998. text. write for info. (*0-323-00149-1*) Mosby Inc.

Brashett, N. V. Planned Management of Forests. 238p. 1985. reprint ed. 150.00 (*0-7855-3070-3*, Pub. by Intl Bk Distr) St Mut.

Brashich, Catherine, ed. World Manual for Group & Incentive Travel. 1000p. 1990. 149.00 (*0-9627465-0-9*) Networld.

Brashinsky, Michael & Horton, Andrew, eds. Russian Critics on the Cinema of Glasnost. LC 93-43590 (Studies in Film). (Illus.). 175p. (C). 1994. text 64.95 (*0-521-44475-6*) Cambridge U Pr.

Brashler, Anne. Getting Jesus in the Mood. LC 90-84011. 106p. (Orig.). (C). 1991. pap. 8.95 (*0-943433-06-1*) Cane Hill Pr.

Brashler, William. The Bingo Long Traveling All-Stars & Motor Kings. LC 92-46723. (Illus.). 280p. 1993. 14.95 (*0-252-06287-6*) U of Ill Pr.

***Brashler, William.** Josh Gibson: A Life in the Negro Leagues. LC 99-57926. (Illus.). 224p. 2000. pap. 14.95 (*1-56663-295-1*, Pub. by I R Dee) Natl Bk Netwk.

Brashler, William. The Story of Negro League Baseball. LC 93-36547. 144p. (J). (gr. 3 up). 1994. 15.95 (*0-395-67169-8*) Ticknor & Flds Bks Yng Read.

— Traders. 1990. reprint ed. mass mkt. 4.95 (*1-55817-460-5*, Pinncle Kensgtn) Kensgtn Pub Corp.

Brasholz, Anton. Lexikon der Anstrichtechnik, Vol. 2. (GER.). 1975. 95.00 (*0-8288-5915-9*, M7280) Fr & Eur.

Brasier, Tim, et al. The Hypocritic Oath: Porno Politics - Puritanism - The President. 112p. 1999. pap. 6.95 (*0-9668993-7-7*) Mardon Pr.

Brasil, Emanuel & Smith, William J., eds. Brazilian Poetry, (1950-1980) LC 83-199745. 197p. reprint ed. pap. 61.10 (*0-7837-0209-4*, 204051700017) Bks Demand.

Brasil, Emanuel, jt. ed. see Bishop, Elizabeth.

Brasile, Frank, et al, eds. Perspectives in Recreational Therapy: Issues of a Dynamic Profession. (Illus.). 550p. 1998. pap. 45.00 (*1-882883-26-8*) Idyll Arbor.

Brasileiro, Ana M., ed. Gender & Sustainable Development. 79p. 1997. pap. 7.95 (*0-912917-45-8*) UNIFEM.

— Women Against Violence: Breaking the Silence. 116p. 1997. pap. 9.95 (*0-912917-32-6*) UNIFEM.

— Women's Leadership in a Changing World. 76p. 1996. pap. 7.95 (*0-912917-40-7*) UNIFEM.

Brasillach, Robert, jt. auth. see Bardeche, Maurice.

Brasington, Bruce C., jt. auth. see Somerville, Robert.

Brasington, Leann, ed. see Chaney, Warren H.

***Brask, K. Alan.** Tiger Success: Thriving in Our Jungle... With Skill Learned in Theirs. 128p. 2000. pap. 12.95 (*0-9701933-0-0*) Paperwhite Pr.

Brask, Ole. Photographs Jazz. 120p. 1995. 65.00 (*3-926048-63-8*) Dist Art Pubs.

Brask, Per. Essays on Kushner's Angels. LC 96-165381. 160p. 1996. pap. text 19.95 (*0-921368-57-7*) Blizzard Publ.

Brask, Per & Morgan, William, eds. Aboriginal Voices: Amerindian, Inuit, & Sami Theater. (PAJ Bks.). (Illus.). 168p. 1992. text 30.00 (*0-8018-4376-6*) Johns Hopkins.

Brask, Per & Szanto, George. Duets. 176p. 1989. pap. 9.95 (*1-55050-000-7*, Pub. by Coteau) Genl Dist Srvs.

Braskamp, Larry A. & Ory, John C. Assessing Faculty Work: Enhancing Individual & Institutional Performance. LC 93-42904. (Higher & Adult Education Ser.). 355p. 1994. text 34.95 (*1-55542-635-2*) Jossey-Bass.

Braskamp, Larry A., et al. Evaluating Teaching Effectiveness. fac. ed. LC 84-9942. (Illus.). 136p. 1984. pap. 42.20 (*0-7837-7703-5*, 204746000007) Bks Demand.

Braskamp, Larry A., jt. ed. see Wergin, Jon F.

Braslavski, W., jt. auth. see Srokovsky, Y.

Braslow, jt. auth. see Goldberg.

Braslow, Joel. Curative Measures: Body Cures for Mental Illness, 1900-1950s. LC 96-39469. (Medicine & Society Ser.). 262p. 1997. 45.00 (*0-520-20547-2*, Pub. by U CA Pr) Cal Prin Full Svc.

Brasmer, Timothy H. The Acutely Traumatized Small Animal Patient. (Major Problems in Veterinary Medicine Ser.: Vol. 2). (Illus.). 192p. 1984. text 69.00 (*0-7216-1917-7*, W B Saunders Co) Harcrt Hlth Sci Grp.

Brasmer, William, ed. see O'Keefe, John & Shield, William.

***Brasner, Shari E.** Advice from a Pregnant Obstetrician: An Insider's Guide. LC 97-36475. 241p. 1998. pap. 12.45 (*0-7868-8339-1*, Pub. by Hyperion) Time Warner.

Brasnett, N. V. Planned Management of Forests. 238p. 1985. pap. 275.00 (*81-7089-024-1*, Pub. by Intl Bk Distr) St Mut.

— Planned Management of Forests. 238p. (C). 1985. 50.00 (*0-7855-3251-X*, Pub. by Scientific) St Mut.

Brasol, Boris. Elements of Crime: Psycho-Social Interpretation. 2nd ed. LC 69-16226. (Criminology, Law Enforcement, & Social Problems Ser.: No. 93). 1969. reprint ed. 28.00 (*0-87585-093-6*) Patterson Smith.

— The World at the Crossroads. 1973. 75.00 (*0-8490-1333-X*) Gordon Pr.

Braspenning, P. J., et al, eds. Artificial Neural Networks: An Introduction to ANN Theory & Practice. (Lecture Notes in Computer Science Ser.: Vol. 931). 1995. write for info. (*0-387-59488-4*) Spr-Verlag.

Brass, Betty & Einsel, Mary. Peanut Butter Delights: Peanut Butter Cookbook - 200 Recipes. LC 86-63090. Orig. Title: Peanut Butter Madness. (Illus.). 174p. 1986. reprint ed. pap. 13.95 (*0-9660552-0-9*) Peanut But Del.

Brass, Danny A. Rabies in Bats: Natural History & Public Health Implications. LC 93-78291. (Illus.). 335p. 1994. 49.95 (*0-9637045-1-6*) Livia Pr CT.

Brass, George, Jr. Mental Illness & the Naked Truth of Life & Sex. 24p. 1999. pap. 6.00 (*0-8059-4397-8*) Dorrance.

Brass, H. & Hammerlin, Gunther, eds. Numerical Integration IV: Proceedings of the Conference at the Mathematical Research Institute at Oberwolfach, November 8-14, 1992. LC 93-5106. (International Series of Numerical Mathematics: Vol. 112). 400p. 1993. 119.00 (*0-8176-2922-X*) Birkhauser.

Brass, H., jt. ed. see Hammerlin, Gunther.

Brass, Lawrence M. & Stys, Peter K. Handbook of Neurological Lists. (Illus.). 397p. 1991. pap. text 37.00 (*0-443-08696-6*) Church.

— Handbook of Neurological Lists. LC 91-10749. (Illus.). 413p. reprint ed. pap. 128.10 (*0-7837-6807-9*, 204663900003) Bks Demand.

Brass, Len. Children First: A Complete Guide for Parenting Through the Elementary School Years. LC 94-32877. 144p. (Orig.). 1994. pap. 14.95 (*0-942963-58-X*) Distinctive Pub.

Brass, Mary C., ed. Village Harmony: Traditional Songs of the Balkans. 2nd rev. ed. (Illus.). 44p. (Orig.). 1995. pap. 8.00 (*0-9627554-5-1*) Nrthn Harmony Pub.

Brass, Paul & Robinson, Frances. The Indian National Congress & India Society, 1885-1985: Social Structure & Political adj Dominance. (C). 1987. 44.00 (*81-7001-026-8*, Pub. by Chanakya) S Asia.

Brass, Paul R. Ethnicity & Nationalism: Theory & Comparison. (Illus.). 300p. 1992. 32.00 (*0-8039-9694-2*); pap. 16.50 (*0-8039-9695-0*) Sage.

— The Politics of India since Independence. 2nd ed. LC 93-30782. (New Cambridge History of India Ser.: No. IV: 1). (Illus.). 423p. (C). 1994. text 69.95 (*0-521-45362-3*); pap. text 24.95 (*0-521-45970-2*) Cambridge U Pr.

— Theft of an Idol: Text & Context in the Representation of Collective Violence. LC 96-9315. (Princeton Studies in Culture, Power & History). 317p. 1997. text 55.00 (*0-691-02651-3*, Pub. by Princeton U Pr); pap. text 17.95 (*0-691-02650-5*, Pub. by Princeton U Pr) Cal Prin Full Svc.

B

Brass, Paul R., ed. Riots & Pogroms. 320p. (C). 1996. text 45.00 (*0-8147-1274-6*) NYU Pr.

— Riots & Pogroms. (C). 1998. pap. text 18.50 (*0-8147-1282-7*) NYU Pr.

Brass, Perry. Albert: or The Book of Man. Laine, Tom, ed. LC 94-74524. (Ki Chronicles Ser.: Bk. 3). 216p. (Orig.). 1995. pap. 11.95 (*0-9627123-5-3*) Belhue Pr.

— Angel Lust: An Erotic Novel of Time Travel. Laine, Tom, ed. 224p. 1999. pap. 12.95 (*1-892149-00-1*, Pub. by Belhue Pr) LPC InBook.

— Circles. Laine, Tom, ed. LC 93-70194. (Ki Chronicles Ser.: Bk. 2). 216p. (Orig.). 1993. pap. 11.95 (*0-9627123-3-7*) Belhue Pr.

— The Harvest. Laine, Tom, ed. LC 96-79452. 224p. (Orig.). 1997. pap. 11.95 (*0-9627123-7-X*) Belhue Pr.

— How to Survive Your Own Gay Life: The Adult Guide to Love, Sex & Relationships. Laine, Tom, ed. LC 98-70408. (Illus.). 224p. (Orig.). 1999. pap. 11.95 (*0-9627123-9-6*) Belhue Pr.

— The Lover of My Soul: A Search for Ecstasy & Wisdom. Laine, Tom, ed. LC 97-73677. (Illus.). 96p. (Orig.). 1997. pap. 8.95 (*0-9627123-8-8*) Belhue Pr.

— Mirage. Laine, Tom, ed. LC 71-73116. (Ki Chronicles Ser.: Bk. 1). 219p. 1991. pap. 10.95 (*0-9627123-1-0*) Belhue Pr.

— Out There: Stories of Private Desires, Horror & the After Life. Laine, Tom, ed. LC 94-70482. 192p. (Orig.). 1994. pap. 10.95 (*0-9627123-4-5*) Belhue Pr.

— Sex-Charge. Hammond, John, ed. LC 90-83699. (Illus.). 76p. (Orig.). 1991. pap. 6.95 (*0-9627123-0-2*) Belhue Pr.

— Works: And Other Smoky George Stories. Laine, Tom, ed. LC 92-71426. 160p. (Orig.). 1992. pap. 9.95 (*0-9627123-2-9*) Belhue Pr.

— Works: And Other Smoky George Stories. 2nd expanded ed. Laine, Tom, ed. LC 96-83493. 192p. (Orig.). 1996. pap. 9.95 (*0-9627123-6-1*) Belhue Pr.

Brass, Richard J., ed. see National Council of Staff, Program & Organizationa.

***Brass, Steve.** Fearless Living: 9 Keys to Get from Where You Are to Where You Truly Want to Be. 193p. 2000. pap. 14.95 (*0-9684055-1-7*) Oct Hse Pub.

***Brass, Tom.** Peasants, Populism & Postmodernism: The Return of the Agrarian Myth. (Library of Peasant Studies: No. 17). 304p. 2000. 52.50 (*0-7146-4940-6*, Pub. by F Cass Pubs); pap. 24.50 (*0-7146-8000-1*, Pub. by F Cass Pubs) Intl Spec Bk.

— Towards a Comparative Political Economy of Unfree Labour: Case Studies & Debates. LC 99-24213. (Library of Peasant Studies: No. 16). 360p. 1999. 52.50 (*0-7146-4938-4*, Pub. by F Cass Pubs); pap. 22.50 (*0-7146-4498-6*, Pub. by F Cass Pubs) Intl Spec Bk.

Brass, Tom, ed. New Farmer's Movements in India. LC 94-31412. 290p. 1994. pap. 19.50 (*0-7146-4134-0*, Pub. by F Cass Pubs) Intl Spec Bk.

Brass, Tom & Byres, T. J., eds. New Farmer's Movements in India. LC 94-31412. 1994. 45.00 (*0-7146-4609-1*) Intl Spec Bk.

Brass, Tom & Van Der Linden, Marcel, eds. Free & Unfree Labour: The Debate Continues. LC 97-47272. (International & Comparative Social History Ser.: Vol. 5). 602p. (C). 1998. text 78.95 (*0-8204-3424-8*) P Lang Pubng.

Brass, Tom & Van der Linden, Marcel, eds. Free & Unfree Labour: The Debate Continues, No. 5. 602p. 1997. 78.95 (*3-906756-87-4*) P Lang Pubng.

***Brass, Tom, et al.** Signpost Guide: New England. 2000. pap. 22.95 (*0-7627-0678-3*) Globe Pequot.

Brass, Tom, ed. see Byres, T. J., et al.

Brass, William, ed. see National Research Council Staff.

Brassai. Henry Miller: The Paris Years. Bent, Timothy, tr. LC 94-39261. (ENG & FRE., Illus.). 224p. 1995. 23.45 (*1-55970-287-7*, Pub. by Arcade Pub Inc) Time Warner.

— Letters to My Parents. 1998. pap. 16.00 (*0-226-07147-2*) U Ch Pr.

*__Brassai, Brassai.__ Proust. 1998. 25.00 (*0-226-07144-8*) U Ch Pr.

Brassard, Ed. Body for Sale: An Inside Look at Medical Research, Drug Testing & Organ Transplants & How You Can Profit from Them. (Illus.). 96p. 1996. pap. 15.00 (*0-87364-858-7*) Paladin Pr.

*__Brassard, Francis.__ The Concept of Bodhicitta in Santideva's Bodhicaryavatara. LC 99-41324. (C). 2000. text 57.50 (*0-7914-4575-5*); pap. text 18.95 (*0-7914-4576-3*) State U NY Pr.

Brassard, G., ed. Advances in Cryptology--CRYPTO '89: Proceedings. (Lecture Notes in Computer Science Ser.: Vol. 435). xiii, 634p. 1990. pap. 60.00 (*0-387-97317-6*) Spr-Verlag.

Brassard, Gilles, et al. Fundamentals of Algorithmics. LC 94-45581. 524p. 1995. 75.00 (*0-13-335068-1*) P-H.

Brassard, Michael. The Memory Jogger Plus: Featuring the Seven Management & Planning Tools. rev. ed. (Illus.). x, 306p. 1997. pap. 29.95 (*1-879364-83-2*) GOAL-QPC.

Brassard, Michael, ed. The Memory Jogger: A Pocket Guide of Tools for Continuous Improvement. 2nd ed. (Illus.). 88p. 1988. pap. 4.50 (*1-879364-03-4*) GOAL-QPC.

Brassard, Michael & Ritter, Diane. The Memory Jogger Vol. II: A Pocket Guide of Tools for Continuous Improvement & Effective Planning. Oddo, Francine, ed. (Illus.). 164p. 1994. spiral bd. 6.95 (*1-879364-44-1*, 1030E) GOAL-QPC.

Brassard, Michael & Tucker, Susan, adapted by. The Educators' Companion to the Memory Jogger Plus+ Featuring the Seven Management & Planning Tools. 56p. 1993. pap. write for info. (*1-879364-33-6*) GOAL-QPC.

Brassard, Ronald E. The Passion of Our Lord Jesus Christ According to John: Arranged for Readers Theatre. 1986. 5.95 (*0-912405-29-5*, Pastoral Press) OR Catholic.

Brassart, Scott, ed. Bar Stories. LC 99-42062. 352p. 1999. pap. 12.95 (*1-55583-536-8*, Pub. by Alyson Pubns) Consort Bk Sales.

Brassart, Scott, jt. ed. see Trevelyan, Julie K.

Brassart, Ugo. Lexique de Commerce International. 225p. 1993. pap. 32.95 (*0-7859-5576-3*, 2010200527) Fr & Eur.

Brasse, William. The Sound of Sirens. 314p. 1998. mass mkt. 5.99 (*0-9667301-0-0*) Rough Magic Pr.

Brasseaux, Carl A. Acadian to Cajun: Transformation of a People, 1803-1877. LC 92-17759. (Illus.). 304p. 1992. pap. 17.95 (*0-87805-583-5*); text 45.00 (*0-87805-582-7*) U Pr of Miss.

— Denis-Nicolas Foucault & the New Orleans Rebellion of 1768. Gilley, Billy H., ed. LC 86-62674. (Monograph). (Illus.). 120p. 1987. 14.95 (*0-940231-01-8*) McGinty Pubns.

— The Foreign French Vol. II: Nineteenth-Century French Immigration into Louisiana, 1840-1848. LC 90-81145. 363p. 1992. 25.00 (*0-940984-71-7*) Univ LA Lafayette.

— Founding of New Acadia: The Beginnings of Acadian Life in Louisiana, 1765-1803. LC 86-20099. 288p. 1996. pap. 16.95 (*0-8071-2099-5*) La State U Pr.

— Nineteenth-Century French Immigration into Louisiana, Vol. 1, 1820-1839. LC 90-81145. (Foreign French Ser.). 569p. 1990. 39.95 (*0-940984-56-3*) Univ LA Lafayette.

Brasseaux, Carl A., ed. A Refuge for All Ages: Immigration in Louisiana History. LC 95-83196. (Louisiana Purchase Bicentennial: Vol. X). 716p. 1996. 40.00 (*1-887366-01-6*) Univ LA Lafayette.

Brasseaux, Carl A. & Conrad, Glenn R. A Bibliography of Scholarly Literature on Colonial Louisiana & New France. 430p. (C). 1992. text 20.00 (*0-940984-73-3*) Univ LA Lafayette.

Brasseaux, Carl A., et al. The Courthouses of Louisiana. 2nd ed. LC 97-69579. (Illus.). 210p. 1998. 25.00 (*1-887366-14-8*) Univ LA Lafayette.

— Creoles of Color in the Bayou Country. LC 94-20383. 192p. 1996. reprint ed. pap. 16.00 (*0-87805-949-0*) U Pr of Miss.

Brasseaux, Carl A., jt. auth. see Conrad, Glenn R.

Brasselet, Jean-Paul, ed. Singularities: Lille 1991. (London Mathematical Society Lecture Note Ser.: No. 201). 435p. (C). 1994. pap. text 47.95 (*0-521-46631-8*) Cambridge U Pr.

Brassens, Georges. La Mauvais Reputation. (FRE.). 210p. 1986. pap. 10.95 (*0-7859-2051-X*, 2070377784) Fr & Eur.

— La Tour des Miracles. (FRE.). 1973. pap. 15.95 (*0-7859-3426-X*, 226400486X) Fr & Eur.

Brasseur, B. French-English--English-French Dictionary of Weaponry. (ENG & FRE.). 864p. 1992. 105.00 (*0-7859-8862-9*) Fr & Eur.

Brasseur, B. & Dobenik, R. French-English - English-French Dictionary of Weaponry. 864p. 1992. 115.00 (*2-85608-046-4*, Pub. by La Maison Du Dict) IBD Ltd.

Brasseur, Guy. Premier Dictionnaire de Pigeon Voyageur a l'Usage des Colombophiles et de Tous Ceux Qui S'Interessent Au Sport Colombophile. (FRE.). 526p. 1991. 145.00 (*0-7859-8178-0*, 2876710870) Fr & Eur.

Brasseur, Guy & Solomon, Susan. Aeronomy of the Middle Atmosphere. rev. ed. 1986. pap. text 68.00 (*90-277-2344-3*) Kluwer Academic.

Brasseur, Guy P., et al, eds. Atmospheric Chemistry & Global Change. LC 98-33483. (Topics in Environmental Chemistry). (Illus.). 688p. (C). 1999. text 75.00 (*0-19-510521-4*) OUP.

Brasseur, Guy P., ed. see NATO Staff.

Brasseur, I., et al. Brasseur & Eisler: To Catch a Dream. (Illus.). 1996. pap. write for info. (*0-7715-7393-6*) Macmillan.

Brasseur, P. & Nihoul, J. C. Data Assimilation: Tools for Modeling the Ocean in a Global Change Perspective. (NATO ASI Series I: Global Environmental Change: No. 19). 1994. 131.95 (*0-387-57909-5*) Spr-Verlag.

Brasseur, Robert, ed. Molecular Description of Biological Membrane Components by Computer Aided Conformational Analysis, Vol. I. (Illus.). 288p. 1990. lib. bdg. 202.00 (*0-8493-6375-6*) CRC Pr.

— Molecular Description of Biological Membrane Components by Computer Aided Conformational Analysis, Vol. II. (Illus.). 224p. 1990. lib. bdg. 202.00 (*0-8493-6376-4*) CRC Pr.

Brassey, M., et al. The New Labour Law: Strikes, Dismissals & the Unfair Labour Practice in South African Law. 510p. 1987. pap. 60.00 (*0-7021-1828-1*, Pub. by Juta & Co) Gaunt.

Brassey, Martin. Employment & Labour Law. 458p. 1998. ring bd. 70.00 (*0-7021-3694-8*, Pub. by Juta & Co) Gaunt.

Brassey, Richard. How To Speak Chimpanzee. LC 94-41389. (J). 1995. write for info. (*0-614-32173-5*) Crown Bks Yng Read.

— Store Detective. 1998. 16.00 (*0-15-201409-8*) Harcourt.

Brassey, T. Index to James' Naval History. (C). 1987. 100.00 (*0-7855-4017-2*) St Mut.

Brasseys Books Staff. IOC Official Olympic Companion: Winter Games, Nagano, 1998. 280p. 1997. pap. text 15.95 (*1-85753-244-9*, Pub. by Brasseys) Brasseys.

Brasseys Inc., Staff. Brassey's Globemac Global Military Aircraft Report, 1996-97. 13th ed. 1997. 590.00 (*1-85753-158-2*, Pub. by Brasseys) Brasseys.

Brasseys Inc. Staff. Northumberland & Tyne & Wear. (Twentieth Century Defence of Britain Ser.). 128p. 1998. pap. text 11.95 (*1-85753-234-1*, Pub. by Brasseys) Brasseys.

Brassfield, Samuel. The Lazarus Generation. 224p. (Orig.). 1994. pap. 10.99 (*1-56043-795-2*, Treasure Hse) Destiny Image.

Brassfield, Sandra M. Profiting from Real Estate Rehab. LC 91-15775. 256p. 1992. pap. 39.95 (*0-471-54858-8*) Wiley.

Brassington, David, jt. auth. see Osenberg, Jens B.

Brassington, Frances & Pettitt, Stephen. Principles of Marketing. (Illus.). xviii, 1086p. 1997. pap. 72.50 (*0-273-60513-5*, Pub. by Pitman Pub) Trans-Atl Phila.

Brassington, Rick. Field Hydrogeology. LC 97-52701. 260p. 1998. pap. 54.95 (*0-471-97347-5*) Wiley.

— Finding Water: A Guide to the Construction & Maintenance of Private Water Supplies. 2nd ed. LC 94-49357. 282p. 1995. pap. 65.00 (*0-471-95711-9*) Wiley.

Brassington, W. S., jt. auth. see Hannett, John.

Brassington, William S. Shakespeare's Homeland. LC 75-39522. reprint ed. 42.50 (*0-404-01068-7*) AMS Pr.

Brassley, Paul. Agricultural Economics & the CAP: An Introduction. LC 96-38522. 160p. (Orig.). 1997. pap. text 32.95 (*0-632-04137-4*) Blackwell Sci.

Brassloff. Religion & Politics in Spain. LC 97-18336. 183p. 1998. text 65.00 (*0-312-21073-6*) St Martin.

Brasted, Howard, jt. auth. see Low, D. A.

Brasted, Howard, jt. ed. see Low, D. A.

Braster, Patrick & De Beer, Pieter. Marking for Telecommunications: A Handbook to the Telecommunications Directives. LC 97-42751. 1997. write for info. (*1-55937-947-2*) IEEE Standards.

Brastow, Lewis O. Representative Modern Preachers. LC 68-57306. (Essay Index Reprint Ser.). 1977. 23.95 (*0-8369-0101-0*) Ayer.

Braswell, A. Glenn. Anti-Aging Pills, I. Q. & Memory Boosters: Life Extension Innovations for a Healthier Longer Life. 335p. 1993. 29.95 (*1-883201-00-4*) Hlth Quest.

— Life Extenders & Memory Boosters! Life Extension Innovations for a Healthier Longer Life. 335p. 1993. 29.95 (*1-883201-01-2*) Hlth Quest.

Braswell, Aaron. Sky Dragon Chronicles: The Sound of Unheard Voices. LC 97-91593. 200p. (Orig.). 1997. pap. 14.95 (*0-9656730-0-6*) Dragons Dream.

Braswell, Alvin L., jt. auth. see Palmer, William M.

Braswell, Bruce K. A Commentary on Pindar: Nemean Nine. LC 98-4904. 204p. 1998. 125.35 (*3-11-016124-9*) De Gruyter.

— A Commentary on the Fourth Pythian Ode of Pindar. (Texte und Kommentare Ser.: Vol. 14). 448p. (C). 1988. lib. bdg. 211.55 (*3-11-010328-1*) De Gruyter.

Braswell, Delores. Back to Basics: A Parent's Guide to Saving Our Children. 214p. (Orig.). 1996. pap. 12.95 (*0-9656043-0-6*) DB Books.

Braswell, George W., Jr. Islam: Its Prophet, Peoples, Politics, & Power. LC 95-44451. 352p. 1996. 24.99 (*0-8054-1169-0*, 4211-69) Broadman.

— Understanding Sectarian Groups in America. rev. ed. LC 93-24941. 400p. 1994. pap. 21.99 (*0-8054-1047-3*, 4210-47) Broadman.

— Understanding World Religions. rev. ed. LC 93-24944. 244p. (Orig.). 1994. pap. 16.99 (*0-8054-1068-6*, 4210-68) Broadman.

— What You Need to Know about Islam & Muslims. LC 99-48857. (Illus.). 192p. 2000. pap. 9.99 (*0-8054-1829-6*) Broadman.

Braswell, James A., ed. Southeastern Journal of Music Education, Vol. 1, 1989. (Orig.). 1990. pap. text. write for info. (*0-9619031-3-9*) U GA GA Ctr Cnt Educ.

— Southeastern Journal of Music Education, 1990, Vol. 2. (Orig.). 1991. pap. text. write for info. (*0-9619031-4-7*) U GA GA Ctr Cnt Educ.

Braswell, John. How You Can Win Like a Pro Two. (Illus.). 40p. (Orig.). 1992. pap. 4.95 (*1-883106-01-X*) Key System.

— How You Can Win Like A Pro Two - Texas Version. (Illus.). 48p. 1992. pap. 4.95 (*1-883106-02-8*) Key System.

— One Thousand & One Ways You Can Win at Greyhound Racing. (Illus.). 163p. (Orig.). 1993. pap. 35.00 (*1-883106-00-1*) Key System.

Braswell, Kermit. Step-by-Step: A Financial Guide for Your Church. 40p. (Orig.). 1995. pap. 7.95 (*0-687-01119-1*) Abingdon.

Braswell, Laurel. The Index of Middle English Prose Handlist IV: Manuscripts in the Douce Collection, Bodleian Library, Oxford. 1987. reprint ed. 60.00 (*0-85991-241-8*) Boydell & Brewer.

Braswell, Lauren, jt. auth. see Kendall, Philip C.

Braswell, Linda. Quest for Respect: A Healing Guide for Survivors of Rape. 3rd ed. Wheeler, Eugene D., ed. LC 89-9274. 80p. 1995. pap. 9.95 (*0-934793-44-1*, Pub. by Pathfinder CA) IPG Chicago.

Braswell, Mary F. The Medieval Sinner: Confession & Characterization in the Literature of the English Middle Ages. LC 81-69040. 220p. 1983. 29.50 (*0-8386-3117-7*) Fairleigh Dickinson.

Braswell, Mary F., ed. Sir Perceval of Galles & Ywain & Gawain. (Teams Middle English Text Ser.). 1995. pap. 10.00 (*1-879288-60-5*) Medieval Inst.

Braswell, Michael, et al. Human Relations & Corrections. 4th rev. ed. LC 99-195798. 201p. (C). 1997. pap. text 16.95 (*0-88133-975-X*) Waveland Pr.

Braswell, Michael, jt. auth. see Bartollas, Clemens.

Braswell, Michael, jt. auth. see Lozoff, Bo.

Braswell, Michael, jt. auth. see Miller, Larry.

Braswell, Michael C., et al. Justice, Crime & Ethics. 3rd ed. LC 98-17914. 424p. (C). 1998. pap., wbk. ed. 41.95 (*0-87084-073-8*) Anderson Pub Co.

— Prison Violence in America. 2nd rev. ed. LC 93-71747. 420p. (C). 1994. pap. 34.95 (*0-87084-094-0*) Anderson Pub Co.

Braszo, Lawrence R. The Inspiration of Christ. 136p. 1999. pap. 13.00 (*0-8059-4555-5*) Dorrance.

Brataas, Anne. The North Country Almanac: A Seasonal Guide to the Great Outdoors. (Illus.). 192p. 1996. pap. 10.95 (*0-8362-1327-0*) Andrews & McMeel.

Bratchel, M. E. Edward Augustus Freeman & the Victorian Interpretation of the Norman Conquest. LC 71-509440. 39 p. 1969. write for info. (*0-7223-0023-9*) A H Stockwell.

— Lucca, 1430-1494: The Reconstruction of an Italian City-Republic. (Illus.). 358p. 1995. text 85.00 (*0-19-820484-1*) OUP.

Bratchell, D. F. Shakespearean Tragedy. LC 89-10506. 176p. (C). 1990. pap. 24.99 (*0-415-03403-5*, A4943) Routledge.

Bratcher, James T. Analytical Index to Publications of the Texas Folklore Society, Vols. 1-36. LC 72-97597. (Illus.). 344p. 1973. 15.95 (*0-87074-135-7*) UNTX Pr.

Bratcher, Jeryl L. Learning & Obeying God's Word with Obedience the Bumblebee. (Illus.). 24p. (Orig.). (J). (ps-4). 1997. pap. write for info. (*1-890192-00-7*) Obedience Ministry.

Bratcher, Joe, ed. see Koziol, Urszula.

Bratcher, Joe, ed. see Marcos, Plinio, et al.

*__Bratcher, Juanita.__ Crooked Curves: The Last of the Red Hot Mamas. (Illus.). 275p. 1999. pap. 9.95 (*0-9635616-5-0*) Bratcher-McMillan.

Bratcher, Juanita. Harold: The Making of a Big City Mayor. (Illus.). 160p. (Orig.). 1993. pap. text 10.00 (*0-9635616-1-8*) Bratcher-McMillan.

— I Cry for a People: In Their Struggle for Justice & Equality. (Illus.). 76p. (Orig.). 1995. pap. text 8.00 (*0-9635616-0-X*) Bratcher-McMillan.

— Short, Sweet & All That: Something to Think About. (Illus.). 94p. (Orig.). 1997. pap. 10.00 (*0-9635616-2-6*) Bratcher-McMillan.

Bratcher-Nelson, Bobby & Wiggers, Carol A. A Practical Approach to Lilly Vol. 1: Traditional Horary Study Guide. (Illus.). 114p. (Orig.). (C). 1990. pap. 20.00 (*1-878935-04-6*) JustUs & Assocs.

Bratcher-Nelson, Bobby. The Complete Course in Predictive Astrology: Self - Taught Version. Wiggers, Carol A., ed. (Illus.). 478p. (Orig.). (C). 1990. student ed. 150.00 (*1-878935-08-9*) JustUs & Assocs.

Bratcher-Nelson, Bobbye & Wiggers, Carol A. Simplified Chart Calculations: Step by Step Instructions. (Illus.). 52p. (C). 1991. student ed. 12.00 (*1-878935-13-5*) JustUs & Assocs.

Bratcher, R. G., ed. Marginal Notes for the New Testament. vi, 125p. 1980. pap. 12.99 (*0-8267-0026-8*, 102701) Untd Bible Soc.

— Marginal Notes for the Old Testament. vi, 186p. 1980. pap. 21.99 (*0-8267-0025-X*, 102700) Untd Bible Soc.

— New Testament Index. vii, 37p. 1963. pap. 4.99 (*0-8267-0003-9*, 102670) Untd Bible Soc.

— Short Bible Reference System. viii, 148p. 1961. pap. 8.99 (*0-8267-0030-6*, 102669) Untd Bible Soc.

Bratcher, R. G. & Thompson, J. A., eds. Bible Index. vi, 136p. 1970. pap. 8.99 (*0-8267-0005-5*, 102674) Untd Bible Soc.

Bratcher, Robert G., ed. Old Testament Quotations in the New Testament. 3rd ed. LC 87-18632. xii, 88p. 1987. pap. 6.99 (*0-8267-0031-4*, 102739) Untd Bible Soc.

Bratcher, Robert G. & Hatton, Howard A. A Handbook on the Revelation to John. LC 92-33639. (UBS Handbook Ser.). viii, 352p. 1993. pap. 13.99 (*0-8267-0174-4*, 104926) Untd Bible Soc.

Bratcher, Robert G. & Newman, Barclay M. A Handbook on the Book of Joshua. LC 92-20510. (UBS Handbook Ser.). Orig. Title: Translator's Handbook on the Book of Joshua. viii, 340p. 1983. pap. 16.99 (*0-8267-0109-4*, 102710) Untd Bible Soc.

Bratcher, Robert G. & Nida, Eugene A. A Handbook on Paul's Letter to the Ephesians. LC 92-40984. (UBS Handbook Ser.). Orig. Title: Translator's Handbook on Paul's Letter to the Ephesians. viii, 199p. 1982. pap. 12.99 (*0-8267-0164-7*, 102765) Untd Bible Soc.

— A Handbook on Paul's Letters to the Colossians & to Philemon. LC 92-20512. (UBS Handbook Ser.). Orig. Title: Translator's Handbook on Paul's Letters to the Colossians & to Philemon. viii, 149p. 1977. pap. 11.99 (*0-8267-0166-3*, 102692) Untd Bible Soc.

— A Handbook on the Gospel of Mark. LC 92-40062. (UBS Handbook Ser.). Orig. Title: Translator's Handbook on the Gospel of Mark. xviii, 534p. 1961. pap. 19.99 (*0-8267-0156-6*, 102666) Untd Bible Soc.

Bratcher, Robert G. & Reyburn, William D. A Handbook on Psalms. LC 92-40983. (UBS Handbook Ser.). Orig. Title: Translator's Handbook on Psalms. (Illus.). xi, 1219p. 1991. pap. 37.99 (*0-8267-0119-1*, 104640) Untd Bible Soc.

Bratcher, Suzanne. Evaluating Children's Writing: A Handbook of Communication Choices for Classroom Teachers. 200p. 2000. pap. 17.50 (*0-8058-8001-1*) L Erlbaum Assocs.

— Evaluating Children's Writing: A Handbook of Communication Choices for Classroom Teachers. 224p. 1994. pap. text 12.00 (*0-312-08121-9*) St Martin.

— The Learning-to-Write Process in Elementary Classrooms. LC 97-8623. 1997. write for info. (*0-8058-2255-0*) L Erlbaum Assocs.

Brate, Adam, jt. auth. see Bunnell, David.

Bratek, Irene E. Yesterday, I Heard the Rain. LC 97-91330. 1998. pap. 14.95 (*0-533-12625-8*) Vantage.

Braten, Ivar. Learning to Spell: Training Orthographic Problem-Solving with Poor Spellers: A Strategy Instructional Approach. 183p. 1991. 18.00 (*82-00-03910-2*) Scandnvan Univ Pr.

Braten, Stein, ed. Intersubjective Communication & Emotion in Early Ontogeny. LC 97-47525. (Studies in Emotion & Social Interaction: No. 3). (Illus.). 488p. (C). 1998. 69.95 (*0-521-62257-3*) Cambridge U Pr.

Bratenwender, Kehrer, ed. see Beer, Johann.

Brater, D. Craig, et al. Rational Therapeutics: A Clinical Pharmacologic Guide for the Health Professional. Williams, Roger L., ed. (Clinical Pharmacology Ser.: Vol. 16). (Illus.). 808p. 1989. text 250.00 (*0-8247-7946-0*) Dekker.

Brater, E. F. Handbook of Hydraulics. 7th ed. LC 95-45662. (Illus.). 640p. 1996. 79.95 (*0-07-007247-7*) McGraw.

Brater, Enoch. The Drama in the Text: Beckett's Late Fiction. LC 93-30405. 248p. 1994. reprint ed. text 55.00 (*0-19-508892-1*) OUP.

Brater, Enoch, ed. Beckett at Eighty: Beckett in Context. LC 85-21523. 192p. 1986. text 25.00 (*0-19-504001-5*) OUP.

— The Theatrical Gamut: Notes for a Post-Beckettian Stage. LC 95-2385. (Theater: Theory - Text - Performance Ser.). 320p. 1995. text 49.50 (*0-472-10583-3*, 10583) U of Mich Pr.

Brater, Enoch, jt. ed. see Schleuter, June.

Brater, Enoch, ed. see Vanden Heuvel, Michael J.

Brater, Meryl. Hidden Agenda. 1991. 18.00 (*0-932526-32-2*) Nexus Pr.

Braterman, P. S. Reactions of Coordinated Ligands, Vol. 1. (Illus.). 1064p. (C). 1987. text 185.00 (*0-306-42201-8*, Kluwer Plenum) Kluwer Academic.

— Reactions of Coordinated Ligands, Vol. 2. (Illus.). 422p. (C). 1989. text 135.00 (*0-306-43094-0*, Kluwer Plenum) Kluwer Academic.

Bratfisch, R. English - German Dictionary of Food Technology. (ENG & GER.). 260p. 1992. lib. bdg. 75.00 (*0-8288-3596-9*, F129930) Fr & Eur.

Brathal, Daniel A. & Langemo, Mark. Planning Conversions to Micrographic Systems. 62p. 1987. pap. 15.00 (*0-933887-19-1*, A4557) ARMA Intl.

Brathwait, Richard. The English Gentleman: Containing Sundry Excellent Rules-How to Demeane or Accommodate Himselfe in the Manage of Publike or Private Affairs. LC 74-28836. (English Experience Ser.: No. 717). 1975. reprint ed. 65.00 (*90-221-0717-5*) Walter J Johnson.

Brathwaite & Phillips. The People Who Came, Bk. 3. 1993. pap. text. write for info. (*0-582-76657-5*, Pub. by Addison-Wesley) Longman.

Brathwaite, Ashton J., see Kwamdela, Odimumba, pseud.

Brathwaite, Barbara C., jt. auth. see Blank, Rolf K.

*__Brathwaite, Christopher.__ There Are No Mistakes, Only Lessons: A Modern Caribbean Story. Akin, Bernetia, ed. (Illus.). 176p. 1999. pap. text 19.95 (*0-9671575-0-1*) C E Brathwaite Assocs.

Brathwaite, Edward K. The Arrivants: New Edition. 286p. (Orig.). 1981. reprint ed. pap. text 15.95 (*0-19-911103-0*) OUP.

Brathwaite, J. Ashton, jt. auth. see Kwamdela, Odimumba, pseud.

Brathwaite, K. S. Information Engineering, 3 vols., Vol. I: Concepts. 1991. 59.95 (*0-8493-7331-X*, QA76) CRC Pr.

— Information Engineering, 3 vols., Vol. II: Analysis & Admin. 1991. 59.95 (*0-8493-7332-8*, QA76) CRC Pr.

— Information Engineering, 3 vols., Vol. III: Development Issues. 1991. 59.95 (*0-8493-7333-6*) CRC Pr.

*__Brathwaite, Kamau.__ Ancestors. rev. expanded ed. 2001. pap. 35.00 (*0-8112-1448-6*, Pub. by New Directions) Norton.

Brathwaite, Kamau. Barabajan Poems 1492-1992. 1995. pap. text 25.00 (*0-9640424-3-6*) Savacou North.

— Black + Blues. LC 95-34695. Vol. 815. 96p. (Orig.). 1995. reprint ed. pap. 9.95 (*0-8112-1313-7*, NDP815, Pub. by New Directions) Norton.

*__Brathwaite, Kamau.__ Conversations with Nathaniel Mackey. 320p. 1999. pap. 20.00 (*0-9668976-0-9*, Pub. by Col St Catherine) SPD-Small Pr Dist.

B

An Asterisk (*) at the beginning of an entry indicates that the title is appearing for the first time.

Brathwaite, Kamau. Middle Passages. 90p. (Orig.). 1993. pap. 15.95 (*1-85224-224-8*, Pub. by Bloodaxe Bks) Dufour.
— MiddlePassages. LC 93-17249. 128p. (Orig.). 1994. pap. 9.95 (*0-8112-1232-7*, NDP776, Pub. by New Directions) Norton.
— Roots. 312p. (C). 1993. reprint ed. pap. text 17.95 (*0-472-06544-0*, 06544) U of Mich Pr.
— Roots. 312p. (C). 1993. reprint ed. text 42.50 (*0-472-09544-7*, 09544) U of Mich Pr.
— Trench Town Rock. (Lost Roads Ser.: No. 40). 88p. (Orig.). 1994. pap. 10.95 (*0-918786-45-2*) Lost Roads.
— Zea Mexican Diary: 7 September, 1926 - 7 September, 1986. LC 92-56924. (Studies in American Autobiography). 112p. (C). 1993. 14.95 (*0-299-13640-X*) U of Wis Pr.
Brathwaite, Karen S. & James, Carl S., eds. Educating African Canadians. (Our Schools/Our Selves Ser.). 328p. pap. 19.95 (*1-55028-500-9*, Pub. by J Lorimer) Formac Dist Ltd.
Brathwaite, Ken S. An Introduction to Plasmas. LC 89-71387. 1990. write for info. (*2-88124-424-6*) Gordon & Breach.
Bratko. Bratko Prolog Programming for Artificial Intelligence. 3rd ed. 600p. (C). 2000. pap. text. write for info. (*0-201-40375-7*) Addison-Wesley.
Bratko, Ivan. PROLOG Programming for Artificial Intelligence. 272p. (C). 1986. pap. text 29.25 (*0-201-14224-4*) Addison-Wesley.
— Prolog Programming for Artificial Intelligence. 2nd ed. 597p. (C). 1990. pap. text 42.19 (*0-201-41606-9*) Addison-Wesley.
Bratley, B. Harlington. Arthritic, Realistic Fantastics & Artistic. 130p. 1986. 45.00 (*0-7223-1970-3*, Pub. by A H S Ltd) St Mut.
Bratley, George H. The Power of Gems & Charms. 198p. 1988. pap. 9.95 (*0-87877-132-8*) Newcastle Pub.
Bratley, P., et al. A Guide to Simulation. 2nd ed. (Illus.). 410p. 1996. 79.95 (*0-387-96467-3*) Spr-Verlag.
Bratman, Fred. Everything You Need to Know When a Parent Dies. rev. ed. (Need to Know Library). (Illus.). 64p. (YA). (gr. 7-12). 1995. lib. bdg. 17.95 (*0-8239-2153-0*) Rosen Group.
— Everything You Need to Know When a Parent Dies. rev. ed. (Illus.). 64p. (gr. 7-12). 1998. 17.95 (*0-8239-2870-5*) Rosen Group.
— War in the Persian Gulf. (Headliners Ser.). (Illus.). 64p. (J). (gr. 5-8). 1991. pap. 6.95 (*1-878841-61-0*) Millbrook Pr.
Bratman, Fred & Lewis, Scott. The Reader's Companion: A Book Lover's Guide to the Most Important Books in Every Field of Knowledge As Chosen by the Experts. 288p. (J). 1995. pap. 9.70 (*0-7868-8095-3*, Pub. by Hyperion) Time Warner.
— The Reader's Companion: A Book Lover's Guide to the Most Important Books in Every Field of Knowledge as Chosen by the Experts. 288p. (J). 1994. 17.45 (*0-7868-6009-X*, Pub. by Hyperion) Time Warner.
Bratman, Michael. Personal Policies. (Working Papers on Risk & Rationality). 1988. 2.50 (*0-318-33324-4*, RR8) IPPP.
Bratman, Michael, jt. ed. see Perry, John.
Bratman, Michael E. Faces of Intention: Selected Essays on Intention & Agency. LC 98-26459. (Studies in Philosophy). 320p. (C). 1999. text 59.95 (*0-521-63131-9*); pap. text 18.95 (*0-521-63727-9*) Cambridge U Pr.
— Intention, Plans, & Practical Reason. 224p. 1987. pap. 15.50 (*0-674-45819-2*) HUP.
— Intention, Plans, & Practical Reason. LC 87-8702. 224p. 1987. 41.50 (*0-674-45818-4*) HUP.
— Intention, Plans, & Practical Reason. LC 99-12134. (David Hume Ser.). 200p. (C). 1999. reprint ed. pap. text 22.95 (*1-57586-192-5*) CSLI.
***Bratman, Stephen.** The Natural Pharmacist: St John's Wort & Depression. LC 98-17492. (Illus.). 179p. 2000. pap. 6.99 (*0-7615-1553-4*) Prima Pub.
Bratman, Stephen. Your Complete Guide to Herbs. LC 98-22156. (Natural Pharmacist Ser.). 274p. 2000. pap. 7.99 (*0-7615-1671-9*) Prima Pub.
Bratman, Steven. Alternative Medicine Ratings Guide: A Expert Rates the Best Treatments & for over 90 Conditions. LC 97-38074. 340p. 1998. per. 19.95 (*0-7615-1278-0*) Prima Pub.
— Alternative Medicine Sourcebook: A Realistic Evaluation of Alternative Healing Method. 2nd ed. LC 99-41600. 272p. 1999. pap. 17.95 (*0-7373-0247-X*, 0247XW) NTC Contemp Pub Co.
— The Alternative Medicine Sourcebook: A Realistic Evaluation of Alternative Healing Methods. LC 96-49550. (Illus.). 272p. 1998. reprint ed. 27.00 (*1-56565-626-1*); reprint ed. pap. 17.00 (*1-56565-855-8*) Lowell Hse.
— Beat Depression with St. John's Wort. LC 97-34408. 224p. 1997. per. 12.00 (*0-7615-1297-7*) Prima Pub.
***Bratman, Steven.** Everything You Need to Know about Valerian & Insomnia. 5th ed. (Natural Pharmacist Ser.). (Illus.). 192p. 2000. pap. 6.99 (*0-7615-1870-3*) Prima Pub.
— The Natural Pharmacist. 8th rev. ed. (Natural Pharmacist Ser.). (Illus.). 2000. pap. 19.99 (*0-7615-2448-7*) Prima Pub.
Bratman, Steven. Your Complete Guide to Illnesses & Their Natural Remedies. LC 98-43896. (Natural Pharmacist Ser.). 305p. 2000. pap. 7.99 (*0-7615-1791-X*) Prima Pub.
Bratman, Steven & DePalma, Angelo. Your Complete Guide to Vitamins & Supplements. LC 99-28105. (Natural Pharmacist Ser.). 321p. 2000. pap. 7.99 (*0-7615-1672-7*) Prima Pub.
***Bratman, Steven & Knight, David.** Health Food Junkies: Orthorexia Nervosa - Overcoming the Obsession with Healthful Eating. 256p. 2000. 23.95 (*0-7679-0630-6*) Broadway BDD.
Bratman, Steven & Kroll, David. Clinical Evaluation of Medicinal Herbs & Other Therapeutic Natural Products. LC 98-25800. 1998. write for info. (*0-7615-1705-7*) Prima Pub.
***Bratman, Steven & Kroll, David.** Natural Health Bible: From the Most Trusted Source in Health Information. LC 99-23813. (Natural Pharmacist Ser.). 495p. 2000. pap. 19.95 (*0-7615-2082-1*) Prima Pub.
Bratnober, John P., jt. auth. see Smith, Michael A.
Braton, N. R., jt. auth. see Lindberg, R. A.
Braton, Norman R. Cryogenic Recycling & Processing. 256p. 1980. 148.00 (*0-8493-5779-9*, TP482, CRC Reprint) Franklin.
Bratos-Anderson, Magda, jt. auth. see Anderson, John.
Bratska, M. & Duric, L. Pedagogicka Psychologia - Terminologicky a Vykladovy Slovnik (Pedagogical Psychology - Dictionary of Terminology) (SLO.). 500p. 1997. pap. 290.00 (*80-08-02498-4*, Pub. by Slov Pegagog Naklad) IBD Ltd.
Bratt, Aimee. Glamour & Turbulence: I Remember Pan Am, 1966-91. LC 96-90242. (Orig.). 1996. pap. 11.95 (*0-533-11972-3*) Vantage.
Bratt, Berneen. No Time for Jello: One Family's Experiences with the Doman-Delacato Patterning Program. 202p. 1989. pap. 17.95 (*0-914797-56-5*) Brookline Bks.
***Bratt, Carolyn S.** Kentucky Intestacy Law. (Illus.). 198p. 1999. pap. 47.00 (*1-58757-027-0*, EM034) Univ of KY.
***Bratt, Holly & Tennenhouse, Dan J.** Risk Prevention Skills: Communicating in Extended & Subacute Care Facilities. iv, 80p. 1998. pap. 21.95 (*1-930548-18-4*) Tennenhouse Prof Pubns.
— Risk Prevention Skills: Record Keeping in Extended & Subacute Care Facilities. iv, 76p. 1998. pap. 21.95 (*1-930548-19-2*) Tennenhouse Prof Pubns.
Bratt, James D. Dutch Calvinism in Modern America: A History of a Conservative Subculture. LC 84-13717. 366p. (Orig.). reprint ed. pap. 113.50 (*0-8357-4356-X*, 203718400007) Bks Demand.
Bratt, James D., ed. Abraham Kuyper: A Centennial Reader. 487p. 1998. pap. 29.00 (*0-8028-4321-2*) Eerdmans.
Bratt, Jean, ed. see Agee, M. J.
Bratt, John. Trails of Yesterday. LC 79-26411. (Illus.). xx, 320p. 1996. pap. 12.00 (*0-8032-6055-5*, Bison Books) U of Nebr Pr.
Bratt, Rachel G. Rebuilding a Low-Income Housing Policy. LC 88-19106. 368p. 1994. pap. text 27.95 (*1-56639-263-2*) Temple U Pr.
Bratt, Rachel G., et al, eds. Critical Perspectives on Housing. LC 85-17274. 646p. 1986. 44.95 (*0-87722-395-5*) Temple U Pr.
Brattain, Michael G., jt. ed. see Mastromarino, Anthony J.
Brattberg, Tim, jt. auth. see Chanson, Hubert.
Bratteland, Eivind, ed. Advances in Berthing & Mooring of Ships & Offshore Structures. (C). 1988. text 260.00 (*90-247-3731-1*) Kluwer Academic.
Bratteli, O. Derivations, Dissipations & Group Actions on C-Algebras. (Lecture Notes in Mathematics Ser.: Vol. 1229). vi, 277p. 1987. 41.95 (*0-387-17199-1*) Spr-Verlag.
Bratteli, O. & Jorgensen, P. E., eds. Positive Semigroups of Operators, & Applications. 1984. text 84.00 (*90-277-1839-3*) Kluwer Academic.
Bratteli, O. & Robinson, D. W. Operator Algebras & Quantum Statistical Mechanics, I: C & W-Algebras, Symmetry Groups, Decomposition of States. 2nd rev. ed. (Texts & Monographs in Physics). 500p. 1987. 106.95 (*0-387-17093-6*) Spr-Verlag.
Bratteli, Ola. Operator Algebras & Quantum Statistical Mechanics: Equilibrium States, Models in Quantum Statistical Mechanics. 2nd ed. xiii, 505p. 1997. 89.95 (*3-540-61443-5*) Spr-Verlag.
Bratteli, Ola & Jrgensen, Palle E. T. Iterated Function Systems & Permutation Representations of the Cuntz Algebra. LC 99-19208. (Memoirs of the Society Ser.). 1999. write for info. (*0-8218-0962-8*) Am Math.
Bratten, John M. The Greatest Wonder of All. 1991. pap. 10.95 (*1-55673-313-5*, 9134) CSS OH.
Bratten, John R., jt. auth. see Hamilton, Donny L.
Bratten, Thomas A. Florida Criminal Procedure: Florida Practice Systems Library Selection. LC 80-80175. 97.50 (*0-317-00565-0*) West Group.
— Florida Criminal Procedure: Florida Practice Systems Library Selection. LC 80-80175. 1989. suppl. ed. 58.00 (*0-317-03204-6*) West Group.
Bratter, Peter & Schramel, Peter, eds. Trace Element Analytical Chemistry in Medicine & Biology Vol. 5: Proceedings of the Fifth International Workshop, Neuherberg, Federal Republic of Germany, April 1988. xx, 666p. (C). 1990. lib. bdg. 235.00 (*3-11-011340-6*) De Gruyter.
Bratter, Thomas E. & Forrest, Gary G., eds. Alcoholism & Substance Abuse: Strategies for Intervention. 640p. (C). 1985. 60.00 (*0-02-904260-7*) Free Pr.
***Bratti, Bruno & Brockwood, Ted.** Linux by Example. (Illus.). 450p. 2000. 24.99 (*0-7897-2260-7*) Que.
Brattin, Barbara. Ohio Online: The Harvest of Ohio's Best Web Sites. LC 97-40012. 288p. 1997. pap. 19.95 (*1-882203-18-6*) Orange Frazer.
Brattina, Anita F. Diary of a Small Business Owner: A Personal Account of How I Built a Profitable Business. 224p. 1995. 21.95 (*0-8144-0291-7*) AMACOM.
Brattle, Sue, jt. auth. see Mackie, Carole.
Bratton, Aileen. Aileen Bratton's Decorative Painting Treasures. LC 97-43101. (Illus.). 128p. 1998. pap. 23.99 (*0-89134-871-9*, North Lght Bks) F & W Pubns Inc.
Bratton, Benjamin, ed. see Bennett, Perry, et al.
Bratton, Daniel. Thirty-Two Short Views of Mazo de la Roche. (Illus.). 200p. 1996. pap. 9.95 (*1-55022-274-0*, Pub. by ECW) LPC InBook.
***Bratton, Daniel.** Years, Ever Affly. 220p. 2000. 39.95 (*0-87013-516-3*) Mich St U Pr.
Bratton, Fred G. The Crime of Christendom. 241p. 1994. pap. 12.95 (*1-56474-122-2*) Fithian Pr.
Bratton, Frederick. Nuts in May. 63p. 1984. 25.00 (*0-7855-1068-0*, Pub. by Regency Pr GBR) St Mut.
Bratton, Heidi. Imagine: A Story about the Beginning. LC 97-7462. (Walking with God Ser.). (Illus.). (J). (ps). 1997. bds. 6.95 (*0-8091-6642-9*) Paulist Pr.
— Spirit! LC 97-7464. (Walking with God Ser.). (Illus.). (J). 1997. bds. 6.95 (*0-8091-6640-2*) Paulist Pr.
— Where Is God? LC 97-7463. (Walking with God Ser.). (J). 1997. pap. 6.95 (*0-8091-6641-0*) Paulist Pr.
— Yes I Can! LC 97-7465. (Walking with God Ser.). (Illus.). (J). (ps). 1997. pap. 6.95 (*0-8091-6639-9*) Paulist Pr.
Bratton, Heidi, photos by. Count Your Blessings. LC 98-32043. (Walking with God II Ser.). (Illus.). 16p. (J). (ps-k). 2000. 5.95 (*0-8091-6659-3*) Paulist Pr.
— The Little Shepherd. LC 98-43547. (Walking with God II Ser.). (Illus.). 16p. (J). (ps-k). 2000. 5.95 (*0-8091-6660-7*) Paulist Pr.
— Little Ways to Give God Praise. LC 98-32046. (Walking with God II Ser.). (Illus.). 16p. (J). 2000. 5.95 (*0-8091-6661-5*) Paulist Pr.
— Rejoice! Jesus Welcomes Me. LC 98-32044. (Walking with God II Ser.). (Illus.). 16p. (J). (ps-k). 2000. 5.95 (*0-8091-6662-3*) Paulist Pr.
Bratton, J. S., ed. Music Hall: Performance & Style. LC 86-12608. (Popular Music in Britain Ser.). 224p. 1987. pap. 33.95 (*0-335-15131-0*) OpUniv Pr.
Bratton, Jacky, et al, eds. Melodrama: Stage Picture Screen. (Illus.). 224p. 1994. text 49.95 (*0-85170-437-9*) Ind U Pr.
Bratton, Jacky & Cook, Jim. Melodrama: Stage Picture Screen. Gledhill, Christine, ed. (Illus.). 224p. 1994. pap. 23.95 (*0-85170-438-7*) Ind U Pr.
Bratton, Jacky, jt. ed. see Carson, Christie.
Bratton, Jacky, ed. & intro. see Pinero, Arthur W.
Bratton, Jacqueline S. Wilton's Music Hall. (Theatre in Focus Ser.). (Illus.). 44p. 1980. pap. text. write for info. incl. sl. (*0-85964-061-2*) Chadwyck-Healey.
Bratton, Jacqueline S. & Traies, Jane. Astley's Amphitheatre. (Theatre in Focus Ser.). 65p. 1980. pap. write for info. incl. sl. (*0-85964-059-0*) Chadwyck-Healey.
***Bratton, John & Gold, Jeffrey.** Human Resource Management: Theory & Practice. 2nd ed. LC 00-33167. 2000. pap. write for info. (*0-8058-3862-7*) L Erlbaum Assocs.
Bratton, John, jt. illus. see Keppler, Rick.
***Bratton, John W. & Gounod, Charles.** The Teddy Bears' Picnic: And Funeral March of a Marionette. (Party Time Ser.: Vol. 2). 27p. 2000. pap. 10.00 (*1-56571-179-3*, PT002) PRB Prods.
Bratton, Mary. From Surviving to Thriving: A Therapist's Guide to Stage II Recovery for Survivors of Childhood Abuse. LC 98-39341. 282p. 1998. 39.95 (*0-7890-0255-8*); pap. 24.95 (*0-7890-0256-6*) Haworth Pr.
Bratton, Michael. Democratic Experiments in Africa: Regime Transitions in Comparative Perspective. LC 96-34865. (Cambridge Studies in Comparative Politics). (Illus.). 328p. (C). 1997. text 59.95 (*0-521-55429-2*); pap. text 19.95 (*0-521-55612-0*) Cambridge U Pr.
— The Local Politics of Rural Development: Peasant & Party State in Zambia. LC 79-56775. (Illus.). 348p. reprint ed. pap. 107.90 (*0-8357-6509-1*, 203588000097) Bks Demand.
Bratton, Robert L. Family Practice Board Review. LC 97-48636. 308p. 1998. 64.95 (*0-683-30504-2*) Lippncott W & W.
***Bratton, Robert L.** Mayo Clinic's Complete Guide for Family Physicians & Residents in Training. (Illus.). 550p. 1999. pap. text 111.25 (*0-07-134683-X*) McGraw-Hill HPD.
***Bratton, William W.** Corporate Law. LC 99-56781. 2000. write for info. (*0-7546-2086-7*, Pub. by Ashgate Pub) Ashgate Pub Co.
Bratton, William W. & Knobler, Peter. Turnaround: How America's Top Cop Reversed the Crime Epidemic. LC 97-28105. 329p. 1998. 25.00 (*0-679-45251-6*) Random.
Bratton, William W., jt. auth. see Brudney, Victor.
Bratton, William W., jt. auth. see Budney, Victor.
Brattsten, L. B. & Ahmed, S. Molecular Aspects of Insect-Plant Associations. LC 87-2236. (Illus.). 358p. (C). 1987. text 105.00 (*0-306-42547-5*, Kluwer Plenum) Kluwer Academic.
Bratukhin, A. G. & Bogolyubov, V. S., eds. Composite Parts & Units Manufacturing Techniques. LC 92-39253. (Russian Composite Materials Ser.). 1993. write for info. (*1-85861-001-X*) Elsevier.
Bratun, Katy. Frogs & Toads: A Nature Sticker Stories Book. (Nature Sticker Stories Ser.). (Illus.). 16p. (J). (ps-1). 1998. mass mkt. 4.99 (*0-448-41859-2*, G & D) Peng Put Young Read.
Bratun, Katy, jt. auth. see Galvin, Laura G.
Bratveit, Kari, et al. Colloquial Norwegian: A Complete Language Course. LC 94-14197. (Colloquials Ser.). 288p. (C). (gr. 13). 1995. audio 22.99 (*0-415-11010-6*, B4034) Routledge.
— Colloquial Norwegian: A Complete Language Course. LC 94-14197. (Colloquials Ser.). (Illus.). 288p. (gr. 13). 1995. pap. 18.99 (*0-415-11009-2*, B4030) Routledge.
— Colloquial Norwegian: A Complete Language Course. LC 94-14197. (Colloquials Ser.). 288p. (gr. 13). 1995. 44.99 incl. audio (*0-415-11011-4*, B4038) Routledge.
Bratvold, Gretchen. Oregon. (Hello U. S. A. Ser.). (Illus.). 72p. (J). (gr. 3-6). 1991. lib. bdg. 19.95 (*0-8225-2704-9*, Lerner Publctns) Lerner Pub.
— Oregon. (Hello U. S. A. Ser.). (Illus.). 72p. (J). 1997. pap. text 5.95 (*0-8225-9765-9*) Lerner Pub.
— Wisconsin. (Hello U. S. A. Ser.). (Illus.). 72p. (J). (gr. 3-6). 1995. lib. bdg. 19.95 (*0-8225-2700-6*, Lerner Publctns) Lerner Pub.
— Wisconsin. (Hello U. S. A. Ser.). (Illus.). 72p. (J). 1997. pap. text 5.95 (*0-8225-9761-6*) Lerner Pub.
Bratvold, Gretchen, ed. see Huegel, Kelly.
Bratz, Gordon T., ed. The Military Engineer: Journal of the Society of American Military Engineers. 80p. 4.00 (*0-318-16536-8*) Soc Am Mil Eng.
Bratzel, John, jt. auth. see Rout, Leslie B.
Brau. Free-Electron Lasers. 1990. pap. text 59.00 (*0-12-126000-3*) Acad Pr.
Brau, E., et al. Recent Multilateral Debt Restructurings with Official & Bank Creditors. (Occasional Paper Ser.: No. 25). 43p. 1983. pap. 5.00 (*1-55775-080-7*) Intl Monetary.
Brau, Eduard, et al. Export Credits: Developments & Prospects. (World Economic & Financial Surveys Ser.). 34p. 1986. pap. 10.00 (*0-939934-69-8*) Intl Monetary.
Brau, Eduard H. & Puckahtikom, Chanpen. Export Credit Cover Policies & Payments Difficulties. (Occasional Papers: No. 37). 51p. 1985. pap. 7.50 (*0-939934-49-3*) Intl Monetary.
Brau, Eduard H., et al. Export Credits: Developments & Prospects. LC 86-15397. (World Economic & Financial Surveys July 1986 Ser.). 40p. reprint ed. pap. 30.00 (*0-608-17941-8*, 202909100058) Bks Demand.
Brau, J., jt. auth. see Parvini, R. S.
Brau, Jean-Louis. Larousse Dictionnaire de l'Astrologie. (FRE.). 222p. 1977. pap. 16.95 (*0-7859-7637-X*, 2030754773) Fr & Eur.
Brauch, Hans G., et al, eds. Controlling the Development & Spread of Military Technology: Lessons from the Past & Challenges for the 1990's. 446p. (Orig.). 1992. pap. text 49.50 (*90-5383-103-7*, Pub. by VU Univ Pr) Paul & Co Pubs.
Brauch, Hans G. & Clarke, Duncan L., eds. Decision Making for Arms Limitation: Assessments & Prospects. LC 82-22773. 368p. 1983. text 35.00 (*0-88410-864-3*, HarpBusn) HarpInfo.
Brauch, Hans G. & Kennedy, Robert F., Jr., eds. Alternative Conventional Defense Postures in the European Theater, Vol. 3: Military Alternatives for Europe after the Cold War. 240p. 1992. 95.00 (*0-8448-1728-7*, Crane Russak) Taylor & Francis.
Brauch, Hans Gunter. Euro-meditarranean Partnership for the 21st Century. text 79.95 (*0-312-23331-0*) St Martin.
***Brauch, Jeffrey A.** Is Higher Law Common Law? Readings on the Influence of Christian Thought in Anglo-American Law. LC 99-35702. xvii, 429p. 1999. lib. bdg. 45.00 (*0-8377-0367-0*, 323560, Rothman) W S Hein.
Brauch, Judy, tr. see Powers, John D.
Brauch, Manfred T. Hard Sayings of Paul. LC 87-31814. (Hard Sayings Ser.). 216p. (Orig.). 1989. pap. 12.99 (*0-8308-1282-2*, 1282) InterVarsity.
Braucher, Antoinette. In Search of Mrs. Barrows. 60p. (Orig.). 1985. pap. 5.95 (*0-933858-07-8*) Kennebec River.
Braucher, Karen. Heaven's Net. 32p. (Orig.). 1997. pap. 5.00 (*0-9637849-9-4*) Bacchae Pr.
Brauchli, Berard, ed. Solo Keyboard Works: Franz Seydelmann. (Music Archive Publications Ser.). 112p. 1997. text 40.00 (*90-5702-060-2*, Harwood Acad Pubs) Gordon & Breach.
Brauchli, Bernard. The Clavichord. LC 97-40897. (Cambridge Musical Texts & Monographs). (Illus.). 450p. (C). 1998. 120.00 (*0-521-63067-3*) Cambridge U Pr.
Brauchli, Bernard, ed. Six Sonatas for Two Persons at One Keyboard: Franz Seydelmann. (Music Archive Publications Ser.). 148p. 1997. pap. text 19.00 (*90-5702-063-7*, Harwood Acad Pubs) Gordon & Breach.
— Six Sonatas for Two Persons at One Keyboard: Franz Seydelmann, 2. (Music Archive Publications Ser.). 148p. 1997. text 48.00 (*90-5702-062-9*, Harwood Acad Pubs) Gordon & Breach.
— Solo Keyboard Works: Franz Seydelmann. (Music Archive Publications Ser.). 112p. 1997. pap. text 18.00 (*90-5702-061-0*, Harwood Acad Pubs) Gordon & Breach.
Braucht, Stephanie. Rashunel Reasoner: A Program to Change Negative Thinking into Positive Thinking. (Illus.). 30p. (Orig.). (J). (ps-5). 1993. pap. 6.95 (*1-884063-56-X*) Mar Co Prods.
Brauckmann-Towns, Krista, jt. auth. see Rowitz, Mary.
Braud, Janice. Through a Glass Darkly. LC 94-70817. (Illus.). 64p. 1994. lib. bdg. 10.00 (*1-878149-26-1*) Counterpoint Pub.
Braud, Janice & Ottenstein, Claire, eds. A Touch of Sunshine. (Illus.). 46p. (Orig.). 1996. pap. 10.00 (*1-878149-34-2*) Counterpoint Pub.
Braud, Philippe & Reid, Jeffrey, trs. The Garden of Democratic Delights: For a Psycho-Emotional Reading of Pluralist Systems. LC 97-38543. 184p. 1998. 59.95 (*0-275-95748-9*, Praeger Pubs) Greenwood.
Braud, William, jt. auth. see Anderson, Rosemarie.
***Braudaway, Douglas.** Val Verde County. (Images of America Ser.). (Illus.). 128p. 1999. pap. 18.99 (*0-7385-0128-X*) Arcadia Publng.
Braude. Pocket Portfolio Jokes. 16p. (C). 1989. pap. text 9.95 (*0-13-683871-5*) P-H.
Braude, Aaron. Carefree Is the Gypsy Life. LC 96-71765. 204p. 1997. pap. 16.95 (*1-57197-049-5*) Pentland Pr.

B

Braude, Ann. News from the Spirit World: A Checklist of American Spiritualist Periodicals, 1847-1900. (Illus.). 63p. 1990. reprint ed. pap. 7.50 (*0-944026-21-4*) Am Antiquarian.
— Radical Spirits: Spiritualism & Women's Rights in Nineteenth-Century America. LC 89-42599. (Illus.). 288p. 1991. pap. 18.50 (*0-8070-7501-9*) Beacon Pr.
— Radical Spirits: Spiritualism & Women's Rights in Nineteenth-Century America. 268p. (C). 1998. pap. text 15.00 (*0-7881-5666-7*) DIANE Pub.
— Women in American Religion. LC 99-32968. (Religion in American Life Ser.). (Illus.). 144p. (YA). 2000. text 22.00 (*0-19-510676-8*) OUP.
Braude, Anne J., ed. Andre Norton: Fables & Futures. 52p. 1989. pap. 5.95 (*0-910619-04-2*) Niekas Pubns.
Braude, Benjamin & Lewis, Bernard, eds. Christians & Jews in the Ottoman Empire: The Functioning of a Plural Society, 2 vols. LC 80-11337. 1982. 94.50 (*0-8419-0519-3*); write for info. (*0-8419-0520-7*) Holmes & Meier.
Braude, Eric. Analyzing & Designing Object-Oriented Systems. 350p. 1997. pap. 329.00 (*0-7803-2324-6*, HL5733) Inst Electrical.
Braude, Eric J., ed. Object-Oriented Analysis & Design: Selected Readings. 500p. 1997. pap. 49.95 (*0-7803-2341-6*, SR107) Inst Electrical.
Braude, Jacob M. Braude's Treasury of Wit & Humor for All Occasions. 300p. (C). 1991. text 27.95 (*0-13-093659-6*); pap. text 10.95 (*0-13-093667-7*) P-H.
— Complete Speaker's & Toastmaster's Library. 2nd ed. 1008p. (C). 1992. text 69.95 (*0-13-161597-1*) P-H.
Braude, Lee. A Sense of Sociology. rev. ed. LC 79-20785. 160p. 1981. reprint ed. pap. 11.50 (*0-89874-016-9*) Krieger.
Braude, Marjorie, ed. Woman, Power, & Therapy. 340p. 1987. pap. 22.95 (*0-918393-36-1*, Harrington Park) Haworth Pr.
— Women, Power & Therapy: Issues for Women. LC 87-14873. (Women & Therapy Ser.: Vol. 6, Nos. 1-2). 340p. 1987. text 49.95 (*0-86656-653-8*) Haworth Pr.
Braude, Monique C. & Szara, Stephen, eds. Pharmacology of Marihuana: Proceedings, Vol. 2. LC 75-14562. 424p. 1976. reprint ed. pap. 131.50 (*0-608-00380-8*, 206109400002) Bks Demand.
Braude, Stephen E. First Person Plural: Multiple Personality & the Philosophy of Mind. rev. ed. LC 94-40570. 320p. 1995. pap. text 23.95 (*0-8476-7996-9*) Rowman.
— The Limit of Influence: Psychokinesis & the Philosophy of Science. 256p. 1986. 39.95 (*0-7102-0556-2*, 05562, Routledge Thoemms) Routledge.
— The Limit of Influence: Psychokinesis & the Philosophy of Science. rev. ed. LC 96-29553. 322p. 1997. 58.50 (*0-7618-0623-7*); pap. 27.50 (*0-7618-0624-5*) U Pr of Amer.
Braude, William G. Tanna Debe Eliyyahu: The Lore of the School of Elijah. 1997. pap. text 29.95 (*0-8276-0634-6*) JPS Phila.
Braude, William G., tr. Midrash on Psalms, 2 vols. (Judaica Ser.: No. 13). 1959. 125.00 (*0-300-00322-6*) Yale U Pr.
— Pesikta Rabbati: Homiletical Discourses for Festal Days & Special Sabbaths, 2 vols. LC 68-27748. (Judaica Ser.: No. 18). (Illus.). 1968. 120.00 (*0-300-01071-0*) Yale U Pr.
Braude, William G., tr. see Bialik, Hayim N. & Ravnitzky, Yehoshua H., eds.
Braudel, Fernand. Afterthoughts on Material Civilization & Capitalism. LC 76-47368. (Johns Hopkins Symposia in Comparative History Ser.: Vol. 7). 134p. 1977. reprint ed. pap. 41.60 (*0-608-03643-9*, 206446900009) Bks Demand.
— Civilization & Capitalism, 15th-18th Century Vol. II: The Wheels of Commerce, 3 vols. Reynolds, Sian, tr. from FRE. LC 92-10173.Tr. of Civilisation Materielle Economie et Capitalisme. (C). 1992. 29.95 (*0-520-08115-3*, Pub. by U CA Pr) Cal Prin Full Svc.
— Civilization & Capitalism, 15th-18th Century Vol. III: The Perspective of the World, 3 vols. Reynolds, Sian, tr. from FRE. LC 92-10173.Tr. of Civilisation Materielle Economie et Capitalisme. (C). 1992. 29.95 (*0-520-08116-1*, Pub. by U CA Pr) Cal Prin Full Svc.
— Civilization & Capitalism, 15th-18th Century Vol. I: The Structure of Everday Life, 3 vols. Reynolds, Sian, tr. from FRE. LC 92-10173.Tr. of Civilisation Materielle Economie et Capitalisme. (C). 1992. pap. 29.95 (*0-520-08114-5*, Pub. by U CA Pr) Cal Prin Full Svc.
— La Dinamica del Capitalismo. (Breviarios Ser.). (SPA.). pap. 6.99 (*968-16-4048-9*, Pub. by Fondo) Continental Bk.
— A History of Civilizations. 624p. 1995. pap. 16.95 (*0-14-012489-6*, Penguin Bks) Viking Penguin.
— The Mediterranean & the Mediterranean World in the Age of Philip II, Vol. I. Reynolds, Sian, tr. LC 95-37581. (Illus.). 642p. 1995. pap. 27.50 (*0-520-20308-9*, Pub. by U CA Pr) Cal Prin Full Svc.
— The Mediterranean & the Mediterranean World in the Age of Philip II, Vol. II. (Illus.). 725p. 1995. pap. 27.50 (*0-520-20330-5*, Pub. by U CA Pr) Cal Prin Full Svc.
— On History. Matthews, Sarah, tr. from FRE. LC 80-11201. 236p. 1982. pap. text 13.00 (*0-226-07151-0*) U Ch Pr.
Braudel, Francoise, tr. see Venturi, Franco.
Braudes, R A. Me 'ayin U-Le'An: Whence & Whither. (Literaria Judaica Section Ser.: No. 7). 47.50 (*0-404-13860-8*) AMS Pr.
— Shete Ha'Qesawot: The Two Extremes Novel. 2nd ed. (Literaria Judaica Section 2 Ser.: No. 5). reprint ed. 47.50 (*0-404-13861-6*) AMS Pr.
Braudet, Jerome. Rainbow Chameleon. 1999. pap. 11.95 (*0-8037-1620-6*, Dial Yng Read) Peng Put Young Read.
Braudis, Bill & Truxaw, Dick. Dr. Katz's Daily Dose: A Board-Certified Collection of Comic Strips Inspired by the Award-Winning Series. LC 99-199260. (Illus.). 1997. pap. 10.00 (*0-671-00758-0*) PB.
Braudy, Leo. Frenzy of Renown. LC 97-5434. 1997. pap. 18.00 (*0-679-77630-3*) Vin Bks.
— Masculinity. 1999. pap. write for info. (*0-679-76830-0*) Knopf.
— Narrative Form in History & Fiction: Hume, Fielding & Gibbon. LC 69-18052. viii, 318 p. 1970. write for info. (*0-691-06168-8*) Princeton U Pr.
— Native Informant: Essays on Film, Fiction, & Popular Culture. 1990. 35.00 (*0-685-38918-9*) OUP.
— The World in a Frame: What We See in Films. LC 84-225. xii, 286p. 1984. reprint ed. pap. text 11.95 (*0-226-07155-3*) U Ch Pr.
Braudy, Leo, ed. Norman Mailer: A Collection of Critical Essays. 1972. pap. 1.95 (*0-13-545541-3*, STC101, Spectrum IN) Macmillan Gen Ref.
Braudy, Leo & Cohen, Marshall. Film Theory & Criticism: Introductory Readings. 5th ed. LC 97-15809. (Illus.). 880p. (C). 1998. pap. text 39.95 (*0-19-510598-2*) OUP.
Braue, Donald A. Maya in Radhakrishnan's Thought: Six Meanings Other Than Illusion. 1985. 15.00 (*0-8364-1129-3*) S Asia.
Braue, Frederick, jt. auth. see Hugard, Jean.
Brauen, Martin. The Mandala: Sacred Circle in Tibetan Buddhism. (Illus.). 152p. 1998. pap. 25.00 (*1-57062-380-5*, Pub. by Shambhala Pubns) Random.
Brauer. Copper, Silver, Gold, Zinc, Cadmium, & Mercury, Vol. 5. Herrmann, W. A., ed. 200p. 1999. 89.00 (*0-86577-662-8*) Thieme Med Pubs.
— Economics for Managers. (HT - Managerial Economics Ser.). Date not set. mass mkt. 56.95 (*0-538-86252-1*); mass mkt., student ed. 18.95 (*0-538-86253-X*) S-W Pub.
Brauer, jt. auth. see Hermann.
Brauer, A. Die Suesswasserfauna Deutchlands. (Illus.). 1961. reprint ed. 250.00 (*3-7682-0045-0*) Lubrecht & Cramer.
Brauer, Alan P., et al. The ESO Ecstasy Program: Better, Safer Sexual Intimacy & Extended Orgasmic Response. LC 82-50863. (Illus.). 228p. 1991. mass mkt. 12.99 (*0-446-39178-6*, Pub. by Warner Bks) Little.
— ESO, Extendended Sexual Orgasm. 1989. mass mkt. 13.99 (*0-446-38645-6*, Pub. by Warner Bks) Little.
Brauer, Amy, jt. auth. see Vermeule, Cornelius C.
Brauer, Anne. F. F. V. - Falmouth - Fredericksburg - Virginia: Legends & Anecdotes. LC 98-70350. (Illus.). 135p. 1998. pap. 20.00 (*1-887648-08-9*) A-A Bks Pub.
Brauer, Anne, ed. & pref. see Brauer, Brooks.
Brauer, Anne B. Ash Flats Murder. LC 99-94739. 250p. 2000. pap. 18.50 (*1-887648-09-7*) A-A Bks Pub.
— The Cactus Fence. LC 94-94147. 234p. pap. 18.50 (*0-9632718-4-9*) A-A Bks Pub.
— The Crazy Eight Murder. 232p. 1999. pap. text 18.50 (*1-887648-04-6*) A-A Bks Pub.
— What Widows Face: Sudden Death of Spouse. LC 97-93590. 120p. (Orig.). (C). 18.00 (*1-887648-07-0*) A-A Bks Pub.
Brauer, Barbara S. Ground Beef Favorites. Herbert, Susan H., ed. LC 81-83356. (Illus.). 64p. 1981. pap. 2.95 (*0-915942-19-4*) SF Design.
— Steam Cooking Now! LC 80-82174. (Illus.). 1980. pap. 2.95 (*0-915942-15-1*) SF Design.
Brauer, Brooks. How to Make Secure Money. Brauer, Anne, ed. & pref. by. LC 95-77396. 88p. (Orig.). 1995. pap. 10.00 (*1-887648-06-2*) A-A Bks Pub.
Brauer, Carl M. The Man Who Built Washington: A Life of John McShain. (Illus.). 300p. 1996. 49.50 (*0-914650-31-9*) Hagley Museum.
Brauer, Carl M., et al. Civil Rights During the Kennedy Administration, 1961-1963: A Collection from the Holdings of the John F. Kennedy Library, Boston, Massachusetts. LC 87-2061. (Black Studies Research Sources). 47 p. 1987. write for info. (*0-89093-364-2*) U Pubns Amer.
Brauer, David, told to. Nellie Stone Johnson: The Life of an Activist. (Illus.). 256p. 2000. 23.00 (*1-886913-35-8*, Pub. by Ruminator Bks) Consort Bk Sales.
Brauer, Denny & Buech, Monte. Denny Brauer's Winning Tournament Tactics. 1991. pap. 12.95 (*1-879206-15-3*) Outdoor World Pr.
Brauer, Denny & Burch, Monte. Denny Brauer's Jig Fishing Secrets. LC 97-67271. (Illus.). 192p. 1997. pap. 14.95 (*1-879206-22-6*) Outdoor World Pr.
Brauer, Douglas C. & Cesarone, John. Total Manufacturing Assurance. (Quality & Reliability Ser.: Vol. 24). (Illus.). 256p. 1991. text 85.00 (*0-8247-8441-3*) Dekker.
Brauer, Erich. Ethnologie der Jemenitischen Juden. LC 77-87611. reprint ed. 37.50 (*0-404-16435-8*) AMS Pr.
— The Jews of Kurdistan. Patai, Raphael, ed. LC 92-46105. (Jewish Folklore & Anthropology Ser.). (Illus.). 430p. 1993. 45.95 (*0-8143-2392-8*) Wayne St U Pr.
Brauer, Erich, jt. auth. see Restany, Pierre.
***Brauer, Fred.** Population Biology: An Introduction to Mathematical Models. (Illus.). 2000. 49.95 (*0-387-98902-1*) Spr-Verlag.
Brauer, Fred & Nohel, John A. Qualitative Theory of Ordinary Differential Equations. 320p. 1994. pap. 8.95 (*0-486-65846-5*) Dover.
Brauer, George, Jr. Taras: Its History & Coinage. (Illus.). xii, 231p. (C). 1986. lib. bdg. 55.00 (*0-89241-377-8*) Caratzas.
Brauer, George C. The Education of a Gentleman. 1959. pap. 14.95 (*0-8084-0115-7*) NCUP.
Brauer, Gunter & Smith, Fred H., eds. Continuity Or Replacement: Controversies in Homo Sapiens Evolution. (Illus.). 328p. (C). 1991. text 123.00 (*90-6191-149-4*, Pub. by A A Balkema) Ashgate Pub Co.
Brauer, H. & Varma, Y. B. Air Pollution Control Equipment. (Illus.). 388p. 1981. 369.95 (*0-387-10463-1*) Spr-Verlag.
Brauer, James L. Meaningful Worship: A Guide to the Lutheran Service. LC 94-6861. 96p. 1994. 10.00 (*0-570-04642-4*, 12-3223) Concordia.
Brauer, Jane Z. Art of Teaching: The Natural Approach Participant's Guide. 1994. pap. text. write for info. (*0-201-53917-9*) Addison-Wesley.
— The Art of Teaching Cooperative Learning: Viewer's Guide. (C). 1996. pap. text. write for info. (*0-201-58708-4*) Addison-Wesley.
— The Art of Teaching Total Physical Response: Viewer's Guide. 1996. pap. text. write for info. (*0-201-58715-7*) Addison-Wesley.
— Art of Teaching Whole Language: Viewer's Guide. (C). 1997. pap. text. write for info. (*0-201-58705-X*) Addison-Wesley.
— Open Sesame Stage C: Cookie Monster's Blue Book Duplicating Masters. 1985. pap. text, teacher ed. 23.95 (*0-19-434193-3*) OUP.
Brauer, Janice K. Safe in His Arms: Moments of Peace in a Hectic World LC 98-49971. 1999. 12.99 (*0-570-05334-X*) Concordia.
Brauer, Janice K., ed. One Cup of Water. (Illus.). 160p. (Orig.). 1997. pap. 6.00 (*0-9614955-6-1*, 23000) Lutheran Womens.
— Rainbow of Saris. (Illus.). 156p. (Orig.). 1996. pap. 6.00 (*0-9614955-5-3*, 22960) Lutheran Womens.
Brauer, Janice K., ed. see Bunkowske, Bernice.
***Brauer, Jeff.** Sexy New York: Annual Guide to N. Y. C. Erotica 2000. (Illus.). 2000. pap. 26.95 (*1-929377-08-8*); pap. 71.95 (*1-929377-09-6*) On Your Own.
— Sexy New York: Annual Guide to N. Y. C. Erotica 2000. 2nd ed. (Illus.). 2000. pap. 8.95 (*1-929377-00-2*) On Your Own.
Brauer, Jeff & Wiles, Veronica. Out & About in Washington, DC: The Insider's Guide. LC 99-203430. (Illus.). 95p. 1999. pap. 7.95 (*0-9643789-2-2*) On Your Own.
Brauer, Jeff, et al. Conozca El Salvador: Spanish Language Version of On Your Own in El Salvador. (On Your Own Travel Guides Ser.). (SPA., Illus.). 270p. 1997. pap. 15.95 (*0-9643789-1-4*) On Your Own.
— On Your Own in El Salvador. (Illus.). 1995. pap. 14.95 (*0-9643789-0-6*) On Your Own.
Brauer, Jerald. Religion & the American Revolution. LC 76-9718. 89p. pap. 30.00 (*0-608-16375-9*, 202688800053) Bks Demand.
Brauer, Jerald C., ed. see Breen, Quirinus & Drake, George A.
Brauer, Jerald C., ed. see Mead, Sidney.
Brauer, John R., ed. WEESKA Finite Element Analysis. 2nd rev. ed. LC 93-12659. (What Every Engineer Should Know Ser.: Vol. 31). (Illus.). 346p. 1993. text 65.00 (*0-8247-8954-7*) Dekker.
Brauer, Jurgen & Gissy, William G., eds. Economics of Conflict & Peace. LC 96-86737. 416p. 1997. text 83.95 (*1-85972-237-7*, Pub. by Avebry) Ashgate Pub Co.
Brauer, Kinley, pref. Austria in the Age of the French Revolution, 1789-1815. (Illus.). xxv, 192p. (Orig.). (C). 1990. pap. text 12.00 (*0-9626990-0-4*) U MN Ctr Austrian Studies.
Brauer, Kinley J. Cotton Versus Conscience: Massachusetts Whig Politics & Southwestern Expansion, 1843-1848. 1967. 15.00 (*0-87018-071-1*) Ross.
Brauer, Markus. Theologie Im Horizont der Geschichte: Fortgang und Schwerpunkte Geschichtstheologischen Denkens in der Theologie des 20. Jahrhunderts und Weiterfuhrende Perspektiven Einer Geschichtstheologischen Systematik. (Europaische Hochschulschriften Ser.: Reihe 23, Bd. 516). (GER.). XVI, 465p. 1994. 66.95 (*3-631-47517-9*) P Lang Pubng.
Brauer, R. W. Boundaries & Frontiers in Medieval Muslim Geography. LC 94-78513. (Transactions Ser.: Vol. 85, Pt. 6). (Illus.). 73p. 1995. pap. 12.00 (*0-87169-856-0*, T856-brr) Am Philos.
Brauer, Richard. Richard Brauer: Collected Papers, 3 vols., 1. Wong, Warren J. & Fong, Paul, eds. 1980. 80.00 (*0-262-02135-8*) MIT Pr.
Brauer, Richard, jt. auth. see Barsky, Robert Franklin.
Brauer, Roger L. Directory of Safety Related Computer Resources, 1994. LC 94-28647. 1994. 9.95 (*1-885581-01-7*) ASSE.
— Facilities Planning. 2nd ed. LC 92-17499. 256p. 1992. 69.95 (*0-8144-5078-4*) AMACOM.
— Safety & Health for Engineering. 1994. pap. 87.95 (*0-442-01856-8*, VNR) Wiley.
— Safety & Health for Engineers. (Industrial Health & Safety Ser.). 672p. 1993. pap. 89.95 (*0-471-28632-X*, VNR) Wiley.
— Safety & Health for Engineers. 2nd ed. 656p. 1994. pap. text 79.95 (*0-442-02040-6*, VNR) Wiley.
Brauer, Roger L. & Vincoli, Jeffrey W. Handbook Safety & Health Engineering. 1999. 89.95 (*1-56670-240-2*) Lewis Pubs.
Brauer, Rose M. My North Dakota Prairie Childhood. LC 94-79031. 138p. 1990. pap. 15.00 (*0-9643204-0-1*) Gregory Pubs.
— Roses in December: The Last Forty Years. LC 94-79032. (Illus.). 243p. 1994. pap. 15.00 (*0-9643204-1-X*) Gregory Pubs.
Brauer, Samuel. Advanced Structural Non-Pyrolyzed Fibers. LC 98-120883. (Report Ser.: No. GB-205). 170p. 1997. 3350.00 (*1-56965-458-1*) BCC.
Brauer, W., et al, eds. KI-95: Advances in Artificial Intelligence: 19th German Annual Conference on Artificial Intelligence, Bielefeld, Germany, September 11-13, 1995 - Proceedings. (Lecture Notes in Computer Science Subseries: Lecture Notes in Artificial Intelligence: Vol. 981). xii, 269p. 1995. pap. 49.00 (*3-540-60343-3*) Spr-Verlag.
— Petri Nets: Applications & Relationships to Other Models of Concurrency. (Lecture Notes in Computer Science Ser.: Vol. 255). x, 516p. 1987. pap. 53.00 (*0-387-17906-2*) Spr-Verlag.
Brauer, W., ed. see De Luca, A. & Varricchio, S.
Brauer, W., ed. see Gergely, T. & Ury, L.
Brauer, W., ed. see Janicki, R. & Lauer, P. E.
Brauer, W., ed. see Jensen, K.
Brauer, W., ed. see Paun, Gheorghe, et al.
Brauer, W., ed. see Schmidt, G. & Stohlein, T.
Brauer, W., ed. see Wechler, W.
Brauer, Wilfried. Foundations of Computer Science: Potential-Theory-Cognition, Vol. 133. Freksa, C. et al, eds. LC 97-39198. (Lecture Notes in Computer Science Ser.: Vol. 1337). xii, 515p. 1997. pap. 75.00 (*3-540-63746-X*) Spr-Verlag.
Braufman, Sheila. Jewish Themes: Northern California Artists. LC 86-82852. (Illus.). 48p. (Orig.). 1987. pap. 9.95 (*0-943376-37-8*) Magnes Mus.
Braukmann, C. J., jt. auth. see Morris, E. K.
Braulik, Georg. The Theology of Deuteronomy: Collected Essays of Georg Braulik, O.S.B. Lindblad, Ulrika, tr. from GER. (Collected Essays Ser.: No. 2). 320p. 1995. pap. 19.95 (*0-941037-30-4*, BIBAL Press) D & F Scott.
Brault, Gerard, tr. see Brault, Gerard J., ed.
Brault, Gerard J. Early Blazon: Heraldic Terminology in the 12th & 13th Centuries with Special Reference to Arthurian Heraldry. 2nd ed. LC 96-52686. (Illus.). 321p. 1998. 75.00 (*0-85115-711-4*, Boydell Pr) Boydell & Brewer.
— The French-Canadian Heritage in New England. LC 85-22512. (Illus.). 298p. 1986. pap. 19.95 (*0-87451-359-6*) U Pr of New Eng.
Brault, Gerard J., ed. Rolls of Arms of Edward I (1272-1307), Vol. II. (Society of Antiquaries Ser.: Vol. III). 1997. 130.00 (*0-85115-676-2*, Boydell Pr) Boydell & Brewer.
— The Song of Roland: An Analytical Edition - Introduction & Commentary, 2 vols., 1. Brault, Gerard, tr. (Illus.). (C). 1978. 40.00 (*0-271-00516-5*) Pa St U Pr.
— The Song of Roland: An Analytical Edition - Oxford Text & English Translation, 2 vols., 2. Brault, Gerard, tr. (Illus.). (C). 1978. 25.00 (*0-271-00204-2*) Pa St U Pr.
Brault, Jacques. Death-Watch, No. 53. Lobdell, David, tr. from FRE. 95p. 1987. reprint ed. pap. 9.95 (*0-88784-154-6*, Pub. by Hse of Anansi Pr) Genl Dist Srvs.
— Within the Mystery, Vol. 1. 50p. pap. 5.00 (*0-919349-62-5*) Guernica Editions.
Brault, Jim. Lessons from the Masters: Seven Keys to Peak Performance & Inner Peace. Resnick, Jennifer, ed. 160p. 1998. pap. 13.50 (*0-9663482-0-6*) Ctr Line Pr.
Brault, Margaret A. & MacDevitt, Margaret L. Chemistry Survival Skills. 128p. (C). 1988. pap. text 7.96 (*0-669-17143-3*) HM Trade Div.
Brault, Pascale-Anne, tr. see Derrida, Jacques.
Brault, Pascale-Anne, tr. see Lyotard, Jean-Francois & Gruber, Eberhard.
Brault, Richard. Best Restaurants in London & England. (Illus.). 256p. 2000. pap. 9.95 (*0-9656956-5-4*, Pub. by Les Edtn R Brault) Seven Hills Bk.
— Best Restaurants in Paris. (FRE., Illus.). 192p. 1997. 6.95 (*0-9656956-0-3*) Les Edtn R Brault.
— Best Restaurants in Paris. (Illus.). 304p. 2000. pap. 9.95 (*0-9656956-4-6*, Pub. by Les Edtn R Brault) Seven Hills Bk.
Brault, Richard, ed. Best Restaurants in New York. (Illus.). 1999. pap. 9.95 (*0-9656956-6-2*, Pub. by Les Edtn R Brault) Seven Hills Bk.
Brauman, J. I. & Streitwieser, Andrew, Jr. Supplemental Tables of Molecular Orbital Calculations, 2 vols. 1965. 707.00 (*0-08-010219-0*, Pub. by Pergamon Repr) Franklin.
Brauman, Ken. Handbook of Drills & Techniques for Coaching High School Track & Field. 1979. pap. 14.95 (*0-13-377226-8*) P-H.
Brauman, Ken & Taylor, Ken. The American Method of Sprinting & Relay Racing. 64p. (Orig.). 1981. pap. 8.95 (*0-932741-96-7*) Championship Bks & Vid Prodns.
Braumiller, Tanya. Visiting Gig Harbor. (Color-A-Story Ser.). (Illus.). (Orig.). (J). (gr. 1-4). 1983. pap. 2.75 (*0-933992-28-9*) Coffee Break.
Braumuller, A. R. & Bulman, James C., eds. Comedy from Shakespeare to Sheridan: Change & Continuity in the English & European Dramatic Tradition. LC 84-40464. 288p. 1986. 42.50 (*0-87413-276-2*) U Delaware Pr.
***Braun.** Blood Storm. 256p. 2000. mass mkt. 5.99 (*0-312-97294-6*) St Martin.
Braun. Gabler Kleines Lexikon Informatik. (GER.). 1993. 49.95 (*0-7859-8340-6*, 3409199284) Fr & Eur.
— Identification of Plastics. 1982. 20.00 (*0-07-007293-0*) McGraw.
— Noble Outlaw. 1996. pap. write for info. (*0-312-95772-6*) St Martin.
— Western, Vol. 1. 1998. 5.99 (*0-312-96600-8*, Pub. by Tor Bks) St Martin.
Braun & Schneider. Historic Costume in Pictures. 2nd ed. (Pictorial Archives Ser.). 1975. 18.05 (*0-606-04248-2*, Pub. by Turtleback) Demco.
— Historic Costumes in Pictures: 1450 Costumes on 125 Plates. 2nd ed. LC 74-12532. (Pictorial Archive Ser.). (Illus.). 256p. reprint ed. pap. 12.95 (*0-486-23150-X*) Dover.
Braun, ed. see Herodotus.
Braun, A. A. & Gilbertson, L. N., eds. Applications of Automation Technology to Fatigue & Fracture Testing & Analysis, Vol. 3. 3rd ed. LC 97-226314. (STP Ser.: No. 1303). (Illus.). 157p. 1997. per. 95.00 (*0-8031-2416-3*, STP1303) ASTM.
Braun, A. A., et al. Applications of Automation to Fatigue & Fracture Testing. LC 90-43922. (Special Technical Publication Ser.: No. 1092). (Illus.). 306p. 1990. text 73.00 (*0-8031-1401-X*, STP1092) ASTM.
Braun, A. C., ed. Plant Tumor Research. (Progress in Experimental Tumor Research Ser.: Vol. 15). 1972. 54.00 (*3-8055-1262-7*) S Karger.

Braun, Alan G., jt. auth. see Longley, Lawrence D.

Braun, Andre M., et al. Photochemical Technology. LC 90-46482. 580p. 1991. 475.00 (*0-471-92652-3*) Wiley.

Braun, Anne R. Wage Determination & Incomes Policy in Open Economies. LC 86-10414. (Illus.). xix, 380p. 1986. pap. 18.50 (*0-939934-75-2*) Intl Monetary.

— Wage Determination & Incomes Policy in Open Economies. LC 86-10414. 400p. reprint ed. pap. 124.00 (*0-608-15305-2*, 202954900061) Bks Demand.

Braun, Armin C. Cancer Problem: A Critical Analysis & Modern Synthesis. LC 77-90432. (Molecular Biology Ser.). (Illus.). 209p. 1969. text 69.50 (*0-231-02938-1*) Col U Pr.

Braun, Aurel. Romanian Foreign Policy since 1965: The Political & Military Limits of Autonomy. LC 78-9516. (Praeger Special Studies). 1978. 62.95 (*0-275-90287-0*, C0287, Praeger Pubs) Greenwood.

Braun, Aurel. Small-State Security in the Balkans. LC 82-6639. (Studies in Russian & East European History). 346p. (C). 1983. text 38.50 (*0-389-20288-6*, 07110) B&N Imports.

— Warsaw Pact: Change & Modernization in the Gorbachev Era. 1999. pap. 34.50 (*0-8133-0381-8*) Westview.

Braun, Aurel & Barany, Zoltan, eds. Dilemmas of Transition: The Hungarian Experience. LC 98-36859. 360p. 1999. 69.00 (*0-8476-9004-0*); pap. 27.95 (*0-8476-9005-9*) Rowman.

Braun, Aurel, ed. see Scheinberg, Stephen.

***Braun, Barbara.** Pre-Columbian Art & the Post-Columbian World: Ancient American Sources of Modern Art. (Illus.). 340p. 2000. pap. 34.95 (*0-8109-2947-3*, Pub. by Abrams) Time Warner.

Braun, Barbara. Pre-Columbian Art & the Post-Columbian World: Ancient Sources of Modern Art. LC 92-29047. (Illus.). 340p. 1993. 75.00 (*0-8109-3723-9*, Pub. by Abrams) Time Warner.

— A Weekend with Diego Rivera. LC 93-38905. 64p. (J). 1994. 19.95 (*0-8478-1749-0*, Pub. by Rizzoli Intl) St Martin.

Braun, Barbara & Roe, Peter. Arts of the Amazon. LC 94-61400. (Illus.). 128p. 1995. pap. 19.95 (*0-500-27824-5*, Pub. by Thames Hudson) Norton.

Braun, Barry. Real Estate Sales: Is It the Career for You? 160p. 1990. pap. 16.95 (*0-7737-5353-2*) Genl Dist Srvs.

***Braun, Beverly Kirschner.** Crafting Your Own Heritage Album. LC 99-33680. (Illus.). 128p. 2000. pap. 23.99 (*1-55870-534-1*, Betrwy Bks) F & W Pubns Inc.

Braun-Blanquet, J. Plant Sociology: The Study of Plant Communities. Fuller, George D. & Conrad, Henry S., eds. & trs. by. (Illus.). xviii, 439p. 1983. reprint ed. 75.00 (*3-87429-208-8*, 002243, Pub. by Koeltz Sci Bks) Lubrecht & Cramer.

Braun, Bonnie & Mitstifer, Dorothy I., eds. Reflective Leading in the Public Interest. 1998. 15.00 (*1-929083-06-8*) Kappa Omi Nu.

Braun, Brad. Learn Digital Photography in a Weekend. LC 98-65966. 350p. 1998. per. 19.99 (*0-7615-1532-1*) Prima Pub.

Braun, Brenda. All about Baby: From Birth to Baptism. (Illus.). 1994. 14.95 (*0-87579-850-0*); ring bd. 24.95 (*0-87579-851-9*) Deseret Bk.

Braun, Brian A. Illinois School Law Survey. 5th rev. ed. 616p. 1998. pap. text 22.00 (*1-880331-09-8*) IL Assn Sch Bds.

Braun, Bruce & Castree, Noel. Remaking Reality: Nature at the Millenium. LC 97-35301. (Illus.). 312p. (C). 1998. pap. 27.99 (*0-415-14494-9*) Routledge.

— Remaking Reality: Nature at the Millenium. LC 97-35301. (Illus.). 312p. (C). 1998. 85.00 (*0-415-14493-0*) Routledge.

Braun, Carl. Looking, Listening & Learning: Observing & Assessing Young Readers. 200p. (Orig.). 1993. pap., teacher ed. 18.00 (*1-895411-55-6*) Peguis Pubs Ltd.

Braun, Carl & Goepfert, Paula S. Along the Line of Smoky Hills. (Strategies Program Ser.). 1991. text 20.12 (*0-8123-6916-5*) McDougal-Littell.

Braun, Cheryl-Lynne. Ice Dance. 192p. mass mkt. 6.99 (*1-55197-490-8*) Picasso Publ.

— Snow Blind. 200p. mass mkt. 3.99 (*1-55197-486-X*) Picasso Publ.

— Wild Rose. 200p. mass mkt. 4.99 (*1-55197-488-6*) Picasso Publ.

Braun, Christian, tr. see Lask, Emil.

Braun, Christoph. UNIX System Security Essentials. LC 94-31241. (C). 1995. pap. text 25.31 (*0-201-42775-3*) Addison-Wesley.

Braun, Christoph-Fried Von, see Von Braun, Christoph-Fried.

Braun, Christopher K., jt. ed. see Malloy, Robin P.

Braun, Connie, jt. auth. see Bazillion, Richard J.

***Braun, Cordula.** Divergentes Bewu & Beta;Tsein: Romanprosa an der Wende Zum 19, Jahrhundert: Interpretationen Zu Schlegels Lucinde, Brentanos Godwi und Jean Pauls Leben Fibels. 456p. 1999. 67.95 (*3-631-35073-2*) P Lang Pubng.

Braun, D., et al. Nuclear Physics with Heavy Ions. Ivin, Kenneth J., tr. from GER. (MMI Press Polymer Monographs: Vol. 4). (C). 1984. 118.95 (*0-685-42165-1*) Gordon & Breach.

Braun, David A. Gathering Speed: Tales of Motorcycles & Life. LC 96-95183. (Illus.). 198p. (Orig.). 1997. pap. 24.95 (*0-9656176-0-2*) Bike Manuscript.

Braun, David B. Over-the-Counter Pharmaceutical Formulations. LC 94-2511. (Illus.). 443p. 1994. 129.00 (*0-8155-1347-X*) Noyes.

— Pharmaceutical Manufacturers: An International Directory. LC 95-21383. 290p. 1995. 109.00 (*0-8155-1384-4*) Noyes.

Braun, David B. & Rosen, Meyer R. Rheology Modifiers. LC 99-32076. 514p. 1999. 285.00 (*0-8155-1441-7*) Noyes.

Braun, David P., et al. The Snyders Mounds & Five Other Mound Groups in Calhoun County, Illinois. LC 82-622498. (University of Michigan, Museum of Anthropology, Anthropological Papers: No. 8). 192p. reprint ed. pap. 59.60 (*0-608-16270-1*, 202623500049) Bks Demand.

Braun, David P., jt. auth. see Braun, Esther K.

Braun, David W., jt. auth. see Roy, William N.

***Braun, Debra S.** The Flintstones Collectibles, An Unauthorized Guide. (Illus.). 144p. 1999. pap. 29.95 (*0-7643-1017-8*) Schiffer.

Braun, Debra S. Garfield Collectibles. LC 98-84277. 152p. 1998. pap. 29.95 (*0-7643-0547-6*) Schiffer.

— Looney Tunes Collectibles: Unauthorized Guide. LC 98-83099. (Illus.). 160p. 1999. pap. 29.95 (*0-7643-0823-8*) Schiffer.

Braun, Dennis D. The Rich Get Richer. 2nd ed. LC 96-47169. 1997. pap. text 37.95 (*0-8304-1433-9*) Thomson Learn.

Braun, Dietmar. Structure & Dynamics of Health Research & Public Funding: An International Institution Comparison. Solomon, Neil, tr. LC 94-7725. 216p. (C). 1994. lib. bdg. 127.50 (*0-7923-2777-2*) Kluwer Academic.

***Braun, Dietmar.** Towards a New Model of Governance for Universities? A Comparative View. 1999. 39.95 (*1-85302-773-1*) Jessica Kingsley.

***Braun, Dietmar & Busch, Andreas, eds.** Public Policy & Political Ideas. LC 99-41927. 240p. 2000. 80.00 (*1-84064-182-7*) E Elgar.

Braun, Dietrich. Metodos Sencillos de Identificacion de Plasticos. 2nd ed. 110p. 1986. 17.50 (*1-56990-007-8*) Hanser-Gardner.

— Simple Methods for Identification of Plastics. 3rd rev. ed. Immergut, Edmund, tr. LC 95-47136. 110p. 1996. 34.95 (*1-56990-204-6*) Hanser-Gardner.

***Braun, Dietrich.** Simple Methods for Identification of Plastics. 4th ed. LC 99-15537. 1999. 29.95 (*1-56990-280-1*) Hanser-Gardner.

Braun, Dietrich, et al, eds. Practical Macromolecular Organic Chemistry, Vol. 2. (MMI Press Polymer Monographs). xiv, 332p. 1984. text 335.00 (*3-7186-0059-5*) Gordon & Breach.

Braun, Dietrich & Cherdron, Harald. Techniques of Polymer Syntheses & Characterization. LC 79-148168. 296p. reprint ed. pap. 91.80 (*0-608-30442-5*, 201196700080) Bks Demand.

Braun, Donna, jt. auth. see Steier, Sarah.

Braun, E. Lucy. The Monocotyledoneae: Cat-Tails to Orchids. LC 66-25170. (Vascular Flora of Ohio Ser.: Vol. 1). (Illus.). 464p. 1967. text 60.00 (*0-8142-0028-1*) Ohio St U Pr.

— The Vegetation of the Mineral Springs Region of Adams County, Ohio. (Bulletin Ser.: No. 15). 1928. pap. text 3.00 (*0-86727-014-4*) Ohio Bio Survey.

Braun, Edmund. Wissenschaftstheoretisches Lexikon. (GER.). 1977. 125.00 (*0-8288-5557-9*, M7688) Fr & Eur.

Braun, Edward. Meyerhold: A Revolution in Theatre. LC 95-60652. (Studies in Theatre History & Culture). (Illus.). 360p. 1998. reprint ed. pap. text 19.95 (*0-87745-633-X*) U of Iowa Pr.

Braun, Eldon M., jt. auth. see Davis, Ronald D.

Braun, Eldon M., ed. see Davis, Ronald D.

Braun, Eliezer. Arquitectura de Solidos y Liquidos. (Ciencia Para Todos Ser.). (SPA.). pap. 6.99 (*968-16-2541-2*, Pub. by Fondo) Continental Bk.

— Caos, Fractales y Cosas Raras. (Ciencia Para Todos Ser.). (SPA.). pap. 6.99 (*968-16-5070-0*, Pub. by Fondo) Continental Bk.

— Electromagnetismo. (Ciencia para Todos Ser.). (SPA.). pap. 6.99 (*968-16-3742-9*, Pub. by Fondo) Continental Bk.

— Un Movimiento en Zigzag. (Ciencia para Todos Ser.). (SPA.). pap. 6.99 (*968-16-2457-2*, Pub. by Fondo) Continental Bk.

— El Saber y los Sentidos. (Ciencia para Todos Ser.). (SPA.). pap. 6.99 (*968-16-3034-3*, Pub. by Fondo) Continental Bk.

Braun, Elisabeth. Portraits in Conservation: Eastern & Southern Africa. (Illus.). 200p. (YA). (gr. 9 up). 1995. text 28.00 (*1-55591-914-6*) Fulcrum Pub.

***Braun, Emily.** Mario Sironi & Italian Modernism: Art & Politics under Fascism. (Illus.). 336p. (C). 2000. 60.00 (*0-521-48015-9*) Cambridge U Pr.

Braun, Emily, et al, eds. Italian Art in the 20th Century: Painting & Sculpture, 1900-1988. (Art in the Twentieth Century Ser.: Vol. 3). (Illus.). 472p. 1989. 85.00 (*3-7913-0907-2*, Pub. by Prestel) te Neues.

Braun, Emily & Pierpont Morgan Library Staff. New York Collects: Drawings & Watercolors, 1900-1950. LC 99-21145. 1999. 45.00 (*0-87598-128-3*) Pierpont Morgan.

Braun, Eric. The Elvis Film Encyclopedia. LC 97-21829. (Illus.). 224p. 1997. pap. 23.95 (*0-87951-814-6*, Pub. by Overlook Pr) Penguin Putnam.

— The History of the Sacramento Monarchs. LC 99-18885. (Women's Pro Basketball Today Ser.). 1999. lib. bdg. 21.30 (*1-58341-016-3*, Creat Educ) Creative Co.

— The History of the Utah Starzz. LC 99-18886. (Women's Pro Basketball Today Ser.). 1999. lib. bdg. 21.30 (*1-58341-017-1*, Creat Educ) Creative Co.

— Tailback U: The USC Trojans Story. LC 98-35316. (College Sports Today Ser.). (Illus.). 32p. (YA). (gr. 4 up). 1999. lib. bdg. 21.30 (*0-88682-985-2*, Creat Educ) Creative Co.

Braun, Ernest. Futile Progress. 1995. 26.00 (*1-85383-243-X*, Pub. by Escan Pubns) Island Pr.

— Technology in Context: Technology Assessment for Managers. LC 97-37967. 144p. (C). 1998. 75.00 (*0-415-18342-1*); pap. 22.99 (*0-415-18343-X*) Routledge.

Braun, Ernst. Wayward Technology, 48. LC 83-22586. (Contributions in Sociology Ser.: No. 48). 215p. 1984. 37.50 (*0-313-24398-0*, BWT/, Greenwood Pr) Greenwood.

Braun, Esther K. & Braun, David P. The First Peoples of the Northeast. LC 93-49328. (Illus.). xv, 144p. (Orig.). 1994. reprint ed. pap. 19.95 (*0-9651476-0-6*) Moccasin Hill.

Braun, Ethel. The New Tripoli. 400p. 1990. 125.00 (*1-85077-147-2*, Pub. by Darf Pubs Ltd) St Mut.

Braun, Eunice. From Vision to Victory: Thirty Years of the Universal House of Justice. (Illus.). 160p. (Orig.). 1993. pap. 24.95 (*0-85398-352-6*) G Ronald Pub.

— A Reader's Guide: The Development of Baha'i Literature in English. 176p. 1986. 17.95 (*0-85398-228-7*); pap. 9.50 (*0-85398-229-5*) G Ronald Pub.

Braun, Eunice & Chance, Hugh E. A Crown of Beauty: The Baha'i Faith & the Holy Land. (Illus.). 104p. 1982. 24.50 (*0-85398-139-6*) G Ronald Pub.

Braun-Falco, O., et al, eds. Lipsome Dermatics: Mit 119 Abbildungen und 48 Tabellen. LC 92-26372. (Griesbach Conference Ser.). (Illus.). xix, 360p. 1992. write for info. (*3-540-55646-X*) Spr-Verlag.

Braun-Falco, O., et al. Dermatology. rev. ed. (Illus.). 1100p. 1991. 272.00 (*0-387-16672-6*) Spr-Verlag.

— Dermatology. 2nd rev. enl. ed. (Illus.). 1600p. 2000. 235.00 (*3-540-59452-3*, B7292) Spr-Verlag.

Braun-Falco, O., jt. auth. see Burg, G.

Braun-Falco, O., ed. see Griesbach Conference Staff.

Braun, Frank X. English Grammar for Language Students. (C). 1947. pap. text 1.25 (*0-914004-03-4*) Ulrich.

Braun, Fred. Determinanten des Landwirtschaftlichen Wachstums in Entwicklungslandern: Eine Analyse unter Verwendung einer Agrarproduktionsfunktion im Landerquerschnitt. (Europaische Hochschulschriften: Reihe 5: Bd. 2022). (GER., Illus.). 163p. 1996. pap. 35.95 (*3-631-30780-2*) P Lang Pubng.

Braun, Friederike. Terms of Address: Problems of Patterns & Usage in Various Languages & Cultures. (Contributions to the Sociology of Language Ser.: No. 50). xiv, 374p. (C). 1988. lib. bdg. 111.55 (*0-89925-432-2*) Mouton.

Braun, George W. Guide to Owning a German Shepherd: AKC Rank #3. LC 99-40532. (Illus.). 64p. 1999. 19.95 (*0-7910-5472-1*) Chelsea Hse.

— Guide to Owning a Rottweiler: AKC Rank #2. (Guide to Owning Ser.). (Illus.). 64p. 1995. pap. 6.95 (*0-7938-1857-5*, RE-301) TFH Pubns.

Braun, Goetz. Norm und Geschichtlichkeit der Dichtung: Klassisch-Romantische Aesthetik und Moderne Literatur. 312p. 1983. 93.10 (*3-11-008238-1*) De Gruyter.

Braun, Guenter & Braun, Waldtraut, eds. Maezenatentum in Berlin: Buergersinn & Kulturelle Kompetenz unter sich Veraendernden Bedingungen. (GER., Illus.). 258p. (C). 1993. lib. bdg. 44.65 (*3-11-013788-7*) De Gruyter.

Braun, H. W. Atmospheric Ionization. 1986. pap. 3.95 (*0-685-24739-2*) Research Analysts.

— Bioenvironmental Research Project: A Preliminary Analysis of the Biological Impact of Specific Environmental Variables. 1986. pap. 2.95 (*0-685-24741-4*) Research Analysts.

— Electromagnetic Radiation (EMR) It's Relationship to Human Health & Productivity. 1987. pap. 5.95 (*0-685-24744-9*) Research Analysts.

— The Phoenix Project. 1987. pap. 3.95 (*0-685-24745-7*) Research Analysts.

— Solar Dish Systems. 1988. pap. 3.50 (*0-685-24746-5*) Research Analysts.

Braun-Haley, Ellie & Haley, Shawn D. War on the Homefront: An Examination of Abuse in the Home. 1999. write for info. (*1-57181-117-6*); pap. write for info. (*1-57181-118-4*) Berghahn Bks.

Braun, Hans J., et al, eds. Wheat Breeding in the 20th Century. LC 97-33651. (Developments in Plant Breeding Ser.). 582p. 1998. text 334.50 (*0-7923-4727-7*) Kluwer Academic.

Braun, Hans-Joachim, ed. see Steinert, Arne.

Braun, Hardo. Bauen Fhur die Wissenschaft: Institute der Max-Planck-Gesellschaft = Building for Science: Architecture of the Max-Planck-Institutes. LC 99-26858. 1999. write for info. (*0-8176-6000-3*) Birkhauser.

***Braun, Hardo, et al.** Building for Science: Architecture of The Max Planck Institutes. LC 99-26858. (Illus.). 216p. 1999. 79.95 (*3-7643-6000-3*) Birkhauser.

Braun, Harold A., et al. Introduction to Respiratory Physiology. 2nd ed. 1980. pap. 17.00 (*0-316-10699-2*, Little Brwn Med Div) Lppncott W & W.

Braun, Harry G. Of Islands & Ships: Life & Times of Captain Harry G. Braun. abr. ed. LC 90-93645. (Illus.). 575p. 1997. pap. 21.95 (*1-879393-01-8*) H G Braun P E.

Braun, Harry W., III. The Phoenix Project: An Energy Transition to Renewable Resources. 272p. (Orig.). 1990. 18.95 (*0-924600-00-4*); pap. 14.95 (*0-924600-01-2*) Research Analysts.

Braun, Helmut J. Funktionelle Histologie der Sekundaeren Sprossachse: Das Holz. (Handbuch der Pflanzenanatomie Encyclopedia of Plant Anatomy - Traite d' Anatomie Vegetale Ser.: Band IX, Teil 1). (GER., Illus.). xi, 190p. 1970. 62.00 (*3-443-14003-3*, Pub. by Gebruder Borntraeger) Balogh.

Braun, Henry, jt. auth. see Wainer, Howard.

Braun, Henry I., ed. see Tukey, John W. & Wilder, John Tukey.

Braun, Hugh. Parish Churches: Their Architectural Development in England. 1970. 18.00 (*0-571-09045-1*) Transatl Arts.

Braun, Irwin. Building a Successful Professional Practice with Advertising. LC 81-66214. 301p. reprint ed. pap. 93.40 (*0-8357-7462-7*, 202349900033) Bks Demand.

Braun, J., et al. Die Behandlung von Herzrhythmusstoerungen bei Nierenkranken. (Illus.). viii, 248p. 1984. pap. 43.50 (*3-8055-3917-7*) S Karger.

Braun, J. K., jt. ed. see McLaren, S. B.

***Braun, Jackie.** One Fiancee to Go, Please. (Romance Ser.: Bk. 1479). 2000. mass mkt. 3.50 (*0-373-19479-X*, 1-19479-4) Silhouette.

Braun, Janet K. Systematic Relationships of the Tribe Phyllotini: Muridae: Sigmodontinae of South America. (Illus.). 50p. (Orig.). 1993. pap. 10.00 (*1-883090-04-0*) OK Museum.

Braun, Janice, jt. auth. see Bringhurst, Robert.

Braun, Jean. Structure & Evolution of the Australian Continent. LC 97-48519. (Geodynamics Ser.: Vol. 26). 1998. 42.00 (*0-87590-528-5*) Am Geophysical.

Braun, Jeffrey. Physics with Modern Physics for Scientists & Engineers. 3rd ed. (C). 1999. pap. text, student ed. write for info. (*0-321-03576-3*) Addison-Wesley.

Braun, Jerome. The Humanized Workplace: A Psychological, Historical, & Practical Perspective. LC 94-31694. 192p. 1994. 59.95 (*0-275-94915-X*, Praeger Pubs) Greenwood.

Braun, Jerome, ed. Psychological Aspects of Modernity. LC 93-20297. 288p. 1993. 69.50 (*0-275-94262-7*, C4262, Praeger Pubs) Greenwood.

— Social Pathology in Comparative Perspective: The Nature & Psychology of Civil Society. LC 95-3332. 304p. 1995. 65.00 (*0-275-94796-3*, Praeger Pubs) Greenwood.

***Braun, Joachim.** Die Musikkultur Altisraels/Palastinas: Studien zu Archaologischen, Schriftlichen und Verleichenden Quellen. (Orbis Biblicus et Orientalis Ser.: Vol. 164). (Illus.). xii, 388p. 1999. text 80.50 (*3-7278-1246-X*, Pub. by Ed Univ Fri) Eisenbrauns.

Braun, Joachim. Studies in Sociol-Musical Sciences LC 98-209832. 272 p. 1998. write for info. (*965-226-200-5*) Bar Ilan U Pr.

Braun, Joachim, et al, eds. Verfemte Musik. 2nd ed. XIV, 460p. 1997. pap. 76.95 (*3-631-31371-3*) P Lang Pubng.

Braun, Joachim Von, see Von Braun, Joachim, ed.

***Braun, Jochen, et al.** Visual Attention & Cortical Circuits. LC 00-39447. 2000. write for info. (*0-262-02493-4*) MIT Pr.

Braun, Johannes. Shenandoah Valley Family Data, 1799-1813. Wust, Klaus, ed. & tr. by. from GER. 1978. pap. 10.00 (*0-917968-05-0*) Shenandoah Hist.

Braun, John A. Come, Take a Seat. 38p. 1997. pap. 5.00 (*0-8100-0766-5*, 06N0710) Northwest Pub.

— Up to Jerusalem. LC 97-69278. 182p. 1997. pap. 9.99 (*0-8100-0795-9*, 06N0711) Northwest Pub.

Braun, John A., ed. His Word Our Delight. LC 97-65698. 247p. 1998. pap. text 10.99 (*0-8100-0713-4*, 06N0708) Northwest Pub.

— Sermon Studies on the Old Testament. LC 95-71846. (Series C). 384p. 1997. 27.99 (*0-8100-0579-4*, 15N0587) Northwest Pub.

Braun, John A. & Inter-Lutheran Commission on Worship. Sermon Studies on the Old Testament. LC 98-65016. 386p. 1998. 27.99 (*0-8100-0797-5*) Northwest Pub.

Braun, Jon E. Divine Energy: The Orthodox Path to Christian Victory. LC 91-21264. 162p. (Orig.). 1991. pap. 9.95 (*0-9622713-1-4*) Conciliar Pr.

Braun, Josef. A Little ABC of the Church Interior. Maloney, Linda M., tr. from GER. LC 97-197755. 32p. (Orig.). 1997. pap. text 3.95 (*0-8146-2413-8*, Litug Pr Bks) Liturgical Pr.

Braun, Joseph A., Jr. Reforming Teacher Education: Issues & New Directions. LC 89-7876. (Source Books on Education: Vol. 20). 380p. 1989. text 61.00 (*0-8240-3712-X*) Garland.

Braun, Joseph A., et al. Technology Tools in the Social Studies Curriculum. LC 97-40537. 1997. pap. 20.95 (*1-887902-06-6*) Franklin Beedle.

Braun, Judith V., jt. auth. see Anderson, Mary Ann.

Braun, Juergen H. Introduction to Pigments. (Illus.). 34p. 1993. pap. 30.00 (*0-934010-26-9*) Fed Soc Coat Tech.

— White Pigments. (Illus.). 43p. 1995. pap. 30.00 (*0-934010-44-7*) Fed Soc Coat Tech.

Braun, K., et al. Deutsch Als Fremdsprache: Neubearbeitung. Incl. Pt. 1. Grundkurs. (GER.). text 19.95 (*3-12-554400-9*); write for info. (*0-318-55655-3*) Schoenhof.

Braun, Karl L., jt. auth. see Keller, Harold W.

Braun, Kathryn, jt. ed. see Perkinson, Margaret A.

Braun, Kazimierz. A History of Polish Theater, 1939-1989: Spheres of Captivity & Freedom, Vol. 64. LC 95-34161. (Contributions in Drama & Theatre Studies: No. 64). 248p. 1996. 65.00 (*0-313-29773-8*, Greenwood Pr) Greenwood.

— Theatre Directing - Art, Ethics, Creativity. LC 99-53748. (Studies in Theatre Arts: Vol. 10). 464p. 2000. 109.95 (*0-7734-7828-0*) E Mellen.

Braun, Lev. Witness of Decline - Albert Camus: Moralist of the Absurd. LC 72-11082. 283p. 1974. 36.50 (*0-8386-1246-6*) Fairleigh Dickinson.

Braun, Lilian Jackson. The Cat Who Ate Danish Modern. 192p. 1986. mass mkt. 6.99 (*0-515-08712-2*, Jove) Berkley Pub.

— The Cat Who Ate Danish Modern. 1986. 11.60 (*0-606-13246-5*, Pub. by Turtleback) Demco.

— The Cat Who Blew the Whistle. 320p. 1996. mass mkt. 6.99 (*0-515-11824-9*, Jove) Berkley Pub.

— The Cat Who Blew the Whistle. 1996. 11.09 (*0-606-12643-0*, Pub. by Turtleback) Demco.

— The Cat Who Blew the Whistle. large type ed. LC 95-2632. 352p. 1995. lib. bdg. 21.95 (*0-7838-1252-3*, G K Hall Lrg Type) Mac Lib Ref.

B

— The Cat Who Blew the Whistle. large type ed. LC 95-2632. 352p. 1996. lib. bdg. 16.95 (*0-7838-1253-1*, G K Hall Lrg Type) Mac Lib Ref.
— The Cat Who Came to Breakfast. 288p. 1995. mass mkt. 6.99 (*0-515-11564-9*, Jove) Berkley Pub.
— The Cat Who Came to Breakfast. 1995. 12.09 (*0-606-12644-9*, Pub. by Turtleback) Demco.
— The Cat Who Could Read Backwards. 250p. 1986. mass mkt. 6.99 (*0-515-09017-4*, Jove) Berkley Pub.
— The Cat Who Could Read Backwards. large type ed. LC 97-25425. (Compass Press Large Print Book Ser.). 1997. 25.95 (*1-56895-470-0*, Compass) Wheeler Pub.
— The Cat Who Had Fourteen Tales. LC 00-3560. 243p. 1988. mass mkt. 6.99 (*0-515-09497-8*, Jove) Berkley Pub.
— The Cat Who Had 14 Tales. 1988. 11.60 (*0-606-13247-3*, Pub. by Turtleback) Demco.
— The Cat Who Knew a Cardinal. 1992. mass mkt. 6.99 (*0-515-10786-7*, Jove) Berkley Pub.
— The Cat Who Knew a Cardinal. 1992. 11.60 (*0-606-12645-7*, Pub. by Turtleback) Demco.
— The Cat Who Knew a Cardinal. large type ed. (General Ser.). 316p. 1992. 18.95 (*0-8161-5279-9*, G K Hall Lrg Type); lib. bdg. 19.95 (*0-8161-5278-0*, G K Hall Lrg Type) Mac Lib Ref.
— The Cat Who Knew Shakespeare. LC 00-3638. 249p. 1988. mass mkt. 6.99 (*0-515-09582-6*, Jove) Berkley Pub.
— The Cat Who Knew Shakespeare. 1991. 11.60 (*0-606-13248-1*, Pub. by Turtleback) Demco.
— The Cat Who Lived High. 1991. mass mkt. 6.99 (*0-515-10566-X*, Jove) Berkley Pub.
— The Cat Who Lived High. 1991. 12.40 (*0-606-12646-5*, Pub. by Turtleback) Demco.

B

Braun, Lilian Jackson. The Cat Who Moved a Mountain. 272p. 1992. mass mkt. 6.99 (*0-515-10950-9*, Jove) Berkley Pub.
Braun, Lilian Jackson. The Cat Who Moved a Mountain. 1992. 11.60 (*0-606-12647-3*, Pub. by Turtleback) Demco.
— The Cat Who Played Brahms. LC 98-193680. 192p. 1987. mass mkt. 6.99 (*0-515-09050-6*, Jove) Berkley Pub.
— The Cat Who Played Brahms. 1990. 12.09 (*0-606-13249-X*, Pub. by Turtleback) Demco.
— The Cat Who Played Post Office. (Cat Who Ser.). 262p. 1987. mass mkt. 6.99 (*0-515-09320-3*, Jove) Berkley Pub.
— The Cat Who Played Post Office. 1987. 11.60 (*0-606-13250-3*, Pub. by Turtleback) Demco.
***Braun, Lilian Jackson.** The Cat Who Played Post Office. large type ed. LC 00-20712. (Illus.). (J). 2000. 26.95 (*1-56895-840-4*) Wheeler Pub.
Braun, Lilian Jackson. The Cat Who Robbed a Bank. LC 99-32581. (Cat Who...Mystery Ser.). 242p. 2000. 23.95 (*0-399-14570-2*) Putnam Pub Group.
***Braun, Lilian Jackson.** The Cat Who Robbed a Bank. LC 99-36458. 2000. 23.95 (*0-375-40878-9*) Putnam Pub Group.
Braun, Lilian Jackson. The Cat Who Said Cheese. 1997. 11.60 (*0-606-12648-1*, Pub. by Turtleback) Demco.
— The Cat Who Said Cheese. large type ed. LC 95-49580. 308p. 1996. 25.95 (*0-7838-1631-6*, G K Hall Lrg Type) Mac Lib Ref.
— The Cat Who Said Cheese. 264p. 1997. reprint ed. mass mkt. 6.99 (*0-515-12027-8*, Jove) Berkley Pub.
— The Cat Who Sang for the Birds. large type ed. LC 98-6709. 1998. 26.95 (*1-56895-555-3*, Wheeler) Wheeler Pub.
— The Cat Who Sang for the Birds. (Illus.). 260p. 1999. reprint ed. mass mkt. 6.99 (*0-515-12463-X*, Jove) Berkley Pub.
— The Cat Who Saw Red. 192p. 1986. mass mkt. 6.99 (*0-515-09016-6*, Jove) Berkley Pub.
— The Cat Who Saw Red. 1986. 12.09 (*0-606-13251-1*, Pub. by Turtleback) Demco.
— The Cat Who Saw Stars. LC 98-24328. 240p. 1999. 22.95 (*0-399-14431-5*) Putnam Pub Group.
— The Cat Who Saw Stars. LC 98-48377. 1999. 26.95 (*1-56895-595-2*) Wheeler Pub.
***Braun, Lilian Jackson.** The Cat Who Saw Stars. 294p. 2000. reprint ed. mass mkt. 6.99 (*0-515-12739-6*, Jove) Berkley Pub.
— The Cat Who Smelled a Rat. (Illus.). (J). 2001. 23.95 (*0-399-14665-2*, G P Putnam) Peng Put Young Read.
— The Cat Who Smelled a Rat. 256p. 2001. 23.95 (*0-399-14675-X*) Putnam Pub Group.
Braun, Lilian Jackson. The Cat Who Sniffed Glue. 278p. 1989. mass mkt. 6.99 (*0-515-09954-6*, Jove) Berkley Pub.
— The Cat Who Sniffed Glue. 1989. 11.60 (*0-606-13252-X*, Pub. by Turtleback) Demco.
— The Cat Who Tailed a Thief. 263p. 1998. mass mkt. 6.99 (*0-515-12240-8*, Jove) Berkley Pub.
— The Cat Who Tailed a Thief. 1998. 12.09 (*0-606-13253-8*, Pub. by Turtleback) Demco.
— The Cat Who Tailed a Thief. large type ed. LC 96-39481. 293p. 1998. pap. 25.95 (*0-7838-8047-2*, G K Hall Lrg Type) Mac Lib Ref.
— The Cat Who Talked to Ghosts. 1990. mass mkt. 6.99 (*0-515-10265-2*, Jove) Berkley Pub.
— The Cat Who Talked to Ghosts. 1990. 11.60 (*0-606-13254-6*, Pub. by Turtleback) Demco.
— The Cat Who Talked to Ghosts. large type ed. (General Ser.). 300p. 1991. 21.95 (*0-8161-5081-8*, G K Hall Lrg Type) Mac Lib Ref.
— The Cat Who Turned on & Off. (Cat Who Ser.). 265p. 1986. mass mkt. 6.99 (*0-515-08794-7*, Jove) Berkley Pub.
— The Cat Who Turned on & Off. 1986. 11.60 (*0-606-13255-4*, Pub. by Turtleback) Demco.
— The Cat Who Wasn't There. 288p. 1993. mass mkt. 6.99 (*0-515-11127-9*, Jove) Berkley Pub.
— The Cat Who Wasn't There. 1993. 11.60 (*0-606-12649-X*, Pub. by Turtleback) Demco.
— The Cat Who Wasn't There. large type ed. LC 92-46712. (General Ser.). 367p. 1993. lib. bdg. 21.95 (*0-8161-5693-X*, G K Hall Lrg Type) Mac Lib Ref.
— The Cat Who Went into the Closet. 288p. 1994. mass mkt. 6.99 (*0-515-11332-8*, Jove) Berkley Pub.
— The Cat Who Went into the Closet. 1994. 11.60 (*0-606-13256-2*, Pub. by Turtleback) Demco.
— The Cat Who Went into the Closet. large type ed. LC 93-43830. 1993. 24.95 (*1-56895-050-0*) Wheeler Pub.
— The Cat Who Went Underground. (Cat Who Ser.). 1989. mass mkt. 5.99 (*0-515-10123-0*, Jove) Berkley Pub.
— The Cat Who Went Underground. 1989. 12.34 (*0-606-13257-0*) Turtleback.
— El Gato Que Leia al Reves.Tr. of Cat Who Could Read Backwards. (SPA.). 1997. pap. 14.58 (*84-01-47431-0*) Lectorum Pubns.
— Lilian Jackson Braun. 1988. pap. 14.00 (*0-515-09901-5*, Jove) Berkley Pub.
— Lilian Jackson Braun. 1989. 14.00 (*0-685-32996-8*, Jove) Berkley Pub.
— Lilian Jackson Braun, 4 vols. 1991. pap. 15.80 (*0-515-10779-4*, Jove) Berkley Pub.
Braun, Lilian Jackson. Lilian Jackson Braun: Three Complete Novels. LC 95-25675. 1996. 12.98 (*0-399-14127-8*, G P Putnam) Peng Put Young Read.
Braun, Lilian Jackson. Lilian Jackson Braun: Three Complete Novels. LC 97-18197. 1998. 12.98 (*0-399-14364-5*, G P Putnam) Peng Put Young Read.
Braun, Lilian Jackson. Lilian Jackson Braun: Three Complete Novels. unabridged ed. LC 94-10502. 608p. 1994. 11.98 (*0-399-13984-2*, G P Putnam) Peng Put Young Read.
— Three Complete Novels: The Cat Who Saw Red; The Cat Who Played Brahms; The Cat Who Played Post Office: Omnibus Edition. LC 93-632. 608p. 1993. 11.98 (*0-399-13885-4*, G P Putnam) Peng Put Young Read.
Braun, Lilian Jackson. Three Complete Novels: The Cat Who Talked to Ghosts; The Cat Who Knew a Cardinal; The Cat Who Lived High, 3 bks. in 1. LC 96-38001. 512p. 1997. 12.98 (*0-399-14258-4*, G P Putnam) Peng Put Young Read.
Braun, Lilly. Selected Writings on Feminism & Socialism. LC 86-45942. 256p. 1987. 12.95 (*0-253-35101-4*) Ind U Pr.
Braun, Lois. Montreal Cats. 226p. 1997. pap. 14.95 (*0-88801-199-7*, Pub. by Turnstone Pr) Genl Dist Srvs.
— The Pumpkin-Eaters. 1997. pap. 10.95 (*0-88801-148-2*, Pub. by Turnstone Pr) Genl Dist Srvs.
— Stone Watermelon. 1997. pap. 10.95 (*0-88801-107-5*, Pub. by Turnstone Pr) Genl Dist Srvs.
Braun, Lutz. Faster Than the Bull. LC 92-37947. (Publish-a-Book Contest Ser.). (Illus.). 32p. (J). (gr. 1-6). 1992. lib. bdg. 22.83 (*0-8114-3580-6*) Raintree Steck-V.
Braun, M. Differential Equations & Their Applications. 335p. 1985. 29.80 (*0-387-90847-1*) Spr-Verlag.
— Differential Equations & Their Applications: An Introduction to Applied Mathematics. 3rd ed. (Applied Mathematical Sciences Ser.: Vol. 15). (Illus.). 546p. 1991. pap. 39.50 (*0-387-90806-4*) Spr-Verlag.
Braun, M., et al. Common Weeds of Central Sudan. (Illus.). 329p. 1991. pap. 51.00 (*3-8236-1201-8*, Pub. by Backhuys Pubs) Balogh.
Braun, Marina & Clothier, Galina. American-Russian Legal Dictionary: Criminal Law. LC 97-43933. 352p. 1998. lib. bdg. 89.50 (*0-313-30455-6*, Greenwood Pr) Greenwood.
Braun, Mark E. Deuteronomy. LC 93-84455. (People's Bible Ser.). 368p. 1994. pap. 12.99 (*0-8100-0492-5*, 15N0498) Northwest Pub.
— Where We Stand. 72p. 1997. pap. text 5.00 (*0-938272-60-8*, 22N2201) WELS Board.
Braun, Mark J. A. M. Stereo & the FCC: Case Study of a Marketplace Shibboleth. LC 93-46342. 216p. 1994. text 73.25 (*0-89391-966-7*) Ablx Pub.
— A. M. Stereo & the FCC: Case Study of a Marketplace Shibboleth. LC 93-46342. (Communication & Information Science Ser.). 216p. 1994. 39.50 (*1-56750-000-5*) Ablx Pub.
— AM Stereo & the FCC: Case Study of a Marketplace Shibboleth. LC 93-46342. (Communication & Information Science Ser.). 206p. 1994. 73.25 (*0-685-72247-3*) Ablx Pub.
Braun, Mark S. Chicago's North Shore Shipwrecks. LC 92-25129. (Illus.). 88p. 1992. pap. 17.00 (*0-933449-18-6*) Transport Trails.
Braun, Marla. Picturing Time: The Work of Etienne-Jules Marey, 1830-1904. (Illus.). xxii, 472p. 1994. pap. text 35.00 (*0-226-07175-8*) U Ch Pr.
Braun, Marta. Picturing Time: The Work of Etienne-Jules Marey, 1830-1904. 1996. 70.00 (*0-226-07173-1*) U Ch Pr.
Braun, Marvin. Daniel's First Deer Hunt. (Illus.). 148p. (J). 1997. pap. write for info. (*1-57579-099-8*) Pine Hill Pr.
Braun, Matt. Black Fox. 1994. mass mkt. 5.99 (*0-312-95355-0*) St Martin.
— Bloodsport. 72p. 1999. pap. 5.99 (*0-312-97176-1*, St Martins Paperbacks) St Martin.
— Bloody Hand. 1996. mass mkt. 5.99 (*0-312-95839-0*, Pub. by Tor Bks) St Martin.
— Brannocks. 1998. mass mkt. 5.99 (*0-312-96490-0*) St Martin.
***Braun, Matt.** Buck Colter. 256p. 2000. mass mkt. 5.99 (*0-312-97405-1*, St Martins Paperbacks) St Martin.
— Deathwalk. 336p. 2000. 5.99 (*0-312-97516-3*) St Martin.
Braun, Matt. Doc Holliday: Gunfighter, Vol. 1. 1997. mass mkt. 5.99 (*0-312-96270-3*) St Martin.
— El Paso. 256p. 1999. mass mkt. 5.99 (*0-312-97074-9*, St Martins Paperbacks) St Martin.
— Gamblers. 1997. mass mkt. 5.99 (*0-312-96215-0*) St Martin.
— High Roller. 1999. mass mkt. 5.99 (*0-312-96827-2*) St Martin.
— Indian Territory. 1999. mass mkt. 5.99 (*0-312-97093-5*, St Martins Paperbacks) St Martin.
— The Kincaids. 512p. 1999. mass mkt. 5.99 (*0-312-96986-4*, Thomas Dunne) St Martin.
***Braun, Matt.** Kinch Riley. 240p. 2000. mass mkt. 5.99 (*0-312-97414-0*) St Martin.
Braun, Matt. Lords of Land. 1996. mass mkt. 5.99 (*0-312-95831-5*, Pub. by Tor Bks) St Martin.
— Matt Braun's Western Cooking. (Illus.). 185p. (Orig.). 1996. reprint ed. pap. 17.95 (*0-87004-374-9*, 037490) Caxton.
— Noble Outlaw. 1996. mass mkt. 5.99 (*0-312-95941-9*) St Martin.
— One Last Town. 1997. mass mkt. 5.99 (*0-312-96236-3*) St Martin.
— Outlaw Kingdom. 1996. mass mkt. 5.99 (*0-312-95618-5*, Pub. by Tor Bks) St Martin.
— Rio Grande, Vol. 1. 352p. 1998. pap. 5.99 (*0-312-96663-6*, Pub. by Tor Bks) St Martin.
— Rio Hondo. 1997. mass mkt. 5.99 (*0-312-96161-8*) St Martin.
— The Savage Land. 1997. mass mkt. 5.99 (*0-312-96004-2*) St Martin.
— Tenbow. large type ed. (Nightingale Ser.). 271p. (Orig.). 1992. pap. 14.95 (*0-8161-5407-4*, G K Hall Lrg Type) Mac Lib Ref.
— Texas Empire. 1996. mass mkt. 5.99 (*0-312-96036-0*) St Martin.
— Wyatt Earp. 2001. mass mkt. 5.99 (*0-312-95325-9*) St Martin.
— Wyatt Earp. large type ed. (Niagara Large Print Ser.). 1995. 29.50 (*0-7089-5800-1*) Ulverscroft.
— You Know My Name. 272p. 1999. mass mkt. 5.99 (*0-312-97245-8*, St Martins Paperbacks) St Martin.
Braun, Matthew. The Save-Your-Life Defense Handbook. (Illus.). 1977. 12.95 (*0-8159-5711-4*) Devin.
Braun, Maximilian, et al, eds. Lieber Prinz: Der Briefwechsel Zwischen Hermann Diels Und Ulrich von Wilamowitz-Moellendorff (1869-1921) (GER.). xxiv, 354p. 1995. 98.00 (*3-615-00173-7*, Pub. by Weidmann) Lubrecht & Cramer.
— Philology & Philosophy: The Letters of Hermann Diels to Theodor & Heinrich Gomperz (1871-1922) xx, 202p. 1995. 68.00 (*3-615-00172-9*, Pub. by Weidmann) Lubrecht & Cramer.
***Braun, Michael, et al.** Stefan Andres. 270p. 1999. 37.95 (*3-631-34626-3*) P Lang Pubng.
Braun, Michael A., et al. Interventional Radiology Procedure Manual. LC 96-53121. 1997. text 75.00 (*0-443-07921-8*) Church.
Braun, Molly, jt. auth. see Waldman, Carl.
Braun, Moshe. Sabbath Peace: A Book of Meditations. 208p. 1997. 24.95 (*0-7657-9957-X*) Aronson.
Braun, Moshe, tr. Pointing the Way: Spiritual Insights from Sfas Emes Rabbi Yehudah Aryeh Leib Alter. LC 96-27842. 216p. 1997. pap. 30.00 (*1-56821-996-2*) Aronson.
Braun, Moshe A. The Heschel Tradition: The Life & Teachings of Rabbi Abraham Joshua Heschel of Apt. 256p. 1997. pap. 30.00 (*1-56821-979-2*) Aronson.
— The Jewish Holy Days: Their Spiritual Significance. LC 95-40428. 456p. 1996. pap. 40.00 (*1-56821-553-3*) Aronson.
— The Sfas Emes: The Life & Teachings of Rabbi Yehudah Aryeh Leib Alter. LC 97-46203. 282p. 1998. pap. 25.00 (*0-7657-6005-3*) Aronson.
Braun-Munzinger, Peter B., ed. Nuclear Physics with Heavy Ions. (Nuclear Science Research Conference Ser.: Vol. 6). 1984. text 477.00 (*3-7186-0196-6*) Gordon & Breach.
Braun, Nora M. Pickle in the Middle. 1997. 9.09 (*0-606-11746-6*, Pub. by Turtleback) Demco.
Braun, Peter. Michael Schumacher. (Illus.). 96p. 1998. pap. 14.95 (*3-89365-732-0*, Pub. by Vloce Pub) Motorbooks Intl.
— Wristwatch Annual 2000. 376p. 1999. pap. text 29.95 (*0-7892-0534-3*) Abbeville Pr.
***Braun, Peter, ed.** Wristwatch Annual 2001. (Illus.). 2000. pap. 29.95 (*0-7892-0666-8*) Abbeville Pr.
Braun, Peter & Fernandes, Luis. Wristwatch Annual. (Illus.). 376p. 1998. pap. 29.95 (*0-7892-0448-7*) Abbeville Pr.
Braun, Rainer. Kohelet und die fruehhellenistische Popularphilosphie. LC 72-76043. (Beiheft zur Zeitschrift fuer die Alttestamentliche Wissenschaft Ser.: No. 130). 187p. (C). 1973. text 89.25 (*3-11-004050-6*) De Gruyter.
Braun, Richard E. Children Passing. LC 62-62491. (Tower Poetry Ser.: No. 2). (Illus.). 1962. 10.00 (*0-87959-000-9*) U of Tex H Ransom Ctr.
— Last Man In. (Illus.). 1990. 20.00 (*0-912330-71-6*) Jargon Soc.
Braun, Richard E., tr. Persius: Satires. 1983. 12.50 (*0-87291-139-X*) Coronado Pr.
Braun, Richard Emil, tr. & intro. see Sophocles.
Braun, Robert E. Compliance Guide to Consumer Credit LC 98-213051. (Compliance & Law Ser.). 1998. write for info. (*1-55827-255-0*) Sheshunoff.
— Compliance Officer's Laws & Regulations Service. LC 98-160681. (Compliance & Law Ser.). 1996. ring bd. write for info. (*1-55827-213-5*) Sheshunoff.
— NAFCU'S Common Compliance Violations LC 98-213163. 1998. write for info. (*1-55827-164-3*) Sheshunoff.
Braun, Robert E. & National Association of Federal Credit Unions Staff. NAFCU's Marketing & Advertising Regulatory Guide for Credit Unions. LC 98-184450. 1995. ring bd. write for info. (*1-55827-183-X*) Sheshunoff.
Braun, Robert J. & Cutilli, Bruce J. Manual of Emergency Medical Treatment for the Dental Team. 2nd ed. LC 98-19198. 139p. 1998. pap. 29.95 (*0-683-30270-1*) Lppncott W & W.
Braun, Roddy. First Chronicles. (Biblical Commentary Ser.: Vol. 14). 29.99 (*0-8499-0213-4*) Word Pub.
Braun, Rudolf. Industrialization & Everyday Life. Hanbury-Tenison, Sarah, tr. (Illus.). 242p. (C). 1990. text 59.95 (*0-521-35311-4*) Cambridge U Pr.
Braun, S. Mechanical Signature Analysis: Theory & Applications. 1986. text 162.00 (*0-12-127255-9*) Acad Pr.
Braun, S., ed. MSA - Mechanical Signature Analysis. 88p. 1983. pap. text 10.00 (*0-317-02630-5*, G00236) ASME.
Braun, Sergei, jt. auth. see Avnir, D.
Braun, Shimon, ed. Long-Acting Nifedipine: End-Organ Protection & Prevention of Cardiovascular Disease: 3rd International Symposium, Berlin, September 1996: Proceedings. (Cardiology Ser.: Vol. 88, Suppl. 3, 1997). (Illus.). iv, 74p. 1997. pap. 34.00 (*3-8055-6620-4*) S Karger.
Braun, Sidney D., ed. Dictionary of French Literature. LC 70-138576. (Illus.). 394p. (C). 1971. reprint ed. lib. bdg. 35.00 (*0-8371-5775-7*, BRDF, Greenwood Pr) Greenwood.
Braun, Siegmar. 150 & More Basic NMR Experiments. 2nd ed. 610p. 1998. pap. 69.95 (*3-527-29512-7*, Wiley-VCH) Wiley.
Braun, Stephen. Buzz: The Science & Lore of Alcohol & Caffeine. LC 95-47790. 214p. 1997. pap. 12.95 (*0-14-026845-6*) Viking Penguin.
— Buzzed: The Science & Lore of Alcohol & Caffeine. (Illus.). 224p. 1996. 30.00 (*0-19-509289-9*) OUP.
***Braun, Stephen.** The Science of Happiness: Unlocking the Mysteries of Mood. LC 99-36213. 208p. 2000. text 24.95 (*0-471-24377-9*) Wiley.
Braun, Steve R., et al. Hitting Drills & Much More. (Illus.). 52p. (Orig.). 1996. pap. 12.95 (*1-890007-00-5*, Instruct Spts) BB Pub.
Braun, T. & Bujdoso, E. Literature of Analytical Chemistry: Scientometric Evaluation. LC 86-6842. 272p. 1986. 154.00 (*0-8493-6591-0*, CRC Reprint) Franklin.
Braun, T., et al. Fullerene Research, 1994-1996: A Computer-Generated Cross-Indexed Bibliography of the Journal Literature. (Advanced Series in Fullerene: Vol. 5). 500p. 1998. 82.00 (*981-02-3345-0*) World Scientific Pub.
— Fullerene Research, 1985-1993. (Advanced Series in Fullerenes: Vol. 3). 480p. 1995. text 93.00 (*981-02-2051-0*) World Scientific Pub.
— Scientometric Indicators: A Thirty-Two Country Comparative Evaluation of Publishing Performance & Citation Impact. 250p. 1985. text 47.00 (*9971-966-69-7*) World Scientific Pub.
Braun, Theodore A. Cuba & Its People - Perspectives. LC 98-54361. (Illus.). 128p. 1999. pap. 11.95 (*0-377-00326-3*) Friendship Pr.
Braun, Tibor, et al, eds. Polyurethane Foam Sorbents in Separation Science & Technology. 232p. 1985. 132.00 (*0-8493-6597-X*, TP1180, CRC Reprint) Franklin.
Braun, Trudi. My Goose Betsy. LC 98-3456. (Illus.). 32p. (J). 1999. text 16.99 (*0-7636-0449-6*) Candlewick Pr.
Braun, Unter Mitarbeit von Karsten, jt. auth. see Heinz, Sabine.
Braun, Uwe. A Monograph of the Erysiphales (Powdery Mildews) (Nova Hedwigia, Beihefte/Supplementary Issues Ser.: Beih 89). (Illus.). 700p. 1987. pap. 199.00 (*3-443-51011-6*, Pub. by Gebruder Borntraeger) Balogh.
— The Powdery Mildews (Erysiphales) of Europe. LC 95-229039. (Illus.). 336p. 1995. 90.00 (*3-334-60994-4*) Balogh.
Braun, Volker. Unvollendete Geschichte. Hollis, Andy, ed. LC 88-12740. (New German Texts Ser.). 160p. 1989. text 19.95 (*0-7190-2402-1*) Manchester Univ Pr.
Braun, W. & Ungar, J., eds. Non-Specific Factors Influencing Host Resistance: A Reexamination. (Illus.). 1973. 116.75 (*3-8055-1598-7*) S Karger.
Braun, Waldtraut, jt. ed. see Braun, Guenter.
Braun, Walter O. Jurisprudence & Informed Consent: Index of Modern Information. LC 88-47583. 150p. 1988. 47.50 (*0-88164-764-0*); pap. 47.50 (*0-88164-765-9*) ABBE Pubs Assn.
Braun, Wernher Von, see Von Braun, Wernher.
Braun, Willi. Feasting & Social Rhetoric in Luke Fourteen. LC 96-33238. (Society for New Testament Studies Monographs: No. 85). 233p. (C). 1995. text 59.95 (*0-521-49553-9*) Cambridge U Pr.
Braun, Willi & McCutcheon, Russell, eds. Critical Guide to The Study of Religion. LC 99-30537. 416p. 1999. 85.00 (*0-304-70175-0*); pap. 35.00 (*0-304-70176-9*) Continuum.
Braun, William E. HLA & Disease: A Comprehensive Review. 160p. 1979. 89.00 (*0-8493-5795-0*, QR184, CRC Reprint) Franklin.
***Braun, Wolfgang.** Applied RHEED: Reflection High-Energy Electron Diffraction During Crystal Growth. Kuhn, J. et al, eds. LC 99-19555. (Tracts in Modern Physics Ser.: Vol. 154). (Illus.). ix, 222p. 1999. 139.00 (*3-540-65199-3*) Spr-Verlag.
Braunagel, Judith S., jt. auth. see Jahoda, Gerald.
***Braunbeck, Gary A.** In Hollow Houses: Dark Matter, Book 1. (Dark Matter Ser.). 320p. 2000. mass mkt. 6.99 (*0-7869-1636-2*) TSR Inc.
— The Indifference of Heaven. 350p. 2000. 29.00 (*1-891480-05-7*) Obsidian Bks.
— The Indifference of Heaven. limited ed. 350p. 2000. 50.00 (*1-891480-06-5*) Obsidian Bks.

An Asterisk (*) at the beginning of an entry indicates that the title is appearing for the first time.

Braunbeck, Gary A. Things Left Behind. aut. limited ed. (Illus.). 570p. 1997. 35.00 (*1-881475-21-2*) Cemetery Dance.

Braunbeck, T., et al, eds. Fish: Ecotoxicology & Ecophysiology. LC 92-45170. 419p. 1993. 158.00 (*3-527-30010-4*, Wiley-VCH) Wiley.

— Fish Ecotoxicology. LC 98-26282. (Experientia Supplementum Ser.: Vol. 86). 300p. 1998. 118.00 (*3-7643-5819-X*) Spr-Verlag.

Braunbeck, T., et al. Fish Ecotoxicology. LC 98-26282. (EXS Ser.). 1998. write for info. (*0-8176-5819-X*) Birkhauser.

Braunbehrens, Volkmar. Maligned Master: The Real Story of Antonio Salieri. Kanes, Eveline L., tr. from GER. LC 92-28067. (Illus.). 264p. 1993. 25.00 (*0-88064-140-1*) Fromm Intl Pub.

— Maligned Master: The Real Story of Antonio Salieri. Kanes, Eveline L., tr. from GER. (Illus.). 264p. 1994. pap. 15.95 (*0-88064-155-X*) Fromm Intl Pub.

Braund, David. Georgia in Antiquity: A History of Colchis & Transcaucasian Iberia, 550 BC-AD 562. LC 93-40486. (Illus.). 378p. 1994. text 75.00 (*0-19-814473-3*) OUP.

— Rulers of Roman Britain: Kings, Queens, Governors & Emperors from Julius Caesar to Agricola. LC 95-52388. 232p. (C). 1996. 65.00 (*0-415-00804-2*) Routledge.

Braund, David, ed. The Administration of the Roman Empire. rev. ed. 116p. 1993. pap. text 14.95 (*0-85989-204-2*, Pub. by Univ Exeter Pr) Northwestern U Pr.

***Braund, Diana T.** Wicked Good Time. LC 98-48246. 240p. 1999. pap. 11.95 (*1-56280-241-0*) Naiad Pr.

Braund, Kathryn. Dog Obedience Training Manual. LC 95-26072. 1996. write for info. (*0-931866-83-9*) Alpine Pubng.

— The New Complete Portuguese Water Dog. 2nd ed. (Illus.). 304p. 1997. 27.95 (*0-87605-261-8*) Howell Bks.

Braund, Kathryn & Miller, Deyanne F. The Complete Portuguese Water Dog. LC 97-1267. (Illus.). 288p. 1986. pap. 27.95 (*0-87605-262-6*) Howell Bks.

Braund, Kathryn E. Deerskins & Duffels: Creek Indian Trade with Anglo-America, 1685-1815. LC 92-26355. (Indians of the Southeast Ser.). (Illus.). xvi, 307p. 1993. pap. 15.00 (*0-8032-6126-8*, Bison Books) U of Nebr Pr.

Braund, Kathryn E., ed. see Bartram, William.

Braund, Kyle G. Clinical Syndromes in Veterinary Neurology. 2nd ed. LC 93-12662. (Illus.). 477p. (gr. 13). 1993. text 70.00 (*0-8016-7354-2*, 07354) Mosby Inc.

Braund, Nathan, jt. ed. see Jakubowski, Maxim.

Braund, Ron, jt. auth. see Voges, Ken.

Braund, Ron L., jt. auth. see Spears, Dana S.

Braund, S. The Roman Satirists & Their Masks. (BCP Classical World Ser.). 96p. 1996. pap. text 18.95 (*1-85399-139-2*, Pub. by Brist Class Pr) Focus Pub-R Pullins.

Braund, Susan H. Beyond Anger: A Study of Juvenal's Third Book of Satires. (Cambridge Classical Studies). 320p. 1989. text 59.95 (*0-521-35637-7*) Cambridge U Pr.

Braund, Susan H., ed. Satire & Society in Ancient Rome. 160p. (C). 1989. pap. 13.95 (*0-85989-331-6*, Pub. by Univ Exeter Pr) Northwestern U Pr.

Braund, Susan M. Satires, Bk. I. (Greek & Latin Classics Ser.). 331p. (C). 1996. pap. text 24.95 (*0-521-35667-9*) Cambridge U Pr.

Braund, Susanna M. & Gill, Christopher, eds. The Passions in Roman Thought & Literature. 276p. (C). 1997. text 64.95 (*0-521-47391-8*) Cambridge U Pr.

Braund, Susanna M., ed. see Juvenal.

Braune, Anna & Sloane, Savilla. The Wonderful Toys. LC 89-77889. (Charlotte Zolotow Bk.). (Illus.). 128p. (J). (gr. 2-5). 1990. 12.95 (*0-06-020618-7*) HarpC Child Bks.

Braune, Beverly. Camouflage. 64p. 1998. pap. 15.95 (*1-85224-271-X*, Pub. by Bloodaxe Bks) Dufour.

Braune, Gabriele. Kustenmusik in Sudarabien: Die Lieder und Tanze an den Jemenitischen Kusten des Arabischen Meeres. (GER., Illus.). 614p. 1997. 95.95 (*3-631-31795-6*) P Lang Pubng.

Braune, W. & Fischer. On the Centre of Gravity of the Human Body. Maquet, P. G. et al, trs. from GER. (Illus.). 115p. 1984. 72.39 (*0-387-13216-3*) Spr-Verlag.

Braune, W. & Fischer, O. Determination of the Moments of Inertia of the Human Body & Its Limbs. (Illus.). 85p. 1988. 68.95 (*0-387-18813-4*) Spr-Verlag.

— The Human Gait. (Illus.). 450p. 1987. 234.00 (*0-387-15270-9*) Spr-Verlag.

Braueneck, Anne-Eva. Fuhlen und Denken. (GER.). 122p. 1996. 32.95 (*3-631-30904-X*) P Lang Pubng.

Brauneck, M., ed. see Birck, Sixt.

Brauneck, Manfred. Lexicon of German Language Literature of the 20th Century: Autorenlexikon Deutschsprachiger Literatur des 20 Jahrhunderts. (GER.). 720p. 1984. pap. 59.95 (*0-8288-1568-2*, M14150) Fr & Eur.

Brauneck, Martin, ed. Spieltexte der Wanderbuehne, 4 vols. Incl. 4. Schau-Buehne Englischen und Frantzosischer Comoedianten, 1670. 1972. 423.10 (*3-11-004001-8*); Vol. 1. Engelische Comedue und Tragedean. (C). 1970. 469.25 (*3-11-002695-3*); Vol. 2. Liebeskampf. (C). 1975. 450.00 (*3-11-005716-6*); Vol. 3. Schau-Buehne Englischen und Frantzosischer Comoedianten, 1670. (C). 1970. 411.55 (*3-11-004685-7*); (Ausgaben Deutscher Literatur des XV bis XVIII Jahrhunderts Ser.). (C). write for info. (*0-318-51649-7*) De Gruyter.

Brauneder, Wilhelm, jt. ed. see Takii, Kazuhiro.

Brauneiss, Leopold. Zahlen Zwischen Struktur und Bedeutung: Zehn Analytische Studien zu Kompositionen von Josquin bis Ligeti und Part. (Europaische Hochschulschriften, Reihe 36: Bd. 169). (GER., Illus.). 153p. 1997. 35.95 (*3-631-32211-9*) P Lang Pubng.

Brauner, Asher. Love Songs of the Tone-Deaf. LC 99-94657. 300p. 1999. pap. 11.95 (*0-9670861-0-8*) Brown Bear Bks.

Brauner, Charles S., ed. see Rossini, Gioachino.

Brauner, Claude-Michel & Schmidt-Laine, Claudine, eds. Mathematical Modeling in Combustion & Related Topics. (C). 1988. text 211.50 (*90-247-3656-0*) Kluwer Academic.

***Brauner, David R., compiled by.** Approaches to Material Culture Research for Historical Archaeologists, 2nd ed. (Illus.). 440p. 2000. pap. text 25.00 (*1-886818-05-3*) Society Hist Arch.

Brauner, Gerhard. Rockbursts in Coal Mines & Their Prevention. LC 99-227029. (Illus.). 144p. (C). 1994. text 91.00 (*90-5410-158-X*, Pub. by A A Balkema) Ashgate Pub Co.

***Brauner, Marygail K.** Making Good Sense: Process Improvement Approach to Logistics Financial Management. LC 00-40306. (J). 2000. write for info. (*0-8330-2854-5*) Rand Corp.

Brauner, Marygail K., et al. ISM-X Evaluation & Policy Implications. LC 97-15245. (Illus.). 105p. 1997. pap. 9.00 (*0-8330-2503-1*, MR-829-A) Rand Corp.

Brauner, N. German-English/English-German Police Dictionary. (ENG & GER.). 1993. 25.00 (*0-7859-9741-5*) Fr & Eur.

Brauner, N., et al. It's All Part of the Job: German-English - English-German Police Dictionary. (ENG & GER.). 282p. 1993. pap. 25.00 (*3-8011-0290-4*, Pub. by Deut Polizeilit) IBD Ltd.

Brauner, Norbert. Woerterbuch Englisch fur die Polizei. (GER.). 282p. 1993. 29.95 (*0-7859-8480-1*, 3801102904) Fr & Eur.

Brauner, Patricia B., ed. see Rossini, Gioachino.

Brauner, Ronald A. Being Jewish in a Gentile World: A Survival Guide. 180p. 1995. 19.95 (*0-9648508-0-X*) Mirkov Pubns.

***Brauner, Ronald A.** Being Jewish in a Gentile World: A Survival Guide. 173p. 2000. reprint ed. pap. 14.95 (*0-9648508-6-9*) Mirkov Pubns.

Brauner, Sigrid. Fearless Wives & Frightened Shrews: The Construction of the Witch in Early Modern Germany. Brown, Robert H., ed. & intro. by. LC 94-39001. (Illus.). 184p. (C). 1995. text 27.50 (*0-87023-767-5*) U of Mass Pr.

***Braunerhjelm, Pontus.** Knowledge Capital & the "New Economy" Firm Size, Performance & Network Production. LC 00-23126. (Economics of Science, Technology & Innovation Ser.). 2000. write for info. (*0-7923-7801-6*) Kluwer Academic.

Braunerhjelm, Pontus & Ekholm, Karolina. The Geography of Multinational Firms Vol. 12: Economics of Science, Technology & Innovation. LC 98-11399. (Economics of Science, Technology, & Innovation Ser.). 225p. 1998. 95.00 (*0-7923-8133-5*) Kluwer Academic.

***Braunerhjelm, Pontus, et al.** Location of Economic Activity in the Eu: Monitoring European Integration. 10th ed. (Monitoring European Integration Ser.). 150p. 2000. pap. text 37.50 (*1-898128-46-4*) Ctr Econ Policy Res.

Braunerhjelm, Pontus B. Regional Integration & the Location of Multinational Corporations: Implications for Comparative Advantage & Welfare of Outsiders & Insiders. (Industrial Institute for Economic & Social Research Report Ser.). 91p. (Orig.). 1996. pap. 42.50 (*91-7204-523-X*) Coronet Bks.

Braunfels, Wolfgang. Monasteries of Western Europe. rev. ed. LC 91-67805. (Illus.). 264p. 1993. reprint ed. pap. 34.95 (*0-500-27201-8*, Pub. by Thames Hudson) Norton.

— Urban Design in Western Europe: Regime & Architecture, 900-1900. Northcott, Kenneth J., tr. (Illus.). xvi, 422p. 1990. pap. text 39.00 (*0-226-07179-0*) U Ch Pr.

— Urban Design in Western Europe: Regime & Architecture, 900-1900. Northcott, Kenneth J., tr. (Illus.). xvi, 408p. 1993. 49.95 (*0-226-07178-2*) U Ch Pr.

***Braungart, Georg, et al, eds.** Lessing Yearbook. 2000. 39.95 (*3-89244-325-4*) Wayne St U Pr.

— The Lessing Yearbook, Vol. XXX. 1999. 39.95 (*0-8143-2847-4*) Lessing Soc.

Braungart, Margaret M., jt. ed. see Braungart, Richard G.

Braungart, Richard G. Research in Political Sociology, Vol. 2. Wasburn, Philo, ed. 332p. 1986. 73.25 (*0-89232-610-7*) Jai Pr.

Braungart, Richard G. & Braungart, Margaret M., eds. Life Course & Generational Politics. LC 92-21177. 218p. (Orig.). (C). 1993. reprint ed. pap. text 21.50 (*0-8191-9006-3*) U Pr of Amer.

— The Political Sociology of the State: Essays on the Origins, Structure, & Impact of the Modern State. 400p. 1991. pap. 25.75 (*1-55938-315-1*) Jai Pr.

Braungart, Richard G., jt. ed. see Wasburn, Philo.

***Braunger, Jane & Lewis, Jan Patricia.** Using the Knowledge Base in Reading: Teachers at Work. 80p. 2000. pap. 12.95 (*0-87207-262-2*, 262) Intl Reading.

Braunger, Jane, jt. auth. see Lewis, Jan P.

Braunig, M. J. The Executive Protection Bible. 2nd rev. ed. (Illus.). 800p. 1999. pap. text 79.95 (*0-9640627-1-2*) ESI Educ Dev.

— The Intelligence Operations Bible: Intelligence Collection, Analysis & Protection. 600p. 1999. pap. text 75.00 (*0-9640627-2-0*) ESI Educ Dev.

***Braunig, M. J.** The New Executive Protection Bible. (Illus.). 785p. 2000. pap. 89.95 (*0-9640627-3-9*) ESI Educ Dev.

Braunig, Martha J. The Executive Protection Bible. (Illus.). 591p. (Orig.). 1993. pap. 69.95 (*0-9640627-0-4*) ESI Educ Dev.

Brauning, Daniel, ed. Atlas of Breeding Birds in Pennsylvania. LC 91-24998. (Pitt Series in Nature & Natural History). (Illus.). 528p. 1993. text 34.95 (*0-8229-3692-5*) U of Pittsburgh Pr.

Brauning, Daniel W., jt. auth. see McWilliams, Gerald M.

***Brauninger, Dallas.** Lectionary Worship Aids: Series V, Cycle B. LC 98-2527. 222p. 1999. pap. 18.50 (*0-7880-1364-5*) CSS OH.

— Lectionary Worship Aids: Series V, Cycle C. LC 98-2527. 222p. 2000. pap. 20.50 (*0-7880-1598-2*); disk 20.50 (*0-7880-1599-0*) CSS OH.

Brauninger, Dallas, compiled by. In the Beginning Was the Word, Cycle B: Scriptures for the Lectionary Speaking Choir, Pt. B. LC 93-6690. 1993. pap. 15.50 (*1-55673-620-7*, 9345) CSS OH.

Brauninger, Dallas A. In the Beginning Was the Word Cycle C: Scriptures for the Lectionary Speaking Choir, Pt. C. LC 94-2458. (Orig.). 1994. pap. 15.50 (*0-7880-0065-9*) CSS OH.

— Lectionary Worship Aids. 1998. pap. 16.95 incl. disk (*0-7880-1212-6*) CSS OH.

— Lectionary Worship Aids Series V, Cycle A. LC 98-2527. 232p. 1998. pap. 16.95 (*0-7880-1209-6*) CSS OH.

— Preaching the Miracles. LC 96-46487. (Series II: Vol. 3). 162p. 1997. pap. 16.75 (*0-7880-1020-4*) CSS OH.

— Preaching the Miracles. 1998. pap. 13.50 (*0-7880-1204-5*) CSS OH.

— Preaching the Miracles, Vol. II, Pt. B. LC 96-5303. (Series II). 1996. pap. 13.50 (*0-7880-0829-3*) CSS OH.

— Preaching the Miracles: Series II, Cycle A. LC 98-2528. 168p. 1998. pap. 13.50 (*0-7880-1201-0*) CSS OH.

— Talking with Your Child about Change. LC 94-7202. (Growing Together Ser.). 32p. (Orig.). 1994. pap. 2.25 (*0-8298-0994-5*) Pilgrim OH.

Braunlich, Phyllis C. Haunted by Home: The Life & Letters of Lynn Riggs. LC 88-4874. (Illus.). 256p. 1988. 24.95 (*0-8061-2142-4*) U of Okla Pr.

Braunmuller, A. R. Natural Fictions: George Chapman's Major Tragedies. LC 89-40764. 192p. 1992. 36.50 (*0-87413-404-8*) U Delaware Pr.

Braunmuller, A. R., comment. A Seventeenth-Century Letter-Book: A Facsimile Editon of Folger MS V.A. 321. LC 81-50652. 464p. 1983. 68.50 (*0-87413-201-0*) U Delaware Pr.

Braunmuller, A. R. & Hattaway, Michael, eds. The Cambridge Companion to English Renaissance Drama. (Cambridge Companions to Literature Ser.). (Illus.). 472p. (C). 1990. pap. text 19.95 (*0-521-38662-4*) Cambridge U Pr.

Braunmuller, A. R., ed. see Shakespeare, William.

Braunrot, Bruno. Francois Rabelais: A Reference Guide, 1950-1990. LC 93-48314. (Reference Guide to Literature Ser.). 456p. 1994. 60.00 (*0-8161-9079-8*, G K Hall & Co) Mac Lib Ref.

Brauns, J., et al, eds. Filters in Geotechnical & Hydraulic Engineering. 414p. 1993. 123.00 (*90-5410-342-6*, Pub. by A A Balkema) Ashgate Pub Co.

***Brauns, Martin.** Poised for Plenty: Moving Your Business to the Web. 2000. 24.95 (*1-886939-43-8*) OakHill Pr VA.

Brauns, Tim, ed. see Chrnalogar, Mary A.

Braunschweig, B., ed. Artificial Intelligence in the Oil Industry: Knowledge Based Systems Neural Networks, Fuzzy Logic. 148p. 1992. 260.00 (*0-7855-2699-4*, Pub. by Edits Technip) Enfield Pubs NH.

Braunschweig, B. & Day, R., eds. Artificial Intelligence in the Petroleum Industry, Vol. 1. 460p. 1996. pap. 145.00 (*2-7108-0688-6*, 06886) Gulf Pub.

***Braunschweig, Thomas & Gotsch, Nikolaus.** Cocoa Biotechnology Research & Issues in Competitiveness: Guidelines for Assessing Potential Economic Impact. 107p. 1999. pap. text 25.95 (*3-8258-2974-X*, Pub. by CE24) Transaction Pubs.

Braunschweiger, Lois. I Wasn't Born Old. Brown, Megan, ed. (Illus.). 312p. (Orig.). 1986. pap. text 8.95 (*0-9615899-0-6*) LZB Pub.

Braunsdorf, Lynn, tr. see Kuprian, Werner.

Braunstein, Baruch. The Chuetas of Majorca. rev. ed. 1971. 25.00 (*0-87068-147-8*) Ktav.

Braunstein, Bruce. The Cars of the Stars. (Orig.). 1980. pap. 10.00 (*0-686-27616-7*) Tetragrammaton.

— The Daily Plan-It R. 180p. (Orig.). 1980. pap. 19.95 (*0-686-27615-9*) Tetragrammaton.

— Disneyland vs. Deutschland - Two Twentieth Century Universes: Good or Evil in Our Time. (Orig.). 1986. 19.95 (*0-685-14664-2*) Tetragrammaton.

— The Magenta or Cyan. (Orig.). 1986. 19.95 (*0-685-14660-X*) Tetragrammaton.

— Prospectus. 1986. 89.95 incl. audio (*0-317-52217-5*) Tetragrammaton.

— Sleepwalking on the Borders of the Apocylapse. (Orig.). 1986. 19.95 (*0-685-14666-9*) Tetragrammaton.

Braunstein, Bruce & Fleisher, M. The Extra Money Book: How to Make Extra Money as an Extra. 1985. 10.00 (*0-685-14662-6*) Tetragrammaton.

Braunstein, Chloe, jt. text see De Bure, Gilles.

Braunstein, H. Terry. Windows. 32p. 1982. 25.00 (*0-942868-01-3*) W Blake Pr.

Braunstein, J., et al, eds. Advances in Molten Salt Chemistry, Vol. 4. LC 78-131884. 456p. 1981. 105.00 (*0-306-40833-3*, Kluwer Plenum) Kluwer Academic.

Braunstein, Jack, ed. see Craig, Sharyn S.

Braunstein, Jerry, ed. see International Symposium on Molten Salts Staff.

Braunstein, Jonathan J. & Toister, Richard P., eds. Medical Applications of the Behavioral Sciences. LC 81-3435. (Illus.). 544p. reprint ed. pap. 168.70 (*0-608-18136-6*, 203279000081) Bks Demand.

Braunstein, Jules, ed. North American Oil & Gas Fields. LC 76-258. (American Association of Petroleum Geologists. Memoir Ser.: 24). 370p. reprint ed. pap. 114.70 (*0-608-12009-X*, 202287800031) Bks Demand.

***Braunstein, Marc.** Deep Branding on the Internet: How to Create a Cohesive & Effective Web Strategy That Integrates Fully with Your Company's Brand Development. 228p. 2000. 25.00 (*0-7615-2532-7*) Prima Pub.

Braunstein, Mark L. & James, John D. A Symptom-Oriented Guide to Adverse Drug Reactions. 560p. pap. write for info. (*0-07-032252-X*) McGraw.

Braunstein, Mark M. Radical Vegetarianism: A Dialectic of Diet & Ethic. 2nd rev. ed. LC 81-4724. 160p. (Orig.). 1993. pap. 9.95 (*0-9635663-1-8*) Panacea Pr CT.

***Braunstein, Mark Mathew.** Sprout Garden. rev. ed. LC 99-14286. 128p. 1999. pap. text 12.95 (*1-57067-073-0*) Book Pub Co.

Braunstein, Mercedes. Drawing & Painting Various Subjects with Mixed Media. (Illus.). 64p. 1996. 13.95 (*0-8120-9748-3*) Barron.

***Braunstein, P., et al, eds.** Metal Clusters in Chemistry, 3 Vols. 1846p. 1999. 850.00 (*3-527-29549-6*) Wiley.

Braunstein, Pierre, ed. Quantum Computing: Where Do We Want To Go Tomorrow? 306p. 1999. 160.00 (*3-527-40284-5*) Wiley.

Braunstein, Terry. A Tale from the Fire. LC 95-2797. 1995. pap. 30.00 (*0-940979-30-6*) Natl Museum Women.

Braunthal, Alfred. Salvation & the Perfect Society: The Eternal Quest. LC 79-4705. 448p. 1979. lib. bdg. 40.00 (*0-87023-273-8*) U of Mass Pr.

Braunthal, Gerard. Parties & Politics in Modern Germany. 224p. (C). 1996. pap. 75.00 (*0-8133-2382-7*, Pub. by Westview); pap. 25.00 (*0-8133-2383-5*, Pub. by Westview) HarpC.

— Political Loyalty & Public Service in West Germany: The 1972 Decree Against Radicals & Its Consequences. LC 89-28435. 272p. (C). 1990. lib. bdg. 32.50 (*0-87023-707-1*) U of Mass Pr.

Braunwald. Essential Atlas of Heart Disease for Primary Care. 400p. (C). 1997. 145.00 (*0-8385-2215-7*, A-2215-0, Apple Lange Med) McGraw.

Braunwald, Dennis K. Gasoline Studies in Health & Disease & Including Carcinogenicity, Auto Workers & MTBE (Methyl Tertiary Butyl Ether) Index of New Information with Authors, Subjects & References. 150p. 1996. 47.50 (*0-7883-1124-7*); pap. 44.50 (*0-7883-1125-5*) ABBE Pubs Assn.

Braunwald, E., jt. ed. see Kellermann, J. J.

Braunwald, Eugene. Atlas of Heart Disease. (C). (gr. 13). 1996. text 1625.00 (*1-878132-21-0*, 30366) Current Med.

— Atlas of Internal Medicine. LC 98-21633. 1998. 125.00 (*1-57340-118-8*) Current Med.

— Diagnosing & Managing Unstable Angina, Quick Reference Guide for Clinicians. 10th ed. 25p. 1994. pap. 22.00 (*0-16-045275-9*) USGPO.

— Unstable Angina: Diagnosis & Management. (Clinical Practice Guidelines: No. 10). 168p. 1994. per. 6.50 (*0-16-045291-0*) USGPO.

— Unstable Angina: Diagnosis & Management - Clinical Practice Guideline. (Illus.). 154p. (C). 1997. pap. text 30.00 (*0-7881-4607-6*) DIANE Pub.

Braunwald, Eugene, ed. CD-Rom for Heart Disease: A Textbook of Cardiovascular Medicine Single User, 2 vols. 5th ed. 1997. write for info. incl. cd-rom (*0-7216-7169-1*, W B Saunders Co) Harcrt Hlth Sci Grp.

— CD-Rom for Heart Disease: A Textbook of Cardiovascular Medicine Single User 5th Edition. 5th ed. 1997. write for info. incl. cd-rom (*0-7216-7171-3*, W B Saunders Co) Harcrt Hlth Sci Grp.

— Chronic Ischemic Heart Disease. (Atlas of Heart Disease Ser.: Vol. 5). 1996. write for info. (*1-57340-060-2*, Pub. by Martin Dunitz) Mosby Inc.

— Heart Disease: A Textbook of Cardiovascular Medicine. 5th ed. LC 95-24767. 1996. text 130.00 (*0-7216-5666-8*, W B Saunders Co) Harcrt Hlth Sci Grp.

— Heart Disease: A Textbook of Cardiovascular Medicine, 2 vols., Set. 5th ed. LC 95-24767. 1996. text 145.00 (*0-7216-5663-3*, W B Saunders Co) Harcrt Hlth Sci Grp.

— Heart Disease Vol. 1: A Textbook of Cardiovascular Medicine, Vol. 1. 5th ed. LC 95-24767. 1996. write for info. (*0-7216-5664-1*, W B Saunders Co) Harcrt Hlth Sci Grp.

— Heart Disease Vol. 2: A Textbook of Cardiovascular Medicine, Vol. 2. 5th ed. LC 95-24767. 1996. write for info. (*0-7216-5665-X*, W B Saunders Co) Harcrt Hlth Sci Grp.

Braunwald, Eugene & Califf, Robert M., eds. Atlas of Heart Diseases Vol. 8: Acute Myocardial Infarction & Other Acute Ischemic Syndromes. (Illus.). 320p. 1996. text 134.00 (*1-878132-32-6*) Current Med.

Braunwald, Eugene & Creager, Mark A., eds. Atlas of Heart Disease: Techniques in Interventional Cardiology, Vol. 13. LC 97-6325. (C). (gr. 13). 1997. 125.00 (*1-878132-55-5*, 26641) Current Med.

Braunwald, Eugene & Freedom, Robert M., eds. Atlas of Heart Disease Vol. 12: Congenital Heart Disease, Vol. 12. LC 96-20464. (Atlas of Heart Diseases Ser.). (Illus.). 284p. (C). (gr. 13). 1996. text 130.00 (*1-878132-33-4*, 26645) Current Med.

Braunwald, Eugene & Rahimtoola, Shahbudin H., eds. Atlas of Heart Disease Vol. 11: Valvular Heart Disease. LC 95-42589. (Atlas of Heart Diseases Ser.: Vol. 11). (Illus.). 336p. 1996. 134.00 (*1-878132-30-X*) Current Med.

Braunwald, Eugene, et al. Atlas of Heart Diseases: Cardiopulmonary Disease & Cardiac Tumors. LC 94-30333. (Atlas of Heart Diseases Ser.: 3). (Illus.). 312p. 1995. text 134.00 (*1-878132-23-7*) Current Med.

Braunwald, Eugene, et al, eds. Heart Disease. 2nd ed. (Illus.). 2365p. Date not set. text. write for info. (*0-7216-8561-7*, W B Saunders Co) Harcrt Hlth Sci Grp.

B

An Asterisk (*) at the beginning of an entry indicates that the title is appearing for the first time.

Braunwald, Eugene, et al. Marcus Cardiac Imaging: A Companion to Braunwald's Heart Disease, 2 vols. 2nd rev. ed. LC 95-19482. (Illus.). 1318p. 1996. text 215.00 (*0-7216-4687-5*, W B Saunders Co) Harcrt Hlth Sci Grp.

Braunwald, Eugene, jt. auth. see Goldman, Lee.

Braunwald, Eugene, jt. auth. see Kaltenbach, M.

Braunwald, Eugene, jt. ed. see Brown, W. Virgil.

Braunwald, Eugene, jt. ed. see Colucci, Wilson S.

Braunwald, Eugene, jt. ed. see Foody, Joanne Micale.

Braunwald, Eugene, jt. ed. see Julian, Desmond.

Braunwald, Eugene, jt. ed. see Lee, Richard T.

Braunwald, Eugene, jt. ed. see Scheinman, Melvin M.

Braunworth, Brent. Blood Guts & Tears: True Stories of Courage, 1. 2000. pap. 14.95 (*1-58501-008-1*) CeShore Pubg.

Braunworth, Brent & Howe, Albert L. Street Scenarios for the EMT & Paramedic. Schlanger, Laurence W., ed. LC 93-14345. 256p. 1993. pap. text 43.00 (*0-89303-976-4*) P-H.

B

Braus, Judy, ed. Biodiversity Basics: An Educators Guide to Exploring the Web of Life. (Illus.). 484p. 1999. teacher ed. 29.95 (*1-881150-03-8*, Acorn Natural) Acorn Grp.

— Biodiversity Basics: Student Book. (Illus.). 230p. 1999. student ed. 11.95 (*1-881150-04-6*, Acorn Natural) Acorn Grp.

Braus, Judy A. & Monroe, Martha C. Designing Effective Workshops. Cappaert, David, ed. (EEToolbox-Workshop Resource Manual Ser.). (Illus.). 36p. 1994. 8.00 (*1-884782-02-7*) Natl Consort EET.

Braus, Judy A. & Wood, David. Environmental Education in the Schools: Creating a Program That Works! rev. ed. (Illus.). 500p. 1994. pap. 25.00 (*1-884008-08-9*) NAAEE.

Braus, Patricia. Marketing Healthcare to Women: Meeting New Demands for Products & Services. (Illus.). 200p. 1997. 42.50 (*0-936889-40-3*) American Demo.

Brausch, Barbra, jt. auth. see Fuleki, Ruth.

Brausch, Georges. Belgian Administration in the Congo. LC 86-22796. 103p. 1986. reprint ed. lib. bdg. 55.00 (*0-313-25282-3*, BRAB, Greenwood Pr) Greenwood.

Brause, Rita S. Enduring Schools: Expedient? Yes. Excellent? No. 224p. 1992. 85.00 (*1-7507-0012-2*, Falmer Pr); pap. 27.00 (*0-7507-0013-0*, Falmer Pr) Taylor & Francis.

***Brause, Rita S.** Writing Your Doctoral Dissertation. LC 99-39560. 2000. pap. write for info. (*0-7507-0744-5*, Falmer Pr) Taylor & Francis.

Brause, Rita S. & Mayher, John S., eds. Search & Re-Search: What the Inquiring Teacher Needs to Know. 224p. 1991. 75.00 (*1-85000-855-8*, Falmer Pr); pap. 29.95 (*1-85000-856-6*, Falmer Pr) Taylor & Francis.

Brautbar, Nachman, ed. Myocardial & Skeletal Muscle Bioenergetics. LC 86-4883. (Advances in Experimental Medicine & Biology Ser.: Vol. 194). 692p. 1986. 130.00 (*0-306-42237-9*, Plenum Trade) Perseus Pubng.

Brauth, S. E. & Hall, W. S., eds. Avian Auditory-Vocal Motor Interfaces, No. 44, No. 4-5. (Journal: Brains, Behavior & Evolution: Vol. 44, No. 4-5). (Illus.). 100p. 1994. pap. 51.50 (*3-8055-6074-5*) S Karger.

Brauth, Steven, et al, eds. Plasticity of Development. 184p. 1991. 38.50 (*0-262-02326-1*, Bradford Bks) MIT Pr.

Brautigam, Bernd & Damerau, Burghard. Offene Formen: Beitrage zur Literatur, Philosophie und Wissenschaft Im 18. Jahrhundert. (Berliner Beitrage zur Neueren Deutschen Literaturgeschichte Ser.: Bd. 22). (GER.). 352p. 1997. 57.95 (*3-631-30163-4*) P Lang Pubng.

Brautigam, Bernd, ed. see Schroeder, Gertrude E.

Brautigam, Dwight D., jt. ed. see Kunze, Bonnelyn Y.

Brautigam, W., et al, eds. First Steps in Psychotherapy. 200p. 1985. 54.95 (*0-387-15042-0*) Spr-Verlag.

Brautigam, Walter, ed. see European Conference on Psychosomatic Research Staf.

***Brautigan, Ianthe Elizabeth.** You Can't Catch Death: A Daughter's Memoir. 176p. 2000. 21.95 (*0-312-25296-X*) St Martin.

Brautigan, Richard. The Edna Webster Collection of Undiscovered Writings. LC 99-32044. 160p. 1999. pap. 12.00 (*0-395-97469-0*, Mariner Bks) HM.

— Revenge of the Lawn: The Abortion: So the Wind Won't Blow It All Away. 516p. 1995. pap. 16.00 (*0-395-70674-2*) HM.

— Richard Brautigan's: A Confederate General from Big Sur, Dreaming of Babylon & the Hawkline Monster. 608p. 1991. pap. 16.95 (*0-395-54703-2*) HM.

— Trout Fishing in America. 122p. Date not set. 17.95 (*0-8488-2578-0*) Amereon Ltd.

— Trout Fishing in America, the Pill Versus the Spring Hill Mine Disaster & in Watermelon Sugar. 416p. 1989. pap. 13.95 (*0-395-50076-1*) HM.

***Brautigan, Richard.** An Unfortunate Woman: A Journey. LC 00-24760. 110p. 2000. 17.95 (*0-312-26243-4*) St Martin.

Brautigan, Richard. Willard & His Bowling Trophies. 168p. 19.95 (*0-8488-0790-1*) Amereon Ltd.

Bravais, A. On the Systems Formed by Points Regularly Distributed on a Plane or in Space. (American Crystallographic Association Monograph Ser.: Vol. 4). 113p. 1969. pap. 15.00 (*0-686-60370-2*) Polycrystal Bk Serv.

Bravata-Brozinsky, Patricia, jt. auth. see Gibson, James Aloysius.

Bravdel, Fernand. El Mediterraneo. San Martin, J. Ignacio, tr. (Nueva Austral Ser.: No. 5). (SPA.). 1991. pap. text 24.95 (*84-239-1805-X*) Elliots Bks.

Brave, B. Ohitika Woman. LC 94-18040. 304p. 1994. pap. 13.50 (*0-06-097583-0*) HarpC.

Brave, Elizabeth, ed. see Jackson, Donna.

Braveboy-Wagner, Jacqueline. Caribbean Diplomacy: Focus on Washington, Cuba & the Post-Cold War Era. 62p. (Orig.). 1995. pap. text 10.00 (*1-878433-15-6*) Caribbean Diaspora Pr.

Braveboy-Wagner, Jacqueline A. Caribbean in World Affairs: The Foreign Policies of the English-Speaking States. 2nd ed. 288p. 2000. pap. 21.95 (*0-8133-2145-X*) Westview.

— Interpreting the Third World: Politics, Economics, & Social Issues. LC 85-16751. 272p. 1985. 69.50 (*0-275-90028-2*, C0028, Praeger Pubs) Greenwood.

Braveboy-Wagner, Jacqueline A. & Gayle, Dennis J. Caribbean Public Policy: Regional, Cultural & Socioeconomic Issues for the 21st Century. LC 97-25026. 288p. (C). 1997. pap. 75.00 (*0-8133-2442-4*, Pub. by Westview) HarpC.

Braveboy-Wagner, Jacqueline A., et al. The Caribbean in the Pacific Century: Prospects for Caribbean-Pacific Cooperation. LC 92-17082. 232p. 1993. lib. bdg. 42.00 (*1-55587-195-X*) L Rienner.

Braveman, Daan. Protecting Constitutional Freedoms: A Role for Federal Courts, 56. LC 89-7531. (Contributions in Legal Studies: No. 56). 217p. 1989. 55.00 (*0-313-26833-9*, BVF, Greenwood Pr) Greenwood.

Braveman, Daan & Banks, William C. Constitutional Law: Structure & Rights in Our Federal System. 1991. write for info. (*0-8205-0337-1*) Bender.

Braveman, Daan & Bender, Leslie. Power, Privilege & Law: A Civil Rights Reader. (American Casebook Ser.). 622p. 1994. pap. 45.50 (*0-314-04577-5*) West Pub.

Braveman, Daan, et al. Constitutional Law: Structure & Rights in Our Federal System. 3rd ed. LC 96-26343. (Casebook Ser.). 1996. 58.00 (*0-8205-2702-5*) Bender.

***Braveman, Daan, et al.** Constitutional Law: Structure & Rights in Our Federal System. 4th ed. LC 99-45250. 2000. write for info. (*0-8205-4374-8*) Bender.

Braveman, Daan, jt. auth. see Bender, Leslie.

Braveman, Dan, et al. Constitutional Law 1992. 2nd ed. (C). 1993. suppl. ed. 8.95 (*0-8205-0338-X*, Irwn McGrw-H) McGrw-H Hghr Educ.

Braveman, Dann & Banks, William. Constitutional Law: Structure & Rights in Our Federal System. 1991. teacher ed. write for info. (*0-8205-0336-3*) Bender.

Braveman, P. A. & Tarimo, E. Screening in Primary Health Care: Setting Priorities with Limited Resources. LC 96-139939. (CHI, ENG, FRE & SPA.). viii, 196p. 1994. pap. text 30.00 (*92-4-154473-2*, 1150424) World Health.

Braveman, Paula & Bennett, Trude. Information for Action: An Advocate's Guide to Using Maternal & Child Health Data. 84p. 1993. pap. 5.95 (*1-881985-03-2*) Childrens Defense.

Bravenec, Lorence L. Federal Taxation of S Corporations & Shareholders. LC 95-80570. 1014p. 1995. text 165.00 (*0-8318-0732-6*) Am Law Inst.

— Federal Taxation of S Corporations & Shareholders. LC 95-80570. 80p. 1997. pap. text 30.00 (*0-8318-0772-5*) Am Law Inst.

***Braver, Gary.** Elixir. LC 99-89057. 352p. 2000. 25.95 (*0-312-87308-5*, Pub. by Forge NYC) St Martin.

— Elixir. 2001. mass mkt. 6.99 (*0-8125-7591-1*) Tor Bks.

Braver, J. C., ed. see Meland, Bernard E.

Braver, Nancy & Jenny, Jane, eds. Splice. (Illus.). 16p. 1997. pap. 7.95 (*0-9666963-1-X*) Side Street Pr.

Braver, Sanford L. & O'Connell, Diane. Divorced Dads: Shattering the Myths. LC 98-23183. 288p. 1998. 24.95 (*0-87477-862-X*, Tarcher Putnam) Putnam Pub Group.

Braverman, jt. auth. see Erdos.

Braverman, Arthur, ed. Warrior of Zen: The Diamond-Hard Wisdom Mind of Suzuki Shosan. LC 94-18320. (Illus.). 128p. 1994. pap. 11.00 (*1-56836-031-2*) Kodansha.

***Braverman, Arthur, tr.** A Quiet Room: Poetry of Zen Master Jakushitsu. 128p. 2000. pap. 14.94 (*0-8048-3213-7*) Tuttle Pubng.

Braverman, Burt A., et al. Getting & Protecting Competitive Business Information: A Business Guide to Using the Freedom of Information Act. 200p. 1997. pap. 99.00 (*1-56726-043-8*) Mgmt Concepts.

***Braverman, Carol.** The Photoshop Retouching Handbook. (Illus.). 256p. 1998. 49.99 incl. cd-rom (*1-55828-599-7*, MIS Pr) IDG Bks.

Braverman, Carole. The Yiddish Trojan Women. 1996. pap. 5.25 (*0-8222-1536-5*) Dramatists Play.

Braverman, Eric. Male Sexual Fitness. (Good Health Guides Ser.). 48p. (Orig.). 1998. pap. 3.95 (*0-87983-762-4*, 37624K, Keats Publng) NTC Contemp Pub Co.

Braverman, Eric R. How to Lower Your Blood Pressure & Reverse Heart Disease Naturally: Dr. Braverman's Revolutionary Drug-Free, No More Hypertension Program, Which Improves Your Sex Life. (Illus.). 230p. 1995. pap. text 18.00 (*0-9640037-3-2*) Pubns for Achieving.

— Hypertension & Nutrition. Bensen, Don R., ed. LC 95-49091. 208p. 1996. pap. 12.95 (*0-87983-688-1*, 36881K, Keats Publng) NTC Contemp Pub Co.

— P. A. T. H. Wellness Manual. (Illus.). 363p. 1993. pap. 25.00 (*0-9638869-0-8*) Pubns for Achieving.

— Path Wellness Manual. 2nd ed. (Illus.). 512p. 1995. text 25.00 (*0-9638869-5-9*) Pubns for Achieving.

— Psalms of the Rabbi Physician. (Illus.). 112p. (Orig.). 1986. pap. 9.95 (*1-55630-003-4*) Brentwood Comm.

Braverman, Eric R., et al. The Healing Nutrients Within. 2nd rev. ed. LC 96-53006. 536p. (Orig.). 1997. pap. 19.95 (*0-87983-706-3*, 37063K, Keats Publng) NTC Contemp Pub Co.

Braverman, Harry. Labor & Monopoly Capital: The Degradation of Work in the Twentieth Century. LC 74-7785. 480p. 1976. pap. 18.00 (*0-85345-370-5*, Pub. by Monthly Rev) NYU Pr.

— Labor & Monopoly Capital: The Degradation of Work in the Twentieth Century. 25th ed. LC 98-46497. 1998. pap. text 19.00 (*0-85345-940-1*, Pub. by Monthly Rev) NYU Pr.

Braverman, Irwin M. Skin Signs of Systemic Disease. 3rd ed. Fletcher, Judy, ed. LC 96-6572. (Illus.). 704p. 1997. text 145.00 (*0-7216-3745-0*, W B Saunders Co) Harcrt Hlth Sci Grp.

Braverman, J. Assessment of Modular Construction for Safety- Related Structures at Advanced Nuclear Power Plants. 212p. 1997. per. 21.00 (*0-16-062823-7*) USGPO.

Braverman, Jay. Jerome's Commentary on Daniel: A Study of Comparative Jewish & Christian Interpretations of the Hebrew Bible. Vawter, Bruce, ed. LC 78-55726. (Catholic Biblical Quarterly Monographs: No. 7). xvi, 162p. 1978. pap. 4.00 (*0-915170-06-X*) Catholic Bibl Assn.

Braverman, Jerome D. Management Decision Making: A Formal-Intuitive Approach. LC 80-65870. 253p. reprint ed. pap. 78.50 (*0-608-12688-8*, 202350900033) Bks Demand.

***Braverman, Kate.** Small Craft Warnings: Stories. LC 98-12952. (Western Literature Ser.). 180p. 1998. pap. 16.00 (*0-87417-321-3*) U of Nev Pr.

Braverman, Lewis E., ed. Diseases of the Thyroid. LC 97-11636. (Contemporary Endocrinology Ser.: Vol. 2). (Illus.). 408p. 1997. 125.00 (*0-89603-414-3*) Humana.

Braverman, Lewis E. & Refetoff, Samuel, eds. Clinical & Molecular Aspects of Diseases of the Thyroid. (Endocrine Reviews Monographs: Vol. 3). 414p. pap. 15.00 (*1-879225-17-4*) Endocrine Soc.

Braverman, Lewis E. & Utiger, Robert D. Werner & Ingbar's the Thyroid: A Fundamental & Clinical Text. 8th ed. 1088p. text 199.00 (*0-7817-2193-8*) Lppncott W & W.

Braverman, Lewis E. & Utiger, Robert D., eds. Werner & Ingbar's the Thyroid: A Fundamental & Clinical Text. 7th ed. LC 95-39527. 1124p. 1996. text 199.00 (*0-397-51406-9*) Lppncott W & W.

Braverman, Libbie. Libbie. (Illus.). 220p. 1986. 16.95 (*0-8197-0504-7*) Bloch.

Braverman, Lisa M., jt. ed. see O'Connor, Kevin.

Braverman, Lois, ed. A Guide to Feminist Family Therapy. LC 87-35180. (Journal of Psychotherapy & the Family Ser.: Vol. 3, No. 4). 180p. 1988. text 19.95 (*0-918393-48-5*, Harrington Park) Haworth Pr.

— Women, Feminism & Family Therapy. LC 87-63475. (Journal of Psychotherapy & the Family: Vol. 3, No. 4). 192p. 1988. text 39.95 (*0-86656-696-1*) Haworth Pr.

Braverman, Marc T., ed. Evaluating Health Promotion Programs. LC 85-644749. (New Directions for Evaluation Ser.: No. PE 43). 1989. pap. 22.00 (*1-55542-854-1*) Jossey-Bass.

Braverman, Mark. Preventing Workplace Violence: A Guide for Employers & Practitioners. LC 98-40177. (Advanced Topics in Organizational Behavior Ser.). 168p. 1999. 36.50 (*0-7619-0614-2*) Sage.

— Preventing Workplace Violence: A Guide for Employers & Practitioners. (Advanced Topics in Organizational Behavior Ser.). 1999. pap. write for info. (*0-7619-0615-0*) Sage.

Braverman, Mark, jt. auth. see Denenberg, Richard V.

Braverman, Melanie. East Justice. LC 95-16897. 176p. 1996. 22.00 (*1-877946-72-9*) Permanent Pr.

Braverman, Michael S. Independent Random Variables & Rearrangement Invariant Spaces. (London Mathematical Society Lecture Note Ser.: No. 194). 124p. (C). 1994. pap. text 32.95 (*0-521-45515-4*) Cambridge U Pr.

Braverman, Mimi. The Spin on Spiner. iv, 93p. 1997. pap. 20.00 (*0-9670972-0-7*) Tornado Pr.

Braverman, Nachum. The Bible in Bytes: Finally, a Guide to Jewish Wisdom for the Embarrassingly Ignorant. (Illus.). 240p. 1998. pap. 16.00 (*1-881927-17-2*, Pub. by Leviathan OH) Natl Bk Netwk.

Braverman, Nachum & Apisdorf, Shimon. The Death of Cupid: Reclaiming the Wisdom of Love, Dating, Romance & Marriage. 160p. 1996. 18.95 (*1-881927-07-5*) Leviathan OH.

Braverman, Terry. When the Going Gets Tough the Tough Lighten Up! How to Be Happy in Spite of It All. unabridged ed. St. George, Vicki, ed. LC 97-93424. (Illus.). v, 167p. (Orig.). 1997. pap. 12.95 (*0-9657395-1-1*) Mental Floss.

Bravin, Jess. Squeaky: The Life & Times of Lynette Alice Fromme. (Illus.). 448p. 1998. pap. 16.95 (*0-312-18762-9*) St Martin.

— Squeaky: The Life & Times of Lynette Alice Fromme - Runaway. LC 96-54514. 1997. text 25.95 (*0-312-15663-4*) St Martin.

Bravman, Bill. Making Ethnic Ways: Communities & the Transformations in Taita, Kenya, 1800-1950. (Social History of Africa Ser.). 304p. 1998. 24.95 (*0-325-00104-9*); 65.00 (*0-325-00105-7*) Greenwood.

Bravman, J. C., et al, eds. Specimen Preparation for Transmission Electron Microscopy of Materials. (Symposium Proceedings Ser.: Vol. 115). 1988. text 17.50 (*0-931837-83-9*) Materials Res.

— Thin Films - Stresses & Mechanical Properties Vol. 130: Materials Research Society Symposium Proceedings. 402p. 1989. text 17.50 (*1-55899-003-8*) Materials Res.

Bravman, J. C. & Paine, D. C., eds. Laser Ablation for Materials Synthesis, Vol. 191. (Symposium Proceedings Ser.: Vol. 1). 241p. 1990. text 30.00 (*1-55899-080-1*) Materials Res.

Bravmann, Scott. Queer Fictions of the Past: History, Culture, & Difference. (Cultural Social Studies). 190p. (C). 1997. text 54.95 (*0-521-59101-5*); pap. text 16.95 (*0-521-59907-5*) Cambridge U Pr.

Bravo. Florida Family Law Practice Manual, No. 98-6. 200p. 1998. ring bd. write for info. (*0-327-00696-X*, 8064933) LEXIS Pub.

— Florida Family Law Practice Manual 99-2, 5 vols. 364p. 1999. ring bd. write for info. (*0-327-01067-3*, 8064935) LEXIS Pub.

***Bravo.** Florida Family Law Practice Manual 99-5. 200p. 1999. ring bd. write for info. (*0-327-01708-2*, 8064938) LEXIS Pub.

— Florida Family Law Practice Manual 99-4, 5 vols., Set. 276p. 1999. ring bd. write for info. (*0-327-01528-4*, 8064937) LEXIS Pub.

Bravo. Florida Family Law Practice Manual 99-1, 5 vols. 806p. 1999. lib. bdg. write for info. (*0-327-01012-6*, 8064934) LEXIS Pub.

Bravo, Armando A. Al Curioso Lector. LC 93-72089. (SPA.). 90p. (Orig.). 1996. pap. 9.95 (*0-89729-696-6*) Ediciones.

— Cabos Sueltos. LC 97-60278. (Coleccion Espejo de Paciencia Ser.). (SPA.). 126p. 1997. pap. 12.00 (*0-89729-830-6*, 830-6) Ediciones.

— La Prisma de la Razon. LC 89-82739. (Coleccion Espejo de Paciencia). (SPA.). 92p. (Orig.). 1990. pap. 15.00 (*0-89729-562-5*) Ediciones.

***Bravo, Armando Alvarez.** El Dia Mas Memorable. LC 99-66891. (Coleccion Caniqui). (SPA.). 91p. 1999. pap. 12.00 (*0-89729-913-2*) Ediciones.

Bravo, Benedetto. Philologie, Histoire, Philosophie de L'Histoire. (Veroffentlichung des Comite des Sciences de la Culture Antique-Academie Polonaise des Sciences Ser.). 410p. 1988. reprint ed. 90.00 (*3-487-09041-4*) G Olms Pubs.

Bravo, Brett. Crystal Healing Secrets: Enhance Your Relationships, Sexuality, Prosperity & Health. (Illus.). 283p. (Orig.). 1988. mass mkt. 10.99 (*0-446-38789-4*, Pub. by Warner Bks) Little.

— Crystal Love Secrets. 348p. 1991. mass mkt. 9.99 (*0-446-39169-7*, Pub. by Warner Bks) Little.

Bravo, Carmine & Schackow, Gerald. Florida Family Law Practice, 5 vols., Set. 202p. 1997. ring bd. 325.00 (*0-409-26047-9*, 80613-10, MICHIE) LEXIS Pub.

Bravo, Ellen. Job-Family. LC 94-45416. 243p. 1995. pap. 12.95 (*0-471-04723-6*) Wiley.

***Bravo, Ellen & Cassedy, Ellen.** The 9 to 5 Guide to Combating Sexual Harassment: Candid Advice from 9 to 5, the National Association of Working Women. 208p. 1999. pap. 15.00 (*0-9673398-0-4*) Nine Five Wrk.

Bravo, Ellen & Cassedy, Ellen. The 9 to 5 Guide to Combating Sexual Harassment: Candid Advice from 9 to 5, the National Association of Working Women. LC 92-9793. 160p. 1992. pap. 12.95 (*0-471-57576-3*) Wiley.

Bravo, Fabiola, tr. see Geraghty, Cynthia W.

Bravo, Francisco B. El Templo Dominico de Osumacinta, Chiapas: Excavaciones Arqueologicas. (SPA., Illus.). 189p. 1996. pap. 17.00 (*968-29-5230-1*, IN89, Pub. by Dir Gen Pubicaiones) UPLAAP.

Bravo-Guzman, Pedro, tr. see Boa, Kenneth.

Bravo-Guzman, Pedro, tr. see Cullen, Murray.

Bravo, Jose Antonio, tr. see Gates, Bill.

Bravo, Juan L. Rodriguez, see Del Mar Martinez Rodriquez, Maria & Rodriguez Bravo, Juan L., eds.

Bravo, Kai, et al. Party Perfect! 40 Original Recipes for 25 Holidays & Celebrations Year-Round. (Illus.). ii, 60p. (Orig.). 1996. pap. 9.95 (*0-9653072-2-0*) Cookbk CA.

Bravo, Lisa, et al. Ma Ke 'Ano Kuloko: Healthy Cooking - Island Style. rev. ed. (Illus.). 188p. 1995. spiral bd. 12.00 (*0-9647939-1-1*) Project LEAN HI.

Bravo, Manuel A. Song of Reality: Latin American Photography. (Illus.). 1998. 65.00 (*84-7782-268-9*, Pub. by Natl Port Gall) Antique Collect.

Bravo, Olga. Olga's Cup & Saucer: A Picture Book with Recipes. (Illus.). 88p. (J). 1995. 15.95 (*0-8050-3301-7*) H Holt & Co.

Bravo Publications Staff. Best Selling Bridal Guide: The Bravo! Bridal Resource Guide. 1992. pap. 9.95 (*1-884471-14-5*) Bravo Pubns.

— Bravo! Bar/Bat Mitzvah Celebration Organizer: A Step-by-Step PLanning Guide for All Events Surrounding the Bar-Bat Mitzvah. 53p. 1992. 22.95 (*1-884471-13-7*) Bravo Pubns.

— Bravo! Event Resource Guide: Designed with the Meeting & Event Planner in Mind. 1992. pap. text 8.95 (*1-884471-15-3*) Bravo Pubns.

***Bravo Publications Staff.** The Bravo! Wedding Organizer: The Professional, Step-by-Step System That Keeps Track of Every Detail. (Illus.). 61p. 1999. 24.95 (*1-884471-22-6*) Bravo Pubns.

Bravo Publications Staff. Seattle. 1997. pap. text 9.95 (*1-884471-16-1*); pap. text 8.95 (*1-884471-17-X*) Bravo Pubns WA.

Bravo, Silvia. Plasma en Todas Partes. (Ciencia para Todos Ser.). (SPA.). pap. 6.99 (*968-16-4366-6*, Pub. by Fondo) Continental Bk.

Bravos, Brooke. Cruise Hosting. 225p. (C). 1992. pap. text 19.95 (*0-9630614-9-6*) Trvl Time.

Braw, Christian. Bucher im Staube: Die Theologie Johann Arndts in ihrem Verhaltnis zur Mystik. (Studies in Medieval & Reformation Thought: Vol. 39). (Illus.). ii, 236p. 1986. 66.50 (*90-04-07815-0*) Brill Academic Pubs.

Braw, Monica. The Atomic Bomb Suppressed: American Censorship in Occupied Japan. LC 90-26211. (Japan in the Modern World Ser.). (Illus.). 214p. (C). (gr. 13). 1991. text 62.95 (*0-87332-628-8*, East Gate Bk) M E Sharpe.

Brawand, Leo B. The Spiegel Story. Bell, Anthea, tr. (GER., Illus.). 80p. 35.50 (*0-08-037257-0*, Pergamon Pr) Elsevier.

Brawarsky, Sandee. How to Meet Men as Smart as You: You Don't Have to Change Yourself to Get a Date, & Other Practical Advice. 128p. 1994. pap. 10.00 (*0-671-86496-3*, Fireside) S&S Trade Pap.

Brawarsky, Sandee & Mark, Deborah, eds. Two Jews, Three Opinions: A Collection of Twentieth-Century American Jewish Quotations. LC 98-35849. 320p. 1998. 22.95 (*0-399-52449-5*, Perigee Bks) Berkley Pub.

An Asterisk (*) at the beginning of an entry indicates that the title is appearing for the first time.

Brawdy, Brian P. & Novick, Patricia M. Somthing to Believe In. viii, 200p. 1997. pap. 19.95 (*0-9658937-4-X*) MindWise.

***Brawer, Arthur E.** Holistic Harmony: A Guide to Choosing a Competent Alternative Medicine Provider. LC 99-71291. 184p. 1999. pap. 16.95 (*1-880254-57-3*) Vista.

Brawer, Catherine, ed. see Rosen, Randy, et al.

Brawer, Catherine C. Chinese Export Porcelain: Ethel Liebmand & Arthur L. Liebman Porcelain Collection. LC 92-52695. (Illus.). 160p. 1992. pap. 29.95 (*0-932900-30-5*) Elvejhem Mus.

Brawer, Florence B. New Perspectives on Personality Development in College Students. LC 73-7150. (Jossey-Bass Higher Education Ser.). 254p. reprint ed. 78.80 (*0-8357-9338-9*, 201379400087) Bks Demand.

Brawer, Florence B., jt. auth. see Cohen, Arthur M.

Brawer, Richard H. The Nurse Wore Black. Dettmore, Diane, ed. LC 94-60684. (Illus.). 180p. 1994. pap. 10.95 (*1-880254-17-4*) Vista.

Brawer, Robert A. Fictions of Business: Insights on Management from Great Literature. LC 98-34826. 256p. 1998. 22.95 (*0-471-17999-X*) Wiley.

— Fictions of Business: Insights on Management from Great Literature. LC 98-34826. 248p. 2000. pap. 16.95 (*0-471-37168-8*) Wiley.

Brawer, Roberta, jt. auth. see Lightman, Alan P.

Brawerman, George, jt. ed. see Belasco, Joel.

Brawick, Theodore. Teacher As World Citizen: A Scenario of the 21st Century. (Education Futures Ser.: No. 5). 1976. 12.95 (*0-88280-042-6*); pap. 12.95 (*0-88280-043-4*) ETC Pubns.

Brawley, B., ed. see Dunbar, Paul Laurence.

***Brawley, Beatrice.** Quiet Moments. 2000. 4.99 (*1-56245-403-X*) Great Quotations.

Brawley, Benjamin. Early Black American Writers. 305p. 1970. pap. 8.95 (*0-486-22623-9*) Dover.

— Early Negro American Writers: Selections. (BCL1-PS American Literature Ser.). 305p. 1993. reprint ed. lib. bdg. 89.00 (*0-7812-6598-3*) Rprt Serv.

— Paul Laurence Dunbar, Poet of His People. (BCL1-PS American Literature Ser.). 159p. 1993. reprint ed. lib. bdg. 69.00 (*0-7812-6960-1*) Rprt Serv.

Brawley, Benjamin G. Doctor Dillard of the Jeanes Fund. LC 73-168511. (Black Heritage Library Collection). 1977. reprint ed. 19.95 (*0-8369-8864-7*) Ayer.

— Early Negro American Writers. LC 68-25601. (Essay Index Reprint Ser.). 1977. reprint ed. 36.65 (*0-8369-0246-7*) Ayer.

— Negro Genius. LC 66-17517. 1966. reprint ed. pap. 27.00 (*0-8196-0184-5*) Biblo.

— The Negro in Literature & Art in the U. S. 1981. lib. bdg. 59.00 (*0-403-00531-0*) Scholarly.

— The Negro in Literature & Art in the U. S. (BCL1 - U. S. History Ser.). 231p. 1991. reprint ed. lib. bdg. 79.00 (*0-7812-6087-6*) Rprt Serv.

— The Negro in Literature & Art in the U. S. 3rd ed. LC 75-144586. (BCL Ser. I). reprint ed. 27.50 (*0-404-00139-4*) AMS Pr.

— A Short History of the American Negro. (History - United States Ser.). 288p. 1993. reprint ed. lib. bdg. 79.00 (*0-7812-4870-1*) Rprt Serv.

— Short History of the English Drama. LC 71-102227. (Select Bibliographies Reprint Ser.). 1977. 26.95 (*0-8369-5112-3*) Ayer.

— A Social History of the American Negro. LC 70-37233. reprint ed. 20.00 (*0-404-00138-6*) AMS Pr.

Brawley, Edward A. Human Services & the Media: Developing Partnerships for Change. (Applied Social Problems & Intervention Ser.: Vol. 2). 362p. 1995. pap. text 27.00 (*3-7186-0574-0*, Harwood Acad Pubs) Gordon & Breach.

— Human Services & the Media: Developing Partnerships for Change, Vol. 1. (Applied Social Problems & Intervention Ser.: Vol. 2). 362p. 1995. text 53.00 (*3-7186-0594-5*, Harwood Acad Pubs) Gordon & Breach.

Brawley, Edward M., ed. Negro Baptist Pulpit. LC 74-154072. (Black Heritage Library Collection). 1977. 22.95 (*0-8369-8783-7*) Ayer.

Brawley, Elizabeth C. Designing for Alzheimer's Disease: Strategies for Creating Better Care Environments. LC 96-33457. (Wiley Series in Healthcare & Senior Living Design). 340p. 1997. 80.00 (*0-471-13920-3*) Wiley.

Brawley, Joel V. & Schnibben, George E. Infinite Algebraic Extensions of Finite Fields. LC 89-14891. (Contemporary Mathematics Ser.: Vol. 95). 104p. 1989. pap. 29.00 (*0-8218-5101-2*, CONM/95) Am Math.

Brawley, John. Anyway, We Won: A Civilian Soldier in World War II. (Illus.). 332p. 1988. 17.95 (*0-929628-00-4*) Scotch Pub.

***Brawley, Mark R.** Afterglow or Adjustment? Domestic Institutions & the Response to Overstretch. LC 98-40997. 1999. pap. text 19.50 (*0-231-11327-7*) Col U Pr.

Brawley, Mark R. Domestic Institutions & Responses to Overstretch. LC 98-40997. 4p. 1999. 49.50 (*0-231-11326-9*) Col U Pr.

— Liberal Leadership: Great Powers & Their Challengers in Peace & War. 224p. 1994. text 39.95 (*0-8014-2808-4*) Cornell U Pr.

— Liberal Leadership: Great Powers & Their Challenges in Peace & War. LC 93-4844. 221p. reprint ed. pap. 68.60 (*0-608-20088-3*, 207136000011) Bks Demand.

— Turning Points: Decisions Shaping the Evolution of the International Political Economy. LC 99-167602. 400p. (C). 1998. pap. 26.95 (*1-55111-152-7*) Broadview Pr.

Brawley, Robert L. Text to Text Pours Forth Speech: Voices of Scripture in Luke-Acts. LC 95-2379. (Indiana Studies in Biblical Literature). 208p. 1995. 27.95 (*0-253-32939-6*) Ind U Pr.

Brawley, Robert L., ed. Biblical Ethics & Homosexuality: Listening to Scriptures. LC 95-46243. 216p. (Orig.). 1996. pap. 19.95 (*0-664-25638-4*) Westminster John Knox.

Brawley, Sean. Beach Beyond: A History of the Palm Beach Surf Club. LC 97-158248. (Illus.). 272p. 1996. 39.95 (*0-86840-357-1*, Pub. by New South Wales Univ Pr) Intl Spec Bk.

— The White Peril: Foreign Relations & Asian Immigration to Australasia & North America 1919-78. 1995. pap. 35.95 (*0-86840-278-8*, Pub. by New South Wales Univ Pr) Intl Spec Bk.

Brawlow, Lisette, ed. see Mitchell, Donald G.

Brawn, Janyce. Angels in the Forest: Cara & Christopher's Day with the Amish. 32p. (Orig.). (J). (gr. 1-4). 1995. pap. 5.00 (*0-9650519-0-0*) T K Moriarty.

***Brawn, Janyce.** Compassion in the City: An Amish Child Finds Love & Friendship. 38p. (J). (gr. 1-5). 2000. pap. 5.00 (*0-9650519-1-9*) T K Moriarty.

Brawn, Nellie L., tr. see Anderson, Winifred, et al.

Brawne, Michael. Kimbell Art Museum. (Architecture in Detail Ser.). (Illus.). 60p. 1993. pap. 29.95 (*0-7148-2745-2*, Pub. by Phaidon Press) Phaidon Pr.

— Museum fur Kunsthandwerk. (Architecture in Detail Ser.). (Illus.). 60p. 1993. pap. 29.95 (*0-7148-2765-7*, Pub. by Phaidon Press) Phaidon Pr.

— University of Virginia: Charlottesville 1817-26 Thomas Jefferson. (Architecture in Detail Ser.). (Illus.). 60p. (C). 1994. pap. 29.95 (*0-7148-2752-5*, Pub. by Phaidon Press) Phaidon Pr.

Brawne, Michael, jt. auth. see Meier, Richard & Partners Staff.

Brawner, C. O., ed. see International Conference of Gold Mining Staff.

Brawner, C. O., ed. see International Conference on Gold Mining (2nd: 1988.

Brawner, C. O., ed. see International Conference on Stability in Open Pit.

Brawner, C. O., ed. see Muskeg Research Conference Staff.

Brawner, Faye, jt. auth. see Becker, Jim.

Brawner, Jim & Brawner, Suzette. Taming the Family Zoo: Maximizing Harmony & Minimizing Family Stress. LC 98-9717. 192p. 1998. pap. 11.00 (*1-57683-058-6*) NavPress.

Brawner, Suzette, jt. auth. see Brawner, Jim.

Brawnstein, Barry. Free Market Analysis: A Reader. (C). 1993. pap. text 41.74 (*0-07-008514-5*) McGraw.

Brax, Ghazi. Madkhal Ila Al-Dahishiyyah. (ARA & ENG.). 135p. 1992. 15.00 (*0-935359-12-5*) Daheshist.

Brax, Najwa. Nasamat. (ARA & ENG., Illus.). 507p. 1994. 40.00 (*0-935359-42-7*) Daheshist.

Brax, Najwa Salam. Ethereal Wings. LC 98-89035. 67 p. 1998. pap. 8.50 (*1-886467-44-7*) WJM Press.

Braxton, Beverly, et al. Math Around the World. Bergman, Lincoln et al, eds. (Great Explorations in Math & Science (GEMS) Ser.). (Illus.). 200p. (Orig.). (J). (gr. 5-8). 1995. teacher ed., spiral bd. 25.50 (*0-912511-94-X*, GEMS) Lawrence Science.

Braxton, E. Paul. Get off My Land! LC 93-80309. 236p. (Orig.). 1994. pap. 9.95 (*0-939017-01-6*) Hermit Pr FL.

— To Kill the Shepherd. 256p. (Orig.). 1996. pap. 9.95 (*0-939017-03-2*) Hermit Pr FL.

— Trail to Riches. 240p. 1995. pap. 9.95 (*0-939017-02-4*) Hermit Pr FL.

Braxton, Hank. The Committee. (Orig.). 1979. mass mkt. 2.25 (*0-89083-484-9*, Zebra Kensgtn) Kensgtn Pub Corp.

Braxton, Joanne & Nicola-McLaughlin, Andree, eds. Wild Women in the Whirlwind: Afra-American Culture & the Contemporary Literary Renaissance. LC 89-30380. 419p. (C). 1990. 50.00 (*0-8135-1441-X*); pap. 17.95 (*0-8135-1442-8*) Rutgers U Pr.

Braxton, Joanne M. Black Women Writing Autobiography: A Tradition Within a Tradition. 240p. (C). 1989. 29.95 (*0-87722-639-3*) Temple U Pr.

— Black Women Writing Autobiography: A Tradition Within a Tradition. (Illus.). 240p. 1990. pap. 22.95 (*0-87722-803-5*) Temple U Pr.

Braxton, Joanne M. & Angelou, Maya. Maya Angelou's I Know Why the Caged Bird Sings: A Casebook. LC 98-13295. (Casebooks in Contemporary Fiction Ser.). (Illus.). 176p. 1998. pap. 13.95 (*0-19-511607-0*) OUP.

Braxton, John M., ed. Perspectives on Scholarly Misconduct in the Sciences. LC 98-50039. (Illus.). 272p. 1999. text 50.00 (*0-8142-0815-0*) Ohio St U Pr.

Braxton, John M. & Bayer, Alan E. Faculty Misconduct in Collegiate Teaching. LC 99-11238. 216p. 1999. 34.95 (*0-8018-6125-X*) Johns Hopkins.

Braxton, Wilbert L. This I Remember. LC 99-61991. (Illus.). 192p. 1999. 15.00 (*0-923687-49-1*) Celo Valley Bks.

Bray. College Algebra & Trig SG - Solution Manual. (C). 1988. pap. text 21.00 (*0-673-18926-0*) Addson-Wesley Educ.

— Poems. (Australian National University Press Ser.). 1979. text 17.50 (*0-08-032934-9*, Pergamon Pr) Elsevier.

— Sainte-Beuve a l'Academie de Lausanne: Chronique du Cours sur Port-Royal (1837-1838) 9.95 (*0-685-34976-4*) Fr & Eur.

Bray, A., et al. Theory & Practice of Force Measurement. (Monographs in Physical Measurement). 380p. 1990. text 142.00 (*0-12-128453-0*) Acad Pr.

Bray, Alan. Homosexuality in Renaissance England. LC 95-31441. (Between Men - Between Women Ser.). 165p. (C). 1996. pap. 14.00 (*0-231-10289-5*) Col U Pr.

— Homosexuality in Renaissance England. 2nd ed. LC 95-31441. (Between Men - Between Women Ser.). 164p. (C). 1996. 39.00 (*0-231-10288-7*) Col U Pr.

Bray, Alison. Hospital Sister. large type ed. (Linford Romance Library). 288p. 1996. pap. 16.99 (*0-7089-7895-9*, Linford) Ulverscroft.

— Nurse at Crag House. large type ed. (Dales Large Print Ser.). 235p. 1997. pap. 18.99 (*1-85389-780-9*, Dales) Ulverscroft.

Bray, Anne. The WoodenBoat Index: Issues 1-100. 115p. 1991. pap. 12.95 (*0-937822-22-1*) WoodenBoat Pubns.

Bray, Anne & Bray, Maynard. Boat Plans at Mystic Seaport. (Illus.). 207p. Date not set. pap. 24.95 (*0-913372-86-2*) Mystic Seaport.

Bray, Aree, ed. see Portland, Charles.

Bray, B. Jean Chapelain, Soixante-Dix-Sept Lettres Inedites a Nicolas Heinsius (1649-1658) Publiees d'Apres le Manuscrit de Leyde avec une Introduction & des Notes. (International Archives of the History of Ideas Ser.: No. 13). 475p. 1965. lib. bdg. 112.50 (*90-247-0189-5*, Pub. by M Nijhoff) Kluwer Academic.

Bray, Barbara, tr. see Bosquet, Alain.

Bray, Barbara, tr. see Caron, Francois.

Bray, Barbara, tr. see Crebillon, Claude P.

Bray, Barbara, tr. see Duby, Georges.

Bray, Barbara, tr. see Duras, Marguerite.

Bray, Barbara, tr. see Flaubert, Gustave & Sand, George.

Bray, Barbara, tr. see Kadare, Ismail.

Bray, Barbara, tr. see Kristeva, Julia.

Bray, Barbara, tr. see Ladurie, Emmanuel L.

Bray, Barbara, tr. see Levi, Jean.

Bray, Barbara, tr. see Roudinesco, Elizabeth.

Bray, Barbara, tr. see Schwarz-Bart, Simone.

Bray, Barbara, tr. see Sollers, Phillipe.

Bray, Barbara, tr. see Starobinski, Jean.

Bray, Barbara, tr. see Tournier, Michel.

Bray, Barbara, tr. see Trefusis, Violet K.

Bray, Barbara, tr. see Zbarsky, Ilya & Hutchinson, Samuel.

Bray, Bonnie, ed. see De Jager, Peter & Smith, Donald.

Bray, Carl. New Villages: Case Studies Christiania, Copenhagen. (C). 1981. 29.00 (*0-7855-3864-X*, Pub. by Oxford Polytechnic) St Mut.

— New Villages: Case Studies New Ash Green, Kent. (C). 1981. 29.00 (*0-7855-3866-6*, Pub. by Oxford Polytechnic) St Mut.

— New Villages: Case Studies South Woodham Ferrers, Essex. (C). 1981. 35.00 (*0-7855-3865-8*, Pub. by Oxford Polytechnic) St Mut.

***Bray, Charles.** A Dictionary of Glass. (Illus.). 224p. 1999. text. write for info. (*976-641-089-5*, Pub. by Craftsman House) Gordon & Breach.

Bray, Charles. A Dictionary of Glass: Materials & Techniques. (Illus.). 240p. (C). 1996. 47.95 (*0-8122-3357-3*, TP788) U of Pa Pr.

Bray, Charles W. Psychology & Military Proficiency. LC 69-13837. 242p. 1969. reprint ed. lib. bdg. 59.75 (*0-8371-1444-6*, BRMI, Greenwood Pr) Greenwood.

Bray, D. E., ed. Nondestructive Evaluation, 1993. (FD Ser.: Vol. 54). 68p. 1993. 36.00 (*0-7918-0951-X*, H00783) ASME.

Bray, Daniel L. Iowa Matrimonial Law. 1995. ring bd. write for info. (*0-86678-347-4*, 81044-10, MICHIE) LEXIS Pub.

Bray, Daniel L. Iowa Matrimonial Law, 1986-1993. 1993. suppl. ed. 41.00 (*1-56257-675-5*, MICHIE) LEXIS Pub.

— Iowa Matrimonial Law, 1986-1993. 400p. 1994. ring bd. 88.00 (*0-86678-348-2*, MICHIE) LEXIS Pub.

Bray, David, jt. ed. see Primack, Richard B.

Bray, David K. & Low, Douglas. The Kahuna Religion of Hawaii: Foundation of Heaven. rev. ed. LC 90-34566. (Illus.). 64p. 1991. pap. 7.95 (*0-945685-05-X*) Borderland Sciences.

Bray, Denis. Brahui Language Introduction & Grammar. 248p. 1986. 39.95 (*0-7859-9819-5*) Fr & Eur.

Bray, Dennis. Cell Movements. LC 91-24911. (Illus.). 450p. 1992. text 49.00 (*0-8153-0404-8*, 3-0404-8); pap. text 31.00 (*0-8153-0717-9*) Garland.

Bray, Dennis, jt. auth. see Alberts, Bruce.

Bray, Denys. Brahui Language: Introduction & Grammar. 248p. 1986. 39.95 (*0-8288-8421-8*) Fr & Eur.

Bray, Denys, ed. see Shakespeare, William.

Bray, Don E., ed. NDE for the Energy Industry, 1995 Proceedings: The Energy & Environmental EXPO '95 - the Energy-Sources Technology Conference & Exhibition (1995: Houston, TX) LC 94-74526. (NDE Ser.: Vol. 13). 91p. 1995. pap. 64.00 (*0-7918-1298-7*, H00930) ASME.

Bray, Don E. & Stanley, Roderic K. Nondestructive Evaluation: A Tool in Design, Manufacturing & Service. rev. ed. LC 96-35233. 608p. 1996. boxed set 99.95 (*0-8493-2655-9*, 2655) CRC Pr.

Bray, Donald E. & McBride, Don, eds. Nondestructive Testing Techniques. LC 91-37970. (New Dimensions in Engineering Ser.). 800p. 1992. 200.00 (*0-471-52513-8*) Wiley.

Bray, Donald E. & Stanley, Roderick K. Nondestructive Evaluation: A Tool in Design, Manufacturing & Service. (Mechanical Engineering Ser.). 672p. 1989. 15.95 (*0-07-007352-X*) McGraw.

Bray, Dorothy, ed. Western Apache-English Dictionary: A Community-Generated Bilingual Dictionary. LC 97-53259. 528p. 1998. pap. 20.00 (*0-927534-79-7*) Biling Rev-Pr.

Bray, Douglas W. Working with Organizations & Their People: A Guide to Human Resources Practice. LC 90-20703. (Professional Practice Ser.). 256p. 1991. 36.95 (*0-89862-475-4*) Guilford Pubns.

Bray, Dwayne. The Gift. 240p. 1999. 22.00 (*1-56352-535-6*) Longstreet.

Bray, Edmund C. Ancient Valleys, Modern Rivers. What the Glaciers Did. (Illus.). 32p. (Orig.). 1985. pap. 4.95 (*0-911338-33-0*) Sci Museum.

— Billions of Years in Minnesota. 2nd ed. (Illus.). 102p. 1985. pap. 7.95 (*0-911338-34-9*) Sci Museum.

Bray, Edmund C. & Colman, Martha, eds. Joseph N. Nicollet on the Plains & Prairies: The Expeditions of 1838-39 with Journals, Letters, & Notes on the Dakota Indians. Coleman, Edmund C. & Bray, Martha C., trs. LC 76-3673. (Illus.). vi, 294p. 1993. pap. 14.95 (*0-87351-290-1*) Minn Hist.

Bray, Elizabeth. The Discovery of the Hebrides: Voyages to the Western Isles, 1745-1883. LC 97-130221. (Illus.). 268p. pap. 24.95 (*1-874744-59-9*, Pub. by Birlinn Ltd) Dufour.

Bray, Emile F. De, see De Bray, Emile F.

Bray, Errol. Playbuilding. LC 94-229338. 142p. 1994. pap. 13.95 (*0-435-08635-9*, 08635) Heinemann.

Bray, F. Sewell. The Interpretation of Accounts. LC 79-22380. 232p. 1979. reprint ed. text 30.00 (*0-914348-29-9*) Scholars Bk.

Bray, Francesca. The Rice Economies: Technology & Development in Asian Societies. LC 93-41318. 1994. 18.95 (*0-520-08620-1*, Pub. by U CA Pr) Cal Prin Full Svc.

— Technology & Gender: Fabrics of Power in Late Imperial China. LC 96-28828. (Illus.). 444p. 1997. 55.00 (*0-520-20685-1*, Pub. by U CA Pr); pap. 22.50 (*0-520-20861-7*, Pub. by U CA Pr) Cal Prin Full Svc.

***Bray, Francesca.** Technology & Society in Ming China (1368-1644) LC 99-58418. (Historical Perspectives on Technology, Society & Culture Ser.). (Illus.). (C). 2000. pap. 8.00 (*0-87229-119-7*) Am Hist Assn.

Bray, Frank S. The Accounting Mission. LC 73-84525. 1973. reprint ed. text 30.00 (*0-914348-01-9*) Scholars Bk.

— Precision & Design in Accountancy. Brief, Richard P., ed. LC 80-1473. (Dimensions of Accounting Theory & Practice Ser.). 1980. reprint ed. lib. bdg. 18.95 (*0-405-13503-3*) Ayer.

Bray, Frank T. & Moodie, Michael. Defense Technology & the Atlantic Alliance: Competition or Collaboration? LC 77-80297. (Foreign Policy Reports). 42p. 1977. 11.95 (*0-89549-000-5*) Inst Foreign Policy Anal.

Bray, G. A., ed. Recent Advances in Obesity Research, Vol. II. 510p. 1978. 71.00 (*0-917678-07-9*) Food & Nut Pr.

Bray, G. A., et al, eds. Diet & Obesity. (Illus.). xiv, 248p. 1989. 139.25 (*3-8055-4980-6*) S Karger.

Bray, G. A., jt. ed. see Bouchard, C.

Bray-Garretson, Helen, jt. auth. see Cook, Kaye V.

Bray, Garth M., jt. ed. see Lam, Dominic M.

Bray, Gary & Pokrass, David. Understanding ADA: A Software Engineering Approach. LC 92-9974. 368p. (C). 1992. reprint ed. lib. bdg. 42.50 (*0-89464-744-X*) Krieger.

Bray, George A. Contemporary Diagnosis & Management of Obesity. LC 98-70972. (Illus.). 298p. 1998. pap. 29.95 (*1-884065-30-9*) Assocs in Med.

Bray, George A., et al, eds. Handbook of Obesity. LC 97-34402. (Illus.). 1032p. 1997. text 225.00 (*0-8247-9899-6*) Dekker.

Bray, George A. & Ryan, Donna H., eds. Molecular & Genetic Aspects of Obesity. LC 95-35680. (Pennington Center Nutrition Ser.: Vol. 5). (Illus.). 712p. (C). 1996. text 95.00 (*0-8071-2025-1*) La State U Pr.

— Nutrition & Reproduction. LC 98-10771. (Pennington Center Nutrition Ser.: Vol. 8). 460p. 1998. text 95.00 (*0-8071-2306-4*) La State U Pr.

— Nutrition, Endocrinology, & Disease. (Pennington Center Nutrition Ser.: Vol. 4). (Illus.). 232p. 1995. text 45.00 (*0-8071-1954-7*) La State U Pr.

— Nutrition, Genetics, & Heart Disease. LC 96-9007. (Pennington Center Nutrition Ser.: Vol. 6). (Illus.). 408p. (C). 1996. text 60.00 (*0-8071-2051-0*) La State U Pr.

— Nutrition, Genetics, & Obesity. LC 98-50606. (Pennington Center Nutrition Ser.: Vol. 9). (Illus.). 574p. 1999. text 95.00 (*0-8071-2407-9*) La State U Pr.

— Science of Food Regulation: Food Intake, Taste, Nutrient Partitioning, & Energy Expenditure. LC 91-29389. (Pennington Center Nutrition Ser.: Vol. 2). 440p. 1992. text 62.50 (*0-8071-1741-2*) La State U Pr.

— Vitamins & Cancer Prevention. LC 92-19677. (Pennington Center Nutrition Ser.: Vol. 3). (Illus.). 456p. (C). 1992. text 62.50 (*0-8071-1789-7*) La State U Pr.

***Bray, George A. & Ryan, Donna H., eds.** Women's Health: Prevention Is the Best Medicine. (Pennington Center Nutrition Ser.: Vol. 11). 302p. 2000. 100.00 (*0-8071-2654-3*) La State U Pr.

Bray, George A., ed. see Ryan, Donna H.

Bray, Gerald. Biblical Interpretation: Past & Present. LC 96-19408. 750p. 1996. 34.99 (*0-8308-1880-4*, 1880) InterVarsity.

***Bray, Gerald.** Biblical Interpretation: Past & Present. 2000. pap. 29.99 (*0-8308-1565-1*) InterVarsity.

Bray, Gerald. Creeds, Councils & Christ. 1997. pap. 15.99 (*1-85792-280-8*, Pub. by Christian Focus) Spring Arbor Dist.

— The Personal God: Is the Classical Understanding of God Tenable? 74p. 1998. reprint ed. pap. 12.99 (*0-85364-909-X*, Pub. by Paternoster Pub) OM Literature.

Bray, Gerald, ed. Ancient Christian Commentary on Scripture: Romans. 404p. 1998. lib. bdg. 40.00 (*1-57958-037-8*) Fitzroy Dearborn.

— The Anglican Canons, 1529-1947. LC 98-157393. (Church of England Record Society Ser.: No. 6). 1104p. 1998. 170.00 (*0-85115-557-X*, 0969-3548, Boydell Pr) Boydell & Brewer.

— Contours of Christian Theology, 4 vols., Set. (Orig.). 1994. pap. 56.97 (*0-8308-1530-9*, 1530) InterVarsity.

— Documents of the English Reformation. LC 95-198665. 674p. 1995. pap. 38.00 (*0-8006-2907-8*, 1-2907) Augsburg Fortress.

B

An Asterisk (*) at the beginning of an entry indicates that the title is appearing for the first time.

Bray, Henry G., et al. Between Nilpotent & Solvable. LC 82-539. 240p. 1982. 22.00 (*0-936428-06-6*) Polygonal Pub.

Bray, J., et al. The Lecture Notes on Human Physiology. 3rd ed. (The Lecture Notes Ser.). (Illus.). 736p. 1994. 29.95 (*0-632-03644-3*, Pub. by Blckwll Scitfc UK) Blackwell Sci.

Bray, J. W. A History of English Critical Terms. 1977. lib. bdg. 59.95 (*0-8490-1974-5*) Gordon Pr.

Bray, J. W., jt. auth. see Hoek, E.

Bray, James & Kelly, John. Stepfamilies: Love, Marriage, & Parenting in the First Ten Years - Based on a Landmark Study. LC 98-3543. 288p. 1998. 25.00 (*0-7679-0102-9*) Broadway BDD.

Bray, James H. & Kelly, John. Stepfamilies: Love, Marriage & Parenting in the First Decade. 288p. 1999. reprint ed. pap. 13.00 (*0-7679-0103-7*) Broadway BDD.

Bray, James H. & Maxwell, Scott E. Multivariate Analysis of Variance. (Quantitative Applications in the Social Sciences Ser.: Vol. 54). 96p. 1985. pap. text 10.95 (*0-8039-2310-4*) Sage.

Bray, James H., jt. ed. see Depner, Charlene E.

Bray, James L. To Burn a Witch. 1963. 3.50 (*0-87129-419-2*, T32) Dramatic Pub.

Bray, Jean & Wright, Sheila, eds. The Use of Technology in the Care of the Elderly & the Disabled. LC 80-17847. 267p. 1980. 55.00 (*0-313-22616-4*, BTC/, Greenwood Pr) Greenwood.

Bray, Jeannette D. The Week Before Christmas; The Most Embarrassing Christmas Tree Ever, 2 vols. in 1. Kenyatta, Imani, ed. LC 98-66316. (Illus.). 96p. (J). (gr. k-6). 1998. 16.95 (*1-886580-43-X*) Pinnacle-Syatt.

Bray, Jeannine D. How My Grandmother Sees. Kenyatta, Imani, ed. LC 98-66325. (Illus.). 64p. (J). (gr. k-6). 1998. 14.95 (*1-886580-39-1*) Pinnacle-Syatt.

— My Poppie. Kenyatta, Imani, ed. LC 98-66324. (Illus.). 80p. (J). (gr. k-6). 1998. 14.95 (*1-886580-62-6*) Pinnacle-Syatt.

— Pop Pop: What Do Armadillos Eat? Kenyatta, Imani, ed. LC 98-66317. (Illus.). 56p. (J). (gr. k-6). 1998. 13.95 (*1-886580-87-1*) Pinnacle-Syatt.

— Rabbie. Kenyatta, Imani, ed. LC 98-66318. (Illus.). 56p. (J). (gr. k-6). 1998. 14.95 (*1-886580-68-5*) Pinnacle-Syatt.

— Superfro. Kenyatti, Imani, ed. LC 98-66323. (Illus.). 72p. (J). (gr. k-6). 1998. 14.95 (*1-886580-10-3*) Pinnacle-Syatt.

Bray, Jeffrey K. Mine Warfare in the Russo-Soviet Navy. (Illus.). 200p. (Orig.). 1996. pap. 34.80 (*0-89412-253-3*, M-22) Aegean Park Pr.

— Ultra in the Atlantic Vol. I: Allied Communications Intelligence & Battle of the Atlantic. 73p. 1994. pap. 16.80 (*0-89412-235-5*) Aegean Park Pr.

— Ultra in the Atlantic Vol. II: U-Boat Operations. 237p. 1994. pap. 24.80 (*0-89412-236-3*) Aegean Park Pr.

— Ultra in the Atlantic Vol. III: German Naval Communications Intelligence. 93p. 1994. pap. 16.80 (*0-89412-237-1*) Aegean Park Pr.

— Ultra in the Atlantic Vol. IV: Technical Intelligence from Allied Communications Intelligence. 73p. 1994. pap. 16.80 (*0-89412-238-X*) Aegean Park Pr.

— Ultra in the Atlantic Vol. V: The German Naval Grid & Its Cipher. LC 97-178148. 75p. 1994. pap. 16.80 (*0-89412-240-1*) Aegean Park Pr.

— Ultra in the Atlantic Vol. VI: Appendices. 281p. 1994. pap. 24.80 (*0-89412-241-X*) Aegean Park Pr.

*__Bray, Jennifer & Sturman, Charles.__ Bluetooth: Connect Without Cables. 400p. 2000. 49.00 (*0-13-089840-6*) P-H.

Bray, Jennifer & Wilks, Michael J., eds. Courts of the Manor of Bandon & Beddington, 1498-1552. Gowans, Hedley M., tr. 130p. 1989. 49.00 (*0-907335-08-X*, Pub. by Sutton Libs & Arts) St Mut.

— One Hundred Years of Public Health in Sutton. 54p. 1987. pap. 20.00 (*0-907335-06-3*, Pub. by Sutton Libs & Arts) St Mut.

Bray, Jeremy. Decision in Government. LC 71-474754. 320p. 1970. write for info. (*0-575-00440-1*) V Gollancz.

Bray, Joan. Border Collies. (Illus.). 104p. (Orig.). 1994. pap. 12.95 (*0-86417-555-8*, Pub. by Kangaroo Pr) Seven Hills Bk.

Bray, Joan & Brack, Lisa. Good Dog: A Guide for the Beginner. (Illus.). 126p. (Orig.). 1993. pap. 7.95 (*0-86417-388-1*, Pub. by Kangaroo Pr) Seven Hills Bk.

Bray, Joan, et al. Biology Laboratory Exercises. 132p. (C). 1997. pap. text, per. 26.95 (*0-7872-3311-0*) Kendall-Hunt.

— Human Biology Laboratory Exercises. 124p. (C). 1997. pap. text, per. 35.95 (*0-7872-3310-2*, 41331001) Kendall-Hunt.

— Organismal Biology Laboratory Exercises. 132p. (C). 1997. pap. text, per. 33.95 (*0-7872-3312-9*, 41331201) Kendall-Hunt.

*__Bray, Joe, et al.__ Ma(r)king the Text: The Presentation of Meaning on the Literary Page. LC 00-34850. 2000. write for info. (*0-7546-0168-4*, Pub. by Ashgate Pub) Ashgate Pub Co.

*__Bray, John.__ Collaborative Inquiry in Practice: Action, Reflection & Making Meaning. LC 00-8152. 162p. 2000. 55.00 (*0-7619-0646-0*) Sage.

Bray, John. The Communications Miracle: The Telecommunications Pioneers from Morse to the Information Superhighway. (Illus.). 400p. (C). 1995. 28.95 (*0-306-45042-9*, Plenum Trade) Perseus Pubng.

— Gallienus: A Study in Reformist & Sexual Politics. LC 97-167915. 1999. 29.95 (*1-86254-337-2*) Wakefield Pr.

*__Bray, John.__ Jon Bray: Collected Poems, 1962-1991. 2000. pap. 29.95 (*0-7022-3171-1*, Pub. by Univ Queensland Pr) Intl Spec Bk.

Bray, John, et al. Mobilising the Organization: Bringing Strategy to Life. LC 95-10147. 320p. (C). 1995. pap. text 24.95 (*0-13-148891-0*) P-H.

Bray, John, jt. auth. see Barker, John N.

Bray, John F. Labour's Wrongs & Labour's Remedy: or The Age of Might & the Age of Right. LC 66-21656. (Reprints of Economic Classics Ser.). 216p. 1968. reprint ed. 35.00 (*0-678-00283-5*) Kelley.

Bray, John J. Lecture Notes on Human Physiology. 4th ed. LC 98-28849. 1999. write for info. (*0-86542-776-3*) Blackwell Sci.

*__Bray, John J., et al.__ Lecture Notes on Human Physiology. 4th ed. LC 98-28849. (Lecture Notes Ser.). (Illus.). 1999. pap. text 34.95 (*0-86542-775-5*) Blackwell Sci.

*__Bray, John N.__ Collaborative Inquiry in Practice: Action, Reflection & Making Meaning. LC 00-8152. 2000. pap. write for info. (*0-7619-0647-9*) Sage.

Bray, John S. Theodore Beza's Doctrine of Predestination. 153p. 1975. 64.50 (*90-6004-334-0*, Pub. by B De Graaf) Coronet Bks.

Bray, Joy. Of Noble Character. 132p. (Orig.). 1988. pap. 5.95 (*0-89827-059-6*, BKD93) Wesleyan Pub Hse.

*__Bray, Libba.__ Sweet Sixteen: Kari, No. 3. LC 99-66680. (Sweet Sixteen Ser.: No. 3). 240p. (YA). (gr. 7-12). 2000. pap. 5.95 (*0-06-440817-5*, HarpTrophy) HarpC Child Bks.

Bray, Lindsay & Arbogast, Nicole. Smithsonian Air & Space Museum Shouldn't Be a Beltway Monopoly. (Issue Papers: No. 5-92). 6p. 1992. pap. write for info. (*1-57655-049-4*) Independ Inst.

Bray, M., jt. ed. see Hooke, J.

Bray, M. A. & Morley, J., eds. The Pharmacology of Lymphocytes. (Handbook of Experimental Pharmacology Ser.: Vol. 85). (Illus.). 700p. 1988. 494.95 (*0-387-18609-3*) Spr-Verlag.

Bray, Madge. Sexual Abuse: The Child's Voice. LC 97-197783. 224p. 1997. pap. 24.95 (*1-85302-487-2*, Pub. by Jessica Kingsley) Taylor & Francis.

Bray, Marian. Lassie: To the Rescue. Harmon, Jeannie, ed. LC 95-31856. (Lassie Bks.: Vol. 3). (Illus.). 144p. (Orig.). (J). (gr. 4-7). 1995. pap. 5.25 (*0-7814-0264-6*) Chariot Victor.

— Lassie: Treasure at Eagle Mountain. Harmon, Jeannie, ed. (Lassie Bks.: Vol. 2). (Illus.). 144p. (Orig.). (J). (gr. 3-6). 1995. pap. 5.25 (*0-7814-0263-8*) Chariot Victor.

— Lassie: Under the Big Top. Harmon, Jeannie, ed. (Lassie Bks.: Vol. 1). (Illus.). 144p. (Orig.). (J). (gr. 3-6). 1995. pap. 5.99 (*0-7814-0262-X*, Lion) Chariot Victor.

— World's Biggest Chicken. LC 92-7556. 96p. (YA). 1992. pap. 4.99 (*1-55513-929-9*) Chariot Victor.

Bray, Mark. Counting the Full Cost: Parental & Community Financing of Education in East Asia. 96p. 1996. pap. 22.00 (*0-8213-3827-7*, 13827) World Bank.

— Decentralization of Education: Community Financing. LC 96-32177. (Directions in Development Ser.). 60p. 1996. pap. 22.00 (*0-8213-3724-6*, 13724) World Bank.

Bray, Mark & Packer, Steve. Education in Small States: Concepts, Challenges, & Strategies. LC 92-36832. (Comparative & International Education Ser.: Vol. 13). 328p. 1993. 89.95 (*0-08-041033-2*, Prgamon Press) Buttrwrth-Heinemann.

— Education in Small States: Concepts, Challenges, & Strategies. LC 92-36832. (Comparative & International Education Ser.: Vol. 13). (Illus.). 325p. reprint ed. pap. 100.80 (*0-608-06261-8*, 206659000008) Bks Demand.

Bray, Martha C. Joseph Nicollet & His Map. LC 79-54278. (American Philosophical Society, Memoirs Ser.: No. 140). (Illus.). 355p. reprint ed. pap. 110.10 (*0-7837-6705-6*, 204633800011) Bks Demand.

Bray, Martha C., tr. see Bray, Edmund C. & Colman, Martha, eds.

Bray, Mayfield. Guide to the Ford Film Collection in the National Archives. LC 71-604432. (Illus.). 118p. 1970. text 20.00 (*0-911333-28-2*, 100008) National Archives & Recs.

Bray, Maynard. Building the Nutshell. (Illus.). 32p. 1991. pap. 7.95 (*0-937822-11-6*) WoodenBoat Pubns.

— How to Build the Haven Twelve & a Half Footer. (Illus.). 64p. 1991. pap. 15.00 (*0-937822-13-2*) WoodenBoat Pubns.

— Mystic Seaport Museum Watercraft. 2nd rev. ed. (Illus.). xx, 300p. 1986. pap. 29.95 (*0-913372-38-2*) Mystic Seaport.

Bray, Maynard, jt. auth. see Bray, Anne.

Bray, Michael A. & Anderson, Wayne, eds. Mediators of Pulmonary Inflammation. (Lung Biology in Health & Disease Ser.: Vol. 54). (Illus.). 688p. 1991. text 255.00 (*0-8247-8442-1*) Dekker.

Bray, Monica. Speech & Language in Clinical Process & Practice. 1998. pap. text 36.95 (*1-86156-094-X*) Whurr Pub.

Bray, N. N. Shifting Sands. LC 70-180321. reprint ed. 39.50 (*0-404-56216-7*) AMS Pr.

Bray, Natalie. Dress Fitting: Basic Principles & Practice. 128p. 1970. pap. 29.95 (*0-8464-0342-0*) Beekman Pubs.

— Dress Fitting: Basic Principles & Practice. (Illus.). 112p. 1988. pap. text 29.95 (*0-8464-1302-7*) Beekman Pubs.

— Dress Fitting: Metric. 2nd ed. 120p. 1982. pap. text 29.50 (*0-632-01879-8*) Sheridan.

— Dress Pattern Designing: Basic Principles of Cut & Fit, Metric System. (Illus.). 160p. 1974. pap. 39.95 (*0-8464-0343-9*) Beekman Pubs.

Bray, Nigel S., ed. The Devizes Branch Line: A Wiltshire Railway Remembered. 92p. (C). 1990. pap. 27.00 (*0-902633-93-7*, Pub. by Picton) St Mut.

Bray, Norman W., ed. International Review of Research in Mental Retardation, Vol. 18. (Illus.). 309p. (C). 1992. text 105.00 (*0-12-366218-4*) Acad Pr.

— International Review of Research in Mental Retardation, Vol. 20. (Illus.). 263p. (C). 1997. text 90.00 (*0-12-366220-6*) Morgan Kaufmann.

— International Review of Research in Mental Retardation, Vol. 21. (Illus.). 268p. (C). 1997. text 95.00 (*0-12-366221-4*) Morgan Kaufmann.

Bray, Norman W., jt. ed. see Ellis, Norman R.

Bray, Olive, ed. Elder or Poetic Edda. LC 76-43949. (Viking Society for Northern Research: Translation Ser.: Vol. 2). (Illus.). 416p. reprint ed. 62.50 (*0-404-60012-3*) AMS Pr.

*__Bray, Patricia.__ Irish Earl. (Regency Romance Ser.). 2000. mass mkt. 4.99 (*0-8217-6536-1*, Zebra Kensgtn) Kensgtn Pub Corp.

Bray, Patricia. A London Season. 208p. 1997. mass mkt. 4.99 (*0-8217-5768-7*, Zebra Kensgtn) Kensgtn Pub Corp.

— Lord Freddie's First Love, 1. 224p. 1999. mass mkt. 4.99 (*0-8217-6322-9*) Kensgtn Pub Corp.

— Unlikely Alliance. (Zebra Regency Romance Ser.). 208p. 1998. mass mkt. 4.99 (*0-8217-6009-2*, Zebra Kensgtn) Kensgtn Pub Corp.

Bray, R. C., et al, eds. Flavins & Flavoproteins: Proceedings of the Eighth International Symposium, Brighton, England, July 9-13, 1984. (Illus.). xxxiv, 923p. (Orig.). 1985. 257.70 (*3-11-009879-2*) De Gruyter.

Bray, R. J., et al. Plasma Loops in the Solar Corona. (Cambridge Astrophysics Ser.: No. 18). (Illus.). 522p. (C). 1991. text 120.00 (*0-521-35107-3*) Cambridge U Pr.

Bray, R. N. & Tatham, P. J. B. Old Waterfront Walls: Management, Maintenance & Rehabilitation. (Illus.). 296p. (C). 1992. 125.00 (*0-419-17640-3*, E & FN Spon) Routledge.

Bray, R. S. Armies of Pestilence: The Effects of Pandemics on History. LC 97-156006. (Illus.). 258p. 1997. 31.95 (*0-7188-2949-2*, Lutterworth-Parkwest) Parkwest Pubns.

Bray, Richard Nicholas. Dredging: A Handbook for Engineers. 2nd ed. LC 97-100972. 434p. 1996. text 129.95 (*0-470-23587-X*) Halsted Pr.

Bray, Robert. Spinning Our Stories: A Media Guide for Lesbian, Gay, Bisexual & Transgender Activists. 1997. pap. text 10.00 (*0-9652779-2-5*) Natl Gay & Lesbian.

— To Have & to Hold: Organizing for Our Right to Marry. 1997. pap. 10.00 (*0-9652779-1-7*) Natl Gay & Lesbian.

Bray, Robert & Independent Media Institute Staff. SPIN Works! A Media Guidebook for Communicating Values & Shaping Opinion. Date not set. write for info. (*0-9633687-9-6*) Inst Alternative Jrnl.

Bray, Robert C. Rediscoveries: Literature & Place in Illinois. LC 81-3353. 184p. (C). 1982. text 24.95 (*0-252-00911-8*) U of Ill Pr.

Bray, Robert C. & Bushnell, Paul E., eds. The Diary of a Common Soldier in the American Revolution, 1775-1783: An Annotated Edition of the Military Journal of Jeremiah Greenman. LC 77-18528. (Illus.). 333p. 1978. pap. 18.00 (*0-87580-528-0*) N Ill U Pr.

Bray, Robert M. & Marsden, Mary E. Drug Use in Metropolitan America. LC 98-19675. 1998. 52.00 (*0-7619-0374-7*); pap. 24.95 (*0-7619-0375-5*) Sage.

Bray, Robert M., jt. ed. see Kerr, Norbert L.

Bray, Robert T. The Utz Site: An Oneota Village in Central Missouri. Yelton, Jeffrey K., ed. (Missouri Archaeologist Ser.: Vol. 52). (Illus.). 146p. (Orig.). 1993. pap. 7.50 (*0-943414-75-X*) MO Arch Soc.

Bray, Robert T., ed. Boone's Lick Salt Works, 1805-33. (Missouri Archaeologist Ser.: Vol. 48). (Illus.). 89p. (C). 1990. pap. 8.00 (*0-943414-70-9*) MO Arch Soc.

— Kansas City Area Archaeology: The Last 1000 Years. (Missouri Archaeologist Ser.: Vol. 49). (Illus.). 187p. 1991. pap. 12.00 (*0-943414-72-5*) MO Arch Soc.

— The Loftin Component, 23SN42. LC 44-14121. (Missouri Archaeologist Ser.: Vol. 44). (Illus.). 134p. (Orig.). 1983. pap. 7.00 (*0-943414-24-5*) MO Arch Soc.

Bray, Robert T., jt. auth. see Waselkov, Gregory A.

Bray, Robert T., jt. auth. see Williams, J. Raymond.

Bray, Robert T., ed. see Chapman, Carl H., et al.

Bray, Robert T., ed. see Geier, Clarence R. & Hamblin, Nancy L.

Bray, Robert T., ed. see Henning, Dale R.

Bray, Robert T., ed. see Keslin, Richard O.

Bray, Robert T., ed. see Martin, Terrell L.

Bray, Robert T., ed. see McMillan, R. Bruce.

Bray, Robert T., ed. see Moselage, John.

Bray, Robert T., ed. see Roberts, Ralph G.

Bray, Robert T., ed. see Schmit, Larry J., et al.

Bray, Robert T., ed. see Schmitts, Larry J.

Bray, Robert T., ed. see Shippee, J. M.

Bray, Robert T., ed. see Stephenson, Robert L.

Bray, Roger, ed. The Blackwell History of Music in Britain Vol. II: Sixteenth Century. (Illus.). 400p. (C). 1995. 121.95 (*0-631-17924-0*) Blackwell Pubs.

*__Bray, Roger & Raitz, Vladimir.__ Flight to the Sun: The Story of the Holiday Revolution. 256p. 2000. write for info. (*0-304-70708-2*); pap. 24.95 (*0-8264-4829-1*) Continuum.

Bray, Rosa A., jt. auth. see Bray, Ruby A.

*__Bray, Rosemary.__ Black Child's Book of Prayer. 96p. (J). 2000. lib. bdg. 18.49 (*0-7868-2502-2*, Pub. by Disney Pr) Little.

Bray, Rosemary. Black Child's Book of Prayer. 96p. 2000. pap. 17.99 (*0-7868-0522-6*, Pub. by Hyprn Ppbks) Little.

Bray, Rosemary L. Martin Luther King. LC 93-41002. (Illus.). 48p. (J). (gr. 2 up). 1995. lib. bdg. 15.93 (*0-688-13132-8*, Grenwillow Bks) HarpC Child Bks.

— Martin Luther King. LC 93-41002. (Illus.). 48p. (J). (gr. 4-7). 1995. 16.00 (*0-688-13131-X*, Grenwillow Bks) HarpC Child Bks.

— Martin Luther King. LC 93-41002. (Illus.). 48p. (J). 1997. mass mkt. 5.95 (*0-688-15219-8*, Wm Morrow) Morrow Avon.

— Martin Luther King. 1997. 11.15 (*0-606-11599-4*, Pub. by Turtleback) Demco.

— Unafraid of the Dark: A Memoir. 304p. 1999. pap. 14.00 (*0-385-49475-0*) Doubleday.

Bray, Ruby A. & Bray, Rosa A. Altizer. Emers Altizer & His Descendants, with Sketches of Connected Families. 164p. 1997. reprint ed. pap. 27.00 (*0-8328-7255-5*); reprint ed. lib. bdg. 37.00 (*0-8328-7254-7*) Higginson Bk Co.

Bray, Ruth G. De, tr. see Reymond, Arnold.

Bray, Sarah H., ed. see McKenna, Barbara.

Bray, SeMia. Love, Loving, & Being Loved: What Men & Women Have to Say about It. Santos-Bray, Wanda et al, eds. (Illus.), 80p. (Orig.). 1996. pap. 14.95 (*0-9653264-0-3*, 1001) Noisemaker Pub.

Bray, Stan. Making Small Workshop Tools. (Workshop Practice Ser.: No. 14). (Illus.). 96p. (Orig.). 1987. pap. 18.50 (*0-85242-886-3*, Pub. by Nexus Special Interests) Trans-Atl Phila.

Bray, Susan R., ed. see Diehl, Cheryl J.

Bray, Tamara L. & Killion, Thomas W., eds. Reckoning with the Dead: The Larsen Bay Repatriation & the Smithsonian Institution. LC 94-2652. (Illus.). 352p. 1994. pap. text 34.95 (*1-56098-365-5*) Smithsonian.

Bray, Thomas J., ed. see Brookes, Warren T.

Bray, W. Case Law on Education. 122p. 1989. pap. 44.00 (*0-409-01338-2*, SA, MICHIE) LEXIS Pub.

Bray, Warwick. Everyday Life of the Aztecs. (Illus.). 208p. 1991. pap. 7.95 (*0-87226-245-6*, 62456B, P Bedrick Books) NTC Contemp Pub Co.

Bray, Warwick & Trump, David. Diccionario de Arqueologia. (SPA.). 276p. 1976. pap. 39.95 (*0-8288-5584-6*, S50363) Fr & Eur.

— Dictionary of Archaeology: Dizionario d'Archeologia. (ENG & ITA.). 336p. 1980. 29.95 (*0-8288-1199-7*, F72520) Fr & Eur.

— Lexikon der Archaeologie, 2 vols., Set. (GER.). 1975. pap. 49.95 (*0-8288-5916-7*, M7276) Fr & Eur.

Bray, Wayne D. Common Law Zone in Panama: A Case Study in Reception. LC 76-23354. (Illus.). 150p. 1976. 20.00 (*0-913480-35-5*) Inter Am U Pr.

Bray, William, jt. auth. see Lam, Joseph.

*__Bray, William O.__ Analysis of Divergence: Control & Management of Divergent Processes. LC 98-44618. 520p. 1999. 79.95 (*0-8176-4058-4*) Birkhauser.

Bray, William O., et al, eds. Fourier Analysis: Analytic & Geometric Aspects. LC 94-1800. (Lecture Notes in Pure & Applied Mathematics Ser.: Vol. 157). (Illus.). 472p. 1994. pap. text 175.00 (*0-8247-9208-4*) Dekker.

Brayboy, Connee. Pembroke in the Twentieth Century, North Carolina. (American Century Ser.). (Illus.). 128p. 1999. pap. 16.99 (*0-7524-0950-6*) Arcadia Publng.

Braybrock, Roy. Supersonic Fighter Developments. (Illus.). 225p. 1987. 24.95 (*0-85429-582-8*, F582, Pub. by GT Foulis) Haynes Manuals.

Braybrook, Julian H. Biocompatiblity: Assessment of Medical Devices & Materials. LC 96-29705. 246p. 1997. 120.00 (*0-471-96597-9*) Wiley.

Braybrook, Roy. The Aircraft Encyclopedia. (Illus.). 192p. (J). (gr. 4 up). 1985. pap. 9.99 (*0-671-55337-2*) S&S Bks Yung.

— Aircraft Weaponry of Today. (Illus.). 168p. 14.98 (*0-85429-634-4*, F634, Pub. by GT Foulis) Haynes Manuals.

— Battle for the Falklands Vol. 3: Air Forces. (Men-at-Arms Ser.: No. 135). (Illus.). 48p. pap. 11.95 (*0-85045-493-X*, 9067, Pub. by Ospry) Stackpole.

Braybrook, Roy R., et al. Russian Warriors. (Osprey Ser.). (Illus.). 128p. 1993. 15.95 (*1-85532-293-5*) MBI Pubg.

Braybrooke, David. Ethics in the World of Business. LC 82-18547. (Philosophy & Society Ser.). 506p. (C). 1983. pap. text 27.95 (*0-8476-7107-0*) Rowman.

— Meeting Needs. LC 86-43130. (Studies in Moral, Political, & Legal Philosophy). 354p. 1987. reprint ed. pap. 109.80 (*0-608-02531-3*, 206317500004) Bks Demand.

— Moral Objectives, Rules & the Forms of Social Change. LC 98-167106. (Toronto Studies in Philosophy). 384p. 1998. text 55.00 (*0-8020-4169-8*); pap. text 21.95 (*0-8020-8031-6*) U of Toronto Pr.

Braybrooke, David, et al. Logic on the Track of Social Change. (Clarendon Library of Logic & Philosophy). 292p. 1996. text 65.00 (*0-19-823530-5*) OUP.

Braybrooke, John. Adamant Eve. LC 96-68132. 372p. (Orig.). 1996. pap. 19.95 (*1-57197-021-5*) Pentland Pr.

*__Braybrooke, M.__ Explorer's Guide to Christianity. 1999. mass mkt. 15.95 (*0-340-71005-5*, Pub. by Hodder & Stought Ltd) Trafalgar.

Braybrooke, Marcus. Children of One God: A History of the Council of Christians & Jews. 1991. text 25.00 (*0-85303-242-4*, Pub. by M Vallentine & Co); pap. text 15.00 (*0-85303-250-5*, Pub. by M Vallentine & Co) Intl Spec Bk.

— Faith & Interfaith in a Global Age. 142p. (Orig.). 1998. pap. 11.50 (*0-9637897-2-4*) CoNexus Pr.

— Inter-Faith Organizations, 1893-1979: An Historical Directory. LC 79-91620. (Texts & Studies in Religion: Vol. 6). xiv, 228p. 1980. lib. bdg. 89.95 (*0-88946-971-7*) E Mellen.

— Time to Meet. LC 90-30880. 192p. (Orig.). (C). 1990. pap. 14.00 (*0-334-02447-1*) TPI PA.

— Wider Vision: A History of the World Congress of Faiths. 1996. pap. 16.95 (*1-85168-119-1*, Pub. by Onewrld Pubns) Penguin Putnam.

Braybrooke, Marcus, jt. auth. see Harpur, James.

Braybrooke, Marcus, jt. ed. see Morgan, Peggy.

Braybrooke, Neville, ed. T. S. Eliot: A Symposium for His Seventieth Birthday. LC 68-58773. (Essay Index Reprint Ser.). 1977. reprint ed. 23.95 (*0-8369-0100-2*) Ayer.

Braybrooke, Patrick. G. K. Chesterton. LC 72-6491. (English Biography Ser.: No. 31). 130p. 1972. reprint ed. lib. bdg. 55.00 (*0-8383-1616-6*) M S G Haskell Hse.

— J. M. Barrie: A Study in Fairies & Mortals. LC 75-174693. (English Biography Ser.: No. 31). 1972. reprint ed. lib. bdg. 75.00 (*0-8383-1349-3*) M S G Haskell Hse.

An Asterisk (*) at the beginning of an entry indicates that the title is appearing for the first time.

— Kipling & His Soldiers. LC 72-3229. (English Literature Ser.: No. 33). 1972. reprint ed. lib. bdg. 75.00 (*0-8383-1506-2*) M S G Haskell Hse.
— Novelists: We Are Seven. LC 67-22075. (Essay Index Reprint Ser.). 1977. 20.95 (*0-8369-1320-5*) Ayer.
— Peeps at the Mighty. LC 67-22076. (Essay Index Reprint Ser.). 1977. 19.95 (*0-8369-1321-3*) Ayer.
— Philosophies in Modern Fiction. LC 67-22077. (Essay Index Reprint Ser.). 1977. 17.95 (*0-8369-1322-1*) Ayer.
— Some Catholic Novelists. LC 67-22078. (Essay Index Reprint Ser.). 1977. 21.95 (*0-8369-1323-X*) Ayer.
— Some Goddesses of the Pen. LC 67-22079. (Essay Index Reprint Ser.). 1977. 19.95 (*0-8369-1324-8*) Ayer.
— Some Thoughts on Hilaire Belloc: 10 Studies. LC 68-1140. (Studies in Irish Literature: No. 16). 1969. reprint ed. lib. bdg. 75.00 (*0-8383-0649-7*) M S G Haskell Hse.
— Some Victorian & Georgian Catholics. LC 67-22080. (Essay Index Reprint Ser.). 1977. 20.95 (*0-8369-1325-6*) Ayer.
— The Subtlety of Shaw. LC 72-2125. (English Literature Ser.: No. 33). 1972. reprint ed. lib. bdg. 75.00 (*0-8383-1465-1*) M S G Haskell Hse.
— Thomas Hardy & His Philosophy. LC 73-9581. (Studies in Thomas Hardy: No. 14). 1973. lib. bdg. 75.00 (*0-8383-1716-2*) M S G Haskell Hse.

Braybrooks, Ann. The Best Thanksgiving Day. LC 97-80713. (Little Golden Bks.). 24p. (J). 1998. 2.29 (*0-307-96009-9*, 96009, Goldn Books) Gldn Bks Pub Co.

***Braybrooks, Ann.** Big Bed for Me! (My Feelings Ser.). (Illus.). (J). 2000. pap. 3.29 (*0-307-13329-X*, Goldn Books) Gldn Bks Pub Co.

Braybrooks, Ann. Disney's Pooh: The Sweetest Christmas. LC 96-75678. (Little Golden Bks.). (J). 1996. 2.29 (*0-307-98788-4*, 98788, Goldn Books) Gldn Bks Pub Co.
— Disney's Sleeping Beauty. LC 97-65590. (Illus.). 32p. (J). 1997. pap. 4.95 (*0-7868-4179-6*, Pub. by Disney Pr) Time Warner.
— The Disney's the Princesses Collection: Stories from the Films. LC 92-56163. (Disney's Collections Ser.). (Illus.). 80p. (J). 1993. 14.95 (*1-56282-497-X*, Pub. by Disney Pr) Time Warner.
— Great Riddle Contest. 24p. 1999. 3.99 (*0-307-16232-X*) Gldn Bks Pub Co.
— Hunny, Funny, Sunny Day. (Pooh Ser.). 24p. 1999. pap. text 2.99 (*0-307-13148-3*) Gldn Bks Pub Co.
— Just Be Nice... And Help a Friend! LC 97-80838. (Super Shape Bks.). 24p. (J). 1998. pap. text 3.29 (*0-307-13312-5*, 13312, Goldn Books) Gldn Bks Pub Co.
— King of the Beasties. (Little Golden Bks.). (Illus.). 24p. (J). 1998. 2.29 (*0-307-98820-1*, 98820, Goldn Books) Gldn Bks Pub Co.

Braybrooks, Ann. Mickey's ABC. 32p. Date not set. write for info. (*0-7868-3088-3*, Pub. by Disney Pr) Little.
— No More Mess. (My Feelings Ser.: No. 3). (Illus.). 24p. (J). (ps-3). 1999. 3.29 (*0-307-13328-1*, 13328, Goldn Books) Gldn Bks Pub Co.
— Plenty of Pockets. LC 98-53784. (Illus.). 34p. (J). (gr. 1-4). 2000. 16.00 (*0-15-202173-6*, Harcourt Child Bks) Harcourt.

Braybrooks, Ann. Pooh Bedtime Stories: Two Tigger Tales. 24p. 1999. pap. text 3.29 (*0-307-13196-3*) Gldn Bks Pub Co.
— Pooh's Best Friend Book & Friendship Bracelet. LC 97-65954. (Illus.). 32p. (J). (gr. 1-4). 1998. 7.95 (*0-7868-3152-9*, Pub. by Disney Pr) Time Warner.
— Pooh's Trick or Treat! LC 97-71235. (Little Golden Bks.). (J). 1997. 2.29 (*0-307-98838-4*, 98838, Goldn Books) Gldn Bks Pub Co.
— The Princess Collection: Stories from the Films. LC 94-80012. (Disney Press Miniature Classics Ser.). (Illus.). 96p. (J). 1996. 5.95 (*0-7868-3076-X*, Pub. by Disney Pr) Time Warner.

***Braybrooks, Ann.** Sweetest Christmas. (Little Golden Storybooks Ser.). (Illus.). (J). 2000. pap. 3.99 (*0-307-16605-8*, Goldn Books) Gldn Bks Pub Co.

Braybrooks, Ann. Tiggers Hate to Lose. LC 98-86080. (Winnie the Pooh First Readers Ser.: No. 8). (Illus.). 40p. (J). (gr. 2-4). 1999. pap. 3.99 (*0-7868-4266-0*, Pub. by Disney Pr) Time Warner.

***Braybrooks, Ann.** Two Best Buddy Tales. (Pooh Bedtime Stories Ser.). (Illus.). (J). 2000. pap. 3.29 (*0-307-13269-2*, Goldn Books) Gldn Bks Pub Co.

Braybrooks, Ann. Walt Disney's Santa's Workshop. LC 94-74819. (Illus.). 32p. (J). (gr. k-3). 1995. 12.95 (*0-7868-3026-3*, Pub. by Disney Pr) Little.
— Walt Disney's Sleeping Beauty. LC 92-56157. (Junior Novelization Ser.). (Illus.). 80p. (J). (gr. 2-6). 1993. pap. 2.95 (*1-56282-368-X*, Pub. by Disney Pr) Time Warner.

***Braybrooks, Ann & Brown, Eliot.** Catdog's Big Idea. LC 99-24001. (Cat Dog Ser.). 32p. 1999. pap. 3.99 (*0-689-83005-X*) S&S Childrens.

Braye, Robert T., et al. The View from Capitol Hill: Lawmakers on Congressional Reform. 78p. (Orig.). (C). 1989. pap. text 10.50 (*0-939715-12-0*) Ctr Politics.

Braye, Suzy & Preston-Shoot, Michael. Empowering Practice in Social Care. LC 94-28838. 208p. 1995. pap. text 31.95 (*0-335-19245-9*) OpUniv Pr.

Brayer, Elizabeth. George Eastman: A Biography. LC 95-9513. (Illus.). 607p. (C). 1996. 39.95 (*0-8018-5263-3*) Johns Hopkins.

Brayer, Herbert O. Pueblo Indian Land Grants of the "Rio Abajo", New Mexico. Bruchey, Stuart, ed. LC 78-56700. (Management of Public Lands in the U. S. Ser.). 1979. reprint ed. lib. bdg. 15.95 (*0-405-11320-X*) Ayer.

Brayer, Herbert O., ed. see Shaw, James C.

Brayer, Menachem M. The Jewish Woman in Rabbinic Literature: A Psychohistorical Perspective. Date not set. 20.00 (*0-88125-073-2*) Yeshiva Univ Pr.
— The Jewish Woman in Rabbinic Literature: A Psychohistorical Perspective, Vol. I. 300p. 1986. pap. text 16.95 (*0-88125-070-8*) Ktav.
— The Jewish Woman in Rabbinic Literature: A Psychohistorical Perspective, 2 vols., Vol. II. 400p. 1986. pap. text 16.95 (*0-88125-072-4*) Ktav.

Brayfield, April A., et al. Caring for Children in Low-Income Families: A Substudy of the National Child Care Survey 1990. LC 93-16112. (Urban Institute Report: No. 93-2). 160p. (Orig.). (C). 1993. pap. text 18.50 (*0-87766-587-7*); lib. bdg. 46.50 (*0-87766-586-9*) Urban Inst.

Brayfield, Celia. Bestseller: Secrets of Successful Writing. 256p. 1997. pap. 13.95 (*1-85702-383-8*, Pub. by Fourth Estate) Trafalgar.

***Brayfield, Celia.** Sunset. large type ed. LC 99-49111. (General Ser.). 2000. pap. 23.95 (*0-7862-2248-4*) Thorndike Pr.

Brayfield, Lelia & Brayfield, William. A Guide for Identifying Florida Fossil Shells & Other Invertebrates. 112p. 1993. pap. 9.95 (*1-883167-02-7*) FL Paleo Soc.

Brayfield, William, jt. auth. see Brayfield, Lelia.

Braylan. Diagnostic Hematopathology. 1997. 145.00 (*0-397-51516-2*, B2827) Lppncott W & W.

Brayles, Anne. Journaling. 13.35 (*0-687-60584-9*) Abingdon.

Brayley, Caroline R. Clinician to Academician: A Handbook for Those Who Aspire to Become Faculty Members. 65p. (Orig.). 1996. pap. 20.00 (*1-56900-031-X*, 1141) Am Occup Therapy.

Brayley, E. W., jt. auth. see Britton, John.

Brayley, Martin. World War II British Women's Uniforms in Color Photographs. (Illus.). 96p. 1997. pap. 19.95 (*1-85915-032-2*, Pub. by W & G) Motorbooks Intl.

Brayley, Martin & Ingrams, Richard. World War II Tommy: British Army Uniforms - European Theatre, 1939-1945 in Colour Photographs. LC 99-531063. (Illus.). 144p. 1999. 44.95 (*1-86126-190-X*, 128248AE) Motorbooks Intl.

Brayley, Russell E., jt. auth. see Searle, Mark S.

Braymer, Daniel H. Electric Motor Repair. (Illus.). 515p. 1991. pap. 18.00 (*1-877767-53-0*) Univ Publng Hse.

Braynard, F. O. World's Greatest Ship: The Story of the S. S. Leviathan, Vol. III. Hamshar, Walter, ed. (Illus.). 400p. 1976. 30.00 (*0-9606204-2-7*) F O Braynard.

Braynard, Frank O. Leviathan, Vol. 4. 424p. 1978. 45.00 (*0-685-34209-3*) F O Braynard.
— Lives of the Liners. LC 48-304. (Illus.). 220p. 1947. reprint ed. pap. 68.20 (*0-608-02462-7*, 206310600004) Bks Demand.
— One Square Mile. (Illus.). 144p. 1986. 14.00 (*0-317-39401-0*) F O Braynard.
— Picture History of the Cunard Line, 1840-1990, Vol. 199. (Illus.). 144p. 1991. pap. 14.95 (*0-486-26550-1*) Dover.
— Picture History of the "Normandie" (Illus.). 144p. 1987. pap. 12.95 (*0-486-25257-4*) Dover.
— Search for the Tall Ships. (Illus.). 144p. 1986. 20.00 (*0-317-39399-5*) F O Braynard.
— Story of the Titanic. 1988. text 4.95 (*0-486-25611-1*) Dover.
— The Tall Ships of Today in Photographs. LC 93-18442. (Illus.). 128p. (Orig.). 1993. pap. 13.95 (*0-486-27163-3*) Dover.
— Worlds Greatest Ship: The Story of the S. S. Leviathan, Vol. I. Hamshar, Walter, ed. (Illus.). 288p. 1972. 50.00 (*0-9606204-0-0*) F O Braynard.
— World's Greatest Ship: The Story of the S. S. Leviathan, Vol. II. Hamshar, Walter, ed. (Illus.). 382p. 1974. 30.00 (*0-9606204-1-9*) F O Braynard.
— World's Greatest Ship: The Story of the S. S. Leviathan, Vol. V. Hamshar, Walter, ed. (Illus.). 424p. (C). 1980. 45.00 (*0-9606204-3-5*) F O Braynard.
— World's Greatest Ship: The Story of the S. S. Leviathan, Vol. VI. (Illus.). 448p. (C). 1983. 59.00 (*0-9606204-5-1*) F O Braynard.

Brayne, Hugh. LPC Case Study: Criminal Litigation. 167p. 1994. pap. 24.00 (*1-85431-387-8*, Pub. by Blackstone Pr) Gaunt.
— LPC Case Study: Criminal Litigation, 1995/96. 202p. 1995. 9.95 (*1-85431-477-7*, Pub. by Blackstone Pr) Gaunt.
— LPC Case Study: Criminal Litigation, 1996/97. 3rd ed. 191p. 1996. pap. 26.00 (*1-85431-578-1*, Pub. by Blackstone Pr) Gaunt.

Brayne, Hugh & Martin, Gerry. Law for Social Workers. 3rd ed. 377p. 1993. 33.00 (*1-85431-288-X*, Pub. by Blackstone Pr) Gaunt.
— Law for Social Workers. 4th ed. 414p. 1995. pap. 30.00 (*1-85431-442-4*, Pub. by Blackstone Pr) Gaunt.
— Law for Social Workers. 5th rev. ed. LC 98-178677. 435p. 1997. pap. 36.00 (*1-85431-684-2*, Pub. by Blackstone Pr) Gaunt.

***Brayne, Hugh & Martin, Gerry.** Law for Social Workers. 6th ed. 479p. 1999. pap. 32.00 (*1-85431-888-8*, Pub. by Blackstone Pr) Gaunt.

Brayne, Hugh & Plowden, Philip. LPC Case Study: Criminal Litigation, 1997/98. 4th rev. ed. 193p. 1997. pap. 28.00 (*1-85431-696-6*, Pub. by Blackstone Pr) Gaunt.
— LPC Case Study: Criminal Litigation, 1998-99. 5th ed. (Legal Practice Course Guides Ser.). 218p. 1998. pap. 36.00 (*1-85431-790-3*) Gaunt.

Brayne, Hugh, et al. Clinical Legal Education: Active Learning in Your Law School. 278p. 1998. pap. 42.00 (*1-85431-831-4*, 15561, Pub. by Blackstone Pr) Gaunt.

Brayshaw, A. Neave. The Quakers: Their Story & Message. 1999. pap. 23.00 (*0-900657-64-2*, Pub. by W Sessions) St Mut.

***Brayshaw, David.** The Road to Beijing. (Illus.). 206p. 2000. pap. 19.95 (*1-85776-403-X*, Pub. by Book Guild Ltd) Trans-Atl Phila.

Brayshaw, Eileen & Wright, Pauline. Antenatal Exercises. 1996. pap. text 19.50 (*1-898507-29-5*) Buttrwrth-Heinemann.

Brayshaw, R. The Concise Guide to Company Finance & Its Management. (Concise Guide Ser.). 160p. 1992. mass mkt. 24.95 (*0-412-35780-1*) Chapman & Hall.

Brayshaw, T. Christopher. Trees & Shrubs of British Columbia. rev. ed. LC 97-124282. (Royal British Columbia Museum Handbook Ser.). (Illus.). 400p. 1996. pap. 25.95 (*0-7748-0564-1*) U of Wash Pr.

Brayshay, Mark, ed. Topographical Writers in South-West England. 216p. 1997. pap. 24.95 (*0-85989-424-X*, Pub. by Univ Exeter Pr) Northwestern U Pr.

Brayton, Isabella & Norton, J. B. Story of Hartford: A History. (Illus.). 212p. 1997. reprint ed. lib. bdg. 29.00 (*0-8328-6889-2*) Higginson Bk Co.

Brayton, Robert K., et al. Logic Minimization Algorithms for VLSI Synthesis. (Kluwer International Series in Engineering & Computer Science). 1984. reprint ed. text 98.50 (*0-89838-164-9*) Kluwer Academic.

Brayton, Robert K., jt. auth. see Lam, William K.

Brayton, Robert K., jt. auth. see McGeer, Patrick C.

Braz, Julio E. En La Oscuridad (In the Darkness) Andreu, Fatima, tr. (SPA., Illus.). (YA). 1993. pap. 6.99 (*968-16-4267-8*, Pub. by Fondo) Continental Bk.
— Saguairu. (SPA.). 80p. (YA). 1991. pap. 6.99 (*968-16-3659-7*, Pub. by Fondo) Continental Bk.

Braza, J., ed. see International Conference on Surface Modifications.

Braza, Jerry. Moment by Moment: The Art & Practice of Mindfulness. LC 97-4179. 112p. 1997. pap. 12.95 (*0-8048-3113-0*) Tuttle Pubng.

Brazaitis, Mark. The River of Lost Voices: Stories from Guatemala. LC 98-24437. (Iowa Short Fiction Award Ser.). 202p. 1998. pap. 16.95 (*0-87745-642-9*) U of Iowa Pr.

***Brazaitis, Mark.** Steal My Heart. LC 99-46825. 275p. 2000. 25.00 (*0-9657639-8-6*) Van Neste.

Brazaitis, Peter & Watanabe, Myrna. The Fight for Survival: Animals in Their Natural Habitats. LC 94-7191. (Illus.). 348p. 1994. 24.98 (*1-56799-094-0*, Friedman-Fairfax) M Friedman Pub Grp Inc.

Brazaitis, Tom, jt. auth. see Clift, Eleanor.

Brazaltis, Peter & Wantanabe, Myrna E. World of Snakes. (Illus.). 176p. 1994. 26.95 (*1-56465-117-7*, 16091) Tetra Pr.

Brazda, Jana L., jt. auth. see Bonilla, Carlos A.

Brazda, Johann, et al. Pioniergenossenschaften: Am Beispiel der Konsumgenossenschaften in Grobbritannien, Schweden & Japan. (Forschungen zur Wirtschafts-, Finanz- und Sozialgeschichte Ser.: Bd. 4). (GER., Illus.). 301p. 1996. pap. 57.95 (*3-631-46488-6*) P Lang Pubng.

Brazdil, James F., jt. ed. see Grasselli, Robert K.

Brazdil, Pavel B., ed. Machine Learning, ECML '93: European Conference on Machine Learning, Vienna, Austria, April 5-7, 1993, Proceedings. LC 93-12645. (Lecture Notes in Computer Science Ser.: Vol. 667). 1993. 65.95 (*0-387-56602-3*) Spr-Verlag.

Brazdil, Pavel B. & Konolige, Kurt, eds. Machine Learning: Meta-Reasoning & Logics. (C). 1989. text 118.50 (*0-7923-9047-4*) Kluwer Academic.

Brazeau, Gayle, jt. ed. see Gupta, Pramod.

Brazeau, Peter, jt. auth. see Fountain, Gary.

Brazee, Mark. Blood, Fire, & Vapor of Smoke. rev. ed. 120p. (Orig.). 1996. pap. 7.00 (*0-934445-06-0*) Eternal Word.
— Does the Problem Look Bigger Than Your Faith. 7th ed. Orig. Title: How to Keep Your Faith Working. 32p. 1985. 1.50 (*0-934445-00-1*) Eternal Word.
— Healing: Choice or Chance. 6th ed. 32p. 1985. 1.50 (*0-934445-01-X*) Eternal Word.

***Brazee, Mark.** Locking Arms for the Harvest: The Power of Partnership. 2nd ed. 46p. 1999. pap. 1.20 (*0-934445-09-5*) Eternal Word.

Brazee, Mark. Prayer, Power, & Prosperity: Three Keys to a Move of God. 119p. 1998. pap. 7.00 (*0-934445-05-2*) Eternal Word.
— Preparing for His Glory. 120p. 1993. pap. 7.00 (*0-934445-02-8*) Eternal Word.

***Brazee, Mark.** Prescription for A Miracle: A Daily Devotional for Divine Health. 1999. pap. text 19.99 (*1-57794-209-4*) Harrison Hse.
— Prescription for A Miracle: A Daily Devotional for Divine Health. 1999. pap. text 15.99 (*1-57794-208-6*) Harrison Hse.

Brazee, Mark. Processing the Plan of God Through Prayer. 107p. 1998. pap. 7.00 (*0-934445-07-9*) Eternal Word.

Brazell, Bill, jt. auth. see Bader, Jenny L.

Brazell, Karen. Traditional Japanese Theater: An Anthology of Plays. Araki, James T., tr. from JPN. LC 97-23964. (Translations from the Asian Classics Ser.). 1997. pap. 18.50 (*0-231-10873-7*) Col U Pr.
— Traditional Japanese Theater: An Anthology of Plays. Araki, James T., tr. LC 97-23964. (Illus.). 464p. 1998. 52.00 (*0-231-10872-9*) Col U Pr.

Brazell, Karen, ed. Twelve Plays of the Noh & Kyogen Theaters. (Cornell East Asia Ser.: No. 50). 272p. 1988. pap. 14.45 (*0-939657-00-7*) Cornell East Asia Pgm.

Brazell, Karen, tr. from JPN. The Confessions of Lady Nijo. 320p. 1973. pap. 15.95 (*0-8047-0930-0*) Stanford U Pr.

Brazell, Karen, jt. auth. see Bethe, Monica.

Brazell, Margaret. Growing Trees on the Great Plains. LC 91-58488. (Illus.). 160p. (Orig.). 1992. pap. 14.95 (*1-55591-096-3*) Fulcrum Pub.

Brazell, Rob, jt. auth. see Hendrix, Roger.

Brazelton, Berry T. Going to the Doctor. (Illus.). 48p. (J). 1996. 15.00 (*0-201-40694-2*) Addison-Wesley.

***Brazelton, Julia K.** A Practical Guide to Tax Issues in Employment. (Illus.). 336p. 1999. reprint ed. text 95.00 (*0-8080-0385-2*, 0-5300-100) CCH INC.

Brazelton, T. Berry. The Earliest Relationship. LC 89-39839. 1991. pap. 13.00 (*0-201-56764-4*) Addison-Wesley.
— Infants & Mothers. rev. ed. 336p. 1983. pap. 18.95 (*0-440-50685-9*) Dell.
— To Listen to a Child. 1986. pap. 9.57 (*0-201-10554-3*) Addison-Wesley.
— To Listen to a Child: Understanding the Normal Problems of Growing Up. 1984. 15.95 (*0-201-10617-5*) Addison-Wesley.
— To Listen to a Child: Understanding the Normal Problems of Growing Up. (Illus.). 192p. 1992. pap. 13.00 (*0-201-63270-5*) Addison-Wesley.
— Toddlers & Parents. rev. ed. 272p. 1989. pap. 18.95 (*0-440-50643-3*) Dell.
— Touchpoints - The Essential Reference: Your Child's Emotional & Behavioral Development. (Illus.). 512p. 1994. pap. 17.00 (*0-201-62690-X*) Addison-Wesley.
— Working & Caring. (Illus.). 224p. 1992. pap. 13.00 (*0-201-63271-3*) Addison-Wesley.

***Brazelton, T. Berry & Greenspan, Stanley.** The Irreducible Needs of Children: What Every Child Must Have to Grow, Learn & Flourish. 160p. 2000. text 23.00 (*0-7382-0325-4*, Pub. by Perseus Pubng) HarpC.

Brazelton, T. Berry & Nugent, J. Kevin, eds. Neonatal Behavioural Assessment Scale. 3rd ed. (Clinics in Developmental Medicine Ser.: No. 137). (Illus.). 159p. (C). 1995. 33.95 (*1-898683-05-0*, Pub. by Mc Keith Pr) Cambridge U Pr.

Brazelton, T. Berry & Yogman, Michael E., eds. Affective Development in Infancy. LC 85-3396. 168p. 1986. text 73.25 (*0-89391-345-6*) Ablx Pub.

Brazelton, T. Berry, jt. auth. see Vaughan, Victor C.

Brazelton, T. Berry, jt. ed. see Barnard, Kathryn E.

Brazelton, T. Berry, jt. ed. see Kobayashi, Noboru.

Brazelton, T. Berry, jt. ed. see Yogman, Michael W.

Brazelton, W. Robert. Alternative Economic Perspectives: A Primer on the Streams of Economic Analysis, 1994-95. 256p. (C). 1994. pap. text, per. 31.95 (*0-8403-9225-7*) Kendall-Hunt.

***Brazelton, W. Robert.** Designing U. S. Economic Policy: An Analytical Biography of Leon H. Keyserling. LC 00-33328. 2000. write for info. (*0-312-23782-0*) St Martin.

Brazendale, Kevin, ed. Encyclopedia of Classic Cars. LC 99-44936. (Illus.). 640p. 1999. 34.98 (*1-57145-182-X*, Thunder Bay) Advantage Pubs.

Brazer, Fuller W., jt. ed. see Sharp, Dan C.

Brazer, Harvey E. City Expenditures in the United States: Supplement, Appendix E. (Occasional Papers: No. 66). 94p. 1959. reprint ed. 24.50 (*0-87014-380-8*) Natl Bur Econ Res.

Braziel, Dennis J. Family-Focused Practice in Out-of-Home Care: A Handbook & Resource Directory. LC 96-23955. 1995. pap. 14.95 (*0-87868-635-5*) Child Welfare.

Braziel, Rick, jt. auth. see Kidd, Virginia.

Brazier, Arthur M. From Milk to Meat. 140p. 1996. pap. 9.99 (*1-56043-278-0*, Treasure Hse) Destiny Image.

Brazier, Chris. Vietnam: The Price of Peace. (Country Profiles Ser.). (Illus.). 64p. (C). 1992. pap. 9.95 (*0-85598-152-0*, Pub. by Oxfam Pub) Stylus Pub VA.

Brazier, David. Beyond Carl Rogers: Towards a Psychotherapy for the 21st Century. 287p. (Orig.). 1998. pap. 19.95 (*0-09-472610-8*, Pub. by Constable & Co) Trafalgar.
— The Feeling Buddha. LC 98-28558. 208p. 1998. 23.00 (*0-88064-198-3*) Fromm Intl Pub.

***Brazier, David.** Feeling Buddha. 2000. pap. 13.00 (*0-88064-223-8*) Fromm Intl Pub.

Brazier, David. Zen Therapy: Transcending the Sorrows of the Human Mind. LC 96-22591. 288p. 1996. 69.95 (*0-471-15563-2*) Wiley.

Brazier, David. Zen Therapy: Transcending the Sorrows of the Human Mind. 288p. 1997. pap. 17.95 (*0-471-19283-X*) Wiley.

Brazier, Gil. Insider Dealing: Law & Regulation. 311p. 1996. pap. 89.90 (*1-874241-02-3*, Pub. by Cavendish Pubng) Gaunt.

Brazier, Margaret. Medicine, Patients & the Law. pap. 29.95 (*0-14-012749-6*, Pub. by Pnguin Bks Ltd) Trafalgar.

Brazier, Margaret. Street on Torts. 9th ed. 632p. 1993. pap. 52.00 (*0-406-00591-5*, U.K., MICHIE) LEXIS Pub.

Brazier, Margaret & Murphy, John. Street on Torts. 10th ed. 1997. pap. write for info. (*0-406-89103-6*, ST10, MICHIE) LEXIS Pub.

Brazier, Margaret, et al. Review for Health Ministers of Current Arrangements for Payments & Regulation: Report of the Review Team. LC 98-223287. 73 p. 1998. 25.00 (*0-10-140682-7*, Pub. by Statnry Office) Bernan Associates.

Brazier, Margaret, ed. see Fletcher, Nina & Holt, Janet.

Brazier, Mary A. A History of Neurophysiology in the 17th & 18th Centuries: From Concept to Experiment. LC 83-23106. (Illus.). 244p. 1984. reprint ed. pap. 75.70 (*0-608-07227-3*, 206745200009) Bks Demand.

Brazier, Mary A. & Coceani, Flavio, eds. Brain Dysfunction in Infantile Febrile Convulsions. LC 75-14564. (International Brain Research Organization Monograph Ser.: Vol. 2). 384p. 1976. reprint ed. pap. 119.10 (*0-608-00351-4*, 206106700007) Bks Demand.

Brazier, Mary A. & Petsche, Hellmuth, eds. Architectonics of the Cerebral Cortex. LC 77-83694. (International Brain Research Organization Monograph Ser.: Vol. 3). 502p. 1978. reprint ed. pap. 155.70 (*0-608-00376-X*, 206108900007) Bks Demand.

B

Brazier, Mary A., ed. see International Symposium on Developmental Neurobiology Staff.

***Brazier, Rodney.** Constitutional Practice: The Foundations of British Government. 3rd ed. LC 98-56186. 1999. write for info. (*0-19-829811-0*) OUP.

Brazier, Rodney. Constitutional Practice: The Foundations of British Government. 3rd ed. LC 98-56186. 348p. 1999. text 70.00 (*0-19-829812-9*) OUP.

— Constitutional Reform. 2nd ed. 204p. 1998. pap. text (*0-19-876523-1*) OUP.

— Constitutional Reform. 2nd ed. 208p. 1998. 75.00 (*0-19-876524-X*) OUP.

— Constitutional Texts: Materials on Government & the Constitution. 640p. 1990. 85.00 (*0-19-876246-1*) OUP.

— Ministers of the Crown. 414p. 1997. text 90.00 (*0-19-825988-3*) OUP.

Brazier, Roy. Empty Fields: The Agricultural Strike of 1914. 1993. pap. 16.00 (*0-86025-427-5*, Pub. by I Henry Pubns) Empire Pub Srvs.

***Brazil-Adelman, Mary Belle.** The German Shepherd Handbook. LC 00-41374. (Illus.). 2000. write for info. (*0-88402-278-1*) Dumbarton Oaks.

B

Brazil, David. A Grammar of Speech. Sinclair, John & Carter, Ronald, eds. (Illus.). 280p. 1995. pap. text 21.95 (*0-19-437193-X*) OUP.

Brazil, James. Cheaters Always Prosper: 50 Ways to Beat the System Without Being Caught. 140p. 1996. pap. text 10.95 (*0-8065-1809-X*, Citadel Pr) Carol Pub Group.

Brazil, June, et al, eds. Clean Needle Technique Manual for Acupuncturists: Guidelines & Standards for the Clean & Safe Clinical Practice. 4th rev. ed. 58p. 1997. 15.00 (*0-9670262-1-0*) Natl Acup Fndt.

— Clean Needle Technique Manual for Acupuncturists: Guidelines & Standards for the Clean & Safe Clinical Practice. 4th rev. ed. (KOR.). 67p. 1997. 15.00 (*0-9670262-3-7*) Natl Acup Fndt.

— Clean Needle Technique Manual for Acupuncturists: Guidelines & Standards for the Clean & Safe Clinical Practice. 4th rev. ed. Wu, Hua, tr. (CHI.). 45p. 1997. 15.00 (*0-9670262-2-9*) Natl Acup Fndt.

Brazil, Mark. A Bird Watcher's Guide to Japan. LC 87-81675. (Illus.). 220p. 1988. pap. 13.95 (*0-87011-849-8*) Kodansha.

***Brazil, Mark.** Wild Asia: Spirit of a Continent. 2000. 49.95 (*1-56554-827-2*) Pelican.

— Wild Asia: Spirit of a Continent. (Illus.). 2000. pap. 5.95 (*1-56554-836-1*) Pelican.

— Wild Asian Birds: Spirit of a Continent. (Illus.). 2000. pap. 5.95 (*1-56554-837-X*) Pelican.

Brazil, Mary J. Building Library Collections on Aging. LC 90-42163. 175p. 1990. lib. bdg. 45.00 (*0-87436-559-7*) ABC-CLIO.

Brazil, Nick. A Journey with Ghosts: Adventures in the Supernatural Heart of Britain & Beyond. (Illus.). 275p. 1999. 29.50 (*1-85776-317-3*, Pub. by Book Guild Ltd) Trans-Atl Phila.

Brazil, Tom. Dances by Mark Morris. (Orig.). 1993. pap. 15.00 (*0-685-67272-7*) Dance Res Found.

Brazil, Wayne D. Effective Approaches to Settlement: A Handbook for Lawyers & Judges. 582p. 1988. 85.00 (*0-13-241423-6*) Aspen Law.

Brazil, Wayne D., et al. Managing Complex Litigation: A Practical Guide to the Use of Special Masters. LC 83-71543. xi, 394p. 1983. 35.00 (*0-910059-03-9*, 304970) W S Hein.

Brazile, Lionel J., Jr. Arithmetic Summary Booklet. (Illus.). 16p. (Orig.). (J). (gr. 1-9). 1990. pap. 12.95 (*0-9624016-0-9*) Scholar Pub Co.

Brazile, Robert. Case Study in C++ 1999. text. write for info. (*0-201-63355-8*) Addison-Wesley.

Brazilian Conference on Mathematical Logic Staff. Mathematical Logic: Proceedings of the First Brazilian Conference, Held 1977. Arruda, Ayda I. et al, eds. LC 78-14488. (Lecture Notes in Pure & Applied Mathematics Ser.: No. 39). 319p. 1978. reprint ed. pap. 98.90 (*0-608-01331-5*, 206207400001) Bks Demand.

Brazilian Conference on Mathematical Logic Staff, et al. Advances in Contemporary Logic & Computer Science: Proceedings of the 11th Brazilian Conference on Mathematical Logic, May 6-10, 1996, Salvador da Bahia, Brazil. LC 99-23309. (Contemporary Mathematics Ser.). 1999. write for info. (*0-8218-1364-1*) Am Math.

Brazill, William J. Young Hegelians. 305p. 1970. 79.50 (*0-300-01275-6*) Elliots Bks.

***Brazill, William P., ed.** Mendocino Artists: An Endangered Species. (Illus.). 48p. 2000. pap. 18.95 (*0-9627007-5-4*) Monday Pr CA.

Brazille, Leonard, ed. see Kellogg, John H.

Brazinsky, Terri C. & Bowden, Kathi, eds. Santa Catalina Cookbook, Vol. II. (Illus.). 400p. 1983. 17.50 (*0-9612300-1-0*) Santa Catalina.

Brazis, Paul W. Loc Clinical Neurology, No. 2. 2nd ed. 1990. 84.95 (*0-316-10743-3*, Little Brwn Med Div) Lppncott W & W.

Brazis, Paul W., et al. Localization in Clinical Neurology. 429p. 1985. 45.00 (*0-316-10721-2*, Little Brwn Med Div) Lppncott W & W.

— Localization in Clinical Neurology. 3rd ed. 384p. 1996. text 105.00 (*0-316-09992-9*) Lppncott W & W.

Brazis, Paul W., jt. auth. see Lee, Andrew G.

***Braznell, William.** An Airman's Odyssey: Walt Braznell & the Pilots He Led into the Jet Age. (Illus.). 256p. 2000. 34.95 (*0-8262-1306-5*) U of Mo Pr.

Brazos. Life of Robert Hall: Indian Fighter & Veteran of Three Great Wars: Also Sketch of Big Foot Wallace. LC 92-28058. (Illus.). 160p. 1992. 24.95 (*0-938349-89-9*) State House Pr.

— Life of Robert Hall: Indian Fighter & Veteran of Three Great Wars: Also Sketch of Big Foot Wallace. LC 92-28058. (Illus.). 160p. 1992. pap. 14.95 (*0-938349-90-2*) State House Pr.

— Life of Robert Hall: Indian Fighter & Veteran of Three Great Wars: Also Sketch of Big Foot Wallace. limited ed. LC 92-28058. (Illus.). 160p. 1992. 60.00 (*0-938349-91-0*) State House Pr.

Brazouski, Antoinette & Klatt, Mary J., eds. Children's Books on Ancient Greek & Roman Mythology: An Annotated Bibliography, 40. LC 93-29896. (Bibliographies & Indexes in World Literature Ser.: No. 40). 208p. (J). 1993. lib. bdg. 59.95 (*0-313-28973-5*, Greenwood Pr) Greenwood.

Brazzil, James W. The House of Coot. LC 94-96547. (Illus.). 96p. 1994. write for info. (*0-9620993-1-7*) J W Brazzil.

— Owl Creek. LC 88-92061. (Illus.). 144p. 1988. 12.50 (*0-9620993-0-9*) J W Brazzil.

Brcic, V. Application of Holography & Hologram Interferometry to Photoelasticity. 2nd ed. (CISM International Centre for Mechanical Sciences Ser.: Vol. 14). (Illus.). 58p. 1975. 16.95 (*0-387-81163-X*) Spr-Verlag.

Brcic, V., ed. see CISM (International Center for Mechanical Sciences.

Brdanovic, D. Modeling Biological Phosphorus Removal in Activated Sludge Systems. (IHE Thesis Ser.: No. 17). 251p. (C). 1998. text 42.00 (*90-5410-415-5*, Pub. by A A Balkema) Ashgate Pub Co.

Brdys, M. A. & Malinowski, K. Computer Aided Control System: Methods, Tools. 560p. 1994. text 105.00 (*981-02-1391-3*) World Scientific Pub.

Brea, Yehuda L., jt. auth. see Sliflein, Nosson.

Breacher, Bob & Fleischmann, Otakar. Liberalism & the New Europe. (Philosophy of Science Ser.). 205p. 1993. 64.95 (*1-85628-538-3*, Pub. by Avebry) Ashgate Pub Co.

Bread & Roses Staff, jt. auth. see Hansen, Joyce.

Bread for the World Institute on Hunger & Developm. Hunger Nineteen Ninety Study Aid. (C). 1990. pap. text 1.50 (*0-9628058-1-5*) Bread for the World.

Bread for the World Institute Staff. Countries in Crisis: Hunger 1996. 113p. 1995. 17.95 (*1-884361-03-X*) Bread for the World.

— Hunger 1990: A Report on the State of World Hunger. (Illus.). 132p. (J). (gr. 3 up). 1990. pap. write for info. (*0-9628058-0-7*) Bread for the World.

Bread Research Institute of Australia Staff. The Australian Breadmaking Handbook. (Illus.). 250p. 1990. pap. 27.95 (*0-908237-36-7*, Pub. by New South Wales Univ Pr) Intl Spec Bk.

Breaden, Radhika S., et al. Prescription for the Boards: A Student-to-Student Guide. LC 95-45312. 512p. 1995. pap. text 29.95 (*0-316-10626-7*) Lppncott W & W.

Breaden, Radhika S., jt. auth. see Feibusch, Kate C.

Breadlove, Buzz. Motor-Vehicle Inspection & Maintenance in California. 42p. 1993. pap. write for info. (*1-58703-013-6*, CRB-93-007) CA St Libry.

Bready, James H. Baseball in Baltimore: The First Hundred Years. LC 97-43217. (Illus.). 272p. 1998. pap. 34.95 (*0-8018-5833-X*) Johns Hopkins.

Bready, Lois L., jt. ed. see Graybar, Gwendolyn B.

Bready, Luis L., et al. Decision Making in Anesthesiology. 3rd ed. LC 99-40692. (Illus.). 540p. (C). (gr. 13). 1999. text 65.95 (*0-8151-2455-4*, 31187) Mosby Inc.

Breag, G. R., et al. Biomass Combustion Systems: Flue Gas Losses & Equipment Efficiency. 1992. pap. 25.00 (*0-85954-304-8*, Pub. by Nat Res Inst) St Mut.

— Wood Carbonization Unit: Design & Development of a Prototype with Recovery of Waste Heat. 1992. pap. 50.00 (*0-85954-306-4*, Pub. by Nat Res Inst) St Mut.

Breag, G. R., jt. auth. see Robinson, A. P.

Breagy, James. Bank CDCs: Instruments for Community Investment. 72p. (Orig.). 1990. pap. 22.50 (*0-317-04831-7*) Natl Coun Econ Dev.

— Commercializing Technology: Linking Research to the Marketplace. Murphy, Jenny, ed. 60p. (Orig.). 1989. pap. 21.50 (*0-317-04915-1*) Natl Coun Econ Dev.

— Community Colleges: An Economic Development Resource. Murphy, Jenny, ed. 38p. (Orig.). 1989. pap. 21.50 (*0-317-04917-8*) Natl Coun Econ Dev.

— Technology Transfer & Economic Development. Murphy, Jenny, ed. 72p. (Orig.). 1990. pap. 22.50 (*0-317-04804-X*) Natl Coun Econ Dev.

— Turning Disadvantaged Youth into an Economic Development Resource: Education & Training Linkages. Murphy, Jenny, ed. 62p. (Orig.). 1991. pap. 22.50 (*0-317-04802-3*) Natl Coun Econ Dev.

Breagy, James & Murphy, Jenny. Utilities As Catalysts in Economic Development. 34p. (Orig.). 1989. pap. 21.50 (*0-317-04805-8*) Natl Coun Econ Dev.

Breagy, James, jt. ed. see Unger, James.

Break, George F. Federal Lending & Economic Stability. LC 79-28549. (Illus.). 185p. 1980. reprint ed. lib. bdg. 59.50 (*0-313-22285-1*, BRFS, Greenwood Pr) Greenwood.

— Financing Government in a Federal System. LC 79-3775. (Studies of Government Finance). 276p. 1980. 32.95 (*0-8157-1068-2*); pap. 12.95 (*0-8157-1067-4*) Brookings.

Break, George F., ed. Metropolitan Financing & Growth Management Policies: Principles & Practice, Proceedings of a Symposium. LC 77-77444. (Publications of the Committee on Taxation, Resources & Economic Development: Vol. 9). 345p. 1978. reprint ed. pap. 107.00 (*0-608-01983-6*, 206263800003) Bks Demand.

— State & Local Finance: The Pressures of the 1980s: Proceedings of a Symposium Sponsored by the Committee on Taxation, Resources & Economic Development (TRED) at the Lincoln Institute of Land Policy, Cambridge MA, 1980. LC 83-47757. (Publications of the Committee on Taxation, Resources & Economic Development: Vol. 12). 255p. 1983. reprint ed. pap. 79.10 (*0-608-01984-4*, 206263900003) Bks Demand.

Break, George F. & Pechman, Joseph A. Federal Tax Reform: The Impossible Dream? LC 75-22391. (Studies of Government Finance). 142p. 1975. pap. 8.95 (*0-8157-1071-2*) Brookings.

Breakefield, Xandra O., jt. ed. see Chiocca, E. Antonio.

Breakell, M. Environmental Planning in Canada. (C). 1986. 45.00 (*0-7855-3833-X*, Pub. by Oxford Polytechnic) St Mut.

— Roads in Central Oxfordshire. (C). 1988. 29.00 (*0-7855-3819-4*, Pub. by Oxford Polytechnic) St Mut.

Breakell, M, et al, eds. Caring for the Countryside: The Proceedings of a Conference Held at Oxford Polytechnic in Conjunction with the Oxfordshire Countryside Group. (C). 1984. 50.00 (*0-7855-3840-2*, Pub. by Oxford Polytechnic) St Mut.

Breakell, M. & Glasson, J., eds. Environmental Impact Assessment - From Theory to Practice: From a Conference Sponsored by South East Branch of the Royal Town Planning Institute. (C). 1981. 55.00 (*0-7855-3867-4*, Pub. by Oxford Polytechnic) St Mut.

Breakenridge, William M. Helldorado: Bringing the Law to the Mesquite. (American Biography Ser.). 256p. 1991. reprint ed. lib. bdg. 69.00 (*0-7812-8037-0*) Rprt Serv.

— Helldorado: Bringing the Law to the Mesquite. Brown, Richard M., ed. & intro. by. LC 92-15378. (Illus.). xxxiii, 448p. 1992. reprint ed. pap. 17.95 (*0-8032-6100-4*, Bison Books) U of Nebr Pr.

***Breakey, Beverly M.** Choose Life! Living Consciously in an Unconscious World. LC 99-91248. (Illus.). xix, 317p. 2000. pap. 19.95 (*0-9674738-0-2*, Pub. by Ashar Pr) Bookpeople.

— Choose Life! The Conscious Living Companion Workbook. (Illus.). 300p. 2001. pap., wbk. ed. 16.95 (*0-9674738-2-9*, Pub. by Ashar Pr) Bookpeople.

— This Is a Brand New Day: A Handbook for Living Consciously. unabridged ed. 366p. 2000. pap. 12.95 (*0-9674738-1-0*, Pub. by Ashar Pr) Bookpeople.

***Breakey, Lise & Thomas, Bruce.** Furry Pirates: Swashbuckling Adventure in the Furry Age of Piracy. (Illus.). 176p. 1999. pap. 22.95 (*1-887801-72-3*) Trident MN.

Breakey, William R., ed. Integrated Mental Health Services: Modern Community Psychiatry. (Illus.). 448p. (C). 1996. text 55.00 (*0-19-507421-1*) OUP.

Breakey, William R. & Thompson, James W., eds. Mentally Ill & Homeless: Special Programs for Special Needs. (Chronic Mental Illness Ser.). 208p. 1998. text 31.00 (*90-5702-557-4*, Harwood Acad Pubs) Gordon & Breach.

Breakstone, David & Jochnowitz, Cindy, eds. The Israel Experience Book. LC 76-56985. (Illus.). 240p. 1985. reprint ed. pap. 8.95 (*0-8197-0021-5*) Bloch.

Breakstone, Steve. Washington Walkabout. Marsh, Jerry & Hurt, Rory, eds. (Illus.). 256p. (Orig.). (YA). 1992. pap. 13.95 (*0-9632724-4-6*) Balance Pubns.

Breakthrough Publications Staff. Flatwork Routines for Every Horse & Rider: Design Your Own Training Program with These 110 Routines. 2000. pap. text 29.95 (*0-914327-79-8*) Breakthrgh NY.

Breakthrough Staff. Draw & Color Beautiful Horses: Including Your Own. 1996. pap. text 14.95 (*0-914327-66-6*) Breakthrgh NY.

Breakwell, Glynis, et al, eds. Research Methods in Psychology. 432p. 1995. 45.00 (*0-8039-7764-6*); pap. 14.99 (*0-8039-7765-4*) Sage.

Breakwell, Glynis M. Coping with Threatened Identities. 280p. 1987. 33.00 (*0-416-37120-5*, 9852) Routledge.

— Facing Physical Violence. (Problems in Practice Ser.). 128p. 1989. 25.00 (*0-901715-96-4*, Pub. by Brit Psychol Soc) Routledge.

Breakwell, Glynis M., ed. Social Psychology of Identity & the Self Concept. (Surrey Seminars in Social Psychology). (Illus.). 271p. 1992. text 94.95 (*0-12-128685-1*) Acad Pr.

— Social Psychology of Political & Economic Cognition. (Surrey Seminars in Social Psychology). (Illus.). 189p. 1991. text 94.95 (*0-12-128680-0*) Acad Pr.

Breakwell, Glynis M., et al, eds. Doing Social Psychology: Laboratory & Field Exercises. (Illus.). 328p. 1988. text 24.95 (*0-521-34015-2*) Cambridge U Pr.

Breakwell, Glynis M. & Canter, David V., eds. Empirical Approaches to Social Representations. LC 92-28703. (Illus.). 358p. 1993. text 98.00 (*0-19-852181-2*, Clarendon Pr) OUP.

Breakwell, Glynis M. & Lyons, Evanthia. Changing European Identities: Social Psychological Analyses of Social Change. LC 96-13486. (International Series in Social Psychology). 460p. 1996. pap. 41.95 (*0-7506-3008-6*) Buttrwrth-Heinemann.

Breakwell, Glynis M. & Lyons, Evanthia, eds. Changing European Identities. (International Series in Experimental Social Psychology: Vol. 29). 360p. 1995. write for info. (*0-08-042412-0*, Pergamon Pr) Elsevier.

Breakwell, Ian. An Actor's Revenge. LC 96-139029. 1996. pap. 10.95 (*0-85170-524-3*, Pub. by British Film Inst) Ind U Pr.

— The Artist's Dream. 120p. 1992. pap. 10.95 (*1-85242-114-2*) Serpents Tail.

Breal, Michel. The Beginnings of Semantics: Essays, Lectures, & Reviews. Wolf, George, tr. from FRE. 320p. 1991. 45.00 (*0-8047-1902-0*) Stanford U Pr.

Brealey. Fundamentals of Corporate Finance. 2nd ed. 1998. pap. 24.06 (*0-07-290987-0*) McGraw.

— Principles of Corporate Finance. 6th ed. 1999. 70.25 (*0-07-290999-4*) McGraw.

— Study Guide Prin Corp Finance. 6th ed. 440p. 1999. pap. 29.38 (*0-07-234658-2*) McGraw.

Brealey, Gena & Hunter, Kay, eds. The Two Worlds of Helen Duncan. 194p. (C). 1988. 35.00 (*0-7212-0730-8*, Pub. by Regency Pr GBR) St Mut.

Brealey, M. Completing the Internal Market of the European Community - 1992 Legislation: Business, 1995 Basic Works. 1000p. (C). 1995. ring bd. 730.00 (*1-85333-850-8*, Pub. by Graham & Trotman) Kluwer Academic.

— Completing the Internal Market of the European Community - 1992 Legislation: Financial Services & Capital Movements - 1994 Basic Works. 1000p. (C). 1995. ring bd. 550.00 (*1-85333-862-1*, Pub. by Graham & Trotman) Kluwer Academic.

— Completing the Internal Market of the European Community - 1992 Legislation: Technical Standards 1995 Basic Work. 1000p. 1995. ring bd. 730.00 (*1-85333-844-3*, Pub. by Graham & Trotman) Kluwer Academic.

— Completing the Internal Market of the European Community - 1992 Legislation: Transport, Customs & Travel 1995 Basic Work & 1995 Supplements. 900p. (C). 1995. ring bd. 550.00 (*1-85333-868-0*, Pub. by Graham & Trotman) Kluwer Academic.

— Completing the Internal Market of the European Community - 1992 Legislation: Veterinary & Phytosanitary Controls 1995 Basic Work. 800p. 1995. ring bd. 730.00 (*1-85333-856-7*, Pub. by Graham & Trotman) Kluwer Academic.

— Completing the Internal Market of the European Community - 1992 Legislation: 1995 Basic Work, 8 vols., Set. 3000p. (C). 1995. ring bd. 1539.00 (*1-85333-838-9*, Pub. by Graham & Trotman) Kluwer Academic.

Brealey, Mark, ed. Environmental Liabilities & Regulations in Europe. 509p. 1993. trans. 120.00 (*0-87179-814-X*) BNA Books.

Brealey, Mark & Quigley, Conor. Completing the Internal Market of the European Communities: 1992 Handbook. 2nd ed. 352p. (C). 1991. lib. bdg. 112.00 (*1-85333-474-X*, Pub. by Graham & Trotman) Kluwer Academic.

— Completing the Internal Market of the European Communities: 1992 Legislation: Transport, Customs, & Travel 1992 Basic Work & 1992 Supplements. 350p. 1992. lib. bdg. 320.50 (*1-85333-679-3*) Kluwer Academic.

— Completing the Internal Market of the European Communities: 1992 Legislation: Transport, Customs, & Travel 1992 Basic Work & 1992 Supplements, Set. 350p. 1992. suppl. ed. 60.00 (*1-85333-680-7*) Kluwer Academic.

— Completing the Internal Market of the European Communities: 1992 Legislation: Veterinary & Phytosanitary Controls 1992 Basic Work & 1992 Supplements, Vols. 1 & 2. 650p. 1992. lib. bdg. 461.00 (*1-85333-691-2*, Pub. by Graham & Trotman) Kluwer Academic.

— Completing the Internal Market of the European Communities: 1992 Legislation: Veterinary & Phytosanitary Controls 1992 Basic Work & 1992 Supplements, Vols. 1 & 2. 650p. 1992. suppl. ed. 70.00 (*1-85333-692-0*) Kluwer Academic.

— Completing the Internal Market of the European Communities: 1992 Legislation: 1992 Basic Work & 1992 Supplements. 1500p. 1992. ring bd. 952.00 (*1-85333-673-4*, Pub. by Graham & Trotman) Kluwer Academic.

— Completing the Internal Market of the European Communities: 1992 Legislation: 1992 Basic Work & 1992 Supplements, Vols. 1-7. 1500p. 1992. suppl. ed. 107.00 (*1-85333-674-2*, Pub. by Graham & Trotman) Kluwer Academic.

— Completing the Internal Market of the European Community: 1992 Basic Work: Financial Services & Capital Movements - 1991 Basic Work & 1991 Supplements. 400p. 1991. 280.00 (*1-85333-532-0*, Pub. by Graham & Trotman) Kluwer Academic.

— Completing the Internal Market of the European Community: 1992 Legislation: Business 1992 Basic work & 1992 Supplements. 650p. 1992. suppl. ed. 70.00 (*1-85333-698-X*, Pub. by Graham & Trotman); ring bd. 575.00 (*1-85333-697-1*, Pub. by Graham & Trotman) Kluwer Academic.

— Completing the Internal Market of the European Community: 1992 Legislation: Financial Services & Capital Movements 1992 Basic Work & 1992 Supplements. 400p. (C). 1992. ring bd. 255.00 (*1-85333-685-8*, Pub. by Graham & Trotman) Kluwer Academic.

— Completing the Internal Market of the European Community: 1992 Legislation: Technical Standards - 1991 Basic Work & 1991 Supplements, Set. 450p. 1991. suppl. ed. 400.00 (*1-85333-526-6*) Kluwer Academic.

— Completing the Internal Market of the European Community: 1992 Legislation: Technical Standards 1992 Basic Work & 1992 Supplements, Vols. 1-3. 650p. 1992. ring bd. 365.00 (*1-85333-703-X*, Pub. by Graham & Trotman) Kluwer Academic.

— Completing the Internal Market of the European Community: 1992 Legislation: Transport, Customs, & Travel - 1991 Basic Work & 1991 Supplements. 350p. 1991. suppl. ed. 280.00 (*1-85333-544-4*) Kluwer Academic.

— Completing the Internal Market of the European Community: 1992 Legislation: Veterinary & Phytosanitary Controls - 1991 Basic Work & 1991 Supplements. 450p. 1991. suppl. ed. 400.00 (*1-85333-520-7*) Kluwer Academic.

— Completing the Internal Market of the European

Community: 1992 Legislation: 1991 Basic Work & 1991 Supplements, Vols. 1-6. 1200p. 1991. 980.00 (*1-85333-550-9*, Pub. by Graham & Trotman) Kluwer Academic.

Brealey, Mark & Quigley, Conor, eds. Completing the Internal Market of the European Communities: 1992 Legislation. (C). 1990. 275.00 (*1-85333-337-9*, Pub. by Graham & Trotman) Kluwer Academic.

— Completing the Internal Market of the European Communities: 1992 Legislation: Basic Work & Supplements, 1990, Set. (C). 1990. pap. text 275.00 (*1-85333-336-0*, Pub. by Graham & Trotman); ring bd. 887.50 (*1-85333-335-2*, Pub. by Graham & Trotman) Kluwer Academic.

— Completing the Internal Market of the European Communities: 1992 Legislation: Basic Work & Supplements, 1990, Vols. 1-6. (C). 1990. 1180.00 (*1-85333-352-2*, Pub. by Graham & Trotman) Kluwer Academic.

— Completing the Internal Market of the European Communities: 1992 Legislation: Business Basic Work & Supplements, 1990. (C). 1990. 275.00 (*1-85333-340-9*, Pub. by Graham & Trotman) Kluwer Academic.

— Completing the Internal Market of the European Communities: 1992 Legislation: Financial Services & Capital Movements, Basic Work, 1989. LC 89-1692. (C). 1989. ring bd. 256.00 (*1-85333-214-3*, Pub. by Graham & Trotman) Kluwer Academic.

— Completing the Internal Market of the European Communities: 1992 Legislation: Technical Standards Basic Work & Supplements, 1990. (C). 1990. 275.00 (*1-85333-339-5*, Pub. by Graham & Trotman) Kluwer Academic.

— Completing the Internal Market of the European Communities: 1992 Legislation: Technical Standards, Supplement 1. 1989. ring bd. 21.25 (*1-85333-210-0*) Kluwer Academic.

— Completing the Internal Market of the European Communities: 1992 Legislation: Veterinary & Phytosanitary Controls Basic Work & Supplements, 1990. (C). 1990. 275.00 (*1-85333-338-7*, Pub. by Graham & Trotman) Kluwer Academic.

— Completing the Internal Market of the European Community: 1992 Legislation: Basic Work, 1989, Vols. 1-3. (C). 1989. pap. text 769.00 (*1-85333-194-5*, Pub. by Graham & Trotman) Kluwer Academic.

— Completing the Internal Market of the European Community: 1992 Legislation: Basic Works, 1989 Veterinary & Phytosanitary Controls. (C). 1989. ring bd. 256.00 (*1-85333-199-6*, Pub. by Graham & Trotman) Kluwer Academic.

— Completing the Internal Market of the European Community: 1992 Legislation: Business - 1991 Basic Work & 1991 Supplements, Set. 450p. 1991. suppl. ed. 400.00 (*1-85333-538-X*) Kluwer Academic.

— Completing the Internal Market of the European Community: 1992 Legislation: Business Basic Work, 1989. (C). 1989. ring bd. 256.00 (*1-85333-219-4*, Pub. by Graham & Trotman) Kluwer Academic.

— Completing the Internal Market of the European Community: 1992 Legislation: Transport, Customs & Travel Basic Works, 1989. LC 89-1690. (C). 1989. ring bd. 256.00 (*1-85333-204-6*, Pub. by Graham & Trotman) Kluwer Academic.

— Completing the International Market of the European Communities: 1992 Legislation: Technical Standards Basic Work, 1989. (C). 1989. ring bd. 256.00 (*1-85333-209-7*, Pub. by Graham & Trotman) Kluwer Academic.

— European Community Internal Market 1992 Legislation Handbook. (C). 1989. lib. bdg. 91.00 (*1-85333-159-7*, Pub. by Graham & Trotman) Kluwer Academic.

***Brealey, Richard & Myers, Stewart C.** Principles of Corporate Finance: Solutions Manual. 6th ed. 384p. (C). 1999. pap. 20.63 (*0-07-234659-0*) McGrw-H Hghr Educ.

***Brealey, Richard, et al.** Fundamentals Corporate Finance: Ready Notes. 2nd ed. (C). 1998. pap. 12.19 (*0-07-304008-8*) McGrw-H Hghr Educ.

— Fundamentals of Corporate Finance from the Wall Street Journal. 2nd ed. 800p. (C). 1998. 103.44 (*0-07-304009-6*) McGrw-H Hghr Educ.

***Brealey, Richard A.** Principles of Corporate Finance. 6th ed. 1999. pap., student ed. 89.69 (*0-07-235236-1*) McGraw.

Brealey, Richard A. & Myers, Stewart C. Principles of Corporate Finance. 5th ed. LC 96-76441. (Illus.). 664p. (C). 1996. text 99.75 (*0-07-007417-8*) McGraw.

— Principles of Corporate Finance. 5th ed. (C). 1996. pap. text, student ed. 29.38 (*0-07-007477-1*) McGraw.

Brealey, Richard A., et al. Fundamentals of Corporate Finance. LC 94-30048. (Finance Ser.). (C). 1994. text 68.00 (*0-07-007461-5*) McGraw.

— Fundamentals of Corporate Finance. 2nd ed. LC 98-10507. 784p. 1998. 86.88 (*0-07-007486-0*) McGraw.

***Brealey, Richard A., et al.** Fundamentals of Corporate Finance. 3rd ed. LC 00-42711. (Series in Finance, Insurance, & Real Estate). 2001. write for info. (*0-07-233777-X*) McGraw Legal.

Brealy, Richard A., et al. Fundamentals of Corporate Finance. (C). 1995. pap. text, student ed. 24.06 (*0-07-007468-2*) McGraw.

Bream, Freda. Anyone Can Murder. large type ed. (Linford Mystery Library). 352p. 1997. pap. 16.99 (*0-7089-5058-2*, Linford) Ulverscroft.

— A Case of Art Failure. large type ed. (Linford Mystery Large Print Ser.). 1994. pap. 16.99 (*0-7089-7636-0*) Ulverscroft.

— Coffin to Let. large type ed. (Mystery Ser.). 1994. pap. 16.99 (*0-7089-7624-7*, Linford) Ulverscroft.

— The Corpse on the Cruise. large type ed. 1990. pap. 16.99 (*0-7089-6896-1*) Ulverscroft.

— Island of Fear. large type ed. (Linford Mystery Library). 1990. pap. 16.99 (*0-7089-6841-4*) Ulverscroft.

— Murder at the Microphone. large type ed. (Linford Mystery Library). 1995. pap. 16.99 (*0-7089-7800-2*) Ulverscroft.

— Murder in the Map Room. large type ed. 1990. pap. 16.99 (*0-7089-6900-3*, Linford) Ulverscroft.

— The Nasty Affair on the Norfolk. large type ed. (Linford Mystery Library .). 320p. 1995. pap. 16.99 (*0-7089-7732-4*, Linford) Ulverscroft.

— The Problem at Piha. large type ed. (Mystery Library). 288p. 1995. pap. 16.99 (*0-7089-7648-4*, Linford) Ulverscroft.

— Sealed & Dispatched. large type ed. (Linford Mystery Large Print Ser.). 288p. 1995. pap. 16.99 (*0-7089-7728-6*, Linford) Ulverscroft.

— The Vica Done It. large type ed. 1990. pap. 16.99 (*0-7089-6904-6*) Ulverscroft.

— The Vicar Investigates. large type ed. (Linford Mystery Library). 1990. pap. 16.99 (*0-7089-6849-X*) Ulverscroft.

— With Murder in Mind. large type ed. 1990. pap. 16.99 (*0-7089-6892-9*) Ulverscroft.

Bream, Howard N. The Apocryphon of John & Other Coptic Translations. 260p. (Orig.). 1987. pap. 18.00 (*0-9613805-3-5*) Halgo Inc.

Brean, Donald J., ed. Taxation in Modern China. LC 98-3094. 320p. (C). 1998. pap. 22.99 (*0-415-92018-3*) Routledge.

— Taxation in Modern China. LC 98-3094. 320p. (C). 1998. 75.00 (*0-415-92017-5*) Routledge.

Brean, Donald J., et al. Taxation of International Portfolio Investment. LC 91-97595. (FRE & ENG., Illus.). 115p. 1991. pap. text 20.00 (*0-88645-123-X*, Pub. by Inst Res Pub) Ashgate Pub Co.

Brean, Joel. Rebels United: The Enduring Reality of James Dean. 2nd ed. Jones, Elbert, ed. (Illus.). 140p. 1987. pap. 10.50 (*0-317-63846-7*) Brean-Jones Pub.

Brear, Holly B. Inherit the Alamo: Myth & Ritual at an American Shrine. LC 94-17220. (Illus.). 192p. 1995. 19.95 (*0-292-70824-6*) U of Tex Pr.

Brear, P. Finance of International Trade. 1986. 90.00 (*0-7855-1824-X*) St Mut.

Breard, Dorothy G., et al. Gardening for Southern Seasons, Vol. I. 3rd ed. (Illus.). 198p. (Orig.). 1988. reprint ed. pap. 14.95 (*0-9652405-0-9*) Monroe Garden.

Brearley, A. & Cox, T. An Outline of Statistical Methods for Use in the Textile Industry. 9th ed. 1980. 60.00 (*0-7855-1020-6*) St Mut.

Brearley, B. & Iredale, I. The Woollen Industry. (C). 1981. 115.00 (*0-7855-6076-9*, Pub. by British Textile Tech) St Mut.

Brearley, Gill. Counseling Children with Special Needs. LC 97-8094. 1997. 29.95 (*0-632-04151-X*) Blackwell Sci.

Brearley, H. Steelmakers & Knotted String. 276p. 1995. 40.00 (*0-901716-65-0*, Pub. by Inst Materials) Ashgate Pub Co.

Brearley, H. C. Homicide in the United States. LC 69-14913. (Criminology, Law Enforcement, & Social Problems Ser.: No. 36). 1969. reprint ed. 24.00 (*0-87585-036-7*) Patterson Smith.

Brearley, Joan M. The Book of the Akita. (Illus.). 272p. 1985. text 39.95 (*0-86622-053-4*, H-1075) TFH Pubns.

— The Book of the Bulldog. (Illus.). 300p. 1984. 39.95 (*0-86622-027-5*, H-1071) TFH Pubns.

— The Book of the Shar-Pei. (TS Ser.). (Illus.). 223p. 1991. text 59.95 (*0-86622-626-5*, TS150) TFH Pubns.

— The Book of the Yorkshire Terrier. LC 84-148045. (Illus.). 300p. 1984. 39.95 (*0-87666-940-2*, H-1066) TFH Pubns.

— The Old English Sheepdog. (Illus.). 356p. 1989. 24.95 (*0-86622-710-5*, PS-817) TFH Pubns.

— The Siberian Husky. (TS Ser.). (Illus.). 512p. 1992. text 59.95 (*0-86622-631-1*, TS148) TFH Pubns.

— This Is the Alaskan Malamute. (Illus.). 415p. 1975. 24.95 (*0-87666-650-0*, PS-737) TFH Pubns.

Brearley, Joan M., jt. auth. see Draper, Samuel.

Brearley, Joan McD. The Book of the Cocker Spaniel. (Illus.). 300p. 1982. 29.95 (*0-87666-737-X*, H-1034) TFH Pubns.

— The Book of the Doberman Pinscher. (Illus.). 576p. 1976. 29.95 (*0-87666-658-6*, H-968) TFH Pubns.

— Book of the Maltese. (Illus.). 288p. 1984. 39.95 (*0-87666-563-6*, H-1067) TFH Pubns.

— The Book of the Pug. (Illus.). 352p. 1980. 23.95 (*0-87666-683-7*, H-1021) TFH Pubns.

Brearley, Joan McD. & Easton, Allen. Book of the Shih Tzu. (Illus.). 304p. 1980. 35.95 (*0-87666-664-0*, H-996) TFH Pubns.

Brearley, Joan McD. & Nicholas, Anna K. This Is the Bichon Frise. (Illus.). 320p. 1973. 24.95 (*0-87666-247-5*, PS-700) TFH Pubns.

Brearley, Judith. Counseling & Social Work. LC 94-22205. (Counselling in Context Ser.). 160p. 1994. write for info. (*0-335-19002-2*, Pub. by OpUniv Pr) Taylor & Francis.

Brearley, K. & McBride, R. Bruce. Nouvelles du Quebec. 2nd ed. 1977. pap. text 19.95 (*0-13-625467-5*) P-H.

Brearley, Kate & Bloch, Selwyn. Brearley & Bloch: Employment Covenants & Confidential Information - Law, Practice & Technique. 2nd ed. 1997. write for info. (*0-406-00220-7*, BBEC2, MICHIE) LEXIS Pub.

— Employment Covenants & Confidential Information: Law, Practice & Technique. 290p. 1993. boxed set 110.00 (*0-614-05554-7*, UK, MICHIE) LEXIS Pub.

Brearley, S. & Tredale, I. The Woolen Industry. rev. ed. 154p. 1982. 85.00 (*0-7855-7314-3*) St Mut.

— The Worsted Industry. rev. ed. 198p. 1982. 60.00 (*0-7855-7315-1*) St Mut.

Brearley, Sue. Talk to Me. (Illus.). 26p. (J). (gr. 1-4). write for info. (*0-7136-3192-9*, Pub. by A & C Blk) Midpt Trade.

Brearley, Sue & Matthews, Jenny. Talk to Me. (J). pap. write for info. (*0-7136-4410-9*, Pub. by A & C Blk) Midpt Trade.

Brearly, Malcom J. Color Atlas of Small Animal Endoscopy. (Illus.). 128p. (C). (gr. 13). 1991. text 78.95 (*0-8151-1195-9*, 21728) Mosby Inc.

Brears, Peter, jt. ed. see Sambrook, Pamela A.

***Brearton, Fran.** The Great War in Irish Poetry: W. B. Yeats to Michael Longley. 340p. 2000. text 74.00 (*0-19-818672-X*) OUP.

***Breashears, David.** High Exposure: An Enduring Passion for Everest & Unforgiving Places. LC 99-31159. (Illus.). 320p. 2000. per. 15.00 (*0-684-86545-9*) S&S Trade.

***Breashears, David F.** High Exposure: An Enduring Passion for Everest & Other Unforgiving Places. LC 99-31159. (Illus.). 319p. 1999. 24.50 (*0-684-85361-2*) S&S Trade.

***Breashears, David F. & Salkeld, Audrey.** Last Climb: The Legendary Everest Expedition of Malloy & Irvine. LC 99-41046. 240p. 1999. pap. 35.00 (*0-7922-7538-1*) Natl Geog.

Breasted, J. H. The Edwin Smith Surgical Papyrus, 2 vols., Vols. I & II. (Oriental Institute Publications: Nos. 3 & 4). (Illus.). xxiv, 596p. 1930. 350.00 (*0-918986-73-7*) Orient Inst.

Breasted, James Henry. Forerunners Byzantine Painting. 1972. lib. bdg. 8.50 (*0-226-07185-5*) U Ch Pr.

Breasted, Mary. Why Should You Doubt Me Now? LC 93-3561. 1993. 23.00 (*0-374-29007-5*) FS&G.

Breasure, Joyce M. C., ed. Nonverbal Communication Skills Handbook. (Professional Handbook Ser.). 49p. (Orig.). 1982. pap. text 10.00 (*0-931975-13-1*) Advanced Dev Sys.

Breathed, Berke. Happy Trails: Bloom County, Selections. (Illus.). 87p. 1998. pap. text 9.00 (*0-7881-5437-3*) DIANE Pub.

***Breathed, Berkeley.** Edwurd Fudwupper Fibbed Big: Explained by Fannie Fudwupper. LC 99-43717. (Illus.). 48p. (J). (ps up). 2000. 15.95 (*0-316-10675-5*) Little.

Breathed, Berkeley. Goodnight Opus. (Illus.). 32p. (J). (gr. k-3). 1996. pap. 7.70 (*0-316-10599-6*) Little.

— Happy Trails. 96p. 1990. pap. 8.95 (*0-316-10741-7*) Little.

***Breathed, Berkeley.** The Last Basselope. (J). 2001. pap. 5.95 (*0-316-12664-0*) Little.

Breathed, Berkeley. The Last Basselope: One Ferocious Story. LC 92-14467. (Illus.). 32p. (J). (gr. k-3). 1992. 14.95 (*0-316-10761-1*) Little.

— Politically, Fashionably & Aerodynamically Incorrect: The First Outland Collection. 1992. pap. 10.95 (*0-316-10701-8*) Little.

— Red Ranger Came Calling. 1997. 12.15 (*0-606-13732-7*, Pub. by Turtleback) Demco.

— Red Ranger Came Calling. (Illus.). 32p. (J). (gr. k-3). 1997. reprint ed. pap. 7.95 (*0-316-10249-0*) Little.

— The Romantic Opus n' Bill. LC 94-925. (Illus.). 1994. pap. 1.40 (*0-316-10879-0*) Little.

— A Wish for Wings That Work. (Illus.). 32p. (J). (gr. k-3). 1995. pap. 5.95 (*0-316-10691-7*) Little.

— Wish for Wings That Work. 1995. 10.15 (*0-606-13923-0*, Pub. by Turtleback) Demco.

— A Wish for Wings That Work: An Opus Christmas Story. 1995. pap. 49.50 (*0-316-11034-5*) Little.

Breathnac. Hold That Thought. 1997. 12.95 (*0-446-91258-1*, Pub. by Warner Bks) Little.

— Sim Abun Spec: Ruby PB, 1 vol. 528p. 1996. 21.00 (*0-446-72902-7*, Pub. by Warner Bks) Little.

Breathnach, Breandan. Folk Music & Dances of Ireland. LC 97-161131. 160p. 1996. pap. 13.95 (*1-900428-65-2*) Dufour.

Breathnach, Padraic. The March Hare. Rosenstock, Gabriel, tr. from IRI. LC 95-115821. 154p. pap. 14.95 (*1-874700-03-6*, Pub. by Clo Iar-Chonnachta) Dufour.

Breathnach, S. M. & Hintner, H. Adverse Drug Reactions & the Skin. (Illus.). 408p. 1992. 150.00 (*0-632-03349-5*) Blackwell Sci.

Breathnach, Sarah Ban. The Simple Abundance Companion: Following Your Authentic Path to Something More. LC 99-49015. 288p. 2000. mass mkt., wbk. ed. 14.95 (*0-446-67333-1*) Warner Bks.

***Breathnach, Sarah Ban.** Something More: Excavating Your Authentic Self. 2000. pap. 12.00 (*0-446-67708-6*) Warner Bks.

***Breathnach, Sarah Ban, et al.** A Man's Journey to Simple Abundance. 2000. 22.00 (*0-7432-0061-6*) Scribner.

Breatnach, Caoilte. Kinvara: A Seaport Town on Galway Bay. LC 97-189424. 119p. 1997. pap. 18.99 (*1-873821-07-7*, Pub. by Tir Eolas) Irish Bks Media.

Breatnach, Mary. Boulez & Mallarme: A Study in Poetic Influence. 170p. 1996. 78.95 (*1-85928-120-6*, Pub. by Scolar Pr) Ashgate Pub Co.

Breatnach, Padraig A., jt. auth. see Bernhard, Michael.

Breau, Lenny, jt. auth. see Knowles, John.

***Breau-Major, Germaine.** Om Revient Toujours Chez Soi - Cocagne. Cormier, Flora & Geoguen, Edna, trs. from ENG.Tr. of We Will Always Return - Cocagne (FRE., Illus.). 7p. 2000. pap. 10.00 (*0-9701316-0-7*) Les Editions Bleuts.

Breaud, Odile, et al. Cultures of the World. LC 97-22766. Orig. Title: Living Around the World. (Illus.). 30p. (J). (gr. 2-9). 1998. lib. bdg. 23.95 (*0-88682-957-7*, Creat Educ) Creative Co.

Breault, Claire, jt. auth. see FitzGerald, Kathleen W.

Breault, Judith C. The Odyssey of a Humanitarian: Emily Howland, 1827-1929. 1981. 38.95 (*0-405-14076-2*) Ayer.

Breault, William. The Ghost in the Mohawk Valley. (Illus.). 243p. 1991. 35.00 (*0-910845-46-8*, 566) Landmark Ent.

— Heart's Impulse: Prayer Reflections. 1999. audio 9.95 (*0-87793-927-6*); audio compact disk 15.95 (*0-87793-928-4*) Ave Maria.

— The Lady from Dublin. (Illus.). 131p. reprint ed. pap. 17.00 (*0-910845-44-1*, 556) Landmark Ent.

— The Miner Was a Bishop: The Pioneer Years of Patrick Manogue in California & Nevada, 1854-1895. (Illus.). 158p. 1988. pap. 20.00 (*0-910845-34-4*, 536) Landmark Ent.

— Power & Weakness. 2nd ed. 69p. 1993. pap. 7.00 (*0-910845-51-4*, 594) Landmark Ent.

— Under the Fig Tree. (Illus.). 95p. 1989. pap. 12.00 (*0-910845-37-9*) Landmark Ent.

***Breault, William J.** John A. Sutter in Hawaii & California, 1838-1839. (Illus.). 94p. 1998. pap. 14.00 (*0-910845-59-X*, 596) Landmark Ent.

Breaux, jt. auth. see Salvo.

***Breaux, Charles.** Journey into Consciousness: The Chakras, Tantra & Jungian Psychology. 254p. 1998. 125.00 (*81-208-1449-5*, Pub. by Motilal Bnarsidass); pap. 100.00 (*81-208-1454-1*, Pub. by Motilal Bnarsidass) St Mut.

Breaux, Charles. The Way of Karma. LC 92-45543. 288p. (Orig.). 1993. pap. 14.95 (*0-87728-773-2*) Weiser.

***Breaux, Magdalene.** The Family Curse. 248p. 2000. pap. 15.00 (*0-9701709-0-4*) Breaux Bks.

— The Family Curse. 248p. 2000. pap. 17.95 (*1-887617-00-0*) St Bart Pr Ltd.

Breaux, Tommy J. Cajun Humor from the Heart. LC 96-43947. (Illus.). 160p. 1997. pap. 8.95 (*1-56554-187-1*) Pelican.

***Breaux, Tommy J.** Cajun Stories My Granpa Tole Me. LC 98-56059. (Illus.). 176p. 1999. pap. 8.95 (*1-56554-416-1*) Pelican.

Breaux, Wayne, Jr. Robotech Strike Force: Robotech Sourcebook. Siembieda, Kevin et al, eds. (Robotech RPG Ser.). (Illus.). 112p. (Orig.). 1995. pap. 11.95 (*0-916211-85-1*, 563) Palladium Bks.

Breaux, Wayne, Jr., jt. auth. see Frater, Jonathan.

Breaux, Wayne, Jr., jt. auth. see Siembieda, Kevin.

Breay, Claire. The Cartulary of Chatteris Abbey. LC 99-36044. (Illus.). 488p. 1999. 90.00 (*0-85115-750-5*) Boydell & Brewer.

Breaza, Michael & Olson, Craig R. Identification & Dating of Round Oak Heating Stoves. (Illus.). 73p. 1995. pap. 10.00 (*1-883228-08-5*) Invictus MI.

Breazeale, Daniel, ed. Fichte: Foundations of Transcendental Philosophy: (Wissenschaftslehre) Nova Methodo (1796-99) Date not set. pap. text 29.95 (*0-8014-8138-4*) Cornell U Pr.

Breazeale, Daniel & Rockmore, Tom, eds. Fichte: Historical Contexts - Contemporary Controversies. LC 93-18260. 248p. (C). 1994. text 55.00 (*0-391-03817-6*) Humanities.

— New Perspectives on Fichte. LC 95-570. 256p. (C). 1996. text 55.00 (*0-391-03917-2*) Humanities.

Breazeale, Daniel, ed. see Nietzsche, Friedrich Wilhelm.

Breazeale, Daniel, ed. & tr. see Fichte, Johann G.

Breazeale, Daniel, ed. & tr. see Nietzsche, Friedrich Wilhelm.

Breazeale, Daniel, tr. see Fichte, Johann G.

Breazeale, J. W. Life As It Is. LC 74-17309. 1969. reprint ed. 60.00 (*0-918450-00-4*) C Elder.

Breazeale, Kennon, jt. auth. see Smuckarn, Snit.

Breazeale, M. A., jt. ed. see Leroy, O.

Breazile, James E., ed. Textbook of Veterinary Physiology. LC 71-135683. (Illus.). 584p. reprint ed. pap. 181.10 (*0-608-18456-X*, 205667700080) Bks Demand.

Breaznell, Gene. The Star of Sutherland. 192p. 1990. 18.95 (*0-8027-5754-5*) Walker & Co.

Breba, Maria L. Dictionary of Metallurgy: Dictionnaire de Metalurgie. (ENG & FRE.). 1984. write for info. (*0-8288-1923-8*, M15832) Fr & Eur.

Brebach, Raymond. Joseph Conrad, Ford Madox Ford, & the Making of Romance. LC 84-14098. (Studies in Modern Literature: No. 46). 137p. reprint ed. pap. 42.50 (*0-8357-1613-9*, 207053300001) Bks Demand.

Brebach, Raymond T., ed. see Gillon, Adam.

Brebbia, C. A., ed. Boundary Element Method XVI. 616p. 1994. 259.00 (*1-85312-283-1*) Computational Mech MA.

— Computational Acoustics & its Environmental Applications. 304p. 1995. 129.00 (*1-85312-308-0*) Computational Mech MA.

Brebbia, C. A., ed. Environmental Coastal Regions: Proceedings of the 2nd International Conference on Coastal Environment Problems. (Environmental Studies: Vol. 1). 456p. 1998. 228.00 (*1-85312-527-X*, 527X, Pub. by WIT Pr) Computational Mech MA.

Brebbia, C. A., ed. The Kobe Earthquake: Geodynamical Aspects. (Advances in Earthquake Engineering Ser.: Vol. 1). 160p. 1996. 138.00 (*1-85312-430-3*, Pub. by WIT Pr) Computational Mech MA.

— Risk Analysis II. (Management Information Systems Ser.). 400p. 2000. 189.00 (*1-85312-830-9*, Pub. by WIT Pr) Computational Mech MA.

Brebbia, C. A., ed. Structural Integrity & Passenger Safety. (Advances in Transport Ser.: Vol. 3). (Illus.). 177p. 1999. 108.00 (*1-85312-784-1*, 7841, Pub. by WIT Pr) Computational Mech MA.

Brebbia, C. A., et al, eds. Advanced Computational Methods in Heat Transfer IV. LC 96-83656. 644p. 1996. 259.00 (*1-85312-402-8*, 4028, Pub. by WIT Pr) Computational Mech MA.

— Air Pollution: Proceedings of the 4th International Conference. LC 96-83666. 888p. 1996. 368.00 (*1-85312-422-2*, 4222, Pub. by WIT Pr) Computational Mech MA.

— Air Pollution VII - Modelling, Monitoring & Management of Air Pollution: Proceedings of the Seventh International Conference on Modelling, Monitoring & Management. (Advances in Air Pollution Ser.: Vol. 7). 1112p. 1999. 480.00 (*1-85312-693-4*, 6934, Pub. by WIT Pr) Computational Mech MA.

— Air Pollution VI: Proceedings of the International Conference on Modelling, Monitoring & Management

B

of Air Pollution. LC 99-195986. (Advances in Air Pollution Ser.: Vol. 5). 996p. 1998. 425.00 (*1-85312-605-5*, 6055, Pub. by WIT Pr) Computational Mech MA.

Brebbia, C. A., et al, eds. Applications of High-Performance Computing in Engineering IV. 344p. 1995. 157.00 (*1-85312-320-X*) Computational Mech MA.

— Boundary Elements XIV Vol. 1: Field Problems & Applications. 708p. 1992. 270.00 (*1-85312-179-7*) Computational Mech MA.

— Boundary Elements XIV Vol. 2: Stress Analysis & Computational Aspects. 736p. 1992. 284.00 (*1-85312-210-6*) Computational Mech MA.

— Boundary Elements XVII. 696p. 1995. 288.00 (*1-85312-324-2*) Computational Mech MA.

Brebbia, C. A., et al, eds. Computational Methods for Smart Structures & Materials. (Structures & Materials Ser.: Vol. 4). 304p. 1998. 158.00 (*1-85312-600-4*, 6004, Pub. by WIT Pr) Computational Mech MA.

Brebbia, C. A. & Aliabadi, M. H., eds. Adaptive Finite & Boundary Element Methods. 380p. 1993. 187.00 (*1-85312-185-1*) Computational Mech MA.

— Industrial Applications of the Boundary Element Method. 200p. 1993. 101.00 (*1-85312-183-5*) Computational Mech MA.

Brebbia, C. A. & Dominguez, J. Boundary Elements: An Introductory Course. 2nd ed. 322p. 1996. reprint ed. 79.00 (*1-85312-160-6*); reprint ed. 122.00 incl. disk (*1-85312-349-8*) Computational Mech MA.

Brebbia, C. A. & Ingber, M. S., eds. Boundary Element Technology VII. 964p. 1992. 337.00 (*1-85312-168-1*) Computational Mech MA.

Brebbia, C. A. & Leftheris, B., eds. Structural Studies of Historical Buildings IV, 2 vols. Incl. Vol. 1. Architectural Studies, Materials & Analysis. LC 95-67477. 464p. 1995. 196.00 (*1-56252-343-0*, 4257); Vol. 1. Architectural Studies, Materials & Analysis. 464p. 1995. 196.00 (*1-85312-425-7*, Pub. by WIT Pr); Vol. 2. Dynamics, Repairs & Restoration. LC 95-67477. 384p. 1995. 163.00 (*1-56252-344-9*, 4265); Vol. 2. Dynamics, Repairs & Restoration. 384p. 1995. 163.00 (*1-85312-426-5*, Pub. by WIT Pr); LC 95-67477. 848p. 1995. 322.00 (*1-56252-238-8*, 3145) Computational Mech MA.

Brebbia, C. A. & Leftheris, B., eds. Structural Studies of Historical Buildings IV, 2 vols. Incl. Vol. 1. Architectural Studies, Materials & Analysis. LC 95-67477. 464p. 1995. 196.00 (*1-56252-343-0*, 4257); Vol. 1. Architectural Studies, Materials & Analysis. 464p. 1995. 196.00 (*1-85312-425-7*, Pub. by WIT Pr); Vol. 2. Dynamics, Repairs & Restoration. LC 95-67477. 384p. 1995. 163.00 (*1-56252-344-9*, 4265); Vol. 2. Dynamics, Repairs & Restoration. 384p. 1995. 163.00 (*1-85312-426-5*, Pub. by WIT Pr); 848p. 1995. 322.00 (*1-85312-314-5*, Pub. by WIT Pr) Computational Mech MA.

Brebbia, C. A. & Partridge, P. W., eds. Boundary Elements in Fluid Dynamics. 806p. 1992. 268.00 (*1-85312-193-2*) Computational Mech MA.

Brebbia, C. A. & Power, H., eds. Applications of Supercomputers in Engineering III. 576p. 1993. 253.00 (*1-85312-236-X*) Computational Mech MA.

Brebbia, C. A. & Rencis, J. J., eds. Boundary Elements XV Vol. 1: Fluid Flow & Computational Aspects. 708p. 1993. 242.00 (*1-85312-273-4*) Computational Mech MA.

— Boundary Elements XV Vol. 2: Stress Analysis. 648p. 1993. 224.00 (*1-85312-274-2*) Computational Mech MA.

Brebbia, C. A. & Sanchez-Galvez, V., eds. Shock & Impact on Structures. 288p. 1994. 100.00 (*1-85312-297-1*, Pub. by WIT Pr) Computational Mech MA.

Brebbia, C. A. & Uso, J.-L., eds. Ecosystems & Sustainable Development II. (Advances in Ecological Sciences Ser.: Vol. 2). 500p. 1999. 287.00 (*1-85312-687-X*, 687X, Pub. by WIT Pr) Computational Mech MA.

Brebbia, C. A., et al. Boundary Element Techniques. 478p. 1984. 110.00 (*1-85312-218-1*) Computational Mech MA.

Brebbia, C. A., jt. ed. see Aliabadi, M. H.

Brebbia, C. A., jt. ed. see Anagnostopoulos, P.

Brebbia, C. A., jt. ed. see Cakmak, A. S.

Brebbia, C. A., jt. ed. see Carlomagno, G. M.

Brebbia, C. A., jt. ed. see Ciskowski, R. D.

Brebbia, C. A., jt. ed. see Escrig, F.

Brebbia, C. A., jt. ed. see Hernandez, S.

Brebbia, C. A., jt. ed. see Jagar, W.

Brebbia, C. A., jt. ed. see Jager, W.

Brebbia, C. A., jt. ed. see Jefferson, C.

Brebbia, C. A., jt. ed. see Murthy, T. K. S.

Brebbia, C. A., jt. ed. see Oliveto, G.

Brebbia, C. A., jt. ed. see Pascolo, P.

Brebbia, C. A., jt. ed. see Pina, H.

Brebbia, C. A., jt. ed. see Power, H.

Brebbia, C. A., jt. ed. see Rajar, R.

Brebbia, C. A., jt. ed. see San Jose, R.

Brebbia, C. A., jt. ed. see Sanchez-Beitia, S.

Brebbia, C. A., jt. ed. see Wrobel, L. C.

Brebbia, C. A., jt. ed. see Zannetti, Paolo.

Brebbia, Carlos A. Finite Element Systems. 3rd rev. ed. 770p. 1985. 206.95 (*0-387-15116-8*) Spr-Verlag.

— Structural Repair & Maintenance of Historical Buildings. 632p. 1989. 295.00 (*0-8176-2302-7*) Birkhauser.

— Viscous Flow Applications. (Topics in Boundary Element Research Ser.: Vol. 5). (Illus.). 200p. 1989. 120.95 (*0-387-50609-8*) Spr-Verlag.

Brebbia, Carlos A., ed. Applications in Geomechanics. (Topics in Boundary Elements Ser.: Vol. 4). 183p. 1987. 57.00 (*1-56252-144-6*) Computational Mech MA.

— Basic Principles & Applications. (Topics in Boundary Elements Ser.: Vol. 1). 270p. 1984. 83.00 (*1-56252-137-3*) Computational Mech MA.

— Boundary Element Method XVI. LC 74-70404. (BEM Ser.: Vol. 16). 616p. 1994. 259.00 (*1-56252-207-8*, 2831) Computational Mech MA.

— Boundary Element Methods X Vol. 1: Mathematical & Computational Aspects. LC 88-71494. (BEM Ser.: Vol. 10). 653p. 1988. 128.00 (*0-945824-00-9*) Computational Mech MA.

— Boundary Element Methods X Vol. 2: Heat Transfer, Fluid Flow & Electrical Applications. LC 88-71494. (BEM Ser.: Vol. 10). 632p. 1988. 106.00 (*0-945824-01-7*) Computational Mech MA.

— Boundary Element Methods X Vol. 3: Stress Analysis. LC 88-71494. (BEM Ser.: Vol. 10). 704p. 1988. 132.00 (*0-945824-02-5*) Computational Mech MA.

— Boundary Element Methods X Vol. 4: Geomechanics, Wave Propagation & Vibrations. LC 88-71494. (BEM Ser.: Vol. 10). 484p. 1988. 92.00 (*0-945824-03-3*) Computational Mech MA.

— Boundary Element Research. (Progress in Engineering Ser.). 100p. 1984. pap. 46.00 (*0-931215-02-1*) Computational Mech MA.

— Boundary Element Research in Europe. LC 98-84466. (Boundary Elements Ser.: Vol. 1). 344p. 1998. 157.00 (*1-85312-594-6*, 5946) Computational Mech MA.

— Boundary Element Techniques in Computer-Aided Engineering. LC 84-16710. 1984. text 206.50 (*90-247-3065-1*) Kluwer Academic.

— Boundary Element Technology VI. LC 91-71739. (BETECH Ser.: Vol. 6). 432p. 1991. 146.00 (*1-56252-067-9*, 1398) Computational Mech MA.

— Boundary Elements V. (BEM Ser.: Vol. 5). 1046p. 1983. 137.00 (*0-931215-46-3*) Computational Mech MA.

— Boundary Elements VI. (BEM Ser.: Vol. 6). 480p. 1984. 87.00 (*0-931215-47-1*) Computational Mech MA.

— Boundary Elements X, 4 vols. 1920p. 1988. 623.95 (*0-387-50095-2*) Spr-Verlag.

— Computational Aspects. (Topics in Boundary Elements Ser.: Vol. 3). 310p. 1987. 95.00 (*1-56252-139-X*) Computational Mech MA.

— Electrical Engineering Applications. (Topics in Boundary Elements Ser.: Vol. 7). 222p. 1990. 67.00 (*1-56252-142-X*) Computational Mech MA.

— Electromagnetic Applications. (Topics in Boundary Elements Ser.: Vol. 6). 246p. 1990. 75.00 (*1-56252-141-1*) Computational Mech MA.

— Finite Element Systems Handbook. 3rd ed. 735p. 1985. 99.00 (*0-931215-28-5*) Computational Mech MA.

— Mathematical & Computational Aspects. (Boundary Elements X Ser.: Vol. 1). 480p. 1988. 190.95 (*0-387-50091-X*) Spr-Verlag.

— Software for Engineering WorkStations: Finite Element Codes. LC 87-70263. (Progress in Engineering Ser.). 102p. 1987. pap. 46.00 (*0-931215-63-3*) Computational Mech MA.

— Stress Analysis. (Boundary Elements X Ser.: Vol. 3). 480p. 1988. 199.95 (*0-387-50093-6*) Spr-Verlag.

— Time Dependent & Vibration Problems. (Topics in Boundary Elements Ser.: Vol. 2). 271p. 1985. 83.00 (*1-56252-138-1*) Computational Mech MA.

— Variational Methods in Engineering. 500p. 1985. 99.00 (*0-931215-50-1*) Computational Mech MA.

— Variational Methods in Engineering. 750p. 1985. 190.95 (*0-387-15496-5*) Spr-Verlag.

— Viscous Flow Applications. (Topics in Boundary Elements Ser.: Vol. 5). 196p. 1990. 60.00 (*1-56252-140-3*) Computational Mech MA.

Brebbia, Carlos A., et al, eds. Advanced Computational Methods in Heat Transfer. LC 90-82732. (Heat Transfer Ser.: Vol. 1). 439p. 1990. 107.00 (*0-945824-68-8*) Computational Mech MA.

— Applications of High-Performance Computing in Engineering IV. LC 95-67472. (HPC Ser.). 344p. 1995. 157.00 (*1-56252-244-2*, 320X) Computational Mech MA.

— Applications of Supercomputers in Engineering II. LC 91-72946. (ASE Ser.). 572p. 1991. 193.00 (*1-56252-052-0*, 1185) Computational Mech MA.

— Boundary Elements XVIII: Proceedings of the 18th International Conference. LC 96-83670. (BEM Ser.: Vol. 18). 667p. 1996. 299.00 (*1-85312-404-4*, 4044) Computational Mech MA.

— Boundary Elements XIV, 2 vols., Set. LC 92-82810. (BEM Ser.: Vol. 14). 1444p. 1992. 549.00 (*1-56252-136-5*, 2114) Computational Mech MA.

— Boundary Elements XX. LC 99-203972. (Advances in Boundary Elements Ser.: Vol. 4). 736p. 1998. 349.00 (*1-85312-592-X*, 592X) Computational Mech MA.

— Computational Acoustics & its Environmental Applications. LC 95-67473. (Acoustics Ser.: Vol. 1). 304p. 1995. 129.00 (*1-56252-232-9*, 3080) Computational Mech MA.

— Computational Acoustics & Its Environmental Applications II. LC 97-67008. (Acoustics Ser.: Vol. 2). 240p. 1997. 138.00 (*1-85312-459-1*, 4591) Computational Mech MA.

— Computational Methods for Smart Structures & Materials II. (Structures & Materials Ser.). 300p. 2000. 149.00 (*1-85312-816-3*, 8163) Computational Mech MA.

— Computational Methods in Subsurface Hydrology: Proceedings of the Eighth International Conference, 11-15 June 1990, Venice, Italy, 2 vols., 1. xiii, 1131p. 1990. 158.95 (*0-387-52701-X*) Spr-Verlag.

— Computational Methods in Subsurface Hydrology: Proceedings of the Eighth International Conference, 11-15 June 1990, Venice, Italy, 2 vols., 2. xiii, 1131p. 1990. 158.95 (*0-387-52702-8*) Spr-Verlag.

— Computational Methods in Subsurface Hydrology: Proceedings of the Eighth International Conference, 11-15 June 1990, Venice, Italy, 2 vols., Set. xiii, 1131p. 1990. 236.00 (*0-387-52700-1*) Spr-Verlag.

— Computer Aided Design in Composite Material Technology. 600p. 1988. 199.95 (*0-387-19024-4*) Spr-Verlag.

— Computer Methods in Water Resources II: Computer Aided Engineering in Water Resources. LC 90-85862. (Computer Methods in Water Resources Ser.: Vol. 3). 347p. 1991. 89.00 (*1-56252-061-X*) Computational Mech MA.

— Computer Modelling of Seas & Coastal Regions II. LC 95-68888. (Coastal Ser.: Vol. 2). 448p. 1995. 192.00 (*1-56252-253-1*, 3293) Computational Mech MA.

— Finite Elements in Water Resources: Proceedings of the 5th International Conference, Burlington, Vermont, June 1984. 800p. 1984. 214.95 (*0-387-13468-9*) Spr-Verlag.

— Hydrosoft '86: Hydraulic Engineering Software. (HYDROSOFT Ser.: No. 2). 1986. 99.00 (*0-931215-31-5*) Computational Mech MA.

— Marine Technology II. LC 97-66367. (Marine Technology Ser.: Vol. 2). 568p. 1997. 268.00 (*1-85312-467-2*, 4672) Computational Mech MA.

— Software Quality Management III, 2 vols., Set. LC 95-67478. (SQM Ser.: Vol. 3). 952p. 1995. 336.00 (*1-56252-233-7*, 3099) Computational Mech MA.

— Software Quality Management III Vol. 1: Quality Management, 2 vols., Set. LC 95-67478. (SQM Ser.: Vol. 3). 494p. 1995. 190.00 (*1-56252-337-6*, 4168) Computational Mech MA.

— Software Quality Management III Vol. 2: Measuring & Maintaining Quality, 2 vols., Set. LC 95-67478. (SQM Ser.: Vol. 3). 458p. 1995. 176.00 (*1-56252-338-4*, 4176) Computational Mech MA.

— Software Quality Management II Vol. 1: Managing Quality Systems. LC 94-70402. (SQM Ser.: No. 2). 800p. 1994. 273.00 (*1-56252-277-9*, 3528) Computational Mech MA.

— Software Quality Management II Vol. 2: Building Quality into Software. LC 94-70402. (SQM Ser.: No. 2). 792p. 1994. 270.00 (*1-56252-278-7*, 3536) Computational Mech MA.

— Soil Dynamics & Earthquake Engineering. (SDEE Ser.: Vol. 2). 700p. 1985. 99.00 (*0-931215-54-4*) Computational Mech MA.

***Brebbia, Carlos A., et al, eds.** The Sustainable City: Urban Regeneration & Sustainability. 616p. 2000. 295.00 (*1-85312-811-2*, 8112) Computational Mech MA.

Brebbia, Carlos A. & Acinas, J. R., eds. Computer Modelling of Seas & Coastal Regions III. LC 97-67009. (Coastal Ser.: Vol. 3). 464p. 1997. 223.00 (*1-85312-499-0*, 4990) Computational Mech MA.

Brebbia, Carlos A. & Aliabadi, M. H., eds. Adaptive Finite & Boundary Element Methods. LC 92-75032. (Computational Engineering Ser.). 380p. 1993. 187.00 (*1-56252-114-4*, 1851) Computational Mech MA.

— Computational Techniques - Contact Mechanics. LC 93-71028. (Contact Mechanics Ser.: Vol. 1). 536p. 1993. 172.00 (*1-56252-163-2*, 2394) Computational Mech MA.

— Industrial Applications of the Boundary Element Method. LC 92-75037. 208p. 1993. 101.00 (*1-56252-112-8*, 1835) Computational Mech MA.

Brebbia, Carlos A. & Anagnostopoulos, P., eds. Coastal Engineering & Marina Developments: Proceedings of the 4th International Conference on Computer Modelling of Seas & Coastal Regions (COASTAL 99) (Environmental Studies: Vol. 3). 668p. 1999. 298.00 (*1-85312-686-1*, 6861, Pub. by WIT Pr) Computational Mech MA.

Brebbia, Carlos A. & Carlomagno, G. M., eds. Computational Methods & Experimental Measurements VI, 2 vols., Set. LC 92-75801. (CMEM Ser.: Vol. 6). 1152p. 1993. 506.00 (*1-56252-155-1*, 2300) Computational Mech MA.

— Computational Methods & Experimental Measurements VI: Heat & Fluid Flow, Vol. 1. LC 92-75801. (CMEM Ser.: Vol. 6). 588p. 1993. 258.00 (*1-56252-152-7*, 2289) Computational Mech MA.

— Computational Methods & Experimental Measurements VI Vol. 2: Stress Analysis. LC 92-75801. (CMEM Ser.: Vol. 6). 562p. 1993. 249.00 (*1-56252-153-5*, 2297) Computational Mech MA.

Brebbia, Carlos A. & Chaudet-Miranda, Mrs., eds. Boundary Elements in Mechanical & Electrical Engineering. LC 90-80853. (EUROBEM Ser.). 1990. 135.00 (*0-945824-44-0*) Computational Mech MA.

Brebbia, Carlos A. & Chaudouet-Miranda, A., eds. Boundary Elements in Mechanical & Electrical Engineering: European Boundary Element Method Symposium, 15-17 May 1990, Nice, France. (Illus.). 580p. 1990. 206.95 (*0-387-52645-5*) Spr-Verlag.

Brebbia, Carlos A. & Connor, J. J., eds. Advances in Boundary Elements, 3 vols. 1350p. 1989. 304.00 (*0-387-51452-X*, 3341) Spr-Verlag.

Brebbia, Carlos A. & Dominguez, J. Boundary Elements: An Introductory Course. 1989. text. write for info. (*0-07-007415-1*) McGraw.

— Boundary Elements: An Introductory Course. 2nd rev. ed. LC 91-77179. 314p. (C). 1992. text 145.00 (*1-56252-087-3*, 1606); text 188.00 incl. disk (*1-56252-273-6*, 3498) Computational Mech MA.

Brebbia, Carlos A. & Frewer, R. J., eds. Structural Repair & Maintenance of Historical Buildings III. LC 93-71023. (Stremah Ser.: Vol. 3). 664p. 1993. 221.00 (*1-56252-167-5*, 2440) Computational Mech MA.

Brebbia, Carlos A. & Gaul, L., eds. Computational Methods in Contact Mechanics IV. (Computational & Experimental Methods Ser.: Vol. 2). 552p. 1999. 235.00 (*1-85312-694-2*, 6942, Pub. by WIT Pr) Computational Mech MA.

Brebbia, Carlos A. & Gipson, G. Steven, eds. Boundary Elements XIII: Boundary Element Methods in Engineering. LC 91-73255. (BEM Ser.: Vol. 13). 1054p. 1991. 268.00 (*1-56252-072-5*, 1452) Computational Mech MA.

Brebbia, Carlos A. & Hernandez, S., eds. Computer Aided Optimum Design of Structure, 2 vols., Set. 800p. 1989. 227.00 (*0-387-51266-7*, 3201) Spr-Verlag.

— Computer Aided Optimum Design of Structures: Recent Advances. LC 86-61075. (OPTI Ser.: Vol. 1). 377p. 1989. 127.00 (*0-945824-09-2*) Computational Mech MA.

— Computer Aided Optimum Design of Structures Vol. 1: Recent Advances. 400p. 1989. 147.95 (*0-387-51263-2*, 3199) Spr-Verlag.

— Computer Aided Optimum Design of Structures Vol. 2: Applications. 400p. 1989. 123.00 (*0-387-51265-9*, 3200) Spr-Verlag.

— Optimization of Structural Systems & Applications: Computer Aided Optimum Design of Structures III. LC 93-71019. (OPTI Ser.: Vol. 3). 696p. 1993. 299.00 (*1-56252-166-7*, 2432) Computational Mech MA.

Brebbia, Carlos A. & Ingber, M. S., eds. Boundary Element Technology VII. LC 92-70437. (BETECH Ser.: Vol. 7). 964p. 1992. 337.00 (*1-56252-097-0*, 1681) Computational Mech MA.

Brebbia, Carlos A. & Kassab, A. J., eds. Boundary Element Technology IX. LC 94-70127. (BETECH Ser.: Vol. 9). 368p. 1994. 161.00 (*1-56252-206-X*, 2823) Computational Mech MA.

Brebbia, Carlos A. & Kenny, J., eds. Surface Treatment IV: Computer Methods & Experimental Measurements. (Computational & Experimental Methods Ser.: No. 3). 416p. 1999. 195.00 (*1-85312-697-7*, 6977, Pub. by WIT Pr) Computational Mech MA.

Brebbia, Carlos A. & Keramidas, G., eds. Reliability & Robustness of Engineering Software. LC 87-62015. (RRES Ser.). 540p. 1987. 138.00 (*0-931215-61-7*) Computational Mech MA.

Brebbia, Carlos A. & Keramidas, G. A., eds. Computational Methods & Experimental Measurements: Proceedings of the 2nd International Conference, on Board the Liner, the Queen Elizabeth 2, New York to Southhampton, June-July 1984. 800p. 1984. 184.95 (*0-387-13419-0*) Spr-Verlag.

Brebbia, Carlos A. & Maier, G., eds. Boundary Elements VII, 2 vols., Set. (BEM Ser.: Vol. 7). 1319p. 1985. 168.00 (*0-931215-05-6*) Computational Mech MA.

Brebbia, Carlos A. & Partridge, P. W., eds. Boundary Elements in Fluid Dynamics & Computer Modelling of Seas & Coastal Regions, 2 vols. 806p. 1992. 268.00 (*1-56252-121-7*) Computational Mech MA.

Brebbia, Carlos A. & Peters, A., eds. Applications of Supercomputers in Engineering, 2 vols., Set. LC 89-62253. (ASE Ser.: Vol. 1). 1989. 175.00 (*0-945824-29-7*, 0464) Computational Mech MA.

— Applications of Supercomputers in Engineering Vol. 1: Algorithms, Computer Systems & User Experience. LC 89-62253. (ASE Ser.: No. 1). 211p. 1989. 91.00 (*0-945824-27-0*, 0448) Computational Mech MA.

— Applications of Supercomputers in Engineering Vol. 2: Fluid Flow & Stress Applications. LC 89-62253. (ASE Ser.). 311p. 1989. 106.00 (*0-945824-28-9*, 0456) Computational Mech MA.

— Applications of Supercomputers in Engineering III. LC 93-71024. (ASE Ser.). 576p. 1993. 253.00 (*1-56252-160-8*, 236X) Computational Mech MA.

Brebbia, Carlos A. & Power, H., eds. Boundary Elements XXI: Proceedings of the International Conference. (Advances in Boundary Elements Ser.: No. 6). 787p. 1999. 344.00 (*1-85312-698-5*, 6985, Pub. by WIT Pr) Computational Mech MA.

— Boundary Elements XXII. (Advances in Boundary Elements Ser.: Vol. 8). 700p. 2000. 338.00 (*1-85312-824-4*, 8244, Pub. by WIT Pr) Computational Mech MA.

Brebbia, Carlos A. & Sanchez-Galvez, V., eds. Shock & Impact on Structures. LC 94-68173. 288p. 1994. 100.00 (*1-56252-221-3*, 2971) Computational Mech MA.

Brebbia, Carlos A. & Selvadural, A. P. S., eds. Damage & Fracture Mechanics VI. (Structures & Materials Ser.: Vol. 6). 632p. 2000. 289.00 (*1-85312-812-0*, 8120) Computational Mech MA.

Brebbia, Carlos A. & Venturini, W. S., eds. Boundary Element Techniques: Applications in Fluid Flow & Computational Aspects. LC 87-70506. (BETECH Ser.: Vol. 3). 260p. (C). 1987. 72.00 (*0-931215-77-3*) Computational Mech MA.

— Boundary Element Techniques: Applications in Stress Analysis & Heat Transfer. LC 87-70777. (BETECH Ser.: Vol. 3). 240p. 1987. 72.00 (*0-931215-76-5*) Computational Mech MA.

Brebbia, Carlos A. & Zamani, N. G., eds. Boundary Element Techniques--Applications in Engineering. LC 89-60747. (BETECH Ser.: Vol. 4). 452p. 1989. 109.00 (*0-945824-08-4*) Computational Mech MA.

Brebbia, Carlos A., et al. Boundary Element Techniques. 478p. 1984. text 110.00 (*1-56252-143-8*, 2181) Computational Mech MA.

— Computational Biomedicine. Held, K. D. et al, eds. LC 93-71017. (BIOMED Ser.: Vol. 2). 366p. 1993. 164.00 (*1-56252-162-4*, 2386) Computational Mech MA.

Brebbia, Carlos A., jt. auth. see Wendland, W. L.

Brebbia, Carlos A., ed. see Aliabaci, M. H., et al.

Brebbia, Carlos A., jt. ed. see Aliabadi, M. H.

Brebbia, Carlos A., ed. see Amini, S., et al.

Brebbia, Carlos A., jt. ed. see Blain, W. R.

Brebbia, Carlos A., ed. see Bruch, E.

Brebbia, Carlos A., jt. ed. see Cakmak, A. S.

Brebbia, Carlos A., ed. see Camp, C. V. & Gipson, G. Steven.

Brebbia, Carlos A., jt. ed. see Carlomagno, G. M.

An Asterisk (*) at the beginning of an entry indicates that the title is appearing for the first time.

Brebbia, Carlos A., jt. ed. see Carpinteri, A.
Brebbia, Carlos A., jt. ed. see Ciskowski, R. D.
Brebbia, Carlos A., jt. ed. see Connor, J. J.
Brebbia, Carlos A., ed. see Deconinck, J., et al.
Brebbia, Carlos A., jt. ed. see Garcia-Martinez, Reinaldo.
Brebbia, Carlos A., ed. see Hayami, K.
Brebbia, Carlos A., jt. ed. see Hernandez, S.
Brebbia, Carlos A., jt. ed. see Jones, N.
Brebbia, Carlos A., jt. ed. see Keramidas, G. A.
Brebbia, Carlos A., jt. ed. see Konrad, A.
Brebbia, Carlos A., jt. ed. see Melli, P.
Brebbia, Carlos A., jt. ed. see Murthy, T. K.
Brebbia, Carlos A., jt. ed. see Olivella, J.
Brebbia, Carlos A., jt. ed. see Ouazar, D.
Brebbia, Carlos A., jt. ed. see Pascolo, P.
Brebbia, Carlos A., jt. ed. see Pina, H.
Brebbia, Carlos A., jt. ed. see Puig-Pey, J.
Brebbia, Carlos A., jt. ed. see Rahman, M.
Brebbia, Carlos A., jt. ed. see Rencis, J. J.
Brebbia, Carlos A., jt. ed. see Silvester, P. P.
Brebbia, Carlos A., jt. ed. see Spanos, P. D.
Brebbia, Carlos A., jt. ed. see Sucharov, L. J.
Brebbia, Carlos A., jt. ed. see Sunden, B.
Brebbia, Carlos A., jt. ed. see Wrobel, L. C.
Brebbia, Carlos A., ed. see Wrobel, L. C., et al.

Brebeck, Theodore R. They Should Have Kept the Bear: The OK Miniature Engine Collector's Reference. (Illus.). 90p. 1995. pap. text 19.95 (*0-9628337-1-1*) Caretaker.

Brebion, Luc, tr. see Martin du Gard, Roger.

Brebler, Reinhard. Integration und Differenzierung Vol. VII: Grundrisse Einer Reformulierten Theorie der Sozialen Konstruktion Wissenschaftlich-Technischer Tatsachen. (Europaische Hochschulschriften: Reihe 22: Bd. 299). (GER.). VII, 342p. 1996. pap. 57.95 (*3-631-30979-1*) P Lang Pubng.

Brebner, C., et al. The Role of Infertility in Adoption. (C). 1989. 60.00 (*0-903534-62-2*, Pub. by Brit Ag for Adopt & Fost) St Mut.

***Brebner, Elaine.** Whispering Winds. 2000. pap. write for info. (*1-58235-431-6*) Watermrk Pr.

Brebner, John B. The Explorers of North America, Fourteen Ninety-Two to Eighteen Hundred Six. LC 83-45719. reprint ed. 67.50 (*0-404-20043-5*) AMS Pr.

— New England's Outpost, Acadia the Conquest of Canada. (BCL1 - History - Canada Ser.). 291p. 1991. reprint ed. lib. bdg. 79.00 (*0-7812-6367-0*) Rprt Serv.

Brebner, John B., tr. see Hansen, Marcus L.

Breborowicz, J. & MacKiewicz, A. Affinity Electrophoresis Principles & Application: Principles & Clinical Application. LC 91-20677. 304p. 1992. 164.00 (*0-8493-6665-8*, QP519, CRC Reprint) Franklin.

Breccia, E., ed. Inscriptiones Graecae Aegypti, No. 2: Alexandria. xxx, 273p. 1978. 30.00 (*0-89005-242-5*) Ares.

Brech, jt. auth. see Ghattas.

Brech, E. F. The Making of Scientific Management, 2 vols., Set. 438p. 1996. 150.00 (*1-85506-354-9*) Bks Intl VA.

Brech, Martha. Analyse Elektroakustischer Musik mit Hilfe von Sonagrammen. (Europaische Hochschulschriften, Reihe 36: Bd. 118). (GER., Illus.). 211p. 1994. 37.00 (*3-631-47427-X*) P Lang Pubng.

Brecheisen, Jerry. How to Prepare for Your Baptism. LC 96-840033. 48p. (Orig.). 1995. pap. 3.95 (*0-89827-129-0*, BKS11) Wesleyan Pub Hse.

— Turning Your Trauma into Triumph - Eight Practical Steps: Personal Insights from a Near Death Experience. (Illus.). 127p. 1996. 12.95 (*0-89827-162-2*, BK938) Wesleyan Pub Hse.

Brecher & Busch, eds. Research, Design & Analysis. LC 99-172014. 1998. text. write for info. (*1-56395-100-2*) Am Assn Blood.

Brecher, et al. Crises in the 20th Century, 2 vols. 1988. text 95.00 (*0-08-035834-9*, Pergamon Pr) Elsevier.

Brecher, jt. auth. see Gaiter.

Brecher, Arline. Bye-Bye Bypass: The Truth about Chelation Therapy. (Illus.). 296p. (Orig.). 1989. pap. 5.95 (*0-927839-58-X*) HlthSavers Pr.

— A Program for Staying Fit after Chelation. Brecher, Harold, ed. 80p. (Orig.). 1989. pap. 29.95 (*0-927839-13-X*) HlthSavers Pr.

Brecher, Arline & Brecher, Harold. Forty Something Forever: A Consumer's Guide to Chelation Therapy & Other Heart-Savers. (Illus.). 377p. 1992. pap. 6.95 (*0-927839-46-6*) HlthSavers Pr.

Brecher, Bob, et al, eds. Nationalism & Racism in the Liberal Order. LC 98-70988. (Avebury Series in Philosophy). 244p. 1998. text 63.95 (*1-84014-148-4*, Pub. by Ashgate Pub) Ashgate Pub Co.

— The University in a Liberal State. (Avebury Series in Philosophy). 160p. 1996. 61.95 (*1-85628-987-7*, Pub. by Avebury) Ashgate Pub Co.

Brecher, Charles. Upgrading Blue Collar & Service Workers. LC 79-186512. (Policy Studies in Employment & Welfare: No. 12). 127p. reprint ed. pap. 39.40 (*0-608-10699-2*, 202049400018) Bks Demand.

Brecher, Charles & Horton, Raymond D., eds. Setting Municipal Priorities, 1981. LC 80-67392. 212p. 1981. text 38.50 (*0-86598-010-1*) Rowman.

Brecher, Charles & Spiezio, Sheila. The Privatization & Public Hospitals: Choosing Wisely for New York City. LC 95-11195. 96p. (C). 1995. pap. 9.95 (*0-87078-371-8*) Century Foundation.

Brecher, Charles, et al. Political Change in New York City: Politics & Policy since 1960. 1993. write for info. (*0-318-69291-0*) OUP.

— Power Failure: New York City Politics & Policy since 1960. 416p. (C). 1993. 35.00 (*0-19-504427-4*) OUP.

Brecher, Charles, jt. ed. see Benjamin, Gerald.

Brecher, Edward. The Sex Researchers. 410p. 1979. 9.50 (*0-317-34150-2*) Specific Pr.

Brecher, Elinor J. Schindler's Legacy: True Stories of the List Survivors. (Illus.). 442p. 1994. pap. 14.95 (*0-452-27353-6*, Plume) Dutton Plume.

Brecher, Erwin. The IQ Booster: Improve Your IQ Performance Dramatically. 128p. 1996. pap. 7.95 (*0-8069-9422-3*) Sterling.

— Lateral Logic Puzzles. LC 94-18776. (Illus.). 96p. 1994. pap. 4.95 (*0-8069-0618-9*) Sterling.

— Surprising Science Puzzles. LC 94-16838. (Illus.). 96p. 1995. 14.95 (*0-8069-0698-7*) Sterling.

— Surprising Science Puzzles. (Illus.). 96p. 1996. pap. 5.95 (*0-8069-0699-5*) Sterling.

— World Class Puzzles. LC 96-28212. (Illus.). 96p. 1996. pap. 5.95 (*0-8069-9458-4*) Sterling.

Brecher, Erwin & Gerrard, Mike. Challenging Science Puzzles. LC 96-49194. (Illus.). 96p. 1997. pap. 5.95 (*0-8069-9610-2*) Sterling.

Brecher, Frank W. Losing a Continent: France's North American Policy, 1753-1763, 62. LC 98-13974. (Contributions to the Study of World History Ser.: Vol. 62). 240p. 1998. 65.00 (*0-313-30786-5*, Greenwood Pr) Greenwood.

— Reluctant Ally: United States Foreign Policy Toward the Jews from Wilson to Roosevelt, 278. LC 91-45. (Contributions in Political Science Ser.: No. 278). 192p. 1991. 52.95 (*0-313-27900-4*, BLU, Greenwood Pr) Greenwood.

Brecher, Harold, jt. auth. see Brecher, Arline.

Brecher, Harold, ed. see Brecher, Arline.

Brecher, Irving. Human Rights, Development & Foreign Policy: Canadian Perspectives. 579p. 1989. 35.95 (*0-88645-101-9*, Pub. by Inst Res Pub) Ashgate Pub Co.

Brecher, Irving, jt. ed. see Savoie, Donald J.

Brecher, James, jt. auth. see Conover, Jim.

Brecher, Jeremy. Strike! 4th rev. ed. Marable, Manning, ed. LC 97-33289. (Classics Ser.: Vol. 1). (Illus.). 420p. 1997. 40.00 (*0-89608-570-8*); pap. 22.00 (*0-89608-569-4*) South End Pr.

Brecher, Jeremy, et al, eds. Global Visions: Beyond the New World Order. 317p. write for info. (*1-895431-75-1*); pap. write for info. (*1-895431-74-3*) Black Rose.

— Global Visions: Beyond the New World Order. 317p. 1993. 40.00 (*0-89608-461-2*); pap. 16.00 (*0-89608-460-4*) South End Pr.

Brecher, Jeremy & Costello, Tim. Global Village or Global Pillage: Economic Reconstruction from the Bottom Up. 2nd ed. LC 98-22232. 237p. 1998. 40.00 (*0-89608-592-9*); pap. 16.00 (*0-89608-591-0*) South End Pr.

— Global Village vs. Global Pillage: A One-World Strategy for Labor. 39p. 1991. pap. 3.75 (*1-880103-02-8*) Intl Labor Rghts.

Brecher, Jeremy & Costello, Tim, eds. Building Bridges: The Emerging Grassroots Coalition of Labor & Community. 320p. 1990. 30.00 (*0-85345-791-3*, Pub. by Monthly Rev); pap. 16.00 (*0-85345-792-1*, Pub. by Monthly Rev) NYU Pr.

***Brecher, Jeremy, et al.** Globalization from Below: The Power of Solidarity. 128p. 2000. 40.00 (*0-89608-623-2*); pap. 12.00 (*0-89608-622-4*) South End Pr.

Brecher, Jeremy, jt. auth. see Dawkins, Kristin.

Brecher, Kenneth & Feirtag, Michael, eds. Astronomy of the Ancients. (Illus.). 1981. pap. text 9.95 (*0-262-52070-2*) MIT Pr.

Brecher, Kenneth & Setti, Giancarlo, eds. High Energy Astrophysics. 1975. pap. text 12.50 (*0-262-52035-4*) MIT Pr.

Brecher, Kenneth S. Too Sad to Sing. LC 87-19679. 1988. pap. 11.95 (*0-15-690465-9*) Harcourt.

— Too Sad to Sing: A Memoir with Postcards. 144p. 1988. 22.95 (*0-318-32726-0*); pap. 11.95 (*0-318-32727-9*) Harcourt.

Brecher, Mark E., et al, eds. Hematopoietic Progenitor Cells: Processing, Standards & Practice. (Illus.). 205p. (C). 1995. 50.00 (*1-56395-050-2*) Am Assn Blood.

Brecher, Mark E. & Jefferies, Leigh C., eds. Orthopedic Transfusion Therapy. LC 95-44616. (Illus.). 107p. (C). 1995. 40.00 (*1-56395-046-4*) Am Assn Blood.

Brecher, Mark E., jt. ed. see Jefferies, Leigh C.

Brecher, Mark E., jt. ed. see Sacher, Ronald A.

Brecher, Michael. Crisis in World Politics: Theory & Reality. LC 92-29898. 694p. 1993. pap. 74.95 (*0-08-041377-3*, Prgamon Press) Buttrwrth-Heinemann.

— Nehru: A Political Biography. (Illus.). 704p. 1999. pap. text 29.95 (*0-19-564756-4*) OUP.

Brecher, Michael, ed. Studies in Crisis Behavior. 384p. (C). 1979. text 44.95 (*0-87855-292-8*) Transaction Pubs.

Brecher, Michael & Wilkenfeld, Jonathan. Crisis, Conflict & Instability: The Analysis of Crises in the Twentieth Century, Vol. 3. 289p. 1989. pap. text 69.95 (*0-08-036502-7*, Prgamon Press) Buttrwrth-Heinemann.

Brecher, Michael & Wilkenfeld, Jonathan. A Study of Crisis. (Illus.). 1088p. (C). pap. text. write for info. (*0-472-08638-3*); pap. text 47.50 incl. cd-rom (*0-472-08707-X*, 08707) U of Mich Pr.

Brecher, Michael & Wilkenfeld, Jonathan. A Study of Crisis. LC 97-6067. 1088p. (C). 1997. text 115.00 (*0-472-10806-9*, 10806) U of Mich Pr.

Brecher, Michael, et al. Crises in the Twentieth Century, 2 vols., Set. 648p. 1988. 299.95 (*0-08-034981-1*, Prgamon Press) Buttrwrth-Heinemann.

Brecher, Paul. Principles of Tai Chi. 1998. pap. 11.00 (*0-7225-3474-4*) Thorsons PA.

— The Way of the Spiritual Warrior. LC 98-48408. (Illus.). 128p. 1998. 19.95 (*0-8069-7079-0*) Sterling.

— Way of the Spiritual Warrior: Soft Style Martial Arts for Body, Mind, & Spirit. LC 98-48408. 1999. pap. text 14.95 (*0-8069-7080-4*) Sterling.

Brecher, Robert. Anselm's Argument: The Logic of Divine Existence. 200p. 1985. 72.95 (*0-566-05022-6*) Ashgate Pub Co.

— Getting What You Want: A Critique of Liberal Morality. LC 97-7484. (Ideas Ser.). 232p. (C). 1997. 70.00 (*0-415-12951-6*); pap. 20.99 (*0-415-12952-4*) Routledge.

***Brecher, W. Puck.** An Investigation of Japan's Relationship to Nature & Environment. LC 00-36161. (Japanese Studies: Vol. 12). 376p. 2000. 99.95 (*0-7734-7768-3*) E Mellen.

Brecher, W. Puck. Nature Watch: Writings from Japan. (ENG & JPN.). 215p. (Orig.). 1999. pap. 18.50 (*1-55212-228-X*, 98-0047, Pub. by Tra3fford) Trafford Pub.

Brechin, Gray A. Imperial San Francisco: Urban Power, Earthly Ruin. LC 98-49052. (Studies in Critical Human Geography: Vol. 3). 402p. 1999. 29.95 (*0-520-21568-0*, Pub. by U CA Pr) Cal Prin Full Svc.

Brechin, Gray A., jt. auth. see Dawson, Robert.

Brechin, Steven R. Planting Trees in the Developing World: A Sociology of International Organizations. LC 96-27636. (Illus.). 280p. 1997. text 48.50 (*0-8018-5439-3*) Johns Hopkins.

Brechin, Steven R., jt. ed. see West, Patrick C.

Brechlin, Earl. A Pocket Guide to Hiking on Mt. Desert Island. LC 95-71936. (Illus.). 72p. (Orig.). 1996. pap. 7.95 (*0-89272-356-4*) Down East.

— A Pocket Guide to Paddling the Waters of Mt. Desert Island. LC 96-83695. (Illus.). 64p. (Orig.). 1996. pap. 7.95 (*0-89272-357-2*) Down East.

Brechling, Frank & Laurence, Louise. Permanent Job Loss & the U. S. System of Financing Unemployment Insurance. LC 95-19352. 116p. 1995. text 30.00 (*0-88099-160-7*) W E Upjohn.

Brechling, Frank P. & Laurence, Louise. Permanent Job Loss & the U. S. System of Financing Unemployment Insurance. LC 95-19352. 116p. 1995. pap. text 11.00 (*0-88099-159-3*) W E Upjohn.

Brechne. Contemporary Math, Business & Consumers. (C). 1997. student ed. write for info. (*0-03-018159-3*) Harcourt Coll Pubs.

— Contemporary Math Business & Consumers. 1996. 246.00 (*0-03-097881-5*) Harcourt Coll Pubs.

— Contemporary Math Business & Consumers. 1997. pap. text 33.50 (*0-03-097877-7*) Harcourt Coll Pubs.

— Contemporary Math for Business. 1996. 246.00 (*0-03-020349-X*, Pub. by Harcourt Coll Pubs) Harcourt.

— Mathematics for Business. (C). 1995. pap. text 37.50 (*0-03-096610-8*) Harcourt Coll Pubs.

Brechner, Irv. Easy to Understand Computer Directions. 1985. pap. 5.95 (*0-684-17803-6*, Scribners Ref) Mac Lib Ref.

Brechner, Irv, jt. auth. see Schwartz, Lester.

***Brechner, Robert A.** Contemporary Mathematics for Business & Consumers. 2nd ed. 1999. pap. text 56.00 (*0-03-026074-4*) HarBrace.

Brechner, Robert A. Contemporary Mathematics for Business & Consumers. 2nd ed. LC 99-60177. (C). 1999. text 74.00 (*0-03-025964-9*) Harcourt.

***Brechner, Robert A.** Contemporary Mathematics for Business & Consumers. 2nd ed. 1999. pap. text 57.50 (*0-03-026249-6*) Harcourt Coll Pubs.

Brechner, Robert A. Contemporary Mathematics for Business & Consumers. 2nd ed. (C). 1999. pap. text 74.00 (*0-03-026077-9*); pap. text 44.50 (*0-03-026078-7*) Harcourt Coll Pubs.

Brechot, Christian. Primary Liver Cancer: Etiology & Progression Factors. 320p. 1994. lib. bdg. 195.00 (*0-8493-4913-3*) CRC Pr.

Brecht, Arnold. The Art & Technique of Administration in German Ministries. LC 70-138205. (Illus.). 191p. 1971. reprint ed. lib. bdg. 55.00 (*0-8371-5557-6*, BRGM, Greenwood Pr) Greenwood.

— Political Theory: The Foundations of Twentieth Century Political Thought. LC 59-5591. 607p. reprint ed. pap. 188.20 (*0-608-30088-8*, 201501100092) Bks Demand.

Brecht, Bertolt. Baal. Willett, John & Manheim, Ralph, eds. Tegel, Peter, tr. from GER. LC 98-72438. 96p. 1998. pap. 10.45 (*1-55970-419-5*, Pub. by Arcade Pub Inc) Time Warner.

— Baal, A Man's A Man, & The Elephant Calf. Bentley, Eric, ed. & tr. by. from GER. Esslin, Martin, tr. from GER. LC 64-13781. 224p. 1989. pap. 9.95 (*0-8021-3159-X*, Grove) Grove-Atltic.

— Bertolt Brecht: Journals 1934-1955. (Illus.). 574p. (C). (gr. 13). 1995. pap. 24.99 (*0-415-91282-2*, C0606) Routledge.

— Bertolt Brecht, Journals 1934 to 1955. 576p. (C). (gr. 13). 1993. text 45.00 (*0-415-90837-X*, Pub. by Tavistock) Routldge.

— Brecht on Theatre. Willett, John, tr. from GER. (Illus.). 352p. 1964. pap. 14.00 (*0-8090-0542-5*) Hill & Wang.

— The Caucasian Chalk Circle. Willett, John & Manheim, Ralph, eds. Stern, James et al, trs. from GER. LC 94-2517. 144p. (C). 1994. pap. 9.70 (*1-55970-253-2*, Pub. by Arcade Pub Inc) Time Warner.

— The Caucasian Chalk Circle. Bentley, Eric, tr. from GER. LC 99-46426. 120p. 1999. pap. 8.95 (*0-8166-3528-5*, Pub. by U of Minn Pr) Chicago Distribution Ctr.

— Collected Stories. Willett, John & Manheim, Ralph, eds. Kapp, Yvonne et al, trs. from GER. LC 97-43476. 256p. 1998. pap. 12.45 (*1-55970-402-0*, Pub. by Arcade Pub Inc) Time Warner.

— Die Dreigroschenoper. Ackermann, Paul K., ed. LC 82-3191. (Suhrkamp/Insel Ser.). (ENG & GER.). xiv, 118p. 1988. pap. 10.00 (*3-518-03049-3*, Pub. by Suhr Verlag) Intl Bk Import.

— Edward the Second. Bentley, Eric, tr. from GER. & intro. by. LC 66-27698. 128p. 1970. pap. 7.95 (*0-8021-5147-7*, Grove) Grove-Atltic.

— Galileo. Bentley, Eric, ed. Laughton, Charles, tr. from GER. LC 66-27699. 160p. 1987. pap. 6.95 (*0-8021-3059-3*, Grove) Grove-Atltic.

— The Good Person of Szechwan. Manheim, Ralph, ed. Willett, John, ed. & tr. by. from GER. LC 93-25407. 160p. 1994. pap. 8.70 (*1-55970-235-4*, Pub. by Arcade Pub Inc) Time Warner.

— The Good Person of Szechwan, Mother Courage & Her Children & Fear & Misery in the Third Reich, Vol. 2. Willett, John, tr. from GER. 320p. (C). 1993. pap. 14.45 (*1-55970-189-7*, Pub. by Arcade Pub Inc) Time Warner.

— The Good Woman of Setzuan. Bentley, Eric, tr. from GER. LC 99-45732. 120p. 1999. pap. 8.95 (*0-8166-3527-7*, Pub. by U of Minn Pr) Chicago Distribution Ctr.

— Der Gute Mensch von Sezuan. (GER.). (C). 1964. 9.95 (*0-8442-2892-3*, X2892-3) NTC Contemp Pub Co.

— Jungle of the Cities & Other Plays: Jungle of the Cities; Drums in the Night; Roundheads & Peakheads. Bentley, Eric, ed. LC 65-23860. 283p. 1966. reprint ed. pap. 10.95 (*0-8021-5149-3*, Grove) Grove-Atltic.

— Der Kaukasische Kreidekreis. (GER.). (C). 1955. 9.95 (*0-8442-2746-3*, X2746-3) NTC Contemp Pub Co.

— Leben des Galilei. 2nd ed. Brookes, H. F. & Fraenkel, C. E., eds. 204p. (Orig.). (C). 1995. pap. text 13.00 (*0-435-38123-7*, 38123) Heinemann.

— Life of Galileo. Willett, John, ed. & tr. by. from GER. Manheim, Ralph, ed. LC 94-4009. 288p. (C). 1994. pap. 10.45 (*1-55970-254-0*, Pub. by Arcade Pub Inc) Time Warner.

— The Life of Galileo, the Resistible Rise of Arturo Uo, the Caucasian Chalk Circle. Willett, John et al, trs. from GER. LC 93-24754. 352p. (Orig.). 1994. pap. 12.45 (*1-55970-190-0*, Pub. by Arcade Pub Inc) Time Warner.

***Brecht, Bertolt.** Man Equals Man & The Elephant Calf. Willett, John & Manheim, Ralph, eds. Nellhaus, Gerald, tr. from GER. LC 99-59183. 160p. 2000. pap. 10.95 (*1-55970-501-9*, Pub. by Arcade Pub Inc) Time Warner.

Brecht, Bertolt. Manual of Piety: Die Hauspostille. Bentley, Eric, tr. from GER. LC 91-20789. 336p. 1970. pap. 11.95 (*0-8021-3245-6*, Grove) Grove-Atltic.

***Brecht, Bertolt.** The Measures Taken & Other Lehrstucke. 2001. reprint ed. pap. 9.95 (*1-55970-544-2*, Pub. by Arcade Pub Inc) Time Warner.

Brecht, Bertolt. Mr. Puntila & His Man Matti. Manheim, Ralph, ed. Willett, John, tr. from GER. & intro. by. LC 94-13982. 176p. 1997. pap. 9.70 (*1-55970-280-X*, Pub. by Arcade Pub Inc) Time Warner.

— The Mother. Baxandall, Lee, tr. from GER. LC 65-14211. 160p. 1989. pap. 7.95 (*0-8021-3160-3*, Grove) Grove-Atltic.

— Mother Courage & Her Children. Manheim, Ralph, ed. Willett, John, ed. & tr. by. from GER. LC 93-25408. 176p. 1994. pap. 8.70 (*1-55970-234-6*, Pub. by Arcade Pub Inc) Time Warner.

— Mother Courage & Her Children. 112p. 1996. pap. 10.45 (*1-55970-361-X*, Pub. by Arcade Pub Inc) Time Warner.

— Mother Courage & Her Children. Bentley, Eric, tr. from GER. & adapted by. by. LC 91-761. 128p. 1987. pap. 6.95 (*0-8021-3082-8*, Grove) Grove-Atltic.

— Mother Courage & Her Children. 1999. text 10.95 (*0-312-54923-7*) St Martin.

— Plays: The Threepenny Opera, The Measures Taken, Galileo, Mother Courage & Her Children, Baal. LC 56-12398. 324p. 1995. pap. 24.95 (*0-8264-0737-4*) Continuum.

— Plays: The Threepenny Opera, The Measures Taken, Galileo, Mother Courage & Her Children, Baal. Grimm, Reinhold & Molina y Vedia, Caroline, eds. LC 76-20409. (German Library: Vol. 75). 324p. (C). 1999. 39.95 (*0-8264-0736-6*) Continuum.

***Brecht, Bertolt.** The Resistible Rise of Arturo Ui. 2001. reprint ed. pap. 10.95 (*1-55970-543-4*, Pub. by Arcade Pub Inc) Time Warner.

Brecht, Bertolt. The Rise & Fall of the City of Mahagony & the Seven Deadly Sins of the Petty Bourgeoisie. Manheim, Ralph, ed. Auden, W. H. & Kallman, Chester, trs. from GER. LC 94-10421. 144p. 1996. pap. 8.70 (*1-55970-279-6*, Pub. by Arcade Pub Inc) Time Warner.

— Saint Joan of the Stockyards. Manheim, Ralph, ed. & tr. by. Willett, John, ed. 160p. 1998. pap. 10.45 (*1-55970-420-9*, Pub. by Arcade Pub Inc) Time Warner.

***Brecht, Bertolt.** Schweyk in the Second World War. Willett, John & Manheim, Ralph, eds. Rowlinson, William et al, trs. from GER. LC 99-58830. 224p. 2000. pap. 11.95 (*1-55970-502-7*, Pub. by Arcade Pub Inc) Time Warner.

Brecht, Bertolt. Short Stories, 1921-1946. Willett, John & Manheim, Ralph, eds. Knapp, Yvonne et al, trs. 1983. 14.95 (*0-413-37050-X*, NO. 3765) Routledge.

— St. Joan of the Stockyards. Jones, Frank, tr. LC 69-16006. 128p. 1970. pap. 8.95 (*0-253-20127-6*, MB 127) Ind U Pr.

— The Three Penny Opera, Baal & the Mother, Vol. 1. Manheim, Ralph et al, trs. from GER. LC 93-16334. 248p. (C). 1993. pap. 11.45 (*1-55970-188-9*, Pub. by Arcade Pub Inc) Time Warner.

Brecht, Bertolt. Threepenny Opera. Date not set. lib. bdg. 17.95 (*0-8488-1668-4*) Amereon Ltd.

Brecht, Bertolt. Threepenny Opera. Vesey, Desmond, tr. from FRE. LC 64-8478. 128p. 1983. pap. 6.95 (*0-8021-5039-X*, Grove) Grove-Atltic.

— The Threepenny Opera. Willett, John & Manheim, Ralph, eds. & trs. by. from GER. LC 94-1775. 144p. (C). 1994. pap. 8.70 (*1-55970-252-4*, Pub. by Arcade Pub Inc) Time Warner.

— The Tutor. Broughton, Pip, tr. from GER. (Old Vic Theatre Collection Ser.: Vol. 2). 86p. 1989. pap. 7.95 (*1-55783-022-3*) Applause Theatre Bk Pubs.

— Two Plays by Bertolt. 1983. pap. 11.95 (*0-452-01055-1*, Mer) NAL.

B

Brecht, Bertolt & Bentley, Eric. The Jewish Wife & Other Short Plays: The Jewish Wife; In Search of Justice; The Informer; The Elephant Calf; The Measures Taken. LC 91-34823. 172p. 1965. reprint ed. pap. 9.95 (0-8021-5098-5, Grove) Grove-Atltic.

Brecht, Bertolt, et al. Essays on the German Theater. Herzfeld-Sander, Margaret, ed. (German Library: Vol. 83). 320p. 1985. 39.50 (0-8264-0296-8) Continuum.

— Happy End. 70p. 1983. pap. 7.95 (0-413-51020-4, NO. 3763) Routledge.

— Happy End. Feingold, Michael, tr. 70p. 1983. 14.95 (0-413-50950-8, NO. 3762) Routledge.

Brecht, Harold. Downfall. 1993. reprint ed. lib. bdg. 89.00 (0-7812-5434-5) Rprt Serv.

Brecht, Kurt. Notes from the Nest. 2nd ed. (Illus.). 41p. 1988. pap. 4.00 (1-879188-00-7) Dirty Rotten Pr.

— See the Loud Feeling. 88p. (Orig.). (C). 1990. pap. 4.00 (1-879188-02-3) Dirty Rotten Pr.

— The Thirty-Day Diarrhea Diet Plan. 86p. (Orig.). (C). 1989. pap. 4.00 (1-879188-01-5) Dirty Rotten Pr.

— Whore Stories. 54p. (Orig.). (C). 1994. pap. 5.00 (1-879188-03-1) Dirty Rotten Pr.

Brecht, Lyle A. America Report: A Common Sense Annual Report to the Citizens of the United States. 32p. 1994. pap. text. write for info. (0-9642575-0-5) Blue Heron MD.

Brecht, Martin. Martin Luther: His Road to Reformation, 1483-1521. Schaaf, James L., tr. 592p. 1985. pap. 29.00 (0-8006-2813-6, 1-2813) Augsburg Fortress.

— Martin Luther: Shaping & Defining the Reformation, 1521-1532. LC 84-47911. 560p. 1994. pap. 29.00 (0-8006-2814-4, 1-2814, Fortress Pr) Augsburg Fortress.

***Brecht, Martin.** Martin Luther: The Preservation of the Church, 1532-1546. 1999. pap. text 29.00 (0-8006-2815-2) Augsburg Fortress.

Brecht, Martin. Martin Luther Vol. 3: The Preservation of the Church, 1532-1546. Schaaf, James L., tr. 544p. 1993. 48.00 (0-8006-2704-0) Augsburg Fortress.

***Brecht, Martin & Zwink, Eberhard.** Eine Glossierte Vulgata Aus Dem Umkreis Martin Luthers: Untersuchungen Zu Dem 1519 in Lyon Gedruckten Exemplar in der Bibelsammlung der Wurttembergischen Landesbibliothek Stuttgart Arbeitsgespräch in der Wurttembergischen Landesbibliothek Stuttgart Vom 20. Bis 22, Februar 1997. (Vestigia Bibliae, Jahrbuch des Deutschen Bibel-Archivs Hamburg Ser.). 407p. 1999. 76.95 (3-906762-86-6, Pub. by P Lang) P Lang Pubng.

Brecht, Martin R. 5-A Process of Programming: Simple Process! Powerful Decisions! Accurate Results! 80p. 1999. pap. 9.00 (0-8059-4645-4) Dorrance.

Brecht, Richard, et al. Russian in the United States: Market Forces, Strategic Capacity, & the National Interest. (C). 1995. pap. text. write for info. (1-880671-04-2) NFLC Pubns.

Brecht, Richard D. Russian: Stage Two : Grammar for Communications, Analysis & Commentaries LC 99-165066. 148p. 1997. write for info. (0-7872-3963-1) Kendall-Hunt.

***Brecht, Richard D. & Rivers, William P.** Language & National Security for the 21st Century: The Role of Title VI-Fulbright-Hays in Supporting National Language Capacity. LC 99-462082. (C). 2000. text 30.00 (1-880671-06-9) NFLC Pubns.

Brecht, S. K., ed. Schwenkfelder, 2 vols. 1752p. 1991. reprint ed. pap. 215.00 (0-8328-2079-2); reprint ed. lib. bdg. 225.00 (0-8328-2078-4) Higginson Bk Co.

Brecht, Stefan. Queer Theatre. 178p. (Orig.). 1985. pap. 9.95 (3-518-02489-2, 9412) Routledge.

— The Theatre of Visions: Robert Wilson. 440p. (Orig.). 1984. pap. 14.95 (3-518-02488-4, 9413) Routledge.

Brechtefeld, Jorg. Mitteleuropa & German Politics: 1848 to the Present. LC 95-52081. 240p. 1996. text 59.95 (0-312-15841-6) St Martin.

Brechtken-Manderscheid, U. An Introduction to the Calculus of Variations. Engstrom, P., tr. from GER. 216p. (gr. 13). 1994. ring bd. 52.95 (0-412-36700-9, A6088, Chap & Hall CRC) CRC Pr.

— Introduction to the Calculus of Variations. Engstrom, P., tr. from GER. 216p. (gr. 13). 1991. ring bd. 89.95 (0-412-36690-8, A6084, Chap & Hall CRC) CRC Pr.

Brecia. Western Heritage Brief, Vol. 1. 1995. pap. text, student ed., wbk. ed. 21.40 (0-13-466806-5) P-H.

Breck, et al. Chemistry for Science & Engineering. 450p. 1982. text 29.95 (0-07-092372-8) McGraw.

Breck, Allen D. From the Rockies to the World: A Companion to the History of the University of Denver, 1864-1995. 2nd ed. (Illus.). 260p. 1996. 25.00 (0-9648871-0-X) Univ Denver.

Breck, Evelyn, ed. see Parker, Elizabeth.

Breck, John. The Power of the Word: Holy Scripture in Orthodox Interpretation, Confession & Celebration. LC 86-24773. 237p. 1987. pap. 10.95 (0-88141-043-8) St Vladimirs.

— The Sacred Gift of Life: Orthodox Christianity & Bioethics LC 98-49629. 1998. write for info. (0-88141-183-3) St Vladimirs.

— The Shape of Biblical Language: Chiasmus in & Beyond the Scriptures. LC 94-30129. 392p. 1994. pap. 16.95 (0-88141-139-6) St Vladimirs.

— The Spirit of Truth. LC 90-23505. (Origins of Johannine Pneumatology). 244p. (Orig.). 1990. pap. 10.95 (0-88141-081-0) St Vladimirs.

Breck, John, tr. see Monk of the Eastern Church Staff.

Breck, Joseph. The Flower Garden. LC 87-28192. (Illus.). 336p. 1988. reprint ed. 24.95 (0-940983-18-4) OPUS Pubns.

— The Young Florist. LC 87-31444. (Illus.). 168p. 1988. reprint ed. 13.95 (0-940983-20-6) OPUS Pubns.

Breck, Michael, tr. see Quenot, Michel.

Breck, Philip. The Beginner's Ancestor Research Kit. (Mature Reader Ser.). 96p. 1990. pap. 9.95 (1-55867-019-X) Bristol Pub Ent CA.

Breck, Richard, ed. ISHM Proceedings, 1990. 23rd ed. (Illus.). 900p. (C). 1990. 75.00 (0-930815-27-0) Intl Soc Hybrid.

Breck, Richard, jt. ed. see Aronson, Bernard.

Brecka, Shawn. The Bean Family Album & Collector's Guide. (Illus.). 160p. 1998. pap. 19.95 (0-930625-95-1, Antique Trader) Krause Pubns.

— The Bean Family Pocket Guide: Fall/ Winter 1999 Values & Trends. (Illus.). 272p. 1999. pap. 12.95 (1-58221-013-6) Krause Pubns.

— Big Book of Little Bears: Identification & Price Guide. LC 99-68990. (Illus.). 160p. 2000. pap. 21.95 (1-58221-021-7, Antique Trader) Krause Pubns.

— Collecting in Cyberspace: A Guide to 2000+ Sites for Antiques & Collectibles. LC 97-72623. (Illus.). 160p. 1997. pap. 14.95 (0-930625-69-2) Krause Pubns.

***Brecke, Ronald F.** A Republic, If You Can Keep It. LC 99-58070. 160p. 2000. 45.00 (0-7391-0101-3) Lxngtn Bks.

Breckenridge, ed. Glacial Lake Missoula & the Channeled Scabland. (IGC Field Trip Guidebooks Ser.). 80p. 1989. 28.00 (0-87590-619-2, T310) Am Geophysical.

***Breckenridge, Jan & Laing, Lesley.** Challenge Silence: Innovative Responses to Sexual & Domestic Violence. 336p. 2000. pap. 24.95 (1-86448-725-9, Pub. by Allen & Unwin Pty) Paul & Co Pubs.

Breckenridge, A., ed. Drugs in the Management of Heart Disease. 1984. text 127.50 (0-85200-724-8) Kluwer Academic.

Breckenridge, A. M. Advanced Medicine: Topics in Therapeutics, No. 1. (Pitman Medical Conference Reports). (Illus.). 200p. 1975. pap. 32.00 (0-8464-0114-2) Beekman Pubs.

— Advanced Medicine: Topics in Therapeutics, No. 3. (Pitman Medical Conference Reports). (Illus.). 1976. pap. 32.00 (0-8464-0115-0) Beekman Pubs.

— Advanced Medicine: Topics in Therapeutics, No. 4. (Pitman Medical Conference Reports). (Illus.). 1977. 32.00 (0-8464-0116-9) Beekman Pubs.

Breckenridge, A. M., ed. see Royal College of Physicians Staff.

Breckenridge, Adam C. Congress Against the Court. LC 79-113168. 170p. reprint ed. pap. 52.70 (0-8357-5593-2, 203523200093) Bks Demand.

— The Right to Privacy. LC 73-88084. 163p. reprint ed. pap. 50.60 (0-8357-3789-6, 203652000003) Bks Demand.

Breckenridge, Carol A., ed. Consuming Modernity: Public Culture in a South Asian World. LC 94-46772. 1995. pap. 18.95 (0-8166-2306-6); text 47.95 (0-8166-2305-8) U of Minn Pr.

***Breckenridge, Carol A., et al, eds.** Cosmopolitanism. 231p. 2000. pap. 12.00 (0-8223-6481-6) Duke.

Breckenridge, Carol A., ed. see Van Der Veer, Peter.

Breckenridge, Donald. Rockaway Wherein. 32p. 1998. pap. 6.95 (0-87376-085-9) Red Dust.

Breckenridge, Jack D. Pumpkins Are Orange. 280p. (Orig.). 1997. pap. 12.95 (0-9656993-0-7) J D Breckenridge.

— Surgeon Fishin' unabridged ed. (Illus.). 320p. 1998. pap. 15.95 (0-9656993-1-5) J D Breckenridge.

Breckenridge, James & Breckenridge, Lillian. What Color Is Your God? Multicultural Education in the Church. LC 94-36907. 288p. (Orig.). (gr. 12). 1995. pap. 16.99 (0-8010-5745-0, Bridgept Bks) Baker Bks.

Breckenridge, Jill. Civil Blood: Poems & Prose. LC 86-60097. (Illus.). 216p. (Orig.). 1986. 19.50 (0-915943-10-7) Milkweed Ed.

— Civil Blood: Poems & Prose. LC 86-60097. (Illus.). 216p. (Orig.). 1995. pap. 9.50 (0-915943-09-3) Milkweed Ed.

Breckenridge, Jill & Kearney, Bob, eds. Walk down the Tiger's Tail. (Illus.). 164p. (Orig.). 1982. pap. 5.00 (0-927663-09-0) COMPAS.

Breckenridge, Judy. 365 More Simple Science Experiments: With Everyday Materials. 320p. 1998. 12.98 (1-57912-035-0) Blck Dog & Leventhal.

Breckenridge, Lillian, jt. auth. see Breckenridge, James.

Breckenridge, Marilyn S. Jesse Tree Devotions: A Family Activity for Advent. 32p. (Orig.). 1985. pap. 6.99 (0-8066-2154-0, 10-3475, Augsburg) Augsburg Fortress.

Breckenridge, Michele, et al. Birthday Galore Birthday Book. (Illus.). (J). (gr. 1-3). 1995. write for info. (0-939979-01-2) Discovery Toys.

— Move over Monet Birthday Book. (Illus.). (J). 1995. write for info. (0-939979-02-0) Discovery Toys.

Breckenridge, Rick. My Favorite Wines. (Illus.). 120p. 1999. 11.95 (0-9669840-0-5) Lexus Pub.

Breckenridge, Robert G. Access to English as a Second Language: Book 1. 1973. pap. text, teacher ed. 1.50 (0-07-007397-X) McGraw.

— Access to English as a Second Language: Book 1, Bk. 1. 1973. pap. text, wbk. ed. 1.40 (0-07-007396-1) McGraw.

— Access to English as a Second Language: Book 2. 1973. pap. text, teacher ed. 1.50 (0-07-007401-1) McGraw.

— Access to English as a Second Language: Book 2, Bk. 2. 1974. pap. text 2.50 (0-07-007399-6); pap. text, wbk. ed. 1.40 (0-07-007400-3) McGraw.

Breckenridge, Roy M. & Bonnichsen, Bill, eds. Guidebook to the Geology of Northern & Western Idaho & Surrounding Area. (Illus.). 156p. (C). 1989. pap. 19.00 (1-55765-027-6) ID Geog Survey.

***Breckenridge, Suzanne & Snyder, Marjorie.** Michigan Herb Cookbook. 300p. 2000. pap. 19.95 (0-472-08694-4, 08694) U of Mich Pr.

Breckenridge, Suzanne & Snyder, Marjorie. The Wisconsin Herb Cookbook. LC 96-23118. (Illus.). 304p. (Orig.). 1996. pap. 19.95 (1-879483-32-7) Prairie Oak Pr.

Brecker, Eric. The Master System: A Visual Guide to the Structure of Music on the Guitar & Bass Fretboards. (Illus.). 62p. 1992. pap. text 19.95 (0-925191-10-8) Omnitek.

Brecker, Stephen, jt. auth. see Timmis, Adam D.

***Breckheimer, Scott.** Smile Now, You May Not Feel Like It Later. 1999. (1-56245-375-0) Great Quotations.

Breckinridge, Elizabeth L. Effective Use of Older Workers. Stein, Leon, ed. LC 79-8661. (Growing Old Ser.). (Illus.). 1980. reprint ed. lib. bdg. 23.95 (0-405-12777-4) Ayer.

Breckinridge, James B., jt. ed. see Bely, Pierre Y.

Breckinridge, Lucy. Lucy Breckinridge of Grove Hill: The Journal of a Virginia Girl, 1862-1864. Robertson, Mary D., ed. LC 79-88609. 251p. reprint ed. pap. 77.90 (0-7837-1979-5, 204225300002) Bks Demand.

Breckinridge, Lucy Gilmer & Robertson, Mary D. Lucy Breckinridge of Grove Hill: The Journal of a Virginia Girl, 1862-1864 ; Edited by Mary D. Robertson. LC 79-88609. xvi, 235 p. 1979. 14.00 (0-87338-234-X) Kent St U Pr.

Breckinridge, Mary. Wide Neighborhoods: A Story of the Frontier Nursing Service. LC 81-50181. (Illus.). 400p. 1981. reprint ed. 36.00 (0-8131-1453-5); reprint ed. pap. 18.00 (0-8131-0149-2) U Pr of Ky.

Breckinridge, Scott D. The CIA & the Cold War: A Memoir. LC 92-46554. 336p. 1993. 57.95 (0-275-94547-2, C4547, Praeger Pubs) Greenwood.

Breckinridge, Sophonisba P. The Family & the State: Select Documents. LC 76-169375. (Family in America Ser.). 584p. 1977. reprint ed. 39.95 (0-405-03851-8) Ayer.

— Women in the Twentieth Century: A Study of Their Political, Social, & Economic Activities. LC 72-2593. (American Women Ser.: Images & Realities). 380p. 1978. reprint ed. 26.95 (0-405-04450-X) Ayer.

Breckinridge, Sophonisba P., ed. Child in the City: A Series of Papers Presented at the Conference Held During the Chicago Child Welfare Exhibit. LC 70-112541. (Rise of Urban America Ser.). (Illus.). 1974. reprint ed. 29.95 (0-405-02437-1) Ayer.

Breckinridge, Sophonisba P. & Abbott, Edith. Delinquent Child & the Home. LC 70-112525. (Rise of Urban America Ser.). 1974. reprint ed. 23.95 (0-405-02438-X) Ayer.

Breckinridge, Sophonisba P., jt. auth. see Abbott, Edith.

Breckle, S. W., jt. auth. see Walter, H.

Breckler & Maull. General Surgery MS Pearls of Wisdom. (Pearls of Wisdom Ser.). 1999. pap. 32.00 (1-890369-19-5) Boston Medical.

— General Surgery Pearls of Wisdom. (Pearls of Wisdom Ser.). 1998. pap. 88.00 (1-890369-11-X) Boston Medical.

Breckler, Rosemary. Pie's in the Oven. LC 95-518. (Illus.). 32p. (J). 1996. 15.95 (0-395-76501-3) HM.

— Sweet Dried Apples: A Vietnamese Wartime Childhood. LC 95-518. (Illus.). 32p. (J). (ps-3). 1996. 15.95 (0-395-73570-X) HM.

***Breckler, Wiggins.** Social Psychology. (Psychology Ser.). 2002. 52.00 (0-534-57834-9) Wadsworth Pub.

Breckling, J. The Analysis of Directional Time Series. (Lecture Notes in Statistics Ser.: Vol. 61). viii, 238p. 1989. 43.95 (0-387-97182-3, 3627) Spr-Verlag.

Breckman, Cynthia G., ed. see Sonday, Arlene.

Breckman, Mel, jt. auth. see Enck, John.

Breckman, Risa S. & Adelman, Ronald D. Strategies for Helping Victims of Elder Mistreatment. (Human Services Guides Ser.: Vol. 53). 160p. (C). 1988. pap. text 18.95 (0-8039-3094-1) Sage.

Breckman, Warren. Marx, the Young Hegelians & the Origins of Radical Social Theory. LC 98-15205. (Modern European Philosophy Ser.). 352p. (C). 1999. text 54.95 (0-521-62440-1) Cambridge U Pr.

Breckner, Fred. Upper Iowa University: Doc Dorman's Peacocks. LC 81-52627. (College Sports Bks.). 1981. 10.95 (0-87397-195-7, Strode Pubs) Circle Bk Service.

Brecknock, Albert. Byron: A Study of the Poet in the Light of New Discoveries. LC 67-30808. (Studies in Byron: No. 5). (Illus.). 1969. reprint ed. lib. bdg. 75.00 (0-8383-0708-6) M S G Haskell Hse.

Brecknock, John L. & Melling, John K. Scaling the High Cs: The Musical Life of Tenor John L. Brecknock. LC 96-17495. 144p. 1996. 44.00 (0-8108-3137-6) Scarecrow.

Breckon. Community Health Education. 4th ed. 1998. teacher ed. 49.00 (0-8342-1153-X) Aspen Pub.

Breckon, A. & Prest, D. Introducing Craft, Design & Technology. (C). 1983. pap. 60.00 (0-09-149541-5, Pub. by S Thornes Pubs) St Mut.

Breckon, Donald J. Discovering the Christ. LC 94-23167. 1994. pap. text 2.00 (0-8309-0682-7) Herald Pub Hse.

— Managing Health Promotion Programs: Leadership Skills for the 21st Century. LC 96-39676. 300p. 50.00 (0-8342-0739-7, 20739) Aspen Pub.

Breckon, Donald J., et al. Community Health Education: Settings, Roles, & Skills for the 21st Century. 4th ed. LC 98-13931. 400p. 1998. 49.00 (0-8342-0987-X, 0987X) Aspen Pub.

Breckon, Garry L., tr. & intro. see De Muralt, Andre.

Breckon, Karen E., jt. auth. see Ferreira, Nico M.

Breckstrom, Gus, compiled by. Florida Criminal Jury Instructions Handbook: Includes Elements & Defenses. 125p. Date not set. pap. 21.95 (0-87526-552-9) Gould.

Brecto, Christina M., ed. see Pastin, Mark J.

Brecy, Robert. Autour de la Muse Rouge. (Songs & Poetry Collection). (FRE.). 256p. 1995. pap. 79.95 (2-86808-047-2) Intl Scholars.

— La Revolution en Chantant. (Songs & Poetry Collection). (FRE., Illus.). 232p. 1995. pap. 89.95 (2-86808-031-6) Intl Scholars.

Breda, Arina Van, see Van Breda, Arina.

Breda, Arina Van, see Strandness, D. Eugene & Van Breda, Arina, eds.

Breda, H. L. Van, see Van Breda, H. L.

Breda, Michael Van, see Hendriksen, Eldon & Van Breda, Michael.

Bredahl, A. Carl, Jr. Ivan Doig. (Western Writers Ser: Vol. 140). (C). pap. 5.95 (0-88430-139-7) Boise St U W Writ Ser.

Bredahl, A. Carl, Jr. New Ground: Western American Narrative & the Literary Canon. LC 88-38938. xii, 196p. 1989. 45.00 (0-8078-1854-2) U of NC Pr.

Bredahl, A. Carl, Jr. & Drake, Susan L. Hemingway's "Green Hills of Africa" As Evolutionary Narrative: Helix & Scimitar. LC 89-14510. (Studies in American Literature: Vol. 5). 168p. 1990. lib. bdg. 79.95 (0-88946-165-1) E Mellen.

Bredahl, Axel C. Melville's Angles of Vision. LC 73-185795. (University of Florida Humanities Monographs: No. 37). 84p. reprint ed. pap. 30.00 (0-7837-0595-6, 204094300019) Bks Demand.

Bredahl, Maury. Agricultural Trade & the Environment: Discovering & Measuring the Critical Linkages. 320p. (C). 1996. pap. 80.00 (0-8133-8896-1, Pub. by Westview) HarpC.

Bredahl, Maury E. Macroeconomic Policy & Agricultural Development Concepts & Case Studies of Egypt, Morocco & Jordan. (Illus.). 70p. (C). 1998. reprint ed. pap. text 20.00 (0-7881-4888-5) DIANE Pub.

Bredahl, Roy D. You, the Safety Manager. (Illus.). 70p. 1997. pap. text 89.95 (0-9660042-0-5) Bredahl Agency.

Bredas, J. L. & Chance, R. R., eds. Conjugated Polymeric Materials: Opportunities in Electronics, Optoelectronics & Molecular Electronics. (C). 1990. text 289.00 (0-7923-0751-8) Kluwer Academic.

Bredas, J. L. & Silbey, R., eds. Conjugated Polymers: The Novel Science & Technology of Highly Conducting & Nonlinear Optically Active Materials. 648p. (C). 1991. text 287.50 (0-7923-1403-4) Kluwer Academic.

Bredas, J.L., et al, eds. Organic Materials for Electronics: Proceedings of Symposium D of the 1994 E-MRS Spring Conference, Strasbourg, France, 24-27 May 1994. (European Materials Research Society Symposia Proceedings Ser.: Vol. 49). 340p. 1994. 228.00 (0-444-82168-6, North Holland) Elsevier.

Bredbeck, Gregory W. Sodomy & Interpretation: Marlowe to Milton. LC 91-55066. 256p. 1991. 39.95 (0-8014-2644-8); pap. 15.95 (0-8014-9945-3) Cornell U Pr.

***Bredbenner, Candice L.** A Nationality of Her Own: Woman, Marriage, & the Law of Citizenship. LC 97-20734. 308p. 1998. 45.00 (0-520-20650-9, Pub. by U CA Pr) Cal Prin Full Svc.

Breddin, H. K., et al, eds. Haemostasis & Thrombosis Abstracts: New Developments in Hemostaseology. (Journal: Haemostasis: Vol. 18, Suppl. 2, 1988). (Illus.). iv, 196p. 1988. pap. 59.25 (3-8055-4796-X) S Karger.

— Low Molecular Weight Heparins: Pharmacology, In-Vivo & Ex-Vivo Effects & Clinical Results - Journal: Haemostasis, Vol. 18, Suppl. 2, 1988. (Illus.). iv, 88p. 1988. pap. 28.00 (3-8055-4787-0) S Karger.

— Recent Advances & New Developments in Hemostaseology: Abstracts. (Journal: Haemostasis: Vol. 16, Suppl. 5, 1986). iv, 148p. 1986. pap. 39.25 (3-8055-4505-3) S Karger.

***Brede, Doug.** Turf Managers Handbook of Maintenance Reduction: Sports, Lawns & Golf. LC 99-87778. (Illus.). 2000. 9.00 (1-57504-106-5) Sleepng Bear.

Brede, Wilhelm. Der Unterschied der Lehren Humes im Treatise und im Inquiry. (GER.). 50p. 1980. reprint ed. write for info. (3-487-06771-4) G Olms Pubs.

Bredehoft, David J., ed. Family Life Education Curriculum Guidelines. rev. ed. 28p. 1995. reprint ed. pap. 15.95 (0-916174-49-2) Natl Coun Family.

Bredehoft, Neila. Collectors Encyclopedia of Heisey Glass. 2nd rev. ed. (Illus.). 463p. 1986. reprint ed. pap. 24.95 (1-888939-11-7) Heisey Collectrs.

— Collector's Encyclopedia of Heisey Glass 1925-1938. (Illus.). 464p. 1996. 24.95 (0-89145-307-5, 1664) Collector Bks.

Bredehoft, Neila & Bredehoft, Tom. Findlay Toothpick Holders. LC 95-211962. (Illus.). 36p. (Orig.). 1994. pap. 11.94 (1-885503-05-9) Cherry H Pubns.

— Hobbs, Brockunier & Co., Glass: Identification & Value Guide. LC 97-192518. (Illus.). 176p. (Orig.). 1997. pap. 19.95 (0-89145-780-1, 4868) Collector Bks.

Bredehoft, Neila, et al. Findlay Flint Glass Co., 1889-1891. LC 95-145588. (American Glass Companies Ser.). (Illus.). 60p. 1994. per. 11.95 (1-885503-04-0) Cherry H Pubns.

— The Melting Pot Pattern Features. (Illus.). 34p. (Orig.). 1996. pap. 12.00 (1-885503-09-1) Cherry H Pubns.

— Pressed Glass Toothpick Holders Identification & Values. LC 99-462674. 208p. 1999. 24.95 (1-57432-127-7) Collector Bks.

Bredehoft, Neila, jt. auth. see Bredehoft, Tom.

Bredehoft, Neila M. & Bredehoft, Thomas H. Heisey's Production Cuttings. 156p. 1991. pap. 15.95 (1-885503-02-4) Cherry H Pubns.

Bredehoft, Neila M., et al. Early Duncan Glassware. 176p. 1987. pap. 19.95 (1-885503-00-8) Cherry H Pubns.

Bredehoft, Thomas H., jt. auth. see Bredehoft, Neila M.

Bredehoft, Tom & Bredehoft, Neila. 50 Years of Collectible Glass, 1920-1970: Easy Identification & Price Guide: Stemware, Decorated Glassware, Glass Decorating Accessories, Vol. II. 2nd ed. (Illus.). 256p. 2000. pap. 26.95 (1-58221-001-2) Krause Pubns.

— 50 Years of Collectible Glass, 1920-1970 Vol. 1: Easy Identification & Price Guide: Tableware, Kitchenware, Barware & Water Sets, 1. (Identification & Price Guide Ser.). (Illus.). 256p. 1997. pap. 26.95 (0-930625-79-X, AT2579) Krause Pubns.

Bredehoft, Tom, jt. auth. see Bredehoft, Neila.

***Bredehorn, George.** Ingenious Puzzles for Word Lovers. (Illus.). 2000. pap. 6.95 (0-8069-3540-5) Sterling.

Bredehorn, George. Word Puzzles, by George! LC 98-205403. (Illus.). 96p. (J). 1999. 5.95 (*0-8069-5962-2*) Sterling.

Bredekamp, Horst. The Lure of the Antique & the Cult of Machine: The Kunstkammer & the Evolution of Nature, Art & Technology. Brown, Allison, tr. from GER. LC 95-16753. (Cultural & Museum Studies). (Illus.). 168p. (C). 1995. pap. text 18.95 (*1-55876-094-6*) Wiener Pubs Inc.

— The Lure of the Antique & the Cult of Machine: The Kunstkammer & the Evolution of Nature, Art & Technology. Brown, Allison, tr. from GER. LC 95-16753. (Cultural & Museum Studies). (Illus.). 168p. (C). 1995. text 42.95 (*1-55876-093-8*) Wiener Pubs Inc.

Bredekamp, Sue, ed. Developmentally Appropriate Practice in Early Childhood Programs Serving Children from Birth Through Age 8. exp. ed. LC 87-62626. 92p. pap. 5.00 (*0-935989-11-0*, NAEYC 224) Natl Assn Child Ed.

Bredekamp, Sue & Copple, Carol, eds. Developmentally Appropriate Practice in Early Childhood Programs. rev. ed. LC 96-71189. (Illus.). 182p. 1997. pap. text 9.00 (*0-935989-79-X*, 234) Natl Assn Child Ed.

Bredekamp, Sue & Rosegrant, Teresa. Reaching Potentials Vol. 2: Transforming Early Childhood Curriculum & Assessment. (Illus.). 1995. pap. 8.00 (*0-935989-73-0*) Natl Assn Child Ed.

Bredekamp, Sue & Rosegrant, Teresa, eds. Reaching Potentials: Appropriate Curriculum & Assessment for Young Children, Vol. 1. LC 92-85332. (Illus.). 169p. 1992. pap. text 7.00 (*0-935989-53-6*, 225) Natl Assn Child Ed.

Bredekamp, Sue & Willer, Barbara, eds. NAEYC Accreditation: A Decade of Learning & the Years Ahead. LC 96-68451. 166p. 1996. pap. text 8.00 (*0-935989-74-9*, NAEYC905) Natl Assn Child Ed.

Bredel, Roland, ed. The Galactic Center, 4th ESO/CTIO Workshop, Vol. 102. (ASP Conference Series Proceedings). 514p. 1996. 34.00 (*1-886733-22-8*) Astron Soc Pacific.

***Bredell, Frank.** Lockport Boy: A Memoir of a Magical Time & Place. LC 99-96410. 210p. 1999. pap. 12.00 (*0-9674846-0-X*, Andiamo Pr) Frank Bredell.

Bredemeier, Brenda J., jt. auth. see Shields, David L.

Bredemeier, Greg. Sins of the Guardians: One Mother's Custody Nightmare. (Illus.). 248p. 1998. pap. 16.00 (*0-8059-4275-0*) Dorrance.

Bredemeier, Harry C. Experience Versus Understanding. 172p. 1997. pap. 16.95 (*1-85756-351-4*, Pub. by Janus Pubng) Paul & Co Pubs.

— Experience vs. Understanding: Understanding Yourself in Twenty-First Century Societies. LC 98-9739. 156p. 1998. text 34.95 (*0-7658-0446-8*) Transaction Pubs.

— The Federal Public Housing Movement: A Case Study of Social Change. Zuckerman, Harriet & Merton, Robert K., eds. LC 79-8978. (Dissertations on Sociology Ser.). 1980. lib. bdg. 18.95 (*0-405-12954-8*) Ayer.

Bredemeier, Mary E. Urban Classroom Portraits: Teachers Who Make a Difference. (American University Studies: Language: Ser. XIV, Vol. 11). 279p. (C). 1988. text 38.50 (*0-8204-0651-1*) P Lang Pubng.

Bredenberg, Alfred R. Advertising by E-Mail - Without Raising Hackles! 11p. 1998. 14.95 (*1-889213-04-7*) A Bredenberg.

— The Smart Business Guide to Internet Marketing: Electronic Version 2.0, ASCIT Text. 70p. 1996. 12.00 (*1-889213-02-0*, SBGIM 2.0) A Bredenberg.

— The Smart Business Guide to Internet Marketing: Version 2.1. Orig. Title: The Small Business Guide to Internet Marketing. (Illus.). 70p. 1997. 20.00 (*1-889213-03-9*, SBGIM 2.1) A Bredenberg.

Bredenberg, Fly & Cichetti, Stephen. Old-Time Country Guitar. (Illus.). 96p. 1976. pap. 17.95 (*0-8256-0167-3*, OK63172, Oak) Music Sales.

Bredenberg, H., ed. Application of Stress-Wave Theory on Piles: Proceedings of the International Seminar, Stockholm, 4-5 June 1980. 350p. (C). 1980. 194.00 (*90-6191-095-1*, Pub. by A A Balkema) Ashgate Pub Co.

***Bredenberg, H., et al.** Dry Mix Methods for Deep Soil Stabilization: Proceedings of the International Conference, Stockholm, Sweden, 13-15 October 1999. (Illus.). 370p. 1999. 95.00 (*90-5809-108-2*, Pub. by A A Balkema) Ashgate Pub Co.

Bredenberg, Jeff. Beat the System! 1200 Tips for Coming Out on Top in Every Deal & Transaction. 1999. mass mkt. 6.99 (*0-425-16756-9*) Berkley Pub.

***Bredenberg, Jeff.** Clean It Fast, Clean It Right. (Illus.). 544p. 2000. pap. text 16.95 (*1-57954-019-8*) Rodale Pr Inc.

Bredenberg, Jeff. The Dream Compass. 192p. (Orig.). 1991. pap. 3.50 (*0-380-75647-1*, Avon Bks) Morrow Avon.

— The Dream Vessel. 240p. (Orig.). 1992. mass mkt. 4.50 (*0-380-76567-5*, Avon Bks) Morrow Avon.

— The Man in the Moon Must Die. 208p. (Orig.). 1993. mass mkt. 4.50 (*0-380-76914-X*, Avon Bks) Morrow Avon.

Bredenberg, Jeff, et al. Food Smart: A Man's Plan to Fuel up for Peak Performance. (Men's Health Life Improvement Guides Ser.: Vol. 1). (Illus.). 176p. 1996. pap. 14.95 (*0-87596-280-7*) Rodale Pr Inc.

Bredenberg, Jeff, ed. see Bennett, Lisa.

Bredenberg, Oscar. Battle of Plattsburgh Bay. 22p. 1978. pap. 4.50 (*1-890402-01-X*) Clinton Cnty Hist.

Bredenkamp, Christian, jt. auth. see Rensburg, Ronel S.

Bredenkamp, Hugh & Schadler, Susan. Economic Adjustment & Reform in Low-Income Countries. LC 98-13352. 1999. write for info. (*1-55775-715-1*) Intl Monetary.

Bredenkamp, I. M. The Small Claims Court. 115p. 1986. pap. 41.00 (*0-409-01336-6*, SA, MICHIE) LEXIS Pub.

Brederlow, G., et al. The High-Power Iodine Laser. (Optical Sciences Ser.: Vol. 34). (Illus.). 182p. 1983. 73.95 (*0-387-11792-X*) Spr-Verlag.

Bredero, Thomas J. Crop Water Management Research. (C). 1991. 40.00 (*81-204-0489-0*, Pub. by Oxford & IBH Pubng) Science Pubs.

***Bredes, Don.** Cold Comfort: A Novel. 2001. 22.00 (*0-609-60687-5*) Harmony Bks.

Bredesen, Eric. Moto Europa: The Complete Guide to European Motoring. 3rd ed. LC 95-70769. (Illus.). 306p. (Orig.). 1996. pap. 15.95 (*0-9641488-3-8*) Seren Pubng.

Bredeson, Carmen. American Writers of the 20th Century. LC 95-34790. (Collective Biographies Ser.). (Illus.). 104p. (YA). (gr. 6 up). 1996. lib. bdg. 20.95 (*0-89490-704-2*) Enslow Pubs.

— The Battle of the Alamo: The Fight for Texas Territory. LC 95-49283. (Spotlight on American History Ser.). (Illus.). 64p. (J). (gr. 4-6). 1996. lib. bdg. 21.90 (*0-7613-0019-8*) Millbrook Pr.

— The Challenger Disaster: Tragic Space Flight. LC 98-46685. (American Disasters Ser.). (Illus.). 48p. (YA). (gr. 4-10). 1999. lib. bdg. 18.95 (*0-7660-1222-0*) Enslow Pubs.

— Fire in Oakland, California: Billion-Dollar Blaze. LC 98-31284. (American Disasters Ser.). (Illus.). 48p. (YA). (gr. 4-10). 1999. lib. bdg. 18.95 (*0-7660-1220-4*) Enslow Pubs.

— Gus Grissom: A Space Biography. LC 97-21343. (Countdown to Space Ser.). (Illus.). 48p. (J). (gr. 4-10). 1998. lib. bdg. 18.95 (*0-89490-974-6*) Enslow Pubs.

***Bredeson, Carmen.** John Glenn: Space Pioneer. LC 99-59775. (Gateway Biography Ser.). (Illus.). (J). 2000. lib. bdg. write for info. (*0-7613-1719-8*) Millbrook Pr.

— John Glenn Returns to Orbit: Life on the Space Shuttle. LC 99-12490. (Illus.). 48p. (J). (gr. 4-10). 2000. lib. bdg. 18.95 (*0-7660-1304-9*) Enslow Pubs.

Bredeson, Carmen. The Mighty Midwest Flood: Raging Rivers. LC 98-11728. (American Disasters Ser.). 48p. (YA). (gr. 4-10). 1999. lib. bdg. 18.95 (*0-7660-1221-2*) Enslow Pubs.

— The Moon. LC 96-40226. (First Bk.). 64p. (J). (gr. 4-6). 1998. 22.00 (*0-531-20308-5*) Watts.

— The Moon. (First Books--The Solar System). (Illus.). 64p. (J). (gr. 4 up). 1998. pap. 6.95 (*0-531-15911-6*) Watts.

***Bredeson, Carmen.** Mount St. Helens Volcano: Violent Eruption. LC 00-9199. (American Disasters Ser.). (Illus.). 2001. write for info. (*0-7660-1552-1*) Enslow Pubs.

— NASA Planetary Spacecraft: Galileo, Magellan, Pathfinder & Voyager. LC 99-50639. (Countdown to Space Ser.). (Illus.). 48p. (YA). (gr. 4-10). 2000. lib. bdg. 18.95 (*0-7660-1303-0*) Enslow Pubs.

Bredeson, Carmen. Neil Armstrong: A Space Biography. LC 97-25449. (Countdown to Space Ser.). (Illus.). 48p. (YA). (gr. 4-10). 1998. lib. bdg. 18.95 (*0-89490-973-8*) Enslow Pubs.

— Our Space Program. LC 98-21693. (I Know America Ser.). (Illus.). 48p. (J). (gr. 2-4). 1999. 20.90 (*0-7613-0952-7*, Copper Beech Bks) Millbrook Pr.

***Bredeson, Carmen.** Our Space Program. (I Know America Ser.). (Illus.). 48p. (J). (gr. 2-4). 2000. pap. text 8.95 (*0-7613-1349-4*, Copper Beech Bks) Millbrook Pr.

— Our Space Program. (I Know America Ser.). (Illus.). (J). 2000. 14.40 (*0-606-18292-6*) Turtleback.

— Pluto. LC 00-35179. (Library). 2001. write for info. (*0-531-11784-7*) Watts.

Bredeson, Carmen. Presidential Medal of Freedom Winners. LC 96-1743. (Collective Biographies Ser.). (Illus.). 104p. (YA). (gr. 6 up). 1996. lib. bdg. 20.95 (*0-89490-705-0*) Enslow Pubs.

— Shannon Lucid: Space Ambassador. LC 97-47147. (Gateway Biography Ser.). (Illus.). 48p. (J). (gr. 3-5). 1998. lib. bdg. 20.90 (*0-7613-0406-1*) Millbrook Pr.

***Bredeson, Carmen.** Shannon Lucid: Space Ambassador. (Gateway Biography Ser.). 48p. (J). (gr. 2-4). 2000. pap. text 8.95 (*0-7613-1375-3*, Copper Beech Bks) Millbrook Pr.

Bredeson, Carmen. The Spindletop Gusher: The Story of the Texas Oil Boom. LC 95-31485. (Spotlight on American History Ser.). (Illus.). 64p. (J). (gr. 4-6). 1996. lib. bdg. 21.90 (*1-56294-916-0*) Millbrook Pr.

— Tide Pools. LC 97-41630. (First Book Ser.). 61p. (J). 1999. 22.00 (*0-531-20368-9*) Watts.

— Tide Pools. (First Books Ser.). 1999. pap. text 6.95 (*0-531-15958-2*) Watts.

Bredeson, Paul V. & Scribner, Jay P., eds. The Professoriate: Challenges & Promises. LC 95-70738. (NCPEA Yearbook Ser.). 285p. 1998. 49.95 (*1-56676-353-3*) Scarecrow.

Bredeson, Paul V., jt. auth. see Hart, Ann W.

Bredeweg, Frank H. U. S. Catholic Elementary & Secondary Schools, 1984-1985. 1985. 6.60 (*0-685-11857-6*) Natl Cath Educ.

— U. S. Catholic Elementary & Secondary Schools, 1986-1987. 1987. 7.30 (*0-317-60173-3*) Natl Cath Educ.

— U. S. Catholic Elementary & Secondary Schools, 1987-1988. 21p. (Orig.). 1988. pap. 7.30 (*1-55833-002-X*) Natl Cath Educ.

— U. S. Catholic Elementary Schools & Their Finances, 1987. 1987. 6.75 (*0-317-60174-1*) Natl Cath Educ.

— United States Catholic Elementary Schools & Their Finances, 1988. (Data Bank Ser.). 14p. 1988. pap. 6.60 (*1-55833-006-2*) Natl Cath Educ.

Bredfeldt, Denise. Great Game Methodology - Appraisal Module. (Illus.). 71p. 1997. pap. text 30.00 (*0-9653067-1-2*) Bizlit.

— The Yo-Yo-Company (The Beginning) 2nd rev. ed. (Illus.). iii, 43p. 1993. wbk. ed. 30.00 (*0-9653067-0-4*) Bizlit.

— The Yo-Yo-Company (The Corporation) (Illus.). 55p. 1999. wbk. ed. 30.00 (*0-9653067-7-1*) Bizlit.

Bredfeldt, Denise & Cantrell, Patty. Great Game Methodology - Financial Planning Module, 4 Vols., Set. (Illus.). 85p. 1998. pap. text. write for info. (*0-9653067-3-9*) Bizlit.

— Great Game Methodology - Huddling Module, 4 Vols., Set. (Illus.). 83p. 1998. pap. text. write for info. (*0-9653067-4-7*) Bizlit.

— Great Game Methodology - Recognition, Bonus & Games Module, 4 Vols., Set. 74p. 1999. pap. text. write for info. (*0-9653067-6-3*) Bizlit.

Bredfeldt, Gary, jt. auth. see Richards, Lawrence O.

Bredhoff, Stacey. Draw! Political Cartoons from Left to Right. LC 91-2559. (Illus.). 144p. (Orig.). 1991. pap. 7.95 (*0-911333-85-1*, 200021) National Archives & Recs.

Bredholt, Russell D., Jr., et al. A Great Commission Movement: The Church of the Nazarene in the 21st Century. 96p. (Orig.). 1993. pap. 7.99 (*0-8341-1454-2*, \) Beacon Hill.

Bredice, Vincent. Complete Book of Guitar Improvisation, Vol. 1. 236p. 1993. spiral bd. 22.95 (*0-87166-663-4*, 93278) Mel Bay.

Bredice, Vincent. Contemporary Model Improvisation for Guitar. 92p. 1997. spiral bd. 19.95 incl. audio compact disk (*0-7866-2777-8*) Mel Bay.

Bredice, Vincent. Deluxe Jazz & Rock Bass Method. 180p. 1981. spiral bd. 14.95 (*1-56222-024-1*, 93766) Mel Bay.

— Deluxe Jazz & Rock Bass Method. 1986. audio 9.98 (*1-56222-600-2*, 93766C) Mel Bay.

— Deluxe Jazz & Rock Bass Method. 1993. 21.95 incl. audio (*0-7866-0932-X*, 93766P) Mel Bay.

— Jazz Guitar Scales & Modes. 156p. 1981. spiral bd. 14.95 (*0-87166-894-7*, 93722) Mel Bay.

Bredin. Women's Issues. (C). 1998. pap. text 16.36 (*0-395-90252-5*) HM.

Bredin, Alice. The Virtual Office Survival Handbook: What Telecommuters & Entrepreneurs Need to Succeed in Today's Non-Traditional Workplace. LC 96-1327. 259p. 1996. 39.95 (*0-471-12061-8*); pap. 16.95 (*0-471-12059-6*) Wiley.

Bredin, Alice & Lagatree, Kirsten. The Home Office Solution: How to Work at Home & Have a Personal Life Too. 2nd ed. LC 97-31545. 221p. 1998. pap. 14.95 (*0-471-19209-0*) Wiley.

Bredin, Henrietta. Christmas Eve. LC 92-1235. (Illus.). 32p. (J). 1992. 5.99 (*0-85953-145-7*) Childs Play.

— The Prince & the Goosegirl. LC 92-260. (Illus.). 32p. (J). 1992. 5.99 (*0-85953-146-5*) Childs Play.

***Bredin, Hugh & Santoro-Brienza, Liberato.** Philosophies of Art & Beauty: Introducing Aesthetics. 240p. 2000. pap. text 23.00 (*0-7486-1191-6*) Col U Pr.

Bredin, Hugh, tr. see Eco, Umberto.

Bredin, Jean-Denis. L' Absence. (FRE.). 192p. 1988. pap. 10.95 (*0-7859-2235-0*, 207037937X) Fr & Eur.

— The Affair: The Case of Alfred Dreyfus. LC 85-22374. 1987. pap. 19.95 (*0-8076-1175-1*) Braziller.

— Un Coupable. (FRE.). 147p. 1986. pap. 10.95 (*0-7859-2054-4*, 2070377849) Fr & Eur.

Brednel, Harold J. Sensuality Sex: To Understand Yourself & Choose to be Your Creative, Released, Sexual Self. 125p. 1987. pap. 5.95 (*0-943073-01-4*) Ctr Creat Lvg.

Bredohl, Thomas M. Class & Religious Identity: The Rhenish Center Party in Wilhelmine, Germany. LC 98-25326. (Studies in Theology). 1998. 40.00 (*0-87462-642-0*) Marquette.

Bredon, Burl. Home to the Hills & Other Poems. LC 94-61994. 57p. 1994. pap. 4.50 (*0-937058-36-X*) West Va U Pr.

Bredon, Glen E. Sheaf Theory. 2nd ed. LC 96-44232. (Graduate Texts in Mathematics Ser.: Vol. 170). 502p. 1997. 59.95 (*0-387-94905-4*) Spr-Verlag.

— Topology & Geometry, Vol. XIV. rev. ed. Ewing, J. H. et al, eds. LC 92-31618. (Graduate Texts in Mathematics Ser.: Vol. 139). (Illus.). 557p. (C). 1997. 69.95 (*0-387-97926-3*) Spr-Verlag.

Bredon, Simon, jt. auth. see Chaucer, Geoffrey.

Bredow, Ilse Von, see Von Bredow, Ilse.

Bredsdorff, Elias, et al. Introduction to Scandinavian Literature. LC 78-98748. 245p. 1970. reprint ed. lib. bdg. 35.00 (*0-8371-2849-8*, BRSL, Greenwood Pr) Greenwood.

Bredthauer, Vanessa. Hands-on Thinking Activities: Centers Through the Year. (Illus.). 160p. (J). (gr. 3-6). 1995. pap. text, teacher ed. 16.95 (*1-55799-370-X*, EMC 388) Evan-Moor Edu Pubs.

Bredvold, Louis I. The Brave New World of the Enlightenment. LC 61-10987. 172p. reprint ed. pap. 53.40 (*0-8357-7383-3*, 205158500004) Bks Demand.

— The Natural History of Sensibility. LC 62-10322. 113p. reprint ed. pap. 35.10 (*0-7837-3645-2*, 204351400009) Bks Demand.

Bredvold, Louis I., ed. see Burke, Edmund.

Bredweg, Frank H. U. S. Catholic Elementary & Secondary Schools, 1985-1986. 21p. 1986. 7.30 (*0-318-20578-5*) Natl Cath Educ.

— United States Catholic Elementary Schools & Their Finances, 1986. 1986. 6.00 (*0-318-20577-7*) Natl Cath Educ.

Bredy, Roy, jt. auth. see Wheeler, Carol Ann.

Bree, Germaine. Camus. rev. ed. LC 72-178591. 289p. reprint ed. pap. 89.60 (*0-8357-7554-2*, 205231800096) Bks Demand.

— Gide. LC 84-27916. 302p. 1985. reprint ed. lib. bdg. 75.00 (*0-313-24797-8*, BRGE, Greenwood Pr) Greenwood.

— Twentieth Century French Literature. Guiney, Louise, tr. from FRE. LC 82-15980. 398p. reprint ed. pap. 123.40 (*0-608-09394-7*, 205413900004) Bks Demand.

— Twentieth-Century French Literature, 1920-1970. Guiney, Louise, tr. LC 82-15980. (Illus.). 398p. (C). 1983. lib. bdg. 36.00 (*0-226-07195-2*) U Ch Pr.

— Twentieth-Century French Literature, 1920-1970. Guiney, Louise, tr. LC 82-15980. (Illus.). 398p. (C). 1984. pap. text 14.50 (*0-226-07196-0*) U Ch Pr.

Bree, Germaine & Markow-Totevy, Georges. Contes et Nouvelles, 1950-1970. rev. ed. LC 72-106166. 378p. (C). 1970. text 26.50 (*0-03-081344-1*) Harcourt Coll Pubs.

Bree, Germaine, ed. see Beckett, Samuel.

Bree, Germaine, ed. see Camus, Albert.

Bree, Germaine, ed. see Dupin, Jacques.

Bree, Germaine, ed. see Flaubert, Gustave.

Bree, Germaine, ed. see Proust, Marcel.

Bree, Germaine, ed. see Reverdy, Pierre.

Bree, Germaine, ed. see Robbe-Grillet, Alain.

Bree, Germaine, tr. see Romains, Jules, pseud.

Bree, Linda. Sarah Fielding. 1996. 32.00 (*0-8057-7051-8*, Twayne) Mac Lib Ref.

Bree, Linda, ed. see Austen, Jane.

***Bree, Loris & Bree, Marlin.** Kid's Travel Fun Book: Play Games. Make Things out of Paper & String. You'll Have a Ball. (Illus.). 96p. (J). (gr. 1-7). 2000. pap. 6.95 (*1-892147-01-7*, Pub. by Marlor Pr) IPG Chicago.

Bree, Loris, jt. auth. see Bree, Marlin.

Bree, Loris T. & Bree, Marlin. Kid's Squish Book: Slimy, Squishy, Sticky Things to Do That Should Only Be Done When Wearing Your Oldest Clothes. (Illus.). 96p. (J). 1993. pap. 8.95 (*0-943400-76-7*) Marlor Pr.

Bree, Malwine. The Groundwork of the Leschetizky Method. LC 68-25284. (Studies in Music: No. 42). (Illus.). 1969. reprint ed. lib. bdg. 75.00 (*0-8383-0290-4*) M S G Haskell Hse.

— The Groundwork of the Leschetizky Method. 1988. reprint ed. lib. bdg. 59.00 (*0-7812-0100-4*) Rprt Serv.

— The Groundwork of the Leschetizky Method. Baker, T., tr. from GER. LC 74-144898. (Illus.). 1972. reprint ed. 39.00 (*0-403-00837-9*) Scholarly.

— The Leschetizky Method: A Guide to Fine & Correct Piano Playing. Elson, Arthur, tr. (Illus.). 96p. 1997. reprint ed. pap. text 8.95 (*0-486-29596-6*, 706640Q) Dover.

Bree, Marlin. Call of the North Wind: Voyages & Adventures on Lake Superior. (Illus.). 232p. 1996. pap. 16.95 (*0-943400-90-2*) Marlor Pr.

— In the Teeth of the Northeaster: A Solo Voyage on Lake Superior. (Illus.). 228p. 1993. pap. 17.95 (*0-943400-72-4*) Marlor Pr.

Bree, Marlin & Bree, Loris. Kids' Trip Diary: Kids! Write about Your Own Adventures & Experiences, Have Fun for Hours! rev. ed. 96p. (J). 1998. pap. 6.95 (*0-943400-98-8*) Marlor Pr.

Bree, Marlin, jt. auth. see Bree, Loris.

Bree, Marlin, jt. auth. see Bree, Loris T.

Breebia, C. A., jt. ed. see VanKeer, R.

Breechen, Carl & Faulkner, Paul. What Every Family Needs: Practical, Biblical Insights into All Areas of Family Life. 1994. pap. 6.99 (*0-89225-424-6*) Gospel Advocate.

***Breecher, Edward V., 3rd, photos by.** A Vision Realized: Stories in Strained Glass of the Episcopal Church of the Good Shepherd. LC 98-88122. (Illus.). 144p. 1998. 39.95 (*0-943335-12-4*) Marblehead Pub.

Breecher, Maury M. & Linde, Shirley M. Healthy Homes in a Toxic World: Preventing, Identifying & Eliminating Hidden Health Hazards in Your Home. LC 91-40600. 256p. 1992. pap. 14.95 (*0-471-54024-2*) Wiley.

Breecher, Maury M., jt. auth. see Anderson, James W.

Breed, Alice G. The Change in Social Welfare from Deregulation: The Case of the Natural Gas Industry. LC 78-22683. (Energy in the American Economy Ser.). (Illus.). 1979. lib. bdg. 18.95 (*0-405-11986-0*) Ayer.

Breed, Charles B. Surveying. 3rd ed. 495p. 1971. text 102.95 (*0-471-10070-6*) Wiley.

Breed, Charles B. & Hosmer, George L. Principles & Practice of Surveying, 2 vols. Incl. Vol. 1. Principles & Pratice of Surveying. 11th ed. 728p. 1977. text 106.95 (*0-471-02979-3*); Vol. 2. Higher Surveying. 8th ed. 543p. 1962. text 102.95 (*0-471-10164-8*); write for info. (*0-318-56436-X*) Wiley.

Breed, David R. The History & Use of Hymns & Hymn Tunes. LC 76-39525. reprint ed. 49.50 (*0-404-09906-8*) AMS Pr.

— Yoking Science & Religion: The Life & Thought of Ralph Wendell Burhoe. LC 91-67648. (Zygon Bks.: No. 2). (Illus.). 150p. (Orig.). 1992. pap. 12.95 (*0-9618233-1-3*) Zygon Jrnl of Rel.

Breed, Donna, jt. auth. see Kahn, David.

Breed, Gary A., ed. see Bullock, Scott R.

Breed, J. Howard. Breed. Record of the Descendants of Allen Bread, Who Came to America from England in 1630. (Illus.). 224p. 1996. reprint ed. pap. 35.00 (*0-8328-5430-1*); reprint ed. lib. bdg. 45.00 (*0-8328-5429-8*) Higginson Bk Co.

Breed, Michael D. Pheromone Communication in Social Insects: Ants, Wasps, Bees & Termites. Vander Meer, Robert K., ed. LC 97-29921. (Westview Studies in Insect Biology). 384p. (C). 1997. text 85.00 (*0-8133-8976-3*, Pub. by Westview) HarpC.

Breed, Nancy L. The Van Wies of Nine Mile Creek: A Story of the Erie Canal. LC 94-36960. (J). 1995. pap. 12.50 (*0-925168-12-2*) North Country.

Breed, Robert & Bunis, Marty. Collector's Guide to Novelty Radios Bk. II: Identification & Values. LC 98-229076. 208p. 1998. pap. 19.95 (*1-57432-088-2*) Collector Bks.

Breed, Warren. The Newspaperman, News & Society. Zuckerman, Harriet & Merton, Robert K., eds. LC 79-8979. (Dissertations on Sociology Ser.). 1980. lib. bdg. 44.95 (*0-405-12955-6*) Ayer.

***Breede, Manfred H.** Handbook of Graphic Arts Equations. (Illus.). 240p. (C). 1999. pap. 65.00 (*0-88362-246-7*, 1702) GATFPress.

Breeden, David. Another Number: A Novel of the 70s. 214p. 1998. pap. 12.95 (*0-9657044-1-6*) Silver Phoenix.

B

— Building a Boat. Bixby, Robert, ed. 21p. (Orig.). 1995. pap. 6.00 (*1-882983-18-1*) March Street Pr.

— The Guiltless Traveler. Bixby, Robert, ed. 33p. 1996. pap. 6.00 (*1-882983-30-0*) March Street Pr.

— Hey, Schliemann. Schultz, Patricia, ed. LC 90-37695. (Poetry Ser.: Vol. 10). 64p. 1990. pap. 14.95 (*0-88946-847-8*) E Mellen.

Breeden, David W. & Edie, Jack. Ethics for a Contemporary Society: A Humanities Course. 1979. 18.50 (*1-881678-19-9*) CSEE.

Breeden, James O., ed. Advice among Masters: The Ideal in Slave Management in the Old South, 51. LC 79-54054. (Contributions in Afro-American & African Studies: No. 51). (Illus.). 350p. 1980. 65.00 (*0-313-20658-9*, BRS/) Greenwood.

— Medicine in the West. (Illus.). 86p. (Orig.). 1982. pap. text 15.00 (*0-89745-025-6*) Sunflower U Pr.

Breeden, James O., ed. A Long Ride in Texas: The Explorations of John Leonard Riddell. LC 93-27569. (Centennial Series of the Association of Former Students: No. 51). (Illus.). 136p. 1994. 25.95 (*0-89096-582-X*) Tex A&M Univ Pr.

Breeden, Joann. Love, Hope & Recovery: Healing the Pain of Addiction. LC 93-36924. 272p. (Orig.). 1993. pap. 12.95 (*0-931892-77-5*) B Dolphin Pub.

Breeden, Stanley & Wright, Belinda. Through the Tiger's Eyes. (Illus.). 192p. 1997. pap. 24.95 (*0-89815-847-8*) Ten Speed Pr.

Breeden, Terri. Teaching the Meaning of Church Ordinances to Children. (Orig.). 1986. pap. 6.95 (*0-89265-097-4*) Randall Hse.

Breeden, Terri & Dillard, Kathryn. The Middle School Mathematician: Empowering Students to Achieve Success in Algebra & Geometry. Britt, Leslie, ed. (Illus.). 128p. (Orig.). (J). (gr. 6-8). 1996. pap. text 12.95 (*0-86530-330-4*, IP 301-1) Incentive Pubns.

Breeden, Terri & Egan, Emalie. Positive Classroom Management. Quinn, Anna, ed. LC 96-78572. (Illus.). 144p. (Orig.). (J). (gr. 5-8). 1997. pap. text, teacher ed. 14.95 (*0-86530-355-X*, 349-4) Incentive Pubns.

— Strategies & Activities to Raise Student Achievement. Britt, Leslie & Noble, Janet, eds. (Illus.). 128p. (J). (gr. 4-8). 1995. pap. text 12.95 (*0-86530-315-0*, 1P315-0) Incentive Pubns.

Breeden, Terri & Mosley, Janice. The Cooperative Learning Companion: Ideas, Activities, & Aids for Middle Grades. (Illus.). 96p. (Orig.). 1992. pap. text, teacher ed. 10.95 (*0-86530-239-1*, 195-5) Incentive Pubns.

— Middle Grades Teacher's Handbook for Cooperative Learning. 160p. (Orig.). (J). (gr. 5-8). 1991. pap. text 14.95 (*0-86530-224-3*, IP 193-8) Incentive Pubns.

Breeden, Terri & Ralph, Sharon. A Is for Algebra: Basic Algebra Concepts. Aldy, Catherine, ed. LC 96-78570. (Illus.). 80p. (J). (gr. k-4). 1997. pap. text 9.95 (*0-86530-354-1*) Incentive Pubns.

Breeden, Terri, ed. see Fletcher, Kathleen.

Breeding, Carolyn. Cost-Effective Recipes for 10 to 100. 222p. 1989. 64.95 (*0-471-29035-1*, VNR) Wiley.

Breeding, John. The Wildest Colts Make the Best Horses. 210p. 1996. pap. text 16.95 (*1-880092-39-5*) Bright Bks TX.

Breeding, Julia G., jt. ed. see Le Blanc, Rufus J.

Breeding, Kenneth J. Digital Design Fundamentals. 2nd ed. 464p. (C). 1991. text 58.60 (*0-13-211277-9*) P-H.

— Microprocessor System Design Fundamentals. LC 94-8257. 408p. 1994. text 69.00 (*0-13-564279-5*) P-H.

Breeding, Marshall. Essential Guide to the Library IBM PC Vol. 13: Integrated Library Systems. (Essential Guide to the Library IBM PC Ser.). 200p. 1993. pap. 34.95 (*0-88736-188-9*) Mecklermedia.

— Integrated Library Systems for PCs & PC Networks: Descriptive & Analytical Reviews of Current Products. LC 94-15132. 464p. 1996. 42.50 (*1-57387-011-0*) Info Today Inc.

— The Official Internet World World-Wide Web Yellow Pages. 912p. 1995. pap. 39.99 (*1-56884-344-5*) IDG Bks.

— TCP/IP for the Internet: The Complete Buyer's Guide to Micro-Based TCP-IP Software. 185p. 1995. pap. 24.95 (*0-88736-980-4*) Mecklermedia.

Breeding, Robert L. Appalachian Haven. LC 81-2312. (Tennessee History Ser.). 280p. 1981. pap., per. 10.95 (*1-880258-00-5*) Thriftecon.

— Footprints in Appalachia. Davidson, Louise, ed. LC 95-2696. (Illus.). 598p. 1996. pap. 16.95 (*1-880258-04-8*) Thriftecon.

— From London to Appalachia. (Illus.). 200p. (J). (gr. 4-7). 1991. pap. 9.95 (*1-880258-03-X*) Thriftecon.

— Tales & Times of Papa Keck. LC 84-14644. 209p. 1984. pap. 7.95 (*1-880258-01-3*) Thriftecon.

***Breedlove, Billie Anita Foutch.** William Foutch & His Descendants' Footprints Across the United States of America: From Virginia, North Carolina to Middle Tennessee & to Points North, South, East & West, 1765-2000. (Illus.). xii, 466p. 2000. 60.00 (*0-944619-61-4*) Gregath Pub Co.

Breedlove, Bob. Web Groupware Developer's Guide. 1999. 59.99 (*1-57521-082-7*) Sams.

— Web Programming Unleashed. LC 96-68248. 1056p. 1996. 49.99 (*1-57521-117-3*) Sams.

Breedlove, Byron. Planned Approach to Community Health: Guide for the Local Coordinator. (Illus.). 311p. (C). 1998. pap. text 50.00 (*0-7881-7262-X*) DIANE Pub.

— Planned Approach to Community Health: Visual Aids. (Illus.). 150p. (C). 1998. pap. text 25.00 (*0-7881-7261-1*) DIANE Pub.

Breedlove, Byron, et al, eds. Hospital Employee Health: Practical Solutions to Current & Potential Problems. 502p. 1982. text 49.00 (*0-9603332-2-3*) Am Health Consults.

Breedlove, Byron & Schwartz, David, eds. Clinical Lasers: Expert Strategies for Practical & Profitable Management. LC 85-70926. (Illus.). 356p. 1985. text 78.00 (*0-9603332-3-1*) Am Health Consults.

Breedlove, Charlene. Uncharted Lines: Poems from the Journal of the American Medical Association. LC 98-29375. 1998. 20.00 (*0-9651879-4-2*) Boaz Pubng.

Breedlove, Charlene, ed. see Benesch, Friedrich & Wilde, Klaus.

Breedlove, Connie M. A Funny Thing Happened on the Way to Heaven. audio 14.99 (*0-310-20977-3*) Zondervan.

Breedlove, Dennis E. Introduction to the Flora of Chiapas. (Flora of Chiapas Ser.: Pt. 1). (Illus.). 1981. pap. 2.50 (*0-940228-00-9*) Calif Acad Sci.

***Breedlove, Dennis E. & Laughlin, Robert M.** The Flowering of Man: A Tzotzil Botany of Zinacantban. abr. ed. LC 99-59833. 2000. write for info. (*1-56098-897-5*) Smithsonian.

Breedlove, Dennis E., ed. see Daniel, Thomas F.

Breedlove, Dennis E., ed. see Frytell, Paul A.

Breedlove, Dennis E., ed. see Smith, Alan R.

Breedlove, Elizabeth A. Public & Academic Library Electronic Access to Information Survey. (Illus.). 80p. (Orig.). 1997. pap. text 30.00 (*0-7881-3884-7*) DIANE Pub.

Breedlove, Greta. The Herbal Home Spa: Naturally Refreshing Wraps, Rubs, Lotions, Masks, Oils & Scrubs. LC 97-44761. (Herbal Body Ser.). 192p. 1997. pap. 14.95 (*1-58017-005-6*, Storey Pub) Storey Bks.

Breedlove, Wanda G. Contemporary Trends in Children's & Young Adults' Literature: Research Perspectives. LC 89-26118. 138p. (Orig.). 1990. pap. text 15.00 (*0-685-32911-9*) SC St Coun Intl Read.

Breedon, F. J. & Fisher, P. G. MO: Causes & Consequences. LC HG0230.3. (Working Papers: No. 20). 44p. 1993. pap. 30.00 (*0-7837-8447-3*, 204925200010) Bks Demand.

Breedon, F. J. & Joyce, M. A. House Prices, Arrears & Possessions: A Three Equation Model for the U. K. fac. ed. LC HG2995.. (Bank of England, Work Paper Ser.: No. 14). (Illus.). 36p. 1994. pap. 30.00 (*0-7837-7650-0*, 204740300007) Bks Demand.

Breedon, F. J., et al. The Bank of England Model 1989: Recent Developments & Simulation Properties. fac. ed. LC HG2996.. (Bank of England, Discussion Papers: No. 29). 148p. 1990. reprint ed. pap. 45.90 (*0-7837-8211-X*, 204796900009) Bks Demand.

Breemen, N. Plant-Induced Soil Changes: Processes & Feedbacks. LC 98-38828. (Developments in Biogeochemistry Ser.). 1998. 108.00 (*0-7923-5216-5*) Kluwer Academic.

Breemen, N. Van, see Van Breemen, N.

Breen. Koreans. LC 99-45599. 1999. text 24.95 (*0-312-24211-5*) St Martin.

— Selected Poems Of Joanna Baill. 206p. 2000. text 69.95 (*0-7190-5474-5*) St Martin.

Breen, Aidan, ed. Ailerani Interpretatio Mystica Progenitorum Domini Iesu Christi. 220p. 1995. 55.00 (*1-85182-193-7*, Pub. by Four Cts Pr) Intl Spec Bk.

Breen, Aidan, ed. De XII Abusivis. 330p. 1998. boxed set 55.00 (*1-85182-192-9*, Pub. by Four Cts Pr) Intl Spec Bk.

Breen, Ann & Rigby, Dick. Fishing Piers: What Cities Can Do. (Illus.). 80p. 1986. pap. 15.00 (*0-935957-01-4*) Waterfront DC.

— The New Waterfront: A Worldwide Urban Success Story. (Illus.). 224p. 1996. 69.95 (*0-07-007454-2*) McGraw.

— Urban Waterfronts '85: Water Makes a Difference! (Illus.). 134p. (Orig.). 1986. pap. 15.00 (*0-935957-02-2*) Waterfront DC.

— Urban Waterfronts '84: Toward New Horizons. (Illus.). 100p. 1985. pap. 15.00 (*0-935957-00-6*) Waterfront DC.

— Urban Waterfronts '87: Water - The Ultimate Amenity. (Illus.). 100p. 1988. pap. 15.00 (*0-935957-04-9*) Waterfront DC.

— Urban Waterfronts '86: Developing Diversity. (Illus.). 100p. (Orig.). 1987. pap. 15.00 (*0-935957-03-0*) Waterfront DC.

Breen, Ann & Thaler-Carter, Ruth E. Keeping Waterfronts Distinctive: Choosing the Right Mix. (Illus.). 100p. 1990. pap. 15.00 (*0-935957-06-5*) Waterfront DC.

Breen, Betty, jt. auth. see Mills, Earl.

Breen, Christine & Williams, Niall. The Pipes Are Calling: Our Jaunts Through Ireland. LC 89-26104. 224p. 1991. pap. 11.00 (*0-939149-52-4*) Soho Press.

Breen, Christine, jt. auth. see Williams, Niall.

Breen, Dale H. Fundamental Aspects of Gear Strength Requirements. (Technical Papers: Vol. P229.17). (Illus.). 11p. 1974. pap. text 30.00 (*1-55589-284-1*) AGMA.

— Physical & Analytical Modeling of Contact Fatigue Pits from Rolling/Sliding Tests. (Nineteen Eighty-Seven Fall Technical Meeting Ser.: Vol. 87FTM8). (Illus.). 18p. 1987. pap. text 30.00 (*1-55589-484-4*) AGMA.

Breen, Dale H. & Cameron, T. Production Testing of a Chromium-Free Carburizing Grade Gear Steel. (Nineteen Eighty-Seven Fall Technical Meeting Ser.: Vol. 87FTM11). (Illus.). 12p. 1987. pap. text 30.00 (*1-55589-487-9*) AGMA.

Breen, Dale H., jt. auth. see Sharma, V. K.

Breen, Dan. My Fight for Irish Freedom. 218p. 1981. reprint ed. pap. 15.95 (*0-947962-33-6*, Pub. by Anvil Books Ltd) Irish Bks Media.

Breen, David H. The Canadian Prairie West & the Ranching Frontier. 312p. 1983. text 35.00 (*0-8020-5548-6*) U of Toronto Pr.

Breen, David H., jt. auth. see House, Donald.

***Breen, Donna L.** Cancer's Gift. Sion, Michael, ed. LC 00-191263. (Illus.). 200p. 2000. pap. 12.95 (*0-9702238-0-3*) Rock Wren.

Breen, Dr. Harold J., jt. auth. see Morin, Gertrude.

Breen, George & Blankenship, A. B. Do-It-Yourself Marketing Research. 3rd ed. (Illus.). 274p. 1998. reprint ed. lib. bdg. 44.95 (*0-7351-0039-X*) Replica Bks.

Breen, J. Women Romantics Writing in Pro. 304p. 1996. 8.50 (*0-460-87793-3*, 665267Q, Everyman's Classic Lib) Tuttle Pubng.

Breen, J. Colleen. Making Changes: Guidebook for Managing Life's Challenges. 192p. 1994. pap. 12.95 (*0-925190-33-0*) Fairview Press.

Breen, Jefferson. You Are a Person of Worth. LC 86-91860. 1988. 12.00 (*0-87212-202-6*) Libra.

Breen, Jennifer, ed. Victorian Women Poets. LC 95-127023. 240p. 1994. pap. 7.50 (*0-460-87457-8*, Everyman's Classic Lib) Tuttle Pubng.

Breen, Jennifer, intro. Women Romantic Poets, 1785-1832: An Anthology. 240p. 1994. pap. 7.50 (*0-460-87456-X*, Everyman's Classic Lib) Tuttle Pubng.

Breen, John. Japanese. LC 98-4198. (Hugo Ser.). 272p. 1998. pap. 29.95 incl. audio (*0-7894-3584-5*) DK Pub Inc.

Breen, John & Teeuwen, Mark. Shinto in Historical Perspective. 300p. (C). 1999. text 55.00 (*0-7007-1170-8*, Pub. by Curzon Pr Ltd); pap. text 27.95 (*0-7007-1172-4*, Pub. by Curzon Pr Ltd) UH Pr.

***Breen, John & Teeuwen, Mark.** Shinto in History: Ways of the Kami. LC 00-24006. 2000. write for info. (*0-8248-2363-X*) UH Pr.

Breen, John, jt. auth. see Hugo's Language Books.

Breen, John F. Encyclopedia of Reptiles & Amphibians. (Illus.). 576p. 1974. text 39.95 (*0-87666-220-3*, H-935) TFH Pubns.

Breen, John J., jt. auth. see Hill, Evan.

Breen, John R., ed. Who's Who of Dogs. LC 94-44826. (Illus.). 504p. 1995. pap. 7.95 (*1-56305-871-5*, 3871) Workman Pub.

Breen, John R. F., ed. Who's Who of Cats. LC 94-1330. (Illus.). 500p. 1994. pap. 7.95 (*1-56305-629-1*, 3629) Workman Pub.

***Breen, Jon L.** The Drowning Icecube & Other Stories. LC 99-45491. 1999. 20.95 (*0-7862-2250-6*) Mac Lib Ref.

Breen, Jon L. Novel Verdicts: A Guide to Courtroom Fiction. 2nd ed. LC 99-35315. 293p. 1999. text 39.50 (*0-8108-3674-2*) Scarecrow.

— What about Murder? A Guide to Books about Mystery Detective Fiction. LC 81-645. 175p. 1981. 26.50 (*0-8108-1413-7*) Scarecrow.

— What about Murder? (1981-1991) A Guide to Books about Mystery & Detective Fiction. 1992. 41.50 (*0-8108-2609-7*) Scarecrow.

Breen, Jon L. & Breen, Rita A. American Murders: Eleven Rediscovered Short Novels from American Magazine, 1934-1954. LC 85-45120. 450p. 1986. text 12.00 (*0-8240-8672-4*, H610) Garland.

Breen, Jon L. & Greenberg, Martin H., eds. Murder off the Rack: Critical Studies of Ten Paperback Masters. LC 89-33085. 188p. 1989. 24.00 (*0-8108-2232-6*) Scarecrow.

— Synod of Sleuths: Essays on Judeo-Christian Detective Fiction. 169p. 1990. 24.00 (*0-8108-2382-9*) Scarecrow.

Breen, Jon L., jt. auth. see Gorman, Ed.

Breen, Joseph J. & Dellarco, Michael J., eds. Pollution Prevention in Industrial Processes: The Role of Process Analytical Chemistry. LC 92-30288. (ACS Symposium Ser.: Vol. 508). (Illus.). 316p. 1992. text 85.00 (*0-8412-2478-1*, Pub. by Am Chemical) OUP.

Breen, Joseph J. & Robinson, Philip E., eds. Environmental Applications of Chemometrics. LC 85-22878. (ACS Symposium Ser.: Vol. 292). 296p. 1985. reprint ed. pap. 91.80 (*0-608-03920-9*, 206436700009) Bks Demand.

Breen, Joseph J. & Stroup, Cindy R., eds. Lead Poisoning: Exposure, Abatement, Regulation. 304p. 1995. lib. bdg. 95.00 (*1-56670-113-9*, L1113) Lewis Pubs.

Breen, Karen, ed. Index to Collective Biographies for Young Readers. 4th ed. 494p. 1988. 48.00 (*0-8352-2348-5*) Bowker.

Breen, Kerry, et al. Ethics, Law & Medical Practice. LC 97-179968. 386p. 1997. pap. 39.95 (*1-86448-407-1*, Pub. by Allen & Unwin Pty) Paul & Co Pubs.

***Breen, Louise A.** Transgressing the Bounds: Subversive Enterprises among the Puritan Elite in Massachusetts, 1630-1692. (Religion in America Ser.). 288p. 2000. text 45.00 (*0-19-513800-7*) OUP.

Breen, Marilyn, jt. ed. see Kay, David C.

***Breen, Mark & Friestad, Kathleen.** The Kids' Book of Weather Forecasting: Build a Weather Station, "Read" the Sky & Make Predictions! LC 99-89954. (Kids Can! Ser.). (Illus.). 160p. (J). (gr. 2-6). 2000. pap. 12.95 (*1-885593-39-2*) Williamson Pub Co.

Breen, Matthew P. Thirty Years of New York Politics, Up-to-Date. LC 73-19132. (Politics & People Ser.). (Illus.). 918p. 1974. reprint ed. 70.95 (*0-405-05857-8*) Ayer.

Breen, Maureen & White, David A. French Through Funetics: Language Learning Through Logos. (Illus.). viii, 231p. 1998. pap. 19.95 (*0-929724-39-9*) Command Performance.

Breen, Michael J. & Altepeter, Thomas S. Disruptive Behavior Disorders in Children: Treatment-Focused Assessment. LC 90-3817. 288p. 1990. lib. bdg. 35.00 (*0-89862-439-8*) Guilford Pubns.

Breen, Michael J. & Fiedler, Craig R., eds. Behavioral Approach to Assessment of Youth with Emotional/Behavioral Disorders: A Handbook for School-Based Practitioners. LC 95-22355. 729p. (C). 1996. pap. text 44.00 (*0-89079-625-4*, 7312) PRO-ED.

Breen, Myles, ed. see Granato, Len, et al.

Breen, Patrick. Diary of Patrick Breen - One of the Donner Party. Teggart, Frederick J., ed. (Illus.). 16p. 1978. reprint ed. pap. 3.95 (*0-89646-048-7*) Vistabooks.

Breen, Paul, jt. auth. see Whitaker, Urban.

Breen, Quirinus & Drake, George A. The Impact of the Church upon Its Culture: Reappraisals of the History of Christianity. Brauer, Jerald C., ed. LC 67-30155. (Essays in Divinity Ser.: Vol. 2). 406p. reprint ed. pap. 125.90 (*0-608-12343-9*, 202408500035) Bks Demand.

Breen, Richard. Regression Models: Censored, Sample Selected, or Truncated Data. (Quantitative Applications in the Social Science Ser.: Vol. 111). 96p. 1996. pap. 10.95 (*0-8039-5710-6*) Sage.

Breen, Rita A., jt. auth. see Breen, Jon L.

Breen, Robert. First to Fight: Australian Diggers, N. Z. Kiwis & U. S. Paratroopers in Vietnam, 1965-66. (Vietnam War Ser.). (Illus.). 332p. 1989. 34.95 (*0-89839-126-1*) Battery Pr.

Breen, Robert S. Chamber Theatre. LC 86-72771. xi, 129p. (C). 1986. reprint ed. pap. 16.95 (*0-940473-00-3*) Wm Caxton.

Breen, Susan. Cloze Reading Wizard, Bk. A. 48p. 1992. student ed. write for info. (*1-881135-00-4*) Wizard Pr.

***Breen, Susan.** Come Play at Home. (Little Sturdy Shape Bks.). (Illus.). 16p. (J). 1999. 4.99 (*0-307-10528-8*, Goldn Books) Gldn Bks Pub Co.

— Come Play at the Park! 16p. 1999. pap. 4.99 (*0-307-10527-X*, Whitman Coin) St Martin.

Breen, T. H. Imagining the Past. 1990. pap. 13.41 (*0-201-52338-8*) Addison-Wesley.

— Imagining the Past: East Hampton Histories. 1989. 19.18 (*0-201-06749-8*) Addison-Wesley.

— Imagining the Past: East Hampton Histories. LC 95-35217. (Illus.). 320p. 1996. pap. 19.95 (*0-8203-1810-8*) U of Ga Pr.

— Puritans & Adventurers: Change & Persistence in Early America. 288p. 1982. pap. text 20.95 (*0-19-503207-1*) OUP.

— Tobacco Culture: The Mentality of the Great Tidewater Planters on the Eve of Revolution. LC 85-42676. (Illus.). 210p. 1985. pap. text 12.95 (*0-691-00596-6*, Pub. by Princeton U Pr) Cal Prin Full Svc.

Breen, T. H., ed. The Power of Words: Documents in American History, Vol. 2. LC 95-18487. Vol. 2. 347p. (C). 1997. pap. text 37.00 (*0-06-501113-9*) Addson-Wesley Educ.

— The Power of Words Vol. 2: Documents in American History. LC 95-18487. Vol. 1. 331p. (C). 1997. pap. text 37.00 (*0-06-501112-0*) Addson-Wesley Educ.

Breen, T. H. & Innes, Stephen. Myne Owne Ground: Race & Freedom on Virginia's Eastern Shore, 1640-1676. (Illus.). 152p. 1982. pap. text 19.95 (*0-19-503206-3*) OUP.

Breen, W. Proof Coins Struck at the U. S. Mints: Updated. 1983. reprint ed. pap. 10.00 (*0-915262-94-0*) S J Durst.

— U. S. Half Cents Encyclopedia. LC 82-73551. (Illus.). 1983. lib. bdg. 75.00 (*0-911021-00-0*) S J Durst.

Breen, Walter. Walter Breen's Complete Encyclopedia of U. S. & Colonial Coins. LC 79-6855. (Illus.). 768p. 1988. 125.00 (*0-385-14207-2*) Doubleday.

— Walter Breen's Encyclopedia of United States & Colonial Proof Coins, 1722-1977. rev. ed. (Illus.). 340p. 1989. pap. 29.95 (*0-943161-21-5*) Bowers & Merena.

Breen, Walter H. Walter Breen's Numisma: The United States Cent, 1793-1814. Vogel, Bruce A., ed. (Illus.). 1998. 250.00 (*1-893055-00-0*) B A Vogel.

— Walter Breen's Numisma: The United States Cent, 1793-1814. Vogel, Bruce A., ed. (Illus.). 1998. reprint ed. pap. 75.00 (*1-893055-02-7*) B A Vogel.

— Walter Green's Numisma: The United States Cent, 1793-1814. Vogel, Bruce A., ed. (Illus.). 1998. pap. 75.00 (*1-893055-01-9*) B A Vogel.

Breen, Walter H. & Sheldon, William H. Walter Breen's Numisma: The United States Cent, 1816-1857. (Illus.). 290p. 1998. pap. 60.00 (*1-893055-03-5*) B A Vogel.

Breen, Walter H, jt. auth. see Highfill, John W.

Breen, William J. Labor Market Politics & the Great War: The Department of Labor, the States, & the First U. S. Employment Service, 1907-1933. LC 96-36067. 1997. 35.00 (*0-87338-559-4*) Kent St U Pr.

— Uncle Sam at Home: Civilian Mobilization, Wartime Federalism, & the Council of National Defense, 1917-1919, 70. LC 83-12576. (Contributions in American Studies: No. 70). 279p. 1984. 65.00 (*0-313-24112-0*, BRU/) Greenwood.

Breene, R. & Belcher, R. Shift & Shape of Spectral Lines. LC 60-14951. (International Series of Monographs on Analytical Chemistry: Vol. 61). 1961. 155.00 (*0-08-009549-6*, Pub. by Pergamon Repr) Franklin.

Breene, R. G., ed. Common Names of Arachnids: Committee on Common Names of Arachnids of the American Arachnological Society. 2nd ed. 74p. 1997. pap. text 9.00 (*1-929427-10-7*) American Tarantula.

Breene, R. G., et al. Tarantulas of Texas: Their Medical Importance, & World-Wide Bibliography. (Illus.). 70p. 1996. 9.00 (*1-929427-04-2*) American Tarantula.

Breene, Robert G., III. All about Fire Ants: What Your Entomologist Will Never Tell You. (ATS Educational Series Manuals). (Illus.). 20p. 1997. 6.00 (*1-929427-07-7*) American Tarantula.

— The ATS Arthropod Medical Manual: Diagnosis & Treatment. (ATS Educational Series Manuals). (Illus.). 38p. 1998. 6.00 (*1-929427-06-9*) American Tarantula.

— Recluse Spiders & the Hobo Spider: Araneae, Sicariidae, Loxosceles, Agelenidae, Tegenaria. (ATS Educational Series Manuals). (Illus.). 28p. 1997. 6.00 (*1-929427-01-8*) American Tarantula.

— Spider Bob's Animal Odysseys I: Tales of Arachnids: Spiders, Scorpions & Others. (Illus.). 66p. 1994. 8.00 (*1-929427-08-5*) American Tarantula.

— Spider Bob's Animal Odysseys II: Tales of Myriapods & Magnificanticent Insects. (Illus.). 82p. 1997. 8.00 (*1-929427-05-0*) American Tarantula.

— Widow Spiders of North America: With a Bibliography. (ATS Educational Series Manuals). (Illus.). 28p. 1997. 6.00 (*1-929427-09-3*) American Tarantula.

An Asterisk (*) at the beginning of an entry indicates that the title is appearing for the first time.

Breene, Robert G., Jr., ed. Latin American Political Yearbook, 1998. 275p. 1999. 49.95 (*1-56000-386-3*) Transaction Pubs.

— Latin American Political Yearbook, 1997. 256p. 1997. text 49.95 (*1-56000-350-2*) Transaction Pubs.

***Breene, Robert G., III & O'Brien, Meip R.** Concise Care Guide: For the 80 Plus Most Common Tarantulas. 67p. 1998. 8.00 (*1-929427-00-X*) American Tarantula.

Breener, Malcolm K. & Moen, Robert C., eds. Gene Therapy in Cancer. (Basic & Clinical Oncology Ser.: Vol. 10). (Illus.). 256p. 1996. text 155.00 (*0-8247-9481-8*) Dekker.

***Breening, Greg.** Compass Minnesota. 2nd ed. 348p. 2000. pap. 19.95 (*0-679-00437-8*) Random.

Breer, Carl. The Birth of Chrysler Corporation & Its Engineering Legacy. LC 94-43487. (Illus.). 238p. 1995. 39.00 (*1-56091-524-2*, R-144) Soc Auto Engineers.

Breer, Dennis. Utah's Green River: A Fly Fisher's Guide to the Flaming George Tailwater. LC 98-209576. (Illus.). 80p. 1998. pap. 19.95 (*1-57188-111-5*) F Amato Pubns.

Breer, H., ed. Neurochemical Techniques in Insect Research. (Experimental Entomology Ser.). (Illus.). 310p. 1985. 129.00 (*0-387-13813-7*) Spr-Verlag.

Breer, Paul. The Spontaneous Self: Viable Alternatives to Free Will. LC 89-84648. 300p. (Orig.). (C). 1989. pap. 20.00 (*0-9623589-0-8*) Inst Naturalistic Philos.

Breer, William. The Adolescent Molester. 2nd ed. LC 95-47296. (Illus.). 234p. 1996. 52.95 (*0-398-06571-3*); pap. 36.95 (*0-398-06572-1*) C C Thomas.

— Diagnosis & Treatment of the Young Male Victim of Sexual Abuse. (Illus.). 236p. 1992. pap. 33.95 (*0-398-06029-0*) C C Thomas.

— Diagnosis & Treatment of the Young Male Victim of Sexual Abuse. (Illus.). 236p. (C). 1992. text 48.95 (*0-398-05816-4*) C C Thomas.

Brees, Samuel C. Railway Practice. (First Ser.). (Illus.). 296p. 1998. reprint ed. pap. 450.00 (*1-85297-013-8*, Pub. by Archival Facs) St Mut.

Breese, B. B. On Inhibition. (Psychology Monographs General & Applied: Vol. 3). reprint ed. 55.00 (*0-8115-1402-1*) Periodicals Srv.

Breese-Biagioni, Janelle. EdPress Membership Roster & Freelance Directory, 1997. 1996. pap. 35.00 (*0-614-05419-2*) EdPress.

Breese, Dave. Seven Men Who Rule the World from the Grave. pap. 12.99 (*0-8024-8448-4*, 284) Moody.

Breese, David. Seven Men Who Rule the World from the Grave. 23p. (Orig.). 1994. pap. 2.95 (*1-879366-63-0*) Hearthstone OK.

Breese, George R. & Creese, Ian, eds. Neurobiology of Central D1-Dopamine Receptors. (Advances in Experimental Medicine & Biology Ser.: Vol. 204). 228p. 1986. 69.50 (*0-306-42383-9*, Plenum Trade) Perseus Pubng.

Breese, Gerald W. & Whiteman, Dorothy E. Approach to Urban Planning. LC 73-90474. 147p. 1969. reprint ed. lib. bdg. 55.00 (*0-8371-2284-8*, BRUP, Greenwood Pr) Greenwood.

Breese, Gillian & Langham, Tony. The Amazing Adventures of Teddy Tum Tum. (Illus.). 32p. (J). (ps-3). 1992. 11.95 (*1-55970-185-4*) Arcade Pub Inc.

Breese, Mark B. H., et al. Materials Analysis Using a Nuclear Microprobe. LC 95-11166. 460p. 1996. 124.00 (*0-471-10608-9*) Wiley.

***Breese, Martin.** Breese's Guide to Modern First Editions & Their Values. 1999. pap. 29.99 (*0-947533-67-2*) Breese Bks.

Breese, Martin, ed. The Titanic Story: The Ocean's Greatest Disaster. abr. ed. LC 99-232576. (Illus.). 118p. 1998. pap. 13.95 (*0-947533-62-1*, Pub. by Breese Bks) Firebird Dist.

Breese, Martin, ed. see Rogers, Terri.

Breese, Mary E. Longsworth Family History: Descendants of Solomon Longsworth, Sr., of Maryland. LC 52-23969. (Illus.). 281p. reprint ed. pap. 87.20 (*0-608-10215-6*, 205167600099) Bks Demand.

Breese, Mikki, ed. see Parker, Dorothy R.

Breese, Sydney S., Jr., jt. ed. see Zacharia, Theodore P.

Breese-Whiting, Kathryn. The Miracle of the Phoenix. 96p. (Orig.). 1995. pap. 14.95 (*0-9647989-0-5*, Voice Phoenix Pr) Phoenix Inst.

Breeskin, Adelyn. Mary Cassatt: A Catalogue Raisonne of the Graphic Work. 2nd ed. (Illus.). 190p. 1979. reprint ed. 150.00 (*1-55660-249-9*) A Wofsy Fine Arts.

Breeskin, Adelyn D. Anne Goldthwaite: A Catalogue Raisonne of the Graphic Work. LC 82-6425. (Illus.). 141p. (J). (ps-12). 1982. pap. 30.00 (*0-89280-019-4*) Montgomery Mus.

Breeskin, Adelyn D., jt. auth. see Brooks, Romaine.

Breesse, Dave & James, William T. Raging into Apocalypse Vol. IV: Essays in Apocalypse IV. LC 95-73132. (Essays in Apocalypse Ser.). 320p. 1996. pap. 11.95 (*0-89221-320-5*) New Leaf.

Breeton, John & Mansfield, Margaret A. Writing on the Job: A Norton Pocket Guide. 176p. 1996. pap. 19.95 (*0-393-03969-2*) Norton.

Breeton, Karen. Australian Cattle Dog: An Owner's Guide to a Happy Healthy Pet. LC 98-146175. 160p. 1998. pap. 12.95 (*0-87605-446-7*) Howell Bks.

Breeur, Roland, jt. auth. see Husserl, Edmund.

Breewer, Linda D. From Me to You Bk. 2: Celebrating the Way We Are Together. LC TXU 743-270. (Illus.). v, 67p. (Orig.). 1996. pap. write for info. (*0-9659366-0-0*) L D Brewer.

Breeze, jt. auth. see Coates.

Breeze, Andrew. Medieval Welsh Literature. 264p. 1996. boxed set 55.00 (*1-85182-229-1*, Pub. by Four Cts Pr) Intl Spec Bk.

***Breeze, Benjamin.** Life after 40. 50p. 1999. 14.95 (*0-9675120-0-X*) Gloom & Doomb Bk.

— Sex after 40. 50p. Date not set. 14.95 (*0-9675120-1-8*) Gloom & Doomb Bk.

Breeze, Carla. The New Modern. LC 94-38699. 1995. 47.50 (*0-86636-327-0*) PBC Intl Inc.

— The New Modern. (Illus.). 160p. 1996. pap. 27.50 (*0-86636-437-4*) St Martin.

Breeze, Claire, jt. auth. see Coates, Jonathan.

***Breeze, David J.** Historic Scotland: People & Places. (Illus.). 144p. 2000. 28.95 (*0-7134-8615-5*) B T B.

Breeze, David J. Historic Scotland: The Historic Scotland Book of Scotland's History. LC 99-205722. (Illus.). 128p. 1998. 29.95 (*0-7134-8394-6*, Pub. by B T B) Branford.

— Roman Forts in Britain. (Shire Archaeology Ser.: No. 37). (Illus.). 72p. 10.50 (*0-85263-654-7*, Pub. by Shire Pubns) Lubrecht & Cramer.

Breeze, David J., jt. auth. see Tabraham, Christopher J.

Breeze, George & Breeze, Linda. Mysteries of the Moon & Star: A Collectors Guide to Moon & Star Pattern Glass with Price Guide. 128p. pap. 29.95 (*0-9649326-0-1*) G & L Breeze.

Breeze, Jean. On the Edge of an Island. LC 97-208847. 96p. 1997. pap. 17.95 (*1-85224-405-4*, Pub. by Bloodaxe Bks) Dufour.

Breeze, Katie. Nekkid Cowboy. 2nd ed. LC 82-73110. 216p. 1991. pap. 9.95 (*0-931722-39-X*) Corona Pub.

Breeze, Lawrence E. The British Experience with River Pollution, 1865-1876. LC 93-22308. (American University Studies: History: Ser. IX, Vols. 139). XVIII, 298p. (C). 1993. text 53.95 (*0-8204-2162-6*) P Lang Pubng.

Breeze, Linda, jt. auth. see Breeze, George.

Breeze, Lynn. Pickle & the Ball. LC 97-76652. (Illus.). (J). 1998. 4.95 (*0-7534-5148-4*, Kingfisher) LKC.

— Pickle & the Blanket. LC 97-76650. (Illus.). (J). 1998. 4.95 (*0-7534-5149-2*) LKC.

— Pickle & the Blocks. LC 97-76468. (J). 1998. 4.95 (*0-7534-5151-4*) LKC.

— Pickle & the Box. LC 97-76651. (Illus.). (J). 1998. 4.95 (*0-7534-5150-6*) LKC.

Breg, Per O., jt. auth. see Alvesson, Mats.

***Brega, Isabella.** Las Vegas. (Illus.). 2000. 9.99 (*0-7858-1240-7*) Bk Sales Inc.

Brega, Isabella. Washington: Pride & Glory of America. (Travel America Ser.). 1997. 14.98 (*0-7651-9401-5*) Smithmark.

***Brega, Isabella.** Washington, D.C. (Illus.). 2000. 9.99 (*0-7858-1236-9*) Bk Sales Inc.

Brega, Julie. Breeding & Youngstock. 1996. pap. 35.00 (*0-85131-647-6*, Pub. by J A Allen) Trafalgar.

— Fitness & Competition. 1996. pap. 40.00 (*0-85131-622-0*, Pub. by J A Allen) Trafalgar.

— The Horse: Physiology. (Open College Ser.: Bk. 4). 1993. pap. text 35.00 (*0-85131-607-7*, Pub. by J A Allen) Trafalgar.

— The Horse: The Foot, Shoeing & Lameness. (Open College Ser.: Bk. 3). 1993. pap. 35.00 (*0-85131-612-3*, Pub. by J A Allen) Trafalgar.

***Brega, Julie.** Horse - General Management. 2000. pap. 14.95 (*0-85131-588-7*, Pub. by J A Allen) Trafalgar.

— Horse-Equestrian Business. 2000. pap. 14.95 (*0-85131-589-5*, Pub. by J A Allen) Trafalgar.

Bregazzi, Josephine, tr. see Baines, John.

Bregel, Yuri. Bibliography of Islamic Central Asia, Set, Pts. I-III. (Uralic & Altaic Ser.: Vol. 160). 2276p. 1995. 299.00 (*0-933070-35-7*) Ind U Res Inst.

— Notes on the Study of Central Asia. (Papers on Inner Asia: No. 28). 1995. 4.50 (*0-614-14924-X*) Res Inst Inner Asian Studies.

Breger, Dee. Journeys in Microspace: Images from a Scanning Electron Microscope. LC 94-37829. (Illus.). 215p. 1995. 41.50 (*0-231-08252-5*) Col U Pr.

Breger, Herbert, jt. auth. see Grosholz, Emily.

Breger, Louis. Dostoevsky: The Author as Psychoanalyst. 320p. (C). 1990. pap. text 17.50 (*0-8147-1151-0*) NYU Pr.

***Breger, Louis.** Freud: Darkness in the Midst of Vision. LC 99-59994. 400p. 2000. pap. 30.00 (*0-471-31628-8*) Wiley.

Breger, Louis, et al. The Effect of Stress on Dreams. LC 74-160287. (Psychological Issues Monographs: No. 27, Vol. 7, No. 3). 214p. 1971. pap. 32.50 (*0-8236-1535-9*) Intl Univs Pr.

Breger, Marshall & Idinopulos, Thomas A. Jerusalem's Holy Places & the Peace Process. LC 97-31999. (Policy Papers Ser.: No. 46). 76p. 1998. pap. 19.95 (*0-944029-73-6*) Wash Inst NEP.

Breger, Marshall J. & Gordis, David M. Vouchers for School Choice: Challenge or Opportunity?: An American Jewish Reappraisal LC 99-194267. viii, 201p. 1998. write for info. (*1-893380-00-9*) Wilstein Inst.

Breger, Rosemary & Hill, Rosanna, eds. Cross-Cultural Marriage: Identity & Choice. LC 98-218569. (Cross-Cultural Perspectives on Women Ser.). 224p. 1998. 55.00 (*1-85973-963-6*, Pub. by Berg Pubs); pap. 19.50 (*1-85973-968-7*, Pub. by Berg Pubs) NYU Pr.

Breggin, Ginger R., jt. auth. see Breggin, Peter.

Breggin, Ginger R., jt. auth. see Breggin, Peter R.

Breggin, Ginger Ross, jt. auth. see Breggin, Peter R.

Breggin, Peter. Brain-Disabling Treatments in Psychiatry: Drugs, Electroshock & the Role of the FDA. LC 97-3969. 320p. 1997. 43.95 (*0-8261-9490-7*) Springer Pub.

— Enough Is Enough: How & When to Stop Taking Psychiatric Drugs. 1998. write for info. (*0-201-32810-0*) Addison-Wesley.

— The Heart of Being Helpful: Empathy & the Creation of a Healing Presence. LC 97-2442. 200p. 1997. 42.95 (*0-8261-9680-2*) Springer Pub.

— Talking Back to Prozac. 1995. mass mkt. 5.99 (*0-312-95606-1*, Pub. by Tor Bks) St Martin.

Breggin, Peter & Breggin, Ginger R. The War Against Children of Color: Psychiatry Targets Inner City Youth. LC 97-13741. 1998. lib. bdg. 29.95 (*1-56751-127-9*) Common Courage.

Breggin, Peter, ed. see Bedillion, A. Mark.

Breggin, Peter R. Electroshock: Its Brain Disabling Effects. 256p. 1979. 32.95 (*0-8261-2710-X*) Springer Pub.

***Breggin, Peter R.** Reclaiming Our Children: A Healing Plan for a Nation in Crisis. 288p. 1999. text 24.00 (*0-7382-0252-5*, Pub. by Perseus Pubng) HarpC.

Breggin, Peter R. Talking Back to Ritalin: What Doctors Aren't Telling You about Stimulants for Children. LC 97-44446. 265p. 1998. 24.95 (*1-56751-129-5*) Common Courage.

— Talking Back to Ritalin: What Doctor's Aren't Telling You about Stimulants for Children. 2nd rev. ed. 450p. 2000. pap. 18.95 (*1-56751-128-7*, Pub. by Common Courage) Login Brothers Bk Co.

— Toxic Psychiatry: Why Therapy, Empathy & Love Must Replace the Drugs, Electroshock Therapy & Biochemical Theories of the "New Psychiatry" 480p. 1994. pap. 17.95 (*0-312-11366-8*) St Martin.

Breggin, Peter R. & Breggin, Ginger R. The War Against Children: How the Drugs, Programs, & Theories of the Psychiatric Establishment Are Threatening America's Children with a Medical "Care" for Violence. 280p. 1994. write for info. (*0-614-24091-3*) Lake Hse Bks.

***Breggin, Peter R. & Breggin, Ginger R.** The War Against Children: How the Drugs, Programs, & Theories of the Psychiatric Establishment Are Threatening America's Children with a Medical "Cure" for Violence. 179p. 1999. reprint ed. text 22.00 (*0-7881-6322-1*) DIANE Pub.

Breggin, Peter R. & Breggin, Ginger Ross. The War Against Children of Color: Psychiatry Targets Inner City Youth. LC 97-13741. 255p. 1999. pap. 18.95 (*1-56751-126-0*, Pub. by Common Courage) SPD-Small Pr Dist.

Breggin, Peter R. & Cohen, David. Your Drug May Be Your Problem: How & Why to Stop Taking Psychiatric Medications. 288p. 1999. 24.00 (*0-7382-0184-7*, Pub. by Perseus Pubng) HarpC.

***Breggin, Peter R. & Cohen, David.** Your Drug May Be Your Problem: How & Why to Stop Taking Psychiatric Medications. 288p. 2000. pap. text 16.00 (*0-7382-0348-3*, Pub. by Perseus Pubng) HarpC.

Breggin, Peter R. & Stern, E. Mark, eds. Psychosocial Approaches to Deeply Disturbed Persons. LC 95-12677. 231p. (C). 1996. 39.95 (*1-56024-841-6*) Haworth Pr.

Breggin, Peter R., jt. auth. see Stein, David B.

Bregman & Evergam. Maryland Landlord & Tenant: 1987 Supplement. 1987. pap. write for info. (*0-87473-326-X*, 60402-10, MICHIE) LEXIS Pub.

Bregman, Rita & Michelman, Barbara. On Amethyst Glass: Two Voices, One Song. 112p. 2000. pap. 11.95 (*0-9664856-2-9*) Manto Pr.

Bregman, Adolph, jt. ed. see Coleman, Satis N.

***Bregman, Ahron.** Israel's Wars, 1947-1993. LC 99-54115. 256p. 2000. pap. write for info. (*0-415-21468-8*) Routledge.

— Israel's Wars, 1947-1993. (Illus.). 256p. 2000. 90.00 (*0-415-21467-X*) Routledge.

Bregman, Ahron. Living & Working in Israel: How to Prepare for a Successful Longterm Stay. (Living & Working Abroad Ser.). 128p. 1996. pap. 22.50 (*1-85703-221-7*, Pub. by How To Bks) Trans-Atl Phila.

Bregman, Ahron & El-Tahri, Jihan. The Fifty Years' War: Israel & the Arabs. (Illus.). 384p. 1999. 29.95 (*1-57500-057-1*, Pub. by TV Bks) HarpC.

***Bregman, Ahron & El-Tahri, Jihan.** Israel & the Arabs: An Eyewitness Account of War & Peace in the Middle East. (Illus.). 384p. 2000. reprint ed. pap. 16.00 (*1-57500-184-5*, Pub. by TV Bks) HarpC.

Bregman, Albert S. Auditory Scene Analysis: The Perpetual Organization of Sound. (Illus.). 792p. 1994. pap. text 34.00 (*0-262-52195-4*, Bradford Bks) MIT Pr.

Bregman, Alice M., jt. auth. see Kohl, Susan.

Bregman, Allyn. Laboratory Investigations in Cell & Molecular Biology. 3rd rev. ed. LC 95-54168. 336p. 1996. pap. 55.95 (*0-471-14809-1*) Wiley.

Bregman, Douglas M. & Everngam, Gary G. Maryland Landlord-Tenant Law: Practice & Procedure. 481p. 1994. 70.00 (*1-55834-125-0*, MICHIE) LEXIS Pub.

Bregman, Douglas M. & Everngam, Gary G. Maryland Landlord-Tenant Law: Practice & Procedure. 2nd ed. 481p. 70.00 (*0-327-01937-9*) LEXIS Pub.

Bregman, Douglas M. & Everngam, Gary G. Maryland Landlord-Tenant Law, 1998 Cumulative Supplement. 2nd ed. 105p. 1998. pap., suppl. ed. write for info. (*0-327-00539-4*, 6040314) LEXIS Pub.

Bregman, J. I., et al. Environmental Compliance Handbook. LC 96-4961. 432p. 1996. lib. bdg. 75.00 (*1-56670-146-5*) Lewis Pubs.

Bregman, Jacob I. Environmental Impact Statements. 304p. 1992. lib. bdg. 95.00 (*0-87371-493-8*, L493) Lewis Pubs.

— Environmental Impact Statements. 2nd ed. LC 98-51739. 248p. 1999. 89.95 (*1-56670-369-7*) Lewis Pubs.

Bregman, Jacob I., jt. auth. see MacKenthun, Kenneth Marsh.

Bregman, Lucy. Beyond Silence & Denial: Death & Dying Reconsidered. LC 98-47299. 216p. 1999. pap. 18.00 (*0-664-25802-6*) Westminster John Knox.

Bregman, Rob. The Genus Matucana: Biology of Systematics of Fascinating Peruvian Cacti. (Illus.). 176p. (C). 1996. text 88.00 (*90-5410-638-7*, Pub. by A A Balkema) Ashgate Pub Co.

Bregman, Robert A. IRMI's Executive Liability Insurance Guide. LC 99-182786. 195p. 1998. pap. 65.00 (*1-886813-39-6*) Intl Risk Mgt.

Bregman, Robert A., et al. Directors & Officiers/Fiduciary Liability Insurance Text & Course Guide 1997. (Registered Professional Liability Underwriter (RPLU) Ser.: Vol. V). 394p. 1997. ring bd. 115.00 (*1-886813-29-9*) Intl Risk Mgt.

— Professional Liability: Insurance Text & Course Guide, 1997. (Registered Professional Liability Underwriter (RPLU) Ser.: Vol. II). 498p. 1997. ring bd. 115.00 (*1-886813-26-4*) Intl Risk Mgt.

— Professional Liability: Medical Text & Course Guide, 1997. (Registered Professional Liability Underwriter (RPLU) Ser.: Vol. IV). 374p. 1997. ring bd. 115.00 (*1-886813-28-0*) Intl Risk Mgt.

— Professional Liability: Non-Medical Text & Course Guide, 1997. (Registered Professional Liability Underwriter (RPLU) Ser.: Vol. III). 540p. 1997. ring bd. 115.00 (*1-886813-27-2*) Intl Risk Mgt.

Bregman, Robert M., et al. The Charlie Parker Discography. 94p. (Orig.). 1994. 14.00 (*1-881993-25-6*) Cadence Jazz.

Bregmann, Lucy & Thiermann, Sara. First Person Mortal: Personal Narratives of Illness, Dying & Grief. 208p. 1995. 19.95 (*1-55778-714-X*); pap. 14.95 (*1-55778-715-8*) Paragon Hse.

Bregnard, Edythe E. How Old Would You Be If You Didn't Have a Mirror & Didn't Know When You Were Born? (Illus.). 96p. (Orig.). 1985. 6.50 (*0-9616565-5-7*, TX1-851-297); pap. 3.50 (*0-9616565-4-9*) Pisces Pr AZ.

— I Am Not an Old Lady (Just a Little Girl with Wrinkles) (Illus.). 96p. 1981. 6.50 (*0-9616565-3-0*, TX 826-426); pap. 3.50 (*0-9616565-2-2*) Pisces Pr AZ.

— Yesterday, Today & Forever. (Illus.). 96p. (Orig.). 1978. 6.50 (*0-9616565-1-4*, TX 641-587); pap. 3.50 (*0-9616565-0-6*) Pisces Pr AZ.

Bregoli-Russo, Mauda. Teatro Del Gonzaga Al Tempo Di Isabella D'Este. (Studies in Italian Culture: No. 21). (ITA.). 131p. (C). 1997. text 36.95 (*0-8204-3124-9*) P Lang Pubng.

Breguet, Emmanuel. Breguet: Watchmakers since 1775: The Life & Legacy of Abraham-louis Breguet, 1747-1823. (Illus.). 364p. 1997. 175.00 (*2-909838-18-8*, Pub. by A Gourcuff) Antique Collect.

Breguet, Jean M., jt. ed. see Nelson, Bradley J.

Bregy, Katherine M. From Dante to Jeanne D'Arc: Adventures in Medieval Life & Letters. LC 78-774. (Science & Culture Ser.). 138p. 1978. reprint ed. lib. bdg. 35.00 (*0-313-20290-7*, BRFD, Greenwood Pr) Greenwood.

Brehal, Nicolas. L' Enfant au Souffle Coupe. (FRE.). 214p. 1989. pap. 11.95 (*0-7859-2121-4*, 2070381595) Fr & Eur.

— Les Etangs De Woodfield. (FRE.). 216p. 1985. pap. 11.95 (*0-7859-2012-9*, 2070376486) Fr & Eur.

— La Paleur et le Sang. (FRE.). 247p. 1988. pap. 11.95 (*0-7859-2101-X*, 2070380726) Fr & Eur.

Brehan, Delle. Kicks Is Kicks. 256p. (Orig.). 1990. mass mkt. 3.95 (*0-87067-319-X*) Holloway.

Brehany, Tony. West Cork: "A Sort of History, Like . . ." LC 97-212400. (Illus.). 138p. 1997. pap. 19.95 (*1-900505-15-0*, Pub. by Kestrel Bks) Irish Bks Media.

Brehaut, Denise & Hay, Paul. Day Skipper Motor Cruising. (Illus.). 128p. 1998. pap. 21.95 (*1-86126-038-5*, Pub. by Crolwood) Motorbooks Intl.

Brehaut, Madeleine. Creative Containers to Make & Decorate. (Illus.). 128p. 1997. pap. 19.95 (*0-8019-8941-8*) Krause Pubns.

Brehaut, Madeleine, jt. auth. see Jones, Bridget.

Brehelin, M., ed. Immunity in Invertebrates. (Proceedings in Life Sciences Ser.). (Illus.). 240p. 1986. 112.95 (*0-387-15871-5*) Spr-Verlag.

Breheney, Colleen, et al. Making Peace at Mayfield: A Whole School Approach to Conflict Resolution. LC 97-101760. 81p. 1996. pap. text 18.00 (*0-435-07229-3*, 07229) Heinemann.

Breheny, Michael & McQuaid, Ronald, eds. The Development of High Technology Industries: An International Survey. 368p. 1987. lib. bdg. 60.00 (*0-7099-3942-6*, Pub. by C Helm) Routldge.

Brehier, E. Chrysippe et L'ancien Stoicisme. (FRE.). 296, vip. 1971. pap. text 109.00 (*0-677-50605-8*) Gordon & Breach.

Brehier, Emile. The History of Philosophy Vol. 3: The Middle Ages & the Renaissance. Thomas, Joseph & Baskin, Wade, trs. LC 63-20912. 272p. reprint ed. pap. 84.40 (*0-608-09395-5*, 205414000003) Bks Demand.

— The History of Philosophy Vol. 4: The Seventeenth Century. Thomas, Joseph & Baskin, Wade, trs. LC 63-20912. 313p. reprint ed. pap. 97.10 (*0-608-09396-3*, 205414000004) Bks Demand.

— The History of Philosophy Vol. 6: The Nineteenth Century: Period of Systems, 1800-1850. Thomas, Joseph & Baskin, Wade, trs. LC 63-20912. 306p. reprint ed. pap. 94.90 (*0-608-09397-1*, 205414000006) Bks Demand.

Brehier, Jean-Pierre & Time-Life Books Editors. Incredible Cuisine with Chef Jean-Pierre Brehier. LC 97-22427. (Illus.). 272p. (YA). (gr. 11). 1999. 24.95 (*0-7835-4946-6*) Time-Life.

Brehier, Louis. L' Eglise et l'Orient au Moyen Age: Les Croisades. 2nd ed. LC 76-29834. (FRE.). reprint ed. 64.50 (*0-404-15413-1*) AMS Pr.

Brehl, J. B., ed. see Danvers, Dennis.

Brehl, J. B., ed. see Silverberg, Robert.

Brehm. Social Psychology, 3 vols. (C). Date not set. text, teacher ed., suppl. ed. 61.16 (*0-395-76069-0*) HM.

— Social Psychology, 3 vols. (C). 1995. pap., teacher ed., suppl. ed. 11.96 (*0-395-74526-8*) HM.

— Social Psychology, 3 vols. 3rd ed. (C). 1995. pap. text, student ed. 19.56 (*0-395-74527-6*) HM.

Brehm, Barbara A. Stress Management: Increasing Your Stress Resistance. LC 97-17767. 1998. write for info. (*0-321-00226-1*) Addson-Wesley Educ.

Brehm, Barbara A., ed. Stress Management: Increasing Your Stress Resistance. LC 97-17767. 380p. (C). 1998. pap. text 48.00 (*0-321-01068-X*) Allyn.

***Brehm, David.** Celebrate the Sunday Readings: Cycle B. 1999. pap. write for info. (*0-15-950607-7*) Harcourt.

Brehm, H. Paul. Flyboys: Wings, Women, War. LC 95-78898. (Illus.). 1995. pap. 19.95 (*0-9647293-0-X*) H P Brehm.

Brehm, Henry P., ed. Medical Care for the Aged: From Social Problem to Federal Program. LC 85-16753. 264p. 1985. 59.95 (*0-275-90021-5*, C0021, Praeger Pubs) Greenwood.

Brehm, Henry P. & Mullner, Ross M., eds. Health Care, Technology, & the Competitive Environment. LC 89-3961. 290p. 1989. 69.50 (*0-275-93033-5*, C3033, Praeger Pubs) Greenwood.

Brehm, J. W., jt. auth. see Wicklund, R. A.

***Brehm, Jack & Nelson, Pete.** That Others May Live: The True Story of a PJ, a Member of America's Most Daring Rescue Force. 2001. pap. 13.95 (*0-609-80676-9*, Three Riv Pr) Crown Pub Group.

Brehm, Jack W., jt. auth. see Nelson, Pete.

Brehm, John. The Phantom Respondents: Opinion Surveys & Political Representation. LC 92-40475. (Michigan Studies in Political Analysis). 280p. (C). 1993. text 44.50 (*0-472-09523-4*, 09523) U of Mich Pr.

Brehm, John & Gates, Scott. Working, Shirking & Sabotage: Bureaucratic Response to a Democratic Public. LC 96-43487. (Studies in Political Analysis). 280p. 1999. pap. text 19.95 (*0-472-08612-X*, 08612) U of Mich Pr.

Brehm, John J. & Mullins, William J. Introduction to the Structure of Matter: A Course in Modern Physics. LC 88-5768. 960p. 1989. text 105.95 (*0-471-60531-X*) Wiley.

Brehm, Madeleine & Tindell, Nancy. Movement with a Purpose: Perceptual Motor-Lesson Plans for Young Children. LC 83-8023. 208p. (C). 1983. text 24.95 (*0-13-604629-0*) P-H.

Brehm, Monica R. & Castro, Jorge Q. The Market for Water Rights in Chile: Major Issues. (World Bank Technical Papers: No. 285). 40p. 1995. pap. 22.00 (*0-8213-3307-0*, 13307) World Bank.

Brehm, Peter, ed. Introduction to Color Bars. 65p. 1992. 43.95 (*0-933505-21-3*) Graph Comm Assn.

— Introduction to Densitometry: User's Guide to Print Production Measurement Using Densitometry. 76p. 1990. 34.25 (*0-933505-10-8*) Graph Comm Assn.

— Tips: Technical Insert Production Specifications. 62p. 1989. 31.75 (*0-933505-08-6*) Graph Comm Assn.

Brehm, Peter, jt. ed. see Strub, William C.

Brehm, Peter, jt. ed. see Youngquist, David.

Brehm, Sharon S. Intimate Relationships. 2nd ed. 576p. (C). 1991. pap. 41.25 (*0-07-007443-7*) McGraw.

Brehm, Sharon S., ed. Seeing Female: Social Roles & Personal Lives, 88. LC 87-15039. (Contributions in Women's Studies: No. 88). 226p. 1988. 42.95 (*0-313-25589-X*, BWN/, Greenwood Pr) Greenwood.

Brehm, Sharon S. & Kassin, Saul M. Social Psychology. (C). 1989. pap. text 2.76 (*0-395-52640-X*); pap. text 2.76 (*0-395-52641-8*); trans. write for info. (*0-318-66707-X*) HM.

— Social Psychology. 3rd ed. 551p. (C). 1996. text. write for info. (*0-395-73630-7*) HM.

Brehm, Victoria, ed. A Fully Accredited Ocean: Essays on the Great Lakes. LC 97-25396. 264p. (C). 1998. text 47.50 (*0-472-10709-7*, 10709) U of Mich Pr.

— Sweetwater, Storms, & Spirits: Stories of the Great Lakes. LC 89-20682. 352p. (Orig.). 1991. pap. 18.95 (*0-472-08151-9*, 08151) U of Mich Pr.

— Sweetwater, Storms & Spirits: Stories of the Great Lakes. LC 89-20682. 352p. 1990. 42.50 (*0-472-10144-7*, 10144) U of Mich Pr.

Brehm, William A., Jr. & Sutter, Thomas H. The Kimberlys: A Glimpse at One Family's Years in North America. LC 89-81827. (Illus.). 304p. (C). 1989. pap. 20.00 (*0-9624758-1-5*) Brehm & Sutter.

Brehmer, Debra, jt. auth. see Bamberger, Tom.

***Brehony, Kathleen & Jones, Karen.** Up the Bestseller Lists! A Hands-On Guide to Successful Book Promotion. 256p. 2000. pap. 12.95 (*1-58062-409-X*) Adams Media.

***Brehony, Kathleen A.** After the Darkest Hour: How Suffering Begins the Journey to Wisdom. LC 00-29577. (Illus.). 288p. 2000. 23.00 (*0-8050-6435-4*) H Holt & Co.

Brehony, Kathleen A. Awakening at Midlife: A Guide to Reviving Your Spirits, Recreating Your Life & Returning to Your Truest Self. 384p. 1997. reprint ed. pap. 14.00 (*1-57322-632-7*, Riverhd Trade) Berkley Pub.

— Ordinary Grace: An Examination of the Roots of Compassion, Altruism & Empathy, & the Ordinary Individuals Who Help Others in Extraordinary Ways. LC 98-31876. 256p. 1999. 24.95 (*1-57322-108-2*, Riverhead Books) Putnam Pub Group.

***Brehony, Kathleen A.** Ordinary Grace: Lessons from Those Who Help Others in Extraordinary Ways. 2000. pap. 12.95 (*1-57322-786-2*, Riverhd Trade) Berkley Pub.

— Untitled Nonfiction on Suffering. 2001. pap. 13.00 (*0-8050-6436-2*) H Holt & Co.

Brehony, Kathleen A., jt. auth. see Gass, Robert.

Brehony, Kathleen A., jt. ed. see Rothblum, Esther D.

Brehony, Kevin J. Nationalisms Old & New. LC 98-49907. 245p. 1999. text 68.00 (*0-312-22052-9*) St Martin.

Brei, D. & Sirkis, J., eds. 1997 International Mechanical Engineering Congress & Exposition, Dallas, Texas, November 16-21, 1997: Adaptive Structures & Material Systems, 1997. LC 97-76721. (AD Ser.: Vol. 54). 252p. 1997. 110.00 (*0-7918-1822-5*, H01103) ASME Pr.

Breiby, Anecia. How to Split, Dry & Smoke Salmon. (Alaska Ser.: Vol. 7). (Illus.). 37p. (Orig.). 1982. pap. 4.95 (*1-878051-20-2*, CP033) Circumpolar Pr.

Breicha, Otto & Loos, Sigrun. Mail Art Anno Klimt: Postcard Art of the Wiener Werkstatte. 320p. pap. 39.95 (*3-201-01320-X*) Moyer Bell.

Breidbach, O., et al, eds. The Nervous System of Invertebrates: An Evolutionary & Comparative Approach. LC 94-35125. Vol. 72. 448p. 1995. 132.00 (*0-8176-5076-8*) Birkhauser.

— The Nervous System of Invertebrates: An Evolutionary & Comparative Approach. 42. (EXS Ser.). vii, 454p. 1995. 132.00 (*3-7643-5076-8*) Birkhauser.

Breidbach, Olaf, et al, contrib. by. Art Forms in Nature: The Prints of Ernst Haeckel. LC 98-231776. (Illus.). 144p. 1998. pap. 25.00 (*3-7913-1990-6*) te Neues.

Breidenbach, Heribert. A Wicking for Natalie. 159p. (Orig.). 1995. pap. 11.95 (*1-882792-08-4*) Proctor Pubns.

***Breidenbach, Monica E.** Career Development: Strategies & Technologies for Career & Life Balance. 4th ed. 220p. 2000. pap. 29.33 (*0-13-086759-4*, Prentice Hall) P-H.

Breidenbach, Stephan & Campbell, Christian, eds. Business Transactions in Eastern Europe. text 405.00 (*0-8205-2477-8*) Bender.

Breidenstein, B. C., jt. auth. see National Live Stock & Meat Board Staff.

Breidenthal, Thomas E. Christian Households: The Sanctification of Nearness. LC 97-9207. 170p. 1997. pap. 11.95 (*1-56101-141-X*) Cowley Pubns.

Breidger, Henry J. How to Harmonize Melodies. 1988. reprint ed. lib. bdg. 59.00 (*0-7812-0740-1*) Rprt Serv.

***Breiding, G. Sutton.** Hallucinating Jenny. limited ed. (Perihelion Signed Limited Edition Broadside Ser.: Vol. 2). (Illus.). 2000. pap. 4.00 (*0-9676666-6-X*) Miniature Sun Pr.

Breiding, G. Sutton. Journal of an Astronaut. (Doubles Ser.). (Illus.). 112p. 1992. pap. 11.95 (*0-938075-40-3*) Ocean View Bks.

— Journal of an Astronaut. limited ed. (Doubles Ser.). (Illus.). 112p. 1992. 59.95 (*0-938075-39-X*) Ocean View Bks.

Breidinger, William J. Shadows of the San Juans. (Illus.). 434p. 1997. pap. 11.95 (*0-9660713-0-1*) Mesa Tioughnioga.

Breidlid, Anders, et al, eds. American Culture: Texts on Civilization. LC 95-21666. 424p. (C). 1996. pap. 24.99 (*0-415-12440-9*) Routledge.

— American Culture: Texts on Civilization. LC 95-21666. (Illus.). 424p. (C). 1996. 80.00 (*0-415-12439-5*) Routledge.

Breier, Alan, ed. The New Pharmacotherapy of Schizophrenia. (Clinical Practice Ser.: No. 36). 272p. 1996. text 33.50 (*0-88048-491-8*, 8491) Am Psychiatric.

Breier, Barbara E., jt. auth. see Barak, Robert J.

Breier, Christine A., ed. Goodles & Oodles: A Collection of Short Stories, Drawings & Poetry of Children. 70p. (J). (ps-12). 1998. pap. 25.95 (*0-7392-0013-5*) Morris Pubng.

***Breier, Mark & Brott, Armin.** The 10-Second Internet Manager: Survive, Thrive & Drive Your Company in the Information Age. 128p. 2000. 18.95 (*0-609-60732-4*, Crown) Crown Pub Group.

Breier, Mignonne, jt. ed. see Prinsloo, Mastin.

Breig, James. The Emotional Jesus: How to Feel Good about Feelings. LC 95-78542. 72p. (Orig.). 1996. pap. 7.95 (*0-89622-669-7*) Twenty-Third.

Breig, James, ed. see Light, Sally.

Breiger, Ronald. Explorations Structural Analysis: Dual & Multiple Networks of Social Interaction. LC 91-9337. (Harvard Studies Sociology Ser.). 197p. 1991. text 20.00 (*0-8240-9271-6*) Garland.

Breighner, Bart. Face-to-Face Selling: Easy & Effective Sales Techniques for New & Experienced Salespeople. LC 94-21279. (Illus.). 228p. (Orig.). 1994. pap. 9.95 (*1-57112-065-3*, FFS) Park Ave.

Breighner, Joe. Does It All Make Sense? Ten Best Guesses about God & Life. 3rd rev. ed. LC 98-60075. (Illus.). 112p. 1998. reprint ed. pap. 9.95 (*0-9662393-0-X*) Tully Inc.

Breighner, Joseph. Father Joe: A Year of Wit, Wisdom & Warmth. LC 94-68116. 216p. 1994. pap. 16.95 (*1-885938-00-4*) Cathdrl Fndtn Pr.

— Stops along the Country Road. LC 96-15862. 232p. (Orig.). 1996. pap. 18.95 (*1-885938-03-9*) Cathdrl Fndtn Pr.

— When Life Doesn't Make Sense. LC 97-66561. 152p. (Orig.). 1997. pap. 10.00 (*1-885938-08-X*) Cathdrl Fndtn Pr.

Breighner, Kathryn & Rohe, Deborah. I Am Amazing Activity Manual. (I Am Amazing Ser.). 1990. 79.95 (*0-88671-370-6*, 4351) Am Guidance.

— My Amazing Body. 1990. teacher ed. 24.95 (*0-88671-371-4*, 4352) Am Guidance.

Breighner, Kathryn W., jt. auth. see Berryman, Judy C.

Breihan, C. W. Outlaws of the Old West. 22.95 (*0-8488-0223-3*) Amereon Ltd.

Breihan, Carl W. Forty Years on the Wild Frontier. large type ed. (Ulverscroft Large Print Ser.). (Illus.). 400p. 1997. 27.99 (*0-7089-3661-X*) Ulverscroft.

— Ride the Razor's Edge: The Younger Brothers Story. LC 91-43547. (Illus.). 288p. 1992. 15.95 (*0-88289-879-5*) Pelican.

Breihan, John R., et al. Martin Aircraft, 1909-1960. LC 92-91184. (American Aircraft Manufacturers Ser.: Vol. 2). (Illus.). 208p. (Orig.). 1995. pap. 33.95 (*0-913322-03-2*) Jonathan T Pub.

Breiling, Brian, ed. see Light Years Ahead Productions Staff.

Breiling, James, jt. ed. see Hawkins, Robert P.

Breimar, A. & Macurda, D. B. The Phylogeny of the Fissiculate Blastoids. (Verhandelingen der Koninklijke Nederlandse Akademie van Wetenschappen, Afd. Natuurkunde Ser.: No. 26(3)). 390p. 1972. pap. text 46.50 (*0-7204-8232-1*) Elsevier.

***Breimer, Stephen F.** The Screenwriter's Legal Guide. 2nd ed. LC 98-74537. 320p. 1999. pap. 19.95 (*1-58115-021-0*) Allworth Pr.

Breimer, T. Environmental Factors & Cultural Measures Affecting the Nitrate of Spinach. 1982. pap. text 73.50 (*90-247-3053-8*) Kluwer Academic.

Breimyer, Harold F. Economics of the Product Markets of Agriculture. LC 75-44220. (Illus.). 218p. 1976. reprint ed. pap. 67.60 (*0-608-00019-1*, 206078500006) Bks Demand.

— Over-Fulfilled Expectations: A Life & an Era in Rural America. LC 90-46633. (Henry A. Wallace Series on Agricultural History & Rural Studies). (Illus.). 316p. 1991. text 49.95 (*0-8138-0856-1*) Iowa St U Pr.

Brein, Michael. Michael Brein's Guide to Amsterdam by the Tram. (Michael Brein's Guides Ser.). (Orig.). 2000. pap. 5.00 (*1-886590-14-1*) Michael Brein.

— Michael Brein's Guide to Barcelona by the Metro. (Michael Brein's Guides Ser.). (Orig.). 1999. pap. 5.00 (*1-886590-04-4*) Michael Brein.

— Michael Brein's Guide to Berlin by the U-Bahn. (Michael Brein's Guides Ser.). (Orig.). 1999. pap. 5.00 (*1-886590-07-9*) Michael Brein.

— Michael Brein's Guide to Honolulu & Oahu by the Bus. rev. ed. (Michael Brein's Guides Ser.). 1p. 1998. pap. 5.00 (*1-886590-01-X*) Michael Brein.

— Michael Brein's Guide to London by the Underground. rev. ed. (Michael Brein's Guides Ser.). 1p. 1998. pap. 5.00 (*1-886590-02-8*) Michael Brein.

— Michael Brein's Guide to Madrid by the Metro. (Michael Brein's Guides Ser.). (Orig.). 1999. pap. 5.00 (*1-886590-05-2*) Michael Brein.

— Michael Brein's Guide to Munich by the U-Bahn. (Michael Brein's Guides Ser.). (Orig.). 1999. pap. 5.00 (*1-886590-06-0*) Michael Brein.

— MIchael Brein's Guide to Paris by the Metro. rev. ed. (Michael Brein's Guides Ser.). 1p. 1999. pap. 5.00 (*1-886590-03-6*) Michael Brein.

— Michael Brein's Guide to Prague by the Metro. (Michael Brein's Guides Ser.). (Orig.). 1999. pap. 5.00 (*1-886590-13-3*) Michael Brein.

***Brein, Michael.** Michael Brein's Guide to Rome by the Metro. (Michael Brein's Travel Guides Ser.). 2001. pap. 5.00 (*1-886590-19-2*, Pub. by Michael Brein) Map Link.

Brein, Michael. Michael Brein's Guide to San Francisco by Public Transit. (Michael Brein's Guides Ser.). (Orig.). 2002. pap. 5.00 (*1-886590-10-9*) Michael Brein.

— Michael Brein's Guide to Sydney by Public Transit. (Michael Brein's Guides Ser.). (Orig.). 1998. pap. 5.00 (*1-886590-11-7*) Michael Brein.

— Michael Brein's Guide to Vienna by the U-Bahn. (Michael Brein's Guides Ser.). (Orig.). 2000. pap. 5.00 (*1-886590-12-5*) Michael Brein.

Brein, Michael & Dickison, Richard. Michael Brein's Guide to Tokyo by the Subway. (Michael Brein's Guides Ser.). (Orig.). 2001. pap. 5.00 (*1-886590-15-X*) Michael Brein.

Brein, Michael & Franklin, Penelope. Michael Brein's Guide to New York by the Subway. (Michael Brein's Guides Ser.). (Orig.). 2001. pap. 5.00 (*1-886590-08-7*) Michael Brein.

— Michael Brein's Guide to Washington by the Metro. (Michael Brein's Guides Ser.). (Orig.). 2000. pap. 5.00 (*1-886590-09-5*) Michael Brein.

Breinburg, Petronella. Doctor Shawn. LC 74-15265. (Illus.). 32p. (J). (gr. k-2). 1975. 12.95 (*0-690-00721-3*); lib. bdg. 12.89 (*0-690-00722-1*) HarpC Child Bks.

— Sally-Ann in the Snow. 1989. pap. 8.95 (*0-370-01809-5*) Random.

***Breinburg, Petronella.** Stories from the Caribbean. (Multicultural Stories Ser.). 48p. 2000. lib. bdg. 25.69 (*0-7398-1334-X*) Raintree Steck-V.

— Stories from the Caribbean. LC 99-48894. (Multicultural Stories Ser.). (Illus.). (J). 2000. 7.95 (*0-7398-2032-X*) Raintree Steck-V.

Breindel, Barbara. Medical Diagnostic Kits & Products. LC 98-100567. (Report Ser.: No. C-045U). 138p. 1997. 3150.00 (*1-56965-386-0*) BCC.

— The New OTC Drug Strategies/Markets. LC 98-120756. 90p. 1997. 2950.00 (*1-56965-371-2*, B-104) BCC.

Breindel, Barbara, contrib. by. Information & Data Handling Developments in Medicine: Highlighting Opportunities for Hardware, Software & Services. 202p. 1995. 2650.00 (*1-56965-071-3*, G-155) BCC.

Breindel, Eric. A Passion for Truth: The Selected Writings Of Eric Breindel. LC 98-51059. 256p. 1999. 25.00 (*0-06-019327-1*) HarpC.

Breindel, Eric & Romerstein, Herbert. The Venona Secrets: The Soviet Union's World War II Espionage Campaign Against the United States - And How America Fought Back: A Story of Espionage, Counterespionage & Betrayal. 400p. 2000. pap. 27.50 (*0-465-09842-8*, Pub. by Basic) HarpC.

Breindel, Eric, jt. auth. see Romerstein, Herbert.

Breindel, Tina Jo. Know That... Quotes from Deaf Women for a Positive Life. 96p. 1999. 5.95 (*1-58121-012-4*) Dawn Sign.

Breiner, Laurence A. An Introduction to West Indian Poetry. LC 97-42231. (Illus.). 282p. (C). 1998. 59.95 (*0-521-58331-4*); pap. 18.95 (*0-521-58712-3*) Cambridge U Pr.

***Breiner, Mark A.** Whole Body Dentistry: Discover the Missing Piece to Better Health. LC 99-70461. (Illus.). 240p. 1999. pap. 19.95 (*0-9678443-0-4*) Quantum Hlth Pr.

Breiner, Peter. Max Weber & Democratic Politics. 1996. text 39.95 (*0-8014-3147-6*) Cornell U Pr.

Breines, Estelle. Functional Assessment Scale. 1983. teacher ed. 21.00 (*0-941930-02-5*) Geri-Rehab.

— Perception: Its Development & Recapitulation. LC 81-81244. (Illus.). 304p. (C). 1981. text 19.00 (*0-941930-01-7*) Geri-Rehab.

Breines, Estelle B. Occupational Therapy Activities from Clay to Computers: Theory & Practice. (Illus.). 245p. pap. text 39.95 (*0-8036-0544-7*) Davis Co.

— Occupational Therapy Activities from Clay to Computers: Theory & Practice. LC 94-6968. (Illus.). 245p. 1994. pap. 41.95 (*0-8036-1145-5*) Davis Co.

— Origins & Adaptations: A Philosophy of Practice. 281p. 1986. text 32.95 (*0-941930-03-3*) Geri-Rehab.

Breines, Wini. Community & Organization in the New Left, 1962-1968: The Great Refusal. 224p. 1982. 55.00 (*0-275-90766-X*, C0766, Praeger Pubs) Greenwood.

— Young, White, & Miserable: Growing up Female in the Fifties. LC 91-28608. 288p. 1994. pap. 17.50 (*0-8070-7503-5*) Beacon Pr.

Breines, Winifred, jt. ed. see Bloom, Alexander.

Breinig, Helmbrecht, jt. ed. see Binder, Wolfgang.

Breinin, C. M. & Siegel, I. M., eds. Advances in Diagnostic Visual Optics. (Optical Sciences Ser.: Vol. 41). (Illus.). 280p. 1983. 62.95 (*0-387-13079-9*) Spr-Verlag.

Breining, Greg. Fishing Minnesota. Linder, Greg, ed. LC 92-43605. (Illus.). (Orig.). 1993. pap. 9.95 (*1-55971-150-7*, NorthWord Pr) Creat Pub Intl.

***Breining, Greg.** The Northern Forest. LC 98-48644. (Ecosystems of North America Ser.). (gr. 4-7). 2000. lib. bdg. 27.07 (*0-7614-0901-7*, Benchmark NY) Marshall Cavendish.

Breining, Greg. Paddling Minnesota. LC 99-14402. (Illus.). 240p. 1999. pap. 14.95 (*1-56044-690-0*) Falcon Pub Inc.

— Return of the Eagle: How America Saved Its National Emblem. LC 94-72402. (Illus.). 126p. (Orig.). 1994. pap. 19.95 (*1-56044-300-6*) Falcon Pub Inc.

— Wild Minnesota. LC 93-49599. (Wild State Ser.). (Illus.). 144p. 1994. 24.95 (*1-55971-226-0*, NorthWord Pr) Creat Pub Intl.

***Breining, Greg.** Wild Shore: Exploring Lake Superior by Kayak. 2000. 24.95 (*0-8166-3141-7*) U of Minn Pr.

— Wild Shore: Exploring Lake Superior by Kayak. LC 00-9081. (Illus.). 2000. pap. write for info. (*0-8166-3142-5*) U of Minn Pr.

Breining, Greg & Sternberg, Dick. Fishing Tips & Tricks. LC 90-3561. (Hunting & Fishing Library). (Illus.). 160p. 1990. 19.95 (*0-86573-033-4*) Creat Pub Intl.

Breining, Greg, jt. auth. see Stebbins, Jerry.

Breinlinger, Sara, jt. auth. see Kelly, Caroline.

Breipohl, Arthur M., jt. auth. see Shanmugan, Sam K.

Breisach, Ernst. Historiography: Ancient, Medieval, & Modern. LC 82-20246. (Illus.). 499p. Date not set. reprint ed. pap. 154.70 (*0-608-20606-7*, 205457400003) Bks Demand.

— Historiography: Ancient, Medieval & Modern. 2nd ed. 494p. 1995. pap. text 16.95 (*0-226-07278-9*) U Ch Pr.

Breisach, Ernst, ed. Classical Rhetoric & Medieval Historiography. LC 85-3055. (Studies in Medieval Culture: No. 19). 1985. pap. 10.95 (*0-918720-57-5*); boxed set 17.95 (*0-918720-56-7*) Medieval Inst.

Breisach, Ernst A. American Progressive History: An Experiment in Modernization. LC 92-31012. 264p. (C). 1993. pap. text 14.95 (*0-226-07277-0*) U Ch Pr.

— American Progressive History: An Experiment in Modernization. LC 92-31012. 264p. (C). 1993. lib. bdg. 40.00 (*0-226-07276-2*) U Ch Pr.

— Historiography: Ancient, Medieval, & Modern. LC 82-20246. 475p. 1983. pap. text 16.95 (*0-226-07275-4*); lib. bdg. 35.00 (*0-226-07274-6*) U Ch Pr.

Breisacher, E. H. & Lorentzen, Sandra, eds. Last Resting Places, Being a Compendium of Fact Pertaining to the Mortal Remains of the Famous & Infamous. LC 79-52704. (Illus.). 400p. 2000. 35.00 (*0-87850-032-4*) Darwin Pr.

Breisch, Eric A. & Greenway, Hubert T. Cutaneous Surgical Anatomy of the Head & Neck. (Practical Manuals in Dermatologic Surgery Ser.). (Illus.). 133p. 1991. pap. text 35.00 (*0-443-08744-X*) Church.

Breisch, Francis, Jr. El Ministerio de Cristo en Jerusalen, Libro 2. (SPA.). 142p. pap. 6.00 (*1-55883-020-0*, 6700-0520C) Libros Desafio.

— El Ministerio de Cristo en Palestina, Libro 1. (SPA.). 192p. pap. 6.00 (*1-55883-019-7*, 6700-0510C) Libros Desafio.

— El Ministerio de Cristo Hasta lo Ultimo de la Tierra, Libro 3. (SPA.). 168p. pap. 6.00 (*1-55883-021-9*, 6700-0530C) Libros Desafio.

Breisch, Kenneth A. Henry Hobson Richardson & the Small Public Library in America: A Study in Typology. LC 96-43752. (Illus.). 366p. 1997. 55.00 (*0-262-02416-0*) MIT Pr.

Breisch, Linda L., et al. Chlorine & the Chesapeake Bay: A Review of Research Literature. 1984. 6.00 (*0-943676-17-7*) MD Sea Grant Col.

Breisch, Linda L., jt. auth. see Kennedy, Victor S.

Breise, Frederic H. Fifty Years of Aviation Knowledge. 108p. 1981. 12.00 (*0-938576-00-3*) F H Breise.

Breit, A., ed. Tumor Response Monitoring & Treatment Planning. (Illus.). 740p. 1992. 180.00 (*0-387-54783-5*) Spr-Verlag.

Breit, Luke. Messages: New & Selected Poems. 136p. 1989. pap. 8.95 (*0-936609-17-6*) QED Ft Bragg.

***Breit, Luke.** Unintended Lessons. LC 98-68388. 88p. 1999. pap. 12.95 (*0-936609-39-7*) QED Ft Bragg.

Breit, Sally, jt. auth. see Hunter, Madeline C.

Breit, William. Academic Scribblers. LC 98-25286. 288p. 1998. pap. text 16.95 (*0-691-05986-1*, Pub. by Princeton U Pr) Cal Prin Full Svc.

— Antitrust Casebook: Milestones. 3rd ed. (C). 1995. text 42.00 (*0-03-016319-6*, Pub. by Harcourt Coll Pubs) Harcourt.

An Asterisk (*) at the beginning of an entry indicates that the title is appearing for the first time.

Breit, William & Culbertson, William P., Jr., eds. Science & Ceremony: The Institutional Economics of C. E. Ayres. LC 76-8238. (Dan Murphy Sports Ser.). 228p. reprint ed. pap. 70.70 (*0-8357-7727-8*, 203608400002) Bks Demand.

Breit, William & Spencer, Roger W., eds. Lives of the Laureates: Thirteen Nobel Economists. 3rd ed. LC 95-16632. 287p. 1995. 30.00 (*0-262-02391-1*) MIT Pr.

— Lives of the Laureates: Thirteen Nobel Economists. 3rd ed. (Illus.). 288p. 1997. reprint ed. pap. text 14.95 (*0-262-52238-1*) MIT Pr.

Breit, William, jt. auth. see Elzinga, Kenneth G.

Breit, William, ed. see Aksoy, Ercument G.

Breit, William, ed. see Brubaker, Earl R.

Breit, William, ed. see Hemenway, David.

Breit, William, ed. see Mercuro, Nicholas & Ryan, Timothy.

Breitbart, Eric, et al. World on Display: Photographs from the St. Louis World's Fair, 1904. LC 95-50174. (Illus.). 108p. 1997. 34.95 (*0-8263-1742-1*) U of NM Pr.

Breitbart, Karen. A-Z Language Games. (Illus.). 128p. (Orig.). (J). (ps-k). 1997. pap. 14.95 (*1-57612-017-1*, MM2047) Monday Morning Bks.

— A-Z Math Games. (Illus.). 128p. (Orig.). (J). 1997. pap. 14.95 (*1-57612-016-3*, MM2048) Monday Morning Bks.

Breitbart, Reinhard, jt. auth. see Tshering, Tashi.

Breitbart, Sidney. God's Challenge to Man: A Theology of Responsibility. 1994. 16.95 (*0-533-10921-3*) Vantage.

Breitbart, William & Holland, Jimmie C., eds. Psychiatric Aspects of Symptom Management in Cancer Patients. LC 92-6969. (Clinical Practice Ser.: No. 25). 278p. 1993. text 14.95 (*0-88048-193-5*, 8193) Am Psychiatric.

Breitbart, William, jt. ed. see Chochinov, Harvey M.

Breitborde, L. B., ed. Alonzo Pond & the Nineteen Thirty Logan Museum Expedition to North Africa: The 1985 Beloit College Symposium. (Logan Museum Bulletin Ser.: Vol. 1, No. 1). 58p. (C). 1991. pap. 10.00 (*1-880763-02-8*) Mus Beloit Coll.

Breitborde, L. B., jt. ed. see White, Randall.

Breitborde, Lawrence B. Speaking & Social Identity: English in the Lives of Urban Africans. LC 97-23313. (Studies in Anthropological Linguistics: No. 11). 227p. 1998. 86.00 (*3-11-014796-3*) De Gruyter.

Breitenbach, Edgar. American Poster: Graphic Communications in the Twentieth Century. Cogswell, Margaret, ed. LC 66-18340. (Illus.). 1968. 17.50 (*0-8079-0002-8*); pap. 9.95 (*0-8079-0003-6*) October.

Breitenbach, Esther & Gordon, Eleanor, eds. Conflicting Interests: The Public Lives of Women in Scotland, 1880-1945. 272p. 1993. pap. text 27.50 (*0-7486-0372-7*, Pub. by Edinburgh U Pr) Col U Pr.

Breitenbach, Esther, jt. auth. see Gordon, Eleanor.

Breitenbach, Esther, jt. ed. see Gordon, Eleanor.

Breitenbach, J. & Kraenzlin, F. W. Fungi of Switzerland; a Contribution to the Knowledge of the Fungal Flora of Switzerland, Vol. 3: Boletes & Agarics, Pt. 1. (Illus.). 350p. 1991. lib. bdg. 150.00 (*3-85604-230-X*, Pub. by Verlag Mykologia) Lubrecht & Cramer.

Breitenbach, J. & Kranzlin, F., eds. Fungi of Switzerland: Ascomycetes, Vol. 1. (Illus.). 313p. 1984. 110.00 (*0-916422-47-X*) Mad River.

Breitenbach, Robert J., et al. Baby Seats, Safety Belts, & You! (Illus.). 52p. 1997. reprint ed. pap. text 30.00 (*0-7881-4032-9*) DIANE Pub.

Breitenbach, Wilhelm. Untersuchungen zur Sprache der Euripideisschen Lyrik. xviii, 293p. 1967. reprint ed. 65.00 (*0-318-70883-3*) G Olms Pubs.

Breitenberg, Mark. Anxious Masculinity in Early Modern England. (Cambridge Studies in Renaissance Literature & Culture: No. 10). 235p. (C). 1996. text 59.95 (*0-521-48141-4*); pap. text 18.95 (*0-521-48588-6*) Cambridge U Pr.

Breitenberg, Maureen. Directory of Federal Government Certification & Related Programs. 497p. 1999. per. 41.00 (*0-16-056869-2*) USGPO.

Breitenberg, Maureen, ed. Directory of European Regional Standards-Related Organizations. 188p. (Orig.). (C). 1994. pap. text 40.00 (*0-7881-0730-5*) DIANE Pub.

***Breitenberg, Maureen, ed.** Directory of Federal Government Certification & Related Programs. 4th ed. 490p. (C). 2000. pap. text 40.00 (*0-7881-8967-0*) DIANE Pub.

Breitenberg, Maureen, ed. Directory of International & Regional Organizations Conducting Standards-Related Activities. 436p. (Orig.). (C). 1993. pap. text 50.00 (*1-56806-481-0*) DIANE Pub.

Breitenberg, Maureen A. The ABC's of the U. S. Conformity Assessment System. 46p. (C). 1998. pap. text 20.00 (*0-7881-7216-6*) DIANE Pub.

Breitenbucher, Cathy. Bonnie Blair: Golden Streak. LC 94-5744. (Sports Achievers Ser.). (Illus.). (J). (gr. 4-9). 1994. pap. 5.95 (*0-8225-9665-2*, First Ave Edns); lib. bdg. 19.93 (*0-8225-2883-5*, Lerner Publctns) Lerner Pub.

Breitenecker, Felix, ed. see EUROSIM Staff.

Breitenfeldt, Dorvan H. & Lorenz, Delores R. Successful Stuttering Management Program. 164p. 1989. student ed. 47.50 (*0-910055-10-6*) East Wash Univ.

***Breitenfeldt, Dorvan H. & Lorenz, Delores R.** Successful Stuttering Management Program (SSMP) For Adolescent & Adult Stutterers 2nd ed. LC 99-13008. 1999. write for info. (*0-910055-55-6*) East Wash Univ.

Breitenkamp, Edward C. & Dabbs. The Church Records of the Pioneer Families of Berlin, Texas. 292p. 1995. 12.50 (*1-57168-241-4*) Sunbelt Media.

Breitenlohner, P., et al, eds. Renormalization of Quantum Field Theories with Non-Linear Field Transformations. (Lecture Notes in Physics Ser.: Vol. 303). vi, 239p. 1988. 34.95 (*0-387-19263-8*) Spr-Verlag.

Breiter, Manfred, ed. see Electrocatalysis of Fuel Cell Reactions Workshop Staff.

***Breiter, Matthias.** The Bears of Katmai, Alaska's Famous Bears. (Illus.). 2000. pap. 29.95 (*1-55868-544-8*) Gr Arts Ctr Pub.

Breiter, Matthias. Kakadu & the Top End. (Illus.). 176p. (Orig.). 1995. pap. 14.95 (*0-86417-647-3*, Pub. by Kangaroo Pr) Seven Hills Bk.

Breiter, Paul. A Still Forest Pool: The Insight Meditation of ACHAAN CHAH. LC 85-40411. (Illus.). 225p. 1985. pap. 13.00 (*0-8356-0597-3*, Quest) Theos Pub Hse.

Breiter-Wu, Denise, ed. see Liang, Shou-Yu & Wu, Wen-Ching.

Breiter-Wu, Denise, ed. & photos by see Liang, Shou-Yu & Wu, Wen-Ching.

Breiter, Yitzchak. Seven Pillars of Faith. Greenbaum, Avraham, tr. from HEB. 64p. 1989. pap. text 3.00 (*0-930213-49-1*) Breslov Res Inst.

Breitfeller, Kurt J. The Mariners Guide to G. M. D. S. S. A Practical Solution. (Illus.). 80p. 1999. pap. 34.95 (*0-7392-0237-5*, PO3279) Morris Pubng.

Breitha, Olivia R. Olivia: My Life of Exile in Kalaupapa. (Illus.). 104p. 1991. reprint ed. pap. 4.95 (*0-9631388-3-9*) AZ Mem Mus.

Breithardt, G., et al, eds. Antiarrhythmic Drugs: Mechanisms of Antiarrhythmic & Proarrhythmic Actions. 1995. write for info. (*0-387-59254-7*) Spr-Verlag.

— Antiarrhythmic Drugs: Mechanisms of Antiarrhythmic & Proarrhythmic Actions. (Illus.). 390p. 1995. 99.00 (*3-540-59254-7*) Spr-Verlag.

Breithaupt, David, ed. see Plymell, Charles.

Breithaupt, Don. Precious & Few. LC 96-24779. (Illus.). 176p. 1996. pap. 9.95 (*0-312-14704-X*) St Martin.

Breithaupt, Douglas J. Pacific Northwest Scholarship Guide: Finding Money for College. 7th ed. 220p. (Orig.). (YA). (gr. 7-12). 1998. pap. 29.95 (*1-880344-09-2*) Col Plan Netwk.

Breithaupt, Douglas J., ed. Pacific Northwest Scholarship Guide: Finding Money for College. 6th rev. ed. 205p. (Orig.). 1996. pap. text 29.95 (*1-880344-06-8*) Col Plan Netwk.

Breithaupt, Douglas J., ed. see Dorn, Ileana.

Breithaupt, James, jt. auth. see Merkow, Mark S.

***Breithaupt, Jim.** Einstein. (Guides for Beginners - Great Lives Ser.). 2000. pap. 11.95 (*0-340-78043-6*, Pub. by Headway) Trafalgar.

Breithaupt, Jim. Key Science: Physics. (Teacher's Guide ser.). (Illus.). 384p. 1994. teacher ed. 33.00 (*0-7487-1720-X*, Pub. by S Thornes Pubs); pap. 33.00 (*0-7487-1674-2*, Pub. by S Thornes Pubs) Trans-Atl Phila.

— Key Science: Physics Extension File. 256p. 1998. pap. 130.00 (*0-7487-3005-2*, Pub. by S Thornes Pubs) Trans-Atl Phila.

— Key Science - Physics. 2nd ed. (Illus.). 406p. (YA). (gr. 9-11). 1998. pap. 29.50 (*0-7487-3008-7*, Pub. by S Thornes Pubs) Trans-Atl Phila.

— Projects & Investigations for Advanced Physics: Teacher's Guide. 1998. pap. 49.50 (*0-7487-2954-2*) St Mut.

— Teach Yourself Cosmology. (Teach Yourself Ser.). 200p. 1999. pap. 12.95 (*0-8442-2681-5*) NTC Contemp Pub Co.

— Understanding Physics for Advanced Level. 3rd ed. 554p. 1994. pap. 49.50 (*0-7487-1579-7*, Pub. by S Thornes Pubs) Trans-Atl Phila.

— Understanding Physics for Advanced Level. 4th ed. (Illus.). 686p. (YA). (gr. 11). 1999. pap. 49.50 (*0-7487-4314-6*, Pub. by S Thornes Pubs) Trans-Atl Phila.

— Upgrad Physics A-Level. 140p. 1996. pap. 25.00 (*0-7487-2385-4*, Pub. by S Thornes Pubs) Trans-Atl Phila.

Breithaupt, Richard H., Jr. Aztec Club of 1847 Military Society of the Mexican War: Sesquicentennial History, 1847-1997. LC 98-96483. (Illus.). 1504p. 1998. 89.95 (*1-886085-05-6*) Walika.

— Centennial Register: Sons of the Revolution in the State of California. LC 95-146713. 1325p. 1994. 49.95 (*1-886085-00-5*) Walika.

Breithaupt, Richard H., Jr., et al. A History of the Order of the Arrow Through Insignia: Arapaho II. 262p. 1993. pap. text 27.00 (*1-886085-02-1*) Walika.

— A History of the Order of the Arrow Through Insignia: Arapaho II. 1994. disk 34.95 (*1-886085-01-3*) Walika.

Breithoff, Connie, ed. see Chapman, John.

Breitinger, Eckhard. The Presidential Campaign, 1976: A Selection of Campaign Speeches. 183p. 1978. 38.00 (*3-261-02605-7*) P Lang Pubng.

Breitinger, Johann J., jt. ed. see Bodmer, Johann J.

Breitkopf, Lyle J. & Bakoulis, Marion G. Coping with Endometriosis. LC 87-43148. (Illus.). 256p. 1988. student ed. 9.50 (*0-929655-63-X*) P-H.

Breitkopf, Piotr, jt. auth. see Kleiber, Michael.

***Breitkreuz, Christoph.** False Friends. 1999. pap. text 22.95 (*3-499-18492-3*) Distribks Inc.

Breitkreuz, Christoph. Das Palaeozoikum in den Kordilleren Nordchiles. (Geotektonische Forschungen Ser.: Vol. 70). (GER.). ii, 88p. 1986. 52.00 (*3-510-50036-9*, Pub. by E Schweizerbartsche) Balogh.

Breitkreuz, Christoph, jt. auth. see Berg, Karsten.

Breitling, Frank, jt. auth. see Dubel, Stefan.

Breitling, Wolf & Mickles, Morgan. Catalogue Raisonnee. 1985. 5.00 (*0-318-18268-8*) Brandon-Lane-Pr.

Breitmaier, E., et al. Atlas of Carbon-Thirteen NMR Data, Vol. 1: Compounds 1-1003. LC 76-2126. 258p. reprint ed. pap. 80.00 (*0-8357-5840-0*, 205569900001) Bks Demand.

Breitmaier, Eberhard. Structure Elucidation by NMR in Organic Chemistry: A Pratical Guide. LC 92-18531. 278p. 1993. pap. 64.95 (*0-471-93381-3*) Wiley.

Breitmaier, Eberhard & Bauer, Gerhard. Thirteen C-NMR Spectroscopy: A Working Manual with Exercises. Cassels, Bruce K., tr. from GER. (MMI Press Polymer Monographs). 431p. 1984. pap. text 96.00 (*3-7186-0473-6*) Gordon & Breach.

Breitmaier, Eberhard & Voelter, Wolfgang. Carbon-13 NMR Spectroscopy: High-Resolution Methods & Applications in Organic Chemistry & Biochemistry. 3rd rev. ed. LC 86-28098. (Illus.). 515p. 1986. 285.00 (*3-527-26466-3*, Wiley-VCH) Wiley.

Breitmaier, Isa. Das Thema der Schopfung in der Okumenischen Bewegung 1948 Bis 1988. (Europaische Hochschulschriften Ser.: Reihe 23, Bd. 530). (GER.). 345p. 1995. 55.95 (*3-631-48287-6*) P Lang Pubng.

Breitman, George. The Last Year of Malcolm X: The Evolution of a Revolutionary. LC 67-20467. 169p. 1967. reprint ed. pap. 14.95 (*0-87348-004-X*) Pathfinder NY.

Breitman, George, et al. The Assassination of Malcolm X. 3rd ed. LC 76-47347. (Illus.). 196p. (C). 1991. reprint ed. pap. 14.95 (*0-87348-632-3*) Pathfinder NY.

— Trotskyism in the United States: Historical Essays & Reconsiderations. LC 95-37066. (Revolutionary Studies Ser.). 352p. (C). 1996. text 60.00 (*0-391-03922-9*) Humanities.

Breitman, George, ed. see Cannon, James P.

Breitman, George, ed. see Malcolm X.

Breitman, George, ed. see Trotsky, Leon.

***Breitman, Patti & Hatch, Connie.** How to Say No Without Feeling Guilty: And Say Yes to More Time, More Joy & What Matters Most to You. 256p. 2000. 23.00 (*0-7679-0379-X*) Broadway BDD.

Breitman, Patti, et al. How to Persuade Your Lover to Use a Condom: And Why You Should. 2nd rev. ed. LC 93-23553. 96p. 1994. pap. 7.95 (*1-55958-437-8*) Prima Pub.

Breitman, Richard. The Architect of Genocide: Himmler & the Final Solution. LC 92-53857. (Tauber Institute Ser.: Vol. 14). 348p. 1992. reprint ed. pap. 22.95 (*0-87451-596-3*) U Pr of New Eng.

— German Socialism & Weimar Democracy. LC 80-21412. 295p. reprint ed. pap. 91.50 (*0-7837-3766-1*, 204358300010) Bks Demand.

— Official Secrets: What the Nazis Planned, What the British & Americans Knew. LC 98-7997. 320p. 1998. 25.00 (*0-8090-3819-6*) Hill & Wang.

***Breitman, Richard.** Official Secrets: What the Nazis Planned, What the British & Americans Knew. 336p. 1999. pap. 13.00 (*0-8090-0184-5*) Hill & Wang.

Breitman, Richard, jt. auth. see Laquer, Walter.

Breitmeier, E., et al. Thirteen NMR Spectroscopy, Vol. 3. (MMI Press Polymer Monographs). x, 356p. 1984. text, wbk. ed. 389.00 (*3-7186-0022-6*) Gordon & Breach.

Breitmeyer, Bruno G. Visual Masking: An Integrative Approach. (Oxford Psychology Ser.). (Illus.). 500p. 1984. 45.00 (*0-19-852105-7*) OUP.

Breitner, Bina, jt. auth. see Perry, Henry B.

Breitowitz, Irving A. Between Civil & Religious Law: The Plight of the Agunah in American Society, 70. LC 92-551. (Contributions in Legal Studies: No. 70). 448p. 1993. 69.50 (*0-313-28471-7*, BZC, Greenwood Pr) Greenwood.

Breitrose, Prudence, ed. see California Project Lean Staff.

Breitrose, Prudence, ed. see Feighery, Ellen, et al.

Breitrose, Prudence, ed. see Howard-Pitney, Beth, et al.

Breitrose, Prudence E., jt. auth. see Fortmann, Stephen P.

Breitrose, Prue, ed. see Mackey, Sally, et al.

Breitsameter. Lexikon der Schulphysik: Elektrizitaet und Magnetismus A-K, Vol. 3A. (GER.). 75.00 (*3-7614-0168-X*, M7224) Fr & Eur.

— Lexikon der Schulphysik: Elektrizitaet und Magnetismus L-Z, Vol. 3B. (GER.). 75.00 (*3-7614-0169-8*, M7225) Fr & Eur.

— Lexikon der Schulphysik Vol. 3A: Elektrizitaet und Magnetismus A-K. (GER.). 75.00 (*0-8288-7623-8*, M7224) Fr & Eur.

Breitschwerdt, D., et al, eds. The Local Bubble & Beyond: Proceedings of the IAU Colloquium No. 166 Held in Garching, Germany, 21-25 April 1997. LC 98-7473. (Lecture Notes in Physics Ser.: Vol. 506). xviii, 603p. 1998. 109.00 (*3-540-64306-0*) Spr-Verlag.

Breitschwerdt, Edward B., ed. Nephrology & Urology. fac. ed. LC 88-4785. (Contemporary Issues in Small Animal Practice Ser.: No. 4). (Illus.). 294p. 1986. reprint ed. pap. 91.20 (*0-7837-7886-4*, 204764200007) Bks Demand.

Breitstein, Ron & Van Leuven, Hendrik. Wine & Dine: California Fine Wines Matched with Gourmet Recipes. LC 96-32400. (Illus.). 266p. (Orig.). 1996. pap. 15.95 (*0-88496-410-8*) Capra Pr.

Breitstein, Stephen, jt. auth. see Nevo, Baruch.

Breitung, E. German-Japanese Dictionary: Deutsch-Japanisches Woerterbuch. (GER & JPN.). 1277p. 1981. 95.00 (*0-8288-1016-8*, F47905) Fr & Eur.

Breitung, Joan C. Caring for Older Adults: Basic Skills & Concepts. (Illus.). 400p. 1987. text 32.00 (*0-7216-1576-7*, W B Saunders Co) Harcrt Hlth Sci Grp.

Breitung, Karl Wilhelm. Asymptotic Approximations for Probability Integrals. (Lecture Notes in Mathematics Ser.: 1592). 1994. pap. write for info. (*0-387-58617-2*) Spr-Verlag.

Breitung, Karl Wilhem. Asymptotic Approximations for Probability Integrals. (Lecture Notes in Mathematics Ser.: 1592). 1994. 35.95 (*3-540-58617-2*) Spr-Verlag.

Breitwieser, Mitchell R. American Puritanism & the Defense of Mourning: Religion, Grief, & Ethnology in Mary White Rowlandson's Captivity Narrative. LC 90-50080. (Wisconsin Project on American Writers Ser.). 224p. (Orig.). (C). 1990. text 40.00 (*0-299-12650-1*); pap. text 18.95 (*0-299-12654-4*) U of Wis Pr.

Breitzter-Kings, Dorothea. Mediation Through the Year: Nature's Cycle of the Seasons in Guilded Visualisation. (Illus.). 96p. 1992. pap. text 13.95 (*1-85398-029-3*, Pub. by Ashgrove Pr) Words Distrib.

Breivik, L. E., et al, eds. Essays on English Language in Honour of Bertil Sundby. (Studia Anglistica Norvegica Ser.: No. 4). xxii, 396p. (Orig.). 1989. pap. 85.00 (*82-7099-144-9*) Coronet Bks.

Breivik, Leiv E. & Jahr, Ernst H., eds. Language Change: Contributions to the Study of Its Causes. (Trends in Linguistics, Studies & Monographs: No. 43). viii, 281p. (C). 1989. lib. bdg. 103.10 (*0-89925-564-7*) Mouton.

Breivik, Patricia S. Student Learning in the Information Age. 2nd ed. LC 97-35183. (Ace/Oryx Series on Higher Education). 240p. 1997. boxed set 34.95 (*1-57356-000-6*) Oryx Pr.

Breivik, Patricia S. & Gee, E. Gordon. Information Literacy: Revolution in the Library. LC 89-2845. (Ace/Oryx Series on Higher Education). 264p. (C). 1989. text 24.95 (*0-02-911440-3*) Oryx Pr.

Breivik, Patricia S. & Senn, J. A. Information Literacy: Educating Children for the 21st Century. (Illus.). 198p. 1997. pap. 18.95 (*0-614-30868-2*, 2975-5) NEA.

— Information Literacy: Educating Children for the 21st Century. 2nd ed. LC 97-51802. 1998. 18.95 (*0-8106-2975-5*) NEA.

Breizman, B. N. & Knyazev, B. A. High-Power Particle Beams (Beams '90) Proceedings of the 8th International Conference, 2 vols. 1404p. 1990. text 251.00 (*981-02-0545-7*) World Scientific Pub.

Breizman, Boris N. & Van Dam, James W., eds. G. I. Budker: Reflections & Remembrances. Breizman, Natasha, tr. from RUS. LC 93-22850.Tr. of Akademik G. I. Budker. (Illus.). 400p. 1993. text 49.95 (*1-56396-070-2*, AIP Pr) Spr-Verlag.

Breizman, Natasha, tr. see Breizman, Boris N. & Van Dam, James W., eds.

Brejcha. Auto Transmission & Transaxles Diagnosis & Service IG. 224p. (C). 1997. pap., teacher ed. 12.95 (*0-8273-8039-9*) Delmar.

Brejcha, Mathias F. Auto Transmission & Transaxles Diagnostics. 4th ed. LC 97-4014. (C). 1997. pap. 79.95 (*0-8273-8038-0*) Delmar.

Brejdak, Jaromir. Philosophia Crucis: Heideggers Beschaftigung Mit Dem Apostel Paulus. (Daedalus - Europaisches Denken in Deutscher Philosophie Ser.: Bd. 8). (GER.). 233p. 1996. 51.95 (*3-631-30706-3*) P Lang Pubng.

Brejla. Biography of Richard Matheson. 1999. text 24.95 (*0-312-86381-0*) St Martin.

***Brejla, Terry.** Senator's Son. 304p. 2000. 22.95 (*1-890768-27-8*, Pub. by Intrigue Press) Midpt Trade.

Brejon de Labergnee, Arnauld & Thiebaut, Dominique. Italie, Espagne, Allemagne, Grande-Bretagne et Divers. (FRE., Illus.). 416p. 1988. pap. 40.00 (*0-317-66905-2*) Abrams.

Breker, Arno. The Collected Writings. Probst, Volker G., ed. Webb, Benjiman D., tr. from GER. (Illus.). 256p. (Orig.). 1990. pap. 15.00 (*0-914301-13-6*) West-Art.

— The Collected Writings. deluxe ed. Probst, Volker G., ed. Webb, Benjiman D., tr. from GER. (Illus.). 256p. (Orig.). 1990. 85.00 (*0-914301-12-8*) West-Art.

— Salute America. (Illus.). 6p. 1985. 120.00 (*0-914301-02-0*) West-Art.

Brekhman, I. I. Man & Biologically Active Substances: Introduction to the Pharmacology of Health. 2nd ed. 90p. 1980. 46.00 (*0-08-023169-1*, Pub. by Pergamon Repr) Franklin.

Brekhovskikh, L. & Goncharov, V. N. Mechanics of Continua & Wave Dynamics. 2nd ed. LC 93-39737. (Wave Phenomena Ser.: No. 1). 1994. 59.95 (*0-387-57336-4*) Spr-Verlag.

Brekhovskikh, L. M. & Godin, O. A. Acoustics of Layered Media, No. 1, Vol. 5. (Illus.). 255p. 1990. 99.00 (*0-387-51038-9*, 2834) Spr-Verlag.

— Acoustics of Layered Media II: Point Source & Bounded Beams. Felsen, L. B. et al, eds. (Wave Phenomena Ser.: Vol. 10). (Illus.). 408p. 1992. 97.95 (*0-387-52646-3*) Spr-Verlag.

— Acoustics of Layered Media I: Plane & Quasi-Plane Waves. LC 98-27950. (Series on Wave Phenomena). 1999. pap. 59.95 (*3-540-64724-4*) Spr-Verlag.

— Acoustics of Layered Media I: Plane & Quasi-Plane Waves. 2nd ed. LC 98-27950. (Series on Wave Phenomena). x, 242p. 1998. pap. write for info. (*3-540-51038-9*) Spr-Verlag.

— Acoustics of Layered Media II: Point Sources & Bounded Beams. 2nd enl. ed. LC 99-12348. (Series on Wave Phenomena). x, 530p. 1999. 139.00 (*3-540-65592-1*) Spr-Verlag.

Brekhovskikh, L. M. & Goncharov, V. N. Mechanics of Continua & Wave Dynamics. (Wave Phenomena Ser.: Vol. 1). (Illus.). 360p. 1985. 93.00 (*0-387-13765-3*) Spr-Verlag.

Brekhovskikh, L. M. & Lysanov, Y. P. Fundamentals of Ocean Acoustics. 2nd ed. Felsen, L. B. & Haus, Herman A., eds. (Wave Phenomena Ser.: Vol. 8). (Illus.). 280p. 1991. 59.95 (*0-387-52976-4*) Spr-Verlag.

— Fundamentals of Oceanic Acoustics. (Electrophysics Ser.: Vol. 8). (Illus.). 250p. 1982. 59.00 (*0-387-11305-3*) Spr-Verlag.

Brekhovskikh, L. M., ed. see Babic, V. M. & Buldyrev, V. S.

Brekhovskikh, L. M., ed. see DeSanto, J. A.

Brekhovskikh, L. M., ed. see Kravtsov, Y. A. & Orlov, Y. I.

Brekhovskikh, L. M., ed. see Kravtsov, Yurii A. & Orlov, Yu I.

Brekhovskikh, L. M., ed. see Oughstun, K. E., et al.

Brekke, A. & Egeland, Alv. The Northern Light: From Mythology to Space Research. (Illus.). 190p. 1983. 119.00 (*0-387-12429-2*) Spr-Verlag.

B

Brekke, B. Copper Coins of Imperial Russia. LC 76-52591. (Illus.). 1977. lib. bdg. 90.00 (*0-85556-00-9*) S J Durst.

Brekke, H., et al, eds. Hydraulic Machinery & Cavitation: Proceedings of the XIX IAHR Symposium Singapore. 700p. 1998. 128.00 (*981-02-3542-9*) World Scientific Pub.

Brekke, Inge B., ed. see Albrechtsen, Dagfinn.

***Brekke, John.** Minnesota Almanac 2000. (Illus.). 2000. pap. 15.95 (*0-942072-05-7*) John L Brekke & Sons.

Brekke, Kjell A. Economic Growth & the Environment: On the Measurement of Income & Welfare. LC 96-35152. 192p. 1997. 85.00 (*1-85898-143-3*) E Elgar.

Brekke, Marsha, jt. auth. see VanNostrand, Shannon.

***Brekke, Nancy & Guglielmi, Sergio.** Prejudice & Discrimination: Stereotypes. 2000. pap. text. write for info. (*1-57259-717-8*) Worth.

Brekus, Catherine A. Strangers & Pilgrims: Female Preaching in America, 1740-1845. LC 98-11394. (Gender & American Culture Ser.). 480p. 1998. 49.95 (*0-8078-2441-0*); pap. 17.95 (*0-8078-4745-3*) U of NC Pr.

***Brelade, S., et al.** Practical Training Strategies for the Future. (Financial Times Management Briefings Ser.). 1998. pap. 89.50 (*0-273-63395-3*, Pub. by F T P-H) Trans-Atl Phila.

Brelade, S., jt. auth. see Miller, T.

Breland & Farmer Designers, Inc. Staff. Home Designs. (Series A). (Illus.). 104p. reprint ed. pap. 5.95 (*0-938007-00-9*); reprint ed. pap. text 5.95 (*0-938007-01-7*) Breland & Farmer.

— House Plans. (Illus.). 104p. reprint ed. pap. text 5.95 (*0-938007-02-5*) Breland & Farmer.

Breland, Charles G. The Breland Families of the Southern States, 1755-1875. 2nd ed. Breland, Hunter M, ed. LC 95-69436. 101p. 1995. 20.00 (*0-9647379-0-6*) Queenstown Pr.

Breland, Hunter M. Assessing Student Characteristics in Admissions to Higher Education: A Review of Procedures. (Research Monographs: No. 9). 144p. (Orig.). 1981. pap. 10.95 (*0-87447-138-9*) College Bd.

— Population Validity & College Entrance Measures. LC 79-51738. (Research Monographs: No. 8). 104p. (Orig.). 1979. pap. 7.50 (*0-87447-110-9*, 270501) College Bd.

Breland, Hunter M., compiled by. Challenges in College Admissions: Report of a Survey of Undergraduate Admissions Policies, Practices & Procedures. LC 95-7713. 1995. 40.00 (*0-929851-37-4*) Am Assn Coll Registrars.

Breland, Hunter M., et al. Assessing Writing Skill. (Research Monographs: No. 11). 128p. (Orig.). 1987. pap. 14.95 (*0-87447-280-6*) College Bd.

Breland, Hunter M, ed. see Breland, Charles G.

Brelich, Mario. The Holy Embrace. Shepley, John, tr. from ITA. LC 93-80764. 248p. 1994. 22.95 (*1-56897-002-1*) Marlboro Pr.

— The Holy Embrace. Shepley, John, tr. from ITA. 229p. 1996. pap. 13.95 (*0-8101-6029-3*, Marlboro) Northwestern U Pr.

— Navigator of the Flood. Shepley, John, tr. from ITA. LC 91-61535. 160p. 1991. 25.95 (*0-910395-79-9*) Marlboro Pr.

— Navigator of the Flood. Shepley, John, tr. from ITA. & frwd. by. LC 91-61535. 160p. 1994. pap. 10.95 (*0-910395-80-2*) Marlboro Pr.

— The Work of Betrayal. Rosenthal, Raymond, tr. from ITA. LC 88-64144. Orig. Title: L'Opera Del Tradimento. 240p. 1989. 29.95 (*0-910395-44-6*) Marlboro Pr.

— The Work of Betrayal. Orig. Title: L'Opera Del Tradimento. 1990. pap. 12.00 (*0-910395-45-4*) Marlboro Pr.

Brelin, Christa & Tyrkus, Michael J., eds. Outstanding Lives: Profiles of Lesbians & Gay Men. LC 97-11522. (Illus.). 454p. 1997. 24.95 (*1-57859-008-6*) Visible Ink Pr.

Brelin, Harvey K., et al. Focused Quality: Managing for Results. 193p. 1995. pap. 18.95 (*0-471-13288-8*) Wiley.

Brelinsky, Paul. How to Play Basic Rhythms for Guitar. 1982. pap. 10.00 (*0-89898-143-3*, F1748JGX) Wrner Bros.

— Jazz Scales for Guitar. 1982. pap. 10.95 (*0-89898-263-4*, F1713JGA) Wrner Bros.

Brelinsky, Paul, ed. see Giuliani, Mauro.

Brelje, H. William, ed. Global Perspectives on the Education of the Deaf. 1999. per. 49.00 (*1-884362-36-2*) Butte Pubns.

Breller, David. Inside a Turnip. Schumake, John P., ed. (Orig.). (C). 1992. pap. 12.95 (*0-9616789-7-6*) Earnest Pubns.

Brellochs, Christel, jt. auth. see Carter, Anjean B.

Brelot, E. & Chocat, B., eds. Innovative Technologies in Urban Storm Drainage (NOVATECH '95) Selected Proceedings on the 2nd NOVATECH Conference on Innovative Technologies in Urban Storm Drainage, held in Lyon, France, 30 May-1 June, 1995. (Water Science & Technology Ser.: Vol. 32). 260p. 1995. pap. text 122.50 (*0-08-042669-7*, Pergamon Pr) Elsevier.

***Brelsford, Harry M.** Active Directory Planning & Design. (Illus.). 400p. 2000. pap. text 29.99 (*0-7645-4713-5*) IDG Bks.

Brelsford, Harry M. NT 5.0 Secrets. LC 99-19196. 1500p. 1999. 59.99 (*0-7645-3130-1*) IDG Bks.

— Teach Yourself Microsoft Small Business Server in 21 Days. (Sams Teach Yourself... in 21 Days Ser.). (Illus.). 738p. 1999. pap. 29.99 incl. cd-rom (*0-672-31513-0*) Sams.

***Brelsford, Harry M.** Windows 2000 Server Secrets. LC 99-52717. (Secrets Ser.). (Illus.). 888p. 1999. pap. 49.99 (*0-7645-4620-1*) IDG Bks.

Brelsford, Lottie K. House Diary: For All Home Owners. 1992. pap. 16.95 (*0-9631632-8-0*) Wow Wadda.

Brelsford, Theodore, jt. auth. see Foster, Charles R.

Brelsford, William M. & Relles, Daniel A. Statlib: A Statistical Computing Library. 448p. (C). 1981. pap. text 48.00 (*0-13-846220-8*) P-H.

Brem, Caroline. Are We on the Same Team Here? Essential Communication Skills to Make Groups Work. 112p. 1995. pap. 14.95 (*1-86373-805-3*, Pub. by Allen & Unwin Pty) IPG Chicago.

Brem, M. M. The Man Caught by a Fish: Book of Jonah. (Arch Bks.: Set 4). 1970. pap. 1.99 (*0-570-06025-7*, 59-1136) Concordia.

— Mary's Story: Luke 1:5-2:18. (Arch Bks.: Set 4). 1967. pap. 1.99 (*0-570-06029-X*, 59-1140) Concordia.

Bremaecker, Jean-Claude De, see De Bremaecker, Jean-Claude.

Breman, Jan. Beyond Patronage & Exploitation: Changing Agrarian Relations in South Gujarat. (India Paperbacks Ser.). (Illus.). 424p. 1994. pap. text 13.95 (*0-19-563087-4*) OUP.

— Footloose Labour: Working in India's Informal Economy. (Contemporary South Asia Ser.: No. 2). 287p. (C). 1996. text 64.95 (*0-521-56083-7*); pap. text 22.95 (*0-521-56824-2*) Cambridge U Pr.

— Labour Migration & Rural Transformation in Colonial Asia. 88p. 1991. pap. 22.95 (*90-6256-873-4*, Pub. by VU Univ Pr) Paul & Co Pubs.

— Of Peasants, Paupers & Migrants: Rural Labour Circulation & Capitalist Production in West India. (Illus.). 500p. 1986. text 48.00 (*0-19-561649-9*) OUP.

— Taming the Coolie Beast: Plantation Society & the Colonial Order in Southeast Asia. (Illus.). 374p. 1989. 28.00 (*0-19-562365-7*) OUP.

— Wage Hunters & Gatherers: Search of Work in the Urban & Rural Economy of South Gujarat. (Illus.). 434p. 1995. text 35.00 (*0-19-563556-6*) OUP.

Breman, Jan, ed. Imperial Monkey Business: Racial Supremacy in Social Darwinist Theory & Colonial Practice. 160p. 1991. pap. 39.95 (*90-6256-931-5*, Pub. by VU Univ Pr) Paul & Co Pubs.

— Rural Transformation in Asia. 560p. 1991. 21.00 (*0-19-562519-6*) OUP.

***Breman, Jan & Das, Arvind N.** Down & Out: Labouring under Global Capitalism. (Illus.). 160p. 2000. text 24.95 (*0-19-565304-1*) OUP.

Breman, Jan, et al. Down & Out: Labouring Under Global Capitalism. (Illus.). 164p. (C). text 25.00 (*90-5356-450-0*, Pub. by Amsterdam U Pr) U of Mich Pr.

Breman, Johanna. Country-Specific State & Local Selective Purchasing Laws. LC 98-192629. 146p. 1997. 45.00 (*1-879775-52-2*) IRRC Inc DC.

— Country-Specific State & Local Selective Purchasing Laws As of June 1998. LC 99-186678. 162p. 1998. 45.00 (*1-879775-62-X*) IRRC Inc DC.

Breman, Paul & Addis, Denise. Guide to Vitruvius Britannicus. Date not set. 259.95 (*0-405-09043-9*) Ayer.

— Guide to Vitruvius Britannicus: An Annotated & Analytic Index to the Plates. LC 67-18052. 1972. 37.95 (*0-405-08303-3*, Pub. by Blom Pubns) Ayer.

Bremann, H. & Kessler, J. J., eds. Woody Plants in Agro-Ecosystems of Semi-Arid Regions: With an Emphasis on the Sahelian Countries. (Advanced Series in Agricultural Sciences: Vol. 23). 330p. 1995. 178.00 (*0-387-58354-8*) Spr-Verlag.

Bremaud, P. Introduction to Probability. (Undergraduate Texts in Mathematics Ser.). (Illus.). 230p. 1997. 47.95 (*0-387-96460-6*) Spr-Verlag.

— Markov Chains: Gibbs Fields, Monte Carlo Simulation & Queues. Marsden, J. E. et al, eds. LC 98-17539. (Texts in Applied Mathematics Ser.: Vol. 31). 550p. 1998. 49.95 (*0-387-98509-3*) Spr-Verlag.

— Point Processes & Queues: Martingale Dynamics. (Series in Statistics). (Illus.). 352p. 1981. 87.95 (*0-387-90536-7*) Spr-Verlag.

Bremaud, P., jt. auth. see Baccelli, Francois L.

Bremaud, Pierre, jt. auth. see Baccelli, Francois L.

Brembeck, Cole S. The Mystery of Bhowal. LC 98-915246. 384p. 1998. write for info. (*81-241-0492-1*) Har-Anand Pubns.

Brembeck, Cole S. Congress, Human Nature, & the Federal Debt: Essays on the Political Psychology of Deficit Spending. LC 90-28077. 192p. 1991. 52.95 (*0-275-93674-0*, C3674, Praeger Pubs) Greenwood.

***Brembeck, Howard S.** In Search of the Fourth Freedom. 2nd ed. (From the Fourth Freedom Forum Ser.). 200p. 2000. 25.00 (*0-268-03151-7*, Pub. by U of Notre Dame Pr); pap. write for info. (*0-268-03152-5*, Pub. by U of Notre Dame Pr) Chicago Distribution Ctr.

Brembeck, Howard S. & Fourth Freedom Forum Staff. In Search of the Fourth Freedom. LC 98-917877. 203 p. 1998. write for info. (*81-241-0100-0*) S Asia.

Breme, J., jt. ed. see Helsen, J.

Bremen, Brian. William Carlos Williams & the Diagnostics of Culture. 248p. 1993. text 65.00 (*0-19-507226-X*) OUP.

Bremen, Christian. Die Eisenhower-Administration und die Zweite Berlinkrise, 1958-1961. 596p. 1998. 186.00 (*3-11-016147-8*) De Gruyter.

Bremen, Jan Van, see Van Bremen, Jan, ed.

Brement, Marshall. Reaching Out to Moscow: From Confrontation to Cooperation. LC 91-18920. 208p. 1991. 55.00 (*0-275-94073-X*, C4073, Praeger Pubs) Greenwood.

Brement, Marshall, tr. & intro. see Johannessen, Matthias.

Bremer, ed. Iurisprudentiae Antehadrianae Pt. I: Liberae rei Publicae Iuris Consulti. (LAT.). 1985. reprint ed. 39.50 (*3-322-00140-7*, T1459, Pub. by B G Teubner) U of Mich Pr.

— Iurisprudentiae Antehadrianae Pt. II, Section 1: Primi Post Principatum Constitutum Saeculi Iuris Consulti. (LAT.). 1985. reprint ed. 46.50 (*3-322-00141-5*, T1460, Pub. by B G Teubner) U of Mich Pr.

— Iurisprudentiae Antehadrianae Pt. II, Section 2: Primi Post Principatum Constitutum Saeculi Iuris Consulti. (LAT.). 1985. reprint ed. 49.50 (*3-322-00142-3*, T1461, Pub. by B G Teubner) U of Mich Pr.

Bremer, Tom. Just Once: Poems. LC 98-49059. 1999. write for info. (*0-89924-093-3*) Lynx Hse.

Bremer, B. A., jt. auth. see Armpriester, K. E.

Bremer, C. Deutsche Lehrtexte Fur Auslander-Medizin. abr. ed. 165p. 1987. 13.00 (*3-324-00142-0*) Langenscheidt.

Bremer, Cornelius D. American Bank Failures. LC 68-58551. (Columbia University. Studies in the Social Sciences: No. 412). reprint ed. 20.00 (*0-404-51412-X*) AMS Pr.

Bremer-David, Charissa. French Tapestries & Textiles in the J. Paul Getty Museum. LC 96-28310. (Getty Trust Publications: J. Paul Getty Museum). (Illus.). 202p. 1997. 85.00 (*0-89236-379-7*, Pub. by J P Getty Trust) OUP.

Bremer-David, Charissa, et al. Decorative Arts: An Illustrated Summary Catalogue of the Collections of The J. Paul Getty Museum. rev. ed. LC 93-9753. (Illus.). 312p. 1993. pap. 49.95 (*0-89236-221-9*, Pub. by J P Getty Trust) OUP.

Bremer, Enrique, tr. see Arnott, John.

Bremer, Ernst & Hildebrandt, Reiner, eds. Stand und Aufgaben der Deutschen Dialektlexikographie Vol. II: Brueder-Grimm-Symposium Zur Historischen Wortforschung. (Historische Wortforschung Ser.). (GER., Illus.). viii, 293p. (C). 1996. lib. bdg. 133.35 (*3-11-014464-6*) De Gruyter.

***Bremer, Frances Winfield.** Running to Paradise. 128p. 2000. pap. write for info. (*1-892668-24-6*) Prospect Pr.

Bremer, Francis J. Congregational Communion: Clerical Friendship in the Anglo-American Puritan Community, 1610-1692. (New England Studies). 352p. 1994. text 47.50 (*1-55553-186-5*) NE U Pr.

— The Puritan Experiment: New England Society from Bradford to Edwards. LC 95-18209. (Illus.). 283p. 1995. pap. 19.95 (*0-87451-728-1*) U Pr of New Eng.

Bremer, Francis J., ed. Anne Hutchinson: Troubler of the Puritan Zion. LC 80-13218. 180p. (Orig.). 1980. pap. text 11.50 (*0-89874-063-0*) Krieger.

— Puritanism: Transatlantic Perspectives on a Seventeenth-Century Anglo-American Faith. LC 93-14428. (Studies in American History & Culture: No. 3). 1993. 45.00 (*0-934909-34-2*, Pub. by Mass Hist Soc); pap. 15.95 (*0-934909-38-5*, Pub. by Mass Hist Soc) NE U Pr.

Bremer, Francis J., jt. ed. see Downey, Dennis B.

Bremer, Frederika. Life, Letters & Posthumous Works of Frederika Bremer. LC 75-37682. (Women of Letters Ser.). reprint ed. 52.50 (*0-404-56708-8*) AMS Pr.

— The Neighbours: A Story of Every Day Life. 4th ed. Howitt, Mary, tr. from SWE. LC 74-150538. (Short Story Index Reprint Ser.). 1977. reprint ed. 26.95 (*0-8369-3835-6*) Ayer.

Bremer, Fredrika. The Colonel's Family. Death, Sarah, tr. from SWE. & frwd. by. 240p. 1996. pap. 24.95 (*1-870041-31-3*, Pub. by Norvik Pr) Dufour.

— The Home: or Family Cares & Family Joys. Howitt, M., tr. from SWE. LC 76-28470. 1978. reprint ed. 45.00 (*0-86527-259-X*) Fertig.

Bremer Gesellschaft fur Wirtschaftsforschung e.V. Massenarbeitslosigkeit Durch Politikversagen? Diskussionsbeitrage. (GER., Illus.). 206p. 1996. 24.95 (*3-631-30708-X*) P Lang Pubng.

Bremer, H. & Clayton, K. M., eds. Coasts: Erosion & Sedimentation. (Annals of Mathematical Chemistry Ser.: Suppl. 73). (Illus.). 180p. 1989. pap. 100.00 (*3-443-21073-2*) Lubrecht & Cramer.

Bremer, H. & Godard, A., eds. Geomorphology of European Massifs. (Annals of Geomorphology Ser.: Suppl. 65). (ENG, FRE & GER., Illus.). 138p. 1987. pap. 80.00 (*3-443-21065-1*, Pub. by Gebruder Borntraeger) Balogh.

Bremer, Hanna. Allgemeine Geomorphologie. Methodik, Grundvorstellungen, Ausblick auf den Landschaftshaushalt. (Boden in Niedersachsen Ser.). (DUT & GER., Illus.). xiv, 450p. 1989. pap. text 35.00 (*3-443-01026-1*, Pub. by Gebruder Borntraeger) Balogh.

— Boden und Relief in den Tropen: Grundvorstellungen und Datenbank. (Relief, Boden, Palaeoklima Ser.: Band 11). (GER., Illus.). xii, 324p. 1995. pap. 70.00 (*3-443-09011-7*, Pub. by Gebruder Borntraeger) Balogh.

— Die Tropen: Geographische Synthese Einer Fremden Welt Im Umbruch.Tr. of Tropical Region: Geographic Synthesis of a Strange, Rapidly Changing World. (GER.). xii, 428p. 1999. 40.00 (*3-443-01040-7*, Pub. by Gebruder Borntraeger) Balogh.

Bremer, Hanna & Loczy, Denes, eds. Geomorphology & Changing Environments in Central Europe: IAG European Regional Geomorphological Conference, Hungary, April 1996. (Zeitschrift fuer Geomorphologie - Annals of Geomorphology Ser.: Supplementband 110). (Illus.). vi, 262p. 1997. pap. 76.00 (*3-443-21110-0*, Pub. by Gebruder Borntraeger) Balogh.

Bremer, Hanna, et al. Zur Morphogenese in den Feuchten Tropen: Verwitterung und Reliefbildung am Beispiel von Sri Lanka. (Relief, Boden, Palaeoklima Ser.: Band 1). (GER., Illus.). x, 296p. 1981. pap. 70.00 (*3-443-09001-X*, Pub. by Gebruder Borntraeger) Balogh.

Bremer, J. Douglas, jt. ed. see Saigh, Philip A.

Bremer, J. M., et al, eds. Hidden Features: Death & Immortality in Ancient Egypt, Anatolia, the Classical, Biblical, & Arabic-Islamic World. (Orig.). (C). 1995. pap. 29.95 (*90-5356-078-5*, Pub. by Amsterdam U Pr) U of Mich Pr.

Bremer, Jackie. Discover Angels: Who They Are & What They Do: Leader's Guide. 44p. 1998. pap., teacher ed. 3.95 (*1-56212-352-1*, 1960-0575) CRC Pubns.

Bremer, Jan M., jt. auth. see Mastronarde, Donald J.

Bremer, Joanna, ed. see Cobb, Carroll.

Bremer, John. Constitution Making in Indiana, Vol. IV. 343p. 1994. pap. 17.95 (*1-885323-03-4*) IN Hist Bureau.

Bremer, Joseph, jt. auth. see Bremer, Kathy.

Bremer, Juan J., ed. see Rulfo, Juan, et al.

Bremer, Kare. Asteraceae: Cladistics & Classification. LC 93-28134. (Illus.). 752p. 1994. 79.95 (*0-88192-275-7*) Timber.

Bremer, Karl D. America's North Coast Gateway: Minneapolis-St. Paul International Airport. (Illus.). 208p. 1993. 34.95 (*1-882933-00-1*) Cherbo Pub Grp.

Bremer, Kathy. Bread Bonanza. (Orig.). 1986. pap. 9.50 (*0-9615766-1-8*, 200) Bremer Bks.

Bremer, Kathy & Bremer, Joseph. First Annual Bremer Almanac. (Illus.). 150p. (Orig.). 1990. pap. 5.00 (*0-9615766-3-4*) Bremer Bks.

Bremer, M. N. Cold Gas at High Redshift. LC 96-9405. (Astrophysiics & Space Science Library). 1996. text 217.50 (*0-7923-4135-X*) Kluwer Academic.

Bremer, M. N., et al, eds. Observational Cosmology with the New Radio Surveys. LC 97-39047. 345p. 1998. lib. bdg. 142.00 (*0-7923-4885-0*) Kluwer Academic.

***Bremer, Michael.** Taming the Electronic Beast: Conquering Computer Fear. LC 99-90827. (Advice from the Neighborhood Nerd Ser.). (Illus.). 144p. 2000. pap. 14.95 (*0-9669949-2-2*) UnTech.

Bremer, Michael. UnTechnical Writing: How to Write about Technical Subjects & Products So Anyone. LC 99-90429. (Press Books for Writers). 1999. pap. 14.95 (*0-9669949-0-6*) UnTech.

— The User Manual Manual: How to Research, Write, Test, Edit & Produce a Software. LC 99-90430. (Press Books for Writers). 1999. pap. 29.95 (*0-9669949-1-4*) UnTech.

Bremer, Ralf. Handel & Umwelt: Statische Wohlfahrtsaspekte & Nachhaltige Entwicklung. (GER., Illus.). 278p. 1996. 54.95 (*3-631-30591-5*) P Lang Pubng.

Bremer, Richard G. Indian Agent & Wilderness Scholar: The Life of Henry Rowe Schoolcraft. LC 88-177898. 1988. 30.00 (*0-916699-13-7*) CMU Clarke Hist Lib.

Bremer, Ronald A. World's Funniest Epitaphs. 2nd rev. ed. 1997. pap. 14.95 (*1-877677-83-3*) Herit Quest.

Bremer, Sidney H. Urban Intersections: Meetings of Life & Literature in United States Cities. 280p. (C). 1992. text 32.50 (*0-252-01886-9*) U of Ill Pr.

Bremer, Stuart & Cusack, Thomas, eds. The Process of War: Advancing the Scientific Study of War. 255p. 1996. text 20.00 (*2-88449-176-7*); pap. text 12.00 (*2-88449-177-5*) Gordon & Breach.

Bremer, Stuart A. Simulated Worlds: A Computer Model of National Decision-Making. LC 76-49547. 267p. reprint ed. pap. 82.80 (*0-8357-7021-4*, 203340500085) Bks Demand.

Bremer, Suzanne W. & Palmatier, Susan M. Long Range Planning: A How-to-Do-It Manual for Public Libraries. LC 94-5841. 109p. 1994. pap. 45.00 (*1-55570-162-0*) Neal-Schuman.

Bremer, Sven. Der Holdingstandort Bundesrepublik Deutschland Vol. XXIV: Eine Vergleichende Analyse der Besteuerung Europaischer Holdingstandorte. (Europaische Hochschulschriften: Reihe 5: Bd. 2006). (GER., Illus.). XXIV, 422p. 1996. pap. 63.95 (*3-631-31044-7*) P Lang Pubng.

Bremeyer, Jay. The Chymical Cook: A True Account of Mystical Initiation in the Georgia Woods. LC 96-37214. 1996. pap. text 13.95 (*1-886449-31-7*) Barrytown Ltd.

Bremger, Jane. Crossings: Helping a Loved One, Vol II. 150p. 1986. pap. 4.95 (*0-931515-08-4*) Triumph Pr.

Bremmer, Francis J. Shaping New Englands. (Twayne's United States Authors Ser.: No. 631). 160p. 1994. 22.95 (*0-8057-4015-5*) Macmillan.

Bremmer, H., jt. auth. see Van Der Pol, Balth.

Bremmer, Ian & Taras, Raymond C., eds. New States, New Politics: Building the Post-Soviet Nations. 2nd ed. 764p. (C). 1996. text 74.95 (*0-521-57101-4*); pap. text 29.95 (*0-521-57799-3*) Cambridge U Pr.

Bremmer, Ian A., et al. Soviet Nationalities Problems. LC 90-24761. (Publications & Reprints). xiv, 137 p. 1990. write for info. (*0-923439-00-5*) Stanford U CFREES.

Bremmer, Jan. A Cultural History of Gesture. Roodenburg, Herman, ed. LC 91-57953. (Illus.). 1992. text 52.50 (*0-8014-2744-4*); pap. text 17.95 (*0-8014-8023-X*) Cornell U Pr.

Bremmer, Jan, ed. From Sappho to de Sade: Moments in the History of Sexuality. 272p. 1989. 45.00 (*0-415-02089-1*, A3625) Routledge.

Bremmer, Jan & Graf, Fritz, eds. Interpretations of Greek Mythology. LC 86-20638. (Illus.). 304p. (C). 1987. pap. 28.00 (*0-389-20871-X*, N8429) B&N Imports.

Bremmer, Jan & Roodenburg, Herman, eds. A Cultural History of Humour: From Antiquity to the Present Day. LC 97-635. (Illus.). 265p. 1997. 66.95 (*0-7456-1535-X*, Pub. by Polity Pr); pap. 28.95 (*0-7456-1880-4*, Pub. by Polity Pr) Blackwell Pubs.

Bremmer, Jan & Van Den Bosch, Lourens. Between Poverty & the Pyre: Movements in the History of Widowhood. LC 94-27018. 352p. (C). (gr. 13). 1995. 90.00 (*0-415-08370-2*, B4461) Routledge.

Bremmer, Michael & Karakotsios, Ken. SimLife: The Official Strategy Guide. (Illus.). 368p. (Orig.). 1993. pap. 18.95 (*1-55958-190-5*) Prima Pub.

Bremmer, R. H. Johannes C. Sikkel: A Pioneer in Social Reform Christian Answers for Labour Unions, Capital & Labour, the Place of Women in Society, Etc. LC 98-42626. 1998. 4.90 (*0-921100-89-2*) Inhtce Pubns.

An Asterisk (*) at the beginning of an entry indicates that the title is appearing for the first time.

Bremmer, Rolf H., Jr. & Van Den Berg, Jan H., eds. Current Trends in West Germanic Etymological Lexicography: Proceedings of the Symposium Held in Amsterdam, 12-13 June 1989. LC 92-31895. x, 164p. 1993. pap. 64.00 (*90-04-09708-2*) Brill Academic Pubs.

Bremmer, Rolf H., Jr., jt. ed. see Aertsen, Ed H.

Bremner. Poultry Mental Hygiene. 1996. text 72.00 (*0-7020-1893-7*, W B Saunders Co) Harcrt Hlth Sci Grp.

***Bremner.** Words on Words: The Columbia Dictionary for Writers. 416p. 1998. 9.98 (*1-56731-282-9*, MJF Bks) Fine Comms.

Bremner, Belinda. Acting in Chicago: H-T Break into Film, TV & Theatre. 120p. 1997. pap. 12.95 (*1-56850-038-6*) Chicago Plays.

Bremner, Cedric G., et al, eds. Modern Approach to Benign Esophageal Disease: Diagnosis & Surgical Therapy. LC 98-114000. (Illus.). 243p. 1995. text 65.00 (*0-942219-96-1*) Quality Med Pub.

Bremner, David. The Industries of Scotland: Their Rise, Progress & Present Condition. LC 69-11242. (Reprints of Economic Classics Ser.). viii, 535p. 1969. reprint ed. 65.00 (*0-678-05583-1*) Kelley.

***Bremner, Gavin & Fogel, Alan.** The Blackwell Handbook of Infant Development. 640p. 2000. 124.95 (*0-631-21234-5*) Blackwell Pubs.

Bremner, Gavin, et al. Infant Development: Recent Advances. LC 97-198292. (Illus.). xii, 339p. 1997. write for info. (*0-86377-462-8*, Pub. by Psychol Pr) Taylor & Francis.

Bremner, J. Douglas & Marmar, Charles R., eds. Trauma, Memory, & Dissociation. LC 97-3211. (Progress in Psychiatry Ser.). 439p. 1998. text 56.00 (*0-88048-753-4*, 8753) Am Psychiatric.

Bremner, J. Gavin. Infancy. 2nd ed. (Illus.). 368p. (C). 1994. pap. 31.95 (*0-631-18466-X*) Blackwell Pubs.

Bremner, John. The Complete IQ Text Book: How to Understand & Measure Each Aspect of Your Intelligence. (Illus.). 128p. 1997. pap. 15.95 (*0-09-185332-X*, Pub. by Ebury Pr) Trafalgar.

— How to Boost Your IQ. LC 96-170770. (Illus.). 128p. 1996. pap. 7.95 (*0-7063-7305-7*, Pub. by WrLock) Sterling.

***Bremner, John.** Mensa Mind Maze Challenge. 1999. pap. 7.99 (*0-7858-1158-3*) Book Sales.

— Mensa Visual Brainteasers. 1999. pap. text 9.95 (*1-85868-548-6*, Pub. by Carlton Bks Ltd) Natl Bk Netwk.

Bremner, John B. Words, Words, Words: A Dictionary for Writers & Others Who Care about Words. LC 80-256. 405p. 1980. pap. text 21.00 (*0-231-04493-3*) Col U Pr.

Bremner, Joseph. Guide to Database Distribution. 2nd ed. 224p. 1994. pap. 75.00 (*0-942308-40-9*) NFAIS.

Bremner, Marilyn J. Background Notes, Lesotho: 1990, November. 4p. 1991. pap. 1.25 (*0-16-028043-5*) USGPO.

Bremner, Moyra. Modern Etiquette. 1995. 8.98 (*0-7858-0116-2*) Bk Sales Inc.

Bremner, Muriel Monsell. The Wolfhound Guide to the Irish Wolfhound. (Illus.). 96p. 1998. pap. 7.95 (*0-86327-636-9*, Pub. by Wolfhound Press) Irish Amer Bk.

Bremner, Robert. Harpsichord or Spinnet Miscellany. Darling, James S., ed. LC 75-165365. 26p. 1972. pap. 7.95 (*0-910412-94-4*) Colonial Williamsburg.

Bremner, Robert, frwd. Giving: Charity & Philanthropy in History. 235p. 1996. pap. text 24.95 (*1-56000-884-9*) Transaction Pubs.

Bremner, Robert H. American Philanthropy. 2nd ed. Boor, Daniel J., ed. LC 87-23739. (Chicago History of American Civilization Ser.). (Illus.). xii, 304p. 1988. pap. text 17.00 (*0-226-07325-4*); lib. bdg. 28.50 (*0-226-07324-6*) U Ch Pr.

— American Social History since 1860. LC 70-146848. (Goldentree Bibliographies Series in American History). (C). 1971. text 19.95 (*0-88295-504-7*); pap. text 13.95 (*0-88295-503-9*) Harlan Davidson.

— Children & Youth in America: A Documentary History, Vol. 3: 1933-1973. Barnard, John et al, eds. LC 73-115473. 2054p. 1974. pap. 65.50 (*0-674-11614-3*) HUP.

— The Discovery of Poverty in the United States. 399p. (C). 1997. pap. text 29.95 (*1-56000-582-3*) Transaction Pubs.

— George & Ohio's Civic Revival: The American Democratic Philosopher Inspired a Successful Fight Against Political Bossism, Ending Many Exactions of the System of Privilege. Lissner, Will & Lissner, Dorothy B., eds. (George Studies Program: Vol. 3). 242p. (Orig.). (C). 1994. pap. 10.00 (*0-911312-89-7*) Schalkenbach.

— Giving: Charity & Philanthropy in History. LC 93-14165. 256p. (C). 1994. text 34.95 (*1-56000-137-2*) Transaction Pubs.

— The Juvenile Court: An Original Anthology. LC 74-1688. (Children & Youth Ser.: Vol. 8). 1977. 28.95 (*0-405-05965-5*) Ayer.

Bremner, Robert H., ed. Care of Dependent Children in the Late Nineteenth & Early Twentieth Century. LC 74-1670. (Children & Youth Ser.). 203p. 1979. reprint ed. 25.95 (*0-405-05950-7*) Ayer.

— Care of Handicapped Children, Vol. 7. LC 74-1671. (Children & Youth Ser.). 1978. 20.95 (*0-405-05951-5*) Ayer.

— The Child Labor Bulletin, 1912, 1913. LC 74-1673. (Children & Youth Ser.: Vol. 5). 314p. 1974. 29.95 (*0-405-05953-1*) Ayer.

— Children & Youth, 53 bks., Set. (Illus.). 1974. 1343.50 (*0-405-05940-X*) Ayer.

— Children in Confinement. LC 74-1675. (Children & Youth Ser.: Vol. 4). 458p. 1977. 21.95 (*0-405-05954-X*) Ayer.

— Children's Bureau Studies. LC 74-1676. (Children & Youth Ser.: Vol. 3). 386p. 1974. 34.95 (*0-405-05955-8*) Ayer.

— The Legal Rights of Children: An Orginal Anthology. LC 74-1692. (Children & Youth Ser.: Vol. 5). 1979. 29.95 (*0-405-05968-X*) Ayer.

— Security & Services for Children: An Original Anthology, Vol. 24. LC 74-1703. (Children & Youth Ser.). 1974. 19.95 (*0-405-05980-9*) Ayer.

Bremner, Robert H., et al, eds. American Choices: Social Dilemas & Public Policy since 1960. LC 85-25833. (U. S. A. 20-21: No. 3). 286p. reprint ed. pap. 88.70 (*0-608-09656-3*, 206977100006) Bks Demand.

— Children & Youth in America: A Documentary History, Vol. 2: 1866-1932. LC 74-115473. 1569p. 1971. 117.00 (*0-674-11612-7*) HUP.

Bremner, Robert H. & Reichard, Gary W., eds. Reshaping America: Society & Institutions, 1945-1960. LC 82-3409. (U. S. A. 20-21: No. 1). 415p. 1982. reprint ed. pap. 128.70 (*0-608-04446-6*, 206497800012) Bks Demand.

Bremner, Robert H., ed. see Comstock, Anthony.

Bremner, Robert H., ed. see National Child Labor Committee.

Bremner, Robert H., ed. see Otey, Elizabeth L.

Bremner, Walter D. Bremner's Bulletins, a Wee Sample. (Illus.). 135p. (Orig.). 1993. pap. 12.95 (*0-931563-13-5*) Wishing Rm.

Bremness, Lesley. The Complete Book of Herbs: A Practical Guide to Growing & Using Herbs. 1988. 32.95 (*0-670-81894-1*, Viking Studio) Studio Bks.

— The Complete Book of Herbs: A Practical Guide to Growing & Using Herbs. (Illus.). 288p. 1994. pap. 19.95 (*0-14-023802-6*, Viking Studio) Studio Bks.

— Herbs. LC 93-26815. (Eyewitness Handbooks Ser.). 304p. (Orig.). 1994. pap. 18.95 (*1-56458-496-8*) DK Pub Inc.

— Herbs. LC 93-26815. (Eyewitness Handbooks Ser.). (Illus.). 304p. (Orig.). 1994. 29.95 (*1-56458-497-6*) DK Pub Inc.

— Pocket Garden Herbs. LC 96-30981. 96p. 1997. pap. 9.95 (*0-7894-1466-X*) DK Pub Inc.

Bremness, Lesley, ed. Herbs. LC 90-8250. (RD Home Handbooks Ser.). (Illus.). 240p. (Orig.). 1990. pap. 16.00 (*0-89577-355-4*, Pub. by RD Assn) Penguin Putnam.

Bremness, Lesley & Moine, Marie-Pierre. Crabtree & Evelyn Fragrant Herbal: Enhancing Your Life with Aromatic Herbs & Essential Oils. LC 97-32701. 256p. (gr. 8). 1998. 35.00 (*0-8212-2471-9*) Little.

Bremness, Leslie. World of Herbs. (Illus.). 176p. 1995. 7.99 (*0-517-12346-0*) Random Hse Value.

Bremond, Claude, et al, eds. Thematics: New Approaches. LC 94-72. (SUNY Series, The Margins of Literature). 229p. (C). 1994. text 49.50 (*0-7914-2167-8*); pap. text 16.95 (*0-7914-2168-6*) State U NY Pr.

Bremond, J. Dictionnaire de la Pensee Politique. (FRE.). 854p. 1989. pap. 45.00 (*0-7859-7785-6*, 2218020076) Fr & Eur.

Bremond, Janine. Dictionnaire des Grands Economistes. (FRE.). 192p. 1992. pap. 32.95 (*0-7859-8251-5*, 2909420027) Fr & Eur.

— Dictionnaire des Theories et Mecanismes Economiques. (FRE.). 1984. pap. 32.95 (*0-7859-7791-0*, 2218071290) Fr & Eur.

— Economics & Social Dictionary (Dictionnaire Economique et Social) 4th ed. (FRE.). 416p. 1990. pap. 24.95 (*0-7859-4701-9*) Fr & Eur.

Bremont, Anna Contesse De, see De Bremont Anna, Contesse.

Brempong, K. O., jt. ed. see Warren, D. Michael.

Brems. Ethics & Professional Practice in the Mental Health Professions. 2002. 29.00 (*0-534-52579-2*) Wadsworth Pub.

— Psychopharmacology for Psychotherapists & Counselors. (Counseling Ser.). 2001. 25.00 (*0-534-53065-6*) Wadsworth Pub.

Brems, Christiane. Basic Skills in Psychotherapy & Counseling. 2000. pap. text 36.00 (*0-534-54942-X*) Thomson Learn.

— The Child Therapist: Markers of Effectiveness. LC 93-25949. 127p. 1993. pap. text 25.00 (*0-205-15521-9*) Allyn.

Brems, Christiane. Comprehensive Guide to Child Psychotherapy. LC 92-24692. 416p. 1993. 93.00 (*0-205-14708-9*) Allyn.

Brems, Christiane. Dealing with Challenges in Psychotherapy & Counseling. LC 99-19539. (Counseling Ser.). 321p. 1999. pap. 45.95 (*0-534-36471-3*) Brooks-Cole.

— Psychotherapy: Processes & Techniques. LC 98-13488. 352p. 1998. 63.00 (*0-205-27532-X*) Allyn.

Brems, Hans. Pioneering Economic Theory, 1630-1980: A Mathematical Restatement. LC 85-19819. 432p. 1986. text 65.00 (*0-8018-2667-5*) Johns Hopkins.

Brems, Marianne. The Fit Swimmer. (Illus.). 128p. (Orig.). 1984. pap. 12.95 (*0-8092-5454-9*, 545490, Contemporary Bks) NTC Contemp Pub Co.

Brems, Marianne, et al. Take Care of Yourself: A Health Care Workbook for Beginning ESL Students. LC 93-7377. 256p. 1993. pap. text 19.93 (*0-13-882317-0*) Prentice ESL.

Bremser, Martha. Fifty Contemporary Choreographers. (Illus.). 304p. (C). 1998. 75.00 (*0-415-10363-0*); pap. 18.99 (*0-415-10364-9*) Routledge.

Bremser, Martha, ed. International Dictionary of Ballet, 2 vols., Set. (Illus.). 1600p. 1993. 240.00 (*1-55862-084-2*, 200157) St James Pr.

Bremser, Ray. The Conquerors: Beat Jazz Poems. 64p. 1998. 12.95 (*0-934953-56-2*) Water Row Pr.

— The Conquerors: Beat Jazz Poems. limited aut. ed. 64p. 1998. 39.95 (*0-934953-57-0*) Water Row Pr.

— The Dying of Children. limited ed. Weinberg, Jeffrey, ed. (Illus.). 1999. 35.00 (*0-934953-62-7*) Water Row Pr.

— Poems of Madness & Angel. LC 86-50905. (Illus.). 90p. 1986. pap. 8.95 (*0-934953-11-2*) Water Row Pr.

Bremser, Sarah E., contrib. by. Chihuly: Courtyards. (Illus.). 16p. 1992. pap. 8.00 (*0-9608382-7-9*) Portland Pr.

Bremser, Sarah E. & Tsai-Lan, Kaohsi. Chihuly: Glass in Architecture. (ENG & JPN., Illus.). 160p. 1997. 40.00 (*1-57684-007-7*) Portland Pr.

Bremyer, Jay. The Dance of Created Lights: A Suf. Tale. LC 96-67335. (Illus.). 256p. (Orig.). 1996. pap. 14.95 (*1-56184-084-X*) New Falcon Pubns.

Bremyer, Jayne. Crossings: Preparing Ahead of Time, Vol I. 200p. 1985. pap. 4.95 (*0-931515-06-8*) Triumph Pr.

— Not Like Other Girls. 162p. (J). (ps up). 1982. pap. 9.95 (*0-944996-09-4*) Carlsons.

— Straight from the Horse's Mouth. (Illus.). 124p. (Orig.). 1991. pap. 13.95 (*0-944996-06-X*) Carlsons.

Bremzen, Anya Von, see Von Bremzen, Anya.

Bren, Valentina, tr. see Phillipps, Mike & Phillipps, Marilyn.

Brenan, jt. auth. see Mandell, Steven L.

Brenan, Dan, ed. see Sears, George Washington.

Brenan, Gerald. The Face of Spain. (Travels Ser.). 176p. 1999. reprint ed. pap. 13.00 (*0-88001-463-6*) HarpC.

— Percy. History of the House of Percy, from the Earliest Times down to the Present Century, 2 vols., Set. Lindsay, W. A., ed. (Illus.). 1996. reprint ed. lib. bdg. 149.00 (*0-8328-5295-3*) Higginson Bk Co.

— Percy. History of the House of Percy, from the Earliest Times Down to the Present Century, 2 vols., Set. Lindsay, W. A., ed. (Illus.). 1996. reprint ed. pap. 129.00 (*0-8328-5296-1*) Higginson Bk Co.

— Personal Record, 1920-1972. LC 75-301961. 38 p. 1974. write for info. (*0-224-01044-1*) Jonathan Cape.

— St. John of the Cross: His Life & Poetry. LC 72-83577. 245p. reprint ed. pap. 69.90 (*0-608-12284-X*, 2024428) Bks Demand.

— South from Granada: 7 Years in an Andalusian Village. LC 97-41978. (Globe Ser.). 304p. 1998. pap. write for info. (*1-56836-184-X*) Kodansha.

— The Spanish Labyrinth: An Account of the Social & Political Background of the Spanish Civil War. (Canto Book Ser.). 404p. 1950. text 95.00 (*0-521-04314-X*) Cambridge U Pr.

— The Spanish Labyrinth: An Account of the Social & Political Background of the Spanish Civil War. (Canto Book Ser.). 404p. (C). 1990. pap. 13.95 (*0-521-39827-4*) Cambridge U Pr.

— Thoughts in a Dry Season: A Miscellany. LC 78-4508. 185p. reprint ed. pap. 52.80 (*0-608-17574-9*, 2030582) Bks Demand.

Brenan, J. P. M., et al. Plants Collected by the Vernay Nyasaland Expedition of 1946: Angiospermae & General Index: Conclusion. (Memoirs Ser.: Vol. 9 (1)). 132p. 1954. pap. 10.00 (*0-89327-028-8*) NY Botanical.

— Plants Collected by the Vernay Nyasaland Expedition of 1946: Angiospermae: Continuation. (Memoirs Ser.: Vol. 8 (5)). 102p. 1954. pap. 10.00 (*0-89327-033-4*) NY Botanical.

Brenan, K. E., et al. Numerical Solution of Initial-Value Problems in Differential-Algebraic Equations. 210p. 1989. 44.95 (*0-444-01511-6*) P-H.

Brenan, Kathleen M. & Mandell, Steven L. Introduction to Computers & BASIC Programming. 2nd ed. 564p. (YA). (gr. 9-12). 1987. pap. text, teacher ed. 15.95 (*0-314-43635-9*); mass mkt. 27.25 (*0-314-32166-7*) West Pub.

— Introduction to Computers & BASIC Programming. 2nd ed. 564p. (YA). (gr. 9-12). 1987. mass mkt., student ed. 8.00 (*0-314-36064-6*) West Pub.

Brenan, Kathleen M., et al. Introduction to Computers & BASIC Programming. 3rd ed. 581p. 1991. mass mkt. 47.50 (*0-314-77483-1*) West Pub.

Brenan, Kathryn E., et al. Numerical Solution of Initial-Value Problems in Differential-Algebraic Equations. LC 95-46482. (Classics in Applied Mathematics Ser.: Vol. 14). x, 256p. 1995. pap. 32.00 (*0-89871-353-6*) Soc Indus-Appl Math.

Brenau College Alumnae Association Staff. Windows: Reflections of Taste. Brenau College Staff, ed. & illus. by. 352p. 1992. text 18.95 (*0-9631804-0-1*) Brenau Coll Alum.

Brenau College Staff, ed. & illus. see Brenau College Alumnae Association Staff.

Brenchley, Chaz. Dead of Light. 330p. 1997. pap. 10.95 (*0-450-61003-9*, Pub. by Hodder & Stought Ltd) Trafalgar.

— Dispossession. 378p. 1997. pap. 10.95 (*0-340-65992-0*, Pub. by Hodder & Stought Ltd) Trafalgar.

— Mall Time. 320p. 1992. text 24.95 (*0-340-52827-3*, Pub. by Hodder & Stought Ltd) Trafalgar.

Brenchley, Frank. Britain & the Middle East: An Economic History 1945-87. 405p. 1991. text 59.50 (*1-870915-07-0*, Pub. by I B T) St Martin.

Brencick, Janice M. & Webster, Glenn A. Philosophy of Nursing: A New Vision for Health Care. LC 99-11409. 288p. (C). 1999. text 59.50 (*0-7914-4379-5*); pap. text 19.95 (*0-7914-4380-9*) State U NY Pr.

Brenckman, Fred. History of Carbon County, PA. (Illus.). 626p. 1994. reprint ed. lib. bdg. 65.00 (*0-8328-3981-7*) Higginson Bk Co.

Brencsan, J. A New Vocabulary of Medical Terms (Uj Magyar Orvosi Szotar) 544p. 1993. 45.00 (*963-05-6497-1*, Pub. by Akade Kiado) St Mut.

Brend, Barbara. The Emperor Akbar's Khamsa of Nizami. (Illus.). (C). 1995. pap. 21.95 (*0-7123-0392-8*, Pub. by B23tish Library) U of Toronto Pr.

— Islamic Art. (Illus.). 240p. 1991. 47.50 (*0-674-46865-1*, BREISL) HUP.

— Islamic Art. (Illus.). 240p. (C). 1992. pap. 28.00 (*0-674-46866-X*) HUP.

Brend, Ruth M. Tagmemic Analysis of Mexican Spanish Clauses. (Janua Linguarum, Ser. Practica: No. 52). 1968. text 73.85 (*90-279-0662-9*) Mouton.

Brend, Ruth M., ed. From Phonology to Discourse: Studies in Six Colombian Languages. LC 82-50643. (Language Data, Amerindian Ser.: No. 9). 133p. (Orig.). 1985. pap. 11.00 (*0-88312-091-7*) S I L Intl.

— Kenneth Lee Pike Bibliography. (Arcadia Bibliographica Virorum Eruditorum Ser.: Fasc. 10). 56p. 1987. 18.00 (*0-931922-28-3*) Eurolingua.

Brend, Ruth M. & Pike, Kenneth L., eds. The Summer Institute of Linguistics: Its Works & Contributions. 1977. pap. 66.15 (*90-279-3355-3*) Mouton.

***Brend, Stephen.** Orangutan. (Natural World Ser.). (Illus.). (J). 2000. 9.95 (*0-7398-3126-7*) Raintree Steck-V.

— Orangutan: Habitats, Life Cycles, Food Chains, Threats. LC 00-27459. (Natural World Ser.). (Illus.). (J). 2000. 27.12 (*0-7398-2765-0*) Raintree Steck-V.

Brenda. El Que Ayuda. (Serie Rompecabezas en Libro - Jigsaw Puzzles in Book Ser.).Tr. of One Who Helped. (SPA.). (J). 1992. pap. 4.99 (*1-56063-308-5*, 490446) Editorial Unilit.

Brendan-Brown, Sean, et al. West Wind Review, Vol. 17. Lewis, Ramana, ed. (Illus.). 182p. 1998. pap. 10.00 (*0-9630694-8-9*) So Oregon.

***Brendan, Mary.** Mr. Trelawney's Proposal. large type ed. 1999. 25.99 (*0-263-15911-6*, Pub. by Mills & Boon) Ulverscroft.

Brende, J., tr. see Curtius Rufus, Quintus.

Brende, J. O. & Parson, E. R. Vietnam Veterans: The Road to Recovery. LC 84-26396. (Illus.). 300p. (C). 1985. 19.95 (*0-306-41966-1*, Plenum Trade) Perseus Pubng.

Brendel. Keyboard: Mailable Letters. 4th ed. 1989. 11.25 (*0-07-007482-8*) McGraw.

***Brendel, Alfred.** Alfred Brendel on Music: Collected Essays. 432p. 2000. pap. 19.95 (*1-55652-408-0*, Pub. by A Cappella Bks) IPG Chicago.

Brendel, Alfred. Musical Thoughts & Afterthoughts. 168p. 1991. pap. 12.95 (*0-374-52278-2*) FS&G.

— One Finger Too Many. LC 98-44869. 80p. 1999. 16.00 (*0-375-50293-9*) Random.

Brendel, Doug, jt. auth. see Anderson, John O.

Brendel, Elke. Die Wahrheit Uber Den Lugner: Eine Philosophische-Logische Analyse der Antinomie des Lugners. (Grundlagen der Kommunikation & Kognition (Foundations of Communication & Cognition) Ser.). (GER.). xiv, 230p. (C). 1992. lib. bdg. 83.10 (*3-11-013684-8*) De Gruyter.

Brendel, H. German-English, English-German Dictionary of Computer Sciences & Economics. (ENG & GER.). 454p. 1992. 125.00 (*0-7859-7467-9*) Fr & Eur.

Brendel, Harold J. Kris & Granpaw: How Adults & Children Can Create Effective Relationships. (Illus.). 54p. (Orig.). 1987. pap. write for info. (*0-943073-00-6*) Ctr Creat Lvg.

Brendel, LeRoy A. & Near, Doris. Punctuation Drills & Exercises. 2nd ed. (gr. 9-12). 1978. text 13.24 (*0-07-007479-8*) McGraw.

— Spelling Drills & Exercises: Programmed for the Typewriter. 3rd ed. (Illus.). 1979. text 13.24 (*0-07-007491-7*) McGraw.

Brendel, LeRoy A., et al. Keyboarding Mailable Letters. 4th ed. 168p. (C). 1989. pap. text 16.47 (*0-07-007481-X*) McGraw.

Brendel, Otto J. Etruscan Art. LC 95-15894. (Pelican History of Art Ser.). 1995. pap. 27.50 (*0-300-06446-2*) Yale U Pr.

Brendel, W. & Messmer, K., eds. European Society for Surgical Research Festschrift, 20 Years. (Journal: European Surgical Research: Vol. 18, No. 3-4, 1986). (Illus.). 144p. 1986. pap. 108.00 (*3-8055-4384-0*) S Karger.

Brendel, W. & Zink, R. A., eds. High Altitude Physiology & Medicine I: Physiology of Adaptation. (Topics in Environmental Physiology & Medicine Ser.). (Illus.). 190p. 1982. 145.00 (*0-387-90482-4*) Spr-Verlag.

***Brendell, Bobby W.** Pieces of the Civil War: The Yankee, the Rebel & the Lighter Side. LC 99-62326. 361p. 1999. pap. 15.95 (*1-884778-65-8*) Old Mountain.

Brendell, Theresa. Willows of the British Isles. (Natural History Ser.: No. 8). (Illus.). 24p. pap. 5.25 (*0-85263-765-9*, Pub. by Shire Pubns) Parkwest Pubns.

Brendemoen, Bernt & Tanrikut, Yasar. Tyrkisk-Norsk Ordbok. 3rd ed. (TUR & NOR.). 271p. 1997. 125.00 (*0-320-02074-6*) Fr & Eur.

Brender. Three Crucial Words. (C). 1995. pap. text 25.00 (*0-15-599883-8*) Harcourt Coll Pubs.

Brender a Brandis, G. White Line. 108p. 1990. pap. write for info. (*0-88984-117-9*) Porcup Quill.

— Wood, Ink & Paper. 160p. 1980. pap. write for info. (*0-88984-029-6*) Porcup Quill.

Brender, J., et al, eds. Medical Informatics, '96. LC 96-77454. (Studies in Health Technology & Informatics: Vol. 34). 1100p. (gr. 12). 1996. 143.00 (*90-5199-278-5*, 278-5) IOS Press.

Brenders, Carl. Wildlife: The Nature Paintings of Carl Brenders. LC 94-6382. (Mill Pond Bk.). (Illus.). 96p. 1994. 29.95 (*0-8109-3977-0*, Pub. by Abrams) Time Warner.

***Brenders, Carl.** Celebration of Nature. 80p. (gr. 13 up). 2000. 20.00 (*0-8010-1198-1*) Baker Bks.

Brenders, David, jt. auth. see Norton, Robert.

Brendle, A. S. Brief History of Schaefferstown. (Illus.). 233p. 1997. reprint ed. lib. bdg. 29.50 (*0-8328-6445-5*) Higginson Bk Co.

Brendle, Albert. Im Prozeh der Konfliktuberwindung: Eine Exegetische Studie zur Kommunikationssituation Zwischen Paulus und Den Korinthern Im 2 Kor 1, 1-2, 13; 7,4-16. (Europaische Hochschulschriften Ser.: Reihe 23, Bd. 533). (GER.). 365p. 1995. 61.95 (*3-631-48513-1*) P Lang Pubng.

B

An Asterisk (*) at the beginning of an entry indicates that the title is appearing for the first time.

Brendle, Thomas R. The Thomas R. Brendle Collection of Pennsylvania German Folklore. Beam, C. Richard, ed. (Illus.). 76p. 1995. pap. 15.95 (*1-880976-11-0*, Historic Schaefferstown) Brookshire Pubns.

Brendler, Charlene, ed. see Clementi, Muzio.

Brendler, John, et al. Madness, Chaos, & Violence: Therapy with Families at the Brink. 220p. (C). 1998. text 20.00 (*0-7881-5667-5*) DIANE Pub.

Brendley, K. W., jt. auth. see Finegold, David.

Brendley, Keith W. & Steeb, Randall. Military Applications of Microelectromechanical Systems. LC 93-18546. 1993. pap. 13.00 (*0-8330-1344-0*, MR-175-OLD/AF/A) Rand Corp.

Brendon, John A. The Age of Chaucer. LC 72-179301. (Illus.). 1975. reprint ed. 39.50 (*0-404-01070-9*) AMS Pr.

— Great Navigators & Discoverers. LC 67-26720. (Essay Index Reprint Ser.). 1977. 20.95 (*0-8369-0248-3*) Ayer.

Brendon, Klaus. Utility Restructuring in Central & Eastern Europe: 2nd Central & Eastern European Energy Workshop. (Series on the Environment in the 21st Century: Vol. II). (Illus.). 56p. 1997. pap. 8.00 (*0-89843-215-4*) The Aspen Inst.

***Brendon, Piers.** Dark Valley: A Panorama of the 1930s. (Illus.). 832p. 2000. 37.50 (*0-375-40881-9*) Knopf.

Brendon, Piers. Eminent Edwardians. (Illus.). 256p. 1996. pap. 16.95 (*0-233-98999-4*, Pub. by Andre Deutsch) Trafalgar.

Brendon, Stuart. Giant Atlas of the World. (J). 1993. pap. 27.95 (*0-528-83589-0*) Rand McNally.

Brendonck, Luc, et al, contrib. by. Advances in Limnology, Heft 52. (Illus.). 1998. 120.00 (*3-510-47054-0*) E Schweizerbartsche.

Brendtro, Larry, et al. Reclaiming Youth at Risk: Our Hope for the Future. (Illus.). 100p. (Orig.). 1990. pap. 21.95 (*1-879639-05-X*) Natl Educ Serv.

***Brendtro, Larry K.** Reclaiming Our Prodigal Sons & Daughters. 1999. pap. 18.95 (*1-879639-69-6*) Natl Educ Serv.

Brendtro, Larry K. & Ness, Arlin E. Re-Educating Troubled Youth: Environments for Teaching & Treatment. LC 83-11787. (Modern Applications of Social Work Ser.). 300p. (C). 1983. pap. text 27.95 (*0-202-36034-2*) Aldine de Gruyter.

Brendtro, Larry K., et al. Positive Peer Culture: A Selected Bibliography. xxi, 172p. (Orig.). (C). 1994. pap. text 19.95 (*0-9639084-1-3*) S D A Pub.

Brendtro, Larry K., jt. auth. see Vorrath, Harry H.

Breneman, Anne. Like Pure Gold: The Story of Louis G. Gregory. LC 97-9451. (Illus.). (J). Date not set. 14.95 (*0-87743-704-1*) Bahai.

Breneman, Bren, jt. auth. see Breneman, Lucille N.

Breneman, Dave. ASHE: Finance in Higher Education. 34.00 (*0-536-05553-X*) Pearson Custom.

Breneman, Dave, et al, eds. ASHE Reader on Finance in Higher Education. 2nd ed. (ASHE Reader Ser.). 578p. (C). 1993. pap. text 48.00 (*0-536-58352-8*) Pearson Custom.

Breneman, David & Nelson, Susan C. Financing Community Colleges: An Economic Perspective. LC 81-17042. (Studies in Higher Education Policy). 222p. 1982. 32.95 (*0-8157-1064-X*) Brookings.

Breneman, David W. Liberal Arts Colleges: Thriving, Surviving, or Endangered? 184p. (C). 1994. 34.95 (*0-8157-1062-3*); pap. 14.95 (*0-8157-1061-5*) Brookings.

Breneman, David W. & Finn, Chester E., eds. Public Policy & Private Higher Education. LC 77-91798. (Studies in Higher Education Policy). 468p. 1978. 29.95 (*0-8157-1066-6*) Brookings.

Breneman, James C. Handbook of Food Allergies. (Immunology Ser.: Vol. 29). (Illus.). 320p. 1986. text 175.00 (*0-8247-7558-9*) Dekker.

Breneman, Lucille N. & Breneman, Bren. Once upon a Time: A Storytelling Handbook. LC 83-10990. (Illus.). 208p. 1983. text 27.95 (*0-8304-1007-4*) Burnham Inc.

Breneman, Mary W. The Land They Possessed. 335p. (Orig.). 1991. pap. 9.95 (*0-9632157-1-X*) SD Human Fnd.

Breneman, Mervin. Ezra, Nehemiah, Esther. (New American Commentary Ser.: Vol. 10). 384p. 1993. 27.99 (*0-8054-0110-5*, 4201-10) Broadman.

Brenenfeld, Florence & Brenenfeld, Mickey. Healthy Baking. 1991. 14.95 (*0-930440-33-1*) Royal Hse.

Brenenfeld, Mickey, jt. auth. see Brenenfeld, Florence.

Brener, Anne. Mourning & Mitzvah: A Guided Journal for Walking the Mourner's Path through Grief to Healing. LC 93-16920. 288p. (Orig.). 1993. pap. 19.95 (*1-879045-23-0*) Jewish Lights.

Brener, Milton. Opera Offstage: Passion & Politics Behind the Great Operas. LC 96-52636. (Illus.). 256p. 1997. pap. 15.95 (*0-8065-1866-9*, Citadel Pr) Carol Pub Group.

— Opera Offstage: Passion & Politics Behind the Great Operas. (Illus.). 256p. 1996. 24.95 (*0-8027-1313-0*) Walker & Co.

Brenes, Edin & Patterson, D. H. Conversemos: First Book for Spanish Conversation. (SPA., Illus.). 1942. text 14.00 (*0-89197-112-2*); pap. text 6.95 (*0-89197-714-7*) Irvington.

Brenet, Michel, pseud. Bibliographie des Bibliographies Musicales. LC 73-125065. (Music Ser.). 1971. reprint ed. lib. bdg. 29.50 (*0-306-70002-6*) Da Capo.

— Diccionario de la Musica: Historico y Tecnico. 4th ed. (SPA.). 566p. 1981. 150.00 (*0-7859-5084-2*) Fr & Eur.

— Haydn. LC 72-80497. 155p. 1972. reprint ed. 23.95 (*0-405-08304-1*, Pub. by Blom Pubns) Ayer.

Brengelman, Fred & Leavenworth, Russ. Puddings from A to Z, Vol. 2. LC 96-104409. 62p. 1995. spiral bd. 14.95 (*0-938911-09-0*) Indiv Ed - Poppy Ln.

Brengle, Elizabeth S. Half Hours with My Guide. 144p. 1994. reprint ed. pap. 9.99 (*0-88019-325-5*) Schmul Pub Co.

— What Hinders You? 112p. 1990. reprint ed. 5.95 (*0-86544-059-X*) Salv Army Suppl South.

Brengle, K. G. Principles & Practices of Dryland Farming. LC 80-70691. 190p. reprint ed. pap. 58.90 (*0-8357-5507-X*, 203512200093) Bks Demand.

Brengle, Richard L., jt. ed. see Bicknell, David L.

Brengle, Samuel L. Ancient Prophets & Modern Problems. 1978. reprint ed. pap. 4.95 (*0-86544-000-X*) Salv Army Suppl South.

— Guest of the Soul. 1978. reprint ed. pap. 4.95 (*0-86544-001-8*) Salv Army Suppl South.

— Heart Talks on Holiness. 1979. pap. 5.99 (*0-88019-037-X*) Schmul Pub Co.

— Heart Talks on Holiness. 1978. reprint ed. pap. 4.95 (*0-86544-002-6*) Salv Army Suppl South.

— Helps to Holiness. 1984. pap. 7.99 (*0-88019-038-8*) Schmul Pub Co.

— Helps to Holiness. 1978. reprint ed. pap. 4.95 (*0-86544-003-4*) Salv Army Suppl South.

— Love Slaves. 104p. 1996. pap. 7.99 (*0-88019-352-2*) Schmul Pub Co.

— Love Slaves. 1960. reprint ed. 4.95 (*0-86544-004-2*) Salv Army Suppl South.

— Resurrection Life & Power. pap. 5.99 (*0-88019-156-2*) Schmul Pub Co.

— Resurrection Life & Power. 1978. reprint ed. 4.95 (*0-86544-005-0*) Salv Army Suppl South.

— The Soul Winner's Secret. pap. 5.99 (*0-88019-155-4*) Schmul Pub Co.

— The Soul Winner's Secret. 1978. reprint ed. pap. 4.95 (*0-86544-007-7*) Salv Army Suppl South.

— The Way of Holiness. 1966. reprint ed. 4.95 (*0-86544-008-5*) Salv Army Suppl South.

— When the Holy Ghost Is Come. 1980. reprint ed. pap. 4.95 (*0-86544-009-3*) Salv Army Suppl South.

Brenholz, Avi. Certain Truth. (Orig.). Date not set. pap. 26.00 (*1-889958-01-8*) A Ben Aur.

— One Known As Seven (Zion) Date not set. pap. 26.00 (*1-889958-02-6*) A Ben Aur.

— A Patient's Guide to Backache Relief Acupressure & Medication. (Illus.). 50p. Date not set. pap. 2.48 (*1-889958-03-4*) A Ben Aur.

— A Patient's Guide to Headache Relief Using Acupressure & Medication. (Illus.). 50p. 1995. 2.48 (*1-889958-05-0*) A Ben Aur.

— A Patient's Midnight Guide to Exercise. (Illus.). 50p. Date not set. pap. 2.48 (*1-889958-09-3*) A Ben Aur.

— A Patient's Midnight Guide to Headache Relief Using Acupressure/Shiatsu. (Illus.). 20p. 1995. pap. 1.95 (*1-889958-07-7*) A Ben Aur.

— A Patient's Midnight Guide to Headache Relief Using Nutrition & Acupressure. (Illus.). 20p. 1996. pap. 1.95 (*1-889958-06-9*) A Ben Aur.

— A Patient's Midnight Guide to Nutrition. (Illus.). 50p. Date not set. pap. 2.48 (*1-889958-08-5*) A Ben Aur.

— A Patient's Midnight Guide to Toothache Relief Using Acupressure & Medication. (Illus.). 50p. 1995. pap. 2.48 (*1-889958-04-2*) A Ben Aur.

— Pro Active Healthful Resistance. (Illus.). 148p. 1994. pap. 18.00 (*1-889958-00-X*) A Ben Aur.

Brenig, W. Statistical Theory of Heat. (Illus.). xii, 296p. 1990. 49.95 (*0-387-51036-2*) Spr-Verlag.

Brenigan, Michelle M. Heart & Soil: Agricultural Folklife. (Illus.). 20p. 1997. pap. 5.00 (*1-890327-01-8*) Longwood Ctr.

Brenk, Frederick E. In Mist Apparelled: Religious Themes in Plutarch's Moralia & Lives. LC 78-323948. (Mnemosyne, Bibliotheca Classica Batava Ser.). 306p. 1977. write for info. (*90-04-05241-0*) Brill Academic Pubs.

Brenke, Donald, ed. John Fitzgerald Kennedy on Worldwide Stamps. 40p. 1995. pap. text 8.00 (*0-935991-23-9*) Am Topical Assn.

— Statue of Liberty on Stamps. 32p. 1988. pap. 5.00 (*0-935991-04-2*) Am Topical Assn.

Brenkman, John. Culture & Domination. LC 87-47343. 256p. (C). 1987. pap. 15.95 (*0-8014-9403-6*) Cornell U Pr.

— Straight, Male, Modern: A Cultural Critique of Psychoanalysis. LC 93-14035. 320p. (C). 1993. pap. 22.99 (*0-415-90218-5*, A3974) Routledge.

— Venue 3. 172p. (C). 1997. 10.00 (*90-5701-391-6*) Dist Art Pubs.

— Venue 2. 172p. (C). 1998. pap. 10.00 (*90-5701-381-9*) Dist Art Pubs.

Brenkman, John, ed. Venue 3: Boy/Girl: An International Literary Magazine. 176p. (C). 1998. pap. 10.00 (*90-5701-371-1*) Gordon & Breach.

Brenlove, Milovan S. The Air Traffic System: A Commonsense Guide. LC 87-2663. (Illus.). 170p. 1987. 29.95 (*0-8138-0061-7*) Iowa St U Pr.

— Vectors to Spare: The Life of an Air Traffic Controller. LC 92-45892. (Illus.). 240p. (C). 1993. 29.95 (*0-8138-0471-X*) Iowa St U Pr.

Brenman, Margaret & Gill, Merton M. Hypnotherapy: A Survey of the Literature. (Menninger Foundation Monograph Ser.: No. 5). 303p. (Orig.). 1971. 40.00 (*0-8236-2420-X*); pap. 24.95 (*0-8236-8073-8*, 022420) Intl Univs Pr.

Brenna, Beverley. Daddy Longlegs at Birch Lane. (Smithsonian's Backyard Ser.). (Illus.). 32p. (J). (ps-2). 1996. 15.95 (*1-56899-321-8*) Soundprints.

Brenna, Beverley. Daddy Longlegs at Birch Lane. (Smithsonian's Backyard Ser.). (Illus.). 32p. (J). (ps-2). 1996. 19.95 incl. audio (*1-56899-325-0*, BC5012) Soundprints.

Brenna, Beverley. Daddy Longlegs at Birch Lane. Incl. large toy. (Smithsonian's Backyard Ser.). (Illus.). 32p. (J). (ps-2). 1996. 32.95 (*1-56899-323-4*) Soundprints.

— Daddy Longlegs at Birch Lane, Micro bk. (Smithsonian's Backyard Ser.). (Illus.). 32p. (J). (ps-2). 1996. 4.95 (*1-56899-322-6*) Soundprints.

— Daddy Longlegs at Birch Lane, Micro bk. & small toy. (Smithsonian's Backyard Ser.). (Illus.). 32p. (J). (ps-2). 1996. 12.95 (*1-56899-324-2*) Soundprints.

Brenna, Duff. Too Cool. LC 98-12924. 272p. 1998. 22.95 (*0-385-48971-4*, N A Talese) Doubleday.

***Brenna, Duff.** Too Cool. 272p. 1999. pap. 12.95 (*0-452-28116-4*, Plume) Dutton Plume.

Brenna, Patricia M. Ten-Minute Marketing. 131p. 1997. pap. 48.00 (*1-885750-03-X*, MM97) Visions Communs.

Brennan. Five Theses on the Feminine. (C). 1999. write for info. (*0-415-05236-X*); pap. write for info. (*0-415-05237-8*) Routledge.

— Process Industry Economics. 1998. 75.00 (*0-85295-391-7*, 53917) Gulf Pub.

— Scitech - Sampler. (College ESL). (J). 1995. mass mkt. 15.95 (*0-8384-5638-3*) Heinle & Heinle.

— Scitech Ch18: Preparing Science on the Job. (College ESL Ser.). 1995. pap. 1.95 (*0-8384-6509-9*) Heinle & Heinle.

— Scitech Ch19: Trends in Science & Technology. (College ESL Ser.). 1995. pap. 1.95 (*0-8384-6510-2*) Heinle & Heinle.

— Scitech Ch17: Scientific Education & Training. (College ESL Ser.). 1995. pap. 1.95 (*0-8384-6508-0*) Heinle & Heinle.

— Scitech Ch16: Career Choices - Science & Technology. (College ESL Ser.). 1995. pap. 2.95 (*0-8384-6507-2*) Heinle & Heinle.

— Scitech Ch25: Professional Behavior for the Scientist. (College ESL Ser.). 1995. pap. 1.95 (*0-8384-6516-1*) Heinle & Heinle.

— Scitech Ch21: Skills on the Job. (College ESL Ser.). 1995. pap. 1.95 (*0-8384-6512-9*) Heinle & Heinle.

— Scitech Ch23: The Scientist & the Community. (College ESL Ser.). 1995. pap. 1.95 (*0-8384-6514-5*) Heinle & Heinle.

— Scitech Ch22: Scientist & Technology. (College ESL Ser.). 1995. pap. 1.95 (*0-8384-6513-7*) Heinle & Heinle.

— SciTech Front Matter. (College ESL Ser.). (J). 1996. mass mkt. 1.75 (*0-8384-4119-X*) Heinle & Heinle.

Brennan, Alice. Castle Mirage. large type ed. (Linford Mystery Library). 1991. pap. 16.99 (*0-7089-7029-X*) Ulverscroft.

Brennan, Andrew. Conditions of Identity: A Study in Identity & Survival. (Illus.). 392p. 1988. text 85.00 (*0-19-824974-8*) OUP.

Brennan, Andrew. Thinking about Nature: An Investigation of Nature, Value, & Ecology. LC 88-13977. 256p. 1988. pap. 17.00 (*0-8203-1088-3*) U of Ga Pr.

Brennan, Andrew, ed. The Ethics of the Environment. (International Research Library of Philosophy). 612p. 1995. text 203.95 (*1-85521-348-6*, Pub. by Dartmth Pub) Ashgate Pub Co.

Brennan, Andrew, ed. see Elder, Crawford.

Brennan, Andrew, jt. ed. see Witoszek, Nina.

Brennan, Ann M. & Lander, James F., eds. Second UJNR Tsunami Workshop (1990) Proceedings. (Illus.). 260p. (C). 1997. reprint ed. pap. text 50.00 (*0-7881-3935-5*) DIANE Pub.

Brennan, Ann Marie, ed. see Berle-Carman, Mary, et al.

Brennan, Anne, jt. auth. see Brewi, Janice.

Brennan, Anthony. Henry the Fifth. LC 92-26948. (Twayne's New Critical Introduction to Shakespeare Ser.: No. 16). 224p. 1992. 33.00 (*0-8057-8731-3*); pap. 13.95 (*0-8057-8732-1*) Macmillan.

— Onstage & Offstage Worlds in Shakespeare's Plays. 352p. 1989. 32.50 (*0-685-26089-5*, A3529) Routledge.

— Shakespeare's Dramatic Structures. 224p. 1988. pap. text 14.95 (*0-415-00269-9*) Routledge.

Brennan, Antoinette. Professional Secrets to Nail Art: Expert Nail Art Techniques-What to Use & How to Use It! LC 93-74394. (Illus.). 190p. (Orig.). 1995. pap. 24.95 (*1-884609-19-8*) Alyssa Prince.

Brennan, Barbara A. Hands of Light. LC 87-47892. (New Age Ser.). (Illus.). 320p. 1988. pap. 24.95 (*0-553-34539-7*, New Age Bks) Bantam.

— Light Emerging: The Experience of Healing Through the Human Energy Field. LC 92-31473. 352p. 1993. pap. 24.95 (*0-553-35456-6*) Bantam.

Brennan, Barrie. Continuing Professional Education. (C). 1990. pap. 55.00 (*0-86431-056-0*, Pub. by Aust Council Educ Res) St Mut.

Brennan, Bill. Irish & Scottish Airs & Ballads for Acoustic Guitar: Intermediate Level. 120p. 1997. spiral bd. 22.95 (*0-7866-1795-0*, 95739BCD) Mel Bay.

— Irish, Scottish & Border Melodies for Flatpicking Guitar. 88p. 1998. 19.95 (*0-7866-3472-3*, 95200BCD) Mel Bay.

Brennan, C. E. Rattler Tales from Northcentral Pennsylvania. (Pitt Series in Nature & Natural History). (Illus.). 176p. (C). 1994. pap. 15.95 (*0-8229-5539-3*); text 29.95 (*0-8229-3856-1*) U of Pittsburgh Pr.

Brennan, Carleen & Brennan, Michael. Custody for Fathers. 4th rev. ed. Date not set. pap. 24.95 (0-9644157-0-4) Brennan Pubg.

A Nationally endorsed book that offers positive approaches for fathers caught up in a brutal custody battle. A 300 page guidebook giving fathers 100 Secret Strategies for winning in court. Fathers learn "how to" Conduct Themselves in Mediation, Deal with a Difficult Judge, Execute Winning Strategies, Master Skills of Testifying, Handle Setbacks & Adversity, Use Court Time Wisely & Skillful Linguistic Techniques. Recommended by: Attorneys, Mediators & Fathers Rights Groups across the U.S. Stocked by Ingram Book Co. Call our office for further questions. (949) 646-9842. *Publisher Paid Annotation.*

Brennan, Carol. Chill of Summer. large type ed. LC 95-47916. (Large Print Ser.). 312p. 1995. lib. bdg. 23.95 (*1-57490-030-7*, Beeler LP Bks) T T Beeler.

— Full Commission: A Liz Wareham Mystery. 256p. 1994. pap. 4.50 (*0-425-14467-4*, Prime Crime) Berkley Pub.

— In the Dark. large type ed. LC 95-41265. 288p. 1995. lib. bdg. 23.95 (*1-57490-029-3*, Beeler LP Bks) T T Beeler.

Brennan, Catherine. Max Weber on Power & Social Stratification: An Interpretation & Critique. LC 97-73613. 336p. 1997. text 78.95 (*1-85628-435-2*, Pub. by Ashgate Pub) Ashgate Pub Co.

Brennan, Charles D., Jr. Proactive Customer Service: Transforming Your Customer Service Department into a Profit Center. LC 97-21788. 208p. 1997. 22.95 (*0-8144-0372-7*) AMACOM.

Brennan, Charles D. Proactive Customer Service: Transforming Your Customer Service Department into a Profit Center. LC 97-21788. 1997. write for info. (*0-8144-7943-X*) AMACOM.

— Sales Questions That Close the Sale: How to Uncover Your Customers Real Needs. LC 94-1054. 160p. 1994. pap. 17.95 (*0-8144-7815-8*) AMACOM.

Brennan, Christine. Edge of Glory: The Inside Story of the Quest for Figure Skating's Olympic Gold Medals. LC 98-9519. (Illus.). 336p. 1998. 25.00 (*0-684-84128-2*) Scribner.

***Brennan, Christine.** Edge of Glory: The Inside Story of the Quest for Figure Skating's Olympic Gold Medals. LC 99-204401. (Illus.). 426p. 1999. pap. 13.95 (*0-14-028065-0*) Viking Penguin.

Brennan, Christine. Inside Edge: A Revealing Journey into the Secret World of Figure Skating. LC 96-38832. 352p. 1997. pap. 12.95 (*0-385-48607-3*, Anchor NY) Doubleday.

Brennan, Colm. Pitchcap & Pike. 84p. 1998. pap. 14.95 (*1-901233-18-9*, Pub. by Dedalus) Dufour.

— Pitchcap & Pike. (Illus.). 84p. 1998. 24.95 (*1-901233-19-7*, Pub. by Dedalus) Dufour.

Brennan, D. D., ed. Tunneling Operations & Equipment: Proceedings of a Session Sponsored by the Construction Division. 37p. 1985. 12.00 (*0-87262-483-8*) Am Soc Civil Eng.

Brennan, Dan. One of Our Bombers Is Missing. large type ed. (Magna Large Print Ser.). 336p. 1998. 29.99 (*0-7505-1217-2*, Pub. by Mgna Lrg Print) Ulverscroft.

***Brennan, Dan.** The Sky Remembers. large type ed. 320p. 1999. 31.99 (*0-7505-1351-9*, Pub. by Mgna Lrg Print) Ulverscroft.

Brennan, Dan. Suicide Squadron. large type ed. (Magna Large Print Ser.). 419p. 1998. 29.99 (*0-7505-1216-4*, Pub. by Mgna Lrg Print) Ulverscroft.

***Brennan, Dan.** Winged Victory. large type ed. 480p. 1999. 31.99 (*0-7505-1350-0*, Pub. by Mgna Lrg Print) Ulverscroft.

Brennan, Daniel C. Admission to the New York State Bar: A Compendium of Statutes & Rules. LC 92-61677. 87p. 1992. ring bd. 60.00 (*0-942954-56-4*) NYS Bar.

***Brennan, David.** Annapolis: Capital Gateway to Maryland. (Postcard History Ser.). (Illus.). 128p. 1999. pap. 18.99 (*0-7385-0323-1*) Arcadia Publng.

Brennan, Deborah. The Politics of Australian Child Care: Philanthropy to Feminism & Beyond. rev. ed. LC 97-52187. (Illus.). 272p. (C). 1998. pap. text 24.95 (*0-521-63510-1*) Cambridge U Pr.

Brennan, Dick, jt. auth. see Brennan, Ella.

Brennan, E. James. Performance Management Workbook. 512p. (C). 1989. text 69.95 (*0-13-658634-1*) P-H.

Brennan, Ed & Weng, Larry. The PE Informant: Your Personal Guide to Becoming a Professional Engineer. 2nd ed. Perry, Susan, ed. (Illus.). 150p. (C). 1998. pap. text 19.95 (*0-9663795-0-0*) Avalon Pr PA.

Brennan, Edward. The Radical Reform of Christianity: A Focus on Catholicism. LC 94-71182. (Church & the World Ser.: Vol. 7). 235p. (Orig.). 1994. pap. 19.95 (0-940121-27-1, P208, Cross Roads Bks) Cross Cultural Pubns.

The purpose & argument of this book is to free the essence of Christian teaching from the historical & cultural limitations to which it has become bound. It challenges intelligent & open-minded Christians to work toward a Christianity free of accustomed but inessential constraints. This book is a gift to all who care about the great traditions of Catholicism. It opens new vistas into which the Church can move in the next millennium. *Publisher Paid Annotation.*

Brennan, Eilis, et al. Nationalism & Unionism: Ireland & British Politics in the Late 19th & Early 20th Centuries. (Irish History in Perspective Ser.). (Illus.). 80p. (C). 1996. pap. 13.95 (*0-521-46605-9*) Cambridge U Pr.

Brennan, Elizabeth, ed. see Webster, John.

Brennan, Elizabeth A. & Clarage, Elizabeth C. Who's Who of Pulitzer Prize Winners. (Illus.). 720p. 1998. 69.00 (*1-57356-111-8*) Oryx Pr.

Brennan, Elizabeth M., ed. see Dickens, Charles.

Brennan, Elizabeth M., ed. see Webster, John.

Brennan, Elizabeth M., ed. & intro. see Dickens, Charles.

Brennan, Elizabeth V. A Singing Wind: Songs & Melodies from Ecuador. rev. ed. (ENG & SPA., Illus.). 48p. 1996. pap. 12.95 incl. audio (*0-937203-60-2*) World Music Pr.

An Asterisk (*) at the beginning of an entry indicates that the title is appearing for the first time.

Brennan, Ella & Brennan, Dick. The Commander's Palace New Orleans Cookbook. (Illus.). 224p. 1984. 25.00 (*0-517-55049-0*) C Potter.

Brennan, Ellen & Brennan, Theodore. Sugar Less for Life! Cookbook & Easy Guide by the Famous Family of Good Food. Orig. Title: Sugar Bust for Life!. (Illus.). 355p. 1998. pap. 14.95 (*0-9663519-1-6*) Shamrock Publ.

***Brennan, Ellen C. & Brennan, Theodore. Sugar Bust for Life!... With the Brennans, Pt. II. 360p. 2000. pap. 14.95 (*0-9663519-2-4*) Shamrock Publ.**

SUGAR BUST FOR LIFE! ... with the Brennans Part II is the Brennans' response to the many Sugar Busters dieters in need of additional recipes & helpful information found in the original best-selling Sugar Bust for Life!. The book includes over 300 new recipes, easy one-dish meals, & updated shopper's brand name guide, new menus, wine list, suggested guidelines & tips for success. Ellen C. Brennan was the foreword, publishing consultant, distribution & sales coordinator for the original edition of Sugar Busters for Life! ... Cut Sugar to Trim Fat, which sold over 200,000 copies. Sugar Bust for Life! ... with the Brennans Part II is a second cookbook & companion guide for an easy, healthy, meal plan. Theodore M. Brennan is co-owner of world famous Brennan's Restaurant in New Orleans & a co-author of the cookbook, Breakfast at Brennan's & Dinner Too. With his wife, Ellen he has blended quality & taste in Sugar Busting recipes that are lacking in unhealthy high glycemic carbohydrates & refined sugar but not in satisfying the most discriminating palates. Sugar Bust for Life! ... with the Brennans Part II is based on the diet principles found in Sugar Busters! Cut Sugar to Trim Fat. This book is not sponsored, affiliated or endorsed by Sugar Busters LLC. The validity of Sugar Busters LLC's claim of federal trademark rights in the term "Sugar Busters" is acknowledged. Ted & Ellen, surrounded by dining opportunities, understand the challenge of Sugar Busters lifestyle & have wisely adjusted their eating habits to maintain their good health. They have taken the guesswork out of making wise choices without relying on counting calories or fat grams. You will discover a new way to eat right, while eating well. Sugar Bust for Life! ... with the Brennans Part II unfolds an easy road to a healthful life for you. ***Publisher Paid Annotation.***

Brennan, Ellen C. & Brennan, Theodore M. Sugar Bust for Life! Cookbook & Companion Guide by the Famous Family of Good Food. 355p. 1998. 14.95 (*0-9663519-0-8*) Shamrock Publ.

Sugar Bust for Life! ... with the Brennans has sold over 150,000 copies. Containing over 400 low sugar recipes, menus, red wine list, shopper's brand name guide, tips for success & more, this helpful cookbook & companion guide is based on the diet principles found in Sugar Busters! Cut Sugar to Trim Fat. Sugar Bust for Life! is the Brennans' response to the many people who need help in implementing the Sugar Busters diet. Ellen C. Brennan was the author of the foreword, publishing consultant, distribution & sales coordinator for the original edition of Sugar Busters! Cut Sugar to Trim Fat, which sold over 200,000 copies. As a result of her initial involvement in the Sugar Busters endeavor, Ellen is eager to share her knowledge of a healthy, low-sugar lifestyle in Sugar Bust for Life!. Theodore M. Brennan is co-owner of the world famous Brennan's Restaurant in New Orleans & co-author of the cookbook, Breakfast at Brennan's & Dinner, Too. Ted shares with you some of Brennan's gastronomic secrets so that you may recreate these very dishes in your own kitchen as you Sugar Bust For Life!. Ellen & Ted have adapted Brennan's recipes to a low sugar lifestyle by eliminating all high glycemic carbohydrates & refined sugar while still maintaining quality & taste. The Brennans have put all their acquired knowledge into a guide to make it easy to follow a healthy meal plan. Sugar Bust For Life! provides an easy way of eating without having to rely on counting calories or fat grams. There are easy menu plans from "soup to nuts," tasty desserts, as well as a suggested red wine list to complement your meal. Although based on the diet principles found in Sugar Busters! Cut Sugar to Trim Fat, this book is not sponsored, affiliated or endorsed by Sugar Busters LLC. The validity of Sugar Busters LLC's claim of federal trademark rights in the term "Sugar Busters" is acknowledged. ***Publisher Paid Annotation.***

Brennan, Ethel. Herbes de Provence: Cooking with the Herbs of Southern France. LC 97-47107. (Artful Kitchen Ser.). (Illus.). 72p. 1999. 12.95 (*0-8118-1933-7*) Chronicle Bks.

Brennan, Ethel & Brennan, Georgeanne. Goat Cheese: 30 Delectable Recipes. LC 96-28039. 1997. 9.95 (*0-8118-1239-1*) Chronicle Bks.

Brennan, Ethel, jt. auth. see Brennan, Georgeanne.

Brennan, Frances C., jt. auth. see Burack-Weiss, Ann.

Brennan, Frank. Does Australia Need a Bill of Rights? LC 98-212725. 1998. pap. 19.95 (*0-7022-3011-1*, Pub. by Univ Queensland Pr) Intl Spec Bk.

— One Land, One Nation. 1995. pap. 18.95 (*0-7022-2729-3*, Pub. by Univ Queensland Pr) Intl Spec Bk.

Brennan, Frank, ed. Wik Debate: The Case for Aborigines, Pastoralists, & Miners. 96p. 1998. pap. 9.95 (*0-86840-409-8*, Pub. by New South Wales Univ Pr) Intl Spec Bk.

Brennan, Frank, Jr., jt. auth. see Brennan, Peggy.

Brennan, G. & Buchanan, James M. The Power to Tax. LC 79-56862. (Illus.). 256p. 1980. text 59.95 (*0-521-23329-1*) Cambridge U Pr.

Brennan, G., et al. Taxation & Fiscal Federalism: Essays in Honour of Russell Mathews. 320p. 1988. 20.00 (*0-08-034401-1*, Pergamon Pr) Elsevier.

Brennan, Gail, jt. auth. see Clare, John.

Brennan, Gale. Earl the Squirrel. (Illus.). 16p. (Orig.). (J). (gr. k-6). 1981. pap. 1.25 (*0-685-02455-5*) Brennan Bks.

— Toulouse the Mouse. (Illus.). 16p. (Orig.). (J). (gr. k-6). 1981. pap. 1.25 (*0-685-02458-X*) Brennan Bks.

Brennan, Gale, jt. auth. see LaFleur, Tom.

***Brennan, Geoffrey & Buchanan, James M.** The Power to Tax: Analytical Foundations of a Fiscal Constitution. LC 99-24061. (Collected Works of James M. Buchanan : Vol. 9). 2000. 20.00 (*0-86597-229-X*); pap. 12.00 (*0-86597-230-3*) Liberty Fund.

— The Reason of Rules: Constitutional Political Economy. LC 99-24060. (Collected Works of James M. Buchanan : Vol. 10). 2000. 20.00 (*0-86597-231-1*); pap. 12.00 (*0-86597-232-X*) Liberty Fund.

***Brennan, Geoffrey & Hamlin, Alan.** Democratic Devices & Desires. (Theories of Institutional Design Ser.). (Illus.). 280p. 2000. 54.95 (*0-521-63020-7*); pap. 22.95 (*0-521-63977-8*) Cambridge U Pr.

Brennan, George, jt. auth. see Milward, Alan S.

Brennan, Georgeanne. Aperitif: Recipes for Simple Pleasures in the French Style. LC 96-28037. 1997. 24.95 (*0-8118-1077-1*) Chronicle Bks.

— Backyard Bouquets: Growing Great Flowers for Simple Arrangements. LC 97-9337. (Illus.). 144p. 1998. pap. 18.95 (*0-8118-1413-0*) Chronicle Bks.

— Casual Outdoor Dining. LC 97-25662. (Williams-Sonoma Lifestyles Ser.). (Illus.). 112p. (YA). (gr. 11). 1999. 14.95 (*0-7835-4613-0*) Time-Life.

— Cooking from the Farmers' Market. Williams, Chuck, ed. LC 98-35969. (Williams-Sonoma Lifestyles Ser.). (Illus.). 112p. (J). (gr. 7). 1999. 14.95 (*0-7370-2013-X*) T-L Custom Pub.

— Easy Roses: Simple Secrets for Glorious Gardens, Indoors & Out. LC 94-13123. (Illus.). 108p. 1995. pap. 12.95 (*0-8118-0749-5*) Chronicle Bks.

***Brennan, Georgeanne.** Family Table: A Journal for Recipes & Memories. 2000. 18.95 (*0-8118-2412-8*) Chronicle Bks.

Brennan, Georgeanne. The Food & Flavors of Haute Provence. LC 97-11389. 336p. 1997. 24.95 (*0-8118-1235-9*) Chronicle Bks.

— Fragrant Flowers: Simple Secrets for Glorious Gardens - Indoors & Out: A Garden Style Book. LC 93-8863. (Illus.). 96p. 1994. pap. 12.95 (*0-8118-0553-0*) Chronicle Bks.

— Garden Dreams: A Scrapbook for Gardeners. (Illus.). 144p. 1999. 19.95 (*0-8118-1684-2*) Chronicle Bks.

***Brennan, Georgeanne.** Holiday Eggs: A Collection of Inspired Recipes, Gifts & Decorations. LC 98-34244. (Holiday Ser.). (Illus.). 112p. 1999. 14.98 (*0-7651-0814-3*) Smithmark.

— Holiday Fruit: A Collection of Inspired Recipes, Gifts & Decorations. LC 99-13385. (Holiday Ser.). (Illus.). 112p. 1999. 14.98 (*0-7651-1662-6*) Smithmark.

— Holiday Pumpkins: A Collection of Inspired Recipes, Gifts & Decorations. LC 98-3363. (Illus.). 112p. 1998. 14.98 (*0-7651-0815-1*) Smithmark.

— Holiday Sweets: A Collection of Inspired Recipes, Gifts & Decorations. LC 99-18271. (Holiday Ser.). (Illus.). 112p. 1999. 14.98 (*0-7651-1663-4*) Smithmark.

Brennan, Georgeanne. In the French Kitchen Garden: The Joys of Cultivating a Potager. LC 97-50335. (Illus.). 120p. 1998. 18.95 (*0-8118-2034-3*) Chronicle Bks.

***Brennan, Georgeanne.** The Mediterranean Herb Cookbook: Fresh & Savory Recipes from the Mediterranean Garden. LC 99-40462. (Illus.). 156p. 2000. pap. 22.95 (*0-8118-1990-6*) Chronicle Bks.

Brennan, Georgeanne. Peppers Hot & Chili. 1988. pap. 9.95 (*0-943186-28-5*) Aris Bks.

— The Vegetarian Table: France. LC 95-12941. (Illus.). 144p. 1995. 22.95 (*0-8118-0474-7*) Chronicle Bks.

Brennan, Georgeanne & Brennan, Ethel. The Children's Kitchen Garden: A Book of Gardening, Cooking & Learning. LC 96-52023. (Illus.). 144p. (J). (gr. 2-7). 1997. pap. 16.95 (*0-89815-873-7*) Ten Speed Pr.

Brennan, Georgeanne & Kleinman, Kathryn. Flowerkeeping: The Lore & Craft of Preserving & Decorating with Dried Flowers. (Illus.). 144p. 1999. pap. text 17.95 (*1-58008-054-5*) Ten Speed Pr.

— The Glass Pantry: Preserving Seasonal Flavors. LC 93-15957. (Illus.). 144p. 1994. 29.95 (*0-8118-0388-0*); pap. 18.95 (*0-8118-0393-7*) Chronicle Bks.

Brennan, Georgeanne & Luebbermann, Mimi. Beautiful Bulbs: Simple Secrets for Glorious Gardens - Indoors & Out. LC 92-27695. (Garden Style Ser.). (Illus.). 96p. 1993. pap. 12.95 (*0-8118-0223-X*) Chronicle Bks.

Brennan, Georgeanne & Luebbermann, Mimi. Little Herb Gardens: Simple Solutions for Great Gardens - Indoors & Out. LC 92-25637. (Illus.). 96p. 1993. pap. 12.95 (*0-8118-0249-3*) Chronicle Bks.

Brennan, Georgeanne & Vaughan, John. Potager: Fresh Garden Cooking in the French Style. (Illus.). 144p. 1992. pap. 19.95 (*0-8118-0127-6*) Chronicle Bks.

Brennan, Georgeanne & Vaughn, John. Potager: Fresh Garden Cooking in the French Style. (Illus.). 144p. 1992. 29.95 (*0-8118-0134-9*) Chronicle Bks.

Brennan, Georgeanne, et al. The American Vegetable Cookbook: The Definitive Guide to America's Exotic & Traditional Vegetables. LC 85-14766. (Illus.). 225p. (Orig.). 1985. 24.95 (*0-943186-24-2*); pap. 14.95 (*0-943186-25-0*) Aris Bks.

— The New American Vegetable Cookbook. write for info. (*0-318-59647-4*) S&S Trade.

Brennan, Georgeanne, jt. auth. see Brennan, Ethel.

Brennan, Gerald. Classical Records: Starting Your Collection. LC 83-70327. 112p. (Orig.). 1983. pap. 6.95 (*0-89708-116-1*) And Bks.

Brennan, Gerald T. Angel Food for Boys & Girls, Vol. I. 125p. (YA). (gr. 5-8). 1997. reprint ed. 14.00 (*0-911845-66-6*) Neumann Pr.

— Angel Food for Boys & Girls, Vol. II. 126p. (YA). (gr. 5-8). 1997. reprint ed. 14.00 (*0-911845-67-4*) Neumann Pr.

Brennan, H. G. & Lomasky, Loren E., eds. Democracy & Decision: The Pure Theory of Electoral Preference. 249p. 1997. pap. text 21.95 (*0-521-58524-4*) Cambridge U Pr.

Brennan, H. Geoffrey & Waterman, A. M., eds. Economics & Religion: Are They Distinct? LC 93-50649. (Recent Economic Thought Ser.). 304p. (C). 1994. lib. bdg. 120.00 (*0-7923-9443-7*) Kluwer Academic.

Brennan, H. George. Aesthetic Facial Surgery: A Clinical & Surgical Atlas. 304p. 1990. text 205.00 (*0-88167-642-X*) Lppncott W & W.

Brennan, Harold G. & Lomasky, Loren E., eds. Democracy & Decision: The Pure Theory of Electoral Preference. (Illus.). 248p. (C). 1989. text 64.95 (*0-521-35043-3*) Cambridge U Pr.

Brennan, Heidi L., et al, eds. Discovering Motherhood. LC 91-43333. (Illus.). 82p. (Orig.). 1991. pap. 9.95 (*0-9631188-0-3*) Mothers at Home.

***Brennan, Herbie.** Atlantis Enigma. 256p. 2000. mass mkt. 6.99 (*0-425-17504-9*) Berkley Pub.

— Eddie the Duck. (Illus.). 64p. (J). pap. 7.95 (*0-14-038632-7*, Pub. by Pnguin Bks Ltd) Trafalgar.

— The Little Book of Nostradamus: Prophecies for the 21st Century. 2000. pap. 8.95 (*0-7225-3984-3*, Pub. by Thorsons PA) HarpC.

— Martian Genesis: The Extraterrestrial Origins of the Human Race. 272p. 2000. mass mkt. 6.50 (*0-440-23557-X*) Dell.

Brennan, Herbie. The Mystery Machine. LC 94-4185. (Illus.). 96p. (J). (gr. 4-7). 1995. per. 14.00 (*0-689-50615-5*) McElderry Bks.

Brennan, Howard & Cherryholmes, J. Edward. One Day in Dallas: The Only Eyewitness Who Saw Lee Harvey Oswald Shoot John F. Kennedy. (Illus.). 224p. 1998. 28.95 (*0-89896-331-1*) Larksdale.

Brennan, Irene J., ed. Fort Mojave, Eighteen Fifty-Nine to Eighteen Ninety: Letter of the Commanding Officers. (Illus.). 222p. (Orig.). 1980. pap. text 36.95 (*0-89126-083-8*) MA-AH Pub.

Brennan, J. G. Food Dehydration: A Dictionary & Guide. LC 94-3051. (Food Control Ser.). 176p. 1994. text 130.00 (*0-7506-1130-8*) Buttrwrth-Heinemann.

Brennan, J. G. Food Dehydration: A Dictionary & Guide. 1994. text 126.00 (*1-85573-360-9*, Pub. by Woodhead Pubng) Am Educ Systs.

Brennan, J. H. Discover Your Past Lives: A Practical Course. LC 93-44450. Orig. Title: Discover Reincarnation. (Illus.). 160p. 1994. reprint ed. pap. 9.95 (*0-8069-0642-1*) Sterling.

***Brennan, J. H.** The Magical I Ching. LC 00-24132 (Illus.). 264p. 2000. pap. 14.95 (*1-56718-087-6*) Llewellyn Pubns.

Brennan, J. H. Nightmares: Terrifying Tales from Beyond the Grave. 144p. 1996. pap. 8.95 (*1-85371-632-4*, Pub. by Poolbeg Pr) Dufour.

— Shiva: An Adventure of the Ice Age. LC 89-77654. 192p. (J). (gr. 5 up). 1990. 13.95 (*0-397-32453-7*) HarpC Child Bks.

— Shiva Accused: An Adventure of the Ice Age. LC 90-25888. 288p. (J). (gr. 5 up). 1991. lib. bdg. 16.89 (*0-06-020742-6*) HarpC Child Bks.

— Shiva Accused: An Adventure of the Ice Age. LC 90-25888. (Trophy Bk.). 288p. (J). (gr. 5 up). 1993. pap. 4.95 (*0-06-440431-5*, HarpTrophy) HarpC Child Bks.

— Shiva's Challenge: An Adventure of the Ice Age. LC 91-40676. 224p. (J). (gr. 5 up). 1992. 17.00 (*0-06-020825-2*) HarpC Child Bks.

— Shiva's Challenge: An Adventure of the Ice Age. LC 91-40676. 224p. (YA). (gr. 5 up). 1992. lib. bdg. 16.89 (*0-06-020826-0*) HarpC Child Bks.

— Shiva's Challenge: An Adventure of the Ice Age. LC 91-40676. (Trophy Bk.). 224p. (J). (gr. 5 up). 1993. pap. 4.95 (*0-06-440460-9*, HarpTrophy) HarpC Child Bks.

— Time Travel: A New Perspective. (Illus.). 224p. (Orig.). 1999. pap. 12.95 (*1-56718-085-X*) Llewellyn Pubns.

Brennan, J. L. Students, Courses & Jobs: The Relationship Between Higher Education & the Labour Market. (Higher Education Policy Ser.: No. 21). 204p. 1993. 55.00 (*1-85302-538-0*) Taylor & Francis.

— What Kind of University. LC 98-55540. 258p. 1999. 120.00 (*0-335-20429-5*) Taylor & Francis.

Brennan, J. William. Regina: An Illustrated History. 224p. 34.95 (*1-55028-250-6*, Pub. by J Lorimer) Formac Dist Ltd.

***Brennan, Jack.** No Quarter, 1 vol. 1999. mass mkt. 5.99 (*0-425-17115-9*) Berkley Pub.

Brennan, James. Activities for the Mind: Memories, Dreams, & Thoughts Revisited. (Illus.). 253p. 1991. 53.50 (*0-929442-09-1*, 2217pp) Prof Prnting & Pub.

— History at a Glance. (Illus.). 153p. 1992. 33.50 (*0-929442-12-1*, 2218pp) Prof Prnting & Pub.

— Marketing for Profitable Results. 1992. 53.00 (*0-929442-10-5*, 2220PP) Prof Prnting & Pub.

Brennan, James. Region & Nation: Politics Economy & Society Twentieth Century. text. write for info. (*0-312-23144-X*) St Martin.

Brennan, James A. Mermaid's Log. Davis, Lisa & Chimera, Mary A., eds. (Illus.). 224p. (Orig.). 1996. pap. 15.95 (*0-9652907-4-3*) J M Brennan.

Brennan, James F. History & Systems of Psychology. 5th ed. LC 97-7922. 374p. 1997. 67.00 (*0-13-857418-9*) P-H.

— Reader: History & Systems of Psychology. 2nd ed. LC 97-7923. 280p. 1997. pap. text 27.60 (*0-13-626797-1*) P-H.

— The Reflection of the Dreyfus Affair in the European Press, 1897-1899. LC 98-9312. (Studies in Modern European History: Vol. 25). IX, 521p. (C). 1998. 68.95 (*0-8204-3844-8*) P Lang Pubng.

Brennan, James F., ed. see Jackson, Creed D.

Brennan, James H. The Astral Projection Workbook. LC 89-29668. (Workbook Ser.). (Illus.). 160p. (Orig.). 1990. pap. 14.95 (*0-8069-7306-4*) Sterling.

Brennan, James P. The Labor Wars in Cordoba, 1955-1976: Ideology, Work, & Labor Politics in an Argentine Industrial City. LC 93-46839. (Harvard Historical Studies: No. 116). 448p. (C). 1994. text 59.95 (*0-674-50851-3*, BRELAB) HUP.

Brennan, James P., et al, eds. Peronism & Argentina. LC 97-46486. (Latin American Silhouette Ser.). 232p. (C). 1998. 50.00 (*0-8420-2706-8*) Scholarly Res Inc.

Brennan, James R. Warranties: Planning Analysis & Implementation. LC 94-4631. 335p. 1992. 49.00 (*0-07-007567-0*) McGraw.

Brennan, Jan. Born Two-Gether. (Illus.). 40p. (Orig.). (J). (ps-2). 1984. pap. 5.95 (*0-9613536-1-9*) J & L Bks.

— Treasured Time with Fives to Tens. LC 97-28820. 1997. pap. text 14.95 (*0-87483-501-1*) August Hse.

— Treasured Time with Your Toddler: A Monthly Guide to Activities. (Illus.). 208p. 1991. pap. 14.95 (*0-87483-127-X*) August Hse.

Brennan, Jeannie I., jt. auth. see Brennan, Robert E.

Brennan, Jennifer. Cuisines of Asia: Nine Great Oriental Cuisines by Technique. (Illus.). 1989. pap. 16.95 (*0-312-66116-9*) St Martin.

— Curries & Bugles: A Memoir & Cookbook of the British Raj. (Illus.). 344p. 2000. pap. 24.95 (*962-593-818-4*) Tuttle Pubng.

— My Illinois Garden: A Gardener's Journal. (Illus.). 128p. 2000. spiral bd. 19.95 (*1-930604-07-6*) Cool Springs Pr.

— Tradewinds & Coconuts: A Reminiscence & Recipes from the Pacific Islands. (Illus.). 344p. 2000. 34.95 (*962-593-819-2*) Tuttle Pubng.

Brennan, J.H. Magic for Beginners: The Power to Change Your World. LC 97-48970. (Llewellyn's for Beginners Ser.). (Illus.). 317p. (Orig.). 1998. pap. 9.95 (*1-56718-086-8*) Llewellyn Pubns.

Brennan, Jill W. Gun Control in the 1990's. 170p. (Orig.). (YA). (gr. 9-12). 1996. pap. 7.95 (*1-57515-093-X*) PPI Pubng.

— Terrorism: Threat & Response. 73p. (YA). (gr. 7-12). 1992. pap. 6.95 (*1-57515-010-7*) PPI Pubng.

Brennan, Jim. Point to the Future: A Principal's Technology Planning Guide. LC 98-194955. 70p. 1997. pap. 12.00 (*1-55833-197-2*) Natl Cath Educ.

— The Road to Success: An Orientation Process for Catholic School Teachers. (Illus.). 52p. (Orig.). 1995. pap. 9.00 (*1-55833-149-2*) Natl Cath Educ.

Brennan, John. Christ, the One Sent. LC 96-40324. 192p. (Orig.). 1997. pap. 15.95 (*0-8146-2445-6*) Liturgical Pr.

Brennan, John, et al, eds. Standards & Quality in Higher Education. (Higher Education Policy Ser.: No. 37). 240p. 1997. pap. 34.95 (*1-85302-423-6*, Pub. by Jessica Kingsley) Taylor & Francis.

Brennan, John, et al. Higher Education & Work. (Higher Education Policy Ser.: No. 23). 250p. 1995. 49.95 (*1-85302-537-2*, Pub. by Jessica Kingsley) Taylor & Francis.

Brennan, John, jt. auth. see Silver, Harold.

Brennan, John M., ed. Buying Guide to California Wines. 3rd ed. (Illus.). 1986. 29.95 (*0-916040-53-4*) Wine Consul Calif.

Brennan, John P. Christian Mission in a Pluralistic World. 144p. (C). 1990. 55.00 (*0-85439-326-9*, Pub. by St Paul Pubns) St Mut.

Brennan, Joseph. Duke: The Life of Duke Kahanamoku. 296p. (Orig.). (YA). (gr. 7-10). 1994. 22.95 (*0-914916-96-3*); pap. 17.95 (*0-914916-97-1*) Ku Paa.

— The Kingdom of Darkness. (Illus.). 95p. 1991. 9.95 (*0-925417-01-7*) Acadian Hse Pub.

— Paniolo. 1995. reprint ed. pap. 9.95 (*0-914916-39-4*) Ku Paa.

— The Parker Ranch. pap. 4.95 (*0-686-79501-6*, PBN 5102) HarpC.

— Social Conditions in Industrial Rhode Island Eighteen

B

Twenty to Eighteen Sixty. LC 78-14597. (Perspectives in American History Ser.: No. 41). ix, 181p. 1978. reprint ed. lib. bdg. 35.00 (*0-87991-365-7*) Porcupine Pr.

Brennan, Joseph P. The Adventures of Lucius Leffing. (Illus.). 1989. 30.00 (*0-937986-95-X*) D M Grant.

— Look Back on Laurel Hills. (Illus.). 54p. (Orig.). 1989. 30.00 (*0-9618918-1-5*); pap. 8.00 (*0-9618918-2-3*) Jwindz Pub.

— Sixty Selected Poems. LC 84-62734. (Illus.). 80p. 1985. 15.00 (*0-932445-11-X*); pap. 5.00 (*0-932445-10-1*) Ganley Pub.

Brennan, Joseph T., jt. auth. see Jackson, Kent S.

Brennan, Karen. Here on Earth. LC 87-36443. (Wesleyan New Poets Ser.). 58p. 1988. pap. 12.95 (*0-8195-1156-0*, Wesleyan Univ Pr); text 25.00 (*0-8195-2155-8*, Wesleyan Univ Pr) U Pr of New Eng.

Brennan, Ken. Rope Rescue for Firefighting. LC 98-2756. 1998. pap. 37.50 (*0-912212-61-6*) Fire Eng.

Brennan, Kevin F. The Physics of Semiconductors: With Applications to Optoelectronic Devices. LC 98-29503. (Illus.). 784p. (C). 1999. text 120.00 (*0-521-59350-6*) Cambridge U Pr.

— The Physics of Semiconductors: With Applications to Optoelectronic Devices. (Studies in Semiconductor Physics & Microelectronic Engineering). (Illus.). 784p. (C). 1999. pap. text 54.95 (*0-521-59662-9*) Cambridge U Pr.

Brennan, Kristine. Scott Hamilton: Figure Skater. LC 98-37285. (Overcoming Adversity Ser.). (Illus.). 128p. (YA). (gr. 4-7). 1999. pap. 9.95 (*0-7910-4945-0*) Chelsea Hse.

— Scott Hamilton: Figure Skater. LC 98-37285. (Overcoming Adversity Ser.). (Illus.). 128p. (YA). (gr. 5 up). 1999. lib. bdg. 19.95 (*0-7910-4944-2*) Chelsea Hse.

***Brennan, Kristine.** Sir Edmund Hillary. (Explorers of the New Worlds Ser.). 2000. 17.95 (*0-7910-5953-7*) Chelsea Hse.

— Sir Edmund Hillary. (Explorers of the New Worlds Ser.). (Illus.). 2000. pap. 8.95 (*0-7910-6163-9*) Chelsea Hse.

— Stock Market Crash of 1929. LC 99-41974. (Great Disasters Ser.). (Illus.). 128p. 2000. 19.95 (*0-7910-5268-0*) Chelsea Hse.

Brennan, Lawrence. Resumes for Better Jobs. 6th ed. 224p. 1994. pap. 10.00 (*0-671-89195-2*) P-H.

Brennan, Lawrence D., et al. Resumes for Better Jobs. 5th ed. 224p. 1992. pap. 9.00 (*0-13-773615-0*, Arco) Macmillan Gen Ref.

***Brennan, Lilli & Helwig, Suzanne.** Designing in Wire! Project Book One. 34p. 1999. write for info. (*0-9650784-3-4*) Helwig Industries.

Brennan, Linda. Welsh Springer Spaniel: AKC Rank No. 117. (Rare Breed Ser.). (Illus.). 96p. 1997. 19.95 (*0-7938-0762-X*, RX-112) TFH Pubns.

Brennan, Linda Crotta. Flannel Kisses. LC 96-2997. (Illus.). 32p. (J). (ps-3). 1997. 16.00 (*0-395-73681-1*) HM.

***Brennan, Linda Crotta.** Marshmellow Kisses. LC 99-36271. (Illus.). 32p. (J). 2000. 15.00 (*0-395-73872-5*) HM.

Brennan, Lisa M. Expression of the Wind. 14p. (Orig.). 1996. pap. 9.95 (*1-885206-38-0*, Iliad Pr) Cader Pubng.

— Read Me a Poem. unabridged ed. 82p. 1999. pap. 12.00 (*0-921249-07-1*) Tyro Publ.

Brennan, Liz. Sewing Her Hand to the Face of the Fleeting. LC 99-185367. 28p. 1998. pap. 4.00 (*0-9656161-3-4*) Quale Pr.

***Brennan, Lynne, et al.** Trade Secrets Practice in California - 12/99 Update. 2nd ed. Brown, Wendy L., ed. LC 96-86519. 476p. 1999. ring bd. 60.00 (*0-7626-0381-X*, BU-32593) Cont Ed Bar-CA.

Brennan, M. F., jt. auth. see Blumgart, L. H.

Brennan, M. H. & Millar, D. D., eds. Today's Science, Tomorrow's Technology. (Illus.). 161p. 1989. pap. text 21.95 (*0-08-040067-1*) Elsevier.

Brennan, M. Rose. Intellectual Virtues According to the Philosophy of St. Thomas. xii, 188p. (C). 1957. pap. text 8.95 (*0-87015-075-8*) Pacific Bks.

Brennan, Maeve. The Long-Winded Lady: Notes from the New Yorker. LC 98-7925. 288p. 1998. pap. 13.00 (*0-395-89363-1*) HM.

***Brennan, Maeve.** The Rose Garden: Short Stories. LC 99-45921. 320p. 1999. text 23.00 (*1-58243-050-0*, Pub. by Counterpt DC) HarpC.

Brennan, Maeve. The Springs of Affection: Stories of Dublin. LC 97-18296. 358p. 1997. 24.00 (*0-395-87046-1*) HM.

— The Springs of Affection: Stories of Dublin. 368p. 1998. pap. 13.00 (*0-395-93759-0*) HM.

***Brennan, Maeve.** The Visitor. 112p. 2000. 18.00 (*1-58243-083-7*, Pub. by Counterpt DC) HarpC.

***Brennan, Maire.** God of Peace Gift Set. 2000. 24.99 (*0-8423-3874-8*) Tyndale Hse.

Brennan, Malcolm. Martyrs of the English Reformation. 174p. (Orig.). 1991. pap. text 9.95 (*0-935952-85-3*) Angelus Pr.

Brennan, Marie, jt. auth. see Popkewitz, Thomas S.

Brennan, Marie, jt. ed. see Popkewitz, Thomas S.

Brennan, Mark, jt. auth. see Cantor, Marjorie H.

Brennan, Martin. Hidden Maya: Understanding Maya Glyphs Through Native American Handsigns. LC 97-42434. (Illus.). 300p. (Orig.). 1998. pap. 20.00 (*1-879181-24-X*) Bear & Co.

— The Stones of Time: Calendars, Sundials, & Stone Chambers of Ancient Ireland. LC 94-4016. (Illus.). 216p. 1994. pap. 19.95 (*0-89281-509-4*) Inner Tradit.

Brennan, Mary. Show Me How: A Manual for Parents of Preschool Visually Impaired & Blind Children. 56p. 1982. pap. 12.95 (*0-89128-113-4*) Am Foun Blind.

Brennan, Mary, ed. see Mayes, Donald S.

Brennan, Mary, ed. see Pardue, Diana.

Brennan, Mary, tr. see Erigena, Johannes Scotus.

Brennan, Mary C. Turning Right in the Sixties: The Conservative Capture of the GOP. LC 95-11799. 224p. 1995. 18.95 (*0-8078-2230-2*) U of NC Pr.

Brennan, Mary E., ed. Public Employees Conference, Dec. 7-10, 1980, Monterey, CA: Proceedings. Incl. Public Employees Conference Proceedings, Nov. 11-14, 1981, Williamsburg. 119p. (Orig.). 1982. pap. 10.00 (*0-89154-173-X*); 114p. (Orig.). 1981. Set pap. 10.00 (*0-89154-151-9*) Intl Found Employ.

Brennan, Mary E., ed. see Harker, Carlton.

Brennan, Mary E., ed. see Horn, Mary E.

Brennan, Mary E., ed. see Johnson, Richard E.

Brennan, Mary E., ed. see McCarthy, John T.

Brennan, Mary E., ed. see Mitzner, Ira R.

Brennan, Mary E., ed. see Sahin, Izzet.

Brennan, Mary E., ed. see Thomas, Norrie, et al.

Brennan, Mary H., jt. auth. see Marshall, Ann E.

Brennan, Mary L. & Eckroate, Norma. The Natural Dog: A Complete Guide for Caring Owners. LC 93-3938. (Illus.). 352p. 1994. pap. 17.95 (*0-452-27019-7*, Plume) Dutton Plume.

Brennan, Matthew. Brennan's War: Vietnam 1965-1969. 304p. 1989. mass mkt. 5.99 (*0-671-70595-4*) PB.

— Headhunters. 1988. mass mkt. 4.99 (*0-671-66013-6*) PB.

— The Music of Exile: Poems by Matthew Brennan. 76p. pap. text 12.00 (*1-55605-250-2*) Wyndham Hall.

— Seeing in the Dark: Poems. 56p. 1993. pap. 8.00 (*0-9635631-1-4*) Hawkhead Pr.

Brennan, Matthew & McCarthy, Paul, eds. Hunter-Killer Squadron. 336p. 1992. reprint ed. mass mkt. 6.50 (*0-671-74453-4*) PB.

Brennan, Matthew, jt. auth. see Foss, Joe.

Brennan, Matthew C. The Gothic Psyche: Disintegration & Growth in Nineteenth-Century English Literature. LC 97-24148. (Studies in English & American Literature, Linguistics, & Culture). 1998. 55.00 (*1-57113-104-3*) Camden Hse.

— Wordsworth, Turner, & Romantic Landscape: A Study of the Traditions of the Picturesque & Sublime. LC 87-70973. (ENGL Ser.: Vol. 5). (Illus.). 166p. 1987. 35.00 (*0-938100-51-3*) Camden Hse.

Brennan, Matthew J. The Resource Guide to Chiropractic: A Bibliography of Chiropractic & Related Areas, 1895-1981. 155p. (C). 1981. pap. text 18.00 (*0-9606618-0-8*, K-12) Am Chiro Assn.

***Brennan, Michael.** Deep Field Painting. Adler, Tracy L., ed. (Illus.). 16p. 2000. pap. 5.00 (*1-885998-22-8*) Hunter College.

Brennan, Michael. Literary Patronage in the English Renaissance: The Pembroke Family. 224p. 1988. lib. bdg. 59.95 (*0-415-00327-X*) Routledge.

Brennan, Michael, jt. auth. see Brennan, Carleen.

Brennan, Michael, jt. ed. see Mendelsohn, Martin.

Brennan, Michael J., Jr. The Economics of Age. Stein, Leon, ed. LC 79-8693. (Growing Old Ser.). (Illus.). 1980. reprint ed. lib. bdg. 25.95 (*0-405-12778-2*) Ayer.

Brennan, Michael J. Financial Markets & Corporate Finance: Selected Papers of Michael J. Brennan. LC 99-11540. (Financial Economists of the Twentieth Century Ser.). 496p. 1999. 120.00 (*1-84064-023-5*) E Elgar.

Brennan, Michael J., ed. Patterns of Market Behavior: Essays in Honor of Philip Taft. LC 65-12932. (Studies in the Fields of General Scholarship). 264p. reprint ed. pap. 81.90 (*0-608-14777-X*, 202564300045) Bks Demand.

— The Theory of Corporate Finance, 2 vols., Set. LC 96-609. (International Library of Critical Writings in Financial Economics: Vol. 1). 1220p. 1996. 440.00 (*1-85898-278-2*) E Elgar.

Brennan, Michael J. & Trigeorgis, Lenos, eds. Project Flexability, Agency & Competition: New Developments in the Theory & Application of Real Options. LC 98-40655. (Illus.). 368p. (C). 1999. text 49.95 (*0-19-511269-5*) OUP.

Brennan, Moya & Briggs, Sarah. NTC's Beginners German & English Dictionary. LC 97-49442. (Here's How Ser.). (Illus.). 192p. 1998. pap. 12.95 (*0-8442-2479-0*) NTC Contemp Pub Co.

Brennan, Moya, jt. auth. see Briggs, Sarah.

Brennan, Murray F. & Pisters, Peter W. Protein & Amino Acid Metabolism in Cancer Cachexia. LC 95-24641. (Medical Intelligence Unit Ser.). 213p. 1995. 99.00 (*1-57059-291-8*) Landes Bioscience.

Brennan, Neil. Anthony Powell. rev. ed. LC 94-49326. (English Authors Ser.: Vol. TEAS 158). 1995. 32.00 (*0-8057-4545-9*, Twyne) Mac Lib Ref.

Brennan, Neil & Redway, A. R. A Bibliography of Graham Greene. (Soho Bibliographies Ser.). (Illus.). 380p. 2001. text 110.00 (*0-19-818187-6*) OUP.

Brennan-Nelson, Denise. Buzzy the Bumblebee. LC 99-37820. (Illus.). 32p. (J). 1999. 15.00 (*1-886947-82-1*) Sleepng Bear.

Brennan, Niall. Damien Parer: Cameraman. 200p. 1994. pap. 29.95 (*0-522-84420-0*, Pub. by Melbourne Univ Pr) Paul & Co Pubs.

Brennan, Niamh, et al. Ireland. (European Financial Reporting Ser.). 256p. (C). (gr. 13). 1992. pap. 114.95 (*0-415-06315-9*, A9721) Thomson Learn.

Brennan, Noel-Anne. Winter Reckoning. (Illus.). 1986. 30.00 (*0-937986-85-2*) D M Grant.

Brennan, P. V. Phased-Locked Loop Principles & Practices. (Illus.). 204p. 1996. 50.00 (*0-07-007568-9*) McGraw.

Brennan, Patricia. I See Moon. 1999. 14.99 (*0-525-45870-0*) NAL.

— I See My Bellybutton. 1999. 14.99 (*0-525-45871-9*) NAL.

Brennan, Patricia, ed. Copyright & the NII: Resources for the Library & Education Community. 145p. 1996. pap. 35.00 (*0-918006-80-5*) Assn Res Lib.

Brennan, Patricia, et al. Licensing Electronic Resources: Strategic & Practical Considerations for Signing Electronic Information Delivery Agreements. 23p. 1997. pap. 10.00 (*0-918006-41-4*) Assn Res Lib.

Brennan, Patricia F., et al. Information Networks for Community Health. LC 96-21900. (Computers in Health Care Ser.). 342p. 1997. 59.00 (*0-387-94697-7*) Spr-Verlag.

Brennan, Patrick. Secessionville: Assault on Charleston. (Illus.). 408p. 1995. 29.95 (*1-882810-08-2*) Savas Pub.

***Brennan, Patrick.** The Way of Forgiveness: How to Heal Life's Hurts & Restore Broken Relationships. 196p. 2000. pap. 10.99 (*1-56955-171-5*, Charis) Servant.

Brennan, Patrick H. Reporting the Nation's Business: Press-Government Relations During the Liberal Years, 1935-1957. 328p. 1993. text 45.00 (*0-8020-2977-9*); pap. text 18.95 (*0-8020-7434-0*) U of Toronto Pr.

Brennan, Patrick J. Parishes That Excel: Models of Excellence in Ministry, Education, & Evangelization. 144p. 1992. 13.95 (*0-8245-1156-5*) Crossroad NY.

— Re-Imagining Evangelization: Vision, Conversion, & Contagion. 176p. (Orig.). 1994. pap. 13.95 (*0-8245-1433-5*) Crossroad NY.

— Sacraments: Celebrations of Conversion. (Illus.). 32p. 1986. pap. text 2.95 (*1-55612-046-X*, LL1046) Sheed & Ward WI.

Brennan, Peggy & Brennan, Frank, Jr. Cranbury. (Images of America Ser.). 1995. pap. 16.99 (*0-7524-0205-6*) Arcadia Publng.

— Cranbury II. (Images of America Ser.). (Illus.). 128p. 1998. pap. 16.99 (*0-7524-0978-6*) Arcadia Publng.

— Hightstown & East Windsor. LC 97-112627. (Images of America Ser.). 1996. pap. 16.99 (*0-7524-0270-6*) Arcadia Publng.

Brennan, R. Lee. Hidden Destination. 1998. pap. 12.99 (*1-892525-00-3*) ACW Press.

***Brennan, Richard.** Alexander Technique: Introductory Guide to Natural Poise for Health & Well-Being. (New Perspectives Ser.). 2000. pap. 9.95 (*1-86204-629-8*, Pub. by Element MA) Penguin Putnam.

Brennan, Richard. Alexander Technique: Natural Poise for Health. (Health Essentials Ser.). 128p. 1997. pap. 9.95 (*1-86204-046-X*, Pub. by Element MA) Penguin Putnam.

— The Alexander Technique Manual: A Step-by-Step Guide to Improve Breathing, Posture & Well-Being at Any Age. LC 96-60635. (Illus.). 144p. 1996. pap. 19.95 (*1-885203-38-1*) Jrny Editions.

— A Practical Introduction: Alexander Technique. LC 98-24793. (Illus.). 144p. 1998. pap. 14.95 (*1-86204-158-X*, Pub. by Element MA) Penguin Putnam.

Brennan, Richard P. Heisenberg Probably Slept Here: The Lives, Times & Ideas of the Great Physicists of the 20th Century. LC 96-42935. (Illus.). 288p. 1996. 22.95 (*0-471-15709-0*) Wiley.

— Heisenberg Probably Slept Here: The Lives, Times & Ideas of the Great Physicists of the 20th Century. (Wiley Popular Science Ser.). 274p. 1998. pap. 14.95 (*0-471-29585-X*) Wiley.

— Levitating Trains & Kamikaze Genes: Technological Literacy for the Future. 262p. 1994. pap. 12.95 (*0-471-07902-2*) Wiley.

— Levitating Trains & Kamikaze Genes: Technological Literacy for the 1990s. LC 90-55492. 1991. pap. 53.70 (*0-06-097374-9*, Perennial) HarperTrade.

Brennan, Robert E., ed. Essays in Thomism. LC 72-1149. (Essay Index Reprint Ser.). 1977. reprint ed. 30.95 (*0-8369-2834-2*) Ayer.

***Brennan, Robert E. & Brennan, Jeannie I.** Sackets Harbor. LC 99-69482. (Images of America Ser.). (Illus.). 128p. 2000. pap. 18.99 (*0-7385-0285-5*) Arcadia Publng.

Brennan, Robert L. Elements of Generalizability Theory. (Illus.). 161p. (Orig.). (C). 1992. pap. text 15.00 (*0-937734-05-5*) ACT.

Brennan, Ruth M. & Hahn, Dan F. Listening for a President: A Citizen's Campaign Methodology. LC 89-29764. 217p. 1990. 55.00 (*0-275-93245-1*, C3245, Greenwood Pr) Greenwood.

Brennan, Shawn, ed. Magill's Cinema Annual, 1995. 95th ed. (Magill's Cinema Annual Ser.). 700p. 1995. 90.00 (*0-7876-0732-0*, 109885) Gale.

Brennan, Stephen C. & Yarbrough, Stephen R. Irving Babbitt. LC 87-420. (Twayne's United States Authors Ser.). 184p. (C). 1987. 32.00 (*0-8057-7499-8*) Macmillan.

Brennan, Stephen J. Competitive Excellence: The Psychology & Strategy of Successful Team Building - Second Edition. 2nd ed. LC 95-92042. 308p. (Orig.). (C). 1995. pap. 23.95 (*0-9619230-5-9*) Peak Perf Pub.

***Brennan, Stephen J.** Competitive Excellence Vol. III: The Psychology & Strategy of Successful Team Building. 3rd large type rev. ed. 175p. 2000. pap. 23.95 (*1-893353-13-3*) Peak Perf Pub.

Brennan, Stephen J. How to Physically & Mentally Toughen Yourself for Your Sport Season: The Workbook. 75p. 1995. pap. 15.95 (*0-9619230-4-0*) Peak Perf Pub.

— The Mental Edge: Basketball's Peak Performance Workbook - Second Edition. 2nd ed. 300p. (C). 1993. reprint ed. pap. 29.95 (*0-9619230-2-4*) Peak Perf Pub.

Brennan, Stephen J., ed. Inside Recruiting: The Master Guide to Successful College Athletic Recruiting, Vol. 1. (Illus.). 200p. 1998. pap. 29.95 (*0-9619230-8-3*) Peak Perf Pub.

— Inside Recruiting: The Master Guide to Successful College Athletic Recruiting, Vol. II. 2nd rev. ed. 138p. 1999. pap. 29.95 (*0-9619230-9-1*) Peak Perf Pub.

— Inside Recruiting Vol. III: The Master Guide to Successful College Athletic Recruiting. 3rd large type rev. ed. 175p. 2000. pap. 29.95 (*1-893353-12-5*) Peak Perf Pub.

***Brennan, Susan E., ed.** Psychological Models of Communication in Collaborative Systems: Papers from the 1999 AAAI Symposium. 145p. 1999. pap. 25.00 (*1-57735-105-3*) AAAI Pr.

Brennan, T. C. & Rosenbaum, Ray. Witness to the Execution: The Odyssey of Amelia Earhart. LC 88-18358. (Illus.). 216p. 1988. pap. 11.95 (*1-55838-108-2*) R H Pub.

***Brennan, T. Corey.** The Praetorship in the Roman Republic. LC 99-35017. 2000. write for info. (*0-19-511459-0*); write for info. (*0-19-511460-4*) OUP.

— The Praetorship in the Roman Republic, 2 vol. 912p. 2000. text 150.00 (*0-19-513867-8*) OUP.

***Brennan, Tad.** Ethics & Epistemology in Sextus Empiricus. LC 00-21519. (Studies in Ethics). 2000. write for info. (*0-8153-3659-4*) Garland.

Brennan, Ted. Breakfast at Brennan's & Dinner, Too. LC 94-178184. 1994. 27.50 (*0-9639819-0-0*) Brennans Rest.

Brennan, Terence. Rooftops. 1989. pap. 3.95 (*0-380-75755-9*, Avon Bks) Morrow Avon.

Brennan, Teresa. Age of Paranoia. Date not set. write for info. (*0-393-03839-4*) Norton.

***Brennan, Teresa.** Exhausting Modernity: Grounds for a New Economy. LC 00-34469. 2000. pap. write for info. (*0-415-23706-8*) Routledge.

Brennan, Teresa. History after Lacan. LC 93-17237. (Opening Out Ser.). 288p. (C). (gr. 13). 1993. pap. 22.99 (*0-415-01117-5*) Routledge.

— The Interpretation of the Flesh: Freud's Theory of Femininity. LC 91-39866. 288p. (C). 1992. pap. 24.99 (*0-415-07449-5*, A7278) Routledge.

— The Interpretation of the Flesh: Freud's Theory of Femininity. LC 91-39866. 288p. (C). (gr. 13). 1992. 80.00 (*0-415-07448-7*, A7274) Routledge.

— Vision in Context: Historical & Contemporary Perspectives on Sight. 245p. (C). 1996. pap. 19.99 (*0-415-91475-2*) Routledge.

Brennan, Teresa, ed. Between Feminism & Psychoanalysis. 224p. 1989. 55.00 (*0-415-01489-1*, A3333) Routledge.

— Vision in Context: Historical & Contemporary Perspectives on Sight. 245p. (C). (gr. 13 up). 1996. 75.00 (*0-415-91474-4*) Routledge.

Brennan, Terry, jt. auth. see Clarkin, Mike.

Brennan, Theodore, jt. auth. see Brennan, Ellen.

Brennan, Theodore, jt. auth. see Brennan, Ellen C.

Brennan, Theodore M., jt. auth. see Brennan, Ellen C.

Brennan, Thomas, ed. Writings on Writing: A Compendium of 1209 Quotations from Authors on Their Craft. LC 93-24477. 189p. 1994. lib. bdg. 28.95 (*0-89950-765-4*) McFarland & Co.

Brennan, Thomas E. Burgundy to Champagne: The Wine Trade in Early Modern France, Vol. 115. LC 97-2188. (Johns Hopkins University Studies in Historical & Political Science Ser.). 375p. 1997. text 39.95 (*0-8018-5567-5*) Johns Hopkins.

— Public Drinking & Popular Culture in Eighteenth-Century Paris. LC 87-29122. 348p. 1988. reprint ed. pap. 107.90 (*0-608-04654-X*, 206534000003) Bks Demand.

Brennan, Thomas F., jt. ed. see Bachtler, Joseph R.

Brennan, Timothy. At Home in the World: Cosmopolitanism Now. LC 97-7299. (Convergences). 384p. 1997. 41.50 (*0-674-05030-4*); pap. 22.95 (*0-674-05031-2*) HUP.

Brennan, Timothy J., et al. A Shock to the System: Restructuring America's Electricity Industry. LC 96-20204. (Illus.). 138p. 1996. pap. text 22.95 (*0-915707-80-2*) Resources Future.

***Brennan, Tom.** Moose Droppings & Other Crimes Against Nature: Funny Stories from Alaska. (Illus.). 128p. 2000. pap. 12.95 (*0-945397-84-4*) Epicenter Pr.

Brennan, Troyen A. Just Doctoring: Medical Ethics in the Liberal State. LC 91-10146. 301p. 1991. 48.00 (*0-520-07333-9*, Pub. by U CA Pr) Cal Prin Full Svc.

Brennan, Troyen A. & Berwick, Donald M. New Rules: Regulation, Markets, & the Quality of American Health Care. (Health Ser.). 416p. 1995. text 40.95 (*0-7879-0149-0*) Jossey-Bass.

Brennan-Whitmore, W. H. Dublin Burning: The Easter Rising from Behind the Barricades. 200p. (Orig.). 1996. pap. 19.95 (*0-7171-2413-4*, Pub. by Gill & MacMill) Irish Bks Media.

Brennan, Wilfred K. Changing Special Education Now. rev. ed. 192p. 1987. reprint ed. pap. 32.95 (*0-335-10277-8*) OpUniv Pr.

— Curriculum for Special Needs. 192p. 1984. pap. 34.95 (*0-335-10421-5*) OpUniv Pr.

Brennan, Will. The Tombstone. large type ed. (Dales Large Print Ser.). 204p. 1997. pap. 18.99 (*1-85389-771-X*, Dales) Ulverscroft.

Brennan, William. The Abortion Holocaust: Today's Final Solution. LC 82-83960. (Illus.). 230p. (Orig.). 1983. pap. 6.95 (*0-911439-01-3*) Landmark Pr.

— Dehumanizing the Vulnerable: When Word Games Take Lives. LC 94-41824. (Values & Ethics Ser.: Vol. 11). 287p. 1995. pap. 13.95 (*0-8294-0821-5*) Loyola Pr.

***Brennan, William.** A Tattered Coat upon a Stick. LC 99-91442. 2000. 25.00 (*0-7388-0784-2*); pap. 18.00 (*0-7388-0785-0*) Xlibris Corp.

Brennan, William J., Jr. Jersey Central Lines in Color. LC 90-63154. (Illus.). 128p. 1991. 45.00 (*1-878887-00-9*) Morning NJ.

— Jersey Central Lines in Color, Vol. 2. LC 90-63154. (Illus.). 128p. 1993. 49.95 (*1-878887-19-X*) Morning NJ.

Brennan, William J. The Lionel Inspiration. LC 97-70600. (Illus.). 128p. 1997. 49.95 (*1-878887-76-9*) Morning NJ.

Brennand, Daniel P. & Tondreau, David P. Configuration Management & Document Control: Fundamentals for Medical Device & Quality Certified Manufacturing. LC 96-93026. x, 284 p. 1997. write for info. (*0-9656032-0-2*) CMDC Systs.

Brennecke, Christof, et al, eds. Logos: Festschrift fuer Luise Abramowski zum 8, Juli 1993. (Beiheft zur Zeitschrift fuer die Neuetestamentliche Wissenschaft Ser.: Vol. 67). (GER.). xiii, 658p. (C). 1993. lib. bdg. 165.30 (*3-11-013985-5*) De Gruyter.

Brennecke, E., ed. see Hardy, Thomas.

Brennecke, Ernest. The Life of Thomas Hardy. LC 72-8648. (Studies in Thomas Hardy). 1973. reprint ed. lib. bdg. 75.00 (*0-8383-1672-7*) M S G Haskell Hse.

— Thomas Hardy's Universe: A Study of a Poet's Mind. LC 68-689. (Studies in Thomas Hardy: No. 14). 1969. reprint ed. lib. bdg. 75.00 (*0-8383-0651-9*) M S G Haskell Hse.

Brennecke, Hanns C. & Ulrich, Jorg, eds. Patristica: Ausgewahlte Aufsatze zur Alten Kirche. 480p. 1998. 155.00 (*3-11-015763-2*) De Gruyter.

Brennecke, Hanns C., ed. see Schaeferdiek, Knut.

Brennecke, Joan F., jt. ed. see Kiran, Erdogan.

Brennecke, Shaun P., jt. ed. see Rice, Gregory E.

Brenneis, C. Brooks. Recovered Memories of Trauma: Transferring the Present to the Past. LC 96-39645. 220p. 1997. 31.50 (*0-8236-5788-4*, BN05788) Intl Univs Pr.

Brenneis, Donald & Macaulay, Ronald K., eds. The Matrix of Language: Contemporary Linguistic Anthropology. LC 95-43947. 352p. (C). 1996. pap. 35.00 (*0-8133-2321-5*, Pub. by Westview) HarpC.

***Brenneis, Lisa.** Final Cut Pro for Macintosh: Visual QuickPro Guide. (Visual Quickpro Guides Ser.). 352p. 1999. pap. 24.99 (*0-201-35480-2*) Peachpit Pr.

Brenneke, Adolf & Leesch, Wolfgang. Archivkunde. 469p. 1988. lib. bdg. 170.00 (*3-598-10785-4*) K G Saur Verlag.

Brenneman, Gerre, jt. auth. see Stewart, Bill F.

Brenneman, Helen. To the New Mother. 16p. 1969. pap. 2.99 (*0-8361-1600-3*) Herald Pr.

Brenneman, Helen G. But Not Forsaken. 1983. pap. 3.95 (*0-87813-954-0*) Christian Light.

— Meditations for the Expectant Mother. LC 68-12025. (Illus.). 78p. 1968. pap. 8.99 (*0-8361-1567-8*) Herald Pr.

— Meditations for the New Mother. rev. ed. LC 53-7585. (Illus.). 78p. 1985. pap. 8.99 (*0-8361-3399-4*) Herald Pr.

Brenneman, James E. Canons in Conflict: Negotiating Texts in True & False Prophecy. LC 96-27946. 256p. 1997. text 45.00 (*0-19-510909-0*) OUP.

Brenneman, Marcia A. Walter: An Airman's Life. (Illus.). 278p. (Orig.). 1989. pap. 21.95 (*0-9625652-0-2*) M Brenneman.

Brenneman, Mary G., jt. auth. see Brenneman, Walter L., Jr.

Brenneman, Richard. Deadly Blessings: Faith Healing on Trial. LC 90-60906. 390p. (C). 1990. 28.95 (*0-87975-580-6*) Prometheus Bks.

***Brenneman, Tim.** Jimmie Boogie Learns about Smoking. LaFlamme, Nicole & Davidson, Don, eds. (Illus.). 12p. (J). (gr. k-7). 2000. mass mkt. 5.99 (*0-9700453-0-1*) T Brenneman.

Brenneman, Walter L., Jr. & Brenneman, Mary G. Crossing the Circle at the Holy Wells of Ireland. LC 94-18909. 1995. 29.95 (*0-8139-1548-1*) U Pr of Va.

Brennen, Bonnie. Picturing the Past: Media,History & Photography. LC 98-58009. (History of Communication Ser.). 320p. 1999. 50.00 (*0-252-02465-6*) U of Ill Pr.

Brennen, Bonnie, jt. ed. see Hardt, Hanno.

***Brennen, Christopher E.** Adventure Hikes & Canyoneering in the San Gabriels. (Illus.). 160p. 1999. ring bd. write for info. (*0-9667409-0-4*) C Brennen.

Brennen, Christopher E. Cavitation & Bubble Dynamics. (Engineering Science Ser.: Vol. 44). (Illus.). 304p. 1995. text 98.00 (*0-19-509409-3*) OUP.

— Hydrodynamics of Pumps. LC 94-70020. (Illus.). 316p. 1994. 95.00 (*0-933283-07-5*) Concepts ETI.

— Hydrodynamics of Pumps. (Concepts ETI Bks.). (Illus.). 336p. (C). 1995. text 120.00 (*0-19-856442-2*) OUP.

Brennen, Moya. Scitech Ch2: Communicating in English about Science & Technology, Chapters 16-25. 208p. 1994. pap. 27.95 (*0-8384-4081-9*) Heinle & Heinle.

Brennenstuhl, W., jt. auth. see Ballmer, T. T.

Brennenstuhl, Waltraud. Control & Ability: Towards a Biocybernetics of Language. (Pragmatics & Beyond Ser.: III: 4). vi, 122p. (Orig.). 1982. pap. 41.00 (*90-272-2522-2*) J Benjamins Pubng Co.

Brenner. Pharmacology. Date not set. pap. text. write for info. (*0-7216-7757-6*, W B Saunders Co) Harcrt Hlth Sci Grp.

— Recent Advances Hematology, Vol. 7. 1993. text 66.00 (*0-443-04689-1*, W B Saunders Co) Harcrt Hlth Sci Grp.

Brenner. Recent Advances in Hemotology, Vol. 8. 1995. text 77.00 (*0-443-05237-9*, W B Saunders Co) Harcrt Hlth Sci Grp.

Brenner & Dascher. Financial Accounting. 4th ed. (SWC-Accounting). 1995. 64.95 (*0-87393-372-9*); pap., student ed. 21.95 (*0-87393-373-7*) Dame Pubns.

— Financial Accounting: Working Papers. 4th ed. 1995. pap. 20.95 (*0-87393-374-5*) Dame Pubns.

Brenner & Stoka. Chaga's Disease Vectors, Vol. III. 168p. 1987. 99.00 (*0-8493-4349-6*, CRC Reprint) Franklin.

Brenner, A. Song of Songs. (Old Testament Guides Ser.). 106p. 1989. pap. 12.50 (*1-85075-242-7*, Pub. by Sheffield Acad) CUP Services.

Brenner, A. L. & Fleming, B. A. James Genealogy. (Illus.). 304p. 1993. reprint ed. pap. 47.50 (*0-8328-3765-2*); reprint ed. lib. bdg. 57.50 (*0-8328-3764-4*) Higginson Bk Co.

Brenner, Alan, jt. ed. see Ames, Karyn R.

Brenner, Alfred. The TV Scriptwriter's Handbook: Dramatic Writing for Television & Film. 325p. 1992. pap. 15.95 (*1-879505-10-X*) Silman James Pr.

Brenner, Anita. Idols Behind Altars. LC 67-19527. (Illus.). 1929. pap. 25.00 (*0-8196-0190-X*) Biblo.

— Influence of Technique on the Decorative Style in the Domestic Pottery of Culhuacan. LC 78-82356. (Columbia Univ. Contributions to Anthropology Ser.: Vol. 13). reprint ed. 27.50 (*0-404-50563-5*) AMS Pr.

Brenner, Anita & Leighton, George R. The Wind That Swept Mexico: The History of the Mexican Revolution of 1910-1942. LC 77-149021. (Texas Pan American Ser.). (Illus.). 320p. (C). 1971. pap. 19.95 (*0-292-79024-4*) U of Tex Pr.

Brenner, Anita, tr. see Frank, Waldo D., ed.

Brenner, Anita, tr. see Lopez y Fuentes, Gregorio.

Brenner, Anita, tr. see Magdaleno, Mauricio.

Brenner, Ann, tr. see Katz, Jacob.

Brenner, Athalya. Colour Terms in the Old Testament. (JSOT Supplement Ser.: No. 21). 296p. 1983. 85.00 (*0-905774-42-6*, Pub. by Sheffield Acad) CUP Services.

Brenner, Athalya. A Feminist Companion To Genesis. (Feminist Companion to the Bible Ser.: Vol. 2). 404p. 1993. pap. 28.50 (*1-85075-420-9*, Pub. by Sheffield Acad) CUP Services.

— A Feminist Companion to the Song of Songs. (Feminist Companion to the Bible Ser.: No. 1). 288p. 1993. pap. 28.50 (*1-85075-291-5*, Pub. by Sheffield Acad) CUP Services.

— The Intercourse of Knowledge: On Gendering Desire & 'Sexuality' in the Hebrew Bible. LC 96-46460. (Biblical Interpretation Ser.: Vol. 26). 200p. 1997. text 72.50 (*90-04-10155-1*, NLG110) Brill Academic Pubs.

Brenner, Athalya, ed. A Feminist Companion to Esther, Judith & Susanna. (Feminist Companion to the Bible Ser.: No. 7). 336p. 1995. pap. 28.50 (*1-85075-527-2*, Pub. by Sheffield Acad) CUP Services.

Brenner, Athalya, ed. The Feminist Companion to Exodus-Deuteronomy. (Feminist Companion to the Bible Ser.: Vol. 6). 269p. 1994. pap. 28.50 (*1-85075-463-2*, Pub. by Sheffield Acad) CUP Services.

— A Feminist Companion to Judges. (Feminist Companion to the Bible Ser.: Vol. 4). 242p. 1993. pap. 28.50 (*1-85075-462-4*, Pub. by Sheffield Acad) CUP Services.

— A Feminist Companion to Ruth. (Feminist Companion to the Bible Ser.: Vol. 3). 292p. 1993. pap. 28.50 (*1-85075-421-7*, Pub. by Sheffield Acad) CUP Services.

— A Feminist Companion to Samuel Kings. (Feminist Companion to the Bible Ser.: Vol. 5). 286p. 1994. pap. 28.50 (*1-85075-480-2*, Pub. by Sheffield Acad) CUP Services.

— A Feminist Companion to the Hebrew Bible in the New Testament. LC 96-183322. (Feminist Companion to the Bible Ser.: No. 10). 384p. 1996. pap. 28.50 (*1-85075-754-2*, Pub. by Sheffield Acad) CUP Services.

Brenner, Athalya, ed. A Feminist Companion to the Latter Prophets. (Feminist Companion to the Bible Ser.: No. 8). 384p. 1995. pap. 28.50 (*1-85075-515-9*, Pub. by Sheffield Acad) CUP Services.

— A Feminist Companion to the Wisdom Literature. (Feminist Companion to the Bible Ser.: No. 9). 264p. 1995. pap. 28.50 (*1-85075-735-6*, Pub. by Sheffield Acad) CUP Services.

Brenner, Athalya, ed. Genesis: A Feminist Companion to the Bible. (Feminist Companion to the Bible Ser.: Vol. 1). 276p. 1998. pap. 28.50 (*1-85075-838-7*, Pub. by Sheffield Acad) CUP Services.

***Brenner, Athalya, ed.** Judges: A Feminist Companion to the Bible. (Feminist Companion to the Bible Ser.: No. 4). 176p. 1999. pap. 28.50 (*1-84127-024-5*, Pub. by Sheffield Acad) CUP Services.

— Ruth & Esther: A Feminist Companion to the Bible. (Feminist Companion to the Bible Ser.: Vol. 3). 294p. 1999. pap. 28.50 (*1-85075-978-2*, Pub. by Sheffield Acad) CUP Services.

Brenner, Athalya & Fontaine, Carole, eds. Wisdom & Psalms: A Feminist Companion to the Bible. (Feminist Companion to the Bible Ser.: Series 2). 332p. 1998. pap. 28.50 (*1-85075-917-0*, Pub. by Sheffield Acad) CUP Services.

***Brenner, Athalya & Fontaine, Carole R., eds.** The Song of Songs: A Feminist Companion to the Bible. (Feminist Companion to the Bible Ser.: No. 6). 226p. 2000. pap. 28.50 (*1-84127-052-0*, Pub. by Sheffield Acad) CUP Services.

Brenner, Athalya & Fontane, Carole, eds. A Feminist Companion to Reading the Bible: Approaches, Methods & Strategies. (Feminist Companion to the Bible Ser.: Vol. 11). 654p. 1997. pap. 39.50 (*1-85075-674-0*, Pub. by Sheffield Acad) CUP Services.

Brenner, Athalya & Van Dijk-Hemmes, Fokkelien. On Gendering Texts: Female & Male Voices in the Hebrew Bible. (Biblical Interpretation Ser.: Vol. I). xiv, 211p. 1996. reprint ed. pap. 39.50 (*90-04-10644-8*) Brill Academic Pubs.

Brenner, Athalya, jt. auth. see Radday, Yehuda T.

Brenner, Athalya, jt. auth. see Van Dijk-Hemmes, Fokkelien.

Brenner, Avis. Helping Children Cope with Stress. LC 97-19819. 1997. pap. 19.95 (*0-7879-3864-5*) Jossey-Bass.

Brenner, Barbara. Beavers Beware! (Illus.). 32p. (J). 1992. pap. 4.50 (*0-553-35386-1*) Bantam.

— Beef Stew. LC 89-36769. (Step into Reading Ser.: A Step 1 Book). (Illus.). 32p. (J). (ps-3). 1990. pap. 3.99 (*0-394-85046-7*, Pub. by Random Bks Yng Read) Random.

Brenner, Barbara. Beef Stew. (Step into Reading Ser.: A Step 1 Book). (J). (ps-1). 1990. 9.19 (*0-606-12183-8*, Pub. by Turtleback) Demco.

Brenner, Barbara. The Boy Who Loved to Draw: Benjamin West. LC 97-5183. (Illus.). 48p. (J). 1999. 15.00 (*0-395-85080-0*) HM.

— A Dog I Know. LC 82-47572. (Illus.). 32p. (J). (gr. k-4). 1983. 11.95 (*0-06-020684-5*) HarpC Child Bks.

***Brenner, Barbara.** Earth Is Painted Green. (Illus.). 96p. (J). (ps-3). 2000. pap. 5.99 (*0-590-45135-9*) Scholastic Inc.

— Earth is Painted Green. (Illus.). (J). 2000. 11.34 (*0-606-18538-0*) Turtleback.

Brenner, Barbara. Hemi: A Mule. LC 73-5479. (I Can Read Bks.). (Illus.). 128p. (J). (ps-3). 1975. pap. 1.25 (*0-06-440063-8*, HarpTrophy) HarpC Child Bks.

***Brenner, Barbara.** If You Lived in Williamsburg in Colonial Days. (If You Lived Ser.). (Illus.). 2000. pap. 5.99 (*0-590-92922-4*) Scholastic Inc.

Brenner, Barbara. If You Were There in 1492. LC 90-24099. (Illus.). 112p. (J). (gr. 3-7). 1991. lib. bdg. 15.00 (*0-02-712321-9*, Bradbury S&S) S&S Childrens.

— If You Were There in 1492: Everyday Life in the Time of Columbus. LC 90-24099. (Illus.). 112p. (J). (gr. 3-7). 1998. per. 5.99 (*0-689-82241-3*) Aladdin.

— If You Were There in 1776. (If You Were There Ser.). (Illus.). 144p. (J). (gr. 3-7). 1994. mass mkt. 17.00 (*0-02-712322-7*, Bradbury S&S) S&S Childrens.

— Mr. Tall & Mr. Small. LC 93-8256. (Illus.). (J). 1995. write for info. (*0-8050-2757-2*) H Holt & Co.

— On the Frontier with Mr. Audubon. LC 97-70578. (Illus.). 96p. (J). (gr. 4 up). 1997. pap. 7.95 (*1-56397-679-X*) Boyds Mills Pr.

Brenner, Barbara. One Small Place: Tree House. 1924. write for info. (*0-688-17180-X*, Wm Morrow) Morrow Avon.

Brenner, Barbara. The Plant That Kept on Growing. LC 95-18798. (Bank Street Ready-to-Read Ser.). (Illus.). (J). (ps-3). 1996. pap. 3.99 (*0-553-09746-6*) Bantam.

— The Plant that Kept on Growing. (Bank Street Ready-to-Read Ser.). (Illus.). 32p. (J). (ps-1). 1996. pap. 4.50 (*0-553-37578-4*) BDD Bks Young Read.

— Si Fueras Una Hormiga. Gonzalez-Prats, Martha, tr. (SPA., Illus.). 32p. (J). (ps-3). 1998. pap. text 4.95 (*1-57255-506-8*) Mondo Pubng.

— A Snake-Lover's Diary. LC 84-43136. 96p. (J). 1970. 12.95 (*0-201-09349-9*) HarpC Child Bks.

— Thinking about Ants. LC 95-45990. (Illus.). (J). (gr. k-5). 1996. 14.95 (*1-57255-210-7*) Mondo Pubng.

— Tide Pool. (One Small Place Ser.). 1924. write for info. (*0-688-17182-6*, Wm Morrow) Morrow Avon.

— Tide Pool. (One Small Place Ser.). (J). 1924. lib. bdg. write for info. (*0-688-17183-4*, Wm Morrow) Morrow Avon.

— Too Many Mice. (Bank Street Ready-to-Read Ser.: No. 33). (Illus.). 32p. (J). 1992. pap. 4.50 (*0-553-35160-5*) Bantam.

— Tree House. (One Small Place Ser.). (J). 1924. lib. bdg. write for info. (*0-688-17181-8*, Wm Morrow) Morrow Avon.

— Tremendous Tree Book. LC 91-73753. (Illus.). 40p. (J). 1998. pap. 7.95 (*1-56397-718-4*, Wordsong) Boyds Mills Pr.

***Brenner, Barbara.** Voices: Poetry & Art from Six Continents. LC 00-20232. (Illus.). 2000. write for info. (*0-7922-7071-1*) Natl Geog.

Brenner, Barbara. Wagon Wheels. LC 92-18780. (I Can Read Bks.). (Illus.). 64p. (J). (ps-3). 1978. 15.95 (*0-06-020668-3*); lib. bdg. 15.89 (*0-06-020669-1*) HarpC Child Bks.

— Wagon Wheels. LC 92-18780. (I Can Read Bks.). (Illus.). 64p. (J). (gr. 2-4). 1984. pap. 3.95 (*0-06-444052-4*, HarpTrophy) HarpC Child Bks.

Brenner, Barbara. Wagon Wheels. (I Can Read Bks.). (J). (gr. 2-4). 1978. 8.95 (*0-606-02372-0*, Pub. by Turtleback) Demco.

— Wagon Wheels. unabridged ed. LC 92-18780. (I Can Read Bks.). (Illus.). 64p. (J). (gr. 2-4). 1995. pap. 8.95 incl. audio (*0-694-70001-0*) HarpC Child Bks.

— What the Elephant Told. 2002. text 15.95 (*0-8050-6442-7*) H Holt & Co.

Brenner, Barbara. Where's That Cat? LC 93-40722. (Hide & Seek Science Ser.). 1995. 10.15 (*0-606-10062-8*, Pub. by Turtleback) Demco.

— Where's That Fish? LC 93-2929. (Hide & Seek Science Book Ser.). 32p. (J). (gr. k-3). 1995. pap. 4.95 (*0-590-45215-0*) Scholastic Inc.

— Where's That Fish? LC 93-2929. (Hide & Seek Science Ser.). 1994. 10.15 (*0-606-10063-6*, Pub. by Turtleback) Demco.

— Where's That Insect? (Hide & Seek Science Book Ser.). 32p. (J). (ps-3). 1995. pap. 4.95 (*0-590-45211-8*) Scholastic Inc.

Brenner, Barbara. Where's That Insect? (Hide & Seek Science Ser.). 1993. 10.15 (*0-606-08376-6*, Pub. by Turtleback) Demco.

— Where's That Reptile? (Hide & Seek Science Ser.). 1993. 10.19 (*0-606-08377-4*, Pub. by Turtleback) Demco.

Brenner, Barbara, ed. The Earth Is Painted Green: A Garden of Poems about Our Planet. LC 93-21466. (Illus.). 96p. (J). 1994. 16.95 (*0-590-45134-0*) Scholastic Inc.

Brenner, Barbara & Chardiet, Bernice. Where's That Cat? LC 93-40722. (Hide & Seek Science Ser.). (Illus.). 32p. (J). (ps-3). 1995. 10.95 (*0-590-45216-9*, Cartwheel) Scholastic Inc.

— Where's That Cat? LC 93-40722. (Hide & Seek Science Ser.). (Illus.). 32p. (J). (gr. k-3). 1996. pap. text 4.95 (*0-590-45217-7*) Scholastic Inc.

— Where's That Fish? LC 93-2929. (Hide & Seek Science Book Ser.). (Illus.). 32p. (J). (ps-3). 1994. 10.95 (*0-590-45214-2*, Cartwheel) Scholastic Inc.

— Where's That Reptile? 32p. (J). (ps-3). 1995. pap. 4.95 (*0-590-45213-4*) Scholastic Inc.

***Brenner, Barbara & Takaya, Julia.** Chibi: A True Story from Japan. LC 94-31082. (Illus.). 64p. (J). (gr. k-4). 1999. 14.95 (*0-395-69623-2*, Clarion Bks) HM.

Brenner, Barbara, et al. Let's Get Dressed! Bank Street College Media Group Staff, ed. (Illus.). 32p. (Orig.). (J). (ps). 1986. write for info. (*0-9617460-0-9*) Levi Strauss.

— Ou' Est Ce Poisson?Tr. of Ou Est Ce Poisson". (FRE., Illus.). (J). pap. 6.99 (*0-590-24226-1*) Scholastic Inc.

— Where's That Bat? LC 98-50527. (Illus.). 1999. write for info. (*0-590-12819-1*) Scholastic Inc.

Brenner, Barbara, jt. auth. see Chardiet, Bernice.

Brenner, Barbara A. The Color Wizard: Level 1. (Illus.). 32p. (J). (ps-3). 1989. pap. 4.50 (*0-553-34690-3*) Bantam.

— Moon Boy. 32p. (J). 1990. pap. 4.50 (*0-553-34851-5*) Bantam.

Brenner, Barbara A. & Chardiet, Bernice. Hide & Seek Science: Where's That Reptile? LC 92-20905. (Illus.). 32p. (J). (ps-3). 1993. 10.95 (*0-590-45212-6*) Scholastic Inc.

Brenner, Barry, jt. auth. see O'Callaghan, Christopher A.

***Brenner, Barry E.** Emergency Asthma. LC 98-56653. (Clinical Allergy & Immunology Ser.: No. 13). (Illus.). 600p. 1999. text 165.00 (*0-8247-1945-X*) Dekker.

Brenner, Barry E., jt. auth. see Simon, Robert R.

Brenner, Barry M. Brenner & Rector's the Kidney, 2 Vols., Set. 5th rev. ed. LC 95-3459. (Illus.). 2592p. 1995. text 350.00 (*0-7216-5075-9*, W B Saunders Co) Harcrt Hlth Sci Grp.

— The Kidney, 2 vols., Set. 6th ed. LC 99-11888. (C). 2000. text 395.00 (*0-7216-7998-6*, W B Saunders Co) Harcrt Hlth Sci Grp.

Brenner, Barry M. & Laragh, John H., eds. Advances in Atrial Peptide Research. LC 88-6730. (American Society of Hypertension Symposium Ser.: Vol. 2). 653p. 1988. reprint ed. pap. 200.00 (*0-608-00310-7*, 206102700007) Bks Demand.

— Biologically Active Atrial Peptides. LC 86-42946. (American Society of Hypertension Symposium Ser.: Vol. 1). (Illus.). 654p. reprint ed. pap. 200.00 (*0-608-09732-2*, 206989500007) Bks Demand.

— Progress in Atrial Peptide Research. LC 89-10468. (American Society of Hypertension Symposium Ser.: No. 3). (Illus.). 715p. 1989. reprint ed. pap. 200.00 (*0-608-00600-9*, 206118700007) Bks Demand.

Brenner, Barry M. & Lazarus, J. Michael. Acute Renal Failure. (Illus.). 837p. 1983. text 179.00 (*0-7216-1964-9*, W B Saunders Co) Harcrt Hlth Sci Grp.

Brenner, Barry M. & Lazarus, J. Michael, eds. Acute Renal Failure. 2nd ed. LC 87-22425. (Illus.). 967p. reprint ed. pap. 200.00 (*0-7837-6260-7*, 204597200010) Bks Demand.

Brenner, Barry M. & Rector, Floyd C., Jr. The Kidney, 2 vols., 1. 4th ed. (Illus.). 1990. text. write for info. (*0-7216-2616-5*, W B Saunders Co) Harcrt Hlth Sci Grp.

— The Kidney, 2 vols., 2. 4th ed. (Illus.). 1990. text. write for info. (*0-7216-2617-3*, W B Saunders Co) Harcrt Hlth Sci Grp.

Brenner, Barry M. & Stein, Jay H., eds. Acute Renal Failure. LC 80-21863. (Contemporary Issues in Nephrology Ser.: No. 6). (Illus.). 308p. reprint ed. pap. 95.50 (*0-8357-6575-X*, 203596100097) Bks Demand.

— Atrial Natriuretic Peptides. fac. ed. LC 89-22191. (Contemporary Issues in Nephrology Ser.: No. 21). (Illus.). 286p. 1989. reprint ed. pap. 88.70 (*0-7837-7897-X*, 204765300008) Bks Demand.

— Body Fluid Homeostasis. (Contemporary Issues in Nephrology Ser.: Vol. 16). (Illus.). 454p. 1986. text 73.00 (*0-443-08530-7*) Church.

— Chronic Renal Failure. LC 81-7636. (Contemporary Issues in Nephrology Ser.: No. 7). 349p. reprint ed. pap. 108.20 (*0-7837-3155-8*, 204283000006) Bks Demand.

— Hormonal Function & the Kidney. LC 79-19204. (Contemporary Issues in Nephrology Ser.: No. 4). 306p. reprint ed. pap. 94.90 (*0-7837-2567-1*, 204272600006) Bks Demand.

— Hypertension. LC 81-10263. (Contemporary Issues in Nephrology Ser.: No. 8). (Illus.). 393p. reprint ed. pap. 121.90 (*0-8357-3066-2*, 203932200012) Bks Demand.

— The Kidney in Diabetes Mellitus. fac. ed. LC 89-809. (Contemporary Issues in Nephrology Ser.: No. 20). (Illus.). 244p. 1989. reprint ed. pap. 75.70 (*0-7837-7903-8*, 204765900008) Bks Demand.

— Modern Techniques of Ion Transport. fac. ed. LC 86-20728. (Contemporary Issues in Nephrology Ser.: No. 15). (Illus.). 352p. 1987. reprint ed. pap. 109.20 (*0-7837-7887-2*, 204764300007) Bks Demand.

— Nephrotic Syndrome. LC 82-9427. (Contemporary Issues in Nephrology Ser.: No. 9). (Illus.). 320p. reprint ed. pap. 99.20 (*0-7837-2568-X*, 204272700006) Bks Demand.

Brenner, Barry M., et al. Renal Physiology in Health & Disease. (Illus.). 190p. 1987. pap. text 36.00 (*0-7216-1973-8*, W B Saunders Co) Harcrt Hlth Sci Grp.

Brenner, Barry M., jt. auth. see Laragh, John H.

Brenner, Barry M., jt. ed. see Tisher, C. Craig.

Brenner, Carla. Weekends with Impressionists. (Illus.). 80p. 1997. 18.95 (*0-7893-0111-3*, Pub. by Universe) St Martin.

Brenner, Carla, ed. see Loveman, Aurelia.

Brenner, Carliene. Integrating Biotechnology in Agriculture: Incentives, Constraints, & Country Experiences. LC 97-120195. 104p. (Orig.). 1996. pap. 19.00 (*92-64-14901-5*, 41-96-05-1, Pub. by Org for Econ) OECD.

Brenner, Carliene & Komen, John. International Initiatives in Biotechnology for Developing Country Agriculture: Promises & Problems. (Illus.). 60p. (Orig.). (C). 1995. pap. text 30.00 (*0-7881-2587-7*) DIANE Pub.

Brenner, Charles. An Elementary Textbook of Psychoanalysis. enl. rev. ed. LC 72-86658. x, 280p. 1973. 45.00 (*0-8236-1621-5*) Intl Univs Pr.

— An Elementary Textbook of Psychoanalysis. rev. ed. 272p. 1974. reprint ed. pap. 11.95 (*0-385-09884-7*, Anchor NY) Doubleday.

— Mind in Conflict. LC 82-21391. v, 266p. (Orig.). 1982. 40.00 (*0-8236-3365-9*) Intl Univs Pr.

— Psychoanalytic Technique & Psychic Conflict. LC 76-15047. 126p. (Orig.). 1976. 32.50 (*0-8236-5054-5*) Intl Univs Pr.

Brenner, Charles, jt. auth. see Arlow, Jacob A.

Brenner, Christine T., jt. ed. see Taebel, Delbert A.

Brenner, Clarence D. Bibliographical List of Plays in the French Language, Seventeen Hundred to Seventeen Eighty-Nine. LC 76-43909. (Music & Theatre in France in the 17th & 18th Centuries Ser.). reprint ed. 64.50 (*0-404-60152-9*) AMS Pr.

Brenner, Claudia & Ashley, Hannah. Eight Bullets: One Woman's Story of Surviving Anti-Gay Violence. LC 95-4327. 216p. 1995. pap. 16.95 (*1-56341-055-9*) Firebrand Bks.

— Eight Bullets: One Woman's Story of Surviving Anti-Gay Violence. LC 95-4327. 216p. 1995. lib. bdg. 26.95 (*1-56341-056-7*) Firebrand Bks.

Brenner, D., jt. auth. see Bilodeau, M.

Brenner, Daeg S., jt. ed. see Meyer, Richard A.

Brenner, Daniel L. Law & Regulation of Common Carriers in the Communications Industry. 2nd ed. (C). 1995. text 79.00 (*0-8133-2740-7*, Pub. by Westview) HarpC.

Brenner, Daniel L., et al. Cable Television & Other Nonbroadcast Media: Law & Policies. LC 85-30946. (Entertainment & Communication Law Ser.). 1986. ring bd. 145.00 (*0-87632-489-8*) West Group.

Brenner, David. The Effective Psychotherapist: Conclusions from Practice & Research. (General Psychology Ser.: No. 105). 160p. 1982. pap. text 16.95 (*0-08-028055-2*, Pergamon Pr) Elsevier.

— Marketing Identities: The Invention of Jewish Ethnicity in Ost und West. LC 97-50452. (Illus.). 256p. 1998. pap. 21.95 (*0-8143-2684-6*) Wayne St U Pr.

Brenner, David J. Radon: Risk & Remedy. LC 88-33529. 225p. 1989. pap. text 9.60 (*0-7167-2030-2*) W H Freeman.

Brenner, David J. & Hall, Eric J. Making the Radiation Therapy Decision. (Illus.). 216p. 1996. 27.00 (*1-56565-333-5*) Lowell Hse.

Brenner, Debbie & Hill, Gary. Credits, 3 Vols., Set. (Orig.). 1985. pap. 75.00 (*0-935469-00-1*) Magpie Pr.

Brenner, Diane, jt. ed. see Rowland, Marilyn.

Brenner, Donald J. The Language of Computer Publishing. 2nd ed. Essman, Dawn M. & Brenner, Robert C., eds. 436p. (Orig.). 1994. pap. 24.95 (*0-929535-14-6*) Brenner Info Group.

Brenner, Donald J., jt. ed. see Brown, Steven R.

Brenner, Eliot & Harwood, William. Desert Storm: The Weapons of War: Air, Land, & Sea Techno-Weapons in the Persian Gulf. (Illus.). 96p. (Orig.). 1997. reprint ed. pap. text 15.00 (*0-7881-5022-7*) DIANE Pub.

Brenner, Eric, jt. auth. see Horn, Wade F.

Brenner, Everett H. Beyond Boolean: New Approaches to Information Retrieval. LC 97-126805. (NFAIS Report Ser.: Vol. 3). 143p. 1996. pap. 75.00 (*0-942308-48-4*) NFAIS.

Brenner, Fred J., jt. ed. see Genoways, Hugh H.

Brenner, Frederic. Exile at Home. LC 98-190119. (Illus.). 80p. 1998. 49.50 (*0-8109-3269-5*, Pub. by Abrams) Time Warner.

Brenner, Frederic, photos by. Jews - America - A Representation. (Illus.). 438p. 1996. 75.00 (*0-8109-3522-8*, Pub. by Abrams) Time Warner.

Brenner, Gabrielle A., jt. auth. see Brenner, Reuven.

Brenner, George D. Plan Smart, Retire Rich! (Illus.). 230p. 1998. 24.95 (*0-07-044464-1*) McGraw.

— Smart Assets: Turning You & Your Business into a Wealth Machine. (Illus.). 176p. 1997. pap. text 14.95 (*0-07-007645-6*) McGraw.

Brenner, George D., et al. Smart Assets: Turning You & Your Business into a Wealth Machine. 2nd rev. ed. LC 98-13345. 1998. 24.95 (*0-07-007652-9*) McGraw.

— Turning You & Your Business into a Wealth Machine. 1996. 29.95 (*0-7863-1102-9*, Irwn Prfssnl) McGraw-Hill Prof.

Brenner, George M. Pharmacology Review. rev. ed. 255p. 1996. pap. text. write for info. (*0-7216-4604-2*, W B Saunders Co) Harcrt Hlth Sci Grp.

Brenner, Gerry. Concealment in Hemingway's Works. LC 83-6283. (Illus.). 291p. reprint ed. pap. 90.30 (*0-608-09657-1*, 206977200006) Bks Demand.

— The Old Man & the Sea: Story of a Common Man. (Twayne's Masterwork Studies: No. 80). 136p. 1991. 29.00 (*0-8057-7991-4*, Twyne) Mac Lib Ref.

Brenner, Gerry & Rovit, Earl H. Ernest Hemingway. rev. ed. (United States Authors Ser.: No.497). 240p. (C). 1986. 32.00 (*0-8057-7455-6*) Macmillan.

***Brenner-Golomb, N. & Brenner, Y. S.** A Theory of Full Employment. 2nd ed. LC 99-28889. 220p. 1999. pap. 24.95 (*0-7658-0608-8*) Transaction Pubs.

Brenner-Golomb, N., jt. auth. see Brenner, Y. S.

Brenner, H. D., et al, eds. Towards a Comprehensive Therapy of Schizophrenia. rev. ed. LC 96-931627. (Illus.). 288p. 1997. text 49.00 (*0-88937-175-X*) Hogrefe & Huber Pubs.

Brenner, Hans Dieter, et al, eds. The Treatment of Schizophrenia: Status & Emerging Trends. (Illus.). 332p. 2000. text 39.00 (*0-88937-195-4*) Hogrefe & Huber Pubs.

Brenner, Howard & Edwards, David A. Macrotransport Processes. (Series in Chemical Physics). 744p. 1993. text 105.00 (*0-7506-9332-0*) Buttrwrth-Heinemann.

Brenner, Howard, et al. Interfacial Transport Processes & Rheology. (Chemical Engineering Ser.). (Illus.). 576p. 1991. text 92.95 (*0-7506-9185-9*) Buttrwrth-Heinemann.

Brenner, Howard, jt. auth. see Churchill, Stuart W.

Brenner, Howard, jt. auth. see Happel, John R.

Brenner, Ira, jt. auth. see Kestenberg, Judith S.

Brenner, Jacques, ed. see Voltaire.

Brenner, James T., ed. Friend Alice: The Civil War Letters of Cpt. David D. Bard, 104th Regiment, Ohio Infantry. 110p. 1996. pap. 7.95 (*0-9675208-0-0*) Old Portage.

Brenner, Jan, jt. auth. see Broadwell, Lynn.

Brenner, Joel F. & Franklin, Herbert M. Rent Control in North America & Four European Countries. 78p. 1977. pap. 14.95 (*0-87855-733-4*) Transaction Pubs.

Brenner, Joel G. The Emperors of Chocolate: Inside the Secret World of Hershey & Mars. LC 99-44715. 384p. 2000. pap. 14.00 (*0-7679-0457-5*) Broadway BDD.

— The Emperors of Chocolate: Inside the Secret World of Hershey & Mars. LC 98-21610. (Illus.). 336p. 1998. 25.95 (*0-679-42190-4*) Random.

***Brenner, Joel G.** Emperors of Chocolate: Inside the Secret World of Hershey & Mars. (Illus.). (J). 2000. 19.35 (*0-606-17997-6*) Turtleback.

Brenner, Johanna. Women & the Politics of Class. LC 99-27817. 1999. pap. 19.95 (*1-58367-010-6*, Pub. by Monthly Rev) NYU Pr.

***Brenner, Johanna.** Women & the Politics of Class. LC 99-27817. 320p. 1999. 50.00 (*1-58367-009-2*, Pub. by Monthly Rev) NYU Pr.

Brenner, Johanna, et al, eds. Rethinking the Political. (Political Science Gender Studies). 300p. 1995. pap. 19.95 (*0-226-07399-8*); lib. bdg. 39.95 (*0-226-07397-1*) U Ch Pr.

***Brenner, John.** Anniversary Reflections: Bible Study. 1999. 37.99 (*0-8100-1140-9*) Northwest Pub.

Brenner, John, tr. see Sanseido Editorial Dept. Staff.

Brenner, Joseph Hayyim. Out of the Depths. 101p. 1992. text. write for info. (*0-8133-8446-X*) Westview.

Brenner, Kerri, jt. auth. see Gordon, Deborah.

Brenner, Kevin & Kelly, Kate. Renovating with a Contractor: The Complete Homeowner's Guide to Updating or Adding on to Your House Using a Home Contractor. LC 95-44167. 200p. 1996. pap. 12.95 (*0-87833-904-3*) Taylor Pub.

Brenner, Lenni. Jews in America Today. 256p. 1986. 17.95 (*0-8184-0379-9*) Carol Pub Group.

— The Lesser Evil: The Democratic Party. 1988. 19.95 (*0-8184-0482-5*) Carol Pub Group.

***Brenner, Leslie.** American Appetite: The Coming of Age of a Cuisine. LC 99-10314. (Illus.). 304p. 1999. 25.00 (*0-380-97336-7*, Avon Bks) Morrow Avon.

— American Appetite: The Coming of Age of a National Cuisine. 384p. 2000. 14.00 (*0-380-78825-X*) Morrow Avon.

Brenner, Leslie. Art of the Cocktail Party: The Complete Guide to Sophisticated Entertaining. (Illus.). 272p. 1994. pap. 13.95 (*0-452-27235-1*, Plume) Dutton Plume.

***Brenner, Leslie.** Greetings from the Golden State: A Novel. 240p. 2001. 23.00 (*0-8050-6564-4*, Owl) H Holt & Co.

Brenner, Leslie & Kinsolving, Katharine. Essential Flavors: The Art of Cooking with Infused Oils, Flavored Vinegars, Essences, & Elixirs. (Illus.). 285p. 1999. text 25.00 (*0-7881-6045-1*) DIANE Pub.

Brenner, Louis. West African Sufi: The Religious Heritage & Spiritual Search of Cerno Bokar Saalif Taal. 214p. 1996. 49.95 (*0-614-21380-0*, 1296) Kazi Pubns.

Brenner, Louis, ed. Muslim Identity & Social Change in Sub-Saharan Africa. LC 93-10131. (Illus.). 260p. (C). 1994. 36.95 (*0-253-31269-8*); pap. 15.95 (*0-253-31271-X*) Ind U Pr.

Brenner, Lynn. Building Your Nest Egg with Your 401(K) A Guide to Help You Achieve Retirement Security. LC 96-173637. 160p. (Orig.). Date not set. pap. 16.95 (*1-885123-09-4*) Investors Pr.

— The Insurance Information Institute's Handbook for Reporters. LC 93-5909. 1993. 22.50 (*0-932387-38-1*) Insur Info.

***Brenner, Lynn.** Smart Questions to Ask Your Financial Adviser. LC 99-461713. 304p. 1999. reprint ed. pap. 12.00 (*0-425-16904-9*) Berkley Pub.

Brenner, Lynn. Smart Questions to Ask Your Financial Advisers. LC 97-29575. (Bloomberg Personal Bookshelf Ser.). 288p. 1997. 19.95 (*1-57660-015-7*, Pub. by Bloomberg NJ) Norton.

Brenner, M., et al, eds. Clustering Phenomena in Atoms & Nuclei: Proceedings of the International Conference on Nuclear & Atomic Clusters 1991, 3-7 June 1991, Turku, Finland. (Series in Nuclear & Particle Physics). (Illus.). 640p. 1992. 107.95 (*0-387-55101-8*) Spr-Verlag.

Brenner, M. Harvey. Mental Illness & the Economy. LC 72-85144. 320p. 1973. 34.00 (*0-674-56875-3*) HUP.

Brenner, M. K., jt. ed. see Hoffbrand, A. Victor.

Brenner, Marcella B. & Lieberman, E. James. Interview Art & Skill. 192p. (C). 1980. pap. text 12.95 (*0-937286-00-1*) Irvington.

Brenner, Marie. Great Dames: What I Learned from Older Women. LC 99-45585. 224p. 2000. 22.00 (*0-609-60612-3*, BIO022000, Crown) Crown Pub Group.

— House of Dreams: The Collapse of an American Dynasty. 432p. 1989. mass mkt. 4.95 (*0-380-70727-6*, Avon Bks) Morrow Avon.

Brenner, Mark. When "No" Gets You Nowhere: Teaching Your Toddler & Child Self-Control. LC 97-1560. 160p. 2000. pap. 14.00 (*0-7615-0954-2*) Prima Pub.

Brenner, Martha. Abe Lincoln's Hat. LC 93-31867. (Step into Reading Ser.: A Step 2 Book). (Illus.). 48p. (J). (gr. 1-3). 1994. pap. 3.99 (*0-679-84977-7*, Pub. by Random Bks Yng Read) Random.

— Abe Lincoln's Hat. LC 93-31867. (Step into Reading Ser.: A Step 2 Book). (Illus.). 48p. (J). (ps-3). 1994. lib. bdg. 11.99 (*0-679-94977-1*, Pub. by Random Bks Yng Read) Random.

Brenner, Martha. Abe Lincoln's Hat. (Step into Reading Ser.: A Step 2 Book). (J). (gr. 1-3). 1994. 9.19 (*0-606-06909-7*, Pub. by Turtleback) Demco.

***Brenner, Martha F.** Stacks of Trouble. LC 99-88839. (Math Matters Ser.). (Illus.). 32p. (J). (gr. 1-3). 2000. pap. 4.95 (*1-57565-098-3*) Kane Pr.

Brenner, Martha L., ed. see Lincoln, Abraham.

Brenner, Martin L. The Song of the Sea; Ex 15: 1-21. (Beiheft zur Zeitschrift fuer die Alttestamentliche Wissenschaft Ser.: Vol. 195). viii, 193p. 1991. lib. bdg. 67.70 (*3-11-012340-1*) De Gruyter.

Brenner, Marty, jt. auth. see Lindberg, Rick.

Brenner, Matthew. Critical Care Medicine, Year 2000 Edition: Current Clinical Strategies. rev. ed. (Current Clinical Strategies Ser.). 100p. 1999. pap. 16.95 (*1-881528-77-4*) Current Clin Strat.

***Brenner, Matthew & Safani, Michael.** Critical Care Medicine: 2000 Edition. rev. ed. (Current Clinical Strategies Ser.). 1999. pap. 32.95 incl. cd-rom (*1-881528-78-2*) Current Clin Strat.

***Brenner, Max.** The Abduction of Harp Adams. LC 99-65309. 192p. 2000. pap. 11.95 (*1-56315-212-6*, Pub. by SterlingHse) Natl Bk Netwk.

Brenner, Michael. After the Holocaust. 1999. pap. 12.95 (*0-691-00679-2*, Pub. by Princeton U Pr) Cal Prin Full Svc.

— After the Holocaust: Rebuilding Jewish Life in Post War Germany. Harshav, Barbara, tr. LC 97-1149. 185p. 1997. 24.95 (*0-691-02665-3*, Pub. by Princeton U Pr) Cal Prin Full Svc.

— The Renaissance of Jewish Culture in Weimar Germany. LC 95-30449. (Illus.). 320p. 1996. 40.00 (*0-300-06262-1*); pap. 18.00 (*0-300-07720-3*) Yale U Pr.

— Spreading Nuclear Capabilities: New Trends. (Research Note Ser.). 1986. 10.00 (*0-86682-071-X*) Ctr Intl Relations.

— Terms of Engagement: The United States & the European Security Identity. 144p. 1998. pap. 19.95 (*0-275-96497-3*, Praeger Pubs) Greenwood.

— Terms of Engagement: The United States & the European Security Identity, 176. (Washington Papers: Vol. 176). 144p. 1998. 49.95 (*0-275-96496-5*, Praeger Pubs) Greenwood.

Brenner, Michael, ed. Multilateralism & Western Strategy. LC 94-25722. 1994. text 55.00 (*0-312-12361-2*) St Martin.

***Brenner, Michael, et al, eds.** Two Nations: British German Jews in Comparative Perspective. LC 99-233269. (Schriftenreihe Wissenschaftlicher Abhandlungen des Leo Baeck Instituts Ser.). 320p. 1999. 97.50 (*3-16-147106-7*, Pub. by JCB Mohr) Coronet Bks.

Brenner, Michael & Penslar, Derek J., eds. In Search of Jewish Community: Jewish Identities in Germany & Austria, 1918-1933. LC 98-8304. 272p. 1998. 39.95 (*0-253-33427-6*); pap. 24.95 (*0-253-21224-3*) Ind U Pr.

Brenner, Michael J. The Iraq-Iran War: Speculations about a Nuclear Rerun. (CISA Working Papers: No. 49). 31p. (Orig.). 1985. pap. 15.00 (*0-86682-062-0*) Ctr Intl Relations.

— The United States-China Nuclear Bilateral Accord. (Pew Case Studies in International Affairs). 50p. (C). 1986. pap. text 3.50 (*1-56927-106-2*) Geo U Inst Dplmcy.

Brenner, Morgan G. College Basketball's National Championship: The Complete Record of Every Tournament Ever Played, Vol. 13. LC 98-41568. (American Sports History Ser.). 1056p. 1998. text 98.50 (*0-8108-3474-X*) Scarecrow.

Brenner, Paul. Health Is a Question of Balance. 2nd ed. 1992. pap. 12.95 (*0-9633554-0-6*) Continuum Pr.

***Brenner, Paul.** If Life is a Game, How Come I'm Not Having Fun? (C). 2001. pap. text 14.95 (*0-7914-4964-5*) State U NY Pr.

— If Life is a Game, How Come I'm Not Having Fun? (C). 2001. text 44.50 (*0-7914-4963-7*) State U NY Pr.

Brenner, Paul. Life Is a Shared Creation. 176p. (Orig.). 1981. pap. 6.95 (*0-87516-454-4*) DeVorss.

— Mi. (Orig.). 1983. pap. 5.00 (*0-914135-00-7*) Rainbow Med Clinic.

***Brenner, Paul & Martin, Donna.** Seeing Your Life Through New Eyes: Insights to Freedom from Your Past. LC 99-88573. (Illus.). 176p. 2000. pap., wbk. ed. 14.95 (*1-58270-022-2*, Pub. by Beyond Words Pub) Publishers Group.

Brenner, Paul F., jt. ed. see Mishell, Daniel R., Jr.

Brenner, Peter. King for One Day. LC 74-151271. (Illus.). 36p. (J). (ps-3). 12.95 (*0-87592-027-6*) Scroll Pr.

Brenner, R. & Merced, Stoka A. Chagas' Disease Vectors: Anatomic & Physiological Aspects. LC 87-13209. 1987. reprint ed. 88.00 (*0-8493-4348-8*, CRC Reprint) Franklin.

— Chagas' Disease Vectors: Taxonomic Ecological & Epidemiological Aspects. LC 87-13209. 168p. 1987. reprint ed. 99.00 (*0-8493-4347-X*, CRC Reprint) Franklin.

Brenner, R. James, jt. auth. see Gorczyca, David P.

Brenner, Rachel F. A. M. Klein, the Father of Canadian Jewish Literature: Essays in the Poetics of Humanistic Politics. LC 89-13775. (Jewish Studies: Vol. 7). 164p. 1990. lib. bdg. 79.95 (*0-88946-259-3*) E Mellen.

— Assimilation & Assertion: The Response to the Holocaust in Mordecai Richler's Writing. (American University Studies: General Literature: Ser. XIX, Vol. 19). X, 219p. (C). 1989. text 35.20 (*0-8204-0811-5*) P Lang Pubng.

— Writing As Resistance: Four Women Confronting the Holocaust, Edith Stein, Simone Weil, Anne Frank & Etty Hillesum. LC 96-20613. 1997. 26.50 (*0-271-01623-X*) Pa St U Pr.

Brenner, Reeve R. The Faith & Doubt of Holocaust Survivors. LC 97-743. 288p. 1997. 35.00 (*0-7657-5993-4*) Aronson.

Brenner, Reuven. Betting on Ideas: Wars, Invention, Inflation. LC 85-8750. (Illus.). xii, 256p. 1986. 38.50 (*0-226-07400-5*) U Ch Pr.

— Betting on Ideas: Wars, Invention, Inflation. LC 85-8750. (Illus.). 260p. 1989. pap. text 16.00 (*0-226-07401-3*) U Ch Pr.

— History-The Human Gamble. LC 83-5780. xiv, 248p. 1983. 17.50 (*0-226-07402-1*) U Ch Pr.

— Labyrinth of Prosperity. LC 94-177. 312p. 1994. pap. text 21.95 (*0-472-06556-4*, 06556) U of Mich Pr.

— Labyrinth of Prosperity. LC 94-177. 312p. 1994. text 51.50 (*0-472-09556-0*, 09556) U of Mich Pr.

Brenner, Reuven & Brenner, Gabrielle A. Gambling & Speculation: A Theory, a History & a Future of Some Human Decisions. 298p. (C). 1990. text 52.95 (*0-521-38180-0*) Cambridge U Pr.

Brenner, Rica. Ten Modern Poets. LC 68-22091. (Essay Index Reprint Ser.). 1977. 20.95 (*0-8369-0249-1*) Ayer.

— Twelve American Poets Before 1900. LC 68-22092. (Essay Index Reprint Ser.). 1977. 20.95 (*0-8369-0250-5*) Ayer.

Brenner, Richard. Baseball Superstars. (J). 1924. write for info. (*0-688-16588-5*, Wm Morrow) Morrow Avon.

***Brenner, Richard.** Basketball Superstars Album 1999. (Illus.). 48p. (gr. 4-7). 1998. pap. 4.50 (*0-688-16230-4*, Wm Morrow) Morrow Avon.

Brenner, Richard. Kobe Bryant. 32p. (J). 1999. write for info. (*0-688-16584-2*, Wm Morrow) Morrow Avon.

— Kobe Bryant. (Illus.). 32p. (J). (gr. 1-4). 1999. pap. 3.95 (*0-688-16585-0*, Wm Morrow) Morrow Avon.

***Brenner, Richard.** Mark McGwire. (Illus.). 32p. (J). (gr. 1-4). 1999. pap. 4.50 (*0-688-17085-4*, Wm Morrow) Morrow Avon.

Brenner, Richard. Michael Jordan. LC 99-160559. (Illus.). 32p. (J). (ps-3). 1999. pap. 3.95 (*0-688-16587-7*, Wm Morrow) Morrow Avon.

— Michael Jordan. (J). 2000. 25.01 (*0-688-16586-9*, Wm Morrow) Morrow Avon.

***Brenner, Richard.** Sammy Sosa. (Illus.). 32p. (gr. 1-4). 1999. pap. 4.50 (*0-688-17084-6*, Wm Morrow) Morrow Avon.

— Superstar Album 1998: Football. LC 98-209960. 48p. 1998. mass mkt. 4.50 (*0-688-16229-0*, Wm Morrow) Morrow Avon.

— Superstar Album 1999: Baseball. 48p. (J). 1999. mass mkt. 4.95 (*0-688-16589-3*, Wm Morrow) Morrow Avon.

Brenner, Robert. Celluloid: Collectibles from the Dawn of Plastics. LC 98-83290. (Illus.). 208p. 1999. 39.95 (*0-7643-0833-5*) Schiffer.

— Christmas Past. rev. ed. (Illus.). 192p. 1996. pap. 29.95 (*0-7643-0172-1*) Schiffer.

— Christmas Revisited. LC 86-61297. (Illus.). 206p. 1986. pap. 24.95 (*0-88740-067-1*) Schiffer.

— Christmas Revisited. 2nd rev. ed. (Illus.). 206p. 1999. pap. 24.95 (*0-7643-0887-4*) Schiffer.

— Christmas Through the Decades. 2nd ed. LC 95-85276. (Illus.). 256p. 1999. 69.95 (*0-88740-545-2*) Schiffer.

— Depression Glass for Collectors. LC 98-85124. 176p. 1998. 24.95 (*0-7643-0670-7*) Schiffer.

— Desktop Production Standards. Hanson, Jenny, ed. 1998. pap. 49.95 (*0-929535-19-7*) Brenner Info Group.

***Brenner, Robert.** Hourly Rates - New York. Hanson, Jenny, ed. 100p. 1999. pap. 24.95 (*0-929535-21-9*, 219) Brenner Info Group.

— Hourly Rates - Southern California. Hanson, Jenny, ed. 76p. 1999. pap. 24.95 (*0-929535-23-5*, 235) Brenner Info Group.

— Hourly Rates - Texas. Hanson, Jenny, ed. 62p. 1999. pap. 19.95 (*0-929535-24-3*, 243) Brenner Info Group.

Brenner, Robert. Maineville, Ohio, History: 100 Years As an Incorporated Town, 1850-1950. (Illus.). 216p. 1997. reprint ed. lib. bdg. 27.50 (*0-8328-7153-2*) Higginson Bk Co.

— Merchants & Revolution: Commercial Change, Political Conflict, & London's Overseas Traders, 1550-1653. LC 90-26252. (Illus.). 754p. reprint ed. pap. 200.00 (*0-608-09106-5*, 206973800005) Bks Demand.

***Brenner, Robert.** Turbulence in the World Economy. 1999. 25.00 (*1-85984-730-7*, Pub. by Verso) Norton.

Brenner, Robert. Valentines. LC 96-36140. 208p. 1997. 49.95 (*0-7643-0195-0*) Schiffer.

Brenner, Robert & Schiffer, Margaret B. Christmas Ornaments: A Festive Study. rev. ed. LC 84-50805. (Illus.). 168p. (Orig.). 1995. pap. 29.95 (*0-88740-878-8*) Schiffer.

***Brenner, Robert C.** Hourly Rates - Mid Atlantic Region. Hanson, Jenny, ed. 152p. 2000. pap. 32.95 (*1-930199-02-3*) Brenner Info Group.

— Hourly Rates - Minnesota. Hanson, Jenny, ed. 1999. pap. 24.95 (*1-930199-00-7*) Brenner Info Group.

— Hourly Rates - Northern California. Hanson, Jenny, ed. 83p. 1999. pap. 24.95 (*0-929535-22-7*, 227) Brenner Info Group.

— How to Price Graphic Design & DTP Services: Pricing Guide for Desktop Services. 5th ed. Hanson, Jenny, ed. (Illus.). 360p. 2000. 34.95 (*1-930199-10-4*) Brenner Info Group.

Brenner, Robert C. Pricing Guide for Desktop Services. 4th ed. Essman, Dawn M., ed. (Illus.). 382p. (YA). (gr. 12). 1995. pap. 34.95 (*0-929535-15-4*) Brenner Info Group.

***Brenner, Robert C.** Pricing Guide for Web Services. 2nd rev. ed. Hanson, Jenny, ed. (Illus.). 320p. 2000. pap. 32.95 (*1-930199-03-1*) Brenner Info Group.

— Pricing Tables - California. 6th ed. Hanson, Jenny, ed. 127p. 1999. ring bd. 49.95 (*0-929535-20-0*, 200) Brenner Info Group.

— Pricing Tables - Canada. 6th ed. Hanson, Jenny, ed. 183p. 1999. ring bd. 49.95 (*0-929535-11-1*, 111) Brenner Info Group.

— Pricing Tables - Mid Atlantic Region. 6th ed. Hanson, Jenny, ed. 1999. pap. 49.95 (*1-930199-01-5*) Brenner Info Group.

— Pricing Tables - Mountain States. Hanson, Jenny, ed. 2000. pap. 49.95 (*1-930199-07-4*) Brenner Info Group.

— Pricing Tables - New England. 6th ed. Hanson, Jenny, ed. 2000. pap. 49.95 (*1-930199-06-6*) Brenner Info Group.

— Pricing Tables - North Central. 6th ed. Hanson, Jenny, ed. 146p. 2000. pap. 49.95 (*1-930199-05-8*) Brenner Info Group.

An Asterisk (*) at the beginning of an entry indicates that the title is appearing for the first time.

— Pricing Tables - Pacific Region. 6th ed. Hanson, Jenny, ed. 2000. 49.95 (*1-930199-08-2*) Brenner Info Group.
— Pricing Tables - South Atlantic. 6th ed. Hanson, Jenny, ed. 136p. 2000. pap. 49.95 (*1-930199-04-X*) Brenner Info Group.
Brenner, Robert C. & Harker, Marisa. Pricing Tables - South Central. 1996. pap. 49.95 (*1-930199-09-0*) Brenner Info Group.
Brenner, Robert C., jt. auth. see Capelo, Gregory R.
Brenner, Robert C., ed. see Brenner, Donald J.
Brenner, Rodolfo R. & Stoka, Angel de la Merced, eds. Chagas' Disease Vectors: Biochemical Aspects & Control, 3 vols., Set. 512p. 1987. 187.00 (*0-8493-4346-1*, RA644, CRC Reprint) Franklin.
Brenner, Roslyn F. Philadelphia's Outdoor Art: A Walking Tour. 2nd ed. LC 86-19989. (Illus.). 128p. (Orig.). 1987. pap. 9.95 (*0-940159-00-7*) Camino Bks.
Brenner, S. & Hanihara, K. Origin & Past of Homo Sapiens. (Human Biology Ser.). 316p. 1995. text 61.00 (*981-02-1912-1*) World Scientific Pub.
Brenner, Sara, jt. ed. see Parish, Lawrence Charles.
Brenner, Saul, ed. American Judicial Behavior. LC 73-10235. 250p. 1974. text 37.50 (*0-8422-5116-2*) Irvington.
Brenner, Saul & Spaeth, Harold J. Stare Indecisis: The Alteration of Precedent on the Supreme Court, 1946-1992. 165p. (C). 1995. text 54.95 (*0-521-45188-4*) Cambridge U Pr.
Brenner, Sayers R. Suffering from Illusion: The Secret Victory of Self-Defeat. LC 94-65657. (Illus.). 341p. 1994. reprint ed. pap. 16.95 (*0-9640827-0-5*) Paradox Bks.
Brenner, Sheila & Tachikawa, H., eds. Representations of Algebras. (London Mathematical Society Lecture Note Ser.: No. 168). (Illus.). 301p. (C). 1992. pap. text 59.95 (*0-521-42411-9*) Cambridge U Pr.
Brenner, Steven, et al. CGI Scripting with Perl. 490p. 1995. pap. 39.95 incl. cd-rom (*1-55851-462-7*, M&T Bks) IDG Bks.
Brenner, Summer. Dancers & the Dance. LC 90-30312. 160p. (Orig.). (YA). 1990. pap. 9.95 (*0-918273-75-7*) Coffee Hse.
— From the Heart to the Center. 1976. pap. 7.50 (*0-935724-84-2*) Figures.
— From the Heart to the Center. deluxe ed. 1976. pap. 10.00 (*0-935724-59-1*) Figures.
***Brenner, Summer.** Ivy: Tale of a Homeless Girl in San Francisco. 2000. pap. 12.95 (*0-88739-287-3*) Creat Arts Bk.
Brenner, Summer. One Minute Movies. 76p. (Orig.). 1996. pap. 9.95 (*0-614-13245-2*) Bay Area Ctr Art & Tech.
— The Soft Room. 1978. pap. 8.00 (*0-935724-80-X*) Figures.
— The Soft Room. deluxe ed. 1978. pap. 10.00 (*0-935724-55-9*) Figures.
Brenner, Susan, jt. auth. see Rosen, Marion.
Brenner, Susan W. Precedent Inflation. 376p. (C). 1991. text 44.95 (*0-88738-440-4*) Transaction Pubs.
Brenner, Susanne & Scott, L. Ridgway. The Mathematical Theory of Finite Element Methods. LC 93-40882. (Texts in Applied Mathematics Ser.: Vol.15). (Illus.). 294p. 1996. 47.95 (*0-387-94193-2*) Spr-Verlag.
Brenner, Suzanne A. The Domestication of Desire: Women, Wealth, & Modernity in Java. LC 97-46124. 336p. 1998. text 55.00 (*0-691-01693-3*, Pub. by Princeton U Pr); pap. text 19.95 (*0-691-01692-5*, Pub. by Princeton U Pr) Cal Prin Full Svc.
Brenner, Sydney, compiled by. Molecular Biology: A Selection of Papers. 622p. 1990. pap. text 52.00 (*0-12-131200-3*) Acad Pr.
Brenner, Sydney & Miller, Jeffrey K., eds. Encyclopedia of Genetics, 4 vols. 2800p. 1999. write for info. (*0-12-227080-0*) Acad Pr.
Brenner, T., et al. Chibi: A True Story from Japan. (Illus.). 64p. (J). (gr. k-4). 1999. pap. 5.95 (*0-395-72088-5*, Clarion Bks) HM.
Brenner, Teddy & Nagler, Barney. Only the Ring Was Square. LC 81-5940. 164p. 1981. 10.95 (*0-685-03883-1*) P-H.
***Brenner, Thomas.** Modelling Learning in Economics. LC 99-14860. 352p. 1999. 100.00 (*1-84064-134-7*) E Elgar.
Brenner, Thomas E. Computational Techniques for Modeling Learning in Economics. LC 99-25823. (Advances in Computational Economics Ser.). xiii, 390p. 1999. write for info. (*0-7923-8503-9*) Kluwer Academic.
— Five Years of Foundation Building: The University of Puerto Rico, 1924-1929. 157p. (C). 1963. 2.50 (*0-8477-0819-5*) U of PR Pr.
Brenner, Vincent C., et al. West's Intermediate Accounting. (Illus.). 1336p. (C). 1983. text. write for info. (*0-314-80324-6*) West Pub.
— West's Intermediate Accounting, Pt. I, Working Papers. (Illus.). 1336p. (C). 1983. pap. text. write for info. (*0-314-72286-6*) West Pub.
— West's Intermediate Accounting, Pt. II, Working Papers. (Illus.). 1336p. (C). 1983. write for info. (*0-314-72287-4*) West Pub.
Brenner, W. & Kolbe, L., eds. The Information Superhighway & Private Households: Case Studies of Business Impacts. (Illus.). x, 427p. 1996. pap. text 99.00 (*3-7908-0907-1*) Spr-Verlag.
Brenner, W., et al. Intelligent Software Agents: Foundations & Applications. LC 98-14462. 260p. 1998. 44.00 (*3-540-63411-8*) Spr-Verlag.
Brenner, Wendy. Large Animals in Everyday Life: Stories. 168p. 1997. pap. 11.00 (*0-393-31648-3*) Norton.
— Large Animals in Everyday Life: Stories. LC 95-21692. 168p. 1996. 22.95 (*0-8203-1794-2*) U of Ga Pr.
Brenner, William H. Logic & Philosophy: An Integrated Introduction. LC 92-56865. (C). 1993. text 34.50 (*0-268-01302-0*); pap. text 18.50 (*0-268-01299-7*) U of Notre Dame Pr.
— Wittgenstein's Philosophical Investigations. LC 98-38226. (SUNY Series in Philosophy). (Illus.). 224p. (C). 1999. text 57.50 (*0-7914-4201-2*); pap. text 18.95 (*0-7914-4202-0*) State U NY Pr.
Brenner, William H., tr. see Schulte, Joachim.
Brenner, Y. S. Agriculture & the Economic Development of Low Income Countries. LC 77-146701. (Publications of the Institute of Social Studies: No. 2). 254p. 1972. pap. text 16.15 (*90-279-1713-2*) Mouton.
— Looking into the Seeds of Time: The Price of Modern Development. 2nd rev. ed. LC 97-30355. 385p. 1997. pap. 24.95 (*1-56000-996-9*) Transaction Pubs.
— The Rise & Fall of Capitalism. 320p. 1991. text 95.00 (*1-85278-527-6*) E Elgar.
Brenner, Y. S., et al, eds. Income Distribution in Historical Perspective. (Illus.). 275p. (C). 1991. text 59.95 (*0-521-35647-4*) Cambridge U Pr.
Brenner, Y. S. & Brenner-Golomb, N. A Theory of Full Employment. LC 95-42650. 232p. (C). 1996. lib. bdg. 109.00 (*0-7923-9651-0*) Kluwer Academic.
Brenner, Y. S., jt. auth. see Brenner-Golomb, N.
Brenner, Zara R. Diagnostic Tests & Procedures. 304p. (C). 1987. pap. text 31.95 (*0-8385-1594-0*, A1594-9) Appleton & Lange.
Brennerbar. Group Soup. 1999. pap. 4.99 (*0-14-054093-8*) NAL.
Brennert, Alan. Her Pilgrim Soul. (Illus.). 256p. 1992. mass mkt. 3.99 (*0-8125-3195-7*, Pub. by Tor Bks) St Martin.
— Kindred Spirits. LC 99-46879. 256p. 1999. pap. text 13.95 (*0-312-87262-3*, Pub. by Forge NYC) St Martin.
— Kindred Spirits. (Illus.). 320p. 1992. mass mkt. 4.99 (*0-8125-2414-4*) Tor Bks.
— Time & Chance. 1990. mass mkt. 4.95 (*0-8125-3188-4*) Tor Bks.
Brennesholtz, Matthew S., jt. auth. see Stupp, Edward H.
Brennglass, Alan C. The Overseas Private Investment Corporation: A Study in Political Risk. LC 83-9566. 291p. 1983. 55.00 (*0-275-90952-2*, C0952, Praeger Pubs) Greenwood.
Brenni, Vito J., compiled by. American English: A Bibliography. LC 81-13412. 221p. 1981. reprint ed. lib. bdg. 35.00 (*0-313-23344-6*, BRAE, Greenwood Pr) Greenwood.
— The Art & History of Book Printing: A Topical Bibliography. LC 83-20696. 147p. 1984. lib. bdg. 49.95 (*0-313-24306-9*, BHI/, Greenwood Pr) Greenwood.
— Book Illustration & Decoration: A Guide to Research. 1. LC 80-1701. (Art Reference Collection Ser.: No. 1). 191p. 1980. lib. bdg. 75.00 (*0-313-22340-8*, BBI/, Greenwood Pr) Greenwood.
— Book Printing in Britain & America: A Guide to the Literature & a Directory of Printers. LC 83-12656. 163p. 1983. lib. bdg. 55.00 (*0-313-23988-6*, BBO/, Greenwood Pr) Greenwood.
— Bookbinding: A Guide to the Literature. LC 82-15810. 199p. 1982. lib. bdg. 47.95 (*0-313-23718-2*, BBB/, Greenwood Pr) Greenwood.
Brennicke, A. & Kuck, U., eds. Plant Mitochondria: With Emphasis on RNA Editing & Cytoplasmic Male Sterility. (Illus.). 432p. 1993. 150.00 (*3-527-30033-3*, Wiley-VCH) Wiley.
Brenning, Lee M., jt. auth. see McMartin, Barbara.
Brenning, N. & Mendillo, M., eds. Active Experiments - Critical Ionization Velocity: Proceedings of Workshop XIII & of the Topical Meeting of the COSPAR Interdisciplinary Scientific Commission D (Meeting D1) of the COSPAR 27th Plenary Meeting Held in Espoo, Finland, 18-29 July, 1988. (Advances in Space Research Ser.: Vol. 10). (Illus.). 190p. 1989. pap. 101.50 (*0-08-040164-3*, Pergamon Pr) Elsevier.
Brenning, Ulrike. Die Sprache der Empfindungen: Der Begriff Vortrag und die Musik des 18. Jahrhunderts. (Europaische Hochschulschriften Ser.: Reihe 36, Bd. 176). (Illus.). 163p. 1998. 31.95 (*3-631-32971-7*) P Lang Pubng.
Brenninkmeijer-Werhohn, Aldegonde, jt. ed. see Demmer, Klaus.
Brennlon, Fred, et al. ALT4.IBM: (Short Reference ALT4.I): New Subsonic & Supersonic Rocket Performance & Drug Programs. (Illus.). 68p. (C). 1989. pap. text 69.00 incl. disk (*0-912468-18-1*) CA Rocketry.
Brennscheidt, Gunnar. Predictive Behavior: An Experimental Study. LC 93-33121. (Lecture Notes in Economics & Mathematical Systems Ser.: Vol. 403). 1993. 55.95 (*0-387-57311-9*) Spr-Verlag.
Brennton, Fred, et al. IBM English Module: Rocket Motor Design & Analysis Program. (Illus.). 68p. (C). 1990. pap. text 49.00 incl. disk (*0-912468-21-1*) CA Rocketry.
Brensilver, Jeffrey M. & Goldberger, Emanuel. A Primer of Water, Electrolyte, & Acid-Base Syndromes. 8th ed. LC 95-11650. (Illus.). 416p. (C). 1996. pap. text 32.50 (*0-8036-0054-2*) OUP.
Brensing, Christian. Daniel Libeskind - The Jewish Museum, Berlin: Between the Lines. LC 99-201714. (Illus.). 64p. 1999. 16.95 (*3-7913-2075-0*) te Neues.
Brensing, Christian, ed. see Balmond, Cecil.
***Brensinger, Terry L.** Judges. LC 99-43081. (Believers Church Bible Commentary Ser.). 264p. 2000. pap. 21.99 (*0-8361-9104-8*) Herald Pr.
Brensinger, Terry L. Simile & Prophetic Language in the Old Testament. LC 96-7048. (Biblical Press Ser.: No. 43). 216p. 1996. 89.95 (*0-7734-2413-X*, Mellen Biblical Pr) E Mellen.
Brensinger, Terry L. & Sider, E. Morris, eds. Within the Perfection of Christ: Essays on Peace & the Nature of the Church. LC 89-82575. vi, 266p. (C). 1990. pap. 14.00 (*0-916035-37-9*) Evangel Indiana.
Brenske, Helmut, jt. auth. see Brenske, Stefan.
***Brenske, Stefan & Brenske, Helmut.** Icons - Windows on Eternity. (Illus.). 52p. 2001. pap. 25.00 (*0-8038-2017-8*, Pub. by Hastings) Midpt Trade.
Brenson, Michael. Joel Shapiro: Sculpture & Drawings. LC 96-139239. (Illus.). 54p. (Orig.). 1996. pap. write for info. (*1-878283-60-X*) PaceWildenstein.
— Magdalena Abakanowicz: Recent Sculpture. LC 93-79991. (Illus.). 68p. 1993. pap. 15.00 (*0-911517-61-8*) Mus of Art RI.
— Tony Smith: Moondog. (Illus.). 20p. 1997. pap. 15.00 (*0-9608210-4-X*) Paula Cooper Gallery.
***Brenson, Michael.** Visionaries & Outcasts. 2001. 22.95 (*1-56584-624-9*, Pub. by New Press NY) Norton.
Brenson, Michael. Where Do We Go from Here? The Place of the Artist & the NEA. 22p. (Orig.). 1995. pap. 3.00 (*0-9637817-2-3*) Schl Art Inst.
Brenson, Michael, et al. Culture in Action: A Public Art Program of Sculpture Chicago. LC 94-78551. (Illus.). 144p. (Orig.). 1995. pap. 20.00 (*0-941920-31-3*) Bay Pr.
— Luis Jimenez: Working-Class Heroes: Images from the Popular Culture. (Illus.). 84p. (Orig.). 1997. pap. 24.00 (*1-882603-05-2*) Mid Am Arts.
Brenson, Michael, jt. auth. see Teicher, Hendel.
Brenson, Michael, jt. ed. see Jacob, Mary J.
Brent. Silence of Isaac Babel. 1994. pap. text 14.95 (*0-226-07396-3*) U Ch Pr.
Brent, et al. Just in Time Algebra for Students of Calculus in Management & the Lifesciences. 192p. (C). 1997. pap. 26.40 (*0-201-31666-8*) Addison-Wesley.
Brent, Allen. Cultural Episcopacy & Ecumenism: Representative Ministry in Church History from the Age of Ignatius of Antioch to the Reformation. LC 92-190. (Studies in Christian Mission: Vol. 6). xiv, 250p. 1992. 82.00 (*90-04-09432-6*) Brill Academic Pubs.
— Hippolytus & the Roman Church in the Third Century: Communities in Tension Before the Emergence of a Monarch-Bishop. LC 95-183489. (Supplements to Vigiliae Christianae Ser.: Vol. 31). 611p. 1997. 186.00 (*90-04-10245-0*, BR1720) Brill Academic Pubs.
***Brent, Allen.** The Imperial Cult & the Development of Church Order. LC 99-36631. (Supplements to Vigilie Christian Ser.). 1999. 124.00 (*90-04-11420-3*) Brill Academic Pubs.
Brent, Bill. Black Book: The Guide for the Erotic Explorer. 4th ed. (Illus.). 224p. 1997. reprint ed. pap. 15.00 (*0-9637401-3-X*) Black Books.
— The Black Book: The Guide for the Erotic Explorer. 5th ed. (Illus.). 224p. (Orig.). 1997. pap. 15.00 (*0-9637401-5-6*) Black Books.
— Make a Zine! A Guide to Self-Publishing Disguised As a Book on How to Produce a Zine. LC 97-70048. (Illus.). 192p. (Orig.). 1997. pap. 10.00 (*0-9637401-4-8*) Black Books.
Brent, Bill & Queen, Carol, eds. Best Bisexual Erotica. 224p. 2000. pap. 16.00 (*1-892723-01-8*) Black Books.
***Brent, Bill & Shows, Rod.** The Black Book: The Guide for the Erotic Explorer. 6th ed. (Illus.). 256p. (Orig.). 2000. pap. 17.00 (*0-9637401-6-4*) Black Books.
Brent, Brian O., jt. auth. see Monk, David H.
Brent, C. H. Brent: Descendants of Col. Giles Brent Capt. George Brent & Robert Brent, Immigrants to Maryland & Virginia. (Illus.). 195p. 1993. reprint ed. pap. 31.00 (*0-8328-3650-8*); reprint ed. lib. bdg. 41.00 (*0-8328-3649-4*) Higginson Bk Co.
Brent, Carol D. Barbecue: The Fine Art of Charcoal & Gas Outdoor Cooking. LC 71-152731. 1971. 5.95 (*0-88351-005-7*) Test Recipe.
— Crepes: The Fine Art of Crepe & Blintz Cooking. LC 76-25350. 1976. 5.95 (*0-685-04875-6*) Test Recipe.
— Eggs: The Fine Art of Egg, Omelet & Souffle Cocking. LC 73-122450. 1970. 5.95 (*0-88351-006-5*) Test Recipe.
— Fondue: The Fine Art of Fondue, Chinese Wok & Chafing Dish Cooking. LC 79-95289. 1969. 5.95 (*0-88351-000-6*) Test Recipe.
— Pancakes - Waffles: The Fine Art of Pancake, Waffle, Crepe & Blintz Cooking. LC 73-122449. 1970. 5.95 (*0-88351-007-3*) Test Recipe.
Brent, Carol D. & Hughes, Betty A. Barbecuing the Weber Covered Way. LC 72-85084. 1980. 7.95 (*0-88351-002-2*) Test Recipe.
Brent, Carolyn, jt. auth. see Giamario, Daniel.
Brent, Charles H. Inspiration of Responsibility, & Other Papers. LC 67-22081. (Essay Index Reprint Ser.). 1977. 18.95 (*0-8369-0251-3*) Ayer.
— The Sixth Sense: Its Cultivation & Use. 1993. reprint ed. pap. 16.95 (*1-872736-47-5*, Pub. by Mandrake Pr) Holmes Pub.
Brent, E. J. & Atkin, E. K., eds. Rational Pesticide Use. (Illus.). 360p. 1987. text 80.00 (*0-521-32068-2*) Cambridge U Pr.
Brent, Edward E., Jr. & Anderson, Ronald E. Computer Applications in the Social Sciences. 384p. (C). 1990. 49.95 (*0-87722-666-0*) Temple U Pr.
Brent, Elizabeth, jt. auth. see Brent, Steve.
Brent, Frances P., tr. see Ratushinskaya, Irina.
Brent, Gary R. Microsoft Projects for Windows 95. LC 96-207443. (C). 1996. pap. text 6.00 (*0-8053-1613-2*) Benjamin-Cummings.
Brent, Gary R. Select Microsoft Windows 95 Projects Module. (C). 1995. pap. text 8.00 (*0-8053-1188-2*) Benjamin-Cummings.
Brent, Gary R. Select Visual Basic 3.O Projects for Windows Module. LC 95-231135. (C). 1995. pap. text 8.00 (*0-8053-1187-4*) Benjamin-Cummings.
— Select Visual Field Guide Microsoft Excel 7 Projects for Windows 95. (C). 1997. pap. text. write for info. (*0-8053-1615-9*) Addison-Wesley.
— Visual Select: Windows 97. (C). 1997. pap. text. write for info. (*0-8053-1637-X*) Benjamin-Cummings.
Brent, Gary R. Windows 95: Lab Series Brief. (C). 1996. pap. text 20.00 (*0-8053-1618-3*) Benjamin-Cummings.
Brent, Gerry. Housing the Pig. (Illus.). 256p. 1986. 32.95 (*0-85236-157-2*, Pub. by Farming Pr) Diamond Farm Bk.
— The Pigman's Handbook. 2nd ed. (Illus.). 256p. 1987. pap. 29.95 (*0-85236-170-X*, Pub. by Farming Pr) Diamond Farm Bk.
Brent, Harry & Lutz, William. Rhetorical Considerations: Essays for Analysis. 4th ed. LC 83-19587. 496p. reprint ed. pap. 153.80 (*0-7837-4745-4*, 204455400004) Bks Demand.
Brent, Harry, jt. auth. see Lutz, William.
Brent, Isabelle. Christmas Record Book. 1992. 16.99 (*1-85145-607-4*, Pavilion Bks) Viking Penguin.
Brent, Isabelle. Christmas Fairy Tales. LC 95-62373. 144p. 1996. 19.99 (*0-670-86805-1*) Viking Penguin.
***Brent, Jonathan.** Silence of Isaac Babel. 1998. 34.00 (*0-226-07395-5*) U Ch Pr.
Brent, Joseph. Charles Sanders Peirce: A Life. LC 92-19888. (Illus.). 412p. 1993. 35.00 (*0-253-31267-1*) Ind U Pr.
— Charles Sanders Peirce: A Life. enl. rev. ed. LC 98-23868. (Illus.). 448p. 1998. 35.00 (*0-253-33350-4*); pap. 18.95 (*0-253-21161-1*) Ind U Pr.
Brent, Joseph, III, jt. auth. see Leffler, Phyllis K.
Brent, Joseph, jt. auth. see Muller, John P.
Brent, Leslie. A History of Transplantation Immunology. LC 96-36685. (Illus.). 488p. 1996. text 54.95 (*0-12-131770-6*) Morgan Kaufmann.
Brent, Linda, pseud. Incidents in the Life of a Slave Girl. Child, L. Maria, ed. LC 72-90506. (Illus.). 228p. (C). 1973. pap. 10.00 (*0-15-644350-3*, Harvest Bks) Harcourt.
Brent, Michael R., ed. Computational Approaches to Language Acquisition. LC 97-11047. (Cognition Special Issues Ser.). (Illus.). 205p. 1997. pap. text 20.00 (*0-262-52229-2*) MIT Pr.
Brent, Nancy J. A Guide to Principles & Applications. Eoyang, Thomas. ed. LC 96-30633. (Illus.). 525p. 1997. pap. text 28.50 (*0-7216-3463-X*, W B Saunders Co) Harcrt Hlth Sci Grp.
Brent, Paul. Beyond the Bay. 352p. 1985. 13.95 (*0-9615014-1-3*) Bay Pubns.
Brent, Rebecca. Simulated Opening of School. (Illus.). 77p. 1998. pap. text 15.00 (*1-880094-29-0*, 1-880094) Assn Advan Comput Educ.
Brent, Richard. Liberal Anglican Politics: Whiggery, Religion & Reform, 1830-1841. LC 87-5567. (Oxford Historical Monographs). (Illus.). 352p. 1987. text 69.00 (*0-19-822942-9*) OUP.
Brent, Robert J. Applied Cost-Benefit Analysis. LC 95-13485. (Illus.). 360p. 1996. 100.00 (*1-85898-285-5*) E Elgar.
— Applied Cost-Benefit Analysis. LC 95-13485. 360p. 1997. pap. text 30.00 (*1-85898-338-X*) E Elgar.
Brent, Robert J. Cost-Benefit Analysis for Developing Countries. LC 97-30628. 320p. 1998. 90.00 (*1-85898-567-6*) E Elgar.
***Brent, Robert J.** Cost-Benefit Analysis for Developing Countries. LC 95-13485. 320p. 2000. pap. 30.00 (*1-84064-442-7*) E Elgar.
Brent, Roger, et al. Current Protocols in Molecular Biology Vol. 3, 3 vols., Vol. 3. Ausubel, Frederick M., ed. 1600p. 1988. 635.00 (*0-471-50338-X*) Wiley.
Brent, Ronald I., jt. auth. see Mueller, Guntram.
Brent, Ruth & Schwarz, Benyamin, eds. Popular American Housing: A Reference Guide. LC 94-47420. (American Popular Culture Ser.). 272p. 1995. lib. bdg. 79.50 (*0-313-28032-0*, Greenwood Pr) Greenwood.
Brent-Smith, Alexander. Schubert: Second Quartet in D Minor & Octet. 55p. 1990. reprint ed. lib. bdg. 59.00 (*0-7812-9166-6*) Rprt Serv.
Brent, Stephen M. & Stiller, Sharon P. Handling Drunk Driving Cases. LC 84-52337. 1985. 120.00 (*0-685-59840-3*) West Group.
Brent, Steve & Brent, Elizabeth. Couple's Guide to the Best of Erotic Video. LC 96-45960. 208p. 1997. pap. 11.95 (*0-312-15081-4*) St Martin.
Brent, Stuart. The Seven Stairs: An Adventure of the Heart. (Illus.). 256p. 1989. per. 11.00 (*0-671-67394-7*) S&S Trade Pap.
Brent, Vickie. . . . That We Might See, Vol. 300. unabridged ed. Phillips, Lorene, ed. 96p. 1998. pap. 10.00 (*0-89754-153-7*, R-01) Dan River Pr.
Brentano. Des Knaben Wunderhorn. unabridged ed. (World Classic Literature Ser.). (GER.). pap. 7.95 (*3-89507-037-8*, Pub. by Bookking Intl) Distribks Inc.
Brentano & Eichendorff. German Romantic Stories. Ryder, Frank G., ed. LC 81-22184. (German Library: Vol. 35). 320p. (C). 1987. 39.50 (*0-8264-0312-3*) Continuum.
Brentano, Carroll, ed. see Clifford, Geraldine J.
Brentano, Carroll, ed. see May, Henry F.
Brentano, Clemens. The Legend of Rosepetal. Bell, Anthea, tr. LC 95-6621.Tr. of Marchen von Rosenblattchen. (Illus.). 32p. (J). (gr. k-3). 1995. 16.95 (*1-55858-484-6*, Pub. by North-South Bks NYC) Chronicle Bks.
Brentano, F. C. On the Existence of God: Lectures Given at the Universities of Wurzburg & Vienna (1868-1891) Krantz, S. F., ed. & tr. by. (Nijhoff International Philosophy Ser.: No. 29). 370p. 1987. lib. bdg. 201.00 (*90-247-3538-6*) Kluwer Academic.
Brentano, Franz. Descriptive Psychology. Mueller, Benito, ed. & tr. by. LC 94-44167. (International Library of Philosophy).Tr. of Deskriptive Psychologie. 232p. (C). (gr. 13). 1995. 75.00 (*0-415-10811-X*, C0403) Routledge.
— Psychology from an Empirical Standpoint. McAlister, Linda L. et al, trs. LC 95-7729. (International Library of Philosophy). 448p. (C). 1995. pap. 27.99 (*0-415-10661-3*, B4322) Routledge.
— Von der Mannigfachen Bedeutung des Seienden Nach Aristoteles. x, 220p. 1983. reprint ed. 40.00 (*3-487-00010-5*) G Olms Pubs.

Brentano, L. English Gilds, Their Statutes & Customs, A. D. 1389, with an Essay on Gilds & Trade-Unions. Smith, Toulmin & Smith, Lucy T., eds. (EETS, OS Ser.: Vol. 40). 1972. reprint ed. 40.00 (*0-8115-3350-6*) Periodicals Srv.

Brentano, L., jt. ed. see Smith, L. Toulmin.

Brentano, Lujo. On the History & Development of Guilds & the Origin of Trade Unions. 1972. 59.95 (*0-8490-0766-6*) Gordon Pr.

— Der Wirtschaftende Mensch in der Geschichte. xii, 498p. 1967. reprint ed. 95.00 (*0-318-70729-2*) G Olms Pubs.

— Das Wirtschaftsleben der Antiken Welt. vii, 242p. 1970. reprint ed. 40.00 (*0-318-70730-6*) G Olms Pubs.

Brentano, Mary B. Nature in the Works of Fray Luis De Granada. LC 75-94164. (Catholic University of American. Studies in Romance Languages & Literatures: No. 15). reprint ed. 37.50 (*0-404-50315-2*) AMS Pr.

Brentano, Robert. The Early Middle Ages: 500-1000. LC 64-21204. 1964. pap. 16.95 (*0-02-904670-X*) Free Pr.

— A New World in a Small Place: Church & Religion in the Diocese of Rieti, 1188-1378. LC 92-35862. 1994. 48.00 (*0-520-08076-9*, Pub. by U CA Pr) Cal Prin Full Svc.

— Rome Before Avignon: A Social History of Thirteenth-Century Rome. (Illus.). 357p. 1991. pap. 18.95 (*0-520-06952-8*, Pub. by U CA Pr) Cal Prin Full Svc.

— Two Churches: England & Italy in the 13th Century. (C). 1988. pap. 18.95 (*0-520-06098-9*, Pub. by U CA Pr) Cal Prin Full Svc.

Brentano, Robyn & Georgia, Olivia. Outside the Frame: Performance & the Object. Mills, Kathleen, ed. (Illus.). 80p. 1994. pap. text 24.95 (*1-880353-06-7*) Cleveland Ctr.

Brentano, Ron. Historic Vehicles in Miniature: The Genius of Ivan Collins. LC 98-14542. 1998. 21.95 (*0-87595-268-2*) Oregon Hist.

Brentano, Ron, pref. Ballou-Wright Automobile Accessories Catalog, 1906. LC 74-635336. (Illus.). 80p. 1971. pap. 2.95 (*0-87595-028-0*) Oregon Hist.

Brentar, Joseph C. The Social & Economic Adjustment of the Croatian Displaced Persons in Cleveland Compared with That of the Earlier Croatian Immigrants. LC 77-155331. 1971. pap. 10.00 (*0-88247-099-X*) Ragusan Pr.

Brentari, Diane. A Prosodic Model of Sign Language Phonology. LC 97-50053. (Language, Speech & Communication Ser.). (Illus.). 384p. 1999. 45.00 (*0-262-02445-4*, Bradford Bks) MIT Pr.

Brentari, Diane, ed. Foreign Vocabulary in Sign Languages: A Cross-Linguistic Investigation of Word Formation. LC 99-89780. 176p. 2000. write for info. (*0-8058-3208-4*) L Erlbaum Assocs.

Brentari, Diane, et al, eds. The Joy of Grammar: A Festschrift in Honor of James D. McCawley. LC 92-7892. xii, 400p. 1992. 89.00 (*1-55619-454-4*); pap. 29.95 (*1-55619-455-2*) J Benjamins Pubng Co.

Brenti, F. Unimodal Log-Concave & Polya Frequency Sequences in Combinatorics. LC 89-15137. (Memoirs Ser.: Vol. 81/413). 106p. 1989. pap. 19.00 (*0-8218-2476-7*, MEMO/81/413) Am Math.

Brentin, Louise, jt. auth. see Sieh, April.

Brentjes, Burchard. The Armenians, Assyrians & the Kurds: Three Nations, One Fate? LC 97-69515. (Illus.). iv, 151p. (C). 1997. pap. 12.00 (*0-9659623-1-8*) Rishi Pubns.

— The Armenians, Assyrians & the Kurds: Three Nations, One Fate? unabridged ed. (Illus.). 150p. 1997. 24.00 (*0-9659623-0-X*) Rishi Pubns.

— Oil, Dollars & Politics. LC 98-68675. (Illus.). 314p. 1999. 28.00 (*0-9659623-3-4*) Rishi Pubns.

Brentlinger, John. The Best of What We Are: Reflections on the Nicaraguan Revolution. LC 95-20330. (Illus.). 384p. 1995. pap. 20.95 (*0-87023-985-6*) U of Mass Pr.

— The Best of What We Are: Reflections on the Nicaraguan Revolution. LC 95-20330. (Illus.). 384p. (C). 1995. text 55.00 (*0-87023-984-8*) U of Mass Pr.

Brentlinger, John A., ed. see Plato.

Brentnall, John M. Just a Talker: Sayings of John ("Rabbi") Duncan. 271p. 1997. pap. 15.99 (*0-85151-726-9*) Banner of Truth.

Brentnall, Margaret. John Hutton: Artist & Glass Engraver. LC 84-45005. (Illus.). 216p. 1987. 55.00 (*0-87982-502-2*) Art Alliance.

Brentnall, Savannah. Object Orientation in Visual FoxPro. 224p. (C). 1996. pap. 19.95 (*0-201-47943-5*) Addison-Wesley.

Brenton. Churchill Plays. 1991. pap. 9.95 (*0-413-33906-8*) Routledge.

Brenton, Albert, et al, eds. Preferences & Democracy: Villa Colombella Papers. LC 92-42163. (International Studies in Economics & Econometrics: Vol. 28). 416p. 1993. lib. bdg. 169.50 (*0-7923-9321-X*) Kluwer Academic.

Brenton, Arthur, Jr. & Taetz, Philip. Elements of Plane Surveying. 420p. (C). 1991. 70.63 (*0-07-004884-3*) McGraw.

***Brenton, Chris.** Mastering Cisco Routers. (Illus.). 800p. 2000. 49.99 (*0-7821-2643-X*) Sybex.

Brenton, Chris. Mastering Network Security. LC 98-87201. (Mastering Ser.). (Illus.). xxvi, 704p. 1998. pap. text 49.99 (*0-7821-2343-0*) Sybex.

— Multiprotocol Network Design & Troubleshooting. LC 97-67760. 848p. 1997. 49.99 (*0-7821-2082-2*) Sybex.

Brenton, Dan. Balancing Act: The Art of Living Out Desired Priorities. (Life Skills Ser.). (Illus.). 4p. (C). 1996. teacher ed., ring bd. 1.25 (*1-57334-020-0*, 742-103t); student ed., ring bd. 3.25 (*1-57334-019-7*, 742-103s) WSN Pr.

Brenton, Howard. Berlin Bertie. 96p. 1992. pap. 11.95 (*1-85459-153-3*, Pub. by N Hern Bks) Theatre Comm.

Brenton, Howard. Berlin Bertie. 96p. 1996. pap. 14.95 (*1-85459-242-4*, Pub. by N Hern Bks) Theatre Comm.

— Brenton: Plays One, Vol. 1. (Methuen World Dramatists Ser.). 390p. (C). 1988. pap. write for info. (*0-413-40430-7*, A0040, Methuen Drama) Methn.

— Brenton: Plays Two. (Methuen World Dramatists Ser.). 399p. (Orig.). (C). 1990. pap. write for info. (*0-413-61490-5*, A0412, Methuen Drama) Methn.

***Brenton, Howard.** Hot Irons. 1998. pap. 16.95 (*0-413-71180-3*) Methn.

Brenton, Howard. Hot Irons: Diaries, Essays & Journalism 1980-1994. 256p. 1995. 34.95 (*1-85459-123-1*, Pub. by N Hern Bks) Theatre Comm.

— Magnificence: A Play. 71p. (C). 1988. pap. write for info. (*0-413-46750-3*, A0163, Methuen Drama) Methn.

— The Romans in Britain: A Play. 103p. (C). 1988. pap. 9.95 (*0-685-63034-X*, A0246) Heinemann.

***Brenton, Howard.** Ugly Rumours. LC 99-232663. 1999. pap. 14.95 (*1-85459-426-5*, Pub. by Theatre Comm) Consort Bk Sales.

Brenton, Howard & Hare, David. Brassneck. 102p. (C). 1974. pap. write for info. (*0-413-31760-9*, A0161, Methuen Drama) Methn.

— Pravda: A Fleet Street Comedy. (Methuen Modern Plays Ser.). 113p. (Orig.). (C). 1988. pap. 9.95 (*0-413-58480-1*, A0228) Heinemann.

Brenton, Howard, tr. see Buchner, Georg.

Brenton, Howard, tr. see Goethe, Johann Wolfgang Von.

Brenton, Jane, tr. see Hassner, Pierre.

Brenton, Lancelot C. Septuagint with Apocrypha: Greek & English. 1386p. 1986. 44.95 (*0-913573-44-2*) Hendrickson MA.

Brenton, Maria. The Voluntary Sector in British Social Services. LC 85-4285. (Social Policy in Modern Britain Ser.). 278p. reprint ed. pap. 86.20 (*0-7837-1604-4*, 204189600024) Bks Demand.

Brenton, Paul & Pelkmans, Jacques, eds. Global Trade & European Workers. LC 98-7077. 240p. 1999. text 69.95 (*0-312-21686-6*) St Martin.

Brenton, Thaddeus R. Bahia: Ensenada & It's Bay; Farce, Fiesta & Frustration in a Small Mexican City. LC 77-26758. (Illus.). 158p. 1978. reprint ed. lib. bdg. 55.00 (*0-313-20173-0*, BRBA, Greenwood Pr) Greenwood.

Brenton, Tony. The Greening of Machiavelli: The Evolution of International Environmental Politics. 282p. (C). 1994. 54.95 (*1-85383-214-6*); pap. 24.95 (*1-85383-211-1*) Brookings.

Brenton, Willis C. According to White Eyes. LC 86-17414. 1988. pap. 13.95 (*0-87949-256-2*) Ashley Bks.

Brentwood/Provident Staff, contrib. by. Celtic Psalms: Music to Soothe the Soul. 16.98 incl. audio compact disk (*0-7601-2583-X*) Brentwood Music.

Brenzel, Barbara M. Daughters of the State: A Social Portrait of the First Reform School for Girls in North America 1856-1905. (Joint Center for Urban Studies). (Illus.). 206p. 1985. pap. text 12.95 (*0-262-52104-0*) MIT Pr.

Brenzinger, Matthias, ed. Language Death: Factual & Theoretical Explorations (with Special Reference to East Africa) (Contributions to the Sociology of Language Ser.: No. 64). (Illus.). viii, 445p. 1992. lib. bdg. 160.00 (*3-11-013404-7*) Mouton.

Breo, Dennis L., jt. auth. see Eliot, Robert S.

Breon, Brad, ed. see Bank, Frank & Twyman, Gib.

Brepether & Sherrill. Contrabandista de Dios. (SPA.). 2000. pap. 5.99 (*0-8297-1697-1*) Vida Pubs.

BREPOLS Staff. Dictionary of the Bible & Its Religions: Judaism, Christianity & Islam: Dictionnaire de la Bible & des Religions du Livre: Judaisme, Christianisme, Islam. (FRE.). 456p. 1985. 175.00 (*0-8288-1202-0*, M7938) Fr & Eur.

Brereton. A Plan for Writing. 3rd ed. (C). 1987. pap. text, teacher ed. 27.50 (*0-03-001433-6*) Harcourt Coll Pubs.

Brereton. Problem Solving in Chemometrics. text. write for info. (*0-471-48977-8*); pap. text. write for info. (*0-471-48978-6*) Wiley.

Brereton, Austin. Life of Henry Irving, 2 vols., 1 bk. LC 74-88604. (Illus.). 1972. 36.95 (*0-405-08305-X*, Pub. by Blom Pubns) Ayer.

— Some Famous Hamlets, from Burbage to Fechter. 74p. 1977. 12.95 (*0-8369-7276-7*) Ayer.

Brereton, Bonnie P. Thai Tellings of Phra Malai: Texts & Rituals Concerning a Popular Buddhist Saint. (Illus.). 231p. (Orig.). 1995. pap. text 24.95 (*1-881044-07-6*) ASU Prog SE Asian.

Brereton, Bridget, ed. The Colonial Caribbean in Transition: Essays on Post-Emancipation Social & Cultural History. 1999. 49.95 (*0-8130-1996-6*) U Press Fla.

Brereton, Bridget & Yelvington, Kevin A. The Colonial Caribbean in Transition: Essays on Post-Emancipation Social & Cultural History. LC 98-53065. 1999. write for info. (*0-8130-1696-7*) U Press Fla.

Brereton, Charles. New Hampshire Notables. (Illus.). 256p. 1986. 5.00 (*0-914339-11-7*) P E Randall Pub.

Brereton, Cloudesley, tr. see Bergson, Henri.

Brereton, Dan. Nocturnals: Black Planet. Rich, Jamie S., ed. (Illus.). 184p. 1998. pap. 19.95 (*0-9667127-0-6*) Oni Pr Inc.

Brereton, Dan & Green, Randy. Buffy the Vampire Slayer. (Illus.). 80p. (YA). (gr. 7 up). 1998. pap. 8.95 (*1-56971-342-1*) Dark Horse Comics.

Brereton, Geoffrey. Principles of Tragedy: A Rational Examination of the Tragic Concept in Life & Literature. LC 69-12459. 1968. 19.95 (*0-87024-104-4*) U of Miami Pr.

Brereton, Geoffrey, tr. & intro. see Froissart, Jean.

Brereton, Georgine E. & Ferrier, Janet M., eds. Le Menagier de Paris: A Critical Edition. 1981. 95.00 (*0-19-815748-7*) OUP.

Brereton, Joel P. The Rigvedic Adityas. (American Oriental Ser.: Vol. 63). x, 356p. 1981. pap. 17.00 (*0-940490-63-3*) Am Orient Soc.

Brereton, John. Chain Mail: The History of the Duke of Lancaster's Own Yeomanry 1798-1991. 320p. 1990. 118.00 (*0-948251-67-0*, Pub. by Picton) St Mut.

— A Plan for Writing. 3rd ed. 264p. (C). 1987. pap. text 36.50 (*0-03-001432-8*, Pub. by Harcourt Coll Pubs) Harcourt.

Brereton, John C. The Origins of Composition Studies in the American College, 1875-1925: A Documentary History. (Series in Composition, Literacy, & Culture). 584p. (C). 1996. pap. 24.95 (*0-8229-5535-0*); text 59.95 (*0-8229-3783-2*) U of Pittsburgh Pr.

***Brereton, John C. & Mansfield, Margaret A.** Writing on the Job: A Norton Pocket Guide. LC 99-27453. 1999. spiral bd. 14.00 (*0-393-97511-8*) Norton.

Brereton, Lewis. The Brereton Diaries. (Politics & Strategy of World War II Ser.). 1976. reprint ed. lib. bdg. 45.00 (*0-306-70766-7*) Da Capo.

— Brereton Diaries. (American Autobiography Ser.). 450p. 1995. reprint ed. lib. bdg. 99.00 (*0-7812-8464-3*) Rprt Serv.

Brereton, Richard G., ed. Multivariate Pattern Recognition in Chemometrics: Illustrated by Case Studies. LC 92-28342. (Data Handling in Science & Technology Ser.: Vol. 2). 326p. (Orig.). 1992. pap. 108.00 (*0-444-89784-4*) Elsevier.

Brereton, Richard G., et al, eds. Chemometrics Tutorials 2. viii,314p. 1992. pap. 180.00 (*0-444-89858-1*) Elsevier.

Brereton, Shannon. Story Rids: Treat Me Wrong & You'll Put Me in a Jar? (Illus.). 32p. (J). (gr. 1-3). 1998. pap. 7.50 (*0-8059-4422-2*) Dorrance.

Brereton, Thomas & Dunaway, James. Exploring the Backcountry of Zion National Park: Off-Trail Routes. rev. ed. (Illus.). 91p. 1996. pap. 7.50 (*0-915630-25-7*) Zion.

***Brereton, Todd R.** Educating the U. S. Army: Arthur L. Wagner & Reform. LC 99-47299. (Illus.). 2000. text 45.00 (*0-8032-1301-8*) U of Nebr Pr.

Brereton, Virginia L. From Sin to Salvation: Stories of Women's Conversions, 1800 to the Present. LC 90-46091. 170p. 1991. 32.00 (*0-253-31213-2*) Ind U Pr.

Bres & Weisshaar. Thinking about Biology. LC 97-30394. 376p. 1997. pap. text 48.00 (*0-13-633033-9*) P-H.

Bres, jt. auth. see Weisshaar.

Bres, B. Confirmed in Love. (C). 1988. 30.00 (*0-85439-125-8*, Pub. by St Paul Pubns) St Mut.

Bres, Mimi & Schiff, Stefan O. Twenty-One Afternoons of Biology: A Laboratory Manual. 208p. (C). 1996. pap. text, spiral bd. write for info. (*0-8403-9680-5*) Kendall-Hunt.

Bres, Mimi & Weisshaar, Arnold. Human Biology. 246p. (C). 1995. text 27.00 (*0-536-58972-0*) Pearson Custom.

Bres, P. Public Health Action in Emergencies Caused by Epidemics: A Practical Guide. 299p. 1986. pap. text 49.00 (*92-4-154207-1*, 1150253) World Health.

Bresc, Genevieve. The Louvre: An Architectural History. LC 95-15362. (Illus.). 224p. 1995. text 75.00 (*0-86565-963-X*) Vendome.

Bresc, Henri. Politique et Societe en Sicile 12e - 15e Siecles. (Collected Studies: No. CS329). 320p. 1991. text 115.95 (*0-86078-285-9*, Pub. by Variorum) Ashgate Pub Co.

Brescher, Antoinette & Abbamont, Gary W. Study Smart! Ready-to-Use Reading-Skill Skills Activities for Grades 5-12. 256p. 1990. pap. text 29.95 (*0-87628-872-7*) Ctr Appl Res.

Brescher, Antoinette, jt. auth. see Abbamont, Gary W.

Breschine, G. S., ed. see Gallegos, Dennis & Kyle, Carolyn.

Breschini, ed. see Porcasi, Judith, et al.

Breschini, G. I., ed. see Elsasser, Albert B. & Rhode, P. T.

Breschini, G. I., ed. see Pastron, Allen G. & Walsh, Michael R.

Breschini, G. S. & Haversat, Trudy. Archaeological Excavations at CA-MNT-108 at Fisherman's Wharf, Monterey County, California. (Archives of California Prehistory Ser.: Vol. 29). (Illus.). 190p. (Orig.). (C). 1989. pap. text 20.63 (*1-55567-067-9*) Coyote Press.

— Archaeological Excavations at CA-SLO-7 & CA-SLO-8, Diablo Canyon, San Luis Obispo County, California. (Archives of California Prehistory Ser.: Vol. 28). (Illus.). 118p. (Orig.). (C). 1988. pap. text 13.13 (*1-55567-064-4*) Coyote Press.

— An Overview of the Esselen Indians of Central Monterey County, California. fac. ed. (Illus.). 43p. (C). 1994. reprint ed. pap. text 4.69 (*1-55567-514-X*) Coyote Press.

Breschini, G. S., et al. Analysis of South-Central California Shell Artifacts, Vol. 23. (Archives of California Prehistory Ser.: No. 23). (Illus.). 106p. (Orig.). (C). 1988. pap. 12.24 (*1-55567-040-7*) Coyote Press.

Breschini, G. S., ed. see Parkman, E. B., et al.

Breschini, Gary S. Models of Population Movements in Central California Prehistory. (Illus.). x, 120p. (Orig.). 1983. pap. text 14.38 (*1-55567-010-5*) Coyote Press.

Breschini, Gary S. & Haversat, Trudy. Archaeological Investigations at CA-FRE-1333 in the White Creek Drainage, Western Fresno County, California. (Archives of California Prehistory Ser.: No. 12). (Illus.). 109p. (Orig.). 1987. pap. 12.19 (*1-55567-045-8*) Coyote Press.

— Archaeological Investigations at CA-SLO-99, Pismo Beach, San Luis Obispo County, California. (Archives of California Prehistory Ser.: Vol. 26). (Illus.). 80p. (Orig.). (C). 1988. pap. text 9.69 (*1-55567-062-8*) Coyote Press.

— La Cueva Pintada CA-MNT-256: A Technical Report on Documenting the Rock Paintings at CA-MNT-256 Site. (Illus.). 40p. (Orig.). (C). 1980. pap. text 4.38 (*1-55567-012-1*) Coyote Press.

— Papers on Central California Prehistory. (Archives of California Prehistory Ser.: No. 3). (Illus.). 90p. (Orig.). (C). 1984. pap. 10.31 (*1-55567-023-7*) Coyote Press.

— The Physical Anthropology of Central California Pt. I: Osteometric Data. fac. ed. 110p. (C). 1980. reprint ed. pap. text 12.19 (*1-55567-511-5*) Coyote Press.

Breschini, Gary S. & Haversat, Trudy, eds. Symposium: A New Look at Some Old Sites. (Archives of California Prehistory Ser.: No. 6). 86p. (Orig.). 1986. pap. 10.00 (*1-55567-037-7*) Coyote Press.

Breschini, Gary S., et al. California Radiocarbon Dates. 8th ed. vi, 120p. (C). 1996. pap. 14.38 (*1-55567-011-3*) Coyote Press.

— Papers on California Prehistory, No. 8, Pt. 1. (Archives of California Prehistory Ser.: No. 8). (Illus.). 98p. (Orig.). 1986. pap. 9.69 (*1-55567-041-5*) Coyote Press.

— Salinas: 10,000 Years on the Salinas Plain. Parks, Lori, ed. LC 99-73083. (Illus.). 300p. 1999. 39.95 (*1-886483-29-9*, Pub. by Heritge Media) Sunbelt Pubns.

Breschini, Gary S., ed. see Berman, Joan.

Breschini, Gary S., ed. see Colten, Roger H.

Breschini, Gary S., ed. see Elsasser, Albert B.

Breschini, Gary S., ed. see Haversat, Trudy, et al.

Breschini, Gary S., ed. see Parsons, Gary A., et al.

Breschini, Gary S., ed. see Stodder, Ann L.

Breschini, Gary S., ed. see Sutton, Mark Q.

Breschini, Gary S., ed. see Towne, Arlean H.

Brescia, Cinina, tr. see Vittorini, Elio.

***Brescia, Martha T.** Another Chance. LC 99-62232. 312p. 1999. pap. 14.95 (*1-56167-520-2*, Five Star Spec Ed) Am Literary Pr.

Brescia, Michael, jt. ed. see Cimino, James E.

Bresciani, Francesco, ed. Perspectives in Steroid Receptor Research. fac. ed. LC 79-5398. (Illus.). 334p. pap. 103.60 (*0-7837-7164-9*, 204713300005) Bks Demand.

Bresciani, Francesco, et al, eds. Hormones & Cancer II: Proceedings of the Second International Congress on Hormones & Cancer. LC 84-11722. (Progress in Cancer Research & Therapy Ser.: No. 31). (Illus.). 735p. reprint ed. pap. 200.00 (*0-608-09637-7*, 205441300001) Bks Demand.

Bresciani, Francesco, ed. see International Congress on Hormones & Cancer Staff.

Bresciani-Turroni, Constantino. The Economics of Inflation: A Study of Currency Depreciation in Post-War Germany. Savers, Millicent E., tr. LC 68-6120. (Illus.). 464p. 1968. reprint ed. 49.50 (*0-678-06030-4*) Kelley.

Bresco, Jose L. Encyclopedie Pratique du Desin et des Arts Decoratifs. (FRE.). 75.00 (*0-7859-0734-3*, M6046) Fr & Eur.

Brescoll, James. Sales. (Opportunities in...Ser.). (Illus.). 128p. 1993. pap. 7.95 (*0-8442-8688-5*, VGM Career) NTC Contemp Pub Co.

Brescoll, James & Dahm, Ralph M. Opportunities in Sales Careers. LC 94-49548. (Opportunities In . . . Ser.). 160p. pap. 11.95 (*0-8442-4439-2*, 44392, VGM Career) NTC Contemp Pub Co.

— Opportunities in Sales Careers. LC 94-49548. (Opportunities in...Ser.). 160p. 1995. 14.95 (*0-8442-4438-4*, 44384, VGM Career) NTC Contemp Pub Co.

Brescoll, James, jt. auth. see Dahm, Ralph.

Bresee, Clyde. How Grand a Flame: A Chronicle of a Plantation Family, 1813-1947. (Illus.). 270p. 1992. 21.95 (*0-945575-55-6*) Algonquin Bks.

— Sea Island Yankee. LC 95-32653. (Illus.). 300p. (C). 1995. reprint ed. pap. 12.95 (*1-57003-095-2*) U of SC Pr.

Bresee, Floyd. Successful Lay Preaching. 137p. 1997. pap. 12.95 (*1-57847-007-2*) Genl Conf Svnth-day.

Bresee, James C., ed. Geothermal Energy in Europe: The Soultz Hot Dry Rock Project. LC 91-36197. 309p. 1992. text 161.00 (*2-88124-523-4*) Gordon & Breach.

***Bresell, Ronald & Ben-Zikri, Abdul.** Radiation Safety for Radiation Workers. DeKock, Leola & North, Ralph, eds. 356p. (C). 2000. pap. text 35.00 (*0-9670043-1-4*) Univ WI.

Bresell, Ronald & Ben-Zikri, Abdul. Radiation Safety for Radiation Workers. 5th rev. ed. DeKock, Leola & North, Ralph, eds. (Illus.). 316p. (C). 1999. pap. text 25.00 (*0-9670043-0-6*) Univ WI.

Bresenhan, Karoline P. & Puentes, Nancy O. Lone Stars Vol. I: A Legacy of Texas Quilts, 1836-1936. (Illus.). 156p. 1986. pap. 27.95 (*0-292-74649-0*) U of Tex Pr.

— Lone Stars Vol. II: A Legacy of Texas Quilts, 1936-1986. (Illus.). 195p. 1990. 39.95 (*0-292-74658-X*); pap. 27.95 (*0-292-74671-7*) U of Tex Pr.

Bresette, Walter, jt. auth. see Whaley, Rick.

Breshko-Breshkovskaia, Ekaterina. The Little Grandmother of the Russian Revolution. (American Biography Ser.). 348p. 1991. reprint ed. lib. bdg. 79.00 (*0-7812-8038-9*) Rprt Serv.

Bresinsky, A. A Colour Atlas of Poisonous Fungi: Handbook for Pharmacists, Doctors, & Biologists. (Illus.). (C). (gr. 13). 1990. 102.00 (*0-7234-1576-5*) Mosby Inc.

Bresinsky, A. & Besl, H. Giftpilze, Mit Einer Einfuehrung in die Pilzbestimmung. Ein Handbuch fuer Apotheker, Aerzte & Biologen. (GER., Illus.). 1985. lib. bdg. 110.00 (*3-8047-0680-0*) Lubrecht & Cramer.

Breskend, Jean S. Backyard Design: Making the Most of the Space Around Your House. (Illus.). 224p. 1991. 35.00 (*0-8212-1776-3*, Pub. by Bulfinch Pr) Little.

— Backyard Design: Making the Most of the Space Around Your House. 224p. 1998. pap. 22.50 (*0-8212-2528-6*, Pub. by Bulfinch Pr) Little.

Breskin, David. Fresh Kills. LC 97-65397. (Poetry Ser.: Vol. LIII). 90p. (Orig.). 1997. 22.50 (*1-880834-32-4*); pap. 12.00 (*1-880834-31-6*) Cleveland St Univ Poetry Ctr.

— Inner Views: Filmmakers in Conversation. expanded ed. LC 97-20013. 409p. 1997. pap. 15.95 (*0-306-80801-3*) Da Capo.

Bresky, Dushan. Literary Practice Vol. 2: Esthetics of Style. (American University Studies: General Literature: Ser. XIX, Vol. 21). 244p. (C). 1989. text 39.00 (*0-8204-1033-0*) P Lang Pubng.

An Asterisk (*) at the beginning of an entry indicates that the title is appearing for the first time.

Bresky, Dushan & Malik, Miroslav. Literary Practice: Esthetic Qualities & Values in Literature; A Humanistic & a Biometric Appraisal, Vol. 1. (American University Studies: General Literature: Ser. XIX, Vol. 1). 215p. (C). 1984. text 25.50 (*0-8204-0199-4*) P Lang Pubng.

***Bresland, Ronald W.** The Backward Glance: C. S. Lewis & Ireland. (Illus.). 144p. 2000. pap. 17.95 (*0-85389-746-8*, Pub. by Inst Irish Studies) Irish Bks Media.

Breslau, Daniel. In Search of the Unequivocal: The Political Economy of Measurement in U. S. Labor Market Policy. LC 98-15647. 160p. 1998. 55.00 (*0-275-96321-7*, Praeger Pubs) Greenwood.

Breslau, Nathan. To Die or Not to Die. (Orig.). 1982. pap. 2.95 (*0-9610716-0-5*) N Breslau.

Breslauer, George, et al. Russia: Political & Economical Development. LC 95-38503. (Monographs: Vol. 9). 1995. pap. write for info. (*0-930607-20-1*) Keck Ctr.

Breslauer, George W. Soviet Strategy in the Middle East. 352p. (C). (gr. 13). 1989. text 62.95 (*0-04-445232-2*) Routledge.

Breslauer, George W., et al, eds. Beyond the Cold War: Conflict & Cooperation in the Third World. LC 91-31527. (Research Ser.: No. 80). x, 410p. (Orig.). 1991. pap. text 19.95 (*0-87725-180-0*) U of Cal IAS.

Breslauer, George W., jt. auth. see Dallin, Alexander.

Breslauer, Jan. The Making of the Rugrats Movie: Behind the Scences at Klasky Csupo. (Rugrats Ser.). (Illus.). 144p. (J). (ps-3). 1998. 25.00 (*0-671-02809-X*, PB Hardcover) PB.

Breslauer, Ken. Fifty Years of Stock Car Racing: A History of Collectibles & Memorabilia. LC 97-35906. (Illus.). 144p. (Orig.). 1998. pap. 24.95 (*0-9649722-5-5*, SCRC) D Bull.

***Breslauer, Ken.** Roadside Paradise: The Golden Age of Florida's Tourist Attractions, 1929-71. (Illus.). 96p. 2000. pap. 21.95 (*0-9678294-0-2*) Retro Florida.

Breslauer, Ken. Sebring: The Official History of America's Great Sports Car Race. Gurney, Dan, ed. (Illus.). 288p. 1996. 79.95 (*0-9649722-0-4*) D Bull.

Breslauer, Martin. Troubles of a Bibliophile or Outpourings from the Heart of a Bookloving Worldling. 1970. 5.00 (*0-910330-16-6*) Grant Dahlstrom.

Breslauer, Martin, ed. Das Deutsche Lied: Geistlich und Weltlich Bis Zum 18 Jahrhundert. xv, 301p. 1966. reprint ed. 65.00 (*0-318-71765-4*) G Olms Pubs.

Breslauer, S. Daniel. Covenant Community in Modern Judaism, 21. LC 88-24631. (Contributions to the Study of Religion Ser.: No. 21). 138p. 1989. 47.95 (*0-313-26605-0*, BRQ, Greenwood Pr) Greenwood.

— The Ecumenical Perspective & the Modernization of Jewish Religion. LC 78-9120. (Brown Judaic Studies: No. 5). 148p. reprint ed. pap. 45.90 (*0-7837-5465-5*, 204523000005) Bks Demand.

— The Hebrew Poetry of Hayyim Nahman Bialik (1873-1934) & a Modern Jewish Theology. LC 91-37226. (Jewish Studies: Vol. 10). 136p. 1991. lib. bdg. 69.95 (*0-7734-9627-0*) E Mellen.

— Judaism & Human Rights in Contemporary Thought: A Bibliographical Survey, 25. LC 92-38996. (Bibliographies & Indexes in Religious Studies: No. 25). 224p. 1993. lib. bdg. 59.95 (*0-313-27994-2*, BJI/, Greenwood.

— Meir Kahane, Ideologue, Hero, Thinker. LC 86-21703. (Jewish Studies: Vol. 1). 168p. 1986. lib. bdg. 79.95 (*0-88946-252-6*) E Mellen.

— A New Jewish Ethics. LC 83-23659. (Symposium Ser.: Vol. 9). 136p. 1983. lib. bdg. 69.95 (*0-88946-700-5*) E Mellen.

— Toward a Jewish Morality: Speaking of a Postmodern Jewish Ethics, 53. LC 97-45658. (Contributions to the Study of Religion: Vol. 53). 184p. 1998. 59.95 (*0-313-30603-6*, Greenwood Pr) Greenwood.

Breslauer, S. Daniel, compiled by. Contemporary Jewish Ethics: A Bibliographical Survey, 6. LC 85-9895. (Bibliographies & Indexes in Religious Studies: No. 6). 213p. 1985. lib. bdg. 59.95 (*0-313-24594-0*, BCJ/, Greenwood Pr) Greenwood.

— Modern Jewish Morality: A Bibliographical Survey, 8. LC 86-12145. 249p. 1986. lib. bdg. 75.00 (*0-313-24700-5*, BJM/, Greenwood Pr) Greenwood.

Breslauer, S. Daniel, ed. The Seductiveness of Jewish Myth: Challenge or Response? LC 97-7430. (Series in Judaica). 317p. (C). 1997. text 59.50 (*0-7914-3601-2*); pap. text 19.95 (*0-7914-3602-0*) State U NY Pr.

Breslaw, Elaine G. Tituba, Reluctant Witch of Salem. 1997. pap. text 18.00 (*0-8147-1307-6*) NYU Pr.

— Tituba, Reluctant Witch of Salem: Devilish Indians & Puritan Fantasies. (American Social Experience Ser.). (Illus.). 296p. (C). 1995. text 42.50 (*0-8147-1227-4*) NYU Pr.

Breslaw, Elaine G., ed. Records of the Tuesday Club of Annapolis, 1745-56. 640p. 1988. text 49.95 (*0-252-01334-4*) U of Ill Pr.

***Breslaw, Elaine G., ed.** Witches of the Atlantic World: An Historical Reader & Primary Sourcebook. 416p. 2000. pap. 24.95 (*0-8147-9851-9*); text 65.00 (*0-8147-9850-0*) NYU Pr.

***Bresler, David E. & Trubo, Richard.** Free Yourself from Pain. 2nd rev. ed. LC 99-73594. (Illus.). 479p. 1999. pap. 19.95 (*1-929295-00-6*) Awareness Pr.

Bresler, E., et al. Saline & Sodic Soils: Principles, Dynamics, Modeling. (Advanced Series in Agricultural Sciences: Vol. 10). (Illus.). 280p. 1982. 109.95 (*0-387-11120-4*) Spr-Verlag.

Bresler, E., ed. see Feigin, A., et al.

***Bresler, Fenton.** Napoleon III: A Life. (Illus.). 300p. 1999. 25.00 (*0-7867-0660-0*) Carroll & Graf.

Bresler, Judith, jt. auth. see Lerner, Ralph E.

Bresler, Michael Jay, jt. auth. see Sternbach, George L.

Bresler, Rob. The Future of Affirmative Action & Some Implications for PA. 16p. 1996. pap. 20.00 (*1-885925-08-5*) Penn State Data Ctr.

***Bresler, Robert J.** Us vs. Them: American Political & Cultural Conflict from WWII to Watergate. LC 99-36066. (American Visions Ser.: No. 2). 262p. 1999. 55.00 (*0-8420-2689-4*); pap. 17.95 (*0-8420-2690-8*) Scholarly Res Inc.

Bresler, Robert J., ed. Contemporary Controversies: An American Government Reader. LC 92-29833. 284p. (C). 1997. pap. text 33.53 (*0-06-501020-5*) Addson-Wesley Educ.

Breslin, John. Banking Law in the Republic of Ireland. LC 98-175038. xcvi, 913 p. 1998. write for info. (*0-7171-2373-1*) Gill & MacMill.

Breslin, Dee. Examining the Claims of Jesus - Chinese Edition. Shyu, Daniel C. & Cheng, Jan-Jan, trs. (CHI.). 64p. 1995. pap. 5.00 (*1-56582-024-X*) Christ Renew Min.

Breslin, Ed, ed. see Brown, Dale.

Breslin, J. William & Rubin, Jeffrey Z., eds. Negotiation: Theory & Practice. 460p. (Orig.). (C). 1991. pap. 20.00 (*1-880711-00-1*, Pon Bks) Prog Negot HLS.

Breslin, James E. Collection of Daily News Columns. 1999. pap. write for info. (*0-670-22912-1*) Viking Penguin.

— From Modern to Contemporary: American Poetry, 1945-1965. LC 83-17869. xvi, 272p. (C). 1985. pap. 9.95 (*0-226-07409-9*) U Ch Pr.

— From Modern to Contemporary: American Poetry, 1945-1965. LC 83-17869. 288p. Date not set. reprint ed. pap. 89.30 (*0-608-20607-5*, 205457500003) Bks Demand.

— Mark Rothco. 700p. 1998. pap. 27.50 (*0-226-07406-4*) U Ch Pr.

— Mark Rothko: A Biography. (Illus.). 712p. (C). 1993. 39.95 (*0-226-07405-6*) U Ch Pr.

— William Carlos Williams: An American Artist. LC 85-16343. xvi, 246p. 1985. pap. 9.95 (*0-226-07407-2*) U Ch Pr.

— William Carlos Williams, am American Artist: With a New Preface. LC 85-16343. 261p. Date not set. reprint ed. pap. 81.00 (*0-608-20608-3*, 205457600003) Bks Demand.

Breslin, Jimmy. The Gang That Couldn't Shoot Straight. LC 97-209902. 256p. 1997. pap. 12.95 (*0-316-11174-0*) Little.

— I Want to Thank My Brain for Remembering Me: A Memoir. 224p. 1997. pap. 12.95 (*0-316-11879-6*) Little.

— I Want to Thank My Brain for Remembering Me: A Memoir. large type ed. LC 96-49644. 1997. 25.95 (*0-7862-0971-2*, G K Hall Lrg Type) Mac Lib Ref.

— The Last Run: A Novel. 288p. 1999. write for info. (*0-316-11845-1*) Little.

***Breslin, Jimmy, et al.** The Story of Eduardo Gutierrez. 2001. 22.00 (*0-609-60827-4*) Crown Pub Group.

Breslin, John P. & Andersen, Poul. Hydrodynamics of Ship Propellers. (Cambridge Ocean Technology Ser.). 583p. 1996. pap. text 52.95 (*0-521-57470-6*) Cambridge U Pr.

Breslin, Jud. Selecting & Installing Software Packages: New Methodology for Corporate Implementation. LC 86-12403. 260p. 1986. 55.00 (*0-89930-158-4*, BSG/, Quorum Bks) Greenwood.

Breslin, Jud & McGann, John. The Business Knowledge Repository: Consolidating & Accessing Your Ways of Working. LC 97-8857. 224p. 1998. 62.95 (*0-89930-484-2*, BFH, Quorum Bks) Greenwood.

Breslin, Judson & Tashenberg, Bradley C. Distributed Processing Systems: End of the Mainframe Era? LC 77-16398. 240p. reprint ed. pap. 74.40 (*0-608-12234-3*, 202389200034) Bks Demand.

***Breslin, Mark.** Control Freaked. 2000. pap. (*1-895837-69-3*) Insomniac.

***Breslin, Mary Lou, ed.** Enforcing the Civil Rights of Air Travelers with Disabilities: Recommendations for the Dept. of Transportation & Congress. 154p. (C). 2000. pap. text 25.00 (*0-7567-0019-1*) DIANE Pub.

Breslin, Nancy, jt. ed. see Wiener, Jerry M.

Breslin, Paul. The Psycho-Political Muse: American Poetry since the Fifties. LC 87-10863. 280p. 1998. 33.00 (*0-226-07410-2*) U Ch Pr.

— The Psycho-Political Muse: American Poetry since the Fifties. LC 87-10863. 278p. reprint ed. pap. 86.20 (*0-608-09439-0*, 205423900005) Bks Demand.

***Breslin, Paul.** You Are Here. 2000. pap. 14.95 (*0-8101-5103-0*) Northwestern U Pr.

Breslin, Rosemary. The Easy Part. 1997. 23.00 (*0-614-19852-6*) Villard Books.

— Not Exactly What I Had in Mind: An Incurable Love Story. 229p. 3.99 (*0-679-42976-8*) Villard Books.

Breslin, Shaun. Mao. LC 98-19456. (Profiles in Power Ser.). 240p. (C). 1998. pap. 24.60 (*0-582-21525-0*) Longman.

Breslin, Shaun G. China in the 1980's: Centre-Province Relations in a Reforming Socialist State. 240p. 1996. text 75.00 (*0-312-16018-6*) St Martin.

Breslin, Susan & Stier, Eleanor. Promoting Poverty: The Shift of Resources away from Low-Income New York City School Districts. LC 89-105213. 110p. 1987. pap. text 10.00 (*0-88156-062-6*) Comm Serv Soc NY.

***Breslin, Theresa.** The Dream Master. 1999. 16.95 (*0-7540-6070-5*) Chivers N Amer.

Breslin, Thomas A., jt. auth. see Crane, Daniel M.

Breslin, W. R. Solar Still. 36p. 1979. 7.25 (*0-86619-030-9*) Vols Tech Asst.

Breslow, Arieh L. Beyond the Closed Door: Chinese Culture & the Creation of T'ai Chi Ch'uan. (Illus.). 397p. (Orig.). 1995. pap. 19.95 (*0-9644730-0-3*, Pub. by Almond Blsm Pr) New Leaf Dist.

— Beyond the Closed Door: Chinese Culture & the Creation of T'ai Chi Ch'uan. 2nd ed. 399p. (Orig.). 1995. reprint ed. mass mkt. 19.95 (*0-9644730-2-X*, Pub. by Almond Blsm Pr) New Leaf Dist.

— When Less Is More: Using the Mind to Exercise the Body. (Illus.). 175p. 1999. mass mkt. 16.95 (*0-9644730-1-1*, Pub. by Almond Blsm Pr) New Leaf Dist.

Breslow, Aron. Happy Birthday America, Every Year Evermore. (Illus.). 1976. 2.00 (*0-918430-00-3*) Happy History.

— Hello Equal Rights! (Illus.). 1988. 2.00 (*0-918430-01-1*) Happy History.

— Nothing Stops a Determined Being! 2000. write for info. (*0-918430-03-8*) Happy History.

— Save the Inch! 2.00 (*0-918430-02-X*) Happy History.

Breslow, Jonathan. Homeopathic Medicine in the Home: A Correspondence Study Course. LC 88-71470. (Illus.). 155p. (C). 1992. pap. 29.95 (*0-9620939-0-4*) Ashwin Pubns.

Breslow, Lester, et al, eds. Annual Review of Public Health, Vol. 1. (Illus.). 1980. text 45.00 (*0-8243-2701-2*) Annual Reviews.

— Annual Review of Public Health, Vol. 2. (Illus.). 1981. text 45.00 (*0-8243-2702-0*) Annual Reviews.

— Annual Review of Public Health, Vol. 3. (Illus.). 1982. text 45.00 (*0-8243-2703-9*) Annual Reviews.

— Annual Review of Public Health, Vol. 4. (Illus.). 1983. text 45.00 (*0-8243-2704-7*) Annual Reviews.

— Annual Review of Public Health, Vol. 5. (Illus.). 1984. text 45.00 (*0-8243-2705-5*) Annual Reviews.

— Annual Review of Public Health, Vol. 6. (Illus.). 1985. text 45.00 (*0-8243-2706-3*) Annual Reviews.

— Annual Review of Public Health, Vol. 7. (Illus.). 1986. text 45.00 (*0-8243-2707-1*) Annual Reviews.

— Annual Review of Public Health, Vol. 8. (Illus.). 1987. text 45.00 (*0-8243-2708-X*) Annual Reviews.

— Annual Review of Public Health, Vol. 9. (Illus.). 1988. text 45.00 (*0-8243-2709-8*) Annual Reviews.

— Annual Review of Public Health, Vol. 10. (Illus.). 1989. text 45.00 (*0-8243-2710-1*) Annual Reviews.

— Annual Review of Public Health, Vol. 11. 1990. text 45.00 (*0-8243-2711-X*) Annual Reviews.

Breslow, Marc, et al, eds. Current Economic Issues: Progressive Perspectives from Dollars & Sense. 3rd ed. (Real World Readers Ser.). (Illus.). 103p. (C) 1998. pap. 11.00 (*1-878585-38-X*) Dollars & Sense.

— Real World Macro. 15th ed. (Real World Readers Ser.). (Illus.). 136p. (Orig.). (C). 1998. pap. 14.50 (*1-878585-13-4*) Dollars & Sense.

Breslow, Marc & Scher, Abby, eds. The Environment in Crisis. (Illus.). 80p. (C). 1997. pap. text 9.50 (*1-878585-79-7*) Dollars & Sense.

Breslow, Mark, et al, eds. Real World International. 4th ed. (Real World Readers Ser.). (Illus.). 80p. (C). Date not set. pap. text 9.50 (*1-878585-12-6*) Dollars & Sense.

Breslow, Marvin, ed. The Political Writings of John Knox: The First Blast of the Trumpet Against the Monstrous Regiment of Women & Other Selected Works. LC 84-47549. 160p. 1985. 29.50 (*0-918016-75-4*) Folger Bks.

Breslow, Marvin A. Mirror of England: English Puritan Views of Foreign Nations, 1618-1640. LC 70-89966. (Historical Studies: No. 84). 189p. 1970. 17.95 (*0-674-57638-1*) HUP.

Breslow, N. E. & Day, N. E. Statistical Methods in Cancer Research: The Design & Analysis of Cohort Studies, Vol. 2. (IARC Scientific Publications: No. 82). (Illus.). 418p. 1994. reprint ed. pap. text 49.50 (*92-832-0182-5*) OUP.

— Statistical Methods in Cancer Research Vol. 1: The Analysis of Case-Control Studies, Vol. 1. (IARC Scientific Publications: No. 32). (Illus.). 352p. (C). 1993. reprint ed. pap. text 39.50 (*92-832-0132-9*, 11877) OUP.

Breslow, Norman. Basic Digital Photography. 216p. 1990. text 49.95 (*0-240-80055-9*, Focal) Buttrwrth-Heinemann.

Breslow, Ronald. Chemistry Today & Tomorrow: The Central, Useful, & Creative Science. LC 96-45078. (Illus.). 144p. 1996. pap. 19.95 (*0-8412-3460-4*) Am Chemical.

— Chemistry Today & Tomorrow: The Central, Useful, & Creative Science. LC 96-45078. (Chemistry Ser.). 117p. 1996. pap. 19.95 (*0-7637-0463-6*) Jones & Bartlett.

Breslow, Ronald. Organic Reaction Mechanisms: An Introduction. 2nd ed. LC 73-80663. (Organic Chemistry Monograph Ser.). xv, 272 p. 1969. write for info. (*0-8053-1252-8*) Benjamin-Cummings.

Breslow, Stephen P. & Sokol, David M. Otto Neumann: A Rediscovered Artist. (Illus.). 85p. (Orig.). (C). 1987. pap. 18.00 (*1-878293-01-X*) Tampa Mus Art.

Breslow, Susan. I Really Want a Dog. (Picture Puffin Ser.). (Illus.). (J). 1993. 10.19 (*0-606-05367-0*, Pub. by Turtleback) Demco.

***Bresman, Jonathan.** The Phantom Menace: Episode 1: The Art of Star Wars. (Star Wars). (Illus.). 1999. 39.95 (*0-345-43108-1*, Del Rey) Ballantine Pub Grp.

Bresnahan, David M. The Larry Nichols Story: Damage Control: How to Get Caught with Your Pants down & Still Get Elected President. LC 98-12618. 228p. 1998. pap. 14.95 (*1-890828-10-6*, 10-6) Camden Ct.

— When the Smoke Clears, Families Are Baptized! A Tool for Missionaries to Help Investigators Quit Smoking. 3rd rev. ed. (Illus.). 70p. 1997. pap. 9.95 (*1-890828-01-7*, 01-7, Pub. by Camden Ct) Origin Bk Sales.

Bresnahan, James. Into the Lion's Mouth. 275p. 1992. pap. 9.95 (*1-881168-25-5*) Red Danceflr.

Bresnahan, Mary I. Finding Our Feet: Understanding Crosscultural Discourse. 228p. (C). 1991. pap. text 26.50 (*0-8191-8208-7*); lib. bdg. 47.50 (*0-8191-8207-9*) U Pr of Amer.

Bresnahan, Michaeline. Parties for Kids. (Art-Crafts-Cooking-Drawing Books for Children Ser.). (Illus.). 64p. (J). (ps up). 1995. lib. bdg. 17.95 (*1-56674-100-9*, HTS Bks) Forest Hse.

Bresnahan, P., et al, eds. Proceedings - 5th International Symposium on Spatial Data Handling, 2 vols., Set. (Illus.). 725p. (Orig.). (C). 1992. pap. text 50.00 (*0-9633532-2-5*) U SC Hum & Soc Sci.

— Proceedings - 5th International Symposium on Spatial Data Handling, 2 vols., Vol. 1. (Illus.). 371p. (Orig.). (C). 1992. pap. text 25.00 (*0-9633532-0-9*) U SC Hum & Soc Sci.

— Proceedings - 5th International Symposium on Spatial Data Handling, 2 vols., Vol. 2. (Illus.). 454p. (Orig.). (C). 1992. pap. text 25.00 (*0-9633532-1-7*) U SC Hum & Soc Sci.

Bresnahan, Roger J. Angles of Vision: Conversations on Philippine Literature. 185p. (Orig.). 1992. pap. 17.50 (*971-10-0420-8*, Pub. by New Day Pub) Cellar.

— Conversations with Filipino Writers. 189p. (Orig.). (C). 1990. pap. 12.50 (*971-10-0380-5*, Pub. by New Day Pub) Cellar.

— In Time of Hesitation: Anti-Imperialists & the Philippine-American War. 216p. 1981. 13.75 (*0-686-32579-6*, Pub. by New Day Pub) Cellar.

Bresnahan, Thomas F., et al. The Sign Maze: Approaches the Development of Signs, Labels, Markings, & Instruction Manuals. LC 93-30075. (Illus.). 70p. (Orig.). 1993. pap. 21.00 (*0-939874-94-6*, 4346) ASSE.

Bresnahan, Timothy F. & Gordon, Robert J., eds. The Economics of New Goods. (Illus.). 456p. 1997. 75.00 (*0-226-07415-3*) U Ch Pr.

Bresnan, Bill. Bill Bresnan Speaks on Tax Planning under the New Tax Law...in Words of One Syllable. (Illus.). 224p. 1987. 20.50 (*0-13-076472-8*) P-H.

— WABC Talkradio 77 AM Financial Expert Bill Bresnan Speaks on Real Estate...In Words of One Syllable. (Illus.). 144p. 1987. 17.50 (*0-13-949629-7*) P-H.

Bresnan, Bill & Gelb, Eric. Getting Started in Asset Allocation. LC 98-46669. (Getting Started In Ser.). (Illus.). 257p. 1999. pap. 18.95 (*0-471-32684-4*) Wiley.

Bresnan, Joan, ed. see Jackendoff, Ray S.

Bresnan, John. From Dominoes to Dynamos: The Transformation of Southeast Asia. LC 94-11497. 115p. 1994. pap. 17.95 (*0-87609-166-4*) Coun Foreign.

— Managing Indonesia: The Modern Political Economy. LC 92-23598. (East Asian Institute Ser.). 375p. (C). 1993. pap. text 23.00 (*0-231-07991-5*) Col U Pr.

Bresnan, Patrick. Awakening: An Introduction to the History of Eastern Thought. LC 97-50033. 422p. (C). 1998. pap. text 41.00 (*0-13-889478-7*) P-H.

Bresnick, David. Management for Attorneys. 160p. 1987. 37.50 (*0-9610834-3-3*) Human Serv Pr.

— Managing Employment & Training Programs. (Managing the Human Services Ser.). 245p. 1986. 27.50 (*0-9610834-1-7*) Human Serv Pr.

— Public Administration: The Execution & Formulation of Public Policy. 240p. (C). 1991. 40.00 (*0-9610834-5-X*) Human Serv Pr.

— Public Organizations & Policy: An Experiential Approach to Public Policy & Its Execution. LC 81-14471. 256p. reprint ed. pap. 79.40 (*0-7837-3012-8*, 204292800006) Bks Demand.

— Youthjobs: Toward a Private-Public Partnership. LC 84-3343. 151p. 1984. 47.95 (*0-89930-093-6*, BYJ/, Quorum Bks) Greenwood.

— Youthjobs: Toward a Private-Public Partnership. 151p. 1986. pap. text 14.95 (*0-9610834-2-5*) Human Serv Pr.

Bresnick, David A. Managing Human Services. 300p. 1989. text 27.50 (*0-9610834-4-1*) Human Serv Pr.

— Managing the Human Services in Hard Times. LC 83-80211. (Managing the Human Services Ser.). 222p. (C). 1983. text 20.00 (*0-9610834-0-9*) Human Serv Pr.

Bresnick, Jan, ed. see Shulman, Jason.

Bresnick, Peggy, ed. Friends Forever: A Book of Quotations. LC 97-71543. 374p. (Orig.). 1997. pap. 5.95 (*0-8362-3559-2*, Arie Bks) Andrews & McMeel.

Bresnick-Perry, Roslyn. Leaving for America. LC 92-8450. (Illus.). 32p. (YA). (ps-3). 1992. 14.95 (*0-89239-105-7*) Childrens Book Pr.

Bresnick, Stephen. Columbia Review Intensive Preparation for the MCAT. LC 95-25627. 825p. 1996. pap. 43.95 (*0-683-01027-1*) Lppncott W & W.

Bresnick, Stephen D. High Yield General Chemistry. (Illus.). 165p. 1996. pap. 12.95 (*0-683-18072-X*) Lppncott W & W.

— High Yield Organic Chemistry. LC 96-20287. (Illus.). 195p. 1996. pap. 12.95 (*0-683-18071-1*) Lppncott W & W.

— High Yield Physics. LC 96-20286. (Illus.). 226p. 1996. pap. 12.95 (*0-683-18070-3*) Lppncott W & W.

Bresnick, Stephen D. & Adams, Gregg A. On Call Procedures. Schmitt, William, ed. LC 98-19200. (On Call Ser.). (Illus.). 220p. 1999. pap. write for info. (*0-7216-7304-X*, W B Saunders Co) Harcrt Hlth Sci Grp.

Bresnick, Stephen D. & Bresnick, William H. Columbia Review MCAT Practice Tests. LC 97-6524. (Illus.). 220p. 1997. pap. 24.95 (*0-683-18099-1*) Lppncott W & W.

— Columbia Review MCAT Verbal Reasoning Powerbuilder. LC 97-3577. 252p. 1997. pap. 14.95 (*0-683-30073-3*) Lppncott W & W.

Bresnick, Stephen D., jt. auth. see Adams, Gregg A.

Bresnick, William H., jt. auth. see Bresnick, Stephen D.

Bress, Helene. Inkle Weaving. (Illus.). 214p. 1991. reprint ed. pap. 19.95 (*0-9620543-1-3*) Flower Valley Pr.

— The Macrame Book. 1999. pap. text 27.95 (*1-886388-15-6*) Flower Valley Pr.

— The Weaving Book: Patterns & Ideas. (Illus.). 548p. 1990. reprint ed. 49.95 (*0-9620543-0-5*) Flower Valley Pr.

Bress, Seymour, ed. see Keasbey, Doramay.

Bress, Seymour, ed. see Nunneley, Faithe S.

Bress, Seymour, ed. see Roche, Nan.

Bress, Seymour, tr. see Bergfeldt, Inga.

B

An Asterisk (*) at the beginning of an entry indicates that the title is appearing for the first time.

*Bressan, Alberto. Hyperbolic Systems of Conservation Laws. (Oxford Lecture Series in Mathematics & Its Applications: Vol. 20). (Illus.). 288p. 2000. text 80.00 (0-19-850700-3) OUP.

*Bressan, Alberto, et al. Well-Posedness of the Cauchy Problem for NXN Systems of Conservation Laws. LC 00-36257. 2000. write for info. (0-8218-2066-4) Am Math.

Bressan, Aldo. A General Interpreted Modal Calculus. LC 77-151568. 355p. reprint ed. pap. 110.10 (0-608-30795-5, 201109600074) Bks Demand.

Bressan, Guido, jt. auth. see Babbibi, Lorenza.

Bressan, O., et al, eds. Relativity, Supersymmetry & Cosmology: Proceedings of the 5th Latin-American Symposium on Relativity & Gravity - SILARG V, Bariloche, Argentina, January 1985. 368p. 1985. 60.00 (9971-5-0003-5) World Scientific Pub.

Bressand, Albert & Nicolaidis, Kalypso, eds. Strategic Trends in Services: An Inquiry into the Global Service Economy. 388p. 1989. text 45.00 (0-88730-317-X, HarpBusn) HarpInfo.

Bressand, Albert, jt. ed. see Cable, Vincent.

Bressani, T., et al, eds. Common Problems & Ideas of Modern Physics. 600p. (C). 1992. text 130.00 (981-02-0711-5) World Scientific Pub.

Bressani, T., et al. Common Problems & Trends of Modern Physics: Proceedings of the 12th Winter Schedule on Hadronic Physics. 512p. 1993. text 116.00 (981-02-1203-8) World Scientific Pub.

Bresser, A. H. & Salomons, W., eds. Acidic Precipitation. (Advances in Environmental Science Ser.: Vol. 5). (Illus.). 352p. 1990. 262.00 (0-387-97111-4, 3198) Spr-Verlag.

Bresser, Jerry. List More, Sell More. 320p. 1983. 33.00 (0-9611574-0-2) Bresser Pub.

Bresser Pereira, Luiz C. Economic Crisis & State Reform in Brazil: Toward a New Interpretation of Latin America. LC 94-28296. 258p. 1996. lib. bdg. 55.00 (1-55587-532-7) L Rienner.

Bresser Pereira, Luiz C. & Spink, Peter. Reforming the State: Managerial Public Administration in Latin America. LC 99-24072. 1999. 55.00 (1-55587-374-X) L Rienner.

Bresser, Rudi K. Strategische Managementtheorie. 728p. 1998. 92.00 (3-11-015787-X); pap. 49.00 (3-11-015786-1) De Gruyter.

Bresser, Rusty. Math & Literature for Grades K-6. (Illus.). 1995. pap. text 15.95 (0-941355-14-4) Math Solns Pubns.

Bresser, Rusty & Holtzman, Caren. Developing Number Sense, Grades 3-6. LC 99-23644. (Illus.). 256p. 1999. pap. 19.95 (0-941355-23-3) Math Solns Pubns.

Bressers, J., et al, eds. Fatigue under Thermal & Mechanical Loading: Mechanism, Mechanics & Modelling: Proceedings of the Symposium Held at Petten, The Netherlands, 22-24 May 1995. LC 96-10840. 505p. 1996. text 217.50 (0-7923-3993-2) Kluwer Academic.

Bressett, K. Collectible American Coins. LC 91-61366. (Illus.). 1991. lib. bdg. 30.00 (0-7853-0684-6) S J Durst.

Bressett, Ken. Guide Book of U. S. Currency: Large Size, Small Size, Fractional. 3rd ed. (Official Whitman Guidebook Ser.). (Illus.). 336p. 1999. pap. 15.95 (0-307-48003-8) Gldn Bks Pub Co.

*Bressett, Kenneth. The Golden Book of Coin Collecting. 1999. pap. 11.95 (0-307-48008-9, Whitman Coin) St Martin.

— Official Whitman Statehood Quarters Collector's Handbook. 96p. 2000. mass mkt. 4.99 (0-312-97804-9) St Martin.

Bressett, Kenneth, ed. see Yeoman, R. S.

Bressett, Kenneth E. Collectible American Coins. (Illus.). 320p. 1993. 19.98 (1-56173-300-8, 3600500) Pubns Intl Ltd.

— Collecting U. S. Coins: A Guide for Beginners. (Illus.). 64p. 1993. spiral bd. 5.98 (1-56173-745-3, 3614900) Pubns Intl Ltd.

Bressi, Todd W., ed. Planning & Zoning New York City: Yesterday, Today, & Tomorrow. LC 92-30574. 278p. (C). 1993. text 19.95 (0-88285-143-8) Ctr Urban Pol Res.

Bressi, Todd W., jt. auth. see Groth, Paul E.

Bressi, Todd W., jt. ed. see Groth, Paul E.

Bressler. Retina. 1996. text. write for info. (0-7216-6731-7, W B Saunders Co) Harcrt Hlth Sci Grp.

*Bressler, Ann Lee. The Universalist Movement in America, 1770-1880. LC 99-58071. (Religion in America Ser.). 224p. 2000. text 35.00 (0-19-512986-5) OUP.

Bressler, Charles E. Literary Criticism: An Introduction to Theory & Practice. 2nd ed. LC 98-33496. 308p. 1998. pap. text 30.80 (0-13-897422-5) P-H.

Bressler, Harry B. Zone Therapy. 173p. 1996. reprint ed. pap. 15.50 (0-7873-1221-5) Hlth Research.

Bressler, Karen W. & Clyde, Art. Workout on the Go: Including a Workout Band. LC 99-231710. 96p. 1998. pap. 10.95 (0-8362-6531-9) Andrews & McMeel.

Bressler, Karen W., jt. auth. see Parker, DeAnsin.

Bressler, Marvin & Lambert, Richard D., eds. American Higher Education: Prospects & Choices. LC 72-85689. (Annals Ser.: 404). 300p. 1972. 28.00 (0-87761-156-4); pap. 18.00 (0-87761-155-6) Am Acad Pol Soc Sci.

Bressler, R., jt. ed. see Brodie, Bernard B.

Bressler-Richardson, Elizabeth J. & Holloran-Hitzel, Sharon M. Cognitive Reorganization: A Stimulus Handbook. 2nd ed. 198p. 1983. spiral bd. 69.00 (0-88120-190-1, 6974) PRO-ED.

Bressler, Rubin & Johnson, David G., eds. Management of Diabetes Mellitus. LC 80-10866. 322p. reprint ed. pap. 99.90 (0-8357-7862-2, 203627900002) Bks Demand.

Bressler, Rubin & Katz, Michael. Geriatric Pharmacology. 2nd ed. (Illus.). 792p. 1999. pap. text 55.00 (0-07-007662-6) McGraw-Hill HPD.

Bressler, Rubin & Katz, Michael D., eds. Geriatric Pharmacology. LC 92-19631. (Illus.). 500p. 1992. text 55.00 (0-07-007660-X) McGraw-Hill HPD.

Bressler, Rubin, jt. ed. see Ewy, Gordon A.

Bressler, Sidney. Reynolds Beal: Impressionist Landscapes & Seacapes. LC 87-45585. (Illus.). 1989. 65.00 (0-8386-3325-0) Fairleigh Dickinson.

*Bressler, Stacey E. & Grantham, Charles. Communities of Commerce: Building Internet Business Communities to Accelerate Growth, Minimize Risk & Increase Customer Loyalty. 300300p. 2000. 24.95 (0-07-136115-4) McGraw-Hill Prof.

Bresson, Henri C., jt. auth. see Bernard, Bruce.

Bresson, Mary A. Contemporary Iowa Opinions Regarding the Influence of Croatians in Waterloo & Vicinity, 1907-1949. LC 70-155647. 1971. pap. 10.00 (0-88247-100-7) Ragusan Pr.

Bresson, Robert. Notes on the Cinematographer. Griffin, Jonathan, tr. (Green Integer Ser.: No. 2). 144p. 1997. pap. 8.95 (1-55713-365-4) Green Integer.

Bressoud, D. M. Factorization & Primality Testing. (Undergraduate Texts in Mathematics Ser.). (Illus.). xiii, 237p. 1997. 49.95 (0-387-97040-1) Spr-Verlag.

— Second Year Calculus: From Celestial Mechanics to Special Relativity. (Undergraduate Texts in Mathematics Ser.). (Illus.). xi, 386p. 1996. reprint ed. 34.95 (0-387-97606-X) Spr-Verlag.

Bressoud, David. A Radical Approach to Real Analysis. (Classroom Resource Materials Ser.). 336p. 1994. pap. text 36.50 (0-88385-701-4, RAN) Math Assn.

Bressoud, David M. Analytic & Combinatorial Generalizations of the Rogers-Ramanujan Identities. LC 79-27622. (Memoirs Ser.: No. 24/227). 54p. 1980. pap. 16.00 (0-8218-2227-6, MEMO/24/227) Am Math.

— Proofs & Confirmations: The Story of the Alternating Sign Matrix Conjecture. LC 99-20232. (Spectrum Ser.). (Illus.). 256p. (C). 1999. 74.95 (0-521-66170-6) Cambridge U Pr.

*Bressoud, David M. Proofs & Confirmations: The Story of the Alternating Sign Matrix Conjecture. (Spectrum Ser.). (Illus.). 256p. (C). 1999. pap. 29.95 (0-521-66646-5) Cambridge U Pr.

*Bressoud, David M. & Wagon, Stan. A Course in Computational Number Theory. 350p. (C). 2000. pap. text 64.95 (1-930190-10-7) Key Coll.

Brest, Albert N., jt. ed. see Dreifus, Leonard S.

Brest, Paul. Processes of Constitutional Decisionmaking: Cases & Materials. 3rd ed. 1632p. 1992. teacher ed. write for info. (0-316-10850-2, 08502) Aspen Law.

— Processes of Constitutional Decisionmaking: Cases & Materials. 3rd ed. 1632p. 1995. suppl. ed. 26.95 (0-316-10625-9, 06259) Aspen Law.

*Brest, Paul. Processes of Constitutional Decisionmaking: Cases & Materials. 4th ed. LC 99-87802. 2000. 64.00 (0-7355-1250-7) Panel Pubs.

Brest, Paul & Levinson, Sanford. Processes of Constitutional Decision Making. 3rd ed. 1632p. 1992. 59.00 (0-316-10787-5, Aspen Law & Bus) Aspen Pub.

— Processes of Constitutional Decision Making, 1986: Supplement. 250p. (C). 1986. pap. text 12.00 (0-316-10789-1, Aspen Law & Bus) Aspen Pub.

Brestensky, Dennis, et al. Patch-Work Voices: The Culture & Lore of a Mining People. LC 91-50104. (Illus.). 96p. 1991. pap. 12.95 (0-8229-5460-5) U of Pittsburgh Pr.

Brestensky, Dennis F., et al. Patchwork Voices: The Culture & Lore of a Mining People. LC 78-23824. 95p. reprint ed. pap. 30.00 (0-608-15897-6, 203079500074) Bks Demand.

Bresticker, Lane, ed. see Celebrity Collection of Recipes Staff.

Bresticker, Robert B. American Manufacturing & Logistics in the Year 2001. (Illus.). 192p. 1992. 24.95 (1-880339-07-2) Brigadoon Bay.

Brestin, Dee. And Then We Were Women. LC 94-11827. (American Family Portrait Ser.). 192p. (Orig.). 1994. pap. 9.99 (1-56476-343-9, 6-3343, Victor Bks) Chariot Victor.

*Brestin, Dee. Believer's Life System. 1999. 8.99 (0-8024-6988-4) Moody.

Brestin, Dee. Examining the Claims of Jesus. (Fisherman Bible Studyguide Ser.). 48p. 1985. pap. 4.99 (0-87788-246-0, H Shaw Pubs) Waterbrook Pr.

*Brestin, Dee. 1, 2 & 3 John - Chinese Edition: How Should a Christian Live. 83p. 1998. pap. 6.00 (1-56582-116-5) Christ Renew Min.

Brestin, Dee. Friendship: Portraits in God's Family Album. (Fisherman Bible Studyguide Ser.). 64p. (Orig.). 1986. pap. 4.99 (0-87788-287-8, H Shaw Pubs) Waterbrook Pr.

— The Friendship of Women. rev. ed. 204p. 1997. 9.99 (1-56476-632-2, Victor Bks) Chariot Victor.

— The Friendships of Women. 184p. 1988. pap. 9.99 (0-89693-432-2, 6-1432, Victor Bks) Chariot Victor.

— The Friendships of Women Workbook. 240p. 1995. pap. 16.99 (1-56476-407-9, 6-3407, Victor Bks) Chariot Victor.

— How Should a Christian Live? 1, 2, & 3 John. (Fisherman Bible Studyguide Ser.). 80p. 1985. pap. 4.99 (0-87788-351-3, H Shaw Pubs) Waterbrook Pr.

— The Joy of Hospitality: Recovering a Lost Art. (Dee Brestin Ser.). 96p. (Orig.). 1993. pap. 6.99 (1-56476-033-2, 6-3033, Victor Bks) Chariot Victor.

— The Joy of Women's Friendships. (Dee Brestin Ser.). 96p. (Orig.). 1993. pap. 6.99 (1-56476-052-9, 6-3052, Victor Bks) Chariot Victor.

— The Lifestyles of Christian Women. 180p. 1991. pap., student ed. 9.99 (0-89693-911-1, 6-1911, Victor Bks) Chariot Victor.

— My Daughter, My Daughter. LC 99-39736. 1999. pap. text 12.99 (1-56476-784-1) SP Pubns.

— Peter: 8 Lessons on Righteous Living Exclusively for Women. 1999. pap. text 6.99 (1-56476-768-X) SP Pubns.

— Proverbs & Parables: God's Wisdom for Living. (Fisherman Bible Studyguide Ser.). 75p. 1975. pap. 4.99 (0-87788-694-6, H Shaw Pubs) Waterbrook Pr.

*Brestin, Dee. Psalms. (Woman's Journey Through... Ser.). 2000. pap. 6.99 (1-56476-767-1) Chariot Victor.

— El Recorrido de una Mujer a Traves de Ester, 1vol. 1999. pap. text 7.99 (0-89922-586-1) Caribe Betania.

— El Recorrido de una Mujer a Traves de Rut: A Woman's Journey Through Ruth. 1999. pap. text 7.99 (0-89922-585-3) Caribe Betania.

Brestin, Dee. We Are Sisters. LC 96-21413. 192p. 1996. pap. 8.99 (1-56476-604-7, Victor Bks) Chariot Victor.

— A Woman of Insight. (Dee Brestin Ser.). 96p. 1995. pap. 5.99 (1-56476-456-7, 6-3456, Victor Bks) Chariot Victor.

— Woman of Joy. 96p. 1995. pap. 5.99 (1-56476-454-0, 6-3454, Victor Bks) Chariot Victor.

— Woman of Value. 96p. 1995. pap. 5.99 (1-56476-455-9, 6-3455, Victor Bks) Chariot Victor.

— A Woman's Journey through Esther: 8 Lessons of Faith Exclusively for Women. LC 98-199442. (Woman's Journey Ser.). 1998. pap. 5.99 (1-56476-731-0, Victor Bks) Chariot Victor.

— A Woman's Journey through Luke. LC 98-199439. (Woman's Journey Ser.). 1998. pap. 5.99 (1-56476-730-2, Victor Bks) Chariot Victor.

— A Woman's Journey through Ruth. LC 98-199445. (Woman's Journey Ser.). 1998. pap. 5.99 (1-56476-732-9, Victor Bks) Chariot Victor.

Brestin, Dee & Johnston, Peggy. The Joy of Eating: Spiritual & Nutritional Principles for Weight Control. LC 92-42311. (Dee Brestin Ser.). 96p. (Orig.). 1993. pap. 5.99 (0-89693-879-4, 6-1879, Victor Bks) Chariot Victor.

Brestin, Dee, jt. auth. see Brestin, Steve.

Brestin, Dee, jt. auth. see Brestin, Steven.

Brestin, Steve & Brestin, Dee. Building Your House on the Lord: Marriage & Parenthood. rev. ed. (Fisherman Bible Studyguide Ser.). 78p. 1979. 4.99 (0-87788-099-9, H Shaw Pubs) Waterbrook Pr.

— Building Your House on the Lord - Chinese Edition: Marriage & Parenthood. Yau, Grace, tr. (CHI.). 71p. 1998. pap. 5.50 (1-56582-026-6) Christ Renew Min.

— First & Second Peter, Jude: Called for a Purpose. (Fisherman Bible Studyguide Ser.). 96p. (Orig.). 1987. pap. text 4.99 (0-87788-703-9, H Shaw Pubs) Waterbrook Pr.

— Higher Ground: Steps Toward Christian Maturity. (Fisherman Bible Studyguide Ser.). 58p. 1978. pap. 4.99 (0-87788-345-9, H Shaw Pubs) Waterbrook Pr.

*Brestin, Steven & Brestin, Dee. 1 & 2 Peter, Jude - Chinese Edition: Called for a Purpose. 86p. 1998. pap. 6.00 (1-56582-117-3) Christ Renew Min.

Brestoff, Richard. The Camera Smart Actor. LC 94-34487. 256p. 1994. pap. 14.95 (1-880399-76-8) Smith & Kraus.

— The Great Acting Teachers & Their Methods. (Career Development Ser.). 224p. 1996. pap. 14.95 (1-57525-012-8) Smith & Kraus.

— Under the Circumstances: Variations on a Theme of Stanislavski: A Step by Step Approach to Playing a Part. LC 99-14281. 224p. 1999. pap. 16.95 (1-57525-187-6) Smith & Kraus.

Brestrup, Craig. Disposable Animals: Ending the Tragedy of Throwaway Pets. LC 97-66622. 240p. (Orig.). 1997. pap. 14.95 (0-9657285-9-5) Camino Bay Bks.

*Bret, David. Freddy Mercury Story: Living on the Edge. 208p. 1999. pap. 13.95 (1-86105-256-1) Robson.

Bret, David. Gracie Fields: The Authorized Biography. (Illus.). 246p. 1996. 27.95 (0-86051-958-9, Robson-Parkwest) Parkwest Pubns.

*Bret, David. Maria Callas: The Tigress & the Lamb. 380p. 1999. pap. 14.95 (1-86105-257-X) Robson.

Bret, David. Maria Callas: The Tigress & the Lamb. LC 98-70052. (Illus.). 380p. 1998. 32.95 (1-86105-110-7, Pub. by Robson Bks) Parkwest Pubns.

— Marlene My Friend: An Intimate Biography. (Illus.). 280p. 1996. pap. 31.95 (0-86051-844-2, Robson-Parkwest) Parkwest Pubns.

— Maurice Chevalier: Up on Top of a Rainbow. (Illus.). 242p. 1993. 26.95 (0-86051-789-6, Robson-Parkwest) Parkwest Pubns.

— Maurice Chevalier: Up on Top of a Rainbow. 2nd large type ed. (Illus.). 336p. 1993. 24.95 (1-85695-165-0, Pub. by ISIS Lrg Prnt) Transaction Pubs.

— Morrissey: Landscapes of the Mind. LC 95-10371. (Illus.). 208p. 1995. pap. 9.95 (0-7867-0218-4) Carroll & Graf.

— On Decoration. LC 91-191539. 1997. 49.95 (0-7188-2801-1, Lutterworth-Parkwest) Parkwest Pubns.

*Bret, David. Piaf: A Passionate Life. 282p. 1999. 30.95 (1-86105-218-9) Robson.

Bret, David. Tallulah Bankhead: A Scandalous Life. (Illus.). 278p. 1998. pap. 18.95 (1-86105-190-5, Pub. by Robson Bks) Parkwest Pubns.

*Bret, David. Valentino: A Dream of Desire. 224p. 1999. 29.95 (1-86105-123-9) Robson.

Bret, Michel. Image Synthesis. 304p. 1991. text 175.00 (0-7923-1488-3) Kluwer Academic.

Bret, P., et al. Radiology of the Small Intestine. (Illus.). 400p. 1989. 350.00 (0-387-59508-2) Spr-Verlag.

Breta, Jeff, jt. auth. see Craig, John C.

Bretagnon, Pierre & Simon, Jean L. Planetary Programs & Tables. LC 86-9099. 160p. 1986. pap. text 19.95 (0-943396-08-5) Willmann-Bell.

Bretall, Robert, ed. A Kierkegaard Anthology. LC 47-827. 528p. 1973. pap. text 19.95 (0-691-01978-9, Pub. by Princeton U Pr) Cal Prin Full Svc.

Bretana, Reinaldo B. La Estacion Equivocada. (SPA.). 192p. (Orig.). 1989. pap. 10.00 (0-917049-20-9) Saeta.

— La Noche Vigilada. (SPA.). 208p. 1999. pap. 15.00 (0-927534-87-8) Biling Rev-Pr.

Bretecher, Claire. Les Frustres, 4 vols., 1. (FRE.). 1987. pap. 10.95 (0-7859-3212-7, 2266019309) Fr & Eur.

— Les Frustres, 4 vols., 2. (FRE.). 1987. pap. 10.95 (0-7859-3213-5, 2266019317) Fr & Eur.

— Les Frustres, 4 vols., 3. (FRE.). 1987. pap. 10.95 (0-7859-3214-3, 2266019325) Fr & Eur.

— Les Frustres, 4 vols., 4. (FRE.). 1987. pap. 10.95 (0-7859-3215-1, 2266019333) Fr & Eur.

— Les Frustres, Vol. 5. (FRE.). 1987. pap. 10.95 (0-7859-3216-X, 2266019341) Fr & Eur.

— Mothers. (Illus.). 70p. (C). 1992. pap. write for info. (0-413-58850-5, A0663, Methuen Drama) Methn.

Breteler, F. J. The Connaraceae: A Taxonomic Study with Emphasis on Africa. (Wageningen Agricultural University Papers: No. 89-6). 407p. 1989. pap. 107.00 (90-6754-158-3, Pub. by Backhuys Pubs) Balogh.

— A Revision of Leucomphalos Including Baphiastrum & Bowringia (Leguminosae-Papilionideae) LC 95-177532. (Wageningen Agricultural University Papers: No. 94-4). (Illus.). 41p. 1994. pap. 11.00 (90-6754-362-4, Pub. by Backhuys Pubs) Balogh.

Breteler, F. J. & Sosef, M. S. Herbarium Vadense, 1896-1996. (Wageningen Agricultural University Papers: No. 96.2). (Illus.). 136p. 1996. pap. 38.00 (90-73348-61-7, Pub. by Backhuys Pubs) Balogh.

Breteler, H., jt. ed. see Van Beek, T. A.

Breternitz, Roger W. Don't Drink & Drive. abr. ed. 1985. pap. 9.95 incl. audio (1-893417-11-5) Vector Studios.

— General Athletics. abr. ed. 1985. pap. 9.95 incl. audio (1-893417-23-9) Vector Studios.

— General Relaxation. abr. ed. 1985. pap. 9.95 incl. audio (1-893417-17-4) Vector Studios.

— Harry the Sixty Lb. Guard Cat. unabridged ed. (Illus.). 50p. (J). (gr. 1-5). 1997. pap. 7.95 (1-893417-00-X) Vector Studios.

— Insomnia Cured. abr. ed. 1985. pap. 9.95 incl. audio (1-893417-12-3) Vector Studios.

— Love Magnetics. abr. ed. 1985. pap. 9.95 incl. audio (1-893417-13-1) Vector Studios.

— Mega Memory. abr. ed. 1985. pap. 9.95 incl. audio (1-893417-22-0) Vector Studios.

— Money Magnetics. abr. ed. 1985. pap. 9.95 incl. audio (1-893417-15-8) Vector Studios.

— Non-Smoking. abr. ed. 1985. pap. 9.95 incl. audio (1-893417-07-7) Vector Studios.

— Permanent Weight Loss. abr. ed. 1985. pap. 9.95 incl. audio (1-893417-08-5) Vector Studios.

— Power Tennis. abr. ed. 1985. pap. 9.95 incl. audio (1-893417-24-7) Vector Studios.

— Power Workout. abr. ed. 1985. pap. 9.95 incl. audio (1-893417-25-5) Vector Studios.

— Self-Confidence. abr. ed. 1985. pap. 9.95 incl. audio (1-893417-18-2) Vector Studios.

— Smart Study. abr. ed. 1985. pap. 9.95 incl. audio (1-893417-20-4) Vector Studios.

— Speed Typing. abr. ed. 1985. pap. 9.95 incl. audio (1-893417-19-0) Vector Studios.

— Stress Management. abr. ed. 1985. pap. 9.95 incl. audio (1-893417-09-3) Vector Studios.

— Stuttering Cured. abr. ed. 1985. pap. 9.95 incl. audio (1-893417-10-7) Vector Studios.

— Super Creativity. abr. ed. 1985. pap. 9.95 incl. audio (1-893417-14-X) Vector Studios.

Breth, Steven, ed. Environment & Agriculture: Proceedings of a Symposium in Honor of Robert D. Havener. LC 94-1828. 1994. 24.95 (0-933595-85-9) Winrock Intl.

Breth, Steven, jt. ed. see Pearlberg, Robert L.

Breth, Steven A., ed. Integration of Sustainable Agriculture & Rural Development Issues in Agricultural Policy. LC 96-191685. 336p. (Orig.). 1996. pap. text 17.95 (0-933595-99-9) Winrock Intl.

*Breth, Steven A., et al. The Future Stakes for U.S. Food & Agriculture in East & Southeast Asia. LC 98-89590. (Illus.). 1999. write for info. (0-89068-146-5) Natl Planning.

Brethauer, Candy K., ed. see Mendel, Kathleen L.

Brethauer, Candy K., ed. & pref. see Mendel, Kathleen L.

*Brethauer, Dale M. The Power of Strategic Costing: Uncover Your Competitors' & Suppliers' Costs. Set Your Company's Target Costs. Maximize Your Profits. LC 99-30854. 250p. 1999. 32.95 (0-8144-0486-3) AMACOM.

*Brethauer, Dave. Stamp in Color: Techniques for Enhancing Your Artwork. (Illus.). 96p. 2000. pap. 21.95 (1-56477-329-9) Martingale & Co.

Bretherick, Dona. Central African Republic. (OIES Country Guide Ser.). 20p. (C). 1995. 20.00 (0-929851-27-7) Am Assn Coll Registrars.

— The Ivory Coast (Cote D'Ivoire) (OIES Country Guide Ser.). (C). 1995. 22.00 (0-929851-29-3) Am Assn Coll Registrars.

— Tanzania. (OIES Country Guide Ser.). (C). 1995. 24.00 (0-929851-31-5) Am Assn Coll Registrars.

*Bretherick, Leslie. Bretherick's Handbook of Reactive Chemical Hazards. 2532p. 1999. text 295.00 (0-7506-3605-X) Buttrwrth-Heinemann.

Bretherick, Sharon. Russian Tea Time. Harrison, Judy, ed. (Illus.). 183p. 1998. pap. 12.95 (1-56325-065-9, TB003) Turnabout.

Bretherton, Barbara A. Prayer Themes & Guided Meditations for Children. LC 97-62343. 96p. (J). 1998. pap. 9.95 (0-89622-896-7) Twenty-Third.

— Ways to Pray with Children: Prayers, Activities, & Services. LC 95-78538. 80p. (Orig.). (J). 1996. pap. 9.95 (0-89622-670-0) Twenty-Third.

Bretherton, C. H. Midas: or The United States & the Future. LC 73-13123. (Foreign Travelers in America, 1810-1935 Ser.). 100p. 1974. reprint ed. 16.95 (0-405-05445-9) Ayer.

An Asterisk (*) at the beginning of an entry indicates that the title is appearing for the first time.

*__Bretherton, Charlotte.__ European Union as a Global Actor. LC 98-31537. 1999. write for info. (*0-415-15052-3*); pap. write for info. (*0-415-15053-1*) Routledge.

Bretherton, Inge & Waters, Everett, eds. Growing Points of Attachment Theory & Research. (Child Development Monographs: No. 209, Vol. 50, Pts. 1 & 2). (Illus.). xii, 336p. 1985. pap. text 19.50 (*0-226-07411-0*) U Ch Pr.

Bretherton, Inge & Watson, Malcolm W., eds. Children's Perspectives on the Family. LC 85-644581. (New Directions for Child Development Ser.: No. CD 48). 1990. pap. 25.00 (*1-55542-825-8*) Jossey-Bass.

Bretherton, Michael & Dunn, Chris. Making Redundancy Work for You. (C). 1988. 510.00 (*0-7855-4551-4*) St Mut.

Brethes, Alain. L' Interpretation Dynamique du Tarot: 462 Assemblages des Arcanes Majeurs. (Illus.). 550p. 1995. 27.95 (*2-920083-95-3*) Edns Roseau.

*__Bretholz, Leo & Olesker, Michael.__ Leap into Darkness: Seven Years on the Run in Wartime Europe. LC 99-31373. 288p. 1999. pap. 12.95 (*0-385-49705-9*, Anchor NY) Doubleday.

Brethower, Dale & Smalley, Karolyn. Performance-Based Instruction: Linking Training to the Workplace. LC 97-45356. 863p. 1998. 44.95 incl. disk (*0-7879-1119-4*) Jossey-Bass.

Brethower, Dale, jt. auth. see LaFleur, Doug.

Bretille, J., jt. auth. see Goris, M.

Bretille, Josiane, jt. auth. see Goris, Michael.

Bretislav, Heinrich, jt. ed. see Bland, J. A.

Bretner, Reginald. The Timeless Tales of Reginald Bretner. Flaman, Fred, ed. LC 98-122614. 224p. 1997. pap. 12.95 (*1-891513-00-1*) Story Bks.

Bretnor, Helen H., tr. see Perlot, Jean-Nicolas.

Bretnor, Reginald. Decisive Warfare: A Study in Military Theory. LC 84-315. (Stokvis Studies in Historical Chronology & Thought: No. 5). 192p. 1986. reprint ed. pap. 21.00 (*0-89370-420-2*) Millefleurs.

— Of Force & Violence & Other Imponderables: Essays on War, Politics & Government. Seldis, Paul D., ed. LC 84-306. (Stokvis Studies in Historical Chronology & Thought: No. 6). 144p. (C). 1992. pap. 19.00 (*0-89370-421-0*, 10375498) Millefleurs.

Bretnor, Reginald, ed. Modern Science Fiction: Its Meaning & Its Future. LC 78-71414. 343p. 1979. 18.00 (*0-911682-23-6*) Advent.

Breton, Albert. Competitive Governments: An Economic Theory of Politics & Public Finance. LC 96-31758. (Illus.). 399p. (C). 1996. text 59.95 (*0-521-48102-3*) Cambridge U Pr.

— Competitive Governments: An Economic Theory of Politics & Public Finance. (Illus.). 384p. (C). 1998. pap. text 19.95 (*0-521-64628-6*) Cambridge U Pr.

— The Economic Constitution of Federal States. LC 77-18526. 176p. reprint ed. pap. 54.60 (*0-608-12848-1*, 202359700033) Bks Demand.

Breton, Albert, et al, eds. The Competitive State. LC 96-20529. (International Studies in Economics & Econometrics). (Illus.). vii, 275p. (C). 1990. lib. bdg. 175.00 (*0-7923-0835-2*) Kluwer Academic.

— Nationalism & Rationality. (Illus.). 341p. (C). 1995. text 59.95 (*0-521-48098-1*) Cambridge U Pr.

Breton, Albert, et al. Understanding Democracy: Economic & Political Perspectives. LC 96-46376. (Illus.). 287p. (C). 1997. text 59.95 (*0-521-58236-9*) Cambridge U Pr.

Breton, Andre. L' Amour Fou. (FRE.). 1976. pap. 10.95 (*0-8288-3659-0*, M11012); pap. 10.95 (*0-7859-1813-2*, 2070367231) Fr & Eur.

— L' Amour Fou. (Folio Ser.: No. 723). (FRE.). pap. 9.25 (*2-07-036723-1*) Schoenhof.

— Anthologie de l'Humour Noir. pap. 14.95 (*0-7859-0784-X*, F89450) Fr & Eur.

— Arcane Seventeen. 12.95 (*0-685-37228-6*, F89460) Fr & Eur.

— Arcanum 17. Rogow, Zack, tr. from FRE. (Sun & Moon Classics Ser.: No. 51). 144p. (Orig.). 1994. pap. 12.95 (*1-55713-170-8*) Sun & Moon CA.

— Automatic Message: The Magnetic Fields & the Immaculate Conception. 224p. 17.99 (*0-947757-99-6*) Serpents Tail.

— Break of Day. Caws, Mary Ann & Polizzotti, Mark, trs. from FRE. LC 99-18321. (French Modernist Library). 160p. 1999. text 35.00 (*0-8032-1259-3*) U of Nebr Pr.

— Clair de Terre. (Poesie Ser.). (FRE.). pap. 9.95 (*2-07-030045-5*) Schoenhof.

Breton, Andre. Claire de Terre, Mont de Piete, le Revolver a Cheveux Blancs, l'Air de l'Eau. (FRE.). 1966. pap. 10.95 (*0-8288-3815-1*, F89480) Fr & Eur.

Breton, Andre. La Cle des Champs. 1991. pap. 19.95 (*0-7859-3164-3*, 2253056545) Fr & Eur.

— Communicating Vessels. Caws, Mary A. & Harris, Geoffrey T., trs. from FRE. LC 90-12123. (French Modernist Library). xxvi, 161p. 1990. text 40.00 (*0-8032-1218-6*) U of Nebr Pr.

— Communicating Vessels. Caws, Mary A. & Harris, Geoffrey T., trs. LC 90-12123. (French Modernist Library). xxiv, 161p. 1990. pap. 12.00 (*0-8032-6135-7*, Bison Books) U of Nebr Pr.

— Earthlight. Zavatsky, Bill & Rogow, Zack, trs. from FRE. (Sun & Moon Classics Ser.: No. 26). 216p. (Orig.). 1990. pap. 12.95 (*1-55713-095-7*) Sun & Moon CA.

— Entretiens -- Gesprache: Dada, Surrealismus, Politik. 400p. 1996. pap. text 24.00 (*90-5705-016-1*) Gordon & Breach.

— Entretiens avec Andre Parinaud (1913-1952) (Coll. Le Point du Jour). (FRE.). 8.95 (*0-7859-0636-3*, M3136); pap. 3.95 (*0-686-66853-7*, M3136) Fr & Eur.

— Free Rein. Parmentier, Michel & D'Amboise, Jacqueline, trs. LC 95-22793. (French Modernist Library). xii, 293p. (Orig.). 1996. text 45.00 (*0-8032-1241-0*) U of Nebr Pr.

— L' Immaculee Conception. Bonnet, M. et al, eds. (FRE.). 288p. 1991. pap. 45.00 (*0-7859-4768-X*) Fr & Eur.

— Lexico Sucinto Del Erotismo. (SPA.). 110p. 1974. pap. 14.95 (*0-7859-0897-8*, S50153) Fr & Eur.

— The Lost Steps. Polizzotti, Mark, tr. & intro. by. LC 96-3479. (French Modernist Library). xxi, 135p. 1996. text 35.00 (*0-8032-1242-9*) U of Nebr Pr.

— Mad Love. Caws, Mary A., tr. from FRE. LC 86-24889. (French Modernist Library). (Illus.). xviii, 129p. 1997. pap. 12.00 (*0-8032-6072-5*, Bison Books) U of Nebr Pr.

— Magritte. (Illus.). 1964. pap. 10.00 (*0-914412-24-8*, Inst Arts Catalogues) Menil Found.

— Les Manifestes du Surrealisme. (FRE.). 1985. pap. 12.95 (*0-7859-2792-1*) Fr & Eur.

— Les Manifestes du Surrealisme. (Folio Essais Ser.: No. 5). (FRE.). 9.95 (*2-07-032279-3*) Schoenhof.

— Manifestoes of Surrealism. Seaver, Richard & Lane, Helen R., trs. from FRE. 316p. 1969. pap. text 17.95 (*0-472-06182-8*, 06182, Ann Arbor Bks) U of Mich Pr.

— Martinique, Charmeuse des Serpents. 1972. 9.95 (*0-7859-0928-1*, M3137) Fr & Eur.

— Nadja. (FRE.). 1972. pap. 10.95 (*0-8288-3660-4*, F89531) Fr & Eur.

— Nadja. Howard, Richard, tr. from FRE. LC 60-7639. 160p. 1988. pap. 11.00 (*0-8021-5026-8*, Grove) Grove-Atltic.

— Nadja. (Folio Ser.: No. 73). (FRE.). pap. 9.25 (*2-07-036073-3*) Schoenhof.

Breton, Andre. Ode a Charles Fourier. Gaulmier, ed. 12.95 (*0-685-37233-2*, F89540) Fr & Eur.

— Oeuvres Complete, Vol. 1. Bonnet, Marguerite, ed. (FRE.). 1988. lib. bdg. 155.00 (*0-7859-3883-4*) Fr & Eur.

— Oeuvres Completes, Tome 1. deluxe ed. (Pleiade Ser.). (FRE.). 1798p. 1988. 99.95 (*2-07-011138-5*) Schoenhof.

— Les Pas Perdus. (FRE.). 1990. pap. 15.95 (*0-7859-2943-6*) Fr & Eur.

— Les Pas Perdus: Essai. (Coll. Soleil). 16.95 (*0-685-37234-0*, S20760); pap. 4.95 (*0-686-66855-3*, F89551) Fr & Eur.

Breton, Andre. Perspectives Cavaliere. Bonnet, ed. 14.50 (*0-685-37235-9*) Fr & Eur.

— Poems of Andre Breton: A Bilingual Anthology. Cauvin, Jean-Pierre & Caws, Mary A., trs. 298p. 1982. text 35.00 (*0-292-76476-6*) U of Tex Pr.

— Point du Jour. (FRE.). 192p. 1992. pap. 10.95 (*0-7859-1680-6*, 2070326489) Fr & Eur.

— Point du Jour. (Idees Ser.). (FRE.). pap. 8.95 (*2-07-035213-7*) Schoenhof.

— Position Politique du Surrealisme. (Bibliotheque Volante Ser.). 1991. pap. 10.95 (*0-7859-3163-5*, 2253056537) Fr & Eur.

— Signe Ascendant. (Poesie Ser.). (FRE.). pap. 9.95 (*2-07-030046-3*) Schoenhof.

Breton, Andre. Signe Ascendant, Fata Morgana, les Etats Generaux des Epingles Tremblantes, Xenophiles, Ode a Charles Fourier, Constellations. (FRE.). 1968. pap. 10.95 (*0-8288-3816-X*, F89600) Fr & Eur.

Breton, Andre. Le Surrealisme au Service de la Revolution. 59.95 (*0-686-51938-8*, S9634) Fr & Eur.

— Les Vases Communicants. (FRE.). 1970. pap. 10.95 (*0-7859-2837-5*) Fr & Eur.

— Les Vases Communicants: Essai. (Idees Ser.). (FRE.). pap. 8.95 (*2-07-035223-4*) Schoenhof.

— What Is Surrealism? LC 74-6446. (Studies in Comparative Literature: No. 35). (C). 1973. reprint ed. lib. bdg. 75.00 (*0-8383-1709-X*) M S G Haskell Hse.

— What Is Surrealism? Selected Writings. Rosemont, Franklin, ed. LC 71-186691. (Illus.). 557p. (C). 1978. reprint ed. pap. 34.95 (*0-87348-822-9*); reprint ed. lib. bdg. 60.00 (*0-913460-59-1*) Pathfinder NY.

Breton, Andre, ed. Anthology of Black Humor. Polizzotti, Mark, tr. from FRE.Tr. of Anthologie de l'Humeur Noir. 200p. (Orig.). 1997. pap. 18.95 (*0-87286-321-2*) City Lights.

— Le Surrealisme au Service de la Revolution, Nos. 1[00ad]6. LC 68-28661. (Contemporary Art Ser.). (FRE., Illus.). 1968. reprint ed. 52.95 (*0-405-00707-8*) Ayer.

Breton, Andre & Eluard, Paul. Dictionnaire Abrege du Surrealisme. (FRE.). 1991. write for info. (*0-7859-7942-5*, 2-7143-0421-4) Fr & Eur.

Breton, Andre & Soupault, Philippe. Les Champs Magnetiques, S'il Vous Plait, Vous M'Oublierez. (FRE.). 1971. pap. 10.95 (*0-8288-3817-8*, F89651) Fr & Eur.

— Champs Magnetiques. S'il Vous Plait. Vous M'Oublierez. (Poesie Ser.). (FRE.). 1971. pap. 9.95 (*2-07-031877-X*) Schoenhof.

Breton, Andre, et al. Automatic Message: The Magnetic Fields & the Immaculate Conception. LC 97-221838. (Anti-Classics of Surrealism Ser.). 223p. 1997. write for info. (*1-900565-01-3*) Atlas Pr.

Breton, Andre, jt. auth. see Eluard, Paul.

Breton, Andre, jt. auth. see Ray, Man.

Breton, Anna L. Le, see Le Breton, Anna L.

Breton, Arthur J. A Guide to the Manuscript Collections of the New York Historical Society, 2 vols. LC 72-7725. 1973. lib. bdg. 185.00 (*0-8371-6073-1*, NYH/, Greenwood Pr) Greenwood.

Breton, Arthur J., ed. A Guide to Archival Sources for Italian-American Art: History in the Archives of American Art. LC 92-82761. 50p. pap. text 10.00 (*1-880193-03-5*) Arch Am Art.

Breton, Bernard. Dictionnaire de la Peche et de l'Eau. (FRE.). 374p. 1988. 32.95 (*0-7859-8646-4*, 273730170x) Fr & Eur.

Breton, Binka Le, see Le Breton, Binka.

Breton, Denise. This Lie Called Evil. LC 82-80906. 134p. (Orig.). 1983. pap. 12.00 (*0-942958-02-0*) Kappeler Inst Pub.

Breton, Denise & Largent, Christopher. Love, Soul & Freedom: Dancing with Rumi on the Mystic Path. Barks, Coleman, tr. LC 97-48972. 320p. 1998. 21.95 (*1-56838-207-3*) Hazelden.

— The Paradigm Conspiracy: How Our Systems of Government, School, & Culture Violate Our Human Potential. 325p. 1998. reprint ed. pap. 13.95 (*1-56838-208-1*) Hazelden.

— The Soul of Economies: Spiritual Evolution Goes to the Marketplace. LC 90-81854. (Illus.). 375p. 1991. pap. 14.95 (*0-9626238-2-2*); lib. bdg. 24.95 (*0-9626238-1-4*) Idea Hse Pub.

Breton, Genevieve. In the Solitude of My Soul: The Diary of Genevieve Breton, 1867-1871. Allen, James S., ed. Palmes, James, tr. LC 93-32344. (ENG & FRE., Illus.). 304p. (C). 1994. 41.95 (*0-8093-1938-1*); pap. 18.95 (*0-8093-1939-X*) S Ill U Pr.

Breton, Harriette Von, see Gebhard, David & Von Breton, Harriette.

Breton, J. & Vermeglio, A. The Photosynthetic Bacterial Reaction Center II Vol. 2: Structure, Spectroscopy & Dynamics. LC 92-36001. (NATO ASI Ser.: Vol. 237). (Illus.). 440p. (C). 1993. text 156.00 (*0-306-44354-6*, Kluwer Plenum) Kluwer Academic.

Breton, Jacques. The Photosynthetic Bacterial Reaction Center: Structure & Dynamics. Vermeglio, Andre, ed. LC 88-12581. (NATO ASI Series A, Life Sciences: Vol. 149). (Illus.). 456p. 1988. 115.00 (*0-306-42917-9*, Plenum Trade) Perseus Pubng.

Breton, Jean-Francois. Arabia Felix from the Time of the Queen of Sheba: Eighth Century to First Century B. C. LaFarge, Albert, tr. from FRE. LC 99-43002.Tr. of Arabie Heureuse Autemps de la Reine de Saba. (Illus.). 248p. 2000. 24.00 (*0-268-02002-7*, Pub. by U of Notre Dame Pr) Chicago Distribution Ctr.

*__Breton, Jean Francois.__ Arabia Felix from the Time of the Queen of Sheba: Eigth Century B. C. to First Century A. D. LaFarge, Albert, tr. from FRE. LC 99-43002. 226p. 2000. reprint ed. pap. 14.95 (*0-268-02004-3*, Pub. by U of Notre Dame Pr) Chicago Distribution Ctr.

*__Breton, Laurie.__ Black Widow. 200p. 1999. pap. 5.99 (*1-893108-36-8*) Neighbrhd Pr Pubng.

Breton, M. & Zaccour, G., eds. Advances in Operations Research in the Oil & Gas Industry: Proceedings of the Workshop Held in HEC-Montreal, June 13 & 14, 1991. 232p. 1991. 365.00 (*2-7108-0610-X*, Pub. by Edits Technip) Enfield Pubs NH.

Breton, M., et al. Treatment Technologies for Solvent Containing Wastes. LC 87-34853. (Pollution Technology Review Ser.: No. 149). (Illus.). 753p. 1988. 64.00 (*0-8155-1158-2*) Noyes.

Breton, Marcos & Villegas, Jose Luis. Away Games: The Life & Times of a Latin Baseball Player. LC 99-12524. (Illus.). 288p. 1999. 22.50 (*0-684-84991-7*) S&S Trade.

Breton, Marcos, jt. auth. see Villegas, Jose Luis.

Breton, Mary Joy. Women Pioneers for the Environment. LC 98-16439. 336p. 1998. text 35.00 (*1-55553-365-5*) NE U Pr.

Breton, Mary Joy. Women Pioneers for the Environment. (Illus.). 336p. Date not set. pap. text 16.95 (*1-55553-426-0*) NE U Pr.

Breton, Nicholas. The Good & the Badde. LC 77-6859. (English Experience Ser.: No. 853). 1977. reprint ed. lib. bdg. 20.00 (*90-221-0853-8*) Walter J Johnson.

— A Mad World, My Masters, & Other Prose Works, 2 vols., Set. (BCL1-PR English Literature Ser.). 1992. reprint ed. lib. bdg. 150.00 (*0-7812-7194-0*) Rprt Serv.

— A Mad World, My Masters, & Other Prose Works, 2 vols., Set. Kentish-Wright, Ursula, ed. LC 30-11771. 1968. reprint ed. 49.00 (*0-403-00108-0*) Scholarly.

— Pasquils Mad-Cap & Mad-Cappes Message. LC 79-25850. (English Experience Ser.: No. 200). 88p. 1969. reprint ed. 25.00 (*90-221-0200-9*) Walter J Johnson.

— Poems by Nicholas Breton. LC 72-161960. 229p. 1952. 39.00 (*0-403-01335-6*) Scholarly.

— Poems by Nicholas Breton. 1988. reprint ed. lib. bdg. 59.00 (*0-7812-0343-0*) Rprt Serv.

— Works in Verse & Prose, 2 vols., Set. (BCL1-PR English Literature Ser.). 1992. reprint ed. lib. bdg. 150.00 (*0-7812-7193-2*) Rprt Serv.

Breton, Raymond. The Governance of Ethnic Communities: Political Structures & Processes in Canada, 26. LC 90-38423. (Contributions in Ethnic Studies: No. 26). 208p. 1990. 55.00 (*0-313-27417-7*, BEN, Greenwood Pr) Greenwood.

Breton, Raymond, et al. Ethnic Identity & Equality: Varieties of Experience in a Canadian City. 408p. 1990. text 50.00 (*0-8020-5860-4*); pap. text 22.50 (*0-8020-6776-X*) U of Toronto Pr.

Breton, Roland J. Atlas of the Languages & Ethnic Communities of South Asia. 2nd ed. LC 96-51603. (Illus.). 230p. 1997. 65.00 (*0-8039-9367-6*) Sage.

Breton, S. Why Worry? How to Stop Worrying & Enjoy Your Life. 1994. pap. 9.95 (*1-85230-556-8*, Pub. by Element MA) Penguin Putnam.

Breton-Smith, Clare. Jenny's Child. large type ed. LC 97-13678. (Nightingale Ser.). 221p. 1997. pap. 17.95 (*0-7838-8218-1*, G K Hall Lrg Type) Mac Lib Ref.

Breton, Sue. Element Guide to Depression: Your Questions Answered. LC 95-42156. (Element Guide Ser.). 144p. 1996. pap. 9.95 (*1-85230-775-7*, Pub. by Element MA) Penguin Putnam.

Bretones, Guy-Jose. Dictionnaire du Francais Fondamental en Image pour les Ruraux. (FRE.). 274p. 1982. pap. 45.00 (*0-7859-8111-X*, 2858022275) Fr & Eur.

Bretonne, Nicholas E. Restif De La, see Restif De La Bretonne, Nicholas E.

Bretscher. Linear Algebra & Application. 1998. pap. text 29.33 (*0-13-576273-1*) P-H.

Bretscher, Otto. Linear Algebra with Applications. LC 96-36942. (Illus.). 587p. (C). 1996. 93.33 (*0-13-190729-8*) P-H.

*__Bretschger, Lucas.__ Growth Theory & Sustainable Development. LC 99-14862. 264p. 1999. 90.00 (*1-84064-135-5*) E Elgar.

Bretschko, G. & Helesic, J., eds. Advances in River Bottom Ecology. (Illus.). viii, 342p. 1998. 136.00 (*90-73348-87-0*, Pub. by Backhuys Pubs) Balogh.

Bretschneider, Arnd. Die Gesellschafterlose Gesellschaft mit Beschrankter Haftung: Regelungen & Gestaltungsmoglichkeiten aus Gesellschaftsrechtlicher, Betriebswirtschaftlicher & Steuerrechtlicher Sicht. (GER.). XXVIII, 374p. 1994. 57.95 (*3-631-48011-3*) P Lang Pubng.

Bretschneider, Charles L. Topics in Ocean Engineering, 3 vols., 1. LC 78-87230. (Illus.). 430p. 1969. reprint ed. pap. 133.30 (*0-608-08513-8*, 203286000001) Bks Demand.

— Topics in Ocean Engineering, 3 vols., 2. LC 78-87230. (Illus.). 372p. 1970. reprint ed. pap. 115.40 (*0-608-08514-6*, 203286000002) Bks Demand.

— Topics in Ocean Engineering, 3 vols., 3. LC 78-87230. (Illus.). 231p. 1976. reprint ed. pap. 71.70 (*0-608-08515-4*, 203286000003) Bks Demand.

*__Bretschneider, E.__ Medieval Researches from Western Asiatic Sources. (Illus.). 716p. 2000. 295.00 (*0-7007-1262-3*, Pub. by Curzon Pr Ltd) Paul & Co Pubs.

Bretschneider, Jeanne, ed. see Kapelos, Joe.

Bretschneider, Peter. Polygyny: A Cross-Cultural Study. LC 96-171037. (Uppsala Studies in Cultural Anthropology: No. 20). 229p. (Orig.). 1995. pap. 46.50 (*91-554-3607-2*) Coronet Bks.

Bretsznajder, S. Prediction of Transport & Other Physical Properties of Fluids. 424p. 1971. 191.00 (*0-08-013412-2*, Pub. by Pergamon Repr) Franklin.

Brett & Younger, Carol. Living with Stress. (Extensions Adult Elective Bible Study Ser.). 59p. pap. 9.00 (*1-880837-43-9*) Smyth & Helwys.

Brett, Mary L. Sweet Offerings. (Illus.). 60p. 2000. pap. 10.95 (*0-935931-36-8*, Gray Matter Pubg) Iberian Pub.

Brett, Alistair, et al, eds. University Spin-Off Companies: Economic Development, Faculty Entrepreneurs, & Technology Transfer. 240p. (C). 1990. lib. bdg. 59.00 (*0-8476-7646-3*) Rowman.

Brett, Ana M., jt. auth. see Brett, Christopher M.

Brett, Annabel S. Liberty, Right & Nature: Individual Rights in Later Scholastic Thought. LC 96-15357. (Ideas in Context Ser.: No. 44). 243p. (C). 1997. text 59.95 (*0-521-56239-2*) Cambridge U Pr.

— William of Ockham on the Power of Emperors & Popes. 180p. 1998. 68.00 (*1-85506-552-5*) Thoemmes Pr.

Brett, Arlene & Provenzo, Eugene F., Jr. Adaptive Technology for Special Human Needs. LC 94-17216. (SUNY Series in Computers in Education). 164p. (C). 1995. pap. text 16.95 (*0-7914-2308-5*) State U NY Pr.

Brett, Arlene, et al. The Complete Playground Book. LC 92-43598. (Illus.). 129p. (C). 1993. pap. 19.95 (*0-8156-0271-5*) Syracuse U Pr.

Brett, Arlene, jt. auth. see Provenzo, Eugene F., Jr.

Brett, Bill. The Stolen Steers: A Tale of the Big Thicket. LC 76-51651. (Illus.). 120p. 1990. pap. 9.95 (*0-89096-452-1*) Tex A&M Univ Pr.

— There Ain't No Such Animal & Other East Texas Tales. LC 78-21777. (Illus.). 128p. 1987. 12.95 (*0-89096-068-2*) Tex A&M Univ Pr.

Brett-Billowitz, JoAnn, ed. see Family Circle Editors.

Brett, C. T. & Waldron, K. Physiology & Biochemistry of Plant Cell Walls. (Topics in Plant Physiology Ser.). 240p. 1989. 49.95 (*0-04-581034-6*) Routledge.

— Physiology & Biochemistry of Plant Cell Walls. (Topics in Plant Physiology Ser.). 240p. (C). 1989. pap. text 24.95 (*0-04-581035-4*) Routledge.

Brett, C. T. & Waldron, K. W. Physiology & Biochemistry of Plant Cell Walls. 1996. text. write for info. (*0-412-72020-5*) Kluwer Academic.

— Physiology & Biochemistry of Plant Cell Walls. 2nd ed. (Topics in Plant Functional Biology Ser.). (Illus.). 256p. 1995. pap. write for info. (*0-412-58060-8*) Kluwer Academic.

Brett, Carlton E., ed. Dynamic Stratigraphy & Depositional Environments of the Hamilton Group (Middle Devonian) in New York State, Pt. I. (Bulletin Ser.: No. 457). (Illus.). 156p. (Orig.). 1986. pap. 12.00 (*1-55557-003-8*) NYS Museum.

Brett, Carlton E. & Baird, Gordon C., eds. Paleontological Events: Stratigraphic, Ecological, & Evolutionary Implications. LC 96-1558. (Illus.). 616p. 1996. 68.50 (*0-231-08250-9*) Col U Pr.

Brett, Carlton E., ed. see Eckert, James D.

Brett, Caroline, ed. The Monks of Redon: Gesta Sanctorum Rotonensium & Vita Conuuoionis. (Studies in Celtic History: No. X). (ENG & LAT.). 270p. 1989. 75.00 (*0-85115-504-9*) Boydell & Brewer.

Brett, Catherine. S. P. Likes A. D. 118p. (YA). pap. 5.95 (*0-88961-142-4*, Pub. by Womens Pr) LPC InBook.

— Things Just Aren't the Same. 100p. (YA). pap. 4.95 (*0-88961-115-7*, Pub. by Womens Pr) LPC InBook.

Brett, Christopher M. & Brett, Ana M. Electroanalysis. LC 98-22282. (Oxford Chemistry Primers Ser.: No. 64). (Illus.). 96p. (C). 1998. pap. text 12.95 (*0-19-854816-8*) OUP.

Brett, Christopher M. & Brett, Maria O. Electrochemistry: Principles, Methods, & Applications. LC 92-29087. (Illus.). 456p. 1993. pap. text 49.95 (*0-19-855388-9*) OUP.

Brett, Colin, jt. auth. see Adler, Alfred.

Brett, Colin, tr. see Adler, Alfred.

Brett, David. C. R. Mackintosh: The Poetics of Workmanship. (Illus.). 152p. 1992. 39.50 (*0-674-54065-4*) HUP.

— The Construction of Heritage. LC 96-161853. 234p. 1996. 49.95 (*1-85918-052-3*, Pub. by Cork Univ); pap. 22.50 (*1-85918-053-1*, Pub. by Cork Univ) Stylus Pub VA.

— C.R. Mackintosh: The Poetics of Workmanship. (Illus.). 152p. (C). 1993. pap. 21.00 (*0-674-54066-2*) HUP.

B

— Poetic Land, Political Territory: Contemporary Art from Ireland. (Illus.). 164p. 1995. pap. 25.00 (*0-9525020-0-3*, Pub. by Lund Humphries) Antique Collect.

Brett, Donna W. & Brett, Edward T. Murdered in Central America: The Stories of Eleven U. S. Missionaries. LC 87-37216. (Illus.). 380p. 1988. reprint ed. pap. 117.80 (*0-7837-9858-X*, 206058700005) Bks Demand.

Brett, Doris. Annie Stories. LC 87-42744. (Illus.). 228p. 1988. pap. 5.95 (*0-89480-528-2*, 1528) Workman Pub.

— More Annie Stories: Therapeutic Storytelling Techniques. LC 91-46084. 224p. 1992. 16.95 (*0-945354-47-9*) Am Psychol.

Brett, E. A. Colonialism & Underdevelopment in East Africa. LC 72-97704. 330p. 1973. pap. 7.95 (*0-88357-001-7*); text 18.95 (*0-88357-000-9*) NOK Pubs.

— Colonialism & Underdevelopment in East Africa: The Politics of Economic Change. (Modern Revivals in African Studies). 330p. 1992. 61.95 (*0-7512-0080-8*, Pub. by Gregg Revivals) Ashgate Pub Co.

— The World Economy since the War: The Politics of Uneven Development. 328p. 1985. 69.50 (*0-275-90197-1*, C0197, Praeger Pubs) Greenwood.

Brett, Edward M. Pediatric Neurology. 3rd ed. LC 97-3033. 1997. text 240.00 (*0-443-05200-X*) Church.

Brett, Edward T. Humbert of Romans. pap. text 27.43 (*0-88844-067-7*) Brill Academic Pubs.

Brett, Edward T., jt. auth. see Brett, Donna W.

Brett, Elaine, ed. see Berk, Diane.

Brett, Elaine, ed. see Bonet, Diana.

Brett, Elaine, ed. see Braham, B.

Brett, Elaine, ed. see DuPont, Kay.

Brett, Elaine, ed. see Haynes, Marion E.

Brett, Elaine, ed. see Luhn, Rebecca.

Brett, Elaine, ed. see Mallory, Charles.

Brett, Elaine, ed. see Mondello, C.

Brett, Elaine, ed. see Nesheim, John L.

Brett, Elaine, ed. see Smith, Debra & Sutton, Helen.

Brett, Elaine, ed. see Swenson, J.

Brett, Felicity. Properties of Love. (Rainbow Romances Ser.: No. 906). 160p. 1994. 14.95 (*0-7090-4989-7*) Parkwest Pubns.

Brett, George & Cameron, Steve. George Brett: From Here to Cooperstown. LC 99-22888. (Illus.). 112p. 1999. 26.95 (*1-886110-79-4*, Pub. by Addax Pubng) Midpt Trade.

Brett, George, jt. auth. see Cameron, Steve.

Brett, George S. The History of Psychology: I. Ancient & Patristic II. Medieval & Early Modern III. Modern, 3 Vol. 1124p. 1998. 350.00 (*1-85506-575-4*) Thoemmes Pr.

Brett, Gerard. English Furniture & Its Setting from the Later Sixteenth to the Early Nineteenth Century. LC NK2529.B7. 127p. reprint ed. pap. 39.40 (*0-608-13629-8*, 201917500011) Bks Demand.

Brett, Guy. Mona Hatoum. (Illus.). 160p. 1997. pap. 29.95 (*0-7148-3660-5*, Pub. by Phaidon Press) Phaidon Pr.

— Transcontinental: Nine Latin American Artists. (Illus.). 112p. (gr. 13). 1990. pap. 23.00 (*0-86091-511-5*, A4983, Pub. by Verso) Norton.

Brett, Guy, et al. Exploding Galaxies: The Art of David Medalla. LC 96-199118. 216p. 1995. 34.95 (*0-947753-06-0*, Pub. by Kala Pr) SPD-Small Pr Dist.

Brett, Hy. How to Survive the New Millennium: Recycled Wisdom for an Age of Diminished Expectations. LC 95-5856. (Illus.). 224p. 1995. 12.95 (*0-9636620-3-1*) Brett Bks.

— The Ultimate New York City Trivia Book. LC 97-26873. 224p. (Orig.). 1997. pap. 6.95 (*1-55853-499-7*) Rutledge Hill Pr.

Brett, J. Alden, jt. auth. see Platt, Rutherford Hayes.

Brett, Jai & Nunn, Nancy. Close, but Not Touching. LC 86-90546. 64p. (Orig.). 1986. pap. write for info. (*0-9617480-0-1*) Spindrift Pr WI.

Brett, James J. The Mountain & the Migration: A Guide to Hawk Mountain. LC 91-14929. (Illus.). 112p. (Orig.). 1991. pap. 15.95 (*0-8014-9613-6*) Cornell U Pr.

Brett, Jan. Annie & the Wild Animals, 001. LC 84-19818. (Illus.). 32p. (J). (gr. k-3). 1985. 15.00 (*0-395-37800-1*) HM.

— Annie & the Wild Animals. LC 84-19818. (Illus.). 32p. (J). (ps-3). 1989. pap. 5.95 (*0-395-51006-6*, Sandpiper) HM.

***Brett, Jan.** Annie & the Wild Animals. (Illus.). 32p. (J). (ps-3). 1999. pap. 9.95 incl. audio (*0-395-95992-6*) HM.

Brett, Jan. Annie & the Wild Animals. (J). 1985. 11.15 (*0-606-04158-3*, Pub. by Turtleback) Demco.

— Armadillo Rodeo. LC 94-42425. (Illus.). 32p. (J). (ps-3). 1995. 15.95 (*0-399-22803-9*, G P Putnam) Peng Put Young Read.

— Beauty & the Beast. LC 88-16965. (Illus.). 48p. (J). (gr. 1-7). 1989. 16.00 (*0-89919-497-4*, Clarion Bks) HM.

— Beauty & the Beast. 32p. (J). (ps-3). 1990. pap. 6.95 (*0-395-55702-X*, Clarion Bks) HM.

— Beauty & the Beast. (J). 1989. 11.15 (*0-606-04614-3*, Pub. by Turtleback) Demco.

— Berlioz the Bear. LC 90-37634. (Illus.). 32p. (J). 1991. 14.95 (*0-399-22248-0*, G P Putnam) Peng Put Young Read.

— Berlioz the Bear. 1996. 11.15 (*0-606-11114-X*, Pub. by Turtleback) Demco.

— Christmas Trolls. LC 93-10106. (Illus.). 32p. (J). (ps-3). 1993. lib. bdg. 15.95 (*0-399-22507-2*, G P Putnam) Peng Put Young Read.

***Brett, Jan.** Christmas Trolls. (Illus.). 32p. (J). (ps-3). 2000. pap. 6.99 (*0-698-11846-4*, PuffinBks) Peng Put Young Read.

Brett, Jan. Comet's Nine Lives. LC 95-11646. (Illus.). 32p. (J). (gr. k-3). 1996. 16.95 (*0-399-22931-0*, G P Putnam) Peng Put Young Read.

— The First Dog. LC 88-2224. (Illus.). 32p. (J). (ps-3). 1988. 16.00 (*0-15-227650-5*) Harcourt.

— The First Dog. LC 88-222. (Illus.). 32p. (J). (ps-3). 1992. pap. 6.00 (*0-15-227651-3*, Voyager Bks) Harcourt.

— The First Dog. (Illus.). 32p. (J). (ps-3). 1999. pap. 24.95 (*0-15-201967-7*) Harcourt.

— Five Lost Chicks. LC 97-148639. 1997. pap. 10.95 (*0-590-13825-1*) Scholastic Inc.

— Fritz & the Beautiful Horses, 001. (Illus.). 32p. (J). (gr. k-3). 1981. 16.00 (*0-395-30850-X*) HM.

— Fritz & the Beautiful Horses. LC 80-26915. (Illus.). 32p. (J). (ps-3). 1987. pap. 5.95 (*0-395-45356-9*) HM.

***Brett, Jan.** Gingerbread Baby. LC 98-52310. (Illus.). 32p. (J). (ps-3). 1999. 16.99 (*0-399-23444-6*, G P Putnam) Peng Put Young Read.

Brett, Jan. Goldilocks & the Three Bears. LC 89-3778. (Illus.). 32p. (J). 1989. 15.95 (*0-399-22033-X*, G P Putnam) Peng Put Young Read.

— Goldilocks & the Three Bears. (J). 1996. 11.15 (*0-606-03397-1*, Pub. by Turtleback) Demco.

— The Hat. LC 96-54015. (Illus.). 32p. (J). (ps-3). 1997. 16.95 (*0-399-23101-3*, G P Putnam) Peng Put Young Read.

***Brett, Jan.** The Hat Board Book & Plush Package. (Illus.). 32p. (J). (ps-k). 1999. 16.99 (*0-399-23463-2*) Peng Put Young Read.

Brett, Jan. The Mitten: A Ukrainian Folktale. (Illus.). 32p. (J). (ps-3). 1989. 15.95 (*0-399-21920-X*, G P Putnam) Peng Put Young Read.

— The Mitten: A Ukrainian Folktale. (Illus.). 36p. (J). (ps). 1996. bds. 7.95 (*0-399-23109-9*, G P Putnam) Peng Put Young Read.

***Brett, Jan.** The Mitten: A Ukrainian Folktale. gif. ed. (Illus.). 32p. (J). 1998. boxed set 14.99 (*0-399-23360-1*) Putnam Pub Group.

— The Surprise. LC 99-20944. (Illus.). 32p. (ps-3). 2000. 20.01 (*0-399-23477-2*) Putnam Pub Group.

Brett, Jan. Town Mouse, Country Mouse. LC 93-41227. (Illus.). 32p. (J). (ps-3). 1994. lib. bdg. 15.95 (*0-399-22622-2*, G P Putnam) Peng Put Young Read.

Brett, Jan. The Trouble with Trolls. LC 91-41061. (Illus.). 32p. (J). (ps-3). 1992. 15.95 (*0-399-22336-3*, G P Putnam) Peng Put Young Read.

Brett, Jan. Twelve Days of Christmas. (Illus.). 32p. (J). 1990. 15.95 (*0-399-22037-2*, G P Putnam) Peng Put Young Read.

— The Twelve Days of Christmas. 1997. 12.15 (*0-606-12833-6*, Pub. by Turtleback) Demco.

— The Wild Christmas Reindeer. (Illus.). 32p. (J). (ps-3). 1990. 15.95 (*0-399-22192-1*, G P Putnam) Peng Put Young Read.

— The Wild Christmas Reindeer. (Illus.). 32p. (J). (ps-3). 1998. pap. 6.99 (*0-698-11652-6*, PapStar) Peng Put Young Read.

Brett, Jan. The Night Before Christmas. LC 98-4998. 32p. (J). 1998. 16.99 (*0-399-23190-0*, G P Putnam) Peng Put Young Read.

Brett, Jan & Lear, Edward. The Owl & the Pussycat. (Illus.). 32p. (J). (ps-3). 1991. 15.95 (*0-399-21925-0*, G P Putnam) Peng Put Young Read.

Brett, Jan, jt. auth. see Bunting, Eve.

Brett, Jane. Animal Noises in the Jungle. 1999. 2.98 (*1-57717-097-0*) Todtri Prods.

— Animal Noises on the Farm. 1999. 2.98 (*1-57717-096-2*) Todtri Prods.

— Going Places. 1999. 3.98 (*1-57717-100-4*) Todtri Prods.

***Brett, Jane.** Hungry Bunny. (Animal Homes Ser.). (Illus.). (J). (ps-k). 1999. 5.98 (*0-7651-1697-9*) Smithmark.

— Little Bear at the Seaside. (Bear Pack Ser.). (Illus.). 12p. (J). (ps-k). 1999. 8.98 (*0-7651-1699-5*) Smithmark.

— Little Bear's Christmas. (Bear Packs Ser.). (Illus.). 12p. (J). (ps-k). 1999. 8.98 (*0-7651-1700-2*) Smithmark.

— Playful Puppy: Including Toy. (Animal Homes Ser.). (Illus.). (J). (ps-k). 1999. 5.98 (*0-7651-1698-7*) Smithmark.

Brett, Jane & Cooke, Andy. In the Country. (Animal Noises Ser.). 2.98 (*1-57717-098-9*) Todtri Prods.

Brett, Jane & Rice, Sally, eds. Public Bodies - Private States: New Views on Women & Representation. (Photography: Critical Views Ser.). (Illus.). 156p. 1994. text 36.00 (*0-7190-4121-X*, Pub. by Manchester Univ Pr) St Martin.

Brett, Jennifer, ed. see Dilendik, John R.

***Brett, Jessica.** Animals on the Go. (Green Light Readers Ser.). (Illus.). 20p. (J). 2000. 10.95 (*0-15-202584-7*) Harcourt.

— Animals on the Go. (Green Light Reader Ser.). (Illus.). (J). 2000. 9.40 (*0-606-18167-9*) Turtleback.

***Brett, Jessica & Cowdrey, Richard.** Animals on the Go. LC 99-6797. (Green Light Readers Ser.). 20p. (J). 2000. pap. 3.95 (*0-15-202590-1*) Harcourt.

Brett, John. Essential Dordogne. (Illus.). 128p. 1996. pap. 7.95 (*0-8442-8891-8*, 88918, Passprt Bks) NTC Contemp Pub Co.

Brett, Judith, ed. Political Lives. (Illus.). 216p. 1998. pap. 19.95 (*1-86448-309-1*, Pub. by Allen & Unwin Pty) Paul & Co Pubs.

Brett, Judith, et al, eds. Developments in Australian Politics. LC 93-204086. 464p. 1994. 64.95 (*0-7329-2010-8*, Pub. by Macmill Educ); pap. 32.95 (*0-7329-2009-4*, Pub. by Macmill Educ) Paul & Co Pubs.

Brett, L. Bible Prayers for Children. 1980. pap. 2.50 (*0-88271-151-2*) Regina Pr.

***Brett, Lily.** Lily Brett: Collected Stories. (Illus.). 1999. pap. 19.95 (*0-7022-3087-1*, Pub. by Univ Queensland Pr) Intl Spec Bk.

— Too Many Men. 2001. write for info. (*0-688-17755-7*, Wm Morrow) Morrow Avon.

Brett, Lily. What God Wants: A Novel. LC 93-2497. (Illus.). 264p. 1993. 18.95 (*1-55972-193-6*, Birch Ln Pr) Carol Pub Group.

Brett, M. The English Church under Henry I. (Oxford Historical Monographs). 1975. 42.50 (*0-19-821861-3*) OUP.

Brett, Maria O., jt. auth. see Brett, Christopher M.

Brett, Mark G. Biblical Criticism in Crisis? The Impact of the Canonical Approach on Old Testament Studies. 251p. (C). 1991. text 69.95 (*0-521-40119-4*) Cambridge U Pr.

Brett, Mark G., ed. Ethnicity & the Bible. LC 95-46888. (Biblical Interpretation Ser.: Vol. 19). 1996. 165.50 (*90-04-10317-1*) Brill Academic Pubs.

Brett, Mary. Tomart's Price Guide to Tin Lithodoll Houses & Plastic Doll House Furniture. Trissel, Rebecca S., ed. LC 97-60705. (Illus.). 72p. 1997. pap. 17.95 (*0-914293-34-6*) Tomart Pubns.

***Brett, Maurice.** Flying the Oregon Trail. (Illus.). 280p. 2000. pap. 29.50 (*1-902807-05-7*, Pub. by Cirrus Assocs) Trans-Atl Phila.

Brett, Michael. Cry Uncle. 2000. pap. 7.00 (*0-671-77490-5*, Pocket Books) PB.

— How to Read the Financial Pages: A Simple Guide to the Way Money Works & the Jargon. 312p. 1992. pap. 24.95 (*0-7126-7560-4*, Pub. by CEN3) Trafalgar.

— Ibn Khaldin & the Medieval Maghrib. LC 98-74331. (Variorum Collected Studies: Vol. 627). 350p. 1999. text 106.95 (*0-86078-772-9*, Pub. by Ashgate Pub) Ashgate Pub Co.

Brett, Michael, ed. Northern Africa: Islam & Modernization. 156p. 1973. 45.00 (*0-7146-2972-3*, Pub. by F Cass Pubs) Intl Spec Bk.

Brett, Michael & Fentress, Elizabeth. The Berbers. Shipton, Parker, ed. (Peoples of Africa Ser.). (Illus.). 352p. (C). 1997. pap. 26.95 (*0-631-20767-8*) Blackwell Pubs.

Brett, Pat. Finding Your "First Real" Job. 192p. (C). 1997. per. 22.95 (*0-7872-3785-X*) Kendall-Hunt.

— Writing for Results: A Resume Workbook. 154p. (C). 1989. pap. write for info. (*0-534-13086-0*) Wadsworth Pub.

Brett, Peter. Building Terminology: An Illustrated Guide for Students. (Illus.). 304p. 1994. pap. 36.95 (*0-7506-1724-1*) Buttrwrth-Heinemann.

— Building Terminology Illustrated. 2nd ed. LC 98-131556. (Illus.). 352p. 1997. pap. 29.95 (*0-7506-3684-X*, Butterwrth Archit) Buttrwrth-Heinemann.

***Brett, Peter.** Canterbury. 64p. 2000. pap. 6.50 (*1-85311-164-3*) Canterbury Press Norwich.

Brett, Peter. Site Carpentry & Joinery. (Illus.). 128p. 1993. pap. 27.50 (*0-7487-1298-4*, Pub. by S Thornes Pubs) Trans-Atl Phila.

Brett, Philip, et al, eds. Cruising the Performative: Interventions into the Representation of Ethnicity, Nationality, & Sexuality. LC 94-47062. (Unnatural Acts Ser.). (Illus.). 288p. 1995. pap. 16.95 (*0-253-20976-5*) Ind U Pr.

— Queering the Pitch: The New Gay & Lesbian Musicology. LC 93-15025. 440p. (C). (gr. 13). 1994. pap. 18.99 (*0-415-90753-5*, B0283) Routledge.

Brett, R. L. Faith & Doubt: Religion & Secularization in Literature, 1800-1980. LC 97-225840. 304p. 1997. text 40.00 (*0-86554-544-8*, H415) Mercer Univ Pr.

— Lyrical Ballads. 1987. pap. 12.00 (*0-416-29720-X*) Routledge.

Brett, R. L. & Jones, A. R., eds. Lyrical Ballads: Wordsworth & Coleridge, 1798-1805. 2nd ed. 1968. pap. 14.95 (*0-415-02790-X*, NO. 2112) Routledge.

Brett, R. L., jt. auth. see Priestley, J. B.

Brett, R. L., ed. see Wordsworth, William & Coleridge, Samuel Taylor.

Brett, Robert J. Mucho gusto! Que gusto! Mucho gusto! Level 1: Textbook. 39.95 (*0-8219-0246-6*) EMC-Paradigm.

— Mucho gusto! Que gusto! Mucho gusto! Level 1: Workbook. 9.50 (*0-8219-0249-0*) EMC-Paradigm.

— Mucho gusto! Que gusto! Que gusto! Level 2: Workbook. 9.95 (*0-8219-0270-9*) EMC-Paradigm.

— Mucho gusto! Que gusto! Que justo!, Level 2: Textbook. 41.95 (*0-8219-0267-9*) EMC-Paradigm.

Brett, Rosalind. The Reluctant Guest. large type ed. 1990. 27.99 (*0-7089-2276-7*) Ulverscroft.

— Spring at the Villa. large type ed. 1991. 27.99 (*0-7089-2404-2*) Ulverscroft.

Brett-Serle, Monica. Journeys Come in Many Colours. (Illus.). 108p. (Orig.). 1997. pap. 10.00 (*1-890702-01-3*) Latitude Ent.

— The Mustard Seed. (Illus.). 30p. (Orig.). 1996. pap. 5.00 (*1-890702-00-5*) Latitude Ent.

Brett, Simon. An Amateur Corpse. large type ed. 1990. pap. 5.00 (*0-7451-1285-4*, Pub. by Chivers N Amer) Chivers N Amer.

— An Amateur Corpse. large type ed. (Nightingale Ser.). 300p. 1990. pap. 13.95 (*0-8161-5040-0*, G K Hall Lrg Type) Mac Lib Ref.

***Brett, Simon.** The Body on the Beach. LC 99-45794. 320p. 2000. 21.95 (*0-425-17500-6*, Prime Crime) Berkley Pub.

Brett, Simon. Corporate Bodies. (Mystery Ser.). 1993. mass mkt. 3.99 (*0-373-26130-6*, 1-26130-4) Harlequin Bks.

— Corporate Bodies: A Charles Paris Mystery. 256p. 1992. text 19.00 (*0-684-19397-3*, Scribners Ref) Mac Lib Ref.

— Crime Writers & Other Animals. large type ed. LC 98-55247. 1999. 30.00 (*0-7862-1820-7*) Mac Lib Ref.

— Dead Room Farce. LC 98-8376. 208p. 1998. text 20.95 (*0-312-19251-7*) St Martin.

— Dead Room Farce. large type ed. LC 98-28871. 1998. 30.00 (*0-7862-1564-X*) Thorndike Pr.

— Mrs. Pargeter's Package. 224p. 1992. mass mkt. 4.99 (*0-446-36204-2*, Pub. by Warner Bks) Little.

— Mrs. Pargeter's Plot. (WWL Mystery Ser.: No. 322). 1999. per. 4.99 (*0-373-26322-8*, 1-26322-7, Wrldwide Lib) Harlequin Bks.

— Mrs. Pargeter's Plot. LC 97-24625. (A Mrs Pargeter Mystery Ser.). 208p. 1998. 21.50 (*0-684-83714-5*) Simon & Schuster.

— Mrs. Pargeter's Plot. large type ed. LC 98-3644. 230p. 1998. 28.95 (*0-7838-0172-6*, G K Hall & Co) Mac Lib Ref.

***Brett, Simon.** Mrs. Pargeter's Point of Honour. (WWL Mystery Ser.). 256p. 2000. mass mkt. 5.99 (*0-373-26361-9*, 1-26361-5, Wrldwide Lib) Harlequin Bks.

— Mrs. Pargeter's Point of Honour. LC 99-32485. 272p. 1999. 22.00 (*0-684-86295-6*) Scribner.

Brett, Simon. Mrs. Pargeter's Pound of Flesh: A Mrs. Pargeter Mystery. large type ed. LC 93-17745. 316p. 1993. lib. bdg. 20.95 (*1-56054-771-5*) Thorndike Pr.

— A Reconstructed Corpse. (WWL Mystery Ser.). 1996. per. 5.50 (*0-373-26194-2*, 1-26194-0, Wrldwide Lib) Harlequin Bks.

— A Reconstructed Corpse. large type ed. LC 94-30492. 234 p. 1994. 23.95 (*1-56895-117-5*) Wheeler Pub.

— A Reconstructed Corpse: A Charles Paris Mystery. LC 93-50797. 192p. 1994. 20.00 (*0-684-19700-6*) S&S Trade.

— Sicken & So Die. LC 96-32448. 1997. 20.50 (*0-684-82459-0*) S&S Trade.

— Sicken & So Die: A Charles Paris Mystery. 1998. per. 5.50 (*0-373-26262-0*, 1-26262-5, Wrldwide Lib) Harlequin Bks.

— Singled Out. LC 94-39141. 1995. 20.00 (*0-684-80248-1*) S&S Trade.

— Singled Out. large type ed. LC 95-17661. 282p. 1995. 24.95 (*0-7838-1377-5*, G K Hall Lrg Type) Mac Lib Ref.

Brett, Simon, ed. see Chapman, Hillary.

Brett-Smith, H. B., ed. see Peacock, Thomas Love.

Brett-Smith, H. F., ed. see Etherege, George.

Brett-Smith, Sarah C. The Making of Bamana Sculpture: Creativity & Gender. (RES Monographs on Anthropology & Aesthetics). (Illus.). 376p. (C). 1995. text 105.00 (*0-521-44484-5*) Cambridge U Pr.

Brett, Stanley, jt. auth. see Brown, Richard.

Brett, Stephen F. Slavery & the Catholic Tradition: Rights in the Balance. LC 93-42798. (Am. Univ. Studies, Series V: Vol. 157). XI, 237p. (C). 1994. text 42.95 (*0-8204-2358-0*) P Lang Pubng.

Brett-Surman, M. K., jt. ed. see Farlow, James O.

Brett-Surman, Michael & Holtz, Thomas. The World of Dinosaurs: A North American Selection. (Illus.). 48p. (J). (gr. 5-8). 1998. 19.95 (*0-86713-046-6*) Greenwich Wrkshop.

***Brett-Surman, Michael, et al.** Dinosaurs. (Time-Life Guides Ser.). (Illus.). 256p. 2000. 24.95 (*0-7370-0081-3*) Time-Life Educ.

Brett, Thomas. Commentaries on the Present Laws of England, 2 vols. 2nd ed. 1294p. 1999. reprint ed. 325.00 (*1-56169-491-6*) Gaunt.

Brett, Virginia, tr. see Steffen, Albert.

***Brett, W., et al, eds.** Surgical Remodeling in Heart Failure: Alternative to Transplantation. (Illus.). 135p. 2000. pap. 49.00 (*3-7985-1223-X*, Pub. by D Steinkopff) Spr-Verlag.

Brett, William F., et al. An Introduction to the History of Mathematics, Number Theory, & Operations Research. 1974. pap. text 19.50 (*0-8422-0379-6*) Irvington.

Brett, William H. Legends & Myths of the Aboriginal Indians of British Guiana. LC 78-67691. (Folktale Ser.). reprint ed. 39.50 (*0-404-16059-X*) AMS Pr.

Brette, Michael N. Raising Capital for Your Business: By Using Private Placement Offerings, Direct Public Offerings. 192p. 1998. pap. text 18.95 (*1-882180-96-8*) Griffin CA.

Brette, Michael N. & Meckes, Richard L. Asset Protection Planning: How to Protect Yourself from the Terror of Lawsuits. 352p. (Orig.). 1997. pap. 26.95 (*1-882180-84-4*) Griffin CA.

Brettel, Caroline B. We Have Already Cried Many Tears: The Stories of Three Portuguese Migrant Women. (Illus.). 170p. 1983. 18.95 (*0-87073-232-3*) Schenkman Bks Inc.

Brettel, Richard, jt. auth. see Selz, Peter H.

Brettell, Caroline. Men Who Migrate, Women Who Wait: Population & History in a Portuguese Parish. LC 86-11270. (Illus.). 346p. reprint ed. pap. 107.30 (*0-608-06439-4*, 206665200008) Bks Demand.

***Brettell, Caroline.** Writing Against the Wind: A Mother's Life History. LC 99-18311. 204p. 1999. 55.00 (*0-8420-2782-3*) Scholarly Res Inc.

Brettell, Caroline B. We Have Already Cried Many Tears: The Stories of Three Portuguese Migrant Women. (Illus.). 151p. (C). 1995. reprint ed. pap. text 11.50 (*0-88133-878-8*) Waveland Pr.

— Writing Against the Wind: A Mother's Life History. LC 99-18311. 204p. 1999. pap. 17.95 (*0-8420-2783-1*) Scholarly Res Inc.

Brettell, Caroline B., ed. When They Read What We Write: The Politics of Ethnography. LC 92-43386. 216p. 1993. 57.95 (*0-89789-325-5*, H325, Bergin & Garvey) Greenwood.

— When They Read What We Write: The Politics of Ethnography. LC 92-43386. 208p. 1996. pap. 20.95 (*0-89789-492-8*, Bergin & Garvey) Greenwood.

***Brettell, Caroline B. & Hollifield, James F., eds.** Migration Theory: Talking Across Disciplines. LC 99-87915. 224p. 2000. write for info. (*0-415-92610-6*); pap. write for info. (*0-415-92611-4*) Routledge.

Brettell, Caroline B. & Sargent, Carolyn F. Gender in Cross-Cultural Perspective. 2nd ed. LC 96-29369. 560p. (C). 1996. pap. text 36.00 (*0-13-533613-9*) P-H.

An Asterisk (*) at the beginning of an entry indicates that the title is appearing for the first time.

***Brettell, Caroline B. & Sargent, Carolyn F.** Gender in Cross-cultural Perspectives. 3rd ed. 592p. 2000. pap. 34.67 (*0-13-017487-4*) P-H.

Brettell, Caroline B., jt. ed. see Sargent, Carolyn F.

***Brettell, Richard.** Modern Art, 1851-1929: Capitalism & Representation. (Oxford History of Art Ser.). (Illus.). 268p. 1999. 39.95 (*0-19-284273-0*); pap. 16.95 (*0-19-284220-X*) OUP.

Brettell, Richard. Pissarro & Pontoise: The Painter in a Landscape. (Illus.). 240p. (C). 1990. 65.00 (*0-300-04336-8*) Yale U Pr.

Brettell, Richard, jt. auth. see Friis-Hansen, Dana.

***Brettell, Richard R.** Impression: Painting Quickly in France, 1860-1890. (Illus.). 240p. 2000. 35.00 (*0-300-08446-3*) Yale U Pr.

Brettell, Richard R. An Impressionist Legacy: The Sara Lee Corporation Collection. (Illus.). 173p. 1997. 50.00 (*0-7892-0450-9*) Abbeville Pr.

— Impressionist Paintings, Drawings, & Sculpture from the Wendy & Emery Reves Collection. (Illus.). 159p. (Orig.). 1995. pap. 18.00 (*0-936227-15-X*) Dallas Mus.

Brettell, Richard R. & Lee, Natalie H. Monet to Moore: The Millennium Gift of Sara Lee Corporation. LC 99-24949. (Illus.). 256p. 1999. 60.00 (*0-300-08134-0*) Yale U Pr.

Brettell, Richard R. & Pissarro, Joachim. The Impressionist & the City: Pissarro's Series. LC 92-50580. (Illus.). 230p. (C). 1992. 65.00 (*0-300-05350-9*) Yale U Pr.

Brettell, Richard R. & Zukowski, Karen. Camille Pissarro in the Caribbean, 1850-1855: Drawings from the Collection at Olana. 2nd ed. (Illus.). 60p. (Orig.). 1998. pap. 15.00 (*0-9655562-0-4*) Hebrew Congreg.

Bretteville, Sheila L. De, see Nodal, Al & De Bretteville, Sheila L.

Bretthauer, E. W., et al, eds. Dioxin Perspectives: A Pilot Study on the International Information Exchange on Dioxins & Related Compounds. (NATO - Challenges of Modern Society Ser.: Vol. 16). (Illus.). 800p. (C). 1991. text 258.00 (*0-306-43916-6*, Kluwer Plenum) Kluwer Academic.

Bretthorst, G. L. Bayesian Spectrum Analysis & Parameter Estimation. (Lecture Notes in Statistics Ser.: Vol. 48). xii, 209p. 1988. 54.95 (*0-387-96871-7*) Spr-Verlag.

Brettle, Jane. Lots To Do. 1999. 3.98 (*1-57717-101-2*) Todtri Prods.

— My Pets. (Animal Noises Ser.). 1999. 2.98 (*1-57717-099-7*) Todtri Prods.

— Nature Is Busy. 1999. 3.98 (*1-57717-103-9*) Todtri Prods.

— Out to Work: A History of Wage-Earning Women in the United States. 1999. 3.98 (*1-57717-102-0*) Todtri Prods.

***Brettle, Mike.** Weather to Sail: The Complete Guide to Sailing Weather. (Illus.). 128p. 2000. pap. 21.95 (*1-86126-295-7*, 130074AE, Pub. by Crolwood) Motorbooks Intl.

Brettler, Marc, jt. ed. see Fishbane, Michael.

Brettler, Marc Z. The Creation of History in Ancient Israel. 272p. (C). 1998. pap. 24.99 (*0-415-19407-5*, D6075) Routledge.

Brettler, Marc Zvi. The Creation of History in Ancient Israel. LC 94-39144. 248p. (C). (gr. 13). 1995. 85.00 (*0-415-11860-3*) Routledge.

Brettler, Marc Zvi. God Is King: Understanding an Israelite Metaphor. (JSOT Supplement Ser.: No. 76). 219p. 1989. 60.00 (*1-85075-224-9*, Pub. by Sheffield Acad) CUP Services.

Brettner, Donald, jt. auth. see Fasser, Yefim.

Bretto, Charlotte C. A Framework for Excellence: A Resource Manual for NLP. LC 96-52560. (Illus.). 150p. (Orig.). 1990. spiral bd. 47.50 (*0-929514-03-3*) Grinder Delozier.

Bretton, Barbara. The Bride Came C. O. D. (American Romance Ser.). 1993. per. 3.50 (*0-373-16505-6*, 1-16505-9) Harlequin Bks.

— Bundle of Joy. (American Romance Ser.: No. 393). 1991. per. 3.25 (*0-373-16393-2*) Harlequin Bks.

— Daddy's Girl. (American Romance Ser.: No. 441). 1992. per. 3.39 (*0-373-16441-6*, 1-16441-7) Harlequin Bks.

***Bretton, Barbara.** The Day We Met. 1999. pap. 6.99 (*0-425-17190-6*) Berkley Pub.

Bretton, Barbara. Destiny's Child. 384p. 1995. per. 4.99 (*1-55166-090-3*, Mira Bks) Harlequin Bks.

— Guilty Pleasures. 1996. per. 5.99 (*1-55166-170-5*, 1-66170-1, Mira Bks) Harlequin Bks.

— I Do, I Do. (To Have & to Hold Ser.: No. 238). 1992. mass mkt. 4.99 (*0-373-83238-9*, 1-83238-5) Harlequin Bks.

— The Invisible Groom. 1994. mass mkt. 3.50 (*0-373-16554-4*, 1-16554-7) Harlequin Bks.

— Maybe This Time. 352p. (Orig.). 1995. mass mkt. 5.99 (*0-425-14724-X*) Berkley Pub.

— Mother Knows Best. (Family Continuity Program Ser.: No. 3). 1999. mass mkt. 4.50 (*0-373-82151-4*, 1-82151-1) Harlequin Bks.

— No Safe Place. (Mira Bks.). 251p. 1995. per. 4.99 (*1-55166-044-X*, 1-66044-8, Mira Bks) Harlequin Bks.

— Nobody's Baby. (Men Made in America Ser.). 1994. per. 3.59 (*0-373-45178-4*, 1-45178-0) Harlequin Bks.

***Bretton, Barbara.** Once Around. 338p. 1998. mass mkt. 6.99 (*0-425-16412-8*) Berkley Pub.

Bretton, Barbara. One & Only. 320p. (Orig.). 1994. pap. text 4.99 (*0-425-14358-9*) Berkley Pub.

— Operation: Baby. 1997. per. 3.75 (*0-373-16689-3*, 1-16689-1) Harlequin Bks.

— Operation: Husband. LC 95-8350. (American Romance Ser.). 250p. 1995. per. 3.50 (*0-373-16581-1*, 1-16581-0) Harlequin Bks.

— Playing for Time. (Men at Work Ser.: Vol. 46). 1998. mass mkt. 4.50 (*0-373-81058-X*, 1-81058-9) Harlequin Bks.

— Renegade Lover. (American Romance Ser.). 1993. mass mkt. 3.50 (*0-373-16493-9*, 1-16493-8) Harlequin Bks.

— Shooting Star. LC 96-3741. 248p. 1995. per. 4.99 (*1-55166-074-1*, 1-66074-5, Mira Bks) Harlequin Bks.

— Sleeping Alone. 320p. 1997. mass mkt. 5.99 (*0-425-15717-2*) Berkley Pub.

— Somewhere in Time. 1992. per. 4.99 (*0-373-83246-X*, 246) Harlequin Bks.

— Starfire. (Mira Bks.). 1996. mass mkt. 5.50 (*0-614-08420-2*, 1-66066-1, Mira Bks) Harlequin Bks.

— Tomorrow & Always. (Promo Ser.). 1994. 15.95 (*0-373-15236-1*, 1-15236-2) Harlequin Bks.

— Tomorrow & Always. 304p. 1994. per. 4.99 (*1-55166-004-0*, 1-66004-2, Mira Bks) Harlequin Bks.

Bretton, Barbara, ed. Once Around. 352p. 1998. mass mkt. 6.99 (*0-425-16555-8*) Berkley Pub.

Bretton, Barbara & McAllister, Anne. New Year's Resolution: Family. (Harlequin Promotion Ser.). 1998. per. 5.99 (*0-373-83332-6*, 1-883332-6) Harlequin Bks.

Bretton-Granatoor, Gary, ed. A Jewish Response to Cults. LC 96-47481. (Orig.). 1997. pap. text 8.95 (*0-8074-0604-X*, 571209) UAHC.

Brettschneider, Marla. Cornerstones of Peace: Jewish Identity Politics & Democratic Theory. LC 95-16068. 250p. (C). 1996. text 48.00 (*0-8135-2215-3*); pap. text 16.95 (*0-8135-2216-1*) Rutgers U Pr.

Brettschneider, Marla, ed. The Narrow Bridge: Jewish Views on Multiculturalism. LC 95-43322. 320p. (C). 1996. text 48.00 (*0-8135-2289-7*); pap. text 18.95 (*0-8135-2290-0*) Rutgers U Pr.

Bretz. Pasajes: Lengua List of Comprehension. 3rd ed. 1992. 14.06 (*0-07-007670-7*) McGraw.

Bretz, Jeff, jt. auth. see Craig, John C.

Bretz, Mary L. Voices, Silences & Echoes: A Theory of the Essay & the Critical Reception of Naturalism in Spain. 148p. (C). 1992. 63.00 (*1-85566-014-8*, Pub. by Tamesis Bks Ltd) Boydell & Brewer.

Bretz, Mary L., et al. Pasajes. 4th ed. LC 96-36735. (ENG & SPA.). 432p. (C). 1996. pap. 45.94 (*0-07-007697-9*) McGraw.

— Pasajes. 4th ed. LC 97-12875. (SPA.). 336p. (C). 1997. pap., student ed. 30.00 (*0-07-007699-5*); pap., student ed. 30.00 (*0-07-007698-7*) McGraw.

— Pasajes: Actividades. 3rd ed. (C). 1992. text 22.00 (*0-07-007667-7*) McGraw.

— Pasajes: Cultura. 3rd ed. (C). 1992. text 21.00 (*0-07-007666-9*) McGraw.

— Pasajes: Gramatica. (C). 1982. 10.00 (*0-685-06749-1*) McGraw.

— Pasajes: Lengua. 3rd ed. (C). 1992. text 33.50 (*0-07-007668-5*) McGraw.

— Pasajes: Lengua. 4th ed. (SPA.). (C). 1997. pap., wbk. ed., lab manual ed. 30.00 (*0-07-007700-2*) McGraw.

— Pasajes: Lengua-Cuaderno de Practica. 3rd ed. (C). 1992. pap. text, wbk. ed. 18.74 (*0-07-007669-3*) McGraw.

— Pasajes: Literatura. 3rd ed. (C). 1992. text 22.75 (*0-07-007665-0*) McGraw.

Bretz, Rudy. Handbook for Producing Educational & Public-Access Programs for Cable Television. LC 75-44365. 160p. 1976. pap. 34.95 (*0-87778-089-7*) Educ Tech Pubns.

— Taxonomy of Communication Media. LC 72-125874. (Illus.). 192p. 1971. 34.95 (*0-87778-012-9*) Educ Tech Pubns.

Bretz, Rudy & Schmidbauer, Michael. Media for Interactive Communication. LC 83-3085. 264p. reprint ed. pap. 81.90 (*0-8357-8479-7*, 203474600091) Bks Demand.

***Bretzger, William, photos by.** Gettysburg: The 2001 Battlefield Calendar. (Illus.). 2000. 12.95 (*0-9678983-0-7*) Solid Shot.

Bretzius, Stephen. Shakespeare in Theory: The Postmodern Academy & the Early Modern Theater. LC 97-33787. 168p. (C). 1997. text 37.50 (*0-472-10853-0*, 10853) U of Mich Pr.

Bretzke, James T. Bibliography on Scripture & Christian Ethics. LC 97-35805. (Studies in Religion & Society). 1997. 99.95 (*0-7734-8460-4*) E Mellen.

— Consecrated Phrases: A Latin Theological Dictionary. LC 97-40204. (LAT.). 152p. 1998. 19.95 (*0-8146-5880-6*) Liturgical Pr.

Breu, R. Algebraic Specification Techniques in Object Oriented Programming Environments. Goos, G. & Hartmanis, J., eds. (Lecture Notes in Computer Science Ser.: Vol. 562). xi, 228p. 1991. 34.00 (*0-387-54972-2*) Spr-Verlag.

Breucker, H. Seasonal Spermatogenesis in the Mute Swan (Cygnus Olor) (Advances in Anatomy, Embryology & Cell Biology Ser.: Vol. 72). (Illus.). 104p. 1982. 39.95 (*0-387-11326-6*) Spr-Verlag.

Breuel, Brian. The Complete Idiot's Guide to Buying Insurance & Annuities. LC 96-84571. 352p. 1996. 16.95 (*0-02-861113-6*) Macmillan Gen Ref.

Breuel, Brian H. Staying Wealthy: Strategies for Protecting Your Assets. LC 98-16525. (Personal Bookshelf Ser.). 288p. 1998. 21.95 (*1-57660-022-X*, Pub. by Bloomberg NJ) Norton.

***Breuel, Brian H.** Staying Wealthy: Strategies for Protecting Your Assets. 2000. reprint ed. pap. 13.95 (*0-425-17273-2*) Berkley Pub.

Breuel, H. P. Clinical Pharmacology in Elderly Subjects: Reference Ranges & Biological Variations after Repeated Measurements. (Illus.). 270p. 1995. pap. 135.00 (*3-540-59495-7*) Spr-Verlag.

Breuer. Crawford Co. & Cuba, Mo. 10.00 (*0-911208-23-2*) Ramfre.

***Breuer.** Undercover Tales of World War II. 256p. 2000. pap. 15.95 (*0-471-37944-1*) Wiley.

Breuer, Alice B. Beauty Plus Utility: How to Decorate Your Home the Smart Money Way. 62p. 1995. pap. 5.95 (*0-9640902-0-1*) Gilleys Pubng.

Breuer, Edward. The Limits of Enlightenment: Jews, Germans, & the Eighteenth-Century Study of Scripture. (Judaic Monographs: Vol. 7). 295p. 1996. 45.00 (*0-674-53426-3*); pap. 17.50 (*0-674-53427-1*) HUP.

Breuer, Eli, et al. Nitrones, Nitronates, & Nitroxides. Patai, Saul & Rappoport, Zvi, eds. LC 88-17388. (Chemistry of Functional Groups Ser.). (Illus.). 445p. reprint ed. pap. 138.00 (*0-608-20171-5*, 205280400012) Bks Demand.

Breuer, Frederica, jt. auth. see Fagre, Janet.

Breuer, Georg. Air in Danger: Ecological Perspectives of the Atmosphere. LC 79-18820. 201p. reprint ed. pap. 57.30 (*0-8357-5280-1*, 2026334) Bks Demand.

***Breuer, H. P., et al, eds.** Open Systems & Measurement in Relativistic Quantum Theory: Proceedings of the Workshop Held at the Istituto Italiano Per Gli Studi Filosofici, Napoli, April 3-4, 1998. (Lecture Notes in Physics Ser.: Vol. 526). viii, 240p. 1999. 68.00 (*3-540-65978-1*) Spr-Verlag.

***Breuer, Hans & Smit, B. J.** Proton Therapy & Radiosurgery. LC 99-35197. (Illus.). 305p. 1999. 146.00 (*3-540-64100-9*) Spr-Verlag.

Breuer, Hans-Peter, ed. The Note-Books of Samuel Butler, 1874-1883, Vol. I. (Complete Note-Books of Samuel Butler). 402p. 1984. lib. bdg. 52.00 (*0-8191-4193-3*) U Pr of Amer.

Breuer, Hans-Peter & Howard, Daniel F., eds. Erewhon: Or Over the Range, by Samuel Butler. 2nd ed. LC 77-92568. 280p. 1982. reprint ed. 38.50 (*0-87413-142-1*) U Delaware Pr.

Breuer, Hans-Peter & Parsell, Roger. Samuel Butler: An Annotated Bibliography of Writings about Him. LC 90-2749. 560p. 1990. text 25.00 (*0-8240-2747-7*, H769) Garland.

Breuer, Hans-Peter, jt. ed. see Lyon, James K.

Breuer, Harry, Jr., jt. auth. see Hassibi, Mahin.

Breuer, Heinz, et al, eds. Methods of Hormone Analysis. LC 75-19225. (Illus.). 545p. reprint ed. pap. 169.00 (*0-7837-3432-8*, 205775300008) Bks Demand.

Breuer, Janos. A Guide to Kodaly. 228p. (C). 1999. pap. 85.00 (*963-13-2908-9*, Pub. by Corvina Bks) St Mut.

Breuer, Josef & Freud, Sigmund. Studies on Hysteria. LC 57-12310. 320p. 1982. pap. 22.00 (*0-465-08276-9*, Pub. by Basic) HarpC.

Breuer, Joseph. Book of Jeremiah. 1988. 22.95 (*0-87306-983-8*) Feldheim.

Breuer, Joseph. The Book of Yechezkel. (ENG & HEB.). 1994. 9.95 (*1-58330-382-0*) Feldheim.

— The Book of Yirmeyahu. (ENG & HEB.). 420p. 1998. 9.95 (*0-87306-876-9*) Feldheim.

Breuer, Joseph, et al. Sefer Yirmeyah (The Book of Yirmeyahu) LC 99-167716. (ENG & HEB.). xv, 419 p. 1998. write for info. (*0-87306-872-6*) Feldheim.

Breuer, Joseph, Foundation Staff, ed. Collected Writings of Samson Raphael Hirsch Vol. I: The Jewish Year, Nissan-Av. (Hirsch Heritage Ser.).Tr. of Gessamelte Schriften. 391p. 1984. 23.95 (*0-87306-364-3*) Feldheim.

— Collected Writings of Samson Raphael Hirsch Vol. III: Jewish Symbolism. (Hirsch Heritage Ser.).Tr. of Gessamelte Schriften. 260p. 1985. 23.95 (*0-87306-924-2*) Feldheim.

Breuer, Joseph M. A Handbook of Assistive Devices for the Handicapped Elderly: New Help for Independent Living. LC 81-20270. (Physical & Occupational Therapy in Geriatrics Ser.: Vol. 1, No. 2). (Illus.). 77p. 1982. text 29.95 (*0-86656-152-8*) Haworth Pr.

Breuer, K. German-English, English-German Technical Pocket Dictionary. 6th ed. (ENG & GER.). 405p. 1971. pap. 53.00 (*3-87749-014-X*) IBD Ltd.

***Breuer, Karin.** An American Focus: The Anderson Graphic Art Collection. (Illus.). 200p. 2000. pap. 29.95 (*0-520-22763-8*) U CA Pr.

— An American Focus: The Anderson Graphic Arts Collection. (Illus.). 200p. 2000. 55.00 (*0-520-22761-1*) U CA Pr.

Breuer, Karl. Pocket Dictionary of Technology & Science: German-English, English-German. 6th ed. (ENG & GER.). 405p. 1971. 75.00 (*0-7859-7117-3*) Fr & Eur.

Breuer, Lee. Sister Suzie Cinema: Collected Poems & Performances 1967-1986. LC 87-1955. (Illus.). 190p. 1987. pap. 10.95 (*0-930452-60-7*) Theatre Comm.

Breuer, Lee, adapted by. The Gospel at Colonus. LC 89-4399. 64p. 1989. pap. 8.95 (*0-930452-94-1*) Theatre Comm.

Breuer, M., ed. Cosmetic Science. 1981. text 176.00 (*0-12-133002-8*) Acad Pr.

Breuer, Melvin A. & Friedman, Arthur D. Diagnosis & Reliable Design of Digital Systems. LC 76-19081. (Digital Systems Design Ser.). 308p. (C). 1976. text 38.40 (*0-7167-8094-1*, Computer Sci Pr) W H Freeman.

Breuer, Miklos M., ed. Milton Harris: Chemist, Innovator, & Entrepreneur. LC 82-13926. 170p. 1982. pap. text 22.00 (*0-8412-0740-2*, Pub. by Am Chemical) OUP.

Breuer, Mordechai. Modernity Within Tradition: The Social History of Orthodox Jewry in Imperial Germany. Petuchowski, Elizabeth, tr. from GER. 514p. 1992. text 57.50 (*0-231-07470-0*) Col U Pr.

Breuer, Peter T., jt. ed. see Kloos, Carlos D.

Breuer, Reinhard. Anthropic Principle: Man As the Focal Point of Nature. 218p. 1990. 42.50 (*0-8176-3482-7*) Birkhauser.

Breuer, Salomon. Chochmo U'Mussar. 1996. 19.95 (*0-87306-753-3*) Feldheim.

Breuer, Shlomo & Zwas, Gideon. Numerical Mathematics: A Laboratory Approach. LC 92-36528. (Illus.). 283p. (C). 1993. text 54.95 (*0-521-44040-8*) Cambridge U Pr.

Breuer, William. Death of a Nazi Army: The Falaise Pocket. 1997. 24.95 (*0-8128-8245-6*) Madison Bks UPA.

— Devil Boats: The PT War Against Japan. LC 86-17062. (Illus.). 256p. 1996. pap. 15.95 (*0-89141-586-5*) Presidio Pr.

Breuer, William B. Feuding Allies: The Private Wars of the High Command. LC 95-11638. 352p. 1995. 30.00 (*0-471-12252-1*) Wiley.

— The Great Raid on Cabanatuan: Rescuing the Doomed Ghosts of Bataan & Corregidor. 258p. 1994. 27.95 (*0-471-03742-7*) Wiley.

— Hoodwinking Hitler: The Normandy Deception. LC 92-31714. 272p. 1993. 29.95 (*0-275-94438-7*, C4438, Praeger Pubs) Greenwood.

— J. Edgar Hoover & His G-Men. LC 94-25967. 280p. 1995. 39.95 (*0-275-94990-7*, Praeger Pubs) Greenwood.

— MacArthur's Undercover War: Spies, Saboteurs, Guerrillas & Secret Missions. LC 94-48706. 257p. 1995. 24.95 (*0-471-11458-8*) Wiley.

— Race to the Moon: America's Duel with the Soviets. LC 92-31849. 232p. 1993. 24.95 (*0-275-94481-6*, C4481, Praeger Pubs) Greenwood.

— Sea Wolf: The Daring Exploits of Navy Legend John D. Bulkeley. 352p. 1998. pap. 16.95 (*0-89141-663-3*) Presidio Pr.

***Breuer, William B.** Secret Weapons of World War II. LC 99-55653. 256p. 2000. 24.95 (*0-471-37287-0*) Wiley.

Breuer, William B. Shadow Warriors: The Covert War in Korea. LC 95-35856. 260p. 1996. 27.95 (*0-471-14438-X*) Wiley.

— Top Secret Tales of World War II. LC 99-27133. (Illus.). 256p. 2000. text 24.95 (*0-471-35382-5*) Wiley.

— Undercover Tales of World War II. LC 98-24119. 242p. 1999. 24.95 (*0-471-31862-0*) Wiley.

***Breuer, William B.** Unexplained Mysteries of World War II. LC 99-55716. (Illus.). 2000. 27.95 (*0-7838-8859-7*, G K Hall & Co) Mac Lib Ref.

— Unexplained Mysteries of World War II. 256p. 1998. pap. 14.95 (*0-471-29107-2*) Wiley.

Breuer, William B. Unexplained Mysteries of World War II: Over 100 Bizarre, Odd, & Puzzling Events & Coincidences. LC 96-29479. (Illus.). 256p. 1997. 24.95 (*0-471-17559-5*) Wiley.

— Vendetta! Fidel Castro & the Kennedy Brothers. LC 97-5029. (Illus.). 278p. 1998. 24.95 (*0-471-18456-X*) Wiley.

— War & American Women: Heroism, Deeds & Controversy. LC 96-9013. 280p. 1997. 24.95 (*0-275-95717-9*, Praeger Pubs) Greenwood.

Breugel, F. Van, see Van Breugel, F.

Breugel, L. Van, see Van Breugel, L.

Breugelmans, Rene. Jacques Perk. LC 74-8658. (Twayne's World Authors Ser.). 210p. (C). 1974. 20.95 (*0-8057-2688-8*) Irvington.

Breugger, Walter. Diccionario de Filosofia. 9th ed. (SPA.). 684p. 1978. pap. 39.95 (*84-254-0146-1*, S50197) Fr & Eur.

Breuil, Henri. Beyond the Bounds of History: Scenes from the Old Stone Age. Boyle, Mary E., tr. LC 76-44694. (Illus.). reprint ed. 49.50 (*0-404-15934-6*) AMS Pr.

Breuil, Henri & Lantier, Raymond. The Men of the Old Stone Age: Palaeolithic & Mesolithic. Rafter, B. B., tr. LC 79-16777. (Illus.). 272p. 1980. reprint ed. lib. bdg. 38.50 (*0-313-21289-9*, BRMO, Greenwood Pr) Greenwood.

Breuil, M. Dictionary Sciences Vie: Terre. (FRE.). 479p. 1997. 35.00 (*0-320-01917-9*) Fr & Eur.

Breuille, J. Dictionnaire de la Sculpture. (FRE.). 1998. 129.00 (*0-320-00178-4*) Fr & Eur.

Breuille, Jean-Philippe. L' Art du XIXe Siecle: Larousse Dictionnaire de Peinture et de Sculpture. (FRE.). 777p. 1993. 225.00 (*0-7859-8610-3*, 203511313x) Fr & Eur.

— L' Art du XXe Siecle Dictionnaire de Peinture et De Sculpture. (FRE.). 896p. 1991. 225.00 (*0-7859-7670-1*, 2035113083) Fr & Eur.

— Larousse Dictionnaire de la Peinture Anglaise et Americaine. (FRE.). 351p. 1991. pap. 79.95 (*0-7859-7695-7*, 2037400659) Fr & Eur.

Breuilly, Elizabeth, jt. tr. see Palmer, Martin.

Breuilly, John. Nationalism & the State. LC 85-8601. x, 422p. 1985. reprint ed. pap. text 13.95 (*0-226-07412-9*) U Ch Pr.

— Nationalism & the State. 2nd ed. LC 93-33180. 407p. 1993. pap. text 18.95 (*0-226-07414-5*) U Ch Pr.

— State of Germany. (C). 1992. text 58.95 (*0-582-07864-4*) Addison-Wesley.

— State of Germany: The National Idea in the Making, Unmaking & Remaking of a Nation State. (C). 1992. pap. text 27.50 (*0-582-07865-2*) Addison-Wesley.

Breuilly, John, jt. auth. see Langewiesche, Dieter.

Breuilly, John, jt. ed. see Fulbrook, Mary.

Breuilly, Liz, jt. auth. see O'Brien, Joanne.

***Breuker, John, Jr.** Study Notes for Vergil's Aeneid. (Illus.). 100p. 2000. pap. text 28.00 (*0-9662763-9-6*, 1672001) Campanian Soc.

Breuker, Keith & Fowler, Pat. The Complete Pocket Guide to Fly Fishing. (Illus.). 136p. 1996. 15.00 (*0-924357-62-2*, 42050-A) Countrysport Pr.

Breul, Frank R. & Diner, Steven J., eds. Compassion & Responsibility: Readings in the History of Social Welfare Policy in the United States. LC 79-56040. 376p. 1985. pap. text 14.50 (*0-226-07413-7*) U Ch Pr.

Breul, Karl, ed. see Cambridge Songs Staff.

Breumer, Lois. Aquarelle. 95p. (C). 1990. 90.00 (*0-86439-121-8*, Pub. by Boolarong Pubns) St Mut.

Breunesse, Caroline. Visiting Vincent Van Gogh. (Adventures in Art Book Ser.). (Illus.). 32p. (J). 1997. 14.95 (*3-7913-1876-4*, Pub. by Prestel) te Neues.

Breunig, LeRoy C., ed. The Cubist Poets in Paris: An Anthology. LC 94-9379. (French Modernist Library). (Illus.). xxviii, 328p. 1995. text 45.00 (*0-8032-1224-0*) U of Nebr Pr.

Breunig, Martin. Integration of Spatial Information for Geo-Information Systems. LC 96-3925. (Lecture Notes in Earth Sciences Ser.: Vol. 61). (Illus.). xi, 171p. 1996. pap. 59.95 (*3-540-60856-7*) Spr-Verlag.

Breunig, Robert C. Houser & Haozous: A Sculptural Retrospective, September 10, 1983-May 1, 1984. Howden, Katharine W., ed. LC 86-177162. (Illus.). 52p. (Orig.). 1983. pap. 7.00 (*0-934351-08-2*) Heard Mus.

Breunig, Robert G. Animal, Bird & Myth in African Art: April 12 Through October 13, 1985, Primitive Art Gallery, the Heard Museum. LC 85-61030. (Illus.). 48p. (Orig.). 1985. pap. 5.00 (*0-934351-06-6*) Heard Mus.

Breuning, E. C., ed. & tr. see Fabri, Friedrich.

Breuning, Gerhard V. Aus dem Schwarzspanierhause: Erinnerungen an Ludwig van Beethoven Aus Meiner Jugendzeit. viii, 221p. 1970. reprint ed. 35.00 (*0-318-71888-X*) G Olms Pubs.

Breuning, M. H., et al, eds. Polycystic Kidney Disease. (Contributions to Nephrology Ser.: Vol. 97). (Illus.). vi, 142p. 1992. 49.75 (*3-8055-5586-5*) S Karger.

Breuning, Marijke A., jt. auth. see Ishiyama, John T.

Breuninger, Michael S. U. S. Military Combat Aircrew Individual Survival Equipment: WW II to Present, a Reference Guide for the Collector. Wise, Alan R., ed. LC 93-90752. (Illus.). 201p. 1994. pap. 29.95 (*0-9638400-0-2*) M Breuninger.

— United States Combat Aircrew Survival Equipment: World War II to the Present - A Reference Guide for Collectors. LC 93-90752. (Illus.). 208p. (Orig.). 1995. pap. 29.95 (*0-88740-791-9*) Schiffer.

Breuninger, Michael S., jt. auth. see Wise, Alan R.

Breunis, Andries. The Nominal Sentence in Sanskrit & Middle Indo-Aryan. LC 89-71270. (Orientalia Rheno-Traiectina Ser.: Vol. 35). vii, 229p. 1989. 63.50 (*90-04-09123-8*) Brill Academic Pubs.

Breunlin, Douglas C. Metaframeworks: Transcending the Models of Family Therapy. LC 97-225287. 1997. pap. 32.95 (*0-7879-1070-8*) Jossey-Bass.

Breur, G. L. Proposed Revision on Tooth Proportions for Enlarged Pinions. (Technical Papers: Vol. P209.10). (Illus.). 17p. 1971. pap. text 30.00 (*1-55589-233-7*) AGMA.

Breur, Joseph. The Jewish Marriage. pap. 5.95 (*0-87306-277-9*) Feldheim.

Breusers, H. N., jt. auth. see Raudkivi, Arved J.

Breuss, Rudolf. The Breuss Cancer Cure: Advice for the Prevention & Natural Treatment of Cancer, Leukemia & Other Seemingly Incurable Diseases. LC 95-910587. 130p. 1995. pap. 11.95 (*0-920470-56-4*) Alive Bks.

Breuste, J., et al, eds. Urban Ecology. LC 98-34103. (Illus.). 680p. 1999. 109.00 (*3-540-64617-5*) Spr-Verlag.

Breva-Claramonte, Manuel. Sanctius' Theory of Language: A Contribution to the History of Renaissance Linguistics. (Studies in the History of Linguistics Sciences : 27). viii, 294p. 1982. 65.00 (*90-272-4505-3*) J Benjamins Pubng Co.

***Brevard, Aleisha.** The Woman I Was Not Born to Be: A Transsexual Journey. 280p. 2001. 69.50 (*1-56639-839-8*); pap. 24.95 (*1-56639-840-1*) Temple U Pr.

Brevard, Joseph. Capital Facilities Planning: A Tactical Approach. LC 85-70761. (Illus.). 408p. 1985. 44.95 (*0-918286-40-9*, Planners Press) Am Plan Assn.

Brevard Music Center Staff. Cooking in Harmony-Opus II. 1996. 16.95 (*0-9648214-0-9*) Brevard Mus Ctr Assn.

Brevda, William. Harry Kemp: The Last Bohemian. LC 84-46102. (Illus.). 280p. 1986. 42.50 (*0-8387-5086-9*) Bucknell U Pr.

Breverton, David. Here Comes Bulldozer. (Pop-up Trucks at Work Ser.). (Illus.). 12p. (J). (ps-1). 1992. 4.95 (*0-448-40590-3*, G & D) Peng Put Young Read.

— Here Comes Fire Truck. LC 91-77449. (Pop-up Trucks at Work Ser.). (Illus.). 12p. (J). (ps-1). 1992. 4.95 (*0-448-40592-X*, G & D) Peng Put Young Read.

*** Breverton, Terry.** A To Z of Wales & the Welsh. 296p. 2000. pap. 34.95 (*0-8464-5187-5*) Beekman Pubs.

Brevilly, John, ed. The State of Germany: The National Idea in the Making, Unmaking & Remaking of a Modern Nation State. 243p. (C). 1992. pap. text 22.75 (*0-685-72534-0*, 79344) Longman.

Brevoort, Eliza H. Gullick. Gullicks & Allied Families, 1653-1948, with Supplement to 1952 & Index. (Illus.). 352p. 1997. reprint ed. pap. 52.00 (*0-8328-8862-1*); reprint ed. lib. bdg. 62.00 (*0-8328-8861-3*) Higginson Bk Co.

Brew, Alec. The History of Black Country Aviation. LC 93-26457. 1993. 13.95 (*0-7509-0404-6*, Pub. by Sutton Pub Ltd) Intl Pubs Mktg.

Brew, Angela, jt. ed. see Society for Research into Higher Education Staff.

Brew, Annie S., jt. auth. see Brew, Lydia E.

Brew, J. O. Archaeology of Alkali Ridge, Southeastern Utah. (HU PMP Ser.: Vol. 21). 1946. 85.00 (*0-527-01250-5*) Periodicals Srv.

***Brew, James.** The Red Book. LC 99-67098. 112p. 2000. 14.95 (*1-56167-534-2*) Am Literary Pr.

Brew, Kwesi. African Panorama. LC 80-66985. 64p. (Orig.). 1981. pap. 3.00 (*0-912678-48-8*, Greenfld Rev Pr) Greenfld Rev Lit.

Brew, Lydia E. & Brew, Annie S. Dr. Edith Irby Jones: A Story of Triumph. (Our Learn Together Book). 58p. (J). (gr. k-2). 1992. pap. text 3.50 (*0-9635351-0-2*) Lydias Educ.

Brew, Susan A., ed. Archaeological Test Excavations in Southern Arizona. (Archaeological Ser.: No. 152). (Illus.). 144p. 1982. pap. 7.95 (*1-889747-29-7*) Ariz St Mus.

Brew, Virginia & McCabe, Michael. Arizona: Studies. rev. ed. (Illus.). 160p. (YA). (gr. 4-6). 2000. text 21.50 (*0-911981-58-6*) Cloud Pub.

Brew, Virginia, jt. auth. see McCabe, Michael.

Breward, Christopher. The Culture of Fashion: A New History of Fashionable Dress. LC 94-5415. Vol. 1. (Illus.). 244p. 1995. pap. 19.95 (*0-7190-4125-2*, Pub. by Manchester Univ Pr) St Martin.

— Hidden Consumer: Masculinities, Fashion & City Life 1860-1914. 1999. pap. text 24.95 (*0-7190-4799-4*, Pub. by Manchester Univ Pr) St Martin.

— The Hidden Consumer: Masculinities, Fashion & City Life 1860-1914. 278p. 1999. 79.95 (*0-7190-4798-6*, Pub. by Manchester Univ Pr) St Martin.

Breward, Christopher, jt. ed. see Kwint, Marius.

Brewater, R. L. Communication Systems & Computer Networks. 1989. text 39.95 (*0-470-21489-9*) P-H.

Brewbaker, Linda. Campbell's 2501 Quiz Questions. 250p. (J). (gr. 5-6). 1999. pap. 15.95 (*0-944322-26-3*) Patricks Pr.

Brewbaker, William S., III, jt. ed. see Hall, Mark A.

Brewer. Biography of Edmund Burke. 1999. write for info. (*0-316-10775-1*) Little.

— Dictionary of Phrase & Fable. (Reference Library). 1200p. 1997. pap. 7.95 (*1-85326-300-1*, 3001WW, Pub. by Wrdsworth Edits) NTC Contemp Pub Co.

— Domestic Plants & Animals: The Ancient Egyptian Origins. (Illus.). 160p. 1994. 95.00 (*0-85668-584-4*, Pub. by Aris & Phillips) David Brown.

— Fish & Fishing in Ancient Egypt: (Formerly-Fishes of Ancient Egypt) (Natural History of Egypt Ser.). 1989. pap. 45.00 (*0-85668-485-6*, Pub. by Aris & Phillips) David Brown.

— Just Friends: A Memoir of Love & Deceit. 1995. 21.95 (*1-879582-07-4*) Platinum Pr.

— Planning a Baby? Complete Guide to Pre-Conceptual Care. 1998. pap. 11.95 (*0-356-21056-1*) Trafalgar.

— The Science of Ecology. 2nd ed. LC 93-87006. (C). 1994. text 89.00 (*0-03-096575-6*, Pub. by Harcourt Coll Pubs) Harcourt.

— Social Psychology: Testbank. Date not set. pap. text, teacher ed., suppl. ed. write for info. (*0-314-03326-2*) West Pub.

Brewer, Alberta & Brewer, Carson. Valley So Wild: A Folk History. 382p. 1975. 15.00 (*0-941199-01-0*) ETHS.

Brewer, Angela M., tr. see Allouache, Merzak.

Brewer, Angela M., tr. see Allouache, Merzak & Naqvi, Tahira.

Brewer, Anne. Breaking Free to Health, Wealth & Happiness: 100s of Powerful Ways to Release Limiting Belief, Vol. 1. 1999. pap. 15.95 (*1-887472-59-2*) Sunstar Pubng.

***Brewer, Anne.** The Power of Twelve: A New Approach to Personal Empowerment. 2nd ed. LC 98-61429. (Illus.). 322p. 2000. pap. 17.95 (*1-887472-70-3*, Pub. by Sunstar Pubng) Midpt Trade.

Brewer, Anne. The Power of Twelve: Achieving 12-Stranded DNA Consciousness. unabridged ed. Mason, Janice, ed. LC 97-62466. 256p. 1998. pap. 19.00 (*1-888604-07-7*) SunShine CO.

Brewer, Anne A., jt. ed. see Feinstein, Robert E.

Brewer, Annie M., ed. Talk Shows & Hosts on Radio: A Directory Including Show Titles & Formats, Biographical Information on Hosts, & Topic/Subject Index. 4th ed. 300p. 1996. 40.00 (*0-9632341-5-3*) Whitefoord.

Brewer, Annie M. & Brewer, Donald E. Auto Suppliers Sourcebook to Japanese Transplants. 187p. 1992. text 148.50 (*0-9632341-2-9*) Whitefoord.

Brewer, Annie M. & Brewer, Donald E., eds. Electric Vehicle Almanac. 200p. 1994. 55.00 (*0-9632341-8-8*) Whitefoord.

Brewer, Annie M., jt. auth. see Brewer, Wesley C.

Brewer, Anthony. Educator's Guide to the Internet: Integrating the Internet into the Classroom. Maguire, Edward J. & Klien, Richard, eds. (Brewers Series on Internet Education: Vol. 1). (Illus.). 1998. pap. 34.95 (*1-889005-02-9*) Temco Publng.

— Marxist Theories of Imperialism. 320p. 1980. pap. 15.95 (*0-415-04307-7*, Routledge Thoemms) Routledge.

— Marxist Theories of Imperialism: A Critical Survey. 2nd ed. 320p. (C). (gr. 13). 1990. pap. 29.99 (*0-415-04469-3*, A5113) Routledge.

Brewer, Bartholomew F. & Furrell, Alfred W. Peregrinaje Desde Roma. Vargas-Caba, Jose M., tr. from ENG. (SPA., Illus.). 194p. 1986. pap. 11.95 (*0-89084-328-7*, 030353) Bob Jones Univ.

— Pilgrimage from Rome. rev. ed. (Illus.). 1986. pap. 11.95 (*0-89084-327-9*, 018036) Bob Jones Univ.

Brewer, Beatrice H. Thru the Years. 1997. pap. write for info. (*1-57553-503-3*) Watermrk Pr.

Brewer, Bill. Perception & Reason. LC 98-45925. 299p. 1999. text 55.00 (*0-19-823567-4*) OUP.

Brewer, Brad & Hosid, Steve. Golf for Everybody: A Lifetime Guide for Learning, Playing & Enjoying the Game. LC 97-77503. 400p. 1998. pap. 19.95 (*1-886284-15-6*, Pub. by Chandler Hse) Natl Bk Netwk.

Brewer, Brent, jt. auth. see Smith, Arlon.

Brewer, Britton W., jt. ed. see Van Raalte, Judy L.

Brewer, Bryan. Eclipse. 2nd ed. (Illus.). 104p. (Orig.). 1991. pap. 14.95 (*0-932898-91-2*) Earth View.

Brewer, Bryan & Key, Edd. The Compact Disc Book: A Complete Guide to the Digital Sound of the Future. LC 87-17706. (Illus.). 1987. pap. 12.95 (*0-15-620050-3*, Harvest Bks) Harcourt.

Brewer, Bryan, jt. auth. see Hester, Debbie.

Brewer, C. & Epstein, G., eds. PVC: Formulation, Compounding & Processing. rev. ed. 230p. 1991. reprint ed. pap. 48.00 (*0-938648-19-5*, 1508) T-C Pr CA.

Brewer, Carson. Great Smoky Mountains National Park. 1997. pap. text 19.95 (*1-55868-408-5*) Gr Arts Ctr Pub.

Brewer, Carson, jt. auth. see Brewer, Alberta.

***Brewer, Charles.** How to Win ROTC Scholarships. LC 99-58458. (Illus.). 112p. (C). 2000. pap. 12.95 (*1-882897-47-1*) Lost Coast.

Brewer, Charles E., ed. see Bertali, Antonio & Dobel, Heinrich.

Brewer, Charles L., jt. ed. see Ware, Mark E.

Brewer, Charlotte. Editing Piers Plowman: The Evolution of the Text. LC 95-26694. (Cambridge Studies in Medieval Literature: No. 28). 474p. (C). 1996. text 74.95 (*0-521-34250-3*) Cambridge U Pr.

Brewer, Charlotte & Minnis, Alastair J., eds. Crux & Controversy in Middle English Textual Criticism. 149p. (C). 1992. 75.00 (*0-85991-321-X*, DS Brewer) Boydell & Brewer.

Brewer, Charlotte & Rigg, A. G., eds. Piers Plowman: A Facsimile of the Z-Text in Bodleian Library, Oxford, MS Bodley 851. (Illus.). 52p. (C). 1994. 150.00 (*0-85991-396-1*, DS Brewer) Boydell & Brewer.

Brewer, Charlotte, ed. see Langland, William.

Brewer, Chris. Artists: Exploring Art Through the Study of Five Great Lives. rev. ed. (Creative Lives Ser.). (Illus.). 88p. 1992. pap., teacher ed. 25.00 (*0-913705-36-5*) Zephyr Pr AZ.

— Bakersfield's Photographic Past. (Illus.). 64p. 1998. pap. 10.95 (*1-892622-00-9*) Brewers Hist.

— Exeter's Photographic History. (Illus.). 80p. 1998. pap. 10.95 (*1-892622-07-6*) Brewers Hist.

— Family Fun in Montana. LC 98-42834. 344p. 1998. pap. 16.95 (*1-56044-554-8*) Falcon Pub Inc.

— The Golden Years - Memorial Hospital at Exeter. (Illus.). 58p. 1998. pap. 6.00 (*1-892622-08-4*) Brewers Hist.

***Brewer, Chris.** Southern San Joaquin Valley Scenes. (Images of America Ser.). (Illus.). 128p. 1999. pap. 18.99 (*0-7385-0245-6*) Arcadia Publng.

Brewer, Chris & Ripkin, Don. Bakersfield & Kern Picture Album. 2nd ed. (Illus.). 96p. 1986. reprint ed. 30.00 (*1-892622-01-7*) Brewers Hist.

Brewer, Chris B. & Campbell, Don G. Rhythms of Learning: Creative Tools for Developing Lifelong Skills. 320p. 1991. pap. text 32.00 (*0-913705-59-4*) Zephyr Pr AZ.

Brewer, Clifton H. History of Religious Education in the Episcopal Church to 1835. LC 73-89152. (American Education: Its Men, Institutions, & Ideas. Series 1). 1978. reprint ed. 18.95 (*0-405-01390-6*) Ayer.

Brewer, Colin, ed. Treatment Options in Addiction: Medical Management of Alcohol & Opiate Abuse. LC 94-137578. 120p. 1993. reprint ed. pap. 37.20 (*0-608-01826-0*, 206247500003) Bks Demand.

Brewer, David I. Techniques & Assumptions in Jewish Exegesis Before 70 C. E. xiii, 299p. 1992. 155.00 (*3-16-145803-6*, Pub. by JCB Mohr) Coronet Bks.

Brewer, David J. The United States: A Christian Nation. (Illus.). 89p. 1996. reprint ed. pap. 8.95 (*0-915815-20-6*) American Vision.

Brewer, Dered. An Introduction to Chaucer. 2nd ed. LC 97-43000. (Longman Medieval & Renaissance Library). 416p. (C). 1998. pap. 39.06 (*0-582-09348-1*) Longman.

Brewer, Derek. Chaucer & His World LC 78-318729. 224p. 1978. write for info. (*0-413-34340-5*) Routledge.

***Brewer, Derek & Gibson, Jonathan, eds.** A Companion to the Gawain-Poet. (Illus.). 456p. 1999. pap. 35.00 (*0-85991-529-8*) Boydell & Brewer.

Brewer, Derek S. Chaucer & His World. 218p. (C). 1992. 60.00 (*0-85991-365-1*, DS Brewer) Boydell & Brewer.

— Chaucer in His Time. LC 77-7517. 243p. 1977. reprint ed. lib. bdg. 65.00 (*0-8371-9649-3*, BRCI, Greenwood Pr) Greenwood.

— Geoffrey Chaucer Vol. 2: 1837-1933. 354p. (C). 1996. 125.00 (*0-415-13398-X*); 160.00 (*0-415-13399-8*) Routledge.

Brewer, Derek S., ed. Chaucer: The Critical Heritage, 2 vols. Incl. Vol. 1. 1385-1837. 1978. 42.50 (*0-7100-0223-8*, 02238); Vol. 2. 1837-1933. 1978. 42.50 (*0-7100-0224-6*); (Critical Heritage Ser.). 1978. 50.00 (*0-7100-8497-8*, Routledge Thoemms) Routledge.

— Medieval Comic Tales. 224p. 1996. pap. 29.95 (*0-85991-485-2*, DS Brewer) Boydell & Brewer.

— Medieval Comic Tales. rev. ed. 224p. 1996. 60.00 (*0-85991-430-5*, DS Brewer) Boydell & Brewer.

— Studies in Medieval English Romances: Some New Approaches. 208p. (Orig.). (C). 1991. pap. 19.95 (*0-85991-324-4*) Boydell & Brewer.

Brewer, Derek S. & Frank, Ernest. Arthur's Britian The Land & the Legend. (C). 1987. text 75.00 (*0-907115-26-8*, Pub. by Pevensey) St Mut.

— Shakespeare's Britain. (C). 1987. text 80.00 (*0-907115-47-0*, Pub. by Pevensey) St Mut.

Brewer, Derek S. & Gibson, Jonathan, eds. A Companion to the Gawain-Poet. LC 96-3210. (Arthurian Studies). (Illus.). 320p. 1998. 90.00 (*0-85991-433-X*) Boydell & Brewer.

Brewer, Derek S., jt. ed. see Alamichel, Marie-Francoise.

Brewer, Derek S., ed. see Malory, Thomas.

Brewer, Derek S., ed. & intro. see James, Henry.

Brewer, Donald. Netscape ONE Sourcebook. LC 97-4049. 416p. 1997. pap. 24.99 (*0-471-18146-3*) Wiley.

Brewer, Donald E., jt. auth. see Brewer, Annie M.

Brewer, Donald E., jt. ed. see Brewer, Annie M.

Brewer, Doug, jt. auth. see Russell, Richard.

Brewer, Douglas J. Domestic Plants & Animals: The Ancient Egyptian Origins. (Illus.). 160p. 1994. pap. 65.00 (*0-85668-585-2*, Pub. by Aris & Phillips) David Brown.

— Fish & Fishing in Ancient Egypt. (Natural History of Egypt Ser.). (Illus.). 128p. 1989. 75.00 (*0-85668-399-X*, Pub. by Aris & Phillips) David Brown.

Brewer, Douglas J. & Teeter, Emily. Egypt & the Egyptians. (Illus.). 218p. (C). 1999. pap. 19.95 (*0-521-44984-7*); text 54.95 (*0-521-44518-3*) Cambridge U Pr.

Brewer, E. Cobham. Dictionary of Miracles: Imitative, Realistic, & Dogmatic. rev. ed. LC 89-28194. 582p. 1992. reprint ed. lib. bdg. 55.00 (*1-55888-900-0*) Omnigraphics Inc.

Brewer, Earl D., ed. Gerontology in Theological Education. LC 89-11077. (Journal of Religion & Aging: Vol. 6, Nos. 1-2). (Illus.). 166p. 1989. text 5.95 (*0-86656-948-0*) Haworth Pr.

— Gerontology in Theological Education: Local Program Development. LC 89-37874. (Journal of Religion & Aging: Vol. 6, Nos. 3-4). (Illus.). 162p. 1989. text 4.95 (*0-86656-958-8*) Haworth Pr.

Brewer, Earl D. & Jackson, Mance C., Jr. Wesleyan Transformations. 87p. (C). 1988. pap. 6.95 (*1-884805-00-0*) Jrnl Interdenom.

***Brewer, Earl J.** The Arthritis Sourcebook. 3rd ed. LC 99-55675. (Illus.). 272p. 2000. pap. 16.95 (*0-7373-0381-6*, 03816W, Pub. by Lowell Hse) NTC Contemp Pub Co.

Brewer, Earl J., Jr. The Arthritis Sourcebook: Everything You Need to Know. Angel, Kathy C., ed. LC 92-39063. 240p. 1994. reprint ed. pap. 12.95 (*1-56565-116-2*) Lowell Hse.

Brewer, Earl J., Jr. & Angel, Kathy C. The Arthritis Sourcebook. LC 92-39063. 252p. 1993. 21.95 (*1-56565-036-0*) Lowell Hse.

— The Arthritis Sourcebook. 240p. 1998. pap. 16.00 (*1-56565-627-X*) Lowell Hse.

— Parenting a Child with Arthritis: A Practical, Empathetic Guide to Help You & Your Child Live with Arthritis. 224p. 1992. 21.95 (*0-929923-55-3*) Lowell Hse.

***Brewer, Earl J., Jr. & Angel, Kathy Cochran.** The Arthritis Sourcebook. 224p. 2000. reprint ed. pap. text 15.00 (*0-7881-6917-3*) DIANE Pub.

Brewer, Ebenezer C. & Evans, Ivor H. Brewer's Dictionary of Phrase & Fable. LC 83-124550. xvi, 1213 p. 1981. write for info. (*0-304-30706-8*) Continuum.

— Brewer's Dictionary of Phrase & Fable. LC 79-107024. xvi, 1175 p. 1970. write for info. (*0-06-010466-X*, HarpBusn) HarpInfo.

Brewer, Edward C., jt. ed. see Campbell, Michael H.

Brewer, Edward S. Understanding Boat Design. 4th ed. 160p. 1994. pap. 16.95 (*0-07-007694-4*) McGraw.

Brewer, Eileen, jt. auth. see Brewer, Phil.

Brewer, Elisabeth. Sir Gawain & the Green Knight: Sources & Analogues. (Arthurian Studies: No. XXVII). 192p. (C). 1992. pap. 24.95 (*0-85991-359-7*) Boydell & Brewer.

— T. H. White's the Once & Future King. (Arthurian Studies: Vol. 30). 246p. (C). 1993. 60.00 (*0-85991-393-7*, DS Brewer) Boydell & Brewer.

Brewer, Elizabeth. The Novel of Entertainment During the Gallant Era: A Study of the Novels of August Bohse, Vol. 13. (Arbeiten zur Mittelern Deutschen Literatur und Sprache Ser.). 145p. 1983. 10.00 (*3-261-03241-3*) P Lang Pubng.

Brewer, Ernest W. 13 Proven Ways to Get Your Message Across: The Essential Reference for Teachers, Trainers, Presenters, & Speakers. LC 97-22291. 128p. 1997. 61.95 (*0-8039-6641-5*); pap. 27.95 (*0-8039-6642-3*) Corwin Pr.

Brewer, Ernest W. & Hollingsworth, Connie. Promising Practices: How Communities Across America Are Working to Meet National Education Goals 2000. LC 98-22238. 243p. 1999. pap. 18.95 (*1-890871-04-4*) Holcomb Hath.

Brewer, Ernest W., et al. Finding Funding: Grantwriting & Project Management from Start to Finish. 2nd ed. (Illus.). 280p. 1995. pap. 39.95 (*0-8039-6202-9*) Corwin Pr.

— Finding Funding: Grantwriting for the Financially Challenged Educator. LC 93-8395. 271p. 1993. pap. 39.95 (*0-8039-6093-X*) Corwin Pr.

— Finding Funding: Grantwriting from Start to Finish, Including Project Management & Internet Use. 3rd ed. LC 97-45257. (Illus.). 320p. 1997. pap. 49.95 (*0-8039-6681-4*) Corwin Pr.

***Brewer, Ernest W., et al.** Foundations of Workforce Education: Historical, Philosophical & Theoretical Applications. 490p. (C). 1999. per. 78.95 (*0-7872-6360-5*, 41636001) Kendall-Hunt.

Brewer, Fay. Scratchin' with Fay. 438p. 1994. 18.00 (*1-885507-01-1*) Fundco Printers.

Brewer, Floyd I. Bethlehem Diary: Stories & Reflections, 1983-1993. Buckley, Teresa A., ed. (Illus.). 1994. 12.50 (*0-9635402-1-1*) Town Beth Bicent.

— A Dutch-English Odyssey: Stories of Brewer & Estey Families in North America, 1636-1996. LC 97-178905. (Illus.). 500p. 1997. 27.00 (*0-9635402-2-X*) Town Beth Bicent.

Brewer, Frances J. James Branch Cabell: A Bibliography of His Writings, Biography & Criticism. 206p. 1977. 18.95 (*0-8369-5785-7*) Ayer.

Brewer, G. Daniel, ed. Hydrogen Aircraft Technology. 448p. 1991. lib. bdg. 239.00 (*0-8493-5838-8*, TL704) CRC Pr.

Brewer, Gail S. Pregnant Vegetarian. 1999. pap. 7.95 (*0-14-008150-X*, Penguin Bks) Viking Penguin.

Brewer, Gail S. & Brewer, Thomas H. The Brewer Medical Diet for Normal & High-Risk Pregnancy: A Leading Obstetrician's Guide to Every Stage of Pregnancy. 1983. 8.95 (*0-671-42635-4*, Fireside) S&S Trade Pap.

Brewer, Gail S., jt. auth. see Notarius, Barbara.

Brewer, Garry D. & Shubik, Martin. The War Game: A Critique of Military Problem Solving. (Illus.). 404p. (C). 1979. 46.50 (*0-674-94600-6*) HUP.

Brewer, Garry D., jt. auth. see Blair, Bruce G.

***Brewer, Gary.** Gary Brewer Guitar - Bluegrass Guitar at Its Best. 64p. 1998. pap. 10.95 (*0-7866-4450-8*, 97329) Mel Bay.

— Journey to the Spring at Crystal Mountain. LC 00-9404. (Illus.). (J). 2000. write for info. (*1-57895-043-0*) Bridge Resources.

Brewer, Gary. Servants of the Mist. Dobson, David, ed. LC 98-16357. 190p. (J). 1998. 6.95 (*1-57895-058-9*) Bridge Resources.

Brewer, Gary J., jt. ed. see Charlet, Laurence D.

An Asterisk (*) at the beginning of an entry indicates that the title is appearing for the first time.

Brewer, Gay. Charles Bukowski. LC 97-5880. (Twayne's United States Authors Ser.: Vol. 684). 1997. 32.00 (*0-8057-4558-0*, Twyne) Mac Lib Ref.

Brewer, Gay. David Mamet & Film: Illusion - Disillusion in a Wounded Land. LC 92-50951. (Illus.). 221p. 1993. lib. bdg. 35.00 (*0-89950-834-0*) McFarland & Co.

— A Detective in Distress: Philip Marlowe's Domestic Dream. LC 90-35522. (Brownstone Mystery Guides Ser.: Vol. 5). 68p. (C). 1989. reprint ed. pap. 13.00 (*0-941028-08-9*) Millefleurs.

— Laughing Like Hell: The Harrowing Satires of Jim Thompson. LC 95-5337. (Mystery Guides Ser.: No. 17). 144p. 1996. pap. 19.00 (*0-941028-22-4*) Millefleurs.

— Predator in the House. 40p. (Orig.). 1996. pap. 9.00 (*0-9628478-7-9*) North Star OH.

— Presently a Beast. 67p. (Orig.). 1996. pap. 8.95 (*0-9647127-4-1*) Coreopsis Bks.

Brewer, Gaylord. Devilfish. 104p. Date not set. pap. 12.95 (*1-888996-15-3*, Red Hen Press) Valentine CA.

***Brewer, Gene.** K-Pax. 2001. pap. write for info. (*0-312-97702-6*, St Martins Paperbacks) St Martin.

Brewer, George, Jr. & Bloch, Bertram. Dark Victory. 1967. pap. 5.25 (*0-8222-0275-1*) Dramatists Play.

Brewer, George E. History of Coosa County, Alabama. 314p. 1990. 35.00 (*0-89308-624-X*, BA 22) Southern Hist Pr.

Brewer, George J. & Sing, Charles F. Introduction to Genetics. (Biology Ser.). (Illus.). 784p. 1983. teacher ed. 8.00 (*0-201-10139-4*) Addison-Wesley.

— Introductory Genetics. (Biology Ser.). (Illus.). 784p. 1983. text. write for info. (*0-201-10138-6*) Addison-Wesley.

Brewer, George R. & Wilson, Robert G. Ion Beams: With Applications to Ion Implantation. LC 79-1345. 512p. 1979. reprint ed. lib. bdg. 51.50 (*0-88275-899-3*) Krieger.

Brewer, Gordon M. How You Played the Game: A History of Intercollegiate Sports at Hope College, 1866-1955. 208p. 1992. text 24.95 (*0-9634061-0-8*) Hope College.

***Brewer, Guy.** Dead Man's Hand. (Diamondback Ser.: Vol. 5). 2000. mass mkt. 5.99 (*0-515-12888-0*) Berkley Pub.

Brewer, Guy. Diamondback: The Novel, 1 vol. (Diamondback Ser.: Vol. 1). 262p. (Orig.). 1999. mass mkt. 5.99 (*0-515-12568-7*, Jove) Berkley Pub.

***Brewer, Guy.** Game of Chance. (Diamondback Ser.: Vol. 4). 197p. 2000. mass mkt. 5.99 (*0-515-12806-6*, Jove) Berkley Pub.

— Ranking in Revenge. (Diamondback Ser.: No. 3). 2000. mass mkt. 5.99 (*0-515-12753-1*, Jove) Berkley Pub.

— Texas Two-Timing, 2. 1999. mass mkt. 5.99 (*0-515-12685-3*, Jove) Berkley Pub.

***Brewer, Harold.** Fig Leaves & Masks: Survival Gear for Sapiens. unabridged ed. (Illus.). 112p. 2000. pap. 15.00 (*0-9675455-0-1*) Toy Piper.

***Brewer, Henry.** R&b Soul Keyboards: The Complete Guide. 64p. 1999. pap. 16.95 incl. audio compact disk (*0-7935-9744-7*) H Leonard.

Brewer, Henry & Clark, Chloe. The Journal of Henry Bridgman Brewer. 141p. 1986. 14.95 (*0-87770-332-9*) Ye Galleon.

Brewer, Hester W. Woolsey: Family of George Wood Woolsey & Sarah Nelson Woolsey. 134p. 1994. reprint ed. pap. 22.00 (*0-8328-4165-X*); reprint ed. lib. bdg. 32.00 (*0-8328-4164-1*) Higginson Bk Co.

Brewer, Ilma M. Learning More & Teaching Less: A Decade of Innovation in Self-Instruction & Small Group Learning. 176p. 1985. 38.00 (*1-85059-003-6*) OpUniv Pr.

Brewer, J. The Common People & Politics, 1750-1790. LC 85-6632. (English Satirical Print Ser.). 304p. 1986. lib. bdg. 100.00 (*0-85964-174-0*) Chadwyck-Healey.

Brewer, J. D. The Danger from Strangers: Confronting the Threat of Assault. LC 93-50220. 284p. (C). 1994. 22.95 (*0-306-44642-1*, Plen Insight) Perseus Pubng.

Brewer, J. Gordon. Guidelines for Learning Resources in Colleges. 167p. 1990. 70.00 (*1-870167-06-6*, Pub. by P Francis) St Mut.

Brewer, J. S., ed. Fr. Rogeri Bacon Opera Quaedam Hactenus Inedita: Opus Tertium, Opus Minus - Compendium Philosophiae. (Rolls Ser.: No. 15). 1969. reprint ed. 70.00 (*0-8115-1020-4*) Periodicals Srv.

Brewer, J. S., et al, eds. Giraldi Cambrensis Opera, 8 vols., Set. Incl. Vol. 1. Invectionum Libellus. 1969. (*0-8115-1027-1*); Vol. 2. Gemma Ecclesiastica. 1969. (*0-8115-1028-X*); Vol. 3. De Invectionibus. 1969. (*0-8115-1029-8*); Vol. 4. Speculum Ecclesiae. 1969. (*0-8115-1030-1*); Vol. 5. Topographia Hibernica. 1969. (*0-8115-1031-X*); Vol. 6. Itinerarium Kambriae. 1969. (*0-8115-1032-8*); Vol. 7. Vita S. Remigii. 1969. (*0-8115-1033-6*); Vol. 8. De Principis Instructione. 1969. (*0-8115-1034-4*); (Rolls Ser.: No. 21). 1969. reprint ed. 560.00 (*0-685-09996-2*) Periodicals Srv.

Brewer, J. S. & Howlett, Richard, eds. Monumenta Franciscana, 2 vols. (Rolls Ser.: No. 4). 1974. reprint ed. 140.00 (*0-8115-1004-2*) Periodicals Srv.

Brewer, J. S. & Martin, Charles T., eds. Registrum Malmesburiense: The Register of Malmesbury Abbey, 2 vols. (Rolls Ser.: No. 72). 1974. reprint ed. 140.00 (*0-8115-1140-5*) Periodicals Srv.

Brewer, J. W., et al. Readings in Insect-Plant Disease Relationships. LC 72-10029. (Illus.). (C). 1973. pap. text 16.25 (*0-8422-0264-1*) Irvington.

***Brewer, James C.** Our Private CIA: A Study in Parapsychology. 192p. 2000. pap. 11.95 (*1-891929-53-4*) Four Seasons.

Brewer, James D. No Bottom: A Masey Baldridge/Luke Williamson Mystery. LC 93-23341. 256p. 1994. 19.95 (*0-8027-3178-3*) Walker & Co.

— No Escape. LC 98-2826. (Masey Baldridge - Luke Williamson Mystery Ser.). 264p. 1998. 22.95 (*0-8027-3318-2*) Walker & Co.

— No Justice: A Masey Baldridge/Luke Williamson Mystery. LC 95-47226. 232p. 1996. 21.95 (*0-8027-3283-6*) Walker & Co.

— No Remorse: A Masey Baldridge/Luke Williamson Mystery. LC 97-4095. 224p. 1997. 22.95 (*0-8027-3302-6*) Walker & Co.

— No Virtue: A Masey Baldridge/Luke Williamson Mystery. LC 94-40125. 232p. (YA). 1995. 20.95 (*0-8027-3259-3*) Walker & Co.

— The Raiders of 1862. LC 96-24333. 224p. 1997. 49.95 (*0-275-95404-8*, Praeger Pubs) Greenwood.

Brewer, James F. & Dressler, Thomas D., eds. Norfolk & Western Railway Standards Drawings. LC 92-81707. (Illus.). 120p. 1996. reprint ed. pap. text 28.50 (*0-9633254-0-X*) Norfolk & Wstrn HS.

Brewer, James F., jt. auth. see Bowers, Robert G.

Brewer, James H. The Confederate Negro: Virginia's Craftsmen & Military Laborers , 1861-1865. LC 75-86479. 234p. reprint ed. pap. 72.60 (*0-608-16185-3*, 202619100048) Bks Demand.

Brewer, James K. Everything You Always Wanted to Know about Statistics but Didn't Know How to Ask. 2nd ed. 136p. 1996. per. 21.95 (*0-7872-2162-7*, 41216201) Kendall-Hunt.

Brewer, James W., Jr. Jerome. rev. ed. Foreman, Ronald J., ed. LC 93-83698. (Illus.). 16p. 1993. pap. 1.50 (*1-877856-31-2*) SW Pks Mnmts.

Brewer, James W. Power Series over Commutative Rings. (Lecture Notes in Pure & Applied Mathematics Ser.: Vol. 64). (Illus.). 112p. 1981. pap. text 115.00 (*0-8247-6952-X*) Dekker.

Brewer, James W. & Bunce, John W. Linear Systems over Commutative Rings. (Lecture Notes in Pure & Applied Mathematics Ser.: Vol. 104). (Illus.). 216p. 1986. pap. text 125.00 (*0-8247-7559-7*) Dekker.

Brewer, James W. & Smith, Martha K., eds. Emmy Noether: A Tribute to Her Life & Work. LC 81-15203. (Monographs & Textbooks in Pure & Applied Mathematics: No. 69). 208p. reprint ed. pap. 64.50 (*0-7837-0908-0*, 204121300019) Bks Demand.

Brewer, Janet N. In God's Image. Watkins, Virginia, ed. LC 98-13165. (Illus.). 32p. (J). (ps). 1998. 14.95 (*1-57895-055-4*) Bridge Resources.

Brewer, Jeannie. A Crack in Forever. 304p. 1996. 21.50 (*0-684-80148-5*) Simon & Schuster.

— A Crack in Forever. large type ed. (Niagara Large Print Ser.). 349p. 1997. pap. 29.50 (*0-7089-5855-9*, Linford) Ulverscroft.

Brewer, Jennifer. Lonely Planet Finland. 3rd ed. 400p. 1999. pap. 19.95 (*0-86442-649-6*) Lonely Planet.

Brewer, Jeutonne P. Anthony Burgess: A Bibiliography. LC 80-413. (Author Bibliographies Ser.: No. 47). 193p. 1980. lib. bdg. 24.00 (*0-8108-1286-X*) Scarecrow.

— The Federal Writer's Project: A Bibliography. LC 94-18246. 160p. 1994. 30.00 (*0-8108-2924-X*) Scarecrow.

Brewer, Jeutonne P., jt. auth. see Davis, Boyd H.

Brewer, Jo & Winter, Dave. Butterflies & Moths: A Companion to Your Field Guide. (Phalarope Bk.). (Illus.). 224p. 1986. 24.45 (*0-13-108861-0*) P-H.

Brewer, Jo Ann. Introduction Early Childhood Education. 3rd ed. LC 97-17754. 543p. 1997. 64.00 (*0-205-26774-2*) P-H.

Brewer, Joe E., jt. ed. see Brown, William D.

Brewer, John. Hong Kong Private Company - A Manual of Practice. 2nd rev. ed. xiv, 370p. 1995. pap. write for info. (*0-409-99784-6*, MICHIE) LEXIS Pub.

— Pleasures of the Imagination: English Culture in the Eighteenth Century. LC 97-60984. (Illus.). 688p. 1997. 40.00 (*0-374-23458-2*) FS&G.

***Brewer, John.** Sentimental Murder. 2002. text. write for info. (*0-374-26103-2*) FS&G.

Brewer, John. The Sinews of Power: War, Money & the English State, 1688-1783. 320p. 1990. pap. 17.95 (*0-674-80930-0*) HUP.

***Brewer, John & Hellmuth, Eckhart, eds.** Rethinking Leviathan: The Eighteenth-Century State in Britain & Germany. (Studies of the German Historical Institute, London Ser.). (Illus.). 412p. 1999. text 95.00 (*0-19-920189-7*) OUP.

Brewer, John & Hunter, Albert. Multimethod Research: A Synthesis of Styles. (Library of Social Research: Vol. 175). 224p. (C). 1989. text 59.95 (*0-8039-3077-1*) Sage.

Brewer, John & Porter, Roy, eds. Consumption & the World of Goods. (Illus.). 592p. (C). 1994. pap. 60.00 (*0-415-11478-0*, B4802) Routledge.

Brewer, John & Staves, Susan, eds. Early Modern Conceptions of Property. LC 94-16164. (Consumption & Culture in the 17th & 18th Century Ser.: Vol. 2). (Illus.). 632p. (C). (gr. 13). 1994. 140.00 (*0-415-10533-1*, B4718) Routledge.

— Early Modern Conceptions of Property. (Consumption & Culture in the 17th & 18th Century Ser.). 632p. (C). 1996. pap. 39.99 (*0-415-15314-X*) Routledge.

Brewer, John & Styles, John, eds. An Ungovernable People: The English & Their Law in the Seventeenth & Eighteenth Centuries. 1980. 50.00 (*0-8135-0891-6*); pap. 15.00 (*0-8135-0976-9*) Rutgers U Pr.

Brewer, John, jt. ed. see Bermingham, Ann.

Brewer, John D. After Soweto: An Unfinished Journey. 416p. 1987. 75.00 (*0-19-827480-7*) OUP.

— Black & Blue: Policing in South Africa. (Illus.). 390p. 1994. text 72.00 (*0-19-827382-7*) OUP.

***Brewer, John D.** Ethnography. LC 00-35625. 2000. pap. write for info. (*0-335-20269-1*, Pub. by OpUniv Pr) Taylor & Francis.

Brewer, John D., ed. Restructuring South Africa. LC 93-29949. 1994. text 59.95 (*0-312-10583-5*) St Martin.

Brewer, John D. & Magee, Kathleen. Inside the RUC: Routine Policing in a Divided Society. 320p. 1991. text 55.00 (*0-19-827846-2*) OUP.

Brewer, John D., et al. Crime in Ireland, 1945-1995: Here Be Dragons. LC 97-225. (Clarendon Studies in Criminology). (Illus.). 288p. (C). 1997. text 78.00 (*0-19-826570-0*, Clarendon Pr) OUP.

Brewer, John M. Negrito: Negro Dialect Poems of the Southwest. LC 78-37585. (Black Heritage Library Collection). (Illus.). 1977. reprint ed. 20.95 (*0-8369-8961-9*) Ayer.

Brewer, John S. Reign of Henry VIII from His Accession to the Death of Wolsey, 2 vols. Gairdner, James, ed. LC 70-52901. reprint ed. 95.00 (*0-404-01072-5*) AMS Pr.

Brewer, Karen & Rushing, Donna. Fun Things to Do with Stickers: 30 Crafts, Games & Activities. Caldwell, Lise, ed. (Illus.). 48p. (J). (gr. 1-6). 1998. pap. 3.99 (*0-7847-0691-3*, 14-03381) Standard Pub.

— More Fun Things to Do with Stickers: 30 Crafts, Games, & Activities. Caldwell, Lise, ed. (Illus.). 48p. (J). (gr. 1-6). 1998. pap. 3.99 (*0-7847-0692-1*, 14-03382) Standard Pub.

Brewer, Karen, ed. see Dunlop, Ed.

Brewer, Kathy. Mother's Sorrow. 130p. 1999. pap. write for info. (*0-7392-0107-7*, PO3002) Morris Pub.

***Brewer, Kathy.** "Mother's Sorrow" 1999. pap. text. write for info. (*0-9676288-0-6*) T Wideman.

Brewer, Kenneth. To Remember What Is Lost. LC 82-13530. (Illus.). 65p. reprint ed. pap. 30.00 (*0-8357-3570-2*, 203460800090) Bks Demand.

Brewer, Kenneth W. The Place in Between. 44p. 1998. pap. 20.00 (*0-931659-50-7*) Limberlost Pr.

— The Place in Between. deluxe ed. 44p. 1998. 60.00 (*0-931659-51-5*) Limberlost Pr.

Brewer, Kristine C. Managing Stress. LC 95-75173. (AMI How-to Ser.). 80p. (Orig.). 1996. pap. text 12.95 (*1-884926-30-4*, STRESS) Amer Media.

Brewer, L. Leigh Hunt & Charles Dickens: The Skimpole Caricature. LC 72-160466. (English Literature Ser.: No. 33). 1971. reprint ed. lib. bdg. 75.00 (*0-8383-1301-9*) M S G Haskell Hse.

Brewer, Lawrence W. & Fagerstone, Kathleen A., eds. Radiotelemetry Applications for Wildlife Toxicology Field Studies. LC 98-4522. (Illus.). 1998. 40.00 (*1-880611-20-1*, SETAC Pr) SETAC.

Brewer, Lewis, jt. auth. see United States Tennis Association Staff.

Brewer, Linda S. Bottom-Line Bidding: A Small Business Guide to Lucrative California-State Contracts. LC 89-60527. 256p. 1989. pap. 45.00 (*0-9622514-0-2*) Columbia San Fran.

Brewer, Linda S., ed. see Hollis, Myrlys L.

Brewer, Lucy, ed. In the Public Interest . . ., Vol. 24:1. 53p. 1996. pap. 15.00 (*0-944285-46-5*) Pol Studies.

— Public Works Administration: Current Public Policy Perspectives. LC 96-10038. 544p. 1996. 48.95 (*0-8039-7178-8*) Sage.

Brewer, Luther A. & Wick, Barthinius L. History of Linn County Iowa, from Its Earliest Settlement to the Present Time, 2 vols. (Illus.). 1376p. 1997. reprint ed. lib. bdg. 129.50 (*0-8328-7093-5*) Higginson Bk Co.

Brewer, Maria M. Claude Simon: Narrativities Without Narrative. LC 94-30413. xxxvi, 185p. 1995. text 50.00 (*0-8032-1261-5*) U of Nebr Pr.

Brewer, Marilyn B. Intergroup Relations. LC 96-45420. (Psychology Ser.). 1997. mass mkt. 48.95 (*0-534-34788-6*) Brooks-Cole.

Brewer, Marilynn B. & Collins, Barry E., eds. Scientific Inquiry & the Social Sciences. LC 81-6023. (Jossey-Bass Social & Behavioral Science Ser.). 543p. reprint ed. pap. 168.40 (*0-8357-4971-1*, 203790400009) Bks Demand.

Brewer, Marilynn B., et al. Ethnocentrism & Intergroup Attitudes: East African Evidence. LC 75-26930. (Cross-Cultural Research & Methodology Ser.). 224p. reprint ed. pap. 69.50 (*0-608-10897-9*, 202187400026) Bks Demand.

Brewer, Marilynn B., jt. auth. see Miller, Norman.

Brewer, Mark. Bembezani. 480p. 1987. 18.95 (*0-88191-050-3*) Freundlich.

Brewer-Marshall, Celia. Genesis. (Interpretation Bible Studies). 124p. 1999. pap. 7.00 (*0-664-50038-2*) Geneva Press.

Brewer, Mary. A Perfect Christmas, Vol. 4. unabridged ed. (Illus.). 16p. 1998. 20.00 (*1-892082-03-9*) Shoestring Pr.

— Sarah Jane Hill Remembered Vol. 5: A Pioneer Woman. unabridged ed. (Illus.). 120p. 1998. 20.00 (*1-892082-04-7*) Shoestring Pr.

Brewer, Mary, jt. auth. see Seed, David.

***Brewer, Mary F.** Race, Sex & Gender in Contemporary Women's Theatre: The Construction of "Woman" LC 98-53080. 224p. 1999. 70.00 (*1-902210-18-2*, Pub. by Sussex Acad Pr); pap. 29.95 (*1-902210-19-0*, Pub. by Sussex Acad Pr) Intl Spec Bk.

Brewer, Melvin E. Sky Ranch: The Denton Years. 250p. (Orig.). 1996. pap. 9.95 (*0-9643885-4-5*) Personal Profiles.

Brewer, Michelle & Francisco, Edward. Book Time for the Family: A Teacher's Kit for Implementing a Family Reading Program. 80p. 1998. teacher ed., per. 15.95 (*0-89390-435-X*) Resource Pubns.

Brewer, Myron L. Noise Investigation Flow Charts. LC 73-85629. (Specialized Ser.). (Illus.). 36p. (Orig.). (C). 1987. pap. text 14.95 (*1-56016-020-9*) ABC TeleTraining.

— Practical Grounding: Theory & Design. LC 73-85629. (ABC of the Telephone Ser.: Vol. 12). (Illus.). 180p. (Orig.). (C). 1987. pap. text 24.95 (*1-56016-011-X*) ABC TeleTraining.

Brewer, Neil & Wilson, Carlene, eds. Psychology & Policing. 504p. 1995. text 89.95 (*0-8058-1478-3*) L Erlbaum Assocs.

Brewer, Pamela B. Lifebook for Relationship Success: 365 (+31!) Daily Necessities. 415p. 1997. mass mkt. 12.00 (*0-9655484-1-4*) Twenty-Six by Two.

— Relationships in Progress: A Pocket Guide to Creating a Healthy Relationship with Yourself & for Yourself, Vol. 1. 167p. (Orig.). 1997. pap. 9.95 (*0-9655484-0-6*) Twenty-Six by Two.

— Relationships in Progress Discussion Group: Facilitator's Guide. (Relationships in Progress Ser.). 39p. (C). 1998. pap., wbk. ed. 19.95 (*0-9655484-2-2*) Twenty-Six by Two.

Brewer, Pamela B., jt. auth. see Ball, Wanda H.

Brewer, Paul. Warfare in the Ancient World. LC 98-4721. (History of Warfare Ser.). 80 p. (YA). (gr. 5-12). 1999. 27.12 (*0-8172-5442-0*) Raintree Steck-V.

— Warfare in the Renaissance World. LC 98-3388. (History of Warfare Ser.). 80p. (YA). (gr. 5-12). 1999. 27.12 (*0-8172-5444-7*) Raintree Steck-V.

Brewer, Paul, compiled by. The Grossest Joke Book Ever. LC 96-51452. (Avon Camelot Bks.). (Illus.). 128p. (J). (gr. 3-7). 1997. pap. 3.99 (*0-380-78702-4*, Avon Bks) Morrow Avon.

***Brewer, Paul & Raintree Steck-Vaughn Publishers Staff.** The American Civil War. LC 98-39042. (History of Warfare Ser.). (Illus.). 80p. (gr. 5-9). 1999. 27.12 (*0-8172-5448-X*) Raintree Steck-V.

Brewer, Phil & Brewer, Eileen. Country Kitchen Collection: Fantastically Delicious & Nutritious Vegetarian Meals. 281p. 1992. pap. 11.95 (*1-878726-20-X*) Fam Hlth Pubns.

***Brewer, Priscilla J.** From Fireplace to Cookstove: Technology & the Domestic Ideal in America. LC 00-29705. (Illus.). 320p. 2000. 29.95 (*0-8156-0650-8*) Syracuse U Pr.

Brewer, Priscilla J. Shaker Communities, Shaker Lives. LC 85-40930. (Illus.). 293p. 1986. pap. 19.95 (*0-87451-400-2*) U Pr of New Eng.

Brewer, R. & Sleeman, J. R. Soil Structure & Fabric. 1988. 50.00 (*0-643-04859-6*, Pub. by CSIRO) Accents Pubns.

Brewer, Richard & McCann, Margaret. Laboratory & Field Manual of Ecology. 325p. (C). 1982. pap. text 45.00 (*0-03-057879-5*, Pub. by SCP) Harcourt.

Brewer, Richard, et al. The Atlas of Breeding Birds of Michigan. 650p. 1991. 39.95 (*0-87013-291-1*) Mich St U Pr.

***Brewer, Richard L., ed.** Roman Legions & Their Fortresses. (Occassional Papers of the Research Committee of the Society of Antiquaries of London : No. 20). (Illus.). 208p. 2000. 54.95 (*0-85431-274-9*, Pub. by Soc Antiquaries) David Brown.

Brewer, Robert F. Design of Experiments for Process Improvement & Quality Assurance. LC 96-14873. (Engineers in Business Ser.: Vol. 2). 280p. 1996. pap. 25.00 (*0-89806-165-2*, BREWER) Eng Mgmt Pr.

***Brewer, Roberta.** Psalms for the Millennium & Wee Words of Wisdom: A Collection of Psalms Paraphrased & Rhymed for New Century Living. LC 00-90012. 96p. 2000. pap. 12.95 (*1-58597-019-0*) Leathers Pub.

Brewer, Robin. Noritake Dinnerware: Identification Made Easy. (Illus.). 144p. 1999. 39.95 (*0-7643-0925-0*) Schiffer.

Brewer, Robyn. Foghorn Outdoors: Colorado Camping. 2nd ed. (Illus.). 420p. 2000. pap. 18.95 (*1-57354-085-4*, Foghorn Outdoors) Avalon Travel.

Brewer, Rogenna. Seal It with a Kiss: In Uniform. (Superromance Ser.: No. 833). 1999. per. 4.25 (*0-373-70833-5*, 1-70833-8, Harlequin) Harlequin Bks.

Brewer, Roger L. The Purging of an Evil. LC 91-91951. 143p. 1991. 16.95 (*0-9628797-0-3*) R L Brewer.

Brewer, Ruth M. Worser Days, Better Times. 1987. mass mkt. write for info. (*0-394-59604-8*) Random.

Brewer, S. Grey. Thistledown. (Illus.). 83p. (Orig.). 1993. pap. 8.00 (*1-879025-07-8*) Christopher-Burghardt.

— Transcending Boundaries: Selected Poems by S. Grey Brewer. 24p. (Orig.). 1996. pap. 7.00 (*1-879025-09-4*) Christopher-Burghardt.

Brewer, Sandra. Murder for Beltene. 309p. 1999. pap. 18.99 (*1-885173-67-9*) Write Way.

Brewer, Sarah. Body Facts. (Pocket Guides Ser.: No. 21). (Illus.). 128p. (J). 1996. pap. 6.95 (*0-7894-1018-4*) DK Pub Inc.

***Brewer, Sarah.** Complete Book of Men's Health. (Illus.). 400p. 1999. pap. 18.00 (*0-7225-3905-3*) Thorsons PA.

— Detox Yourself: A Comprehensive Programme to Cleanse Your Mind & Body. (Illus.). 128p. 2000. pap. 18.95 (*1-85868-964-3*, Pub. by Carlton Bks Ltd) Natl Bk Netwk.

— Increase Your Sex Drive in 12 Weeks. 1999. pap. 13.00 (*0-7225-3697-6*) Thorsons PA.

— Irritable Bowel Syndrome. 1997. pap. 9.95 (*0-7225-3392-6*) Thorsons.

Brewer, Sarah. Menopause. 1997. pap. 9.95 (*0-7225-3389-6*) Thorsons PA.

— Planning a Baby? A Complete Guide to Pre-Conceptual Care. 296p. 1996. pap. 11.95 (*0-09-181256-9*, Pub. by Optima) Trafalgar.

***Brewer, Sarah.** Pregnancy the Natural Way. 2000. pap. 13.95 (*0-285-63511-5*) Souvenir Pr Ltd.

— Saw Palmetto: Natural Prostate Relief. (Illus.). 2000. pap. 11.00 (*0-7225-3960-6*) Thorsons PA.

— Simply Relax: An Illustrated Guide to Slowing Down & Enjoying Life. (Illus.). 144p. 2000. pap. 15.95 (*1-56975-213-3*, Pub. by Ulysses Pr) Publishers Group.

Brewer, Sarah. Super Baby: Boost Your Baby's Potential from Conception to Year 1. (Illus.). 304p. 1998. pap. 14.00 (*0-7225-3597-X*, Pub. by Thorsons MD) Natl Bk Netwk.

Brewer, Sarah, ed. The Early Letters of Bishop Richard Hurd, 1739 to 1762. (Church of England Record Society Ser.: Vol. 3). 550p. (C). 1995. 120.00 (*0-85115-653-3*, Boydell Pr) Boydell & Brewer.

***Brewer, Sarah & Webb, Tim.** The Bluffer's Guide to Sex: Bluff Your Way in Sex. (Bluffer's Guides Ser.). 64p. 1999. pap. 5.95 (*1-902825-61-6*) Oval Bks.

B

Brewer, Sarah S. Southport: The War Years: An Island Remembers. unabridged ed. (Illus.). ix, 389p. 1996. 33.00 (0-9655925-0-2) Cozy Harbor.

Brewer, Scott, ed. The Philosophy of Legal Reasoning: A Collection of Essays by Philosophers & Legal Scholars, 5 vols. LC 98-5169. 2048p. 1998. 375.00 (0-8153-2654-8) Garland.

Brewer, Scott & Nozick, Robert, eds. Evolution & Revolution in Theories of Legal Reasoning: Nineteenth Century Through the Present. LC 98-5167. (Philosophy of Legal Reasoning Ser.: No. 4). 400p. 1998. reprint ed. text 75.00 (0-8153-2658-0) Garland.

— Logic, Probability, & Presumptions in Legal Reasoning. LC 98-5169. (Philosophy of Legal Reasoning Ser.: No. 1). 416p. 1998. reprint ed. text 75.00 (0-8153-2655-6) Garland.

— Moral Theory & Legal Reasoning. LC 98-5171. (Philosophy of Legal Reasoning Ser.: No. 3). 408p. 1998. reprint ed. text 75.00 (0-8153-2657-2) Garland.

— Precedents, Statutes, & Analysis of Legal Concepts: Interpretation. LC 98-5170. (Philosophy of Legal Reasoning Ser.: No. 2). 400p. 1998. reprint ed. text 75.00 (0-8153-2656-4) Garland.

— Scientific Models of Legal Reasoning: Economics, Artificial Intelligence, & the Physical Sciences. LC 98-5168. (Philosophy of Legal Reasoning Ser.: No. 5). 424p. 1998. reprint ed. text 75.00 (0-8153-2757-9) Garland.

Brewer, Sonny. Rembrandt the Rocker. (Illus.). 1994. 14.95 (0-9643727-0-3) Over the Transom.

— A Yin for Change: Awakening Imagination for More Life in Your Living. 134p. (Orig.). 1996. pap. 9.95 (0-9643727-1-1) Over the Transom.

Brewer, Sonny, jt. ed. see Wolff, Robbie.

***Brewer, Steve.** Baby Face. (Bubba Mabry Mysteries Ser.). 256p. 2000. mass mkt. 5.95 (1-890768-20-0) Intrigue Press.

Brewer, Steve. Baby Face. (Illus.). (J). 1995. mass mkt. 5.50 (0-671-74735-5) PB.

— Dirty Pool. LC 98-50731. 272p. 1999. text 23.95 (0-312-20203-2) St Martin.

***Brewer, Steve.** End Run: A Drew Gavin Mystery. 304p. 2000. 22.95 (1-890768-25-1, Pub. by Intrigue Press) Midpt Trade.

— Lonely Street. (Bubba Mabry Mystery Ser.: No. 1). 256p. 1999. mass mkt. 5.95 (1-890768-19-7) Intrigue Press.

Brewer, Steve. Lonely Street. Grad, Doug, ed. 224p. 1994. mass mkt. 4.99 (0-671-74734-7) PB.

— Witchy Woman: A Bubba Mabry P. I. Mystery. 256p. 1999. reprint ed. mass mkt. 5.95 (1-890768-13-8) Intrigue Press.

Brewer, Susan A. To Win the Peace: British Propaganda in the United States During World War II. LC 97-15057. (Illus.). 240p. 1997. text 39.95 (0-8014-3367-3) Cornell U Pr.

Brewer, Suzette. 1997 Book of Lists. 1997. 32.50 (0-932439-11-X) Denver Busn Media.

— 1996 Book of Lists. 1996. 30.00 (0-932439-10-1) Denver Busn Media.

Brewer, Sydney G. BBC BASIC Programming for Young Mathematicians. 1991. pap. text 25.00 (0-7486-0254-2, Pub. by Edinburgh U Pr) Col U Pr.

Brewer, T. S., ed. Precambrian Crustal Evolution in the North Atlantic Region. (Geological Society Special Publication Ser.: No. 112). (Illus.). 376p. 1996. 115.00 (1-897799-62-4, 245, Pub. by Geol Soc Pub Hse) AAPG.

***Brewer, Talbot.** The Bounds of Choice: Unchosen Virtues, Unchosen Commitments. LC 00-21518. (Studies in Ethics). 2000. write for info. (0-8153-3667-5) Garland.

Brewer, Ted. Czech & Slovak Republics Guide. 2nd ed. 552p. 1999. pap. text 18.95 (1-892975-02-5) Open Rd Pub.

***Brewer, Ted.** Prague Guide. 2nd ed. (Illus.). 280p. 1999. pap. 14.95 (1-892975-21-1) Open Rd Pub.

Brewer, Ted. Understanding Boat Design. 4th ed. 1993. pap. 16.95 (0-87742-392-X) Intl Marine.

Brewer, Teri, ed. The Marketing of Tradition: Perspectives on Folklore, Tourism & the Heritage Industry. 1994. pap. 19.50 (1-874312-21-4, Pub. by Hisarlik Pr) Intl Spec Bk.

Brewer, Thomas. Experiments in Analog & Digital Electronics: Laboratory Manual for EE3741. 176p. (C). 1997. pap. text, per. 19.95 (0-7872-3382-X) Kendall-Hunt.

— An Introduction to Electrical Measurements. 368p. (C). 1997. spiral bd. 32.95 (0-7872-4370-1) Kendall-Hunt.

***Brewer, Thomas.** An Introduction to Electrical Measurements. 2nd ed. 368p. (C). 2000. ring bd. 42.95 (0-7872-7209-4) Kendall-Hunt.

Brewer, Thomas, jt. auth. see Leach, W., Jr.

***Brewer, Thomas A.** Searching for the Good: A Young Man's Journey to War & Back. LC 00-91390. (Illus.). 300p. 2000. 24.95 (0-9701339-0-1) Quaise.

Brewer, Thomas H., jt. auth. see Brewer, Gail S.

Brewer, Thomas L., ed. Political Risks in International Business: New Directions for Research, Management & Public Policy. LC 84-24801. 384p. 1985. 75.00 (0-275-90066-5, C0066, Praeger Pubs) Greenwood.

— Trade & Investment Policy, 2 vols. LC 98-33208. 1072p. 1999. 395.00 (1-85898-704-0) E Elgar.

***Brewer, Thomas L. & Boyd, Gavin, eds.** Globalizing America: The U. S. A. in World Integration. LC 99-44832. (New Horizons in International Business Ser.). 320p. 2000. 100.00 (1-85898-981-7) E Elgar.

***Brewer, Thomas L. & Young, Stephen.** The Multilateral Investment System & Multinational Enterprises. (Illus.). 320p. 2000. pap. 24.95 (0-19-924110-4) OUP.

Brewer, Thomas L. & Young, Stephen. Multilateral Investment System Rules & Multinational Enterprises. (Illus.). 320p. 1998. text 75.00 (0-19-829315-1) OUP.

Brewer, Tony G. Catfish Don't Jump Vol. 1: And Other Stories of the South. large type ed. (Illus.). 1p. (Orig.). (YA). (gr. 8 up). 1996. 15.95 (1-889005-00-2, 101) Temco Publng.

Brewer, Vernon E., 2nd. Frenchy's Whore. LC 94-60593. 192p. 1994. pap. 12.00 (1-55787-121-3, Empire State Bks) Hrt of the Lakes.

Brewer, W. Alabama: Her History, Resources, War Record & Public Men, from 1540 to 1872. 712p. 1997. reprint ed. lib. bdg. 74.50 (0-8328-6590-7) Higginson Bk Co.

Brewer, W. D., tr. see Haken, H. & Wolf, H. C.

Brewer, Waldo L. Factors Affecting Student Achievement & Change in a Physical Science Survey Course. LC 70-176691. (Columbia University. Teachers College. Contributions to Education Ser.: No. 868). reprint ed. 37.50 (0-404-55868-2) AMS Pr.

Brewer-Ward, Daniel A. The House of Habsburg: A Genealogy of the Descendants of Empress Maria Theresia. LC 96-203853. 466p. 1997. pap. 37.50 (0-8063-4644-2, 9139) Clearfield Co.

Brewer, Warren A., jt. auth. see Anttila, Raimo.

Brewer, Wesley C. & Brewer, Annie M. The Glove Box Auto Reviver. (Illus.). 350p. (Orig.). spiral bd. 24.95 (0-938641-01-8) Chaparral Prodns.

Brewer, William D. The Shelley-Byron Conversation. LC 94-11299. 216p. 1994. 42.95 (0-8130-1300-3) U Press Fla.

Brewer, William D., jt. auth. see Losey, Jay.

Brewer, William D., tr. see Haken, Hermann & Wolf, Hans C.

Brewer, William D., tr. see Haken, Hermann, et al.

Brewer, William E. Winning in Small Claims Court: A Step-by-Step Guide for Citizen Litigators. 215p. (Orig.). 1995. pap. 22.95 (0-9646787-6-4) Law Works.

— Winning in Small Claims Court: A Step-by-Step Guide for Trying Your Own Small Claims Cases. LC 98-30415. 224p. 1998. pap. 17.99 (1-56414-374-0) Career Pr Inc.

Brewer, William H. Up & down California in Eighteen Sixty to Eighteen Sixty-Four: The Journal of William H. Brewer. Farquhar, Francis P., ed. LC 66-26246. (Illus.). 1974. reprint ed. pap. 22.50 (0-520-02762-0, Pub. by U CA Pr) Cal Prin Full Svc.

— Up & down California in Eighteen Sixty to Eighteen Sixty-Four: The Journal of William H. Brewer. 3rd ed. Farquhar, Francis P., ed. LC 66-26246. 625p. reprint ed. pap. 193.80 (0-608-18068-8, 202904000058) Bks Demand.

— Up & down in California, 1860-1864: The Journal of William H. Brewer. (American Biography Ser.). 583p. 1991. reprint ed. lib. bdg. 99.00 (0-7812-8039-7) Rprt Serv.

Brewer, William H., et al. Such a Landscape! A Narrative of the 1864 California Geological Survey Exploration of Yosemite, Sequoia & Kings Canyon from the Diary, Fieldnotes, Letters & Reports of William Henry Brewer. LC 98-27798. (Illus.). 124p. 1998. pap. 29.95 (0-939666-91-X) Yosemite Assn.

Brewer, Wilmon. Shakespeare's Influence on Sir Walter Scott. reprint ed. 64.50 (0-404-01075-X) AMS Pr.

Brewers Publications Staff, compiled by. Evaluating Beer. (Illus.). 244p. 1993. pap. 19.95 (0-937381-37-3) Brewers Pubns.

Brewerton, Derrick. All about Arthritis. LC 92-11557. (Illus.). 320p. (C). 1992. text 29.95 (0-674-01615-7) HUP.

— All about Arthritis. (Illus.). 328p. (C). 1995. pap. 15.95 (0-674-01616-5) HUP.

Brewerton, G. Douglas. The War in Kansas. LC 74-164381. (Black Heritage Library Collection). reprint ed. 31.95 (0-8369-8840-X) Ayer.

Brewerton, George D. Overland with Kit Carson: A Narrative of the Old Spanish Trail in '48. LC 93-10688. (Illus.). xxiii, 301p. (C). 1993. pap. 12.95 (0-8032-6113-6, Bison Books) U of Nebr Pr.

Brewerton, Kevin. Warrior Within: Mental Approach of a Champion. (Illus.). 140p. 1998. pap. 14.95 (0-86568-168-6, 450) Unique Pubns.

Brewi, Janice & Brennan, Anne. Mid-Life Spirituality & Jungian Archetypes. LC 99-32541. 304p. 1999. pap. 18.95 (0-89254-046-X) Nicolas-Hays.

— Passion for Life: Lifelong Psychological & Spiritual Growth. LC 80-5342. 176p. 1998. 17.95 (0-8264-1181-9) Continuum.

Brewin, Chris R., jt. auth. see Power, Michael J.

Brewin, Chris R., jt. auth. see Power, Mick.

Brewin, Chris R., jt. ed. see Antaki, Charles.

***Brewin, Christopher.** The European Union & Cyprus. 156p. 1999. pap. 29.95 (0-906719-24-0, Pub. by Eothen) Paul & Co Pubs.

Brewin, T. B., jt. ed. see Caird, F. I.

Brewin, Thurstan B. & Sparshott, Margaret. Relating to the Relatives: Breaking Bad News, Communication & Support. LC 96-42946. 177p. 1996. pap. 24.95 (1-85775-081-0, Radcliffe Med Pr) Scovill Paterson.

Brewington, Dorothy, jt. auth. see Brewington, Marion V.

Brewington, Dorothy E. Dictionary of Marine Artists. (Illus.). 431p. 1982. 40.00 (0-913372-24-2, PEMP119, Pub. by Mystic Seaport) Peabody Essex Mus.

— Marine Paintings & Drawings in Mystic Seaport Museum. (Illus.). ix, 219p. 1982. 40.00 (0-913372-25-0) Mystic Seaport.

Brewington, Marion V. Check List of the Paintings, Drawings & Prints at the Kendall Whaling Museum. (Illus.). 74p. 1957. pap. 2.00 (0-937854-02-6) Kendall Whaling.

— Chesapeake Bay Log Canoes & Bugeyes. LC 62-18218. (Illus.). 182p. 1963. 35.95 (0-87033-011-X, Tidewtr Pubs) Cornell Maritime.

— Chesapeake Bay Sailing Craft. (Illus.). 1966. pap. 2.50 (0-614-04340-9) Ches Bay Mus.

— The Peabody Museum Collection of Navigating Instruments: With Notes on Their Makers. (Illus.). xii, 144p. 1996. reprint ed. 75.00 (1-888262-00-1) Martino Pubng.

Brewington, Marion V. & Brewington, Dorothy. Marine Paintings & Drawings in the Peabody Museum of Salem. rev. ed. (Illus.). xvii, 530p. 1981. 125.00 (0-87577-066-5, PEMP140, Peabody Museum) Peabody Essex Mus.

Brewis. Lives on Line. LC 95-76341. (C). 1995. pap. text 23.50 (0-15-501969-4) Harcourt Coll Pubs.

— Polymer Handbook. 1997. write for info. (0-582-03409-4, Pub. by Addison-Wesley) Longman.

Brewis, A. A., jt. auth. see Cambie, R. C.

Brewis, D. M. & Briggs, D., eds. Industrial Adhesion Problems. 298p. 1985. 265.00 (0-471-84005-X) Wiley.

Brewis, D. M. & Comyn, J., eds. Advances in Adhesives: Application, Materials, & Safety. 306p. 1983. 76.00 (0-938648-32-2) T-C Pr CA.

Brewis, Henry. Chewing the Cud. (Illus.). 128p. 1990. pap. 8.95 (0-85236-211-0, Pub. by Farming Pr) Diamond Farm Bk.

— Clarts & Calamities: The Diary of a Peasant Farmer. (Illus.). 256p. 1988. pap. 8.95 (0-85236-187-4, Pub. by Farming Pr) Diamond Farm Bk.

— Country Dance. (Illus.). 208p. 1992. pap. 12.95 (0-85236-244-7, Pub. by Farming Pr) Diamond Farm Bk.

— Don't Laugh till He's Out of Sight. (Illus.). 160p. (Orig.). 1984. pap. 12.95 (0-85236-153-X, Pub. by Farming Pr) Diamond Farm Bk.

— Funny Way t'mekalivin' (Illus.). 128p. (Orig.). 1983. pap. 8.95 (0-85236-142-4, Pub. by Farming Pr) Diamond Farm Bk.

— Goodbye Clartiehole. (Illus.). 228p. 1994. pap. 8.95 (0-85236-290-0, Pub. by Farming Pr) Diamond Farm Bk.

— The Handy Lads. (Illus.). 48p. (J). (gr. 2-5). 1996. 18.95 (0-85236-345-1, Pub. by Farming Pr); pap. 12.95 (0-85236-356-7, Pub. by Farming Pr) Diamond Farm Bk.

— The Magic Peasant. (Illus.). 128p. 1986. pap. 8.95 (0-85236-162-9, Pub. by Farming Pr) Diamond Farm Bk.

***Brewis, Joanna & Linstead, Stephen.** Sex, Work & Sex Work: Eroticizing Organization. LC 99-59923. 2000. pap. write for info. (0-415-20757-6) Routledge.

Brewis, R. A. Respiratory Medicine, 2 vols. 2nd ed. 1995. text 275.00 (0-7020-1641-1, W B Saunders Co) Harcrt Hlth Sci Grp.

Brewis, R. A. L., jt. auth. see Bourke, S. J.

Brewitt, Ross. Clear the Track: The Eddie Shack Story. LC 98-110869. 256p. 1998. 22.95 (0-7737-3049-4) Stoddart Publ.

— Clear the Track: The Eddie Shack Story. 1998. pap. text 13.95 (0-7737-5994-8) Stoddart Publ.

— Sabres: 26 Seasons in Buffalo's Memorial Auditorium. 1997. 36.00 (0-87833-125-5) Taylor Pub.

— Sabres: 26 Seasons in Buffalo's Memorial Auditorium. limited ed. 1997. 75.00 (0-87833-126-3) Taylor Pub.

Brewitt-Taylor, C. H., tr. see Guanzhong, Lou.

Brewka, Gerhard. Nonmonotonic Reasoning: From Theoretical Foundation to Efficient Computation. (Tracts in Theoretical Computer Science Ser.: No. 12). 182p. (C). 1991. text 42.95 (0-521-38394-3) Cambridge U Pr.

Brewka, Gerhard, ed. Principles of Knowledge Representation. LC 96-23338. (Studies in Logic, Language & Information). 334p. (C). 1996. pap. text 25.95 (1-57586-056-2) Cambridge U Pr.

Brewka, Gerhard, et al. Nonmonotonic & Inductive Logic: Second International Workshop, Reinhardsbrunn Castle, Germany, December 2-6, 1991, Proceedings. LC 92-46636. (Lecture Notes in Computer Science Ser.: Vol. 659). 1993. write for info. (3-540-56433-0) Spr-Verlag.

— Nonmonotonic Reasoning: An Overview. LC 96-46540. (Lecture Notes Ser.). 192p. (C). 1996. 49.95 (1-881526-84-4); pap. 22.95 (1-881526-83-6) CSLI.

Brewka, Gerhard E., et al, eds. KI-97: Advances in Artificial Intelligence, Vol. 130. LC 97-34487. (Lecture Notes in Artificial Intelligence: Vol. 1303). xi, 413p. 1997. pap. 67.00 (3-540-63493-2) Spr-Verlag.

Brews, John R., jt. auth. see Nicollian, Edward H.

Brewster. Cosmopolites Journey: Episodes from a Life. LC 98-226162. 224p. 1998. text 39.50 (1-86064-262-4, Pub. by I B T) St Martin.

— Economics of Business Decision Making. 1998. pap. 19.99 (1-86152-425-0) Thomson Learn.

***Brewster, et al.** Human Resource Management Europe. 352p. 2001. 37.95 (0-7506-4717-5) Buttrwrth-Heinemann.

Brewster, jt. auth. see Haines.

***Brewster, Charles W.** Rambles about Portsmouth. 378p. 2000. pap. 27.35 (0-7884-1484-4, 1484) Heritage Bk.

Brewster, Anne. Literary Formations: Postcolonialism, Nationalism, Globalism. Ruthven, Ken, ed. LC 96-139398. (Interpretations Ser.). 160p. 1995. pap. 19.95 (0-522-84534-7, Pub. by Melbourne Univ Pr) Paul & Co Pubs.

***Brewster, Anne, et al, eds.** Those Who Remain Will Always Remember: An Anthology of Aboriginal Writing. 328p. 2000. pap. 19.95 (1-86368-291-0, Pub. by Fremantle Arts) Intl Spec Bk.

Brewster, B. Chris, ed. The United States Lifesaving Association Manual of Open Water Lifesaving. LC 95-11842. 352p. 1995. pap. text 23.40 (0-8359-4919-2) P-H.

Brewster, Barbara M. Down under All Over: A Love Affair with Australia. (Illus.). 240p. (Orig.). 1991. pap. 14.95 (0-9628608-0-8) Four Winds OR.

— Journey to Wholeness: And the Day Came When the Risk to Remain Tight in a Bud Was More Painful Than the Risk It Took to Bloom. 256p. 1992. pap. text 14.95 (0-9628608-1-6) Four Winds OR.

Brewster, Ben & Jacobs, Lea. Theatre to Cinema: Stage Pictorialism & the Early Feature Film. (Illus.). 256p. 1998. text 95.00 (0-19-818267-8) OUP.

— Theatre to Cinema: Stage Pictorialism & the Early Feature Film. (Illus.). 256p. 1998. pap. text 19.95 (0-19-815950-1) OUP.

Brewster, Ben, ed. & tr. see Burch, Noel.

Brewster, Ben, tr. see Althusser, Louis.

Brewster, Betty. Stories That Rhyme: Reading Fun Time. (Illus.). 20p. (J). (ps-2). 1998. pap. write for info. (1-57579-120-X) Pine Hill Pr.

Brewster, Betty J. Beyond the Past. 1996. 8.95 (0-533-11702-X) Vantage.

***Brewster, Bill & Broughton, Frank.** Last Night a DJ Saved My Life: The History of the Disc Jockey. 336p. 2000. pap. 14.00 (0-8021-3688-5, Pub. by Grove-Atltic) Publishers Group.

***Brewster, Bob.** Income Surfing: The New Way to Get Rich! 1998. pap. 24.95 (1-892044-00-5) Eagle Team.

***Brewster, Bonnie.** Family Portrait. large type ed. 115p. 1999. pap. 12.50 (1-885631-36-7, 36-7, Family Of Man Pr) G F Hutchison.

Brewster, C. Ray. The Cluster of Jesse Mercer. (Illus.). 226p. 1983. 12.00 (0-914707-01-9) Ren Pr GA.

Brewster, Charles. Rambles about Portsmouth, 2 vols., Vol. 1. LC 70-181350. 1971. reprint ed. write for info. (0-912274-12-3) Picton Pr.

Brewster, Charles E. Sophia's Unfaithful Lovers: How Philosophers Have Seduced the Church. (Illus.). 288p. (Orig.). 1996. pap. 10.99 (1-57502-189-7, P0813) Morris Pubng.

Brewster, Charles H. When This Cruel War Is Over: The Civil War Letters of Charles Harvey Brewster. Blight, David W., ed. LC 91-38861. (Illus.). 376p. (C). 1992. lib. bdg. 40.00 (0-87023-773-X) U of Mass Pr.

***Brewster, Chris.** New Challenges for Human Resource Management. LC 99-88128. 1999. text 69.95 (0-312-22872-4) St Martin.

***Brewster, Chris, ed.** Human Resource Management in Northern Europe: Trends, Dilemmas & Strategy. 272p. 2000. 89.95 (0-631-21777-0); pap. 52.95 (0-631-19715-X) Blackwell Pubs.

Brewster, Chris, et al, eds. The European Human Resource Management Guide. (Illus.). 672p. 1992. text 179.95 (0-12-133130-X) Acad Pr.

Brewster, Chris & Harris, Hilary. International HRM: Contemporary Issues in Europe. LC 98-18992. 1999. 100.00 (0-415-19489-X) Routledge.

Brewster, Chris & Hegewisch, Ariane, eds. Policy & Practice in European Human Resource Management. LC 93-43235. 432p. (C). 1994. pap. 36.95 (0-415-06530-5) Thomson Learn.

Brewster, Chris & Teague, Paul. European Community Social Policy: Its Impact on the U. K. 376p. (C). 1989. 210.00 (0-85292-408-9, Pub. by IPM Hse) St Mut.

Brewster, Christene, ed. see Harter, Lynda L.

Brewster, D. E. London "General" Motor Buses. (C). 1985. 39.00 (0-85361-305-2) St Mut.

— Motor Buses in Wales, 1898-1932. 52p. (C). 1985. 50.00 (0-7855-3367-2) St Mut.

Brewster, Dan. Only Paralyzed from the Neck Down: The Life & Ministry of Tom Brewster. LC 98-132230. 324p. 1997. pap. 15.95 (0-87808-275-1, WCL275-1) William Carey Lib.

Brewster, Daniel. Me & Mine. 31p. 1997. pap. 15.95 (0-9666484-0-4) Dimby Co.

Brewster, Dorothy. Aaron Hill: Poet, Dramatist, Projector. LC 13-21690. reprint ed. 32.50 (0-404-01076-8) AMS Pr.

— Virginia Woolf's London. LC 78-26590. 120p. 1979. reprint ed. lib. bdg. 35.00 (0-313-20788-7, BRVW, Greenwood Pr) Greenwood.

Brewster, Dorothy & Burrell, Angus. Adventure or Experience: Four Essays on Certain Writers & Readers of Novels. LC 67-23185. (Essay Index Reprint Ser.). 1977. reprint ed. 19.95 (0-8369-0252-1) Ayer.

— Dead Reckonings in Fiction. LC 76-90614. (Essay Index Reprint Ser.). 1977. 21.95 (0-8369-1248-9) Ayer.

— Modern Fiction. LC 75-86732. (Essay Index Reprint Ser.). 1977. 26.95 (0-8369-1123-7) Ayer.

Brewster, Dorothy P. Discovering Torrance: A Guide & Coloring Book. Haggott, Mikko, tr. (Illus.). 52p. (Orig.). (J). (gr. 3). 1987. teacher ed. 8.00 (0-9619944-1-X); pap. 4.50 (0-9619944-0-1); write for info. (0-9619944-2-8) Rodor & Co.

Brewster, Earl H., compiled by. The Life of Gotama Buddha (Compiled Exclusively from the Pali Canon) LC 78-72380. reprint ed. 34.50 (0-404-17229-6) AMS Pr.

***Brewster, Gail.** The Voucher System Behavior Management Program for Home. (Illus.). 77p. 2000. pap. 37.95 (0-9679443-0-9) Crisara Pubng.

— The Voucher System Behavior Management Program for Home Schoolers. (Illus.). 37p. 2000. pap. 19.95 (0-9679443-3-3) Crisara Pubng.

— The Voucher System Behavior Management Program for Managed Care. (Illus.). 2000. pap. 37.95 (0-9679443-2-5) Crisara Pubng.

— The Voucher System Behavior Management Program for Schools. 36p. 2000. pap. 37.95 (0-9679443-1-7) Crisara Pubng.

Brewster, George A. Little Inventions That Made Big Money. 155p. (Orig.). 1983. pap. text. write for info. (1-877782-11-4) MGM & Assocs.

Brewster, Harold P. Saints & Festivals of the Christian Church. LC 89-43339. (Illus.). 558p. 1990. reprint ed. lib. bdg. 45.00 (1-55888-878-0) Omnigraphics Inc.

An Asterisk (*) at the beginning of an entry indicates that the title is appearing for the first time.

Brewster, Harry. Classical Anatolia: The Glory of Hellenism. 224p. 1994. text 49.50 (*1-85043-773-4*, Pub. by I B T) St Martin.

Brewster, Harry & Levi, Peter. River Gods of Greece: Myths & Mountain Waters in the Hellenic World. LC 97-38381. (Illus.). 224p. 1997. text 39.95 (*1-86064-207-1*, Pub. by I B T) St Martin.

Brewster, Hoyt W., Jr. Behold, I Come Quickly: The Last Days & Beyond. LC 94-22203. xxi, 246p. 1994. 15.95 (*0-87579-865-9*) Deseret Bk.

— Doctrine & Covenants Encyclopedia. 1998. 20.95 (*0-88494-669-X*) Bookcraft Inc.

— Isaiah Plain & Simple: The Message of Isaiah in the Book of Mormon. LC 95-37716. xiv, 281p. 1995. 14.95 (*1-57345-084-7*) Deseret Bk.

— Prophets, Priesthood Keys, & Succession. LC 91-32110. 154p. 1991. 10.95 (*0-87579-560-9*) Deseret Bk.

***Brewster, Hugh.** Anastasia's Album: The Last Tsar's Youngest Daughter. 64p. (J). 1999. pap. 7.99 (*0-7868-1395-4*, Pub. by Disney Pr) Little.

Brewster, Hugh. Inside the Titanic: A Giant Cut-Away Book. LC 97-382. (Illus.). 32p. (J). (gr. k-3). 1997. 18.95 (*0-316-55716-1*) Little.

Brewster, Hugh & Coulter, Laurie. 882 1/2 Amazing Answers to Questions about the Titanic. LC 98-27558. (Illus.). 96p. (J). (gr. 3-7). 1998. 16.95 (*0-590-18730-9*) Scholastic Inc.

Brewster, Hugh, jt. auth. see Sauder, Eric.

Brewster, Hugh, jt. auth. see Tanaka, Shelley.

Brewster, J. Leland. Kentucky Corporation Law & Practice. LC 92-33885. (National Corporation Law Ser.). 1992. 110.00 (*0-13-514910-X*) Aspen Law.

Brewster, James. Sketches of Southern Mystery, Treason, & Murder. LC 70-39529. reprint ed. 39.50 (*0-404-00006-1*) AMS Pr.

Brewster, James L. Onions & Other Vegetable Alliums. (Illus.). 256p. 1994. pap. text 45.00 (*0-85198-753-2*) OUP.

Brewster, James L., jt. ed. see Rabinowitch, Haim D.

Brewster, Janet B. A Bradham Family History & Genealogy. LC 86-71079. (Illus.). 700p. 1986. 30.00 (*0-9616934-0-1*) J B Brewster.

Brewster, Janet B., ed. see Brewster, Marcus V.

***Brewster, Janice.** Log Cabins. LC 99-12756. (Architecture & Design Library Ser.). (Illus.). 96p. 1999. text 17.95 (*1-56799-723-6*) M Friedman Pub Grp Inc.

Brewster, Jennifer, tr. & intro. see Sanuki no Suke & Fujiwara no Nagako.

Brewster, Jim. Wild League on Ice. 1998. pap. text 5.95 (*0-9683303-4-7*) Tumbleweed Pr.

Brewster, John. Meditations on Aging for the Christian Woman: Revised Selections from "Meditations for the Aged - Adapted to the Progress of Human Life" abr. rev. ed. Rutherford, Anne, ed. LC 98-67305. iii, 58p. 1998. reprint ed. pap. 5.95 (*1-889298-50-6*) Rhwymbooks.

— Turning Fifty - Meditations on Aging: Selections from "Meditations for the Aged - Adapted to the Progress of Human Life" abr. rev. ed. LC 98-67304. i, 58p. 1998. reprint ed. pap. 5.95 (*1-889298-49-2*) Rhwymbooks.

Brewster, John, et al. Four Fife Poets: Fower Brigs Ti a Kinrik. 148p. 1988. pap. text 14.00 (*0-08-036417-9*, Pub. by Aberdeen U Pr) Macmillan.

Brewster, Kingman, Jr. Antitrust & American Business Abroad. Bruchey, Stuart & Bruchey, Eleanor, eds. LC 76-4768. (American Business Abroad Ser.). 1976. reprint ed. 47.95 (*0-405-09266-0*) Ayer.

Brewster, Kingman Staff & Atwood, James. Antitrust & American Business Abroad, 2 vols., Set. 2nd ed. LC 81-1504. (International Practice Ser.). 770p. 1981. text 220.00 (*0-07-002435-9*) Shepards.

Brewster, Lawrence F. Summer Migrations & Resorts of South Carolina Low-Country Planters. LC 76-115992. (Trinity College Historical Papers: No. 26). reprint ed. 39.50 (*0-404-51776-5*) AMS Pr.

Brewster, Lawrence G. Primer to California Politic. LC 95-73317. 304p. 1996. pap. text 24.95 (*0-312-13699-4*) St Martin.

— The Public Agenda. LC 97-65178. 341p. 1997. pap. text 21.95 (*0-312-15394-5*) St Martin.

Brewster, M. I. Fraser: Descendants of Simon Fraser of Laggan, Inverness-shire, Scotland, & Allied Families in Scotland, Canada & U. S. (Illus.). 219p. 1993. reprint ed. pap. 34.00 (*0-8328-3319-3*); reprint ed. lib. bdg. 44.00 (*0-8328-3318-5*) Higginson Bk Co.

Brewster, M. Quinn. Thermal Radiative Transfer Properties. LC 91-12888. 568p. 1992. 140.00 (*0-471-53982-1*) Wiley.

Brewster, Marcus V. Mark Brewster of Hull England & Allied Families in America Including: Atkey, Carpenter, Dare, Fowler, Hiscock, Hewitt, Potter & Yelf. Brewster, Janet B., ed. (Biographical & Genealogical Ser.). (Illus.). 340p. 1990. 30.00 (*0-89308-449-2*) J B Brewster.

***Brewster, Margaret.** Straight from My Heart. 1999. pap. write for info. (*1-58235-206-2*) Watermrk Pr.

***Brewster, Marge A.** Self-Assessment in Clinical Laboratory Science. 3rd rev. ed. Wu, Alan H. B. et al, eds. LC 00-23225. 2000. pap. 37.00 (*1-890883-25-5*, 347) Am Assn Clinical Chem.

Brewster, Maryjane. Eye of the Wind: A Poet's Journal of the Eighties, 1980-1991. LC 93-14297. 1993. pap. 10.00 (*0-934172-28-5*) WIM Pubns.

— Verses in the Wind. LC 84-50316. (Illus.). 48p. 1984. pap. 5.00 (*0-934172-10-2*) WIM Pubns.

Brewster, Nancy P., jt. ed. see Poor, Janet M.

Brewster, Patience. Rabbit Inn, Vol. 1. (J). (ps-3). 1991. 14.95 (*0-316-10747-6*) Little.

— Too Many Puppies. (Hello Reader! Ser.). 1997. 3.50 (*0-590-60276-4*) Scholastic Inc.

Brewster, Patience. Too Many Puppies. (Hello, Reader! Ser.). (J). 1997. 8.70 (*0-606-11997-3*, Pub. by Turtleback) Demco.

Brewster, Patience, jt. auth. see Bateman, Teresa.

Brewster, Patience, jt. auth. see Hurwitz, Johanna.

Brewster, Paul G., ed. Children's Games & Rhymes. LC 75-35063. (Studies in Play & Games: Vol. 1). 1980. reprint ed. 18.95 (*0-405-07914-1*) Ayer.

Brewster, Quinn M. Thermal Radiative Transfer Properties. 1991. pap. text. write for info. (*0-471-54922-3*) Wiley.

Brewster, R. L. Telecommunications Technology. LC 85-27347. (Electrical & Electronic Engineering Ser.). 200p. 1986. text 36.95 (*0-470-20270-X*) P-H.

— Telecommunications Technology. 1989. pap. text 24.95 (*0-470-21454-6*) P-H.

Brewster, R. L., ed. Data Communications & Networks. 3rd ed. (Telecommunications Ser.: No. 31). 252p. 1994. boxed set 77.00 (*0-85296-804-3*, TE031) INSPEC Inc.

***Brewster, Scott.** In Human Reflections. 2000. text. write for info. (*0-7190-5337-4*, Pub. by Manchester Univ Pr) St Martin.

Brewster, Susan. To Be an Anchor in the Storm: A Guide for Families & Friends of Abused Women. LC 97-18577. 240p. 1997. pap. 12.95 (*0-345-41719-4*) Ballantine Pub Grp.

***Brewster, Susan.** To Be an Anchor in the Storm: A Guide for Families & Friends of Abused Women. 256p. 2000. pap. 12.95 (*1-58005-037-9*, Pub. by Seal Pr WA) Publishers Group.

Brewster, Tara, ed. see Sobel, Robert.

Brewster, Ted. Biological Remediation, 001. 2000. lib. bdg. 59.95 (*0-8493-4126-4*); ring bd. 59.95 (*1-56670-471-5*) CRC Pr.

Brewster, Todd, jt. auth. see Jennings, Peter.

Brewster, Townsend, tr. see Bemba, Sylvain, et al.

Brewster, Townsend, tr. see Zinsou, Senouvo A., et al.

Brewster, Townsend T., tr. see Dadie, Bernard B.

Brewster, William. History of the Certified Township of Kingston, Pennsylvania, 1769 to 1929. (Illus.). 580p. 1997. reprint ed. lib. bdg. 59.50 (*0-8328-7167-2*) Higginson Bk Co.

Brewster, Yvonne. Black Plays Three. 256p. 1995. pap. 17.95 (*0-413-69130-6*, A0727, Methuen Drama) Methn.

Brewton, Barney. California Studies. (J). (gr. 4). 1987. student ed. 229.00 (*0-318-41079-6*) Southwinds Pr.

Brewton, John E. & Brewton, Sara W. Index to Children's Poetry. 966p. 1942. 63.00 (*0-8242-0021-7*) Wilson.

— Index to Children's Poetry. 405p. 1954. suppl. ed. 40.00 (*0-8242-0022-5*) Wilson.

— Index to Children's Poetry. 453p. 1965. suppl. ed. 40.00 (*0-8242-0023-3*) Wilson.

Brewton, John E., jt. auth. see Brewton, Sara W.

Brewton, John E., ed. see Blackburn, G. Meredith, III & Blackburn, Lorraine A.

Brewton, John E., ed. see Brewton, Sara W. & Blackburn, G. Meredith, III.

Brewton, Sara W., et al, eds. Of Quarks, Quasars, & Other Quirks: Quizzical Poems for the Supersonic Age. LC 76-54747. (Illus.). 128p. (YA). (gr. 5 up). 1990. lib. bdg. 13.89 (*0-690-04885-8*) HarpC Child Bks.

Brewton, Sara W. & Blackburn, G. Meredith, III. Index to Poetry for Children & Young People: 1964-1969. Brewton, John E., ed. LC 71-161574. 574p. 1972. 53.00 (*0-8242-0435-2*) Wilson.

Brewton, Sara W. & Brewton, John E. Laughable Limericks. LC 65-16179. (Illus.). 160p. (J). (gr. 3-6). 1990. lib. bdg. 12.89 (*0-690-04887-4*) HarpC Child Bks.

Brewton, Sara W., jt. auth. see Brewton, John E.

Brewton, Sara Westbrook. My Tangs Tungled. (J). 1973. 12.95 (*0-690-57223-9*) HarpC Child Bks.

Brewyn, William. A Fifteenth Century Guidebook to the Principal Churches of Rome. Woodruff, C. Eveleigh, tr. LC 78-63451. (Crusades & Military Orders Ser.: Second Series). reprint ed. 34.50 (*0-404-16374-2*) AMS Pr.

Brey, Barry B. Assembly Language Programming, 8086-8088, 80286, 80386, 80486. LC 93-93. 448p. (C). 1993. pap. text 42.00 (*0-02-314247-2*, Macmillan Coll) P-H.

— The 8085A Microprocessor: Software, Programming & Architecture. 2nd ed. 432p. 1993. text 69.80 (*0-13-090804-5*) P-H.

— Embedded Controllers: 80186 & 80386. LC 97-18174. 804p. (C). 1997. 106.00 (*0-13-400136-2*) P-H.

— The Intel Microprocessors 8086/8088, 80186/80188, 80286, 80386, 80486... 5th ed. LC 98-51137. (Illus.). 966p. 1999. 105.00 (*0-13-995408-2*) P-H.

Brey, Barry B. The Intel 32-Bit Microprocessors: 80386, 80486 & Pentium Microprocessors. LC 94-14162. 576p. (C). 1994. 115.00 (*0-02-314260-X*, Macmillan Coll) P-H.

Brey, Barry B. Microprocessors & Peripherals: Hardware, Software, Interfacing & Applications. 2nd ed. 512p. (C). 1990. text 61.60 (*0-675-20884-X*, Merrill Coll) P-H.

— Programming the 80286, 80386, 80486, & Pentium-Based Personal Computer. LC 95-32795. 786p. 1995. 115.00 (*0-02-314263-4*, Macmillan Coll) P-H.

Brey, Barry B., jt. auth. see Forbes, Mark M.

Brey, Catherine F. & Reed, Lena F. The New Complete Bloodhound. 2nd rev. ed. (Illus.). 256p. 1992. 27.95 (*0-87605-077-1*) Howell Bks.

***Brey, Hans-Michael.** Doppelstaat Ddr: Menschenrechtsverletzungen der Deutschen Volkspolizei. (Illus.). 387p. 1999. 56.95 (*3-631-34655-7*) P Lang Pubng.

Brey, Marie, jt. auth. see Brey, William.

Brey, Paul T. & Hultmark, Dan E., eds. Molecular Mechanisms of Immune Responses in Insects. (Illus.). 256p. 1997. write for info. (*0-412-71280-6*) Kluwer Academic.

Brey, Robin L., jt. auth. see Levine, Steven R.

Brey, Ronald G., jt. auth. see Hudspeth, DeLayne R.

Brey, Wallace S., ed. Pulse Methods in ID & IID Liquid Phase NMR. 561p. 1988. text 146.00 (*0-12-133155-5*) Acad Pr.

Brey, William. John Carbutt on the Frontiers of Photography. (Illus.). 218p. (Orig.). 1985. pap. 19.95 (*0-9613955-0-8*) Willowdale Pr.

Brey, William & Brey, Marie. Philadelphia Photographers, 1840-1900. 180p. (Orig.). 1992. pap. text 14.95 (*0-9613955-1-6*) Willowdale Pr.

Breyel, Janine M. Improving State Programs for Pregnant Women & Children: Conference Proceedings. Miller, Mark, ed. 90p. (Orig.). 1990. pap. text 15.00 (*1-55877-110-7*) Natl Governor.

Breyel, Janine M., ed. Gaining Ground: State Initiatives for Pregnant Women & Children. 76p. (Orig.). 1992. pap. text 15.00 (*1-55877-152-2*) Natl Governor.

Breyel, Janine M. & Hill, Ian T. Creating Systems of Care for Substance-Using Pregnant Women & Their Children. Glass, Karen, ed. 96p. (Orig.). 1993. pap. text 15.00 (*1-55877-214-6*) Natl Governor.

Breyel, Janine M., jt. auth. see Hill, Ian T.

Breyel, Janine M., jt. auth. see Volpe, L. Carl.

Breyer. The Design of Wood Structures. 2000. 79.95 (*0-07-134873-5*) McGraw.

— Design Wood Struct (sol Mnl) 2000. 79.95 (*0-07-135073-X*) McGraw.

— Design Wood Structures. 3rd ed. 1993. student ed. write for info. (*0-07-007695-2*) McGraw.

Breyer, Betty J., ed. see Trollope, Anthony.

Breyer, Betty J., ed. & intro. see Trollope, Anthony.

Breyer-Brandwijk, Maria G., jt. auth. see Watt, John M.

***Breyer, Chloe.** The Close: A Young Woman's First Year in a Seminary. 2000. 23.00 (*0-465-00714-7*, Pub. by Basic) HarpC.

Breyer, Donald E., et al. Design of Wood Structures: ASD. 4th ed. LC 98-35386. (Illus.). 950p. 1999. 69.95 (*0-07-007716-9*) McGraw.

Breyer, Friedrich, jt. auth. see Zweifel, Peter.

Breyer, Michelle. Ancient Civilizations Brain Teasers. (Brain Teasers Ser.). 80p. (J). (gr. 5-8). 1998. pap. 9.95 (*1-57690-215-3*) Tchr Create Mat.

— Ancient Egypt. (Interdisciplinary Units Ser.). 224p. (J). (gr. 5-8). 1997. pap. 16.95 (*1-55734-574-0*) Tchr Create Mat.

— Ancient Greece. (Interdisciplinary Units Ser.). 176p. (J). (gr. 5-8). 1997. pap. 15.95 (*1-55734-575-9*) Tchr Create Mat.

— Ancient India. (Thematic Unit Ser.). 80p. (J). (gr. 5-8). 1997. pap. 9.95 (*1-55734-577-5*) Tchr Create Mat.

***Breyer, Michelle.** Ancient Japan: Thematic Unit. Welly, Barbara M., ed. (Illus.). 80p. (J). 1999. pap., teacher ed. 9.95 (*1-55734-579-1*, TCM579) Tchr Create Mat.

Breyer, Michelle. Ancient Rome. (Interdisciplinary Units Ser.). 176p. (J). (gr. 5-8). 1997. pap. 15.95 (*1-55734-576-7*) Tchr Create Mat.

— Early Humans. (Illus.). 224p. 1998. pap., teacher ed. 14.95 (*1-55734-572-4*) Tchr Create Mat.

***Breyer, Michelle.** How to Give a Presentation: Grades 6-8. (Illus.). 48p. 1999. pap., teacher ed. 7.95 (*1-57690-501-2*, TCM 2501) Tchr Create Mat.

— How to Punctuate. Buehler, Stephanie J., ed. 48p. (YA). (gr. 6-8). 1999. pap., teacher ed. 7.95 (*1-57690-488-1*, TCM2488) Tchr Create Mat.

Breyer, Michelle. The Middle East. (Thematic Unit Ser.). 80p. (J). (gr. 5-8). 1997. pap. 9.95 (*1-55734-573-2*) Tchr Create Mat.

Breyer, Michelle A., jt. auth. see Teacher Created Materials Staff.

Breyer, Pamela. Grammarwork: English Exercise in Context, Bk. 1. 2nd ed. Vol. 1. 160p. 1995. pap. text 19.13 (*0-13-340241-X*) P-H.

— Grammarwork: English Exercise in Context, Bk. 2. 2nd ed. Vol. 2. 160p. 1995. pap. text 19.13 (*0-13-340258-4*) P-H.

Breyer, Pamela. Grammarwork 3: English Exercise in Context, Bk. 3. 2nd ed. 160p. 1996. pap. text 19.13 (*0-13-340266-5*) P-H.

Breyer, Pamela Peterson. Grammar, Bk. 4. 2nd ed. 160p. 1996. pap. text, wbk. ed. 19.13 (*0-13-340274-6*) P-H.

Breyer, Ralph F. The Marketing Institution. Assael, Henry, ed. LC 78-245. (Century of Marketing Ser.). 1979 reprint ed. lib. bdg. 31.95 (*0-405-11160-6*) Ayer.

— Quantitative Systemic Analysis & Control. Assael, Henry, ed. LC 78-250. (Century of Marketing Ser.). 1979 reprint ed. lib. bdg. 33.95 (*0-405-11164-9*) Ayer.

Breyer, Robert A. Switched, Fast & Gigabit Ethernet. 3rd ed. LC 98-85496. 1998. pap. 45.00 (*1-57870-073-5*) Macmillan Tech.

Breyer, Siegfried. Aircraft Carrier: Graf Zeppelin. LC 90-60481. (Illus.). 48p. 1990. pap. 9.95 (*0-88740-242-9*) Schiffer.

— Battleship: Gneisenau. LC 90-62989. (Illus.). 48p. 1991. pap. 9.95 (*0-88740-290-9*) Schiffer.

— Battleship: Scharnhorst. LC 90-62990. (Illus.). 48p. 1991. pap. 9.95 (*0-88740-291-7*) Schiffer.

— Battleship: Tirpitz. LC 89-84174. (Illus.). 48p. 1989. pap. 9.95 (*0-88740-184-8*) Schiffer.

— German U-Boat Type XXI. LC 99-184248.Tr. of Marine Arsenal Wunderwaffe Elektro-UBoot Type XXI. (Illus.). 48p. (Orig.). 1999. pap. 9.95 (*0-7643-0787-8*) Schiffer.

— Pocket Battleship: The Admiral Graf Spee. LC 89-84177. (Illus.). 48p. 1989. pap. 9.95 (*0-88740-183-X*) Schiffer.

Breyer, Siegfried & Koop, Gerhard. The German Navy at War Vol. I: The Battleships. LC 89-63851. (Illus.). 192p. 1990. 39.95 (*0-88740-220-8*) Schiffer.

— The German Navy at War, 1935-1945 Vol. II: The U-Boat. LC 89-63595. (Illus.). 188p. 1990. 39.95 (*0-88740-218-6*) Schiffer.

Breyer, Stephen G. Administrative Law & Regulatory Policy. 4th ed. LC 98-8231. xiii, 1054 p. 1998. boxed set 60.00 (*0-7355-0015-0*) Aspen Law.

— Breaking the Vicious Circle: Toward Effective Risk Regulation. (Illus.). 160p. (C). 1993. 29.00 (*0-674-08114-5*) HUP.

— Breaking the Vicious Circle: Toward Effective Risk Regulation. (Illus.). 144p. 1995. pap. text 16.50 (*0-674-08115-3*, BREBRX) HUP.

— Regulation & Its Reform. LC 81-6753. (Illus.). 486p. 1982. 46.50 (*0-674-75375-5*) HUP.

— Regulation & Its Reform. 486p. 1984. pap. 25.50 (*0-674-75376-3*) HUP.

— Supplement to Administrative Law '88. 1988. 10.95 (*0-316-10786-7*, Aspen Law & Bus) Aspen Pub.

Breyer, Stephen G. & Stewart, Richard B. Administrative Law & Regulatory Policy: Problems, Text, & Cases. 3rd ed. 1208p. 1992. teacher ed. write for info. (*0-316-10847-2*, 08472) Aspen Law.

— Administrative Law & Regulatory Policy: Problems, Text, & Cases. 3rd ed. 1208p. 1996. suppl. ed. write for info. (*0-316-11106-6*, 11066) Aspen Law.

Breyfogle, Forrest W. Smarter Six Sigma Solutions: Statistics Methods for Testing, Development, Manufacturing, & Service. 2nd ed. LC 98-31917. 832p. 1999. 90.00 (*0-471-29659-7*) Wiley.

— Statistical Methods for Testing, Development & Manufacturing. LC 91-14539. 544p. 1992. 140.00 (*0-471-54035-8*) Wiley.

***Breyfogle, Forrest W., et al.** Managing Six Sigma: A Practical Guide to Understanding, Assessing & Implementing the Strategy That Yields Bottom Line Success. LC 00-43301. 2000. write for info. (*0-471-39673-7*) Wiley.

***Breyfogle, Todd.** Literary Imagination: Ancient & Modern. LC 98-50892. 405p. 1999. pap. text 19.00 (*0-226-07425-0*) U Ch Pr.

— Literary Imagination, Ancient & Modern: Essays in Honor of David Grene. LC 98-50892. 1999. lib. bdg. 50.00 (*0-226-07424-2*) U Ch Pr.

Breyman, Steven. Movement Genesis: Social Movement Theory & the West German Peace Movement. LC 98-113391. 256p. (C). 1997. pap. 69.00 (*0-8133-8811-2*, Pub. by Westview) HarpC.

***Breyman, Steven.** Why Movements Matter: The West German Peace Movement & U.S. Arms Control Policy. LC 99-59161. (C). 2000. pap. text 23.95 (*0-7914-4656-5*) State U NY Pr.

— Why Movements Matter: The West German Peace Movement & U.S. Arms Control Policy. LC 99-59161. (C). 2000. text 71.50 (*0-7914-4655-7*) State U NY Pr.

***Breymann, Ulrich.** Designing Components with the C++ STL: A New Approach to Programming. 2nd rev. ed. (Illus.). 304p. 1999. 39.95 (*0-201-67488-2*) Addison-Wesley.

Breymer, Sylvia, ed. see Birdseye, Harvey E.

Breymeyer, Alicia I., ed. Managed Grasslands: Regional Studies. (Ecosystems of the World Ser.: No. 17A). xii,388p. 1991. 262.50 (*0-444-42998-0*) Elsevier.

Breymeyer, Alicia I., ed. see Van Dyne, G. M.

Breymeyer, Alicja, ed. see National Research Council Staff.

Breyner, Sophia D. Log Book: Selected Poems. 144p. 1998. pap. 17.95 (*1-85754-364-5*, Pub. by Carcanet Pr) Paul & Co Pubs.

Breyrer, Chris. War in the Blood: Sex, Politics & AIDS in Southeast Asia, Vol. 1. LC 98-178656. 1998. pap. text 62.50 (*1-85649-531-0*, Pub. by Zed Books) St Martin.

Breysig, A., ed. see Caesar, Germanicus.

Breysse, D., ed. Probabilities & Materials: Tests, Models & Applications - Proceedings of the NATO Advanced Research Workshop on PROBAMAT, Cachan, France, November 23-25, 1993. LC 94-16935. (NATO ASI Series E: Applied Sciences: Vol. 269). 552p. (C). 1994. text 332.00 (*0-7923-2876-0*) Kluwer Academic.

Breytenbach, Breyten. Dog Heart. LC 98-47017. 192p. (C). 1999. 22.00 (*0-15-100458-7*) Harcourt.

— In Africa Even the Flies Are Happy. 144p. 1983. 13.95 (*0-7145-3696-2*) Riverrun NY.

— The Memory of Birds in Time of Revolution: Essays. LC 95-47982. 169p. 1996. 22.00 (*0-15-100168-5*) Harcourt.

— Return to Paradise. LC 93-8721. 1993. 22.95 (*0-15-177086-7*) Harcourt.

— A Season in Paradise. Vaughan, Rike, tr. from AFR. LC 94-20364. (Illus.). 288p. (J). 1994. pap. 12.95 (*0-15-600133-0*, Harvest Bks) Harcourt.

— The True Confessions of an Albino Terrorist. LC 94-12789. (Harvest Book Ser.). 400p. 1994. pap. 14.95 (*0-15-600134-9*) Harcourt.

***Breytenbach, Breyton.** Dog Heart: A Memoir. 2000. pap. write for info. (*0-15-601153-0*) Harcourt.

Breytenbach, Cilliers. Paulus und Barnabas in der Provinz Galatien: Studien Zu Apostelgeschichte 13f.; 16,6; 18,23 und Den Adressaten Des Galaterbriefes. (GER.). xvi, 215p. 1996. 94.00 (*90-04-10693-6*) Brill Academic Pubs.

Breza, Greg. Unexpected Rendezvous. 109p. Date not set. mass mkt. 5.99 (*1-55197-728-1*) Picasso Publ.

Brezany, Peter, et al, eds. Input/Output Intensive Massively Parallel Computing: Language Support, Automatic Parallelization, Advanced Optimization, & Runtime Systems, Vol. 122. LC 97-13205. (Lecture Notes in Computer Science Ser.: No. 1220). 302p. 1997. pap. 44.95 (*3-540-62840-1*) Spr-Verlag.

Brezden, Mike, jt. auth. see Spear, Barbara.

Brezear, Winifred. A Childhood in Havering-at-the-Bower. 1993. pap. 10.00 (*0-86025-810-6*, Pub. by I Henry Pubns) Empire Pub Srvs.

Brezee, Fran. Modular C-LECT Occupational Modules User's Guide, 1996-97. rev. ed. 32p. (YA). (gr. 9-12). 1996. pap. text 19.00 (*1-55631-256-3*) Chron Guide.

Brezee, Fran, ed. Counselor-Administrator's Guide for Chronicle Occ Briefs on Diskette. 8p. (YA). (gr. 9-12). 1996. pap. text. write for info. (*1-55631-255-5*) Chron Guide.

B

Brezen-Block, Tamara & Robinson, William. Sales Promotion Handbook. 8th ed. LC 95-136999. 910p. 1994. 69.95 (*0-85013-212-6*) Dartnell Corp.

Brezen-Block, Tamara & Robinson, William A., eds. Sales Promotion Handbook. 8th ed. 910p. 1997. pap. 69.95 (*0-85013-315-7*) Dartnell Corp.

***Brezet, Han.** Ecodesign: A Promising Approach to Sustainable Production & Consumption. 346p. 1998. 150.00 (*92-807-1631-X*) UN.

Brezhner, Alexander, et al. American Universities, Colleges & English Language Programs. (CIES-USA Guide for International Students Ser.). (RUS., Illus.). 266p. 1997. 12.00 (*0-9656433-0-1*) CIES-USA.

Brezhnev, D. D., ed. see Ivanov, A. I.

***Brezhnev, L. I.** Following Lenin's Course. 504p. 2000. pap. 26.25 (*0-89875-050-4*) U Pr Pacific.

Brezhnev, Leonid I. Peace, Detente, Cooperation. LC 80-25943. 213p. 1981. reprint ed. pap. 66.10 (*0-608-05406-2*, 206587500006) Bks Demand.

Brezhnev, Leonid I., ed. Leonid I. Brezhnev: His Life & Work, 1906-1982. LC 82-19510. (Illus.). 214p. 1982. 29.95 (*0-943071-03-8*) Sphinx Pr.

***Brezianu, Andrei.** Historical Dictionary of the Republic of Moldova, No. 37. (European Historical Dictionaries Ser.). 336p. 2000. 60.00 (*0-8108-3734-X*) Scarecrow.

Brezik, Victor B., ed. One Hundred Years of Thomism: Aeterni Patris & Afterwards: A Symposium. LC 80-70377. (Center for Thomistic Studies). 210p. 1981. pap. 9.95 (*0-268-01498-1*) Ctr Thomistic.

— Thomistic Papers, No. I. LC 83-73623. 176p. 1984. 20.95 (*0-685-31936-9*); pap. 10.95 (*0-685-31937-7*) Ctr Thomistic.

— Thomistic Papers, No. I. LC 85-18508. 176p. 1984. text 24.50 (*0-268-01850-2*); pap. text 13.00 (*0-268-01851-0*) U of Notre Dame Pr.

Brezillon, Michel. Larousse Dictionnaire de la Prehistoire. (FRE.). 250p. 1969. pap. 16.95 (*0-7859-7636-1*) Fr & Eur.

***Brezillon, Patrick, et al, eds.** Reasoning in Context for AI Applications: Papers from the AAAI Workshop. (Technical Reports: Vol. WS-99-14). (Illus.). 118p. 1999. spiral bd. 25.00 (*1-57735-098-7*) AAAI Pr.

Brezin, E. & Wadia, S. R. The Large N Expansion in Quantum Field Theory & Statistical Physics. 600p. 1993. text 162.00 (*981-02-0455-8*); pap. text 86.00 (*981-02-0456-6*) World Scientific Pub.

Brezin, E. & Zinn-Justin, J., eds. Fields, Strings, Critical Phenomena. (Houches Summer School Proceedings Ser.: Vol. 49). xxx,642p. 1990. 177.50 (*0-444-88440-8*) Elsevier.

Brezin, Jonathan. Unitary Representation Theory for Solvable Lie Groups. LC 52-42839. (Memoirs Ser.: No. 79). 122p. 1968. pap. 16.00 (*0-8218-1279-3*, MEMO/1/79) Am Math.

Brezina, Okokar. Hidden History. 150p. 1997. pap. 18.50 (*80-902171-2-5*, Pub. by Twisted Spoon) SPD-Small Pr Dist.

Brezina, Paul B., et al, eds. Seeing Society: Perspectives on Social Life. 2nd ed. LC 93-9936. 509p. 1993. pap. text 44.00 (*0-205-14348-2*) Allyn.

Brezinka, Wolfgang. Basic Concepts of Educational Science: Analysis, Critique, Proposals. Brice, James S., tr. 290p. (C). 1993. lib. bdg. 53.50 (*0-8191-9257-0*) U Pr of Amer.

— Educational Aims, Educational Means, Educational Success: Contributions to a System of Science of Education. Brice, James S., tr. LC 96-79839. 368p. 1997. 83.95 (*1-85972-511-2*, Pub. by Avebry) Ashgate Pub Co.

— Philosophy of Educational Knowledge: An Introduction to the Foundations of Science of Education, Philosophy of Education & Practical Pedagogics. (Philosophy & Education Ser.). 320p. (C). 1991. lib. bdg. 145.00 (*0-7923-1522-7*, Pub. by M Nijhoff) Kluwer Academic.

— Socialization & Education: Essays in Conceptual Criticism, 63. LC 93-47087. (Contributions to the Study of Education Ser.: No. 63). 232p. 1994. 59.95 (*0-313-29258-2*, Greenwood Pr) Greenwood.

Brezinra, Wolfgang. Belief, Morals & Education: Collected Essays on the Philosophy of Education. (Avebury Series in Philosophy). 288p. 1994. 87.95 (*1-85628-873-0*, Pub. by Avebry) Ashgate Pub Co.

Brezinski, C. History of Continued Fractions & Pade Approximants. Graham, R. L., et al, eds. (Computational Mathematics Ser.: Vol. 12). viii, 560p. 1990. 169.95 (*0-387-15286-5*) Spr-Verlag.

— Pade-Typed Approximation & General Orthogonal Polynomials. (International Series of Numerical Mathematics: No. 50). 250p. 1980. 84.00 (*0-8176-1100-2*) Birkhauser.

Brezinski, C., et al, eds. Polynomes Orthogonaux et Applications. (Lecture Notes in Mathematics Ser.: Vol. 1171). (FRE & GER.). 584p. 1985. 77.95 (*0-387-16059-0*) Spr-Verlag.

Brezinski, C. & Kulisch, Ulrich W., eds. Computational & Applied Mathematics I: Algorithms & Theory. LC 92-24965. x,502p. 1992. 189.00 (*0-444-89701-1*, North Holland) Elsevier.

Brezinski, C. & Redivo, Zaglia M. Extrapolation Methods. (Studies in Computational Mathematics: Vol. 2). x,464p. 1991. 169.50 incl. disk (*0-444-88814-4*, North Holland) Elsevier.

Brezinski, Claude. Projection Methods for Systems of Equations. LC 97-43588. (Studies in Computational Mathematics). 408p. 1997. 143.50 (*0-444-82777-3*) Elsevier.

Brezinski, Claude, ed. Biorthogonality & Its Applications to Numerical Analysis. (Pure & Applied Mathematics Ser.: Vol. 156). (Illus.). 184p. 1991. text 125.00 (*0-8247-8616-5*) Dekker.

Brezinski, Horst. Shadow Economy: An Assessment. (WVSS in International Economics Ser.). (C). 1996. pap. text 23.00 (*0-8133-7589-4*) Westview.

Brezinski, Horst & Fritsch, Michael, eds. The Economic Impact of New Firms in Post-Socialist Countries: Bottom-up Transformation in Eastern Europe. LC 95-30783. (Illus.). 288p. 1996. text 95.00 (*1-85898-121-2*) E Elgar.

— The Emergence & Evolution of Markets. LC 97-25024. (European Association for Comparative Economic Studies Ser.). 240p. (C). 1997. text 85.00 (*1-85898-659-1*) E Elgar.

Brezinski, Horst, jt. ed. see Fritsch, Michael.

Brezinski, Horst D., ed. see Franck, Egon.

Brezinski, John, ed. Manual on Determination of Volatile Organic Compound (VOC) Content in Paints, Inks, & Related Coating Products, MNL 4. 2nd ed. LC 93-20769. (ASTM Manual Ser.: No. MNL 4). 175p. 1993. text 39.00 (*0-8031-2054-0*, MNL4) ASTM.

Brezinski, Mark H., jt. auth. see Gordon, Robert T.

Brezis. Nonlinear Partial Differential Equation. Date not set. text. write for info. (*0-582-02181-2*, Pub. by Addison-Wesley) Longman.

***Brezis, Elise S. & Temin, Peter, eds.** Elites, Minorities & Economic Growth. 266p. 1999. 95.00 (*0-444-82848-6*, North Holland) Elsevier.

Brezis, Haim, et al, eds. Variational Methods for Discontinuous Structures: Applications to Image Segmentation, Continuum Mechanics, Homogenization : Villa Olmo, Como, 8-10 September 1994, Vol. 25. LC 96-35953. (Progress in Nonlinear Differential Equations & Their Applications Ser.). 208p. 1996. 89.50 (*3-7643-5273-6*) Birkhauser.

Brezis, Haim & Lions, J. L., eds. Nonlinear Partial Differential Equations & Their Applications: College de France Seminar, Vol. 10. LC 90-8426. (Pitman Research Notes in Mathematics Ser.: Vol. 220). 407p. 1991. reprint ed. pap. 126.20 (*0-608-03596-3*, 206441900009) Bks Demand.

***Breznik, Marko.** Storage Reservoirs & Deep Wells in Karst Regions. LC 99-496407. (Illus.). 268p. 1998. 69.00 (*90-5410-688-3*, Pub. by A A Balkema) Ashgate Pub Co.

Breznik, Melitta. Night Duty: A Novel. Theobold, Roslyn, tr. from GER. LC 99-12851. 131p. 1999. pap. 12.00 (*1-883642-85-X*) Steerforth Pr.

Breznitz, Shlomo. Cry Wolf: The Psychology of False Alarms. 280p. 1984. text 49.95 (*0-89859-296-8*) L Erlbaum Assocs.

— Education for Change. Date not set. 19.95 (*0-465-01837-8*, Pub. by Basic); pap. 18.00 (*0-465-01818-1*, Pub. by Basic) HarpC.

Breznitz, Shlomo, ed. The Denial of Stress. LC 82-13044. xiv, 316p. 1983. 50.00 (*0-8236-1185-X*) Intl Univs Pr.

Breznitz, Shlomo, jt. ed. see Goldberger, Leo.

Brezny, Robert, ed. see Zakis, Girts F.

Brezonik, Patrick L. Chemical Kinetics & Process Dynamics in Aquatic Systems. 784p. 1993. lib. bdg. 85.00 (*0-87371-431-8*, L431) Lewis Pubs.

***Brezovszky, Peter, et al.** Multikulturalitat und Multiethnizitat in Mittel-, Ost- und Sudosteuropa. 342p. 1999. 48.95 (*3-631-35162-3*) P Lang Pubng.

***Brezsny, Rob.** The Televisionary Oracle. 300p. 1999. pap. 16.95 (*1-58394-000-6*) Frog Ltd CA.

Brezzi, F., ed. Numerical Methods in Fluid Dynamics. (Lecture Notes in Mathematics Ser.: Vol. 1127). vii, 333p. 1985. 46.95 (*0-387-15225-3*) Spr-Verlag.

Brezzi, F., jt. auth. see Fortin, M.

Brezzi, Paolo. La Diplomazia Pontificia. 449p. reprint ed. write for info. (*0-318-71583-X*) G Olms Pubs.

Brezzi, Paolo & Lee, Egmont. Sources of Social History. Lee, E., ed. pap. text 36.57 (*0-88844-805-8*) Brill Academic Pubs.

***Brhauer, Gerd.** Writing Across Languages LC 99-38370. (Advances in Foreign & Second Language Pedagogy Ser.). 1999. pap. write for info. (*1-56750-479-5*) Ablx Pub.

Brhuntrup, Godehard, ed. see Tacelli, Ronald K.

Bria, Gina. The Art of Family: Rituals, Play, & Everyday Spirituality. LC 97-39217. 224p. 1998. pap. 12.95 (*0-440-50772-3*) Dell.

Bria, William F. & Rydell, Richard L. The Physician-Computer Connection: A Practical Guide to Physician Involvement in Health Care Information Systems. rev. ed. LC 96-26417. 124p. 1996. pap. 42.50 (*1-55648-166-7*, 093106) AHPI.

Briaddy, Katherine Q. Around Ballston Lake. (Images of America Ser.). 1997. pap. 16.99 (*0-7524-0576-4*) Arcadia Publng.

— Around Burnt Hills. LC 98-86606. (Images of America Ser.). (Illus.). 128p. 1998. pap. 16.99 (*0-7524-1248-5*) Arcadia Publng.

Brian. Murderers Die, Vol. 1. 1990. mass mkt. 5.95 (*0-312-92472-0*) St Martin.

***Brian.** Pulitzer. 400p. 2000. 30.00 (*0-471-33200-3*) Wiley.

Brian, Bridget. Orla. 112p. 1984. 40.00 (*0-7212-0641-7*, Pub. by Regency Pr GBR) St Mut.

— Shannondene. 73p. 1984. 25.00 (*0-7212-0591-7*, Pub. by Regency Pr GBR) St Mut.

— Why Damien, Oh Why? 152p. 1984. 39.00 (*0-7212-0662-X*, Pub. by Regency Pr GBR) St Mut.

Brian, Danielle, ed. Tripwired? Document Trial of Faulty Airplane Wiring Demonstrates Need for Comprehensive Review. (Illus.). 94p. (C). 1999. pap. text 25.00 (*0-7881-7668-4*) DIANE Pub.

Brian, Denis. Einstein: A Life. LC 95-12075. 528p. 1996. 30.00 (*0-471-11459-6*) Wiley.

— Einstein: A Life. LC 95-12075. (Illus.). 528p. 1997. pap. 19.95 (*0-471-19362-3*) Wiley.

— Genius Talk: Conversations with Nobel Scientists & Other Luminaries. LC 95-31823. (Illus.). 436p. (C). 1995. 28.95 (*0-306-45089-5*, Plenum Trade) Perseus Pubng.

Brian, Gayle & Wilhelm, Emogene C. The Executor's Handbook: A Practical Guide to Settling Connecticut Estates. 2nd rev. ed. 166p. 1993. pap. text 14.95 (*0-9637764-0-1*) Chase Pubng.

***Brian-Johnson, Donald & Pina, Leslie.** Moss Lamps, Lighting the 50's. (Illus.). 192p. 1999. 49.95 (*0-7643-1002-X*) Schiffer.

Brian, Nancy J. River to Rim: A Guide to Place Names along the Colorado River in Grand Canyon from Lake Powell to Lake Mead. LC 92-90263. (Illus.). 176p. (Orig.). 1992. pap. 14.95 (*1-881438-00-7*) Earthquest.

Brian, Rob. Parliamentary Libraries & Information Services of Asia & the Pacific: Papers Prepared for the 62cnd Conference, Beijing, China, August 25-31, 1996. (IFLA Publications: 83). iv, 106p. 1997. write for info. (*3-598-21808-7*) K G Saur Verlag.

Brian, Robert F. Bangwa Kinship & Marriage. LC 70-166945. 209p. reprint ed. pap. 59.60 (*0-8357-5957-1*, 2027286) Bks Demand.

Brian, Sarah J. Funtastic Math: Probability. 64p. 1998. pap. 9.95 (*0-590-37367-6*) Scholastic Inc.

— Funtastic Math! Problem Solving & Logic. 64p. (J). 1998. pap. text 9.95 (*0-590-37368-4*) Scholastic Inc.

***Brian, Sarah Jane.** Polar Bear. (All-Star Readers Ser.). (Illus.). 48p. (J). (gr. 2-3). 2000. pap. 3.99 (*1-57584-660-8*, Pub. by Rdrs Digest) S&S Trade.

— Way to Go: Exploring Nature with Tools. (See for Yourself Guides Ser.). (Illus.). 48p. (J). (gr. 3-6). Date not set. spiral bd. write for info. (*1-57584-427-3*, Pub. by Rdrs Digest) S&S Trade.

Brian, William L., II. Moongate: Suppressed Findings of the U. S. Space Program: The NASA-Military Cover-Up. LC 81-69211. (Illus.). 119p. (C). 1982. spiral bd. 49.95 (*0-941292-00-2*) Future Sci Res.

Brianberg Grant, Diana, et al. China. 96p. 1999. pap. 12.95 (*0-590-76987-1*) Scholastic Inc.

Brianchaninov, Ignatius. Bodily & Spiritual Labor. 1996. pap. 0.50 (*0-89981-159-0*) Eastern Orthodox.

— Following Our Lord Jesus Christ. 1994. pap. 0.75 (*0-89981-154-X*) Eastern Orthodox.

— On Tears. 1993. pap. 0.75 (*0-89981-121-3*) Eastern Orthodox.

— On the Prayer of Jesus: With Introduction & "The Prayer Rope" by an Exiled Athonite Monk. Williams, Gregory, ed. Moore, Lazarus, tr. from RUS. 112p. 1995. 15.00 (*0-912927-61-5*, X047) St John Kronstadt.

— Prayer Life for the Beginner. 1994. pap. 0.50 (*0-89981-156-6*) Eastern Orthodox.

— Purity. 1994. pap. 0.75 (*0-89981-155-8*) Eastern Orthodox.

Brianchianinov, Ignatius. The Arena. Archimandrite Lazarus Moore, tr. from RUS. 300p. (Orig.). 1982. 15.00 (*0-88465-009-X*); pap. 12.00 (*0-88465-011-1*) Holy Trinity.

— Asketitcheskije Opiti: Tom 1, Tom 1.Tr. of Ascetic Experiences. 468p. reprint ed. 25.00 (*0-317-28935-7*) Holy Trinity.

— Asketitcheskije Opiti Tom 3, Tom 3.Tr. of Ascetic Experiences. 315p. reprint ed. 20.00 (*0-317-28957-8*); reprint ed. pap. 15.00 (*0-317-28958-6*) Holy Trinity.

— Fasting. 1980. pap. 0.25 (*0-89981-024-1*) Eastern Orthodox.

— Sin & Repentance. 1991. pap. 1.00 (*0-89981-119-1*) Eastern Orthodox.

— Three Essays: On Reading the Gospel, on Reading the Holy Fathers, on Shunning Reading of Books Containing False Teachings. 1976. pap. 0.50 (*0-89981-103-5*) Eastern Orthodox.

Briand, Jean P., ed. Atoms in Unusual Situations. LC 86-22495. (NATO ASI Series B, Physics). 450p. 1986. 110.00 (*0-306-42399-5*, Plenum Trade) Perseus Pubng.

Briand, Lo C. & Roy, Daniel. Meeting Deadlines In Real-Time Systems: A Practical Introduction to Design with Rate Monotonic Analysis. LC 99-33707. 250p. 1997. pap. 59.00 (*0-8186-7406-7*) IEEE Comp Soc.

Briand, Michael K. Dialogue in Williamsburg: The Turning Point for South Africa? LC 89-28989. 1989. pap. 19.95 (*1-55815-068-4*) ICS Pr.

— Practical Politics: Five Principles for a Community That Works. LC 98-58010. 320p. 1999. 44.95 (*0-252-02460-5*); pap. text 15.95 (*0-252-06766-5*) U of Ill Pr.

Briand, Michael K., ed. A Way Out: Federalist Options for South Africa. 144p. 1987. pap. 19.95 (*0-917616-90-1*) ICS Pr.

Briand, Paul L., Jr. In Search of Paradise. LC 52-5010. 395p. 1987. reprint ed. mass mkt. 5.95 (*0-935180-48-6*) Mutual Pub HI.

***Briandet, Benjamin.** Sams Teach Yourself Qt Programming in 24 Hours. (Teach Yourself... in 24 Hours Ser.). (Illus.). 456p. 2000. pap. 29.99 (*0-672-31869-5*) Sams.

Briandet, Philippe A., jt. auth. see Goris, Michael L.

Brians. Comp Resrch Soc Schl CB. (C). 1998. pap. text 14.06 (*0-201-32242-0*) Addison-Wesley.

Brians, Paul. Nuclear Holocausts: Atomic War in Fiction, 1895-1984. LC 86-10685. 410p. 1987. 29.50 (*0-87338-335-4*) Kent St U Pr.

— Nuclear Holocausts: Atomic War in Fiction, 1895-1984. LC 86-10685. 410p. reprint ed. pap. 127.10 (*0-608-10528-7*, 207114800009) Bks Demand.

Briansky, Oleg, tr. & intro. see Kostrovitskaya, Vera S.

Briant, Anthony. The Samurai. (Elite Ser.: No. 23). (Illus.). 64p. pap. 12.95 (*0-85045-897-8*, 9423, Pub. by Osprey) Stackpole.

Briant, C. Impurities in Engineering Materials: Impact, Reliability & Control. LC 99-17273. (Materials Engineering Ser.). (Illus.). 320p. 1999. text 150.00 (*0-8247-9965-8*) Dekker.

Briant, C. L. Metallurgy of Environmental Fracture. No. 12. 300p. 1984. write for info. (*0-318-57814-X*) Elsevier.

Briant, C. L., et al, eds. Interfacial Engineering for Optimized Properties. LC 97-23549. (Materials Research Society Symposium Proceedings Ser.: No. 458). 510p. 1997. text 75.00 (*1-55899-362-2*) Materials Res.

Briant, Jean, et al. Rheological Properties of Lubricants. (Illus.). 296p. (C). 1989. 530.00 (*2-7108-0564-2*, Pub. by Edits Technip) Enfield Pubs NH.

***Briant, John H.** Adirondack Detective. LC 99-96188. 200p. 2000. pap. 14.95 (*0-9648327-2-0*) Chalet Pubng.

Briant, John H. One Cop's Story: A Life Remembered. LC 95-71016. (Illus.). 182p. 1995. 21.95 (*0-9648327-1-2*); pap. 14.95 (*0-9648327-0-4*) Chalet Pubng.

Briant, Pierre. Alexander the Great: Man of Action-Man of Spirit. Leggatt, Jeremy, tr. (Discoveries Ser.). (Illus.). 176p. 1996. pap. 12.95 (*0-8109-2833-7*, Pub. by Abrams) Time Warner.

Briant, Pierre. From Cyrus to Alexander: A History of the Persian Empire, 2 vols. 69.50 (*1-57506-031-0*) Eisenbrauns.

Briant, Pierre. Histoire de le Empire Perse: De Cyrus a Alexander, 2 vols. (FRE.). 1247p. 1996. pap. 66.50 (*90-6258-410-1*, Pub. by Netherlands Inst) Eisenbrauns.

Brianza, David. Beginning Technical Mathematics Made Easy. (Illus.). 140p. 1989. pap. 8.95 (*0-8306-3383-9*) McGraw-Hill Prof.

***Briar, Arielle.** Seasons of Desire: Lesbian Love Stories from New England. 200p. 1999. pap. 13.95 (*0-9665917-2-0*, Pub. by Nocturnis Prodns) Alamo Sq Dist.

Briar, Celia. Working for Women? Gendered Work & Welfare Policies in Twentieth Century Britain. (Gender & Society Ser.). 192p. 1997. 74.95 (*0-7484-0552-6*, Pub. by Tay Francis Ltd); pap. 24.95 (*0-7484-0553-4*, Pub. by Tay Francis Ltd) Taylor & Francis.

Briar, Katharine H. Social Work & the Unemployed. LC 87-34846. 222p. 1988. 21.95 (*0-87101-153-0*) Natl Assn Soc Wkrs.

Briarcliff Press Staff. New York Area Golf Guide, 1992: A Guide to Facilities Open to the Public. 1992. pap. 12.95 (*0-9631658-0-1*) Briarcliff NY.

— Powers Northeast Region Golf Guide, 1994. 1993. pap. 14.95 (*0-9631658-2-8*) Briarcliff NY.

— Powers 1995 Northeast Region Golf Guide. 1994. pap. 16.95 (*0-9631658-3-6*) Briarcliff NY.

— Powers 1996 Northeast Region Golf Guide. 1995. pap. text 16.95 (*0-9631658-4-4*) Briarcliff NY.

Briassoulis, Helen & Van Der Straaten, Jan, eds. Tourism & the Environment: Regional, Economic, & Policy Issues. LC 92-31871. (Environment & Assessment Ser.: Vol. 2). 176p. (C). 1992. text 141.50 (*0-7923-1986-9*) Kluwer Academic.

Briat, Martine, et al, eds. Legal Aspects of International Art Trade: Aspects Juridiques Du Commerce International De l'Art. LC 93-32026. (International Sales of Works of Art - la Vente Internationale d'Oeuvres d'Art Ser.: Vol. 4). 1993. 109.00 (*90-6544-691-5*) Kluwer Law Intl.

Briat, Martine, et al. Legal Aspects of International Trade in Art: Les Aspects Juridiques du Commerce International de l'Art. LC 96-36288. (ENG & FRE.). 1996. pap. 150.00 (*90-411-0295-7*) Kluwer Law Intl.

Briat, Rene. Rideaux et Tentures. (FRE.). 1993. lib. bdg. 195.00 (*0-7859-3620-3*, 270590322) Fr & Eur.

Briatico, Debra, ed. see Beecher, Margaret.

Briaud, Jean-Louis. The Pressuremeter. (Illus.). 336p. (C). 1992. text 128.00 (*90-6191-125-7*, Pub. by A A Balkema) Ashgate Pub Co.

Briaud, Jean-Louis, ed. Foundations for Transmission Line Towers. 192p. 1987. 21.00 (*0-87262-588-5*) Am Soc Civil Eng.

Briaud, Jean-Louis & Audibert, M. E., eds. The Pressuremeter & Its Marine Applications: Second International Symposium, STP 950. LC 86-3337. (Special Technical Publication Ser.). (Illus.). 505p. 1986. text 64.00 (*0-8031-0454-5*, STP950) ASTM.

Briaud, Jean-Louis & Gibbens, Robert, eds. Predicted & Measured Behavior of Five Spread Footings on Sand: Proceedings of a Prediction Symposium Sponsored by the Federal Highway Administration at the Occasion of the Settlement of the '94 ASCE Conference at Texas A&M University, June 16-18, 1994. LC 94-19960. (Geotechnical Special Publications: No. 41). 260p. 1994. 32.00 (*0-7844-0025-3*) Am Soc Civil Eng.

Briaudo, Richard J. & Macintosh, Jeffrey G. Competitive Industrial Development in the Age of Information: The Role of Co-Operation in the Technology Sector. LC 98-26660. 1999. 99.99 (*0-415-17854-1*) Routledge.

Briazack, Norman J. & Mennick, Simon. The UFO Guidebook. 1978. pap. 4.95 (*0-8065-0763-2*, Citadel Pr) Carol Pub Group.

Briber, R. M., et al, eds. Morphological Control in Multiphase Polymer Mixtures. LC 97-6800. (Materials Research Society Symposium Proceedings Ser.: No. 461). 241p. 1997. text 75.00 (*1-55899-365-7*) Materials Res.

Bricard, Nancy, ed. Ravel/Gaspard de la Nuit. (Alfred Masterworks Ser.). 64p. 1990. pap. 10.95 (*0-7390-0327-5*) Alfred Pub.

Bricaud, Pierre, jt. auth. see Keating, Michael.

Bricault, G. C. Credit Control Letter. 1984. pap. text 77.00 (*0-86010-477-X*) Kluwer Academic.

— Sunday Telegraph Business Finance Directory 1987. Carr, J., ed. (C). 1987. pap. text 167.50 (*0-86010-827-9*, Pub. by Graham & Trotman) Kluwer Academic.

— Sunday Telegraph Business Finance Directory 1987. Carr, J., ed. (C). 1987. lib. bdg. 215.00 (*0-86010-828-7*, Pub. by Graham & Trotman) Kluwer Academic.

Bricault, G. C., ed. Financial Services in Wales, 1991. 3rd rev. ed. 234p. 1991. lib. bdg. 85.00 (*1-85333-559-2*, Pub. by Graham & Trotman) Kluwer Academic.

— Major Transportation Companies of the Arab World, 1987-1988. (C). 1987. pap. text 146.50 (*0-86010-737-X*, Pub. by Graham & Trotman) Kluwer Academic.

Briccetti, Rebecca. Herb Gardens: For Your Garden. 1997. pap. text 12.95 (*1-56799-452-0*, Friedman-Fairfax) M Friedman Pub Grp Inc.

***Briccetti, Rebecca A.** Cold Climate Gardening: How to Select & Grow the Best Vegetables & Ornamental Plants for the North. LC 99-28989. (Taylor's Weekend Gardening Guides Ser.). (Illus.). 128p. 2000. pap. 14.00 (*0-395-86044-X*) HM.

— Sunflowers. (Illus.). 72p. 2000. 6.98 (*1-58663-066-0*) M Friedman Pub Grp Inc.

Briccetti, Rebecca W. Sunflowers. LC 97-13133. 1997. 15.00 (*1-56799-536-5*, Friedman-Fairfax) M Friedman Pub Grp Inc.

Brice, Albert G. Masonry - The Great Gift to Man. 38p. 1995. reprint ed. pap. 7.00 (*1-887560-23-8*) M Poll Pub.

***Brice, Andrew.** E-Commerce Concepts & Practices: A4, Version 4.07. McKenna, Jill, ed. (CIW E-Commerce Professional Track A4 Ser.). (Illus.). 1999. pap. write for info. (*1-58143-093-0*) Prosoft I-net.

— E-Commerce Concepts & Practices: Version 4.07. McKenna, Jill, ed. (CIW E-Commerce Professional Track Ser.). (Illus.). 1999. pap. write for info. (*1-58143-057-4*) Prosoft I-net.

— E-Commerce Strategies & Solutions: Version 3.07. McKenna, Jill, ed. (CIW E-Commerce Professional Track Ser.). (Illus.). 1999. pap. write for info. (*1-58143-058-2*) Prosoft I-net.

Brice-Baker, Janet, jt. auth. see Gopaul-McNicol, Sharon.

***Brice, Carleen.** Lead Me Home: An African American's Guide Through the Grief Journey. LC 99-33771. 192p. 1999. pap. 12.00 (*0-380-79608-2*, Avon Bks) Morrow Avon.

Brice, Carleen. Walk Tall: Affirmations for People of Color. 384p. (Orig.). 1997. reprint ed. pap. 12.00 (*0-8070-2811-8*) Beacon Pr.

Brice, Cecil. A Different World. 49p. 1998. pap. 6.00 (*0-8059-4292-0*) Dorrance.

Brice, Donald. Robin Hood. (Learning & Coloring Bks.). (Illus.). 28p. (J). (gr. k up). 1991. pap. 3.95 (*1-878452-04-5*, Tory Corner) Quincannon.

Brice, Donaly E., jt. auth. see Crouch, Barry A.

Brice, Donna. Step-by-Step Guide for Making Busts & Masks (Cold-Cast Bronze or Plaster/Hydrocal) 2nd ed. LC 82-15703. (Illus.). 52p. 1982. 24.95 (*0-910733-00-7*); pap. 16.95 (*0-910733-01-5*) ICTL Pubns.

Brice-Finch, Jacquelyn, ed. see Spencer-Walters, Tom.

Brice, J., et al. Onion Storage in the Tropics: A Practical Guide to the Methods of Storage & Their Selection. 120p. 1997. pap. 90.00 (*0-85954-487-7*, Pub. by Nat Res Inst) St Mut.

***Brice, James, et al.** Laboratory Studies in Earth History. 7th ed. 288p. (C). 2000. pap. 41.25 (*0-07-366130-9*) McGraw-H Hghr Educ.

Brice, James C., et al. Lab Studies in Earth History. 5th ed. 256p. (C). 1992. text. write for info. (*0-697-12176-3*, WCB McGr Hill) McGraw-H Hghr Educ.

Brice, James S., tr. see Brezinka, Wolfgang.

Brice, Jennifer. The Last Settlers. LC 97-45310. (Emerging Writers in Creative Nonfiction Ser.). (Illus.). 190p. 1998. 24.95 (*0-8207-0290-0*) Duquesne.

Brice, Joseph. The Crowd for Christ. 1993. reprint ed. pap. 8.99 (*0-88019-303-4*) Schmul Pub Co.

— Pentecost. 1983. 9.99 (*0-88019-092-2*) Schmul Pub Co.

Brice, Joseph. The Shadow of Cliff College. pap. 5.99 (*0-88019-172-4*) Schmul Pub Co.

Brice, Nancy, ed. see Bachay, Judith.

***Brice, R. Andrew.** E-Commerce Concepts & Practices: A4, Version 3.07. McKenna, Jill, ed. (CIW E-Commerce Professional Track A4 Ser.). (Illus.). 1999. pap. write for info. (*1-58143-094-9*) Prosoft I-net.

***Brice, R. Andrew & Koenen, Frank.** Advanced Internet System Management: A4, Version 2.07. McKenna, Jill & Oberman, David, eds. (CIW Server Administrator Track A4 Ser.). (Illus.). 1999. pap. write for info. (*1-58143-084-1*) Prosoft I-net.

— Advanced Internet System Management: Version 2.07. McKenna, Jill & Oberman, David, eds. (CIW Server Administrator Track Ser.). (Illus.). 1999. pap. write for info. (*1-58143-048-5*) Prosoft I-net.

Brice, Raphaelle. From Oil to Plastic. Matthews, Sarah, tr. from FRE. LC 87-31753. (Illus.). 38p. (J). (gr. k-5). 1991. 5.95 (*0-944589-17-0*, 170) Young Discovery Lib.

— Rice: The Little Grain That Feeds the World. Bogard, Vicki, tr. from FRE. LC 90-50775. (Young Discovery Library). (Illus.). 38p. (J). (gr. k-5). 1991. 5.95 (*0-944589-30-8*, 308) Young Discovery Lib.

Brice, Regina A. A Martial Artist's Guide to American Law. (Illus.). 537p. 1994. ring bd. 65.00 (*0-9643872-1-2*) Sanshin Consulting.

Brice, Richard. Multimedia & the Virtual Reality Engineering. LC 97-219489. 320p. 1997. text 48.95 (*0-7506-2987-8*) Buttrwrth-Heinemann.

***Brice, Richard.** Music Engineering. 416p. 2001. pap. 37.95 (*0-7506-5040-0*, Newnes) Buttrwrth-Heinemann.

— Newnes Guide to Digital Television. 258p. 2000. 49.95 (*0-7506-4586-5*, Newnes) Buttrwrth-Heinemann.

Brice, Richard. The Technology of Music & Recording. LC 99-179458. (Illus.). 368p. 1998. pap. text 34.95 (*0-7506-3903-2*, Newnes) Buttrwrth-Heinemann.

***Brice, Tracy & De Vos, Robert, eds.** Fuel Finder: Guide to North American Diesel Locations. 5th rev. ed. (Illus.). 1999. pap. 9.95 (*1-890141-07-0*, FF99) TR Info Pubs.

— The RVer's Friend: National Diesel & Parking Directory. 5th rev. ed. (Illus.). 1999. pap. 9.95 (*1-890141-08-9*, RV99) TR Info Pubs.

— The Trucker's Friend: National Truck Stop Directory. annuals 13th rev. ed. (Illus.). 1999. pap. 9.95 (*1-890141-06-2*, TF99) TR Info Pubs.

Brice, Virginia L., ed. see Smith, Bernard T.

Brice, W. Inscriptions in the Minoan Linear Script of Class A. (Illus.). 51p. 1961. reprint ed. 20.00 (*0-85431-188-2*, Pub. by Soc Antiquaries) David Brown.

Brice, Wallace A. History of Fort Wayne: From the Earliest Known Accounts to the Present Period (1868), with a Sketch of the Life of General Anthony Wayne; Together with Short Sketches of...the Early Pioneer Settlers of Ft. Wayne. (Illus.). 1997. reprint ed. lib. bdg. 42.50 (*0-8328-6651-2*) Higginson Bk Co.

Brice, William. William Brice: Notations, 1982. (Illus.). 120p. 1984. 45.00 (*0-942642-06-6*) Twelvetrees Pr.

Brice, William C., ed. Europa: Studien zur Geschichte und Epigraphik der fruehen Aegaeis Festschrift fuer Ernst Grumach. (GER., Illus.). (C). 1967. 150.00 (*3-11-005182-6*) De Gruyter.

Brice, William R. Cornell Geology Through the Years. 240p. 1989. write for info. (*0-918531-03-9*) Cornell Coll Eng.

Briceno, R. Daniel & Eberhard, William G. The Functional Morphology of Male Cerci & Associated Characters in 13 Species of Tropical Earwigs: Dermaptera: Forficulidae, Labiidae, Carcinophoridae, Pygidicranidae. LC 94-1220. (Smithsonian Contributions to Zoology Ser.: Vol. 555). 67p. 1995. reprint ed. pap. 30.00 (*0-608-00507-X*, 206132700008) Bks Demand.

Briceno, Salvano & Pitt, David, eds. New Ideas in Environmental Education. 256p. 1988. lib. bdg. 59.00 (*0-7099-5042-X*, Pub. by C Helm) Routldge.

Brich, Steve & Knops, Bob. Fishing the Mississippi Pools 5A, 6, 7, 8. (Mississippi River Ser.). (Illus.). 88p. 1990. pap. 9.95 (*0-939314-10-X*) Fishing Hot.

Brich, Steve, et al. Chicagoland's Top 30 Fishing Trips. LC 94-78416. (Illus.). 1994. write for info. (*0-939314-53-3*) Fishing Hot.

Brich, Steve, jt. auth. see Laasch, Jack.

***Brichacek, Lisa & Saunders County Historical Society Staff.** Images of Saunders County: A Pictorial History. LC 00-31560. (Illus.). 2000. write for info. (*1-57864-109-8*) Donning Co.

Brichant, Collette D. French Grammar: The Key to Reading. (Orig.). (C). 1968. pap. text 27.40 (*0-13-331264-X*) P-H.

Brichard, Pierre. Book of Cichlids & All Other Fishes of Lake Tanganyika. (Illus.). 512p. 1989. 139.95 (*0-86622-667-2*, TS-116) TFH Pubns.

Brichtn, Ira, ed. see Shellenberger, Martin B.

Brichto, Stanley. Jewish Life, Jewish Humor, 1. 1999. 22.95 (*1-56649-020-0*) Welcome Rain.

Brichto, Herbert C. The Names of God: Poetic Readings of Biblical Beginnings. LC 96-10381. (Illus.). 480p. 1998. text 65.00 (*0-19-510965-1*) OUP.

***Brichto, Mira Pollak.** The God Around Us Vol. 2: Unending Wonder. (Illus.). (J). 2000. 12.95 (*0-8074-0738-0*) UAHC.

***Brichto, Sidney.** Jewish Life, Jewish Humor: A Guide to Jews & Jewish Life. (Illus.). 188p. 1999. 22.95 (*1-929074-01-8*, Benford Bks) IBM Ltd.

Bricianer, Serge. Pannekoek & the Workers' Councils. Carroll, Malachy, tr. from FRE. LC 78-50978. (C). 1978. 28.00 (*0-914386-17-4*) Telos Pr.

Brick. Age of Contradiction: American Thought & Culture in the 1960's. 1997. pap. 15.95 (*0-8057-9081-0*, Twyne) Mac Lib Ref.

— Age of Contradiction: American Thought & Culture in the 1960's. LC 98-18965. 242p. 1998. 29.95 (*0-8057-9080-2*, Twyne) Mac Lib Ref.

Brick, Andrew, et al. Mongolia: An Assessment of the Election to the Great People's Hural. ii, 22p. 1992. pap. 4.00 (*1-879720-68-X*) Intl Fndt Elect.

Brick, Andy. The Global Songbook. (Illus.). 72p. (Orig.). 1995. pap. 21.95 incl. audio compact disk (*1-57623-262-X*, BMR05121CD); pap. 19.95 incl. audio (*1-57623-263-8*, BMR05121AT) Wrner Bros.

Brick, Anita R. How to Market Yourself for Career Success: Secrets for Positioning Yourself. 1997. pap. text 15.95 (*0-02-861493-3*) Macmillan.

Brick, Douglas, tr. see Borch-Jacobsen, Mikkel.

Brick, Douglas, tr. see Henry, Michel.

Brick, Edgar W. Helping Employees Plan for Financial Security: An Approach to Educating the Entire Work Force. (Building Blocks Ser.: Vol. 21). (Illus.). 16p. (Orig.). 1995. pap. 24.95 (*1-57963-024-3*, A0041) Am Compensation.

Brick, Gary. Ace's Exambuster Japanese Study. 2nd ed. Burchard, Elizabeth R., ed. (Exambusters Ser.). 384p. (YA). (gr. 7 up). 2000. reprint ed. pap. 10.95 (*1-881374-96-3*, Exambusters) Ace Acad.

***Brick, Howard.** Age of Contradiction: American Thought & Culture in the 1960s. 2000. reprint ed. pap. 16.95 (*0-8014-8700-5*) Cornell U Pr.

Brick, Howard. Daniel Bell & the Decline of Intellectual Radicalism: Social Theory & Political Reconciliation in the 1940s. LC 85-40757. (History of American Thought & Culture Ser.). 296p. 1986. text 35.00 (*0-299-10550-4*) U of Wis Pr.

Brick, J. Michael. Adjusting for Coverage Bias Using Telephone Service Interruption Data. 36p. 1996. pap. 5.00 (*0-16-048917-2*) USGPO.

— Feasibility of Conducting Followup Surveys in the National Household Education Survey. 27p. 1997. pap. 4.25 (*0-16-049082-0*) USGPO.

Brick, James W., jt. auth. see Adams, Walter.

Brick, Jennie, jt. auth. see Brick, Jim.

Brick, Jim. For the Love of Carmel, Monterey & Pacific Grove: Scenic Address Book. 64p. 1990. 9.95 (*1-878525-01-8*) Visual Impressions.

— For the Love of San Francisco: Scenic Address Book. (Illus.). 64p. 1991. 10.95 (*1-878525-03-4*) Visual Impressions.

Brick, Jim & Brick, Jennie. For the Love of Carmel, Monterey & Pacific Grove: Scenic Natural Cookbook. 64p. 1990. 9.95 (*1-878525-00-X*) Visual Impressions.

— For the Love of San Francisco: A Scenic Natural Cookbook. (Illus.). 64p. 1993. 10.95 (*1-878525-02-6*) Visual Impressions.

Brick, John & Erickson, Carlton K. Drugs, the Brain, & Behavior: The Pharmacology of Abuse & Dependence. LC 97-39232. xv, 186 p. 1998. 49.95 (*0-7890-0274-4*, Hawrth Medical) Haworth Pr.

— Drugs, the Brain, & Behavior: The Pharmacology of Abuse & Dependence. LC 97-39232. 1998. pap. 19.95 (*0-7890-0275-2*, Hawrth Medical) Haworth Pr.

Brick, Lynne G. Fitness Aerobics. LC 95-49231. (Fitness Spectrum Ser.). (Illus.). 176p. (Orig.). 1996. pap. 14.95 (*0-87322-471-X*, PBRI0471) Human Kinetics.

Brick, M. L., ed. see Krieger, Leonard.

Brick, Peggy. Bodies, Birth & Babies: Sexuality Education in Early Childhood Programs. (Illus.). 38p. 1989. 15.00 (*0-9609366-9-6*) Plan Parenthood.

— The New Teaching Safer Sex. 129p. 1998. 25.00 (*0-9609366-1-0*) Plan Parenthood.

— Positive Images: Teaching Abstinence, Contraception & Sexual Health. 158p. 1995. 25.00 (*0-9609366-5-3*) Plan Parenthood.

Brick, Peggy, et al. Healthy Foundations - The Teacher's Book: Responding to Young Children's Questions & Behaviors. (Illus.). 23p. 1993. 5.00 (*0-9609366-7-X*) Plan Parenthood.

Brick, Peggy, jt. auth. see Montfort, Sue.

***Brick, Philip, et al, eds.** Across the Great Divide: Explorations in Collaborative Conservation & the American West. (Illus.). 256p. 2000. 50.00 (*1-55963-810-9*, Shearwater Bks); pap. 25.00 (*1-55963-811-7*, Shearwater Bks) Island Pr.

Brick, Philip & Cawley, R. McGreggor, eds. A Wolf in the Garden: The Land Rights Movement & the Renewal of the American Environmental Movement. LC 96-433. 334p. 1996. pap. text 25.95 (*0-8476-8185-8*) Rowman.

— A Wolf in the Garden: The Land Rights Movement & the Renewal of the American Environmental Movement. LC 96-433. 334p. (C). 1996. lib. bdg. 66.00 (*0-8476-8184-X*) Rowman.

Brick, R. M., et al. Structure & Properties of Engineering Materials. 4th ed. (McGraw-Hill Series in Materials Science & Engineering). (Illus.). 512p. (C). 1977. 103.44 (*0-07-007721-5*) McGraw.

Bricke, John. Hume's Philosophy of Mind. LC 79-43025. 184p. 1980. reprint ed. pap. 57.10 (*0-7837-8577-1*, 204939200011) Bks Demand.

Bricke, John. Mind & Morality: An Examination of Hume's Moral Psychology. LC 95-46828. 274p. (C). 1996. text 45.00 (*0-19-823589-5*, Clarendon Pr) OUP.

***Bricke, John.** Mind & Morality: An Examination of Hume's Moral Psychology. 2000. pap. 19.95 (*0-19-825011-8*) OUP.

Brickell, Christopher. A to Z Encyclopedia of Garden Plants. 1997. 479.00 (*0-7894-3203-X*) DK Pub Inc.

***Brickell, Christopher.** Garden Plants: The Expert Guide to over 500 Plants for All Seasons. (Illus.). 2000. pap. 24.95 (*0-7063-7851-2*) WrLock.

Brickell, Christopher. Pruning & Training LC 98-32292. (Eyewitness Garden Handbks.). 160p. 1999. 18.95 (*0-7894-4148-9*) DK Pub Inc.

— To Z Encyclopedia of Garden Plants. 1997. 479.00 (*0-7894-2339-1*) DK Pub Inc.

Brickell, Christopher, et al, eds. The American Horticultural Society Encyclopedia of Gardening: The Definitive Practical Guide to Gardening Techniques, Planning & Maintenance. LC 93-3042. (AHS Practical Guides Ser.). (Illus.). 648p. 1993. 59.95 (*1-56458-291-4*) DK Pub Inc.

Brickell, Christopher & Joyce, David. The American Horticultural Society Pruning & Training: A Fully Illustrated Plant-by-Plant Manual. LC 96-1086. (AHS Practical Guides Ser.). 336p. 1996. 34.95 (*1-56458-331-7*) DK Pub Inc.

Brickell, Christopher & Zuk, Judy D., eds. American Horticultural Society A to Z Encyclopedia of Garden Plants. LC 97-10941. (Illus.). 1096p. 1997. 79.95 (*0-7894-1943-2*) DK Pub Inc.

Brickell, Christopher D., ed. The American Horticultural Society Encyclopedia of Garden Plants. (Illus.). 608p. 1989. 59.95 (*0-02-557920-7*) Macmillan.

Brickell, Ernest F., ed. Advances in Cryptology - CRYPTO '92: Twelfth Annual International Cryptology Conference, Santa Barbara, California, U. S. A., August 16-20, 1992, Proceedings. LC 93-37164. (Lecture Notes in Computer Science Ser.: Vol. 740). 1993. 87.95 (*0-387-57340-2*) Spr-Verlag.

Brickell, G. Project Management for Product Development. Date not set. write for info. (*0-8247-9931-3*) Dekker.

Brickell, G. & Mathews, P. Photoelectric Sensors & Controls. 2nd ed. (Mechanical Engineering Ser.). Date not set. write for info. (*0-8247-9919-4*) Dekker.

Brickell, Henry M., jt. auth. see Aslanian, Carol B.

Brickell, Sean, jt. auth. see Woodall, Allen.

***Brickenkamp.** D2 Test Manual: Test of Attention. 8th ed. 1998. 45.00 (*0-88937-172-5*) Hogrefe & Huber Pubs.

Bricker, Audrey, ed. see Greenberg, Morrie.

Bricker, David C. Classroom Life as Civic Education: Individual Achievement & Student Cooperation in Schools. (Professional Ethics in Education Ser.: No. 2). 152p. 1989. text 22.00 (*0-8077-2959-0*) Tchrs Coll.

Bricker, Diane, jt. auth. see Squires, Jane.

Bricker, Diane B. & Pretti-Frontczak, Kristie, eds. Assessment, Evaluation, & Programming System (AEPS) Measurement for 3 to 6 Years, Vol. 3. (Assessment, Evaluation & Program System Ser.). (Illus.). 560p. (Orig.). 1996. spiral bd. 57.00 (*1-55766-187-1*, 1871) P H Brookes.

Bricker, Diane D. AEPS Child Progress Record, 3-6 Years. (Illus.). 6p. (Orig.). 1996. 21.00 (*1-55766-251-7*, 2517) P H Brookes.

— AEPS Data Recording Forms, Three to Six Years. 36p. (Orig.). 1996. 24.00 (*1-55766-249-5*, 2495) P H Brookes.

— AEPS Family Report, 3-6 Years. (Illus.). 28p. (Orig.). 1996. 23.00 (*1-55766-250-9*, 2509) P H Brookes.

***Bricker, Diane D.** Ages & Stages Questionnaires: A Parent-Completed, Child-Monitoring System. 2nd ed. LC 98-43538. 1999. text 165.00 (*1-55766-368-8*) P H Brookes.

Bricker, Diane D., ed. Assessment, Evaluation, & Programming System for Infants & Children, Vol. 1: Measurement for Birth to Three Years. 352p. (C). 1992. spiral bd. 43.95 (*1-55766-095-6*) P H Brookes.

— Assessment, Evaluation, & Programming System for Infants & Children, Vol. 1: Measurement for Birth to Three Years, AEPS Child Progress Record, 02/1994, pkg. of 30. 352p. (C). 1994. lp 18.00 (*1-55766-165-0*) P H Brookes.

— Assessment, Evaluation, & Programming System for Infants & Children, Vol. 1: Measurement for Birth to Three Years, Data Recording Forms, pkg. of 10. 36p. (C). 1992. 23.00 (*1-55766-097-2*) P H Brookes.

— Assessment, Evaluation, & Programming System for Infants & Children, Vol. 1: Measurement for Birth to Three Years, Family Report, pkg. of 10. 352p. (C). 1993. 17.00 (*1-55766-099-9*) P H Brookes.

Bricker, Diane D. & Wilderstrom, Anne. Preparing Personnel to Work with Infants & Young Children & Their Families: A Team Approach. LC 95-39289. 1996. 45.00 (*1-55766-237-1*) P H Brookes.

Bricker, Diane D., et al. An Activity-Based Approach to Early Intervention. 1995. VHS 45.00 (*1-55766-186-3*) P H Brookes.

— An Activity-Based Approach to Early Intervention. 2nd ed. LC 98-24852. 1998. 34.00 (*1-55766-351-3*) P H Brookes.

— Activity-Based Intervention & an Activity-Based Approach to Early Intervention. (Illus.). 1995. 56.00 incl. VHS (*0-614-03674-7*) P H Brookes.

***Bricker, Diane D., et al.** Ages & Stages Questionnaires: A Parent-Completed, Child-Monitoring System. 2nd ed. LC 98-43538. 1999. text 165.00 (*1-55766-369-6*) P H Brookes.

Bricker, Diane D., et al. The Complete ASQ System. 1995. boxed set 135.00 (*0-614-02521-4*, SQU) P H Brookes.

Bricker, Diane D., jt. auth. see Twombly, Liz.

Bricker, Douglas, jt. auth. see Gossel, Thomas A.

Bricker, George H., jt. ed. see Yrigoyen, Charles, Jr.

Bricker, Harvey M., Jr. & David, Nicholas. Excavation of the Abri Pataud, Les Eyzies (Dordogne) The Perigordian VI (Level 3) Assemblage. Movius, Hallam L., Jr., ed. LC 82-62718. (American School of Prehistoric Research Bulletins Ser.: No. 34). (Illus.). 110p. 1984. pap. 28.00 (*0-87365-537-0*) Peabody Harvard.

Bricker, Herschel L., ed. Our Theatre Today. LC 79-128213. (Essay Index Reprint Ser.). 1977. 35.95 (*0-8369-1823-1*) Ayer.

Bricker-Jenkins, Mary & Hooyman, Nancy R., eds. Not for Women Only: Social Work Practice for a Feminist Future. LC 85-28532. 127p. 1986. 18.95 (*0-87101-131-X*) Natl Assn Soc Wkrs.

Bricker-Jenkins, Mary, et al. Feminist Social Work Practice in Clinical Settings. (Sourcebooks for the Human Services Ser.: Vol. 19). (Illus.). 320p. 1991. text 56.00 (*0-8039-3625-7*); pap. text 26.00 (*0-8039-3626-5*) Sage.

***Bricker, Kathryn.** Traditional Aerobics. American Council on Exercise Staff, ed. (Illus.). 75p. 2000. pap. 14.95 (*1-890720-08-9*) Am Coun Exer.

Bricker, Owen P., ed. Carbonate Cements. LC 70-123524. (Johns Hopkins University Studies in Geology: No. 19). (Illus.). 398p. reprint ed. pap. 123.40 (*0-608-04057-6*, 206479300011) Bks Demand.

Bricker, Owen P. & Teasley, John I., eds. Geological Aspects of Acid Deposition. (Acid Precipitation Ser.: Vol. 7). 160p. 1984. 79.95 (*0-250-40572-5*) Buttrwrth-Heinemann.

Bricker, Phillip & Hughes, R. I., eds. Philosophical Perspectives on Newtonian Science. LC 89-29465. (Johns Hopkins Series on the History & Philosophy of Science). 250p. 1990. 37.50 (*0-262-02301-6*, Bradford Bks) MIT Pr.

Bricker, Richard W. Wooden Ships from Texas: A World War I Saga. LC 98-13742. (Centennial Series of the Association of Former Students, Texas A&M University: Vol. 77). (Illus.). 272p. 1998. 29.95 (*0-89096-827-6*) Tex A&M Univ Pr.

Bricker, Sandra D. Challenger. Parker, Liz, ed. (Take Ten Bks.). 47p. (YA). (gr. 6-12). 1993. pap. text 3.95 (*1-56254-096-3*) Saddleback Pubns.

***Bricker, Sandra D.** Challenger. rev. ed. (Take Ten Ser.). (Illus.). 47p. (YA). (gr. 4-12). 1999. pap. 3.95 (*1-58659-021-9*) Artesian.

Bricker, Sandra D. Freeze Frame. Parker, Liz, ed. (Take Ten Bks.). (Illus.). 45p. (J). (gr. 6-12). 1992. pap. text 3.95 (*1-56254-050-5*) Saddleback Pubns.

***Bricker, Sandra D.** Freeze Frame. rev. ed. (Take Ten Ser.). (Illus.). 45p. (YA). (gr. 4-12). 1999. pap. 3.95 (*1-58659-005-7*) Artesian.

Bricker, Steven L., et al. Oral Diagnosis, Oral Medicine & Treatment Planning. 2nd ed. (Illus.). 854p. 1994. pap. text 59.95 (*0-8121-1605-4*) Lppncott W & W.

Bricker, Victoria R. El Cristo Indegena, el Rey Nativo. (SPA.). pap. 16.99 (*968-16-3161-7*, Pub. by Fondo) Continental Bk.

— A Grammar of Mayan Hieroglyphs. LC 85-60766. (Publications: No. 56). 214p. 1986. 30.00 (*0-939238-86-1*) Tulane MARI.

— The Indian Christ, the Indian King: The Historical Substrate of Maya Myth & Ritual. LC 81-7436. (Illus.). 382p. 1981. text 45.00 (*0-292-73824-2*) U of Tex Pr.

— The Indian Christ, the Indian King: The Historical

B

Substrate of Maya Myth & Ritual. LC 81-7436. (Illus.). 382p. reprint ed. pap. 118.50 (0-608-08648-7, 2069170003) Bks Demand.
— A Morpheme Concordance of the Book of Chilam Balam of Chumayel. LC 89-9359. (Publications: No. 59). viii, 638p. 1991. 45.00 (0-939238-90-X) Tulane MARI.
— A Morpheme Concordance of the Book of Chilam Balam of Tizimin. LC 89-9360. (Publications: No. 58). viii, 483p. 1991. 35.00 (0-939238-89-6) Tulane MARI.
— Ritual Humor in Highland Chiapas. LC 73-6501. (Texas Pan-American Ser.). 293p. 1973. reprint ed. pap. 83.60 (0-8357-7728-6, 2036085) Bks Demand.
Bricker, Victoria R., ed. Supplement to the Handbook of Middle American Indians Vol. 5: Epigraphy. LC 91-14769. (Illus.). 203p. 1992. text 40.00 (0-292-77650-0) U of Tex Pr.
Bricker, Victoria R. & Gossen, Gary H., eds. Ethnographic Encounters in Southern Mesoamerica: Essays in Honor of Evon Zartman Voght, Jr. (Studies on Culture & Society: Vol. 3). (Illus.). 366p. (Orig.). 1989. pap. text 25.00 (0-942041-12-7) Univ Albany IFMS.
Bricker, Victoria R. & Vail, Gabrielle, eds. Papers on the Madrid Codex. LC 97-37003. (Publication Ser.: No. 64). 1997. write for info. (0-939238-94-2) Tulane MARI.
Bricker, Victoria R., et al. A Dictionary of the Maya Language: As Spoken in Hocaba, Yucatan. LC 98-25171. (Illus.). 416p. 1998. pap. 65.00 (0-87480-569-4) U of Utah Pr.
Brickey, Kathleen F. Corporate & White Collar Crime: Cases & Materials. LC 90-60591. xxx, 663 p. 1990. write for info. (0-316-10849-9, Aspen Law & Bus) Aspen Pub.
— Corporate & White Collar Crime: Cases & Materials. 2nd ed. 864p. 1995. teacher ed. write for info. (0-316-11029-9, 10299) Aspen Law.
Brickey, Kathleen F. Corporate & White Collar Crime: Cases & Materials: With Teacher's Manual. 2nd ed. 864p. 1995. teacher ed. write for info. (0-7355-0623-X, 0623X) Panel Pubs.
Brickey, Kathleen F. Corporate & White Collar Crime: Selected Statutes: 1997 Edition. LC 97-179069. 200p. 1997. pap. text 16.95 (1-56706-574-0, 65740) Panel Pubs.
Brickey, Kathy. Conflict of Law. 4th ed. 1024p. 1995. 53.00 (0-316-10883-9, Aspen Law & Bus) Aspen Pub.
— Corporate Criminal Liability, 3 vols. LC 84-9465. 1990. 350.00 (0-685-09046-9) West Group.
— Corporate Criminal Liability, 3 vols. annuals 1990. suppl. ed. write for info. (0-318-58076-4) West Group.
— White Collar Crime. 2nd ed. 864p. 1995. 52.00 (0-316-10880-4) Little.
Brickey, Louise. Pouche: Assistant to the Easter Bunny. rev. ed. (Illus.). 20p. (J). (gr. k-3). 1991. bds. write for info. (0-9624767-1-4) Cottontail Creations.
— Pouche: The Assistant to the Easter Bunny. rev. ed. (Illus.). 36p. (J). (gr. k-3). 1989. reprint ed. write for info. (0-9624767-0-6) Cottontail Creations.
***Brickey, Michael P.** Defy Aging: Develop the Mental & Emotional Vitality to Live Longer, Healthier & Happier Than You Ever Imagined. LC 00-91404. (Illus.). 395p. 2000. 24.95 (0-9701555-0-6) New Resour.
Brickham, Richard. The Fate of the Dead: Studies on Jewish & Christian Apocalypses. LC 98-16848. (Supplements to Novum Testamentum Ser.). xvi, 425p. 1998. write for info. (90-04-11203-0) Brill Academic Pubs.
Brickhill, Paul. The Great Escape. 21.95 (0-8488-1359-6) Amereon Ltd.
Brickhill, Paul. The Great Escape. 224p. 1986. mass mkt. 5.99 (0-449-21068-5) Fawcett.
Brickhill, Paul. The Great Escape. (Bulls-Eye Ser.). (C). 1981. 35.00 (0-09-141021-5) St Mut.
— The Great Escape. 1998. lib. bdg. 21.95 (1-56723-024-5) Yestermorrow.
— The Great Escape. large type ed. LC 96-5901. 359 p. 1996. 22.95 (0-7838-1816-5, G K Hall Lrg Type) Mac Lib Ref.
Brickhill, Paul. The Great Escape. 256p. 1993. reprint ed. lib. bdg. 37.95 (1-56849-188-3) Buccaneer Bks.
— Reach for the Sky. (Illus.). 346p. 1992. reprint ed. lib. bdg. 37.95 (0-89966-910-7) Buccaneer Bks.
Brickhouse, Jack, et al. Thanks for Listening! LC 86-2103. (Illus.). 264p. 1995. pap. 12.95 (0-912083-92-1) Diamond Communications.
Brickhouse, John. Business Math Using Calculator. Saris, Eleanor M., ed. 105p. (C). 1989. text 14.95 (0-318-42434-7) EIT VA.
Brickhouse, Thomas C. & Smith, Nicholas D. Plato's Socrates. 256p. 1996. reprint ed. pap. 18.95 (0-19-510111-1) OUP.
— Socrates on Trial. 350p. 1989. pap. text 17.95 (0-691-01900-2, Pub. by Princeton U Pr) Cal Prin Full Svc.
Brickhouse, Thomas C., jt. auth. see Smith, Nicholas D.
Brickley. Managerial Economics & Organizational Architecture. (C). 1996. pap., student ed. 23.75 (0-256-17232-3) McGraw.
Brickley, James, et al. Managerial Economics & Organizational Architecture. 576p. (C). 1996. text 66.50 (0-256-15825-8, Irwn McGrw-H) McGrw-H Hghr Educ.
— Organizational Architecture: A Managerial Economics Approach. 448p. (C). 1995. text 21.95 (0-256-20224-9, Irwn McGrw-H) McGrw-H Hghr Educ.
***Brickley, James A., et al.** Managerial Economics & Organizational Architecture. LC 00-36959. 2001. write for info. (0-07-231447-8) McGraw.
Brickley, James E. The Dear Old Book of Hattie Thomas. LC 83-90777. 247p. 1983. 21.95 (0-9611514-0-4) J E Brickley.
Brickley, Susan G., jt. ed. see Henry, Marcia K.
Bricklin. Pets Letters to God pap. 49.75 (1-57954-223-9) Rodale Pr Inc.
Bricklin, Barry. Custody Evaluation: Problems & Solutions. LC 95-32936. 304p. 1995. text 47.95 (0-87630-775-6) Brunner-Mazel.
Bricklin, Mark. Best of Prevention. LC 96-47050. (Illus.). 320p. 1997. pap. 12.95 (0-87596-419-2) Rodale Pr Inc.
— Lose Weight Naturally. 374p. 1993. 9.98 (1-56731-027-3, MJF Bks) Fine Comms.
***Bricklin, Mark.** Pets Letters to God. LC 99-35543. 96p. 1999. 9.95 (1-57954-208-5) Rodale Pr Inc.
Bricklin, Mark. The Practical Encyclopedia of Natural Healing. 1992. 10.98 (1-56731-005-2, MJF Bks) Fine Comms.
— The Practical Encyclopedia of Natural Healing. (Illus.). 592p. 1990. pap. 14.95 (0-14-013864-1, Penguin Bks) Viking Penguin.
Bricklin, Mark & Editors of Pets: Part of the Family Magazine. Pets: Part of the Family: The Total Care Guide for All the Pets in Your Life. (Illus.). 1999. 27.95 (1-57954-125-9) Rodale Pr Inc.
Bricklin, Mark & Konner, Linda. Prevention's Your Perfect Weight: Diet-Free Weight Loss Method Developed by the World's Leading Health Magazine. LC 94-5318. 1995. text 27.95 (0-87596-229-7) Rodale Pr Inc.
— Prevention's Your Perfect Weight: Diet-Free Weight Loss Method Developed by the World's Leading Health Magazine. LC 94-5318. 1997. pap. 14.95 (0-87596-452-4) Rodale Pr Inc.
Bricklin, Mark & Maleskey, Gale. Prevention's Fight Fat: The Best New Ways to Cut Fat--from Your Plate & Your Waist. LC 96-27692. 1997. pap. 9.95 (0-87596-420-6) Rodale Pr Inc.
Bricklin, Mark & Pets: Part of the Family Magazine Editors. Pets: Part of the Family: The Total Care Guide for All the Pets in Your Life. LC 98-32094. (Illus.). 1999. pap. 16.95 (1-57954-136-4) Rodale Pr Inc.
Bricklin, Mark, jt. auth. see Prevention Magazine Editors.
Brickman, Brenda, jt. auth. see Joyce, Peter.
Brickman, Danette, jt. auth. see Johnson, Charles A.
Brickman, Hal. The Thin Book: Hypnotherapy Trance Scripts for Weight Mangement. 108p. 2000. pap. 24.95 (1-891944-09-6) Zeig Tucker.
Brickman, Julie. What Birds Can Only Whisper: A Novel about Recovered Memory & Surviving Sexual Abuse. LC 98-138679. 320p. 1997. pap. text 14.95 (0-88801-214-4, Pub. by Turnstone Pr) Genl Dist Srvs.
Brickman, L. A Mathematical Introduction to Linear Programming & Game Theory. (Undergraduate Texts in Mathematics Ser.). (Illus.). ix, 130p. 1989. 42.95 (0-387-96931-4) Spr-Verlag.
Brickman, Nancy A. Supporting Young Learners 2: Ideas for Child Care Providers & Teachers. LC 96-18555. 328p. 1996. 25.95 (1-57379-006-0, P1105) High-Scope.
Brickman, Nancy A. & Taylor, Lynn S., eds. Supporting Young Learners 1: Ideas for Preschool & Day Care Providers. LC 91-21317. 314p. 1991. pap. 25.95 (0-929816-34-X, P1083) High-Scope.
Brickman, Patti L., ed. How to Own & Operate a Card & Gift Shop. 260p. 1988. pap. text 50.00 (0-938369-05-9) Greeting Card Assn.
Brickman, Ronald, et al. Controlling Chemicals: The Politics of Regulation in Europe & the United States. LC 84-29340. 336p. (C). 1985. 45.00 (0-8014-1677-9) Cornell U Pr.
— Controlling Chemicals: The Politics of Regulation in Europe & the United States. LC 84-29340. 344p. reprint ed. pap. 106.70 (0-608-20876-0, 207197500003) Bks Demand.
***Brickman, Sarah.** The Reflection of Memories. 1999. pap. write for info. (1-58235-247-X) Watermrk Pr.
Brickman, Twyla. Leading Cell Worship. 1997. ring bd. 79.95 incl. Beta (1-880828-01-4) Touch Pubns.
Brickman, William W. Educational Roots & Routes in Western Europe. LC 85-70176. viii, 404p. (Orig.). 1986. pap. 22.00 (0-943694-01-9) Emeritus Inc.
Brickman, William W. & Lehrer, Stanley, eds. Religion, Government & Education. LC 77-24684. 292p. 1977. reprint ed. lib. bdg. 65.00 (0-8371-9749-X, BRRG, Greenwood Pr) Greenwood.
Brickman, William W. & Zepper, John T. Russian & Soviet Education, 1731-1989: A Multilingual Annotated Bibliography. LC 91-45874. (Reference Books in International Education: Vol. 9). 556p. 1992. text 98.00 (0-8240-9052-7, SS200) Garland.
Brickman, William W., jt. ed. see Cordasco, Francesco.
***Brickner.** Electrician's Portable Handbook. 1999. 49.95 (0-07-134167-6) McGraw.
Brickner, Bryan W. The Promise Keepers: Politics & Promises. LC 99-10349. 160p. 1999. 59.00 (0-7391-0008-4); pap. 22.95 (0-7391-0059-9) Lxngtn Bks.
Brickner, Colleen J. Inside Out. LC 92-81111. 152p. 1992. 24.50 (0-9638399-0-X); pap. 16.50 (0-9638399-1-8) R Brickner Trust.
Brickner, Dale, jt. auth. see Traister, John E.
Brickner, Dale C., ed. see Traister, John E.
Brickner, David. Future Hope: A Jewish Christian Look at the End of the World. Rosen, Ruth, ed. (Illus.). 185p. 1999. pap. 10.00 (1-881022-41-2, BK071) Purple Pomegranate.
— Mishpochah Matters. LC 96-3075. 1996. pap. 7.00 (1-881022-24-2) Purple Pomegranate.
Brickner, Philip W. Under the Safety Net: The Health & Social Welfare of the Homeless in the United States. 1990. 27.95 (0-393-02885-2) Norton.
Brickner, Philip W., et al, eds. Geriatric Home Health Care: The Collaboration of Physicians, Nurses, & Social Workers. LC 96-26154. (Illus.). 320p. 1996. 49.95 (0-8261-9450-8) Springer Pub.
Brickner, William. An Entrepreneur & Businessman Looks Business & Success. 1993. text. write for info. (1-880075-01-6) Alamo Pub.
Brickson, Betty. The Central Valley Project. McClurg, Sue, ed. (Layperson's Guide Ser.). (Illus.). 20p. 1994. pap. 5.00 (1-893246-51-5) Water Educ.
— The Central Valley Project. McClurg, Sue & McCarthy, Elizabeth, eds. (Layperson's Guide Ser.). (Illus.). 20p. 1998. pap. 15.00 (1-893246-18-3) Water Educ.
Brickson, Betty, et al. California Water. McClurg, Sue, ed. (Layperson's Guide Ser.). (Illus.). 24p. 1997. pap. 5.00 (1-893246-57-4) Water Educ.
Bricktop & Haskins, Jim. Bricktop. (Illus.). 300p. 2000. reprint ed. pap. 14.00 (1-56649-114-2) Welcome Rain.
Bricmont, Jean, jt. auth. see Sokal, Alan.
Bricogne, Gerard & Carter, Charles W., eds. Likelihood, Bayesian, Inference & Their Application to the Solution of New Structures. (Transactions of the American Crystallographic Association Ser.: Vol. 30). 166p. (C). 1997. pap. text 25.00 (0-937140-39-2) Am Crystallographic.
Briconnet, Guillaume, ed. see Marguerite d'Angouleme.
Bricose, Jill. Here Am I: Send Aaron! rev. ed. 1989. teacher ed. 1.20 (0-88207-982-4, 6-2982, Victor Bks) Chariot Victor.
Bricout, N. Breast Surgery. LeVay, D., tr. (Illus.). 445p. 1996. pap. 175.00 (2-287-59632-1) Spr-Verlag.
Bricusse, Leslie. Great Movie Songs - Leslie Bricusse. Okun, Milton, ed. pap. 9.95 (0-89524-700-3) Cherry Lane.
— Leslie Bricusse Movie Songbook. pap. 19.95 (0-685-75232-1) Cherry Lane.
— Sammy Davis Jr., Songbook (Piano - Vocal) Okun, Milton, ed. (Illus.). 176p. (Orig.). (YA). 1992. pap. 19.95 (0-89524-717-8) Cherry Lane.
— Willy Wonka & the Chocolate Factory: Easy Piano. (Easy Play Ser.). 48p. 1991. pap. 6.95 (0-7935-0649-2, 00222530) H Leonard.
Bricuth, John. The Heisenberg Variations. 112p. 1976. pap. 6.95 (0-8018-2654-3) Johns Hopkins.
— Just Let Me Say This about That: A Narrative Poem. LC 98-6483. (Sewanee Writers Ser.). 128p. 1998. text 22.95 (0-87951-902-9, Pub. by Overlook Pr) Penguin Putnam.
Bridal, Tessa. The Tree of Red Stars. LC 96-40156. 304p. 1997. 21.95 (1-57131-013-4) Milkweed Ed.
— The Tree of Red Stars. 304p. 1998. pap. 13.95 (1-57131-023-1) Milkweed Ed.
Bridal, Tessa & McCormick, Susan, eds. Science on Stage Anthology. (Illus.). 116p. 1991. pap. 14.00 (0-944040-26-8) AST Ctrs.
Bridbury, A. R. Economic Growth: England in the Later Middle Ages. LC 83-8540. 115p. 1983. reprint ed. lib. bdg. 57.50 (0-313-24066-3, BREG, Greenwood Pr) Greenwood.
— The English Economy from Bede to the Reformation. 334p. (C). 1992. 75.00 (0-85115-305-4) Boydell & Brewer.
***Briddell, Dan.** Love Bug & Other Tales of Psychotherapy. LC 00-27327. 272p. 2000. text 24.95 (0-312-24249-2) St Martin.
***Briddick, Richard W.** The Demon Exorcised. LC 99-175220. 1998. write for info. (0-9664585-0-8) R W Briddick.
Bride, Johnny M. Horse Thieves. large type ed. 224p. 1998. pap. 17.99 (0-7089-5323-9) Ulverscroft.
— The Men & the Boys. large type ed. (Linford Western Library). 208p. 1993. pap. 16.99 (0-7089-7314-0, Linford) Ulverscroft.
Bride, Johnny M. Renegade Blood. large type ed. 224p. pap. 18.99 (0-7089-5414-6) Ulverscroft.
Bride, Johnny M. Ride for Your Life. large type ed. (Linford Western Large Print Ser.). 224p. 1997. pap. 16.99 (0-7089-5001-9, Linford) Ulverscroft.
— Riders of the Plugged Nickel. large type ed. (Linford Western Large Print Ser.). 256p. 1998. pap. 17.99 (0-7089-5282-8, Linford) Ulverscroft.
— This Savage Land. large type ed. (Western Ser.). 1994. pap. 16.99 (0-7089-7596-8, Linford) Ulverscroft.
Bride, Mac. HTML: Publishing on the World Wide Web. 2nd ed. (Teach Yourself Ser.). 208p. 1998. pap. 11.95 (0-8442-0218-5, 02185, Teach Yrslf) NTC Contemp Pub Co.
— HTML Publishing on the World Wide Web. (Teach Yourself Ser.). (Illus.). 208p. 1997. pap. 11.95 (0-8442-3060-X) NTC Contemp Pub Co.
— Teach Yourself the Internet. 214p. 1996. pap. 9.95 (0-8442-3700-0, M3700-0, NTC Business Bks) NTC Contemp Pub Co.
Bride of Christ. Love Letter from God. (Illus.). 77p. 1997. mass mkt. 8.95 (1-885351-77-1) Cheval Intl.
Bridel, ed. see Bernanos, Georges.
Bridel, Pascal. Money & General Equilibrium Theory: From Walras to Pareto (1870-1923) LC 97-12052. 224p. 1997. 85.00 (1-85898-623-0) E Elgar.
Bridenbaugh, Carl. The Colonial Craftsman. 1990. pap. 6.95 (0-486-26490-4) Dover.
Bridenbaugh, Carl. The Colonial Craftsman. LC 50-7479. 1962. pap. text 3.95 (0-226-07436-6, P80) U Ch Pr.
Bridenbaugh, Carl. The Colonial Craftsman. LC 50-7479. 240p. reprint ed. pap. 74.40 (0-608-16531-X, 202676700052) Bks Demand.
— Myths & Realities: Societies of the Colonial South. LC 80-25280. (Walter Lynwood Fleming Lectures in Southern History). 208p. 1981. reprint ed. lib. bdg. 55.00 (0-313-22770-5, BRMR) Greenwood.
— Silas Downer - Forgotten Patriot: His Life & Writings. LC 74-83462. (Rhode Island Revolutionary Heritage Ser.: Vol. 1). (Illus.). 1974. 8.95 (0-917012-01-1) RI Pubns Soc.
Bridenbaugh, Carl & Bridenbaugh, Jessica. Rebels & Gentlemen: Philadelphia in the Age of Franklin. LC 78-657. (Illus.). 393p. 1978. reprint ed. lib. bdg. 38.50 (0-313-20300-8, BRRE, Greenwood Pr) Greenwood.
Bridenbaugh, Carl, ed. see Pynchon, John.
Bridenbaugh, Jessica, jt. auth. see Bridenbaugh, Carl.
Bridenhagen, Keith & Spielman, Patrick. Realistic Decoys: Carving, Texturing, Painting & Finishing. LC 84-8608. (Illus.). 232p. (Orig.). 1986. pap. 17.95 (0-8069-7908-9) Sterling.
Bridenthal. Becoming Visible, 3 vols. 3rd ed. LC 97-72450. (C). 1997. pap. text 35.96 (0-395-79625-3) HM.
Bridenthal, Renate, et al. Becoming Visible: Women in European History, 2 vols. 2nd ed. LC 86-81542. 528p. (C). 1987. pap. text 35.96 (0-395-41950-6) HM.
Bride's Magazine Editors. Bride's All-New Book of Etiquette. 320p. 1994. pap. 16.95 (0-399-51834-7, Perigee Bks) Berkley Pub.
— Bride's Book of Etiquette. rev. ed. LC 98-40024. (Illus.). 320p. 1999. pap. 16.95 (0-399-52471-1, Perigee Bks) Berkley Pub.
— Bride's Little Book of Bouquets & Flowers. LC 92-23644. (Illus.). 47p. 1993. 10.00 (0-517-59295-9) C Potter.
— Bride's Little Book of Cakes & Toasts. LC 92-23017. (Illus.). 48p. 1993. 10.00 (0-517-59296-7) C Potter.
— Bride's Little Book of Customs & Keepsakes. LC 93-25805. 1994. 10.00 (0-517-59679-2) C Potter.
— Bride's Little Book of Vows & Rings. LC 93-25802. 1994. 10.00 (0-517-59678-4) C Potter.
— Bride's Shortcuts & Strategies for a Beautiful Wedding. 1986. pap. 8.95 (0-399-51224-1, Perigee Bks) Berkley Pub.
— The Bride's Wedding Planner. rev. ed. 192p. 1990. pap. 15.00 (0-449-90467-9, Columbine) Fawcett.
Bride's Magazine Staf, ed. The Bride's Wedding Planner: The Perfect Guide to the Perfect Wedding. rev. ed. 240p. 1997. pap. 16.00 (0-449-91129-2) Fawcett.
Brideson, Jane, jt. auth. see Moorey, Teresa.
Bridewell, David A. & Nauts, Charles. The Lawyer's Guide to Retirement. 3rd ed. LC 98-30656. 1998. 74.95 (1-57073-612-X) Amer Bar Assn.
— Reverse Mortgages & Other Senior Housing Options. LC 96-42998. 1997. pap. 79.95 (1-57073-406-2) Amer Bar Assn.
Bridge, et al, eds. United Kingdom National Committee of Comparative Law: United Kingdom Law in the Mid 1990s, Vol. 15. 661p. 1994. pap. 105.00 (0-904281-05-1, Pub. by UK Natl Committee) St Mut.
Bridge, Antony. Theodora: Portrait in a Byzantine Landscape. 194p. 1993. reprint ed. pap. 10.00 (0-89733-394-2) Academy Chi Pubs.
Bridge, B. & Salt, S. Access & Delivery in Continuing Education & Training. (C). 1992. 50.00 (1-85041-066-6, Pub. by Univ Nottingham) St Mut.
Bridge, Brian. Employment Services for the Disadvantaged: Research Paper. 1977. 45.00 (0-7855-0576-8, Pub. by Natl Inst Soc Work) St Mut.
***Bridge Builder Company Staff.** Prima's Guide to Seagate Crystal Reports, No. 8. 2000. pap. 39.99 (0-7615-2483-5) Prima Pub.
Bridge, Carl, ed. Manning Clark: Essays on His Place in History. LC 95-105052. 184p. 1994. pap. 29.95 (0-522-84640-8, Pub. by Melbourne Univ Pr) Paul & Co Pubs.
— Munich to Vietnam: Australia's Relations with Britain & the United States since the 1930s. 220p. 1991. pap. 19.95 (0-522-84436-7, Pub. by Melbourne Univ Pr) Paul & Co Pubs.
Bridge, Chris. Appletime, Vol. I. (Illus.). 36p. (Orig.). (J). 1996. pap. 3.00 (0-9653438-0-4) U S Chart.
Bridge, David R. Sea Light: A Photographic Essay by Paul Liebhardt. LC 97-75323. (Illus.). 160p. 1997. text 45.00 (0-9659227-0-7) Inst Shipboard.
Bridge, David R., jt. auth. see Anderson, David S.
***Bridge, Diana.** The Girls on the Wall. 64p. 1999. pap. 14.95 (1-86940-209-X, Pub. by Auckland Univ) Paul & Co Pubs.
Bridge, Donald. Jesus, the Man & His Message. pap. 8.50 (1-85792-117-8, Pub. by Christian Focus) Spring Arbor Dist.
— Spiritual Gifts & the Church. 8.99 (1-85792-141-0, Pub. by Christian Focus) Spring Arbor Dist.
— Why Four Gospels? unabridged ed. 208p. 1996. 15.99 (1-85792-225-5, Pub. by Christian Focus) Spring Arbor Dist.
Bridge, F. R. The Habsburg Monarchy among the Great Powers, 1815-1918. LC 89-28947. (Illus.). 430p. 1991. 19.95 (0-85496-413-4) Berg Pubs.
Bridge, Frank H. The Council of Europe French-English Legal Dictionary. LC 94-238649. 315p. (Orig.). 1994. pap. 56.00 (92-871-2496-5, Pub. by Council of Europe) Manhattan Pub Co.
Bridge, Frederick. The Old Cryes of London. LC 74-24050. 1976. reprint ed. 36.50 (0-404-12872-6) AMS Pr.
— Shakespearean Music in the Plays & Early Operas. LC 68-358. (Studies in Shakespeare: No. 24). 1969. reprint ed. lib. bdg. 59.00 (0-8383-0513-X) M S G Haskell Hse.
***Bridge, Gary & Watson, Sophie, eds.** A Companion to the City. (Illus.). 500p. 2000. 99.95 (0-631-21052-0) Blackwell Pubs.
Bridge, Gillian. Parents As Care Managers: The Experiences of Those Caring for Young Children with Cerebral Palsy. LC 99-72593. 324p. 1999. text 69.95 (1-84014-973-6, Pub. by Ashgate Pub) Ashgate Pub Co.
Bridge, Helena. Natural Way: Back Pain. 128p. 1995. pap. 5.95 (1-85230-581-9, Pub. by Element MA) Penguin Putnam.
Bridge, Horatio. Journal of an African Cruiser. LC 78-92421. 1853. 19.00 (0-403-00154-4) Scholarly.
— Journal of an African Cruiser. (Works of Horatio). 1989. reprint ed. lib. bdg. 79.00 (0-7812-2061-0) Rprt Serv.

An Asterisk (*) at the beginning of an entry indicates that the title is appearing for the first time.

— Journal of an African Cruiser. (American Biography Ser.). 179p. 1991. reprint ed. lib. bdg. 79.00 (*0-7812-8040-0*) Rprt Serv.

— Personal Recollections of Nathaniel Hawthorne. LC 68-24931. (Studies in Hawthorne: No. 15). 1969. reprint ed. lib. bdg. 75.00 (*0-8383-0916-X*) M S G Haskell Hse.

— Personal Recollections of Nathaniel Hawthorne. (Works of Horatio). 1989. reprint ed. lib. bdg. 79.00 (*0-7812-2062-9*) Rprt Serv.

— The Works of Horatio Bridge. 1989. reprint ed. lib. bdg. 63.00 (*0-685-27304-0*) Rprt Serv.

***Bridge Information Systems AME.** CRB Commodity Yearbook, 1999 Edition. 384p. 1999. 99.95 (*0-471-32704-2*) Wiley.

Bridge, James H. The Inside History of the Carnegie Steel Company. LC 73-38274. (Evolution of Capitalism Ser.). 390p. 1979. reprint ed. 37.95 (*0-405-04112-8*) Ayer.

— Inside History of the Carnegie Steel Company: A Romance of Millions. LC 91-50106. (Social & Labor History Ser.). (Illus.). 432p. 1991. reprint ed. pap. 19.95 (*0-8229-6095-8*) U of Pittsburgh Pr.

— Millionaires & Grub Street: Comrades - Contacts in the Last Half Century. LC 68-8441. (Essay Index Reprint Ser.). (Illus.). 1977. reprint ed. 23.95 (*0-8369-0253-X*) Ayer.

— Uncle Sam at Home. LC 73-13153. (Foreign Travelers in America, 1810-1935 Ser.). (Illus.). 248p. 1974. reprint ed. 20.95 (*0-405-05446-7*) Ayer.

Bridge, James H., ed. The Trust: Its Book. LC 73-1995. (Big Business; Economic Power in a Free Society Ser.). 1973. reprint ed. 20.95 (*0-405-05077-1*) Ayer.

Bridge, Jane, et al. The Children's Act 1989. 384p. 1990. pap. 39.00 (*1-85431-058-5*, Pub. by Blackstone Pr) Gaunt.

***Bridge, Janet.** Decorating with Nature. LC 98-86814. (Illus.). 128p. 1999. 24.95 (*1-57076-142-6*) Trafalgar.

Bridge, John. Economics in Personnel Management. 272p. (C). 1981. 60.00 (*0-85292-260-4*) St Mut.

Bridge, John F. Shakespearean Music in the Plays & Early Operas. LC 75-153307. reprint ed. 29.50 (*0-404-07808-7*) AMS Pr.

Bridge, John P. Ceramic Tile Setting. 1992. 16.95 (*0-07-007738-X*) McGraw.

— Ceramic Tile Setting. (Illus.). 240p. 1992. 24.95 (*0-8306-2573-9*, 2803); pap. 14.95 (*0-8306-2572-0*, 2803) McGraw-Hill Prof.

Bridge, Mark. Encyclopedia of Desks. 1989. 12.98 (*1-55521-271-9*) Bk Sales Inc.

***Bridge, Michael.** The International Sale of Goods: Law & Practice. LC 99-25368. 592p. 1999. text 215.00 (*0-19-876490-1*) OUP.

Bridge, Michael. Moses Goodleaf Learns to Walk: A Short Tale of Discovery. (Illus.). 32p. (J). 2000. pap. 16.95 (*0-944963-19-6*); pap. 7.95 incl. audio (*0-944963-33-1*); lib. bdg. 22.95 (*0-944963-18-8*) Glastonbury CA.

— Personal Property Law. 182p. 1993. pap. 36.00 (*1-85431-254-5*, Pub. by Blackstone Pr) Gaunt.

— Personal Property Law. 2nd ed. 170p. 1996. pap. 26.00 (*1-85431-581-1*, Pub. by Blackstone Pr) Gaunt.

— Pillow Mountain: Notes on Inhabiting a Living Planet. LC 91-35970. (Illus.). 192p. (Orig.). 1991. pap. 10.95 (*0-87810-039-3*) Times Change.

— The Sale of Goods. 2nd ed. 708p. 1997. text 155.00 (*0-19-825871-2*) OUP.

Bridge, P. D., et al, eds. Applications of PCR Mycology. LC 97-43094. (A CAB International Publication). (Illus.). 384p. (C). 1998. text 110.00 (*0-85199-233-1*) OUP.

Bridge, P. D., et al. Molecular Variability of Fungal Pathogens. LC 98-14967. (CAB International Publication). 350p. 1999. text 100.00 (*0-85199-266-8*) OUP.

Bridge, P. D., jt. auth. see Paterson, R. R.

Bridge, Paul, et al, eds. Information Technology, Plant Pathology & Biodiversity. LC 98-159399. (A CAB International Publication). (Illus.). 496p. 1998. text 90.00 (*0-85199-217-X*) OUP.

Bridge, Peter J. The Calculation of Genetic Risks: Worked Examples in DNA Diagnostics. 2nd ed. LC 97-20471. (Illus.). 400p. 1997. text 50.00 (*0-8018-5744-9*) Johns Hopkins.

Bridge Publications Staff. L. Ron Hubbard Presents Writers of the Future, Vol. XII. 496p. 1996. mass mkt. 6.99 (*1-57318-027-0*) Bridge Pubns Inc.

— While Martha Told the Hours. (C). 1989. 80.00 (*0-947934-18-9*, Pub. by Bridge Pubns); pap. 45.00 (*0-947934-17-0*, Pub. by Bridge Pubns) St Mut.

Bridge Publishing Staff. Research & Discovery Series, Vol. 10. 860p. 1996. 150.00 (*1-57318-044-0*) Bridge Pubns Inc.

— Research & Discovery Series, Vol. 11. 761p. 1997. 150.00 (*1-57318-022-X*) Bridge Pubns Inc.

— Research & Discovery Series, Vol. 12. 763p. 1997. 150.00 (*1-57318-098-X*) Bridge Pubns Inc.

— Research & Discovery Series, Vol. 13. 1998. 150.00 (*1-57318-099-8*) Bridge Pubns Inc.

***Bridge, Ruth.** Love with a Difference. large type ed. 272p. 1999. pap. 18.99 (*0-7089-5520-7*, Linford) Ulverscroft.

Bridge, Steve. The Communal Family: Model for Change. (Illus.). 108p. (Orig.). 1991. pap. 9.95 (*0-9631099-0-1*) Loquat Press.

***Bridge, Stuart.** Assured Tenancies. 265p. 1999. pap. 45.00 (*1-85431-978-7*, Pub. by Blackstone Pr) Gaunt.

Bridge, Stuart. Blackstone's Statutes on Landlord & Tenant. (C). 1991. text 33.00 (*1-85431-118-2*, Pub. by Blackstone Pr) Gaunt.

— Blackstone's Statutes on Landlord & Tenant. 2nd ed. Date not set. 16.00 (*1-85431-493-9*, Pub. by Blackstone Pr) Gaunt.

— The Housing Act 1988. 400p. 1989. pap. 34.00 (*1-85431-045-3*, Pub. by Blackstone Pr) Gaunt.

Bridge, Susan. Monitoring the News: The Brilliant Launch & Sudden Collapse of the Monitor Channel. LC 98-10021. (Illus.). 264p. (YA). (gr. 13). 1998. text 38.95 (*0-7656-0315-2*) M E Sharpe.

***Bridge, Susan.** Monitoring the News: The Brilliant Launch & Sudden Collapse of the Monitor Channel. (Illus.). 264p. 1999. pap. text 21.95 (*0-7656-0316-0*) M E Sharpe.

Bridge, T. Peter, et al, eds. Psychological, Neuropsychiatric, & Substance Abuse Aspects of AIDS. fac. ed. LC 87-42723. (Advances in Biochemical Psychopharmacology Ser.: No. 44). (Illus.). 281p. 1988. pap. 87.20 (*0-7837-7271-8*, 204703400005) Bks Demand.

Bridge, Tom. 200 Classic Sauces: Guaranteed Recipes for Every Occasion. LC 96-29684. (Illus.). 127p. 1996. 29.95 (*0-470-23679-5*) Wiley.

***Bridge, Tom.** The Ultimate Game Cookbook. (Illus.). 192p. 2000. 19.95 (*0-7499-1988-4*, Pub. by Piatkus Bks) London Brdge.

Bridge, Tom. What's Cooking: Chicken. LC 98-56393. 1999. 15.98 (*1-57145-180-3*, Thunder Bay) Advantage Pubs.

— What's Cooking? Pasta. LC 98-3259. 1998. 15.98 (*1-57145-147-1*, Thunder Bay) Advantage Pubs.

Bridge, Ursula, ed. see Yeats, William Butler.

Bridge, William. A Lifting up for the Downcast. (Puritan Paperbacks Ser.). 1979. pap. 7.50 (*0-85151-298-4*) Banner of Truth.

Bridge, William F. An Account of the Descendants of John Bridge, Cambridge, 1632. (Illus.). 122p. 1988. reprint ed. pap. 22.00 (*0-8328-0317-0*); reprint ed. lib. bdg. 32.00 (*0-8328-0316-2*) Higginson Bk Co.

Bridgeforth, Dennis. The Life & Death of Solitude. 184p. 1997. pap. 8.95 (*1-878561-62-6*) Seacoast AL.

Bridgeforth, Med. Another Chance. LC 73-18569. reprint ed. 20.00 (*0-404-11379-6*) AMS Pr.

Bridgeland, Michael, tr. see Kaup, Ludger & Kaup, Burchard.

Bridgeland, William M. Diversity & Change in American Society. 1995. write for info. (*1-57074-220-0*) Greyden Pr.

— Society & the Individual. 160p. (C). 12.25 (*1-57074-202-2*) Greyden Pr.

Bridgeland, William M. & Duane, Edward A., eds. Young Children & Social Policy. (Annals of the American Academy of Political & Social Science Ser.: Vol. 461). (Illus.). 224p. 1982. 26.00 (*0-8039-1831-3*); pap. 17.00 (*0-8039-1832-1*) Sage.

***Bridgeman, Brian & Barnsley, Mike.** Junction Railway Midland & Southwestern. (Transport Ser.). 1999. pap. 18.99 (*0-7524-0016-9*) Arcadia Publng.

Bridgeman, Bruce, jt. ed. see Prinz, Wolfgang.

Bridgeman, Cunningham, jt. auth. see Cellier, Francois.

Bridgeman, George B. Bridgman's Life Drawing. 1990. 22.25 (*0-8446-0038-5*) Peter Smith.

Bridgeman, J. C., jt. auth. see Davis, H. C.

Bridgeman, Jo & Millns, Susan, eds. Law & Body Politics: Regulating the Female Body. LC 95-102. 328p. 1995. 87.95 (*1-85521-515-2*, Pub. by Dartmth Pub) Ashgate Pub Co.

***Bridgeman, Peter & Davis, Glyn.** Australian Policy Handbook. 2nd ed. (Illus.). 208p. 2000. pap. 29.95 (*1-86508-260-0*, Pub. by Allen & Unwin Pty) Paul & Co Pubs.

Bridgeman, Rae, jt. auth. see Glassen, Irene.

Bridgeman, Rae, jt. auth. see Glasser, Irene.

***Bridgeman, Teresa.** Queneau: Exercices de Style. 96p. 1999. pap. 35.00 (*0-85261-464-0*, Pub. by U of Glasgow) St Mut.

Bridgeman, Teresa. Unconventional Interactions: Genre, Author, & Audience in the French Novel. LC 97-43281. 288p. (C). 1998. pap. 27.99 (*0-415-13126-X*) Routledge.

— Unconventional Interactions: Genre, Author, & Audience in the French Novel. LC 97-43281. 288p. (C). 1998. 85.00 (*0-415-13125-1*) Routledge.

Bridgeman, William & Hazard, Jacqueline. The Lonely Sky. Gilbert, James B., ed. LC 79-7232. (Flight: Its First Seventy-Five Years Ser.). (Illus.). 1980. reprint ed. lib. bdg. 30.95 (*0-405-12148-2*) Ayer.

Bridgemon, Rondal R. & Lindsley, Karen B., eds. South China Caves. (Illus.). 62p. (Orig.). 1991. pap. 7.95 (*0-939748-27-4*) Cave Bks MO.

Bridgen, John, ed. Collected Poems - Humphrey Moore: With a Memoir by John Bridgen. LC 98-111670. 288p. 1998. 47.95 (*0-7188-2959-X*, Lutterworth-Parkwest) Parkwest Pubns.

Bridgeo, W. A. & Eisenhauer, H. R., eds. Arctic Water Pollution Research: Applications of Science & Technology: Proceedings of an IAWPRC Conference Held in Yellowknife, Canada, 28 April-1 May 1985. LC 82-645900. (Illus.). 194p. 1986. pap. 52.00 (*0-08-034149-7*, Pub. by PPL) Elsevier.

Bridger. Altering Houses. 192p. 1998. pap. 34.95 (*0-7506-3444-8*) Buttrwrth-Heinemann.

— Women & Political Change: Perspectives from East-Central Europe. LC 98-28243. 206p. 1999. text 65.00 (*0-312-21847-8*) St Martin.

Bridger, Ann & Bridger, Colin. Altering Houses & Small Scale Residential Development. LC 98-218982. 353p. 1998. 34.95 (*0-7506-4100-2*) Buttrwrth-Heinemann.

Bridger, Bobby. A Ballad of the West: Seekers of the Fleece. 2nd ed. 156p. reprint ed. pap. 15.00 (*0-9636882-0-0*) Augustine TX.

Bridger, Charles. An Index to Printed Pedigrees: Contained in County & Local Histories, the Heralds' Visitations, & in the More Important Genealogical Collections. 384p. 1997. pap. 35.00 (*0-8063-0049-3*) Clearfield Co.

Bridger, Colin, jt. auth. see Bridger, Ann.

Bridger, Darren, jt. auth. see Lewis, David.

Bridger, David. Hebrew & Heritage: Language, No. 1. Fishman, Priscilla, ed. (Modern Language Ser.). (Illus.). 1995. pap. 6.95 (*0-87441-254-4*) Behrman.

— Hebrew & Heritage: Language, No. 2. Fishman, Priscilla, ed. (J). 1995. pap., wbk. ed. 4.95 (*0-87441-373-7*) Behrman.

— Hebrew & Heritage: Language, No. 3. Fishman, Priscilla, ed. (J). 1995. pap., wbk. ed. 4.95 (*0-87441-374-5*) Behrman.

— Hebrew & Heritage Language, 4 vols. LC 75-1812. (Modern Language Ser.). (Illus.). 1976. teacher ed., vinyl bd. 14.95 (*0-685-00731-6*) Behrman.

— Hebrew & Heritage Language, Level 1. Fishman, Priscilla, ed. LC 75-1812. (Illus.). 1976. teacher ed., vinyl bd. 14.95 (*0-87441-253-6*) Behrman.

— Hebrew & Heritage Language, Level 2. Fishman, Priscilla, ed. LC 75-1812. (Illus.). 1976. teacher ed., vinyl bd. 14.95 (*0-87441-258-7*) Behrman.

— Hebrew & Heritage Language, Level 3. Fishman, Priscilla, ed. LC 75-1812. (Illus.). 1976. teacher ed., vinyl bd. 14.95 (*0-87441-260-9*) Behrman.

— Hebrew & Heritage Language, Level 4. Fishman, Priscilla, ed. LC 75-1812. (Illus.). 1976. teacher ed., vinyl bd. 14.95 (*0-87441-438-5*) Behrman.

— Hebrew & Heritage Language, Vol. 2. Fishman, Priscilla, ed. LC 75-1812. (Modern Language Ser.). (Illus.). 1976. pap. 6.95 (*0-87441-252-8*) Behrman.

— Hebrew & Heritage Language, Vol. 3. Fishman, Priscilla, ed. LC 75-1812. (Modern Language Ser.). (Illus.). 1976. pap. 6.95 (*0-87441-259-5*) Behrman.

— Hebrew & Heritage Language, Vol. 4. Fishman, Priscilla, ed. LC 75-1812. (Modern Language Ser.). (Illus.). 1976. pap. 6.95 (*0-87441-274-9*) Behrman.

Bridger, David, ed. Programmed Hebrew Series, 2 vols. Incl. Vol. 1. 1971. pap. text 3.50 (*0-87441-079-7*); 62p. pap. write for info. (*0-318-51048-0*) Behrman.

Bridger, David & Wolk, Samuel. The New Jewish Encyclopedia. rev. ed. LC 76-15251. (Illus.). 542p. 1976. 24.95 (*0-87441-120-3*) Behrman.

Bridger, G. Patrick, jt. ed. see Smee, Robert.

Bridger, Geoff. Neuve Chapelle: La Bassee. (Battleground Europe Ser.). 1999. pap. text 16.95 (*0-85052-648-5*) Leo Cooper.

Bridger, Gordon. First Corinthians-Galatians. (Bible Study Commentaries Ser.). 95p. 1985. pap. 4.95 (*0-87508-172-X*) Chr Lit.

***Bridger, Jake.** Acts of the Apostles. LC 98-90873. 2000. 21.95 (*0-533-12969-9*) Vantage.

Bridger, M., jt. auth. see Auslander, M.

Bridger, Michael, ed. Hybridity. (Performing Arts International Ser.). 105p. 1997. pap. text 15.00 (*90-5702-056-4*, Harwood Acad Pubs) Gordon & Breach.

Bridger, R.S. Introduction to Ergonomics. LC 94-24688. 576p. (C). 1995. 90.00 (*0-07-007741-X*) McGraw.

Bridger, Sue, et al. No More Heroines? Russia, Women & the Market. LC 95-19881. (Women in Politics Ser.). 240p. (C). 1995. pap. 22.99 (*0-415-12460-3*) Routledge.

— No More Heroines? Russia, Women & the Market. LC 95-19881. (Women in Politics Ser.). 240p. (C). (gr. 13). 1995. 90.00 (*0-415-12459-X*) Routledge.

Bridger, Sue, jt. ed. see Riordan, Jim.

Bridger, Susan. Women in the Soviet Countryside: Women's Role in Rural Development in the U. S. S. R. (Cambridge Russian, Soviet & Post-Soviet Studies: No. 56). (Illus.). 288p. 1988. text 69.95 (*0-521-32862-4*) Cambridge U Pr.

Bridger, Susan, jt. auth. see Pine, Frances.

Bridger, Zandra. Dear Stupid. LC 98-92991. 272p. (Orig.). 1998. 19.50 (*0-9664176-5-8*) Bainbrdge TX.

— Dear Stupid: Letters to My Wounded Child Within. LC 98-92991. 272p. (Orig.). 1998. pap. 18.50 (*0-9664176-6-6*) Bainbrdge TX.

Bridgers, John D. What's Right with Football. (Illus.). 400p. 1995. 24.95 (*1-57168-016-0*, Eakin Pr) Sunbelt Media.

Bridgers, Karen, jt. auth. see Crabtree, Cheryl.

***Bridgers, Lee.** Moab: An Atlas of Moab, Utah's Greatest Off-Road Bicycle Rides. (Mountain Bike America Guidebks.). (Illus.). 288p. 2000. pap. 17.95 (*0-7627-0702-X*) Globe Pequot.

Bridgers, Lee. Mountain Bike Utah: An Atlas of Southern Utah's Greatest Off-Road Bicycle Rides. (Mountain Bike America Ser.). 224p. 1998. pap. 15.95 (*1-882997-13-1*) Beachway Pr.

Bridgers, Lynn. Death's Deceiver: The Life of Joseph P. Machebeuf. LC 97-4620. 268p. 1997. 50.00 (*0-8263-1803-7*); pap. 21.95 (*0-8263-1810-X*) U of NM Pr.

Bridgers, Robert S., ed. Confederate Military History: Cumulative Index, 2 vols. 1159p. 1988. 150.00 (*1-56837-003-2*) Broadfoot.

Bridgers, Robert S., et al, eds. State Magazine Index, 1966-1986. 300p. 1989. 59.50 (*0-916107-75-2*) Broadfoot.

Bridgers, Sue E. All We Know of Heaven. LC 96-84201. 212p. 1996. 22.00 (*0-9635967-4-8*) Banks Channel.

— Home Before Dark. 186p. (J). 1998. reprint ed. 29.95 (*0-7351-0053-5*) Replica Bks.

— Keeping Christina. 290p. 1998. reprint ed. lib. bdg. 29.95 (*0-7351-0042-X*) Replica Bks.

— Notes for Another Life. 258p. (YA). 1998. lib. bdg. 29.95 (*0-7351-0044-6*) Replica Bks.

— Permanent Connections. 272p. 1998. reprint ed. lib. bdg. 29.95 (*0-7351-0043-8*) Replica Bks.

— Sara Will. (J). 1986. 14.95 (*0-06-020691-8*) HarpC Child Bks.

Bridges. Biology 101. 128p. (C). 1998. pap. text 13.60 (*0-536-01475-2*) Pearson Custom.

— En Pos de la Santidad.Tr. of Pursuit of Holiness. (SPA.). 1995. pap. write for info. (*0-614-27038-3*) Editorial Unilit.

Bridges, jt. auth. see Brambilla, F.

Bridges, jt. auth. see Lunsford, Andrea.

Bridges & Dunn-Raskin, LPP Staff & Culpepper & Associates Staff. Financial Operating Ratios for Software Companies: A Benchmark of the Software Industry's Financial Performance & Accounting Practices. (Illus.). 290p. 1997. 895.00 (*1-58128-008-4*, OR) Culpepper.

Bridges, Alan. The Construction Net: Online Information Sources for the Construction Industry. (Illus.). 256p. 1996. pap. 39.99 (*0-419-21780-0*, E & FN Spon) Routledge.

Bridges, Amy. Morning Glories. (Princeton Studies in American Politics). 264p. 1999. pap. 19.95 (*0-691-01009-9*, Pub. by Princeton U Pr) Cal Prin Full Svc.

— Morning Glories: Municipal Reform in the Southwest. LC 96-45262. 258p. 1997. text 35.00 (*0-691-02780-3*, Pub. by Princeton U Pr) Cal Prin Full Svc.

Bridges, Anne B. & Williams, Roy. St. James Santee, Plantation Parish: History & Records, 1685-1925. LC 96-43877. 1997. 37.50 (*0-87152-504-6*) Reprint.

Bridges, B. A. & Harnden, D. G., eds. Ataxia Telangiectasia: A Cellular & Molecular Link Between Cancer, Neuropathology & Immune Deficiency. LC 81-13146. (Wiley-Medical Publication). (Illus.). 422p. reprint ed. pap. 130.90 (*0-8357-6031-6*, 203421500089) Bks Demand.

Bridges, Barbara J. Therapeutic Caregiving: A Practical Guide for Caregivers of Persons with Alzheimer's & Other Dementia Causing Diseases. rev. ed. LC 95-94060. (Illus.). 256p. (Orig.). 1996. reprint ed. pap. 19.95 (*0-9645178-0-9*) BJB Pub.

Bridges, Ben. Aces Wilde. large type ed. (Dales Western Ser.). 218p. 1993. pap. 18.99 (*1-85389-407-9*, Dales) Ulverscroft.

— Blood Canyon. large type ed. (Dales Western Ser.). 272p. 1998. pap. 19.99 (*1-85389-791-4*, Dales) Ulverscroft.

— Gunsmoke Is Grey. large type ed. (Dales Large Print Ser.). 237p. 1997. pap. 18.99 (*1-85389-758-2*, Dales) Ulverscroft.

— Hard As Nails. large type ed. (Dales Western Ser.). 1993. pap. 13.95 (*1-85389-382-X*, Dales) Ulverscroft.

— Linford Western Library. large type ed. (Linford Western Large Pr. Ser.). 1995. pap. 16.99 (*0-7089-7756-1*, Linford) Ulverscroft.

— Marked for Death. large type ed. (Linford Western Library). 272p. 1994. pap. 16.99 (*0-7089-7581-X*, Linford) Ulverscroft.

— Rattler Creek. large type ed. (Dales Large Print Ser.). (Illus.). 246p. 1996. pap. 18.99 (*1-85389-643-8*) Ulverscroft.

Bridges, Bill. Book of the Weaver. (Werewolf Ser.). 1996. 12.00 (*1-56504-311-1*, 3402) White Wolf.

***Bridges, Bill.** Croatan Song. 2000. pap. 17.95 (*1-56504-388-X*) White Wolf.

Bridges, Bill. Dark Between the Stars. (Illus.). 128p. 1997. pap. 18.00 (*1-888906-08-1*) Holistic Design.

— Fading Suns Players Companion. (Illus.). 224p. 1997. pap. 25.00 (*1-888906-07-3*) Holistic Design.

— Forbidden Lore: Technology. (Fading Suns Ser.: Vol. 225). 1996. pap. text 15.00 (*1-888906-03-0*) Holistic Design.

— The Great Chili Book: 101 Variations on "The Perfect Bowl of Red" 219p. 1998. pap. text 16.00 (*0-7881-5380-3*) DIANE Pub.

— The Great Chili Book: 101 Variations on "The Perfect Bowl of Red" LC 93-33993. 224p. 1994. pap. 13.95 (*1-55821-281-7*) Lyons Pr.

***Bridges, Bill.** Litany of the Tribes, Vol. 4. 2000. pap. text 22.95 (*1-56504-305-7*) White Wolf.

Bridges, Bill. Merchants of the Jumpweb. (Fading Suns: Vol. 231). 1997. pap. 20.00 (*1-888906-09-X*) Holistic Design.

— Rage Across the World, Vol. 1. (Werewolf Ser.). (Illus.). 288p. (Orig.). 1996. pap. 20.00 (*1-56504-319-7*, 3069) White Wolf.

— Rage Across the World, Vol. 2. (Werewolf Ser.). (Illus.). 272p. (Orig.). 1996. pap. 20.00 (*1-56504-320-0*, 3070) White Wolf.

***Bridges, Bill.** War in the Heavens: Lifeweb. (Illus.). 128p. 1999. pap. 20.00 (*1-888906-12-X*) Holistic Design.

Bridges, Bill. Weird Places. (Illus.). 80p. 1997. pap. 12.95 (*1-888906-05-7*) Holistic Design.

— Wendigo: Tribebook. (Werewolf Ser.). (Illus.). 1998. pap. 10.00 (*1-56504-334-0*, 3078) White Wolf.

***Bridges, Bill, ed.** Gamemasters Screen & Complete Pandemonium. (Illus.). 32p. 1999. pap. 12.95 (*1-888906-19-7*) Holistic Design.

— Legions of the Empire. (Illus.). 128p. 1999. pap. 19.95 (*1-888906-16-2*) Holistic Design.

— The Sinful Stars. (Illus.). 400p. 1998. pap. 15.95 (*1-888906-14-6*) Holistic Design.

***Bridges, Bill & Greenberg, Andrew.** Fading Suns. 2nd ed. (Illus.). 312p. 1999. 34.95 (*1-888906-18-9*) Holistic Design.

Bridges, Bill & Greenberg, Daniel. War of Ages: Elysium/Anarch Cookbook. (Vampire Ser.). (Illus.). 1998. reprint ed. pap. 16.00 (*1-56504-243-3*, 2022) White Wolf.

Bridges, Bill, jt. auth. see Moore, Jim.

Bridges, Bill, ed. see Greenberg, Andrew.

Bridges, Bill, ed. see Howard, Christopher.

Bridges, Bill, ed. see Quaide, Rustin.

***Bridges, Brian.** Europe & the Challenge of the Asia Pacific: Change, Continuity & Crisis. LC 98-45785. 240p. 1999. 90.00 (*1-85898-497-1*) E Elgar.

Bridges, Brian. Japan & Korea in the 1990s: From Antagonism to Adjustment. 196p. 1993. 85.00 (*1-85278-681-7*) E Elgar.

— Korea & the West. 1987. 12.95 (*0-7102-1110-4*, Routledge Thoemms) Routledge.

B

Bridges, Brian N., ed. Innovative Advances in the Forest Products Industries. LC 98-36295. (Symposium Ser.: Vol. 94). 1998. pap. 90.00 (*0-8169-0775-7*, S-319) Am Inst Chem Eng.

Bridges, Bryn A. & Weinstein, I. Bernard, eds. Indicators of Genotoxic Exposure. LC 82-12972. (Banbury Reports: Vol. 13). 580p. 1982. 62.50 (*0-87969-212-X*) Cold Spring Harbor.

Bridges, Byron & Metzger, Melanie. Deaf Tend Your: Non-Manual Signals in American Sign Language. LC 96-70907. 67 p. 1996. write for info. (*0-9654871-1-3*) Calliope MD.

Bridges, C. R., et al, eds. EBO - Experimental Biology Online Annual, 1998. 200p. 1999. 139.00 incl. cd-rom (*3-540-65441-0*) Spr-Verlag.

Bridges, C. R., et al. EBO - Experimental Biology Online Annual, 1996-1997. 450p. 1998. 129.00 incl. cd-rom (*3-540-64146-7*) Spr-Verlag.

Bridges, Carol. Medicine Woman Deck-Book Set. (Illus.). 256p. 1992. pap. 29.00 (*0-88079-537-9*, MWS99) US Games Syst.

— The Medicine Woman Inner Guidebook. LC 91-75047. (Illus.). 256p. 1992. pap. 12.95 (*0-88079-512-3*, BK114) US Games Syst.

— The Medicine Woman Inner Guidebook: A Woman's Guide to Her Unique Powers. rev. ed. (Illus.). 279p. (Orig.). 1987. pap., student ed. 21.00 (*0-945111-00-2*) Earth Nation.

— Medicine Woman Tarot. 1989. pap. 15.00 (*0-88079-419-4*, MW78) US Games Syst.

— The Medicine Woman's Guide to Being in Business for Yourself: How to Live by Your Spiritual Vision in a Money-Based World. 3rd ed. (Illus.). 160p. (Orig.). 1996. reprint ed. pap. 14.95 (*0-945111-08-8*) Earth Nation.

— Secrets Stored in Ecstasy. 192p. (Orig.). 1991. pap. 12.95 (*0-945111-07-X*) Earth Nation.

— A Soul in Place: Reclaiming Home As Sacred Space. (Illus.). 256p. (Orig.). 1996. pap. 15.00 (*0-945111-11-8*) Earth Nation.

Bridges, Catina, ed. see Reynolds, Patrice.

Bridges, Charles. The Christian Ministry. 390p. 1991. reprint ed. 29.99 (*0-85151-087-6*) Banner of Truth.

— Ecclesiastes. 319p. 1981. reprint ed. 19.99 (*0-85151-322-0*) Banner of Truth.

— Proverbs. (Geneva Commentaries Ser.). 1979. 29.99 (*0-85151-088-4*) Banner of Truth.

— Psalm 119. 1977. 24.99 (*0-85151-176-7*) Banner of Truth.

Bridges, Christina. The Hero. (Illus.). 29p. (J). (gr. k-6). 1981. pap. text 14.95 (*0-917002-39-3*) Joyce Media.

Bridges, D. & Mehta, G. Representations of Preference Orderings. Fandel, Gunter U. & Trockel, W., eds. (Lecture Notes in Economics & Mathematical Systems Ser.: Vol. 422). x, 162p. 1995. 52.00 (*3-540-58839-6*) Spr-Verlag.

Bridges, D. S. Foundations of Real & Abstract Analysis. LC 97-10649. (Graduate Texts in Mathematics Ser.: Vol. 174). 1997. 44.95 (*0-387-98239-6*) Spr-Verlag.

Bridges, D. S., et al, eds. Combinatorics, Complexity, & Logic: Proceedings of the 1st International Conference: DMTCS '96. LC 96-45243. 350p. 1997. pap. 59.95 (*981-3083-14-X*) Spr-Verlag.

Bridges, David. Education, Autonomy & Democratic Citizenship: Philosophy in a Changing World. LC 97-1287. 296p. (C). 1997. 85.00 (*0-415-15334-4*) Routledge.

— Education, Democracy & Discussion. 184p. (C). 1988. reprint ed. pap. text 19.50 (*0-8191-7051-8*) U Pr of Amer.

Bridges, David & Husbands, Chris, eds. Consorting & Collaborating in the Education Marketplace. LC 95-8947. 186p. 1995. 85.00 (*0-7507-0449-7*, Falmer Pr); pap. 27.95 (*0-7507-0450-0*, Falmer Pr) Taylor & Francis.

Bridges, David & Kerry, Trevor, eds. Developing Teachers Professionally: Reflections for Initial & In-Service Trainers. LC 93-6981. 192p. 1993. pap. write for info. (*0-415-09296-5*) Routledge.

Bridges, David & McLaughlin, Terence H., eds. Education & the Market Place. LC 94-24821. 154p. 1994. 85.00 (*0-7507-0348-2*, Falmer Pr); pap. 27.95 (*0-7507-0349-0*, Falmer Pr) Taylor & Francis.

Bridges, Douglas, et al, eds. Computability: A Mathematical Sketchbook. LC 93-21313. (Graduate Texts in Mathematics Ser.: Vol. 146). (Illus.). 192p. (C). 1994. 47.95 (*0-387-94174-6*) Spr-Verlag.

Bridges, Douglas & Mehta, Ghanshyam. Representations of Preference Orderings. LC 94-45869. (Lecture Notes in Economics & Mathematical Systems Ser.: Vol. 422). 1995. write for info. (*0-387-58839-6*) Spr-Verlag.

Bridges, Douglas & Richman, Fred. Varieties of Constructive Mathematics. LC 85-26904. (London Mathematical Society Lecture Note Ser.: No. 97). 159p. 1987. pap. text 31.95 (*0-521-31802-5*) Cambridge U Pr.

Bridges, Douglas, jt. auth. see Bishop, E.

Bridges, E. Lucas. Uttermost Part of the Earth. 1988. pap. 13.95 (*0-486-25751-7*) Dover.

Bridges, E. R. & Butler, P. J., eds. Techniques in Comparative Respiratory Physiology. (Society for Experimental Biology Seminar Ser.: No. 37). 368p. (C). 1989. text 90.00 (*0-521-34568-5*) Cambridge U Pr.

Bridges, Edwin M. The Incompetent Teacher: Managerial Responses. 2nd ed. LC 92-2285. (Stanford Series on Education & Public Policy). 282p. 1992. pap. 24.95 (*0-7507-0050-5*, Falmer Pr) Taylor & Francis.

— Managing the Incompetent Teacher. 2nd ed. LC 90-80371. x, 98p. 1990. pap. 7.95 (*0-86552-102-6*) U of Oreg ERIC.

— PBL Project One: Time Management - Work of the Principal. viii, 112p. 1994. pap., teacher ed., ring bd. 15.00 (*0-86552-122-0*) U of Oreg ERIC.

— PBL Project One: Time Management: Work of the Principal. vii, 112p. 1994. pap., student ed., ring bd. 14.00 (*0-86552-127-1*) U of Oreg ERIC.

— PBL Project Three: Write Right! vii, 22p. 1994. pap., teacher ed., ring bd. 6.00 (*0-86552-125-5*); pap., student ed., ring bd. 5.50 (*0-86552-129-8*) U of Oreg ERIC.

— Problem-Based Learning for Administrators. LC 92-71619. xi, 160p. (C). 1992. pap. 10.95 (*0-86552-117-4*) U of Oreg ERIC.

— Surveying Derelict Land. (Monographs on Soil & Resources Survey: No. 13). (Illus.). 146p. 1987. 65.00 (*0-19-854566-5*) OUP.

— World Geomorphology. 270p. (C). 1990. pap. text 32.95 (*0-521-28965-3*) Cambridge U Pr.

Bridges, Edwin M. & Davidson, D. A., eds. Principles & Applications of Soil Geography. LC 80-41509. (Illus.). 309p. reprint ed. pap. 95.80 (*0-8357-2983-4*, 203924600011) Bks Demand.

Bridges, Edwin M. & Hallinger, Philip. Implementing Problem-Based Learning in Leadership Development. LC 95-5124. xii, 194p. 1995. pap. 14.95 (*0-86552-131-X*) U of Oreg ERIC.

Bridges, Francis J. So You Want to Be a Manager? LC 93-8230. 123p. (Orig.). 1993. pap. 9.95 (*0-9623126-2-2*) ESM Bks.

Bridges, Francis J. & Roquemore, Libby L. Management: Principles, Theory & Practice. (Illus.). 480p. (C). 1996. pap. text. write for info. (*0-9623126-4-9*) ESM Bks.

— Management for Athletic/Sport Administration: Theory & Practice. 2nd ed. (Illus.). 448p. (Orig.). (C). 1996. pap. text. write for info. (*0-9623126-5-7*) ESM Bks.

***Bridges, Francis J. & Roquemore, Libby L.** Management for Athletic/Sport Administration: Theory & Practice. 3rd rev. ed. LC 00-133048. (Illus.). 410p. (Orig.). 2000. pap. 45.00 (*0-9623126-6-5*) ESM Bks.

***Bridges, Frank.** Everything You Need to Know about Physics. LC 99-46971. 176p. 1999. per. 12.00 (*0-671-53490-4*) PB.

Bridges, Fraser. Alaska-Yukon Adventures. (Illus.). 368p. 1996. pap. 16.95 (*0-7615-0226-2*) Prima Pub.

— Alaska-Yukon Adventures: The Driver's Guide. 3rd ed. 1994. pap. 14.95 (*1-883470-02-1*) Amer Traveler.

— Alaska-Yukon Adventures: The Driver's Guide, Vol. 1. 1992. pap. 12.95 (*0-9694136-4-5*) Amer Traveler.

— Gulf Coast & Texas Adventures. (Illus.). 400p. Date not set. pap. 17.00 (*0-7615-0571-7*) Prima Pub.

— Natural Places of the Gulf Coast from Florida to Texas: A Traveler's Guide to the Culture . . . (Illus.). 352p. 1996. pap. text 18.00 (*0-7615-0570-9*) Prima Pub.

— Natural Places of the Southwest. (Natural Places Ser.). (Illus.). 432p. 1996. pap. 17.95 (*0-7615-0158-4*) Prima Pub.

— New England Adventures: The Driver's Guide. (Illus.). 352p. (Orig.). 1993. pap. 14.95 (*1-883470-01-3*) Amer Traveler.

— Pacific Coast Adventures: The Driver's Guide. 1991. pap. 12.95 (*0-9694136-3-7*) Amer Traveler.

— Pacific Coast Adventures: The Driver's Guide. 2nd enl. rev. ed. (Fraser Bridges Driver's Guide Ser.). (Illus.). 352p. 1993. pap. 14.95 (*1-883470-00-5*) Amer Traveler.

— Rocky Mountain Adventures: The Driver's Guide, Vol. 1. 1992. pap. 14.95 (*0-9694136-5-3*) Amer Traveler.

— Sierra Adventures. (Driver's Guide Ser.). (Illus.). 352p. pap. 14.95 (*0-9694136-7-X*) Amer Traveler.

— Southwest Adventures: The Complete Road Guide. LC 95-10894. (Illus.). 400p. 1995. pap. 16.95 (*0-7615-0134-7*) Prima Pub.

— Southwest Adventures: The Driver's Guide. (Illus.). 1992. pap. 14.95 (*0-9694136-6-1*) Amer Traveler.

Bridges, Fraser & Stone, Donald. Pacific Coast Adventures. LC 95-17208. (Illus.). 400p. 1995. pap. 16.95 (*0-7615-0135-5*) Prima Pub.

Bridges, G. Wilson. Annals of Jamaica, 2 vols., Set. 1968. reprint ed. 95.00 (*0-7146-1931-0*, Pub. by F Cass Pubs) Intl Spec Bk.

Bridges, Geoffrey G. Identity & Distinction in Petrus Thomae. (Philosophy Ser.). ix, 186p. 1959. pap. 10.00 (*1-57659-102-6*) Franciscan Inst.

Bridges, George. IBM Personal Computer Program Writing Workbook. 96p. 1983. 4.95 (*0-86668-818-8*) ARCsoft.

Bridges, George S. Understanding Social Deviance: A Lecture & Study Guide. 2nd ed. 128p. 1995. per. 19.95 (*0-8403-8916-7*) Kendall-Hunt.

Bridges, Hal. Lee's Maverick General: Daniel Harvey Hill. 323p. 1961. 30.00 (*1-56013-004-0*) Olde Soldier Bks.

— Lee's Maverick General: Daniel Harvey Hill. LC 91-13093. (Illus.). xxii, 323p. 1991. reprint ed. pap. 13.95 (*0-8032-6096-2*, Bison Books) U of Nebr Pr.

Bridges, Helice. Who I Am Makes a Difference: Stories That Connect People Heart-To-Heart & Ignite the Human Spirit. 1997. pap. 14.95 (*0-9660686-0-2*) Difference Makers.

Bridges, Herb. The Filming of Gone with the Wind. LC 98-231426. (Illus.). viii, 283p. 1998. reprint ed. pap. 21.95 (*0-86554-621-5*, P180) Mercer Univ Pr.

— Frankly, My Dear. . . Gone with the Wind Memorabilia. 2nd ed. (Illus.). 192p. (C). 1995. 34.95 (*0-86554-487-5*, MUP/H382) Mercer Univ Pr.

***Bridges, Herb.** Gone with the Wind: The Three-Day Premiere in Atlanta. LC 99-38010. (Illus.). 256p. 1999. 32.95 (*0-86554-672-X*) Mercer Univ Pr.

Bridges, Herb & Boodman, Terryl C. Gone with the Wind: The Definitive, Illustrated History of the Book, the Movie, the Legend. 256p. 1989. pap. 17.00 (*0-671-68387-X*, Fireside) S&S Trade Pap.

Bridges, Holly. Circle of Prayer: Coming Together to Find Spirit, Caring, & Community. LC 96-30055. 224p. 1997. pap. 12.95 (*1-885171-17-X*) Wldcat Canyon.

Bridges, Horace J. As I Was Saying. LC 70-121451. (Essay Index Reprint Ser.). 1977. 21.95 (*0-8369-1698-0*) Ayer.

— Criticisms of Life. LC 75-99684. (Essay Index Reprint Ser.). 1977. 23.95 (*0-8369-1342-6*) Ayer.

— God of Fundamentalism & Others Studies. LC 79-86733. (Essay Index Reprint Ser.). 1977. 21.95 (*0-8369-1249-7*) Ayer.

— Humanity on Trial. LC 74-142609. (Essay Index Reprint Ser.). 1977. 23.95 (*0-8369-2039-2*) Ayer.

— Taking the Name of Science in Vain. LC 72-86734. (Essay Index Reprint Ser.). 1977. 20.95 (*0-8369-1168-7*) Ayer.

Bridges, Horace J., ed. Aspects of Ethical Religion: Essays in Honor of Felix Adler. 1977. lib. bdg. 59.95 (*0-8490-1459-X*) Gordon Pr.

— Aspects of Ethical Religion: Essays in Honor of Felix Adler on the Fiftieth Anniversary of His Founding of the Ethical Movement. LC 68-29190. (Essay Index Reprint Ser.). 1977. reprint ed. 23.95 (*0-8369-0161-4*) Ayer.

Bridges, J. En Pos de la Santidad.Tr. of Pursuit of Holiness. (SPA.). 173p. 1995. 4.99 (*0-7899-0166-8*, 497283) Editorial Unilit.

— Gracia Transformadora.Tr. of Transforming Grace. (SPA.). 240p. 1995. pap. 10.99 (*0-8297-1969-5*) Vida Pubs.

Bridges, J. L., Jr., jt. auth. see Turner, J. Kelly.

***Bridges, James.** The Adventures of Elmo in Grouchland: Movie Storybook. LC 98-52321. (Illus.). 48p. (J). (ps-3). 1999. 6.99 (*0-375-80162-6*, Pub. by Random Bks Yng Read) Random.

Bridges, James E. Mortgage Loans: What's Right for You? 4th ed. LC 96-54243. 144p. 1997. pap. 14.99 (*1-55870-434-5*, Betrwy Bks) F & W Pubns Inc.

Bridges, James J. Structure & History in John Eleven: A Methodological Study Comparing Structuralist & Historical Critical Approaches. LC 90-28591. (Distinguished Dissertations Ser.: Vol. 4). 332p. 1991. lib. bdg. 99.95 (*0-7734-9942-3*) E Mellen.

Bridges, James P. The Academic Adventures of Laura Bridges: An Introduction to Educational Architecture Therapy. LC 99-62325. (Educational Architecture Therapy Ser.). 100p. 2000. 34.50 (*0-945741-03-0*); pap. 24.50 (*0-945741-05-7*); spiral bd. 24.50 (*0-945741-06-5*) New Philosopher Pr.

— The Academic Adventures of Laura Bridges: An Introduction to Educational Architecture Therapy. LC 99-62325. (Educational Architecture Therapy Ser.). 171p. 2000. lib. bdg. 39.95 (*0-945741-04-9*) New Philosopher Pr.

Bridges, James S. & Dempsey, Clyde R., eds. Pesticide Waste Disposal Technology. LC 87-31548. (Pollution Technology Review Ser.: No. 148). (Illus.). 331p. 1988. 89.00 (*0-8155-1157-4*) Noyes.

Bridges, James W. An Experimental Study of Decision Types & Their Mental Correlates. (Psychology Monographs General & Applied: Vol. 17). 1972. reprint ed. pap. 55.00 (*0-8115-1416-1*) Periodicals Srv.

Bridges, James W. & Chasseaud, L. F., eds. Progress in Drug Metabolism, 1. LC 75-19446. (Illus.). 300p. reprint ed. pap. 85.50 (*0-608-18830-1*, 2030485) Bks Demand.

— Progress in Drug Metabolism, 2. LC 75-19446. (Illus.). 360p. reprint ed. pap. 102.60 (*0-608-18831-X*, 2030485) Bks Demand.

— Progress in Drug Metabolism, 3. LC 75-19446. (Illus.). 385p. reprint ed. pap. 109.80 (*0-608-18832-8*, 2030485) Bks Demand.

— Progress in Drug Metabolism, 4. LC 75-19446. (Illus.). 347p. reprint ed. pap. 98.90 (*0-608-18833-6*, 2030485) Bks Demand.

— Progress in Drug Metabolism, 5. LC 75-19446. (Illus.). 372p. reprint ed. pap. 106.10 (*0-608-18834-4*, 2030485) Bks Demand.

— Progress in Drug Metabolism, 6. LC 75-19446. (Illus.). 331p. reprint ed. pap. 94.40 (*0-608-18835-2*, 2030485) Bks Demand.

***Bridges, Jennifer M. & Jensen, Randall.** Kinesiology Laboratory Manual. (Illus.). 281p. (C). 1999. spiral bd., lab manual ed. 19.95 (*0-87563-911-9*) Stipes.

Bridges, Jerry. The Crisis of Caring: Recovering the Meaning of True Fellowship. LC 92-14842. 1992. pap. 8.99 (*0-87552-110-X*) P & R Pubng.

— Crisis of Caring Study Guide: Recovering the Meaning of True Fellowship. 95p. 1992. pap. 4.99 (*0-87552-109-6*) P & R Pubng.

— The Discipline of Grace: God's Role & Our Role in the Pursuit of Holiness. LC 94-31041. 1994. pap. 12.00 (*0-89109-883-6*) NavPress.

— The Discipline of Grace Discussion Guide. 96p. (Orig.). 1995. pap., student ed. 6.00 (*0-89109-884-4*) NavPress.

***Bridges, Jerry.** The Joy of Fearing God. LC 98-228472. 288p. 1998. 19.95 (*1-57856-029-2*) Waterbrook Pr.

— The Joy of Fearing God: The Fear Of The Lord Is a Life-Giving Fountain, Proverbs 14:27. 288p. 1999. pap. 12.95 (*1-57856-254-6*) Waterbrook Pr.

— The Joy of Fearing God Study Guide. 96p. 1998. pap., student ed. 6.95 (*1-57856-059-4*) Waterbrook Pr.

Bridges, Jerry. Podemos Confiar en Dios. (Serie Realidades - Realities Ser.).Tr. of You Can Trust God. (SPA.). 90p. 1994. 1.99 (*1-56063-927-X*, 498131) Editorial Unilit.

— The Practice of Godliness. (NavClassics Ser.). 1996. pap. 10.00 (*0-89109-941-7*) NavPress.

— The Practice of Godliness: Bible Study. 72p. 1996. pap. 5.00 (*0-89109-498-9*) NavPress.

— The Pursuit of Holiness. (NavClassics Ser.). 1996. pap. 8.00 (*0-89109-940-9*) NavPress.

— The Pursuit of Holiness. large type ed. 172p. 1985. pap. 13.95 (*0-8027-2507-4*) Walker & Co.

— The Pursuit of Holiness: Bible Study. 64p. 1996. pap. 5.00 (*0-89109-025-8*) NavPress.

— Transforming Grace: Living Confidently in God's Unfailing Love. LC 91-61390. 224p. 1993. pap. 12.00 (*0-89109-656-6*) NavPress.

— Transforming Grace Discussion Guide: Living Confidently in God's Unfailing Love. 224p. 1993. pap. 7.00 (*0-89109-644-2*) NavPress.

— Trusting God: Even When Life Hurts. LC 88-60825. 216p. 1988. pap. 12.00 (*0-89109-617-5*) NavPress.

— Trusting God (Study Guide) Even When Life Hurts. 120p. (Orig.). 1990. pap. 7.00 (*0-89109-241-2*) NavPress.

— You Can Trust God. 1991. pap. 2.50 (*0-89109-571-3*) NavPress.

Bridges, Jim, jt. auth. see Bridges, Olga.

Bridges, John. How to Be a Gentleman: A Contemporary Guide to Common Courtesy. LC 98-10379. (Illus.). 150p. 1998. 12.95 (*1-55853-596-9*) Rutledge Hill Pr.

— Keeping Up: Blue Blazers, Iced Tea, & Everything Else Worthwhile in Life. LC 93-37424. 134p. 1993. pap. 11.95 (*0-9638616-0-3*) City Press.

Bridges, John, illus. see Appel, Shannon, et al.

Bridges, John C. Making Violence Part of the Game. LC 97-40873. 259p. 1998. pap. 35.00 (*1-56072-506-0*, Nova Kroshka Bks) Nova Sci Pubs.

Bridges, John H. The Life & Work of Roger Bacon. Jones, H. Gordon, ed. LC 79-8597. reprint ed. 27.50 (*0-404-18450-2*) AMS Pr.

— The Life & Work of Roger Bacon: An Introduction to the Opus Majus. Jones, H. Gordon, ed. LC 76-1120. 1977. reprint ed. lib. bdg. 15.00 (*0-915172-14-3*) Richwood Pub.

Bridges-Johns, Cheryl. Pentecostal Formation: A Pedagogy among the Oppressed. (JPT Supplement Ser.: No. 2). 154p. 1993. pap. 13.95 (*1-85075-438-1*, Pub. by Sheffield Acad) CUP Services.

Bridges, Joseph L. A Guide to the Internet for Mass Communication Students. LC 97-114956. 144p. (C). 1997. text. write for info. (*0-697-35273-0*) Brown & Benchmark.

Bridges, Josephine. The Only Word There Is. 72p. 1999. pap. 12.00 (*0-9670716-0-7*) Mall Street.

Bridges, Joyce, jt. auth. see Bpuet, Jeanie.

Bridges, Joyce S. & Head, Wanda V. Mississippi Roots & Records Vol. I: Claiborne, Co. 100p. 1994. pap. text 16.00 (*1-57088-035-2*) J&W Ent.

— Mississippi Roots & Records Vol. 2: Tishomingo County. 100p. 1995. pap. text 16.00 (*1-57088-036-0*) J&W Ent.

— Mississippi Roots & Records - Copiah County, Vol. 3. 97p. 1994. pap. text 16.00 (*1-57088-037-9*) J&W Ent.

— Mississippi Roots & Records - Franklin County, Vol. 4. 104p. 1994. pap. text 16.00 (*1-57088-038-7*) J&W Ent.

— Mississippi Roots & Records - Madison County, Vol. 5. 102p. 1994. pap. text 16.00 (*1-57088-039-5*) J&W Ent.

— Mississippi Roots n' Records - WPA County Maps, Vol. 6. 81p. 1997. pap. 16.00 (*1-57088-047-6*) J&W Ent.

Bridges, Ken. Succeeding in the World Without Being of the World. LC 93-90236. 71p. (Orig.). (C). 1993. pap. 5.95 (*0-9636330-0-7*) Bridge PA.

Bridges, L. T. Flags of Louisiana. (J). (ps-8). 1971. 6.95 (*0-87511-010-X*) Claitors.

Bridges, Lee, et al. Judicial Review in Perspective. 2nd ed. 236p. 1995. pap. 40.00 (*1-85941-203-3*, Pub. by Cavendish Pubng) Gaunt.

— Legality & Local Politics. LC 87-366. 150p. 1987. text 87.95 (*0-566-05430-2*, Pub. by Dartmth Pub) Ashgate Pub Co.

Bridges, Lee, jt. ed. see McConville, Michael.

Bridges, Linda & Rickenbacker, William F. The Art of Persuasion: A National Review Rhetoric for Writers. (Illus.). 144p. 1991. 19.95 (*0-9627841-0-9*) Natl Review.

Bridges, Linda McKinnish. The Church's Portraits of Jesus. LC 97-8701. 128p. 1997. pap. 12.00 (*1-57312-003-0*) Smyth & Helwys.

Bridges, Lois. Assessment: Continuous Learning. (Strategies for Teaching & Learning Ser.). 112p. (C). 1996. reprint ed. pap. text 15.00 (*1-57110-048-2*) Stenhse Pubs.

— Creating Your Classroom Community. (Strategies for Teaching & Learning Ser.). 112p. (C). 1996. reprint ed. pap. text 15.00 (*1-57110-049-0*) Stenhse Pubs.

— Writing As a Way of Knowing. LC 97-16320. (Strategies for Teaching & Learning Ser.). 144p. 1997. pap. text 15.00 (*1-57110-062-8*) Stenhse Pubs.

Bridges, Margaret P. If I Were Your Father. LC 98-24131. (Illus.). 32p. (J). (ps-3). 1999. 16.00 (*0-688-15192-2*, Wm Morrow) Morrow Avon.

***Bridges, Margaret P.** If I Were Your Father. LC 98-24132. (Illus.). 32p. (J). (ps-3). 1999. lib. bdg. 15.89 (*0-688-15193-0*, Wm Morrow) Morrow Avon.

Bridges, Margaret P. Will You Take Care of Me. LC 97-32917. (Illus.). 32p. (J). (ps-k). 1998. 16.00 (*0-688-15194-9*, Wm Morrow) Morrow Avon.

***Bridges, Margaret P.** Will You Take Care of Me. LC 97-32917. (Illus.). 32p. (J). (ps-k). 1998. 15.89 (*0-688-15195-7*, Wm Morrow) Morrow Avon.

***Bridges, Margaret Park.** Am I Big or Little? (Illus.). (J). 2000. 14.95 (*1-58717-019-1*) SeaStar.

Bridges, Margaret Park. If I Were Your Mother. LC 98-24132. (Illus.). 32p. (J). (ps-3). 1999. 15.95 (*0-688-15190-6*, Wm Morrow) Morrow Avon.

***Bridges, Margaret Park.** If I Were Your Mother. (Illus.). 32p. (J). (ps up). 1999. lib. bdg. 15.89 (*0-688-15191-4*, Wm Morrow) Morrow Avon.

***Bridges, Margaret Park & Dockray, Tracy A.** Am I Big or Little? LC 00-25825. (Illus.). (J). 2000. pap. 14.88 (*1-58717-020-5*) SeaStar.

Bridges, Marilyn. Markings: Aerial Views of Sacred Landscapes. (Illus.). 96p. 1986. 60.00 (*0-89381-228-5*) Aperture.

— Planet Peru. (Illus.). 108p. 1991. 53.00 (*0-89381-469-5*) Aperture.

— This Land Is Your Land. LC 96-78749. 1997. 76.00 (*0-89381-604-3*) Aperture.

Bridges, Mark & Dineen, Joe, compiled by. Gig Bag Book of Arpeggios for All Guitarists. (Illus.). 245p. 1998. pap. text 12.95 (*0-8256-1659-X*, AM946902) Music Sales.

An Asterisk (*) at the beginning of an entry indicates that the title is appearing for the first time.

Bridges, Mark & Dineen, Joe, eds. The Encyclopedia of Guitar Tab Chords. LC 99-180642. (Illus.). 269p. 1998. pap. text 19.95 (*0-8256-1690-5*, AM948772) Music Sales.

Bridges, Mary, ed. see International Festivals & Events Assoc. Staff.

Bridges, Moe & L-W Book Sales (Firm). Better Electric Lamps of the 20's & 30's. LC 97-153165. (Illus.). 1997. write for info. (*0-89538-087-0*) L-W Inc.

Bridges, Nancy S. Bible Discovery - Words of Wisdom - Job, Psalms & Proverbs: Student Workbook. Clark, Virginia A. & Constance, Tom M., eds. (J). (gr. 3-6). 1998. pap., wbk. ed. 18.95 (*1-889015-25-3*) Explrs Bible.

Bridges, Olga & Bridges, Jim. Losing Hope: The Environment & Health in Russia. LC 95-83401. (Avebury Studies in Green Research). 288p. 1996. 78.95 (*1-85972-144-3*, Pub. by Avebury) Ashgate Pub Co.

Bridges, Olga, et al. Teach Yourself Business Russian: A Complete Course for Beginners. (RUS., Illus.). 320p. 1995. pap. 14.95 (*0-8442-3784-1*, Teach Yrslf) NTC Contemp Pub Co.

— Teach Yourself Russian Business. (RUS.). 320p. 1995. pap. 24.95 incl. audio (*0-8442-3876-7*, Teach Yrslf) NTC Contemp Pub Co.

Bridges, Robert. Collected Essays, Papers, Etc. 30 Parts in 1. 1972. reprint ed. 142.25 (*3-487-04382-3*) Adlers Foreign Bks.

— Influence of the Audience on Shakespeare's Drama. LC 74-100795. (Studies in Shakespeare: No. 24). 1970. reprint ed. pap. 39.95 (*0-8383-0085-5*) M S G Haskell Hse.

— John Keats. LC 72-1976. (Studies in Keats: No. 19). 1972. reprint ed. lib. bdg. 75.00 (*0-8383-1453-8*) M S G Haskell Hse.

— Robert Bridges: (A Collection of Poems) Thompson, Edward, ed. (Augustan Books of Modern Poetry Ser.). 36p. 1998. reprint ed. 10.00 (*0-89904-736-X*, Silhouette Imprints); reprint ed. pap. 5.00 (*0-89904-737-8*, Silhouette Imprints) Crumb Elbow Pub.

Bridges, Robert, ed. The Chilswell Book of English Poetry. LC 74-168774. (Granger Index Reprint Ser.). 1977. reprint ed. 20.95 (*0-8369-6294-X*) Ayer.

Bridges, Robert S. Milton's Prosody with a Chapter on Accentual Verse & Notes. (BCL1-PR English Literature Ser.). 119p. 1992. reprint ed. lib. bdg. 69.00 (*0-7812-7380-3*) Rprt Serv.

— Poetical Works of Robert Bridges, Excluding the 8 Dramas. 2nd ed. LC 75-41036. (BCL Ser. II). reprint ed. 72.50 (*0-404-14511-6*) AMS Pr.

— The Testament of Beauty: A Poem in Four Books. (BCL1-PR English Literature Ser.). 175p. 1992. reprint ed. lib. bdg. 69.00 (*0-7812-7450-8*) Rprt Serv.

Bridges, Roger D., ed. see Grant, Ulysses S.

Bridges, Ronald F., jt. auth. see Weigle, Luther A.

***Bridges, Roy.** Imperialism, Decolonization, & Africa: Studies Presented to John Hargreaves. LC 99-32867. 2000. text 65.00 (*0-312-22395-1*) St Martin.

***Bridges, Roy G.** How to Calculate & Use Drip Constants. LC 99-90919. (Illus.). 71p. 1999. pap. 10.00 (*0-9666974-1-3*) R Bridges Enter.

Bridges, Roy G. Roy's Pocket Guide - Medication Drip Constants & Reference Tables. LC 98-92100. (Illus.). 106p. 1998. pap. 14.95 (*0-9666974-0-5*) R Bridges Enter.

Bridges, Roy G., jt. auth. see Beach, David P.

Bridges, Ruby. Through My Eyes. LC 98-49242. (Illus.). 63p. (J). (gr. 3-7). 1999. 16.95 (*0-590-18923-9*, Pub. by Scholastic Inc) Penguin Putnam.

Bridges, Ruth. Versified Inspirations. 1998. pap. write for info. (*1-57553-871-7*) Watermrk Pr.

Bridges, Thomas. The Culture of Citizenship: Inventing Postmodern Civic Culture. LC 93-48374. (SUNY Series in Social & Political Thought). 267p. (C). 1994. text 21.50 (*0-7914-2033-7*) State U NY Pr.

Bridges, Thomas, et al. Travel Industry World Yearbook: The Big Picture. (Illus.). 180p. (Orig.). 1996. pap. write for info. (*0-614-12929-X*) Child & Waters Inc.

Bridges, Thomas, et al. Travel Industry World Yearbook Vol. 42: The Big Picture. annuals annot. ed. Date not set. pap. 95.00 (*1-883933-05-6*, 99-42) Travel Industry Pubg.

Bridges, Thomas, ed. see Waters, Somerset R.

Bridges, Thomas C. & Tiltman, Hubert H. Heroes of Modern Adventure. LC 76-152160. (Essay Index Reprint Ser.). 1977. reprint ed. 24.95 (*0-8369-2216-6*) Ayer.

— Kings of Commerce. LC 68-8442. (Essay Index Reprint Ser.). 1977. 20.95 (*0-8369-0102-9*) Ayer.

— Master Minds of Modern Science. LC 68-57307. (Essay Index Reprint Ser.). 1977. 20.95 (*0-8369-0064-2*) Ayer.

— More Heroes of Modern Adventure. LC 76-86735. (Essay Index Reprint Ser.). 1977. 23.95 (*0-8369-1343-4*) Ayer.

Bridges, Thomas J. & Furter, Jacques E. Singularity Theory & Equivariant Symplectic Maps. LC 93-37171. (Lecture Notes in Mathematics Ser.: Vol. 1558). 1993. 45.95 (*0-387-57296-1*) Spr-Verlag.

Bridges, Toby. Advanced Black Powder Hunting. 1998. pap. 21.95 (*0-88317-209-7*) Stoeger Pub Co.

***Bridges, Toby.** Complete Book of Whitetail Hunting. Jarrett, Bill, ed. (Illus.). 320p. 2000. pap. 21.95 (*0-88317-222-4*) Stoeger Pub Co.

— The Complete Hunter Muzzleloading. 2000. 21.95 (*0-86573-127-6*) Creat Pub Intl.

Bridges, Toby. Muzzleloading. LC 97-3876. (Hunting & Fishing Library). (Illus.). 128p. 1997. 19.95 (*0-86573-066-0*) Creat Pub Intl.

— Muzzleloading for Whitetails. Helgeland, Glenn, ed. LC 94-49359. (On Target Ser.: No. 12). (Illus.). 156p. 1995. pap. 12.95 (*0-913305-12-X*) Target Comm.

Bridges, Tom, jt. ed. see Hoy, Anne H.

Bridges, Tyler. The Rise of David Duke. LC 93-43873. (Illus.). 308p. 1994. text 24.95 (*0-87805-678-5*) U Pr of Miss.

— The Rise of David Duke. LC 93-43873. (Illus.). 320p. 1995. pap. 15.95 (*0-87805-684-X*) U Pr of Miss.

Bridges, W. P. & Villemez, W. J. The Employment Relationship: Causes & Consequences of Modern Personnel Administration. (Studies in Work & Industry). (Illus.). 256p. (C). 1994. 39.50 (*0-306-44744-4*, Plenum Trade) Perseus Pubng.

Bridges, William. The Character of Organizations: Using Jungian Type in Organizational Development. LC 91-42122. 152p. 1992. pap. 13.95 (*0-89106-052-9*, 7375, Davies-Black Pub) Consulting Psychol.

***Bridges, William.** The Character of Organizations: Using Personality Type in Organization Development. Updated Edition. LC 00-35877. 160p. 2000. pap. 18.95 (*0-89106-149-5*, Davies-Black Pub) Consulting Psychol.

Bridges, William. Creating You & Co. Learn to Think Like the CEO of Your Own Career. LC 98-87225. 208p. 1998. pap. text 14.00 (*0-7382-0032-8*) Perseus Pubng.

— Job Shift: How to Prosper in a Workplace Without Jobs. 272p. 1995. pap. 14.00 (*0-201-48933-3*) Addison-Wesley.

— JobShift: How To Prosper in a Workplace Without Jobs. 240p. 1995. 11.66 (*0-201-62667-5*) Addison-Wesley.

— Managing Transitions: Making the Most of Change. (Illus.). 276p. 1991. pap. 19.00 (*0-201-55073-3*) Addison-Wesley.

— Transitions: Making Sense of Life's Changes. 160p. 1980. pap. 13.00 (*0-201-00082-2*) Addison-Wesley.

Bridges, William F. Health Care Reform: The Dilemma & a Pathway for the Health Care System. 1993. text 31.95 (*1-878060-07-4*) GW Medical.

Bridges, William P., jt. auth. see Nelson, Robert L.

Bridgestone Management Publishing Staff, contrib. by. Captain Bible: Dome of Darkness. 1994. 39.95 (*1-56371-159-1*, F1300) Brdgstn Multimed Grp.

— Giants of the Faith. 1998. cd-rom 39.95 (*1-56371-461-2*) Brdgstn Multimed Grp.

— God's Word for Windows. 1997. cd-rom 19.95 (*1-56371-413-2*) Brdgstn Multimed Grp.

Bridget. The Magnificent Prayers of Saint Bridget of Sweden. (Illus.). 19p. 1994. reprint ed. pap. 2.00 (*0-89555-220-5*) TAN Bks Pubs.

Bridgett, Christopher, et al. Atopic Skin Disease: A Manual for Practitioners. LC 97-204482. 176p. 1996. 49.50 (*1-871816-32-7*, Pub. by Wrightson Biomed) Taylor & Francis.

Bridgewater, Alan. Easy-to-Make Decorative Kites: Sixteen Designs with Full-Scale Templates. (Illus.). 48p. 1986. pap. 3.95 (*0-486-24981-6*) Dover.

— Handles, Hinges, Knobs, & Latches. LC 97-51569. (Illus.). 144p. 1998. 17.95 (*0-8069-1335-5*) Sterling.

— I Made It Myself: Kids Craft Projects. (Illus.). 192p. (J). 1990. 19.95 (*0-8306-8339-9*, 3339); pap. 11.95 (*0-8306-3339-1*) McGraw-Hill Prof.

Bridgewater, Alan & Bridgewater, Gill. Basics: Woodcarving Basics. LC 95-44153. (Illus.). 128p. 1996. pap. 10.95 (*0-8069-1334-7*) Sterling.

— The Beastly Book of Dinosaur Action Toys. 224p. 1992. 24.95 (*0-8306-2162-8*, 3994); pap. 14.95 (*0-8306-2161-X*, 3994) McGraw-Hill Prof.

— Beautiful Wooden Gifts You Can Make in a Weekend. LC 97-34530. (Illus.). 128p. 1998. pap. 22.99 (*1-55870-452-3*, Betrwy Bks) F & W Pubns Inc.

— Boxes & Chests: How to Make & Decorate 15 Traditional Country Projects. LC 96-27435. (Illus.). 192p. 1997. pap. 19.95 (*0-8117-2559-6*) Stackpole.

— Building Doors & Gates. LC 98-27518. viii, 168p. 1999. 19.95 (*0-8117-2678-9*) Stackpole.

***Bridgewater, Alan & Bridgewater, Gill.** Building Shelves in a Weekend. (Illus.). 80p. 2000. pap. 16.99 (*1-55870-548-1*, Popular Woodwking Bks) F & W Pubns Inc.

Bridgewater, Alan & Bridgewater, Gill. Carving Figureheads & Other Nautical Designs. LC 94-47294. (Illus.). 176p. 1995. pap. 14.95 (*0-8069-8706-5*) Sterling.

— Carving Totem Poles & Masks: Native American Folk Art. LC 91-726. (Illus.). 192p. 1991. pap. 14.95 (*0-8069-8214-4*) Sterling.

— Craft for One Another: Projects for the Young & the Young at Heart. LC 93-8531. 1993. 14.60 (*0-8306-3761-3*) McGraw-Hill Prof.

— Holiday Crafts: More Year-Round Crafts Kids Can Make. (Illus.). 256p. (J). 1990. pap. 16.95 (*0-8306-3409-6*) McGraw-Hill Prof.

— How to Use & Care for Woodworking Tools. LC 98-9266. (Illus.). 224p. 1998. 19.95 (*0-8117-2794-7*) Stackpole.

— Making Marble-Action Games, Gadgets, Mazes, & Contraptions: Designs for 10 Outlandish, Ingenious, & Intricate Woodworking Projects. LC 99-11796. (Illus.). 144p. 1999. pap. 19.95 (*0-8117-2855-2*) Stackpole.

***Bridgewater, Alan & Bridgewater, Gill.** Making More Wooden Mechanical Models. LC 99-21732. (Illus.). 128p. 1999. pap. 24.99 (*1-55870-508-2*, 70444, Popular Woodwking Bks) F & W Pubns Inc.

Bridgewater, Alan & Bridgewater, Gill. Making Traditional Pull-Along Toys in Wood. (Illus.). 159p. 1998. pap. text 13.00 (*0-7881-5898-8*) DIANE Pub.

— Making Wooden Mechanical Models: 15 Designs with Visible Wheels, Cranks, Pistons, Cogs & Cams. LC 95-14143. (Illus.). 144p. (Orig.). 1995. pap. 21.99 (*1-55870-381-0*, Betrwy Bks) F & W Pubns Inc.

— Marquetry & Inlay: Twenty Decorative Projects. (Illus.). 192p. 1991. 24.95 (*0-8306-8426-3*, 3426); pap. 15.95 (*0-8306-3426-6*) McGraw-Hill Prof.

— Mastering Hand Tool Techniques. (Illus.). 144p. 1997. 27.99 (*1-55870-457-4*, Betrwy Bks) F & W Pubns Inc.

— 100 Keys to Preventing & Fixing Woodworking Mistakes. (Illus.). 64p. 1996. 17.99 (*1-55870-429-9*, Betrwy Bks) F & W Pubns Inc.

— 100 Keys to Woodshop Safety. (Illus.). 64p. 1996. 17.99 (*1-55870-430-2*, Betrwy Bks) F & W Pubns Inc.

***Bridgewater, Alan & Bridgewater, Gill.** Outdoor Stonework: 16 Easy-to-Build Projects for Your Yard & Garden. 96p. 2001. pap. 17.95 (*1-58017-333-0*) Storey Bks.

— Outdoor Water Features: 16 Easy-to-Build Projects for Your Yard. 96p. 2001. pap. 17.95 (*1-58017-334-9*) Storey Bks.

Bridgewater, Alan & Bridgewater, Gill. Painted Wood Projects in the Pennsylvania Folk Art Style. LC 95-14927. (Illus.). 144p. 1995. 27.95 (*0-8069-0508-5*) Sterling.

— Painted Wood Projects in the Pennsylvania Folk Art Style. (Illus.). 144p. 1997. pap. 14.95 (*0-8069-0509-3*) Sterling.

— Power Tool Woodcarving: Projects & Techniques. LC 93-41044. (Illus.). 164p. 1994. pap. 14.95 (*0-8069-8710-3*) Sterling.

— Teddy Bear Treasures: Making Movable Wooden Toys. LC 92-41248. 1993. 14.60 (*0-8306-2168-7*) McGraw-Hill Prof.

— Treasury of Woodcarving Designs from Around the World. LC 98-51586. (Illus.). 1999. pap. text. write for info. (*0-486-40480-3*) Dover.

— Wood Carving: Twenty-Three Traditional Decorative Projects. (Illus.). 272p. 1988. 22.95 (*0-8306-0979-2*); pap. 14.95 (*0-8306-2979-3*) McGraw-Hill Prof.

— Woodturning Traditional Folk Toys. LC 94-16756. (Illus.). 128p. 1994. pap. 14.95 (*0-8069-8708-1*) Sterling

— The Woodworker's Solution Book. (Illus.). 128p. 1998. pap. 26.99 (*1-55870-496-5*, Popular Woodwking Bks) F & W Pubns Inc.

— Woodworking Together: Projects for Kids & Their Families. (Illus.). 200p. 1992. pap. 15.95 (*0-8306-2164-4*, 3995) McGraw-Hill Prof.

Bridgewater, Allan, jt. auth. see Bridgewater, Gill.

Bridgewater Book Co. Pastries & Puddings. (Victorian Kitchen Ser.). 41p. 1995. write for info. (*1-57215-050-5*) World Pubns.

— Pickles & Preserves. (Victorian Kitchen Ser.). 41p. 1995. write for info. (*1-57215-049-1*) World Pubns.

Bridgewater Book Co., Staff. Cakes & Cookies. (Victorian Kitchen Ser.). 41p. 1995. write for info. (*1-57215-052-1*) World Pubns.

— Candies & Confections. (Victorian Kitchen Ser.). 41p. 1995. write for info. (*1-57215-051-3*) World Pubns.

— Jams & Jellies. (Victorian Kitchen Ser.). 41p. 1995. write for info. (*1-57215-048-3*) World Pubns.

— Milk & Honey. (Victorian Kitchen Ser.). 41p. 1995. write for info. (*1-57215-053-X*) World Pubns.

Bridgewater, Earl Edward, ed. see Charles, Homer N.

Bridgewater, Gill & Bridgewater, Allan. Traditional & Folk Designs. (Illus.). 64p. (Orig.). 1990. pap. 9.95 (*0-85532-654-9*, 654-9, Pub. by Srch Pr) A Schwartz & Co.

Bridgewater, Gill, jt. auth. see Bridgewater, Alan.

Bridgewater, Lucy. Treasures from the Well: Memories of Three Generations. 116p. 1997. pap. write for info. (*1-57502-637-6*, P01810) Morris Pubng.

Bridgewater, Patrick, jt. auth. see Coustillas, Pierre.

Bridgewater, Peter & Woods, Gerald. Halftone Effects: A Complete Visual Guide to Enhancing & Transforming Halftone Images. LC 92-26802. (Illus.). 144p. 1993. pap. 19.95 (*0-8118-0326-0*) Chronicle Bks.

Bridgewater, Shirlene, ed. see Potts, Nancy D.

Bridgewater, Susan. Innovation in Marketing. 224p. 1999. pap. text 39.95 (*0-7506-4121-5*) Buttrwrth-Heinemann.

Bridgewaters, Alan. How to Make Simple Wooden Puzzles & Jigsaws. (Illus.). 48p. 1994. pap. 11.95 (*0-85532-759-6*, 759-6, Pub. by Srch Pr) A Schwartz & Co.

Bridgewaters Staff. How to Make Simple Wooden Puzzles & Jigsaws. (Illus.). 48p. (YA). 1994. pap. 11.95 (*0-85532-779-0*, Pub. by Srch Pr) A Schwartz & Co.

Bridgford, Jeff. The Politics of French Trade Unionism. 206p. 1992. text 59.00 (*0-7185-1350-9*, Pub. by Leicester U Pr) Cassell & Continuum.

— The Politics of French Trade Unionism. 208p. 1994. pap. 17.95 (*0-7185-1487-4*, Pub. by Leicester U Pr) Cassell & Continuum.

Bridgford, Jeff & Stirling, John. Employee Relations in Europe: New Developments in European Human Resource Policies. LC 93-16874. (Human Resource Management in Action Ser.). (Illus.). 320p. 1994. pap. 43.95 (*0-631-18683-2*) Blackwell Pubs.

Bridgforth, Glinda. The Basic Money Management Workbook: A Twelve Month Program for Financial Peace of Mind. (Illus.). 230p. (Orig.). 1994. pap. 20.00 (*0-9659133-0-9*) Bridgforth Fin.

***Bridgforth, Glinda.** Girl, Get Your Money Straight. 2000. 20.95 (*0-7679-0487-7*) Broadway BDD.

Bridgforth, Sharon. Bull-Jean Stories. LC 99-191227. 111p. 1998. pap. 12.00 (*0-9656659-1-7*) RedBone Pr.

Bridgham, Fred. A Friendly German-English Dictionary: A Guide to German Language, Culture & Society Through Faux-Amis, Literary Illustration & Other Diversions. LC 96-166675. (ENG & GER.). 320p. pap. 26.95 (*1-870352-67-X*, Pub. by Libris) Paul & Co Pubs.

— A Friendly German-English Dictionary: A Guide to German Language, Culture & Society Through Faux-Amis, Literary Illustration & Other Diversions. LC 96-166675. (ENG & GER.). 320p. 1996. 67.50 (*1-870352-65-3*, Pub. by Libris) Paul & Co Pubs.

Bridgham, Fred, tr. see Geiss, Imanuel.

Bridgland, D. R., jt. auth. see Preece, R. C.

Bridgland, Tony. Field Gun Jack vs. the Boers. 1998. 39.95 (*0-85052-580-2*, Pub. by Leo Cooper) Trans-Atl Phila.

***Bridgland, Tony.** Sea Killers in Disguise: Q Ships & Raiders of World War I. 1999. 34.95 (*1-55750-895-X*) Naval Inst Pr.

Bridgman, Anne, ed. see National Research Council Staff & Institute of Medicine Staff.

Bridgman, Beth. Binary Fusion & the Millennium Bug. (Binary Fusion Ser.). 386p. 1999. pap. 20.00 (*0-9669444-0-2*) BTwo Pub.

Bridgman, Beth, contrib. by. Adjectives & Adverbs. rev. ed. (Horizons Grammar Ser.). (Illus.). 24p. (J). (gr. 4-9). 1998. pap. 5.95 (*1-58086-062-1*, Usborne) EDC.

— Apostrophe, Colon, Hyphen. rev. ed. (Horizons Grammar Ser.). (Illus.). 24p. (J). (gr. 4-9). 1998. pap. 5.95 (*1-58086-059-1*, Usborne) EDC.

— Capital Letters. rev. ed. (Horizons Grammar Ser.). (Illus.). 24p. (J). (gr. 4-9). 1998. pap. 5.95 (*1-58086-070-2*, Usborne) EDC.

— Comma. rev. ed. (Horizons Grammar Ser.). (Illus.). 24p. (J). (gr. 4-9). 1998. pap. 5.95 (*1-58086-061-3*, Usborne) EDC.

— Context Clues. rev. ed. (Horizons Grammar Ser.). (Illus.). 24p. (J). (gr. 4-9). 1998. pap. 5.95 (*1-58086-068-0*, Usborne) EDC.

— Dictionary Skills. rev. ed. (Horizons Grammar Ser.). (Illus.). 24p. (J). (gr. 4-9). 1998. pap. 5.95 (*1-58086-071-0*, Usborne) EDC.

— Figures of Speech. rev. ed. (Horizons Grammar Ser.). (Illus.). 24p. (J). (gr. 4-9). 1998. pap. 5.95 (*1-58086-067-2*, Usborne) EDC.

— Nouns & Pronouns. rev. ed. (Horizons Grammar Ser.). (Illus.). 24p. (J). (gr. 4-6). 1998. pap. 5.95 (*1-58086-065-6*, Usborne) EDC.

— Paragraph & Topic Sentence. rev. ed. (Horizons Grammar Ser.). (Illus.). 24p. (J). (gr. 4-9). 1998. pap. 5.95 (*1-58086-072-9*, Usborne) EDC.

— Period, Question Mark, Exclamation Mark. rev. ed. (Horizons Grammar Ser.). (Illus.). 24p. (J). (gr. 4-9). 1998. pap. 5.95 (*1-58086-058-3*, Usborne) EDC.

— Prefixes, Bases, Suffixes. rev. ed. (Horizons Grammar Ser.). (Illus.). 24p. (J). (gr. 4-9). 1998. pap. 5.95 (*1-58086-066-4*, Usborne) EDC.

— Prepositions & Conjunctions. rev. ed. (Horizons Grammar Ser.). (Illus.). 24p. (J). (gr. 4-9). 1998. pap. 5.95 (*1-58086-063-X*, Usborne) EDC.

— Quotation Marks, Underlining. rev. ed. (Horizons Grammar Ser.). (Illus.). 24p. (J). (gr. 4-9). 1998. pap. 5.95 (*1-58086-060-5*, Usborne) EDC.

— Synonyms, Antonyms, Homonyms. rev. ed. (Horizons Grammar Ser.). (Illus.). 24p. (J). (gr. 4-9). 1998. pap. 5.95 (*1-58086-069-9*, Usborne) EDC.

— Teacher's Guide. rev. ed. (Horizons Grammar Ser.). (Illus.). 24p. (J). (gr. 4-9). 1998. pap. 1.00 (*1-58086-113-X*, Usborne) EDC.

— Verbs. rev. ed. (Horizons Grammar Ser.). (Illus.). 24p. (J). (gr. 4-9). 1998. pap. 5.95 (*1-58086-064-8*, Usborne) EDC.

Bridgman, Beth, rev. Distinguishing Between Fact & Opinion. rev. ed. (Horizons Concepts Ser.: Level 1). (Illus.). 24p. (J). (gr. 4-9). 1998. pap. 5.95 (*1-58086-042-7*, Usborne) EDC.

— Distinguishing Between Fact & Opinion. rev. ed. (Horizons Concepts Ser.: Level 2). (Illus.). 24p. (J). (gr. 4-9). 1998. pap. 5.95 (*1-58086-052-4*, Usborne) EDC.

— Drawing Conclusions. rev. ed. (Horizons Concepts Ser.: Level 1). (Illus.). 24p. (J). (gr. 4-9). 1998. pap. 5.95 (*1-58086-043-5*, Usborne) EDC.

— Drawing Conclusions. rev. ed. (Horizons Concepts Ser.: Level 2). (Illus.). 24p. (J). (gr. 4-9). 1998. pap. 5.95 (*1-58086-053-2*, Usborne) EDC.

— Establishing Sequence. rev. ed. (Horizons Concepts Ser.: Level 1). (Illus.). 24p. (J). (gr. 4-9). 1998. pap. 5.95 (*1-58086-040-0*, Usborne) EDC.

— Establishing Sequence. rev. ed. (Horizons Concepts Ser.: Level 2). (Illus.). 24p. (J). (gr. 4-9). 1998. pap. 5.95 (*1-58086-050-8*, Usborne) EDC.

— Finding the Main Idea. rev. ed. (Horizons Concepts Ser.: Level 1). (Illus.). 24p. (J). (gr. 4-9). 1998. pap. 5.95 (*1-58086-039-7*, Usborne) EDC.

— Finding the Main Idea. rev. ed. (Horizons Concepts Ser.: Level 2). (Illus.). 24p. (J). (gr. 4-9). 1998. pap. 5.95 (*1-58086-049-4*, Usborne) EDC.

— Following Directions. rev. ed. (Horizons Concepts Ser.: Level 1). (Illus.). 24p. (J). (gr. 4-9). 1998. pap. 5.95 (*1-58086-041-9*, Usborne) EDC.

— Following Directions. rev. ed. (Horizons Concepts Ser.: Level 2). (Illus.). 24p. (J). (gr. 4-9). 1998. pap. 5.95 (*1-58086-051-6*, Usborne) EDC.

— Horizons Concepts, Level 1. rev. ed. (Illus.). (J). (gr. 4-9). 1998. pap. 54.95 (*1-58086-073-7*, Usborne) EDC.

— Horizons Concepts, Level 2. rev. ed. (Illus.). (J). (gr. 4-9). 1998. pap. 54.95 (*1-58086-074-5*, Usborne) EDC.

— Horizons Grammar. rev. ed. (Illus.). (J). (gr. 4-9). 1998. pap. 84.95 (*1-58086-075-3*, Usborne) EDC.

— Making Judgments. rev. ed. (Horizons Concepts Ser.: Level 1). (Illus.). 24p. (J). (gr. 4-9). 1998. pap. 5.95 (*1-58086-047-8*, Usborne) EDC.

— Making Judgments. rev. ed. (Horizons Concepts Ser.: Level 2). (Illus.). 24p. (J). (gr. 4-9). 1998. pap. 5.95 (*1-58086-057-5*, Usborne) EDC.

— Predicting Outcomes. rev. ed. (Horizons Concepts Ser.: Level 1). (Illus.). 24p. (J). (gr. 4-9). 1998. pap. 5.95 (*1-58086-045-1*, Usborne) EDC.

— Predicting Outcomes. rev. ed. (Horizons Concepts Ser.: Level 2). (Illus.). 24p. (J). (gr. 4-9). 1998. pap. 5.95 (*1-58086-055-9*, Usborne) EDC.

— Recalling Details. rev. ed. (Horizons Concepts Ser.: Level 1). (Illus.). 24p. (J). (gr. 4-9). 1998. pap. 5.95 (*1-58086-038-9*, Usborne) EDC.

— Recalling Details. rev. ed. (Horizons Concepts Ser.: Level 2). (Illus.). 24p. (J). (gr. 4-9). 1998. pap. 5.95 (*1-58086-048-6*, Usborne) EDC.

B

— Recognizing Cause & Effect. rev. ed. (Horizons Concepts Ser.: Level 1). (Illus.). 24p. (J). (gr. 4-9). 1998. pap. 5.95 (*1-58086-044-3*, Usborne) EDC.

— Recognizing Cause & Effect. rev. ed. (Horizons Concepts Ser.: Level 2). (Illus.). 24p. (J). (gr. 4-9). 1998. pap. 5.95 (*1-58086-054-0*, Usborne) EDC.

— Recognizing Plot, Character, Mood. rev. ed. (Horizons Concepts Ser.: Level 1). (Illus.). 24p. (J). (gr. 4-9). 1998. pap. 5.95 (*1-58086-046-X*, Usborne) EDC.

— Recognizing Plot, Character, Mood. rev. ed. (Horizons Concepts Ser.: Level 2). (Illus.). 24p. (J). (gr. 4-9). 1998. pap. 5.95 (*1-58086-056-7*, Usborne) EDC.

— Teacher's Guide. rev. ed. (Horizons Concepts Ser.: Level 1). (Illus.). 24p. (J). (gr. 4-9). 1998. pap. 1.00 (*1-58086-111-3*, Usborne) EDC.

— Teacher's Guide. rev. ed. (Horizons Concepts Ser.: Level 2). (Illus.). 24p. (J). (gr. 4-9). 1998. pap. 1.00 (*1-58086-112-1*, Usborne) EDC.

Bridgman, C. A. My Hawaiian Smile. (J). 14.95 (*0-681-32826-6*) Booklines Hawaii.

— My Hawaiian Smile. LC TXU645-473. (Illus.). 32p. (J). (ps-4). 1996. 14.95 (*0-9659382-1-2*) Immanuel Pr.

— Santa's Hawaiian Vacation. (J). 14.95 (*0-681-32827-4*) Booklines Hawaii.

— Santa's Hawaiian Vacation. LC GB033229537. (Illus.). 32p. (J). (ps-4). 1996. 14.95 (*0-9659382-0-4*) Immanuel Pr.

Bridgman, Charles F., jt. auth. see Telford, Ira R.

Bridgman, Dianne, contrib. by. Richard O. Barnes: An Oral History. (Illus.). xii, 97p. (Orig.). 1994. pap. write for info. (*1-889320-00-5*) WA St Oral Hist.

— Robert C. Bailey: An Oral History. (Illus.). xiv, 210p. (Orig.). 1996. pap. write for info. (*1-889320-02-1*) WA St Oral Hist.

Bridgman, George B. Book of One-Hundred Hands. (Illus.). 175p. 1971. reprint ed. pap. 6.95 (*0-486-22709-X*) Dover.

— Bridgman's Complete Guide to Drawing from Life. (Illus.). 352p. 1992. reprint ed. 14.99 (*0-517-25546-4*) Random Hse Value.

— Bridgman's Life Drawings. (Illus.). 192p. 1971. reprint ed. pap. 5.95 (*0-486-22710-3*) Dover.

— Constructive Anatomy. (Illus.). 170p. (C). 1973. reprint ed. pap. 6.95 (*0-486-21104-5*) Dover.

— Heads, Features, & Faces. LC 74-78681. (Illus.). 64p. 1974. reprint ed. pap. 3.95 (*0-486-22708-1*) Dover.

— The Human Machine: The Anatomical Structure & Mechanism of the Human Body. LC 70-187018. (Illus.). 143p. (C). 1972. reprint ed. pap. 5.95 (*0-486-22707-3*) Dover.

Bridgman, Howard. Global Air Pollution: Problems for the 1990s. 288p. 1991. 30.95 (*1-85293-099-3*, Pub. by P P Pubs); text 61.95 (*1-85293-094-2*, Pub. by P P Pubs) CRC Pr.

Bridgman, Howard, et al. Urban Biophysical Environments. LC 96-177896. (Meridian Australian Geographical Perspectives Ser.). (Illus.). 168p. (C). 1996. pap. text 29.95 (*0-19-553611-8*) OUP.

Bridgman, Leonard. Jane's Fighting Aircraft of WW II. (Illus.). 320p. 1994. 29.99 (*0-517-67964-7*) Random Hse Value.

Bridgman, Percy Williams. Collected Experimental Papers, 7 Vols, Set. LC 64-16060. (Illus.). 4800p. 1964. 355.00 (*0-674-13750-7*) HUP.

— The Logic of Modern Physics. Cohen, I. Bernard, ed. LC 79-3117. (Three Centuries of Science in America Ser.). 1980. reprint ed. lib. bdg. 29.95 (*0-405-12594-1*) Ayer.

— Philosophical Writings of Percy William Bridgman: An Original Anthology, 2 vols. Cohen, I. Bernard, ed. LC 79-7952. (Three Centuries of Science in America Ser.). 1980. lib. bdg. 21.95 (*0-405-12532-1*) Ayer.

— Reflections of a Physicist. 2nd ed. Cohen, I. Bernard, ed. LC 79-3118. (Three Centuries of Science in America Ser.). 1980. reprint ed. lib. bdg. 53.95 (*0-405-12595-X*) Ayer.

Bridgman, Peter & Davis, Glyn. Australian Policy Handbook. (Illus.). 176p. 1998. pap. 24.95 (*1-86448-608-2*, Pub. by Allen & Unwin Pty) Paul & Co Pubs.

Bridgman, R., ed. Concord Lectures in Philosophy 1883-1969: Comprising Outlines of All the Lectures at the Concord Summer School of Philosophy in 1882. 100p. 1969. text 15.00 (*0-87556-006-7*) Saifer.

Bridgman, R. F. Rural Hospital: Its Structure & Organization. (Monographs: No. 21). (ENG & FRE., Illus.). 162p. 1955. pap. text 20.00 (*92-4-140021-8*, 1140021) World Health.

Bridgman, R. F. & Roemer, M. I. Hospital Legislation & Hospital Systems. (Public Health Papers: No. 50). 1973. pap. text 12.00 (*92-4-130050-7*, 1110050) World Health.

***Bridgman, Rae, et al, eds.** Feminist Fields: Ethnographic Insights. 320p. 1999. pap. 22.95 (*1-55111-195-0*) Broadview Pr.

Bridgman, Raymond L. The First Book of World Law: A Compilation of the International Conventions to Which the Principle Nations Are Signatory, with a Survey of Their Significance, No. 1. iv, 308p. 1999. reprint ed. 94.50 (*1-56169-457-6*) Gaunt.

— Master Idea (1899) 354p. 1998. reprint ed. pap. 27.95 (*0-7661-0575-X*) Kessinger Pub.

Bridgman, Richard. Dark Thoreau. LC 81-4788. 322p. 1982. reprint ed. pap. 99.90 (*0-608-02381-7*, 206302300004) Bks Demand.

— Traveling in Mark Twain. (Quantum Bks.: No. 30). (Illus.). 176p. 1987. 40.00 (*0-520-05952-2*, Pub. by U CA Pr) Cal Prin Full Svc.

Bridgman, Richard W. Reflections on the Study of the Law: In Two Parts - Addressed First, to the Nobility & Gentry, As the Hereditary & Elective Senators of the Nation, & Secondly, to Those Gentlemen Who Propose to Study the Law, with a View to Professional Practice. xiv, 143p. 1996. reprint ed. 35.00 (*0-8377-1980-1*, Rothman) W S Hein.

— Short View of Legal Bibliography: Bridgman's Legal Bibliography. xviii, 430p. 1958. reprint ed. 55.00 (*0-89941-353-6*, 502140) W S Hein.

Bridgman, Roger. Electronics. LC 93-863. (Eyewitness Books). (Illus.). 64p. (J). (gr. 4-7). 1993. 15.95 (*1-56458-324-4*) DK Pub Inc.

***Bridgman, Roger.** Electronics. (Eyewitness Books). 64p. (J). (gr. 4-7). 2000. 15.95 (*0-7894-5598-6*, D K Ink) DK Pub Inc.

Bridgman, Shari L. In Heavenly Arms: Grieving the Loss, Healing the Wounds of Miscarriage. 1997. pap. 12.95 (*0-9657698-3-6*) Black Hawk Canyon.

Bridgman, Thomas. Inscriptions on the Grave Stones in the Grave Yards of Northampton & of Other Towns in the Valley of the Connecticut, As Springfield, Amherst, Hadley, Hatfield, Deerfield, & with Brief Annals of Northampton. 227p. 1996. reprint ed. pap. 21.00 (*0-7884-0590-X*, B632) Heritage Bk.

Bridgman, Thomas, jt. auth. see Singhal, Sandeep.

Bridgmont, Peter. Liberation of the Actor. 160p. 1992. pap. 16.95 (*0-904693-33-3*, Pub. by Temple Lodge) Anthroposophic.

Bridgstock, Martin, et al. Science, Technology & Society: An Introduction. LC 97-30209. (Illus.). 288p. (C). 1998. text 64.95 (*0-521-58320-9*); pap. text 22.95 (*0-521-58735-2*) Cambridge U Pr.

***Bridgwater, A., et al.** Fast Pyrolysis of Biomass: A Handbook. (Illus.). 196p. 1999. 70.00 (*1-872691-07-2*, CPL Pr) CPL Sci Pub.

Bridgwater, Beth. Bridgwater's Cambridgeshire. (Bridgwater's Ser.). (Illus.). 224p. 1996. pap. text 19.95 (*1-897924-14-3*, Pub. by Encompass Pr) Distribks Inc.

— Bridgwater's Norfolk. (Bridgwater's Ser.). (Illus.). 224p. 1996. pap. text 19.95 (*1-897924-04-6*, Pub. by Encompass Pr) Distribks Inc.

— Bridgwater's Suffolk. (Bridgwater's Ser.). (Illus.). 224p. 1996. pap. text 19.95 (*1-897924-09-7*, Pub. by Encompass Pr) Distribks Inc.

Bridgwater, David, ed. Fluid Movements - Element Transport & the Composition of the Deep Crust. (C). 1989. text 213.50 (*0-7923-0335-0*) Kluwer Academic.

Bridgwater, J. Fifty Years Young: Products & Processes--The Future of Chemical Engineering. (Illus.). 33p. (C). 1996. pap. text 8.95 (*0-521-56779-3*) Cambridge U Pr.

Bridgwater, J., ed. Developments in Chemical Engineering: A Festschrift for P. V. Danckwerts. (Illus.). 190p. 1983. pap. 39.00 (*0-08-030251-3*, Pergamon Pr) Elsevier.

Bridgwater, John, jt. auth. see Benbow, John.

Bridgwater, Patrick. Arthur Schopenhauer's English Schooling. 416p. (C). 1988. lib. bdg. 77.00 (*0-415-00743-7*, A2467) Routledge.

— Poet of Expressionist Berlin: The Life & Work of Georg Heym. (Illus.). 320p. 1992. text 59.95 (*1-870352-75-0*, Pub. by Libris) Paul & Co Pubs.

Bridson, D. & Forman, L., eds. The Herbarium Handbook. 3rd rev. ed. (Illus.). xii, 334p. 1998. pap. 30.00 (*1-900347-43-1*, Pub. by Royal Botnic Grdns) Balogh.

Bridson, G. D., ed. B-P-H - S: Botanico-Periodicum-Huntianum-Supplementum. 1068p. 1991. text 95.00 (*0-913196-54-1*) Hunt Inst Botanical.

Bridson, G. D. & Wendel, D. E. Printmaking in the Service of Botany. (Illus.). 166p. 1986. pap. 20.00 (*0-913196-49-5*) Hunt Inst Botanical.

Bridson, Gavin & Wakeman, Geoffrey. Printmaking & Picture Printing: A Bibliographical Guide to Artistic & Industrial Techniques in Britain, 1750-1900. 1984. 55.00 (*0-916271-00-5*) BkPr Ltd.

Bridson, M. & Haefliger, A. Metric Spaces of Non-Positive Curvature. Chern, S. S. et al, eds. LC 99-38163. xv, 575p. 1999. 106.00 (*3-540-64324-9*) Spr-Verlag.

Bridson, Rory. The Making of a Para. (Illus.). 192p. 1995. 19.95 (*1-85367-222-X*, Pub. by Greenhill Bks) Stackpole.

Bridwell. Herbaceous Plants. (Agriculture Ser.). 1996. teacher ed. 10.00 (*0-8273-6536-5*) Delmar.

— Herbaceous Plants. (Agriculture Ser.). 1997. text 44.95 (*0-8273-6535-7*) Delmar.

Bridwell & Ingles. Residential Landscape Design. (Agriculture Ser.). 1997. teacher ed., wbk. ed. 13.95 (*0-8273-6540-3*) Delmar.

Bridwell, et al. Identity Matters: Rhetorics of Difference. LC 97-30620. 592p. 1997. pap. text 37.60 (*0-13-243288-9*) P-H.

Bridwell-Bowles, Lillian & Batchelder, Susan, eds. Diversity & Writing: Dialogue Within a Modern University: Proceedings First Annual Conference, April 1990. (Monographs: Vol. 2). 41p. (Orig.). 1992. pap. 4.50 (*1-881221-01-6*) U Minn Ctr Interdis.

Bridwell-Bowles, Lillian & Olson, Mark, eds. Abstracts of CISW Grants: Completed Projects & Works in Progress 1989-93. 2nd ed. (Monographs: Vol. 4). 62p. 1994. 5.50 (*1-881221-09-1*) U Minn Ctr Interdis.

Bridwell-Bowles, Lillian & Prior, Paul, eds. Abstracts of CISW Grants: Completed Projects & Works in Progress. (Monographs: Vol. 4). 42p. (Orig.). 1992. pap. 3.50 (*1-881221-03-2*) U Minn Ctr Interdis.

Bridwell-Bowles, Lillian, et al. Writing-Intensive Courses: Possible Criteria, National Patterns, & Resources. (Technical Reports: No. 11). 25p. (Orig.). (C). 1994. pap. 3.00 (*1-881221-18-0*) U Minn Ctr Interdis.

Bridwell-Bowles, Lillian, ed. see Bazerman, Charles.

Bridwell-Bowles, Lillian, ed. see Evans, Carolyn & Miller, Carol.

Bridwell-Bowles, Lillian, ed. see Fang, Irving E.

Bridwell-Bowles, Lillian, ed. see Ganguli, Aparna B. & Henry, Richard.

Bridwell-Bowles, Lillian, ed. see Homstad, Torild & Thorson, Helga.

Bridwell-Bowles, Lillian, ed. see Kassner, Linda A. & Collins, Terence.

Bridwell-Bowles, Lillian, ed. see Lunsford, Andrea A.

Bridwell-Bowles, Lillian, ed. see Martin, Roger, et al.

Bridwell-Bowles, Lillian, ed. see McLeod, Susan.

Bridwell-Bowles, Lillian, ed. see McNaron, Toni A. & Olano, Pamela J.

Bridwell-Bowles, Lillian, ed. see Miller, Carol.

Bridwell-Bowles, Lillian, ed. see Miller, Hildy & Ashcroft, Mary E.

Bridwell-Bowles, Lillian, ed. see Nereson, Sally.

Bridwell-Bowles, Lillian, ed. see Prell, Riv-Ellen.

Bridwell-Bowles, Lillian, ed. see Smitherman, Geneva.

Bridwell-Bowles, Lillian, ed. see Young, Art.

Bridwell, Ferrell, jt. auth. see Ingels.

Bridwell, Ferrell M. Landscape Plants: Their Identification, Culture & Use. LC 93-28665. (C). 1994. mass mkt. 54.00 (*0-8273-6017-7*) Delmar.

Bridwell, J., jt. auth. see Kazeck, Melvin.

Bridwell, Jim & Peall, Keith. Climbing Adventures: A Climber's Passion. Moser, Sally, ed. LC 92-17929. (Illus.). 214p. (Orig.). 1992. pap. 16.50 (*0-934802-22-X*) Globe Pequot.

Bridwell, Keith H., et al, eds. The Textbook of Spinal Surgery, 2 vols., Set. 2nd ed. LC 96-7784. 2,632p. 1996. text 375.00 (*0-397-51384-4*) Lppncott W & W.

— The Textbook of Spinal Surgery, Vol. 1. 2nd ed. LC 96-7784. 8p. 1996. write for info. (*0-395-75179-9*) Lppncott W & W.

— The Textbook of Spinal Surgery, Vol. 2. 2nd ed. LC 96-7784. 1996. write for info. (*0-397-51800-5*) Lppncott W & W.

Bridwell, Lillian S., jt. ed. see Beach, Richard.

Bridwell, Nelson, jt. auth. see Shooter, Jim.

Bridwell, Norman. The Adventures of Clifford the Big Red Dog. (Comes to Life Bks.). 16p. (J). (ps-2). 1994. write for info. (*1-883366-42-9*) YES Ent.

— Las Buenas Acciones de Clifford. Palacios, Argentina, tr. from ENG. (Clifford, the Big Red Dog Ser.).Tr. of Clifford's Good Deeds. (SPA., Illus.). 32p. (J). (gr. k-2). 1987. pap. 3.25 (*0-590-40179-3*) Scholastic Inc.

Bridwell, Norman. Las Buenas Acciones de Clifford. (Clifford, the Big Red Dog Ser.).Tr. of Clifford's Good Deeds. (SPA.). (J). (gr. k-2). 1980. 8.15 (*0-606-03108-1*, Pub. by Turtleback) Demco.

— Cat & the Bird. (Hello, Reader! Ser.). (Illus.). (J). 2000. 9.44 (*0-606-18531-3*) Turtleback.

— The Cat & the Bird in the Hat. (Hello Reader! Ser.). (Illus.). 32p. (J). (ps-3). 2000. pap. 3.99 (*0-439-15433-2*) Scholastic Inc.

— Clifford al Rescate. (Clifford, the Big Red Dog Ser.).Tr. of Clifford to the Rescue. (SPA., Illus.). 28p. (J). (ps-1). 2000. pap. 3.25 (*0-439-12956-7*) Scholastic Inc.

— Clifford al Rescate.Tr. of Clifford to the Rescue. (SPA., Illus.). (J). 2000. 8.70 (*0-606-18534-8*) Turtleback.

Bridwell, Norman. Clifford & the Big Parade. (Clifford, the Big Red Dog Ser.). (Illus.). 32p. (J). (gr. k-2). 1998. pap. 2.99 (*0-590-10811-5*) Scholastic Inc.

***Bridwell, Norman.** Clifford & the Big Parade. (Clifford, the Big Red Dog Ser.). (J). (gr. k-2). 1998. 8.19 (*0-606-13284-8*, Pub. by Turtleback) Demco.

Bridwell, Norman. Clifford & the Big Storm. (Clifford, the Big Red Dog Ser.). (Illus.). 32p. (J). (gr. k-1). 1995. pap. 2.99 (*0-590-25756-0*, Cartwheel) Scholastic Inc.

— Clifford & the Big Storm. LC 95-182786. (Clifford, the Big Red Dog Ser.). (Illus.). 32p. (J). (gr. k-2). 1995. pap. 2.99 (*0-590-25755-2*, Cartwheel) Scholastic Inc.

Bridwell, Norman. Clifford & the Big Storm. (Clifford, the Big Red Dog Ser.). (J). (gr. k-2). 1995. 8.19 (*0-606-07377-9*, Pub. by Turtleback) Demco.

Bridwell, Norman. Clifford & the Grouchy Neighbors. (Clifford, the Big Red Dog Ser.). (Illus.). 32p. (J). (ps-3). 1985. pap. 2.99 (*0-590-44261-9*) Scholastic Inc.

— Clifford & the Grouchy Neighbors. (Clifford, the Big Red Dog Ser.). (Illus.). 32p. (J). (gr. k-2). 1989. pap. text 6.95 incl. audio (*0-590-63437-2*) Scholastic Inc.

Bridwell, Norman. Clifford & the Grouchy Neighbors. (Clifford, the Big Red Dog Ser.). (J). (gr. k-2). 1985. 8.19 (*0-606-03399-8*, Pub. by Turtleback) Demco.

— Clifford & the Halloween Parade. LC 98-53951. (Clifford, the Big Red Dog Ser.). (Illus.). 32p. (J). (ps-1). 2000. pap. 3.99 (*0-439-09834-3*) Scholastic Inc.

— Clifford & the Halloween Parade. (Hello, Reader! Ser.). (Illus.). (J). 2000. 9.44 (*0-606-18867-3*) Turtleback.

Bridwell, Norman. Clifford at the Circus. (Clifford, the Big Red Dog Ser.). (Illus.). (J). (gr. k-2). pap. 6.95 incl. audio (*0-590-68639-9*) Scholastic Inc.

— Clifford at the Circus. (Clifford, the Big Red Dog Ser.). (Illus.). 32p. (J). (gr. k-2). 1985. pap. 2.99 (*0-590-44293-7*) Scholastic Inc.

— Clifford at the Circus. (Clifford, the Big Red Dog Ser.). (Illus.). 32p. (J). (gr. k-2). 1989. pap. 6.95 incl. audio (*0-590-63340-6*) Scholastic Inc.

Bridwell, Norman. Clifford at the Circus. (Clifford, the Big Red Dog Ser.). (J). (gr. k-2). 1985. 8.19 (*0-606-03422-6*, Pub. by Turtleback) Demco.

Bridwell, Norman. Clifford Barks! (Clifford, the Big Red Dog Ser.). (Illus.). 16p. (J). (ps-k). 1996. bds. 7.95 (*0-590-67093-X*, Cartwheel) Scholastic Inc.

***Bridwell, Norman.** Clifford Barks! (Clifford, the Big Red Dog Ser.). (Illus.). 16p. (J). (ps-k). 2000. bds. 3.95 (*0-439-14999-1*, Cartwheel) Scholastic Inc.

Bridwell, Norman. Clifford Counts Bubbles. LC 91-45140. (Clifford, the Big Red Dog Ser.). (Illus.). 16p. (J). (ps-k). 1992. bds. 3.95 (*0-590-45872-8*, 035, Cartwheel) Scholastic Inc.

— Clifford Counts 1-2-3. (Clifford, the Big Red Dog Ser.). (Illus.). 14p. (J). (ps-k). 1998. bds. 5.99 (*0-590-37928-3*, Pub. by Scholastic Inc) Penguin Putnam.

— Clifford el Gran Perro Colorado. Leos, Frances, tr. from ENG. (Clifford, the Big Red Dog Ser.).Tr. of Clifford the Big Red Dog. (SPA., Illus.). 32p. (J). (gr. k-2). 1988. pap. 2.99 (*0-590-41380-5*) Scholastic Inc.

— Clifford el Gran Perro Colorado. (Clifford, the Big Red Dog Ser.).Tr. of Clifford the Big Red Dog. (SPA.). (J). (ps-2). 1997. pap. text 5.99 (*0-590-38178-4*) Scholastic Inc.

Bridwell, Norman. Clifford el Gran Perro Colorado. (Clifford, the Big Red Dog Ser.).Tr. of Clifford the Big Red Dog. (SPA.). (J). (gr. k-2). 1985. 8.19 (*0-606-03759-4*, Pub. by Turtleback) Demco.

Bridwell, Norman. Clifford, El Pequeno Perro Colorado. (Clifford, the Big Red Dog Ser.). Orig. Title: Clifford the Small Red Puppy. (SPA.). (J). (gr. k-2). 1998. pap. 3.25 (*0-590-04311-0*) Scholastic Inc.

Bridwell, Norman. Clifford El Perro Bombero. (Clifford, the Big Red Dog Ser.).Tr. of Clifford the Firehouse Dog. (SPA.). (J). (gr. k-2). 1994. 8.19 (*0-606-06281-5*, Pub. by Turtleback) Demco.

Bridwell, Norman. Clifford Follows His Nose. (Clifford, the Big Red Dog Ser.). 24p. (J). (ps-k). 1992. bds. 5.95 (*0-590-44345-3*) Scholastic Inc.

— Clifford Gets a Job. (Clifford, the Big Red Dog Ser.). (Illus.). 32p. (J). (gr. k-2). 1985. pap. 2.99 (*0-590-44296-1*) Scholastic Inc.

Bridwell, Norman. Clifford Gets a Job. (Clifford, the Big Red Dog Ser.). (J). (gr. k-2). 1965. 8.19 (*0-606-01044-0*, Pub. by Turtleback) Demco.

Bridwell, Norman. Clifford Goes to Hollywood. (Clifford, the Big Red Dog Ser.). (Illus.). 32p. (J). (gr. k-2). 1986. pap. 2.99 (*0-590-44289-9*) Scholastic Inc.

— Clifford Goes to Hollywood. (Clifford, the Big Red Dog Ser.). (Illus.). 32p. (J). (gr. k-2). 1990. pap. 6.95 incl. audio (*0-590-63435-6*) Scholastic Inc.

Bridwell, Norman. Clifford Goes to Hollywood. (Clifford, the Big Red Dog Ser.). (J). (gr. k-2). 1980. 8.19 (*0-606-03090-5*, Pub. by Turtleback) Demco.

Bridwell, Norman. Clifford Grow Chart. (Clifford, the Big Red Dog Ser.). (J). (gr. k-2). 1990. pap. 2.95 (*0-590-63637-5*) Scholastic Inc.

— Clifford Grows Up. LC 98-54107. (Clifford, the Big Red Dog Ser.). (Illus.). 32p. (J). (gr. k-2). 1999. pap. text 3.25 (*0-439-08233-1*) Scholastic Inc.

— Clifford Keeps Cool. LC 99-36901. (Clifford, the Big Red Dog Ser.). (Illus.). 32p. (J). (ps-3). 1999. pap. 3.25 (*0-439-04394-8*) Scholastic Inc.

— Clifford Makes a Friend. LC 98-14076. (Clifford, the Big Red Dog Ser.). (J). (gr. k-2). 1998. 3.50 (*0-590-37930-5*) Scholastic Inc.

***Bridwell, Norman.** Clifford Plush Face Book. (Clifford, the Big Red Dog Ser.). (Illus.). 8p. (J). (gr. k-2). 1999. pap. 7.95 (*0-439-06131-8*) Scholastic Inc.

Bridwell, Norman. Clifford Takes a Trip. (Clifford, the Big Red Dog Ser.). (Illus.). 32p. (J). (gr. k-2). 1985. pap. 2.99 (*0-590-44260-0*) Scholastic Inc.

— Clifford Takes a Trip. (Clifford, the Big Red Dog Ser.). 32p. (J). (gr. k-2). 1991. pap. 7.95 incl. audio (*0-590-63823-8*, Cartwheel) Scholastic Inc.

Bridwell, Norman. Clifford Takes a Trip. (Clifford, the Big Red Dog Ser.). (J). (gr. k-2). 1966. 8.19 (*0-606-01045-9*, Pub. by Turtleback) Demco.

Bridwell, Norman. Clifford the Big Red Dog. LC 86-31502. (Clifford, the Big Red Dog Ser.). (Illus.). 28p. (J). (gr. k-2). 1985. pap. 2.99 (*0-590-44297-X*) Scholastic Inc.

— Clifford the Big Red Dog. (Clifford, the Big Red Dog Ser.). (Illus.). 32p. (J). (gr. k-2). 1988. pap. 7.95 incl. audio (*0-590-63212-4*) Scholastic Inc.

— Clifford the Big Red Dog. LC 86-31502. (Clifford, the Big Red Dog Ser.). (Illus.). 32p. (J). (ps-3). 1988. 10.95 (*0-590-40743-0*, Scholastic Hardcover) Scholastic Inc.

— Clifford the Big Red Dog. (Clifford, the Big Red Dog Ser.). (J). (gr. k-2). 1997. 15.99 (*0-590-27359-0*) Scholastic Inc.

— Clifford the Big Red Dog. (Clifford, the Big Red Dog Ser.). (Illus.). 32p. (J). (ps-k). 1997. bds. 5.99 (*0-590-34125-1*) Scholastic Inc.

Bridwell, Norman. Clifford, the Big Red Dog. (Clifford, the Big Red Dog Ser.). (J). (gr. k-2). 1963. 8.19 (*0-606-01116-1*, Pub. by Turtleback) Demco.

Bridwell, Norman. Clifford the Big Red Dog With Puppet. (Clifford, the Big Red Dog Ser.). (J). (gr. k-2). 1997. 23.99 (*0-590-27449-X*) Scholastic Inc.

— Clifford the Firehouse Dog. (Clifford, the Big Red Dog Ser.). (FRE., Illus.). (J). (gr. k-2). pap. 5.99 (*0-590-24375-6*) Scholastic Inc.

— Clifford the Firehouse Dog. LC 00-4691. (Clifford, the Big Red Dog Ser.). (SPA., Illus.). 32p. (J). (gr. k-2). 1994. pap. 2.99 (*0-590-48808-2*, Cartwheel) Scholastic Inc.

— Clifford the Firehouse Dog. LC 94-233657. (Clifford, the Big Red Dog Ser.). (Illus.). 30p. (J). (ps-3). 1994. pap. 2.99 (*0-590-48419-2*, Cartwheel) Scholastic Inc.

Bridwell, Norman. Clifford the Firehouse Dog. (Clifford, the Big Red Dog Ser.). (J). (gr. k-2). 1994. 8.19 (*0-606-06282-3*, Pub. by Turtleback) Demco.

Bridwell, Norman. Clifford the Small Red Puppy. (Clifford, the Big Red Dog Ser.). 32p. (J). (gr. k-3). 1988. 5.95 incl. audio (*0-590-63211-6*) Scholastic Inc.

— Clifford the Small Red Puppy. (Clifford, the Big Red Dog Ser.). 32p. (J). (gr. k-2). 1990. 10.95 (*0-590-43496-9*) Scholastic Inc.

Bridwell, Norman. Clifford the Small Red Puppy. (Clifford, the Big Red Dog Ser.). (J). (gr. k-2). 1972. 8.19 (*0-606-01046-7*, Pub. by Turtleback) Demco.

Bridwell, Norman. Clifford the Small Red Puppy. anniversary ed. LC 86-102123. (Clifford, the Big Red Dog Ser.). (Illus.). 32p. (J). (ps-3). 1985. pap. 2.99 (*0-590-44294-5*) Scholastic Inc.

An Asterisk (*) at the beginning of an entry indicates that the title is appearing for the first time.

*Bridwell, Norman. Clifford to the Rescue. LC 99-36901. (Clifford, the Big Red Dog Ser.). (Illus.). 32p. (J). (ps-1). 2000. mass mkt. 3.25 (0-439-14038-2, Cartwheel) Scholastic Inc.

— Clifford to the Rescue. (Illus.). (J). 2000. 8.70 (0-606-18535-6) Turtleback.

Bridwell, Norman. Clifford Treasury Boxed Set: Clifford the Small Red Puppy; Clifford the Big Red Dog; Clifford's Pals; Clifford & the Grouchy Neighbors, 4 vols., No. 1. (Clifford, the Big Red Dog Ser.). (J). (ps-3). 1991. pap., boxed set 9.00 (0-590-63953-6) Scholastic Inc.

— Clifford Treasury Boxed Set: Clifford's Birthday Party; Clifford's Puppy Days; Clifford's Family; Clifford's Kitten, 4 vols., No. 2. (Clifford, the Big Red Dog Ser.). (J). (ps-3). 1991. pap., boxed set 9.00 (0-590-63952-8) Scholastic Inc.

— Clifford Va a la Escuela. (Clifford, the Big Red Dog Ser.).Tr. of Clifford's First School Day. (SPA.). (J). (ps-k). 1999. pap. text 3.25 (0-439-08729-5) Scholastic Inc.

*Bridwell, Norman. Clifford Va a la Escuela.Tr. of Clifford's First School Day. 1999. 9.35 (0-606-17052-9, Pub. by Turtleback) Demco.

— Clifford Va de Viaje. (Clifford, the Big Red Dog Ser.).Tr. of Clifford Takes a Trip. (SPA.). (J). (gr. k-2). 1987. 8.19 (0-606-03188-X, Pub. by Turtleback) Demco.

Bridwell, Norman. Clifford Va de Viaje. rev. ed. Palacios, Argentina, tr. from ENG. (Clifford, the Big Red Dog Ser.).Tr. of Clifford Takes a Trip. (SPA., Illus.). 32p. (J). (gr. k-2). 1987. pap. 2.99 (0-590-40844-5) Scholastic Inc.

*Bridwell, Norman. Clifford Visits the Hospital. LC 99-55200. (Clifford, the Big Red Dog Ser.). (Illus.). 32p. (J). (gr. k-2). 2000. 3.25 (0-439-14096-X) Scholastic Inc.

— Clifford Visits the Hospital. (Illus.). (J). 2000. 8.70 (0-606-18868-1) Turtleback.

— Clifford Vista el Hospital. (SPA., Illus.). (J). 2000. 8.70 (0-606-18869-X) Turtleback.

Bridwell, Norman. Clifford Wants a Cookie. (Clifford, the Big Red Dog Ser.). (Illus.). 16p. (J). (gr. k-2). 1988. pap. 3.95 (0-590-63282-5) Scholastic Inc.

— Clifford, We Love You. (Clifford, the Big Red Dog Ser.). 32p. (J). (gr. k-2). 1991. pap. 6.95 incl. audio (0-590-63604-9) Scholastic Inc.

— Clifford, We Love You. LC 94-4005. (Clifford, the Big Red Dog Ser.). 32p. (J). (ps-3). 1991. pap. 2.99 (0-590-43843-3) Scholastic Inc.

— Clifford, We Love You. LC 94-4005. (Clifford, the Big Red Dog Ser.). (J). (gr. k-2). 1994. 10.95 (0-590-48612-8) Scholastic Inc.

Bridwell, Norman. Clifford, We Love You. (Clifford, the Big Red Dog Ser.). (J). (gr. k-2). 1991. 8.19 (0-606-04638-0, Pub. by Turtleback) Demco.

— Clifford y el Dia de Halloween. LC 99-87629. (Clifford, the Big Red Dog Ser.).Tr. of Clifford's Halloween. (SPA., Illus.). 32p. (J). (ps-3). 2000. pap. text 3.25 (0-439-17451-1) Scholastic Inc.

— Clifford y el Dia de Halloween.Tr. of Clifford's Halloween. (SPA., Illus.). (J). 2000. 8.70 (0-606-18870-3) Turtleback.

Bridwell, Norman. Clifford y el Dia de Pascua. (Clifford, the Big Red Dog Ser.).Tr. of Clifford's Happy Easter. (SPA.). (J). (gr. k-2). 1998. pap. text 2.99 (0-590-11740-8, Little Apple) Scholastic Inc.

— Clifford y el Gran Desfile. (Clifford, the Big Red Dog Ser.).Tr. of Clifford & the Big Parade. (SPA.). (J). (gr. k-2). 1998. pap. text 2.99 (0-590-50663-3, Cartwheel) Scholastic Inc.

*Bridwell, Norman. Clifford y el Gran Desfile. (Clifford, the Big Red Dog Ser.).Tr. of Clifford & the Big Parade. (SPA.). (J). (gr. k-2). 1998. 8.19 (0-606-13285-6, Pub. by Turtleback) Demco.

Bridwell, Norman. Clifford y el Verano Caluroso. Mlawer, Teresa, tr. from ENG. (Clifford, the Big Red Dog Ser.).Tr. of Clifford Keeps Cool. (SPA., Illus.). (J). (gr. k-2). 1999. pap. 3.25 (0-439-05014-6) Scholastic Inc.

— Clifford y la Limpieza de Primavera. (Clifford, the Big Red Dog Ser.).Tr. of Clifford's Spring Cleaning. (SPA.). (J). (gr. k-2). 1997. pap. 2.99 (0-590-04158-4, 691735Q) Scholastic Inc.

Bridwell, Norman. Clifford y la Limpieza de Primavera. (Clifford, the Big Red Dog Ser.).Tr. of Clifford's Spring Cleaning. (J). (gr. k-2). 1997. 8.44 (0-606-11211-1) Turtleback.

Bridwell, Norman. Clifford y la Tormenta. (Clifford, the Big Red Dog Ser.).Tr. of Clifford & the Big Storm. (SPA.). (J). (gr. k-2). 1995. 8.19 (0-606-07378-7, Pub. by Turtleback) Demco.

— Clifford's ABC. (Clifford, the Big Red Dog Ser.). 32p. (J). (gr. k-2). 1986. pap. 2.99 (0-590-44286-4) Scholastic Inc.

— Clifford's ABC. LC 94-9787. (Clifford, the Big Red Dog Ser.). (J). (gr. k-2). 1994. 10.95 (0-590-48694-2) Scholastic Inc.

Bridwell, Norman. Clifford's ABC. (Clifford, the Big Red Dog Ser.). (J). (gr. k-2). 1983. 8.19 (0-606-03087-5, Pub. by Turtleback) Demco.

Bridwell, Norman. Clifford's Animal Sounds. LC 91-7725. (Clifford, the Big Red Dog Ser.). 16p. (J). (ps-k). 1991. bds. 3.95 (0-590-44734-3) Scholastic Inc.

— Clifford's Bag of Fun. (Clifford, the Big Red Dog Ser.). 16p. (J). (gr. k-2). 1993. pap. 5.95 (0-590-69010-8) Scholastic Inc.

— Clifford's Bathtime. LC 91-7964. (Clifford, the Big Red Dog Ser.). 16p. (J). (ps-k). 1991. bds. 3.95 (0-590-44735-1) Scholastic Inc.

— Clifford's Bedtime. LC 91-2169. (Clifford, the Big Red Dog Ser.). 16p. (J). (ps-k). 1991. bds. 3.95 (0-590-44736-X) Scholastic Inc.

*Bridwell, Norman. Clifford's Best Friend: A Story about Emily Elizabeth. (Clifford, the Big Red Dog Ser.). (Illus.). 32p. (J). (ps-1). 2000. 3.25 (0-439-21997-3) Scholastic Inc.

Bridwell, Norman. Clifford's Big Book of Stories. LC 93-31367. (Clifford, the Big Red Dog Ser.). (Illus.). 64p. (J). (gr. k-2). 1994. bds. 9.95 (0-590-47925-3, Cartwheel) Scholastic Inc.

— Clifford's Big Book of Things to Know: A Book of Fun Facts. LC 97-45800. (Clifford, the Big Red Dog Ser.). (Illus.). 40p. (J). (ps-1). 1999. 10.95 (0-590-00385-2, Pub. by Scholastic Inc) Penguin Putnam.

— Clifford's Birthday Party. (Clifford, the Big Red Dog Ser.). (Illus.). 32p. (J). (gr. k-2). 1988. pap. 6.95 incl. audio (0-590-63237-X); pap. 2.99 (0-590-44279-1) Scholastic Inc.

Bridwell, Norman. Clifford's Birthday Party. (Clifford, the Big Red Dog Ser.). (J). (gr. k-2). 1988. 8.19 (0-606-03561-3, Pub. by Turtleback) Demco.

Bridwell, Norman. Clifford's Christmas. (Clifford, the Big Red Dog Ser.). (Illus.). 32p. (J). (gr. k-2). 1984. pap. 2.99 (0-590-44288-0) Scholastic Inc.

— Clifford's Christmas. (Clifford, the Big Red Dog Ser.). (Illus.). 32p. (J). (gr. k-2). 1987. pap. 5.95 incl. audio (0-590-63210-8) Scholastic Inc.

— Clifford's Christmas. (Clifford, the Big Red Dog Ser.). (J). (gr. k-2). 1984. 8.19 (0-606-03088-3, Pub. by Turtleback) Demco.

— Clifford's Family. (Clifford, the Big Red Dog Ser.). (Illus.). 32p. (J). (gr. k-2). 1985. pap. 2.99 (0-590-44290-2) Scholastic Inc.

Bridwell, Norman. Clifford's Family. (Clifford, the Big Red Dog Ser.). (J). (gr. k-2). 1985. 8.19 (0-606-03373-4, Pub. by Turtleback) Demco.

Bridwell, Norman. Clifford's First Autumn. LC 97-199914. (Clifford, the Big Red Dog Ser.). (Illus.). 32p. (J). (ps-3). 1997. pap. 2.99 (0-590-34130-8) Scholastic Inc.

Bridwell, Norman. Clifford's First Autumn. (Clifford, the Big Red Dog Ser.). (J). (gr. k-2). 1997. 8.19 (0-606-11212-X, Pub. by Turtleback) Demco.

Bridwell, Norman. Clifford's First Christmas. (Clifford, the Big Red Dog Ser.). (FRE., Illus.). (J). (gr. k-2). pap. 5.99 (0-590-24374-8) Scholastic Inc.

— Clifford's First Christmas. (Clifford, the Big Red Dog Ser.). (Illus.). 32p. (J). (gr. k-2). 1994. pap. 2.99 (0-590-48420-6, Cartwheel) Scholastic Inc.

— Clifford's First Christmas. (Clifford, the Big Red Dog Ser.). (SPA., Illus.). 32p. (J). (ps-3). 1994. pap. 2.50 (0-590-48852-X, Cartwheel) Scholastic Inc.

Bridwell, Norman. Clifford's First Christmas. (Clifford, the Big Red Dog Ser.). (J). (gr. k-2). 1994. 8.19 (0-606-06283-1, Pub. by Turtleback) Demco.

Bridwell, Norman. Clifford's First Easter. LC 95-126913. (Clifford, the Big Red Dog Ser.). (Illus.). 20p. (J). (ps-k). 1995. 7.95 (0-590-22241-4, Cartwheel) Scholastic Inc.

— Clifford's First Halloween. LC 00-3033. (Clifford, the Big Red Dog Ser.). (Illus.). 32p. (J). (ps-3). 1995. pap. 2.50 (0-590-50317-0, Cartwheel) Scholastic Inc.

— Clifford's First Halloween. (Clifford, the Big Red Dog Ser.). (FRE., Illus.). 32p. (J). (gr. k-2). 1996. pap. 5.99 (0-590-16034-6) Scholastic Inc.

Bridwell, Norman. Clifford's First Halloween. (Clifford, the Big Red Dog Ser.). (J). (gr. k-2). 1995. 8.19 (0-606-07379-5, Pub. by Turtleback) Demco.

Bridwell, Norman. Clifford's First School Day. LC 99-12688. (Clifford, the Big Red Dog Ser.). (Illus.). 32p. (J). (ps-3). 1999. bds. 3.25 (0-439-08284-6, Pub. by Scholastic Inc) Penguin Putnam.

— Clifford's First Snow Day. LC 99-165909. (Clifford, the Big Red Dog Ser.). (Illus.). 32p. (J). (gr. k-2). 1998. pap. 2.99 (0-590-03480-4, Pub. by Scholastic Inc) Penguin Putnam.

— Clifford's First Valentine's Day. LC 97-135099. (Clifford, the Big Red Dog Ser.). (Illus.). 32p. (J). (ps-3). 1997. 2.99 (0-590-92162-2, Cartwheel) Scholastic Inc.

Bridwell, Norman. Clifford's First Valentine's Day. (Clifford, the Big Red Dog Ser.). (J). (gr. k-2). 1997. 7.94 (0-606-10774-6, Pub. by Turtleback) Demco.

Bridwell, Norman. Clifford's Furry Friends. (Clifford, the Big Red Dog Ser.). (J). (ps-k). Date not set. 8.95 (0-614-19201-3, Blue Ribbon Bks) Scholastic Inc.

— Clifford's Furry Friends. LC 96-224724. (Clifford, the Big Red Dog Ser.). (Illus.). 16p. (J). (ps-k). 1996. 8.95 (0-590-86402-5, Cartwheel) Scholastic Inc.

— Clifford's Good Deeds. (Clifford, the Big Red Dog Ser.). (Illus.). 32p. (J). (gr. k-2). 1985. pap. 2.99 (0-590-44292-9) Scholastic Inc.

— Clifford's Good Deeds. (Clifford, the Big Red Dog Ser.). 32p. (J). (gr. k-2). 1991. pap. 6.95 incl. audio (0-590-63824-6) Scholastic Inc.

Bridwell, Norman. Clifford's Good Deeds. (Clifford, the Big Red Dog Ser.). (J). (gr. k-2). 1975. 8.19 (0-606-01047-5, Pub. by Turtleback) Demco.

Bridwell, Norman. Clifford's Halloween. LC 67-23536. (Clifford, the Big Red Dog Ser.). (Illus.). 32p. (J). (ps-3). 1986. pap. 2.99 (0-590-44287-2) Scholastic Inc.

— Clifford's Halloween. (Clifford, the Big Red Dog Ser.). (Illus.). (J). (gr. k-2). 1994. pap. 6.95 (0-590-66159-0) Scholastic Inc.

— Clifford's Halloween. (Clifford, the Big Red Dog Ser.). (J). (gr. k-2). 1986. 8.19 (0-606-03091-3, Pub. by Turtleback) Demco.

— Clifford's Happy Christmas Lacing Book. LC 96-159913. (Clifford, the Big Red Dog Ser.). (Illus.). 24p. (J). (gr. k-2). 1995. 8.95 (0-590-60494-5, Cartwheel) Scholastic Inc.

— Clifford's Happy Days: A Pop-up Book. (Clifford, the Big Red Dog Ser.). (Illus.). 12p. (J). (ps-k). 1990. bds. 12.95 (0-590-42926-4) Scholastic Inc.

— Clifford's Happy Easter. LC 94-186641. (Clifford, the Big Red Dog Ser.). (Illus.). 32p. (J). (ps-3). 1994. pap. 2.99 (0-590-47782-X, Cartwheel) Scholastic Inc.

Bridwell, Norman. Clifford's Happy Easter. (Clifford, the Big Red Dog Ser.). (J). (gr. k-2). 1994. 8.19 (0-606-05790-0, Pub. by Turtleback) Demco.

Bridwell, Norman. Clifford's Kitten. (Clifford, the Big Red Dog Ser.). (Illus.). 32p. (J). (gr. k-2). 1984. pap. 2.99 (0-590-44280-5) Scholastic Inc.

Bridwell, Norman. Clifford's Kitten. (Clifford, the Big Red Dog Ser.). (J). (gr. k-2). 1984. 8.19 (0-606-03372-6, Pub. by Turtleback) Demco.

Bridwell, Norman. Clifford's Manners. (Clifford, the Big Red Dog Ser.). (Illus.). 32p. (J). (ps-3). 1987. pap. 2.99 (0-590-44285-6) Scholastic Inc.

— Clifford's Manners. LC 94-4004. (Clifford, the Big Red Dog Ser.). (J). (gr. k-2). 1994. 10.95 (0-590-48697-7) Scholastic Inc.

Bridwell, Norman. Clifford's Manners. (Clifford, the Big Red Dog Ser.). (J). (gr. k-2). 1987. 8.19 (0-606-01309-1, Pub. by Turtleback) Demco.

Bridwell, Norman. Clifford's Noisy Day. LC 91-45116. (Clifford, the Big Red Dog Ser.). (Illus.). (J). (ps-k). 1992. bds. 3.95 (0-590-45737-3, 036, Cartwheel) Scholastic Inc.

*Bridwell, Norman. Clifford's Opposites. (Clifford, the Big Red Dog Ser.). (Illus.). 16p. (J). (ps-k). 2000. bds. 3.95 (0-439-15000-0, Cartwheel) Scholastic Inc.

Bridwell, Norman. Clifford's Pals. (Clifford, the Big Red Dog Ser.). (Illus.). 32p. (J). (ps-3). 1985. pap. 2.99 (0-590-44295-3) Scholastic Inc.

Bridwell, Norman. Clifford's Pals. (Clifford, the Big Red Dog Ser.). (J). (gr. k-2). 1985. 8.19 (0-606-03423-4, Pub. by Turtleback) Demco.

Bridwell, Norman. Clifford's Peek-&-Seek Animal Riddles. (Clifford, the Big Red Dog Ser.). (Illus.). 24p. (J) (ps-k). 1997. bds. 7.95 (0-590-05704-9) Scholastic Inc.

— Clifford's Peekaboo. LC 91-7911. (Clifford, the Big Red Dog Ser.). 16p. (J). (ps-k). 1991. bds. 3.95 (0-590-44737-8) Scholastic Inc.

— Clifford's Puppy Days. (Clifford, the Big Red Dog Ser.). (J). (gr. k-2). 1989. pap. 1.95 (0-590-42189-1) Scholastic Inc.

— Clifford's Puppy Days. LC 89-10625. (Clifford, the Big Red Dog Ser.). (Illus.). 31p. (J). (ps-3). 1989. pap. 2.99 (0-590-44262-7) Scholastic Inc.

— Clifford's Puppy Days. LC 93-1802. (Clifford, the Big Red Dog Ser.). (Illus.). 32p. (J). (ps-3). 1994. 10.95 (0-590-43339-3, Cartwheel) Scholastic Inc.

— Clifford's Puppy Days. (Clifford, the Big Red Dog Ser.). (J). (ps-k). 1999. bds. 6.99 (0-590-63608-1, Cartwheel) Scholastic Inc.

Bridwell, Norman. Clifford's Puppy Days. (Clifford, the Big Red Dog Ser.). (J). (gr. k-2). 1989. 8.19 (0-606-04188-5, Pub. by Turtleback) Demco.

Bridwell, Norman. Clifford's Riddles. (Clifford, the Big Red Dog Ser.). (Illus.). 32p. (J). (gr. k-2). 1984. pap. 2.99 (0-590-44282-1) Scholastic Inc.

Bridwell, Norman. Clifford's Riddles. (Clifford, the Big Red Dog Ser.). (J). (gr. k-2). 1974. 8.19 (0-606-03089-1, Pub. by Turtleback) Demco.

— Clifford's Schoolhouse. (Clifford, the Big Red Dog Ser.). (Illus.). (J). (gr. k-2). 2000. 87.60 (0-439-21185-9) Scholastic Inc.

— Clifford's Schoolhouse. (Clifford, the Big Red Dog Ser.). (Illus.). 10p. (J). (ps-k). 2000. bds. 10.95 (0-439-16252-1) Scholastic Inc.

Bridwell, Norman. Clifford's Sports Day. (Clifford, the Big Red Dog Ser.). (Illus.). 32p. (J). (gr. k-2). pap. 5.59 (0-590-16002-8) Scholastic Inc.

— Clifford's Sports Day. LC 96-140880. (Clifford, the Big Red Dog Ser.). (Illus.). 32p. (J). (gr. k-2). 1996. mass mkt. 2.99 (0-590-62971-9, Cartwheel) Scholastic Inc.

Bridwell, Norman. Clifford's Sports Day. (Clifford, the Big Red Dog Ser.). (J). (gr. k-2). 1996. 8.19 (0-606-08715-X, Pub. by Turtleback) Demco.

Bridwell, Norman. Clifford's Spring Clean-Up. (Clifford, the Big Red Dog Ser.). (Illus.). 32p. (J). (gr. k-2). 1997. pap. 2.99 (0-590-06012-0, Cartwheel) Scholastic Inc.

Bridwell, Norman. Clifford's Spring Clean-Up. (Clifford, the Big Red Dog Ser.). (J). (gr. k-2). 1997. 8.19 (0-606-11213-8, Pub. by Turtleback) Demco.

Bridwell, Norman. Clifford's Sticker Book. (Clifford, the Big Red Dog Ser.). (Illus.). 24p. (J). (gr. k-2). 1995. pap. 3.95 (0-590-33657-6) Scholastic Inc.

— Clifford's Thanksgiving Visit. LC 94-205318. (Clifford, the Big Red Dog Ser.). (Illus.). 32p. (J). (ps-3). 1993. pap. 2.99 (0-590-46987-8, Cartwheel) Scholastic Inc.

Bridwell, Norman. Clifford's Thanksgiving Visit. (Clifford, the Big Red Dog Ser.). (J). (gr. k-2). 1993. 8.19 (0-606-05208-9, Pub. by Turtleback) Demco.

Bridwell, Norman. Clifford's Tricks. (Clifford, the Big Red Dog Ser.). (FRE., Illus.). (J). (gr. k-2). pap. 5.99 (0-590-73954-9) Scholastic Inc.

— Clifford's Tricks. (Clifford, the Big Red Dog Ser.). (Illus.). 32p. (J). (gr. k-2). 1986. pap. 2.99 (0-590-44291-0) Scholastic Inc.

Bridwell, Norman. Clifford's Tricks. (Clifford, the Big Red Dog Ser.). (J). (gr. k-2). 1969. 8.19 (0-606-01048-3, Pub. by Turtleback) Demco.

Bridwell, Norman. Clifford's Valentine Bag of Fun. (Clifford, the Big Red Dog Ser.). (Illus.). 32p. (J). (ps-3). 1999. pap. 6.95 (0-590-00380-1, Cartwheel) Scholastic Inc.

*Bridwell, Norman. Clifford's Valentines. LC 99-52812. (Clifford, the Big Red Dog Ser.). (Illus.). (J). (gr. k-2). 2001. write for info. (0-439-18300-6) Scholastic Inc.

Bridwell, Norman. Clifford's Word Book. (Clifford, the Big Red Dog Ser.). (Illus.). 32p. (J). (gr. k-2). 1990. pap. 2.50 (0-590-43095-5) Scholastic Inc.

— Clifford's Word Book. LC 94-4003. (Clifford, the Big Red Dog Ser.). (J). (gr. k-2). 1994. 10.95 (0-590-48696-9) Scholastic Inc.

Bridwell, Norman. Clifford's Word Book. (Clifford, the Big Red Dog Ser.). (J). (gr. k-2). 1990. 7.70 (0-606-04639-9, Pub. by Turtleback) Demco.

Bridwell, Norman. Clifford's Work Book.Tr. of Mots Preferes de Bertrand. (FRE., Illus.). (J). pap. 5.99 (0-590-74326-0) Scholastic Inc.

— Cooking with Clifford. (Clifford, the Big Red Dog Ser.). 24p. (J). (gr. k-2). 1999. pap. 9.95 (0-590-68931-2, Cartwheel) Scholastic Inc.

— Count on Clifford. (Clifford, the Big Red Dog Ser.). (Illus.). 32p. (J). (gr. k-2). 1985. 5.95 (0-590-33614-2) Scholastic Inc.

— Count on Clifford. (Clifford, the Big Red Dog Ser.). (Illus.). 32p. (J). (gr. k-2). 1987. pap. 2.99 (0-590-44284-8) Scholastic Inc.

Bridwell, Norman. Count on Clifford. (Clifford, the Big Red Dog Ser.). (J). (gr. k-2). 1985. 8.19 (0-606-03762-4, Pub. by Turtleback) Demco.

Bridwell, Norman. Count on Clifford. (Clifford, the Big Red Dog Ser.). (Illus.). 32p. (J). (gr. k-2). 1987. reprint ed. pap. 2.25 (0-685-67546-7) Scholastic Inc.

— Cuenta Con Clifford. (Clifford, the Big Red Dog Ser.).Tr. of Count on Clifford. (SPA.). (J). (gr. k-2). 1999. pap. text 3.25 (0-590-87589-2) Scholastic Inc.

*Bridwell, Norman. Cuenta Con Clifford.Tr. of Count on Clifford. 1999. 8.70 (0-606-16907-5, Pub. by Turtleback) Demco.

Bridwell, Norman. El Dia Deportivo de Clifford. (Clifford, the Big Red Dog Ser.).Tr. of Clifford's Sports Day. (SPA.). 32p. (J). (ps-3). 1996. pap. 2.99 (0-590-69070-1) Scholastic Inc.

Bridwell, Norman. El Dia Deportivo de Clifford. (Clifford, the Big Red Dog Ser.).Tr. of Clifford's Sports Day. (SPA.). (J). (gr. k-2). 1996. 8.44 (0-606-08735-4) Turtleback.

B

Bridwell, Norman. La Familia de Clifford. (Clifford, the Big Red Dog Ser.).Tr. of Clifford's Family. (SPA.). (J). (gr. k-2). 1989. 19.95 (0-590-73228-5) Scholastic Inc.

— La Familia de Clifford. (Clifford, the Big Red Dog Ser.).Tr. of Clifford's Family. (SPA.). 32p. (J). (gr. k-2). 1989. pap. 2.99 (0-590-41992-7) Scholastic Inc.

*Bridwell, Norman. La Familia de Clifford.Tr. of Clifford's Family. (SPA., Illus.). (J). 1999. mass mkt. 8.70 (0-606-17004-9) Turtleback.

— My Dog Clifford Plush Book. (Clifford, the Big Red Dog Ser.). (Illus.). 12p. (J). (ps-k). 2000. bds. 7.95 (0-439-06046-X, Cartwheel) Scholastic Inc.

— Oops, Clifford! LC 98-42693. (Clifford, the Big Red Dog Ser.). (Illus.). 32p. (J). (ps-3). 1999. pap. 15.95 (0-590-63117-9, Cartwheel) Scholastic Inc.

Bridwell, Norman. El Primer Halloween de Clifford. Mlawer, Teresa, tr. from ENG. (Clifford, the Big Red Dog Ser.).Tr. of Clifford's First Halloween. (SPA.). 32p. (J). (gr. k-2). 1995. pap. 2.50 (0-590-50928-4) Scholastic Inc.

Bridwell, Norman. El Primer Halloween de Clifford. (Clifford, the Big Red Dog Ser.).Tr. of Clifford's First Halloween. (SPA.). (J). (gr. k-2). 1995. 7.70 (0-606-07475-9, Pub. by Turtleback) Demco.

Bridwell, Norman. El Primer Otono de Clifford. (Clifford, the Big Red Dog Ser.).Tr. of Clifford's First Autumn. (SPA.). (J). (ps-3). 1997. pap. text 2.99 (0-590-37332-3) Scholastic Inc.

Bridwell, Norman. El Primer Otono de Clifford. (Clifford, the Big Red Dog Ser.).Tr. of Clifford's First Autumn. (SPA.). (J). (gr. k-2). 1997. 8.19 (0-606-11295-2, Pub. by Turtleback) Demco.

Bridwell, Norman. El Primer San Valentin de Clifford. LC 49-242900. (Clifford, the Big Red Dog Ser.).Tr. of Clifford's First Valentine's Day. (SPA.). 32p. (J). (gr. k-2). 1997. pap. text 2.99 (0-590-97469-6) Scholastic Inc.

— El Primer San Valentin de Clifford. (Clifford, the Big Red Dog Ser.).Tr. of Clifford's First Valentine's Day. (SPA.). (J). (gr. k-2). 1996. 8.19 (0-606-10799-1, Pub. by Turtleback) Demco.

Bridwell, Norman. La Primera Navidad de Clifford. (Clifford, the Big Red Dog Ser.).Tr. of Clifford's First Christmas. (SPA.). (J). (gr. k-2). 1994. 8.19 (0-606-06516-4, Pub. by Turtleback) Demco.

Bridwell, Norman. A Tiny Family. LC 98-8689. 32p. (J). (ps-1). 1999. 3.99 (0-439-04019-1, Pub. by Scholastic Inc) Penguin Putnam.

— Los Trucos de Clifford. Palacios, Argentina, tr. from ENG. (Clifford, the Big Red Dog Ser.).Tr. of Clifford's Tricks. (SPA.). 32p. (J). (ps-3). 1986. pap. 2.99 (0-590-40123-8) Scholastic Inc.

— Los Trucos de Clifford. (Clifford, the Big Red Dog Ser.).Tr. of Clifford's Tricks. (SPA.). (J). (gr. k-2). 1981. 8.19 (0-606-03109-X, Pub. by Turtleback) Demco.

— What Time Is It, Clifford? Book & Clock Set. (Clifford, the Big Red Dog Ser.). (Illus.). 32p. (J). (gr. k-2). 1998. pap. 9.95 (0-590-76338-5) Scholastic Inc.

— Where Is Clifford? A Lift-a-Flap Book. (Clifford, the Big Red Dog Ser.). 10p. (J). (ps-k). 1989. 11.95 (0-590-42925-6) Scholastic Inc.

*Bridwell, Norman. Where Is the Big Red Doggie? LC 98-235172. (Clifford, the Big Red Dog Ser.). (Illus.). 14p. (J). (ps-k). 1998. bds. 5.99 (0-590-04710-8, Pub. by Scholastic Inc) Penguin Putnam.

Bridwell, Norman. The Witch Goes to School. LC 92-12091. (Hello Reader! Ser.). (J). (ps-3). 1992. pap. 3.50 (0-590-45831-0) Scholastic Inc.

— Witch Goes to School. (Hello Reader! Level 3 Ser.). (J). 1992. 8.70 (0-606-01981-2, Pub. by Turtleback) Demco.

— The Witch Next Door. LC 66-7278. (Illus.). 32p. (J). (ps-3). 1986. pap. 2.99 (0-590-40433-4) Scholastic Inc.

Bridwell, Norman. The Witch Next Door. (J). 1986. 8.19 (0-606-03148-0, Pub. by Turtleback) Demco.

Bridwell, Norman. The Witch's Christmas. (Illus.). (J). (gr. k-3). 1972. pap. 1.50 (0-590-09216-2) Scholastic Inc.

— The Witch's Christmas. (Illus.). 32p. (J). (gr. k-3). 1986. pap. 2.50 (*0-590-40434-2*) Scholastic Inc.

Bridwell, Norman. Witch's Christmas. (J). 1986. 7.70 (*0-606-03150-2*, Pub. by Turtleback) Demco.

Bridwell, Norman. The Witch's Vacation. (Illus.). 32p. (J). (gr. k-3). 1987. pap. 2.50 (*0-590-40558-6*) Scholastic Inc.

Bridwell, R. & Quirk, William. Judicial Dictatorship. 158p. 1996. pap. text 18.95 (*1-56000-926-8*) Transaction Pubs.

*__Bridwell, R. Randall.__ The Power: Government by Consent & Majority Rule in America. LC 98-18655. 291p. 1998. 75.00 (*1-57292-114-5*) Austin & Winfield.

Bridwell, R. Randall, jt. auth. see Quirk, William J.

Bridwell, Raymond. Hydroponic Gardening: The Magic of Hydroponics for the Home Gardener. rev. ed. (Illus.). 216p. 1990. pap. 12.95 (*0-88007-176-1*) Woodbridge Pr.

Brie, F., ed. The Brut, or the Chronicle of England, Pt. 1. (EETS, OS Ser.: Vol. 131). 1972. reprint ed. 54.00 (*0-8115-0151-5*) Periodicals Srv.

Brie, Henry G. La, see La Brie, Henry G.

Brie, Vicki G. La, see La Brie, Vicki G.

Briedenbach, Monica. Career Development. 3rd ed. LC 97-39572. 199p. 1997. pap. text 33.33 (*0-13-576588-9*) P-H.

Brief, Arthur P. Attitudes in & Around Organizations. LC 98-19719. (Foundations for Organizational Science Ser.). 280p. 1998. 35.00 (*0-7619-0096-9*) Sage.

B

*__Brief, Arthur P.__ Attitudes in & Around Organizations. LC 98-19719. (Foundations for Organizational Science Ser.). 1998. pap. 16.99 (*0-7619-0097-7*) Sage.

Brief, Arthur P., ed. Productivity Research in the Behavioral & Social Sciences. LC 84-5877. 301p. 1984. 59.95 (*0-275-91132-2*, C1132, Praeger Pubs) Greenwood.

Brief, Richard. The History of the Financial Control Function of Local Government Accounting in the United Kingdom. LC 91-43227. (New Works in Accounting History). 192p. 1992. text 15.00 (*0-8153-0686-5*) Garland.

— Local Authority Accounting Methods: Problems & Solutions, 1909-1934. LC 90-25398. (New Works in Accounting History). 384p. 1992. text 10.00 (*0-8153-0685-7*) Garland.

Brief, Richard P. Corporate Financial Reporting & Analysis in the Early 1900s. (Accounting Ser.). 210p. 1986. text 10.00 (*0-8240-7856-X*) Garland.

— Nineteenth Century Capital Accounting & Business Investment. LC 75-18459. (History of Accounting Ser.). 1977. 18.95 (*0-405-07543-X*) Ayer.

Brief, Richard P., ed. The American Association of Public Accountants: Its First Twenty Years, 1886-1906. LC 77-87292. (Development of Contemporary Accounting Thought Ser.). 1978. reprint ed. lib. bdg. 37.95 (*0-405-10919-9*) Ayer.

— Carman G. Blough: His Professional Career & Accounting Thought. LC 77-87319. (Development of Contemporary Accounting Thought Ser.). 1978. lib. bdg. 37.95 (*0-405-10931-8*) Ayer.

— The Development of Contemporary Accounting Thought Series, 57 bks., Set. (Illus.). 1978. lib. bdg. 1701.00 (*0-405-10891-5*) Ayer.

— Dicksee's Contribution to Accounting Theory & Practice. LC 80-1454. (Dimensions of Accounting Theory & Practice Ser.). 1980. lib. bdg. 44.95 (*0-405-13476-2*) Ayer.

— Dimensions of Accounting Theory & Practice Ser., 70 vols., Set. 1981. lib. bdg. 2079.50 (*0-405-13475-4*) Ayer.

— The Etiquette of the Accountancy Profession & the Ethical Problems of Modern Accountancy: Lectures Delivered in 1932 on the William Vawter Foundation on Business Ethics, 2 vols. LC 80-1491. (Dimensions of Accounting Theory & Practice Ser.). 1980. reprint ed. lib. bdg. 28.95 (*0-405-13521-1*) Ayer.

— The Herwood Library of Accountancy: A Catalogue of Books Printed Between 1494 to 1900. LC 80-1495. (Dimensions of Accounting Theory & Practice Ser.). 1980. reprint ed. lib. bdg. 28.95 (*0-405-13525-4*) Ayer.

— The Institute of Chartered Accountants in England & Wales Library Catalogue, 1913, 2 vols., Set. LC 80-1501. (Dimensions of Accounting Theory & Practice Ser.). 1980. reprint ed. lib. bdg. 101.95 (*0-405-13526-2*) Ayer.

— The Institute of Chartered Accountants in England & Wales Library Catalogue, 1937, 2 vols. LC 80-1502. (Dimensions of Accounting Theory & Practice Ser.). 1980. reprint ed. lib. bdg. 56.95 (*0-405-13527-0*) Ayer.

— A Landmark in Accounting Theory: The Work of Gabriel A. D. Preinreich. LC 95-46235. (New Works in Accounting History). 216p. 1996. text 55.00 (*0-8153-2250-X*) Garland.

— The Story of the Firm, 1864-1964. LC 89-23275. (Accounting History & Thought Ser.). 172p. 1990. text 15.00 (*0-8240-3610-7*) Garland.

Brief, Richard P. & Peasnell, K. V., eds. Clean Surplus: A Link Between Accounting & Finance. LC 95-26375. (New Works in Accounting History). 324p. 1996. text 66.00 (*0-8153-2251-8*) Garland.

Brief, Richard P. & Previts, Gary J., eds. Early Twentieth Century Developments in American Accounting Thought: A Pre-Classical School. LC 77-87316. (Development of Contemporary Accounting Thought Ser.). 1978. lib. bdg. 30.95 (*0-405-10929-6*) Ayer.

Brief, Richard P., ed. see Amer Institute of Accountants Staff.

Brief, Richard P., ed. see American Association of University Instructors in.

Brief, Richard P., ed. see Baily, Francis.

Brief, Richard P., ed. see Baldwin, Harry G. & Holz, William B.

Brief, Richard P., ed. see Baxter, William T.

Brief, Richard P., ed. see Beckett, Thomas.

Brief, Richard P., ed. see Blough, Carman G.

Brief, Richard P., ed. see Bray, Frank S.

Brief, Richard P., ed. see Brinton, Willard C.

Brief, Richard P., ed. see Broaker, Frank & Chapman, Richard M.

Brief, Richard P., jt. ed. see Brooks, Collin.

Brief, Richard P., ed. see Burns, Thomas J. & Coffman, Edward N.

Brief, Richard P., ed. see Canning, John B.

Brief, Richard P., ed. see Carey, John L.

Brief, Richard P., ed. see Cerboni, Giuseppe.

Brief, Richard P., jt. ed. see Chatfield, Michael.

Brief, Richard P., ed. see Cleveland, Frederick A.

Brief, Richard P., ed. see Cocke, Hugh.

Brief, Richard P., ed. see Cole, William M. & Geddes, Anne E.

Brief, Richard P., ed. see Congress of Accountants, World Fair, St Louis, Sep.

Brief, Richard P., ed. see Cotter, Arundel.

Brief, Richard P., ed. see Courcelle-Seneuil, J. G.

Brief, Richard P., ed. see Cronhelm, Frederick W.

Brief, Richard P., ed. see Daniels, Mortimer B.

Brief, Richard P., ed. see Davidson, Sydney.

Brief, Richard P., ed. see De Motte Green, Catherine.

Brief, Richard P., ed. see De Paula, Frederic & Zeff, Stephen A.

Brief, Richard P., ed. see DeMond, C. W.

Brief, Richard P., ed. see Devine, Carl T.

Brief, Richard P., ed. see Dicksee, Lawrence R.

Brief, Richard P., ed. see Edwards, J. R.

Brief, Richard P., ed. see Epstein, Marc J.

Brief, Richard P., ed. see Esquerre, Paul-Joseph.

Brief, Richard P., ed. see Ficker, Nicholas T.

Brief, Richard P., ed. see Fitzgerald, Adolf A.

Brief, Richard P., ed. see Goldberg, Louis.

Brief, Richard P., ed. see Green, David, Jr.

Brief, Richard P., ed. see Hain, Hans P.

Brief, Richard P., ed. see Haskins, Charles W.

Brief, Richard P., ed. see Hawawini, Gabriel A. & Vora, Ashok.

Brief, Richard P., ed. see Hein, Leonard W.

Brief, Richard P., ed. see Hendriksen, Eldon S.

Brief, Richard P., ed. see Hepworth, Samuel R.

Brief, Richard P., ed. see Holmes, William, et al.

Brief, Richard P., ed. see Horngren, Charles T.

Brief, Richard P., jt. ed. see Horrigan, James O.

Brief, Richard P., ed. see International Accountants Congress Staff.

Brief, Richard P., ed. see Johnson, Thomas H.

Brief, Richard P., ed. see Jones, Edward T.

Brief, Richard P., ed. see King, George.

Brief, Richard P., ed. see Lamden, Charles W.

Brief, Richard P., ed. see Langenderfer, Harold Q.

Brief, Richard P., ed. see Langer, Russell D.

Brief, Richard P., ed. see Leake, Percy D.

Brief, Richard P., ed. see Leautey, Eugene & Guilbaut, Adolfe.

Brief, Richard P., ed. see Lee, Thomas A.

Brief, Richard P., ed. see Levy, Saul.

Brief, Richard P., ed. see Lewis, J. Slater.

Brief, Richard P., jt. ed. see Lisle, George.

Brief, Richard P., ed. see Lubell, Myron S.

Brief, Richard P., ed. see Mair, John.

Brief, Richard P., ed. see Mann, Helen S.

Brief, Richard P., ed. see Marchi, Francesco.

Brief, Richard P., ed. see Markus, Hugh B.

Brief, Richard P., ed. see Marsh, Christopher C.

Brief, Richard P., ed. see Merino, Barbara D.

Brief, Richard P., ed. see Mitchell, William.

Brief, Richard P., ed. see Montgomery, Robert H.

Brief, Richard P., ed. see Moonitz, Maurice.

Brief, Richard P., jt. ed. see Moonitz, Maurice.

Brief, Richard P., ed. see Murray, David.

Brief, Richard P., ed. see Nicholson, Jerome L.

Brief, Richard P., ed. see Norris, Harry.

Brief, Richard P., ed. see O'Neill, Michael T.

Brief, Richard P., ed. see Parker, R. H.

Brief, Richard P., ed. see Paton, William A. & Stevenson, Russell A.

Brief, Richard P., ed. see Perera, M. H.

Brief, Richard P., ed. see Pixley, Francis W.

Brief, Richard P., ed. see Preinreich, Gabriel A.

Brief, Richard P., ed. see Previts, Gary J.

Brief, Richard P., ed. see Rich, Wiley D.

Brief, Richard P., jt. ed. see Richardson, Alphyn P.

Brief, Richard P., ed. see Roberts, Alfred R.

Brief, Richard P., ed. see Ronen, Joshua & Sorter, George H.

Brief, Richard P., ed. see Saliers, Earl A.

Brief, Richard P., ed. see Schiff, Michael.

Brief, Richard P., ed. see Schmalenbach, Eugen.

Brief, Richard P., ed. see Scovell, Clinton H.

Brief, Richard P., ed. see Simpson, Kemper.

Brief, Richard P., ed. see Sneed, Florence R.

Brief, Richard P., ed. see Solomons, David & Inst Chart Accountants Staff.

Brief, Richard P., ed. see Sorter, George H.

Brief, Richard P., ed. see Sprague, Thomas B.

Brief, Richard P., ed. see Stacey, Nicholas A.

Brief, Richard P., ed. see Stamp, Edward, et al.

Brief, Richard P., ed. see Staubus, George J.

Brief, Richard P., ed. see Sweeney, Henry W.

Brief, Richard P., ed. see Taylor, R. Emmett.

Brief, Richard P., ed. see Todhunter, Ralph.

Brief, Richard P., ed. see Van De Linde, Gerald.

Brief, Richard P., ed. see Vatter, William J.

Brief, Richard P., ed. see Walker, R. G.

Brief, Richard P., ed. see Walker, Stephen P.

Brief, Richard P., ed. see Wells, Murry C.

Brief, Richard P., jt. ed. see Wells, Murry C.

Brief, Richard P., ed. see Wildman, John R. & Powell, Weldon.

Brief, Richard P., ed. see Williams, Robert B.

Brief, Richard P., ed. see Worthington, Beresford.

Brief, Richard P., ed. see Yamey, Basil S.

Brief, Richard P., ed. see Yang, Ju Mei.

Brief, Richard P., ed. see Zeff, Stephen A.

Brief, Richard S. Basic Industrial Hygiene: A Training Manual. 250p. 1975. 25.00 (*0-932627-01-3*) Am Indus Hygiene.

Brief, Rita B., ed. see Ibbotson Associates Staff.

Briefe. Die Neueste Litteratur Betreffend, 4 vols. Nicolai, Friedrich et al, eds. (GER., Illus.). 4578p. 1974. reprint ed. write for info. (*3-487-05074-9*) G Olms Pubs.

Briefel, Liliana C. Racconti Simpatici: Intermediate. (ITA.). 136p. (C). Date not set. pap. 12.65 (*0-8442-8049-6*, X8049-6) NTC Contemp Pub Co.

— Raccontini Simpatici: Advanced Beginning. (ITA.). (C). Date not set. pap. 12.65 (*0-8442-8048-8*, X8048-8) NTC Contemp Pub Co.

Briefings Publishing Group Staff, ed. Negotiation Techniques You Can Use in the Workplace--Or Anyplace. 40p. 1998. pap. 12.50 (*1-878604-28-7*) Briefings Pub Grp.

Briefings Publishings Group Staff, ed. Teamwork: Proven Solutions to Frustrating Problems. LC 99-222914. 44p. 1998. pap. 25.00 (*1-878604-29-5*) Briefings Pub Grp.

Briefs-Elgin, Gina, ed. see Brown, Catherine R., et al.

Briefs, Goetz A. The Proletariat: A Challange to Western Civilization. LC 74-25742. (European Sociology Ser.). 320p. 1975. reprint ed. 26.95 (*0-405-06498-5*) Ayer.

Briefs, U., et al, eds. Computerization & Work. viii, 180p. 1985. pap. 49.95 (*0-387-15367-5*) Spr-Verlag.

Briege, M. & Dittrich, H., eds. Semiconductor Processing & Characterization with Lasers. (Materials Science Forum Ser.: Vols. 173-174). (Illus.). 394p. (C). 1995. 166.00 (*0-87849-683-1*, Pub. by Trans T Pub) Enfield Pubs NH.

Brieger, Daniela. Charakterisierung der Blaetter Von Ilex Paraguariensis Saint Hilaire und Moeglicher Verfaelschungen Mit Hilfe Botanischer und Phytochemischer Methoden. (Dissertationes Botanicae Ser.: Band 240). (Illus.). viii, 270p. 1995. pap. 71.00 (*3-443-64152-0*, Pub. by Gebruder Borntraeger) Balogh.

Brieger, Friedrich, et al, eds. Rudolf Schlechter's "Die Orchideen" Band I: Beschreibung, Kultur und Zuechtung. Handbuch fuer Orchideenliebhaber, Zuechter und Botaniker, Band I/B, Lfg. 16-31. (Illus.). xx, 1031p. 1996. 343.00 (*3-8263-3084-6*, Pub. by Blckwell Wissenschafts) Balogh.

— Rudolf Schlechter's "Die Orchideen" Band I: Botanische Grundlagen der Orchideenforschung. Taxonomische Beschreibung der Orchideen (Botanical Basis for Orchid Research. Taxonomic Descriptions of Orchids), Band I/A, Lfg. 1-15. (Illus.). 976p. 1992. 323.00 (*3-8263-2609-1*, Pub. by Blckwell Wissenschafts) Balogh.

— Rudolf Schlechter's "Die Orchideen" Band I: Lieferung 32, Band I/C, Lfg. 32. (Illus.). 80p. 1996. pap. 29.00 (*3-8263-3106-0*, Pub. by Blckwell Wissenschafts) Balogh.

— Rudolf Schlechter's "Die Orchideen" Band I: Lieferung 33/34/35/36, Band I/C, Lfg. 33-36. (Illus.). 252p. 1997. pap. 79.00 (*3-8263-3156-7*, Pub. by Blckwell Wissenschafts) Balogh.

— Rudolf Schlechter's "Die Orchideen" Band I: Subtribus Oncidiinae. Verwandtschaft Oncidium - Odontoglossum - Miltonia - Cyrotochilum - Brassia, ect. Dr. Karlheinz Sengas, Band I/C. (Illus.). 240p. 1997. pap. 79.00 (*3-8263-3182-6*, Pub. by Blckwell Wissenschafts) Balogh.

— Rudolf Schlechter's "Die Orchideen" Band II: Orchideen Im Erwerbsgartenbau. Die Orchideenpflege Im Zimmer, Freilandorchideen. Krankheiten der Orchideen. Orchideen und Naturschutz (Orchid Propagation & Diseases. Orchids in Nature & Protection) (Illus.). 743p. 1985. 252.00 (*3-8263-2608-3*, Pub. by Blckwell Wissenschafts) Balogh.

Brieger, Gert H., ed. Medical America in the Nineteenth Century: Readings from the Literature. LC 76-165053. 348p. reprint ed. pap. 107.90 (*0-8357-8217-4*, 203413400088) Bks Demand.

*__Brieger, Gottfried.__ Pontiac, Michigan: A Postcard Album. (Postcard History Ser.). (Illus.). 128p. 2000. pap. 18.99 (*0-7385-0714-8*) Arcadia Publng.

Brieger, Nick & Sweeney, Simon. Descriptive Language: Reference & Practice. LC 93-30937. (C). 1994. pap. 11.50 (*0-13-042516-8*) P-H Intl.

Briehl, Susan. Come, Lord Jesus: Devotions for the Home Advent, Christmas, Epiphany. LC 96-21186. 64p. 1996. pap. 5.99 (*0-8066-2982-7*, 10-29827) Augsburg Fortress.

Briel, Holger M. Adorno und Derrida: Oder Wo Liest Das Ende Der Moderne? LC 92-39169. (American University Studies: Germanic Languages & Literature: Ser. I, Vol. 102). (GER.). X, 174p. (C). 1993. text 42.95 (*0-8204-2025-5*) P Lang Pubng.

Briel, Pat, jt. ed. see Fuller, Anne.

Brieland, Donald & Lemmon, John A. Social Work & the Law. 2nd ed. (Illus.). 621p. 1985. text 61.00 (*0-314-77848-9*) West Pub.

Briem, Gunnlaugur S. E., jt. auth. see Sassoon, Rosemary.

Brieman, Leo. Probability. LC 92-1381. (Classics in Applied Mathematics Ser.: No. 7). xiii, 421p. 1992. pap. 45.00 (*0-89871-296-3*) Soc Indus-Appl Math.

Briemberg, Mordecai, ed. It Was, It Was Not: Essays & Art on the War Against Iraq. 366p. 1992. pap. 14.95 (*0-921586-21-3*, Pub. by New Star Bks) Genl Dist Srvs.

Briemle, G. Farbatlas Kraeuter und Graeser (Color Atlas of Weeds & Grasses) (GER.). 288p. 1996. 27.00 (*3-8001-4125-6*, Pub. by Eugen Ulmer) Balogh.

Brien, Dolores E., ed. see Digney, Marita.

Brien, Joanna & Fairbairn, Ida. Pregnancy & Abortion Counselling. LC 96-6101. 216p. (C). 1996. 75.00 (*0-415-12278-3*); pap. 24.99 (*0-415-12010-1*) Routledge.

Brien, Kevin M. Marx, Reason & the Art of Freedom. LC 86-24048. 288p. 1987. 37.95 (*0-87722-466-8*) Temple U Pr.

*__Brien, Nell.__ Lioness. 408p. 2000. mass mkt. 5.99 (*1-55166-598-0*, 1-66598-3, Mira Bks) Harlequin Bks.

Brien, Nell. A Veiled Journey. 408p. 1999. per. 5.99 (*1-55166-528-X*, Mira Bks) Harlequin Bks.

Brien, R. J. The Shaping of Scotland: Eighteenth Century Patterns of Land Use & Settlement. (Illus.). 150p. 1989. pap. text 17.90 (*0-08-036572-8*, Pub. by Aberdeen U Pr) Macmillan.

Brien, Robert & Eastmond, Nick. Cognitive Science & Instruction. LC 93-40707. 192p. 1994. 34.95 (*0-87778-272-5*) Educ Tech Pubns.

Brienza, Susan D. Samuel Beckett's New Worlds: Style in Metafiction. LC 86-24919. (Illus.). 312p. 1987. 32.95 (*0-8061-2047-9*) U of Okla Pr.

Brienzo, Gary. Willa Cather's Transforming Vision: New France & the American Northeast. LC 94-17434. 1995. 28.50 (*0-945636-66-0*) Susquehanna U Pr.

Brier. Who Built America. write for info. (*1-57259-302-4*) Worth.

Brier, Alan & Lovelock, Robin, eds. Communication & Community: Anglo-German Perspectives. 272p. 1997. text 77.95 (*1-85972-138-9*, Pub. by Avebry) Ashgate Pub Co.

*__Brier, Bob.__ Ancient Egyptian Magic. LC 80-15608. (Illus.). 320p. 1999. reprint ed. pap. 15.00 (*0-688-00796-1*, Quil) HarperTrade.

Brier, Bob. El Asesinato de Tutankamon. 1999. pap. text 24.95 (*84-08-02788-3*) Planeta.

— Egyptian Mummies: Unraveling the Secrets of an Ancient Art. 1996. pap. 14.00 (*0-688-14624-4*, Quil) HarperTrade.

— Encyclopedia of Mummies. LC 97-16588. (Illus.). 248p. 1997. 35.00 (*0-8160-3108-8*) Facts on File.

— The Encyclopedia of Mummies. (Illus.). 256p. 1998. pap. 17.95 (*0-8160-3906-2*, Checkmark) Facts on File.

— The Murder of Tutankhamen: A True Story. LC 97-49193. 288p. 1998. pap. 24.95 (*0-399-14383-1*, Perigee Bks) Berkley Pub.

— The Murder of Tutankhamen: A True Story. 288p. 1999. reprint ed. pap. 14.00 (*0-425-16689-9*) Berkley Pub.

Brier, Bob & Hobbs, Hoyt. Daily Life of the Ancient Egyptians. LC 99-10137. (Daily Life Through History Ser.). 272p. 1999. 45.00 (*0-313-30313-4*) Greenwood.

Brier, David. International Typographic Design 2. (Illus.). 192p. 1994. 49.95 (*0-942604-39-3*) Madison Square.

— Typographic Design: Promotion. (Illus.). 192p. 1993. 45.00 (*0-942604-25-3*) Madison Square.

Brier, David, ed. Typographic Design. 256p. 1992. 49.95 (*0-942604-23-7*) Madison Square.

Brier, DeJoly La, see La Brier, DeJoly.

Brier, Ellen M., jt. auth. see Hiemstra, Roger.

Brier, Peter. Howard Mumford Jones & the Dynamics of Liberal Humanism. LC 93-47306. 200p. (C). 1994. 32.50 (*0-8262-0944-0*) U of Mo Pr.

Brier, Steven. Primary Care Orthopaedics in Chiropractic. (Illus.). 494p. (C). (gr. 13). 1999. text 59.00 (*0-8016-6381-4*, 06381) Mosby Inc.

Briercliffe, Harold. Illustrated History of Douglas Motorcycles. (Illus.). 112p. 1991. 19.95 (*0-85429-799-5*, Pub. by GT Foulis) Haynes Manuals.

Briere, Daniel D. Internet Telephony for Dummies. LC 96-77077. 384p. 1996. pap. 24.99 (*0-7645-0019-8*) IDG Bks.

— Long Distance Services: A Buyer's Guide. LC 90-42994. (Artech House Telecommunications Library). 310p. 1990. reprint ed. pap. 96.10 (*0-608-00557-6*, 206144000008) Bks Demand.

— Virtual Networks: A Buyer's Guide. (Telecom Management Library). 200p. 1989. text. write for info. (*0-89006-411-3*) Artech Hse.

— Virtual Networks: A Buyer's Guide. LC 89-48433. (Artech House Materials Science Library). 213p. 1989. reprint ed. pap. 66.10 (*0-608-02078-8*, 206273100003) Bks Demand.

*__Briere, Danny.__ Smart Homes for Dummies. (For Dummies Ser.). 384p. 1999. pap. 19.99 (*0-7645-0527-0*) IDG Bks.

Briere, Elizabeth, tr. see Vaseleios, Archimandrite.

Briere, Elizabeth, tr. see Yannaras, Christos.

Briere, Emile. The Power of Love: For Uncomplicated Christians. 158p. 1990. pap. 11.95 (*0-921440-17-0*) Madonna Hse.

Briere, Eugene J. Psycholinguistic Study of Phonological Interference. LC 68-13339. (Janua Linguarum, Ser. Minor: No. 66). 1968. pap. text 42.35 (*90-279-0594-0*) Mouton.

Briere, Euphemia. The Nativity of Our Lord: The Birth of the Messiah. (Illus.). (J). (gr. 1-3). 1993. pap. 5.00 (*0-913026-38-7*) St Nectarios.

Briere, Euphemia J. The Baptism of the Lord. (Illus.). 28p. (Orig.). (J). (gr. k-3). 1995. pap. 6.00 (*0-913026-44-1*) St Nectarios.

Briere, Gaston, jt. ed. see Vitry, Paul.

Briere, Jean-Francois, jt. auth. see Wylie, Laurence.

Briere, Jean-Francois, tr. see Gregoire, Henri.

Briere, John. Psychological Assessment of Adult Posttraumatic States. LC 96-52132. (Psychotherapy Practitioner Resource Ser.). 251p. 1997. pap. text 24.95 (*1-55798-403-4*, 431-7840) Am Psychol.

— Therapy for Adults Molested As Children: Beyond Survival. 2nd expanded rev. ed. LC 96-8221. (Illus.). 272p. 1996. 36.95 (*0-8261-5641-X*) Springer Pub.

An Asterisk (*) at the beginning of an entry indicates that the title is appearing for the first time.

Briere, John, ed. Assessing & Treating Victims of Violence. LC 87-646993. (New Directions for Mental Health Services Ser.: No. MHS 64). Orig. Title: Violent Victimization. 110p. (Orig.). 1994. pap. 25.00 (*0-7879-9991-1*) Jossey-Bass.
— Treating Victims of Child Sexual Abuse: Implications for Clinical Practice. LC 87-646993. (New Directions for Mental Health Services Ser.: No. MHS51). 1991. 25.00 (*1-55542-775-8*) Jossey-Bass.
Briere, John N. Child Abuse Trauma: Theory & Treatment of the Lasting Effects. (Interpersonal Violence: the Practice Ser.: Vol. 2). 200p. (C). 1992. 48.00 (*0-8039-3712-1*); pap. 21.50 (*0-8039-3713-X*) Sage.
Briere, John N., et al, eds. The APSAC Handbook on Child Maltreatment. 449p. 1996. 69.95 (*0-8039-5596-0*); pap. 32.95 (*0-8039-5597-9*) Sage.
Briere, O. Fifty Years of Chinese Philosophy: Eighteen Ninety-Eight to Nineteen Fifty. Thompson, Laurence G., tr. LC 78-31391. 159p. 1979. reprint ed. lib. bdg. 55.00 (*0-313-20650-3*, BRFY, Greenwood Pr) Greenwood.
Brierley, Anthony. Explorers of the Ancient World. LC 96-1261. (Voyages of Discovery Ser.). (Illus.). 48p. (YA). (gr. 4-7). 1996. 18.95 (*0-87226-485-8*, 64858B, P Bedrick Books) NTC Contemp Pub Co.
Brierley, Anthony, tr. see Bertela, Giovanna G.
Brierley, Anthony, tr. see Micheletti, Emma.
Brierley, Anthony, tr. see Olivari, Mariolina.
Brierley, Barry. Wasichu. (Illus.). 1996. pap. 15.00 (*1-889657-02-6*) Bear Bks AZ.
— Wasichu. 345p. 1993. 21.95 (*0-9637792-0-6*); pap. write for info. (*0-9637792-1-4*) Lagare.
— Wasichu. limited ed. 345p. 1993. 75.00 (*0-9637792-9-X*) Lagare.
— Wasichu's Return. (Illus.). 336p. (Orig.). Date not set. 23.95 (*1-889657-19-0*) Bear Bks AZ.
— Wasichu's Return. (Illus.). 336p. (Orig.). 1996. pap. 14.00 (*1-889657-20-4*) Bear Bks AZ.
— White Horse, Red Rider. 188p. (Orig.). 1996. pap. 11.95 (*1-889657-27-1*); pap. 11.95 (*0-933025-49-1*) Bear Bks AZ.
Brierley, Brooks. Magic Motors, 1930. (Illus.). 160p. (C). 1996. 34.95 (*0-9615791-2-9*) Garrett & String.
Brierley, Brooks T. Auburn, Reo, Franklin & Pierce-Arrow Versus Cadillac, Chrysler, Lincoln & Packard. (Illus.). 160p. 1994. 49.95 (*0-9615791-1-0*) Garrett & String.
***Brierley, Cornelia.** Tales of Taliesin: A Memoir of Fellowship. (Illus.). 176p. 2000. boxed set 29.95 (*0-7649-1335-2*, A539) Pomegranate Calif.
Brierley, David. Health & Safety in Schools. 240p. 1991. pap. 30.00 (*1-85396-130-2*, Pub. by P Chapman) Taylor & Francis.
Brierley, Eric. Visual Basic. LC 98-84685. 1998. pap. text 39.99 (*1-57169-153-7*) Sams.
Brierley, Harry. Transvestism: A Handbook for Psychologists, Psychiatrists & Counsellors. (Illus.). 160p. 1979. 126.00 (*0-08-022268-4*, Pub. by Pergamon Repr) Franklin.
Brierley, Jane, tr. see Sioui, Georges E.
Brierley, John. Give Me a Child Until He Is Seven: Brain Studies & Early Childhood Education. 2nd ed. LC 94-16346. 1994. 24.95 (*0-7507-0319-9*, Falmer Pr) Taylor & Francis.
— Give Me a Child until He Is 7. 2nd ed. 134p. 1994. 75.00 (*0-7507-0318-0*, Falmer Pr) Taylor & Francis.
— Growth in Children. Wragg, C. E., ed. (Education Matters Ser.). 192p. 1992. text 90.00 (*0-304-32601-1*); pap. text 29.95 (*0-304-32581-3*) Continuum.
Brierley, John K. Biology & the Social Crisis. LC 71-120071. (Illus.). 260p. 1975. 28.50 (*0-8386-7719-3*) Fairleigh Dickinson.
— A Natural History of Man. 184p. 1975. 28.50 (*0-8386-7819-X*) Fairleigh Dickinson.
— The Thinking Machine. LC 72-14220. 195p. 1973. 18.50 (*0-8386-1364-0*) Fairleigh Dickinson.
Brierley, John S. & Todd, Daniel. Prairie Small-Town Survival: The Challenge of Agro-Manitoba. LC 89-13551. (Canadian Studies: Vol. 7). 88p. 1990. lib. bdg. 49.95 (*0-88946-211-9*) E Mellen.
Brierley, Louise. The Twelve Days of Christmas. 2nd ed. LC 94-19705. (Illus.). (J). (ps-3). 1995. pap. 5.99 (*1-56402-525-X*) Candlewick Pr.
Brierley, Ned F., tr. see Chapa, Juan B.
Brierley, Peter. New Perspectives on Microsoft Windows NT Server 4.0. 1997. pap. text 49.99 (*0-7600-5604-8*) Course Tech.
— New Perspectives on Microsoft Windows NT 4.0 Server. 600p. 1997. write for info. (*0-7600-5384-7*) Course Tech.
— New Perspectives on Microsoft Windows NT 4.0 Server. 10th ed. (New Perspectives Ser.). 600p. (C). 1997. pap. 53.95 (*0-7600-5254-9*) Course Tech.
Brierley, Peter & Wright. The Atlas of World Christianity: The Comprehensive Guide 2000 Years. LC 98-45389. 1998. 24.99 (*0-7852-0991-3*) Nelson.
Brierley, Sean. The Advertising Handbook. LC 94-48378. (Media Practice Ser.). (Illus.). 304p. (C). (gr. 13). 1995. 75.00 (*0-415-10713-X*) Routledge.
— Advertising Handbook. (Media Practice Ser.). (Illus.). 304p. (C). 1995. pap. 22.99 (*0-415-10714-8*) Routledge.
Brierley, Walter. Sandwichman. (Radical Fiction Ser.). 304p. 1990. reprint ed. lib. bdg. 25.00 (*0-929587-41-3*) I R Dee.
Brierly, Anthony, tr. see Letta, Elisabetta M.
Brierly, Cornelia. Tales of Taliesin: A Memoir of Fellowship. (Illus.). 196p. 1999. 25.00 (*1-884320-18-X*); pap. 19.95 (*1-884320-19-8*) ASU Herberger Ctr.
Brierly, Eric, jt. auth. see Jerke, Noel.
Brierly, James L. Law of Nations: An Introduction to the International Law of Peace. 6th ed. Waldock, Humphrey, ed. 460p. 1978. text 54.95 (*0-19-825105-X*) OUP.
Brierly, John E., jt. auth. see David, Rene.
Brierly, Ken, ed. see Berry, Glen.
Brierre De Boismont, Alexandre-Jacques-Francois. Hallucinations. LC 75-16689. (Classics in Psychiatry Ser.). 1976. reprint ed. 46.95 (*0-405-07419-0*) Ayer.
Brierre, Jean F. Les Horizons sans Ciel. (B. E. Ser.: No. 57). (FRE.). 1935. 35.00 (*0-8115-3008-6*) Periodicals Srv.
Briers, A. True Stories about Greek Coins. (Illus.). 48p. 6.95 (*0-907849-56-3*, Pub. by Ashmolean Mus) A Schwartz & Co.
— True Stories about Roman Coins. (Illus.). 48p. 6.95 (*0-907849-12-1*, Pub. by Ashmolean Mus) A Schwartz & Co.
Briers, Audrey. Eat, Drink & Be Merry: Food & Drink in the Roman World. (Illus.). 48p. 1995. pap. 6.95 (*0-907849-93-8*, 93-8, Pub. by Ashmolean Mus) A Schwartz & Co.
— Sporting Success in Ancient Greece & Rome. 48p. (Orig.). 1996. pap. 8.95 (*1-85444-055-1*, 0551, Pub. by Natl Mus Scotland) A Schwartz & Co.
Briers, M., et al. Australian Financial Markets Association (AFMA) Report. 160p. 1998. pap. 25.00 (*0-86840-497-7*) Intl Spec Bk.
***Briers, Richard.** Coward & Company. 152p. 1999. pap. 12.95 (*1-86105-232-4*) Robson.
— A Little Light Weeding LC 99-169967. 256p. 1998. write for info. (*0-86051-883-3*, Robson-Parkwest) Parkwest Pubns.
Briers, Richard. A Little Light Weeding: Evergreen Reading for the Perennial Gardener. LC 99-169967. (Illus.). 256p. 1995. pap. 12.95 (*0-86051-936-8*, Robson-Parkwest) Parkwest Pubns.
— A Little Light Weeding: Gardening Tips. large type ed. 23.95 (*1-85695-047-6*, Pub. by ISIS Lrg Prnt); pap. 19.95 (*1-85695-038-7*, Pub. by ISIS Lrg Prnt) Transaction Pubs.
Brierton, Joan M. Victorian: American Restoration Style. LC 98-43575. (American Restoration Style Ser.: No. 2). (Illus.). 128p. 1999. pap. 21.95 (*0-87905-887-0*) Gibbs Smith Pub.
Brierty, Edward G., et al. Business Marketing. 3rd ed. LC 97-23946. 683p. (C). 1997. 93.00 (*0-13-757378-2*) P-H.
Briery, Traci. Vampire Journals. 352p. 1998. mass mkt. 4.99 (*0-8217-6024-6*, Zebra Kensgtn) Kensgtn Pub Corp.
Briesath, Jerry. Billiards: The Official Rules & Record Book. rev. ed. (Illus.). 160p. (C). 1995. pap. 6.95 (*1-878493-01-9*) Billiard Congress of Amer.
Briese, K. English-German Dictionary. (ENG & GER.). 624p. 1986. 65.00 (*0-569-06892-4*, Pub. by Collets) St Mut.
Briese, Russell J. Foundations of a Lutheran Theology of Evangelism. LC 95-106825. (Regensburger Studien Zur Theologie Ser.: Bd. 42). IX, 304p. 1994. pap. 54.95 (*3-631-46392-8*) P Lang Pubng.
Brieskorn, E. & Knorrer, Horst. Plane Algebraic Curves. 864p. 1986. 137.00 (*0-8176-1769-8*) Birkhauser.
Brieskorn, Egbert, et al. Singularities: The Brieskorn Anniversary Volume. LC 98-18099. (Progress in Mathematics Ser.). 1998. 98.00 (*0-8176-5913-7*) Birkhauser.
Briesmeister, James M. & Schaefer, Charles E., eds. Handbook of Parent Training: Parents As Co-Therapists for Children's Behavior. 2nd ed. LC 97-20446. (Problems Ser.). 608p. 1997. 69.50 (*0-471-16343-0*) Wiley.
Briessen, Fritz Van, see Van Briessen, Fritz.
Briet, E., ed. Liber Amicorum for Emil Alfred Loeliger. (Journal: Haemostasis: Vol. 15, No. 4, 1985). (Illus.). 72p. 1985. pap. 51.50 (*3-8055-4146-5*) S Karger.
Briet, Henri. Savoir Accorder le Verbe. (FRE.). 94p. 1986. pap. 19.95 (*0-8288-3353-2*) Fr & Eur.
Briet, Philippe, ed. see Corman, Cid.
Brietzke, Paul H. Law, Development, & the Ethiopian Revolution. LC 80-65574. 600p. 1982. 50.00 (*0-8387-5008-7*) Bucknell U Pr.
Brievingh, R. P. Van Wijk van, see Van Wijk van Brievingh, R. P.
Briffa, John. Better Health Through Natural Supplements. LC 99-27421. (Health Factfiles Ser.). 112p. 1999. pap. 12.95 (*0-7370-1612-4*) T-L Custom Pub.
***Briffa, John.** Food for Health. LC 99-26890. (Health Factfiles Ser.). (Illus.). 112p. 1999. pap. 12.95 (*0-7370-1603-5*) T-L Custom Pub.
Briffa, Merice. A Ballet Lesson. (C). 1990. pap. 35.00 (*0-908175-98-1*, Pub. by Boolarong Pubns) St Mut.
Briffa, Salvino. That I May See: A Prayerful Discovery Through Imagination. 140p. 1986. pap. 8.95 (*0-87193-251-2*) Dimension Bks.
Briffault, tr. see Racine, Jean.
Briffault, Herma, tr. see Mallet, Francoise.
Briffault, R. Sin & Sex. LC 72-6300. (Studies in Philosophy: No. 40). 228p. 1972. reprint ed. lib. bdg. 75.00 (*0-8383-1631-X*) M S G Haskell Hse.
Briffault, Richard & Twentieth Century Fund Staff. Balancing Acts: The Reality Behind State Balanced Budget Requirements. LC 96-21838. (Balanced Budget Debate Ser.). 1996. pap. 9.95 (*0-87078-394-7*) Century Foundation.
Briffault, Richard, jt. auth. see Kramer, Orin.
Briffault, Robert. The Mothers: The Matriarchal Theory of Social Origins. LC 90-34114. 451p. 1993. reprint ed. lib. bdg. 45.00 (*0-86527-398-7*) Fertig.
— Reasons for Anger. LC 68-58774. (Essay Index Reprint Ser.). 1977. 20.95 (*0-8369-1024-9*) Ayer.
— Sin & Sex. LC 72-9623. (Human Sexual Behavior Ser.). reprint ed. 37.50 (*0-404-57418-1*) AMS Pr.
Briffault, Robert & Malinowski, Bronislaw. Marriage: Past & Present: A Debate Between Robert Briffault & Bronislaw Malinowksi. (Extending Horizons Ser.). 90p. (C). 1956. reprint ed. 3.95 (*0-87558-027-0*); reprint ed. pap. 2.45 (*0-87558-028-9*) Porter Sargent.
Briffett, Clive. The Birds of Singapore. LC 92-41708. (Images of Asia Ser.). (Illus.). 122p. (C). 1994. text 38.00 (*0-19-588606-2*) OUP.
Briffett, Clive, ed. Building Maintenance Technology in Tropical Climates. (Illus.). 216p. 1995. pap. 47.50 (*9971-69-190-6*, Pub. by Sngapore Univ Pr) Coronet Bks.
Briffett, David. Sussex Murders, County Murders & Mysteries. (C). 1989. 45.00 (*1-85455-045-4*, Pub. by Ensign Pubns & Print) St Mut.
***Brig, Milly.** Eyes of Grass: Ojos de Hierba LC 98-92260. 89p. 1999. write for info. (*0-9667328-0-4*) M Brig.
Brigance, Albert H. Brigance Genealogy, 2 vols., Vol. 1. LC 95-75717. (Illus.). 250p. 1995. 40.00 (*0-9619971-2-5*) Brigance Pub.
— Brigance Genealogy, 2 vols., Vol. 2. LC 95-75717. (Illus.). 250p. 1995. 40.00 (*0-9619971-3-3*) Brigance Pub.
— Building Reading Skills, 18 vols., Student Bks. A-H. (Illus.). 1998. pap. text 208.44 (*0-9619971-4-1*) Brigance Pub.
— Christenberry/ Christenbury Genealogy. LC 87-73529. (Illus.). 231p. 1988. 40.00 (*0-9619971-0-9*) Brigance Pub.
Brigance, Pat H. Blythe. LC 94-94262. (Illus.). 400p. 1994. 60.00 (*0-9619971-1-7*) Brigance Pub.
Brigandi. My Favorite Martian. 96p. (J). 1999. pap. 4.95 (*0-7868-4239-3*, Pub. by Hyperion) Time Warner
Brigandi, Pat. One Hundred & One Valentine Jokes. 96p. (J). (gr. 4-6). 1994. pap. 1.95 (*0-590-47141-4*) Scholastic Inc.
Brigandi, Pat, jt. auth. see Black, Sonia W.
***Brigandi, Phil.** 100 Years of Headline News. Whiting, David, ed. (Illus.). 256p. 2000. pap. 19.95 (*0-9635868-7-4*, Pub. by OC Register) Sunbelt Pubns.
Brigandi, Phil. Orange: The City 'Round the Plaza. Parks, Lori, ed. LC 97-71127. (Illus.). 200p. 1997. 39.95 (*1-886483-11-6*) Heritge Media.
— Temecula: At the Crossroads of History. LC 97-77577. (Illus.). 1998. 39.95 (*1-886483-14-0*) Heritge Media.
Briganti, Louis A. & Wacker, Steven C. Fatty Acid Profiling (FAP) & the Identification of Environmental Bacteria for Drinking Water Utilities. LC 96-173622. (Illus.). 89p. 1995. pap. 48.00 (*0-89867-823-4*, 90698) Am Water Wks Assn.
Brigdale, Martin, jt. auth. see Harris, Valentina.
Brigden, John. The Sporting Minis: Mini Cooper, Mini Coopers 1275GT. (Illus.). 128p. 1990. 27.95 (*0-947981-40-3*, Pub. by Motor Racing) Motorbooks Intl.
***Brigden, Paul & Lowe, R.** Welfare Policy under the Conservatives, 1951-1964. (PRO Handbks.: No. 30). (Illus.). 343p. 1999. pap. 39.95 (*1-873162-46-4*, Pub. by PRO Pubns) Midpt Trade.
Brigden, Roy. Agricultural Hand Tools. (Album Ser.: No. 100). (Illus.). 32p. 1985. reprint ed. pap. 5.25 (*0-85263-630-X*, Pub. by Shire Pubns) Parkwest Pubns.
Brigden, Roy. Ploughs & Ploughing. (Album Ser.: No. 125). (Illus.). 32p. 1998. pap. 6.25 (*0-85263-695-4*, Pub. by Shire Pubns) Parkwest Pubns.
Brigden, Roy, ed. Harvesting Machinery. 1989. pap. 25.00 (*0-85263-979-1*, Pub. by Shire Pubns) St Mut.
Brigel, J. Grammar of the Tulu Language. 139p. 1982. 25.00 (*0-88431-916-4*) IBD Ltd.
Brigel, J. A. Grammar of the Tulu Language. 148p. 1982. 39.95 (*0-8288-8422-6*) Fr & Eur.
Brigermann, Chuck. Corvette Essentials: A Collector's Guide, 1956-1967. (Illus.). 243p. 1993. pap. 19.95 (*0-89709-207-4*) Liberty Pub.
— Record Collector's Fact Book, Vol. I. LC 82-73474. (Illus.). 96p. 1983. pap. 7.95 (*0-89709-037-3*) Liberty Pub.
Brigg, Peter. J. G. Ballard. Schlobin, Roger C., ed. LC 85-2724. (Starmont Reader's Guide Ser.: Vol. 26) (Illus.). 138p. 1985. lib. bdg. 29.00 (*0-916732-84-3*) Millefleurs.
— Shanghai Year: A Westerner's Life in the New China. LC 87-1949. (Illus.). x, 115p. 1987. pap. 17.00 (*0-930261-89-5*) Millefleurs.
Briggaman, Robert A., jt. ed. see Wojnarowska, Fenella.
Briggeman, Kim. Year of the Griz. (Saga of the Sierras Ser.). 1996. pap. text 2.95 (*1-56037-101-3*) Am Wrld Geog.
Briggs. Riparian Ecosystem Recovery: Strategies & References. LC 96-9957. (Illus.). 159p. 1996. pap. 19.95 (*0-8165-1644-8*) U of Ariz Pr.
— World of Herman Kahn. 1997. 22.95 (*0-02-904841-9*) Free Pr.
Briggs & Cobley. The Media an Introduction. (C). 1997. pap. text 23.44 (*0-582-27798-1*, Pub. by Addison-Wesley) Longman.
Briggs & Courtney. Agriculture & Environment. 1989. pap. text. write for info. (*0-582-00413-6*, Pub. by Addison-Wesley) Longman.
Briggs, et al. Create Your Own! Early Childhood Activities. 224p. (C). 2000. pap. text 25.95 (*0-7668-1610-9*) Delmar.
— Fundamentals of Physical Geography. 2nd ed. 1993. pap. text. write for info. (*0-7730-5173-2*) Addison-Wes.
Briggs, jt. auth. see Bennett.
Briggs, Dean. God Spot, 1. LC 99-12078. 1999. pap. text 12.99 (*0-8499-3734-5*) Word Pub.
Briggs, A. D. Alexander Pushkin: A Critical Study. LC 82-16242. 258p. (C). 1983. text 44.00 (*0-389-20340-8*, 07184) B&N Imports.
— A Comparative Study of Pushkin's "The Bronze Horseman", Nekrasov's "Red-Nosed Frost", & Blok's "The Twelve" The Wild World. LC 90-42249. (Studies in Slavic Language & Literature: Vol. 5). 288p. 1990. lib. bdg. 89.95 (*0-88946-082-5*) E Mellen.
Briggs, A. D., ed. English Sonnets. 1999. pap. 3.50 (*0-460-87990-1*) Tuttle Pubng.
Briggs, A. D. & Unbegaun, Boris O., eds. Pushkin: Tales of the Late Ivan Petrovich Belkin (Povesti Pokoinogo Ivana Petrovicha Belkina) (Russian Texts Ser.). (RUS.). 167p. 1994. pap. 20.95 (*1-85399-402-2*, Pub. by Brist Class Pr) Focus Pub-R Pullins.
Briggs, A. D., ed. see Dostoyevsky, Fyodor.
Briggs, A. D., ed. see Dostoyevsky, Fyodor & Tolstoy, Leo.
Briggs, A. D., ed. see Pushkin, Aleksandr.
Briggs, A. D., tr. see Medvedev, Roy.
Briggs, Adrian. Norton Rose on Civil Jurisdiction & Judgments. Rees, Peter & Rose, Norton, eds. 350p. 1993. 124.00 (*1-85044-500-1*) LLP.
Briggs, Alma W. Don't Give Up! How to Live the Christian Life Joyously, Victoriously & Successfully. LC 97-60709. 160p. 1997. pap. 10.95 (*0-9657749-0-2*, 7904) Eagles Nst Pubns.
Briggs, Alys, jt. ed. see Harris, Anne.
Briggs, Amy Thompson, see Thompson Briggs, Amy.
Briggs, Andrew. Acoustic Microscopy. (Monographs on the Physics & Chemistry of Materials: No. 46). (Illus.). 364p. 1992. text 110.00 (*0-19-851377-1*) OUP.
Briggs, Andrew & Arnold, Walter, eds. Advances in Acoustic Microscopy, Vol. 2. (Illus.). 287p. (C). 1996. text 90.00 (*0-306-45344-4*, Kluwer Plenum) Kluwer Academic.
Briggs-Anigboh, Comfort, jt. auth. see Ikein, Augustine.
Briggs, Anna M., ed. see Bower, Bill & Werner, David B.
Briggs, Anne. Circumcision: What Every Parent Should Know. (Illus.). 183p. 1985. pap. 4.95 (*0-9615484-0-1*) Birth & Parenting.
Briggs, Asa. AGE IMPROVEMENT1783 1867. (History of England Ser.). (Illus.). 550p. (C). 1989. pap. text 42.00 (*0-582-49100-2*, 73478) Longman.
***Briggs, Asa.** The Age of Improvement, 1783-1867. 2nd ed. LC 99-22388. (History of England Ser.). 486p. (C). 1999. pap. 30.73 (*0-582-36959-2*) Longman.
Briggs, Asa. Chartism. LC 99-163548. (Pocket Histories Ser.). 128p. 1998. pap. 9.95 (*0-7509-1916-7*, Pub. by Sutton Pub Ltd) Intl Pubs Mktg.
— Collected Essays of Asa Briggs Vol. I: Words, Numbers, Places, People. LC 84-24484. 272p. 1985. pap. text 16.95 (*0-252-06004-0*) U of Ill Pr.
— Collected Essays of Asa Briggs Vol. II: Images, Problems, Standpoints & Forecasts. LC 84-24484. 352p. pap. text 16.95 (*0-252-06005-9*) U of Ill Pr.
— Collected Essays of Asa Briggs Vol. II: Images, Problems, Standpoints & Forecasts. LC 84-24484. 352p. 1985. text 37.50 (*0-252-01217-8*) U of Ill Pr.
— The Collected Essays of Asa Briggs, Vol. III Vol. III: Serious Pursuits: Communications & Education. 480p. 1991. text 44.95 (*0-252-01872-9*) U of Ill Pr.
***Briggs, Asa.** Go to It! Victory on the Home Front, 1939-1945. (Illus.). 128p. 2000. pap. 26.95 (*1-84000-262-X*, Pub. by Mitchell Beazley) Antique Collect.
Briggs, Asa. History of Broadcasting in the U. K. Vol. IV: Sound & Vision, Vol. IV. (Illus.). 1028p. 1979. text 79.00 (*0-19-212967-8*) OUP.
— History of Broadcasting in the U. K. Vol. V: Competition. (Illus.). 1,160p. 1995. 90.00 (*0-19-215964-X*) OUP.
— The History of Broadcasting in the United Kingdom, 3 vols. Incl. Vol. 1. History of Broadcasting in the U. K. Vol. I: The Birth of Broadcasting. (Illus.). 414p. 1995. 79.00 (*0-19-212926-0*); Vol. 2. History of Broadcasting in the U. K. Vol. II: The Golden Age of Wireless. (Illus.). 654p. 1995. 79.00 (*0-19-212930-9*); Vol. 3. History of Broadcasting in the U. K. Vol. III: The War of Words. (Illus.). 716p. 1995. 79.00 (*0-19-212956-2*); (Illus.). (C). write for info. (*0-318-54836-4*) OUP.
— The Power of Steam: An Illustrated History of the World's Steam Age. LC 82-40321. (Illus.). 208p. Date not set. reprint ed. pap. 64.50 (*0-608-20609-1*, 205457700003) Bks Demand.
— The Power of Steam: An Illustrated History of the World's Steam Age. LC 82-40321. (Illus.). 208p. (C). 1983. reprint ed. pap. 10.00 (*0-226-07497-8*) U Ch Pr.
— Social History & Human Experience. (Grace A. Tanner Lecture in Human Values Ser.). 22p. 1984. 7.50 (*0-910153-02-7*) E T Woolf.
— A Social History of England. (Illus.). 352p. 1995. 45.00 (*0-297-83262-X*, Pub. by Weidenfeld & Nicolson) Trafalgar.
— Victorian Cities. LC 92-30443. (Classics in Urban History Ser.: Vol. 2). 1993. 17.95 (*0-520-07922-1*, Pub. by U CA Pr) Cal Prin Full Svc.
— Victorian People: A Reassessment of Persons & Themes, 1851-67. rev. ed. LC 55-5118. (Chicago Collectors Editions Ser.). (Illus.). x, 368p. 1975. reprint ed. pap. text 16.95 (*0-226-07488-9*, P365) U Ch Pr.
— Victorian Things. LC 88-30633. (Illus.). 464p. 1989. 35.95 (*0-226-07483-8*) U Ch Pr.
— Wine for Sale: Victoria Wine & the Liquor Trade, 1860-1984. LC 85-20877. (Illus.). x, 208p. 1986. lib. bdg. 30.00 (*0-226-07485-4*) U Ch Pr.
Briggs, Asa, ed. A Dictionary of Twentieth-Century World Biography. 624p. 1992. 30.00 (*0-19-211679-7*) OUP.
Briggs, Asa, frwd. Longman Dictionary of Twentieth Century Biography. 480p. 1900. pap. text 16.95 (*0-582-89213-9*, TV3862) Longman.
Briggs, Asa & Clavin, Patricia. Modern Europe, 1789-1989. LC 96-10174. (History of Europe Ser.). 512p. (C). 1996. pap. text 22.50 (*0-582-49405-2*, Pub. by Addison-Wesley) Longman.
— Modern Europe Since 1789. LC 96-10174. (History of Europe Ser.). 512p. (C). 1996. 74.00 (*0-582-49406-0*) Addison-Wesley.
Briggs, Asa & Saville, John. Essays in Labour History, 1918-1939. 1977. 69.50 (*0-85664-239-8*) Elliots Bks.

B

Briggs, Asa & Snowman, Daniel, eds. Fins de Siecle: How Centuries End, 1400-2000. LC 96-19885. (Illus.). 288p. 1996. 40.00 (*0-300-06687-2*) Yale U Pr.

Briggs, Asa, jt. auth. see Burke, Peter.

Briggs, Asa, ed. see Alford, B. W.

Briggs, Asa, ed. see Bennett, Martyn.

Briggs, Asa, ed. see Green, Vivian.

Briggs, Asa, ed. see Hamilton, Bernard.

Briggs, Asa, ed. see Maclay, Michael.

Briggs, Asa, ed. see Shukman, Harold.

Briggs, Asa, ed. see Watterson, Barbara.

Briggs, Austin. Flash Gordon: Dailies 1940-1942. Schreiner, Dave, ed. (Flash Gordon Ser.: Vol. 2). (Illus.). 112p. 1993. pap. 10.95 (*0-87816-187-2*) Kitchen Sink.

— Flash Gordon Dailies 1940-1942. Schreiner, Dave, ed. LC 92-25057. (Flash Gordon Ser.). (Illus.). 96p. 1992. pap. 10.95 (*0-87816-172-4*) Kitchen Sink.

***Briggs, Betty.** Quality Concealed. (Illus.). 203p. 1999. pap. 9.95 (*0-9656307-1-4*, Pub. by Sunrise Selections) Evans Bk Dist.

Briggs, Betty Savidge, ed. see Storter, Rob.

Briggs, Bob. Around Hallowell. LC 97-112633. (Images of America Ser.). 1999. pap. 16.99 (*0-7524-0480-6*) Arcadia Publng.

Briggs, Bob, jt. auth. see Wright, Debra.

Briggs, Bonnie-Anne & Petersen, Catherine Fish. Brief Review in United States History & Government. LC 98-234519. vi, 418 p. 1997. 8.50 (*0-13-433282-2*) P-H.

Briggs, Bruce B. World of Herman Kahn. 416p. 1996. 30.00 (*0-684-82775-1*) Free Pr.

Briggs-Bunting, Jane. Laddie of the Light. LC 97-93003. (Illus.). 48p. (J). (gr. 3-6). 1997. teacher ed. 17.00 (*0-9649083-1-X*) Blck Riv Trad.

— Legal Guidelines for Reporters in Michigan. rev. ed. LC 98-73481. 58 p. (C). 1998. pap. text 8.00 (*0-9649083-2-8*) Blck Riv Trad.

— Whoop for Joy: A Christmas Wish. LC 95-95152. (Barnyard Tales Ser.). (Illus.). 32p. (J). (gr. 1-5). 1995. 13.95 (*0-9649083-0-1*) Blck Riv Trad.

Briggs-Bunting, Jane, ed. Federal, Regional & Michigan Press Law: A Compilation of Cases Pertinent to Media. (C). 1998. pap. text 80.00 (*0-9649083-3-6*) Blck Riv Trad.

***Briggs, Carl & Smith, Barbara.** Barbour County. (Images of America Ser.). (Illus.). 128p. 2000. pap. 18.99 (*0-7385-0570-6*) Arcadia Publng.

Briggs, Carl M. Instructor's Manual with Test Bank & Transparency Masters to Accompany Martin - Parker, Mastering Today's Software Database Management with Paradox 4.0. 2nd ed. 115p. (C). 1994. pap. text, teacher ed. 84.00 (*0-03-002903-1*) Dryden Pr.

Briggs, Carole S. Women in Space. LC 98-2916. (A&E Biographies Ser.). 128p. (J). (gr. 6-9). 1998. 23.93 (*0-8225-4937-9*, Lerner Publctns) Lerner Pub.

Briggs, Charles, ed. Disorderly Discourse: Narrative, Conflict & Inequality. (Oxford Studies in Anthropological Linguistics: No. 7). 256p. 1996. text 65.00 (*0-19-508776-3*) OUP.

— Disorderly Discourse No. 7: Narrative, Conflict & Inequality. (Oxford Studies in Anthropological Linguistics). 256p. 1996. pap. text 29.95 (*0-19-508777-1*) OUP.

Briggs, Charles & Briggs, Emile G. Psalms: Critical & Exegetical Commentary, Vol. 1. Driver, Samuel R. et al, eds. (International Critical Commentary Ser.). 532p. 1993. 39.95 (*0-567-05011-4*, Pub. by T & T Clark) Bks Intl VA.

— Psalms: Critical & Exegetical Commentary, Vol. 2. Driver, Samuel R. et al, eds. (International Critical Commentary Ser.). 580p. 1999. 39.95 (*0-567-05012-2*, Pub. by T & T Clark) Bks Intl VA.

Briggs, Charles, ed. see Driver, Samuel R.

Briggs, Charles A. Inaugural Address & Defense, Eighteen Ninety-One to Eighteen Ninety-Three. LC 70-38442. (Religion in America, Ser. 2). 336p. 1972. reprint ed. 24.95 (*0-405-04062-8*) Ayer.

Briggs, Charles A., ed. see Burton, Ernest De Witt.

Briggs, Charles A., ed. see Charles, R. H.

Briggs, Charles A., ed. see Frame, James E.

Briggs, Charles A., ed. see Plummer, Alfred.

Briggs, Charles A., ed. see Plummer, Alfred & Robertson, Archibald T.

Briggs, Charles A., ed. see Vincent, Marvin R.

Briggs, Charles F. The Adventures of Harry Franco: A Tale of the Great Panic. 1972. reprint ed. 29.50 (*0-8422-8010-3*) Irvington.

— The Adventures of Harry Franco: A Tale of the Great Panic. (C). 1986. reprint ed. pap. text 7.95 (*0-8290-1898-0*) Irvington.

— Giles of Rome's "De Regimine Principum" Reading & Writing Politics at Court & University, c. 1275-c. 1525. LC 97-47553. (Cambridge Studies in Palaeography & Codicology: No. 5). (Illus.). 222p. (C). 1999. text 69.95 (*0-521-57053-0*) Cambridge U Pr.

— Working a Passage: or Life on a Liner. 1972. reprint ed. lib. bdg. 28.00 (*0-8422-8009-X*) Irvington.

— Working a Passage: or Life on a Liner. 1986. reprint ed. pap. text 6.95 (*0-8290-1947-2*) Irvington.

Briggs, Charles L. Competence in Performance: The Creativity of Tradition in Mexicano Verbal Art. LC 88-14427. (University of Pennsylvania Press Conduct & Communication Ser.). 448p. 1988. pap. 138.90 (*0-608-04815-1*, 206547200004) Bks Demand.

— Competence in Performance: The Creativity of Tradition in Mexicano Verbal Art. LC 88-14427. (Conduct & Communication Ser.). (Illus.). 448p. (C). 1988. pap. text 23.95 (*0-8122-1260-6*) U of Pa Pr.

Briggs, Charles L. Learning How to Ask: A Sociolinguistic Appraisal of the Role of the Interview in Social Science Research. (Studies in the Social & Cultural Foundations of Language: No. 1). (Illus.). 175p. 1986. pap. text 17.95 (*0-521-31113-6*) Cambridge U Pr.

Briggs, Charles L. The Lost Gold Mine of Juan Mondragon: A Legend from New Mexico Performed by Melaquias Romero. Vigil, Julian J., ed. LC 89-32119. 270p. 1990. 49.95 (*0-8165-0977-8*) U of Ariz Pr.

Briggs, Charles L. & Van Ness, John R., eds. Land, Water, & Culture: New Perspectives on Hispanic Land Grants. LC 87-10957. (New Mexico Land Grant Ser.). (Illus.). 432p. reprint ed. pap. 134.00 (*0-7837-5860-X*, 204557900006) Bks Demand.

Briggs, Charlie, ed. see Munson, Will.

Briggs, Clyde. Nina's War. LC 95-76887. 224p. 1996. text 12.95 (*1-885487-13-4*) Brownell & Carroll.

Briggs Company, Ltd. Staff. Designs & Patterns for Embroiderers & Craftsmen: Five Hundred & Twelve Motifs from "Album of Transfer Patterns" Nichols, Marion, ed. LC 73-93081. (Illus.). 160p. 1974. reprint ed. pap. 8.95 (*0-486-23030-9*) Dover.

Briggs, Constance. Encyclopedia of Angels. 1999. text 22.95 (*0-525-94251-3*) Viking Penguin.

— The Encyclopedia of Angels: The A-to-Z Guide with Nearly 4000 Entries. LC 97-17193. 352p. 1997. pap. 14.95 (*0-452-27921-6*, Plume) Dutton Plume.

Briggs, D. Surface Analysis of Polymers by XPS & Static SIMS. LC 97-26059. (Solid State Science Ser.). (Illus.). 212p. (C). 1998. text 69.95 (*0-521-35222-3*) Cambridge U Pr.

Briggs, D., et al, eds. Linkage Methods for Environment & Health Analysis: General Guidelines. 136p. (Orig.). 1996. pap. text 16.20 (*0-614-17676-X*, 1930089) World Health.

Briggs, D. & Seah, M. P., eds. Practical Surface Analysis: Auger & X-Ray Photoelectron Spectroscopy, Vol. 1, Auger and X-ray Photoelectron Spectroscopy. 2nd ed. 674p. 1996. pap. 175.00 (*0-471-95340-7*) Wiley.

— Practical Surface Analysis, 2E, Vol. 2, Ion & Neutral Spectroscopy, Vol. 2, Ion and Neutral Spectroscopy. 2nd ed. LC 90-12172. 756p. 1992. 438.00 (*0-471-92082-7*) Wiley.

Briggs, D. & Walters, S. M. Plant Variation & Evolution. 3rd ed. LC 96-39293. (Illus.). 536p. (C). 1997. text 80.00 (*0-521-45295-3*); pap. text 37.95 (*0-521-45918-4*) Cambridge U Pr.

Briggs, D., et al. Hdbk Of Static Secondary Ion M. 164p. 1989. text 995.00 (*0-471-91627-7*) Wiley.

Briggs, D., jt. ed. see Brewis, D. M.

Briggs, D., ed. see European Conference on Applications of Surface & I.

Briggs, D. E. Barley. 1978. text 200.50 (*0-412-11870-X*, NO.6043) Chapman & Hall.

Briggs, D. E. & Young, Tom W. Malting & Brewing Science, Vol. 2. 536p. 1982. 135.00 (*0-8342-1684-1*) Aspen Pub.

Briggs, D. E., jt. auth. see Allison, P. A.

***Briggs, D. E. G. & Crowther, Peter R.** Palaeobiology II. LC 00-31211. 2001. write for info. (*0-632-05147-7*) Blackwell Sci.

Briggs, Daphne, tr. see Eluere, Christiane.

Briggs, David & Smithson, Peter. Fundamentals of Physical Geography. LC 93-8067. 1993. write for info. (*0-415-08394-X*) Routledge.

Briggs, David & Smithson, Peter, eds. Fundamentals of the Physical Environment. 2nd ed. (Illus.). 600p. (C). 1997. 110.00 (*0-415-10890-X*); pap. 34.99 (*0-415-10891-8*) Routledge.

Briggs, David, et al. Assessing Sexual Offenders. LC 98-129378. 172p. 1997. pap. 29.95 (*1-85302-435-X*, Pub. by Jessica Kingsley) Taylor & Francis.

Briggs, David J., et al, eds. Environmental Health for All: Risk Assessment & Risk Communication for National Environmental Health Action Plans - Proceedings. LC 98-40849. (NATO Science Ser.: Vol. 49). 278p. 1998. 129.00 (*0-7923-5452-4*, RA566) Kluwer Academic.

Briggs, David J., et al. Environmental Health for All: Risk Assessment & Risk Communication for National Environmental Health Action Plans. LC 98-40849. (NATO Science Ser.). 1998. write for info. (*0-7923-5453-2*) Kluwer Academic.

Briggs, Dennie. A Class of Their Own: When Children Teach Children. LC 97-41000. 144p. 1998. 49.95 (*0-89789-550-9*, Bergin & Garvey); pap. 16.95 (*0-89789-563-0*, Bergin & Garvey) Greenwood.

Briggs, Dennie, jt. ed. see Maher, John.

Briggs, Derek E. & Crowther, Peter R., eds. Palaeobiology: A Synthesis. (Illus.). 608p. 1992. pap. 85.00 (*0-632-03311-8*) Blackwell Sci.

Briggs, Derek E., et al. The Fossils of the Burgess Shale. LC 93-198. (Illus.). 272p. 1994. text 45.00 (*1-56098-364-7*) Smithsonian.

— The Fossils of the Burgess Shale. (Illus.). 272p. 1995. pap. text 24.95 (*1-56098-659-X*) Smithsonian.

Briggs, Diane. 52 Programs for Preschoolers: The Librarian's Year-Round Planner. LC 96-52415. 200p. 1997. 30.00 (*0-8389-0705-9*) ALA.

— Flannel Board Fun: A Collection of Stories, Songs & Poems. (Illus.). 153p. 1992. pap. 29.00 (*0-8108-2616-X*) Scarecrow.

***Briggs, Diane.** 101 Fingerplays, Stories & Songs to Use with Finger Puppets. LC 98-42136. 144p. 1999. 25.00 (*0-8389-0749-0*) ALA.

Briggs, Diane. Toddler Storytime Programs. (School Library Media Programs Ser.: No. 2). (Illus.). 198p. 1993. pap. 31.00 (*0-8108-2777-8*) Scarecrow.

Briggs, Donald C. & Alisky, Marvin. Historical Dictionary of Mexico. LC 80-27320. (Latin American Historical Dictionaries Ser.: No. 21). 275p. 1981. lib. bdg. 34.50 (*0-8108-1391-2*) Scarecrow.

***Briggs, Donald R.** Ground Lease Practice - 9/99 Update. LC 78-63464. 121p. 1999. ring bd. 40.00 (*0-7626-0357-7*, RE-30525) Cont Ed Bar-CA.

Briggs, Donald R. & Castro, Leonard E. Selecting & Forming Business Entities. LC 96-85264. (Calf. Business Start-Up Ser.). 498p. 1997. ring bd. 45.00 (*0-7626-0128-0*, BU-32571) Cont Ed Bar-CA.

Briggs, Donald R., ed. see Ankenmann, C. Gregg, et al.

Briggs, Donald R., ed. see Berk, Michael D. & Zipser, Dean J.

Briggs, Donald R., ed. see Bernhardt, Roger & Tour-Sarkissian, Christine.

Briggs, Donald R., ed. see Brockmeyer, Neal H. & Trussell, Elizabeth S.

Briggs, Donald R., ed. see Burchett, Marjorie F., et al.

Briggs, Donald R., ed. see Castro, Leonard E., et al.

Briggs, Donald R., ed. see Cohen, Hilary H. & Gummerman, Doug.

Briggs, Donald R., ed. see Edwards, Margaret H.

Briggs, Donald R., ed. see Enkelis, Richard L., et al.

Briggs, Donald R., ed. see Keligian, David L., et al.

Briggs, Donald R., ed. see Kostka, Stephen L. & Zischke, Michael H.

Briggs, Donald R., ed. see London, Michael E.

Briggs, Donald R., ed. see Martin, Neil B.

Briggs, Donald R., ed. see Matteoni, Norman E. & Veit, Henry.

Briggs, Donald R., ed. see McBride, Keith R.

Briggs, Donald R., ed. see McBride, Keith W.

Briggs, Donald R., ed. see Schug, Charles.

Briggs, Donald R., ed. see Sher, Malcolm & Minnard, Carla V.

Briggs, Donald R., ed. see Sproul, Curtis C. & Rosenberry, Katharine N.

Briggs, Donald R., ed. see Tufts, Robert R. & Foster, Twila L.

Briggs, Donald R., ed. see Wagner, Jeffrey G., et al.

Briggs, Donald R., ed. see Williams, Charles J.

Briggs, Dorothy C. Celebrate Yourself: Enhancing Your Own Self-Esteem. LC 85-29260. 240p. 1986. pap. 13.95 (*0-385-13105-4*) Doubleday.

— Your Child's Self-Esteem: The Key to His Life. LC 70-121948. 368p. 1988. pap. 12.95 (*0-385-04020-2*) Doubleday.

Briggs, Doug. I'm OK...Even If You're Not! The Personal Protection Handbook. (Illus.). 512p. 1995. 24.95 (*1-881287-09-2*) Beverly Bk.

— I'm OK...Even If You're Not! The Personal Protection Handbook. rev. ed. (Illus.). 384p. pap. 16.95 (*1-881287-10-6*) Beverly Bk.

— A Matter of Personal Protection: The Weapons & Self-Defense Laws of Texas. 3rd ed. (Illus.). 256p. 1994. pap. 12.95 (*1-881287-07-6*) Beverly Bk.

— Old Black. limited ed. LC 97-72767. (Illus.). 387p. 1997. 24.95 (*1-881287-12-2*) Beverly Bk.

— Personal Protection: The Weapons & Self-Defense Laws of the United States. LC 93-71047. (Illus.). 640p. (Orig.). 1993. 19.95 (*1-881287-02-5*) Beverly Bk.

— The Writer's Complete Guide to Firearms: Get Your Facts Straight on Revolvers & Pistols, Shotguns, Machine Guns, Rifles, Silencers, Ammunition... (Illus.). 224p. 1993. 14.95 (*1-881287-03-3*) Beverly Bk.

Briggs, Ellis. Proud Servant: The Memoirs of a Career Ambassador. LC 97-36506. (Illus.). 464p. 1998. 45.00 (*0-87338-588-8*) Kent St U Pr.

Briggs, Emile G., jt. auth. see Briggs, Charles.

Briggs, Erasmus. History of the Original Town of Concord, Being the Present Towns of Concord, Collons, North Collons, Sardinia, Erie County. 977p. 1996. reprint ed. lib. bdg. 95.00 (*0-8328-5078-0*) Higginson Bk Co.

Briggs-Erickson, Carol, jt. auth. see Murphy, Toni.

Briggs, Everett F. Across the Bridge Vol. 1: Selected Poems. (ENG & JPN., Illus.). 365p. (Orig.). 1996. 14.95 (*0-9615976-4-X*) E F Briggs.

— A Briggs Memorial. LC 97-226508. 506p. 1997. write for info. (*0-9654355-1-2*) Fmly History.

Briggs, Everett F., tr. see Noguchi, Kaku C.

Briggs, F., et al, eds. Warped Disks & Inclined Rings Around Galaxies. 309p. (C). 1991. text 74.95 (*0-521-40184-4*) Cambridge U Pr.

Briggs, Frank. Complete Modern Drum Set. 160p. 1994. pap. 23.95 incl. audio (*0-7866-1289-4*, 95366P); pap. 29.95 incl. audio compact disk (*0-7866-1288-6*, 95366CDP) Mel Bay.

— Drum Set Dailies/Rudimental Book. 32p. 2000. pap. 5.95 incl. audio compact disk (*0-7866-5248-9*, 98581BCD) Mel Bay.

— The Good Foot. 40p. 1999. 14.95 (*0-7866-3505-3*, 97216BCD) Mel Bay.

Briggs, Frank. Mel Bay's Complete Modern Drum Set. 158p. 1994. spiral bd. 17.95 (*0-7866-0259-7*) Mel Bay.

Briggs, Frank M., Sr. Glossary of Thoroughbred Racing. Roberts, Eddie, ed. (Illus.). 180p. 1987. pap. 9.95 (*0-937529-03-6*); text 14.95 (*0-937529-04-4*) Big Hse Pub.

Briggs, Freda. Developing Personal Safety Skills in Children with Disabilities. 200p. 1995. write for info. (*0-614-03434-5*, Pub. by Jessica Kingsley) P H Brookes.

— Developing Personal Safety Skills in Children with Disabilities. 350p. 1995. pap. 34.00 (*1-55766-184-7*, Pub. by Jessica Kingsley) P H Brookes.

— Developing Personal Safety Skills in Children with Disabilities. LC 93-40464. 1994. 24.95 (*1-85302-245-4*) Taylor & Francis.

— From Victim to Offender: How Child Abuse Victims Become Offenders. LC 95-147540. 192p. 1995. pap. 20.00 (*1-86373-759-6*, Pub. by Allen & Unwin Pty) IPG Chicago.

— Why My Child? Supporting the Families of Victims of Child Sexual Abuse. (Illus.). 233p. 1998. pap. text 15.00 (*0-7881-5543-1*) DIANE Pub.

Briggs, Freda, ed. Children & Families: Australian Perspectives. 224p. 1995. pap. 22.95 (*1-86373-626-3*, Pub. by Allen & Unwin Pty) Paul & Co Pubs.

Briggs, Freda & Hawkins, Russell. Child Protection: A Guide for Teachers & Child Care Professionals. 256p. 1997. pap. 29.95 (*1-86448-221-4*, Pub. by Allen & Unwin Pty) Paul & Co Pubs.

Briggs, G. A. Loudspeakers: The Why & How of Good Reproduction. LC 90-81199. (Illus.). 88p. 1990. pap. text 6.95 (*0-9624191-3-3*) Audio Amateur.

— Plume Rise. LC 77-603261. (AEC Critical Review Ser.). 81p. 1969. pap. 10.00 (*0-87079-304-7*, TID-25075); fiche 9.00 (*0-87079-305-5*, TID-25075) DOE.

Briggs, G. Andrew, ed. Advances in Acoustic Microscopy, Vol. 1. (Illus.). 382p. (C). 1995. text 89.50 (*0-306-44798-3*, Kluwer Plenum) Kluwer Academic.

Briggs, G. G., ed. Advances in the Chemistry of Insect Control III: Proceedings of the 3rd International Symposium, Cambridge, UK, 1993. 256p. 1994. 94.00 (*0-85186-992-0*, R6992) CRC Pr.

***Briggs, Geneva Clark.** Ambulatory Care Clinical Skills Program: Dyslipidemia Management Module. 250p. 2000. pap. text. write for info. (*1-58528-010-0*) Am Soc Hlth-Syst.

Briggs, George, jt. auth. see Byrd, Gary.

Briggs, George B. & Calvin, Clyde L. Indoor Plants. 99th ed. LC 86-4070. 528p. 1987. text 105.95 (*0-471-03298-0*) Wiley.

***Briggs, George W.** Gorakhnatha & the Kanphata Yogis. 1998. 19.50 (*81-208-0563-1*, Pub. by Motilal Bnarsidass); pap. 12.50 (*81-208-0564-X*, Pub. by Motilal Bnarsidass) S Asia.

Briggs, Gerald G. Drugs in Pregnancy & Lactation: A Guide to Fetal & Neonatal Risk. 4th ed. 1008p. 1994. 85.00 (*0-683-01060-3*) Lppncott W & W.

Briggs, Gerald G., et al. Drugs in Lactation. 2nd ed. LC 97-13538. 1997. write for info. (*0-683-30394-5*) Lppncott W & W.

Briggs, Gerald G., et al. Drugs in Pregnancy & Lactation: A Reference Guide to Fetal & Neonatal Risk. 5th ed. 1,200p. 149.00 (*0-683-30715-0*) Lppncott W & W.

***Briggs, Gerald G., et al.** Drugs in Pregnancy & Lactation: A Reference Guide to Fetal & Neonatal Risk. 5th ed. LC 97-42686. 1200p. 1998. 89.00 (*0-683-30262-0*) Lppncott W & W.

Briggs, H. M., intro. More Reflections of a Prairie Daughter. (Illus.). 200p. 1993. pap. 10.00 (*0-9623066-1-4*) Prairie Daughter.

Briggs, Henry. Arithmetica logarithmica. (GER.). 1997. reprint ed. write for info. (*3-487-06012-4*) G Olms Pubs.

Briggs, Homer, jt. auth. see Bass, James.

Briggs, I. Lesley. Poems, 1942-1992. LC 92-73124. 1994. 10.95 (*0-8158-0489-X*) Chris Mass.

Briggs, J., jt. auth. see Leigh, J.

Briggs, J. C. Biogeography & Plate Tectonics. (Developments in Palaeontology & Stratigraphy Ser.: Vol. 10). xii,204p. 1987. 150.00 (*0-444-42743-0*) Elsevier.

Briggs, J. Robert & Kosy, Eugene J. Electronic Calculators & Office Machines with Business Math Applications & Simulation. 4th ed. (C). 1983. text. write for info. (*0-538-13600-6*, M60) S-W Pub.

Briggs, J. Robert, et al. Electronic Calculators & Office Machines with Business Math Applications. 5th ed. 668p. (C). 1989. mass mkt. 27.75 (*0-538-13610-3*, M61) S-W Pub.

— Electronic Calculators with Business Math Applications. 5th ed. 474p. (C). 1989. mass mkt. 24.50 (*0-538-13700-2*, M70) S-W Pub.

Briggs, J. S., et al, eds. Fundamental Processes of Atomic Dynamics. LC 88-21804. (NATO ASI Series B, Physics: Vol. 181). (Illus.). 706p. 1988. 155.00 (*0-306-42988-8*, Plenum Trade) Perseus Pubng.

Briggs, Jack, tr. see Kamal, Mustapha.

Briggs, Jacqueline E. Strikes in Politicisation. LC 97-30131. 215p. 1997. text 68.95 (*1-85521-937-9*, Pub. by Ashgate Pub) Ashgate Pub Co.

Briggs, Jean L. Inuit Morality Play: The Emotional Education of a Three-Year-Old. LC 97-32605. (Illus.). xix, 275p. 1998. 35.00 (*0-300-07237-6*) Yale U Pr.

***Briggs, Jean L.** Inuit Morality Play: The Emotional Education of a Three-Year-Old. 304p. 1999. 17.00 (*0-300-08064-6*) Yale U Pr.

Briggs, Jean L. Never in Anger: Portrait of an Eskimo Family. LC 75-105368. (Illus.). 379p. 1971. pap. 18.95 (*0-674-60828-3*) HUP.

Briggs, Jeanine & Engel-Doyle, Beate T. Alles in Allem: An Intermediate German Course. LC 94-1529. (GER.). 288p. (C). 1994. pap. 40.63 (*0-07-007832-7*) McGraw.

— Alles in Allem: An Intermediate German Course (Grammar Manual) LC 94-4402. (ENG & GER.). 1994. pap. text 33.13 (*0-07-007837-8*) McGraw.

— Alles in Allem: Guide to Audio Cassette Program. LC 94-1529. (GER.). (C). 1994. pap., teacher ed. 29.38 (*0-07-007833-5*) McGraw.

Briggs, Jeanine, et al. Alles Gute! Basic German for Communication. 3rd ed. (GER.). (C). 1990. text, teacher ed. 81.56 (*0-07-909499-6*) McGraw.

— Alles Gute! Basic German for Communication. 3rd ed. (GER.). 1990. write for info. (*0-07-909500-3*) McGraw.

— Alles Gute! Basic German for Communication. 3rd ed. (GER.). (C). 1990. pap. text 35.50 (*0-07-540831-7*) McGraw.

— Alles Gute! Basic German for Communication. 4th ed. LC 93-36233. 448p. (C). 1994. 61.25 (*0-07-007864-5*) McGraw.

— Alles Gute: Basic German for Communication. 4th ed. (GER.). (C). 1994. pap., lab manual ed. 23.44 (*0-07-007867-X*) McGraw.

— Alles Gute: Basic German for Communication. 4th ed. (GER.). (C). 1994. pap., wbk. ed. 23.44 (*0-07-007866-1*) McGraw.

Briggs, Jeff & American Radio Relay League. Dxing on the Edge: The Thrill of 160 Meters. LC 98-195203. xi, 224 p. 1997. write for info. (*0-87259-635-4*) Am Radio.

Briggs, Jeff, jt. auth. see Healy, Tom.

Briggs, Jeffrey M. The Inventor's Sales Kit. (Illus.). 80p. 1999. pap. text 39.95 (*0-9670382-0-0*) N P R.

Briggs, Jennifer, compiled by. Strive to Excel: The Will & Wisdom of Vince Lombardi. LC 97-33623. 160p. 1997. 12.95 (*1-55853-550-0*) Rutledge Hill Pr.

Briggs, Jennifer, jt. auth. see Pingel, D. Kent.

Briggs, Joe B. Iron Joe Bob. LC 92-30426. 259p. 1993. pap. 12.00 (*0-87113-553-1*, Atlntc Mnthly) Grove-Atltic.

Briggs, John. Crime & Punishment in England, 1100-1990: An Introductory History. LC 96-20019. 288p. 1996. pap. 21.95 (*0-312-16331-2*); text 59.95 (*0-312-16330-4*) St Martin.

***Briggs, John.** Fire in the Crucible: Understanding the Process of Creative Genius. (Illus.). 382p. 2000. pap. 17.95 (*1-890482-77-3*); pap. 35.00 (*1-890482-78-1*) Phanes Pr.

Briggs, John. Fractals: The Patterns of Chaos. LC 92-16886. 128p. 1992. pap. 20.00 (*0-671-74217-5*, Touchstone) S&S Trade Pap.

Briggs, John & Monaco, Richard. Metaphor: The Logic of Poetry. rev. ed. (Illus.). 304p. (C). 1990. lib. bdg. 46.50 (*0-944473-03-2*) Pace Univ Pr.

Briggs, John & Peat, David. Turbulent Mirror: An Illustrated Guide to Chaos Theory & the Science of Wholeness. LC 88-45567. (Illus.). 224p. 1990. reprint ed. pap. 15.00 (*0-06-091696-6*, Perennial) HarperTrade.

Briggs, John & Peat, F. David. Seven Life Lessons of Chaos: Spiritual Wisdom from the Science of Change. LC 97-52983. (Illus.). 224p. 1999. 25.00 (*0-06-018246-6*) HarpC.

— Seven Life Lessons of Chaos: Spiritual Wisdom from the Science of Change. 224p. 2000. pap. 13.00 (*0-06-093073-X*, Perennial) HarperTrade.

Briggs, John C. Francis Bacon & the Rhetoric of Nature. LC 89-31279. (Thomas J. Wilson Prize Ser.). 336p. 1989. 49.95 (*0-674-31743-2*) HUP.

— Global Biogeography. LC 95-30597. 472p. 1995. 210.00 (*0-444-88297-9*) Elsevier.

— Global Biogeography. 472p. 1996. pap. 92.00 (*0-444-82560-6*) Elsevier.

Briggs, John W. An Italian Passage: Immigrants to Three American Cities, 1890-1930. LC 77-22006. (Illus.). 348p. 1978. 50.00 (*0-300-02095-3*) Yale U Pr.

***Briggs, Jonathan.** S-4: Roswell Was Only the Beginning! 577p. 1999. pap. 11.95 (*0-9700544-0-8*) Port Town Pubng.

Briggs, Julia. This Stage-Play World: Texts & Contexts, 1580-1625. 2nd ed. LC 97-5258. 372p. 1997. pap. 14.95 (*0-19-289286-X*) OUP.

— A Woman of Passion: The Life of E. Nesbit, 1858-1928. LC 87-11215. (Illus.). 473p. (C). 1987. 27.95 (*0-941533-03-4*, NAB) I R Dee.

Briggs, Julia, ed. & intro. see Woolf, Virginia.

Briggs, Julie. Telephone Triage Protocols for Nurses. LC 96-39097. 416p. 1997. spiral bd. 38.95 (*0-397-55410-9*, Lippnctt) Lppncott W & W.

Briggs, K. Holy Siege. pap. 14.00 (*0-685-68964-6*, Perennial) HarperTrade.

Briggs, Karen. Understanding Equine Nutrition: Your Guide to Horse Health Care & Management. (Horse Health Care Library). (Illus.). 108p. 1998. pap. 14.95 (*0-939049-97-X*) Blood-Horse.

***Briggs, Karen.** Understanding the Pony: Your Guide to Horse Health Care & Management. 120p. 2000. 34.95 (*1-58150-055-6*, Pub. by Blood-Horse) IPG Chicago.

Briggs, Katherine M. The Anatomy of Puck: An Examination of Fairy Beliefs among Shakespeare's Contemporaries & Successors. Dorson, Richard M., ed. LC 77-70581. (International Folklore Ser.). 1977. reprint ed. lib. bdg. 24.95 (*0-405-10082-5*) Ayer.

— An Encyclopedia of Fairies: Hobgoblins, Brownies, Bogies, & Other Supernatural Creatures. LC 76-12939. (Illus.). (J). (gr. 4 up). 1978. 12.95 (*0-394-40918-3*) Pantheon.

— Pale Hecates Team: Examination of the Beliefs on Witchcraft & Magic Among Shakespeare's Contemporaries & His Immediate Succesors. Dorson, Richard M., ed. LC 77-70582. (International Folklore Ser.). (Illus.). 1977. lib. bdg. 26.95 (*0-405-10083-3*) Ayer.

Briggs, Katherine M. & Tongue, Ruth L., eds. Folktales of England. LC 65-18341. (Folktales of the World Ser.). 208p. (C). 1968. pap. text 15.95 (*0-226-07494-3*, FW3) U Ch Pr.

Briggs, Kelly P. Island Alphabet: An ABC of Maine Islands. LC 95-36512. (Illus.). 32p. (J). (gr. 2 up). 1995. 15.95 (*0-89272-369-6*) Down East.

Briggs, Kenneth. Ziggurat: How Ur Gave Birth. LC 97-94731. 332p. 1998. 23.50 (*0-9661945-0-0*, Z-01) Chora Hse.

Briggs, L. V. Genealogy of the Different Families Bearing the Name of Kent in the United States, Their Possible English Ancestry, 1295-1898. (Illus.). 346p. reprint ed. pap. 52.00 (*0-8328-0726-5*); reprint ed. lib. bdg. 60.00 (*0-8328-0725-7*) Higginson Bk Co.

Briggs, L. Vernon. Cabot: History & Genealogy of the Cabot Family, 1475-1927. (Illus.). 885p. 1992. reprint ed. pap. 135.00 (*0-8328-2278-7*); reprint ed. lib. bdg. 145.00 (*0-8328-2277-9*) Higginson Bk Co.

— The Manner of Man That Kills. (Historical Foundations of Forensic Psychiatry & Psychology Ser.). (Illus.). 444p. 1983. reprint ed. lib. bdg. 45.00 (*0-306-76182-3*) Da Capo.

— Occupation As a Substitute for Restraint in the Treatment of the Mentally Ill: A History of the Passage of Two Bills Through the Massachusetts Legislature. LC 72-2387. (Mental Illness & Social Policy; the American Experience Ser.). 1973. reprint ed. 21.95 (*0-405-05195-6*) Ayer.

Briggs, L. Vernon, et al. History of the Psychopathic Hospital, Boston, Massachusetts. LC 73-2386. (Mental Illness & Social Policy; the American Experience Ser.). 1973. reprint ed. 23.95 (*0-405-05194-8*) Ayer.

Briggs, Larry. The Comprehensive Encyclopedia of United States Seated Liberty Quarters. Smith, Harry, ed. (Illus.). 264p. (Orig.). (C). 1992. pap. 39.95 (*0-9631667-0-0*); text 49.95 (*0-9631667-1-9*) L Briggs Rare Coins.

Briggs, Larry J. Songs. 1998. pap. write for info. (*1-57553-924-1*) Watermrk Pr.

Briggs, Le Baron R. College Life: Essays Reprinted from "School, College, & Character," & "Routine & Ideals" (Select Bibliographies Reprint Ser.). 1977. 19.95 (*0-8369-5039-9*) Ayer.

Briggs, Leslie J., et al, eds. Instructional Design: Principles & Applications. 2nd rev. ed. LC 90-23255. (Illus.). 512p. 1991. 49.95 (*0-87778-230-X*) Educ Tech Pubns.

Briggs, Leslie J. & Wager, Walter W. Handbook of Procedures for the Design of Instruction. 2nd ed. LC 80-20920. 272p. 1981. pap. 39.95 (*0-87778-177-X*) Educ Tech Pubns.

Briggs, Leslie J., jt. auth. see Martin, Barbara L.

Briggs, Lloyd C. Tribes of the Sahara. LC 60-7988. 328p. reprint ed. pap. 101.70 (*0-608-11569-X*, 200600900054) Bks Demand.

Briggs, Lloyd V. Two Years' Service on the Reorganized State Board of Insanity in Massachusetts, August, 1914 to August, 1916. Grob, Gerald N., ed. LC 78-22551. (Historical Issues in Mental Health Ser.). (Illus.). 1980. reprint ed. lib. bdg. 50.95 (*0-405-11905-4*) Ayer.

— A Victory for Progress in Mental Medicine. Grob, Gerald N., ed. LC 78-22552. (Historical Issues in Mental Health Ser.). 1980. reprint ed. lib. bdg. 25.95 (*0-405-11906-2*) Ayer.

***Briggs, Lynn Craigue & Woolbright, May, eds.** Stories from the Center. LC 99-52503. 144p. 2000. 25.95 (*0-8141-4746-1*) NCTE.

Briggs, M. H. Vitamins in Human Biology & Medicine. 272p. 1981. 152.00 (*0-8493-5673-3*, QP771, CRC Reprint) Franklin.

Briggs, M. H., ed. Recent Vitamin Research. 224p. 1984. 130.00 (*0-8493-5618-0*, QP771, CRC Reprint) Franklin.

Briggs, Margaret H. Building Early Intervention Teams: Working Together for Children & Families. LC 96-30178. 250p. 1996. 48.00 (*0-8342-0638-2*); write for info. (*0-8342-0639-0*) Aspen Pub.

***Briggs, Margaret Luellen.** Romantic Days & Nights in Houston: Romantic Diversions in & Around the City. (Romantic Days & Nights Ser.). (Illus.). 256p. 2000. pap. 15.95 (*0-7627-0710-0*) Globe Pequot.

Briggs, Marie. Cocos Island Venture. 1950. 4.95 (*0-87505-120-0*) Borden.

Briggs, Mark, ed. see Gant, Charles.

Briggs, Mark K. Riparian Ecosystem Recovery in Arid Lands: Strategies & References. LC 96-9957. (Illus.). 159p. 1996. 46.00 (*0-8165-1642-1*) U of Ariz Pr.

Briggs, Martha W. The Compass Windows of Old Blandford Church: A Tribute in Tiffany Glass. 16p. 1992. 9.95 (*0-9633240-0-4*) Dory Pr.

— The Little Ferry's Christmas. LC 97-68566. (Illus.). (Orig.). (J). 1997. pap. 6.50 (*0-9633240-3-9*, LFC-97) Dory Pr.

— Travels with Virginia, the Little Ferry Bk. 2: The Little Ferry Goes to the Paper Mill. LC 98-93235. (Illus.). 18p. (J). (gr. 3-7). 1998. pap. 6.50 (*0-9633240-4-7*, LFPM-98) Dory Pr.

Briggs, Martha W. & Pittman, April C. Circle & Square Tracts of the Nottoway Indians. LC 95-92575. (Illus.). 13p. (Orig.). 1996. pap. 5.25 (*0-9633240-1-2*) Dory Pr.

***Briggs, Martha Wren.** Travels wih Virginia, the Little Ferry Bk. 3: The Little Ferry, a Ham Sandwich & a Virginia Tradition. large type ed. LC 99-94742. (Illus.). 18p. (J). (gr. 3-7). 1999. pap. 6.95 (*0-9633240-5-5*, LFH) Dory Pr.

— Travels with Virginia, the Little Ferry Vol. 4: The Little Ferry Meets the Colonial Ships. LC 99-94743. (Illus.). 18p. (J). (gr. 3-8). 1999. pap. 6.95 (*0-9633240-6-3*) Dory Pr.

Briggs, Martin S. Muhammadan Architecture in Egypt & Palestine. LC 74-1280. (Architecture & Decorative Art Ser.). (Illus.). 255p. 1974. reprint ed. lib. bdg. 39.50 (*0-306-70590-7*) Da Capo.

***Briggs, Matt.** The Remains of River Names. 1999. 22.95 (*0-930773-56-X*, Pub. by Black Heron Pr) Midpt Trade.

Briggs, Matt, jt. auth. see Blench, Roger.

Briggs, Mike, et al, eds. Decommissioning, Mothballing, & Revamping. 1997. text 60.00 (*0-85295-325-9*, 53259, Pub. by IChemE) Gulf Pub.

Briggs Morrow, Barbara. Sisters: Words from the Heart. LC 97-176760. (Illus.). 71p. 1997. write for info. (*0-7853-2287-6*) Pubns Intl Ltd.

Briggs, Nancy E., jt. auth. see Galdikas, Birute M.

Briggs, Noreen V. Bugaboo Words. (Illus.). 160p. (J). (gr. 3 up). 1989. 26.95 (*0-937857-13-0*, 1570) Speech Bin.

Briggs, Noreen V., ed. Finishing Touches. 80p. 1992. student ed. 16.95 (*0-937857-31-9*, 1598) Speech Bin.

Briggs Nursery, Inc. Staff & Henny, Thomas, Nursery Staff. Color Portraits of Outstanding Plants. 1986. ring bd. 15.00 (*0-910013-01-2*) Offshoot Pub.

Briggs, Patricia. Giant Book of the Horse. 1999. 29.99 (*0-7858-1049-8*) Bk Sales Inc.

— Steal the Dragon. 288p. (Orig.). 1995. mass mkt. 4.99 (*0-441-00273-0*) Ace Bks.

— When Demons Walk. 1998. mass mkt. 5.99 (*0-441-00534-9*) Ace Bks.

Briggs, Patrick. Physics Lab Manual. 114p. (C). 1997. lab manual ed. 20.00 (*1-886855-79-X*) Tavenner Pub.

Briggs, Peter D. Principles of International Trade & Payments. Brooke, Michael Z., ed. LC 94-15853. (Principles of Export Guidebooks Ser.). 256p. (C). 1994. pap. text 43.95 (*0-631-19163-1*) Blackwell Pubs.

Briggs, Philip. East & Southern Africa: The Backpacker's Manual. LC 98-10100. (Illus.). 514p. 1998. pap. 21.95 (*1-898323-60-7*, Pub. by Bradt Pubns) Globe Pequot.

— Guide to Ethiopia. 2nd ed. LC 98-5273. (Bradt Guides Ser.). (Illus.). 354p. 1998. pap. 18.95 (*1-898323-56-6*, Pub. by Bradt Pubns) Globe Pequot.

— Guide to Mozambique. 2nd ed. LC 96-15660. (Illus.). 240p. 1997. pap. text 27.50 (*1-898323-45-3*, Pub. by Bradt Pubns) Globe Pequot.

— Guide to South Africa. 3rd rev. ed. LC 97-15899. (Bradt Guides Ser.). (Illus.). 310p. 1998. pap. 17.95 (*1-898323-52-6*, Pub. by Bradt Pubns) Globe Pequot.

— Malawi: The Bradt Travel Guide. 2nd ed. LC 99-13956. (Illus.). 272p. 1999. pap. 17.95 (*1-898323-84-4*, Pub. by Bradt Pubns) Globe Pequot.

— Tanzania: The Bradt Travel Guide. LC 99-24571. (Illus.). 336p. 1999. pap. text 17.95 (*1-898323-86-0*, Pub by Bradt Pubns) Globe Pequot.

— Uganda: The Bradt Travel Guide. 3rd ed. LC 98-35318. 1998. pap. text 17.95 (*1-898323-79-8*, Pub. by Bradt Pubns) Globe Pequot.

— Visitors' Guide to Kenya & East Africa. LC 95-16145. 236p. 1995. pap. 17.95 (*1-86812-533-5*) Menasha Ridge.

Briggs, Philip J. Making American Foreign Policy: President - Congress Relations from the Second World War to the Post-Cold War Era. 2nd ed. LC 94-16780. 251p. 1994. reprint ed. pap. 24.95 (*0-8476-7946-2*); reprint ed. lib. bdg. 62.50 (*0-8476-7945-4*) Rowman.

— Making American Foreign Policy: President - Congress Relations from the Second World War to Vietnam. 292p. (Orig.). (C). 1991. pap. text 28.00 (*0-8191-8113-7*); lib. bdg. 48.00 (*0-8191-8112-9*) U Pr of Amer.

Briggs, Phillip. Guide to Ghana. LC 98-27865. (Illus.). 262p. 1998. pap. 18.95 (*1-898323-69-0*, Pub. by Bradt Pubns) Globe Pequot.

Briggs, R., ed. Instrumentation, Control & Automation of Water & Wastewater Treatment & Transport Systems, 1997: Selected Proceedings of the 7th International Workshop on Instrumentation, Control & Automation of Water & Wastewater Treatment & Transport Systems, held at Brighton, U. K., 6-9 July 1997. 404p. 1998. pap. 159.00 (*0-08-043388-X*, Pergamon Pr) Elsevier.

Briggs, R. H. Credit Insurance. (C). 1988. 400.00 (*0-7855-4188-8*, Pub. by Witherby & Co) St Mut.

Briggs, Raymond. The Bear. (Illus.). 40p. (J). (gr. k-3). 1998. pap. 7.99 (*0-679-89465-9*) Random.

— The Bear. LC 94-8734. (Illus.). 48p. (J). (ps up). 1994. lib. bdg. 20.99 (*0-679-96944-6*, Pub. by Random Bks Yng Read) Random.

— Ethel & Ernest: A True Story. LC 99-33343. (Illus.). 103p. (YA). 1999. 21.00 (*0-375-40758-8*) Knopf.

— Father Christmas. LC 97-5667. (J). 1997. 18.99 (*0-679-88776-8*, Pub. by Random Bks Yng Read) Random.

— Father Christmas. 32p. (J). text 4.95 (*0-241-02260-6*, H Hamilton) Viking Penguin.

Briggs, Raymond. Father Christmas It's a Bloomin' It's a Bloomin' pap. 5.95 (*0-14-037354-3*, Pub. by Pnguin Bks Ltd) Trafalgar.

Briggs, Raymond. Jim & the Beanstalk. LC 99-158170. (Illus.). 40p. (J). (ps-3). 1997. pap. 5.99 (*0-698-11577-5*, PapStar) Peng Put Young Read.

— The Snowman. LC 94-69689. (Illus.). 22p. (J). 1995. 3.99 (*0-679-87273-6*) Random.

— The Snowman. LC 97-76063. (Nifty Lift-And-Look Bks.). (Illus.). 10p. (J). (ps). 1998. bds. 5.99 (*0-679-88896-9*) Random.

— The Snowman. LC 78-55904. (Illus.). 32p. (J). (ps-3). 1978. 17.00 (*0-394-83973-0*, Pub. by Random Bks Yng Read) Random.

— The Snowman. LC 78-55904. (Illus.). 32p. (J). (ps-2). 1986. pap. 7.99 (*0-394-88466-3*, Pub. by Random Bks Yng Read) Random.

***Briggs, Raymond.** Snowman. (Bright & Early Bks.). (Illus.). 24p. (J). (ps-k). 2000. 4.99 (*0-375-81067-6*, Pub. by Random Bks Yng Read) Random.

Briggs, Raymond. Snowman. (J). 1978. 11.15 (*0-606-03472-2*, Pub. by Turtleback) Demco.

— Snowman: Songbook. (J). 1987. pap. 7.95 (*0-7935-1831-8*, 50489170) H Leonard.

— The Snowman Cuddle Cloth Book. (Cuddle Cloth Bks.). (Illus.). 12p. (J). (ps). 1993. 4.99 (*0-679-82696-3*, Pub. by Random Bks Yng Read) Random.

— Snowman Shaped Board Book. (J). 1999. 4.99 (*0-375-80085-9*, Pub. by Random Bks Yng Read) Random.

— Snowman Storybook. LC 96-16076. (Picturebacks Ser.). 24p. (J). (ps-3). 1997. pap. 3.25 (*0-679-88343-6*) Random.

— Snowman Storybook. (Pictureback Ser.). (J). 1997. lib. bdg. 8.99 (*0-679-98343-0*, Pub. by Random Bks Yng Read) Random.

Briggs, Raymond. Snowman Storybook. (Random House Pictureback Ser.). (J). 1997. 8.45 (*0-606-12815-8*, Pub. by Turtleback) Demco.

Briggs, Raymond & Knudsen, Michelle. Raymond Briggs' The Snowman. 1 vol. LC 99-19328. (Early Step into Reading Ser.). (J). (ps-k). 1999. pap. 3.99 (*0-679-89443-8*) Random.

— Raymond Briggs' The Snowman. LC 99-19328. (Early Step into Reading Ser.). (Illus.). 32p. (J). (ps-3). 1999. lib. bdg. 11.99 (*0-679-99443-2*) Random.

Briggs, Raymond P., jt. auth. see Freed, Donald.

***Briggs, Rex.** Transforming Anxiety, Transcending Shame. LC 99-41648. 280p. 1999. pap. 11.95 (*1-55874-722-2*) Health Comm.

***Briggs, Richard.** It's Been a Quiet Week in the Global Village. 1999. pap. 9.95 (*0-281-05196-8*) Society Prom Christ Know.

Briggs, Richard, ed. see OM Staff.

Briggs, Rick. Caregiving Daughters: Accepting the Role of Caregiver for Elderly Parents. rev. ed. LC 97-35312. (Studies on the Elderly in America). (Illus.). 192p. 1998. text 48.00 (*0-8153-3027-8*) Garland.

Briggs, Robert. The American Emergency. LC 88-38176. 1989. pap. 8.95 (*0-89087-546-4*) Celestial Arts.

***Briggs, Robert A.** Jewish Temple Imagery in the Book of Revelation. LC 97-50625. (Studies in Biblical Literature: Vol. 10). xvi, 275p. (C). 1999. text 52.95 (*0-8204-3999-1*) P Lang Pubng.

Briggs, Robert E. Principles of the New Covenant: A Study Contrasting the Old & New Covenants. (Illus.). 58p. (Orig.). 1997. pap. 4.59 (*0-9657749-5-3*) Eagles Nst Pubns.

Briggs, Robert L., jt. auth. see Hayes, Jonathan.

Briggs, Robin. Communities of Belief: Cultural & Social Tension in Early Modern France. (Illus.). 432p. 1995. pap. text 29.95 (*0-19-820603-8*) OUP.

— Communities of Belief: Cultural & Social Tensions in Early Modern France. (Illus.). 440p. 1989. text 95.00 (*0-19-821981-4*) OUP.

***Briggs, Robin.** Early Modern France 1560-1715. 2nd ed. (Illus.). 256p. 1998. pap. 13.95 (*0-19-289284-3*) OUP.

Briggs, Robin. Witches & Neighbors: The Social & Cultural Context of European Witchcraft. 480p. 1998. pap. 15.95 (*0-14-014438-2*, Penguin Bks) Viking Penguin.

Briggs, Rod. Working on Contract Worldwide: How to Triple Your Earnings by Working As an Independent Contractor Anywhere in the World. (Living & Working Abroad Ser.). 160p. 1996. pap. 19.95 (*1-85703-429-5*, Pub. by How To Bks) Trans-Atl Phila.

Briggs, Roger C., ed. see Champion, Joe E.

Briggs, Roger C., ed. see Champion, Joe E. & Thompson, Michael R.

Briggs, Rose T. Plymouth Rock: History & Significance. 1968. 5.95 (*0-940628-03-1*) Pilgrim Soc.

Briggs, Russell. Men, Women & Colleges. LC 73-167313. (Essay Index Reprint Ser.). 1977. reprint ed. 19.95 (*0-8369-2308-1*) Ayer.

Briggs, S., jt. auth. see Freedland, R. A.

Briggs, Sandra J. Grammar: Strategies & Practice. 208p. 1997. pap. text, teacher ed. 11.83 (*0-673-19599-6*) Addison-Wesley.

Briggs, Sarah. The University of Michigan Examination for the Certificate of Proficiency in English: Official Papers: Student's Book (without Answers) 104p. 1997. pap. text 15.95 (*0-19-453362-X*) OUP.

— The University of Michigan Examination for the Certificate of Proficiency in English: Official Past Papers: Answer Book (with Teaching Notes) 40p. 1997. pap. text 9.95 (*0-19-453361-1*) OUP.

***Briggs, Sarah, et al, eds.** The International Teaching Assistant: An Annotated Critical Bibliography. 2nd ed. (Illus.). 198p. (C). 1998. pap. text 20.00 (*0-472-59008-1*) U of Mich Pr.

Briggs, Sarah & Brennan, Moya. How to Apply to American Colleges & Universities. (Illus.). 194p. 1994. pap. 12.95 (*0-8442-0747-0*, VGM Career) NTC Contemp Pub Co.

Briggs, Sarah, jt. auth. see Brennan, Moya.

Briggs, Sharon L. & Sorrell, Ginny O. How to Rescue At-Risk Students. 2nd rev. ed. LC 90-91906. (J). (gr. 4-12). 1991. 20.00 incl. audio (*0-9627409-2-6*) Sound Reading.

Briggs, Shirley. Basic Guide to Pesticides: Their Characteristics & Hazards. 320p. 1992. 52.95 (*1-56032-253-5*) Taylor & Francis.

Briggs, Shirley A., ed. see Barnes, Irston R. & Gude, Gilbert.

Briggs, Stephanie B., jt. auth. see Bunchman, Janis.

Briggs, Stephen. Growth & Risk in Infancy. LC 97-140715. 280p. 1996. pap. 24.95 (*1-85302-398-1*, Pub. by Jessica Kingsley) Taylor & Francis.

Briggs, Stephen, jt. auth. see Pratchett, Terry.

Briggs, Steven. The Municipal Grievance Process. (Monograph & Research Ser.: No. 36). 185p. 1984. 9.00 (*0-89215-118-8*) U Cal LA Indus Rel.

Briggs, Steven M. Who's Where in the John Rigg Family. (Illus.). 276p. 1997. write for info. (*1-57579-095-5*) Pine Hill Pr.

Briggs, Susan. Successful Tourism Marketing. (Marketing & Sales Ser.). 1997. pap. 24.95 (*0-7494-2123-1*) Kogan Page Ltd.

Briggs, T. Biochemistry. 2nd ed. Chandler, A. M., ed. (Oklahoma Notes Ser.). (Illus.). 224p. 1992. 16.95 (*0-387-97781-3*) Spr-Verlag.

Briggs, T. & Chandler, A. M., eds. Biochemistry. (Oklahoma Notes Ser.). 250p. (C). 1991. pap. 15.95 (*0-387-96341-3*) Spr-Verlag.

Briggs, Tami, et al. Do's & Taboos Around the World for Women in Business. Axtell, Roger E., ed. LC 96-35911. 252p. 1997. pap. 17.95 (*0-471-14364-2*) Wiley.

Briggs, Thomas. A Funny Thing Happened at the Doctor's Office. Adams, Milton, ed. (Illus.). 80p. 1998. pap. 6.95 (*1-890676-07-1*) Beavers Pond.

Briggs, Thomas & Chandler, Albert M. Biochemistry. 3rd ed. LC 95-14197. (Oklahoma Notes Ser.). (Illus.). 287p. 1995. 17.95 (*0-387-94398-6*) Spr-Verlag.

B

Briggs, Thomas F. Briggs' Banjo Instructor of 1855. LC 92-61249. (Illus.). 54p. (Orig.). 1992. pap. 16.00 (*0-9633593-0-4*) Tuckahoe Music.

Briggs, Tom, jt. auth. see Weidlich, Joseph.

Briggs, Toni A. I'm a Lucky Person Just to Be Here on Earth: A Collection of Inspirational Poems. 48p. pap. 5.95 (*0-9637029-0-4*) Cactus Rose.

Briggs, Tony, ed. Alexander Pushkin. (Everyman's Poetry Ser.). 1997. 3.50 (*0-460-87862-X*, Everyman's Classic Lib) Tuttle Pubng.

Briggs, Vernon, Jr. Mass Immigration & the National Interest. LC 92-16927. (Labor & Human Resources Ser.). 287p. (gr. 13). 1992. pap. text 34.95 (*1-56324-171-4*) M E Sharpe.

Briggs, Vernon M., Jr. Immigration Policy & the American Labor Force. LC 84-7850. 312p. (C). 1985. text 49.95 (*0-8018-3168-7*) Johns Hopkins.

— Mass Immigration & the National Interest. LC 92-16927. (Labor & Human Resources). 287p. (C). (gr. 13). 1992. text 74.95 (*1-56324-170-6*) M E Sharpe.

— Mass Immigration & the National Interest. 2nd ed. LC 96-2929. (Labor & Human Resources Ser.). 296p. (gr. 13). 1996. pap. text 36.95 (*1-56324-830-1*) M E Sharpe.

— Mass Immigration & the National Interest. 2nd ed. LC 96-2929. (Labor & Human Resources Ser.). 296p. (YA). (gr. 13). 1996. text 77.95 (*1-56324-829-8*) M E Sharpe.

Briggs, Vernon M., Jr. & Moore, Stephen. Still an Open Door? U. S. Immigration Policy & the American Economy. LC 94-19180. 175p. (Orig.). 1994. pap. text 18.00 (*1-879383-32-2*); lib. bdg. 55.00 (*1-879383-31-4*) Am Univ Pr.

Briggs, Vernon M., Jr., et al. The Chicano Worker. LC 76-28237. 145p. 1977. pap. text 5.95 (*0-292-71055-0*) U of Tex Pr.

Briggs, Vernon M., et al. Chicano Worker. LC 76-28237. 143p. reprint ed. pap. 44.40 (*0-8357-7729-4*, 203608600002) Bks Demand.

Briggs, Vernon M., jt. auth. see Marshall.

Briggs, Vernon M., Jr., jt. auth. see Marshall, F. Ray.

Briggs, Virginia L., jt. auth. see Kushner, Michael G.

Briggs, W. R., ed. Annual Review of Plant Physiology, Vol. 38. LC 51-1660. (Illus.). 1987. text 40.00 (*0-8243-0638-4*) Annual Reviews.

Briggs, W. R., et al, eds. Annual Review of Plant Physiology, Vol. 26. LC 51-1660. (Illus.). 1975. text 40.00 (*0-8243-0626-0*) Annual Reviews.

— Annual Review of Plant Physiology, Vol. 27. LC 51-1660. (Illus.). 1976. text 40.00 (*0-8243-0627-9*) Annual Reviews.

— Annual Review of Plant Physiology, Vol. 28. LC 51-1660. (Illus.). 1977. text 40.00 (*0-8243-0628-7*) Annual Reviews.

— Annual Review of Plant Physiology, Vol. 29. LC 51-1660. (Illus.). 1978. text 40.00 (*0-8243-0629-5*) Annual Reviews.

— Annual Review of Plant Physiology, Vol. 31. LC 51-1660. (Illus.). 1980. text 40.00 (*0-8243-0631-7*) Annual Reviews.

— Annual Review of Plant Physiology, Vol. 32. LC 51-1660. (Illus.). 1981. text 40.00 (*0-8243-0632-5*) Annual Reviews.

— Annual Review of Plant Physiology, Vol. 33. LC 51-1660. (Illus.). 1982. text 40.00 (*0-8243-0633-3*) Annual Reviews.

— Annual Review of Plant Physiology, Vol. 34. LC 51-1660. (Illus.). 1983. text 40.00 (*0-8243-0634-1*) Annual Reviews.

— Annual Review of Plant Physiology, Vol. 35. (Illus.). 1984. text 40.00 (*0-8243-0635-X*) Annual Reviews.

— Annual Review of Plant Physiology, Vol. 36. LC 51-1660. (Illus.). 1985. text 40.00 (*0-8243-0636-8*) Annual Reviews.

— Annual Review of Plant Physiology, Vol. 37. LC 51-1660. (Illus.). 1986. text 40.00 (*0-8243-0637-6*) Annual Reviews.

— Annual Review of Plant Physiology & Plant Molecular Biology, Vol. 39. LC 51-1660. (Illus.). 1988. text 40.00 (*0-8243-0639-2*) Annual Reviews.

— Annual Review of Plant Physiology & Plant Molecular Biology, Vol. 40. (Illus.). 1989. text 40.00 (*0-8243-0640-6*) Annual Reviews.

— Annual Review of Plant Physiology & Plant Molecular Biology, Vol. 41. 1990. text 40.00 (*0-8243-0641-4*) Annual Reviews.

Briggs, Wallace N. Riverside Remembered. LC 92-16397. (Illus.). 248p. (C). 1992. 21.00 (*0-8131-1807-7*) U Pr of Ky.

Briggs, Ward, ed. see Dawe, Roger D.

Briggs, Ward W. Biographical Dictionary of North American Classicists. LC 94-4785. 880p. 1994. lib. bdg. 145.00 (*0-313-24560-6*, Greenwood Pr) Greenwood.

***Briggs, Ward W.** Pre 19th Century British Bibliographers. LC 99-33325. (Dictionary of Literary Biography Ser.). 400p. 1999. text 155.00 (*0-7876-3105-1*) Gale.

Briggs, Ward W., ed. Cato - Concordantia in Catonis Librum de Agri Cultura. (Alpha-Omega, Reihe A Ser.: Bd. LXX). (GER.). viii, 166p. 1983. 70.00 incl. 3.5 hd (*3-487-06696-3*) G Olms Pubs.

Briggs, Ward W., Jr., ed. The Selected Classical Papers of Basil Lanneau Gildersleeve. LC 92-35986. (American Philological Association, American Classical Studies: No. 30). 355p. 1992. pap. 39.95 (*1-55540-807-9*, 400430) OUP.

Briggs, Ward W. & Benario, Herbert W., eds. Basil Lanneau Gildersleeve. LC 85-25619. (American Journal of Philology Monographs: No. 1). 128p. 1986. text 29.95 (*0-8018-3117-2*) Johns Hopkins.

Briggs, Ward W. & Kopff, E. Christian, eds. The Roosevelt Lectures of Paul Shorey, 1913-14. Reinke, Edgar C., tr. from GER. & anno. by. LC 96-185000. xxxii, 416p. 1995. write for info. (*3-487-09982-9*) G Olms Pubs.

Briggs, Ward W., Jr., ed. see Gildersleeve, Basil L.

Briggs, Ward W., ed. see Varro.

Briggs, Warren. Brass Facts. 192p. 1999. pap. 11.95 (*1-56315-148-0*) SterlingHse.

Briggs, William. Law of International Copyright with Special Sections on the Colonies & the United States of America. xx, 850p. 1986. reprint ed. 85.00 (*0-8377-1941-0*, Rothman) W S Hein.

Briggs, William L. A Multigrid Tutorial. LC 87-62333. (Miscellaneous Bks.: No. 17). (Illus.). ix, 90p. (C). 1987. pap. text 21.50 (*0-89871-221-1*) Soc Indus-Appl Math.

Briggs, William L. & Henson, Van E. The DFT: An Owner's Manual for the Discrete Fourier Transform. LC 95-3232. (Miscellaneous Bks.: No. 45). xv, 434p. 1995. pap. 40.50 (*0-89871-342-0*) Soc Indus-Appl Math.

***Briggs, William L., et al.** A Multigrid Tutorial. 2nd ed. (Miscellaneous Bks.: Vol. 72). 2000. pap. 39.00 (*0-89871-462-1*) Soc Indus-Appl Math.

Briggs, William L., jt. auth. see Bennett, Jeffrey O.

Briggs, Winslow R., et al, eds. Annual Review of Plant Physiology & Plant Molecular Biology, Vol. 42. 1991. text 40.00 (*0-8243-0642-2*) Annual Reviews.

— Annual Review of Plant Physiology & Plant Molecular Biology, Vol. 43. 1992. text 44.00 (*0-8243-0643-0*) Annual Reviews.

— Annual Review of Plant Physiology & Plant Molecular Biology, Vol. 44. (Illus.). 1993. text 44.00 (*0-8243-0644-9*) Annual Reviews.

Brigham. Comprehensive Lecture Notes - Fund Finance. 7th ed. (C). 1994. teacher ed. 33.75 incl. 3.5 hd (*0-03-000599-X*) Harcourt Coll Pubs.

— The Constitution. (C). 2000. pap. text 42.50 (*0-15-501295-9*); pap. text 42.50 (*0-15-501296-7*) Harcourt.

— The Constitution: Law, Politics. (C). 1999. pap. text 61.50 (*0-15-501294-0*, Pub. by Harcourt Coll Pubs) Harcourt.

Brigham. The Constitution of Interests. pap. text 20.00 (*0-8147-1286-X*) NYU Pr.

Brigham. Contemporary Issues in Social Psychology. 2nd ed. (Psychology Ser.). 1973. pap. 8.00 (*0-8185-0071-9*) Brooks-Cole.

— Contemporary Issues in Social Psychology. 3rd ed. (Psychology Ser.). 1977. mass mkt. 14.75 (*0-8185-0210-X*) Brooks-Cole.

— Encyclopedia of Mormonism, Vol. 1. 1992. 90.00 (*0-02-879600-4*) Macmillan.

— Encyclopedia of Mormonism, Vol. 2. 1992. 90.00 (*0-02-879601-2*) Macmillan.

— Encyclopedia of Mormonism, Vol. 3. 1992. 90.00 (*0-02-879602-0*) Macmillan.

— Encyclopedia of Mormonism, Vol. 4. 1992. 90.00 (*0-02-879603-9*) Macmillan.

— Encyclopedia of Mormonism, Vol. 5. 1992. 90.00 (*0-02-879604-7*) Macmillan.

— Financial. 8th ed. (C). 1996. pap. text, teacher ed. 28.00 (*0-03-018697-8*) Harcourt Coll Pubs.

— Financial Management. 8th ed. (C). 1996. pap. text, student ed. 26.50 (*0-03-018689-7*) Harcourt Coll Pubs.

— Financial Management. 9th ed. (C). 1998. pap. text 106.00 (*0-03-024399-8*, Pub. by Harcourt Coll Pubs) Harcourt.

— Financial Management: Theory & Practice. 8th ed. (C). 1996. text 5.75 (*0-03-020928-5*); pap. text 7.55 (*0-03-021143-3*) Harcourt Coll Pubs.

— Financial Management: Theory & Practice. 9th ed. (C). 1998. pap. text, student ed. 34.00 (*0-03-023367-4*) Harcourt.

— Financial Management Technical. 8th ed. (C). 1997. pap. text, suppl. ed. 15.50 (*0-03-018687-0*) Harcourt Coll Pubs.

— Fundamentals of Financial Management. (C). 1995. pap. text, teacher ed., suppl. ed. 43.50 (*0-03-015963-6*, Pub. by Harcourt Coll Pubs) Harcourt.

Brigham. Fundamentals of Financial Management. (C). 1995. pap. text, student ed. 24.50 (*0-03-015962-8*) Harcourt Coll Pubs.

Brigham. Fundamentals of Financial Management. 2nd ed. (C). 1998. pap. text, student ed. 33.00 (*0-03-022322-9*) Harcourt.

— Fundamentals of Financial Management. 2nd ed. (C). 1998. text 58.50 (*0-03-022319-9*, Pub. by Harcourt Coll Pubs) Harcourt.

— Fundamentals of Financial Management. 5th ed. (C). 1995. pap. text, teacher ed. 36.75 (*0-03-015959-8*) Harcourt Coll Pubs.

— Fundamentals of Financial Management. 7th ed. (C). 1994. pap. text, teacher ed. 36.75 (*0-03-094871-1*) Harcourt Coll Pubs.

— Fundamentals of Financial Management. 8th ed. 1997. student ed. 125.50 (*0-03-024231-2*, Pub. by Harcourt Coll Pubs) Harcourt.

— Fundamentals of Financial Management. 8th ed. 1997. 82.00 (*0-03-024437-4*) Harcourt Coll Pubs.

— Intermediate Financial Management. (C). 1995. text 44.95 (*0-03-015958-X*) Harcourt Coll Pubs.

— Intermediate Financial Management. 6th ed. (C). 1999. pap. text, student ed. 33.50 (*0-03-023461-1*) Harcourt.

— Intermediate Financial Management. 6th ed. (C). 1998. pap. text 40.50 (*0-03-023479-4*, Pub. by Harcourt Coll Pubs) Harcourt.

— Intermediate Financial Management. 6th ed. LC 98-73893. (C). 1999. text 97.00 (*0-03-023451-4*, Pub. by Harcourt Coll Pubs) Harcourt.

— Intermediate Financial Management: Test Bank. 5th ed. (C). 1995. pap. text, suppl. ed. 43.50 (*0-03-015942-3*, Pub. by Harcourt Coll Pubs) Harcourt.

— Intermediate Financial Manual. 5th ed. (C). 1995. pap. text, student ed. 28.50 (*0-03-015939-3*) Harcourt Coll Pubs.

— Kit Fundamental Financial Management, 8th ed. 8th ed. 1997. 137.50 (*0-03-024187-1*) H Holt & Co.

Brigham, A. P. Glacial Geology & Geographic Conditions of the Lower Mohawk Valley. 133p. 1993. reprint ed. lib. bdg. 69.00 (*0-7812-5139-7*) Rprt Serv.

Brigham, Amariah. An Inquiry Concerning the Diseases & Functions of the Brain, the Spinal Cord the Nerves. LC 73-2388. (Mental Illness & Social Policy; the American Experience Ser.). 1973. reprint ed. 25.95 (*0-405-05196-4*) Ayer.

— Observations on the Influence of Religion upon the Health & Physical Welfare of Mankind. LC 73-2389. (Mental Illness & Social Policy; the American Experience Ser.). 1973. reprint ed. 23.95 (*0-405-05197-2*) Ayer.

— Observations on the Influence of Religion upon the Health & Physical Welfare of Mankind, 1835: Remarks on the Influence of Mental Cultivation & Mental Excitement Upon Health, 2 vols. in 1. LC 73-17271. (History of Psychology Ser.). 478p. 1973. 75.00 (*0-8201-1125-2*) Schol Facsimiles.

Brigham, Amariah, et al. The Beginnings of Mental Hygiene in America: Three Selected Essays, 1833-1850. (Mental Illness & Social Policy; the American Experience Ser.). 1973. 35.95 (*0-405-05193-X*) Ayer.

Brigham, Arthur J., jt. auth. see Little, J. Wesley.

Brigham, Besmilr. Agony Dance: Death of the Dancing Dolls. 30p. (Orig.). 1969. pap. 15.00 (*0-932264-11-5*) Trask Hse Bks.

Brigham, Beth. Incredible Kids' Edibles. LC 98-93795. (Illus.). 128p. 1999. pap. write for info. (*0-9667135-0-8*) ABCD Pr.

Brigham, Carl. Two Studies in Mental Tests. (Psychology Monographs General & Applied: Vol. 24). 1974. reprint ed. pap. 55.00 (*0-8115-1423-4*) Periodicals Srv.

Brigham, Christopher, et al. The Independent Medical Evaluation Report Vol. 1: A Step-by-Step Guide with Models. (Illus.). x, 200p. (Orig.). 1996. pap. 99.00 (*0-9652197-0-4*) SEAK.

Brigham, Clarence S. Bibliography of American Editions of Robinson Crusoe to 1830. 1958. pap. 3.00 (*0-912296-21-6*) Am Antiquarian.

— History & Bibliography of American Newspapers, 1690-1820, 2 vols., Set. LC 75-40215. 1976. reprint ed. lib. bdg. 165.00 (*0-8371-8677-3*, BRAN) Greenwood.

— History & Bibliography of American Newspapers, 1690-1820, 2 vols., Vol. 1. LC 75-40215. 1976. reprint ed. lib. bdg. 85.00 (*0-8371-8681-1*, BRANA) Greenwood.

— History & Bibliography of American Newspapers, 1690-1820, 2 vols., Vol. 2. LC 75-40215. 1976. reprint ed. lib. bdg. 85.00 (*0-8371-8682-X*, BRANB) Greenwood.

Brigham, David E. How to Study Independently: A Study Guide for Adult College Students. 2nd rev. ed. 44p. (Orig.). 1996. pap. text 9.95 (*1-889403-00-8*) Regnts College.

— Statistics. (Illus.). 68p. (Orig.). (YA). 1996. pap. text, student ed. 12.95 (*1-889403-01-6*) Regnts College.

Brigham, David R. Public Culture in the Early Republic: Peale's Museum & Its Audience. LC 94-7705. (Illus.). 240p. 1995. text 45.00 (*1-56098-416-3*) Smithsonian.

Brigham, David R. & Worcester Art Museum Staff. American Impressionism: Paintings of Promise. LC 97-14725. (Illus.). 88p. (Orig.). 1997. pap. 25.00 (*0-7649-0359-4*, A900) Pomegranate Calif.

Brigham, Deidre. Imagery for Getting Well. 464p. 1996. pap. 20.00 (*0-393-70225-1*) Norton.

Brigham, Don L. Focus on Fine Arts: Visual Arts. 80p. 1989. 9.00 (*0-8106-0304-7*) Natl Art Ed.

Brigham, E. Oran. Fast Fourier Transform & Applications. LC 88-1029. (C). 1988. text 67.00 (*0-13-307505-2*) P-H.

***Brigham, Emma E.** Neal Family. fac. ed. 378p. 1999. reprint ed. 67.00 (*0-8328-9913-5*); reprint ed. pap. 57.00 (*0-8328-9914-3*) Higginson Bk Co.

Brigham, Eugene F. Financial Management: Theory & Practice. 8th ed. 1997. 99.00 (*0-03-024053-0*) Dryden Pr.

— Financial Management: Theory & Practice. 9th ed. (C). 1998. pap. text 35.00 (*0-03-023373-9*) Harcourt Coll Pubs.

— Financial Management: Theory & Practice. 9th ed. 1998. 106.00 (*0-03-021029-1*, Pub. by Harcourt Coll Pubs) Harcourt.

— Fundamentals of Financial Management. 2nd ed. (C). 1998. pap. text 51.50 (*0-03-022327-X*) Harcourt Coll Pubs.

— Fundamentals of Financial Management. 7th ed. 168p. (C). 1995. pap. text, suppl. ed. write for info. (*0-614-18304-9*) Harcourt Coll Pubs.

— Intermediate Financial Management. 6th ed. 1999. 106.00 (*0-03-021028-3*, Pub. by Harcourt Coll Pubs) Harcourt.

Brigham, Eugene F. & Gapenski, Louis C. Cases in Financial Management: Directed Versions. LC 93-70608. 357p. (C). 1993. pap. text 32.00 (*0-03-055024-6*) Dryden Pr.

— Cases in Financial Management: Non-Directed Versions. LC 93-71260. 139p. (C). 1993. pap. text 21.75 (*0-03-098329-0*) Dryden Pr.

— Financial Management: Theory & Practice. 8th ed. (Blueprints: A Problem Notebook Ser.). 526p. (C). 1996. pap. text 10.50 (*0-03-018708-7*) Dryden Pr.

— Financial Management - Theory & Practice: Blueprints, a Problem Notebook. 272p. (C). 1993. student ed. 10.00 (*0-03-098771-7*) Dryden Pr.

— Intermediate Financial Management. 4th ed. LC 92-20738. 1122p. (C). 1993. disk 59.75 (*0-03-075482-8*) Dryden Pr.

Brigham, Eugene F. & Houston, Joel F. Fundamentals of Financial Management. 2nd ed. LC 98-71883. 672p. (C). 1998. text 95.50 (*0-03-021337-1*) Harcourt Coll Pubs.

— Fundamentals of Financial Management. 8th ed. LC 96-80089. 928p. (C). 1997. text 104.50 (*0-03-024418-8*) Dryden Pr.

— Fundamentals of Financial Management: Blueprints: A Problem Notebook. 8th ed. 424p. (C). 1997. pap. text 14.00 (*0-03-024433-1*) Dryden Pr.

Brigham, Eugene F. & Pappas, James L. Liberalized Depreciation & the Cost of Capital. LC 77-631430. (MSU Public Utilities Studies: Vol. 1970). (Illus.). 136p. reprint ed. pap. 42.20 (*0-608-20491-9*, 207174300002) Bks Demand.

Brigham, Eugene F., et al. Fundamentals of Financial Management. 8th ed. 424p. (C). 1997. pap. text, student ed. 35.00 (*0-03-024434-X*) Dryden Pr.

Brigham, Frederick H. U. S. Catholic Elementary & Secondary Schools, 1989-1990: Annual Statistical Report on Schools, Enrollment & Staffing. (Illus.). 1990. pap. 8.00 (*1-55833-050-X*) Natl Cath Educ.

Brigham, Frederick H., Jr. United States Catholic & Secondary Schools Finance, 1994. (Illus.). 35p. (Orig.). 1995. pap. 13.30 (*1-55833-159-X*) Natl Cath Educ.

— United States Catholic Elementary & Secondary Schools, 1990-91: Annual Statistical Report on Schools, Enrollment & Staffing. 1991. 9.00 (*1-55833-100-X*) Natl Cath Educ.

— United States Catholic Elementary & Secondary Schools, 1992-1993. 62p. (Orig.). 1993. pap. text 10.00 (*1-55833-098-4*) Natl Cath Educ.

— United States Catholic Elementary & Secondary Schools, 1993-1994. (Illus.). 32p. (Orig.). 1994. pap. 12.00 (*1-55833-134-4*) Natl Cath Educ.

Brigham, James A., jt. auth. see Thomas, Alan G.

Brigham, Janet. Dying to Quit: Why We Smoke & How We Stop. LC 98-17906. 308p. Date not set. 29.95 (*0-309-06409-0*) Natl Acad Pr.

Brigham, Jay L. Empowering the West: Electrical Politics Before FDR. LC 98-19379. (Development of Western Resources Ser.). xi, 211 p. 1998. 35.00 (*0-7006-0920-2*) U Pr of KS.

Brigham, John. The Constitution of Interests: Beyond the Politics of Rights. 336p. (C). 1996. text 40.00 (*0-8147-1285-1*) NYU Pr.

— Constitutional Language: An Interpretation of Judicial Decision, 17. LC 78-4020. (Contributions in Political Science Ser.: No. 17). 182p. 1978. 49.95 (*0-313-20420-9*, BCO/, Greenwood Pr) Greenwood.

— The Cult of the Court. 248p. 1991. pap. 22.95 (*0-87722-828-0*) Temple U Pr.

Brigham, John & Brown, Don W., eds. Policy Implementation: Penalties or Incentives? LC 80-16765. (Sage Focus Editions Ser.: Vol. 25). 271p. 1980. reprint ed. pap. 84.10 (*0-608-03378-2*, 205964200008) Bks Demand.

Brigham, John & Kevelson, Roberta, eds. States, Citizens, & Questions of Significance: 10th Round Table on Law & Semiotics. LC 97-3291. (Semiotics & the Human Sciences Ser.: Vol. 11). 263p. (C). 1997. text 48.95 (*0-8204-3020-X*) P Lang Pubng.

Brigham, Johnson. History of Des Moines & Polk County, Iowa, Vol. 1. (Illus.). 746p. 1994. reprint ed. lib. bdg. 75.00 (*0-8328-3823-3*) Higginson Bk Co.

— History of Des Moines & Polk County, Iowa, Vol. 2. (Illus.). 1448p. 1994. reprint ed. lib. bdg. 145.00 (*0-8328-3822-5*) Higginson Bk Co.

Brigham, Judith. A Historical Study of the Educational Agencies of the Southern Baptist Convention, 1845-1945. LC 77-177047. (Columbia University. Teachers College. Contributions to Education Ser.: No. 974). reprint ed. 37.50 (*0-404-55974-3*) AMS Pr.

Brigham, Karen. Money Without Madness: Organize Your Budget & Stop Money Stress on Any Income. LC 98-33531. 288p. 1998. pap. text 9.95 (*1-58062-050-7*) Adams Media.

Brigham, Kenneth L. Endotoxin & the Lungs. (Lung Biology in Health & Disease Ser.: Vol. 77). (Illus.). 575p. 1994. text 210.00 (*0-8247-9222-X*) Dekker.

— Gene Therapy for Diseases of the Lung. LC 97-7151. (Lung Biology in Health & Disease Ser.: Vol. 104). (Illus.). 416p. 1997. text 180.00 (*0-8247-0060-0*) Dekker.

Brigham, Mary F., jt. auth. see Fredericks, Anthony D.

Brigham, Nancy, et al. How to Do Leaflets, Newsletters & Newspapers. 2nd ed. LC 91-90152. (Illus.). 176p. (Orig.). 1991. pap. 14.95 (*0-9629067-6-X*, 10258, Pub. by PEP Pubs) F & W Pubns Inc.

Brigham, R. Mark, jt. auth. see Nagorsen, David W.

Brigham, Richard. Snowy Owls & Battered Bulbuls. (Illus.). 128p. 1996. 29.95 (*1-873580-27-4*, Pub. by Whittet Bks) Diamond Farm Bk.

— Snowy Owls & Battered Bulbuls. large type ed. (Isis Large Print Ser.). 1997. 25.95 (*0-7531-5040-9*) T T Beeler.

Brigham, Robert K. Guerrilla Diplomacy: The NLF's Foreign Relations & the Vietnam War. LC 98-29109. (Illus.). 224p. 1999. 33.50 (*0-8014-3317-7*) Cornell U Pr.

Brigham, Steven & DeMarche, Deborah, eds. Roadmap to Resources: Sources & Tools for CQI Implementation. 130p. 1996. pap. 20.00 (*1-56377-037-7*, CQ9601) Am Assn Higher Ed.

Brigham, Thomas A. Managing Everyday Problems. LC 88-19031. (Treatment Manuals for Practitioners Ser.). 172p. 1988. pap. text 18.95 (*0-89862-508-4*) Guilford Pubns.

— Self-Management for Adolescents: A Skills Training Program. LC 88-19031. (Treatment Manuals for Practitioners Ser.). 161p. 1988. pap. text 27.95 (*0-89862-202-6*) Guilford Pubns.

B

An Asterisk (*) at the beginning of an entry indicates that the title is appearing for the first time.

Brigham, W. I. The History of the Brigham Family, 1603-1653. (Illus.). 636p. 1988. reprint ed. pap. 95.00 (*0-8328-0321-9*); reprint ed. lib. bdg. 103.00 (*0-8328-0320-0*) Higginson Bk Co.

— Tyler Genealogy: The Descendants of Job Tyler of Andover, Massachusetts, 1619-1700, 2 vols. in 1. 891p. 1989. reprint ed. pap. 153.50 (*0-8328-1191-2*); reprint ed. lib. bdg. 161.50 (*0-8328-1190-4*) Higginson Bk Co.

Brigham, W. Parks. Senseless Misconceptions. 228p. 1997. mass mkt. 14.95 (*0-9664962-0-5*) W Parks Brig.

Brigham, William. Compact with the Charter & Laws of the Colony of New Plymouth. Helmholz, R. H. & Bernard, Reams, eds. LC 86-62939. (Historical Writings in Law & Jurisprudence Ser.: No. 7). ix, 357p. 1986. reprint ed. lib. bdg. 45.00 (*0-89941-522-9*, 304580) W S Hein.

Brigham, William T. Guatemala: The Land of the Quetzal. LC 65-14894. (Latin American Gateway Ser.). 528p. reprint ed. pap. 163.70 (*0-7837-5015-3*, 204468200004) Bks Demand.

Brigham, William T., tr. see Remy, M. Jules.

Brigham Young University College of Humanities Staff, jt. auth. see Bradford, Miles Gerald.

Brigham Young University, Provo, Utah, Law Library. Legal Research Manual for Law Students, 1988. 1988. pap. write for info. (*0-318-63119-9*, BYU Law) Brigham.

Brigham Young University Staff. Religion C234: LDS Marriage & Family Relations. LC 99-180382. 358p. (C). 1998. student ed., per. 15.95 (*0-7872-2738-2*, 41273801) Kendall-Hunt.

Brighman, Frederick H., Jr., et al. Catholic School & Society. (National Congress Catholic Schools for the 21st Century Ser.). 61p. 1991. pap. 2.00 (*1-55833-068-2*) Natl Cath Educ.

Brighouse. Making Schools Effective. (C). Date not set. write for info. (*0-415-10587-0*); pap. text. write for info. (*0-415-10588-9*) Routledge.

— Managing the Curriculum. 1989. pap. text. write for info. (*0-582-05309-9*, Pub. by Addison-Wesley) Longman.

***Brighouse, David.** The Financial Services Environment: An Advanced Guide to Regulation & Legislation. 80p. 1999. pap. 80.00 (*0-85297-514-7*, Pub. by Chartered Bank) St Mut.

— Introduction to the Financial Services Environment. 188p. 1999. pap. 80.00 (*0-85297-520-1*, Pub. by Chartered Bank) St Mut.

***Brighouse, Harry.** School Choice & Social Justice. LC 99-53195. 232p. 2000. 29.95 (*0-19-829586-3*) OUP.

Brighouse, Tim & Woods, David. How to Improve Your School. LC 98-34525. viii, 176p. 1999. pap. 17.99 (*0-415-19444-X*) Routledge.

Bright. Edificando un Hogar en un Mundo Desintegrado - Building a Home in a Pull-Apart World. write for info. (*0-7899-0181-1*) Editorial Unilit.

— Ha Hecho Usted el Maravilloso Descubrimiento de la Vida Llena del Espiritu?Tr. of Have You Made the Wonderful Discovery of the Spirit-Filled Life?. (SPA.). 16p. 1996. 6.99 (*0-7899-0249-4*, 492323) Editorial Unilit.

— Manual Del Maestro - A Handbook for Christian Maturity. (Diez Grados Basicos - Ten Basic Steps Ser.). (SPA.). teacher ed. write for info. (*1-56063-470-7*) Editorial Unilit.

— Una Vida Sin Igual.Tr. of Life Without Equal. (SPA.). 129p. 1995. write for info. (*0-614-27155-X*) Editorial Unilit.

Bright, et al. Calculator Quest: Exploring Number Concepts. 96p. 1994. pap. 19.95 (*0-939765-64-0*, G164) Janson Pubns.

Bright, jt. auth. see Carlson.

Bright, Allan H. New Lights on Piers Plowman. 1984. reprint ed. 19.00 (*0-403-01320-8*) Scholarly.

Bright, Arthur A., Jr. The Electric-Lamp Industry: Technological Change & Economic Development from 1800 to 1947. LC 72-5037. (Technology & Society Ser.). 554p. 1979. reprint ed. 45.95 (*0-405-04690-1*) Ayer.

Bright, B. La Aventura Cristiana. (Diez Grados Basicos - Ten Basic Steps Ser.: No. 1).Tr. of Christian Adventure. (SPA.). 1995. 3.99 (*1-56063-650-5*, 492308) Editorial Unilit.

— Como Caminar en el Espiritu Santo. (Serie Conceptos Transferibles (Transferable Concepts) Ser.).Tr. of How You Can Walk in the Spirit. (SPA.). 43p. 1995. 1.99 (*1-56063-858-3*, 492334) Editorial Unilit.

— Como Puede Ayudar a Cumplir la Gran Comision. (Serie Conceptos Transferibles (Transferable Concepts) Ser.).Tr. of How You Can Fulfill Great Commission. (SPA.). 43p. 1995. 1.99 (*1-56063-863-X*, 492339) Editorial Unilit.

— Como Puede Estar Seguro de Conocer a Dios. (Serie Conceptos Transferibles (Transferable Concepts) Ser.).Tr. of How You Can Be Sure You Are a Christian. (SPA.). 47p. 1995. 1.99 (*1-56063-856-7*, 492332) Editorial Unilit.

— Como Puede Experimentar Amor y Perdon de Dios. (Serie Conceptos Transferibles (Transferable Concepts) Ser.).Tr. of How You Can Experience God's Love & Forgiveness. (SPA.). 45p. 1995. 1.99 (*1-56063-855-9*, 492331) Editorial Unilit.

— Como Puede Ser Lleno del Espiritu Santo. (Serie Conceptos Transferibles (Transferable Concepts) Ser.).Tr. of How You Can Be Filled with the Holy Spirit. (SPA.). 43p. 1995. 1.99 (*1-56063-857-5*, 492333) Editorial Unilit.

— Como Puede Usted Amar por Fe. (Serie Conceptos Transferibles (Transferable Concepts) Ser.).Tr. of How You Can Love by Faith. (SPA.). 41p. 1995. 1.99 (*1-56063-859-1*, 492335) Editorial Unilit.

— Como Puede Usted Dirigir a Otros a Cristo. (Serie Conceptos Transferibles (Transferable Concepts) Ser.).Tr. of How You Introduce Others to Christ. (SPA.). 43p. 1995. 1.99 (*1-56063-861-3*, 492337) Editorial Unilit.

— Como Puede Usted Experimentar la Aventura de Dar. (Serie Conceptos Transferibles (Transferable Concepts) Ser.).Tr. of How You Can Experience the Adventure of Giving. (SPA.). 65p. 1995. 1.99 (*1-56063-864-8*, 492340) Editorial Unilit.

— Como Puede Usted Orar con Confianza. (Serie Conceptos Transferibles (Transferable Concepts) Ser.).Tr. of How You Can Pray with Confidence. (SPA.). 45p. 1995. 1.99 (*1-56063-860-5*, 492336) Editorial Unilit.

— Como Puede Usted Ser un Testigo Fructifero. (Serie Conceptos Transferibles (Transferable Concepts) Ser.).Tr. of How You Can Be a Fruitful Witness. (SPA.). 41p. 1995. 1.99 (*1-56063-862-1*, 492338) Editorial Unilit.

— El Cristiano y el Espiritu Santo. (Diez Grados Basicos - Ten Basic Steps Ser.: No. 3).Tr. of Christian & the Holy Spirit. (SPA.). 1995. 3.99 (*1-56063-652-1*, 492310) Editorial Unilit.

— El Cristiano y la Biblia. (Diez Grados Basicos - Ten Basic Steps Ser.: No. 5).Tr. of Christian & the Bible. (SPA.). 1995. 3.99 (*1-56063-654-8*, 492312) Editorial Unilit.

— El Cristiano y la Evangelizacion. (Diez Grados Basicos - Ten Basic Steps Ser.: No. 7).Tr. of Christian & Witnessing. (SPA.). 1995. 3.99 (*1-56063-656-4*, 492314) Editorial Unilit.

— El Cristiano y la Mayordomia. (Diez Grados Basicos - Ten Basic Steps Ser.: No. 8).Tr. of Christian & Giving. (SPA.). 1995. 3.99 (*1-56063-657-2*, 492315) Editorial Unilit.

— El Cristiano y la Obediencia. (Diez Grados Basicos - Ten Basic Steps Ser.: No. 6).Tr. of Christian & the Obedience. (SPA.). 3.99 (*1-56063-655-6*, 492313) Editorial Unilit.

— El Cristiano y la Oracion. (Dies Grados Basicos - Ten Basic Steps Ser.: No. 4).Tr. of Christian & Prayer. (SPA.). 3.99 (*1-56063-653-X*, 492311) Editorial Unilit.

— El Cristiano y la Vida Abundante. (Diez Grados Basicos - Ten Basic Steps Ser.: No. 2).Tr. of Christian & the Abundant Life. (SPA.). 3.99 (*1-56063-651-3*, 492309) Editorial Unilit.

— Explorando el Antiguo Testamento. (Diez Grados Basicos - Ten Basic Steps Ser.: No. 9).Tr. of Exploring the Old Testament. (SPA.). 3.99 (*1-56063-658-0*, 492316) Editorial Unilit.

— Explorando el Nuevo Testamento. (Diez Grados Basicos - Ten Basic Steps Ser.: No. 10).Tr. of Exploring the New Testament. (SPA.). 3.99 (*1-56063-659-9*, 492317) Editorial Unilit.

— How Fufill Great Commiss. 1991. pap. text 1.99 (*0-8407-4539-7*) New Life Pubns.

— How to Be Filled with the Holy Spirit. 1991. pap. text 1.99 (*0-8407-4537-0*) NewLife Pubns.

— How to Experience Giving. 1991. pap. text 1.99 (*0-8407-4536-2*) NewLife Pubns.

— How to Experience God's Love. 1991. pap. text 1.99 (*0-8407-4538-9*) NewLife Pubns.

— How to Introduce Others to Christ. 1991. pap. text 1.99 (*0-8407-4541-9*) NewLife Pubns.

— How to Pray with Confidence. 1991. pap. text 1.99 (*0-8407-4535-4*) New Life Pubns.

— How Walk in the Spirit. 1991. pap. write for info. (*0-8407-4533-8*) New Life Pubns.

— Mojor Leccion de Mi Vida.Tr. of Greatest Lesson I Have Learned. (SPA.). 128p. 1994. pap. 7.99 (*0-8297-1847-8*) Vida Pubs.

— 7 Pasos Basicos para Ayunar y Orar con Exito.Tr. of 7 Basic Steps to Successful Fasting & Prayer. (SPA.). 24p. 1995. 1.99 (*0-7899-0190-0*, 492319) Editorial Unilit.

— La Singularidad de Jesus: Introduccion. (Diez Grados Basicos - Ten Basic Steps Ser.).Tr. of Uniqueness of Jesus: Introduction. (SPA.). 1995. 3.99 (*1-56063-472-3*, 492307) Editorial Unilit.

— Testificando Sin Temor.Tr. of Witnessing Without Fear. (SPA.). 100. pap. 8.99 (*1-56063-920-2*, 492326) Editorial Unilit.

Bright, B. Una Vida Sin Igual.Tr. of Life Without Equal. (SPA.). 3.99 (*1-56063-545-2*, 498586) Editorial Unilit.

Bright, Barry, ed. Theory & Practice in Adult Education: The Epistemological Debate. 288p. 1989. 49.95 (*0-415-02446-3*, A3534); pap. 18.50 (*0-415-03909-6*, A3538) Routledge.

Bright, Beatrice. Shades of the Battlefield. limited ed. LC 96-92083. (Illus.). 64p. (Orig.). 1996. 11.00 (*1-888578-00-9*) R E F Typesetting Pub.

Bright, Betty. Completing the Circle: Artists' Books on the Environment. (Illus.). 35p. 1992. pap. 7.00 (*1-879832-01-1*) MN Ctr Book Arts.

Bright, Betty, et al. Incoming Tide: Works by Clare Chanler Forster. (Illus.). 36p. 1998. pap. 10.00 (*1-879832-16-X*) MN Ctr Book Arts.

Bright, Betty T., contrib. by. A Kelmscott Centennial - William Morris & His Heirs: Leonard Baskin, Claire Van Vliet & Victor Hammer. 1991. 11.00 (*1-879832-00-3*) MN Ctr Book Arts.

Bright, Bill. El Abivamiento Que Viene.Tr. of Coming Revival. (SPA.). pap. 8.99 (*0-7899-0180-3*, 497286) Editorial Unilit.

— Beginning Your Journey of Joy. 1997. pap. 5.99 (*1-56399-093-8*) New Life Pubns.

***Bright, Bill.** Building a Home in a Pull-Apart World. (Illus.). 2000. pap. 5.99 (*5-550-03073-X*) Nairi.

Bright, Bill. The Christian Adventure, Step 1: Beginning the Exciting Journey of Faith. rev. ed. Tanner, Don et al, eds. (Ten Basic Steps Toward Christian Maturity Ser.). (Illus.). 80p. (Orig.). 1994. pap. 4.99 (*1-56399-030-X*) NewLife Pubns.

— The Christian & Giving, Step 8: Rejoicing in His Abundance, Sharing His Resources. rev. ed. Tanner, Don et al, eds. (Ten Basic Steps Toward Christian Maturity Ser.). (Illus.). 80p. (Orig.). 1994. pap. 4.99 (*1-56399-037-7*) NewLife Pubns.

— The Christian & Obedience, Step 6: Living Daily in God's Grace. rev. ed. Tanner, Don et al, eds. (Ten Basic Steps Toward Christian Maturity Ser.). (Illus.). 64p. (Orig.). 1994. pap. 4.99 (*1-56399-035-0*) NewLife Pubns.

— The Christian & Prayer, Step 4: Unlocking the Secrets of a Successful Prayer Life. rev. ed. Tanner, Don et al, eds. (Ten Basic Steps Toward Christian Maturity Ser.). (Illus.). 64p. (Orig.). 1994. pap. 4.99 (*1-56399-033-4*) NewLife Pubns.

— The Christian & the Abundant Life, Step 2: Focusing on New Priorities. rev. ed. Tanner, Don et al, eds. (Ten Basic Steps Toward Christian Maturity Ser.). (Illus.). 64p. (Orig.). 1994. pap. 4.99 (*1-56399-031-8*) NewLife Pubns.

— The Christian & the Bible, Step 5: Growing Through the Study of God's Word. rev. ed. Tanner, Don et al, eds. (Ten Basic Steps Toward Christian Maturity Ser.). (Illus.). 80p. (Orig.). 1994. pap. 4.99 (*1-56399-034-2*) NewLife Pubns.

— The Christian & the Holy Spirit, Step 3: Moving Beyond Discouragement & Defeat. rev. ed. Tanner, Don et al, eds. (Ten Basic Steps Toward Christian Maturity Ser.). (Illus.). 80p. (Orig.). 1994. pap. 4.99 (*1-56399-032-6*) NewLife Pubns.

— The Christian & Witnessing, Step 7: Bringing Words of Hope to the World Around You. rev. ed. Tanner, Don et al, eds. (Ten Basic Steps Toward Christian Maturity Ser.). (Illus.). 80p. (Orig.). 1994. pap. 4.99 (*1-56399-036-9*) NewLife Pubns.

— Cinco Pasos para el Crecimiento del Cristiano/Estudiante.Tr. of Five Steps of Christian Growth/Student. (SPA.). 47p. student ed. 3.29 (*0-7899-0224-9*, 492346) Editorial Unilit.

— Cinco Pasos para el Crecimiento del Cristiano/Lider.Tr. of Five Steps of Christian Growth/Leader. (SPA.). 111p. teacher ed. 4.50 (*1-56063-474-X*, 492345) Editorial Unilit.

— La Clave para una Vida Vistoriosa.Tr. of Key to Dynamic Living. (SPA.). 1995. 3.99 (*0-7899-0094-7*, 492329) Editorial Unilit.

***Bright, Bill.** Come Help Change the World. 3rd ed. LC 99-32774. 320p. 1999. pap. 11.99 (*1-56399-132-2*) NewLife Pubns.

Bright, Bill. The Coming Revival: America's Call to Fast, Pray & "Seek God's Face" LC 94-46680. 224p. 1995. pap. 9.99 (*1-56399-064-4*) NewLife Pubns.

— Cuatro Leyes Espirituales.Tr. of Four Spiritual Laws. (SPA.). 65p. 6.99 (*1-56063-928-8*, 492321) Editorial Unilit.

— Exploring the New Testament Step 10: Discover the Mystery of God's Plan. rev. ed. Tanner, Don et al, eds. (Ten Basic Steps Toward Christian Maturity Ser.). (Illus.). 80p. (Orig.). 1994. pap. 4.99 (*1-56399-039-3*) NewLife Pubns.

— Exploring the Old Testament Step 9: Discover God's Pattern of Promise & Blessing. rev. ed. Tanner, Don et al, eds. (Ten Basic Steps Toward Christian Maturity Ser.). (Illus.). 80p. (Orig.). 1994. pap. 4.99 (*1-56399-038-5*) NewLife Pubns.

***Bright, Bill.** 50 Steps to Discovering God's Character. 112p. 2000. pap. 5.99 (*1-56399-142-X*); pap. 3.99 (*1-56399-143-8*) New Life AZ.

Bright, Bill. 5 Steps of Christian Growth. (Five Steps Ser.). 1994. pap., student ed. 3.99 (*1-56399-021-0*) NewLife Pubns.

— 5 Steps of Christian Growth. (Five Steps Ser.). (Illus.). 112p. 1994. pap., teacher ed. 5.99 (*1-56399-022-9*) NewLife Pubns.

— Five Steps to Fasting & Prayer. 48p. pap., student ed. 3.99 (*1-56399-116-0*) NewLife Pubns.

— Five Steps to Fasting & Prayer: Leader's Guide. 112p. pap. 5.99 (*1-56399-115-2*) NewLife Pubns.

— 5 Steps to Knowing God's Will. Whims, Joette, ed. (Five Steps Ser.). 112p. 1997. pap., teacher ed. 5.99 (*1-56399-082-2*); pap., student ed. 3.99 (*1-56399-083-0*) NewLife Pubns.

— 5 Steps to Making Disciples. Whims, Joette, ed. (Five Steps Ser.). 112p. 1997. pap., teacher ed. 5.99 (*1-56399-055-5*); pap., student ed. 3.99 (*1-56399-056-3*) NewLife Pubns.

***Bright, Bill.** God: Discover His Character. 336p. 2000. pap. 14.99 (*1-56399-125-X*) NewLife Pubns.

Bright, Bill. God: Discover His Character, Renew Your Passion. LC 99-33089. 336p. 1999. 19.99 (*1-56399-121-7*) NewLife Pubns.

***Bright, Bill.** God: Discover His Character, Renew Your Passion, Leader's Guide ed. 1999. pap. text 4.99 (*1-56399-123-3*) New Life Pubns.

— God: 13 Steps to Discovering His Attributes. 32p. 1999. pap. 0.99 (*1-56399-126-8*) NewLife Pubns.

Bright, Bill. A Great Adventure. (Illus.). 32p. (Orig.). 1959. pap. 0.99 (*1-56399-015-6*) NewLife Pubns.

— Le Gustaria Conocer a Dios... ?Tr. of Would You Like to Know God Personally?. (SPA.). 16p. pap. 6.99 (*1-56063-923-7*, 492328) Editorial Unilit.

— Ha Oido Usted las Cuatro Leyes Espirituales?, 25 Vols. (SPA.). 32p. 1996. pap. 6.99 (*1-56399-080-6*) NewLife Pubns.

— A Handbook for Christian Maturity. Tanner, Don et al, eds. (Ten Basic Steps Toward Christian Maturity Ser.). (Illus.). 448p. (Orig.). 1994. pap. 16.99 (*1-56399-040-7*) NewLife Pubns.

— A Handbook for Christian Maturity: Leading an Effective Bible Study. Tanner, Don et al, eds. (Ten Basic Steps Toward Christian Maturity Ser.). (Illus.). 552p. (Orig.). 1994. pap., teacher ed. 14.99 (*1-56399-028-8*) NewLife Pubns.

— Have You Heard of the Four Spiritual Laws?, 50 Vols. 1993. pap. 9.99 (*1-56399-019-9*) NewLife Pubns.

— Have You Made the Wonderful Discovery of the Spirit-Filled Life?, 25 Vols. 1990. pap. 6.99 (*1-56399-020-2*) NewLife Pubns.

— The Holy Spirit: The Key to Supernatural Living. (Illus.). 292p. 1980. mass mkt. 7.99 (*1-56399-053-9*) NewLife Pubns.

— Un Hombre Sin Igual.Tr. of Man Without Equal. (SPA.). 126p. 1992. pap. 3.99 (*1-56063-366-2*, 498534) Editorial Unilit.

— How Can You Be Filled with the Holy Spirit, No. 3. (Transferable Concepts Ser.: Bk. 3). (Illus.). 64p. (Orig.). 1971. pap. 1.99 (*1-56399-002-4*) NewLife Pubns.

— How Can You Be Fruitful Witness, No. 5. (Transferable Concepts Ser.: Bk. 5). (Illus.). 64p. (Orig.). 1971. pap. 1.99 (*1-56399-004-0*) NewLife Pubns.

— How to Reach Your World: Through A New Life Group. Orig. Title: Five Steps to Sharing Your Faith. (Illus.). 48p. (Orig.). 1993. 3.99 (*1-56399-027-X*) NewLife Pubns.

— How You Can Be a Fruitful Witness. 1998. pap. 3.99 (*1-56399-105-5*) New Life Pubns.

— How You Can Be Filled with the Holy Spirit. 1998. pap. 3.99 (*1-56399-103-9*) New Life Pubns.

— How You Can Be Sure You Are a Christian. 1998. pap. 3.99 (*1-56399-101-2*) New Life Pubns.

— How You Can Experience God's Love & Forgiveness. 1998. pap. 3.99 (*1-56399-102-0*) New Life Pubns.

— How You Can Experience God's Love & Forgiveness, No. 2. (Transferable Concepts Ser.: Bk. 2). 58p. 1991. reprint ed. pap. 1.99 (*1-56399-001-6*) NewLife Pubns.

— How You Can Experience the Adventure of Giving. 1998. pap. 3.99 (*1-56399-110-1*) New Life Pubns.

— How You Can Experience the Adventure of Giving, No. 10. (Transferable Concepts Ser.: Bk. 10). (Illus.). 64p. 1991. pap. 1.99 (*1-56399-009-1*) NewLife Pubns.

— How You Can Help Fulfill the Great Comission. 1998. pap. 3.99 (*1-56399-107-1*) New Life Pubns.

— How You Can Introduce Others to Christ. 1998. pap. 3.99 (*1-56399-106-3*) New Life Pubns.

— How You Can Introduce Others to Christ, No. 6. (Transferable Concepts Ser.: Bk. 6). 64p. 1972. pap. 1.99 (*1-56399-005-9*) NewLife Pubns.

— How You Can Love by Faith. 1998. pap. 3.99 (*1-56399-108-X*) New Life Pubns.

— How You Can Love by Faith, No. 8. (Transferable Concepts Ser.: Bk. 8). 64p. 1971. pap. 1.99 (*1-56399-007-5*) NewLife Pubns.

— How You Can Pray with Confidence. 1998. pap. 3.99 (*1-56399-109-8*) New Life Pubns.

— How You Can Pray with Confidence, No. 9. (Transferable Concepts Ser.: Bk. 9). (Illus.). 64p. 1971. pap. 1.99 (*1-56399-008-3*) NewLife Pubns.

***Bright, Bill.** How You Can Study the Bible Effectively. (Illus.). 48p. 1999. pap. 3.99 (*1-56399-127-6*) NewLife Pubns.

Bright, Bill. How You Can Walk in the Spirit. 1998. pap. 3.99 (*1-56399-104-7*) New Life Pubns.

— How You Can Walk in the Spirit, No. 4. (Transferable Concepts Ser.: Bk. 4). 1991. pap. 1.99 (*1-56399-003-2*) NewLife Pubns.

— Jesus & the Intellectual. (Illus.). 64p. (Orig.). 1959. pap. 1.99 (*1-56399-016-4*) NewLife Pubns.

— Life Without Equal: Discover Purpose, Peace & Power for Living. (Uniqueness of Jesus Ser.: Bk. 2). 128p. 1992. mass mkt. 4.99 (*1-56399-011-3*) NewLife Pubns.

— A Man Without Equal: Jesus, the Man Who Changed the World. LC 91-28459. (Uniqueness of Jesus Ser.: Bk. 1). 128p. 1992. mass mkt. 4.99 (*1-56399-012-1*) NewLife Pubns.

— Preparing for the Coming Revival: How to Lead a Successful Fasting & Prayer Gathering. 48p. 1995. pap., teacher ed. 3.99 (*1-56399-075-X*) NewLife Pubns.

— Promises: A Daily Guide to Supernatural Living. 384p. 1998. reprint ed. 14.99 (*1-56399-043-1*) NewLife Pubns.

— Promises Daily Devotions for Supernatural Living. 400p. 1996. pap. 14.99 (*1-56399-054-7*) NewLife Pubns.

— Quiet Moments with Bill Bright. LC 99-32268. 140p. 1999. 15.99 (*1-56955-167-7*, Vine Bks) Servant.

— Reaching Your World Through Witnessing without Fear. 64p. 1998. pap., teacher ed. 4.99 (*1-56399-060-1*) NewLife Pubns.

— Reaching Your World Through Witnessing Without Fear: How to Share Your Faith with Confidence. 1995. pap., teacher ed. 29.99 incl. VHS (*1-56399-061-X*) NewLife Pubns.

— Red Sky in the Morning: Leaders Guide. 1998. pap. text 5.99 (*1-56399-098-9*) New Life Pubns.

— The Secret. LC 93-10169. 1993. pap. 8.99 (*0-8407-4435-8*) Nelson.

— 7 Basic Steps to Successful Fasting & Prayer. 24p. 1995. pap. 0.99 (*1-56399-073-3*) NewLife Pubns.

— Seven Promises of a Promise Keeper, Revised & Expanded Edition. LC 99-11090. 1999. pap. text 12.99 (*0-8499-3730-2*) Word Pub.

— The Transforming Power of Fasting & Prayer: Personal Accounts of Spiritual Renewal. LC 97-16983. 208p. 1997. pap. 9.99 (*1-56399-090-3*) NewLife Pubns.

***Bright, Bill.** Two Bills from Boston: Making the American Dream Come True. LC 99-44987. (Illus.). 224p. 2000. pap. 15.95 (*1-58151-049-7*, Pub. by BookPartners) Midpt Trade.

Bright, Bill. The Uniqueness of Jesus: The Life & Teachings of Jesus Introduction. rev. ed. Tanner, Don et al, eds. (Ten Basic Steps Toward Christian Maturity Ser.). (Illus.). 80p. (Orig.). 1994. pap. 4.99 (*1-56399-029-6*) NewLife Pubns.

— Witnessing Without Fear. LC 87-45. 215p. 1992. pap. 9.99 (*0-8407-4401-3*) Nelson.

B

— Would You Like to Belong to God's Family. 1998. pap. 7.99 (*1-56399-081-4*) New Life Pubns.
— Would You Like to Know God Personally?, 50 Vols. pap. 9.99 (*1-56399-018-0*) NewLife Pubns.
— Your Most Important Investment, 10. (Illus.). 8p. 1999. pap. text 6.99 (*1-56399-119-5*) NewLife Pubns.
— Your New Life: Steps to Strengthening Your New Relationship with Christ. rev. ed. 36p. 1.95 (*1-57229-054-4*) FamilyLife.
***Bright, Bill, ed.** The Greatest Lesson I've Ever Learned (for Men) 2000. pap. 12.99 (*1-56399-084-9*) New Life AZ.
— Living Supernaturally in Christ. 256p. 2000. 19.99 (*1-56399-145-4*) New Life AZ.
Bright, Bill & Bright, Vonette. Building a Home in a Pull-Apart World: Powerful Principles for a Happier Marriage: Four Steps That Work. LC 94-45053. 1995. pap. 7.99 (*1-56399-058-X*) NewLife Pubns.
Bright, Bill & Damoose, John N. Red Sky in the Morning: How You Can Help Prevent America's Gathering Storms. LC 98-24200. 1998. 17.99 (*1-56399-095-4*) NewLife Pubns.
***Bright, Bill & Peterson, Dan.** Change Your World Through Prayer & Fasting: An Interactive Prayer Seminar. 96p. 1999. pap., teacher ed. 5.99 (*1-56399-134-9*); pap., student ed. 3.99 (*1-56399-133-0*) NewLife Pubns.
Bright, Bill, et al. The Seven Promises of a Promise Keeper. LC 94-4124. 200p. 1994. 17.99 (*1-56179-222-5*) Focus Family.
Bright, Brenda J. & Bakewell, Liza, eds. Looking High & Low: Art & Cultural Identity. LC 94-48508. (Illus.). 210p. 1995. 43.00 (*0-8165-1311-2*); pap. 18.95 (*0-8165-1516-6*) U of Ariz Pr.
***Bright, Brenda Jo, et al.** Customized: Art Inspired by Hot Rods, Low Riders & American Car Culture. (Illus.). 160p. 2000. 34.95 (*0-8109-5727-2*, Pub. by Abrams) Time Warner.
Bright, Charles. The Powers That Punish: Prison & Politics in the Era of the "Big House," 1920-1955. LC 96-9954. (Law, Meaning, & Violence Ser.). 336p. (C). 1996. text 49.50 (*0-472-10732-1*, 10732) U of Mich Pr.
— Sea Serpents. (Illus.). 112p. (C). 1991. 17.95 (*0-87972-539-7*) Bowling Green Univ Popular Press.
Bright, Charles D. Submarine Telegraphs: Their History, Construction & Working. LC 74-4669. (Telecommunications Ser.). (Illus.). 744p. 1974. reprint ed. 63.95 (*0-405-06035-1*) Ayer.
Bright, Charles D., ed. Historical Dictionary of the U. S. Air Force. LC 91-25461. 768p. 1992. lib. bdg. 99.50 (*0-313-25928-3*, BHD, Greenwood Pr) Greenwood.
Bright, Chris. Life Out of Bounds: Bioinvasion in a Borderless World. LC 99-163011. (Illus.). 288p. 1998. pap. 13.00 (*0-393-31814-1*) Norton.
Bright, Christopher, ed. A Guide to the European Economic Area. (Illus.). 406p. 1994. text 79.00 (*0-19-825911-5*) OUP.
Bright, Chuck. University of Iowa Football: The Hawkeyes. LC 82-50031. (College Sports Bks.). 1982. 10.95 (*0-87397-233-3*, Strode Pubs) Circle Bk Service.
Bright, Courtney, ed. see Skarlinski, Robert W.
Bright, David, ed. see Hay, Jean.
Bright, David. F. The Miniature Epic in Vandal Africa. LC 87-40211. 320p. 1987. 37.50 (*0-8061-2075-4*) U of Okla Pr.
Bright, Deborah. The Official Criticism Manual: Perfecting the Art of Giving & Receiving Criticism. 132p. 1991. 23.35 (*0-9635783-0-8*) Bright Ent.
— On the Edge & in Control: A Proven 8-Step Program for Getting the Most Out of Life. 288p. 1998. pap. 15.95 (*0-07-007916-1*) McGraw.
— Passionate Camera: Photography & the Bodies of Desire. LC 98-12079. (Illus.). 456p. 1998. pap. 30.00 (*0-415-14582-1*) Routledge.
— Passionate Camera: Photography & the Bodies of Desire. LC 98-12079. (Illus.). 456p. (C). 1998. 85.00 (*0-415-14581-3*) Routledge.
— The Positive Power of Criticism. 1990. wbk. ed. 79.95 incl. audio (*0-9615400-7-9*) Intl Ctr Creat Think.
Bright, Deborah, et al. Image & Enterprise: The Photography of Adolphe Braun. O'Brien, Maureen & Bergstein, Mary, eds. LC 99-70952. (Illus.). 159p. 2000. text 50.00 (*0-500-54232-5*, Pub. by Thames Hudson) Norton.
Bright, Donald E. The Insects of Arachnids of Canada, Pt. 21: The Weevils of Canada & Alaska: Vol. 1, Cleoptera: Curculionoidean, Excluding Scolytidae & Curculionida, Pt. 21, Vol. 1. (FRE.). 217p. (Orig.). 1993. pap. 45.45 (*0-660-14433-6*, Pub. by Canadian Govt Pub) Accents Pubns.
Bright, Donald E., Jr., ed. A Catalog of Scolytidae & Platypodidae (Coleoptera) Vols. A & B, Pt. 2: Taxonomic Index. (Great Basin Naturalist Memoirs Ser.: Vol. 13). iv, 1553p. 1992. 120.00 (*0-8425-2310-3*, Friends of the Library) Brigham.
Bright, Donald E. & Skidmore, Robert E. A Catalog of Scolytidae & Platypodidae (Coleoptera), 1990-1994, Suppl. 1. 368p. 1997. pap. 56.50 (*0-660-16709-3*, Pub. by NRC Res Pr) Accents Pubns.
Bright, Edna. God Uses Ordinary People: A Memoir of Church Planting. LC 98-67738. (Illus.). 112p. 1998. pap. 10.95 (*1-57736-117-2*) Providence Hse.
Bright, Elise M. Tactics for Preserving Open Space: A Survey & Analysis of Local Governments' Park Land Acquisition Techniques. 51p. 1990. pap. text 5.00 (*0-936440-80-5*) U TX SUPA.
Bright-Fey, John. Mystique Poetica: Living Philosophy Through Revealed Wisdom. LC 98-96499. (Illus.). xii, 190p. 1998. 23.00 (*0-9665247-0-5*) Rubrica.
Bright, Frank V. & McNally, Mary E., eds. Supercritical Fluid Technology: Theoretical & Applied Approaches to Analytical Chemistry. LC 92-11434. (ACS Symposium Ser.: No. 488). (Illus.). 374p. 1992. text 95.00 (*0-8412-2220-7*, Pub. by Am Chemical) OUP.
Bright, Franklyn F. Planning for a Movable Compact Shelving System. LC 91-14261. (Library Administration & Management Association Ser.: No. 1). (Illus.). 80p. 1991. reprint ed. pap. 30.00 (*0-608-02968-8*, 206343600006) Bks Demand.
Bright, Freda. Parting Shots. large type ed. LC 93-15831. 599p. 1993. 18.95 (*1-56054-763-4*) Thorndike Pr.
***Bright, G. A.** Forestry Budgets & Accounts. (CABI Publishing Ser.). 250p. 1999. pap. text 45.00 (*0-85199-328-1*) OUP.
Bright, George. Basic Math Games, Bk. 1. 1997. text 10.50 (*0-86651-264-0*) Seymour Pubns.
— Basic Math Games, Bk. 2. 1997. text 10.50 (*0-86651-342-6*) Seymour Pubns.
Bright, George W., et al, eds. Impact of Calculators on Mathematics Instruction. 144p. (Orig.). (C). 1994. lib. bdg. 48.50 (*0-8191-9308-9*) U Pr of Amer.
Bright, George W. & Joyner, Jeane M., eds. Classroom Assessment in Mathematics: Views from a National Science Foundation Working Conference. LC 97-51761. 320p. (C). 1998. 62.00 (*0-7618-1027-7*); pap. 39.50 (*0-7618-1028-5*) U Pr of Amer.
Bright, George W., et al. Mathematics Programs: A Guide to Evaluation. (Essential Tools for Educators Ser.). 144p. 1993. pap. 27.95 (*0-8039-6044-1*) Corwin Pr.
Bright, George W., jt. ed. see Friel, Susan N.
Bright, Greg. The Great Maze Book. rev. ed. LC 74-26198. (Illus.). 96p. 1987. pap. 7.95 (*0-394-75234-1*) Pantheon.

Bright, Harry G. I Lived on Air... For Forty Years. LC 81-81752. 96p. 1981. pap. 5.00 (*0-87012-424-2*) McClain.

Bright, Hugh. Complete Marine Radion Control Manual. 192p. 1999. 36.95 (*1-55750-198-X*) Naval Inst Pr.
Bright, J. B. The Brights of Suffolk, England. (Illus.). 365p. 1988. reprint ed. pap. 57.50 (*0-8328-0323-5*); reprint ed. lib. bdg. 67.50 (*0-8328-0322-7*) Higginson Bk Co.
Bright, J. Clayton, ed. see Sharp, David B., Jr.
***Bright, J. E.** All or Nothing. (NASCAR Racers Novelizations Ser.: Vol. 5). 2000. pap. 4.50 (*0-06-107197-8*) HarpC.
— Digimon: Andromon's Attack, No. 3. (Digimon Ser.: No. 3). 96p. 2000. pap. 4.50 (*0-06-107188-9*, HarpEntertain) Morrow Avon.
— The Fast Lane. (NASCAR Racers Ser.: No. 1). 128p. (gr. 2-6). 2000. mass mkt. 4.50 (*0-06-107228-1*) HarpC.
— Nascar Racers: Daredevil, No. 4. (Nascar Racers Ser.: No. 4). 128p. 2000. pap. 4.50 (*0-06-107191-9*, HarpEntertain) Morrow Avon.
Bright, J. S. The Dictionary of Palmistry. 237p. 1984. 9.95 (*0-318-36394-1*) Asia Bk Corp.
— Palmistry Made Easy. 261p. 1983. 8.95 (*0-318-36393-3*) Asia Bk Corp.
Bright, James F. Maria Theresa. LC 71-154145. (Select Bibliographies Reprint Ser.). 1977. reprint ed. 20.95 (*0-8369-5761-X*) Ayer.
Bright, James L. Home Repair: Illustrated Deluxe Edition. 378p. 1991. write for info. (*0-89434-130-8*) Ferguson.
Bright, James R. A Brief Introduction to Technology Forecasting: Concepts & Exercises. 2nd ed. LC T 0174.B7. 266p. reprint ed. pap. 82.50 (*0-8357-7403-1*, 200710600061) Bks Demand.
— Practical Technology Forecasting. 110p. 1978. pap. 25.00 (*1-884154-09-3*) Tech Futures.
Bright, James W., ed. Evangelium Secundum Iohannem: The Gospel of Saint John in West-Saxon. LC 71-144447. (Belles Lettres Ser., Section 1: No. 4). reprint ed. 35.00 (*0-404-53605-0*) AMS Pr.
— Evangelium Secundum Lucam: The Gospel of Saint Luke in West-Saxon. LC 75-144448. (Belles Lettres Ser., Section 1: No. 3). reprint ed. 27.50 (*0-404-53602-6*) AMS Pr.
— Evangelium Secundum Marcum: The Gospel of Saint Mark in West-Saxon. LC 74-144445. (Belles Lettres Ser., Section 1: No. 2). reprint ed. 27.50 (*0-404-53603-4*) AMS Pr.
— Evangelium Secundum Mattheum: The Gospel of Saint Matthew in West Saxon. LC 78-144446. (Belles Lettres Ser., Section 1: No. 1). reprint ed. 27.50 (*0-404-53604-2*) AMS Pr.
Bright, Jennifer. At the Sea. (Illus.). 72p. 1996. 12.98 (*1-56799-289-7*, MetroBooks) M Friedman Pub Grp Inc.
— At the Sea: Celebrations in Art. (Celebrations in Art Ser.). 1996. write for info. (*0-614-96418-0*, MetroBooks) M Friedman Pub Grp Inc.
— Dance. LC 95-51984. (Celebrations in Art Ser.). (Illus.). 72p. 1996. 12.98 (*1-56799-293-5*, MetroBooks) M Friedman Pub Grp Inc.
Bright, Jessie, tr. see Corti, Maria.
Bright, Jessie, tr. see Sgorlon, Carlo.
Bright, Jessie, tr. & intro. see Messina, Annie.
Bright, Jessie, tr. & intro. see Sgorlon, Carlo.
Bright, Jo A. 60 Minute Museum Visits: New York City. 2nd rev. ed. Haseman, Jan, ed. LC 96-92158. (Illus.). 181p. 1998. reprint ed. pap. 15.95 (*0-9650580-2-6*) Quick View.
Bright, JoAnn. 60 Minute Museum Visits: Washington, D. C. (Forthcoming) Early 1999. Museum Curators & PR Associates Staff, ed. (Illus.). 180p. 2000. pap. write for info. (*0-9650580-4-2*) Quick View.
— 60-Minute Museum Visits Bk. 1: New York City. Wigglesworth, Zeke & Museum Curators, P. R. Assocs. Staff, eds. LC 96-92158. (Illus.). 164p. (Orig.). 1996. pap. 14.95 (*0-9650580-3-4*) Quick View.
Bright, John. The Authority of the Old Testament. (Biblical & Theological Classics Library: Vol. 18). 272p. 1997. reprint ed. pap. 9.99 (*0-85364-807-7*, Pub. by Paternoster Pub) OM Literature.
— A History of Israel. 3rd ed. LC 80-22774. (Illus.). 528p. (C). 1981. 39.95 (*0-664-21381-2*) Westminster John Knox.
***Bright, John.** History of Israel. 4th ed. (Illus.). 2000. pap. 34.95 (*0-664-22068-1*) Westminster John Knox.
Bright, John. Kingdom of God. rev. ed. (Series A). 1980. pap. 12.95 (*0-687-20908-0*) Abingdon.
Bright, John, tr. Jeremiah. LC 65-13603. (Anchor Bible Ser.: Vol. 21). 528p. 1964. 35.00 (*0-385-00823-6*, Anchor NY) Doubleday.
Bright, Jon. Crime Prevention in America: A British Perspective. LC 91-51072. 128p. (C). 1992. 14.95 (*0-942511-52-2*) OICJ.
Bright, Joseph E. To Will or Not to Will. xii, 72p. 1939. lib. bdg. 30.00 (*0-89941-597-0*, 500260) W S Hein.
Bright, Laren. Laughter Is the Best Meditation: The Best of the Inner Jester. LC 78-4491. 1979. pap. 5.00 (*0-686-10176-6*) Mandeville LA.
Bright, Larry K. Guidelines for Writing in a Computer Lab Using WordPerfect. 48p. (C). 1993. per. 10.95 (*0-8403-8819-5*) Kendall-Hunt.
Bright, Laurence & Clements, Simon, eds. The Committed Church. 1966. 69.50 (*0-317-27423-6*) Elliots Bks.
Bright, Laurey. An Interrupted Marriage. 1994. per. 3.50 (*0-373-09916-9*, 1-09916-7) Harlequin Bks.
— The Kindness of Strangers. (Special Edition Ser.). 1993. per. 3.50 (*0-373-09820-0*, 5-09820-7) Silhouette.
— The Mother of His Child (Conveniently Wed) (Intimate Moments Ser.: No. 918). 1999. per. 4.25 (*0-373-07918-4*, 1-07918-5) Harlequin Bks.
— A Perfect Marriage. (Intimate Moments Ser.). 1995. per. 3.75 (*0-373-07621-5*, 1-07621-5) Silhouette.
Bright, Leila. Reincarnation & You: A Beginner's Guide. (Illus.). 96p. 1997. pap. 11.95 (*0-340-70517-5*, Pub. by Headway) Trafalgar.
— Teach Yourself Dream Interpretation. (Teach Yourself Ser.). 192p. 1999. pap. 9.95 (*0-8442-2679-3*, Teach Yrslf) NTC Contemp Pub Co.
Bright, Leonard D. The Gifted Kids Guide to Puzzles & Mind Games. (Illus.). 143p. (J). 1985. pap. 7.95 (*0-936750-15-4*) Paradon Pub Co.
Bright, Marjorie B. Nellie's Boarding House: A Dual Biography of Nellie Coffman & Palm Springs. 1981. 19.95 (*0-88280-068-X*) ETC Pubns.
Bright, Martha, ed. see Baer, Emo.
Bright, Michael. Barks, Roars & Siren Songs: How Animals Talk to Us & How We Talk Back. (Illus.). 1991. 17.95 (*1-55972-086-7*, Birch Ln Pr) Carol Pub Group.
***Bright, Michael.** Bears & Pandas. Anness Publishing Staff, ed. (Nature Watch Ser.). (Illus.). 64p. (J). (gr. 3-7). 1999. 12.95 (*1-85967-642-1*, Lorenz Bks) Anness Pub.
Bright, Michael. The Living World. large type ed. 367p. 1990. 20.95 (*1-85089-360-8*, Pub. by ISIS Lrg Prnt) Transaction Pubs.
***Bright, Michael.** Looking into Nature's Secrets. LC 98-68766. (Looking into Our World Ser.). (Illus.). 14p. (J). (ps-2). 1999. bds. 11.99 (*1-57584-316-1*, Pub. by Rdrs Digest) S&S Trade.
— Man Eaters: An Enthralling Study of the Animals That Prey on People. (Illus.). 2000. 24.95 (*1-58574-197-3*) Lyons Pr.
Bright, Michael. Nature's Masterpieces. Reader's Digest Editors, ed. LC 97-22868. (Earth, Its Wonders, Its Secrets Ser.). (Illus.). 160p. 1997. 19.95 (*0-89577-914-5*, Pub. by RD Assn) Penguin Putnam.
***Bright, Michael.** Private Life of Sharks: The Truth Behind the Myth. 260p. 1999. 31.95 (*1-86105-157-3*) Robson.
— The Private Life of Sharks: The Truth Behind the Myth. LC 99-56906. 2000. 17.95 (*0-8117-2875-7*) Stackpole.
Bright, Michael. Robert Browning's Rondures Brave. LC 95-33244. 279p. (Orig.). (C). 1995. text 34.95 (*0-8214-1125-X*) Ohio U Pr.
***Bright, Michael.** Sharks. (Illus.). 64p. (J). 2000. 12.95 (*1-85967-524-7*, Lorenz Bks) Anness Pub.
— Talking with Animals: An Intriguing Account of How Humans Talk to Animals & How They Talk Back. (Illus.). 250p. 1999. pap. 12.95 (*1-86105-183-2*) Robson.
Bright, Mynors, tr. see Pepys, Samuel.
Bright, Myron. Objections at Trial: National Edition. 1993. 29.95 (*0-614-06016-8*, 31105) Natl Prac Inst.
Bright, Myron H., et al. California Objections at Trial. LC 92-36115. 191p. (Orig.). 1992. pap. 39.50 (*1-56257-344-6*, 83065-10, MICHIE) LEXIS Pub.
Bright, Myron H., jt. auth. see Carlson, Ronald L.
Bright, Nancee O. Mothers of Steel: The Women of Um Gargur, an Eritrean Refugee Settlement in the Sudan. 330p. 1997. 79.95 (*1-56902-063-9*) Red Sea Pr.
— Mothers of Steel: The Women of Um Gargur, an Eritrean Refugee Settlement in the Sudan. (Illus.). 330p. 1997. pap. 21.95 (*1-56902-064-7*) Red Sea Pr.
***Bright, Nancy.** Poems, Litanies & Meditations. (Illus.). 80p. 1999. lib. bdg. 22.00 (*0-9650485-2-7*) Phoenix Intl AR.
Bright, Pam, jt. ed. see Arnold, Duane W.
Bright, Pamela, tr. from FRE. Augustine & the Bible. LC 97-20807. 1999. 50.00 (*0-268-00654-7*); pap. 30.00 (*0-268-00655-5*) U of Notre Dame Pr.
Bright, Poppy. The Best American Erotica, 1993. 1997. per. 12.00 (*0-684-84514-8*) S&S Trade.
Bright, Preston & Johnson, Clarence. Proceedings of a National Conference on Preventing Alcohol & Drug Abuse in Black Communities. 257p. (C). 1997. reprint ed. pap. text 50.00 (*0-7881-4188-0*) DIANE Pub.
Bright, Richard K. Coinage of Kutch. 71p. 1975. pap. 4.00 (*1-889172-05-7*) Numismatic Intl.
Bright, Robert. Georgie. LC 99-10646. (Illus.). 48p. (YA). (ps-3). 1999. pap. 4.95 (*0-374-42539-6*, Sunburst Bks) FS&G.
— Georgie. Scholastic, Inc. Staff, ed. (J). 1990. pap. 2.50 (*0-590-42126-3*) Scholastic Inc.
— Georgie & the Robbers. LC 99-10643. (Illus.). 32p. (YA). (ps-3). 1999. pap. 4.95 (*0-374-42542-6*, Sunburst Bks) FS&G.
— Jorgito: Georgie. Palacios, Argentina, tr. (SPA.). 48p. (J). (ps-3). 1991. pap. 3.95 (*0-590-42127-1*) Scholastic Inc.
Bright, Robin. Writing Instruction in the Intermediate Grades: What Is Said, What Is Done, What Is Understood. 134p. 1995. pap. 14.95 (*0-87207-124-3*, 124-3) Intl Reading.
***Bright, Robin M., et al.** From Your Child's Teacher: Helping Your Child Learn to Read, Write & Speak. 160p. 1999. spiral bd. 15.95 (*0-9682970-3-X*) FPH Pub.
Bright, Roy. Smart Cards: Principles, Practice, Applications. 1989. text 39.95 (*0-470-21159-8*) P-H.
Bright, Ruth. Grief & Powerlessness: Helping People Regain Control of Their Lives. 160p. 1996. pap. 24.95 (*1-85302-386-8*, Pub. by Jessica Kingsley) Taylor & Francis.
— Music Therapy & the Dementias: Improving the Quality of Life. (Horizon Ser.: No. 4). 80p. (Orig.). (C). 1988. pap. 9.75 (*0-918812-56-9*, ST 178) MMB Music.
— Wholeness in Later Life. LC 97-198660. 272p. 1997. pap. 27.95 (*1-85302-447-3*, Pub. by Jessica Kingsley) Taylor & Francis.
Bright, Sigrid. Hardanger Embroidery: A Complete & Practical Course. LC 77-87845. (Illus.). 32p. 1978. reprint ed. pap. 3.95 (*0-486-23592-0*) Dover.
Bright, Spencer. Peter Gabriel: An Authorized Biography. 2nd rev. ed. (Illus.). 524p. 1999. 32.50 (*0-283-06187-1*, Pub. by S1 & J) Trans-Atl Phila.
Bright, Susan. Altar. 24p. 1984. 6.00 (*0-911051-10-4*) Plain View.
— Atomic Basket: Occasional Poems. (Illus.). 100p. (Orig.). 1985. pap. text 10.00 (*0-935430-10-5*) In Between.
— Bunny. (Illus.). 62p. Date not set. 10.00 (*0-911051-53-8*) Plain View.
— House of the Mother. (Illus.). 129p. (Orig.). 1995. pap. 13.95 (*0-911051-79-1*) Plain View.
— Land Law: Themes & Perspectives. 620p. 1998. pap. text (*0-19-876455-3*) OUP.
Bright, Susan. Landlord & Tenant Law: The Nature of Tenancies. (Illus.). 844p. 1995. pap. text 41.00 (*0-19-876349-2*) OUP.
Bright, Susan. Pewter Wheel. 1982. 3.00 (*0-911051-04-X*); VHS. write for info. (*0-318-56961-2*) Plain View.
— Swimming the English Channel. (Fastbook 1985 Ser.). 20p. 1985. 6.00 (*0-685-10808-2*) Plain View.
— Tirades & Evidence of Grace. 164p. 1992. pap. 13.95 (*0-911051-58-9*) Plain View.
Bright, Susan & Dewar, John, eds. Land Law: Themes & Perspectives. LC 98-3193. 620p. 1998. text 90.00 (*0-19-876454-5*) OUP.
Bright, Susan & Gilbert, Geoffrey. Landlord & Tenant Law: The Nature of Tenancies. (Illus.). 848p. 1995. text 79.00 (*0-19-876348-4*) OUP.
Bright, Susan & LaGattuta, Margo, eds. Wind Eyes: A Women's Reader & Writing Source. (New Voices Ser.). Date not set. 16.95 (*0-911051-90-2*) Plain View.
Bright, Susan, ed. see Artemis, Deuce, et al.
Bright, Susan, ed. see Askhami, Mahnaz, et al.
Bright, Susan, ed. see Book, Lana, et al.
Bright, Susan, ed. see Greer, Scott.
Bright, Susan S. Union Bride: A Story about Workers, Unions, Employers, & the Changing Labor Scene. LC 95-61075. 368p. (Orig.). 1996. pap. 10.95 (*1-896560-06-7*) Tll Pubng.
Bright, Susie. The Best American Erotica, 1997. 256p. 1997. per. 12.00 (*0-684-81823-X*, Touchstone) S&S Trade Pap.
— Best American Erotica 1996. 256p. 1996. per. 12.00 (*0-684-81830-2*) S&S Trade.
— The Best American Erotica, 1995. annuals 256p. 1995. per. 12.00 (*0-684-81829-9*, Touchstone) S&S Trade Pap.
— Full Exposure: Opening up to Sexual Creativity & Erotic Expression. LC 99-23097. 176p. 1999. 22.00 (*0-06-251554-3*, Pub. by Harper SF) HarpC.
***Bright, Susie.** Full Exposure: Opening up to Sexual Creativity & Erotic Expression. LC 99-23097. 176p. 2000. reprint ed. pap. 14.00 (*0-06-251591-8*) Harper SF.
— Full Exposure: Opening up to Sexual Creativity & Erotic Expression, Set. unabridged ed. 1999. audio 18.00 (*0-694-52230-9*) HarperAudio.
Bright, Susie. Nothing but the Girl: The Blatant Lesbian Image. Posener, Jill, ed. 1996. 29.95 (*0-304-33482-0*, Pub. by Cassell) LPC InBook.
— Nothing but the Girl: The Blatant Lesbian Image. 1996. pap. 29.95 (*1-86047-001-7*, Pub. by Cassell) LPC InBook.
— Nothing but the Girl: The Blatant Lesbian Image. 1997. pap. text 24.95 (*1-86047-002-5*) Continuum.
— The Sexual State of the Union. LC 96-44603. 251p. 1997. 23.00 (*0-684-80023-3*) S&S Trade.
— The Sexual State of the Union. 1998. per. 12.00 (*0-684-83850-8*, Touchstone) S&S Trade Pap.
— Susie Bright's Sexwise: America's Favorite X-Rated Intellectual Does Dan Quayle, Catharine MacKinnon, Stephen King, Camille Paglia, Nicholson Baker, Madonna, the Black Panthers & the GOP. LC 94-47330. 180p. 1995. pap. 10.95 (*1-57344-002-7*) Cleis Pr.
— Susie Sexpert's Lesbian Sex World. 2nd ed. 175p. 1998. pap. 14.95 (*1-57344-077-9*) Cleis Pr.
Bright, Susie, ed. The Best American Erotica. 304p. 2000. per. 13.00 (*0-684-84396-X*) S&S Trade.
— The Best American Erotica 1999. 288p. 1999. per. 12.00 (*0-684-84395-1*) S&S Trade Pap.
***Bright, Susie, ed.** Best American Erotica 2001. 2001. pap. 13.00 (*0-684-86914-4*, Touchstone) S&S Trade Pap.
Bright, Susie, ed. The Best American Erotica 1993. 241p. 1993. pap. 12.00 (*0-02-079262-X*) Macmillan.
— The Best American Erotica, 1994. 272p. 1994. per. 12.00 (*0-671-89942-2*) S&S Trade.

— Herotica: A Collection of Women's Erotic Fiction. 10th anniversary ed. LC 98-72962. 160p. 1998. pap. 11.00 (*0-940208-24-5*) Down There Pr.

Bright, Susie, intro. Herotica Three: A Collection of Women's Erotic Fiction. 224p. (Orig.). 1994. pap. 12.95 (*0-452-27180-0*, Plume) Dutton Plume.

Bright, Susie & Blank, Joani, eds. Herotica Two: A Collection of Women's Erotic Fiction. 176p. (Orig.). 1992. pap. 12.95 (*0-452-26787-0*, Plume) Dutton Plume.

Bright, Timothy. A Treatise Wherein Is Declared the Sufficiencie of English Medicines, for Cure of All Diseases, Cured with Medicine. LC 77-6860. (English Experience Ser.: No. 854). 1977. reprint ed. lib. bdg. 15.00 (*90-221-0854-6*) Walter J Johnson.

Bright, Tom, et al. Peace with God the Creator, Peace with All Creation. 53p. 1995. 7.95 (*1-55586-032-X*) US Catholic.

Bright, Velma. The Story of the Little Round Barn. LC 81-65540. (Illus.). 48p. (Orig.). (J). (gr. 2-3). 1981. 10.00 (*0-9605968-2-8*); pap. 5.00 (*0-9605968-3-6*) Bright Bks.

— What Would You Like to Be? (Illus.). 32p. (J). (gr. 1). 1976. reprint ed. lib. bdg. 10.00 (*0-9605968-0-1*) Bright Bks.

Bright, Victor M. Selected Papers on Optical Mems. LC 98-45576. (Milestone Ser.). 644p. 1999. 110.00 (*0-8194-3129-X*) SPIE.

Bright, Vonette & Ball, Barbara. The Joy of Hospitality: Fun Ideas for Evangelistic Entertaining. 256p. 1996. pap. 10.99 (*1-56399-057-1*) NewLife Pubns.

Bright, Vonette & Ball, Barbara, eds. The Joy of Hospitality Cookbook: Favorite Recipes from the Campus Crusade for Christ Family. 480p. 1996. pap. 17.99 (*1-56399-077-6*) NewLife Pubns.

Bright, Vonette & Bell, Barbara. The Joy of Hospitality: Fun Ideas for Evangelistic Entertaining. LC 95-46627. 1996. 16.99 (*1-56399-079-2*) NewLife Pubns.

Bright, Vonette, jt. auth. see Bright, Bill.

***Bright, Vonette Zachary, ed.** The Greatest Lesson I've Ever Learned (for Women) 2000. pap. 12.99 (*1-56399-085-7*) New Life AZ.

Bright, William. Age of the Fathers, 2 vols. LC 77-113564. reprint ed. 115.00 (*0-404-01077-6*) AMS Pr.

— American Indian Linguistics & Literature. LC 83-24949. 159p. (Orig.). 1984. 65.40 (*3-11-009846-6*); pap. 20.00 (*3-11-010241-2*) Mouton.

— Ancient Collects: A Facsimilie of the Fifth Edition 1875. 254p. 1993. boxed set 16.95 (*0-88028-142-1*, 1220) Forward Movement.

— Bibliography of the Languages of Native California: Including Closely Related Languages of Adjacent Areas. LC 82-3331. (Native American Bibliography Ser.: No. 3). 234p. 1982. 21.00 (*0-8108-1547-8*) Scarecrow.

— A Coyote Reader. LC 92-32640. (C). 1993. pap. 16.95 (*0-520-08062-9*, Pub. by U CA Pr) Cal Prin Full Svc.

Bright, William, ed. American Indian Languages 1, Vol. 5. (Collected Works of Edward Sapir). 584p. (C). 1989. lib. bdg. 120.00 (*0-89925-654-6*) Mouton.

— The Collected Works of Edward Sapir Vol. 10: Southern Paiute & Ute Linguistics & Ethnography. (Illus.). 932p. 1992. lib. bdg. 290.00 (*3-11-013543-4*) Mouton.

— International Encyclopedia of Linguistics, 4 vols., Set. (Illus.). 1856p. 1992. text 475.00 (*0-19-505196-3*) OUP.

Bright, William & Gudde, Erwin G. 1,500 California Place Names: Their Origin & Meaning. 4th ed. LC 97-43147. 172p. 1998. pap. 12.95 (*0-520-21271-1*, Pub. by U CA Pr) Cal Prin Full Svc.

Bright, William & Kahn, Saeed A. The Urdu Writing System. LC 76-40672. 48p. (C). 1976. reprint ed. pap. 5.00 (*0-87950-256-8*) Spoken Lang Serv.

Bright, William & Sapir, Philip, eds. The Collected Works of Edward Sapir Vol. VII: Wishram Texts & Ethnography, 16 vols. 518p. (C). 1990. lib. bdg. 117.00 (*3-11-012328-2*) Mouton.

Bright, William, jt. auth. see Gudde, Erwin G.

Bright, William, jt. ed. see Daniels, Peter T.

Bright, William E. Avocations. 100p. 1984. pap. 10.00 (*0-911051-12-0*) Plain View.

Bright, William R. How to Know the Will of God in Your Life. 6p. Date not set. pap. 0.32 (*1-57902-107-7*) Integrtd Res.

Brightbill, Frederick S. Corneal Surgery: Theory, Technique & Tissue. 3rd ed. LC 99-19068. (Illus.). 848p. (C). (gr. 13). 1999. text 225.00 (*0-8151-1229-7*, 27235) Mosby Inc.

Brightbill, Frederick S., ed. Corneal Surgery: Theory, Technique & Tissue. 2nd ed. LC 92-23630. (Illus.). 763p. (C). (gr. 13). 1992. text 225.00 (*0-8016-6487-X*, 06487) Mosby Inc.

Brightbill, Frederick S., jt. auth. see Albert, Daniel M.

***Brighter Child Publishing Staff.** The Story of Easter. (J). 1999. cd-rom 9.95 (*5-550-17737-4*) Nairi.

***Brighter Vision Publishing Staff.** About Colors, Shapes & Sizes. (My Discovery Bks.). (Illus.). (J). 2000. pap. text 2.95 (*1-55254-208-4*) Brighter Vision.

— About Nursery Rhymes Activity Book. (My Discovery Bks.). (Illus.). (J). 2000. pap. text 2.95 (*1-55254-206-8*) Brighter Vision.

— About the Farm. (My Discovery Bks.). (Illus.). (J). 2000. pap. text 2.95 (*1-55254-202-5*) Brighter Vision.

— About the Neighborhood. (My Discovery Bks.). (Illus.). (J). 2000. pap. text 2.95 (*1-55254-203-3*) Brighter Vision.

— Alphabet - Pre-K. (Primary Skills Ser.). (Illus.). (J). (ps-3). 2000. pap. 2.25 (*1-55254-174-6*) Brighter Vision.

— Alphabet Activities Activity Book. (Illus.). (J). 2000. pap. 1.39 (*1-55254-151-7*) Brighter Vision.

— Caring. (Character Counts Ser.). (Illus.). (J). 2000. pap. 2.75 (*1-55254-218-1*) Brighter Vision.

— Character Counts. (Illus.). (J). 2000. pap. 3.99 (*1-55254-220-3*) Brighter Vision.

— Christmas Crafts to Make. (Illus.). (J). 2000. pap. 3.95 (*1-55254-179-7*) Brighter Vision.

— Citizenship. (Character Counts Ser.). (Illus.). (J). 2000. pap. 2.75 (*1-55254-219-X*) Brighter Vision.

— Color & Shapes Activity Book. (Illus.). (J). 2000. pap. 1.39 (*1-55254-148-7*) Brighter Vision.

— Crossword Puzzles Activity Book. (Illus.). (J). 2000. pap. 1.39 (*1-55254-153-3*) Brighter Vision.

— Dinosaurs. (Illus.). (J). 2000. pap. text 2.25 (*1-55254-147-9*) Brighter Vision.

— Everday Crafts to Make. (Illus.). (J). 2000. pap. 3.95 (*1-55254-176-2*) Brighter Vision.

— Fairness. (Character Counts Ser.). (Illus.). (J). 2000. pap. 2.75 (*1-55254-217-3*) Brighter Vision.

— First Grade Skills Review. (Skills Review Workbks.). (Illus.). (J). (gr. 1). 2000. pap. 3.95 (*1-55254-198-3*) Brighter Vision.

— Fun with Friends. (Learning Adventures Ser.). (Illus.). (J). 2000. pap. text 2.25 (*1-55254-062-6*) Brighter Vision.

— Halloween & Thanksgiving. (Illus.). (J). 2000. pap. 3.95 (*1-55254-178-9*) Brighter Vision.

— Home & School Success, Grade K. (Illus.). (J). (gr. k). 2000. pap. 3.99 (*1-55254-169-X*) Brighter Vision.

— Home & School Success, Grade 1. (Illus.). (J). (gr. 1). 2000. pap. 3.99 (*1-55254-170-3*) Brighter Vision.

— Home & School Success, Grade 3. (Illus.). (J). (gr. 3). 2000. pap. 3.99 (*1-55254-172-X*) Brighter Vision.

— Home & School Success, Grade 2. (Illus.). (J). (gr. 2). 2000. pap. 3.99 (*1-55254-171-1*) Brighter Vision.

— Kindergarten Skills Review. (Skills Review Workbks.). (Illus.). (J). (gr. k). 2000. pap. 3.95 (*1-55254-197-5*) Brighter Vision.

— Let's Go. (Little Books to Make & Read). (Illus.). (J). 2000. pap. 1.49 (*1-55254-067-7*) Brighter Vision.

— Look & Find Activity Book. (Illus.). (J). 2000. pap. 1.39 (*1-55254-149-5*) Brighter Vision.

— Math-a-Magic Grade 1. (Illus.). (J). 1999. pap. text 2.25 (*1-55254-110-X*) Brighter Vision.

— Math-a-Magic Grade 3. (Illus.). (J). (gr. 3). 1999. pap. 2.25 (*1-55254-112-6*) Brighter Vision.

— Math-a-Magic Grade 2. (Illus.). (J). 1999. pap. text 2.25 (*1-55254-111-8*) Brighter Vision.

— Math-a-Magic Grades 3-4. (Illus.). (J). (gr. 3-4). 1999. pap. 2.25 (*1-55254-113-4*) Brighter Vision.

— Math-a-Magic Kindergarten. (Illus.). (J). (gr. k). 2000. pap. 2.25 (*1-55254-156-8*) Brighter Vision.

— Math-a-Magic Phonics Magic. (Illus.). (J). (gr. k). 2000. pap. 2.25 (*1-55254-157-6*) Brighter Vision.

— Math-a-Magic Phonics Magic. (Illus.). (J). (gr. 3). 2000. pap. 2.25 (*1-55254-160-6*) Brighter Vision.

— Math-a-Magic Phonics Magic. (Illus.). (J). (ps-3). 2000. pap. 2.25 (*1-55254-158-4*); pap. 2.25 (*1-55254-159-2*) Brighter Vision.

— Math K: And Thinking Activities. (Primary Skills Ser.). (Illus.). (J). 1999. pap. 2.25 (*1-55254-114-2*) Brighter Vision.

— Math-1: And Thinking Activities. (Primary Skills Ser.). (Illus.). (J). 1999. pap. 2.25 (*1-55254-116-9*) Brighter Vision.

— Math-3: And Thinking Activities. (Primary Skills Ser.). (Illus.). (J). 1999. pap. 2.25 (*1-55254-120-7*) Brighter Vision.

— Math-2: And Thinking Activities. (Primary Skills Ser.). (Illus.). (J). 1999. pap. 2.25 (*1-55254-118-5*) Brighter Vision.

— Numbers - Pre-K. (Primary Skills Ser.). (Illus.). (J). (ps-3). 2000. pap. 2.25 (*1-55254-173-8*) Brighter Vision.

— Numbers & Counting Activity Book. (Illus.). (J). 2000. pap. 1.39 (*1-55254-150-9*) Brighter Vision.

— Ocean Life. (Kindergarten Learning Adventure Bks.). (J). 1999. pap. 2.25 (*1-55254-056-1*) Brighter Vision.

— Rain Forest. (Kindergarten Learning Adventure Bks.). (Illus.). (J). 1999. pap. 2.25 (*1-55254-057-X*) Brighter Vision.

— Reading Skills-K: And Language Activities. (Primary Skills Ser.). (Illus.). (J). 1999. pap. 2.25 (*1-55254-115-0*) Brighter Vision.

— Reading Skills-1: And Language Activities. (Primary Skills Ser.). (Illus.). (J). 1999. pap. 2.25 (*1-55254-117-7*) Brighter Vision.

— Reading Skills-3: And Language Activities. (Primary Skills Ser.). (Illus.). (J). 1999. pap. 2.25 (*1-55254-121-5*) Brighter Vision.

— Reading Skills-2: And Language Activities. (Primary Skills Ser.). (Illus.). (J). 1999. pap. 2.25 (*1-55254-119-3*) Brighter Vision.

— Respect. (Character Counts Ser.). 2000. pap. 2.75 (*1-55254-215-7*) Brighter Vision.

— Responsibility. (Character Counts Ser.). (Illus.). (J). 2000. pap. 2.75 (*1-55254-216-5*) Brighter Vision.

— Second Grade Skills Review. (Illus.). (J). (gr. 2). 2000. pap. 3.95 (*1-55254-199-1*) Brighter Vision.

— Space & the Planets. (Illus.). (J). 2000. pap. text 2.25 (*1-55254-146-0*) Brighter Vision.

— Summertime Crafts to Make. (Illus.). (J). 2000. pap. 3.95 (*1-55254-177-0*) Brighter Vision.

— Teaching House: A Parent's Guide to Early Learning Activities Around the House. (Learning Everywhere Ser.). (Illus.). (J). 1999. pap. 3.99 (*1-55254-139-8*) Brighter Vision.

— Teaching Town: A Parent's Guide to Early Learning Activities Around the Town. (Learning Everywhere Ser.). (Illus.). 1999. pap. 3.99 (*1-55254-140-1*) Brighter Vision.

— Teaching Trips: A Parent's Guide to Early Learning Activities on Short Trips. (Learning Everywhere Ser.). (Illus.). 1999. pap. 3.99 (*1-55254-141-X*) Brighter Vision.

— Third Grade Skills Review. (Skills Review Workbks.). (Illus.). (J). (gr. 3). 2000. pap. 3.95 (*1-55254-200-9*) Brighter Vision.

— Trustworthiness. (Character Counts Ser.). (Illus.). (J). 2000. pap. 2.75 (*1-55254-214-9*) Brighter Vision.

— Wipe Away Christmas. (Illus.). (J). 2000. pap. 2.95 (*1-55254-184-3*) Brighter Vision.

— Wipe Away Halloween-Alpha. (Illus.). (J). 2000. pap. 2.95 (*1-55254-183-5*) Brighter Vision.

— Wipe Away Halloween-Numbers. (Illus.). (J). 2000. pap. 2.95 (*1-55254-182-7*) Brighter Vision.

— Word Games & Puzzles Activity Book. (Illus.). (J). 2000. pap. 1.39 (*1-55254-152-5*) Brighter Vision.

***Brighter Vision Staff.** About Dinosaurs. (Illus.). 20p. (ps). 1999. pap. text 3.99 (*1-55254-055-3*) Brighter Vision.

— About Dinosaurs. (My Discovery Bks.). (Illus.). (J). 2000. pap. text 2.95 (*1-55254-207-6*) Brighter Vision.

— About Me. (My Discovery Bks.). (Illus.). (J). 2000. pap. text 2.95 (*1-55254-209-2*) Brighter Vision.

— About Numbers. 32p. (J). (ps). 1998. pap. text 3.99 (*1-55254-004-9*) Brighter Vision.

— About Numbers. (Illus.). (J). 2000. pap. text 2.95 (*1-55254-205-X*) Brighter Vision.

— About Nursery Rhymes. 1999. pap. text 3.99 (*1-55254-054-5*) Brighter Vision.

— About the Farm. (My Discovery Bks.). 32p. (J). (ps). 1998. pap. text 3.99 (*1-55254-001-4*) Brighter Vision.

— About the Neighborhood. (My Discovery Bks.). 32p. (J). (ps). 1998. pap. text 3.99 (*1-55254-002-2*) Brighter Vision.

— About the Zoo. (J). 1998. pap. text 7.95 (*1-55254-035-9*) Brighter Vision.

— About the Zoo. (My Discovery Bks.). 32p. (J). (ps). 1998. pap. text 3.99 (*1-55254-003-0*) Brighter Vision.

— About the Zoo. (My Discovery Bks.). (Illus.). (J). 2000. pap. text 2.95 (*1-55254-204-1*) Brighter Vision.

— Animal Families. (Learning Adventures Preschool Ser.). (J). 1998. pap. text 2.25 (*1-55254-006-5*) Brighter Vision.

— Balloons. 1999. pap. text 2.50 (*1-55254-069-3*) Brighter Vision.

— Bible Story Math 2. (J). 1998. pap. text 2.25 (*1-55254-028-6*) Brighter Vision.

— Birds. (Illus.). (gr. k-1). 1999. pap. text 2.25 (*1-55254-059-6*) Brighter Vision.

— Bugs. 1999. pap. text 2.50 (*1-55254-068-5*) Brighter Vision.

— Cars & Trains, Ships & Planes. (Learning Adventures Preschool Ser.). (J). 1998. pap. text 2.25 (*1-55254-008-1*) Brighter Vision.

— Easter Bunny Activity Book. (Illus.). (J). 2000. pap. text 1.59 (*1-55254-076-6*) Brighter Vision.

— First Grade Skills Review. (Skills Review Workbks.). (J). 1998. pap. text 5.99 (*1-55254-010-3*) Brighter Vision.

— First Grade Skills Review. 48p. (J). (gr. 1-2). 1998. pap. text 5.95 (*1-55254-048-0*) Brighter Vision.

— Fun in the City & Country. (Illus.). (J). 2000. pap. text 2.25 (*1-55254-064-2*) Brighter Vision.

— Fun with Seasons Activity Book. (Illus.). (J). 2000. pap. text 2.25 (*1-55254-065-0*) Brighter Vision.

— Kindergarten Skills Review. (Skills Review Workbks.). 96p. (J). (gr. k). 1998. pap. text 5.99 (*1-55254-009-X*) Brighter Vision.

— Mittens. 1999. pap. text 2.50 (*1-55254-070-7*) Brighter Vision.

— My Body. (Learning Adventure Preschool Bks.). 32p. (J). 1998. pap. text 2.25 (*1-55254-005-7*) Brighter Vision.

— Our Earth. (Learning Adventures Ser.). (Illus.). (J) (gr. k-1). 1999. pap. text 2.25 (*1-55254-061-8*) Brighter Vision.

— Reading Skills Grade 3. (Illus.). 32p. (J). 1998. pap. text 2.25 (*1-55254-032-4*) Brighter Vision.

— Second Grade Skills Review. (Skills Review Workbks.). (J). 1998. pap. text 5.99 (*1-55254-011-1*) Brighter Vision.

— Second Grade Skills Review. (J). (gr. 2-3). 1998. pap. text 5.95 (*1-55254-049-9*) Brighter Vision.

— Senses. (Learning Adventures Ser.). (J). (gr. k). 1999. pap. text 2.25 (*1-55254-060-X*) Brighter Vision.

— Springtime Activity Book. (Illus.). (J). 2000. pap. text 1.59 (*1-55254-077-4*) Brighter Vision.

— Things That Grow. (Learning Adventures Preschool Ser.). (J). 1998. pap. text 2.25 (*1-55254-007-3*) Brighter Vision.

— Third Grade Skills Review. (Skills Review Workbks.). (J). 1998. pap. text 5.99 (*1-55254-012-X*) Brighter Vision.

— Third Grade Skills Review. 48p. (J). (gr. 3-4). 1998. pap. text 5.95 (*1-55254-050-2*) Brighter Vision.

— Weather: A Skill-builder Workbook. 1999. pap. text 2.25 (*1-55254-058-8*) Brighter Vision.

— Zoo. (Illus.). (J). 2000. pap. text 2.25 (*1-55254-063-4*) Brighter Vision.

***Brighter Vision Staff, ed.** Pets. (Little Books to Make & Read). (Illus.). 2000. pap. 1.49 (*1-55254-066-9*) Brighter Vision.

Brightfield, Myron F. Issue in Literary Criticism. LC 68-23278. 1968. reprint ed. lib. bdg. 75.00 (*0-8371-0029-1*, BRLC, Greenwood Pr) Greenwood.

— Theodore Hook & His Novels. (BCL1-PR English Literature Ser.). 381p. 1992. reprint ed. lib. bdg. 89.00 (*0-7812-7564-4*) Rprt Serv.

***Brightfield, R.** Mystic Knights: Water Around, Earth Below!, No. 3. (Mystic Knights Ser.: No. 3). 96p. (J). (gr. 1-5). 1999. mass mkt. 3.99 (*0-06-107162-5*) HarpC.

Brightfield, Richard. African Safari. (Young Indiana Jones Chronicles Choose Your Own Adventure Ser.: No 5). (YA). (gr. 5-8). 1993. 8.35 (*0-606-03004-2*, Pub. by Turtleback) Demco.

— Island of Doom. (Choose Your Own Nightmare Ser.: No. 3). (J). (gr. 4-8). 1995. 8.60 (*0-606-07367-1*, Pub. by Turtleback) Demco.

— Master of Judo. (Choose Your Own Adventure Ser.: No. 148). (J). (gr. 4-8). 1994. 8.60 (*0-606-06560-1*, Pub. by Turtleback) Demco.

— Master of Tae Kwon Do. (Choose Your Own Adventure Ser.: No. 102). (J). (gr. 4-8). 1990. 8.60 (*0-606-04553-8*, Pub. by Turtleback) Demco.

— Something's in the Woods. (Choose Your Own Nightmare Ser.: No. 12). (J). (gr. 4-8). 1996. pap. 4.75 (*0-553-54278-8*) BDD Bks Young Read.

— Your Maze Adventure, No. 6. 1986. 1.95 (*0-8125-6046-9*, Pub. by Tor Bks) St Martin.

Brightling. Multiple Choice Questions Vet. (C). 1996. pap. text 35.00 (*0-7020-2084-2*) Harcourt.

— Stock Diseases. 328p. 1997. 135.00 (*0-409-30476-X*) Buttrwrth-Heinemann.

Brightling, George B. History of Carshalton. 128p. 1989. 35.00 (*0-9503224-6-6*, Pub. by Sutton Libs & Arts) St Mut.

Brightman. Data Analysis for Busy Managers. LC 98-28206. 1998. pap. 43.95 (*0-534-52650-0*) Brooks-Cole.

Brightman & Schneider. Statistics for Business Problem Solving. 2nd ed. 1994. 68.00 incl. 3.5 hd (*0-538-83141-3*) Brooks-Cole.

— Statistics for Business Problem Solving. 2nd ed. 1996. teacher ed. 36.75 (*0-538-83139-1*) Brooks-Cole.

Brightman, Becky, jt. auth. see Radd, Tommie R.

Brightman, Carol. Sweet Chaos: The Grateful Dead's American Adventure. LC 98-11826. 356p. 1998. 27.50 (*0-517-59448-X*) C Potter.

— Sweet Chaos: The Grateful Dead's American Adventure. 368p. 1999. per. 15.00 (*0-671-01117-0*, PB Trade Paper) PB.

— Writing Dangerously: Mary McCarthy & Her World. LC 94-60359. (Illus.). 736p. 1994. pap. 18.95 (*0-15-600067-9*) Harcourt.

Brightman, Edgar S. Personality & Religion. LC 75-3084. (Philosophy in America Ser.). reprint ed. 37.50 (*0-404-59083-7*) AMS Pr.

— Philosophy of Religion. LC 72-95112. 556p. 1969. reprint ed. lib. bdg. 85.00 (*0-8371-2468-9*, BRPR, Greenwood Pr) Greenwood.

— The Problem of God. LC 75-3085. (Philosophy in America Ser.). reprint ed. 37.50 (*0-404-59084-5*) AMS Pr.

— The Spiritual Life. LC 75-3086. (Philosophy in America Ser.). reprint ed. 37.50 (*0-404-59085-3*) AMS Pr.

Brightman, Edgar S., ed. Personalism in Theology. LC 75-3088. (Philosophy in America Ser.). reprint ed. 37.50 (*0-404-59086-1*) AMS Pr.

Brightman, F. E., tr. & intro. see Andrewes, Lancelot.

Brightman, Frank H., jt. ed. see Best, Michael R.

Brightman, Harvey J. Statistics in Plain English. (C). 1985. pap. 19.75 (*0-538-13210-8*, M21) S-W Pub.

Brightman, Robert. Grateful Prey: Rock Cree Human-Animal Relationships. 412p. (C). 1993. 50.00 (*0-520-07053-4*, Pub. by U CA Pr) Cal Prin Full Svc.

Brightman, Robert, jt. auth. see Brown, Jennifer S.

Brightman, Schneider. Statistics for Business: Problem Solving. 2nd ed. (C). 1994. 4100.00 (*0-538-83133-2*) Thomson Learn.

Brighton, Andrew. Introducing Picasso. (Illus.). 176p. 1996. pap. 9.95 (*1-874166-29-3*, Pub. by Totem Bks) Natl Bk Netwk.

Brighton, C. T. & Pollack, S. R., eds. Electromagnetics in Medicine & Biology. (Illus.). 1991. 37.50 (*0-911302-65-4*) San Francisco Pr.

Brighton, Carl T., et al, eds. Bone Formation & Repair. (Illus.). 542p. 1994. 105.00 (*0-89203-116-6*) Amer Acad Ortho Surg.

Brighton, Carl T., jt. auth. see Amstutz, Harlan C.

***Brighton, Catherine.** The Bronte's: Scenes from the Childhood of Charlotte, Branwell, Emily & Anne. (Illus.). (J). (gr. 1-5). 1999. pap. text 7.99 (*0-7112-0882-4*) F Lincoln.

Brighton, Catherine. The Fossil Girl: Mary Anning's Dinosaur Discovery. LC 98-36180. 32p. (J). (gr. k-3). 1999. lib. bdg. 21.40 (*0-7613-1468-7*, Copper Beech Bks) Millbrook Pr.

— My Napoleon. LC 96-7663. (Illus.). 32p. (J). (gr. k-4). 1997. 16.95 (*0-7613-0106-2*) Millbrook Pr.

Brighton Genealogical Society Staff. History of Brighton Colorado. (Illus.). 698p. 1987. 50.00 (*0-88107-086-6*) Curtis Media.

Brighton, John B., ed. see Wise, Murray R.

***Brighton, Louis A.** Revelation. LC 99-43448. (Commentary Ser.). 1999. write for info. (*0-570-06312-4*) Concordia.

Brighton, Ray. The Checkered Career of Tobias Lear. LC 84-18105. (Portsmouth Marine Society Ser.: No. 4). (Illus.). 320p. 1984. 20.00 (*0-915819-03-1*) Portsmouth Marine Soc.

— Clipper Ships from the Port of Portsmouth & the Men Who Built Them. LC 84-18128. (Portsmouth Marine Society Ser.: No. 5). (Illus.). 175p. 1985. 25.00 (*0-915819-05-8*) Portsmouth Marine Soc.

— Port of Portsmouth Ships & the Cotton Trade, 1783-1829. (Portsmouth Marine Society Ser.: No. 10). (Illus.). 236p. 1985. 24.95 (*0-915819-09-0*) Portsmouth Marine Soc.

— Rambles about Portsmouth. LC 93-7851. (Portsmouth Marine Society Ser.: No. 20). (Illus.). 288p. 1993. 25.00 (*0-915819-18-X*) Portsmouth Marine Soc.

— Tall Ships of the Piscataqua, 1830-1877. (Portsmouth Marine Society Ser.: Vol. 15). (Illus.). 410p. 1989. 25.00 (*0-915819-14-7*, 15) Portsmouth Marine Soc.

Brighton, Raymond A. They Came to Fish. (Illus.). 912p. 1994. reprint ed. 35.00 (*0-914339-48-6*) P E Randall Pub.

***Brighton, Terry.** The Last Charge: The 21st Lancers & the Battle of Omdurman. (Illus.). 128p. 2000. 62.00 (1-86126-189-6, 129761AE, Pub. by Crolwood) Motorbooks Intl.

Brightwell, D. B. Concordance to Tennyson. LC 72-124396. (Studies in Tennyson: No. 27). 1970. reprint ed. lib. bdg. 75.00 (0-8383-1099-0) M S G Haskell Hse.

***Brightwell, Emily.** Ghost & Mrs. Jeffries. large type ed. LC 99-12938. 285p. 1999. pap. text 23.95 (0-7838-8602-0, G K Hall & Co) Mac Lib Ref.

Brightwell, Emily. The Inspector & Mrs. Jeffries. 192p. 1993. mass mkt. 5.99 (0-425-13622-1) Berkley Pub.

— The Inspector & Mrs. Jeffries. large type ed. LC 98-45066. 1999. 30.00 (0-7838-0417-2) Mac Lib Ref.

***Brightwell, Emily.** Mrs. Jeffries Dusts for Clues. LC 99-35727. (Orig.). 1999. pap. 23.95 (0-7838-8721-3, G K Hall Lrg Type) Mac Lib Ref.

Brightwell, Emily. Mrs. Jeffries on the Ball. large type ed. LC 95-2472. (Nightingale Ser.). 282p. 1995. reprint ed. pap. 18.95 (0-7838-1284-1, G K Hall Lrg Type) Mac Lib Ref.

— Mrs. Jeffries on the Ball: A Victorian Mystery. 208p. (Orig.). 1994. mass mkt. 5.99 (0-425-14491-7, Prime Crime) Berkley Pub.

— Mrs. Jeffries on the Trail. 240p. (Orig.). 1995. mass mkt. 5.50 (0-425-14691-X, Prime Crime) Berkley Pub.

— Mrs. Jeffries Plays the Cook. 1995. mass mkt. 5.50 (0-425-15053-4) Berkley Pub.

— Mrs. Jeffries Questions the Answer. 240p. 1997. mass mkt. 5.99 (0-425-16093-9, Prime Crime) Berkley Pub.

— Mrs. Jeffries Reveals Her Art. 1998. mass mkt. 5.99 (0-425-16243-5, Prime Crime) Berkley Pub.

***Brightwell, Emily.** Mrs. Jeffries Reveals Her Art. large type ed. LC 00-39598. 264p. 2000. 23.95 (0-7838-9104-0, G K Hall & Co) Mac Lib Ref.

Brightwell, Emily. Mrs. Jeffries Rocks the Boat, 1 vol., Vol. 12. 198p. 1999. mass mkt. 5.99 (0-425-16934-0) Berkley Pub.

— Mrs. Jeffries Stands Corrected. 224p. (Orig.). 1996. mass mkt. 5.99 (0-425-15580-3, Prime Crime) Berkley Pub.

— Mrs. Jeffries Take the Stage. 1997. mass mkt. 5.99 (0-425-15724-5, Prime Crime) Berkley Pub.

— Mrs. Jeffries Takes Stock. 208p. (Orig.). 1994. pap. 4.99 (0-425-14282-5, Prime Crime) Berkley Pub.

— Mrs. Jeffries Takes the Cake. 240p. 1998. pap. 5.99 (0-425-16569-8, Prime Crime) Berkley Pub.

***Brightwell, Emily.** Mrs. Jeffries Takes the Cake. large type ed. LC 99-45562. (G. K. Hall Paperback Ser.). 1999. pap. 23.95 (0-7838-8798-1, G K Hall Lrg Type) Mac Lib Ref.

— Mrs. Jeffries Takes the Stage. large type ed. LC 00-27602. (Paperback Ser.). 290p. 2000. pap. 23.95 (0-7838-9035-4, G K Hall & Co) Mac Lib Ref.

Brighurst, Newell G., ed. Reconsidering "No Man Knows My History" Fawn M. Brodie & Joseph Smith in Retrospect. 192p. 1996. pap. 17.95 (0-87421-214-6) Utah St U Pr.

— Reconsidering "No Man Knows My History" Fawn M. Brodie & Joseph Smith Jr. in Retrospect. 192p. 1996. 34.95 (0-87421-205-7) Utah St U Pr.

Brigidi, Stephen. Remarkable People: A Rhode Island Family Album. 230p. (Orig.). 1996. pap. write for info. (0-9629642-0-4) Bristol Wkshps.

Briginshaw, Valerie, et al. Dance Analysis: Theory & Practice. Adshead, Janet, ed. 200p. 1995. pap. 24.95 (1-85273-003-X, Dance Horizons) Princeton Bk Co.

Brigman. Close Relationships: Developong Skills & Making Choices. 32p. (C). 1998. write for info. (0-02-314510-2, Macmillan Coll) P-H.

Brignac, Margie. Southern Spice a la Microwave. LC 81-19241. (Illus.). 240p. (Orig.). 1982. spiral bd. 13.95 (0-88289-318-1) Pelican.

Brignano, Mary. The Frick Art & Historical Center: The Art & Life of a Pittsburgh Family. (Illus.). 48p. (Orig.). 1993. pap. 19.95 (1-881403-01-7) Frick Art Mus.

Brignano, Russell. Black Americans in Autobiography: An Annotated Bibliography of Autobiographies & Autobiographical Books Written since the Civil War. LC 73-92535. 126p. reprint ed. pap. 39.10 (0-8357-7282-9, 202337300033) Bks Demand.

Brignano, Russell C. Richard Wright: An Introduction to the Man & His Works. LC 72-81667. (Critical Essays in Modern Literature Ser.). 217p. 1970. reprint ed. pap. 67.30 (0-608-00900-8, 206169400010) Bks Demand.

Brignell, John & White, Neil. Intelligent Sensor Systems. rev. ed. LC 96-20100. (Sensors Ser.). 280p. 1996. pap. 66.00 (0-7503-0389-1) IOP Pub.

Brignoli, Christine J. & Brignoli, Frank J. Lhasa, Tibet's Forbidden City. LC 89-108700. (Illus.). 107p. 1987. 25.00 (0-9622122-0-2) Creative Focus.

Brignoli, Frank J., jt. auth. see Brignoli, Christine J.

Brigstocke, Hugh. William Buchanan & the Nineteenth Century Art Trade: 100 Letters to His Agents in London & Italy. 525p. 1982. 25.00 (0-685-38945-6) Yale Ctr Brit Art.

Brigstocke, Hugh & Somerville, John. Italian Paintings from Burghley House. LC 94-36386. 1995. pap. 29.95 (0-88397-114-3) Art Srvc Intl.

Briguglio, Lino, et al, eds. Sustainable Tourism in Islands & Small States: Case Studies, Vol. 2. (Island Studies). (Illus.). 352p. 1996. 90.00 (1-85567-371-1) Bks Intl VA.

— Sustainable Tourism in Islands & Small States: Issues & Policies, Vol. 1. (Island Studies). (Illus.). 256p. 1996. 90.00 (1-85567-370-3) Bks Intl VA.

Brihaye, J., et al, eds. Pain. (Acta Neurochirugica - Supplementum Ser.: No. 38). (Illus.). 200p. 1987. 180.00 (0-387-81990-8) Spr-Verlag.

Brihaye, J., jt. ed. see Samii, Madjid.

Brijabasi. Khajuraho. 1993. 14.95 (0-945475-03-9); 14.95 (0-9564750-3-5) Mandala Pub Grp.

Brijbhushan, J. Muslim Women: In Purdah & Out of It. 133p. 1980. 14.95 (0-318-37060-3) Asia Bk Corp.

Brijbhushan, Jamila. Masterpieces of Indian Jewellery. (Illus.). 142p. 1979. 34.95 (0-318-36272-4) Asia Bk Corp.

Bril, Vera & Said, Gerard, eds. Emerging Opportunities in Peripheral Neuropathy Vol. I, 1999: ENS Satellite Symposium, Nice, June 1998. (European Neurology Ser.: Vol. 41). (Illus.). iv, 44p. 1999. pap. 25.25 (3-8055-6843-6) S Karger.

Briles, Judith. The Confidence Factor: How Self-Esteem Can Change Your Life. 1990. 18.95 (0-942361-15-6) MasterMedia Pub.

***Briles, Judith.** Smart-Money Moves for Kids: The Parent's Complete Guide. Maling, John E., ed. LC 99-75221. (Smart-Money Moves Ser.: Vol. 1). (Illus.). 300p. 2000. pap. 19.95 (1-885331-03-7) Briles Grp.

Briles, Judith. 10 Smart Money Moves for Women. LC 99-17807. 256p. 1999. pap. 14.95 (0-8092-2783-5, 278350, Contemporary Bks) NTC Contemp Pub Co.

— When God Says No: Finding the "Yes" in Pain & Disappointment. 160p. 1994. pap. text, per. 16.95 (0-8403-9820-4) Kendall-Hunt.

— Woman to Woman 2000: Becoming Sabotage Savvy in the New Millennium. 216p. 1999. 26.95 (0-88282-171-7, Pub. by New Horizon NJ) Natl Bk Netwk.

Briles, Judith, et al. The Dollars & Sense of Divorce. LC 98-7416. 256p. 1998. pap. text 17.95 (0-7931-2763-7) Dearborn.

Briley, Alice, ed. Encore, Encore. LC 75-30253. (Poetry Ser.: No. 5). (Illus.). 1976. 8.00 (0-910042-25-X); pap. 3.00 (0-910042-26-8) Allegheny.

— Second Encore II. (Illus.). 128p. 1985. pap. 6.95 (0-910042-54-3) Allegheny.

Briley, Ann. Lonely Pedestrian: Francis Marion Streamer. 174p. 1986. 18.95 (0-87770-534-8) Ye Galleon.

Briley, B. E. An Introduction to Fiber Optics System Design. 332p. 1990. reprint ed. pap. 88.00 (0-444-88708-3) Elsevier.

Briley, Dorothy, ed. see Wiesner, David.

Briley, J. M., Jr. Pediatric Ward. LC 82-39991. 1986. pap. 13.95 (0-87949-229-5) Ashley Bks.

Briley, M. New Concepts in Anxiety. File, S. E., ed. 1991. 107.00 (0-8493-7105-8, QP) CRC Pr.

***Briley, M. & Nutt, David J.** Anxiolytics. LC 00-33748. (Milestones in Drug Therapy Ser.). 2000. write for info. (3-7643-6032-1) Birkhauser.

***Briley, Mike.** Antidepressant Therapy. 368p. 1998. write for info. (1-85317-517-X) Martin Dunitz.

Briley, Rebecca L. You Can Go Home Again: The Focus on Family in the Works of Horton Foote. LC 92-45641. (American University Studies: American Literature: Ser. XXIV, Vol. 45). (Illus.). 214p. (C). 1993. text 43.95 (0-8204-2004-2) P Lang Pubng.

Briley, Richard, 3rd. Nightriders: Inside Story of the West & Kimbrell Clan. 102p. 1992. reprint ed. pap. 10.00 (0-9646846-3-2) Dogwood TX.

Briley, Richard G. Everything I Needed to Know about Success, I Learned in the Bible (& So Can You!) 144p. (Orig.). 1993. pap. 14.95 (1-882988-05-1) Pub-in-the-Glen.

— Pray & Grow Rich: Seven Overlooked Secrets from the Bible That Control Your Wealth, Success & Happiness. 145p. 1998. pap. 12.99 (1-882988-07-8) Pub-in-the-Glen.

Briley, Rita, jt. illus. see Stodghill, Pat.

***Briley, Terry R.** Isaiah. LC 99-59033. 2000. write for info. (0-89900-890-9) College Pr Pub.

Brilhart, John K. & Galanes, Gloria J. Effective Group Discussion. 9th ed. LC 97-12935. 400p. (C). 1997. text. write for info. (0-697-32726-4, WCB McGr Hill) McGrw-H Hghr Educ.

Brilhart, John K. & Gillanes, Gloria J. Effective Group Discussion. 8th ed. LC 93-74332. 400p. (C). 1994. text. write for info. (0-697-20129-5) Brown & Benchmark.

Brilhart, John K., jt. auth. see Galanes, Gloria J.

Brill, jt. auth. see Herschfelt.

Brill, A. A. Basic Principles of Psychoanalysis. LC 85-7407. 316p. 1985. reprint ed. pap. text 22.00 (0-8191-4665-X) U Pr of Amer.

— Fundamental Conceptions of Psychoanalysis. LC 73-2390. (Mental Illness & Social Policy; the American Experience Ser.). 1973. reprint ed. 24.95 (0-405-05198-0) Ayer.

— Psychoanalysis, Its Theories & Practical Application. LC 78-180559. (Medicine & Society in America Ser.). 346p. 1972. reprint ed. 23.95 (0-405-03939-5) Ayer.

Brill, A. A., tr. see Freud, Sigmund.

Brill, A. Bertrand. Low Level Radiation Effects: A Fact Book. 2nd ed. Adelstein, James et al, eds. LC 82-16939. 153p. 1982. ring bd. 20.00 (0-932004-14-8) Soc Nuclear Med.

***Brill, Alan E., et al.** Cybercrime & Security, 3 vols. LC 98-14524. 1998. ring bd. 295.00 (0-379-01281-2) Oceana.

Brill, Alida. Nobody's Business. 1991. pap. 9.57 (0-201-56754-7) Addison-Wesley.

— Nobody's Business: The Paradoxes of Privacy. 1990. 17.26 (0-201-06745-5) Addison-Wesley.

Brill, Alida, ed. A Rising Public Voice: Women in Politics Worldwide. LC 95-13894. (Illus.). 294p. 1995. 35.00 (1-55861-110-X); pap. 17.95 (1-55861-111-8) Feminist Pr.

Brill, Alida, jt. auth. see McClosky, Herbert.

Brill, Amy, ed. The Digital Directory: Art & Technology Resources in New York State. 179p. 1999. pap. 15.00 (0-9669869-0-3) NY Found Art.

Brill, Betsy, jt. see Kobre, Kenneth.

Brill, Bill. Back to Back. 1992. pap. 21.95 (0-8223-1318-9) Duke.

Brill, Charles. Indian & Free: A Contemporary Portrait of Life on a Chippewa Reservation. LC 73-91450. (Illus.). 144p. reprint ed. pap. 44.70 (0-8357-8918-7, 203320700085) Bks Demand.

— Red Lake Nation: Portraits of Ojibwe Life. 2nd rev. ed. (Illus.). 192p. (C). 1992. reprint ed. 27.95 (0-8166-1906-9) U of Minn Pr.

Brill, David. As Far As the Eye Can See: Reflections of an Appalachian Trail Hiker. LC 90-45387. 187p. 1996. pap. text 9.95 (1-55853-401-6) Rutledge Hill Pr.

— Brilliant Origami: A Collection of Original Designs by David Brill. 232p. (Orig.). 17.00 (1-56836-896-8) FS&G.

— Brilliant Origami: A Collection of Original Designs by David Brill. (Illus.). 232p. (Orig.). 1996. pap. 20.00 (0-87040-896-8) Japan Pubns USA.

***Brill, David.** A Separate Place: A Family, a Cabin in the Woods & a Journey of Love & Spirit. LC 00-23993. 240p. 2000. 23.95 (0-525-94497-4) NAL.

***Brill de Ramirez, Susan Berry.** Contemporary American Indian Literatures & the Oral Tradition. LC 98-40233. 272p. 1999. pap. 19.95 (0-8165-1957-9) U of Ariz Pr.

Brill, Earl H. The Christian Moral Vision. (Church's Teaching Ser.: Vol. 6). 254p. 1984. 5.95 (0-8164-0423-2) Harper SF.

Brill, Edith. Ehrfurcht und Zweifel: Das Theodizeeproblem Im Denken und Dichten P. B. Shelleys. (Europaische Hochschulschriften Ser.: Reihe 23, Bd. 470). (GER.). VIII, 187p. 1992. 44.80 (3-631-45394-9) P Lang Pubng.

Brill, Ernie. I Looked over Jordan & Other Stories. LC 80-51042. 294p. 1980. 25.00 (0-89608-118-4); pap. 6.00 (0-89608-117-6) South End Pr.

Brill, Ethel C. Copper Country Adventure. LC 87-31485. 213p. (J). (gr. 4 up). 1988. 26.00 (0-933249-05-5) Mid-Peninsula Lib.

— Madeleine Takes Command. LC 96-83472. (Living History Library). (Illus.). 208p. (YA). (gr. 6 up). 1996. reprint ed. pap. 11.95 (1-883937-17-5, 17-5) Bethlehem ND.

Brill, Gerhard W. The New Creole: Gulf Coast to Pacific Rim. Barnette, David C. & Barnette, Ashley S., eds. 182p. (Orig.). 1998. pap. 12.95 (1-888769-50-5) Pub One Hund One.

Brill, Hal, et al. Investing with Your Values: Making Money & Making a Difference. LC 99-17947. (Bloomberg Personal Bookshelf Ser.). 363p. 1999. 23.95 (1-57660-026-2, Pub. by Bloomberg NJ) Norton.

***Brill, Hal, et al.** Investing with Your Values: Making Money & Making a Difference. 400p. 2000. pap. 18.95 (0-86571-422-3, Pub. by New Soc Pubs) Consort Bk Sales.

Brill, Henry, jt. auth. see Mule, S. J.

Brill, James E. Texas Probate System. 2nd rev. ed. LC 93-84172. 852p. 1993. ring bd. 160.00 (0-938160-76-1, 6224) State Bar TX.

Brill, James E., ed. see State Bar of Texas Probate System Committee.

Brill Koln, E. J. Alo Raun Bibliography. (Arcadia Bibliographica Virorum Eruditorum Ser.: Fasc. 2). 29p. 1980. 18.00 (0-931922-02-X) Eurolingua.

— Erich Kunze Bibliographie: Mit Unterstutzung der Friedrich-Ebert-Stiftung. (Arcadia Bibliographica Virorum Eruditorum Ser.: Fasc. 3). (GER.). 33p. 1980. 11.00 (0-931922-07-0) Eurolingua.

— Felix Johannes Oinas Bibliography. (Arcadia Bibliographica Virorum Eruditorum Ser.: Fasc. 4). 51p. 1981. 18.00 (0-931922-03-8) Eurolingua.

Brill, Laura. Sales Letters That Sell. LC 97-2279. 208p. (Orig.). 1997. pap. 17.95 (0-8144-7945-6) AMACOM.

Brill, Leon & Harms, Ernest, eds. The Yearbook of Drug Abuse, Vol. I. LC 70-174271. (Illus.). 386p. 1973. 52.00 (0-87705-060-0, Kluwer Acad Hman Sci) Kluwer Academic.

Brill, Leon & Winick, Charles. The Yearbook of Substance Use & Abuse, Vol. II. LC 70-174271. 360p. 1980. 52.00 (0-87705-487-8, Kluwer Acad Hman Sci) Kluwer Academic.

Brill, Leon & Winick, Charles, eds. The Yearbook of Substance Use & Abuse, Vol. III. 351p. 1985. 52.00 (0-89885-216-1, Kluwer Acad Hman Sci) Kluwer Academic.

Brill, Leon, jt. ed. see Chambers, Carl D.

Brill, Lesley. John Huston's Filmmaking. (Studies in Film). (Illus.). 283p. (C). 1997. text 59.95 (0-521-58359-4); pap. text 18.95 (0-521-58670-4) Cambridge U Pr.

Brill, Lynda D. & Luster, J. Scott. The Net Result: A Working Guide to Recruiting for Student-Athletes. 119p. (Orig.). (YA). (gr. 7-12). 1996. pap. 13.95 (0-9653051-0-4) Classic Kaleidoscope.

Brill, Marlene T. Allen Jay & the Underground Railroad. LC 92-25279. (Illus.). (J). (gr. k-3). 1993. lib. bdg. 18.60 (0-87614-776-7, Carolrhoda) Lerner Pub.

— Allen Jay & the Underground Railroad. LC 92-25279. (Illus.). 32p. (J). (ps-3). 1993. pap. 5.95 (0-87614-605-1, Carolrhoda) Lerner Pub.

— Building the Capital City. LC 95-40518. (Cornerstones to Freedom Ser.). (Illus.). 32p. (J). (gr. 4-7). 1996. lib. bdg. 19.50 (0-516-06633-1) Childrens.

— Building the Capital City. (J). 1996. pap. 5.95 (0-516-20066-6) Childrens.

— Extraordinary Young People. (Extraordinary People Ser.). (Illus.). 208p. (J). (gr. 6 up). 1996. lib. bdg. 37.00 (0-516-00587-1) Childrens.

— Extraordinary Young People. (YA). (gr. 6 up). 1996. pap. 16.95 (0-516-26044-8) Childrens.

— James Buchanan. LC 88-10884. (Encyclopedia of Presidents Ser.). (Illus.). 100p. (J). (gr. 3 up). 1988. lib. bdg. 24.00 (0-516-01358-0) Childrens.

— John Adams. (Encyclopedia of Presidents Ser.). (Illus.). 100p. (J). (gr. 3 up). 1986. lib. bdg. 24.00 (0-516-01384-X) Childrens.

— Keys to Parenting a Child with Down Syndrome. (Parenting Keys Ser.). 208p. 1993. pap. 5.95 (0-8120-1458-8) Barron.

— Keys to Parenting the Child with Autism. (Parenting Keys Ser.). 208p. 1994. pap. 6.95 (0-8120-1679-3) Barron.

— Let Women Vote! (Spotlight on American History Ser.). (Illus.). 64p. (J). (gr. 4-6). 1995. lib. bdg. 21.90 (1-56294-589-0) Millbrook Pr.

— Tooth Tales: From Around the World. LC 97-14275. (Illus.). 32p. (J). (ps-3). 1998. 15.95 (0-88106-398-3) Charlesbridge Pub.

— Tooth Tales: From Around the World. LC 97-14275. (Illus.). 32p. (J). (ps-4). 1998. pap. 6.95 (0-88106-399-1) Charlesbridge Pub.

***Brill, Marlene T.** Tooth Tales from Around the World. (J). 1998. 12.15 (0-606-13856-0, Pub. by Turtleback) Demco.

Brill, Marlene T. The Trail of Tears: The Cherokee Journey from Home. LC 94-16988. (Spotlight on American History Ser.). (Illus.). 64p. (J). (gr. 4-6). 1995. lib. bdg. 21.90 (1-56294-486-X) Millbrook Pr.

— Women for Peace. LC 96-28945. (Women Then - Women Now Ser.). 1997. lib. bdg. 24.00 (0-531-11328-0) Watts.

Brill, Marlene T., et al. Infertility & You. (Illus.). 40p. 1991. pap. 3.60 (0-317-59856-2) Budlong.

Brill, Marlene Targ. Diary of a Drummer Boy. LC 97-22022. (Illus.). 48p. (J). (gr. 4-6). 1998. lib. bdg. 21.90 (0-7613-0118-6) Millbrook Pr.

***Brill, Marlene Targ.** Diary of a Drummer Boy. (I Know America Ser.). 48p. (J). (gr. 4-6). 2000. pap. 8.95 (0-7613-1388-5) Millbrook Pr.

— Keys to Parenting the Child with Autism. 2nd ed. LC 00-39821. (Parenting Keys Ser.). 2001. write for info. (0-7641-1292-9) Barron.

— Winning Women in Basketball. LC 99-88679. (Sport Success Ser.). (Illus.). 112p. (J). (gr. 5). 2000. pap. write for info. (0-7641-1232-5) Barron.

— Winning Women in Ice Hockey. LC 99-24682. (Sport Success Ser.). 90p. 1999. pap. text 6.95 (0-7641-1115-9) Barron.

Brill, Marlene Targ. Winning Women in Soccer. LC 99-41583. 90p. 1999. pap. text 6.95 (0-7641-1116-7) Barron.

***Brill, Marlene Targ & Friar, Joanne H.** Margaret Knight. LC 99-45145. (J). 2000. lib. bdg. write for info. (0-7613-1756-2) Millbrook Pr.

Brill, Michael. No One Will Marry a Princess with a Tree Growing Out of Her Head: A Musical. 67p. 1996. pap. 6.50 (0-87602-348-0) Anchorage.

Brill, Michael E. Bamboozled. (J). (gr. 6 up). 1985. pap. 6.00 (0-87602-240-9) Anchorage.

— The Masque of Beauty & the Beast. (J). 1979. 6.00 (0-87602-156-9) Anchorage.

Brill, Naomi, compiled by. Working with People: The Helping Process. 5th ed. LC 94-44036. 1995. write for info. (0-614-03331-4) Longman.

Brill, Naomi I. Working with People. 4th rev. ed. 321p. (C). 1990. pap. text 34.66 (0-8013-0282-X, 75932) Longman.

— Working with People: The Helping Process. 6th ed. LC 97-16304. 252p. (C). 1997. pap. text 48.00 (0-8013-1799-1) Allyn.

Brill, Norman Q. Being Black in America Today: A Multiperspective Review of the Problem. LC 98-37451. (American Series in Behavioral Science & Law). 194p. 1999. text 43.95 (0-398-06917-4); pap. text 30.95 (0-398-06918-2) C C Thomas.

***Brill, Norman Q.** Cultural Roots of the Education Problem. 2000. pap. 14.95 (0-533-13544-3) Vantage.

Brill, Patricia, ed. see Center for Innovation in Education Staff.

Brill, Patricia, ed. see Childs, Leigh & Choate, Laura.

Brill, Ralph L. & American Bar Association Staff. Sourcebook on Legal Writing Programs. LC 98-164871. xi, 174 p. 1997. write for info. (1-57073-530-1) Amer Bar Assn.

Brill, Richard G. The Conference of Educational Administrators Serving the Deaf: A History. LC 86-9868. 189p. reprint ed. pap. 58.60 (0-7837-1851-9, 204205100001) Bks Demand.

— International Congresses on Education of the Deaf: An Analytical History, 1878-1980. LC 83-16578. 479p. reprint ed. pap. 148.50 (0-7837-1854-3, 204205400001) Bks Demand.

Brill, Robert H. Chemical Analyses of Early Glasses Vol. 1: The Catalogues, Set. LC 98-73595. 553p. 1998. 116.00 (0-87290-142-4) Corning.

— Chemical Analyses of Early Glasses Vol. 2: The Tables, Set. LC 98-73595. 335p. 1998. 116.00 (0-87290-143-2) Corning.

***Brill, Ronald R.** Emotional Honesty & Self-Acceptance: Education Strategies for Preventing Violence. LC 00-190859. 319p. 2000. 25.00 (0-7388-1806-2); pap. 18.00 (0-7388-1807-0) Xlibris Corp.

Brill, Sharon, jt. auth. see Herschfelt, Diane.

Brill, Steve & Dean, Evelyn. Identifying & Harvesting Edible & Medicinal Plants in Wild (& Not So Wild) Places. LC 93-31796. 317p. 1994. pap. 18.95 (0-688-11425-3, Hearst) Hearst Commns.

Brill, Susan B. Wittgenstein & Critical Theory: Beyond Postmodernism & Toward Descriptive Investigations. LC 94-31577. 180p. (C). 1994. text 40.00 (0-8214-1092-X); pap. text 16.95 (0-8214-1093-8) Ohio U Pr.

Brill, T. B. Light - Its Interaction with Art & Antiquities: Its Interaction with Art & Antiquities. LC 80-16975. (Illus.). 298p. (C). 1980. text 65.00 (0-306-40416-8, Kluwer Plenum) Kluwer Academic.

Brill, Thomas B., et al, eds. Decomposition, Combustion, & Detonation Chemistry of Energetic Materials Vol. 418: Materials Research Society Symposium Proceedings. (MRS Symposium Proceedings Ser.: Vol. 418). 454p. 1996. 83.00 (1-55899-321-5) Materials Res.

An Asterisk (*) at the beginning of an entry indicates that the title is appearing for the first time.

Brill, Thomas M. & Kitchens, John G., eds. Gator Country Cooks. 5th ed. LC 75-12456. (Illus.). 1981. pap. 9.95 (*0-9606616-0-3*); pap. 5.97 (*0-685-02777-5*) Jr League Gainesville.

Brill, Toni. Date with a Dead Doctor. 1992. per. 3.99 (*0-373-26109-8*, 1-26109-8) Harlequin Bks.

— Date with a Plummeting Publisher. (WWL Mystery Ser.). 1995. per. 3.99 (*0-373-26161-6*, 1-26161-9) Harlequin Bks.

***Brillat-Savarin, Jean Anthelme.** The Physiology of Taste. Fisher, M. F. K., tr. 2000. pap. 23.00 (*1-58243-103-5*, Pub. by Counterpt DC) HarpC.

Brillat-Savarin, Jean Anthelme. The Physiology of Taste: Or, Meditations on Transcendental Gastronomy. Fisher, M. F. K., tr. from FRE. (Illus.). 376p. 1995. 55.00 (*1-887178-09-0*, Pub. by Counterpt DC) HarpC.

— The Physiology of Taste: Or, Meditations on Transcendental Gastronomy. Fisher, M. F. K., tr. & pref. by. LC TX637.B8613 1999. 464p. 1999. text 35.00 (*1-58243-008-X*, Pub. by Counterpt DC) HarpC.

— The Physiology of Taste: Or, Meditations on Transcendental Gastronomy. Drayton, Anne, tr. & intro. by. 384p. 1994. pap. 13.95 (*0-14-044614-1*, Penguin Classics) Viking Penguin.

— The Physiology of Taste: Or, Meditations on Transcendental Gastronomy. (Illus.). 350p. 1982. reprint ed. pap. 9.95 (*0-918172-11-X*) Leetes Isl.

Briller, Margaret, ed. see Thomas, John E. & Thomas, Danita.

Brillhart, Allen T. Arthroscopic Laser Surgery: Clinical Implications. LC 93-38570. (Illus.). 288p. 1994. 157.00 (*0-387-94186-X*) Spr-Verlag.

Brillhart, David. System Manager's Bible. (C). 2001. pap. text 52.00 (*0-13-443680-6*) P-H.

Brillhart, J. A. Brillhart: A Pictorial History of the Brillharts of America. (Illus.). 268p. 1991. reprint ed. pap. 42.00 (*0-8328-1894-1*); reprint ed. lib. bdg. 52.00 (*0-8328-1893-3*) Higginson Bk Co.

Brillhart, John, et al. Factorizations of BN Plus-Minus 1, B Equals 2, 3, 4, 5, 6, 7, 10, 11, 12 up to High Powers. rev. ed. LC 88-6407. (Contemporary Mathematics Ser.: No. 22). 236p. 1988. pap. 40.00 (*0-8218-5078-4*, CONM/22) Am Math.

Brillhart, Julie. When Daddy Came to School. LC 94-25981. (Illus.). 24p. (J). (ps-k). 1995. lib. bdg. 13.95 (*0-8075-8878-4*) A Whitman.

— When Daddy Took Us Camping. LC 96-27302. (Illus.). 24p. (J). (ps-1). 1997. lib. bdg. 13.95 (*0-8075-8879-2*) A Whitman.

Brilliant, Alan, tr. see Garcia Lorca, Federico.

Brilliant, Ashleigh. All I Want Is a Warm Bed & a Kind Word & Unlimited Power. LC 85-17973. (Brilliant Thoughts Ser.: No. 5). (Illus.). 168p. 1985. 17.95 (*0-88007-155-9*); pap. 9.95 (*0-88007-156-7*) Woodbridge Pr.

— Appreciate Me Now & Avoid the Rush. LC 81-11582. (Brilliant Thoughts Ser.: No. 3). (Illus.). 160p. 1981. 17.95 (*0-912800-97-6*); pap. 9.95 (*0-912800-94-1*) Woodbridge Pr.

— Be a Good Neighbor & Leave Me Alone: Wry & Riotous Writings. LC 91-26655. (Illus.). 224p. 1992. 24.95 (*0-88007-191-5*); pap. 12.95 (*0-88007-192-3*) Woodbridge Pr.

— The Great Car Craze: How Southern California Collided with the Automobile in the 1920's. LC 89-5453. (Illus.). 240p. 1989. 19.95 (*0-88007-172-9*) Woodbridge Pr.

— I Feel Much Better, Now That I've Given up Hope. LC 84-2284. (Brilliant Thoughts Ser.: No. 4). (Illus.). 168p. (Orig.). 1984. 17.95 (*0-88007-145-1*); pap. 9.95 (*0-88007-147-8*) Woodbridge Pr.

— I Have Abandoned My Search for Truth, & Am Now Looking for a Good Fantasy. LC 80-22852. (Brilliant Thoughts Ser.: No. 2). (Illus.). 160p. (Orig.). 1981. 17.95 (*0-912800-89-5*); pap. 9.95 (*0-912800-90-9*) Woodbridge Pr.

— I May Not Be Totally Perfect, but Parts of Me Are Excellent. LC 79-10052. (Brilliant Thoughts Ser.: No. 1). (Illus.). 160p. 1979. 17.95 (*0-912800-66-6*) Woodbridge Pr.

— I May Not Be Totally Perfect, but Parts of Me Are Excellent. LC 79-10052. (Brilliant Thoughts Ser.: No. 1). (Illus.). 160p. 1979. pap. 9.95 (*0-88007-216-4*) Woodbridge Pr.

— I Try to Take One Day at a Time, but Sometimes Several Days Attack Me at Once. LC 87-23145. (Brilliant Thoughts Ser.: No. 6). (Illus.). 168p. (Orig.). 1988. 17.95 (*0-88007-161-3*); pap. 9.95 (*0-88007-162-1*) Woodbridge Pr.

— I Want to Reach Your Mind...Where Is It Currently Located? LC 93-36992. (Brilliant Thoughts Ser.: No. 8). (Illus.). 168p. (Orig.). 1993. 17.95 (*0-88007-203-2*); pap. 9.95 (*0-88007-204-0*) Woodbridge Pr.

— I'm Just Moving Clouds Today -- Tomorrow I'll Try Mountains: And Other More or Less Blissfully Brilliant Thoughts. LC 98-37805. (Brilliant Thoughts Ser.: No. 9). (Illus.). 168p. 1999. pap. 9.95 (*0-88007-221-0*) Woodbridge Pr.

— We've Been Through So Much Together, & Most of It Was Your Fault. LC 90-12357. (Brilliant Thoughts Ser.: No. 7). (Illus.). 168p. (Orig.). 1990. 17.95 (*0-88007-182-6*); pap. 9.95 (*0-88007-183-4*) Woodbridge Pr.

Brilliant Beginnings, LLC Staff. Baby Brain Basics Guidebook. (Illus.). 144p. 1999. write for info. (*0-9665815-1-2*) Brllnt Begnngs.

— Baby Brain Basics Toy Buying Guide. (Illus.). 1999. write for info. (*0-9665815-2-0*) Brllnt Begnngs.

— Friendly Faces: Baby's Rhyming Photo Book. (Illus.). (J). 1999. write for info. (*0-9665815-4-7*) Brllnt Begnngs.

***Brilliant Beginnings Staff.** Baby Brain Basics Value Pak. (Illus.). 144p. 1999. (*0-9665815-5-5*) Brllnt Begnngs.

— Brilliant Beginnings Toddler Brain Basics Parent Kit. (Illus.). 176p. 1999. 39.95 (*0-9665815-7-1*) Brllnt Begnngs.

— Furry Friends & Merry Melodies Follow-Along Picture Book. (Illus.). 1999. write for info. (*0-9665815-9-8*) Brllnt Begnngs.

— Toddler Brain Basics Activities Toyguide. 1999. write for info. (*1-929651-01-5*) Brllnt Begnngs.

— Toddler Brain Basics Guidebook. (Illus.). 176p. 1999. (*1-929651-00-7*) Brllnt Begnngs.

— Toddler Brain Basics Value Pak. (Illus.). 176p. 1999. (*1-929651-02-3*) Brllnt Begnngs.

***Brilliant, Eleanor L.** Private Charity & Public Inquiry: A History of the Filer & Peterson Commissions. LC 00-39647. (Philanthropic Studies). 2000. write for info. (*0-253-33751-8*) Ind U Pr.

Brilliant, Eleanor L. The United Way: Dilemmas of Organized Charity. 382p. (C). 1993. pap. text 22.50 (*0-231-05623-0*) Col U Pr.

Brilliant, Kelly A., jt. auth. see McLaughlin, Karen A.

Brilliant, Kelly J., jt. auth. see McLaughlin, Karen A.

Brilliant, Richard. Facing the New World: Jewish Portraits in Colonial & Federal America. LC 97-33276. 128p. 1997. 49.95 (*3-7913-1863-2*, Pub. by Prestel) te Neues.

— Gesture & Rank in Roman Art: The Use of Gestures to Denote Status in Roman Sculpture & Coinage. Vol. 14. 1963. pap. 75.00 (*0-685-22857-6*) Elliots Bks.

***Brilliant, Richard.** My Laocohon, or Yours, or Theirs. LC 99-41240. (Discovery Ser.). 160p. 2000. 45.00 (*0-520-21682-2*, Pub. by U CA Pr) Cal Prin Full Svc.

Brilliant, Richard. Portraiture. (Essays in Art & Culture Ser.). (Illus.). 192p. (C). 1992. 41.50 (*0-674-69175-X*) HUP.

— Portraiture. (Essays in Art & Culture Ser.). (Illus.). 192p. (C). 1993. pap. 22.95 (*0-674-69176-8*) HUP.

— Visual Narratives: Storytelling in Etruscan & Roman Art. LC 83-18869. (Illus.). 208p. 1984. 47.50 (*0-8014-1558-6*) Cornell U Pr.

— Visual Narratives: Storytelling in Etruscan & Roman Art. LC 83-18869. (Illus.). 202p. 1984. reprint ed. pap. 62.70 (*0-608-05315-5*, 206585300001) Bks Demand.

Brilliant, Richard & F., Voss. Faces of Time: Premium Edition. 1998. 1.28 (*0-8212-2542-1*, Pub. by Bulfinch Pr) Little.

Brilliant, Richard & Voss, Fredrick. Faces of Time: 75 Years of Time Cover Portraits. LC 97-77748. (Illus.). 176p. (gr. 8). 1998. 40.00 (*0-8212-2498-0*) Little.

Brilliant, Richard, jt. auth. see Borgatti, Jean M.

Brilliant, Richard L. Essentials of Low Vision Practice. LC 98-4114. 480p. 1998. text 85.00 (*0-7506-9307-X*) Buttrwrth-Heinemann.

Brillinger, ed. The Collected Works of John W. Tukey: Time Series 1965-1984, Vol. 2. (Statistics-Probability Ser.). (Illus.). 642p. 1986. ring bd. 83.95 (*0-412-99561-1*, Chap & Hall CRC) CRC Pr.

Brillinger, David R., et al, eds. New Directions in Time Series Analysis, Pt. 1. LC 92-22697. (Mathematics & Its Applications Ser.: Vol. 45). (Illus.). 408p. 1992. 74.95 (*0-387-97896-8*) Spr-Verlag.

Brillinger, David R. & Krishnaiah, P. R. Handbook of Statistics: Time Series in the Frequency Domain. (Handbook of Statistics Ser.: Vol. 3). xiv,486p. 1984. 170.00 (*0-444-86726-0*, I-461-83) Elsevier.

Brillinger, David R., ed. see Hardel, W.

Brillinger, David R., ed. see Ross, G. J.

Brillinger, Jeff. Collected Works of John W. Tukey. 792p. 1984. ring bd. 83.95 (*0-412-74240-3*) CRC Pr.

Brillman, Judith C. & Quenzer, Ronald W. Infectious Disease in Emergency Medicine. 2nd ed. LC 97-25512. (Illus.). 975p. 1997. text 179.00 (*0-316-10950-9*) Lppncott W & W.

Brillman, Judith C. & Quenzer, Ronald W., eds. Infectious Disease in Emergency Medicine. LC 92-17541. 1992. 150.00 (*0-316-10838-3*, Little Brwn Med Div) Lppncott W & W.

Brillson, L. J. Frontiers in Electronic Materials & Processing. Lucovsky, Gerald, ed. LC 86-70108. (AIP Conference Processings No. 138, American Vacum Society Ser.: No. 1). 358p. 1986. lib. bdg. 65.00 (*0-88318-337-4*) Am Inst Physics.

Brillson, Leonard J., ed. Contacts to Semiconductors: Fundamentals & Technology. LC 93-26692. (Illus.). 680p. 1993. 125.00 (*0-8155-1336-4*) Noyes.

Brillstein, Bernie & Rensin, David. Where Did I Go Right? You're No One in Hollywood Unless Someone Wants You Dead. LC 99-21072. 400p. (gr. 8). 1999. 24.95 (*0-316-11885-0*) Little.

***Brillstein, Bernie & Rensin, David.** Where Did I Go Right? You're No One in Hollywood Unless Someone Wants You Dead. 2001. pap. write for info. (*0-446-67665-9*) Warner Bks.

Brillstein, Richard. A Problem Solving Approach to Mathematics for Elementary School Teachers. 6th ed. Guardino, Karen, ed. LC 96-26205. 928p. (C). 1999. 92.00 (*0-201-56649-4*) Addison-Wesley.

Brilmayer, Lea. American Hegemony: Political Morality in a One-Superpower World. LC 94-11807. 304p. 1994. 40.00 (*0-300-06033-5*) Yale U Pr.

— American Hegemony: Political Morality in a One-Superpower World. 304p. 1996. pap. 19.00 (*0-300-06853-0*) Yale U Pr.

— Conflict of Laws. 368p. 1995. 24.95 (*0-316-10893-6*, Aspen Law & Bus) Aspen Pub.

— Justifying International Acts. LC 89-7121. (Illus.). 160p. 1989. 29.95 (*0-8014-2278-7*) Cornell U Pr.

— Justifying International Acts. LC 89-7121. 176p. reprint ed. pap. 54.60 (*0-608-20877-9*, 207197600003) Bks Demand.

Brilon, W., ed. Intersections Without Traffic Signals. (Illus.). xvii, 328p. 1988. 66.00 (*0-387-18890-8*) Spr-Verlag.

— Intersections Without Traffic Signals II: Proceedings of an International Workshop 18-19 July, 1991, Bochum. (Illus.). 343p. 1991. 103.95 (*0-387-54180-2*) Spr-Verlag.

***Brilon, W., et al, eds.** Traffic & Mobility: Simulation - Economics - Environment. LC 99-48774. x, 450p. 1999. 89.95 (*3-540-66295-2*) Spr-Verlag.

Brilvitch, Charles. Walking Through History: The Seaports of Black Rock & Southport. (Illus.). 1977. pap. 3.50 (*0-614-05155-X*) Fairfield Hist.

Brim, Billye. The Blood & the Glory. 1995. pap. 9.99 (*1-57794-058-X*) Harrison Hse.

Brim, Frank M. The Christian Approach To Spiritual Warfare, Vol. 1. Shoemaker, Connie, ed. 280p. 1990. spiral bd. 35.00 (*0-9612676-2-3*) World Wide Mini.

— Satan's Secret Revealed: From the Files of a Christian Exorcist. 176p. 1983. pap. 5.00 (*0-9612676-0-7*) World Wide Mini.

Brim, John A., et al. Research Design in Anthropology: Paradigms & Pragmatics in the Testing of Hypotheses. 123p. (C). 1982. reprint ed. pap. text 16.95 (*0-8290-0583-8*) Irvington.

***Brim, L., et al, eds.** Mathematical Foundations of Computer Science, 1998: 23rd International Symposium, MFCS '98, Brnmo, Czech Republic August 24-28, 1998. (Lecture Notes in Computer Science Ser.: Vol. 1450). xvii, 846p. 1998. pap. 90.00 (*3-540-64827-5*) Spr-Verlag.

Brim, Orville G., Jr. & Kagan, Jerome, eds. Constancy & Change in Human Development. (Illus.). 760p. 1980. 58.50 (*0-674-16625-6*) HUP.

Brim, Orville G., Jr., et al. American Beliefs & Attitudes about Intelligence. LC 75-76746. 292p. 1969. 40.00 (*0-87154-152-1*) Russell Sage.

— The Dying Patient. LC 80-20141. 390p. (C). 1981. reprint ed. pap. 24.95 (*0-87855-684-2*) Transaction Pubs.

Brim, Orville G., Jr., ed. see Freeman, Howard E.

Brimacomb, John. The Complete Idiot's Guide to Microsoft Excel 97. 2nd ed. 1998. 19.99 (*0-7897-1693-3*) Que.

Brimacomb, Jon. Easy Office: Small Business Edition. 1998. pap. text 19.99 (*0-7897-1638-0*) Que.

Brimacombe, J. K., et al. Continuous Casting Vol. II: Heat Flow, Solidification & Crack Formation, Vol. II. LC 83-81654. 238p. 1984. 70.00 (*0-89520-160-7*) Iron & Steel.

Brimacombe, J. K., ed. see Savard-Lee International Symposium on Bath Smeltin.

Brimacombe, J. R., et al. The Laryngeal Mask Airway: A Review & Practical Guide. (Illus.). 314p. 1997. pap. text 68.00 (*0-7020-2321-3*, Pub. by Harcourt) Saunders.

Brimacombe, J. S., ed. Carbohydrate Chemistry, Vols. 1-11. Incl. 1967 Literature. LC 79-67610. 1968. 31.00 (*0-85186-002-8*); 1968 Literature. LC 79-67610. 1969. 31.00 (*0-85186-012-5*); 1969 Literature. LC 79-67610. 1970. 34.00 (*0-85186-022-2*); 1970 Literature. LC 79-67610. 1971. 34.00 (*0-85186-032-X*); 1971 Literature. LC 79-67610. 1972. 36.00 (*0-85186-042-7*); 1972 Literature. LC 79-67610. 1973. 38.00 (*0-85186-052-4*); 1973 Literature. LC 79-67610. 1975. 56.00 (*0-85186-062-1*); 1974 Literature. LC 79-67610. 1976. 61.00 (*0-85186-072-9*); 1975-76 Literature. LC 79-67610. 1977. 82.00 (*0-85186-082-6*); 1976-77 Literature. LC 79-67610. 1978. 82.00 (*0-85186-092-3*); 1977-78 Literature. LC 79-67610. 1979. 97.00 (*0-85186-102-4*); LC 79-67610. write for info. (*0-318-50464-2*) Am Chemical.

Brimacombe, J. William. Ready, Set, Retire! How Much Money You Need & the Tax-Smart Way to Get It & Keep It. LC 94-66841. 210p. 1994. 24.99 (*0-9641532-3-8*) Financial Freedom.

— Ready, Set, Retire! How Much Money You Need & the Tax-Smart Way to Get It & Keep It. LC 94-66841. 210p. 1995. pap. 12.95 (*0-9641532-4-6*) Financial Freedom.

***Brimacombe, Peter.** All the Queen's Men: The World of Elizabeth. LC 00-21022. (Illus.). 240p. 2000. text 35.00 (*0-312-23251-9*) St Martin.

Brimacombe, Peter. The Charm of the Cotswolds: With Stratford-Upon-Avon & Bath. (English Tourist Board Souvenir Ser.). (Illus.). 36p. 1996. pap. 15.00 (*0-11-300086-3*) Statnry Office.

***Brimax, S.** Fairy Tales. (J). 1998. 80.00 (*81-86982-75-2*, Pub. by Business Pubns) St Mut.

— My First Dictionary. (J). 1998. 60.00 (*81-86982-64-7*, Pub. by Business Pubns) St Mut.

— My First Word Book. (J). 1998. pap. 40.00 (*81-86982-65-5*, Pub. by Business Pubns) St Mut.

Brimax Staff. Christmas Teddy Bear. Date not set. 5.98 (*1-85854-534-X*) Brimax Bks.

Brimberry, Alexis, et al. Tao Cards. (CHI & ENG.). x, 104p. 1996. spiral bd. 29.99 (*1-889890-00-6*) Wellness Inst of Res.

Brimblecombe, Peter. Air Composition & Chemistry. 2nd ed. (Cambridge Environmental Chemistry Ser.: No. 1). (Illus.). 267p. (C). 1996. text 74.95 (*0-521-45366-6*); pap. text 26.95 (*0-521-45972-9*) Cambridge U Pr.

— The Big Smoke. 1987. 42.50 (*0-416-90080-1*) Routledge.

Brimblecombe, Peter & Lein, Alla Yu, eds. Evolution of the Global Biogeochemical Sulphur Cycle. LC 89-5806. 276p. 1989. 400.00 (*0-471-92251-X*) Wiley.

Brimblecombe, Peter & Maynard, Robert L. The Urban Atmosphere & Its Effects, Vol. 1. 300p. 1999. text 48.00 (*1-86094-064-1*) World Scientific Pub.

Brimelow, Judith M., ed. see Heisser, David C.

Brimelow, Judith M., ed. see Helsley, Alexia J. & Stauffer, Michael E.

Brimelow, Judith M., ed. see Hornsby, Benjamin F., Jr.

Brimelow, Judith M., ed. see McCawley, Patrick J.

Brimelow, Judith M., ed. see Power, J. Tracy.

Brimelow, Judith M., ed. see Rowland, Lawrence S.

Brimelow, Peter. Alien Nation: Common Sense about America's Immigration Disaster. 384p. 1996. pap. 14.00 (*0-06-097691-8*) HarpC.

— Alien Nation: Common Sense about America's Immigration Disaster. 327p. 1995. 24.00 (*0-614-32302-9*) Random.

— The Patriot Game: Canada & the Canadian Question Revisited. (Publication Ser.: No. 368). 310p. 1987. 10.78 (*0-8179-8681-2*); pap. text 6.78 (*0-8179-8682-0*) Hoover Inst Pr.

— The Wall Street Gurus: How You Can Profit From Investment Newsletters. 238p. 1988. 19.95 (*0-9620125-1-3*) Minerva Bks.

Brimer. Educating Students with Learning Disabilities. (Special Education Ser.). 1994. teacher ed. 12.00 (*0-8273-5883-0*) Delmar.

Brimer, Leon, et al, eds. Natural Resources & Social Conflicts in the Sahel: Proceedings of the 5th Sahel Workshop 4-6 January 1993. (Illus.). 232p. (C). 1994. pap. 25.00 (*87-984671-0-7*, Pub. by Aarhus Univ Pr) David Brown.

Brimer, Mark A. Health Care Management in Physical Therapy. (Illus.). 328p. 1990. pap. 45.95 (*0-398-06032-0*) C C Thomas.

Brimer, Mark A. Health Care Management in Physical Therapy. (Illus.). 328p. (C). 1990. text 62.95 (*0-398-05642-0*) C C Thomas.

Brimer, Mark A. & Moran, Michael L. Clinical Cases in Physical Therapy. LC 95-13055. 103p. 1995. pap. text 27.50 (*0-7506-9637-0*) Buttrwrth-Heinemann.

Brimfield Town Committee, compiled by. Historical Celebration of the Town of Brimfield, Mass., Including Genealogies. (Illus.). 487p. 1989. reprint ed. lib. bdg. 49.00 (*0-8328-0812-1*, MA0026) Higginson Bk Co.

Brimhall. Basic Keyboard Chords. (Keyboard Chords Ser.). 1990. 3.95 (*0-685-32019-7*, P031) Hansen Ed Mus.

— Best of Pop Waltzes. 1990. 6.95 (*0-685-32043-X*, H440) Hansen Ed Mus.

— The Best of Sacred Music. 1990. 6.95 (*0-685-32047-2*, H446) Hansen Ed Mus.

— Best of Top Classics. 1990. 6.95 (*0-685-32044-8*, H442) Hansen Ed Mus.

— Classics Made Easy: Level One. (Made Easy Ser.). 1990. 7.95 (*0-685-32065-0*, 8415) Hansen Ed Mus.

— Complete Picture Chords. (Keyboard Chords Ser.). 1990. 5.95 (*0-685-32021-9*, 77-100) Hansen Ed Mus.

— Duets Made Easy. (Made Easy Ser.). 1990. 7.95 (*0-685-32066-9*, 8416) Hansen Ed Mus.

— Fifty Selected Children's Classics. 1990. 5.95 (*0-685-32117-7*, 0526); 5.95 (*0-685-37383-5*, O527) Hansen Ed Mus.

— Fun-Way Instruction Method. (Beginning Band Ser.). 1990. teacher ed. 0.75 (*0-685-32004-9*, G004) Hansen Ed Mus.

— Fun-Way Pre-Band Instrument Method: Recorder & Song Flute. (Beginning Orchestra Ser.). 1990. 4.95 (*0-685-32000-6*, G028) Hansen Ed Mus.

— Fun-Way Pre-Band Instrument Method: Recorder & Song Flute, No. 1. 1990. 4.95 (*0-685-32160-6*, G028) Hansen Ed Mus.

— Fun-Way Tooter: Tonette, Song Flute, Flutophone & Recorder, No. 2. 1990. 3.95 (*0-685-32159-2*, G005) Hansen Ed Mus.

— Fun-Way Tutor: Harmonica. (Uke & Harmonica Ser.). 1990. 3.95 (*0-685-32012-X*, G139) Hansen Ed Mus.

— Fun-Way Tutor: Recorder. (Beginning Orchestra Ser.). 1990. 3.95 (*0-685-31999-7*, G136) Hansen Ed Mus.

— How to Play the Recorder. 1990. 7.95 (*0-685-31456-1*, 85-39) Hansen Ed Mus.

— My Favorite Classics, Bk. 1. (Children's Classics Ser.). 1990. 13.95 (*0-685-32040-5*, O114) Hansen Ed Mus.

— One Hundred Children's Classics. (Children's Classics Ser.). 1990. 12.95 (*0-685-32041-3*, O109) Hansen Ed Mus.

— The Popular Chord Instructor. (Keyboard Chords Ser.). 1990. 6.95 (*0-685-32022-7*, T059) Hansen Ed Mus.

— Three Thousand Three Hundred Keyboard Chords. (Keyboard Chords Ser.). 1990. 9.95 (*0-685-32020-0*, P030) Hansen Ed Mus.

Brimhall & Abrill. The Complete Book of Scales, Cadences & Arpeggios. (Beginning Skills Ser.). 1990. 7.95 (*0-685-32028-6*, T386) Hansen Ed Mus.

Brimhall, John. Americana for Autoharp. (Miscellaneous Ser.). 1990. 2.95 (*0-685-32016-2*, G076) Hansen Ed Mus.

— Best of Folk-Pop-Rock. 1990. 6.95 (*0-685-32045-6*, H443) Hansen Ed Mus.

— Brimhall Piano Method, Bk. 1. (Piano Method Ser.). 40p. (Orig.). 1985. pap. text 6.95 (*0-8494-2768-1*, T101) Hansen Ed Mus.

— Brimhall Piano Method, Bk. 2. (Piano Method Ser.). 40p. (Orig.). 1985. pap. text 6.95 (*0-8494-2769-X*) Hansen Ed Mus.

— Brimhall Piano Method, Bk. 3. (Piano Method Ser.). 40p. (Orig.). 1985. pap. text 6.95 (*0-8494-2770-3*, T103) Hansen Ed Mus.

— Brimhall Piano Method, Bk. 4. (Piano Method Ser.). 40p. (Orig.). 1985. pap. text 6.95 (*0-8494-2771-1*, T104) Hansen Ed Mus.

— Children's Piano Method. (Illus.). 64p. (J). (gr. 1-6). 1984. pap. text 6.95 (*0-8494-2887-4*, T430) Hansen Ed Mus.

— Children's Songs for Piano. 96p. (J). (gr. 1-6). 1985. pap. text 8.95 (*0-8494-2264-7*, 0496) Hansen Ed Mus.

— How to Play Easy Organ. (Self Improvement Ser.). 96p. (Orig.). 1985. pap. text 7.95 (*0-8494-1706-6*, 85-27) Hansen Ed Mus.

— John Brimhall's Adult Piano Course Complete. 96p. (Orig.). 1985. pap. text 13.95 (*0-8494-2915-3*, T564) Hansen Ed Mus.

— My Favorite Classics Level One. 120p. (J). (gr. 3-6). pap. text 13.95 (*0-8494-2180-2*, 0114) Hansen Ed Mus.

— My Favorite Classics Level Two. 120p. (Orig.). 1985. pap. text 13.95 (*0-317-39977-2*, 0124); 13.95 (*0-8494-2184-5*) Hansen Ed Mus.

B

Brimhall, John. Piano Magic. 9.95 (*0-7692-9204-6*) Warner Bros.

Brimhall, John. Pre-Band Instrument Method. Cavalier, Debbie, ed. 32p. (YA). 1997. pap. text 4.95 (*0-7692-1695-1*, 0189B) Wrner Bros.

— Pre-Band Instrument Method. Cavalier, Debbie, ed. (C). 1997. pap. text. write for info. (*0-7692-1776-1*, 0196B) Wrner Bros.

— Theory Notebook Complete. 96p. (Orig.). 1985. pap. text 13.95 (*0-8494-0028-7*, M465) Hansen Ed Mus.

— Young Adult Piano Course, Bk. 1. (Piano Course Ser.). 32p. (Orig.). 1985. pap. text 6.95 (*0-8494-1356-7*, T561) Hansen Ed Mus.

— Young Adult Piano Course, Bk. 2. (Piano Course Ser.). 32p. (Orig.). 1984. pap. text 6.95 (*0-8494-1357-5*, T562) Hansen Ed Mus.

Brimhall, John, ed. The Wedding Book. 32p. (YA). 1995. pap. text 6.95 (*0-89724-849-X*, BMP507) Wrner Bros.

Brimhall, John & Edging, Vicki. How to Start Your Child on Piano. (Self Improvement Ser.). 96p. (Orig.). 1985. pap. text 7.95 (*0-8494-1712-0*, 85-28) Hansen Ed Mus.

Brimley, Dawn B. Waking Moments. (Illus.). 50p. (Orig.). 1989. pap. write for info. (*0-318-64718-4*) D B Brimley.

Brimley, Herbert H. North Carolina Naturalist, H. H. Brimley. Odum, Eugene P., ed. LC 78-134058. (Essay Index Reprint Ser.). 1977. 20.95 (*0-8369-2145-3*) Ayer.

Brimley, Vern, Jr., jt. auth. see Burrup, Percy E.

Brimlow, Robert W., jt. ed. see Budde, Michael L.

Brimm, Mark, ed. The Royal Vagrant Review, Vol. 1, No. 1, Issue 1. 32p. 1997. 4.00 (*1-889717-01-0*, RVP1) Royal Vagrant.

Brimm, Mark, ed. see Locklin, Gerald.

Brimm, Mark, ed. see Rochette, Joe.

Brimmell, R. A., jt. auth. see Roscoe, S.

Brimmer, Andrew F. Economic Development: International & African Perspectives. (YA). 1990. 15.95 (*0-87498-093-3*) Assoc Pubs DC.

Brimmer, Larry D. Brave Mary. (Rookie Readers Ser.). (Illus.). 32p. (J). (ps-2). 1996. lib. bdg. 17.00 (*0-516-02056-0*) Childrens.

— Country Bear's Surprise. LC 97-70361. (Illus.). 32p. (J). (ps-1). 1997. pap. text 7.95 (*1-56397-674-9*) Boyds Mills Pr.

— E-Mail. LC 96-29053. (True Bks.). (J). 1997. lib. bdg. 21.00 (*0-516-20332-0*) Childrens.

Brimmer, Larry Dane. Jupiter. (True Bks.). (Illus.). 48p. (gr. 2-4). 1999. lib. bdg. 6.95 (*0-516-26495-8*) Childrens.

— Neptune. (True Books: Continents Ser.). 1999. lib. bdg. 6.95 (*0-516-26496-6*) Childrens.

— Pluto. (True Bks.). 1999. lib. bdg. 6.95 (*0-516-26499-0*) Childrens.

Brimmicombe-Wood, Lee. Aliens: Colonial Marines Technical Manual. Hughes, Dave, ed. LC 96-4232. 160p. 1996. pap. 18.00 (*0-06-105343-0*, HarperPrism) HarpC.

Brimmicombe-Wood, Leo. Aliens Colonial Marines Technical Manual. 1996. pap. 17.00 (*0-614-97805-X*, HarperPrism) HarpC.

Brimner, Larry. Merry Christmas Old Armadillo. LC 94-79155. (Illus.). 32p. (J). (ps-1). 1995. 15.95 (*1-56397-354-5*) Boyds Mills Pr.

Brimner, Larry D. Aggie & Will. LC 97-40054. (Rookie Readers Ser.). (Illus.). (J). 1998. 17.00 (*0-516-20754-7*) Childrens.

— Aggie & Will. (Rookie Readers Ser.). (Illus.). 32p. (YA). (gr. k-3). 1999. pap. text 4.95 (*0-516-26409-5*) Childrens.

— Being Different: Lambda Youths Speak Out. LC 95-7679. (Lesbian & Gay Experience Ser.). (Illus.). 160p. (YA). (gr. 9 up). 1995. lib. bdg. 24.00 (*0-531-11222-5*) Watts.

— Bobsledding & the Luge. LC 97-2271. (True Bks.). (J). 1997. lib. bdg. 21.00 (*0-516-20436-X*) Childrens.

— Dinosaurs Dance. Rau, Dana, ed. (Rookie Readers Ser.). (Illus.). 32p. (J). 1998. pap. 4.95 (*0-516-26358-7*) Childrens.

— Earth. LC 97-48867. (True Bks.). (Illus.). 48p. (J). (gr. 2-4). 1998. lib. bdg. 21.00 (*0-516-20620-6*) Childrens.

— Earth. (True Bks.). (Illus.). 48p. (J). (gr. 3-5). 1999. pap. text 6.95 (*0-516-26431-1*) Childrens.

— Elliot Fry's Goodbye. LC 92-72993. (Illus.). 32p. (J). 1998. pap. text 7.95 (*1-56397-715-X*) Boyds Mills Pr.

— Figure Skating. LC 97-9014. (True Bks.). (Illus.). 48p. (J). (gr. 2-4). 1997. lib. bdg. 21.00 (*0-516-20440-8*) Childrens.

— Firehouse Sal. LC 96-2087. (Rookie Readers Ser.). (Illus.). 32p. (J). (gr. k-2). 1996. lib. bdg. 17.00 (*0-516-20010-0*) Childrens.

— Firehouse Sal. (Rookie Readers Ser.). (Illus.). 32p. (J). (gr. 3-5). 1997. pap. 4.95 (*0-516-26077-4*) Childrens.

— How Many Ants? LC 96-48573. (Rookie Readers Ser.). (Illus.). 32p. (J). (gr. k-2). 1997. lib. bdg. 17.00 (*0-516-20398-3*) Childrens.

— How Many Ants? (Rookie Readers Ser.). (Illus.). 32p. (J). (gr. k-2). 1998. pap. text 4.95 (*0-516-26251-3*) Childrens.

— If Dogs Had Wings. LC 95-80776. (Illus.). 32p. (J). (ps-1). 1996. 14.95 (*1-56397-146-1*) Boyds Mills Pr.

— Jupiter. LC 98-2951. (Space Ser.). 47p. (J). 1999. 21.50 (*0-516-21153-6*) Childrens.

— Lightning Liz. LC 97-13835. (Rookie Readers Ser.). (Illus.). 32p. (J). (gr. k-2). 1998. 17.00 (*0-516-20753-9*) Childrens.

— Lightning Liz. Rau, Dana, ed. (Rookie Readers Ser.). (Illus.). 32p. (J). 1998. pap. 4.95 (*0-516-26360-9*) Childrens.

— Mars. LC 97-42072. (True Bks.). (J). 1998. 21.00 (*0-516-20618-4*) Childrens.

— Mars. LC 97-42072. (True Books: Space (Paper) Ser.). (Illus.). 48p. (J). (gr. 3-5). 1999. pap. text 6.95 (*0-516-26435-4*) Childrens.

— Max & Felix. LC 91-77611. (Illus.). 32p. (J). (ps-1). 1995. pap. 5.95 (*1-56397-519-X*) Boyds Mills Pr.

— Mercury. LC 97-38648. (True Bks.). (J). 1998. 21.00 (*0-516-20619-2*) Childrens.

— Mercury. (True Bks.). (Illus.). 48p. (J). (gr. 3-5). 1999. pap. text 6.95 (*0-516-26436-2*) Childrens.

— Merry Christmas, Old Armadillo. LC 94-79155. (Illus.). 32p. (J). (ps-1). 1997. pap. 7.95 (*1-56397-678-1*) Boyds Mills Pr.

— A Migrant Family. (In My Shoes Ser.). (Illus.). 40p. (J). (gr. 4-8). 1992. lib. bdg. 19.93 (*0-8225-2554-2*, Lerner Publctns) Lerner Pub.

— Mountain Biking. (First Bks.). 64p. (J). 1997. pap. 6.95 (*0-531-15814-4*); lib. bdg. 22.00 (*0-531-20243-7*) Watts.

— The Names Project. LC 98-49434. (Cornerstones to Freedom Ser.). 32p. (J). (gr. 4-6). 1999. 20.00 (*0-516-20999-X*) Childrens.

— Nana's Hog. LC 97-40045. (Rookie Readers Ser.). (Illus.). (J). 1998. 17.00 (*0-516-20755-5*) Childrens.

— Neptune. LC 98-22039. (Space Ser.). 47p. (J). 1999. 21.50 (*0-516-21157-9*) Childrens.

— The Official "M&M's" Book of the Millennium. LC 99-19359. (Illus.). 32p. (YA). (ps up). 1999. 15.95 (*0-88106-071-2*); pap. 6.95 (*0-88106-072-0*) Charlesbridge Pub.

— Pluto. LC 98-26740. (Space Ser.). 47p. (J). 1999. 21.50 (*0-516-21155-2*) Childrens.

— Polar Mammals. LC 96-34192. (True Bks.). 48p. (J). 1997. pap. 6.95 (*0-516-26112-6*) Childrens.

— Raindrops. LC 98-19036. (Rookie Readers Ser.). (Illus.). 32p. (J). (gr. 1-2). 1999. 17.50 (*0-516-21203-6*) Childrens.

— Rock Climbing. LC 96-28943. (First Bk.). (J). 1997. lib. bdg. 22.00 (*0-531-20269-0*) Watts.

— Rock Climbing. (First Bks.). (J). 1997. pap. text 6.95 (*0-531-15860-8*) Watts.

— Saturn. LC 98-14006. (Space Ser.). 47p. (J). 1999. 21.50 (*0-516-21154-4*) Childrens.

— Skiing. LC 97-12829. (True Bks.). (J). 1997. 21.00 (*0-516-20449-1*) Childrens.

— Snowboarding. LC 97-8962. (First Bks.). (J). (gr. 4-6). 1997. lib. bdg. 21.00 (*0-531-20313-1*) Watts.

— Snowboarding. (First Bks.). 1998. pap. 6.95 (*0-531-15890-X*) Watts.

— Speed Skating. LC 97-2920. (True Bks.). (Illus.). 48p. (J). (gr. 2-4). 1997. 21.00 (*0-516-20451-3*) Childrens.

— Surfing. LC 97-9428. (First Book Ser.). (J). 1997. lib. bdg. 22.00 (*0-531-20315-8*) Watts.

— Surfing. (First Bks.). 1998. pap. 6.95 (*0-531-15891-8*) Watts.

— Unusual Friendships: Symbiosis in the Animal World. LC 92-24953. (First Bks.). (Illus.). 64p. (J). (gr. 4-6). 1993. lib. bdg. 22.00 (*0-531-20106-6*) Watts.

— Unusual Friendships: Symbiosis in the Animal World. large type ed. (First Bks.). (Illus.). 64p. (J). (gr. 5-8). 1993. pap. 6.95 (*0-531-15675-3*) Watts.

— Uranus. LC 98-22451. (Space Ser.). 47p. (J). 1999. 21.50 (*0-516-21156-0*) Childrens.

— Venus. LC 97-52144. (True Bks.). (J). 1998. 21.00 (*0-516-21158-7*) Childrens.

— Venus. (True Bks.). (Illus.). 48p. (J). (gr. 3-5). 1999. pap. text 6.95 (*0-516-26443-5*) Childrens.

— Voices from the Camps: Japanese Americans During World War II. LC 93-31956. (International Affairs Ser.). (Illus.). 144p. (YA). (gr. 9-12). 1994. lib. bdg. 24.00 (*0-531-11179-2*) Watts.

— What Good Is a Tree? LC 97-40053. (Rookie Readers Ser.). (Illus.). (J). 1998. 17.00 (*0-516-20953-1*) Childrens.

— The Winter Olympics. LC 97-2272. (True Bks.). (J). (gr. 2-4). 1997. 21.00 (*0-516-20456-4*) Childrens.

Brimner, Larry Dane. Baby Bear. 32p. (ps-3). pap. 15.95 (*0-06-029039-0*); pap. 5.95 (*0-06-443703-5*); lib. bdg. 15.89 (*0-06-029040-4*) HarpC.

— Bees. (True Bks.). (J). 2000. pap. text 6.95 (*0-516-26755-8*) Childrens.

Brimner, Larry Dane. Bees & Other Stinging Insects. LC 99-13835. (Animals Ser.). (J). 1999. 21.50 (*0-516-21160-9*) Childrens.

— Butterflies & Moths. LC 99-13839. (Animals Ser.). (J). 1999. 21.50 (*0-516-21162-5*) Childrens.

***Brimner, Larry Dane.** Butterflies & Moths. (True Bks.). (J). 2000. pap. text 6.95 (*0-516-26756-6*) Childrens.

— A Cat on Wheels. LC 99-63865. (Illus.). 32p. (gr. k-3). 2000. 15.95 (*1-56397-747-8*) Boyds Mills Pr.

— Caves. LC 99-58037. (Illus.). (J). 2000. 22.00 (*0-516-21567-1*) Childrens.

Brimner, Larry Dane. Cockroaches. LC 99-13838. (Animals Ser.). (J). 1999. 21.50 (*0-516-21159-5*) Childrens.

***Brimner, Larry Dane.** Cockroaches. (True Bks.). (J). 2000. pap. text 6.95 (*0-516-26758-2*) Childrens.

Brimner, Larry Dane. Cory Coleman: Grade 2. (Redfeather Bks.). 1991. 11.15 (*0-606-12226-5*, Pub. by Turtleback) Demco.

— Cowboy Up! LC 98-22307. (Rookie Readers Ser.). (Illus.). 31p. (J). (gr. k-3). 1999. lib. bdg. 4.95 (*0-516-26475-3*) Childrens.

— Cowboy Up! LC 98-22307. (Rookie Readers Ser.). (Illus.). 32p. (J). (gr. 1-2). 1999. 17.50 (*0-516-21199-4*) Childrens.

— Flies. LC 99-13836. (Animals Ser.). (J). 1999. 21.50 (*0-516-21161-7*) Childrens.

***Brimner, Larry Dane.** Flies. (True Bks.). (J). 2000. pap. text 6.95 (*0-516-26761-2*) Childrens.

— Gatitos. (Rookie Espanol Ser.). (SPA., Illus.). (J). 2000. 15.00 (*0-516-22024-1*) Childrens.

— Geysers. LC 99-58038. (True Bks.). (Illus.). (J). 2000. 22.00 (*0-516-20669-9*) Childrens.

— Glaciers. LC 99-58047. (True Bks.). (Illus.). (J). 2000. 22.00 (*0-516-20670-2*) Childrens.

— Long Way Home. (Rookie Readers Ser.). (Illus.). (J). 2000. 18.00 (*0-516-22011-X*) Childrens.

— Mountains. LC 99-58039. (True Bks.). (Illus.). (J). 2000. 22.00 (*0-516-21568-X*) Childrens.

— Names Project. (Cornerstones to Freedom Ser.). (J). 2000. pap. text 5.95 (*0-516-26517-2*) Childrens.

Brimner, Larry Dane. Nana's Hog. (Rookie Readers Ser.). (Illus.). 32p. (YA). (gr. k-3). 1999. pap. text 4.95 (*0-516-26412-5*) Childrens.

— Praying Mantises. LC 99-13837. (Animals Ser.). (J). 1999. 21.50 (*0-516-21163-3*) Childrens.

***Brimner, Larry Dane.** Praying Mantises. (True Bks.). (J). 2000. pap. text 6.95 (*0-516-26769-8*) Childrens.

Brimner, Larry Dane. Raindrops. (Rookie Readers Ser.). 1999. lib. bdg. 4.95 (*0-516-26477-X*) Childrens.

— Saturn. (True Bks.). 1999. lib. bdg. 6.95 (*0-516-26501-6*) Childrens.

— Uranus. (True Bks.). (Illus.). 48p. (gr. 2-4). 1999. lib. bdg. 6.95 (*0-516-26508-3*) Childrens.

— What Good Is a Tree? (Rookie Readers Ser.). (Illus.). 32p. (YA). (gr. k-3). 1999. pap. text 4.95 (*0-516-26414-1*) Childrens.

Brimnes, Niels. Constructing the Colonial Encounter: Right & Left Hand Castes in Early Colonial South India. (NIAS Monographs: Vol. 81). 288p. 1998. text 49.00 (*0-7007-1106-6*, Pub. by Curzon Pr Ltd) UH Pr.

Brims, Bernagh & Smith, Duncan. Seven Potato, More LC 93-102663. 78 p. (J). 1992. write for info. (*0-86281-345-X*) Appletree Pr.

Brimsek, Tobi A. From the Top: Profiles of U. S. & Canadian Corporate Libraries & Information Centers. LC Z 0731.B745. (SLA Research Ser.: Vol. 4). 308p. 1989. reprint ed. pap. 95.50 (*0-608-00760-9*, 206155800010) Bks Demand.

Brimsek, Tobi A., ed. Inside Information: Profiles of Association Libraries & Information Centers. (SLA Research Ser.). 1991. 19.00 (*0-87111-372-4*) SLA.

Brimson. Activity-Based Management. 364p. (C). 1998. pap. 42.95 (*0-471-33158-9*) Wiley.

Brimson, Dougie & Brimson, Eddy. Everywhere We Go: Behind the Matchday Madness. mass mkt. 13.95 (*0-7472-5225-4*, Pub. by Headline Bk Pub) Trafalgar.

Brimson, Eddy, jt. auth. see Brimson, Dougie.

Brimson, James A. Activity Accounting: An Activity-Based Costing Approach. LC 90-21506. 214p. 1991. 90.00 (*0-471-53985-6*) Wiley.

— Activity Accounting: An Activity-Based Costing Approach. LC 90-21506. 214p. 1997. pap. 39.95 (*0-471-19628-2*) Wiley.

Brimson, James A., et al. Driving Value Using Activity-Based Budgeting. LC 98-28231. 288p. 1998. 69.95 (*0-471-08631-2*) Wiley.

Brimson, Terence J. The Health & Safety Survival Guide: A Comprehensive Handbook for Managers. LC 95-9896. 1995. 39.95 (*0-07-709049-7*) McGraw.

Brin, David. Brightness Reef. LC 95-17601. (Uplift Trilogy Ser.). 528p. 1995. write for info. (*0-614-07797-4*) Bantam.

— Brightness Reef. (Uplift Trilogy Ser: Bk. 1). 528p. 1995. 22.95 (*0-553-89015-8*) Bantam.

— Brightness Reef. (Uplift Trilogy Ser.: Bk. 1). 688p. 1996. mass mkt. 6.99 (*0-553-57330-6*) Bantam.

— Dr. Pak's Pre-School. deluxe limited ed. (Illus.). 84p. 1989. boxed set 105.00 (*0-941826-19-8*) Cheap St.

— Earth. 704p. 1991. mass mkt. 6.99 (*0-553-29024-X*, Spectra) Bantam.

***Brin, David.** Foundation's Triumph. Vol. 3. 400p. 2000. mass mkt. 6.99 (*0-06-105639-1*, Torch) HarpC.

Brin, David. Glory Season. 784p. 1994. mass mkt. 6.99 (*0-553-56767-5*) Bantam.

— Heaven's Reach. (Uplift Trilogy Ser.). 557p. 1999. reprint ed. mass mkt. 6.99 (*0-553-57473-6*) Bantam.

— Infinity's Shore. LC 96-32346. (Uplift Trilogy Ser.: Vol. 2). 644p. 1997. mass mkt. 6.99 (*0-553-57777-8*) Bantam.

— Otherness: Collected Stories by a Modern Master of Science Fiction. 368p. 1994. mass mkt. 6.99 (*0-553-29528-4*) Bantam.

— The Postman. 336p. 1997. mass mkt. 6.99 (*0-553-27874-6*, Bantam Classics) Bantam.

— The Postman. 1986. 11.60 (*0-606-03120-0*, Pub. by Turtleback) Demco.

— The Practice Effect. 288p. (Orig.). 1995. mass mkt. 6.99 (*0-553-26981-X*, Bantam Classics) Bantam.

— Secret Foundation: The Second Foundation Trilogy, Volume 3, Vol. 3. LC 98-52683. (Second Foundation Trilogy Ser.: Vol. 3). 336p. 1999. 25.00 (*0-06-105241-8*, HarperPrism) HarpC.

— Startide Rising. (Uplift Trilogy Ser.). 496p. 1984. mass mkt. 6.99 (*0-553-27418-X*, Bantam Classics) Bantam.

— Sundiver. (Uplift Trilogy Ser.). 368p. 1985. mass mkt. 6.99 (*0-553-26982-8*, Bantam Classics) Bantam.

— The Transparent Society: Will Technology Force Us to Choose Between Privacy & Freedom? LC 99-61238. 384p. 1999. pap. text 15.00 (*0-7382-0144-8*, Pub. by Perseus Pubng) HarpC.

— The Uplift War. (Uplift Trilogy Ser.). 672p. 1995. mass mkt. 6.99 (*0-553-27971-8*, Bantam Classics) Bantam.

— The Uplift War. 1987. 22.00 (*0-932096-44-1*) Phantasia Pr.

Brin, David, jt. auth. see Benford, Gregory.

Brin, David, jt. auth. see Jackson, Steve.

Brin, Gershon. Studies in Biblical Law: From the Hebrew Bible to the Dead Sea Scrolls. LC 94-213161. (Journal for the Study of the Old Testament Supplement Ser.: Vol. 176). 309p. 1994. 85.00 (*1-85075-484-5*, Pub. by Sheffield Acad) CUP Services.

Brin, Herb. ICH Bin Ein Jude. LC 81-15256. 146p. 1983. 9.95 (*0-8246-0275-7*) Jonathan David.

— Where Are the Children? 200p. 1991. 17.95 (*0-8246-0351-6*) Jonathan David.

Brin, M. & Thickstun, T. Three-Manifolds Which Are End One-Movable. LC 89-15146. (Memoirs Ser.: Vol. 81/411). 73p. 1989. pap. 17.00 (*0-8218-2474-0*, MEMO/81/411) Am Math.

Brin, Ruth. Harvest: Collected Poems. 1986. 16.95 (*0-935457-38-0*) Reconstructionist Pr.

***Brin, Ruth F.** Bittersweet Berries: Growing up Jewish in Minnesota. LC 98-47111. 215p. 1999. pap. text 14.95 (*0-930100-83-2*) Holy Cow.

Brin, Ruth F. Harvest: Collected Poems & Prayers. 2nd ed. LC 99-22745. 246p. 1999. pap. text 16.95 (*0-930100-89-1*, Pub. by Holy Cow) Consort Bk Sales.

Brin, Susannah. Alien Encounter. Hagerty, Carol, ed. (Chillers & Thrillers Ser.). 64p. (J). (gr. 4-10). 1998. pap. text 3.95 (*1-56254-232-X*, SP232X) Saddleback Pubns.

***Brin, Susannah.** Alien Encounter. rev. ed. (Take Ten Ser.). 64p. (YA). (gr. 4-12). 1999. pap. 3.95 (*1-58659-051-0*) Artesian.

Brin, Susannah. Bronco Buster. Hagerty, Carol, ed. (Chillers & Thrillers Ser.). 64p. (J). (gr. 4-10). 1998. pap. text 3.95 (*1-56254-225-7*, SP2257) Saddleback Pubns.

***Brin, Susannah.** Bronco Buster. rev. ed. (Take Ten Ser.). 64p. (YA). (gr. 4-12). 1999. pap. 3.95 (*1-58659-041-3*) Artesian.

Brin, Susannah. The Climb. Hagerty, Carol, ed. (Chillers & Thrillers Ser.). 64p. (J). (gr. 4-10). 1998. pap. text 3.95 (*1-56254-226-5*, SP2265) Saddleback Pubns.

***Brin, Susannah.** The Climb. rev. ed. (Take Ten Ser.). 61p. (YA). (gr. 4-12). 1999. pap. 3.95 (*1-58659-042-1*) Artesian.

Brin, Susannah. Ghost in the Desert. Hagerty, Carol, ed. (Chillers & Thrillers Ser.). 64p. (J). (gr. 4-10). 1998. pap. text 3.95 (*1-56254-233-8*, SP2338) Saddleback Pubns.

***Brin, Susannah.** Ghost in the Desert. rev. ed. (Take Ten Ser.). 64p. (YA). (gr. 4-12). 1999. pap. 3.95 (*1-58659-052-9*) Artesian.

Brin, Susannah. The Haunted Beach House. Hagerty, Carol, ed. (Chillers & Thrillers Ser.). 64p. (J). (gr. 4-10). 1998. pap. text 3.95 (*1-56254-234-6*, SP2346) Saddleback Pubns.

***Brin, Susannah.** The Haunted Beach House. rev. ed. (Take Ten Ser.). 63p. (YA). (gr. 4-12). 1999. pap. 3.95 (*1-58659-053-7*) Artesian.

Brin, Susannah. Mean Waters. (Orig.). 1992. 9.40 (*0-606-11609-5*) Turtleback.

— The Seal Killers. Parker, Liz, ed. (Take Ten Bks.). (Illus.). 45p. (J). (gr. 6-12). 1992. pap. text 3.95 (*1-56254-051-3*) Saddleback Pubns.

***Brin, Susannah.** The Seal Killers. rev. ed. (Take Ten Ser.). (Illus.). 50p. (YA). (gr. 4-12). 1999. pap. 3.95 (*1-58659-014-6*) Artesian.

Brin, Susannah. Search & Rescue. Hagerty, Carol, ed. (Chillers & Thrillers Ser.). 64p. (J). (gr. 4-10). 1998. pap. text 3.95 (*1-56254-227-3*, SP2273) Saddleback Pubns.

***Brin, Susannah.** Search & Rescue. rev. ed. (Take Ten Ser.). 62p. (YA). (gr. 4-12). 1999. pap. 3.95 (*1-58659-043-X*) Artesian.

Brin, Susannah. Timber. Hagerty, Carol, ed. (Chillers & Thrillers Ser.). 64p. (J). (gr. 4-10). 1998. pap. text 3.95 (*1-56254-228-1*, SP2281) Saddleback Pubns.

***Brin, Susannah.** Timber. rev. ed. (Take Ten Ser.). 64p. (YA). (gr. 4-12). 1999. pap. 3.95 (*1-58659-044-8*) Artesian.

Brin, Susannah. Touch Guy. Hagerty, Carol, ed. (Chillers & Thrillers Ser.). 64p. (J). (gr. 4-10). 1998. pap. text 3.95 (*1-56254-229-X*, SP229X) Saddleback Pubns.

***Brin, Susannah.** Tough Guy. rev. ed. (Take Ten Ser.). 62p. (YA). (gr. 4-12). 1999. pap. 3.95 (*1-58659-045-6*) Artesian.

Brin, Susannah. Trapped in the Sixties. Hagerty, Carol, ed. (Chillers & Thrillers Ser.). 64p. (J). (gr. 4-10). 1998. pap. text 3.95 (*1-56254-235-4*, SP2354) Saddleback Pubns.

***Brin, Susannah.** Trapped in the Sixties. rev. ed. (Take Ten Ser.). 64p. (YA). (gr. 4-12). 1999. pap. 3.95 (*1-58659-054-5*) Artesian.

Brin, Susannah. The Water Witch. Hagerty, Carol, ed. (Chillers & Thrillers Ser.). 64p. (J). (gr. 4-10). 1998. pap. text 3.95 (*1-56254-236-2*, SP2362) Saddleback Pubns.

***Brin, Susannah.** The Water Witch. rev. ed. (Take Ten Ser.). 64p. (YA). (gr. 4-12). 1999. pap. 3.95 (*1-58659-055-3*) Artesian.

Brin, Susannah, ed. see Peters, V. A. Pete.

Brina, Grace. A Time to Wait. 84p. 1997. pap. write for info. (*1-57579-069-6*) Pine Hill Pr.

Brinacesco, Eduardo, ed. see Kienzler, Klaus.

Brinberg, D. & Jaccard, J., eds. Dyadic Decision Making. (Illus.). xii, 351p. 1988. 155.00 (*0-387-96749-4*) Spr-Verlag.

Brinberg, D. & Lutz, R., eds. Perspectives on Methodology in Consumer Research. (Illus.). 325p. 1986. 88.95 (*0-387-96238-7*) Spr-Verlag.

Brinberg, D., jt. auth. see Axelson, M. L.

Brinberg, David & McGrath, Joseph E. Validity & the Research Process. 1985. pap. 19.95 (*0-8039-3376-2*) Sage.

— Validity & the Research Process. LC 85-1903. (Illus.). 175p. 1985. reprint ed. pap. 54.30 (*0-608-04301-X*, 206508000012) Bks Demand.

***Brincat & Wike.** Morality & the Prof Life. LC 98-56099. 434p. 1999. pap. text 31.00 (*0-13-915729-8*) P-H.

***Brincat, M.** Hormone Replacement Therapy & the Skin. (Illus.). 150p. 2001. 78.00 (*1-85070-810-X*) Prthnon Pub.

Brinch Hansen, Per. Programming for Everyone in Java. LC 98-51800. (Illus.). 238p. 1999. pap. 29.95 (*0-387-98683-9*) Spr-Verlag.

An Asterisk (*) at the beginning of an entry indicates that the title is appearing for the first time.

— Studies in Computational Science: Parallel Programming Paradigms. LC 94-47128. 400p. (C). 1995. 76.00 (*0-13-439324-4*) P-H.

Brinck, Gretchen. Boy Next Door. 384p. 1999. mass mkt. 5.99 (*0-7860-1011-8*) Kensgtn Pub Corp.

Brinck, Ingar. The Indexical 'I' The First Person in Thought & Language. LC 97-34178. (Synthese Library: No. 265). 192p. 1997. text 87.00 (*0-7923-4741-2*) Kluwer Academic.

Brinck, Wolfgang. The Aleutian Kayak: Origins, Construction, & Use of the Traditional Seagoing Baidarka. LC 94-43165. (Illus.). 192p. 1995. pap. text 19.95 (*0-07-007893-9*, Ragged Mntain) McGraw-Hill Prof.

***Brinckerhoff, Deborah.** Weaving for the Gods: Textiles of the Ancient Andes. (Illus.). 1999. pap. 14.95 (*0-9665144-4-0*) Bruce Museum.

Brinckerhoff, Loring C., et al. Promoting Postsecondary Education for Students with Learning Disabilities: A Handbook for Practitioners. LC 93-9576. 440p. 1993. text 41.00 (*0-89079-589-4*, 6687) PRO-ED.

***Brinckerhoff, Peter C.** Faith-Based Management: Leading Organizations That Are Based on More Than Just Mission. LC 99-22087. (Nonprofit Law, Finance, & Management Ser.). 250p. 1999. 49.95 (*0-471-31544-3*) Wiley.

Brinckerhoff, Peter C. Financial Empowerment. LC 96-11813. (Mission-Based Management Ser.). 1996. 34.95 (*0-931712-19-X*) Wiley.

***Brinckerhoff, Peter C.** Financial Empowerment: More Money for More Mission. LC 98-25937. (Nonprofit Law, Finance, & Management Ser.). 256p. 1998. 52.95 (*0-471-29692-9*) Wiley.

Brinckerhoff, Peter C. Financial Empowerment Discussion Leader's Guide. (Mission-Based Management Ser.). 51p. 1996. ring bd. 21.95 (*0-931712-20-3*) Wiley.

***Brinckerhoff, Peter C.** Mission-Based Management: Leading Your Not-for-Profit in the 21st Century. 2nd ed. 300p. 2000. 34.95 (*0-471-39013-5*) Wiley.

Brinckerhoff, Peter C. Mission-Based Management: Leading Your Not-for-Profit into the 21st Century. LC 94-28766. 272p. 1994. 29.95 (*0-931712-15-7*) Wiley.

***Brinckerhoff, Peter C.** Mission-Based Management: Leading Your Not-for-Profit into 21st Century. LC 98-25938. (Nonprofit Law, Finance, & Management Ser.). 272p. 1998. 52.95 (*0-471-29691-0*) Wiley.

Brinckerhoff, Peter C. Mission-Based Management Discussion Leader's Guide. (Mission-Based Management Ser.). 37p. 1995. spiral bd. 19.95 (*0-931712-17-3*) Wiley.

— Mission-Based Marketing. LC 97-29488. (Mission-Based Management Ser.). 1997. 34.95 (*0-931712-23-8*) Wiley.

***Brinckerhoff, Peter C.** Mission-Based Marketing: How Your Not-for-Profit Can Succeed in a More Competitive World. LC 98-25934. (Nonprofit Law, Finance, & Management Ser.). 224p. 1998. 52.95 (*0-471-29693-7*) Wiley.

— Social Entrepreneurship: The Art of Mission-Based Venture Development. LC 99-58144. (Nonprofit Law, Finance, & Management Ser.). 270p. 2000. text 44.95 (*0-471-36282-4*) Wiley.

Brinckloe, Julie. Fireflies! 1986. 10.19 (*0-606-00876-4*, Pub. by Turtleback) Demco.

Brinckloe, Julie. Fireflies. LC 85-26767. (Illus.). 32p. (J). (gr. k-2). 1986. reprint ed. mass mkt. 4.99 (*0-689-71055-0*) Aladdin.

Brinckman, F. E. & Bellama, J. Michael, eds. Organometals & Organometalloids: Occurrence & Fate in the Environment. LC 78-24316. (ACS Symposium Ser.: No. 82). 1978. 49.95 (*0-8412-0461-6*) Am Chemical.

— Organometals & Organometalloids: Occurrence & Fate in the Environment. LC 78-24316. (ACS Symposium Ser.: Vol. 82). 463p. 1978. reprint ed. pap. 143.60 (*0-608-03944-6*, 206439100009) Bks Demand.

Brinckman, F. E., jt. auth. see Thayer, J. S.

Brinckmann, Caren, et al. Beforderung. (GER., Illus.). 40p. (YA). (gr. 7 up). 1990. pap. text 25.00 incl. audio (*0-939990-71-7*) Intl Linguistics.

Brind. Lying Abroad. 2000. text 39.50 (*1-86064-377-9*) I B T.

Brind'Amour, Lucie & Vance, Eugene, eds. Archeologie du Signe. (ENG & FRE.). xii, 369p. pap. text 39.43 (*0-88844-803-1*) Brill Academic Pubs.

***Brindis, Claire, et al.** Protection As Prevention: Contraception for Sexually Active Teens. 35p. 2000. pap. 5.00 (*1-58671-028-1*) Natl Cpgn Teen Preg.

Brindis, Claire D. Adolescent Pregnancy Prevention: A Guidebook for Communities. (Illus.). 280p. (Orig.). 1991. pap. 24.50 (*1-879552-00-0*) SCRDP.

Brindle, J. V., compiled by. Talking in Flowers: Japanese Botanical Art. (Illus.). 96p. 1982. pap. 3.00 (*0-913196-40-1*) Hunt Inst Botanical.

Brindle, J. V. & White, J. J. Reflections from the Third Day: Photographic Revelations of Plant Design. (Illus.). 60p. (Orig.). 1978. pap. 6.00 (*0-913196-20-7*) Hunt Inst Botanical.

Brindle, J. V., jt. ed. see White, J. J.

Brindle, Jane. No Mercy. large type ed. (Dales Large Print Ser.). 1995. pap. 18.99 (*1-85389-540-7*, Dales) Ulverscroft.

Brindle, Kevin M., et al, eds. Advances in Molecular & Cell Biology Vol. 11: Enzymology in Vivo. 288p. 1995. 128.50 (*1-55938-844-7*) Jai Pr.

Brindle, Margaret A. & Mainiero, Lisa A. Managing Power Relationships in the New Lateral Organization. LC 99-27822. 192p. 2000. 59.95 (*1-56720-334-5*, Quorum Bks) Greenwood.

Brindle, Reginald S. The New Music: The Avant-Garde since 1945. 2nd ed. (Illus.). 224p. 1987. pap. text 27.95 (*0-19-315468-4*) OUP.

Brindle, Stephen, jt. auth. see Tyack, Geoffrey.

Brindle, Susan A. & Lademan, Miriam A. The Fish in the Fountain (El Pez de la Fuente) A Story of Baptism (Un Cuento Acerca del Bautisma) Emmanuelli Klosterman, Carmen A., tr. (Seven Sacraments Ser.). (ENG & SPA., Illus.). 56p. (gr. k-10). 1997. pap. 9.95 (*1-889733-05-9*, 01007) Precious Life Bks.

— The Little Creatures' Crusade (La Cruzada de las Criaturitas) A Story of Confirmation (Un Cuentro Acerca de la Confirmacion) Emmanuelli Klosterman, Carmen A., tr. (Seven Sacraments Ser.). (ENG & SPA., Illus.). 56p. (gr. k-10). 1999. pap. 9.95 (*1-889733-07-5*, 01009) Precious Life Bks.

Brindle, Susan A., et al. Children's Stations of the Cross (Estaciones de la Cruz por los Ninos) Andrews, William X., tr. (Stories of the Faith Ser.). (ENG & SPA., Illus.). 56p. (gr. k-10). 1997. pap. 9.95 (*1-889733-04-0*, 01006) Precious Life Bks.

— The Little Caterpillar That Finds Jesus (La Oruguita que Encuentra a Jesus) A Parable of the Eucharist (Una Parabola Acerca de la Eucaristia) Emmanuelli Klosterman, Carmen A., tr. (Seven Sacraments Ser.). (ENG & SPA., Illus.). 72p. (gr. k-10). 1999. pap. 9.95 (*1-889733-08-3*, 01011) Precious Life Bks.

Brindle, Susan A., jt. auth. see Hooker, Irene H.

Brindle, Susan A., jt. auth. see Lademan, Miriam A.

Brindley. Compuserve Made Simple. 160p. Date not set. pap. text 29.95 (*0-7506-3512-6*) Buttrwrth-Heinemann.

— Word for Windows 95 Made Simple. 160p. Date not set. pap. text 19.95 (*0-7506-2815-4*) Buttrwrth-Heinemann.

Brindley, Anna. Irish Prehistory: An Introduction. (Treasures of the National Museum of Ireland Ser.). (Illus.). 48p. (Orig.). 1995. pap. 7.95 (*0-946172-38-2*, Pub. by Town Hse) Roberts Rinehart.

Brindley, Caroline, et al. Pediatric Oral Skills Package. 80p. 1996. spiral bd. 300.00 (*1-56593-572-1*, 0762) Singular Publishing.

Brindley, David N., ed. Phosphatidate Phosphohydrolase, 2 vols., Vol. I. 160p. 1988. 85.00 (*0-8493-4359-3*, QP609, CRC Reprint) Franklin.

— Phosphatidate Phosphohydrolase, 2 vols., Vol. II. 136p. 1988. 136.00 (*0-8493-4360-7*, QP609, CRC Reprint) Franklin.

Brindley, J., jt. auth. see Kapitaniak, Tomasz.

Brindley, James C. The Irish Landscape. (Appletree Pocket Guides Ser.). (Illus.). 72p. (Orig.). 1992. pap. 7.95 (*0-86281-310-7*, Pub. by Appletree Pr) Irish Bks Media.

Brindley, Keith. Electronics Engineer's Pocket Book. (Illus.). 319p. 1993. text 34.95 (*0-7506-0937-0*) Buttrwrth-Heinemann.

— Modern Electronic Test Equipment. 1988. 27.00 (*0-434-90567-4*) CRC Pr.

— Newnes Radio & Electronic Engineer's Pocket Book. 1988. 27.00 (*0-434-90179-2*) CRC Pr.

***Brindley, Keith.** Starting Electronics. 2nd ed. 256p. 1999. pap. text 19.95 (*0-7506-4435-4*, Newnes) Buttrwrth-Heinemann.

Brindley, Keith. Starting Electronics: All You Need to Get a Grounding in Practical Electronics. (Maplin Ser.). (Illus.). 240p. 1999. pap. text 24.95 (*0-7506-2053-6*) Buttrwrth-Heinemann.

— Word for Windows 95. LC 96-83476. (Clear & Simple Ser.). 160p. 1996. pap. text 10.95 (*0-7506-9803-9*, Digital DEC) Buttrwrth-Heinemann.

Brindley, Keith & Carr, Joseph. Newnes Electronics Engineer's Pocket Book. 2nd ed. (Illus.). 368p. 2000. 28.95 (*0-7506-3972-5*, Newnes) Buttrwrth-Heinemann.

Brindley, Keith, jt. auth. see Judd, Mike.

Brindley, Louise. Autumn Comes to Mrs. Hazell. 256p. 1996. 22.00 (*0-7278-5180-2*) Severn Hse.

— Indian Summer. 256p. 1998. 25.00 (*0-7278-5235-3*) Severn Hse.

***Brindley, Louise.** Indian Summer. large type ed. 400p. 1999. 31.99 (*0-7505-1306-3*, Pub. by Mgna Lrg Print) Ulverscroft.

— Lizzie. large type ed. 384p. 1999. 31.99 (*0-7505-1396-9*, Pub. by Mgna Lrg Print) Ulverscroft.

— Tantalus. 1999. 25.00 (*0-7278-5497-6*, Pub. by Severn Hse) Chivers N Amer.

— Tantalus. LC 00-28686. 2000. write for info. (*0-7862-2568-8*) Thorndike Pr.

Brindley, N. Phosphatidate Phosphohydrolase, 2 vols., Set. LC 87-20867. 1988. reprint ed. 220.00 (*0-8493-4358-5*, CRC Reprint) Franklin.

***Brindley, Thomas A.** The China Youth Corps in Taiwan. LC 98-44637. (American University Studies XIV: Vol. 46). xi, 155p. (C). 1999. text 38.95 (*0-8204-4296-8*) P Lang Pubng.

Brindley, Tim & Rydin, Yvonne. Remaking Planning: Politics of Urban Change. 2nd ed. (Illus.). 240p. (C). 1996. pap. 25.99 (*0-415-09874-2*) Routledge.

Brindley, Tim, et al. Remaking Planning: The Politics of Urban Change in the Thatcher Years. 192p. (C). (gr. 13). 1989. text 65.00 (*0-04-711021-X*) Routledge.

Brindze, Ruth. Not to Be Broadcast: The Truth about the Radio. LC 73-19802. (Civil Liberties in American History Ser.). 310p. 1974. reprint ed. lib. bdg. 37.50 (*0-306-70598-2*) Da Capo.

Brine. Islam. 1989. pap. text. write for info. (*0-582-31786-X*, Pub. by Addison-Wesley) Longman.

— Islam. 1991. pap. text. write for info. (*0-582-02967-8*, Pub. by Addison-Wesley) Longman.

Brine, D. Undereducating Women: Globalizing Inequality. LC 98-18439. (Feminist Educational Thinking Ser.). 178p. 1998. pap. 95.00 (*0-335-19739-6*) OpUniv Pr.

— Undereducating Women: Globalizing Inequality. LC 98-18439. (Feminist Educational Thinking Ser.). 1998. pap. 29.95 (*0-335-19738-8*) OpUniv Pr.

Brine, Adrian & York, Michael. A Shakespearean Actor Prepares. LC 99-48900. 288p. 1999. pap. 16.95 (*1-57525-189-2*) Smith & Kraus.

Brine, Charles J., jt. ed. see Furda, Ivan.

Brine, Jenny. Comecon: The Rise & Fall of an International Socialist Organization. 250p. (C). 1992. 54.95 (*1-56000-080-5*) Transaction Pubs.

Brine, Kevin, jt. ed. see Cannon, Garland.

***Brine, Lindesay.** Travels Amongst American Indians, Their Ancient Earthworks & Temples: Including a Journey in Guatemala, Mexico & Yucatan, & a Visit to Ruins of Patinamit, Utatlan, Palenque & Uxmal. (LC History-America-E). 429p. 1999. reprint ed. lib. bdg. 99.00 (*0-7812-4240-1*) Rprt Serv.

Brine, Mary. Hopwood Street to Wellington Lane. (C). 1989. text 35.00 (*0-948929-16-2*) St Mut.

Brinegar, George K. & Fettig, Lyle P. Some Measures of the Quality of Agricultural Credit. (Technical Papers: No. 19). 66p. 1968. reprint ed. 20.00 (*0-87014-493-6*) Natl Bur Econ Res.

Brinegar, Jerry L. Breaking Free from Domestic Violence. 158p. (Orig.). 1992. pap. 12.95 (*1-56838-288-X*) Hazelden.

Briner. Project Leadership 2nd Edition. 176p. 1996. pap. 29.95 (*0-566-07785-X*) Ashgate Pub Co.

Briner, Bob. Business Basics from the Bible: More Ancient Wisdom for Modern Business. LC 96-30608. 1996. 15.99 (*0-310-21320-7*) Zondervan.

***Briner, Bob.** The Final Roar. 224p. 2000. 17.99 (*0-8054-2361-3*) Broadman.

Briner, Bob. The Management Methods of Jesus: Ancient Wisdom for Modern Business. 128p. 1996. 14.99 (*0-7852-7681-5*) Nelson.

— The Management Methods of Jesus: Ancient Wisdom for Modern Business. abr. ed. 1998. 15.99 incl. audio (*0-8054-1265-4*) Broadman.

— Men in Leadership: One Minute Bible. LC 99-15732. (One Minute Bible Ser.). 1999. 14.99 (*0-8054-9153-8*) Broadman.

— Roaring Lambs: A Gentle Plan to Radically Change Your World. 192p. 1995. pap. 10.99 (*0-310-59111-2*) Zondervan.

— Squeeze Play: Caught Between Business & Home Practical Devotions for Men. LC 93-8943. 160p. 1993. pap. 8.99 (*0-310-40021-X*) Zondervan.

— Women in Leadership. LC 99-15731. (One Minute Bible Ser.). 1999. 14.99 (*0-8054-9193-7*) Broadman.

Briner, Bob & Pritchard, Ray. Jesus el Lider Modelo: Su Ejemplo y Ensenanza para Hoy.Tr. of Leadership Lessons of Jesus. (SPA.). 144p. 1997. pap. text 9.99 (*0-311-46165-4*, Edit Mundo) Casa Bautista.

— The Leadership Lessons of Jesus: Timeless Insights for Today's Leaders. LC 97-13207. 250p. 1997. 14.99 (*0-8054-6356-9*) Broadman.

— More Leadership Lessons of Jesus: A Timeless Model for Todays Leaders. LC 98-24153. 176p. 1998. 14.99 (*0-8054-1687-0*) Broadman.

Briner, Elaine. A Collection of Children's Stories. (Illus.). (J). 1996. pap. 4.95 (*0-7880-0659-2*, Fairway Pr) CSS OH.

— Fairytales of the Wentny Kind. (Illus.). 38p. (J). (gr. 2-5). pap. write for info. (*0-9641429-2-9*) Versary Pubns.

Briner, Elaine, jt. auth. see Kovach, George D.

Briner, Patricia J., ed. see Blair, John S. & Tindall, Barry S.

***Briner, Rob B.** Emotion at Work. 1999. pap. text 39.95 (*0-86377-991-3*) L Erlbaum Assocs.

Briner, Wendy, et al. Project Leadership. 2nd ed. 175p. 1996. 59.95 (*0-566-07714-0*, Pub. by Gower) Ashgate Pub Co.

Brines, Steven F., ed. see Willcutt, J. Robert & Ball, Kenneth R.

Briney, Doug. The Home Machinist's Handbook. 288p. (Orig.). 1984. pap. 19.95 (*0-07-155653-2*) McGraw.

— The Home Machinist's Handbook. (Illus.). 228p. (Orig.). 1983. 21.95 (*0-8306-0573-8*, 1573); pap. 18.95 (*0-8306-1573-3*) McGraw-Hill Prof.

Bring, Ove, ed. Current International Law Issues: Nordic Perspectives Essays in Honour of Jerzy Sztucki. LC 94-6909. 220p. (C). 1994. lib. bdg. 92.00 (*0-7923-2762-4*) Kluwer Academic.

Bringa, Tone. Being Muslim the Bosnian Way: Identify & Community in a Central Bosnian Village. 288p. (C). 1996. pap. text 18.95 (*0-691-00175-8*, Pub. by Princeton U Pr) Cal Prin Full Svc.

Bringans, R. D., et al, eds. Atomic Scale Structure of Interfaces Vol. 159: Materials Research Society Symposium Proceedings. 478p. 1990. text 17.50 (*1-55899-047-X*) Materials Res.

Bringas, Ernie. Going by the Book: Past & Present Tragedies of Biblical Authority. LC 96-157078. 224p. (Orig.). 1995. pap. 12.95 (*1-57174-022-8*) Hampton Roads Pub Co.

Bringe, Julie, et al. East Asia: Regional Economic Integration & Implications for the U. S. (Illus.). 151p. (C). 1997. reprint ed. pap. text 35.00 (*0-7881-4160-0*) DIANE Pub.

Bringeus, Nils-Arvid, ed. Man & Picture: Papers from the First International Symposium for Ethnological Research. (Illus.). 264p. (Orig.). 1986. pap. text 52.00 (*91-22-00794-6*) Coronet Bks.

— Religion in Everyday Life: Papers Given at a Symposium in Stockholm, 1993. (Konferenser Ser.: No. 31). (Illus.). 224p. 1994. 44.50 (*91-7402-250-4*) Coronet Bks.

Bringgold, Diane. Life Instead. 128p. 1984. reprint ed. pap. 4.95 (*0-9614225-0-5*) Howard Pub.

Bringham. Encouragement. 1997. pap. 6.99 (*1-85792-317-0*, Pub. by Christian Focus) Spring Arbor Dist.

Bringhurst, Bob. WordPerfect 8 Answers! Certified Tech Support. LC 98-127048. 496p. 1997. pap. text 24.99 (*0-07-882449-4*) Osborne-McGraw.

Bringhurst, Bruce. Antitrust & Oil Monopoly: The Standard Oil Cases, 1890-1911, 8. LC 78-67908. (Contributions in Legal Studies: No. 8). (Illus.). 296p. 1979. 55.00 (*0-313-20642-2*, BRA/, Greenwood Pr) Greenwood.

Bringhurst, John. Planes, Jets & Helicopters. (Illus.). 160p. 1994. pap. 11.95 (*0-07-007904-8*) McGraw.

Bringhurst, John R. Fifty Great Paper Airplanes. LC 93-8272. (Illus.). 142p. 1993. pap. 8.95 (*0-8306-4451-2*) McGraw-Hill Prof.

Bringhurst, Newell G. Brigham Young & the Expanding American Frontier. 240p. (C). 1997. pap. 20.20 (*0-673-39322-4*) Addson-Wesley Educ.

***Bringhurst, Newell G.** Fawn McKay Brodie: A Biographer's Life. LC 99-34845. 448p. 1999. 37.95 (*0-8061-3181-0*) U of Okla Pr.

Bringhurst, Newell G. Saints, Slaves, & Blacks: The Changing Place of Black People Within Mormonism, 4. LC 81-1093. (Contributions to the Study of Religion Ser.: No. 4). (Illus.). 254p. 1981. 65.00 (*0-313-22752-7*, BSB/, Greenwood Pr) Greenwood.

***Bringhurst, Newell G.** Visalia's Fabulous Fox: A Theater Story. unabridged ed. Allen, William R. et al, eds. LC 99-76059. (Illus.). 200p. 1999. 39.95 (*0-9675482-0-9*) Visalian Friends.

Bringhurst, Robert. The Beauty of the Weapons: Selected Poems 1972-82. 160p. 1985. reprint ed. pap. 10.00 (*0-914742-90-6*) Copper Canyon.

***Bringhurst, Robert.** Elements Of Typographic Style. (Illus.). 254p. 2000. reprint ed. pap. text 20.00 (*0-7881-6454-6*) DIANE Pub.

Bringhurst, Robert. Elements Of Typographic Style. 2nd rev. ed. LC 96-910471. (Illus.). 320p. 1996. pap. 24.95 (*0-88179-132-6*); text 34.95 (*0-88179-133-4*) Hartley & Marks.

— Pieces of Map, Pieces of Music. LC 86-73199. 128p. (Orig.). 1987. reprint ed. pap. 9.00 (*1-55659-003-2*) Copper Canyon.

***Bringhurst, Robert.** A Story As Sharp As a Knife: The Classical Haida Mythtellers & Their World. (Illus.). 527p. 2000. pap. 24.95 (*0-8032-6179-9*, Bison Books); text 45.00 (*0-8032-1314-X*) U of Nebr Pr.

Bringhurst, Robert. Tzuhalem's Mountain. 1982. text 50.00 (*0-88982-044-9*, Pub. by Oolichan Bks) Genl Dist Srvs.

Bringhurst, Robert. Word 97 Essentials: Level II. LC 97-65613. 224p. 1997. 22.99 (*1-57576-801-1*) Sams.

Bringhurst, Robert. Word 97 Essentials Level II. 1997. 49.99 (*1-57576-806-2*) Que Educ & Trng.

***Bringhurst, Robert, tr.** Nine Visits to the Mythworld: Ghandl of the Qayahl Llaanas. 224p. 2000. 29.95 (*0-8032-1316-6*) U of Nebr Pr.

Bringhurst, Robert & Braun, Janice. Peter Koch, Printer: Cowboy Surrealists, Maverick Poets & Pre-Socratic Philosophers. (Illus.). 65p. 1995. pap. 25.00 (*0-87104-439-0*) NY Pub Lib.

Bringhurst, Robert, jt. auth. see Chappell, Warren.

Bringhurst, Robert, jt. auth. see Reid, Bill.

***Bringi, V. N. & Chandrasekar, V.** Polarimetric Doppler Weather Radar: Principles & Applications. (Illus.). 500p. 2000. write for info. (*0-521-62384-7*) Cambridge U Pr.

Bringle. Universities as Citizens. LC 98-31361. 210p. (C). 1999. 26.99 (*0-205-28696-8*, Macmillan Coll) P-H.

Bringman, Dale. A Star Is Born. (Orig.). 1987. pap. 4.95 (*0-89536-881-1*, 7867) CSS OH.

Bringmann, Wolfgang G., et al, eds. A Pictorial History of Psychology. LC 96-24728. (Illus.). 656p. 1997. 78.00 (*0-86715-292-3*); pap. 38.95 (*0-86715-330-X*) Quint Pub Co.

Bringmann, Wolfgang G. & Tweney, Ryan D., eds. Wundt Studies: A Centennial Collection. 350p. (C). 1980. pap. text 28.00 (*0-88937-001-X*) Hogrefe & Huber Pubs.

Brings, Allen, et al. A New Approach to Keyboard Harmony. (Illus.). 181p. (C). 1979. pap. text 23.00 (*0-393-95001-8*) Norton.

***Brings, Felicia & Winter, Susan.** Older Women, Younger Men: New Options for Love & Romance. LC 00-132571. 208p. 2000. pap. 14.95 (*0-88282-200-4*, Pub. by New Horizon NJ) Natl Bk Netwk.

Brings, Lawrence M. Clever Introductions for Chairmen: A Compilation of Practical Speeches & Stories. LC 99-26981. 1999. 40.00 (*0-7808-0302-7*) Omnigraphics Inc.

Bringsjord, Selmer. Abortion: A Dialogue. LC 97-22044. 96p. (C). 1997. pap. text 5.95 (*0-87220-366-2*); lib. bdg. 24.95 (*0-87220-367-0*) Hackett Pub.

— What Robots Can & Can't Be. 394p. (C). 1992. lib. bdg. 175.00 (*0-7923-1662-2*, Pub. by Kluwer Academic) Kluwer Academic.

Bringsjord, Selmer & Ferrucci, David. Artificial Intelligence & Literary Creativity: Inside the Mind of BRUTUS, a Storytelling Machine. LC 99-13748. 320p. 1999. pap. write for info. (*0-8058-1987-8*) L Erlbaum Assocs.

— Artificial Intelligence & Literary Creativity: Inside the Mind of Brutus, a Storytelling Machine. LC 99-13748. 320p. 1999. write for info. (*0-8058-1986-X*) L Erlbaum Assocs.

Bringuier, Carlos J. Operacion Judas. LC 93-72086. (Coleccion Caniqui). (SPA.). 185p. (Orig.). 1993. pap. 19.00 (*0-89729-694-X*) Ediciones.

Bringuier, J. Dictionnaire Pratique de Droit Funeraire. (FRE.). 1998. 195.00 (*0-320-00239-X*) Fr & Eur.

Bringuier, Jean-Claude. Conversations with Jean Piaget. Gulati, Basia M., tr. (Illus.). xiv, 160p. 1989. pap. text 13.95 (*0-226-07505-2*, Midway Reprint) U Ch Pr.

— Conversations with Jean Piaget. Gulati, Basia M., tr. LC 79-15669. (C). 1982. reprint ed. pap. 6.95 (*0-226-07504-4*) U Ch Pr.

Brini, A., et al. Oncology of the Eye & Adnexa: Atlas of Clinical Pathology. (Monographs in Ophthalmology). (C). 1990. text 304.50 (*0-7923-0409-8*) Kluwer Academic.

Brinig, Brian P., et al. A Guide to Litigation Support Services, 3 vols. Incl. Vol. 3. Guide to Litigation Support Services. 1997. ring bd. 165.00

(*0-7646-0094-X*); Vol. 1. 1997. ring bd. (*0-7646-0092-3*); Vol. 2. 1997. ring bd. (*0-7646-0093-1*); 156.00 (*0-7646-0091-5*) Prctnrs Pub Co.

***Brinig, Brian P., et al.** Guide to Litigation Support Services, 3 vols. 1999. ring bd. 175.00 (*0-7646-0859-2*) Prctnrs Pub Co.

Brinig, Brian P., et al. Guide to Litigation Support Services, 2 vols. Incl. Vol. 1. Guide to Litigation Support Services. 1998. ring bd. 175.00 (*0-7646-0522-4*); Vol. 2. Guide to Litigation Support Services. 1998. ring bd. 175.00 (*0-7646-0523-2*); Vol. 3. Guide to Litigation Support Services. 1998. ring bd. 175.00 (*0-7646-0524-0*); 156.00 (*1-56433-847-9*) Prctnrs Pub Co.

Brinig, Brian P., et al. Guide to Litigation Support Services, 3 vols. Incl. Vol. 1. Guide to Litigation Support Services. 1998. ring bd. 175.00 (*0-7646-0522-4*); Vol. 2. Guide to Litigation Support Services. 1998. ring bd. 175.00 (*0-7646-0523-2*); Vol. 3. Guide to Litigation Support Services. 1998. ring bd. 175.00 (*0-7646-0524-0*); 175.00 (*0-7646-0521-6*) Prctnrs Pub Co.

— Guide to Litigation Support Services, Vol. 1. 1999. ring bd. write for info. (*0-7646-0860-6*) Prctnrs Pub Co.

— Guide to Litigation Support Services, Vol. 2. 1999. ring bd. write for info. (*0-7646-0861-4*) Prctnrs Pub Co.

— Guide to Litigation Support Services, Vol. 3. 1999. ring bd. write for info. (*0-7646-0862-2*) Prctnrs Pub Co.

Brinig, Brian P., et al. Developing & Managing a Litigation Services Practice. 98th ed. 300p. 1999. pap. text 79.00 (*0-15-606076-0*) Harcourt.

Brinig, Liz. Bridge Bidding: The Golden Rules. (Illus.). 149p. 1992. pap. 16.95 (*1-85223-282-X*, Pub. by Crolwood) Trafalgar.

Brinig, Margaret. Virginia Domestic Relations Handbook, 1996. 3rd ed. LC 96-77723. 554p. 1996. text 90.00 (*1-55834-399-7*, 60666-11, MICHIE) LEXIS Pub.

***Brinig, Margaret F.** From Contract to Covenant: Beyond the Law & Economics of the Family. 2000. 47.50 (*0-674-00216-4*) HUP.

Brinig, Margaret F. Virginia Domestic Relations Handbook. 2nd ed. 472p. 1991. 90.00 (*0-87473-815-6*, MICHIE) LEXIS Pub.

***Brinig, Margaret F.** Virginia Domestic Relations Handbook, 1999 Cumulative Supplement: Pocketpart. 155p. 1999. write for info. (*0-327-01592-6*, 6066716) LEXIS Pub.

***Brinig, Margaret F., et al.** Family Law in Action: A Reader. 1999. pap. 29.95 (*1-58360-750-1*) Anderson Pub Co.

Brinig, Margaret F., jt. auth. see Crafton, Steven M.

Brinig, Margaret F., ed. see Schneider, Carl E.

Brinig, Myron. Singermann. LC 74-27968. (Modern Jewish Experience Ser.). 1975. reprint ed. 40.95 (*0-405-06698-8*) Ayer.

— Wide Open Town: A Novel. rev. ed. LC 93-4645. (Sweetgrass Bks.). 192p. 1993. reprint ed. pap. 12.95 (*1-56037-034-3*) Am Wrld Geog.

Brininstool, E. A. Troopers with Custer. (Custer Library). (Illus.). 368p. 1994. 19.95 (*0-8117-1742-9*) Stackpole.

— Troopers with Custer: Historic Incidents of the Battle of the Little Big Horn. LC 88-31143. (Illus.). xii, 343p. 1989. reprint ed. pap. 13.95 (*0-8032-6101-2*, Bison Books) U of Nebr Pr.

Brininstool, E. A., jt. auth. see Hebard, Grace R.

Brininstool, E. A., ed. see Spotts, David L.

Brininstool, E. A., ed. see Standing Bear, Luther.

Brininstool, Earl A., jt. auth. see Hebard, Grace R.

***Brink.** Devil's Valley. 2000. pap. write for info. (*0-15-601208-1*) Harcourt.

Brink. Texas Election Update-american Government. (Political Science). 1997. 1.00 (*0-534-53986-6*) Wadsworth Pub.

Brink & Mellish, J. M. Teaching the Practice of Nursing. 3rd ed. 1991. pap. text 45.00 (*0-409-11154-6*) Buttrwrth-Heinemann.

Brink, A. W., ed. see Trosse, George.

***Brink, Andre Philippus.** Devil's Valley. LC 98-40513. 416p. 1999. 24.00 (*0-15-100440-4*) Harcourt.

Brink, Andre Philippus. A Dry White Season. 256p. 1984. pap. 13.95 (*0-14-006890-2*, Penguin Bks) Viking Penguin.

— Imaginings of Sand. LC 96-19316. 352p. 1996. 24.00 (*0-15-100224-X*) Harcourt.

— Imaginings of Sand. (C). 1999. pap. 14.00 (*0-15-600658-8*, Harvest Bks) Harcourt.

— The Novel: Language & Narrative from Cervantes to Calvino. LC 97-48400. 388p. 1998. text 30.00 (*0-8147-1330-0*) NYU Pr.

***Brink, Andre Philippus.** Reinventing a Continent: Writing & Politics in South Africa, 1982-1998. LC 98-13859. 288p. 1998. reprint ed. 25.00 (*0-944072-89-5*) Zoland Bks.

— Reinventions: Old Literature; New Climates. 28p. 1997. pap. 12.00 (*1-884381-10-3*) W Drenttel Ed.

Brink, Andrea. Parents: Help Your Preschooler Now! LC 97-65971. (Illus.). 91p. (Orig.). 1997. pap. 11.95 (*1-883122-09-0*) Pearce Pub.

— Parents: Help Your Preschooler Now! Home Activities for Learning & Growing. rev. ed. (Illus.). 96p. (J). (ps). 1998. pap. 11.95 (*1-58112-898-3*) Dissertation.

***Brink, Andrew.** The Creative Matrix: Anxiety & the Origin of Creativity. LC 99-17536. (Reshaping of Psychoanalysis Ser.: No. 10). 232p. 2000. text 50.95 (*0-8204-4480-4*) P Lang Pubng.

Brink, Andrew. Obsession & Culture: A Study of Sexual Obsession in Modern Fiction. LC 95-30472. 256p. (C). 1996. 39.50 (*0-8386-3596-2*) Fairleigh Dickinson.

Brink, B. Language of Metre of Chaucer. LC 68-24899. (Studies in Chaucer: No. 6). 1969. reprint ed. lib. bdg. 75.00 (*0-8383-0917-8*) M S G Haskell Hse.

Brink, Ben. David's Story: A Book about Surgery. (Meeting the Challenge Ser.). (J). 1996. lib. bdg. 21.27 (*0-8225-2577-1*, Lerner Publctns) Lerner Pub.

Brink, Benjamin M. Early History of Saugerties, 1660-1825. (Illus.). 364p. 1997. reprint ed. lib. bdg. 42.00 (*0-8328-6225-8*) Higginson Bk Co.

— Olde Ulster, 1905, Vol. I. 384p. 1988. 29.95 (*0-941567-00-1*) J C & A L Fawcett.

— Palatines of Olde Ulster. 80p. (Orig.). 1996. pap. 9.95 (*0-910746-20-6*) Hope Farm.

Brink, Bernhard. The Language & Metre of Chaucer. Smith, M. Bentinck, tr. LC 69-13838. 280p. 1970. reprint ed. lib. bdg. 65.00 (*0-8371-1927-8*, BRLM, Greenwood Pr) Greenwood.

Brink, Bernhard A. The Language & Metre of Chaucer. (BCL1-PR English Literature Ser.). 280p. 1992. reprint ed. lib. bdg. 79.00 (*0-7812-7170-3*) Rprt Serv.

Brink, Bernhard A. Ten. History of English Literature, 3 vols. LC 73-154132. reprint ed. 110.00 (*0-404-09210-1*) AMS Pr.

Brink, Beverly E. Wyoming: Land of Echoing Canyons. LC 85-80478. (Old West Region Ser.: Vol. 3). (Illus.). 180p. 1986. 21.95 (*0-918532-15-9*, Flyng Diamond) Hlthy Wght Network.

Brink-Budgen, Roy Van den, see Van den Brink-Budgen, Roy.

Brink, C. & Schmidt, W. Kahl, eds. Relational Methods in Computer Science. (Advances in Computing Science Ser.). (Illus.). xv, 288p. 1997. pap. 49.95 (*3-211-82971-7*) Spr-Verlag.

Brink, Carla J., ed. Cocaine: A Symposium. LC 85-17797. (Illus.). 69p. (Orig.). 1985. pap. text 10.00 (*0-9615363-0-6*) Wis Inst Drug Abuse.

Brink, Carol. Harps in the Wind: The Story of The Singing Hutchinsons. LC 80-11626. (Illus.). v, 312p. 1980. reprint ed. lib. bdg. 39.50 (*0-306-76024-X*) Da Capo.

Brink, Carol A. Dare to Dream! A Handbook for the Empowered Dreamer. large type ed. LC 95-94515. 148p. (Orig.). 1995. pap. 12.95 (*0-9646759-6-X*) Brink Publns.

Brink, Carol R. Baby Island. LC 92-45577. (Illus.). 160p. (J). (gr. 3-7). 1993. reprint ed. mass mkt. 4.50 (*0-689-71751-2*) Aladdin.

— Baby Island. 160p. 1992. reprint ed. 25.95 (*0-89968-304-5*, Lghtyr Pr) Buccaneer Bks.

— Buffalo Coat. LC 93-17131. (Washington State University Press Reprint Ser.). 421p. 1993. reprint ed. pap. 19.95 (*0-87422-095-5*) Wash St U Pr.

— Caddie Woodlawn. LC 89-18357. (Illus.). 288p. (J). (gr. 4-6). 1990. mass mkt. 4.50 (*0-689-71370-3*) Aladdin.

— Caddie Woodlawn. LC 73-588. (Illus.). 288p. (J). (gr. 4-6). 1973. text, lib. bdg. 16.00 (*0-02-713670-1*, Mac Bks Young Read) S&S Childrens.

— Caddie Woodlawn. (Scholastic Literature Guide Ser.). (Illus.). 16p. (J). 1997. pap. text 3.95 (*0-590-37359-5*) Scholastic Inc.

— Caddie Woodlawn. (J). 1970. 9.60 (*0-606-02490-5*, Pub. by Turtleback) Demco.

Brink, Carol R. Caddie Woodlawn. 2nd ed. LC 97-1416. 242p. (J). (gr. 3-7). 1997. pap. 4.50 (*0-689-81521-2*) Aladdin.

Brink, Carol R. Caddie Woodlawn, Vol. 1. 1999. pap. 2.99 (*0-689-82969-8*) Aladdin.

— A Chain of Hands. LC 93-6908. 200p. 1993. pap. 17.95 (*0-87422-098-X*) Wash St U Pr.

— Goody O'Grumpity. LC 94-5103. (Illus.). 32p. (J). (gr. k-3). 1994. pap. 6.95 (*1-55858-614-8*, Pub. by North-South Bks NYC) Chronicle Bks.

Brink, Carol R. Magical Melons. (J). 1990. 9.05 (*0-606-04473-6*, Pub. by Turtleback) Demco.

Brink, Carol R. Magical Melons. LC 90-144. (Illus.). 208p. (J). (gr. 4-6). 1990. reprint ed. mass mkt. 3.95 (*0-689-71416-5*) Aladdin.

— Pink Motel. (J). 1993. 9.05 (*0-606-05545-2*, Pub. by Turtleback) Demco.

— The Pink Motel. LC 92-17953. (Illus.). 224p. (J). (gr. 3-7). 1993. reprint ed. mass mkt. 3.95 (*0-689-71677-X*) Aladdin.

— Snow in the River. LC 92-46243. (Washington State University Press Reprint Ser.). 308p. 1993. reprint ed. pap. 19.95 (*0-87422-097-1*) Wash St U Pr.

— Strangers in the Forest. LC 93-12731. (Washington State University Press Reprint Ser.). 314p. 1993. reprint ed. pap. 19.95 (*0-87422-096-3*) Wash St U Pr.

Brink, Carol Ryrie. Baby Island. 1993. 9.05 (*0-606-05132-5*, Pub. by Turtleback) Demco.

Brink, Charles O. Klassische Student in England: Historische Reflexionen Uber Bentley, Porson Und Housman. Deufert, M., tr. (Illus.). 297p. (C). 1997. text 63.50 (*3-519-07441-9*) B G Teubner.

Brink, D. M. & Mulvey, J., eds. Progress in Nuclear Physics. Incl. Vol. 10. 1969. 98.00 (*0-08-012682-0*); Vol. 11. 1970. 98.00 (*0-08-006360-8*); Vol. 12, Pt. 1. 1970. pap. 24.00 (*0-08-015766-1*); Vol. 12, Pt. 2. 1970. pap. 24.00 (*0-08-016394-7*); write for info. (*0-318-55214-0*) Elsevier.

Brink, D. M. & Satchler, George R. Angular Momentum. 3rd ed. LC 93-32190. (Illus.). 182p. (Orig.). 1994. pap. text 32.95 (*0-19-851759-9*, Clarendon Pr) OUP.

Brink, Daniel. Giacomo Puccini's Tosca. (Black Dog Opera Library). 144p. 1998. 19.98 (*1-57912-048-2*) Blck Dog & Leventhal.

— Giuseppe Verdi's Rigoletto. (Black Dog Opera Library). 144p. 1998. 19.98 (*1-57912-047-4*) Blck Dog & Leventhal.

Brink, Daniel S. Madama Butterfly. (Black Dog Opera Library). 144p. 1998. 19.98 (*1-57912-019-9*) Blck Dog & Leventhal.

— La Traviata. (Black Dog Opera Library). 144p. 1998. 19.98 (*1-57912-017-2*) Blck Dog & Leventhal.

Brink, Daniel T., jt. ed. see Adams, Karen L.

Brink, David O. Moral Realism & the Foundations of Ethics. (Cambridge Studies in Philosophy). 352p. (C). 1989. text 80.00 (*0-521-35080-8*); pap. text 25.95 (*0-521-35937-6*) Cambridge U Pr.

Brink, Emily R. & Polman, Bertus F. Psalter Hymnal Handbook. LC 97-39977. 1998. 59.95 (*1-56212-269-X*) CRC Pubns.

Brink, Gary. Captains Guide I: Lake Michigan, Pentwater to Mackinac Island. 1992. pap. text 9.95 (*0-681-79914-5*) Waldenbooks Co Inc.

— Captains Guide V: Lower Lake Huron. 1992. pap. text 9.95 (*0-681-79918-8*) Waldenbooks Co Inc.

Brink, Gijsbert Van Den, jt. ed. see Sarot, Marcel.

Brink, H. L., jt. ed. see Mashaba, T. G.

Brink, Henriette Maassen van den, see Maassen van den Brink, Henriette.

Brink, Hilla. Fundamentals of Research Methodology for Health Care Professionals. 232p. 1996. pap. 36.00 (*0-7021-3719-7*, Pub. by Juta & Co) Gaunt.

Brink, J. M. Van, see Van Brink, J. M., ed.

Brink, James, jt. auth. see Spillman, Richard.

Brink, James A., jt. auth. see Silverman, Paul M.

Brink, Jean R. Michael Drayton, Revisited. (Twayne's English Authors Ser.: No. 476). 168p. (C). 1990. text 25.95 (*0-8057-6989-7*, Twyne) Mac Lib Ref.

Brink, Jean R., ed. Privileging Gender in Early Modern England. (Sixteenth Century Essays & Studies: Vol. 23). 250p. 1993. 40.00 (*0-940474-24-7*, SCJP) Truman St Univ.

Brink, Jean R. & Gentrup, William F., eds. Renaissance Culture in Context: Theory & Practice. LC 93-7203. 240p. 1993. 86.95 (*0-85967-950-0*, Pub. by Scolar Pr) Ashgate Pub Co.

Brink, Judy & Mencher, Joan, eds. Mixed Blessings: Gender & Religious Fundamentalism Cross Culturally. 264p. (C). 1996. pap. 20.99 (*0-415-91186-9*) Routledge.

Brink, K. Interfacing Control & Software Engineering: A Formal Approach. (Illus.). 200p. 1997. pap. 49.50 (*90-407-1456-8*, Pub. by Delft U Pr) Coronet Bks.

Brink, Kenneth H. & Robinson, Allan R. The Sea: The Global Coastal Ocean: Processes & Methods, Vol. 10. (Ideas & Observations on Progress in the Study of the Seas Ser.). 624p. 1997. 200.00 (*0-471-11544-4*) Wiley.

Brink, Kenneth H., jt. auth. see Robinson, Allan R.

Brink, Kurt. Overcoming Pastoral Pitfalls. LC 97-176583. 1997. pap. 13.00 (*0-570-04969-5*, 12-3319) Concordia.

Brink, L., et al, eds. Nobel Symposium '67: Unification of Fundamental Interactions. 212p. (C). 1989. text 86.00 (*9971-5-0942-3*); pap. text 33.00 (*9971-5-0943-1*) World Scientific Pub.

— Physics & Mathematics of Strings. 608p. (C). 1990. text 86.00 (*9971-5-0980-6*); pap. text 40.00 (*9971-5-0981-4*) World Scientific Pub.

Brink, L. & Henneaux, M. Principles of String Theory. LC 87-29815. (Centro de Estudios Cientificos de Santiago Ser.). (Illus.). 312p. (C). 1988. text 89.50 (*0-306-42657-9*, Kluwer Plenum) Kluwer Academic.

Brink, L. & Marnelius, R. Pathways to Fundamental Theories. 376p. 1993. text 109.00 (*981-02-1411-1*) World Scientific Pub.

***Brink, Lars & Marnelius, R.** Novelties in String Theory: Proceedings of the Johns Hopkins Workshop on Current Problems in Particle Theory 22, Ghoteborg, 1998 (August 20-22) LC 99-41242. 370p. 1999. write for info. (*981-02-4084-8*) World Scientific Pub.

Brink, Pamela J. & Wood, Marilyn J. Basic Steps Nursing Research. 5th ed. (Nursing Ser.). 416p. Date not set. 43.75 (*0-7637-0538-1*) Jones & Bartlett.

Brink, Pamela J. & Wood, Marilynn J. Advanced Design in Nursing Research. 336p. (C). 1989. text 48.00 (*0-8039-2742-8*) Sage.

— Advanced Design in Nursing Research. 2nd ed. LC 97-33824. 1997. write for info. (*0-8039-5800-5*) Sage.

— Basic Steps in Planning Nursing Research: From Question to Proposal. 4th ed. LC 93-41640. 400p. 1994. text 43.75 (*0-86720-677-2*) Jones & Bartlett.

Brink, Pamela J. & Wood, Marilynn T. Basic Steps in Planning Nursing Research. 2nd ed. LC 82-17426. 304p. (C). 1983. pap. text 22.50 (*0-534-01241-8*) Jones & Bartlett.

Brink, Randall. Lost Star: The Search for Amelia Earhart. (Illus.). 224p. 1995. pap. 12.95 (*0-393-31311-5*, Norton Paperbks) Norton.

— Nimitz: The Man & His Wars. LC 95-50254. 368p. 1999. pap. 24.95 (*1-55611-478-8*) D I Fine.

Brink, Raymond W. College Algebra. 2nd ed. (Century Mathematics Ser.). 1951. text 16.95 (*0-89197-084-3*) Irvington.

Brink, Rita A. Playing & Praying with God: Guided Meditations for Children. LC 96-28991. 112p. (Orig.). (J). 1997. pap. 12.95 (*0-8091-3679-1*) Paulist Pr.

Brink, Satya, ed. see International Federation on Aging Staff.

Brink, Susan. A Data Book of Child & Adolescent Injury. (Illus.). 68p. (C). 1999. reprint ed. pap. text 15.00 (*0-7881-7714-1*) DIANE Pub.

Brink, T. L. Mental Health in the Nursing Home. LC 90-4667. (Clinical Gerontologist Ser.: Vol. 9, Nos. 3-4). 226p. 1990. pap. text 19.95 (*1-56024-011-3*) Haworth Pr.

— Mental Health in the Nursing Home. LC 90-4667. (Clinical Gerontologist Ser.: Vol. 9, Nos. 3-4). 226p. 1990. text 39.95 (*1-56024-010-5*) Haworth Pr.

Brink, T. L., ed. Clinical Gerontology: A Guide to Assessment & Intervention. LC 86-240. (Clinical Gerontologist Ser.: Vol. 5, Nos. 1-4). 517p. 1986. 79.95 (*0-86656-536-1*) Haworth Pr.

— The Elderly Uncooperative Patient. LC 86-26997. (Clinical Gerontologist Ser.: Vol. 6, No. 2). 194p. 1987. text 39.95 (*0-86656-604-X*) Haworth Pr.

— Hispanic Aged Mental Health. LC 92-1473. 207p. 1992. 49.95 (*1-56024-107-1*) Haworth Pr.

— Hispanic Aged Mental Health. LC 92-1473. 207p. 1992. pap. 19.95 (*1-56024-217-5*) Haworth Pr.

Brink, T. L., intro. The Forgotten Aged: Ethnic, Psychiatric & Societal Minorities. LC 93-40823. (Clinical Gerontologist Ser.). (Illus.). 133p. 1994. lib. bdg. 39.95 (*1-56024-572-7*) Haworth Pr.

— Holocaust Survivors' Mental Health. LC 94-4500. (Clinical Gerontologist Ser.). (Illus.). 117p. 1994. lib. bdg. 39.95 (*1-56024-669-3*) Haworth Pr.

Brink, Terry L. Geriatric Psychotherapy. LC 78-26232. 318p. 1979. 45.95 (*0-87705-344-8*, Kluwer Acad Hman Sci); pap. 24.95 (*0-87705-346-4*, Kluwer Acad Hman Sci) Kluwer Academic.

Brink, Victor Z. & Dittenhofer, Mortimer. Case Studies in Internal Auditing, Vol. 2. 300p. 1994. 75.00 (*0-89413-139-7*, A871) Inst Inter Aud.

Brink, W. J. Van den, see Kuiper, J. & Van den Brink, W. J., eds.

Brink, W. Van den, see Van den Brink, W.

Brink, William D. Priming the Anabolic Environment: A Practical, Scientific Guide to the Art & Science of Building Muscle. (Illus.). viii, 120p. 1996. pap. 14.95 (*1-55210-003-0*, Pub. by MuscleMag Intl) BookWorld.

Brinker. Primary Orthopedics. LC 97-43313. (Illus.). xiii, 390p. 1999. pap. text 35.00 (*0-7216-6698-1*, W B Saunders Co) Harcrt Hlth Sci Grp.

Brinker, Barry J. Emerging Practices in Cost Management. LC 90-71250. xvii, 507 p. 1990. write for info. (*0-7913-0782-4*) Warren Gorham & Lamont.

— Emerging Practices in Cost Management. LC 93-234514. 1993. write for info. (*0-7913-1597-5*) Warren Gorham & Lamont.

— Emerging Practices in Cost Management. LC 95-231993. 1995. write for info. (*0-7913-2404-4*) Warren Gorham & Lamont.

— Guide to Cost Management. LC 99-43409. 733p. 2000. text 140.00 (*0-471-31579-6*) Wiley.

Brinker, Barry J., ed. Handbook of Cost Management. 1993. ring bd. 145.00 (*0-685-69590-5*, HBM) Warren Gorham & Lamont.

— Handbook of Cost Management. 1994. ring bd. 135.00 (*0-685-69591-3*) Warren Gorham & Lamont.

Brinker, C. J., et al, eds. Better Ceramics Through Chemistry IV Vol. 180: Symposium Proceedings Ser. 1113p. 1990. text 17.50 (*1-55899-069-0*) Materials Res.

Brinker, C. Jeffrey & Scherer, George W., eds. Sol-Gel Science: The Physics & Chemistry of Sol-Gel Processing. 928p. 1990. text 212.00 (*0-12-134970-5*) Acad Pr.

Brinker, Claudia, et al. Contemplata Aliis Tradere: Studien zum Verhaltnis von Literatur und Spiritualitat Fur Alois M. Haas. (GER.). 1995. 62.95 (*3-906753-91-3*) P Lang Pubng.

Brinker, Francis. Formulas for Healthful Living. Rosson, Kathryn, ed. LC 95-83568. (Illus.). 240p. 1996. pap. 12.95 (*1-888483-00-8*) Eclectic Med.

— Formulas for Healthful Living, Vol. 2. 2nd rev. ed. Rosson, Kathryn, ed. LC 97-78424. (Illus.). 244p. 1998. pap. 12.95 (*1-888483-01-6*) Eclectic Med.

— Herb Contraindications & Drug Interactions: With Appendices Addressing Certain Conditions & Medicines. Stodart, Nancy, ed. LC 97-61558. 148p. 1997. pap. 14.95 (*0-9659135-0-3*) Eclectic Inst.

— Herb Contraindications & Drug Interactions: With Appendices Addressing Certain Conditions & Medicines. 2nd rev. ed. Stodart, Nancy, ed. LC 98-73743. 268p. 1998. pap. 19.95 (*1-888483-06-7*) Eclectic Med.

Brinker-Gabler, Gisela, ed. Encountering the Other(s) Studies in Literature, History, & Culture. LC 94-30706. 378p. (C). 1995. text 69.50 (*0-7914-2159-7*); pap. text 23.95 (*0-7914-2160-0*) State U NY Pr.

Brinker-Gabler, Gisela & Smith, Sidonie, eds. Writing New Identities: Gender, Nation, & Immigration in Contemporary Europe. 384p. (C). 1996. pap. 22.95 (*0-8166-2461-5*); text 57.95 (*0-8166-2460-7*) U of Minn Pr.

Brinker, Helen B., ed. see Grosse, W. Jack.

Brinker, Helmut. Shussan Shaka-Darstellungen in der Malerei Ostasiens. (Schweitzer Asiatische Studien: Vol. 3). (GER., Illus.). 145p. 1983. 13.00 (*3-261-04806-9*) P Lang Pubng.

Brinker, Helmut & Fischer, Eberhard. Treasures from the Rietberg Museum. LC 80-12528. (Illus.). 176p. 1980. 19.95 (*0-87848-055-2*) Asia Soc.

Brinker, Helmut & Kanazawa, Hiroshi. Zen Masters of Meditation in Images & Writings. Leisinger, Andreas, tr. (Illus.). 384p. 1996. text 79.00 (*3-907070-62-3*, Pub. by Artibus Asiae) UH Pr.

Brinker, Julie. Rachel's Night. 44p. (J). (gr. k-5). 1999. mass mkt. 4.00 (*1-58193-174-3*) Brown Bag Prods.

Brinker, Mark R. Review of Orthopaedic Trauma. 350p. 2000. pap. text. write for info. (*0-7216-8191-3*, W B Saunders Co) Harcrt Hlth Sci Grp.

Brinker, Nancy & Harris, Catherine M. The Race Is Run One Step at a Time: Every Woman's Guide to Taking Charge of Breast Cancer. LC 95-24204. 224p. 1995. pap. 13.95 (*1-56530-182-X*, Pub. by Summit TX) BookWorld.

Brinker, Nancy, jt. auth. see Chihal, Jane.

Brinker, Norman & Phillips, Donald T. On the Brink: The Life & Leadership of Norman Brinker. (Illus.). 234p. 1996. 24.95 (*1-56530-212-5*) Summit TX.

Brinker, Russell C. Four Thousand Five Hundred Sixty-Seven Questions for Surveyors. (Illus.). 408p. 1978. reprint ed. pap. 50.00 (*0-910845-38-7*, 712) Landmark Ent.

— Surveying Handbook. LC 87-8217. (Illus.). 1100p. 1987. text 105.00 (*0-442-21423-5*) Chapman & Hall.

— Surveying Handbook. 2nd ed. 1993. text 129.95 (*0-442-01062-1*) Chapman & Hall.

Brinker, Russell C., et al. Noteforms for Surveying Measurements. LC 80-13406. (Illus.). 63p. 1981. pap. 15.00 (*0-910845-09-3*, 441) Landmark Ent.

Brinker, Russell C., jt. auth. see Wolf, Paul R.

Brinker, Udo H. Advances in Carbene Chemistry, Vol. 2. 1998. 109.50 (*1-55938-837-4*) Jai Pr.

Brinker, Udo H., ed. Advances in Carbene Chemistry, Vol. 1. 228p. 1994. 109.50 (*1-55938-545-6*) Jai Pr.

***Brinker, Udo H., ed.** Advances in Carbene Chemistry, Vol. 3. 1999. 109.50 (*0-7623-0493-6*) Jai Pr.

Brinker, Wade O., et al, eds. Manual of Internal Fixation in Small Animals. (Illus.). 304p. 1983. 266.00 (*0-387-10629-4*) Spr-Verlag.

— Manual of Internal Fixation in Small Animals. (Illus.). 304p. 1984. 316.00 (*0-387-92118-4*) Spr-Verlag.

Brinkerhoff. Sociology. 3rd ed. Date not set. pap. text, teacher ed. 16.50 (*0-314-81739-5*) West Pub.

— Sociology. 3rd ed. 1991. pap., student ed. 18.50 (*0-314-81740-9*) West Pub.

Brinkerhoff & White. Essentials of Sociology. 3rd ed. (Sociology - Intro Level Ser.). 1995. pap., student ed. 15.75 (*0-314-04977-0*) West Pub.

— S.g. Essentials Of Sociology. 4th ed. (Sociology - Intro Level). 1998. pap., student ed. 15.25 (*0-534-55550-0*) Wadsworth Pub.

— Sociology. 4th ed. (Sociology - Intro Level Ser.). 1997. mass mkt., student ed. 17.25 (*0-314-20869-0*) West Pub.

Brinkerhoff, et al. Essentials Of Sociology. 4th ed. (Sociology - Intro Level). 1998. pap. 31.50 (*0-534-55559-4*) Wadsworth Pub.

***Brinkerhoff, et al.** Essentials of Sociology. 5th ed. 2001. pap. 32.75 (*0-534-55605-1*) Thomson Learn.

Brinkerhoff, et al. Essentials of Sociology with Infotrac. 4th ed. LC 98-15988. (Sociology-Introduction Level Ser.). 1998. pap. 31.50 (*0-534-55548-9*) Wadsworth Pub.

Brinkerhoff, Audrey, jt. auth. see Teasdale, Carrie.

Brinkerhoff, Audrey, ed. see Davies, Diana.

Brinkerhoff, Brian. Best Easy Day Hikes Salt Lake City. LC 99-25152. (Illus.). 96p. 1999. pap. 6.95 (*1-56044-854-7*) Falcon Pub Inc.

Brinkerhoff, David B. Sociology. 4th ed. LC 96-26108. 1996. 78.95 (*0-314-02562-6*) West Pub.

Brinkerhoff, David B. & White, Lynn K. Sociology. 3rd ed. Perlee, Clyde, ed. 681p. (C). 1990. pap. 54.75 (*0-314-74128-3*) West Pub.

Brinkerhoff, David B., et al. Essentials of Sociology. 2nd ed. Perlee, Clyde, ed. 375p. (C). 1991. pap. 37.00 (*0-314-89294-X*) West Pub.

— Essentials of Sociology. 3rd ed. LC 94-32591. 386p. (C). 1995. pap. 35.50 (*0-314-04176-1*) West Pub.

Brinkerhoff, Derek W. Improving Development Program Performance: Guidelines for Managers. (Studies in Development Management). 224p. 1996. pap. 22.50 (*1-55587-753-2*) L Rienner.

Brinkerhoff, Derick W. La Gestion Efficace des Projets de Developpement: Un Guide a l'Execution et l'Evaluation. 2nd ed. LC 91-29248. (Kumarian Press Library of Management for Development). (FRE.). 160p. (Orig.). reprint ed. pap. 49.60 (*0-608-20807-8*, 207190600003) Bks Demand.

Brinkerhoff, Derick W. & Garcia-Zamor, Jean-Claude, eds. Politics, Projects, & People: Institutional Development in Haiti. LC 85-16979. 304p. 1985. 69.50 (*0-275-90035-5*, C0035, Praeger Pubs) Greenwood.

Brinkerhoff, Derick W. & Goldsmith, Arthur A., eds. Institutional Sustainability in Agriculture & Rural Development: A Global Perspective. LC 90-34369. 272p. 1990. 65.00 (*0-275-93373-3*, C3373, Praeger Pubs) Greenwood.

Brinkerhoff, Donna & Rippy, Susan. The Cupboard Cookbook. (Illus.). 155p. (Orig.). (C). 1981. pap. 11.95 (*0-9613676-0-1*) Cupbd Cookbk.

Brinkerhoff, Donna C. Cooking in a New Dimension. large type ed. 245p. 1991. spiral bd. 25.00 (*1-881594-02-5*) Horiz For the Blind.

Brinkerhoff, Jim. I Would If I Could, But. (Illus.). 128p. 1997. pap. 9.95 (*0-9653327-2-1*, Pub. by BF Publng) Origin Bk Sales.

Brinkerhoff, Jim. You Know You're a Mormon If... LC 96-225998. (Illus.). 164p. 1996. pap. 12.95 (*0-9653327-0-5*, Pub. by BF Publng) Origin Bk Sales.

Brinkerhoff, Jim. You Know You're a Mormon Mother If... (Illus.). 96p. 1997. pap. 10.95 (*0-9653327-4-8*) BF Publng.

Brinkerhoff, John R. 101 Commonsense Rules for the Office: How to Get along & Get Ahead. LC 91-27344. (Illus.). 176p. 1992. pap. 9.95 (*0-8117-2418-2*) Stackpole.

— 101 Commonsense Rules for Making Things Happen: How to Make Plans & Implement Projects. LC 93-1215. (Illus.). 256p. 1993. pap. 9.95 (*0-8117-2419-0*) Stackpole.

***Brinkerhoff, Linda E.** Vital Records Computer Databases. 44p. 1998. pap. 10.00 (*0-940764-71-7*) Genealog Inst.

— Why Maps Are Important. (Illus.). 36p. 1998. pap. 10.00 (*0-940764-73-3*) Genealog Inst.

Brinkerhoff, Linda E., jt. auth. see Eakle, Arlene H.

Brinkerhoff, Merlin B., ed. Family & Work: Comparative Convergences, 8. LC 83-10721. (Contributions in Family Studies: No. 8). (Illus.). 221p. 1984. 49.95 (*0-313-23703-4*, BRF/, Greenwood Pr) Greenwood.

— Work, Organizations, & Society: Comparative Convergences, 53. LC 84-6676. (Contributions in Sociology Ser.: No. 53). (Illus.). 200p. 1984. 49.95 (*0-313-23704-2*, BWO/, Greenwood Pr) Greenwood.

Brinkerhoff, Richard F. One Minute Readings Issues in Science, Technology, & Society. 1993. pap. 12.50 (*0-201-23157-3*) Addison-Wesley.

Brinkerhoff, Robert. Strategic Employee Development Guide: Group Facilitation Guide. 16p. 1998. pap. 19.95 (*0-7879-4399-1*, Pfffr & Co) Jossey-Bass.

Brinkerhoff, Robert O. High Impact Learning Systems: Fundamentals. (Illus.). 41p. 1998. pap. 14.95 (*1-57740-067-4*, ILW169) Intl LrningWrk.

— High Impact Learning Systems: Impact Scenerios Collection. (Illus.). 52p. 1998. spiral bd. 895.00 (*1-57740-068-2*, ILW065) Intl LrningWrk.

— High Impact Learning Systems: Leaders Guide. 1997. teacher ed., ring bd. 895.00 (*1-57740-059-3*, ILW144) Intl LrningWrk.

— High Impact Learning Systems: Learner's Workbook. 46p. 1997. student ed., spiral bd. 895.00 (*1-57740-061-5*, ILW143) Intl LrningWrk.

— High Impact Learning Systems: Trainer's Guide. 37p. 1997. teacher ed., ring bd. 895.00 (*1-57740-060-7*, ILW142) Intl LrningWrk.

— Strategic Employee Development Guide: Employee Workbook. 24p. 1998. pap., wbk. ed. 19.95 (*0-7879-4403-3*, Pfffr & Co) Jossey-Bass.

— Strategic Employee Development Guide: Manager's Guidebook. LC 99-184700. 32p. 1998. pap. 29.95 (*0-7879-4400-9*, Pfffr & Co) Jossey-Bass.

Brinkerhoff, Robert O. & Dressler, Dennis E. Productivity Measurement: A Guide for Managers & Evaluators. (Applied Social Research Methods Ser.: Vol. 19). (Illus.). 160p. (C). 1989. text 42.00 (*0-8039-3151-4*); pap. text 18.95 (*0-8039-3152-2*) Sage.

Brinkerhoff, Robert O. & Gill, Stephen J. The Learning Alliance: Systems Thinking in Human Resource Development. LC 94-11716. (Management Ser.). 208p. 1994. text 29.95 (*1-55542-711-1*) Jossey-Bass.

Brinkerhoff, Shirley. Balancing Act. LC 98-35174. (Nikki Sheridan Ser.). 1998. pap. 5.99 (*1-56179-559-3*) Bethany Hse.

— Choice Summer. LC 96-5783. (Nikki Sheridan Ser.: Bk. 1). 192p. (YA). (gr. 9-13). 1998. pap. 5.99 (*1-56179-484-8*) Focus Family.

— Mysterious Love. (Nikki Sheridan Ser.: Bk. 2). 192p. (YA). (gr. 9-13). 1998. pap. 5.99 (*1-56179-485-6*) Focus Family.

— Narrow Walk. LC 97-24439. (Nikki Sheridan Ser.: Bk. 3). 192p. (YA). (gr. 9-13). 1998. pap. 5.99 (*1-56179-539-9*) Focus Family.

***Brinkerhoff, Shirley.** Second Choices. (Nikki Sheridan Ser.: Vol. 6). (Illus.). 160p. (J). (gr. 9 up). 2000. pap. 5.99 (*1-56179-880-0*) Bethany Hse.

Brinkerhoff, Shirley. Tangled Web, Vol. 5. LC 99-53733. (Nikki Sheridan Ser.: Vol. 5). 160p. (gr. 9). 1999. pap. text 5.99 (*1-56179-737-5*) Bethany Hse.

Brinkerhoff, T. Van. Brinkerhoff, Family of Joris Dircksen Brinckerhoff, 1638. 188p. 1993. reprint ed. pap. 29.50 (*0-8328-3609-5*); reprint ed. lib. bdg. 39.50 (*0-8328-3608-7*) Higginson Bk Co.

***Brinkerhoff, Val, photos by.** Architecture of the Ancient Ones. LC 99-57372. (Illus.). 80p. 2000. pap. 19.95 (*0-87905-955-9*) Gibbs Smith Pub.

Brinkerhoff, Val, jt. auth. see Gardner, A. Dudley.

Brinkernoff, Sidney, jt. ed. see Crowe, Rosalie.

***Brinkgreve, Ronald B. J., ed.** Beyond 2000 in Computational Geotechnics: Ten Years of PLAXIS International. (Illus.). 23p. (C). 1999. 135.00 incl. cd-rom (*90-5809-040-X*, Pub. by A A Balkema) Ashgate Pub Co.

Brinkhurst, R. O. A Guide for the Identification of British Aquatic Oligochaeta. 2nd ed. 1971. 39.00 (*0-900386-15-0*) St Mut.

Brinkhurst, R. O. & Diaz, R. J., eds. Aquatic Oligochaeta. (Developments in Hydrobiology Ser.). (C). 1987. lib. bdg. 253.50 (*90-6193-641-1*) Kluwer Academic.

Brinkkemper, S., jt. auth. see Wijers, G.

***Brinkkemper, Sjaak, et al.** Information Systems Engineering: State of the Art & Research Themes. LC 00-32971. 2000. write for info. (*1-85233-317-0*) Spr-Verlag.

Brinkley. American History. 9th ed. 1994. pap., student ed. 70.94 (*0-07-912114-4*) McGraw.

— American History, 2 vols. 10th ed. 1998. 55.50 (*0-07-232472-4*) McGraw.

— American History: A Survey, Vol. 2. 10th ed. 1998. 41.00 (*0-07-303392-8*) McGraw.

— American History: From 1865, Vol. 2. 10th ed. 1998. 41.00 (*0-07-232471-6*) McGraw.

— American History: Survey & Maps. 9th ed. 1995. (*0-07-074614-1*) McGrw-H Hghr Educ.

— American History: With Map, Vol. 1. 10th ed. 1998. 41.00 (*0-07-232470-8*) McGraw.

— American History Vol. 2: Survey, Vol. 2. 9th ed. 1995. pap., student ed. 13.75 (*0-07-007959-5*) McGraw.

— American History Survey. 1995. pap. 119.68 (*0-07-007991-9*) McGraw.

— Caught off Guard. LC 98-46508. 283p. (C). 1999. pap. 33.95 (*0-205-18529-0*) P-H.

Brinkley, Alan. American History: A Survey. 10th expanded rev. ed. LC 98-16235. 1056p. 1999. write for info. (*0-07-303390-1*, McGrw-H College) McGrw-H Hghr Educ.

— American History: A Survey, Vol. 1. 10th ed. LC 98-15454. 1998. 51.22 (*0-07-303391-X*) McGraw.

— American History Vol. I: A Survey. 10th ed. 224p. 1998. pap., student ed. 15.94 (*0-07-303404-5*) McGraw.

***Brinkley, Alan.** Culture & Politics in the Great Depression. LC 99-62124. (Charles Edmondson Historical Lectures). 46p. 1999. pap. 5.95 (*0-918954-72-X*) Baylor Univ Pr.

Brinkley, Alan. End of Reform. LC 94-21478. 1995. 27.50 (*0-394-53573-1*) Knopf.

— The End of Reform. 371p. 1995. 27.50 (*0-614-32266-9*) Knopf.

— The End of Reform: New Deal Liberalism in Recession & War. 384p. 1996. pap. 15.00 (*0-679-75314-1*) Vin Bks.

— Liberalism & Its Discontents. LC 97-40654. 384p. 1999. text 29.00 (*0-674-53017-9*) HUP.

***Brinkley, Alan.** Liberalism & Its Discontents. 2000. pap. 16.95 (*0-674-00185-0*) HUP.

Brinkley, Alan. The New Federalist Papers: Essays in Defense of the Constitution. 192p. 1997. pap. 13.95 (*0-393-31737-4*) Norton.

— Prosperity, Depression, & War, 1920-1945. 2nd expanded rev. ed. (New American History Ser.). 26p. (C). 1997. reprint ed. pap. 5.00 (*0-87229-090-5*) Am Hist Assn.

— The Unfinished Nation. 2nd ed. 1997. 50.00 (*0-679-45459-4*) Knopf.

— Unfinished Nation. 3rd ed. LC 99-19682. 1176p. 1999. 40.00 (*0-07-229559-7*); pap. 33.75 (*0-07-229558-9*) McGraw.

— Unfinished Nation. 3rd ed. 374p. 1999. pap., student ed. 20.30 (*0-07-229562-7*) McGraw.

— Unfinished Nation, Vol. II. 3rd ed. 704p. 1999. pap. 26.86 (*0-07-229561-9*) McGraw.

— The Unfinished Nation: A Concise History of the American People, 2 vols., Set. LC 92-26666. 1993. 12.76 (*0-685-61105-1*) McGraw.

— The Unfinished Nation: A Concise History of the American People, Vol. 1. 2nd ed. (C). 1996. text 52.25 (*0-07-913182-4*) McGraw.

— The Unfinished Nation: A Concise History of the American People, Vol. 1: To 1877. LC 92-26666. (C). 1993. text. write for info. (*0-07-007871-8*) McGraw.

— The Unfinished Nation: A Concise History of the American People, Vol. 3. 2nd ed. LC 96-1210. 152p. 1996. pap. 33.75 (*0-07-008216-2*) McGraw.

— The Unfinished Nation: A Concise History of the American People, Vol. 4. (C). 1993. text 34.25 (*0-07-007873-4*) McGraw.

— The Unfinished Nation: A Concise History of the American People from 1865, Vol. 3. 2nd ed. 640p. (C). 1996. pap. 26.55 (*0-07-008218-9*) McGraw.

— The Unfinished Nation: A Concise History of the American People: From 1865, Vol. 3. 2nd ed. (C). 1996. pap., student ed. 15.00 (*0-07-008221-9*) McGraw.

— The Unfinished Nation: A Concise History of the American People: From 1865 with Documents, Vol. 3. 2nd ed. (C). 1996. pap. text 30.50 (*0-07-913180-8*) McGraw.

— The Unfinished Nation: A Concise History of the American People from 1877, Vol. 2. 2nd ed. 576p. (C). 1996. pap. 26.55 (*0-07-008217-0*) McGraw.

— The Unfinished Nation: A Concise History of the American People to 1877, Vol. 2. 2nd ed. (C). 1996. pap., student ed. 15.00 (*0-07-008220-0*) McGraw.

— The Unfinished Nation: A Concise History of the American People to 1877, Vol. 2. 2nd ed. (C). 1996. pap. text 30.50 (*0-07-913179-4*) McGraw.

— The Unfinished Nation Combined Edition: A Concise History of the American People, Vol. 1. 2nd ed (C). 1996. pap. text, student ed. 19.36 (*0-07-015105-9*) McGraw.

— The Unfinished Nation Commbined Edition: A Concise History of the American People, Vol. 1. 2nd ed (C). 1996. pap. text 45.00 (*0-07-913181-6*) McGraw.

— The Unfinished Nation Vol. 3: A Concise History of the American People, Vol. 3. (C). 1993. text 21.50 (*0-07-015033-8*) McGraw.

— Voices of Protest: Huey Long, Father Coughlin, & the Great Depression. 1983. pap. text. write for info. (*0-07-544450-X*) McGraw.

— Voices of Protest: Huey Long, Father Coughlin, & the Great Depression. LC 83-3496. 1983. pap. 14.00 (*0-394-71628-0*) Vin Bks.

Brinkley, Alan & Dyer, Davis, eds. The Reader's Companion to the American Presidency. LC 99-59638. (Illus.). 576p. 2000. 40.00 (*0-395-78889-7*) HM.

Brinkley, Alan & Fitzpatrick, Ellen. America in Modern Times: Since 1890, Vol. 1. LC 96-34842. 640p. (C). 1996. pap. 43.75 (*0-07-007933-1*) McGraw.

— America in Modern Times: Since 1941, Vol. 1. LC 96-34841. 352p. (C). 1996. pap. 26.25 (*0-07-007962-5*) McGraw.

Brinkley, Alan, et al. American History: A Survey, Vol. 3. 9th ed. LC 94-12795. (C). 1994. text. write for info. (*0-07-007955-2*) McGraw.

— American History Vol. I: A Survey, Vol. 2. 8th ed. (C). 1991. text 44.50 (*0-07-015027-3*) McGraw.

— American History, A Survey, 1. 9th ed. (C). 1994. pap. text. write for info. (*0-07-007956-0*) McGraw.

— American History, A Survey, No. 1. 9th ed. (C). 1994. pap., student ed. 13.75 (*0-07-007958-7*) McGraw.

— American History, A Survey, Vol. I. 9th ed. (C). 1994. pap. text 52.50 (*0-07-912118-7*) McGraw.

— American History, A Survey, Vol. 1. 9th ed. 1995. mac hd 27.00 (*0-07-843368-1*) McGraw.

— American History, A Survey, Vol. 1. 9th ed. 1995. 3.5 hd 21.25 (*0-07-843367-3*); 5.25 hd 20.00 (*0-07-843366-5*) McGraw.

— American History, A Survey, Vol. 2. 9th ed. (C). 1994. pap. 44.69 (*0-07-007957-9*) McGraw.

— American History, A Survey, Vol. 2. 9th ed. (C). 1994. pap. text 41.00 (*0-07-912119-5*) McGraw.

— The Chicago Handbook for Teachers: A Practical Guide to the College Classroom. LC 99-36617. 144p. 1999. lib. bdg. 25.00 (*0-226-07511-7*) U Ch Pr.

— The Chicago Handbook for Teachers: A Practical Guide to the College Classroom. LC 99-36617. 178p. 1999. pap. 9.00 (*0-226-07512-5*) U Ch Pr.

— The New Federalist Papers: Essays. LC 96-48355. 1996. write for info. (*0-87078-404-8*) Century Foundation.

— New Federalist Papers: Essays in Defense of the Constitution. 179p. 1997. 23.00 (*0-393-04619-2*) Norton.

Brinkley, B. R., et al, eds. Cellular & Molecular Aspects of Fiber Carcinogenesis. (Current Communications in Cell & Molecular Biology Ser.: No. 2). (Illus.). 260p. (C). 1991. text 36.00 (*0-87969-361-4*) Cold Spring Harbor.

Brinkley, B. R. & Porter, Keith R., eds. International Cell Biology, 1976-1977. LC 77-79991. (Illus.). 694p. 1977. text 15.00 (*0-87470-027-2*) Rockefeller.

Brinkley, B. R., jt. ed. see Hyams, Jeremy S.

Brinkley, Dannion. At Peace in the Light: At Peace in the Light. 240p. 1996. mass mkt. 5.99 (*0-06-109446-3*, Harp PBks) HarpC.

Brinkley, Dannion & Perry, Paul. Saved by the Light. large type ed. LC 94-31536. xiii, 169 p. 1994. 24.95 (*1-56895-119-1*) Wheeler Pub.

— Saved by the Light: The True Story of a Man Who Died Twice & the Profound Revelations He Received. 224p. 1995. mass mkt. 6.50 (*0-06-100889-3*) HarpC.

Brinkley, David. David Brinkley: 11 Presidents, 4 Wars, 22 Political Conventions, 1 Moon Landing, 3 Assassinations, 2,000 Weeks of News & Other Stuff on Television & 18 Years of Growing Up in North Carolina. LC PN4874.B6695B75. (Illus.). 288p. 1996. pap. 12.00 (*0-345-37402-9*) Ballantine Pub Grp.

— David Brinkley: 11 Presidents, 4 Wars, 22 Political Conventions, 1 Moon Landing, 3 Assassinations, 2,000 Weeks of News & Other Stuff on Television & 18 Years of Growing Up in North Carolina. large type ed. LC 95-22852. 560p. 1995. pap. 25.00 (*0-679-76506-9*) Random Hse Lrg Prnt.

— Everyone Is Entitled to My Opinion. LC 96-77571. 176p. 1996. 20.00 (*0-679-45071-8*) Knopf.

— Everyone is Entitled to My Opinion. LC E169.12.B697. 192p. 1997. pap. 10.95 (*0-345-40952-3*) Ballantine Pub Grp.

— Everyone Is Entitled to My Opinion. large type ed. LC 96-11944. 1996. pap. 21.00 (*0-679-75905-0*) Random.

— Washington Goes to War. LC D769.85.D6B75. (Illus.). 352p. 1996. pap. 12.00 (*0-345-40730-X*) Ballantine Pub Grp.

Brinkley, Douglas. The American Heritage History of the United States. LC 98-7337. (Illus.). 640p. 1998. 50.00 (*0-670-86966-X*) Viking Penguin.

— Dean Acheson: The Cold War Years. (Illus.). 512p. 1994. pap. 20.00 (*0-300-06075-0*) Yale U Pr.

— Dean Acheson & the Making of U. S. Foreign Policy. 1993. text 49.95 (*0-312-05016-X*) St Martin.

— Jimmy Carter: Citizen for Peace. LC 95-36969. 1996. 25.00 (*0-614-95709-5*) Random.

— Jimmy Carter: The Post-Presidential Years. LC 95-36969. (Illus.). 320p. 1998. 25.00 (*0-679-44742-3*) Random.

***Brinkley, Douglas.** Rosa Parks. LC 00-35916. 160p. 2000. 19.95 (*0-670-89160-6*, Viking) Viking Penguin.

— Unfinished Presidency. 1999. 99.95 (*0-7861-1502-5*) Blckstn Audio.

Brinkley, Douglas. The Unfinished Presidency: Jimmy Carter's Journey Beyond the White House. 624p. 1999. pap. 15.95 (*0-14-027616-5*) Viking Penguin.

Brinkley, Douglas & Ambrose, Stephen, eds. Witness to America: An Illustrated Documentary History of the United States from the Revolution to Today. LC E173.W78 1999. 624p. 1999. 39.95 (*0-06-271611-5*) HarpC.

Brinkley, Douglas & Griffiths, Richard T., eds. John F. Kennedy & Europe. LC 98-56145. (Eisenhower Center Studies on War & Peace). 304p. 1999. text 60.00 (*0-8071-2332-3*) La State U Pr.

Brinkley, Douglas, jt. auth. see Abbey, Edward.

Brinkley, Douglas, jt. auth. see Ambrose, Stephen E.

Brinkley, Douglas, jt. auth. see Hoopes, Townsend.

Brinkley, Douglas, ed. see Thompson, Hunter S.

***Brinkley, Edward.** Birds. LC 99-87130. (Pathfinders Ser.). (Illus.). (J). 2000. write for info. (*1-57584-382-X*, RD Childrens) Rdrs Digest.

Brinkley, George A. The Volunteer Army & Allied Intervention in South Russia, 1917-1921: A Study in the Politics & Diplomacy of the Russian Civil War. LC 66-15501. (International Studies of the Committee on International Relations, University of Notre Dame). 464p. reprint ed. pap. 143.90 (*0-608-13835-5*, 202207700024) Bks Demand.

Brinkley, Ginny & Sampson, Sherry. Baby & Me. (Illus.). 30p. (J). (gr. 5-7). 1997. wbk. ed. 6.95 (*0-9622585-9-8*) Pink Inc.

— Joven y Embarazada: Un Libro Para Usted. Salmon, Otilia & Rodriquez, Judy, trs. from ENG. (SPA., Illus.). 80p. (YA). (gr. 7-12). 1992. pap. text 4.95 (*0-9622585-3-9*) Pink Inc.

— Promises: A Teen's Guide to Pregnancy. (Illus.). 48p. (YA). (gr. 7-12). 1993. pap. text. write for info. (*0-9622585-4-7*) Pink Inc.

— Usted y Su Nuevo Bebe: Un Libro Para Madres Jovenes. Salmon, Otilia & Rodriquez, Judy, trs. from ENG. LC 92-80146. (SPA., Illus.). 80p. (YA). (gr. 7-12). 1992. pap. text 4.95 (*0-9622585-2-0*) Pink Inc.

— What's Right for Me? A Guide to Decision Making for Young Women. (Illus.). 10p. (J). (gr. 6-7). 1995. pap. 1.00 (*0-9622585-6-3*) Pink Inc.

— You & Your New Baby: A Book for Young Mothers. (Illus.). 70p. (Orig.). 1991. pap. text 3.95 (*0-9622585-1-2*) Pink Inc.

— You're What? Stories from Sexually Active Young Men. (Illus.). 10p. (J). (gr. 6-7). 1994. pap. 1.00 (*0-9622585-5-5*) Pink Inc.

Brinkley, Ginny, et al. Pregnancy to Parenthood: Your Personal Step-by-Step Journey Through the Childbirth Experience. LC 97-46507. (Illus.). 336p. 1999. pap. 12.95 (*0-89529-635-7*, Avery) Penguin Putnam.

Brinkley, Ginny, jt. auth. see Sampson, Sherry.

Brinkley, J. H., et al. Teen Guide to Homemaking. 4th ed. 1976. text 33.88 (*0-07-007840-8*) McGraw.

Brinkley, Jeanne, jt. auth. see Aletti, Ann.

Brinkley, Jeanne, jt. auth. see Lyle, Dorothy S.

Brinkley, Joel. Defining Vision. rev. expanded ed. LC 98-17794. 416p. 1998. pap. 15.00 (*0-15-600597-2*) Harcourt.

— Defining Vision: The Battle for the Future of Television. LC 96-31923. 402p. (C). 1997. 27.00 (*0-15-100087-5*, Harvest Bks) Harcourt.

***Brinkley, Joel.** U. S. V. Microsoft: The Inside Story of the Landmark Case. (Illus.). 400p. 2000. 24.95 (*0-07-136438-2*) McGraw.

Brinkley, John L. On This Hill: A Narrative History of Hampden-Sydney College, 1774-1994. (Illus.). 896p. 1995. 39.95 (*1-886356-06-8*) Hampden-Sydney.

Brinkley, M. Kent & Chappell, Gordon W. The Gardens of Colonial Williamsburg. (Illus.). 168p. 1996. 29.95 (*0-87935-158-6*, Pub. by Colonial Williamsburg) Antique Collect.

Brinkley, Richard N. Thy Strong Word: The Enduring Legacy of Martin Franzmann. LC 93-28284. 1993. 9.95 (*0-570-01347-X*, 99-1480) Concordia.

Brinkley, Robert & Hanley, Keith, eds. Romantic Revisions. (Illus.). 384p. (C). 1992. text 85.00 (*0-521-38074-X*) Cambridge U Pr.

Brinkley, Roberta F. Arthurian Legend in the Seventeenth Century. (BCL1-PR English Literature Ser.). 228p. 1992. reprint ed. lib. bdg. 79.00 (*0-7812-7038-3*) Rprt Serv.

Brinkley, Velma Howell & Malone, Mary Huddleston. African-American Life in Sumner County, Tennessee. (Images of America Ser.). (Illus.). 128p. 1998. pap. 16.99 (*0-7524-0541-1*) Arcadia Publng.

Brinkley, William. Don't Go near the Water. 380p. Date not set. 26.95 (*0-8488-2217-X*) Amereon Ltd.

— Don't Go Near the Water. 1993. reprint ed. lib. bdg. 27.95 (*1-56849-144-1*) Buccaneer Bks.

— The Last Ship. 1989. pap. 12.95 (*0-345-35982-8*) Ballantine Pub Grp.

Brinklow, Henry. Henry Brinklow's Complaynt of Roderyck Mors, Sometyme a Gray Fryre unto the Parliament Howse of England His Natural Cuntry. (EETS, ES Ser.: No. 22). 1969. reprint ed. 45.00 (*0-527-00236-4*) Periodicals Srv.

Brinklow, Laurie. Prince Edward Island: A Color Guidebook. (Illus.). 200p. 1995. pap. 16.95 (*0-88780-318-0*, Pub. by Formac Publ Co) Formac Dist Ltd.

Brinklow, Laurie, ed. Prince Edward Island. 2nd ed. 200p. 1998. pap. 16.95 (*0-88780-438-1*, Pub. by J Lorimer) Formac Dist Ltd.

Brinkman, Alexander R. Pascal Programming for Music Research. 986p. 1990. lib. bdg. 45.00 (*0-226-07507-9*) U Ch Pr.

— Pascal Programming for Music Research. 896p. 1994. pap. text 39.95 (*0-226-07508-7*) U Ch Pr.

Brinkman, C. R. & Duffy, S. F., eds. Life Prediction Methodologies & Data for Ceramic Materials. LC 93-44605. (ASTM Special Technical Publication Ser.: Vol. 1201). (Illus.). 425p. 1994. text 59.00 (*0-8031-1864-3*, STP1201) ASTM.

Brinkman, C. R. & Garvin, H. W., eds. Properties of Austenitic Stainless Steels & Their Weld Metals: Influence of Slight Chemistry Variations - STP 679. 153p. 1979. pap. 13.50 (*0-8031-0537-1*, STP679) ASTM.

Brinkman, D., ed. Jane's Avionics, 98-99. 1998. text 350.00 (*0-7106-1792-5*) Janes Info Group.

Brinkman, Edna E. Epperson: The Story of David Epperson & His Family of Albemarle Co., Va., with Supplementary Notes on the Epperson Family in America. (Illus.). 304p. 1997. reprint ed. pap. 46.50 (*0-8328-8488-X*); reprint ed. lib. bdg. 56.50 (*0-8328-8487-1*) Higginson Bk Co.

Brinkman, Harold D. Dear Companion: The Civil War Letters of Silas I. Shearer. 164p. (Orig.). 1996. pap. text 9.95 (*0-9635812-9-5*) Sigler Print.

***Brinkman, Henk-Jan.** Explaining Prices in the Global Economy: A Post Keynesian Model. LC 99-30948. (New Directions in Modern Economics Ser.). 240p. 1999. 80.00 (*1-84064-044-8*) E Elgar.

Brinkman, J. A. A Catalogue of Cuneiform Sources Pertaining to Specific Monarchs of the Kassite Dynasty. LC 76-44965. (Materials & Studies for Kassite History (MSKH): Vol. 1). (Illus.). xxiv, 469p. 1977. pap. 30.00 (*0-918986-00-1*) Orient Inst.

Brinkman, John A. Prelude to Empire. (Occasional Publications of the Babylonian Fund: No. 7). xii, 159p. 1984. 25.00 (*0-934718-62-8*) U Museum Pubns.

Brinkman, John T. Simplicity: A Distinctive Quality of Japanese Spirituality. (Berkeley Insights in Linguistics & Semiotics Ser.: Vol. 23). XI, 275p. (C). 1996. pap. 33.95 (*0-8204-2726-8*) P Lang Pubng.

Brinkman, K. Kluwer's Computer Dictionary. (DUT & ENG.). 75.00 (*0-8288-9439-6*) Fr & Eur.

Brinkman, Karen & Walker, Joanie. Start Right: A Positive Approach to Literacy. 176p. (C). 1991. pap. text 20.00 (*0-13-068271-3*, 640302) P-H.

Brinkman, L. Turn-of-the-Century Cooking. (Illus.). 150p. 1998. spiral bd. 9.95 (*1-57166-107-7*) Hearts N Tummies.

Brinkman, L. & Faaborg, B. Indiana Prairie Skirts. (Illus.). 154p. 1996. pap. 9.95 (*1-57166-026-7*) Quixote Pr IA.

Brinkman, Marilyn. Bringing Home the Cows: Family Dairy Farming in Stearns County 1853-1986. Green, Ellen, ed. LC 87-62588. (Illus.). 88p. (Orig.). (C). 1988. pap. write for info. (*0-929049-00-4*) Stearns Hist Mus.

Brinkman, Marilyn S. & Morgan, William T. Light from the Hearth: Central Minnesota Pioneers & Early Architecture. (Illus.). 144p. (Orig.). 1983. pap. 9.95 (*0-87839-038-3*) North Star.

Brinkman, Martien E. Progress In Unity Vol. 18: Fifty Years of Theology within the World Council of Churches, 1945-1995. (Louvain Theological & Pastoral Monographs). 188p. 1995. pap. 25.00 (*0-8028-0557-4*) Eerdmans.

***Brinkman, Matt.** Teratoid Heights. 2000. pap. 12.95 (*0-9665363-2-0*) Highwater Bks.

Brinkman, Patricia. A Journey in Psalms: Life Stories in Poetry. 1997. pap. 15.95 (*1-887918-11-6*) Brockton Pubng.

***Brinkman, Paula.** A Dog Is Your Best Friend. (Charming Petites Ser.). 80p. 2000. 4.95 (*0-88088-398-7*) Peter Pauper.

Brinkman, Paula. Shop 'Til You Drop. (Charming Petites Ser.). 80p. 1998. 4.95 (*0-88088-380-4*) Peter Pauper.

Brinkman, Rick. Dealing with People You Can't Stand: How to Bring Out the Best in People At Their Worst. 208p. 1994. pap. 12.95 (*0-07-007838-6*) McGraw.

Brinkman, Rick & Kirschner, Rick. Dealing with People You Can't Stand: How to Bring Out the Best in People at Their Worst. 199p. 1994. 19.95 (*0-07-007839-4*) McGraw.

Brinkman, Rick, jt. auth. see Kirschner, Rick.

Brinkman, Sally, et al. Tales from the Springs. (Illus.). 150p. (Orig.). 1994. pap. 10.00 (*0-938572-07-5*) Bunny Crocodile.

Brinkman, U. A., jt. auth. see Frei, R. W.

***Brinkman, Udo A.Th., ed.** Hyphenation: Hype & Fascination. 540p. 1999. 200.50 (*0-444-50190-8*) Elsevier.

Brinkmann, ed. Alexandri Lycopolitani. (GRE.). 1989. reprint ed. pap. 37.50 (*3-519-01024-0*, T1024, Pub. by B G Teubner) U of Mich Pr.

Brinkmann, B., jt. ed. see Carracedo, A.

Brinkmann, K. & Schmidt, R. Data Processing Dictionary: Woerterbuch der Datentechnik, 1989. 4th rev. ed. (ENG & GER.). 904p. 1989. 150.00 (*0-8288-0240-8*, M7117) Fr & Eur.

Brinkmann, Karl-Heinz. Data Systems & Communications Dictionary, English-German/German-English. 5th ed. (ENG & GER.). 1108p. 1997. 195.00 (*0-7859-9630-3*) Fr & Eur.

Brinkmann, Klaus. Aristoteles: Allgemeine und Spezielle Metaphysik, Vol. 12. (Peripatoi Ser.). (C). 1979. 105.40 (*3-11-007578-4*) De Gruyter.

Brinkmann, Klaus, ed. Proceedings of the Twentieth World Congress of Philosophy Vol. 1: Ethics, Vol. 1. 288p. (C). 1999. 45.00 (*1-889680-05-2*) Philos Document.

Brinkmann, Reinhold. Late Idyll: The Second Symphony of Johannes Brahms. Palmer, Peter, tr. LC 94-29128. 256p. 1995. text 56.00 (*0-674-51175-1*, BRILAT) HUP.

— Late Idyll: The Second Symphony of Johannes Brahms. Palmer, Peter, tr. LC 94-29128. 256p. 1997. reprint ed. pap. 22.95 (*0-674-51176-X*) HUP.

***Brinkmann, Reinhold & Wolff, Christoph.** Driven into Paradise: The Musical Migration from Nazi Germany to the United States. LC 98-28956. 413p. 1999. 55.00 (*0-520-21413-7*, Pub. by U CA Pr) Cal Prin Full Svc.

Brinkmann, Ron. The Art & Science of Digital Compositing. (Illus.). 400p. 1999. pap. text 54.95 incl. cd-rom (*0-12-133960-2*) Morgan Kaufmann.

Brinkmann, Rudiger. Vom Schopfungsglauben Zum Umweltbhandeln - Umwelterziehung Im Religionsunterricht: Okologische, Biblisch-Theologische, Umweltethische und Padagogisch-Didaktische Beitrage Fur Einen Handlungsorientierten Unterricht. (GER.). 293p. 1996. 41.95 (*3-631-30141-3*) P Lang Pubng.

Brinkmann, Ursula. The Locative Alternation in German: Its Structure & Acquisition. LC 97-26692. (Language Acquisition & Language Disorders (LALD) Ser.: Vol. 15). x, 289p. 1997. lib. bdg. 79.00 (*1-55619-778-0*) J Benjamins Pubng Co.

Brinkmann, Wolfgang, et al, eds. Physical Processes in Hot Cosmic Plasmas. (C). 1990. text 226.50 (*0-7923-0665-1*) Kluwer Academic.

Brinkmeier, Hermina, jt. auth. see Bingam, Stephen.

Brinkmeier, Michaela. Die Buhnenwelt des Achim Freyer: Ansatz & Umfeld Seines Theaters der Langsamkeit. (GER., Illus.). 301p. 1997. 57.95 (*3-631-31933-9*) P Lang Pubng.

Brinkmeyer, Robert & March, Stephen, eds. Festival: Celebrating Southern Literature. (Southern Exposure Ser.). (Illus.). 112p. (Orig.). (C). 1981. pap. 4.00 (*0-943810-11-6*) Inst Southern Studies.

Brinkmeyer, Robert H., Jr. The Art & Vision of Flannery O'Connor. LC 89-34063. (Southern Literary Studies). xviii, 201p. (C). 1993. pap. text 15.95 (*0-8071-1853-2*) La State U Pr.

— Katherine Anne Porter's Artistic Development: Primitivism, Tradition, & Totalitarianism. LC 92-37039. (Southern Literary Studies). 224p. 1993. text 30.00 (*0-8071-1822-2*) La State U Pr.

***Brinkmeyer, Robert H., Jr.** Remapping Southern Literature: Contemporary Southern Writers & the West. LC 99-43731. (Mercer University Lamar Memorial Lectures: Vol. 42). 152p. 2000. 28.00 (*0-8203-2189-3*) U of Ga Pr.

Brinko, Kathleen & Menges, Robert J. Practically Speaking: A Sourcebook for Instructional Consultants. (Faculty Development Ser.). 360p. 1997. pap. 39.95 (*0-913507-87-3*) New Forums.

***Brinks, Dave.** The Snow Poems: First Snow. (Illus.). 28p. 2000. pap. 5.00 (*0-9663846-8-7*) Lavender Ink.

Brinks, Herbert J., ed. Dutch American Voices: Letters from the United States, 1850-1930. (Documents in American Social History Ser.). (Illus.). 520p. 1995. text 37.50 (*0-8014-3063-1*) Cornell U Pr.

***Brinks, Jan Herman.** Children of a New Fatherland: Germany's Post-War Right-Wing Politics. Smith, Ewan, ed. Vincent, Paul, tr. (Illus.). 200p. 2000. 35.00 (*1-86064-458-9*, Pub. by I B T) St Martin.

Brinks, Jim & Culpepper & Associates Staff. Software Industry Job Descriptions: The Job Description You Need to Structure Performance & Reward Systems for an Effective Software Company. 3rd ed. 330p. 1996. 795.00 (*1-58128-002-5*, JR) Culpepper.

— Software Industry Small Company Job Descriptions: The Job Descriptions You Need to Structure Performance & Reward Systems for an Effective Software Company. 222p. 1996. 450.00 (*1-58128-006-8*, JU) Culpepper.

Brinksma, E., et al, eds. Tools & Algorithms for the Construction & Analysis of Systems: First International Workshop, TACAS '95, Aarhus, Denmark, May 19-20, 1995, Selected Papers. LC 95-47444. (Lecture Notes in Computer Science Ser.: No. 1019). 291p. 1995. 49.00 (*3-540-60630-0*) Spr-Verlag.

Brinksma, Ed. Tools & Algorithms for the Construction & Analysis of Systems: Third International Workshop, Tacas 97, Enschede, The Netherlands, April 2-4, 1997: Proceedings, Vol. 121. LC 97-11043. (Lecture Notes in Computer Science Ser.). 1997. pap. write for info. (*3-540-62790-1*) Spr-Verlag.

Brinkworth, Judy, et al. Troika Four: Funny How You Remember Things; Pulling up the Dawn; Hidden Seed. 96p. 1992. 5.95 (*0-939395-18-5*) Thorntree Pr.

Brinkworth, M. Andrology: Male Reproductive Health & Dysfunction. Nieschlag, E. & Behre, H. M., eds. LC 96-45653. (Illus.). 424p. 1997. 119.00 (*3-540-61616-0*) Spr-Verlag.

Brinkworth, Marida. The Complete Great Falls Climbing Guide: The Climber's Guide to Great Falls, Virginia That Makes It Easy to Find the Climbs from the Trails. LC 98-92534. (Illus.). 80p. 1998. pap. 10.00 (*0-9663431-0-7*) Dog Days.

Brinley, D., jt. auth. see Lamb.

Brinley, Douglas A. Strengthening Your Marriage & Family. 1997. pap. 9.95 (*1-57008-308-8*) Bookcraft Inc.

Brinley, Douglas E. Marital Relationships Seminar. 24p. 1988. pap. 2.95 (*1-55503-064-5*, 0111812) Covenant Comms.

— Together Forever: Gospel Perspectives for Marriage & Family. LC 98-73234. 1998. 16.95 (*1-57008-540-4*) Bookcraft Inc.

Brinley, Douglas E. & Judd, Daniel K., eds. Eternal Companions. 1995. 16.95 (*0-88494-972-9*) Bookcraft Inc.

— Eternal Families. 1996. 15.95 (*1-57008-227-8*) Bookcraft Inc.

Brinley, Francis. Life of William T. Porter. LC 79-125680. (American Journalists Ser.). 1978. reprint ed. 23.95 (*0-405-01655-7*) Ayer.

Brinley, George. Catalogue of the American Library of George Brinley, 5 pts. in 2 vols. Trumbull, J. Hammond, ed. LC 68-54529. reprint ed. lib. bdg. 125.00 (*0-404-01081-4*) AMS Pr.

Brinley-Higgins, John. Joe's Cafe, a Santa Barbara Old Town Tradition. LC 83-145951. 88p. 1983. write for info. (*0-87461-949-1*) McNally & Loftin.

Brinley, Maryann B. The Everything Pregnancy Book. 1999. pap. 12.95 (*1-58062-146-5*) Adams Media.

Brinley, Maryann B., jt. auth. see Willis, Kay.

Brinley, Maryann Bucknum, jt. auth. see Hill, Tamara.

Brinn, Ross. To the Woods & Waters Wild: A Collection of Irish Writings. LC 90-80516. 150p. (Orig.). (YA). 1990. pap. 9.95 (*0-944638-02-3*) EduCare Pr.

Brinn, Ruth E. Jewish Holiday Games for Little Hands. (Illus.). 112p. (J). (ps-2). 1995. pap. text 14.95 (*0-929371-86-0*) Kar-Ben.

Brinn, Ruth Esrig. Jewish Holiday Crafts for Little Hands. LC 92-39638. (Illus.). 128p. (J). (ps-2). 1993. pap. 12.95 (*0-929371-47-X*) Kar-Ben.

***Brinn, Ruth Esrig & Springer, Sally.** Bible Story Crafts for Little Hands. LC 00-22217. (Illus.). 96p. (J). (ps-2). 2000. pap. text 18.95 (*1-58013-064-X*) Kar-Ben.

Brinner, Benjamin. Knowing Music, Making Music: Javanese Gamelan & the Study of Musical Competence & Interaction. LC 95-30177. (Chicago Studies in Ethnomusicology). (Illus.). 388p. 1995. pap. text 22.50 (*0-226-07510-9*); lib. bdg. 59.95 (*0-226-07509-5*) U Ch Pr.

Brinner, William M., intro. An Elegant Composition Concerning Relief Adversity. LC 49-9495. (Judaica Ser.: No. 20). 1977. 45.00 (*0-300-01952-1*) Yale U Pr.

Brinner, William M., tr. The History of al-Tabari Vol. 2: Prophets & Patriarchs. LC 84-97. (SUNY Series in Near Eastern Studies). 207p. (C). 1986. text 57.50 (*0-87395-921-3*) State U NY Pr.

— The History of al-Tabari Vol. 2: Prophets & Patriarchs. LC 84-97. (SUNY Series in Near Eastern Studies). 207p. (C). 1987. pap. text 20.95 (*0-88706-313-6*) State U NY Pr.

— The History of al-Tabari, Ta'rikh al-rusul wa'l-muluk Vol. 3: The Children of Israel. LC 90-10264. (SUNY Series in Near Eastern Studies). 180p. (C). 1991. text 49.50 (*0-7914-0687-3*) State U NY Pr.

— The History of al-Tabari, Ta'rikh al-rusul wa'l-muluk Vol. 3: The Children of Israel. LC 90-10264. (SUNY Series in Near Eastern Studies: Vol. 3). 180p. (C). 1991. pap. text 20.95 (*0-7914-0688-1*) State U NY Pr.

Brinner, William M. & Rischin, Moses, eds. Like All the Nations? The Life & Legacy of Judah L. Magnes. LC 86-29992. 256p. (C). 1987. pap. text 14.95 (*0-88706-508-2*) State U NY Pr.

Brinner, William M., tr. see Al-Tabari.

Brinner, William M., tr. & intro. see Ben Jacob Ibn Shahin, Nissim.

***Brinnin, John M.** Dylan Thomas in America. (Lost Treasures Ser.). 2000. pap. 17.95 (*1-85375-378-5*, Pub. by Prion) Trafalgar.

Brinnin, John M. Sorrows of Cold Stone: Poems, 1940-1950. LC 73-110817. 109p. 1971. reprint ed. lib. bdg. 35.00 (*0-8371-3220-7*, BRSO, Greenwood Pr) Greenwood.

— Travel & the Sense of Wonder. LC 92-2906. 3.95 (*0-8444-0743-7*) Lib Congress.

— William Carlos Williams. LC 63-62710. (University of Minnesota Pamphlets on American Writers Ser.: No. 24). 48p. (Orig.). reprint ed. pap. 30.00 (*0-7837-2897-2*, 205755800006) Bks Demand.

Brinon, Pierre, et al. Flower Arranging in the French Style. LC 98-11748. (Illus.). 144p. 1998. pap. 29.95 (*2-08-013651-8*, Pub. by Flammarion) Abbeville Pr.

Brinsbury, Wolf. The World Before Man: In Search of the Circle. Cassady, William A., ed. & illus. by. 256p. (Orig.). 1997. mass mkt. 29.95 (*1-882637-55-0*) SJL Pub.

***Brinsden, P. R.** An Atlas of in Vitro Fertilization. (Illus.). 2001. write for info. (*1-84214-025-6*) Prthnon Pub.

Brinsden, P. R., ed. A Textbook of In Vitro Fertilization & Assisted Reproduction: The Bourn Hall Guide to Clinical & Laboratory Practice. 2nd ed. LC 99-14782. (Illus.). 564p. 1999. 110.00 (*1-85070-000-1*) Prthnon Pub.

Brinser, A. The Respectability of Mr. Bernard Shaw. LC 75-22167. (Studies in George Bernard Shaw: No. 92). 1975. lib. bdg. 49.00 (*0-8383-2082-1*) M S G Haskell Hse.

Brinser, Marlin. Dictionary of Twentieth Century Italian Violin Makers & Import Dealers Scrapbook. 2nd ed. 1978. pap. 22.50 (*0-9602298-1-7*) Timberwood.

— Labels, Addresses & Signatures of Twentieth Century Italian Violin Makers. 1986. pap. 3.50 (*0-317-39573-4*) Timberwood.

Brinsfield, John W. Religion & Politics in Colonial South Carolina. (Illus.). 204p. 1983. 25.00 (*0-89308-333-X*, SC 69) Southern Hist Pr.

Brinsley, John. A Consolation for Our Grammar Schools. LC 71-177. (English Experience Ser.: No. 203). 84p. 1969. reprint ed. 40.00 (*90-221-0203-3*) Walter J Johnson.

Brinsley, Richard & McDonough, Jerome. Arrivals. 1995. 3.50 (*0-87129-521-0*, A60) Dramatic Pub.

Brinsmade, Akbar F. Travel to the Stars. limited ed. (Illus.). 169p. 1996. 30.00 (*1-889930-15-6*) J M Phillips Pub.

Brinsmade, Herman H. Utopia Achieved: A Novel of the Future. LC 74-154431. (Utopian Literature Ser.). 1975. reprint ed. 24.95 (*0-405-03514-4*) Ayer.

Brinsmead, Ann-Marie. Strategies of Resistance in "Les Liaisons Dangereuses" Heroines in Search of "Authority" LC 88-32603. (Studies in French Civilization). 194p. 1989. lib. bdg. 79.95 (*0-88946-639-4*) E Mellen.

Brinsmead, E. History of the Pianoforte, Ancient Musical Instruments: 1870-80. (Illus.). 120p. 1983. pap. 15.00 (*0-87556-572-7*) Saifer.

Brinson, Boone, jt. auth. see Romo, Richard.

Brinson, Charmian. The Strange Case of Dora Fabian & Mathilde Wurm: A Study of German Political Exiles in London During the 1930's. 418p. 1996. pap. 57.95 (*3-906756-27-0*, Pub. by P Lang) P Lang Pubng.

Brinson, Erik. Reflections from a Liquid Mirror: Poems. LC 96-90394. 57p. (Orig.). 1997. pap. 8.95 (*0-533-12025-X*) Vantage.

Brinson, Hal F., et al, eds. Adhesion Science Review 1987. (Illus.). 328p. 1988. 40.00 (*0-9619517-1-0*) HF Brinson.

***Brinson, J. Dianne & Radcliffe, Mark F.** Internet Law & Business Handbook: A Practical Guide. 600p. 2000. pap. 44.95 (*0-9639173-3-1*, Pub. by Ladera Pr) IPG Chicago.

Brinson, J. Dianne & Radcliffe, Mark F. Internet Legal Forms for Business. LC 97-71372. 140p. (Orig.). 1997. pap. 24.95 (*0-9639173-4-X*) Ladera Pr.

— Multimedia Contracts. 1996. 680p. (Orig.). 1996. pap. 89.95 (*0-9639173-1-5*); disk 99.95 (*0-9639173-5-8*) Ladera Pr.

— Multimedia Law & Business Handbook: A Practical Guide for Developers & Publishers. LC 96-75898. 468p. (Orig.). 1996. pap. 44.95 (*0-9639173-2-3*) Ladera Pr.

Brinson, Jean S. Cry in Night. 1996. mass mkt. 5.99 (*0-312-95785-8*, Pub. by Tor Bks) St Martin.

— Murderous Memories: One Woman's Hellish Real-Life Struggle to Save Herself. LC 94-66755. 288p. 1994. 22.95 (*0-88282-126-1*) New Horizon NJ.

***Brinson, Josef.** Oracle8 DBA: Performance Tuning Exam Cram. (Exam Cram Ser.). (Illus.). 2000. pap. 29.99 (*1-57610-602-0*) Coriolis Grp.

Brinson, L. C. & Moran, B., eds. Mechanics & Materials for Electronic Packaging Vol. 1: Design & Process Issues in Electronic Packaging: 1994 International Mechanical Engineering Congress & Exposition, Chicago, Illinois - November 6-11, 1994. LC 94-79149. (AMD Ser.: Vol. 195). 236p. 1994. 88.00 (*0-7918-1449-1*, G00944) ASME.

— Mechanics of Phase Transformations & Shape Memory Alloys: 1994 International Mechanical Engineering Congress & Exposition, Chicago, Illinois - November 6-11, 1994. (AMD - PVP Ser.: Vol. 189, Vol. 292). 224p. 1994. 80.00 (*0-7918-1437-8*, G00932) ASME.

Brinson, Peter. Background to European Ballet. LC 79-7754. (Dance Ser.). (Illus.). 1980. reprint ed. lib. bdg. 23.95 (*0-8369-9279-2*) Ayer.

— Dance As Education. 1991. pap. 29.95 (*1-85000-717-9*, Falmer Pr) Taylor & Francis.

Brinson, Rebecca, tr. see Mitchell, Pearline W.

Brinson, Robert J. FisCAL: Business Analysis Software. 1990. student ed. 50.00 (*1-878870-01-7*) Halcyon Grp SC.

— Profiting from Financial Statements: A Business Analysis System. (Orig.). 1992. pap. text 25.00 (*1-878870-04-1*) Halcyon Grp SC.

— Profiting from Financial Statements: Fiscal Key Disk & Manual. (C). 1995. pap. text 25.00 incl. disk (*1-878870-03-3*) Halcyon Grp SC.

— Profiting from Financial Statements: Fiscal Key Disk & Manual, 3.5 Inch Disk. (C). 1990. pap. text 15.00 (*1-878870-02-5*) Halcyon Grp SC.

B

— Maximize Your Martial Arts Training: The Martial Arts Training Diary. (Illus.). 256p. 1996. otabind 14.95 (*1-880336-09-X*) Turtle CT.

Brisbane. The Developing Child: Understanding Children & Parenting: Teacher's Wraparound Edition. 7th rev. ed. 619p. 1999. teacher ed. 49.75 (*0-02-647731-9*) Glencoe.

Brisbane, jt. auth. see Riker.

Brisbane, Albert. Association: Or, a Concise Exposition of the Practical Part of Fourier's Social Science. LC 72-2947. (Communal Societies in America Ser). reprint ed. 29.50 (*0-404-10713-3*) AMS Pr.

— Social Destiny of Man: Or Association & Reorganization of Industry. LC 68-18217. (Reprints of Economic Classics Ser.). xiv, 480p. 1969. reprint ed. 57.50 (*0-678-00471-4*) Kelley.

— The Social Destiny of Mankind. 1972. 300.00 (*0-87968-025-3*) Gordon Pr.

Brisbane, Art, et al. Celebrating Greater Kansas City. LC 98-30775. (Urban Tapestry Ser.). (Illus.). 1998. 49.95 (*1-881096-61-0*) Towery Pub.

Brisbane, Frances L. & Womble, Maxine, eds. Treatment of Black Alcoholics. LC 85-13975. (Alcoholism Treatment Quarterly Ser.: Vol. 2, No. 3-4). 270p. 1985. text 49.95 (*0-86656-403-9*) Haworth Pr.

Brisbane, Holly E. Developing Child. rev. ed. (Illus.). (gr. 9-12). 1971. text 20.64 (*0-02-663220-9*) Glencoe.

Brisbane, Katharine. Entertaining Australia. 360p. (C). 1990. 75.00 (*0-86819-286-4*, Pub. by Currency Pr) Accents Pubns.

— Entertaining Australia. 360p. (C). 1991. pap. 39.95 (*0-86819-367-4*, Pub. by Currency Pr) Accents Pubns.

Brisbane, Katharine, ed. Critical Perspectives. 1997. pap. 24.95 (*0-86819-502-2*, Pub. by Currency Pr) Accents Pubns.

***Brisbane, Katharine, ed.** Plays of the 70's, Vol. 1. LC 99-196480. (Orig.). 1998. pap. 24.95 (*0-86819-548-0*, Pub. by Currency Pr) Accents Pubns.

— Plays of the 60's, Vol. 3. (Orig.). pap. 24.95 (*0-86819-562-6*, Pub. by Currency Pr) Accents Pubns.

Brisbane, Katherine, ed. Australia Plays. 336p. 1989. pap. 18.95 (*1-85459-056-1*, Pub. by N Hern Bks) Theatre Comm.

Brisbane, Robert H. The Black Vanguard: Origins of the Negro Social Revolution, 1900-1960. LC 69-18900. 285p. reprint ed. 88.40 (*0-8357-9356-7*, 201486800094) Bks Demand.

Brisbin, I. Lehr, jt. ed. see Adriano, Domy C.

Brisbin, Richard A., Jr. Justice Antonin Scalia & the Conservative Revival. LC 96-22883. 464p. 1997. text 39.95 (*0-8018-5432-6*) Johns Hopkins.

Brisbin, Richard A. Justice Antonin Scalia & the Conservative Revival. 488p. 1998. pap. 19.95 (*0-8018-6094-6*) Johns Hopkins.

Brisbin, Richard A., Jr., et al. West Virginia Politics & Government. LC 96-14437. (Politics & Governments of the American States Ser.). xx, 218p. 1996. pap. text 20.00 (*0-8032-6128-4*) U of Nebr Pr.

Brisbin, Richard A., Jr., et al. West Virginia Politics & Government. LC 96-14437. (Politics & Governments of the American States Ser.). (Illus.). xx, 218p. 1996. text 50.00 (*0-8032-1271-2*) U of Nebr Pr.

Brisbin, Robert E., jt. auth. see Grant, Carol B.

***Brisbin, Shelly.** Adobe Golive 5 for Macintosh & Windows: Visual Quickstart Guide. 352p. 2000. pap. text 18.99 (*0-201-70841-8*) Peachpit Pr.

— Adobe GoLive 4 for Macintosh & Windows: Visual QuickStart Guide. (Illus.). 352p. 1999. pap. text 18.99 (*0-201-35477-2*) Peachpit Pr.

— Mac Answers! 2nd ed. 1999. pap. 24.99 (*0-07-212399-0*) McGrw-H Intl.

Brisbin, Shelly, jt. auth. see LeVitus, Bob.

Brisbin, Terri. A Love Through Time. (Time Passages Romance Ser.). 532p. 1998. mass mkt. 5.99 (*0-515-12403-6*, Jove) Berkley Pub.

***Brisbin, Terri.** Matter of Time. 1999. mass mkt. 5.99 (*0-515-12683-7*, Jove) Berkley Pub.

— Queen's Man. (Time Passages Romance Ser.). 2000. mass mkt. 5.99 (*0-515-12906-2*, Jove) Berkley Pub.

Brisbois, Roy. California Products Liability Law & Practice. 1985. im. lthr. write for info. (*0-327-00066-X*) LEXIS Pub.

***Brisbois, Roy M.** California Products Liability Law & Practice. 2nd ed. 100p. 1999. 120.00 (*0-327-01668-X*, 6865011) LEXIS Pub.

Brisby, Linda-Sue, et al. Logic: A "Hands On" Approach to Teaching . . . (Illus.). 180p. 1989. teacher ed. 17.95 (*0-927726-02-5*) Hands On CA.

— Number & Operations: A "Hands On" Approach to Teaching . . . (Illus.). 218p. 1991. teacher ed. 17.95 (*0-927726-07-6*) Hands On CA.

Brisby, Stewart. A Death in America: Or, The Life Expectancy of Your Nearest Living Relative Depends on How Fast You Fill out This Form. LC 85-51535. (Illus.). 83p. (Orig.). 1986. 13.95 (*0-685-43127-4*); pap. 7.95 (*0-9615395-6-9*) Wolverine Pr.

***Brisch, J. H., et al.** Masonry: Materials, Testing & Applications. LC 99-36980. (STP Ser.: No. 1356). (Illus.). 170p. 1999. pap. text 46.00 (*0-8031-2600-X*) ASTM.

Brisco, Norris A. Economic Policy of Robert Walpole. LC 07-36150. (Columbia University. Studies in the Social Sciences: No. 72). reprint ed. 29.50 (*0-404-51072-8*) AMS Pr.

Brisco, Paula. Asthma: Questions You Have...Answers You Need. LC 94-23176. 192p. (Orig.). 1994. pap. 10.95 (*1-882606-16-7*) Peoples Med Soc.

— Diabetes: Questions You Have, Answers You Need. rev. ed. LC 96-49561. 192p. 1997. pap. 12.95 (*1-882606-53-1*) Peoples Med Soc.

Brisco, Paula & Morales, Karla. The Hormone Replacement Handbook. (Illus.). 256p. 1996. pap. 16.95 (*1-882606-20-5*) Peoples Med Soc.

***Brisco, Thomas V.** Holman Bible Atlas: A Complete Guide to the Expansive Geography of Biblical History. 256p. 1999. 39.99 (*1-55819-709-5*) Broadman.

Briscoa, Alan K. Your Guide to Emergency Home Storage. 96p. 1999. pap. 7.98 (*0-88290-660-7*) Horizon Utah.

Briscoe, ed. Livi, Titi, Libri XLI-XLV. (LAT.). 1986. 95.00 (*3-519-01491-2*, T1491, Pub. by B G Teubner) U of Mich Pr.

— Livi, Titi Tom. I, Libri XXXI-XXXV: Libri XXXI-XL. (LAT.). 1991. 89.50 (*3-519-01492-0*, T1492, Pub. by B G Teubner) U of Mich Pr.

— Livi, Titi Tom. II, Libri XXXVI-XL: Libri XXXI-XL. (LAT.). 1991. 110.00 (*3-519-01493-9*, T1493, Pub. by B G Teubner) U of Mich Pr.

Briscoe, Alan. Home Garden Hints. 30p. 1975. pap. 5.98 (*0-88290-049-8*) Horizon Utah.

Briscoe, Alan K. Soybean Granule Recipes. 24p. 1974. pap. 4.98 (*0-88290-040-4*) Horizon Utah.

Briscoe, B. J. & Adams, M. J., eds. Tribology in Particulate Technology. (Illus.). 496p. 1987. 225.00 (*0-85274-425-0*) IOP Pub.

Briscoe, Bobby. The Jungle Warriors. 160p. 1994. reprint ed. pap. 12.95 (*1-890549-00-2*, 940601) Alpha Pub Grp.

***Briscoe, Bobby.** The Jungle Warriors. 2nd rev. ed. J. T. Advertising & Graphics Staff, ed. & prod. by. 160p. 2000. pap. 15.95 (*0-9676518-1-6*) B Briscoe Pub.

Briscoe, Connie. Big Girls Don't Cry. 1997. pap. 12.00 (*0-345-41362-8*) Ballantine Pub Grp.

— Big Girls Don't Cry. 1998. mass mkt. 6.99 (*0-449-00258-6*, GM) Fawcett.

— Big Girls Don't Cry. 416p. 1999. mass mkt. 6.99 (*0-449-00564-X*, GM) Fawcett.

— Big Girls Don't Cry. LC 96-33927. 384p. 1996. 23.00 (*0-06-017277-0*) HarpC.

— Big Girls Don't Cry. large type ed. LC 96-22467. Date not set. 25.95 (*1-56895-346-1*) Wheeler Pub.

***Briscoe, Connie.** A Long Way from Home. 416p. 2000. mass mkt. 6.99 (*0-06-103021-X*, Avon Bks) Morrow Avon.

Briscoe, Connie. A Long Way Home. LC 98-52053. 368p. 1999. 25.00 (*0-06-017278-9*) HarpC.

— Sisters & Lovers. 1996. pap. 12.00 (*0-345-40969-8*) Ballantine Pub Grp.

— Sisters & Lovers. 409p. 1995. mass mkt. 6.99 (*0-8041-1334-3*) Ivy Books.

Briscoe, Connie. Sisters & Lovers: A Novel, Set. abr. ed. 1994. audio 17.00 (*1-55994-987-2*, 391588) HarperAudio.

Briscoe, D. Romans. (Mastering the Old & New Testament Ser.: Vol. 6). pap. 14.99 (*0-8499-3322-6*) Word Pub.

Briscoe, D. Stuart. The Fruit of the Spirit: Cultivating Christian Character. rev. ed. (Foundations of the Faith Ser.). 176p. 1993. pap. 8.99 (*0-87788-366-1*, H Shaw Pubs) Waterbrook Pr.

— Genesis. (Communicator's Commentary Ser.: Vol. 1). 414p. 22.99 (*0-8499-0406-4*) Word Pub.

— Romans. (Communicator's Commentary Ser.: Vol. 6). 264p. 22.99 (*0-8499-0159-6*) Word Pub.

— Secrets of the Heart: Lessons from the Psalms. LC 98-55388. 155p. 1999. pap. 10.99 (*0-87788-767-5*, H Shaw Pubs) Waterbrook Pr.

Briscoe, David & Mahoney-Briscoe, Charlotte. A Personal Peace: Macrobiotic Reflections on Mental & Emotional Recovery. 212p. 1989. 18.95 (*0-87040-698-1*) Japan Pubns USA.

Briscoe, E. J. Modelling Human Speech Comprehension: A Computational Approach. (Cognitive Science Ser.). 272p. 1987. text 69.95 (*0-470-21032-X*) P-H.

Briscoe, G. & Wilson, R. A. Employment Forecasting in the Construction Industry. 176p. 1993. 66.95 (*1-85628-564-2*, Pub. by Avebry) Ashgate Pub Co.

Briscoe, Gordon & Australian Institute of Aboriginal & Torres Strait Islander Studies Staff. Queensland Aborigines & the Spanish Influenza Pandemic of 1918-1919. LC 97-108211. 20 p. 1996. write for info. (*0-85575-282-3*) AIB & TSIS.

***Briscoe, Jack, Jr.** Secrets to Marketing Your Products to Catalog Companies. Owens, James, ed. 112p. 1998. pap. 29.95 (*0-7392-0462-9*, PO2771) Morris Pubng.

Briscoe, James R. Contemporary Anthology of Music by Women. 1997. pap. 29.95 (*0-253-21102-6*) Ind U Pr.

***Briscoe, James R.** Debussy in Performance. LC 99-38223. (Illus.). 288p. 1999. 35.00 (*0-300-07626-6*) Yale U Pr.

Briscoe, James R., ed. Historical Anthology of Music by Women. LC 85-45987. (Illus.). 414p. 1987. spiral bd. 29.95 (*0-253-21296-0*) Ind U Pr.

Briscoe, Jill. Before You Say "Amen" (Jill Briscoe Inductive Bible Study Ser.). 108p. 1989. pap. 7.99 (*0-89693-637-6*, 6-1637, Victor Bks) Chariot Victor.

— Eight Choices That Can Change a Woman's Life. LC 98-20193. 180p. 1998. pap. 10.99 (*0-87788-208-8*, H Shaw Pubs) Waterbrook Pr.

— Fight for the Family. (Orig.). 1981. pap. 3.95 (*0-310-21841-1*, 9259P) Zondervan.

— Harrow Sparrow. (Illus.). 143p. (J). (gr. 6). 1989. reprint ed. pap. write for info. (*0-318-66527-1*) Jilcoe.

— The Heartbeat of Jesus. (Jill Briscoe Inductive Bible Study Ser.). 96p. (Orig.). 1993. pap. 7.99 (*1-56476-102-9*, 6-3102, Victor Bks) Chariot Victor.

— Heartstrings. LC 97-33490. 1997. 10.99 (*0-8423-1461-X*) Tyndale Hse.

— Hush, Hush. 1978. pap. 6.70 (*0-310-21831-4*, 9258P) Zondervan.

— In a Quiet Place: Daily Devotions with Jill & Stuart Briscoe. LC 97-15985. 370p. 1997. 17.99 (*0-87788-065-4*, H Shaw Pubs) Waterbrook Pr.

— It Had to Be a Monday. LC 95-17024. 230p. 1995. pap. 10.99 (*0-8423-8393-X*) Tyndale Hse.

— Jonah & the Worm. (Illus.). 143p. (J). (gr. 6). 1989. reprint ed. pap. write for info. (*0-318-66528-X*) Jilcoe.

***Briscoe, Jill.** Mujer, Cambia Tu Mundo: Como Dios USA A las Mujeres Para Hacer una Difference. (SPA.). 96p. 2000. pap. 6.00 (*0-311-04660-6*) Baptist Spanish.

Briscoe, Jill. The One Year Book of Devotions for Kids, Vol. 3. (J). 1997. pap. 10.99 (*0-8423-4662-7*) Tyndale Hse.

***Briscoe, Jill.** Prayer That Works. LC 00-21837. 2000. pap. 10.99 (*0-8423-1919-0*) Tyndale Hse.

Briscoe, Jill. Prime Rib & Apple. 1976. pap. 6.95 (*0-310-21811-X*, 9257P) Zondervan.

— Psalms for a Woman's Life 7 Studies to Better Understand Our God, Ourselves & Our World. 1999. pap. text 6.99 (*1-56476-774-4*) SP Pubns.

— Renewal on the Run: Encouragement for Wives Who Are Partners in Ministry. 164p. (Orig.). 1992. pap. 8.99 (*0-87788-719-5*, H Shaw Pubs) Waterbrook Pr.

— Running on Empty: Refilling Your Spirit at the Low Points of Life. 168p. 1995. pap. 8.99 (*0-87788-739-X*, H Shaw Pubs) Waterbrook Pr.

— Solid Ground. (Jill Briscoe Inductive Bible Study Ser.). 96p. 1992. pap. 7.99 (*0-89693-884-0*, 6-1884) Chariot Victor.

— Thank You for Being a Friend. 192p. (Orig.). 1981. reprint ed. pap. 7.99 (*0-310-21851-9*, 9261P) Zondervan.

— Thank You for Being a Friend: My Personal Journey. rev. expanded ed. 215p. 1999. pap. 10.99 (*0-8024-8547-2*) Moody.

— There's a Snake in My Garden. 205p. 1996. pap. 8.99 (*0-87788-811-6*, H Shaw Pubs) Waterbrook Pr.

— There's a Snake in My Garden. 1977. pap. 4.70 (*0-310-21821-7*, 9256P) Zondervan.

— Women in the Life of Jesus. (Jill Briscoe Inductive Bible Study Ser.). 96p. 1986. pap. 7.99 (*0-89693-254-0*, 6-2254, Victor Bks) Chariot Victor.

***Briscoe, Jill.** Women in the Life of Jesus: 8 Studies on the Significance of Women in Christ's Life & Ministry. 1999. pap. text 6.99 (*1-56476-775-2*) SP Pubns.

Briscoe, Jill. Women Who Changed the World 8 Studies on Women of Influence in the Old Testament. 1999. pap. text 6.99 (*1-56476-773-6*) SP Pubns.

— Women Who Changed Their World. (Jill Briscoe Inductive Bible Study Ser.). 108p. 1991. pap. 7.99 (*0-89693-001-7*, 6-1001, Victor Bks) Chariot Victor.

***Briscoe, Jill.** Your Gift of Friendship: Selections from Thank You for Being a Friend. 96p. 2000. 12.99 (*0-8024-6691-5*) Moody.

Briscoe, Jill, ed. Daily Study Bible for Men. 1999. pap. text 19.99 (*0-8423-3329-0*) Tyndale Hse.

Briscoe, Jill & Briscoe, Stuart D., eds. Daily Study Bible for Men. 1999. 26.99 (*0-8423-3328-2*) Tyndale Hse.

Briscoe, Jill, jt. auth. see Briscoe, Stuart.

Briscoe, John. A Commentary on Livy, Bks. 31-33. 400p. 1990. reprint ed. pap. 39.95 (*0-19-814738-4*) OUP.

— A Commentary on Livy, Bks. 34-37. (Illus.). 462p. 1981. text 85.00 (*0-19-814455-5*) OUP.

— Surveying the Courtroom: A Land Expert's Guide to Evidence & Civil Procedure. 199p. 1985. 75.00 (*0-910845-21-2*, 958) Landmark Ent.

***Briscoe, John.** Surveying the Courtroom: A Land Expert's Guide to Evidence & Civil Procedure. 2nd ed. LC 99-11597. 216p. 1999. 59.95 (*0-471-31840-X*) Wiley.

Briscoe, John, ed. Valerius Maximus, Vol. I. 9th ed. (LAT.). 434p. 1999. 140.00 (*3-519-01916-7*, T1916, Pub. by B G Teubner) U of Mich Pr.

— Valerius Maximus, Vol. II. 9th ed. (LAT.). 454p. 1999. 130.00 (*3-519-01917-5*, T1917, Pub. by B G Teubner) U of Mich Pr.

Briscoe, John, jt. ed. see Koester, C. Thomas.

***Briscoe, Keith G.** The Siebens' Family Saga. (Illus.). 52p. 2000. write for info. (*0-9678576-2-7*) S & T Pubng.

Briscoe, M. H. A Researcher's Guide to Scientific & Medical Illustrations. (Contemporary Bioscience Ser.). (Illus.). xi, 290p. 1990. pap. 19.95 (*0-387-97199-8*) Spr-Verlag.

Briscoe, Marianne G. Ethics in Fundraising, Philanthropy, & Organizational Culture: Putting Values into Practice. (New Directions for Philanthropic Fundraising Ser.: No. PF6). (Orig.). 1994. pap. 25.00 (*0-7879-9995-4*) Jossey-Bass.

Briscoe, Marianne G., ed. Ethics in Fundraising: Advancing Philanthropy. (New Directions for Philanthropic Fundraising Ser.: No. PF 5). 110p. (Orig.). 1994. pap. 25.00 (*0-7879-9994-6*) Jossey-Bass.

Briscoe, Marianne G. & Coldewey, John C., eds. Contexts for Early English Drama. LC 88-45099. 272p. 1989. reprint ed. pap. 84.40 (*0-608-01049-9*, 205935700001) Bks Demand.

Briscoe, Mary H. Preparing Scientific Illustrations: A Guide to Better Posters, Presentations, & Publications. 2nd ed. LC 95-34366. (Illus.). 204p. 1996. 29.95 (*0-387-94581-4*) Spr-Verlag.

Briscoe, Mary L., et al, eds. American Autobiography, 1945-1980: A Bibliography. LC 82-70547. 379p. 1982. reprint ed. pap. 117.50 (*0-608-01859-7*, 206251000003) Bks Demand.

Briscoe, Oliver E., ed. Asphalt Rheology Relatonship to Mixture. LC 87-1835. (Special Technical Publication Ser.: No. 941). (Illus.). viii, 200p. 1987. 34.00 (*0-8031-0938-5*, STP941) ASTM.

Briscoe, Peter, tr. see Cabanis, Jose.

Briscoe, Stuart. The Apostles' Creed: Beliefs That Matter. LC 93-41884. 250p. 1994. pap. 8.99 (*0-87788-052-2*, H Shaw Pubs) Waterbrook Pr.

— David: A Heart for God. 180p. 1988. pap. 8.99 (*0-89693-466-7*, 6-1466, Victor Bks) Chariot Victor.

— Discipleship for Ordinary People. (Christianity in Practice Ser.). 208p. 1995. pap. 8.99 (*0-87788-176-6*, H Shaw Pubs) Waterbrook Pr.

— The Fruit of the Spirit: Christian Character. (Fisherman Bible Studyguide Ser.). 64p. 1995. pap. 4.99 (*0-87788-258-4*, H Shaw Pubs) Waterbrook Pr.

— Genuine People: Living & Relating As a Real Christian. (Christianity in Practice Ser.). 176p. 1995. pap. 8.99 (*0-87788-844-2*, H Shaw Pubs) Waterbrook Pr.

— 9 Attitudes That Keep a Christian Going & Growing. 144p. 1995. pap. 8.99 (*0-87788-581-8*, H Shaw Pubs) Waterbrook Pr.

— Secrets of Spiritual Stamina: Healthy Habits for a Lasting Faith. LC 94-2438. 208p. 1994. pap. 8.99 (*0-87788-757-8*, H Shaw Pubs) Waterbrook Pr.

— The Sermon on the Mount: Daring to Be Different. (Foundations of the Faith Ser.: No. 4). 224p. 1995. pap. 8.99 (*0-87788-758-6*, H Shaw Pubs) Waterbrook Pr.

— The Ten Commandments: God's Rules for Living. (Fisherman Bible Studyguide Ser.). 80p. 1995. pap. 4.99 (*0-87788-803-5*, H Shaw Pubs) Waterbrook Pr.

— The Ten Commandments: Playing by the Rules. rev. ed. (Foundations of the Faith Ser.). 198p. 1993. pap. 8.99 (*0-87788-805-1*, H Shaw Pubs) Waterbrook Pr.

— Titus: Living As God's Very Own People. LC 94-2437. (Understanding the Bk.). 136p. 1994. pap. 8.99 (*0-87788-813-2*, H Shaw Pubs) Waterbrook Pr.

— Transforming the Daily Grind: Life with God Is an Adventure. 128p. 1995. pap. 8.99 (*0-87788-504-4*, H Shaw Pubs) Waterbrook Pr.

Briscoe, Stuart & Briscoe, Jill. The Family Book of Christian Values: Timeless Stories for Today's Family. 512p. 1995. 24.99 (*0-7814-0245-X*) Chariot Victor.

— Life, Liberty, & the Pursuit of Holiness. 192p. (Orig.). 1993. pap. 8.99 (*1-56476-064-2*, 6-3064, Victor Bks) Chariot Victor.

— Living Love: What Can Happen When We Learn to Love God's Way. 220p. (Orig.). 1993. pap. 9.99 (*0-87788-488-9*, H Shaw Pubs) Waterbrook Pr.

— Marriage Matters! Growing Together Through the Differences & Surprises of Life Together. LC 93-40582. 272p. 1994. pap. 9.99 (*0-87788-532-X*, H Shaw Pubs) Waterbrook Pr.

— Meet Him at the Manger: Discovering the Heart of Christmas. 160p. 1996. 15.99 (*0-87788-557-5*, H Shaw Pubs) Waterbrook Pr.

Briscoe, Stuart D. What Works When Life Doesn't. LC 98-23468. 176p. 1998. pap. write for info. (*0-87788-854-X*, H Shaw Pubs) Waterbrook Pr.

Briscoe, Stuart D., jt. ed. see Briscoe, Jill.

Briscoe, Ted, et al, eds. Default Inheritance Within Unification-Based Approaches to the Lexicon. (Studies in Natural Language Processing). (Illus.). 306p. (C). 1994. text 59.95 (*0-521-43027-5*) Cambridge U Pr.

Briscoe, Ted, jt. ed. see Boguraev, Bran.

Briscoe, Walter A. Byron the Poet: A Collection of Essays & Addresses by Contemporary Critics. LC 67-30803. (Studies in Byron: No. 5). (Illus.). 1969. reprint ed. lib. bdg. 75.00 (*0-8383-0694-2*) M S G Haskell Hse.

Briscomb, Christine. Gentlemen's Agreement. large type ed. (Romance Ser.). 288p. 1995. pap. 16.99 (*0-7089-7674-3*, Linford) Ulverscroft.

***Briscomb, Christine.** Three Tall Tamarisks. large type ed. 272p. 1999. pap. 18.99 (*0-7089-5484-7*, Linford) Ulverscroft.

— Visions of the Heart. large type ed. 272p. pap. 18.99 (*0-7089-5448-0*) Ulverscroft.

Briscombe, Christine. Gentlemen's Agreement. (Rainbow Romances Ser.). 160p. 1993. 14.95 (*0-7090-4925-0*) Parkwest Pubns.

Briscombe, Richard. Training for IT: Library Training Guide. 71p. 1997. pap. 40.00 (*1-85604-186-7*, LAP1867, Pub. by Library Association) Bernan Associates.

Brisdon, Alan K. Inorganic Spectroscopic Methods. (Oxford Chemistry Primers Ser.: No. 62). (Illus.). 96p. (C). 1998. pap. text 12.95 (*0-19-855949-6*) OUP.

Brisebarre, Jean-Jacques, ed. see Gefen, Gerard.

Brisebois, Mireille. St. Paul. (C). 1988. 45.00 (*0-85439-243-2*, Pub. by St Paul Pubns) St Mut.

Brisendine, jt. auth. see Kovanda.

Brisindine, Karen, jt. auth. see Kovanda.

Brisk, Katherine. Hot Tips for College Freshmen: or Try Not to Learn the Hardway. (Illus.). (Orig.). 1990. pap. text 6.95 (*0-614-04156-2*) Goldray Pub.

Brisk, Maria E. Bilingual Education: From Compensatory to Quality Education. 204p. 1997. write for info. (*0-8058-2494-4*); pap. 29.95 (*0-8058-2495-2*) L Erlbaum Assocs.

Brisk, Maria E. & Harrington, Margaret M. Literacy & Bilingualism: A Handbook for All Teachers. LC 99-31664. 160p. 1999. pap. write for info. (*0-8058-3165-7*) L Erlbaum Assocs.

Brisk, Marion. 1001 Ideas for Science Projects. 3rd ed. LC 97-81089. (Illus.). 256p. 1998. 12.95 (*0-02-862513-7*, Arc) IDG Bks.

Brisk, Marion, jt. auth. see Bosworth, Stefan.

Brisk, Marion A. Environmental Science. 1999. 22.00 (*0-07-007986-2*) McGraw.

— 50 Simple Things: Science. (Illus.). 192p. 1997. 11.95 (*0-02-861935-8*) Macmillan.

— One Thousand & One Ideas for Science Projects. 2nd ed. 272p. 1994. 12.95 (*0-671-89029-8*) Prntice Hall Bks.

— 1001 Ideas for Science Projects on the Environment. (Illus.). 256p. 1997. pap. 12.95 (*0-02-861707-X*, Arc) IDG Bks.

— One Thousand One Ideas for Science Projects. (Illus.). 224p. 1991. pap. 12.00 (*0-13-633769-4*, Arco) Macmillan Gen Ref.

Brisk Publishing Staff, jt. auth. see Bisk, Nathan M.

Brisk, William J. & Talis, William G. Legal Planning for the Elderly in Massachusetts. 530p. 1994. spiral bd. 125.00 (*0-88063-775-7*, MICHIE) LEXIS Pub.

Brisk, William J., et al. Massachusetts Elder Law, 1998. LC 98-89532. 900p. 1998. 135.00 (*0-327-00810-5*, 8153411) LEXIS Pub.

Brisk, William J., tr. see Bidart Campos, German J.

Briskey, Ernest J., et al, eds. The Physiology & Biochemistry of Muscle As a Food, Vol. 1. LC 66-22849. (Illus.). 453p. reprint ed. pap. 140.50 (*0-7837-7020-0*, 204683600001) Bks Demand.

— The Physiology & Biochemistry of Muscle As a Food, Vol. 2. LC 66-22849. (Illus.). 859p. reprint ed. pap. 200.00 (*0-7837-7021-9*, 204683600002) Bks Demand.

Briskin, Alan. The Stirring of Soul in the Workplace. LC 97-53319. 300p. 1998. pap. 16.95 (*1-57675-040-X*) Berrett-Koehler.

Briskin, Alan. The Stirring of Soul in the Workplace. LC 96-9975. (Business & Management Ser.). 300p. 1996. reprint ed. pap. 29.95 (*0-7879-0281-0*) Jossey-Bass.

***Briskin, Alan & Peppers, Cheryl.** Bringing Your Soul to Work: An Everyday Practice. 260p. 2000. pap. 16.95 (*1-57675-111-2*, Pub. by Berrett-Koehler) Publishers Group.

Briskin, Jacqueline. The Onyx. large type ed. LC 94-31285. 739p. 1995. 24.95 (*0-7838-1133-0*, G K Hall Lrg Type) Mac Lib Ref.

— Rich Friends. large type ed. LC 94-32355. 704p. 1994. lib. bdg. 25.95 (*0-7838-1132-2*, G K Hall Lrg Type) Mac Lib Ref.

Briskin, Linda, ed. Union Sisters: Women in the Labour Movement. 2nd ed. 424p. reprint ed. pap. 10.95 (*0-88961-079-7*, Pub. by Womens Pr) LPC InBook.

***Briskin, Linda & Eliasson, Mona.** Women's Organizing & Public Policy in Canada & Sweden. 408p. 2000. pap. 27.95 (*0-7735-1891-6*, Pub. by McG-Queens Univ Pr) CUP Services.

***Briskin, Linda & Eliasson, Mona, eds.** Women's Organizing & Public Policy in Canada & Sweden. 408p. 2000. text 65.00 (*0-7735-1855-X*, Pub. by McG-Queens Univ Pr) CUP Services.

Briskin, Linda & McDermott, Patricia, eds. Women Challenging Unions: Feminism, Democracy, & Militancy. 346p. 1993. text 50.00 (*0-8020-2872-1*); pap. text 19.95 (*0-8020-7376-X*) U of Toronto Pr.

Brisky, Jeffrey. Money Agency Planning Guide. 8th ed. 192p. 1996. pap. 25.00 (*1-56150-191-3*) Intl Wealth.

— Money Agency Planning Guide. 9th ed. 192p. 1998. pap. 25.00 (*1-56150-241-3*) Intl Wealth.

— Money Agency Planning Guide. 10th ed. 192p. 1999. pap. 25.00 (*1-56150-292-8*) Intl Wealth.

***Brisky, Jeffrey.** Money Agency Planning Guide. 11th ed. 192p. 2000. pap. 25.00 (*1-56150-352-5*) Intl Wealth.

Brisky, Michael. Mastering SMT Manufacturing. 265p. (C). 1992. text 249.95 (*1-882812-08-5*) SMT Plus.

Brisky, Richard. How to Be a Second Mortgage Loan Broker. 9th ed. 94p. 1998. pap. 25.00 (*1-56150-231-6*) Intl Wealth.

— How to Be a Second Mortgage Loan Broker. 8th ed. 94p. 1996. pap. 25.00 (*1-56150-181-6*) Intl Wealth.

— How to Be a Second Mortgage Loan Broker. 10th ed. 94p. 1999. pap. 25.00 (*1-56150-282-0*) Intl Wealth.

***Brisky, Richard.** How to Be a Second Mortgage Loan Broker. 11th ed. 94p. 2000. pap. 25.00 (*1-56150-342-8*) Intl Wealth.

Brislain, Michael. Bugging the Atlantic Salmon. (Illus.). 104p. 1995. pap. 12.95 (*0-86492-161-6*, Pub. by Goose Ln Edits) Genl Dist Srvs.

***Brisley, Joyce Lakester.** The Big Milly-Molly-Mandy Storybook. (Milly-Molly-Mandy Ser.). (Illus.). 80p. (J). (gr. k-3). 2000. 18.95 (*0-7534-5331-2*) LKC.

Brisley, Joyce Lakester. Milly-Molly-Mandy Storybook. LC 97-76184. (Milly-Molly-Mandy Ser.). (Illus.). 224p. (J). (gr. k-3). 1998. 13.95 (*1-85697-493-6*) LKC.

***Brisley, Joyce Lakester.** More Milly-Molly-Mandy. (Milly-Molly-Mandy Ser.). 224p. (J). (gr. k-3). 1999. 13.95 (*0-7534-0200-9*) LKC.

Brislin. Under Cultures Inflate Behavior V. (C). 1993. pap. text 51.50 (*0-03-075897-1*, Pub. by Harcourt Coll Pubs) Harcourt.

Brislin, Joann & McDonald, Doug S., eds. Championship Swimming Results, 1990. 474p. (Orig.). 1991. pap. 21.95 (*0-9628642-0-X*) Golf Eighties.

Brislin, Joseph A. Multiemployer Plans: A Guide for New Trustees. Brzezinski, Mary Jo, ed. LC 95-78933. 159p. (Orig.). 1995. pap. 29.00 (*0-89154-491-7*) Intl Found Employ.

— The WARN Act: A Manager's Compliance Guide to Workforce Reductions. LC 90-2133. 1990. 195.00 (*1-55871-171-6*, BSP 173) BNA PLUS.

Brislin, Ralph F. Effective Report Writing for the Security Officer. LC 94-21030. 166p. 1994. pap. 36.95 (*0-7506-9609-5*, BH Security) Buttrwrth-Heinemann.

— The Effective Security Officer Training Manual. LC 94-25959. 432p. 1994. pap. 34.95 (*0-7506-9610-9*) Buttrwrth-Heinemann.

— The Effective Security Supervision Manual. LC 94-25958. 256p. 1994. pap. 34.95 (*0-7506-9611-7*) Buttrwrth-Heinemann.

Brislin, Ralph F. & Lewis, Eric C. The Effective Security Officer's Training Manual. 2nd ed. LC 98-5581. 1998. 36.95 (*0-7506-7090-8*) Buttrwrth-Heinemann.

Brislin, Richard & Tomoko Yoshida. Intercultural Communication Training: An Introduction. LC 93-43061. (Communicating Effectively in Multicultural Contexts Ser.: Vol. 2). 222p. (C). 1994. text 39.95 (*0-8039-5074-8*); pap. text 18.50 (*0-8039-5075-6*) Sage.

Brislin, Richard, jt. ed. see Cushner, Kenneth.

Brislin, Richard W. The Art of Getting Things Done: A Practical Guide to the Use of Power. LC 90-47542. 272p. 1991. 22.95 (*0-275-93761-5*, C3761, Praeger Pubs) Greenwood.

— Intercultural Interactions: A Practical Guide. LC 85-18464. (Cross-Cultural Research & Methodology Ser.: Vol. 9). 310p. 1986. 49.95 (*0-8039-2558-1*); pap. 24.00 (*0-8039-3441-6*) Sage.

Brislin, Richard W., ed. Applied Cross-Cultural Psychology. (Cross-Cultural Research & Methodology Ser.: Vol. 14). (Illus.). 368p. (C). 1990. text 54.00 (*0-8039-3785-7*) Sage.

— Applied Cross-Cultural Psychology. 14th ed. (Cross-Cultural Research & Methodology Ser.: Vol. 14). (Illus.). 368p. (C). 1990. pap. text 26.00 (*0-8039-3786-5*) Sage.

— Culture Learning: Concepts, Applications, & Research. LC 77-5111. (East-West Center Bk.). 369p. reprint ed. pap. 114.40 (*0-7837-3988-5*, 204381900011) Bks Demand.

Brislin, Richard W., et al, eds. Cross-Cultural Perspectives on Learning. LC 73-91353. (Cross-Cultural Research & Methodology Ser.). 346p. reprint ed. pap. 107.30 (*0-608-10892-8*, 202187500026) Bks Demand.

Brislin, Richard W. & Yoshida, Tomoko, eds. Improving Intercultural Interactions: Modules for Cross-Cultural Training Programs. LC 93-35561. (Multicultural Aspects of Counseling Ser.: Vol. 3). (C). 1993. text 58.00 (*0-8039-5409-3*) Sage.

— Improving Intercultural Training Interactions: Modules for Cross-Cultural Training Programs. 3rd ed. LC 93-35561. (Multicultural Aspects of Counseling Ser.: Vol. 3). (C). 1993. pap. text 27.50 (*0-8039-5410-7*) Sage.

Brislin, Richard W., jt. auth. see Cushner, Kenneth.

***Brislin, Tom.** 30-Day Keyboard Workout. (National Keyboard Workshop Ser.). 96p. 1999. 9.95 (*0-7390-0230-9*, 18511) Alfred Pub.

Brislin, Tom, ed. Teaching Media Ethics: A Special Issue of the Journal of Mass Media Ethics. 64p. 1998. pap. 20.00 (*0-8058-9843-3*) L Erlbaum Assocs.

***BRISMAN, ANDREW.** American Mensa Guide to Casino Gambling: Winning Ways. LC 99-44616. 255p. 2000. pap. text 17.95 (*0-8069-4837-X*) Sterling.

Brisman, Leslie. The Voice of Jacob: On the Composition of Genesis. LC 89-45194. (Indiana Studies in Biblical Literature). 144p. 1990. 27.50 (*0-253-31264-7*) Ind U Pr.

— The Voice of Jacob: On the Composition of Gensis. LC 89-45194. (Indiana Studies in Biblical Literature). 142p. Date not set. reprint ed. pap. 44.10 (*0-608-20534-6*, 205444800002) Bks Demand.

Brisman, Ronald, ed. Neurosurgical & Medical Management of Pain: Trigeminal Neuralgia, Chronic Pain & Cancer Pain. (C). 1989. text 145.00 (*0-89838-405-2*) Kluwer Academic.

***Brisman, Shimeon.** A History & Guide to Judaic Dictionaries & Concordances. LC 99-11033. (Jewish Research Literature Ser.). 1999. 79.50 (*0-88125-658-7*) Ktav.

Brisman, Shimeon. A History & Guide to Judaic Encyclopedias & Lexicons: Jewish Research Literature, Vol. II. (Bibliographica Judaica Ser.: No. 11). 498p. 1987. 25.00 (*0-87820-909-3*) Hebrew Union Coll Pr.

Brison, Fred R., jt. auth. see Adriance, Guy W.

Brison, Karen J. Just Talk: Gossip, Meetings, & Power in a Papua New Guinea Village. (Studies in Melanesian Anthropology: No. 11). (C). 1992. 50.00 (*0-520-07700-8*, Pub. by U CA Pr) Cal Prin Full Svc.

Brisou, Jean. Biofilms Methods for Enzymatic Release of Microorganisms. LC 95-14237. 224p. 1995. boxed set 149.95 (*0-8493-4791-2*, 4791) CRC Pr.

Brissac, Elvire De, see De Brissac, Elvire.

Brissaud, J. B. History of French Private Law. (Continental Legal History Ser.: Vol. 3). (Illus.). xlvii, 922p. 1999. reprint ed. 85.00 (*0-8377-1931-3*, Rothman) W S Hein.

Brissaud, Jean B. History of French Public Law. Garner, James W., tr. from FRE. (Continental Legal History Ser.: Vol. 9). lviii, 581p. 1969. reprint ed. 85.00 (*0-8377-1932-1*, Rothman) W S Hein.

Brisseau, Janine. Children. LC 99-19872. 1999. 9.95 (*0-7641-5189-4*) Barron.

Brissenden. Whale in Darkness. (Australian National University Press Ser.). 1980. text 21.00 (*0-08-032933-0*, Pergamon Pr) Elsevier.

Brissenden, Alan, ed. Aspects of Australian Fiction. 1991. pap. 19.95 (*0-85564-312-9*, Pub. by Univ of West Aust Pr) Intl Spec Bk.

— Rolf Boldrewood. (UQP Australian Authors Ser.). 519p. 1979. pap. 16.95 (*0-7022-1277-6*) Intl Spec Bk.

Brissenden, Alan, ed. see Middleton, Thomas.

Brissenden, Alan, ed. see Shakespeare, William.

Brissenden, Constance. Whistler. (Altitude SuperGuides Ser.). pap. text 9.95 (*1-55153-029-5*) Altitude Publ.

***Brissenden, Constance, ed.** Vancouver & Victoria: A Colourguide. (Illus.). 2000. pap. 16.95 (*0-88780-520-5*, Pub. by Formac Dist Ltd) Seven Hills Bk.

Brissenden, Paul F. Launching of the I. W. W. LC 78-169188. (American History & Americana Ser.: No. 47). 1971. reprint ed. lib. bdg. 75.00 (*0-8383-1275-6*) M S G Haskell Hse.

— The Settlement of Labor Disputes on Rights in Australia. (Monograph & Research Ser.: No. 13). 131p. 1966. 5.00 (*0-89215-014-9*) U Cal LA Indus Rel.

Brissenden, T. H. Mathematics Teaching: Theory in Practice. 192p. (C). 1980. pap. 45.00 (*0-7855-2375-8*) St Mut.

Brisset, Annie. A Sociocritique of Translation Theatre & Alterity in Quebec, 1968-1988. (Theory/Culture Ser.). 272p. 1996. text 45.00 (*0-8020-0533-0*) U of Toronto Pr.

Brissett-Chapman, Sheryl & Issacs-Shockley, Mareasa, compiled by. Children in Social Peril: A Community Vision for Preserving Family Care of African American Children & Youths. LC 97-141794. 64p. (Orig.). 1997. pap. 5.95 (*0-87868-685-1*, CWLA Pr) Child Welfare.

Brissett-Chapman, Sheryl, jt. ed. see Jackson, Sandra.

Brissett, Dennis & Edgley, Charles, eds. Life As Theater: A Dramaturgical Sourcebook. 2nd ed. (Communication & Social Order Ser.). 477p. (C). 1990. pap. text 34.95 (*0-202-30363-2*); lib. bdg. 56.95 (*0-202-30362-4*) Aldine de Gruyter.

Brissman, Charles P., jt. auth. see Walton, Wesley S.

Brisson, Barbara S. Such Is the Way of the World: A Journey Through Grief. 64p. (Orig.). 1997. pap. 5.95 (*0-8091-3691-0*) Paulist Pr.

Brisson, Claire, tr. see Minnaar, Phillip & Minnaar, Maria.

Brisson, Jean Paul. Autonomisme et Christianisme dans l'Afrique Romaine de Septime Severe a L'invasion Vandale. LC 82-45808. (Orthodoxies & Heresies in the Early Church Ser.). 1983. reprint ed. 49.50 (*0-404-62377-8*) AMS Pr.

Brisson, Luc. Orphee et l'Orphisme dans l'Antiquite Greco-Romaine. (Collected Studies: Vol. CS476). 320p. 1995. 109.95 (*0-86078-453-3*, Pub. by Variorum) Ashgate Pub Co.

Brisson, Luc. Plato the Myth Maker. 1997. pap. text 12.95 (*0-226-07519-2*) U Ch Pr.

Brisson, Luc. Plato the Myth Maker. LC 98-8641. 176p. 1999. 27.50 (*0-226-07518-4*) U Ch Pr.

Brisson, Luc & Meyerstein, F. Walter. Inventing the Universe: Plato's Timaeus, the Big Bang, & the Problem of Scientific Knowledge. LC 95-18054. (SUNY Series in Ancient Greek Philosophy). 193p. (C). 1995. text 44.50 (*0-7914-2691-2*); pap. text 14.95 (*0-7914-2692-0*) State U NY Pr.

Brisson, Lynn. Across the Board: Bulletin Boards, Activities, & Awards to Reinforce Basic Content Skills. Britt, Leslie, ed. & intro. by. (Illus.). 80p. (Orig.). (J). (gr. 1-3). 1995. pap. text 9.95 (*0-86530-312-6*, IP312-6) Incentive Pubns.

— Bulletin Board Activities to Reinforce Basic Skills Throughout the Year. Quinn, Anna, ed. (Illus.). 80p. (Orig.). (J). (ps-k). 1995. pap. text 9.95 (*0-86530-318-5*, 318-5) Incentive Pubns.

— Easy Art Projects to Teach Global Awareness. Keeling, Jan, ed. (Illus.). 64p. (Orig.). (J). (gr. k-6). 1993. pap. text 8.95 (*0-86530-266-9*, 266-9) Incentive Pubns.

— Environmental Bulletin Boards: Patterns, Plans & Instructions. Britt, Leslie, ed. (Illus.). 80p. (J). (gr. k-3). 1993. pap. text, teacher ed. 8.95 (*0-86530-277-4*, 270-0) Incentive Pubns.

— Exploring Our Faith Through Crafts. 64p. 1989. pap. 3.57 (*0-687-12427-1*) Abingdon.

— Exploring Our Faith Through Crafts, No. 2. 64p. 1991. pap. 5.95 (*0-687-12429-8*) Abingdon.

— Hablo Espanol! Creative Activities to Teach Basic Spanish. Britt, Leslie & Westerman, Karla, eds. (Illus.). 64p. (Orig.). (J). (gr. k-3). 1995. pap. text 7.95 (*0-86530-311-8*, IP311-8) Incentive Pubns.

— Quick & Easy Holiday Activities for Early Learners: Arts & Crafts for Beginning Skills & Concepts. (Illus.). 80p. (Orig.). (J). (ps). 1991. pap. text 8.95 (*0-86530-195-6*, 195-6) Incentive Pubns.

Brisson, Lynn. Small Projects for Small Hands: Arts & Crafts for Beginning Skills Programs. (Illus.). 80p. (Orig.). (J). (ps-1). 1991. pap. text 9.95 (*0-86530-187-5*, IP 193-4) Incentive Pubns.

Brisson, Lynn. The Teacher's Holiday Helper. Lewis, Sherri Y., ed. (Illus.). 96p. (Orig.). (J). (gr. k-6). 1990. pap. text 10.95 (*0-86530-172-7*, 190-9) Incentive Pubns.

— 3-D Art Projects That Teach. (Illus.). 80p. (J). (gr. k-6). 1989. pap. text 9.95 (*0-86530-084-4*, IP 166-1) Incentive Pubns.

— 3-D Bulletin Boards. Sharpe, Sally D., ed. (Illus.). 80p. 1988. pap. text 9.95 (*0-86530-164-6*, IP 28-4) Incentive Pubns.

Brisson, Mark. Barn Swallows. (Stories We Tell Ser.). 37p. 1993. pap. 4.00 (*1-884983-01-4*) Homegrown Bks.

Brisson, N., jt. ed. see Verma, Desh P.

Brisson, Pat. Benny's Pennies. (J). 1995. mass mkt. 6.99 (*0-440-91060-9*) BDD Bks Young Read.

— Benny's Pennies. (Illus.). 32p. (J). (ps-1). 1995. pap. 5.99 (*0-440-41016-9*, YB BDD) BDD Bks Young Read.

— Benny's Pennies. 1995. 11.19 (*0-606-07275-6*, Pub. by Turtleback) Demco.

***Brisson, Pat.** Bertie's Picture Day. LC 00-22431. (Illus.). 80p. (gr. 1-3). 2000. text 14.95 (*0-8050-6281-5*) St Martin.

Brisson, Pat. Hot Fudge Hero. LC 96-32511. 80p. (J). (gr. 1-4). 1995. 14.95 (*0-8050-4551-1*) H Holt & Co.

— Kate Heads West. LC 89-27590. (Illus.). 40p. (J). (gr. k-3). 1990. lib. bdg. 14.00 (*0-02-714345-7*, Bradbury S&S) S&S Childrens.

— Kate on the Coast. LC 91-17046. (Illus.). 40p. (J). (gr. k-3). 1992. lib. bdg. 13.95 (*0-02-714341-4*, Bradbury S&S) S&S Childrens.

— Little Sister, Big Sister. LC 98-33905. (Illus.). (J). (gr. 1-3). 1999. 15.95 (*0-8050-5887-7*) H Holt & Co.

***Brisson, Pat.** Sky Memories. LC 98-38962. (Illus.). 80p. 1999. 14.95 (*0-385-32606-8*) Dela Pr.

Brisson, Pat. Summer My Father Was Ten. LC 97-72769. (Illus.). 32p. (J). 1998. 15.95 (*1-56397-435-5*) Boyds Mills Pr.

— The Summer My Father Was Ten. LC 97-72769. (Illus.). 32p. (J). 1999. pap. 7.95 (*1-56397-829-6*) Boyds Mills Pr.

— Wanda's Roses. LC 93-72916. (Illus.). 32p. (J). (ps-3). 1994. 14.95 (*1-56397-136-4*) Boyds Mills Pr.

***Brisson, Pat.** Wanda's Roses. LC 93-72916. (Illus.). 32p. (J). (ps-3). 2000. pap. 7.95 (*1-56397-925-X*) Boyds Mills Pr.

Brisson, Renee, tr. see Minnaar, Phillip & Minnaar, Maria.

Brissot De Warville, Jean P. New Travels in the United States: Performed in 1788. LC 74-11214. (On America Ser.: Vol. 1). 483p. 1970. reprint ed. lib. bdg. 57.50 (*0-678-04028-1*) Kelley.

Brissot De Warville, Jean P. & Claviere, Etienne. The Commerce of America with Europe: Particularly with France & Great Britain. LC 74-11218. (On America Ser.: Vol. 2). lxiv, 348p. 1970. reprint ed. lib. bdg. 57.50 (*0-678-04029-X*) Kelley.

Bristeau, M. O., et al, eds. Computational Science for the 21st Century. 896p. 1997. 195.00 (*0-471-97298-3*, Q174) Wiley.

Bristen, Darryl. The Monster Within. Cramberg, JoAnne, ed. 48p. 1998. pap. 6.00 (*0-9657706-7-2*) Phos Pub.

Brister, Barbara, tr. see Saubin, Beatrice.

Brister, Bob. Moss, Mallards & Mules: And Other Hunting & Fishing Stories. LC 98-45553. (Illus.). 216p. 1998. reprint ed. 30.00 (*0-924357-73-8*) Countrysport Pr.

— Shotgunning: The Art & the Science. LC 82-62603. 1976. 18.95 (*0-8329-1840-7*, Winchester Pr) New Win Pub.

Brister, C. W. Change Happens: Finding Your Way Through Life's Transitions. LC 96-38532. 128p. 1997. 20.00 (*1-57312-091-X*) Smyth & Helwys.

Brister, Darryl S. Exposing the Enemy. Peacock, Jimmy, ed. 112p. 1997. pap. 11.95 (*0-9657706-4-8*) Phos Pub.

Brister, David M., jt. auth. see Brister, Phyllis D.

Brister, Elaine H. Once upon a River: His, Pineville, Louisiana. 1968. 17.50 (*0-87511-578-0*) Claitors.

Brister, Judith, tr. see Galeano, Eduardo.

Brister, Phyllis D. & Brister, David M. The Vicious Circle Phenomenon: Our Battle for Self-Control - How to Win the War. LC 87-15434. (Illus.). 304p. (C). 1987. 19.95 (*0-939977-69-9*) Diadem Pub.

Brister, Robert D., jt. auth. see Langjahr, Stephen W.

Brister, Ronald C., jt. ed. see Dye, David H.

Brister, Shirley J. Comprehensive Physical Therapy Assistant Board Review. LC 95-31273. (Illus.). 304p. (C). (gr. 13). 1995. pap. text 39.95 (*0-8151-1010-3*, 26358) Mosby Inc.

Bristol, Claude M. The Magic of Believing. 1991. per. 5.99 (*0-671-74521-2*) PB.

— The Magic of Believing. 180p. 1991. pap. 10.00 (*0-671-76412-8*, Fireside) S&S Trade Pap.

Bristol, Claude M. & Sherman, Harold. TNT: The Power Within You. 238p. 1974. per. 10.00 (*0-671-76546-9*) S&S Trade Pap.

Bristol Conference on Critical Philosophy Staff. Practical Reason: Papers & Discussions by G. E. M. Anscombe . . . et al. Khorner, Stephan, ed. LC 74-77066. 272p. reprint ed. pap. 84.40 (*0-8357-8281-6*, 203378900087) Bks Demand.

Bristol, David. Paradise & Cash. LC 80-50064. (Series Five). 50p. 1980. pap. 7.00 (*0-931846-14-5*) Wash Writers Pub.

Bristol, Evelyn, ed. Russian Literature & Criticism: Selected Papers from the Second World Congress for Soviet & East European Studies. 254p. 1983. pap. 12.00 (*0-933884-27-3*) Berkeley Slavic.

Bristol, Evelyn, ed. East European Literature: Papers from the Second World Congress for Soviet & East European Studies. 106p. 1982. pap. 6.00 (*0-933884-26-5*) Berkeley Slavic.

Bristol, George L. Visual Voices: Between Mountains & Me. LC 91-614915. (Illus.). 96p. 1991. 34.95 (*1-879234-24-6*) State House Pr.

Bristol, Hollace. The "I Really Like It When You..." Cards. (C). 1997. pap. text 28.95 (*0-7872-4656-5*) Kendall-Hunt.

Bristol, Horace. Stories from Life: The Photography of Horace Bristol. (Illus.). 187p. 1995. pap. text 35.00 (*0-915977-20-6*, TR500) Georgia Museum of Art.

Bristol House Staff. Communion: Jesus' Love for Us Student. 44p. 1992. pap. 6.95 (*0-917851-55-2*) Bristol Hse.

— Communion: Jesus' Love for Us Teacher. 54p. 1992. pap. 7.95 (*0-917851-49-8*) Bristol Hse.

— The Order of St. George: Bible Memory. 47p. 1992. pap. 29.95 (*0-917851-32-3*) Bristol Hse.

Bristol, James A., ed. Annual Reports in Medicinal Chemistry, Vol. 29. Vol. 29. (Illus.). 397p. 1994. pap. text 78.00 (*0-12-040529-6*) Acad Pr.

— Annual Reports in Medicinal Chemistry, Vol. 30. (Illus.). 400p. 1995. pap. text 74.00 (*0-12-040530-X*) Acad Pr.

— Annual Reports in Medicinal Chemistry, Vol. 31. (Illus.). 413p. 1996. pap. text 70.00 (*0-12-040531-8*) Acad Pr.

— Annual Reports in Medicinal Chemistry, Vol. 32. (Illus.). 378p. 1997. pap. text 70.00 (*0-12-040532-6*) Morgan Kaufmann.

Bristol, James E. McCarthyism: The Seed Is in Us. LC 54-9201. (C). 1954. pap. 4.00 (*0-87574-076-6*) Pendle Hill.

— Stand Fast in Liberty. LC 61-18784. (C). 1961. pap. 4.00 (*0-87574-119-3*) Pendle Hill.

***Bristol, Larsh K. & Maas, Curt, photos by.** Iowa: Simply Beautiful. (Illus.). 120p. 2000. 29.95 (*1-56037-160-9*) Am Wrld Geog.

Bristol, Leigh. Angel. 352p. (Orig.). 1992. mass mkt. 4.99 (*0-446-35078-8*) Warner Bks.

— Legacy. 352p. 1993. mass mkt. 4.99 (*0-446-35081-8*) Warner Bks.

— Legacy. large type ed. LC 93-22679. 413p. 1993. lib. bdg. 21.95 (*0-8161-5828-2*, G K Hall Lrg Type) Mac Lib Ref.

Bristol, Lorin W. Revelation Paralleled. 220p. (Orig.). 1990. 12.95 (*0-9626302-0-9*); pap. 8.95 (*0-9626302-3-3*) Bristol CA.

Bristol, Michael D. Big-Time Shakespeare. 272p. (C). 1996. 90.00 (*0-415-06016-8*); pap. 24.99 (*0-415-06017-6*) Routledge.

— Carnival & Theatre: Plebian Culture & the Structure of Authority in Renaissance England. 256p. 1989. pap. 13.95 (*0-415-90138-3*, A2730) Routledge.

— Shakespeare's America, America's Shakespeare. LC 89-6057. 247p. reprint ed. pap. 76.60 (*0-608-20319-X*, 207157200002) Bks Demand.

Bristol, Michael D., jt. ed. see Marotti, Arthur F.

Bristol-Myers Squibb Symposium on Pain Research St. Current & Emerging Issues in Cancer Pain Research & Practice: The Bristol-Myers Squibb Symposium on Pain

B

Research. Chapman, C. Richard & Foley, Kathleen M., eds. LC 93-3669. (Illus.). 461p. 1993. reprint ed. pap. 143.00 (*0-608-07195-1*, 206742000009) Bks Demand.

— Hyperalgesia & Allodynia: The Bristol-Myers Squibb Symposium on Pain Research, 2nd, Galveston, Texas, 1991. Willis, William D., Jr., ed. LC 92-6601. (Bristol-Myers Squibb Symposium on Pain Research Ser.). (Illus.). 414p. reprint ed. pap. 128.40 (*0-608-09759-4*, 206993200007) Bks Demand.

— Pain & Central Nervous System Disease: The Central Pain Syndromes. Casey, Kenneth L., ed. LC 91-10602. (Bristol-Myers Squibb Symposium on Pain Research Ser.). (Illus.). 304p. 1991. reprint ed. pap. 94.30 (*0-608-07240-0*, 206746500009) Bks Demand.

Bristol-Myers/Zimmer Orthopaedic Symposium (4th: 1. Articular Cartilage & Knee Joint Function: Basic Science & Arthroscopy. Ewing, J. Whit, ed. LC 89-10451. (Bristol-Myers/Zimmer Orthopaedic Symposium Ser.). (Illus.). 403p. reprint ed. pap. 125.00 (*0-608-05848-3*, 205981500007) Bks Demand.

Bristol-Myers/Zimmer Orthopaedic Symposium (5th, 1989, Scottsdale, AZ) Staff. Controversies of Total Knee Arthroplasty. Goldberg, Victor M., ed. LC 91-18288. (Illus.). 335p. reprint ed. pap. 103.90 (*0-608-05854-8*, 205982100007) Bks Demand.

Bristol, Olivia. Six Victorian & Edwardian Board Games. (Illus.). 12p. (J). 1995. bds. write for info. (*1-85479-713-1*, Pub. by M OMara) Assoc Pubs Grp.

Bristol, Olivia & Geddes-Brown, Leslie. Dolls' Houses: Domestic Life & Architectural Styles in Miniature from the 16th Century to the Present Day. LC 99-234938. (Illus.). 168p. 1997. 45.00 (*1-85732-824-8*, Pub. by Mitchell Beazley) Antique Collect.

Bristol Polytechnic Staff. Ideas on Training, Vol. 1: Self Management. (C). 1989. text 750.00 (*0-89771-038-X*, Pub. by B Polytechnic) St Mut.

— Ideas on Training, Vol. 2: Leadership. (C). 1989. text 750.00 (*0-89771-335-4*, Pub. by B Polytechnic) St Mut.

— Ideas on Training, Vol. 3: Motivation. (C). 1989. text 750.00 (*0-89771-334-6*, Pub. by B Polytechnic) St Mut.

— Ideas on Training, Vol. 4: Getting. (C). 1989. text 750.00 (*0-89771-333-8*, Pub. by B Polytechnic) St Mut.

— Ideas on Training, Vol. 5: Communication. (C). 1989. text 750.00 (*0-89771-332-X*, Pub. by B Polytechnic) St Mut.

— Ideas on Training, Vol. 6: Problem Solving. (C). 1990. text 750.00 (*0-89771-331-1*, Pub. by B Polytechnic) St Mut.

Bristol, Sherlock. The Pioneer Preacher: Incidents of Interest, & Experiences in the Author's Life. (Illus.). 240p. 1989. reprint ed. pap. text 14.95 (*0-252-06091-1*) U of Ill Pr.

Bristol, Steve. Distilled Logic: Drinking. (Inter Acta Ser.). (Illus.). 6p. (C). 1995. teacher ed., ring bd. 1.25 (*1-885702-11-6*, 741-006t, Inter Acta); student ed., ring bd. 3.25 (*1-885702-10-8*, 741-006s, Inter Acta) WSN Pr.

— Shades of Gray. (Inter Acta Ser.). (Illus.). 6p. (C). 1994. teacher ed., ring bd. 1.25 (*1-885702-15-9*, 741-007t, Inter Acta); student ed., ring bd. 3.25 (*1-885702-14-0*, 741-007s, Inter Acta) WSN Pr.

Bristol, Stewart J. Hunting Wild Turkeys in New England. LC 86-21777. (Illus.). 170p. (Orig.). 1986. pap. 8.95 (*0-89621-099-5*) Nrth Country Pr.

Bristol, Terry. Study Guide to Accompany Jacob & Francone's Elements of Anatomy & Physiology. 2nd ed. (Illus.). 183p. 1992. pap. text 17.95 (*0-7216-3644-6*, W B Saunders Co) Harcrt Hlth Sci Grp.

Bristol, Terry. Zeno's Paradise. (C). 1998. write for info. (*0-201-48961-9*) Addison-Wesley.

***Bristol, Terry.** Zeno's Paradise. 2000. 22.00 (*0-7382-0192-8*, Pub. by Perseus Pubng) HarpC.

Bristol Wagon & Carriage Works Co., Ltd. Staff. Bristol Wagon & Carriage Illustrated Catalog, 1900. LC 94-13893. (Illus.). 160p. 1994. reprint ed. pap. 9.95 (*0-486-28123-X*) Dover.

Bristol. Plastic Films. 3rd ed. 1996. (*0-582-01490-5*) Addison-Wesley.

Briston, J. H. Rigid & Semi-Rigid Plastic Containers. 1996. 64.95 (*0-582-01491-3*) Addison-Wesley.

Briston, J. H., jt. auth. see Miles, D. C.

Briston, Patrick & Weidner, Dennis. Boys' Preparatory Schools: A Photographic Essay. (Illus.). 136p. 1990. 24.95 (*0-9624570-0-0*) Apertures.

Bristor, Martha. Individuals & Family Systems in Their Environments. 2nd ed. 464p. (C). 1995. pap. text, per. 54.95 (*0-7872-1493-0*, 41149301) Kendall-Hunt.

Bristow, Adrian. A Serious Disappointment: The Battle of Aubers Ridge, 1915, & the Subsequent Munitions Scandal. 202p. 1995. 31.95 (*0-85052-462-8*, Pub. by Leo Cooper) Trans-Atl Phila.

Bristow, Alex. Orchids. (Wisley Handbooks Ser.). (Illus.). 64p. (Orig.). 1989. pap. 5.95 (*0-304-31097-2*, Pub. by Cassell) Sterling.

Bristow, Barbara J. It All Adds Up. rev. ed. 200p. 1998. pap. 30.50 (*1-57753-286-4*, 322LM1) Corn Coop Ext.

Bristow, Bennie & Bristow, Gwen. Living for Eternity. 1991. pap. 7.75 (*0-89137-451-5*) Quality Pubns.

Bristow, Benny. From Kneepants to Romance. 1978. pap. 3.15 (*0-89137-810-3*) Quality Pubns.

Bristow, Benny. Self Teaching New Testament, Vol. II. unabridged ed. 387p. 1996. 29.95 (*0-89137-214-8*, 7213X) Quality Pubns.

— Self Teaching New Testament, Vol. III. unabridged ed. 343p. 1998. 29.95 (*0-89137-215-6*, 72156) Quality Pubns.

Bristow, Benny. Ten Commandments for Husbands. 1985. pap. 6.95 (*0-89137-623-2*) Quality Pubns.

— Ten Commandments for Wives. 1983. pap. 6.95 (*0-89137-430-2*) Quality Pubns.

Bristow, Benny B. Calm Out of the Storms: Stresses of Lilfe. 1986. pap. 6.35 (*0-89137-321-7*) Quality Pubns.

— Charts & Sermons for Overhead Projectors. 1985. pap. 9.85 (*0-89137-622-4*) Quality Pubns.

— Commentary on Ephesians. 1987. pap. 6.15 (*0-89137-571-6*) Quality Pubns.

— Invitations for Mid-Week Services. 1990. pap. 6.95 (*0-89137-625-9*) Quality Pubns.

— Self Teaching New Testament, Vol. 1. 506p. 1996. 29.95 (*0-89137-213-X*) Quality Pubns.

— Sermons to See & Hear. 1990. pap. 8.75 (*0-89137-624-0*) Quality Pubns.

— Thinking with Solomon. 1992. pap. 8.75 (*0-89137-134-6*) Quality Pubns.

— Youth Power for God. (YA). 1994. pap. 6.15 (*0-89137-831-6*) Quality Pubns.

Bristow, C. R., et al. The Wincanton District - A Concise Account of the Geology: Memoir for 1:50 000 Geological Sheet 297 (England & Wales) (British Geological Survey Memoirs Ser.). (Illus.). x, 110p. 75.00 (*0-11-884551-9*, Pub. by Statnry Office) Balogh.

Bristow, C. S., jt. ed. see Best, J. L.

Bristow, Catherine. Annabelle's Rescue. large type ed. (Illus.). 36p. (J). (gr. k-3). 1997. 12.95 (*0-9645531-2-0*) Nadan Pubns.

— The Golden Horse: An American Fairy Tale. (Illus.). 32p. (J). (ps-6). 1995. 12.95 (*0-9645531-0-4*) Nadan Pubns.

— The Golden Horse: The Journey West. large type ed. (Illus.). 32p. (J). (gr. 2-6). 1998. 12.95 (*0-9645531-1-2*) Nadan Pubns.

Bristow, Christopher, ed. see Defoe, Daniel.

***Bristow, David L.** A Dirty, Wicked Town: Tales of 19th Century Omaha. Cornell, Wayne, ed. (Illus.). 318p. 2000. pap. 16.95 (*0-87004-398-6*, 039860) Caxton.

Bristow, Diana E. Titanic R. I. P. 216p. 1989. per. 7.95 (*0-8187-0113-7*) Harlo Press.

Bristow, Edward W., ed. No Religion is an Island: The Nostra Aetate Dialogues. LC 98-38054. xi, 184p. 1998. 35.00 (*0-8232-1824-4*); pap. 18.00 (*0-8232-1825-2*) Fordham.

Bristow, Eugene K., ed. see Chekhov, Anton.

Bristow, George. Rip Van Winkle. (Earlier American Music Ser.: No. 25). 297p. 1990. 49.50 (*0-306-76124-6*) Da Capo.

***Bristow, George Frederick & Hardenbrook, William.** George Frederick Bristow: The Oartorio of Daniel, Opus 42. Griggs-Janower, David, ed. (Recent Researches in American Music Ser.). (Illus.). xviii, 444p. 1999. pap. 145.00 (*0-89579-443-8*, A34) A-R Eds.

***Bristow, Gwen.** Celia Garth: A Story of Charleston in the Revolution. LC 99-59319. 320p. 1999. reprint ed. 24.95 (*1-877853-58-5*) Nautical & Aviation.

Bristow, Gwen. Deep Summer. 310p. 1979. reprint ed. lib. bdg. 29.95 (*0-89966-025-8*) Buccaneer Bks.

— From Pigtails to Wedding Bells. 1978. pap. 3.15 (*0-89137-811-1*) Quality Pubns.

— Handsome Road. 320p. 1979. reprint ed. lib. bdg. 31.95 (*0-89966-028-2*) Buccaneer Bks.

— This Side of Glory. 278p. 1979. reprint ed. lib. bdg. 29.95 (*0-89966-026-6*) Buccaneer Bks.

— Tomorrow Is Forever. 320p. 1976. lib. bdg. 27.95 (*0-89966-027-4*) Buccaneer Bks.

Bristow, Gwen, jt. auth. see Bristow, Bennie.

Bristow, Ian C. Architectural Colour in British Interiors, 1615-1840. LC 95-45152. (Illus.). 288p. 1996. 110.00 (*0-300-03866-6*) Yale U Pr.

— Interior House-Painting Colours & Technology, 1615-1840. LC 95-43941. (Illus.). 288p. 1996. 100.00 (*0-300-03867-4*) Yale U Pr.

Bristow, J. A Local Historians Glossary & Vade Mecum. (C). 1989. 100.00 (*0-7855-6424-1*, Pub. by Univ Nottingham) St Mut.

Bristow, J. Anthony. Paper Structure & Properties. Kolseth, Peter, ed. (International Fiber Science & Technology Ser.: Vol. 8). (Illus.). 416p. 1986. text 235.00 (*0-8247-7560-0*) Dekker.

Bristow, Jacqueline. Memory & Learning: A Practical Guide for Teachers, Vol. 1. (Resource Materials for Teachers Ser.). 1999. pap. 27.95 (*1-85346-594-1*) David Fulton.

Bristow, Jenny. Cookin' in the Kitchen. (Illus.). 128p. 1995. pap. 15.95 (*0-86281-581-9*, Pub. by Appletree Pr) Irish Bks Media.

— Jenny Bristow's Country Cooking. (Illus.). 140p. 1996. pap. 15.95 (*0-86281-645-9*, Pub. by Appletree Pr) Irish Bks Media.

— Jenny Bristow's Country Cooking 2. (Illus.). 128p. 1997. pap. 15.95 (*0-86281-697-1*, Pub. by Appletree Pr) Irish Bks Media.

Bristow, Joan. Cathedral Meditations. LC 99-171090. 128p. 1998. pap. text 7.95 (*0-281-05130-5*) Intl Pubs Mktg.

Bristow, John A. The Bulgarian Economy in Transition. LC 95-36671. (Studies of Communism in Transition). (Illus.). 264p. (C). 1996. 85.00 (*1-85278-994-8*) E Elgar.

Bristow, John T. What Paul Really Said About Women: The Apostle's Liberating Views on Equality in Marriage, Leadership, & Love. LC 87-46200. 144p. 1991. reprint ed. pap. 13.00 (*0-06-061063-8*, Pub. by Harper SF) HarpC.

— What the Bible Really Says about Love, Marriage, & Family. 152p. (Orig.). 1994. pap. 12.99 (*0-8272-4232-8*) Chalice Pr.

Bristow, Joseph. Effeminate England: Homoerotic Writing after 1885. LC 95-10836. (Between Men - Between Women Ser.). 193p. 1995. 44.00 (*0-231-10348-4*); pap. 17.00 (*0-231-10349-2*) Col U Pr.

— Effeminate England: Homoerotic Writing after 1885. Flint, Kate, ed. (Gender in Writing Ser.). 208p. 1995. 9.00 (*0-335-09666-2*); pap. 2.00 (*0-335-09665-4*) OpUniv Pr.

— Sexuality. LC 96-32461. (The New Critical Idiom Ser.). 256p. (C). 1997. 50.00 (*0-415-12268-6*); pap. 12.99 (*0-415-08494-6*) Routledge.

— The Victorian Poet: Poetics & Persona. (World & Word Ser.). 256p. 1987. 65.00 (*0-7099-3925-6*, Pub. by C Helm) Routldge.

***Bristow, Joseph, ed.** The Cambridge Companion to Victorian Poetry. (Cambridge Companions to Literature Ser.). 353p. (C). 2000. Price not set. (*0-521-64115-2*); pap. Price not set. (*0-521-64680-4*) Cambridge U Pr.

Bristow, Joseph, ed. The Oxford Book of Adventure Stories. 436p. 1995. 35.00 (*0-19-214214-3*) OUP.

— Sexual Sameness: Textual Differences in Lesbian & Gay Writing. LC 91-28659. (Illus.). 272p. (C). (gr. 13). 1992. text 59.95 (*0-415-06936-X*, A7199) Routledge.

— Victorian Women Poets: Emily Bronte, Elizabeth Barrett Browning, Christina Rossetti. LC 95-8581. 1995. text 45.00 (*0-312-12735-9*) St Martin.

Bristow, Joseph, intro. Collected Works of Oscar Wilde, 15 vols., Set. (Collected Works Ser.). 4918p. (C). (gr. 13). 1993. text, boxed set 1320.00 (*0-415-10584-6*, B3682) Routledge.

Bristow, Joseph & Broughton, Trev L. Infernal Desires Of Angela Carter. LC 96-29641. (Studies in Twentieth Century Literature Ser.). 227p. (C). 1997. pap. text 28.00 (*0-582-29191-7*) Addison-Wesley.

Bristow, Joseph & Wilson, Angie, eds. Activating Theory: Lesbian, Gay, Bisexual Politics. 256p. (C). 1993. pap. 19.50 (*0-85315-790-1*, Pub. by Lawrence & Wishart) NYU Pr.

Bristow, Joseph, ed. & intro. see Schreiner, Olive.

Bristow, Joy, compiled by. The Local Historian's Glossary & Vade Mecum. 288p. 1998. pap. 36.00 (*1-85041-069-0*, Pub. by U of Nottingham) St Mut.

***Bristow, Julian P. & Tang, Suning, eds.** Optoelectronic Interconnects VI. 394p. 1999. pap. text 84.00 (*0-8194-3102-8*) SPIE.

Bristow, Julian P., jt. ed. see Chen, Ray T.

***Bristow, Julie.** If Only We Would Listen: Tales of a Tasmanian Goat Farm. (Illus.). 204p. 1999. pap. 14.95 (*1-929492-03-0*) Stringalong.

Bristow, K. D., et al. Habitat Use & Movements of Desert Bighorn Sheep Near the Silver Bell Mine, Arizona. (Technical Reports: No. 25). (Illus.). 57p. (Orig.). 1996. pap. 5.00 (*0-917563-32-8*) AZ Game & Fish.

Bristow, Linda K. Bread & Breakfast. LC 92-30279. (One Hundred One Productions Ser.). 134p. (Orig.). 1993. reprint ed. pap. 11.95 (*1-56426-551-X*, One Hund One Prods) Cole Group.

Bristow, Lois. Will I Be Next? Bea Gorman's Life Story - The Terror of Living with Familial Alzheimer's Disease. 260p. (Orig.). 1995. pap. 12.00 (*0-9648885-0-5*) HopeWarren Pr.

***Bristow, M. J., ed.** State Songs of America. 169p. 2000. 35.00 (*0-313-29298-1*, Greenwood Pr) Greenwood.

Bristow, M. J., ed. see Reed, W. L.

Bristow, M. R., jt. ed. see Feldman, A. M.

Bristow, Nancy K. Making Men Moral. 1998. pap. text 19.50 (*0-8147-1308-4*) NYU Pr.

— Making Men Moral: Social Engineering During the Great War. (American Social Experience Ser.). (Illus.). 298p. (C). 1996. text 45.00 (*0-8147-1220-7*) NYU Pr.

Bristow, Nigel J. Building Communities of Learning: How to Harness the Collective Genius of the People in Your Organization. Orig. Title: Coaching for Teams: Building Communities of Learning in Organizations. 238p. 1997. pap. 20.00 (*1-886662-10-X*, Cascde Pr) Alexanders Pub.

Bristow, P. A. Liquid Chromatography in Practice. 28.00 (*0-9504833-1-1*); pap. 20.00 (*0-9504833-0-3*); fiche 10.00 (*0-9504833-2-X*) Lab Data Control.

Bristow, Peggy, ed. see Brand, Dionne, et al.

Bristow, Philip. Famous Ways to Grow Old. (C). 1989. 39.00 (*0-86242-087-3*, Pub. by Age Concern Eng) St Mut.

***Bristow, Philip.** Through the French Canals. 9th ed. 304p. 1999. pap. text 27.50 (*0-7136-4921-6*) Sheridan.

Bristow, Philip. Through the German Waterways. (Illus.). 158p. 1996. pap. 24.50 (*0-7136-5770-7*) Sheridan.

Bristow, Roger. Hong Kong's New Towns: A Selected Review. (Illus.). 400p. 1990. text 39.95 (*0-19-584210-3*) OUP.

Bristow, Sujata, jt. auth. see Stern, Malcolm.

Bristow, Walter S., III. The Charitable Forest Vol. 1: The Path to Security During Retirement. (Illus.). 100p. (Orig.). 1989. pap. 10.00 (*0-317-93891-6*) Hayden Bridge.

— Comprehensive Split Dollar Kit. (Illus.). 100p. (Orig.). 1989. pap. 20.00 (*0-317-93893-2*) Hayden Bridge.

— The Moving Company: An Easy-to-Understand Guide to Estate Planning, Wills & Trusts. LC 92-71620. (Illus.). 176p. (Orig.). 1992. pap. 20.00 (*0-685-61658-4*); student ed. 50.00 (*0-685-61659-2*); 20.00 (*0-685-61660-6*); audio 10.00 (*0-685-61661-4*); audio 10.00 (*0-685-61662-2*) Hayden Bridge.

— The Moving Company: An Easy Way to Explain Estate Planning. 2nd rev. ed. LC 89-92022. (Illus.). 150p. 1989. pap. 20.00 (*1-877763-00-4*) Hayden Bridge.

— The Moving Company: How to Explain Estate Planning Concepts. (Illus.). 56p. (Orig.). 1988. pap. 10.00 (*0-317-93894-0*) Hayden Bridge.

Bristow, Wayne. Total Life. 104p. (Orig.). 1996. pap. 10.00 (*1-57087-216-3*) Prof Pr NC.

Bristowe, P. D., et al, eds. Defects in Materials Vol. 209: Materials Research Society Symposium Proceedings. 920p. 1991. text 17.50 (*1-55899-101-8*) Materials Res.

— Materials Theory & Modelling. (Materials Research Society Symposium Proceedings Ser.: Vol. 291). 663p. 1993. text 30.00 (*1-55899-186-7*) Materials Res.

Britain, Bret. Hunting from Sculling Boats: A Complete Manual. 115p. 1992. 25.00 (*0-9632564-7-5*) More to Life.

Britain, Ian. Once an Austalian: Journeys with Barry Humphries, Clive James, Germaine Greer & Robert Hughes. LC DU121.B75 1997. (Illus.). 304p. 1998. text 29.95 (*0-19-553742-4*) OUP.

***Britain, Kristen.** Green Rider. 471p. 2000. mass mkt. 6.99 (*0-88677-858-1*, Pub. by DAW Bks) Penguin Putnam.

— Green Rider. (Illus.). (J). 2000. 12.34 (*0-606-18094-X*) Turtleback.

Britain, Kristin. Green Rider. LC 99-165898. 512p. 1998. 23.95 (*0-88677-824-7*, Pub. by DAW Bks) Penguin Putnam.

Britain, Lory, jt. auth. see Chaille, Christine.

Britain, Radie. Ridin' Herd to Writing Symphonies: An Autobiography. LC 95-6267. (Composers of North America Ser.: No. 12). 444p. 1996. 75.00 (*0-8108-2733-6*) Scarecrow.

Britain, Stuart. The Oxford Illustrated History of Tudor & Stuart Britain. Morrill, John, ed. (Oxford Illustrated Histories Ser.). (Illus.). 464p. 1996. 49.95 (*0-19-820325-X*) OUP.

Britan, Maya, jt. auth. see Tarostar.

Britanico, Jose D., jt. auth. see Mintz, Malcolm W.

Britch, Carroll, jt. ed. see Lewis, Cliff.

Britcher, Robert. The Limits of Software: People, Project & Perspectives. LC 99-24951. (Illus.). 240p. (C). 1999. pap. text 24.95 (*0-201-43323-0*) Addison-Wesley.

Brite, Poppy. Courtney Love. LC 97-35819. (Illus.). 253p. 1999. 25.00 (*0-684-84506-7*) S&S Trade.

— The Crow: The Lazarus Heart. (Crow Ser.). 336p. 1999. mass mkt. 6.99 (*0-06-102009-5*, Pub. by Harper SF) HarpC.

Brite, Poppy & Greenberg, Martin H., eds. Love in Vein II. 448th ed. 544p. 1998. mass mkt. 5.99 (*0-06-105657-X*, HarperPrism) HarpC.

***Brite, Poppy Z.** Are You Loathsome Tonight? A Collection of Short Stories. 2000. pap. 16.95 (*1-887368-25-6*) Gauntlet.

Brite, Poppy Z. Are You Loathsome Tonight? A Short Story Collection by Poppy Z. Brite. (Illus.). 193p. 1998. 40.00 (*1-887368-16-7*) Gauntlet.

— Courtney Love: The Real Story. (Illus.). 256p. 1998. pap. 12.00 (*0-684-84800-7*) S&S Trade.

— The Crow: The Lazarus Heart. LC 97-48896. (Crow Ser.). 224p. 1998. pap. 13.00 (*0-06-105824-6*, HarperPrism) HarpC.

— Drawing Blood. 416p. 1994. mass mkt. 6.50 (*0-440-21492-0*) Delacorte.

— Exquisite Corpse. 240p. 1997. per. 11.00 (*0-684-83627-0*) S&S Trade Pap.

— The Lazarus Heart. aut. limited ed. (Illus.). 213p. 1999. 50.00 (*1-887368-19-1*) Gauntlet.

— Lost Souls. 384p. 1993. mass mkt. 6.99 (*0-440-21281-2*) Dell.

— Love in Vein (MM) 416p. 1995. mass mkt. 6.50 (*0-06-105490-9*) HarpC.

***Brite, Poppy Z.** Love in Vein II: 18 More Original Tales of Vampire Erotica. 2000. 9.99 (*0-7858-1211-3*) Bk Sales Inc.

Brite, Robert L. Introduction to Business Statistics. LC 76-17717. (Illus.). (C). 1977. text. write for info. (*0-201-00593-X*) Addison-Wesley.

Brite, Z. Wormwood. 256p. 1995. mass mkt. 6.50 (*0-440-21798-9*) Dell.

Brites, Jose. Coisas e Loisas das Nossas Terras: Cronicas. unabridged ed. Peregrinacao Publications Staff, ed. (Prosa Ser.: No. 2). (POR.). 160p. 1996. 12.95 (*1-889358-03-7*, 05) Peregrinacao.

— De Casa para o Inferno No. II: Partir e Ficar um Pouco. unabridged ed. Peregrinacao Publications Staff, ed. (Prosa Ser.: No. 6). (POR.). 190p. 1999. 18.00 (*1-889358-06-1*, 14) Peregrinacao.

— Do Ribatejo Ao Alem-Tejo: Partir e Ficar um Pouco I. unabridged ed. Peregrinacao Publications Staff, ed. (Prosa Ser.: No. 5). (POR.). 160p. 1998. 14.95 (*1-889358-11-8*, 09) Peregrinacao.

— Estorias para a Historia de Alcorochel: Cronicas e Contos. unabridged ed. Peregrinacao Publications Staff, ed. (Prosa Ser.: No. 1). (POR.). 190p. 1994. text, boxed set 12.00 (*1-889358-00-2*, 0001) Peregrinacao.

***Brites, Jose.** Poems Without Poetry: Twenty Five Years of Poetry. abr. ed. Peregrinacao Publications Staff, ed. (Poetry/ Poesia Ser.: No. 7). Orig. Title: Poemas Sem Poesia; Imigramar; Vinte e Cinco Anos de Poesia. (ENG & POR.). 192p. 2001. reprint ed. boxed set 18.00 (*1-889358-13-4*, 26) Peregrinacao.

— Trinta Anos de Poesia: Poemas. unabridged ed. Peregrinacao Publications Staff, ed. (Poetry/ Poesia Ser.: No. 8). 160p. 2001. boxed set 15.95 (*1-889358-29-0*, 30) Peregrinacao.

Brites, Jose. Vinte e Cinco Anos de Poesia: E Meio Seculo de Vida. unabridged ed. Peregrinacao Publications Staff, ed. (Poetry/ Poesia Ser.: No. 1). (POR.). 160p. 1995. text 12.00 (*1-889358-01-0*, 02) Peregrinacao.

***Brites, Jose, ed.** Cantigas Ao Desafio, Na Diaspora: Na Nova Inglaterra E Acores. unabridged ed. (Poetas Populares Ser.: Vol. 6). (POR.). 192p. 2000. boxed set 18.00 (*1-889358-24-X*) Peregrinacao.

Brites, Jose, ed. Dia de Portugal, em Verso: De Camoes e das Comunidades Portuguesas. unabridged ed. (Poetas Populares Ser.: No. 1). (POR.). 128p. 1998. boxed set 12.00 (*1-889358-12-6*, 11) Peregrinacao.

***Brites, Jose, ed.** Portugal E Asaudade, Em Verso: Versos. unabridged ed. (Poetas Populares Ser.: Vol. 4). (POR.). 128p. 2000. boxed set 12.95 (*1-889358-20-7*, 21) Peregrinacao.

Britians. Top 4000 Private Companies. pap. text 97.00 (*0-00-033504-5*) Kluwer Academic.

— Top 4000 Private Companies. 2nd ed. pap. text 97.00 (*0-00-033503-7*) Kluwer Academic.

British Academy. 1992 Lectures & Memoirs. (Proceedings of the British Academy Ser.: Vol. 82). (Illus.). 532p. 1994. text 95.00 (*0-19-726132-9*) OUP.

— Proceedings of the British Academy: 1994 Lectures & Memoirs, Vol. 8. (Proceedings of the British Academy Ser.). (Illus.). 528p. (C). 1996. text 115.00 (*0-19-726162-0*) OUP.

British Academy, Major Research Project in the Ear. Papers in Economic Prehistory: Studies. Higgs, E. S., ed. LC 78-180019. 229p. reprint ed. pap. 65.30 (*0-608-16447-X*, 2026342) Bks Demand.

British Academy Staff. 1993 Lectures & Memoirs, Vol. 84. (Proceedings of the British Academy Ser.: Vol. LXXXIV). (Illus.). 604p. 1995. text 95.00 (*0-19-726149-3*) OUP.

— Proceedings of the British Academy. (British Academy: Vol. 97). (Illus.). 540p. 1999. text 115.00 (*0-19-726192-2*) OUP.

— Proceedings of the British Academy: 1995 Lectures & Memoirs, Vol. 90. (Proceedings of the British Academy Ser.). (Illus.). 576p. 1997. text 135.00 (*0-19-726169-8*) OUP.

— Proceedings of the British Academy: 1996 Lectures & Memoirs, Vol. 94. (Proceedings of the British Academy Ser.). (Illus.). 776p. 1998. text 140.00 (*0-19-726180-9*) OUP.

— Proceedings of the British Academy, 1991 Vol. 80: Lectures & Memoirs, Vol. 80. (British Academy Ser.). (Illus.). 512p. 1993. text 95.00 (*0-19-726124-8*) OUP.

British Academy Staff, jt. auth. see National Academies Policy Advisory Group (Great Britain) Staff.

British Agencies for Adoption & Fostering Editors. The Adoption Triangle Training Pack. (C). 1989. 500.00 (*0-903534-90-8*, Pub. by Brit Ag for Adopt & Fost) St Mut.

— In Touch with Children Training Pack. (C). 1989. 39.00 (*0-903534-53-3*, Pub. by Brit Ag for Adopt & Fost) St Mut.

— Taking a Stand: Child Psychiatrists in Custody, Access & Disputed Adoption Cases. (C). 1989. 39.00 (*0-903534-55-X*, Pub. by Brit Ag for Adopt & Fost) St Mut.

British Agencies for Adoption & Fostering Editors, ed. Aid & After: Papers from BAAF, BASW & a Scottish Working Party. (C). 1989. 39.00 (*0-903534-50-9*, Pub. by Brit Ag for Adopt & Fost) St Mut.

British Air Historical Branch Staff. The Royal Air Force in the Great War. (Great War Ser.: No. 52). 504p. 1996. reprint ed. 39.95 (*0-89839-251-9*) Battery Pr.

British Association for Applied Linguistics Staff & Hunston, Susan. Language at Work: Papers from the Annual Meeting of the British Association for Applied Linguistics Held at the University of Birmingham, September, 1997. LC 98-24776. (British Studies in Applied Linguistics). 1998. pap. 39.95 (*1-85359-427-X*, Pub. by Multilingual Matters) Taylor & Francis.

British Association for Applied Linguistics Staff, et al. Evolving Models of Language: Papers from the Annual Meeting of the British Association for Applied Linguistics Held at the University of Wales, Swansea, September 1996. LC 97-25056. (British Studies in Applied Linguistics). 124p. 1997. pap. 39.95 (*1-85359-398-2*, Pub. by Multilingual Matters) Taylor & Francis.

British Association for the Advancement of Science. Economics & Technical Change. Hugh-Jones, E. M., ed. LC 71-93848. xii, 179p. 1969. lib. bdg. 37.50 (*0-678-06265-X*) Kelley.

— The Management of Science: Proceedings of Section F (Economics) of the British Association for the Advancement of Science, Sheffield, 1989. Hague, Douglas C., ed. LC 90-8895. 190p. 1991. text 65.00 (*0-312-05323-1*) St Martin.

British Association For The Advancement Of Science. March of Science: A First Quinquennial Review, 1931-1935. LC 68-55841. (Essay Index Reprint Ser.). 1977. 19.95 (*0-8369-0254-8*) Ayer.

British Association for the Advancement of Science. Public Sector Economics. Prest, A. R., ed. LC 68-6526. vii, 206p. 1968. 37.50 (*0-678-06765-1*) Kelley.

British Association for the Advancement of Science, jt. auth. see Sahay, Arun.

British Association for the Advancement of Science Staff & Prest, A. R. Public Sector Economics: Papers Presented at the 1967 Section F Meeting of the British Association for the Advancement of Science. LC 79-406507. vii, 206p. 1968. write for info. (*0-7190-0330-X*) Manchester Univ Pr.

British Association for the Advancement of Science Staff, jt. auth. see Roll, Eric.

British Broadcasting Company Staff. Getting by in German. 2nd ed. LC 96-1459. (Getting by Ser.). (GER.). 160p. 1996. pap. 18.95 (*0-8120-8441-1*) Barron.

— More Short Trips. 1999. mass mkt. 5.95 (*0-563-55565-3*, Pub. by BBC Bks) Genl Dist Srvs.

British Broadcasting Company Staff, ed. BBC World Glossary of Current Affairs. 500p. 1991. 85.00 (*1-55862-108-3*) St James Pr.

British Broadcasting Corporation Staff. Why Is Britain Becoming Harder to Govern? King, Anthony Stephen, ed. LC 76-364956. 144p. 1976. write for info. (*0-563-10999-8*) BBC.

British Broadcasting Corporation Staff & Mitchell, Carolyn B. Getting by in Greek. (Getting by Ser.). (Illus.). 90p. 1983. pap. 3.95 (*0-8120-2663-2*) Barron.

British Broadcasting Corporation Staff, jt. auth. see Harrod, Dominick.

British Cast Iron Research Association Staff. Effects of Copper on Iron. 65p. 1965. 9.75 (*0-317-34518-4*, 82) Intl Copper.

British Chambers Staff. International Trade Manual. 352p. 1998. text 75.00 (*0-7506-3822-2*) Buttrwrth-Heinemann.

British Chemical Dist. & Trade Association Directo. Where to Buy Chemicals & Chemical Plant. (C). 1989. 200.00 (*0-7855-4937-4*, Pub. by Fuel Metallurgical Jrnl) St Mut.

British Columbia Staff. BC FAS Community Action Guide. 1998. (*0-7726-3483-1*) GovofBC.

***British Commission for Military History Staff.** Look to Your Front: Studies in the First World War. Bond, Brian, ed. 224p. 2000. pap. 60.00 (*1-86227-065-1*, Pub. by Spellmnt Pubs) St Mut.

British Committee for Standards in Haematology, jt. auth. see Wood, Keith.

British Computer Society Staff. Algebra of Communicating Processes: Proceedings of the First Workshop on the Algebra of Communicating Processes, Utrecht, the Netherlands, 16-17 May 1994. Ponse, Alban et al, eds. LC 94-39829. (Workshops in Computing Ser.). 357p. 1994. pap. 69.00 (*0-387-19909-8*) Spr-Verlag.

— Control & Audit of Minicomputer Systems. LC QA0076.9.A25. 58p. reprint ed. pap. 30.00 (*0-608-18453-5*, 203267300080) Bks Demand.

— Functional Programming, Glasgow 1995: Proceedings of the 1995 Glasgow Workshop on Functional Programming, Ullapool, Scotland, 10-12 July 1995. Turner, David N., ed. LC 96-22045. (Electronic Workshops in Computing Ser.). 9p. 1996. pap. 54.50 (*3-540-14580-X*) Spr-Verlag.

— Miro 95: Proceeding of the Final Workshop on Multimedia Information Retrieval : Glasgow, Scotland, 18-20 September 1995. Ruthven, Ian, ed. LC 96-22046. (Electronic Workshops in Computing Ser.). 9p. 1996. pap. 54.50 (*3-540-14582-6*) Spr-Verlag.

— U. K. Parallel, '96: Proceedings of the BCS PPSG Annual Conference, 3-5 July 1996. Jesshope, C. R. & Shafarenko, A. V., eds. LC 96-24166. 205p. 1996. pap. 69.95 (*3-540-76068-7*) Spr-Verlag.

— Water Resource Management: An Annotated Bibliography. Newell, R. A., ed. LC 81-40231. (Use of Computers for National Development Ser.). 79p. reprint ed. pap. 30.00 (*0-608-18452-7*, 203266800080) Bks Demand.

British Computer Society Staff, ed. Glossary Computing Terms. 8th ed. (Illus.). 380p. (C). 1996. pap. text 39.50 (*0-582-27544-X*, Pub. by Addison-Wesley) Trans-Atl Phila.

British Computer Society Staff, et al. Database Programming Languages (DBPL-5) Proceedings of the Fifth International Workshop on Database Programming Languages, Gubbio, Umbria, Italy, 6-8 September 1995. Atzeni, Paolo & Tannen, Val, eds. LC 96-27602. (Electronic Workshops in Computing Ser.). 20p. 1996. pap. 54.50 (*3-540-76086-5*) Spr-Verlag.

— Interfaces to Databases (IDS-3) Proceedings of the 3rd International Workshop on Interfaces to Databases, Napier University, Edinburgh, 8-10 July, 1996. Kennedy, Jessie & Barclay, Peter J., eds. LC 96-30965. (Electronic Workshops in Computing Ser.). 16p. 1996. pap. 54.50 (*3-540-76066-0*) Spr-Verlag.

— Methods Integration: Proceedings of the Methods Integration Workshop, Leeds, 25-26 March 1996. Bryant, Antony & Semmens, Lesley, eds. LC 96-3337. (Electronic Workshops in Computing Ser.). 16p. 1996. 54.50 (*3-540-76065-2*) Spr-Verlag.

***British Council Staff.** Lost & Found: Critical Voices in New British Design. LC 99-42385. (Illus.). 128p. 1999. pap. 35.00 (*3-7643-6095-X*, Pub. by Birkhauser); pap. 35.00 (*3-7643-5998-6*, Pub. by Birkhauser); pap. 35.00 (*3-7643-6096-8*, Pub. by Birkhauser) Princeton Arch.

British Council Staff. Management & Diseases of Sheep. 467p. 1980. 75.00 (*0-85198-451-7*) OUP.

— Studying & Living in Britain: The British Council's Guide. LC 96-40398. 1997. write for info. (*0-87805-986-5*); pap. 15.00 (*0-87805-987-3*) U Pr of Miss.

British Council Staff, ed. English As an International Language. (English Language Teaching Documents Ser.: Vol. 102). 72p. 1987. pap. 5.75 (*0-08-029480-4*) Alemany Pr.

— Studying & Living in Britain: A Guide for International Students & Visitors. (Illus.). 158p. 1998. pap. 14.95 (*0-7463-0902-3*, Pub. by Northcote House) Trans-Atl Phila.

British Council Staff & Scott-Kilvert, Ian, eds. British Writers, Vol. II. LC 78-23483. (British Council Pamphlet Ser.). 1979. 120.00 (*0-684-16407-8*, Scribners Ref) Mac Lib Ref.

British Council Staff, jt. auth. see Barley, Nick.

***British Design & Art Directors Staff, ed.** British Design & Art Direction 1999. (Illus.). 656p. 2000. 89.95 (*1-85669-176-4*, Pub. by L King Pubng) Gingko Press.

British Diabetic Association Staff, jt. auth. see Day, John L.

British Ecological Society Staff, et al. Dynamics of Tropical Communities. LC 97-28569. 1998. 125.00 (*0-632-04944-8*) Blackwell Sci.

***British Ecological Society Staff, et al.** The Ecological Consequences of Environmental Heterogeneity: The 40th Symposium of the British Ecological Society, Held at the University of Sussex, 23-25 March, 1999. LC 00-27087. 2000. write for info. (*0-632-05713-0*) Blackwell Sci.

British Ecological Society Staff, et al. Herbivores: The 38th Symposium of the British Ecological Society 1997. LC 98-8024. 1998. write for info. (*0-632-05155-8*); pap. write for info. (*0-632-05204-X*) Blackwell Sci.

***British Ecological Society Staff, et al.** Physiological Plant Ecology: The 39th Symposium of the British Ecological Society, Held at the University of York, 7-9 September 1998. LC 99-29393. (British Ecological Society Symposium Ser.: Vol. 39). (Illus.). 2000. pap. 49.95 (*0-632-05491-3*) Blackwell Sci.

British Electrical & Allied Manufacturers Staff. Combines & Trusts in the Electrical Industry: The Position in Europe in 1927. Wilkins, Mira, ed. LC 76-29775. (European Business Ser.). (Illus.). 1977. reprint ed. lib. bdg. 25.95 (*0-405-09787-5*) Ayer.

British Electricity International Staff, ed. Modern Power Station Practice: Incorporating Modern Power System Practice, 12 vols. LC 90-43748. (British Electricity International Ser.). (Illus.). 6500p. 1992. 1350.00 (*0-08-040746-3*, Pergamon Pr); 1503.50 (*0-08-040747-1*, Pergamon Pr) Elsevier.

— Modern Power Station Practice: Incorporating Modern Power System Practice, 12 vols. 3rd ed. LC 90-43748. (British Electricity International Ser.). (Illus.). 6500p. 1992. 2570.50 (*0-08-040510-X*, Pergamon Pr) Elsevier.

British Feminism & Nonviolence Study Group Staff. Piecing It Together: Feminism & Nonviolence. (Illus.). 60p. 1983. 3.00 (*0-9508602-0-4*) J Tiffany.

British Film Institute Book Library Staff. Catalogue of the Book Library of the British Film Institute, Supplement 1. 1983. suppl. ed. 305.00 (*0-8161-1435-8*, G K Hall & Co) Mac Lib Ref.

British Film Institute Staff. The BFI Companion to Horror. Newman, Kim, ed. LC 97-131165. (Cassell Film Studies). (Illus.). 352p. 1997. 85.00 (*0-304-33213-5*); pap. 27.95 (*0-304-33216-X*) Continuum.

— Cassell Film Guides: France. Vincendeau, Ginette, ed. LC 96-218912. (Film Studies). (Illus.). 192p. 1997. 19.95 (*0-304-34157-6*) Continuum.

— Cassell Film Guides: Italy. Smith, Geoffrey N., ed. LC 96-219335. (Film Studies). (Illus.). 192p. 1996. 19.95 (*0-304-34197-5*) Continuum.

— Cassell Film Guides: United Kingdom. Caughie, John & Rocket, Kevin, eds. LC 96-218911. (Film Studies). (Illus.). 192p. 1996. 22.50 (*0-304-34158-4*) Continuum.

British Gas Staff. Combustion Engineering & Gas Utilisation. 3rd ed. 1000p. 1992. 145.95 (*0-442-30886-8*) Chapman & Hall.

— Combustion Engineering & Gas Utilisation. 3rd ed. (Illus.). 895p. (C). 1992. 260.00 (*0-419-17670-5*, E & FN Spon) Routledge.

British Gen. Staff. British Trench Warfare, 1917-1918: A Reference Manual. Battery Press, Inc. Staff, ed. (Reference Ser.: Vol. 15). (Illus.). 214p. 1997. 34.95 (*0-89839-267-5*) Battery Pr.

British General Staff. Handbook of German Military & Naval Aviation, 1918. (Reference Ser.: No. 9). (Illus.). 160p. 1995. reprint ed. 39.95 (*0-89839-236-5*) Battery Pr.

— Handbook of the German Army at War, April 1918. (Reference Ser.: No. 10). (Illus.). 217p. 1996. reprint ed. 39.95 (*0-89839-244-6*) Battery Pr.

British Geological Society Staff. Geology of the Country Around Aberdaron, Including Bardsey Island: Memoir for 1:50,000 Geological Sheet 133 (England & Wales) Gibbons, W., ed. (Illus.). viii, 88p. 1994. pap. 35.00 (*0-11-884487-3*, HM44873, Pub. by Statnry Office) Balogh.

British Geological Survey Staff. Geology of the Malin-Hebrides Sea Area: United Kingdom Offshore Regional Report. Fyfe, J. A., ed. (Illus.). viii, 95p. 1994. pap. 40.00 (*0-11-884494-6*, HM44946, Pub. by Statnry Office) Balogh.

British Government Staff. The Report on the Loss of the SS Titanic. (Illus.). 92p. 1998. text 19.95 (*0-312-21487-1*, Picador USA) St Martin.

British Haiku Society Staff. The Genius of Haiku: Readings from R. H. Blyth on Poetry, Life, & Zen. (Illus.). 154p. 1997. pap. 17.95 (*4-590-00988-9*, Pub. by Hokuseido Pr) Book East.

British Horse Society Staff. The BHS Complete Manual of Stable Management. Auty, Islay, ed. (Illus.). 408p. 1998. pap. 44.95 (*1-872119-03-4*) Half Halt Pr.

British Hotels, Restaurants, & Caterers Associatio. Hotels & Restaurants in Britain: The Offical Guide, 1985. write for info. (*0-318-58205-8*) P-H.

British Institute of International & Comparative Law Staff. Joint Development of Offshore Oil & Gas, Vol. 1. 272p. 1990. pap. 74.00 (*0-903067-32-3*, Pub. by Brit Inst ICL) St Mut.

British Institute of International & Comparative Law Staff. The Role & Future of the European Court of Justice. LC 97-192691. 154p. 1996. pap. write for info. (*0-903067-70-6*, Pub. by Brit Inst ICL) St Mut.

British Institute of International & Comparative Law Staff. Theory & International Law: An Introduction. 144p. 1992. pap. 54.00 (*0-903067-34-X*, Pub. by Brit Inst ICL) St Mut.

***British Institute of International & Comparative Law Staff, ed.** The International Law Commission & the Future of International Law. 239p. 1998. pap. 90.00 (*0-903067-95-1*, Pub. by Brit Inst ICL) St Mut.

British Intelligence Branch, ed. Handbook of the German Army, 1940. (Reference Ser.: Vol. 13). (Illus.). 417p. 1996. reprint ed. 49.95 (*0-89839-258-6*) Battery Pr.

British Intelligence Sub-Committee. People's Car: An Investigation into the Design & Performance of Civilian & Military Volkswagens 1938-1946. (Illus.). 156p. 1997. pap. 34.95 (*0-11-290555-2*, Pub. by Statnry Office) Seven Hills Bk.

British Iris Society, Species Group Staff, ed. A Guide to Species Irises: Their Identification & Cultivation. LC 95-23954. (Illus.). 386p. (C). 1997. text 110.00 (*0-521-44074-2*) Cambridge U Pr.

British Juvenile & Family Courts Society Staff, jt. auth. see Cavadino, Paul.

British Leyland Motors. The Land Rover Series II, 1959-1970, Pts. 1 & 2. (Illus.). (Orig.). student ed. 100.00 (*0-8376-0529-6*) Bentley Pubs.

— The Land Rover Series 1 Workshop Manual, 1948-1958: Gasoline & Diesel. (Illus.). 384p. (Orig.). 65.00 (*0-8376-0516-4*) Bentley Pubs.

— MGB Driver's Handbook: 1965 Edition. (Illus.). 68p. 16.00 (*0-8376-0530-X*) Bentley Pubs.

— MGB Tourer & GT Parts Catalogue, 1977-1980. (Illus.). 170p. 40.00 (*0-8376-0500-8*) Bentley Pubs.

— MGB Tourer & GT Tuning Handbook, 1975-1980. (Illus.). 50p. (Orig.). 16.00 (*0-8376-0504-0*) Bentley Pubs.

— MGB Tourer, GT & V8 Parts Catalogue, 1962-1976. (Illus.). 440p. (Orig.). 60.00 (*0-8376-0505-9*) Bentley Pubs.

— MGB Tuning Handbook (1800cc), 1962-1974. (Illus.). 50p. (Orig.). 16.00 (*0-8376-0506-7*) Bentley Pubs.

— Midget MK 2 & MK 3 Parts Catalogue, 1962-74. (Illus.). 280p. 1988. 55.00 (*0-8376-0513-X*) Bentley Pubs.

— Morris Minor Workshop Manual: All Models, 1956-1971. (Illus.). 460p. (Orig.). 50.00 (*0-8376-0520-2*) Bentley Pubs.

— Triumph GT6 Mk III Driver's Handbook (1973) 66p. (Orig.). 16.00 (*0-8376-0536-9*) Bentley Pubs.

— Triumph GT6 Mk III Parts Catalogue, 1971-1973: 1971-1973. 140p. (Orig.). 40.00 (*0-8376-0523-7*) Bentley Pubs.

— Triumph Spitfire MK IV & 1500 1971-1974 Parts Catalogue. 112p. (Orig.). 40.00 (*0-8376-0515-6*) Bentley Pubs.

— Triumph Spitfire MK III Driver's Handbook (1964) 80p. (Orig.). 16.00 (*0-8376-0527-X*) Bentley Pubs.

— Triumph TR4 Driver's Handbook, 1961-1965. 68p. 16.00 (*0-8376-0517-2*) Bentley Pubs.

— Triumph TR4 Spare Parts Catalogue, 1961-1964. 319p. 55.00 (*0-8376-0546-6*) Bentley Pubs.

— Triumph TR4A Driver's Handbook, 1965-1967. 64p. (Orig.). 16.00 (*0-8376-0511-3*) Bentley Pubs.

— Triumph TR4A Spare Parts Catalogue, 1965-1967. 336p. (Orig.). 55.00 (*0-8376-0556-3*) Bentley Pubs.

— Triumph TR7 Driver's Handbook, 1976 (U.S. Spec) 16.00 (*0-8376-0514-8*) Bentley Pubs.

— Triumph TR6 Driver's Handbook (U. S. Spec), 1975. 72p. 16.00 (*0-8376-0550-4*) Bentley Pubs.

— The Triumph TR2 & TR3 Spare Parts Catalogue, 1953-1963. 374p. (Orig.). 55.00 (*0-8376-0533-4*) Bentley Pubs.

— Triumph TR250 Driver's Handbook, 1968. 72p. (Orig.). 16.00 (*0-8376-0559-8*) Bentley Pubs.

— Triumph TR250 Spare Parts Catalogue, 1968. 259p. (Orig.). 55.00 (*0-8376-0507-5*) Bentley Pubs.

British Leyland Motors Staff. Austin-Healey Complete Official 100-Six & 3000, 1956-1968. LC 77-72588. (Illus.). 416p. (Orig.). 1977. pap. 45.00 (*0-8376-0133-9*) Bentley Pubs.

British Leyland Motors, Staff. Austin-Healey Sprite MK 1 Driver's Handbook (1958-1961) (Illus.). 16.00 (*0-8376-0545-8*) Bentley Pubs.

British Leyland Motors Staff. Austin-Healey 3000 MK3 Bk. 3: Handbook. 1994. 25.00 (*0-8376-0575-X*) Bentley Pubs.

— The Complete Official MGB: 1975-1980. LC 80-65229. (Illus.). 304p. (Orig.). 1978. pap. 40.00 (*0-8376-0112-6*) Bentley Pubs.

— Jaguar "E" Complete Official Workshop Manual: 1961 to 1971, 6 Cylinder. 2nd rev. ed. LC 73-94377. (Illus.). 416p. (Orig.). 1974. pap. 50.00 (*0-8376-0136-3*) Bentley Pubs.

— The MG MGA 1500 Parts Catalogue, 1955-1959. (Illus.). 60.00 (*0-8376-0570-9*) Bentley Pubs.

— MG Midget 1500 Driver's Handbook. (Illus.). 64p. 1979. 16.00 (*0-8376-0590-3*) Bentley Pubs.

— The MG Midget MK3 Driver's Handbook (1974) (Illus.). 1979. pap. 16.00 (*0-8376-0549-0*) Bentley Pubs.

— MGA 1600 Parts Catalogue, 1959-1962. (Illus.). (Orig.). 65.00 (*0-8376-0569-5*) Bentley Pubs.

— MGB Model Years 1962-1974, the Complete Official: Comprising the Official Driver's Handbook, Workshop Manual, Special Tuning Manual. 4th rev. ed. LC 75-7766. (Illus.). 480p. (Orig.). 1975. pap. 50.00 (*0-8376-0115-0*) Bentley Pubs.

— MGC Driver's Handbook: 1967-1969. (Illus.). 64p. 16.00 (*0-8376-0503-2*) Bentley Pubs.

— Range Rover Workshop Manual, 1986-1989. (Illus.). pap. 90.00 (*0-8376-0606-3*, YVW3) Bentley Pubs.

— Range Rover Workshop Manual, 1990-1994. (Illus.). pap. 90.00 (*0-8376-0607-1*, YVW4) Bentley Pubs.

— Sprite-MG Midget Service Repair Handbook: Comprising the Official Driver's Handbook, Workshop Manual, Emission Control Supplement. LC 75-37232. (Illus.). 400p. (Orig.). 1975. pap. 45.00 (*0-8376-0127-4*) Bentley Pubs.

— Austin-Healy Sprite-Midget 948cc & 1098cc, 1961-1966, the Complete Official: Comprising the Official Driver's Handbook, Workshop Manual, Special Tuning Manual. LC 67-28432. (Illus.). 256p. (Orig.). 1968. pap. 40.00 (*0-8376-0023-5*) Bentley Pubs.

— Triumph Spitfire 1500, Model Years 1975-1980, the Complete Official: Comprising the Official Driver's Handbook & Workshop Manual. LC 79-53184. (Illus.). 520p. (Orig.). 1980. pap. 55.00 (*0-8376-0122-3*) Bentley Pubs.

— Triumph Spitfire MK I Driver's Handbook, 1964. (Orig.). 16.00 (*0-8376-0560-1*) Bentley Pubs.

— Triumph Spitfire MK I, MK II, MK III, Herald Vitesse Workshop Manual, 1959-1970. (Orig.). 70.00 (*0-8376-0564-4*) Bentley Pubs.

— Triumph Stag Workshop Manual: 1971-1973. (Illus.). 640p. 70.00 (*0-8376-0508-3*) Bentley Pubs.

— Triumph TR4 & TR4A, 1961-1968: Official Driver's Handbook, Workshop Manual, Competition Preparation Manual. LC 74-21354. (Illus.). 408p. (Orig.). 1975. pap. 55.00 (*0-8376-0121-5*) Bentley Pubs.

— Triumph TR7, 1975-1981, the Complete Official: Comprising the Official Driver's Handbook & Repair Operation Manual. LC 78-73515. (Illus.). 544p. (Orig.). 1979. pap. 55.00 (*0-8376-0116-9*) Bentley Pubs.

— Triumph TR7 Parts Catalogue, 1975-1978. 288p. 55.00 (*0-8376-0544-X*) Bentley Pubs.

— Triumph TR7 Spare Parts Catalogue, 1979-1981. (Illus.). 420p. 60.00 (*0-8376-0567-9*) Bentley Pubs.

B

— Triumph TR6 & TR250, 1967-1976, the Complete Official: Comprising the Official Driver's Handbook & Workshop Manual. LC 77-91592. (Illus.). 608p. (Orig.). 1978. pap. 60.00 (*0-8376-0108-8*) Bentley Pubs.

— Triumph TR6 Driver's Handbook (U. S. Spec), 1970. 16.00 (*0-8376-0562-8*) Bentley Pubs.

— Triumph TR6 Driver's Handbook (1973) 16.00 (*0-8376-0558-X*) Bentley Pubs.

— Triumph TR6 Spare Parts Catalogue, 1974-1976. 280p. 55.00 (*0-8376-0553-9*) Bentley Pubs.

— Triumph TR6 Spare Parts Catalogue, 1969-1973. 264p. 1988. 55.00 (*0-8376-0540-7*) Bentley Pubs.

British Leyland Motors Staff, jt. auth. see Bentley, Robert, Inc. Staff.

British Library & Whitehead, H. G. Short-title Catalogue of Eighteenth-century Spanish Books in the British Library., Vol. 3. LC 95-118550. 1994. write for info. (*0-7123-0374-X*) B23tish Library.

British Library, jt. auth. see Dale, Peter.

British Library Business Information Research Serv, ed. Sources of European Economic & Business Information. 6th ed. LC 94-11836. 352p. 1995. 253.95 (*0-566-07487-7*, Pub. by Gower) Ashgate Pub Co.

British Library, Department of Manuscript Staff, ed. Index of Manuscripts in the British Library, 10 vols. 5603p. 1985. lib. bdg. write for info. (*0-85964-140-6*) Chadwyck-Healey.

British Library Document Supply Centre Staff, ed. Index of Conference Proceedings Received 1964-1988. 12500p. 1989. lib. bdg. 6415.00 (*0-86291-870-7*) U Pubns Amer.

British Library, Manuscript Staff & Cotton, Nero A. The Complete Works of the Gawain-Poet. LC 65-17291. (Illus.). 359p. reprint ed. pap. 111.30 (*0-608-09307-6*, 205418100004) Bks Demand.

British Library Manuscripts Staff, ed. see Cross, James E. & Hill, Thomas D.

British Library of Political & Economic Science St. International Bibliography of the Social Sciences Vol. 34: Anthropology, 1988. 242p. (C). 1992. 230.00 (*0-415-06471-6*) Routledge.

— International Bibliography of the Social Sciences Vol. 37: Economics, 1988. (International Bibliography of the Social Sciences Ser.). 520p. (C). (gr. 13 up). 1992. 230.00 (*0-415-06472-4*) Routledge.

— International Bibliography of the Social Sciences Vol. 37: Political Science, 1988. 322p. (C). 1992. 230.00 (*0-415-06473-2*) Routledge.

British Library of Political & Economic Science St, compiled by. Complete International Bibliography of the Social Sciences: Anthropology, Economics, Political Science, Sociology, 166 vols. 19840.00 (*0-415-12696-7*) Routledge.

— International Bibliography of Anthropology: International Bibliography of the Social Sciences, 1997. (International Bibliography of the Social Sciences Ser.: Vol. 43). 428p. (C). (gr. 13). 1999. 250.00 (*0-415-19298-6*, D6185) Routledge.

— International Bibliography of Economics: International Bibliography of the Social Sciences, 1997. (International Bibliography of the Social Sciences Ser.: Vol. 46). 684p. (C). (gr. 13). 1999. 250.00 (*0-415-19299-4*, D6186) Routledge.

— International Bibliography of Political Science, 1997: International Bibliography of the Social Sciences, 1997. (International Bibliography of the Social Sciences Ser.: Vol. 46). 500p. (C). 1999. 250.00 (*0-415-19300-1*, D6187) Routledge.

— International Bibliography of Sociology, 1997: International Bibliography of the Social Sciences, 1997. (International Bibliography of the Social Sciences Ser.: Vol. 47). 500p. (C). 1999. 250.00 (*0-415-19301-X*, D6188) Routledge.

— A London Bibliography of the Social Sciences Vol. 32: Ninth Supplement, 1974. 461p. 1975. 180.00 (*0-7201-0524-2*) Continuum.

— A London Bibliography of the Social Sciences Vol. 33: Tenth Supplement, 1975. 418p. 1976. 180.00 (*0-7201-0634-6*) Continuum.

— A London Bibliography of the Social Sciences Vol. 34: Eleventh Supplement, 1976. LC 31-9970. 458p. 1977. lib. bdg. 180.00 (*0-7201-0721-0*) Continuum.

— A London Bibliography of the Social Sciences Vol. 36: Thirteenth Supplement, 1978. 416p. 1979. lib. bdg. 180.00 (*0-7201-0929-9*) Continuum.

— A London Bibliography of the Social Sciences Vol. 41: Eighteenth Supplement, 1983. 928p. 1984. text 160.00 (*0-7201-1695-3*) Continuum.

— A London Bibliography of the Social Sciences Vol. 42: Nineteenth Supplement, 1984. 1056p. 1985. 160.00 (*0-7201-1726-7*) Continuum.

— A London Bibliography of the Social Sciences Vol. 43: Twentieth Supplement, 1985. 976p. 1986. text 200.00 (*0-7201-1771-2*) Continuum.

— A London Bibliography of the Social Sciences Vol. 45: Twenty-Second Supplement, 1987. 1128p. 1988. text 220.00 (*0-7201-1958-8*) Continuum.

— A London Bibliography of the Social Sciences Vol. 47: Twenty-Fourth Supplement, 1989. 1024p. 1990. text 250.00 (*0-7201-2034-9*) Continuum.

British Library of Political & Economic Science Staff. International Bibliography of Social Sciences: Anthropology, 1996, 42. (International Bibliography of the Social Sciences Ser.). 428p. (C). 1998. 250.00 (*0-415-16080-4*) Routledge.

— International Bibliography of Social Sciences: Economics, 1996, 45. (International Bibliography of the Social Sciences Ser.). 636p. (C). 1998. 250.00 (*0-415-16082-0*) Routledge.

— International Bibliography of Social Sciences: Political Science, 1996. (International Bibliography of the Social Sciences Ser.). 588p. (C). 1998. 250.00 (*0-415-16081-2*) Routledge.

— International Bibliography of Social Sciences: Sociology, 1996, 46. (International Bibliography of the Social Sciences Ser.). 628p. (C). 1998. 250.00 (*0-415-16079-0*) Routledge.

British Library of Political Science Staff, ed. International Bibliography of Social Sciences: Economics, 1995, Vol. 44. 676p. (C). 1997. 250.00 (*0-415-15215-1*) Routledge.

British Library Staff. The British Library Catalogue of Additions to the Manuscripts: New Series, 1976-1980, 2 vols., Set. 702p. 1996. 170.00 (*0-7123-0429-0*, Pub. by B23tish Library) U of Toronto Pr.

— Catalogue of Additions to MSS: 1986-1990, 3 Vol. Set. (Catalogues of the British Library Collections). 1993. 250.00 (*0-7123-0305-7*, Pub. by B23tish Library) U of Toronto Pr.

— The Illuminated Haggadah: Featuring Medieval Illuminations from the Haggadah Collection of the British Library. LC 97-30520. (ENG & HEB.). 64p. 1998. pap. 15.00 (*1-55670-724-X*) Stewart Tabori & Chang.

— The Illuminated Haggadah: Featuring Medieval Illuminations from the Haggadah Collection of the British Library. LC 97-30520. (ENG & HEB., Illus.). 1998. write for info. (*1-55670-704-5*); 25.00 (*1-55670-800-9*) Stewart Tabori & Chang.

— The Lindisfarne Gospels Address Book. (Illus.). 96p. 1997. pap. 9.95 (*0-7123-4550-7*) U of Toronto Pr.

— The Lindisfarne Gospels Book of Days. (Illus.). 96p. 1998. pap. 9.95 (*0-7123-4551-5*) U of Toronto Pr.

— Location Register of Twentieth Century English Literary Manuscripts & Letters: A Union List of Papers of Modern English, Irish, Scottish & Welsh Authors in the British Isles. 1200p. (C). 1988. 190.00 (*0-8161-8981-1*, Hall Reference) Macmillan.

— A Medieval Illuminated Address Book. (Illus.). 96p. 1997. pap. 9.95 (*0-7123-4549-3*) U of Toronto Pr.

— A Medieval Illuminated Book of Days. (Illus.). 96p. 1997. pap. 9.95 (*0-7123-4548-5*) U of Toronto Pr.

British Library Staff, ed. The British Library General Catalogue of Printed Books to 1975, 360 vols. 1987. write for info. (*3-598-31000-5*) K G Saur Verlag.

— The British Library General Catalogue of Printed Books to 1975: Supplement, 6 vols. 1988. 9660.00 (*3-598-31390-X*) K G Saur Verlag.

— The British Library General Catalogue of Printed Books, 1976-1982, 50 Vols. 1983. lib. bdg. 9660.00 (*0-86291-485-X*) U Pubns Amer.

— The British Library General Catalogue of Printed Books, 1982-1985, 26 vols. 1987. lib. bdg. 6175.00 (*0-86291-540-6*) U Pubns Amer.

— The British Library General Catalogue of Printed, Books 1986-1987. (British Library General Catalogue Ser.). 8500p. 1988. lib. bdg. 6175.00 (*3-598-32740-4*) K G Saur Verlag.

— The British Library General Catalogue of Printed Books, 1988-1989, 28 vols., Set. 13440p. 1990. lib. bdg. 6350.00 (*3-598-33050-2*) K G Saur Verlag.

— The British Library General Subject Catalogue, 1975-1985, 75 vols. 1987. lib. bdg. write for info. (*3-598-32191-0*) K G Saur Verlag.

— The British Library General Subject Catalogue, 1986-1990, 42 vols. 1991. lib. bdg. write for info. (*3-598-31810-3*) K G Saur Verlag.

British Library Staff & Wolf, Melvin H. Catalogue & Indexes to the Title-Pages of English Printed Books Preserved in the British Library's Bagford Collection LC 76-367359. xxvii, 505 p. 1974. write for info. (*0-7141-0335-7*) BRI5.

British Library Staff, et al. Catalogue of Early Armenian Books, 1512-1850 LC 81-457014. 172p. 1980. write for info. (*0-904654-35-4*) Br Library Bd.

— Imagining the West: A Guide to Printed Materials in the British Library on the Literature of the American West. LC 97-174884. 60p. 1997. write for info. (*0-7123-4413-6*) Brit Lib R & D.

British Library Staff, jt. auth. see Lees, Nigel.

British Mechanical Engineering Confederation Staff. The European Economic Community & United Kingdom Engineering Companies. 57p. 1980. 78.75 (*0-89771-002-9*) St Mut.

British Medical Association Library Staff. Catalogue of Films & Videos in the British Medical Association Library. LC 93-240711. 349p. 1993. reprint ed. pap. 108.20 (*0-608-02469-4*, 206311300004) Bks Demand.

British Medical Association Staff. Human Genetics: Choice & Responsibility. (Illus.). 250p. 1998. pap. text 26.50 (*0-19-288055-1*) OUP.

***British Medical Association Staff.** The Medical Profession & Human Rights: A Handbook for a Changing. 2000. pap. 29.95 (*1-85649-612-0*, Pub. by Zed Books) St Martin.

— The Medical Profession & Human Rights: Handbook for a Changing. 2000. text 69.95 (*1-85649-611-2*, Pub. by Zed Books) St Martin.

British Medical Association Staff. Medicine Betrayed: The Participation of Doctors in Human Rights Abuses. LC 92-28909. 288p. (C). 1992. pap. 19.95 (*1-85649-104-8*, Pub. by Zed Books); text 55.00 (*1-85649-103-X*, Pub. by Zed Books) St Martin.

— Pesticides, Chemicals & Health. (Illus.). 224p. 1992. pap. text 29.95 (*0-340-54924-6*, A6602, Pub. by E A) Routldge.

— Therapeutic Uses of Cannabis. 144p. 1998. text 23.00 (*90-5702-317-2*, Harwood Acad Pubs); pap. text 11.00 (*90-5702-318-0*, Harwood Acad Pubs) Gordon & Breach.

British Medical Association Staff, ed. The Misuse of Drugs. 160p. 1997. text 24.00 (*90-5702-259-1*, Harwood Acad Pubs); pap. text 20.00 (*90-5702-260-5*, Harwood Acad Pubs) Gordon & Breach.

British Medical Association Staff, jt. auth. see Ellis, Norman.

British Motor Corporation Ltd., MG Car Division. MGA 1500, 1600, 1600 (MK II) Workshop Manual, 1955-1962. (Illus.). 272p. (Orig.). 55.00 (*0-8376-0510-5*) Bentley Pubs.

British Museum, Department of Egyptian & Assyrian. Annals of the Kings of Assyria. LC 78-72730. (Ancient Mesopotamian Texts & Studies). reprint ed. 95.00 (*0-404-18165-1*) AMS Pr.

— Babylonian Boundary-Stones & Memorial Tablets in the British Museum, 2 vols., Set. King, L. W., ed. LC 78-72731. (Ancient Mesopotamian Texts & Studies). reprint ed. 85.00 (*0-404-18166-X*) AMS Pr.

British Museum, Geological Department Staff. Man's Place in Evolution. 2nd ed. (Illus.). 103p. (YA). (gr. 7 up). 1991. pap. 14.95 (*0-521-40864-4*) Cambridge U Pr.

— Nature at Work: Introducing Ecology. LC 78-66795. (Illus.). 96p. (YA). (gr. 7 up). 1978. pap. 12.95 (*0-521-29469-X*) Cambridge U Pr.

British Museum of Natural History Staff. British Caenozoic Fossils: Tertiary & Quaternary. 5th ed. (British Fossils Ser.). vi, 132p. 1975. pap. write for info. (*0-11-310024-8*, Pub. by Statnry Office) Balogh.

— British Palaeozoic Fossils. 4th ed. (British Fossils Ser.). vi, 203p. 1975. pap. write for info. (*0-11-310026-4*, Pub. by Statnry Office) Balogh.

British Museum Staff. Ancient Egyptian Art Postcards in Full Color. 1991. pap. text 4.95 (*0-486-26703-2*) Dover.

— Medallic Illustrations of the History of Great Britain & Ireland. (Illus.). 1980. 150.00 (*0-88000-001-5*) Quarterman.

British Museum Staff & Higgins, Reynold A. Catalogue of the Terracottas in the Department of Greek & Roman Antiquities, British Museum. LC 72-175593. 1969. reprint ed. write for info. (*0-7141-1225-9*, Pub. by British Mus Pr) Art Media Resources.

British Museum Staff, jt. auth. see Bailey, Donald M.

***British National Conference on Database Staff, et al.** Advances in Databases: 17th British National Conference on Databases, Bncod 17, Exeter, Uk, July 3-5, 2000 Proceedings. LC 00-55632. 2000. pap. write for info. (*3-540-67743-7*) Spr-Verlag.

British National Conference on Databases. Directions in Databases: Proceedings of the 12th British National Conference on Databases, BNCOD 12, Guildford, United Kingdom, July 6-8, 1994. Bowers, David S., ed. (Lecture Notes in Computer Science Ser.: Vol. 826). 234p. 1994. 39.95 (*0-387-58235-5*) Spr-Verlag.

British Non-Ferrous Metals Research Association St. Clear Lacquers for Copper & Copper Alloys. 75p. 1965. 11.25 (*0-317-34498-6*, 5) Intl Copper.

— Energy Requirements in the Electrode-Position of Copper, including a Summary of Work on the Deposition of Copper for Direct Working to Wire. 54p. 1965. 8.10 (*0-317-34521-4*, 42) Intl Copper.

— Physical Studies of Water-Formed Corrosion Products on Copper & Proposals for an Alternative Mechanism of Pitting Corrosion. 73p. 10.95 (*0-317-34539-7*, 34) Intl Copper.

British-North American Committee. Higher Oil Prices: Worldwide Financial Implications. LC 75-29675. 64p. 1975. 3.00 (*0-902594-27-3*) Natl Planning.

— Mineral Development in the 80s: Prospects & Problems. LC 76-53628. 64p. 1977. 3.00 (*0-902594-29-X*) Natl Planning.

British-North American Committee Staff. On Preserving Shared Values. 16p. (Orig.). 1989. pap. text 2.00 (*0-902594-49-4*, BN 37 (NPA 240)) Natl Planning.

***British Nutrition Foundation Staff.** Obesity: The Report of the British Nutrition Foundation Task Force. LC 99-88087. 2000. pap. write for info. (*0-632-05298-8*) Blackwell Sci.

British Nutrition Foundation Staff. Unsaturated Fatty Acids in Foods: The Report of the British Nutrition Foundation's Task Force. 300p. 1992. 89.95 (*0-442-31621-6*) Chapman & Hall.

British Nutrition Foundation Staff, jt. auth. see Arens, Ursula.

British Patent Office Staff, ed. Patents for Inventions: Class 119 (Small Arms), 1855-1930, 7 vols. (Illus.). 2013p. 1994. reprint ed. boxed set 250.00 (*0-939683-08-3*) Armory Pubns.

British Record Society Staff. Abstracts of Inquisitiones Post Mortem for Gloucestershire Returned into the Court of Chancery During the Plantagenet Period, Pt. VI: 33 Edward III to 14 Henry IV, 1359-1413. (Index Library: Vol. 47). 1972. reprint ed. pap. 25.00 (*0-8115-1492-7*) Periodicals Srv.

— Abstracts of Inquisitiones Post Mortem for Wiltshire Returned into the Court of Chancery During the Plantagenet Period: 21 Edward II to 51 Edward III, 1327-1377. (Index Library: Vol. 48). 1972. reprint ed. pap. 36.00 (*0-8115-1493-5*) Periodicals Srv.

British Small Animal Vet Assoc. Staff, ed. BSAVA Manual of Small Animal Fracture Repair & Management. LC 98-167590. 348p. 1998. 94.95 (*0-905214-37-4*) Brynwood Publishing Co.

British Small Animal Veterinary Association Staff, jt. auth. see Gorman, Neil T.

British Small Animal Veterinary Association Staff, jt. auth. see Jones, Bruce V.

British Society for Developmental Biology Staff. The Early Development of Mammals: Symposium of the British Society for Developmental Biology, 2nd. Balls, M. & Wild, A. E., eds. LC 75-2728. 462p. reprint ed. pap. 131.70 (*0-608-18733-X*, 2029214) Bks Demand.

— Vertebrate Limb & Somite Morphogenesis: The Third Symposium of the British Society for Developmental Biology. Ede, D. A. et al, eds. LC 76-30451. (British Society for Developmental Biology Symposium Ser.: No. 3). 508p. reprint ed. pap. 144.80 (*0-608-15716-3*, 2031644) Bks Demand.

British Society of Gerontology Staff, et al, eds. Social Policy & Elderly People: The Role of Community Care. (Avebury Community Care Ser.). 304p. 1992. 69.95 (*1-85628-303-8*, Pub. by Avebry) Ashgate Pub Co.

British Standards Institution Staff. Film Editing Room Handbook: How to Avoid the Near-Chaos of the Cutting Room. 3rd ed. LC 98-30708. 1998. write for info. (*0-580-65000-6*) B S I Stndrds.

British Textile Tech Group Editorial Staff. Guide to the Identification of Animal Fibres. (C). 1978. 170.00 (*0-900820-11-X*, Pub. by British Textile Tech) St Mut.

British Textile Tech. Group Staff. Woven Structure & Design Pt. 2: Compound Structures. 140p. (C). 1989. 165.00 (*0-903669-51-X*, Pub. by British Textile Tech) St Mut.

British Tourist Authority Staff. The British on Holiday: A Summary of Regular Surveys on the Taking of Holidays of Four Nights or More by British Adults 1951-1972. LC 74-162258. 1973. write for info. (*0-85630-035-7*) British Tour.

British Tourist Authority Staff. European Architectural Heritage Year, 1975. LC 75-332062. 24 p. 1975. write for info. (*0-85630-079-9*) British Tour.

British Tourist Authority Staff & Great Britain. Historic Houses Survey. LC 70-528407. 56 p. 1970. write for info. (*0-900225-68-8*) British Tour.

British Tourist Authority Staff, jt. auth. see Conference on Tourism & the Environment Staff.

British Tourist Board Staff. Britain: Camping & Caravan Parks 1998 Edition. (Where to Stay Ser.). 1998. pap. text 10.95 (*0-7095-6789-8*, Pub. by British Tour) Seven Hills Bk.

— Leisure Guide: Horse Riding. 1994. pap. text 30.00 (*1-85253-294-7*, Pub. by Quiller Pr) St Mut.

British War Office General Staff. The Austro-Hungarian Forces in the Field, October 1918. (Reference Ser.: No. 3). 225p. 1994. reprint ed. 39.95 (*0-89839-209-8*) Battery Pr.

British War Office Staff, contrib. by. Course in Cryptanalysis: Explanatory Text & Short Exercises, S. I. Course, 2 vols., Vol. I. enl. rev. ed. 72p. 1981. pap. 18.80 (*0-89412-052-2*) Aegean Park Pr.

— Course in Cryptanalysis: Figures & Cipher Texts, S. I. Course, 2 vols., Vol. II. enl. rev. ed. 69p. 1981. pap. 18.80 (*0-89412-053-0*) Aegean Park Pr.

British War Office Staff, ed. Armies of the Balkan States, 1914-1918: The Military Forces of Bulgaria, Greece, Montenegro, Rumania, & Servia. (Reference Ser.: Vol. 14). (Illus.). 425p. 1996. reprint ed. 49.95 (*0-89839-262-4*) Battery Pr.

British Welding Research Association Staff. The Welding of Sand Cast Incramet 800. 75p. 1965. 11.25 (*0-317-34556-7*, 57) Intl Copper.

British Writers & Their Work Staff. British Writers & Their Work, No. 10. LC 63-63096. (Bison Bk.). 146p. reprint ed. pap. 45.30 (*0-7837-1764-4*, 200576800010) Bks Demand.

***Britnell, Charlie.** The Newlyweds: Forty-eight Inspirational Stories of the Britnell Family from Writings in the Family Tree. LC 98-211039. (Illus.). 1998. write for info. (*0-89315-402-4*) Lambert Bk.

Britnell, Jennifer. Jean Bouchet. 360p. 1986. 67.50 (*0-85224-533-5*, Pub. by Edinburgh U Pr) Col U Pr.

***Britnell, Jennifer & Britnell, Richard H.** Vernacular Literature & Current Affairs in the Early Sixteenth Century France, England & Scotland. LC 99-87400. (Studies in European Cultural Transition). 2000. 70.95 (*0-7546-0093-9*, Pub. by Ashgate Pub) Ashgate Pub Co.

Britnell, R. H. The Commercialisation of English Society, 1000-1500. 2nd ed. LC 96-38816. (Manchester Medieval Sources Ser.). 304p. 1997. text 59.95 (*0-7190-5042-1*) St Martin.

Britnell, R. H. & Pollard, A. J. The McFarlane Legacy: Studies in Late Medieval Politics & Society. LC 95-12671. 1995. text 59.95 (*0-312-12590-9*) St Martin.

Britnell, R. H. & Pollard, A. J., eds. The McFarlane Legacy: Studies in Late Medieval Politics & Society. (Fifteenth Century Ser.: No. 1). 240p. 1997. 72.00 (*0-7509-0626-X*, Pub. by Sutton Pub Ltd) Intl Pubs Mktg.

Britnell, Richard, ed. Daily Life in Late Medieval England. (Medieval History Ser.). (Illus.). 234p. 1998. 39.95 (*0-7509-1587-0*, Pub. by Sutton Pub Ltd) Intl Pubs Mktg.

— Pragmatic Literacy, East & West, 1200-1330. LC 96-38238. (Illus.). 274p. 1997. 90.00 (*0-85115-695-9*) Boydell & Brewer.

Britnell, Richard & Campbell, Bruce M. S., eds. A Commercialising Economy: England 1086 to c. 1300. LC 94-17562. 228p. 1995. text 79.95 (*0-7190-3994-0*) Manchester Univ Pr.

Britnell, Richard & Hatcher, John, eds. Progress & Problems in Medieval England: Essays in Honour of Edward Miller. (Illus.). 344p. (C). 1996. text 64.95 (*0-521-55036-X*) Cambridge U Pr.

Britnell, Richard H. The Closing of the Middle Ages? England, 1471-1529. LC 96-51565. (History of Medieval Britain Ser.). (Illus.). 288p. 1997. pap. 26.95 (*0-631-20540-3*); text 62.95 (*0-631-16598-3*) Blackwell Pubs.

Britnell, Richard H., jt. auth. see Britnell, Jennifer.

Britney, Robert R., jt. auth. see Kuzdrall, Paul J.

Britnieva, Mary, tr. see Benois, Alexandre.

Brito, Alan. Infructuoso Mendoza. Arango, Alfredo, tr. (SPA.). 154p. 1998. pap. 14.95 (*0-9664690-0-3*) Editorial La Gaveta.

An Asterisk (*) at the beginning of an entry indicates that the title is appearing for the first time.

Brito, Aristeo. The Devil in Texas: El Diablo en Texas. Foster, David W., tr. LC 90-80917. (Clasicos Chicanos - Chicano Classics Ser.: No. 5). 224p. 1990. 26.00 (*0-927534-05-3*); pap. 16.00 (*0-927534-06-1*) Biling Rev-Pr.

***Brito, Armando.** Voces Hispanicas: Historias Personales. (SPA.). 168p. (C). 1999. pap. 18.75 (*0-07-290418-6*) McGrw-H Hghr Educ.

Brito, D. L. & Intriligator, Michael D. Formal Models of Arms Races. (CISA Working Papers: No. 2). 24p. (Orig.). 1976. pap. 15.00 (*0-86682-001-9*) Ctr Intl Relations.

Brito, Dagobert L. & Intriligator, Michael D. Dettering Nuclear Weapons Proliferation. (New Ser.: No. 16). 1998. pap. 15.00 (*0-86682-103-1*) Ctr Intl Relations.

Brito-Millard, Chris. Low Fat Finales: Reduced Fat Dessert Recipes Collected by Chris Brito-Millard, Certified Personal Trainer. rev. ed. (Illus.). 92p. 1995. 12.95 (*0-9649659-1-7*) B A Brito.

— Take a Bite . . . It's Light! Low Fat Recipes Collected by Chris Brito-Millard, Certified Personal Trainer. rev. ed. (Illus.). 168p. 1995. 14.95 (*0-9649659-0-9*) B A Brito.

Brito, Silvester J. The Way of a Peyote Roadman. (American University Studies: Regional Studies: Ser. XX, Vol. 1). XVI, 183p. (C). 1989. text 36.00 (*0-8204-1064-0*) P Lang Pubng.

Briton, Derek. The Modern Practice of Adult Education: A Postmodern Critique. LC 95-38597. (SUNY Series, Teacher Empowerment & School Reform). 156p. (C). 1996. text 44.50 (*0-7914-3025-1*); pap. text 16.95 (*0-7914-3026-X*) State U NY Pr.

Britsch, Barbara M. & Dennison-Tansey, Amy. One Voice: Music & Stories in the Classroom. LC 95-11838. (Illus.). xxiv, 175p. 1995. pap. text 18.50 (*1-56308-049-4*) Teacher Ideas Pr.

Britsch, Eckart. Bernd Koberling: Paintings 1991-1993. (Illus.). 90p. 55.00 (*3-928762-19-2*) Dist Art Pubs.

Britsch, R. Lanier. From the East: The History of the Latter-Day Saints in Asia. LC 97-36785. 1997. 29.95 (*1-57345-268-8*) Deseret Bk.

— Moramona: The Mormons in Hawaii. LC 89-37402. (Mormons in the Pacific Ser.). (Illus.). 256p. (Orig.). 1989. pap. 12.95 (*0-939154-46-3*) Inst Polynesian.

***Britsch, R. Lanier.** Nothing More Heroic: A Pioneer Missionary Memoir of Courage & Faith LC 99-35842. 1999. write for info. (*1-57345-565-2*) Deseret Bk.

Britt, Alan. Amnesia Tango. 90p. 1998. pap. 10.00 (*1-891812-14-9*, 98-009) Cedar Hill Pubns.

— Bodies of Lightening: Poems. 66p. 1995. pap. 8.95 (*0-9647754-8-4*) CypressBks.

Britt, Alan, ed. see Crawford, Roberta.

Britt, Albert. Great Biographers. LC 71-84300. (Essay Index Reprint Ser.). 1977. 20.95 (*0-8369-1077-X*) Ayer.

— Great Indian Chiefs. LC 76-76895. (Essay Index Reprint Ser.). 1980. 23.95 (*0-8369-0006-5*) Ayer.

— Great Indian Chiefs. LC 76-76895. (Essay Index Reprint Ser.). 280p. reprint ed. lib. bdg. 19.50 (*0-8290-0792-X*) Irvington.

Britt, Beverly A., ed. Malignant Hyperthermia. (C). 1987. text 147.50 (*0-89838-960-7*) Kluwer Academic.

Britt, Brian. Walter Benjamin & the Bible. 200p. 1996. 29.95 (*0-8264-0879-6*) Continuum.

Britt, Chris. Britt Happens. 128p. 1995. pap. text 13.95 (*0-7872-1687-9*) Kendall-Hunt.

Britt, Christa & Schutte, Lilith E. Wiley's English-German, German-English Business Dictionary. LC 95-37977. (ENG & GER.). 343p. 1995. 49.95 (*0-471-13401-5*); pap. 19.95 (*0-471-12140-1*) Wiley.

Britt, Christa B., tr. see Von LaRoche, Sophie.

Britt, D. P. Research Review (Ethical) Committees for Animal Experimentation. 1985. 30.00 (*0-7855-1123-7*) St Mut.

Britt, David, ed. Modern Art: Impressionism to Post-Modernism. LC 99-70796. (Illus.). 416p. 1999. pap. 24.95 (*0-500-28126-2*, Pub. by Thames Hudson) Norton.

Britt, David, tr. from GER. Friedrich Gilly: Essays on Architecture, 1796-1799. LC 93-23386. (Texts & Documents Ser.). (Illus.). 240p. 1994. 39.95 (*0-89236-280-4*, Pub. by J P Getty Trust); pap. 24.95 (*0-89236-281-2*, Pub. by J P Getty Trust) OUP.

Britt, David, jt. auth. see Gercken, Gunther.

Britt, David, tr. see Beaumont-Maillet, Laure.

Britt, David, tr. see Beckmann, Max.

Britt, David, tr. see Frank, Isabelle, ed.

Britt, David, tr. see Le Camus de Mezieres, Nicolas.

Britt, David, tr. see Lindinger, Herbert, ed.

Britt, David, tr. see Pacht, Otto.

Britt, David, tr. see Richter, Gerhard.

Britt, David, tr. see Richter, Hans.

Britt, David, tr. see Stachelhaus, Heiner.

Britt, David, tr. see Tiege, Karel.

Britt, David, tr. see Von Kalnein, Wend.

Britt, David W. A Conceptual Introduction to Modeling: Qualitative & Quantitative Perspectives. 224p. (C). 1997. text 49.95 (*0-8058-1937-1*); pap. text 19.95 (*0-8058-1938-X*) L Erlbaum Assocs.

Britt, Dorothy. The Happiness Handbook of Love Those Worry Birds. (Illus.). 46p. (Orig.). 1992. pap. 6.95 (*1-881809-01-3*) Gabriel TX.

— The Water Bug Story. (Illus.). 10p. (Orig.). (J). 1992. pap. 4.95 (*1-881809-32-3*) Gabriel TX.

Britt, Dorothy, ed. see Caradja, Catherine.

Britt, George, jt. auth. see Broun, Heywood.

Britt, Grant. Charlie Sifford. LC 97-48657. (Great Athletes Ser.). (Illus.). 64p. (YA). (gr. 3 up). 1998. lib. bdg. 17.95 (*1-883846-27-7*) M Reynolds.

Britt, Greg, jt. auth. see Endahl, Carol F.

***Britt-Hay, Deborah.** Jack Russel Terriers for Dummies. (For Dummies (Lifestyles) Ser.). (Illus.). 334p. 2000. pap. 15.99 (*0-7645-5268-6*) IDG Bks.

Britt-Hay, Deborah. Owning, Raising & Training a Jack Russell Terrier. LC 99-10109. (Illus.). 302p. 1999. pap. text. write for info. (*1-58245-042-0*) Macmillan Gen Ref.

Britt, Helen. Ye Gods. (J). 1987. pap. text 11.16 (*0-88334-196-4*, 76161) Longman.

Britt, James P., et al. Sport A. S. I. S. T. A Student Athlete's Guide to Collegiate Athletics. rev. ed. LC 96-92001. 140p. 1996. pap. 19.95 (*1-881013-11-1*) Sports Sci.

***Britt, Jim.** Authentic Power. 250p. 2000. pap. 11.95 (*1-55874-760-5*) Health Comm.

Britt, Jim. Rings of Truth: A True-to-Life Story That Will Invigorate Your Mind, Open Your Heart & Touch Your Soul. unabridged ed. Hogan, Eve & Flood, Cloudsifter, eds. (Illus.). 368p. 1998. 24.95 (*0-9662171-0-1*) Master Key Prodns.

***Britt, Jim & Hogan, Eve Eschner.** Rings of Truth. LC 99-40759. 350p. 1999. pap. 12.95 (*1-55874-724-9*) Health Comm.

Britt, John. John Henry Newman's Rhetoric: Becoming a Discriminating Reader. 2nd ed. (American University Studies: Language: Ser. XIV, Vol. 21). X, 218p. (C). 1992. text 40.00 (*0-8204-1065-9*) P Lang Pubng.

Britt, John F. Rhetorical Mosaic for a Kaleidoscope of Sound: Poetry As a Road to Understanding the Prose Voice. LC 93-40295. (Am. Univ. Studies, V: Vol. 159). XIII, 192p. (C). 1994. text 37.95 (*0-8204-2383-1*) P Lang Pubng.

Britt, Judith S. Nothing More Agreeable: Music in George Washington's Family. LC 84-20735. (Illus.). 120p. 1984. pap. 4.95 (*0-931917-10-7*) Mt Vernon Ladies.

Britt, Leslie, ed. see Beadles, Gloria.

Britt, Leslie, ed. see Bickert, Grace.

Britt, Leslie, ed. see Breeden, Terri & Dillard, Kathryn.

Britt, Leslie, ed. see Breeden, Terri & Egan, Emalie.

Britt, Leslie, ed. see Brisson, Lynn.

Britt, Leslie, ed. see Bushey, Jeanne.

Britt, Leslie, ed. see Cochran, Judith.

Britt, Leslie, ed. see Cook, Shirley.

Britt, Leslie, ed. see Crosby, Diane.

Britt, Leslie, ed. see Duguran, Debbie & Hopkins, Margot.

Britt, Leslie, ed. see Fletcher, Kathleen.

Britt, Leslie, ed. see Forle, Imogene & MacKenzie, Joy.

Britt, Leslie, ed. see Forte, Imogene.

Britt, Leslie, ed. see Forte, Imogene & MacKenzie, Joy.

Britt, Leslie, ed. see Forte, Imogene & Schurr, Sandra.

Britt, Leslie, ed. see Forte, Imogene, et al.

Britt, Leslie, ed. see Frank, Marjorie.

Britt, Leslie, ed. see Frender, Gloria.

Britt, Leslie, ed. see Gork, Mardi.

Britt, Leslie, ed. see Graham, Leland & Ledbetter, Darriel.

Britt, Leslie, ed. see March, Deborah & Canull, Nancy.

Britt, Leslie, ed. see Michener, Dorothy.

Britt, Leslie, ed. see Mussain, Donna.

Britt, Leslie, ed. see Philpot, Jan G.

Britt, Leslie, ed. see Philpot, Jan & Philpot, Ed.

Britt, Leslie, ed. see Ralph, Sharon.

Britt, Leslie, ed. see Seguin, Marilyn, et al.

Britt, Leslie, ed. see Ullinskey, Nancy & Hibbert, Lorri.

Britt, Leslie, ed. see Wright, Sue.

Britt, Leslie, ed. & intro. see Blankenhorn, Kathy & Richards, Joanne.

Britt, Leslie, ed. & intro. see Brisson, Lynn.

Britt, Leslie, ed. & intro. see Maben, Laura.

Britt, Linda, tr. see Fares, Gustavo & Hermann, Eliana C., eds.

Britt, Linda, tr. & intro. see Naranjo, Carmen.

Britt, Lora S. My Gold Coast: South Florida in Earlier Years. (Illus.). 245p. 1984. 10.95 (*0-9613982-0-5*) Brittany Hse.

Britt, Melissa, jt. auth. see Haugen, Janie.

Britt, Melissa, ed. see Haugen, Janie.

Britt, N. Wilson. Biology of Two Species of Lake Erie Mayflies. (Bulletin New Ser.: Vol. 1, No. 5). 1962. pap. text 4.00 (*0-86727-047-0*) Ohio Bio Survey.

Britt, N. Wilson, et al. Limnological Studies of the Island Area of Western Lake Erie. (Bulletin New Ser.: Vol. 4, No. 3). 1973. pap. text 3.00 (*0-86727-062-4*) Ohio Bio Survey.

Britt, Nancy, ed. see Kennedy, D. James.

Britt, Peggy, jt. auth. see Biggs, Nancy.

Britt, Peggy, jt. auth. see Tourtillot, Leeann.

Britt, Rachael. Wildflower Studio, No. 1. (Illus.). 80p. 1999. pap. 10.50 (*1-56770-457-3*) S Scheewe Pubns.

Britt, Richard W. The Princess & the P. O. W. 2nd ed. (Illus.). 283p. 1988. pap. 11.95 (*1-881809-25-0*) Gabriel TX.

Britt, Ruby B. Flutterings. 1997. pap. write for info. (*1-57553-527-0*) Watermrk Pr.

Britt, Stan. Dexter Gordon: A Musical Biography. (Quality Paperbacks Ser.). (Illus.). 192p. 1989. pap. 12.95 (*0-306-80361-5*) Da Capo.

Britt, Stephanie. My Little Bible Blue. (Illus.). 98p. (Orig.). (J). (ps-k). 1993. 5.99 (*0-8499-1078-1*) Tommy Nelson.

— My Name is Peter. 1999. pap. text 3.95 (*0-687-05328-5*) Abingdon.

Britt, Stephanie, jt. auth. see Pingry, Patricia.

Britt, Stephanie M. My Little Bible, Pink. (My Little Bible Ser.). (Illus.). 98p. (J). (ps-k). 1993. 5.99 (*0-8499-1077-3*) Tommy Nelson.

— My Little Bible, White. (My Little Bible Ser.). (Illus.). 98p. (J). (ps-k). 1993. 5.99 (*0-8499-0824-8*) Tommy Nelson.

— My Little Bible Promises. LC 94-17707. (My Little Bible Ser.). (Illus.). 98p. (J). (ps-k). 1994. 5.99 (*0-8499-1145-1*) Tommy Nelson.

— My Little Memory Verses. (My Little Bible Ser.). (Illus.). 98p. (J). (ps-k). 1994. 5.99 (*0-8499-1140-0*) Tommy Nelson.

— My Little Prayers. LC 93-578. (My Little Bible Ser.). (Illus.). 98p. (J). (ps-k). 1995. 5.99 (*0-8499-1064-1*) Tommy Nelson.

— My Little Psalms. LC 95-1446. (My Little Bible Ser.). (Illus.). 98p. (J). (ps-k). 1995. 5.99 (*0-8499-1193-1*) Tommy Nelson.

Britt, Steuart H., jt. auth. see Graeber, Isacque.

Britt, Suzanne. A Writer's Rhetoric. 463p. (C). 1988. teacher ed. write for info. (*0-15-597661-3*) Harcourt Coll Pubs.

Britt, Teri, et al. Managed Care & Capitation: Issues in Nursing. LC 98-3607. 30p. 1998. pap. 15.95 (*1-55810-141-1*) Am Nurses Pub.

Britt, Viola L. Discipline in Family Resource Management. 179p. 1998. pap. 8.95 (*0-89228-132-4*) Impact Christian.

— Family Planner: Companion Workbook to Discipline in Family Resource Management. 64p. 1999. pap., wbk. ed. 5.95 (*0-89228-137-5*) Impact Christian.

— Raising Responsible Children in a Single Parent Home. 224p. 1997. pap. 8.95 (*0-89228-124-3*) Impact Christian.

Britta, Albert J. Della, see Loudon, David L. & Della Britta, Albert J.

Brittain. The Wizards & the Monster. LC 93-47077. 96p. (J). (gr. 2-5). pap. 4.25 (*0-06-442003-5*) HarpC Child Bks.

Brittain, ed. Polymorphism in Pharmaceutical Solids. LC 99-11315. (Drugs & the Pharmaceutical Sciences Ser.). (Illus.). 448p. 1999. text 185.00 (*0-8247-0237-9*) Dekker.

Brittain, A. & Morton, P. Engraving on Precious Metals. (Illus.). 228p. 1988. 35.00 (*0-7198-0022-6*, Pub. by NAG Press) Antique Collect.

Brittain, Angela K. Don't Forget to Look Up: A Christian's Guide to Overcoming Anxiety & Panic Attacks. LC 97-94922. 105p. (Orig.). 1998. pap. 10.95 (*0-9662003-0-6*) Brittain Communs.

Brittain, Bill. All the Money in the World. LC 77-25635. (Trophy Bk.). (Illus.). 160p. (J). (gr. 4-7). 1982. pap. 4.95 (*0-06-440128-6*, HarpTrophy) HarpC Child Bks.

— All the Money in the World. 1982. 10.05 (*0-606-01068-8*, Pub. by Turtleback) Demco.

— Devil's Donkey. LC 80-7907. (Illus.). 128p. (J). (gr. 3-7). 1981. lib. bdg. 14.89 (*0-06-020683-7*) HarpC Child Bks.

— Dr. Dredd's Wagon of Wonders. (J). 1990. mass mkt. 3.50 (*0-06-107011-4*, Harp PBks) HarpC.

— Dr. Dredd's Wagon of Wonders. LC 86-45775. (Illus.). 192p. (J). (gr. 4-7). 1987. lib. bdg. 15.89 (*0-06-020714-0*) HarpC Child Bks.

— Dr. Dredd's Wagon of Wonders. LC 86-45775. (Trophy Bk.). (Illus.). 192p. (J). (gr. 4-7). 1989. pap. 4.95 (*0-06-440289-4*, HarpTrophy) HarpC Child Bks.

— Dr. Dredd's Wagon of Wonders. (J). 1987. 9.60 (*0-606-04135-4*, Pub. by Turtleback) Demco.

— The Fantastic Freshman. LC 87-35051. 160p. (J). (gr. 5-9). 1988. 11.95 (*0-06-020718-3*) HarpC Child Bks.

— The Fantastic Freshman. LC 87-35051. (Trophy Keypoint Bk.). 160p. (YA). (gr. 7 up). 1990. mass mkt. 3.25 (*0-06-447016-4*, HarpTrophy) HarpC Child Bks.

— Ghost from Beneath the Sea. LC 92-1091. 1994. 9.60 (*0-606-06408-7*, Pub. by Turtleback) Demco.

— My Buddy, the King. LC 88-35704. (Trophy Bk.). 144p. (J). (gr. 5-8). 1992. pap. 3.95 (*0-06-440339-4*, HarpTrophy) HarpC Child Bks.

— The Mystery of the Several Sevens. LC 93-47076. (Illus.). 88p. (J). (gr. 2-5). 1994. lib. bdg. 12.89 (*0-06-024462-3*) HarpC Child Bks.

— Professor Popkin's Prodigious Polish: A Tale of Coven Tree. LC 89-78221. (Illus.). 160p. (J). (gr. 3-7). 1991. 13.95 (*0-06-020726-4*) HarpC Child Bks.

— Shape-Changer. LC 93-27268. (Trophy Bk.). 112p. (J). (gr. 3-7). 1995. pap. 4.95 (*0-06-440514-1*, HarpTrophy) HarpC Child Bks.

— Shape-Changer. (J). 1995. 9.60 (*0-606-08453-3*, Pub. by Turtleback) Demco.

— Who Knew There'd Be Ghosts? (J). 1988. 9.60 (*0-606-03677-6*, Pub. by Turtleback) Demco.

— Who Knew There'd Be Ghosts. LC 84-48496. (Trophy Bk.). (Illus.). 128p. (J). (gr. 4-7). 1988. pap. 4.95 (*0-06-440224-X*, HarpTrophy) HarpC Child Bks.

— Wings. LC 90-19785. 128p. (J). (gr. 4-7). 1991. 13.95 (*0-06-020648-9*) HarpC Child Bks.

— Wings. LC 90-19785. (Trophy Bk.). 144p. (J). (gr. 4-7). 1995. pap. 4.95 (*0-06-440612-1*, HarpTrophy) HarpC Child Bks.

— Wings A Novel. 1995. 9.60 (*0-606-08457-6*, Pub. by Turtleback) Demco.

— The Wish Giver: Three Tales of Coven Tree. LC 82-48264. (Illus.). 192p. (J). (gr. 3-7). 1983. 14.00 (*0-06-020686-1*) HarpC Child Bks.

— The Wish Giver: Three Tales of Coven Tree. LC 82-48264. (Illus.). 192p. (J). (gr. 4-7). 1983. lib. bdg. 15.89 (*0-06-020687-X*) HarpC Child Bks.

— The Wish Giver: Three Tales of Coven Tree. LC 82-48264. (Trophy Bk.). (Illus.). 192p. (J). (gr. 4-7). 1986. pap. 5.95 (*0-06-440168-5*, HarpTrophy) HarpC Child Bks.

— The Wish Giver: Three Tales of Coven Tree. (J). 1983. 10.05 (*0-606-01967-7*, Pub. by Turtleback) Demco.

Brittain, C. Dale. A Bad Spell in Yurt. 320p. 1991. mass mkt. 5.99 (*0-671-72075-9*) Baen Bks.

— Daughter of Magic. 352p. 1996. mass mkt. 5.99 (*0-671-87720-8*) Baen Bks.

***Brittain, C. Dale.** Is This Apocalypse Necessary? LC 00-32054. 2000. write for info. (*1-888683-06-6*, Wooster Bk.

Brittain, C. Dale. Mage Quest. 368p. (Orig.). 1993. mass mkt. 4.99 (*0-671-72169-0*) Baen Bks.

— The Witch & the Cathedral. 352p. (Orig.). 1995. mass mkt. 5.99 (*0-671-87661-9*) Baen Bks.

— The Wood Nymph & the Cranky Saint. 320p. 1993. mass mkt. 4.99 (*0-671-72156-9*) Baen Bks.

Brittain, C. Dale & Bouchard, Robert. Count Scar. 352p. 1997. per. 5.99 (*0-671-87801-8*) Baen Bks.

***Brittain, Charles.** Philo of Larissa: The Last of the Academic Sceptics. (Oxford Classical Monographs). 280p. 2001. text 70.00 (*0-19-815298-1*) OUP.

***Brittain, Colin.** Scuba Diving. 1999. pap. 29.95 (*1-86126-279-5*, Pub. by Crolwood) Trafalgar.

Brittain, Cynthia G. General Chemistry Experiments for the Allied Health Student: A Prescription for Common Laboratory Ailments. 2nd ed. 88p. (C). 1995. pap. text, per. 16.95 (*0-8403-7338-4*) Kendall-Hunt.

***Brittain, David.** Creative Camera: Thirty Years of Writing. (Illus.). 300p. 2000. pap. 29.95 (*0-7190-5805-8*, Pub. by Manchester Univ Pr); text 69.95 (*0-7190-5804-X*, Pub. by Manchester Univ Pr) St Martin.

Brittain, Grady B. Platy: The Child in Us. LC 81-6503. (Illus.). 53p. (Orig.). (J). (ps-8). 1981. pap. 5.00 (*0-86663-761-3*) Ide Hse.

Brittain, H. G. Analytical Applications of Circular Dichroism. Purdie, N., ed. LC 93-38647. (Techniques & Instrumentation in Analytical Chemistry Ser.: Vol. 14). 358p. 1993. 246.50 (*0-444-89508-6*) Elsevier.

Brittain, Harry G. Physical Characterization of Pharmaceutical Solids. (Drugs & the Pharmaceutical Sciences Ser.: Vol. 70). (Illus.). 440p. 1995. text 175.00 (*0-8247-9372-2*) Dekker.

Brittain, Harry G., ed. Analytical Profiles of Drug Substances & Excipients, Vol. 23. (Illus.). 691p. 1993. text 116.00 (*0-12-260822-4*) Acad Pr.

— Analytical Profiles of Drug Substances & Excipients, Vol. 23. (Illus.). 611p. 1994. text 105.00 (*0-12-260823-2*) Acad Pr.

Brittain, Harry G., ed. Analytical Profiles of Drug Substances & Excipients, Vol. 24. (Illus.). 619p. 1996. text 99.00 (*0-12-260824-0*) Acad Pr.

— Analytical Profiles of Drug Substances & Excipients Vol. 26. 650p. 1999. 99.00 (*0-12-260826-7*) Acad Pr.

Brittain, Harry G., et al, eds. Analytical Profiles of Drug Substances & Excipients, Vol. 25. (Illus.). 582p. 1998. text 99.00 (*0-12-260825-9*) Morgan Kaufmann.

Brittain, J. R. J. Oversized Air Handling Plant. 1997. pap. 40.00 (*0-86022-463-5*, Pub. by Build Servs Info Assn) St Mut.

— Oversized Cooling & Pumping Plant. 1997. pap. 40.00 (*0-86022-464-3*, Pub. by Build Servs Info Assn) St Mut.

— Oversized Heating Plant. 1997. pap. 40.00 (*0-86022-469-4*, Pub. by Build Servs Info Assn) St Mut.

Brittain, James E. Alexanderson: Pioneer in American Electrical Engineering. (Studies in the History of Technology: No. 12). 374p. 1992. text 55.00 (*0-8018-4228-X*) Johns Hopkins.

Brittain, Janelle. Star Team Dynamics: 12 Lessons Learned from Experienced Team Builders. LC 98-33952. (Illus.). 224p. 1998. pap. 16.95 (*1-886939-28-4*) OakHill Pr VA.

Brittain, Joan T. Laurence Stallings. Bowman, Sylvia E., ed. LC 74-23831. (Twayne's United States Authors Ser.). 127p. (C). 1975. 17.95 (*0-8057-0686-0*) Irvington.

Brittain, John A. Corporate Dividend Policy. LC 66-15642. (Studies of Government Finance). 272p. reprint ed. pap. 84.40 (*0-608-16787-8*, 202640000049) Bks Demand.

— Inheritance & the Inequality of Material Wealth. LC 77-91814. (Brookings Institution Studies in Social Experimentation). 111p. reprint ed. pap. 34.50 (*0-608-14530-0*, 202536500043) Bks Demand.

— The Inheritance of Economic Status. LC 76-56369. (Brookings Institution Studies in Social Experimentation). 199p. reprint ed. pap. 61.70 (*0-608-12150-9*, 202536600043) Bks Demand.

***Brittain, John N.** The Backside of God: And Other Occasional Sermons. LC 99-52794. 2000. pap. 9.95 (*0-7880-1558-3*) CSS OH.

— Living Vertically: Gospel Sermons for Lent/Easter, Cycle C. LC 00-35799. 2000. disk 10.95 (*0-7880-1732-2*) CSS OH.

***Brittain, John Neal.** Living Vertically: Gospel Sermons for Lent/Easter, Cycle C. LC 00-35799. 110p. 2000. pap. 10.95 (*0-7880-1731-4*) CSS OH.

Brittain, Mary A. A Snake Called George. (Illus.). 32p. (Orig.). (gr. 1-12). 1987. pap. 0.50 (*0-917134-13-3*) NC Natl Sci.

Brittain, Mary Ann. A Whale Called Trouble. (Illus.). 24p. (J). (gr. 1-12). 1985. pap. 0.50 (*0-917134-08-7*) NC Natl Sci.

Brittain, P., jt. auth. see Cox, R.

Brittain, Robert E. & Griffith, Benjamin W. A Pocket Guide to Correct Punctuation. 3rd ed. LC 97-634. 128p. 1997. pap. 6.95 (*0-8120-9814-5*) Barron.

Brittain, Vera. Testament of Friendship: The Story of Winifred Holtby LC 80-54510. xxxii, 442p. 1985. 7.95 (*0-87223-680-3*) Playboy Ent.

— Testament of Friendship: The Story of Winifred Holtby. LC 80-54516. xxxii, 442 p. 1981. write for info. (*0-87223-679-X*) Playboy Ent.

— Testament of Youth. 672p. 1994. pap. 16.95 (*0-14-018844-4*, Penguin Classics) Viking Penguin.

— Vera Brittain's Diary, 1939-1945. large type ed. 512p. 1993. 27.99 (*0-7089-8716-8*) Ulverscroft.

Brittain, Vera, et al. Letters from a Lost Generation: First World War Letters of Vera Brittain & Four Friends. LC 98-42383. (Illus.). 448p. 1999. text 29.95 (*1-55553-379-5*) NE U Pr.

Brittain, Victoria. The Death of Dignity: Angola's Civil War. LC 97-30309. 1998. write for info. (*0-7453-1252-7*, Pub. by Pluto GBR) Stylus Pub VA.

— Death of Dignity: Angola's Civil War. LC 97-30309. 200p. 1998. 49.95 (*0-86543-635-5*); 16.95 (*0-86543-636-3*) Africa World.

B

— Death of Dignity: Angola's Civil War. 1998. pap. text 14.95 (0-7453-1247-0, Pub. by Pluto GBR) Stylus Pub VA.

Brittain, Victoria & Omaar, Rakiya, eds. States of Africa, Issue 7. 224p. 1998. pap. 19.50 (0-85315-849-5, Pub. by Lawrence & Wishart) NYU Pr.

Brittain, Virginia T. The Berryhill Family History. (Illus.). 338p. 1982. reprint ed. 25.00 (0-89308-293-7, FH 16) Southern Hist Pr.

Brittain, W. Bruce, jt. auth. see Cleveland, Harold Van B.

Brittain, W. Lambert, jt. auth. see Lowenfeld, Viktor.

Brittan, Arthur. Meanings & Situations. (International Library of Sociology Ser.). 222p. 1973. 19.95 (0-7100-7509-X, Routledge Thoemms) Routledge.

Brittan, D. The People of Thailand. LC 96-47347. (Celebrating the Peoples & Civilizations of Southeast Asia Ser.). (J). 1997. lib. bdg. 15.93 (0-8239-5126-X, PowerKids) Rosen Group.

Brittan, Dolly. The Hmong. LC 97-10184. (Celebrating the Peoples & Civilizations of Southeast Asia Ser.). (J). 1997. lib. bdg. 15.93 (0-8239-5128-6, PowerKids) Rosen Group.

— The People of Cambodia. LC 97-7982. (Celebrating the Peoples & Civilizations of Southeast Asia Ser.). (J). 1997. lib. bdg. 15.93 (0-8239-5129-4, PowerKids) Rosen Group.

— The People of Laos. LC 97-5879. (Celebrating the Peoples & Civilizations of Southeast Asia Ser.). (J). 1997. lib. bdg. 15.93 (0-8239-5124-3, PowerKids) Rosen Group.

— The People of the Philippines. LC 97-8377. (Celebrating the Peoples & Civilizations of Southeast Asia Ser.). (Illus.). 24p. (J). (gr. k-4). 1997. lib. bdg. 15.93 (0-8239-5127-8, PowerKids) Rosen Group.

— The People of Vietnam. LC 96-39805. (Celebrating the Peoples & Civilizations of Southeast Asia Ser.). (J). 1997. lib. bdg. 15.93 (0-8239-5125-1, PowerKids) Rosen Group.

Brittan, Gordon G. Kant's Theory of Science. LC 77-85531. 228p. reprint ed. pap. 70.70 (0-8357-4674-7, 203762000008) Bks Demand.

Brittan, Gordon G., Jr., ed. Causality, Method, & Modality: Essays in Honor of Jules Vuillemin. (University of Western Ontario Series in Philosophy of Science). 248p. 1990. lib. bdg. 129.50 (0-7923-1045-4, Pub. by Kluwer Academic) Kluwer Academic.

Brittan, Gordon G., Jr., jt. auth. see Lambert, Karel.

Brittan, Leon. European Competition Policy: Keeping the Playing Field Level. 120p. 1992. 37.00 (1-85753-077-2, Pub. by Brasseys) Brasseys.

— Globalisation vs. Sovereignty? The European Response: The 1997 Rede Lecture & Related Speeches. LC 98-150734. 86p. 1998. pap. text 14.95 (0-521-63884-4) Cambridge U Pr.

Brittan, Martin R. Rasboras: Keeping & Breeding Them in Captivity. 64p. 1998. pap. 6.95 (0-7938-0375-6, RE626) TFH Pubns.

Brittan, Samuel. Capitalism with a Human Face. LC 94-28484. 320p. 1995. 90.00 (1-85278-446-6); pap. 25.00 (1-85278-449-0) E Elgar.

— Capitalism with a Human Face. (Illus.). 320p. 1996. pap. 19.95 (0-674-09492-1) HUP.

Brittan, Samuel & Hamlin, Alan, eds. Market Capitalism & Moral Values: Proceedings of Section F (Economics) of the British Association for the Advancement of Science, 1993. 168p. 1995. 85.00 (1-85898-080-1) E Elgar.

Brittan, Samuel & Webb, Steven. Beyond the Welfare State: An Examination of Basic Incomes in a Market Economy. (David Hume Papers: No. 17). 78p. 1990. pap. text 14.00 (0-08-040915-6, Pub. by Aberdeen U Pr) Macmillan.

Brittany, Lynn. Ancient Greece: 4,000 Years of History & Mythology to Unolck & Discover. (Treasure Chest Ser.). (Illus.). 32p. (J). 1998. pap. 19.95 (0-7624-0193-1) Running Pr.

Britten, A. F., et al, eds. Blood Transfusion: A Basic Text. (WHO Regional Publications: No. 7). xi, 171p. 1994. pap. text 15.00 (92-9021-181-4, 1440007) World Health.

Britten, A. F., jt. ed. see Gibbs, W. N.

Britten, B. & Britten, C. Amor y Matrimonio.Tr. of Love & Marriage. (SPA.). 4.99 (0-7899-0405-5, 498199) Editorial Unilit.

Britten, B. & Britten, C. Respuestas Matrimoniales.Tr. of Answers for Your Marriage. (SPA.). 6.99 (0-7899-0404-7, 498198) Editorial Unilit.

Britten, Benjamin. Peter Grimes & Gloriana. John, Nicholas, ed. (English National Opera Guide Series: Bilingual Libretto, Articles: No. 24). (Illus.). 128p. (Orig.). 1984. pap. 9.95 (0-7145-3856-6) Riverrun NY.

Britten, C., jt. auth. see Britten, B.

Britten, D. J., et al, eds. Lie Algebras & Related Topics: Conference Proceedings of the Canadian Mathematical Society, Vol. 5. LC 85-26818. 382p. 1986. reprint ed. pap. 57.00 (0-8218-6009-7, CMSAMS/5) Am Math.

Britten, Emma H. Ghost Land: Researches into the Mysteries of Occultism. 355p. 1996. reprint ed. spiral bd. 21.00 (0-7873-0120-5) Hlth Research.

— Nineteenth Century Miracles: or Spirits & Their Work in Every Country of the Earth. LC 75-36831. (Occult Ser.). (Illus.). 1976. reprint ed. 47.95 (0-405-07943-5) Ayer.

Britten, F. J. Watch & Clockmakers' Handbook, Dictionary & Guide. (Illus.). 500p. 1976. 29.50 (1-85149-192-9) Antique Collect.

— Watch & Clockmakers' Handbook, Dictionary & Guide. (Illus.). 500p. 1976. reprint ed. 29.50 (0-902028-46-4) Antique Collect.

Britten, F. W. Horological Hints & Helps. (Illus.). 375p. 1977. reprint ed. 29.50 (0-902028-64-2) Antique Collect.

Britten, Helen. Food Preparation Essentials. 2nd ed. 114p. (C). 1996. spiral bd. 16.95 (0-7872-2758-7) Kendall-Hunt.

Britten, James. Old Country & Farming Words: Gleaned from Agricultural Books. (English Dialect Society Publications: No. 30). 1974. reprint ed. pap. 25.00 (0-8115-0457-3) Periodicals Srv.

Britten, James, ed. The Names of Herbes: A. D. 1548. (English Dialect Society Publications: No. 34). 1974. reprint ed. pap. 25.00 (0-8115-0460-3) Periodicals Srv.

Britten, James, ed. see Aubrey, John.

Britten-Jones, Mark. Fixed Income & Interest Rate Derivative Analysis. LC 99-164256. 220p. 1998. text 64.95 (0-7506-4012-X) Buttrwrth-Heinemann.

Britten, Michael J., jt. auth. see Eggland, Steven A.

Britten, Thomas A. American Indians in World War I. 254p. 1999. pap. 18.95 (0-8263-2090-2) U of NM Pr.

***Britten, Thomas A.** A Brief History of the Seminole-Negro Indian Scouts. LC 99-29551. (Native American Studies: Vol. 7). 140p. 1999. text 69.95 (0-7734-7963-5) E Mellen.

Britten, Walter S. & DeArman, J. Sold: A Biography by Legendary Auctioneer. (Illus.). 200p. 1988. 21.00 (0-9619686-0-5) Britten Trust.

Brittenham, Dean & Brittenham, Greg. Stronger Abs & Back. LC 96-48346. (Illus.). 248p. (Orig.). 1997. pap. 16.95 (0-88011-558-0, PBRI0558) Human Kinetics.

Brittenham, Greg. Complete Conditioning for Basketball. LC 95-13033. (Illus.). 264p. (Orig.). 1995. pap. 15.95 (0-87322-881-2, PBRI0881) Human Kinetics.

Brittenham, Greg, et al. Safe Plyometrics for Soccer: Field & Goalie Play. unabridged ed. (Illus.). 36p. 1997. pap. 5.95 (1-891200-05-4) Performance Conditioning.

— 3-Step Approach to Better Jumping: Beginning Program. unabridged ed. (Illus.). 28p. 1996. pap. 5.95 (1-891200-03-8) Performance Conditioning.

Brittenham, Greg, jt. auth. see Brittenham, Dean.

Brittenham, Jill, ed. see Bjelland, Harley.

Brittenham, Jill C., ed. see Hayden, Shila.

Brittian, L. W. Roadway Illumination Electrical Exam Course. 1998. 34.58 (1-56870-301-5) RonJon Pub.

Brittin. International Law for Seagoing Officers. 5th ed. 503p. 1994. pap. text 29.95 (1-55750-074-6) Naval Inst Pr.

Brittin, Helen C. Food Preparations Essentials. 3rd ed. 118p. (C). 1998. spiral bd. 20.95 (0-7872-5332-4, 41533201) Kendall-Hunt.

Brittin, Norman A. Edna St. Vincent Millay. rev. ed. (United States Authors Ser.: No. 116). 184p. 1982. 32.00 (0-8057-7362-2) Macmillan.

Brittin, Robert P. Central Vermont: The South End: Remembering the Banana Belt. (Illus.). 84p. 1995. pap. 20.95 (0-942035-32-1) South Platte.

Brittin, Wesley E., et al, eds. Air & Water Pollution: Proceedings of the Summer Workshop, August 3 to August 15, 1970, University of Colorado. LC 72-165367. (Illus.). 631p. reprint ed. pap. 195.70 (0-8357-5514-2, 203513000093) Bks Demand.

— Boulder Lecture Notes in Theoretical Physics, 1963, Vol. 6. x, 516p. 1964. text 557.00 (0-677-13030-9) Gordon & Breach.

— Boulder Lecture Notes in Theoretical Physics, 1964: Vol. 7-B, Elementary Particles, Vol. 7. viii, 472p. 1968. text 613.00 (0-677-13050-3) Gordon & Breach.

— Boulder Lecture Notes in Theoretical Physics, 1965: Vol. 8-A, Statistical Physics & Solid State Physics. 364p. 1966. 418.00 (0-685-01946-2) Gordon & Breach.

— Boulder Lecture Notes in Theoretical Physics, 1965: Vol. 8-C, Nuclear Structure Physics, Vol. 8. x, 678p. 1966. text 779.00 (0-677-13090-2) Gordon & Breach.

Brittin, Wesley E. & Odabasi, Halis, eds. Topics in Modern Physics: A Tribute to Edward U. Condon. LC 70-135286. (Illus.). 392p. reprint ed. pap. 121.60 (0-8357-5524-X, 203514000093) Bks Demand.

Brittin, Wesley E., jt. ed. see Barut, Asim O.

Brittin, Wesley E., ed. see Conference on De Sitter & Conformal Groups & Their.

Brittingham, Angela, et al. National Household Survey on Drug Abuse: Main Findings, 1996. (Illus.). 328p. (C). 1998. pap. text 45.00 (0-7881-7419-3) DIANE Pub.

Brittingham, Barbara E. & Pezzullo, Thomas R. The Campus Green: Fund Raising in Higher Education. Fife, Jonathan D., ed. LC 90-60889. (ASHE-ERIC Higher Education Reports: No. 90-1). 128p. (Orig.). (C). 1990. pap. text 24.00 (0-9623882-8-9) GWU Grad Schl E&HD.

Brittingham, Geoffrey H. Illustrated Children's Bible. LC 94-32772. 256p. (J). 1995. 14.95 (1-57102-018-7, Ideals Child) Hambleton-Hill.

— 'Twas the Week Before Christmas Coloring Book. 32p. (Orig.). (J). (ps-3). 1996. pap. 2.49 (1-57102-093-4, Ideals Child) Hambleton-Hill.

Brittingham, Hazel D. Lantern on Lewes: Where the Past Is Present. Ippolito, Elaine, ed. & illus. by. LC 99-191660. 96p. 1998. pap. 9.95 (0-9663956-0-3) Lewestown Pubs.

Brittingham, Janet R. Census Index of Bucks County, Pennsylvania, 1810. LC 84-60426. 266p. 1984. spiral bd. 18.00 (0-9613351-0-6) J R Brittingham.

— Eighteen Eighty Census Index of Bucks County, PA. LC 85-70527. (Illus.). 182p. 1985. spiral bd. 14.00 (0-9613351-1-4) J R Brittingham.

Brittker, Boris, et al. Supplement to Federal Income Taxation, 1985. (C). 1985. pap. text. write for info. (0-318-59076-X, Aspen Law & Bus) Aspen Pub.

Brittlebank, Kate. Tipu Sultan's Search for Legitimacy: Islam & Kingship in a Hindu Domain. LC 98-164288. (Illus.). 206p. 1998. text 26.00 (0-19-563977-4) OUP.

Brittney, Lynne. Ancient Rome Treasure Chest. LC 97-76122. (Treasure Chest Ser.). (Illus.). 32p. (J). (gr. 3-8). 1998. 19.95 (0-7624-0351-9) Running Pr.

Britto, A. M. & Gunn, M. J. Critical State Soil Mechanics Via Finite Elements. LC 86-33791. (Civil & Mechanical Engineering Ser.). 488p. 1987. text 157.00 (0-470-20816-3) P-H.

Britto, Anthony. Tattoo. LC 96-45540. 400p. 1997. 24.95 (0-312-15220-5, Thomas Dunne) St Martin.

Britto, Francis. Diglossia: A Study of the Theory with Application to Tamil. LC 86-14902. 384p. (Orig.). reprint ed. pap. 119.10 (0-7837-6307-7, 204602200010) Bks Demand.

Britto, Frank. Once upon a Cross: A Group of Short Christian Stories to Manifest God's Presence in You. LC 95-3990. 1995. 10.00 (1-877633-27-5) Luthers.

Britto, J. A. & Dalrymple-Hay, M. J. Pathways Through Surgical Finals. LC 93-12293. 200p. 1993. pap. text 25.00 (0-443-04806-1) Church.

Britto, Karen. Negotiations for a North American Free Trade Agreement. (State-Federal Issue Brief Ser.: Vol. 4, No. 5). 11p. 1991. pap. text 6.50 (1-55516-894-9, 8500-0405) Natl Conf State Legis.

Britto, Paul H., tr. see Sussekind, Flora.

Britto, Paulo H., tr. see Costa-Lima, Luiz.

Britto, Paulo H., tr. see Lima, Luiz C.

Britton, ed. see De Quevedo, F. DeQuevedo.

Britton, Alison & Margetts, Martina, contrib. by. The Raw & the Cooked: New Wokkin Clay in Britain. 96p. 1993. pap. 60.00 (0-905836-79-0, Pub. by Museum Modern Art) St Mut.

Britton, Alison, jt. auth. see Mclean, Sheila.

Britton, Allen P., et al. American Sacred Music Imprints, 1698-1810. 814p. 1990. 160.00 (0-912296-95-X, 42173) Am Antiquarian.

Britton, Andrew. Macroeconomic Policy in Britain, 1974-1987. (NIESR Economic & Social Studies: No. 34). (Illus.). 400p. (C). 1991. 65.00 (0-521-41004-5) Cambridge U Pr.

— Macroeconomic Policy in Britain, 1974-1987. (National Institute of Economic & Social Research Occasional Papers: No. 34). (Illus.). 384p. (C). 1994. pap. text 24.95 (0-521-47833-2) Cambridge U Pr.

— Policymaking with Macroeconomic Models. 282p. 1989. text 82.95 (0-566-05748-4, Pub. by Dartmth Pub) Ashgate Pub Co.

— Talking Films: The Best of the Guardian Film Lectures. 266p. 1992. 29.95 (1-872180-17-5, Pub. by Fourth Estate) Trafalgar.

Britton, Andrew & Mayes, David. Achieving Monetary Union in Europe. 160p. (C). 1992. 69.95 (0-8039-8718-8); pap. 22.95 (0-8039-8719-6) Sage.

Britton, Ann H. & Reed, Thomas J., eds. To My Beloved Wife & Boy at Home: The Letters & Diaries of Orderly Sergeant John F. L. Hartwell. LC 95-31189. (Illus.). 416p. 1997. 55.00 (0-8386-3675-6) Fairleigh Dickinson.

***Britton, Ann H. & Rohs, Timothy H.** Law & Mental Health Professionals: Delaware. LC 99-86786. 2000. 59.95 (1-55798-686-X) Am Psychol.

Britton, Anne. Essentials of Finance for Managers. (C). 2000. pap. text. write for info. (0-201-39834-6) Addison-Wesley.

Britton, Anne, jt. auth. see Waterston, Christopher.

Britton, B. K. & Pellegrini, Anthony D., eds. Narrative Thought & Narrative Language. 296p. (C). 1989. text 79.95 (0-8058-0099-9) L Erlbaum Assocs.

***Britton, Benjamin, prod.** Moon. limited ed. (Illus.). 12p. 1999. write for info. incl. cd-rom (0-9677388-1-4) Britton & Assocs.

Britton, Betty L. Promises! Promises! Adventures of Sargento Tico, Cataluna to California, 1766-1802. LC 96-95504. (ENG & SPA., Illus.). 302p. 1997. lib. bdg. 28.50 (0-9655914-0-9) Juanez Bks.

Britton, Bruce K. Executive Control Processes in Reading. (Reading & Comprehension Rand Spiro Ser.). 328p. 1987. 65.00 (0-89859-883-4) L Erlbaum Assocs.

Britton, Bruce K., et al, eds. Learning from Textbooks: Theory & Practice. 208p. 1993. text 49.95 (0-8058-0677-6) L Erlbaum Assocs.

Britton, Bruce K. & Black, John B., eds. Understanding Expository Text: A Theoretical & Practical Handbook for Analyzing Explanatory Text. LC 84-13807. (Psychology of Reading & Reading Instruction Ser.). (Illus.). 421p. reprint ed. pap. 130.60 (0-8357-4207-5, 203698400003) Bks Demand.

Britton, Bruce K. & Glynn, Shawn M., eds. Computer Writing Environments: Theory, Research & Design. 184p. (C). 1989. text 32.50 (0-89859-961-X) L Erlbaum Assocs.

Britton, Bruce K. & Graesser, Arthur C., eds. Models of Understanding Text. (Publication of the Cognitive Studies Group of the Institute for Behavioral Research at the University of Georgia). 376p. 1995. text 79.95 (0-8058-1848-0) L Erlbaum Assocs.

— Models of Understanding Text. (Publication of the Cognitive Studies Group & the Institute for Behavioral Research at the University of Georgia). 376p. 1996. pap. 36.00 (0-8058-1849-9) L Erlbaum Assocs.

Britton, Bruce K., jt. ed. see Foltz, Peter W.

***Britton, Burnett.** Gandhi Arrives in South Africa. (Illus.). 744p. 1999. 30.00 (0-934676-96-8) Greenlf Bks.

Britton, Carol & Doake, Jill. Software System Development: A Gentle Introduction. 2nd ed. LC 96-9028. (International Series In Software E). 1996. write for info. (0-07-709224-4) McGraw.

— Software Systems Development: A Gentle Introduction. LC 92-26809. (International Series in Software Engineering). 240p. 1993. 30.00 (0-07-707712-1) McGraw.

Britton, Celia. Edouard Glissant & Postcolonial Theory: Strategies of Language & Resistance. LC 98-48754. (New World Studies). 256p. 1999. text 55.00 (0-8139-1848-0); pap. text 19.50 (0-8139-1849-9) U Pr of Va.

Britton, Celia, intro. Claude Simon. LC 92-28025. (Modern Literatures in Perspective Ser.). (C). 1993. text 63.50 (0-582-08160-2, 79752); pap. text 28.50 (0-582-08161-0, 79751) Longman.

Britton, Celia, tr. see Metz, Christian.

Britton, Chris, jt. auth. see Worthington, Ian.

Britton, Coburn. An Abecedarium. 64p. 1990. pap. 8.95 (0-86316-001-8) Writers & Readers.

— Lesser Goods & Other Poems. 64p. 1988. pap. 8.95 (0-86316-106-5) Writers & Readers.

Britton, Colleen. Celebrate Communion. 79p. (J). (gr. 1-6). 1984. pap. 9.95 (0-940754-26-6) Ed Ministries.

— Create & Use Bulletin Boards That Teach. 1990. pap. 12.95 (0-940754-96-7, 5410) Ed Ministries.

— Palestine 30 A. D. You Are There. (Illus.). 73p. (Orig.). (J). (ps-6). 1987. pap. 12.95 (0-940754-38-X) Ed Ministries.

***Britton, Crystal A.** African American Art: The Long Struggle. (Illus.). 1998. 16.95 (1-880908-72-7) Todtri Prods.

Britton, Dana. Changing Habits. rev. ed. 18p. 1989. ring bd. 2.00 (0-944478-09-3) Dock Pub Co.

— Hidden Treasures Cookbook: Recipes for Health & Healing. 45p. 1994. spiral bd. 5.00 (0-944478-13-1) Dock Pub Co.

— How to Enjoy Better Health: A Self Help Guide to Health & Healing. 2nd ed. LC 89-71428. 98p. 1990. pap. 12.95 (0-944478-10-7) Dock Pub Co.

— Meditation: Quieting the Conscious Mind. 23p. 1989. ring bd. 2.00 (0-944478-08-5) Dock Pub Co.

— The Original Vegetarian Food Combining Cookbook: Recipes for Health & Healing. Orig. Title: Hidden Treasures Cookbook. (Illus.). 55p. (Orig.). 1997. pap., spiral bd. 6.00 (0-944478-14-X) Dock Pub Co.

— Understanding Communication: Hidden Insight into Human Communication. 35p. (Orig.). 1987. pap. 5.00 (0-944478-00-X) Dock Pub Co.

Britton, David. The Adventures of Meng & Ecker. (Illus.). (Orig.). 1997. pap. 20.95 (0-86130-099-8, Pub. by Savoy Bks) AK Pr Dist.

Britton, Denis K., ed. Agriculture in Britain: Changing Pressures & Policies. 214p. (Orig.). 1990. pap. text 45.00 (0-85198-655-2) OUP.

Britton, Denis K., ed. see Marks, Hilary F.

Britton, Dennis & Gun, Terry. The Complete Handbook of Flyfishing Knots, Lines, Leaders & Rigs. 288p. 1999. pap. 34.95 (0-07-079339-5) McGraw.

Britton, Derek. Lady Chatterley: The Making of the Novel. 256p. 1988. 44.95 (0-04-800075-2) Routledge.

Britton, Derek, ed. English Historical Linguistics 1994: Papers from the 8th International Conference on English Historical Linguistics (8 ICEHL, Edinburgh, 19-23 September 1994) LC 96-667. (Current Issues in Linguistic Theory Ser.: Vol. 135). viii, 403p. 1996. lib. bdg. 84.00 (1-55619-590-7) J Benjamins Pubng Co.

Britton, Diane F., jt. ed. see Britton, J. D.

Britton, Dorothy, tr. see Basho, Matsu.

Britton, Dorothy, tr. see Kuroyanagi, Tetsuko.

Britton, Dorothy, tr. see Princess Chichibu, et al.

Britton, E. B., jt. auth. see Lawrence, John.

Britton, Edward C. & Winans, J. Merritt. Growing from Infancy to Adulthood: A Summary of the Changing Characteristics of Children & Youth. LC 58-7149. (Illus.). (Orig.). 1958. pap. text 7.95 (0-89197-193-9) Irvington.

Britton, Edward D., ed. Examining the Examinations: An International Comparison of Science & Mathematics Examinations for College-Bound Students. (Evaluation in Education & Human Services Ser.). 320p. (C). 1996. lib. bdg. 97.00 (0-7923-9692-8) Kluwer Academic.

***Britton, Edward D., et al.** Connecting Mathematics & Science to Workplace Contexts: A Guide to Curriculum Materials. LC 99-6183. (1-Off Ser.). (Illus.). 272p. 1999. lib. bdg. 69.96 (0-8039-6866-3) Sage.

— Connecting Mathematics & Science to Workplace Contexts: A Guide to Curriculum Materials. LC 99-6183. (1-Off Ser.). (Illus.). 272p. 1999. pap. 32.95 (0-8039-6867-1) Sage.

Britton, Edward D., jt. auth. see Raizen, Senta A.

Britton, Eudine M. John Morgan (b. 1784 NJ) & His Family of Georgia: His Sons: William, Richard, James J., Samuel J., & John B. Morgan; His Daughters: Lucinda M. Cannon, Nancy M. Vickery, Emma M. Adams, Lodoizky M. Boss & Deidama M. Jackson. LC 89-62036. (Illus.). 320p. (Orig.). 1989. 35.00 (0-685-26992-2) E M Britton.

Britton, F. J. The Escapements: Their Action Construction & Proportion. LC 84-16875. (Illus.). 66p. 1984. reprint ed. pap. 6.95 (0-930163-22-2) Arlington Bk.

Britton, Frances. Basic Nursing Skills. (Illus.). 272p. 1981. pap. text 7.95 (0-87619-921-X) P-H.

Britton, Frank. English Delftware in the Bristol Collection. (Illus.). 332p. 1983. 95.00 (0-85667-152-5) Sothebys Pubns.

Britton, Frank L. Behind Communism. 97p. (Orig.). 1979. reprint ed. pap. 3.50 (0-911038-82-5, 0230, Noontide Pr) Legion Survival.

Britton, G., et al, eds. Carotenoids: Volumes 1A & 1B, 2 vols. Incl. Carotenoids Vol. 1B: Spectroscopy. (Illus.). 384p. 1994. 129.00 (0-8176-2909-2); 1995. 198.00 (0-8176-2910-6) Birkhauser.

— Carotenoids Vol. 2: Synthesis. 384p. 1996. 139.50 (3-7643-5297-3) Birkhauser.

— Carotenoids Vol. 3. 432p. 1998. 149.00 (3-7643-5829-7) Birkhauser.

— Carotenoids Vols. 1A & 1B: Isolation & Analysis; Spectroscopy. LC 94-40358. (Illus.). 368p. 1994. 129.00 (0-8176-2908-4) Birkhauser.

— Carotenoids Vols. 1A & 1B: "Key to Carotenoids", 3 vols. 1996. text 234.00 (0-8176-2936-X) Birkhauser.

Britton, Gregory, jt. auth. see Runde, Raymond E.

Britton, J. D. & Britton, Diane F., eds. History Outreach: Programs for Museums, Historical Organizations, & Academic History Departments. LC 93-26829. 214p. (C). 1994. lib. bdg. 25.50 (0-89464-586-2) Krieger.

An Asterisk (*) at the beginning of an entry indicates that the title is appearing for the first time.

Britton, J. L. Collected Works of A. M. Turing Vol. 2: Pure Mathematics. 286p. 1992. 132.00 (*0-444-88059-3*, North Holland) Elsevier.

Britton, Jack R., jt. auth. see Bello, Ignacio.

Britton, Jade & Kircher, Tamara. The Complete Book of Home Herbal Remedies: A Holistic Guide to Understanding & Treating Common Ailments with Herbs. (Illus.). 160p. (J). 1998. pap. 19.95 (*1-55209-176-7*) Firefly Bks Ltd.

Britton, James N. Language & Learning: The Importance of Speech in Children's Development. 2nd ed. LC 93-22156. 330p. 1993. pap. text 25.00 (*0-86709-335-8*, 0335, Pub. by Boynton Cook Pubs) Heinemann.

— Literature in Its Place. LC 92-24089. 136p. (J). 1993. pap. text 17.50 (*0-86709-315-3*, 0315, Pub. by Boynton Cook Pubs) Heinemann.

— Prospect & Retrospect: Selected Essays of James Britton. Pradl, Gordon M., ed. LC 82-14608. 218p. (C). 1982. pap. text 21.50 (*0-86709-043-X*, 0043, Pub. by Boynton Cook Pubs) Heinemann.

Britton, James N., et al, eds. Teaching & Learning English Worldwide. 356p. 1990. 99.00 (*1-85359-065-7*, Pub. by Multilingual Matters); pap. 39.95 (*1-85359-064-9*, Pub. by Multilingual Matters) Taylor & Francis.

Britton, James, pseud. The House on Remington Street. 527p. (Orig.). 1992. pap. 13.95 (*0-9634027-0-6*) Southern CA.

Britton, Jan, ed. see Cooper, Sally.

Britton, Janice F. Tales of an Uncommon Man: Uncle Ort's Keepsakes. LC 95-145389. 296p. 1994. pap. 14.95 (*0-9643940-0-6*) Slow Loris Pr.

Britton, Jill. Explorations with TesselMania! Activities for Math & Art Classrooms. Gideon, Joan, ed. (Illus.). 92p. (Orig.). 1996. pap. text 24.95 (*1-57232-270-5*, 21808) Seymour Pubns.

***Britton, Jill.** Symmetry & Tesselations: Investigation Patterns. (Illus.). 1999. pap. 14.95 (*0-7690-0083-5*) Seymour Pubns.

Britton, John. Remarks on the Life & Writings of William Shakespeare. LC 79-39531. reprint ed. 24.50 (*0-404-01086-5*) AMS Pr.

— Revolution & Ideology: Images of the Mexican Revolution in the United States. (Illus.). 288p. 1995. text 35.00 (*0-8131-1896-4*) U Pr of Ky.

Britton, John & Brayley, E. W. Memoirs of the Tower of London: Comprising Historical & Descriptive Accounts of That National Fortress & Palace. xvi, 374p. 1994. reprint ed. 52.50 (*0-8377-1977-1*, Rothman) W S Hein.

Britton, John & Harris, Richard. Tree-Pruning Guidelines. (Illus.). 14p. 1994. pap. 6.00 (*1-881956-07-5*) Int Soc Arboricult.

Britton, John, jt. auth. see Shepherd, Thomas H.

Britton, John A. The United States & Latin America: A Select Bibliography. LC 96-42962. (Magill Bibliographies Ser.). 1997. 38.00 (*0-8108-3248-8*) Scarecrow.

Britton, John A., ed. Molding the Hearts & Minds: Education, Communications, & Social Change in Latin America. LC 93-41937. (Jaguar Books on Latin America: No. 4). 275p. 1994. 55.00 (*0-8420-2489-1*) Scholarly Res Inc.

— Molding the Hearts & Minds: Education, Communications, & Social Change in Latin America, Vol. 4. LC 93-41937. (Jaguar Books on Latin America: No. 4). 275p. 1994. pap. 18.95 (*0-8420-2490-5*) Scholarly Res Inc.

Britton, John N. Canada & the Global Economy: The Geography of Structural & Technological Change. LC 97-160433. 472p. (C). 1996. pap. text 32.95 (*0-7735-1356-6*, Pub. by McG-Queens Univ Pr) CUP Services.

Britton, John N., ed. Canada & the Global Economy: The Geography of Structural & Technological Change. LC 97-160433. (Canadian Association of Geographers Series in Canadian Geography). 472p. 1996. 75.00 (*0-7735-0927-5*, Pub. by McG-Queens Univ Pr) CUP Services.

Britton, John N., et al. The Weakest Link: A Technological Perspective on Canadian Industrial Underdevelopment. LC 79-321656. (Background Study Ser.). 215 p. 1978. write for info. (*0-660-10100-9*, Pub. by Can7 Govern Pub) Intl Spec Bk.

Britton, Joseph C. & Morton, Brian. Shore Ecology of the Gulf of Mexico. (Illus.). 403p. 1989. 55.00 (*0-292-77610-1*); pap. 27.95 (*0-292-77626-8*) U of Tex Pr.

Britton, K., jt. ed. see Donato, L.

Britton, Karen G. Bale o' Cotton: The Mechanical Art of Cotton Ginning. LC 92-14229. (Centennial Series of the Association of Former Students: No. 43). (Illus.). 160p. (C). 1992. 29.95 (*0-89096-510-2*) Tex A&M Univ Pr.

Britton, Kimberly, ed. see Sill, Robert, et al.

***Britton, Laurence G.** Avoiding Static Ignition Hazards in Chemical Operations. LC 99-35855. 282p. 1999. 74.95 (*0-8169-0800-1*) Am Inst Chem Eng.

Britton, Lesley. Montessori Play & Learn: A Practical Guide for Parents & Children. (Illus.). 144p. (J). 1992. pap. 19.95 (*0-517-59182-0*, Crown) Crown Pub Group.

Britton, M. Decennial Supplements No. 12: Health of Adult Britain 1841-1994, 2 vols. (OPCS Series DS: No. 12). 246p. 1997. pap. 130.00 (*0-11-620909-7*, HM09097, Pub. by Statnry Office) Bernan Associates.

— Dicennial Supplements. (English Life Tables Ser.: No. 15). 246p. 1997. pap. 55.00 (*0-11-620925-9*, Pub. by Statnry Office) Bernan Associates.

Britton, N. F. Reaction-Diffusion Equations & Their Applications to Biology. 1986. text 128.00 (*0-12-135140-8*) Acad Pr.

Britton, Nan. The President's Daughter. 1977. 30.95 (*0-8369-7132-9*, 7966) Ayer.

Britton, Nathaniel L. & Brown, Addison. Illustrated Flora of the Northern United States & Canada, 3 vols., Vol. 1. (Illus.). 1970. reprint ed. pap. 16.95 (*0-486-22642-5*) Dover.

— Illustrated Flora of the Northern United States & Canada, 3 vols., Vol. 2. (Illus.). 1970. reprint ed. pap. 16.95 (*0-486-22643-3*) Dover.

— Illustrated Flora of the Northern United States & Canada, 3 vols., Vol. 3. (Illus.). 1970. reprint ed. pap. 16.95 (*0-486-22644-1*) Dover.

— Illustrated Flora of the Northern United States & Canada, Vols. 1-3. 2nd enl. rev. ed. (Illus.). 1990. 83.25 (*0-8446-0514-X*) Peter Smith.

Britton, Nathaniel L. & Rose, J. N. Cactaceae: Descriptions & Illustrations of Plants of the Cactus Family, 4 vols. in 2, Vol. 1. 2nd ed. (Illus.). 1963. 37.50 (*0-486-21191-6*) Dover.

— Cactaceae: Descriptions & Illustrations of Plants of the Cactus Family, 4 vols. in 2, Vol. 2. 2nd ed. (Illus.). 1963. 37.50 (*0-486-21192-4*) Dover.

***Britton, Pamela.** My Fallen Angel. 352p. 2000. mass mkt. 5.99 (*0-06-101431-1*) HarpC.

Britton, Patricia A. California Legal Filing Directory. LC 98-169485. 1998. write for info. (*0-07-172266-1*) McGraw.

***Britton, Paul.** Jigsaw Man. 2000. 29.95 (*0-593-04066-X*, Pub. by Transworld Publishers Ltd) Trafalgar.

Britton, Paul R. & Stallings, John W. Leadership Is Empowering People. LC 86-9193. 374p. (Orig.). (C). 1986. pap. text 31.50 (*0-8191-5410-5*) U Pr of Amer.

Britton, R. K., ed. see De Quevedo, Francisco.

Britton, Richard B., ed. see Siebenmann, Veronique.

Britton, Rick, et al. Albemarle Archives Famous, Infamous & Unforgettable: People & Events That Shaped Central Virginia. Swinson, Hilary, ed. 120p. 1997. pap. 11.95 (*1-891524-00-3*) Carden Jennings.

Britton, Ronald. Belief & Imagination: Explorations in Psychoanalysis. LC 98-19593. 240p. (C). 1998. 90.00 (*0-415-19437-7*) Routledge.

— Belief & Imagination: Explorations in Psychoanalysis. LC 98-19593. 240p. 1999. pap. 29.99 (*0-415-19438-5*) Routledge.

— Introduction to Engineering. (C). 2000. pap. text. write for info. (*0-201-65444-X*) Addison-Wesley.

Britton, Ronald, et al. The Oedipus Complex Today: Clinical Implications. 160p. 1989. reprint ed. pap. text 25.00 (*0-946439-55-9*, Pub. by H Karnac Bks Ltd) Other Pr LLC.

Britton, Scott G. Practical Coal Mine Management. LC 81-11426. 248p. 1986. reprint ed. 40.50 (*0-471-09035-2*, (JW)) Krieger.

***Britton, Tamara L.** Iraq. LC 00-26643. (Countries Ser.). (Illus.). 2000. write for info. (*1-57765-392-0*) ABDO Pub Co.

Britton, Tamara L. LeeAnn Rimes. LC 98-40385. (Young Profiles Ser.). 1998. 13.95 (*1-57765-325-4*) ABDO Pub Co.

— Prince William. LC 98-38113. (J). 1999. 13.98 (*1-57765-324-6*) ABDO Pub Co.

***Britton, Tamara L., contrib. by.** Mary-Kate & Ashley Olsen. LC 99-27235. (Young Profiles Ser.). (Illus.). 32p. (J). 2000. lib. bdg. write for info. (*1-57765-351-3*, Checkerboard Library) ABDO Pub Co.

***Britton, Tom & Cummins, Kent.** The Magic of Change: The Illusion... The Excitement... The Reward. LC 00-90420. 192p. 2000. 21.95 (*0-9651376-5-1*, Pub. by Bullion Bks) Midpt Trade.

Britton, Tom, jt. auth. see Andersson, Hjakan.

Britton, Vanessa. All about Rugs. (Allen Photographic Guides Ser.). (Illus.). 24p. 2000. pap. 10.95 (*0-85131-675-1*, Pub. by J A Allen) Trafalgar.

— Basic Tack. (Crowood Equestrian Guides Ser.). (Illus.). 96p. 1995. pap. 17.95 (*1-85223-800-3*, Pub. by Cro1wood) Trafalgar.

— Equiz Advanced. 1996. pap. 25.00 (*0-85131-655-7*, Pub. by J A Allen) Trafalgar.

— Equiz Intermediate. 1996. pap. 25.00 (*0-85131-654-9*, Pub. by J A Allen) Trafalgar.

— Equiz Newcomer. 1996. pap. 25.00 (*0-85131-652-2*, Pub. by J A Allen) Trafalgar.

— Equiz Novice. 1996. pap. 25.00 (*0-85131-653-0*, Pub. by J A Allen) Trafalgar.

— Foal to First Ridden. (Illus.). 160p. 1998. 35.00 (*1-85223-939-5*, Pub. by Cro1wood) Trafalgar.

— Horse Owner's Problem Solver. (Illus.). 160p. 1998. 27.95 (*0-7153-0614-6*, Pub. by D & C Pub) Sterling.

— Horse Rider's Problem Solver. LC 98-120870. (Illus.). 160p. 1998. 27.95 (*0-7153-0613-8*, Pub. by D & C Pub) Sterling.

— Keeping a Horse at Grass. (Illus.). 160p. 1996. 35.00 (*1-85223-862-3*, Pub. by Cro1wood) Trafalgar.

— Photographic Guide to Buying & Selling Horses. LC 97-214688. (Illus.). 160p. 1997. 29.95 (*0-7153-0377-5*) Sterling.

— Showing Masterclass: With Allister Hood & Wendy King. (Illus.). 160p. 1996. 27.95 (*0-7153-0310-4*, Pub. by D & C Pub) Sterling.

Britton, Vickie. The Dangerous Cliffs of Severon. 352p. 1993. mass mkt. 3.99 (*0-8217-4373-2*, Zebra Kensgtn) Kensgtn Pub Corp.

— Legend of the Sea Wolf. 358p. 1984. 11.95 (*0-89697-193-7*) Intl Univ Pr.

Britton, Vickie, jt. auth. see Jackson, Loretta.

Britton, W. Conjugate Duality & the Exponential Fourier Spectrum. (Lecture Notes in Statistics Ser.: Vol. 18). (Illus.). 226p. 1983. 58.95 (*0-387-90826-9*) Spr-Verlag.

Britton, Wayne E., jt. ed. see Fry, Albert J.

Britton, Wiley. The Civil War on the Border Vol. 1: 1861-1862. (Illus.). 473p. (C). 1995. pap. 22.95 (*1-878882-09-0*) KS Heritage Pr.

— The Civil War on the Border Vol. 2: 1863-1865. (Illus.). 546p. (C). 1995. pap. 22.95 (*1-878882-10-4*) KS Heritage Pr.

— Memoirs of the Rebellion on the Border, 1863. LC 86-82410. 463p. 1986. reprint ed. 26.00 (*0-940435-01-2*) Inland Print Ltd.

— Memoirs of the Rebellion on the Border, 1863. LC 93-1330. 458p. 1993. reprint ed. text 50.00 (*0-8032-1231-3*) U of Nebr Pr.

— Memoirs of the Rebellion on the Border, 1863. LC 93-1330. (Illus.). 458p. 1993. reprint ed. pap. 14.95 (*0-8032-6109-8*, Bison Books) U of Nebr Pr.

— The Union Indian Brigade in the Civil War. (Illus.). 474p. (C). 1995. text 40.00 (*1-878882-06-6*) KS Heritage Pr.

Britton, William N. The Adventures of Carlos the Coyote. (Illus.). 116p. (Orig.). (J). (gr. 3-6). 1995. pap. 8.50 (*0-9645018-1-3*) Savannah Pub.

— The Legend of Rainbow Bridge. (Illus.). 24p. (Orig.). 1994. pap. 9.95 (*0-9645018-0-5*) Savannah Pub.

Britts, Malcolm M. Motor Accidents Law NSW. LC 94-191207. 1994. pap. 35.00 (*0-455-21268-6*, Pub. by LawBk Co) Gaunt.

— Pleading Precedents. 5th ed. LC 95-103131. 359p. 1994. pap. 69.00 (*0-455-21267-8*, Pub. by LawBk Co) Gaunt.

— Traffic Law. vii, 397p. 1990. pap. 28.00 (*0-455-20988-X*, Pub. by LawBk Co) Gaunt.

— Traffic Law: NSW. 3rd ed. 445p. 1992. pap. 41.00 (*0-455-21166-3*, Pub. by LawBk Co) Gaunt.

— Traffic Law: NSW. 4th ed. 1994. pap. 35.00 (*0-455-21259-7*, Pub. by LawBk Co) Gaunt.

Britts, Maurice W. & Allen, Phyllis W. Safari: African American Stories, Parables & Tales. Knight, Ginny, ed. & illus. by. LC 98-70462. 68p. 1998. pap., teacher ed. 10.00 (*0-940248-50-6*) Guild Pr.

Britts, Paul, et al. The Historical Organ in America: A Documentary of Recent Organs Based on European & American Models. Edwards, Lynn, ed. 223p. 1992. pap. 48.00 (*0-9616755-5-1*) Westfield Ctr.

Brittsan, Allison & Shelley, Clarene. Surviving: A Guide for Victims, Families, Friends & Professionals. 175p. (Orig.). 1994. pap. 14.95 (*0-9626437-4-2*) Biblic Unlimited.

Britvec, S. J. Stability & Optimization of Flexible Space Structures. LC 93-16441. (Illus.). 312p. 1995. 134.00 (*3-7643-2864-9*) Birkhauser.

Britz, jt. auth. see Pohland, Frederick G.

Britz, Andrew & Maier, Zita. Preparing Sunday Without the Eucharist. LC 96-52680. (Preparing for Liturgy Ser.). 1997. pap. 3.95 (*0-8146-2479-0*) Liturgical Pr.

Britz-Crecelius, Heidi. Children at Play: Using Waldorf Principles to Foster Childhood Development. LC 96-4205. (Illus.). 128p. 1996. pap. 9.95 (*0-89281-629-5*) Inner Tradit.

Britz, D. Digital Simulation in Electrochemistry. 2nd rev. ed. (Illus.). 235p. 1988. 61.95 (*0-387-18979-3*) Spr-Verlag.

Britz, Joan & Richard, Norma. Problem Solving in the Early Childhood Classroom. 96p. 1992. pap. 10.95 (*0-8106-0360-8*) NEA.

Britz, Marjie, jt. auth. see Barker, Thomas.

Britzius, O. A Practical Guide to Meetings. 125p. 1991. pap. 39.00 (*0-409-01340-4*, SA, MICHIE) LEXIS Pub.

Britzke, Ron. Speed King, Rudy Kling: Triumph & Tragedy in Air Racing's "Golden Age" LC 94-37920. 1995. pap. 20.00 (*0-912526-74-2*) Lib Res.

Britzman, Deborah P. Lost Subjects, Contested Objects: Toward a Psychoanalytic Inquiry of Learning. LC 97-35166. 256p. (C). 1998. text 59.50 (*0-7914-3807-4*); pap. text 19.95 (*0-7914-3808-2*) State U NY Pr.

— Practice Makes Practice: A Critical Study of Learning to Teach. LC 90-37229. (SUNY Series, Teacher Empowerment & School Reform). 283p. (C). 1991. pap. text 24.95 (*0-7914-0569-9*) State U NY Pr.

Britzman, Mark J. Life: From Surviving to Thriving. 100p. (Orig.). 1997. pap. 4.95 (*0-9657284-0-4*) M J Britzman.

Britzolakis, Christina. Sylvia Plath & the Theatre of Mourning. LC 99-45928. 264p. 2000. text 60.00 (*0-19-818373-9*) OUP.

Briuer, Elke. Young Scientist's Introduction to Wetlands. 20p. 1994. pap. 2.00 (*0-16-061268-3*) USGPO.

Briusova, V. G. Russian Painting of the 17th Century. (RUS., Illus.). 338p. 1984. 300.00 (*0-7855-1660-3*) St Mut.

Brivati, Brian. Contemporary History Handbook. 560p. 1996. pap. 32.00 (*0-7190-4836-2*) St Martin.

— Hugh Gaitskell: A Biography. LC 96-214415. (Illus.). 492p. 1997. 50.00 (*1-86066-073-8*, Pub. by R Cohen Bks) Trafalgar.

Brivati, Brian & Bale, Tim. New Labour in Power. LC 97-30749. 224p. (C). 1998. 70.00 (*0-415-17972-6*); pap. 20.99 (*0-415-17973-4*) Routledge.

***Brivati, Brian & Heffernan, Richard.** The Labour Party: A Centenary History. LC 00-27833. 2000. write for info. (*0-312-23458-9*) St Martin.

Brivati, Brian & Jones, Harriet, eds. From Reconstruction to Integration: Britain & Europe since 1945. 256p. 1993. 59.00 (*0-7185-1482-3*, Pub. by Leicester U Pr) Cassell & Continuum.

— What Difference Did the War Make? (Themes in Contemporary British History Ser.). 240p. 1995. pap. 25.95 (*0-7185-2263-X*) Bks Intl VA.

— What Difference Did the War Make? The Impact of the Second World War on British Institutions & Culture. (Contemporary British History Ser.). 240p. (C). 1993. text 54.00 (*0-7185-1446-7*) St Martin.

Brivati, Brian, et al. Anatomy of Decline: The Political Writings of Peter Jenkins. 256p. 1996. pap. 19.95 (*0-575-40051-X*, Pub. by V Gollancz) Trafalgar.

Brivic, Sheldon. Joyce the Creator. LC 84-40492. 192p. 1985. reprint ed. pap. 59.60 (*0-608-07456-X*, 206768300009) Bks Demand.

— Joyce's Waking Women: An Introduction to Finnegans Wake. LC 95-6475. 176p. 1995. pap. 17.95 (*0-299-14804-1*) U of Wis Pr.

— The Veil of Signs: Joyce, Lacan, & Perception. 224p. 1991. text 29.95 (*0-252-01765-X*); pap. text 13.95 (*0-252-06159-4*) U of Ill Pr.

Brivin. Gun Down the Young. 136p. 1998. pap. text 15.75 (*0-536-01460-4*) Pearson Custom.

Brivois, Jules. Bibliographie Des Ouvrages Illustres Du Nineteenth Siecle. (Principalement Des Livres A Gravures Sur Bois Ser.). xiv, 468p. 1974. reprint ed. 145.00 (*3-487-05419-1*) G Olms Pubs.

Briwnant-Jones, Gwyn. Railway Through Talerddig. 144p. 1990. pap. 35.00 (*0-86383-813-8*, Pub. by Gomer Pr) St Mut.

— Railway Through Talerddig. 144p. (C). 1990. 36.00 (*0-86383-662-3*, Pub. by Gomer Pr) St Mut.

Briwnant-Jones, Gwyn, jt. auth. see Jenkins, David.

Brix, H., jt. auth. see Kadlec, R. H.

Brix, V., jt. auth. see Martynov, A.

Brixen, Peter, jt. auth. see Tarp, Finn.

***Briys, Eric C.** Modern Finance. 128p. 2000. pap. 18.95 (*0-471-88961-X*) Wiley.

Briys, Eric C. Options, Futures & Exotic Derivatives Assets. LC 97-44712. (Frontiers in Finance Ser.). 472p. 1998. 89.95 (*0-471-96909-5*) Wiley.

Briys, Eric C. & Bellalah, Mondher. Options, Futures & Exotic Derivative Assets. LC 97-44712. 472p. 1998. pap. 64.95 (*0-471-96908-7*) Wiley.

Brizee, Robert. Eight Paths to Forgiveness. 136p. 1998. pap. 12.99 (*0-8272-0811-1*) Chalice Pr.

— The Gift of Listening. LC 92-32061. 128p. (Orig.). 1993. pap. 10.99 (*0-8272-1237-2*) Chalice Pr.

Brizee, Sandra L., tr. see Mayer, Karl H.

Brizendine, William, jt. auth. see Illo, Maria.

Brizer, David. Addiction & Recovery for Beginners. (Illus.). 160p. 1995. pap. 11.00 (*0-86316-198-7*) Writers & Readers.

— Babies for Beginners. (Illus.). 192p. 1994. pap. 9.95 (*0-86316-169-3*) Writers & Readers.

— Health Care for Beginners. (Illus.). 192p. 1994. pap. 9.95 (*0-86316-170-7*) Writers & Readers.

Brizer, David A. Psychiatry for Beginners. 2nd ed. (Illus.). 176p. 1993. pap. 9.95 (*0-86316-166-9*) Writers & Readers.

Brizga, S. O. & Finlayson, B. L. River Management: The Australisian Experience. LC 99-35924. 310p. 2000. 105.00 (*0-471-96976-1*) Wiley.

Briziarelli, Susan. Enrico Annibale Butti: The Predicament of the Minor Writer. LC 94-8009. 1994. 58.50 (*1-882528-08-5*) Scripta.

Brizius, Jack A. & Campbell, Michael D. Getting Results: A Guide for Government Accountability. 135p. (Orig.). (C). 1991. pap. 17.95 (*0-934842-12-4*) CSPA.

Brizius, Jack A. & Foster, Susan. Enhancing Adult Literacy. 182p. 1987. 12.95 (*0-934842-96-5*) CSPA.

Brizius, Jack A., jt. auth. see Popovich, Mark G.

Brizova, Joza, et al. Czechoslovak Cookbook. Adams, C., ed. Vahalla, A., tr. (International Cookbook Ser.). 1965. 12.00 (*0-517-50547-9*, Crown) Crown Pub Group.

***Brizuela, Barbara, et al, eds.** Acts of Inquiry in Qualitative Research. (Reprint Ser.: No. 34). 450p. 2000. pap. 29.95 (*0-916690-36-9*) Harvard Educ Rev.

Brizuela, E. F. Barro Docil en Sus Manos. (Serie Creciendo - Growing Ser.).Tr. of Clay in the Potter's Hands. (SPA.). 47p. 1995. 2.50 (*1-56063-553-3*, 493036) Editorial Unilit.

Brizzi, Enrico. Jack Frusciante Has Left the Band: A Love Story - With Rock 'n' Roll. Luczkiw, Stash, tr. LC 97-25065. 192p. 1997. pap. 12.00 (*0-8021-3521-8*, Grove) Grove-Atltic.

Brizzi, Ginny, jt. auth. see Fischer, William L.

Brizzi, Mary T. Philip Jose Farmer. Schlobin, Roger C., ed. LC 79-17691. (Starmont Reader's Guide Ser.: Vol. 3). (Illus.). ii, 80p. 1980. pap. 15.00 (*0-916732-05-3*) Millefleurs.

Brkic, Svetozar. Serbocroatian-English Dictionary: Srpskohrvatsko-Engelski Recnik. 2nd ed. (CRO, ENG & SER.). 416p. 1990. pap. 29.95 (*0-8288-4714-2*, M9631) Fr & Eur.

Brletich, Nancy R., et al. Worldwide Chemical Detection Equipment Handbook. (Illus.). 482p. 1995. pap. text 299.95 (*1-888727-00-4*, HB-95-02) CBIAC.

— Worldwide NBC Mask Handbook. (Illus.). 433p. 1992. pap. text 299.95 (*1-888727-01-2*, HB-92-01) CBIAC.

Brna, Paul, et al, eds. Learning to Build & Comprehend Complex Information Structures: Prolog as a Case Study. LC 98-43570. (Contemporary Studies in Cognitive Science & Technology: Vol. 3). 430p. 1999. 73.25 (*1-56750-434-5*); pap. 39.50 (*1-56750-435-3*) Ablx Pub.

Bro, Harmon H. Edgar Cayce on Dreams. Cayce, Hugh L., ed. 224p. 1988. mass mkt. 5.99 (*0-446-35108-3*, Pub. by Warner Bks) Little.

— A Seer Out of Season: The Life of Edgar Casey, Vol. 1. 1996. mass mkt. 6.99 (*0-312-95988-5*) St Martin.

Bro, Lu. Figure & Form, 2 vols., Vol. I. 288p. (C). 1992. text. write for info. (*0-697-03059-8*) Brown & Benchmark.

Bro, P. & Levy, S. C. Quality & Reliability Methods for Primary Batteries. (Electrochemical Society Ser.). 302p. 1990. 179.00 (*0-471-52427-1*) Wiley.

Bro, P., jt. auth. see Levy, S. C.

Broach, James R., et al, eds. Cell Cycle & Cell Biology Vol. 3: The Molecular & Cellular Biology of the Yeast Saccharomyces. (Monographs: No. 21B). (Illus.). 650p. (C). 1997. text 118.00 (*0-87969-356-8*); pap. text 77.00 (*0-87969-364-9*) Cold Spring Harbor.

— Gene Expression Vol. 2: The Molecular & Cellular

B

Biology of the Yeast Saccharomyces. (Monographs: No. 21C). (Illus.). 725p. (C). 1992. pap. text 77.00 (*0-87969-365-7*) Cold Spring Harbor.

— Genome Dynamics, Protein Synthesis & Energetics Vol. 1: The Molecular & Cellular Biology of the Yeast Saccharomyces. (Monographs: No. 21A). (Illus.). 826p. (C). 1991. text 108.00 (*0-87969-355-X*); pap. text 77.00 (*0-87969-363-0*) Cold Spring Harbor.

Broach-Sowels, Holly. Childhood Sexual Abuse 101: Not an Elective. large type ed. Phillips, Ron, ed. 164p. 1998. pap. 14.95 (*0-9637441-7-8*) Kehori.

— Daddy, Don't: Letters to My Father, A Story of Incest. Giblin, Gary L., ed. 144p. (Orig.). 1993. pap. 4.99 (*0-9637441-0-0*) Kehori.

— The Preaching Machine: The Biography of Bishop Paul A. Bowers. Daniel, Jean E., ed. (Illus.). 240p. (Orig.). 1994. pap. 14.95 (*0-9637441-1-9*) Kehori.

— Ten Years of Heat: The Paula Duncan Story "It Can Happen to You" large type ed. Daniel, Jean, ed. (Illus.). 192p. (Orig.). 1995. pap. 19.95 (*0-9637441-4-3*) Kehori.

Broad, Bob. Young People Leaving Care: Life after the Children Act, 1989. LC 98-137818. 281p. 1997. pap. write for info. (*1-85302-412-0*, Pub. by Jessica Kingsley) Taylor & Francis.

Broad, C. D. Berkeley's Argument. LC 75-1069. (Studies in Philosophy: No. 40). 1975. lib. bdg. 59.95 (*0-8383-0113-4*) M S G Haskell Hse.

— Ethics. Lewyt, C., ed. 328p. 1985. lib. bdg. 184.00 (*90-247-3088-0*, Pub. by M Nijhoff) Kluwer Academic.

*__Broad, C. D.__ Examination of McTaggart's Philosophy, 3 vols. 8th ed. (Idealism Ser.). 1388p. 2000. 365.00 (*1-85506-852-4*) Thoemmes Pr.

Broad, C. D. Induction Probability & Causation: Selected Papers. (Synthese Library). 307p. 1967. text 169.50 (*90-277-0012-5*, D Reidel) Kluwer Academic.

— Scientific Thought: 1923 Edition. 560p. 1996. reprint ed. 75.00 (*1-85506-230-5*) Bks Intl VA.

Broad, C. Lewis. Dictionary to the Plays & Novels of Bernard Shaw: With Bibliography of His Works. 1988. reprint ed. lib. bdg. 49.00 (*0-7812-0555-7*) Rprt Serv.

Broad, C. Lewis & Broad, Violet M. Dictionary to Plays & Novels of Shaw. LC 75-92947. (Studies in Irish Literature: No. 16). 1969. reprint ed. lib. bdg. 75.00 (*0-8383-0961-5*) M S G Haskell Hse.

— Dictionary to the Plays & Novels of Bernard Shaw: With Bibliography of His Works & of the Literature Concerning Him with the Record of the Principle Shawian Play Production. LC 76-131645. (Illus.). 1972. reprint ed. 39.00 (*0-403-00532-9*) Scholarly.

Broad, Dave & Foster, Lori, eds. The New World Order & The Third World. LC 91-72978. 160p. 1991. pap. 19.99 (*1-895431-16-6*, Pub. by Black Rose) Consort Bk Sales.

— The New World Order & the Third World. LC 91-72978. 160p. 1991. 48.99 (*1-895431-17-4*, Pub. by Black Rose) Consort Bk Sales.

Broad, John. Buckinghamshire Dissent & Parish Life, 1669-1712. LC 95-163380. (Buckinghamshire Record Society Ser.). xlvi, 293p. 1993. write for info. (*0-901198-28-5*) Bucks Record.

Broad, Kendall, jt. auth. see Jenness, Valerie.

Broad, Laura P. The Playgroup Handbook. 3rd ed. 1991. pap. 12.95 (*0-312-05494-7*) St Martin.

Broad, Mary, jt. auth. see Newstrom, John W.

Broad, Mary L. & Phillips, Jack J., eds. Transfering Learning to the Workplace. LC 97-70842. 331p. 1997. pap. 50.00 (*1-56286-059-3*) Am Soc Train & Devel.

Broad Minds Collective Staff. Ourselves As Students: Multicultural Voices in the Classroom. LC 96-15621. 176p. (C). 1996. 34.95 (*0-8093-2087-8*) S Ill U Pr.

Broad Minds Collective Staff, ed. Ourselves As Students: Multicultural Voices in the Classroom. LC 96-15621. 176p. (C). 1996. pap. 16.95 (*0-8093-2088-6*) S Ill U Pr.

Broad, R. A. Punishment under Pressure: The Probation Service in the Inner City. 200p. 1991. 39.95 (*1-85302-090-7*) Taylor & Francis.

Broad, Robin. Plundering Paradise: The Struggle for the Environment in the Philippines. 1994. pap. 16.95 (*0-520-08921-9*, Pub. by U CA Pr) Cal Prin Full Svc.

— Unequal Alliance: The World Bank, the International Monetary Fund & the Philippines. (Studies in International Political Economy: Vol. 19). 1988. pap. 16.95 (*0-520-06953-6*, Pub. by U CA Pr) Cal Prin Full Svc.

Broad, Violet M., jt. auth. see Broad, C. Lewis.

Broad, William J. Star Warriors: A Penetrating Look into the Lives of the Young Scientists Behind Our Space Age Weaponry. (Illus.). 245p. 1997. reprint ed. text 15.00 (*0-7881-5115-0*) DIANE Pub.

— The Universe Below: Discovering the Secrets of the Deep Sea. (Illus.). 432p. 1998. per. 15.00 (*0-684-83852-4*, Touchstone) S&S Trade Pap.

Broadbent. Design in Architecture. 1997. 49.95 (*0-419-16830-3*, E & FN Spon) Routledge.

— Multilingual Glossary of Automatic Control. (ENG, FRE, GER, ITA & JPN.). 212p. 1981. 150.00 (*0-8288-7629-0*, M15653) Fr & Eur.

Broadbent, Bill & Rosenberg, George. Owner Will Carry: How to Take Back a Mortgage Without Being Taken. Orig. Title: Sell Your Property Fast. 176p. 1993. pap. 25.00 (*0-9637838-0-7*) Whos Who Creat.

Broadbent, Brooke. Using the Internet. (Professional Ser.). (Illus.). 96p. 1998. pap. 14.95 (*1-56052-493-6*) Crisp Pubns.

Broadbent, Donald E. Behaviour. LC 86-4661. 215p. 1986. reprint ed. lib. bdg. 59.50 (*0-313-25216-5*, BBEH, Greenwood Pr) Greenwood.

— Perception & Communication. (Illus.). 352p. 1987. pap. text 29.95 (*0-19-852171-5*) OUP.

— Perception & Communication. 3rd ed. LC 58-11832. 1969. 192.00 (*0-08-009090-7*, Pub. by Pergamon Repr) Franklin.

Broadbent, Donald E. & Reason, J. T., eds. Human Factors in Hazardous Situations. (Illus.). 154p. 1990. text 75.00 (*0-19-852191-X*) OUP.

Broadbent, E. H. The Pilgrim Church. 422p. 1987. pap. 12.95 (*0-310-55171-4*, 19017P) Zondervan.

*__Broadbent, E. H.__ Pilgrim Church. 456p. 1999. 21.99 (*1-882701-53-4*, Gospel Folio Pr) Uplook Min.

Broadbent, Eliot K., ed. Tungsten & Other Refractory Metals for VLSI Applications II, Vol. 2. 1987. text 17.50 (*0-931837-66-9*, Vol. V-2) Materials Res.

Broadbent, Geoffrey. Deconstruction - A Student Guide: UIA Journal. (Academy Editions Ser.). (Illus.). 96p. (Orig.). 1991. pap. 25.00 (*0-312-06229-X*) St Martin.

— Emerging Concepts in Urban Design. (Illus.). 392p. (gr. 13). 1996. text 57.95 (*0-7476-0025-2*) Chapman & Hall.

— Emerging Concepts in Urban Space Design. (Illus.). 392p. (C). 1995. pap. 45.00 (*0-419-16150-3*, E & FN Spon) Routledge.

Broadbent, James & Hughes, Joy, eds. The Age of Macquarie. 208p. 1992. pap. 29.95 (*0-522-84460-X*, Pub. by Melbourne Univ Pr) Paul & Co Pubs.

Broadbent, James S. Right-of-Way Man: Clearing the Path for Our Nation's Highways. LC 98-85362. 192p. 1999. pap. 11.95 (*1-56315-094-8*, Pub. by SterlingHse) Natl Bk Netwk.

Broadbent, Jeffrey. Environmental Politics in Japan: Networks of Power & Protest. LC 97-24297. (Illus.). 432p. (C). 1998. text 59.95 (*0-521-56424-7*) Cambridge U Pr.

*__Broadbent, Jeffrey.__ Environmental Politics in Japan: Networks of Power & Protest. (Illus.). 440p. (C). 1999. pap. 22.95 (*0-521-66574-4*) Cambridge U Pr.

Broadbent, John, ed. see Milton, John.

Broadbent, K. Dictionary of China's Rural Economy. (CHI & ENG.). 406p. 1978. 125.00 (*0-8288-5169-7*, M9712) Fr & Eur.

Broadbent, K. P. Tourism & the Leisure Industry: International Problems & Prospects [1963-1973]. LC 74-170496. (Annotated Bibliography Ser.). 40p. 1973. write for info. (*0-85198-279-4*) C A B Intl.

Broadbent, Marianne, jt. auth. see Weill, Peter.

Broadbent, Michael. Michael Broadbent's Wine Tasting: How to Approach & Appreciate Wine. 1997. 14.95 (*1-85732-761-6*, Pub. by Mitchell Beazley) Antique Collect.

— Michael Broadbent's Wine Vintages. (Mitchell Beazley Pocket Guides Ser.). 208p. 1998. 14.95 (*1-84000-090-2*, Pub. by Mitchell Beazley) Antique Collect.

— Michael Broadbent's Winetasting: How to Approach & Appreciate Wine. (Mitchell Beazley Pocket Guides Ser.). (Illus.). 176p. 1998. 14.95 (*1-84000-091-0*, Pub. by Mitchell Beazley) Antique Collect.

— Wine Vintages. 1997. 14.95 (*1-85732-762-4*, Pub. by Mitchell Beazley) Antique Collect.

Broadbent, Michael & Cullen, John. Managing Financial Resources. 2nd ed. LC 97-199477. (Institute of Management Ser.). 480p. 1997. pap. text 35.95 (*0-7506-3392-1*, HG) Buttrwrth-Heinemann.

Broadbent, Michael, jt. auth. see Duijker, Hubrecht.

Broadbent, Mick, jt. auth. see Cullen, John.

Broadbent, Noel D., ed. Readings in Saami History, Culture & Language. (Center for Arctic Cultural Research Ser.: No. 7). (Illus.). 152p. (Orig.). 1989. pap. 67.50 (*0-685-40929-5*) Coronet Bks.

Broadbent, Pamela J., et al. The End of the Professions? The Restructuring of Professional Work. LC 96-19119. 200p. (C). 1997. 75.00 (*0-415-14300-4*) Routledge.

Broadbent, Peter. Charlie Christian. (Illus.). 120p. 1997. 19.95 (*0-614-29479-7*, Pub. by Ashley Mark Pub) H Leonard.

— Charlie Christian. 120p. 1997. pap. 19.95 (*1-872639-21-6*, Pub. by Ashley Mark Pub) H Leonard.

Broadbent, R. J. Annals of the Liverpool Stage. LC 70-83872. (Illus.). 1972. 30.95 (*0-405-08306-8*, Pub. by Blom Pubns) Ayer.

— A History of Pantomime. LC 64-14694. 226p. 1972. 23.95 (*0-405-08307-6*, Pub. by Blom Pubns) Ayer.

Broadberry, Richard E., jt. auth. see Nelson, Ethel R.

Broadberry, S. N. The Productivity Race: British Manufacturing in International Perspective, 1850-1990. LC 96-49929. (Illus.). 478p. (C). 1997. text 74.95 (*0-521-58440-X*) Cambridge U Pr.

Broadberry, S. N. & Crafts, N. F., eds. Britain in the International Economy, 1870-1939. 440p. (C). 1992. text 69.95 (*0-521-41859-3*) Cambridge U Pr.

Broadbridge, Edward, tr. see Nielsen, Kirsten.

Broadbridge, Seymour. Industrial Dualism in Japan: A Problem of Economic Growth & Structural Change. 105p. 1966. 35.00 (*0-7146-1208-1*, Pub. by F Cass Pubs) Intl Spec Bk.

— Studies in Railway Expansion & the Capital Market in England, 1825-73. 216p. 1970. 45.00 incl. sl. (*0-7146-1287-1*, Pub. by F Cass Pubs) Intl Spec Bk.

Broadcast Dessign Assoc. Staff, jt. auth. see Books Nippan Staff.

Broaddus, Dorothy C. Genteel Rhetoric: Writing High Culture in 19th Century Boston. LC 98-19678. (Studies in Rhetoric/Communication). 1999. 24.95 (*1-57003-244-0*) U of SC Pr.

Broaddus, James W. Spenser's Allegory of Love: Social Vision in Books III, IV & V of The Faerie Queene. LC 95-1119. 192p. 1996. 33.50 (*0-8386-3632-2*) Fairleigh Dickinson.

Broadfoot, Barry. Ten Lost Years, 1929-1939: Memories of Canadians Who Survived the Depression. (Illus.). 464p. 1997. pap. text 15.95 (*0-7710-1652-2*) McCland & Stewart.

Broadfoot, James W. Investing In Emerging Groth St. LC 88-29021. 240p. 1989. 45.00 (*0-471-61844-6*) Wiley.

Broadfoot, Patricia. Education, Assessment, & Society: A Sociological Analysis. (Assessing Assessment Ser.). 256p. 1996. pap. 33.95 (*0-335-19601-2*) OpUniv Pr.

*__Broadfoot, Patricia.__ Promoting Quality in Learning: Does England Have the Answer? (Illus.). 2000. pap. 31.95 (*0-304-70684-1*) Continuum.

Broadfoot, Patricia, et al, eds. Policy Issues in National Assessment. LC 92-38545. (BERA Dialogues Ser.: No. 7). 1992. 69.00 (*1-85359-171-8*, Pub. by Multilingual Matters); pap. 24.95 (*1-85359-170-X*, Pub. by Multilingual Matters) Taylor & Francis.

Broadfoot, Patricia, et al. Perceptions of Teaching: Primary School Teachers in England & France. (Education Ser.). (Illus.). 160p. 1994. 70.00 (*0-304-32773-5*) Continuum.

Broadfoot, Tom. Civil War Books: A Price Checklist with Advice. 4th rev. ed. LC 97-174213. 936p. 1996. 50.00 (*1-56837-320-1*) Broadfoot.

Broadhead. The Worlds We Have Lost. (C). 1996. pap. text 12.25 (*0-07-024568-1*) McGraw.

Broadhead, B. L. Updated Nuclear Criticality Slide Rule: Technical Basis. 95p. 1997. per. 8.50 (*0-16-062831-8*) USGPO.

— Verification & Validation of the Scale-4 Radiation Shielding Software. 53p. 1996. pap. 8.00 (*0-16-062790-7*) USGPO.

Broadhead, Edward. Ceran St. Vrain. 2nd ed. 56p. (Orig.). 1986. pap. 4.00 (*0-915617-13-7*) Pueblo Co Hist Soc.

— Fort Pueblo. (Illus.). 32p. 1981. pap. 4.00 (*0-915617-01-3*) Pueblo Co Hist Soc.

— George Semmes Simpson, the Wayward Pioneer, 1818-1885. (Illus.). 40p. (Orig.). 1985. pap. 3.50 (*0-915617-07-2*) Pueblo Co Hist Soc.

— John Simpson Smith, 1810-1871. (Illus.). 30p. (Orig.). 1985. pap. 3.50 (*0-915617-10-2*) Pueblo Co Hist Soc.

Broadhead, Edwin K. Demand & Grace: The Sermon on the Mount. 128p. 1999. pap. 11.00 (*1-57312-269-6*) Smyth & Helwys.

— Naming Jesus: Titular Christology in the Gospel of Mark. (JSNTS Ser.: Vol. 175). 193p. 1999. 57.50 (*1-85075-929-4*, Pub. by Sheffield Acad) CUP Services.

— Prophet, Son, Messiah: Narrative Form & Function in Mark 14-16. LC 94-212245. (JSNTS Ser.: Vol. 97). 336p. 1994. 85.00 (*1-85075-476-4*, Pub. by Sheffield Acad) CUP Services.

— Teaching with Authority: Miracles & Christology in the Gospel of Mark. (JSNT Supplement Ser.: No. 74). 235p. (C). 1992. 70.00 (*1-85075-366-0*, Pub. by Sheffield Acad) CUP Services.

Broadhead, Fred C. Here Comes Whirlaway! (Illus.). 236p. 1995. pap. text 19.95 (*0-89745-181-3*) Sunflower U Pr.

Broadhead, G. F. Orchestral & Band Instruments. 1976. lib. bdg. 49.00 (*0-403-03788-3*) Scholarly.

— Orchestral & Band Instruments. 1988. reprint ed. lib. bdg. 49.00 (*0-7812-0256-6*) Rprt Serv.

Broadhead, Glenn J. & Freed, Richard C., eds. Variables of Composition: Process & Product in a Business Setting. LC 85-14239. (Studies in Writing & Rhetoric). 184p. (Orig.). (C). 1986. pap. text 14.95 (*0-8093-1262-X*) S Ill U Pr.

Broadhead, H. D. Latin Prose Rhythm: A New Method of Investigation. (C). 1995. reprint ed. pap. text 14.95 (*0-89341-755-6*) Hollowbrook.

Broadhead, J. & Scrosati, B., eds. Lithium Polymer Batteries. LC 97-137472. (Proceedings Ser.: Vol. 96-17). (Illus.). 304p. 1997. 59.00 (*1-56677-167-6*) Electrochem Soc.

Broadhead, Marjorie S. Portrait of a Woman's Soul. LC 98-90041. xvi, 64p. 1998. 17.95 (*0-9663074-7-X*, 1657725) Whippersnap OH.

Broadhead, Pat, ed. Researching the Early Years Continuum. (BERA Dialogues Ser.: No. 12). 194p. 1995. 79.00 (*1-85359-312-5*, Pub. by Multilingual Matters); pap. 29.95 (*1-85359-311-7*, Pub. by Multilingual Matters) Taylor & Francis.

Broadhead, Richard, ed. see Lafargue, Paul.

Broadhead, Robert S. The Private Lives & Professional Identity of Medical Students. LC 82-19502. 140p. 1983. 34.95 (*0-87855-478-5*) Transaction Pubs.

Broadhead, Steve. NetWare Lite. 178p. (C). 1993. pap. text 45.00 (*0-201-63193-8*) Addison-Wesley.

Broadhead, Susan H. Historical Dictionary of Angola. 2nd ed. LC 91-44889. (African Historical Dictionaries Ser.: No. 52). (Illus.). 344p. 1992. 45.00 (*0-8108-2532-5*) Scarecrow.

Broadhead, T. W., ed. Foraminifera: Notes for a Short Course Organized by M. A. Buzas & B. K. Sen Gupta. (Studies in Geology). (Illus.). iv, 219p. (C). 1982. pap. 12.00 (*0-910249-05-9*) U of Tenn Geo.

— Hollusks: Notes for a Short Course Organized by D. J. Bottjer, C. S. Hickman & P. D. Ward. (Studies in Geography: No. 13). (Illus.). 305p. (Orig.). 1985. pap. 12.00 (*0-910249-12-1*) U of Tenn Geo.

— Land Plants: Notes for a Short Course. (Studies in Geology). (Illus.). vi, 226p. pap. 12.00 (*0-910249-14-8*) U of Tenn Geo.

— Lophophorates: Notes for a Short Course Organized by J. T. Dutro, Jr. & R. S. Boardman. (Studies in Geology). (Illus.). iv, 251p. 1981. pap. 12.00 (*0-910249-03-2*) U of Tenn Geo.

— Mammals: Notes for a Short Course Organized by P. D. Gingerich & C. E. Badgley. (Studies in Geology). (Illus.). 234p. (C). 1984. pap. 12.00 (*0-910249-07-5*) U of Tenn Geo.

— Sponges & Spongiomorphs: Notes for a Short Course Organized by J. K. Rigby & C. W. Stearn. (Studies in Geology). (Illus.). 220p. (C). 1983. pap. 12.00 (*0-910249-06-7*) U of Tenn Geo.

Broadhead, T. W. & Waters, J. A., eds. Echinoderms: Notes for a Short Course. (Studies in Geology). (Illus.). iv, 235p. 1980. pap. 12.00 (*0-910249-01-6*) U of Tenn Geo.

Broadhouse, John. Musical Acoustics or the Phenomena of Sound As Connected with Music. 425p. 1990. reprint ed. lib. bdg. 89.00 (*0-7812-9126-7*) Rprt Serv.

— Musical Acoustics: or The Phenomena of Sound As Connected with Music. LC 72-181115. 425p. 1926. reprint ed. 35.00 (*0-403-01630-4*) Scholarly.

Broadhurst, Alan. The Great Cross-Country Race. (J). 1965. 7.00 (*0-87602-133-X*) Anchorage.

— Young Dick Whittington. (J). (gr. 1-7). 1964. 6.00 (*0-87602-224-7*) Anchorage.

Broadhurst, Alison. The Health & Safety at Work Act in Practice. LC 81-468929. (Illus.). 253p. reprint ed. pap. 78.50 (*0-8357-6652-7*, 203532100094) Bks Demand.

Broadhurst, Anne, jt. ed. see Feldman, M. Philip.

Broadhurst, Arlene Idol, jt. auth. see Ledgerwood, Grant.

Broadhurst, C. Leigh. All about Preventing Diabetes: Frequently Asked Questions. (FAQs All about Health Ser.). 1999. mass mkt. 2.99 (*0-89529-962-3*, Avery) Penguin Putnam.

*__Broadhurst, C. Leigh.__ Diabetes: Prevention & Cure. 1999. pap. 12.00 (*1-57566-471-2*, Knsington) Kensgtn Pub Corp.

Broadhurst, Claire. Harrap's Ingles Starter Pack. 1995. 27.00 (*0-671-52082-2*) S&S Trade.

Broadhurst, John, ed. Ouo Vaditis. 160p. 1997. pap. 14.95 (*0-85244-382-X*, 958, Pub. by Gra1cewing) Morehouse Pub.

Broadhurst, Kent. The Eye of the Beholder. 1982. pap. 3.25 (*0-8222-0375-8*) Dramatists Play.

— The Habitual Acceptance of the Near Enough. 1983. pap. 3.25 (*0-8222-0490-8*) Dramatists Play.

— Lemons. 1984. pap. 5.25 (*0-8222-0651-X*) Dramatists Play.

Broadhurst, Phil. Law & Practice for Mortgage Lenders. 1997. pap. 110.00 (*0-85297-424-8*, Pub. by Chartered Bank) St Mut.

Broadhurst, Phil, ed. Law & Practice for Mortgage Lenders. 350p. 1990. pap. 125.00 (*0-85297-388-8*, Pub. by Chartered Bank) St Mut.

*__Broadhurst, Susan.__ Liminal Acts: A Critical Overview of Contemporary Performance & Theory LC 99-20180. 1999. 26.95 (*0-304-70586-1*) Continuum.

Broadie, Alexander. The Circle of John Mair: Logic & Logicians in Pre-Reformation Scotland. 288p. 1985. text 45.00 (*0-19-824735-4*) OUP.

— Introduction to Medieval Logic. 2nd ed. LC 92-33382. 228p. 1993. text 59.00 (*0-19-824026-0*, Clarendon Pr) OUP.

— The Scottish Enlightenment Reader: An Anthology. (Canongate Scottish Classics Ser.). 840p. 1998. pap. 16.00 (*0-86241-738-4*, Pub. by Canongate Books) Interlink Pub.

— The Shawdow of Scotus: Philosophy & Faith in Pre-Reformation Scotland. LC 96-209831. 128p. 37.95 (*0-567-09734-X*, Pub. by T & T Clark); pap. 19.95 (*0-567-29295-9*, Pub. by T & T Clark) Bks Intl VA.

— The Tradition of Scottish Philosophy. 1990. 20.00 (*0-7486-6029-1*, Pub. by Polygon) Subterranean Co.

— The Tradition of Scottish Philosophy: A New Perspective on the Enlightenment. 192p. (C). 1990. lib. bdg. 53.00 (*0-389-20921-X*) Rowman.

Broadie, Alexander, ed. see Paul of Venice.

Broadie, Kim, et al. BASIC Programming Two: Course Code 393-1. McDonald, Kathy, ed. (Illus.). 96p. 1989. reprint ed. pap. text 9.95 (*0-917531-91-4*) CES Compu-Tech.

— BASIC Programming Two: Course Code 393-2. McDonald, Kathy, ed. (Illus.). 85p. (gr. 6). 1989. reprint ed. pap. text 9.95 (*0-917531-92-2*) CES Compu-Tech.

Broadie, Sarah. Ethics with Aristotle. 480p. (C). 1993. reprint ed. pap. text 29.95 (*0-19-508560-4*) OUP.

Broadley, K. J. Autonomic Pharmacology. 500p. 1996. text 160.00 (*0-7484-0556-9*, Pub. by Tay Francis Ltd) Taylor & Francis.

Broadley, Nancy. Waiting for the Sun. 120p. (Orig.). 1999. pap. 8.99 (*1-57532-253-6*, Pub. by Press-Tige Pub) Barnes & Noble Inc.

Broadman & Holman. Alphabet & Numbers Poster Set. 1998. 3.99 (*0-8054-0419-8*) Broadman.

— Months of the Year, Days of the Week Poster Set. 1998. 3.99 (*0-8054-0420-1*) Broadman.

— Mothers' Memories: Padded Cover with Photo Frame Onlay, Inspirational Verse on Each Page. 1998. 7.99 (*0-8054-0358-2*) Broadman.

*__Broadman & Holman.__ One Minute Bible for Starters: A 90 Days Journey for New Christians, Vol. 1. LC 99-15734. (One Minute Bible Ser.). 1999. pap. 1.99 (*0-8054-9386-7*, DoorWay TN) Broadman.

Broadman & Holman Publishers Staff. Concise Bible Dictionary. LC 97-22283. 1997. pap. text 14.99 (*1-55819-694-3*) Broadman.

*__Broadman & Holman Publishers Staff.__ Grade 1. (Learning Activities from the Bible Ser.). (Illus.). (J). 2000. pap. 15.99 (*0-8054-0984-X*) Broadman.

Broadman & Holman Publishers Staff. Holman Ultimate Bible Dictionary & Concordance. large type ed. 1998. 16.99 (*0-8054-9266-6*) Broadman.

*__Broadman & Holman Publishers Staff.__ Kindergarten. (Learning Activities from the Bible Ser.). (Illus.). (J). 2000. pap. 15.99 (*0-8054-0983-1*) Broadman.

— Pocket-Size Classic Bible. 1999. 35.99 (*1-55819-840-7*) Broadman.

— Preschool. (Learning Activities from the Bible Ser.). (Illus.). (J). 2000. pap. 15.99 (*0-8054-0982-3*) Broadman.

— 2nd Grade. (Learning Activities from the Bible Ser.). (Illus.). (J). 2000. pap. 15.99 (*0-8054-0985-8*) Broadman.

— Tips for the New Mom: Tiptionary Journal. (Illus.). 1999. 11.99 (*0-8054-0354-X*) Broadman.

— Ultrathin Large Print Reference Bible. large type ed. 1996. 55.99 (1-55819-655-2) Broadman.

***Broadman & Holman Publishing Staff.** El Antiguo Testamento. (SPA.). 2000. pap. 5.95 (0-8054-9424-3) Broadman.

— Basic Christian Beliefs. LC 99-54864. (Shepherd's Notes Bible Summary Ser.). 1999. pap. 5.95 (0-8054-9380-8) Broadman.

— Celebrate Jesus New Testament. (SPA.). 1999. pap. text 72.00 (1-55819-836-9) Broadman.

Broadman & Holman Publishing Staff. Christy Daily Journal. 1995. 7.99 incl. VHS (0-8054-7700-4, 4348-78) Broadman.

***Broadman & Holman Publishing Staff.** Concise Holman Bible Atlas. 2000. pap. 7.99 (0-8054-9419-7) Broadman.

— Cornerstone Hand Size Giant Print Reference Bible. 1999. 31.97 (1-55819-797-4) Broadman.

— Grandmother's Memories Journal. 1999. pap. 9.99 (0-8054-0662-X) Broadman.

— Here's Hope Bible. 2000. pap. 4.99 (1-55819-856-3) Broadman.

— Holman Ultrathin Classic Bible. 2000. 36.99 (1-55819-850-4); 36.99 (1-55819-851-2); 42.99 (1-55819-852-0); 42.99 (1-55819-853-9); 42.99 (1-55819-854-7) Broadman.

— Large Print Special Reference Bible. large type ed. 1999. 28.99 (1-55819-834-2) Broadman.

— Life & Letters of Paul. LC 99-54866. (Shepherd's Notes Bible Summary Ser.). 1999. pap. 5.95 (0-8054-9385-9) Broadman.

— Life & Teachings of Jesus. LC 99-54018. (Shepherd's Notes Bible Summary Ser.). 1999. pap. 5.95 (0-8054-9384-0) Broadman.

— Manners & Customs of Bible Times. LC 99-54865. (Shepherd's Notes Bible Summary Ser.). 1999. pap. 5.95 (0-8054-9376-X) Broadman.

— New Testament. LC 99-54017. (Shepherd's Notes Bible Summary Ser.). 1999. pap. 5.95 (0-8054-9378-6) Broadman.

— El Nuevo Testamento. (SPA.). 2000. pap. 5.95 (0-8054-9425-1) Broadman.

— Old Testament. LC 99-53654. (Shepherd's Notes Bible Summary Ser.). 1999. pap. 5.95 (0-8054-9377-8) Broadman.

— Pocket Bible. (SPA.). 1999. 31.99 (1-55819-997-7); 31.99 (1-55819-998-5); 31.99 (1-55819-999-3) Broadman.

— Pregnancy Journal. 1999. 11.99 (0-8054-0590-9) Broadman.

— The Super Giant Print Reference Bible. large type ed. 1999. 42.99 (1-55819-796-6) Broadman.

— Tips for the New Bride: Tiptionary Journal. (Illus.). 1999. 11.99 (0-8054-0355-8) Broadman.

— Ultrathin Classic Bible. 2000. 42.99 (1-55819-858-X); 49.99 (1-55819-859-8); 42.99 (1-55819-860-1); 49.99 (1-55819-861-X) Broadman.

— Ultrathin Reference Bible. 2000. 25.97 (1-55819-872-5); 25.97 (1-55819-873-3); 25.97 (1-55819-874-1); 25.97 (1-55819-875-X) Broadman.

— Water for the Soul. 1999. pap. 14.99 (0-8054-3309-0) Broadman.

Broadman & Holman Staff. 1 & 2 Tesalonicenzes (1 & 2 Thessalonians) 100p. 1999. pap. 5.95 (0-8054-9360-3) Broadman.

— Galatians, Ephesians, Philippians & Colossians, Vol. 8. (Holman New Testament Commentary Ser.). 400p. 1999. 16.99 (0-8054-0208-X) Broadman.

— Mark. LC 99-11542. (Shepherd's Notes Ser.). 100p. 1999. pap. 5.95 (0-8054-9071-X) Broadman.

— Mere Christianity. LC 99-37906. (Shepherd's Notes Ser.). 1999. pap. 5.95 (0-8054-9347-6) Broadman.

***Broadman & Holman Staff.** Psalms 51-100. LC 99-11544. (Shepherd's Notes Ser.). 100p. 1999. pap. 5.95 (0-8054-9340-9) Broadman.

Broadman & Holman Staff. Read to Me Bible 4 Kids. 1999. 16.99 (1-55819-844-X); 16.99 (1-55819-845-8) Broadman.

Broadman & Holman Staff. So That's in the Bible? LC 97-6436. 1997. pap. 14.99 (1-55819-474-6) Broadman.

Broadman & Holman Staff, ed. Stories of Jesus: The Greatest Stories of the New Testament. 1998. 9.99 (0-8054-9342-5) Broadman.

Broadman, Harry G. Meeting the Challenge of Chinese Enterprise Reform. LC 95-10466. (Discussion Paper Ser.: Vol. 283). 60p. 1995. pap. 22.00 (0-8213-3223-6, 13223) World Bank.

— Policy Options for Reform of Chinese State-Owned Enterprises. (World Bank Discussion Papers: No. 335). 248p. 1996. pap. 22.00 (0-8213-3686-X, 13686) World Bank.

Broadman, Harry G., ed. Case-by-Case Privatization in the Russian Federation: Lessons from International Experience. (Discussion Papers Ser.: No. 385R). (RUS.). 108p. 1998. pap. 22.00 (0-8213-4231-2, 14324) World Bank.

***Broadman, Harry G., ed.** Russian Enterprise Reform: Policies to Further the Transition. LC 98-51010. (Discussion Paper Ser.: No. 400). 159p. 1998. pap. 25.00 (0-8213-4405-6, 14405) World Bank.

Broadman, Harry G., ed. Russian Trade Policy Reform for World Trade Organization Accession. LC 98-51347. (Discussion Paper Ser.: No. 401). 95p. 1998. pap. 22.00 (0-8213-4406-4, 14406) World Bank.

Broadman, Harry G., et al. Natural Gas Markets after Deregulation: Methods of Analysis & Research Needs. LC 83-42907. 96p. 1983. pap. 11.00 (0-8018-3125-3) Resources Future.

Broadman, Henry. The Higher Life Doctrine of Sanctification Tried by the Word of God. 1994. pap. 21.99 (0-87377-179-6) GAM Pubns.

Broadman, Holman. Broadman Comments, Annual 1998-1999 ed. 1998. pap. text 12.99 (0-8054-1755-9) Broadman.

— First Christmas. 1999. 19.95 (0-88271-676-X) Regina Pr.

***Broadman Holman Publishing Staff.** Holman Ultrathin Classic Bible. 2000. 36.99 (1-55819-750-8) Broadman.

Broadman Holman Publishing Staff. Joshua. (New American Commentary Ser.). 1998. 29.99 (0-8054-0105-9) Broadman.

Broadman, Joseph. Bee Venom: The Natural Curative for Arthritis & Rheumatism. rev. ed. 220p. 1997. pap. 27.95 (1-890708-01-1) Health Res Pr.

Broadman, Muriel, jt. auth. see Yakim, Moni.

Broadman Publishing Staff. Share Jesus Without Fear. 1998. 12.99 (1-55819-793-1) Broadman.

Broadman, Ted, et al. Fundamentals of 3D Studio Max 1.0 Instructor Guide. (Version 1.0 Ser.). (Illus.). 1997. pap. text, teacher ed., spiral bd. 150.00 (1-890484-29-6, KnowledgeWorks) HTR Inc.

Broadmeadow, Mark S. J. & Freer-Smith, Peter H. Urban Woodland & the Benefits for Local Air Quality. ix, 89p. 1996. 50.00 (0-11-753191-X, Pub. by Statnry Office) Balogh.

Broadnax. Diversity & Affirmative Action. LC 99-48881. 2000. text 70.00 (0-8133-6691-7); pap. text 29.00 (0-8133-6690-9) Westview.

Broadnax, Derek A. The Black Entrepreneurs Guide to Million Dollar Business Opportunities. 75p. 1990. pap. 15.00 (1-56028-004-2) Blk Entrepreneurs.

— Black Entrepreneurs Guide to Money: How to Make, Keep It, & Grow Rich! rev. ed. 57p. 1989. pap. 13.00 (1-56028-001-8) Blk Entrepreneurs.

— The Black Entrepreneurs Guide to Money Sources: Where to Get It! 50p. 1992. pap. 15.00 (1-56028-006-9) Blk Entrepreneurs.

— The Black Entrepreneurs Guide to Money Sources Vol. 1: How to Get Your Share! 50p. 1992. pap. 15.00 (1-56028-003-4) Blk Entrepreneurs.

— The Black Entrepreneurs Guide to Starting & Building a Million Dollar Business of Your Own. 57p. 1990. pap. 17.00 (1-56028-002-6) Blk Entrepreneurs.

— What Every Black African-American Should Know to Gain Financial Success in the 90's. 60p. 1991. pap. 14.00 (1-56028-007-7) Blk Entrepreneurs.

Broadribb, Donald. The Dream Story. 246p. (Orig.). pap. 4.95 (0-85564-263-7, Pub. by Univ of West Aust Pr) Intl Spec Bk.

— Dream Story. 256p. 1995. pap. 20.00 (0-919123-45-7, Pub. by Inner City Bks) BookWorld.

— The Mystical Chorus: Jung & the Religious Dimension. LC 95-193988. 276p. (Orig.). 1996. pap. 12.95 (1-86429-019-6, Pub. by Millennium Bks) Morehouse Pub.

Broadribb, Violet. Introductory Pediatric Nursing. 3rd ed. (Illus.). 392p. 1982. text 26.00 (0-397-54330-1, 64-02739, Lppncott W & W.

Broadrick, Anette, et al. Help Wanted - Angel: A Loving Spirit, Earth Angel, Angel for Hire. (By Request Ser.). 1995. per. 5.50 (0-373-20118-4) Harlequin Bks.

Broadrick, Annette. Bachelor Father. (Desire Ser.). 1991. pap. 2.79 (0-373-15159-4) Silhouette.

— Choices. (Men Made in America Ser.). 1994. mass mkt. 3.59 (0-373-45175-X, 1-45175-6) Silhouette.

— Courtship Texas Style! (Desire Ser.). 1992. pap. 2.89 (0-373-05739-3, 5-05739-3) Silhouette.

— Daddy's Angel: Fabulous Father, under the Mistletoe. (Romance Ser.). 1993. per. 2.75 (0-373-08976-7, 5-08976-8) Silhouette.

***Broadrick, Annette.** Daughters of Texas: Megan's Marriage, Instant Mommy, The Groom, I Presume? 2000. mass mkt. 6.99 (0-373-20170-2, 1-20170-6) Harlequin Bks.

Broadrick, Annette. Despues de Tantos Anos. (SPA.). 1996. per. 3.50 (0-373-35159-3, 1-35159-2) Harlequin Bks.

— The Gemini Man. (Romance Ser.: No. 796). 1991. per. 2.50 (0-373-08796-9) Silhouette.

— Groom, I Presume? large type ed. (Romance (Large Print) Ser.). 1998. 21.95 (0-373-59928-5) Silhouette.

— Groom, I Presume? (Daughters of Texas) (Desire Ser.). 1996. per. 3.50 (0-373-05992-2, 1-05992-2) Silhouette.

— Hunter's Prey. (Western Lovers Ser.). 1995. per. 3.99 (0-373-88527-X, 1-88527-6) Harlequin Bks.

— Instant Mommy, Vol. 113. large type ed. (Silhouette Romance Ser.). 1998. 21.95 (0-373-59922-6) Harlequin Bks.

— Instant Mommy (Bundles of Joy, Daughters of Texas) LC 96-7285. (Romance Ser.). 186p. 1996. per. 3.25 (0-373-19139-1, 1-19139-4) Silhouette.

— Irresistible. (And the Winner Is...Ser.). 1997. mass mkt. 3.99 (0-373-48345-7, 1-48345-2) Harlequin Bks.

— Lean, Mean & Lonesome: Man of the Month Anniversary. (Desire Ser.: No. 1237). 1999. mass mkt. 3.75 (0-373-76237-2, 1-76237-6) Silhouette.

***Broadrick, Annette.** Marriage Prey. (Desire Ser.: Bk. 1327). 2000. mass mkt. 3.99 (0-373-76327-1, 1-76327-5) Silhouette.

Broadrick, Annette. Married? (Here Come the Grooms Ser.: No. 27). 1996. per. 3.99 (0-373-30127-8, 1-30127-4) Harlequin Bks.

— Married? (Romance Ser.: No. 742). 1990. per. 2.25 (0-373-08742-X) Silhouette.

***Broadrick, Annette.** Maximum Marriage: Men on a Mission (Hunter's Prey; Bachelor Father; Hawk's Flight), 3 bks. (Thirty-Six Hours Ser.). 2000. mass mkt. 6.99 (0-373-48411-9) Silhouette.

Broadrick, Annette. Megan's Marriage. (Desire Ser.). 1996. per. 3.50 (0-373-05979-5, 1-05979-9) Silhouette.

— Megan's Marriage. large type ed. (Large Print Ser.). 1998. 20.95 (0-373-59855-6) Harlequin Bks.

— Mysterious Mountain Man: Man of the Month. (Desire Ser.). 1995. mass mkt. 3.25 (0-373-05925-6, 1-05925-2) Silhouette.

— Mystery Wife. (Special Edition Ser.). 1994. per. 3.50 (0-373-09877-4, 5-09877-7) Silhouette.

— The President's Daughter. 1999. per. 4.25 (0-373-24226-3, Harlequin) Harlequin Bks.

— Quien es el Novio (The Groom, I Presume?) (Deseo Ser.). (SPA.). 1997. per. 3.50 (0-373-35172-0, 1-351725) Harlequin Bks.

— Return to Yesterday. (Western Lovers Ser.). 1995. per. 3.99 (0-373-88536-9, 1-88536-7) Harlequin Bks

***Broadrick, Annette.** Sons of Texas: Callaway Country. 2000. per. 5.99 (0-373-48407-0) Silhouette.

Broadrick, Annette. Sons of Texas: Cowboys & Wedding Bells, 2 bks. in 1. (By Request Ser.). 1999. per. 5.99 (0-373-20157-5, 1-20157-3) Harlequin Bks.

— Sons of Texas: Love & Courtship!, 2 bks. in 1. 1998. per. 5.99 (0-373-20148-6, 1-20148-2) Harlequin Bks.

— Sons of Texas: Rogues & Ranchers. 1996. per. 4.99 (0-373-48336-8) Harlequin Bks.

— The Sound of Summer. (Men at Work Ser.: Vol. 19). 1998. per. 4.50 (0-373-81031-8) Harlequin Bks.

— Surprise, Surprise! 1993. mass mkt. 4.99 (0-373-43262-0, 5-48262-5) Silhouette.

— Tall, Dark & Texan: Man of the Month/50th Book (Desire Ser.). 1999. per. 3.75 (0-373-76261-5, 1-76261-6) Silhouette.

— Temptation Texas Style! 1994. mass mkt. 2.99 (0-373-05883-7, 1-05883-3) Harlequin Bks.

— Unforgettable Bride. (Silhouette Romance Ser.). 1998. per. 3.50 (0-373-19294-0, 0-19294-8) Silhouette.

— Unheavenly Angel. (Family Continuity Program Ser.: No. 16). 1999. per. 4.50 (0-373-82164-6, 1-82164-4) Harlequin Bks.

— Where There Is Love. (Desire Ser.: No. 714). 1992. pap. 2.89 (0-373-05714-8, 5-05714-6) Harlequin Bks.

— Zeke. (Desire Ser.). 1993. per. 2.99 (0-373-05793-3, 5-05793-0) Silhouette.

Broadrick, Annette & Davis, Justine. Love Child: Where There Is Love: Upon the Storm, 2 vols. in 1. (By Request 2's Ser.). 2000. per. 4.99 (0-373-21704-8, 1-21704-1) Harlequin Bks.

Broadrick, Annette, et al. Silhouette Summer Sizzlers, 1994. 1994. mass mkt. 4.99 (0-373-48321-X) Harlequin Bks.

— Solution: Marriage. 1993. mass mkt. 5.50 (0-373-20096-X, 1-20096-3) Silhouette.

— Wanted: Mother. 1996. per. 4.99 (0-373-48318-X, 1-48318-9) Harlequin Bks.

Broadskaya, Natalia. Henri Rousseau. (Masters of World Painting Ser.). (C). 1983. text 100.00 (0-569-08791-3, Pub. by Collets) St Mut.

Broadstock, Havey, jt. auth. see Farrugia, Dennis.

Broadstreet, Sarah. Of Life Immense. LC 91-42542. 507p. 1992. 25.00 (0-933532-84-9) BkMk.

Broadus. 95-96 Federal Audit Update Service. 1995. 129.00 (0-15-602139-0) Harcourt Legal.

— 95-96 Federal Audit Update Service. 95th ed. 1995. 79.00 (0-15-601993-0) Harcourt Legal.

— Single Audits. 96th ed. 1995. pap. text. write for info. (0-15-602179-X) Harcourt Coll Pubs.

Broadus, Boyce. History of First Baptist Church Russellville. 1967. 15.00 (0-317-13830-8); pap. 7.00 (0-685-09691-2) Banner Pr AL.

Broadus, Calvin. The Dynamics of Time & Stress. 24p. 1998. pap. 4.95 (0-913507-57-1) New Forums.

Broadus, Debbie, ed. see Raynes, Bert.

Broadus, Edmund K. Laureateship. LC 67-22082. (Essay Index Reprint Ser.). 1977. 21.95 (0-8369-1326-4, Ayer.

— Saturday & Sunday. LC 67-23186. (Essay Index Reprint Ser.). 1977. 19.95 (0-8369-0255-6) Ayer.

Broadus, J. A. Tratado Sobre la Predicacion: On the Preparation & Delivery of Sermons. Barocio, Ernesto, tr. 336p. 1963. reprint ed. pap. 11.99 (0-311-42034-5) Casa Bautista.

Broadus, James & Vartanov, Raphael. The Oceans & Environmental Security: Shared U. S. & Russian Perspectives. LC 93-48894. 320p. 1994. text 60.00 (1-55963-235-6); pap. text 40.00 (1-55963-236-4) Island Pr.

Broadus, John A. Commentary on Matthew. LC 89-77852. 664p. 1989. pap. 26.99 (0-8254-2283-3, Kregel Class) Kregel.

— On the Preparation & Delivery of Sermons: Fourth Edition. 4th ed. LC 78-20602. 368p. 1979. 25.00 (0-06-061112-X, Pub. by Harper SF) HarpC.

Broadus, Loren. Ethics for Real People: A Guide for the Morally Perplexed. 144p. (Orig.). 1996. pap. 14.99 (0-8272-0809-X) Chalice Pr.

***Broadus, Loren.** Responses to Suffering. 2001. pap. 14.99 (0-8272-3222-5) Chalice Pr.

Broadus, W. A., Jr., et al. Guide to Single Audits, 3 vols. Incl. Vol. 1. Guide to Single Audits. 1998. ring bd. 168.00 (0-7646-0442-2); Vol. 2. Guide to Single Audits. 1998. ring bd. 168.00 (0-7646-0443-0); Vol. 3. Guide to Single Audits. 1998. ring bd. 168.00 (0-7646-0444-9); 168.00 (0-7646-0441-4) Prctnrs Pub Co.

***Broadus, W. A., Jr., et al.** Guide to Single Audits, 3 vols. 1999. ring bd. 168.00 (0-7646-0743-X) Prctnrs Pub Co.

Broadus, W. A., Jr., et al. Guide To Single Audits, 3 vols. Incl. Vol. 1. 1997. ring bd. Not sold separately (0-7646-0192-X); Vol. 2. 1997. ring bd. Not sold separately (0-7646-0193-8); Vol. 3. 1997. ring bd. Not sold separately (0-7646-0194-6); 150.00 (0-7646-0191-1) Prctnrs Pub Co.

***Broadus, W. A., Jr., et al.** Guide to Single Audits, Vol. 1. 1999. ring bd. write for info. (0-7646-0744-8) Prctnrs Pub Co.

— Guide to Single Audits, Vol. 2. 1999. ring bd. write for info. (0-7646-0745-6) Prctnrs Pub Co.

— Guide to Single Audits, Vol. 3. 1999. ring bd. write for info. (0-7646-0746-4) Prctnrs Pub Co.

***Broadview Media, Inc. Staff.** Fearless Flying: A Complete Program to Help You Overcome Your Fear of Flying. unabridged ed. (Illus.). 2000. 69.95 incl. audio, VHS (0-9679724-0-X) Broadview Media.

Broadview Press Staff, ed. see LePan, Don.

***Broadwater, Andrea.** Marian Anderson: Singer & Humanitarian. LC 99-36258. (African-American Biographies Ser.). (Illus.). 128p. (gr. 6 up). 2000. lib. bdg. 20.95 (0-7660-1211-5) Enslow Pubs.

***Broadwater, Deborah.** English Skills Practice & Apply: Grade 4. (Illus.). 128p. 2000. pap. text 10.95 (1-58037-119-1, Pub. by M Twain Media) Carson-Dellos.

— English Skills Practice & Apply: Grade 5. (Illus.). 128p. 2000. pap. text 10.95 (1-58037-120-5, Pub. by M Twain Media) Carson-Dellos.

— English Skills Practice & Apply: Grade 6. (Illus.). 128p. 2000. pap. text 10.95 (1-58037-121-3, Pub. by M Twain Media) Carson-Dellos.

— English Skills Practice & Apply: Grade 7. (Illus.). 128p. 2000. pap. text 10.95 (1-58037-122-1, Pub. by M Twain Media) Carson-Dellos.

Broadwater, Jeff. Adlai Stevenson & American Politics: The Odyssey of a Cold War Liberal. LC 93-43000. (Twayne's Twentieth-Century American Biography Ser.). 304p. 1994. 27.95 (0-8057-7798-9, Twyne); pap. 14.95 (0-8057-7799-7, Twyne) Mac Lib Ref.

— Eisenhower & the Anti-Communist Crusade. LC 91-32011. (Illus.). xiii, 291p. (C). 1992. 45.00 (0-8078-2015-6) U of NC Pr.

***Broadwater, Robert.** Desperate Deliverance: The Story of African-Americans in the Civil War. Mitchell, Patrica & Gowan, Judy, eds. 72p. 1998. 6.50 (0-9670553-0-X) Daisy Pubg.

Broadwater, Robert P. Of Men of Muskets Vol. XI: Stories of the Civil War. LC 98-7161. (Civil War Heritage Ser.). 80p. 1998. pap. 7.95 (1-57249-105-1, Burd St Pr) White Mane Pub.

Broadway, Beth A. Board Orientation Training Design Handbook. Carlin, Chip, ed. LC 95-100650. 1988. pap. text 4.00 (0-930713-59-1) Lit Vol Am.

Broadway, David, et al. Clinical Examination Cases in Ophthalmology. LC 99-25521. (Illus.). 336p. 1999. pap. text 85.00 (0-7506-2500-7) Buttrwrth-Heinemann.

Broadway, Frank. State Intervention in British Industry, 1964-68. LC 79-115974. 191p. 1975. 25.00 (0-8386-7690-1) Fairleigh Dickinson.

Broadway, Robin, jt. ed. see Banting, Keith S.

Broadwell, John M. Practical Guide to Particle Counting: A Guide for Drinking Water Treatment. 224p. 1999. 49.95 (1-56670-306-9) Lewis Pubs.

Broadwell, Lynn. Here Comes the Guide: Northern California: Exceptional Locations for Weddings & Special Events. 6th ed. (Here Comes the Guide Ser.). 856p. 1999. pap. text 19.95 (1-885355-04-1) Hopscotch Pr.

***Broadwell, Lynn & Brenner, Jan.** Here Comes the Guide: Southern California: Locations & Services for Weddings & Special Events. 6th ed. (Here Comes the Guide Ser.). (Illus.). 700p. 1999. pap. 19.95 (1-885355-06-8) Hopscotch Pr.

Broadwell, Martin M. The Lecture Method of Instruction. Langdon, Danny G., ed. LC 79-23528. (Instructional Design Library). 116p. 1980. 27.95 (0-87778-147-8) Educ Tech Pubns.

— Moving up to Supervision. 2nd ed. LC 85-29411. (Training & Development Ser.). 256p. 1986. pap. 70.95 (0-471-83677-X) Wiley.

— New Supervisor. 3rd ed. 1984. pap. text 18.95 (0-201-10353-2) Addison-Wesley.

— The New Supervisor: How to Thrive in Your First Year As a Manager. 5th ed. LC 98-14806. 304p. 1998. pap. 15.00 (0-201-33992-7) Addison-Wesley.

— Supervisor: On the Job Training. 4th ed. 1995. pap. 23.00 (0-201-56363-0) Addison-Wesley.

Broadwell, Martin M., jt. auth. see Dieckelmann, Nancy L.

Broadwell, Martin M., jt. auth. see Simpson, W. F.

Broadwell, R. G. & Hickey, C. F., eds. Toughness & Fracture Behavior of Titanium - STP 651. 294p. 1978. 28.50 (0-8031-0591-6, STP651) ASTM.

Broadwell, Richard D., ed. Neuroscience, Memory, & Language: Papers Presented at a Symposium Series Cosponsored by the National Institute of Mental Health & the Library of Congress. LC 94-37346. (Decade of the Brain Ser.: Vol. 1). 1995. pap. write for info. (0-8444-0847-6) Lib Congress.

— Neuroscience, Memory, & Language: Papers Presented at a Symposium Series Cosponsored by the National Institute of Mental Health & the Library of Congress. LC 94-37346. (Decade of the Brain Ser.: Vol. 1). (Illus.). 160p. 1995. 26.00 (0-8444-0815-8) Lib Congress.

Broadwin, David A. Negotiating & Documenting Business Acquisitions. LC 97-70290. 374p. 1997. text 189.50 (0-8318-0690-7) Am Law Inst.

Broadwin, John, tr. see Hoffmann, Hilmar.

Broadwin, John, tr. see Liepman, Ruth.

Broadwin, John A., tr. see Schipperges, Heinrich.

Broadwin, John A., tr. see Scholz, Piotr O.

Broadwin, Judith, et al. Solutions, A. P. Calculus Problems, 1984-1998, Pt. II, AB & BC. (Illus.). 165p. 1998. pap. text 12.00 (1-882144-06-6) Math Olympiads.

Broady, Dorothy. Brownville Nebraska Territory: Story of a Town. 176p. 1996. pap. 24.95 (1-886225-30-3) Dageforde Pub.

Broady, Elspeth, jt. auth. see Carpenter, Catrine.

Broady, P. A. The Terrestrial Algae of Signy Island, South Orkney Islands. (British Antarctic Survey Report Ser.: No. 98). 120p. 1979. 30.00 (0-85665-056-0, Pub. by Brit Antarctic Surv) Balogh.

B

Broaker, Frank & Chapman, Richard M. The American Accountants' Manual: Examinations Questions Together with Answers, Vol. 1. Brief, Richard P., ed. LC 77-87264. (Development of Contemporary Accounting Thought Ser.). 1978. reprint ed. lib. bdg. 23.95 (0-405-10893-1) Ayer.

Broan, David & Broan, Freda. Upholstery: A Practical Guide. (Illus.). 119p. 1987. 13.95 (0-900873-48-5, Pub. by Bishopsgte Pr); pap. 11.95 (0-900873-49-3, Pub. by Bishopsgte Pr) Intl Spec Bk.

Broan, Freda, jt. auth. see Broan, David.

Broatch, Joanne, ed. see Ruhe, Pia & Ruhe, Brian.

Broatch, Stuart. Vauxhall. LC 98-145631. (Photographic History of Transport Ser.). (Illus.). 160p. 1998. pap. 19.95 (0-7509-1561-7, Pub. by Sutton Pub Ltd) Intl Pubs Mktg.

Broback, Steve, jt. auth. see Williams, Robin.

Brobeck, John R., et al, eds. History of the American Physiological Society: The First Century, 1887-1987. (American Physiological Society Book). (Illus.). 542p. 1988. text 45.00 (0-19-520697-5) OUP.

Brobeck, Stephen, ed. Encyclopedia of the Consumer Movement. LC 97-41345. 659p. 1997. lib. bdg. 99.50 (0-87436-987-8, RF-1781) ABC-CLIO.

Broberg, K. Bertram. Cracks & Fracture. LC 00-265839. (Illus.). 768p. (C). 1999. 99.95 (0-12-134130-5) Acad Pr.

Broberg, Carl M. Local Government in Ohio. LC 95-79975. (Illus.). 220p. (Orig.). (J). (gr. 8). 1995. pap. text 24.95 (0-9647908-0-7) Amer Legal Pubng.

Broberg, Gunnar & Roll-Hansen, Nils. Eugenics & the Welfare State: Norway, Sweden, Denmark, & Finland. LC 95-17633. 300p. 1996. 39.95 (0-87013-413-2) Mich St U Pr.

Broberg, Hal. Experiments in Electronic Communication. 2nd ed. 224p. (C). 1990. pap. text 26.60 (0-675-21257-X, Merrill Coll) P-H.

Broberg, Merle. Barbados: Major World Nations. (Major World Nations Ser.). (Illus.). 144p. (YA). (gr. 5 up). 1999. lib. bdg. 19.95 (0-7910-4756-3) Chelsea Hse.

Broberg, Morten P. The European Commission's Jurisdiction to Scrutinise Mergers. LC 97-51737. (European Monographs Ser.). 408p. 1998. pap. 81.00 (90-411-0549-2) Kluwer Law Intl.

Broberg, Rose F. Stories & Games for Easy Lipreading Practice. 2nd ed. LC 71-14203. 114p. reprint ed. pap. 35.40 (0-7837-1253-7, 204139000020) Bks Demand.

Brobst, Lee & Beddoe, A. F. U. S. of A. the Republic: How You Lost It, How You Get It Back. (Illus.). 96p. (Orig.). 1992. pap. 15.00 (1-881201-03-1) S & J Unltd.

Brobst, William A. Comparison of Nineteen Eighty-Five & Nineteen Seventy-Three IAEA Transport Safety Regulations. 1985. 17.00 (0-9608112-2-2) Transport Env.

— Pulling Your Tail: A Primer on the Art of Motorcycle Trailering. LC 82-90072. (Illus.). 64p. 1982. pap. 5.65 (0-9608112-0-6) Transport Env.

Brobyn, Anne & Cecceralo, Julius. Independence: A Lifeskills Guide for Teens. 96p. (YA). 1990. pap. 14.95 (0-87868-350-X, 3500) Child Welfare.

Broc, Numa. Dictionnaire Illustre des Explorateurs et Grands Voyageurs Francais du XIX Siecle Vol. 1: Afrique. (FRE.). 346p. 1988. 150.00 (0-7859-7994-8, 2735501582) Fr & Eur.

— Dictionnaire Illustre des Explorateurs et Grands Voyageurs Francais du XIX Siecle Vol. 2: Asie. (FRE.). 452p. 1992. 175.00 (0-7859-7995-6, 2735502333) Fr & Eur.

Brocas, Anne-Marie, et al. Women & Social Security: Progress Towards Equality of Treatment. v, 116p. (Orig.). 1990. 31.50 (92-2-106518-9); pap. 22.50 (92-2-105559-0) Intl Labour Office.

Brocato, Rick C., et al. Empowering the Leader Within: Four Essential Virtues: A Process for Achieving Peak Leadership Performance. LC 95-90765. (Illus.). 128p. (Orig.). 1996. pap. 14.95 (0-9648722-0-X) Virtus Pr Pubns.

Brocchi, Paul. Mission Scientifique au Mexique et dans l'Amerique Centrale . . . Recherches Zoologiques: Etude des Batraciens de l'Amerque Centrale. Sterling, Keir B., ed. LC 77-81099. (Biologists & Their World Ser.). (Illus.). 1978. reprint ed. lib. bdg. 19.95 (0-405-10681-5) Ayer.

Broccoli, Cubby & Zec, Donald. When the Snow Melts: The Autobiography. (Illus.). 352p. 1999. 29.50 (0-7522-1162-5) Trans-Atlantic Des.

Broccoli, Matthew, ed. see Griffin, Alice.

Broccolo, Bernadette M. & Niles, Kathleen M. Tax-Exempt Status of Health Care Organizations. (BNA's Health Law & Business Ser.: No. 1900). 1996. 125.00 (1-55871-340-9) BNA.

Broce, Gerald. History of Anthropology. LC 72-97620. (Basic Concepts in Anthropology Ser.). 48p. (C). reprint ed. pap. 30.00 (0-8357-9051-7, 201587800097) Bks Demand.

Broce, Thomas E. Fund Raising: The Guide to Raising Money from Private Sources. 2nd enl. rev. ed. LC 85-40948. (Illus.). 288p. 1986. 27.95 (0-8061-1988-8) U of Okla Pr.

Broce, Thomas E. & Junkin, Daniel P. Directory of Oklahoma Foundations. 2nd rev. ed. LC 82-6984. 304p. 1982. 29.95 (0-8061-1827-X) U of Okla Pr.

Broch. Selected Essays. 1993. lib. bdg. 34.95 (0-226-07517-6) U Ch Pr.

Broch-Due, Vigdis, et al, eds. Carved Flesh - Cast Selves: Gendered Symbols & Social Practices. 288p. 1993. 49.50 (0-85496-725-7, Pub. by Berg Pubs) NYU Pr.

— Carved Flesh - Cast Selves: Gendered Symbols & Social Practices. 288p. (C). 1993. pap. 19.50 (0-85496-868-7, Pub. by Berg Pubs) NYU Pr.

Broch-Due, Vigdis, jt. ed. see Anderson, David M.

Broch, E., et al, eds. Hydropower '97: Proceedings of the 3rd International Conference, Trondheim, Norway, 30 June-2 July 1997. (Illus.). 724p. (C). 1997. text 126.00 (90-5410-888-6, Pub. by A A Balkema) Ashgate Pub Co.

Broch, E. & Lysne, D. K., eds. Hydropower, 1992: Proceedings of the Second International Conference on Hydropower, Lillehammer, Norway, 16-18 June 1992. (Illus.). 800p. (C). 1992. text 149.00 (90-5410-054-0, Pub. by A A Balkema) Ashgate Pub Co.

Broch, Harald B. Growing up Agreeably: Bonerate Childhood Observed. LC 89-49006. (Illus.). 200p. 1990. reprint ed. pap. 62.00 (0-608-04393-1, 206517400001) Bks Demand.

— Woodland Trappers: Hare Indians of Northwestern Canada. (Bergen Studies in Social Anthropology: No. 35). 224p. (Orig.). 1987. pap. text 13.95 (0-936508-68-X, Pub. by Bergen Univ Dept Social Anthro) MBIPubg.

Broch, Hermann. Death of Virgil. 1990. 17.50 (0-8446-1742-3) Peter Smith.

— The Death of Virgil. Untermeyer, Jean S., tr. LC 94-34712. 1995. pap. 16.00 (0-679-75548-9) Vin Bks.

***Broch, Hermann.** The Guiltless. (Orig.). 2000. pap. 18.95 (0-8101-6078-1) Northwestern U Pr.

Broch, Hermann. Hugo Von Hofmannsthal & His Time: The European Imagination, 1860-1920. Steinberg, Michael P., ed. LC 84-76. 216p. 1984. pap. text 17.00 (0-226-07516-8) U Ch Pr.

— Hugo von Hofmannsthal & His Time: The European Imagination, 1860-1920. Steinberg, Michael P., ed. & tr. by. LC 84-76. 214p. reprint ed. pap. 66.40 (0-608-09398-X, 205414300004) Bks Demand.

— The Sleepwalkers: A Trilogy. Muir, Willa & Muir, Edwin, trs. LC 95-35201. 656p. 1996. pap. 18.00 (0-679-76406-2) Random.

***Broch, Hermann.** The Unknown Quantity. 2000. pap. 17.95 (0-8101-6082-X) Northwestern U Pr.

Broch, Hermann. The Unknown Quantity. Muir, Willa & Muir, Edwin, trs. from GER. LC 87-63049. 240p. 1988. reprint ed. pap. 10.95 (0-910395-36-5) Marlboro Pr.

Broch, Ingvild, jt. ed. see Jahr, Ernst H.

Broch, Tica, tr. see Donnet, Pierre-Antoine.

Broch, Yitzhak I. The Book of Ruth. 1975. 9.95 (0-87306-328-7); pap. 7.95 (0-87306-329-5) Feldheim.

Brochen, A. Les Mots de la Maison: English, French, German Vocabulary of Home Buying, Construction, Restoration. (ENG, FRE & GER.). 339p. 1995. pap. 79.95 (0-7859-9636-2) Fr & Eur.

Brocher, Tobias. Lexikon der Sozialerziehung. (GER.). 1972. 17.95 (0-8288-6410-1, M7221) Fr & Eur.

Brocheriou, C., et al. CD-ROM Atlas of Pathology: Stomatology - ENT. (ENG & FRE.). 1998. 149.00 incl. cd-rom (3-540-14654-7) Spr-Verlag.

Brochert, Adam, jt. auth. see Brochert, Bruno.

***Brochert, Bruno & Brochert, Adam.** Crush the Boards: The Ultimate USMLE Step 2 Review. LC 99-42852. (Illus.). 224p. (C). 1999. pap. text 28.00 (1-56053-366-8, Pub. by Hanley & Belfus) Mosby Inc.

Broches, Aaron. Selected Essays: World Bank, ICSID, & Other Subjects of Public & Private International Law. LC 94-19430. 563p. (C). 1995. lib. bdg. 160.00 (0-7923-2906-6) Kluwer Academic.

Broches, Aron. Commentary on the UNCITRAL Model Law on International Commercial Arbitration. 240p. 1990. pap. 60.00 (90-6544-507-2) Kluwer Law Intl.

Broches, Charles F. & Spranger, Michael S., eds. The Politics & Economics of Columbia River Water. LC 85-11506. (Orig.). 1985. pap. 10.00 (0-934539-02-2, WSG-WO) Wash Sea Grant.

Brocheux, Pierre. Indochina: The Ambiguous Colonization, 1858-1954. (Illus.). (C). text. write for info. (0-472-10951-0) U of Mich Pr.

Brocheux, Pierre. The Mekong Delta: Ecology, Economy, & Revolution, 1860-1960. LC 94-69001. 269p. Date not set. 45.00 (1-881261-12-3); pap. 19.95 (1-881261-13-1) U Wisc Ctr SE Asian.

Brochmann, Grete. European Integration & Immigration from Third Countries. 1995. pap. 26.00 (82-00-22721-9) Scandnvan Univ Pr.

Brochmann, Grete & Hammar, Tomas, eds. Mechanisms of Immigration Control: A Comparative Analysis of European Regulation Policies. 316p. 1999. 65.00 (1-85973-267-4, Pub. by Berg Pubs); pap. 19.50 (1-85973-272-0, Pub. by Berg Pubs) NYU Pr.

Brochner, Jessie, tr. see Lagerlof, Selma.

Brochon, Pierre. Eugene Pottier: Naissance de Pinternationale. (FRE.). 310p. 1997. pap. 74.95 (2-86808-109-6) Intl Scholars.

Brochu, Jim. Lucy in the Afternoon: An Intimate Memoir of Lucille Ball. large type ed. (General Ser.). 367p. 1991. lib. bdg. 21.95 (0-8161-5077-X, G K Hall Lrg Type) Mac Lib Ref.

Brochu, S. Bear's Big Day. (Illus.). 24p. (ps-3). 1998. pap. text 5.25 (0-9681925-1-3) Hushion Hse.

Brock. Cost Accounting Principles. 5th ed. 1989. student ed. 26.82 (0-07-008153-0) McGraw.

Brock. Great Reform Acts. 416p. 1993. 68.95 (0-7512-0238-X) Ashgate Pub Co.

Brock, et al. Quarterly Review of Literature: The 1960s, Poetry, Vol. XV, Nos. 1-2. 1960. pap. 15.00 (1-888545-32-1) Quarterly Rev.

Brock & Company Staff. A Brock Feast: Celebrating 70 Years of Cooking. Brock, Claudie J., ed. (Illus.). 240p. 1997. text, spiral bd. 20.00 (0-9660002-1-8, 1000) Brock & Co.

Brock, Alice M. How to Massage Your Cat. (Illus.). 32p. 1992. 8.95 (0-8118-0203-5) Chronicle Bks.

Brock, Anita. Divorce Recovery. 192p. 1991. reprint ed. pap. 7.95 (0-940999-80-3, C2182) Star Bible.

Brock, Arthur J., ed. Greek Medicine, Being Extracts Illustrative of Medical Writing from Hippocrates to Galen. LC 76-179302. (Library of Greek Thought: No. 8). reprint ed. 36.50 (0-404-07806-0) AMS Pr.

***Brock, Avril.** Into the Enchanted Forest. 130p. 1999. pap. 22.50 (1-85856-132-9, Trentham Bks) Stylus Pub VA.

Brock, B. Peter, et al, eds. Inorganic Chemical Nomenclature: Principles & Practice. LC 90-760. (Illus.). 148p. 1990. text 65.00 (0-8412-1697-5, Pub. by Am Chemical) OUP.

— Inorganic Chemical Nomenclature: Principles & Practice. LC 90-760. (Illus.). 148p. 1990. pap. 39.95 (0-8412-1698-3) Am Chemical.

***Brock, Barbara, et al.** Reality Comprehension Clock Test: RCCT, 2 vols. (Illus.). 4p. 1999. pap. 1.09 (0-9677014-1-4, 2331) RCCT Pr.

— Reality Comprehension Clock Test Manual Vol. 2: RCCT Manual. (Illus.). 45p. 1999. pap. text 49.95 (0-9677014-0-6) RCCT Pr.

Brock, Barbara H. The Development of Public Utility Accounting in New York. LC 81-81934. (MSU Public Utilities Papers: Vol. 1981). (Illus.). 319p. reprint ed. pap. 98.90 (0-608-20492-7, 207174400002) Bks Demand.

Brock, Barbara L. & Grady, Marilyn L. From First-Year to First-Rate: Principals Guiding Beginning Teachers. LC 96-51205. (Illus.). 120p. 1997. 43.95 (0-8039-6418-8); pap. 18.95 (0-8039-6419-6) Corwin Pr.

— From First-Year to First-Rate: Principals Guiding Beginning Teachers. 120p. 1997. 40.00 (2-8106-6418-8); pap. 18.00 (2-8106-6419-6) NEA.

— Principals in Transition: Tips for Surviving Succession. LC 95-7973. (RTS Ser.). 64p. 1995. pap. 14.95 (0-8039-6238-X, 7694) Corwin Pr.

Brock, Bernard L., ed. Kenneth Burke & Contemporary European Thought: Rhetoric in Transition. LC 94-35290. (Rhetoric & Communication Ser.). 296p. (C). 1995. text 39.95 (0-8173-0731-1) U of Ala Pr.

— Kenneth Burke & the 21st Century. LC 98-10475. (Series in Speech Communication). 288p. (C). 1998. text 65.50 (0-7914-4007-9); pap. text 21.95 (0-7914-4008-7) State U NY Pr.

Brock, Bernard L., et al, eds. Methods of Rhetorical Criticism: A Twentieth-Century Perspective. 3rd rev. ed. LC 89-35152. 520p. (C). 1990. pap. text 24.95 (0-8143-2300-6) Wayne St U Pr.

Brock, Betty. No Flying in the House. LC 79-104755. (Trophy Bk.). (Illus.). 144p. (J). (gr. 3-7). 1982. pap. 4.95 (0-06-440130-8, HarpTrophy) HarpC Child Bks.

— No Flying in the House. (Harper Trophy Book Ser.). 1982. 10.05 (0-606-13665-7, Pub. by Turtleback) Demco.

***Brock, Bill, et al.** The Beginner's Guide to Becoming a Complete Trader - Trading Stock Options. 53p. 1999. pap. 25.00 (0-9673555-0-8) Complete Trader.

Brock-Broido, Lucie. A Hunger. LC 87-46036. 80p. 1988. pap. 18.00 (0-394-75852-8) Knopf.

— The Master Letters. 96p. 1997. pap. 14.00 (0-679-76599-9) Knopf.

— The Master Letters. LC 95-30284. 96p. 1995. 21.00 (0-679-44174-3) Random.

Brock, Bryn J. The Woman Clothed with the Sun: A Story from the Book of Revelation. Childs, Karin A., ed. LC 99-72286. (Illus.). 32p. 1999. 15.95 (0-9659164-1-3) Fountain Publ.

Brock, C. Control of Restrictive Practices from 1956. 1969. 6.95 (0-07-094038-X) McGraw.

Brock, Carolyn. Asante Africa. 250p. 1990. pap. 10.00 (0-8309-0580-4) Herald Pub Hse.

Brock, Carolyn & Brock, David. The Gift of Peace. LC 93-35808. (Orig.). 1994. pap. 2.00 (0-8309-0643-6) Herald Pub Hse.

Brock, Charles. Boas Novas para Vocu.Tr. of Good News for You. (POR.). 28p. 1987. pap. 1.00 (1-885504-09-8) Church Gwth.

— Bonne Nouvelle pour Vous. Balzora, Renaud, tr.Tr. of Good News for You. (FRE.). 28p. (Orig.). 1993. pap. 1.00 (1-885504-06-3) Church Gwth.

— Buenas Nuevas para Ti. Vargas, Ruby, tr.Tr. of Good News for You. (SPA.). 28p. 1986. pap. 1.00 (1-885504-05-5) Church Gwth.

— Como Dirigir un Biblico Estudio por Metodos Indirectos. Vargas, Ruby, tr.Tr. of Leading a Bible Study by Indirect Methods. (SPA.). 19p. (Orig.). 1985. pap. 1.00 (1-885504-01-2) Church Gwth.

— Conduire une Etude Biblique par des Methodes Indirectes. Balzora, Renaud, tr.Tr. of Leading a Bible Study by Indirect Methods. (FRE.). 16p. (Orig.). 1993. pap. 1.00 (1-885504-03-9) Church Gwth.

— E Agora?Tr. of I Have Been Born Again, What Next?. (POR.). 56p. 1987. pap. 3.00 (1-885504-19-5) Church Gwth.

— Galatians, from Law to Grace: A Bible Study Guide. rev. ed. 28p. 1993. pap. 1.50 (1-885504-23-3) Church Gwth.

— Good News for You. 28p. (Orig.). 1973. pap. 1.00 (1-885504-04-7) Church Gwth.

— Good News for You. (CAM.). 28p. (Orig.). 1985. pap. 1.00 (1-885504-10-1) Church Gwth.

— Good News for You. (CHI.). 37p. (Orig.). 1989. pap. 1.00 (1-885504-07-1) Church Gwth.

— Good News for You. (RUS.). 30p. (Orig.). 1994. pap. 1.00 (1-885504-33-0) Church Gwth.

— Good News For You: Prison Edition. 28p. 1998. pap. 1.00 (1-885504-44-6) Church Gwth.

— He Nacido De Nuevo Ahora Que? Mussiett, Salomon, tr.Tr. of I Have Been Born Again, What Next?. (SPA.). 92p. 1986. pap. 3.00 (1-885504-16-0) Church Gwth.

— Huong Dan Mot Lop Hoc Kinh Thanh Bang Phuong Phap Gian Tiep.Tr. of Leading a Bible Study by Indirect Methods. (VIE.). 16p. (Orig.). 1985. pap. 1.00 (1-885504-02-0) Church Gwth.

— I Have Been Born Again, What Next? (CHI.). 83p. (Orig.). 1989. pap. 3.00 (1-885504-18-7) Church Gwth.

— I Have Been Born Again, What Next? rev. ed. 100p. (Orig.). 1994. pap. 3.00 (1-885504-15-2) Church Gwth.

— Indigenous Church Planting, a Practical Journey. 272p. 1990. pap., student ed. 10.00 (1-885504-27-6) Church Gwth.

— Indigenous Church Planting in Review. 28p. 1996. pap. 1.00 (1-885504-38-1) Church Gwth.

— Je Suis Ne de Nouveau. Balzora, Renaud, tr.Tr. of I Have Been Born Again, What Next?. (FRE.). 80p. (Orig.). 1993. pap. 3.00 (1-885504-17-9) Church Gwth.

— John, Behold the Lamb: A Bible Study Guide. 164p. 1994. pap. 5.00 (1-885504-24-1) Church Gwth.

— Leading a Bible Study by Indirect Methods. 16p. 1975. pap. 1.00 (1-885504-00-4) Church Gwth.

— Plantar Iglesias Autoctonas: Un Viaje Practico. Armengol, Norma C., tr.Tr. of Indigenous Church Planting: A Practical Journey. (SPA.). 262p. 1996. pap. 10.00 (1-885504-35-7) Church Gwth.

— Questions People & Churches Ask. rev. ed. 228p. 1997. pap. 10.00 (1-885504-43-8) Church Gwth.

— Romans: The Road to Righteousness. 120p. (Orig.). 1996. pap. 5.00 (1-885504-26-8) Church Gwth.

— Tin Mung Cho Ban.Tr. of Good News for You. (VIE.). 28p. 1987. pap. 1.00 (1-885504-08-X) Church Gwth.

Brock, Charles, compiled by. Good News in Song. 23p. (Orig.). 1989. pap. 1.00 (1-885504-28-4) Church Gwth.

Brock, Charles D. Principles & Practice of Indigenous Church Planting. 96p. 1981. pap. 6.00 (1-885504-45-4) Church Gwth.

Brock, Claude L. & Budd, Thomas. Farming Once Upon a Time: More Remarkable Photographs by J. C. Allen & Son. LC 96-84463. (Illus.). 160p. (J). 1996. 24.95 (0-9643429-2-8) Concord Pubs.

Brock, Claudie, ed. see Philadelphia Rotary Club Members & Wives.

Brock, Claudie J., ed. see Brock & Company Staff.

Brock, Clifton. Americans for Democratic Action: Its Role in National Politics. LC 85-7976. 229p. 1985. reprint ed. lib. bdg. 65.00 (0-313-24284-4, BRAD, Greenwood Pr) Greenwood.

— The Literature of Political Science: A Guide for Students, Librarians, & Teachers. LC 79-79426. 244p. reprint ed. pap. 75.70 (0-608-11188-0, 201758600007) Bks Demand.

Brock, Colin, ed. Caribbean in Europe: Aspects of the West Indian Experience in Britain, France & the Netherlands. (Legacies of West Indian Slavery Ser.: No. 4). 224p. 1987. 39.50 (0-7146-3263-5, Pub. by F Cass Pubs) Intl Spec Bk.

Brock, Colin & Clarkson, Donald, eds. Education in Central America & the Caribbean. 256p. (C). 1988. lib. bdg. 49.95 (0-415-00569-8) Routledge.

Brock, Colin & Lawlor, Hugh, eds. Education in Latin America. LC 84-3750. 208p. 1985. 37.50 (0-7099-3273-1, Pub. by C Helm) Routldge.

Brock, Colin & Tulasiewicz, Witold. Education in Single Europe. 2nd ed. LC 99-26322. 1999. pap. write for info. (0-415-16441-9) Routledge.

***Brock, Colin & Tulasiewicz, Witold, eds.** Education in Single Europe. 2nd ed. LC 99-26322. 432p. (C). 2000. text. write for info. (0-415-16440-0) Routledge.

Brock, Colin, jt. ed. see Tulasiewicz, Witold.

Brock, D. Heyward, ed. The Culture of Biomedicine. LC 82-40438. (Studies in Science & Culture: Vol. 1). 200p. 1984. 32.50 (0-87413-229-0) U Delaware Pr.

Brock, D. J. Molecular Genetics for the Clinician. LC 92-9574. (Illus.). 301p. (C). 1993. text 74.95 (0-521-41179-3); pap. text 31.95 (0-521-42325-2) Cambridge U Pr.

Brock, Dan W. Life & Death: Philosophical Essays in Biomedical Ethics. LC 92-20921. (Studies in Philosophy & Public Policy). 449p. (C). 1993. pap. text 23.95 (0-521-42833-5) Cambridge U Pr.

— Life & Death: Philosophical Essays in Biomedical Ethics. LC 92-20921. (Studies in Philosophy & Public Policy). 449p. (C). 1993. text 74.95 (0-521-41785-6) Cambridge U Pr.

Brock, Dan W., jt. auth. see Buchanan, Allen.

Brock, Daniel G. Recollections of DGB, 1843: Rural Rides in South Australia. (C). 1981. 50.00 (0-7855-0327-7, Pub. by Royal Geograp Soc) St Mut.

— To the Desert with Stuart - 1844. 240p. (C). 1989. pap. text 40.00 (0-89771-021-5, Pub. by Bob Mossel) St Mut.

— To the Desert with Sturt: A Diary of the 1844 Expedition SA Government Printer & RGSA (SA) 222p. (C). 1989. 39.00 (0-7855-0328-5, Pub. by Royal Geograp Soc) St Mut.

***Brock, Darryl.** Havana Heat. LC 00-100099. 260p. 2000. 24.95 (1-892129-23-X) Total Sprts.

***Brock, Daryl.** If I Never Get Back. 2001. reprint ed. pap. 14.95 (1-892129-96-5) Total Sprts.

Brock, David. The Seduction of Hillary Rodham. 432p. 1996. 26.00 (0-684-83451-0) Free Pr.

— The Seduction of Hillary Rodham. 464p. 1998. per. 14.00 (0-684-83770-6) Free Pr.

***Brock, David, et al, eds.** Restructuring Professional Organisation: Accounting Healthcare & Law. LC 99-12839. 248p. (C). 1999. text. write for info. (0-415-19216-1) Routledge.

***Brock, David, et al.** Restructuring the Professional Organisation: Accounting Healthcare & Law. LC 99-12839. 1999. pap. write for info. (0-415-19217-X) Routledge.

Brock, David, jt. auth. see Brock, Carolyn.

Brock, Dean. Mastering Tools, Taming Demons: UNIX for the Wizard Apprentice. 350p. (C). 1995. pap. text 34.00 (0-13-228016-7) P-H.

Brock, Debbie. God, Metaphysics, & You. 56p. 1997. pap. 8.00 (0-8059-4104-5) Dorrance.

An Asterisk (*) at the beginning of an entry indicates that the title is appearing for the first time.

Brock, Deborah R. Making Work, Making Trouble: Prostitution as a Social Problem. LC 98-219071. 224p. 1998. text 45.00 (*0-8020-0976-X*); pap. text 18.95 (*0-8020-7935-0*) U of Toronto Pr.

Brock, Dee, jt. auth. see Resnik, Linda.

***Brock, Derek.** Glorious Poverty. large type unabridged ed. 1999. 25.95 (*0-7531-5094-8*, 150948, Pub. by ISIS Lrg Prnt) ISIS Pub.

Brock, E., ed. Morte Arthure (Alliterative Version from Thornton MS.) (EETS Original Ser.: No. 8). 228p. 1963. reprint ed. text 20.00 (*0-19-722008-8*, Pub. by EETS) Boydell & Brewer.

Brock, E., jt. ed. see Cockayne, O.

Brock, Earl E. Devotional Interpretation of Familiar Hymns. LC 72-93319. (Essay Index Reprint Ser.). 1977. 17.95 (*0-8369-1395-7*) Ayer.

***Brock, Edwin.** And Another Thing. 64p. 1999. pap. (*1-900564-36-X*, Pub. by Enitha Pr) Dufour.

Brock, Edwin. The Blocked Heart. LC 75-6528. 64p. 1976. 7.25 (*0-8112-0577-0*, Pub. by New Directions) Norton.

Brock, Edwin. The Blocked Heart. LC 75-6528. 64p. 1976. pap. 2.45 (*0-8112-0578-9*, NDP399, Pub. by New Directions) Norton.

Brock, Edwin. Five Ways to Kill a Man: New & Selected Poems. 134p. (Orig.). 1990. 38.00 (*1-870612-21-3*, Pub. by Enitha Pr); pap. 18.95 (*1-870612-16-7*, Pub. by Enitha Pr) Dufour.

— Here. Now. Always. LC 76-54314. 1977. 8.50 (*0-8112-0638-6*, Pub. by New Directions); pap. 2.95 (*0-8112-0639-4*, NDP429, Pub. by New Directions) Norton.

— Invisibility Is the Art of Survival. LC 72-80979. 96p. 1972. 7.50 (*0-8112-0450-2*, Pub. by New Directions); pap. 1.95 (*0-8112-0451-0*, NDP342, Pub. by New Directions) Norton.

— Paroxisms: A Guide to the Isms. LC 74-8647. (Illus.). 96p. 1974. 5.95 (*0-8112-0549-5*, Pub. by New Directions) Norton.

— The Portraits & the Poses. LC 73-78783. 64p. 1973. 6.95 (*0-8112-0486-3*, Pub. by New Directions); pap. 1.95 (*0-8112-0487-1*, NDP360, Pub. by New Directions) Norton.

— The River & the Train. LC 78-27463. 1979. 7.95 (*0-8112-0722-6*, Pub. by New Directions); pap. 3.75 (*0-8112-0723-4*, NDP478, Pub. by New Directions) Norton.

Brock, Emi N. Rural Development: Financial Condition of the Rural Utilities Service's Loan Portfolio. (Illus.). 48p. 1997. pap. text 25.00 (*0-7881-4639-4*) DIANE Pub.

***Brock, Eric J.** Centenary College of Louisiana. (College History Ser.). (Illus.). 128p. 2000. pap. 19.99 (*0-7385-0558-7*) Arcadia Publng.

Brock, Eric J. A Necrology of Graves at the Old Oakland Cemetery. 107p. 1988. pap. 16.50 (*1-57088-055-7*) J&W Ent.

***Brock, Eric J.** New Orleans. (Images of America Ser.). (Illus.). 128p. 1999. pap. 18.99 (*0-7385-0223-5*) Arcadia Publng.

— New Orleans Cemeteries. (Images of America Ser.). (Illus.). 128p. 1999. pap. 18.99 (*0-7385-0126-3*) Arcadia Publng.

— Shreveport in the Twentieth Century. LC 98-88696. (American Century Ser.). (Illus.). 128p. 1998. pap. 18.99 (*0-7385-0042-9*) Arcadia Publng.

Brock, Eric J. Shreveport, LA. (Images of America Ser.). (Illus.). 128p. 1998. pap. 16.99 (*0-7524-1245-0*) Arcadia Publng.

***Brock, Eric J. & Joiner, Gary.** Red River Steamboats. (Images of America Ser.). (Illus.). 128p. 1999. pap. 18.99 (*0-7385-0168-9*) Arcadia Publng.

Brock, Erica. Scotland for Backpackers: 1999 Edition. 1999. pap. text 14.95 (*0-9524913-3-8*) Reel Pubng.

Brock, Erica, ed. Scotland for Backpackers, 1997. (Illus.). 280p. (Orig.). 1997. pap. 14.95 (*0-9524913-9-7*, Pub. by Reel Pubng) Seven Hills Bk.

— Scotland for Backpackers '98. 290p. 1998. pap. 14.95 (*0-9524913-1-1*, Pub. by Reel Pubng) Seven Hills Bk.

Brock, Geoffrey E., ed. Metallurgy of Advanced Electronic Materials: Proceedings of a Technical Conference. LC 63-13589. (Metallurgical Society Conference Ser.: Vol. 19). 365p. reprint ed. pap. 113.20 (*0-608-30597-9*, 200150700079) Bks Demand.

Brock, Gerald W. Telecommunication Policy for the Information Age: From Monopoly to Competition. LC 94-3911. (Illus.). 336p. 1994. text 55.50 (*0-674-87277-0*, BROTEP) HUP.

— Telecommunication Policy for the Information Age: From Monopoly to Competition. (Illus.). 336p. 1998. pap. 22.95 (*0-674-87326-2*) HUP.

— The Telecommunications Industry: The Dynamics of Market Structure. LC 80-25299. (Economic Studies: No. 151). (Illus.). 348p. (C). 1981. 24.95 (*0-674-87285-1*) HUP.

Brock, Gerald W., ed. Toward a Competitive Telecommunications Industry: Selected Papers from the 1994 Telecommunications Policy Research Conference. (Telecommunications Ser.). 400p. 1995. pap. 39.95 (*0-8058-2031-0*); text 79.95 (*0-8058-2030-2*) L Erlbaum Assocs.

Brock, Gerald W. & Rosston, Gregory L., eds. Selected Papers from the 1995 Telecommunications Policy Research Conference. LC 96-23166. (Telecommunications Ser.). 328p. 1996. 69.95 (*0-8058-2418-9*); pap. 36.00 (*0-8058-2419-7*) L Erlbaum Assocs.

Brock, Gillian, ed. Necessary Goods: Our Responsibilities to Meet Others' Needs. LC 97-45733. (Studies in Social, Political, & Legal Philosophy). 288p. 1998. 63.00 (*0-8476-8818-6*) Rowman.

— Necessary Goods: Our Responsibilities to Meet Others' Needs. LC 97-45733. (Studies in Social, Political, & Legal Philosophy). 288p. 1998. pap. 23.95 (*0-8476-8819-4*) Rowman.

Brock, Glen T. Inside the Green Circle. 208p. (Orig.). 1988. mass mkt. 2.50 (*0-87067-299-1*) Holloway.

— Truth Killers. 240p. (Orig.). 1991. mass mkt. 3.50 (*0-87067-576-1*) Holloway.

Brock, Gregory & Barnard, Charles P. Procedures in Marriage & Family Therapy. 252p. 1988. text 43.00 (*0-205-11310-9*, H13105) Allyn.

Brock, Gregory W. & Barnard, Charles P. Procedures in Marriage & Family Therapy. 3rd ed. LC 98-13583. 228p. 1998. pap. text 53.00 (*0-205-28782-4*) Allyn.

Brock, Gregory W., jt. auth. see Vesper, Joyce H.

Brock, H. I., ed. Little Book of Limericks. LC 71-84351. (Granger Index Reprint Ser.). 1977. 19.95 (*0-8369-6053-X*) Ayer.

Brock, Hal. The Associated Press Pictorial History of Baseball. 208p. 1994. write for info. (*0-9640034-1-4*) World Pubns.

***Brock, Harold L.** The Fords in My Past. LC 00-26531. (Illus.). 2000. write for info. (*0-7680-0599-X*) Soc Auto Engineers.

Brock, Horace, ed. Game Theory, Social Choice & Ethics. 1979. lib. bdg. 31.50 (*0-686-26826-1*) Kluwer Academic.

***Brock, Horace & Herrington, Linda.** Cost Accounting: Principles & Applications. 6th ed. 564p. 1998. text 56.13 incl. disk (*0-02-803435-X*) Glencoe.

Brock, Horace R. & Herrington, Linda A. Cost Accounting: Principles & Applications. 6th ed. LC 97-50268. 1998. 41.50 (*0-02-803428-7*) Glencoe.

Brock, Horace R., et al. Accounting: Basic Principles. 5th ed. LC 84-12578. 432p. 1985. text 48.50 (*0-07-008262-6*) McGraw.

— Accounting: Principles & Applications. 6th ed. (Illus.). 1168p. (C). 1990. student ed. 1.50 (*0-07-008754-7*) McGraw.

— Accounting: Principles & Applications. 6th ed. (Illus.). 1168p. (C). 1990. student ed. 30.54 (*0-07-008744-X*) McGraw.

— Accounting: Principles & Applications, Pt. 1. 6th ed. (Illus.). 1168p. (C). 1990. text 87.56 (*0-07-008736-9*) McGraw.

— Accounting: Principles & Applications, Pt. 2. 6th ed. (Illus.). 1168p. (C). 1990. text 33.60 (*0-07-008739-3*) McGraw.

— Brookside Real Estate: A Sole Proprietorship Service Business Practice Set. rev. ed. 216p. 1990. pap. text 21.33 (*0-07-008747-4*) McGraw.

— Cost Accounting: Principles & Applications. 5th ed. 592p. (C). 1989. text 46.05 (*0-07-008152-2*) McGraw.

— Petroleum Accounting: Principles, Procedures, & Issues. LC 85-60604. 1000p. 1996. text 125.00 (*0-940966-24-7*) Pro Dev Inst.

***Brock, Horace R., et al.** Petroleum Accounting: Principles, Procedures & Issues. 5th ed. (Illus.). 1150p. 2000. write for info. (*0-940966-25-5*) Pro Dev Inst.

Brock, J., jt. ed. see Hidy, George M.

Brock, J. H., et al, eds. Plant Invasions: Studies from North America & Europe. (Illus.). 224p. 1997. pap. 53.00 (*90-73348-23-4*, Pub. by Backhuys Pubs) Balogh.

***Brock, Jack L., Jr., ed.** Executive Guide: Information Security Management - Learning from Leading Organizations. (Illus.). 68p. 1999. pap. text 25.00 (*0-7881-8010-X*) DIANE Pub.

— Information Security Management: Learning from Leading Organizations. (Illus.). 68p. (C). 2000. reprint ed. pap. text 20.00 (*0-7881-8998-0*) DIANE Pub.

Brock, Jack L., Jr., et al. Business Process Reengineering Assessment Guide. 74p. (Orig.). (C). 1997. pap. text 30.00 (*0-7881-4638-6*) DIANE Pub.

Brock, James. Contributions in Petroleum Geology & Engineering: Applied Open-Hole Log Analysis. LC 85-30604. (Illus.). 284p. 1986. 65.00 (*0-87201-638-2*) Gulf Pub.

***Brock, James.** "nearly Florida" (Florida Poetry Ser.: Vol. 3). xiv, 80p. 2000. pap. 12.00 (*0-938078-67-4*) Anhinga Pr.

Brock, James. Sunshine Mine Disaster: A Book of Poetry. 82p. 1995. pap. 12.95 (*0-89301-181-9*) U of Idaho Pr.

Brock, James, et al. A Cultural Resources Assessment of the Hansen Dam Flood Control Basin, City of Los Angeles, California. (Technical Ser.: No. 5). (Illus.). v, 66p. 1993. pap. 12.95 (*1-881844-00-5*) Archaeol Adv.

***Brock, James, et al.** Investigations at the Burning Dune Site (CA-RIV-475A), La Quinta, Calif. (AAG Monograph Ser.). (Illus.). 104p. 1999. pap. 15.87 (*1-881844-01-3*) Archaeol Adv.

Brock, James A. & Main, Kevan L. A Guide to the Common Problems & Diseases of Cultured Penaeus Vannamei. (Illus.). 242p. (C). 1996. reprint ed. pap. text 45.00 (*1-886608-00-8*) World Aquaculture.

Brock, James L. A Forecast for the Grocery Retailing Industry in the 1980s. Dufey, Gunter, ed. LC 81-16498. (Research for Business Decisions Ser.: No. 45). 171p. 1981. reprint ed. pap. 53.10 (*0-8357-1259-1*, 207012400064) Bks Demand.

***Brock, James P.** The Evolution of Adaptive Systems: The General Theory of Evolution. 450p. 2000. 69.95 (*0-12-134740-0*) Acad Pr.

Brock, James P., jt. auth. see Bailowitz, Richard A.

Brock, James W. & Elzinga, Kenneth G., eds. Antitrust, the Market, & the State: The Contributions of Walter Adams. LC 90-32017. 320p. (C). (gr. 13). 1992. text 78.95 (*0-87332-854-X*) M E Sharpe.

Brock, James W. & Elzinga, Kenneth G., eds. Antitrust, the Market, & the State: The Contributions of Walter Adams. LC 90-32017. 320p. (C). (gr. 13). 1992. pap. text 39.95 (*0-87332-855-8*) M E Sharpe.

Brock, James W., jt. auth. see Adams, Walter E.

Brock, Jeanette M. The Mobile Scot: Emigration & Migration, 1861-1911. 190p. 1998. pap. 75.00 (*0-85976-453-2*, Pub. by J Donald) St Mut.

Brock, Jeremy H., et al, eds. Iron Metabolism: In Health & Disease. (Illus.). 495p. 1994. text 94.00 (*0-7020-1732-9*, Pub. by W B Saunders) Saunders.

Brock, Jim. Applied Open-Hole Log Analysis. LC 85-30604. (Contributions in Petroleum Geology & Engineering Ser.: Vol. 2). (Illus.). 292p. 1986. reprint ed. pap. 90.60 (*0-608-07950-2*, 206792300012) Bks Demand.

Brock, Jim, et al. Idaho Plus: Contemporary Poetry from the American West. O'Brien, Kathleen, ed. LC 87-61388. (Illus.). 96p. (Orig.). 1987. pap. 10.95 (*0-961893-0-0*) Painted Smiles.

Brock, John M. An Illustrated History of Kern County. (Illus.). 83p. (J). (gr. 3-8). 1976. pap. 5.00 (*0-943500-05-2*) Kern Historical.

Brock, Jonathan. Bargaining Beyond Impasse: Joint Resolution of Public Sector Labor Disputes. LC 81-20652. 301p. 1982. 55.00 (*0-86569-110-X*, Auburn Hse) Greenwood.

— Managing People in Public Agencies: Personnel & Labor Relations. LC 88-36475. (Illus.). 440p. (C). 1989. reprint ed. pap. text 32.00 (*0-8191-7277-4*) U Pr of Amer.

***Brock, Juliet C.** Cat. (Eyewitness Books). (Illus.). (J). (gr. 4-7). 2000. 19.99 (*0-7894-6578-7*) DK Pub Inc.

— Dog. (Illus.). 2000. 19.99 (*0-7894-6581-7*) DK Pub Inc.

— Horse. (Eyewitness Books). (Illus.). (J). (gr. 4-7). 2000. 19.99 (*0-7894-6582-5*) DK Pub Inc.

Brock, Juliet C. The Walking Larder: Patterns of Domestication Pastoralism, & Predation. (One World Archaeology Ser.: No. 2). (Illus.). 384p. 1988. text 75.00 (*0-04-445013-3*) Routledge.

Brock, Kenneth J. Birds of the Indiana Dunes. 2nd rev. ed. LC 97-61101. (Illus.). 240p. 1997. pap. write for info. (*0-9659358-0-9*) S Heinze.

Brock, Kenneth W. Question! LC 98-90247. 1998. pap. 9.95 (*0-533-12745-9*) Vantage.

Brock, L. M., ed. Defects & Anelasticity in the Characterization of Crystalline Solids. (AMD Ser.: Vol. 148). 176p. 1992. 50.00 (*0-7918-1102-6*, G00746) ASME.

Brock, Lee, ed. see Barrish, Seth.

Brock, Leslie V. The Currency of the American Colonies, Seventeen Hundred to Seventeen Sixty-Four: A Study in Colonial Finance & Imperial Relations. LC 75-2576. (Dissertations in American Economic History Ser.). (Illus.). 1978. 63.95 (*0-405-07257-0*) Ayer.

Brock, Lillie & Salerno, Mary Ann. The Change Cycle: Managing Life Means Managing Changes. (Successful Changes Ser.). (Illus.). 256p. 1994. 24.00 (*0-9638959-0-7*) Bridge Builder.

Brock, Lisa & Fuertes, Digna Castraneda, eds. Between Race & Empire: African-Americans & Cubans Before the Cuban Revolution. LC 97-20278. (Illus.). 256p. (C). 1998. text 59.95 (*1-56639-586-0*); pap. text 22.95 (*1-56639-587-9*) Temple U Pr.

Brock, Loise. How to Develop the Mind of Christ in You. LC 96-108614. 112p. 1995. 7.99 (*0-89274-787-6*, HH-787) Harrison Hse.

Brock, Louis M., ed. Thermoelastic Problems & the Thermodynamics of Continua Vol. 198: Thermoelastic Problems & the Thermodynamics of Continua. LC 95-75743. (1995 Joint ASME Applied Mechanics & Materials Summer Meeting Ser.: Vol. 198). 76p. 1995. 64.00 (*0-7918-1312-6*, H00944) ASME.

***Brock, Lucile Reid.** Taos Then: Only-In Taos Stories from a Bride Who Lived Them. (Illus.). 150p. 1999. pap. write for info. (*0-7392-0443-2*, 3725) Morris Pubng.

Brock, Luther A. How to Communicate by Letter & Memo. (Illus.). 304p. 1974. text 62.43 (*0-07-008043-7*) McGraw.

Brock, M., ed. Modern Neurosurgery, Vol. I. (Illus.). 400p. 1982. 79.95 (*0-387-10972-2*) Spr-Verlag.

Brock, M., et al. The Artificial Disc. (Illus.). 104p. 1991. 58.95 (*0-387-51857-6*) Spr-Verlag.

Brock, M., jt. ed. see Boon, P. I.

Brock, M., jt. ed. see Mayer, H. M.

***Brock, M. G. & Curthoys, M. C., eds.** The History of the University of Oxford Volume Vii: The Nineteenth Century, Part 2. (Illus.). 980p. 2000. text 130.00 (*0-19-951017-2*) OUP.

Brock, M. G. & Curthoys, M. C., eds. The Nineteenth Century, Pt. I. (The History of the University of Oxford Ser.). (Illus.), 880p. 1998. text 145.00 (*0-19-951016-4*) OUP.

Brock, M. Louise & Brock, Thomas. The Application of Micro-Autoradiographic Techniques to Ecological Studies. (International Association of Theoretical & Applied Limnology, Communications Ser.: No. 15). (Illus.). 29p. 1968. pap. 15.00 (*3-510-52015-7*, Pub. by E Schweizerbartsche) Balogh.

Brock, Malcolm. Biotechnology in Japan. 144p. 1989. 55.00 (*0-415-03495-7*, A3695) Routledge.

Brock, Mark N. & Walters, Larry, eds. Teaching Composition Around the Pacific Rim: Politics & Pedagogy. LC 92-13741. 1992. 89.00 (*1-85359-151-0*, Pub. by Multilingual Matters); pap. 34.95 (*1-85359-160-2*, Pub. by Multilingual Matters) Taylor & Francis.

Brock, Michael L., jt. auth. see Glenn, H. Stephen.

Brock, Nathalie, tr. see Sotillos, Eugenio.

Brock, P. Cisplatin Toxicity in Infants & Children. No. 102. 157p. (Orig.). 1994. 44.50 (*90-6186-651-0*, Pub. by Leuven Univ) Coronet Bks.

Brock, Pat D. Fire Protection Hydraulics & Water Supply Analysis. Brakhage, Cynthia, ed. LC 90-83716. (Illus.). 326p. (C). 1990. text 50.00 (*0-87939-088-3*) IFSTA.

***Brock, Pat D.** Fire Protection Hydraulics & Water Supply Analysis. (Illus.). 336p. (C). 1999. pap. write for info. (*0-87939-171-5*) IFSTA.

Brock, Patricia A. Educational Technology in the Classroom. LC 93-23417. 250p. 1994. 39.95 (*0-87778-269-5*) Educ Tech Pubns.

Brock, Peggy. Outback Ghettos: Aboriginal Institutionalisation & Survival. LC 93-16329. (Studies in Australian History). (Illus.). 256p. (C). 1993. pap. write for info. (*0-521-44708-9*) Cambridge U Pr.

— Outback Ghettos: Aboriginal Institutionalisation & Survival. LC 93-16329. (Studies in Australian History). (Illus.). 190p. (C). 1993. text 59.95 (*0-521-43435-1*) Cambridge U Pr.

Brock, Peggy, ed. Women, Rites & Sites: Aboriginal Women's Cultural Knowledge. 208p. (Orig.). 1989. pap. text 14.95 (*0-04-370186-8*, Pub. by Allen & Unwin Pty) Paul & Co Pubs.

Brock, Penelope. Excellent Prose, Sensitive Poetry. 70p. (Orig.). 1990. pap. 4.95 (*0-913412-38-4*) Brandon Hse.

Brock, Peter. Folk Cultures & Little People: Aspects of National Awakening in East Central Europe. 250p. 1993. text 54.50 (*0-88033-243-3*, 346, Pub. by East Eur Monographs) Col U Pr.

— Freedom from Violence: Sectarian Nonresistance from the Middle Ages to the Great War. 448p. 1991. text 55.00 (*0-8020-5879-5*) U of Toronto Pr.

— Freedom from War: Nonsectarian Pacifism, 1814-1914. 512p. 1991. text 60.00 (*0-8020-5883-3*) U of Toronto Pr.

— Mahatma Gandhi As a Linguistic Nationalist. (C). 1995. pap. 9.00 (*0-945921-30-6*, Pub. by S Asia Pubs) S Asia.

— One Hundred Walks Around Bristol. (Illus.). 256p. 1994. pap. 22.95 (*1-85158-606-7*, Pub. by Mainstream Pubng) Trafalgar.

— Pacifism in Europe to 1914. LC 75-166362. (History of Pacifism Ser.: Vol. 1). 566p. 1972. reprint ed. pap. 175.50 (*0-7837-9305-7*, 206004500004) Bks Demand.

— Polish Revolutionary Populism: A Study in Agrarian Socialist Thought from the 1830s to the 1850s. LC 77-2840. 134p. reprint ed. pap. 41.60 (*0-608-18024-6*, 202648400049) Bks Demand.

— The Quaker Peace Testimony, 1660-1914. 400p. 1991. text 40.00 (*1-85072-074-6*, Pub. by Ebor Pr) Syracuse U Pr.

— The Quaker Peace Testimony, 1660-1914. 400p. 1999. pap. 45.00 (*1-85072-065-7*, Pub. by W Sessions) St Mut.

— Records of Conscience. (C). 1989. pap. 21.00 (*0-7855-7022-5*, Pub. by W Sessions) St Mut.

— The Slovak National Awakening: An Essay in the Intellectual History of East Central Europe. LC 75-42013. 114p. reprint ed. pap. 35.40 (*0-608-15390-7*, 202932600060) Bks Demand.

— Studies in Peace History. 112p. 1999. pap. 21.00 (*1-85072-090-8*, Pub. by W Sessions) St Mut.

— Varieties of Pacifism: A Survey from Antiquity to the Outset of the Twentieth Century. 4th ed. 111p. 1998. pap. 15.95 (*0-8156-8124-0*) Syracuse U Pr.

Brock, Peter, ed. Records of Conscience. 72p. 1999. pap. 21.00 (*1-85072-117-3*, Pub. by W Sessions) St Mut.

Brock, Peter & Skilling, H. Gordon, eds. The Czech Renascence of the Nineteenth Century: Essays Presented to Otakar Odlozilik in Honour of His Seventieth Birthday. LC 76-18281. 359p. reprint ed. pap. 111.30 (*0-608-14378-2*, 201944700011) Bks Demand.

Brock, Peter & Socknat, Thomas P., eds. Challenge to Mars: Pacifism from 1918 to 1945. 560p. 1999. text 75.00 (*0-8020-4371-2*) U of Toronto Pr.

Brock, Peter & Young, Nigel. Pacifism in the Twentieth Century: A Survey from Antiquity to the Outset of the Twentieth Century. LC 99-201765. 452p. 1999. pap. 29.95 (*0-8156-8125-9*) Syracuse U Pr.

Brock, Peter, et al. Daytona Cobra Coupes: Carroll Shelby's 1965 World Champions. (Illus.). 532p. 1995. 100.00 (*0-9648193-0-9*) Stauffer Pub.

Brock, Philip L., et al, eds. Latin American Debt & Adjustment: External Shocks & Macroeconomic Policies. LC 88-25021. 283p. 1989. 59.95 (*0-275-93123-4*, C3123, Praeger Pubs) Greenwood.

Brock, Pope. Indiana Gothic: A Story of Adultery & Murder in an American Family. LC 98-41736. 384p. 1999. 24.95 (*0-385-48509-3*) Doubleday.

Brock, Pope, jt. auth. see Patterson, L. Ray.

Brock, R. A., ed. see Grigsby, Hugh B.

Brock, R. A., ed. see Spotswood, Alexander.

Brock, R. A., ed. see Virginia Company of London, 1619-1624 Staff.

Brock, R. A., ed. see Virginia Historical Society Annual Meeting Staff.

Brock, Ray. Go Fly a Kite. (Illus.). (J). (gr. 4 up). 1976. pap. 10.00 (*0-912846-17-8*) Bookstore Pr.

Brock, Raymond. No Trump Play. Sowter, Tony, ed. LC 98-39175. (How to Play Bridge Ser.). (Illus.). 96p. 1998. pap. 8.95 (*0-8442-0078-6*, 00786, Natl Textbk Co) NTC Contemp Pub Co.

***Brock, Raymond & Brock, Sally.** Defence. (Bridge Quiz Bks.). 128p. 1999. pap. 15.95 (*0-7134-8509-4*) B T B.

— Slams. (Bridge Quiz Bks.). 128p. 1999. pap. 15.95 (*0-7134-8504-3*) B T B.

Brock, Raymond T. Facing Midlife Challenges. (Spiritual Discovery Ser.). 110p. 1996. pap., teacher ed. 9.95 (*0-88243-215-X*, 02-0215); pap., student ed. 4.95 (*0-88243-115-3*, 02-0115) Gospel Pub.

— Parenting the Elementary Child. (Spiritual Discovery Ser.). 128p. 1996. pap., teacher ed. 9.95 (*0-88243-209-5*); pap., student ed. 4.95 (*0-88243-109-9*) Gospel Pub.

Brock, Rebecca. Designing Object-Oriented Software. 341p. 1990. pap. 60.00 (*0-13-629825-7*) P-H.

Brock, Rita N. Journeys by Heart: A Christology of Erotic Power. 130p. 1991. reprint ed. pap. 14.95 (*0-8245-1082-8*, Pub. by Crossroad NY) Natl Bk Netwk.

Brock, Rita N., et al, eds. Setting the Table: Women in Theological Conversation. 300p. (Orig.). 1995. pap. 19.99 (*0-8272-3433-3*) Chalice Pr.

B

An Asterisk (*) at the beginning of an entry indicates that the title is appearing for the first time.

Brock, Rita N. & Thistlewaite, Susan B. Casting Stones: Prostitution & Liberation in Asia & the United States. 320p. 1996. pap. 25.00 (*0-8006-2979-5*, 1-2979, Fortress Pr) Augsburg Fortress.

Brock, Robert A., compiled by. Documents, Chiefly Unpublished, Relating to the Huguenot Emigration to Virginia & the Settlement at Manakin-Town. LC 72-14424. (Virginia Historical Society. Collections First Ser.: No. 5). reprint ed. 38.50 (*0-404-57655-9*) AMS Pr.

Brock, Robert A., ed. Miscellaneous Papers, 1672-1865: Now First Printed from the Manuscript in the Collections of the Virginia Historical Society. LC 72-14425. (Virginia Historical Society. Collections First Ser.: No. 6). reprint ed. 27.50 (*0-404-57656-7*) AMS Pr.

Brock, Robert A., jt. auth. see Lewis, Virginia A.

Brock, Robert R. Lire, Enfin, Robbe-Grillet. LC 90-46510. (American University Studies: Romance Languages & Literature: Ser. II, Vol. 163). 152p. (C). 1991. text 31.95 (*0-8204-1451-4*) P Lang Pubng.

***Brock, Roger & Hodkinson, Stephen, eds.** Alternatives to Athens: Varieties of Political Organization & Community in Ancient Greece. (Illus.). 500p. 2001. text 110.00 (*0-19-815220-5*) OUP.

Brock, S. L., jt. auth. see Wood, W. Raymond.

Brock, S. P. The Old Testament in Syriac According to the Peshitta Version Pt. III, Fasc. 1: Isaiah. LC 78-339247. xxxix, 121p. 1993. reprint ed. 86.00 (*90-04-07766-9*) Brill Academic Pubs.

***Brock, Sabine.** White Amnesia - Black Memory? American Women's Writing & History. 195p. 1999. pap. 37.95 (*3-631-33545-8*) P Lang Pubng.

Brock, Sabine. White Amnesia - Black Memory? American Women's Writing & History. LC 99-30573. (Bremer Beitrage Zur Literatur-und Ideengeschichte Ser.: Vol. 25). 195p. 1999. pap. 37.95 (*0-8204-3605-4*) P Lang Pubng.

Brock, Sally. The Complete Book of Bols Bridge Tips. 1998. pap. text 17.95 (*0-9698461-6-9*) Master Pt Pr.

— Playing with Trumps. LC 97-39105. (How to Play Bridge Ser.). (Illus.). 96p. 1998. pap. 8.95 (*0-8442-2565-7*) NTC Contemp Pub Co.

— Suit Combinations in Bridge. 1998. pap. text 17.95 (*0-7134-8164-1*, Pub. by B T B) Branford.

Brock, Sally, jt. auth. see Brock, Raymond.

Brock, Sarah. Syzygy. 32p. 1995. pap. 10.00 (*0-930502-42-6*) Pine Pr.

Brock, Sebastian. From Ephrem to Romanos: Interactions Between Syriac & Greek in Late Antiquity. (Variorum Collected Studies Ser.: Vol. CS664). 350p. 1999. text 101.95 (*0-86078-800-8*, Pub. by Ashgate Pub) Ashgate Pub Co.

— The Luminous Eye: The Spiritual World Vision of St. Ephrem the Syrian. 2nd ed. (Cistercian Studies: No. 124). 250p. 1992. 36.95 (*0-87907-524-4*); pap. 15.95 (*0-87907-624-0*) Cistercian Pubns.

— Studies in Syriac Christianity: History, Literature & Theology. (Collected Studies: No. CS357). 350p. 1992. text 109.95 (*0-86078-305-7*, Pub. by Variorum) Ashgate Pub Co.

— Syriac Perspectives on Late Antiquity. (Collected Studies: No. CS199). 336p. (C). 1984. reprint ed. lib. bdg. 109.95 (*0-86078-147-X*, Pub. by Variorum) Ashgate Pub Co.

Brock, Sebastian, tr. see St. Ephrem the Syrian.

Brock, Sebastian P. Holy Women of the Syrian Orient. (Transformation of the Classical Heritage Ser.). 1998. pap. text 15.95 (*0-520-21366-1*, Pub. by U CA Pr) Cal Prin Full Svc.

Brock, Stephen E., et al. Preparing for Crises in the Schools: A Manual for Building School Crises Response Teams. 200p. 1996. 64.95 (*0-471-16212-4*) Wiley.

***Brock, Stephen E., et al.** Preparing for Crises in the Schools: A Manual for Building School Crises Response Teams. 2nd ed. 320p. 2001. 45.00 (*0-471-38423-2*) Wiley.

Brock, Stephen E., et al. Preparing for Crises in the Schools: Manual for Building School Crisis Response Teams. LC 95-4474. 1995. write for info. (*0-88422-156-3*) Clinical Psych.

Brock, Stephen L. Action & Conduct: Thomas Aquinas & the Theory of Action. 288p. 47.95 (*0-567-08547-3*, Pub. by T & T Clark) Bks Intl VA.

Brock, Steve. Strength for Today & Bright Hope for Tomorrow: Let God Guide You Through Your Pain & Grief. LC 97-2907. 224p. (Orig.). 1997. pap. 12.99 (*0-7852-7557-6*, J Thoma Bks) Nelson.

Brock, Stuart. Killer's Choice. large type ed. (Linford Mystery Large Print Ser.). 1995. pap. 16.99 (*0-7089-7808-8*, Linford) Ulverscroft.

Brock, Susan & Cabbell, Sally. How to Write a Staff Manual. 2nd ed. (Better Management Skills Ser.). 1995. pap. 12.95 (*0-7494-1545-2*) Kogan Page Ltd.

Brock, Susan & Pringle, Marian J. Shakespeare Memorial Theatre, 1919-1945. (Theatre in Focus Ser.). (Illus.). 120p. 1984. pap. write for info. incl. sl. (*0-85964-157-0*) Chadwyck-Healey.

Brock, Susan A., jt. auth. see Allen, Judy.

Brock, Susan L. Better Business Writing: Techniques for Improving Correspondence. 3rd rev. ed. Crisp, Michael, ed. LC 96-85351. (Fifty-Minute Ser.). (Illus.). 97p. 1996. pap. 10.95 (*1-56052-396-4*) Crisp Pubns.

— Writing Business Proposals & Reports: Key Strategies for Success. Manber, Beverly, ed. LC 91-76247. (Fifty-Minute Ser.). (Illus.). 85p. 1992. pap. 10.95 (*1-56052-122-8*) Crisp Pubns.

Brock, Ted, ed. see Greenwald, Hank.

Brock, Thomas, jt. auth. see Brock, M. Louise.

Brock, Thomas D. The Emergence of Bacterial Genetics. (Illus.). 346p. 1990. 55.00 (*0-87969-350-9*) Cold Spring Harbor.

— A Eutrophic Lake. (Ecological Studies: Vol. 55). (Illus.). xii, 308p. 1985. 135.00 (*0-387-96184-4*) Spr-Verlag.

— Robert Koch: A Life in Medicine & Bacteriology. (Illus.). 364p. 1998. reprint ed. 39.95 (*1-55581-143-4*) ASM Pr.

Brock, Thomas D., ed. Milestones in Microbiology. 2nd rev. ed. 274p. 1998. pap. 29.95 (*1-55581-142-6*) ASM Pr.

Brock, Thomas D., et al. Basic Microbiology with Application. 3rd ed. (Illus.). 688p. (C). 1986. text 67.60 (*0-13-065244-X*) P-H.

Brock-Utne. Near Misses in Pediatric Anesthesia. 128p. 1998. pap. text 35.00 (*0-7506-7018-5*) Buttrwrth-Heinemann.

Brock-Utne, Birgit. Educating for Peace: A Feminist Perspective. (Athene Ser.). 192p. (C). 1985. pap. text 16.95 (*0-8077-6217-2*) Tchrs Coll.

— Educating for Peace: A Feminist Perspective on Peace Research & Action. (Athene Ser.). 180p. 1985. text 47.50 (*0-08-032370-7*, Pergamon Pr); pap. text 16.95 (*0-08-032369-3*, Pergamon Pr) Elsevier.

— Feminist Perspectives on Peace & Peace Education. (Athene Ser.). 256p. 1989. text 43.00 (*0-08-036568-X*, Pergamon Pr); pap. text 15.95 (*0-08-036567-1*, Pergamon Pr) Elsevier.

— Feminist Perspectives on Peace & Peace Education. (Athene Ser.). 224p. (C). 1989. pap. text 17.95 (*0-8077-6204-0*) Tchrs Coll.

***Brock-Utne, Birgit.** Whose Education for All? Recolonization of the African Mind. LC 99-35515. (Studies in Education/Politics : Vol. 6). 360p. 1999. 50.00 (*0-8153-3478-8*, SS1445) Garland.

Brock, Van K. The Hard Essential Landscape. LC 79-21071. (University of Central Florida Contemporary Poetry Ser.). 93p. 1979. 13.95 (*0-8130-0659-7*) U Press Fla.

— Spelunking. 1978. 1.50 (*0-936814-04-7*) New Collage.

— Unspeakable Strangers: Poems about the Holocaust. Campbell, Rick, ed. LC 95-83122. 108p. (Orig.). 1996. pap. 12.00 (*0-938078-42-9*) Anhinga Pr.

Brock, Van K., et al, eds. Cafe at Saint Marks. 1973. pap. 5.00 (*0-938078-03-8*) Anhinga Pr.

Brock, Veronica E. The Valley of Flowers: Story of a T.B. Sanitorium. large type ed. 360p. 1995. pap. 17.95 (*1-55050-084-8*, Pub. by Coteau) Genl Dist Srvs.

Brock, Veronica Eddy. The Valley of Flowers: A Story of a TB Sanatorium. 296p. 1987. reprint ed. mass mkt. 7.95 (*0-919926-74-6*, Pub. by Coteau) Genl Dist Srvs.

Brock, Vilmut, et al. Gewaesserfauna des Norddeutschen Tieflandes. Bestimmungsschluessel fuer Aquatische Makroinvertebraten (Aquatic Fauna of North German Lowlands) (Illus.). 225p. 1995. pap. 25.00 (*3-8263-3044-7*, Pub. by Blckwell Wissenschafts) Balogh.

Brock, Vivian. The Complete Colorado Raspberry Story. LC 97-93953. (Illus.). 110p. 1997. pap. write for info. (*0-9657668-4-5*) Mountain Media.

Brock, W. A. & Malliaris, A. G. Differential Equations, Stability & Chaos in Dynamic Economics. (Advanced Textbooks in Economics Ser.: Vol. 27). xvi,390p. 1989. 110.50 (*0-444-70500-7*, North Holland) Elsevier.

Brock, William. Justus von Liebig: The Chemical Gatekeeper. (Illus.). 390p. (C). 1997. text 80.00 (*0-521-56224-4*) Cambridge U Pr.

Brock, William A. Global Economy. Hormats, Robert, ed. LC 89-15972. (American Assembly Book Ser.). 264p. (Orig.). (C). 1989. pap. text 13.25 (*0-393-95945-7*) Norton.

Brock, William A. & Evans, David S. The Economics of Small Businesses. LC 84-25138. (Illus.). 256p. 1986. 54.50 (*0-8419-0848-6*) Holmes & Meier.

Brock, William A. & Hsieh, David A. Nonlinear Dynamics, Chaos & Instability. (Illus.). 346p. 1991. 46.50 (*0-262-02329-6*) MIT Pr.

Brock, William A., jt. auth. see Hsieh, David A.

Brock, William H. The Chemical Tree: A History of Chemistry. (Illus.). 784p. pap. 19.95 (*0-393-32068-5*) Norton.

Brock, William H. Norton History of Chemistry. Porter, Roy, ed. (History of Science Ser.). (Illus.). 768p. 1993. pap. 19.95 (*0-393-31043-4*) Norton.

— Science for All: Studies in the History of Victorian Science & Education. LC 95-41842. (Collected Studies: No. CS518). 320p. 1996. 101.95 (*0-86078-542-4*, Pub. by Variorum) Ashgate Pub Co.

Brock, William R. Lord Liverpool & Liberal Toryism, 1820-1827. 2nd ed. (Illus.). 300p. 1967. 35.00 (*0-7146-1457-2*, Pub. by F Cass Pubs) Intl Spec Bk.

— Scotus Americanus: A Study of 18th Century Sources. 293p. 1982. 60.00 (*0-85224-420-7*, Pub. by Edinburgh U Pr) Col U Pr.

— Welfare, Democracy & the New Deal. 384p. 1988. text 69.95 (*0-521-33379-2*) Cambridge U Pr.

Brocka, Bruce, ed. Automation in Quality Assurance. 2nd ed. (Illus.). 206p. 1988. write for info. (*0-9623395-0-4*) Exec Sci Inst.

Brocka, Bruce & Brocka, M. Suzanne. Quality Management: Implementing the Best Ideas of the Masters. 300p. 1992. text 44.95 (*1-55623-540-2*, Irwn Prfssnl) McGraw-Hill Prof.

Brocka, M. Suzanne, jt. auth. see Brocka, Bruce.

Brockbank, Anne & McGill, Ian. Facilitating Reflective Learning in Higher Education. LC 97-47445. 1998. 35.95 (*0-335-19685-3*); pap. 99.50 (*0-335-19686-1*) OpUniv Pr.

Brockbank, Kevin G., ed. Principle of Autologous, Allogenic & Cyropreserved Venous Transplantation. LC 95-19008. (Medical Intelligence Unit Ser.). 110p. 1995. text 79.00 (*1-57059-221-7*) Landes Bioscience.

Brockbank, Philip, ed. Players of Shakespeare: Essays in Shakespearean Performance by Twelve Players with the Royal Shakespeare Company, No. 1. (Illus.). 192p. 1988. pap. text 20.95 (*0-521-36817-0*) Cambridge U Pr.

Brockbank, Philip, ed. see Jonson, Ben.

Brockbank, Philip, ed. see Shakespeare, William.

Brockbank, Reed, jt. ed. see Settlage, Calvin F.

Brockdorff, T. Graf, et al, eds. Japanese Information in Science, Technology & Commerce: Proceedings of the 2nd International Conference, Berlin, F. R. Germany, 1989. 629p. (gr. 12). 1990. pap. 97.00 (*90-5199-022-7*, Pub. by IOS Pr) IOS Press.

Brockdorff, T. Graf, ed. see Talas, B.

Brocke, Bernhard Vom, see Vom Brocke, Bernhard, ed.

Brocke, Burkhard, jt. ed. see Netter, Petra.

Brockelman, Paul. Cosmology & Creation: The Spiritual Significance of Contemporary Cosmology. LC 98-28273. 208p. 1999. 23.00 (*0-19-511990-8*) OUP.

— The Inside Story: A Narrative Approach to Religious Understanding & Truth. LC 91-4092. 204p. (C). 1992. text 21.50 (*0-7914-1019-6*) State U NY Pr.

Brockelman, Paul T. Existential Phenomenology & the World of Ordinary Experience: An Introduction. LC 80-67208. 83p. 1980. pap. text 14.50 (*0-8191-1192-9*) U Pr of Amer.

Brockelman, Paul T., tr. see Gusdorf, Georges.

Brockelman, Thomas, tr. see Lang, Hermann.

Brockelmann, C. Geschichte der Arabischen Litteratur, 4 vols., Set. (GER.). 1996. reprint ed. 1194.50 (*90-04-10407-0*) Brill Academic Pubs.

— History of the Islamic Peoples. 1980. pap. 17.95 (*0-7100-0521-0*, Routledge Thoemms) Routledge.

Brockelmann, Carl. Geschichte der Islamischen Volker und Staaten. (Illus.). xii, 495p. 1977. reprint ed. 110.00 (*3-487-06343-3*) G Olms Pubs.

— Grundriss der Vergleichenden Grammatik der Semitischen Sprachen, 2 vols., Set. (GER.). xl, 1374p. 1982. reprint ed. 270.00 (*3-487-00061-X*) G Olms Pubs.

— History of Islamic Peoples. Carmichael, Joel & Perlmann, Mose, trs. from GER. (Illus.). 600p. (Orig.). 1995. 49.50 (*81-215-0694-8*, Pub. by M Manoharial) Coronet Bks.

***Brockelmann, Carl.** History of the Islamic Peoples. LC 99-53540. (Orientalism Ser.). 2000. write for info. (*0-415-20909-9*) Routledge.

Brockemann, Suzanne. Embraced by Love. 224p. 1995. mass mkt. 4.99 (*0-8217-0091-X*, Zebra Kensgtn) Kensgtn Pub Corp.

Brocken, H. & Ryckbost, D., eds. The Codification of Environmental Law: Proceedings of the International Conference in Ghent, February 21 & 22, 1995. LC 96-6410. (International Environmental Law & Policy Ser.). 1996. 155.00 (*90-411-0888-2*) Kluwer Law Intl.

Brockenbrough, Roger L. Structural Steel Designer's Handbook. 2nd ed. 1056p. 1992. 99.95 (*0-07-008776-8*) McGraw.

***Brockenbrough, Roger L.** Structural Steel Designer's Handbook. 3rd ed. 1208p. 1999. 125.00 (*0-07-008782-2*) McGraw.

Brockenbrough, Roger L. & Boedecker, Kenneth J., Jr. Highway Engineering Handbook: Building & Rehabilitating the Infrastructure. 1100p. 1996. 110.00 (*0-07-008777-6*) McGraw.

Brocker, James H. A Portrait of Molokai: Collectors' Edition. LC 95-201358. 1994. pap. text 19.95 (*0-9642197-0-0*) Molokai Fish & Dive.

Brocker, Susan. Sharks Vol. 2: Animals of the Ocean. (Animals of the Ocean Ser.: No. 3). (Illus.). 32p. (J). (gr. 2-6). 1998. lib. bdg. 14.95 (*1-56674-232-3*) Forest Hse.

Brocker, Susan, jt. auth. see Hodge, Judith.

Brocker, T. & Dieck, Tom T. Representations of Compact Lie Groups. (Graduate Texts in Mathematics Ser.: Vol. 98). (Illus.). x, 313p. 1995. 49.95 (*0-387-13678-9*) Spr-Verlag.

Brockes, Jeremy, ed. Neuroimmunology. LC 82-3679. (Current Topics in Neurobiology Ser.). 272p. 1982. 65.00 (*0-306-40955-0*, Plenum Trade) Perseus Pubng.

Brocket. Theatre: An Introduction. 4th ed. 1979. text 73.00 (*0-03-021676-1*, Pub. by Harcourt Coll Pubs) Harcourt.

Brockett. The Essential Theatre. 7th ed. (C). 1999. text 65.00 (*0-15-507229-3*, Pub. by Harcourt Coll Pubs) Harcourt.

— Plays for the Theatre. 7th ed. LC 98-75702. 640p. (C). 1999. text 51.00 (*0-15-507230-7*, Pub. by Harcourt Coll Pubs) Harcourt.

Brockett, Adrian, tr. The History of al-Tabari Vol. 16: The Community Divided: The Caliphate of Ali I, A. D. 656-657-A. H. 35-36. LC 96-17177. (SUNY Series in Near Eastern Studies). 288p. (C). 1996. pap. text 21.95 (*0-7914-2392-1*) State U NY Pr.

— The History of al-Tabari Vol. 16: The Community Divided: The Caliphate of Ali I, A. D. 656-657-A. H. 35-36. LC 96-17177. (SUNY Series in Near Eastern Studies). 288p. (C). 1997. text 59.50 (*0-7914-2391-3*) State U NY Pr.

Brockett, Adrian, tr. see Al-Tabari.

Brockett, C. W. Antiphons, Responsories & Other Chants from the Mozarabic Rite. (Wissenschaftliche Abhandlungen-Musicological Studies: Vol. 15). 300p. 1968. lib. bdg. 80.00 (*0-912024-85-2*) Inst Mediaeval Mus.

Brockett, Charles D. Land, Power, & Poverty: Agrarian Transformation & Political Change in Central America. (Thematic Studies in Latin America). 240p. (C). 1990. text 39.95 (*0-04-497027-7*); pap. text 16.95 (*0-04-445754-5*) Routledge.

— Land, Power & Poverty: Agrarian Transformation & Political Conflict in Central America. 2nd ed. LC 98-5451. (Thematic Studies in Latin America). 288p. (C). 1998. pap. 25.00 (*0-8133-8695-0*, Pub. by Westview) HarpC.

Brockett, Edward J., et al. The Descendants of John Brockett of New Haven Colony. (Illus.). 266p. 1988. reprint ed. pap. 40.00 (*0-8328-0325-1*); reprint ed. lib. bdg. 50.00 (*0-8328-0324-3*) Higginson Bk Co.

Brockett, Henry E. Riches of Holiness. pap. 4.99 (*0-88019-169-4*) Schmul Pub Co.

— Scriptural Freedom from Sin. 1980. pap. 6.99 (*0-88019-107-4*) Schmul Pub Co.

Brockett, Joseph R. Myths of Wyoming Vol. I: Jackson Hole. (Myths of Wyoming Ser.). (Illus.). 32p. 1985. pap. 1.50 (*0-942345-19-3*) Dovehaven Pr Ltd.

Brockett, L. P. Woman: Her Rights, Wrongs, Privileges, & Responsibilities. LC 70-114869. (Select Bibliographies Reprint Ser.). 1977. 35.95 (*0-8369-5274-X*) Ayer.

Brockett, Oscar G. The Essential Theatre. 5th ed. LC 91-13499. (Illus.). 480p. (C). 1992. pap. text 57.00 (*0-03-055353-9*, Pub. by Harcourt Coll Pubs) Harcourt.

— Perspectives on Contemporary Theatre. LC 75-154268. 166p. reprint ed. pap. 51.50 (*0-608-09818-3*, 206998600007) Bks Demand.

Brockett, Oscar G., ed. Studies in Theatre & Drama. (De Proprietatibus Litterarum, Ser. Major: No. 23). 217p. 1972. text 56.95 (*90-279-2112-1*) Mouton.

Brockett, Oscar G. & Findlay, Robert R. Century of Innovation: A History of European & American Theatre & Drama, 1870-1970. 2nd ed. 480p. 1991. 83.00 (*0-205-12878-5*, H28780) Allyn.

Brockett, Oscar G. & Pape, Mark. World Drama. 656p. (C). 1984. pap. text 49.00 (*0-03-057668-7*, Pub. by Harcourt Coll Pubs) Harcourt.

Brockett, Oscar G., ed. see Chaudhuri, Una.

Brockett, Oscar G., ed. see Dahl, Mary K.

Brockett, Oscar G., ed. see Dolan, Jill.

Brockett, Oscar G., ed. see Frick, John W.

Brockett, Oscar G., ed. see Ilson, Carol.

Brockett, Oscar G., ed. see Johnson, Stephen B.

Brockett, Oscar G., ed. see Kiebuzinska, Christine.

Brockett, Oscar G., ed. see Larlham, Peter F.

Brockett, Oscar G., ed. see Mason, Jeffrey.

Brockett, Oscar G., ed. see Nelson, Stephen.

Brockett, Oscar G., ed. see Prevots, Naima.

Brockett, Oscar G., ed. see Rokem, Freddie.

Brockett, Oscar G., ed. see Rouse, John.

Brockett, Oscar Gross. History of the Theatre. 8th ed. LC 98-17349. 708p. 1998. 74.00 (*0-205-28171-0*) P-H.

— Plays for the Theatre. 6th ed. (C). 1996. pap. text 43.50 (*0-15-504462-1*) Harcourt Coll Pubs.

Brockett, Patrick & Levine, Arnold. Statistics & Probability & Their Applications. 624p. (C). 1985. text 81.00 (*0-03-053406-2*) SCP.

Brockett, Paul. Bibliography of Aeronautics. 1966. reprint ed. 85.00 (*1-55888-932-9*) Omnigraphics Inc.

— Bibliography of Aeronautics, Vol. 1. 954p. 1997. reprint ed. 95.00 (*1-57898-040-2*) Martino Pubng.

***Brockett, Paul.** Bibliography of Aeronautics, Vol. 2. 1493p. 1998. reprint ed. 100.00 (*1-57898-100-X*) Martino Pubng.

Brockett, R., ed. Robotics. LC 90-1220. (Proceedings of Symposia in Applied Mathematics Ser.: Vol. 41). 196p. 1990. text 53.00 (*0-8218-0163-5*, PSAPM/41) Am Math.

Brockett, R. W., ed. see NATO Advanced Study Institute Staff.

Brockett, Ralph G. Ethical Issues in Adult Education. LC 88-1233. 229p. (Orig.). reprint ed. pap. 71.00 (*0-608-08637-1*, 206916000003) Bks Demand.

Brockett, Ralph G., jt. auth. see Merriam, Sharan B.

Brockett, Ralph G., jt. ed. see Hiemstra, Roger.

Brockett, William A., et al. Effective Direct & Cross Examination. LC 86-70031. 375p. 1986. suppl. ed. 75.00 (*0-88124-143-1*, CP-32330) Cont Ed Bar-CA.

Brockhaus. Brockhaus, 3 vols. 2nd ed. (GER.). 2064p. 1995. 595.00 (*0-320-00104-0*) Fr & Eur.

— Brockhaus. 7th ed. (GER.). 1024p. 1996. 95.00 (*0-320-00103-2*) Fr & Eur.

— Brockhaus, 5 vols. 8th ed. (GER.). 3500p. 1993. 1095.00 (*0-320-00107-5*) Fr & Eur.

— Brockhaus Dictionary in One Volume: Der Brockhaus in Einem Band Neu von A-Z. 2nd ed. (GER.). 1020p. 1985. write for info. (*0-8288-1967-X*, M15502) Fr & Eur.

— Brockhaus Enzklopaedie, 20 vols. & 5 suppl. vols., Set. 19th ed. (GER.). 19200p. 1986. 3995.00 (*0-8288-1966-1*, M7315) Fr & Eur.

— Brockhaus Enzyklopadie, 24 vols. 20th ed. (GER.). 1996. 1495.00 (*0-320-00105-9*) Fr & Eur.

Brockhaus. Brockhaus Grosdruckausgabe, 4 vols. large type ed. (GER.). 432p. 1995. 350.00 (*0-320-00106-7*) Fr & Eur.

Brockhaus. Brockhaus Jugend (Young Teens), 3 vols. 3rd ed. (GER.). 1200p. (YA). 1996. 150.00 (*0-320-00115-6*) Fr & Eur.

— Brockhaus Kinder (Children), 4 vols. (GER.). 648p. (J). 1997. 150.00 (*0-320-00116-4*) Fr & Eur.

— Brockhaus of Natural Sciences: Brockhaus der Naturwissenschaften und der Technik, 5 vols., Set. (GER.). 832p. 1983. 250.00 (*0-7859-0845-5*, M7314) Fr & Eur.

— Brockhaus Pflichtabnahme, 15 vols. (GER.). 7200p. 1997. write for info. (*0-320-00108-3*) Fr & Eur.

— Dictionary of Spoken German: Deutsches Bildwoerterbuch der Sprache Brockhaus. 8th ed. (ENG & GER.). 972p. 1981. 59.95 (*0-8288-1971-8*, M9299) Fr & Eur.

— Der Grosse Brockhaus, 12 vols., Set. 18th ed. (GER.). 1977. 2250.00 (*0-8288-5444-0*, M7326) Fr & Eur.

— Neue Brockhaus, 5 vols. 7th ed. (GER.). 700p. 1992. boxed set 595.00 (*0-7859-4856-2*) Fr & Eur.

— The Spoken Brockhaus, Germany Dictionary: Der Sprach Brockhaus: Deutsches Bildwoerterbuch von A-Z. 9th ed. (GER.). 972p. 1984. 85.00 (*0-8288-1970-X*, M15507) Fr & Eur.

— Sport-Brockhaus. 4th ed. (GER.). 576p. 1984. 110.00 (*0-8288-2346-4*, M7626) Fr & Eur.

— The Two Volume Brockhaus: Der Brockhaus in 2 Banden, 2 vols. (GER.). 1440p. 1984. 295.00 (*0-8288-4412-7*, M7327) Fr & Eur.

An Asterisk (*) at the beginning of an entry indicates that the title is appearing for the first time.

B

An Asterisk (*) at the beginning of an entry indicates that the title is appearing for the first time.

— Beaker, Version 2.1 DOS: Expert System for the Organic Chemistry Student. (Chemistry Ser.). 1995. pap. text 45.00 (0-534-13410-6) Brooks-Cole.
— Beaker 2.1 DOS User Guide. (Chemistry Ser.). 1995. mass mkt. 13.25 (0-534-13413-0) Brooks-Cole.
Brockwell, Maurice W. Van Eyck Problem. LC 78-138101. (Illus.). 102p. 1971. reprint ed. lib. bdg. 35.00 (0-8371-5677-7, BRVE, Greenwood Pr) Greenwood.
Brockwell, P. J. & Davis, R. A. ITSM: An Interactive Time Series Modelling Package for the PC. (Illus.). ix, 53p. 1991. disk 49.95 (0-387-97482-2) Spr-Verlag.
— ITSM: An Interactive Time Series Modelling Package for the PC. 16p. 1992. 135.00 (0-387-14210-X) Spr-Verlag.
— ITSM for Windows: A User's Guide to Time Series Modeling & Forecasting. (Illus.). 118p. 1996. 54.95 (0-387-94337-4) Spr-Verlag.
— Time Series: Theory & Methods. (Series in Statistics). (Illus.). 520p. 1986. 49.00 (0-387-96406-1) Spr-Verlag.
— Time Series: Theory & Methods. 2nd ed. 1989. disk 24.00 (0-387-14204-5) Spr-Verlag.
— Time Series: Theory & Methods. 2nd ed. (Series in Statistics). xvi, 577p. 1993. write for info. (3-540-97429-6) Spr-Verlag.
Brockwell, P. J., et al. Time Series: Theory & Methods. 2nd ed. Berger, J. O. et al, eds. (Series in Statistics). (Illus.). 544p. 1996. 60.95 (0-387-97429-6) Spr-Verlag.
Brockwell-Tillman, Elizabeth & Wolf, Earl. Discovering Great Lakes Dunes. Swinehart, Carol, ed. (Illus.). 32p. 1998. 4.95 (1-885756-10-0) MI Sea Grant.
Brockwood, Ted, jt. auth. see Bratti, Bruno.
Brod, jt. auth. see Lewis.
Brod, Charles. Apus & Incas: A Cultural Walking & Trekking Guide to Cuzco, Peru. 2nd ed. Boush, Karen, ed. LC 88-83843. (Illus.). 160p. (Orig.). 1989. pap. 10.95 (0-9618296-1-3) Inca Expedns.
Brod, D. C. Brothers in Blood: A Quint McCauley Mystery. LC 93-3636. 288p. 1993. 21.95 (0-8027-3239-9) Walker & Co.
Brod, D. C. Error in Judgment. 192p. 1990. 18.95 (0-8027-5763-4) Walker & Co.
— Error in Judgment. large type ed. (General Ser.). 544p. 1993. 27.99 (0-7089-2855-2) Ulverscroft.
Brod, D. C. Masquerade in Blue. 208p. 1991. 19.95 (0-8027-5792-8) Walker & Co.
Brod, D. C. Murder in Store. large type ed. 1991. 27.99 (0-7089-2548-0) Ulverscroft.
***Brod, D. C.** Paid in Full. LC 00-30847. (Standard Print Mystery Ser.). 2000. write for info. (0-7862-2673-0) Five Star.
Brod, Evelyn F. & Brady, Carol J. VIAJEMOS 2001 Workbook: Repaso y Progreseo. 416p. (C). 1989. text, wbk. ed. 41.20 (0-13-948670-4) P-H.
— VIAJEMOS 2001 Workbook: Repaso y Progreseo. 173p. (C). 1990. pap. text 17.80 (0-13-948688-7) P-H.
Brod, Harry, ed. The Making of Masculinities: The New Men's Studies. LC 86-28796. 304p. 1987. text 44.95 (0-04-497035-8); pap. text 22.95 (0-04-497036-6) Routledge.
Brod, Harry & Kaufman, Michael, eds. Theorizing Masculinities. LC 94-7490. (Research on Men & Masculinities Ser.: Vol. 5). 1994. 58.00 (0-8039-4903-0); pap. 26.00 (0-8039-4904-9) Sage.
Brod, Harry & Levin, Michael. Sexual Preference & Human Rights. LC 99-28622. (Point/Counterpoint Ser.). 192p. 1998. 58.00 (0-8476-8769-4); pap. 18.95 (0-8476-8770-8) Rowman.
Brod, J., et al, eds. Proteinuria. (Contributions to Nephrology Ser.: Vol. 1). (Illus.). 250p. 1975. 29.75 (3-8055-2183-9) S Karger.
Brod, J. & Knell, A. J. Diagnose in der Inneren Medizin. 2nd ed. (GER., Illus.). xiv, 362p. 1985. pap. 24.50 (3-8055-4148-1) S Karger.
Brod, J., jt. ed. see Bahlmann, J.
Brod, J., jt. ed. see Eisenbach, G. M.
Brod, Jan, jt. ed. see Eisenbach, G. M.
Brod, Max. Franz Kafka: A Biography. 2nd ed. Roberts, G. Humphreys & Winston, Richard, trs. LC 95-4828. (Illus.). 295p. 1995. reprint ed. pap. 16.00 (0-306-80670-3) Da Capo.
— Kafka. (FRE.). 307p. 1991. pap. 12.95 (0-7859-1679-2, 2070326373) Fr & Eur.
Brod, Max, ed. see Kafka, Franz.
Brod, Richard I., ed. Language Study for the 1980s: Reports of the MLA-ACLS Language Task Forces. LC 79-87582. 106p. reprint ed. pap. 32.90 (0-608-17986-8, 202912200058) Bks Demand.
Brod, Richard I. & Franklin, Phyllis. Profession '85. 54p. (Orig.). 1985. pap. text 7.50 (0-87352-320-2) Modern Lang.
— Profession '83. 52p. (Orig.). 1983. pap. text 7.50 (0-87352-318-0) Modern Lang.
Brod, Richard I. & Franklin, Phyllis, eds. Profession '84. iv, 43p. (Orig.). 1984. pap. text 7.50 (0-87352-319-9) Modern Lang.
Brod, Richard I., ed. see Modern Language Association of America Staff.
Brod, Shirley. Ideas At Work: Techniques for Effective Communication Minibook A. (Work Styles Ser.). 38p. 1987. teacher ed. 3.95 (0-940723-01-8) SIIS.
Brod, Shirley, compiled by. Melt Bibliography. 285p. 1987. teacher ed. 20.00 (0-940723-03-4) SIIS.
***Broda, Aldo.** Administrando Bien la Vida. (SPA.). 2000. pap. 8.99 (0-7899-0760-7) Spanish Hse Distributors.
Broda, Engelbert. Ludwig Boltzmann: Man, Physicist, Philosopher. LC 82-80707. (Illus.). 179p. (C). 1983. 27.50 (0-918024-24-2) Ox Bow.
Broda, Johanna, et al. The Great Temple of Tenochtitlan: Center & Periphery in the Aztec World. 1988. pap. 22.50 (0-520-06597-2, Pub. by U CA Pr) Cal Prin Full Svc.
Broda, Krysia, ed. ALPUK'92: Proceedings of the 4th U. K. Annual Conference on Logic Programming, London, 30 March - 01 April 1992. LC 92-39256. (Workshops in Computing Ser.). 1993. 79.00 (0-387-19783-4); 57.00 (3-540-19783-4) Spr-Verlag.
Broda, Paul, et al, eds. The Eukaryotic Genome: Organisation & Regulation. (Society for General Microbiology Symposium Ser.: No. 50). (Illus.). 407p. (C). 1993. text 125.00 (0-521-44364-4) Cambridge U Pr.
Brodal, Alf. Neurological Anatomy in Relation to Clinical Medicine. 3rd ed. (Illus.). 1053p. 1981. text 89.00 (0-19-502694-2) OUP.
Brodal, Per. The Central Nervous System: Structure & Function. 2nd ed. LC 96-40369. (Illus.). 688p. 1997. text 54.50 (0-19-511741-7) OUP.
Brodatz, Phil. Textures: A Photographic Album for Artists & Designers. LC 99-28805. 128p. 1999. pap. text 13.95 (0-486-40699-7) Dover & Greer.
Brodbeck, Andreas, jt. auth. see Schlogl, Hermann A.
Brodbeck, Arthur J., jt. ed. see Burdick, Eugene.
Brodbeck, David. Brahms: Symphony No. 1. (Cambridge Music Handbooks Ser.). (Illus.). 125p. (C). 1997. text 39.95 (0-521-47432-9); pap. text 12.95 (0-521-47959-2) Cambridge U Pr.
Brodbeck, David, ed. Brahms Studies. (Brahms Studies: Vol. 1). x, 198p. 1995. text 65.00 (0-8032-1243-7) U of Nebr Pr.
— Brahms Studies 2. (Illus.). vii, 208p. 1998. text 75.00 (0-8032-1287-9, BRAST2) U of Nebr Pr.
Brodbeck, John E., ed. Motor Fleet Safety Manual. 4th rev. ed. LC 95-33267. 207p. 1995. 48.95 (0-87912-188-2, 22133-0000) Natl Safety Coun.
Brodbeck, May, et al. American Non-Fiction, 1900-1950. LC 70-106668. 198p. 1970. reprint ed. lib. bdg. 55.00 (0-8371-3420-X, BRNF, Greenwood Pr) Greenwood.
Brodber, Erna. Louisiana: A Novel. LC 97-21363. 168p. (Orig.). 1997. pap. 17.00 (1-57806-031-1) U Pr of Miss.
Brodd, Jeffrey. World Religions: A Voyage of Discovery. 356p. (YA). 1998. teacher ed., spiral bd. 24.95 (0-88489-487-8) St Marys.
— World Religions: A Voyage of Discovery. (Illus.). 272p. (YA). 1998. pap., student ed. 19.50 (0-88489-486-X) St Marys.
— World Religions: A Voyage of Discovery. 272p. 1998. pap. 27.95 (0-88489-370-7) St Marys.
Brodd, R. J., ed. see Electrochemical Society Staff.
Broddle, S. Merrow, ed. see Philalethes, Eirenaeus.
Brode, Anthony. A Hampshire Album: 1900-1940. 80p. 1987. pap. 30.00 (0-905392-27-2) St Mut.
— The Hampshire Village Books. 192p. 1987. pap. 30.00 (0-905392-06-X) St Mut.
— The Southampton Blitz. 96p. 1987. 50.00 (0-905392-15-9) St Mut.
Brode, Bernice. Tales of Los Alamos: Life on the Mesa, 1943-1945. Storms, Barbara G., ed. & pref. by. LC 97-29558. (Illus.). 158p. 1997. pap. 12.95 (0-941232-17-4) Los Alamos Hist Soc.
Brode, Douglas. Denzel Washington: His Films & Career. (Illus.). 288p. 1996. 22.50 (1-55972-381-5, Birch Ln Pr) Carol Pub Group.
— The Films of Dustin Hoffman. (Illus.). 256p. 1983. 18.95 (0-8065-0869-8, Citadel Pr) Carol Pub Group.
— The Films of Dustin Hoffman. (Illus.). 224p. 1988. reprint ed. pap. 14.95 (0-8065-1085-4, Citadel Pr) Carol Pub Group.
— The Films of Jack Nicholson. (Illus.). 256p. 1987. 19.95 (0-8065-1047-1, Citadel Pr) Carol Pub Group.
— The Films of Jack Nicholson. 1990. pap. 15.95 (0-8065-1192-3, Citadel Pr) Carol Pub Group.
— The Films of Jack Nicholson. rev. ed. LC 93-45774. (Illus.). 1994. 17.95 (0-8065-1524-4, Citadel Pr) Carol Pub Group.
— Films of Jack Nicholson. rev. ed. LC 96-36129. (Illus.). 288p. 1996. pap. text 19.95 (0-8065-1834-0) Carol Pub Group.
— The Films of Robert De Niro. rev. ed. LC 96-36130. (Illus.). 288p. 1996. pap. 19.95 (0-8065-1779-4, Citadel Pr) Carol Pub Group.
— The Films of Robert De Niro. 4th rev. ed. LC 99-21058. (Illus.). 320p. 1999. pap. 22.50 (0-8065-2110-4, Citadel Pr) Carol Pub Group.
— The Films of Steven Spielberg. LC 94-17783. (Illus.). 254p. 1994. pap. 18.95 (0-8065-1540-6, Citadel Pr) Carol Pub Group.
— The Films of Steven Spielberg. rev. ed. LC 98-20239. (Illus.). 288p. 1997. pap. text 21.95 (0-8065-1951-7) Carol Pub Group.
— The Films of the Eighties. (Illus.). 286p. (Orig.). 1990. pap. 15.95 (0-8065-1162-1, Citadel Pr) Carol Pub Group.
— The Films of the Sixties. (Illus.). 1980. pap. 15.95 (0-8065-0798-5, Citadel Pr) Carol Pub Group.
— The Films of Woody Allen. LC 97-17177. (Illus.). 320p. 1997. write for info. (0-8065-1902-9) Carol Pub Group.
— Lost Films of the Fifties. (Illus.). 288p. (Orig.). (YA). 1988. pap. 15.95 (0-8065-1092-7, Citadel Pr) Carol Pub Group.
— Money, Women & Guns: Crime Movies from Bonnie & Clyde to the Present. (Citadel Film Ser.). (Illus.). 256p. (Orig.). 1995. pap. 17.95 (0-8065-1608-9, Citadel Pr) Carol Pub Group.
— Once Was Enough: Celebrities (& Others) Who Appeared a Single Time on the Screen. (Illus.). 256p. 1996. pap. 16.95 (0-8065-1735-2, Citadel Pr) Carol Pub Group.
***Brode, Douglas.** Shakespeare in the Movies: From the Silent Era to Shakespeare in Love. 272p. 2000. 25.00 (0-19-513958-5) OUP.
Brode, Douglas. Shakespeare in the Movies: From the Silent Era to the Present Day. LC 98-56152. (Illus.). 320p. 1999. 24.95 (1-55972-514-1, Birch Ln Pr) Carol Pub Group.
— Woody Allen: His Films & Career. 1987. 19.95 (0-8065-0959-7, Citadel Pr); pap. 14.95 (0-8065-1067-6, Citadel Pr) Carol Pub Group.
— Woody Allen: His Films & Career. (Illus.). 1991. pap. 17.95 (0-8065-1259-8, Citadel Pr) Carol Pub Group.
Brode, George, Jr. Tax Planning for Corporate Acquisitions. (Illus.). 770p. 1995. pap. text, suppl. ed. 87.00 (1-884673-04-X) Brode Pubns.
— Tax Planning for Corporate Acquisitions. 2nd ed. (Illus.). 1200p. 1997. 245.00 (1-884673-07-4) Brode Pubns.
— Tax Planning for Corporate Acquisitions: (With Current Supplement) (Illus.). 1995. 175.00 (1-884673-03-1) Brode Pubns.
Brode, Heinrich. British & German East Africa: Their Economic & Commercial Relations. Wilkins, Mira, ed. LC 76-29766. (European Business Ser.). (Illus.). 1977. reprint ed. lib. bdg. 18.95 (0-405-09780-8) Ayer.
Brode, Patrick. Casual Slaughters & Accidental Judgments: Canadian War Crimes Prosecutions, 1944-1948. LC 98-166419. 352p. 1997. text 39.95 (0-8020-4204-X) U of Toronto Pr.
— The Odyssey of John Anderson. (Publications of the Osgoode Society). 176p. 1989. pap. 15.95 (0-8020-6748-4); text 35.00 (0-8020-5840-X) U of Toronto Pr.
— Sir John Beverley Robinson: Bone & Sinew of the Compact. (Publications of the Osgoode Society). 344p. 1984. pap. 17.95 (0-8020-3419-5) U of Toronto Pr.
— Sir John Beverley Robinson: Bone & Sinew of the Compact. LC 85-133805. (Illus.). 342p. reprint ed. pap. 106.10 (0-7837-0538-7, 204086600019) Bks Demand.
Brode, Wallace R., ed. Science in Progress. LC 78-37534. (Essay Index Reprint Ser.: 12). 1977. reprint ed. 25.95 (0-8369-7275-9) Ayer.
— Science in Progress. LC 78-37534. (Essay Index Reprint Ser.: 14). 1977. reprint ed. 23.95 (0-8369-7274-0) Ayer.
Brode, Wallace R., ed. see Waterman, Alan T., et al.
Brodelius, Peter, jt. ed. see Miller, Ian M.
***Brodell, James D. & Occhiogrosso, Peter.** Gregory Perillo: And the Masters of American Western Art. LC 99-67486. (Illus.). 200p. 2000. write for info. (0-9676196-0-2) JDB.
Broder, Aaron J. Trial Handbook for New York Lawyers. 2nd ed. LC 85-82119. 1986. 115.00 (0-318-19876-2) West Group.
— Trial Handbook for New York Lawyers. 2nd ed. LC 85-82119. 1991. suppl. ed. 40.00 (0-317-03286-0) West Group.
— Trial Handbook for New York Lawyers. 3rd ed. LC 96-75045. (New York Practice Library). 980p. 1996. text. write for info. (0-7620-0040-6) West Group.
Broder, Aaron J., jt. auth. see Baer, Harold.
Broder, Adam, jt. auth. see Abrams, Tony.
Broder, Christopher C., jt. auth. see Dimitrov, Dimiter S.
***Broder, David S.** Democracy Derailed: The Initiative Movement & the Power of Money. LC 99-54190. (Illus.). 256p. 2000. 23.00 (0-15-100464-1) Harcourt.
Broder, David S., jt. auth. see Johnson, Haynes.
Broder, Eric. The Below-the-Belt Manager. LC 97-34344. 128p. 1998. mass mkt. 9.99 (0-446-67310-2, Pub. by Warner Bks) Little.
***Broder, Eric.** The Great Indoors: Favorites from 1987-1996. LC 99-50452. (Illus.). 224p. 1999. pap. 13.95 (1-886228-34-5) Gray & Co Pubs.
Broder, James F. Risk Analysis & the Security Survey. 2nd ed. LC 99-31487. 352p. 1999. 39.95 (0-7506-7089-4) Buttrwrth-Heinemann.
Broder, James F. & Schur, Peyton B. Investigation of Substance Abuse in the Workplace. 192p. 1990. pap. 29.95 (0-409-90121-0) Buttrwrth-Heinemann.
Broder, Lawrence E. & Carter, Stephen K. Meningeal Leukemia. LC 74-190394. 140p. reprint ed. pap. 43.40 (0-608-30231-7, 202070600018) Bks Demand.
Broder, Michael S. Art of Living Single. Claflin, Edward B., ed. 352p. 1990. mass mkt. 6.99 (0-380-70933-3, Avon Bks) Morrow Avon.
— The Art of Staying Together. 256p. 1994. reprint ed. mass mkt. 5.50 (0-380-72263-1, Avon Bks) Morrow Avon.
***Broder, Michael S., et al.** Uterine Artery Embolization: A Systematic Review of the Literature & Proposal for Research. 58p. (C). 2000. 6.00 (0-8330-2808-1, MR-1158-CIRREF) Rand Corp.
Broder, Nathan. The Collector's Bach. LC 77-28265. (Keystone Books in English). 192p. 1978. reprint ed. lib. bdg. 55.00 (0-313-20240-0, BRBAC, Greenwood Pr) Greenwood.
— Samuel Barber. LC 85-14803. (Illus.). 111p. 1985. reprint ed. lib. bdg. 55.00 (0-313-24984-9, BRSB, Greenwood Pr) Greenwood.
Broder, Nathan, ed. Mozart's Symphony in G Minor, K.550. (Critical Scores Ser.). (C). 1967. pap. text 15.50 (0-393-09775-7) Norton.
Broder, Nathan, tr. see Einstein, Alfred.
Broder, Patricia J. Shadows on Glass: The Indian Photographs of Ben Wittick. 1991. 49.95 (0-8476-7631-5) Rowman.
— Shadows on Glass: The Indian World of Ben Wittick. 160p. 1991. pap. 24.95 (0-8476-7701-X) Rowman.
***Broder, Patricia Janis.** Dean Cornwell: Dean of Illustrators. (Illus.). 240p. 2000. reprint ed. 75.00 (1-888054-43-3, 54433, Pub. by Collectors Pr) Universe.
Broder, Patricia Janis. Earth Songs, Moon Dreams: Paintings by American Indian Women. LC 99-22181. (Illus.). 286p. 1999. pap. 60.00 (0-312-20534-1) St Martin.
Broder, Samuel, ed. AIDS: Modern Concepts & Therapeutic Challenges. 386p. 1986. text 125.00 (0-8247-7649-6) Dekker.
Broder, Samuel, et al, eds. Textbook of AIDS Medicine. LC 93-8436. (Illus.). 944p. 1994. 155.00 (0-683-01072-7) Lppncott W & W.
Broderic, Damien, ed. Not the Only Planet: Travel Stories from Science Fiction. 350p. 1998. pap. 12.95 (0-86442-582-1) Lonely Planet.
Broderick, Albert, ed. French Institutionalists: Maurice Hauriou, Georges Renard, Joseph T. Delos. Welling, Mary, tr. from FRE. (Twentieth Century Legal Philosophy Ser.: No. 8). 396p. 1970. 46.50 (0-674-32125-1) HUP.
— Law & the Liberal Arts. LC 67-20497. 261p. reprint ed. pap. 81.00 (0-608-30186-8, 200521800051) Bks Demand.
Broderick, Amanda, jt. ed. see Picton, David.
Broderick, Bill. Groundwork for College Reading. 2nd ed. 467p. (C). 1997. pap. text 16.00 (0-944210-27-9) Townsend NJ.
***Broderick, Bill.** Groundwork for College Reading. 3rd rev. ed. 576p. (C). 1999. 18.00 (0-944210-48-1) Townsend NJ.
Broderick, Bill. Ten Steps to Building College Reading Skills, Form B. 2nd ed. 1994. pap. text 16.00 (0-944210-67-8, Form B) Townsend NJ.
Broderick, Carlfred B. My Parents Married on a Dare & Other Favorite Essays on Life. LC 96-19270. viii, 150p. 1996. 14.95 (1-57345-190-8) Deseret Bk.
— The Therapeutic Triangle: A Sourcebook on Marital Therapy. LC 82-23062. 184p. 1983. reprint ed. pap. 57.10 (0-608-01507-5, 205955100001) Bks Demand.
— Understanding Family Process: The Basics of Family Systems Theory. (Illus.). 296p. 1993. 55.00 (0-8039-3777-6); pap. 26.00 (0-8039-3778-4) Sage.
Broderick, Carlfred B. & Bernard, Jessie, eds. The Individual, Sex & Society. LC 69-11934. (Illus.). 422p. reprint ed. pap. 130.90 (0-608-14670-6, 202583600046) Bks Demand.
Broderick, Damien. The Architecture of Babel: Discourses of Literature & Science. (Interpretations Ser.). 160p. 1994. pap. 19.95 (0-522-84614-9, Pub. by Melbourne Univ Pr) Paul & Co Pubs.
***Broderick, Damien.** The Last Mortal Generation. 272p. 2000. pap. 14.95 (1-86436-440-8, Pub. by New Holland) BHB Intl.
Broderick, Damien. Reading by Starlight: Postmodern Science Fiction. LC 94-9505. (Popular Fiction Ser.). 224p. (Orig.). (C). 1994. pap. 22.99 (0-415-09789-4, B4755) Routledge.
— Reading by Starlight: Postmodern Science Fiction. LC 94-9505. (Popular Fiction Ser.). 224p. (Orig.). (C). (gr. 13). 1994. 85.00 (0-415-09788-6, B4751) Routledge.
— The Sea's Furthest End. 192p. (Orig.). 1993. pap. 10.00 (1-875346-07-4, Pub. by Aphelion) Firebird Dist.
— Striped Holes. 1988. pap. 2.95 (0-380-75377-4, Avon Bks) Morrow Avon.
***Broderick, Damien.** Transrealist Fiction: Writing in the Slipstream of Science, 90. LC 99-49691. (Contributions to the Study of Science Fiction & Fantasy Ser.). 208p. 2000. 65.00 (0-313-31121-8, Greenwood Pr) Greenwood.
Broderick, Damien. The White Abacus. LC 96-23764. 352p. 1997. pap. 12.50 (0-380-78559-5, Avon Bks); mass mkt. 23.00 (0-380-97476-2, Avon Bks) Morrow Avon.
— The White Abacus. 352p. 1998. reprint ed. mass mkt. 5.99 (0-380-79615-5, Avon Bks) Morrow Avon.
— Zones. LC 97-211214. (Illus.). 232p. (YA). (gr. 7-12). 1998. pap. 7.95 (0-7322-5760-3) HarpC.
Broderick, Damien, jt. ed. see Hartwell, David G.
Broderick, Damient, ed. Theory & Its Discontents. LC 97-183611. 1996. pap. text 70.00 (0-949823-65-1, Pub. by Deakin Univ) St Mut.
Broderick, David. An Early Toll-Road: The Dublin-Dunleer Turnpike, 1731-1855. 64p. 1996. pap. 9.95 (0-7165-2595-X, Pub. by Irish Acad Pr) Intl Spec Bk.
Broderick, Dorothy M., ed. The VOYA Reader. LC 90-37812. 320p. 1990. 34.50 (0-8108-2331-4) Scarecrow.
Broderick, Dorothy M., jt. auth. see Curley, Arthur.
Broderick, Dorothy M., jt. ed. see Chelton, Mary K.
Broderick, Dorothy M., ed. see Makowski, Silk.
Broderick, Francis L. Progressivism at Risk: Electing a President in 1912, 134. LC 88-38547. (Contributions in American History Ser.: No. 134). 244p. 1989. 59.95 (0-313-26400-7, BPX, Greenwood Pr) Greenwood.
— W. E. B. Du Bois: Negro Leader in a Time of Crisis. xii, 259p. 1959. 35.00 (0-8047-0558-5) Stanford U Pr.
— W. E. B. Du Bois: Negro Leader in a Time of Crisis. fac. ed. LC 59-7422. (Illus.). 277p. 1959. pap. 30.00 (0-7837-7265-3, 204704000005) Bks Demand.
Broderick, George, jt. auth. see Niedhart, Gottfried.
Broderick, Glenn. Official Deathtrap Dungeon: Strategy Guide. LC 98-106489. 1997. pap. text 19.95 (0-911295-44-5) Air Age.
Broderick, James. The Economic Morals of the Jesuits. LC 76-38248. (Evolution of Capitalism Ser.). 168p. 1977. reprint ed. 15.95 (0-405-04113-6) Ayer.
— The Origin of the Jesuits. LC 96-31317. 274p. (C). 1997. reprint ed. pap. 13.95 (0-8294-0930-0, Jesuit Way) Loyola Pr.
— Saint Ignatius of Loyola: The Pilgrim Years. LC 97-76861. 346p. 1998. pap. 14.95 (0-89870-683-1) Ignatius Pr.
Broderick, John. Chameleons. 1961. 10.95 (0-8392-1010-8) Astor-Honor.
— Don Juaneen. 1965. 12.95 (0-8392-1156-2) Astor-Honor.
— Fugitives. 1962. 10.95 (0-8392-1036-1) Astor-Honor.
— The Irish Magdalen. 265p. 1990. 21.95 (0-7145-2906-0) M Boyars Pubs.
— A Prayer for Fair Weather. LC 83-6341. 192p. 1984. 13.95 (0-7145-2796-3) M Boyars Pubs.
— The Rose Tree. (Fiction Ser.). 192p. 1985. 14.95 (0-7145-2824-2) M Boyars Pubs.
— The Trial of Father Dillingham. 224p. 1981. 14.95 (0-7145-2747-5) M Boyars Pubs.

An Asterisk (*) at the beginning of an entry indicates that the title is appearing for the first time.

Broderick, John, ed. The Flood: A Novel. 320p. 1987. 22.95 (*0-7145-2867-6*) M Boyars Pubs.

Broderick, John C., ed. Journal, 1837-1844, Vol. 1. 712p. 1981. text 69.50 (*0-691-06361-3*, Pub. by Princeton U Pr) Cal Prin Full Svc.

Broderick, M. & Morton, A. A. Concise Dictionary of Egyptian Archaeology. vii, 193p. 1979. reprint ed. pap. 15.00 (*0-89005-303-0*) Ares.

Broderick, Maria, et al, eds. For Teachers about Teaching. LC 88-81479. (Reprint Ser.: No. 20). 96p. 1988. pap. 14.95 (*0-916690-22-9*) Harvard Educ Rev.

Broderick, Maureen E. Love Waits. 256p. 1999. 25.00 (*0-9664483-6-7*); pap. write for info. (*0-9664483-5-9*) Baxter Bks.

Broderick, Mick, ed. Hibakusha Cinema: Hiroshima, Nagaski & the Nuclear Image in Japanese Film. (Japanese Studies). (Illus.). 256p. 1996. 110.00 (*0-7103-0529-X*, Pub. by Kegan Paul Intl) Col U Pr.

Broderick, Orla. Dash of Mustard. 128p. 1995. 14.98 (*0-7858-0351-3*) Bk Sales Inc.

***Broderick, Orla.** Great Soups. (Illus.). 64p. 1999. 17.50 (*0-8478-2205-2*, Pub. by Rizzoli Intl) St Martin.

Broderick, Orla. Pickles, Relishes, & Chuntneys. 128p. 1995. 14.98 (*0-7858-0352-1*) Bk Sales Inc.

Broderick, Renae F. & National Research Council Staff, eds. Issues in Civilian Outplacement Strategies: Proceedings of a Workshop. LC 96-69970. 112p. 1996. pap. text 34.00 (*0-309-05544-X*) Natl Acad Pr.

Broderick, Richard. Night Sale. LC 82-61652. (Minnesota Voices Project Ser.: No. 8). (Illus.). 135p. 1982. pap. 0.75 (*0-89823-040-3*) New Rivers Pr.

***Broderick, Richard.** Woman Lake. LC 99-68468. (Minnesota Voices Project Ser.: Vol. 95). 76p. 2000. pap. 13.95 (*0-89823-201-5*, Pub. by New Rivers Pr) Consort Bk Sales.

Broderick, Robert C. Catholic Encyclopedia. rev. ed. 1990. pap. 19.99 (*0-8407-3175-2*) Nelson.

Broderick, Sean F. & Switzer, James F. The Original Plane Watcher's Mini Field Guide. 2nd rev. ed. 2p. 1997. pap. 4.95 (*0-9649462-1-1*) FishBelly White.

— The Original Plane Watchers Mini-Field Guide: D. C./Baltimore Edition. 1995. 3.95 (*0-9649462-0-3*) FishBelly White.

Broderick, Warren F., ed. Brunswick: A Pictorial History. (Illus.). (Orig.). 1978. pap. 9.95 (*0-686-26173-9*) Brunswick Hist Soc.

Broderick, Warren F. & Bouck, William. Pottery Works: Potteries of New York State's Capital District & Upper Hudson Region. LC 92-55116. (Illus.). 288p. (C). 1995. 59.50 (*0-8386-3538-5*) Fairleigh Dickinson.

Broderidge, Tom. Fly-Fishing the Gulf Coast. LC 95-61821. (Illus.). 101p. 1996. pap. 14.95 (*0-9632059-3-5*) Woodland Prods.

***Brodersen, Brian.** The Gifts of the Holy Spirit. 50p. 2000. pap. 2.99 (*0-9700218-1-X*) Calvary Dist.

Brodersen, Brian. Spiritual Warfare. Smith, Chuck, ed. (Calvary Basics Ser.). 73p. 1995. pap. 3.50 (*0-936728-54-X*) Word for Today.

Brodersen, Kai. Terra Cognita. (Spudasmata Ser.: Vol. 59). (GER.). 354p. 1995. write for info. (*3-487-10008-8*) G Olms Pubs.

Brodersen, Momme. Walter Benjamin: A Biography. 352p. 1998. pap. 19.00 (*1-85984-082-5*) Norton.

— Walter Benjamin: A Biography. LC 96-48951. (Illus.). 316p. 1996. 35.00 (*1-85984-967-9*, Pub. by Verso) Norton.

Brodersen, Robert, jt. auth. see Chandrakasan, Anantha P.

Brodersen, Robert W. Technologies for Wireless Computing. Chandrakasan, Anantha P., ed. LC 96-35750. 200p. (C). 1996. text 133.00 (*0-7923-9785-1*) Kluwer Academic.

Brodersen, Robert W., ed. Anatomy of a Silicon Compiler. LC 92-10809. (International Series in Engineering & Computer Science, VLSI, Computer Architecture, & Digital Screen Processing). 384p. (C). 1992. text 139.50 (*0-7923-9249-3*) Kluwer Academic.

Brodersen, Robert w., jt. auth. see Sheng, Samuel.

Broderson, Robert W., jt. auth. see Chandrakasan, Anantha P.

Broderson, Steve, jt. auth. see Sharpe, Sally D.

Brodetsky, Tessa. Elizabeth Gaskell. LC 86-1045. (Women's Ser.). (Illus.). 113p. (C). 1987. pap. 16.50 (*0-907582-83-4*) Berg Pubs.

Brodeur, Adrienne, ed. see Coppola, Francis Ford.

Brodeur, Claude, jt. auth. see Devisch, Rene.

Brodeur, Jean-Paul. Comparisons in Policing: An International Perspective. (Economists of the Twentieth Century Ser.). 256p. 1995. 73.95 (*1-85972-091-9*, Pub. by Avebry) Ashgate Pub Co.

— How to Recognize Good Policing: Problems & Issues. LC 98-9032. 1998. 58.00 (*0-7619-1613-X*) Sage.

Brodeur, Jean-Paul, ed. How to Recognize Good Policing: Problems & Issues. LC 98-9032. 272p. 1998. pap. 27.95 (*0-7619-1614-8*) Sage.

Brodeur, Karen. MaxNotes 1984. (MaxNotes Ser.). 128p. 1995. pap. text 3.95 (*0-87891-996-1*) Res & Educ.

Brodeur, Paul. Secrets: A Writer in the Cold War. LC 96-43622. 360p. 1997. 24.95 (*0-571-19907-0*) Faber & Faber.

Brodey, Jerry, jt. auth. see Brodey, Kim.

Brodey, Jim. Heart of the Breath: Poems, 1979-1992. Coolidge, Clark, ed. LC 96-2100. 381p. 1996. pap. 15.95 (*0-9638433-7-0*) Hard Pr MA.

Brodey, Kim & Brodey, Jerry. Can You Hear My Voice? Teacher's Activity Guide. 1994. pap. text, teacher ed. 11.00 (*0-9695319-3-1*, Pub. by K & J Brodey) Consort Bk Sales.

Brodey, Vivana, ed. Coplas de Mingo Revulgo. (Spanish Ser.: No. 30). viii, 312p. 1986. 25.00 (*0-942260-74-0*) Hispanic Seminary.

Brodhead, B. North Central Coll 98 Freshman. 1998. pap. text 18.00 (*0-07-428955-1*) McGraw.

Brodhead, B. & Brodhead, Mindy. Sacked: The Darkside of Sports at Louisiana State University. 221p. 1987. 19.95 (*0-318-23877-2*) Beauregard Pr.

Brodhead, John R., et al, eds. Documents Relative to the Colonial History of the State of New York, 15 vols. reprint ed. 3915.00 (*0-404-19516-4*) AMS Pr.

— Documents Relative to the Colonial History of the State of New York, 15 vols., Set. reprint ed. 3915.00 (*0-404-01090-3*) AMS Pr.

Brodhead, Michael J. David J. Brewer: The Life of a Supreme Court Justice, 1837-1910. LC 93-16866. 262p. (C). 1994. 41.95 (*0-8093-1909-8*) S Ill U Pr.

Brodhead, Michael J., jt. auth. see Cutright, Paul R.

Brodhead, Michael J., ed. see Woodhouse, S. W.

Brodhead, Mindy, jt. auth. see Brodhead, B.

Brodhead, Richard H. Cultures of Letters: Scenes of Reading & Writing in Nineteenth-Century America. LC 92-30967. (Illus.). 256p. (C). 1994. pap. text 15.95 (*0-226-07526-5*) U Ch Pr.

— Cultures of Letters: Scenes of Reading & Writing in Nineteenth-Century America. LC 92-30967. (Illus.). 256p. (C). 1997. 27.50 (*0-226-07525-7*) U Ch Pr.

— Hawthorne, Melville & the Novel. LC PS1888.B7. (Midway Reprint Ser.). 224p. Date not set. reprint ed. pap. 69.50 (*0-608-20610-5*, 205457800003) Bks Demand.

Brodhead, Richard H., ed. see Chesnutt, Charles Waddell.

Brodia, Rick, jt. auth. see Johnson, Dave.

***Brodie.** Canada in the 21st Century. 2000. pap. write for info. (*0-13-082634-0*) P-H.

Brodie, jt. ed. see Campbell.

Brodie, Antonia, et al. Directory of British Architects, 1834-1914. 2nd ed. LC 99-26477. 1072p. 1999. 330.00 (*0-7201-2352-6*) Continuum.

Brodie, B. B., jt. auth. see Marks, R. J.

Brodie, B. B., ed. see Conference on Bioavailability of Drugs, Washington.

Brodie, Barry, ed. see Mills, Kenneth G.

Brodie, Bernard. The Development of Nuclear Strategy. (CISA Working Papers: No. 11). 30p. (Orig.). 1978. pap. 15.00 (*0-86682-010-8*) Ctr Intl Relations.

— Escalation & the Nuclear Option. LC 66-23765. 159p. reprint ed. pap. 49.30 (*0-608-30756-4*, 200088600050) Bks Demand.

— On Clarifying Objectives of Arms Control. (CISA Working Papers: No. 1). 33p. (Orig.). 1976. pap. 15.00 (*0-86682-000-0*) Ctr Intl Relations.

— Strategy in the Missile Age. LC 58-6102. 439p. 1965. reprint ed. pap. 136.10 (*0-7837-8163-6*, 204786800008) Bks Demand.

— War & Politics. 514p. (C). 1974. pap. write for info. (*0-685-28575-8*) Macmillan.

— War & Politics. 514p. (C). 1974. pap. text 66.00 (*0-02-315020-3*, Macmillan Coll) P-H.

Brodie, Bernard & Brodie, Fawn M. From Crossbow to H-Bomb. enl. rev. ed. LC 72-90408. (Illus.). 320p. 1973. pap. 12.95 (*0-253-20161-6*, MB 161) Ind U Pr.

Brodie, Bernard B. & Bressler, R., eds. Minireviews of the Neurosciences from Life Sciences, Vols. 13-15. LC 75-8733. 493p. 1975. 225.00 (*0-08-019724-8*, Pub. by Pergamon Repr) Franklin.

Brodie, Carolyn S. Exploring the Plains States Through Literature. LC 93-42065. (Exploring the United States Through Literature Ser.). 136p. 1994. pap. 27.50 (*0-89774-762-3*) Oryx Pr.

Brodie, Carolyn S., et al. The Bookmark Book. (Cut 'n Clip Ser.). 115p. 1996. pap. text 25.00 (*1-56308-300-0*) Libs Unl.

Brodie, Carolyn S., jt. auth. see Manna, Anthony L.

Brodie, Carolyn S., ed. see Virginia Hamilton Conference Staff.

Brodie, D., ed. see Oneal, Zibby.

Brodie, David A. Research Methods for the Health Sciences. xii, 210p. 1994. text 52.00 (*3-7186-5609-4*, Harwood Acad Pubs) Gordon & Breach.

Brodie, David A., ed. A Reference Manual for Human Performance Measurement in the Field of Physical Education & Sports Sciences. LC 95-47646. (Mellen Studies in Education: Vol. 26). 252p. 1996. text 89.95 (*0-7734-8788-3*) E Mellen.

Brodie, David A. & McConnell, Rachel, eds. Selected Sermons for Christian Students on Campus. LC 93-12553. 248p. 1993. text 89.95 (*0-7734-9247-X*) E Mellen.

Brodie, David A., et al. Research Methods for Health Sciences. LC 94-1258. xii, 210p. 1994. pap. text 27.00 (*3-7186-5527-6*) Gordon & Breach.

Brodie, Deborah. Writing Changes Everything. LC 96-40453. 1997. text 18.95 (*0-312-15432-1*) St Martin.

Brodie, Deborah, ed. Untying the Knot: Ex-Husbands, Ex-Wives & Other Experts on the Passage of Divorce. LC 98-48160. 160p. 1998. pap. 9.95 (*0-312-20042-0*) St Martin.

Brodie, Donald W. Individual Employment Disputes: Definite & Indefinite Term Contracts. LC 90-40701. 280p. 1991. 65.00 (*0-89930-512-1*, BIJ, Quorum Bks) Greenwood.

Brodie, Douglas S. & Culbert, Michael. Cancer & Common Sense: Combining Science & Nature to Control Cancer. Engstrom, Paul L., ed. 1997. pap. 12.95 (*1-884367-03-8*) Winning St Paul.

Brodie, Edmund D. Venomous Animals, 300 Animals in Full Color. (Golden Guide Ser.). 1989. 11.05 (*0-606-12038-6*, Pub. by Turtleback) Demco.

Brodie, Faithe. When "The Other Woman" Is His Mother: Book I: Boys & Incest Victims, & Male Multiple Personality Disorder. LC 90-70218. 181p. 1992. pap. 13.95 (*0-9626009-0-3*) Winged Eagle Pr.

Brodie, Fawn M. The Devil Drives: A Life of Sir Richard Burton. (Illus.). 408p. 1984. reprint ed. pap. 12.95 (*0-393-30166-4*) Norton.

— No Man Knows My History. LC 90-50139. 576p. 1995. pap. 17.00 (*0-679-73054-0*) Random.

— No Man Knows My History: The Life of Joseph Smith. (Illus.). 1971. 35.00 (*0-394-46967-4*) Knopf.

— Thomas Jefferson: An Intimate History. 832p. 1981. mass mkt. 7.99 (*0-553-27335-3*, Bantam Classics) Bantam.

— Thomas Jefferson: An Intimate History. (Illus.). 608p. 1998. pap. 14.95 (*0-393-31752-8*) Norton.

Brodie, Fawn M., jt. auth. see Brodie, Bernard.

Brodie, Harold J. The Bird's Nest Fungi. LC 75-18476. 1975. pap. 12.95 (*0-8020-6766-2*) U of Toronto Pr.

— The Bird's Nest Fungi. LC 75-19476. (Illus.). 216p. reprint ed. pap. 67.00 (*0-8357-3774-8*, 203650400003) Bks Demand.

— Fungi: Delight of Curiosity. LC 77-25204. 143p. reprint ed. pap. 44.40 (*0-608-17117-4*, 202645000049) Bks Demand.

Brodie, Henry, et al. South Asia in the World Today. Talbot, Phillips, ed. LC 78-161774. (BCL Ser. I). reprint ed. 22.50 (*0-404-09042-7*) AMS Pr.

Brodie, Howard. Drawing Fire: A Combat Artist at War. LC 95-33748. (Illus.). 168p. (Orig.). 1996. pap. 16.95 (*0-9641932-1-3*) Portola Press.

Brodie, I. & Muray, Julius J. The Physics of Micro/Nano-Fabrication. (Microdevices: Physics & Fabrication Technologies Ser.). (Illus.). 670p. (C). 1993. text 110.00 (*0-306-44146-2*, Kluwer Plenum) Kluwer Academic.

Brodie, Ian, jt. auth. see Goodman, Di.

Brodie-Innes, J. W. The Astrology of the Golden Dawn. Kuntz, Darcy, ed. (Golden Dawn Studies: No. 10). (Orig.). 1996. pap. 8.95 (*1-55818-345-0*) Holmes Pub.

Brodie, Isabelle. School Exclusion. Date not set. 14.95 (*1-86020-013-3*, Pub. by U of Luton Pr) Bks Intl VA.

Brodie, Isabelle, jt. auth. see Berridge, David.

Brodie, Ivor & Muray, Julius J. The Physics of Microfabrication. LC 82-3835. (Illus.). 522p. (C). 1982. 144.00 (*0-306-40863-5*, Plenum Trade) Perseus Pubng.

Brodie, J. P., jt. ed. see Smith, G. H.

Brodie, Jack. A Treasury of Nebraska Pioneer Folklore. LC 66-10876. xviii, 391p. 1966. reprint ed. pap. 16.95 (*0-8032-9707-6*, Bison Books) U of Nebr Pr.

Brodie, James M., jt. auth. see Curry, Barbara K.

Brodie, Jan. Earth Dance: A Year of Pagan Rituals. (Illus.). 137p. (Orig.). 1995. pap. 19.95 (*1-898307-35-0*) Holmes Pub.

— Magical Incenses & Perfumes. (Orig.). 1999. pap. 22.95 (*1-898307-59-8*, Pub. by Capall Bann Pubng) Holmes Pub.

— Moon Mysteries. (Orig.). 1997. pap. 21.95 (*1-898307-81-4*, Pub. by Capall Bann Pubng) Holmes Pub.

— Psychic Self Defense: Real Solutions. (Illus.). (Orig.). 1995. pap. 19.95 (*1-898307-36-9*, Pub. by Capall Bann Pubng) Holmes Pub.

Brodie, Janet F. Contraception & Abortion in Nineteenth-Century America. (Illus.). 360p. 1996. pap. text 17.95 (*0-8014-8433-2*) Cornell U Pr.

Brodie, Janine, et al. Abortion Politics. 224p. 1992. pap. text 22.00 (*0-19-540866-7*) OUP.

Brodie, Jessie L. Doctor Jessie, the Odyssey of a Woman Physician. (Illus.). 395p. (Orig.). (C). 1991. 22.50 (*0-945490-03-8*); pap. 12.50 (*0-945490-04-6*) Carolina Pacific.

Brodie, Jim, jt. auth. see Plum, Thomas.

Brodie, John & Houston, James D. Open Field. (San Francisco Ser.). 1974. 7.95 (*0-395-19882-8*) HM.

Brodie, Joseph W. & Beeharry, Girindre K. School Enrollment Decline in Sub-Saharan Africa: Beyond the Supply Constraint. LC 98-34812. (Discussion Paper Ser.: No. 395). 43p. 1998. pap. 22.00 (*0-8213-4312-2*, 14312) World Bank.

Brodie, Keith & Banner, Leslie. Keeping an Open Door: Passages in a University Presidency. LC 96-8678. (Illus.). 200p. 1996. text 22.95 (*0-8223-1862-8*) Duke.

***Brodie, Laura Fairchild.** Breaking Out: VMI & the Coming of Women. LC 99-49937. (Illus.). 384p. 2000. 26.00 (*0-375-40614-X*) Pantheon.

Brodie, Louise, jt. auth. see Stone, Jean.

Brodie, M. L. & Mylopoulos, John, eds. On Knowledge Base Management Systems. (Topics in Information Systems Ser.). (Illus.). 690p. 1986. 87.95 (*0-387-96382-0*) Spr-Verlag.

Brodie, M. L., jt. ed. see Schmidt, J. William.

Brodie, Malcolm. The Tele: A History of the Belfast Telegraph. LC 95-198773. 300p. 1995. pap. 33.00 (*0-85640-547-7*, Pub. by Blackstaff Pr) Dufour.

Brodie, Martin J. & Harrison, P. Ian, eds. Practical Prescribing. LC 85-20926. (Illus.). 295p. 1986. text 51.00 (*0-443-03304-8*) Church.

Brodie, Michael, jt. ed. see Mylopoulos, John.

Brodie, Michael L. & Stonebraker, Michael. Migrating Legacy Systems: Gateways, Interfaces, & the Incremental Approach. LC 95-19699. 210p. 1995. pap. text 42.95 (*1-55860-330-1*) Morgan Kaufmann.

Brodie, Peter. Dictionary of Shipping Terms. Vlassopulos, John S., tr. (ENG & GRE.). 174p. 1989. pap. 65.00 (*1-85044-173-1*) LLP.

— Dictionary of Shipping Terms. (ENG & FRE.). 192p. 1989. pap. 65.00 (*1-85044-245-2*) LLP.

— Dictionary of Shipping Terms. 2nd ed. 207p. 1994. pap. 45.00 (*1-85044-531-1*) LLP.

— Illustrated Dictionary of Cargo Handling. (Illus.). 176p. 1991. 90.00 (*1-85044-340-8*) LLP.

Brodie, Peter & Possemiers, Marc. Dictionary of Shipping Terms Spanish-English. (ENG & SPA.). 205p. 1988. pap. 65.00 (*1-85044-153-7*) LLP.

Brodie, Peter & Vincenzini, Enrico. Dictionary of Shipping Terms Italian-English. (ENG & ITA.). 171p. 1988. pap. 65.00 (*1-85044-174-X*) LLP.

Brodie, Richard. Getting Past OK: A Straightforward Guide to Having a Fantastic Life. (Illus.). 256p. (Orig.). 1993. pap. 9.95 (*0-9636001-0-9*) Integral Pr.

— Virus of the Mind: The New Science of the Meme. LC 95-79421. (Illus.). 1996. 22.00 (*0-9636001-1-7*) Integral Pr.

***Brodie, Robert & Randall, Warren.** The Log of the "Gloria Scott" LC 99-234417. (Sherlockian Scholarship Ser.). 1998. 36.00 (*1-55246-057-6*) Battered Silicon.

Brodie, Thomas G. Bombs & Bombings: A Handbook to Detection, Disposal, & Investigation for Police & Fire Departments. 2nd ed. (Illus.). 290p. 1995. 60.95 (*0-398-06551-9*); pap. 36.95 (*0-398-06552-7*) C C Thomas.

***Brodie, Thomas L.** The Crucial Bridge: The Elijah - Elisha Narrative As an Interpretive Synthesis of Genesis - Kings & a Literary Model for the Gospels. LC 99-41107. 120p. 2000. pap. 11.95 (*0-8146-5942-X*, M Glazier) Liturgical Pr.

Brodie, Thomas L. The Gospel According to John: A Literary & Theological Commentary. 640p. 1997. reprint ed. pap. 29.95 (*0-19-511811-1*) OUP.

— The Quest for the Origin: A Source-Oriented Approach. (Illus.). 208p. 1993. pap. text 24.95 (*0-19-507588-9*) OUP.

Brodie, Walter. Pitcairn's Island, & the Islanders in 1850. 3rd ed. LC 75-3441. reprint ed. 34.50 (*0-404-14445-4*) AMS Pr.

Brodin, G. Multilingual Dictionary of Music: Musiikisanakirja. (ENG, FIN, FRE, GER & ITA.). 375p. 1987. 85.00 (*0-8288-2187-9*, F15060) Fr & Eur.

— Music Dictionary: Musikordboken. (SWE.). 306p. 1985. 95.00 (*0-8288-2185-2*, F17030) Fr & Eur.

— Presences Contemporaines: Auteurs Francais du XXe Siecle. 9.95 (*0-685-37147-6*) Fr & Eur.

Brodin, Katarina. Nordic Security: Issues & Prospects. (CISA Working Papers: No. 67). 25p. (Orig.). 1989. pap. 15.00 (*0-86682-086-8*) Ctr Intl Relations.

Brodin, Mark S., jt. auth. see Bloom, Robert M.

Brodin, Michael. Over Counter Drug Book. LC 99-195314. 1998. mass mkt. 6.99 (*0-671-01380-7*) S&S Trade.

— Skin Game. 1990. mass mkt. 4.50 (*0-8217-3214-5*, Zebra Kensgtn) Kensgtn Pub Corp.

Brodin, Micheal B. The Encyclopedia of Medical Tests. 1997. per. 6.99 (*0-671-53537-4*) S&S Trade.

Brodin, Y. W. & Henrikson, L. Liming of Acidified Surface Waters: A Swedish Synthesis. 1994. write for info. (*0-387-58505-2*) Spr-Verlag.

— Liming of Acidified Surface Waters: A Swedish Synthesis. 1995. 108.95 (*3-540-58505-2*) Spr-Verlag.

Brodine, Janine & Isaacs, Judith. Journals in the Classroom: A Complete Guide for the Elementary Teacher. (Illus.). 144p. 1994. pap., teacher ed. 17.00 (*1-895411-69-6*) Peguis Pubs Ltd.

Brodine, Karen. Illegal Assembly. 1980. pap. 6.00 (*0-914610-17-1*) Hanging Loose.

— Slow Juggling. 48p. (Orig.). 1975. pap. 9.95 (*0-917658-02-7*) BPW & P.

— Woman Sitting at the Machine, Thinking: Poems. LC 87-83121. 100p. (Orig.). 1990. pap. 8.95 (*0-932323-01-4*) Red Letter Pr.

Brodine, Virginia W. Seed of the Fire. 310p. 1996. 18.95 (*0-7178-0721-5*); pap. 9.95 (*0-7178-0722-3*) Intl Pubs Co.

Brodish, H., ed. see International Symposium on Brain-Pituitary-Adrenal.

Brodkey, Florence, tr. see Barron's Educational Editors.

Brodkey, Florence A., tr. see Potter, Beatrix & Pomaska, Anna.

Brodkey, Harold. First Love & Other Sorrows. LC 98-21213. 288p. 1998. pap. 14.00 (*0-8050-6010-3*, Owl) H Holt & Co.

— My Venice. LC 97-28899. 1998. 20.00 (*0-8050-4833-2*) H Holt & Co.

— Profane Friendship. 1994. 23.00 (*0-374-23544-9*) FS&G.

— The Runaway Soul. 835p. 1991. 30.00 (*0-374-25286-6*) FS&G.

— The Runaway Soul. LC 97-23052. 848p. 1997. 17.00 (*0-8050-5503-7*) H Holt & Co.

Brodkey, Harold. The Runaway Soul. 1991. write for info. (*0-224-03001-9*, Pub. by Random) Random House.

Brodkey, Harold. Sea Battles on Dry Land: Essays. LC 98-46248. 452p. 1999. 30.00 (*0-8050-6052-9*, Pub. by H Holt & Co) VHPS.

— Sea Battles on Dryland. Date not set. pap. 13.00 (*0-8050-6051-0*) H Holt & Co.

— Short Stories. 1996. write for info. (*0-8050-4832-4*) H Holt & Co.

— Stories in an Almost Classical Mode. 1989. pap. 18.00 (*0-679-72431-1*) Vin Bks.

— This Wild Darkness: The Story of My Death. 192p. 1997. pap. 12.95 (*0-8050-5511-8*, Owl) H Holt & Co.

— The World Is the Home of Love & Death: Stories. LC 97-16459. 384p. 1997. 25.00 (*0-8050-5513-4*) H Holt & Co.

***Brodkey, Harold.** The World Is the Home of Love & Death: Stories. 384p. 1998. pap. 14.00 (*0-8050-5999-7*, Owl) H Holt & Co.

Brodkey, Linda. Writing Permitted in Designated Areas Only. (Pedagogy & Cultural Practices Ser.: Vol. 4). (C). 1996. pap. 21.95 (*0-8166-2807-6*); text 54.95 (*0-8166-2806-8*) U of Minn Pr.

Brodkey, Robert S. The Phenomena of Fluid Motions. LC 95-2346. (Illus.). 752p. 1995. pap. text 21.95 (*0-486-68605-1*) Dover.

B

An Asterisk (*) at the beginning of an entry indicates that the title is appearing for the first time.

B

Brodkey, Robert S. & Hershey, H. C. Transport Phenomena: A Unified Approach. (Chemical Engineering Ser.). 847p. (C). 1987. 103.44 (*0-07-007963-3*) McGraw.

Brodkin, Adele M. The Lonely Only Dog. LC 98-7782. (Hello Reader! Ser.). (Illus.). 32p. (J). (gr. 1-3). 1998. 3.99 (*0-590-52280-9*) Scholastic Inc.

Brodkin, Karen. How Jews Became White Folks & What That Says about Race in America. LC 98-22606. 272p. (C). 1999. 48.00 (*0-8135-2589-6*); pap. 18.00 (*0-8135-2590-X*) Rutgers U Pr.

Brodland, Donna A. Awakened: The Account of David Anderson. LC 98-60794. 192p. 1998. pap. 12.99 (*1-57921-127-5*, Pub. by WinePress Pub) BookWorld.

***Brodley, Inger.** Rediscovering Natsume Soseki. 2000. 24.95 (*1-901903-30-3*) Global Oriental.

Brodlie, K. W., et al, eds. Scientific Visualization: Techniques & Applications. (Illus.). xxv, 284p. 1992. 91.95 (*0-387-54565-4*) Spr-Verlag.

Brodman, Estelle. The Development of Medical Bibliography. 226p. 1981. reprint ed. 8.25 (*0-912176-00-8*) Med Lib Assn.

Brodman, Estelle, ed. The Development of Medical Bibliography. (Medical Library Association). 236p. 1954. pap. 6.00 (*0-8108-2423-X*) Scarecrow.

Brodman, James. Charity & Welfare: Hospitals & the Poor in Medieval Catalonia. LC 97-45102. (Middle Ages Ser.). 256p. 1998. 39.95 (*0-8122-3436-7*) U of Pa Pr.

Brodmann, Aliana. Gift. (Illus.). 40p. (J). (ps-3). 1993. per. 15.00 (*0-671-75110-7*) S&S Bks Yung.

— The Gift: A Hanukkah Story. LC 92-7887. (Illus.). 40p. (J). (gr. k-3). 1998. per. 5.99 (*0-689-82240-5*) Aladdin.

— Que Ruido! (What Noise!) Krohn, Hildegard M., tr. from GER. (Coleccion Barril Sin Fondo Ser.). (SPA., Illus.). 26p. (J). (gr. 3 up). 1990. 13.95 (*968-6465-08-1*) Hispanic Bk Dist.

— Such a Noise! Fillingham, David, tr. from GER.Tr. of Ein Wunderlicher Rat. (Illus.). 32p. (J). (gr. k-3). 1989. 11.95 (*0-916291-25-1*) Kane-Miller Bk.

Brodmann, E. T., tr. see Hoffmann, E. T. A.

Brodmann, M. P. & Sharp, R. Y. Local Cohomology: An Algebraic Introduction with Geometric Applications. LC 97-29059. (Studies in Advanced Mathematics: No. 60). (Illus.). 432p. (C). 1998. text 69.95 (*0-521-37286-0*) Cambridge U Pr.

Brodnax, Elizabeth. The Marquis of Carabas. 224p. 1991. 18.95 (*0-8027-1130-8*) Walker & Co.

— The Marquis of Carabas. large type ed. LC 91-16987. 270p. 1991. reprint ed. lib. bdg. 19.95 (*1-56054-188-1*) Thorndike Pr.

— A Splendid Scheme. 208p. 1994. reprint ed. mass mkt. 3.99 (*0-515-11406-5*, Jove) Berkley Pub.

Brodnax, Ken. If Nax Can Write, Bubba Can, Too. Kirkham, Kim, ed. (Illus.). 192p. (Orig.). 1994. pap. text 12.95 (*0-9642634-0-8*) Odessa Amer.

***Brodniewicz-Stawick, Margaret.** For Your Freedom & Ours: The Polish Army in the Second World War. (Illus.). 304p. 1999. write for info. (*1-55125-035-7*) Vanwell Publ.

Brodnitz, Friedrich S. Keep Your Voice Healthy: A Guide to the Intelligent Use & Care of the Speaking & Singing Voice. 2nd ed. LC 90-21693. (Illus.). 158p. 1988. reprint ed. pap. text 26.00 (*0-316-10902-9*, 1624) PRO-ED.

Brodoff, Ami S. Can You See Me? A Novel. LC 99-61935. 365p. 1999. 25.00 (*0-7388-0366-9*); pap. 15.00 (*0-7388-0367-7*) Xlibris Corp.

Brodoff, Douglas. Spirit Stones Vol. I: Cornerstones. 35p. (Orig.). 1988. pap. 4.25 (*0-317-91169-4*) Spirit Stone Bks.

***Brodova, I. G., et al.** Liquid Metal Processing: Applications to Aluminium Alloy Production. (Advances in Metallic Alloys Ser.: Vol. 1). 288p. 2000. text 110.00 (*90-5699-229-5*, G & B Science) Gordon & Breach.

Brodow, Ed. Negotiate with Confidence. LC 95-83970. (How-to Book Ser.). 97p. (Orig.). 1996. pap. 12.95 (*1-884926-50-9*, NEGOT) Amer Media.

Brodowsky, H. & Schaller, H. J. Thermochemistry of Alloys. (C). 1989. text 287.50 (*0-7923-0434-9*) Kluwer Academic.

Brodribb, Somer. Nothing Mat(t)ers: A Feminist Critique of Postmodernism. 208p. 1992. text 50.00 (*1-875559-10-8*) NYU Pr.

— Nothing Mat(t)ers: A Feminist Critique of Postmodernism. 208p. (C). 1992. text 50.00 (*0-87555-910-7*, 559108) NYU Pr.

***Brodribb, Somer, ed.** Reclaiming the Future: Women's Strategies for the 21st Century. 296p. 1999. pap. 24.95 (*0-921881-51-7*) gynergy Bks.

Brodrick, Alan H. Little China: The Annamese Lands. LC 74-179173. (South & Southeast Asia Studies). reprint ed. 21.50 (*0-404-54803-2*) AMS Pr.

— Man & His Ancestors. LC 74-502456. (Radius Book Ser.). ix, 238 p. 1971. write for info. (*0-09-107690-0*) Hutchinson.

Brodrick, George C. English Land & English Landlords: An Enquiry into the Origin & Character of the English Land System. LC 67-29495. (Reprints of Economic Classics Ser.). viii, 501p. 1968. reprint ed. 57.50 (*0-678-00360-2*) Kelley.

Brodrick, George C. & Fotheringham, John K. History of England from Addington's Administration to the Close of William Fourth's Reign. LC 71-5624. (Political History of England Ser.). reprint ed. 45.00 (*0-404-50781-6*) AMS Pr.

Brodrick, James. The Origin of the Jesuits. LC 83-45590. reprint ed. 33.50 (*0-404-19883-X*) AMS Pr.

— The Origin of the Jesuits. LC 70-138604. 274p. 1971. reprint ed. lib. bdg. 65.00 (*0-8371-5523-1*, BROJ, Greenwood Pr) Greenwood.

— Procession of Saints. LC 72-5436. (Biography Index Reprint Ser.). 1977. reprint ed. 22.95 (*0-8369-8134-0*) Ayer.

— The Progress of the Jesuits (1556-79) LC 86-2864. 357p. (C). 1986. reprint ed. 12.95 (*0-8294-0523-2*, Jesuit Way) Loyola Pr.

— Saint Peter Canisius, S. J., 1521-1597. LC 83-45589. reprint ed. 65.00 (*0-404-19882-1*) AMS Pr.

Brodrick, James P. Saint Peter Canisius. LC 98-9861. (Illus.). 880p. 1998. pap. 19.95 (*0-8294-1048-1*) Loyola Pr.

Brodrogligeti, A. J., jt. ed. see Decsy, Gyula.

Brodsgaard, Kjeld E. & Strand, David, eds. Reconstructing Twentieth Century China. LC 99-163558. (Studies on Contemporary China). 360p. 1998. text 79.00 (*0-19-829311-9*) OUP.

***Brodsgaard, Kjeld Eric & Young, Susan, eds.** State Capacity in East Asia: China, Taiwan, Vietnam, & Japan. 300p. 2000. text 72.00 (*0-19-829763-7*) OUP.

Brodshaug, Melvin. Buildings & Equipment for Home Economics in Secondary Schools. LC 75-176592. (Columbia University. Teachers College. Contributions to Education Ser.: No. 502). reprint ed. 37.50 (*0-404-55502-0*) AMS Pr.

Brodskaya, Natalia. Auguste Renoir. (Great Painters Ser.). (Illus.). 176p. 1996. 40.00 (*1-85995-142-2*) Parkstone Pr.

— Fauves: The Masters Who Shook the World of Art. (Schools & Movements Ser.). (Illus.). 288p. 1996. 55.00 (*1-85995-190-2*) Parkstone Pr.

— Naive Art. (Schools & Movements Ser.). (Illus.). 272p. 2000. 55.00 (*1-85995-335-2*) Parkstone Pr.

Brodskii, M. S. Triangular & Jordan Representations of Linear Operators. LC 74-162998. (Translations of Mathematical Monographs: Vol. 32). 246p. 1971. text 47.00 (*0-8218-1582-2*, MMONO/32) Am Math.

Brodskii, M. S., et al. Nine Papers on Number Theory & Operator Theory. LC 51-5559. (Translations Ser.: Series 2, Vol. 13). 346p. 1960. reprint ed. pap. 62.00 (*0-8218-1713-2*, TRANS2/13) Am Math.

— Thirteen Papers on Functional Analysis & Partial Differential Equations. LC 51-5559. (Translations Ser.: Series 2, Vol. 47). 299p. 1965. 36.00 (*0-8218-1747-7*, TRANS2/47) Am Math.

Brodskii, Mikhail S., et al. Nine Papers on Partial Differential Equations & Functional Analysis. LC 51-5559. (American Mathematical Society Ser.: Series 2, 65). 300p. 1987. pap. 93.00 (*0-608-05171-3*, 205259200001) Bks Demand.

Brodsky. Smoke Signals: From Eminence to Exile. LC 98-189091. 225p. 1997. text 39.50 (*1-86064-150-4*, Pub. by I B T) St Martin.

Brodsky, A. Series in Radiation Meaurement & Protection, No. 2. LC 78-10558. 1982. reprint ed. 781.00 (*0-8493-3750-X*, CRC Reprint) Franklin.

Brodsky, Allen, ed. Handbook of Radiation Measurement & Protection, Vol. I: Physical Science & Engineering Data. 720p. 1979. 384.00 (*0-8493-3756-9*, QC795, CRC Reprint) Franklin.

— Handbook of Radiation Measurement & Protection, Vol. II: Biological & Mathematical Data. 736p. 1982. 398.00 (*0-8493-3757-7*, QC795, CRC Reprint) Franklin.

***Brodsky, Alyn.** Grover Cleveland: A Study in Character. (Illus.). 512p. 2000. 35.00 (*0-312-26883-1*, Truman Talley) St Martin.

Brodsky, Alyn. Imperial Charade: A Biography of Emperor Napoleon III & Empress Eugenie. LC 78-55665. 1978. 12.95 (*0-672-52346-9*, Bobbs) Macmillan.

Brodsky, Andrei K. The Evolution of Insect Flight. (Illus.). 244p. 1997. pap. 55.00 (*0-19-850089-0*) OUP.

Brodsky, Annette M., ed. The Female Offender. LC 75-27014. (Sage Contemporary Social Science Issues Ser.: No. 19). 108p. reprint ed. pap. 33.50 (*0-608-10116-8*, 202187600026) Bks Demand.

Brodsky, Annette M. & Hare-Mustin, Rachel, eds. Women & Psychotherapy: An Assessment of Research & Practice. LC 80-14842. 428p. 1986. pap. text 30.00 (*0-89862-909-8*) Guilford Pubns.

Brodsky, Annette M., jt. auth. see Bates, Carolyn M.

Brodsky, Archie, jt. auth. see Edelwich, Jerry.

Brodsky, Archie, jt. auth. see Peele, Stanton.

Brodsky, Archie, jt. auth. see Powell, David J.

***Brodsky, B. E. & Darkhovsky, B. S.** Non-Parametric Statistical Diagnosis: Problems & Methods. LC 00-38933. (Mathematics & Its Applications Ser.). (Illus.). 2000. write for info. (*0-7923-6328-0*, Kluwer Plenum) Kluwer Academic.

Brodsky, B. E. & Darkhovsky, B. S. Nonparametric Methods in Change Point Problems. LC 92-43810. (Mathematics & Its Applications Ser.: No. 243). 224p. (C). 1993. text 129.50 (*0-7923-2122-7*) Kluwer Academic.

Brodsky, Bart & Geis, Janet. Finding Your Niche... Marketing Your Professional Service. LC 91-70347. (Illus.). 272p. (Orig.). 1992. pap. 15.95 (*0-9628464-1-4*) Cmnty Resc Inst.

— The Teaching Marketplace: Make Money with Freelance Teaching, Corporate Trainings, & on the Lecture Circuit. (Illus.). 176p. (Orig.). 1991. pap. 14.95 (*0-9628464-0-6*) Cmnty Resc Inst.

Brodsky, Bernard. Anti-Haiku. 48p. 1985. pap. 9.95 (*0-931896-05-3*) Cove View.

— Closure: Last Poems & Pages. LC 98-53035. 120p. 1998. pap. 9.95 (*0-931896-18-5*) Cove View.

— The Will to Go On. 64p. (Orig.). 1981. pap. 9.95 (*0-931896-01-0*) Cove View.

Brodsky, Beverley. Secret Places. LC 77-16391. (Illus.). (J). (gr. 1-3). 1979. 9.82 (*0-397-31790-5*) HarpC Child Bks.

Brodsky, David M. & Kramer, Daniel J. Federal Securities Litigation: Commentary & Forms: A Deskbook for the Practitioner. LC 97-31984. 516p. 1997. ring bd. 195.00 (*1-57400-032-2*) Data Trace Pubng.

Brodsky, Edward. A Practical Guide to Tax Shelter Litigation. 600p. 1985. ring bd. 70.00 (*0-318-21434-2*, 00577) NY Law Pub.

Brodsky, Edward & Adamski, M. Patricia. Law of Corporate Officers & Directors: Rights, Duties, & Liabilities. LC 84-14310. 1990. 130.00 (*0-685-09579-7*) West Group.

***Brodsky, Eric.** Poetry of the Angels: Inspiration For Us All. 2nd ed. 53p. 2000. pap. 8.00 (*0-9676406-0-1*) Universal One.

Brodsky, Estrellita, ed. see Alegria, Ricardo E., et al.

Brodsky, G. W. Gentlemen of the Blade: A Social & Literacy History of the British Army Since 1660, 70. LC 87-23692. (Contributions in Military Studies Ser.: No. 70). 220p. 1988. 57.95 (*0-313-26067-2*, BGB/, Greenwood Pr) Greenwood.

Brodsky, Gary. Art of Getting Even. 1995. 5.98 (*1-55521-663-3*) Bk Sales Inc.

— Mind of the Cat. 1990. 5.98 (*1-55521-698-6*) Bk Sales Inc.

Brodsky, Harold, ed. Land & Community: Geography in Jewish Studies. LC 97-46204. (Studies & Texts in Jewish History & Culture: Vol. 3). 1998. 40.00 (*1-883053-30-7*) Univ Pr MD.

Brodsky, Ira. Wireless: The Revolution in Personal Telecommunications. LC 95-6097. (Mobile Communications Ser.). 276p. 1995. 59.00 (*0-89006-717-1*) Artech Hse.

— Wireless Computing: A Manager's Guide to Wireless Networking. (Communications Ser.). 416p. 1997. pap. 34.95 (*0-471-28656-7*, VNR) Wiley.

Brodsky, Ira. Wireless Computing: A Manager's Guide to Wireless Networking. LC 97-14572. (Communications Ser.). (Illus.). 369p. 1997. pap. 34.95 (*0-442-01912-2*, VNR) Wiley.

Brodsky, Jeff. Stepping into Adulthood. 158p. 1997. pap. 10.00 (*0-9656749-2-4*) ACW Press.

***Brodsky, Joseph.** Collected Poems in English. 400p. 2000. 30.00 (*0-374-12545-7*) FS&G.

— Discovery. LC 98-74220. (Illus.). 24p. (J). 1999. 16.00 (*0-374-31793-3*) FS&G.

— Less Than One: Selected Essays. 501p. 1986. text 30.00 (*0-374-18503-4*) FS&G.

Brodsky, Joseph. Less Than One: Selected Essays. 448p. 1987. pap. 16.00 (*0-374-52055-0*) FS&G.

— Marbles: A Play in Three Acts. Myers, Alan, tr. (Noonday Ser.). 80p. 1990. pap. 11.00 (*0-374-52116-6*) FS&G.

***Brodsky, Joseph.** Nativity Poems. 2000. text. write for info. (*0-374-21940-0*) FS&G.

Brodsky, Joseph. Novye Stansy K. Avguste: Stikhotvoreniia K. M. B. (RUS.). 144p. 1983. pap. 15.95 (*0-88233-776-9*) Ardis Pubs.

— On Grief & Reason: Essays. LC 94-10872. 458p. 1996. 24.00 (*0-374-23415-9*) FS&G.

— On Grief & Reason: Essays. 496p. 1997. pap. text 16.00 (*0-374-52509-9*) FS&G.

— A Part of Speech. Hecht, Anthony et al, trs. from RUS. LC 80-613. 160p. 1980. 15.95 (*0-374-22987-2*) FS&G.

— A Part of Speech. Hecht, Anthony et al, trs. from RUS. LC 80-613. 160p. 1981. pap. 11.00 (*0-374-51633-2*) FS&G.

— Peizazh S Navodneniem - Landscape with Flood. (RUS.). 1996. pap. 13.95 (*0-87501-094-6*) Ardis Pubs.

— So Forth: Poems. LC 94-24631. 132p. 1996. 18.00 (*0-374-26641-7*) FS&G.

— So Forth: Poems. 144p. 1998. pap. text 12.00 (*0-374-52553-6*, Noonday) FS&G.

— To Urania. 174p. 1992. pap. 13.00 (*0-374-52333-9*) FS&G.

— Watermark. 135p. 1993. pap. 11.00 (*0-374-52382-7*) FS&G.

Brodsky, Joseph, et al. Homage to Robert Frost. 94p. 1996. text 18.00 (*0-374-17246-3*) FS&G.

— Homage to Robert Frost. LC 96-15654. (Illus.). 117p. 1997. 30.00 (*0-374-14814-7*) FS&G.

— Homage to Robert Frost. 128p. 1997. pap. text 11.00 (*0-374-52524-2*) FS&G.

— Mandelstam Centenary Conference - Stoletle Mandelshtama. Aizlewood, Robin & Myers, Diana, eds. LC 93-50155. (ENG & RUS.). 352p. (Orig.). 1994. pap. 25.00 (*1-55779-058-2*) Hermitage Pubs.

Brodsky, Joseph, ed. & intro. see Hardy, Thomas.

Brodsky, K. A. Mountain Torrent of the Tien Shan: An Ecology-Faunistic Essay. (Monographiae Biologicae: No. 39). (Illus.). 311p. 1980. text 211.50 (*90-6193-091-X*) Kluwer Academic.

Brodsky, Linda, jt. ed. see Arvedson, Joan C.

Brodsky, Louis D. The Capital Cafe: Poems of Redneck, U. S. A. LC 93-24238. 111p. 1993. 18.95 (*1-877770-48-5*); pap. 12.50 (*1-877770-49-3*) Time Being Bks.

— Disappearing in Mississippi Latitudes Vol. 2: A Mississippi Trilogy. LC 94-28822. 121p. 1994. 18.95 (*1-877770-80-9*); pap. 12.50 (*1-877770-81-7*) Time Being Bks.

— The Easy Philosopher. LC 95-35282. 84p. 1995. spiral bd. 9.95 (*1-56809-024-2*) Time Being Bks.

— The Eleventh Lost Tribe: Poems of the Holocaust. LC 97-49672. 105p. 1998. 22.00 (*1-56809-041-2*); pap. 14.50 (*1-56809-042-0*) Time Being Bks.

— Five Facets of Myself. LC 95-35283. 104p. 1995. spiral bd. 9.95 (*1-56809-023-4*) Time Being Bks.

— Forever, for Now: Poems for a Later Love. LC 90-72137. 103p. 1991. 18.95 (*1-877770-28-0*); pap. 12.50 (*1-877770-29-9*); audio 12.95 (*1-877770-31-0*) Time Being Bks.

— The Foul Rag-&-Bone Shop. LC 95-25042. 67p. 1995. spiral bd. 9.95 (*1-56809-027-7*) Time Being Bks.

— Four & Twenty Blackbirds Soaring. LC 89-50804. 91p. 1989. 18.95 (*1-877770-07-8*); pap. 12.50 (*1-877770-72-8*); pap. 19.95 incl. audio (*1-877770-10-8*); audio 12.95 (*1-877770-09-4*) Time Being Bks.

— Gestapo Crows: Holocaust Poems. LC 92-60745. 108p. 1993. 18.95 (*1-877770-76-0*); pap. 12.50 (*1-877770-77-9*); audio 19.95 (*1-877770-78-7*) Time Being Bks.

— A Gleam in the Eye: Poems for a First Baby. LC 90-72136. 86p. 1992. 18.95 (*1-877770-40-X*); pap. 12.50 (*1-877770-41-8*) Time Being Bks.

— A Hard Coming of It & Other Poems. 70p. 1995. spiral bd. 9.95 (*1-56809-025-0*) Time Being Bks.

— Mississippi Vistas. LC 90-70684. (Mississippi Trilogy Ser.: Vol. 1). 91p. 1990. pap. 12.50 (*1-877770-73-6*); pap. 19.95 incl. audio (*1-877770-15-9*); audio 12.95 (*1-877770-14-0*) Time Being Bks.

— Mississippi Vistas Vol. 1: A Mississippi Trilogy. LC 90-70684. 91p. 1990. 18.95 (*1-877770-12-4*) Time Being Bks.

— Mistress Mississippi. LC 90-72139. (Mississippi Trilogy Ser.: Vol. 3). 125p. 1992. pap. 12.50 (*1-877770-37-X*) Time Being Bks.

— Mistress Mississippi Vol. 3: A Mississippi Trilogy. LC 90-72139. 125p. 1992. 18.95 (*1-877770-36-1*) Time Being Bks.

***Brodsky, Louis D.** Mondays Child Poems. 2nd ed. LC 98-45900. 1998. spiral bd. 9.95 (*1-56809-054-4*) Time Being Bks.

Brodsky, Louis D. Paper-Whites for Lady Jane. LC 95-42905. 74p. 1995. pap. 12.50 (*1-877770-96-5*) Time Being Bks.

— Paper-Whites for Lady Jane: Poems of a Midlife Love Affair. LC 95-42905. 74p. 1995. 18.95 (*1-877770-95-7*) Time Being Bks.

— Point of Americas II: Poems. LC 98-21767. 1998. spiral bd. 9.95 (*1-56809-049-8*) Time Being Bks.

— Points in Time. LC 95-35333. 106p. 1995. spiral bd. 9.95 (*1-56809-026-9*) Time Being Bks.

***Brodsky, Louis D.** Preparing for Incarnations: Poems. 2nd rev. expanded ed. LC 99-35469. 1999. spiral bd. 9.95 (*1-56809-058-7*) Time Being Bks.

Brodsky, Louis D. Taking the Back Road Home. LC 97-8183. 76p. 1997. spiral bd. 9.95 (*1-56809-038-2*) Time Being Bks.

— The "Talking Machine" & Other Poems. LC 97-32033. 69p. 1997. spiral bd. 9.95 (*1-56809-040-4*) Time Being Bks.

— This Here's a Merica: Short Fictions. LC 99-25320. 2000. pap. 16.95 (*1-56809-056-0*) Time Being Bks.

— The Thorough Earth. LC 89-50805. 52p. 1989. 18.95 (*1-877770-03-5*); pap. 12.50 (*1-877770-04-3*); pap. 19.95 incl. audio (*1-877770-06-X*); audio 12.95 (*1-877770-05-1*) Time Being Bks.

— Three Early Books of Poems, 1965-1969: The Easy Philosopher, "A Hard Coming of It" & Other Poems, & the Foul Rag-&-Bone Shop. Vandermolen, Sheri L., ed. LC 96-17150. 205p. 1997. pap. 16.95 (*1-56809-031-5*) Time Being Bks.

— Tiffany Shade. LC 97-47563. 71p. 1997. spiral bd. 9.95 (*1-56809-043-9*) Time Being Bks.

— Toward the Torah, Soaring: Poems of the Renascence of Faith. LC 98-27106. 1998. 22.00 (*1-56809-046-3*); pap. 14.50 (*1-56809-047-1*) Time Being Bks.

— Trilogy: A Birth Cycle; Poems. 2nd ed. LC 98-6899. 1998. spiral bd. 9.95 (*1-56809-048-X*) Time Being Bks.

— Trip to Tipton & Other Compulsions. LC 97-33421. 85p. 1997. spiral bd. 9.95 (*1-56809-039-0*) Time Being Bks.

— William Faulkner, Life Glimpses. (Illus.). 224p. 1990. 27.50 (*0-292-79048-1*) U of Tex Pr.

— You Can't Go Back, Exactly. LC 89-50806. 57p. 1989. 18.95 (*1-877770-00-0*); pap. 19.95 incl. audio (*1-877770-02-7*); audio 12.95 (*1-877770-01-9*) Time Being Bks.

Brodsky, Louis D. & Heyen, William. Falling from Heaven: Holocaust Poems of a Jew & a Gentile. LC 90-70683. 109p. 1991. 18.95 (*1-877770-16-7*); pap. 12.50 (*1-877770-75-2*); pap. 19.95 incl. audio (*1-877770-19-1*); audio 12.95 (*1-877770-18-3*) Time Being Bks.

Brodsky, Louis D., jt. auth. see Hamblin, Robert W.

Brodsky, Louis D., ed. see Faulkner, William.

Brodsky, Louis Daniel. Catchin' the Drift O' the Draft: Short Fictions. LC 99-24791. 1999. pap. 16.95 (*1-56809-052-8*) Time Being Bks.

— Cold Companionable Streams: Poems. LC 98-52424. 1999. spiral bd. 9.95 (*1-56809-055-2*) Time Being Bks.

— Preparing for Incarnations: Poems. LC 99-24793. 1999. spiral bd. 9.95 (*1-56809-057-9*) Time Being Bks.

— Yellow Bricks: Short Fictions By. LC 99-24792. 1999. pap. 16.95 (*1-56809-053-6*) Time Being Bks.

Brodsky, M., ed. see AIP Conference Staff.

Brodsky, M. H., ed. Amorphous Semiconductors. 2nd ed. (Topics in Applied Physics Ser.: Vol. 36). (Illus.). 370p. 1986. 47.95 (*0-387-16008-6*) Spr-Verlag.

Brodsky, M. S., et al. Nine Papers in Analysis. LC 51-5559. (Translations Ser.: Series 2, Vol. 103). 203p. 1974. 55.00 (*0-8218-3053-8*, TRANS2/103) Am Math.

Brodsky, Marc D. The Courthouse at Edenton: A History of the Chowan County Courthouse of 1767. LC 89-60832. (Illus.). 142p. (Orig.). 1989. 22.00 (*0-9622742-0-8*); pap. 16.00 (*0-9622742-1-6*) Chowan County.

Brodsky, Merwyn B., ed. see Materials Research Society Staff, et al.

Brodsky, Michael. * * * A Novel. LC 93-40969. 368p. 1994. 26.95 (*1-56858-000-2*); pap. 13.95 (*1-56858-001-0*) FWEW.

— Circuits. 170p. 1991. reprint ed. pap. 11.95 (*0-941062-58-9*) Begos & Rosenberg.

— Detour. 1990. pap. 14.25 (*0-941062-59-7*) Begos & Rosenberg.

— Dyad. LC 89-36339. 300p. 1989. 23.95 (*0-941423-30-1*); pap. 11.95 (*0-941423-31-X*) FWEW.

— Project. (Illus.). 224p. 1991. reprint ed. pap. 10.95 (*0-941062-51-1*) Begos & Rosenberg.

An Asterisk (*) at the beginning of an entry indicates that the title is appearing for the first time.

— Southernmost & Other Stories. LC 96-1449. 342p. 1996. 25.00 (*1-56858-064-9*); pap. 14.95 (*1-56858-065-7*) FWEW.

— Three Goat Songs. LC 90-49706. 166p. 1991. 18.95 (*0-941423-46-8*); pap. 9.95 (*0-941423-47-6*) FWEW.

— We Can Report Them. LC 99-36040. 365p. 1999. pap. 16.95 (*1-56858-144-0*) FWEW.

— X in Paris. 192p. 1988. 18.95 (*0-941062-44-9*) Begos & Rosenberg.

— Xman. LC 87-7389. 540p. 1987. 21.95 (*0-941423-01-8*); pap. 11.95 (*0-941423-02-6*) FWEW.

Brodsky, Michael, tr. see Beckett, Samuel.

Brodsky, Michael C., et al. Pediatric Neuroophthalmology. LC 95-16249. (Illus.). 552p. 1995. 160.00 (*0-387-94464-8*) Spr-Verlag.

Brodsky, Patricia P. Rainer Maria Rilke. (Twayne's World Authors Ser.: Vol. 796). 192p. (C). 1988. 26.95 (*0-8057-8226-5*, Twayne) Mac Lib Ref.

Brodsky, Paul A. Corporate Fairy Tales. LC 97-97098. (Illus.). 64p. 1998. pap. 8.95 (*0-9661165-5-0*) IMOCO Pub.

Brodsky, S. & Moniz, E., eds. Nuclear Chromodynamics, Quarks & Gluons in Particles & Nuclei: Proceedings of the Workshop on Nuclear Chromodynamics, Santa Barbara, California, August 12-23, 1985. 532p. 1986. pap. 52.00 (*9971-5-0056-6*); text 131.00 (*9971-5-0055-8*) World Scientific Pub.

***Brodsky, Stanley L.** The Expert Expert Witness: More Maxims & Guidelines for Testifying in Court. LC 99-27655. 197p. 1999. pap. 19.95 (*1-55798-597-9*) Am Psychol.

Brodsky, Stanley L. Psychological Adjustment & Well-Being. (C). 1988. pap. text, teacher ed. 42.00 (*0-03-013369-6*) Harcourt Coll Pubs.

— The Psychology of Adjustment & Well-Being. 480p. (C). 1988. pap. text 67.00 (*0-03-013368-8*) Harcourt Coll Pubs.

— Testifying in Court: Guidelines & Maxims for the Expert Witness. LC 91-16296. (Illus.). 208p. (Orig.). 1991. pap. 19.95 (*1-55798-128-0*) Am Psychol.

Brodsky, Stanley L. & Smitherman, H. O'Neal. Handbook of Scales for Research in Crime & Delinquency. LC 82-18142. (Perspectives in Law & Psychology Ser.: Vol. 5). 642p. 1983. 89.50 (*0-306-40792-2*, Plenum Trade) Perseus Pubng.

Brodsky, Stanley L., jt. ed. see Fischer, Constance T.

***Brodsky, Steven.** Mastering XMI: Java Programming with the XMI Toolkit, XML & UML. (Illus.). 416p. 2000. text 49.99 (*0-471-38429-1*) Wiley.

Brodt, Pnina. Cell Adhesion & Invasion Mechanisms in Cancer Metastasis. LC 95-12647. (Medical Intelligence Unit Ser.). 258p. 1996. 99.00 (*1-57059-263-2*) Landes Bioscience.

Brodt, Susan E., jt. auth. see Whitener, Ellen M.

Brodtkorb, Milka K. De, see De Brodtkorb, Milka K.

Brodwer. Andre Breton, Arbiter of Surrealism. 29.95 (*0-7859-0637-1*, F89730) Fr & Eur.

Brodwin, Paul. Medicine & Morality in Haiti: The Contest for Healing Power. (Cambridge Studies in Medical Anthropology: No. 3). (Illus.). 256p. (C). 1996. text 64.95 (*0-521-57029-8*); pap. text 23.95 (*0-521-57543-5*) Cambridge U Pr.

Brodwin, Stanley, ed. The Old & New World Romanticism of Washington Irving. LC 86-3168. 201p. 1986. 52.95 (*0-313-25441-9*, BWG/, Greenwood Pr) Greenwood.

Brodxinsky, David M. Psychology of Adoption. (Illus.). 416p. 1993. pap. text 39.95 (*0-19-508273-7*) OUP.

Brody. Massachusetts Tort Law. 1993. 105.00 (*1-880637-99-5*, 81499-10, MICHIE) LEXIS Pub.

Brody, jt. auth. see Campbell.

Brody, jt. auth. see Cornfeld.

Brody, jt. auth. see Henretta.

Brody, ed. see Goldberg, P. & Roberts, J.

Brody, Aaron L. Modified Atmosphere food Packaging. (Illus.). 275p. (C). 1994. pap. 75.00 (*1-930268-11-4*) Packaging Prof.

Brody, Aaron L., ed. Controlled-Modified Atmosphere-Vacuum Packaging of Foods. 190p. 1989. 84.95 (*0-917678-24-9*) Technomic.

***Brody, Aaron L. & Lord, John B., eds.** Developing New Food Products for a Changing Marketplace. LC 99-66882. 500p. 1999. text 79.95 (*1-56676-778-4*) Technomic.

Brody, Aaron L. & Marsh, Kenneth S., eds. The Wiley Encyclopedia of Packaging Technology. 2nd ed. LC 96-44725. 1040p. 1997. 190.00 (*0-471-06397-5*) Wiley.

Brody, Alan, jt. auth. see Burton, Edward.

Brody, Alvin & Brody, Betty. Massachusetts Tort Law. LC 94-26585. 300p. 1994. spiral bd. 95.00 (*0-88063-799-4*, MICHIE) LEXIS Pub.

Brody, Andrew. Slowdown: Global Economic Maladies. LC 84-15040. (Studies in Economic Development & Planning: Vol. 36). 151p. 1985. reprint ed. pap. 46.90 (*0-608-00816-8*, 206160400010) Bks Demand.

Brody, Angela. Been There, Done That, Vol. II. 185p. 1998. per. 11.95 (*0-9662743-1-8*) Tysseland Pub.

Brody, Annie & Schultz, Patricia. Made in Italy: A Shopper's Guide to Florence, Milan, Rome & Venice. LC 86-40544. (Illus.). 560p. (Orig.). 1987. pap. 14.95 (*0-89480-305-0*, 1305) Workman Pub.

Brody, Arnold G., jt. auth. see Stuhlman, Daniel D.

Brody, Baruch A. Ethical Issues in Drug Testing, Approval & Pricing: The Clot-Dissolving Drugs. (Illus.). 280p. 1995. text 39.50 (*0-19-508831-X*) OUP.

— Ethics & Its Applications. 200p. (C). 1983. pap. text 20.00 (*0-15-524510-4*) Harcourt Coll Pubs.

— The Ethics of Biomedical Research: An International Perspective. 400p. 1998. text 49.95 (*0-19-509007-1*) OUP.

— Identity & Essence. LC 80-7511. 175p. reprint ed. pap. 54.30 (*0-7837-6494-4*, 204658400003) Bks Demand.

— Life & Death Decision-Making. 274p. (C). 1988. text 39.95 (*0-19-505007-X*) OUP.

— Readings in the Philosophy of Religion: An Analytic Approach. 2nd ed. 672p. (C). 1991. text 36.80 (*0-13-756206-3*, 660801) P-H.

Brody, Baruch A., ed. Moral Theory & Moral Judgments in Medical Ethics. (Philosophy & Medicine Ser.: No. 32). 238p. 1988. text 120.00 (*1-55608-060-3*) Kluwer Academic.

Brody, Baruch A. & Engelhardt, H. Tristram, eds. Mental Illness: Law & Public Policy. (Philosophy & Medicine Ser.: No. 5). 272p. 1980. text 94.00 (*90-277-1057-0*) Kluwer Academic.

Brody, Baruch A. & Englehardt, Tris. Bioethics: Reading & Cases. 448p. (C). 1987. 52.00 (*0-13-076522-8*) P-H.

Brody, Betty, jt. auth. see Brody, Alvin.

Brody, Brian. Lessons from Littleton: Levelling: A Guide to Positive Parenting. Institute for Integration Therapy Staff, ed. (Illus.). 109p. 1985. pap. text 27.00 (*0-9618074-8-2*) IFIT.

***Brody, Brian & Petersen, Sandy.** Lessons from Littleton: Levelling - A Guide to Positive Parenting. (Illus.). 145p. 2000. pap. 19.95 (*0-9618074-9-0*, Pub. by IFIT) Partners Pubs Grp.

Brody, Cathy, jt. auth. see Brody, Steve.

Brody, Celeste, et al. Gender Consciousness & Privilege. LC 99-28035. (Illus.). 160p. 1999. 90.00 (*0-7507-0999-5*, Pub. by Falmer Pr UK); pap. 28.95 (*0-7507-0998-7*, Pub. by Falmer Pr UK) Taylor & Francis.

Brody, Celeste M. & Davidson, Neil, eds. Professional Development for Cooperative Learning: Issues & Approaches. LC 97-37732. (Illus.). 320p. (C). 1998. text 59.50 (*0-7914-3849-X*); pap. text 19.95 (*0-7914-3850-3*) State U NY Pr.

Brody, Celeste M. & Wallace, James, eds. Ethical & Social Issues in Professional Education. LC 93-26783. 285p. (C). 1994. text 64.50 (*0-7914-1915-0*); pap. text 21.95 (*0-7914-1916-9*) State U NY Pr.

Brody, Claire. Women's Therapy Groups: Paradigms of Feminist Treatment. (Women's Ser.). 288p. 1987. 35.95 (*0-8261-5570-7*) Springer Pub.

Brody, Claire, ed. Women Therapists Working with Women: New Theory & Process of Feminist Therapy. (Focus on Women Ser.: Vol. 7). 192p. 1984. 42.95 (*0-8261-4550-7*) Springer Pub.

Brody, Claire M. & Semel, Vicki G. Strategies for Therapy with the Elderly: Living with Hope & Meaning. LC 93-3273. 200p. 1993. 32.95 (*0-8261-8010-8*) Springer Pub.

Brody, David. The American Labor Movement. LC 85-7482. 168p. 1985. reprint ed. pap. 15.00 (*0-8191-4667-6*) U Pr of Amer.

— The Banjo Picker's Fakebook. (Illus.). 216p. 1985. pap. 24.95 (*0-8256-0271-8*, OK64261, Oak) Music Sales.

— Butcher Workmen: A Study of Unionization. LC 64-21240. (Wertheim Publications in Industrial Relations). 332p. 1964. 29.95 (*0-674-08925-1*) HUP.

— Fiddler's Fake Book. 1983. pap. 24.95 (*0-8256-0238-6*, OK63925, Oak) Music Sales.

— The Guitar Picker's Fakebook. (Illus.). 248p. 1984. pap. 22.95 (*0-8256-0272-6*, OK64279, Oak) Music Sales.

— Labor in Crisis: The Steel Strike of 1919. LC 86-30880. 224p. 1987. pap. text 12.95 (*0-252-01373-5*) U of Ill Pr.

— Labor in Crisis: The Steel Strike of 1919. LC 82-11746. (Critical Periods of History Ser.). 208p. 1982. reprint ed. lib. bdg. 59.50 (*0-313-23499-X*, BROL, Greenwood Pr) Greenwood.

— Main Chapters in American Labor History: From Origins to the Present. LC 92-42134. 272p. 1993. text 57.95 (*0-19-506790-8*); pap. text 21.95 (*0-19-506791-6*) OUP.

— Mandolin Picker's Fake Book. 1984. pap. 24.95 (*0-8256-0239-4*, OK64352, Oak) Music Sales.

— Steelworkers in America: The Non-Union Era. LC 98-23404. 1998. pap. 19.95 (*0-252-06713-4*) U of Ill Pr.

— Workers in Industrial America: Essays on the Twentieth Century Struggle. 2nd ed. LC 92-366. 288p. (C). 1993. pap. text 21.95 (*0-19-504504-1*) OUP.

Brody, David & Koslow-Miller, Francine, frwds. David Brody, Selected Paintings 1985-1994. (Illus.). 60p. 1995. pap. 20.00 (*0-9674593-0-3*) Evil Monkey.

Brody, David & Thaler, Dena. Ani Tefilati. LC 97-174738. (Illus.). (Orig.). 1996. pap. text, teacher ed. 15.00 (*0-8074-0606-6*, 208043) UAHC.

— Ani Tefilati. (Illus.). 64p. (Orig.). (J). (gr. k-3). 1996. pap. text 8.00 (*0-8074-0602-3*, 101092) UAHC.

***Brody, David C., et al.** Criminal Law: A Contemporary Perspective. LC 00-44220. 2000. write for info. (*0-8342-1083-5*) Aspen Pub.

Brody, David C., jt. auth. see Acker, James R.

Brody, David E. The American Legal System. 585p. (C). 1978. text 63.56 (*0-669-01439-7*) HM Trade Div.

Brody, Deborah, jt. ed. see Wayman, Adele.

Brody, Dorje C. & Hughston, Lane P. The Geometry of Statistical Physics. 220p. 1999. 34.00 (*1-86094-140-0*) World Scientific Pub.

Brody, Dylan. A Tale of a Hero & the Song of Her Sword. LC 97-198168. (YA). (gr. 7 up). 1997. pap. 9.99 (*0-88092-412-8*) Royal Fireworks.

***Brody, Dylan.** A Warm Hello. 190p. (Orig.). 1999. pap. 7.99 (*1-928767-05-2*) Silk Label Bks.

Brody, E. D., jt. auth. see Farrell, R. J.

Brody, E. W. The Business of Public Relations. LC 86-30552. 343p. 1987. 69.50 (*0-275-92333-9*, C2333, Praeger Pubs); pap. 17.95 (*0-275-92649-4*, B2649, Praeger Pubs) Greenwood.

— Communicating for Survival: Coping with Diminishing Human Resources. LC 87-11774. 275p. 1987. 65.00 (*0-275-92652-4*, C2652, Praeger Pubs); pap. 14.95 (*0-275-92808-X*, B2808, Praeger Pubs) Greenwood.

— Communication Tomorrow: New Audiences, New Technologies, New Media. LC 89-16175. 308p. 1990. 59.95 (*0-275-93280-X*, C3280, Praeger Pubs); pap. 21.95 (*0-275-93281-8*, B3281, Praeger Pubs) Greenwood.

— Managing Communication Processes: From Planning to Crisis Response. LC 90-23751. 248p. 1991. 57.95 (*0-275-93467-5*, C3467, Praeger Pubs); pap. 22.95 (*0-275-93468-3*, B3468, Praeger Pubs) Greenwood.

— Professional Practice Development: Meeting the Competitive Challenge. LC 88-28574. 273p. 1989. 69.50 (*0-275-93102-1*, C3102, Praeger Pubs) Greenwood.

— Public Relations Programming & Production. LC 87-24626. 328p. 1988. 59.95 (*0-275-92677-X*, C2677, Praeger Pubs); pap. 24.95 (*0-275-92682-6*, B2682, Praeger Pubs) Greenwood.

— Public Relations Writing. LC 89-22983. 288p. 1990. 65.00 (*0-275-92895-0*, C2895, Greenwood Pr); pap. 22.95 (*0-275-92896-9*, B2896, Greenwood Pr) Greenwood.

Brody, E. W. & Stone, Gerald C. Public Relations Research. LC 88-29270. 295p. 1989. 55.00 (*0-275-92870-5*, C2870, Praeger Pubs); pap. 18.95 (*0-275-92871-3*, B2871, Praeger Pubs) Greenwood.

Brody, Elaine. Long-Term Care of Older People: A Practical Guide. LC 77-5944. 402p. 1977. 52.00 (*0-87705-274-3*, Kluwer Acad Hman Sci) Kluwer Academic.

Brody, Elizabeth G. Genetic Basis at Spontaneous Activity in the Albino Rat. (Comparative Psychology Monographs). 1942. pap. 40.00 (*0-527-24924-6*) Periodicals Srv.

Brody, Ervin C. Demetrius Legend & Its Literary Treatment in the Age of the Baroque. LC 73-141869. 323p. 1975. 37.50 (*0-8386-7969-2*) Fairleigh Dickinson.

***Brody, Esther.** The 250 Best Muffin Recipes. (Illus.). 192p. 1999. pap. 17.95 (*0-7788-0014-8*, Pub. by R Rose Inc) Firefly Bks Ltd.

***Brody, Esther.** Another 250 Best Muffin Recipes. (Illus.). 192p. 2000. pap. 18.95 (*0-7788-0020-2*, Pub. by R Rose Inc) Firefly Bks Ltd.

Brody, Eugene B. Biomedical Technology & Human Rights. LC 93-175. (Unesco Ser.). 326p. 1993. 69.95 (*1-85521-373-7*, Pub. by Dartmth Pub) Ashgate Pub Co.

— Biomedical Technology & Human Rights. 325p. 1993. 39.95 (*92-3-102806-5*, U2806, Pub. by UNESCO) Bernan Associates.

— Psychoanalytic Knowledge. 250p. 1990. 35.00 (*0-8236-4447-2*) Intl Univs Pr.

— Sex, Contraception, & Motherhood in Jamaica. LC 81-4133. (Commonwealth Fund Publications). (Illus.). 288p. (C). 1981. 37.95 (*0-674-80277-2*) HUP.

Brody, Eugene B. & Redlich, Frederick C., eds. Psychotherapy with Schizophrenics. (Monograph Series on Schizophrenia: No. 3). 246p. (Orig.). 1964. 35.00 (*0-8236-5420-6*) Intl Univs Pr.

Brody, Eugene B., jt. ed. see Schlesinger, Herbert J.

Brody, Evelyn & Bryant, M. Kevin. Partnerships: Complete Tax Practice & Planning Guide. 900p. 1996. ring bd. 135.00 (*1-886035-02-4*) Pro Tax & Business.

Brody, Evelyn, et al. Partnership Tax Practice Manual: 1991 Edition. 467p. 1990. text 99.00 (*0-916592-99-5*) Panel Pubs.

Brody, F. & Vamos, T., eds. The Neumann Compendium. LC 95-1809. (Series in 20th Century Mathematics: Vol. 1). 850p. 1995. text 86.00 (*981-02-2201-7*) World Scientific Pub.

Brody, G. & Sigel, Irving E., eds. Methods of Family Research: Biographies of Research Projects, Vol. II. 296p. 1990. 69.95 (*0-89859-827-3*) L Erlbaum Assocs.

Brody, Gene H., ed. see Dunn, Judy, et al.

Brody, H., ed. Synthetic Fibre Materials. (Polymer Science & Technology Ser.). 384p. 1994. pap. 162.75 (*0-582-06267-5*) Longman.

Brody, Harold D., ed. see Metallurgical Society of AIME Staff.

Brody, Harold J. Chemical Peeling. 2nd ed. LC 97-120805. (Illus.). 256p. (C). (gr. 13). 1997. text 99.00 (*0-8151-1261-0*, 26992) Mosby Inc.

Brody, Harold J., et al. Human Pharmacology: Molecular to Clinical. 3rd ed. Larner, Joseph, ed. LC 97-22474 (Illus.). 1024p. (C). (gr. 13). 1997. pap. text 52.95 (*0-8151-2456-2*, 31204) Mosby Inc.

Brody, Helen & Morris, Patricia. Cooking with Fire. 100p. 1993. pap. 10.00 (*0-9638885-0-1*) Fairfield Hist.

Brody, Howard. The Healer's Power. 324p. (C). 1993. pap. 17.00 (*0-300-05783-0*) Yale U Pr.

***Brody, Howard.** The Placebo Response: How You Can Release the Body's Inner Pharmacy for Better Health. 336p. 2000. 25.00 (*0-06-019493-6*, Cliff Street) HarperTrade.

Brody, Howard. Placebos & the Philosophy of Medicine: Clinical, Conceptual, & Ethical Issues. LC 79-18481. 171p. Date not set. reprint ed. pap. 53.10 (*0-608-20611-3*, 205457900003) Bks Demand.

— Tennis Science for Tennis Players. LC 86-30735. (Illus.). 168p. (Orig.). 1987. pap. 19.95 (*0-8122-1238-X*) U of Pa Pr.

Brody, Howard, et al. Final Report of the Michigan Commission on Death & Dying. 205p. 1997. reprint ed. pap. text 35.00 (*0-7881-4681-5*) DIANE Pub.

Brody, Hugh. The Living Arctic: Hunters of the Canadian North. LC 90-32419. (Illus.). 270p. 1990. pap. 16.95 (*0-295-97002-2*) U of Wash Pr.

— Maps & Dreams: Indians & the British Columbia Frontier. (Illus.). 294p. (C). 1997. reprint ed. pap. text 14.95 (*0-88133-965-2*) Waveland Pr.

Brody, Ilene N., jt. ed. see Vardin, Patricia A.

Brody, J. J. The Chaco Phenomenon. (Illus.). 32p. 1983. pap. 6.25 (*0-912535-01-6*) Max Mus.

— A Day with a Mimbres. LC 98-35121. (Day with Ser.). (Illus.). 48p. (J). (gr. 5-7). 1999. lib. bdg. 22.60 (*0-8225-1917-8*, Runestone Pr) Lerner Pub.

— Pueblo Indian Painting: Tradition & Modernism in New Mexico, 1900-1930. LC 96-50100. (Illus.). 238p. 1997. 60.00 (*0-933452-45-4*); pap. 30.00 (*0-933452-46-2*) Schol Am Res.

Brody, J. J. & Allen, Rebecca. Beauty from the Earth: Pueblo Indian Pottery from the University Museum of Archaeology & Anthropology. (Illus.). xii, 84p. 1990. pap. 19.95 (*0-924171-05-7*) U Museum Pubns.

Brody, J. J., et al. Mimbres Pottery: Ancient Art of the American Southwest. LC 83-10812. (Illus.). 132p. 1983. 39.95 (*0-933920-46-6*, Pub. by Hudson Hills) Natl Bk Netwk.

— To Touch the Past: The Painted Pottery of the Mimbres People. LC 95-44485. (Illus.). 120p. 1996. 29.95 (*1-55595-128-7*) Hudson Hills.

Brody, J. J., jt. auth. see Szabo, Joyce M.

***Brody, J. Kenneth.** The Avoidable War, 2 vols. 1999. 95.00 (*1-56000-435-5*); pap. 40.00 (*0-7658-0628-2*) Transaction Pubs.

Brody, J. Kenneth. The Avoidable War: Lord Cecil & the Policy of Principle, 1932-1935. 438p. 1998. 59.95 (*1-56000-374-X*) Transaction Pubs.

— The Avoidable War: Lord Cecil & the Policy of Principle, 1932-1935. 438p. 1999. pap. 24.95 (*0-7658-0498-0*) Transaction Pubs.

— The Avoidable War Vol. 2: Pierre Laval & the Politics of Reality, 1935-1936. 389p. 1999. pap. 24.95 (*0-7658-0622-3*) Transaction Pubs.

— The Avoidable War Vol. 2: Pierre Laval & The Politics Of Reality, 1935-1936. LC 99-43673. 389p. 1999. 59.95 (*1-56000-375-8*) Transaction Pubs.

Brody, Jacob A., jt. ed. see Butler, Robert N.

Brody, Jane. Jane Brody's Cold & Flu Fighter. 88p. 1995. 10.95 (*0-393-03913-7*) Norton.

***Brody, Jane.** Jane Brody's Cold Flu Fighter. 2000. 5.99 (*0-7858-1253-9*) Bk Sales Inc.

Brody, Jane & Flaste, Richard. Jane Brody's Good Seafood Book. LC 94-16482. (Illus.). 1994. 27.50 (*0-393-03687-1*) Norton.

— Jane Brody's Good Seafood Cookbook: A Guide to Healthy Eating with More Than 200 Low-Fat Recipes. (Illus.). 592p. 1995. pap. 16.00 (*0-449-91021-0*) Fawcett.

Brody, Jane A., et al. 1001 Great Gift Ideas. 168p. 1999. 12.99 (*1-57866-064-5*) Galahad Bks.

Brody, Jane E. Jane Brody's Allergy Fighter. LC 96-34499. 128p. 1998. pap. 10.00 (*0-393-31635-1*) Norton.

— Jane Brody's Cold & Flu Fighter. LC 95-10236. Orig. Title: Cold & Flu Fighter. 88p. 1995. pap. 5.95 (*0-393-31353-0*) Norton.

— Jane Brody's Good Food Book. LC 86-47600. 736p. 1987. pap. 17.95 (*0-553-34618-0*) Bantam.

— Jane Brody's Good Food Book: Living the High Carbohydrate Way. (Illus.). 621p. 1985. 25.00 (*0-393-02210-2*) Norton.

— Jane Brody's Good Food Gourmet: Recipes & Menus for Delicious & Healthful Entertaining. LC 91-22127. 624p. 1992. pap. 16.95 (*0-553-35295-4*) Bantam.

— Jane Brody's Good Food Gourmet: Recipes & Menus for Delicious & Healthful Entertaining. (Illus.). 1990. 25.00 (*0-393-02878-X*) Norton.

— Jane Brody's Nutrition. 576p. 1982. pap. 17.95 (*0-553-34721-7*) Bantam.

— Jane Brody's Nutrition Book: A Lifetime Guide to Good Eating for Better Health & Weight Control by the Personal Health Columnist for the New York Times. LC 80-25117. (Illus.). 576p. 1981. 29.95 (*0-393-01429-0*) Norton.

— Jane Brody's The New York Times Guide to Personal Health. 736p. 1982. 19.95 (*0-686-95972-8*, Times Bks) Crown Pub Group.

— Jane Brody's the New York Times Guide to Personal Health. 752p. 1983. pap. 15.00 (*0-380-64121-6*, Avon Bks) Morrow Avon.

— New York Times Book of Health. 464p. 1998. pap. 15.00 (*0-8129-3012-6*, Times Bks) Crown Pub Group.

***Brody, Jane E. & Reporters of the New York Times Staff.** The New York Times Book of Women's Health: The Latest on Feeling Fit, Eating Right & Healthy Living. Grady, Denise, ed. (Illus.). 356p. 2000. 29.95 (*0-86730-806-0*) Lebhar Friedman.

***Brody, Janis.** Bringing Home the Laundry: Effective Parenting for College & Beyond. 2000. pap. 14.95 (*0-87833-184-0*) Taylor Pub.

— Your Body: The Girls Guide. 256p. (gr. 4-11). 2000. mass mkt. 4.99 (*0-312-97563-5*) St Martin.

Brody, Jean. Cleo. 368p. 1997. pap. 14.95 (*0-312-15078-4*) St Martin.

— Elephants: An Affectionate Portrait. Leon, Vicki, ed. LC 94-30880. (Close up: A Focus on Nature Ser.). (Illus.). 48p. (YA). (gr. 5 up). 1994. pap. 7.95 (*0-382-24877-5*); lib. bdg. 14.95 (*0-382-24876-7*) Silver Burdett Pr.

Brody, Jean P. Braille Me. 64p. (Orig.). 1984. pap. 5.95 (*0-941374-02-5*) Grapetree Prods.

Brody, Jeffrey, jt. auth. see Picard, Robert G.

Brody, Jennifer D. Impossible Purities: Blackness, Femininity & Victorian Culture. LC 98-23196. 1998. 49.95 (*0-8223-2105-X*); pap. 17.95 (*0-8223-2120-3*) Duke.

Brody, Jerome S. The Lung: Molecular Basis of Disease. Fletcher, Judy, ed. LC 97-27841. (Illus.). 240p. (C). 1998. text 50.00 (*0-7216-6814-3*, W B Saunders Co) Harcrt Hlth Sci Grp.

Brody, Jerome S., et al, eds. Current Concepts in Respiratory Cell & Molecular Biology. (Current Concepts Ser.). 144p. 1991. 39.95 (*0-915116-18-9*) Am Lung Assn.

Brody, Jerome S. & Snider, Gordon L., eds. Current Topics in the Management of Respiratory Diseases, Vol. 1. LC 81-10264. (Illus.). 192p. reprint ed. pap. 59.60 (*0-7837-2559-0*, 204271800003) Bks Demand.

B

Brody, Jerome S., et al. Signal Transduction in Lung Cells. Tkacuk, Vsevolod A., ed. (Lung Biology in Health & Disease Ser.: Vol. 65). (Illus.). 704p. 1993. text 260.00 (*0-8247-8813-3*) Dekker.

Brody, Jules. Du Style a la Pensee: Trois Etudes Sur les Caracteres de la Bruyere. LC 80-66328. (French Forum Monographs: No. 20). (FRE.). 88p. (Orig.). 1980. pap. 9.95 (*0-917058-19-4*) French Forum.

— Fate in Oedipus Tyrannus: A Textual Approach. (Arethusa Monographs: No. 11). 94p. (C). 1985. pap. 10.00 (*0-930881-08-7*) Dept Classics.

— Lectures Classiques. (FRE.). 368p. 1996. lib. bdg. 49.95 (*1-886365-01-6*) Rookwood Pr.

— Lectures de Montaigne. LC 82-82428. (French Forum Monographs: No. 39). 181p. (Orig.). 1982. pap. 14.95 (*0-917058-38-0*) French Forum.

Brody, Jules, ed. see Edelman, Nathan.

Brody, Karen & Trickett, Shirley. Candida: A Natural Approach. (Natural Approach Health Ser.). (Illus.). 208p. 1999. reprint ed. pap. 11.95 (*1-56975-153-6*) Ulysses Pr.

Brody, Kenneth D. Building American Prosperity in the 21st Century: U. S. Trade & Investment in the Asia Pacific Region. (Illus.). 133p. (C). 1998. pap. text 35.00 (*0-7881-4336-0*) DIANE Pub.

Brody, Lawrence, jt. auth. see Cormfeld, Dave L.

Brody, Lawrence, jt. auth. see Cornfeld, Dave L.

Brody, Lawrence, jt. auth. see Richey, Louis R.

Brody, Leslie. Gender, Emotion & the Family. LC 98-32351. vi, 359p. 1999. 45.00 (*0-674-34186-4*) HUP.

— Red Star Sister: Between Madness & Utopia. LC 98-71628. 211p. 1998. pap. 15.00 (*1-886913-15-3*) Ruminator Bks.

Brody, Leslie, ed. Daughters of Kings: Growing up As a Jewish Woman in America. LC 97-14069. 224p. 1997. 26.95 (*0-571-19919-4*) Faber & Faber.

Brody, Leslie G. Effective Fund Raising: Tools & Techniques for Success. 158p. 1994. pap. 39.95 (*0-87411-692-9*) Copley Pub.

Brody, Linda, ed. see Hyman Blumberg Symposium on Research in Early Chil.

Brody, Lora. Basic Baking: Everything You Need to Know to Start Baking Plus 101 Lucious Dessert Recipes. LC 00-38025. 320p. 2000. 25.00 (*0-688-16724-1*, Wm Morrow) Morrow Avon.

***Brody, Lora.** Lora Brody Plugged In: The Definitive Guide to the Best Kitchen Appliances. Hoenig, Pam, ed. LC 97-17682. 384p. 1998. 25.00 (*0-688-14961-8*, Wm Morrow) Morrow Avon.

— The Slow Cooker Gourmet 2001. write for info. (*0-688-17471-X*, Wm Morrow) Morrow Avon.

Brody, Lora & Brody, Max. Stuff It! Hoenig, Pam, ed. LC 97-47320. 160p. 1998. pap. 12.00 (*0-688-15868-4*, Wm Morrow) Morrow Avon.

Brody, Lora A. Chocolate. Wertz, Laurie, ed. LC 93-17990. (Williams-Sonoma Kitchen Library). (Illus.). 108p. 1993. lib. bdg. write for info. (*0-7835-0242-7*) Time-Life.

— Chocolate. Wertz, Laurie, ed. LC 93-17990. (Williams-Sonoma Kitchen Library). (Illus.). 108p. (gr. 11). 1999. 14.95 (*0-7835-0241-9*) Time-Life.

— Desserts from Y Brea. LC 93-42503. 1994. pap. 22.00 (*0-688-13071-2*, Wm Morrow) Morrow Avon.

— The Kitchen Survival Guide: A Hand-Holding Kitchen Primer with 140 Recipes to Get You Started. LC 91-40663. 308p. 1992. pap. 22.00 (*0-688-10587-4*, Hearst) Hearst Commns.

— Pizza, Focaccia, Flat & Filled Breads from Your Bread Machine: Perfect Every Time. LC 94-26833. 320p. 1995. pap. 23.00 (*0-688-13752-0*, Wm Morrow) Morrow Avon.

— Survival-Entertainin. LC 94-7761. 404p. 1994. pap. 20.00 (*0-688-12295-7*, Wm Morrow) Morrow Avon.

Brody, Lora A. & Apter, Millie. Rev. Bread Machine B. 1996. pap. 24.00 (*0-688-14565-5*, Wm Morrow) Morrow Avon.

Brody, M. Jill & Thomas, John S., eds. The Tojolabal Maya: Ethnographic & Linguistic Approaches. LC 88-81803. (Geoscience & Man Ser.: Vol. 26). (Illus.). 84p. (Orig.). (C). 1988. pap. text 18.00 (*0-938909-61-4*) Geosci Pubns LSU.

***Brody, Marjorie.** Power Marketing for Consultants. 1999. pap. 19.99 (*1-57472-310-3*) Archer-Ellison.

— Speaking Is an Audience-Centered Sport. Roddy, Miryam S. & Alfaro, Aren, eds. (Illus.). 262p. 1998. pap. 19.95 (*0-9654827-2-3*) Career Skills Brody.

Brody, Marjorie. Speaking Your Way to the Top: Making Powerful Business Presentations. LC 97-27883. 170p. 1997. pap. text 12.00 (*0-205-26814-5*) Allyn.

***Brody, Marjorie.** 21st Century Pocket Guides to Proper Business Protocol: Creating First Impressions That Can Lead to Lasting Impressions. Roddy, Miryam S., ed. (Illus.). 41p. 1999. pap. 8.00 (*0-9654827-7-4*) Career Skills Brody.

— 21st Century Pocket Guides to Proper Business Protocol: Have Office Will Travel: Doing Business in Social Settings. Roddy, Miryam S., ed. (Illus.). 41p. 1999. pap. 8.00 (*0-9654827-9-0*) Career Skills Brody.

— 21st Century Pocket Guides to Proper Business Protocol: Make the Work Environment Work for You. Roddy, Miryam S., ed. (Illus.). 37p. 1999. pap. 8.00 (*0-9654827-8-2*) Career Skills Brody.

— 21st Century Pocket Guides to Proper Business Protocol: Rules for the Wired. Roddy, Miryam S., ed. (Illus.). 45p. 1999. pap. 8.00 (*0-9654827-6-6*) Career Skills Brody.

— 21 Ways to Springboard Your Speaking, Training & Consulting Career. Roddy, Miryam Strassberg, ed. (Illus.). 75p. 1997. pap. 14.95 (*0-9654827-0-7*) Career Skills Brody.

Brody, Marjorie & Kent, Shawn. Power Presentations: How to Connect with Your Audience & Sell Your Ideas. LC 92-10949. 224p. 1992. pap. 19.95 (*0-471-55961-X*) Wiley.

Brody, Marjorie & Pachter, Barbara. Business Etiquette. LC 94-7620. (Business Skills Express Ser.). 144p. 1994. text 10.95 (*0-7863-0323-9*, Irwn Prfssnl) McGraw-Hill Prof.

— Minding Your Business Manners: Etiquette Tips for Presenting Yourself Professionally in Every Business Situation. Scanlon, Kelly, ed. LC 95-71779. (Illus.). 110p. 1996. pap. 12.95 (*1-57294-014-X*, 12-0026) SkillPath Pubns.

Brody, Marjorie, jt. auth. see Pachter, Barbara.

Brody, Max, jt. auth. see Brody, Lora.

Brody, Michael. Immunization Dice. (Twentieth Century Fund Papers). 77p. (Orig.). (C). 1987. pap. text 10.00 (*0-87078-211-8*) Century Foundation.

— Lexico-Logical Form: A Radically Minimalist Theory. LC 95-8254. (Linguistic Inquiry Monographs: No. 27). 168p. 1995. 40.00 (*0-262-02390-3*); pap. text 20.00 (*0-262-52203-9*) MIT Pr.

Brody, Michal, ed. Are We There Yet? A Continuing History of "Lavender Woman" A Chicago Lesbian Newpaper 1971-1976. 188p. 1985. pap. 8.95 (*0-918040-07-8*) Inst Lesbian.

Brody, Miriam. Manly Writing: Gender, Rhetoric, & the Rise of Composition. LC 92-32129. 272p. (C). 1993. 29.95 (*0-8093-1691-9*) S Ill U Pr.

Brody, Nathan. Intelligence. 2nd ed. (Illus.). 395p. 1992. text 69.95 (*0-12-134251-4*) Acad Pr.

— Personality: In Search of Individuality. 270p. 1988. text 69.95 (*0-12-134845-8*) Acad Pr.

Brody, Nathan & Ehrlichman, Howard. Personality Psychology: The Science of Individuality. LC 97-20128. 446p. 1997. 83.00 (*0-13-146903-7*) P-H.

Brody, Philip J. The Technology Planning & Management Handbook: A Guide for School District Educational Technology Leaders. LC 95-6388. 178p. 1995. pap. 37.95 (*0-87778-287-3*) Educ Tech Pubns.

Brody, Ralph. Effectively Managing Human Service Organizations. LC 92-33061. (Sourcebooks for the Human Services Ser.: Vol. 23). (Illus.). 320p. (C). 1993. text 56.00 (*0-8039-5028-4*); pap. text 26.00 (*0-8039-5029-2*) Sage.

***Brody, Ralph.** Effectively Managing Human Service Organizations. 2nd ed. LC 00-8041. (Sourcebooks for the Human Services Ser.). (Illus.). 2000. pap. write for info. (*0-7619-2143-5*) Sage.

Brody, Ralph. Problem Solving: Concepts & Methods for Community Organizations. LC 81-7221. 240p. (C). 1982. pap. 20.95 (*0-89885-079-7*, Kluwer Acad Hman Sci) Kluwer Academic.

Brody, Ralph & Goodman, Marcie. Fund Raising Events: Strategies & Programs for Success. LC 86-27433. 291p. 1987. 35.95 (*0-89885-362-1*, Kluwer Acad Hman Sci); pap. 20.95 (*0-89885-390-7*, Kluwer Acad Hman Sci) Kluwer Academic.

Brody, Ralph & Nair, Murali D. Macro Practice: A Generalist Approach. 214p. 1999. pap. 30.00 (*0-911541-61-6*) Gregory Pub.

Brody, Ralph, jt. auth. see Nair, Murali D.

Brody, Reed. Contra Terror in Nicaragua: Report of a Fact-Finding Mission: September 1984-January 1985. 200p. (Orig.). 1985. 30.00 (*0-89608-313-6*); pap. 8.50 (*0-89608-312-8*) South End Pr.

***Brody, Reed & Ratner, Michael.** The Pinochet Papers: The Case of Augusto Pinochet Ugarte in Spain & Britain. LC 00-33090. 2000. write for info. (*90-411-1404-1*) Kluwer Law Intl.

Brody, Richard A. Assessing the President: The Media, Elite Opinion, & Public Support. 208p. 1991. 32.50 (*0-8047-1907-1*) Stanford U Pr.

Brody, Richard J. Effective Partnering: A Report to Congress on Federal Technology Partnerships. (Illus.). 76p. (C). 1997. pap. text 25.00 (*0-7881-4601-7*) DIANE Pub.

Brody, Robert. The Geonim of Babylonia & the Shaping of Medieval Jewish Culture. LC 97-2879. (Illus.). 384p. 1997. 42.00 (*0-300-07047-0*) Yale U Pr.

Brody, Robert & Wiesenberg, E. J. A Hand-List of Rabbinic Manuscripts in the Cambridge Genizah Collections Vol. 1: Taylor-Schechter New Series. (Cambridge University Library Genizah Ser.: No. 5). (Illus.). 368p. (C). 1999. text 150.00 (*0-521-58400-0*) Cambridge U Pr.

Brody, Robert, jt. auth. see Richler, Binyamin.

Brody, S. Legal Drafting. LC 93-80291. 416p. 1994. pap. text 28.95 (*0-316-10908-8*, Aspen Law & Bus) Aspen Pub.

Brody, Sara. The Brody Reading Manual: An Implementation Guide for Teachers. (Brody Reading Method). 69p. 1987. pap. text, teacher ed. 8.00 (*1-886042-02-0*) Larc Pubg.

— Brody Reading Method: Complete Set. (Brody Reading Method Ser.). pap. text 68.00 (*1-886042-11-X*) Larc Pubg.

— Study Skills: Teaching & Learning Strategies for Mainstream & Specialized Classrooms. 69p. 1987. pap. text, teacher ed. 8.00 (*1-886042-00-4*) Larc Pubg.

— Teaching Reading: Language, Letters & Thought. 402p. (Orig.). (C). 1994. pap. text 28.00 (*1-886042-12-8*) Larc Pubg.

Brody, Seth, jt. auth. see Solomon, Ezra B.

Brody, Steve. Renew Your Marriage at Midlife. LC 98-36483. 275p. 1999. 21.95 (*0-399-14457-9*) Putnam Pub Group.

***Brody, Steve & Brody, Cathy.** Renew Your Marriage at Midlife. 2000. reprint ed. pap. 13.95 (*0-399-52570-X*, Perigee Bks) Berkley Pub.

Brody, Steven A., jt. auth. see Edwards, Robert G.

Brody, Stuart. Sex at Risk: Lifetime Number of Partners, Frequency of Intercourse, & the Low AIDS Risk of Vaginal Intercourse. LC 97-12110. 120p. 1997. text 32.95 (*1-56000-309-X*) Transaction Pubs.

Brody, Susan, et al. Legal Drafting. 416p. 1994. teacher ed. write for info. (*0-316-10425-6*, 04256) Aspen Law.

Brody, Susan, ed. see Hoyt, Erich.

Brody, Sylvia. Passivity: A Study of Its Development & Expression in Boys. LC 64-18623. 184p. 1964. 28.50 (*0-8236-4020-5*) Intl Univs Pr.

— Patterns of Mothering: A Study of Maternal Influence During Infancy. LC 56-8839. 446p. (Orig.). 1970. reprint ed. 65.00 (*0-8236-4040-X*) Intl Univs Pr.

Brody, Sylvia & Axelrad, Sidney. Anxiety & Ego Formation in Infancy. 432p. (C). 1993. reprint ed. pap. 24.95 (*0-8236-8003-7*) Intl Univs Pr.

Brody, Sylvia & Siegel, Miriam G. The Evolution of Character: Birth to 18 Years, a Longitudinal Study. LC 91-8952. 556p. (C). 1992. 82.50 (*0-8236-1518-9*) Intl Univs Pr.

Brody, T. A. The Philosophy Behind Physics. De la Pena, L. & Hodgson, P. E., eds. (Illus.). 368p. 1994. 39.95 (*0-387-57952-4*) Spr-Verlag.

Brody, Thomas A. The Philosophy Behind Physics. Hodgson, P. E. & De La Pena, L., eds. LC 93-17950. (Illus.). 350p. 1994. 59.00 (*0-387-55914-0*) Spr-Verlag.

Brody, Tom. Nutritional Biochemistry. (Food Science & Technology Ser.). (Illus.). 658p. 1994. text 83.00 (*0-12-134835-0*) Acad Pr.

— Nutritional Biochemistry. 2nd ed. LC 98-40384. (Illus.). 1006p. (C). 1998. text 79.95 (*0-12-134836-9*) Acad Pr.

Brody, Viola A. The Dialogue of Touch: Developmental Play Therapy. LC 97-9432. (Master Works Ser.). 400p. (C). 1997. pap. text 45.00 (*0-7657-0088-3*) Aronson.

— The Dialogue of Touch: Developmental Play Therapy. 373p. (C). 1993. pap. text 20.00 (*0-9646232-0-X*) V A Brody.

***Brody, Wendy.** Prince Harry. (Illus.). (Orig.). 2000. mass mkt. 5.99 (*0-7860-1145-9*, Pinncle Kensgtn) Kensgtn Pub Corp.

Brody, William R. Digital Radiography. LC 83-21246. 239p. 1984. reprint ed. pap. 74.10 (*0-608-03391-X*, 206408800008) Bks Demand.

Brody, Ziporah, tr. see Katz, Jacob.

Brodyanbsky, V. M., et al. The Efficiency of Industrial Processes: Energy Analysis & Optimization. LC 94-11390. (Energy Research Ser.: Vol. 9). 512p. 1994. 316.50 (*0-444-89996-0*) Elsevier.

Brodzikowski, K. & Van Loon, A. J. Glacigenic Sediments. (Developments in Sedimentology Ser.: No. 49). xiv,674p. 1991. 179.50 (*0-444-88307-X*) Elsevier.

Brodzinsky, Anne B. The Mulberry Bird: An Adoption Story. rev. ed. LC 95-2460. (Illus.). 48p. (J). (gr. k-5). 1996. 16.00 (*0-944934-15-3*) Perspect Indiana.

Brodzinsky, David, et al. Children's Adjustment to Adoption: Developmental & Clinical Issues. LC 97-45404. (Developmental Clinical Psychology & Psychiatry Ser.). 150p. 1998. 30.00 (*0-7619-0515-4*); pap. 12.99 (*0-7619-0516-2*) Sage.

Brodzinsky, David M., et al. Being Adopted: The Lifelong Search for Self. LC 92-38103. 224p. 1993. pap. 14.00 (*0-385-41426-9*, Anchor NY) Doubleday.

Brodzinsky, David M., jt. ed. see Ashmore, Richard D.

Broe, Mary L., ed. Silence & Power: A Reevaluation of Djuna Barnes. LC 89-56358. (Illus.). 384p. (C). 1991. 36.95 (*0-8093-1250-6*); pap. 17.95 (*0-8093-1255-7*) S Ill U Pr.

Broe, Michael & Pierrehumbert, Janet, eds. Papers in Laboratory Phonology V: Language Acquisition & the Lexicon. (Papers in Laboratory Phonology). (Illus.). 408p. (C). 2000. 64.95 (*0-521-64363-5*) Cambridge U Pr.

Broeck, Andre Vanden, see Vanden Broeck, Andre.

Broeck, Fabricio Vanden, see Vanden Broeck, Fabricio.

Broecke, M. P. Van den, see Cohen, A. & Van den Broecke, M. P., eds.

Broecke, M. Van der, see Van Heuven, Vincent J. & Van der Broecke, M., eds.

Broeckelmann, Russ. All Inventory Is Not Created Equal: Inventory Management for Multi-Branch Distributors & Suppliers. LC 98-42135. 256p. 1998. boxed set 54.95 (*1-57444-237-6*) St Lucie Pr.

Broecker, Michael. Die Metamorphe- Vulkano-Sedimentaere Abfolge der Insel Tinos (Kykladen, Griechenland) (Geotektonische Forschungen Ser.: Vol. 74). (GER.). 108p. 1990. 44.00 (*3-510-50040-7*, Pub. by E Schweizerbartsche) Balogh.

Broecker, W. S., jt. ed. see Bard, E.

Broecker, Wallace S. How to Build a Habitable Planet. (Illus.). 291p. (C). 1986. text 20.00 (*0-9617511-1-8*) Eldigio Pr.

Broecker, William L., ed. see Hufnagel, James A.

Broeckhove, J., et al, eds. Dynamics of Wave Packets in Molecular & Nuclear Physics. (Lecture Notes in Physics Ser.: Vol. 256). viii, 187p. 1986. 34.95 (*0-387-16772-2*) Spr-Verlag.

Broeckhove, J. & Lathouwers, L. Time-Dependent Quantum Molecular Dynamics. LC 92-28749. (NATO ASI Ser.: Vol. 299). (Illus.). 436p. (C). 1992. text 135.00 (*0-306-44305-8*, Kluwer Plenum) Kluwer Academic.

Broeder, Frederick Den, see Den Broeder, Frederick.

Broeder, P. Talking about People: A Multiple Case Study on Adult Language Acquisition. (European Studies on Multilingualism: Vol. I). x, 198p. 1991. pap. 32.75 (*90-265-1211-2*) Swets.

Broeder, Peter. Language, Ethnicity & Education: Case Studies on Immigrant Minority Groups. LC 98-45024. (Multilingual Matters Ser.). 1998. 44.95 (*1-85359-430-X*) Taylor & Francis.

***Broeder, Peter & Murre, Jaap, eds.** Models of Language Acquisition: Inductive & Deductive Approaches. (Illus.). 320p. 2000. text 85.00 (*0-19-824138-0*) OUP.

Broeders, Mario. Tangos a los Maestros. 106p. 1996. 20.00 (*0-9654944-1-1*) Music Pub NY.

— 20 Poemas de Amor y Una Cancion Desesperada. (SPA.). 1996. 40.00 (*0-9654944-0-3*) Music Pub NY.

Broeg, Bob. Bob Broeg: Memories of a Hall of Fame Sportswriter. LC 95-67285. (Illus.). 378p. 1995. 22.95 (*1-57167-010-6*) Sports Pub.

— Ol' Mizzou: A Century of Tiger Football. Missouri Editing Group Staff & Anderson, Kelly, eds. (Illus.). 1992. write for info. (*1-56166-028-0*) Walsworth Pub.

***Broeg, Bob.** One Hundred Greatest Moments in St. Louis Sports. (Illus.). 240p. 2000. write for info. (*1-883982-31-6*, Pub. by MO Hist Soc) Booksource.

Broeg, Bob. Redbirds: The Centennial Celebration of Cardinal Baseball. Missouri Editing Group Staff & Anderson, Kelly, eds. (Illus.). 1992. write for info. (*1-56166-075-2*) Walsworth Pub.

Broeg, Bob & Miller, William J., Jr. Baseball from a Different Angle. LC 88-9556. 1989. pap. 12.95 (*0-912083-27-1*) Diamond Communications.

Broeg, Bob & Vickery, Jerry. St. Louis Cardinals Encyclopedia. LC 98-15508. (Illus.). 352p. 1998. pap. 35.00 (*1-57028-171-8*, 81718H, Mstrs Pr) NTC Contemp Pub Co.

Broehl, John & Faruqui, Ahmad. The Changing Structure of American Industry & Energy Use Patterns: Issues, Scenarios, & Forecasting Models. LC 86-17488. 512p. 1987. 44.50 (*0-935470-33-6*) Battelle.

Broehl, Wayne G., Jr. Cargill: Going Global. LC 97-35033. (Illus.). 437p. 1998. 30.00 (*0-87451-854-7*) U Pr of New Eng.

— Cargill: Trading the World's Grain. LC 91-31608. (Illus.). 1027p. 1992. 39.95 (*0-87451-572-6*) U Pr of New Eng.

Broehl, Wayne G. Crisis of the Raj: The Revolt of 1857 Through British Lieutenants' Eyes. LC 86-4067. (Illus.). 381p. reprint ed. pap. 118.20 (*0-8357-6510-5*, 203588100097) Bks Demand.

Broehl, Wayne G., Jr. Precision Valley: The Machine Tool Companies of Springfield, Vermont. LC 75-41748. (Companies & Men: Business Enterprises in America Ser.). (Illus.). 1976. reprint ed. 31.95 (*0-405-08065-4*) Ayer.

— Trucks, Trouble & Triumph: The Norwalk Truck Line Company. LC 75-41749. (Companies & Men: Business Enterprises in America Ser.). (Illus.). 1976. reprint ed. 31.95 (*0-405-08066-2*) Ayer.

— Tuck & Tucker: The Origin of the Graduate Business School. LC 98-52853. (Illus.). 122p. 1999. 19.95 (*0-87451-916-0*) U Pr of New Eng.

— The Village Entrepreneur: Change Agents in India's Rural Development. LC 77-18880. 228p. 1978. 37.95 (*0-674-93915-8*) HUP.

Broek, Aart, jt. auth. see Berrian, Brenda.

Broek, David. Elementary Engineering Fracture Mechanics. rev. ed. 1982. pap. text 85.00 (*90-247-2656-5*) Kluwer Academic.

— Elementary Engineering Fracture Mechanics. 4th rev. ed. 1982. lib. bdg. 238.00 (*90-247-2580-1*) Kluwer Academic.

— Fracture Control for the Chemical Process Industries. LC TA0409.B77. (MTI Manual Ser.: No. 8). (Illus.). 582p. 1983. reprint ed. pap. 180.50 (*0-608-06737-7*, 206693400009) Bks Demand.

— The Practical Use of Fracture Mechanics. (C). 1988. lib. bdg. 216.00 (*90-247-3707-9*) Kluwer Academic.

— The Practical Use of Fracture Mechanics. (C). 1989. pap. text 75.00 (*0-7923-0223-0*) Kluwer Academic.

***Broek, Floris V.** Management of International Networks: Cost-Effective Strategies for the New Telecom Regulations & Services. LC 99-32369. 208p. 1999. boxed set 69.95 (*0-8493-0739-2*) CRC Pr.

Broek, G. Van Den, see Schefstrom, D. & Van Den Broek, G., eds.

Broek, G. Van Den, see Van Den Broek, G.

Broek, Gonny Van den, see Ricketts, Marijane G. & Van den Broek, Gonny, eds.

Broek, Jacobus Ten, see Ten Broek, Jacobus.

***Broek, Jon Ten.** Fingerstyle Pattern Picking - 150 Patterns. 32p. 1999. pap. 9.95 incl. audio compact disk (*0-7866-0854-4*, 96936BCD) Mel Bay.

Broek, L. & Sikkel, A. J., eds. Health Cards '97. (Studies in Health Technology & Informatics). 213p. 1998. 86.00 (*90-5199-379-X*) IOS Press.

Broek, Lyle D. Vander, see Bailey, James L. & Vander Broek, Lyle D.

Broek, Paulus Van den, see Van den Broek, Paulus.

Broek, R. Van Den, see Van Den Broek, R.

Broek, Silvere Van den, see Van den Broek, Silvere, ed.

Broekaert, J. A., et al, eds. Metal Speciation in the Environment. (NATO ASI Series G: Ecological Sciences: Vol. 23). (Illus.). 660p. 1990. 272.95 (*0-387-50423-0*) Spr-Verlag.

Broeke, P. W. Van den, see Van den Broeke, P. W.

Broekel, Ray. Dangerous Fish. LC 82-4464. (New True Books Ser.). (J). (gr. k-4). 1982. pap. 5.50 (*0-516-41635-9*) Childrens.

— Dangerous Fish. LC 82-4464. (New True Books Ser.). (Illus.). 48p. (J). (ps-3). 1982. lib. bdg. 21.00 (*0-516-01635-0*) Childrens.

— Experiments with Straws & Paper. LC 90-2173. (New True Books Ser.). (Illus.). 48p. (J). (ps-3). 1990. lib. bdg. 21.00 (*0-516-01104-9*) Childrens.

— Snakes. LC 81-38487. (New True Books Ser.). (Illus.). 48p. (J). (gr. k-4). 1982. pap. 5.50 (*0-516-41649-9*) Childrens.

— Snakes. LC 81-38487. (New True Books Ser.). (Illus.). 48p. (J). (ps-3). 1982. lib. bdg. 21.00 (*0-516-01649-0*) Childrens.

An Asterisk (*) at the beginning of an entry indicates that the title is appearing for the first time.

— Sound Experiments. LC 82-17869. (New True Books Ser.). (Illus.). 48p. (J). (gr. 3-5). 1983. lib. bdg. 21.00 (*0-516-01686-5*) Childrens.

— Trains. (New True Books Ser.). (Illus.). 48p. (J). (gr. k-4). 1981. pap. 5.50 (*0-516-41652-9*) Childrens.

Broekel, Ray & White, Laurence B., Jr. Abra-Ca-Dazzle: Easy Magic Tricks. Fay, Ann, ed. LC 81-11578. (Illus.). 48p. (YA). (gr. 3 up). 1982. lib. bdg. 13.95 (*0-8075-0121-2*) A Whitman.

Broekel, Ray & White, Laurence B. 512 Ants on Sullivan Street, Level 4. LC 97-5295. (Hello Reader! Ser.). (Illus.). (J). (gr. k-2). 1980. reprint ed. 1.50 (*0-590-30876-9*) Scholastic Inc.

Broekel, Ray & White, Laurence B., Jr. Hocus Pocus: Magic You Can Do. Fay, Ann, ed. LC 83-26096. (Illus.). 48p. (J). (gr. 3 up). 1984. lib. bdg. 13.95 (*0-8075-3350-5*) A Whitman.

Broekel, Ray, jt. auth. see White, Larry.

Broekel, Ray, jt. auth. see White, Laurence B.

***Broekhuizen, Marius.** Islands. LC 99-90998. 1999. 25.00 (*0-7388-0564-5*); pap. 18.00 (*0-7388-0565-3*) Xlibris Corp.

Broekhuizen, Richard J. Graphic Communications. large type ed. 612p. 153.00 (*0-614-20547-6*, L-31621-00 APHB) Am Printing Hse.

— Graphic Communications. 4th ed. (Illus.). 624p. (YA). (gr. 6-12). 1999. student ed. 34.47 (*0-02-676305-2*); student ed., wbk. ed. 7.92 (*0-02-676307-9*) Glencoe.

— Graphic Communications: Instructor's Resource Guide. 4th ed. 100p. 1999. teacher ed. 9.51 (*0-02-676306-0*) Glencoe.

Broekhuysen, Arthur, ed. Inspired Wisdom in Practice: Quotations from Paul Brunton. 64p. (Orig.). 1992. pap. 4.95 (*0-943914-57-4*) Larson Pubns.

Broekman, J. Intertwinements of Law & Medicine. LC 98-209285. (Law Ser.: Vol. 7). 248p. (Orig.). 1996. pap. 67.50 (*90-6186-778-9*, Pub. by Leuven Univ) Coronet Bks.

***Broekman, J. M.** A Philosophy of European Union Law. (On the Making of Europe Ser.). 1999. 40.00 (*90-429-0728-2*, Pub. by Peeters Pub) Bks Intl VA.

Broekman, Jan M. Structuralism, Moscow, Prague, Paris. Beekman, J. F. & Helm, B., trs. from GER. LC 74-79570. (Synthese Library: No. 67). Orig. Title: Strukturalismus. 125p. 1974. text 85.50 (*90-277-0478-3*, D Reidel) Kluwer Academic.

Broekman, Jan M. & Knopf, J. Konkrete Reflexion: Festschrift fur Hermann Wein zum 60. Geburtstag. 240p. 1975. pap. text 106.00 (*90-247-1679-9*, Pub. by M Nijhoff) Kluwer Academic.

Broekmeyer, M. E., et al, eds. European Forest Reserves: Proceedings of the European Forest Reserves. Workshop, Wageningen, Netherlands, 6-8 May, 1992. 306p. 1994. 120.00 (*90-220-1082-1*, Pub. by Pudoc Sci Pubs) Balogh.

Broekmeyer, M. J., ed. see Yugoslav Workers' Self-Management Symposium Staff.

Broekstra, Robbert. Nude World. Bensen, Don & Loibl, Bernard J., eds. (Illus.). 120p. (Orig.). 1997. pap. text 29.95 (*0-9636805-2-8*) Events Unltd.

Broell, H. & Dambacher, M., eds. Osteoporosis: A Guide to Diagnostic & Treatment. (Rheumatology Ser.: Vol. 18). (Illus.). viii, 292p. 1996. 259.25 (*3-8055-5624-1*) S Karger.

Broell, H. & Dambacher, M. A., eds. Osteoporose: Grundlagen, Diagnostik und Therapiekonzepte. (Illus.). viii, 314p. 1995. 259.25 (*3-8055-6192-X*) S Karger.

Broelsch-Houssin, Christoph E. Atlas of Liver Surgery. (Surgical Practice Illustrated Ser.). (Illus.). 248p. 1993. text 176.00 (*0-443-08733-4*) Church.

Broelsch-Houssin, Christoph E., ed. Cholestatic Liver Diseases in Children & Adults. (Falk Symposium Ser.). 128p. (C). 1997. text 60.00 (*0-7923-8710-4*) Kluwer Academic.

Broelsch-Houssin, Christoph E. & Zelder, O., eds. Experimental & Clinical Hepatology. 1986. text 178.50 (*0-85200-929-1*) Kluwer Academic.

Broemeling, Lyle D. & Tsurumi, Hiroki. Econometrics & Structural Change. (Statistics: Textbooks & Monographs: Vol. 74). (Illus.). 280p. 1986. text 125.00 (*0-8247-7500-7*) Dekker.

Broenner, Herbert. Berlin Promotion Law in Its Version of February 18, 1976 Including a Brief Commentary. 2nd ed. (C). pap. 13.85 (*3-11-007037-5*) De Gruyter.

Broer, A. & Daigneault, Aubert. Representation Theories & Algebraic Geometry. LC 98-28196. (NATO ASI, Series C, Mathematical & Physical Sciences). 1998. 205.00 (*0-7923-5193-2*) Kluwer Academic.

Broer, D. P. Neoclassical Theory & Empirical Models of Aggregate Firm Behavior. (Advanced Studies in Theoretical & Applied Econometrics). 1986. lib. bdg. 168.00 (*90-247-3412-6*) Kluwer Academic.

Broer, D. P. & Lassila, J., eds. Pension Policies & Public Debt in Dynamic CGE Models. LC 98-208537. (Illus.). x, 189p. 1997. pap. 69.95 (*3-7908-0970-5*) Spr-Verlag.

Broer, H. Geometry & Analysis in Nonlinear Dynamics. 1992. pap. 42.95 (*0-582-06081-8*, Pub. by Addison-Wesley) Longman.

Broer, H. W., et al, eds. Nonlinear Dynamical Systems & Chaos. LC 95-47179. (Progress in Nonlinear Differential Equations & Their Applications Ser.: Vol. 19). 459p. 1996. 149.00 (*0-8176-5346-5*) Birkhauser.

— Nonlinear Dynamical Systems & Chaos. (Progress in Nonlinear Differential Equations & Their Applications Ser.: 19). 459p. 1996. 149.00 (*3-7643-5346-5*) Spr-Verlag.

Broer, H. W., et al. Quasi-Periodic Motions in Families of Dynamical Systems: Order Amidst Chaos, Vol. XI. LC 96-39689. (Lecture Notes in Mathematics Ser.: Vol. 1645). 195p. 1996. pap. 43.00 (*3-540-62025-7*) Spr-Verlag.

— Unfoldings & Bifurcations of Quasi-Periodic Tori. LC 89-18093. (Memoirs Ser.). 175p. 1990. pap. 24.00 (*0-8218-2483-X*, MEMO/83/421) Am Math.

Broer, Hendrik W. & Takens, F., eds. Geometry & Analysis in Nonlinear Dynamics. LC 89-13198. (Pitman Research Notes in Mathematics Ser.: No. 222). (Illus.). 148p. 1992. pap. 45.90 (*0-608-05232-9*, 206576900001) Bks Demand.

Broer, K. H. & Turanli, I., eds. New Trends in Reproductive Medicine. LC 95-44731. 448p. 1996. 139.00 (*3-540-58981-3*) Spr-Verlag.

Broer, Lawrence R. Rabbit Tales: Poetry & Politics in John Updike's Rabbit Novels. LC 97-40344. 280p. 1998. text 34.95 (*0-8173-0899-7*) U of Ala Pr.

***Broer, Lawrence R.** Rabbit Tales: Poetry & Politics in John Updike's Rabbit Novels. 264p. 2000. pap. text 19.95 (*0-8173-1037-1*) U of Ala Pr.

Broer, Lawrence R. Sanity Plea: Schizophrenia in the Novels of Kurt Vonnegut. Scholes, Robert, ed. LC 88-39248. (Studies in Speculative Fiction: No. 18). 226p. reprint ed. 70.10 (*0-8357-1885-9*, 207069800004) Bks Demand.

— Sanity Plea: Schizophrenia in the Novels of Kurt Vonnegut. rev. ed. LC 94-1075. 264p. 1994. pap. text 19.95 (*0-8173-0752-4*) U of Ala Pr.

Broer, Lawrence R. & Walther, John D., eds. Dancing Fools & Weary Blues: The Great Escape of the Twenties. LC 89-61587. 194p. (C). 1990. 34.95 (*0-87972-457-9*); pap. 17.95 (*0-87972-458-7*) Bowling Green Univ Popular Press.

Broer, Lawrence R., et al. The First Time: Initial Sexual Experiences in Fiction. LC 74-9903. 298p. 1975. pap. 8.95 (*0-672-61355-7*, Bobbs) Macmillan.

Broer, Michael, et al. The Neutron Bomb & the Premises of Power: President Carter's Neutron Bomb Decision. (Pew Case Studies in International Affairs). 50p. (C). 1995. pap. text 3.50 (*1-56927-318-9*) Geo U Inst Dplmcy.

Broer, Sharon. Train Up Your Children in the Way They Should Eat, Vol. 1. 1999. pap. 12.99 (*0-88419-663-1*) Creation House.

***Broer, Ted.** A. D. H. D. - Attention Deficit Hyperactivity Disorder: A Natural Approach to Help & Heal a Hyperactive Child. 2000. 19.99 (*0-88419-719-0*) Creation House.

Broer, Ted. Maximum Energy: Top Ten Foods Never to Eat: Top Ten Health Strageties to Feel Great. 1999. 19.99 (*0-88419-643-7*) Creation House.

Broere, jt. auth. see Bode.

Broere, jt. auth. see De Bode.

Broering, Naomi, ed. High-Performance Medical Libraries: Advances in Information Management for the Virtual Era. (Medical Information Management & Libraries: No. 68). 175p. 1993. pap. 39.50 (*0-88736-878-6*) Mecklermedia.

Broerman, Bruce M. The German Historical Novel in Exile after 1933: Calliope Contra Clio. LC 85-21712. (Studies in German Literature). 139p. 1986. 28.50 (*0-271-00421-5*) Pa St U Pr.

***Broerman, Joan.** Weekend Get-a-Ways in Alabama. LC 00-35966. (Illus.). 2000. pap. write for info. (*1-56554-676-8*) Pelican.

Broers, A. & Smith, J. Dutch-English Dictionary: Nederlands-Engels Woordenboek. (DUT & ENG.). 725p. 1981. pap. 29.95 (*0-8288-0449-4*, M10060) Fr & Eur.

— English-Dutch Dictionary: Engels-Nederlands Woordenboek. (DUT & ENG.). 674p. 1980. pap. 29.95 (*0-8288-0448-6*, M9748) Fr & Eur.

Broers, B. C. Mysticism in the Neo-Romanticists. LC 68-767. (Studies in Comparative Literature: No. 35). 1969. reprint ed. lib. bdg. 75.00 (*0-8383-0514-8*) M S G Haskell Hse.

Broers, Michael. Europe after Napoleon: Revolution, Reaction & Romanticism, 1814-1848. 172p. 1996. text 79.95 (*0-7190-4722-6*) Manchester Univ Pr.

Broers, Michael. Europe under Napoleon 1799-1815. LC 96-3010. 304p. 1996. text 49.95 (*0-340-66265-4*, Pub. by E A); pap. text 19.95 (*0-340-66264-6*, Pub. by E A) OUP.

Broers, Michael, ed. Napoleonic Imperialism & the Savoyard Monarchy, 1773-1821: State Building in Piedmont. LC 97-20840. (Studies in French Civilization: Vol. 12). 596p. 1997. text 119.95 (*0-7734-8609-7*) E Mellen.

Broerse, J. J., ed. Ion Chambers for Neutron Dosimetry, Vol. 3. (European Applied Research Reports Special Topics Ser.). viii, 352p. 1980. text 389.00 (*3-7186-0048-X*) Gordon & Breach.

Broerse, J. J. & MacVittie, T. J., eds. Response of Different Species to Total Body Irradiation. (Radiology Ser.). 1984. text 141.50 (*0-89838-678-0*) Kluwer Academic.

Broerse, Jacqueline E., jt. ed. see Bunders, Joske F.

Broes, Arthur T. Lectures on Modern Novelists. Carnegie Institute of Technology, Department of En, ed. LC 72-1312. (Essay Index Reprint Ser.). 1977. reprint ed. 18.95 (*0-8369-2835-0*) Ayer.

Broesamle, John J. Reform & Reaction in Twentieth Century American Politics, 137. LC 89-11751. (Contributions in American History Ser.: No. 137). 500p. 1990. 75.00 (*0-313-26799-5*, BTB/, Greenwood Pr) Greenwood.

Broesch, James D. Practical Programmable Circuits: A Guide to PLDs, State Machines, & Microcontrollers. (Illus.). 286p. (C). 1991. text 65.00 (*0-12-134885-7*) Acad Pr.

Broesch, James O. Digital Signal Processing Demystified. LC 97-70388. (Illus.). 232p. 1997. pap. 49.95 incl. cd-rom (*1-878707-16-7*) LLH Tech Pub.

Broeske, Pat H., jt. auth. see Brown, Peter Harry.

Broeze, Frank. Containerisation: The Globalisation of Liner Shipping. 270p. 1999. 110.00 (*0-7103-0652-0*, Pub. by Kegan Paul Intl) Col U Pr.

— Island Nation: A History of Australians & the Sea. 304p. 1998. pap. 24.95 (*1-86448-424-1*, Pub. by Allen & Unwin Pty) Paul & Co Pubs.

— Mr. Brooks & the Australian Trade: Imperial Business in the Nineteenth Century. 384p. 1993. 49.95 (*0-522-84574-6*, Pub. by Melbourne Univ Pr) Paul & Co Pubs.

Broeze, Frank, ed. Gateways of Asia: Port Cities of Asia in the 13th-20th Centuries. 320p. 1996. 110.00 (*0-7103-0554-0*, Pub. by Kegan Paul Intl) Col U Pr.

— Private Enterprise, Government & Society. (Studies in Western Australian History: Vol. XIII). pap. 20.00 (*0-86422-206-8*, Pub. by Univ of West Aust Pr) Intl Spec Bk.

Broeze, Frank J., ed. & tr. see Boelan, Jacobus.

Brofka, Maria A. & Bowers, Maria. Benvenuti All' Italiano: Activity Book. (ITA., Illus.). 120p. (YA). (gr. 7-9). 1994. student ed. 12.95 (*0-9645107-1-5*) Cima Publ.

***Brogan, Brian.** The Hailing Light of Bees: Surreal Poems. 88p. 1999. pap. 10.00 (*1-881604-49-7*) Scopcraeft.

Brogan, D. W. American Character. 1990. 16.50 (*0-8446-1746-6*) Peter Smith.

— Development of Modern France 1870-1939, Vol. 2. rev. ed. 1990. 18.50 (*0-8446-0515-8*) Peter Smith.

Brogan, Daniel. FullWrite Professional: Power Word Processing. (Illus.). 256p. (Orig.). 1989. pap. 17.60 (*0-8306-3163-1*) McGraw-Hill Prof.

Brogan, David, et al, eds. Visual Search Two. 448p. 1993. 125.00 (*0-7484-0010-9*, Pub. by Tay Francis Ltd) Taylor & Francis.

Brogan, Denis W. America in the Modern World. LC 79-25851. 117p. 1980. reprint ed. lib. bdg. 55.00 (*0-313-22254-1*, BRAW, Greenwood Pr) Greenwood.

— American Themes. (History - United States Ser.). 284p. 1993. reprint ed. lib. bdg. 79.00 (*0-7812-4847-7*) Rprt Serv.

— U. S. A., an Outline of the Country, Its People & Institutions. (History - United States Ser.). 143p. 1993. reprint ed. lib. bdg. 69.00 (*0-7812-4850-7*) Rprt Serv.

Brogan, Hugh. All Honorable Men: Huey Long, Robert Moses, Estes Kefauver, Richard J. Daley. LC 92-39809. 352p. 2000. 25.00 (*0-19-507502-1*) OUP.

— History of the U.S.A. 1991. pap. 17.95 (*0-14-013460-3*) Viking Penguin.

Brogan, Hugh. Kennedy. (Profiles in Power Ser.). 249p. (C). 1997. 75.00 (*0-582-02889-2*) Addison-Wesley.

Brogan, J. C. Nitrogen Losses & Surface Run-Off from Landspreading of Manures: Proceedings of a Workshop in the EEC Programme of Co-Ordination & Research on Effluents from Livestock. 487p. 1981. text 141.50 (*90-247-2471-6*) Kluwer Academic.

Brogan, Jacqueline V. Part of the Climate: American Cubist Poetry. LC 90-34743. 290p. 1990. 60.00 (*0-520-06848-3*, Pub. by U CA Pr) Cal Prin Full Svc.

Brogan, Jacqueline V., et al, eds. Women Poets of the Americas: Toward a Pan-American Gathering. LC 98-45417. 312p. 1999. pap. 27.00 (*0-268-01955-X*) U of Notre Dame Pr.

Brogan, Jacqueline V. & Candelaria, Cordelia C., eds. Women Poets of the Americas: Toward a Pan-American Gathering. LC 98-45417. 312p. 1999. 50.00 (*0-268-01956-8*) U of Notre Dame Pr.

Brogan, James. Light in Architecture. (Architectural Design Ser.: Vol. 126). (Illus.). 112p. (Orig.). 1997. pap. 29.95 (*1-85490-501-5*) Academy Ed UK.

Brogan, James A., jt. auth. see Wolff, William H., Jr.

Brogan, Jim. Casey: The Bi-Coastal Kid. LC 81-69478. 175p. (Orig.). 1986. pap. 7.95 (*0-941362-01-9*) Equanimity.

— A Time to Live. LC 97-174893. 235p. (Orig.). 1997. pap. 13.95 (*1-879194-22-8*) GLB Pubs.

Brogan, John A. Clear Technical Writing. (C). 1973. text 66.80 (*0-07-007974-9*) McGraw.

— Grab Your Readers' Attention & Hold It for Powerful Government, Technical & Business Writing: Learn Interactively the Six Guidelines for Dynamic Instructions, E-Mail, Reports, Letters. (Illus.). viii, 220p. 1998. pap. 49.95 (*0-9660754-0-4*, 1007) Brogan Clear-Writing.

Brogan, Joseph, jt. auth. see Bland, Randall W.

Brogan, Joseph V., jt. auth. see Bland, Randall Walton.

Brogan, Kathleen. Cultural Haunting: Ghosts & Ethnicity in Recent American Literature. LC 98-8419. 224p. 1999. 39.50 (*0-8139-1826-X*); pap. 16.50 (*0-8139-1827-8*) U Pr of Va.

Brogan, Martha L., compiled by. Research Guide to Libraries & Archives in the Low Countries, 5. LC 91-12598. (Bibliographies & Indexes in Library & Information Science: No. 5). 560p. 1991. lib. bdg. 99.50 (*0-313-25466-4*, BNR, Greenwood Pr) Greenwood.

Brogan, Meg, et al. No Problem. 50p. 1996. pap. 3.50 (*0-87129-683-7*, N43) Dramatic Pub.

***Brogan, Mike.** Business to Kill For. 2000. 19.95 (*0-615-11570-5*) Lghthse MI.

Brogan, Patricia B. Above the Waves' Calligraphy: A Collection of Poems & Etchings. (Illus.). 112p. 1995. pap. 19.95 (*1-897648-23-5*, Pub. by Poolbeg Pr) Dufour.

— Eclipsed. 80p. 1995. pap. 14.95 (*1-897648-34-0*) Dufour.

Brogan, Patrick. The Captive Nations: Eastern Europe, 1945-1990. 1990. pap. 8.95 (*0-380-76304-4*, Avon Bks) Morrow Avon.

***Brogan, Patrick.** Introducing American Politics. 176p. 1999. pap. 10.95 (*1-84046-098-9*, TOTM) Topaz Maps.

Brogan, Patrick. Spiked: The Short Life & Death of the National News Council - A Twentieth Century Fund Paper. 129p. 1985. pap. text 8.00 (*0-87078-162-6*) Century Foundation.

— World Conflicts: A Comprehensive Guide to World Strife since 1945. 600p. 1999. text 49.50 (*0-8108-3551-7*) Scarecrow.

Brogan, Patrick, jt. auth. see Milano, James V.

Brogan, Peggy, ed. see Domjan, Evelyn A.

Brogan, Roy. A Signature of Power & Patronage: The Medici Coat of Arms, 1299-1492. LC 93-25229. (Currents in Comparative Romance Languages & Literatures Ser.: Vol. 20). (Illus.). 349p. (C). 1994. text 49.95 (*0-8204-2213-4*) P Lang Pubng.

Brogan, T., ed. The Princeton Handbook of Multicultural Poetries. 352p. 1996. text 49.50 (*0-691-01089-7*, Pub. by Princeton U Pr) Cal Prin Full Svc.

Brogan, T. V. Verseform: A Comparative Bibliography. LC 88-45406. 160p. (C). 1989. text 32.50 (*0-8018-3362-0*) Johns Hopkins.

Brogan, T. V., ed. The New Princeton Handbook of Poetic Terms. LC 93-43944. 360p. (C). 1994. text 49.50 (*0-691-03671-3*, Pub. by Princeton U Pr); pap. text 18.95 (*0-691-03672-1*, Pub. by Princeton U Pr) Cal Prin Full Svc.

— The Princeton Handbook of Multicultural Poetries. LC 95-30610. 352p. (C). 1996. pap. text 18.95 (*0-691-00168-5*, Pub. by Princeton U Pr) Cal Prin Full Svc.

Brogan, T. V., jt. ed. see Preminger, Alex.

Brogan, Terry V. English Versification, 1570-1980: A Reference Guide with a Global Appendix. LC 80-8861. 824p. reprint ed. pap. 200.00 (*0-7837-2653-8*, 204300700006) Bks Demand.

— The New Princeton Handbook of Poetic Terms. LC 93-43944. 355p. 1994. reprint ed. pap. 110.10 (*0-608-07173-0*, 206739800009) Bks Demand.

***Brogan, Walter & Risser, James.** American Continental Philosophy: A Reader. LC 99-88427. (Illus.). 464p. 2000. lib. bdg. 45.00 (*0-253-33729-1*) Ind U Pr.

***Brogan, Walter & Risser, James, eds.** American Continental Philosophy: A Reader. LC 99-88427. (Studies in Continental Thought). (Illus.). 464p. 2000. pap. 19.95 (*0-253-21376-2*) Ind U Pr.

Brogan, Walter, tr. see Heidegger, Martin & Aristotle.

Brogan, Walter J. Donuts Aren't Ughly Eny Mor: Simpler Spelling for th 2000z. xii, 132p. 1997. 18.00 (*0-9658595-0-9*); pap. 8.00 (*0-9658595-1-7*) R P Mudgett.

Brogan, Whit. The Work of Placement Officers in Teacher Training Institutions. LC 79-176593. (Columbia University. Teachers College. Contributions to Education Ser.: No. 434). reprint ed. 37.50 (*0-404-55434-2*) AMS Pr.

Brogan, William L. Modern Control Theory. 3rd ed. 736p. 1990. 105.00 (*0-13-589763-7*) P-H.

Brogden, John V., jt. ed. see Crowson, Noel.

Brogden, Michael. On the Mersey Beat: Policing Liverpool Between the Wars. 192p. 1991. 32.00 (*0-19-825430-X*) OUP.

— The Police: Autonomy & Consent. (Law, State & Society Ser.). 1983. text 109.00 (*0-12-135180-7*) Acad Pr.

Brogden, Michael & Shearing, Clifford D. Policing for a New South Africa. LC 92-47078. 256p. (C). (gr. 13). 1997. 85.00 (*0-415-08321-4*) Routledge.

***Brogden, Mike & Nijhar, Preeti.** Crime, Abuse & the Elderly. 200p. 2000. 67.50 (*1-903240-03-4*, Pub. by Willan Pubg); pap. 25.50 (*1-903240-02-6*, Pub. by Willan Pubg) Intl Spec Bk.

Brogden, Mike & Nijhar, Saranjit. Crime & the Elderly. (Longman Criminology Series). 224p. 1998. pap. 24.50 (*0-582-30597-7*) Gaunt.

Brogden, Stanley. Sky Diggers: Aces of the R. A. A. F. 1944. 15.00 (*0-913076-02-3*) Beachcomber Bks.

Brogden, W. A. Aberdeen: An Illustrated Architectural Guide. (Illus.). 152p. (C). 1986. pap. 40.00 (*1-873190-26-3*, Pub. by Rutland Pr) St Mut.

Brogdon, B. G. Forensic Radiology. LC 97-43645. 1998. lib. bdg. 84.95 (*0-8493-8105-3*) CRC Pr.

Brogdon, Bill. Boat Navigation for the Rest of Us: Finding Your Way by Eye & Electronics. 1995. pap. 18.95 (*0-07-008164-6*) Intl Marine.

— Java 2 Exam Cram: Exam 310-025. LC 98-26340. (Exam Cram Ser.). (Illus.). 388p. 1999. pap. 29.99 (*1-57610-291-2*) Coriolis Grp.

Brogdon, Jennie L. & Olsen, Wallace C., eds. The Contemporary & Historical Literature of Food Science & Human Nutrition. (Literature of the Agricultural Sciences Ser.). 304p. 1995. text 75.00 (*0-8014-3096-8*) Cornell U Pr.

Brogdon, Philip R. Sherlock in Black. (Illus.). 29p. (Orig.). 1995. pap. 8.00 (*1-896032-45-1*) Battered Silicon.

***Brogen, Kim A.** Virulence Mechanisms of Bacterial Pathogens. 3rd rev. ed. 384p. 2000. 84.95 (*1-55581-174-4*) ASM Pr.

Broger, Achim. The Day Chubby Became Charles. Cañero, Renee V., tr. from GER. LC 89-13112. (Illus.). 96p. (J). (gr. 2-5). 1990. 12.95 (*0-397-32144-9*); lib. bdg. 12.89 (*0-397-32145-7*) HarpC Child Bks.

— Fantasmas Escolares (School Ghosts) Arruti, Maria O., tr. (SPA.). (J). (gr. 5-6). 1994. pap. 5.99 (*968-16-4591-X*, Pub. by Fondo) Continental Bk.

Broger, Achim & Duden Editorial Staff. Kinderduden. 192p. 1994. 17.50 (*3-411-04494-2*, Pub. by Bibliogr Inst Brockhaus) Langenscheidt.

Broger, John C. Instructor's Guide for the Self-Confrontation Course. 1992. text 15.00 (*1-878114-02-6*) Biblical Counseling.

— Self-Confrontation: Syllabus for Biblical Counseling Training Program, Course I. 2nd rev. ed. 1992. pap. text 24.95 (*1-878114-01-8*) Biblical Counseling.

Brogger, A. W. Nazare. (C). 1997. pap. text 19.00 (*0-15-504381-1*) Harcourt Coll Pubs.

Brogger, Jan. Nazare: Men & Women in a Prebureaucratic Portuguese Village. Spindler, Louise S. & Spindler, George D., eds. LC 91-32074. (Spindler Ser. (Anthropology)). (Illus.). xii, 135p. (C). 1992. pap. text 13.50 (*0-03-043382-7*) Harcourt Coll Pubs.

B

An Asterisk (*) at the beginning of an entry indicates that the title is appearing for the first time.

Brogger, Suzanne & Allemano, Marina. A Fighting Pig's Too Tough to Eat. LC 97-179081. 282p. 1997. pap. 19.95 (*1-870041-35-6*, Pub. by Norvik Pr) Dufour.

Brogger, Yoli, jt. auth. see Barnes, Emilie.

Broggi, Alberto, et al. Argo Autonomous Vehicle. 250p. 1999. pap. text 26.00 (*981-02-3721-9*) World Scientific Pub.

Broggi, G., ed. Craniopharyngioma: Surgical Treatment. (Illus.). 160p. 1995. pap. 102.00 (*4-431-75001-0*) Spr-Verlag.

Broggi, G., et al, eds. Advances in Stereotactic & Functional Neurosurgery, Vol. 8. (Illus.). 130p. 1989. 112.00 (*0-387-82120-1*) Spr-Verlag.

Broggi, Giovanni. The Rational Basis for the Surgical Treatment of Epilepsy. (Current Problems in Epilepsy Ser.: Vol. 5). 350p. 1986. 64.95 (*0-86196-099-8*, Pub. by J Libbey Med) Bks Intl VA.

Broggie, Michael. Walt Disney's Railroad Story: The Small-Scale Fascination That Led to a Full-Scale Kingdom. 2nd ed. LC 98-33742. (Illus.). 432p. 1998. 59.95 (*1-56342-009-0*, B926) Pentrex Media.

Broghamer, E. L., jt. auth. see Dolan, T. J.

Broghaus-Ephron. Entsiklopedicheskii Slovar, 86 vols., Set. (GER.). reprint ed. 2500.00 (*0-317-05091-5*) Szwede Slavic.

— Jewish Encyclopedia (Evreiskaia Entsiklopedia), 16 vols., Set. (RUS.). 1981. reprint ed. 560.00 (*0-317-05090-7*) Szwede Slavic.

— Rossiia-Entsiklopedicheski Slovar. 874p. reprint ed. 75.00 (*0-317-05089-3*) Szwede Slavic.

Brogiato, Heinz P. Tschechoslowakei - Tschechien - Slowakei: Literatur in Westlichen Sprachen, 1975-1995. (Wiener Osteuropa Studien: Band 6). (GER.). 511p. 1997. pap. 73.95 (*3-631-32654-8*) P Lang Pubng.

Brogila, Ricardo A., et al, eds. Nuclear Structure, 1985: Proceeding of the Niels Bohr Centennial Conference, Copenhagen, Denmark, May 20-25, 1985, Set. 614p. 1985. 146.00 (*0-317-38671-9*, North Holland) Elsevier.

Brogila, Ricardo A. & Bertsch, G., eds. The Response of Nuclei under Extreme Conditions. LC 87-32747. (Ettore Majorana International Science Series, Life Sciences: Vol. 28). (Illus.). 422p. 1988. 95.00 (*0-306-42571-8*, Plenum Trade) Perseus Pubng.

Brogila, Ricardo A. & Winther, Aage. Heavy Ion Reactions, Pts. I & II. (Frontiers in Physics Advanced Book Program Ser.: Vol. 84). (Illus.). 528p. (C). 1990. text 49.50 (*0-685-47207-8*) Addison-Wesley.

Brogila, Ricardo A., jt. auth. see Bertsch, George F.

Brogiolo, Gian P. & Ward-Perkins, Bryan. The Idea & Ideal of the Town Between Late Antiquity & the Early Middle Ages. LC 98-52661. (Transformation of the Roman World Ser.). 1999. write for info. (*90-04-10901-3*) Brill Academic Pubs.

***Brogiolo, G. P., et al, eds.** Towns & Their Territories Between Late Antiquity & the Early Middle Ages. (Transformation of the Roman World Ser.). 406p. 2000. text 125.00 (*90-04-11869-1*) Brill Academic Pubs.

Broglia, Fabrizio, ed. Lectures in Real Geometry. LC 96-31731. (Expositions in Mathematics Ser.: Vol. 23). xiv, 268p. (C). 1996. lib. bdg. 98.95 (*3-11-015095-6*) De Gruyter.

Broglia, Fabrizio, et al, eds. Real Analytic & Algebraic Geometry: Proceedings of the International Conference on Real Analytic & Algebraic Geometry (1992: Trento, Italy) LC 94-42179. 294p. (C). 1995. 129.95 (*3-11-013778-X*) De Gruyter.

Broglia, Ricardo A. Heavy on Physics - Probing the Nuclear Paradigm: Proceedings of the International School. (Science & Culture Series - Physics). 532p. 1995. text 104.00 (*981-02-1886-9*) World Scientific Pub.

Broglia, Ricardo A., et al, eds. Perspectives in Many-Particle Physics: Varenna on Lake Como, Villa Monastero, 7-17 July 1992. LC 94-6889. (Proceedings of the International School of Physics "Enrico Fermi" Ser.: Vol.121). 306p. 1994. 184.00 (*0-444-82004-3*, North Holland) Elsevier.

Broglia, Ricardo A. & Hansen, P. Gregers, eds. Exotic Nuclei: Proceedings of the 4th Course of the International School of Heavy Ion Physics Erice, Italy 11 - 20 May 1997. LC 98-216892. (Science & Culture Ser.). 400p. 1998. 86.00 (*981-02-3444-9*) World Scientific Pub.

Brogliato, Bernard. Nonsmooth Impact Mechanics: Models, Dynamics, & Control. LC 96-26963. (Lecture Notes in Control & Information Sciences: Vol. 220). 400p. 1996. pap. 76.00 (*3-540-76079-2*) Spr-Verlag.

— Nonsmooth Mechanics: Models, Dynamics & Control. 2nd ed. Dickinson, B. W. et al, eds. LC 98-53322. xx, 556p. 1999. 119.00 (*1-85233-143-7*) Spr-Verlag.

Broglie, Louis De, see De Broglie, Louis.

Broglie, M. & Smith, D. Gear Hardness Technology. (1991 Fall Technical Meeting Ser.: Vol. 91FTM15). (Illus.). 12p. 1991. pap. text 30.00 (*1-55589-612-X*) AGMA.

Broglin, Jana. Roster of Ohio Soldiers in the Mexican War. 1991. 25.00 (*0-935057-63-3*) OH Genealogical.

Broglin, Jana, compiled by. Ohio Records & Pioneer Families: Surname Index, 1985-1994. 1996. per. 15.00 (*0-935057-83-8*) OH Genealogical.

Brogno, Karen, jt. ed. see Umbaugh, Robert E.

Brogran, Patrick, jt. auth. see Milano, James V.

Brogyany, Gabriel J., tr. see Diderot, Denis.

Brogyanyi, Bela, ed. Prehistory, History, & Historiography of Language, Speech, & Linguistic Theory: Papers in Honor of Oswald Szemerenyi I. LC 92-8921. (Current Issues in Linguistic Theory Ser.: No. 64). x, 414p. 1992. 124.00 (*1-55619-064-6*) J Benjamins Pubng Co.

— Studies in Diachronic, Synchronic & Typological Linguistics: Festschrift for Oswald Szemerenyi on the Occasion of His 65th Birthday, 2 vols., Set. (Current Issues in Linguistic Theory Ser.: No. 11). 1979. 177.00 (*90-272-3504-X*) J Benjamins Pubng Co.

Brogyanyi, Bela & Krommelbein, Thomas, eds. Germanic Dialects: Linguistic & Philological Investigations. LC 86-8213. (Current Issues in Linguistic Theory Ser.: No. 38). ix, 693p. 1986. 140.00 (*90-272-3526-0*) J Benjamins Pubng Co.

Brogyanyi, Bela & Lipp, Reiner, eds. Comparative-Historical Linguistics: Indo-European & Finno-Ugric Papers in Honour of Oswald Szemerenyi III. LC 92-45266. (Current Issues in Linguistic Theory Ser.: No. 97). xii, 566p. 1993. 148.00 (*1-55619-159-6*) J Benjamins Pubng Co.

— Historical Philology. Greek, Latin & Romance: Papers in Honour of Oswald Szemerenyi II. LC 92-20724. (Current Issues in Linguistic Theory Ser.: No. 87). xii, 386p. 1992. 112.00 (*1-55619-144-8*) J Benjamins Pubng Co.

Brogyanyi, Bela, jt. ed. see Untermann, Jurgen.

Brogyanyi, Eugene. DramaContemporary: Hungary. 1991. 34.50 (*1-55554-053-8*); pap. 16.95 (*1-55554-054-6*) PAJ Pubns.

Brohaugh, Bill & Lucyszyn, Andrew, eds. 2000 Writer's Market--The Electronic Edition: Instant Access to 8,000 Editors Who Buy What You Write. LC 31-20772. 1120p. 1999. pap. 49.99 incl. cd-rom (*0-89879-916-3*, 10614, Wrtrs Digest Bks) F & W Pubns Inc.

Brohaugh, Catherine, ed. see Wolfe, J. Kevin.

Brohaugh, William. English Through the Ages. LC 97-40771. 608p. 1998. 24.99 (*0-89879-655-5*, Wrtrs Digest Bks) F & W Pubns Inc.

Brohawn, Dawn K., ed. see ESOP Association Staff.

Brohi, A. K. Iqbal & the Concept of Islamic Socialism. 1984. pap. 3.00 (*1-56744-061-4*) Kazi Pubns.

— Islam in the Modern World. 322p. 1992. 29.50 (*0-933511-18-3*) Kazi Pubns.

Brohl, Kathryn. Working with Traumatized Children: A Handbook for Healing. LC 96-24093. 105p. 1996. pap. 19.95 (*0-87868-633-9*) Child Welfare.

Brohl, Kathryn & Case, Joyce. When Your Child Has Been Molested: A Parent's Guide to Healing & Recovery. LC 97-38475. 190p. 1998. pap. 14.95 (*0-7879-4073-9*) Jossey-Bass.

Brohman, James. Popular Development: Rethinking the Theory & Practice of Development. LC 95-42639. 352p. (C). 1996. 66.95 (*1-55786-315-6*); pap. text 28.95 (*1-55786-316-4*) Blackwell Pubs.

Brohmer, J. Urgen. State Immunity & the Violation of Human Rights, Vol. ISHR 47. LC 96-47876. (International Studies in Human Rights). 1997. 107.00 (*90-411-0322-8*) Kluwer Law Intl.

Broich, Ulrich. The Eighteenth-Century Mock-Heroic Poem. Wilson, David H., tr. (European Studies in English Literature). 298p. (C). 1990. text 69.95 (*0-521-30965-4*) Cambridge U Pr.

Broida, H. P., jt. ed. see Badash, Lawrence.

***Broida, Marian.** The Ancient Egyptians & Their Neighbors: An Activity Guide. LC 99-22707. (Illus.). 186p. (YA). (gr. 4-8). 1999. pap. 16.95 (*1-55652-360-2*) Chicago Review.

— Natural Treatments for Insomnia. (Natural Pharmacist Ser.). 2000. pap. 9.99 (*0-7615-3011-8*) Prima Pub.

***Broida, Peter.** A Guide to Federal Labor Relations Authority Law & Practice: 2000 Edition. 13th ed. 2800p. 2000. pap. 250.00 (*1-878810-58-8*) Dewey Pubns.

— A Guide to Merit Systems Protection Board Law & Practice: 2000 Edition. annuals 17th ed. 3374p. 2000. pap. 275.00 (*1-878810-57-X*) Dewey Pubns.

Broide, Deborah, jt. auth. see Fox, Molly.

Broido, Bing. Spalding Book of Rules. rev. ed. (Illus.). 352p. 1993. pap. 14.95 (*0-940279-82-7*, Mstrs Pr) NTC Contemp Pub Co.

— Spalding Book of Rules. 3rd rev. ed. LC 97-44547. 448p. 1997. pap. 14.95 (*1-57028-149-1*, 81491H, Mstrs Pr) NTC Contemp Pub Co.

Broido, Ethel, tr. see Gil, Moshe.

Broido, Lucy, jt. auth. see Cheret, Jules.

***Broido, Vera.** Daughter of Revolution. 224p. 1999. 35.00 (*0-09-479110-4*, Pub. by Constable & Co) Trafalgar.

Broikos, Chrysanthe B., jt. ed. see Albrecht, Donald.

Broili, June. Church's Greenland Odyssey. unabridged ed. Oliver, Sally, ed. (Illus.). 92p. 1997. pap. 16.95 (*0-9615557-6-9*) Anthony Pr NV.

— Easy Cookin' in Nevada & Tales of the Sagebrush State. 2nd rev. ed. (Illus.). 208p. 1985. 24.00 (*0-9615557-3-4*, TX 1-519-376) Anthony Pr NV.

— Easy Cookin' in Nevada & Tales of the Sagebrush State. 4th ed. (Illus.). 210p. 1995. reprint ed. pap. 19.95 (*0-9615557-5-0*) Anthony Pr NV.

Broin. In Great Haste: Letters of Mich. 256p. 1998. text 39.95 (*0-7171-2398-7*) St Martin.

Broinowski, Alison. The Yellow Lady: Australian Impressions of Asia. (Illus.). 280p. 1994. reprint ed. pap. 26.00 (*0-19-553452-2*) OUP.

Brok, Rolv, ed. see SDL Forum Staff.

Brokate, Martin. Functional Analysis with Current Applications in Science, Technology & Industry. 1997. 73.95 (*0-582-31260-4*, Pub. by Addison-Wesley) Longman.

— Functional Analysis with Current Applications in Science, Technology & Industry. 5th ed. 1998. write for info. (*0-201-36042-X*) Addison-Wesley.

Brokate, Martin & Sprekels, J. Hysteresis & Phase Transitions. 357p. 1996. 64.95 (*0-387-94763-9*) Spr-Verlag.

Brokate, Martin & Visintin, Augusto, eds. Phase Transitions & Hysteresis. LC 94-22894. (Lecture Notes in Mathematics Ser.). 1994. 62.00 (*0-387-58386-6*) Spr-Verlag.

Brokate, Martin, et al. Phase Transitions & Hysteresis. Visintin, Augusto, ed. LC 94-22894. (Lecture Notes in Mathematics Ser.: Vol. 1584). 1994. 52.95 (*3-540-58386-6*) Spr-Verlag.

Brokaw. Skippy Peanut Butter Birthday Party Book. 1993. per. 5.00 (*0-671-88649-5*, Fireside) S&S Trade Pap.

***Brokaw, Brian.** Pokemon Trading Card Game Player's Guide. (Illus.). (YA). 2000. pap. 12.95 (*1-884364-53-5*) Sandwich Islands.

***Brokaw, Brian & Arnold, J. Douglas.** Pokemon Trading Card Game - Fossil Expansion - Player's Guide Vol. 2: Fossil Expansion & Japanese Card. (Illus.). 144p. 2000. pap. 12.95 (*1-884364-39-X*, Pub. by Sandwich Islands) Login Pubs Consort.

Brokaw, Brian, jt. auth. see Arnold, J Douglas.

Brokaw, Cynthia J. The Ledgers of Merit & Demerit: Social Change & Moral Order in Late Imperial China. LC 90-9059. 299p. reprint ed. pap. 92.70 (*0-608-09112-X*, 206974400005) Bks Demand.

Brokaw, Leslie, ed. 301 Great Management Ideas from America's Most Innovative Small Companies. 2nd rev. ed. 360p. 1997. pap. 14.95 (*1-880394-21-9*) Thomson Learn.

Brokaw, Lynn, jt. auth. see Walker, Velma.

Brokaw, Meredith. The Penny Whistle Any Day Is a Holiday Book. 1996. 25.50 (*0-684-83192-9*) S&S Trade.

— The Penny Whistle Every Day Is a Holiday Party Book. LC 96-15083. 256p. 1996. pap. 13.00 (*0-684-80917-6*) S&S Trade.

Brokaw, Meredith & Gilbar, Annie. The Penny Whistle Birthday Party Book. (Illus.). 256p. (Orig.). 1992. per. 14.00 (*0-671-73795-3*) S&S Trade.

— The Penny Whistle Christmas Party Book: Including Hanukkah, New Year's, & Twelfth Night Family Parties. (Illus.). 128p. (Orig.). 1991. per. 13.00 (*0-671-73794-5*, Fireside) S&S Trade Pap.

— The Penny Whistle Halloween Book. (Illus.). 80p. 1991. per. 11.00 (*0-671-73791-0*, Fireside) S&S Trade Pap.

— The Penny Whistle Lunch Box Book. (Illus.). 96p. 1991. pap. 11.00 (*0-671-73793-7*, Fireside) S&S Trade Pap.

— The Penny Whistle Party Planner. (Illus.). 256p. 1991. per. 13.00 (*0-671-73792-9*, Fireside) S&S Trade Pap.

— The Penny Whistle Sick-in-Bed Book: What to Do with Kids When They're Home for a Day, a Week, a Month or More. LC 92-44300. (Illus.). 160p. 1993. pap. 12.00 (*0-671-78691-1*, Fireside) S&S Trade Pap.

— The Penny Whistle Traveling with Kids Book: Whether by Boat, Train, Car, or Plane - How to Take the Best Trip Ever with Kids of All Ages. LC 94-3604. (Illus.). 160p. 1995. 24.50 (*0-671-88135-3*, Fireside) S&S Trade Pap.

Brokaw, Nancy Steele. Leaving Emma. LC 98-22688. 144p. (J). (gr. 4-7). 1999. 15.00 (*0-395-90699-7*, Clarion Bks) HM.

Brokaw, Tom. Can We Get Along. 1992. write for info. (*1-55614-134-3*) U of SD Gov Res Bur.

— The Greatest Generation. 352p. 1998. 24.95 (*0-375-50202-5*) Random.

— The Greatest Generation. large type ed. LC 98-45842. (Illus.). 511p. 1998. pap. 24.95 (*0-375-70569-4*) Random.

***Brokaw, Tom.** The Greatest Generation Speaks: Letters & Reflections. 288p. 1999. 19.95 (*0-375-50394-3*) Random.

— The Greatest Generation Speaks: Letters & Reflections. large type ed. 288p. 1999. 19.95 (*0-375-40922-X*) Random.

Broke, Arthur. Brooke's Romeus & Juliet, Being the Original of Shakespeare's Romeo & Juliet. Munro, J. J., ed. LC 74-134609. reprint ed. 21.50 (*0-404-04539-1*) AMS Pr.

— The Tragicall Historye of Romeus & Juliet. LC 78-26035. (English Experience Ser.: No. 134). 168p. 1969. reprint ed. 21.00 (*90-221-0134-7*) Walter J Johnson.

Brokenleg, Martin & Hoover, Herbert T. Yanktonai Sioux Water Colors: Cultural Remembrances of John Saul. (Illus.). 66p. 1992. 12.95 (*0-931170-53-2*) Ctr Western Studies.

Brokenmouth, Robert. Nick Cave: The Birthday Party & Other Epic Adventures. (Illus.). 96p. (Orig.). 1996. pap. 17.95 (*0-7119-5601-4*, OP47826) Omnibus NY.

Brokensha, David, ed. A River of Blessings: Essays in Honor of Paul Baxter. LC 94-3061. (Foreign & Comparative Studies, African Ser.: Vol. 44). 1994. write for info. (*0-915984-69-5*) Maxwell Schl Citizen.

Brokensha, David, et al. The Cultural Dimension of Development: Indigenous Knowledge Systems. 640p. 1995. pap. 39.95 (*1-85339-251-0*, Pub. by Intermed Tech); text 75.00 (*1-85339-264-2*, Pub. by Intermed Tech) Stylus Pub VA.

Brokensha, David, jt. auth. see Riley, Bernard W.

Brokenshire, Doug. Washington State Place Names: From Alki to Yelm. LC 93-18926. 336p. (Orig.). 1993. pap. 14.95 (*0-87004-356-0*) Caxton.

Broker, Ignatia. Night Flying Woman: An Ojibway Narrative. LC 83-13360. (Illus.). xiv, 135p. (Orig.). 1983. pap. 9.50 (*0-87351-167-0*) Minn Hist.

Brokering, Herb. Angels Love Children: Stories, Poems & Prayers to Share. LC 97-44721. 128p. 1997. pap. 10.99 (*0-8066-3333-6*, 9-3333, Augsburg) Augsburg Fortress.

— Wholly Holy. 96p. (Orig.). 1981. pap. 3.95 (*0-942562-00-3*) Brokering Pr.

Brokering, Herbert. Love, Dad: Letters of Faith to My Children. LC 98-9577. 1998. pap. text 10.99 (*0-8066-3619-X*, 9-3619, Augsburg) Augsburg Fortress.

— Unto Us Is Born: Christmas Conversations with the Mother of Jesus. LC 99-29517. 96p. 1999. pap. 9.99 (*0-8066-3897-4*, Augsburg) Augsburg Fortress.

Brokering, Herbert F. Hello, Night! Healing Thoughts for Sleepless Nights. LC 98-43673. 112p. 1999. pap. text 9.99 (*0-8066-3837-0*, 9-3837, Augsburg) Augsburg Fortress.

— I'm Thinking of You: Spiritual Letters of Hope & Healing. 128p. 1996. pap. 10.99 (*0-8066-1999-6*, 9-1999) Augsburg Fortress.

— The Night Before Jesus. 36p. (J). (ps-4). 1983. 7.99 (*0-570-04084-1*, 56-1439) Concordia.

Brokering, Herbert F., ed. Luther's Prayers. LC 94-24889. 1994. pap. 10.99 (*0-8066-2755-7*, 9-2755, Augsburg) Augsburg Fortress.

Brokering, Lois. Rainbow Bags: Instructions for Making Six Colorful Bags of Soft Toys for a Young Child in Church. 2nd ed. (Illus.). 48p. 1990. reprint ed. pap. 7.00 (*0-8066-2256-3*) Brokering Pr.

— Resources for Dramatic Play. (J). (ps). 1990. pap. 11.99 (*0-8224-5811-X*) Fearon Teacher Aids.

Brokhoff, Barbara. Grapes of Wrath or Grace? Sermons for Pentecost, First Third - First Lesson. LC 94-1002. (Orig.). 1994. pap. 9.75 (*0-7880-0035-7*) CSS OH.

Brokhoff, John. Lectionary Preaching Workbook, Cycle B. 1984. pap. 28.75 (*0-89536-645-2*) CSS OH.

Brokhoff, John R. Grace Words from the Cross. 1991. pap. 5.75 (*1-55673-382-8*, 9200) CSS OH.

— Lectionary Preaching Workbook: Revised for Use with Revised Common, Episcopal, Luterhan, & Roman Catholic Lectionaries, Small Version, Series IV, Cycle B. LC 93-5725. 1993. wbk. ed. 23.95 (*1-55673-624-X*, 9349) CSS OH.

— Pray Like Jesus: Sermons & Bible Study on Prayer. LC 94-227. (Orig.). 1994. pap. 14.50 (*0-7880-0105-1*) CSS OH.

— This You Can Believe: Faith Seeking Understanding, Vol. 2. LC 98-48040. 238p. 1999. pap. 19.95 (*0-7880-1333-5*) CSS OH.

— This You Can Believe: Participant. (Orig.). 1987. pap. 2.75 (*0-89536-893-5*, 7879) CSS OH.

— Wrinkled Wrappings: Sermons for Advent & Christmas. 1995. 8.75 (*0-7880-0700-9*) CSS OH.

Brokke, Cees. Beware the Bequest. 261p. Date not set. mass mkt. 4.99 (*1-55197-090-2*) Picasso Publ.

Brokken, Jan. The Rainbird: A Central African Journey. Garrett, Sam, tr. from DUT. (Illus.). 300p. 1997. pap. 10.95 (*0-86442-469-8*) Lonely Planet.

Brokmeyer, Ron, et al. The Fetish of High Tech & Karl Marx's Unknown Mathematical Manuscripts. 28p. 1985. pap. 1.00 (*0-914441-25-6*) News & Letters.

Brokmeyer, Ron, jt. auth. see Moon, Terry.

Brokoph-Mauch, Gudrun, ed. Thunder Rumbling at My Heels: Tracing Ingeborg Bachmann. LC 97-13187. (Studies in Austrian Literature, Culture & Thought). 224p. 1998. 29.50 (*1-57241-043-4*) Ariadne CA.

***Brokopp, John G.** Thrifty Gambling: More Casino Fun for Less Risk. 175p. 2000. pap. 13.95 (*1-56625-150-8*) Bonus Books.

Brolander, Glen E. An Historical Survey of the Augustana College Campus. rev. ed. 125p. 1992. pap. 15.00 (*0-910184-41-0*) Augustana.

***Brolin, Brent C.** Architectural Ornament. LC 99-88788. (Illus.). 304p. 2000. pap. 26.95 (*0-393-73046-8*) Norton.

Brolin, Donn E. Career Education: A Functional Life Skills Approach. 3rd ed. LC 94-45749. (Illus.). 525p. 1995. 83.00 (*0-02-315062-9*, Macmillan Coll) P-H.

— Life Centered Career Education: Competency Assessment Knowledge Batteries. LC 93-11908. 152p. 1992. ring bd. 125.00 (*0-86586-239-7*, P370K) Coun Exc Child.

— Life Centered Career Education: Competency Assessment Performance Batteries. LC 93-11908. 683p. 1992. ring bd. 225.00 (*0-86586-240-0*, P370P) Coun Exc Child.

— Life Centered Career Education: Competency Units for Daily Living Skills. LC 92-17690. 1556p. 1992. ring bd. 400.00 (*0-86586-224-9*, P367) Coun Exc Child.

— Life Centered Career Education: Competency Units for Personal-Social Skills. LC 92-17680. 1348p. 1992. ring bd. 400.00 (*0-86586-225-7*, P368) Coun Exc Child.

Brolin, Donn E., ed. Exceptional Individuals: A Special Issue of Journal of Career Development. 73p. 1987. pap. 14.95 (*0-89885-370-2*, Kluwer Acad Hman Sci) Kluwer Academic.

Brolin, Donn E. & Council for Exceptional Children Staff. Life Centered Career Education: A Competency Based Approach. 5th ed. LC 97-3894. 175p. 1997. pap. text 30.00 (*0-86586-292-3*, P180G) Coun Exc Child.

Brolin, Donn E., jt. auth. see Loyd, Robert J.

Brolin, Donn E., jt. auth. see Roessler, Richard T.

Brolin, Hans, jt. auth. see Bjork, Lars-Eric.

Broll, James, ed. see Perry, Susan & O'Hanlon, Katherine.

Brollier, Chestina & Cromwell, Florence S. The Occupational Therapy Manager's Survival Handbook. LC 87-37486. (Occupational Therapy in Health Care Ser.: Vol. 5, No. 1). (Illus.). 221p. 1988. text 39.95 (*0-86656-686-4*) Haworth Pr.

Brollier, Chestina, jt. auth. see Watts, Janet H.

Brolmann, Catherine, et al, eds. Peoples & Minorities in International Law. LC 93-13379. 384p. (C). 1993. lib. bdg. 123.50 (*0-7923-2315-7*) Kluwer Academic.

Brolsma, Jody, ed. Pray & Play Bible for Young Children. LC 96-40288. 176p. (Orig.). (J). 1997. pap. 16.99 (*0-7644-2024-0*) Group Pub.

Brolsma, Jody, et al. Fun-to-Learn Bible Lessons Grades 4 & Up: 20 Easy-to-Use Programs. LC 94-49160. (J). (gr. 4 up). 1995. 16.99 (*1-55945-604-3*) Group Pub.

Brolsma, Jody, ed. see Cope, Sandy & Dillbeck, Sandy.

Brolsma, Jody, ed. see Reazin, Ruth.

Brolsma, Jody, ed. see Temple, Bonnie & Wolf, Beth R.

***Brom.** Darkwerks: The Art of Brom. (Illus.). 2000. pap. 21.95 (*1-85585-836-3*, Pub. by Paper Tiger) Sterling.

Brom, Elgar. What Earth Has Done to You: The Wisdom of Noel. Moteka, Patricia, ed. (Brom Ser.: Vol. III). (Illus.). (Orig.). (C). 1989. pap. write for info. (*0-9624381-0-3*) Masters Ink.

*Brom, Shlomo & Shapir, Yiftah, eds. The Middle East Military Balance, 1999-2000. LC 99-49269. (BCSIA Studies in International Security). (Illus.). 480p. 2000. 37.50 (0-262-02478-0) MIT Pr.

Bromage, Arthur W. A Councilman Speaks. 1951. pap. 5.00 (0-911586-04-0) Wahr.

— Councilmen at Work. 1954. pap. 5.00 (0-911586-05-9) Wahr.

— Introduction to Municipal Government & Administration. 2nd ed. LC 57-7072. (Illus.). 1957. 32.50 (0-89197-243-9) Irvington.

Bromage, Bernard. The Occult Arts of Ancient Egypt. 205p. 1996. pap. 17.00 (0-89540-219-X, SB-219) Sun Pub.

Bromage, Nial, jt. auth. see Shepherd, Jonathan.

Bromage, Niall R. & Roberts, R. J. Broodstock Management & Egg & Larval Quality. 1994. pap. 100.00 (0-632-03591-9) Blackwell Sci.

Bromage, Niall R., jt. auth. see Shepherd, C. Jonathan.

Bromage, Timothy G. & Schrenk, Friedmann, eds. African Biogeography, Climate Change & Human Evolution. LC 98-21953. (Human Evolution Ser.). (Illus.). 496p. 1999. text 115.00 (0-19-511437-X) OUP.

Broman, Arne. Introduction to Partial Differential Equations. (Illus.). 192p. 1989. pap. 6.95 (0-486-66158-X) Dover.

Broman, Mickey. Nevada Ghost Town Trails. LC 72-94635. 1989. 5.95 (0-935182-09-8) Gem Guides Bk.

Broman, Sarah H., et al, eds. Low Achieving Children: The First Seven Years. 184p. (C). 1985. text 36.00 (0-89859-637-8) L Erlbaum Assocs.

Broman, Sarah H. & Fletcher, Jack M., eds. The Changing Nervous System: Neurobehavioral Consequences of Early Brain Disorders. LC 98-45750. (Illus.). 428p. 1999. text 65.00 (0-19-512193-7) OUP.

Broman, Sarah H. & Grafman, Jordan, eds. Atypical Cognitive Deficits in Developmental Disorders: Implications for Brain Function. LC 93-12499. 352p. 1994. text 89.95 (0-8058-1180-X) L Erlbaum Assocs.

Broman, Sarah H. & Michel, Mary E., eds. Traumatic Head Injury in Children. (Illus.). 320p. 1995. text 49.50 (0-19-509428-X) OUP.

Broman, Sarah H., et al. Retardation in Young Children: A Developmental Study of Cognitive Deficit. 376p. 1987. text 69.95 (0-89859-989-X) L Erlbaum Assocs.

Broman, Sven. Chinese Shadow Theatre. (Ethnographical Museum of Sweden Monograph: No. 15). (Illus.). 250p. 1981. 83.50 (91-22-01370-9) Coronet Bks.

Broman, Thomas H. The Transformation of German Academic Medicine, 1750-1820. (Cambridge History of Medicine Ser.). 220p. (C). 1996. text 54.95 (0-521-55231-1) Cambridge U Pr.

Bromann, Mark. The Design & Layout of Fire Sprinkler Systems. LC 97-60653. 405p. 1997. pap. text 84.95 (1-56676-474-2) Technomic.

Brombacher, A. C. Reliability by Design: CAE Techniques for Electronic Components & Systems. 294p. 1992. 260.00 (0-471-93193-4) Wiley.

Bromberg, A. Y. Rebbes of Ger: Sfas emes & Imrei Emes. Kaploun, Uri, tr. from HEB. (ArtScroll History Ser.). (Illus.). 302p. 1987. 20.99 (0-89906-484-1); pap. 17.99 (0-89906-485-X) Mesorah Pubns.

Bromberg, Alan R. Partnership, 2 vols., 1. 1988. 162.50 (0-316-10927-4, Aspen Law & Bus) Aspen Pub.

— Partnership, 2 vols., 2. 1988. 162.50 (0-316-10928-2, Aspen Law & Bus) Aspen Pub.

— Partnership, Chapter 5. 1991. 75.00 (0-316-10937-1, Aspen Law & Bus) Aspen Pub.

— Partnership, Vol. 3. 1993. 162.50 (0-316-10934-7, Aspen Law & Bus) Aspen Pub.

— Partnership, Vol. 4. 1993. 162.50 (0-316-10923-1, Aspen Law & Bus) Aspen Pub.

— Partnership: 1994 Supplement. 1994. 150.00 (0-316-10942-8) Little.

— Partnership '95. 1995. 175.00 (0-316-11046-9, Aspen Law & Bus) Aspen Pub.

Bromberg, Alan R. & Lowenfels, Lewis D. Securities Fraud & Commodities Fraud, 7 vols. (Securities Law Publications). 5027p. 1980. text 420.00 (0-07-008016-X) Shepards.

Bromberg, Alan R. & Ribstein, Larry E. Bromberg & Ribstein on Limited Liability Partnerships & the Revised Uniform Partnership Act. 600p. pap. 130.00 (0-316-11137-6, 11376) Aspen Law.

*Bromberg, Alan R. & Ribstein, Larry E. Bromberg & Ribstein on Limited Liability Partnerships & the Revised Uniform Partnership Act. LC 98-180727. xx, 634 p. 1998. 135.00 (0-7355-0148-3) Panel Pubs.

Bromberg, Alan R. & Ribstein, Larry E. Bromberg & Ribstein on Partnership, 2 vols., Set. 1904p. 1988. 595.00 (0-316-10925-8, Aspen Law & Bus) Aspen Pub.

Bromberg, Anna B., jt. auth. see Felder, Mira B.

Bromberg, Anne R. & Kilinski, Karl, II. Gods, Men & Heroes: Ancient Art at the Dallas Museum of Art. LC 96-22975. (Illus.). 144p. (Orig.). 1996. pap. 24.95 (0-936227-18-4) Dallas Mus.

Bromberg, Conrad. Actors & at Home: Two Short Plays. 1975. pap. 5.25 (0-8222-0008-2) Dramatists Play.

— Transfers: Three Plays. 1970. pap. 5.25 (0-8222-1166-1) Dramatists Play.

Bromberg, Eleanor M., jt. ed. see Aronowitz, Eugene.

Bromberg, Erik. The Hopi Approach to the Art of Kachina Doll Carving. LC 86-70331. (Illus.). 94p. (Orig.). 1992. pap. 9.95 (0-88740-062-0) Schiffer.

Bromberg, J. Philip. Physical Chemistry. 2nd ed. (C). 1983. teacher ed. 10.00 (0-685-07781-0, H80203) P-H.

Bromberg, Joan L. Fusion: Science, Politics & the Invention of a New Energy Source. (Illus.). 376p. 1982. 46.50 (0-262-02180-3) MIT Pr.

— The Laser in America 1950 to 1970. (Illus.). 326p. 1991. 38.50 (0-262-02318-0) MIT Pr.

Bromberg, Joan L. NASA & the Space Industry. LC 98-44795. (New Series in NASA History). 1999. write for info. (0-8018-6050-4) Johns Hopkins.

*Bromberg, Joan L. NASA & the Space Industry. (New Series in NASA History). (Illus.). 256p. 2000. pap. 18.95 (0-8018-6532-8) Johns Hopkins.

Bromberg, Mark B. Handbook on Motor Unit Number Estimation for Nerve & Muscular Disorders: Methods, Cautions, Clinical, & Research Uses. 1999. 99.00 (0-89603-559-X) Humana.

Bromberg, Murray & Gale, Cedric. Vocabulary Success. 3rd ed. LC 97-27775. 250p. 1998. pap. 11.95 (0-7641-0311-3) Barron.

Bromberg, Murray & Gordon, Melvin. 1100 Words You Need to Know. 3rd ed. LC 93-1014. 280p. 1993. pap. 10.95 (0-8120-1620-3) Barron.

*Bromberg, Murray & Gordon, Melvin. 1100 Words You Need to Know. 4th ed. 280p. 2000. pap. 11.95 (0-7641-1365-8) Barron.

Bromberg, Murray & Liebb, Julius. The English You Need to Know. 2nd ed. LC 97-1384. 208p. 1997. pap. 10.95 (0-7641-0164-1) Barron.

— Hot Words for the SAT I. 3rd rev. ed. LC 97-41266. 196p. 1998. pap. 8.95 (0-7641-0465-9) Barron.

— 601 Words You Need to Know to Pass Your Exam. 3rd ed. LC 96-28700. 256p. 1997. pap. 9.95 (0-8120-9645-2) Barron.

Bromberg, Murray, et al. 504 Absolutely Essential Words. 4th ed. 164p. 1996. pap. 10.95 (0-8120-9530-8) Barron.

Bromberg, Nicolette. Wisconsin Revisited. LC 99-191125. (Illus.). 80p. 1998. pap. 20.00 (0-87020-307-X) State Hist Soc Wis.

Bromberg, Norbert & Small, Verna V. Hitler's Psychopathology. LC 83-261. xi, 335p. 1984. 50.00 (0-8236-2345-9) Intl Univs Pr.

Bromberg, Philip M. Standing in the Spaces: Essays on Clinical Process, Trauma & Dissociation. LC 98-29429. 376p. 1998. 55.00 (0-88163-246-5) Analytic Pr.

Bromberg, Ruth. Canaletto's Etchings: Catalogue Raisonne. rev. ed. (Illus.). 244p. 1993. 150.00 (1-55660-214-6) A Wofsy Fine Arts.

*Bromberg, Ruth & Sickert, Walter. Walter Sickert: Prints: A Catalogue Raisonne. LC 99-59502. (Illus.). 320p. 2000. 120.00 (0-300-08161-8) Yale U Pr.

Bromberg, S. Erik. The Evolution of Ethics: An Introduction to Cybernetic Ethics. 2nd rev. ed. Seriguchi, Karen, ed. (Evolution of Ethics Ser.). 118p. (Orig.). (C). 1999. pap. text 4.00 (0-9610450-0-0) Dianic Pubns.

Bromberg, Sarah. Homosexuality Ethics & Military Policy No. 2: The Introduction. Draheim, Alan et al, eds. 20p. (Orig.). (C). 1997. pap. 4.80 (0-9610450-6-X) Dianic Pubns.

Bromberg, Walter. Crime & the Mind, an Outline of Psychiatric Criminology. LC 77-170192. 219p. 1982. reprint ed. lib. bdg. 86.50 (0-8371-6249-1, BRCM, Greenwood Pr) Greenwood.

— Psychiatry Between the Wars, 1918-1945: A Recollection, 10. LC 82-6153. (Contributions in Medical History Ser.: No. 10). 184p. 1982. 49.95 (0-313-23460-4, BWN/, Greenwood Pr) Greenwood.

— The Uses of Psychiatry in the Law: A Clinical View of Forensic Psychiatry. LC 78-22724. (Illus.). 442p. 1979. 75.00 (0-89930-000-6, BRP/, Quorum Bks) Greenwood.

Bromberger, Jacqueline. Nul N'est Cense Ignorer la Loi: Petit Dictionnaire Juridique. 3rd ed. (FRE.). 494p. 1977. pap. 39.95 (0-7859-7937-9, 2711100588) Fr & Eur.

Bromberger, Sylvain. On What We Don't Know: Explanation, Theory, Linguistics, & How Questions Shape Them. LC 92-10906. viii, 240p. (C). 1992. pap. text 18.95 (0-226-07540-0) U Ch Pr.

— On What We Don't Know: Explanation, Theory, Linguistics, & How Questions Shape Them. LC 92-10906. viii, 240p. (C). 1992. lib. bdg. 47.50 (0-226-07539-7) U Ch Pr.

— On What We Know We Don't Know: Explanation, Theory, Linguistics, & How Questions Shape Them. LC 92-10906. 1992. 39.95 (0-937073-89-X); pap. 16.95 (0-937073-88-1) CSLI.

Brombert, Beth A. Cristina: Portraits of a Princess. (Illus.). xii, 402p. 1983. pap. 10.95 (0-226-07551-6) U Ch Pr.

— Edouard Manet: Rebel in a Frock Coat. LC 97-3321. xx, 506p. 1997. pap. 19.95 (0-226-07544-3) U Ch Pr.

Brombert, Victor. The Hidden Reader: Stendhal, Balzac, Hugo, Baudelaire, Flaubert. LC 87-26115. 256p. 1988. 42.50 (0-674-39012-1) HUP.

— Victor Hugo & the Visionary Novel. (Illus.). 320p. 1986. pap. 18.00 (0-674-93551-9) HUP.

Brombert, Victor, ed. see Flaubert, Gustave.

*Brombert, Victor H. In Praise of Antiheroes. LC 98-36832. 1999. 29.00 (0-226-07552-4) U Ch Pr.

Brombert, Victor H. The Novels of Flaubert: A Study of Themes & Techniques. LC PQ2247.B68. 311p. pap. 96.50 (0-8357-8974-8, 205228500085) Bks Demand.

— The Romantic Prison: The French Tradition. LC 77-85532. 250p. 1978. reprint ed. pap. 77.50 (0-7837-9492-4, 206023600004) Bks Demand.

Bromby, Len. To the Gutter & Back. (C). 1989. text 35.00 (0-948929-36-7) St Mut.

*Bromcie, Alec. Complete Book of Farting. 160p. 2000. pap. 4.95 (1-85479-440-X) M OMara.

Brome, Alexander. Poems, Vol 1. Dubinski, Roman R., ed. LC 83-107902. 407p. reprint ed. pap. 126.20 (0-7837-1231-6, 204136800001) Bks Demand.

— Poems, Vol. 2. Dubinski, Roman R., ed. LC 83-107902. 156p. reprint ed. pap. 48.40 (0-7837-1232-4, 204136800002) Bks Demand.

Brome, Richard. The Antipodes. Haaker, Ann, ed. LC 66-13403. (Regents Renaissance Drama Ser.). 160p. 1966. pap. 49.60 (0-7837-8444-9, 204924800010) Bks Demand.

— Dramatic Works of Richard Brome, 3 vols. Shepherd, R. H., ed. reprint ed. 165.00 (0-404-01110-1) AMS Pr.

— A Jovial Crew. LC 68-10433. (Regents Renaissance Drama Ser.). 166p. 1968. reprint ed. pap. 51.50 (0-8357-6660-8, 203532900094) Bks Demand.

Brome, Richard, tr. see Horace.

Brome, Vincent. Frank Harris. LC 79-8057. reprint ed. 27.50 (0-404-18368-9) AMS Pr.

— H. G. Wells: A Biography. LC 78-133515. (Select Bibliographies Reprint Ser.). 1977. reprint ed. 18.95 (0-8369-5547-1) Ayer.

— H. G. Wells, a Biography. LC 70-109284. 255p. 1970. reprint ed. lib. bdg. 38.50 (0-8371-3827-2, BRHW, Greenwood Pr) Greenwood.

— Six Studies in Quarrelling. LC 72-6176. 197p. 1973. reprint ed. lib. bdg. 59.50 (0-8371-6484-2, BRSQ, Greenwood Pr) Greenwood.

Bromek, Tadeusz & Pleszczynska, Elzbieta, eds. Statistical Inference: Theory & Practice. (C). 1991. text 278.50 (0-7923-0718-6) Kluwer Academic.

Bromeliad Society of Australia Staff. Growing Bromeliads. 2nd ed. Williams, Barry E., ed. (Growing Ser.). (Illus.). 112p. 1993. pap. 11.95 (0-86417-336-9, Pub. by Kangaroo Pr) Seven Hills Bk.

Bromeling, Lyle D. Bayesian Analysis of Linear Models. (Statistics: Textbooks & Monographs: Vol. 60). (Illus.). 472p. 1984. text 160.00 (0-8247-8582-7) Dekker.

Bromell, Nicholas K. By the Sweat of the Brow: Literature & Labor in Antebellum America. LC 93-17247. 286p. 1993. 32.95 (0-226-07554-0) U Ch Pr.

— By the Sweat of the Brow: Literature & Labor in Antebellum America. (Literary Studies). 288p. 1995. pap. text 15.95 (0-226-07555-9) U Ch Pr.

Bromfiel, Andrew, tr. see Pelevin, Victor.

Bromfield & Nugent. Atlas of Adult EEG Rhythms. 176p. 1997. 42.95 (0-7506-9619-2) Buttrwrth-Heinemann.

Bromfield, Andrew, tr. see Latynin, Leonid.

Bromfield, Andrew, tr. see Pelevin, Victor.

Bromfield, Ann & Juan, Don. From Pimp Stick to Pulpit - "It's Magic" The Life Story of Don "Magic" Juan. 1994. 21.95 (0-533-10873-X) Vantage.

Bromfield, Avery P. OLIO Large Print Crossword Puzzle Book. 64p. 1984. spiral bd. 4.00 (0-934381-00-3) Olio Pubs.

Bromfield, Betsy B. Behind the Scenes at the Casa: Sketches. 80p. (Orig.). 1995. pap. 10.00 (1-56474-134-6) Fithian Pr.

Bromfield, David. Essays on Art & Architecture in Western Australia. LC 89-180596. 99p. 1988. 17.25 (0-86422-070-7) Intl Spec Bk.

Bromfield, Derek, jt. auth. see Pitt, Leyland F.

Bromfield, Ellen G. Heritage. Date not set. lib. bdg. 21.95 (0-8488-1760-5) Amereon Ltd.

Bromfield, K. R., ed. Soybean Rust. (APS Monographs). 65p. 1984. 20.00 (0-89054-062-4) Am Phytopathol Soc.

Bromfield, Louis. Animals & Other People. Date not set. lib. bdg. 23.95 (0-8488-1758-3) Amereon Ltd.

— La Colline Aux Cypres. (FRE.). 448p. 1973. pap. 10.95 (0-7859-1768-3, 2070365131) Fr & Eur.

— Colorado. 22.95 (0-88411-509-7) Amereon Ltd.

*Bromfield, Louis. Early Autumn. 224p. 2000. pap. 14.00 (1-888683-31-7) Wooster Bk.

Bromfield, Louis. Early Autumn. 264p. reprint ed. lib. bdg. 22.95 (0-88411-508-9) Amereon Ltd.

— The Farm. vi, 346p. 1976. reprint ed. lib. bdg. 25.95 (0-88411-501-1) Amereon Ltd.

— The Farm. 1993. reprint ed. lib. bdg. 39.95 (1-56849-189-1) Buccaneer Bks.

— The Farm. 1993. reprint ed. lib. bdg. 89.00 (0-7812-5342-X) Rprt Serv.

— The Farm. LC 99-35559. (Illus.). 300p. 1999. reprint ed. pap. 14.00 (1-888683-33-3) Wooster Bk.

— From My Experience. 355p. reprint ed. lib. bdg. 26.95 (0-88411-540-2) Amereon Ltd.

— From My Experience: The Pleasures & Miseries of Life on a Farm. LC 99-35558. (Illus.). 300p. 1999. reprint ed. pap. 14.00 (1-888683-55-4) Wooster Bk.

— Green Bay Tree. 20.95 (0-8488-0689-1) Amereon Ltd.

— Green Bay Tree. 1993. reprint ed. lib. bdg. 89.00 (0-7812-5343-8) Rprt Serv.

*Bromfield, Louis. The Green Bay Tree, Set. unabridged ed. (YA). (gr. 8 up). 1999. 47.95 incl. audio (1-55685-591-5) Audio Bk Con.

Bromfield, Louis. Malabar Farm. 1976. reprint ed. lib. bdg. 28.95 (0-88411-506-2) Amereon Ltd.

— Malabar Farm. LC 98-33594. (Illus.). 375p. 1999. reprint ed. pap. 14.00 (1-888683-84-8) Wooster Bk.

— Man Who Had Everything. 278p. reprint ed. lib. bdg. 22.95 (0-88411-510-0) Amereon Ltd.

— Mr. Smith. Date not set. lib. bdg. 23.95 (0-8488-1958-6) Amereon Ltd.

— Mrs. Parkington. large type ed. 592p. 1992. lib. bdg. 21.95 (1-56054-354-X) Thorndike Pr.

— Mrs. Parkington. 1976. reprint ed. lib. bdg. 25.95 (0-88411-502-X) Amereon Ltd.

— Mrs. Parkington. 1994. reprint ed. lib. bdg. 39.95 (1-56849-546-3) Buccaneer Bks.

— New Pattern for a Tired World. LC 72-174234. (Right Wing Individualist Tradition in America Ser.). 1972. reprint ed. 25.95 (0-405-00416-8) Ayer.

— Night in Bombay. 1976. reprint ed. lib. bdg. 25.95 (0-88411-503-8) Amereon Ltd.

— Out of the Earth. 305p. reprint ed. lib. bdg. 24.95 (0-88411-541-0) Amereon Ltd.

— Pleasant Valley. LC 97-18639. (Illus.). 320p. 1997 pap. 14.00 (1-888683-56-2) Wooster Bk.

— Pleasant Valley. 1976. reprint ed. lib. bdg. 25.95 (0-88411-504-6) Amereon Ltd.

— Possession. 31.95 (0-8488-0690-5) Amereon Ltd.

— The Rains Came. 1976. reprint ed. lib. bdg. 34.95 (0-88411-505-4) Amereon Ltd.

— The Rains Came. 1993. reprint ed. lib. bdg. 45.95 (1-56849-190-5) Buccaneer Bks.

— Until the Day Break. 25.95 (0-8488-0250-0) Amereon Ltd.

— Wild Country. 274p. reprint ed. lib. bdg. 23.95 (0-88411-542-9) Amereon Ltd.

— Wild Is the River. 332p. reprint ed. lib. bdg. 25.95 (0-88411-507-0) Amereon Ltd.

— The World We Live In. 347p. Date not set. 27.95 (0-8488-1759-1) Amereon Ltd.

Bromfield, Richard. Doing Child & Adolescent Psychotherapy: The Ways & Whys. LC 99-12391. 1999. 40.00 (0-7657-0220-7) Aronson.

*Bromfield, Richard. Handle with Care: Children & Teachers, Hearts & Mind. LC 00-44334. 2000. pap. write for info. (0-8077-3994-4) Tchrs Coll.

Bromfield, Richard. Playing for Real: Exploring the World of Child Therapy & the Inner Worlds of Children. LC 97-13376. 256p. 1997. reprint ed. pap. 35.00 (0-7657-0129-4, RA1) Aronson.

Bromhall, A. J. Hudson Taylor & China's Open Century, Bk. 7: It Is Not Death to Die. 1989. pap. 5.95 (0-340-50270-3) OMF Bks.

Bromham, A. A. & Bruzzi, Zara. The Changeling & the Years of Crisis, 1619-1624: A Hieroglyph of Britain. 220p. 1993. pap. 14.95 (1-85567-163-8) St Martin.

Bromham, A. A. & Bruzzi, Zara A. The Changeling Decoded. 224p. 1990. text 42.50 (0-86187-703-9) St Martin.

Bromham, David R., et al, eds. Ethics in Reproductive Medicine. (Illus.). 232p. 1992. 89.95 (0-387-19698-6) Spr-Verlag.

Bromhead. Life in Modern America. LC 97-107887. 1989. pap. text. write for info. (0-582-01838-2, Pub. by Addison-Wesley) Longman.

— Life in Modern Britain. 1991. pap. text. write for info. (0-582-03642-9, Pub. by Addison-Wesley) Longman.

— Life in Modern Britain. 6th ed. 1985. pap. text. write for info. (0-582-74919-0, Pub. by Addison-Wesley) Longman.

Bromhead, Alison, jt. auth. see McLagan, Patricia.

Bromhead, E. N. The Stability of Slopes. (Illus.). 450p. 1992. 125.00 (0-216-93175-4, A9753, Pub. by B Acad & Prof) Routldge.

*Bromhead, E. N. The Stability of Slopes. 2nd ed. 411p. (C). (gr. 13). 1998. text 150.00 (0-7514-0275-3) B Acad & Prof.

Bromhead, Eddie, jt. auth. see Ward, Tim.

Bromige, David. A Cast of Tens. Chadwick, Cydney, ed. 96p. (Orig.). 1994. pap. text 9.50 (1-880713-01-2) AVEC Bks.

— Desire: Selected Poems, 1963-1987. LC 88-3409. 232p. 1988. 20.00 (0-87685-724-1) Black Sparrow.

— Desire: Selected Poems, 1963-1987, signed ed. deluxe ed. LC 88-3409. 232p. 1988. 30.00 (0-87685-725-X) Black Sparrow.

— The Harbormaster of Hong Kong. (Sun & Moon Classics Ser.: No. 32). 88p. 1993. pap. 10.95 (1-55713-027-2) Sun & Moon CA.

— Men, Women & Vehicles: Prose Works. LC 90-1061. 176p. 1990. 20.00 (0-87685-798-5); pap. 10.00 (0-87685-797-7) Black Sparrow.

— Men, Women & Vehicles: Prose Works, signed ed. deluxe ed. LC 90-1061. 176p. 1990. 30.00 (0-87685-799-3) Black Sparrow.

*Bromige, David. T as in Tether. LC 98-50514. 1999. write for info. (0-925904-23-6) Chax Pr.

Bromige, David. Tiny Courts in a World Without Scales. 64p. 1991. pap. 9.95 (0-919626-53-X, Pub. by Brick Bks) Genl Dist Srvs.

Bromige, Iris. A New Life for Joanna. large type ed. 1986. 15.95 (0-7089-1538-8) Ulverscroft.

— The Years Between. large type ed. (General Ser.). 304p. 1993. 27.99 (0-7089-2837-4) Ulverscroft.

Bromiley, G. W., ed. & tr. see Barth, Karl.

Bromiley, Geoffrey. Children of Promise: The Case for Baptizing Infants. 127p. 1996. pap. 15.00 (1-57910-148-8) Wipf & Stock.

Bromiley, Geoffrey W. Historical Theology. 1995. pap. 34.95 (0-567-22357-4, Pub. by T & T Clark) Bks Intl VA.

*Bromiley, Geoffrey W. Historical Theology: An Introduction. 494p. 1998. pap. 40.00 (1-57910-172-0) Wipf & Stock.

Bromiley, Geoffrey W. The International Standard Bible Encyclopedia, 4 vols. rev. ed. (International Standard Bible Encyclopedia Ser.). 1995. 280.00 (0-8028-3785-9) Eerdmans.

— The International Standard Bible Encyclopedia Vol. 2: E-J, Vol. 2. rev. ed. (International Standard Bible Encyclopedia Ser.). 1175p. 1995. 70.00 (0-8028-3782-4) Eerdmans.

— The International Standard Bible Encyclopedia Vol. 3: K-P, Vol. 3. rev. ed. (International Standard Bible Encyclopedia Ser.). 1080p. 1995. 70.00 (0-8028-3783-2) Eerdmans.

— International Standard Bible Encyclopedia Vol. 4: Q-Z, Vol. 4. rev. ed. (International Standard Bible Encyclopedia Ser.). 1995. 70.00 (0-8028-3784-0) Eerdmans.

— An Introduction to the Theology of Karl Barth. 268p. (Orig.). 1990. pap. 24.95 (0-567-29054-9, Pub. by T & T Clark) Bks Intl VA.

*Bromiley, Geoffrey W. Sacramental Teaching & Practice in the Reformation Churches. 112p. 1998. pap. 14.00 (1-57910-173-9) Wipf & Stock.

Bromiley, Geoffrey W., ed. The International Standard Bible Encyclopedia Vol. 1: A-D, Vol. 1. rev. ed. (International Standard Bible Encyclopedia Ser.). 1006p. 1995. 70.00 (0-8028-3781-6) Eerdmans.

B

— Zwingli & Bullinger. LC 53-1533. (Library of Christian Classics). 360p. 1979. pap. 28.95 (*0-664-24159-X*) Westminster John Knox.

Bromiley, Geoffrey W., ed. see Barth, Karl.

Bromiley, Geoffrey W., ed. see Thielicke, Helmut.

Bromiley, Geoffrey W., ed. & tr. see Barth, Karl.

Bromiley, Geoffrey W., tr. see Barth, Karl.

Bromiley, Geoffrey W., tr. see Bockmuehl, Klaus.

Bromiley, Geoffrey W., tr. see Ellul, Jacques.

Bromiley, Geoffrey W., tr. see Kasemann, Ernst.

Bromiley, Geoffrey W., tr. see Kittel, Gerhard & Friedrich, Gerhard, eds.

Bromiley, Geoffrey W., tr. see Pannenberg, Wolfhart.

Bromiley, Geoffrey W., tr. see Thielicke, Helmut.

Bromiley, Geoffrey William, jt. auth. see Fahlbusch, Erwin.

Bromiley, Mary. Massage for Horses, Vol. 38. (Threshold Picture Guides Ser.). (Illus.). 24p. (YA). 1996. pap. 12.00 (*1-872082-87-4*, Pub. by Kenilworth Pr) Half Halt Pr.

Bromiley, Mary W. Natural Methods for Equine Health. (Illus.). 256p. 1995. pap. 28.95 (*0-632-03818-7*, Pub. by Blckwll Scitfc UK) Blackwell Sci.

Bromilow, William E. Twenty Years among Primitive Papuans. LC 75-32800. reprint ed. 41.50 (*0-404-14103-X*) AMS Pr.

Bromily, Jill, tr. see Kaai, Anneke.

Bromka, Gregg. Mountain Biking Colorado. 1998. pap. 14.95 (*1-56044-840-7*) Falcon Pub Inc.

— Mountain Biking Utah. (Illus.). 450p. 1999. pap. 19.95 (*1-56044-824-5*) Falcon Pub Inc.

— Mountain Biking Utah's Brian Head - Bryce Country. LC 98-67191. (Illus.). 224p. 1998. pap. 14.95 (*0-9624374-3-3*) Off-Road Pubns.

— Mountain Biking Utah's Wasatch & Uinta Mountains. (Illus.). 364p. 1996. pap. 18.95 (*0-9624374-2-5*) Off-Road Pubns.

Bromke, Adam. Eastern Europe. 1985. text 47.50 (*0-88033-076-7*, 183, Pub. by East Eur Monographs) Col U Pr.

— The Meaning & Uses of Polish History. (East European Monographs: No. 212). 244p. 1987. text 46.50 (*0-88033-109-7*, Pub. by East Eur Monographs) Col U Pr.

— Poland: The Protracted Crisis. 280p. 1994. pap. 14.95 (*0-88962-194-2*) Mosaic.

— Poland's Politics: Idealism vs. Realism. LC 66-21331. (Harvard University, Russian Research Center Studies: Vol. 51). 330p. reprint ed. pap. 102.30 (*0-608-10068-4*, 201775400007) Bks Demand.

Bromlei, Iulian V. & D'Iakov, Vladimir A., eds. Slavianovedenie v SSSR: Izuchenie Iuzhnykh I Zapadnykh Slavian: Biobibliograficheskii Slovar' - A Biobibliographical Dictionary of Slavicists in the U. S. S. R. Specializing in Southern & Western Slavic Studies. LC 92-60509. (RUS.). xii, 528p. 1993. lib. bdg. 54.00 (*0-88354-356-7*) N Ross.

Bromley. Behavioural Gerontology: Central Issues in the Psychology of Aging. 420p. 1995. pap. text 71.95 (*0-471-96082-9*) Wiley.

— Retail Change. 1993. 75.00 (*1-85728-059-8*, Pub. by UCL Pr Ltd); pap. 25.00 (*1-85728-060-1*, Pub. by UCL Pr Ltd) Taylor & Francis.

Bromley, Kirk W. Icarus & Aria. Gracia, Chad, ed. (Bromley Plays Ser.: No. 2). 100p. 1997. pap. 15.00 (*1-893194-01-9*, 002) Inverse Theater.

— Life's Loss's Loved. Gracia, Chad, ed. (Bromley Plays Ser.: No. 3). 95p. 1998. pap. 15.00 (*1-893194-02-7*, 003) Inverse Theater.

— Want's Unwished Work: A Birthday Play. Gracia, Chad, ed. & intro. by. (Bromley Plays Ser.: No. 1). 90p. 1996. pap. 15.00 (*1-893194-00-0*, 001) Inverse Theater.

Bromley, A. K., jt. auth. see White, M. K.

Bromley, Anne. Midwinter Transport. LC 85-70429. (Poetry Ser.). 80p. 1985. 20.95 (*0-88748-016-0*); pap. 11.95 (*0-88748-017-9*) Carnegie-Mellon.

Bromley, Anne C. Scenes from the Light Years. LC 94-70460. (Poetry Ser.). 72p. 1995. pap. 11.95 (*0-88748-197-3*) Carnegie-Mellon.

***Bromley, Carl, ed.** Cinema Nation: The Best Writing on Film from "The Nation," 1913-2000. (Illus.). 2000. pap. 15.95 (*1-56025-286-3*, Thunders Mouth) Avalon NY.

Bromley, D. A. Treatise on Heavy Ion Science Vol. 8: Nuclei Far from Stability. (Illus.). 752p. (C). 1989. text 155.00 (*0-306-42949-7*, Kluwer Plenum) Kluwer Academic.

Bromley, D. A., jt. auth. see Greiner, Walter.

Bromley, D. A., ed. see International Conference on Nuclear Structure Staf.

Bromley, D. Allan. The President's Scientists: Reminiscences of a White House Science Advisor. LC 94-10424. Vol. 47. (Illus.). 232p. 1994. 37.00 (*0-300-06006-8*) Yale U Pr.

— Treatise on Heavy-Ion Science Vol. 4: Extreme Nuclear States. (Illus.). 721p. (C). 1985. text 186.00 (*0-306-41574-7*, Kluwer Plenum) Kluwer Academic.

Bromley, D. Allan, ed. Treatise on Heavy-Ion Science Vol. 1: Elastic & Quasi-Elastic Phenomena. LC 84-8384. (Illus.). 775p. (C). 1984. text 186.00 (*0-306-41571-2*, Kluwer Plenum) Kluwer Academic.

— Treatise on Heavy-Ion Science Vol. 2: Fusion & Quasi-Fusion Phenomena. (Illus.). 762p. (C). 1985. text 186.00 (*0-306-41572-0*, Kluwer Plenum) Kluwer Academic.

— Treatise on Heavy-Ion Science Vol. 3: Compound Systems Phenomena. (Illus.). 609p. (C). 1985. text 174.00 (*0-306-41573-9*, Kluwer Plenum) Kluwer Academic.

— Treatise on Heavy-Ion Science Vol. 5: High-Energy Atomic Physics. (Illus.). 518p. (C). 1985. text 162.00 (*0-306-41575-5*, Kluwer Plenum) Kluwer Academic.

— Treatise on Heavy-Ion Science Vol. 6: Astrophysics, Chemistry & Condensed Matter. (Illus.). 452p. (C). 1985. text 150.00 (*0-306-41786-3*, Kluwer Plenum) Kluwer Academic.

— Treatise on Heavy Ion Science Vol. 7: Instrumentation & Techniques. (Illus.). 492p. (C). 1985. text 156.00 (*0-306-41787-1*, Kluwer Plenum) Kluwer Academic.

Bromley, D. B., jt. auth. see Livesley, W. J.

Bromley, Daniel W. Handbook of Environmental Economics. (Illus.). 672p. 1995. pap. 44.95 (*1-55786-641-4*) Blackwell Pubs.

***Bromley, Daniel W.** Sustaining Development: Environmental Resources in Developing Countries. LC 98-45767. 304p. 1999. 95.00 (*1-85898-888-8*) E Elgar.

Bromley, Daniel W., ed. Making the Commons Work: Theory, Practice, & Policy. LC 92-24880. 339p. 1992. 44.95 (*1-55815-198-2*) ICS Pr.

— The Social Response to Environmental Risk: Policy Formulation in an Age of Uncertainty. (Recent Economic Thought Ser.). 240p. (C). 1992. lib. bdg. 120.00 (*0-7923-9208-6*) Kluwer Academic.

Bromley, Daniel W. & Cernea, Michael M. The Management of Common Property Natural Resources: Some Conceptual & Operational Fallacies, No. 57. (Discussion Paper Ser.). 76p. 1989. pap. 22.00 (*0-8213-1249-9*, 11249) World Bank.

Bromley, Daniel W., jt. auth. see Buse, Rueben C.

Bromley, Daniel W., ed. see Blomquist, William A.

Bromley, David, ed. see Augendre, Jacque.

Bromley, David G. Religion & the Social Order, Vol. 3, Pt. A. 292p. 1993. 73.25 (*1-55938-714-9*) Jai Pr.

Bromley, David G., ed. Falling from the Faith: Causes & Consequences of Religious Apostasy. LC 87-19281. (Sage Focus Editions Ser.: No. 95). 266p. reprint ed. pap. 82.50 (*0-7837-6590-8*, 204615500011) Bks Demand.

— The Politics of Religious Apostasy: The Role of Apostates in the Transformation of Religious Movements. LC 97-34747. (Religion in the Age of Transformation Ser.). 256p. 1998. 62.50 (*0-275-95508-7*, Praeger Pubs) Greenwood.

— Religion & the Social Order, Vol. 3, Pt. A. 292p. 1993. 73.25 (*0-614-24145-6*) Jai Pr.

— Religion & the Social Order, Vol. 3, Pt. B. 229p. 1993. 73.25 (*1-55938-715-7*) Jai Pr.

— Religion & the Social Order, Vol. 7. 1998. 73.25 (*0-7623-0215-1*) Jai Pr.

— Religion & the Social Order: Between Sacred & Secular, Vol. 4. 321p. 1994. 73.50 (*1-55938-763-7*) Jai Pr.

— Religion & the Social Order: New Developments in Theory & Research, Vol. 1. 283p. 1991. 73.25 (*1-55938-291-0*) Jai Pr.

— Religion & the Social Order: Sex, Lies & Sanctity, Vol. 5. 269p. 1995. 73.25 (*1-55938-904-4*) Jai Pr.

— Religion & the Social Order: The Handbook on Cults & Sects in America, 2 vols., Vol. 3. 1993. 146.50 (*1-55938-477-8*) Jai Pr.

— Religion & the Social Order: The Issue of Authenticity in the Study of Religions, Vol. 6. 279p. 1996. 73.25 (*0-7623-0038-8*) Jai Pr.

— Religion & the Social Order: Vatican II & U. S. Catholicism, Vol. 2. 284p. 1991. 73.25 (*1-55938-388-7*) Jai Pr.

Bromley, David G. & Cutchin, Diane G. Satanism: An Annotated Bibliography. Melton, John G., ed. (Sects & Cults in America Ser.). Date not set. text 40.00 (*0-8153-0037-9*) Garland.

Bromley, David G. & Richardson, James T., eds. The Brainwashing-Deprogramming Controversy: Sociological, Psychological, Legal & Historical Perspectives. LC 83-4346. (Studies in Religion & Society: Vol. 5). 376p. 1983. lib. bdg. 99.95 (*0-88946-868-0*) E Mellen.

Bromley, David G. & Shinn, Larry D., eds. Krishna Consciousness in the West. LC 87-47975. (Illus.). 296p. 1989. 39.50 (*0-8387-5144-X*) Bucknell U Pr.

Bromley, David G. & Shupe, Anson D. Moonies in America: Cult, Church, & Crusade. LC 79-16456. (Sage Library of Social Research: No. 92). 269p. reprint ed. pap. 83.40 (*0-8357-4771-9*, 203770800009) Bks Demand.

Bromley, David G., jt. ed. see Shupe, Anson.

Bromley, David W. & Allott, Angela M., eds. British Librarianship & Information Work, 1981-1985 Vol. 1: General Libraries & the Profession. LC 88-22625. (Illus.). 373p. reprint ed. pap. 115.70 (*0-608-08893-5*, 206953000001) Bks Demand.

— British Librarianship & Information Work, 1981-1985 Vol. 2: Special Libraries, Materials & Processes. LC 88-22625. (Illus.). 368p. reprint ed. pap. 114.10 (*0-608-08894-3*, 206953000002) Bks Demand.

— British Librarianship & Information Work, 1986-1990 Vol. 1: General Libraries & the Profession. LC 92-45605. 331p. reprint ed. pap. 102.70 (*0-608-08895-1*, 206953100001) Bks Demand.

— British Librarianship & Information Work, 1986-1990 Vol. 2: Special Libraries, Materials & Processes. LC 93-19580. 363p. reprint ed. pap. 112.60 (*0-608-08896-X*, 206953100002) Bks Demand.

Bromley, Dennis B. Personality Description in Ordinary Language. LC 76-40293. 288p. reprint ed. pap. 89.30 (*0-608-17615-X*, 203046700069) Bks Demand.

Bromley, Dudley. Guide to Kaypro Computers. 1984. 13.95 (*0-671-52828-9*) S&S Trade.

— North to Oak Island. (Bestsellers II Ser.). (J). 1977. 16.60 (*0-606-02423-9*, Pub. by Turtleback) Demco.

Bromley, Eileen. Christianity: An Activity & Resource Pack. (Illus.). 1992. teacher ed., spiral bd. 72.50 (*0-7487-1396-4*, Pub. by S Thornes Pubs) Trans-Atl Phila.

Bromley, Hank. LISP LORE: A Guide to Programming the LISP Machine. 1986. text 89.00 (*0-89838-220-3*) Kluwer Academic.

Bromley, Hank & Apple, Michael W., eds. Education/Technology/Power: Educational Computing As a Social Practice. LC 97-35887. (SUNY Series, Frontiers in Education). (Illus.). 263p. (C). 1998. text 59.50 (*0-7914-3797-3*); pap. text 19.95 (*0-7914-3798-1*) State U NY Pr.

Bromley, Hank & Lamson, Richard. LISP LORE: A Guide to Programming the LISP Machine. 2nd rev. ed. (C). 1987. text 110.50 (*0-89838-228-9*) Kluwer Academic.

Bromley, Ida. Tetraplegia & Paraplegia: A Guide for Physiotherapists. 5th ed. LC 97-41290. (C). 1998. text 45.00 (*0-443-05872-5*) Church.

Bromley, J. S. Corsairs & Navies, 1660-1760. 517p. 1988. 75.00 (*0-907628-77-X*) Hambledon Press.

***Bromley, K.** 50 Graphic Organizers. 112p. 1999. pap. 14.95 (*0-590-00484-0*) Scholastic Inc.

Bromley, Karen D. Webbing with Literature: Creating Story Maps with Children's Books. 2nd ed. 304p. 1995. pap. text 37.00 (*0-205-16975-9*) Allyn.

Bromley, Karen D'Angelo. Journaling: Engagement in Reading, Writing, & Thinking. LC 94-175172. 128p. (gr. k-9). 1993. pap. 14.95 (*0-590-49478-3*) Scholastic Inc.

— Language Arts. 3rd ed. LC 97-27515. 528p. 1997. 77.00 (*0-205-26812-9*) P-H.

***Bromley, Kirk Wood, et al.** Plays & Playwright for the New Millenium. Denton, Martin, ed. 366p. 2000. pap. 14.00 (*0-9670234-1-6*) NY Theatre Exp.

Bromley, Larry, ed. see Frederic, Harold.

Bromley, Lynn. Monkeys, Apes & Other Primates. (Illus.). 64p. 1981. pap. 3.95 (*0-88388-069-5*) Bellerophon Bks.

Bromley, Michael. Spirit Stones: Use the Positive Energies of Native American Sacred Animal Spirit Stones to Balance Your Life. (Illus.). 128p. 1998. pap. 29.95 (*1-885203-51-9*) Jrny Editions.

Bromley, Michael & O'Malley, Tom. A Journalism Reader. LC 97-9914. (Communication & Society Ser.). 416p. (C). 1997. 85.00 (*0-415-14135-4*); pap. 25.99 (*0-415-14136-2*) Routledge.

Bromley, Michael & Stephenson, Hugh. Sex, Lies & Democracy: The British Press & the Public. LC 97-26175. (C). 1998. pap. text 16.95 (*0-582-29332-4*, Pub. by Addison-Wesley) Longman.

Bromley, P. Countryside Management. (Illus.). 384p. (C). 1990. pap. 45.00 (*0-419-15140-0*, E & FN Spon) Routledge.

— Countryside Recreation: A Handbook for Managers. LC 94-146375. (Illus.). 168p. (C). 1993. 70.00 (*0-419-18200-4*, E & FN Spon) Routledge.

— Nature Conservation in Europe: Policy & Practice. LC 97-189879. (Illus.). 240p. (C). 1998. 60.00 (*0-419-21610-3*, E & FN Spon) Routledge.

Bromley, P. M., et al, eds. Butterworths Family Law Service, 3 vols. 1991. ring bd. 550.00 (*0-406-10720-3*, UK, MICHIE) LEXIS Pub.

Bromley, Richard. Trace Fossils: Biology & Taphonomy. (Special Topics in Palaeontology Ser.). (Illus.). 310p. (C). 1990. pap. 40.95 (*0-04-445686-7*) Thomson Learn.

— Trace Fossils: Biology & Taphonomy. (Special Topics in Palaeontology Ser.). (Illus.). 310p. (C). 1990. pap. 103.50 (*0-04-445303-5*) Thomson Learn.

Bromley, Robin. The Official Smokey Bear Book. (Illus.). (J). 1996. 15.99 (*0-614-19332-X*, Ladybrd) Penguin Putnam.

Bromley, Roger. Lost Narratives: Popular Fictions, Politics & Recent History. 204p. 1989. pap. 14.95 (*0-415-01873-0*) Routledge.

— Lost Narratives: Popular Fictions, Politics & Recent History. LC 88-14883. (Popular Fiction Ser.). 246p. reprint ed. pap. 76.30 (*0-608-20321-1*, 207157400002) Bks Demand.

Bromley, Simon. American Hegemony & World Oil: The Industry, the State System & the World Economy. 300p. 1991. 45.00 (*0-271-00746-X*) Pa St U Pr.

— Rethinking Middle East Politics. LC 93-34723. 216p. (Orig.). (C). 1994. pap. 16.95 (*0-292-70816-5*); text 39.50 (*0-292-70815-7*) U of Tex Pr.

Bromley, Viola A. Bromley Genealogy. (Illus.). 452p. 1989. reprint ed. pap. 69.50 (*0-8328-0329-4*); reprint ed. lib. bdg. 79.50 (*0-8328-0328-6*) Higginson Bk Co.

Bromley, Yu, ed. Soviet Ethnology & Anthropology Today. (Studies in Anthropology: No. 1). 401p. 1974. pap. text 84.65 (*90-279-2725-1*) Mouton.

Bromling, Brad T. Be Sure! A Study in Christian Evidences. 120p. (Orig.). (YA). (gr. 7 up). 1995. pap. 4.00 (*0-932859-23-2*) Apologetic Pr.

***Bromma, Hubert F.** Real Estate Investments in Your Self Directed Retirement Plan: A Guide. Gudmundson, Lori et al, eds. (Illus.). iii, 316p. 1999. 149.00 (*1-929141-00-9*) Entrust Adm Inc.

Bromme, Rainer, jt. ed. see Ben-Peretz, Miriam.

Brommel, Bernard J. Eugene V. Debs, Spokesman for Labor & Socialism. LC 75-23910. (Illus.). 265p. 1978. 19.95 (*0-88286-006-2*); pap. 12.00 (*0-88286-024-0*) C H Kerr.

Brommel, Bernard J., jt. auth. see Galvin, Kathleen M.

Brommelhorster, Jorn & Frankenstein, John, eds. Mixed Motives, Uncertain Outcomes: Defense Conversion in China. LC 96-27539. 280p. 1996. lib. bdg. 58.00 (*1-55587-710-9*, 877109) L Rienner.

Brommelle, Norman S. & Smith, Perry, eds. Urushi: Proceedings of the 1985 Urushi Study Group. LC 85-21394. (Illus.). 260p. 1988. pap. 50.00 (*0-89236-096-8*, Pub. by J P Getty Trust) OUP.

Brommer, Frank. Heracles: The Twelve Labors of the Hero in Ancient Art & Literature. Schwarz, Shirley J., tr. (Illus.). 128p. (C). 1986. 25.00 (*0-89241-375-1*) Caratzas.

— Odysseus: The Deeds & Sufferings of the Hero in Ancient Greek Art & Literature. (Illus.). 192p. text 50.00 (*0-89241-433-2*) Caratzas.

— Theseus: The Deeds & Sufferings of the Greek Hero in Ancient Art & Literature. (Illus.). 208p. text 50.00 (*0-89241-438-3*) Caratzas.

Brommer, Gerald F. Collage Techniques: A Guide for Artists & Illustrators. LC 94-7775. (Illus.). 160p. 1994. pap. 27.50 (*0-8230-0655-7*) Watsn-Guptill.

— Discovering Art History. 3rd ed. LC 95-68098. (Illus.). 656p. (YA). (gr. 9-12). 1997. text, teacher ed. 57.70 (*0-87192-300-9*) Davis Mass.

— Exploring Drawing. LC 88-130593. (Illus.). 240p. (YA). (gr. 9-12). 1988. text 28.60 (*0-87192-192-8*) Davis Mass.

— Understanding Transparent Watercolor. LC 92-72328. (Illus.). 192p. (YA). (gr. 9-12). 1993. 31.15 (*0-87192-245-2*) Davis Mass.

— Watercolor & Collage Workshop. (Illus.). 144p. 1986. 27.50 (*0-8230-5652-X*) Watsn-Guptill.

— Watercolor & Collage Workshop: Make Better Paintings Through Mastery of Collage Techniques. (Illus.). 144p. 1997. pap. text 19.95 (*0-8230-5643-0*) Watsn-Guptill.

Brommer, Gerald F. & Gatto, Joseph A. Carrers in Art: An Illustrated Guide, 2nd rev. ed. LC 98-71023. (Illus.). 256p. (YA). (gr. 7-12). 1998. text 29.95 (*0-87192-377-7*, Pub. by Davis Mass) Sterling.

Brommer, Gerald F. & Kinne, Nancy. Exploring Painting. rev. ed. LC 93-74642. (Illus.). 256p. (YA). (gr. 9-12). 1995. text 35.35 (*0-87192-287-8*) Davis Mass.

Brompton Books Staff. Gaudi. 1993. 15.98 (*1-55521-930-6*) Bk Sales Inc.

— Who Was Who in the Twentieth Century? 1993. 17.98 (*1-55521-929-2*) Bk Sales Inc.

Broms, Bengt, ed. Geomechanics in Tropical Soils: Proceedings of the Second International Conference, Singapore, 12-14 December, 1988, 2 vols., Set. 700p. (C). 1988. text 210.00 (*90-6191-816-2*, Pub. by A A Balkema) Ashgate Pub Co.

Broms, Bengt B. Precast Piling Practice. 132p. 1981. 25.00 (*0-7277-0121-5*, Pub. by T Telford) RCH.

Bromwell, H. P. Restorations of Masonic Geometry & Symbolry Being a Dissertation on the Lost Knowledge of the Lodge (1905) 617p. 1993. reprint ed. pap. 60.00 (*1-56459-417-3*) Kessinger Pub.

Bromwell, Perry & Gensler, Howard. The Student Athlete's Handbook: The Complete Guide for Success. LC 97-19049. 256p. 1997. pap. 14.95 (*0-471-14975-6*) Wiley.

Bromwell, William J. History of Immigration to the United States. LC 69-18760. (American Immigration Collection. Series 1). 1969. reprint ed. 15.95 (*0-405-00508-3*) Ayer.

— History of Immigration to the United States. LC 68-27676. (Reprints of Economic Classics Ser.). 225p. 1969. reprint ed. 12.50 (*0-678-00533-8*) Kelley.

Bromwich, ed. PeopleSoft HRMS Reporting. LC 99-48943. 464p. 1999. pap. 55.00 (*0-13-021612-7*) P-H.

Bromwich, David. Choice of Inheritance: Self & Community from Edmund Burke to Robert Frost. LC 88-30411. 336p. 1989. 46.50 (*0-674-12775-7*) HUP.

— Disowned by Memory: Wordworth's Poetry of the 1790s. LC 98-3704. 192p. 1998. 25.00 (*0-226-07556-7*) U Ch Pr.

***Bromwich, David.** Disowned by Memory: Wordworth's Poetry of the 1790s. (Illus.). 2000. pap. 15.00 (*0-226-07557-5*) U Ch Pr.

— Hazlitt: The Mind of a Critic. LC 99-30873. 496p. 1999. pap. text 18.00 (*0-300-07989-3*) Yale U Pr.

Bromwich, David. Politics by Other Means: Higher Education & Group Thinking. 296p. (C). 1992. pap. 14.00 (*0-300-05920-5*) Yale U Pr.

Bromwich, David, jt. auth. see Burke, Edmund.

Bromwich, David, ed. see James, Henry.

Bromwich, David H. & Stearns, Charles R., eds. Antarctic Meteorology & Climatology: Studies Based on Automatic Weather Stations. LC 94-3154. (Antarctic Research Ser.: Vol. 61). 207p. 1994. 70.00 (*0-87590-839-X*) Am Geophysical.

Bromwich, James. The Roman Remains of Southern France. 272p. 1996. pap. 18.95 (*0-415-13817-5*) Routledge.

— Roman Remains of Southern France: A Guide Book. (Illus.). 368p. (C). 1996. pap. 27.99 (*0-415-14358-6*) Routledge.

Bromwich, Michael. Accounting for Overheads: Critique & Reforms. LC 97-149993. (Studia Oeconomiae Negotiorum Ser.: No. 41). 102p. (Orig.). 1997. pap. 39.50 (*91-554-3885-7*, Pub. by Uppsala Universitet) Coronet Bks.

— Financial Reporting, Information & Capital Markets. 376p. (Orig.). 1992. pap. 62.50 (*0-273-03464-2*, Pub. by Pitman Pub) Trans-Atl Phila.

Bromwich, Michael R. Allegations of Racial & Criminal Misconduct at the Good O' Boy Roundup. (Illus.). 300p. (Orig.). 1996. pap. text 35.00 (*0-7881-2983-X*) DIANE Pub.

— The FBI Laboratory: An Investigation into Laboratory Practices & Alleged Misconduct in Explosives-Related & Other Cases. 530p. (C). 1998. pap. text 60.00 (*0-7881-7087-2*) DIANE Pub.

Bromwich, Rachel. Dafydd ap Gwilym: Poems. 1998. pap. 37.95 (*0-8464-4799-1*) Beekman Pubs.

— Medieval Celtic Literature: A Select Bibliography. LC 74-82287. (Toronto Medieval Bibliographies Ser.: No. 5). 128p. reprint ed. pap. 39.70 (*0-608-16924-2*, 202641800049) Bks Demand.

Bromwich, Rachel, ed. Dafydd Ap Gwilym Vol. 1: Poems. 207p. 1982. 45.00 (*1-85902-091-7*, Pub. by Gomer Pr) St Mut.

— Trioedd Ynys Prydein: The Welsh Triads. 598p. 1998. write for info. (*0-7083-1386-8*, Pub. by Univ Wales Pr) Paul & Co Pubs.

An Asterisk (*) at the beginning of an entry indicates that the title is appearing for the first time.

B

An Asterisk (*) at the beginning of an entry indicates that the title is appearing for the first time.

Bronner, Simon J., ed. see Schlereth, Thomas J.

Bronner, Simon J., jt. ed. see Vlach, John M.

Bronner, Simon J., ed. see Yoder, Don.

Bronner, Stephen A. A Beggar's Tales. 136p. 1977. text 11.00 (0-918618-07-X); pap. text 6.00 (0-918618-08-8) Pella Pub.

Bronner, Stephen E. Camus: Portrait of a Moralist. 172p. 1999. 37.95 (0-8166-3283-9); pap. 14.95 (0-8166-3284-7) U of Minn Pr.

— Ideas in Action: Political Tradition in the Twentieth Century. LC 98-52021. 368p. 1999. pap. 24.95 (0-8476-9387-2); text 69.00 (0-8476-9386-4) Rowman.

— Leon Blum. (World Leaders Past & Present Ser.). (Illus.). 120p. (YA). (gr. 5 up). 1987. lib. bdg. 19.95 (0-87754-511-1) Chelsea Hse.

— Moments of Decision: Political History & the Crises of Radicalism. LC 91-18169. 224p. (C). 1991. pap. 21.99 (0-415-90465-X, A6277) Routledge.

— Of Critical Theory & Its Theorists. 380p. 1994. pap. 28.95 (0-631-18738-3) Blackwell Pubs.

— Rosa Luxemburg: A Revolutionary for Our Time. 1997. pap. 14.95 (0-271-01685-X) Pa St U Pr.

Bronner, Stephen E. & Kellner, Douglas M., eds. Critical Theory & Society: A Reader. 304p. 1989. 49.50 (0-415-90040-9, A2329) Routledge.

— Critical Theory & Society: A Reader. 320p. (C). 1989. pap. 23.99 (0-415-90041-7, A2333) Routledge.

— Passion & Rebellion: The Expressionist Heritage. (Morningside Bk.). 468p. 1988. pap. text 21.00 (0-231-06763-1, King's Crown Paperbacks) Col U Pr.

— Passion & Rebellion: The Expressionist Heritage. LC 81-40492. 480p. 1983. 32.95 (0-87663-356-4, Bergin & Garvey) Greenwood.

Bronner, Stephen E. & Wagner, F. Peter, eds. Vienna, the World of Yesterday 1889-1914. 279p. (C). 1996. text 49.95 (0-391-03987-3) Humanities.

Bronner, Stephen E., ed. see Pachter, Henry.

***Bronner, Stephen Eric.** A Rumor about the Jews: Reflections on Antisemitism & the Protocols of the Learned Elders of Zion. LC 99-42576. 160p. 2000. 24.95 (0-312-21804-4) St Martin.

Bronnimann, Herve, tr. see Boissonnat, Jean-Daniel & Yvinec, Mariette.

Bronosted, A. An Introduction to Convex Polytopes. (Graduate Texts in Mathematics Ser.: Vol. 90). (Illus.). 160p. 1982. 59.95 (0-387-90722-X) Spr-Verlag.

Bronowski, Alexander. They Were Few. LC 91-21675. (Studies in the Shoah: Vol. 2). (C). 1992. text 44.95 (0-8204-1629-0) P Lang Pubng.

Bronowski, Jacob. The Ascent of Man. LC 73-20446. (Illus.). 448p. 1976. pap. 29.95 (0-316-10933-9) Little.

— The Common Sense of Science. LC 53-9924. 158p. 1978. pap. text 10.50 (0-674-14651-4) HUP.

— The Origins of Knowledge & Imagination. LC 77-13209. (Silliman Lectures: Vol. 44). 1979. pap. 12.00 (0-300-02409-6) Yale U Pr.

— Science & Human Val. LC 89-45631. 144p. 1990. reprint ed. pap. 11.00 (0-06-097281-5, Perennial) HarperTrade.

— Science & Human Values. 1959. pap. text 6.95 (0-06-130505-7, TB505, Torch) HarpC.

— Science & Human Values. 1992. 24.00 (0-8446-6518-5) Peter Smith.

— Science & Human Values. enl. rev. ed. (Illus.). 142p. 1972. mass mkt. 4.95 (0-06-080269-3, P269, Perennial) HarperTrade.

— The Visionary Eye: Essays in the Arts, Literature, & Science. Ariotti, Piero & Bronowski, Rita, eds. 1978. 22.50 (0-262-02129-3) MIT Pr.

— The Visionary Eye: Essays in the Arts, Literature, & Science. Ariotti, Piero & Bronowski, Rita, eds. 1981. pap. text 12.50 (0-262-52068-0) MIT Pr.

— William Blake: A Man Without a Mask. 1976. lib. bdg. 250.00 (0-8490-1300-3) Gordon Pr.

— William Blake: A Man Without a Mask. LC 67-30809. (Studies in Blake: No. 3). 1969. reprint ed. lib. bdg. 75.00 (0-8383-0709-4) M S G Haskell Hse.

Bronowski, Jacob & Mazlish, Bruce. Western Intellectual. 544p. 1962. pap. 18.00 (0-06-133001-9, TB 3001, Torch) HarpC.

— The Western Intellectual Tradition: From Leonardo to Hegel. LC 70-167315. (Essay Index Reprint Ser.). 1977. reprint ed. 40.95 (0-8369-2448-7) Ayer.

Bronowski, Rita, ed. see Bronowski, Jacob.

Brons, Martha P. Journal Index, 1972 to 1988. 1990. 6.25 (0-89917-592-9) Am String Tchrs.

Brons, Morten, et al, eds. Progress in Industrial Mathematics at ECMI '94. LC 98-139547. 449 p. 1997. write for info. (3-519-02607-4) B G Teubner.

Brons, Penney R., jt. auth. see Kinucan, Edith S.

Brons, Rijnko. Facial Harmony: Standards for Orthognathic Surgery & Orthodontics. LC 98-10901. (Illus.). 166p. 1998. text 78.00 (0-86715-331-8) Quint Pub Co.

***Bronsard, Marie.** In Memoriam Cassiopee. Alland, Sonia, tr. from FRE. (French Ser.). (Illus.). 24p. 2000. pap. 8.95 (0-87376-088-3) Red Dust.

Bronsen, Hugo H. Gymnastics & Variations: Index of New Information Including Practices, Injury, Theory & Medical Applications. 147p. 1997. 47.50 (0-7883-1544-7); pap. 44.50 (0-7883-1545-5) ABBE Pubs Assn.

— Sports: Guidebook for Reference & Research. LC 88-47627. 150p. 1988. 47.50 (0-88164-652-0); pap. 44.50 (0-88164-653-9) ABBE Pubs Assn.

— Sports - Mental Health, Psychic Stress & Emotional Reactions: Index of New Information with Authors, Subjects, Research Categories & References. rev. ed. 147p. 1997. 47.50 (0-7883-1560-9); pap. 44.50 (0-7883-1561-7) ABBE Pubs Assn.

— Sports--It's Shoes & Sole: Quality, Action, Choices, Safety, Problems & Shoe Therapy: Index of New Information with References. 150p. 1999. 47.50 (0-7883-2162-5); pap. 44.50 (0-7883-2163-3) ABBE Pubs Assn.

— Sports & Anabolic Steroids: Index of Modern Information. LC 88-47866. 150p. 1988. 37.50 (0-88164-924-4); pap. 34.50 (0-88164-925-2) ABBE Pubs Assn.

— Sports & Psycho-Physiology: Index of Modern Information with Guide for Rapid Research. LC 92-26129. 1992. 47.50 (1-55914-754-7); pap. 44.50 (1-55914-755-5) ABBE Pubs Assn.

— Sports & Psychological Influences: Index of Modern Authors & Subjects with Guide for Rapid Research. rev. ed. LC 94-34382. 145p. 1994. 47.50 (0-7883-0250-7); pap. 44.50 (0-7883-0251-5) ABBE Pubs Assn.

— Sports, Drugs & Doping: Index of Modern Information. LC 89-77608. 175p. 1990. 47.50 (1-55914-126-3); pap. 44.50 (1-55914-127-1) ABBE Pubs Assn.

— Sports Encyclopedia: Index & Reference Books of New Information Vol. 3: Sports, Drugs & Doping, Vol. 3. Bartone, John C., ed. 150p. 1996. 44.50 (0-7883-1082-8); pap. 39.50 (0-7883-1083-6) ABBE Pubs Assn.

— Sports Encyclopedia: Index & Reference Books of New Information Vol. 4: Sports & Psychological Influences, Vol. 4. Bartone, John C., ed. 150p. 1996. 44.50 (0-7883-1084-4); pap. 39.50 (0-7883-1085-2) ABBE Pubs Assn.

— Sports Encyclopedia: Index & Reference Books of New Information Vol. 6: Sports & Psycho-Physiology, Vol. 6. Bartone, John C., ed. 150p. 1996. 44.50 (0-7883-1088-7); pap. 39.50 (0-7883-1089-5) ABBE Pubs Assn.

— Sports Encyclopedia: Index & Reference Books of New Information Vol. 9: Sports, Prevention & Control of Athletic Injuries, Vol. 9. Bartone, John C., ed. 150p. 1996. 44.50 (0-7883-1094-1); pap. 39.50 (0-7883-1095-X) ABBE Pubs Assn.

— Sports, Prevention & Control of Athletic Injuries: Index of New Information with Authors & Subjects. rev. ed. LC 94-24773. 157p. 1994. 47.50 (0-7883-0264-7); pap. 44.50 (0-7883-0265-5) ABBE Pubs Assn.

— Sports Report - Baseball: Index of New Information with Authors, Subjects & References. rev. ed. 171p. 1997. 47.50 (0-7883-1460-2); pap. 44.50 (0-7883-1461-0) ABBE Pubs Assn.

— Sports Report - Football: Index of New Information with Authors, Subjects & References. 1994. 47.50 (1-55914-730-X); pap. 44.50 (1-55914-731-8) ABBE Pubs Assn.

— Sports Report - Soccer: Index of New Information with Authors, Subjects & References. 1994. 47.50 (1-55914-732-6); pap. 44.50 (1-55914-733-4) ABBE Pubs Assn.

— Sports Report - Swimming: Index of New Information with Authors, Subjects & References. 1994. 47.50 (1-55914-734-2); pap. 44.50 (1-55914-735-0) ABBE Pubs Assn.

— Sports Report - Tennis: Index of New Information with Authors, Subjects & References. 1994. 47.50 (1-55914-736-9); pap. 44.50 (1-55914-737-7) ABBE Pubs Assn.

— Sports Report - Tennis Elbow: Index of New Information with Authors, Subjects & References. 1994. 47.50 (1-55914-738-5); pap. 44.50 (1-55914-739-3) ABBE Pubs Assn.

— Sports Report - Track & Field: Index of New Information with Authors, Subjects, & References. 160p. 1995. 47.50 (0-7883-0456-9); pap. 44.50 (0-7883-0457-7) ABBE Pubs Assn.

— Sports with Racquets (Badminton, Lacross, Racquetball & Squash) Index of New Information. rev. ed. 123p. 1998. 47.50 (0-7883-1898-5); pap. 44.50 (0-7883-1899-3) ABBE Pubs Assn.

Bronshtein, I. N. & Semendyayev, K. A. Guidebook to Mathematics for Technologists & Engineers. LC 60-16788. (International Series of Monographs on Pure & Applied Mathematics: Vol. 36). 1964. 338.00 (0-08-010019-8, Pub. by Pergamon Repr) Franklin.

— Handbook of Mathematics. 3rd ed. 990p. 1997. 59.95 (3-540-62130-X) Spr-Verlag.

Bronshtein, Z. S. Fresh-Water Ostracoda: Fauna of the U.S.S.R., Crustaceans, Vol. II, No. 1. Nayar, Indira, tr. (Russian Translation Ser.: No. 64). (Illus.). 485p. (C). 1989. text 188.00 (90-6191-916-9, Pub. by A A Balkema) Ashgate Pub Co.

Bronski, Michael. Culture Clash: The Making of Gay Sensibility. LC 84-50941. 249p. 1984. 30.00 (0-89608-218-0) South End Pr.

***Bronski, Michael.** Flashpoint. 2000. pap. 9.95 (1-873741-36-7) Millivres Bks.

Bronski, Michael. The Pleasure Principle. LC 97-7983. 304p. 1998. text 24.95 (0-312-15625-1) St Martin.

***Bronski, Michael.** Pleasure Principle: Sex, Backlash, & the Struggle for Gay Freedom. 304p. 2000. pap. 13.95 (0-312-25287-0) St Martin.

Bronski, Michael, ed. Flashpoint: Gay Male Sexual Writing. (Orig.). 1996. pap. 12.95 (1-56333-424-0, R Kasak Bks) Masquerade.

— Flashpoint: Gay Male Sexual Writing. (Orig.). 1998. reprint ed. mass mkt. 7.95 (1-56333-687-1, Badboy) Masquerade.

Bronsky, Eric, ed. see Plachno, Larry.

Bronson. Finite Mathematics: Explorations in Finite Math. 1996. text 15.50 (0-314-09332-X) West Pub.

— Finite Mathematics with Calculus. LC 99-38894. 1122p. 1999. pap. 90.95 (0-534-35652-4) Brooks-Cole.

***Bronson.** Finite Mathematics with Calculus: A Modeling Approach. (Mathematics Ser.). 1999. text 15.00 (0-534-36840-9) Brooks-Cole.

— A First Book of ANSI C: Fundamentals of C Programming. 3rd ed. (Computer Science Ser.). (C). 2000. text 45.00 (0-534-37964-8) Brooks-Cole.

Bronson. First Book of Visual C++ LC 99-56139. (West Computer Science Ser.). 993p. 1999. 62.95 (0-534-95313-1) PWS Pubs.

— First Book of C++ From Here to There. 2nd ed. LC 99-14647. (West Computer Science Ser.). 1999. text 54.95 (0-534-36801-8) PWS Pubs.

***Bronson.** A First Book of Web Design & Development. 2001. pap. 45.00 (0-534-37792-0) Thomson Learn.

Bronson & Sims. Pushcart War Activity Book. 160p. 1997. spiral bd. 22.95 (0-7872-3570-9) Kendall-Hunt.

Bronson, Gary. Introduction to Programming Using Visual Basic 6. 2nd ed. (Illus.). 700p. (C). 1999. pap. text 63.54 (1-57676-031-6) Scott Jones Pubng.

***Bronson, Gary & Walter, Kenneth.** Modern Fortran 77-9-2000. (Illus.). 757p. (C). 1999. pap. 60.65 (1-57676-038-3) Scott Jones Pubng.

Bronson, A. & Warren, G. W., eds. Techniques for Corrosion Measurement. (Illus.). 276p. 1992. 25.00 (1-877914-47-9) NACE Intl.

Bronson, B. H., et al. Studies in the Comic. LC 76-29415. reprint ed. 23.50 (0-404-15324-0) AMS Pr.

Bronson, Bertrand H. In Search of Chaucer. LC 60-4242. (Alexander Lectureship Ser.: 1958-59). 127p. reprint ed. pap. 39.40 (0-608-16265-5, 202651600050) Bks Demand.

— The Traditional Tunes of the Child Ballads: With Their Texts According to the Extant Records of Great Britain & America, Vol. 1. LC 57-5468. 503p. 1959. reprint ed. pap. 143.40 (0-608-02231-4, 2011482) Bks Demand.

— The Traditional Tunes of the Child Ballads: With Their Texts According to the Extant Records of Great Britain & America, Vol. 2. LC 57-5468. 585p. 1959. reprint ed. pap. 181.40 (0-608-02232-2, 201148200002) Bks Demand.

Bronson, Bertrand H., ed. The Singing Tradition of Child's Popular Ballads. LC 75-2980. 576p. reprint ed. pap. 178.60 (0-7837-4324-6, 204402800012) Bks Demand.

Bronson, Bertrand H., et al. Five Studies in Literature. LC 78-58253. (Essay Index in Reprint Ser.). 1978. reprint ed. 30.00 (0-8486-3015-7) Roth Pub Inc.

Bronson, Bertrand H., ed. & intro. see Johnson, Samuel.

Bronson, Bill. Sexual Paradises of Earth: A Single Man's Guide to International Travel. (Illus.). 240p. (Orig.). 1993. pap. 18.95 (0-9633966-0-9) BB Pr.

Bronson, Carol E. A History of Christ the King Catholic Church. LC 96-97009. (Illus.). 133p. (Orig.). 1996. pap. 15.00 (0-9654471-1-1) C E Bronson.

Bronson, Charles W. Extent of the Atonement. 1992. mass mkt. 4.00 (1-56186-513-3) Pilgrim Pubns.

Bronson, Denise F., et al. Computerizing Your Agency's Information System. (Human Services Guides Ser.: Vol. 54). (Illus.). 160p. (C). 1988. pap. text 18.95 (0-8039-2653-7) Sage.

Bronson, Edgar B. Reminiscences of a Ranchman. LC 62-8407. (Bison Bk.: No. BB127). 384p. reprint ed. pap. 119.10 (0-8357-6633-0, 203528600094) Bks Demand.

Bronson, F. H. Mammalian Reproductive Biology. (Illus.). 336p. 1989. pap. text 22.00 (0-226-07559-1) U Ch Pr.

— Mammalian Reproductive Biology. (Illus.). 336p. 1992. lib. bdg. 45.00 (0-226-07558-3) U Ch Pr.

Bronson, Fred. The Billboard Book of Number One Hits. expanded rev. ed. LC 97-41864. (Illus.). 912p. 1997. pap. 24.95 (0-8230-7641-5, Billboard Bks) Watsn-Guptill.

— Billboard Hottest Hot 100 Hits. enl. rev. ed. LC 95-6044. (Illus.). 512p. 1995. pap. 21.95 (0-8230-7646-6, Billboard Bks) Watsn-Guptill.

***Bronson, Fred.** Billboard's Hottest Hot 100 Hits. 3rd expanded rev. ed. (Illus.). 544p. 2000. pap. 21.95 (0-8230-7738-1) Watsn-Guptill.

Bronson, Fred, jt. auth. see Clark, Dick.

Bronson, Gary J. Algorithm Development & Program Design Using C. 600p. (C). 1996. mass mkt. 63.95 (0-314-06987-9) West Pub.

— C for Engineers & Scientists: An Introduction to Programming with ANSI C. Mixter, ed. LC 92-21688. 500p. (C). 1992. mass mkt. 43.75 (0-314-00816-0) West Pub.

— C++ for Engineers & Scientists. (Electrical Engineering Ser.). (C). 1998. pap. 57.95 (0-534-95060-4) PWS Pubs.

— Finite Math. 1996. mass mkt., student ed. 16.50 (0-314-09485-7) West Pub.

— Finite Mathematics. Date not set. pap. text, teacher ed. write for info. (0-314-09484-9) West Pub.

— First Book of C Plus Plus: From Here to There. LC 94-28503. 676p. (C). 1994. mass mkt. 38.25 (0-314-04236-9) West Pub.

— FORTRAN for Scientists & Engineers. 2nd ed. 652p. (C). 1995. pap. text 50.54 (1-881991-39-3) Scott Jones Pubng.

— Intro to Programming Using Visual Basic. (Illus.). 604p. (Orig.). (C). 1997. pap. text 53.43 (1-881991-47-4) Scott Jones Pubng.

— Program Design & Development Using C++ LC 96-47078. (Illus.). 991p. 1997. pap. 69.95 (0-314-20338-9) West Pub.

Bronson, Gary J. & Menconi, Stephen J. A First Book of ANSI C: Fundamentals of C Programming. 2nd ed. LC 95-44977. 550p. (C). 1996. mass mkt. 63.95 (0-314-07336-1) West Pub.

Bronson, Gary J. & Silver, Howard I. Thirty-Two-Bit Microprocessors: A Primer Plus. Van Heest, Rose & Menconi, Stephen J., eds. (AT&T Advanced Technology Ser.: Vol. 1). (Illus.). 568p. (C). 1988. text 24.95 (0-932764-10-X, 311-027) AT&T Customer Info.

Bronson, Gary J., jt. auth. see Bronson, Richard.

Bronson, Gordon. Scanning Patterns of Human Infants: Implications for Visual Learning. LC 81-20543. (Monographs on Infancy: Vol. 2). 136p. 1982. text 73.25 (0-89391-114-3) Ablx Pub.

Bronson, Harrison A. Treatise on the Law of Fixtures. LC 98-26712. xii, 508p. 1998. reprint ed. 65.00 (0-8377-1989-5, Rothman) W S Hein.

Bronson, J. & Bronson, R. Early American Weaving & Dyeing: The Domestic Manufacturer's Assistant, & Family Directory in the Arts of Weaving & Dyeing. (Illus.). 204p. 1977. reprint ed. pap. 7.95 (0-486-23440-1) Dover.

Bronson, James Graham. Willie & Esther. LC 98-232327. 70 p. 1997. pap. write for info. (0-573-60310-3) French.

Bronson, Judith G., ed. see Kaye, Keith W.

Bronson, Julien L. Parrots. Orig. Title: Parrot Family: Their Training, Care, & Breeding. (Illus.). 80p. 1985. pap. text 6.95 (0-86622-874-8, PB-120) TFH Pubns.

***Bronson, Linda.** Circus Alphabets: 100 Complete Fonts. 2001. text 16.95 (0-8050-6294-7) H Holt & Co.

Bronson, M. Dictionary in Assamese & English. (ASM & ENG.). 1987. 59.95 (0-8288-1595-X, F136031) Fr & Eur.

Bronson, Marsha. Amnesty International. LC 93-26367. (Organizations That Help the World Ser.). 64p. (J). 1994. pap. 7.95 (0-614-09465-8, New Dscvry Bks); lib. bdg. 13.95 (0-02-714550-6, New Dscvry Bks) Silver Burdett Pr.

Bronson, Martha B. The Right Stuff for Children Birth to Eight: Selecting Play Materials to Support Development. (Illus.). 1995. pap. 8.00 (0-935989-72-2) Natl Assn Child Ed.

Bronson, Martha B. Self-Regulation in Early Childhood: Nature & Nurture. LC 99-57183. 286p. Date not set. lib. bdg. 45.00 (1-57230-532-0, C0532) Guilford Pubns.

***Bronson, Orval.** Burning Brightly: John Steinbeck on Stage. (Illus.). xviii, 117p. 2000. 45.00 (0-933994-24-9) Comstock Bon.

Bronson, Po. Bombardiers. 336p. 1996. pap. 12.95 (0-14-025450-1, Viking) Viking Penguin.

— Bombardiers. 319p. 1997. reprint ed. text 20.00 (0-7881-5047-2) DIANE Pub.

***Bronson, Po.** Bombardiers. 434p. 2000. reprint ed. pap. 15.00 (0-7881-9367-8) DIANE Pub.

— The First $20 Million Is Always the Hardest: A Novel. 304p. 2000. pap. 13.00 (0-380-81624-5, Perennial) HarperTrade.

Bronson, Po. The First $20 Million Is Always the Hardest: A Silicon Valley Novel. LC 96-33143. 352p. 1998. mass mkt. 6.99 (0-380-73155-X, Avon Bks) Morrow Avon.

***Bronson, Po.** The Nudist on the Late Shift. LC 00-27416. 256p. 2000. pap. 14.95 (0-7679-0603-9) Broadway BDD.

Bronson, Po. The Nudist on the Late Shift: And Other True Tales of Silicon Valley. LC 98-32381. 288p. 1999. 25.00 (0-375-50277-7) Random.

Bronson, R., jt. auth. see Bronson, J.

Bronson, Richard. Linear Algebra: An Introduction. (Illus.). 504p. 1995. pap. text 45.00 (0-12-135245-5) Acad Pr.

— Matrix Methods: An Introduction. 2nd ed. 503p. (C). 1991. text 48.00 (0-12-135251-X) Acad Pr.

— Schaum's Outline of Differential Equations. 2nd ed. (Schaum's Outline Ser.). 358p. (C). 1994. pap. 15.95 (0-07-008019-4) McGraw.

— Schaum's Outline of Matrix Operations. (Schaum's Outline Ser.). 230p. 1988. pap. 15.95 (0-07-007978-1) McGraw.

Bronson, Richard & Bronson, Gary J. Finite Mathematics: A Modeling Approach. LC 95-33545. 650p. (C). 1996. mass mkt. 102.95 (0-314-06394-3) West Pub.

Bronson, Richard & Naadimuthu, Govindsami. Schaum's Outline of Theory & Problems of Operations Research. 2nd ed. LC 97-9538. (Illus.). 456p. (C). 1997. pap. 15.95 (0-07-008020-8) McGraw.

Bronson, Richard, et al. Reproductive Immunology. 1000p. 1996. 235.00 (0-86542-367-9) Blackwell Sci.

Bronson, Richard, jt. auth. see Jacobsen, Chanoch.

***Bronson, Tammy Carter.** Tiny Snail. (Illus.). 32p. (J). (ps-3). 2000. pap. 10.95 (0-9678167-0-X) Bookaroos Pubng Inc.

Bronson, Tan, jt. auth. see Bolinger, Don.

Bronson, Wade A. Boothill Brand. large type ed. (Western Ser.). 1994. pap. 16.99 (0-7089-7597-6, Linford) Ulverscroft.

— The Marshal of Twisted Fork. large type ed. 221p. 1994. pap. 18.99 (1-85389-440-0, Dales) Ulverscroft.

Bronson, Walter C. American Education Series, No. 2. LC 75-165708. (American Education Ser, No. 2). 1972. reprint ed. 27.95 (0-405-03697-3) Ayer.

— English Poems. LC 70-109135. (Granger Index Reprint Ser.). 424p. 1982. reprint ed. lib. bdg. 17.00 (0-8290-0527-7) Irvington.

Bronson, Walter C., ed. American Prose. LC 71-121525. (Short Story Index Reprint Ser.). 1977. 35.95 (0-8369-3481-4) Ayer.

— English Essays. LC 74-111817. (Essay Index Reprint Ser.). 1977. 26.95 (0-8369-1595-X) Ayer.

— English Poems: Four Fifty to Fifteen Fifty. LC 70-109135. (Granger Index Reprint Ser.). 1977. 20.95 (0-8369-6119-6) Ayer.

— English Poems: Sixteen Sixty to Eighteen Hundred. LC 70-109135. (Granger Index Reprint Ser.). 1977. 26.95 (0-8369-6195-1) Ayer.

— English Poems: The Nineteenth Century. LC 76-38595. (Granger Index Reprint Ser.). 1977. reprint ed. 31.95 (0-8369-6327-X) Ayer.

Bronson, Wanda C. Toddler's Behavior with Agemates: Issues of Interaction, Cognition & Affect. LC 81-12896. (Monographs on Infancy: Vol. 1). 128p. (C). 1981. text 73.25 (0-89391-080-5) Ablx Pub.

An Asterisk (*) at the beginning of an entry indicates that the title is appearing for the first time.

Bronson, William. Earth Shook, the Sky Burned: A Photographic Record of the 1996 San Francisco Earthquake & Fire. (Illus.). 1997. pap. 16.95 (0-8118-1667-2) Chronicle Bks.

Bronsted, H. & Kerkut, G. A. Planarian Regeneration. LC 70-75454. (International Series of Monographs on Pure & Applied Mathematics: Vol. 42). 1969. 134.00 (0-08-012876-9, Pub. by Pergamon Repr) Franklin.

Bronstein, jt. auth. see Sloane.

Bronstein, A., jt. ed. see Yemin, Edward.

***Bronstein, Alan & Hofer, Stephen C.** Forever Brillant: The Aurora Collection of Colored Diamonds. rev. ed. LC 00-132823. (Illus.). 92p. 2000. write for info. (0-9659410-2-7) Ashland Press.

Bronstein, Alvin C. & Currance, Phillip L. Emergency Care for Hazardous Materials Exposure, Vol. 2. 2nd ed. (Illus.). 656p. (C). (gr. 13). 1994. pap. text 25.95 (0-8016-7813-7, 07813) Mosby Inc.

Bronstein, Alvin C., jt. auth. see Currance, Phillip L.

Bronstein, Arna. Making Progress in Russian: A Second Year Course. 2nd ed. LC 96-29535. (RUS.). 584p. 1996. pap. 80.95 (0-471-14810-5) Wiley.

Bronstein, Arthur J. & American Dialect Society Staff. Conference Papers on American English & the International Phonetic Alphabet. LC 97-51467. (Publications of the American Dialect Society). 1998. pap. text 15.00 (0-8173-0929-2) U of Ala Pr.

Bronstein, Arturo & Thomas, Constance, eds. European Labour Courts: International & European Labour Standards in Labour Court Decisions, & Jurisprudence on Sex Discrimination. vii, 115p. 1995. pap. 18.00 (92-2-108012-9) Intl Labour Office.

Bronstein, Daniel A. Law for the Expert Witness. 256p. 1993. boxed set 85.00 (0-87371-906-9, L906) Lewis Pubs.

— Law for the Expert Witness. 2nd ed. LC 98-49963. 230p. 1999. 49.95 (0-8493-8135-5) CRC Pr.

Bronstein, Daniel A., ed. Demystifying Law: An Introduction for Professionals. (Illus.). 176p. 1990. lib. bdg. 49.95 (0-87371-324-9, L324) Lewis Pubs.

Bronstein, Daniel A., jt. ed. see Vanclay, Frank.

Bronstein, Daniel J. & Schulweis, Harold M., eds. Approaches to the Philosophy of Religion. LC 77-93320. (Essay Index Reprint Ser.). 1977. 36.95 (0-8369-1344-2) Ayer.

***Bronstein, David.** Invitation to the King's Indian Defence. 1999. pap. text 19.95 (1-85744-265-2) Cadogan Pubns.

Bronstein, David. The Modern Chess Self-Tutor. 144p. 1996. pap. 17.95 (1-85744-136-2) Macmillan.

— The Sorcerer's Apprentice. 256p. 1995. pap. text 19.95 (1-85744-151-6) S&S Trade.

— Two Hundred Open Games. (Illus.). 240p. 1991. pap. 7.95 (0-486-26857-8) Dover.

— Zurich International Chess Tournament, 1953. Marfia, Jim, tr. from RUS. LC 78-74881. (Illus.). 349p. 1979. pap. 10.95 (0-486-23800-8) Dover.

Bronstein, David & Smolyan, Georgy. Chess in the Eighties. Neat, Kenneth P., tr. (Russian Chess Ser.). 120p. 1982. 19.90 (0-08-024126-3, Pergamon Pr) Elsevier.

Bronstein, Henri A., tr. see Gurvich, L. V. & Veyts, I., eds.

Bronstein, Henri A., tr. see Lokshin, V. A., et al, eds.

Bronstein, Herbert, ed. A Passover Haggadah. rev. ed. LC 74-33161. (Illus.). 123p. 1974. pap. 13.95 (0-916694-05-4) Central Conf.

Bronstein, Herbert & Friedlander, Albert, eds. The Five Scrolls. deluxe limited ed. LC 84-12183. (Illus.). 383p. 1984. ring bd. 375.00 (0-916694-82-8) Central Conf.

Bronstein, Howard, jt. auth. see Ray, Darrell W.

Bronstein, I. U. Extensions of Minimal Transformation Groups. 327p. 1979. lib. bdg. 129.50 (90-286-0368-9) Kluwer Academic.

Bronstein, I. U. & Kopanskii, A. Ya. Smooth Invariant Manifolds & Normal Forms. 396p. 1994. text 74.00 (981-02-1572-X) World Scientific Pub.

Bronstein, I. U., et al. Eleven Papers on Logic, Algebra, Analysis & Topology. LC 51-5559. (Translations Ser.: Series 2, Vol. 97). 258p. 1971. 45.00 (0-8218-1797-3, TRANS2/97) Am Math.

Bronstein, Jamie L. Land Reform & Working-Class Experience in Britain & the United States, 1800-1862. LC 98-28068. viii, 372 p. 1999. write for info. (0-8047-3451-8) Stanford U Pr.

Bronstein, Leo. El Greco. (Masters of Art Ser.). (Illus.). 128p. 1990. 24.95 (0-8109-0873-5, Pub. by Abrams) Time Warner.

— Fragments of Life, Metaphysics & Art. 2nd ed. (Illus.). 224p. (C). 1995. text 69.95 (1-56000-249-2) Transaction Pubs.

— Kabbalah & Art. 2nd ed. LC 97-31334. 129p. 1997. text 49.95 (1-56000-353-7) Transaction Pubs.

— A Romantic Homage to Greece & Spain. (Illus.). 290p. 1991. 30.00 (0-933858-24-8) Kennebec River.

— A Romantic Homage to Greece & Spain: My Fable, Their Art. LC 93-9949. (Illus.). 317p. (C). 1993. text 79.95 (1-56000-117-8) Transaction Pubs.

— Space in Persian Painting. (Illus.). 142p. (C). 1994. 59.95 (1-56000-197-6) Transaction Pubs.

Bronstein, Leona B. & McGrain, Eleanore. Chemistry Flipper. 49p. (J). (gr. 7 up). 1989. reprint ed. 6.95 (1-878383-06-X) C Lee Pubns.

Bronstein, M., ed. see Timor-Tritsch, I. E.

Bronstein, Manuel. Symbolic Integration: Transcendental Functions, Vol. 1. LC 96-41956. 299p. 1997. 49.00 (3-540-60521-5) Spr-Verlag.

Bronstein, Manuel, et al, eds. Symbolic Rewriting Techniques. LC 98-11497. (Progress in Computer Science & Applied Logic Ser.: Vol. 15). 296p. 1998. 98.00 (3-7643-5901-3) Birkhauser.

Bronstein, Manuel, et al. Symbolic Rewriting Techniques. LC 98-11497. (Progress in Computer Science & Applied Logic Ser.). 1998. write for info. (0-8176-5901-3) Birkhauser.

***Bronstein, Marty.** Coaching & Mentoring for Dummies. 256p. 2000. pap. 19.99 (0-7645-5223-6) IDG Bks.

***Bronstein, Mel.** A Voice in the Clouds: Healing Words for the Heart. viii, 88p. 2000. pap. 10.00 (0-9700208-0-5) Lightworks Earth.

Bronstein, Nikki. Praise the Lord with Bells, Bk. I. 31p. (J). (gr. k-7). 1992. spiral bd. 15.00 (1-880892-14-6) Com Sense FL.

— Praise the Lord with Bells, Bk. II. 38p. (J). (gr. k-7). 1992. spiral bd. 15.00 (1-880892-15-4) Com Sense FL.

Bronstein, Phyllis & Cowan, Carolyn P., eds. Fatherhood Today: Men's Changing Role in the Family. LC 88-144615. (Personality Processes Ser.). 364p. 1988. 150.00 (0-471-83627-3) Wiley.

Bronstein, Phyllis & Quina, Kathryn, eds. Teaching a Psychology of People: Resources for Gender & Sociocultural Awareness. LC 88-16715. 220p. 1988. pap. 29.95 (1-55798-039-X) Am Psychol.

Bronstein, Robert. Just a Moment, Soldier! A Story in Play Format. LC 93-74141. (Illus.). 205p. (YA). (gr. 8-12). 1994. 17.95 (0-9638960-3-2); pap. 12.95 (0-9638960-2-4) Bronfam Pr.

Bronstein, Sidney L., jt. ed. see Thomas, Mohan.

Bronston, Edythe L. Obtaining Appointment of a Receiver (And Monitoring the Receivership) Winter, 1993, Action Guide. Stein, Carolyn J., ed. 142p. 1993. pap. text 52.00 (0-88124-605-0, CP-11242) Cont Ed Bar-CA.

Bronston, Roger Z. Adults with Self Concepts about Health, Disorders & Disease: Index of New Information. 1998. 47.50 (0-7883-1808-X); pap. 44.50 (0-7883-1809-8) ABBE Pubs Assn.

***Bronstone, Adam.** European Bank for Reconstruction & Development. 1999. 69.95 (0-7190-5551-2, Pub. by Manchester Univ Pr) St Martin.

— European Security into the 21st Century: Beyond Traditional Theories of International Relations. 282p. 1999. text 69.95 (1-84014-752-0, Pub. by Ashgate Pub) Ashgate Pub Co.

Bront, David D., et al. Teach Yourself Photoshop in 14 Days. 4th ed. 464p. 1997. 39.99 (1-56830-403-X) Hayden.

***Bronte & Peterson.** Wuthering Heights. 2nd ed. 2001. pap. text. write for info. (0-312-25686-8) St Martin.

Bronte, Anne. Agnes Grey. Marsden, Hilda & Inglesfield, Robert, eds. (Clarendon Edition of the Novels of the Brontes Ser.). 252p. 1988. 85.00 (0-19-812693-X) OUP.

— Agnes Grey. Inglesfield, Robert & Marsden, Hilda, eds. (Oxford World's Classics Ser.). 240p. 1998. pap. 7.95 (0-19-283478-9) OUP.

— Agnes Grey. Goreau, Angeline, ed. & intro. by. 272p. 1989. pap. 8.95 (0-14-043210-8, Penguin Classics) Viking Penguin.

— Agnes Grey. (Classics Library). 150p. 1998. pap. 3.95 (1-85326-216-1, 2161WW, Pub. by Wrdsworth Edits) NTC Contemp Pub Co.

Bronte, Anne. Agnes Grey. ed. 1.99 (1-58627-209-8) Electric Umb OR.

Bronte, Anne. Agnes Grey & Poems. 208p. 1994. pap. 4.95 (0-460-87121-8, Everyman's Classic Lib) Tuttle Pubng.

— Complete Poems. 1971. reprint ed. 49.00 (0-403-01758-0) Scholarly.

— Complete Poems of Anne Bronte. 1988. reprint ed. lib. bdg. 59.00 (0-7812-0137-3) Rprt Serv.

— The Tenant of Wildfell Hall. LC 97-14200. 548p. 1997. 19.00 (0-679-60279-8) Modern Lib NY.

— The Tenant of Wildfell Hall. 416p. 1998. pap. 3.95 (1-85326-092-4) NTC Contemp Pub Co.

— The Tenant of Wildfell Hall. Rosengarten, Herbert, ed. (Clarendon Edition of the Novels of the Brontes Ser.). 570p. 1992. text 160.00 (0-19-812596-8) OUP.

— The Tenant of Wildfell Hall. Davies, Steve, ed. & intro. by. LC 96-164052. 1996. pap. 7.95 (0-14-043474-7) Viking Penguin.

— The Tenant of Wildfell Hall. (Classics Ser.). 1996. pap. 3.95 (1-85326-488-1, 4881WW, Pub. by Wrdsworth Edits) NTC Contemp Pub Co.

— The Tenant of Wildfell Hall. large type ed. (Isis Clear Type Classic Ser.). 512p. 1990. 22.95 (1-85089-363-2, Pub. by ISIS Lrg Prnt) Transaction Pubs.

— The Tenant of Wildfell Hall. large type ed. 799p. 1997. 27.99 (0-7089-8951-9) Ulverscroft.

— The Tenant of Wildfell Hall. Rosengarten, Herbert, ed. (Oxford World's Classics Ser.). 520p. 1998. reprint ed. pap. 6.95 (0-19-283462-2) OUP.

— The Tenant of Wildfell Hall. LC 79-4122. (Banquo Bks.). 389p. 1979. reprint ed. pap. 4.95 (0-912800-70-4) Woodbridge Pr.

Bronte, Charlotte. Charlotte & Emily Bronte. deluxe ed. 1200p. 1995. 19.99 (0-517-14779-3) Random Hse Value.

— Charlotte Bronte's High Life in Verdopolis: A Story from the Glass Town Saga. Alexander, Christine, ed. (Illus.). 140p. 1996. 24.95 (0-7123-0408-8) U of Toronto Pr.

— Complete Poems of Charlotte Bronte. 1988. reprint ed. lib. bdg. 59.00 (0-7812-0136-5) Rprt Serv.

— Complete Poems of Charlotte Bronte. LC 73-131647. (Literature Ser.). 266p. 1972. reprint ed. 49.00 (0-403-00534-5) Scholarly.

— An Edition of the Early Writings of Charlotte Bronte: The Rise of Angria, 1834-1835, Vol. II, Pts. 1. Alexander, Christine, ed. 448p. 1991. 207.95 (0-631-12989-8) Blackwell Pubs.

— Jane Eyre. (YA). (gr. 9 up). 1963. mass mkt. 4.95 (0-8049-0017-5, CL-17) Airmont.

— Jane Eyre. Date not set. lib. bdg. 28.95 (0-8488-1269-7) Amereon Ltd.

— Jane Eyre. 1998. pap. text 14.95 (1-55701-233-4) BNI Pubns.

— Jane Eyre. 464p. (YA). (gr. 7-12). 1983. mass mkt. 4.95 (0-553-21140-4, Bantam Classics) Bantam.

— Jane Eyre. Kendrick, Walter, ed. (Macdonald Classics Ser.). 508p. (C). 1980. 19.95 (0-8464-1070-2) Beekman Pubs.

— Jane Eyre. Nemesvari, Richard, ed. (Literary Texts Ser.). 680p. 1999. pap. 7.95 (1-55111-180-2) Broadview Pr.

— Jane Eyre. Cockcroft, Susan, ed. (Cambridge Literature Ser.). 528p. 1996. pap. 11.95 (0-521-56865-X) Cambridge U Pr.

— Jane Eyre. Luaces, Juan G., tr. (Nueva Austral Ser.: No. 59). (SPA.). 1991. pap. text 19.95 (84-239-1859-9) Elliots Bks.

— Jane Eyre. 640p. 1991. 20.00 (0-679-40582-8) Everymns Lib.

— Jane Eyre. 1997. text 8.25 (0-03-051488-6) Holt R&W.

— Jane Eyre. (Cloth Bound Pocket Ser.). 240p. 1998. 7.95 (3-89508-259-7) Konemann.

— Jane Eyre. write for info. (0-614-22110-2, Sig Classics) NAL.

— Jane Eyre. 464p. (C). 1999. mass mkt. 4.95 (0-451-52655-4) NAL.

— Jane Eyre, 4 vols. 40.00 (0-614-30527-6) NAVH.

— Jane Eyre. Smith, Margaret, ed. & intro. by. LC 98-218821. (Oxford World's Classics Ser.). 532p. 1998. pap. 6.95 (0-19-283356-1) OUP.

***Bronte, Charlotte.** Jane Eyre. (Oxford World's Classics Hardcovers Ser.). 544p. 2000. 15.00 (0-19-210042-4) OUP.

Bronte, Charlotte. Jane Eyre. 1997. per. 5.99 (0-671-01479-X) PB.

— Jane Eyre. Farr, Naunerle C., ed. (Illus.). (J). (gr. 4-12). 1977. student ed. 1.25 (0-88301-290-1); pap. text 2.95 (0-88301-266-9) Pendulum Pr.

— Jane Eyre. (Illustrated Junior Library). (Illus.). 576p. (J). (gr. 4 up). 1983. 16.95 (0-448-06031-0, G & D) Peng Put Young Read.

— Jane Eyre. (Puffin Classics Ser.). (Illus.). 656p. (YA). (gr. 5 up). 1995. pap. 4.99 (0-14-036678-4, PuffinBks) Peng Put Young Read.

***Bronte, Charlotte.** Jane Eyre. 1998. pap. 12.95 (84-08-01725-X) Planeta.

— Jane Eyre. 200p. 1999. cd-rom 8.99 (1-57646-162-9) QVision.

Bronte, Charlotte. Jane Eyre. 700p. 1993. 19.95 (0-679-42472-5) Random.

— Jane Eyre. LC 97-10488. (Step into Classics Ser.). 99p. (J). (gr. 2-7). 1997. pap. 3.99 (0-679-88618-4) Random.

***Bronte, Charlotte.** Jane Eyre. (Unabridged Classics Ser.). 336p. (YA). 2000. pap. 5.98 (0-7624-0547-3, Courage) Running Pr.

Bronte, Charlotte. Jane Eyre. write for info. (0-318-58795-5) S&S Trade.

— Jane Eyre. Newman, Beth, ed. LC 94-31302. (Case Studies in Contemporary Criticism). 592p. 1996. text 39.95 (0-312-12795-2) St Martin.

***Bronte, Charlotte.** Jane Eyre. LC 99-218183. 96p. 1999. pap. 14.95 (1-85459-329-3, Pub. by Theatre Comm) Consort Bk Sales.

Bronte, Charlotte. Jane Eyre. 512p. 1994. mass mkt. 3.99 (0-8125-2337-7, Pub. by Tor Bks) St Martin.

— Jane Eyre. (YA). (gr. 8 up). 1996. pap. 3.99 (0-614-15793-5) Tor Bks.

— Jane Eyre. 1997. pap. 2.95 (0-89375-779-9) Troll Communs.

— Jane Eyre. 1960. 10.05 (0-606-00892-6, Pub. by Turtleback) Demco.

Bronte, Charlotte. Jane Eyre. 1981. 9.05 (0-606-13533-2, Pub. by Turtleback) Demco.

Bronte, Charlotte. Jane Eyre. (Bullseye Step into Classics Ser.). 1997. 9.09 (0-606-11517-X, Pub. by Turtleback) Demco.

— Jane Eyre. 474p. 1991. pap. 6.95 (0-460-87085-8, Everyman's Classic Lib) Tuttle Pubng.

***Bronte, Charlotte.** Jane Eyre. 2000. pap. 6.95 (0-460-87596-5, Everyman's Classic Lib) Tuttle Pubng.

Bronte, Charlotte. Jane Eyre. Mason, Michael, ed. & intro. by. LC 96-204575. 576p. 1996. pap. 7.95 (0-14-043400-3) Viking Penguin.

— Jane Eyre. (Classics Library). 405p. 1997. pap. 3.95 (1-85326-020-7, 0207WW, Pub. by Wrdsworth Edits) NTC Contemp Pub Co.

— Jane Eyre. Hedge, Tricia, ed. (Illus.). 110p. 1991. pap. text 5.95 (0-19-421632-2) OUP.

— Jane Eyre. large type ed. 1997. pap. 21.95 (1-55701-207-5) BNI Pubns.

— Jane Eyre. large type ed. LC 94-31302. 689p. 1994. lib. bdg. 23.95 (0-7838-1135-7, G K Hall Lrg Type) Mac Lib Ref.

— Jane Eyre. large type ed. 740p. 1997. 27.99 (0-7089-8015-5) Ulverscroft.

— Jane Eyre. 599p. 1984. reprint ed. lib. bdg. 27.95 (0-89966-493-8) Buccaneer Bks.

— Jane Eyre. 550p. 1998. reprint ed. lib. bdg. 24.00 (1-58287-089-6) North Bks.

— Jane Eyre. unabridged ed. (Wordsworth Classics). (YA). (gr. 6-12). 1998. 5.27 (0-89061-020-7, R0207WW, Jamestwn Pub) NTC Contemp Pub Co.

— Jane Eyre. 2nd ed. Dunn, Richard J., ed. LC 86-21716. 497p. (C). 1987. pap. text 14.00 (0-393-95589-3) Norton.

***Bronte, Charlotte.** Jane Eyre. 2nd ed. (Norton Critical Editions Ser.). (C). 1999. pap. text 28.00 (0-393-98061-8) Norton.

— Jane Eyre. 2nd ed. Smith, Margaret, ed. (Oxford World's Classics Ser.). 544p. 2000. pap. 6.95 (0-19-283965-9) OUP.

Bronte, Charlotte. Jane Eyre. 2nd ed. Howe, D. H., ed. (Illus.). 62p. 1993. pap. text 5.95 (0-19-585275-3) OUP.

— Jane Eyre. 2nd ed. (Illustrated Classic Book Ser.). (Illus.). 61p. (J). (gr. 3 up). 1998. reprint ed. pap. text 4.95 (1-56767-267-1) Educ Insights.

Bronte, Charlotte. Jane Eyre: Bloom,&Claire, Set. abr. ed. 1996. audio 18.00 (0-694-51769-0) HarperAudio.

Bronte, Charlotte. Jane Eyre Readalong. (Illustrated Classics Collection 3). 64p. 1994. pap. 14.95 incl. audio (0-7854-0739-1, 40458) Am Guidance.

***Bronte, Charlotte.** The Letters of Charlotte Bronte 1848-1851, Vol. II. Smith, Margaret, ed. (Illus.). 650p. 2000. text 110.00 (0-19-818598-7) OUP.

Bronte, Charlotte. The Letters of Charlotte Bronte, 1829-1847, Vol. I. Smith, Margaret, ed. (Illus.). 644p. 1995. text 98.00 (0-19-818597-9) OUP.

— Life & Works of the Sisters Bronte, 7 vols. LC 77-148757. reprint ed. 510.00 (0-404-08830-9) AMS Pr.

***Bronte, Charlotte.** The Professor. (Twelve-Point Ser.). 250p. 1999. lib. bdg. write for info. (1-58287-095-0) North Bks.

Bronte, Charlotte. The Professor. Smith, Margaret & Rosengarten, Herbert, eds. (Clarendon Edition of the Novels of the Brontes Ser.). (Illus.). 390p. 1987. 110.00 (0-19-812694-8) OUP.

— The Professor. Smith, Margaret & Rosengarten, Herbert, eds. (World's Classics Ser.). 336p. 1991. pap. 5.95 (0-19-282741-3) OUP.

— The Professor. Smith, Margaret & Rosengarten, Herbert, eds. (Oxford World's Classics Ser.). 330p. 1998. pap. 6.95 (0-19-283511-4) OUP.

— The Professor. Glen, Heather, ed. & intro. by. 320p. 1989. pap. 8.95 (0-14-043311-2, Penguin Classics) Viking Penguin.

— The Professor. (Classics Library). 215p. 1998. pap. 3.95 (1-85326-208-0, 2080WW, Pub. by Wrdsworth Edits) NTC Contemp Pub Co.

— Sarah Miles. 1996. 24.00 (0-679-45715-1) Random.

— Shirley. LC 97-9954. 688p. 1997. 19.50 (0-679-60275-5) Modern Lib NY.

— Shirley. Smith, Margaret & Rosengarten, Herbert, eds. (Oxford World's Classics Ser.). 718p. 1998. pap. 6.95 (0-19-283378-2) OUP.

— Shirley. Hook, Andrew & Hook, Judith, eds. (English Library). 624p. 1974. pap. 7.99 (0-14-043095-4, Penguin Classics) Viking Penguin.

— Shirley. (Classics Library). 656p. 1998. pap. 3.95 (1-85326-064-9, 0649WW, Pub. by Wrdsworth Edits) NTC Contemp Pub Co.

— The Unfinished Novels. LC 93-26286. (Pocket Classics Ser.). 1993. pap. 6.95 (0-7509-0481-X, Pub. by Sutton Pub Ltd) Intl Pubs Mktg.

***Bronte, Charlotte.** Vilette. (Classics Library). 1998. pap. 3.95 (1-85326-072-X, 072XWW, Pub. by Wrdsworth Edits) NTC Contemp Pub Co.

Bronte, Charlotte. Villette. 512p. 1986. mass mkt. 5.95 (0-553-21243-5) Bantam.

— Villette. 1992. 20.00 (0-679-40988-2) McKay.

***Bronte, Charlotte.** Villette. (Twelve-Point Ser.). 1999. lib. bdg. 24.00 (1-58287-114-0) North Bks.

Bronte, Charlotte. Villette. Smith, Margaret & Rosengarten, Herbert, eds. LC 98-195483. (Oxford World's Classics Ser.). 698p. 1998. pap. 9.95 (0-19-283433-9) OUP.

— Villette. Kemp, Sandra, ed. 576p. 1993. pap. 5.95 (0-460-87247-8, Everyman's Classic Lib) Tuttle Pubng.

— Villette. Lilly, Mark, ed. (English Library). 624p. 1980. pap. 10.95 (0-14-043118-7, Penguin Classics) Viking Penguin.

— Villette. large type ed. (Isis Clear Type Classic Ser.). 601p. 1992. 24.95 (1-85089-449-3, Pub. by ISIS Lrg Prnt) Transaction Pubs.

— Villette. 1992. reprint ed. lib. bdg. 24.95 (0-89966-998-0) Buccaneer Bks.

***Bronte, Charlotte.** Villette. 2nd ed. Smith, Margaret & Rosengarten, Herbert, eds. (Oxford World's Classics Ser.). 704p. 2001. pap. 9.95 (0-19-283964-0) OUP.

Bronte, Charlotte & Bronte, Emily Jane. The Belgian Essays. Lonoff, Sue, ed. & tr. by. from FRE. LC 95-48323. 576p. (C). 1996. 37.00 (0-300-06489-6) Yale U Pr.

— The Brontes' Christmas. (Illus.). 128p. 1997. pap. 17.95 (0-7509-1424-6, Pub. by Sutton Pub Ltd) Intl Pubs Mktg.

— Charlotte & Emily Bronte: The Complete Novels. 1200p. 1993. 15.99 (0-517-09292-1) Random Hse Value.

— Works of Charlotte & Emily Bronte. (Classics - Bonded Leather Fibers Ser.). 502p. 1990. 24.95 (0-681-41000-0) Borders Pr.

— The Works of the Brontes. 703p. 1995. pap. write for info. (1-57215-130-7) World Pubns.

Bronte, Charlotte & Milton, Joyce. Jane Eyre. (Barron's Book Notes Ser.). (C). 1984. pap. 2.95 (0-8120-3422-8) Barron.

Bronte, Charlotte, et al. The Bronte Sisters: Selected Poems of Charlotte, Emily & Anne Bronte. Davies, Stevie, ed. 1990. pap. 7.50 (0-85635-131-8) Carcanet Pr.

— The Brontes: Three Great Novels. 942p. 1994. pap. 19.95 (0-19-282285-3) OUP.

— Selected Poems. 182p. 1993. pap. 6.95 (0-460-87282-6, Everyman's Classic Lib) Tuttle Pubng.

Bronte, Charlotte, jt. auth. see Austen, Jane.

Bronte, Charlotte, jt. auth. see Center for Learning Network Staff.

Bronte, Charlotte, jt. auth. see Johanson, Robert.

Bronte, Charlotte, jt. auth. see Rhys, Jean.

***Bronte, Emily.** Wuthering Heights. 2000. mass mkt. 6.95 (0-375-75644-2) Random.

— Wuthering Heights. large type ed. 473p. 2000. 27.95 (0-7838-9062-1) Mac Lib Ref.

— Wuthering Heights, Vol. 1. Bloom, Harold, ed. (Bloom's Reviews Comprehensive Research & Study Guide Ser.). 80p. (YA). (gr. 8-11). 1999. pap. 4.95 (0-7910-4170-0) Chelsea Hse.

B

An Asterisk (*) at the beginning of an entry indicates that the title is appearing for the first time.

Bronte, Emily Jane. The Complete Poems of Emily Jane Bronte. Hatfield, C. W., ed. LC 41-21750. 262p. 1941. text 46.00 (*0-231-01222-5*) Col U Pr.

— The Complete Poems of Emily Jane Bronte. Hatfield, C. W., ed. LC 97-100951. 288p. 1995. pap. 16.00 (*0-231-10347-6*) Col U Pr.

***Bronte, Emily Jane.** Cumbres Borrascosas. 1998. pap. 9.95 (*84-320-4038-X*) Planeta.

Bronte, Emily Jane. Hurlevant. Bellour, Raymond, ed. (FRE.). 469p. 1991. pap. 16.95 (*0-7859-2152-4*, 2070383059) Fr & Eur.

— Monarch Notes on Bronte's Wuthering Heights. (C). 3.95 (*0-671-00603-7*, Arco) Macmillan Gen Ref.

— Monarch Quick & Easy Notes: "Wuthering Heights" by Emily Bronte. write for info. (*0-318-58789-0*) S&S Trade.

— No Coward Soul Is Mine: Emily Bronte Poems. LC 92-62239. 160p. 1992. lib. bdg. 21.95 (*0-9634340-0-4*) Odessa.

— Poems: Emily Bronte. LC 96-140866. 254p. 1996. 12.50 (*0-679-44725-3*) Random.

Bronte, Emily Jane. The Poems of Emily Bronte. Lloyd-Evans, Barbara, ed. 224p. (C). 1992. text 54.50 (*0-389-20977-5*) B&N Imports.

Bronte, Emily Jane. The Poems of Emily Bronte. Roper, Derek & Chitham, Edward, eds. (English Texts Ser.). 326p. 1996. text 74.00 (*0-19-812641-7*) OUP.

— Selected Poems of Emily Bronte. (Bloomsbury Classic Poetry Ser.). 128p. 1995. text 9.95 (*0-312-13438-X*) St Martin.

— Wuthering Heights. 1991. pap. text. write for info. (*0-17-556575-9*) Addison-Wesley.

— Wuthering Heights. 320p. Date not set. 24.95 (*0-8488-2218-8*) Amereon Ltd.

— Wuthering Heights. 1998. pap. text 14.95 (*1-55701-238-5*) BNI Pubns.

— Wuthering Heights. 320p. (YA). (gr. 7-12). 1983. mass mkt. 4.95 (*0-553-21258-3*, Bantam Classics) Bantam.

***Bronte, Emily Jane.** Wuthering Heights. (Literature Made Easy Ser.). 96p. (YA). 1999. pap. 4.95 (*0-7641-0829-8*) Barron.

— Wuthering Heights. Seely, Elizabeth & Seely, John, eds. LC 99-25635. (Classic Novels). 368p. 1999. pap. text 8.95 (*0-7641-1148-5*) Barron.

Bronte, Emily Jane. Wuthering Heights. Kendrick, Walter, ed. (Classics Ser.). 400p. (C). 1990. 19.95 (*0-8464-1072-9*) Beekman Pubs.

— Wuthering Heights. Hoyes, Richard, ed. LC 97-183620. (Cambridge Literature Ser.). 416p. (C). 1997. pap. 11.95 (*0-521-58949-5*) Cambridge U Pr.

— Wuthering Heights. 416p. 1991. 17.00 (*0-679-40543-7*) Everymns Lib.

Bronte, Emily Jane. Wuthering Heights, 001. Pritchett, V. S., ed. LC 56-14017. (YA). (gr. 9 up). 1956. pap. 13.96 (*0-395-05102-9*, RivEd) HM.

Bronte, Emily Jane. Wuthering Heights. 1997. text 8.25 (*0-03-051489-4*) Holt R&W.

— Wuthering Heights. 240p. 1998. 7.95 (*3-89508-208-2*) Konemann.

— Wuthering Heights. Blatchford, Roy, ed. (Literature Ser.). 1993. pap. 5.95 (*0-582-07782-6*, TG7655) Longman.

— Wuthering Heights. LC 96-214026. 448p. 1994. 16.50 (*0-679-60135-X*) Modern Lib NY.

— Wuthering Heights. Stoneman, Patsy & Jack, Ian, eds. LC PR4172.W7 1998b. (Oxford World's Classics Ser.). (Illus.). 428p. 1998. pap. 5.95 (*0-19-283354-5*) OUP.

— Wuthering Heights. LC 99-462504. (Oxford World's Classics Hardcovers Ser.). 384p. 1999. 15.50 (*0-19-210027-0*) OUP.

— Wuthering Heights. Peters, Sally, ed. 352p. 1992. mass mkt. 4.99 (*0-671-79022-6*) PB.

— Wuthering Heights. 1997. per. 5.99 (*0-671-01480-3*) PB.

— Wuthering Heights. (Classics for Young Readers Ser.). (Illus.). 448p. (YA). (gr. 5 up). 1995. pap. 4.99 (*0-14-036694-6*, PuffinBks) Peng Put Young Read.

***Bronte, Emily Jane.** Wuthering Heights. 1999. pap. 2.99 (*0-14-130547-9*, PuffinBks) Peng Put Young Read.

Bronte, Emily Jane. Wuthering Heights. Nestor, Pauline, ed. (Penguin Ser.). 353p. (C). 1995. pap. 5.99 (*0-14-043418-6*) Penguin Books.

— Wuthering Heights. LC 81-15786. (Illus.). 48p. (gr. 4-7). 1998. pap. text 6.95 (*0-8114-6847-X*) Raintree Steck-V.

***Bronte, Emily Jane.** Wuthering Heights. (Unabridged Classics Ser.). 256p. (YA). 2000. pap. 5.98 (*0-7624-0559-7*, Courage) Running Pr.

Bronte, Emily Jane. Wuthering Heights. (Thornes Classic Novels Ser.). (Illus.). 354p. 1997. pap. 16.95 (*0-7487-2978-X*, Pub. by S Thornes Pubs) Trans-Atl Phila.

— Wuthering Heights. Murfin, Ross C. & Peterson, Linda H., eds. LC 90-71625. (Case Studies in Contemporary Criticism). 467p. (C). 1991. pap. text 11.95 (*0-312-03547-0*) St Martin.

— Wuthering Heights. 224p. (YA). 1989. pap. 2.99 (*0-8125-0516-6*, Pub. by Tor Bks) St Martin.

— Wuthering Heights. 1997. pap. 2.95 (*0-89375-706-3*) Troll Communs.

Bronte, Emily Jane. Wuthering Heights. (Signet Classics). 1959. 10.05 (*0-606-01582-5*, Pub. by Turtleback) Demco.

Bronte, Emily Jane. Wuthering Heights. (Classics Library). 246p. 1997. pap. 3.95 (*1-85326-001-0*, 0010WW, Pub. by Wrdsworth Edits) NTC Contemp Pub Co.

— Wuthering Heights. abr. ed. 1993. write for info. incl. audio compact disk (*0-7871-0064-1*) NewStar Media.

— Wuthering Heights. abr. ed. Farr, Naunerle C., ed. (Now Age Illustrated III Ser.). (Illus.). (J). (gr. 4-12). 1977. pap. text 2.95 (*0-88301-272-3*) Pendulum Pr.

— Wuthering Heights. large type ed. 1997. pap. 19.95 (*1-55701-208-3*) BNI Pubns.

***Bronte, Emily Jane.** Wuthering Heights. large type ed. 464p. 2000. pap. 22.00 (*0-06-095570-8*) HarpC.

Bronte, Emily Jane. Wuthering Heights. large type ed. (Large Print Heritage Ser.). 536p. 1997. lib. bdg. 35.95 (*1-58118-003-9*, 21964) LRS.

— Wuthering Heights. large type ed. (Large Print Ser.). 566p. 1992. lib. bdg. 24.00 (*0-939495-28-7*) North Bks.

— Wuthering Heights. large type ed. LC 97-30817. 440p. 1998. text 24.95 (*1-56000-527-0*) Transaction Pubs.

— Wuthering Heights. large type ed. 551p. 1997. 27.99 (*0-7089-8950-0*) Ulverscroft.

— Wuthering Heights. 320p. 1986. reprint ed. lib. bdg. 25.95 (*0-89966-520-9*) Buccaneer Bks.

— Wuthering Heights. LC 88-62416. (Signet Classics Ser.). 320p. (YA). (gr. 10 up). 2000. reprint ed. mass mkt. write for info. (*0-451-52338-5*) NAL.

***Bronte, Emily Jane.** Wuthering Heights. 350p. 1998. reprint ed. lib. bdg. 24.00 (*1-58287-083-7*) North Bks.

Bronte, Emily Jane. Wuthering Heights. unabridged ed. LC 96-20636. (Thrift Editions Ser.). 256p. 1996. reprint ed. pap. 2.00 (*0-486-29256-8*) Dover.

— Wuthering Heights. unabridged ed. (Classics Ser.). (YA). (gr. 9 up). 1963. mass mkt. 4.95 (*0-8049-0011-6*, CL-11) Airmont.

— Wuthering Heights. 3rd rev. ed. Sale, William M., Jr. & Dunn, Richard J., eds. LC 88-8543. (Critical Editions Ser.). 396p. (YA). (gr. 9-12). 1990. pap. text 11.25 (*0-393-95760-8*) Norton.

— Wuthering Heights: And Poems. Drabble, Margaret, ed. 432p. 1993. pap. 4.95 (*0-460-87311-3*, Everyman's Classic Lib) Tuttle Pubng.

— Wuthering Heights: The Story of Catherine & Heathcliff. LC 74-157756. (Hallmark Editions Ser.). 61p. (J). 1971. write for info. (*0-87529-213-5*) Hallmark.

***Bronte, Emily Jane.** Wuthering Heights: With a Preface by Charlotte Bronte. (Signature Classics Ser.). 384p. 1999. 24.95 (*1-58279-033-7*) Trident Pr Intl.

— Wuthering Heights: With a Preface by Charlotte Bronte. deluxe ed. 384p. 1999. 29.95 (*1-58279-045-0*) Trident Pr Intl.

Bronte, Emily Jane. Wuthering Heights Readalong. (Illustrated Classics Collection 3). 64p. 1994. pap. 14.95 incl. audio (*0-7854-0745-6*, 40476) Am Guidance.

Bronte, Emily Jane & Geary, Rick. Wuthering Heights. (Classics Illustrated Ser.). (Illus.). 52p. (YA). pap. 4.95 (*1-57209-011-1*) Classics Int Ent.

Bronte, Emily Jane, et al. Best Poems of the Bronte Sisters. Ward, Candace, ed. LC 96-38774. (Thrift Editions Ser.). 64p. (Orig.). 1997. pap. 1.00 (*0-486-29529-X*) Dover.

Bronte, Emily Jane, jt. auth. see Bronte, Charlotte.

Bronte, Emily Jane, jt. auth. see Center for Learning Network Staff.

Bronte, Emily Jane, jt. auth. see Vance, Charles C.

Bronte, Erica. Lust, Inc. (Orig.). 1996. mass mkt. 6.50 (*1-56333-467-4*) Masquerade.

— Slave to Her Desires. 1998. mass mkt. 6.95 (*1-56333-699-5*) Masquerade.

Bronte, Lydia, jt. ed. see Pifer, Alan.

Bronte, Patrick. Bronteana: The Rev. Patrick Bronte, His Collected Works & Life. LC 77-148320. reprint ed. 38.00 (*0-404-08920-8*) AMS Pr.

Bronvoll, Hilde. Andrea Moves to America. (NOR & SPA., Illus.). 32p. (J). 1999. pap. 14.95 (*1-57532-137-8*) Press-Tige Pub.

Bronx County Historical Society Staff & Hermalyn, Gary. The Beautiful Bronx: Nineteen Twenty to Nineteen Fifty. (Life in the Bronx Ser.). (Illus.). 192p. 1979. text 25.00 (*0-517-54800-3*) Bronx County.

Bronz, Ruth A. Third Coast, Gulf Coast. 1924. write for info. (*0-688-17090-0*, Wm Morrow) Morrow Avon.

Bronzaft, Arline L. Top of the Class: Guiding Children along the Smart Path to Happiness. (Creative Research Monographs). (Illus.). 206p. 1996. pap. 39.50 (*1-56750-185-0*); text 73.25 (*1-56750-184-2*) Ablx Pub.

Bronzan, JoAnn P. Siri-Along Norwegian Winter. LC 99-63874. 80p. 2000. pap. 13.95 (*0-88739-294-6*) Creat Arts Bk.

Bronze, Lewis & Brown, Peter. Blue Peter Action Book. (Illus.). 65p. (YA). 1994. 9.95 (*0-563-36495-5*, Pub. by BBC) Parkwest Pubns.

Bronzert, Kathleen & Sherwin, Bruce, eds. The Glory of the Garden. (Illus.). 320p. (Orig.). 1993. pap. 10.00 (*0-380-76854-2*, Avon Bks) Morrow Avon.

Bronzetti, G., et al. Antimutagenesis & Anticarcinogenesis Mechanisms 3. (Basic Life Sciences Ser.: Vol. 61). (Illus.). 504p. (C). 1993. text 135.00 (*0-306-44577-8*, Kluwer Plenum) Kluwer Academic.

Bronzino, Joseph & Smith, Vincent K. Medical Technology & Society: An Interdisciplinary Perspective. (Sloan NLA Ser.). (Illus.). 580p. 1990. 50.00 (*0-262-02300-8*) MIT Pr.

Bronzino, Joseph, et al. Medical Technology, Ethics & Economics. (C). 1990. text 46.00 (*0-07-008002-X*) McGraw.

Bronzino, Joseph D. The Biomedical Engineering Handbook. 2nd ed. (Electrical Engineering Handbook Ser.). 1999. 139.95 (*0-8493-8594-6*) CRC Pr.

***Bronzino, Joseph D.** Biomedical Engineering Handbook, Vol. 1. 2nd ed. (Electrical Engineering Handbook Ser.). 1656p. 1999. 94.98 (*0-8493-0461-X*) CRC Pr.

Bronzino, Joseph D., ed. The Biomedical Engineering Handbook. (Electrical Engineering Handbook Ser.). 2896p. 1995. boxed set 159.95 (*0-8493-8346-3*, 8346) CRC Pr.

Bronzino, Joseph D. & Roosa, Vernon. Management of Medical Technology: A Primer for Clinical Engineers. Austin-LaFrance, Robert J., ed. LC 92-21070. (Biomedical Engineering Ser.). 451p. 1992. 64.95 (*0-7506-9252-9*) Buttrwrth-Heinemann.

Bronzino, Joseph D., jt. auth. see Smith, Vincent H.

***Bronzite, Michael.** System Development: A Strategic Framework. LC 99-59971. xvi, 248p. 2000. pap. 39.95 (*1-85233-176-3*) Spr-Verlag.

Bronznick, jt. auth. see Uveeler.

Broock, Sabra, ed. see Webby & Chang.

***Broodbank, Cyprian.** An Island Archaeology of theEarly Cyclades. (Illus.). 352p. (C). 2000. text Price not set. (*0-521-78272-4*) Cambridge U Pr.

Brooding Heron Press, jt. auth. see Genoways, Ted.

Broodthaers, Marcel. Broodthaers: Catalogue Raisonne of Prints & Drawings. 1996. pap. 35.00 (*3-89322-836-5*, Pub. by Edition Cantz) Dist Art Pubs.

Brook, et al. The Fascination of Statistics. (Popular Statistics Ser.: Vol. 4). (Illus.). 456p. 1986. text 55.00 (*0-8247-7329-2*) Dekker.

Brook, Adele. Bread & Tears. 1993. 12.95 (*0-533-10506-4*) Vantage.

Brook, Alan J., jt. auth. see Lind, Edna M.

Brook, Alexander B. The Hard Way: The Odyssey of a Weekly Newspaper Editor. LC 92-39425. (Illus.). 306p. 1993. 19.95 (*1-882593-00-6*) Bridge Wrks.

***Brook, Alexander B.** The Hard Way: The Odyssey of a Weekly Newspaper Editor. LC 92-39425. 328p. 2000. reprint ed. pap. 15.00 (*1-882593-37-5*) Bridge Wrks.

Brook, Andrew. Kant & the Mind. 341p. (C). 1994. text 74.95 (*0-521-45036-5*) Cambridge U Pr.

— Kant & the Mind. 341p. 1997. pap. text 20.95 (*0-521-57441-2*) Cambridge U Pr.

***Brook, Andrew & Stainton, Robert J.** Knowledge & Mind: A Philosophical Introduction LC 99-38797. 2000. pap. write for info. (*0-262-52269-1*) MIT Pr.

— Knowledge & Mind: A Philosophical Introduction. LC 99-38797. (Illus.). 269p. 2000. 27.95 (*0-262-02475-6*, Bradford Bks) MIT Pr.

Brook, Andrew T., tr. see Gindely, Anton.

***Brook, Barbara.** Feminist Perspectives on the Body. LC 98-52841. (Feminist Perspectives Ser.). 200p. 1999. pap. 24.95 (*0-582-35639-3*) Longman.

Brook, Barry S., ed. Ringmacher Thematic Catalogue (1773) (Thematic Catalogues Ser.: No. 14). (Illus.). 150p. 1988. lib. bdg. 70.00 (*0-918728-91-6*) Pendragon NY.

— The Symphony in Norway, Vol. I. LC 81-13252. (Symphony 1720-1840 Ser.: Vol. 11, Series F). 320p. 1981. 25.00 (*0-8240-3810-X*) Garland.

Brook, Barry S. & Viano, Richard J. Thematic Catalogues in Music: An Annotated Bibliography. 2nd ed. LC 97-2411. (Rilm Retro Ser.: No. 5). 602p. 1997. 68.00 (*0-918728-86-X*) Pendragon NY.

Brook, Benjamin. The Lives of the Puritans, 3 vols. 1543p. 1994. reprint ed. 105.00 (*1-877611-79-4*) Soli Deo Gloria.

— Lives of the Puritans, Vol. 2. 507p. 1994. 35.00 (*1-877611-81-6*) Soli Deo Gloria.

— Lives of the Puritans, Vol. 3. 556p. 1994. 35.00 (*1-877611-82-4*) Soli Deo Gloria.

Brook, Bonnie, jt. auth. see Kraus, Robert.

Brook, Bonnie, ed. see Amerikaner, Susan.

Brook, Bonnie, ed. see Arnold, Caroline.

Brook, Bonnie, ed. see Ashley, Jill.

Brook, Bonnie, ed. see Ball, Jacqueline.

Brook, Bonnie, ed. see Barkan, Joanne.

Brook, Bonnie, ed. see Binnamin, Vivian.

Brook, Bonnie, ed. see Boynton, Alice B.

Brook, Bonnie, ed. see Calder, S. J.

Brook, Bonnie, ed. see Carter, Polly.

Brook, Bonnie, ed. see Himmelman, John.

Brook, Bonnie, ed. see Hoobler, Dorothy & Hoobler, Thomas.

Brook, Bonnie, ed. see Kraus, Robert.

Brook, Bonnie, ed. see Kuhn, Dwight.

Brook, Bonnie, ed. see Pearce, Querida L. & Pearce, W. L.

Brook, Bonnie, ed. see Please Touch Museum Staff.

Brook, Bonnie, ed. see Poskanzer, Susan C.

Brook, Bonnie, ed. see Woodson, Jacqueline.

Brook, Bonnie, ed. see Young, Robert.

***Brook, Bryan.** Love Styles: Re-Engineering Marriage for the New Millennium. 92p. 2000. pap. 9.95 (*0-9637285-3-9*) Prose Assocs.

Brook, C. Clinical Paediatric Endocrinology. 3rd ed. (Illus.). 864p. 1995. 295.00 (*0-632-03632-X*) Blackwell Sci.

Brook, C. & Hanstead, P. D., eds. Impact of Non-Destructive Testing NDT, 1989: Proceedings of the 28th Annual British Conference on Non-Destructive Testing, Sheffield, UK, 18-21 September 1989. (Illus.). 323p. 1990. pap. 35.00 (*0-08-040192-9*, Pergamon Pr) Elsevier.

— Reliability in Non-Destructive Testing: Proceedings of the 27th Annual British Conference on Non-Destructive Testing, Portsmouth, UK, 12-15 September 1988. (Illus.). 521p. 1989. pap. 27.00 (*0-08-036961-8*, Pergamon Pr) Elsevier.

Brook, C. & Marshall, N. Essentials of Endocrinology. 3rd ed. (Essentials Ser.). (Illus.). 256p. 1996. pap. 36.95 (*0-632-03622-2*, Pub. by Blckwll Scitfc UK) Blackwell Sci.

Brook, Carol L. Tortured by Sound: Beyond Human Endurance. 320p. 1999. 25.95 (*0-9664620-0-9*) Roaring Prodns.

Brook, Charles G. A Guide to the Practice of Paediatric Endocrinology. (Illus.). 191p. (C). 1993. text 54.95 (*0-521-43179-4*) Cambridge U Pr.

Brook, Christopher, jt. ed. see McGrew, Anthony.

Brook, Claire, jt. ed. see Clinkscale, Edward.

Brook, D. & Wynne, R. J. Signal Processing: Principles & Applications. (Illus.). 288p. (C). 1988. pap. text 19.95 (*0-7131-3564-6*, Pub. by E A) Routldge.

Brook, David L. A Lasting Gift of Heritage: A History of the North Carolina Society for the Preservation of Antiquities, 1939-1974. LC 98-141858. (Illus.). 205p. 1997. 24.00 (*0-86526-274-8*) NC Archives.

Brook, Diane L. Georgia: A Geography. 1996. text 35.00 (*0-86531-615-5*) Westview.

— Georgia: A Geography. (C). 1996. pap. text 20.00 (*0-86531-616-3*) Westview.

Brook, Donald. Composer's Gallery: Biographical Sketches of Contemporary Composers. LC 76-136641. (Biography Index Reprint Ser.). 1977. 20.95 (*0-8369-8036-0*) Ayer.

— Composers' Gallery: Biographical Sketches of Contemporary Composers: Music Book Index. 218p. 1993. reprint ed. lib. bdg. 79.00 (*0-7812-9569-6*) Rprt Serv.

— Conductors' Gallery. LC 70-136642. (Biography Index Reprint Ser.). 1977. 26.95 (*0-8369-8037-9*) Ayer.

— Five Great French Composers: Berlioz, Cesar Franck, Saint-Saens, Debussy, Ravel; Their Lives & Works. LC 77-160916. (Biography Index Reprint Ser.). 1977. reprint ed. 23.95 (*0-8369-8079-4*) Ayer.

— Five Great French Composers: Music Book Index. 1993. reprint ed. lib. bdg. 79.00 (*0-7812-9580-7*) Rprt Serv.

— Masters of the Keyboard. LC 75-114479. 184p. 1971. reprint ed. lib. bdg. 45.00 (*0-8371-4768-9*, BRMK, Greenwood Pr) Greenwood.

— Masters of the Keyboard. 2nd ed. LC 76-148206. (Biography Index Reprint Ser.). 1977. 21.95 (*0-8369-8053-0*) Ayer.

— Masters of the Keyboard: Music Book Index. 183p. 1993. reprint ed. lib. bdg. 69.00 (*0-7812-9571-8*) Rprt Serv.

— Pageant of English Actors. LC 71-38315. (Biography Index Reprint Ser.). 1977. reprint ed. 20.95 (*0-8369-8116-2*) Ayer.

— Singers of Today. LC 70-160917. (Biography Index Reprint Ser.). 1977. reprint ed. 22.95 (*0-8369-8080-8*) Ayer.

— Six Great Russian Composers. LC 73-136643. (Biography Index Reprint Ser.). 1977. reprint ed. 27.95 (*0-8369-8038-7*) Ayer.

— Six Great Russian Composers: Music Book Index. 193p. 1993. reprint ed. lib. bdg. 69.00 (*0-7812-9570-X*) Rprt Serv.

— Violinists of Today. LC 74-38313. (Biography Index Reprint Ser.). 1977. reprint ed. 18.95 (*0-8369-8117-0*) Ayer.

— Violinists of Today: Music Book Index. 192p. 1993. reprint ed. lib. bdg. 69.00 (*0-7812-9583-1*) Rprt Serv.

Brook, Donald E. AP Calculus AB. 1999. pap. text 17.95 (*0-87891-282-7*) Res & Educ.

Brook, Donna. The Journey of English. LC 95-52354. (Illus.). 48p. (J). (gr. 5 up). 1998. 17.00 (*0-395-71211-4*) Lerner Pub.

— A More Human Face. 1999. 21.00 (*1-882413-59-8*); pap. 13.00 (*1-882413-58-X*) Hanging Loose.

— Notes on Space-Time. 1977. pap. 5.00 (*0-914610-11-2*) Hanging Loose.

— What Being Responsible Means to Me. 1988. 15.00 (*0-914610-50-3*); pap. 7.00 (*0-914610-49-X*) Hanging Loose.

Brook, Douglas Alan, jt. auth. see Pfiffner, James P.

Brook, Elaine. The Land of the Snow Lion. large type ed. (Illus.). 448p. 1988. 27.99 (*0-7089-1908-1*) Ulverscroft.

Brook, Eve & Davis, Ann, eds. Women, the Family & Social Work. (Tavistock Library of Social Work Practice). 192p. (Orig.). 1985. 27.50 (*0-422-77940-7*, 9484, Pub. by Tavistock); pap. text 13.95 (*0-422-77950-4*, 9485, Pub. by Tavistock) Routldge.

Brook, G. B., jt. ed. see Brandes, E. A.

Brook, G. L. & Leslie, R. F., eds. Layamon's Brut Vol. II: Text (Lines 8021-End), Vol. II, Text (lines 8021-end) (EETS Original Ser.: Vol. 277). 1978. 39.50 (*0-19-722279-X*) OUP.

Brook, George & Heyl, Royle J. Introduction to Landforms. 3rd ed. (Illus.). 220p. (C). 1993. lab manual ed. 36.95 (*0-89892-118-X*) Contemp Pub Co of Raleigh.

Brook-Hart, Denys. British Nineteenth Century Marine Painting. (Illus.). 370p. 1976. 69.50 (*0-902028-32-4*) Antique Collect.

***Brook, Itzhak.** Atlas of Upper Respiratory & Head & Neck Infections. 2nd ed. LC 99-462026. 2000. write for info. (*1-57340-140-4*) Current Med.

Brook, Itzhak, jt. ed. see Mandell, Gerald L.

Brook, J. Sales & Leases. LC 94-75927. 592p. 1994. 25.95 (*0-316-10985-1*, Aspen Law & Bus) Aspen Pub.

Brook, Jack & Kohen, James. The Parramatta Institution & the Black Town: A History. 295p. 1991. 42.95 (*0-86840-300-8*, Pub. by New South Wales Univ Pr) Intl Spec Bk.

Brook, Jack, et al. Attorney's Guide to Oncology Cases, 2. (Personal Injury Library: Vol. 2). 962p. 1994. boxed set 255.00 (*0-471-11209-7*) Wiley.

***Brook, Jacqueline.** Our Rock Who Art in Heaven, Hallowed Be Thy Name. (Illus.). 592p. 1999. per. 18.00 (*0-9676656-0-4*) Sinclair Pr.

Brook, James. Sales & Leases: Examples & Explanations. 2nd ed. LC 98-56171. 580p. 1999. pap. text 33.95 (*0-7355-0056-8*) Panel Pubs.

— Secured Transactions: Examples & Explanations. LC 98-42019. 490p. 1999. pap. text 32.95 (*0-7355-0058-4*) Panel Pubs.

Brook, James, et al, eds. Reclaiming San Francisco: History Politics & Culture. LC 97-22799. (Illus.). 384p. 1998. pap. 17.95 (*0-87286-335-2*) City Lights.

Brook, James & Boal, Iain, eds. Resisting the Virtual Life: The Culture & Politics of Information. (Illus.). 256p. (Orig.). 1995. pap. 15.95 (*0-87286-299-2*) City Lights.

Brook, James, tr. see Debord, Guy.

Brook, James, tr. see Naum, Gellu.

Brook, James, tr. see Savinio, Alberto.

B

Brook, James, tr. see Serge, Victor.

Brook, Jasmine. Over the Moon Bear. (Illus.). 12p. (J). 1998. 7.95 (*0-7641-5071-5*) Barron.

— Top to Tail Bear. (Illus.). 12p. (J). 1998. 7.95 (*0-7641-5072-3*) Barron.

Brook, Jasmine, jt. auth. see McCabe, Lianne.

Brook, John. School of Prayer: An Introduction to the Divine Office for All Christians. 480p. 1992. pap. text 17.95 (*0-8146-2028-0*) Liturgical Pr.

— A Shorter Morning & Evening Prayer: The Psalter of the Liturgy of the Hours. 562p. (C). 1989. pap. 17.95 (*0-8146-1939-8*) Liturgical Pr.

Brook, Judith S., et al, eds. Alcohol & Substance Abuse in Adolescence. LC 84-29004. (Advances in Alcohol & Substance Abuse Ser.: Vol. 4, Nos. 3 & 4). 206p. 1985. text 49.95 (*0-86656-333-4*) Haworth Pr.

Brook, Julie H., ed. see Coats, Susan S. & DeRonde, John A., Jr.

Brook, Kevin A. The Jews of Khazaria. LC 98-38767. 1999. 35.00 (*0-7657-6032-0*) Aronson.

Brook, Larry. Daily Life in Ancient & Modern Timbuktu. LC 98-18314. (Cities Through Time Ser.). (Illus.). 64p. (J). (gr. 4-7). 1999. lib. bdg. 23.93 (*0-8225-3215-8*, Runestone Pr) Lerner Pub.

— How to Develop a Curriculum: For Christian Education Materials in Your Culture. 116p. 1995. pap. text 25.00 (*1-884752-14-4*, 44446) Cook Min Intl.

— How to Write a Lesson: For Christian Education Materials Developed in Your Own Culture. 2nd ed. 99p. 1996. pap. text 25.00 (*1-884752-47-0*, 44487) Cook Min Intl.

Brook, Leeanne. The Great Big, Enormous, Gigantic Cardboard Box. LC 92-29957. (Illus.). (J). (gr. 3 up). 1993. 14.00 (*0-383-03571-6*) SRA McGraw.

Brook, Liz, jt. auth. see Knight, Bill.

Brook, Martin D. Estimating & Tendering for Construction Work. 2nd ed. LC 98-221619. (Illus.). 288p. 1998. pap. text 39.95 (*0-7506-3407-3*) Buttrwrth-Heinemann.

Brook, Mary & Brook, Ray. Synthy. Mind & Body. 1981. pap. 90.00 (*0-9513312-0-5*, Pub. by R Brooks Pubns) St Mut.

Brook, Michael & Rubinstein, Sarah P. Supplement to Reference Guide to Minnesota History: A Subject Bibliography, 1970-80. LC 83-5438. 69p. 1983. pap. 6.95 (*0-87351-160-3*) Minn Hist.

Brook, Michael, ed. see Bengston, Henry.

Brook, Michael A. Silicon in Organic, Organometallic, & Polymer Chemistry. LC 98-49722. 680p. 1999. 125.00 (*0-471-19658-4*) Wiley.

Brook, Nancy O. & Krainin, Cynthia E. Thriving at Work: A Guidebook for Survivors of Childhood Abuse. (Illus.). 107p. 1998. pap., spiral bd., wbk. ed. 15.95 (*0-9664766-0-3*) Career Res Bk.

Brook, Norman. Endurance Running. (Illus.). 93p. 1989. pap. 19.95 (*1-85223-125-4*, Pub. by Crolwood) Trafalgar.

Brook, Paula. Work Less Live More. 256p. 1997. pap. 21.95 (*0-385-25654-X*) Doubleday.

Brook, Penelope. Freedom at Work: The Case for Reforming Labour Law in New Zealand. 206p. 1991. pap. text 29.95 (*0-19-558220-9*, 12297) OUP.

Brook, Peter. Between Two Silences: Talking with Peter Brook. Moffitt, Dale, ed. LC 99-25841. (Illus.). 224p. 1999. 14.95 (*0-87074-443-7*) SMU Press.

— The Empty Space: A Book About the Theatre: Deadly, Holy, Rough, Immediate. LC 68-12531. 142p. (C). 1978. pap. 9.00 (*0-689-70558-1*, 237) Atheneum Yung Read.

— Empty Space: A Book About the Theatre; Deadly, Holy, Rough, Immediate. 1995. per. 10.00 (*0-684-82957-6*) S&S Trade.

— Evoking Shakespeare. LC 99-18472. (Dramatic Contexts Ser.). 48p. 1999. pap. 7.95 (*1-55936-169-7*, Pub. by Theatre Comm) Consort Bk Sales.

— The Open Door: Thoughts on Acting & Theatre. 160p. (Orig.). 1995. pap. 10.95 (*1-55936-102-6*) Theatre Comm.

— The Shifting Point: Theatre, Film, Opera, 1946-1987. LC 94-2600. (Illus.). 272p. 1994. pap. 10.95 (*1-55936-081-X*) Theatre Comm.

— Threads of Time: Recollections. LC 97-52007. (Illus.). 388p. 1998. 25.00 (*1-887178-35-X*, Pub. by Counterpt DC) HarpC.

— Threads of Time: Recollections. (Cornelia & Michael Bessie Book Ser.). (Illus.). 224p. 1999. pap. text 14.00 (*1-58243-018-7*, Pub. by Counterpt DC) HarpC.

Brook, Peter, ed. A Midsummer Night's Dream: Authorized Acting Edition. 193p. 1974. pap. 14.95 (*0-87129-737-X*, M26) Dramatic Pub.

Brook, R. C., jt. auth. see Peart, R. M.

Brook, R. J. Berkeley's Philosophy of Science. (International Archives of the History of Ideas Ser.: No. 65). 210p. 1974. lib. bdg. 106.00 (*90-247-1555-5*) Kluwer Academic.

Brook, R. J., ed. Concise Encyclopedia of Advanced Ceramic Materials. (Advances in Materials Science & Engineering Ser.: No. 6). (Illus.). 604p. 1991. 206.25 (*0-08-034720-7*, Pergamon Pr) Elsevier.

Brook, Ray, jt. auth. see Brook, Mary.

Brook, Richard. Applied Regression Analysis & Experimental Design. (Statistics: Textbooks & Monographs: Vol. 62). (Illus.). 256p. 1985. text 69.75 (*0-8247-7252-0*) Dekker.

Brook, Richard J., ed. Concise Encyclopedia of Advanced Ceramic Materials. 400p. 1991. 150.00 (*0-262-02304-0*) MIT Pr.

Brook, Robert & Whitehead, Paul. Drug-Free Therapeutic Community: An Evaluation. LC 79-20477. 158p. 1980. 32.95 (*0-87705-383-9*, Kluwer Acad Hman Sci) Kluwer Academic.

Brook, Roy. The Stress of Combat - The Combat of Stress: Caring Strategies Towards Ex-Service Men & Women. 248p. 1998. 35.00 (*1-898595-26-7*, Pub. by Fremantle Arts); pap. 17.95 (*1-898595-27-5*, Pub. by Fremantle Arts) Intl Spec Bk.

Brook-Shepherd, Gordon. The Austrians: A Thousand-Year Odyssey. (Illus.). 512p. 1998. pap. 16.95 (*0-7867-0520-5*) Carroll & Graf.

— The Storm Birds: Soviet Postwar Defectors: The Dramatic True Stories: 1945-1985. (Illus.). 384p. 1997. reprint ed. pap. text 10.00 (*0-7881-5135-5*) DIANE Pub.

Brook, Stephen. A Bibliography of the Gehenna Press, 1942-1975. 2nd ed. 1976. 40.00 (*0-686-18219-7*) J P Dwyer.

— God's Army: The Story of the Salvation Army. 1999. 32.95 (*0-7522-1322-9*, Pub. by Boxtree) Trans-Atl Phila.

— Honkytonk Gelato: Travels through Texas. large type ed. 448p. 1987. 27.99 (*0-7089-1580-9*) Ulverscroft.

— Maple Leaf Rag. large type ed. 1989. 27.99 (*0-7089-2100-0*) Ulverscroft.

— Pauillac: The Wines & Estates of a Renowned Bordeaux Commune. (Illus.). 192p. 1998. 45.00 (*1-85732-352-1*, Pub. by Mitchell Beazley) Antique Collect.

— Sauternes: And Other Sweet Wines of Bordeaux. 192p. 1995. pap. 15.95 (*0-571-17317-9*) Faber & Faber.

— The Wines of California. 656p. 1999. text 40.00 (*0-571-19029-4*) Faber & Faber.

***Brook, Stephen.** The Wines of California. 656p. 1999. pap. 20.00 (*0-571-19030-8*) Faber & Faber.

***Brook, Stephen, ed.** A Century of Wine: The Biography of Wine by a Selection of the World's Finest Wine Writers. (Illus.). 192p. 2000. 40.00 (*1-84000-253-0*, Pub. by Mitchell Beazley) Antique Collect.

Brook, Stephen, jt. auth. see Radford, John.

***Brook-Taylor, Tim.** I'm Sorry I Haven't a Clue. 1999. pap. 13.95 (*0-7528-2680-8*, Pub. by Orion Pubng Grp) Trafalgar.

— I'm Sorry I Haven't a Clue. 1998. 22.95 (*0-7528-1775-2*, Pub. by Orion Pubng Grp) Trafalgar.

Brook, Timothy. The Confusions of Pleasure: Commerce & Culture in Ming China. LC 97-8838. 345p. 1998. 45.00 (*0-520-21091-3*, Pub. by U CA Pr) Cal Prin Full Svc.

— The Confusions of Pleasure: Commerce & Culture in Ming China. LC 97-8838. 352p. 1999. pap. 18.95 (*0-520-22154-0*, Pub. by U CA Pr) Cal Prin Full Svc.

— Praying for Power: Buddhism & the Formation of Gentry Society in Late-Ming China. LC 93-5407. (Harvard-Yenching Institute Monographs: No. 38). 400p. 1994. 35.00 (*0-674-69775-8*) HUP.

— Quelling the People: The Military Suppression of the Beijing Democracy Movement. LC 98-46955. 1999. pap. text 16.95 (*0-8047-3638-3*) Stanford U Pr.

Brook, Timothy, ed. The Asiatic Mode of Production in China. LC 89-4247. (Chinese Studies on China). 216p. (gr. 13). 1989. text 85.95 (*0-87332-542-7*) M E Sharpe.

***Brook, Timothy, ed.** Documents on the Rape of Nanking. LC 99-54728. (Illus.). 320p. (C). 1999. text 39.50 (*0-472-11134-5*, 11134); pap. text 15.95 (*0-472-08662-6*, 08662) U of Mich Pr.

Brook, Timothy, et al, eds. Civil Society in China. LC 97-16586. (Studies on Contemporary China). 256p. (C). (gr. 13). 1997. pap. text 30.95 (*0-7656-0092-7*, East Gate Bk) M E Sharpe.

Brook, Timothy & Blue, Gregory, eds. China & Historical Capitalism: Genealogies of Sinological Knowledge. LC 98-38596. (Studies in Modern Capitalism). 304p. (C). 1999. text 64.95 (*0-521-64029-6*) Cambridge U Pr.

Brook, Timothy & Frolic, B. Michael, eds. Civil Society in China. LC 97-16586. (Studies on Contemporary China). 256p. (C). (gr. 13). 1997. text 72.95 (*0-7656-0091-9*, East Gate Bk) M E Sharpe.

Brook, Timothy & Luong, Hy V. Culture & Economy: The Shaping of Capitalism in Eastern Asia. LC 97-3281. 312p. 1999. pap. text 19.95 (*0-472-08598-0*, 08598) U of Mich Pr.

Brook, Timothy & Schmid, Andre, eds. Nation Work: Asian Nationalisms since 1850. LC 99-6574. 280p. 2000. text 49.50 (*0-472-11032-2*, 11032) U of Mich Pr.

Brook, Timothy & Van Luong, Hy, eds. Culture & Economy: The Shaping of Capitalism in Eastern Asia. LC 97-3281. 312p. (C). 1997. text 52.50 (*0-472-10776-3*, 10776) U of Mich Pr.

***Brook, Timothy & Wakabayashi, Bob T.** Opium Regimes: China, Britain & Japan, 1839-1952. LC 99-35149. (Illus.). 456p. 2000. pap. 22.95 (*0-520-22236-9*, Pub. by U CA Pr) Cal Prin Full Svc.

***Brook, Timothy & Wakabayashi, Bob Tadashi.** Opium Regimes: China, Britain & Japan, 1839-1952. LC 99-35149. (Illus.). 456p. 2000. 60.00 (*0-520-22009-9*, Pub. by U CA Pr) Cal Prin Full Svc.

Brook, Timothy, jt. ed. see Kuhn, Philip A.

Brook, Tom. Getting Elected in Canada. 274p. pap. 14.95 (*0-920544-84-3*, Pub. by Mercury Bk) LPC InBook.

Brook, W. & MacLeod, R. Natural Knowledge in Social Context: The Journals of Thomas Archer Hirst FRS, 1845-1892. 1980. 500.00 incl. fiche (*0-7201-0373-8*) Continuum.

Brookal. Idioms for Everyday Use. 1994. pap., teacher ed. 9.33 (*0-8442-0749-7*) NTC Contemp Pub Co.

Brookbank, George. The Desert Gardener's Calendar: Your Month-by-Month Guide. LC 99-26175. (Illus.). 168p. 1999. pap. 17.95 (*0-8165-1894-7*) U of Ariz Pr.

— Desert Gardening: Fruits & Vegetables. rev. ed. LC 91-225. (Illus.). 288p. (Orig.). 1991. pap. 17.95 (*1-55561-002-1*) Fisher Bks.

— Desert Landscaping: How to Start & Maintain a Healthy Landscape in the Southwest. LC 91-21559. (Illus.). 247p. (Orig.). 1992. pap. 22.00 (*0-8165-1201-9*) U of Ariz Pr.

Brookbank, John W., ed. see Southern Conference on Gerontology Staff.

Brookbush, Virginia. Preproduction Planning for Video Taped Television: Grassroots Handbook. LC 87-71787. 51p. 1990. 10.00 (*0-9619120-0-6*) Cmnt TV Agcy.

Brooke. Bussy D'ambois: George Chapman. 169p. 1999. pap. 19.95 (*0-7190-5696-9*) St Martin.

Brooke, A. Method for Flute. Pappoutsakis, James, ed. 211p. 1962. pap. 23.50 (*0-8258-0145-1*, CU-20) Fischer Inc NY.

Brooke, A. D. Sketches in Spain & Morocco, Vol. 1. 400p. 1987. 320.00 (*1-85077-153-7*, Pub. by Darf Pubs Ltd) St Mut.

— Sketches in Spain & Morocco, Vol. 2. 416p. 1987. 320.00 (*1-85077-154-5*, Pub. by Darf Pubs Ltd) St Mut.

Brooke, A. E. The Johannine Epistles: Critical & Exegetical Commentary. Driver, Samuel R. et al, eds. LC 13-170. (International Critical Commentary Ser.). 336p. 1998. 39.95 (*0-567-05037-8*, Pub. by T & T Clark) Bks Intl VA.

Brooke, A. Lindsay & Gaylin, David. Triumph Motorcycles in America. LC 93-13166. (Illus.). 224p. 1993. pap. 24.95 (*0-87938-746-7*) MBI Pubg.

Brooke, A. M., jt. auth. see Amber, R. B.

Brooke, Anthony. Towards Human Unity. 133p. 1976. pap. 7.50 (*0-7051-0234-3*) Attic Pr.

Brooke, Anthony, et al. GAMS Release 2.25: A User's Guide. 289p. 1992. pap. text 45.50 incl. 3.5 hd (*0-89426-215-7*) Course Tech.

— GAMS Release 2.25: A User's Guide. 289p. 1992. pap. 34.00 (*0-89426-213-0*) Course Tech.

Brooke, Arthur. Romeus & Iuliet. Daniel, P. A., ed. (New Shakespeare Society, London, Ser.: Ser. 3, No. 1). 1974. reprint ed. pap. 35.00 (*0-8115-0237-6*) Periodicals Srv.

Brooke, Avery. Finding God in the World: Reflections on a Spiritual Journey. LC 93-44081. 157p. 1994. reprint ed. pap. 10.95 (*1-56101-089-8*) Cowley Pubns.

— Healing in the Landscape of Prayer. 160p. (Orig.). 1996. pap. 10.95 (*1-56101-125-8*) Cowley Pubns.

— Plain Prayers for a Complicated World. LC 93-22817. (Illus.). 160p. 1993. pap. 10.95 (*1-56101-084-7*) Cowley Pubns.

— Plain Prayers for a Complicated World. 1984. 6.20 (*0-8164-3501-4*) Harper SF.

— Plain Prayers for a Complicated World. 124p. 1983. reprint ed. 5.95 (*0-8164-0501-8*) Harper SF.

Brooke, Betty. Saturday Extra Special! (C). 1990. pap. text 24.00 (*0-85305-301-4*, Pub. by Arthur James) St Mut.

— Tovey - A Free Range Dog. (C). 1990. pap. 35.00 (*0-85305-294-8*, Pub. by Arthur James) St Mut.

Brooke, Betty, tr. Saturday Special. (C). 1990. pap. 24.00 (*0-85305-286-7*, Pub. by Arthur James) St Mut.

Brooke, Bob. Solar Energy. (Earth at Risk Ser.). (Illus.). 128p. (YA). (gr. 5 up). 1992. lib. bdg. 19.95 (*0-7910-1590-4*) Chelsea Hse.

Brooke, C. N., ed. see John of Salisbury.

Brooke, C. N., ed. see Map, Walter.

Brooke, C. N., tr. see Knowles, David.

Brooke, C. W. Notaries Public in England since the Reformation. 160p. 1998. pap. 165.00 (*1-85297-034-0*, Pub. by Erskine Press) St Mut.

Brooke, Charles F. The Reputation of Christopher Marlowe. (Connecticut Academy of Arts & Sciences Ser., Trans.: Vol. 25). 1922. pap. 49.50 (*0-685-22824-X*) Elliots Bks.

— William Gager's Pyramis. (Connecticut Academy of Arts & Sciences Ser., Trans.: Vol. 32). 1936. pap. 49.50 (*0-685-22918-1*) Elliots Bks.

Brooke, Charles F., ed. Shakespeare's Plutarch, 2 vols., Set. 441p. (C). 1966. reprint ed. lib. bdg. 150.00 (*0-8383-0516-4*) M S G Haskell Hse.

Brooke, Charlotte. Reliques of Irish Poetry 1789: A Memoir of Miss Brooke, 1816. Seymour, A. C., ed. LC 76-13332. 544p. 1970. 75.00 (*0-8201-1082-5*) Schol Facsimiles.

Brooke, Cheryl, ed. see Manak, Frank C.

***Brooke, Christopher.** Europe in the Central Middle Ages, 962-1154. 470p. 1999. pap. 28.60 (*0-582-36904-5*) Addison-Wesley.

Brooke, Christopher. The History of Gonville & Caius College. (Illus.). 400p. 1996. reprint ed. 55.00 (*0-85115-423-9*) Boydell & Brewer.

— History of the University of Cambridge, Vol. 4: 1870-1990. (Illus.). 678p. (C). 1993. text 100.00 (*0-521-34350-X*) Cambridge U Pr.

— Jane Austen: Illusion & Reality. LC 99-33905. 240p. 1999. 45.00 (*0-85991-557-3*, DS Brewer) Boydell & Brewer.

***Brooke, Christopher N.** Churches & Churchmen in Medieval Europe. LC 99-52269. 1999. 70.00 (*1-85285-183-X*) Hambledon Press.

Brooke, Christopher N., et al, eds. Church & Government in the Middle Ages: Essays Presented to C. R. Cheney on His 70th Birthday. LC 75-41614. 332p. reprint ed. pap. 94.70 (*0-608-17076-3*, 2027285) Bks Demand.

Brooke, David S. Master Drawings: Sterling & Francine Clark As Collectors. LC 95-18873. (Illus.). 40p. (Orig.). 1995. pap. 10.95 (*0-931102-34-0*) S & F Clark Art.

Brooke, Deborah, jt. ed. see Adshead, Gwen.

Brooke, E. L. A Tale of Two Spiders: Not for Children. (Illus.). 104p. 1996. pap. 9.95 (*1-887922-09-1*) Orange Cty Univ Pr.

— Who Is My Father? (Illus.). 80p. 1996. write for info. (*1-887922-06-7*) Orange Cty Univ Pr.

Brooke, E. M., ed. Suicide & Attempted Suicide. (Public Health Papers: No. 58). 1974. pap. text 8.00 (*92-4-130058-2*, 1110058) World Health.

Brooke, Edward, jt. compiled by see Worrall, John.

Brooke, Eileen M. Current & Future Use of Registers in Health Information Systems. (Offset Publications: No. 8). 1974. pap. text 14.00 (*92-4-170008-4*, 1120008) World Health.

Brooke, Elisabeth. A February Cuckoo. 192p. 1997. pap. 13.95 (*0-7043-4516-1*, Pub. by Womens Press) Trafalgar.

— Herbal Therapy for Women. 160p. 1993. 10.00 (*0-7225-2722-5*) Thorsons PA.

— Medicine Women: A Pictorial History of Women Healers. LC 96-44733. (Illus.). 128p. 1997. pap. 20.00 (*0-8356-0751-8*, Quest) Theos Pub Hse.

— Woman's Book of Herbs. 258p. 1999. pap. 17.95 (*0-7043-4296-0*, Pub. by Womens Press) Trafalgar.

— Women Healers: Portraits of Herbalists, Physicians & Midwives. LC 95-23433. 176p. 1995. pap. 12.95 (*0-89281-548-5*, Heal Arts VT) Inner Tradit.

Brooke, Elizabeth. A Wise Woman's Guide to Spells, Rituals, & Goddess Love. (Illus.). 262p. 1995. pap. 12.95 (*0-89594-779-X*) Crossing Pr.

***Brooke, Felicity & Litchfield, Jo.** Birthday Surprise. (Illus.). 16p. (ps-3). 2000. lib. bdg. 13.95 (*1-58086-189-X*) EDC.

— Missing Cat. (Illus.). 16p. (ps-3). 2000. lib. bdg. 13.95 (*1-58086-226-8*) EDC.

— Runaway Orange. (Illus.). 16p. (ps-3). 2000. lib. bdg. 13.95 (*1-58086-230-6*) EDC.

Brooke, Frances. The Excursion. Backscheider, Paula R. & Cotton, Hope D., eds. (Eighteenth-Century Novels by Women Ser.). 240p. 1997. pap. 16.95 (*0-8131-0881-0*); text 40.00 (*0-8131-1979-0*) U Pr of Ky.

— The History of Emily Montague. (New Canadian Library). 368p. 1995. mass mkt. 8.95 (*0-7710-3457-1*) McCland & Stewart.

Brooke, Francis T. A Family Narrative: Being the Reminiscences of a Revolutionary Officer, Afterwards Judge of the Court Appeals. LC 74-140856. (Eyewitness Accounts of the American Revolution Ser.). 1971. reprint ed. 14.95 (*0-405-01196-2*) Ayer.

— A Family Narrative: Being the Reminiscences of a Revolutionary Officer, Afterwards Judge of the Court Appeals. (American Biography Ser.). 43p. 1991. reprint ed. lib. bdg. 59.00 (*0-7812-8042-7*) Rprt Serv.

Brooke, Fulke G. Poems & Dramas of Fulke Greville First Lord Brooke, 2 vols. reprint ed. 95.00 (*0-403-04210-0*) Somerset Pub.

— Works in Verse & Prose Complete, 4 vols., Set. (BCL1-PR English Literature Ser.). 1992. reprint ed. lib. bdg. 360.00 (*0-7812-7195-9*) Rprt Serv.

— The Works in Verse & Prose Complete of the Right Honourable Fulke Greville, 4 vols., Set. LC 79-181918. (Fuller Worthies' Library). reprint ed. 306.00 (*0-404-02940-X*) AMS Pr.

Brooke, G. C. English Coins - From 7th Century. 1977. 40.00 (*0-932106-60-9*) S J Durst.

Brooke, Gabriella. The Words of Bernfrieda: A Chronicle of Hauteville. LC 98-42114. 1998. write for info. (*0-910055-50-5*); pap. 18.95 (*0-910055-49-1*) East Wash Univ.

Brooke, Gabriella, jt. ed. see Marotti, Maria Ornella.

Brooke, George J. Exegesis at Qumran 4Q: Florilegium in Its Jewish Context. (JSOT Supplement Ser.: No. 29). 390p. 1985. 85.00 (*0-905774-76-0*, Pub. by Sheffield Acad) CUP Services.

Brooke, George J. Temple Scroll Studies. (Journal for the Study of the Pseudepigrapha Supplement Ser.: No. 7). 299p. 1989. 85.00 (*1-85075-200-1*, Pub. by Sheffield Acad) CUP Services.

Brooke, George J., ed. Women in the Biblical Tradition. LC 92-40883. (Studies in Women & Religion: Vol. 31). 302p. 1992. text 99.95 (*0-7734-9216-X*) E Mellen.

Brooke, George J., et al, eds. Ugarit & the Bible: Proceedings of the International Symposium on Ugarit & the Bible, Manchester, September 1992. LC 96-177059. (Ugaritisch-Biblische Literatur Ser.). ix, 470p. 1994. text 78.00 (*3-927120-22-7*, Pub. by UGARIT) Eisenbrauns.

Brooke, George J. & Martinez, Florentino G., eds. New Qumran Texts & Studies: Proceedings of the First Meeting of the International Organization for Qumran Studies, Paris, 1992. LC 94-18402. (Studies on the Texts of the Desert of Judah: Vol. 15). ix, 328p. 1994. 109.00 (*90-04-10093-8*) Brill Academic Pubs.

Brooke, George M. John M. Brooke, Naval Scientist & Educator. LC 79-18559. 388p. reprint ed. pap. 120.30 (*0-608-08559-6*, 206908200002) Bks Demand.

Brooke, Geroge, et al. Qumran Cave 4 Pt. 3: Parabiblical Texts, Pt. 3. (Discoveries in the Judaean Desert Ser.: No. XXII). (Illus.). 362p. 1997. text 150.00 (*0-19-826936-6*) OUP.

Brooke, Helynna & Short, Ann. First Moon: Passage to Womanhood: A Celebration of a Young Woman's First Menses. unabridged ed. 72p. 1997. pap. 49.00 (*0-9660811-0-2*, First Moon) Brooke Co.

Brooke, Henry. Institute Cargo Clauses (Air) (C). 1986. 110.00 (*0-900886-27-7*, Pub. by Witherby & Co) St Mut.

Brooke-Houghton, Julian. Dinghy Crewing. 64p. (C). 1990. text 59.00 (*0-906754-16-X*, Pub. by Fernhurst Bks) St Mut.

Brooke House Staff. Jingle Bells: Glitter Glow. (Illus.). 12p. (J). (ps-3). 1996. mass mkt. 4.99 (*0-689-80931-X*) S&S Childrens.

— Silent Night: Glitter Glow. (Illus.). 12p. (J). (ps-3). 1996. mass mkt. 4.99 (*0-689-80932-8*) S&S Childrens.

Brooke-Hunt, Violet. Story of Westminster Abbey. 1977. lib. bdg. 59.95 (*0-8490-2692-X*) Gordon Pr.

Brooke, I. English Costume of the 18th Century. (Illus.). 86p. 1977. reprint ed. 7.25 (*0-7136-0158-2*) Dufour.

***Brooke, Ian.** Trees. (Collins Gem Ser.). (Illus.). 256p. 2000. pap. 7.95 (*0-00-472268-X*, Pub. by HarpC) Trafalgar.

Brooke, Iris. Costume in Greek Classic Drama. LC 73-3010. (Illus.). 112p. 1973. reprint ed. lib. bdg. 35.00 (*0-8371-6828-7*, BRGC, Greenwood Pr) Greenwood.

— Dress & Undress, the Restoration & Eighteenth Century. LC 73-3011. (Illus.). 161p. 1973. reprint ed. lib. bdg. 38.50 (*0-8371-6829-5*, BRDU, Greenwood Pr) Greenwood.

B

An Asterisk (*) at the beginning of an entry indicates that the title is appearing for the first time.

B

***Brooke, Iris.** English Costume from the Early Middle Ages Through the Sixteenth Century. LC 00-31399. (Illus.). 2000. pap. write for info. (*0-486-41238-5*) Dover.

Brooke, Iris. History of English Costume. LC 72-85476. (Illus.). 1973. pap. 10.95 (*0-87830-569-6*, Thtre Arts Bks) Routledge.

— Western European Costume & Its Relation to the Theatre. Incl. Vol. 2. 17th Through 19th Centuries. LC 63-18334. 1963. pap. 10.95 (*0-87830-514-9*, Thtre Arts Bks); LC 63-18334. (Illus.). (Orig.). pap. write for info. (*0-318-55926-9*, Thtre Arts Bks) Routledge.

Brooke, Iris & Landes, William-Alan. Western European Costume Thirteenth to Seventeenth Century. LC 93-36612. (Illus.). 192p. 1993. pap. 15.00 (*0-88734-635-9*) Players Pr.

***Brooke, Iris & Laver, James.** English Costume from the Seventeenth Through the Nineteenth Centuries. LC 00-31460. 2000. pap. write for info. (*0-486-41239-3*) Dover.

Brooke, Jan. Machine Applique. 96p. (C). 1989. 100.00 (*1-85368-059-1*, Pub. by New5 Holland) St Mut.

***Brooke, Jeffrey R.** Hard Right Turn: The New Face of Neo-Conservatism in Canada. 472p. 2000. 29.95 (*0-00-255762-2*) HarpC.

***Brooke, Jerome.** Cave of Shadows. (Sulu Sea Bks.). 42p. 1999. pap. 6.00 (*0-9674487-9-4*) Good SAMAR.

— Hunters of Stone. 42p. 1999. pap. 6.00 (*1-930714-04-1*) Good SAMAR.

— Mirage: Dance of the Sun. 2nd ed. (Mirage Bks.). 42p. 1999. pap. 4.00 (*0-9674487-0-0*) Good SAMAR.

— Shadows: Verse from the Mirage. Date not set. pap. 9.00 (*0-9674487-6-X*) Good SAMAR.

— Sulu: Empire of the Lost. 36p. 1999. pap. 3.00 (*0-9674487-1-9*) Good SAMAR.

***Brooke, Jerome & Lee, Jarita Ador.** Fire. 26p. 1999. pap. 7.00 (*0-9674487-5-1*) Good SAMAR.

Brooke, Jocelyn. The Scapegoat. LC 96-60142. 174p. (Orig.). 1998. pap. 12.95 (*1-885983-09-3*) Turtle Point Pr.

***Brooke, John & Cantor, Geoffrey.** Reconstructing Nature: The Engagement of Science & Religion. LC 99-59053. (Illus.). 384p. 1999. pap. 25.00 (*0-19-513706-X*) OUP.

Brooke, John & Cantor, Geoffrey. Reconstructing Nature: The Engagement of Science & Religion. 352p. 1998. 49.95 (*0-567-08600-3*, Pub. by T & T Clark) Bks Intl VA.

Brooke, John & Sorensen, Mary, eds. W. E. Gladstone I: Autobiographical. (Prime Ministers' Papers). 270p. 1971. 10.00 (*0-11-440015-6*, HM00156, Pub. by Statnry Office) Bernan Associates.

— W. E. Gladstone II: Autobiographical Memoranda, 1832-1845. (Prime Ministers' Papers). 309p. 1972. 10.00 (*0-11-440033-4*, HM00334, Pub. by Statnry Office) Bernan Associates.

— W. E. Gladstone III: Autobiographical Memoranda, 1845-1866. (Prime Ministers' Papers). 309p. 1978. 10.00 (*0-11-440086-5*, HM00865, Pub. by Statnry Office) Bernan Associates.

Brooke, John, ed. see Walpole, Horace.

Brooke, John H. Science & Religion: Some Historical Perspectives. (Cambridge History of Science Ser.). (Illus.). 434p. (C). 1991. text 59.95 (*0-521-23961-3*); pap. text 21.95 (*0-521-28374-4*) Cambridge U Pr.

— Thinking about Matter: Studies in the History of Chemical Philosophy. LC 95-10977. (Collected Studies: Vol. CS502). 304p. 1995. 101.95 (*0-86078-464-9*, Pub. by Variorum) Ashgate Pub Co.

Brooke, John L. The Heart of the Commonwealth: Society & Political Culture in Worcester County, Massachusetts, 1713-1861. (Illus.). 468p. (C). 1990. text 57.95 (*0-521-37029-9*) Cambridge U Pr.

— The Heart of the Commonwealth: Society & Political Culture in Worcester County, Massachusetts, 1713-1861. LC 92-14828. (Illus.). 472p. 1993. pap. 19.95 (*0-87023-826-4*) U of Mass Pr.

— The Refiner's Fire: The Making of Mormon Cosmology, 1644-1844. LC 93-37366. (Illus.). 443p. (C). 1994. text 49.95 (*0-521-34545-6*) Cambridge U Pr.

— The Refiner's Fire: The Making of Mormon Cosmology, 1644-1844. (Illus.). 443p. 1996. pap. 18.95 (*0-521-56564-2*) Cambridge U Pr.

Brooke, L. T., et al, eds. Acute Toxicities of Organic Chemicals to Fathead Minnows (Pimephales promelas), Vol. 1. LC 85-116909. (Toxicity of Organic Chemicals Ser.). (Illus.). 414p. (Orig.). 1984. pap. 75.00 (*0-9614968-0-0*) Lke Superior Res.

***Brooke, Lauren.** After the Storm. (Heartland Ser.: Vol. 2). (Illus.). 128p. (J). (gr. 3-7). 2000. pap. 4.50 (*0-439-13022-0*) Scholastic Inc.

— Breaking Free. (Heartland Ser.: Vol. 3). (Illus.). (J). 2000. pap. 4.50 (*0-439-13024-7*) Scholastic Inc.

— Coming Home. (Heartland Ser.: Vol. 1). (Illus.). 144p. (J). (gr. 3-7). 2000. pap. 4.50 (*0-439-13020-4*) Scholastic Inc.

Brooke, Lindsay. Triumph Racing Motorcycles in America. (Illus.). 160p. 1996. pap. 24.95 (*0-7603-0174-3*) MBI Pubg.

Brooke-Little, J. P. An Heraldic Alphabet. LC 97-66444. (Illus.). 218p. 1987. pap. 12.95 (*1-86105-077-1*, Robson-Parkwest) Parkwest Pubns.

Brooke-Little, J. P., jt. auth. see Neubecker, Ottfried.

***Brooke, Marcus.** Insight Pocket Guide Boston with Map. 6th rev. ed. (Illus.). 96p. 2000. pap. 12.95 (*1-58573-012-2*, Insight Guides) Langenscheidt.

Brooke, Michael. The Concrete Wave: The History of Skateboarding. (Illus.). 200p. 1999. pap. 19.95 (*1-894020-54-5*) Warwick Publ.

Brooke, Michael Z. International Management: A Review of Strategies & Operations. 3rd ed. 328p. 1999. pap. 52.50 (*0-7487-2245-9*, Pub. by S Thornes Pubs) Trans-Atl Phila.

— Le Play: Engineer & Social Scientist. LC 98-11406. 224p. 1998. pap. text 22.95 (*0-7658-0425-5*) Transaction Pubs.

Brooke, Michael Z. & Skilbeck, John M. Licensing: The International Sale of Patents & Technical Knowhow. 452p. 1994. 131.95 (*0-566-07461-3*, Pub. by Gower) Ashgate Pub Co.

Brooke, Michael Z., jt. auth. see Witt, Stephen F.

Brooke, Michael Z., ed. see Briggs, Peter D.

Brooke, Michael Z., ed. see Conlan, James.

Brooke, Michael Z., ed. see Kouladis, Nicholas.

Brooke, Nicholas. Horrid Laughter in Jacobean Tragedy. LC 79-53305. 135p. 1979. text 42.00 (*0-06-490701-5*, 06367) B&N Imports.

— Shakespeare: Richard II. LC 73-172876. (Casebook Ser.). 256p. 1973. write for info. (*0-333-00218-0*) Macmillan.

Brooke, Nicholas & Curtis, Michael. Brooke & Curtis: Commercial Leasing. 1997. write for info. (*0-406-08137-9*, CL, MICHIE) LEXIS Pub.

Brooke, Nicholas, ed. see Chapman, George.

Brooke, Nicholas, ed. see Shakespeare, William.

Brooke, Odo. Studies in Monastic Theology. (Cistercian Studies: No. 37). 1980. 8.95 (*0-87907-837-5*) Cistercian Pubns.

Brooke, P. A., jt. auth. see Johnson, P. N.

Brooke, Pamela. Communicating Through Story Characters. (Illus.). 174p. (Orig.). (C). 1995. pap. text 24.50 (*0-8191-9925-7*); lib. bdg. 48.00 (*0-8191-9924-9*) U Pr of Amer.

— Traditional Media for Gender Communication. (Illus.). 78p. (Orig.). 1996. pap. 15.00 (*1-888753-06-4*) PACT Pubns.

Brooke, Patricia S., ed. see Cincinnati Zoo Volunteer Program Staff.

Brooke, Paul. Strings: The Lives of Two Yakama Women in the 1800's. (Illus.). 36p. 1998. pap. 3.00 (*1-888431-20-2*) ASGP.

***Brooke, Peggy.** Jake's Orphan. LC 99-46466. 272p. (J). 2000. 16.95 (*0-7894-2628-5*, D K Ink) DK Pub Inc.

Brooke, Robert & Hendricks, John. Audience Expectations & Teacher Demands. LC 88-31210. (Studies in Writing & Rhetoric). 148p. (Orig.). (C). 1989. pap. 14.95 (*0-8093-1514-9*) S Ill U Pr.

Brooke, Robert Z., tr. see Ogrizek, Michel & Guillery, Jean-Michel.

***Brooke, Roger.** Pathways Into Jungian World: Phenomenology & Analytical Psychology. LC 98-56540. 1999. pap. 29.99 (*0-415-16999-2*) Routledge.

***Brooke, Roger, ed.** Pathways into the Jungian World: Phenomenology & Analytical Psychology. LC 98-56540. 274p. (C). 1999. text. write for info. (*0-415-16998-4*) Routledge.

Brooke, Rosalind B., ed. Scripta Leonis, Rufini, et Angeli Sociorum S. Franciscii: The Writings of Leo, Rufino, & Angelo, Companions of St. Francis. (Oxford Medieval Texts Ser.). (Illus.). 380p. 1993. text 85.00 (*0-19-822214-9*) OUP.

Brooke-Rose, Christine. Amalgamemnon. LC 93-21194. 144p. 1994. reprint ed. pap. 11.95 (*1-56478-050-3*) Dalkey Arch.

— Remake. 160p. 1996. pap. 18.95 (*1-85754-222-3*, Pub. by Carcanet Pr) Paul & Co Pubs.

— Stories, Theories & Things. 317p. (C). 1991. text 74.95 (*0-521-39181-4*) Cambridge U Pr.

— A Structural Analysis of Pound's Usura Canto: Jakobson's Method Extended & Applied to Free Verse. (De Proprietatibus Litterarum Ser.: No. 26). 76p. 1976. pap. text 36.15 (*90-279-3361-8*) Mouton.

***Brooke-Rose, Christine.** Subscript. 224p. 2000. pap. 19.95 (*1-85754-441-2*, Pub. by Carcanet Pr) Paul & Co Pubs.

Brooke-Rose, Christine. Textermination. LC 92-17328. 192p. 1992. pap. 10.95 (*0-8112-1216-5*, NDP756, Pub. by New Directions) Norton.

— Textermination. LC 92-17328. 192p. 1992. 21.95 (*0-8112-1230-0*, Pub. by New Directions) Norton.

— Xorander. 224p. 1988. mass mkt. 2.95 (*0-380-70407-2*, Avon Bks) Morrow Avon.

Brooke, Rupert. Complete Poems. 1992. reprint ed. lib. bdg. 21.95 (*0-89968-286-3*, Lghtyr Pr) Buccaneer Bks.

Brooke, Rupert. The Complete Poems of Rupert Brooke. 2nd ed. LC 75-41038. (BCL Ser. II). reprint ed. 19.50 (*0-404-14647-3*) AMS Pr.

— John Webster & the Elizabethan Drama. (BCL1-PR English Literature Ser.). 282p. 1992. reprint ed. lib. bdg. 79.00 (*0-7812-7315-3*) Rprt Serv.

Brooke, Rupert. Lithuania. unabridged ed. Landes, William-Alan, ed. LC 97-29922. 55p. (Orig.). 1997. pap. 6.00 (*0-88734-341-4*) Players Pr.

Brooke, Rupert. The Poetical Works of Rupert Brooke. 20.95 (*0-8488-0351-5*) Amereon Ltd.

— The Poetical Works of Rupert Brooke. Keynes, Geoffrey, ed. 216p. 1970. pap. 14.95 (*0-571-04704-1*) Faber & Faber.

— Rupert Brooke. (Pocket Poet Ser.). 1968. pap. 3.95 (*0-8023-9042-0*) Dufour.

Brooke, Rupert & Strachey, James. Friends & Apostles: The Correspondence of Rupert Brooke & James Strachey, 1905-1914. Hale, Keith, ed. LC 98-7353. (Illus.). 320p. 1998. 35.00 (*0-300-07004-7*) Yale U Pr.

Brooke, Sandy. Hooked on Drawing! Ready-to-Use Lessons & Exercises. LC 96-12022. (Illus.). 272p. (YA). (gr. 4 up). 1996. pap. text 27.95 (*0-13-231853-9*) P-H.

— Hooked on Painting! Illustrated Lessons & Exercises for Grades 4 & Up. LC 98-41859. (Illus.). 320p. 1998. pap. 32.95 (*0-13-918152-0*) P-H.

Brooke-Shepherd, Gordon. Prelude to Infamy. 1962. 12.95 (*0-8392-1086-8*) Astor-Honor.

Brooke, Stephanie L. Art Therapy with Sexual Abuse Survivors. LC 97-22272. (Illus.). 188p. 1997. text 42.95 (*0-398-06805-4*); pap. text 26.95 (*0-398-06806-2*) C C Thomas.

— A Therapist's Guide to Art Therapy Assessments: Tools of the Trade. LC 96-11642. (Illus.). 164p. 1996. 34.95 (*0-398-06618-3*); pap. 24.95 (*0-398-06619-1*) C C Thomas.

Brooke, Stephen. Labour's War. (Illus.). 384p. 1992. 95.00 (*0-19-820285-7*) OUP.

***Brooke, Steven.** Historic Washington, Arkansas. LC 00-26826. (Illus.). 2000. write for info. (*1-56554-652-0*) Pelican.

— Majesty of Natchez Postcard Book. (Illus.). 1998. pap. 9.95 (*1-56554-340-8*) Pelican.

Brooke, Steven. Seaside. LC 94-20911. (Illus.). 128p. 1995. 29.95 (*0-88289-996-1*); pap. 19.95 (*0-88289-997-X*) Pelican.

Brooke, Steven, photos by. Views of Jerusalem & the Holy Land. LC 98-27186. (Illus.). 224p. 2000. 60.00 (*0-8478-1995-7*, Pub. by Rizzoli Intl) St Martin.

Brooke, Steven, photos by. The Majesty of Natchez. 2nd ed. LC 98-48354. (Majesty Architecture Ser.). (Illus.). 96p. 1999. pap. 16.95 (*1-56554-158-8*) Pelican.

***Brooke, Steven, photos by.** Seaside Postcard Book. (Illus.). 1999. pap. 9.95 (*1-56554-639-3*) Pelican.

Brooke, Steven & Cerwinske, Laura. The Gardens of Florida. LC 97-85. 128p. 1997. 29.95 (*1-56554-184-7*) Pelican.

Brooke, Steven, et al. Views of Rome. LC 95-999. (Illus.). 224p. 1995. 60.00 (*0-8478-1881-0*, Pub. by Rizzoli Intl) St Martin.

Brooke, Stopford A. Four Victorian Poets: A Study of Clough, Arnold, Rossetti, Morris, with an Introduction on the Course of Poetry from 1822-1852. (BCL1-PR English Literature Ser.). 299p. 1992. reprint ed. lib. bdg. 79.00 (*0-7812-7094-4*) Rprt Serv.

— History of Early English Literature, Being the History of English Poetry from Its Beginnings to the Accession of King Aelfred. LC 70-114905. (Select Bibliographies Reprint Ser.). 1977. 35.95 (*0-8369-5309-6*) Ayer.

— Milton. LC 70-39534. reprint ed. 19.50 (*0-404-01108-X*) AMS Pr.

— Naturalism in English Poetry. (BCL1-PR English Literature Ser.). 289p. 1992. reprint ed. lib. bdg. 79.00 (*0-7812-7078-2*) Rprt Serv.

— Naturalism in English Poetry. 289p. reprint ed. 39.00 (*0-403-03079-X*) Somerset Pub.

— On Ten Plays of Shakespeare. LC 72-149655. reprint ed. 32.50 (*0-404-01109-8*) AMS Pr.

— Poetry of Robert Browning. LC 02-24748. reprint ed. 29.50 (*0-404-01114-4*) AMS Pr.

— Tennyson: His Art & Relation to Modern Life. LC 74-123761. reprint ed. 29.50 (*0-404-01115-2*) AMS Pr.

— Theology in the English Poets. 1972. 59.95 (*0-8490-1189-2*) Gordon Pr.

— Theology in the English Poets: Cowper, Coleridge, Wordsworth & Burns. 6th ed. LC 79-129367. reprint ed. 29.50 (*0-404-01116-0*) AMS Pr.

***Brooke, Tal.** Avatar of Night. 3rd unabridged ed. (Illus.). 405p. 1999. pap. 16.95 (*1-930045-00-X*) End Run.

Brooke, Tucker. The Marlowe Canon. 51p. (Orig.). (C). 1922. reprint ed. pap. 39.95 (*0-8383-0010-3*) M S G Haskell Hse.

— Shakespeare of Stratford. LC 79-128883. (Select Bibliographies Reprint Ser.). 1977. 20.95 (*0-8369-5503-X*) Ayer.

Brooke, Tucker, et al, eds. Shakespeare's Principal Plays. 3rd ed. (Illus.). 1935. 62.50 (*0-89197-402-4*) Irvington.

Brooke, William J. A Is for AARRGH! LC 99-14827. 249p. (YA). (gr. 5-9). 1999. 14.95 (*0-06-023393-1*) HarpC Child Bks.

— A Is for AARRGH! LC 99-14827. 256p. (YA). (gr. 5-9). 1999. lib. bdg. 14.89 (*0-06-023394-X*) HarpC Child Bks.

***Brooke, William J.** A Is for AARRGH! LC 99-14827. 256p. (J). (gr. 5 up). 2000. mass mkt. 5.95 (*0-06-440889-2*, HarpTrophy) HarpC Child Bks.

Brooke, William J. OperAntics: Fun & Games for the Opera Buff. (Illus.). 96p. (Orig.). 1986. pap. 7.95 (*0-930753-02-X*) Spect Ln Pr.

— Teller of Tales. LC 93-43421. (Trophy Bk.). 176p. (J). (gr. 3-7). 1995. pap. 5.95 (*0-06-440511-7*, HarpTrophy) HarpC Child Bks.

— Teller of Tales. (J). 1995. 11.05 (*0-606-08456-8*, Pub. by Turtleback) Demco.

— A Telling of the Tales: Five Stories. LC 89-36588. (Trophy Bk.). (Illus.). 144p. (J). (gr. 3-7). 1993. pap. 5.95 (*0-06-440467-6*, HarpTrophy) HarpC Child Bks.

— Untold Tales. LC 91-4179. 160p. (J). (gr. 5 up). 1992. 15.00 (*0-06-020271-8*) HarpC Child Bks.

Brooke, Xanthe. Mantegna to Rubens: The Weld-Blundell Drawings Collection. LC 98-205350. (Illus.). 208p. 1998. 65.00 (*1-85894-052-4*, Pub. by Merrell Holberton) U of Wash Pr.

Brooke, Xanthe, et al. Mantegna to Rubens: The Weld-Blundell Drawings Collection. LC 98-205350. 208p. 1998. pap. write for info. (*1-85894-053-2*) Merrell Holberton.

Brooke, Zachary N. The English Church & the Papacy, from the Conquest to the Reign of John. LC 80-2228. reprint ed. 42.00 (*0-404-18756-0*) AMS Pr.

Brooker. Serious Mental Health Problems. 1998. pap. text 29.00 (*0-7020-2127-X*, W B Saunders Co) Harcrt Hlth Sci Grp.

Brooker, jt. auth. see Eliot.

Brooker, Alan M. & Puglisi, Catherine R. Bad Blood. LC 98-87513. 325p. 1998. 25.00 (*0-7388-0107-0*) Xlibris Corp.

Brooker, Alan M., jt. auth. see Puglisi, Catherine R.

Brooker, Anthony. Dataplan: A Databased Language. LC 96-3191. (Advanced Topics in Computer Science Ser.). 1996. write for info. (*0-07-709296-1*) McGraw.

Brooker, Barbara R. Dead Mother Pt. 1: Anger. 37p. 1995. pap. 9.95 (*0-943485-01-0*, DM1) Ren Sound Pubns.

Brooker, Blake. Ilsa, Queen of the Nazi Love Camp & Other Plays. Doolittle, Joyce, ed. LC 97-17565. 160p. (Orig.). 1994. pap. 10.95 (*0-88734-627-8*, Pub. by Red Deer) Empire Pub Srvs.

Brooker, Charles, ed. Community Psychiatric Nursing: A Research Perspective. 320p. 1990. 40.50 (*0-412-34790-3*, A4880) Chapman & Hall.

Brooker, Charles & White, E. Community Psychiatric Nursing, Vol. 3. 256p. 1995. pap. 38.25 (*1-56593-354-0*, 0678) Singular Publishing.

Brooker, Gary, et al, eds. Advances in Cyclic Nucleotide Research: Current Methodology, Vol. 10. fac. ed. LC 71-181305. (Illus.). 271p. pap. 84.10 (*0-7837-7237-8*, 204706200010) Bks Demand.

Brooker-Gross, Susan, ed. see Lee, T., et al.

Brooker, James H. The Lands of Father Damien: Kalaupapa, Molokai, Hawaii. (Illus.). 135p. (Orig.). 1998. 24.95 (*0-9642197-3-5*) Molokai Fish & Dive.

Brooker, Jewel S. Mastery & Escape: T. S. Eliot & the Dialectic of Modernism. LC 93-45634. 288p. 1996. pap. 18.95 (*1-55849-040-X*) U of Mass Pr.

Brooker, Jewel S., ed. Approaches to Teaching Eliot's Poetry & Plays. LC 88-13158. (Approaches to Teaching World Literature Ser.: No. 19). xii, 203p. (Orig.). 1988. pap. 18.00 (*0-87352-514-0*, AP19P); lib. bdg. 37.50 (*0-87352-513-2*, AP19C) Modern Lang.

— Conversations with Denise Levertov. LC 98-15893. (Literary Conversation Ser.). 256p. 1998. pap. 17.00 (*1-57806-074-5*); text 45.00 (*1-57806-073-7*) U Pr of Miss.

Brooker, Jewel S. & Bentley, Joseph. Reading "The Waste Land" Modernism & the Limits of Interpretation. LC 89-36484. 256p. (C). 1990. pap. 18.95 (*0-87023-803-5*) U of Mass Pr.

Brooker, M. P., jt. auth. see Edwards, R. W.

Brooker, P. I. A Geostatistical Primer. 104p. (C). 1991. text 37.00 (*981-02-0547-3*) World Scientific Pub.

Brooker, Paul. Defiant Dictatorships. LC 97-15332. 1997. text 42.50 (*0-8147-1311-4*) NYU Pr.

— The Faces of Fraternalism: Nazi Germany, Fascist Italy, & Imperial Japan. (Illus.). 416p. 1991. 75.00 (*0-19-827319-3*) OUP.

***Brooker, Paul.** Non-Democratic Regimes: Theory, Government & Politics. LC 99-36064. (Comparative Government & Politics Ser.). 2000. pap. 21.95 (*0-312-22755-8*); text 59.95 (*0-312-22754-X*) St Martin.

Brooker, Paul. Twentieth-Century Dictatorships: The Ideological One-Party States. 311p. (C). 1994. text 45.00 (*0-8147-1233-9*) NYU Pr.

— Twentieth-Century Dictatorships: The Ideological One-Party States. 311p. (C). 1995. pap. text 19.50 (*0-8147-1251-7*) NYU Pr.

Brooker, Peter. Bertolt Brecht: Dialectics, Poetry, Politics. 240p. 1988. lib. bdg. 57.50 (*0-7099-5015-2*, Pub. by C Helm) Routldge.

***Brooker, Peter.** Cultural Theory: A Concise Glossary. LC 98-26308. (Arnold Publications). 256p. 1999. pap. text 18.95 (*0-340-69147-6*) OUP.

Brooker, Peter. Cultural Theory: A Glossary. LC 98-20411. (Arnold Publication Ser.). 304p. 1998. text 65.00 (*0-340-69146-8*) OUP.

— New York Fictions: Modernity, Postmodernism, the New Modern. Smith, Stan, ed. LC 95-24903. (Studies in Twentieth Century Literature Ser.). 256p. (C). 1996. pap. text 30.94 (*0-582-09954-4*, Pub. by Addison-Wesley) Longman.

Brooker, Peter. New York Fictions: Modernity, Postmodernism, the New Modern. Smith, Stan, ed. LC 95-24903. (Studies in Twentieth Century Literature). 256p. (C). 1996. 90.00 (*0-582-09955-2*) Longman.

Brooker, Peter, ed. Modernism - Postmodernism. (Critical Readers Ser.). 280p. (C). 1995. pap. 49.00 (*0-582-06357-4*, 79264) Longman.

— Modernism& Postmodernism. (Critical Readers Ser.). 268p. (C). 1992. text 63.50 (*0-582-06358-2*, 79263) Longman.

Brooker, Peter & Brooker, Will, eds. Postmodern After-Images: A Reader in Film, Television, & Video. LC 96-48152. (An Arnold Publication). 304p. 1997. text 60.00 (*0-340-67692-2*, Pub. by E A); pap. text 19.95 (*0-340-67691-4*, Pub. by E A) OUP.

Brooker, Peter & Humm, Peter, eds. Dialogue & Difference: English for the 1990s. 256p. 1989. 49.95 (*0-415-01643-6*, A3622) Routledge.

Brooker, Peter, jt. auth. see Widdowson, Peter.

Brooker, Richard & Corder, Matthew. Environmental Economy. 200p. 1986. text 47.50 (*0-419-13300-3*, 9930, E & FN Spon) Routledge.

Brooker, Robert J. Principles Genetics. LC 98-34247. 761p. (C). 1998. 92.00 (*0-8053-9175-4*) Benjamin-Cummings.

Brooker, S. G., et al. Economic Native Plants of NZ. 1988. 18.35 (*0-477-02526-9*, Pub. by Manaaki Whenua) Balogh.

Brooker, Wendell. Storyweaving: You & Your Faith Journey. LC 90-888902. 96p. 1990. pap., student ed. 7.00 (*0-8170-1157-9*) Judson.

— Storyweaving: You & Your Faith Journey. 55p. 1990. pap. 6.00 (*0-8170-1158-7*); pap., teacher ed. 6.00 (*0-8170-1167-6*) Judson.

***Brooker, Will.** Batman Unmasked: Analyzing a Cultural Icon. 256p. 2000. 27.95 (*0-8264-4949-2*) Continuum.

— Teach Yourself Cultural Studies. 192p. 1999. pap. 12.95 (*0-8442-2641-6*, Teach Yrslf) NTC Contemp Pub Co.

Brooker, Will, jt. ed. see Brooker, Peter.

Brookes. The Road More Traveled. Date not set. pap. 10.00 (*0-8050-5367-0*) H Holt & Co.

— The Road More Traveled. 1998. 20.00 (*0-8050-5366-2*) H Holt & Co.

— Ten Steps. 3rd ed. (C). 1995. pap. text, teacher ed. 6.00 (*0-13-460015-0*) P-H.

Brookes, Alan. Cladding of Buildings. 3rd ed. LC 97-66022. (Illus.). 208p. (C). 1998. pap. 45.00 (*0-419-22170-0*, E & FN Spon) Routledge.

Brookes, Alan J. Building Envelope & Connections. 2nd ed. LC 96-229223. 288p. 1996. pap. text 66.95 (*0-7506-3096-5*) Buttrwrth-Heinemann.

— Claddings of Buildings. LC 90-20268. 224p. 1990. reprint ed. pap. 69.50 (*0-608-03615-3*, 206443900009) Bks Demand.

Brookes, Alan J. & Grech, Chris. The Building Envelope: Applications of New Technology Cladding. (Illus.). 144p. 1995. pap. text 41.95 (*0-7506-1790-X*) Buttrwrth-Heinemann.

***Brookes, Andrew.** Air War over Italy. (Illus.). 2000. 34.95 (*0-7110-2690-4*, Pub. by Ian Allan) Combined Pub.

Brookes, Andrew. Channelized Rivers: Perspectives for Environmental Management. LC 85-5647. 342p. 1989. 280.00 (*0-471-91979-9*) Wiley.

Brookes, Andrew & Shields, F. Douglas, eds. River Channel Restoration: Guiding Principles for Sustainable Projects. 458p. 1996. 200.00 (*0-471-96139-6*) Wiley.

***Brookes, Arthur & Grundy, Peter.** Beginning to Write: Writing Activities for Elementary & Intermediate Learners. LC 98-44372. 1998. write for info. (*0-521-58979-7*) Cambridge U Pr.

Brookes, Arthur & Grundy, Peter. Writing for Study Purposes: A Teacher's Guide to Developing Individual Writing Skills. 172p. (C). 1991. pap. text 19.95 (*0-521-35853-1*) Cambridge U Pr.

Brookes, Barbara. Abortion in England, 1900-1967. 256p. 1988. lib. bdg. 55.00 (*0-7099-5046-2*, A1773) Routledge.

Brookes, C. Avery. Sea Breezes, Salt Air LC 98-74691. 53 p. 1999. 6.95 (*0-9666246-0-2*, Bunny Express) C A Brookes Ltd.

Brookes, C. E., jt. auth. see Andersdatter, Karla.

Brookes, Christopher. When the Doctor Drops the Bomb. 104p. (Orig.). 1997. pap. 9.95 (*0-9655207-0-6*) Cutters Rig Bks.

Brookes, Clive & Smith, Peter B., eds. A History of Southampton in Picture Postcards. (C). 1989. 39.00 (*1-85455-031-4*, Pub. by Ensign Pubns & Print) St Mut.

Brookes, Derek R. Thomas Reid, an Inquiry into the Human Mind on the Principles of Common Sense. 340p. 1997. 55.00 (*0-271-01702-3*) Pa St U Pr.

***Brookes, Derek R., ed.** Thomas Reid: Essays on the Intellectual Powers of Man; Edinburgh Edition. 340p. 2000. 55.00 (*0-271-02069-5*) Pa St U Pr.

Brookes, Derek R., jt. auth. see Reid, Thomas.

Brookes, Diane. All Alone. (Illus.). (J). (ps-2). 1999. pap. 7.95 (*0-9683640-9-8*) RRP.

— David's Day. (Illus.). (J). (gr. 1-5). 1998. pap. 7.95 (*0-9683640-6-3*) RRP.

***Brookes, Diane.** A General Novel Study for Primary Students Listening to a Teacher-Selected Novel. 1998. pap. text, teacher ed. 7.95 (*0-9683449-8-4*) RRP.

— How the Leopard Got Its Spots. large type ed. (Illus.). 24p. (J). (ps-5). 1999. pap. 7.95 (*1-894303-00-8*) RRP.

— It Was a Lemon. large type ed. (Illus.). 24p. (J). (ps-3). 1999. pap. 5.95 (*1-894303-03-2*) RRP.

Brookes, Diane. Kailee & the Frog Prince. (Illus.). (J). (ps-5). 1999. pap. 7.95 (*0-9683640-2-0*) RRP.

***Brookes, Diane.** The Man in the Moon. 32p. 1998. pap. 7.95 (*0-9683234-0-5*) RRP.

Brookes, Diane. Passing the Peace: A Counting Book for Kids. (ENG & FRE., Illus.). 24p. (J). 1990. pap. 8.95 (*0-921254-20-2*, Pub. by Penumbra Pr) U of Toronto Pr.

***Brookes, Diane.** Said the Raven. 24p. (J). 1999. pap. 5.95 (*1-894303-18-0*) RRP.

— Spring Blizzard. large type ed. (Illus.). 24p. (J). (ps-3). 1999. pap. 7.95 (*1-894303-04-0*) RRP.

— The Story of Spot, the School Cat. large type ed. (Illus.). 16p. (J). (ps-3). 1999. pap. 5.95 (*1-894303-02-4*) RRP.

Brookes, Diane. Su Lin & the Dragon. (Illus.). 24p. (J). (ps-5). 1999. pap. 7.95 (*0-9683640-0-4*) RRP.

Brookes, Diane. The Tough Little Tugboat. (Illus.). 8p. (J). bds. 7.95 (*1-894303-16-4*) RRP.

***Brookes, Diane & Adler, David A.** A Novel Study for Grades Two & Three Based on Cam Jensen & the Mystery of the Dinosaur Bones. 1998. pap. text, teacher ed. 7.95 (*0-9683234-8-0*) RRP.

***Brookes, Diane & Baird, Alison.** A Novel Study for Grades Three & Four Based on The Dragon's Egg. 1998. pap. text, teacher ed. 7.95 (*0-9683234-7-2*) RRP.

Brookes, Diane & Brandenburg, Franz J. A Novel Study for Grades Two & Three Based on Cam Jensen & the Mystery of the Dinosaur Bones, 23 vols. (Raven Rock Primary Novel Study Collection). 1998. pap. 7.95 (*0-9683640-3-9*) Raven Rocks Pr.

Brookes, Diane & Dahl, Roald. A Novel Study for Grades One & Two Based on Esio Trot. 1998. pap. text, teacher ed. 7.95 (*0-9683449-3-3*) RRP.

— A Novel Study for Grades One & Two Based on Fantastic Mr. Fox. 1998. pap. text, teacher ed. 7.95 (*0-9683449-5-X*) RRP.

— A Novel Study for Grades One & Two Based on the Twits. 1998. pap. text, teacher ed. 7.95 (*0-9683449-6-8*) RRP.

— A Novel Study for Grades Two & Three Based on the Magic Finger. 1998. pap. text, teacher ed. 7.95 (*0-9683449-4-1*) RRP.

Brookes, Diane & Gardiner, John R. A Novel Study for Grade Three Based on Stone Fox. 1998. pap. text, teacher ed. 7.95 (*0-9683449-1-7*) RRP.

***Brookes, Diane & Glimmerveen, Ulco.** A Novel Study for Grades One & Two Based on a Tale of Antarctica. 1998. pap. text, teacher ed. 7.95 (*0-9683449-0-9*) RRP.

***Brookes, Diane & Leonard, Marcia.** A Novel Study for Grades One & Two Based on When the Giants Came to Town. 1998. pap. text, teacher ed. 7.95 (*0-9683234-5-6*) RRP.

***Brookes, Diane & Lobel, Arnold.** A Novel Study for Grades One & Two Based on Frog & Toad Are Friends. 1998. pap. text, teacher ed. 7.95 (*0-9683234-2-1*) RRP.

***Brookes, Diane & McGovern, Ann.** A Novel Study for Grades Three & Four Based on Playing with Penguins & Other Adventures in Antarctica. 1998. pap. text, teacher ed. 7.95 (*0-9683449-2-5*) RRP.

Brookes, Diane & Osborne, Mary Pope. A Novel Study for Grade Two Based on Dolphins at Daybreak. (Illus.). 1998. pap. text, teacher ed. 7.95 (*0-9683640-1-2*) RRP.

***Brookes, Diane & Osborne, Mary Pope.** A Novel Study for Grades Two & Three Based on Dinosaurs Before Dark. 1998. pap. text, teacher ed. 7.95 (*0-9683234-6-4*) RRP.

***Brookes, Diane & Wood, Audrey.** A Novel Study for Grades One & Two Based on Little Penguin's Tale. 1998. pap. text, teacher ed. 7.95 (*0-9683234-3-X*) RRP.

***Brookes, Diane, et al.** A Novel Study for Grades One or Grades Three & Four Based on Mr. Popper's Penguins. 1998. pap. text, teacher ed. 7.95 (*0-9683449-7-6*) RRP.

Brookes, Diane, jt. auth. see Parish, Peggy.

Brookes, Diane, ed. see Dahl, Roald.

Brookes, Edgar H. America in Travail. LC 68-8590. (C). 1968. pap. 4.00 (*0-87574-159-2*) Pendle Hill.

— The City of God & the Politics of Crisis. LC 80-11820. 111p. 1980. reprint ed. lib. bdg. 55.00 (*0-313-22385-8*, BRGD, Greenwood Pr) Greenwood.

— Colour Problem of South Africa: Being the Phelps-Stokes Lectures, 1933, Delivered at the University of Cape Town. LC 79-111565. 237p. 1970. reprint ed. lib. bdg. 49.50 (*0-8371-4586-4*, BCP&) Greenwood.

— Three Letters from Africa. LC 65-12948. (Orig.). 1965. pap. 4.00 (*0-87574-139-8*) Pendle Hill.

— White Rule in South Africa, 1830-1910. 230p. 1974. 14.95 (*0-86980-031-0*, Pub. by Univ Natal Pr) Intl Spec Bk.

Brookes, Edgar H. & Webb, Colin D. A History of Natal. 2nd ed. (Illus.). 394p. 1987. pap. 24.95 (*0-86980-579-7*, Pub. by Univ Natal Pr) Intl Spec Bk.

Brookes, Gavon I. Tolley's Practice Development Handbook. 70p. (C). 1994. 175.00 (*0-85459-857-X*, Pub. by Tolley Pubng) St Mut.

Brookes, Gay & Withrow, Jean. Ten Steps: Controlled Composition for Beginning & Intermediate Language Development. 2nd rev. ed. Munch, Helen, ed. 72p. (gr. 7-12). 1988. pap. text 6.25 (*0-88084-253-9*) Alemany Pr.

— Ten Steps: Controlled Composition for Beginning & Intermediate Language Development. 2nd rev. ed. Munch, Helen, ed. 72p. (YA). (gr. 7-12). 1990. pap. text, teacher ed. 7.67 (*0-13-904111-7*) Alemany Pr.

— Ten Steps: Controlled Composition for Language Development. 3rd ed. (Illus.). 64p. 1995. pap. text 14.00 (*0-13-456989-X*, Pub. by P-H) S&S Trade.

Brookes, George S. Cascades & Courage: The History of the Town of Vernon & the City of Rockville (Connecticut) (Illus.). 529p. 1993. reprint ed. lib. bdg. 53.00 (*0-8328-2902-1*) Higginson Bk Co.

Brookes, H. F., ed. see Brecht, Bertolt.

Brookes, Ian A. & Weatherston, Jamie. Business Enviroment: Challenges & Changes. 384p. 1997. pap. 45.00 (*0-13-376716-7*) P-H.

Brookes, Ivan S. The Lower St. Lawrence. (Illus.). 1974. 10.75 (*0-912514-13-2*) Freshwater.

Brookes, James H. Salvation: The Way Made Plain. pap. 4.99 (*0-87377-015-3*) GAM Pubns.

Brookes, John. The Book of Garden Design. (Illus.). 352p. 1991. 45.00 (*0-02-516695-6*) Macmillan.

— Complete Gardner. (Illus.). 577p. 1994. 29.99 (*0-517-10287-0*) Random Hse Value.

— Country Garden. (Illus.). 208p. 1987. 40.00 (*0-517-56704-0*, Crown) Crown Pub Group.

— Garden Book: Designing, Creating & Maintaining Your Garden. 1992. 24.00 (*0-517-58948-6*, Crown) Crown.

— Gardens of Paradise: The History & Design of the Great Islamic Gardens. LC 87-12229. (Illus.). 240p. (C). 1987. 36.00 (*0-941533-07-7*, NAB) I R Dee.

— The Indoor Garden Book: The Complete Guide to the Creative Use of Plants & Flowers in the Home. LC 93-34262. (Illus.). 288p. 1994. reprint ed. pap. 19.95 (*1-56458-527-1*) DK Pub Inc.

— John Brookes' Garden Design Workbook. LC 94-242325. (Illus.). 72p. 1994. wbk. ed. 17.95 (*1-56458-559-X*) DK Pub Inc.

— John Brookes' Natural Landscapes: How to Design, Build, & Plant Your Garden With Nature in Mind. LC 97-14827. (Illus.). 168p. 1998. 29.95 (*0-7894-1995-5*) DK Pub Inc.

Brookes, John. A Place in the Country. LC 83-51677. (Illus.). 240p. 1984. 24.95 (*0-500-01327-6*, Pub. by Thames Hudson) Norton.

Brookes, John. Planting the Country Way: A Hands-On Approach. LC 97-74411. (Illus.). 192p. 1997. 32.95 (*0-563-36799-7*, BBC-Parkwest) Parkwest Pubns.

Brookes, John, ed. House Plants. LC 89-70332. (RD Home Handbooks Ser.). (Illus.). 204p. (Orig.). 1990. pap. 16.00 (*0-89577-349-X*, Pub. by RD Assn) Penguin Putnam.

***Brookes, Kate.** Ancient Times: A Journey from the Dawn of History to the Glory of Rome. 1999. 9.99 (*1-84100-271-2*) Quadrillion Pubng.

— Biblical Times: A Comprehensive History of the People, Places & Events of the Old & New Tes. 1999. 9.99 (*1-84100-269-0*) Quadrillion Pubng.

— Little Farmyard Adventures Carry Case. LC 98-235715. (Illus.). 24p. (J). (ps-1). 1998. 7.98 (*0-7651-0700-7*) Smithmark.

— Middle Ages: Turbulent Centuries: From the Dark Ages to the New World. 1999. 9.99 (*1-84100-270-4*) Quadrillion Pubng.

Brookes, Kate. Spooky Activity Box: Book, Spider, Vampire Teeth, Bat & Werewolf Marks, & Skeleton. (Illus.). (J). (ps up). 1997. pap. 11.95 (*1-85479-215-6*) Trans-Atl Phila.

— The Spooky Activity Box: Color Book, Bat Mask, Werewolf Mask, & Skeleton. (Illus.). (J). (ps up). 1997. boxed set 11.95 (*1-85479-219-9*) Trans-Atl Phila.

***Brookes, Kate.** World War II: Turning Points in the Global Conflict That Shaped Our World. 1999. 9.99 (*1-84100-272-0*) Quadrillion Pubng.

***Brookes, Kate & Songhurst, Hazel.** Potty Tales: Lulu's a Big Girl Now; Now Wash Your Hands!; Where's Max's Potty; Lulu's Su, 4 bks. (Carry Cases Ser.). (Illus.). 10p. (J). (ps-k). 1998. bds. 7.98 (*0-7651-0805-4*) Smithmark.

Brookes, Keith. The Complete Video Course. 176p. (C). 1990. 60.00 (*1-85283-269-X*, Pub. by Boxtree) St Mut.

Brookes, Kenneth. Battle Thunder: The Story of Britain's Artillery. (Illus.). 256p. 1973. 29.95 (*0-8464-0185-1*) Beekman Pubs.

Brookes, Kenneth J. Hardmetals & Other Hard Materials. 198p. 1992. pap. 60.00 (*0-9508995-3-4*) Metal Powder.

Brookes, Kenneth J. World Directory & Handbook of Hardmetals & Hard Materials. 750p. 1997. 395.00 (*0-9508995-4-2*, 9040D) Metal Powder.

Brookes, M. What's the Big Idea? Genetics. (Illus.). (J). mass mkt. 8.95 (*0-340-70877-8*, Pub. by Hodder & Stought Ltd) Trafalgar.

Brookes, Martin. Get a Grip on Genetics. LC 98-28745. (Get a Grip On . . . Ser.). 192p. (gr. 7). 1998. pap. 14.95 (*0-7370-0035-X*) T-L Custom Pub.

Brookes, Mona. Drawing for Older Children & Teens: A Creative Method for Adult Beginners, Too. (Illus.). 256p. (Orig.). 1991. pap. 15.95 (*0-87477-661-9*, Tarcher Putnam) Putnam Pub Group.

— Drawing with Children: A Creative Method for Adult Beginners, Too. annuals 10th anniversary expanded ed. LC 95-49072. (Illus.). 272p. 1996. pap. 15.95 (*0-87477-827-1*, Tarcher Putnam) Putnam Pub Group.

Brookes, Murray & Revell, William J. Blood Supply of Bone: Scientific Aspects. LC 97-31214. (Illus.). xx, 359p. 1997. 119.00 (*3-540-76204-3*) Spr-Verlag.

Brookes, Murray & Zietman, Anthony L. A Clinical Embryology Color Atlas & Text. LC 98-22967. 341p. 1998. lib. bdg. 39.95 (*0-8493-1255-8*) CRC Pr.

Brookes, Naomi J., jt. auth. see Backhouse, Christopher J.

Brookes, Naomi J., jt. ed. see Backhouse, Christopher J.

Brookes, Paul. Electronic Surveillance Devices. (Illus.). 208p. 1996. pap. 39.95 (*0-7506-2582-1*) Buttrwrth-Heinemann.

Brookes, R. F., tr. see Kulaev, Igor S.

Brookes, R. F., tr. see Kurganov, Boris I.

Brookes, Richard. The New Marketing. 200p. 1988. text 65.95 (*0-566-02677-5*, Pub. by Gower) Ashgate Pub Co.

Brookes, Samuel O., jt. ed. see Peacock, Evan.

Brookes, Stephen D., ed. Mathematical Foundations of Programming Semantics: Ninth International Conference, New Orleans, LA, U. S. A., April 1993. No. 802. 1994. write for info. (*0-318-72717-X*) Spr-Verlag.

Brookes, Stephen D., et al, eds. Seminar on Concurrency. (Lecture Notes in Computer Science Ser.: Vol. 197). xi, 523p. 1985. 49.00 (*0-387-15670-4*) Spr-Verlag.

Brookes, Tim. Catching My Breath: An Asthmatic Explores His Illness. 291p. 1998. text 22.00 (*0-7881-5713-2*) DIANE Pub.

***Brookes, Tim.** A Hell of a Place to Lose a Cow: My American Hitchhiking Odyssey. (Illus.). 304p. 2000. 26.00 (*0-7922-7683-3*) Natl Geog.

Brookes, Tim. Signs of Life: A Memoir of Hospice, Home & Hope. LC 96-30576. 1997. 23.00 (*0-8129-2468-1* Times Bks) Crown Pub Group.

Brookes, Tony. CO2 Powered Model Aircraft. (Illus.). 76p. (Orig.). 1998. pap. 24.50 (*1-85486-172-7*) Nexus Special Interests.

Brookes, Virginia. British Keyboard Music to Circa 1660: Sources & Thematic Index. (Illus.). 430p. 1996. text 150.00 (*0-19-816425-4*) OUP.

Brookes, Virginia. Sir William Dunch's Pavan & Galliard for Five Viols. (Charney Manor Ser.: No. 6). i, 15p. 1993. pap. text 10.00 (*1-56571-073-8*, CM006) PRB Prods.

Brookes, Virginia, ed. Priscilla Bunbury's Virginal Book: A Collection of Keyboard Music for a Young Lady of the Seventeenth Century. (Illus.). xi, 40p. 1993. pap. text 30.00 (*1-56571-052-5*, EK003) PRB Prods.

Brookes, Virginia, ed. see Cranford, William.

Brookes, Virginia, ed. see Dering, Richard.

Brookes, Virginia, ed. see Gibbons, Orlando.

Brookes, Virginia, ed. see Ravenscroft, Thomas.

Brookes, Virginia, ed. see Ward, John.

Brookes, W. S. & Yarrow, P. J. The Dramatic Criticism of Elizabeth Charlotte, Duchesse D'Orleans, with an Annotated Chronology of Performances of the Popular & Court Theatres in France (1671-1722), Reconstructed from Her Letters. LC 95-22909. (Studies in French Civilization). 372p. 1996. 99.95 (*0-7734-8834-0*) E Mellen.

Brookes, Warren T. Better Schools Through Wider Choice: Market Discipline, Not Spending, Is the Key. 16p. 1988. pap. text 8.00 (*1-57655-109-1*) Independ Inst.

— Unconventional Wisdoms: The Best of Warren Brookes. Bray, Thomas J., ed. LC 97-13938. 1997. pap. text 16.95 (*0-936488-83-2*) PRIPP.

Brookesmith, Peter, jt. auth. see Devereux, Paul.

Brookfield, Cornelia, tr. see Durkheim, Emile.

Brookfield, F. M. Law & Practice of Conveyancing with Precedents. 4th ed. 593p. 1980. boxed set 108.00 (*0-409-60029-6*, NZ, MICHIE) LEXIS Pub.

Brookfield, F. M., ed. see Brownlie, Ian.

Brookfield, Frances M. Cambridge "Apostles" LC 70-148758. reprint ed. 34.50 (*0-404-08729-9*) AMS Pr.

Brookfield, H., et al. In Place of the Forest: Environmental Change in Borneo & the Eastern Malay. LC 96-211982. 300p. 1995. pap. text 30.00 (*92-808-0893-1*) UN.

Brookfield, Harold. South-East Asia's Environmental Future: The Search for Sustainability. 456p. (C). 1993. write for info. (*92-808-0823-0*, Pub. by UN Univ Pr) Brookings.

Brookfield, Harold, ed. Transformation with Industrialization in Peninsular Malaysia. (South-East Asian Social Science Monographs). (Illus.). 344p. (C). 1994. 60.00 (*967-65-3030-1*, 8940) OUP.

Brookfield, Harold & Byron, Yvonne, eds. South-East Asia's Environmental Future: The Search for Sustainability. LC 93-10193. 1993. 58.00 (*0-685-65144-4*) OUP.

Brookfield, Harold, et al. The City in the Village: The In-Situ Urbanization of Villages & their Land Around Juala. (Illus.). 212p. 1991. text 59.00 (*0-19-588976-2*, 12239) OUP.

Brookfield, Harold, jt. auth. see Blaikie, Piers.

Brookfield, John. Mastery of Hand Strength. LC 95-78894. 120p. (Orig.). 1995. pap. 14.95 (*0-926888-03-X*) IronMind Enterprises.

***Brookfield, Karen.** Book. (Eyewitness Books). (J). (gr. 4-7). 2000. 15.95 (*0-7894-5892-6*) DK Pub Inc.

Brookfield, Karen, ed. Scholarly Communication & Serials Prices. (British Library Research). 160p. 1991. lib. bdg. 45.00 (*0-86291-478-7*) Bowker-Saur.

Brookfield, S. Independent Adult Learning. (C). 1988. text 32.00 (*0-7855-6015-7*, Pub. by Univ Nottingham) St Mut.

Brookfield, Stephen D. Adult Learners, Adult Education & the Community. 240p. 1983. pap. 39.95 (*0-335-10409-6*) OpUniv Pr.

Brookfield, Stephen D. Becoming a Critically Reflective Teacher. LC 95-12699. (Higher & Adult Education Ser.). 320p. 1995. text 32.45 (*0-7879-0131-8*) Jossey-Bass.

Brookfield, Stephen D. Developing Critical Thinkers: Challenging Adults to Explore Alternative Ways of Thinking & Acting. 312p. 1987. pap. 34.00 (*0-335-15551-0*) OpUniv Pr.

— Developing Critical Thinkers: Challenging Adults to Explore Alternative Ways of Thinking & Acting. fac. ed. LC 87-45411. (Jossey-Bass Higher Education & the Jossey-Bass Management Ser.). 311p. 1987. reprint ed. pap. 96.50 (*0-7837-8046-X*, 204779900008) Bks Demand.

— Developing Critical Thinkers: Challenging Adults to Explore Alternative Ways of Thinking & Acting. LC 87-45411. (Higher & Adult Education-Management Ser.). 311p. 1991. reprint ed. pap. text 27.95 (*1-55542-356-6*) Jossey-Bass.

***Brookfield, Stephen D.** Discussion as a Way of Teaching: Tools & Techniques for Democratic Classrooms. LC 98-53903. (Jossey-Bass Higher & Adult Education Ser.). 5p. 1999. 32.95 (*0-7879-4458-0*) Jossey-Bass.

Brookfield, Stephen D. The Skillful Teacher: On Technique, Trust, & Responsiveness in the Classroom. LC 90-40387. (Higher Education Ser.). 255p. 1990. text 32.95 (*1-55542-267-5*) Jossey-Bass.

— Understanding & Facilitating Adult Learning: A Comprehensive Analysis of Principles & Effective Practices. 375p. 1986. 39.95 (*0-335-15226-0*) OpUniv Pr.

— Understanding & Facilitating Adult Learning: A Comprehensive Analysis of Principles & Effective Practices. LC 85-23861. (Higher & Adult Education-Management Ser.). 393p. 1991. reprint ed. text 28.95 (*1-55542-355-8*) Jossey-Bass.

Brookhart, Clint. Go Figure! LC 97-48461. 160p. 1998. 22.95 (*0-8092-2882-3*, 288230, Contemporary Bks) NTC Contemp Pub Co.

— Go Figure! 160p. 1999. pap. 14.95 (*0-8092-2608-1*, 260810, Contemporary Bks) NTC Contemp Pub Co.

Brookhart, Mary. Internet Terms & Computer Acronyms: A Useful Guide. LC 98-85554. 161p. (Orig.). 1998. pap. 19.95 (*0-9654348-1-8*) SE Consulting.

***Brookhart, Susan M.** The Art & Science of Classroom Assessment: The Missing Part of Pedagogy. LC 99-63955. (ASHE-ERIC Higher Education Report: Vol. 27). 121p. 1999. 24.00 (*1-878380-89-3*) GWU Grad Schl E&HD.

Brookhaven National Laboratory Staff, ed. Protein Data Bank CD-ROM. 1992. 798.95 (*0-387-14101-4*); 325.00 (*0-387-14102-2*) Spr-Verlag.

Brookheart, Brian. A Prisoner: Released. unabridged ed. 133p. 1997. pap. 10.00 (*0-9661038-0-7*) B Brookheart.

***Brookheiser, Richard.** Alexander Hamilton, American. 256p. 2000. per. 13.00 (*0-684-86331-6*) S&S Trade.

Brookhiser, Richard. Alexander Hamilton, American. LC 98-46846. (Illus.). 240p. 1999. 24.50 (*0-684-83919-9*) Free Pr.

***Brookhiser, Richard.** Alexander Hamilton, American. large type ed. LC 99-25955. (Americana Series). (Illus.). 454p. 1999. 30.00 (*0-7862-1987-4*) Thorndike Pr.

Brookhiser, Richard. Founding Father: Rediscovering George Washington. 240p. 1996. 24.50 (*0-684-82291-1*) Free Pr.

— Founding Father: Rediscovering George Washington. 240p. 1997. per. 12.00 (*0-684-83142-2*) Free Pr.

— The Rules of Civility: The 110 Precepts That Guided Our First President in War & Peace. LC 96-6521. (Illus.). 96p. 1997. 15.50 (*0-684-83723-4*) Free Pr.

— The Way of the Wasp: How It Made America, & How It Can Save It, So to Speak. 261p. 1990. text 24.95 (*0-02-904721-8*) Free Pr.

Brookhouse, Christopher. Dear Otto. LC 94-31749. 133p. 1995. 22.00 (*1-877946-63-X*) Permanent Pr.

— The Light Between the Fields. LC 98-19403. (Signature Poets Ser.). 69p. 1998. 18.00 (*0-930095-34-0*) Signal Bks.

B

***Brookhouse, Christopher.** Passing Game. LC 00-190466. 160p. 2000. 19.95 (*0-9665798-2-8*, Pub. by Safe Harbor Bks) Enfield Pubs NH.

Brookhouse, Shaun. Hypnotherapy Training: An Investigation into the Development of Clinical Hypnosis Training Post, 1971. 60p. 1998. spiral bd. 24.95 (*1-899836-17-9*, Pub. by Crown Hse) LPC Group.

Brooking. Intellect Capital: Core Assets. 1998. pap. 19.99 (*1-86152-408-0*) Thomson Learn.

— Psychiatric Nursing. (Illus.). 640p. (Orig.). 1992. pap. text 54.00 (*0-443-03461-3*) Church.

Brooking, Annie. Corporate Memory: Strategies for Knowledge Management. LC 99-187820. 224p. 1998. pap. 19.99 (*1-86152-268-1*) Thomson Learn.

— Dream Ticket: Corporate Strategy with Intellectual Capital. 224p. 1999. pap. 19.95 (*1-86152-267-3*, Pub. by ITBP) Thomson Learn.

— Intellectual Capital: Core Assets for the Third Millenium. LC 96-38887. 224p. 1996. pap. 19.99 (*1-86152-023-9*) Thomson Learn.

Brooking, Tom. Lands for the People? The Highland Clearances & the Colonisation of New Zealand: A Biography of John McKenzie. (Illus.). 300p. 1996. pap. 39.95 (*1-877133-21-3*, Pub. by Univ Otago Pr) Intl Spec Bk.

Brookings Conference on the Effects of Tax Policy. Tax Incentives & Capital Spending: Proceedings of Brookings Conference on the Effects of Tax Policy on Investment, Brooking Institution, 1967. Fromm, Gary, ed. LC 79-115225. (Brookings Institution Staff Papers). 319p. reprint ed. pap. 98.90 (*0-608-12199-1*, 202537900043) Bks Demand.

Brookings, Eugene. Memories of the Windswept Plains. (Illus.). 300p. 1995. 14.95 (*0-9649583-0-9*) E Brookings.

Brookings Institution Staff. Domestic Economic Policies in the Industrial Countries: A Tripartite Report by Fourteen Economists from Japan, Europe & North America. LC 78-308154. 17p. reprint ed. pap. 30.00 (*0-608-12170-3*, 202537100043) Bks Demand.

— Economic Effects of Fundamental Tax Reform. Aaron, Henry J. et al, eds. LC 96-27074. 521p. 1996. 52.95 (*0-8157-0058-X*); pap. 24.95 (*0-8157-0057-1*) Brookings.

— Economic Prospects & Policies in the Industrial Countries: A Tripartite Report by Sixteen Economists from the European Community, Japan, & North America. LC 77-354856. 16p. reprint ed. pap. 30.00 (*0-608-12190-8*, 202537500043) Bks Demand.

— Economic Relations Between East & West--Prospects & Problems: A Tripartite Report by Fifteen Experts from the European Community, Japan & North America. LC 78-109561. 41p. reprint ed. pap. 30.00 (*0-608-12192-4*, 202537600043) Bks Demand.

— International Linkages under Flexible Exchange Rates: A Tripartite Report by Seventeen Economists from Japan, the European Community, & North America. LC 79-105240. 39p. reprint ed. pap. 30.00 (*0-608-12701-9*, 202538200043) Bks Demand.

— Service Monographs of the United States Government, No. 1-66. reprint ed. write for info. (*0-404-57100-X*) AMS Pr.

— The U. S. Geological Survey: Its History, Activities & Organization. LC 72-3014. (Service Monographs of the U. S. Government: No. 1). reprint ed. 21.50 (*0-404-57101-8*) AMS Pr.

— The U. S. Reclamation Service: Its History, Activities & Organization. LC 72-3015. (Service Monographs of the U. S. Government: No. 2). reprint ed. 24.50 (*0-404-57102-6*) AMS Pr.

Brookings, Jeff D., jt. auth. see McEvoy, Alan W.

Brookings, Publishing. Blueprint for Restructuring America's Financial Institutions: Report of a Task Force. 48p. 1989. pap. 6.95 (*0-8157-5275-X*) Brookings.

Brookings, Robert S. Industrial Ownership: Its Economic & Social Significance. LC 74-37872. (Select Bibliographies Reprint Ser.). 1977. reprint ed. 17.95 (*0-8369-6709-7*) Ayer.

Brookings, Warren, jt. auth. see Stone, David.

***Brookins, Carl.** Inner Passages. 320p. 2000. pap. 14.95 (*1-929976-01-1*, Pub. by Top Pubns) Herveys Bklink.

Brookins, Chris, jt. auth. see Holly, Kristina.

Brookins, Chris, jt. auth. see Holly, Krisztina.

Brookins, Donald G., jt. auth. see Gorrell, Robert P., Jr.

Brookins, Douglas G. Eh-pH Diagrams for Geochemistry. (Illus.). 200p. 1988. 147.95 (*0-387-18485-6*) Spr-Verlag.

— Geochemical Aspects of Radioactive Waste Disposal. (Illus.). 420p. 1984. 152.00 (*0-387-90916-8*) Spr-Verlag.

— The Indoor Radon Problem. 228p. 1990. text 48.00 (*0-231-06748-8*) Col U Pr.

— Mineral & Energy Resources. 2nd ed. (C). 1996. 44.00 (*0-02-315081-5*, Macmillan Coll) P-H.

Brookins-Fisher, Jodi, jt. auth. see Reagan, Patricia A.

Brookins-Fisher, Jodi, jt. ed. see Bensley, Robert J.

Brookins, Gary & Gorrell, Bob. Pen Pals: A Cartoon Collection. 132p. (Orig.). 1992. pap. 9.95 (*0-9635288-0-7*) Richmnd-Times-Dispatch.

Brookins, Terrie. The Care She Needs. 66p. 1998. pap. 5.00 (*1-57502-793-3*, PO2193) Morris Pubng.

— Visions & Revisions. 70p. (Orig.). 1997. pap. 5.00 (*1-57502-474-8*, P01419) Morris Pubng.

Brookler, K., jt. auth. see Rubin, W.

Brookline Books Staff, jt. auth. see Kamen, Daniel R.

Brooklyn. Natural Insect Control: The Ecological Gardener's Guide to Foiling Pests. 1995. pap. text 6.95 (*0-945325-28-2*) Perf Pr OR.

Brooklyn Art Museum Staff, jt. auth. see Harwood, Barry R.

Brooklyn Botanic Garden Botanists. Get Ready, Set, Grow. 1997. 29.95 incl. VHS (*0-945352-51-4*, 0300K) Bklyn Botanic.

Brooklyn Botanic Garden Botanists & Lewis, Alcinda C., eds. Butterfly Gardens: Luring Nature's Loveliest Pollinators to Your Yard. (21st-Century Gardening Ser.). (Illus.). 112p. 1995. pap., per. 9.95 (*0-945352-88-3*) Bklyn Botanic.

Brooklyn Botanic Garden Botanists, jt. ed. see Burrell, C. Colston.

Brooklyn Botanic Garden Botanists, jt. ed. see Cutler, Karan D.

Brooklyn Botanic Garden Botanists, jt. ed. see Hyland, Bob.

Brooklyn Botanic Garden Botanists, jt. ed. see Kress, Stephen W.

Brooklyn Botanic Garden Botanists, jt. ed. see Scanniello, Stephen.

Brooklyn Business Library Staff. Business Rankings Annual, 1991. 91st ed. 1991. 199.00 (*0-8103-4294-4*) Gale.

— Business Rankings Annual, 1992. 92nd ed. 1992. 199.00 (*0-8103-4295-2*) Gale.

— Business Rankings Annual, 1993. 93rd ed. 1993. 199.00 (*0-8103-5347-4*) Gale.

— Business Rankings Annual, 1995: Lists of Companies, Products, Services, & Activities Compiled from a Variety of Published Sources. 95th ed. 800p. 1995. 199.00 (*0-8103-8953-3*) Gale.

— Business Rankings Annual, 1996. 96th ed. 1995. 199.00 (*0-8103-0200-4*) Gale.

— Business Rankings Annual, 1997. 97th ed. 1996. 199.00 (*0-7876-0065-2*) Gale.

Brooklyn Chamber of Commerce Staff. Brooklyn@tlas. deluxe ed. (Atlas: Vol. 2). (Illus.). 100p. 1998. 7.95 (*0-931141-89-3*) VanDam Inc.

Brooklyn Dodgers Organization Staff. Brooklyn Dodgers in Their Original Voices: Ebbets Field - 1956 - Baseball Greats - How They Played the Game. LC 99-195179. (Illus.). 74p. 1998. 29.95 (*0-9664181-0-7*) Frank II.

Brooklyn Eagle Staff. Brooklyn Eagle Index: July 1, 1891 to December 31, 1902, 3 vols., Set. 1980. lib. bdg. 79.95 (*0-8490-3102-8*) Gordon Pr.

Brooklyn Institute of Arts & Sciences Museum Staff, et al. Egyptian Sculpture of the Late Period, 700 BC to AD 100. 1969. 26.95 (*0-405-00872-4*, 11174) Ayer.

Brooklyn Museum Staff. Brooklyn Museum of Art. LC 96-40100. 1997. write for info. (*0-87273-136-7*) Bklyn Mus.

***Brooklyn Museum Staff.** The Native American Look Book: Art & Activities for Kids. 2000. pap. 12.95 (*1-56584-604-4*, Pub. by New Press NY) Norton.

Brooklyn Museum Staff. Two Dutch Houses: Tradition & Change in Early New York: The Schenck Houses at the Brooklyn Museum. Date not set. write for info. (*0-87273-123-5*) Bklyn Mus.

Brooklyn Museum Staff & Bolton, Richard. Culture Wars: Documents from the Recent Controversies in the Arts. LC 95-51358. (Portfolio Ser.). (Illus.). 1996. pap. 19.95 (*1-56584-006-2*, Pub. by New Press NY) Norton.

Brooklyn Public Library Business Staff, compiled by. Business Book of Lists: A Ranking of the Biggest, Smallest, Best & Worst. 1991. pap. 15.00 (*0-8103-9410-3*) Visible Ink Pr.

***Brooklyn Public Library Literacy Program Staff, Brooklyn Public Library.** Technology Toolkit: A Library Literacy Approach. (Illus.). 82p. 1999. spiral bd. write for info. (*1-891001-03-5*) Brooklyn Pub Lib.

***Brookman, Adam L.** Trademark Law: Protection, Enforcement & Licensing. LC 99-42621. 1999. ring bd. 160.00 (*0-7355-0649-3*) Panel Pubs.

Brookman, Al, Sr. Sitka Man. LC 84-6430. 172p. (Orig.). 1984. pap. 7.95 (*0-88240-263-3*, Alaska NW Bks) Gr Arts Ctr Pub.

Brookman, Fiona & Wincup, Emma, eds. Qualitative Research in Criminology. LC 98-74933. (Cardiff Papers in Qualitative Research). 190p. 1999. 59.95 (*1-84014-571-4*, Pub. by Ashgate Pub) Ashgate Pub Co.

Brookman, Kenneth E., ed. Refractive Management of Ametropia. (Illus.). 240p. 1996. pap. text 39.50 (*0-7506-9569-2*) Buttrwrth-Heinemann.

Brookman, Lester G. The United States Postage Stamps of the Nineteenth Century, 3 vols., I. LC 89-62408. (Illus.). 882p. 1989. reprint ed. write for info. (*1-877998-01-X*) D G Phillips.

— The United States Postage Stamps of the Nineteenth Century, 3 vols., II. LC 89-62408. (Illus.). 882p. 1989. reprint ed. write for info. (*1-877998-02-8*) D G Phillips.

— The United States Postage Stamps of the Nineteenth Century, 3 vols., III. LC 89-62408. (Illus.). 882p. 1989. reprint ed. write for info. (*1-877998-03-6*) D G Phillips.

— The United States Postage Stamps of the Nineteenth Century, 3 vols., Set. LC 89-62408. (Illus.). 882p. 1989. reprint ed. text 120.00 (*0-685-28852-8*) D G Phillips.

***Brookman, Philip.** Arnold Newman. 2000. 39.99 (*3-8228-7193-1*) Taschen Amer.

Brookman Stamp Co., ed. First Day Cover Price Guide: 1988 Edition, Vol. II. (Illus.). 128p. 1988. pap. 5.95 (*0-936937-09-2*) Brookman Stamp.

Brookmeyer, Ron & Gail, Mitchell H. AIDS Epidemiology: A Quantitative Approach. LC 92-48337. (Monographs in Epidemiology & Biostatistics: Vol. 22). (Illus.). 376p. (C). 1994. text 54.50 (*0-19-507641-9*) OUP.

Brookner, Anita. Altered States. 1998. pap. 12.00 (*0-679-77325-8*) Vin Bks.

Brookner, Anita. Altered States. large type ed. LC 96-51783. 350p. 1997. 25.95 (*0-7862-0977-1*) Thorndike Pr.

Brookner, Anita. Brief Lives. 1992. pap. 12.00 (*0-679-73733-2*) Vin Bks.

***Brookner, Anita.** Brief Lives. large type ed. LC 99-56102. 312p. 2000. lib. bdg. 27.95 (*1-58547-018-X*) Ctr Point Pubg.

Brookner, Anita. A Closed Eye. LC 92-56358. (Contemporaries Ser.). 1993. pap. 11.00 (*0-679-74340-5*) Vin Bks.

— A Closed Eye. large type ed. LC 93-16778. 346p. 1993. pap. 17.95 (*0-8161-5592-5*, G K Hall Lrg Type) Mac Lib Ref.

— The Debut. 1985. pap. 5.95 (*0-07-545286-3*) McGraw.

— The Debut. (Vintage Contemporaries Ser.). 1990. pap. 12.00 (*0-679-72712-4*) Vin Bks.

— Dolly. LC 93-14537. 1995. pap. 12.00 (*0-679-74578-5*) Random.

— Falling Slowly. 2000. pap. 12.00 (*0-375-70424-8*) Knopf.

— Falling Slowly. LC 98-12964. 240p. 1998. 24.00 (*0-375-50189-4*) Random.

— Family & Friends. 1986. 6.95 (*0-317-53641-9*, WSP) PB.

— Family & Friends. 1998. pap. 12.00 (*0-679-78164-1*) Vin Bks.

— Fraud. 1994. pap. 13.00 (*0-679-74308-1*) Random.

— A Friend from England. large type ed. (General Ser.). 293p. 1989. lib. bdg. 19.95 (*0-8161-4656-X*, G K Hall Lrg Type) Mac Lib Ref.

— Hotel du Lac. 1995. pap. text. write for info. (*0-582-25406-X*, Pub. by Addison-Wesley) Longman.

— Hotel du Lac. 1995. pap. 11.00 (*0-679-75932-8*) Random.

— Incidents in the Rue Laugier. 1997. pap. 12.00 (*0-679-76512-3*) Vin Bks.

— Incidents in the Rue Laugier. large type ed. 1996. 24.95 (*1-56895-301-1*, Compass) Wheeler Pub.

— Latecomers. (Vintage Contemporaries Ser.). 1990. pap. 12.00 (*0-679-72668-3*) Vin Bks.

— Latecomers. large type ed. (General Ser.). 259p. 1990. lib. bdg. 19.95 (*0-8161-4892-9*, G K Hall Lrg Type) Mac Lib Ref.

— Lewis Percy. LC 90-50482. 272p. 1991. pap. 14.00 (*0-679-72944-5*) Vin Bks.

— Look at Me. 1997. pap. 12.00 (*0-679-73813-4*) Vin Bks.

— A Private View. 256p. 1996. pap. 12.00 (*0-679-75443-1*) Random.

— Providence. 1994. pap. 12.00 (*0-679-73814-2*) Knopf.

***Brookner, Anita.** Romanticism & Its Discontents. (Illus.). 208p. 2000. 25.00 (*0-374-25159-2*) FS&G.

Brookner, Anita. Soundings. LC 98-165900. 224p. 1999. pap. 15.00 (*1-86046-510-2*, Pub. by Harvill Press) FS&G.

— Soundings: Studies in Art & Literature. (Illus.). 224p. 1998. 26.00 (*1-86046-388-6*, Pub. by Harvill Press) FS&G.

— Start in Life. 1982. pap. 4.95 (*0-586-05505-3*) HarpC.

***Brookner, Anita.** Undue Influence: A Novel. LC 99-36282. 240p. 1999. 24.00 (*0-375-50334-X*) Random.

— Undue Influence: A Novel. large type ed. LC 00-24303. (Core Ser.). 2000. 29.95 (*0-7838-9001-X*, G K Hall Lrg Type) Mac Lib Ref.

Brookner, Anita. Visitors. 242p. 1999. pap. 12.00 (*0-679-78147-1*) Vin Bks.

— Visitors. large type ed. LC 98-9304. 301p. 1998. write for info. (*0-7540-2099-1*) Chivers N Amer.

Brookner, Anita, ed. see Wharton, Edith.

Brookner, Eli. Tracking & Kalman Filtering Made Easy. LC 97-33122. 504p. 1998. 85.00 (*0-471-18407-1*, Wiley-Interscience) Wiley.

Brookner, Eli, ed. Aspects of Modern Radar. 576p. 1988. text. write for info. (*0-89006-263-3*) Artech Hse.

— Practical Phased-Array Antenna Systems. (Antenna Library). 258p. 1991. text. write for info. (*0-89006-563-2*) Artech Hse.

Brookover, J. Lois. Bible Oriented Puzzles: For Teens & Adults. (Illus.). 32p. 1996. pap. text 6.95 (*1-878579-08-8*) SUN Pub Co.

Brookover, W. B. Effective Secondary Schools. 36p. 1981. pap. 7.95 (*1-56602-001-8*) Research Better.

Brooks. Academic Women. LC 96-47866. 1997. 116.00 (*0-335-19600-4*) OpUniv Pr.

— Academic Women. LC 96-47866. (Illus.). 192p. 1997. pap. 36.95 (*0-335-19599-7*) OpUniv Pr.

— Come Back, Energy Man. 224p. (J). Date not set. 14.95 (*0-06-020670-5*); lib. bdg. 14.89 (*0-06-020671-3*) HarperTrade.

Brooks. Come Back Energy Man. 1996. pap. write for info. (*0-06-440513-3*) HarpC Child Bks.

Brooks. Computerizing for Personal Productivity: A Guide for the High Performance Lawyer. 216p. 1989. 63.00 (*0-409-80906-3*, MICHIE) LEXIS Pub.

— Consultamation Including Word Processing. 2nd ed. 1988. 34.62 (*0-07-008110-7*) McGraw.

— Contemporary Debates in Education. 1991. pap. text. write for info. (*0-582-05797-3*, Pub. by Addison-Wesley) Longman.

Brooks. Dictionary. (ORI & ENG.). 157p. 79.95 (*0-320-03414-3*) Fr & Eur.

Brooks. Environmental Medicine: Principles & Practice. (Illus.). 864p. (C). (gr. 13). 1995. text 96.00 (*0-8016-6469-1*, 06469) Mosby Inc.

— Ethics Accountants. Date not set. pap. text, teacher ed. write for info. (*0-314-04982-7*) West Pub.

— Instrumentation. 5th ed. LC 98-53249. 384p. 1999. spiral bd. 43.00 (*0-323-00350-8*) Mosby Inc.

— Marketing. 6th ed. 1995. pap. text, student ed. 28.60 (*0-13-207853-8*) P-H.

— Mary Will Not Watch Moon. 32p. (ps-1). 14.95 (*0-06-024491-7*) HarpC.

— Mary Will Not Watch the Moon. 32p. (ps-1). lib. bdg. 14.89 (*0-06-024492-5*) HarpC.

— Media Science Before the Great War. LC 96-7159. 220p. 1996. text 55.00 (*0-312-16019-4*) St Martin.

— Midpoint Key to Chiron. 98p. 1992. 13.00 (*0-86690-407-7*) Am Fed Astrologers.

— Modern Rhetoric. 4th ed. (C). 1979. pap. text, teacher ed. 4.75 (*0-15-562816-X*) Harcourt Coll Pubs.

Brooks. 101 Spreadsheet Exercises. (One Hundred One Ser.). Date not set. teacher ed. write for info. (*0-02-800759-X*) Glencoe.

— 101 Word Processing Exercises. (One Hundred One Ser.). 1992. teacher ed. write for info. (*0-02-800755-7*) Glencoe.

Brooks. Professional Ethics for Accountants. 2nd ed. LC 99-38151. (SWC-Accounting). 316p. 1999. pap. 40.95 (*0-324-01316-7*) Thomson Learn.

— 7 Secrets of Successful Women. 256p. 1999. 14.95 (*0-07-134264-8*) McGraw.

— Soft Tissue Tumors. (C). 1995. text. write for info. (*0-7216-6696-5*, W B Saunders Co) Harcrt Hlth Sci Grp.

— Soils & Geomorphological Processes. 1212p. 84.95 (*0-471-96602-9*) Wiley.

— Work with Words. 3rd ed. 1996. pap. text, wbk. ed. 29.25 (*0-312-10014-0*) St Martin.

— Working with Words. 4th ed. 1999. pap. text 32.95 (*0-312-20176-1*) St Martin.

Brooks & Levy, Haim. Introduction to Investments. (C). 1996. pap. text, student ed. write for info. (*0-201-84614-4*) Addison-Wesley.

***Brooks & Pinson.** Working with Words. 4th ed. 1999. pap. text, wbk. ed. 16.95 (*0-312-20982-7*) St Martin.

Brooks, et al. Medical Microbiology: Jawtz, Melnick & Adelberg's Medical Microbiology. 21st ed. (Illus.). 740p. (C). 1998. pap. 44.95 (*0-8385-6316-3*, A-6316-2, Apple Lange Med) McGraw.

— Poems & Annotations. 31p. (Orig.). 1994. pap. 18.00 (*1-887648-05-4*) A-A Bks Pub.

Brooks, A. Taeko, jt. tr. see Brooks, E. Bruce.

Brooks, Abbie M., see Sunshine, Silvia, pseud.

Brooks, Al. Cat Owner's Survival Guide. (Illus.). 224p. 1994. pap. 4.95 (*0-9633921-3-1*) Humor Bks.

— Dog Owner's Survival Guide. (Illus.). 224p. 1994. pap. 4.95 (*0-9633921-4-X*) Humor Bks.

Brooks, Al, jt. auth. see Warfield, Allen.

***Brooks, Alan.** Frogs Jump. (Illus.). 48p. (ps-1). 1999. pap. 6.99 (*0-590-45529-X*) Scholastic Inc.

Brooks, Alan. Frogs Jump! A Counting Book. LC 95-35917. (Illus.). 40p. (J). (ps-3). 1996. 15.95 (*0-590-45528-1*, Scholastic Hardcover) Scholastic Inc.

Brooks, Alan & Nielsen, Nancy L. Living on Salt & Stone: Poems from Straight Bay. (Illus.). 24p. (Orig.). 1984. pap. 5.00 (*0-914473-00-X*) Stone Man Pr.

Brooks, Alden. Will Shakespeare: A Factotum & Agent. LC 77-39536. reprint ed. 41.50 (*0-404-01117-9*) AMS Pr.

Brooks, Alexander D. Law, Psychiatry & the Mental Health System. 1974. 54.00 (*0-316-10970-3*, Aspen Law & Bus) Aspen Pub.

— Law, Psychiatry & the Mental Health System. 1980. pap., suppl. ed. 13.00 (*0-316-10971-1*, Aspen Law & Bus) Aspen Pub.

Brooks, Alfred H. Blazing Alaska's Trails. LC 73-88211. (Illus.). 567p. 1973. 12.50 (*0-912006-01-3*) U of Alaska Pr.

Brooks, Alfred M. Gloucester Recollected: A Familiar History. Garland, Joseph E., ed. (Illus.). 1990. 15.50 (*0-8446-5012-9*) Peter Smith.

Brooks, Alice. Clenched Fist. (American Autobiography Ser.). 206p. 1995. reprint ed. lib. bdg. 79.00 (*0-7812-8465-1*) Rprt Serv.

Brooks, Alison. Thicker Than Blood. (Cyberpunk Ser.). 48p. 1993. pap. 9.00 (*1-887801-40-5*, Atlas Games) Trident MN.

— With a Long Spoon: An over the Edge Adventure. (Over the Edge Ser.). 48p. 1994. pap. 8.95 (*1-887801-10-3*, Atlas Games) Trident MN.

Brooks, Alison, jt. auth. see Masters, Phil.

Brooks, Allan, et al. Ducks of the World in Full-Color Paintings. (Illus.). 80p. 1989. pap. 10.95 (*0-486-26120-4*) Dover.

Brooks, Allen H., ed. Projects pour un Stade Olympique Bagdad & Other Buildings & Projects 1953. (Le Corbusier Archive Ser.). 1984. text 95.00 (*0-8240-5076-2*) Garland.

Brooks, Ann. Postfeminisms: Feminism, Cultural Theory, & Cultural Forms. LC 96-47498. 256p. (C). 1997. pap. 22.99 (*0-415-11475-6*) Routledge.

— Postfeminisms: Feminism, Cultural Theory, & Cultural Forms. LC 96-47498. 256p. (C). 1997. 75.00 (*0-415-11474-8*) Routledge.

Brooks, Ann & Watkins, Karen E., eds. The Emerging Power of Action Inquiry Technologies. LC 85-644750. (New Directions for Adult & Continuing Education Ser.: No. ACE 63). 110p. (Orig.). 1994. pap. 22.00 (*0-7879-9980-6*) Jossey-Bass.

***Brooks, Anne M.** The Grieving Time: A Year's Account of Recovery from Loss. 4th ed. LC 99-34684. 64p. 1999. reprint ed. pap. 11.00 (*1-928746-04-7*) Herodias.

Brooks, Anne T. Fire in the Wind. large type ed. 1991. 27.99 (*0-7089-2440-9*) Ulverscroft.

— Island Neighbor. large type ed. 1991. 27.99 (*0-7089-2494-8*) Ulverscroft.

— One Enchanted Summer. large type ed. 1990. 27.99 (*0-7089-2277-5*) Ulverscroft.

— Smoke on the River. large type ed. (Historical Romance Ser.). 496p. 1992. 27.99 (*0-7089-2655-X*) Ulverscroft.

— White Camellias. large type ed. (Romance Ser.). 256p. 1993. 27.99 (*0-7089-2889-7*) Ulverscroft.

Brooks, Arthur, et al. Weapon Mix & Exploratory Analysis: A Case Study. LC 97-220526. 53 p. 1997. pap. 6.00 (*0-8330-2535-X*) Rand Corp.

Brooks, Ashley & Matthews, Hodin. Gastrointestinal & Hepatobiliary Surgery: The Requisites. (Illus.). 544p. 2000. text 65.00 (*0-8151-4386-9*, 31680) Mosby Inc.

Brooks, Aubrey L. Selected Addresses of a Southern Lawyer. ix, 165p. 1954. 24.95 (*0-8078-0657-9*) U of NC Pr.

An Asterisk (*) at the beginning of an entry indicates that the title is appearing for the first time.

— A Southern Lawyer: Fifty Years at the Bar. LC 50-10879. 224p. reprint ed. pap. 69.50 (*0-7837-5240-7*, 204497400005) Bks Demand.

Brooks, Aubrey L., ed. see Clark, Walter.

Brooks, Audrey, jt. auth. see Sutherland, Lynn.

Brooks, B. David & Dalby, Rex K. Manual De Reparacion y Mantenimiento Del Autoestima. Hunter, Paula J., ed. Martinez, Adolfo, tr.Tr. of Self-Esteem Repair & Maintenance Manual. (ENG & SPA., Illus.). 143p. 1991. reprint ed. pap. 14.95 (*968-38-0251-6*, Pub. by Panorama Edit) Routldge.

— The Self-Esteem Repair & Maintenance Manual. Hunter, Paula J., ed. LC 89-36692. (Illus.). 122p. (Orig.). 1990. pap. 9.95 (*0-943793-27-0*) Kincaid Hse.

— Self Esteem Repair & Maintenance Manual. 123p. 1990. pap. text 9.95 (*0-9635491-0-3*) Reda Pr.

Brooks, B. David & Goble, Frank. The Case for Character Education: The Role of the School in Teaching Values & Virtue. LC 95-971127. 161p. 1995. 18.95 (*1-882349-02-4*) Studio Four Prods.

— The Case for Character Education: The Role of the School in Teaching Values & Virtue. LC 83-70068. 161p. 1998. pap. 11.95 (*1-882349-01-6*) Studio Four Prods.

Brooks, Barbara. The Seminole. (Native American People Ser.). (Illus.). 32p. (J). (gr. 5-8). 1989. 11.95 (*0-685-58584-0*) Rourke Corp.

— The Seminole. (Native American People Ser.: Set I). (Illus.). 32p. (J). (gr. 4-8). 1989. lib. bdg. 22.60 (*0-86625-377-7*) Rourke Pubns.

— The Sioux. (Native American People Ser.). (Illus.). 32p. (J). (gr. 5-8). 1989. 11.95 (*0-685-58585-9*) Rourke Corp.

— The Sioux. (Native American People Ser.: Set I). (Illus.). 32p. (J). (gr. 4-8). 1989. lib. bdg. 22.60 (*0-86625-382-3*) Rourke Pubns.

Brooks, Barbara & Siegel, Paula M. The Scared Child: Helping Kids Overcome Traumatic Events. LC 96-10330. 176p. 1996. pap. 16.95 (*0-471-08284-8*) Wiley.

Brooks, Barbara, et al. Native American People, 6 bks., Reading Level 4. (Illus.). 192p. (J). (gr. 5-8). 1989. lib. bdg. 71.70 (*0-685-58768-1*) Rourke Corp.

— Native American People, 6 bks., Set. (Illus.). 192p. (J). (gr. 5-8). 1989. lib. bdg. 95.64 (*0-86625-375-0*) Rourke Pubns.

Brooks, Barbara A. & Wallis, Sherry E. The Alaskan Malamute Yesterday & Today. LC 98-9655. (Illus.). 322p. 1998. 59.95 (*0-931866-96-0*, Blue Rib Books) Alpine Pubns.

***Brooks, Barbara J.** Japan's Imperial Diplomacy: Consuls, Treaty Ports & War in China, 1895-1938. LC 00-21819. 2000. pap. write for info. (*0-8248-2325-7*) UH Pr.

Brooks, Barbera. Fine Flowers By Phone: The Essential Guide to Ordering Flowers by Phone. 2nd ed. 1997. pap. text 19.95 (*0-9656082-0-4*) Wyatt Grp.

Brooks, Bearl. Jumbo Cursive Handwriting Yearbook. (Jumbo Handwriting Ser.). 96p. (gr. 3). 1978. student ed. 18.00 (*0-8209-0019-2*, JHWY-3) ESP.

— Jumbo Phonics Yearbook. (Jumbo Phonics Ser.). 96p. (gr. 1-3). 1977. 18.00 (*0-8209-0049-4*, JPY 1) ESP.

— Jumbo Reading Yearbook: Kindergarten. (Jumbo Reading Ser.). 96p. (J). (gr. k). 1980. 18.00 (*0-8209-0011-7*, JRY R) ESP.

— My Fifth Grade Yearbook. (My Yearbook Ser.). 832p. (gr. 5). 1981. 18.00 (*0-8209-0085-0*, MFG-5) ESP.

— My First Grade Yearbook. (My Yearbook Ser.). 544p. (gr. 1). 1979. 18.00 (*0-8209-0081-8*, MFG-1) ESP.

— My Fourth Grade Yearbook. (My Yearbook Ser.). 832p. (gr. 4). 1979. 18.00 (*0-8209-0084-2*, MFG-4) ESP.

— My Kindergarten Yearbook. (My Yearbook Ser.). 544p. (gr. k). 1980. 18.00 (*0-8209-0080-X*, MKY_K) ESP.

— My Second Grade Yearbook. (My Yearbook Ser.). 640p. (gr. 2). 1979. 18.00 (*0-8209-0082-6*, MSG-2) ESP.

— My Sixth Grade Yearbook. (My Yearbook Ser.). 832p. 1981. 18.00 (*0-8209-0086-9*, MSG-6) ESP.

— My Third Grade Yearbook. (My Yearbook Ser.). 768p. (gr. 3). 1979. 18.00 (*0-8209-0083-4*, MTG-3) ESP.

Brooks, Bearl, et al. Jumbo Word Games Yearbook. (Jumbo Vocabulary Ser.). 96p. (gr. 3). 1980. 18.00 (*0-8209-0059-1*, JWG 1) ESP.

Brooks, Ben. The Icebox. LC 86-72594. (Amelia Chapbooks Ser.). 90p. (Orig.). 1986. pap. 10.95 (*0-936545-04-6*) Amelia.

Brooks, Benjamin. Lives of the Puritans, 3, Vol. 1. 480p. 1994. 35.00 (*1-877611-80-8*) Soli Deo Gloria.

***Brooks, Benjamin & Cook, Tim.** The Waterfalls of South Carolina. (Illus.). 64p. 1999. pap. 12.95 (*0-9679016-0-X*, Pub. by Palmetto Conservat) Parnassus Bk Dist.

Brooks, Benjamin L. & Sabatino, David A., eds. Personal Perspectives on Emotional Disturbance - Behavioral Disorders. LC 94-45064. 495p. (Orig.). (C). 1996. pap. text 38.00 (*0-89079-618-1*, 6929) PRO-ED.

Brooks, Benjamin L., jt. auth. see Sabatino, David A.

Brooks, Beth. Animals of the Zoo. 1993. 5.95 (*1-55708-447-5*, MCJ804) McDonald Pub Co.

Brooks, Betty. Always a Bride. 352p. 1999. mass mkt. 5.99 (*0-8217-6222-2*) Kensgtn Pub Corp.

— Comanche Sunset. 320p. 1998. mass mkt. 4.99 (*0-8217-5848-9*, Zebra Kensgtn) Kensgtn Pub Corp.

— Jade. 320p. 1997. mass mkt. 4.99 (*0-8217-5642-7*, Zebra Kensgtn) Kensgtn Pub Corp.

— Place in My Heart. 1999. mass mkt. 4.99 (*0-8217-6179-X*, Zebra Kensgtn) Kensgtn Pub Corp.

— Sweet Words of Love. 304p. 1998. pap. 4.99 (*0-8217-5952-3*) Kensgtn Pub Corp.

***Brooks, Betty.** Texas Treasure. 2000. mass mkt. 4.99 (*0-8217-6575-2*, Zebra Kensgtn) Kensgtn Pub Corp.

Brooks, Betty. Warrior's Destiny. 384p. 1995. pap. 4.99 (*0-8217-4999-4*) NAL.

***Brooks, Betty.** Wayward Heart. (Zebra Splendor Historical Romances Ser.). 320p. 1999. mass mkt. 4.99 (*0-8217-6415-2*, Zebra Kensgtn) Kensgtn Pub Corp.

Brooks, Bill. The Badmen. 192p. 1992. 18.95 (*0-8027-4129-0*) Walker & Co.

— Buscadero. large type ed. LC 93-20784. 331p. 1993. lib. bdg. 19.95 (*0-8161-5858-4*, G K Hall Lrg Type) Mac Lib Ref.

— Deadwood. 352p. 1997. mass mkt. 4.99 (*0-7860-0356-1*, Pinncle Kensgtn) Kensgtn Pub Corp.

— Dust on the Wind. 352p. 1998. mass mkt. 4.99 (*0-7860-0471-1*, Pinncle Kensgtn) Kensgtn Pub Corp.

— The Last Law There Was. 288p. 1995. mass mkt. 3.99 (*0-8217-4908-0*, Pinncle Kensgtn) Kensgtn Pub Corp.

— Leaving Cheyenne. 1999. mass mkt. 5.99 (*0-440-22652-X*) Dell.

— Old Times. 1995. mass mkt. 4.50 (*0-8217-5109-3*, Zebra Kensgtn) Kensgtn Pub Corp.

***Brooks, Bill.** Return to No Man's Land. 2000. mass mkt. 5.99 (*0-440-22653-8*) Dell.

Brooks, Brad, et al. Four Down Here. 1994. pap. 20.00 (*0-932526-38-1*) Nexus Pr.

Brooks, Bradford O. Understanding Indoor Air Quality. 189p. 1991. lib. bdg. 79.95 (*0-8493-8846-5*, TD883) CRC Pr.

Brooks, Brian S. Journalism in Information Age. LC 96-26357. 166p. 1996. pap. text 23.00 (*0-205-26411-5*) Allyn.

Brooks, Brian S. News Reporting & Writing. LC 80-50144. 542 p. 1980. write for info. (*0-312-57202-6*) St Martin.

— Working with Words. 3rd ed. LC 95-73211. 272p. 1996. pap. text 32.95 (*0-312-13760-5*) St Martin.

Brooks, Brian S. & Pinson, James L. Working with Words: A Concise Handbook for Media Writers & Editors. Lambert, Jane, ed. 256p. (Orig.). 1999. reprint ed. 20.00 (*0-7881-6187-3*) DIANE Pub.

***Brooks, Brian S., et al.** The Art of Editing. 7th ed. LC 00-35572. 2000. write for info. (*0-205-31957-2*) Allyn.

Brooks, Brian S., et al. News Reporting & Writing. 4th ed. LC 90-71645. 192p. (C). 1992. pap. text, teacher ed. 0.84 (*0-312-06246-X*) St Martin.

Brooks, Bruce. Asylum for Nightface. LC 95-40645. 144p. (YA). (gr. 7 up). 1996. lib. bdg. 13.89 (*0-06-027061-6*) HarpC Child Bks.

— Asylum for Nightface. LC 95-40645. 144p. (YA). (gr. 12 up). 1996. 13.95 (*0-06-027060-8*) HarpC Child Bks.

— Asylum for Nightface. LC 95-40645. (Illus.). 160p. (YA). (gr. 7-12). 1999. pap. 4.95 (*0-06-447214-0*) HarpC Child Bks.

— Barry. LC 98-49467. (Wolfbay Wings Ser.: No. 10). (J). (gr. 4-7). 1999. pap. 4.50 (*0-06-440727-6*) HarpC Child Bks.

***Brooks, Bruce.** Barry. LC 98-49467. (Wolfbay Wings Ser.: No. 11). (J). (gr. 4-7). 1999. lib. bdg. 14.89 (*0-06-028056-5*) HarpC Child Bks.

Brooks, Bruce. Billy. LC 98-14228. (Wolfbay Wings Ser.: Vol. 7). (Illus.). 128p. (J). (gr. 3-7). 1998. lib. bdg. 14.89 (*0-06-027899-4*) HarpC.

— Billy. (Wolfbay Wings Ser.: No. 7). (J). (gr. 4-7). 1998. 9.60 (*0-606-13927-3*, Pub. by Turtleback) Demco.

— Boot. LC 97-39674. (Wolfbay Wings Ser.: No. 4). (Illus.). 144p. (J). (gr. 3-7). 1998. lib. bdg. 14.89 (*0-06-027569-3*) HarpC.

— Boot. LC 97-39674. (Wolfbay Wings Ser.: No. 4). (Illus.). 144p. (J). (gr. 4-7). 1998. pap. 4.50 (*0-06-440680-6*) HarpC.

— Boot. (Wolfbay Wings Ser.: No. 4). (J). (gr. 4-7). 1998. 9.60 (*0-606-13071-3*, Pub. by Turtleback) Demco.

— Boys Will Be. 144p. (YA). (gr. 6 up). 1995. 14.95 (*0-8050-2420-4*, Bks Young Read) H Holt & Co.

— Boys Will Be. LC 94-3599. 144p. (J). (gr. 5-9). 1995. pap. 4.50 (*0-7868-1026-2*, Pub. by Hyprn Ppbks) Little.

— Boys Will Be. 1995. 9.60 (*0-606-07318-3*, Pub. by Turtleback) Demco.

— Cody. LC 97-2052. (Wolfbay Wings Ser.: No. 3). 128p. (J). (gr. 3-7). 1997. pap. 4.50 (*0-06-440599-0*, HarpTrophy) HarpC Child Bks.

— Cody. LC 97-2052. (Wolfbay Wings Ser.: No. 3). (Illus.). 128p. (J). (gr. 4-7). 1997. lib. bdg. 14.89 (*0-06-027541-3*) HarpC Child Bks.

Brooks, Bruce. Cody. (Wolfbay Wings Ser.: No. 3). (J). (gr. 4-7). 1997. 9.60 (*0-606-12113-7*, Pub. by Turtleback) Demco.

Brooks, Bruce. The Dolores Stories. 160p. (J). (gr. 3-7). Date not set. 14.95 (*0-06-027818-8*) HarpC Child Bks.

— Dooby. LC 98-24715. (Wolfbay Wings Ser.: No. 8). (Illus.). 128p. (J). (gr. 3-7). 1998. lib. bdg. 14.89 (*0-06-027898-6*) HarpC.

— Dooby. LC 98-24715. (Wolfbay Wings Ser.: No. 8). (Illus.). 128p. (J). (gr. 4-7). 1998. pap. 4.50 (*0-06-440708-X*) HarpC.

— Everywhere. LC 90-4073. 80p. (J). (gr. 4-7). 1990. lib. bdg. 15.89 (*0-06-020729-9*) HarpC Child Bks.

— Everywhere. LC 90-4073. 80p. (J). (gr. 4 up). 1990. 13.00 (*0-06-020728-0*) HarpC Child Bks.

— Making Sense: Animal Perception & Communication. LC 93-10474. (Knowing Nature Ser.). 80p. (J). 1993. 17.00 (*0-374-34742-5*) FS&G.

— Midnight Hour Encores. LC 86-45035. 288p. (YA). (gr. 7 up). 1986. 14.00 (*0-06-020709-4*) HarpC Child Bks.

Brooks, Bruce. Midnight Hour Encores. LC 86-45035. (Trophy Keypoint Bk.). 272p. (YA). (gr. 12 up). 1988. mass mkt. 4.95 (*0-06-447021-0*, HarpTrophy) HarpC Child Bks.

Brooks, Bruce. The Moves Make the Man. LC 83-49476. 208p. (YA). (gr. 7-12). 1984. lib. bdg. 15.89 (*0-06-020698-5*) HarpC Child Bks.

— The Moves Make the Man. LC 83-49476. 320p. (YA). (gr. 7 up). 1984. 15.00 (*0-06-020679-9*) HarpC Child Bks.

— The Moves Make the Man. LC 83-49476. 256p. (J). (gr. 7-12). 1987. mass mkt. 5.95 (*0-06-447022-9*, HarpTrophy) HarpC Child Bks.

Brooks, Bruce. The Moves Make the Man. LC 83-49476. (Trophy Bk.). 288p. (YA). (gr. 12 up). 1996. pap. 5.95 (*0-06-440564-8*, HarpTrophy) HarpC Child Bks.

Brooks, Bruce. The Moves Make the Man. 1987. 10.05 (*0-606-09638-8*, Pub. by Turtleback) Demco.

Brooks, Bruce. The Moves Make the Man. 1987. 10.30 (*0-606-07894-0*) Turtleback.

Brooks, Bruce. Nature by Design. (Knowing Nature Ser.). (Illus.). 80p. (J). (gr. 5 up). 1991. bds. 13.95 (*0-374-30334-7*) FS&G.

— NBA by the Numbers. LC 96-27327. (J). 1997. 10.95 (*0-590-97578-1*) Scholastic Inc.

— No Kidding. LC 88-22057. 224p. (YA). (gr. 7 up). 1989. 14.00 (*0-06-020722-1*) HarpC Child Bks.

— Predator! (Knowing Nature Ser.). 80p. (J). (gr. 5 up). 1991. bds. 13.95 (*0-374-36111-8*) FS&G.

— Predator! 80p. (J). (gr. 10 up). 1994. 8.95 (*0-374-35112-6*) FS&G.

— Prince. LC 97-40265. (Wolfbay Wings Ser.: No. 5). (Illus.). 144p. (J). (gr. 3-7). 1998. pap. 4.50 (*0-06-440600-8*) HarpC.

— Prince. LC 97-40265. (Wolfbay Wings Ser.: No. 5). (Illus.). 144p. (J). (gr. 4-7). 1998. lib. bdg. 14.89 (*0-06-027542-1*) HarpC.

— Prince. (Wolfbay Wings Ser.: No. 5). (J). (gr. 4-7). 1998. 9.60 (*0-606-13925-7*, Pub. by Turtleback) Demco.

— The Red Wasteland. LC 97-42568. 143p. (J). (gr. 9 up). 1995. 15.95 (*0-8050-4495-7*) H Holt & Co.

— Reed. LC 98-36709. (Wolfbay Wings Ser.: No. 9). 144p. (J). (gr. 4-7). 1998. lib. bdg. 14.89 (*0-06-028055-7*) HarpC.

— Shark. LC 97-40270. (Wolfbay Wings Ser.: No. 6). (Illus.). 128p. (J). (gr. 3-7). 1998. lib. bdg. 14.89 (*0-06-027570-7*) HarpC.

— Shark. LC 97-40270. (Wolfbay Wings Ser.: No. 6). (Illus.). 128p. (J). (gr. 4-7). 1998. pap. 4.50 (*0-06-440681-4*) HarpC.

— Shark. (Wolfbay Wings Ser.: No. 6). (J). (gr. 4-7). 1998. 9.60 (*0-606-13926-5*, Pub. by Turtleback) Demco.

Brooks, Bruce. Sports Essays: Bruce Books. 1995. text (*0-8050-3479-X*) H Holt & Co.

Brooks, Bruce. Subtle. LC 98-49473. (Wolfbay Wings Ser.: No. 10). 128p. (J). (gr. 5-9). 1999. pap. 4.50 (*0-06-440728-4*, HarpTrophy) HarpC Child Bks.

— Subtle. 11th ed. LC 98-49473. (Wolfbay Wings Ser.: No. 10). 128p. (J). (gr. 4-7). 1999. lib. bdg. 14.89 (*0-06-028057-3*, HarpTrophy) HarpC Child Bks.

***Brooks, Bruce.** Throwing Smoke. LC 99-59555. 144p. (J). (gr. 5 up). 2000. mass mkt. 4.95 (*0-06-440774-8*, L Geringer) HarpC Child Bks.

— Throwing Smoke. LC 99-59555. 144p. (J). (gr. 4-7). 2000. 15.89 (*0-06-028320-3*); 15.95 (*0-06-028972-4*) HarpC Child Bks.

Brooks, Bruce. Vanishing. LC 99-11743. 112p. (YA). (gr. 5-9). 1999. 14.95 (*0-06-028236-3*); lib. bdg. 14.89 (*0-06-028237-1*) HarpC Child Bks.

***Brooks, Bruce.** Vanishing. (J). 2000. pap. 4.95 (*0-06-440754-3*) HarpC Child Bks.

— Vanishing. LC 99-11743. 112p. (YA). 2000. mass mkt. 6.95 (*0-06-447234-5*) Morrow Avon.

Brooks, Bruce. What Hearts. LC 92-5305. (Laura Geringer Bks.). 208p. (YA). (gr. 5 up). 1992. 16.95 (*0-06-021131-8*) HarpC Child Bks.

— What Hearts. LC 92-5305. (Laura Geringer Bks.). 208p. (YA). (gr. 7-12). 1992. pap. 5.95 (*0-06-447127-6*) HarpC Child Bks.

— What Hearts. 1995. 9.60 (*0-606-08362-6*, Pub. by Turtleback) Demco.

— Woodsie. LC 97-2048. (Wolfbay Wings Ser.: No. 1). 128p. (J). (gr. 3-7). 1997. pap. 4.50 (*0-06-440597-4*, HarpTrophy); lib. bdg. 14.89 (*0-06-027349-6*) HarpC Child Bks.

Brooks, Bruce. Woodsie. (Wolfbay Wings Ser.: No. 1) (J). (gr. 4-7). 1997. 9.60 (*0-606-12111-0*, Pub. by Turtleback) Demco.

Brooks, Bruce. Woodsie, Again. (Wolfbay Wings Ser.: No. 12). 128p. (J). (gr. 4-7). 1999. pap. 4.50 (*0-06-440729-2*, HarpTrophy) HarpC Child Bks.

— Woodsie, Again. LC 98-41707. (Wolfbay Wings Ser.: No. 12). 128p. (J). (gr. 4-7). 1999. lib. bdg. 14.89 (*0-06-028058-1*, Pub. by Harper SF) HarpC.

— Zip. LC 97-2049. (Wolfbay Wings Ser.: No. 2). 144p. (J). (gr. 4-7). 1997. pap. 4.50 (*0-06-440598-2*, HarpTrophy) HarpC Child Bks.

— Zip. LC 97-2049. (Wolfbay Wings Ser.: No. 2). 128p. (J). (gr. 4-7). 1997. lib. bdg. 14.89 (*0-06-027350-X*) HarpC Child Bks.

Brooks, Bruce. Zip. (Wolfbay Wings Ser.: No. 2). (J). (gr. 4-7). 1997. 9.60 (*0-606-12112-9*, Pub. by Turtleback) Demco.

***Brooks, Bruce, ed.** The Red Wasteland: A Personal Selection of Writings about Nature for Young Readers. 143p. (YA). (gr. 6-8). 2000. text 16.00 (*0-7881-9058-X*) DIANE Pub.

Brooks, Bruce, jt. auth. see Rivers, Glenn.

Brooks, Bryant A., jt. auth. see Brooks, Lloyd D.

Brooks, C. Harry. The Practice of Autosuggestion by the Method of Emile Coue. 120p. 1981. pap. 12.00 (*0-89540-076-6*, SB-076) Sun Pub.

Brooks, C. Harry & Charles, Ernest. Christianity & Autosuggestion. 158p. 1996. pap. 12.00 (*0-89540-198-3*, SB-198) Sun Pub.

Brooks, Calvin. Introduction to Science. 1986. spiral bd. 23.35 (*0-88252-129-2*) Paladin Hse.

***Brooks, Carellin.** Carnal Nation: New Sex Fictions. 2000. pap. 16.95 (*1-55152-083-4*) Arsenal Pulp.

Brooks, Carellin, ed. Bad Jobs: My Last Shift at Albert Wong's Pagoda & Other Ugly Tales of the Workplace. 275p. 1998. pap. 14.95 (*1-55152-055-9*, Pub. by Arsenal Pulp) LPC InBook.

Brooks, Carl N., jt. auth. see Silvern, Leonard C.

Brooks, Carol C., ed. see Perry, Donald G.

Brooks, Carol C., ed. see Queen, Phillip L.

Brooks, Carolyn & Kvist, Darlene. Picture Book for Zone Cooks. (Illus.). 94p. 1997. pap. 18.95 (*0-9661630-8-7*) Nutrit Weight.

Brooks, Carolyn S. & Rice, Kathleen F. Familes in Recovery: Coming Full Circle. LC 96-19846. 352p. (Orig.). 1996. pap. 34.00 (*1-55766-264-9*, 2649) P H Brookes.

Brooks, Caryl. Empty Summer. 192p. (gr. 7-9). 1995. mass mkt. 3.50 (*0-590-45864-7*) Scholastic Inc.

— Empty Summer. 1993. 8.60 (*0-606-07481-3*, Pub. by Turtleback) Demco.

Brooks, Catherine M., jt. auth. see McCarthy, Michael.

Brooks, Cecil, jt. auth. see Adams, Bill.

Brooks, Cecil, ed. see Keisling, William & Kearns, Richard.

***Brooks, Chandler & Cranefield, Paul, eds.** Historical Development of Physiological Thought. 401p. 2000. 65.00 (*1-57898-196-4*) Martino Pubng.

***Brooks, Charles.** A+ Certification: Concepts & Practice. 2nd ed. 804p. (C). 1998. pap. text 46.67 (*1-58076-191-7*) Que Educ & Trng.

Brooks, Charles. A+ Certification Training Guide. 1998. 59.00 (*1-58076-007-4*) Que Educ & Trng.

— Best Editorial Cartoons of the Year: 1998 Edition. (Illus.). 208p. 1998. pap. text 14.95 (*1-56554-339-4*) Pelican.

***Brooks, Charles.** Best Editorial Cartoons of the Year 1999. (Illus.). 208p. 1999. pap. 14.95 (*1-56554-464-1*) Pelican.

Brooks, Charles. Network & Certification Training Guide. (Training Guides Ser.). 800p. 1999. 89.95 (*0-7357-0077-X*) New Riders Pub.

Brooks, Charles, ed. Best Editorial Cartoons of the Year: 1987 Edition. (Best Editorial Cartoons of the Year Ser.). (Illus.). 160p. (Orig.). 1987. pap. 14.95 (*0-88289-638-5*) Pelican.

— Best Editorial Cartoons of the Year: 1990 Edition. (Best Editorial Cartoons of the Year Ser.). (Illus.). 160p. (Orig.). 1990. pap. 14.95 (*0-88289-781-0*) Pelican.

— Best Editorial Cartoons of the Year: 1991 Edition. (Best Editorial Cartoons of the Year Ser.). (Illus.). 176p. (Orig.). 1991. reprint ed. pap. 14.95 (*0-88289-837-X*) Pelican.

— Best Editorial Cartoons of the Year: 1992 Edition. (Best Editorial Cartoons of the Year Ser.). (Illus.). 176p. 1992. pap. 14.95 (*0-88289-910-4*) Pelican.

— Best Editorial Cartoons of the Year: 1993 Edition. LC 86-645456. (Best Editorial Cartoons of the Year Ser.). (Illus.). 192p. 1993. pap. 14.95 (*0-88289-968-6*) Pelican.

— Best Editorial Cartoons of the Year: 1994 Edition. LC 74-29707. (Best Editorial Cartoons of the Year Ser.). (Illus.). 192p. 1994. text 14.95 (*1-56554-011-5*) Pelican.

— Best Editorial Cartoons of the Year: 1995 Edition. (Best Editorial Cartoons of the Year Ser.). (Illus.). 246p. 1995. pap. 14.95 (*1-56554-117-0*) Pelican.

— Best Editorial Cartoons of the Year: 1996 Edition. 24th ed. LC 86-645456. (Best Editorial Cartoons of the Year Ser.). (Illus.). 208p. 1996. pap. 14.95 (*1-56554-201-0*) Pelican.

— Best Editorial Cartoons of the Year: 1997 Edition. (Best Editorial Cartoons of the Year Ser.). (Illus.). 208p. 1997. pap. 14.95 (*1-56554-262-2*) Pelican.

***Brooks, Charles, ed.** Best Editorial Cartoons of the Year: 2000 Edition. (Illus.). 208p. 2000. pap. 14.95 (*1-56554-742-X*) Pelican.

Brooks, Charles B. Disaster at Lisbon: The Great Earthquake of 1755. LC 95-101565. (Illus.). xxviii, 249p. (Orig.). 1994. pap. 20.00 (*0-9667578-1-5*) Brooks Hse.

— The Girl, the Street, the Song. (Illus.). xx, 119p. 1997. pap. 15.00 (*0-9667578-2-3*) Brooks Hse.

— The Old Man's Money. vii, 277p. 1998. pap. 17.50 (*0-9667578-3-1*) Brooks Hse.

Brooks, Charles B. Pierian Spring: The True Account of the Case of John Toiro. . . LC 93-152071. x, 179p. 1991. pap. 17.50 (*0-9667578-0-7*) Brooks Hse.

Brooks, Charles E. Fishing Yellowstone Waters. (Illus.). 144p. 1984. pap. 18.95 (*1-55821-017-2*) Lyons Pr.

— Frontier Settlement & Market Revolution: The Holland Land Purchase. (Illus.). 272p. 1996. text 45.00 (*0-8014-3120-4*) Cornell U Pr.

— Nymph Fishing for Larger Trout. (Illus.). 192p. 1988. pap. 18.95 (*0-941130-90-8*) Lyons Pr.

Brooks, Charles H. Official History & Manual of the Grand United Order of Odd Fellows in America. LC 74-157362. (Black Heritage Library Collection). 1977. 25.95 (*0-8369-8800-0*) Ayer.

Brooks, Charles J. Microcomputer System Theory Service: MC-3000. rev. ed. (Illus.). 1991. pap. text, teacher ed. 27.00 (*1-884268-02-1*) Marcraft Intl.

— Microcomputer System Theory Service: MC-3000. 3rd ed. (Illus.). (C). 1991. pap. text, lab manual ed. 25.00 (*1-884268-01-3*) Marcraft Intl.

— Microcomputer System Theory Service: MC-3000. 3rd rev. ed. (Illus.). (C). 1991. pap. text 27.00 (*1-884268-00-5*) Marcraft Intl.

— Microcomputer Systems Theory & Service. 7th ed. Tonda, Anthony, ed. 1998. teacher ed., ring bd. 35.00 (*1-58122-006-5*) Marcraft Intl.

— Microcomputer Systems Theory & Service: MC-6000. rev. ed. (Illus.). (C). 1996. teacher ed., ring bd. 35.00 (*1-884268-98-6*) Marcraft Intl.

— Microcomputer Systems Theory & Service: MC-6000. 5th rev. ed. (Illus.). (C). 1996. pap. text 59.95 (*1-884268-96-X*) Marcraft Intl.

— Microcomputer Systems Theory & Service - IC-Level Theory/Lab Guide. 7th ed. 1998. pap. text 20.00 (*1-58122-005-7*) Marcraft Intl.

— Microcomputer Systems Theory & Service - Lab Guide. 7th ed. Freeman, Whitney G., ed. 1998. pap. text 59.95 (*1-58122-009-X*) Marcraft Intl.

B

— Microcomputer Systems Theory & Service - Theory. 7th ed. Freeman, Whitney G., ed. 1998. pap. text 59.95 (*1-58122-008-1*) Marcraft Intl.

Brooks, Charles J. The New A+ Certification Training Guide. Freeman, Whitney G., ed. Hall, Michael R. & Boulay, Cathy J., trs. (Illus.). 1998. pap. text 59.95 (*1-58122-000-6*); pap. text, teacher ed. 35.00 (*1-58122-002-2*); pap. text, lab manual ed. 59.95 (*1-58122-001-4*) Marcraft Intl.

***Brooks, Charles J.** The New A+ Certification Training Guide. LC 99-39274. 2000. write for info. (*0-13-017549-8*) P-H.

Brooks, Charles J. & Whittington, Todd. Microcomputer Systems Theory & Service: MC-6000. (Illus.). (C). 1996. pap. text, lab manual ed. 59.95 (*1-884268-97-8*) Marcraft Intl.

Brooks, Charles L., et al. Proteins: A Theoretical Perspective of Dynamics, Structure & Thermodynamics. LC 87-15993. (Advances in Chemical Physics Ser.). 259p. 1988. 169.00 (*0-471-62801-8*) Wiley.

Brooks, Charles L., et al. Proteins: A Theoretical Perspective of Dynamics, Structure & Thermodynamics. (Advances in Chemical Physics Ser.). 259p. 1990. pap. 79.95 (*0-471-52977-X*) Wiley.

Brooks, Charles M., Jr., jt. auth. see Barr, Alfred H., Jr.

B

Brooks, Charles R. The Hare Krishnas in India. LC 88-22655. (Illus.). 277p. 1989. reprint ed. pap. 85.90 (*0-608-07143-9*, 206736900009) Bks Demand.

— Metallurgical Failure Analysis. 409p. 1992. 59.95 (*0-07-008078-X*) McGraw.

Brooks, Charles T. Poems, Original & Translated. Andrews, W. P., ed. LC 72-4952. (Romantic Tradition in American Literature Ser.). 256p. 1972. reprint ed. 21.95 (*0-405-04624-3*) Ayer.

— Puck's Nightly Pranks, 1870. (Illus.). 20p. 1998. reprint ed. pap. 25.00 (*0-87556-860-2*) Saifer.

Brooks, Charles V. W. Sensory Awareness: Rediscovery of Experiencing Through the Workshops & Classes of Charlotte Selver. (Illus.). 256p. 1986. reprint ed. pap. 12.95 (*0-9615659-2-6*) F Morrow.

Brooks, Charles W. America in France's Hopes & Fears, 1890-1920, 2 Vols., Set. (Modern European History Ser.). 9680p. 1987. text 20.00 (*0-8240-8031-9*) Garland.

Brooks, Charlie R. Heat Treatment, Structure & Properties of Nonferrous Alloys. (Illus.). 420p. 1982. 176.00 (*0-87170-138-3*, 6516) ASM.

— Principles of the Heat Treatment of Plain Carbon & Low Alloy Steel. 490p. 1996. 134.00 (*0-87170-538-9*, 6456) ASM.

— Principles of the Surface Treatment of Steel. LC 91-67902. 290p. 1992. pap. text 49.95 (*0-87762-796-7*) Technomic.

Brooks, Chelsea. California Dreams, Vol 13. (J). 1995. pap. 2.95 (*0-689-80090-8*) Aladdin.

Brooks, Chris. Gothic Revival. 1999. pap. 24.95 (*0-7148-3480-7*) Phaidon Press.

***Brooks, Chris, ed.** The Albert Memorial: The Prince Consort National Memorial, Its History, Contexts & Conservation. (Illus.). 480p. 2000. 65.00 (*0-300-07311-9*) Yale U Pr.

Brooks, Chris & Evans. The Great East Window of Exeter Cathdral: A Glazing History. (Illus.). 208p. 1989. text 120.00 (*0-85989-317-0*, Pub. by Univ Exeter Pr) Northwestern U Pr.

Brooks, Chris & Faulkner, Peter, eds. The White Man's Burden: An Anthology of British Poetry of the Empire. LC 96-143913. 176p. 1996. text 50.00 (*0-85989-492-4*, Pub. by Univ Exeter Pr); pap. text 19.95 (*0-85989-450-9*, Pub. by Univ Exeter Pr) Northwestern U Pr.

Brooks, Chris, ed. see De Sivry.

Brooks, Christine. Sports Marketing: Competitive Business Strategies for Sport. 352p. 1994. 67.00 (*0-13-835893-1*) P-H.

Brooks, Christopher W. Lawyers, Litigation & English Society, 1450-1900. LC 97-45673. 250p. 1997. 55.00 (*1-85285-156-2*) Hambledon Press.

Brooks, Christopher W. & Lobran, Michael. Communities & Courts in Britain, 1150-1900. 256p. 1997. 60.00 (*1-85285-151-1*) Hambledon Press.

Brooks, Cleanth. Community, Religion & Literature: Essays. LC 94-43049. 352p. 1995. 34.95 (*0-8262-0993-9*) U of Mo Pr.

— Historical Evidence & the Reading of Seventeenth-Century Poetry. 184p. (C). 1991. text 27.50 (*0-8262-0775-8*) U of Mo Pr.

— On the Prejudices, Predilections & Firm Beliefs of William Faulkner. LC 87-2968. (Southern Literary Studies). 168p. 1987. 16.95 (*0-8071-1391-3*) La State U Pr.

— The Well Wrought Urn: Studies in the Structure of Poetry. LC 47-3143. 300p. (Orig.). (YA). (gr. 7 up). 1956. pap. 14.00 (*0-15-695705-1*, Harvest Bks) Harcourt.

— William Faulkner: First Encounters. LC 83-3634. 224p. 1985. reprint ed. pap. 16.00 (*0-300-03399-0*, Y-523) Yale U Pr.

— William Faulkner: Toward Yoknapatawpha & Beyond. LC 89-13317. 445p. 1990. pap. 18.95 (*0-8071-1602-5*) La State U Pr.

Brooks, Cleanth, ed. Tragic Themes in Western Literature: Seven Essays by Bernard Knox & Others. LC 55-5516. 184p. reprint ed. pap. 57.10 (*0-8357-8769-9*, 203368200087) Bks Demand.

Brooks, Cleanth & Faulkner, William. William Faulkner: The Yoknapatawpha Country. LC 63-17023. 520p. 1990. pap. 22.95 (*0-8071-1601-7*) La State U Pr.

Brooks, Cleanth & Tate, Allen. Cleanth Brooks & Allen Tate: Collected Letters, 1933-1976. Vinh, Alphonse, ed. LC 98-34156. 312p. 1998. 34.95 (*0-8262-1207-7*) U of Mo Pr.

Brooks, Cleanth & Warren, Robert Penn. Understanding Poetry. 4th ed. 602p. (C). 1976. pap. text 43.50 (*0-03-076980-9*, Pub. by Harcourt Coll Pubs) Harcourt.

Brooks, Cleanth, jt. auth. see Wimsatt, William K., Jr.

Brooks, Cleanth, ed. see Percy, Thomas.

Brooks, Cleanth, jt. ed. see Warren, Robert Penn.

Brooks, Clem, jt. auth. see Manza, Jeff.

***Brooks, Clifford.** Setting Objectives: For College Reading & Learning Prodiciency. 3rd ed. 214p. 1998. pap. 38.95 (*0-945483-96-1*) E Bowers Pub.

Brooks, Clifford, et al. Music! Words! Opera!, 4 vols., Level 2. LC 91-45210. (Illus.). 460p. (J). (gr. 3-5). 1991. teacher ed. 82.50 (*0-918812-66-6*, SE 0706) MMB Music.

— Music! Words! Opera!, 3 vols., Set, Level 2. LC 91-45210. (Illus.). (J). (gr. 3-5). 1991. student ed. 4.95 (*0-918812-68-2*, SE 0707, SE 0708, SE 0709) MMB Music.

Brooks, Clifford W. Essentials for Ophthalmic Lens Work. (Illus.). 267p. 1983. text 65.00 (*0-7506-9248-0*) Buttrwrth-Heinemann.

— Lens Surfacing Handbook. (Illus.). 144p. 1992. spiral bd. 37.50 (*0-7506-9186-7*) Buttrwrth-Heinemann.

— Understanding Lens Surfacing. (Illus.). 416p. 1991. text 90.00 (*0-7506-9177-8*) Buttrwrth-Heinemann.

— Understanding Lens Surfacing Laboratory Exercises: A Laboratory Manual in Lens Surfacing. (Illus.). 118p. 1995. pap. text, lab manual ed. 30.00 (*0-7506-9617-6*) Buttrwrth-Heinemann.

Brooks, Clifford W. & Borish, Irving M. System for Ophthalmic Dispensing. 2nd ed. (Illus.). 583p. 1996. text 80.00 (*0-7506-9481-5*) Buttrwrth-Heinemann.

Brooks, Clifton R. Hints on the Allergy Diet: A Manual for Patents. 2nd ed. Brooks, Herbert B., ed. 29p. 1978. reprint ed. pap. 3.00 (*0-9620104-0-5*) Brooks Enterprises.

Brooks, Clyde S., et al. Metal Recovery from Industrial Waste. 288p. 1991. lib. bdg. 84.95 (*0-87371-456-3*, L456) Lewis Pubs.

Brooks, Colin. Governors & Government: A Political & Public History of Early Modern England 1550-1850. (An Arnold Publication). 256p. 1999. pap. 19.95 (*0-340-52129-5*, A9523, Pub. by E A); text 70.00 (*0-340-52130-9*, A9519, Pub. by E A) OUP.

Brooks, Collin, ed. The Royal Mail Case: Rex vs. Lord Kylsant, & Another. (Notable British Trials Ser.). xlii, 276p. 1995. reprint ed. 86.00 (*1-56169-178-X*) Gaunt.

Brooks, Collin & Brief, Richard P., eds. The Royal Mail Case: Rex vs. Lord Kylsant, & Another. LC 80-1475. (Dimensions of Accounting Theory & Practice Ser.). 1980. reprint ed. lib. bdg. 35.95 (*0-405-13505-X*) Ayer.

Brooks, Connie. The Last Cowboys: Closing the Open Range in Southeastern New Mexico, 1890s-1920s. LC 92-33399. (Illus.). 144p. 1993. reprint ed. pap. 44.70 (*0-608-07275-3*, 206750300009) Bks Demand.

Brooks, Constance. Preservation Planning Program Resource Guides: Disaster Preparedness. 184p. 1993. pap. 15.00 (*0-918006-65-1*) ARL.

Brooks, Cora. Sky Blew Blue. LC 87-60700. 80p. (C). 1987. pap. text 4.95 (*0-934678-13-8*) New Victoria Pubs.

Brooks, Cora V. Rinds, Roots & Stars: A Woman's Journal from the Great Flood. LC 96-26027. 64p. 1996. pap. 14.95 (*0-7734-2708-2*, Mellen Poetry Pr) E Mellen.

Brooks, Courtaney. The Case of the Stolen Dinosaur: A Play in Two Versions: Stage & Radio. (Illus.). 26p. (Orig.). (J). (gr. 4 up). 1983. pap. text 4.00 (*0-941274-02-0*) Belnice Bks.

— Eight Steps to Choral Reading. (Illus.). (Orig.). (J). (gr. 1 up). 1983. pap. text 3.00 (*0-941274-01-2*) Belnice Bks.

— Little Red & the Wolf: A Puppet Play. (Illus.). (J). (gr. k up). 1983. pap. text 2.50 (*0-941274-04-7*) Belnice Bks.

— Pardner & Freddie: A Puppet Play. (Illus.). (J). (gr. k up). 1983. pap. text 2.50 (*0-941274-03-9*) Belnice Bks.

— Plays & Puppets &cetera. 7th ed. LC 81-68933. (Illus.). 100p. (Orig.). (J). (gr. k up). 1981. pap. text 14.95 (*0-941274-00-4*) Belnice Bks.

Brooks, Courtaney & Pollock, Kenna. How to Teach Children Kindness & Manners with Puppets: Including Stories, Plays, Puppets & Props. (Illus.). 100p. (Orig.). (J). 1995. pap. 14.95 (*0-941274-06-3*) Belnice Bks.

Brooks, Cristen, ed. see Mowat, Farley.

Brooks, Cristen, ed. see Newfield, Nancy L. & Nielsen, Barbara.

Brooks, Cuyler W., Jr., ed. see Machen, Arthur.

Brooks, Cyril. Grace Triumphant: Autobiography. 266p. (Orig.). 1985. pap. 10.00 (*0-937396-66-4*) Walterick Pubs.

Brooks, Cyrus, tr. see Kastner, Erich.

Brooks, D. C Programming: The Essentials for Engineers & Scientists. Gries, D. & Schneider, F. B., eds. LC 98-31041. (Undergraduate Texts in Computer Science Ser.). 380p. 1999. 49.95 (*0-387-98632-4*) Spr-Verlag.

Brooks, D. C., ed. Current Review of Laparoscopy. 3rd ed. (Illus.). 232p. 1998. text 150.00 (*0-387-98338-4*) Spr-Verlag.

Brooks, D. H. The Unity of the Mind. LC 93-37499. 1994. text 69.95 (*0-312-12017-6*) St Martin.

Brooks, Dale, ed. Who's Who in Karate, 1982-83. (Illus.). 112p. 1983. pap. 17.95 (*0-931981-00-X*) Am Martial Arts Pub.

— Who's Who in the Martial Arts. (Illus.). 180p. (Orig.). 1985. pap. 12.95 (*0-931981-04-2*) Am Martial Arts Pub.

Brooks, Dana D. & Althouse, Ronald C. The African American Athlete Resource Directory. LC 96-86494. 212p. (Orig.). 1997. pap. text 19.00 (*1-885693-07-9*) Fit Info Tech.

Brooks, Dana D. & Althouse, Ronald C., eds. Racism in College Athletics. LC 92-73667. 319p. (C). 1993. 38.00 (*0-9627926-2-4*) Fit Info Tech.

— Racism in College Athletics: The African-American Athlete's Experience. 2nd rev. ed. 400p. 1999. text. write for info. (*1-885693-19-2*) Fit Info Tech.

Brooks, Daniel & Verdecchia, Guillermo. The Noam Chomsky Lectures. 96p. 1991. pap. 10.95 (*0-88910-413-1*) Genl Dist Srvs.

***Brooks, Daniel & Verdecchia, Guillermo.** The Noam Chomsky Lectures: A Play. 2nd ed. 92p. 1998. pap. 10.95 (*0-88922-405-6*) Talonbks.

Brooks, Daniel, jt. auth. see MacIvor, Daniel.

Brooks, Daniel J. Musil's Socratic Discourse in "Der Mann Ohne Eigenschaften" A Comparative Study of Ulrich & Socrates. (American University Studies: Germanic Languages & Literature: Ser. I, Vol. 81). IX, 169p. (C). 1989. text 32.95 (*0-8204-0923-5*) P Lang Pubng.

Brooks, Daniel M., ed. see IUCN/SSC Tapir Specialist Group Staff.

Brooks, Daniel R. & McLennan, Deborah A. Parascript: Parasites & the Language of Evolution. LC 92-20822. (Series in Comparative Evolutionary Biology). (Illus.). 448p. (C). 1993. text 69.00 (*1-56098-215-2*); pap. text 25.00 (*1-56098-285-3*) Smithsonian.

— Phylogeny, Ecology, & Behavior: A Research Program in Comparative Biology. (Illus.). xii, 392p. 1990. pap. text 23.95 (*0-226-07572-9*); lib. bdg. 54.00 (*0-226-07571-0*) U Ch Pr.

Brooks, Daniel R. & Wiley, Edward O. Evolution As Entropy: Toward a Unified Theory of Biology. 2nd ed. (Science & Its Conceptual Foundations Ser.). (Illus.). 432p. 1988. pap. text 24.00 (*0-226-07574-5*) U Ch Pr.

— Evolution As Entropy: Toward a Unified Theory of Biology. 2nd ed. (Science & Its Conceptual Foundations Ser.). (Illus.). 432p. 1996. lib. bdg. 72.00 (*0-226-07573-7*) U Ch Pr.

Brooks, David. The Age of Upheaval: Edwardian Politics, 1899-1914. LC 94-36786. 1995. text 27.95 (*0-7190-3696-8*, Pub. by Manchester Univ Pr) St Martin.

***Brooks, David.** Bobos in Paradise: The New Upper Class & How They Got There. LC 99-88094. 288p. 2000. 24.50 (*0-684-85377-9*) S&S Trade.

Brooks, David. Current Techniques in Laparoscopy. (Illus.). 224p. 1993. text 149.95 (*1-878132-05-9*) Current Med.

— Problem Solving with FORTRAN 90: For Scientists & Engineers. LC 97-10929. (Undergraduate Texts in Computer Science Ser.). 640p. 1997. text 49.95 (*0-387-98229-9*) Spr-Verlag.

— Right Livelihood. (Chapbook Award Ser.: No. 3). (Illus.). 40p. 1998. pap. 5.00 (*1-886350-80-9*) Pavement Saw.

***Brooks, David, ed.** The Double Looking Glass: New & Classic Essays on A. D. Hope. 2000. pap. 32.95 (*0-7022-3148-7*, Pub. by Univ Queensland Pr) Intl Spec Bk.

Brooks, David, ed. Urinary Tract Infections. LC 87-4115. (Practical Clinical Medicine Ser.). (C). 1987. pap. text 73.50 (*0-85200-695-0*) Kluwer Academic.

Brooks, David & Dunbar, Edward M. Infectious Diseases. (Management of Common Diseases in Family Practice Ser.). 1986. text 82.00 (*0-85200-760-4*) Kluwer Academic.

Brooks, David & Walker, Brenda, eds. Poetry & Gender: Statements & Essays on Australian Women Poets. 1989. pap. 14.95 (*0-7022-2240-2*, Pub. by Univ Queensland Pr) Intl Spec Bk.

Brooks, David, jt. auth. see Lonergan, Stephen.

Brooks, David, jt. auth. see Meister, Cari.

Brooks, David B. Low-Grade & Nonconventional Sources of Manganese. LC 66-24411. 135p. reprint ed. pap. 41.90 (*0-608-12256-4*, 202378700034) Bks Demand.

Brooks, David B, ed. Resource Economics: Selected Works of Orris C. Herfindahl. LC 74-6814. 316p. 1974. 27.50 (*0-8018-1645-9*) Resources Future.

Brooks, David B., et al, eds. Management of Water Demand in Africa & the Middle East: Current Practices & Future Needs. LC 98-700393. xi, 78p. 1997. pap. 17.50 (*0-88936-844-9*, Pub. by IDRC Bks) Stylus Pub VA.

Brooks, David B. & Krutilla, John V. Peaceful Use of Nuclear Explosives: Some Economic Aspects. LC 69-15904. 55p. reprint ed. pap. 30.00 (*0-608-12239-4*, 202378800034) Bks Demand.

***Brooks, David B. & Mehmet, Ozay, eds.** Water Balances in the Eastern Mediterranean. 160p. 2000. pap. 17.95 (*0-88936-907-0*, Pub. by IDRC Bks) Stylus Pub VA.

Brooks, David C. Current Review of Laparoscopy. 2nd ed. (Illus.). 248p. 1995. text 99.00 (*1-878132-61-X*) Rapid Science.

Brooks, David L., ed. From Magna Carta to the Constitution: Documents in the Struggle for Liberty. 104p. 1993. pap. 9.95 (*0-930073-07-X*) Fox & Wilkes.

Brooks, David W. Web-Teaching: A Guide to Designing Interactive Teaching for the World Wide Web. LC 97-1861. (Innovations in Science Education & Technology Ser.). (Illus.). 236p. (C). 1997. pap. 25.00 (*0-306-45552-8*, Plenum Trade) Perseus Pubng.

Brooks-Davies, Douglas, ed. Alexander Pope. (Everyman's Poetry Ser.). 116p. 1997. pap. 1.95 (*0-460-87798-4*, Everyman's Classic Lib) Tuttle Pubng.

— Four Metaphysical Poets. (Everyman's Poetry Ser.). 1997. pap. 3.50 (*0-460-87857-3*, Everyman's Classic Lib) Tuttle Pubng.

Brooks-Davies, Douglas, ed. Silver Poets of the Sixteenth Century. 512p. 1994. 9.50 (*0-460-87440-3*, Everyman's Classic Lib) Tuttle Pubng.

Brooks-Davies, Douglas, ed. see Spenser, Edmund.

Brooks-Davies, Doulgas, ed. Robert Herrick. (Everyman's Poetry Ser.). 116p. 1997. pap. 1.95 (*0-460-87799-2*, Everyman's Classic Lib) Tuttle Pubng.

***Brooks, De Vita.** Mythatypes: Signatures & Signs of African/Diaspora & Black Goddesses, 198. LC 99-56463. (Contributions in Afro-American & African Studies: Vol. 198). 200p. 2000. 59.95 (*0-313-31068-8*, Greenwood Pr) Greenwood.

***Brooks, Deirdre.** Aberrants Worldwide. (Aberrant Ser.). 2000. pap. 21.95 (*1-56504-684-6*) White Wolf.

Brooks, Delores W., ed. The Poems of Life. (Illus.). 60p. (Orig.). 1987. pap. 9.95 (*0-932471-10-2*) Falsoft.

Brooks, Dennis. Breaking with Tradition: Introducing a New Concept in Reading Improvement. 241p. 1999. pap. 18.95 (*0-7414-0036-7*) Buy Books.

***Brooks, Dennis.** Read, Write, Speak Correct English in 90 Days: A Self-Teaching Course. 285p. 1999. pap. 20.95 (*0-7414-0083-9*) Buy Books.

Brooks, Dennis L. & Henley, Arthur. Don't Be Afraid of Cataracts. (Illus.). 1978. 8.95 (*0-8184-0272-5*) Carol Pub Group.

— Don't Be Afraid of Cataracts. 128p. 1983. reprint ed. pap. 5.95 (*0-8065-0823-X*, Citadel Pr) Carol Pub Group.

Brooks, Diane L. Literature for Visual & Performing Arts: Kindergarten Through Grade Twelve. 66p. (C). 1998. reprint ed. pap. text 25.00 (*0-7881-3920-7*) DIANE Pub.

***Brooks, Dierdre.** Mage: The Ascension. 2000. 29.95 (*1-56504-405-3*); 69.95 (*1-56504-438-X*) White Wolf.

***Brooks, Dierdre & McCandliss, Adam.** Masters of the Art. (Mage Ser.). (Illus.). 88p. 1999. pap. 13.95 (*1-56504-427-4*, 4017) White Wolf.

Brooks, Don. Anhydrous Ammonia Safety. LC 81-730680. 1982. student ed. 7.00 (*0-8064-0031-5*, 266) Bergwall.

— Chain Saw Safety. 1983. student ed. 7.00 (*0-8064-0035-8*, 268) Bergwall.

Brooks, Donald W. Prop Talk: Understanding & Optimizing Propeller Performance for Model Electric Aircraft. unabridged ed. (Illus.), v, 98p. (Orig.). 1997. pap., spiral bd. 17.95 (*0-9657014-0-9*, ARPI-0100) ARPI Bks.

Brooks, Donna & Brooks, Lynn. 7 Secrets of Successful Women. 1997. 19.95 (*0-614-28012-5*) McGraw.

— Seven Secrets of Successful Women. LC 97-5058. 256p. 1997. 19.95 (*0-07-008229-4*) McGraw.

Brooks, Doris W. The Old Eagle-Nester: The Lost Legends of the Catskills. LC 92-73745. (Illus.). 128p. 1992. pap. 13.95 (*0-9628523-5-X*) Blk Dome Pr.

Brooks, Douglas. America Looks to the Sea. 1984. 19.95 (*0-685-14505-0*) Viking Penguin.

— A Practical Approach to Professional Writing: Technical & Business. 240p. (C). 1996. per. 37.95 (*0-7872-2894-X*, 41289401) Kendall-Hunt.

— Program Design for Personal Trainers: Bridging Theory into Application. LC 98-25930. (Illus.). 328p. 1998. 30.00 (*0-7360-0079-8*, BBRO0079) Human Kinetics.

— Your Personal Trainer: The Expert Training Companion for Total Fitness. LC 98-54744. 264p. 1999. pap. 19.95 (*0-88011-861-X*) Human Kinetics.

***Brooks, Douglas A.** From Playhouse to Printing House: Drama & Authorship in Early Modern England. LC 99-16686. (Cambridge Studies in Renaissance Literature & Culture: No. 36). (Illus.). 318p. (C). 2000. 59.95 (*0-521-77117-X*) Cambridge U Pr.

***Brooks, Douglas H. & Queisser, Monika, eds.** Financial Liberalisation in Asia: Analysis & Prospects. (Development Centre Seminars Ser.). 200p. 1999. pap. 34.00 (*92-64-16974-1*, 41 1999 02 1 P, Pub. by Org for Econ) OECD.

Brooks, Douglas H., jt. ed. see Thant, Myo.

Brooks, Douglas L. America Looks to the Sea: Ocean Use & the National Interest. (Marine Science Ser.). 266p. 1984. 30.00 (*0-86720-250-5*) Jones & Bartlett.

Brooks, Douglas M. A Nation of Learners: Building a New Learning America. 1995. 69.95 (*0-590-49386-8*) Scholastic Inc.

Brooks, Douglas R. Auspicious Wisdom: The Texts & Traditions of Srividya Sakta Tantrism in South India. LC 91-31730. (SUNY Series in Tantric Studies). 301p. (C). 1992. pap. text 18.95 (*0-7914-1146-X*) State U NY Pr.

— Meditation Revolution: A History & Theology of the Siddha Yoga Lineage. LC 97-73501. (Illus.). 711 p. 1997. 24.95 (*0-9654096-0-0*) Agama Pr.

— The Secret of the Three Cities: An Introduction to Hindu Sakta Tantrism. (Illus.). 328p. 1990. lib. bdg. 57.00 (*0-226-07569-9*) U Ch Pr.

— The Secret of the Three Cities: An Introduction to Hindu Sakta Tantrism. (Illus.). 328p. 1998. pap. text 19.95 (*0-226-07570-2*) U Ch Pr.

Brooks, Drex. Sweet Medicine: Sites of Indian Massacres, Battlefields, & Treaties. LC 94-6689. (Illus.). 163p. (C). 1995. pap. 26.95 (*0-8263-1538-0*) U of NM Pr.

Brooks, E., jt. auth. see Beaven, Donald W.

Brooks, E. Bruce & Brooks, A. Taeko, trs. Original Analects: Sayings of Confucius & His Successors. LC 97-25748. 368p. 1997. 29.50 (*0-231-10430-8*) Col U Pr.

Brooks, E. S. The Story of New York. 1991. lib. bdg. 79.95 (*0-8490-4495-2*) Gordon Pr.

Brooks, Edward, Jr., jt. ed. see Ross, Thomas W.

Brooks, Elaine & Fox, Len. Making Peace: A Reading/Writing/Thinking Text on Global Community. 295p. (C). 1995. pap. text 19.95 (*0-521-65780-6*) Cambridge U Pr.

— Making Peace: A Reading/Writing/Thinking Text on Global Community: Instructor's Manual. 26p. (C). 1995. pap., teacher ed. 6.00 (*0-521-65779-2*) Cambridge U Pr.

Brooks, Ellen. Just-Right Books for Beginning Readers: Leveled Booklists & Strategies. LC 96-182349. 1996. pap. text 12.95 (*0-590-49243-8*) Scholastic Inc.

Brooks, Ellen, jt. auth. see Kirton, Jim.

Brooks, Elmer. Elmer's Tune. LC 97-90706. 54p. 1998. pap. 8.95 (*0-533-12463-8*) Vantage.

Brooks, Elmore L. Georgia. Genealogical Record & History of the Georgia Family in America, Being the Children & Descendants of William & Sarah (Cable) Georgia & the Children & Descendants of Elijah Burr (1st) & Keziah (Stewart) Georgia. (Illus.). 314p. 1997. reprint ed. pap. 46.50 (*0-8328-8720-X*); reprint ed. lib. bdg. 56.50 (*0-8328-8719-6*) Higginson Bk Co.

An Asterisk (*) at the beginning of an entry indicates that the title is appearing for the first time.

***Brooks, Erik.** The Practically Perfect Pajamas. LC 99-16879. (Illus.). 32p. (J). (ps-3). 2000. 16.95 (*1-890817-22-8*, Pub. by Winslow Pr) Publishers Group.

Brooks, F. Clothes & Fashion. (Explainers Ser.). (Illus.). 24p. (J). (gr. 2-4). 1990. lib. bdg. 12.95 (*0-88110-400-0*, Usborne) EDC.

— Food & Eating. (Explainers Ser.). (Illus.). 24p. (J). (gr. 2-4). 1989. lib. bdg. 12.95 (*0-88110-399-3*, Usborne) EDC.

Brooks, F. Food & Eating. (Explainers Ser.). (Illus.). 24p. (J). (gr. 2-4). 1989. pap. 4.95 (*0-7460-0452-4*, Usborne) EDC.

Brooks, F. King Arthur. (Library of Fantasy & Adventure). (Illus.). 64p. (J). (gr. 5 up). 1995. pap. 8.95 (*0-7460-2061-9*, Usborne) EDC.

— King Arthur. (Library of Fantasy & Adventure). (Illus.). 84p. (J). (gr. 5 up). 1999. lib. bdg. 16.95 (*0-88110-751-4*, Usborne) EDC.

— Protecting Endangered Species. (Conservation Guides Ser.). (Illus.). 24p. (J). (gr. 2-5). 1991. lib. bdg. 12.95 (*0-88110-500-7*, Usborne) EDC.

— Protecting Our World. (Conservation Guides Ser.). (Illus.). 72p. (J). (gr. 2-5). 1992. pap. 10.95 (*0-7460-1082-6*, Usborne) EDC.

— Protecting Rivers & Seas. (Conservation Guides Ser.). (Illus.). 24p. (J). (gr. 2-5). 1992. pap. 4.50 (*0-7460-0687-X*, Usborne); lib. bdg. 12.95 (*0-88110-529-5*, Usborne) EDC.

Brooks, F., et al. Ornithology. (Science & Nature Ser.). (Illus.). 48p. (J). (gr. 5-11). 1993. pap. 7.95 (*0-7460-0685-3*, Usborne); lib. bdg. 15.95 (*0-88110-514-7*, Usborne) EDC.

Brooks, F., jt. auth. see Edom, H.

Brooks, F. T. Plant Diseases. (C). 1981. text 210.00 (*0-89771-569-1*, Pub. by Intl Bk Distr) St Mut.

— Plant Diseases. 386p. 1981. reprint ed. 150.00 (*0-7855-3069-X*, Pub. by Intl Bk Distr) St Mut.

Brooks, Felicity. Dracula. (Library of Fear & Fantasy). (J). (gr. 5 up). 1996. pap. 9.95 (*0-7460-2365-0*, Usborne) EDC.

— Dracula. (Library of Fear & Fantasy). 96p. (J). (gr. 5 up). 1999. lib. bdg. 17.95 (*0-88110-811-1*, Usborne) EDC.

***Brooks, Felicity.** First Encyclopedia of Our World. (Illus.). 64p. (ps-3). 2000. lib. bdg. 17.95 (*1-58086-265-9*) EDC.

Brooks, Felicity. Jason & the Argonauts. (Library of Myths & Legends Ser.). (Illus.). 112p. (Orig.). (YA). (gr. 5-9). 1997. pap. 10.95 (*0-7460-2733-8*, Usborne) EDC.

— Jason & the Argonauts. (Library of Myths & Legends Ser.). (Illus.). 112p. (Orig.). (J). (gr. 5 up). 1997. lib. bdg. 18.95 (*0-88110-930-4*, Usborne) EDC.

— Seas & Oceans. (Understanding Geography Ser.). (Illus.). 32p. (J). (gr. 6-11). 1994. pap. 7.95 (*0-7460-0986-0*, Usborne) EDC.

— Seas & Oceans. (Understanding Geography Ser.). (Illus.). 32p. (J). (gr. 6-11). 1999. lib. bdg. 15.95 (*0-88110-593-7*, Usborne) EDC.

***Brooks, Felicity, ed.** First Encyclopedia of Our World. (First Encyclopedia Ser.). (Illus.). 64p. (ps-3). 2000. pap. 9.95 (*0-7460-2839-3*) Usbrne Pbng UK.

— The Runaway Orange. (Easy Reading Ser.). (Illus.). 16p. (J). (ps-3). 2000. pap. 5.95 (*0-7460-3029-0*, Pub. by Usbrne Pbng UK) EDC.

Brooks, Felicity & Claybourne, Anna, eds. King Arthur & His Knights. (Illus.). 180p. (YA). (gr. 5 up). 1999. text 24.95 (*0-7460-3387-7*, Usborne) EDC.

***Brooks, Felicity & Litchfield, Jo.** Tales from Littletown. (Easy Reading Ser.). (Illus.). 48p. (J). (ps up). 2000. 9.95 (*0-7460-3474-1*, Usborne) EDC.

***Brooks, Felicity & Litchfield, Jo, eds.** The Birthday Surprise. (Easy Reading Ser.). (Illus.). 16p. (J). (ps-3). 2000. pap. 5.95 (*0-7460-3031-2*, Pub. by Usbrne Pbng UK) EDC.

— The Missing Cat. (Easy Reading Ser.). (Illus.). 16p. (J). (ps-3). 2000. pap. 5.95 (*0-7460-3027-4*, Pub. by Usbrne Pbng UK) EDC.

Brooks, Fern F. Letters to My Husband. LC 93-81264. (Illus.). 250p. 1993. pap. 14.95 (*0-9638683-0-6*) Hall-Sloane.

Brooks, Fonzie E. & Brooks, William D. Forever Spring: An Autobiography of a Pilgrim's Journey. (Illus.). 160p. 1995. 10.00 (*0-913719-95-1*, High Coo Pr) Brooks Books.

Brooks, Frank H., ed. The Individualist Anarchists: An Anthology of Liberty (1881-1908) LC 93-30303. 310p. (C). 1993. text 44.95 (*1-56000-132-1*) Transaction Pubs.

Brooks, Fred O. Principles & Practices in Classroom Evaluation. 152p. (C). 1990. pap. 30.60 (*0-536-57728-5*) Pearson Custom.

Brooks, Frederick P., Jr. The Mythical Man-Month: Essays on Software Engineering. anniversary ed. (Illus.). 336p. (C). 1995. pap. text 24.95 (*0-201-83595-9*) Addison-Wesley.

Brooks, Frederick P., et al. Automatic Data Processing: System-360 Edition. LC 68-31293. 490p. reprint ed. pap. 151.90 (*0-8357-5914-8*, 205509700008) Bks Demand.

Brooks, Frederick P., Jr., jt. auth. see Blaauw, Gerrit A.

Brooks, G. T. & Roberts, T., eds. Pesticide Chemistry & Biosciences: The Food-Environment Challenge. (Special Publication Ser.: Vol. 233). 400p. 1999. 100.00 (*0-85404-709-3*) Royal Soc Chem.

Brooks, Gary D., jt. ed. see Burns, Richard W.

Brooks, Gary R. The Centerfold Syndrome: Now Men Can Overcome Objectification & Achieve Intimacy with Women. LC 95-8838. (Psychology Ser.). 262p. 1995. mass mkt. 22.50 (*0-7879-0104-0*) Jossey-Bass.

***Brooks, Gary R.** New Handbook of Psychotherapy & Counseling with Men: A Comprehensive Guide for All Settings. 2001. 69.95 (*0-7879-5155-2*) Jossey-Bass.

Brooks, Gary R. A New Psychotherapy for Traditional Men. LC 97-45455. 288p. 1998. 36.95 (*0-7879-4123-9*) Jossey-Bass.

Brooks, Gary R., jt. auth. see Levant, Ronald F.

Brooks, Gennifer B. Praise the Lord: Litanies, Prayers & Occasional Services. LC 96-10672. (Orig.). 1996. pap. 12.75 (*0-7880-0851-X*) CSS OH.

Brooks, Geoffrey, tr. see Furbringer, Werner.

Brooks, Geoffrey, tr. see Greger, Rene.

Brooks, Geoffrey, tr. see Koop, Bernard & Schmolke, Klaus-Peter.

Brooks, Geoffrey, tr. see Koop, Gerhard & Schmolke, Klaus-Peter.

***Brooks, George A.** Exercise Physiology: Human Bioenergetics & Its Applications. 3rd ed. LC 99-16015. xxi, 851p. 1999. text 61.95 (*0-7674-1024-6*, 1024-6) Mayfield Pub.

Brooks, George E., Jr. The Kru Mariner in the Nineteenth Century: An Historical Compendium. (Liberian Research Working Papers: No. 1). (Illus.). 121p. 1972. 8.50 (*0-916712-05-2*) Arden Assocs.

— Themes in African & World History: A Schema for Integrating Africa into World History; Tropical Africa: The Colonial Heritage; The African Heritage & the Slave Trade. rev. ed. (African Humanities Ser.). 59p. 1983. pap. text 5.00 (*0-941934-06-3*) Indiana Africa.

Brooks, George E. Western Africa to 1860 A.D. A Provisional Historical Schem Based on Climate Periods. (African Studies Working). 231p. 1985. pap. text 15.00 (*0-941934-67-5*) Indiana Africa.

Brooks, George F. Tell Us Another. 44p. 1970. 6.60 (*3-296-50100-2*, Pub. by Weidmann) Lubrecht & Cramer.

Brooks, George S. Friend Anthony Benezet. 1993. reprint ed. lib. bdg. 89.00 (*0-7812-5435-3*) Rprt Serv.

Brooks, George S., ed. see Durand, James R.

Brooks, Geraldine. Building Blocks of Leadership. 63p. 1998. spiral bd. 12.00 (*0-9667498-0-4*) Gerald Brooks Minist.

— Dames & Daughters of Colonial America. (Women in America Ser.). 1977. 29.95 (*0-405-06080-7*) Ayer.

— Dames & Daughters of Colonial Days. 284p. 1982. reprint ed. 24.95 (*0-87928-109-X*) Corner Hse.

— Dames & Daughters of the French Colonies. (Essay Index Reprint Ser.). 1977. 21.95 (*0-8369-0256-4*) Ayer.

— Emotion of a Leader. 64p. 1998. spiral bd. 12.00 (*0-9667498-1-2*) Gerald Brooks Minist.

— Foreign Correspondence: A Pen Pal's Journey from down under to All Over. LC 97-15413. (Illus.). 224p. 1997. 22.95 (*0-385-48269-8*, Anchor NY) Doubleday.

— Foreign Correspondence: A Pen Pal's Journey from down under to All Over. 240p. 1999. pap. 12.95 (*0-385-48373-2*, Anchor NY) Doubleday.

— Foreign Correspondence: A Pen Pal's Journey from down under to All Over. large type ed. LC 98-56114. 1999. 30.00 (*0-7862-1840-1*) Thorndike Pr.

— Nine Parts of Desire: The Hidden World of Islamic Women. 272p. 1995. reprint ed. pap. 14.00 (*0-385-47577-2*) Doubleday.

— Prophet's Daughters. 1992. write for info. (*0-679-41245-X*) McKay.

Brooks, Geraldine, jt. auth. see Courtney-Clarke, Margaret.

Brooks, Glenwood C., Jr., jt. auth. see Sedlacek, William E.

Brooks, Graham, ed. Trial of Captain Kidd, No. 1. (Notable British Trials Ser.). x, 223p. 1995. reprint ed. 70.00 (*1-56169-116-X*) Gaunt.

Brooks, Greg. Queen Live: A Concert Documentary. (Illus.). 176p. (Orig.). (C). 1995. pap. 24.95 (*0-7119-4814-3*, OP 47752) Omnibus NY.

Brooks Group, NASRI Staff. Superior Selling Master Guide. 24p. 1993. spiral bd. 3.00 (*0-8403-9108-0*) Kendall-Hunt.

Brooks-Gunn, J. & Peterson, A. C. Girls at Puberty: Biological & Psychosocial Perspectives. (Illus.). 370p. (C). 1983. 75.00 (*0-306-41144-X*, Plenum Trade) Perseus Pubng.

Brooks-Gunn, Jeanne, ed. Helping Children Take Healthy Steps: Abstracts of Selected Articles on Early Childhood Interventions. 147p. (C). 1999. reprint ed. pap. text 30.00 (*0-7881-7662-5*) DIANE Pub.

Brooks-Gunn, Jeanne, et al, eds. Neighborhood Poverty: Context & Consequences for Children. Vol. 1. LC 97-7864. (Illus.). 432p. (C). 1997. 49.95 (*0-87154-145-9*) Russell Sage.

— Neighborhood Poverty: Policy Implications in Studying Neighborhoods, 2 vols., Vol. 2. LC 97-7864. (Illus.). 288p. (C). 1997. 39.95 (*0-87154-146-7*) Russell Sage.

Brooks-Gunn, Jeanne, jt. auth. see Duncan, Greg.

Brooks-Gunn, Jeanne, jt. ed. see Chase-Lansdale, P. Lindsay.

Brooks-Gunn, Jeanne, jt. ed. see Cox, Martha J.

Brooks-Gunn, Jeanne, jt. ed. see Duncan, Greg.

Brooks, Guy & Brooks, Victoria. Costa Rica: A Kick Start Guide for Business Travelers. 160p. 1996. pap. 9.95 (*1-55180-025-X*) Self-Counsel Pr.

— Hong Kong: A Kick Start Guide for Business Travelers. (Travel Ser.). 168p. (Orig.). 1995. pap. 9.95 (*1-55180-043-8*) Self-Counsel Pr.

— Indonesia: A Kick Start Guide for Business Travelers. 160p. 1995. pap. 9.95 (*0-88908-844-6*) Self-Counsel Pr.

— Malaysia: A Kick Start Guide for Business Travelers. 160p. 1995. pap. 9.95 (*0-88908-845-4*) Self-Counsel Pr.

— Vietnam: A Kick Start Guide for Business Travelers. 160p. (Orig.). 1995. pap. 9.95 (*0-88908-843-8*) Self-Counsel Pr.

Brooks, Gwen H., jt. auth. see Regan, Helen B.

Brooks, Gwendolyn. Aloneness. LC 74-147270. (J). (gr. 1 up). 1971. pap. 5.00 (*0-910296-55-3*) Broadside Pr.

— Beckonings. 1975. pap. 5.00 (*0-910296-37-5*) Broadside Pr.

— Blacks. 1991. 36.95 (*0-88378-139-5*); pap. 19.95 (*0-88378-105-0*) Third World.

— Bronzeville Boys & Girls. LC 56-8152. (Illus.). 48p. (J). (gr. 3-6). 1967. lib. bdg. 15.89 (*0-06-020651-9*) HarpC Child Bks.

— Family Pictures. LC 70-139494. 1970. pap. 7.00 (*0-910296-43-X*) Broadside Pr.

— Maud Martha. LC 92-63012. 192p. 1993. reprint ed. pap. 9.95 (*0-88378-061-5*) Third World.

— The Near Johannesburg Boy & Other Poems. 1991. 4.00 (*0-88378-055-0*) Third World.

— Primer for Blacks. 16p. 1991. 4.00 (*0-88378-056-9*) Third World.

— Report from Part One: An Autobiography. LC 72-77308. 192p. (YA). (gr. 12). 1972. 22.95 (*0-910296-82-0*) Broadside Pr.

— Report from Part Two. 170p. 21.95 (*0-88378-164-6*) Third World.

Brooks, Gwendolyn. Report from Part Two. 170p. 1996. pap. text 14.95 (*0-88378-162-X*) Third World.

— Selected Poems. LC 98-54645. 160p. 1999. pap. 12.00 (*0-06-093174-4*) HarpC.

Brooks, Gwendolyn. Selected Poems. LC 63-16503. 1963. 17.10 (*0-606-03463-3*, Pub. by Turtleback) Demco.

— The Tiger Who Wore White Gloves: Or What You Are You Are. LC 74-75589. (J). 1974. pap. 8.00 (*0-88378-031-3*) Third World.

— To Disembark. 70p. 1992. pap. 8.00 (*0-88378-102-6*) Third World.

— Very Young Poets. 32p. 1991. pap. 4.00 (*0-88378-046-1*) Third World.

— Winnie. 1991. 4.00 (*0-88378-050-X*) Third World.

Brooks, H. Allen. Frank Lloyd Wright & the Prairie School. LC 83-15621. (Illus.). 120p. (Orig.). (C). 1984. pap. 18.95 (*0-8076-1084-4*) Braziller.

— Le Corbusier's Formative Years: Charles-Edouard Jeanneret at La Chaux-de-Fonds. LC 96-22865. 588p. 1997. 65.00 (*0-226-07579-6*) U Ch Pr.

— Le Corbusier's Formative Years: Charles-Edouard Jeanneret at La Chaux-de-Fonds. 1999. pap. text 35.00 (*0-226-07582-6*) U Ch Pr.

— The Prairie School: Frank Lloyd Wright & His Midwest Contemporaries. rev. ed. (Illus.). 400p. 1996. pap. 22.50 (*0-393-31439-1*, Norton Paperbks) Norton.

Brooks, H. Allen, ed. Chandigarh: City & Musee. LC 83-11607. (Le Corbusier Archive Ser.). 1983. text 95.00 (*0-8240-5074-6*) Garland.

— Unite d'Habitation, Reze-les-Nantes. LC 83-9074. (Le Corbusier Archive Ser.). 1983. lib. bdg. 95.00 (*0-8240-5070-3*) Garland.

— Writings on Wright: Selected Comment on Frank Lloyd Wright. (Illus.). 249p. 1983. pap. text 14.00 (*0-262-52086-9*) MIT Pr.

Brooks, H. Allen, jt. auth. see Marvel, Thomas S.

Brooks, H. C. Compendiosa Bibliografia de Edizioni Bodoniane. (ITA., Illus.). 366p. 1994. reprint ed. 100.00 (*1-888262-40-0*) Martino Pubng.

Brooks, Harold A. The Prairie School: Frank Lloyd Wright & His Midwest Contemporaries. LC 72-151363. 398p. reprint ed. pap. 123.40 (*0-608-16930-7*, 2026419000049) Bks Demand.

Brooks, Harold A., ed. Prairie School Architecture: Studies from "The Western Architect" LC 73-91567. 351p. reprint ed. pap. 108.90 (*0-608-13717-0*, 2020459000018) Bks Demand.

Brooks, Harold F., ed. see Shakespeare, William.

***Brooks-Harris, Jeff E.** Workshops: Designing & Facilitating Experiential Learning. LC 99-6167. 188p. 1999. 42.00 (*0-7619-1020-4*) Sage.

Brooks-Harris, Jeff E. & Stock-Ward, Susan R. Workshops: Designing & Facilitating Experiential Learning. LC 99-6167. 1999. 24.95 (*0-7619-1021-2*) Sage.

Brooks, Harry F. Risk Management & Insurance for Equipment Lessors. 260p. 1988. pap. text 110.00 (*0-912413-02-6*) Am Assn Equip Lessors.

Brooks, Harvey, et al, eds. Public-Private Partnership: New Opportunities for Meeting Social Needs. LC 83-27564. (American Academy of Arts & Sciences Ser.). 392p. 1984. text 34.95 (*0-88410-482-6*, HarpBusn) HarpInfo.

Brooks, Harvey, ed. see Barbour, Ian G.

Brooks-Heath. Speech Communication. 7th ed. 1992. teacher ed. 25.00 (*0-697-12916-0*) McGraw.

Brooks, Helen. And the Bride Wore Black. LC 95-4554. (Romance Ser.). 189p. 1995. per. 2.99 (*0-373-03350-8*, 1-03350-5) Harlequin Bks.

— Angels Do Have Wings. large type ed. (Harlequin Romance Ser.). 283p. 1995. 19.95 (*0-263-14150-0*) Mac Lib Ref.

— Angels Do Have Wings: Sealed with a Kiss. 1995. per. 2.99 (*0-373-03378-8*) Harlequin Bks.

***Brooks, Helen.** The Baby Secret. large type ed. 288p. 1999. 25.99 (*0-263-16101-3*, Pub. by Mills & Boon) Ulverscroft.

Brooks, Helen. The Baby Secret: Expecting. 1998. per. 3.75 (*0-373-12004-4*, 1-12004-7, Mira Bks) Harlequin Bks.

— Bitter Honey. large type ed. (Harlequin Romance Ser.). 1994. lib. bdg. 19.95 (*0-263-13819-4*) Thorndike Pr.

***Brooks, Helen.** Boss in a Million. (Presents Ser.). 2000. per. 3.99 (*0-373-12095-8*) Harlequin Bks.

— Boss in a Million. large type ed. (Harlequin Romance Ser.). 2000. 22.95 (*0-263-16306-7*) Mills & Boon.

Brooks, Helen. The Bride's Secret. 1999. per. 3.75 (*0-373-12047-8*, 1-12047-6) Harlequin Bks.

— Cold Fire. large type unabridged ed. (Harlequin Ser.). 1993. lib. bdg. 19.95 (*0-263-13577-2*) Mac Lib Ref.

***Brooks, Helen.** A Convenient Proposal: Marry Me? (Harlequin Presents Ser.). 2000. mass mkt. 3.99 (*0-373-12118-0*, 1121185) Harlequin Bks.

— Dark Oasis. large type ed. 304p. 1999. 31.99 (*0-7505-1347-0*, Pub. by Mgna Lrg Print) Ulverscroft.

Brooks, Helen. Deceitful Lover. large type ed. (Magna Large Print Ser.). 279p. 1997. 27.50 (*0-7505-1128-1*) Thorndike Pr.

— Dream Wedding. 1996. per. 3.25 (*0-373-03434-2*, 1-03434-7) Harlequin Bks.

— Dream Wedding. large type ed. 1996. per. 3.25 (*0-373-15680-4*) Harlequin Bks.

— For a Mother's Love. large type ed. (Ulverscroft Large Print Ser.). 672p. 1997. 27.99 (*0-7089-3841-8*) Ulverscroft.

— A Heartless Marriage. (Presents Ser.). 1996. per. 3.50 (*0-373-11844-9*, 1-11844-7) Harlequin Bks.

— Husband by Contract. large type ed. (Mills & Boon Large Print Ser.). 288p. 1997. 22.50 (*0-263-15288-X*, Pub. by Mills & Boon) Ulverscroft.

— Husband by Contract: Husbands & Wives. (Presents Ser.: No. 1934). 1998. per. 3.50 (*0-373-11934-8*, 1-11934-6) Harlequin Bks.

— Lace & Satin. large type ed. 288p. 1995. 23.99 (*0-263-14290-6*, Pub. by Mills & Boon) Ulverscroft.

— Lovers Not Friends. large type ed. (Harlequin Romance Ser.). 284p. 1995. lib. bdg. 18.95 (*0-263-14125-X*) Mac Lib Ref.

— Man Worth Waiting For. large type ed. 1998. 21.95 (*0-263-15590-0*, G K Hall & Co) Mac Lib Ref.

***Brooks, Helen.** The Marriage Quest. large type ed. 288p. 1999. 25.99 (*0-263-16204-4*, Pub. by Mills & Boon) Ulverscroft.

Brooks, Helen. The Marriage Solution. (Presents Ser.: Vol. 1987). 1998. per. 3.75 (*0-373-11987-9*, 1-11987-4) Harlequin Bks.

— Mistletoe Mistress. 1999. 21.95 (*0-263-15953-1*, G K Hall & Co) Mac Lib Ref.

***Brooks, Helen.** Mistress to a Millionaire. large type ed. (Thorndike Harlequin Romance (Large Print) Ser.). 2000. 22.95 (*0-263-16440-3*) Mac Lib Ref.

Brooks, Helen. The Price of a Wife. 1997. per. 3.50 (*0-373-11914-3*, 1-11914-8) Harlequin Bks.

— The Price of a Wife. large type ed. (Mills & Boon Large Print Ser.). 288p. 1997. 23.99 (*0-263-15120-4*, Pub. by Mills & Boon) Ulverscroft.

— Satisfaction Guaranteed. large type ed. (Mills & Boon Large Print Ser.). 288p. 1998. 24.99 (*0-263-15431-9*, Pub. by Mills & Boon) Ulverscroft.

— Second Marriage. (Presents Ser.: No. 1939). 1998. per. 3.75 (*0-373-11939-9*, 1-11939-5) Harlequin Bks.

— Second Marriage. large type ed. (Mills & Boon Large Print Ser.). 288p. 1998. 24.99 (*0-263-15372-X*, Pub. by Mills & Boon) Ulverscroft.

***Brooks, Helen.** The Sicilian's Mistress. 1999. per. 3.75 (*0-373-12071-0*) Harlequin Bks.

Brooks, Helen. Sultan's Favourite. large type ed. 1995. lib. bdg. 18.95 (*0-263-13963-8*) Thorndike Pr.

***Brooks, Helen.** A Suspicious Proposal: Marry Me? (Presents Ser.: Bk. 2112). 2000. per. 3.99 (*0-373-12112-1*, 1-12112-8) Harlequin Bks.

Brooks, Helen. Sweet Betrayal. large type ed. 1994. lib. bdg. 19.95 (*0-263-13647-7*) Thorndike Pr.

— Venganza Privada. (Bianca Ser.: Vol. 159).Tr. of Private Revenge. (SPA.). 1999. per. 3.50 (*0-373-33509-1*, 1-33509-0) Harlequin Bks.

***Brooks, Helen.** A Very Private Revenge. 1999. per. 3.75 (*0-373-12021-4*, 1-12021-1, Harlequin) Harlequin Bks.

Brooks, Helen. Web of Darkness. large type ed. (Harlequin Romance Ser.). 1995. lib. bdg. 18.95 (*0-263-14072-5*) Mac Lib Ref.

Brooks, Henry M. Olden-Time Music. LC 70-39537. reprint ed. 42.50 (*0-404-09919-X*) AMS Pr.

Brooks, Herbert B., ed. see Brooks, Clifton R.

Brooks, Hindi. Captain Noah: A Musical for the Whole Family. (Illus.). 36p. 1989. pap. 4.50 (*0-88680-317-9*) I E Clark.

— Captain Noah: (Piano - Vocal Score) (Illus.). 36p. (Orig.). (J). (gr. 1 up). 1989. 15.00 (*0-88680-318-7*) I E Clark.

— Computer Pals: A Short Comedy. (Illus.). 8p. 1998. pap. 3.50 (*0-88680-452-3*, C4523) I E Clark.

— Making It! A Play in 3-Acts. 60p. 1984. pap. 4.00 (*0-88680-216-4*) I E Clark.

Brooks, Hollace P., jt. auth. see Chill, Paul.

Brooks, Hugh. Building & Construction Resource Directory. 304p. 1992. pap. 29.95 (*0-9623910-2-6*) HBA Pubns.

— The Tilt-Up Design & Construction Manual. (Illus.). 263p. 1989. ring bd. 87.50 (*0-9623910-1-8*) HBA Pubns.

— The Tilt-Up Design & Construction Manual. (Illus.). 324p. 1994. ring bd. 92.00 (*0-9623910-3-4*) HBA Pubns.

— The Tilt-Up Design & Construction Manual. 4th ed. (Illus.). 382p. 1997. ring bd. 92.00 (*0-9623910-5-0*) HBA Pubns.

Brooks, Hugh, ed. Illustrated Encyclopedic Dictionary of Building & Construction Terms. (Illus.). 320p. 1975. 29.95 (*0-13-451013-5*, Busn) P-H.

Brooks, Hugh C. & El-Ayouty, Yassin, eds. Refugees South of the Sahara: An African Dilemma, 4. LC 71-105994. (Contributions in Afro-American & African Studies: No. 14). 307p. 1970. 69.50 (*0-8371-3324-6*, BSS&, Greenwood Pr) Greenwood.

***Brooks, I. & Weatherston, Jamie.** The Business Environment: Challenges & Changes. 2nd ed. LC 99-59112. 2000. write for info. (*0-273-64690-7*) F T P H.

***Brooks, Ian.** Organisational Behaviour: Individual, Group & Organisation. 320p. 1999. pap. 38.50 (*0-273-63286-8*, Pub. by F T P-H) Trans-Atl Phila.

Brooks, III, Lewis C. A Mindful Abyss Springing in the Distance. unabridged ed. Wegeng, Lana M., ed. (Illus.). 26p. 1998. pap. 8.50 (*1-892651-01-7*) Columbia Pubns.

Brooks, Ilsley D. Jennifer Ilsley Deering Brooks. Stearns, Helen M., ed. (Illus.). 48p. (J). (ps up). 1987. 12.95 (*0-9614281-3-9*, 1475, Cricketfld Pr) Picton Pr.

B

Brooks Institute Staff. Profile in Photography. Corbell, Tony, ed. (Illus.). 224p. 1991. boxed set 50.00 (*0-9628858-0-0*) Serbin Commns.

Brooks, J., ed. Classic Petroleum Provinces. (Geological Society Special Publications: No. 50). (Illus.). 576p. 1990. 140.00 (*0-903317-48-6*, 236, Pub. by Geol Soc Pub Hse) AAPG.

Brooks, J. & Glennie, K. W., eds. Petroleum Geology of Northwestern Europe. (C). 1988. lib. bdg. 535.50 (*0-86010-703-5*, Pub. by Graham & Trotman) Kluwer Academic.

Brooks, J. & Strantzen, J. Blaschke's Rolling Theorem in RN. LC 89-7017. (MEMO Ser.: Vol. 80/405). 101p. 1989. pap. 20.00 (*0-8218-2466-X*, MEMO 80/405) Am Math.

Brooks, J. A. The Good Ghost Guide: A Gazetteer of over a Thousand British Hauntings. (Jarrold Ghost Ser.). (Illus.). 288p. (Orig.). 1994. pap. 18.95 (*0-7117-0669-7*) Seven Hills Bk.

Brooks, J. L., ed. Benito Perez Galdos: Torquemada en la Hoguera. 100p. (C). 1973. 6.30 (*0-08-016917-1*, Pergamon Pr); pap. text 5.25 (*0-08-016918-X*, Pergamon Pr) Elsevier.

Brooks, J. R. King Alfred School & the Progressive Movement 1898-1998. (Illus.). 384p. 1998. write for info. (*0-7083-1453-8*, Pub. by Univ Wales Pr) Paul & Co Pubs.

Brooks, J. R., ed. see Tawney, R. H.

***Brooks, Jacki.** The Complete Encyclopedia of Teddy Bears (1903-1990) (Illus.). 191p. 2000. reprint ed. text 30.00 (*0-7881-9042-3*) DIANE Pub.

***Brooks, Jacqueline G. & Brooks, Martin G.** In Search of Understanding: The Case for Constructivist Classrooms. rev. ed. LC 99-6468. 136p. 1999. pap. 16.95 (*0-87120-358-8*, 199234) ASCD.

Brooks, James. Wounded Underneath: God's Power Shows up Best in the Suffering Person. 120p. (Orig.). 1996. pap. 10.00 (*1-57502-362-8*, PO1166) Morris Pubng.

Brooks, James, jt. auth. see Draper, James.

Brooks, James A. Mark. (New American Commentary Ser.: Vol.23). 288p. 1991. 27.99 (*0-8054-0123-7*) Broadman.

Brooks, James A. & Winbery, Carlton L. A Morphology of New Testament Greek: A Review & Reference Grammar. LC 94-1376. 478p. (Orig.). 1994. pap. text 39.50 (*0-8191-9491-3*); lib. bdg. 65.00 (*0-8191-9490-5*) U Pr of Amer.

— Syntax of New Testament Greek. LC 78-51150. 186p. 1978. pap. text 15.50 (*0-8191-0473-6*) U Pr of Amer.

Brooks, James E. My Great-Grandfather's House in Exeter, New Hampshire. (Illus.). 64p. 1997. reprint ed. pap. 13.00 (*0-8328-5991-5*) Higginson Bk Co.

Brooks, James W. History of the Court of Common Pleas of the City & County of New York, with Full Reports of All Important Proceedings. 253p. 1979. reprint ed. 40.00 (*0-8377-0308-5*, Rothman) W S Hein.

Brooks, Jane. Midlife Orphan: Facing Life's Changes Now That Your Parents Are Gone. LC 99-191736. 228p. (Orig.). 1999. pap. 13.00 (*0-425-16693-7*) Berkley Pub.

Brooks, Jane B. Parenting. 2nd ed. LC 97-20105. xvi, 345p. 1997. pap. text 26.95 (*1-55934-937-9*, 1937) Mayfield Pub.

***Brooks, Jane B.** Parenting. 3rd ed. LC 00-55044. 2000. write for info. (*0-7674-1797-6*) Mayfield Pub.

Brooks, Jane B. The Process of Parenting. 5th rev. ed. LC 98-39378. (Illus.). 556p. 1999. pap. text 47.95 (*0-7674-0215-4*, 0215-4) Mayfield Pub.

— The Process of Parenting Instructor's Manual. 5th rev. ed. 147p. (C). 1999. pap. text, teacher ed. write for info. (*0-7674-1044-0*, 1044-0) Mayfield Pub.

Brooks, Jay R. & Knezevich, Karen. The Bars of Santa Clara County: A Beer Drinker's Guide to Silicon Valley. 296p. (Orig.). 1992. pap. 13.95 (*0-9631587-0-8*) Zero CA.

Brooks, Jean O. & Dalfonso, Deborah. Christina Olson: Her World Beyond the Canvas. LC 98-22320. (Illus.). 112p. 1998. pap. 10.95 (*0-89272-404-8*) Down East.

Brooks, Jean S. & Reich, David L. The Public Library in Non-Traditional Education. LC 73-21903. (Illus.). 256p. 1974. 24.95 (*0-88280-008-6*) ETC Pubns.

Brooks, Jeanice, ed. see De Castro, Jean & Ronsard, Pierre De.

Brooks, Jeffrey. Thank You, Comrade Stalin! Soviet Public Culture from Revolution to Cold War. LC 99-25331. 312p. 1999. 35.00 (*0-691-00411-0*, Pub. by Princeton U Pr) Cal Prin Full Svc.

Brooks, Jennifer. Hand in Hand Around God's World. LC 97-43519. (J). (ps-2). 1998. bds. 7.99 (*1-57673-307-6*, Gold n Honey) Zondervan.

— Princess Jessica Rescues a Prince. Ridley, Chas, ed. LC 93-92628. (Illus.). 40p. (J). (ps-2). 1994. 15.95 (*0-9636335-0-3*) Nadja Pub.

Brooks, Jennifer & Engstrom, Kim. How Sweet the Sound. LC 96-48363. (Illus.). 48p. (Orig.). (J). (ps-3). 1997. pap. 10.99 incl. audio (*1-57673-056-5*, Gold n Honey) Zondervan.

Brooks, Jennifer J., jt. auth. see Bishop, Carter G.

Brooks, Jeremy, tr. see Euripides.

Brooks, Jeremy, tr. see Gorky, Maxim.

***Brooks, Jerome.** Tobacco: Its History Illustrated by the Books & Manuscripts in the Library of George Arents, 5 vols. (Illus.). 2465p. 1999. reprint ed. 495.00 (*1-57898-099-2*) Martino Pubng.

Brooks, Jerome E. Green Leaf & Gold: Tobacco in North Carolina. (Illus.). vi, 39p. 1997. reprint ed. pap. 5.00 (*0-86526-078-8*) NC Archives.

Brooks, Jessica. Career after Cosmetology School: Step-by-Step Guide to a Lucrative Career & Salon Ownership. LC 94-65047. 320p. (Orig.). 1997. 29.95 (*1-884573-07-X*); pap. 19.95 (*1-884573-12-6*) S-By-S Pubns.

Brooks, Jim & Welte, Dietrich H. Advances in Petroleum Geochemistry, Vol. 1. (Serial Publication Ser.). 1984. text 135.00 (*0-12-032001-0*) Acad Pr.

Brooks, Jo Gabeler. Background Notes, Namibia: 1991, Apr. 7p. 1991. pap. 1.25 (*0-16-033813-1*) USGPO.

Brooks, Joan. Desert Padre: The Life & Writings of Father John J. Crowley, 1891-1940. LC 97-70406. (Illus.). 401p. (Orig.). 1997. pap. 19.95 (*0-9656521-4-9*) Mesquite Pr.

Brooks, Joan, jt. auth. see Budlong, Tom.

Brooks, Joanne L. Caron-Nadeau Family History: 1612-1986. (Illus.). 380p. 1987. pap. 45.00 (*0-941216-36-5*) Cay-Bel.

Brooks, Joe. Salt Water Fly Fishing. (Blue Water Classics Ser.). 240p. lthr. 65.00 (*1-56416-146-3*) Derrydale Pr.

— Salt Water Fly Fishing. LC 00-25870. (Illus.). 224p. 2000. pap. 21.95 (*1-58667-007-X*, Pub. by Derrydale Pr) Natl Bk Netwk.

Brooks, John. The Go-Go Years. LC 73-76567. vi, 375p. 1973. write for info. (*0-679-40038-9*) Random.

— The Go-Go Years: The Drama & Crashing Finale of Wall Street's Bullish 60s. LC 99-33867. (Wiley Investment Classics Ser.). 384p. 1999. 34.95 (*0-471-35755-3*) Wiley.

— The Go-Go Years: The Drama & Crashing Finale of Wall Street's Bullish 60's. LC 99-33867. (Wiley Investment Classics Ser.). 374p. 1999. pap. 19.95 (*0-471-35754-5*) Wiley.

— Once in Golconda: A True Drama of Wall Street, 1920-1938. LC 99-33868. (Wiley Investment Classics Ser.). 320p. 1999. 34.95 (*0-471-35753-7*) Wiley.

— The Takeover Game: The Men, the Moves & the Wall Street Money Behind Today's Nationwide Merger Wars. LC 99-44355. 1999. write for info. (*1-893122-36-0*) Beard Bks.

Brooks, John G. An American Citizen: The Life of William Henry Baldwin Jr. Bruchey, Stuart, ed. LC 80-1295. (Railroads Ser.). 1981. reprint ed. lib. bdg. 33.95 (*0-405-13765-6*) Ayer.

— American Syndicalism. LC 78-86170. reprint ed. 31.50 (*0-404-01118-7*) AMS Pr.

— American Syndicalism. LC 70-89722. (American Labor, from Conspiracy to Collective Bargaining Ser., No. 1). 264p. 1970. reprint ed. 17.95 (*0-405-02107-0*) Ayer.

— American Syndicalism: The I.W.W. LC 78-107407. (Civil Liberties in American History Ser.). 1970. reprint ed. lib. bdg. 32.50 (*0-306-71887-1*) Da Capo.

Brooks, John I., III. The Eclectic Legacy: Academic Philosophy & the Human Sciences in Nineteenth-Century France. LC 97-32351. 328p. 1998. 49.50 (*0-87413-648-2*) U Delaware Pr.

Brooks, John L., II. Balloons, Sea Creatures, Me. large type ed. LC TXU838-153. (Illus.). 20p. (J). (gr. k-3). 1999. pap. 7.00 (*0-9661789-1-2*) Lone Wolf Prodns.

— The Sundarbans Tiger. (Illus.). 44p. (Orig.). (YA). (gr. 4-6). 1997. pap. 5.50 (*0-9661789-0-4*) Lone Wolf Prodns.

Brooks, John L. The Systematics of North American Daphnia. (Connecticut Academy of Arts & Sciences Ser., Trans.: Vol. 13). 1957. pap. 100.00 (*0-685-22858-4*) Elliots Bks.

Brooks, John R. Surgery of the Pancreas. (Illus.). 528p. 1983. text 142.00 (*0-7216-2082-5*, W B Saunders Co) Harcrt Hlth Sci Grp.

Brooks, John R. & Wiant, Harry V., Jr. Introduction to BASIC Programming for Foresters. Cooney, Timothy & Allen, Sherhonda, eds. 79p. (Orig.). 1986. pap. text 8.95 (*0-9615391-4-3*) Forest Res Syst.

Brooks, John S. & Pietra, Giuseppe G. Atlas of Microscopic Artifacts & Foreign Materials. Yeh, I-Tien, ed. LC 96-50067. (Illus.). 224p. 1997. text. write for info. (*0-89640-331-9*) Igaku-Shoin.

Brooks, John S., jt. auth. see Weiss, Sharon W.

Brooks, John W. Passport Pal: The Pacific Rim: A Business Traveler's Guide to Fifteen Pacific Rim Destinations, 1999 Edition. 4th ed. (Illus.). viii, 68p. 1998. pap. 19.95 (*0-9655022-2-8*) Passport Pal Pr.

— Passport Pal - The Pacific Rim: A Business Traveler's Guide to Fourteen Pacific Rim Countries, 1998 Edition. 3rd ed. (Illus.). viii, 63p. 1997. pap. 19.95 (*0-9655022-1-X*) Passport Pal Pr.

***Brooks, Jonathan Oswald.** Attributes of the Unified Field & Quantum Gravity. LC 99-94962. 2000. 24.95 (*0-533-13239-8*) Vantage.

Brooks, Joyce. Golden Nuggets (From the Books of Psalms & Proverbs & John) Trust in the Lord. 1998. pap. 7.00 (*0-9654480-8-8*) Gam-Jam Pub.

Brooks, Juanita. Emma Lee. 2nd rev. ed. (Illus.). 108p. 1984. pap. 12.95 (*0-87421-121-2*) Utah St U Pr.

— The History of the Jews in Utah & Idaho, 1853-1950. 252p. 1973. 15.00 (*0-914740-12-1*) Western Epics.

— John Doyle Lee: Zealot, Pioneer Builder, Scapegoat. LC 92-36969. (Illus.). 404p. 1992. reprint ed. pap. 19.95 (*0-87421-162-X*) Utah St U Pr.

— The Mountain Meadows Massacre. LC 62-18053. (Illus.). 352p. 1991. pap. 17.95 (*0-8061-2318-4*) U of Okla Pr.

— Quicksand & Cactus: A Memoir of the Southern Mormon Frontier. LC 92-36970. (Western Experience Ser.). (Illus.). 342p. 1992. reprint ed. pap. 19.95 (*0-87421-163-8*) Utah St U Pr.

Brooks, Juanita, ed. see Stout, Hosea.

Brooks, Judith G. Allergy & Immunology: A Practical Guide for Health Care Professionals. LC 96-39477. 150p. 1997. text 42.95 (*0-398-06735-X*); pap. text 29.95 (*0-398-06736-8*) C C Thomas.

Brooks, Judith K., jt. auth. see Chriss, Michael.

Brooks, Karen. Cuisine of the Rain: Oregon's Extraordinary Foods & Recipes. LC 92-34431. 1993. pap. 14.38 (*0-201-63282-9*) Addison-Wesley.

Brooks, Karen, et al. Agricultural Reform in Russia: A View from the Farm Level. (Discussion Paper Ser.: No. 327). 100p. 1996. pap. 22.00 (*0-8213-3655-X*, 13655) World Bank.

— Atomic Cocktails: Mixed Drinks for Modern Times. LC 97-34026. (Illus.). 96p. 1998. 12.95 (*0-8118-1926-4*) Chronicle Bks.

***Brooks, Karen, et al.** Dude Food: Recipes for the Modern Guy. LC 99-40022. (Illus.). 96p. 2000. 14.95 (*0-8118-1679-6*) Chronicle Bks.

Brooks, Karen G. & Bosker, Gideon. The Global Kitchen. LC 81-12803. 550p. 1981. 19.95 (*0-8362-2104-4*) Andrews & McMeel.

***Brooks, Katherine H.** But Will the the Toilet Flush? A Dear John Letter in Three Acts. (Illus.). 23p. 1998. pap. 3.00 (*1-886467-40-4*) WJM Press.

— Florida Vacation: The Adventures of Marty, Mimmie, Mary & John. 16p. 1998. pap. 3.00 (*1-886467-46-3*) WJM Press.

Brooks, Katherine H. The Last Dinosaur. 40p. (Orig.). 1996. pap. 4.00 (*1-886467-12-9*) WJM Press.

— The Nine Lives of Frank & Natalie. 2nd rev. ed. LC 98-84839. 52p. (Orig.). 1998. pap. 5.00 (*1-886467-33-1*) WJM Press.

— Off Limits. LC 95-61179. 52p. (Orig.). 1995. pap. 4.00 (*1-886467-05-6*) WJM Press.

— Unsung Creatures from A to Z. (Illus.). 44p. (Orig.). 1996. pap. 4.00 (*1-886467-09-9*) WJM Press.

Brooks, Kathleen R. Little Bits of Whimsy: A Pattern Book. Feece, Debra, ed. LC 97-22066. (Illus.). 32p. (Orig.). 1997. pap. 12.95 (*1-885588-15-1*) Chitra Pubns.

— A Pocketful of Whimsy: Five Patchwork Gifts. Feece, Debra, ed. LC 99-32787. (Illus.). 32p. 1999. pap. 12.95 (*1-885588-27-5*) Chitra Pubns.

Brooks, Kaye P. Saved from the Very Start: Growing up in New Jersey Projects. 102p. (YA). 1995. pap. 3.95 (*1-886663-04-1*) Chatman Pub.

Brooks, Keith L. Acts. (Teach Yourself the Bible Ser.). pap. 5.99 (*0-8024-0125-2*, 523) Moody.

— Basic Bible Study. (Teach Yourself the Bible Ser.). pap. 5.99 (*0-8024-0478-2*, 538) Moody.

— Bible Summarized Handbook. 300p. 1990. pap. 13.99 (*0-529-06935-0*, BSH) World Publng.

— Christian Character Course. (Teach Yourself the Bible Ser.). pap. 5.99 (*0-8024-1301-3*, 539) Moody.

— Colossians & Philemon. (Teach Yourself the Bible Ser.). 81p. pap. 5.99 (*0-8024-1525-3*, 530) Moody.

— Ephesians. (Teach Yourself the Bible Ser.). pap. 5.99 (*0-8024-2333-7*, 528) Moody.

— First & Second Thessalonians. (Teach Yourself the Bible Ser.). pap. 5.99 (*0-8024-2645-X*, 531) Moody.

— First Corinthians. (Teach Yourself the Bible Ser.). pap. 5.99 (*0-8024-2649-2*, 525) Moody.

— Galatians. (Teach Yourself the Bible Ser.). pap. 5.99 (*0-8024-2925-4*, 527) Moody.

— Great Prophetic Themes. (Teach Yourself the Bible Ser.). pap. 5.99 (*0-8024-3320-0*, 540) Moody.

— Hebrews: Beauty of Christ Unveiled. (Teach Yourself the Bible Ser.). pap. 5.99 (*0-8024-3507-6*, 534) Moody.

— How to Pray. (Teach Yourself the Bible Ser.). pap. 5.99 (*0-8024-3708-7*, 542) Moody.

— James. (Teach Yourself the Bible Ser.). pap. 5.99 (*0-8024-4227-7*, 534) Moody.

— Luke: Gospel of God's Man. (Teach Yourself the Bible Ser.). pap. 5.99 (*0-8024-5047-4*, 521) Moody.

— Mark. (Teach Yourself the Bible Ser.). pap. 5.99 (*0-8024-5200-0*, 520) Moody.

— Matthew: Gospel of God's King. (Teach Yourself the Bible Ser.). pap. 5.99 (*0-8024-5212-4*, 519) Moody.

— Philippians. (Teach Yourself the Bible Ser.). 1964. pap. 5.99 (*0-8024-6506-4*) Moody.

— Practical Bible Doctrine. (Teach Yourself the Bible Ser.). pap. 5.99 (*0-8024-6733-4*, 543) Moody.

— Revelation. (Teach Yourself the Bible Ser.). pap. 5.99 (*0-8024-7308-3*, 537) Moody.

— Romans. (Teach Yourself the Bible Ser.). pap. 5.99 (*0-8024-7372-5*, 524) Moody.

Brooks, Ken. The Last Rebel Yell. 146p. (Orig.). 1986. pap. 7.95 (*0-9616447-0-2*) Seneca Pk Pub.

Brooks, Kenneth. African-Americans & Other Myths: Confusing Racism with Cultural Diversity. LC 93-73899. 160p. (Orig.). 1993. pap. 13.98 (*0-9639042-3-X*) Amper Pubng.

— Cultural Diversity Without Prejudice: A Guide for Critical Thinking in the 21st Century. LC 95-75515. 110p. (Orig.). 1995. pap. 16.95 (*0-9639042-2-1*) Amper Pubng.

Brooks, Kenneth, jt. auth. see Robinson, Clarence.

Brooks, Kenneth N. Hydrology & the Management of Watersheds. 2nd ed. LC 97-319. (Illus.). 1997. 62.95 (*0-8138-2287-4*) Iowa St U Pr.

Brooks, Kimberly & Brooks, Reggie. Shadows on the Horizon. (Illus.). 136p. 1998. pap. 12.95 (*1-880047-62-4*) Creative Des.

Brooks, Kirsty. Hitching: Tales from the Byways & Superhighways. 1999. pap. text 12.95 (*1-86254-362-3*) Wakefield Pr.

Brooks, L. Anathea. Saving the Seas: Values, Scientists & International Governance. LC 96-78428. 1997. 30.00 (*0-943676-62-2*) MD Sea Grant Col.

Brooks, L. B. This Thousand Years. LC 94-71926. 392p. (Orig.). 1994. pap. 11.99 (*0-88270-711-6*) Bridge-Logos.

***Brooks, Larry.** Darkness Bound. 2000. mass mkt. 6.99 (*0-451-40945-0*, Onyx) NAL.

Brooks, Laura. Country Roads. LC 99-15188. 1999. 16.98 (*1-56799-829-1*, MetroBooks) M Friedman Pub Grp Inc.

***Brooks, Laura.** Greek Isles. LC 00-39340. (Timeless Places Ser.). (Illus.). 2000. write for info. (*1-56799-989-1*, Friedman-Fairfax) M Friedman Pub Grp Inc.

— Monuments. 1998. pap. 10.98 (*1-57717-033-4*) Todtri Prods.

— Palaces. 1999. 10.95 (*1-57717-146-2*) Todtri Prods.

Brooks, Laura. Windmills. LC 99-18048. (Great Architecture Ser.). (Illus.). 120p. 1999. text 16.98 (*1-56799-756-2*) M Friedman Pub Grp Inc.

Brooks, Laurence F. & Babson, W. Warren. As They May Need: A History of the Addison Gilbert Hospital, 1889-1989. LC 89-16395. (Illus.). 360p. 1989. 18.00 (*0-914659-43-X*) Phoenix Pub.

Brooks, Lee. First Ladies of the White House: Washington Thru Nixon. LC 76-86857. (Illus.). 156p. 1969. 9.95 (*0-87319-022-X*) Hallberg Pub Corp.

Brooks, Leigh. Late Bloomer. 1999. mass mkt. 4.99 (*0-8217-5074-7*) NAL.

Brooks, Leonard J. Professional Ethics in Accounting. LC 95-1648. 300p. (C). 1995. pap. 28.75 (*0-314-04603-8*) West Pub.

Brooks-Leonard, John, jt. ed. see Bernstein, Eleanor.

Brooks, Leonard L. & Soule, Margaret W. Celebrating Waynflete: One Hundred Years in the Life of a School. LC 98-60845. (Illus.). 200p. 1998. pap. 27.50 (*0-9664235-0-X*) Waynflete Schl.

Brooks, Leroy, II. PC Fingame: Participant's Manual. 2nd ed. 168p. (C). 1995. per. 30.45 incl. disk (*0-256-13611-4*, Irwn McGrw-H) McGrw-H Hghr Educ.

***Brooks, Leroy D.** Fingame Online 3.0: The Financial Management Decision Game: Participant's Manual 3rd ed. LC 99-31794. 160p. 1999. pap. 38.44 (*0-256-13613-0*) McGraw.

Brooks, Leroy D., II. PC Fingame: The Financial Management Decision Game Participant's Manual. 2nd ed. 204p. (C). 1995. text, per. 30.45 incl. disk (*0-256-20989-8*, Irwn McGrw-H) McGrw-H Hghr Educ.

Brooks, Les, et al. Elric! Gamemaster Screen: Gruesome Gamemaster Gobbets! (Elric Roleplaying Game Ser.). (Illus.). (Orig.). 1994. pap. 14.95 (*1-56882-011-9*, 2902) Chaosium.

Brooks, Les, ed. see Behrendt, Fred, et al.

Brooks, Les, ed. see Dutton, Rick & Freitao, Walter O.

Brooks, Lester. African Achievements: Leaders, Civilizations & Cultures of Ancient Africa. rev. ed. LC 75-105341. (Illus.). 275p. (YA). (gr. 8-12). 1992. reprint ed. pap. 18.95 (*0-9626946-2-2*) De Gustibus Pr.

Brooks, Lester, jt. auth. see Brooks, Pat.

Brooks, Lewis E. Black Genealogy: A Record Keeping Book. 198p. 1992. student ed. 19.95 (*0-9635328-0-4*) L E Brooks.

Brooks, Linda. Rebounding to Better Health: A Practical Guide to the Ultimate Exercise. 96p. (Orig.). 1995. pap. 5.95 (*0-9647265-0-5*) KE Pub.

Brooks, Linda & Haring-Hidor, Marilyn. Career Interventions with Women: A Special Issue of Journal of Career Development. 68p. 1988. pap. 14.95 (*0-89885-431-8*, Kluwer Acad Hman Sci) Kluwer Academic.

Brooks, Linda, jt. auth. see Brown, Duane.

Brooks, Linda, jt. ed. see Brown, Duane.

Brooks, Linda M. The Menace of the Sublime to the Individual Self in Kant, Schiller & Coleridge: The Disintegration of Identity in Romanticism. LC 96-8613. 248p. 1996. text 89.95 (*0-7734-8752-2*) E Mellen.

Brooks, Linton F., jt. ed. see Kanter, Arnold L.

Brooks, Lisa & Freedman, Matt. Renewable Energy Sourcebook Section II: Federal Government R & D-Wind & Ocean Thermal. (Illus.). 24p. (Orig.). 1996. pap. 15.00 (*0-937188-28-X*) Pub Citizen.

Brooks, Lisa, jt. auth. see Riccio, James.

Brooks, Liz, ed. see Nasset, William J.

Brooks, Lloyd D. Business Math. 3rd ed. 1994. text, student ed. 16.95 (*1-56118-869-7*); pap. text, student ed. 8.95 (*1-56118-662-7*) Paradigm MN.

— Business Math. 3rd ed. LC 94-21341. 666p. 1995. pap. text 36.95 (*1-56118-657-0*); pap. text, teacher ed. 36.95 (*1-56118-658-9*) Paradigm MN.

— College Business Mathematics Comprehensive Text. 2nd ed. 428p. 1988. student ed. 5.80 (*0-574-20087-8*) SRA.

— Consultamation, Inc. Word Processing Practice & Applications. 192p. 1982. text 33.00 (*0-07-008081-X*) McGraw.

— Intermediate Word Processing Applications: Job-Based Tasks. 1992. teacher ed. 9.95 (*1-56118-383-0*); student ed. 13.95 (*1-56118-382-2*) Paradigm MN.

— Math: Skill Enhancement. LC 92-44949. 224p. 1994. 10.95 (*1-56118-261-3*) Paradigm MN.

— Math for Workplace Success. 363p. (C). 1991. pap. text 17.95 (*1-56118-257-5*); pap. text, teacher ed. 8.00 (*1-56118-258-3*) Paradigm MN.

— One Hundred & One Spreadsheet Exercises. 144p. 1986. pap. text 15.56 (*0-07-008135-2*) McGraw.

— One Hundred One Advanced Spreadsheet Exercises (Using Lotus 1-2-3, VP-Planner, or Twin) 1990. pap., wbk. ed. 18.64 (*0-07-008186-7*) McGraw.

— One Hundred One Word Processing Exercises. 128p. 1986. pap. text 15.56 (*0-07-008118-2*) McGraw.

Brooks, Lloyd D. & Brooks, Bryant A. Business Presentations Using Harvard Graphics with Version 3.0 Tutorial. LC 92-33029. 1993. 19.50 (*0-02-800407-8*) Glencoe.

— Business Presentations Using Harvard Graphics with Version 3.0 Tutorial. large type ed. 1995. 38.50 (*0-614-09551-4*, L-31428-00) Am Printing Hse.

Brooks, Lloyd D., et al. Business Mathematics. 10th ed. 576p. (YA). (gr. 9-12). 1987. text 24.96 (*0-07-008166-2*) McGraw.

— Reading: Skill Enhancement, Instructor's Guide. LC 92-44949. 98p. 1994. teacher ed. 8.00 (*1-56118-208-7*) Paradigm MN.

***Brooks, Lonnie, et al.** Blues for Dummies. (For Dummies Ser.). 400p. 1998. pap. 24.99 incl. audio compact disk (*0-7645-5080-2*) IDG Bks.

Brooks, Louise. Early History of Divine Science. 1963. 6.95 (*0-686-24363-3*) Divine Sci Fed.

***Brooks, Louise.** Lulu in Hollywood. expanded ed. 2000. pap. 19.95 (*0-8166-3731-8*) U of Minn Pr.

Brooks, Lynn. The History of the National Court Reporters Association: The 7th Decade. 36p. 1995. pap. text 6.95 (*1-881859-09-6*) Natl Ct Report.

Brooks, Lynn, jt. auth. see Brooks, Donna.

Brooks, M., jt. auth. see Kearey, Philip.

Brooks, M., jt. ed. see Barter, V. C.

Brooks, M., ed. see European Geological Societies Staff.

Brooks Manufacturing Co. Arts & Crafts Furniture: The Complete Brooks Catalog of 1912. LC 92-44407. (Illus.). 80p. 1993. reprint ed. pap. 7.95 (*0-486-27471-3*) Dover.

Brooks, Marc D., ed. see Paralan Staff.

Brooks, Maree, ed. see Oman, Lela K.

Brooks, Maria Z. Polish Reference Grammar. LC 74-78500. (Slavistic Printings & Reprintings Ser.: No. 2). 580p. 1976. text 123.10 (*90-279-3313-8*) Mouton.

Brooks, Marilyn, ed. see Hays, Mary.

Brooks, Marlo, ed. see Parvin, Rose A.

Brooks, Marshall. A Brief Illustrated History of the Bookshelf. (Illus.). 64p. 1998. pap. 15.00 (*0-913559-40-7*) Birch Brook Pr.

— A Brief Illustrated History of the Bookshelf. aut. limited num. ed. (Illus.). 64p. 1998. 50.00 (*0-913559-41-5*) Birch Brook Pr.

— A Visit to Pinky Ryder's. deluxe ed. (Illus.). 20p. (Orig.). 1991. 35.00 (*0-933292-19-8*) Arts End.

— A Visit to Pinky Ryder's: A Book to Read Inside a Whale. LC 94-66399. 48p. 1995. bds. 15.00 (*1-882986-18-0*) Smith.

Brooks, Marshall & Smith, Harry. Snow Poems. 12p. 1985. 15.00 (*0-933292-15-5*, Baguette Bks); pap. 5.00 (*0-933292-14-7*, Baguette Bks) Arts End.

Brooks, Marshall, ed. see Baldwin, et al.

Brooks, Marshall, ed. see Mangan, Sherry.

***Brooks, Martha.** Being with Henry. 224p. (YA). (gr. 7-12). 2000. 17.95 (*0-7894-2588-2*, D K Ink) DK Pub Inc.

Brooks, Martha. Bone Dance. 192p. (YA). 1999. mass mkt. 4.50 (*0-440-22791-7*) BDD Bks Young Read.

— Bone Dance. 192p. (YA). (gr. 7 up). Date not set. pap. write for info. (*0-88899-336-6*, Pub. by Gro1undwood-Douglas) Publishers Group.

— Bone Dance. LC 97-10230. (Illus.). 192p. (YA). (gr. 7 up). 1997. 16.95 (*0-531-30021-8*); lib. bdg. 17.99 (*0-531-33021-4*) Orchard Bks Watts.

— Traveling on into the Light: And Other Stories. LC 94-9136. 144p. (YA). (gr. 7 up). 1994. 15.95 (*0-531-06863-3*); lib. bdg. 16.99 (*0-531-08713-1*) Orchard Bks Watts.

— Traveling on into the Light: And Other Stories. 1996. 9.09 (*0-606-09988-3*, Pub. by Turtleback) Demco.

— Two Moons in August. (YA). (gr. 7 up). 1992. 15.95 (*0-316-10979-7*) Little.

— Two Moons in August. (YA). (gr. 8 up). 1998. pap. text 5.95 (*0-88899-170-3*) Publishers Group.

Brooks, Martin G., jt. auth. see Brooks, Jacqueline G.

Brooks, Marvene. The Promise of His Glory. LC 98-90369. 1998. 13.95 (*0-533-12769-6*) Vantage.

Brooks, Mary & Engmann-Hartung, Deedra. Your Child's Speech & Language: Guidelines for Parents. 52p. 1978. pap. text 14.00 (*0-89079-039-6*, 1070) PRO-ED.

Brooks, Mary L. Retirement Communities in Florida: A Consumer's Guide & Directory to Service-Oriented Facilities. LC 92-33930. 164p. 1993. pap. 12.95 (*1-56164-024-7*) Pineapple Pr.

Brooks, Mary R. & Kindred, Hugh M. Multimodal Transport Rules. LC 96-54219. 1997. 102.00 (*90-411-0360-0*) Kluwer Law Intl.

Brooks, Maureen & Ritchie, Joan. Tassie Terms: A Glossary of Tasmanian Words. (Illus.). 192p. (C). 1996. pap. text 29.95 (*0-19-553812-9*) OUP.

Brooks, Maurice. The Appalachians. LC 75-3897. (Illus.). 346p. 1995. pap. 18.95 (*0-89092-005-2*) Seneca Bks.

Brooks, Mazie C. Marriage Records Marshall County Alabama, 1849-1869. fac. ed. iv, 86p. 1982. spiral bd. 15.00 (*0-944619-19-3*) Gregath Pub Co.

Brooks, Meade, et al. How to Make Secure Money: After Experience Years. LC 95-77396. 88p. (Orig.). (C). 1995. pap. 10.00 (*0-9632718-6-5*) A-A Bks Pub.

— Poems & Annotations. limited ed. 31p. (C). pap. 15.00 (*0-9632718-5-7*) A-A Bks Pub.

Brooks, Mel. All American: Musical. 1962. pap. 5.95 (*0-87129-312-9*, A02) Dramatic Pub.

— The 2000-Year-Old Man in the Year 2000: The Book. LC 97-24142. (Illus.). 160p. 1998. pap. 10.00 (*0-06-092992-8*, HarperFlamingo) HarpC.

Brooks, Mel & Henry, Buck. Get Smart. 1967. 5.50 (*0-87129-260-2*, G14) Dramatic Pub.

Brooks, Mel & Reiner, Carl. The 2000 Year Old Man in the Year 2000. LC 97-24142. 160p. 1997. 20.00 (*0-06-017480-3*) HarpC.

Brooks, Mel, jt. auth. see Bradshaw, John.

Brooks, Michael. Instant Rapport. 224p. 1990. mass mkt. 12.99 (*0-446-39133-6*, Pub. by Warner Bks) Little.

— John Ruskin & Victorian Architecture. 356p. (C). 1987. text 40.00 (*0-8135-1205-0*) Rutgers U Pr.

— Quantum Computing & Communications. LC 99-19975. (Illus.). 152p. 1999. pap. 44.95 (*1-85233-091-0*) Spr-Verlag.

Brooks, Michael, ed. Stock Perqs Monitor: A Guide to Popular Benefits for Shareholders of America's Leading Businesses. LC 94-79879. 400p. (Orig.). Date not set. ring bd. 150.00 incl. disk (*0-9641544-3-9*, SPM-P1) Monitor Pubns.

— Stock Perqs Monitor - a Guide to Popular Benefits: For Shareholders of America's Leading Businesses. rev. ed. LC 94-79879. 400p. (Orig.). Date not set. ring bd. 90.00 (*0-9641544-1-2*, SPM-B1) Monitor Pubns.

Brooks, Michael E. In Search of Perfection: Studies from Job. 168p. 1992. pap. 6.95 (*0-945441-13-4*) Res Pubns AR.

Brooks, Michael J., jt. ed. see Horn, Berthold K.

Brooks, Michael W. Subway City: Riding the Trains, Reading New York. LC 96-39309. (Illus.). 295p. 1997. 35.00 (*0-8135-2396-6*) Rutgers U Pr.

Brooks, Miguel F., ed. Kebra Nagast: The Glory of Kings. LC 99-461891. (True Ark of the Covenant Ser.). 193p. 1996. 59.95 (*1-56902-032-9*); pap. 18.95 (*1-56902-033-7*) Red Sea Pr.

Brooks, Mildred J. Southern Stuff. 224p. (Orig.). 1992. pap. 9.00 (*0-380-76491-1*, Avon Bks) Morrow Avon.

Brooks, Nan. Twelve Days of Christmas. (Rebus Sticker Storybks.). (Illus.). 16p. (J). (ps-3). 1998. pap. 3.99 (*0-689-81805-X*) Litle Simon.

— Wee Sing Sleepy-Time Lullabies: With Cassette, 1. (Wee Sing Ser.). (Illus.). 12p. (J). (ps). 1999. pap. 9.99 (*0-8431-7507-9*, Price Stern) Peng Put Young Read.

***Brooks, Nan.** Friendly Farm. (Animals All Around Ser.). 18p. (J). (ps-1). 2000. bds. 5.99 (*1-57584-387-0*) Rdrs Digest.

Brooks, Nan. The Nutcracker, Story Book Set & Advent Calendar. 4p. 1993. bds. 16.95 (*1-56305-503-1*, 3503) Workman Pub.

Brooks, Nan, jt. auth. see Aber, Linda.

Brooks, Nan, jt. auth. see Muldrow, Diane.

Brooks, Nan, ed. see Fischer, Jean.

Brooks, Nancy, ed. see Colantuono, Susan L.

Brooks, Nancy A., jt. auth. see Deegan, Mary Jo.

Brooks, Nancy C., et al. Ocho Siglos de Cuentos y Narraciones de Espana. (gr. 12 up). 1976. pap. text 5.95 (*0-88345-280-4*, 18465) Prentice ESL.

Brooks, Nancy C., jt. tr. see Spindler, Frank M.

Brooks, Nancy G. Arlington House: The Robert E. Lee Memorial. LC 85-18925. (Official National Park Handbook Ser.: No. 133). (Illus.). 48p. 1986. pap. 3.50 (*0-912627-23-9*) Natl Park Serv.

Brooks, Nancy G., ed. see Smith, Jane W.

Brooks, Neal A., et al. A History of Baltimore County. LC 78-31598. (Illus.). 1979. 15.95 (*0-9602326-1-3*) Friends Towson Lib.

Brooks, Neal A., jt. auth. see Parsons, Richard.

Brooks, Ned, et al. Quest for the Green Hills of Earth. (Illus.). 28p. (Orig.). 1995. pap. 5.00 (*0-9603300-4-6*) Purple Mouth.

***Brooks, Nicholas.** Communities & Warfare, 700-1400. LC 99-55759. (Illus.). 2000. 70.00 (*1-85285-155-4*) Hambledon Press.

Brooks, Nicholas. The Early History of the Church of Canterbury. 366p. 1996. pap. 29.95 (*0-7185-0041-5*) Bks Intl VA.

Brooks, Nicholas & Cubitt, Catherine. St. Oswald of Worcester: Life & Influence. LC 95-23869. (Studies in the Early History of Britain: No. 2). (Illus.). 352p. 1998. 95.00 (*0-7185-0003-2*) Bks Intl VA.

Brooks, Nicholas, jt. ed. see Bassett, Steven.

***Brooks, Nigel & Horner, Abigail.** Country Mouse Cottage: How We Lived One Hundred Years Ago. (Illus.). 32p. (J). (gr. k-3). 2000. write for info. (*0-8027-8752-5*) Walker & Co.

— Town Mouse House: How We Lived One Hundred Years Ago. LC 99-55403. (Illus.). 32p. (J). (gr. k-2). 2000. 15.95 (*0-8027-8732-0*) Walker & Co.

Brooks, Noah. Abraham Lincoln & the Downfall of American Slavery. LC 73-14436. (Heroes of the Nations Ser.). reprint ed. 49.50 (*0-404-58254-0*) AMS Pr.

— Lincoln Observed: The Civil War Dispatches of Noah Brooks. Burlingame, Michael, ed. LC 97-41950. 240p. 1998. 25.95 (*0-8018-5842-9*) Johns Hopkins.

— Tales of the Maine Coast. 1980. 8.50 (*0-686-64301-1*) Bookfinger.

Brooks, Noel. Charismatic Ministries in the New Testament. (Orig.). 1988. pap. 5.00 (*0-945478-00-3*) Holmes Coll Bible.

— Ephesians. 1984. pap. 5.95 (*0-911866-02-7*) LifeSprings Res.

— Let There Be Life. 1975. pap. 3.95 (*0-911866-88-4*) LifeSprings Res.

Brooks, Noel, ed. see DiMattio, Joe.

Brooks, Norman E., ed. see Webster, Alan C. & Perry, Paul E.

Brooks, P. M., et al, eds. Basis for Variability of Response to Anti-Rheumatic Drugs. (AAS: Agents & Actions Supplements Ser.: Vol. 24). 300p. 1988. 75.00 (*0-8176-1959-3*) Birkhauser.

Brooks, Pamela, ed. see Allen, Theresa C.

Brooks, Pamela, ed. see Puckett, Ron.

Brooks, Pat. Climb Mount Moriah. 128p. 1974. mass mkt. 5.99 (*0-88368-024-6*) Whitaker Hse.

Brooks, Pat & Brooks, Lester. Spain, 1985. Fisher, Robert C., ed. (Fisher Annotated Travel Guides Ser.). 384p. 1984. 12.95 (*0-8116-0063-7*) NAL.

***Brooks, Patricia.** But for the Grace. 256p. 2000. mass mkt. 5.99 (*0-440-22608-2*) Bantam Dell.

Brooks, Patricia. Connecticut's Best Dining & Wining, 1998. 240p. 1997. pap. 10.95 (*1-889900-00-1*) De Gustibus Pr.

— Falling from Grace: A Molly Piper Mystery. 1998. mass mkt. 5.99 (*0-440-22607-4*) Dell.

***Brooks, Paul.** Rachel Carson: The Writer at Work. 1999. 26.25 (*0-8446-6989-X*) Peter Smith.

Brooks, Paul. Speaking for Nature. LC 82-16997. (Sierra Club Guides Ser.). (Illus.). 320p. 1983. reprint ed. pap. 8.95 (*0-87156-332-0*, Pub. by Sierra) Random.

— The View from Lincoln Hill: Man & the Land in a New England Town. (Illus.). 273p. 1986. reprint ed. 14.95 (*0-944856-05-5*) Lincoln Hist Soc.

Brooks-Pazmany, Kathleen. United States Women in Aviation, 1919-1929. LC 82-10812. Orig. Title: Smithsonian Studies in Air & Space Number 5. (Illus.). 62p. 1991. pap. 13.95 (*0-87474-378-8*) Smithsonian.

Brooks, Peggy, ed. see Travis, Carole A.

Brooks, Penelope, et al, eds. Learning & Cognition in the Mentally Retarded. LC 84-10289. 576p. 1984. text 115.00 (*0-89859-374-3*) L Erlbaum Assocs.

Brooks, Perry. Piero Della Francesca. (Rizzoli Art Ser.). 24p. 1992. pap. 7.95 (*0-8478-1513-7*, Pub. by Rizzoli Intl) St Martin.

Brooks, Peter. Body Work: Objects of Desire in Modern Narrative. LC 92-34163. (Illus.). 384p. 1993. 57.50 (*0-674-07724-5*); pap. 23.50 (*0-674-07725-3*) HUP.

— History, Painting & Narrative: Delacroix's "Moments" (Legenda Special Lecture Ser.: 2). (Orig.). 1998. pap. 49.95 (*1-900755-21-1*, Pub. by E H R C) David Brown.

— The Melodramatic Imagination. (C). 1976. pap. 17.00 (*0-300-06553-1*) Yale U Pr.

— The Novel of Worldliness: Crebillon, Marivaux, Laclos, Stendhal. LC 68-56303. 305p. reprint ed. pap. 94.60 (*0-608-17854-3*, 203264100080) Bks Demand.

— Psychoanalysis & Storytelling. (Bucknell Lectures in Literary Theory). 176p. 1994. pap. 19.95 (*0-631-19008-2*) Blackwell Pubs.

— Reading for the Plot: Design & Intention in Narrative. 363p. 1992. pap. 16.95 (*0-674-74892-1*) HUP.

***Brooks, Peter.** Troubling Confessions: Speaking Guilt in Law & Literature. LC 99-59060. 2000. 24.00 (*0-226-07585-0*) U Ch Pr.

Brooks, Peter. World Elsewhere: A Novel. LC 98-28230. 226p. 1999. 22.00 (*0-684-85333-7*) S&S Trade.

Brooks, Peter & Gewirtz, Paul, eds. Law's Stories: Narrative & Rhetoric in the Law. LC 95-26410. 302p. (C). 1996. 40.00 (*0-300-06675-9*) Yale U Pr.

— Law's Stories: Narrative & Rhetoric in the Law. LC 95-26410. 302p. 1998. pap. 16.00 (*0-300-07490-5*) Yale U Pr.

***Brooks, Peter & Woloch, Alex.** Whose Freud? The Place of Psychoanalysis in Contemporary Culture. LC 00-27261. (Illus.). 352p. 2000. 40.00 (*0-300-08116-2*) Yale U Pr.

***Brooks, Peter & Woloch, Alex, eds.** Whose Freud? The Place of Psychoanalysis in Contemporary Culture. (Illus.). 352p. 2000. pap. 19.95 (*0-300-08745-4*) Yale U Pr.

Brooks, Peter, jt. auth. see Balzac, Honore de.

Brooks, Peter, ed. & intro. see James, Henry.

Brooks, Peter M., et al, eds. Variability in Response to Anti-Rheumatic Drugs. LC 93-2005. (Agents & Actions Supplements Ser.: Vol. 44). xi, 227p. 1993. 81.50 (*0-8176-2869-X*) Birkhauser.

Brooks, Peter N., ed. Reformation Principles & Practice: Essays in Honour of A. G. Dickens. 1980. 83.95 (*0-85967-579-3*, Pub. by Scolar Pr) Ashgate Pub Co.

— Seven-Headed Luther: Essays in Commemoration of Quincentenary, 1483-1983. (Illus.). 1983. 65.00 (*0-19-826648-0*) OUP.

Brooks, Peter Newman. Hymns as Homilies. LC 95-233005. 272p. 1997. pap. 12.95 (*0-85244-281-5*, 1989, Pub. by Gra1cewing) Morehouse Pub.

Brooks, Peter W. Modern Airliner. 2nd ed. (Illus.). 194p. 1982. 18.50 (*0-89745-011-6*); pap. text 12.00 (*0-89745-028-0*) Sunflower U Pr.

Brooks, Philip. Dikembe Mutombo: Mount Mutombo. LC 95-14018. (Sports Stars Ser.). 48p. (J). (gr. 2-8). 1995. lib. bdg. 19.00 (*0-516-04392-7*) Childrens.

— Extraordinary Jewish Americans. LC 97-37535. (Extraordinary People Ser.). 288p. (gr. 5-9). 1998. lib. bdg. 27.75 (*0-516-20609-5*) Childrens.

— Extraordinary Jewish Americans. (Extraordinary People Ser.). (Illus.). (J). (gr. 5-9). 1998. pap. 16.95 (*0-516-26350-1*) Childrens.

— Invaders from Outer Space: Real-Life Stories of UFOs. LC 98-41848. (Eyewitness Readers). (J). (gr. 2-3). 1999. 12.95 (*0-7894-3999-9*); pap. 3.95 (*0-7894-3998-0*) DK Pub Inc.

— Japan. LC 95-1791. (Games People Play Ser.). (Illus.). 64p. (J). (ps-2). 1995. lib. bdg. 23.50 (*0-516-04438-9*) Childrens.

— Michael Jordan: Beyond Air. LC 94-24336. (Sports Stars Ser.). 48p. (J). (gr. 2-8). 1995. lib. bdg. 19.00 (*0-516-04391-9*) Childrens.

— Michael Jordan: Beyond Air. (Sports Stars Ser.). (J). 1995. pap. 5.95 (*0-516-44391-7*) Childrens.

— Oprah Winfrey: A Voice for the People. LC 98-35382. (Book Report Biography Ser.). 128p. (J). (gr. 6-8). 1999. 22.00 (*0-531-11563-1*) Watts.

***Brooks, Philip.** Oprah Winfrey: A Voice for the People. (Illus.). 2000. pap. 6.95 (*0-531-16406-3*) Watts.

Brooks, Philip. Steffi Graf: Tennis Champ. LC 95-40244. (Sports Stars Ser.). (Illus.). 48p. (J). (gr. 3-4). 1996. lib. bdg. 19.00 (*0-516-04397-8*) Childrens.

— The U. S. Holocaust Memorial Museum. LC 95-18633. (Cornerstones to Freedom Ser.). (Illus.). 32p. (J). (gr. 4-7). 1996. lib. bdg. 19.50 (*0-516-20007-0*) Childrens.

— United States. LC 95-49450. (Games People Play Ser.). (Illus.). 64p. (J). (gr. 4-6). 1996. lib. bdg. 23.50 (*0-516-04442-7*) Childrens.

— The United States Holocaust Memorial Museum. (Cornerstones to Freedom Ser.). 32p. (J). (gr. 4-6). 1997. pap. 5.95 (*0-516-26071-5*) Childrens.

Brooks, Philip C. Research in Archives: The Use of Unpublished Primary Sources. LC 69-19273. (Midway Reprint Ser.). 138p. reprint ed. pap. 42.80 (*0-608-18233-8*, 205664100078) Bks Demand.

Brooks, Philip R. & Hayes, Edward F., eds. State-to-State Chemistry. LC 77-14164. (ACS Symposium Ser.: No. 56). 1977. 35.95 (*0-8412-0386-5*) Am Chemical.

— State-to-State Chemistry. LC 77-14164. (ACS Symposium Ser.: Vol. 56). 271p. 1977. reprint ed. pap. 84.10 (*0-608-03939-X*, 206438600009) Bks Demand.

Brooks, Phillips. The Joy of Preaching. LC 89-2549. 240p. 1989. pap. 12.99 (*0-8254-2276-0*, Kregel Class) Kregel.

— Selected Sermons. Scarlett, William, ed. LC 79-142610. (Essay Index Reprint Ser.). 1977. 22.95 (*0-8369-2146-1*) Ayer.

***Brooks, Phyllis & Guy, Basil, eds.** That Infernal Affair. Loy, J. Robert, tr. from FRE. LC 98-18697. (Eighteenth-Century French Intellectual History Ser.: Vol. 8). XII, 292p. (C). 1999. text 54.95 (*0-8204-4004-3*) P Lang Pubng.

Brooks, Phyllis, jt. ed. see Wyant, Susan.

Brooks, Phyllis, tr. see Faure, Bernard.

Brooks, Phyllis, tr. see Robinet, Isabelle.

Brooks, Phyllis, tr. see Stein, Rolf A.

Brooks, Pierce R. Officer down Code Three. LC 75-23841. 1975. 9.95 (*0-916070-01-8*, MTI Film & Video) Coronet.

Brooks, Polly S. Cleopatra: Goddess of Egypt, Enemy of Rome. LC 95-10688. (Illus.). 160p. (YA). (gr. 7 up). 1995. lib. bdg. 16.89 (*0-06-023608-6*) HarpC Child Bks.

***Brooks, Polly Schoyer.** Beyond the Myth: The Story of Joan of Arc. 178p. (YA). (gr. 7 up). 1999. pap. 8.95 (*0-395-98138-7*) HM.

— Queen Eleanor: Independent Spirit of the Medieval World: A Biography of Eleanor of Aquitaine. 192p. (YA). (gr. 7). 1999. pap. 8.95 (*0-395-98139-5*) HM.

Brooks, R. G. Site Planning. (Illus.). 512p. (C). 1987. text 64.60 (*0-13-811258-4*) P-H.

Brooks, R. R., et al, eds. Williamstown: The First Two Hundred Years, 1753-1953. (Illus.). 458p. 1996. reprint ed. lib. bdg. 48.00 (*0-8328-5039-X*) Higginson Bk Co.

Brooks, R. R., jt. auth. see Malaisse, F.

Brooks, R. R., ed. see Kovalevsky, A. L.

Brooks, R. T. A Place to Start: The Bible As a Guide for Today. 120p. 1983. reprint ed. 4.95 (*0-86683-708-6*) Harper SF.

Brooks, R. T., ed. Ask the Bible. LC 83-3841. 400p. 1983. write for info. (*0-672-52765-0*) Macmillan.

Brooks, Rachelle, jt. auth. see Daniels, Cynthia R.

Brooks, Randy. Barbwire Holds Its Ground. 32p. 1981. pap. 3.50 (*0-913719-16-1*, High Coo Pr) Brooks Books.

— Me Too! (Chapbks.: No. 17). 40p. 1985. 10.00 (*0-913719-83-8*, High Coo Pr); pap. 3.50 (*0-913719-82-X*, High Coo Pr) Brooks Books.

— The Rosebud Bursts. 40p. 1979. pap. 3.50 (*0-913719-67-6*, High Coo Pr) Brooks Books.

Brooks, Randy & Brooks, Shirley. In Her Blue Eyes: Jessica Poems. (Brooks Books Chapbooks Ser.). (Illus.). 32p. 1998. pap. 5.00 (*0-913719-96-X*, High Coo Pr) Brooks Books.

Brooks, Randy & Brooks, Shirley, eds. Haiku Review '84. 76p. (Orig.). 1984. pap. 5.00 (*0-913719-71-4*, High Coo Pr) Brooks Books.

— Haiku Review '87. 72p. (Orig.). 1987. pap. 5.00 (*0-913719-87-0*, High Coo Pr) Brooks Books.

Brooks, Randy & Gurga, Lee, eds. Midwest Haiku Anthology. 128p. 1992. 15.00 (*0-913719-94-3*, High Coo Pr) Brooks Books.

Brooks, Randy, ed. see Swede, George.

Brooks, Randy M., ed. see Gurga, Lee.

Brooks, Ray. Blowing Zen: Finding an Authentic Life. LC 99-34947. 288p. 2000. pap. 12.00 (*0-915811-85-5*, Pub. by H J Kramer Inc) Publishers Group.

Brooks, Raymond C., VI. Winging It with the Flying Colonel. LC 97-77528. (Illus.). 176p. 1997. write for info. (*0-944641-28-8*) Greenwich Pub Group.

Brooks, Rebecca. Inside Art: Culture History Expression, Bk. 1. Crawford, A. F., ed. (Illus.). 224p. (J). (gr. 7). 1992. teacher ed. 40.00 (*0-87443-103-4*); text 44.40 (*0-87443-101-8*) Benson.

— Inside Art: Culture History Expression, Bk. 2. Crawford, A. F., ed. (Illus.). 240p. 1992. teacher ed. 40.00 (*0-87443-104-2*); text 44.40 (*0-87443-102-6*) Benson.

Brooks, Rebecca, et al. Healthcare Controller's Manual. Barcus, Sam W., III, ed. 464p. 1995. 150.00 (*0-7913-2589-X*) Warren Gorham & Lamont.

— Through Their Eyes, Intermediate Level: A Sequentially Developed Art Program, Grades 4-6. Crawford, Ann F., ed. (Illus.). 288p. 1989. ring bd., suppl. ed. 99.92 (*0-87443-087-9*) Benson.

— Through Their Eyes, Primary Level: A Sequentially Developed Art Program, Grades 1-3. Crawford, Ann F., ed. (Illus.). 280p. 1989. ring bd., suppl. ed. 99.92 (*0-87443-086-0*) Benson.

Brooks, Reggie, jt. auth. see Brooks, Kimberly.

***Brooks, Richard.** Definitive Data Window. LC 99-55658. 704p. (C). 2000. pap. text 39.95 incl. cd-rom (*0-201-70224-X*) Addson-Wesley Educ.

Brooks, Richard. Great Is Your Faithfulness (Lamentations) 1989. pap. 10.99 (*0-85234-257-8*, Pub. by Evangelical Pr) P & R Pubng.

— Lamb Is All the Glory (Revelation) (Welwyn Commentary Ser.). 1986. pap. 11.99 (*0-85234-229-2*, Pub. by Evangelical Pr) P & R Pubng.

— PFC Programmar's Reference Manual. LC 98-3861. 368p. 1998. pap. 37.95 (*1-884777-55-4*) Manning Pubns.

— Song Of Songs. 1999. pap. text 12.99 (*1-85792-486-X*) Christian Focus.

— String of Pearls. 1990. pap. 8.99 (*0-85234-280-2*, Pub. by Evangelical Pr) P & R Pubng.

Brooks, Richard A., ed. Critical Bibliography of French Literature Vol. 4A: The 18th Century-Supplement. LC 47-3282. 1968. 75.00 (*0-8156-2009-8*) Syracuse U Pr.

Brooks, Richard A., jt. ed. see Alden, Douglas W.

Brooks, Richard A., jt. ed. see Hall, H. Gaston.

Brooks, Richard A., jt. ed. see LaCharite, Raymond C.

B

Brooks, Richard E., pref. Country-U. S. A. Twenty-Four Hours in Rural America. (Illus.). 192p. 1989. 29.95 (*0-9624617-0-9*) Silver Image.

Brooks, Richard H., et al. An Archeological Inventory Report of the Owlshead/Amargosa-Mojave Basin Planning Units of the Southern California Desert Area. (Illus.). 176p. (C). 1981. reprint ed. pap. text 18.75 (*1-55567-396-1*) Coyote Press.

Brooks, Richard M., jt. auth. see Kasavana, Michael L.

Brooks, Richard O. Green Justice: The Environment & the Courts. 2nd ed. Hoban, Thomas M., ed. (C). 1996. pap. text 26.00 (*0-8133-2603-6*, Pub. by Westview) HarpC.

Brooks, Richard R. & Iyengar, Sundararaja. Multi-Sensor Fusion. LC 97-29569. 416p. (C). 1997. text 89.00 incl. disk (*0-13-901653-8*) P-H.

***Brooks, Risa.** Political-military Relations & the Stability of Arab Regimes. LC 99-219926. (Adelphi Papers: 324). (Illus.). 92p. 1999. pap. text 25.95 (*0-19-922420-X*) OUP.

Brooks, Robert. So That's How I Was Born! LC 81-20859. (Illus.). 48p. (J). (ps-3). 1993. pap. 5.95 (*0-671-78344-0*) S&S Bks Yung.

Brooks, Robert, et al, eds. Differential Geometry: Proceedings, Special Year, Maryland 1981-1982. (Progress in Mathematics Ser.: Vol. 32). 263p. 1983. 45.00 (*0-8176-3134-8*) Birkhauser.

— Geometry of the Spectrum: 1993 Joint Summer Research Conference on Spectral Geometry, July 17-23, 1993, University of Washington, Seattle. LC 94-26306. (Contemporary Mathematical Society Ser.: Vol. 173). 299p. 1994. pap. 58.00 (*0-8218-5185-3*, CONM/173) Am Math.

Brooks, Robert, jt. auth. see Gup, Benton E.

Brooks, Robert A. Ennis & Roman Tragedy. Connor, W. R., ed. LC 81-2642. (Monographs in Classical Studies). 1981. reprint ed. lib. bdg. 38.95 (*0-405-14030-4*) Ayer.

— Roman Epistle. LC 83-21044. 72p. (Orig.). 1984. pap. 8.95 (*0-87233-072-9*) Bauhan.

Brooks, Robert A., compiled by. Gods & Heroes of Ancient Greece: An Illustrated Wallchart. 1995. bds. 19.95 (*0-8078-6500-1*) U of NC Pr.

Brooks, Robert C. Bibliography of Municipal Problems & City Conditions. LC 78-112527. (Rise of Urban America Ser.). 1973. reprint ed. 25.95 (*0-405-02439-8*) Ayer.

— Corruption in American Politics & Life. LC 73-19133. (Politics & People Ser.). 326p. 1974. reprint ed. 24.95 (*0-405-05858-6*) Ayer.

— Deliver Us from Dictators. 1977. 17.95 (*0-8369-7154-X*, 7986) Ayer.

Brooks, Robert E. The Brain People & the New Humans: A History. LC 86-70386. 340p. 1986. pap. 9.95 (*0-936339-07-1*) Circa Pr Portland.

— Free Will: An Ultimate Illusion. LC 86-72701. 136p. 1987. 14.95 (*0-936339-10-1*); pap. 9.95 (*0-936339-09-8*) Circa Pr Portland.

— The Human Position. Lehnhoff, Nora, ed. LC 87-30935. 149p. 1988. 14.95 (*0-936339-12-8*); pap. 9.95 (*0-936339-11-X*) Circa Pr Portland.

***Brooks, Robert Edwin.** Building Financial Derivatives Applications with C++ LC 99-45994. 232p. 2000. write for info. (*1-56720-287-X*, Quorum Bks) Greenwood.

Brooks, Robert L. The Arthur Site: Settlement & Subsistence Structure at a Washita River Phase Village. (Studies in Oklahoma's Past: Vol. 15). (Illus.). 170p. (C). 1987. pap. text 6.50 (*1-881346-08-0*) Univ OK Archeol.

— The Talihina Project: Survey & Testing of the Proposed Talihina Wastewater Treatment Plant Improvements, LeFlore County, Oklahoma. (Archeological Resource Survey Report: Vol. 15). (Illus.). 82p. (C). 1982. pap. text 5.00 (*1-881346-10-2*) Univ OK Archeol.

Brooks, Robert L., et al. Prehistoric Farmers of the Washita River Valley: Settlement & Subsistence Patterns During Plains Village Period. (Archeological Resource Survey Report: No. 23). (Illus.). 172p. (C). 1985. pap. text 6.00 (*1-881346-16-1*) Univ OK Archeol.

Brooks, Robert L., jt. auth. see Wyckoff, Don G.

Brooks, Robert P. Agrarian Revolution in Georgia, 1865-1912. LC 73-129939. 129p. 1970. reprint ed. lib. bdg. 35.00 (*0-8371-1603-1*, BRG&) Greenwood.

Brooks, Robert P. The Agrarian Revolution in Georgia, 1865-1912. LC 72-181919. reprint ed. 31.50 (*0-404-00007-X*) AMS Pr.

— Georgia Studies, Selected Writings of Robert Preston Brooks. LC 69-17565. (Essay Index Reprint Ser.). 1977. 21.95 (*0-8369-1025-7*) Ayer.

Brooks, Robert R. Noble Metals & Biological Systems. 416p. 1992. lib. bdg. 179.00 (*0-8493-6164-8*, QP532) CRC Pr.

— When Labor Organizes. LC 76-156407. (American Labor Ser., No. 2). (Illus.). 1971. reprint ed. 25.95 (*0-405-02916-0*) Ayer.

Brooks, Robert R., ed. Plants That Hyperaccummulate Heavy Metals. LC 97-43257. (A CAB International Publication). (Illus.). 392p. 1998. text 100.00 (*0-85199-236-6*) OUP.

Brooks, Robert W. Systematics & Bionomics of Anthophora: The Bomboides Group & Species Groups of the New World (Hymenoptera: Apoidea, Anthophoridae) fac. ed. LC 82-40445. (University of California Publications in Entomology: No. 98). (Illus.). 96p. 1983. reprint ed. pap. 30.00 (*0-7837-8128-8*, 204793500008) Bks Demand.

Brooks, Robin R. Latin for Elementary School Students. 16p. 1991. pap. text 3.05 (*0-939507-23-4*, B8) Amer Classical.

Brooks, Rodney, jt. ed. see Steels, Luc.

Brooks, Rodney A. Cambrian Intelligence. LC 99-17220. (Illus.). 225p. 1999. pap. text 25.00 (*0-262-52263-2*, Bradford Bks) MIT Pr.

— Cambrian Intelligence: The Early History of the New AI. 1999. 60.00 (*0-262-02468-3*) MIT Pr.

— Model-Based Computer Vision. LC 84-2416. (Computer Science: Artificial Intelligence Ser.: No. 14). (Illus.). 162p. reprint ed. pap. 50.30 (*0-8357-1526-4*, 207035100088) Bks Demand.

Brooks, Rodney A. & Maes, Pattie, eds. Artificial Life IV: Proceedings of the Fourth International Workshop on the Synthesis & Simlulation of Living Systmes. (Bradford Series in Complex Adaptive Systems). (Illus.). 740p. 1994. pap. text 65.00 (*0-262-52190-3*, Bradford Bks) MIT Pr.

Brooks, Roger, ed. Unanswered Questions: Theological Views of Jewish-Catholic Relations. LC 87-40353. (C). 1995. reprint ed. pap. text 14.95 (*0-268-01902-9*) U of Notre Dame Pr.

Brooks, Roger, jt. auth. see Noble, James.

Brooks, Roger, tr. see Neusner, Jacob, ed.

Brooks, Roger B. & Wilson, Larry W. Inventory Record Accuracy: Unleashing the Power of Cycle Counting. LC 92-60660. 175p. 1993. 107.00 (*0-939246-28-7*) Wiley.

— Inventory Record Accuracy: Unleashing the Power of Cycle Counting. 192p. 1995. 45.00 (*0-471-13224-1*) Wiley.

Brooks, Romaine. Portraits, Tableaux, Dessins. LC 75-12306. (Homosexuality Ser.). (Illus.). 1980. reprint ed. 13.95 (*0-405-07396-8*) Ayer.

Brooks, Romaine & Breeskin, Adelyn D. Romaine Brooks, "Thief of Souls" LC 79-150515. (Illus.). 144p. reprint ed. pap. 44.70 (*0-608-11100-7*, 205119700086) Bks Demand.

Brooks, Ron, et al. The Effective Teaching of History. LC 92-44657. (Effective Teacher Ser.). 1993. pap. text. write for info. (*0-582-05915-1*) Longman.

Brooks, Ron, jt. auth. see Geisler, Norman L.

Brooks, Ron, jt. illus. see Wild, Margaret.

Brooks, Ronald K. A Flint, a Sponge or a Honeycomb. 1994. pap. 7.95 (*1-55673-583-9*, 7982) CSS OH.

Brooks, Ronald M., jt. auth. see Geisler, Norman L.

Brooks, Rosetta, contrib. by. William T. Wiley: One Man's Moon . . . (Illus.). 24p. (Orig.). 1992. pap. 20.00 (*1-879173-09-3*) Locks Gallery.

Brooks, Rosetta & Whitney Museum of American Art Staff. Kienholz: A Retrospective. (Illus.). 304p. 1996. 85.00 (*1-881616-68-1*) Dist Art Pubs.

Brooks, Rosetta, jt. auth. see Foulkes, Lynn.

Brooks, Roy L. Basic Law Text: Civil Procedure. (Winning in Law School Ser.). 200p. (Orig.). (C). 1992. pap. text 12.95 (*0-915667-19-3*) Spectra Pub Co.

— Critical Procedure. LC 98-13881. 284p. 1998. 35.00 (*0-89089-693-3*) Carolina Acad Pr.

— Integration or Separation? A Strategy for Racial Equality. LC 96-16935. 352p. 1996. 37.95 (*0-674-13295-5*) HUP.

— Integration or Separation? A Strategy for Racial Equality, Vol. 1. 348p. 1999. pap. 18.95 (*0-674-45645-9*) HUP.

— Questions & Answers: Civil Procedure. (Winning in Law School Ser.: Bk. 5). 152p. (Orig.). 1988. pap. text 12.95 (*0-915667-10-X*) Spectra Pub Co.

— Rethinking the American Race Problem. 240p. 1990. 45.00 (*0-520-06886-6*, Pub. by U CA Pr) Cal Prin Full Svc.

— Rethinking the American Race Problem. 1992. pap. 17.95 (*0-520-07878-0*, Pub. by U CA Pr) Cal Prin Full Svc.

Brooks, Roy L., ed. When Sorry Isn't Enough: The Controversy over Apologies & Reparations for Human Injustice. LC 99-6248. (Critical America Ser.). 416p. 1999. pap. 22.95 (*0-8147-1332-7*); text 60.00 (*0-8147-1331-9*) NYU Pr.

Brooks, Roy L., et al. Civil Rights Litigation. 150p. (C). 1996. pap. text, suppl. ed. 12.50 (*0-89089-004-8*) Carolina Acad Pr.

— Civil Rights Litigation: Cases & Perspectives. LC 94-73848. 1550p. (C). 1995. boxed set 90.00 (*0-89089-692-5*) Carolina Acad Pr.

***Brooks, Roy L., et al.** Civil Rights Litigation: Cases & Perspectives. 1250p. 2000. boxed set. write for info. (*0-89089-691-7*) Carolina Acad Pr.

Brooks, Roy L., et al. Civil Rights Litigation: Constitution & Statuatory Supplement. (Orig.). 1996. pap. 15.00 (*0-614-30901-8*) Carolina Acad Pr.

Brooks, Rusty, jt. auth. see Moore, Allen B.

Brooks, Sandra. I Can Pray to God. Beegle, Shirley, ed. LC 82-80031. (Happy Day Bks.). (Illus.). 24p. (Orig.). (J). (ps). 1994. reprint ed. pap. 1.99 (*0-7847-0258-6*, 04208) Standard Pub.

— Yes, You Can, Moses! (Happy Day Bks.). (Illus.). 24p. (J). (ps). 1995. pap. 1.99 (*0-7847-0355-8*, 04235) Standard Pub.

Brooks, Sandra A. Obedience Will Bring the Rain. 38p. 1997. pap. 2.00 (*0-9665108-0-1*) Keeping Word.

Brooks, Sandra H., jt. auth. see Gentz, William H.

Brooks, Sarah W. English Poetry & Poets. LC 72-37511. (Essay Index Reprint Ser.). 1977. reprint ed. 26.95 (*0-8369-2537-8*) Ayer.

Brooks-Scott, Sandra. Handbook of Mobilization in the Management of Children with Neurological Disorders. LC 98-32457. 112p. 1999. text 27.50 (*0-7506-7025-8*) Buttrwrth-Heinemann.

— Mobilization for the Neurologically Involved Child: Assessment & Application Strategies for Pe. 1997. pap. text 54.00 (*0-12-785061-9*) Acad Pr.

Brooks, Sean & Knowles, Alison, eds. Education for Action: Undergraduate & Graduate Programs That Focus on Social Change. 3rd expanded ed. 136p. 1995. pap. 8.95 (*0-935028-64-1*) Inst Food & Develop.

Brooks, Sherry. 101 Plus Great Gift-Giving Ideas: For Special Friends, Secret Pals...To Show You Care. (Giftables Ser.). 1998. pap. 5.99 (*0-932081-61-4*) Victory Hse.

Brooks, Shirley, jt. auth. see Brooks, Randy.

Brooks, Shirley, jt. auth. see Winters, Sandy.

Brooks, Shirley, jt. ed. see Brooks, Randy.

***Brooks, Shirley Lomax.** Argentina Cooks! Treasured Recipes from the Nine Regions of Argentina. 330p. 2000. 24.95 (*0-7818-0829-4*) Hippocrene Bks.

Brooks Staff. Using Maple for College Algebra. (Mathematics Ser.). 1996. mass mkt., student ed. 16.00 (*0-534-34757-6*) Brooks-Cole.

Brooks, Stella. The Boy Who Ate Too Slowly. (Illus.). 10p. (J). (gr. 3). 1998. pap. 5.99 (*1-57532-160-2*) Press-Tige Pub.

— The Boy Who Would Not Go to Bed. (Illus.). 10p. (J). (gr. 3). 1998. pap. 5.99 (*1-57532-159-9*) Press-Tige Pub.

Brooks, Stephen. Canadian Democracy: An Introduction. 2nd ed. (Illus.). 398p. 1996. pap. text 39.95 (*0-19-541205-2*) OUP.

***Brooks, Stephen.** Canadian Democracy: An Introduction. 3rd ed. (Illus.). 416p. 2000. pap. text 35.00 (*0-19-541503-5*) OUP.

Brooks, Stephen. Public Policy in Canada: An Introduction. 3rd ed. LC 99-182452. (Illus.). 312p. 1998. pap. text 29.95 (*0-19-541272-9*) OUP.

Brooks, Stephen & Gagnon, Alain G. Social Scientists & Politics in Canada: Between Clerisy & Vanguard. 168p. (C). 1988. text 60.00 (*0-7735-0663-2*, Pub. by McG-Queens Univ Pr) CUP Services.

— Social Scientists, Policy & the State. LC 89-22771. 193p. 1990. 57.95 (*0-275-93449-7*, C3449, Greenwood Pr) Greenwood.

Brooks, Stephen & Gagnon, Alain-G., eds. The Political Influence of Ideas: Policy Communities & the Social Sciences. LC 93-23680. 256p. 1994. 65.00 (*0-275-94333-X*, Praeger Pubs) Greenwood.

Brooks, Stephen, jt. auth. see Mound, Laurence A.

Brooks, Stephenson H. Matthew's Community: The Evidence of his Special Sayings Material. (JSNTS Ser.: Vol. 16). 1987. pap. 23.75 (*1-85075-108-0*, Pub. by Sheffield Acad) CUP Services.

Brooks, Steve. Phillip Blanc in San Francisco. (Illus.). 20p. 1972. pap. 3.00 (*0-915572-12-5*) Panjandrum.

Brooks, Stewart M., et al. Handbook of Infectious Diseases. 1980. 14.00 (*0-316-10968-1*, Little Brwn Med Div) Lppncott W & W.

***Brooks, Sue.** Fun with African Animals Stencils. (Little Activity Bks.). (Illus.). (J). 1999. pap. 1.00 (*0-486-40758-6*) Dover.

Brooks, Sue. Nature Stencil Designs. LC 95-49191. (Illus.). 80p. 1996. pap. 6.95 (*0-486-29092-1*) Dover.

Brooks, Sue M., jt. auth. see Anderson, M. G.

Brooks, Susan. Any Girl Can Rule the World. LC 98-2519. 224p. (YA). (gr. 9 up). 1998. pap. 12.95 (*1-57749-068-1*) Fairview Press.

— The Geography of the Earth. (J). (gr. 3-7). 1996. 17.95 (*0-614-15687-4*) OUP.

***Brooks, Susan & Schumacher, Udo, eds.** Metastasis Methods & Protocols. (Methods in Molecular Medicine Ser.). 500p. 2000. 99.50 (*0-89603-610-3*) Humana.

***Brooks, Susan Leigh.** TV & Me: A Beginning Book of Activities to Help Middle School Students. 96p. (YA). (gr. 7-10). 2000. pap. 18.95 (*1-877673-40-4*) Cottonwood Pr.

Brooks, Susan W. & Senatori, Susan M. See the Paintings: A Handbook for Art Appreciation in the Classroom. 95p. (Orig.). 1988. pap. 12.95 (*0-935493-13-1*, RRB 369) Modern Learn Pr.

Brooks, Suzanne, ed. see Tutashinda, Lazima.

Brooks, T. Open Sesame Octet. 1995. pap. text 23.00 (*0-7935-4828-4*, 00000678) H Leonard.

***Brooks, T. & Marsh, E.** Complete Directory Prime Time. 1999. pap. 24.95 (*0-345-42923-0*) Ballantine Pub Grp.

***Brooks, Ted.** I Was a Flakey Preacher. 152p. 1999. pap. 12.00 (*1-894169-79-4*, Guardian Bks) Essence Publ.

***Brooks, Terri.** Words' Worth: A Handbook on Writing & Selling Nonfiction. 224p. (C). 1999. pap. 13.95 (*1-57766-095-1*) Waveland Pr.

***Brooks, Terry.** Angel Fire East. LC 99-26026. (Trolltown Ser.). 336p. 1999. pap. 25.95 (*0-345-37964-0*, Del Rey) Ballantine Pub Grp.

— Angel Fire East. 2000. mass mkt. 6.99 (*0-345-43525-7*, Del Rey) Ballantine Pub Grp.

Brooks, Terry. The Black Unicorn. 320p. 1988. mass mkt. 6.99 (*0-345-33528-7*, Del Rey) Ballantine Pub Grp.

— The Black Unicorn. (Magic Kingdom of Landover Novel Ser.). 1988. 12.09 (*0-606-01234-6*, Pub. by Turtleback) Demco.

— The Druid of Shannara. 384p. 1992. mass mkt. 6.99 (*0-345-37559-9*, Del Rey) Ballantine Pub Grp.

— The Druid of Shannara. (Heritage of Shannara Ser.: Bk. 2). 1997. pap. 6.99 (*0-345-91131-8*, Del Rey) Ballantine Pub Grp.

— The Druid of Shannara. (Heritage of Shannara Ser.). 1992. 12.09 (*0-606-01237-0*, Pub. by Turtleback) Demco.

— The Elf Queen of Shannara. (Heritage of Shannara Ser.: Bk. 3). 1993. mass mkt. 6.99 (*0-345-37558-0*, Del Rey) Ballantine Pub Grp.

— The Elf Queen of Shannara. (Heritage of Shannara Ser.: Bk. 3). 1997. pap. 6.99 (*0-345-91132-6*, Del Rey) Ballantine Pub Grp.

— The Elf Queen of Shannara. (Heritage of Shannara Ser.). 1993. 12.09 (*0-606-02627-4*, Pub. by Turtleback) Demco.

— The Elfstones of Shannara. (Shannara Ser.: Bk. 2). 480p. 1983. mass mkt. 6.99 (*0-345-28554-9*, Del Rey) Ballantine Pub Grp.

— The Elfstones of Shannara. (Shannara Ser.: Bk. 2). 1996. mass mkt. 6.99 (*0-345-90956-9*, Del Rey) Ballantine Pub Grp.

— The Elfstones of Shannara. (Shannara Ser.: Bk. 2). 1997. mass mkt. 6.99 (*0-345-91128-8*, Del Rey) Ballantine Pub Grp.

— The Elfstones of Shannara. LC 81-69187. (Shannara Ser.: Bk. 2). 1982. 12.09 (*0-606-03402-1*, Pub. by Turtleback) Demco.

— First King of Shannara, Vol.. 8. 1997. mass mkt. 6.99 (*0-345-39653-7*, Del Rey) Ballantine Pub Grp.

— The King of Shannara. (Shannara Ser.). (YA). (gr. 9 up). 1996. 23.00 (*0-614-15579-7*, Del Rey) Ballantine Pub Grp.

***Brooks, Terry.** A Knight of the Word. LC 98-5471. 309p. 1998. 25.95 (*0-345-37963-2*, Del Rey) Ballantine Pub Grp.

— A Knight of the Word Num. 2: Trolltown. 1999. mass mkt. 6.99 (*0-345-42464-6*) Ballantine Pub Grp.

Brooks, Terry. Magic Kingdom for Sale - Sold! 324p. 1986. 16.95 (*0-345-31757-2*, Ballantine) Ballantine Pub Grp.

— Magic Kingdom for Sale - Sold! 320p. 1987. mass mkt. 6.99 (*0-345-31758-0*, Ballantine) Ballantine Pub Grp.

— Magic Kingdom for Sale - Sold! 1986. 12.09 (*0-606-02550-2*, Pub. by Turtleback) Demco.

***Brooks, Terry.** Menace Fantome. 1999. pap. 12.95 (*2-265-06849-7*) Midwest European Pubns.

Brooks, Terry. Running with the Demon. 434p. 1998. mass mkt. 6.99 (*0-345-42258-9*, Del Rey) Ballantine Pub Grp.

— The Scions of Shannara. 432p. 1991. mass mkt. 6.99 (*0-345-37074-0*, Del Rey) Ballantine Pub Grp.

— The Scions of Shannara. (Heritage of Shannara Ser.: Bk. 1). 1997. pap. 6.99 (*0-345-91130-X*, Del Rey) Ballantine Pub Grp.

Brooks, Terry. The Scions of Shannara. (Heritage of Shannara Ser.). 1991. 12.09 (*0-606-01236-2*, Pub. by Turtleback) Demco.

Brooks, Terry. The Shannara Trilogy: The Sword of Shannara, The Elfstone of Shannara, & Wishsong of Shannara, 3 vols., Set. 1988. pap., boxed set 17.97 (*0-345-35833-3*, Del Rey) Ballantine Pub Grp.

— Star Wars: Episode I: The Phantom Menace. (Star Wars Ser.). 1999. write for info. (*0-345-43754-3*) Ballantine Pub Grp.

***Brooks, Terry.** Star Wars: Episode I: The Phantom Menace. LC 98-96827. (Star Wars Ser.). 324p. 1999. 25.00 (*0-345-42765-3*, Del Rey) Ballantine Pub Grp.

— Star Wars: Episode I: The Phantom Menace. (Star Wars Ser.). 2000. mass mkt. 7.50 (*0-345-43411-0*) Ballantine Pub Grp.

Brooks, Terry. The Sword of Shannara. (Shannara Ser.: Bk. 1). 736p. 1983. mass mkt. 6.99 (*0-345-31425-5*, Ballantine) Ballantine Pub Grp.

— The Sword of Shannara. (Shannara Ser.: Bk. 1). 1996. mass mkt. 6.99 (*0-345-90957-7*, Del Rey) Ballantine Pub Grp.

— The Sword of Shannara. (Shannara Ser.: Bk. 1). 1997. mass mkt. 6.99 (*0-345-91127-X*, Del Rey) Ballantine Pub Grp.

— Sword of Shannara. (J). 1977. 12.09 (*0-606-01377-6*, Pub. by Turtleback) Demco.

— The Talismans of Shannara. 448p. 1994. mass mkt. 6.99 (*0-345-38674-4*, Del Rey) Ballantine Pub Grp.

— The Talismans of Shannara. (Heritage of Shannara Ser.: Bk. 4). 1997. pap. 6.99 (*0-345-91133-4*, Del Rey) Ballantine Pub Grp.

— The Tangle Box: A Magic Kingdom of Landover Novel. 352p. 1995. reprint ed. mass mkt. 6.99 (*0-345-38700-7*, Del Rey) Ballantine Pub Grp.

— The Voyage of the Jerle Shannara Ilse Witch. 464p. 2000. 26.95 (*0-345-39654-5*, Del Rey) Ballantine Pub Grp.

— The Wishsong of Shannara. (Shannara Ser.: Bk. 3). 512p. 1988. mass mkt. 6.99 (*0-345-35636-5*, Del Rey) Ballantine Pub Grp.

— The Wishsong of Shannara. (Shannara Ser.: Bk. 3). 1996. mass mkt. 5.99 (*0-345-90959-3*, Del Rey) Ballantine Pub Grp.

— The Wishsong of Shannara. (Shannara Ser.: Bk. 3). 1997. mass mkt. 6.99 (*0-345-91129-6*, Del Rey) Ballantine Pub Grp.

Brooks, Terry. The Wishsong of Shannara. 1992. 12.70 (*0-606-01232-X*, Pub. by Turtleback) Demco.

Brooks, Terry. Witches' Brew. 1996. mass mkt. 6.99 (*0-345-38702-3*) Ballantine Pub Grp.

— Wizard at Large. (Magic Kingdom Ser.). 320p. 1989. mass mkt. 6.99 (*0-345-36227-6*, Del Rey) Ballantine Pub Grp.

— Wizard at Large. (Magic Kingdom of Landover Novel Ser.). 1989. 12.09 (*0-606-01235-4*, Pub. by Turtleback) Demco.

Brooks, Terry J., ed. Comparison of the Features of Mandatory Continuing Legal Education Rules in Effect As of July 1993. 65p. 1997. pap. text 25.00 (*0-614-03087-0*) NYS Bar.

Brooks, Theo. Accountability: It All Depends on What You Mean. rev. ed. (Illus.). 176p. (Orig.). 1995. 19.50 (*0-9645322-5-5*); pap. 13.50 (*0-9645322-6-3*) Akkad Pr.

***Brooks, Theo.** From Fairbanks to Florida: Taking Accountability Across America. LC 99-65050. (Illus.). 132p. 1999. pap. 14.00 (*0-9645322-7-1*) Akkad Pr.

Brooks, Theo. 17th Century Wisdom for 21st Century Problems. LC 95-80432. 112p. 1995. pap. 5.95 (*0-9645322-4-7*) Akkad Pr.

Brooks, Thomas. Complete Works of Thomas Brooks, 6 vols. Grosart, Alexander B., ed. LC 74-39538. reprint ed. lib. bdg. 405.00 (*0-404-01120-9*) AMS Pr.

— Heaven on Earth. (Puritan Paperbacks Ser.). 320p. 1983. pap. 8.99 (*0-85151-356-5*) Banner of Truth.

— Precious Remedies Against Satan's Devices. 253p. 1984. reprint ed. pap. 7.50 (*0-85151-002-7*) Banner of Truth.

***Brooks, Thomas.** Remedios Preciosos Contra las Artimanas del Diablo. abr. ed. Montgomery, Thomas & Negrete, Omar Ibanez, trs. Orig. Title: Resist the Devil. (SPA.). 70p. 1999. pap. 1.59 (*1-928980-03-1*) Pub Faro.

Brooks, Thomas. Smooth Stones from Ancient Brooks. 269p. 1995. 24.95 (*1-57358-027-9*) Soli Deo Gloria.

Brooks, Thomas, et al. Test Taking: Lan.-Re. 1997. 4.95 (*1-55708-229-4*, R851) McDonald Pub Co.

— Test Taking: Math. 1979. 4.95 (*1-55708-230-8*, R853) McDonald Pub Co.

Brooks, Thomas R. The War North of Rome: June 1944 - May 1945. 432p. 1997. 80.00 (*1-873376-67-7*, Pub. by Spellmnt Pubs) St Mut.

Brooks, Thomas R. The War North of Rome: June, 1944-May, 1945. LC 96-17257. (Illus.). 408p. 1996. 27.50 (*1-885119-26-7*) Sarpedon.

Brooks, Thomas R., jt. auth. see Mayden, Bronwyn.

Brooks, Tilford. America's Black Musical Heritage. (Illus.). 384p. (C). 1983. pap. text 39.75 (*0-13-024307-8*) P-H.

Brooks, Tim. The Columbia Master Book Discography Vol. I: U. S. Matrix Series 1 Through 4999, 1901-1910: With a History of the Columbia Phonograph Company to 1934, Vol. 1. LC 99-12630. (Documentary Reference Collections: Vol. 78). 560p. 1999. lib. bdg. 115.00 (*0-313-30821-7*, Greenwood Pr) Greenwood.

Brooks, Tim, jt. auth. see Rust, Brian.

***Brooks, Tony.** The Diaries of Black Men. LC 99-72397. 112p. 1999. pap. 12.95 (*0-9656739-1-X*) BYE Pub Servs.

Brooks, Traci. Stepping Into Womanhood: A Black Woman's Poetic Journey. LC 98-96738. (Illus.). 80p. 1999. pap. 14.95 (*0-9668023-0-6*) Black Buttafly.

Brooks, Tucker, ed. EPA's Chemical Safety Audit Protocol: A Guide for Team Members. (Illus.). 96p. 1998. reprint ed. pap. text 25.00 (*0-7881-7211-5*) DIANE Pub.

Brooks, Tucker, intro. General Information on Applying for Registration of Pesticides in the U. S. (Illus.). 290p. (C). 1996. reprint ed. pap. text 50.00 (*0-7881-3174-5*) DIANE Pub.

Brooks, Turner, et al. Turner Brooks Work. (Illus.). 152p. 1995. pap. 27.95 (*1-56898-031-0*) Princeton Arch.

Brooks, Val, et al. The Good Mentor Guide: Initial Teacher Education in Secondary Schools. LC 96-42217. 188p. 1997. pap. 28.95 (*0-335-19758-2*) OpUniv Pr.

— The Mentoring Experience: Options for School-Based Initial Teacher Education. LC 96-42217. 192p. 1997. 94.00 (*0-335-19759-0*) OpUniv Pr.

Brooks, Valerie, jt. auth. see Maiorano, Robert.

Brooks, Van Wyck. America's Coming-of-Age. 20.95 (*0-8488-0433-3*) Amereon Ltd.

— Emerson & Others. (BCL1-PS American Literature Ser.). 250p. 1992. reprint ed. lib. bdg. 79.00 (*0-7812-6609-2*) Rprt Serv.

— The Flowering of New England, 1815-1865. LC 80-2898. reprint ed. 45.00 (*0-404-18007-8*) AMS Pr.

— Flowering of New England, 1815-1865. 27.95 (*0-8488-0251-9*) Amereon Ltd.

— John Addington Symonds: A Biographical Study. 1988. reprint ed. lib. bdg. 59.00 (*0-7812-0368-6*) Rprt Serv.

— John Addington Symonds: A Biographical Study. LC 77-121648. 1971. reprint ed. 49.00 (*0-403-00535-3*) Scholarly.

— The Life of Emerson. LC 80-2528. reprint ed. 37.00 (*0-404-19252-1*) AMS Pr.

— New England: Indian Summer, 1865-1915. LC 84-8545. xii, 558p. 1985. reprint ed. pap. text 14.95 (*0-226-07578-8*) U Ch Pr.

— On Literature Today. (BCL1-PS American Literature Ser.). 290p. 1993. reprint ed. lib. bdg. 59.00 (*0-7812-6578-9*) Rprt Serv.

— The Ordeal of Mark Twain. LC 75-41039. (BCL Ser. II). reprint ed. 37.50 (*0-404-14512-4*) AMS Pr.

— The Pilgrimage of Henry James. (BCL1-PS American Literature Ser.). 170p. 1992. reprint ed. lib. bdg. 69.00 (*0-7812-6770-6*) Rprt Serv.

— The World of H. G. Wells. 190p. 1973. reprint ed. lib. bdg. 59.95 (*0-8490-1334-8*) Gordon Pr.

— The World of H. G. Wells. LC 72-92949. (English Literature Ser.: No. 33). 1969. reprint ed. lib. bdg. 75.00 (*0-8383-0962-3*) M S G Haskell Hse.

Brooks, Van Wyck, see Wyck Brooks, Van.

Brooks, Vernon, tr. see Von Franz, Marie-Louise.

Brooks, Vernon B. The Neural Basis of Motor Control. (Illus.). 344p. 1986. pap. text 49.50 (*0-19-503684-0*) OUP.

Brooks, Vernon B., ed. Handbook of Physiology: Section 1; The Nervous System, Set, Vol. II, Pts. 1 & 2: Motor Control. (American Physiological Society Book). (Illus.). 1548p. 1988. text 245.00 (*0-19-520659-2*) OUP.

Brooks, Veronica. A New Beginning. 70p. 1999. pap. 10.00 (*0-7392-0160-3*, PO3110) Morris Pubng.

***Brooks, Victor.** The Fredericksburg Campaign: November - December 1862. (Illus.). 2000. 29.95 (*1-58097-033-8*) Combined Pub.

Brooks, Victor D. African Americans in the Civil War. LC 99-52502. (Illus.). 64p. 1999. 19.95 (*0-7910-5435-7*) Chelsea Hse.

— The Boston Campaign. 1999. 24.95 (*1-58097-007-9*) Combined Pub.

— Civil War Forts. LC 99-52101. (Illus.). 64p. 1999. 19.95 (*0-7910-5438-1*) Chelsea Hse.

***Brooks, Victor D.** Marye's Heights: Fredericksburg. 2000. pap. 16.95 (*1-58097-036-2*, 970362) Combined Pub.

— Secret Weapons in the Civil War. LC 99-52111. (Illus.). 64p. 1999. 19.95 (*0-7910-5433-0*) Chelsea Hse.

Brooks, Victor D. & Hohwald, Robert. How America Fought Its Wars: Military Strategy from Lexington to Appomattox. LC 99-25572. 1998. 29.95 (*1-58097-002-8*, 970028) Combined Pub.

Brooks, Victoria. Ministering to God: The Reach of the Heart. 166p. 1995. pap. 8.00 (*1-886296-10-3*, VB1-001) Arrow Publications.

***Brooks, Victoria & Ignatius, Alex.** Literary Trips: Following in the Footsteps of Fame. 2000. pap. 19.95 (*0-9686137-0-5*) GE com.

Brooks, Victoria, jt. auth. see Brooks, Guy.

Brooks, Virginia. Introduction to Law. 96.95 (*0-7546-2038-7*) Ashgate Pub Co.

Brooks, W. F. History of the Fanning Family: A Genealogical Record to 1900 of the Descendants of Edmund Fanning, Who Settled in Connecticut in 1655. (Illus.). 872p. 1989. reprint ed. pap. 131.00 (*0-8328-0535-1*); reprint ed. lib. bdg. 139.00 (*0-8328-0534-3*) Higginson Bk Co.

Brooks, W. Hal. Your Life in Christ. 1971. 3.99 (*0-8054-2520-9*, 4225-20) Broadman.

Brooks, Walter. Freddy Detective Sel Poe. unabridged ed. LC 81-740215. (J). 1982. audio 10.50 (*0-89845-153-1*, CP 1698, Caedmon) HarperAudio.

Brooks, Walter H. The Pastor's Voice. (Illus.). 1990. 25.00 (*0-87498-016-X*) Assoc Pubs DC.

***Brooks, Walter R.** Freddy & Mr. Camphor. LC 00-24839. (Illus.). 239p. (J). (gr. 3-7). 2000. 23.95 (*1-58567-027-8*, Pub. by Overlook Pr) Penguin Putnam.

Brooks, Walter R. Freddy & the Baseball Team from Mars. (Illus.). 256p. (YA). (gr. 3 up). 1999. 23.95 (*0-87951-942-8*, Pub. by Overlook Pr) Penguin Putnam.

***Brooks, Walter R.** Freddy & the Bean Home News. (Freddy Ser.). (Illus.). 230p. (J). (gr. 3 up). 2000. 23.95 (*1-58567-081-2*) Overlook Pr.

— Freddy & the Dragon. (Illus.). 239p. (YA). 2000. 23.95 (*1-58567-026-X*, Pub. by Overlook Pr) Penguin Putnam.

Brooks, Walter R. Freddy & the Flying Saucer Plans. (Illus.). 256p. (J). (gr. 3 up). 1998. 23.95 (*0-87951-883-9*, Pub. by Overlook Pr) Penguin Putnam.

***Brooks, Walter R.** Freddy & the Ignormus. (Illus.). 288p. (J). (gr. 3 up). 1998. 23.95 (*0-87951-882-0*, Pub. by Overlook Pr) Penguin Putnam.

Brooks, Walter R. Freddy Goes to Florida. LC 97-10219. (Illus.). 208p. (YA). (gr. 3 up). 1997. 22.95 (*0-87951-808-1*, Pub. by Overlook Pr) Penguin Putnam.

— Freddy Plays Football. (J). 1992. reprint ed. lib. bdg. 28.95 (*0-89968-302-9*, Lghtyr Pr) Buccaneer Bks.

— Freddy Rides Again. (J). 1992. reprint ed. lib. bdg. 28.95 (*0-89968-300-2*, Lghtyr Pr) Buccaneer Bks.

— Freddy the Cowboy. (J). 1992. reprint ed. lib. bdg. 28.95 (*0-89968-301-0*, Lghtyr Pr) Buccaneer Bks.

— Freddy the Detective. LC 97-10214. (Illus.). 256p. (J). (gr. 3 up). 1997. 22.95 (*0-87951-809-X*, Pub. by Overlook Pr) Penguin Putnam.

***Brooks, Walter R.** Freddy the Pilot. (Illus.). 288p. (YA). (gr. 3 up). 1999. 23.95 (*0-87951-941-X*, Pub. by Overlook Pr) Penguin Putnam.

— Freddy the Politician. (Freddy Ser.). (Illus.). 253p. (gr. 3 up). 2000. 23.95 (*1-58567-080-4*) Overlook Pr.

Brooks, Walter R. Wiggins for President. Date not set. lib. bdg. 22.95 (*0-8488-1707-9*) Amereon Ltd.

***Brooks, Walter R.** The Wit & Wisdom of Freddy. (Illus.). 192p. (gr. 3). 1999. text 19.95 (*0-87951-725-5*, Pub. by Overlook Pr) Penguin Putnam.

Brooks, Wayne. Active Server Developers: A Developer's Guide. LC 97-46333. 480p. 1998. pap. 39.95 (*1-55851-576-3*, M&T Bks) IDG Bks.

***Brooks, Wayne.** FrontPage 2000. (Short Order Ser.). 320p. 1999. pap. 19.99 (*0-7897-2050-7*) Que.

Brooks, Wayne & Klander, Lars. Access 2000 Programming Blue Book. LC 98-32428. (Illus.). 639p. 1999. pap. 39.99 (*1-57610-328-5*) Coriolis Grp.

Brooks, Wayne F. Frontpage 97 Sourcebook. LC 97-4463. 446p. 1997. pap. 29.95 (*0-471-16505-0*) Wiley.

Brooks, William D. & Heath, Robert W. Speech Communication. 7th ed. 400p. (C). 1992. text. write for info. (*0-697-12915-2*) Brown & Benchmark.

Brooks, William D., jt. auth. see Brooks, Fonzie E.

Brooks, William E. Grant of Appomattox, a Study of the Man. LC 73-138577. (Illus.). 347p. 1971. reprint ed. lib. bdg. 65.00 (*0-8371-5776-5*, BRGR, Greenwood Pr) Greenwood.

— Lee of Virginia: A Biography. LC 75-16842. (Illus.). 361p. 1975. reprint ed. lib. bdg. 35.00 (*0-8371-8270-0*, BRLV, Greenwood Pr) Greenwood.

Brooks, William E., III, jt. auth. see Henderson, Richard.

Brooks, William H. Grizzly: The Spirit Bear. (Illus.). 96p. 1999. pap. 12.00 (*0-7392-0142-5*, PO3011) Morris Pubng.

Brooks, William K. The Oyster. (Maryland Paperback Bookshelf Ser.). (Illus.). 230p. (C). 1996. reprint ed. pap. 14.95 (*0-8018-5391-5*) Johns Hopkins.

Brooks, William T. High Impact Selling: Power Strategies for Successful Selling. 208p. 1987. 19.50 (*0-13-387663-2*) P-H.

— Niche Selling: How to Find Your Customer in a Crowded Market. 225p. 1991. text 30.00 (*1-55623-499-6*, Irwn Prfssnl) McGraw-Hill Prof.

Brooks, William T., et al. You're Working Too Hard to Make the Sale! More Than 100 Insider Tools to Sell Faster & Easier! LC 94-42726. 272p. 1995. text 22.95 (*0-7863-0395-6*, Irwn Prfssnl) McGraw-Hill Prof.

***Brooks, Xan.** Choose Life: Ewan McGregor & the British Film Revival. (Illus.). 2000. pap. 17.95 (*0-233-99410-6*, Pub. by Chameleon) Trafalgar.

Brooks, Yuvonne. Introduction to Algebra with Natural Resources Emphasis. 300p. (C). 1998. spiral bd. 29.95 (*0-7872-5363-4*) Kendall-Hunt.

Brooks, Yuvonne C. Slicing Through Your Emotional Luggage. 3rd ed. 64p. (C). 1996. pap. text, per. 17.95 (*0-7872-1906-1*) Kendall-Hunt.

Brooks, Zelda & Garcia, Santos J. The Splendor of Spain: A Serious Scientific Study of Grammar. (C). 1994. pap. text 20.50 (*0-07-008112-3*) McGraw.

Brooks, Zelda I. Poet, Mystic, Modern Hero: Fernando Rielo Pardal. 200p. 1991. 49.50 (*0-916379-85-X*) Scripta.

— The Poetry of Gabriel Celaya. 26.00 (*0-916379-27-2*) Scripta.

— Struggle for Being: An Interpretation of the Poetry of Ana Maria Fagundo. LC 93-84477. (Illus.). 215p. (Orig.). 1994. pap. 19.00 (*0-89729-725-3*) Ediciones.

***Brooksbank.** Samba Administrator's Handbook. LC 99-52732. (Administrator's Handbook). 550p. 1999. 24.99 (*0-7645-4636-8*) IDG Bks.

Brooksbank & Nice. County-Vocational School. 1989. pap. text. write for info. (*0-582-03341-1*, Pub. by Addison-Wesley) Longman.

Brooksbank, Angela. I've Lost My Yellow Zebra. (Illus.). 20p. (J). 1996. 11.95 (*0-8120-6635-9*) Barron.

***Brooksbank, Angela.** I've Lost My Yellow Zebra. (Illus.). 32p. (J). (ps-k). 1999. pap. 6.95 (*0-7641-0875-1*) Barron.

***Brooksbank, David & Wilson, John.** Security Manual. 7th ed. LC 99-462488. 300p. 1999. pap. 19.95 (*0-566-08174-1*, Pub. by Ashgate Pub) Ashgate Pub Co.

Brooksby, L. J. Queen of the Strip. LC 98-89794. 240p. 2000. pap. 14.95 (*0-88739-234-2*) Creat Arts Bk.

***Brooksby, L. J.** The Strip Outlaw. LC 99-74693. 340p. 1999. pap. 14.95 (*1-882792-86-6*) Proctor Pubns.

Brooksfield Historical Society Staff, compiled by. Vital Statistics Copied from Town Records, Penobscot, Maine, 1787 to 1875. 216p. 1998. reprint ed. pap. 25.00 (*0-8328-7037-4*) Higginson Bk Co.

***Brookshear.** Computer Science: An Overview for Suffolk Community College. 1999. pap. write for info. (*0-201-67704-0*) Addison-Wesley.

Brookshear, Glenn. Lab Mnl Ver C Expe Cmput. 4th ed. (C). 1994. pap. text, lab manual ed. 16.95 (*0-8053-4629-5*) Addison-Wesley.

Brookshear, J. Glenn. Computer Science. 4th ed. 506p. (C). 1996. pap. text 29.20 (*0-201-83309-3*) Addison-Wesley.

Brookshear, J. Glenn. Computer Science: An Overview. 3rd ed. (C). 1993. pap. text. write for info. (*0-201-59483-8*) Addison-Wesley.

— Computer Science: An Overview. 4th ed. (C). 1994. pap. text 39.75 (*0-8053-4627-9*) Benjamin-Cummings.

— Computer Science: An Overview. 6th ed. LC 99-29326. (Illus.). 609p. (C). 1999. pap. 60.00 (*0-201-35747-X*) Addison-Wesley.

— Teoria de la Computacion Lenguages Formales, Automatas & Complejidad. (SPA.). 360p. (C). 1993. pap. text 23.33 (*0-201-60119-2*) Addison-Wesley.

Brooksher, William R., II. Bloody Hill: The Civil War Battle of Wilson's Creek. 296p. 1995. 24.95 (*1-57488-018-7*) Brasseys.

Brooksher, William R. War along the Bayous: The 1864 Red River Campaign in Louisiana. LC 98-15747. (Illus.). 304p. 1998. 27.50 (*1-57488-139-6*) Brasseys.

Brooksher, William R. & Snider, David K. Glory at a Gallop: Tales of the Confederate Cavalry. 288p. (Orig.). 1993. 23.95 (*0-02-881081-3*) Brasseys.

Brookshire, LaJoyce. Web of Deception. limited ed. 269p. 1998. pap. 15.00 (*1-58441-000-0*, 001) Retnuh.

Brookshire, Lajoyce. Soul Food. 256p. 1997. mass mkt. 5.99 (*0-06-101298-X*) HarpC.

Brookshire, Robert H. An Introduction to Neurogenic Communication Disorders. 5th ed. (Illus.). 512p. 1997. pap. text 48.00 (*0-8151-1014-6*, 29387) Mosby Inc.

— An Introduction to Neurogenic Communication Disorders. 5th ed. LC 96-53118. (Illus.). 378p. 1998. text 79.95 (*0-8151-3609-9*, 31840) Mosby Inc.

Brookshire, Velma P. God Still Speaks in the Midnight Hours. LC 95-69544. (Illus.). 104p. (Orig.). (C). 1995. pap. 11.95 (*1-882792-14-9*) Proctor Pubns.

Brookshire, Wanda S. Scripture Cryptograms. Ramirez, Cecillee & Starr, Jean, eds. (Illus.). iv, 47p. (Orig.). 1997. pap. write for info. (*0-9656802-0-7*) Brooks Pub OK.

— The Way It Was: An Indian Girl Living Thru the Depression. Starr, Jean, ed. (Illus.). 56p. 1999. ring bd. 10.00 (*0-9656802-1-5*) Brooks Pub OK.

***Brookson, Stephen.** Managing Budgets. (Illus.). 72p. 2000. pap. 6.95 (*0-7894-5969-8*) DK Pub Inc.

Brooksville Historical Society Staff, compiled by. Vital Statistics from Town Records, Penobscot, 1787 to 1875. (Illus.). 217p. 1997. reprint ed. lib. bdg. 29.00 (*0-8328-5892-7*) Higginson Bk Co.

Brookwood Guild Staff. Cooking up a Storm. LC 93-73243. 192p. 1993. 13.95 (*0-87197-390-1*) Favorite Recipes.

Broom, Barbara. Geoffrey Broom's War. (C). 1989. text 59.00 (*1-85821-008-9*, Pub. by Pentland Pr) St Mut.

Broom, Betty L., jt. auth. see Novak, Julie C.

Broom, Brian. Psychosomatic Illnesses. 1997. 55.00 (*1-85343-379-9*, Pub. by Free Assoc Bks); pap. 21.50 (*1-85343-381-0*, Pub. by Free Assoc Bks) NYU Pr.

***Broom, Dave.** Connoisseur's Book of Spirits & Cocktails. 1999. 24.95 (*1-85868-837-X*, Pub. by Carlton Bks Ltd) Natl Bk Netwk.

Broom, Dave. Whiskey: A Connoisseur's Guide. 1. 95p. 1999. 14.95 (*1-85868-706-3*, Pub. by Carlton Bks Ltd) Natl Bk Netwk.

Broom, Dorothy, ed. Double Bind: Women Affected by Alcohol & Other Drugs. 235p. 1995. pap. 24.95 (*1-86373-724-3*, Pub. by Allen & Unwin Pty) Paul & Co Pubs.

Broom, Dorothy H. Damned If We Do: Contradictions in Women's Health Care. 208p. (Orig.). 1992. pap. text 19.95 (*1-86373-054-0*, Pub. by Allen & Unwin Pty) Paul & Co Pubs.

Broom, Eric F., ed. see International Symposium on Comparative Physical Ed.

Broom, Herbert. Commentaries on the Common Law: Designed As Introductory to Its Study. LC 97-25767. li, 674p. 1997. reprint ed. 125.00 (*0-8377-1987-9*, Rothman) W S Hein.

— Constitutional Law Viewed in Relation to Common Law & Exemplified by Cases. xxviii, 1012p. 1998. reprint ed. 210.00 (*1-56169-367-7*) Gaunt.

— Philosophy of Law: Being Notes of Lectures Delivered During Twenty-Three Years (1852-1875) in the Inner Temple Hall. xi, 338p. 1980. reprint ed. 40.00 (*0-8377-0310-7*, Rothman) W S Hein.

***Broom, Herbert.** A Selection of Legal Maxims, Classified & Illustrated: Eighth American, from the Fifth London Edition, with References. 5th fac. ed. LC 99-49329. lxxviii, 993p. 2000. 125.00 (*1-58477-052-X*) Lawbk Exchange.

***Broom, Herbert & Hadley, Edward A.** Commentaries on the Laws of England, 4 vols. 2430p. 1999. 610.00 (*1-56169-466-5*) Gaunt.

Broom, Leonard & Kitsuse, John. The Managed Casualty: The Japanese-American Family in World War II. LC 57-9006. (University of California Publications in Social Welfare: Vol. 6). 232p. reprint ed. pap. 72.00 (*0-608-13941-6*, 202139400022) Bks Demand.

***Broom, Michael & Rook, Derek, photos by.** Lucio Fulci's "Zombie" We Are Going to Eat You! deluxe ed. (Illus.). 120p. 2000. pap. 24.99 (*0-9667514-1-8*) Blackest Heart.

Broom, Michael F. & Klein, Donald. Power: Infinite Game. LC 96-209693. 1995. pap. text 24.95 (*0-87425-296-2*) HRD Press.

Broom, Neil D. How Blind Is the Watchmaker? LC 98-72801. (Avebury Series in Philosophy). xv, 207 p. 1998. text 63.95 (*1-84014-517-X*, Pub. by Avebury) Ashgate Pub Co.

Broom, Robert & Robinson, J. T. Swartkrans Ape-Man: Paranthropus Crassidens. LC 76-44697. reprint ed. 47.50 (*0-404-15911-7*) AMS Pr.

Broom, Robert & Schepers, G. W. The South African Fossil Ape-Man: The "Australopithecinae" LC 76-44698. reprint ed. 67.50 (*0-404-15910-9*) AMS Pr.

Broom, Steven H. Tame Game: One Hundred Twenty-Eight Deer & Elk Recipes to Tame Your Wild Game. LC 92-81420. (Illus.). 137p. (Orig.). 1992. pap. 14.95 (*0-9632946-0-1*) Teven Pr.

Broomal, Robert, ed. see Hill, Anita.

Brooman. A Caring People. 1994. pap. text. write for info. (*0-582-24597-4*, Pub. by Addison-Wesley) Longman.

— A Changing Nation. 1994. pap. text. write for info. (*0-582-24594-X*, Pub. by Addison-Wesley) Longman.

— Communication & Culture. 1994. pap. text. write for info. (*0-582-25159-1*, Pub. by Addison-Wesley) Longman.

— People at Work. 1994. pap. text. write for info. (*0-582-24595-8*, Pub. by Addison-Wesley) Longman.

— People in Change. 1994. pap. text. write for info. (*0-582-22665-1*, Pub. by Addison-Wesley) Longman.

— Twentieth Century World. 1995. pap. text. write for info. (*0-582-24975-9*, Pub. by Addison-Wesley) Longman.

Brooman, E. W., et al, eds. Electrochemical Technology Applied to Environmental Problems. LC 95-60530. (Proceedings Ser.: Vol. 95-12). 306p. 1995. pap. 46.00 (*1-56677-106-4*) Electrochem Soc.

Brooman, Josh. Imperial China: From the First Emperor to Kublai Khan. (Longman Origin Ser.). 1991. pap. text 10.64 (*0-582-08249-8*) Longman.

— Revolution in France: The Era of the French Revolution & Napoleon 1789-1815. (Longman Origin Ser.). 1992. pap. text 10.64 (*0-582-08254-4*) Longman.

— The World since 1900. (J). 1989. pap. text 16.00 (*0-582-00989-8*, 78443) Longman.

Brooman, Josh, ed. The End of Old Europe: Causes of the First World War, 1914-18. (Longman 20th Century History Ser.). (Illus.). 32p. (Orig.). (J). (gr. 4-12). 1985. pap. text 10.92 (*0-582-22368-7*, 70921) Longman.

— The Great War: The First World War, 1914-18. (Twentieth Century History Ser.). (Illus.). 40p. (Orig.). (J). (gr. 4-12). 1985. pap. text 10.92 (*0-582-22369-5*, 70922) Longman.

— Hitler's Germany. (Twentieth Century History Ser.). (Illus.). 32p. (Orig.). 1985. pap. text 10.92 (*0-582-22373-3*, 70926) Longman.

— Weimar Germany: Germany 1918-33. (Twentieth Century History Ser.). (Illus.). 32p. (Orig.). 1985. pap. text 10.92 (*0-582-22372-5*, 70925) Longman.

— The World Re-Made: The Results of the First World War. (Twentieth Century History Ser.). (Illus.). 32p. (Orig.). (YA). (gr. 4-12). 1985. pap. text 10.92 (*0-582-22370-9*, 70923) Longman.

Brooman, Simon & Legge, Debbie. Law Relating to Animals. 462p. 1997. pap. 49.00 (*1-85941-238-6*, Pub. by Cavendish Pubng) Gaunt.

Broomberg, E. B. & Kruger, Des. Tax Strategy 3rd ed. LC 99-186811. xxiv, 267p. 1998. write for info. (*0-409-07528-0*) Buttrwrth-Heinemann.

Broome. Chiropractic Peripheral Joint Technique. LC 99-17378. 256p. 2000. pap. text 75.00 (*0-7506-3289-5*) Buttrwrth-Heinemann.

Broome, Annabel K. Health Psychology: Processes & Applications. (Illus.). 440p. 1990. pap. 47.50 (*0-412-33210-8*, A4057) Chapman & Hall.

Broome, Annabel K. & Llewellyn, S. P., eds. Health Psychology: Processes & Applications. 2nd ed. 448p. 1994. pap. text 65.00 (*1-56593-226-9*, 0559) Singular Publishing.

Broome, Annabel K. & Llewelyn, Sue, eds. Health Psychology: Process & Applications. 2nd ed. LC 94-71819. 1995. pap. 44.95 (*0-412-55120-9*) Chapman & Hall.

Broome, Annabel K. & Wallace, Louise. Psychology & Gynaecological Problems. 320p. (Orig.). 1984. pap. 14.95 (*0-422-78590-3*, 9251, Pub. by Tavistock) Routldge.

Broome, Benjamin. Understanding Relationships: Selected Readings in Interpersonal Communication. 2nd ed. 192p. (C). 1994. pap. text, per. 25.95 (*0-8403-9139-0*) Kendall-Hunt.

Broome, Benjamin J. Exploring the Greek Mosaic: A Guide to Intercultural Communication in Greece. LC 95-52223. (InterAct Ser.). 192p. (Orig.). 1996. pap. text 18.95 (*1-877864-39-0*, 1414) Intercult Pr.

Broome, Betsy & Cummings, Cynthia. Bag It! Distinctive Gift Ideas Using Bags! Coy, Stanley C., ed. (Illus.). 148p. (Orig.). 1992. pap. 10.95 (*1-881459-02-0*) Eagle Pr SC.

B

An Asterisk (*) at the beginning of an entry indicates that the title is appearing for the first time.

Broome, C. E., jt. auth. see Berkeley, M. J.

Broome, Claire V. Youth Risk Behavior Surveillance: United States, 1997. (Illus.). 90p. (C). 1999. pap. text 20.00 (*0-7881-8148-3*) DIANE Pub.

Broome, Errol. Tough Luck. 1998. pap. 8.95 (*1-86368-228-7*, Pub. by Fremantle Arts) Intl Spec Bk.
— What a Goat! LC 97-157898. 74p. 1997. pap. 8.95 (*1-86368-171-X*, Pub. by Fremantle Arts) Intl Spec Bk.

Broome, Francis. Prayers to the Little Flower with Novena. 21p. 1973. 1.25 (*0-911988-95-5*, 48789) AMI Pr.

Broome, H. B. The Meanest Man in West Texas. 192p. 1988. pap. 2.95 (*0-671-66184-1*) PB.

Broome, John. Counting the Cost of Global Warming. 150p. pap. 19.95 (*1-874267-00-6*, Pub. by White Horse Pr) Paul & Co Pubs.
— Counting the Cost of Global Warming. 150p. 1993. 50.00 (*1-874267-01-4*, Pub. by White Horse Pr) Paul & Co Pubs.
— Ethics Out of Economics. LC 98-35992. (Illus.). 275p. (C). 1999. text 64.95 (*0-521-64275-2*); pap. text 24.95 (*0-521-64491-7*) Cambridge U Pr.

***Broome, John.** The Flash Archives, Vol. 2. (Illus.). 224p. (YA). 2000. 49.95 (*1-56389-606-0*, Pub. by DC Comics) Time Warner.

Broome, John. Green Lantern Annual, 1963, No. 1. (Illus.). 80p. 1998. pap. 4.95 (*1-56389-451-3*) DC Comics.

***Broome, John.** Green Lantern Archives. 224p. 2000. 49.95 (*1-56389-566-8*, Pub. by DC Comics) Time Warner.

Broome, John. Weighing Goods: Equality, Uncertainty & Time. Hamun, Alan & Pettit, Philip, eds. (Economics & Philosophy Ser.). 255p. 1996. pap. 31.95 (*0-631-19972-1*) Blackwell Pubs.

Broome, John, et al. The Flash Archives, Vol. 1. Kahan, Bob, ed. LC 97-148158. (Illus.). 224p. (J). 1996. 49.95 (*1-56389-139-5*, Pub. by DC Comics) Time Warner.

Broome, Linda, jt. auth. see Mansergh, Ian.

Broome, Margaret R., ed. see Goddard, Neville W.

Broome, Marion. Children & Families in Health & Illness. LC 97-45403. 1998. 79.95 (*0-8039-5902-8*); pap. 39.95 (*0-8039-5903-6*) Sage.

Broome, Marion, jt. auth. see Clayton, Gloria.

Broome, Marion E. & Rollins, Judy A., eds. Core Curriculum for the Nursing Care of Children & Their Families. LC 99-226706. 500p. 1998. text 69.00 (*0-9655310-3-1*) Jannetti Pubns.

Broome, Marion E., ed. see Albers, Anne C., et al.

Broome, Peter. Andre Frenaud, dans la Crique: Du Lieu du Poeme a l'Univers. LC 97-49655. (Studies in French Literature: Vol. 28). 176p. 1997. text 79.95 (*0-7734-8464-7*) E Mellen.

Broome, Richard. Aboriginal Australians: Black Response to White Dominance 1788-1994. 2nd ed. (Illus.). 272p. 1996. pap. 19.95 (*1-86373-760-X*, Pub. by Allen & Unwin Pty) Paul & Co Pubs.

Broome, Susannah. The Pearl Pagoda. large type ed. 505p. 1982. 27.99 (*0-7089-0765-2*) Ulverscroft.

Broome, T. From Ruth to Ryan: Unbeatable Card Buys. LC 93-80093. (Illus.). 160p. 1993. pap. 6.95 (*0-87341-289-3*, BV01) Krause Pubns.

Broomell, Anna P. Friendly Story Caravan. LC 89-28984. 1990. reprint ed. pap. 11.00 (*0-87574-913-5*) Pendle Hill.
— Poets Walk In. LC 54-8405. (C). 1954. pap. 4.00 (*0-87574-077-4*) Pendle Hill.

Broomer, Stuart. Good Timing: The Paul Molitor Story. (Illus.). 144p. 1994. pap. 9.95 (*1-55022-207-4*, Pub. by ECW) LPC InBook.

Broomfield, Andrea & Mitchell, Sally. Prose by Victorian Women: An Anthology. LC 95-24400. (Garland Reference Library of the Humanities: Vol. 1893). 752p. 1995. reprint ed. text 95.00 (*0-8153-1970-3*, H1893) Garland.

Broomfield, Andrea & Mitchell, Sally, eds. Prose by Victorian Women: An Anthology. LC 95-24400. 752p. 1995. pap. text 32.95 (*0-8153-1967-3*, H1893) Garland.

Broomfield, Hilary & Combley, Margaret. Overcoming Dyslexia: A Practical Handbook for the Classroom. LC 97-138107. 238p. 1996. pap. 49.95 (*1-56593-836-4*, 1634) Thomson Learn.

Broomfield, Janet. A Fallen Land. large type ed. (Romance Ser.). 848p. 1992. 27.99 (*0-7089-2656-8*) Ulverscroft.

Broomfield, John. Other Ways of Knowing: Recharting Our Future with Ageless Wisdom. LC 97-7876. 224p. 1997. pap. 14.95 (*0-89281-614-7*) Inner Tradit.

Broomfield, John P. Corrosion of Steel in Concrete: Understanding, Investigation & Repair. LC 96-70579. (Illus.). 264p. (C). 1996. 90.00 (*0-419-19630-7*, E & FN Spon) Routledge.

Broomhall, A. J. Hudson Taylor & China's Open Century, Bk. 3: If I Had a Thousand Lives, Bk. III. 1983. pap. 5.95 (*0-340-32392-2*) OMF Bks.
— Hudson Taylor & China's Open Century, Bk. 6: Assault on the Nine. 1988. pap. 5.95 (*0-340-42629-2*) OMF Bks.

Broomhall, B. A. Islam in China. 352p. 1987. 300.00 (*1-85077-151-0*, Pub. by Darf Pubs Ltd) St Mut.

***Broomhall, Marshall.** Hudson Taylor's Legacy: Daily Meditations from Devotional Articles & Letters. 1999. pap. 7.99 (*1-85792-492-4*) Christian Focus.

Broomham, Rosemary. Steady Revolutions: The Australian Institute of Marine & Power Engineers 1881-1990. (Illus.). 296p. 41.95 (*0-86840-324-5*, Pub. by New South Wales Univ Pr) Intl Spec Bk.

***Broomhead, David S., et al, eds.** Stochastic & Chaotic Dynamics in the Lakes: Stochaos. LC 99-69566. (AIP Conference Proceedings Ser.: Vol. 502). (Illus.). xviii, 678p. 2000. 175.00 (*1-56396-915-7*) Am Inst Physics.

Broomhead, Frank. The Book Illustrations of Orlando Jewitt. (Illus.). 272p. 1996. 90.00 (*0-900002-36-0*, 44059) Oak Knoll.
— The Zaehnsdorfs, 1842-1947: Craft Bookbinders. 110p. 1986. 40.00 (*0-900002-74-3*, Pub. by Priv Lib Assn) Oak Knoll.

Broomhill, Ray. Unemployed Workers: A Social History of the Great Depression in Adelaide. LC 79-313789. xiv, 220p. 1978. write for info. (*0-7022-1235-0*) Intl Spec Bk.

Broomhill, Ray, jt. auth. see Sharp, Rhonda.

Brooms, John, ed. Welcome Back to the House of Mystery. (Illus.). 96p. 1998. pap. 5.95 (*1-56389-452-1*) DC Comics.

Broonzy, William. Big Bill Blues: William Broonzy's Story. LC 92-18376. (Illus.). 176p. 1992. reprint ed. pap. 10.95 (*0-306-80490-5*) Da Capo.

Broos, Ben. Intimacies & Intrigues: History Paintings in the Mauritshuis. (Exhibitions International Ser.). (Illus.). 446p. 1994. 125.00 (*90-5349-097-3*) U of Wash Pr.

Broos, Kees, et al. Dutch Graphic Design: A Century. LC 93-77256. (Illus.). 224p. 1997. reprint ed. pap. text 35.00 (*0-262-52250-0*) MIT Pr.

Broos, Ton J., ed. Publications of the American Association for Netherlandic Studies: Papers from the Third Interdisciplinary Conference on Netherlandic Studies. 342p. (C). 1988. lib. bdg. 52.00 (*0-8191-7056-9*) U Pr of Amer.

Brooten, Bernadette J. Love Between Women: Early Christian Responses to Female Homoeroticism. (Illus.). 416p. 1996. 34.95 (*0-226-07591-5*) U Ch Pr.
— Love Between Women: Early Christian Responses to Female Homoeroticism. 1998. pap. 19.00 (*0-226-07592-3*) U Ch Pr.

Brooten, Dorothy A., et al. Leadership for Change: An Action Guide for Nurses. 2nd ed. LC 64-5153. 192p. 1988. text 19.95 (*0-397-54597-5*, Lippncott) Lppncott W & W.

Brooten, Dorothy A., jt. auth. see Downs, Florence.

Broown, J., jt. ed. see Davies, P. C.

Brophy, Ann. John Ericson & the Inventions of War. Gallin, Richard, ed. (History of the Civil War Ser.). (Illus.). 160p. (YA). (gr. 5 up). 1990. pap. 7.95 (*0-382-24052-9*) Silver Burdett Pr.

Brophy, Anthony B. Foundlings on the Frontier: Racial & Religious Conflict in Arizona Territory, 1904-1905. LC 79-187824. (Southwest Chronicle Ser.). (Illus.). 141p. reprint ed. pap. 43.80 (*0-608-15583-7*, 202964900062) Bks Demand.

Brophy, Brigid. The Finishing Touch. 1995. per. 6.95 (*0-85449-059-0*, Pub. by Gay Mens Pr) LPC InBook.
— Mozart the Dramatist. (Quality Paperbacks Ser.). 336p. 1990. pap. 12.95 (*0-306-80389-5*) Da Capo.

Brophy, Catherine. The Liberation of Margaret McCabe. 168p. 1992. pap. 9.95 (*0-86327-067-0*) Dufour.

***Brophy, Donald F., ed.** Word & Worship Desk Calendar 2001. 128p. 2000. pap. 11.95 (*0-8091-3918-9*) Paulist Pr.
— Word & Worship Pocket Calendar 2001. 128p. 2000. pap. 4.95 (*0-8091-3919-7*) Paulist Pr.

Brophy, Elizabeth B. Samuel Richardson: The Triumph of Craft. LC 74-3248. 152p. 1974. reprint ed. pap. 47.20 (*0-608-05699-5*, 206621400007) Bks Demand.
— Women's Lives & the Eighteenth-Century English Novel. 312p. 1991. 49.95 (*0-8130-1036-5*) U Press Fla.

Brophy, G. R., jt. auth. see Wickende, T. H.

Brophy, Holly E., jt. auth. see Honig, Alice S.

Brophy, James. Perspectives from the Past: From Early Modern Era through Contemporary Times, Vol. 2. LC 98-13551. 1998. pap. text. write for info. (*0-393-95879-5*) Norton.

Brophy, James, et al. Perspectives from the Past: Primary Sources in Western Civilizations, 1. LC 98-13551. 1998. pap. text. write for info. (*0-393-95876-0*) Norton.

Brophy, James D. & Grennan, Eamon. New Irish Writing. 242p. 1988. 28.95 (*0-8057-9025-X*, Twayne) Mac Lib Ref.

Brophy, James J. Basic Electronics for Scientists. 5th ed. 480p. (C). 1989. text 37.50 (*0-07-008148-4*) McGraw.
— Basic Electronics for Scientists. 5th ed. 462p. (C). 1989. 90.63 (*0-07-008147-6*) McGraw.

Brophy, James J., jt. auth. see Azaroff, Leonid V.

Brophy, James M. Capitalism, Politics & Railroads in Prussia, 1830-1870. LC 97-29251. (Historical Perspectives on Business Enterprise Ser.). 1998. text 52.50 (*0-8142-0751-0*) Ohio St U Pr.

Brophy, Jere. Teaching Problem Students. LC 96-19772. 466p. 1996. lib. bdg. 50.00 (*1-57230-144-9*, 0144) Guilford Pubns.

Brophy, Jere, ed. Advances in Research on Teaching Vol. 7: Expectations in the Classroom. 1998. 78.50 (*0-7623-0261-5*) Jai Pr.
— The Value Aspects of Motivation in Education: A Special Issue of Educational Psychologist. 64p. 1999. pap. 20.00 (*0-8058-9792-5*) L Erlbaum Assocs.

Brophy, Jere, jt. auth. see Good, Thomas L.

Brophy, Jere E. Motivating Students to Learn. LC 97-1283. 320p. 1997. pap. 30.00 (*0-07-008198-0*) McGraw.

Brophy, Jere E., ed. Advances in Research on Teaching, Vol. 1. 384p. 1989. 78.50 (*0-89232-845-2*) Jai Pr.
— Advances in Research on Teaching, Vol. 5. 400p. 1995. 78.50 (*1-55938-771-8*) Jai Pr.
— Advances in Research on Teaching, Vol. 6. 336p. 1996. 78.50 (*0-7623-0104-X*) Jai Pr.
— Advances in Research on Teaching: Case Studies of Teaching & Learning in Social Studies, Vol. 4. 248p. 1994. 78.50 (*1-55938-742-4*) Jai Pr.
— Advances in Research on Teaching: Planning & Managing Learning Tasks & Activities, Vol. 3. 304p. 1992. 78.50 (*1-55938-437-9*) Jai Pr.
— Advances in Research on Teaching: Teachers Knowledge of Subject Matter As It Relates to Their Teaching Practice, Vol. 2. 384p. 1991. 78.50 (*1-55938-034-9*) Jai Pr.

Brophy, Jere E. & Van Sledright, Bruce A. Teaching & Learning History in Elementary School. LC 96-52833. 304p. (C). 1997. text 56.00 (*0-8077-3608-2*); pap. text 27.95 (*0-8077-3607-4*) Tchrs Coll.

Brophy, Jere E., et al. Structure & Properties of Materials, Vol. 2: Thermodynamics of Structure. LC TA0403.B7. 228p. 1964. reprint ed. pap. 70.70 (*0-608-08387-9*, 205576900002) Bks Demand.

Brophy, Jere E., jt. auth. see Good, Thomas L.

Brophy, Jim, jt. auth. see Flynn, Arthur.

Brophy, John. Fun with the Drums. (Fun Bks.). 32p. 1973. pap. 5.95 (*0-87166-440-2*, 93326) Mel Bay.

Brophy, John & Partridge, Eric. The Long Trail: Soldiers Songs & Slang, 1914-18. LC 72-8462. (Select Bibliographies Reprint Ser.). 1977. reprint ed. 20.95 (*0-8369-6966-9*) Ayer.

Brophy, Keith. Teach Yourself Visual Basic Script in 21 Days. LC 96-68236. 720p. 1996. pap. text 39.99 incl. cd-rom (*1-57521-120-3*) Sams.
— Visual Basic Language. 1999. pap. text 29.99 (*0-672-31479-7*) Sams.

Brophy, Keith & Koets, Tim. Visual Basic 4 Performance Tuning & Optimization. LC 95-70087. (Illus.). 784p. (Orig.). 1995. 49.99 (*0-672-30796-0*) Sams.

Brophy, Kevin. Almost Heaven: A Love That Could Not Be. 320p. 1997. pap. 21.95 (*1-86023-051-2*, Pub. by Martello Bks) Irish Amer Bk.
— Creativity: Psychoanalysis, Surrealism & Creative Writing. LC 98-227751. 216p. 1998. pap. 29.95 (*0-522-84786-2*, Pub. by Melbourne Univ Pr) Paul & Co Pubs.

Brophy, Kevin T. Walking the Line: Scenes from an Army Childhood. (Illus.). 189p. 1995. 29.95 (*1-85158-638-5*, Pub. by Mainstream Pubng) Trafalgar.

Brophy, Leo P., et al. U. S. Army Chemical Warfare Service: From Laboratory to Field. (Illus.). 498p. 1997. text 60.00 (*0-7881-4496-0*) DIANE Pub.

***Brophy, Mike.** Curtis Joseph: The Goaltender. LC 99-66341. (Sport Snaps Ser.). (Illus.). 56p. (YA). 2000. pap. 12.95 (*1-892920-07-7*) G H B Pubs.

Brophy, Negy. Introduction to Psychology. 5th ed. 1999. 35.00 (*0-07-235495-X*) McGraw.

Brophy, P. Perspectives from the Past. 1998. pap. text. write for info. (*0-393-97387-5*) Norton.

***Brophy, Patrick.** Bushwhackers of the Border: The Civil War Period in Western Missouri. 2nd rev. ed. LC 00-132992. (Illus.). 96p. 2000. pap. 9.95 (*1-893046-02-8*) Vernon Cty Hist Soc.
— Past Perfect: True Tales of Town & 'Round - Nevada & Vernon County, Missouri. LC 99-75655. (Illus.). 375p. 1999. pap. 19.95 (*1-893046-12-5*, Bushwacker Mus) Vernon Cty Hist Soc.

Brophy, Patrick. Three Hundred Years: Historical Highlights of Nevada & Vernon County, Missouri. (Illus.). 350p. (Orig.). 1993. pap. 12.95 (*0-9614944-2-5*) DGL InfoWrite.

Brophy, Patrick, ed. In the Devil's Dominions: A Union Soldier's Adventures in "Bushwhacker Country" LC 98-74036. 215p. 1998. pap. 14.95 (*1-893046-10-9*) Vernon Cty Hist Soc.

Brophy, Paul, jt. auth. see Shabecoff, Alice.

Brophy, Peter. Management Information & Decision Support Systems in Libraries. 200p. 1986. text 54.95 (*0-566-03551-0*) Ashgate Pub Co.

Brophy, Peter & Coulling, Kate. Quality Management for Information & Library Managers. 206p. 1996. 74.95 (*0-566-07725-6*, Pub. by Gower) Ashgate Pub Co.

Brophy, Peter, et al. Dobis-Libis: A Guide for Librarians & Systems Managers. (Illus.). 210p. 1990. text 58.95 (*0-566-05590-2*, Pub. by Gower) Ashgate Pub Co.

Brophy, Robert J. Robinson Jeffers. LC 75-29982. (Western Writers Ser.: No. 19). (Illus.). 50p. (Orig.). 1975. pap. 4.95 (*0-88430-018-8*) Boise St U W Writ Ser.

Brophy, Robert J., ed. Robinson Jeffers: The Dimensions of a Poet. (Illus.). xvii, 248p. (C). 1995. pap. 16.95 (*0-8232-1566-0*); text 30.00 (*0-8232-1565-2*) Fordham.

Brophy, Susan. The Fighting Ground: A Study Guide. (Novel-Ties Ser.). (J). (gr. 4-6). 1988. pap. text, teacher ed. 15.95 (*0-88122-082-5*) Lrn Links.

Brophy, Thomas G. The Mechanism Demands a Mysticism: An Exploration of Spirit, Matter & Physics. LC 99-17722. 360p. 1999. pap. 19.95 (*1-891850-12-1*) Med Bear.

***Brophy, Timothy S.** Assessing the Developing Child Musician: A Guide for General Music Teachers. LC 00-37631. 2000. pap. write for info. (*1-57999-090-8*) GIA Pubns.

Brophy, William S. The Krag Rifle. 35.00 (*0-88227-025-7*) Gun Room.
— L. C. Smith Shotguns. 35.00 (*0-88227-046-X*) Gun Room.
— Marlin Firearms: A History of the Guns & the Company That Made Them. LC 88-38768. (Illus.). 704p. 1989. 75.00 (*0-8117-0877-2*) Stackpole.
— The Springfield 1903 Rifles. LC 84-16154. (Illus.). 624p. 1985. 75.00 (*0-8117-0872-1*) Stackpole.

Brophy, William S., compiled by. Arsenal of Freedom - The Springfield Armory, 1890-1948: A Year-by-Year Account Drawn from Official Records. LC 91-77399. (Illus.). 400p. 1992. pap. 29.95 (*0-917218-51-5*) A Mowbray.

Bropson, Eileen, jt. auth. see Levin, Linda.

Broquard, Vic. Intermediate MFC for Windows 95 & NT. LC 97-26440. 704p. (C). 1997. pap. text 39.95 (*0-13-848276-4*) P-H.

***Broqueville, Paulette R.** The Answer to Sun Tzu, Bk. 3. (Illus.). 96p. (Orig.). 2000. pap. 20.00 (*0-9669024-7-5*) Broqueville Pubg.
— The Answer to Sun Tzu Bk. 1: A Story of Growth Through Questions. 2nd ed. (Illus.). 96p. 1999. reprint ed. pap. 20.00 (*0-9669024-0-8*) Broqueville Pubg.
— The Answer to Sun Tzu Bk. 2: A Story of Growth Through Questions. (Illus.). 96p. 1999. reprint ed. pap. 20.00 (*0-9669024-3-2*) Broqueville Pubg.
— Gentle Breeze: The Carrying the Scent of Flowers, Bk. 1. 2nd ed. (Illus.). 80p. (Orig.). 1999. reprint ed. pap. 20.00 (*0-9669024-1-6*) Broqueville Pubg.
— Gentle Breeze Bk. 2: Carrying the Scent of Flowers. (Illus.). 96p. 2000. pap. 20.00 (*0-9669024-5-9*) Broqueville Pubg.
— Running Water Bk. 1: Kissed by the Sun. (Illus.). 96p. (Orig.). 2000. pap. 20.00 (*0-9669024-4-0*) Broqueville Pubg.
— Unraveling Your Past: To Get into the Present, Bk. 1. 2nd ed. 200p. 1999. reprint ed. spiral bd. 25.00 (*0-9669024-2-4*) Broqueville Pubg.
— Unraveling Your Past Bk. 2: To Get into the Present. large type ed. 150p. 2000. spiral bd. 25.00 (*0-9669024-6-7*) Broqueville Pubg.

Brorson, Kerstin. Sing the Cows Home. 2nd abr. rev. ed. Ekstrand, Florence, ed. (Illus.). 176p. 1985. reprint ed. pap. 9.95 (*0-916871-07-X*) Welcome Pr.

Bros, Peter. Human Nature: How the Mind Generates Behavior. (Copernican Ser.: Vol. 8). 217p. 1998. pap. 18.95 (*0-9627769-9-8*) Fin Bk Partners.

Bros, Peter K. At the Gates of the Citadel: The Subjugation of Modern Science. (Copernican Ser.: Vol. 1). 264p. (Orig.). 1994. pap. 14.95 (*0-9627769-5-5*) Fin Bk Partners.
— Atoms, Stars & Minds: Synthesizing an Elementary Particle That Comprehends Itself. (Copernican Ser.: Vol. 3). 334p. (Orig.). 1992. pap. 14.95 (*0-9627769-1-2*) Fin Bk Partners.
— The Cooling Continuum: The Rise & Fall of Species on Earth. LC 95-116765. (Copernican Ser.: Vol. 2). 474p. 1994. pap. 14.95 (*0-9627769-3-9*) Fin Bk Partners.
— The Credit Union: Its Position in the Consumer Financial Marketplace. 186p. (C). 1989. 29.95 (*0-9627769-0-4*) Fin Bk Partners.
— How the Weather Really Works! (Copernican Ser.: Vol. 5). 188p. 1994. pap. 14.95 (*0-9627769-4-7*) Fin Bk Partners.
— Light: Replacing Three Centuries of Misconceptions. LC 97-123169. (Copernican Ser.: Vol. 6). 332p. (Orig.). 1996. pap. 16.95 (*0-9627769-6-3*) Fin Bk Partners.
— The Model Mind: How the Mind Moves Matter. (Copernican Ser.: Vol. 4). 370p. (Orig.). 1993. pap. 14.95 (*0-9627769-2-0*) Fin Bk Partners.
— The Model Mind: What the Mind Is & How It Works. 2nd rev. ed. (Copernican Ser.: Vol. 4). Orig. Title: Model Mind: How the Mind Moves Matter. 114p. 1998. pap. 14.95 (*0-9627769-8-X*) Fin Bk Partners.

Brosch, Dieter. Der Hafturlaub von Strafgefangenen unter Beruecksichtigung des Strafvollzugsziels. (European University Studies: Law: Ser. 2, Vol. 332). (GER.). 206p. 1983. 39.25 (*3-8204-7687-3*) P Lang Pubng.

Brosch, Ernie. How to Cable the Home Office - Small Office: A Complete Guide. 200p. 1995. per. 24.95 (*0-936648-72-4*) Telecom Bks.

Brosch, Robert A. Horror, Science Fiction, Fantasy Movie Posters & Lobby Cards, Vol. II, 1925-1970. Sevitch, Kren, ed. (Color Collector's Guide Ser.). (Illus.). 80p. (Orig.). 1993. pap. 12.95 (*0-9632794-0-8*) Archival Photo.

Broschart, Jacob. Ornamental Designs. (Illus.). 96p. 1992. pap. 9.95 (*0-486-27039-4*) Dover.

Broschat, T. K., jt. ed. see Chase, A. R.

***Broschat, Timothy K. & Meerow, Alan W.** Ornamental Palm Horticulture. LC 00-36403. 2000. write for info. (*0-8130-1804-8*) U Press Fla.

Brosche, P. & Suendermann, J., eds. Tidal Friction & the Earth's Rotation: Proceedings, Bielefeld, FRG, 1981. (Illus.). 345p. 1982. 54.95 (*0-387-12011-4*) Spr-Verlag.

Broschek, Anja. Michel Erhart: Ein Beitrag zur Schwaebischen Plastik der Spaetgotik. LC 72-81548. (Beitraege zur Kunstgeschichte Ser.: Vol. 8). (C). 1973. 192.35 (*3-11-001765-2*) De Gruyter.

Broschek, Erika, et al. Kursstrukturen: Syllabi & Course Descriptions for Business German in American Colleges & Universities. (Illus.). 106p. 1995. pap. 16.00 (*0-942017-25-0*) Amer Assn Teach German.

Broschek, Erika, jt. auth. see Kind, Uwe.

Broscious, John A., jt. auth. see Niaki, Shahzad.

Brose, David S. The Archaeology of Summer Island: Changing Settlement Systems in Northern Lake Michigan. LC 71-633183. (Museum of Anthropology, University of Michigan, Anthropological Papers: No. 41). (Illus.). 281p. reprint ed. pap. 87.20 (*0-7837-4773-X*, 204452800003) Bks Demand.
— Northwest Florida Expeditions of Clarence Bloomfield Moore. LC 99-6364. (Classics in Southeastern Archaeology Ser.). 1999. pap. 49.95 (*0-8173-0992-6*) U of Ala Pr.
— Yesterday's River: The Archaeology of Ten Thousand Years along the Tennessee-Tombigbee Waterway. (Illus.). 160p. (YA). (gr. 10). 1990. pap. 9.75 (*1-878600-00-1*) Cleve Mus Nat Hist.

Brose, David S., ed. The Late Prehistory of the Lake Erie Drainage Basin: A 1972 Symposium Revised. (Illus.). 355p. (Orig.). (C). 1976. pap. 5.00 (*1-878600-01-X*) Cleve Mus Nat Hist.

Brose, David S. & Greber, Nomi, eds. Hopewell Archaeology: The Chillicothe Conference. LC 79-88607. (MCJA Special Paper: No. 3). (Illus.). 323p. reprint ed. pap. 100.20 (*0-8357-6423-0*, 203579100097) Bks Demand.

Brose, E. F. Twenty New Ways to Get the Minister Out of Moneyraising. 1976. pap. 2.50 (*0-941500-18-7*) Sharing Co.

Brose, Eric D. Christian Labor & the Politics of Frustration in Imperial Germany. LC 83-25172. 420p. 1985. reprint ed. pap. 130.20 (*0-7837-9190-9*, 204989100004) Bks Demand.
— German History 1789-1871: From the Holy Roman

An Asterisk (*) at the beginning of an entry indicates that the title is appearing for the first time.

Empire to the Bismarckian Reich. LC 97-11757. (Illus.). 392p. (Orig.). (C). 1997. 65.00 (*1-57181-055-2*); pap. 19.50 (*1-57181-056-0*) Berghahn Bks.

— Out of the Shadow of Antiquity: The Politics of Technological Change in Prussia, 1809-1848. 312p. 1992. text 49.50 (*0-691-05685-4*, Pub. by Princeton U Pr) Cal Prin Full Svc.

— Technology & Science in Industrializing Nations 1500-1914. LC 97-22720. (Control of Nature Ser.). (C). 1997. 39.95 (*0-391-03973-3*); pap. 12.50 (*0-391-03974-1*) Humanities.

— Technology & Science in the Industrializing Nations, 1500-1914. (Control of Nature Ser.). 114p. 1999. 39.95 (*1-57392-536-5*, Humanity Bks); pap. 14.95 (*1-57392-537-3*, Humanity Bks) Prometheus Bks.

***Brose, John, et al.** The Guide to EKG Interpretation. 2nd rev. ed. (White Coat Pocket Guide Ser.). (Illus.). 150p. 2000. 20.00 (*0-8214-1328-7*) Ohio U Pr.

Brose, Margaret, ed. see White, Hayden V.

Brose, Michael J., et al. The Wisconsin Rules of Evidence: A Courtroom Handbook. 5th ed. 390p. 1997. ring bd. 75.00 (*0-945574-99-1*) State Bar WI.

Broselow, Ellen, et al, eds. Perspectives on Arabic Linguistics Vol. IV: Papers from the 4th Annual Symposium on Arabic Linguistics. Detroit, Michigan 1990. (Current Issues in Linguistic Theory Ser.: No. 85). viii, 282p. 1992. 71.00 (*1-55619-140-5*) J Benjamins Pubng Co.

***Brosen, Kim, ed.** A Guide to Training in Clinical Pharmacology in Europe. (Illus.). 340p. 1999. pap. 25.00 (*87-7838-459-1*, Pub. by Odense Univ) Intl Spec Bk.

Brosens. Diagnostic Imaging-Endoscopy. 1997. text 136.50 (*0-7020-2105-9*) Bailliere Tindall.

Brosens, I. & Donnez, J., eds. The Current Status of Endometriosis: Research & Management: Proceedings of the 3rd World Congress of Endometriosis, Brussels, 1992. LC 93-18078. (Illus.). 1993. 85.00 (*1-85070-454-6*) Prthnon Pub.

***Brosens, I. A. & Lunenfeld, Bruno.** Pathogenesis & Medical Management of Uterine Fibroids. LC 99-35362. (Illus.). 158p. 1999. 59.95 (*1-85070-098-2*) Prthnon Pub.

Brosheer, J. C., ed. see Munson, Robert D.

***Brosi, Brian.** Golf by the Numbers. (By the Numbers Ser.). (Illus.). 112p. (J). 2000. pap. 4.95 (*1-58261-184-X*) Sprts Pubng.

Brosi, Brian, jt. auth. see Ratermann, Dale.

Brosio, Georgio & Hochman, Harold M. Economic Justice, 2 vols. LC 98-36012. (International Library of Critical Writings in Economics: No. 97). 1208p. 1999. 400.00 (*1-85898-676-1*) E Elgar.

Brosio, Richard A. A Radical Democratic Critique of Capitalist Education. LC 93-24033. (Counterpoints Studies in the Postmodern Theory of Education Ser.: Vol. 3). XIX, 635p. (Orig.). (C). 1994. text 39.95 (*0-8204-2189-8*) P Lang Pubng.

Brosius, Christians & Butcher, Melissa. Image Journeys: Audio-visual Media & Cultural Change in India. LC 99-11082. 1999. write for info. (*0-7619-9326-6*) Sage.

Brosius, G. Excel 3.0 Professionell Klassikerreihe. (GER.). (C). 1991. text. write for info. (*0-201-55929-3*) Addison-Wesley.

Brosius, Hans-Bernd & Holtz-Bacha, Christina, eds. The German Communication Yearbook. LC 99-36332. 336p. 1999. text 67.50 (*1-57273-295-4*); pap. text 27.50 (*1-57273-296-2*) Hampton Pr NJ.

Brosius, Hans-Bernd, jt. auth. see Zillmann, Dolf.

Brosius, J. Peter & Hutterer, Karl L. After Duwagan: Deforestation, Succession & Adaptation in Upland Luzon, Philippines. LC 89-81764. (Michigan Studies on South & Southeast Asia: No. 2). (Illus.). 188p. (Orig.). 1990. pap. 16.95 (*0-89148-061-7*) Ctr S&SE Asian.

Brosius, Karen & Walker, Lisa. Philip Morris & the Arts: Thirty-Five Year Report. 128p. (Orig.). 1993. pap. text. write for info. (*0-934037-07-8*) P Morris.

Brosius, Lewis W. Brosius, Genealogy of Henry & Brosius & Their Descendants: Also Some Short Accounts of Other Families Bering the Brosius Name. (Illus.). 472p. 1993. reprint ed. pap. 63.00 (*0-8328-3595-1*); reprint ed. lib. bdg. 73.00 (*0-8328-3594-3*) Higginson Bk Co.

***Brosius, maria.** Women in Ancient Persia, 559-331 BC. (Oxford Classical Monographs). (Illus.). 278p. 1998. reprint ed. pap. text 24.95 (*0-19-815255-8*) OUP.

Broskowski, Anthony, et al, eds. Linking Health & Mental Health. LC 81-8875. (Sage Annual Reviews of Community Mental Health Ser.: No. 2). 296p. reprint ed. pap. 91.80 (*0-8357-8480-0*, 203474700091) Bks Demand.

Brosky, Kerriann F. Huntington's Past Revisited. (Illus.). 192p. 1997. 21.95 (*0-930545-17-6*) Maple Hill Pr.

Broslavick, Chris, jt. compiled by see Pichler, Tony.

Brosler, Lauren. New Ways of Working with Local Laws to Prevent Crime. Kirby, Judy, ed. (Special Focus Ser.). 80p. (Orig.). 1996. pap. 14.95 (*0-934513-10-4*, LAW1) Natl Crime DC.

Brosler, Lauren & O'Neil, Jean. Reducing Gun Violence: What Communities Can Do. Kirby, Judy, ed. 42p. (Orig.). 1995. pap. 9.95 (*0-934513-04-X*) Natl Crime DC.

Brosman, Catharine S. French Novelists, 1930-1960. (Dictionary of Literary Biography Ser.: Vol. 72). 400p. 1988. text 155.00 (*0-8103-4550-1*) Gale.

Brosman, Catharine S. Jean-Paul Sartre. (World Authors Ser.: No. 697). 168p. 1983. 23.95 (*0-8057-6544-1*, Twyne) Mac Lib Ref.

— Journeying from Canyon de Chelly. LC 90-33362. 64p. 1990. pap. 7.95 (*0-8071-1627-0*); text 15.95 (*0-8071-1626-2*) La State U Pr.

— Malraux, Sartre, & Aragon As Political Novelists. LC 65-63876. (University of Florida Humanities Monographs: No. 17). 71p. reprint ed. pap. 30.00 (*0-7837-5829-4*, 204554800006) Bks Demand.

— Passages: Poems. LC 95-44605. (C). 1996. pap. 9.95 (*0-8071-2050-2*); text 16.95 (*0-8071-2049-9*) La State U Pr.

— Simone de Beauvoir Revisited. (Twayne's World Authors Ser.: No. 820). 190p. 1991. 32.00 (*0-8057-8269-9*) Macmillan.

— Visions of War in France: Fiction, Art, Ideology. LC 98-50884. (Illus.). 240p. 1999. text 50.00 (*0-8071-2346-3*) La State U Pr.

Brosman, Catharine S., ed. Dictionary of Twentieth-Century Culture Vol. 2: French Culture, Vol. 2. 449p. 1995. 99.00 (*0-8103-8482-5*) Gale.

— Dictionary of Twentieth-Century Culture Vol. 5: African American Culture, Vol. 5. (Dictionary of 20th Century Culture Ser.: No. 2). 531p. 1996. 99.00 (*0-8103-8485-X*) Gale.

Brosman, Catharine S., ed. French Novelists, 1900-1930. (Dictionary of Literary Biography Ser.: Vol. 65). 450p. 1987. text 155.00 (*0-8103-1743-5*) Gale.

— Nineteenth Century French Fiction Writers: Romanticism & Realism, 1800-1860. LC 92-17232. (Dictionary of Literary Biography Ser.: Vol. 119). 400p. 1992. text 155.00 (*0-8103-7596-6*) Gale.

***Brosman, Catharine Savage.** Places in Mind. LC 99-59204. 80p. 2000. 22.50 (*0-8071-2546-6*); pap. 14.95 (*0-8071-2547-4*) La State U Pr.

Brosman, Catherine S. An Annotated Bibliography on the Criticism of Andre Gide, 1973-1988. LC 89-16846. 368p. 1989. text 20.00 (*0-8240-7973-6*, H959) Garland.

— Art as Testimony: The Work of Jules Roy. 237p. 1989. pap. 24.95 (*0-8130-0915-4*) U Press Fla.

— Shimmering Maya & Other Essays. LC 94-6065. 168p. 1994. 24.95 (*0-8071-1874-5*) La State U Pr.

Brosman, Paul W. The Rhine Franconian Element in Old French. LC 98-30529. (Studies in Old Germanic Languages & Literatures: Vol. 5). XI, 311p. (C). 1999. pap. text 55.95 (*0-8204-4189-9*) P Lang Pubng.

Brosnac, Donald. The AMP Book: A Guitarists Introductory Guide to Tube Amps. (Illus.). 64p. (C). 1987. reprint ed. pap. 13.95 (*0-933224-05-2*, T004) Bold Strummer Ltd.

— The Electric Guitar: Its History & Construction. (Illus.). 96p. (C). 1975. pap. 7.95 (*0-915572-00-1*) Panjandrum.

— Guitar Electronics for Musicians. LC 95-187906. (Illus.). 128p. 1983. pap. 22.95 (*0-7119-0232-1*, OP42324) Omnibus NY.

— Guitar History Vol. 1: Guitars Made by the Fender Company. (Illus.). 60p. 1986. reprint ed. pap. text 13.95 (*0-933224-06-0*, T016) Bold Strummer Ltd.

— An Introduction to Scientific Guitar Design. Clarke, Nicholas, ed. LC 79-50925. (Illus.). 1979. reprint ed. pap. text 19.95 (*0-933224-01-X*, T023) Bold Strummer Ltd.

— The Steel String Guitar: Its History & Construction. 2nd rev. ed. (Illus.). 112p. (C). 1976. pap. 7.95 (*0-915572-26-5*) Panjandrum.

Brosnac, Donald. Tuning Your Guitar. LC 77-82816. (Illus.). 32p. 1977. pap. 5.95 (*0-8256-2180-1*, AM35858) Music Sales.

Brosnahan, Leonard F. The Sounds of Language: An Inquiry into the Role of Genetic Factors in the Development of Sound Systems. LC 82-975. 250p. 1982. reprint ed. lib. bdg. 59.50 (*0-313-23353-5*, BRSOL, Greenwood Pr) Greenwood.

Brosnahan, Thomas. Dollarwise Guide to New England. 408p. 1986. pap. 11.95 (*0-317-37801-5*) S&S Trade.

— Israel on $35 a Day. 360p. 1986. pap. 10.95 (*0-671-55631-2*) S&S Trade.

Brosnahan, Tom. Frommer's Comprehensive Travel Guide New England, 1996. 1996. pap. 17.00 (*0-671-51888-7*) S&S Trade.

— Lonely Planet Bali et Lombok. 2nd ed. (FRE.). 1997. 24.95 (*2-84070-057-3*) Lonely Planet.

— Lonely Planet Istanbul: City Guides. (Illus.). 260p. 1997. pap. 12.95 (*0-86442-388-8*) Lonely Planet.

— Lonely Planet Istanbul: City Guides. 2nd ed. (Lonely Planet City Guides). (Illus.). 176p. 1999. pap. text 14.95 (*0-86442-585-6*) Lonely Planet.

— Lonely Planet New England: Travel Survival Kit. (Illus.). 528p. 1996. pap. 19.95 (*0-86442-265-2*) Lonely Planet.

— Lonely Planet Turquie. (FRE.). 1997. 29.95 (*2-84070-054-9*) Lonely Planet.

— Lonely Planet Turquie. 2nd ed. 800p. 1999. pap. 31.95 (*2-84070-096-4*) Lonely Planet.

— Turkish Phrasebook. (TUR., Illus.). 160p. 1990. pap. 3.95 (*0-86442-069-2*) Lonely Planet.

— Turkish Phrasebook. 2nd ed. (Lonely Planet Phrasebooks). 256p. 1999. pap. text 6.95 (*0-86442-436-1*) Lonely Planet.

Brosnahan, Tom, contrib. by. Lonely Planet Turkey Travel Atlas. (Illus.). 112p. 1997. pap. 14.95 (*0-86442-272-5*) Lonely Planet.

Brosnahan, Tom & Keller, Nancy. Lonely Planet Guatemala, Belize & Yucatan: La Ruta Maya. 3rd ed. (Illus.). 584p. 1997. pap. 19.95 (*0-86442-424-8*) Lonely Planet.

Brosnahan, Tom & Yale, Pat. Lonely Planet Turkey. 5th ed. (Illus.). 752p. 1996. pap. 19.95 (*0-86442-364-0*) Lonely Planet.

— Lonely Planet Turkey. 6th ed. 848p. 1999. pap. 21.95 (*0-86442-599-6*) Lonely Planet.

***Brosnahan, Tom, et al.** New England. 2nd ed. (Illus.). 544p. 1999. pap. 19.95 (*0-86442-570-8*) Lonely Planet.

Brosnan, C. F., ed. Heat Shock Proteins & Gamma-Delta T Cells. (Chemical Immunology Ser.: Vol. 53). (Illus.). viii, 132p. 1992. 108.00 (*3-8055-5508-3*) S Karger.

Brosnan, Cornelius J. Jason Lee: Prophet of the New Oregon. LC 84-71620. (Illus.). 376p. 1985. reprint ed. pap. text 12.00 (*0-685-10039-1*) Academy Bks.

Brosnan, James. The Long Season. 1981. reprint ed. 19.95 (*0-941372-01-4*) Holtzman Pr.

Brosnan, Julia. Lesbians Talk Detonating the Nuclear Family. 1996. pap. 8.95 (*1-85727-028-2*, Pub. by Scarlet Pr) LPC InBook.

Brosnan, Leila. Reading Virginia Woolf's Essays & Journalism. LC 98-131484. 200p. 1998. 70.00 (*0-7486-0852-4*, Pub. by Edinburgh U Pr) Col U Pr.

Brosnan, Mark J. Technophobia: The Psychological Impact of Information Technology. LC 97-39321. (Illus.). 232p. (C). 1998. 75.00 (*0-415-13596-6*); pap. 22.99 (*0-415-13597-4*) Routledge.

Brosnan, Michael. Against the Current: How One School Struggled & Succeeded with At-Risk Teens. 1997. 24.95 (*0-614-27997-6*); pap. 24.95 (*0-435-08140-3*, 08140) Heinemann.

— Telecom Professionals Complete Guide to the Internet Saves Hours of Time in Finding the Most Us, 1. 1999. pap. text 24.95 (*1-57820-030-X*) Telecom Bks.

Brosnan, William J. God & Reason: Some Theses from Natural Theology. LC 33-1364. 224p. reprint ed. pap. 69.50 (*0-7837-5575-9*, 204535700005) Bks Demand.

Brosowske, Scott D. & Bement, Leland C. Pedestrian Survey of Playa Lake Environments in Beaver & Texas Counties, Oklahoma: Project 40-12040.021. (Archeological Resource Survey Report: No. 39). (Illus.). 68p. 1998. pap. 4.00 (*1-881346-32-3*) Univ OK Archeol.

Brosowski, Bruno, ed. see Hao, Dinh Nho.

Brosowski, Bruno, ed. see Nho Hao, Dinh.

Brosowski, Bruno, ed. see Wu Li.

Brosowski, F. & Deutsch, F., eds. Parametric Optimization & Approximation. (International Series of Numerical Mathematics: No. 72). 264p. 1985. 86.50 (*0-8176-1671-3*) Birkhauser.

Bross, et al, eds. Handbook of Semiconductor Interconnect Technology. LC 97-38710. (Illus.). 592p. 1997. text 175.00 (*0-8247-9966-6*) Dekker.

Bross & Walsh, eds. International Patents for Electronic Cooling Technology, 6 vols., Set. 6112p. 1994. 995.00 (*0-8247-9588-1*) Dekker.

Bross, A. D., et al, eds. SciFi97: Workshop on Scintillating Fiber Detectors. LC 98-87810. (Conference Proceedings Ser.: Vol. 450). (Illus.). 640p. 1998. 165.00 (*1-56396-792-8*) Am Inst Physics.

Bross, Arthur & Martinez, Anthony. Auditing Guidelines in the Semiconductor Industry: Assessing Quality. Date not set. write for info. (*0-8247-9944-5*) Dekker.

Bross, Arthur & Walsh, Thomas J., eds. International Patents for Electronic Cooling Technology, Master Index. (Illus.). 594p. 1994. text 995.00 (*0-8247-9207-6*) Dekker.

— International Patents for Electronic Cooling Technology, 6 vols., Vol. 1. (Illus.). 1100p. 1994. text 995.00 (*0-8247-9202-5*) Dekker.

— International Patents for Electronic Cooling Technology, 6 vols., Vol. 2. (Illus.). 1114p. 1994. text 995.00 (*0-8247-9203-3*) Dekker.

— International Patents for Electronic Cooling Technology, 6 vols., Vol. 4. (Illus.). 1108p. 1994. text 995.00 (*0-8247-9205-X*) Dekker.

— International Patents for Electronic Cooling Technology, 6 vols., Vol. 5. (Illus.). 1108p. 1994. text 995.00 (*0-8247-9206-8*) Dekker.

Bross, D., et al. Scintillating Fiber Detectors: Proceedings of the SCIFI '93 Workshop, 2 vols. 684p. 1995. text 129.00 (*981-02-1818-4*) World Scientific Pub.

Bross, Donald C., et al. The New Child Protection Team Handbook. LC 88-2542. 658p. 1988. text 30.00 (*0-8240-8519-1*) Garland.

Bross, Donald G., jt. auth. see Taylor, Jimmy D.

Bross, Irwin D. Crimes of Official Science: A Casebook. rev. ed. 106p. (C). 1988. 25.00 (*0-317-92308-0*); pap. 12.50 (*0-317-92309-9*) Biomed Metatech.

— Fifty Years of Folly & Fraud "In the Name of Science" From Crossroads to the Health Care Crisis. 195p. (C). 1994. pap. 15.00 (*0-9621418-6-0*) Biomed Metatech.

***Bross, Jean E., et al.** Quick Takes Rituals & Retreats. 120p. (Orig.). 1999. pap. text 16.95 (*1-889108-43-0*) Liv Good News.

Bross, Jean E., jt. auth. see Piercy, Robert W.

Bross, Louise S., ed. see Rubin, David S.

Bross, Olive J. Church & Parliament: The Reshaping of the Church of England, 1828-1860. LC 59-7423. 249p. 1959. reprint ed. pap. 30.00 (*0-608-08248-1*, 202399200035) Bks Demand.

Bross, Richard & Walsh, Thomas J., eds. International Patents for Electronic Cooling Technology, 6 vols., Vol. 3. (Illus.). 1112p. 1994. text 995.00 (*0-8247-9204-1*) Dekker.

Bross, Ruth M. Always in Season Florida: Your Florida Gulfcoast Newcomer & Relocation Guide. 2nd rev. ed. (Illus.). 128p. 1997. pap. 7.00 (*0-9659469-0-8*) SPACOC.

Bross, U., et al. Bio-Technology Audit in Hungary: Guidelines, Implementation, Results. (Technology, Innovation & Policy Ser.: Vol. 7). (Illus.). xiv, 221p. 1998. pap. 63.00 (*3-7908-1092-4*) Spr-Verlag.

Brossa, Joan. Bosc a Casa: Con Cinco Litografias Orieinales y dos Agua Fuertes Firmados por Perejaume. deluxe limited ed. (Ediciones Especiales y de Bibliofilo Ser.). (CAT., Illus.). 74p. 1993. 4750.00 (*0-614-00144-7*) Elliots Bks.

— Cabaleta. limited ed. (CAT., Illus.). 1993. 3750.00 (*0-614-00246-X*) Elliots Bks.

— Cabaleta: Con Doce Litografias Originales Firmados por Moises Villelia. limited ed. (CAT., Illus.). 1993. 3750.00 (*0-614-00141-2*) Elliots Bks.

— Nocturn Matinal. deluxe limited ed. (Ediciones Especiales y de Bibliofilo Ser.). (CAT., Illus.). 1993. 4750.00 (*84-343-0110-5*) Elliots Bks.

— Oda a Joan Miro. limited ed. (Ediciones Especiales y de Bibliofilo Ser.). (CAT., Illus.). 1993. 1000.00 (*84-343-0183-0*) Elliots Bks.

— Tal I Tant. (CAT., Illus.). 1993. bds. 250.00 (*0-614-00244-3*) Elliots Bks.

— Tal I Tant. limited ed. (Ediciones Especiales y de Bibliofilo Ser.). (CAT., Illus.). 1993. 150.00 (*84-343-0282-9*) Elliots Bks.

— U No Es Ningu. (Ediciones Especiales y de Bibliofilo Ser.). (CAT., Illus.). 100p. 1993. 750.00 (*84-343-0302-7*); pap. 475.00 (*0-614-00140-4*) Elliots Bks.

Brossa, Joan, ed. see Miro, Joan.

Brossard. Dictionary of Music. Gruber, Albion, ed. (Musical Theorists in Translation Ser.: Vol. 12). 280p. 1983. lib. bdg. 74.00 (*0-931902-15-0*) Inst Mediaeval Mus.

Brossard, Chandler. As the Wolf Howls at My Door. LC 91-28630. 21.95p. 1992. 21.95 (*0-916583-97-X*) Dalkey Arch.

***Brossard, Chandler.** The Bold Saboteurs. 4th ed. 352p. 2001. reprint ed. pap. 15.00 (*1-928746-18-7*) Herodias.

Brossard, Chandler. Did Christ Make Love? LC 72-89690. 1973. 6.95 (*0-672-51730-2*, Bobbs) Macmillan.

***Brossard, Chandler.** Who Walk in Darkness. 3rd ed. 256p. 2000. reprint ed. pap. 14.00 (*1-928746-12-8*) Herodias.

Brossard, Chandler, ed. see Poe, Edgar Allan.

Brossard, Emma. Petroleum Research & Venezuela's Intevep: The Clash of the Giants. LC 93-13661. 250p. 1993. 25.00 (*0-87814-399-8*) PennWell Bks.

Brossard, Jean. Grammatica Pratica dell'Inglese dalla A alla Z. (ENG & ITA.). 244p. 1992. pap. 39.95 (*0-7859-9600-1*) Fr & Eur.

Brossard, Judith & Cowles Creative Publishing Staff. Deck the Halls: A Treasury of Christmas Crafts. LC 97-205174. 160 p. 1997. write for info. (*0-86573-196-9*) Creat Pub Intl.

Brossard, Nicole. The Aerial Letter. Wildeman, Marlene, tr. 165p. pap. 9.95 (*0-88961-123-8*, Pub. by Womens Pr) LPC InBook.

— French Kiss: or A Pang's Progress. 1986. pap. 9.95 (*0-88910-158-2*, Pub. by Talonbks) Genl Dist Srvs.

— Lovhers. 96p. 1987. pap. 5.00 (*0-919349-93-5*) Guernica Editions.

— Picture Theory. 186p. pap. 12.00 (*0-920717-22-5*) Guernica Editions.

— Picture Theory. Goddard, Barbara, tr. LC 90-63921. (Roof Bks.). (Illus.). 160p. 1991. pap. text 75.00 (*0-937804-40-1*) Segue NYC.

— Typhon Dru. Bergvall, Caroline, tr. 44p. 1997. 11.00 (*1-874400-11-3*, Pub. by Reality St Edits) SPD-Small Pr Dist.

Brossard, Nicole, et al. Yefief 2: Health & Human Rights, a View Along the Running Edge. abr. rev. ed. (Yefief Asia Editions Ser.). (Illus.). 100p. 2002. pap. 24.95 (*1-884434-02-9*) Images For Media.

Brossard, Sebastien De, see De Brossard, Sebastien.

Brossart, Judith, ed. A Treasury of Christmas Ornaments by the Editors of Crafts Magazine. (Illus.). 96p. 1991. text. write for info. (*0-9621148-4-7*); pap. text. write for info. (*0-9621148-5-5*) PRMDIA Spcl Intrst.

Brosse, Olivier de la, see De la Brosse, Olivier.

Brosseau, Christian. Fundamentals of Polarized Light: A Statistical Optics Approach. LC 98-10444. 424p. 1998. 98.95 (*0-471-14302-2*) Wiley.

Brosseau, Maurice, et al, eds. China Review, 1997. 430p. (C). 1997. 64.50 (*962-201-774-6*, Pub. by Chinese Univ) U of Mich Pr.

— China Review, 1996. (Illus.). 453p. (C). 1997. 64.50 (*962-201-735-5*, Pub. by Chinese Univ) U of Mich Pr.

Brosselin, Arlette. Les Forets de la Cote D'or Au XIX Siecle, et L'utilisation de Leurs Produits. Bruchey, Stuart, ed. LC 77-81822. (Dissertations in European Economic History Ser.). (FRE., Illus.). 1978. lib. bdg. 41.95 (*0-405-10775-7*) Ayer.

Brossi, Arnold & Benson, Richard E., eds. Organic Syntheses: An Annual Publication of Satisfactory Methods for the Preparation of Organic Chemicals, Vol. 53. LC 21-17747. 207p. reprint ed. pap. 64.20 (*0-608-13716-2*, 205528300013) Bks Demand.

Brossi, Mario & Mariano, Joseph N. Multilevel Marketing: A Legal Primer: A Handbook for Executives, Entrepreneurs, Managers & Distributors. 78p. (Orig.). 1991. text. write for info. (*0-9630469-0-X*) Direct Selling.

Brossman, Douglas, jt. auth. see Prescott, Michael K.

Brossman, Sandra C. Co-Creating Oneness: Choosing a Path to Inner Peace & Universal Harmony. 1999. pap. 20.99 (*0-9671540-1-4*) Universal Vision.

***Brost, Gerald, ed.** Containing Costs in Minnesota's Health Care System: A Report to Governor Arne H. Carlson & the Minnesota Legislature. 177p. (C). 1999. reprint ed. pap. text 30.00 (*0-7881-8320-6*) DIANE Pub.

Brost, Leif, jt. auth. see Dahlstrom, Ake.

***Brostek, Michael.** Equal Employment Opportunity: Complaint Caseloads Rising, with Effects of New Regulations on Future Trends Unclear. (Illus.). 50p. (C). 2000. pap. text 20.00 (*0-7881-8721-X*) DIANE Pub.

Brosten, Olga. The Mystic Eye-Manifestations of Psychic Phenomenon. Ashton, Sylvia, ed. LC 78-54162. 1981. 22.95 (*0-87949-122-1*) Ashley Bks.

Brosterman, Norman. Inventing Kindergarten: Nineteenth-Century Children, Twentieth-Century Art. LC 96-27191. (Illus.). 160p. 1997. 39.95 (*0-8109-3526-0*, Pub. by Abrams) Time Warner.

***Brosterman, Norman.** Out of Time: Designs for the 20th-Century Future. (Illus.). 96p. 2000. pap. 19.95 (*0-8109-2939-2*, Pub. by Abrams) Time Warner.

Brosterman, Robert. The Complete Estate Planning Guide. 1994. pap. 6.99 (*0-451-62877-2*, Ment) NAL.

Brosterman, Robert, jt. auth. see Adams, Kathleen.

B

Brostof. Immunology Case Studies. 1997. 17.00 (*0-7234-2945-6*) Wolfe Pubng AZ.

Brostoff, J. Clinical Immunology Outline. 1994. 20.00 (*1-56375-664-1*) Gower-Mosby.

***Brostoff, Jonathan & Gamlin, Linda.** Asthma: The Complete Guide to Integrative Therapies. (Illus.). 512p. 2000. pap. 19.95 (*0-89281-932-4*) Inner Tradit.

— Food Allergies & Food Intolerance: The Complete Guide to Their Identification & Cure. LC 99-56018. (Illus.). 480p. 2000. pap. 19.95 (*0-89281-875-1*, Inner Trad Espanol) Inner Tradit.

***Brostoff, Teresa & Sinsheimer, Ann.** American Legal English: An Introduction to the Legal Language & Culture of the United States. LC 00-32643. 2000. write for info. (*0-379-21424-5*) Oceana.

Brostow, ed. Mechanical & Thermophysical Properties of Polymer Liquid Crystals. (Polymer Liquid Crystals Ser.). (Illus.). 448p. 1998. 169.95 (*0-412-60900-2*, Chap & Hall NY) Chapman & Hall.

Brostow, Witold. Failure of Plastics. 1986. 135.00 (*0-02-947510-4*) Free Pr.

***Brostow, Witold.** Performance of Plastics. LC 00-21005. 2000. write for info. (*1-56990-277-1*) Hanser-Gardner.

Brostow, Witold. Science of Materials. LC 84-15484. 460p. (C). 1985. reprint ed. lib. bdg. 55.50 (*0-89874-780-5*) Krieger.

Brostow, Witold & Corneliussen, Roger D. Failure of Plastics. 486p. 1986. 159.00 (*1-56990-008-6*) Hanser-Gardner.

B

Brostrom & Kasinec. Literary Criticism from 1400 to 1800, Vol. 31. 500p. 1996. text 150.00 (*0-8103-9276-3*) Gale.

Brostrom, David C. A Guide to Homeschooling for Librarians. (Handbook Ser.). 85p. 1995. pap. text 19.00 (*0-917846-46-X*, 95625) Highsmith Pr.

Brostrom, Jennifer, ed. Literature Criticism from 1400 to 1800 Vol. 29: 18th Century Scottish Poetry. 500p. 1995. text 140.00 (*0-8103-8945-2*, 001413) Gale.

Brostrom, Jennifer & Kasinec. Criticism from 1400 to 1800, Vol. 32. 500p. 1996. text 150.00 (*0-8103-9277-1*) Gale.

— Literary Criticism from 1400 to 1800, Vol. 30. 500p. 1995. text 150.00 (*0-8103-9275-5*) Gale.

— Literature Criticism from 1400 to 1800, Vol. 33. 500p. 1996. text 150.00 (*0-8103-9975-X*, GML00597-001582) Gale.

Brostrom, Kenneth, ed. Russian Literature & American Critics. (Papers in Slavic Philology: No. 4). 412p. 1984. pap. 15.00 (*0-930042-58-1*) Mich Slavic Pubns.

Brostrom, Kenneth, tr. see Bakhtin, Mikhail M.

Brostrom, Kenneth N., ed. Archpriest Avvakum: The Life Written by Himself. LC 79-19639. (Michigan Slavic Translations Ser.: No. 4). 1979. 20.00 (*0-930042-33-6*); pap. 10.00 (*0-930042-37-9*) Mich Slavic Pubns.

Broszat, Martin. Hitler & the Collapse of Weimar Germany. Berghahn, Volker R., tr. LC 86-26857. 166p. 1987. 39.00 (*0-85496-509-2*); pap. 16.50 (*0-85496-517-3*, Pub. by Berg Pubs) NYU Pr.

— The Hitler State: The Foundation & Development of the Internal Structure of the Third Reich. Hiden, John, tr. from GER. (Illus.). 378p. (C). 1989. pap. 45.00 (*0-582-48997-0*, 73439) Longman.

Broszeit, E., et al, eds. Plasma Surface Engineering: Proceedings of the 1st International Conference, 1988, 2 vols. (Illus.). 1310p. 1989. lib. bdg. 178.00 (*0-685-44884-3*, Pub. by DGM Metallurgy Info) IR Pubns.

— Plasma Surface Engineering: Proceedings of the 1st International Conference, 1988, 2 vols., Vol. 1. (Illus.). 1310p. 1989. write for info. (*3-88355-150-3*, Pub. by DGM Metallurgy Info) IR Pubns.

— Plasma Surface Engineering: Proceedings of the 1st International Conference, 1988, 2 vols., Vol. 2. (Illus.). 1310p. 1989. write for info. (*3-88355-151-1*, Pub. by DGM Metallurgy Info) IR Pubns.

Brotchi, Jacques & Fischer, Georges, eds. Intramedullary Spinal Cord Tumors. (Illus.). 128p. 1996. text 119.00 (*0-86577-593-1*) Thieme Med Pubs.

Brotchie, jt. auth. see Mathews.

Brotchie, Alastair & Jones, Richard G., eds. This Fish Is Loaded! The Book of Surreal Humor. 256p. (Orig.). 1991. 17.95 (*0-8065-1262-8*, Citadel Pr); pap. 10.95 (*0-8065-1270-9*, Citadel Pr) Carol Pub Group.

Brotchie, Alastair, ed. see Roussel, Raymond.

Brotchie, Alastair, tr. see Jarry, Alfred.

Brotchie, Alistair, jt. auth. see Gooding, Mel.

Brotchie, John, et al, eds. Cities in Competition: Productive & Sustainable Cities for the 21st Century. LC 95-186192. (Illus.). 532p. (Orig.). 1995. pap. 52.50 (*0-582-80106-0*) Trans-Atl Phila.

— East West Perspectives on the 21st Century Urban Development: Sustainable Eastern & Western Cities in the New Millennium. LC 98-74506. 4p. 1999. text 78.95 (*1-84014-317-7*) Ashgate Pub Co.

— The Spatial Impact of Technological Change. 336p. 1987. lib. bdg. 55.00 (*0-7099-5006-3*, Pub. by C Helm) Routldge.

Brotemarkle, Benjamin D. Beyond the Theme Parks: Exploring Central Florida. LC 98-46870. (Illus.). 242p. 1999. 24.95 (*0-8130-1657-6*) U Press Fla.

***Brotemarkle, Benjamin D.** Beyond the Theme Parks: Exploring Central Florida. 2000. reprint ed. pap. 16.95 (*0-8130-1825-0*) U Press Fla.

Brotemarkle, Diane. Cross Cultural Mythology. 2nd ed. LC 97-140745. 171p. (C). 1997. pap. text 13.95 (*0-943025-96-6*) Cummngs & Hath.

— Imagination & Myths in John Keat's Poetry. LC 93-18843. 176p. 1993. 79.95 (*0-7734-2214-5*) E Mellen.

Brother Andrew. For the Love of My Brothers. 256p. 1998. pap. 10.99 (*0-7642-2074-8*, 212074) Bethany Hse.

Brother Andrew & DeVore Williams, Susan. And God Changed His Mind. 2nd ed. LC 99-30464. 192p. 1999. reprint ed. pap. 9.99 (*0-8007-9272-6*) Chosen Bks.

Brother Anthony of Taize & Kim, Young-moo, trs. from KOR. The Sound of My Waves: Selected Poems by Ko Un. (Cornell East Asia Ser.: No. 68). 124p. (C). 1993. pap. 14.00 (*0-939657-68-6*) Cornell East Asia Pgm.

Brother Anthony of Taize, tr. see Ch'on Sang Pyong.

Brother Anthony of Taize, tr. see Kwang-kyu, Kim.

Brother Anthony of Taize, tr. see Kyong-Nim, Shin.

Brother Anthony of Taize, tr. see Sang, Ku.

Brother Bob. Please Remind Me I Am the Presence of Love: Awakening to the Awareness of Love. LC 94-69510. (Illus.). 159p. (Orig.). 1995. pap. 12.95 (*0-9644021-5-7*) Peaceful Express.

— Real Feelings: Heaven on Earth. LC 95-71962. (Illus.). 126p. (Orig.). 1996. pap. 10.95 (*0-9644021-3-0*) Peaceful Express.

Brother Craig. Humor Helps! The Benefits of Humor, Laughter & Being Funny. LC 98-14694. (Illus.). 160p. 1998. pap. 9.95 (*0-88007-219-9*) Woodbridge Pr.

— Love Yourself, So . . . Hate the Weight! 100 Practical Tips That Really Work - You Can Feel Better, Look Better, Even Be Better. LC 96-34357. (Illus.). 128p. (Orig.). 1996. pap. 9.95 (*0-88007-215-6*) Woodbridge Pr.

Brother Ephraim. Rains of the Late Season: The Holy Spirit at the Birth of a New Community. 136p. (C). 1990. 49.00 (*0-85439-417-6*, Pub. by St Paul Pubns) St Mut.

***Brother John of Taize.** The Adventure of Holiness: Biblical Foundations & Present-Day Perspectives. LC 99-28261. xviii, 168p. 1999. pap. 12.95 (*0-8189-0877-7*) Alba.

Brother John of Taize. The Pilgrim God: A Biblical Journey. 220p. 1985. reprint ed. pap. 13.95 (*0-912405-18-X*, Pastoral Press) OR Catholic.

— Praying the Our Father Today. 64p. 1992. pap. 7.95 (*0-912405-91-0*, Pastoral Press) OR Catholic.

— The Way of the Lord: A New Testament Pilgrimage. 200p. (Orig.). 1990. pap. 13.95 (*0-912405-69-4*, Pastoral Press) OR Catholic.

Brother Lawrence. Daily Readings with Brother Lawrence. Llewelyn, Robert, ed. (Daily Readings Ser.). 96p. 1986. pap. 4.95 (*0-87243-144-4*) Templegate.

— The God-Illuminated Cook: The Practice of the Presence of God. Dawes, Robin, ed. LC 74-84399. (Illus.). 144p. 1975. pap. 3.95 (*0-914896-00-8*) East Ridge Pr.

— The Kitchen Saint & the Heritage of Islam. Douglas, Elmer H., tr. from FRE. LC 88-35793. (Princeton Theological Monographs: No. 18).Tr. of La/Pratique de la Presence de Dieu. (Illus.). (Orig.). 1989. pap. 10.00 (*1-55635-003-1*) Pickwick.

— The Practice of the Presence of God. DeMeester, Conrad, ed. Sciurba, Salvatore, tr. from FRE. LC 93-2444. (Illus.). 240p. (Orig.). 1994. pap. 9.95 (*0-935216-21-9*) ICS Pubns.

— The Practice of the Presence of God. 112p. (YA). (gr. 10). 1989. mass mkt. 4.99 (*0-8007-8599-1*, Spire) Revell.

***Brother Lawrence.** The Practice of the Presence of God. rev. ed. Chadwick, Harold J., ed. (Pure Gold Classics). (Illus.). 2000. pap. 9.99 (*0-88270-793-0*) Bridge-Logos.

Brother Lawrence. The Practice of the Presence of God: Updated in Today's Language. 64p. 1998. 5.97 (*1-57748-243-3*) Barbour Pub.

Brother Lawrence & Laubach, Frank C. Practicing His Presence. 3rd ed. Edwards, Gene, ed. 1973. pap. 8.95 (*0-940232-01-4*) Seedsowers.

Brother, Marvin, jt. auth. see Rosen, Paul.

Brother Michael of the Holy Trinity. The Third Secret of Fatima. Gardiner, Anne B., tr. from FRE. LC 91-65429. 53p. (Orig.). 1992. pap. 1.50 (*0-89555-435-6*) TAN Bks Pubs.

Brother Nectario. Christopher Columbus a Jew. 1992. lib. bdg. 79.95 (*0-8490-5345-5*) Gordon Pr.

Brother Nectario M. Juan Colon Alias Christopher Columbus. Josephson, Emanuel M., ed. LC 72-166573. (Blacked-Out History Ser.). 1971. pap. 10.00 (*0-686-29300-2*) A-albionic Res.

Brother Ramon. Forty Days & Forty Nights: A Guide for Spending Time Alone with God. (Illus.). 176p. 1993. 12.00 (*0-551-02738-X*, Pub. by M Pickering) Harper SF.

***Brother Ramon.** The Prayer Mountain: Exploring the High Places of Prayer. 144p. 1999. 12.95 (*1-85311-225-9*, 6112, Pub. by Canterbury Press Norwich) Morehouse Pub.

Brother Robert J. Kealey. Curriculum in the Catholic School. 61p. 1986. 6.00 (*0-318-20568-8*) Natl Cath Educ.

Brother Roger. Peace of Heart in All Things: Meditations for Each Day of the Year. LC 96-53041. 1996. 9.95 (*0-941050-96-3*) GIA Pubns.

Brother Roger of Taize. Life from Within: Prayers by Brother Roger of Taize. 32p. (Orig.). 1990. pap. 9.95 (*0-664-25162-5*) Westminster John Knox.

— The Wonder of a Love. (Illus.). 24p. (Orig.). 1996. pap. 6.95 (*0-664-25685-6*) Westminster John Knox.

Brotherhead, William. Forty Years Among the Old Booksellers of Philadelphia: With Bibliographical Remarks. LC 72-5538. (Select Bibliographies Reprint Ser.). 1977. reprint ed. 18.95 (*0-8369-6900-6*) Ayer.

Brotherlin, Wendy. Monsters in the M. A. C. Monster's Athletic Club. (Illus.). 31p. (J). 1996. pap. 15.95 (*0-9655704-0-1*) Three Dog Prods.

Brothers, ed. see Terence.

Brothers, A. J., ed. see Terence.

Brothers, Al & Ray, Murphy E., Jr. Producing Quality Whitetails. 3rd rev. ed. McTee, Charly, ed. (Illus.). 1997. 29.95 (*0-9661411-0-5*); pap. 19.95 (*0-9661411-1-3*); lthr. 99.95 (*0-9661411-2-1*) Tex Wildlife.

Brothers Andrew Staff. Calling. pap. 9.99 (*0-8297-2150-9*) Vida Pubs.

***Brothers, Barbara.** British Travel Writers, 1840-1999. LC 98-51321. 400p. 1999. text 155.00 (*0-7876-3098-5*) Gale.

Brothers, Barbara & Gergits, Julia, eds. British Travel Writers, 1837-1875: Victorian Period. LC 96-16075. (Dictionary of Literary Biography Ser.: Vol. 166). 400p. 1996. text 155.00 (*0-8103-9361-1*) Gale.

Brothers, Barbara & Neyrohr, Deborah. Ten Classical Myths. (LAT.). 23p. 1992. spiral bd. 3.25 (*0-939507-34-X*, B733) Amer Classical.

Brothers, Barbara J. Couples on Coupling. LC 90-33921. (Journal of Couples Therapy: Vol. 1, No. 2). 95p. 1990. text 3.95 (*1-56024-049-0*) Haworth Pr.

— Virginia Satir: Foundational Ideas. LC 90-26287. (Journal of Couples Therapy). (Illus.). 204p. 1991. text 39.95 (*1-56024-104-7*) Haworth Pr.

Brothers, Barbara J., ed. Attraction & Attachment: Understanding Styles of Relationships. LC 93-42448. (Journal of Couples Therapy). (Illus.). 160p. 1994. lib. bdg. 39.95 (*1-56024-620-0*) Haworth Pr.

— Couples: Building Bridges. LC 96-12678. (Journal of Couples Therapy: Vol. 5, No. 4). 109p. (C). 1996. 29.95 (*1-56024-802-5*) Haworth Pr.

— Couples: Building Bridges. LC 96-12678. (Journal of Couples Therapy: Vol. 5, No. 4). 109p. (C). 1997. pap. 14.95 (*0-7890-0222-1*) Haworth Pr.

— Couples & Change. LC 96-25514. 192p. 1996. 39.95 (*1-56024-828-9*) Haworth Pr.

— Couples & Countertransference. LC 95-22643. 1995. 24.95 (*1-56024-746-0*) Haworth Pr.

— Couples & the Tao of Congruence. LC 96-38931. (Journal of Couples Therapy Monograph: Vol. 6, Nos. 3-4). 168p. (C). 1997. 39.95 (*0-7890-0018-0*); pap. text 19.95 (*0-7890-0301-5*) Haworth Pr.

— Coupling ... What Makes Permanance: A Feminine Perspective. LC 91-123880. (Journal of Couples Therapy). (Illus.). 109p. 1991. text 24.95 (*1-56024-186-1*) Haworth Pr.

— Equal Partnering: A Feminine Perspective. LC 92-13454. (Journal of Couples Therapy Ser.). (Illus.). 109p. 1992. pap. 9.95 (*1-56023-017-7*, Harrington Park); text 24.95 (*1-56024-260-4*) Haworth Pr.

— Intimate Autonomy: Autonomous Intimacy. LC 90-25177. (Journal of Couples Therapy). 146p. 1991. text 39.95 (*1-56024-089-X*) Haworth Pr.

— Peace, War, & Mental Health: Couples Therapists Look at the Dynamics. LC 93-18004. (Journal of Couples Therapy: Vol. 3, No. 4). (Illus.). 181p. 1993. lib. bdg. 39.95 (*1-56024-437-2*) Haworth Pr.

— When One Partner Is Willing & the Other Is Not. LC 96-51966. 106p. 1997. pap. 9.95 (*0-7890-0342-2*) Haworth Pr.

— When One Partner Is Willing & the Other Is Not. LC 96-51966. (Journal of Couples Therapy Monograph Ser.: Vol. 7, No. 1). 122p. (C). 1997. 29.95 (*0-7890-0038-5*) Haworth Pr.

Brothers, Barbara J., ed. Surpassing Threats & Rewards: Newer Plateaus for Couples & Coupling. LC 94-44765. (Journal of Couples Therapy). (Illus.). 144p. 1995. lib. bdg. 39.95 (*1-56024-723-1*) Haworth Pr.

Brothers, Barbara J., intro. Couples Therapy, Multiple Perspectives: In Search of Universal Threads. LC 92-32943. (Journal of Couples Therapy). (Illus.). 181p. 1993. lib. bdg. 39.95 (*1-56024-374-0*) Haworth Pr.

Brothers, Barbara J., pref. Spirituality & Couples Therapy: Heart & Soul in the Therapy Process. LC 93-4262. (Journal of Couples Therapy: Vol. 3, No.1). (Illus.). 158p. 1993. lib. bdg. 39.95 (*1-56024-312-0*) Haworth Pr.

Brothers, Barbara-Jo. Couples, Trauma, & Catastrophes. LC 98-35597. 1998. 19.95 (*0-7890-0546-8*) Haworth Pr.

Brothers, Barbara Jo, ed. Couples: A Medley of Models. LC 98-8114. 157p. 1998. 29.95 (*0-7890-0531-X*) Haworth Pr.

— Couples & Change. 192p. 1996. pap. 19.95 (*0-7890-0213-2*, Hawrth Medical) Haworth Pr.

***Brothers, Barbara Jo, ed.** Couples & Pregnancy: Welcome, Unwelcome, & In-Between. LC 99-38461. (Journal of Couples Therapy Ser.: Vol. 8, No. 2). 99p. 1999. 39.95 (*0-7890-0787-8*, Hawrth Medical) Haworth Pr.

— Couples & Pregnancy: Welcome, Unwelcome & In-Between, No. 2. LC 99-38461. (Journal of Couples Therapy: Vol. 8). 109p. 1999. pap. 13.95 (*0-7890-0822-X*) Haworth Pr.

— Couples Therapy in Managed Care: Facing the Crisis. LC 99-51401. (Journal of Couples Therapy Monograph Ser.: Vol. 8, Nos. 3/4). 130p. 1999. pap. 15.95 (*0-7890-0823-8*) Haworth Pr.

— Couples Therapy in Managed Care: Facing the Crisis. LC 99-51401. (Journal of Couples Therapy Monograph Ser.: Vol. 8, Nos. 3/4). 130p. 1999. 39.95 (*0-7890-0788-6*) Haworth Pr.

Brothers, Barbara Jo, ed. Couples, Trauma & Catastrophes. 157p. 1998. 29.95 (*0-7890-0532-8*) Haworth Pr.

— Power & Partnering. LC 95-3596. 1995. 39.95 (*1-56024-720-7*) Haworth Pr.

Brothers, Caroline. War & Photography: Cultural History. LC 97-147656. (Illus.). 304p. (C). 1997. 65.00 (*0-415-13099-9*) Routledge.

Brothers, Chet, jt. ed. see Miller, Rathe.

Brothers, David, jt. ed. see Reida, Clara M.

Brothers, David L., ed. see Haga, Michael W.

Brothers, Don. South Africa. (Let's Visit Places & Peoples of the World Ser.). (Illus.). 120p. (YA). (gr. 5 up). 1989. lib. bdg. 16.95 (*1-55546-790-3*) Chelsea Hse.

Brothers, Doris. Falling Backwards: An Exploration of Trust & Self-Experience. 272p. 1995. 30.00 (*0-393-70177-8*) Norton.

Brothers, Doris, jt. auth. see Ulman, Richard B.

Brothers, Fletcher A. Rock Report. LC 87-91288. 160p. 1987. pap. 6.95 (*0-914984-13-6*) Starburst.

Brothers Halamandaris Staff, ed. Caring Quotes: A Compendium of Caring Thoughts. 465p. 1994. per. 15.00 (*1-886450-00-5*) Caring Pub.

Brothers, Jay. Ox. LC 74-17683. 240p. 1975. 7.95 (*0-672-52076-1*, Bobbs) Macmillan.

Brothers, Joyce. Positive Plus: The Practical Plan for Liking Yourself Better. 288p. 1995. mass mkt. 5.99 (*0-425-14949-8*) Berkley Pub.

— What Every Woman Should Know about Men. 288p. 1987. mass mkt. 6.99 (*0-345-35372-2*) Ballantine Pub Grp.

— Widowed. 1992. mass mkt. 5.99 (*0-345-37400-2*) Ballantine Pub Grp.

— Widowed. large type ed. 274p. 1991. 13.95 (*1-56054-984-X*) Thorndike Pr.

— Widowed. large type ed. 274p. 1991. reprint ed. lib. bdg. 21.95 (*1-56054-165-2*) Thorndike Pr.

Brothers, Leslie. Friday's Footprint: How Society Shapes the Human Mind. LC 97-13482. (Illus.). 208p. 1997. 25.00 (*0-19-510103-0*) OUP.

Brothers, Leslie A. & High, Steven S. Private Stories. 16p. 1991. 7.00 (*0-935519-13-0*) Anderson Gal.

Brothers, Leslie A., et al. Anonymity & Identity. (Illus.). 40p. 1993. 8.00 (*0-935519-15-7*) Anderson Gal.

Brothers, Theresa & Miranda, Elizabeth, eds. Sustaining Total Quality. (Report: No. 1025). 54p. (Orig.). 1993. pap. text 100.00 (*0-8237-0473-4*) Conference Bd.

Brothers, Theresa, jt. ed. see Friedman, Dana E.

Brothers, Thomas. Chromatic Beauty in the Late Medieval Chanson: An Interpretation of Manuscript Accidentals. LC 96-50936. 235p. (C). 1997. text 64.95 (*0-521-55051-3*) Cambridge U Pr.

Brothers, Thomas, ed. see Armstrong, Louis.

***Brothers, William P.** The Sabbatical. LC 99-93980. 2000. pap. 18.95 (*0-533-13215-0*) Vantage.

Brothers, William S. 13 Diseases That Can Be Spread by Intimate Contact. 1996. 12.50 (*0-9651755-0-2*) Bros Enter.

Brotherson, D. E., ed. Roofing Systems - STP 603. 148p. 1987. pap. 21.00 (*0-8031-0559-2*, STP603) ASTM.

Brotherston, Gordon. The Book of the Fourth World: Reading the Native Americas Through Their Literature. (Illus.). 494p. (C). 1993. text 69.95 (*0-521-30760-0*) Cambridge U Pr.

— Book of the Fourth World: Reading the Native Americas Through Their Literature. (Illus.). 494p. 1995. pap. 24.95 (*0-521-31493-3*) Cambridge U Pr.

Brotherston, Gordon, ed. Spanish-American Modernista Poets: A Critical Anthology. 2nd ed. (Bristol Spanish Texts Ser.). (SPA.). 1995. pap. 18.95 (*1-85399-463-4*, Pub. by Brist Class Pr) Focus Pub-R Pullins.

Brotherston, Gordon & Vargas Llosa, Mario, eds. Seven Stories from Spanish America. (Bristol Spanish Texts Ser.). (SPA.). 1995. pap. 18.95 (*1-85399-464-2*, Pub. by Brist Class Pr) Focus Pub-R Pullins.

— Seven Stories from Spanish America. 1968. pap. text 4.60 (*0-08-012675-8*, Pergamon Pr) Elsevier.

Brotherston, Gordon, jt. auth. see Dorn, Edward.

***Brotherston, Naida Edgar.** Adolescence & Myalgic Encephalomyelitis/Chronic Fatigue Syndrome: Journeys with the Dragon. LC 00-38836. 186p. 2000. pap. 24.95 (*0-7890-1208-1*); lib. bdg. 49.95 (*0-7890-0874-2*) Haworth Pr.

Brotherstone, Terry, ed. Covenant, Charter & Party: Traditions of Revolt & Protest in Modern Scottish History. 1989. pap. text 19.95 (*0-08-037736-X*, Pergamon Pr) Elsevier.

Brotherstone, Terry & Dukes, Paul, eds. The Trotsky Reappraisal. 240p. 1992. 75.00 (*0-7486-0317-4*, Pub. by Edinburgh U Pr) Col U Pr.

Brotherton. Social Psychology in Management: Issues for a Changing Society. LC 98-22226. 1999. 85.00 (*0-335-19800-7*); pap. 29.95 (*0-335-19799-X*) OpUniv Pr.

Brotherton, A., tr. see Vestdijk, Simon.

Brotherton, Bob. The Handbook of Contemporary Hospitality Management Research. LC 98-39462. 562p. 1999. 85.00 (*0-471-98395-0*) Wiley.

***Brotherton, Bob.** Introduction to the U. K. Hospitality Industry: A Comparative Approach. 256p. 2000. pap. 32.95 (*0-7506-4711-6*) Buttrwrth-Heinemann.

Brotherton, Chris. New Developments in Research on Adult Cognition. (C). 1991. 35.00 (*1-85041-036-4*, Pub. by Univ Nottingham) St Mut.

Brotherton, Christopher J., jt. ed. see Stephenson, Geoffrey M.

Brotherton, James S. Dino-Man: The Untold Story. 224p. 1996. pap. 12.95 (*1-888701-19-6*) Jarrett Pr.

Brotherton, John. The Pastor-Bobo in the Spanish Theatre Before the Time of Lope de Vega. (Monagrafias A Ser.: No. 51). 210p. (C). 1975. pap. 51.00 (*0-7293-0011-0*, Pub. by Tamesis Bks Ltd) Boydell & Brewer.

Brotherton, Marvin K. Lake Norman - Piedmont History. LC 94-78239. 200p. 1995. write for info. (*1-886057-01-X*) Warren Pubg NC.

Brotherton, Miner. The Twelve-Volt Bible for Boats. (Illus.). 174p. 1987. pap. text 14.95 (*0-07-156091-2*) Intl Marine.

Brotherton, Sue, tr. see Ferrone, Vincenzo.

Brotherton, Susan J. Counselor Education for the Twenty-First Century. LC 95-39389. (Contributions to the Study of Music & Dance Ser.: Vol. 43). 152p. 1996. 55.00 (*0-89789-471-5*, Bergin & Garvey) Greenwood.

***Brotherton, Velda.** Washington County. (Images of America Ser.). (Illus.). 128p. 1999. pap. 18.99 (*0-7385-0008-9*) Arcadia Publng.

Brotherton, Velda, ed. see Caudle, C. Edd.

Brotherus, V. F. Contribution to the Broyological Flora of N. W. Himalaya. (C). 1988. 35.00 (*0-7855-3256-0*, Pub. by Scientific) St Mut.

An Asterisk (*) at the beginning of an entry indicates that the title is appearing for the first time.

— Contribution to the Broyological Flora of Southern India. (C). 1988. 35.00 (*0-7855-3257-9*, Pub. by Scientific) St Mut.
— Hawaiian Mosses. (BMB Ser.: No. 40). 1969. reprint ed. pap. 25.00 (*0-527-02143-1*) Periodicals Srv.
— Die Laubmoose Fennoskandias. (Flora Fennica Ser.: Vol. 1). (GER., Illus.). 635p. 1974. reprint ed. 150.00 (*3-87429-078-6*, 002455, Pub. by Koeltz Sci Bks) Lubrecht & Cramer.
Brotherwood, Clive. Haynes Honda 100 & 125 Singles Roads & Trails Owner's Workshop Manual, No. M188: '70-'76. 1979. 16.95 (*0-85696-188-4*) Haynes Manuals.
— Haynes Triumph 350 & 500 Unit Twins Owners Workshop Manual, No. 137: '58-'73. 1979. 23.95 (*0-85696-137-X*) Haynes Manuals.
Brothwell, Don R. Biosocial Man: Studies Related to the Interaction of Biological & Cultural Factors in Human Populations. LC 80-511608. viii, 296 p. 1977. 4.00 (*0-900490-09-8*) Inst Biol.
Brothwell, Don R. The Bog Man & the Archaeology of People. LC 87-8435. (Illus.). 136p. 1987. pap. text 16.50 (*0-674-07732-6*) HUP.
— Digging up Bones. 3rd rev. ed. LC 80-66914. (Illus.). 196p. 1981. pap. 32.50 (*0-8014-9875-9*) Cornell U Pr.
— Skeletal Biology of Earlier Human Populations. LC 68-14720. (Symposia of the Society for the Study of Human Biology Ser.: Vol. 8). 1968. 137.00 (*0-08-013187-5*, Pub. by Pergamon Repr) Franklin.
Brothwell, Don R. & Brothwell, Patricia. Food in Antiquity: A Survey of the Diet of Early Peoples. LC 97-18406. 248p. 1998. reprint ed. pap. text 15.95 (*0-8018-5740-6*) Johns Hopkins.
Brothwell, Don R. & Sandison, A. T. Diseases in Antiquity: A Survey of the Diseases, Injuries & Surgery of Early Populations. (Illus.). 792p. 1967. 125.95 (*0-398-00233-9*) C C Thomas.
— Diseases in Antiquity: A Survey of the Diseases, Injuries & Surgery of Early Populations. fac. ed. (Illus.). 792p. 1967. pap. 79.95 (*0-398-06034-7*) C C Thomas.
Brothwell, Patricia, jt. auth. see Brothwell, Don R.
Brothwood, John, ed. see Institute of Petroleum, London Staff.
Brotman. Legal Aspects of Global Information Infrastructure. Date not set. write for info. (*90-411-0965-X*) Kluwer Law Intl.
Brotman, Juliano. Raw. Date not set. pap. Price not set. (*0-06-098863-0*, ReganBks) HarperTrade.
***Brotman-Leve, Barbara & Fleifeld, Julia.** Lifelines: Collected Poems Created at the Jewish Community Center of Wake County, N. C. (Illus.). 92p. 1999. pap. 9.95 (*1-880849-16-X*) Chapel Hill NC.
Brotman, R., et al. Delivering Health Care Comprehensively. LC 89-20966. (Illus.). 180p. (Orig.). 1990. pap. text 10.00 (*0-9627072-0-1*) Ctr CHP.
Brotman, Richard, et al. Delivering Health Care Comprehensively. LC 91-1952. 192p. 1991. 49.95 (*0-275-93999-5*, C3999, Praeger Pubs) Greenwood.
Brotman, Stuart, jt. auth. see Hamburg, Morton I.
Brotman, Stuart N. The Telecommunications Deregulation Sourcebook. 225p. 1987. text. write for info. (*0-89006-205-6*) Artech Hse.
Brotman, Stuart N., ed. The Telecommunications Deregulation Sourcebook. LC 87-1012. (Artech House Telecommunications Library). 355p. 1987. reprint ed. pap. 110.10 (*0-608-00212-7*, 206099500006) Bks Demand.
***Broto, Carles.** Apartment Buildings. (Architecture Collection Ser.). (Illus.). 238p. 1998. 85.00 (*84-89861-04-8*, Pub. by Links Inter) Bks Nippan.
Broto, Carles. Architecture: An Overview. LC 97-171909. (Architectural Design Ser.). (Illus.). 230p. 1997. 85.00 (*84-921606-3-2*, Pub. by Links Inter) Bks Nippan.
— Architecture for Education & Culture. LC 98-103956. (Architectural Design Ser.). (Illus.). 230p. 1997. 85.00 (*84-921606-5-9*, Pub. by Links Inter) Bks Nippan.
***Broto, Carles.** Building for the Elderly. (Architecture Collection Ser.). (Illus.). 238p. 1998. 85.00 (*84-89861-05-6*, Pub. by Links Inter) Bks Nippan.
— Home Offices. (Illus.). 180p. 45.00 (*84-89861-10-2*, Pub. by Links Inter) Bks Nippan.
Broto, Carles. Houses. Mostaedi, Arian, ed. LC 97-171858. (Architectural Design Ser.). (Illus.). 238p. 1997. 85.00 (*84-921606-2-4*, Pub. by Links Inter) Bks Nippan.
— Single Family Houses. (Illus.). 180p. 1999. 45.00 (*84-89861-11-0*, Pub. by Links Inter) Bks Nippan.
Broto, Carles. Town Houses. (Illus.). 180p. 45.00 (*84-89861-09-9*, Pub. by Links Inter) Bks Nippan.
Broto, Carles, et al, eds. Algebraic Topology: New Trends in Localization & Periodicity: Barcelona Conference on Algebraic Topology, Sant Feliu de Guixols, Spain, June 1-7, 1994. LC 95-47180. (Progress in Mathematics Ser.: Vol. 136). 400p. 1995. 94.50 (*0-8176-5333-3*) Birkhauser.
***Broto, Carles & Mostaedi, Arian.** Home Interiors. (Illus.). 180p. 2000. 69.95 (*3-931884-64-3*, Pub. by Nippon Shuppan) Bks Nippan.
— New Commercial Spaces. (Illus.). 180p. 2000. 69.95 (*3-931884-55-4*, Pub. by Nippon Shuppan) Bks Nippan.
— New Houses. (Illus.). 180p. 2000. 69.95 (*3-931884-65-1*, Pub. by Nippon Shuppan) Bks Nippan.
— Transformed Buildings. (Illus.). 180p. 2000. 69.95 (*3-931884-56-2*, Pub. by Nippon Shuppan) Bks Nippan.
Brott, Ardyth. Jeremy's Decision. (Illus.). 32p. (J). (ps-3). 1996. pap. 6.95 (*0-916291-65-0*) Kane-Miller Bk.
— Olivier Ne Sait Pas. (Droles D'Histories Ser.). (FRE., Illus.). 24p. (J). (ps up). 1995. pap. 6.95 (*2-89021-230-0*, Pub. by La Courte Ech) Firefly Bks Ltd.
Brott, Armin. A Dad's Guide to the Toddler Years. (Illus.). 224p. 1998. 15.95 (*0-7892-0480-0*); pap. 10.95 (*0-7892-0396-0*) Abbeville Pr.
— The New Father Boxed Set. (Illus.). 224p. 1998. pap. 35.00 (*0-7892-0494-0*) Abbeville Pr.
Brott, Armin, jt. auth. see Breier, Mark.
Brott, Armin A. A Dad's Guide to the First Year. (New Father Ser.). (Illus.). 224p. 15.95 (*0-7892-0418-5*) Abbeville Pr.
— A Dad's Guide to the First Year. LC 97-32876. (New Father Ser.). (Illus.). 224p. 1998. pap. 10.95 (*0-7892-0275-1*) Abbeville Pr.
— The Single Father: A Dad's Guide to Parenting without a Partner. LC 98-49531. (New Father Ser.). (Illus.). 300p. 1999. 18.95 (*0-7892-0518-1*) Abbeville Pr.
— The Single Father: A Dad's Guide to Parenting without a Partner. LC 98-49531. (New Father Ser.: No. 4). (Illus.). 300p. 1999. pap. 12.95 (*0-7892-0520-3*) Abbeville Pr.
Brott, Armin A. & Ash, Jennifer. The Expectant Father: Facts, Tips & Advice for Dads-to-Be. (Illus.). 224p. 15.95 (*0-7892-0417-7*) Abbeville Pr.
Brott, Armin A., jt. auth. see Ash, Jennifer.
Brott, Armin A., jt. auth. see Parke, Ross D.
Brott, L. J., ed. see Nichole, Brianna.
Brottman, May & Loe, Mary, eds. The LIRT Library Instruction Book. 175p. 1990. lib. bdg. 26.50 (*0-87287-664-0*) Libs Unl.
Brottman, Mikita. Hollywood Hex: An Illustrated History of Cursed Movies. (Cinema Collection). (Illus.). 256p. 1999. pap. 19.95 (*1-871592-85-2*, Pub. by Creation Books) Subterranean Co.
— Meat Is Murder! An Illustrated Guide to Cannibal Culture. (Creation Cinema Collection: Vol. 9). (Illus.). 224p. 1998. pap. 19.95 (*1-871592-90-9*) Creation Books.
— Offensive Films: Toward an Anthropology of Cinema Vomitif, 72. LC 96-49734. (Contributions to the Study of Science Fiction & Fantasy: Vol. 72). 224p. 1997. 55.00 (*0-313-30033-X*, Greenwood Pr) Greenwood.
***Brottman, Mikita, ed.** Jack Nicholson Vol. 6: Movie Top Ten. (Illus.). 160p. 2000. pap. 17.95 (*1-871592-98-4*, Pub. by Creation Books) Subterranean Co.
***Brottman, Stuart.** Sax Scales. 64p. 1998. pap. 9.95 (*0-7866-4067-7*, 97742) Mel Bay.
Brotton, Jerry. Trading Territories: Mapping the Early Modern World. LC 97-37603. (Illus.). 256p. 1998. 35.00 (*0-8014-3499-8*) Cornell U Pr.
Brotton, Jerry, jt. auth. see Jardine, Lisa.
Brotz, Howard, ed. African - American Social & Political Thought, 1850-1920. 641p. (C). 1991. pap. text 24.95 (*1-56000-563-7*) Transaction Pubs.
Brotzma. Orthopaedic. 1996. text 130.00 (*0-8151-1011-1*, 29167) Mosby Inc.
Brotzman, Ellis R. Old Testament Textual Criticism: A Practical Introduction. LC 93-42726. (Illus.). 208p. 1993. pap. 10.99 (*0-8010-1065-9*) Baker Bks.
Brotzman, Robert L. Love for Life. 63p. 1999. pap. 9.95 (*0-7414-0109-6*) Buy Books.
Brotzman, S. Brent, ed. Clinical Orthopaedic Rehabilitation. LC 95-42300. (Illus.). 416p. (C). (gr. 13). 1995. text 89.95 (*0-8151-1034-0*, 24183) Mosby Inc.
— Handbook of Orthopaedic Rehabilitation. LC 95-42301. (Illus.). 400p. (C). (gr. 13). 1996. text 44.95 (*0-8151-1102-9*, 24215) Mosby Inc.
***Brouald, Ken C.** Silent Towns on the Prairie: North Dakota's Disappearing Towns & Farms. LC 99-70024. (Illus.). 134p. 1999. pap. 19.95 (*1-57510-048-7*) Pictorial Hist.
Brouard, F., et al. Notes on Observations of Daily Rings on Otoliths of Deepwater Snappers. (ICLARM Translations Ser.: No. 3). Orig. Title: Note sur les lectures de stries journalieres observees sur les otolithes de poissons. (Illus.). 8p. (Orig.). 1984. pap. 2.00 (*971-10-2207-9*, Pub. by ICLARM) Intl Spec Bk.
Brouard, M. Reaction Dynamics. (Oxford Chemistry Primers Ser.: No. 61). (Illus.). 96p. (C). 1998. pap. text 12.95 (*0-19-855907-0*) OUP.
Broucek, Francis J. Shame & the Self. LC 91-6797. 167p. 1991. lib. bdg. 33.00 (*0-89862-444-4*) Guilford Pubns.
Brouch, Kathy, ed. Modifiers Made Easy. 200p. (C). 1999. pap. 99.95 (*1-56329-536-9*) Thomson Learn.
— St. Anthony's Three-in-One Code Book for ENT: 1993 Edition. 1992. 167.00 (*1-56329-110-X*, SEN) St Anthony Pub.
Brouch, Virginia M., ed. Microcomputers in Art Education. 48p. (C). 1988. pap. 7.00 (*0-937652-39-3*) Natl Art Ed.
Brouchey, Stuart, ed. see Ibrahim A. Al-Moneef.
Broucke, Pieter B. The Archaeology of Architecture: Charles Robert Cockerell in Southern Europe & the Levant, 1810-1817. LC 93-60063. (Illus.). 23p. 1993. pap. 4.95 (*0-930606-69-8*) Yale Ctr Brit Art.
Broude, Gwen J. Growing Up: A Cross-Cultural Encyclopedia. LC 95-44079. (Human Experience Ser.). 376p. 1995. lib. bdg. 55.00 (*0-87436-767-0*) ABC-CLIO.
— Marriage Family & Relationships: A Cross-Cultural Encyclopedia. (Human Experience Ser.). 372p. 1995. lib. bdg. 49.50 (*0-87436-736-0*) ABC-CLIO.
Broude, Henry W. Steel Decisions & the National Economy. LC 63-13958. (Yale Studies in Economics: No. 16). 347p. reprint ed. pap. 107.60 (*0-608-14190-9*, 202198300024) Bks Demand.
Broude, Inna. Ot Khodasevicha do Nabokova. LC 90-49449. (RUS.). 180p. (Orig.). 1990. pap. 10.00 (*1-55779-024-8*) Hermitage Pubs.
Broude, Norma. The Macchiaioli: Italian Painters of the Nineteenth Century. LC 86-28270. 306p. 1988. 75.00 (*0-300-03547-0*) Yale U Pr.
Broude, Norma & Garrard, Mary D., eds. Expanding Discourse. LC 91-58341. (Illus.). 512p. 1992. pap. 40.00 (*0-06-430207-5*, Perennial) HarperTrade.
— Feminism & Art History. LC 81-48062. (Icon Editions Ser.). (Illus.). 336p. 1982. pap. 30.00 (*0-06-430117-6*, IN117, Icon Edns) HarpC.
Broude, Norma & Garrard, Mary D., eds. The Power of Feminist Art: The American Movement of the 1970s, History & Impact. (Illus.). 320p. 1996. pap. 24.95 (*0-8109-2659-8*, Pub. by Abrams) Time Warner.
Broude, Norma, ed. see Bernstein, Roberta.
***Broude, Richard F.** International Business Insolvency Guide. LC 99-46502. 1999. 275.00 (*0-8205-3909-7*) Bender.
Broude, Richard F. Reorganizations under Chapter 11 of the Bankruptcy Code. 800p. 1986. ring bd. 110.00 (*0-317-05387-6*, 00595) NY Law Pub.
— Reorganizations under Chapter 11 of the Bankruptcy Code. 500p. 1986. ring bd. 85.00 (*0-318-19265-9*, 00595) NY Law Pub.
Broude, Richard F., ed. Insolvency & Finance in the Transportation Industry. 290p. 1993. 145.00 (*1-85044-492-7*) LLP.
Broude, V. L., et al. Spectroscopy of Molecular Excitons. (Chemical Physics Ser.: Vol. 16). (Illus.). 290p. 1985. 117.95 (*0-387-12409-8*) Spr-Verlag.
Broudy, Charles E., jt. auth. see Baarr, Vilma.
***Broudy, David.** Personalized & Database Printing: The Complete Guide. 1999. pap. 49.95 (*0-941845-24-9*) Micro Pub Pr.
Broudy, David, jt. auth. see Romano, Frank J.
Broudy, Eric. The Book of Looms: A History of the Handloom from Ancient Times to the Present. LC 93-13617. (Illus.). 176p. 1993. reprint ed. pap. 22.95 (*0-87451-649-8*) U Pr of New Eng.
Broudy, Harry S. Enlightened Cherishing: An Essay on Aesthetic Education. LC 93-11498. 128p. 1994. pap. text 9.95 (*0-252-06374-0*) U of Ill Pr.
— Enlightened Cherishing: An Essay on Aesthetic Education. LC 79-182032. (Kappa Delta Pi Lecture). 126p. reprint ed. pap. 39.10 (*0-608-15366-4*, 205637500061) Bks Demand.
— The Role of Imagery in Learning. LC 88-21521: (Occasional Paper Ser.: Vol. 1). 56p. 1987. pap. 15.00 (*0-89236-145-X*, Pub. by J P Getty Trust) OUP.
— The Uses of Schooling. 160p. 1988. text 19.95 (*0-415-00176-5*) Routledge.
— What Do Professors of Education Profess? (DeGarmo Lectures: No. 4). 1979. 10.00 (*0-933669-28-3*) Soc Profs Ed.
Broudy, Harry S., et al. Philosophy of Education: An Organization of Topics & Selected Sources. LC 67-27774. 299p. (C). reprint ed. pap. 92.70 (*0-8357-9693-0*, 201905000010) Bks Demand.
Brouers, M., jt. ed. see Sironval, C.
Brough, D. K. The Passing of Marine Griffiths. 1981. 35.00 (*0-7223-1413-2*, Pub. by A H S Ltd) St Mut.
Brough, D. R., ed. Logic Programming - New Frontiers. (Diverse Ser.). 300p. (C). 1992. text 141.50 (*0-7923-1546-4*) Kluwer Academic.
Brough, Holly, jt. auth. see Durning, Alan B.
Brough, John B., ed. Philosophical Knowledge. LC 80-69505. (Proceedings of the American Catholic Philosophical Association Ser.: Vol. 54). 250p. (Orig.). 1980. pap. 20.00 (*0-918090-14-8*) Am Cath Philo.
Brough, John B., tr. see Husserl, Edmund.
Brough, Judith, jt. ed. see Irvin, Judith L.
Brough, Matthew. The Angel Who Fell from the Sky. (Illus.). (Orig.). (J). (gr. k-4). 1997. pap. 7.95 (*0-929537-06-8*) Herit Pub Inc.
Brough, Michael B. & Green, Philip P., Jr. The Zoning Board of Adjustment in North Carolina. rev. ed. 128p. (C). 1984. pap. text 9.50 (*1-56011-150-X*, 84.21) Institute Government.
Brough, Peggy, jt. auth. see Cready, Bonnie.
Brough, R. Clayton. The Lost Tribes: History, Doctrine, Prophecies & Theories about Israel's Lost Ten Tribes. 1992. 14.98 (*0-88290-441-8*) Horizon Utah.
— Teaching of the Prophets: Statements of the LDS Leaders on Contemporary Issues. 1993. 14.98 (*0-88290-461-2*, 1010) Horizon Utah.
— They Who Tarry: A Doctrine of Translated Beings. 97p. 1976. 10.98 (*0-88290-069-2*) Horizon Utah.
Brough, R. Clayton & Grassley, Thomas W. Understanding Patriarchal Blessings. LC 84-81233. 81p. 1984. 12.98 (*0-88290-253-9*) Horizon Utah.
Brough, R. Clayton & Griffin, Rodney D. Scientific Support for Scriptural Stories. 1992. 18.98 (*0-88290-450-7*) Horizon Utah.
Brough, S. Langenscheidts Handworterbucher: Deutsch-Englisch. 736p. 1997. pap. write for info. (*3-468-04128-4*) Langenscheidt.
Brough, S., jt. auth. see Puckering, R. D.
Brough, Sherman & Weber, Darrell. Trees in Idaho. LC 98-196836. (Illus.). 315p. (YA). (gr. k up). 1997. pap. 19.00 (*0-9635617-1-5*) Brstlecone Pr.
Brough, Sherman & Weber, Darrell J. Trees of Utah. (Illus.). 148p. (Orig.). (YA). (gr. k up). 1993. pap. 10.00 (*0-9635617-0-7*) Brstlecone Pr.
Brougham, Henry. An Inquiry into the Colonial Policy of the European Powers, 2 vols., Set. LC 75-118017. (Reprints of Economic Classics Ser.). 1970. reprint ed. 125.00 (*0-678-00658-X*) Kelley.
Brougham, Henry, et al. Popularizing Classical Economics. LC 94-27002. (Studies in the History of Economics). 1994. text 65.00 (*0-312-12383-3*) St Martin.
Brougham, John. The Irish Emigrant: Temptation. Meserve, Walter J. & Meserve, Mollie A., eds. (When Conscience Trod the Stage Ser.). 1998. pap., spiral bd. 3.95 (*0-937657-41-7*) Feedbk Theabks & Prospero.
Broughel, Barbara. Poetic Resemblance. (Illus.). 24p. 1986. pap. 5.00 (*0-936739-00-2*) Hallwalls Inc.
Brougher, Kerry. Art & Film since 1945: Hall of Mirrors. LC 95-52679. 1996. pap. 50.00 (*0-914357-45-X*) Los Angeles Mus Contemp.
***Brougher, Kerry, et al.** Ed Ruscha. LC 00-39662. 2000. pap. write for info. (*3-908247-37-3*) Dist Art Pubs.
Brougher, Kerry, et al. Jeff Wall. LC 96-47704. 1997. write for info. (*0-914357-47-6*) Los Angeles Mus Contemp.
Brougher, Nora H. & Belloli, Andrea P., eds. Selected Works from the Frederick R. Weisman Art Foundation. (Illus.). 50p. (Orig.). 1988. write for info. (*0-9614537-2-9*) F R Weisman Collect.
Brougher, Valentina, tr. see Ivanov, Vsevolod.
Brougher, William E. South to Bataan, North to Mukden: The Prison Diary of Brigadier General W. E. Brougher. James, D. Clayton, ed. LC 77-135182. 247p. reprint ed. pap. 76.60 (*0-608-15808-9*, 203118100073) Bks Demand.
***Broughman, Stephen P.** Private School Universe Survey, 1995-96. 96p. 1998. pap. 7.50 (*0-16-049499-0*) USGPO.
— Private School Universe Survey, 1997-98. 100p. 1999. pap. 9.00 (*0-16-050184-9*) USGPO.
Broughtn, Geoffrey, et al, eds. Teaching English As a Foreign Language. 2nd ed. (Education Bks.). 256p. 1981. 24.50 (*0-7100-0642-X*, Routledge Thoemms) Routledge.
Broughton. Basic Writing: Paragraphs to Portfolio - Writers Workshop, Vol. II. (C). 1999. write for info. (*0-321-40638-9*) Addison-Wesley.
— Governess. LC 97-30125. 226p. 1998. text 45.00 (*0-312-21089-2*) St Martin.
***Broughton.** Miracle of the Loaves & Fishes. 20p. (J). 2000. pap. text. write for info. (*0-307-16036-X*) Gldn Bks Pub Co.
Broughton. Pediatric Orthopedics. 1996. text 99.00 (*0-7020-1962-3*, W B Saunders Co) Harcrt Hlth Sci Grp.
Broughton, jt. auth. see Collins1.
Broughton, Alan. Preparing to Be Happy. LC 87-71456. (Poetry Ser.). 1988. pap. 11.95 (*0-88748-061-6*) Carnegie-Mellon.
— Preparing to Be Happy. LC 87-71456. (Poetry Ser.). 1988. 20.95 (*0-88748-060-8*) Carnegie-Mellon.
Broughton, Bradford B. Dictionary of Medieval Knighthood & Chivalry: Concepts & Terms. LC 84-29036. (Illus.). 614p. 1986. lib. bdg. 85.00 (*0-313-24552-5*, BKD/, Greenwood Pr) Greenwood.
— Dictionary of Medieval Knighthood & Chivalry: People, Places, & Events. LC 87-18163. (Illus.). 795p. 1988. lib. bdg. 55.00 (*0-313-25347-1*, BPN/, Greenwood Pr) Greenwood.
Broughton, Carrie L. Marriage & Death Notices: From Raleigh Register & North Carolina State Gazette, 1799-1825. LC 66-26935. 178p. 1995. reprint ed. pap. 18.50 (*0-8063-0052-3*) Clearfield Co.
***Broughton, Carrie L.** Marriage & Death Notices in "Raleigh Register & North Carolina State Gazette," 1826-1845. LC 68-17004. 402p. 1999. reprint ed. pap. 32.50 (*0-8063-0053-1*) Clearfield Co.
Broughton, David. Public Opinion Polling & Politics in Britain. LC 95-10435. (Contemporary Political Studies). 216p. (C). 1995. pap. text 29.00 (*0-13-433921-5*) P-H.
Broughton, David, et al, eds. British Elections & Parties Yearbook. 304p. 1995. 60.00 (*0-7146-4620-2*, Pub. by F Cass Pubs); pap. 30.00 (*0-7146-4150-2*, Pub. by F Cass Pubs) Intl Spec Bk.
Broughton, David & Donovan, Mark, eds. Changing Party Systems in Western Europe. LC 98-15093. 320p. 1998. 75.00 (*1-85567-327-4*); pap. 24.95 (*1-85567-328-2*) P P Pubs.
Broughton, David, jt. ed. see Berger, Stefan.
Broughton, Frank. Time Out Interviews, 1968-1998. 320p. 1999. pap. 19.95 (*0-14-027963-6*, Penguin Bks) Viking Penguin.
Broughton, Frank, jt. auth. see Brewster, Bill.
Broughton, Hugh. An Epistle to the Learned Nobility of England: Touching Translating the Bible. LC 77-6862. (English Experience Ser.: No. 855). 1977. reprint ed. lib. bdg. 25.00 (*90-221-0855-4*) Walter J Johnson.
— Madrid. (Architecture Guides Ser.). (Illus.). 320p. 1998. pap. 5.95 (*3-89508-640-1*, 520203) Konemann.
Broughton, Irv. The Art of Interviewing for Television, Radio & Film. LC 79-9399. (Illus.). 1981. 18.95 (*0-8306-9743-8*) McGraw-Hill Prof.
— The Blessing of the Fleet. LC 77-8971. (Lost Roads Poetry Ser.: No. 6). 1978. pap. 3.00 (*0-918786-11-8*) Lost Roads.
— Hangar Talk: Interviews with Fliers, 1920's-1990's. LC 97-33389. (Illus.). 502p. 1998. pap. 35.00 (*0-910055-40-8*) East Wash Univ.
Broughton, J. The Past in Pictures: A Further Collection of Photographs of the London Borough of Sutton over the Last Century. 1986. 20.00 (*0-907335-03-9*, Pub. by Sutton Libs & Arts) St Mut.
Broughton, J., ed. All Our Yesterdays: A Pictorial Record of the London Borough of Sutton Over the Last Century. 58p. 1988. 29.00 (*0-9503224-2-3*, Pub. by Sutton Libs & Arts) St Mut.
Broughton, J. M. Critical Theories of Psychological Development. LC 86-30383. (PATH in Psychology Ser.). (Illus.). 338p. (C). 1987. 62.50 (*0-306-42431-2*, Plenum Trade) Perseus Pubng.
***Broughton, Jack.** Going Downtown: The War Against Hanoi & Washington. (Illus.). 360p. 1999. reprint ed. pap. 16.95 (*1-888237-28-7*) Baxter Pr.
Broughton, Jack, ed. Process Utility Systems: Introduction to Design, Operation, & Maintenance. 282p. 1994. 55.00 (*0-85295-322-4*, 9CH89) Gulf Pub.
***Broughton, Jack M.** Resource Depression & Intensification During the Late Holocene, San Francisco [i.e. Francisco] Bay: Evidence from the Emeryville Shellmound Vertebrate Fauna. LC 99-11333. (Anthropological Records Ser.: Vol. 32). 160p. 1999. pap. 32.00 (*0-520-09828-5*, Pub. by U CA Pr) Cal Prin Full Svc.
Broughton, James. A to Z. 20p. (Orig.). (C). 1986. pap. 3.00 (*0-9608372-4-8*) Syzygy Pr.
— Coming Unbuttoned: A Memoir. (Illus.). 160p. (Orig.). 1993. pap. 11.95 (*0-87286-280-1*) City Lights.

— Ecstasies. LC 83-61663. 128p. 1983. 20.00 (*0-9608372-3-X*); pap. 7.00 (*0-9608372-2-1*) Syzygy Pr.

Broughton, James. Graffiti for the Johns of Heaven. LC 82-60091. (Illus.). 80p. 1982. pap. 6.00 (*0-9608372-1-3*) Syzygy Pr.

Broughton, James. Hooplas: A Collection of Celebratory Verse. 94p. 1988. pap. 8.95 (*0-938631-02-0*) Pennywhistle Pr.

— Little Sermons of the Big Joy. 25p. (Orig.). 1994. pap. 7.00 (*1-882827-05-8*) Insight to Riot.

— Making Light of It. (Illus.). 124p. (Orig.). 1992. pap. 7.95 (*0-87286-265-8*) City Lights.

— Packing up for Paradise: Selected Poems, 1946-1996. Cory, Jim, ed. LC 97-41887. 331p. 1997. 27.50 (*1-57423-053-0*); pap. 16.00 (*1-57423-052-2*) Black Sparrow.

— Packing up for Paradise: Selected Poems, 1946-1996. limited ed. Cory, Jim, ed. LC 97-41887. 331p. 1997. 35.00 (*1-57423-054-9*) Black Sparrow.

— Tidings. 70p. 1965. boxed set 10.00 (*0-931757-03-7*) Pterodactyl Pr.

***Broughton, Jeffrey L.** The Bodhidharma Anthology: The Earliest Records of Zen. LC 98-18245. 197p. 1999. pap. 17.95 (*0-520-21972-4*, Pub. by U CA Pr) Cal Prin Full Svc.

Broughton, Jeffrey L., jt. auth. see Bodhidharma.

Broughton, John C. Recollections of a Long Life: With Additional Extracts from His Private Diaries, 6 vols., Set. Lady Dorchester, ed. LC 09-25987. reprint ed. 459.00 (*0-404-03320-2*) AMS Pr.

Broughton, John M. & Freeman-Moir, John D. Cognitive-Development Psychology of James Mark Baldwin: Current Theory & Research in Genetic Epistemology. LC 81-7885. (Publications for the Advancement of Theory & History in Psychology, the PATH Ser.). 386p. 1982. text 73.25 (*0-89391-043-0*) Ablx Pub.

Broughton, Kate. Textile Dyeing: The Step-by-Step Guide & Showcase. (Illus.). 144p. 1996. 29.99 (*1-56496-213-X*) Rockport Pubs.

Broughton, Kelly M., rev. The Philosopher's Index Thesaurus. 2nd rev. ed. 105p. 1998. pap. 26.00 (*0-912632-67-4*) Philos Document.

Broughton, Leslie N. A Concordance to the Poems of Robert Browning, 4 vols., Set. (BCL1-PR English Literature Ser.). 1992. reprint ed. lib. bdg. 390.00 (*0-7812-7461-3*) Rprt Serv.

Broughton, Leslie N. & Stetler, Benjamin F. A Concordance to the Poems of Robert Browning 1924-1925, 4 Vols. LC 77-92950. (Studies in Browning: No. 4). 1388p. 1970. reprint ed. lib. bdg. 325.00 (*0-8383-1101-6*) M S G Haskell Hse.

Broughton, N. J., ed. Life on the Red Rock Ranch, 1904-1965: An Interview with Lawrence A. Dickinson. (Illus.). 198p. 1986. lib. bdg. 41.50 (*1-56475-304-2*); fiche. write for info. (*1-56475-305-0*) U NV Oral Hist.

— Life on the Red Rock Ranch, 1931-1965: An Interview with Judie Dickinson. (Illus.). 243p. 1986. lib. bdg. 45.50 (*1-56475-302-6*); fiche. write for info. (*1-56475-303-4*) U NV Oral Hist.

Broughton, Panthea Reid. William Faulkner: The Abstract & the Actual. LC 74-77324. 240p. 1974. pap. 74.40 (*0-7837-8460-0*, 204926500010) Bks Demand.

Broughton, Panthea Reid, ed. The Art of Walker Percy: Stratagems for Being. LC 78-27494. (Southern Literary Studies). 333p. reprint ed. pap. 103.30 (*0-608-09823-X*, 206999100007) Bks Demand.

Broughton, Peter. Joshua & Samuel. (Bible Study Commentaries Ser.). 126p. 1984. pap. 4.95 (*0-87508-154-1*) Chr Lit.

Broughton, Peter & Ndumbaro, Paul. Analysis of Cable & Catenary Structures. 94p. 1994. 48.00 (*0-7277-2008-2*) Am Soc Civil Eng.

Broughton, Pip, tr. see Brecht, Bertolt.

Broughton-Pipkin, Fiona, jt. auth. see Chamberlain, Geoffrey.

Broughton, Rhoda. Belinda: A Novel. LC 78-108463. 460p. 1884. 39.00 (*0-403-00448-9*) Scholarly.

— Cometh up as a Flower: An Autobiography, 2 vols., 1 bk. LC 79-8240. reprint ed. 44.50 (*0-404-61794-8*) AMS Pr.

— Fifteenth Century England, 1399-1509: Studies in Politics & Society. Chrimes, Stanley B. et al, eds. (Fifteenth Century Ser.). 208p. 1996. pap. 17.95 (*0-7509-0923-4*, Pub. by Sutton Pub Ltd) Intl Pubs Mktg.

Broughton, Richard. English Protestants Plea. LC 76-57380. (English Experience Ser.: No. 798). 1977. reprint ed. lib. bdg. 25.00 (*90-221-0798-1*) Walter J Johnson.

Broughton, Robert. The Dumbest Kid in the 3rd Grade. rev. ed. Wightman, Christina C., ed. (Illus.). 350p. 1999. pap. write for info. (*1-888911-12-3*) Benson Smythe.

Broughton, Roger J., jt. ed. see Dinges, David F.

Broughton, Roger J., jt. ed. see Miles, Laughton E.

Broughton, Roger J., ed. see Ogilvie, Robert D.

Broughton, Rosemary. Praying with Teresa of Avila. Koch, Carl, ed. (Companions for the Journey Ser.). (Illus.). 120p. (Orig.). 1990. pap. 8.95 (*0-88489-249-2*) St Marys.

Broughton, Rosemary, jt. auth. see Allaire, James.

Broughton, Simon, ed. see Rough Guides Staff.

Broughton, Sue. Lion Handbook: The Library & Information Organizations & Networks Handbook. 220p. 1998. 65.00 (*1-85604-126-3*, LAP1263) Library Association.

Broughton, T. Alan. Dreams Before Sleep. LC 81-71589. 1982. pap. 11.95 (*0-915604-69-8*) Carnegie-Mellon.

— Dreams Before Sleep. LC 81-71589. 1982. 20.95 (*0-915604-68-X*) Carnegie-Mellon.

— In the Country of Elegies. LC 94-70461. (Poetry Ser.). 120p. 1995. pap. 11.95 (*0-88748-198-1*) Carnegie-Mellon.

— The Jesse Tree. (Voyages to the Inland Sea Ser.: No. 5). 160p. (Orig.). (C). 1988. pap. text 12.00 (*1-55780-100-2*) Juniper Pr ME.

Broughton, T. Robert. Candidates Defeated in Roman Elections: Some Ancient Roman "Also-Rans" LC 90-56339. (Transactions Ser.: Vol. 81, Pt. 4). 64p. (Orig.). (C). 1991. pap. 10.00 (*0-87169-814-5*, T814-BRT) Am Philos.

— The Magistrates of the Roman Republic. (American Philological Association Philological Monographs). 578p. 1974. 67.95 (*0-89130-706-0*, 40 00 15) OUP.

— The Magistrates of the Roman Republic, Vol. III: Supplement. (American Philological Association Philological Monographs). 294p. 1974. 44.95 (*0-89130-811-3*, 40-00-15) OUP.

Broughton, T. Robert, ed. see Mommsen, Theodor.

Broughton, Thomas D. Letters in a Mahratta Camp During the Year, 1809. (C). 1995. reprint ed. 28.00 (*81-206-1008-3*, Pub. by Asian Educ Servs) S Asia.

Broughton, Thomas R. The Romanization of Africa Proconsularis. LC 78-64276. (Johns Hopkins University. Studies in the Social Sciences. Thirtieth Ser. 1912: 5). reprint ed. 37.50 (*0-404-61377-2*) AMS Pr.

Broughton, Trev L. Men of Letters, Writing Lives: Masculinity & Literary Auto Biography in the Late-Victorian Period. LC 98-30505. 1999. 90.00 (*0-415-08211-0*); pap. 29.99 (*0-415-08212-9*) Routledge.

Broughton, Trev L. & Anderson, Linda, eds. Women's Lives/Women's Times: New Essays on Auto/Biography. LC 96-27662. (SUNY Series, Feminist Theory in Education). 291p. (C). 1997. text 59.50 (*0-7914-3397-8*); pap. text 19.95 (*0-7914-3398-6*) State U NY Pr.

Broughton, Trev L., jt. auth. see Bristow, Joseph.

Broughton, Vanda, jt. ed. see Mills, Jack.

Brouha, L. & Zapp, J. Physiology in Industry: Eval. Ind. Stresses Physiological Reactions of the Worker, Vol. 4. 2nd ed. LC 60-8058. (International Series of Monographs on Pure & Applied Mathematics). 1960. 79.00 (*0-08-011703-1*, Pub. by Pergamon Repr) Franklin.

Brouillard, Anne. The Bathtub Prima Donna. LC 98-53970. (Illus.). 32p. (J). (gr. k-2). 1999. 12.95 (*0-8109-4093-0*, Pub. by Abrams) Time Warner.

Brouillard, F., ed. Atomic Processes in Electron-Ion & Ion-Ion Collisions. (NATO ASI Series B, Physics: Vol. 145). 502p. 1986. 125.00 (*0-306-42413-4*, Plenum Trade) Perseus Pubng.

Brouillet, Chrystine. Le Cameleon. (Novels in the Roman Jeunesse Ser.). (FRE., Illus.). 96p. (J). (gr. 4-7). 1988. pap. 8.95 (*2-89021-072-3*, Pub. by La Courte Ech) Firefly Bks Ltd.

— Les Chevaux Enchantes. (Novels in the Roman Jeunesse Ser.). (FRE.). 96p. (J). (gr. 4-7). 1994. pap. 8.95 (*2-89021-221-1*, Pub. by La Courte Ech) Firefly Bks Ltd.

— The Chinese Puzzle. Gaboriau, Linda, tr. (Illus.). 96p. (J). (gr. 3-7). 1998. pap. 6.95 (*0-921556-60-8*, Pub. by Gynergy-Ragweed) U of Toronto Pr.

— Le Complot. (Novels in the Roman Jeunesse Ser.). (FRE.). 96p. (J). (gr. 4-7). 1985. pap. 8.95 (*2-89021-052-9*, Pub. by La Courte Ech) Firefly Bks Ltd.

— Le Corbeau. (Novels in the Roman Jeunesse Ser.). (FRE.). 96p. (J). (gr. 4-7). 1990. pap. 8.95 (*2-89021-132-0*, Pub. by La Courte Ech) Firefly Bks Ltd.

— Un Crime Audacieux. (Novels in the Roman Plus Ser.). (FRE., Illus.). 160p. (YA). (gr. 8 up). 1995. pap. 8.95 (*2-89021-235-1*, Pub. by La Courte Ech) Firefly Bks Ltd.

— The Enchanted Horses. Gaboriau, Linda, tr. (FRE., Illus.). 96p. (J). (gr. 3-7). 1998. pap. 6.95 (*0-921556-63-2*, Pub. by Gynergy-Ragweed) U of Toronto Pr.

— Un Jeu Dangereux. (Novels in the Roman Plus Ser.). (FRE.). 160p. (YA). (gr. 8 up). 1989. pap. 7.95 (*2-89021-105-3*, Pub. by La Courte Ech) Firefly Bks Ltd.

— La Montagne Noire. (Novels in the Roman Jeunesse Ser.). (FRE.). 96p. (J). (gr. 4-7). 1988. pap. 8.95 (*2-89021-080-4*, Pub. by La Courte Ech) Firefly Bks Ltd.

— Mysteres de Chine. (Novels in the Roman Jeunesse Ser.). (FRE.). 96p. (J). (gr. 4-7). 1993. pap. 8.95 (*2-89021-189-4*, Pub. by La Courte Ech) Firefly Bks Ltd.

— No Orchids for Andrea! Gaboriau, Linda, tr. (FRE., Illus.). 96p. (J). (gr. 3-7). 1998. pap. 6.95 (*0-921556-62-4*, Pub. by Gynergy-Ragweed) U of Toronto Pr.

— Une Nuit Tres Longue. (Novels in the Roman Plus Ser.). (FRE.). 160p. (YA). (gr. 8 up). 1992. pap. 8.95 (*2-89021-174-6*, Pub. by La Courte Ech) Firefly Bks Ltd.

— Pas d'Orchidees pour Miss Andrea! (Novels in the Roman Jeunesse Ser.). (FRE.). 96p. (J). (gr. 4-7). 1994. pap. 8.95 (*2-89021-207-6*, Pub. by La Courte Ech) Firefly Bks Ltd.

— Les Pirates. (Novels in the Roman Jeunesse Ser.). (FRE.). 96p. (J). (gr. 4-7). 1992. pap. 8.95 (*2-89021-180-0*, Pub. by La Courte Ech) Firefly Bks Ltd.

— Une Plage Trop Chaude. (Novels in the Roman Plus Ser.). (FRE.). 160p. (YA). (gr. 8 up). 1991. pap. 8.95 (*2-89021-148-7*, Pub. by La Courte Ech) Firefly Bks Ltd.

— Un Rendez-Vous Troublant. (Novels in the Roman Plus Ser.). (FRE.). 160p. (YA). (gr. 8 up). 1993. pap. 8.95 (*2-89021-193-2*, Pub. by La Courte Ech) Firefly Bks Ltd.

— Secrets D'Afrique. (Novels in the Roman Jeunesse Ser.). (FRE., Illus.). 96p. (J). (gr. 4-7). 1996. pap. 8.95 (*2-89021-248-3*, Pub. by La Courte Ech) Firefly Bks Ltd.

— Le Ventre du Serpent. (Roman Jeunesse Ser.). (FRE., Illus.). 96p. (J). (gr. 4 up). 1996. pap. 8.95 (*2-89021-262-9*, Pub. by La Courte Ech) Firefly Bks Ltd.

— La Veuve Noire. (Novels in the Roman Jeunesse Ser.). (FRE., Illus.). 96p. (J). (gr. 4-7). 1995. pap. 8.95 (*2-89021-237-8*, Pub. by La Courte Ech) Firefly Bks Ltd.

— Le Vol du Siecle. (Novels in the Roman Jeunesse Ser.). (FRE.). 96p. (J). (gr. 4-7). 1991. pap. 8.95 (*2-89021-160-6*, Pub. by La Courte Ech) Firefly Bks Ltd.

Brouillet, Claire, jt. ed. see Vary, Andree.

Brouillet, Monique S., ed. From Hannibal to Saint Augustine: Ancient Art of North Africa from the Musee de Louvre. LC 94-197766. (EUMILOP Ser.: No. 6). (Illus.). 176p. 1994. pap. text 29.95 (*0-9638169-1-8*) M C Carlos Mus.

Brouillette, Liane. A Geology of School Reform: The Successive Restructurings of a School District. LC 95-33411. (SUNY Series, Restructuring & School Change). 251p. (C). 1996. text 59.50 (*0-7914-2989-X*); pap. text 19.95 (*0-7914-2990-3*) State U NY Pr.

Broukal. Weaving It Together. (College ESL Ser.: Bk. 4). (J). 1996. mass mkt., student ed. 7.95 (*0-8384-6595-1*) Heinle & Heinle.

Broukal, Milada. A.K. Weaving It Together, Bk. 3. (College Esl Ser.). (J). 1994. mass mkt. 7.75 (*0-8384-5415-1*) Wadsworth Pub.

— A First Look at the U. S. A. A Cultural Reader. LC 96-48752. 96p. 1997. pap. text 17.58 (*0-201-69512-X*) Addison-Wesley.

— The Heinle & Heinle TOEFL Test Assistant: Grammar. (YA). 1995. mass mkt. 26.95 (*0-8384-4252-8*) Heinle & Heinle.

— The Heinle & Heinle TOEFL Test Assistant: Listening. LC 94-37203. 176p. (J). 1995. pap. 26.95 (*0-8384-4697-3*) Heinle & Heinle.

— Heinle & Heinle Toefl Test Assistant: Listening. 1995. text 27.00 incl. audio (*0-8384-4699-X*) Heinle & Heinle.

— The Heinle & Heinle TOEFL Test Assistant: Reading. (YA). 1994. mass mkt. 26.95 (*0-8384-4276-5*) Heinle & Heinle.

Broukal, Milada. The Heinle & Heinle TOEFL Test Assistant: Vocabulary. LC 94-12306. 182p. (J). 1994. pap. 26.95 (*0-8384-4280-3*) Heinle & Heinle.

Broukal, Milada. Idioms for Everyday Use: The Basic Text for Learning & Communicating with English Idioms. (Illus.). 112p. 1995. pap. 13.25 (*0-8442-0748-9*, 07489) NTC Contemp Pub Co.

— NTC's Practice Test Kit for the TOEFL. 2nd ed. (Illus.). 168p. 1997. pap. text 13.95 (*0-8442-0495-1*, 04951) NTC Contemp Pub Co.

— NTC's Preparation Book for the TOEFL. 2nd ed. (Illus.). 352p. 1997. pap. text 15.95 (*0-8442-0483-8*, 04838) NTC Contemp Pub Co.

***Broukal, Milada.** TOEFL Grammar Flash 2001. 224p. 2000. pap. 9.95 (*0-7689-0509-5*) Petersons.

— TOEFL Reading Flash 2001. 224p. 2000. pap. 9.95 (*0-7689-0511-7*) Petersons.

Broukal, Milada. TOEFL Word Flash: The Quick Way to Build Vocabulary Power. LC 97-24011. 176p. 1997. 8.95 (*1-56079-950-1*) Petersons.

***Broukal, Milada.** TOEFL Word Flash 2001. 224p. 2000. pap. 9.95 (*0-7689-0510-9*) Petersons.

Broukal, Milada. Weaving It Together, No. 4. (College ESL Ser.: Bk. 4). 250p. (J). 1996. pap. 26.95 (*0-8384-6594-3*) Heinle & Heinle.

— Weaving It Together - 1. (College ESL Ser.). (J). 1994. mass mkt., suppl. ed. 6.95 (*0-8384-5414-3*) Heinle & Heinle.

— Weaving It Together - 1, No. 1. (College ESL Ser.). 144p. (J). 1994. mass mkt. 17.50 (*0-8384-4221-8*) Heinle & Heinle.

— Weaving It Together - 3, No. 3. (College ESL Ser.). 160p. (J). 1994. mass mkt. 17.50 (*0-8384-4222-6*) Heinle & Heinle.

— Weaving It Together Two, No. 2. 145p. (J). 1993. mass mkt. 17.50 (*0-8384-3977-2*) Heinle & Heinle.

— Weaving It Together Two, No. 2. (J). 1993. mass mkt., teacher ed. 9.95 (*0-8384-4201-3*) Heinle & Heinle.

***Broukal, Milada.** What a Life! Stories of Amazing People. LC 99-59443. 128p. 2000. pap. text 18.60 (*0-201-61996-2*) Addison-Wesley.

Broukal, Milada & Flynn, Kathleen. The TOEFL Assistant Test of Written English. LC 93-47011. (J). 1994. mass mkt. 21.95 (*0-8384-4281-1*) Heinle & Heinle.

Broukal, Milada & Milhomme, Janet. More about the U. S. A. LC 95-24398. 1995. pap. text 17.59 (*0-201-87679-5*) Longman.

Broukal, Milada & Murphy, Peter. All about the U. S. A. A Cultural Reader. 2nd ed. LC 98-19385. 128p. 1998. 17.27 (*0-201-34673-7*) Addison-Wesley.

— Introducing the U.S.A. A Cultural Reader. LC 92-35468. (Illus.). 1993. pap. text 17.59 (*0-8013-0984-0*, 79275) Longman.

Broukal, Milada & Nolan-Woods, Enid. NTC's Practice Test Kit for the TOEFL. 160p. 1994. pap. 9.95 (*0-8442-0743-8*, Natl Textbk Co) NTC Contemp Pub Co.

— NTC's Practice Test Kit for the TOEFL. 2nd ed. 168p. 1997. pap. 39.95 incl. audio (*0-8442-0496-X*, 0496X) NTC Contemp Pub Co.

— NTC's Preparation Kit for the TOEFL. 352p. 1994. pap. 11.95 (*0-8442-0738-1*, Natl Textbk Co) NTC Contemp Pub Co.

— NTC's Preparation Kit for the TOEFL, Set. 352p. 1995. 39.95 incl. audio (*0-8442-0739-X*, Natl Textbk Co) NTC Contemp Pub Co.

— NTC's Preparation Kit for the TOEFL, 3 cass., Set. 2nd ed. 352p. 1997. pap. 39.95 incl. audio (*0-8442-0482-X*, 0482X) NTC Contemp Pub Co.

Brouke, Ben. Hill Tauk. (Illus.). 112p. 1997. pap. write for info. (*0-9658565-0-X*) Whisper Hope.

Broumas, Olga. Beginning with O. LC 76-49697. (Younger Poets Ser.: Vol. 72). 74p. 1977. pap. 11.00 (*0-300-02111-9*) Yale U Pr.

***Broumas, Olga.** Olga Broumas: A Listener's Guide. (Listener's Guides for Poetry Ser.). 32p. 2000. 12.00 incl. cd-rom (*1-55659-997-8*) Copper Canyon.

Broumas, Olga. Perpetua. LC 89-61455. 96p. (Orig.). 1989. pap. 11.00 (*1-55659-025-3*) Copper Canyon.

***Broumas, Olga.** Rave: Poems 1975-1999. LC 99-6370. 375p. 1999. 28.00 (*1-55659-127-6*, Pub. by Copper Canyon); pap. 16.00 (*1-55659-126-8*, Pub. by Copper Canyon) SPD-Small Pr Dist.

Broumas, Olga & Begley, T. Helen Groves. deluxe ed. 36p. 1994. 75.00 (*1-888553-01-4*) Kore Pr.

— Helen Groves. deluxe limited ed. 36p. 1994. pap. 55.00 (*1-888553-00-6*) Kore Pr.

— Ithaca - Little Summer in Winter. (Wind Room Ser.). 16p. (Orig.). 1996. pap. 4.00 (*1-887853-08-1*) Radiolarian.

— Sappho's Gymnasium. LC 94-31304. 200p. 1994. pap. 12.00 (*1-55659-071-7*) Copper Canyon.

Broumas, Olga, tr. see Elytis, Odysseus.

Broun, Daniel, ed. see Collins, Michael, et al.

***Broun, Dauvit.** The Irish Identity of the Kingdom of the Scots in the 12th & 13th Centuries. LC 98-50019. (Studies in Celtic History: Vol. 0261-9865). 256p. 1999. 75.00 (*0-85115-375-5*) Boydell & Brewer.

***Broun, Dauvit & Clancy, Thomas Owen, eds.** Spes Scotorum Hope of Scots: Saint Columba, Lona & Scotland. 338p. 1999. pap. 29.95 (*0-567-08682-8*) T&T Clark Pubs.

Broun, Elizabeth, frwd. National Museum of American Art, Smithsonian Institution. LC 94-37723. 1995. pap. write for info. (*0-937311-20-0*); text. write for info. (*0-937311-24-3*) Natl Mus Amer Art.

Broun, Elizabeth, et al. Images on Stone: Two Centuries of Artist's Lithographs. (Illus.). 150p. (Orig.). 1987. pap. 12.00 (*0-941193-00-4*) U Houst Sarah.

Broun, Elizabeth, jt. auth. see Shoemaker, Innis H.

Broun, H. H., ed. see Broun, Heywood C.

Broun, Heywood & Britt, George. Christians Only: A Study in Prejudice. LC 73-19688. (Civil Liberties in American History Ser.). 333p. 1974. reprint ed. lib. bdg. 39.50 (*0-306-70599-0*) Da Capo.

Broun, Heywood C. Collected Edition of Heywood Broun. Broun, H. H., ed. LC 70-90615. (Essay Index Reprint Ser.). 1977. 39.95 (*0-8369-1345-0*) Ayer.

Broun, Heywood H. A Studied Madness. 1999. lib. bdg. 25.95 (*1-56723-206-X*) Yestermorrow.

Broun, Kenneth. Brandis - North Carolina Evidence: 1991 Supplement. 3rd ed. 103p. 1991. write for info. (*0-87473-862-8*, 60671-10, MICHIE) LEXIS Pub.

***Broun, Kenneth S.** Black Lawyers, White Courts: The Soul of South African Law. LC 99-16923. (Illus.). 304p. 1999. 45.00 (*0-8214-1285-X*) Ohio U Pr.

— Black Lawyers, White Courts: The Soul of South African Law. LC 99-16923. 304p. 1999. pap. 19.95 (*0-8214-1286-8*) Ohio U Pr.

Broun, Kenneth S. Brandis & Broun on North Carolina Evidence, 2 vols., Set. 4th ed. 1993. 160.00 (*1-55834-135-8*, 60668-11, MICHIE) LEXIS Pub.

— Brandis & Broun on North Carolina Evidence Vol. 1: 1998 Replacement Volume. 5th ed. LC 98-88470. 1998. 160.00 (*0-327-00498-3*, 6067312) LEXIS Pub.

— Brandis & Broun on North Carolina Evidence Vol. 2: 1998 Replacement Volume. 5th ed. LC 98-88470. 1998. 160.00 (*0-327-00499-1*, 6067312) LEXIS Pub.

— Green vs. Hall & Rose. 4th rev. ed. 134p. 1996. pap. 22.95 (*1-55681-548-4*) Natl Inst Trial Ad.

Broun, Kenneth S. & Blakey, Walker J. Evidence. 2nd ed. (Black Letter Ser.). 265p. (C). 1994. pap., pap. text 24.50 incl. disk (*0-314-02900-1*) West Pub.

Broun, Kenneth S. & Seckinger, James H. Potter v. Shrackle: Wrongful Death. 4th rev. ed. 162p. 1992. pap. 22.95 (*1-55681-313-9*) Natl Inst Trial Ad.

— United States v. Peters: Cocaine Distribution. 4th rev. ed. 126p. 1992. pap. 22.95 (*1-55681-307-4*) Natl Inst Trial Ad.

Broun, Kenneth S., et al. Hornbook on Evidence, 2 vols. 4th ed. Strong, John W., ed. (Hornbook Ser.). 672p. (C). 1992. reprint ed. 42.50 (*0-314-90350-X*) West Pub.

— Problems in Evidence. (American Casebook Ser.). 238p. 1992. reprint ed. pap. text, teacher ed. write for info. (*0-314-46936-2*) West Pub.

— Problems in Evidence. 3rd ed. (American Casebook Ser.). 238p. (C). 1988. reprint ed. pap. 25.50 (*0-314-42363-X*) West Pub.

***Broun, Maurice.** Hawks Aloft: The Story of Hawk Mountain. (Illus.). 288p. 1999. pap. 12.95 (*0-8117-2790-4*) Stackpole.

Brouns, Fred. Nutritional Needs of Athletes. LC 93-11818. 174p. 1994. 75.00 (*0-471-94079-8*) Wiley.

Brounstein, Marty. Handling Difficult Employees. Manber, Beverly, ed. LC 92-54370. (Fifty-Minute Ser.). 76p. (Orig.). 1993. pap. 10.95 (*1-56052-179-1*) Crisp Pubns.

***Brounstein, Paul J. & Zweig, Janine M.** Understanding Substance Abuse Prevention Toward the 21st Century: A Primer on Effective Programs. (Illus.). 80p. (C). 2000. pap. text 20.00 (*0-7567-0164-3*) DIANE Pub.

Brounstein, Paul J., et al. Substance Use & Delinquency among Inner City Adolescent Males. LC 90-11970. (Reports: No. 90-3). (Illus.). 156p. (C). 1990. pap. text 17.00 (*0-87766-475-7*) Urban Inst.

An Asterisk (*) at the beginning of an entry indicates that the title is appearing for the first time.

Brourman, Sherri & Rodman, Randy. Walk Yourself Well: Eliminate Back, Shoulder, Knee, Hip & Other Structural Pain Forever - Without Surgery or Drugs. LC 97-17885. (Illus.). 292p. (J). 1998. 22.45 (*0-7868-6293-9*, Pub. by Hyperion) Time Warner.

Brourman, Sherry & Rodman, Randy. Walk Yourself Well: Eliminate Back, Neck, Shoulder, Knee, Hip, & Other Structural Pain Forever - Without Surgery or Drugs. (Illus.). 304p. 1999. pap. 12.95 (*0-7868-8362-6*, Pub. by Hyperion) Time Warner.

***Brourman, Sherry & Rodman, Randy.** Walk Yourself Well: Eliminate Back, Neck, Shoulder, Knee, Hip & Other Structural Pain Forever - Without Surgery or Drugs. (Illus.). 292p. 1999. reprint ed. text 23.00 (*0-7881-6701-4*) DIANE Pub.

***Brous, Elizabeth.** Seventeen: How to Be Gorgeous: The Ultimate Beauty Guide to Makeup, Hair, & More. (Seventeen Ser.). 160p. (YA). (gr. 7 up). 2000. pap. 14.95 (*0-06-440871-X*, HarpTrophy) HarpC Child Bks.

Broussalis, Martin. Castaneda for Beginners. 1999. pap. text 11.95 (*0-86316-281-9*) Writers & Readers.

Broussard, Albert S. African-American Odyssey: The Stewarts, 1853-1963. LC 98-23811. (Illus.). 272p. 1998. 29.95 (*0-7006-0916-4*) U Pr of KS.

— Black San Francisco: The Struggle for Racial Equality in the West, 1900-1954. LC 92-30597. 336p. 1994. pap. 17.95 (*0-7006-0684-X*) U Pr of KS.

Broussard, Anne E., ed. see Mekz, Andrew K.

Broussard, Anne E., ed. see Merz, Andrew K.

Broussard, Antoinette. African-American Holiday Traditions: Celebrating with Passion, Style & Grace. 1999. 17.95 (*1-55972-532-X*, Birch Ln Pr) Carol Pub Group.

Broussard, Bernard & Broussard, Raymond. Cajun Reunion. 143p. (Orig.). 1989. write for info. (*0-318-64550-5*) Cypress Bks.

Broussard, Bernard B. A Ripple of Hope: White Couple's Struggle for Civil Rights in 60's & 70's. 200p. reprint ed. pap. 10.00 (*0-924798-09-2*) Cypress Bks.

Broussard, Cheryl D. The Black Woman's Guide to Financial Independence: Money Management Strategies for the 1990s. LC 90-81992. (Illus.). 184p. (Orig.). 1991. pap. 19.95 (*0-9627507-2-7*) Hyde Park CA.

— The Black Woman's Guide to Financial Independence: Smart Ways to Take Charge of Your Money, Build Wealth, & Achieve Financial Security. LC 95-36770. 1996. pap. 15.95 (*0-14-025283-5*, Penguin Bks) Viking Penguin.

— Sister CEO: The Black Woman's Guide to Starting Your Own Business. 1998. pap. 12.95 (*0-14-025302-5*) Viking Penguin.

***Broussard, Cheryl D.** Sister CEO: The Black Woman's Guide to Starting Your Own Business. 273p. 2000. reprint ed. text 22.00 (*0-7881-9122-5*) DIANE Pub.

Broussard, Ella. An Act of Love. 1998. mass mkt. 5.95 (*0-352-33240-9*, Pub. by BLA4) London Brdge.

— Black Lace: A Secret Place. 1999. mass mkt. 6.95 (*0-352-33307-3*) London Brdge.

— Black Lace: Searching for Venus. 1998. mass mkt. 6.95 (*0-352-33284-0*, Pub. by BLA4) London Brdge.

Broussard, James H., ed. see Ritter, Charles & Wakelyn, Jon L.

Broussard, Lucretia-del J., jt. auth. see Johnson, Zenobia M.

Broussard, Mark, jt. ed. see Carter, Craig.

Broussard, Peter A. Energy Security for Industrial Facilities. LC 93-45911. 200p. 1994. 34.95 (*0-87814-412-9*) PennWell Bks.

Broussard, Raymond, jt. auth. see Broussard, Bernard.

Broussard-Simmons, Vanessa & Shay, Wendy A. Register of the Hills Bros. Coffee, Inc. Collections, Ca. 1856-1988. 1996. write for info. (*0-614-10099-2*) Natl Mus Am.

Brousse, Adeline, jt. auth. see Verge, Roger.

Brousse, G. Dictionnaire Foucher de Stenographie. (FRE.). 346p. 1980. pap. 24.95 (*0-8288-4692-8*, M6699) Fr & Eur.

Brousseau, Francine, et al. Jean-Paul Lemieux: His Canada. LC 99-197992. (Illus.). 48p. 1999. pap. 23.95 (*0-660-10797-X*) Groupe Commn CAN.

Brousseau, Guy. Theory of Didactical Situations in Mathematics: Didactique des MathEmatiques, 1970-1990. Balacheff, Nicolas, ed. & tr. by. from FRE. LC 97-12155. (Mathematics Education Library). 1997. lib. bdg. 147.00 (*0-7923-4526-6*) Kluwer Academic.

Brousseau, J., et al. Reference Point, Mesh Stiffness & Dynamic Behavior of Solid, Semi-Solid & Thin-Rimmed Spur Gears. (Nineteen Ninety-Four Fall Technical Meeting Ser.: Vol. 94FTM8). (Illus.). 7p. 1994. pap. text 30.00 (*1-55589-643-X*) AGMA.

Brouthers, Dianna W. & Turcotte, Roger. Buyer Representation in Real Estate. LC 97-8527. 1997. 59.00 (*0-7931-2513-8*, 1520-4401) Dearborn.

Broutin, Christian. Arbre. (Gallimard - Mes Premieres Decouvertes Ser.: No. 6). (FRE.). (J). (ps-1). 1989. 12.95 (*2-07-035712-0*) Schoenhof.

— Boats. LC 92-41644.Tr. of Le Bateau. 24p. (J). (ps-3). 1993. 11.95 (*0-590-47131-7*) Scholastic Inc.

Broutman, L. J., jt. auth. see Agarwal, Bhagwan D.

Broutzas, Sharon, et al. Paper Crafts. (Drawing, Paper Folding & Craft Books for Children). (Illus.). 48p. (J). (gr. k-5). 1998. lib. bdg. 17.95 (*1-56674-229-3*) Forest Hse.

Brouwer, A. General Palaeontology. Kaye, R. H., tr. LC 67-18435. (Illus.). 1968. pap. text 5.00 (*0-226-07602-4*) U Ch Pr.

Brouwer, A. E., et al. Distance Regular Graphs. (Ergebnisse der Mathematik und Ihrer Grenzgebiete Ser.: Vol. 18). xvii, 495p. 1989. 150.95 (*0-387-50619-5*) Spr-Verlag.

Brouwer, Arie R. Ecumenical Testimony. Bruggink, Donald J., ed. (Historical Series of the Reformed Church in America). xx, 332p. (Orig.). 1991. pap. 17.00 (*0-8028-0610-4*) Eerdmans.

Brouwer, Bob. Coherence & Conflict. 1993. pap. text 42.00 (*90-6544-681-8*) Kluwer Academic.

Brouwer, D. & De Haan, D., eds. Women's Language Socialization & Self-Image. (Women's Studies). ix, 228p. 1986. pap. 50.00 (*90-6765-275-X*) Mouton.

Brouwer, Dede. Gender Variation in Dutch: A Sociolinguistic Study of Amsterdam Speech. (Topics in Sociolinguistics Ser.). xvi, 125p. (Orig.). (C). 1990. pap. 50.00 (*90-6765-440-X*) Mouton.

***Brouwer, Douglas J.** Remembering the Faith: What Christians Believe. LC 99-28086. 188p. 1999. pap. 12.00 (*0-8028-4621-1*) Eerdmans.

Brouwer, Douglas J., ed. The Pastor's Appreciation Book of Wit & Wisdom. 96p. 1995. mass mkt. 5.99 (*0-87788-641-5*, H Shaw Pubs) Waterbrook Pr.

Brouwer, Elizabeth C. Womanhood in the Making: Domestic Ritual & Public Culture in South India. LC 98-47288. 304p. 1999. text 55.00 (*0-8133-3583-3*, Pub. by Westview) HarpC.

Brouwer, Elizabeth C., ed. see World Bank Staff.

***Brouwer, F. J. & Lowe, P., eds.** Cap Regimes & the European Countryside. LC 99-57217. (CABI Publishing Ser.). 320p. 1999. text 85.00 (*0-85199-354-0*) OUP.

Brouwer, F. M., et al, eds. Land Use Changes in Europe: Processes of Change, Environmental Transformations & Future Patterns. (C). 1991. text 234.00 (*0-7923-1099-3*) Kluwer Academic.

Brouwer, Floor & Crabtree, Bob, eds. Environmental Indicators & Agricultural Policy. LC 98-27951. (CABI Publishing Ser.). (Illus.). 320p. 1999. text 90.00 (*0-85199-289-7*) OUP.

Brouwer, Frans & Leaver, Robin A., eds. Ars Et Musica in Liturgia: Essays Presented to Casper Harders on His Seventieth Birthday. (Studies in Liturgical Musicology: No. 1). 214p. 1994. 35.00 (*0-8108-2948-7*) Scarecrow.

Brouwer, H. H. Bona Dea. xxviii, 507p. 1989. 171.00 (*90-04-08606-4*, EPRO, 110) Brill Academic Pubs.

Brouwer, Hans, et al, eds. Biotechnology & Farmer's Rights. 140p. (Orig.). 1993. pap. text 25.00 (*90-5383-193-2*, Pub. by VU Univ Pr) Paul & Co Pubs.

Brouwer, J. & Helbig, Klaus. Shallow High-Resolution Reflection Seismics. LC 97-51967. (Handbook of Geophysical Exploration Ser.: 19). 396p. 1998. 143.75 (*0-08-043197-6*) Elsevier.

Brouwer, Jan. The Makers of the World: Caste, Craft & Mind of South Indian Artisans. (Illus.). 626p. 1995. text 55.00 (*0-19-563091-2*) OUP.

Brouwer-Janse, M. D. & Harrington, T. L., eds. Human-Machine Communication for Educational Systems Design. (NATO ASI Series F: Computer & Systems Science). x, 342p. 1994. 85.95 (*0-387-57748-3*) Spr-Verlag.

***Brouwer, Joel.** Exactly What Happened. LC 99-27481. 1999. pap. 12.95 (*1-55753-158-7*) Purdue U Pr.

Brouwer, Joel. This Just In, Vol. 21, No. 2. 43p. 1998. pap. 5.00 (*1-892184-05-2*) Beyond Baroque.

Brouwer, Kurt. Kurt Brouwer's Guide to Mutual Funds: How to Invest with the Pros. LC 90-34328. 214p. 1990. pap. 16.95 (*0-471-52128-0*) Wiley.

Brouwer, Maria. Schumpeterian Puzzles: Technological Competition & Economic Evolution. 272p. 1991. text 59.50 (*0-472-10254-0*, 10254) U of Mich Pr.

Brouwer, Norman J. International Register of Historic Ships. 2nd ed. (Illus.). 392p. 57.75 (*0-930248-04-X*); pap. 37.75 (*0-930248-05-8*) Sea Hist Pr.

Brouwer, Norman J., jt. auth. see Hellman, Nina.

Brouwer, Ruth C. New Women for God: Canadian Presbyterian Women & India Missions, 1876-1914. (Social History of Canada Ser.). 376p. 1990. text 50.00 (*0-8020-2718-0*); pap. text 19.95 (*0-8020-6750-6*) U of Toronto Pr.

Brouwer, Ruth C., et al, eds. Structure & Function of Plant Roots: Proceedings of the International Symposium, 2nd, Bratislava, September, 1980. 1981. text 214.50 (*90-247-2510-0*) Kluwer Academic.

Brouwer, S. Cesta de Luna. (Serie el Jinete Fantasma - The Ghost Rider Ser.).Tr. of Moon Basket. (SPA.). 5.99 (*0-7899-0178-1*, 497285) Editorial Unilit.

Brouwer, Sigmund. All-Star Pride. LC 95-19380. (Lightening on Ice Ser.: Vol. 2). 128p. (J). (gr. 5-9). 1995. pap. 5.99 (*0-8499-3638-1*) Tommy Nelson.

— Barbarians from the Isle. (Winds of Light Ser.: No. 2). 132p. (J). (gr. 5-8). 1992. pap. 5.99 (*0-89693-116-1*, 6-1116, Victor Bks) Chariot Victor.

— Blazer Drive. LC 96-42062. (Lightning on Ice Ser.: Vol. 5). (Illus.). 128p. (Orig.). (J). (gr. 5-9). 1996. pap. 5.99 (*0-8499-3983-6*) Tommy Nelson.

— Blood Ties. 304p. 1996. 19.99 (*0-8499-1294-6*) Word Pub.

Brouwer, Sigmund. Blood Ties. 1996. audio 23.00 (*0-8499-6230-7*) Word Pub.

— Can the Real Jesus Still Be Found? (Truth Is Out There Ser.). 225p. 2000. pap. 9.99 (*0-7369-0274-0*) Harvest Hse.

Brouwer, Sigmund. The Carpenter's Cloth. (Illus.). 128p. 1998. 12.99 (*0-8499-5366-9*) Word Pub.

— Chief Honor. LC 96-48592. (Lightning on Ice Ser.: Vol. 6). 128p. (Orig.). (J). (gr. 5-9). 1997. pap. 5.99 (*0-8499-3984-4*) Tommy Nelson.

— Cobra Threat. LC 98-23259. (Sigmund Brouwer's Sports Mystery Ser.). (J). (gr. 5-9). 1998. pap. 5.99 (*0-8499-5815-6*) Tommy Nelson.

***Brouwer, Sigmund.** Cyberquest: The Complete Virtual Adventure. LC 00-20019. (Cyberquest Ser.). (Illus.). 336p. (J). (gr. 5-9). 2000. pap. 6.99 (*0-8499-7577-8*) Tommy Nelson.

Brouwer, Sigmund. Dance of Darkness. LC 97-202859. 124p. (J). 1997. write for info. (*1-56476-274-2*, Chariot Bks) Chariot Victor.

— The Disappearing Jewel of Madagascar. (Accidental Detective Ser.: Vol. 4). 132p. (J). (gr. 3-7). 1994. pap. 4.99 (*1-56476-373-0*, 6-3373, Victor Bks) Chariot Victor.

— Double Helix: A Novel. LC 95-10690. 320p. 1995. 19.99 (*0-8499-1215-6*) Word Pub.

— Double Helix: Conversion. 320p. 1996. pap. 10.99 (*0-8499-3938-0*) Word Pub.

— The Downtown Desperados. LC 94-24747. (Accidental Detective Ser.: Vol. 8). 132p. (J). (gr. 3-7). 1995. pap. 5.99 (*1-56476-377-3*, 6-3377, Victor Bks) Chariot Victor.

***Brouwer, Sigmund.** Evening Star. 320p. 2000. pap. 8.99 (*0-7642-2366-6*) Bethany Hse.

Brouwer, Sigmund. The Forsaken Crusade. LC 96-3454. (Winds of Light Ser.: No.3). 127p. (Orig.). (J). 1992. pap. 5.99 (*0-89693-118-8*, 6-1118, Victor Bks) Chariot Victor.

— Hurricane Power. LC 98-51078. (Sigmund Brouwer's Sports Mystery Ser.). 128p. (J). (gr. 5-9). 1999. pap. 5.99 (*0-8499-5818-0*) Tommy Nelson.

***Brouwer, Sigmund.** Into His Arms: Seeing Jesus Through Children's Eyes. 1999. 12.99 (*0-8499-5467-3*) Word Pub.

Brouwer, Sigmund. The Legend of Burning Water. LC 96-3452. (Winds of Light Ser.: No.1). 130p. (Orig.). (J). 1992. pap. 5.99 (*0-89693-117-X*, 6-1117, Victor Bks) Chariot Victor.

— Lost Beneath Manhattan. (Accidental Detective Ser.: Vol. 1). 132p. (J). (gr. 3-7). 1994. pap. 5.99 (*1-56476-370-6*, 6-3370, Victor Bks) Chariot Victor.

— Magnus. LC 94-13611. (Illus.). 500p. 1994. pap. 11.99 (*1-56476-296-3*, 6-3296, Victor Bks) Chariot Victor.

— Maverick Mania. LC 98-14576. (Sigmund Brouwer's Sports Mystery Ser.). 128p. (J). 1998. 5.99 (*0-8499-5813-X*) Tommy Nelson.

— Merlin's Destiny. LC 96-29181. (Winds of Light Ser.: No. 6). (Illus.). 132p. (Orig.). (J). (gr. 4-8). 1993. pap. 5.99 (*1-56476-049-9*, 6-3049, Victor Bks) Chariot Victor.

— The Missing Map of Pirate's Haven. (Accidental Detective Ser.: Vol. 5). 132p. (J). (gr. 3-7). 1995. pap. text 5.99 (*1-56476-374-9*, 6-3374, Victor Bks) Chariot Victor.

— Morning Star. LC 94-7591. (Ghost Rider Ser.). 312p. (Orig.). 1994. pap. 9.99 (*1-56476-340-4*, 6-3340, Victor Bks) Chariot Victor.

— Mountain Biking . . . to the Extreme - Cliff Dive. LC 96-34928. (Short Cuts Sports Mysteries Ser.: Vol. 2). 64p. (J). (gr. 5-9). 1996. mass mkt. 3.99 (*0-8499-3952-6*) Tommy Nelson.

— The Mystery Tribe of Camp Blackeagle. rev. ed. (Accidental Detective Ser.: Vol. 2). 132p. (J). (gr. 3-7). 1994. pap. 4.99 (*1-56476-371-4*, 6-3371, Victor Bks) Chariot Victor.

— Phantom Outlaw at Wolf Creek. (Accidental Detective Ser.). 132p. (J). (gr. 3-7). 1990. pap. text 4.99 (*0-89693-013-0*, Victor Bks) Chariot Victor.

***Brouwer, Sigmund.** Pony Express Christmas. 2000. 12.99 (*0-8423-4018-1*) Tyndale Hse.

Brouwer, Sigmund. Race for the Part Street Treasure. (Accidental Detective Ser.). 132p. (J). (gr. 3-7). 1991. pap. 4.99 (*0-89693-859-X*) Chariot Victor.

— Rebel Glory. (Lightning on Ice Sports Mysteries Ser.: Vol. 1). 128p. (J). (gr. 5-9). 1995. pap. 5.99 (*0-8499-3637-3*) Tommy Nelson.

— Scarlet Thunder, 1. LC 98-40559. (Simund Brouwer Sports Mystery Ser.). 128p. (J). (gr. 5-9). 1998. pap. 5.99 (*0-8499-5817-2*) Tommy Nelson.

— Scuba Diving... To the Extreme-Off the Wall. LC 96-44834. (Short Cuts Sports Mysteries Ser.: Vol. 4). 64p. (J). (gr. 5-9). 1997. mass mkt. 3.99 (*0-8499-3954-2*) Tommy Nelson.

— Short Cuts. LC 93-26411. (Accidental Detective Ser.: Vol. 11). 132p. (J). (gr. 3-7). 1993. pap. 4.99 (*1-56476-158-4*, Victor Bks) Chariot Victor.

***Brouwer, Sigmund.** Silver Moon. 320p. 2000. pap. 8.99 (*0-7642-2365-8*) Bethany Hse.

Brouwer, Sigmund. Sky Diving to the Extreme 'Chute Roll. LC 96-38593. (Short Cuts Ser.). 96p. (J). (gr. 5-9). 1997. pap. 3.99 (*0-8499-3953-4*) Tommy Nelson.

— Snowboarding... To the Extreme - Rippin. LC 96-18646. (Short Cuts Sports Mysteries Ser.: Vol. 1). 64p. (J). (gr. 5-9). 1996. mass mkt. 3.99 (*0-8499-3951-8*) Tommy Nelson.

— Sunrise at the Mayan Temple. (Accidental Detective Ser.: Vol. 10). (J). (gr. 3-7). 1992. pap. 4.99 (*0-89693-057-2*, Victor Bks) Chariot Victor.

— Thunderbird Spirit. LC 95-19410. (Lightening on Ice Ser.: Vol. 3). 128p. (J). (gr. 5-9). 1996. pap. 5.99 (*0-8499-3639-X*) Tommy Nelson.

— Tiger Heat. LC 98-14584. (Sigmund Brouwer's Sports Mystery Ser.). 128p. (J). 1998. 8.99 (*0-8499-5814-8*) Tommy Nelson.

— Titan Clash: Basketball. LC 98-33708. (Sigmund Brouwer's Sports Mystery Ser.). (J). (gr. 5-9). 1998. pap. text 5.99 (*0-8499-5816-4*) Tommy Nelson.

— Tyrant of the Badlands. (Accidental Detective Ser.: Vol. 13). 132p. (J). (gr. 3-7). 1996. mass mkt. 5.99 (*1-56476-160-6*, Victor Bks) Chariot Victor.

— The Weeping Chamber: A Novel. LC 98-11033. 350p. 1998. pap. 12.99 (*0-8499-3703-5*) Word Pub.

— Wings of an Angel. LC 96-3451. (Winds of Light Ser.: No. 1). 132p. (J). (gr. 5-8). 1992. pap. 5.99 (*0-89693-115-3*, 6-1115, Victor Bks) Chariot Victor.

— Wings of Dawn. (Illus.). 1999. pap. text 12.99 (*1-56476-756-6*, Victor Bks) Chariot Victor.

***Brouwer, Sigmund.** Wings of the Dawn. LC 98-21780. 1999. write for info. (*0-7459-4083-8*) Chariot Victor.

Brouwer, Sigmund. Winterhawk Star. (Lightening on Ice Ser.: Vol. 4). 128p. (J). (gr. 5-9). 1996. pap. 5.99 (*0-8499-3640-3*) Tommy Nelson.

***Brouwer, Sigmund, et al.** Fiction Starter Kit. (Illus.). (J). (gr. 3-9). 1999. 9.97 (*0-8499-7539-5*) Tommy Nelson.

Brouwer, Steve. Conquest & Capitalism 1492-1992. (Illus.). 120p. (Orig.). (C). 1992. pap. 10.00 (*0-9622152-3-6*) Big Picture Bks.

— Sharing the Pie. LC 97-43523. (Illus.). 180p. 1998. pap. 12.95 (*0-8050-5206-2*) St Martin.

— Sharing the Pie: A Disturbing Picture of the U. S. Economy. (Illus.). 88p. (Orig.). (C). 1992. pap. 8.00 (*0-9622152-2-8*) Big Picture Bks.

— Sharing the Pie: A Disturbing Picture of the U. S. Economy in the 1980s. (Illus.). 240p. (C). 1988. 7.95 (*0-317-93354-X*) Big Picture Bks.

Brouwer, Steve, ed. Exporting the American Gospel. LC 96-8439. 344p. (C). 1996. 75.00 (*0-415-91711-5*); pap. 23.99 (*0-415-91712-3*) Routledge.

***Brouwer, Wayne.** Being a Believer in an Unbelieving World. 1999. pap. 12.95 (*1-56563-455-1*) Hendrickson MA.

Brouwer, Wayne. Hear Me, O God: Meditations on the Psalms. LC 95-30412. 303p. 1995. pap. 13.95 (*1-56212-119-7*) CRC Pubns.

***Brouwer, Wayne.** Humming Till the Music Returns: Second Lesson Sermons for Advent/Christmas/Epiphany, Cycle B. LC 99-16010. 160p. 1999. pap. 16.50 (*0-7880-1506-0*) CSS OH.

Brouwer, Wayne. Moving Day: Funeral Mediations. 1997. pap. text 8.50 (*0-936497-15-7*) Seven Worlds.

Brouwer, Wayne. Walking on Water: Faith & Doubt in the Christian Life. LC 94-3931. 135p. 1994. pap. 9.95 (*1-56212-055-7*) CRC Pubns.

Brouwer, Wayne. With New & Open Eyes. 160p. 1994. pap. 11.95 (*0-936497-10-6*) Seven Worlds.

Brouwer, Wiebo H., jt. auth. see Van Zomeren, Adriaan H.

B

Brouwers, Jeroen. Sunken Red. Dixon, Adrienne, tr. from DUT. LC 88-19502. 131p. (C). 1988. 15.95 (*0-941533-19-0*, NAB) I R Dee.

— Sunken Red. 131p. 1992. reprint ed. pap. 9.95 (*1-56131-025-5*, NAB) I R Dee.

Brouwers, P., jt. ed. see Mohr, E.

Brouwers, Ruud. Yearbook of Architecture in the Netherlands, 1996-1997. (Illus.). 176p. 1997. pap. 49.50 (*90-5662-040-1*) Dist Art Pubs.

***Brouws, Jeffrey T. & Delvers, Ed.** Starlight on the Rails. LC 00-31319. (Illus.). 136p. 2000. 39.95 (*0-8109-4167-8*, Pub. by Abrams) Time Warner.

Broux, Jane De, see Demco, Inc. Staff & De Broux, Jane.

***Brovarski, Edward.** The Senedjemib Complex Pt. 1: The Mastabas of Senedjemib Inti (G2370), Khnumenti (G2374) Der Manuelian, Peter & Kelly Simpson, William, eds. (Illus.). (C). 2000. 150.00 (*0-87846-479-4*, Pub. by Mus Fine Arts Boston) D Brown Bk Co.

***Brovelli, Tito A.** La Nubecita Panza de Agua (Water Belly, the Little Cloud) Cuentos Bilingues (Bilingual Stories) Anderson, Kirk, tr. (ENG & SPA., Illus.). 24p. (J). (ps-6). 2000. 14.00 (*0-9673032-0-6*, Pub. by Sweet Dreams Bilingual Pubs) IPG Chicago.

***Brovelli, Tito Alberto.** Kiko, el Dragon Desobediente (Kiko, the Disobedient Dragon) Cuentos Bilingues (Bilingual Stories) Anderson, Kirk, tr. (SPA & ENG., Illus.). 24p. (J). (ps-6). 2000. 14.00 (*0-9673032-2-2*, Pub. by Sweet Dreams Bilingual Pubs) IPG Chicago.

— Mary, la Ostra Timida (Mary, the Shy Oyster) Cuentos Bilingues (Bilingual Stories) Anderson, Kirk, tr. (ENG & SPA., Illus.). 24p. (J). (ps-6). 2000. 14.00 (*0-9673032-1-4*, Pub. by Sweet Dreams Bilingual Pubs) IPG Chicago.

Broven, John. Rhythm & Blues in New Orleans. LC 77-13351. Orig. Title: Walking To New Orleans. (Illus.). 328p. 1983. pap. 13.95 (*0-88289-433-1*) Pelican.

— South to Louisiana: The Music of the Cajun Bayous. LC 82-11247. (Illus.). 384p. 1983. pap. 14.95 (*0-88289-608-3*) Pelican.

Brovender, Jacqueline G., tr. see Clastres, Helene.

Broverman, Samuel A. Mathematics of Investment & Credit. 2nd ed. (Illus.). 391p. (C). 1996. pap. text 55.00 (*1-56698-218-9*) Actex Pubns.

***Brovick, Ed, et al.** Windows 2000 Active Directory. 525p. 2000. 44.95 (*0-7357-0870-3*) New Riders Pub.

Brovkin, Vladimir N. Behind the Front Line of the Civil War: Political Parties & Social Movements in Russia, 1918-1922. 472p. 1994. text 65.00 (*0-691-03278-5*, Pub. by Princeton U Pr) Cal Prin Full Svc.

— Behind the Front Lines of the Civil War: Political Parties & Social Movements in Russia, 1918-1922. LC 93-5299. (Illus.). 469p. reprint ed. pap. 145.40 (*0-608-20149-9*, 207142100011) Bks Demand.

— The Bolsheviks in Russian Society: The Revolution & the Civil Wars. LC 96-47127. 320p. 1997. 35.00 (*0-300-06706-2*) Yale U Pr.

— The Mensheviks after October: Socialist Opposition & the Rise of the Bolshevik Dictatorship. LC 87-47952. 352p. 1991. reprint ed. pap. text 18.95 (*0-8014-9976-3*) Cornell U Pr.

— Russia after Lenin: Politics, Culture & Society. LC 97-39751. 266p. (C). 1998. 85.00 (*0-415-17991-2*) Routledge.

— Russia after Lenin: Politics, Culture & Society. LC 97-39751. (Illus.). 280p. (C). 1998. pap. 27.99 (*0-415-17992-0*) Routledge.

Brovkin, Vladimir N., ed. Dear Comrades: Menshevik Reports on the Bolshevik Revolution & the Civil War. (Publication Series: Archival Documentaries: No. 398). 296p. 1991. pap. 21.95 (*0-8179-8982-X*) Hoover Inst Pr.

Brow. Dictionary Catalog of the Harris Collection of American Poetry & Plays. 1977. 420.00 (*0-8161-1453-6*, G K Hall & Co) Mac Lib Ref.

***Brow, Fred & McDonald, Jeanne.** The Serpent Handler's: Three Families & Their Faith. (Illus.). 352p. 2000. 19.95 (*0-89587-191-2*) Blair.

Brow, James. Agrarian Change in Sri Lanka. Weeraamunda, Joe, ed. 400p. (C). 1992. text 39.95 (*0-8039-9415-X*) Sage.

An Asterisk (*) at the beginning of an entry indicates that the title is appearing for the first time.

— Vedda Villages of Anuradhapura: The Historical Anthropology of a Community in Sri Lanka. LC 77-16663. (Publications on Asia of the School of International Studies: No. 33). (Illus.). 288p. 1978. 35.00 (*0-295-95585-6*) U of Wash Pr.

Brow, James B. Demons & Development: The Struggle for Community in a Sri Lankan Village. LC 96-9982. (Hegemony & Experience Ser.). (Illus.). 318p. 1996. 45.00 (*0-8165-1638-3*); pap. 19.95 (*0-8165-1639-1*) U of Ariz Pr.

Brow, Robert C., jt. auth. see Pinnock, Clark H.

Broward, Robert C. The Architecture of Henry John Klutho: The Prairie School in Jacksonville. LC 83-6460. (Illus.). 379p. 1984. 49.95 (*0-8130-0731-3*) U Press Fla.

Browder. Developmental Biology. 4th ed. (C). 1998. text 44.00 (*0-03-096836-4*) Harcourt Coll Pubs.

Browder, Andrew. Mathematical Analysis: An Introduction. Axler, S. et al, eds. LC 95-44877. (Undergraduate Texts in Mathematics Ser.). (Illus.). 333p. (C). 1996. 39.95 (*0-387-94614-4*) Spr-Verlag.

Browder, Anne, ed. see Browder, Atlantis T. & Browder, Anthony T.

Browder, Anne E., ed. see Browder, Atlantis T. & Browder, Anthony T.

Browder, Anthony T. From the Browder File: Twenty-Two Essays on the African American Experience. Peterson, Zelma, ed. LC 89-80061. (From the Browder File Ser.). (Illus.). (Orig.). 1989. pap. 10.00 (*0-924944-00-5*) Inst Karmic.

— Nile Valley Contributions to Civilization: Exploding the Myths, Vol. 1. LC 92-73935. (Illus.). 296p. 1992. 39.95 (*0-924944-04-8*); pap. 16.95 (*0-924944-03-X*) Inst Karmic.

— Survival Strategies for Africans in America: 13 Steps to Freedom. LC 89-80061. (From the Browder File Ser.: Vol. II). (Illus.). 172p. (Orig.). 1996. pap. 15.00 (*0-924944-10-2*) Inst Karmic.

Browder, Anthony T., et al. Nile Valley Contributions to Civilization. (Illus.). 64p. 1994. pap., student ed. 10.00 (*0-924944-05-6*) Inst Karmic.

Browder, Anthony T., jt. auth. see Browder, Atlantis T.

Browder, Atlantis T. & Browder, Anthony T. Africa on My Mind: Reflections of My Second Trip. Browder, Anne E., ed. (Illus.). 98p. 1995. 24.99 (*0-924944-09-9*); pap. 11.99 (*0-924944-08-0*) Inst Karmic.

— My First Trip to Africa. Browder, Anne, ed. LC 91-70328. (Illus.). 38p. (Orig.). (J). 1991. pap. 16.95 (*0-924944-02-1*); pap. 8.95 (*0-924944-01-3*) Inst Karmic.

Browder, Catherine. The Clay That Breathes: A Novella & Stories. LC 90-26184. (Illus.). 164p. (Orig.). 1991. pap. 9.95 (*0-915943-63-8*) Milkweed Ed.

— The Heart: A Story. 15p. (Orig.). 1995. pap. 3.50 (*1-884235-11-5*) Helicon Nine Eds.

Browder, Clifford. The Money Game in Old New York: Daniel Drew & His Times. LC 85-17938. 335p. reprint ed. pap. 103.90 (*0-7837-5799-9*, 204546500006) Bks Demand.

Browder, Dewey A. Americans in Post-World War II Germany: Teachers, Tinkers, Neighbors & Nuisances. LC 98-11846. 212p. 1998. text 89.95 (*0-7734-2245-5*) E Mellen.

Browder, Diane M. & Lim, Levan. Improving Work Efficiency: Job Training Based on Engineering Principles. (Innovations Ser.). (Illus.). 28p. (Orig.). 1996. pap. 21.95 (*0-940898-40-3*) Am Assn Mental.

Browder, Diane M., ed. see Agran, Martin & Moore, Stephen C.

Browder, Diane M., ed. see Bambara, Linda M. & Koger, Freya.

Browder, Diane M., ed. see Demchak, MaryAnn & Bossert, Karen W.

Browder, Diane M., ed. see Dyer, Kathleen & Luce, Stephen C.

Browder, Diane M., ed. see Test, David W. & Spooner, Fred.

Browder, Dustin. Diablerie: Britain/Mexico. (FRE.). 1997. pap. text 12.00 (*1-56504-238-7*) White Wolf.

— House Call: An Adventure Resource for Over the Edge. (Over the Edge Ser.). 16p. 1993. pap. 4.95 (*1-887801-05-7*, Atlas Games) Trident MN.

Browder, Earl. Marx & America. LC 73-16734. 146p. 1974. reprint ed. lib. bdg. 65.00 (*0-8371-7218-7*, BRMA, Greenwood Pr) Greenwood.

Browder, Earl, jt. auth. see Bowers, Claude G.

Browder, Felix, ed. The Mathematical Heritage of Henri Poincare, 2 Pts., Set. LC 83-2774. (Proceedings of Symposia in Pure Mathematics Ser.: Vol. 39). 905p. 1984. reprint ed. pap. 49.00 (*0-8218-1442-7*, PSPUM/39) Am Math.

Browder, Felix E., ed. The Mathematical Heritage of Henri Poincare, 2 Pts., Pt. 1. LC 83-2774. (Proceedings of Symposia in Pure Mathematics Ser.: Vol. 39). 435p. 1984. reprint ed. pap. 58.00 (*0-8218-1448-6*, PSPUM/39.2) Am Math.

— The Mathematical Heritage of Henri Poincare, 2 Pts., Pt. 2. LC 83-2774. (Proceedings of Symposia in Pure Mathematics Ser.: Vol. 39). 470p. 1984. reprint ed. pap. 58.00 (*0-8218-1449-4*, PSPUM/39.1) Am Math.

— Mathematics into the Twenty-First Century. LC 91-22093. (Centennial Publications: Vol. II). 491p. 1992. text 165.00 (*0-8218-0167-8*, HMBROWDER) Am Math.

— Nonlinear & Global Analysis. LC 92-36618. (Reprints from the Bulletin of the American Mathematical Society Ser.: Vol. 1). 625p. 1992. pap. 73.00 (*0-8218-8500-6*, BULLRE/1) Am Math.

— Nonlinear Functional Analysis, Pt. 1. LC 74-34154. (Proceedings of Symposia in Pure Mathematics Ser.: Vol. 18). 296p. 1970. pap. 50.00 (*0-8218-0243-7*, PSPUM/18.1) Am Math.

— Nonlinear Functional Analysis, Pt. 2. LC 74-34154. (Proceedings of Symposia in Pure Mathematics Ser.: Vol. 18). 308p. 1970. pap. 75.00 (*0-8218-0244-5*, PSPUM/18.2) Am Math.

— Nonlinear Functional Analysis, Set, Pts. 1 & 2. LC 74-34154. (Proceedings of Symposia in Pure Mathematics Ser., Humboldt State University, Arcata, CA, July 29-August 16, 1974: Vol. 18). 604p. 1970. pap. 110.00 (*0-8218-1418-4*, PSPUM/18) Am Math.

— Nonlinear Functional Analysis & Its Applications, 2 pts., Pt. 1. LC 85-28725. (Proceedings of Symposia in Pure Mathematics Ser.: Vol. 45). 540p. (Orig.). 1986. text 82.00 (*0-8218-1471-0*, PSPUM/45.1) Am Math.

— Nonlinear Functional Analysis & Its Applications, 2 pts., Pt. 2. LC 85-28725. (Proceedings of Symposia in Pure Mathematics Ser.: Vol. 45). 577p. (Orig.). 1986. text 89.00 (*0-8218-1472-9*, PSPUM/45.2) Am Math.

— Nonlinear Functional Analysis & Its Applications, 2 pts., Set. LC 85-28725. (Proceedings of Symposia in Pure Mathematics Ser.: Vol. 45). 1117p. (Orig.). 1986. text 160.00 (*0-8218-1467-2*, PSPUM/45) Am Math.

Browder, Felix E., tr. see Sobolev, Sergei L.

Browder, George C. Foundations of the Nazi Police State: The Formation of SIPO & SD. LC 89-22618. (Illus.). 376p. 1990. 39.95 (*0-8131-1697-X*) U Pr of Ky.

— Hitler's Enforcers: The Gestapo & the Security Service in the Nazi Revolution. (Illus.). 384p. (C). 1996. text 65.00 (*0-19-510479-X*) OUP.

Browder, Joan A., ed. Aquatic Organisms As Indicators of Environmental Pollution. LC QH0096.8.A65. (American Water Resources Association Monograph Ser.: No. 12). (Illus.). 94p. reprint ed. pap. 30.00 (*0-8357-3161-8*, 203942400012) Bks Demand.

Browder, John O. & Godfrey, Brian J. Rainforest Cities: The Urban Transformation of Amazonia. LC 96-33481. 1997. 49.50 (*0-231-10654-8*); pap. 24.00 (*0-231-10655-6*) Col U Pr.

Browder, L. W. The Cellular Basis of Morphogenesis, Vol. 2. LC 85-3406. (Developmental Biology Ser.). (Illus.). 668p. (C). 1986. text 120.00 (*0-306-42164-X*, Kluwer Plenum) Kluwer Academic.

— Developmental Biology Vol. 1: A Comprehensive Synthesis; Oogenesis. LC 85-3406. (Illus.). 644p. (C). 1985. text 120.00 (*0-306-41866-5*, Kluwer Plenum) Kluwer Academic.

— The Molecular Biology of Cell Determination & Cell Differentiation. LC 85-3406. (Developmental Biology Ser.). (Illus.). 460p. (C). 1988. text 105.00 (*0-306-42735-4*, Kluwer Plenum) Kluwer Academic.

Browder, Laura. Rousing the Nation: Radical Culture in Depression America. LC 97-33358. (Illus.). 240p. 1998. 29.95 (*1-55849-125-2*) U of Mass Pr.

***Browder, Laura.** Slippery Characters: Ethnic Impersonators & American Identities. LC 99-53732. (Cultural Studies of the United States). (Illus.). 368p. 2000. pap. 18.95 (*0-8078-4859-X*); lib. bdg. 49.95 (*0-8078-2546-8*) U of NC Pr.

Browder, Leon W., et al. Developmental Biology. 3rd ed. 754p. (C). 1991. text 90.50 (*0-03-013514-1*, Pub. by SCP) Harcourt.

Browder, Olin L. Property: Adaptable to Courses Utilizing Materials by Browder. 2nd ed. LC 87-130233. (Legalines Ser.). 355p. 13.50 (*0-685-19023-4*) Harcourt.

Browder, Olin L., et al. Basic Property Law. 5th ed. (American Casebook Ser.). 369p. (C). 1989. pap. text, teacher ed. write for info. (*0-314-67335-0*) West Pub.

— Property Law. 5th ed. (American Casebook Ser.). 1386p. (C). 1989. reprint ed. text 55.00 (*0-314-54012-1*) West Pub.

Browder, Robert P. & Kerensky, Alexander F., eds. The Russian Provisional Government, 1917: Documents, 3 vols., Set. 1949p. 1961. 129.50 (*0-8047-0023-0*) Stanford U Pr.

— The Russian Provisional Government, 1917: Documents, Vol. 1. LC 60-9052. (Hoover Institution Publications). 507p. 1961. reprint ed. pap. 30.00 (*0-7837-9059-7*, 204981000001) Bks Demand.

— The Russian Provisional Government, 1917: Documents, Vol. 2. LC 60-9052. (Hoover Institution Publications). 742p. 1961. reprint ed. pap. 30.00 (*0-7837-9060-0*, 204981000002) Bks Demand.

— The Russian Provisional Government, 1917: Documents, Vol. 3. LC 60-9052. (Hoover Institution Publications). 701p. 1961. reprint ed. pap. 30.00 (*0-7837-9061-9*, 204981000003) Bks Demand.

Browder, Robin, ed. see Feeney, Agnes M. & Leckel, John L.

Browder, Sue. The New Age Baby Name Book. LC 86-40549. (Illus.). 360p. 1987. pap. 7.95 (*0-89480-309-3*, 1309) Workman Pub.

— The New Age Baby Name Book. rev. ed. 320p. 1987. mass mkt. 5.99 (*0-446-32004-8*, Pub. by Warner Bks) Little.

— The New Age Baby Name Book. rev. ed. 1997. mass mkt. write for info. (*0-446-60391-0*) Warner Bks.

— The New Age Baby Name Book. rev. ed. 480p. 1998. mass mkt. 6.99 (*0-446-60607-3*, Pub. by Warner Bks) Little.

— New Age Baby Name Book. 3rd ed. LC 97-53250. 512p. 1998. pap. 9.95 (*0-7611-0232-9*) Workman Pub.

***Browder, Sue Ellin.** The Power: How Women Just Like You Become Weight-Loss Winners. 272p. 2000. 22.95 (*0-471-37968-9*) Wiley.

Browder, Sue Ellin & Browder, Walter. 101 Secrets a Good Dad Knows. LC 99-44983. (Illus.). 224p. 1999. text 14.95 (*1-55853-719-8*) Rutledge Hill Pr.

Browder, T. Maldive Islands Money. (Illus.). 1997. lib. bdg. 8.00 (*0-932106-06-4*) S J Durst.

Browder, T. E., et al, eds. B Physics & CP Violation: Proceedings of the 2nd International Conference Honolulu, Hawaii, U. S. A., 24-27 March, 1997. 500p. 1998. 108.00 (*981-02-3370-1*) World Scientific Pub.

Browder, T. E. & Sahu, S. K., eds. Backgrounds at Machine-Detector Interface. 240p. 1997. text 56.00 (*981-02-3222-5*) World Scientific Pub.

Browder, W. Surgery on Simply-Connected Manifolds. LC 70-175907. (Ergebnisse der Mathematik und Ihrer Grenzgebiete Ser.: Vol. 65). 140p. 1972. 42.95 (*0-387-05629-7*) Spr-Verlag.

Browder, Walter, jt. auth. see Browder, Sue Ellin.

Browdy, Craig L. & Hopkins, J. Stephen, eds. Swimming Through Troubled Water, Proceedings of the Special Session on Shrimp Culture, Aquaculture '95. (Illus.). 253p. (C). 1995. pap. text 35.00 (*0-9624529-8-X*) World Aquaculture.

Browe, Gary. We Are No Longer "A Couple" LC 92-81968. (Illus.). 128p. (Orig.). 1992. pap. 9.95 (*0-8187-0162-5*) Harlo Press.

Browell, Felicia. Breyer Animal Collector's Guide. 2nd ed. LC 00-265504. 208p. 1999. pap. text 19.95 (*1-57432-135-8*) Collector Bks.

Brower. World in the 20th Century: From Empires to Nations. 4th ed. LC 98-28880. 399p. 1998. pap. text 36.80 (*0-13-095917-0*) P-H.

— The World since 1945: A Brief History. LC 98-50894. (Illus.). 258p. 1999. pap. text 32.00 (*0-13-434465-0*) P-H.

— World War II in Europe: The Final Year. LC 97-44886. 320p. 1998. text 55.00 (*0-312-21133-3*) St Martin.

— World 20th Century. 3rd ed. 1995. text, teacher ed. write for info. (*0-13-443649-0*) Allyn.

Brower, Aaron & Zanzig, Ann. The Clue Book. 96p. (C). 1995. pap. text, per. 16.95 (*0-7872-1366-7*, 41136601) Kendall-Hunt.

Brower, Aaron M. Social Cognition & Individual Change: A Cognitive-Ecological Approach to Practice. LC 93-29475. (Sourcebooks for the Human Services Ser.: Vol. 26). 1993. 56.00 (*0-8039-3883-7*); pap. 26.00 (*0-8039-3884-5*) Sage.

Brower, Aaron M. & Rose, Sheldon D., eds. Advances in Group Work Research. LC 89-77595. (Journal of Social Service Research: Vol. 13, No. 2). 124p. 1990. text 39.95 (*0-86656-983-9*) Haworth Pr.

Brower, Aaron M., jt. ed. see Nye, Judith L.

Brower, Alexandra & Wright, Thomas L. Working in Hollywood. 560p. 1991. reprint ed. pap. 14.00 (*0-380-71500-7*, Avon Bks) Morrow Avon.

Brower, Anne C. Arthritis in Black & White Vol. 2. 2nd ed. Bralow, Lesteet, ed. 400p. 1996. text 83.00 (*0-7216-5152-6*, W B Saunders Co) Harcrt Hlth Sci Grp.

Brower, Barbara. Linking to the Church. (Core Value Ser.). 62p. 1998. pap. 2.95 (*1-56212-335-1*, 1960-0054) CRC Pubns.

— The Sherpa of Khumbu: People, Livestock & Landscape. (C). 1991. text 75.00 (*0-7855-0160-6*, Pub. by Ratna Pustak Bhandar) St Mut.

— The Sherpa of Khumbu: People, Livestock & Landscape. (Illus.). 226p. 1993. reprint ed. pap. text 10.95 (*0-19-563137-4*) OUP.

Brower, Bob. Presidents of the LDS Church Coloring Book. (Coloring Bks.). 50p. (Orig.). (J). (gr. 2-6). 1993. pap. 5.95 (*0-910523-21-5*) Grandin Bk Co.

Brower, Brock, jt. auth. see Abshire, David M.

***Brower, Carol & Brower, Steven.** I Love It! The Best Way to Get Great Gifts from Your Man. LC 99-91497. iv, 163p. 2000. pap. 14.95 (*0-9675642-0-4*) Utopia CA.

Brower, Carol, jt. auth. see Wilhelm, Henry.

Brower, Charles D. Fifty Years below Zero: A Lifetime of Adventure in the Far North. (Classic Reprint Ser.: No. 3). (Illus.). xxii, 324p. 1994. reprint ed. pap. 20.00 (*0-912006-68-4*) U of Alaska Pr.

Brower, Charles N. & Brueschke, Jason D. The Iran - United States Claims Tribunal. LC 98-5149. 1998. 270.00 (*90-411-0627-8*) Kluwer Academic.

Brower, Charles N. & Marks, Lee R. International Commercial Arbitration. vi, 362p. write for info. (*0-318-57663-5*) Harcourt.

Brower, Charles N., jt. ed. see Lillich, Richard B.

Brower, Daniel R. The Russian City Between Tradition & Modernity, 1850-1900. 1990. 55.00 (*0-520-06764-9*, Pub. by U CA Pr) Cal Prin Full Svc.

Brower, Daniel R. & Lazzerini, Edward J., eds. Russia's Orient: Imperial Borderlands & Peoples, 1700-1917. LC 96-39473. (Indiana-Michigan Series in Russian & East European Studies). 1997. 39.95 (*0-253-33274-5*); pap. 19.95 (*0-253-21113-1*) Ind U Pr.

***Brower, David.** Reading the Earth. (Illus.). 48p. (ps-3). 2000. 16.00 (*1-893163-15-6*) Berkeley Hills.

***Brower, David & Chapple, Steve.** Let the Mountains Talk, Let the Rivers Run: A Call to Those Who Would Save the Earth. 208p. 2000. reprint ed. pap. 14.95 (*0-86571-411-8*, Pub. by New Soc Pubs) Consort Bk Sales.

Brower, David, jt. auth. see Beatley, Timothy.

Brower, David, ed. see Porter, Eliot.

Brower, David J., et al, eds. Understanding Growth Management: Critical Issues & a Research Agenda. LC 89-51662. 198p. (Orig.). 1989. pap. text 43.95 (*0-87420-691-X*, U99) Urban Land.

Brower, David J. & Carol, Daniel S., eds. Managing Land-Use Conflicts: Case Studies in Special Area Management. LC 86-19881. (Duke Press Policy Studies). ix, 323p. 1987. text 59.95 (*0-8223-0560-7*) Duke.

Brower, Harriette M. Modern Masters of the Keyboard. LC 70-86736. (Essay Index Reprint Ser.). 1977. 21.95 (*0-8369-1124-5*) Ayer.

— Story-Lives of Master Musicians. LC 74-167316. (Essay Index Reprint Ser.). 1977. reprint ed. 26.95 (*0-8369-2338-3*) Ayer.

Brower, Harriette M. & Cooke, James F. Great Singers on the Art of Singing. (Illus.). 160p. (Orig.). 1996. pap. text 7.95 (*0-486-29190-1*) Dover.

Brower, James E., ed. Hazard Communication: Issue & Implementations. LC 86-22228. (Special Technical Publication Ser.: No. 932). (Illus.). 237p. 1986. text 37.00 (*0-8031-0933-4*, STP932) ASTM.

***Brower, Kathy, et al.** The Australian Blouse. LC 98-66729. 64p. 1998. 19.95 (*1-878048-15-5*) M Pullen.

Brower, Keith H. Contemporary Latin American Fiction. (Magill Bibliographies Ser.). 218p. 1989. 42.00 (*0-8108-2810-3*) Scarecrow.

***Brower, Keith H., et al.** Jorge Amado: New Critical Essays. (Latin American Studies: 18). 300p. 2000. 45.00 (*0-8153-2083-3*) Garland.

Brower, Kenneth. Starship & The Canoe. LC 82-48519. 272p. 1983. pap. 13.50 (*0-06-091030-5*, CN 1030, Perennial) HarperTrade.

— With Their Islands Around Them. LC 74-4455. (Illus.). 1974. 8.95 (*0-03-013121-9*) Friends of Earth.

***Brower, Kent E.** Eschatology in Bible & Theology: Evangelical Essays at the Dawn of a New Millennium. LC 99-25216. 347p. 1999. pap. 24.99 (*0-8308-1582-1*) InterVarsity.

Brower, Lincoln P. Mimicry & the Evolutionary Process. (Illus.). 136p. 1988. pap. text 18.00 (*0-226-07608-3*) U Ch Pr.

— Mimicry & the Evolutionary Process. (Illus.). 136p. 1996. lib. bdg. 36.00 (*0-226-07607-5*) U Ch Pr.

Brower, Michael, et al. Consumer's Guide to Effective Environmental Choices. LC 98-27570. 1999. pap. 15.00 (*0-609-80281-X*) Random Hse Value.

— The Next Texas Energy Boom: Power Choices for the 21st Century. (Illus.). 71p. 1997. reprint ed. pap. text 30.00 (*0-7881-4579-7*) DIANE Pub.

Brower, Michael C. Cool Energy: Renewable Solutions to Environmental Problems. rev. ed. (Illus.). 215p. 1992. 32.00 (*0-262-02349-0*); pap. text 16.00 (*0-262-52175-X*) MIT Pr.

Brower, Neal. Mayberry 101, 3 vols., vol. 1. LC 98-28733. (Behind the Scenes of a TV Classic Ser.: Vol. 1). (Illus.). 507p. 1998. pap. 14.95 (*0-89587-218-8*) Blair.

Brower, Pauline. Missions of the Inland Valleys. (J). (gr. 4-7). pap. 5.95 (*0-8225-9833-7*) Lerner Pub.

— Missions of the Inland Valleys. LC 95-2844. (California Missions Ser.). (J). 1996. lib. bdg. 23.93 (*0-8225-1929-1*, Lerner Publctns) Lerner Pub.

Brower, Pauline, ed. see Behrens, June.

Brower, Reuben A. Alexander Pope: The Poetry of Allusion. 384p. 1986. pap. 19.95 (*0-19-881149-7*) OUP.

— The Fields of Light: An Experiment in Critical Reading. LC 80-19289. 218p. 1980. reprint ed. lib. bdg. 59.50 (*0-313-22653-9*, BRFI, Greenwood Pr) Greenwood.

— Mirror on Mirror: Translation, Imitation, Parody. LC 74-80442. (Studies in Comparative Literature: No. 34). 224p. 1974. 28.00 (*0-674-57645-4*) HUP.

Brower, Reuben A., ed. Twentieth Century Literature in Retrospect. LC 76-168430. (English Studies: No. 2). 371p. 1971. pap. 8.95 (*0-674-91424-4*) HUP.

Brower, Reuben A., et al, eds. Beginning with Poems. (C). 1966. pap. text 16.75 (*0-393-09509-6*) Norton.

— Beginning with Poems. (C). 1966. text 22.25 (*0-393-09685-8*) Norton.

Brower, Reuben A., ed. see Shakespeare, William.

Brower, Robert H. Fujiwara Teika's "Superior Poems of Our Time" A Thirteenth-Century Poetic Treatise & Sequence. Miner, Earl, tr. ix, 148p. 1967. 27.50 (*0-8047-0171-7*) Stanford U Pr.

Brower, Robert H., tr. from JPN. Conversations with Shotetsu. LC 90-2433. (Michigan Monographs in Japanese Studies: No. 7).Tr. of Shotetsu Monogatari. x, 225p. 1992. 35.00 (*0-939512-43-2*) U MI Japan.

Brower, Robert H. & Miner, Earl. Japanese Court Poetry. (Illus.). xvi, 527p. 1961. 65.00 (*0-8047-0536-4*); pap. 24.95 (*0-8047-1524-6*) Stanford U Pr.

Brower, Ross D. & Visocky, Adrian P. Evaluation of Underground Injection of Industrial Waste in Illinois. (Illus.). 176p. (C). 1998. reprint ed. pap. text 30.00 (*0-7881-7457-6*) DIANE Pub.

Brower, Sidney. Design in Familiar Places: What Makes Home Environments Look Good. LC 87-27889. 203p. 1988. 57.95 (*0-275-92686-9*, C2686, Praeger Pubs) Greenwood.

Brower, Sidney. Good Neighborhoods: A Study of In-Town & Suburban Residential Environments. LC 95-26519. 232p. 1996. 59.95 (*0-275-95181-2*, Praeger Pubs) Greenwood.

***Brower, Sidney.** Good Neighborhoods: A Study of In-Town & Suburban Residential Environments. LC 95-26519. 232p. 2000. pap. 22.95 (*0-275-96921-5*, Praeger Pubs) Greenwood.

Brower, Steven, jt. auth. see Brower, Carol.

Brower, T. J., jt. auth. see Mier, R. J.

Brower, Walter, et al. Systems for Administrative Office Support. 4th ed. 1994. teacher ed. 20.00 (*0-02-801026-4*) Glencoe.

Brower, Walter A., Jr., et al. Systems for Administrative Office Support. 4th ed. LC 93-4814. 1993. 54.95 (*0-02-801025-6*) Glencoe.

Brower, Wilbur L. A Little Book of Big Principles: Values & Virtues for a More Successful Life. rev. ed. LC 97-65513. 80p. (Orig.). 1998. 14.95 (*1-887798-07-2*) WriteMore Pubns.

Brower, William B., Jr. A Primer in Fluid Mechanics. LC 98-34265. 1998. 69.95 (*0-8493-9368-X*, HE9368) CRC Pr.

Brower, William B., Jr., compiled by. Theory, Tables & Data for Compressible Flow. (Illus.). 288p. 1990. 120.00 (*1-56032-065-6*) Hemisp Pub.

Browing, Graeme. Electronic Democracy: Using the Internet to Influence American Politics. LC 96-213162. (Illus.). 186p. (Orig.). 1996. pap. 19.95 (*0-910965-20-X*) Info Today Inc.

Browitt, C. W., jt. ed. see Merriman, P. A.

Browler, Kenneth & National Geographic Society (U. S.) Staff. American Legacy: Our National Forests. LC 96-37341. 1997. write for info. (*0-7922-3650-5*); write for info. (*0-7922-4230-0*) Natl Geog.

Browlie, Ian & Crawford, James, eds. The British Year Book of International Law 1997: Sixty-Seventh Year of Issue, Vol. 68. 700p. 1999. text 180.00 (*0-19-826086-5*) OUP.

Browm, Alfred E., jt. auth. see Atlas, Ronald M.

Browman, David L., ed. Advances in Andean Archaeology. (World Anthropology Ser.). (Illus.). xvi, 580p. 1978. 66.15 (*90-279-7550-7*) Mouton.

— Cultural Continuity in Mesoamerica. (World Anthropology Ser.). (Illus.). xiv, 438p. 1978. 57.70 (*90-279-7560-4*) Mouton.

— Early Native Americans: Prehistoric Demography, Ecology & Technology. (World Anthropology Ser.). xiv, 486p. 1979. text 71.55 (*90-279-7940-5*) Mouton.

Browman, David L. & Schwartz, Ronald A., eds. Peasants, Primitives, & Proletariats: The Struggle for Identity in South America. (World Anthropology Ser.). xiv, 430p. 1980. text 63.10 (*90-279-7880-8*) Mouton.

Browman, David L., ed. see Scwartz, Ronald A.

Brown. Administration of Wills, Trusts & Estates. 2nd ed. (Paralegal Law Library). 1997. teacher ed. 14.95 (*0-8273-7565-4*, VNR) Wiley.

— Advanced Math. Date not set. pap., student ed. 11.96 (*0-395-42170-5*) HM.

— Advanced Math. 1988. pap., teacher ed. 36.84 (*0-395-46138-3*); text, student ed. 65.96 (*0-395-46137-5*) HM.

— Advanced Math. 1991. text, teacher ed. 77.80 (*0-395-55210-9*) HM.

— Advanced Math. 1991. text, student ed. 67.36 (*0-395-55189-7*) HM.

— Advanced Math. (C). 1993. pap., suppl. ed. 27.76 (*0-395-64954-4*) HM.

— Advanced Math. 1993. text, teacher ed. 89.20 (*0-395-42169-1*) HM.

— Advanced Math. 1994. text, teacher ed. 79.36 (*0-395-64953-6*) HM.

Brown. Advanced Math, 001. rev. ed. 1983. text 65.44 (*0-395-32073-9*) HM.

Brown. Advanced Mathematics. 1986. text, student ed. 63.60 (*0-395-42379-1*) HM.

— Adventure Play. LC 99-182794. 200p. (C). 1998. pap. text 11.50 (*0-536-01420-5*) Pearson Custom.

— Alcuin of York. 1998. 23.95 (*0-8057-4555-6*, Twyne) Mac Lib Ref.

— America's Garden Book. 1997. pap. 50.00 (*0-02-517971-3*) Macmillan.

— Analysis of Medical Data Using Mixed Models. LC 99-14216. 428p. 2000. 110.00 (*0-471-96554-5*) Wiley.

***Brown.** Anthony Van Dyck. 1999. text 75.00 (*0-8478-2196-X*) Rizzoli Intl.

Brown. Architectural Drawing Constr. (C). 1996. pap. text 33.00 (*0-03-069327-6*) Harcourt Coll Pubs.

— Astronomy in Color. 6.95 (*0-02-567700-4*) Macmillan.

— Basic Algebra, 001. 1987. text, student ed. 57.80 (*0-395-41188-2*) HM.

Brown. Basic Algebra, 001. 1987. text, teacher ed. 79.76 (*0-395-41189-0*) HM.

Brown. Basic Algebra. 1989. text, teacher ed. 72.00 (*0-395-50113-X*) HM.

— Basic Algebra. 1991. pap., teacher ed., suppl. ed. 25.16 (*0-395-50114-8*) HM.

— Basic Algebra. 1992. text, teacher ed. 72.00 (*0-395-63747-3*); text, student ed. 54.08 (*0-395-56480-8*) HM.

— Basic Algebra. (C). 1992. pap., suppl. ed. 25.16 (*0-395-63748-1*) HM.

— Basic Drug Calculations. 6th ed. 1999. pap. text 28.00 (*0-323-01004-0*) Mosby Inc.

— Biology of the Timber Rattlesnake. 1993. pap. write for info. (*0-916984-29-X*) SSAR.

— Brown Asian Economic & Legal D. LC 98-192188. 1997. lib. bdg. 148.00 (*90-411-0934-X*) Kluwer Law Intl.

— Business Law UCC, Applications. 8th ed. 1992. student ed. 21.93 (*0-02-800654-2*) McGraw.

— Casebook in Abnormal Psychology: An Integrative Approach. 2nd ed. (Psychology Ser.). 2000. mass mkt. 15.50 (*0-534-36316-4*) Brooks-Cole.

Brown. Chemistry. 7th ed. 1997. pap. text 30.00 (*0-13-578329-1*); pap. text 30.00 (*0-13-578337-2*) Allyn.

— Chemistry. 7th ed. 1997. pap. text, teacher ed. write for info. (*0-13-578287-2*) Allyn.

— Chemistry: The Central Science & Media Companion. 8th ed. 1999. pap. 106.33 (*0-13-086640-7*, Prentice Hall) P-H.

Brown. Clotel. 2000. pap. text 11.95 (*0-312-15265-5*) St Martin.

***Brown.** The Clotel. 2000. text 39.95 (*0-312-22758-2*) St Martin.

Brown. Coal Country Christmas. LC 99-31891. (J). 2000. 16.00 (*0-689-80705-8*) S&S Childrens.

— The Complete Oracle 8 Training Course. (C). 1999. pap. text 99.99 (*0-13-096276-7*) P-H.

Brown. Crazy Charlie. 1993. write for info. (*0-905478-51-7*, Pub. by Andersen Pr) Trafalgar.

Brown. Democracy Challenged: United States Since WWII. 192p. (C). 1997. pap. 18.00 (*0-673-99297-7*) Addson-Wesley Educ.

— Dental Radiography, Lessons 1-14: Student Workbooks. (C). (gr. 13). 1985. spiral bd. 42.95 (*0-8016-2374-X*, 02374) Mosby Inc.

— Digital Electronics. 288p. 1997. write for info. (*0-412-73500-8*, Chap & Hall NY) Chapman & Hall.

***Brown.** Early Medieval. 1999. pap. text. write for info. (*0-582-03392-6*) Addison-Wesley.

Brown. Early Prediction & Prevention of Child Abuse. 1988. pap. text 84.00 (*0-471-91636-6*) Wiley.

— Econometrics. Date not set. pap. text, wbk. ed. 20.50 (*0-314-80896-5*) West Pub.

— Economic Restructuring & Social: A New Europe? 224p. 1994. 75.00 (*1-85728-149-7*, Pub. by UCL Pr Ltd); pap. 27.50 (*1-85728-150-0*, Pub. by UCL Pr Ltd) Taylor & Francis.

— Elder Law. (American Casebook Ser.). Date not set. text. write for info. (*0-314-06643-8*) West Pub.

***Brown.** Emergency Dysrhythmias & Electrocardiograph Injury Patterns. 2nd ed. (C). 2000. pap. 25.95 (*0-7668-1988-4*) Delmar.

— Engineering Rope Rescue System. LC 99-56517. (Illus.). 352p. (C). 2000. pap. 34.95 (*0-7668-0197-7*) Delmar.

Brown. Entrepreneurship & Technology. 1986. pap. text. write for info. (*0-582-90122-7*, Pub. by Addison-Wesley) Longman.

— The Episcopal Church in Texas, Vol. II. (Illus.). 304p. 1988. 24.95 (*0-89015-505-4*) Sunbelt Media.

— Ethics & Religions. 1991. pap. text. write for info. (*0-582-03307-1*, Pub. by Addison-Wesley) Longman.

— The Evolution of Customer Care: A Strategic Approch to Increasing Customer Value & Profitability. 320p. (C). 1999. 34.95 (*0-471-64342-4*) Wiley.

— Experiments in Exploring Electricity. 1995. pap. text 32.80 (*0-13-207580-6*) P-H.

***Brown.** Fay. 2001. write for info. (*0-7432-0538-3*) S&S Trade.

Brown. Feeding Scotland. (Scottish Life, Past & Present Ser.). (Illus.). 88p. (Orig.). Date not set. pap. 6.95 (*0-948636-84-X*, 684X, Pub. by Natl Mus Scotland) A Schwartz & Co.

— Fierce Yellow Pumpkin. (Illus.). 32p. (J). (ps-1). 5.95 (*0-06-443534-2*) HarpC Child Bks.

Brown. The Fierce Yellow Pumpkin. 32p. (J). (ps-1). 15.95 (*0-06-024479-8*); lib. bdg. 15.89 (*0-06-024481-X*) HarpC Child Bks.

Brown. Flying Mouse. (J). Date not set. 13.99 (*0-7868-3065-4*, Pub. by Disney Pr) Little.

***Brown.** Foseco Foundryman's Handbook. 352p. 2000. text 85.00 (*0-7506-4284-X*) Buttrwrth-Heinemann.

Brown. General Organic & Biochemistry. (Chemistry Ser.). 1980. 25.50 (*0-87150-732-3*); teacher ed. 1.00 (*0-87150-493-6*); student ed. 7.25 (*0-87150-733-1*); lab manual ed. 10.50 (*0-87150-745-5*) PWS Pubs.

— General, Organic & Biochemistry. 2nd ed. (Chemistry Ser.). Date not set. 37.75 (*0-87150-762-5*); teacher ed. 1.00 (*0-87150-774-9*); student ed. 12.75 (*0-87150-772-2*) PWS Pubs.

— Get the Job You Want. (C). 1991. text, teacher ed. 3.16 (*0-395-60595-4*) HM.

Brown. God Talk, Science Talk. 1997. pap. 55.00 (*0-7459-3132-4*, Pub. by Lion Pubng) Trafalgar.

Brown. A Guide to Teaching Phonics. (C). 1999. pap. text. write for info. (*0-15-508048-2*) Harcourt Coll Pubs.

— Help with Finding a Job. (C). 1989. pap. text 13.96 (*0-395-53489-5*) HM.

— Help with Finding a Job. (C). 1990. pap. 3.16 (*0-395-53856-4*) HM.

— Herpetology of the North American Deserts. 1995. pap. 29.95 (*1-885209-02-9*) Serpents Tale.

— Hopes & Shadows: East Europe after Communism. 1994. pap. text. write for info. (*0-582-24407-2*, Pub. by Addison-Wesley) Longman.

***Brown.** Human Rights & World Politics. LC 99-37780. 195p. (C). 1999. pap. text 25.00 (*0-321-02547-4*) Addison-Wesley Educ.

Brown. Human Sexuality, No. 2. 1990. 41.00 (*0-697-11638-7*, WCB McGr Hill) McGrw-H Hghr Educ.

— Iner the Dreamer. (J). 1996. 14.95 (*0-02-714931-5*) Macmillan.

— Intro to Organic Chemistry. (C). 1996. teacher ed. 441.50 (*0-03-018723-0*) Harcourt.

— Introduction to Construction. 1996. 73.00 (*0-07-008239-1*) McGraw.

— Introduction to Organic & Biochemistry. (Chemistry Ser.). 1972. 14.75 (*0-87150-487-1*) PWS Pubs.

— Introduction to Organic & Biochemistry. 3rd ed. (Chemistry Ser.). Date not set. student ed. 10.50 (*0-87150-739-0*) PWS Pubs.

— Introduction to Organic & Biochemistry. 3rd ed. (Chemistry Ser.). 1980. 34.00 (*0-87150-738-2*) PWS Pubs.

— An Introduction to Organic Chemistry. LC 96-67860. (C). 1996. text 88.50 (*0-03-016914-3*, Pub. by Harcourt Coll Pubs) Harcourt.

— An Introduction to Organic Chemistry. (C). 1996. pap. text, student ed. 35.50 (*0-03-018304-9*, Pub. by Harcourt Coll Pubs) Harcourt.

— Introduction to Organic Chemistry. (C). 1996. pap. text, teacher ed. 44.50 (*0-03-018737-0*) Harcourt.

— Introduction to Organic Chemistry. (Chemistry Ser.). Date not set. 14.75 (*0-87150-709-9*) PWS Pubs.

— Introduction to Organic Chemistry. 2nd ed. (Chemistry Ser.). Date not set. 20.75 (*0-87150-725-0*) PWS Pubs.

— Introduction to Organic Chemistry. 3rd ed. (Chemistry Ser.). 1981. 36.50 (*0-87150-747-1*); student ed. 11.25 (*0-87150-748-X*) PWS Pubs.

Brown. Lab Experiment Chemistry. 7th annot. ed. 1996. pap. text, teacher ed. write for info. (*0-13-578352-6*) Allyn.

— Little Lost Lamb. 40p. (J). (ps-3). Date not set. 14.95 (*0-06-027290-2*); lib. bdg. 14.89 (*0-06-027291-0*) HarpC Child Bks.

— Malaria & Development, Vol. 17. 124p. 1997. pap. text 28.00 (*90-5699-603-7*) Gordon & Breach.

Brown. Marital Therapy. 2001. 40.00 (*0-534-52732-9*) Wadsworth Pub.

— MCQ Tutor in Radiology. 1996. pap. text 25.00 (*0-443-05464-9*, W B Saunders Co) Harcrt Hlth Sci Grp.

***Brown.** Miner's Canary. 2001. pap. text. write for info. (*0-7167-3390-0*) W H Freeman.

Brown. Modern Latin America, Vol. 1. (C). 2000. pap. text 26.50 (*0-03-055387-3*, Pub. by Harcourt Coll Pubs) Harcourt.

— The Modern Seafood Cookbook. Date not set. pap. write for info. (*0-517-88507-7*) Crown Pub Group.

— Multiple Choice Questions in Pathology. 3rd ed. pap. text. write for info. (*0-340-55164-X*, Pub. by E A) Routldge.

— Nehru. LC 98-39397. 224p. (C). 1998. pap. 24.60 (*0-582-04284-4*) Longman.

— Nehru. LC 98-39397. (C). 1999. text 63.95 (*0-582-04285-2*) Longman.

— A New Introduction to Organic Chemistry. Date not set. pap. text. write for info. (*0-582-35128-6*, Pub. by Addison-Wesley) Longman.

— New Vistas, Bk. 4. 2nd ed. 1998. pap., wbk. ed. 10.27 (*0-13-908328-6*) P-H.

— New Vistas Student 2nd ed. 1999. pap. text 10.95 (*0-13-908237-9*) S&S Trade.

— New Vistas Student, 4. 2nd ed. 1998. pap. 15.33 (*0-13-908310-3*) S&S Trade.

— No More Chernobyls. 1996. lib. bdg. 12.95 (*0-8057-3880-0*, Twyne) Mac Lib Ref.

— Nursing Administration Quarterly Series: Operations & the Working Environment, Vol. 2. 224p. 1993. 42.00 (*0-8342-0508-4*, 20508) Aspen Pub.

— Nutrition, Unit 3. Date not set. 2.75 (*0-314-06267-X*) West Pub.

— Nutrition, Unit 4. Date not set. 2.75 (*0-314-06268-8*) West Pub.

— Nutrition, Unit 5. Date not set. 2.75 (*0-314-06269-6*) West Pub.

— Nutrition, Unit 6. Date not set. 2.75 (*0-314-06270-X*) West Pub.

— Nutrition, Unit 7. Date not set. 2.75 (*0-314-06271-8*) West Pub.

— Nutrition, Unit 8. Date not set. 3.00 (*0-314-06272-6*) West Pub.

— Nutrition, Unit 9. Date not set. 2.75 (*0-314-06273-4*) West Pub.

— Nutrition, Unit 10. Date not set. 2.75 (*0-314-06274-2*) West Pub.

— Nutrition, Unit 11. Date not set. 2.75 (*0-314-06275-0*) West Pub.

— Nutrition, Unit 13. Date not set. 2.75 (*0-314-06277-7*) West Pub.

— Nutrition, Unit 14. Date not set. 3.00 (*0-314-06278-5*) West Pub.

— Nutrition, Unit 15. Date not set. 2.00 (*0-314-06279-3*) West Pub.

— Nutrition, Unit 16. Date not set. 2.00 (*0-314-06280-7*) West Pub.

— Nutrition, Unit 17. Date not set. 2.75 (*0-314-06281-5*) West Pub.

— Nutrition, Unit 18. Date not set. 2.00 (*0-314-06282-3*) West Pub.

— Nutrition, Unit 19. Date not set. 2.00 (*0-314-06283-1*) West Pub.

— Nutrition, Unit 20. Date not set. 2.75 (*0-314-06284-X*); 2.75 (*0-314-06285-8*) West Pub.

— Nutrition, Unit 22. Date not set. 3.00 (*0-314-06286-6*) West Pub.

— Nutrition, Unit 23. Date not set. 2.00 (*0-314-06287-4*) West Pub.

— Nutrition, Unit 24. Date not set. 3.50 (*0-314-06288-2*) West Pub.

— Nutrition, Unit 25. Date not set. 2.00 (*0-314-06289-0*) West Pub.

— Nutrition, Unit 26. Date not set. 2.00 (*0-314-06290-4*) West Pub.

— Nutrition, Unit 27. Date not set. 2.75 (*0-314-06291-2*) West Pub.

— Nutrition, Unit 28. Date not set. 2.75 (*0-314-06292-0*) West Pub.

— Nutrition, Unit 29. Date not set. 3.50 (*0-314-06293-9*) West Pub.

— Nutrition, Unit 30. Date not set. 2.75 (*0-314-06294-7*) West Pub.

— Nutrition, Unit 31. Date not set. 2.00 (*0-314-06295-5*) West Pub.

— Nutrition, Unit 32. Date not set. 2.75 (*0-314-06296-3*) West Pub.

— Nutrition, Unit 33. Date not set. 2.00 (*0-314-06297-1*) West Pub.

— Nutrition, Unit 34. Date not set. 2.00 (*0-314-06298-X*) West Pub.

— Nutrition Appendices. 1995. pap. text. write for info. (*0-314-06299-8*) West Pub.

— Nutrition Now. 2nd ed. (Health Sciences Ser.). 1998. 59.95 (*0-534-56439-9*) Wadsworth Pub.

— Nutrition Now. 2nd ed. (Health Sciences Ser.). 1999. pap. text 27.00 (*0-534-76796-6*) Wadsworth Pub.

***Brown.** Nutrition Now. 3rd ed. (Health Sciences Ser.). 2001. 43.00 (*0-534-58005-X*) Wadsworth Pub.

Brown. Nutrition Unit 1 & 2, Unit 1&2. Date not set. write for info. (*0-314-06266-1*) West Pub.

— Nutrition Unit Twelve, Unit 12. Date not set. 2.75 (*0-314-06276-9*) West Pub.

— Object-Oriented Analysis. 2nd ed. text. write for info. (*0-471-37137-8*) Wiley.

***Brown.** On Hegel. 2000. pap. 8.25 (*0-534-58357-1*) Wadsworth Pub.

Brown. Operating Systems Survey. 2nd ed. 400p. (C). 1998. pap. text 38.00 (*0-536-01203-2*) S&S Trade.

***Brown.** Oracle 7 Administration in a Box. (C). 1998. pap. text 145.00 (*0-13-011932-6*) P-H.

Brown. Organic Chemistry. 2nd ed. (C). 1997. pap. 114.00 (*0-03-023137-X*); pap. 114.00 (*0-03-023144-2*) Harcourt.

— Organic Chemistry. 2nd ed. (C). 1997. 118.50 (*0-03-023182-5*) Harcourt.

— Organic Chemistry. 2nd ed. (C). 1997. 441.50 (*0-03-020694-4*) Harcourt.

— Organic Chemistry. 2nd ed. (C). 1997. pap. text 31.00 (*0-03-024301-7*, Pub. by Harcourt Coll Pubs) Harcourt.

— Organic Chemistry. 2nd ed. 848p. (C). 1997. text, student ed. 60.50 (*0-03-020453-4*, Pub. by SCP) Harcourt.

Brown. Organic Chemistry. 7th ed. 1997. text. write for info. (*0-13-578378-X*) Allyn.

— Palm Computing. (Bible Ser.). 816p. 2000. 39.99 (*0-7645-3408-4*) IDG Bks.

Brown. Pediatric Pain Pt. 1: A Special Issue of "Children's Health Care", Vol. 25, No. 4, 1996. 1996. pap. 20.00 (*0-8058-9887-5*) L Erlbaum Assocs.

***Brown.** Perestroika in Perspectve. 2000. 59.95 (*0-8133-2629-X*, Pub. by Westview) HarpC.

Brown. Physical Chemistry. 3rd ed. Date not set. pap. text. write for info. (*0-582-35365-3*, Pub. by Addison-Wesley) Longman.

***Brown.** Picathartes to Oxpeckers, Vol. 6. (Birds of Africa Ser.). 600p. 2000. write for info. (*0-12-137306-1*) Acad Pr.

Brown. Posing Mathematically, 6 vols., Vol. 6. 1996. pap. text 20.00 (*0-435-07112-2*) Heinemann.

— Postmodern Marketing. (ITBP Textbooks Ser.). 1998. pap. 19.99 (*1-86152-483-8*) Thomson Learn.

— Practice Guide to Language Learning. 2nd ed. 2001. 11.50 (*0-07-365518-X*) McGraw.

— Profiting from IPOs & Small Cap Stocks. (C). 1998. 24.95 (*0-13-679804-7*, Macmillan Coll) P-H.

— Public Services Broadcasting in Four English-Speaking Countries: A Special Issue of the "Journal of Media Economics", Vol. 9, No. 1, 1996. 1996. pap. 20.00 (*0-8058-9914-6*) L Erlbaum Assocs.

— Reading Relationships. (C). 1998. pap. text 27.57 (*0-395-88977-4*) HM.

— Resource & Environmental Economics. (HB - Economics Ser.). (C). 2002. mass mkt. 59.95 (*0-538-83108-1*) S-W Pub.

— Scottish Electorate. LC 98-15609. 1999. text 69.95 (*0-312-21614-9*) St Martin.

— Setswana-English, English-Setswana Dictionary. (ENG.). write for info. (*0-7859-7470-9*) Fr & Eur.

— S/G PURSUIT LIBERTY VOL1. 3rd ed. (C). 1996. pap. text, student ed. 21.56 (*0-673-99531-3*) Addson-Wesley Educ.

— S/G PURSUIT LIBERTY VOL2. 3rd ed. 240p. (C). 1997. pap. text, student ed. 26.40 (*0-673-99532-1*) Addison-Wesley Educ.

Brown. Sleepy ABC. LC 93-36398. 32p. (J). (ps-2). pap. 4.95 (*0-06-443370-6*) HarpC Child Bks.

Brown. Sneakers. (Illus.). 32p. (J). (ps-3). 5.95 (*0-06-443622-5*) HarpC.

Brown. Sneakers. (Illus.). 32p. (J). (ps-3). 15.95 (*0-06-028692-X*) HarpC.

Brown. Social Psychology. 2001. 53.00 (*0-07-230796-X*) McGraw.

— Soldier Boys. (J). (gr. 4-6). 2000. 16.00 (*0-689-81748-7*) S&S Childrens.

— Spectroscopic Multicomponent Analysis. 250p. 1999. write for info. (*0-12-136680-4*) Acad Pr.

— Storyworlds. 1988. pap. text. write for info. (*0-05-004201-7*) Addison-Wesley.

***Brown.** Strategic Operations Management. 2000. pap. 47.95 (*0-7506-4257-2*) Buttrwrth-Heinemann.

Brown. Stress & Policing: Sources & Strategies. 214p. 1995. pap. text 51.00 (*0-471-96176-0*) Wiley.

Brown. Studying Psychology: A Manual for Success. 4th ed. 62p. 1990. pap. text 4.00 (*0-205-13027-5*, H3027-3) Allyn.

Brown. Testbank Pursuit Liberty: 3rd Edition. 3rd ed. (C). 1997. 24.00 (*0-673-55764-2*) Addson-Wesley Educ.

— Texas Politics Brief. 6th ed. LC 98-72003. 1998. pap. text 27.87 (*0-395-90608-3*) HM.

— Trick Train Ride. (Kate & Tracy Ser.). (J). (gr. 4-8). 1989. lib. bdg. 8.49 (*0-685-70384-3*) Jan Prods.

— 2 Little Trains. 32p. (J). (ps-1). 2001. pap. 6.95 (*0-06-443568-7*) HarpC Child Bks.

— 2 Little Trains. 32p. (J). (ps-1). 2001. 15.95 (*0-06-028376-9*); lib. bdg. 15.89 (*0-06-028377-7*) HarpC Child Bks.

— Understanding Youth & Crime: Listening to Youth? LC 97-47447. (Crime & Justice Ser.). 144p. 1998. 85.00 (*0-335-20004-4*) OpUniv Pr.

— Uninterrupted Interrupts. (C). 1994. 49.95 (*0-201-40966-6*) Addson-Wesley Educ.

— Using Chemoffice With Organic Chemistry. (C). 1995. pap. text 8.50 (*0-03-017959-9*) Harcourt Coll Pubs.

***Brown.** Vital Signs 1999. 200p. 1999. pap. 13.00 (*0-393-31893-1*) Norton.

Brown. Webster White Devil. LC 95-21693. (Revels Student Editions Ser.). 1996. pap. write for info. (*0-7190-4354-9*) Manchester Univ Pr.

— Where Have You Been? 32p. (J). (ps-1). Date not set. 15.95 (*0-06-028378-5*); pap. 6.95 (*0-06-443569-5*) HarpC Child Bks.

— Wills, Trusts & Estates. 96p. 1997. pap. text 16.95 (*0-8273-8283-9*) Delmar.

— Workbook Challenges. (C). 1993. pap. text 10.80 (*0-13-009093-X*) P-H.

— Workbook Vistas. 1993. pap. text, wbk. ed. 10.40 (*0-13-650375-6*); pap. text, wbk. ed. 10.40 (*0-13-650383-7*) P-H.

***Brown.** Wound Care for Health Professionals. 2000. 35.00 (*0-8342-1665-5*) Aspen Pub.

Brown, ed. Human Rights & World Politics. (C). 1999. text. write for info. (*0-673-98037-5*) Addison-Wesley.

— Landslides in Central California, No. T381. (IGC Field Trip Guidebooks Ser.). 104p. 1989. 28.00 (*0-87590-640-0*) Am Geophysical.

B

Brown & Christoph. Mastering German. (Foreign Service Institute Language Ser.). (GER & ENG.). 1985. pap. 16.95 (0-8120-2210-6) Barron.
— Mastering German, 15 CD. (Mastering Ser.). (ENG & GER.). 1992. pap. 120.00 incl. audio compact disk (0-8120-7869-1) Barron.
Brown & Christoph, contrib. by. Mastering German. (Foreign Service Institute Language Ser.). (GER & ENG.). 1985. 79.95 incl. audio (0-8120-7352-5) Barron.
Brown & Clapp. General, Organic & Biochemistry. 2nd ed. (Chemistry Ser.). Date not set. lab manual ed. 18.25 (0-87150-773-0) PWS Pubs.
Brown & DeNicola, Alejandro F. Copyright Law: 1998 Statutory Supplement. 7th ed. 1998. write for info. (1-56662-640-4) Foundation Pr.
Brown & Dunning. Brown In-Terra-Active: West's Physical Geology Interactive. 1996. 26.00 (0-314-04731-X) West Pub.
Brown & Foote. Organic Chemistry. 2nd ed. LC 97-65257. (Illus.). 1232p. (C). 1997. text 106.00 (0-03-020458-5, Pub. by SCP) Harcourt.
— Organic Chemistry (Preview Edition) 2nd ed. 320p. 1997. text. write for info. (0-03-024563-X) SCP.
Brown & Fuller. Statistical Analysis of Measurement Error Models & Applications. LC 90-44278. (Contemporary Mathematics Ser.: Vol. 112). 248p. 1990. pap. 55.00 (0-8218-5117-9, CONM/112) Am Math.
Brown & Grushka, eds. Advances in Chromatography, Vol. 39. (Illus.). 384p. 1998. text 175.00 (0-8247-0159-3) Dekker.
— Advances in Chromatography, Vol. 39. LC 98-41888. (Illus.). 832p. 1998. text 235.00 (0-8247-0160-7) Dekker.
Brown & Melrose. Easter Storykeepers. (Storykeepers Ser.). (J). 1998. 14.99 incl. VHS (0-310-21777-6) Zondervan.
***Brown & Miller.** Concise Encyclopedia of Grammatical Categories. 1999. 191.50 (0-08-043164-X, Pergamon Pr) Elsevier.
Brown & Moore. Spanish for Life-answer Key. (C). 2000. pap. text 39.00 (0-8384-0933-4) Heinle & Heinle.
— Spanish for Life-business Worktext. (C). 2000. pap. text 25.00 (0-8384-0765-X) Heinle & Heinle.
— Spanish for Life-communications Worktext. (C). 2000. pap. text 25.00 (0-8384-0738-2) Heinle & Heinle.
— Spanish for Life-health Worktext. (C). 2000. pap. text 25.00 (0-8384-0747-1) Heinle & Heinle.
— Spanish for Life-instr Annotated Ed. (C). 2000. pap. text 39.00 (0-8384-0711-0) Thomson Learn.
— Spanish for Life-law Worktext. (C). 2000. pap. text 25.00 (0-8384-0756-0) Heinle & Heinle.
Brown & Mugglestone. The Aral Sea. 1994. pap. text. write for info. (0-582-07556-4, Pub. by Addison-Wesley) Longman.
Brown & Pryzwansky. Psychological Consultation: Introduction to Theiry & Practice. 4th ed. LC 97-39540. 448p. 1997. 62.00 (0-205-26830-7) P-H.
Brown & Sherbert, Donald R. Linear Algebra with Business Applications. 2nd ed. (C). 1993. pap. text 31.00 (0-07-056966-5) McGraw.
Brown & Stein. Music in the Renaissance. 2nd ed. LC 98-12248. 396p. 1998. pap. 41.00 (0-13-400045-5) P-H.
Brown & Stewart. Manual of Nursing Staff Development. (Illus.). 432p. (C). (gr. 13). 1995. text 98.00 (0-8016-6609-0, 06609) Mosby Inc.
Brown & Sunderman, F. William. Progress in Nickel Toxicology. 1991. 55.00 (0-632-01355-9) CRC Pr.
Brown & Sweetow, Linda. The Visual Arts Major's College Guide. 1996. pap. 20.00 (0-671-51731-7) S&S Trade.
Brown & Young. Famous Florida Restaurants & Recipes. LC 81-90604. (Famous Florida Ser.). (Illus.). 320p. (Orig.). 1986. reprint ed. pap. 14.95 (0-932855-26-1) Winner Enter.
Brown, et al. Camouflage Cuisine: Wildgame & Seafood Cookery. 1998. spiral bd. 9.95 (0-941162-20-6) D Gibson.
— Essentials of Cell Biology. 250p. write for info. (1-55664-228-8) Mosby Inc.
— Higher Education & Corporate Re: Class, Culture & the Decline of Graduate Careers. LC 94-12564. 208p. 1994. 65.00 (1-85728-103-9, Pub. by UCL Pr Ltd); pap. 24.95 (1-85728-104-7, Pub. by UCL Pr Ltd) Taylor & Francis.
***Brown, et al.** Ohio Corporation Law, 2 vols. Set. 1999. 220.00 (0-87084-802-X) Anderson Pub Co.
— Operations Management: A New Approach. 352p. 2001. pap. 37.95 (0-7506-4995-X) Buttrwrth-Heinemann.
Brown, et al. Prerequisites for Community Wellbeing. 1972. pap. 1.50 (0-910420-20-3) Comm Serv OH.
— Rip, Strip & Row: A Builder's Guide to the Cosine Wherry. LC 85-51141. 1985. pap. 19.95 (0-917436-02-4) Tamal Vista.
— Spellfire: Master the Magic Card Game. 3rd ed. (Collector's Cards (Tsr)). 1994. 8.95 (0-7869-0229-9, Pub. by TSR Inc) Random.
— Texas Government. 2nd ed. 1997. pap. 19.95 (0-87393-639-6) Dame Pubns.
Brown, jt. auth. see Boyd.
Brown, jt. auth. see Brown, Beverly S.
Brown, jt. auth. see Cooney, Thomas J.
Brown, jt. auth. see French.
Brown, jt. auth. see Hoek, E.
Brown, jt. auth. see Irby.
Brown, jt. auth. see Meyer.
Brown, jt. auth. see Nishiyama, Hidetaka.
Brown, jt. auth. see Osborne.
Brown, jt. auth. see Presley, Bruce.
Brown, jt. auth. see Rund.
Brown, jt. auth. see Sutton.
Brown, jt. auth. see Thompson, James R.
Brown, jt. auth. see Tighe.
Brown, jt. auth. see Volhard.
Brown, jt. auth. see Wolverton.
Brown, ed. see Townsley, David & Bjork, Russell.
***Brown.** Medical Insurance Made Easy. 2001. pap. text. write for info. (0-7216-9187-0) Harcourt.
***Brown, Austen.** Genomes. LC 99-12241. 608p. 1999. pap. 69.95 (0-471-31618-0) Wiley.
Brown, Chris R. The Effective Teaching of Biology. LC 94-33256. (Effective Teacher Ser.). 1995. 31.95 (0-582-09505-0) Longman.
Brown, Kim. Dalton & Whitfield County-Legendary. (Illus.). 150p. 1999. 39.95 (1-890291-10-2) Platinum Pubng.
Brown & Benchmark Staff. Abnormal Psychology. 2nd ed. (C). 1995. vdisk. write for info. (0-697-24266-8) Brown & Benchmark.
— Base Map Collection. 80p. (C). 1996. text. write for info. (0-697-37957-4) Brown & Benchmark.
— Basketball. (Elements of Learning Ser.). 120p. 1997. per. write for info. (0-697-29455-2) Brown & Benchmark.
— Bowling. (Elements of Learning Ser.). 120p. (C). 1997. text. write for info. (0-697-29461-7) Brown & Benchmark.
— Golf. (Elements of Learning Ser.). 120p. 1997. per. write for info. (0-697-29459-5) Brown & Benchmark.
— Weight Training. LC 97-11006. (Elements of Learning Ser.). 120p. (C). 1997. text. write for info. (0-697-29463-3) Brown & Benchmark.
Brown, A. Cabell - the Cabells & Their Kin: A Memorial Volume of History, Biography & Genealogy. (Illus.). 708p. 1991. reprint ed. pap. 99.00 (0-8328-1704-X); reprint ed. lib. bdg. 109.00 (0-8328-1703-1) Higginson Bk Co.
Brown, A. Dog of My Own. (J). mass mkt. 7.95 (0-340-68658-8, Pub. by Hodder & Stought Ltd) Trafalgar.
— Humbugs. (Illus.). (J). 1998. text 22.95 (0-340-70960-X, Pub. by Hodder & Stought Ltd); pap. text 11.95 (0-340-70961-8, Pub. by Hodder & Stought Ltd) Trafalgar.
— King of the Dark Tower. 1996. mass mkt. 7.95 (0-340-66733-8, Pub. by Hodder & Stought Ltd) Trafalgar.
Brown, A. Late Night Extra. Date not set. 8.99 (1-871676-73-8, Pub. by Christian Focus) Spring Arbor Dist.
— Runaway. (Freestyle Ser.). 1995. 4.99 (1-85792-101-1, Pub. by Christian Focus) Spring Arbor Dist.
— Save Sam. (J). (gr. 2-5). 4.99 (1-85792-021-X, Pub. by Christian Focus) Spring Arbor Dist.
***Brown, A.** Sword & Sorcery. (Illus.). (J). 1998. mass mkt. 8.95 (0-340-69806-3, Pub. by Hodder & Stought Ltd) Trafalgar.
Brown, A. To Illustrate That. 1995. 8.50 (0-906731-85-2, Pub. by Christian Focus) Spring Arbor Dist.
Brown, A., ed. Creating a Business-Based IT Strategy. LC 92-26878. (UNICOM Applied Information Technology Ser.: Vol. 14). 1992. write for info. (0-442-31643-7) Routledge.
Brown, A. & Pearcy, Carl M. Introduction to Operator Theory Vol. 1: Elements of Functional Analysis. LC 77-23438. (Graduate Texts in Mathematics Ser.: Vol. 55). (Illus.). 1977. 59.95 (0-387-90257-0) Spr-Verlag.
Brown, A., tr. see Ljapin, E. S.
Brown, A. A., tr. see Botvinnik, Mikhael M.
Brown, A. A., tr. see Palamodov, V. P.
Brown, A. A., tr. see Petrov, V. V.
Brown, A. C. & Crounse, Robert G., eds. Hair: Trace Elements & Human Illness. LC 80-10280. 360p. 1980. 95.00 (0-275-91337-6, C1337, Praeger Pubs) Greenwood.
Brown, A. C. & McLachlan, N. A., eds. Ecology of Sandy Shores. 340p. 1990. 168.00 (0-444-88661-3) Elsevier.
Brown, A. D. Microbial Water Stress Physiology: Principles & Perspectives. LC 89-70451. 328p. 1990. 270.00 (0-471-92579-9) Wiley.
Brown, A. E., ed. Roman Small Towns in Eastern England & Beyond. (Oxbow Monographs in Archaeology: No. 52). (Illus.). 208p. 1995. pap. 50.00 (0-946897-90-5, Pub. by Oxbow Bks) David Brown.
Brown, A. E. & Jeffcott, H. A., Jr. Absolutely Mad Inventions. Orig. Title: Beware of Imitations. (Illus.). 125p. 1970. reprint ed. pap. 3.95 (0-486-22596-8) Dover.
Brown, A. G. Australian Tree Species Research in China. 226p. 1994. pap. 105.00 (1-86320-095-9, Pub. by ACIAR) St Mut.
Brown, A. G. The Kettle. 284p. mass mkt. 4.99 (1-55197-418-5) Picasso Publ.
Brown, A. G. Nerve Cells & Nervous Systems: An Introduction to Neuroscience. (Illus.). xi, 265p. 1994. 54.95 (0-387-19637-4) Spr-Verlag.
— Organization in the Spinal Cord. (Illus.). 260p. 1983. 157.00 (0-387-10549-2) Spr-Verlag.
Brown, A. G., ed. Geomorphology & Groundwater. LC 95-6587. 224p. 1996. 190.00 (0-471-95754-2) Wiley.
Brown, A. H., et al, eds. The Use of Plant Genetic Resources. 400p. (C). 1989. pap. text 26.95 (0-521-36886-3) Cambridge U Pr.
— The Use of Plant Genetic Resources. 400p. (C). 1989. text 74.95 (0-521-34584-7) Cambridge U Pr.
Brown, A. H., ed. see 7th C.O.S.P.A.R International Space Science Symposium, et al.
Brown, A. J. History of Newton County, Mississippi. (Illus.). 472p. 1993. reprint ed. lib. bdg. 49.50 (0-8328-2942-0) Higginson Bk Co.
— History of Newton County, Mississippi, from 1834-1894. xvi, 494p. 1991. reprint ed. pap. text 30.00 (1-55613-440-1) Heritage Bk.
Brown, A. Peter. The First Golden Age of the Viennese Symphony: Haydn, Mozart, Beethoven & Schubert. LC 98-26549. (Symphonic Repertoire Ser.: Vol. 2). 816p. 1998. 59.95 (0-253-33487-X) Ind U Pr.
— The French Music Publisher Guera of Lyon. LC 87-3511. (Detroit Studies in Music Bibliography: No. 57). xxiii, 115p. 1987. 30.00 (0-89990-033-X) Harmonie Park Pr.
— Joseph Haydn's Keyboard Music: Sources & Style. LC 85-45029. (Illus.). 476p. 1986. 59.95 (0-253-33182-X) Ind U Pr.
— Performing Haydn's "The Creation" Reconstructing the Earliest Renditions. LC 84-43053. (Music: Scholarship & Performance Ser.). (Illus.). 142p. 1986. 12.95 (0-253-38820-1) Ind U Pr.
— The Symphonic Repertoire Vol. 4: The Second Golden Age of the Viennese Symphony: Brahms, Bruckner, Dvorak, Mahler, & Selected. (Published with the Kind Support of Allen W. Clowes Ser.). 816p. 1998. text 59.95 (0-253-33488-8) Ind U Pr.
Brown, A. Peter, ed. see D'Ordonez, Carlo.
Brown, A. S. The Publishing List: The Self-Publishers' Book of Essential Information. 256p. 1999. pap. 14.95 (0-9665306-1-6) New Park Pr.
Brown, A. W. & Pal, R. Insecticide Resistance in Arthropods. 2nd ed. (Monographs: No. 38). (Illus.). 491p. 1971. pap. text 41.00 (92-4-140038-2, 1140038) World Health.
Brown, A. Winnifred, jt. auth. see Howells, John G.
Brown, Aaron V. Oregon Territory. 24p. 1968. reprint ed. pap. 4.95 (0-87770-034-6, A825) Ye Galleon.
Brown, Abbie F. The Lantern & Other Plays for Children. LC 77-94333. (One-Act Plays in Reprint Ser.). (Illus.). 1978. reprint ed. 20.00 (0-8486-2033-X) Roth Pub Inc.
Brown, Abbie Farwell. Christmas Angel. LC 99-32202. (Focus on the Family Great Stories). 1999. pap. text 9.99 (1-56179-762-6) Focus Family.
Brown, Abiel. W. Simsbury Genealogical History, with Short Sketches & Family Records of the Early Settlers of West Simsbury, Now Canton, Connecticut. 151p. 1997. reprint ed. pap. 19.00 (0-8328-5696-7) Higginson Bk Co.
Brown, Abigail. And Don't Tell Anyone: Healing from Incest Through Poetry & Art. (Illus.). 64p. 1997. 14.95 (0-87839-109-6) North Star.
Brown, Abram E. Glimpses of Old New England Life: Legends of Old Bedford, Massachusetts. (Illus.). 198p. 1993. reprint ed. lib. bdg. 25.00 (0-8328-3132-8) Higginson Bk Co.
— History of the Town of Bedford, MA. (Illus.). 158p. 1993. reprint ed. lib. bdg. 23.00 (0-8328-3147-6) Higginson Bk Co.
— History of the Town of Bedford...to 1891...with a Genealogical Register of Old Families. (Illus.). 110p. 1992. reprint ed. lib. bdg. 40.00 (0-8328-2264-7) Higginson Bk Co.
Brown, Adam. Fanatics: Power, Identity, & Fandom in Football. LC 98-14911. (Illus.). 312p. (C). 1998. 80.00 (0-415-18103-8); pap. 24.99 (0-415-18104-6) Routledge.
— Nuclear Weapons. (World Issues Ser.). (Illus.). 48p. (J). (gr. 5 up). 1987. 13.95 (0-685-67572-6) Rourke Corp.
— Pronunciation Models. 135p. 1991. pap. 28.50 (9971-69-157-4, Pub. by Sngapore Univ Pr) Coronet Bks.
Brown, Adan. Nuclear Weapons, Set II. (World Issues Ser.). (Illus.). 48p. (J). (gr. 5 up). 1987. lib. bdg. 25.27 (0-86592-278-0) Rourke Enter.
Brown, Addie. Seeds of Inspiration. 1997. pap. 56.95 (1-57553-542-4) Watermrk Pr.
Brown, Addie, jt. auth. see Primus, Rebecca.
Brown, Addison, jt. auth. see Britton, Nathaniel L.
Brown, Adele. So What about Sewing, 2 vols., Set. large type ed. pap. 15.00 (0-317-01861-2) Cath Guild Blind.
Brown, Aggrey. Color, Class & Politics in Jamaica. LC 76-58231. 250p. 1980. text 39.95 (0-87855-099-2) Transaction Pubs.
Brown, Agnes, ed. see Jagoe, John R.
Brown, Alan. Audrey Hepburn's Neck. 1997. pap. 12.00 (0-671-52672-3, WSP) PB.
— Audrey Hepburn's Neck: A Novel. Ng, Donna, ed. 320p. 1996. 21.00 (0-671-52671-5, PB Hardcover) PB.
— The Face in the Window & Other Alabama Ghostlore. LC 95-33572. (Illus.). 176p. (Orig.). 1996. pap. 19.95 (0-8173-0813-X) U of Ala Pr.
— The How to Study Book. 2000. pap. 10.00 (1-56980-143-6) Barricade Bks.
— Literary Levees of New Orleans. 1998. pap. text 8.95 (0-913515-44-2, Starrhill Press) Black Belt Communs.
***Brown, Alan.** Nikki & the Rocking Horse. (Illus.). (J). (ps-3). 1999. pap. 9.95 (0-00-664517-8, Pub. by HarpC) Trafalgar.
Brown, Alan. Princess. 1990. 17.95 (1-55972-017-4, Birch Ln Pr) Carol Pub Group.
***Brown, Alan.** Shadows & Cypress: Southern Ghost Stories. LC 00-21350. 240p. 2000. pap. 18.00 (1-57806-271-3); lib. bdg. 45.00 (1-57806-270-5) U Pr of Miss.
Brown, Alan. Wheelchair Willie & Other Plays: Brown Ale with Gertie & O'Conner. (Orig.). 1980. pap. 6.95 (0-7145-3655-5) Riverrun NY.
— Wind up the Willow. 1989. pap. 8.95 (0-7145-3734-9) Riverrun NY.
— The Windhover. LC 96-48759. (Illus.). (J). (gr. k-3). 1997. 17.00 (0-15-201187-0) Harcourt.
Brown, Alan, ed. Active Games for Children with Movement Problems. 256p. (C). 1987. 45.00 (0-7855-2376-6) St Mut.
***Brown, Alan & Langley, Andrew.** What I Believe: A Young Person's Guide to the Religions of the World. LC 98-33120. 64p. (J). (gr. 3-5). 1999. lib. bdg. 23.90 (0-7613-1501-2) Millbrook Pr.
Brown, Alan & Taylor, David Conrad, eds. Gabr'l Blow Sof' Sumter County, Alabama Slave Narratives. (Illus.). 124p. (Orig.). 1997. 20.50 (0-942979-37-0, 942979); pap. 10.50 (0-942979-38-9, 942979) Livingston U Pr.
Brown, Alan, et al. Lighting Secrets for the Professional Photographer. (Illus.). 134p. 1990. pap. 26.99 (0-89879-412-9, Wrtrs Digest Bks) F & W Pubns Inc.
Brown, Alan, jt. auth. see Brown, Leslie.
Brown, Alan, jt. ed. see Friday, Kathryn.
Brown, Alan, ed. see Tartt, Ruby P.
Brown, Alan, tr. see Aquin, Hubert.
Brown, Alan, jt. tr. see Boucher, Denise.
Brown, Alan, tr. see Cendrars, Blaise.
Brown, Alan, tr. see Hemon, Louis.
Brown, Alan A., ed. see Conference on International Trade & Central Planni.
Brown, Alan E., jt. auth. see Hodges, Graham R.
Brown, Alan K. The Aboriginal Population of the Santa Barbara Channel. fac. ed. (Reports of the University of California Archaeological Survey: No. 69). (Illus.). 106p. 1967. reprint ed. pap. 11.88 (1-55567-385-6) Coyote Press.
Brown, Alan L. Power Pitches: How to Produce Winning Presentations Using Charts, Slides, Video & Multimedia. LC 96-48063. 208p. 1997. text 39.95 (0-7863-0972-5, Irwn Prfssnl) McGraw-Hill Prof.
Brown, Alan S. Hard Work & Integrity: The Witco Story. LC 95-81658. (Illus.). 108p. 1995. write for info. (0-944641-16-4) Greenwich Pub Group.
***Brown, Alan W.** Component-based Development: Building Enterprise Scale Applications. 308p. 2000. pap. 49.99 (0-13-088720-X, Prentice Hall) P-H.
Brown, Alan W. Invitation to Sailing. 224p. 1971. per. 11.00 (0-671-21134-X, Fireside) S&S Trade Pap.
Brown, Alan W., ed. Component Based Software Engineering: Selected Papers from the Software Engineering Institute. LC 96-77860. 152p. 1996. pap. 26.00 (0-8186-7718-X, BP07718) IEEE Comp Soc.
— Integrated Project Support Environments: The Aspect Project. (APIC Ser.). 291p. 1990. text 84.00 (0-12-136740-1) Acad Pr.
Brown, Alan W., et al. Principles of CASE Tool Integration. (Illus.). 288p. 1994. text 65.00 (0-19-509478-6) OUP.
Brown, Albert F., jt. auth. see Isham, Norman M.
Brown, Albert J. High Performance Bank: Insights & Advice on How to Make Your Bank a Consistent. rev. ed. 225p. 1994. text 39.95 (1-55738-743-5, Irwn Prfssnl) McGraw-Hill Prof.
— High Performance Banking: How to Improve Earnings in Any Bank. 1991. text 47.50 (1-55520-128-8, Irwn Prfssnl) McGraw-Hill Prof.
Brown, Albert M. The Camp Wise Story, Nineteen Hundred Seven to Nineteen Eighty-Eight. Guralnik, David B. & Rubinstein, Judah, eds. (Illus.). 185p. (Orig.). 1989. pap. 12.95 (0-9624787-0-9) Jewish Community.
Brown, Alec, tr. see Cocteau, Jean.
Brown, Alec, tr. see Leonov, Leonid.
Brown, Aletha. Dear God, Help Us to Know You. 90p. (Orig.). 1996. pap. 7.75 (1-888813-03-2, 004) Brghtside.
Brown, Alexander, ed. The Genesis of the United States: A Narrative of the Movement in England, 1605-1616, Which Resulted in the Plantation of North America by Englishmen... (Illus.). 1157p. 1994. pap. text 56.00 (0-7884-0104-1) Heritage Bk.
Brown, Alexander, tr. see Lis, Catharina & Soly, Hugo.
Brown, Alexander C. The Good Ships of Newport News: An Informal Account of Ships, Shipping, & Shipbuilding in the Lower Chesapeake Bay Region, Together with the Story of the Last Terrible Voyage of the Yarmouth Castle. LC 76-12100. (Illus.). 255p. 1976. reprint ed. pap. 79.10 (0-7837-9077-5, 204982600003) Bks Demand.
— Steam Packets on the Chesapeake: A History of the Old Bay Line since 1840. LC 61-12580. (Illus.). 208p. reprint ed. pap. 64.50 (0-7837-6726-9, 204635400011) Bks Demand.
Brown, Alexander C., ed. Longboat to Hawaii: An Account of the Voyage of the Clipper Ship Hornet of New York, Bound for San Francisco in 1886, As Recorded in the Journals in Captain Josiah A. Mitchell, Master, Henry Ferguson, Passenger, Samuel Ferguson, Passenger Together with Observations on the Burning of the Vessel by Mark Twain. LC 74-22317. 256p. 1974. reprint ed. pap. 79.40 (0-608-02468-6, 206311200004) Bks Demand.
Brown, Alexander M., ed. Utah P. R. Finder Binder: 1997. xxxiv, 638p. 1997. lib. bdg. 130.00 (0-9650510-3-X); vinyl bd. 110.00 (0-9650510-2-1) J Brown & Assocs.
— Utah P. R. Finder Binder, 1998. 685p. 1997. lib. bdg. write for info. (0-9650510-5-6) J Brown & Assocs.
— Utah P. R. Finder Binder, 1998. 3rd ed. 685p. 1997. write for info. (0-9650510-4-8) J Brown & Assocs.
— Utah P.R. Finder Binder: 1996. xvi, 421p. 1996. 110.00 (0-9650510-0-5); lib. bdg. 125.00 (0-9650510-1-3) J Brown & Assocs.
Brown, Alexandra R. The Cross & Human Transformation: Paul's Apocalyptic Word in 1 Corinthians. LC 95-11829. 208p. 1995. pap. 19.00 (0-8006-2677-X, 1-2677) Augsburg Fortress.
Brown, Alfred B., ed. Great Democrats. LC 70-128216. (Essay Index Reprint Ser.). 1977. 39.95 (0-8369-1942-4) Ayer.
— Great Democrats. LC 70-128216. (Essay Index Reprint Ser.). 704p. reprint ed. lib. bdg. 37.50 (0-8290-0791-1) Irvington.
***Brown, Alfred T., Jr.** South Florida Ecosystem Restoration: An Overall Strategic Plan & a Decision-Making Process Are Needed to Keep the Effort on Track. (Illus.). 79p. (C). 1999. pap. text 20.00 (0-7881-8431-8) DIANE Pub.
Brown, Alice. The County Road. LC 68-23713. (Americans in Fiction Ser.). lib. bdg. 19.50 (0-8398-0172-6) Irvington.
— The County Road. LC 68-23713. (Americans in Fiction Ser.). reprint ed. pap. text 4.50 (0-89197-715-5) Irvington.
— The Empire of Death. 1989. lib. bdg. 25.00 (0-910489-21-1) Scream Pr.

An Asterisk (*) at the beginning of an entry indicates that the title is appearing for the first time.

— High Noon. LC 75-121526. (Short Story Index Reprint Ser.). 1977. 21.95 (*0-8369-3482-2*) Ayer.

— Meadow-Grass: Tales of New England Life. 1972. reprint ed. lib. bdg. 18.00 (*0-8422-8011-1*) Irvington.

— Meadow-Grass: Tales of New England Life, Vol. 1. LC 72-4456. (Short Story Index Reprint Ser.). 1977. reprint ed. 23.95 (*0-8369-4172-1*) Ayer.

— Mercy Warren. LC 67-30159. (Illus.). 328p. 1968. reprint ed. 20.00 (*0-87152-042-7*) Reprint.

— Tiverton Tales. LC 67-29259. (Americans in Fiction Ser.). 339p. 1968. reprint ed. lib. bdg. 32.50 (*0-8398-0173-4*) Irvington.

— Tiverton Tales. (Americans in Fiction Ser.). 339p. (C). 1986. reprint ed. pap. text 6.95 (*0-8290-2042-X*) Irvington.

— Vanishing Points. LC 71-106250. (Short Story Index Reprint Ser.). 1977. 21.95 (*0-8369-3287-0*) Ayer.

Brown, Alice, et al, eds. Politics & Society in Scotland. 272p. 1996. text 59.95 (*0-312-16040-2*) St Martin.

Brown, Alice & Fairley, John, eds. The Manpower Services Commission in Scotland. (Edinburgh Education & Society Ser.). 324p. 1990. 55.00 (*0-7486-0126-0*, Pub. by Edinburgh U Pr) Col U Pr.

— The Manpower Services Commission in Scotland. 324p. 1991. pap. 20.00 (*0-7486-0141-4*, Pub. by Edinburgh U Pr) Col U Pr.

Brown, Alice & McCrone, David, eds. The Scottish Government Yearbook, 1991. 272p. 1991. text 39.00 (*0-7486-0264-X*, Pub. by Edinburgh U Pr) Col U Pr.

Brown, Alice & Parry, Richard, eds. The Scottish Government Yearbook, 1990. 323p. 1990. 39.00 (*0-7486-0174-0*, Pub. by Edinburgh U Pr) Col U Pr.

Brown, Alison. Bartolomeo Scala, Chancellor of Florence, 1430-1497: The Humanist As Bureaucrat. LC 78-70280. 379p. 1979. reprint ed. pap. 117.50 (*0-608-03355-3*, 206406700008) Bks Demand.

— On Foucault. (Wadsworth Notes Ser.). 1999. pap. text 13.95 (*0-534-57614-1*) Thomson Learn.

— The Renaissance. 2nd ed. LC 99-24864. 160p. (C). 1999. pap. 14.66 (*0-582-30781-3*) Addison-Wesley.

Brown, Alison, ed. Bartolomeo Scala: Humanistic & Political Writings. LC 96-25584. (Medieval & Renaissance Texts & Studies: Vol. 159). 608p. 1997. 60.00 (*0-86698-199-3*, MR159) MRTS.

— Language & Images of Renaissance Italy. (Illus.). 354p. 1995. text 59.00 (*0-19-820318-7*) OUP.

Brown, Alison, ed. see Guicciardini, Francesco.

Brown, Alison L. Subjects of Deceit: A Phenomenology of Lying. LC 97-11798. 173p. (C). 1998. text 59.50 (*0-7914-3673-X*); pap. text 19.95 (*0-7914-3674-8*) State U NY Pr.

***Brown, Alistair R.** Interpretation of Three-Dimensional Seismic Data. 5th ed. (Memoir Ser.: Vol. 42). (Illus.). xiv, 514p. 1999. 109.00 (*0-89181-352-7*, 630) AAPG.

Brown, Alister J., et al, eds. Protein Synthesis & Targeting in Yeast. LC 93-903. (NATO ASI Series H: Cell Biology: Vol. 71). 1993. 255.95 (*0-387-56521-3*) Spr-Verlag.

Brown, Allan. The Burden of Jonah ben Amittai. 64p. 1991. pap. 12.95 (*1-55082-022-2*, Pub. by Quarry Pr) LPC InBook.

— By Green Mountains. 48p. 1980. 5.95 (*0-920806-14-7*, Pub. by Penumbra Pr) U of Toronto Pr.

— Consultation: An Aid to Successful Social Work. (Community Care Practice Handbook Ser.). xiv, 104p. 1984. pap. text 18.95 (*0-435-82092-3*, Pub. by Gower) Ashgate Pub Co.

— Groupwork. 3rd ed. 239p. 1992. pap. 24.95 (*1-85742-087-X*, Pub. by Arena) Ashgate Pub Co.

Brown, Allan & Bourne, Iain. The Social Work Supervisor: Supervision in Community, Day Care & Residential Settings. LC 95-14730. (Supervision in Context Ser.). 192p. 1995. 91.95 (*0-335-19459-1*); pap. 29.95 (*0-335-19458-3*) OpUniv Pr.

Brown, Allan & Caddick, Brian. Groupwork with Children. 180p. 1992. 70.00 (*1-871177-52-9*, Pub. by Whiting & Birch) Paul & Co Pubs.

Brown, Allan, et al. Training Social Workers for Groupwork. (C). 1987. text 35.00 (*0-902789-50-3*, Pub. by Natl Inst Soc Work) St Mut.

Brown, Allan, jt. auth. see Kraak, M. J.

Brown, Allan, jt. ed. see Mistry, Tara.

Brown, Allan C., ed. Anesthesia for Extracranial Surgery of the Head & Neck. (Illus.). 352p. Date not set. text 59.00 (*0-07-008312-6*) McGraw-Hill HPD.

Brown, Allan E. & Brown, Nancy L. National Speedway Directory, Vol. 19. 19th rev. ed. 496p. 1998. pap. 8.00 (*0-931105-50-1*) Slideways Pubns.

— National Sprint Car Annual. rev. ed. 64p. 1999. pap. text 5.00 (*0-931105-51-X*) Slideways Pubns.

Brown, Allan E. & Brown, Nancy L., eds. National Speedway Directory. 532p. 1999. pap. 8.00 (*0-931105-52-8*) Slideways Pubns.

Brown, Allan E. & Davis, Wilson. The History of America's Speedways Past & Present. LC 95-157597. (Illus.). 596p. 1994. 20.00 (*0-931105-42-0*) Slideways Pubns.

***Brown, Allen, Jr.** Buying a Personal Computer: How to Choose the Right Equipment to Meet Your Needs. 3rd ed. (Illus.). 176p. (Orig.). 1999. pap. 19.95 (*1-85703-432-5*, Pub. by How To Bks) Trans-Atl Phila.

Brown, Allen, Jr., jt. auth. see Teller, Edward.

Brown, Allen T., photos by. Dominion of Shadow. (Illus.). 32p. 1996. 20.00 (*0-9655504-0-0*); pap. 15.00 (*0-9655504-1-9*) AT Brown.

Brown, Allison, tr. see Beck, Gad & Heibert, Frank.

Brown, Allison, tr. see Bredekamp, Horst.

Brown, Allison, tr. see Busse, Heribert.

Brown, Allison, tr. see Diner, Dan.

Brown, Allison, tr. see Halm, Heinz.

Brown, Allison, tr. see Schippmann, Klaus.

Brown, Allison, tr. see Schoppman, Claudia.

Brown, Alma C. Hold Fast This Beauty. Mynatt, Elizabeth B., ed. (Orig.). 1991. 12.95 (*0-9622568-4-6*) Earthtide Pubns.

Brown, Alonzo L. History of the Fourth Regiment of Minnesota Infantry Volunteers During the Great Rebellion, 1861-65. (Illus.). 592p. 1995. reprint ed. lib. bdg. 61.50 (*0-8328-4701-1*) Higginson Bk Co.

Brown, Alvin, jt. auth. see Maxfield, Clive.

Brown, Amy. Earthworms Unlimited. (Illus.). 80p. (Orig.). 1995. pap. 7.95 (*0-86417-631-7*) Seven Hills Bk.

Brown, Amy, et al. Primary Dictionary, No. 1. 96p. 1987. mass mkt. 3.99 (*0-515-09093-X*, Jove) Berkley Pub.

— Primary Dictionary, No. 4. 432p. 1987. mass mkt. 4.99 (*0-515-09096-4*, Jove) Berkley Pub.

Brown, Amy Benson. Island Summer Love. large type ed. LC 92-44778. (General Ser.). 382p. 1993. reprint ed. lib. bdg. 17.95 (*1-56054-664-6*) Thorndike Pr.

— Rewriting the Word: American Women Writers & the Bible, 172. LC 98-37718. (Contributions in Women's Studies: Vol. 172). 208p. 1999. 49.95 (*0-313-30865-9*) Greenwood.

Brown, Amy Benson & McPherson, Kathryn Read, eds. The Reality of Breastfeeding: Reflections by Contemporary Women. LC 97-32977. 256p. 1998. pap. 16.95 (*0-89789-577-0*, Pub. by Greenwood) Natl Bk Netwk.

Brown, Amy C. The Fast Food Freeway Guide: A Map to Lower Fat & Calories at Fast Food Restaurants. LC 98-96281. (Illus.). x, 250p. 1998. pap. 5.95 (*0-9664096-0-4*) Mtn Top Prodns.

Brown, Andreas, ed. A Creative Century: Selections from the Twentieth-Century Collections. (Illus.). 1970. pap. 8.00 (*0-87959-004-1*) U of Tex H Ransom Ctr.

Brown, Andrew. Amazing Sea Creatures. LC 96-46984. (Extraordinary Animals Ser.). (Illus.). 32p. (J). (gr. 1-7). 1997. pap. 7.95 (*0-86505-569-6*) Crabtree Pub Co.

Brown, Andrew. Amazing Sea Creatures. LC 96-46984. (Extraordinary Animals Ser.). (Illus.). 32p. (J). (gr. 2-3). 1997. lib. bdg. 20.60 (*0-86505-561-0*) Crabtree Pub Co.

Brown, Andrew. Armored Animals. LC 96-46983. (Extraordinary Animals Ser.). (Illus.). 32p. (J). (gr. 2-3). 1997. pap. 7.95 (*0-86505-566-1*) Crabtree Pub Co.

Brown, Andrew. Armored Animals. LC 96-46983. (Extraordinary Animals Ser.). (Illus.). 32p. (J). (gr. 2-3). 1997. lib. bdg. 20.60 (*0-86505-558-0*) Crabtree Pub Co.

Brown, Andrew. Baby Animals. LC 96-47204. (Extraordinary Animals Ser.). (Illus.). 32p. (J). (gr. 2-3). 1997. pap. 7.95 (*0-86505-567-X*) Crabtree Pub Co.

Brown, Andrew. Baby Animals. LC 96-47204. (Extraordinary Animals Ser.). (Illus.). 32p. (J). (gr. 2-3). 1997. lib. bdg. 20.60 (*0-86505-559-9*) Crabtree Pub Co.

Brown, Andrew. Dangerous Animals. LC 96-46982. (Extraordinary Animals Ser.). (Illus.). 32p. (J). (gr. 2-3). 1997. pap. 7.95 (*0-86505-568-8*); lib. bdg. 20.60 (*0-86505-560-2*) Crabtree Pub Co.

— The Neutron & the Bomb: A Biography of Sir James Chadwick. LC 97-200691. (Illus.). 402p. (C). 1997. 35.00 (*0-19-853992-4*) OUP.

— New Zealand Intellectual Property. 744p. 1989. boxed set 192.00 (*0-409-78736-1*, NZ, MICHIE) LEXIS Pub.

— Organisational Culture. 2nd ed. 320p. 1998. pap. 54.50 (*0-273-63147-0*, Pub. by Pitman Pub) Trans-Atl Phila.

— Popular Piety in Late Medieval England: The Diocese of Salisbury, 1250-1550. (Oxford Historical Monographs). (Illus.). 308p. 1995. text 59.00 (*0-19-820521-X*) OUP.

— Roland Barthes: The Figures of Writing. 314p. 1992. text 80.00 (*0-19-815171-3*) OUP.

— Secret City. Bixby, Robert, ed. 18p. 1994. pap. text 6.00 (*1-882983-12-2*) March Street Pr.

Brown, Andrew & Dowling, Paul. Reading Research - Doing Research. LC 98-122085. (Master Classes in Education Ser.). 150p. 1997. pap. 24.95 (*0-7507-0719-4*, Falmer Pr) Taylor & Francis.

— Reading Research - Doing Research: A Mode of Interrogation for Education. LC 98-122085. (Master Classes in Education Ser.). 186p. 1998. 79.00 (*0-7507-0728-3*, Falmer Pr) Taylor & Francis.

Brown, Andrew & Grant, Anthony. The Law of Intellectual Property in New Zealand. 716p. 1989. pap. 90.00 (*0-409-78884-8*, NZ, MICHIE) LEXIS Pub.

Brown, Andrew, jt. auth. see Boghanni, Ashok.

Brown, Andrew, jt. auth. see Hoffman, Noel.

Brown, Andrew, ed. & intro. see Eliot, George, pseud.

Brown, Andrew, ed. & tr. see Sophocles.

***Brown, Andy, ed.** Binary Myths, No. 2. 108p. 1999. pap. 16.95 (*1-900152-62-2*, Pub. by Stride Pubns) SPD-Small Pr Dist.

***Brown, Andy & Garratt, Tim.** Discovery Road. (Illus.). 384p. 2000. pap. 15.95 (*0-9530575-3-4*, Pub. by Travellerseye Ltd) Midpt Trade.

***Brown, Andy, et al.** Vital Movement. (Four Packs Ser.: No. 2). 80p. 1998. pap. 8.95 (*1-874400-14-8*, Pub. by Reality St Edits) SPD-Small Pr Dist.

Brown, Andy R. Political Languages of Race & the Politics of Exclusion. LC 98-73857. (Research in Migration & Ethnic Relations Ser.). 7p. 1999. text 74.95 (*1-84014-516-1*) Ashgate Pub Co.

Brown, Angela. Prayers That Avail Much for Children. (Illus.). 32p. (Orig.). (J). (gr. 1-3). 1983. pap. 4.99 (*0-89274-296-8*) Harrison Hse.

Brown, Angela, et al, eds. Computing in Local & Regional History. (Leicester University Press Bk.). 256p. 1993. text. write for info. (*0-7185-1416-5*) St Martin.

***Brown, Angela McHaney.** Produce Manager. LC 99-51703. (Workers You Know Ser.). 32p. (J). 2000. lib. bdg. 22.83 (*0-8172-5594-X*) Raintree Steck-V.

Brown, Ann. Arthur Evans & the Palace at Minos. (Illus.). 110p. 1995. pap. 15.95 (*0-900090-92-8*, 0928, Pub. by Ashmolean Mus) A Schwartz & Co.

— Arthur Evans & the Palace at Minos. (Illus.). 110p. 1995. 19.95 (*0-907849-50-4*, 9504, Pub. by Ashmolean Mus) A Schwartz & Co.

— Before Knossos: Arthur Evans' Travels in the Balkans & Crete. (Illus.). 112p. 1994. 19.95 (*1-85444-030-6*, 0306) A Schwartz & Co.

— Before Knossos: Arthur Evans' Travels in the Balkans & Crete. (Illus.). 112p. 1995. pap. 15.95 (*1-85444-029-2*, 0292, Pub. by Ashmolean Mus) A Schwartz & Co.

Brown, Ann, ed. Consumer's Resource Handbook (1998-99) 142p. 1999. pap. text 25.00 (*0-7881-7152-6*) DIANE Pub.

Brown, Ann, jt. auth. see Remenyi.

Brown, Ann, ed. see Klein, Ken.

Brown, Ann C. Stay Love until Autumn. 245p. 1989. pap. 9.95 (*0-89697-288-7*) Intl Univ Pr.

Brown, Ann L. Eighteen Fifty Hillsborough County, New Hampshire Census, Pts. I & II. (Illus.). 695p. (Orig.). 1992. pap. 40.00 (*1-55613-576-9*) Heritage Bk.

Brown, Ann L., jt. ed. see Lamb, Michael E.

Brown, Ann L. Nichols, see Nichols Brown, Ann L.

Brown, Ann M. Foghorn Outdoors: California Waterfalls: Your Key to Accessing the State's Most Spectacular Falls. 2nd ed. (Illus.). 410p. 2000. pap. 17.95 (*1-57354-070-6*, Foghorn Outdoors) Avalon Travel.

— Foghorn Outdoors: 101 Great Hikes of the San Francisco Bay Area. (Illus.). 318p. 2000. pap. 15.95 (*1-57354-068-4*, Foghorn Outdoors) Avalon Travel.

***Brown, Ann M.** No Greater Love: Bl. Gianna: Physician, Mother, Martyr. (Illus.). 32p. 1999. pap. 3.00 (*1-892875-03-9*, 3007, Remnant Israel) New Hope Publicatns.

Brown, Ann Marie. Foghorn Outdoors: Day-Hiking California's National Parks: Exploring Mountains Deserts, Volcanos, Island & Redwood Forests. (Illus.). 550p. 1999. pap. 18.95 (*1-57354-055-2*, Foghorn Outdoors) Avalon Travel.

— Foghorn Outdoors: Easy Biking in Northern California: More Than 100 Places Anyone Can Bike This Weekend. 2nd ed. (Illus.). 260p. 1999. pap. 12.95 (*1-57354-061-7*, Foghorn Outdoors) Avalon Travel.

— Foghorn Outdoors: Easy Camping in Southern California: 100 Places Anyone Can Camp This Weekend. (Illus.). 200p. 1998. pap. text 12.95 (*1-57354-004-8*, Foghorn Outdoors) Avalon Travel.

— Foghorn Outdoors: Easy Hiking in Northern California: More Than 100 Places Anyone Can Hike This Weekend. 2nd ed. LC 99-461776. (Illus.). 260p. 1999. pap. 12.95 (*1-57354-062-5*, Foghorn Outdoors) Avalon Travel.

— Foghorn Outdoors: Easy Hiking in Southern California: 100 Places Anyone Can Hike This Weekend. (Illus.). 240p. 1998. pap. text 12.95 (*1-57354-006-4*, Foghorn Outdoors) Avalon Travel.

Brown, Ann Marie, jt. auth. see Stienstra, Tom.

Brown, Anna R. What Is Worth While? 32p. 1997. pap. 9.95 (*1-56849-515-3*) Buccaneer Bks.

Brown, Anne. A la Decouverte du "Petit Prince" An Enrichment Workbook for Exploring Languages & Themes. (FRE.). 128p. (C). pap., student ed. 13.95 (*0-8442-1386-1*, VF1386-1) NTC Contemp Pub Co.

— Communiquons. (SPA.). (C). 1997. pap. text. write for info. (*0-201-89272-3*) Addison-Wesley.

— A Player's Guide to Greyhawk. 1998. 13.95 (*0-7869-1248-0*, Pub. by TSR Inc) Random.

Brown, Anne B. Khourane Domain Sourcebook. 1995. 7.95 (*0-7869-0397-X*, Pub. by TSR Inc) Random.

Brown, Anne E. & Gooze, Marianne E., eds. International Women's Writing: New Landscapes of Identity, 47. LC 94-27950. (Contributions in Women's Studies: Vol. 147). 320p. 1995. 65.00 (*0-313-29045-8*, Greenwood Pr) Greenwood.

Brown, Anne H. The Colonial South. LC 93-49008. (American Food Library). (J). 1994. write for info. (*0-86625-509-5*) Rourke Pubns.

— Colonial South. (American Food Library). 48p. (J). (gr. 3-6). Date not set. lib. bdg. 19.93 (*1-57103-509-5*) Rourke Pr.

Brown, Anne S., jt. auth. see Lachouque, Henry.

***Brown, Anne W.** New York Marble Cemetary Interrments, 1830-1937: With Additional Biographical Information. (Illus.). 238p. 1999. lib. bdg. 37.95 (*1-56012-157-2*, 161) Kinship Rhinebeck.

Brown, Annette N., ed. When Is Transition Over? LC 99-24188. 150p. 1999. 33.00 (*0-88099-196-8*) W E Upjohn.

— When Is Transition over? LC 99-24188. 6p. 1999. pap. 14.00 (*0-88099-195-X*) W E Upjohn.

Brown, Anthony C. The Last Hero: Wild Bill Donovan. 768p. 1982. 24.95 (*0-686-95975-2*, Times Bks) Crown Pub Group.

Brown, Anthony Cave. Oil, God, & Gold: The Story of Aramco & the Saudi Kings. LC 98-39654. (Illus.). 480p. 1999. 30.00 (*0-395-59220-8*) HM.

— Secret History of the Atomic Bomb. 1977. 16.95 (*0-8037-8164-4*, Dial Yng Read) Peng Put Young Read.

Brown, Anthony E. The Politics of Airline Deregulation. LC 86-30888. 240p. 1987. reprint ed. pap. 74.40 (*0-608-07983-9*, 206794800012) Bks Demand.

Brown, Anthony E., ed. Boswellian Studies: A Bibliography. 3rd ed. 176p. 1992. 75.00 (*0-7486-0303-4*, Pub. by Edinburgh U Pr) Col U Pr.

Brown, Anthony F. Accident & Emergency: Diagnosis & Management. 3rd ed. 432p. 1996. pap. text 40.00 (*0-7506-2233-4*) Buttrwrth-Heinemann.

***Brown, Anthony G.** Persons, Animals, Ships & Cannons in the Aubrey-Maturin Sea Novels of Patrick O'Brian. LC 99-30996. (Illus.). 350p. 1999. pap. 35.00 (*0-7864-0684-4*) McFarland & Co.

Brown, Anthony V., et al. African-American Architectural Presence in Arizona. 2nd ed. 44p. 1993. spiral bd. 20.00 (*1-884320-00-7*) ASU Herberger Ctr.

Brown, Antony. Hazard Unlimited. (C). 1987. 160.00 (*0-7855-4157-8*, Pub. by Witherby & Co); pap. 75.00 (*0-7855-4158-6*, Pub. by Witherby & Co) St Mut.

— Hazard Unlimited: The Story of Lloyd's. 3rd ed. 1987. 60.00 (*1-85044-137-5*); pap. 35.00 (*1-85044-131-6*) LLP.

— Three Hundred Years of Lloyd's: A Lloyd's List Special Supplement. 1988. pap. 43.00 (*1-85044-188-X*) LLP.

***Brown, Antony & Quine, Timothy.** Fluvial Processes & Environmental Change. (British Geomorphological Research Group Symposia Ser.). 426p. 1999. 160.00 (*0-471-98548-1*) Wiley.

Brown, Arch. Freeze: A Comedy of Bad Manners. LC 98-61480. 86p. 1998. pap. 8.95 (*1-886586-05-5*) T n T Class.

Brown, Arch & Langworth, Richard M. Great Cars of the 20th Century LC 97-67603. 436 p. 1998. write for info. (*0-7853-2523-9*) Pubns Intl Ltd.

Brown, Archibald. New Law Dictionary & Institute of the Whole Law: For the Use of Students, the Legal Profession, & the Public. lxviii, 391p. 1987. reprint ed. 47.50 (*0-8377-1949-6*, Rothman) W S Hein.

Brown, Archie. The Gorbachev Factor. (Illus.). 444p. 1996. 30.00 (*0-19-827344-4*) OUP.

— The Gorbachev Factor. LC 97-8830. (Illus.). 426p. 1997. reprint ed. pap. 16.95 (*0-19-288052-7*) OUP.

Brown, Archie & Gray, Jack, eds. Political Culture & Political Change in Communist States. 2nd rev. ed. LC 76-41832. 375p. (C). 1979. reprint ed. 35.00 (*0-8419-0508-8*) Holmes & Meier.

Brown, Aren & Pearcy, Carl M. An Introduction to Analysis: A Local Search Approach. LC 94-22509. (Graduate Texts in Mathematics Ser.: Vol. 154). (Illus.). 297p. 1994. 49.95 (*0-387-94369-2*) Spr-Verlag.

Brown, Arlene. Booklinks: Writing Connections to Children's Literature. 96p. 1993. pap. text 13.95 (*0-944459-61-7*) ECS Lrn Systs.

— Math Whiz Kids, 4 vols. Durst, Shirley, ed. (Illus.). 80p. (J). (gr. 3-5). 1997. pap., wbk. ed. 43.80 (*1-57022-132-4*, ECS1324) ECS Lrn Systs.

— Math Whiz Kids: Math Whiz Kids at Home. Durst, Shirley J., ed. (Illus.). 80p. (J). (gr. 3-5). 1997. pap., wbk. ed. 10.95 (*1-57022-105-7*, ECS1057) ECS Lrn Systs.

— Math Whiz Kids: Math Whiz Kids at the Amusement Park. Durst, Shirley J., ed. (Illus.). 80p. (J). (gr. 3-5). 1997. pap. 10.95 (*1-57022-103-0*, ECS1030) ECS Lrn Systs.

— Math Whiz Kids: Math Whiz Kids at the Mall. Durst, Shirley J., ed. (Illus.). 80p. (J). (gr. 3-5). 1997. pap. 10.95 (*1-57022-106-5*, ECS1065) ECS Lrn Systs.

— Math Whiz Kids: Math Whiz Kids at the Zoo. Durst, Shirley J., ed. (Illus.). 80p. (J). (gr. 3-5). 1997. pap., wbk. ed. 10.95 (*1-57022-104-9*, ECS1049) ECS Lrn Systs.

Brown, Arnethea H., ed. see Brown, Nan M.

Brown, Arnold. Physiological & Psychological Considerations in the Management of Stroke. LC 72-7682. 160p. 1976. 12.50 (*0-87527-094-8*) Green.

Brown, Arnold S. The Social Process of Aging & Old Age. 2nd ed. LC 95-19370. 406p. 1995. pap. text 49.00 (*0-13-449604-3*) P-H.

Brown, Arthur. Police Governance in England & Wales. LC 98-196562. xxvi, 193p. 1998. pap. 36.00 (*1-85941-395-1*, Pub. by Cavendish Pubng) Gaunt.

Brown, Arthur C. Iwain: Study of the Origin of the Arthurian Romance. LC 68-8365. (Arthurian Legend & Literature Ser.: No. 1). 1969. reprint ed. lib. bdg. 75.00 (*0-8383-0515-6*) M S G Haskell Hse.

***Brown, Arthur S.** V2K - Vegetarian Dining, 2000: In New York City - Of Course. 1999. pap. 12.95 (*0-9635338-3-5*, Callaloo Pr) Vegetarian Dining.

Brown, Arthur S. & Holmes, Barbara. Vegetarian Dining in New York City: (And Not Just the Places the Yuppies Like) 3rd ed. (Illus.). 96p. 1993. pap. 8.95 (*0-9635338-1-9*, Callaloo Pr) Vegetarian Dining.

— Vegetarian Dining in New York City: (And Not Just the Places the Yuppies Like) 4th ed. (Illus.). 132p. 1994. pap. 8.95 (*0-9635338-2-7*, Callaloo Pr) Vegetarian Dining.

Brown, Arthur W. Always Young for Liberty: A Biography of William Ellery Channing. LC 56-9464. 280p. 1956. reprint ed. pap. 86.80 (*0-608-06940-X*, 206714800009) Bks Demand.

— Margaret Fuller. Bowman, Sylvia E., ed. LC 63-20612. (Twayne's United States Authors Ser.). 155p. (C). 1964. text 17.95 (*0-8290-1712-7*) Irvington.

Brown, Ashland. Servant of the Dead. Zagury, Carolyn S., ed. LC 96-61493. 328p. 1997. pap. 14.95 (*1-880254-40-9*) Vista.

***Brown, Ashley.** Icons of Jazz. 2000. 17.98 (*1-57145-268-0*, Thunder Bay) Advantage Pubs.

Brown, Ashley & Haller, Robert S., eds. The Achievement of Wallace Stevens. LC 73-189246. 287p. 1973. reprint ed. 50.00 (*0-87752-161-1*) Gordian.

Brown, Audrey. A Matter of Timing: Alzheimer's - A Carer's Journey. (Illus.). 166p. 1998. 29.50 (*1-85776-331-9*, Pub. by Book Guild Ltd) Trans-Atl Phila.

Brown, Audrey & Gross, Toby. Pediatricians, Families & Child Care. McCracken, Janet B., ed. (Pediatric Round Table Ser.: No. 15). 110p. (Orig.). 1993. pap. text 10.00 (*0-931562-17-1*) J & J Consumer Prods.

Brown, Audrey I. Alive...but Alone. 130p. (Orig.). 1996. pap. 7.95 (*0-9654635-0-8*) Aubro Publns.

Brown, Avis L. My Friend, My Lover, My Husband. LC 96-95415. 132p. (Orig.). 1997. pap. 12.99 (*0-9656554-0-7*) Lamb Pub TX.

Brown-Azarowicz, Marjory, et al. Yes! You Can Learn a Foreign Language. 128p. 1993. pap. 4.95 (*0-8442-9514-0*, Natl Textbk Co) NTC Contemp Pub Co.

B

Brown-Azarowicz, Marjory F. Individual & Group Procedures in Reading: For the Classroom Teacher in Grades 4-7. LC 81-40095. (Illus.). 310p. (Orig.). (C). 1982. pap. text 27.00 (*0-8191-2264-5*) U Pr of Amer.

***Brown, Azby.** Japanese Dream House: How Technology & Tradition Are Shaping New Home Design. (Illus.). 2001. 55.00 (*4-7700-2611-0*) Kodansha.

Brown, Azby. Small Spaces: Stylish Ideas for Making More of Less in the Home. (Illus.). 96p. 1996. pap. 19.95 (*4-7700-2084-8*) Kodansha.

Brown, Azby, et al. Japan: A Living Portrait. (Illus.). 80p. 1999. 25.00 (*4-7700-2478-9*, Pub. by Kodansha Intl) Kodansha.

***Brown-Azorowicz, Majory Frances.** The Hobbyist's Guide to Playing the Piano. 223p. 2000. 23.95 (*0-7541-0892-9*, Pub. by Minerva Pr) Unity Dist.

Brown, B. Learn Biochemistry! (Illus.). 304p. 1993. pap. text 25.00 (*0-412-48220-7*) Chapman & Hall.

Brown, B. C., ed. The History of Panty Hose in America. (Illus.). ii, 18p. 1999. 10.00 (*0-9672466-0-1*) Espresso Pr.

Brown, B. F., et al, eds. Corrosion & Metal Artifacts: A Dialogue Between Conservators & Archaeologists & Corrosion Scientists. (Illus.). 240p. 1991. reprint ed. text 20.00 (*1-877914-21-5*) NACE Intl.

Brown, B. Frank. Crisis in Secondary Education: Rebuilding America's High Schools. LC 84-6923. 163p. 1984. 16.95 (*0-13-193517-8*, Busn) P-H.

— The Reform of Elementary School Education: A Report on Elementary Schools in America & How They Can Be Changed to Improve Teaching & Learning. 168p. 1992. 22.50 (*0-89464-475-0*) Krieger.

***Brown, B. H.** Medical Physics & Biomedical Engineering. LC 99-23505. 1999. 180.00 (*0-7503-0367-0*) IOP Pub.

***Brown, B. H., et al.** Medical Physics & Biomedical Engineering. LC 99-23505. (Illus.). 800p. 1999. pap. text 60.00 (*0-7503-0368-9*) IOP Pub.

Brown, B. T. Comprehensive Rock Engineering Vol. 1: Fundamentals. 1993. 411.75 (*0-08-040614-9*, Pergamon Pr) Elsevier.

Brown Bag Poets Staff. Brown Bag Lunch: Bite-Sized Poems for Snacking On. Sherrill, Peter, ed. 80p. (Orig.). 1993. pap. 5.95 (*1-889216-01-1*) Meadowcroft.

Brown, Barbara. Barns of Yesteryear & More. (Illus.). 64p. (Orig.). 1993. pap. 8.95 (*0-87961-223-1*) Naturegraph.

***Brown, Barbara.** The Exam Secret: How to Make the Grade. 160p. 2000. pap. 7.95 (*0-7160-2121-8*, Pub. by Elliot RW Bks) Midpt Trade.

Brown, Barbara. Hematology: Principles & Procedures. 6th ed. (Illus.). 453p. 1993. text 48.00 (*0-8121-1643-7*) Lppncott W & W.

— The Low Vision Handbook. LC 97-10169. (Basic Bookshelf for Eyecare Professionals Ser.). (Illus.). 160p. 1997. pap. text 30.00 (*1-55642-329-2*, 63292) SLACK Inc.

Brown, Barbara A., et al. Women's Rights & the Law: The Impact of the ERA on State Laws. LC 77-9961. 432p. 1977. 75.00 (*0-275-90257-9*, C0257, Praeger Pubs) Greenwood.

Brown, Barbara A. Knezevich, see Knezevich Brown, Barbara A.

Brown, Barbara B. Infinite Well-Being. 400p. 1985. 16.95 (*0-8290-1158-7*) Irvington.

Brown, Barbara B., jt. auth. see Seymour, Richard T.

***Brown, Barbara D.** By the Color of Our Skin: The Illusion of Integration & the Reality of Race. 256p. 2000. pap. 13.95 (*0-452-27873-2*) NAL.

Brown, Barbara F. & Brown, Jane L. Life & Health Insurance Underwriting. LC 98-73106. (Underwriting Life & Health Insurance Ser.). 392p. pap. text 74.95 (*1-57974-019-7*, Pub. by Life Office) PBD Inc.

***Brown, Barbara F. & Burger, John.** Agency Administration Course Manual. rev. ed. (C). 2000. pap. text 39.95 (*1-57974-083-9*, Pub. by Life Office) PBD Inc.

Brown, Barbara F. & Martin, Ernest L. Intro to Life Insurance Sales Illustrations: Complying with the Model Regulation. (Step One Ser.). 75p. spiral bd. 29.95 (*1-57974-065-0*, Pub. by Life Office) PBD Inc.

Brown, Barbara F., et al. Prep Pak for FLMI 301: Insurance Administration. (FLMI Insurance Education Program Ser.). 227p. 1997. spiral bd. 24.00 (*0-939921-95-2*) Life Office.

Brown, Barbara J. The Good Detective's Guide to Library Research. LC 95-30640. (Illus.). 111p. 1995. 29.95 (*1-55570-197-3*) Neal-Schuman.

— Programming for Librarians: A How-to-Do-It Manual. (How-to-Do-It Ser.). 130p. 1992. 45.00 (*1-55570-112-4*) Neal-Schuman.

Brown, Barbara J., ed. Dynamics of Administration, Vol. 1. LC 93-24273. 230p. 1993. 42.00 (*0-8342-0507-6*, 20507) Aspen Pub.

— Nursing Administration Quarterly Series, 3 vols., Set. (Brown Ser.). 736p. 1993. 100.00 (*0-8342-0386-3*, 20386) Aspen Pub.

— Research, Education & Public Policy, Vol. 3. LC 93-24268. (Nursing Administration Quarterly Ser.). 304p. 1993. 42.00 (*0-8342-0509-2*, 20509) Aspen Pub.

Brown, Barbara L., jt. auth. see Kenney, David.

Brown, Barbara W., jt. auth. see Rose, James M.

Brown, Barclay, tr. see Russolo, Luigi.

Brown, Barron. Comanche. (Illus.). 1941. 19.50 (*0-914074-02-4*, J M C & Co); pap. 12.95 (*0-685-73714-4*, J M C & Co) Amereon Ltd.

Brown, Barry & MacGregor, Douglas S. Massachusetts Condominium Law, 2 vols., Set. 2nd ed. 800p. 1993. spiral bd. 180.00 (*1-56257-311-X*, 81442-10, MICHIE) LEXIS Pub.

Brown, Barry, et al. Massachusetts Condominium Law, 2 vols. 2nd ed. 1993. suppl. ed. 49.00 (*0-685-74463-9*, MICHIE) LEXIS Pub.

Brown, Barry L. & Dobson, Pauline R., eds. Cell Signalling: Biology & Medicine of Signal Transduction. LC QP0625.N8C4. (Advances in Second Messenger & Phosphoprotein Research Ser.: Vol. 28). (Illus.). 319p. reprint ed. pap. 98.90 (*0-608-07367-9*, 206759500009) Bks Demand.

Brown, Barry S. 50 Strategies for Substance Abuse Treatment. 148p. 1998. pap. text 30.00 (*0-7881-2761-6*) DIANE Pub.

Brown, Barry S., ed. Handbook on AIDS, IV Drug Users, & Sexual Behavior in the United States. LC 92-35550. 632p. 1993. lib. bdg. 105.00 (*0-313-28374-5*, BKL, Greenwood Pr) Greenwood.

Brown, Bartram S. The United States & the Politicization of the World Bank: Issues of International Law & Policy. 350p. 1992. 89.95 (*0-7103-0424-2*, A6709) Routledge.

***Brown, Basil.** Law Sports at Gray's Inn (1594) Including Shakespeare's Connection with the Inn's of Court, the Origin of the Capias Utlegatum Re Coke & Bacon, Francis Bacon's Connection with Warwickshire, Together with a Reprint of the Gesta Grayorum. fac. ed. LC 99-49829. 2000. write for info. (*1-58477-056-2*) Lawbk Exchange.

***Brown Bear.** Loyalty, Betrayal & Other Contact Sports. LC 99-95057. v, 347p. 1999. pap. 12.00 (*0-9673933-0-2*) Erzse.

Brown, Beatrice C. Anthony Trollope. 2nd ed. LC 71-877420. (The European Novelists Ser.). 107 p. 1969. write for info. (*0-213-17902-4*) Art Barker.

Brown, Bellmore H. Guns & Gunning. fac. ed. Beard, Dan, ed. (Shorey Lost Arts Ser.). (Illus.). 109p. 1908. reprint ed. pap. 4.95 (*0-8466-6014-8*, U-14) Shoreys Bkstore.

Brown, Ben. All Things Considered: A Comedy LC 99-165617. 73 p. 1997. write for info. (*0-573-01720-4*) S French Trade.

— Practical Accounting for Farm & Rural Business. 192p. 1991. text 34.95 (*0-85236-224-2*, Pub. by Farming Pr) Diamond Farm Bk.

Brown, Ben R. The Organic Chemistry of Aliphatic Nitrogen Compounds. LC 93-31645. (International Series of Monographs on Chemistry: No. 28). (Illus.). 794p. 1994. text 225.00 (*0-19-855783-3*, Clarendon Pr) OUP.

Brown, Benjamin H. Tariff Reform Movement in Great Britain, 1881-1895. reprint ed. 12.50 (*0-404-01119-5*) AMS Pr.

Brown, Berit I. Nordic Experiences: Exploration of Scandinavian Cultures, 71. LC 96-18203. (Contributions to the Study of World Literature Ser.). 336p. 1997. 75.00 (*0-313-29954-4*) Greenwood.

***Brown, Bernadeane & Strole, James R.** Living Without Death: The Experience of Physical Immortality. 164p. 1999. pap. 14.95 (*0-9673813-0-4*) People Unlimit.

Brown, Bernard E. Intellectuals & Other Traitors. 196p. 1980. 27.95 (*0-935764-01-1*) Irvington.

— Socialism of a Different Kind: Reshaping the Left in France, 85. LC 82-6125. (Contributions in Political Science Ser.: No. 85). 201p. 1982. 57.95 (*0-313-23377-2*, BFL/, Greenwood Pr) Greenwood.

Brown, Bernard E., ed. Eurocommunism & Eurosocialism: The Left Confronts Modernity. LC 78-71538. 400p. reprint ed. text 39.50 (*0-8290-0394-0*); reprint ed. pap. text 22.95 (*0-8290-0395-9*) Irvington.

— Great American Political Thinkers Vol. 1: Creating America: From Settlement to Mass Democracy. 464p. 1983. mass mkt. 5.95 (*0-380-83915-6*, Avon Bks) Morrow Avon.

— Great American Political Thinkers Vol. II: Modern America since Civil War & Industrialization. 432p. 1983. mass mkt. 4.95 (*0-380-83923-7*, 83923-7, Avon Bks) Morrow Avon.

Brown, Bernard O. Ideology & Community Action: The West Side Organization of Chicago, 1964-1967. LC 77-91842. (Studies in Religion & Society). 99p. 1978. 19.95 (*0-913348-16-3*) Ctr Sci Study.

— Ideology & Community Action: The West Side Organization of Chicago, 1964-1967. LC 77-91842. (Studies in Religion & Society). 99p. 1978. pap. 12.95 (*0-913348-17-1*) Ctr Sci Study.

Brown, Bernice. The Magic Caterpillar. Eberspacher, Jeff, ed. (Illus.). 48p. (J). (gr. k-3). 1992. pap. 6.95 (*1-877740-20-9*); lib. bdg., boxed set 11.95 (*1-877740-19-5*) Nel-Mar Pub.

— Men of Earth. LC 70-122692. (Short Story Index Reprint Ser.). 1977. 20.95 (*0-8369-3525-X*) Ayer.

Brown, Bernita J. Snowbird Mating Season. large type ed. Davis, Jerra & Long, Jean, eds. (Illus.). 200p. (Orig.). 1992. pap. 10.95 (*0-9632555-0-9*) Snowbird Pub.

Brown, Bertram S., ed. see Willie, Charles V., et al.

Brown, Beth. Lightyears. LC 81-82663. 75p. 1982. per. 5.00 (*0-916418-36-7*) Lotus.

— Satin Tunnels. LC 87-46317. 127p. 1989. per. 8.50 (*0-916418-69-3*) Lotus.

Brown, Beth, compiled by. Fairy Tales of Birds & Beasts, Vol. 1. (Illus.). 128p. (J). (gr. 3-7). 1999. lib. bdg. 15.95 (*0-87460-375-7*) Lion Bks.

Brown, Beth, jt. auth. see Presley, Bruce.

Brown, Betsy. Esmerelda. 24p. (J). (gr. 1-3). 1995. write for info. (*1-888479-03-5*) Tarpley Pubng.

— Hooper the Hopping Hero. (Illus.). 14p. (Orig.). (J). (gr. 1-2). 1996. pap. write for info. (*1-888479-04-3*) Tarpley Pubng.

— Pippa. (Illus.). (J). (gr. 1-2). 1996. pap. write for info. (*1-888479-06-X*) Tarpley Pubng.

— The Q That Lost Its Tail. (Illus.). 14p. (Orig.). (J). (gr. 1-2). 1996. pap. write for info. (*1-888479-05-1*) Tarpley Pubng.

— Rollo & the Wishee. 16p. (J). (gr. 1-3). 1995. write for info. (*1-888479-00-0*) Tarpley Pubng.

— Squeaky Blue & the Cat. 16p. (J). (gr. 1-3). 1995. write for info. (*1-888479-01-9*) Tarpley Pubng.

— Tommy. 16p. (J). (gr. 1-3). 1995. write for info. (*1-888479-02-7*) Tarpley Pubng.

Brown, Betty A. How to Survive I. R. S. Impossible Real Situations. Milligan, Letica, ed. 267p. 1999. pap. 15.00 (*0-7392-0225-1*, PO3253) Morris Pubng.

Brown, Betty A., jt. auth. see Burns, Jim.

Brown, Betty B. & Edwards, Margaret. Developmental Disorders of Language. (Illus.). 234p. (Orig.). (C). 1990. pap. 39.95 (*1-879105-06-3*, A011) Thomson Learn.

***Brown, Betty D.** University of Wisconsin - Green Bay: From the Beginning. (Illus.). 256p. 2000. 18.75 (*0-9702129-0-9*) Univ of WI.

Brown, Betty J. Introduction to Business: Our Business & Economic World. 1991. 36.40 (*0-02-800055-2*) Glencoe.

— Teaching General Business. (Rapid Reader Ser.: No. 1). (Illus.). 34p. (C). 1977. pap. text 5.00 (*0-9603064-6-3*) Delta Pi Epsilon.

Brown, Betty J. & Clow, Betty J. Introduction to Business: Our Business & Economic World. 1997. teacher ed. write for info. (*0-02-814150-4*) Glencoe.

Brown, Beverley, et al. Sex Crimes on Trial: The Use of Sexual Evidence in Scottish Courts. (Edinburgh Law & Society Ser.). 234p. 1994. text 60.00 (*0-7486-0408-1*, Pub. by Edinburgh U Pr) Col U Pr.

Brown, Beverly. Erick Hawkins: Theory & Training. 39p. 1979. 7.00 (*0-317-64499-8*) Am Dance Guild.

— Law & the Sexual Politics of Interpretation. 220p. (C). 1997. 85.00 (*0-485-11475-5*, Pub. by Athlone Pr); pap. 29.95 (*0-485-12114-X*, Pub. by Athlone Pr) Humanities.

— Rays of Light by Jean Blome. 1998. pap. write for info. (*1-57553-986-1*) Watermrk Pr.

— The Traveling Pillow. LC 94-75990. (Illus.). 32p. (J). (ps-2). 1994. 12.95 (*1-880851-12-1*) Greene Bark Pr.

Brown, Beverly A. In Timber Country: Working People's Stories of Environmental Conflict & Urban Flight. LC 94-21274. (Conflicts in Urban & Regional Development Ser.). (Illus.). 336p. (C). 1995. text 69.95 (*1-56639-272-1*); pap. text 22.95 (*1-56639-273-X*) Temple U Pr.

Brown, Beverly A., jt. auth. see Brown, Richard E.

Brown, Beverly L., jt. ed. see Aikema, Bernard.

Brown, Beverly S. Mouse's Baby Blanket. (Illus.). 8p. (J). (gr. k-1). 1996. pap. 3.75 (*1-880612-51-8*) Seedling Pubns.

— Oliver's High Five. LC 97-35089. (Illus.). 32p. (J). (gr. k-3). 1997. pap. 8.95 (*0-929173-26-0*) Health Press.

— Panda's Birthday Surprise. (Illus.). 8p. (J). (gr. k-2). 1998. pap. 3.75 (*1-880612-80-1*) Seedling Pubns.

— The Secret at Morgan Manor. unabridged ed. (Kate & Tracy Series: We Love a Mystery!). (J). (gr. 4-8). 1989. lib. bdg. 16.99 incl. audio (*0-87386-060-8*); pap. 9.95 incl. audio (*0-87386-064-0*) Jan Prods.

Brown, Beverly S. & Brown. The House on Winchester Lane. unabridged ed. (Kate & Tracy Series: We Love a Mystery!). (J). (gr. 4-8). 1989. pap. 9.95 incl. audio (*0-87386-062-4*) Jan Prods.

— The Springtime Ghost. unabridged ed. (Kate & Tracy Series: We Love a Mystery!). (J). (gr. 4-8). 1989. lib. bdg. 16.99 incl. audio (*0-87386-059-4*); pap. 9.95 incl. audio (*0-87386-063-2*) Jan Prods.

— The Tricky Train-Ride Mystery. unabridged ed. (Kate & Tracy Series: We Love a Mystery!). (J). (gr. 4-8). 1989. lib. bdg. 16.99 incl. audio (*0-87386-061-6*); pap. 9.95 incl. audio (*0-87386-065-9*) Jan Prods.

Brown, Bill. The Art of Dying. (Illus.). 64p. 1996. 20.00 (*1-885912-11-0*) Sows Ear Pr.

— The Art of Dying: Poems. (Illus.). 64p. (Orig.). 1996. pap. 12.00 (*1-885912-08-0*) Sows Ear Pr.

— The Material Unconscious: American Amusement, Stephen Crane, & the Economies of Play. LC 96-26028. (Illus.). 384p. 1996. 48.95 (*0-674-55380-2*) HUP.

— The Material Unconscious: American Amusement, Stephen Crane, & the Economies of Play. LC 96-26028. (Illus.). 384p. 1997. reprint ed. pap. 23.95 (*0-674-55381-0*) HUP.

— Reading the West: An Anthology of Dime Westerns. LC 96-86764. 507p. 1997. text 35.00 (*0-312-16373-8*); pap. text 19.95 (*0-312-13761-3*) St Martin.

— We Are, Are We? (Orig.). 1992. pap. 12.00 (*0-940556-06-5*) Coyote.

— What the Night Told Me: Poems. LC 92-40363. 64p. 1993. pap. 14.95 (*0-7734-0035-4*, Mellen Poetry Pr) E Mellen.

Brown, Bill & Glass, Malcolm. Important Words: A Book for Poets & Writers. LC 91-122. 198p. (Orig.). (YA). (gr. 9-12). 1991. pap. text 20.00 (*0-86709-271-8*, 0271, Pub. by Boynton Cook Pubs) Heinemann.

Brown, Bill, jt. auth. see Brown, Joanie.

Brown, Bill, ed. see Dichmann, Kurt.

Brown, Bill W. A Casebook on Administration & Supervision in Industrial-Technical Education. LC 76-127888. (Illus.). 119p. reprint ed. pap. 36.90 (*0-608-11379-4*, 201158000078) Bks Demand.

— Successful Technical Writing: Documentation for Business & Industry. LC 99-33158. 349p. 2000. 34.64 (*1-56637-696-3*) Goodheart.

Brown, Blain. The Filmmaker's Pocket Reference. (Illus.). 264p. 1994. pap. 29.95 (*0-240-80058-3*, Focal) Buttrwrth-Heinemann.

— Motion Picture & Video Lighting. rev. ed. (Illus.). 226p. 1995. pap. 37.95 (*0-240-80249-7*, Focal) Buttrwrth-Heinemann.

Brown, Blake Adele, jt. auth. see Ames, Adele Z.

Brown, Blanche R. Royal Portraits in Sculpture & Coins: Pyrrhos & the Successors of Alexander the Great. LC 94-13113. (Hermeneutics of Art Ser.: Vol. 5). 192p. (C). 1995. 48.95 (*0-8204-2577-X*) P Lang Pubng.

Brown, Blythe. The Bald Book. LC 98-201788. 64p. 1998. pap. 5.99 (*0-7860-0519-X*, Pinncle Kensgtn) Kensgtn Pub Corp.

Brown, Bob. More Science for You: One Hundred Twelve Illustrated Experiments. (Illus.). 128p. (J). (ps-8). 1988. 12.95 (*0-8306-9125-1*, 3125); pap. 7.95 (*0-8306-3125-9*, 3125) McGraw-Hill Prof.

***Brown, Bob.** Not One Shred of Decency: A Historical Novel Based on Actual Events. 2000. pap. 12.95 (*0-9675673-0-0*) River City Bks.

Brown, Bob. The Turtle's Darshan for All the Animals. (Illus.). 32p. (J). (gr. 2 up). 1973. pap. 5.00 (*0-913078-17-4*) Sheriar Pr.

— 200 Illustrated Science Experiments for Children. (J). 1987. 18.05 (*0-606-00263-4*, Pub. by Turtleback) Demco.

Brown, Bob & Still, Bill. The Little Brown Book of Restaurant Success. LC 94-94450. (Illus.). 142p. 1994. pap. 17.95 (*0-9640485-1-5*) Reinhardt & Still.

Brown, Bob, et al. South American Cook Book: Including Central America, Mexico & the West Indies. LC 72-166427. 1971. reprint ed. pap. 7.95 (*0-486-20190-2*) Dover.

Brown, Bob, jt. auth. see Brown, Eleanor.

Brown, Bob W. It's Been One of Those Days, Lord. 144p. (Orig.). 1985. pap. 2.70 (*0-310-28912-2*, 12773P) Zondervan.

Brown, Bobbi. Bobbi Brown Beauty. (Illus.). 256p. 1998. pap. 16.00 (*0-06-092976-6*, Cliff Street) HarperTrade.

***Brown, Bobbi.** Bobbi Brown Teenage Beauty: Everything You Need to Look Pretty, Natural, Sexy & Awesome. (Illus.). 224p. (YA). 2000. 25.00 (*0-06-019636-X*) HarpC.

Brown, Bobbi & Iverson, Annemarie. Bobbi Brown Beauty: The Ultimate Beauty Resource. LC 96-23880. (Illus.). 256p. 1997. 30.00 (*0-06-270167-3*, HarperStyle) HarpC.

Brown, Bonaventure A. The Numerical Distinction of Sins According to the Franciscan School of the Seventeenth & Eighteenth Centuries. xviii, 114p. 1948. pap. 3.50 (*1-57659-112-3*) Franciscan Inst.

Brown, Bonnie M. Stress Busters for Kids: A Parent's Guide to Helping Kids Cope with Stress. LC 89-91558. (Illus.). 74p. (Orig.). 1990. pap. 8.95 (*0-9624705-0-3*) B M Brown.

Brown, Bradley J., ed. Second International Applied Statistics in Industry Conference Proceedings, 1994. (Illus.). 480p. (Orig.). 1994. pap. 29.95 (*0-9642033-0-8*) ACG Pr.

***Brown, Brenda.** Black Oaks. 72p. (YA). 2000. pap. 9.00 (*0-8059-4777-9*) Dorrance.

Brown, Brenda, jt. auth. see Brown, Robert F.

Brown, Brenda L., ed. Bringing It Home: Women Talk about Feminism in Their Lives. LC 97-120040. 347p. (Orig.). 1997. pap. 16.95 (*1-55152-034-6*, Pub. by Arsenal Pulp) LPC InBook.

Brown, Brenda W., jt. auth. see Brown, Robert F.

Brown, Brendan. Economists & the Financial Markets. LC 96-12239. 208p. (C). 1996. 25.99 (*0-415-02080-8*) Routledge.

— The Flight of International Capital: A Contemporary History. 480p. 1989. 57.50 (*0-7099-5036-5*, A1063); pap. 21.50 (*0-415-02585-0*, A3263) Routledge.

— The Flight of International Capital: A Contemporary History. LC 87-8988. 475p. reprint ed. pap. 147.30 (*0-608-20322-X*, 207157500002) Bks Demand.

Brown, Brent W., jt. ed. see Herzik, Eric B.

Brown, Brent W., jt. ed. see Herzik, Eric.

***Brown, Brett V.** Trends in the Well Being of America's Children & Youth. 505p. 2000. per. 45.00 (*0-16-042781-9*) USGPO.

Brown, Brian. Chinese Nights Entertainment: Stories of Old China. 1972. lib. bdg. 250.00 (*0-87968-491-7*) Krishna Pr.

***Brown, Brian.** Complete Storykeepers Collection. (Illus.). 302p. (J). (gr. k-3). 1998. reprint ed. 17.99 (*1-85608-395-0*, Pub. by Hunt GBR) OM Literature.

Brown, Brian. Storykeepers Activity Book, No. 1. (Storykeepers Ser.). (Illus.). 80p. (J). (gr. k-5). 1996. pap. 1.99 (*0-310-20236-1*) Zondervan.

— The Wisdom of Hindus. (C). 1991. 28.50 (*81-7026-171-6*, Pub. by Heritage IA) S Asia.

— The Wisdom of the Chinese: Their Philosophy in Sayings & Proverbs. 1974. lib. bdg. 250.00 (*0-87968-138-1*) Krishna Pr.

— The Wisdom of the Hindus. 320p. 1981. pap. 27.00 (*0-89540-093-6*, SB-093) Sun Pub.

Brown, Brian & Melrose, Andres. Roar in the Night: A. D. 64. (Story Keepers A.D.64: Bk. 7). 64p. (J). (gr. 2-5). 1997. pap. 3.99 (*0-310-20344-9*) Zondervan.

Brown, Brian & Melrose, Andrew. Breakout! (Storykeepers Ser.: Vol. 1). (Illus.). 64p. (J). (gr. 2-5). 1996. pap. 3.99 (*0-310-20214-0*) Zondervan.

— Breakout! (Storykeepers Ser.: Vol. 1). (Illus.). 24p. (J). (ps-3). 1996. pap. 3.99 (*0-310-20213-2*) Zondervan.

— Captured. 64p. (J). (gr. 2-5). 1997. pap. 3.99 (*0-310-20347-3*) Zondervan.

— Captured. 32p. (J). (ps-3). 1997. pap. 3.99 (*0-310-20349-X*) Zondervan.

— The Catacomb Rescue. (Storykeepers Ser.: Vol. 3). (Illus.). 24p. (J). (ps-3). 1996. pap. 3.99 (*0-310-20333-3*) Zondervan.

— Raging Waters. (Storykeepers Ser.: Vol. 2). (Illus.). 64p. (J). (gr. 2-5). 1996. pap. 3.99 (*0-310-20327-9*) Zondervan.

— Raging Waters. (Storykeepers Ser.: Vol. 2). (Illus.). 64p. (J). (ps-3). 1996. pap. 3.99 (*0-310-20329-5*) Zondervan.

— Roar in the Night. (Storykeepers Ser.: Vol. 7). (J). 1997. 14.99 incl. VHS (*0-310-20629-4*) Zondervan.

— Roar in the Night: A. D. 64. (Storykeepers Easy Reader Ser.: Vol. 7). 32p. (J). (ps-3). 1997. pap. 3.99 (*0-310-20346-5*) Zondervan.

— Sink or Swim. (Storykeepers Ser.: Vol. 5). (J). 1996. 12.99 incl. VHS (*0-310-20619-7*) Zondervan.

— Starlight Escape. (Storykeepers Ser.: Vol. 6). (J). (gr. 1-7). 1996. 14.99 incl. VHS (*0-310-20609-X*) Zondervan.
— Trapped. 32p. (J). (ps-3). 1997. pap. 3.99 (*0-310-20354-6*) Zondervan.
— Trapped. (Storykeepers Ser.: Vol. 9). (J). 1997. 14.99 incl. VHS (*0-310-20649-9*) Zondervan.
— Trapped! (Storykeepers Ser.). 64p. (J). (ps-3). 1997. pap. 3.99 (*0-310-20352-X*) Zondervan.
Brown, Brian & Melrose, Andrew, adapted by. Ready, Aim, Fire! (Storykeepers Easy Reader Ser.: Bk. 4). (J). (ps-3). 1997. pap. 3.99 (*0-310-20336-8*) Zondervan.
— Starlight Escape. (Storykeepers Easy Reader Ser.: Bk. 6). (J). (ps-3). 1997. pap. 3.99 (*0-310-20339-2*) Zondervan.
Brown, Brian, jt. auth. see Melrose, Andrew.

Brown, Brian A. Your Neighbor As Yourself: Race, Religion & Region: North America into the Twenty First Century. LC 96-71406. 300p. (Orig.). 1997. pap. 19.95 (*0-940121-41-7*, P311) Cross Cultural Pubns. This book is a watershed undertaking on Canadian-American relations & was written by a Canadian author who is well known for his earlier work concerned with the national unity issue in Canada. This work explores area of economic stability which lead to a good society in all its aspects. Racism, nationalism & religious bigotry are still the greatest challenges in the regional neighborhoods that make up the world of the twenty-first century. North Americans will soon tear down these "walls that divide" & at the same time, establish appropriate new ethical standards for their society in the Information Age. In a FOREWORD BY John Kenneth Galbraith it is pointed out that "an economic system that is inclusive of all elements of society is simply good business." *Publisher Paid Annotation.*

Brown, Brian E. The Buddha Nature: A Study of the Tathagatagarbha. 1991. 28.00 (*81-208-0631-X*, Pub. by Motilal Bnarsidass) S Asia.
***Brown, Brian E.** Religion, Law & the Land: Native Americans & the Judicial Interpretation of Sacred Land, 94. LC 99-33830. (Contributions in Legal Studies: No. 94). 208p. 1999. 59.95 (*0-313-30972-8*) Greenwood.
***Brown, Brian V. & Donahue, Julian P.** Butterfly Gardening in Southern California. (Illus.). 32p. 1999. pap. 4.00 (*0-938644-35-1*) Nat Hist Mus.
***Brown, Brown & Maschino Staff.** Early Ozarks. (Images of America Ser.). 128p. 1999. pap. 18.99 (*0-7385-0267-7*) Arcadia Publng.
Brown, Bruce. The Cheap Date Handbook: The Complete How-to Guide to Successful Inexpensive Dating. (Illus.). 176p. 1982. pap. 12.95 (*0-941256-00-6*) New Lifestyle.
— The Complete Roommate Handbook: How to Sucessfully Find, Live with & Lose a Roommate. (Illus.). 32p. (Orig.). 1982. pap. 5.00 (*0-941256-01-4*) New Lifestyle.
— Desert Duel. LC 98-85367. 192p. 1999. pap. 11.95 (*1-56315-182-0*, Pub. by SterlingHse) Natl Bk Netwk.
— Experience Las Vegas. (Illus.). 586p. 1995. reprint ed. pap. 20.00 (*0-9649035-2-0*); reprint ed. pap. 20.00 (*0-9649035-3-9*) ACT Access.
Brown, Bruce, et al. The Windows 95 Bug Collection: Fixes & Work-Arounds for Nearly 1,000 Pesky Problems When Running Windows 95. LC 95-38809. 256p. 1995. pap. 14.95 (*0-201-48995-3*) Addison-Wesley.
Brown, Bruce, jt. auth. see Gallant, Aprile.
Brown, Bruce A. W. A. Mozart: Cosi Fan Tutte. (Opera Handbooks Ser.). (Illus.). 220p. (C). 1995. text 49.95 (*0-521-43134-4*); pap. text 19.95 (*0-521-43735-0*) Cambridge U Pr.
Brown, Bruce C. Mountain in the Clouds: A Search for the Wild Salmon. LC 95-13392. (Illus.). 240p. (C). 1995. reprint ed. pap. 12.95 (*0-295-97475-3*) U of Wash Pr.
***Brown, Bruce E.** 101 Drills & Games for Youth Basketball. (Illus.). 150p. 2000. pap. 16.95 (*1-57167-441-1*) Coaches Choice.
Brown, Bruce E., jt. ed. see Larousse, Jean.
Brown, Bryan, et al. Birds of the Grand Canyon Region: An Annotated Checklist. 2nd ed. LC 84-80860. 54p. 1985. pap. 15.00 (*0-938216-22-8*) GCA.
Brown, Bryant T., et al. Grand Canyon Birds: Historical Notes, Natural History & Ecology. LC 86-27208. (Illus.). 302p. 1987. 24.95 (*0-8165-0930-1*) U of Ariz Pr.
Brown, Burnell R., Jr., jt. ed. see Prys-Roberts, Cedric.
Brown, Byron. The People of Forrs. 443p. (Orig.). mass mkt. 4.99 (*1-55197-364-2*) Picasso Publ.
Brown, Byron. Soul Without Shame: A Guide to Liberating Yourself from the Judge Within. LC 98-23402. 336p. 1998. pap. 17.95 (*1-57062-383-X*, Pub. by Shambhala Pubns) Random.
Brown, Byron W., Jr. & Hollander, Myles. Statistics: A Biomedical Introduction. (Probability & Mathematical Statistics Ser.). 480p. 1977. 169.95 (*0-471-11240-2*) Wiley.
Brown, C. Broths to Bannocks. pap. text 24.95 (*0-7195-4988-4*, Pub. by John Murray) Trafalgar.
Brown, C. & Montz, G. Bald Cypress. (Illus.). 1986. 20.00 (*0-87511-780-5*) Claitors.
Brown, C., et al. Introduction to Biotechnology. 1987. pap. 34.95 (*0-632-01139-4*) Blackwell Sci.
Brown, C. Ann. AppleWorks 5 for Windows & Macintosh: Visual QuickStart Guide. (Visual QuickStart Guide Ser.). 224p. (C). 1998. pap. text 17.99 (*0-201-35403-9*) Peachpit Pr.
— ClarisWorks 5 for Windows & Macintosh: Visual QuickStart Guide. 3rd ed. LC 98-142455. 224p. (C). 1997. pap. text 16.95 (*0-201-69660-6*) Peachpit Pr.
Brown, C. C., tr. Sejarah Melayu or Malay Annals. (Oxford in Asia Historical Reprints Ser.). 1970. 10.50 (*0-19-638106-1*) OUP.
Brown, C. E., et al. Cost & Management Accounting I. (Illus.). 151p. (Orig.). (C). 1994. pap. text 23.00 (*0-7021-3218-7*, Pub. by Juta & Co) Intl Spec Bk.
Brown, C. G., jt. auth. see Longworth, J. W.
Brown, C. Gilles, ed. see Hardy, Edward.
Brown, C. Gilles, ed. see Kaufman, Beth A.
Brown, C. H. Genealogical Record of Nathaniel Babcock, Simeon Main, Isaac Miner, Ezekiel Main. (Illus.). 362p. 1988. reprint ed. pap. 57.00 (*0-8328-0153-4*); reprint ed. lib. bdg. 67.00 (*0-8328-0152-6*) Higginson Bk Co.
Brown, C. Harmon, jt. ed. see Puhl, Jacqueline L.
Brown, C. J. Catalogue of Coins in the Provincial Museum Lucknow: Coins of the Mughal Emperors. 560p. 1986. 150.00 (*0-9511308-1-1*, Pub. by R C Senior) St Mut.
— Cattle on a Thousand Hills: A History of Cattle in Arkansas. LC 96-11631. 1996. 40.00 (*1-55728-439-3*) U of Ark Pr.
— The Coins of India. (C). 1988. reprint ed. 14.50 (*81-206-0345-1*, Pub. by Asian Educ Servs) S Asia.
Brown, C. Lloyd, ed. Federal-Type Solutions & European Integration. 672p. 1994. lib. bdg. 75.00 (*0-8191-9549-9*) U Pr of Amer.
Brown, C. Mackenzie. The Devi Gita: The Song of the Goddess: A Translation, Annotation, & Commentary. LC 98-15227. 384p. (C). 1998. text 73.50 (*0-7914-3939-9*); pap. text 24.95 (*0-7914-3940-2*) State U NY Pr.
— The Triumph of the Goddess: The Canonical Models & Theological Visions of the "Devi-Bhagavata Purana" LC 89-21974. (SUNY Series in Hindu Studies). 327p. (C). 1990. pap. text 21.95 (*0-7914-0364-5*) State U NY Pr.
— The Triumph of the Goddess: The Canonical Models & Theological Visions of the "Devi-Bhagavata Purana" LC 89-21974. (SUNY Series in Hindu Studies). 327p. (C). 1990. text 64.50 (*0-7914-0363-7*) State U NY Pr.
Brown, C. Marlin. Human-Computer Interface Design Guidelines. LC 99-474247. 11p. 1998. pap. 24.95 (*1-871516-54-4*, Pub. by Intellect) Intl Spec Bk.
Brown, C. N. Modern English-Greek Dictionary. (ENG & GRE.). 420p. 1976. 35.00 (*0-8288-5743-1*, M9592) Fr & Eur.
Brown, C. P. English-Telugu Dictionary. 1367p. 1992. reprint ed. 31.95 (*0-7859-7469-5*, 8420600398) Fr & Eur.
— A Grammar of the Telugu Language. (ENG & TEL.). 363p. 1992. 24.95 (*0-7859-7468-7*, 812060041X) Fr & Eur.
— A Grammar of the Telugu Language. 392p. 1986. reprint ed. 22.00 (*0-8364-1692-9*, Pub. by Usha) S Asia.
— A Grammar of the Telugu Language. 2nd ed. (ENG & TEL.). 432p. 1981. 21.95 (*0-7859-9816-0*) Fr & Eur.
— Primary Commodity Control. (Illus.). 1977. pap. text 18.50 (*0-19-580304-3*) OUP.
— Telugu English Dictionary. 1424p. 1986. reprint ed. 32.00 (*0-8364-1690-2*, Pub. by Usha) S Asia.
— Telugu-English Dictionary. (ENG & TEL.). 1986. reprint ed. 59.95 (*0-8288-1149-0*, M15174) Fr & Eur.
Brown, C. R., jt. ed. see Maxwell, W. Harold.
Brown, C. Reynolds. American Paintings from the Collection of Mr. & Mrs. Charles H. Wampold, Jr. LC 84-20613. (Illus.). 20p. (J). (ps-12). 1984. pap. 5.00 (*0-89280-023-2*) Montgomery Mus.
— Montgomery Museum of Fine Arts: A Handbook to the Collection. LC 80-80053. (Illus.). 68p. (J). (ps-12). 1980. pap. 3.00 (*0-89280-014-3*) Montgomery Mus.
Brown, C. V. & Jackson, P. M. Public Sector Economics. 4th ed. (Illus.). 500p. (C). 1992. pap. text 37.95 (*0-631-16208-9*) Blackwell Pubs.
***Brown, C. W. & Schneider, Edward.** Subduing Science: The Reformation of Natural Philosophy. 208p. 1999. pap. 14.95 (*0-7392-0358-4*, PO3551) E Schneider.
Brown, Cal. Masters Memories. LC 98-30971. 133p. 1998. 19.95 (*1-886947-46-5*) Sleepng Bear.
Brown, Cal, jt. auth. see Christian, Frank.
Brown, Cal, jt. auth. see Fazio, Tom.
Brown, Cal, jt. auth. see Sommers, Robert.
***Brown, Calef.** Dutch Sneakers & Flea Keepers: 14 More Stories. LC 99-53722. (Illus.). 32p. (J). 2000. 15.00 (*0-618-05183-X*) HM.
Brown, Calef. Polka-bats & Octopus Slacks: 14 Stories. LC 97-12011. 32p. (J). 1998. 15.00 (*0-395-85403-2*) HM.
Brown, Callum. Religion & Society in Scotland since 1707. 224p. 1997. pap. 25.00 (*0-7486-0886-9*, Pub. by Edinburgh U Pr) Col U Pr.
Brown, Callum. The Social History of Religion in Modern Scotland. McLeod, Hugh & Scribner, Bob, eds. (Christianity & Society in the Modern World Ser.). 288p. 1987. lib. bdg. 65.00 (*0-416-36980-4*) Routledge.
Brown, Callum G. Up-Helly-AA: Custom, Culture & Community in Shetland. LC 98-54612. (Illus.). 224p. 1999. pap. 17.95 (*1-901341-07-0*, Pub. by Manchester Univ Pr) St Martin.
— Up-Helly-AA: Custom, Culture & Community in Shetland. LC 98-54612. (Illus.). 224p. 1999. text 59.95 (*0-7190-5332-3*) St Martin.
Brown, Calvin S. Archaeology of Mississippi. LC 72-5011. (Antiquities of the New World Ser.: Vol. 16). (Illus.). reprint ed. 76.50 (*0-404-57316-9*) AMS Pr.
— Archaeology of Mississippi. LC 92-28657. (Illus.). 384p. 1992. reprint ed. text 43.00 (*0-87805-602-5*) U Pr of Miss.
— A Glossary of Faulkner's South. LC 75-43308. 249p. reprint ed. pap. 77.20 (*0-7837-3284-8*, 205768600006) Bks Demand.
— Music & Literature: A Comparison of the Arts. fac. ed. LC 86-28914. (Illus.). 303p. 1987. reprint ed. pap. 94.00 (*0-7837-8195-4*, 204790000008) Bks Demand.
Brown, Campbell, Jr. Retire at 55: A Road Map to Retirement. Brown, Mary C., ed. (Illus.). 20p. (C). 1998. pap. 3.00 (*0-939900-84-X*) Soc Human Resc Mgmt.
— Retire at 55: Campbell Brown's Guide to Early Retirement. Brown, Mary C., ed. (Orig.). 1997. pap. write for info. (*0-614-28380-9*) C Brown.
Brown, Candice L. The Body of Dancers. LC 93-70996. 207p. 1993. 18.00 (*1-880909-07-3*) Baskerville.
Brown, Canter, Jr. African Americans on the Tampa Bay Frontier. (Reference Library Ser.: No. 3). (Illus.). 76p. (Orig.). 1997. pap. 4.95 (*0-9658451-2-5*) T B H C.
— Children on the Tampa Bay Frontier. (Reference Library Ser.: No. 1). (Illus.). 1996. pap. 4.95 (*0-9658451-0-9*) T B H C.
— Children on the Tampa Bay Frontier. 2nd ed. (Reference Library Ser.: No. 1). (Illus.). 50p. 1997. pap. 4.95 (*0-9658451-3-3*) T B H C.
Brown, Canter. Florida's Black Public Officials, 1867-1924. LC 97-43612. 312p. 1998. text 44.95 (*0-8173-0915-2*); pap. text 22.95 (*0-8173-0916-0*) U of Ala Pr.
Brown, Canter, Jr. Florida's Peace River Frontier. (Illus.). 504p. 1991. 37.95 (*0-8130-1037-3*) U Press Fla.
— Fort Meade, 1849-1900. LC 94-25623. (Illus.). 222p. (Orig.). 1995. pap. text 19.95 (*0-8173-0763-X*) U of Ala Pr.
— The Founding of the Children's Home of Tampa, 1892-1899. (Reference Library Ser.: No. 6). (Illus.). 11p. 1997. pap. 4.95 (*0-9658451-6-8*) T B H C.
***Brown, Canter, Jr.** Genealogical Records of the African American Pioneers of Tampa & Hillsborough County. (Reference Library Ser.: No. 8). (Illus.). 80p. 2000. pap. 4.95 (*1-930148-00-3*) T B H C.
Brown, Canter, Jr. Jewish Pioneers of the Tampa Bay Frontier. large type ed. (Reference Library Ser.). Date not set. pap. 4.95 (*0-9658451-9-2*) T B H C.
— Ossian Bingley Hart, Florida's Loyalist Reconstruction Governor. LC 97-16763. (Southern Biography Ser.). (Illus.). 336p. 1997. text 40.00 (*0-8071-2137-1*) La State U Pr.
— Reminiscences of Judge Charles E. Harrison: Pictures from the Past in Tampa & South Florida. (Reference Library Ser.: No. 5). (Illus.). 78p. 1997. pap. 14.95 (*0-9658451-5-X*) T B H C.
***Brown, Canter.** Tampa Before the Civil War. Mathews, Richard, ed. LC 99-6980. (Illus.). 197p. 1999. 25.00 (*1-879852-64-0*) Univ Tampa.
Brown, Canter, Jr. Teachers & Schools on the Tampa Bay Frontier. (Reference Library Ser.: Vol. 4). (Illus.). 76p. 1997. pap. 4.95 (*0-9658451-4-1*) T B H C.
— Women on the Tampa Bay Frontier. (Reference Library Ser.: No. 2). (Orig.). pap. 4.95 (*0-9658451-1-7*) T B H C.
Brown, Canter, jt. auth. see Brady, Rowena F.
Brown, Canter, Jr., jt. auth. see Rogers, William W.
Brown, Caralyn C. Forbid Them Not Year B: Involving Children in Sunday Worship. 208p. (Orig.). 1993. pap. 19.95 (*0-687-13256-8*) Abingdon.
Brown, Carl. Law & Martial Arts. 1999. pap. text 38.95 (*1-58133-142-8*) Black Belt Mag.
— Law & Martial Arts. LC 97-69903. 1998. pap. 13.95 (*0-89750-134-9*, 466) Ohara Pubns.
Brown, Carl F. Abuse from My Mind: A Book of Poetry to Ease Your Mind. LC 97-93117. 51p. (Orig.). 1997. pap. 13.00 (*1-890259-00-4*) Brown Palace.
Brown, Carla & Thomas-Osborne, Valerie. Accent African: Traditional & Contemporary Hairstyles for the Black Woman. 3rd ed. 72p. 1991. pap. 8.95 (*0-9629827-0-9*) Cult Express.
Brown, Carla L., ed. see Lowenberg, Carlton.
Brown, Carleton F. A Register of Middle English Religious & Didactic Verse. 1977. 57.95 (*0-8369-7155-8*, 7987) Ayer.
Brown, Carleton F. & Robbins, Rossell H. The Index of Middle English Verse. fac. ed. LC 43-16653. 808p. 1943. reprint ed. pap. 200.00 (*0-7837-8026-5*, 204778200008) Bks Demand.
Brown, Carlyle. The African Company Presents Richard III. 1994. pap. 5.25 (*0-8222-1378-8*) Dramatists Play.
— Buffalo Hair. 1995. pap. 5.25 (*0-8222-1463-6*) Dramatists Play.
— The Little Tommy Parker Celebrated Colored Minstrel Show. 1992. pap. 5.25 (*0-8222-0679-X*) Dramatists Play.
Brown, Carol, et al. An American History Reader, 1. 3rd ed. 368p. (C). 1995. pap. text, per. 20.95 (*0-7872-0426-9*, 41042601) Kendall-Hunt.
— The Art Student's College Guide. LC 96-11290. 256p. 1996. 18.95 (*0-02-860580-2*, Arc) IDG Bks.
— Introducing God's Word: A First Look at the Bible, for Groups & Individuals. (Illus.). 96p. 1999. pap. 12.00 (*1-880573-54-7*) Bible Search Pubns.
Brown, Carol, ed. see Darnell, Michael N.
Brown, Carol E. & Philips, Mary E. Expert Systems for Management Accounting Tasks. Barth, Claire, ed. (Illus.). 212p. 1995. pap. 40.00 (*0-86641-236-0*, 94299) Inst Mgmt Account.
Brown, Carol R. Planning Library Interiors: The Selection of Furnishings for the 21st Century. 2nd ed. LC 94-30430. (Illus.). 176p. 1994. pap. 29.95 (*0-89774-850-6*) Oryx Pr.
Brown, Carol S., jt. auth. see Glazer, Susan M.
***Brown, Carol V. & Topi, Heikki.** IS Management Handbook. 7th ed. LC 99-41254. 808p. 1999. boxed set 95.00 (*0-8493-9820-7*) CRC Pr.
***Brown, Caroline Shields, ed.** Shooting Star: Writings & Images of Caroline Shields Brown. (Illus.). 160p. 1999. pap. write for info. (*0-9663764-2-0*) Reivers Pr.
***Brown, Carolyn.** All the Way from Texas. LC 00-190017. 192p. 2000. 18.95 (*0-8034-9414-9*, Avalon Bks) Bouregy.
Brown, Carolyn. Contrary Things: Exegesis, Dialectic, & the Poetics of Didacticism. LC 98-17381. (Figurae Ser.). 246p. 1998. 45.00 (*0-8047-3009-1*) Stanford U Pr.
***Brown, Carolyn.** A Falling Star. LC 99-91309. 192p. 2000. 18.95 (*0-8034-9396-7*, Avalon Bks) Bouregy.
— Love Is. LC 99-94443. 192p. 1999. 18.95 (*0-8034-9366-5*, Avalon Bks) Bouregy.
Brown, Carolyn, et al. Decide for Yourself: A Book to Help You Make End of Life Decisions:Life Support, Living Will, Durable Power of Attorney for Health Care. Hull, Nancy R., ed. LC 92-19858. (Illus.). 40p. 1993. pap. text 7.95 (*0-939838-34-6*) Pritchett & Hull.
Brown, Carolyn, jt. auth. see Sheedy, Kevin.
Brown, Carolyn, jt. ed. see Schuster, Eleanor.
Brown, Carolyn C. Developing Christian Education in a Smaller Church. LC 81-17563. (Griggs Educational Resources Ser.). 96p. (Orig.). 1982. pap. 12.95 (*0-687-10508-0*) Abingdon.
— Forbid Them Not Year A: Involving Children in Sunday School Worship. 208p. (Orig.). 1992. pap. 19.95 (*0-687-13255-X*) Abingdon.
— Forbid Them Not-Year C: Involving Children in Sunday Worship. 208p. (Orig.). 1994. pap. 19.95 (*0-687-13265-7*) Abingdon.
— Gateways to Worship: A Year of Worship Experiences for Young Children. 1989. pap. 21.95 (*0-687-14020-X*) Abingdon.
— You Can Preach to the Kids Too! Designing Sermons for Adults & Children. LC 97-26777. 160p. 1997. pap. 13.95 (*0-687-06157-1*) Abingdon.
— Youth Ministries: Thinking Big with Small Groups. LC 83-15891. (Griggs Educational Resources Ser.). 96p. 1984. pap. 10.95 (*0-687-47203-2*) Abingdon.
Brown, Carolyn J. Curriculum Connections. (Illus.). 179p. 1995. teacher ed., spiral bd. 25.00 (*1-890891-06-1*) Breakthrough Inc.
— Foundations in Reading. (Illus.). 272p. 1995. teacher ed., ring bd. 60.00 (*1-890891-03-7*) Breakthrough Inc.
— Report Connections. (Illus.). 68p. 1995. spiral bd. 25.00 (*1-890891-07-X*) Breakthrough Inc.
— Student Connections. (Illus.). 22p. 1995. teacher ed., spiral bd. 25.00 (*1-890891-05-3*) Breakthrough Inc.
— Teacher Connections. (Illus.). 80p. 1995. spiral bd. 25.00 (*1-890891-04-5*) Breakthrough Inc.
***Brown, Carolyn M.** The Millionaires' Club: How to Start & Run Your Own Investment Club - And Make Your Money Grow! 256p. 2000. pap. 19.95 (*0-471-36938-1*) Wiley.
— Nobody's Business but Your Own: A Business Start-Up Guide with Advice from Today's Most Successful Young Entrepreneurs. LC 98-41065. (Illus.). 352p. (Orig.). 1999. pap. 14.95 (*0-7868-8301-4*, Pub. by Hyperion) Time Warner.
Brown, Carolyn S. The Tall Tale in American Folklore & Literature. LC 86-25125. (Illus.). 186p. 1987. pap. 16.95 (*0-87049-627-1*) U of Tenn Pr.
Brown, Carolyn S., jt. auth. see Brown, Joseph H.
Brown, Carolyn S., jt. auth. see Rodricks, Dan.
***Brown, Carrie.** The Hatbox Baby. 368p. 2000. 22.95 (*1-56512-299-2*) Algonquin Bks.
Brown, Carrie. Lamb in Love. LC 98-44580. 348p. 1999. 21.95 (*1-56512-203-8*, 72203) Algonquin Bks.
***Brown, Carrie.** Lamb in Love. large type ed. LC 99-22156. (Large Print Book Ser.). 1999. write for info. (*1-56895-732-7*) Wheeler Pub.
— Lamb in Love. 336p. 2000. reprint ed. pap. 11.95 (*0-553-38085-0*) Bantam.
Brown, Carrie. Rose's Garden. LC 97-41082. 252p. 1998. 20.95 (*1-56512-174-0*, 72174) Algonquin Bks.
— Rose's Garden. large type ed. LC 98-6906. 1998. 23.95 (*1-57490-141-9*, Beeler LP Bks) T T Beeler.
— Rose's Garden. 243p. 1999. reprint ed. pap. 11.95 (*0-553-38028-1*) Bantam.
Brown, Carroll. Food-Fit for the King! LC 94-1639. 84p. (Orig.). 1994. pap. 6.00 (*1-880573-18-0*) Bible Search Pubns.
Brown, Carroll N. The Glory That Was Greese. Date not set. 30.95 (*0-8369-4793-2*) Ayer.
Brown, Carroll N., tr. see Andreades, Andreas M. & Finley, Moses, eds.
Brown, Carter. The Aseptic Murders. 1979. mass mkt. 2.50 (*0-451-11701-8*, AE1701, Sig) NAL.
— The Blonde. 1979. mass mkt. 2.50 (*0-451-11703-4*, AE1703, Sig) NAL.
— The Brazen. 1981. mass mkt. 2.50 (*0-451-11704-2*, AE1704, Sig) NAL.
— The Coven. 1978. mass mkt. 2.50 (*0-451-11697-6*, AE1697, Sig) NAL.
— The Dance of Death. 1982. mass mkt. 2.75 (*0-451-11926-6*, AE1926, Sig) NAL.
— The Dream Is Deadly. 1981. mass mkt. 2.50 (*0-451-09776-9*, E9776, Sig) NAL.
— The DumDum Murder. 1982. mass mkt. 2.95 (*0-451-11873-1*, AE1873, Sig) NAL.
— The Lover. 1980. mass mkt. 1.75 (*0-451-09121-3*, E9121, Sig) NAL.
— The Sad-Eyed Seductress. 1982. mass mkt. 2.50 (*0-451-11520-1*, AE1520, Sig) NAL.
— Sex Clinic. 1978. mass mkt. 2.50 (*0-451-11698-4*, AE1698, Sig) NAL.
— The Tigress. 1981. mass mkt. 2.50 (*0-451-11027-7*, AE1027, Sig) NAL.
— Walk Softly, Witch. 1980. mass mkt. 1.75 (*0-451-09418-2*, E9418, Sig) NAL.
Brown-Casey, Marcia. Who's That Bitch in the Mirror? Hogan, Sherrie & Hempstead, Valerie, eds. (Illus.). 253p. 1998. pap., per. 12.00 (*0-9652459-2-6*) TSFP.
Brown, Cassie. Death on the Ice. 256p. 1988. pap. 11.95 (*0-385-25179-3*) Doubleday.
— Winter's Tale. 304p. 1988. mass mkt. 12.00 (*0-385-25181-5*) Doubleday.

B

Brown, Catana, et al. Mental Health Protocols for Occupational Therapy. 32p. (C). 1993. pap. text 6.50 (*0-935273-06-9*) Chess Pub.

Brown, Catherine. A Year in a Scots Kitchen. (Illus.). 212p. 1999. pap. 15.00 (*1-897784-79-1*) Interlink Pub.

Brown, Catherine C., ed. Childhood Learning Disabilities & Prenatal Risk. (Pediatric Round Table Ser.: No. 9). 109p. 1983. 10.00 (*0-931562-11-2*) J & J Consumer Prods.

— Infants at Risk. (Pediatric Round Table Ser.: No. 5). 132p. (Orig.). 1981. pap. text 10.00 (*0-931562-06-6*) J & J Consumer Prods.

— Play Interactions. (Pediatric Round Table Ser.: No. 11). 209p. (Orig.). (C). 1985. pap. text 10.00 (*0-931562-13-9*) J & J Consumer Prods.

Brown, Catherine C., et al. The Many Facets of Touch. (Pediatric Round Table Ser.: No. 10). 207p. 1984. 10.00 (*0-931562-12-0*) J & J Consumer Prods.

Brown, Catherine F., jt. auth. see Benedek, Elissa P.

Brown, Catherine L., compiled by. The Urban South: A Bibliography, 12. LC 89-2151. (Bibliographies & Indexes in American History Ser.: No. 12). 465p. 1989. lib. bdg. 89.50 (*0-313-26154-7*, BRJ/, Greenwood Pr) Greenwood.

Brown, Catherine L. & Wheeler, James O., compiled by. A Bibliography of Geographical Thought: Bibliographies & Indexes in Geography, 1. LC 89-25958. 520p. 1989. lib. bdg. 99.50 (*0-313-26899-1*, BBJ/, Greenwood Pr) Greenwood.

Brown, Catherine R. Jack Russell Terrier: Courageous Companion. LC 98-11631. 224p. 1998. 27.95 (*0-87605-195-6*) Howell Bks.

Brown, Catherine R., et al. Building for the Arts: A Guidebook for the Planning & Design of Cultural Facilities. Briefs-Elgin, Gina, ed. LC 89-40275. (Illus.). 1989. pap. 29.95 (*0-9611710-4-9*) Western States.

Brown, Catherine R., jt. auth. see Morrish, William R.

Brown-Cathers, Barbara. Bobio: A Fairy Tale for All Ages. (Illus.). 36p. (Orig.). (J). (gr. 5). 1994. pap. 7.95 (*0-9640122-0-0*) Pen & Pr United.

Brown, Cathey, et al. Kids' Power, Too: Words to Grow By. (Illus.). 386p. (Orig.). (J). (gr. 4-8). 1996. pap. 12.95 (*0-9653789-0-X*) ImaginWorks.

Brown, Cathy. The World's Most Forgotten Grandmother, Granny Goose. (Illus.). (J). (ps-4). 1998. 10.95 (*1-892089-55-6*); pap. 5.95 (*1-892089-52-1*) Our Kids Pubn.

Brown, Cathy J. & Paterson, Debi. Bouncy Bunny's Birthday: A Family Story about Bravery. LC 86-61065. (Illus.). 32p. (Orig.). (J). (gr. 1-3). 1985. pap. 8.75 (*0-9614796-0-4*) C J Brown.

— Bouncy Bunny's Birthday: A Family Story about Bravery. (Illus.). 32p. (Orig.). (J). (gr. 1-3). 1985. pap. 8.75 (*0-318-19386-8*) Offset Hse.

Brown, Catrina & Jasper, Karin, eds. Consuming Passions: Feminist Approaches to Eating Disorders & Weight Preoccupations. LC 98-106909. 250p. (Orig.). 1993. pap. 16.95 (*0-929005-42-2*, Pub. by Sec Story Pr) LPC InBook.

Brown, Cecil. Coming up down Home: A Memoir of a Southern Childhood. 240p. 1995. pap. 40.00 (*0-88001-414-8*) HarpC.

— Coming up down Home: Memoir of a Sharecropper's Son. 1993. 24.95 (*0-88001-293-5*) HarpC.

Brown, Cecil H. Language & Living Things: Uniformities in Folk Classification & Naming. LC 83-3238. 322p. reprint ed. pap. 99.90 (*0-8357-7942-4*, 205701500002) Bks Demand.

— Lexical Acculturation in Native American Languages. LC 98-13835. (Oxford Studies in Anthropological Linguistics: No. 19). 272p. 1999. text 55.00 (*0-19-512161-9*) OUP.

Brown, Cedric C. John Milton: A Literary Life. LC 94-24505. (Literary Lives Ser.). 256p. 1995. text 45.00 (*0-312-12514-3*) St Martin.

— John Milton's Aristocratic Entertainments. (Illus.). 220p. 1985. 69.95 (*0-521-30440-7*) Cambridge U Pr.

Brown, Cedric C., ed. Patronage Politics & Literary Traditions in England, 1558-1658. 310p. (C). 1993. pap. 19.95 (*0-8143-2417-7*) Wayne St U Pr.

— The Poems & Masques of Aurelian Townshend: With Music by Henry Lawes & William Webb. 126p. 1983. 37.00 (*0-7049-0108-0*, WK1) Pegasus Pr.

Brown, Cedric C. & Marotti, Arthur F. Texts & Cultural Change in Early Modern England. LC 97-24801. (Early Modern Literature in History Ser.). 256p. 1997. text 55.00 (*0-312-17728-3*) St Martin.

Brown, Celia. Doctor's Little Book of Answers: 600 Medical Facts Everyone Should Know. LC 95-39609. 176p. 1996. pap. 9.95 (*0-7615-0325-0*) Prima Pub.

***Brown, Celia.** Mending the Skies: Poems. LC 99-50657. 96p. 2000. pap. 12.00 (*1-56474-338-1*) Fithian Pr.

Brown, Celia, tr. see Avitabile, Gunhild, et al.

***Brown, Chad & Eisenstock, Alan.** Inside The Meat Grinder. 272p. 2000. mass mkt. 6.99 (*0-312-97653-4*) St Martin.

Brown, Chad & Eisenstock, Alan. Inside the Meatgrinder: An NFL Official's Life in the Trenches. LC 99-35780. 226p. 1999. text 24.95 (*0-312-24658-7*) St Martin.

Brown, Chamberlain, jt. ed. see Bonitsis, Theologos H.

Brown, Chappell, jt. auth. see Johnson, R. Colin.

Brown, Charlene B. The Art of Framing. Sprague, Sydney, ed. (Artist's Library). (Illus.). 64p. (Orig.). 1991. pap. 7.95 (*1-56010-070-2*, AL19) W Foster Pub.

Brown, Charles & Brown, Mary B. Coloniality in the Cliff Swallow: The Effect of Groups Size on Social Behavior. LC 95-44561. 552p. (C). 1996. pap. text 34.95 (*0-226-07626-1*) U Ch Pr.

Brown, Charles, et al. Employers Large & Small. (Illus.). 144p. 1990. 30.50 (*0-674-25162-8*) HUP.

Brown, Charles A. Shakespeare's Autobiographical Poems. 1972. 59.95 (*0-8490-1038-1*) Gordon Pr.

— Shakespeare's Autobiographical Poems. LC 76-39541. reprint ed. 47.50 (*0-404-01127-6*) AMS Pr.

Brown, Charles Brockden. An Address to the Congress of the United States on the Restrictions upon Foreign Commerce. (Works of Charles Brockden Brown). 1989. reprint ed. lib. bdg. 79.00 (*0-7812-2075-0*) Rprt Serv.

— An Address to the Congress of the United States on the British Treaty. (Works of Charles Brockden Brown). 1989. reprint ed. lib. bdg. 79.00 (*0-7812-2074-2*) Rprt Serv.

— An Address to the Government of the United States on the Cession of Louisiana. (Works of Charles Brockden Brown). 1989. reprint ed. lib. bdg. 79.00 (*0-7812-2071-8*) Rprt Serv.

— Alcuin. Kierner, Cynthia, ed. (Masterworks of Literature Ser.). 1994. pap. 12.95 (*0-8084-0448-2*) NCUP.

— Alcuin: A Dialogue. (Works of Charles Brockden Brown). 1989. reprint ed. lib. bdg. 79.00 (*0-7812-2065-3*) Rprt Serv.

— Arthur Mervyn. Gabo, Frank, ed. (Masterworks of Literature Ser.). 1991. pap. 17.95 (*0-8084-0446-6*) NCUP.

— Arthur Mervyn, 2 vols., Set. 1993. reprint ed. lib. bdg. 150.00 (*0-7812-5436-1*) Rprt Serv.

— Arthur Mervyn: Or the Memoirs of the Year 1793. (Works of Charles Brockden Brown). 1989. reprint ed. lib. bdg. 79.00 (*0-7812-2069-6*) Rprt Serv.

— Arthur Mervyn: or Memoirs of the Year 1793: Bicentennial Edition. LC 79-27061. (Novels & Related Works of Charles Brockden Brown Ser.: Vol. 3). 557p. reprint ed. pap. 172.70 (*0-608-08076-4*, 206903500002) Bks Demand.

— The Bilouist & Other American Tales & Pieces. (Works of Charles Brockden Brown). 1989. reprint ed. lib. bdg. 79.00 (*0-7812-2077-7*) Rprt Serv.

— Clara Howard. (Works of Charles Brockden Brown). 1989. reprint ed. lib. bdg. 79.00 (*0-7812-2070-X*) Rprt Serv.

— Edgar Huntley: Or Memoirs of a Sleepwalker. (Works of Charles Brockden Brown). 1989. reprint ed. lib. bdg. 79.00 (*0-7812-2068-8*) Rprt Serv.

— Edgar Huntly. 22.95 (*0-8488-0923-8*) Amereon Ltd.

— Edgar Huntly. Stineback, David, ed. (Masterworks of Literature Ser.). 1973. write for info. (*0-8084-0359-1*); pap. 11.95 (*0-8084-0360-5*) NCUP.

— Edgar Huntly: Memoirs of a Sleep Walker. Grabo, Norman S., ed. & intro. by. 288p. 1988. pap. 12.95 (*0-14-039062-6*, Penguin Classics) Viking Penguin.

— Edgar Huntly: Memoirs of a Sleep-Walker. Krause, Sydney J. & Reid, S. W., eds. LC 86-21055. 344p. (C). 1987. reprint ed. pap. 10.00 (*0-87338-342-7*) Kent St U Pr.

— Edgar Huntly: Or, Memoirs of a Sleepwalker, 3 vols. LC 79-144587. reprint ed. 125.00 (*0-404-01130-6*) AMS Pr.

— Jane Talbot. 1927. 15.00 (*0-87556-042-3*) Saifer.

— Jane Talbot. (Works of Charles Brockden Brown). 1989. reprint ed. lib. bdg. 79.00 (*0-7812-2072-6*) Rprt Serv.

— The Novels & Related Works of Charles Brockden Brown: Clara Howard & Jane Talbot. Krause, Sydney J. & Reid, S. W., eds. LC 85-8102. (C.S.E. Edition Ser.: Vol. 5). 539p. 1986. 35.00 (*0-87338-320-6*) Kent St U Pr.

— The Novels & Related Works of Charles Brockden Brown: Edgar Huntly; or, Memoirs of a Sleep-Walker. Krause, Sydney J. & Reid, S. W., eds. LC 84-4376. (C.S.E. Edition Ser.: No. 4). 510p. 1985. 35.00 (*0-87338-305-2*) Kent St U Pr.

— Ormond. Chapman, Mary, ed. (Literary Texts Ser.). 400p. 1999. pap. 12.95 (*1-55111-091-1*) Broadview Pr.

— Ormond: or The Secret Witness. (Works of Charles Brockden Brown). 1989. reprint ed. lib. bdg. 79.00 (*0-7812-2067-X*) Rprt Serv.

Brown, Charles Brockden. Ormond: or The Secret Witness: Bicentennial Edition. LC 82-14904. (Novels & Related Works of Charles Brockden Brown Ser.: Vol. 2). 492p. 1982. reprint ed. pap. 152.60 (*0-608-07346-6*, 206757400009) Bks Demand.

Brown, Charles Brockden. A Prospectus of a System of General Geography. (Works of Charles Brockden Brown). 1989. reprint ed. lib. bdg. 79.00 (*0-685-44731-6*) Rprt Serv.

— The Rhapsodist & Other Uncollected Writings. LC 43-9591. 176p. 1977. 50.00 (*0-8201-1203-8*) Schol Facsimiles.

— Selected Prose Fiction of Charles Brockden Brown. Barnard, Philip, ed. (Masterworks of Literature Ser.). 1999. pap. 16.95 (*0-8084-0487-3*) NCUP.

— Three Gothic Novels: Wieland; Arthur Mervyn; Edgar Huntly. Krause, Sydney J., ed. LC 97-46701. 914p. 1998. 35.00 (*1-883011-57-4*, Pub. by Library of America) Penguin Putnam.

— A View of the Soil & Climate of the United States of America. (Works of Charles Brockden Brown). 1989. reprint ed. lib. bdg. 79.00 (*0-7812-2073-4*) Rprt Serv.

— Wieland. 22.95 (*0-8488-0922-X*) Amereon Ltd.

— Wieland: Or, the Transformation. Pattee, F. L., ed. LC 58-13328. 408p. 1969. reprint ed. pap. 13.00 (*0-15-696680-8*, Harvest Bks) Harcourt.

— Wieland & "Memoirs of Carwin" Krause, Sydney J. & Reid, S. W., eds. LC 78-15330. 310p. 1978. pap. 14.00 (*0-87338-220-X*) Kent St U Pr.

— Wieland & Memoirs of Carwin the Biloquist. Fliegelman, Jay, ed. & intro. by. 416p. 1991. pap. 10.95 (*0-14-039079-0*, Penguin Classics) Viking Penguin.

— Wieland: or The Transformation. LC 97-26695. (Literary Classics Ser.). 234p. 1997. pap. text 7.95 (*1-57392-175-0*) Prometheus Bks.

— Wieland: or The Transformation. (Works of Charles Brockden Brown). 1989. reprint ed. lib. bdg. 79.00 (*0-7812-2066-1*) Rprt Serv.

***Brown, Charles Brockden.** Wieland; or the Transformation & Memoirs of Carwin, the Biloquist. Elliott, Emory, ed. & intro. by. (Oxford World's Classics Ser.). 336p. 1999. pap. 9.95 (*0-19-283680-3*) OUP.

Brown, Charles C. Niebuhr & His Age: Reinhold Niebuhr's Prophetic Role in the Twentieth Century. LC 92-25356. 334p. 1992. 35.00 (*1-56338-042-0*) TPI PA.

— Perak Malays: Papers on Malay Subjects. LC 77-87481. 128p. reprint ed. 32.50 (*0-404-16797-7*) AMS Pr.

Brown, Charles D. Spacecraft Mission Design. LC 92-17976. 210p. (C). 1992. text 69.95 (*1-56347-041-1*, 41-1) AIAA.

— Spacecraft Mission Design Second Edition. 2nd ed. LC 98-12675. 183p. 1998. write for info. (*1-56347-262-7*) AIAA.

— Spacecraft Propulsion. (AIAA Education Ser.). 1995. 74.95 (*1-56347-128-0*, 28-0) AIAA.

Brown, Charles E. Applied Multivariate Statistics in Geohydrology & Related Sciences. LC 97-30060. (Illus.). 348p. 1998. 79.95 (*3-540-61827-9*) Spr-Verlag.

— The Meaning of Sanctification. 1980. pap. 7.99 (*0-88019-079-5*) Schmul Pub Co.

Brown, Charles E., IV. Reference Guide for Allied Video Corporation's Video Production of The Greenhouse Effect. 24p. 1994. pap. 5.95 (*1-56913-022-1*) Allied Video.

Brown, Charles E. The Self in Time: Retrieving Existential Theology & Freud. LC 96-42212. 328p. 1996. 44.00 (*0-7618-0516-8*) U Pr of Amer.

Brown, Charles E., jt. auth. see Currie, Nicholas C.

Brown, Charles F. Letters of Artemus Ward to Charles E. Wilson, 1858-1861. 1971. 59.95 (*0-8490-0511-6*) Gordon Pr.

Brown, Charles G. First Get Mad, Then Get Justice: The Handbook for Crime Victims. LC 92-39829. 1993. 18.95 (*1-55972-170-7*, Birch Ln Pr) Carol Pub Group.

Brown, Charles H. Agents of Manifest Destiny: The Lives & Times of the Filibusters. LC 79-383. (Illus.). 545p. 1980. reprint ed. pap. 169.00 (*0-7837-9026-0*, 204977700003) Bks Demand.

***Brown, Charles H.** Dark Sky, Black Sea: Aircraft Carrier Night & All-Weather Operations. LC 99-28613. 1999. 34.95 (*1-55750-185-8*) Naval Inst Pr.

Brown, Charles H. Handbook of Drug Therapy Monitoring. (Illus.). 352p. 1990. 32.00 (*0-683-01091-3*) Lppncott W & W.

Brown, Charles H., jt. auth. see Meyer, C. Kenneth.

Brown, Charles J. The Divine Glory of Christ. 95p. 1982. pap. 4.99 (*0-85151-342-5*) Banner of Truth.

Brown, Charles J. & Lago, Armando M. The Politics of Psychiatry in Revolutionary Cuba. LC 91-7537. 215p. (C). 1991. 39.95 (*1-56000-020-1*); pap. 24.95 (*1-56000-585-8*) Transaction Pubs.

Brown, Charles N. I Always Put the Seat Down. (Illus.). 70p. 1996. pap. 10.95 (*1-57502-258-3*, P0940) Morris Pubng.

Brown, Charles N. & Contento, William G. Science Fiction, Fantasy & Horror, 1986. (Science Fiction, Fantasy & Horror Ser.: No. 2). 347p. 1987. 45.00 (*0-9616629-3-X*) Locus Pr.

— Science Fiction, Fantasy & Horror, 1986. 347p. 1987. 45.00 (*0-88736-071-8*) Locus Pr.

— Science Fiction, Fantasy & Horror, 1987. (Science Fiction, Fantasy & Horror Ser.: No. 3). 420p. 1987. 45.00 (*0-9616629-4-8*) Locus Pr.

— Science Fiction, Fantasy & Horror, 1984. (Science Fiction, Fantasy & Horror Ser.: No. 4). 300p. 1990. 50.00 (*0-9616629-5-6*) Locus Pr.

— Science Fiction, Fantasy & Horror, 1988. 1989. 50.00 (*0-9616629-6-4*) Locus Pr.

— Science Fiction, Fantasy & Horror, 1989. 515p. 1990. 50.00 (*0-9616629-7-2*) Locus Pr.

— Science Fiction, Fantasy & Horror, 1990. 587p. 1991. 50.00 (*0-9616629-8-0*) Locus Pr.

— Science Fiction, Fantasy, & Horror, 1991: A Comprehensive Bibliography of Books & Short Fiction Published in the English Language. 1992. 60.00 (*0-9616629-9-9*) Locus Pr.

— Science Fiction in Print: 1985. 237p. 1986. 35.00 (*0-9616629-2-1*) Locus Pr.

Brown, Charles P. Dictionary of Telugu & English: Explaining English Idioms & Phrases in Telugu, 2 Vols. (ENG & TEL.). 1977. reprint ed. 214.95 (*0-518-19008-0*) Ayer.

— English Telugu Dictionary. 1416p. 1986. reprint ed. 32.00 (*0-8364-1691-0*, Pub. by Usha) S Asia.

— English-Telugu Dictionary. (TEL & ENG.). 1367p. (C). 1986. reprint ed. 44.00 (*81-206-0039-8*, Pub. by Asian Educ Servs) S Asia.

Brown, Charles P., tr. The Wars of the Rajas: Being the History of Anantapuram: Written in Telugu: in or about the Years 1750-1810. (C). 1988. reprint ed. 17.50 (*81-206-0365-6*, Pub. by Asian Educ Servs) S Asia.

Brown, Charles P., et al. Together Forever: An Invitation to Physical Immortality. LC 89-82414. (Illus.). 176p. (Orig.). 1990. pap. 9.95 (*0-9625346-0-9*) People Forever Intl.

Brown, Charles R. Swallow Summer. LC 98-4551. (Illus.). xiii, 377p. 1998. pap. 16.95 (*0-8032-6145-4*, Bison Books) U of Nebr Pr.

— They Were Giants. LC 68-54332. (Essay Index Reprint Ser.). 1977. 20.95 (*0-8369-0257-2*) Ayer.

— They Were Giants. LC 68-54332. (Essay Index Reprint Ser.). 285p. 1982. reprint ed. lib. bdg. 20.00 (*0-8290-0835-7*) Irvington.

Brown, Charles R. & Brown, Mary B. Coloniality in the Cliff Swallow: The Effect of Groups Size on Social Behavior. LC 95-44561. (C). 1996. lib. bdg. 95.00 (*0-226-07625-3*) U Ch Pr.

Brown, Charles R., jt. auth. see Gabriel, Ralph H.

Brown, Charles T. The Art of Rock & Roll. 3rd ed. 352p. (C). 1992. pap. text 34.60 (*0-13-044892-3*) P-H.

— Country & Western Music. (Illus.). 250p. (C). 1985. pap. 12.95 (*0-685-10424-9*); text 22.95 (*0-685-10423-0*) P-H.

— Music U. S. A. America's Country & Western Tradition. 1986. 14.95 (*0-13-608167-3*) P-H.

— The Rock & Roll Story. (Illus.). 128p. 1986. 13.50 (*0-13-782227-8*) P-H.

***Brown, Charles Thomas.** The Gospel & Ignatius of Antioch. LC 98-37321. (Studies in Biblical Literature Ser.: No. 12). 264p. (C). 2000. text 51.95 (*0-8204-4132-5*) P Lang Pubng.

Brown, Charles V. The Nigerian Banking System. LC 66-19192. 212p. reprint ed. pap. 65.80 (*0-608-13176-8*, 201528900001) Bks Demand.

Brown, Charles W. American Star Speaker. LC 79-139755. (Granger Index Reprint Ser.). 1977. 39.95 (*0-8369-6209-5*) Ayer.

— The Church That's More Than a Place: Insights from Ephesians for Today's Church. 144p. (Orig.). 1996. pap. 12.95 (*0-9652483-0-5*, 011) New Century Pub.

Brown, Charles W., ed. Comic Recitations & Readings. LC 72-139756. (Granger Index Reprint Ser.). 1977. 18.95 (*0-8369-6210-9*) Ayer.

Brown, Charlie, jt. auth. see Scherer, Pat.

***Brown, Charlotte.** Bundle of Joy. 2000. pap. text 4.99 (*1-56245-408-0*) Great Quotations.

Brown, Charlotte A. ClarisWorks 4 for Macintosh: Visual QuickStart Guide. (Illus.). 256p. (C). 1995. pap. text 16.95 (*0-201-88407-0*) Peachpit Pr.

— FileMaker Pro 3 for Macintosh: Visual QuickStart Guide. (Illus.). 250p. (C). 1996. pap. text 16.95 (*0-201-88357-0*) Peachpit Pr.

Brown, Charlotte H. Mammy: An Appeal to the Heart of the South; &, The Correct Thing to Do--to Say--to Wear. LC 94-42137. (African American Women Writers, 1910-1940 Ser.). 1995. 25.00 (*0-8161-1632-6*, G K Hall & Co) Mac Lib Ref.

— Mammy: An Appeal to the Heart of the South; &, The Correct Thing to Do--to Say--to Wear. Gates, Henry Louis, Jr., ed. LC 94-42137. (African American Women Writers 1910-1940 Ser.). 149p. 1995. 15.95 (*0-7838-1395-3*, Hall Reference) Macmillan.

Brown, Charlotte V., et al. The Humanities: Cultural Roots & Continuities, 2 vols. 4th ed. (C). 1993. 11.96 (*0-669-27580-8*); sl. 35.16 (*0-669-27582-4*) HM Trade Div.

— The Humanities: Cultural Roots & Continuities, 2 vols., Vol. I. 4th ed. (C). 1993. student ed. 18.76 (*0-669-27578-6*) HM Trade Div.

— The Humanities: Cultural Roots & Continuities, Vol. I. 5th ed. (C). 1997. pap. text, student ed. 18.76 (*0-669-41659-2*) HM Trade Div.

— The Humanities: Cultural Roots & Continuities, 2 vols., Vol. I: Three Cultural Roots. 4th ed. 448p. (C). 2000. pap. text 51.56 (*0-669-27575-1*) HM Trade Div.

— The Humanities: Cultural Roots & Continuities, 2 vols., Vol. II. 4th ed. (C). 1993. student ed. 18.76 (*0-669-27579-4*) HM Trade Div.

— The Humanities: Cultural Roots & Continuities, Vol. II. 5th ed. (C). 1996. pap. text, student ed. 18.76 (*0-669-41660-6*) HM Trade Div.

— The Humanities: Cultural Roots & Continuities, 2 vols., Vol. II: The Humanities & the Modern World. 4th ed. 608p. (C). 1993. pap. text 51.56 (*0-669-27576-X*) HM Trade Div.

— The Humanities Vol. II: Cultural Roots & Continuities: The Humanities & the Modern World. 5th ed. 624p. (C). 1996. pap. text 51.56 (*0-669-41658-4*) HM Trade Div.

— The Humanities: Cultural Roots & Continuities Vol. I: Three Cultural Roots. 5th ed. 544p. (C). 1996. pap. text 51.56 (*0-669-41657-6*) HM Trade Div.

— The Humanities: Cultural Roots & Continuities Vol. I: Three Cultural Roots. 5th ed. (C). 1997. pap. text, teacher ed. 11.96 (*0-669-41661-4*) HM Trade Div.

Brown, Cherie R. The Art of Coalition Building: A Guide for Community Leaders. LC 84-70911. 56p. 1984. pap. 3.50 (*0-87495-053-8*) Am Jewish Comm.

— Face to Face: Black-Jewish Campus Dialogues. LC 87-71222. 31p. (Orig.). 1987. pap. 5.00 (*0-87495-092-9*) Am Jewish Comm.

Brown, Cherie R. & Mazza, George J. Healing into Action: A Leadership Guide for Creating Diverse Communities. LC 97-92381. 98p. 1997. pap. 14.95 (*0-9659731-0-7*) Natl Coal Build.

Brown, Cheryl & Ruddell, Anita. Fancy Dressing. LC 95-60778. (Fun to Do Ser.). (Illus.). 32p. (J). (gr. 3 up). 1995. lib. bdg. 15.95 (*1-887238-01-8*) Fitzgerald.

Brown, Cheryl, jt. auth. see Hatch, Evelyn.

Brown, Cheryl L. & Olson, Karen, eds. Feminist Criticism: Essays on Theory, Poetry & Prose. LC 78-8473. 383p. 1978. 29.00 (*0-8108-1143-X*) Scarecrow.

Brown, Chester. Little Man: Short Strips, 1979-1994. 1998. pap. text 14.95 (*1-896597-13-0*, Pub. by Drawn & Quarterly) LPC InBook.

Brown, Chip. Afterwards, You're a Genius: Faith, Medicine, & the Metaphysics of Healing. LC 98-36015. 416p. 1998. 24.95 (*1-57322-113-9*, Riverhead Books) Putnam Pub Group.

***Brown, Chip.** Afterwards, You're a Genius: Faith, Medicine, & the Metaphysics of Healing. LC 98-63015. 2000. reprint ed. pap. 13.95 (*1-57322-776-5*, Riverhd Trade) Berkley Pub.

Brown, Chris. International Relations Theory: New Normative Approaches. 272p. (C). 1993. pap. 20.50 (*0-231-08151-0*); text 61.50 (*0-231-08150-2*) Col U Pr.

***Brown, Chris.** The Revised Edition of the Completely Unauthorized Saga of the Life & Times of Mary Swarthout: A Collection of Poems. rev. ed. Wightman, Christina C., ed. 55p. 1999. pap. 14.95 (*1-888911-15-8*) Benson Smythe.

An Asterisk (*) at the beginning of an entry indicates that the title is appearing for the first time.

Brown, Chris. Selected Experiments in College Physics. (C). 1996. pap. text 12.22 (*1-56870-261-2*) RonJon Pub.

***Brown, Chris.** The Spiritual Revolution: A Possible Spiritual Path for the New Millennium. Wightman, Christina C., ed. 2000. pap. write for info. (*1-888911-16-6*) Benson Smythe.

Brown, Chris. Understand International Relationship. LC 96-50057. 288p. 1997. pap. 19.95 (*0-312-17338-5*) St Martin.

Brown, Chris & Earley, Dave. The Pledge: Calling Adolescents to Maturity, Purity, & Ministry. Spear, Cindy G., ed. 127p. 1997. ring bd. 99.95 incl. audio (*1-57052-081-X*) Chrch Grwth VA.

Brown, Chris J. & Nielsen, J., eds. Silos: Fundamentals of Theory Behaviour & Design. 856p. (C). 1998. pap. 150.00 (*0-419-21580-8*) Thomson Learn.

Brown, Chris W., III. Cruising Guide to New York Waterways & Lake Champlain. Young, Claiborne S., ed. LC 98-17842. (Illus.). 480p. 1999. pap. 28.95 (*1-56554-250-9*) Pelican.

Brown, Christopher. Discovering Bows for the Double Bass. Otis, Caroline, ed. Deligny, Annick, tr. (ENG & FRE.). 275p. 300.00 (*0-9642895-0-4*); lib. bdg. 500.00 (*0-9642895-1-2*) Beaux Arts Edits.

***Brown, Christopher.** Dutch Genre Paintings from the Maseritshuis. 1999. pap. 29.95 (*1-85444-126-4*, Pub. by Ashmolean Mus) A Schwartz & Co.

Brown, Christopher. Dutch Painting. (Color Library). (Illus.). 128p. (C). 1993. pap. 14.95 (*0-7148-2865-3*, Pub. by Phaidon Pres) Phaidon Pr.

— Money & Consumer Durable Spending. rev. ed. LC 92-34573. (Financial Sector of the American Economy Ser.). 192p. 1992. text 20.00 (*0-8153-1211-3*) Garland.

— The Paintings of Carel Fabritius: Complete Edition with a Catalogue Raisonne. LC 80-69741. (Illus.). 168p. 1981. text 105.00 (*0-8014-1394-X*) Cornell U Pr.

— Rembrandt: The Master & His Workshop, Paintings. LC 91-65959. (Illus.). 360p. 1991. 75.00 (*0-300-05149-2*) Yale U Pr.

— Riley's Search, Vol. 1. Wightman, Kimberly J., ed. (Illus.). 90p. 1998. pap. write for info. (*1-888911-10-7*) Benson Smythe.

***Brown, Christopher.** The Royal Society of Painter-Printmakers: Dutch Genre Paintings from the Mauritshuls Collection. (Illus.). 96p. 1999. pap. 24.95 (*1-85444-119-1*, Pub. by Ashmolean Mus) A Schwartz & Co.

Brown, Christopher. Rubens's Landscapes: Making & Meaning. (Illus.). 128p. 1997. 35.00 (*0-300-06947-2*); pap. 19.95 (*0-300-07794-7*) Yale U Pr.

— The Tao of Travel: A Traveler's Tale of Oriental Wisdom for the Road. Wightman, Kimberly J., ed. LC 98-60762. 90p. 1998. pap. 21.00 (*1-888911-08-5*) Benson Smythe.

— Van Dyck Drawings. (Illus.). 294p. 1991. 95.00 (*0-8109-3914-2*, Pub. by Abrams) Time Warner.

— Web Site Construction Kit for Windows NT. 500p. 1996. 49.99 (*1-57521-047-9*) Sams.

Brown, Christopher, ed. Advances in Computer Vision, Vol. I. 240p. (C). 1988. text 49.95 (*0-89859-648-3*) L Erlbaum Assocs.

Brown, Christopher, et al, eds. Rembrandt: The Master & His Workshop, 2 vols. (Illus.). 640p. (C). 1991. 145.00 (*0-300-05191-3*) Yale U Pr.

— Rembrandt: The Master & His Workshop - Drawings & Etchings. LC 91-65961. (Illus.). 360p. (C). 1991. 70.00 (*0-300-05151-4*) Yale U Pr.

Brown, Christopher & Bertone, Joseph. The 5 Minute Veterinary Consult: Equine. 1,184p. 85.00 (*0-683-30605-7*) Lppncott W & W.

Brown, Christopher & Wright, Richard D. Directory of Spatial Datasets to Support Environmental Research along the United States-Mexico Border. LC 96-118553. 116p. 1995. text 5.00 (*0-925613-15-0*) SDSU Inst Reg Studies.

Brown, Christopher, jt. auth. see Traub-Dargatz, Josie L.

***Brown, Christopher K.** Encyclopedia of Travel Literature. 2000. lib. bdg. 75.00 (*0-87436-940-1*) ABC-CLIO.

Brown, Christopher L. & Zimmerman, Scott. Web Site Construction Kit for Windows 95. LC 95-72942. 560p. 1996. 49.99 (*1-57521-072-X*) Sams.

Brown, Christopher M. Problems in Equine Medicine. LC 88-27255. (Illus.). 302p. 1989. text 50.00 (*0-8121-1171-0*) Lppncott W & W.

Brown, Christopher M., ed. Advances in Computer Vision, Vol. 2. 200p. 1987. 49.95 (*0-8058-0092-1*) L Erlbaum Assocs.

Brown, Christopher M. & Terzopoulos, Demetri, eds. Real-Time Computer Vision. LC 96-26688. (Publications of the Newton Institute: No. 3). (Illus.). 248p. (C). 1995. text 57.95 (*0-521-47278-4*) Cambridge U Pr.

Brown, Christopher P. The Political & Social Economy of Commodity Control. LC 79-88568. 394p. 1980. 75.00 (*0-275-90458-X*, C0458, Praeger Pubs) Greenwood.

Brown, Christopher W., jt. auth. see Kahru, Mati.

Brown, Christopher W., jt. ed. see Kahru, Mati.

Brown, Christy. Down All the Days. 266p. (C). 1991. pap. 9.95 (*0-7493-9179-0*, A0570) Heinemann.

— My Left Foot. 192p. (C). 1995. reprint ed. pap. 9.95 (*0-7493-9177-4*, A0571) Heinemann.

— A Shadow on Summer. 274p. (C). 1991. pap. 9.95 (*0-685-63036-6*, A0573) Heinemann.

— A Shadow on Summer. LC 74-79420. 228p. 1974. pap. 9.95 (*0-8128-8530-9*, Scrbrough Hse) Madison Bks UPA.

— Wild Grow the Lilies. 304p. (C). 1991. pap. 9.95 (*0-7493-9183-9*, A0574) Heinemann.

— Wild Grow the Lilies. LC 75-37905. 304p. 1976. reprint ed. pap. 9.95 (*0-8128-2470-9*, Scrbrough Hse) Madison Bks UPA.

Brown, Cindy & Houghton, Bill, eds. Bi-State Bicycle Tours: Bicycle Tours in & Around the St. Louis Metropolitan Area. 4th rev. ed. (Illus.). 116p. 1997. pap. 12.00 (*0-9661322-0-3*) Hostelling Intl.

Brown, Cindy, ed. see Cornell, Gary & Strain, Troy.

Brown, Cindy K. Vermont Wildlife Viewing Guide. LC 94-19270. (Falcon Guides Ser.). (Illus.). 64p. (Orig.). 1994. pap. 8.95 (*1-56044-291-3*) Falcon Pub Inc.

Brown, Cinita D. The Black Kettle Ride. LC 96-27665. (Illus.). (J). 1997. write for info. (*1-56763-291-2*); pap. write for info. (*1-56763-292-0*) Ozark Pub.

Brown, Clair. American Standards of Living: 1918-1988. 384p. 1995. 43.95 (*1-55786-371-7*) Blackwell Pubs.

— Louisiana Trees & Shrubs. 1965. pap. 20.00 (*0-87511-012-6*) Claitors.

Brown, Clair & Pechman, Joseph A., eds. Gender in the Workplace. LC 87-668. 316p. 1987. 36.95 (*0-8157-1170-0*); pap. 18.95 (*0-8157-1169-7*) Brookings.

Brown, Clair, et al. Work & Pay in the United States & Japan: Employment & Pay Systems in Japan & the United States. LC 96-39268. (Illus.). 256p. 1997. 39.95 (*0-19-511521-X*) OUP.

Brown, Claire D., et al, eds. Conflict & Diversity. LC 97-21692. (Communication Ser.). (Illus.). 320p. (C). 1997. text 65.00 (*1-57273-070-6*); pap. text 26.50 (*1-57273-071-4*) Hampton Pr NJ.

***Brown, Clare & Brown, Karen.** Karen Brown's Austria: Charming Inns & Itineraries. LC 00-37938. (Karen Brown's Country Inn Ser.). (Illus.). 2001. pap. write for info. (*1-928901-00-X*) K Browns Guides.

— Karen Brown's Italy: Charming Inns & Itineraries. LC 00-39734. (Karen Brown's Country Inn Ser.). (Illus.). 2001. pap. write for info. (*1-928901-13-1*) K Browns Guides.

Brown, Clare & Brown, Karen. Karen Brown's Portugal Charming Inns & Itineraries. LC 97-31220. (Karen Brown's Country Inn Ser.). (Illus.). 250p. 1998. 25.00 (*0-930328-70-1*) Travel Print.

***Brown, Clare & Wearden, Jennifer.** Samplers: From the Victoria & Albert Museum. (Illus.). 144p. 2000. 45.00 (*1-85177-309-6*, Pub. by V&A Ent) Antique Collect.

Brown, Clare, jt. auth. see Brown, Karen.

Brown, Clare, jt. auth. see Sauvage, Cynthia.

Brown, Clarence, ed. The Portable Twentieth-Century Russian Reader. rev. ed. LC 92-39863. 624p. 1993. pap. 15.95 (*0-14-015107-9*, Penguin Bks) Viking Penguin.

Brown, Clarence, tr. & intro. see Zamyatin, Yevgeny.

Brown, Clarence A. & Zoellner, Ronald. The Strategy of Composition: A Rhetoric with Readings. LC 68-13470. 704p. reprint ed. pap. 200.00 (*0-608-30130-2*, 201247000081) Bks Demand.

Brown, Clarence D., et al. Vocational Evaluation Systems & Software: A Consumer's Guide. LC 94-199233. 180p. (C). 1993. pap. 24.00 (*0-916671-99-2*) TRR.

***Brown, Claud L. & Kirkman, L. Katherine.** Trees of Georgia & Adjacent States. (Illus.). 384p. 2000. pap. 24.95 (*0-88192-480-6*) Timber.

Brown, Claude. Manchild in the Promised Land. 416p. 1990. 55.00 (*0-02-517325-1*, Hudson Rvr Edtn) S&S Trade.

— Manchild in the Promised Land. LC 90-34905. 416p. 1999. per. 12.00 (*0-684-86418-5*, Touchstone) S&S Trade Pap.

Brown, Claudia. Chinese Cloisonne: The Clague Collection. LC 80-80709. (Illus.). 181p. (Orig.). 1980. 30.00 (*0-910407-05-3*) Phoenix Art.

Brown, Claudia & Chou, Ju-Hsi. Heritage of the Brush: The Roy & Marilyn Papp Collection of Chinese Painting. Rabiner, Donald, ed. (Illus.). 128p. (Orig.). 1989. pap. 29.00 (*0-910407-22-3*) Phoenix Art.

— Transcending Turmoil: Painting at the Close of China's Empire, 1796-1911. LC 92-50375. (Illus.). 368p. 1992. pap. 49.95 (*0-910407-26-6*) Phoenix Art.

Brown, Claudia, et al. Minol Araki. LC 98-50148. 1999. write for info. (*0-910407-36-3*) Phoenix Art.

Brown, Claudia, jt. auth. see Chou, Ju-hsi.

Brown, Claudia, jt. auth. see Shangraw, Clarence F.

Brown, Claudia, ed. see Mowry, Robert D.

Brown, Claudia, ed. see Phoenix Art Museum Staff & Eden Siu-Hung Yu.

Brown, Clementina, tr. see Mina, Hanna.

Brown, Clementina R., tr. see Kabbani, Nizar.

Brown, Cliff. Racial Conflicts & Violence in the Labor Market: Roots in the 1919 Steel Strike. rev. ed. LC 98-35310. (Studies in the History of American Labor). 225p. 1998. 60.00 (*0-8153-3176-2*) Garland.

Brown, Cliff, jt. auth. see Jarrett, Michael.

Brown, Clifford. Leibniz & Strawson. (Introductiones Ser.). 120p. 1990. 33.00 (*0-685-38867-0*) Philosophia Pr.

Brown, Clifford M. Engraved Gems: Survivals & Revivals. (Illus.). 1996. 50.00 (*0-300-07697-5*) Yale U Pr.

— Our Accustomed Discourse on the Antique: Cesare Gonzaga & Gerolamo Garimberto, Two Renaissance Collectors of Greco-Roman Art. LC 92-29917. (Reference Library of the Humanities: Vol. 1438). 336p. 1993. text 35.00 (*0-8153-0228-2*) Garland.

Brown, Clifford M., ed. Engraved Gems: Survivals & Revivals. LC 97-225325. (Studies in the History of Art Ser.: No. 54). (Illus.). 300p. 1997. 50.00 (*0-89468-271-7*) Natl Gallery Art.

Brown, Clifford M. & Delmarcel, Guy. Tapestries for the Courts of Federico II, Ercole, & Ferrante Gonzaga, 1522-63. LC 95-25130. (College Art Association Monograph on the Fine Arts Ser.: Vol. LII). (Illus.). 232p. 1996. text 50.00 (*0-295-97513-X*) U of Wash Pr.

Brown, Clifford W. & Brown, Clifford W. Music at West Virginia University, 1897-1987: The West Virginia School of Music, 1897. Luchok, John & Wilson, C. B., eds. (Illus.). 100p. (Orig.). 1989. pap. write for info. (*0-925500-00-3*) WV Univ Pubns Servs.

Brown, Clifford W., Jr. & Walker, Robert J., compiled by. A Campaign of Ideas: The Nineteen Eighty Anderson-Lucey Platform, 76. LC 84-6564. (Contributions in American Studies: No. 76). 486p. 1984. 65.00 (*0-313-24535-5*, BCA/) Greenwood.

Brown, Clifford W., Jr., et al. Serious Money: Fundraising & Contributing in Presidential Nomination Campaigns. (Illus.). 198p. (C). 1995. text 59.95 (*0-521-44058-0*); pap. text 19.95 (*0-521-49780-9*) Cambridge U Pr.

Brown, Clifford W., jt. auth. see Brown, Clifford W.

Brown, Clifton F., compiled by. Ethiopian Perspectives: A Bibliographical Guide to the History of Ethiopia, 5. LC 77-89111. (African Special Bibliographic Ser.: No. 5). 264p. 1978. lib. bdg. 65.00 (*0-8371-9850-X*, BET/) Greenwood.

Brown, Clifton F., jt. auth. see Williams, Ethel L.

***Brown, Clint.** Make My Baby Jump. Doggett, Gerald, ed. 138p. 1998. 10.00 (*0-9672114-0-9*, BK MMBJ 4000) Tribe Music.

Brown, Clint, ed. Artist to Artist: Inspiration & Advice from Artists Past & Present. (Illus.). 272p. 1998. 24.95 (*0-943097-05-3*); pap. 14.95 (*0-943097-04-5*) Jackson Creek Pr.

Brown, Clint & McLean, Cheryl. Drawing from Life. 2nd ed. LC 96-76313. 272p. (C). 1996. pap. text 57.50 (*0-15-501511-7*) Harcourt Coll Pubs.

— Economics/Macroeconomics: Principles & Policies. 7th ed. 272p. (C). 1997. pap. text 33.50 (*0-03-011727-5*, Pub. by Harcourt Coll Pubs) Harcourt.

Brown, Clint, jt. auth. see McLean, Cheryl.

Brown, Clint, jt. auth. see Parsley, Rod.

Brown, Clive. Classical & Romantic Performing Practice, 1750-1900. LC 97-50572. (Illus.). 680p. 2000. text 110.00 (*0-19-816165-4*) OUP.

— Jessonda. (Selected Works of Louis Spohr, 1784-1859: Vol. 2). 300p. 1989. text 30.00 (*0-8240-1501-0*) Garland.

Brown, Clive, ed. Concertos: Concertante for Violin & Cello, Vol. 7. (Selected Works of Louis Spohr, 1784-1859). 200p. 1987. text 25.00 (*0-8240-1506-1*) Garland.

— Des Heilands Letzte Stunden: Des Heilands Letzte Stunden, Vol. 5. (Selected Works of Louis Spohr, 1784-1859). 260p. 1987. text 25.00 (*0-8240-1504-5*) Garland.

— Die Letzten Dinge, Vol. 4. LC 87-75818. (Selected Works of Louis Spohr, 1784-1859). 248p. 1987. text 25.00 (*0-8240-1503-7*) Garland.

— Pietro Von Abano. (Selected Works of Louis Spohr, 1784-1859: Vol. 3). 500p. 1989. reprint ed. text 45.00 (*0-8240-1502-9*) Garland.

— Symphonies, Vol. 6: Symphony No. 1 in E-flat, op. 20; Symphony No. 2 in D Minor, op. 49; Symphony No. 5 in C Minor, op. 102. (Selected Works of Louis Spohr, 1784-1859). 440p. 1988. text 45.00 (*0-8240-1505-3*) Garland.

Brown, Cockerell. Prospects for the British Economy. 59.95 (*1-85628-844-7*) Ashgate Pub Co.

***Brown, Coen.** Understanding of Microstation. LC 98-34139. 524p. (C). 1998. pap. text 57.00 (*0-13-792680-4*) P-H.

Brown, Colin. Christianity & Western Thought - a History of Philosophers, Ideas & Movements Vol. 1: From the Ancient World to the Age of Enlightenment. LC 89-48564. 447p. 1990. 29.99 (*0-8308-1752-2*, 1752) InterVarsity.

— Crash Course on Christian Ethics. 1998. pap. 13.95 (*0-340-72150-2*, Pub. by Hodder & Stought Ltd) Trafalgar.

— Haynes Honda Accord Owners Workshop Manual, No. 1221: 1984-1989. (Illus.). 1986. pap. 17.95 (*1-85010-615-0*) Haynes Manuals.

— History & Faith: A Personal Exploration. 128p. (Orig.). 1987. pap. 8.95 (*0-310-21961-2*, 11127P) Zondervan.

***Brown, Colin.** Independent Film Channel's Guide to Cinema's New Outsiders. 250p. 1999. pap. text 19.95 (*1-57859-097-3*) Visible Ink Pr.

— Karl Barth & the Christian Message. 164p. 1998. pap. 18.00 (*1-57910-204-2*) Wipf & Stock.

Brown, Colin. Philosophy & the Christian Faith. LC 68-58083. 320p. (Orig.). 1969. pap. 18.99 (*0-87784-712-6*, 712) InterVarsity.

Brown, Colin. That You May Believe: Miracles & Faith Then & Now. 230p. 1996. pap. 26.00 (*0-9653517-4-2*) Wipf & Stock.

Brown, Colin, ed. Indonesia. LC 96-175737. 216p. 1997. pap. text 24.95 (*1-86448-068-8*, Pub. by Allen & Unwin Pty) Paul & Co Pubs.

— The New International Dictionary of New Testament Theology, 4 vols. 1986. 169.99 (*0-310-33238-9*, 11137) Zondervan.

Brown, Colin, jt. auth. see Brown, Diana.

Brown, Colin, jt. auth. see Chadwick-Jones, J. K.

Brown, Colin, jt. auth. see Cribb, Robert.

Brown, Colin, tr. see Von Weizsacker, Ernst U.

Brown, Colin D. Dictionary of Metallurgy. LC 97-27383. 316p. 1997. 150.00 (*0-471-96155-8*) Wiley.

Brown, Colin H. Stalemate in Korea & How We Coped. (Illus.). 150p. 1997. 35.00 (*0-646-22368-2*) Letter of Marque.

Brown, Colin M. & Hagoort, Peter, eds. The Neurocognition of Language. LC 98-50252. (Illus.). 430p. 1999. text 95.00 (*0-19-852448-X*) OUP.

Brown, Constance. Aerodynamic Trading. LC 95-74771. (Illus.). 312p. 1995. 35.00 (*0-932750-42-7*) New Classics Lib.

— Technical Analysis for the Trading Professional: Strategies & Techniques for Today's Turbulent Financial Markets. LC 95-15906. (Irwin Trader's Edge Ser.). 341p. 1999. 49.95 (*0-07-012062-5*) McGraw.

***Brown, Corrie & Bolin, Carole A.** Emerging Diseases of Animals. LC 00-40167. 2000. write for info. (*1-55581-201-5*) ASM Pr.

Brown, Cory. A Warm Trend. LC 88-64018. 54p. (Orig.). 1989. pap. 7.95 (*0-930501-18-7*); pap. 7.95 (*0-930501-19-5*) Swallows Tale Pr.

Brown County Historical Society Staff & Bailey, Dorothy. History & Families of Brown County, Indiana, 1836-1991. LC 90-71731. (Illus.). 336p. 1991. 55.00 (*1-56311-025-3*) Turner Pub KY.

Brown, Courtney. Ballots of Tumult: A Portrait of Volatility in American Voting. (Illus.). 248p. 1991. text 42.50 (*0-472-10250-8*, 10250) U of Mich Pr.

— Chaos & Catastrophe Theories: Nonlinear Modeling in the Social Sciences. (Quantitative Applications in the Social Science Ser.: Vol. 107). 96p. (C). 1995. pap. 10.95 (*0-8039-5847-1*) Sage.

— Cosmic Explorers: Scientific Remote Viewing, Extraterrestrials & a Message for Mankind. LC 98-53341. (Illus.). 260p. 1999. 24.95 (*0-525-94430-3*) NAL.

***Brown, Courtney.** Cosmic Explorers: Scientific Remote Viewing, Extraterrestrials & a Message for Mankind. 400p. 2000. mass mkt. 6.99 (*0-451-20105-1*) Signet.

Brown, Courtney. Cosmic Voyage. 400p. 1997. mass mkt. 6.99 (*0-451-19026-2*, Sig) NAL.

— Serpents in the Sand: Essays on the Nonlinear Nature of Politics & Human Destiny. LC 95-11859. 192p. (C). 1995. text 39.50 (*0-472-10643-0*, 10643) U of Mich Pr.

Brown, Courtney C. The Dean Meant Business. LC 83-20625. 288p. (Orig.). 1985. 17.50 (*0-9612584-0-3*) Grad Sch Bus NY.

Brown, Craig. Animals at Home. (Illus.). 32p. (J). (ps-3). 1996. pap. 6.95 (*1-57098-077-2*) Roberts Rinehart.

***Brown, Craig.** Little Book of Chaos: Tips to Irritate. LC 98-56277. 96p. 1999. pap. 7.95 (*1-57322-759-5*, Riverhead Books) Putnam Pub Group.

— Optimum Healing. 1998. pap. 19.95 (*0-7126-7107-2*, Pub. by Random) Trafalgar.

Brown, Craig. Tractor. LC 94-19367. (Illus.). 24p. (J). (ps-3). 1995. 16.00 (*0-688-10499-1*, Grenwillow Bks) HarpC Child Bks.

***Brown, Craig.** Working in the Voluntary Sector: How to Find Rewarding Work in Charities & Voluntary Organizations. (Illus.). 144p. (Orig.). 1998. pap. 19.95 (*1-85703-367-1*) How To Bks.

Brown, Craig, ed. La Historia Ilustrada de Canada (The Illustrated History of Canada) (SPA.). 664p. 1994. 30.99 (*968-16-4019-5*, Pub. by Fondo) Continental Bk.

***Brown, Craig, ed.** The Illustrated History of Canada. 3rd ed. (Illus.). 600p. 2000. pap. 19.95 (*1-55263-146-X*, Pub. by Key Porter) Firefly Bks Ltd.

Brown, Craig McFarland, jt. auth. see Krudwig, Vickie L.

***Brown-Crocker, Sandra.** Intuition Handbook: A Reminder for the Curious. (Illus.). 44p. 1999. pap. 12.00 (*0-9676397-0-0*) S Brown-Crocker.

Brown, Crosland. Tombley's Walk. 416p. 1991. mass mkt. 4.50 (*0-380-76097-5*, Avon Bks) Morrow Avon.

Brown, Curtis. Dog Locomotion & Gait Analysis. deluxe ed. 160p. 1995. pap. 25.00 (*0-614-04520-7*) Donald R Hoflin.

Brown, Curtis, jt. auth. see Luper-Foy, Steven.

Brown, Curtis, jt. auth. see Luper, Steven.

Brown, Curtis, jt. ed. see Luper-Foy, Steven.

Brown, Curtis L. From a Brown Study, Set. (Illus.). (Orig.). 1993. pap. write for info. (*1-882900-02-2*) Tech Trans Bur.

— From a Brown Study, Vol. 1: Preaching Is Easy - Living Is Tough. (Illus.). (Orig.). 1993. pap. 9.95 (*1-882900-00-6*) Tech Trans Bur.

— From a Brown Study, Vol. 2: Poems That Rhyme - Most of the Time. (Illus.). (Orig.). 1993. pap. 9.95 (*1-882900-01-4*) Tech Trans Bur.

Brown, Curtis M., et al. Brown's Boundary Control & Legal Principles. 4th ed. LC 94-46173. 432p. 1995. 99.00 (*0-471-04312-5*) Wiley.

— Evidence & Procedures for Boundary Location. 3rd ed. LC 00-639. 528p. 1993. 99.00 (*0-471-55219-4*) Wiley.

Brown, Cynthia & Reid, Jill. Twenty Years On: New Federal & State Roles to Achieve Equity in Education. 130p. 1987. 14.95 (*0-89788-099-4*) CPA Washington.

Brown, Cynthia A., jt. auth. see Purdom, Paul W.

Brown, Cynthia J. Poets, Patrons, & Printers: Crisis of Authority in Late Medieval France. (Illus.). 320p. 1995. text 42.50 (*0-8014-3071-2*) Cornell U Pr.

— The Shaping of History & Poetry in Late Medieval France. LC 85-61597. 215p. 1986. 18.95 (*0-917786-10-6*) Summa Pubns.

Brown, Cynthia S. Alexander Meiklejohn: Teacher of Freedom. Ginger, Ann Fagan, ed. LC 81-81355. (Studies in Law & Social Change: No. 2). (Illus.). 304p. 1981. 13.95 (*0-913876-16-X*, 176); pap. 7.95 (*0-913876-17-8*, 177) Meiklejohn Civ Lib.

— Like It Was: A Complete Guide to Writing Oral History. (Illus.). 144p. (Orig.). (C). 1988. pap. 13.95 (*0-915924-12-9*) Tchrs & Writers Coll.

Brown, Cynthia S., ed. Ready from Within: A First Person Narrative: Septima Clark & the Civil Rights Movement. LC 90-80668. (Illus.). 145p. (C). 1990. reprint ed. 29.95 (*0-86543-173-6*); reprint ed. pap. 9.95 (*0-86543-174-4*) Africa World.

Brown, Cynthia S., jt. auth. see Jorgensen, Karen.

Brown, D. Capetown Ambush Quintet. 1995. pap. text 20.00 (*0-7935-4824-1*, 00000570) H Leonard.

— Land Acquisition. 3rd ed. 186p. 1991. boxed set 126.00 (*0-409-49102-0*, Austral, MICHIE) LEXIS Pub.

— Land Acquisition. 4th ed. LC 97-157537. 1996. write for info. (*0-409-31063-8*, MICHIE) LEXIS Pub.

Brown, D. 150 Solitaire Games. 144p. 1991. pap. 10.00 (*0-06-092315-6*) HarpC.

— A Practical Guide to Competency Related Pay. (Financial Times Management Briefings Ser.). 1998. pap. 89.50 (*0-273-63751-7*, Pub. by F T P-H) Trans-Atl Phila.

Brown, D. Principles of Art Therapies. 1998. pap. 11.00 (*0-7225-3495-7*) Thorsons PA.

— Traffic Offences & Accidents. 3rd ed. 350p. 1996. pap. write for info. (*0-409-31090-5*, MICHIE) LEXIS Pub.

Brown, D. & Rothery, P. Computing Examples Supplement to Models in Biology: Mathematics, Statistics, & Computing. LC 92-41229. 708p. 1993. pap. 84.95 (*0-471-93322-8*) Wiley.

Brown, D. & Smirnov, V. I. Course in Higher Mathematics Vol. 5: Integration & Functional Analysis. LC 63-10134. (International Series of Monographs on Pure & Applied Mathematics: Vol. 62). 1964. 282.00 (*0-08-010211-5*, Pub. by Pergamon Repr) Franklin.

— Course in Higher Mathematics, Pt. 2 Vol. 3: Complex Variables Special Functions. LC 63-10134. (International Series of Monographs on Pure & Applied Mathematics: Vol. 60). 314.00 (*0-08-010209-3*, Pub. by Pergamon Repr) Franklin.

— Course of Higher Math, Vol. 5. LC 63-10134. (Adiwes International Series in Math: Vol. 62). 1964. 282.00 (*0-08-013719-9*, Pub. by Pergamon Repr) Franklin.

— Course of Higher Mathematics, Vol. 1. LC 63-10134. (International Series of Monographs on Pure & Applied Mathematics: Vol. 57). 1964. 241.00 (*0-08-010206-9*, Pub. by Pergamon Repr) Franklin.

— Course of Higher Mathematics, Vol. 2. LC 63-10340. (International Series of Monographs on Pure & Applied Mathematics: Vol. 58). 1964. 292.00 (*0-08-010207-7*, Pub. by Pergamon Repr) Franklin.

— Course of Higher Mathematics Series, 6 vols., Set. 1964. 1637.00 (*0-08-010212-3*, Pub. by Pergamon Repr) Franklin.

Brown, D., jt. auth. see Belousov, S.

Brown, D., jt. auth. see Berman, Gerald.

Brown, D., jt. auth. see Bermant, A.

Brown, D., jt. auth. see Smirnov, V. I.

***Brown, D. A. G.** CAD for Model Engineers. (Workshop Practice Ser.: No. 29). (Illus.). 95p. 1999. pap. 19.95 (*1-85486-189-1*, Pub. by Nexus Special Interests) Trans-Atl Phila.

Brown, D. C., jt. ed. see McKersie, B. D.

Brown, D. Catherine. Pastor & Laity in the Theology of Jean Gerson. 420p. 1987. 85.00 (*0-521-33029-7*) Cambridge U Pr.

Brown, D. Clayton. Dwight D. Eisenhower. LC 97-4368. (United States Presidents Ser.). (Illus.). 128p. (YA). (gr. 5 up). 1998. lib. bdg. 20.95 (*0-89490-940-1*) Enslow Pubs.

— Electricity for Rural America: The Fight for the REA, 29. LC 79-8287. (Contributions in Economics & Economic History Ser.: No. 29). (Illus.). 178p. 1980. 52.95 (*0-313-21478-6*, BEF/, Greenwood Pr) Greenwood.

Brown, D. F. A Monographic Study of the Fern Genus Woodsia. (Illus.). 1964. 48.00 (*3-7682-5416-X*) Lubrecht & Cramer.

Brown, D. G., ed. see Gilbert, Michael J.

Brown, D. H., ed. Lichen Physiology & Cell Biology. LC 85-24452. 374p. 1985. 85.00 (*0-306-42200-X*, Plenum Trade) Perseus Pubng.

Brown, D. J. Fused Pyrimidines: Pteridines, Vol. 24, Pt. 3, Pteridines. LC 68-4274. (Chemistry of Heterocyclic Compounds, a Series of Monographs: Vol. 24, Pt. 3). 730p. 1988. 595.00 (*0-471-83041-0*) Wiley.

***Brown, D. J.** The Pyridazines. LC 99-28985. (Chemistry of Heterocyclic Compounds, a Series of Monographs). 672p. 2000. text 450.00 (*0-471-25137-2*, Wiley-Interscience) Wiley.

Brown, D. J. Quinazolines Supplement I, Vol. 55. LC 96-6182. (Chemistry of Heterocyclic Compounds Ser.: Vol. 55). 756p. 1996. 385.00 (*0-471-14565-3*) Wiley.

Brown, D. J., et al. The Pyrimidines, Vol. 52. LC 92-35909. (Chemistry of Heterocyclic Compounds, a Series of Monographs: vOL. 52). 1509p. 1994. 599.00 (*0-471-50656-7*) Wiley.

Brown, D. J., jt. auth. see Taylor, C. E.

***Brown, D K.** Grand Fleet: Warship Design & Development, 1906-1922. 1999. 59.95 (*1-55750-315-X*) Naval Inst Pr.

Brown, D. K. Paddle Warships: The Earliest Steam Powered Fighting Ships, 1815-1850. (Conway's Ship Type Ser.). (Illus.). 128p. 1995. 41.95 (*0-85177-616-7*) Naval Inst Pr.

Brown, D. R. & Keith-Smith, J. E., eds. Frontiers of Mathematical Psychology: Essays in Honor of Clyde Coombs. (Recent Research in Psychology Ser.). (Illus.). xxvi, 202p. 1990. 63.95 (*0-387-97451-2*) Spr-Verlag.

Brown, D. R. & Veroff, J., eds. Frontiers of Motivational Psychology. (Recent Research in Psychology Ser.). xviii, 194p. 1986. pap. 38.00 (*0-387-96444-4*) Spr-Verlag.

Brown, D. S., et al. The Geological Evolution of Australia & New Zealand. 1968. 189.00 (*0-08-012278-7*, Pub. by Pergamon Repr) Franklin.

Brown, Dakota B. Data on Some Virginia Families. (Illus.). 282p. 1979. 25.00 (*0-686-63646-5*) VA Bk.

Brown, Dale. Battle Born. LC 99-38390. 416p. 1999. 1.11 (*0-553-11123-X*) Bantam.

***Brown, Dale.** Battle Born. LC 99-36763. 1999. 24.95 (*0-375-40861-4*) Wheeler Pub.

Brown, Dale. Chains of Command. 528p. 1994. reprint ed. mass mkt. 7.99 (*0-425-14207-8*) Berkley Pub.

— Day of the Cheetah. 528p. 1990. mass mkt. 7.99 (*0-425-12043-0*) Berkley Pub.

— Fatal Terrain. 474p. 1998. mass mkt. 7.99 (*0-425-16260-5*) Berkley Pub.

— Flight of the Old Dog. Breslin, Ed, ed. 416p. 1988. reprint ed. mass mkt. 7.99 (*0-425-10893-7*) Berkley Pub.

— Hammerheads. 560p. 1991. mass mkt. 6.99 (*0-425-12645-5*) Berkley Pub.

— Night of the Hawk. 576p. 1993. mass mkt. 7.99 (*0-425-13661-2*) Berkley Pub.

— Night of the Hawk. large type ed. LC 92-33396. 906p. 1994. reprint ed. lib. bdg. 22.95 (*1-56054-586-0*) Thorndike Pr.

— Shadows of Steel. 384p. 1997. mass mkt. 7.99 (*0-425-15716-4*) Berkley Pub.

— Shadows of Steel. LC 96-24248. 400p. 1996. 24.95 (*0-399-14139-1*) Thorndike Pr.

— Shadows of Steel. large type ed. LC 96-24248. 1996. 26.95 (*0-7862-0779-5*) Thorndike Pr.

— Shadows of Steel. large type ed. 1997. pap. 24.95 (*0-7862-0780-9*) Thorndike Pr.

— Silver Tower. 1989. mass mkt. 6.99 (*0-425-11529-1*) Berkley Pub.

— Sky Masters. 496p. 1992. mass mkt. 7.99 (*0-425-13262-5*) Berkley Pub.

— Storming Heaven. 496p. 1995. mass mkt. 7.99 (*0-425-14723-1*) Berkley Pub.

— Storming Heaven. large type ed. LC 94-34298. 732p. 1994. lib. bdg. 25.95 (*0-7862-0334-X*) Thorndike Pr.

— The Tin Man: He's Fighting a New War & the Last Thing He Needs Is a Heart. LC 98-44850. (Large Print Book Ser.). 1998. 25.95 (*1-56895-684-3*) Wheeler Pub.

— The Tin Man: He's Fighting a New War & the Last Thing He Needs Is a Heart. 464p. 1999. reprint ed. mass mkt. 6.99 (*0-553-58000-0*, Bantam Classics) Bantam.

Brown, Dale, ed. Africa's Glorious Legacy. LC 94-916. (Lost Civilizations Ser.). (Illus.). 168p. 1994. lib. bdg. 25.93 (*0-8094-9026-9*) Time-Life.

— Aztecs: Reign of Blood & Splendor. (Lost Civilizations Ser.). (Illus.). 168p. 1992. lib. bdg. 19.45 (*0-8094-9855-3*) Time-Life.

— Celts: Europe's People of Iron. (Lost Civilizations Ser.). (Illus.). 168p. 1994. lib. bdg. 25.93 (*0-8094-9030-7*) Time-Life.

— China's Buried Kingdoms. LC 93-15068. (Lost Civilizations Ser.). (Illus.). 168p. 1993. lib. bdg. 25.93 (*0-8094-9892-8*) Time-Life.

— Egypt: Land of the Pharaohs. (Lost Civilizations Ser.). (Illus.). 168p. 1992. lib. bdg. 18.95 (*0-8094-9851-0*) Time-Life.

— Greece: Temples, Tombs, & Treasures. (Lost Civilizations Ser.). (Illus.). 168p. 1994. lib. bdg. 25.93 (*0-8094-9021-8*) Time-Life.

— The Holy Land. (Lost Civilizations Ser.). (Illus.). 168p. 1992. lib. bdg. 25.93 (*0-8094-9867-7*) Time-Life.

— Incas: Lords of Gold & Glory. (Lost Civilizations Ser.). (Illus.). 168p. 1992. lib. bdg. 25.93 (*0-8094-9871-5*) Time-Life.

— The Magnificent Maya. (Lost Civilizations Ser.). (Illus.). 168p. 1993. lib. bdg. 25.93 (*0-8094-9880-4*) Time-Life.

— Mesopotamia: The Mighty Kings. LC 94-24305. (Lost Civilizations Ser.). (Illus.). 168p. 1995. lib. bdg. write for info. (*0-8094-9042-0*) Time-Life.

— Pompeii: The Vanished City. (Lost Civilizations Ser.). (Illus.). 168p. 1992. lib. bdg. 19.45 (*0-8094-9863-4*) Time-Life.

— Rome: Echoes of Imperial Glory. LC 93-37766. (Lost Civilizations Ser.). (Illus.). 168p. 1994. lib. bdg. 25.93 (*0-8094-9017-X*) Time-Life.

— Sumer: Cities of Eden. LC 92-38367. (Lost Civilizations Ser.). (Illus.). 168p. 1993. lib. bdg. 25.93 (*0-8094-9888-X*) Time-Life.

— Vikings: Raiders from the North. LC 93-14028. (Lost Civilizations Ser.). (Illus.). 168p. 1993. lib. bdg. 25.93 (*0-8094-9896-0*) Time-Life.

Brown, Dale & Yaeger, Don. Tiger in a Lion's Den: Adventures in LSU Basketball. (Illus.). 192p. 1994. 22.45 (*0-7868-6044-8*, Pub. by Hyperion) Time Warner.

Brown, Dale, ed. see Time-Life Books Editors.

Brown, Dale E. Elements of Business Computing: A Beginners Guide to PC Computer Systems. 224p. (C). 1993. spiral bd. 16.95 (*0-8403-8611-7*) Kendall-Hunt.

Brown, Dale S. I Know I Can Climb the Mountain. (Learning Disability Ser.). (Illus.). 88p. 1995. pap. 8.95 (*1-881650-04-9*) Mntn Bks.

***Brown, Dale S.** Learning a Living: A Guide to Planning Your Career & Finding a Job for People with Learning Disabilities, Attention Deficit Disorder & Dyslexia. LC 99-53658. 256p. 2000. pap. 18.95 (*0-933149-87-5*) Woodbine House.

Brown, Dale S., jt. ed. see Gerber, Paul J.

Brown, Dale Susan, jt. auth. see Bolles, Richard Nelson.

Brown, Dale W. Biblical Pacifism: A Peace Church Perspective. fac. ed. LC 85-30636. 224p. 1994. pap. 69.50 (*0-7837-7341-2*, 204729400007) Bks Demand.

— Understanding Pietism. rev. ed. 125p. 1996. pap. 10.00 (*0-916035-64-6*) Evangel Indiana.

Brown, Dale W., ed. What about the Russians? A Christian Approach to U. S. - Soviet Conflict. LC 84-6169. 160p. reprint ed. pap. 49.60 (*0-7837-5927-4*, 204572600007) Bks Demand.

Brown, Damian, jt. auth. see Johne, Axel.

Brown, Dan. Angels & Demons. LC 99-87852. 448p. 2000. 24.95 (*0-671-02735-2*, PB Hardcover) PB.

— Digital Fortress. LC 97-33118. 384p. 1998. text 24.95 (*0-312-18087-X*) St Martin.

***Brown, Dan.** Digital Fortress. 2000. pap. 14.95 (*0-312-26312-0*) St Martin.

Brown, Dan. Matter. LC 95-90583. 64p. 1996. 14.00 (*0-9647581-0-5*); pap. 9.00 (*0-9647581-1-3*) Crosstown Bks.

***Brown, Dan, et al.** In-Touch Science: Fiber & Animals. (Illus.). 114p. 1999. pap. 12.00 (*1-57753-267-8*) Corn Coop Ext.

Brown, Dan, jt. illus. see Adler, David A.

***Brown, Dani.** An Untimely Death. LC 99-93746. 221p. 2000. pap. 12.95 (*0-533-13128-6*) Vantage.

Brown, Daniel. The Beautiful Beast: The Life & Crimes of SS-Aufseherin Irma Grese. LC 96-19330. (Illus.). 96p. 1996. pap. 11.75 (*0-930860-14-4*) Golden West Hist.

— Bukang y Kim: 1987-1997. (Illus.). 16p. (Orig.). 1997. mass mkt. write for info. (*1-891122-00-2*) Spfld Mus Art.

— Das Geschaft mit dem Staat, die Uberschneidung des Politischen und des Privaten im Corpus Demosthenicum. 357p. 1974. 80.00 (*3-487-05132-X*) G Olms Pubs.

— Heaven. LC 99-15625. 239p. 1999. pap. 9.99 (*0-8307-2341-2*, Regal Bks) Gospel Lght.

— Hopkins' Idealism: Philosophy, Physics, Poetry. LC 96-35164. (Illus.). 360p. (C). 1997. text 85.00 (*0-19-818353-4*) OUP.

— Memory, Trauma Treatment, & the Law. LC 97-25902. 960p. 1998. 100.00 (*0-393-70254-5*) Norton.

***Brown, Daniel.** Rethinking Tradition in Modern Islamic Thought. (Middle East Studies: No. 5). 250p. (C). 1999. pap. text 19.95 (*0-521-65394-0*) Cambridge U Pr.

Brown, Daniel. Schools with Heart: Voluntarism & Public Education. LC 98-18416. (C). 1998. pap. 69.00 (*0-8133-9084-2*, Pub. by Westview) HarpC.

— Unlock the Power of Family: Discover God's Design for Lasting Relationships. LC 94-17643. 1994. 10.95 (*0-917143-30-2*) Sparrow TN.

Brown, Daniel, jt. auth. see Fraser, Hilary.

Brown, Daniel, jt. ed. see Bosworth, Brian.

Brown, Daniel, jt. ed. see Fass, Margot L.

Brown, Daniel A. The Other Side of Pastoral Ministry: Using Process Leadership to Transform Your Church. LC 96-22620. 160p. 1996. pap. 9.99 (*0-310-20602-2*) Zondervan.

Brown, Daniel E., jt. auth. see Kormondy, Edward J.

Brown, Daniel J. Decentralization: The Administrator's Guidebook to School District Change. LC 90-26172. (Illus.). 128p. 1991. 43.95 (*0-8039-6005-0*) Corwin Pr.

— Decentralization: The Administrator's Guidebook to School District Change. LC 90-26172. (Illus.). 128p. 1994. pap. 18.95 (*0-8039-6187-1*) Corwin Pr.

— Decentralization & School-Based Management. 250p. 1989. pap. 39.95 (*1-85000-601-6*, Falmer Pr) Taylor & Francis.

Brown, Daniel P. Giovanni's Europe. LC 83-81929. (Illus.). 50p. (Orig.). 1983. pap. 6.95 (*0-9612528-0-4*) Giovanni's Tour.

— The Protectorate & the Northumberland Conspiracy: Political Intrigue in the Reign of Edward VI. LC 80-65156. (European History Ser.: No. I-1001). (Illus.). 74p. (Orig.). 1982. reprint ed. pap. 4.15 (*0-930860-02-0*) Golden West Hist.

— The Tragedy of Libby & Andersonville Prison Camps. 5th ed. LC 79-54263. (U. S. History Civil War Ser.: No. III102). (Illus.). 1991. reprint ed. pap. 3.95 (*0-930860-01-2*) Golden West Hist.

Brown, Daniel P. & Fromm, Erika. Hypnosis & Behavioral Medicine. 296p. 1987. text 59.95 (*0-89859-925-3*) L Erlbaum Assocs.

— Hypnotherapy & Hypnoanalysis. 392p. 1986. text 59.95 (*0-89859-783-8*) L Erlbaum Assocs.

Brown, Danielle. 187 Men to Avoid. LC 95-190728. 96p. (Orig.). 1995. pap. 7.95 (*0-425-14783-5*) Berkley Pub.

Brown, Danny. A Guide to Pigeons, Doves & Quail. (Illus.). 178p. 1995. pap. 29.95 (*0-646-23058-1*) Avian Pubns.

Brown, Danny & Bumbeck, David. David Bumbeck: Prints. (Illus.). (Orig.). 1989. pap. 15.00 (*0-685-31756-0*) Middlebury Coll Mus.

Brown, Darlene, jt. auth. see Brown, Jack.

Brown, Darlene, ed. see Lindland, Frances K.

Brown, Darlene E. & Brown, Jack. The Legend of Pan Phillips. 5th rev. ed. (Illus.). 198p. (Orig.). 1986. reprint ed. pap. 11.95 (*0-9617572-1-3*) Times Journal Pub.

Brown, Darrell. Seven Steps to Renewing the Mind Study Guide. Date not set. write for info. (*1-893558-98-3*) Rhema Word Pub.

***Brown, Darrell.** Spiritually Armed & Dangerous. 2nd variorum ed. Brown, Tanya, ed. 1999. pap. 14.95 (*1-893558-55-X*) Rhema Word Pub.

Brown, Darrell. Spiritually Armed & Dangerous Study Guide. Date not set. write for info. (*1-893558-86-X*) Rhema Word Pub.

Brown, Darrell. Tearing down Strongholds & Destroying Yokes Study Guide. Date not set. write for info. (*1-893558-97-5*) Rhema Word Pub.

— Thine Kingdom Come: Vital Keys to Kingdom Living for the Next Millennium. 1999. pap. 14.95 (*1-893558-64-9*) Rhema Word Pub.

Brown, Darren, ed. For the Love of a Dog: Classic Sporting Dog Stories. LC 99-35725. 1999. 24.95 (*1-885106-80-7*) Wild Adven Pr.

Brown, Davana, ed. see Irani, Mehera J.

Brown, Dave. Bristlecone Peak. LC 97-78165. (Legend of the Golden Feather Ser.: Vol. 1). 320p. 1998. pap. 14.95 (*1-878406-13-2*) Parker Dstb.

Brown, Dave & Crane, Paula. Who Killed Alaska? LC 90-50876. 336p. 1991. 21.95 (*0-88282-069-9*) New Horizon NJ.

Brown, Dave & Meadowcroft, Sam. The Modern Shepherd. (Illus.). 240p. 1989. 32.95 (*0-85236-188-2*, Pub. by Farming Pr) Diamond Farm Bk.

— The Veterinary Book for Sheep Farmers. (Illus.). 240p. 1990. 49.95 (*0-85236-189-0*, Pub. by Farming Pr) Diamond Farm Bk.

Brown, Dave & Mitchell, Ian. Mountain Days & Bothy Nights. LC 99-185040. (Illus.). 192p. 1999. pap. 12.95 (*0-946487-15-4*, Pub. by Luath Pr Ltd) Midpt Trade.

Brown, Dave, jt. auth. see Williams, Mitch.

Brown, David. Beat Your Ticket: Go to Court & Win! LC 98-56031. (Quick & Legal Ser.). 275p. (Orig.). 1999. pap. 19.95 (*0-87337-465-7*) Nolo com.

— The California Landlord's Law Book: Evictions, Vol. 2. 1999. 44.95 (*0-87337-543-2*) Nolo com.

***Brown, David.** Contemporary Nationalism: Civic, Ethnocultural & Multicultural Politics. LC 00-20053. (Illus.). 2000. pap. write for info. (*0-415-17139-3*) Routledge.

— Cybertrends: Chaos, Power & Accountability in the Information Age. 288p. 1998. pap. 17.95 (*0-14-024673-8*, Pub. by Pnguin Bks Ltd) Trafalgar.

Brown, David. Degrees of Control: A Sociology of Educational Expansion & Occupational Credentialism. 240p. (C). 1995. text 36.00 (*0-8077-3452-7*) Tchrs Coll.

***Brown, David.** Discipleship & Imagination: Christian Tradition & Truth. (Illus.). 300p. 2000. text 39.95 (*0-19-827018-6*) OUP.

Brown, David. The Divine Trinity. LC 85-18941. 328p. (C). 1984. 36.95 (*0-87548-439-5*) Open Court.

— Electronic Publishing & Libraries: Planning for the Impact & Growth to 2003. 600p. 1996. 50.00 (*1-85739-166-7*) Bowker-Saur.

— 50 Popular Topics. 240p. 1995. pap. 35.95 (*1-85742-163-9*, Pub. by Arena) Ashgate Pub Co.

— The Four Gospels. 486p. 1993. reprint ed. 35.99 (*0-85151-016-7*) Banner of Truth.

— Glinka, Borodin, Balakirev, Musorgshky & Tchaikovsky. (New Grove Composer Biography Ser.). 1997. pap. 16.95 (*0-393-31585-1*) Norton.

— Goldmine, 1995-96: Finding Free & Low-Cost Resources for Teaching. 5th ed. (Popular Cultural Studies). 336p. 1993. pap. 29.95 (*1-85742-137-X*, Pub. by Arena) Ashgate Pub Co.

— I Would Rather Be Audited by the IRS Than Give a Speech. LC 94-73465. 176p. 1995. pap. text, per. 19.95 (*0-7872-0314-9*) Kendall-Hunt.

— An Introduction to Object-Oriented Analysis: Objects in Plain English. LC 96-49130. 736p. 1997. text 84.95 (*0-471-11028-0*) Wiley.

***Brown, David.** Learn to Draw Dogs. (Learn to Draw Ser.). (Illus.). 64p. 1999. pap. 14.95 (*0-00-413356-0*, Pub. by HarpC) Trafalgar.

— Learn to Draw Horses. (Learn to Draw Ser.). (Illus.). 64p. 1999. pap. 14.95 (*0-00-413360-9*, Pub. by HarpC) Trafalgar.

Brown, David. Life Is Hard, but God Is Good! LC 98-171508. (Illus.). 128p. 1997. pap. 6.95 (*0-9659263-0-3*) D Brown Pub.

— Mikhail Glinka. LC 84-19878. (Music Reprint Ser.). (Illus.). 342p. 1985. reprint ed. lib. bdg. 39.50 (*0-306-76247-1*) Da Capo.

***Brown, David.** Naval Operations of the Campaign in Norway, April-June, 1940. LC 00-31708. (Whitehall Histories Ser.). 2000. write for info. (*0-7146-5119-2*, Pub. by F Cass Pubs) Intl Spec Bk.

Brown, David. Obstetrics, Contraception & Gynecology. 208p. 1976. pap. 42.95 (*0-8464-1430-9*) Beekman Pubs.

— The Planter: or 13 Years in the South. LC 75-104423. 276p. reprint ed. pap. text 6.95 (*0-89197-888-7*); reprint ed. lib. bdg. 14.25 (*0-8398-0174-2*) Irvington.

— Power of QuarkXPress for the Mac. LC 94-39390. 900p. 1994. pap. 34.95 (*1-55828-381-1*, MIS Pr) IDG Bks.

***Brown, David.** Producer Responsibility: Packaging Law. 224p. 2000. pap. write for info. (*1-902558-12-X*, Pub. by Palladian Law) Gaunt.

Brown, David. The Rest of Your Life Is the Best of Your Life. 128p. 1993. pap. 9.95 (*0-942637-93-3*) Barricade Bks.

— The Rest of Your Life Is the Best of Your Life: David Brown's Guide to Growing Gray Disgracefully. LC 91-19324. 128p. 1991. 14.95 (*0-942637-35-6*) Barricade Bks.

— Ride the Money Wave on the Web: Four On-Line Investing Techniques Used by the Pros. 2002. 24.95 (*0-07-134498-5*) McGraw.

— Royal Navy & the Falklands. (C). 1996. text 32.50 (*0-8133-0771-6*) Westview.

— The State Ethnic Politics in Southeast Asia. 376p. (C). 1997. pap. 29.99 (*0-415-12792-0*) Routledge.

***Brown, David.** Tchaikovsky Remembered. (Illus.). 248p. 1999. reprint ed. pap. text 21.00 (*0-7881-6785-5*) DIANE Pub.

Brown, David. Thomas Weelkes. LC 79-10068. 1979. reprint ed. lib. bdg. 32.50 (*0-306-79523-X*) Da Capo.

***Brown, David.** Tradition & Imagination: Revelation & Change. LC 99-12411. 432p. 2000. text 45.00 (*0-19-826991-9*) OUP.

Brown, David. Warship Losses of World War Two. (Illus.). 256p. (Orig.). 1995. pap. 19.95 (*1-55750-914-X*) Naval Inst Pr.

— Welcome to the Word Worksheets. 142p. 1993. pap. 25.95 (*0-225-66650-2*, 810, Pub. by G Chapman) Morehouse Pub.

Brown, David, ed. St. Ives, 1939-64: Twenty-Five Years of Painting, Sculpture, & Pottery. (Illus.). 248p. 1996. 75.00 (*1-85437-190-8*, Pub. by Tate Gallery) U of Wash Pr.

Brown, David & Brown, Virginia. Whitman Juvenile Books: Reference & Value Guide. LC 96-212974. (Illus.). 744p. (Orig.). 1996. pap. 17.95 (*0-89145-740-2*, 4733) Collector Bks.

Brown, David & Carmony, Neil B., eds. Aldo Leopold's Southwest. LC 94-48678. (Illus.). 250p. 1995. pap. 17.95 (*0-8263-1580-1*) U of NM Pr.

Brown, David & Chandrasekaran, B. Design Problem Solving: Knowledge Structures & Control Strategies. (Design Problem Service ser.). (Illus.). 200p. (Orig.). 1989. pap. text 34.95 (*0-934613-07-9*) Morgan Kaufmann.

Brown, David & Fuller, David, eds. Signs of Grace: Sacraments in Poetry & Prose. LC 96-1298. 224p. 1996. 19.95 (*0-8192-1654-2*) Morehouse Pub.

***Brown, David & Knowles, Trudy.** Understanding Young Adolescents: The Key to Successful Middle School. 2000. pap. text 18.00 (*0-325-00266-5*) Heinemann.

An Asterisk (*) at the beginning of an entry indicates that the title is appearing for the first time.

Brown, David & Loades, Ann, eds. The Sense of the Sacramental: Movement & Measure in Art & Music, Place & Time. 224p. 1995. pap. 22.95 (*0-687-06615-8*) Abingdon.

Brown, David & Warner, Ralph E. The Landlord's Law Book Vol. 1: Rights & Responsibilities. 6th rev. ed. (Illus.). 336p. 1998. pap. 34.95 (*0-87337-443-6*) Nolo com.

Brown, David, et al. Criminal Laws: Materials & Commentary on Criminal Law & Process in New South Wales. 1464p. 1990. pap. 98.00 (*1-86287-024-1*, Pub. by Federation Pr) Gaunt.

— Criminal Laws: Materials & Commentary on Criminal Law & Process of NSW. 2nd ed. pap. 54.00 (*1-86287-212-0*, Pub. by Federation Pr) Gaunt.

— Criminal Laws: Materials & Commentary on Criminal Law & Process of NSW. 2nd ed. 1996. pap. 54.00 (*1-86287-213-9*, Pub. by Federation Pr) Gaunt.

Brown, David, jt. auth. see Berman, Michael.

Brown, David, jt. auth. see Goddard, Larry.

Brown, David, jt. auth. see McDonnell, S. N.

Brown, David, jt. auth. see Ortiz, Fernando.

Brown, David A. Leonardo da Vinci: Origins of a Genius. LC 98-15164. (Illus.). 248p. 1998. 55.00 (*0-300-07246-5*) Yale U Pr.

Brown, David A., compiled by. History of Penacook from Its First Settlement in 1734 up to 1900. (Illus.). 570p. 1997. reprint ed. lib. bdg. 59.00 (*0-8328-6017-4*) Higginson Bk Co.

Brown, David A., et al. The Legacy of Leonardo: Painters in Lombardy, 1480-1530. (Illus.). 304p. 1999. 90.00 (*88-8118-463-X*, Pub. by Skira IT) Abbeville Pr.

— Lorenzo Lotto: Rediscovered Master of the Renaissance. LC 97-26418. 1997. write for info. (*0-89468-257-1*) Natl Gallery Art.

— Lorenzo Lotto: Rediscovered Master of the Renaissance. (Illus.). 272p. 1997. 55.00 (*0-300-07331-3*) Yale U Pr.

Brown, David A., jt. auth. see Morrow, Raymond A.

Brown, David A., tr. see Sobolev, N. V.

Brown, David B. The Art of J. M. W. Turner. (Illus.). 192p. 1998. pap. 25.95 (*1-57715-030-9*) Knckerbocker.

— Tchaikovsky: The Final Years, 1885-1983. 544p. 1992. 40.00 (*0-393-03099-7*) Norton.

— Technimanagement: Empowering the Organization by Liberating Your People. (C). 1995. 27.80 (*0-13-180811-7*) P-H.

Brown, David B., ed. Mixed-Valence Compounds: Theory & Applications in Chemistry, Physics, Geology & Biology. (NATO Advanced Study Institute, C. Mathematical & Physical Sciences Ser.: No. 58). 525p. 1980. text 234.00 (*90-277-1152-6*) Kluwer Academic.

Brown, David B. & Herbanek, Jeffrey A. Systems Analysis for Applications: Software Design. (Illus.). 466p. (C). 1984. text 39.95 (*0-8162-1160-4*) Holden-Day.

Brown, David B., et al. Benjamin Robert Haydon. 196p. (C). 1996. pap. text 29.95 (*0-8135-2391-5*) Rutgers U Pr.

Brown, David C. A Guide to the Salem Witchcraft Hysteria of 1692. LC 84-164658. (Illus.). 132p. (Orig.). 1984. pap. 9.95 (*0-9613415-0-5*) D C Brown.

Brown, David C., jt. auth. see Gatter, Kevin.

Brown, David E. Arizona Game Birds. LC 88-27797. (Illus.). 307p. 1989. 29.95 (*0-8165-1019-9*) U of Ariz Pr.

— Arizona Wetlands & Waterfowl. LC 85-20890. (Illus.). 169p. 1985. 33.50 (*0-8165-0904-2*) U of Ariz Pr.

***Brown, David E.** Arizona Wetlands & Waterfowl. (Illus.). 169p. 1999. reprint ed. text 25.00 (*0-7881-6726-X*) DIANE Pub.

Brown, David E. The Grizzly in the Southwest: Documentary of an Extinction. LC 84-28027. (Illus.). 280p. 1985. 29.95 (*0-8061-1930-6*) U of Okla Pr.

— The Grizzly in the Southwest: Documentary of an Extinction. (Illus.). 304p. 1996. pap. 15.95 (*0-8061-2880-1*) U of Okla Pr.

***Brown, David E.** Home to Kentucky. (Legend of the Golden Feather Ser.: Vol. 3). 300p. 1999. pap. 14.95 (*1-878406-22-1*) Parker Dstb.

Brown, David E. It's Natural to Be Gay. 96p. (Orig.). 1994. pap. 7.95 (*0-9640801-0-9*, 8010-9) Jireh Pubns.

— Meeting the Needs of Out-of-School Youth. 32p. 1997. pap. 15.00 (*1-55877-276-6*) Natl Governor.

— The Protectors. LC 98-93975. (Legend of the Golden Feather Ser.: Vol. 2). 270p. 1998. pap. 14.95 (*1-878406-20-5*) Parker Dstb.

***Brown, David E.** Vampiro: The Vampire Bat in Fact & Fantasy. LC 99-13760. 1999. pap. text 10.95 (*0-87480-601-1*) U of Utah Pr.

Brown, David E., ed. Biotic Communities: Southwestern United States & Northwestern Mexico. LC 94-20777. (Illus.). 344p. 1994. reprint ed. pap. 24.95 (*0-87480-459-0*) U of Utah Pr.

— The Wolf in the Southwest: The Making of an Endangered Species. LC 82-17399. 195p. 1983. pap. 14.95 (*0-8165-0796-1*) U of Ariz Pr.

***Brown, David E. & Carmony, Neil B.** Gila Monster: Facts & Folklore of America's Aztec Lizard. LC 99-13759. (Illus.). 129p. 1999. pap. 10.95 (*0-87480-600-3*) U of Utah Pr.

Brown, David E. & Murray, John A., eds. The Last Grizzly & Other Southwestern Bear Stories. LC 88-14819. 184p. 1988. 22.50 (*0-8165-1067-9*) U of Ariz Pr.

Brown, David E. & Neumann, Randall D. Orthopedic Secrets. 2nd rev. ed. LC 99-11421. (Secrets Ser.). (Illus.). 400p. 1999. pap. text 39.00 (*1-56053-302-1*) Hanley & Belfus.

Brown, David E. & Neumann, Randall D., eds. Orthopedic Secrets: Questions You Will Be Asked on Rounds, in the Clinic, on Oral Exams. (Secrets Ser.). (Illus.). 400p. (Orig.). 1994. pap. text 39.00 (*1-56053-106-1*) Hanley & Belfus.

Brown, David E., et al. A Classification of North American Biotic Communities. LC 97-53661. 141p. 1998. pap. 19.95 (*0-87480-562-7*) U of Utah Pr.

— North American Biotic Communities: Book & Map Set. 1998. pap. 34.95 (*0-87480-568-6*) U of Utah Pr.

Brown, David E., jt. ed. see Carmony, Neil B.

Brown, David F. Birds of Prey Aircraft, Nose Art & Mission Markings of the Operation Desert Shield/Storm. LC 92-62609. (Illus.). 160p. (Orig.). 1993. pap. 29.95 (*0-88740-472-3*) Schiffer.

— Tomcat Alley: A Photographic Roll Call of the Grumman F-14 Tomcat. LC 97-81278. (Illus.). 256p. 1998. 59.95 (*0-7643-0477-1*) Schiffer.

***Brown, David G.** Always in Touch: A Practical Guide to Ubiquitous Computing. 84p. 1999. pap. text 10.00 (*0-9644070-2-7*) Wake Forest Univ.

Brown, David G. Boatbuilding with Baltek DuraKore. 1994. 29.95 (*0-07-008212-X*) McGraw.

— Complete Guide to Boat Maintenance & Repair. LC 93-3394. 1993. pap. 16.00 (*0-688-11932-8*, Hearst) Hearst Commns.

— Gold Buckle Dreams, The Rodeo Life Story of Chris LeDoux. (Illus.). 228p. 1989. reprint ed. pap. 11.95 (*0-941875-08-3*) Wolverine Distrib.

***Brown, David G.** Last Log of the Titanic. 224p. 2000. 19.95 (*0-07-136447-1*) McGraw.

***Brown, David G., ed.** Electronically Enhanced Education: A Case Study of Wake Forest University. (Illus.). 126p. 1999. pap. write for info. (*0-9644070-3-5*) Wake Forest Univ.

Brown, David H. & Porter, Robin, eds. Management Issues in China: Domestic Enterprises. LC 95-12696. 240p. (C). 1995. pap. 22.50 (*0-415-13002-6*) Thomson Learn.

— Management Issues in China: Domestic Enterprises. LC 95-12696. 288p. (C). (gr. 13). 1995. pap. 69.95 (*0-415-13001-8*) Thomson Learn.

Brown, David J. Brainchild. LC 88-81440. 130p. (Orig.). 1988. pap. 9.95 (*0-941404-92-7*) New Falcon Pubns.

— Bridges. LC 93-9747. (Illus.). 176p. 1993. 30.00 (*0-02-517455-X*) Macmillan.

***Brown, David J.** The Impact of Electronic Publishing: The Future for Libraries & Publishers. 300p. 1999. 72.00 (*1-85739-237-X*) Bowker-Saur.

Brown, David J. Roy Lichtenstein: Man Hit by the 21st Century. LC 97-43096. (Illus.). 48p. 1997. pap. 19.95 (*0-917562-70-4*) Contemp Arts.

***Brown, David J.** Virus: The Alien Strain. LC 99-64783. 144p. 1999. pap. 14.95 (*1-56184-144-7*) New Falcon Pubns.

Brown, David J. Voices from the Edge: More Conversations for the New Millienium. (Illus.). 402p. 1995. pap. 14.95 (*0-89594-732-3*) Crossing Pr.

Brown, David J., et al. Innuendo Non Troppo: The Work of Gregory Barsamian. LC 98-34639. 1998. pap. write for info. (*0-917562-71-2*) Contemporary Arts.

Brown, David K. Before the Ironclad: The Development of Ship Design, Propulsion, & Armament in the Royal Navy. LC 89-64155. (Illus.). 256p. 1990. 49.95 (*0-87021-784-4*) Naval Inst Pr.

— The Future of British Surface Fleet. LC 90-70787. (Illus.). 224p. 1991. 42.50 (*1-55750-275-7*) Naval Inst Pr.

— Introduction to Public Policy: An Aging Perspective. LC 96-8816. 278p. 1996. 42.50 (*0-7618-0414-5*) U Pr of Amer.

— Warrior to Dreadnought: Warship Development, 1860-1905. LC 97-177475. (Illus.). 208p. 1997. 59.95 (*1-86176-022-1*) Naval Inst Pr.

Brown, David L. Atlas of Regional Anesthesia. (Illus.). 1991. text 132.00 (*0-7216-3177-0*, W B Saunders Co) Harcrt Hlth Sci Grp.

— Atlas of Regional Anesthesia. 2nd ed. Ross, Allan, ed. LC 98-18198. (Illus.). 300p. (C). 1998. text. write for info. (*0-7216-7004-0*, W B Saunders Co) Harcrt Hlth Sci Grp.

— Cardiac Intensive Care. LC 96-28909. (Illus.). 860p. 1998. 125.00 (*0-7216-6006-1*, W B Saunders Co) Harcrt Hlth Sci Grp.

— Cyber-Investing: Cracking Wall Street with Your Personal Computer. LC 96-47737. (Wiley Investing Ser.). 336p. 1997. pap., pap. text 29.95 incl. disk (*0-471-16986-2*) Wiley.

— Cyber-Investing: Cracking Wall Street with Your Personal Computer. LC 96-47737. (Wiley Investing Ser.). 309p. 1997. text 59.95 incl. disk (*0-471-16987-0*) Wiley.

— Regional Anesthesia & Analgesia. Zorab, Richard, ed. (Illus.). 800p. 1996. text 146.00 (*0-7216-5654-4*, W B Saunders Co) Harcrt Hlth Sci Grp.

— Three Years in the Rocky Mountains. 28p. 1975. pap. 5.95 (*0-87770-151-2*) Ye Galleon.

Brown, David L., ed. Risk & Outcome in Anesthesia. 2nd ed. LC 91-31228. (Illus.). 621p. 1992. reprint ed. pap. 192.60 (*0-608-05871-3*, 205978200007) Bks Demand.

Brown, David L. & Bentley, Kassandra. Getting Started in Online Investing. LC 98-51037. (Getting Started Ser.). (Illus.). 272p. 1999. pap. 18.95 (*0-471-31703-9*) Wiley.

— Wall Street City: Your Guide to Investing on the Web. LC 97-12706. (Illus.). 351p. 1997. pap. 29.95 incl. cd-rom (*0-471-17878-0*) Wiley.

Brown, David O., ed. & anno. see John Paul, II, pseud.

***Brown, David Paul.** The Forum: Forty Years Full Practice at the Philadelphia Bar, 2 vols. 1109p. 2000. reprint ed. 225.00 (*1-56169-588-2*) Gaunt.

Brown, David R. How to Win Your Lover Back & Keep the One You Love. LC 98-100495. 184p. (Orig.). 1997. per. 14.95 (*0-9656440-0-6*) Randall Pub.

Brown, David R., ed. Gastrointestinal Regulatory Peptides. LC 92-49563. (Handbook of Experimental Pharmacology Ser.: Vol. 106). 1993. 485.00 (*0-387-55970-1*) Spr-Verlag.

Brown, David S. Freshwater Snails of Africa & Their Medical Importance. 2nd ed. 550p. 1994. 175.00 (*0-7484-0026-5*, Pub. by Tay Francis Ltd) Taylor & Francis.

— Managing the Large Organization: Issues, Ideas, Precepts, Innovations. 300p. 1982. 27.50 (*0-912338-31-8*); fiche 19.50 (*0-912338-34-2*) Lomond.

— Thomas Jefferson: A Biographical Companion. LC 98-7991. (Biographical Companion Ser.). 266p. (J). 1998. lib. bdg. 55.00 (*0-87436-949-5*) ABC-CLIO.

Brown, David T., ed. Cannabis: The Genus Cannabis. (Medicinal & Aromatic Plants - Industrial Profiles Ser.: Vol. 4). 296p. 1998. text 100.00 (*90-5702-291-5*, ECU113, Harwood Acad Pubs) Gordon & Breach.

Brown, David W. Fight Your Ticket--& Win! 8th ed. LC 99-21021. 336p. 1999. pap. 24.95 (*0-87337-524-6*) Nolo com.

— Information Sources for Teachers. LC 96-85392. 334p. 1996. text 54.95 (*1-85742-231-7*, Pub. by Arena) Ashgate Pub Co.

— Surviving the Year 2000 Computer Crash: It's Too Late to Fix All the Software! 186p. 1998. pap. 15.57 (*1-55212-224-7*, 98-0043) Trafford Pub.

— When Strangers Cooperate: Using Social Conventions to Govern Ourselves. 1995. 25.00 (*0-02-904875-5*) Free Pr.

Brown, David W. & Goldoftas, Lisa. The Guardianship Book: How to Become a Child's Guardian in California 2.2. LC 95-13181. (Illus.). 304p. 1997. pap. 24.95 (*0-87337-302-2*) Nolo com.

***Brown, David W. & Warner, Ralph E.** The Landlord's Law Book. 7th ed. LC 99-86063. 2000. write for info. (*0-87337-581-5*) Nolo com.

Brown, David W., et al. Organic Spectroscopy. fac. ed. LC 87-36005. (Illus.). 258p. 1988. reprint ed. pap. 80.00 (*0-608-00984-9*, 206184000012) Bks Demand.

Brown, David W., jt. auth. see Goldoftas, Lisa.

Brown, David W., jt. auth. see Loeb, David.

Brown, David Wayne, jt. auth. see Loeb, David V.

Brown, Dawn. Dawn Brown's Complete Guide to Step Aerobics. (Fitness & Health Ser.). 1992. pap. text 16.25 (*0-86720-269-6*) Jones & Bartlett.

Brown, Dawny. A Guide to Pheasants & Waterfowl. (Illus.). 140p. 1998. pap. 44.95 (*0-9587102-3-6*) Avian Pubns.

Brown, De Soto. Hawaii Recalls. LC 82-83322. (Illus.). 134p. 1982. pap. 18.00 (*0-9607938-2-8*); text 22.50 (*0-9607938-3-6*) Editions Ltd.

***Brown, De Soto, ed.** Hawaii Recalls: Nostalgic Images. LC 99-83322. (Illus.). 134p. 1998. pap. 16.95 (*0-8159-5724-6*) Devin.

Brown, Dean R. Simply Science: Discovering the Fascinations of Our World. (Illus.). 206p. (YA). (gr. 7-12). 1993. pap. text 24.95 (*1-880293-02-1*) A aken.

Brown, Deanna, tr. see Sullivan, Sean, et al.

Brown, Deaver. Tax Survival Kit: For Filing Your 1998 Taxes. (Illus.). 101p. 1998. pap. 7.99 (*1-893177-00-9*) Simply Media.

Brown, Deb A. Lessons from the Rocking Chair: Timeless Stories for Teaching Character. 70p. 1997. pap. 8.95 (*0-9653163-3-5*) Character Dev.

***Brown, Deb Austin.** Lessons from the Beach Chair: Nature's Wisdom for Teaching Character. 75p. 1999. pap. 9.95 (*1-892056-05-4*) Character Dev.

Brown, Debbie. Favorite Character Cakes. (Illus.). 96p. 1999. pap. 9.95 (*3-8290-1480-5*, 520918) Konemann.

— Lovable Character Cakes. (Illus.). 1999. 14.95 (*1-85391-727-3*) Tuttle Pubng.

Brown, Debbie T. Johnny & the Gnome: The Beginning of an Ordian Adventure. LC 98-84390. (Illus.). 134p. (J). (gr. k-6). 1998. pap. 5.95 (*0-9640537-9-9*) Monterey Pubng.

***Brown, Deborah.** Minnesota Gardening, 2000. Cleberg, Kathleen, ed. (Illus.). 30p. 1999. pap. 9.95 (*1-888440-07-4*) U MN Ext Serv.

***Brown, Deborah, ed.** Christianity in the Twenty-First Century. 244p. 2000. pap. 19.95 (*0-8245-1842-X*, Pub. by Crossroad NY) Natl Bk Netwk.

Brown, Deborah, jt. auth. see Freer, Ian.

Brown, Deborah, jt. auth. see Gust, Katharine.

Brown, Deborah, ed. see Headen-Anthony, Shirley.

Brown, Deborah A. Turmoil in Hong Kong on the Eve of Communist Rule: The Fate of the Territory & Its Anglican Church. LC 93-23579. 472p. 1993. 109.95 (*0-7734-2242-0*) E Mellen.

***Brown, Deborah Singley, et al.** R. S. V. P. Recipes & Suggestion for Various Parties. 2nd ed. (Illus.). 259p. (Orig.). 1999. pap. 14.95 (*0-9666804-1-3*) RSVP.

***Brown, Debra Lee.** Virgin Spring. (Historical Ser.: Vol. 506). 2000. per. 4.99 (*0-373-29106-X*) Harlequin Bks.

Brown, Dee. American West. (Illus.). 304p. 1994. 25.00 (*0-02-517421-5*, Scribners Ref) Mac Lib Ref.

— The American West. (Illus.). 448p. 1995. per. 14.00 (*0-684-80441-7*, Pub. by Macmillan) S&S Trade.

— Bury My Heart at Wounded Knee. 1992. reprint ed. lib. bdg. 49.95 (*0-89966-975-1*) Buccaneer Bks.

— Bury My Heart at Wounded Knee: An Indian History of the American West. (Illus.). 487p. (C). 1991. pap. 14.95 (*0-8050-1730-5*, Owl) H Holt & Co.

— Bury My Heart at Wounded Knee: An Indian History of the American West. LC 70-121633. (Illus.). 512p. 1995. 27.50 (*0-8050-1045-9*) H Holt & Co.

***Brown, Dee.** Bury My Heart at Wounded Knee: An Indian History of the American West. (Illus.). 512p. 2001. pap. 16.00 (*0-8050-6669-1*, Owl) H Holt & Co.

Brown, Dee. Bury My Heart at Wounded Knee: An Indian History of the American West. 1991. 20.05 (*0-606-12853-0*, Pub. by Turtleback) Demco.

— Dee Brown's Civil War Anthology. Bahash, Stan, ed. LC 98-5448. (Illus.). 272p. 1998. pap. 14.95 (*1-57416-010-9*) Clear Light.

— Dee Brown's Civil War Anthology. Bahash, Stan, ed. LC 98-5448. (Illus.). 272p. 1998. 24.95 (*1-57416-009-5*) Clear Light.

— Dee Brown's Folktales of the Native American Indian: Retold for Our Times. LC 93-12449. Orig. Title: Tepee Tales of the American Indian. (Illus.). 176p. 1995. reprint ed. pap. 9.95 (*0-8050-2607-X*) H Holt & Co.

— The Fetterman Massacre. LC 83-19805. (Illus.). 259p. 1971. reprint ed. pap. 11.95 (*0-8032-5730-9*, Bison Books) U of Nebr Pr.

— The Galvanized Yankees. LC 85-23219. (Illus.). 255p. 1986. pap. 12.95 (*0-8032-6075-X*, Bison Books) U of Nebr Pr.

— The Gentle Tamers: Women of the Old Wild West. LC 81-3428. (Illus.). 335p. 1981. pap. 10.00 (*0-8032-5025-8*, Bison Books) U of Nebr Pr.

— Satanic Ritual Abuse: A Handbook for Therapists. (Illus.). 136p. (Orig.). 1994. pap. 16.95 (*0-9642200-8-3*) Blue Moon CO.

— Wave High the Banner: A Novel of Davy Crockett. LC 99-19825. 367p. 1999. 35.00 (*0-8263-2012-0*); pap. 15.95 (*0-8263-2013-9*) U of NM Pr.

— The Way to Bright Star. 1999. mass mkt. 6.99 (*0-8125-8913-0*, Pub. by Forge NYC) St Martin.

— The Way to Bright Star. LC 98-14621. 352p. (YA). (gr. 10 up). 1998. text 24.95 (*0-312-86612-7*) St Martin.

— When the Century Was Young: A Writer's Notebook. LC 93-25232. (Illus.). 223p. 1993. 23.00 (*0-87483-267-5*) August Hse.

— Wondrous Times on the Frontier. 320p. 1991. 23.95 (*0-87483-137-7*) August Hse.

— Wounded Knee: An Indian History of the American West. (Illus.). 224p. (YA). (gr. 7 up). 1995. pap. 9.95 (*0-8050-2700-9*, Bks Young Read) H Holt & Co.

Brown, Dee, jt. ed. see Banash, Stan.

Brown, Dee A. Dee Brown's Folktales of the Native American: Retold for Our Times. (J). 1993. 15.05 (*0-606-02591-X*, Pub. by Turtleback) Demco.

— Grierson's Raid: A Cavalry Adventure of the Civil War. LC 54-9661. 261p. 1981. reprint ed. 24.95 (*0-89029-061-X*) Morningside Bkshop.

Brown, Deirdre, et al. Life in Victorian Ireland. (Primary History Ser.). 48p. 1996. pap. 10.95 (*0-85640-556-6*, Pub. by Blackstaff Pr) Dufour.

Brown, Delmer M., ed. The Cambridge History of Japan Vol. 1: Ancient Japan. (Illus.). 628p. (C). 1993. text 125.00 (*0-521-22352-0*) Cambridge U Pr.

Brown, Delmer M., tr. see Muraoka, Tsunetsugu.

***Brown, Delores Anderson.** I Believe in Myself--I Don't Have to Cry Anymore. LC 00-90923. 2000. 18.95 (*0-533-13540-0*) Vantage.

Brown, Delores M., jt. auth. see Wiles, Gary H.

Brown, Delwin. Boundaries of Our Habitations: Tradition & Theological Construction. LC 93-27411. (SUNY Series in Religious Studies). 215p. (C). 1994. text 49.50 (*0-7914-1965-7*); pap. text 16.95 (*0-7914-1966-5*) State U NY Pr.

Brown, Delwin, et al. Process Philosophy & Christian Thought. LC 74-127586. 1971. pap. 17.50 (*0-672-60799-9*, Bobbs) Macmillan.

Brown, Delwin, jt. auth. see Pinnock, Clark H.

Brown, Demetra V. Haremlik: Some Pages from the Life of Turkish Women. LC 77-87626. reprint ed. 37.50 (*0-404-16451-X*) AMS Pr.

Brown, Demetra V. & Phoutrides, Aristides, trs. Modern Greek Stories. LC 79-136414. reprint ed. 24.50 (*0-404-01134-9*) AMS Pr.

Brown, Deming. The Last Years of Soviet Russian Literature: Prose Fiction, 1975-1991. LC 92-44724. 218p. (C). 1994. pap. text 18.95 (*0-521-40865-2*) Cambridge U Pr.

— Soviet Attitudes Toward American Writing. LC 62-11954. 350p. reprint ed. pap. 108.50 (*0-608-16190-X*, 201464000096) Bks Demand.

Brown, Deni. 4 Gardens in One. Bennell, Alan P. & Gregory, Norma M., eds. (Illus.). viii, 212p. 1992. 51.00 (*1-872291-08-2*, Pub. by Royal Botanic Edinburgh) Balogh.

Brown, Denis. Sarah Vaughan: A Discography, 47. LC 91-27632. (Discographies Ser.: No. 47). 184p. 1991. lib. bdg. 52.95 (*0-313-28005-3*, BVG/, Greenwood Pr) Greenwood.

Brown, Denise. Massage. (Headway Lifeguides Ser.). (Illus.). 88p. 1995. pap. 15.95 (*0-340-55949-7*, Pub. by Headway) Trafalgar.

Brown, Denise, jt. auth. see Carroll, Amy.

Brown, Denise S., et al. The Highway. LC 75-313584. (Illus.). 48p. 1970. pap. 6.00 (*0-939594-49-8*) Menil Found.

Brown, Denise W. Massage. (Teach Yourself Ser.). 192p. 1996. pap. 9.95 (*0-8442-3108-8*, Teach Yrslf) NTC Contemp Pub Co.

— Teach Yourself Aromatherapy. (Illus.). 160p. 1996. pap. 9.95 (*0-8442-3102-9*, Teach Yrslf) NTC Contemp Pub Co.

Brown, Denise Whichello. Hand Reflexology: A Practical Introduction. LC 99-57401. (Alternative Health Ser.). (Illus.). 112p. 1999. 9.95 (*1-57145-214-1*, Thunder Bay) Advantage Pubs.

— Reflexology: A Practical Introduction. LC 99-55190. (Alternative Health Ser.). (Illus.). 112p. 1999. 9.98 (*1-57145-216-8*, Thunder Bay) Advantage Pubs.

— Sensual Massage: A Practical Introduction. LC 99-56843. (Alternative Health Ser.). (Illus.). 112p. 1999. 9.98 (*1-57145-213-3*, Thunder Bay) Advantage Pubs.

— Therapeutic Massage: A Practical Introduction. LC 99-55321. (Alternative Health Ser.). (Illus.). 112p. 1999. 9.98 (*1-57145-212-5*, Thunder Bay) Advantage Pubs.

***Brown, Dennis.** Actors Talk: Profiles & Stories from the Acting Trade. (Illus.). 288p. 1999. 25.00 (*0-87910-287-X*) Limelight Edns.

B

An Asterisk (*) at the beginning of an entry indicates that the title is appearing for the first time.

— John Betjeman. (Writers & Their Works Ser.). 96p. 1999. pap. text 19.00 (*0-7463-0895-7*, Pub. by Northcote House) U Pr of Miss.

Brown, Dennis. The Poetry of Modernity: Anglo-American Encodings. LC 93-48922. 1994. text 55.00 (*0-312-12093-1*) St Martin.

— Shoptalk: Conversations about Theater & Film with Twelve Writers, One Producer - & Tennessee Williams' Mother. LC 92-2975. (Illus.). 224p. 1992. 19.95 (*1-55704-128-8*, Pub. by Newmarket) Norton.

— Shoptalk: Conversations about Theater & Film with Twelve Writers, One Producer - & Tennessee Williams' Mother. LC 92-2975. (Illus.). 224p. 1993. pap. 10.95 (*1-55704-170-9*, Pub. by Newmarket) Norton.

Brown, Dennis & Toussaint, Pamela A. Mama's Little Baby: The Black Woman's Guide to Pregnancy, Childbirth, & Baby's First Year. 512p. 1998. pap. 16.95 (*0-452-27419-2*, Plume) Dutton Plume.

Brown, Dennis G. & Pedder, Jonathan R. Introduction to Psychotherapy: An Outline to Psychodynamic Principles & Practice. 1979. 10.95 (*0-422-76670-4*, NO.2049, Pub. by Tavistock) Routldge.

Brown, Dennis G. & Zinkin, Louis, eds. The Psyche & the Social World: Developments in Group-Analytic Theory. LC 93-3918. (International Library of Group Psychotherapy & Group Process Ser.). 272p. (C). 1993. text 79.95 (*0-415-08708-2*, B0877) Routledge.

— The Psyche & the Social World: Developments in Group-Analytic Theory. LC 93-3918. (International Library of Group Psychotherapy & Group Process Ser.). 288p. (C). 1994. pap. 27.99 (*0-415-08709-0*, B0881) Routledge.

Brown, Denny L. Master Painters' Biblical History & Destiny of the World. LC 97-47719. 1998. 39.95 (*1-57345-371-4*, Shadow Mount) Deseret Bk.

Brown, Derek. Explaining Bread & Wine, Vol. 49. (Explaining Ser.). 1999. pap. text 5.99 (*1-85240-162-1*) SOV5.

***Brown, Derrick.** Upside Brown. (Pale Ale Poets Ser.). 59p. 1999. pap. 6.95 (*1-929250-00-2*) FarStarFire Pr.

***Brown, Derrick, et al.** Beyond the Valley of the Contemporary Poets: 1999 Anthology. O'Halloran, Jamie, ed. 72p. 2000. pap. 10.00 (*0-9670715-3-4*) Valley Contemp.

Brown, Derrick C., jt. auth. see Lee, William S.

Brown, Deryck F., jt. auth. see Watt, David A.

Brown, Desmond H. The Genesis of the Canadian Criminal Code of 1892. (Publications of the Osgoode Society). 272p. 1989. text 35.00 (*0-8020-5833-7*) U of Toronto Pr.

Brown, Desmond H., ed. A Documentary History of the Canadian Criminal Code of 1892. (Illus.). 505p. 1993. text 115.00 (*0-8020-3472-1*) U of Toronto Pr.

Brown, DeSoto. Aloha Waikiki. (Illus.). 96p. (Orig.). 1985. pap. 12.00 (*0-9607938-9-5*) Editions Ltd.

— Hawaii Goes to War. (Illus.). 160p. (C). 1989. pap. 17.00 (*0-915013-12-6*); text 24.95 (*0-915013-11-8*) Editions Ltd.

— Hawaii Recalls: Nostalgic Images of the Hawaiian Islands, 1910-1950. (Illus.). 134p. 1986. pap. 15.95 (*0-7103-0194-4*, 01944) Routledge.

Brown, DeSoto & Burlingame, Burl. Coverama - The Collector's Guide to Antique Hawaiian Milk Covers. 1994. pap. 4.80 (*0-9629227-4-9*) Pacific Mono.

Brown, Diana & Brown, Colin. The Whaler & the Privateer: The Story of Two Ships, 1795-1807. LC 93-86010. (Illus.). 270p. (Orig.). 1993. pap. 23.50 (*0-9638208-0-X*) Letter of Marque.

Brown, Diana D. Umbanda: Religion & Politics in Urban Brazil. LC 94-17210. 1994. reprint ed. pap. 19.00 (*0-231-10005-1*) Col U Pr.

Brown, Diane, jt. auth. see Geffert, Annette W.

Brown, Diane, ed. see Evans, Margaret.

Brown, Diane, ed. see Whittlesey, Lisa.

Brown, Diane B., jt. auth. see Hawthorne, Terri B.

Brown, Diane E. CorelDRAW! 5.0 for Windows at a Glance. LC 94-23965. (At a Glance Ser.). 128p. 1995. pap. 15.95 (*1-55622-451-6*) Wordware Pub.

Brown, Dick. Bonefish Fly Patterns: Tying, Selecting, & Fishing the Best Bonefish Flies. (Illus.). 256p. 1996. 45.00 (*1-55821-392-9*) Lyons Pr.

— Fly Fishing for Bonefish. (Illus.). 352p. 1993. 35.00 (*1-55821-203-5*) Lyons Pr.

Brown, Dollene P., ed. see Hammond, Judy.

Brown, Dolores. White Squaw, Adventures of a Lady Woodsman. 19.95 (*1-879356-13-9*) Wolfe Pub Co.

Brown, Don. Alice Ramsey's Grand Adventure. LC 96-31783. (Illus.). 32p. (J). (ps-3). 1997. 15.00 (*0-395-70127-9*) HM.

***Brown, Don.** Alice Ramsey's Grand Adventure. (Illus.). (J). 2000. pap. 5.95 (*0-618-07316-7*) HM.

Brown, Don. Herbal Prescriptions for Better Health. LC 95-32966. (Illus.). 368p. 1996. text 22.95 (*0-7615-0114-2*) Prima Pub.

— One Giant Leap: The Story of Neil Armstrong. LC 97-42152. 32p. (J). (gr. k-3). 1998. 16.00 (*0-395-88401-2*) HM.

***Brown, Don.** Rare Treasure: Mary Anning & Her Remarkable Discoveries. LC 98-32372. (Illus.). 32p. (J). (gr. k-3). 1999. 15.00 (*0-395-92286-0*) HM.

Brown, Don. Ruth Law Thrills a Nation. (Illus.). 32p. (J). 1995. pap. 5.95 (*0-395-73517-3*) H Holt & Co.

***Brown, Don.** Uncommon Traveler: Mary Kingsley in Africa. LC 99-87823. 2000. 16.00 (*0-618-00273-1*) HM.

Brown, Don. Ruth Law Thrills a Nation. LC 92-45701. 32p. (J). (ps-2). 1993. 15.00 (*0-395-66404-7*) Ticknor & Flds Bks Yng Read.

Brown, Don & Cohen, Andrew. Overview of the Indigent Health Care System in Texas. (Working Paper Ser.: No. 67). 76p. 1992. pap. 5.50 (*0-89940-549-5*) LBJ Sch Pub Aff.

Brown, Don W., jt. ed. see Brigham, John.

Brown, Dona. Inventing New England: Regional Tourism in the Nineteenth Century. LC 94-23220. (Illus.). 256p. 1995. 29.95 (*1-56098-473-2*) Smithsonian.

— Inventing New England: Regional Tourism in the Nineteenth Century. 254p. 1997. pap. 17.95 (*1-56098-799-5*) Smithsonian.

— A Tourist's New England: Travel Fiction, 1820-1920. LC 98-48769. (Hardscrabble Bks.). 227p. 1999. pap. 17.95 (*0-87451-900-4*) U Pr of New Eng.

Brown, Donald. Basic Metallurgy. LC 80-68584. (Mechanical Ser.). (Illus.). 323p. (Orig.). (C). 1981. teacher ed. 12.95 (*0-8273-1770-0*); mass mkt. 52.95 (*0-8273-1769-7*) Delmar.

Brown, Donald A. & Clary, Chanda. Sexuality in America: Contemporary Perspectives on Sexual Identity, Dysfunction & Treatment. LC 81-81824. 1981. 24.50 (*0-87650-132-3*) Pierian.

Brown, Donald A., jt. ed. see Lemons, John.

Brown, Donald B. & White, Chelsea, III, eds. Operations Research & Artificial Intelligence: The Integration of Problem-Solving Strategies. (C). 1990. lib. bdg. 157.00 (*0-7923-9106-3*) Kluwer Academic.

Brown, Donald E. Hierarchy, History, & Human Nature: The Social Origins of Historical Consciousness. LC 88-15287. 384p. 1988. 49.95 (*0-8165-1060-1*) U of Ariz Pr.

— Human Universals. 160p. (C). 1991. pap. 22.19 (*0-07-008209-X*) McGraw.

Brown, Donald E., ed. Intelligent Scheduling Systems. (Operations Research - Computer Science Interface Ser.). 272p. (C). 1994. lib. bdg. 148.50 (*0-7923-9515-8*) Kluwer Academic.

Brown, Donald E., et al. The Penis Inserts of Southeast Asia: An Annotated Bibliography with an Overview & Comparative Perspectives. LC 88-71425. (Occasional Papers: Vol. 15). (Illus.). 60p. (Orig.). (C). 1988. pap. text 6.00 (*0-944613-05-5*) UC Berkeley Ctrs SE Asia.

Brown, Donald G. Action. LC 68-132946. 164p. reprint ed. pap. 50.90 (*0-8357-5084-1*, 201414600090) Bks Demand.

Brown, Donald J. Herbal Prescriptions for Better Health: Your Everyday Guide to Prevention, Treatment & Care. (Illus.). 368p. 1997. pap. 16.00 (*0-7615-1001-X*) Prima Pub.

***Brown, Donald J.** Herbal Prescriptions for Health & Healing: Your Everyday Guide to Using Herbs Safely & Effectively. 8th ed. (Illus.). 2000. pap. 19.95 (*0-7615-2410-X*) Prima Pub.

Brown, Donald M. The White Umbrella: Indian Political Thought from Manu to Ghandi. LC 81-13391. (Illus.). 203p. 1982. reprint ed. lib. bdg. 59.50 (*0-313-23210-5*, BRWU, Greenwood Pr) Greenwood.

Brown, Donald N., jt. auth. see Parman, Ray, Jr.

Brown, Donald R., ed. The Role & Status of Women in the Soviet Union. LC 68-27326. 151p. reprint ed. pap. 46.90 (*0-608-14968-3*, 202599500048) Bks Demand.

Brown, Donald R. & Mathews, Wendell G. Real Estate Advertising Handbook. Berlin, Helene, ed. LC 81-51380. (Illus.). 96p. 1981. reprint ed. 10.00 (*0-686-73397-5*, 340) Realtors Natl.

Brown, Donald R., jt. auth. see Harvey, Donald F.

Brown, Donn W. Facility Maintenance: The Manager's Practical Guide & Handbook. LC 96-14639. 256p. 1996. 49.50 (*0-8144-0322-0*) AMACOM.

Brown, Donna. The History of Oklahoma. ii, 68p. 1985. teacher ed. 4.95 (*0-8061-1969-1*); pap. 0.75 (*0-8061-1971-3*); pap., wbk. ed. 4.95 (*0-8061-1970-5*) U of Okla Pr.

Brown, Doris V. & MacDonald, Pauline. Creative Art for Home & School. (Illus.). 1974. pap. 3.95 (*0-87505-060-3*) Borden.

***Brown, Dorothy H.** Christian Humanism in the Late English Morality Plays LC 99-28370. 1999. 49.95 (*0-8130-1701-7*) U Press Fla.

Brown, Dorothy H. & Ewell, Barbara C., eds. Louisiana Women Writers: New Essays & a Comprehensive Bibliography. LC 92-48. (Southern Literary Studies). 328p. (C). 1992. text 45.00 (*0-8071-1743-9*) La State U Pr.

Brown, Dorothy M. Mabel Walker Willebrandt: A Study of Power, Loyalty, & Law. LC 83-6651. (Illus.). 348p. 1984. 42.50 (*0-87049-402-3*) U of Tenn Pr.

***Brown, Dorothy M.** Poor Belong to Us: Catholic Charities & American Welfare. 304p. 2000. pap. 18.95 (*0-674-00401-9*) HUP.

Brown, Dorothy M. & McKeown, Elizabeth. The Poor Belong to Us: Catholic Charities & American Welfare. LC 97-25736. 352p. 1998. 45.00 (*0-674-68973-9*) HUP.

Brown, Dorothy S. Books for a Small Planet: A Multicultural-Intercultural Bibliography for Young English Language Learners. LC 93-61812. 94p. 1994. pap. 18.95 (*0-939791-53-6*) Tchrs Eng Spkrs.

— Handle with Care: A Question of Alzheimer's. 120p. 1984. pap. 8.95 (*0-932910-47-5*) Potentials Development.

— Handle with Care: A Question of Alzheimer's. LC 84-61253. 120p. 1984. pap. 17.95 (*0-87975-272-6*) Prometheus Bks.

— A World of Books. 2nd rev. ed. 70p. 1988. pap. 12.95 (*0-939791-32-3*) Tchrs Eng Spkrs.

Brown, Dorris D. Agricultural Development in India's Districts. LC 71-131467. (Center for International Affairs Ser.). 182p. 1971. 26.95 (*0-674-01230-5*) HUP.

Brown, Dottie. Alabama. LC 93-37796. (Hello U. S. A. Ser.). (Illus.). 72p. (J). (gr. 3-6). 1994. lib. bdg. 19.93 (*0-8225-2741-3*, Lerner Publctns) Lerner Pub.

— Delaware. LC 92-44845. (Illus.). 72p. (J). (gr. 3-6). 1994. lib. bdg. 19.93 (*0-8225-2733-2*, Lerner Publctns) Lerner Pub.

Brown, Dottie. Kentucky. Lerner Geography Department Staff, ed. (Hello U. S. A. Ser.). (Illus.). 72p. (J). (gr. 3-6). 1992. lib. bdg. 19.93 (*0-8225-2715-4*, Lerner Publctns) Lerner Pub.

— Kentucky. (Hello U. S. A. Ser.). (Illus.). 72p. (J). (gr. 3-6). 2000. pap. 5.95 (*0-8225-9687-3*, First Ave Edns) Lerner Pub.

Brown, Dottie. New Hampshire. LC 92-28662. (Hello U. S. A. Ser.). (Illus.). 72p. (J). (gr. 3-6). 1993. lib. bdg. 19.95 (*0-8225-2730-8*, Lerner Publctns) Lerner Pub.

— New Hampshire. (Hello U. S. A. Ser.). (Illus.). 72p. (J). (gr. 3-6). 1998. pap. 5.95 (*0-8225-9789-6*) Lerner Pub.

— Ohio. Lerner Geography Department Staff, ed. (Hello U. S. A. Ser.). (Illus.). 72p. (J). (gr. 3-6). 1992. lib. bdg. 19.95 (*0-8225-2725-1*, Lerner Publctns) Lerner Pub.

— Ohio. (Illus.). 72p. (J). 1995. pap. 5.95 (*0-8225-9708-X*) Lerner Pub.

Brown, Doug, jt. auth. see Satir, Gregory.

Brown, Douglas. Thomas Hardy. LC 79-19057. (Illus.). 196p. 1980. reprint ed. lib. bdg. 35.00 (*0-313-22105-7*, BRTH, Greenwood Pr) Greenwood.

— Traffic Offences: An Examination of the Principles of Law Governing Offences Committed by Motorists on the Roads of Australia. 2nd ed. 302p. 1988. 75.00 (*0-409-49517-4*, AT, MICHIE) LEXIS Pub.

Brown, Douglas A., jt. ed. see Hansen, Gerald E.

***Brown, Douglas E. & Brown, Kaori A.** Bad Dog! True Tales of Trouble Only a Best Friend Could Get Away With. LC 99-48250. 192p. 2000. pap. 14.95 (*1-58245-164-8*) Howell Bks.

Brown, Douglas H. An Interactive Course in English. 160p. (C). 1993. pap. text 14.40 (*0-13-471152-1*) P-H.

— Vistas No. 1: An Interactive Course in English. 144p. (C). 1991. pap. text 14.40 (*0-13-650326-8*) P-H.

— Vistas No. 2: An Interactive Course in English. 144p. (C). 1991. pap. text 14.40 (*0-13-650334-9*, 640802) P-H.

— Vistas No. 3: An Interactive Course in English. 144p. (C). 1992. pap. text 14.40 (*0-13-471160-2*) P-H.

Brown, Douglas H., et al. Challenges: A Process Writing Course in English. 256p. (C). 1990. pap. text 30.07 (*0-13-009085-9*) P-H.

Brown, Douglas M. Thorstein Veblen in the Twenty-First Century: A Commemoration of the Theory of the Leisure Class, 1899-1999. LC 98-29683. 256p. 1998. 80.00 (*1-85898-613-3*) E Elgar.

Brown, Douglas M. & Fry, Earl H., eds. States & Provinces in the International Economy. LC 92-44595. 248p. (C). 1993. pap. 24.95 (*0-87772-335-4*) UCB IGS.

Brown, Douglas M. & Smith, Murray G. Canadian Federalism: Meeting Global Economic Challenges? 300p. 1991. pap. 15.00 (*0-88911-574-5*, Pub. by Inst Res Pub) Ashgate Pub Co.

Brown, Douglas M., jt. ed. see Fafard, Patrick C.

Brown, Douglas M., jt. ed. see Watts, Ronald L.

Brown, Douglas R. The Restaurant Manager's Handbook: How to Set up, Operate, & Manage a Financially Successful Restaurant. 3rd rev. ed. Montgomery, Robert, ed. LC 88-84047. (Illus.). 300p. 1992. 59.95 (*0-910627-08-8*) Atlantic FL.

Brown, Douglas S. Lynchburg's Pioneer Quakers & Their Meeting House. 3rd rev. ed. (Illus.). 125p. 1997. reprint ed. 14.95 (*1-890306-06-1*) Warwick Hse.

Brown, Douglas T. & Prout, H. Thompson. Counseling & Psychotherapy with Children & Adolescents: Theory & Practice for School & Clinic Settings. 2nd ed. LC 89-62094. (Illus.). 434p. (C). 1989. text 49.50 (*0-88422-104-0*) Clinical Psych.

Brown, Douglas T., jt. auth. see Prout, H. Thompson.

Brown, Douglas V., et al. The Economics of the Recovery Program. LC 70-163644. (FDR & the Era of the New Deal Ser.). 1971. reprint ed. lib. bdg. 27.50 (*0-306-70197-9*) Da Capo.

Brown, Douglass V. Economics of the Recovery Program. LC 68-29202. (Essay Index Reprint Ser.). 1977. reprint ed. 18.95 (*0-8369-0400-1*) Ayer.

Brown, Dovid. Mysteries of the Creation. (Illus.). 400p. 1987. 19.99 (*0-939833-24-7*) Mosdos Pubs.

— Mysteries of the Creation: A Cosmology Derived from the Tanuch & Chazal. 402p. 1997. 21.95 (*1-56871-145-X*) Targum Pr.

Brown, Drollene p. Belva Lockwood Wins Her Case. Levine, Abby, ed. LC 87-2114. (Albert Whitman Biography Ser.). (Illus.). 48p. (J). (gr. 3-7). 1987. lib. bdg. 13.95 (*0-8075-0630-3*) A Whitman.

Brown, Drollene P. Remembering Daddy: A Daughter's Biography of Wilson William Plattner (Nov. 5, 1912-Dec. 30, 1987) (Illus.). 145p. 1999. pap. text 9.95 (*0-9641216-4-6*) RitAmelia Pr.

— Thomas & Launia - Their Ancestors & Descendants: A History of One Branch of the Lincoln County, West Virginia, McClures. Reynolds, Sharon E., ed. LC 94-20856. (Illus.). 192p. (Orig.). 1994. pap. 24.95 (*0-9641216-0-3*) RitAmelia Pr.

Brown, Drollene P., jt. auth. see Goldman, Abe.

Brown, Drollene P., ed. see King, Charles.

Brown, Duane. Dropping out or Hanging In: What you Should Know Before Dropping Out of School. (Illus.). 88p. 1994. pap. 7.95 (*0-8442-8687-7*, VGM Career) NTC Contemp Pub Co.

— Dropping-Out or Hanging In: What You Should Know Before Dropping-Out of School. 88p. Date not set. pap., teacher ed. 4.95 (*0-8442-8691-5*, VGM Career) NTC Contemp Pub Co.

— Dropping Out or Hanging In: What You Should Know Before Dropping Out of School. 2nd ed. 128p. 1998. teacher ed. 5.95 (*0-8442-4538-0*, VGM Career) NTC Contemp Pub Co.

— Dropping Out or Hanging In: What You Should Know Before Dropping Out of School. 2nd ed. LC 97-48614. (Illus.). 112p. 1998. pap., student ed. 8.95 (*0-8442-4537-2*, 45372, VGM Career) NTC Contemp Pub Co.

— Flying Without Fear. LC 95-72224. 176p. 1996. pap. 13.95 (*1-57224-042-3*) New Harbinger.

— How to Find a New Career upon Retirement. (Professional Careers Ser.). (Illus.). 160p. 1994. pap. 9.95 (*0-8442-4392-2*, VGM Career) NTC Contemp Pub Co.

— Proven Strategies for Improving Learning & Achievement. 307p. 1999. pap. text 26.95 (*1-56109-086-7*, EC 237) CAPS Inc.

Brown, Duane & Brooks, Linda. Career Counseling Techniques. 308p. 1990. text 76.00 (*0-205-12874-2*, H28749) Allyn.

Brown, Duane & Brooks, Linda, eds. Career Choice & Development. 3rd rev. ed. (Psychology Ser.). 560p. 1996. 37.95 (*0-7879-0204-7*) Jossey-Bass.

***Brown, Duane & Pryzwansky, Walter B.** Psychological Consultation: Introduction to Theory & Practice. 5th ed. 384p. 2000. 60.00 (*0-205-32210-7*) Allyn.

Brown, Duane & Srebalus, David J. An Introduction to the Counseling Profession. 2nd ed. LC 95-33253. 448p. 1995. 79.00 (*0-205-16204-5*) Allyn.

Brown, Duane, et al. Career Choice & Development. LC 83-49258. (Jossey-Bass Social & Behavioral Science Ser.). (Illus.). 527p. reprint ed. pap. 150.20 (*0-8357-4870-7*, 2037802) Bks Demand.

Brown, Duane, jt. auth. see Srebalus, David J.

Brown, Dub, ed. see Cate, Michael, et al.

Brown, Duncan. The Monkey's Constitution. LC 97-68483. (Illus.). 88p. (J). (gr. 4-8). 1997. pap. 7.95 (*1-57960-030-1*) Disc Enter Ltd.

***Brown, Duncan.** Oral Literature & Performance in Southern Africa. LC 99-16622. 256p. 2000. pap. 22.95 (*0-8214-1309-0*, Ohio U Ctr Intl) Ohio U Pr.

Brown, Duncan. Voicing the Text: South African Oral Poetry & Performance. LC 99-164985. 304p. 1999. pap. text 18.95 (*0-19-571632-9*) OUP.

— Zenlux: Architecture & Electronics. (Illus.). 64p. (Orig.). 1997. pap. 15.00 (*0-930829-39-5*) Lumen Inc.

***Brown, Duncan, ed.** Oral Literature & Performance in Southern Africa. LC 99-16622. 256p. 2000. text 44.95 (*0-8214-1308-2*, Ohio U Ctr Intl) Ohio U Pr.

***Brown, Duncan & Armstrong, Michael.** Paying for Contribution: Real Performance Related Pay Strategies. 435p. 1998. 34.95 (*0-7494-2899-6*) Kogan Page Ltd.

Brown, Duncan & VanDyk, Bruno, eds. Exchanges: South African Writing in Transition. x, 125 p. 1991. pap. 22.50 (*0-86980-789-7*, Pub. by Univ Natal Pr) Intl Spec Bk.

Brown, Dwight. Living in the Biosphere: Production, Pattern, Population, & Diversity. (Active Learning Modules on the Human Dimensions of Global Change Ser.). (Illus.). 158p. (C). 1997. pap., teacher ed. 20.00 (*0-89291-231-6*); pap., student ed., wbk. ed. 8.75 (*0-89291-232-4*) Assn Am Geographers.

Brown, E. Beyond the Winter Night. 6.99 (*1-85792-180-1*, Pub. by Christian Focus) Spring Arbor Dist.

— Learning to Live with Depression. 1997. pap. 2.99 (*1-85792-186-0*, Pub. by Christian Focus) Spring Arbor Dist.

Brown, E. D. The International Law of the Sea, 2 vols., Set. LC 94-21352. 950p. 1994. 179.95 (*1-85521-306-0*, Pub. by Dartmth Pub) Ashgate Pub Co.

— The International Law of the Sea, Set: Vols. I & II. LC 94-21352. (Illus.). 960p. 1994. pap. 89.95 (*1-85521-330-3*, Pub. by Dartmth Pub) Ashgate Pub Co.

Brown, E. D. & Churchill, Robin, eds. The U. N. Convention on the Law of the Sea: Impact & Implementation, 19th Annual Conference Proceedings. 654p. 1988. 38.50 (*0-911189-16-5*) Law Sea Inst.

***Brown, E. Don, ed.** Breaking Ranks: Changing an American Institution. (Illus.). 114p. (C). 1999. reprint ed. pap. text 40.00 (*0-7881-8355-9*) DIANE Pub.

Brown, E. H., ed. Geography Yesterday & Tomorrow. (Illus.). 312p. 1980. text 43.00 (*0-19-874096-4*) OUP.

Brown, E. I. Silam Irrusia (Weather Conditions) (ESK.). 23p. 1976. pap. 3.00 (*0-933769-64-4*) Alaska Native.

Brown, E. Jane, et al. The Official Book of the Polish Lowland Sheepdog. (Illus.). 160p. 1996. 39.95 (*0-7938-2084-7*, TS247) TFH Pubns.

Brown, E. Lynn. The Disciple - Pastor: Enabling & Equipping the Church for Discipleship. LC 93-78819. (Reader Resource Ser.). 100p. (Orig.). 1993. pap. text 6.00 (*1-883667-01-1*) Christian Meth.

Brown, E. M. & Simione, F. P., eds. ATCC Guide to Packaging & Shipping of Biological Materials. rev. ed. (Illus.). 32p. 1994. pap. text. write for info. (*0-930009-55-X*) ATCC.

Brown, E. M., jt. ed. see Simione, F. P.

Brown, E. Parker, II, et al. Contesting New York State Tax Assessments. 2nd ed. LC 89-61582. 117p. 1989. 30.00 (*0-942954-24-6*) NYS Bar.

Brown, E. R. The Twenty-Seventh Indiana Volunteer Infantry. 1988. 47.00 (*0-934085-04-8*) Amereon Ltd.

Brown, E. R., ed. New Pavement Materials. (Sessions Proceedings Ser.). 112p. 1988. 5.00 (*0-87262-638-5*) Am Soc Civil Eng.

Brown, E. Richard. Rockefeller Medicine Men: Medicine & Capitalism in America. LC 78-65461. (Illus.). 295p. 1979. 17.95 (*0-520-04269-7*, Pub. by U CA Pr) Cal Prin Full Svc.

Brown, E. Richard, et al. The Uninsured in California: Causes, Consequences & Solutions. 44p. 1997. pap. write for info. (*1-929008-06-6*) CA HlthCare Fnd.

Brown, E. T., ed. Rock Characterization, Testing & Monitoring: ISRM Suggested Methods. LC 80-49711. 200p. 1981. 97.00 (*0-08-027308-4*, Pub. by Pergamon Repr) Franklin.

Brown, E. T., jt. auth. see Brady, B. H.

Brown Eakley, Barbara. The Browns of Bedford County, VA, 1784-1840: A Collection of Brown Surname Records Extracted from Primary & Secondary Sources. LC 98-215559. 186p. 1998. pap. 18.50 (*0-7884-0922-0*, E044) Heritage Bk.

Brown, Earl A. Law of Oil & Gas Leases, 2 vols. 2nd ed. 1958. ring bd. 250.00 (*0-8205-1160-9*) Bender.

An Asterisk (*) at the beginning of an entry indicates that the title is appearing for the first time.

Brown, Earl J. Basic Concepts in Pathology: A Student's Survival Guide. LC 97-35643. (Basic Concepts Ser.). (Illus.). 456p. 1997. pap. text 25.95 (*0-07-008321-5*) McGraw-Hill HPD.

— Pathology. 9th ed. (Basic Sciences: Pretest Self Assessment & Review Ser.). (Illus.). 1998. pap. 18.95 (*0-07-052686-9*) McGraw-Hill HPD.

Brown, Earl J., ed. Integrated Basic Sciences: PreTest Self-Assessment & Review. LC 98-49307. (Illus.). 304p. 1999. pap. text 29.00 (*0-07-052551-X*) McGraw-Hill HPD.

Brown, Earl K. Women of Mr. Wesley's Methodism. LC 83-22010. (Studies in Women & Religion: Vol. 11). 270p. 1989. lib. bdg. 89.95 (*0-88946-538-X*) E Mellen.

Brown, Earl L. Why Race Riots? LC 74-22734. (Labor Movement in Fiction & Non-Fiction Ser.). reprint ed. 29.50 (*0-404-58486-1*) AMS Pr.

Brown, Earl L. & Leighton, George R. Negro & the War. LC 75-172045. reprint ed. 32.50 (*0-404-00194-7*) AMS Pr.

Brown, Ed, et al. Official Guide to Corel VENTURA 7, Vol. 7. LC 97-185331. 656p. (Orig.). 1997. pap. text 34.99 (*0-07-882169-X*) Osborne-McGraw.

Brown, Edgar & Behrens, Kaye. Humanetics Testing Procedure. (Illus.). 12p. (Orig.). 1985. pap. 2.95 (*0-9613697-2-8*) Madison Ave Pub.

— Your Body's Response. LC 82-90165. (Illus.). 192p. (Orig.). 1985. 22.95 (*0-9613697-1-X*); pap. 16.95 (*0-9613697-0-1*) Madison Ave Pub.

***Brown, Edi.** A Pirate Treasure. ii, 232p. (YA). (gr. 5-10). 2000. 5.95 (*0-9677953-0-3*) Red Fox OR.

Brown, Edmund G. Mea Culpa: Money, Lies & the Killing of Democracy. 144p. 1994. pap. 7.95 (*1-882206-05-3*) Argonaut Pr.

Brown, Edmund R. The Twenty-Seventh Indiana Volunteer Infantry. 640p. 1985. reprint ed. 40.00 (*0-942211-43-X*) Olde Soldier Bks.

Brown, Edna, tr. see Kahn, Lisa.

Brown, Edward. Account of Some Travels. (Illus.). 179p. 1971. 20.95 (*0-405-01728-6*) Arno Press.

— Arabian Medicine. 1992. 19.95 (*0-935782-19-2*) Kazi Pubns.

— Just Around the Corner in New Jersey. (Illus.). 112p. (J). (gr. 6 up). 1987. pap. 7.95 (*0-912608-17-X*) Mid Atlantic.

Brown, Edward & Boehm, Arthur. The Modern Seafood Cookbook: New Tastes, New Techniques New Ease. 352p. 1995. 30.00 (*0-517-70241-X*) C Potter.

Brown, Edward E. Tassajara Bread Book. (Orig.). 1974. pap. 5.95 (*0-394-73003-8*) Random.

— The Tassajara Bread Book. 25th anniversary ed. (Illus.). 160p. 1995. pap. 12.95 (*1-57062-089-X*, Pub. by Shambhala Pubns) Random.

— Tassajara Cooking. 1974. pap. 8.95 (*0-394-70949-7*) Random.

— Tassajara Cooking. LC 85-8185. 1986. pap. 17.00 (*0-87773-344-9*, Pub. by Shambhala Pubns) Random.

— The Tassajara Recipe Book: Favorites of the Guest Season. LC 84-23576. (Illus.). 160p. 1985. pap. 17.00 (*0-87773-308-2*, Pub. by Shambhala Pubns) Random.

***Brown, Edward E.** The Tassajara Recipe Book: Favorites of the Guest Season. rev. ed. LC 00-21721. 256p. 2000. pap. 16.95 (*1-57062-580-8*, Pub. by Shambhala Pubns) Random.

Brown, Edward E. Tomato Blessings & Radish Teachings: Recipes & Reflections. LC 96-43994. 320p. 1998. pap. 15.95 (*1-57322-673-4*, Riverhd Trade) Berkley Pub.

Brown, Edward E. & Madison, Deborah. The Greens Cookbook: Extraordinary Vegetarian Cuisine from the Celebrated Restaurant. LC 86-47884. 416p. 1987. 29.95 (*0-553-05195-4*) Bantam.

Brown, Edward G., Jr., tr. see Rocard, Marcienne.

Brown, Edward J. Russian Literature since the Revolution. enl. rev. ed. (Illus.). 424p. 1982. 49.95 (*0-674-78203-8*); pap. 21.50 (*0-674-78204-6*) HUP.

Brown, Edward J., ed. see Vroon, Ronald.

Brown, Edward K. Studies in the Text of Matthew Arnold's Prose Works. 1972. 59.95 (*0-8490-1151-5*) Gordon Pr.

Brown, Edward S. A Badge Without Blemish: Avoiding Police Corruption. 66p. 1997. pap. 6.95 (*1-57502-510-8*, PO1515) Morris Pubng.

***Brown, Edward S., III.** The Liberating Factor: Unmasking the Truth about Life. 2nd ed. LC 99-98074. (Illus.). 110p. 1999. pap. 9.95 (*0-9678208-0-4*) ESB Pubng.

Brown, Edward W., III. The Liberating Factor. (Illus.). 136p. (Orig.). 1997. pap. 10.95 (*1-57502-440-3*, PO1331) Morris Pubng.

Brown, Edwin G., jt. auth. see Feinstein, Barbara.

Brown, Edwin H., jt. ed. see Evans, Bernard W.

Brown, Edwin J., et al. Managing the Classroom: The Teacher's Part in School Administration. 2nd ed. LC 87-5983. (Douglass Series in Education). 262p. reprint ed. pap. 81.30 (*0-608-08658-4*, 206918100003) Bks Demand.

Brown, Edwin L. It Is Union & Liberty: Alabama Coal Miners, 1898-1998. LC 99-6205. 1999. 39.95 (*0-8173-0999-3*) U of Ala Pr.

***Brown, Edwin L. & Davis, Colin J., eds.** It Is Union & Liberty: Alabama Coal Miners, 1898-1998. LC 99-6205. 184p. 1999. pap. 19.95 (*0-8173-1000-2*) U of Ala Pr.

Brown, Edwin P. In the Wake of Whales. 61.95 (*0-8488-0873-8*) Amereon Ltd.

Brown, Edwin R., compiled by. Old Historic Homes of Cheshire, with an Account of the Early Settlement of the Town, Etc. (Illus.). 138p. 1997. reprint ed. lib. bdg. 25.00 (*0-8328-5627-4*) Higginson Bk Co.

Brown, Edwina & Parfrey, Patrick, eds. Complications of Long-Term Dialysis. LC 98-22503. (Oxford Clinical Nephrology Ser.). (Illus.). 354p. 1999. text 139.50 (*0-19-262829-1*) OUP.

Brown, Elaine. A Taste of Power. (Illus.). 464p. 1993. pap. 16.95 (*0-385-47107-6*, Anchor NY) Doubleday.

Brown, Elaine S. Secret Songs of Sara. LC 97-66172. 221p. 1997. pap. 13.95 (*1-878647-37-7*) APU Pub Grp.

Brown, Eleanor. Maiden Speech. LC 96-210361. 64p. 1996. pap. 15.95 (*1-85224-351-1*, Pub. by Bloodaxe Bks) Dufour.

— Readings, Issues, & Questions in Public Finance. (C). 1988. pap. text 26.95 (*0-256-06316-8*, Irwn McGrw-H) McGrw-H Hghr Educ.

Brown, Eleanor & Brown, Bob. Culinary Americana: Cookbooks Published in the Cities & Towns of the U. S. 431p. 1996. reprint ed. 60.00 (*1-888262-21-4*) Martino Pubng.

Brown, Eleanor, jt. auth. see Cluff, Sheila.

Brown, Eleanor, jt. auth. see Rosen, Harvey S.

Brown, Eleanor A. Recipes for Fitness for Very Busy People. rev. ed. (Illus.). 89p. 1985. pap. 6.95 (*0-9618805-1-1*) Fitness Ojai.

Brown, Eleanor F. Bibliotherapy & Its Widening Applications. LC 74-28187. 414p. 1975. 37.00 (*0-8108-0782-3*) Scarecrow.

Brown, Eli M., jt. ed. see Brown, Morris.

Brown, Elijah. The Real America. LC 73-13124. (Foreign Travelers in America, 1810-1935 Ser.). 308p. 1974. reprint ed. 26.95 (*0-405-05447-5*) Ayer.

Brown, Elinor L. Cherish Your Health. (Illus.). 220p. 1997. pap. 19.95 (*0-918798-30-2*) Midwest Pub NE.

— A Consumer's Guide for Aluminum Products, Their Effects on Humans, Animals, & Plants with Alternatives & Commentary. (Illus.). 144p. (Orig.). 1987. pap. 24.95 (*0-918798-04-3*) Midwest Pub NE.

Brown, Eliot, jt. auth. see Braybrooks, Ann.

Brown, Elisabeth P. & Stuard, Susan M., eds. Witness for Change: Quaker Women over Three Centuries. LC 88-27157. 200p. (C). 1989. pap. text 17.00 (*0-8135-1448-7*) Rutgers U Pr.

Brown, Elizabeth. In a Nutshell: Alternative Medicine: A Step-by-Step Guide. (In a Nutshell Ser.). 64p. 1997. 7.95 (*1-86204-155-5*, Pub. by Element MA) Penguin Putnam.

Brown, Elizabeth, et al. Making Residential Care Work: Structure & Culture in Children's Homes. LC 98-70907. (Dartington Social Research Ser.: No. 1). (Illus.). 200p. 1998. pap. 16.95 (*1-84014-457-2*) Ashgate Pub Co.

— Marking Residential Care Work: Structure & Culture in Children's Homes. LC 98-70907. (Dartington Social Research Ser.: Vol. 1). 176p. 1998. text 51.95 (*1-84014-499-8*, Pub. by Ashgate Pub) Ashgate Pub Co.

Brown, Elizabeth, jt. auth. see Brown, Fan.

Brown, Elizabeth A. The Anne Frank Project. (Illus.). 12p. 1993. pap. 15.00 (*0-942006-24-0*) U of CA Art.

— Customary Aids & Royal Finance in Capetian France: The Marriage Aid of Philip the Fair. (Medieval Academy Bks.: No. 100). (Illus.). xvi, 331p. 1992. 45.00 (*0-915651-00-9*) Medieval Acad.

— Franks, Burgundians, & Aquitanians & the Royal Coronation Ceremony in France. LC 92-70404. (Transactions Ser.: Vol. 82, Pt. 7). (Illus.). 217p. (C). 1993. pap. 20.00 (*0-87169-827-7*, T827-BRE) Am Philos.

— Guys Who Sew. (Illus.). 15p. 1994. pap. 3.00 (*0-942006-45-3*) U of CA Art.

— The Monarchy of Capetian France & Royal Ceremonial. (Collected Studies: No. CS 345). 350p. 1991. text 115.95 (*0-86078-279-4*, Pub. by Variorum) Ashgate Pub Co.

— The Oxford Collection of the Drawings of Roger de Gagnieres & the Royal Tombs of Saint-Denis. LC 87-72867. (Transactions Ser.: Vol. 78, Pt. 5). (Illus.). (C). 1988. pap. 12.00 (*0-87169-785-8*, T785-BRE) Am Philos.

— Politics & Institutions in Capetian France. (Collected Studies: No. CS 350). 336p. 1991. text 109.95 (*0-86078-298-0*, Pub. by Variorum) Ashgate Pub Co.

***Brown, Elizabeth A. & Dini, Jane, eds.** Afterglow in the Desert: The Art of Fernand Lungren. (Illus.). 96p. 2000. pap. 23.00 (*0-942006-70-4*) U of CA Art.

Brown, Elizabeth A. R., ed. Jean Du Tillet & the French Wars of Religion: Five Tracts, 1562-1569. (Medieval & Renaissance Texts & Studies: Vol. 108). 248p. 1994. 25.00 (*0-86698-155-1*, MR108) MRTS.

Brown, Elizabeth B. No More Walking on Eggshells: Living Successfully with Screw. LC 99-25171. 256p. 1999. pap. 11.99 (*0-8007-5708-4*) Revell.

Brown, Elizabeth D., et al, eds. Accrediation Guide for Substance Abuse Programs. LC 96-51238. 224p. (C). 1997. pap. 19.95 (*0-7619-0564-2*, 05642) Sage.

Brown, Elizabeth G. British Statutes in American Law. LC 73-21605. (American Constitutional & Legal History Ser). 1974. reprint ed. lib. bdg. 42.50 (*0-306-70610-5*) Da Capo.

— British Statutes in American Law, 1776-1836. LC 64-64845. (Michigan Legal Publications). xii,377p. 1984. reprint ed. lib. bdg. 45.00 (*0-89941-321-8*, 303130) W S Hein.

Brown, Elizabeth K. Sticker Paper Dolls Bunny Rabbit Family. 50th ed. (Illus.). (J). (gr. k-3). 1990. pap. 3.95 (*0-486-26503-X*) Dover.

Brown, Elizabeth M. New Haven: A Guide to Architecture & Urban Design. LC 75-18166. (Illus.). 228p. 1976. pap. 14.00 (*0-300-01993-9*) Yale U Pr.

Brown, Elizabeth W. Parents Stop! Don't Give up, There Is Hope. 96p. 1998. pap. 8.95 (*0-89228-116-2*) Impact Christian.

Brown, Ellen. All Wrapped Up. LC 97-36111. (Illus.). 160p. 1998. pap. 12.00 (*0-7679-0137-1*) Broadway BDD.

— Great Chefs of the East. Miller, Carolyn, ed. LC 94-77617. (Illus.). 257p. 1995. 29.95 (*0-929714-65-2*) Great Chefs TV.

— Great Chefs of the East. Miller, Carolyn, ed. LC 94-77617. (Illus.). 257p. 1995. pap. 24.95 (*0-929714-66-0*) Great Chefs TV.

— Southwest Tastes. 4th ed. LC 87-14865. (Illus.). 212p. 1990. reprint ed. pap. 24.95 (*0-929714-24-5*) Great Chefs TV.

— Southwest Tastes. 6th ed. LC 87-14865. (Illus.). 212p. 1987. reprint ed. 29.95 (*0-929714-04-0*) Great Chefs TV.

Brown, Ellen & Walker, Lynn. Menopause & Estrogen: Natural Alternatives to Hormone Replacement Therapy. 2nd ed. LC 96-53863. (Illus.). 197p. (Orig.). 1997. pap. 14.95 (*1-883319-53-6*) Frog Ltd CA.

Brown, Ellen H. Forbidden Medicine: Is Effective Non-Toxic Cancer Treatment Being Suppressed? LC 98-203415. x, 329p. 1998. write for info. (*1-879854-28-7*) Christian Servs Pub.

Brown, Ellen H. & Walker, Lynn P. The Alternative Pharmacy: Break the Drug Cycle with Safe, Natural Alternative Treatments for Over 200 Common Health Conditions. LC 98-21512. 432p. (C). 1998. text write for info. (*0-13-907254-3*) P-H.

— Informed Consumer's Pharmacy: The Complete Guide to Prescription & Over-the-Counter Drugs. 308p. 1990. pap. 12.95 (*0-88184-586-8*) Carroll & Graf.

Brown, Ellen H. & Walker, Lynne P. The Alternative Pharmacy. LC 98-21512. 400p. 1998. pap. text 22.00 (*0-7352-0021-1*) PH Pr.

— Breezing Through the Change: Managing Menopause Naturally. LC 93-26662. 197p. 1994. pap. 14.95 (*1-883319-12-9*) Frog Ltd CA.

Brown, Elmer C. 100 Bible Studies You Need: A Layperson's Guide for Growth. LC 97-78180. 99p. 1998. 24.95 (*0-9661986-1-1*) Avalon Valley.

— Sharing the Road: Experiences of Touring Bicyclists: on North Carolina's Outer Banks, on the Blue Ridge Parkway, in the People's Trepublic of China. LC 98-93504. 190p. 1999. write for info. (*0-9661986-2-X*) Avalon Valley.

Brown, Elmer C., jt. auth. see Thompson, James R.

Brown, Elmer E. Making of Our Middle Schools. LC 77-89153. (American Education: Its Men, Institutions, & Ideas. Series 1). 1977. reprint ed. 35.95 (*0-405-01391-4*) Ayer.

Brown, Emily C. Har Dayal: Hindu Revolutionary & Rationalist. LC 74-16895. 335p. 1975. pap. 103.90 (*0-608-05649-9*, 206610300006) Bks Demand.

— Soviet Trade Unions & Labor Relations. LC 66-21332. 406p. reprint ed. pap. 125.90 (*0-608-14302-2*, 201726000006) Bks Demand.

Brown, Emily I. The Tales of Ticasuk: Eskimo Legends & Stories. Bedford, Jimmy & Morack, K. Fiedler, eds. LC 87-81286. (Illus.). 134p. 1987. lib. bdg. 15.00 (*0-912006-24-2*) U of Alaska Pr.

— Tales of Ticasuk: Eskimo Legends & Stories. LC 87-81286. (Illus.). 134p. 1990. reprint ed. pap. 8.95 (*0-912006-45-5*) U of Alaska Pr.

***Brown, Emily M.** Affairs: A Guide to Working through the Repercussions of Infidelity. LC 99-6189. 256p. 1999. 25.00 (*0-7879-5004-1*) Jossey-Bass.

Brown, Emily M. Patterns of Infidelity & Their Treatment. LC 90-25925. (Frontiers in Couples & Family Therapy Ser.: No. 3). (Illus.). 304p. 1991. text 40.95 (*0-87630-631-8*) Brunner-Mazel.

Brown, Enid. Suriname & the Netherlands Antilles: An Annotated English-Language Bibliography. LC 92-10786. 293p. 1992. 36.00 (*0-8108-2576-7*) Scarecrow.

Brown, Eric. Different Shades of Courage: A Coloring & Activities Book of African American Achievement, Vol. 1. Sheen, Jen, ed. (Illus.). 53p. (Orig.). (J). (gr. 4 up). 1993. pap. 9.95 (*0-9636468-0-X*) Little Tike.

***Brown, Eric.** News of the World Football Annual 1999-2000. 1999. pap. 10.95 (*0-00-218883-X*, Pub. by HarpC) Trafalgar.

— Ring Nitrogen & Key Biomolecules: The Biochemistry of N-Heterocycles. LC 98-70669. 256p. 1998. write for info. (*0-412-83570-3*) Kluwer Academic.

Brown, Eric. That's Edutainment! A Parents Guide to Educational Software. 400p. 1995. pap. text 29.95 (*0-07-882083-9*) Osborne-McGraw.

— Wings of the Luftwaffe. (Illus.). 176p. 1993. pap. 28.95 (*1-85310-413-2*) Airlife Publishing.

— Wings of the Navy: Flying Allied Carrier Aircraft of World War II. LC 86-62670. (Illus.). 176p. 1987. 28.95 (*0-87021-995-2*) Naval Inst Pr.

— Wings of the Weird & Wonderful. (Illus.). 160p. 1987. 19.95 (*0-8306-9404-8*, 2404) McGraw-Hill Prof.

Brown, Eric, jt. ed. see CCH Editorial Staff.

Brown, Eric, jt. ed. see CCH Editors.

Brown, Eric H., ed. see Vaughan-Brown, Joy.

Brown, Eric M. Duels in the Sky: WWII Naval Aircraft in Combat. LC 88-15258. (Illus.). 288p. 1988. 29.95 (*0-87021-063-7*) Naval Inst Pr.

***Brown, Erica.** Loss, Change & Grief: An Educational Perspective. 1998. pap. 25.95 (*1-85346-465-1*) Taylor & Francis.

Brown, Erica. Provence Gastronomique. (Illus.). 160p. 1996. 29.95 (*0-7892-0038-4*) Abbeville Pr.

— Religious Education for All LC 96-142008. viii, 104 p. 1996. write for info. (*1-85346-392-2*) David Fulton.

Brown, Erik. Seat in a Wild Place: Seasons on a New Hampshire Pond. LC 81-15017. (Illus.). 128p. 1993. pap. 10.00 (*0-87233-059-1*) Bauhan.

***Brown, Erika.** How to Think Like the Worlds Greatest High-Tech Titans. (Leader's Edge Ser.). 224p. 2000. 18.95 (*0-07-136068-9*) McGraw.

Brown, Ernest & Hedrick, Henry B. Tables of the Motion of the Moon, 3 vols., Set. 1920. pap. 750.00 (*0-685-89789-3*) Elliots Bks.

***Brown, Ernest C.** California Public Works Projects: Managing Contracts & Resolving Disputes. LC 99-65953. (Illus.). 200p. 1999. pap. 29.95 (*1-929170-00-9*) Pubs Design.

Brown, Ernest D., Jr. Lozi. LC 96-45306. (Heritage Library of African Peoples: Set 4). (Illus.). 64p. (YA). (gr. 7-12). 1996. lib. bdg. 16.95 (*0-8239-2015-1*, D2015-1) Rosen Group.

Brown, Ernest F. Joseph Hawley: Colonial Radical. LC 31-29646. reprint ed. 20.00 (*0-404-01128-4*) AMS Pr.

Brown, Errol, et al. Managing Environmental Risks in Texas: Background Papers, Vol. 1. (Working Paper Ser.: Vol. 78). 166p. 1994. pap. 10.50 (*0-89940-565-7*) LBJ Sch Pub Aff.

Brown, Esther L. Lawyers & the Promotion of Justice. (Russell Sage Foundation Reprint Ser.). reprint ed. lib. bdg. 39.00 (*0-697-00201-2*) Irvington.

— Lawyers, Law Schools & the Public Service. (Russell Sage Foundation Reprint Ser.). reprint ed. lib. bdg. 37.00 (*0-697-00200-4*) Irvington.

— Newer Dimensions of Patient Care, 3 pts. Incl. Pt. 1. Use of the Physical & Social Environment of the General Hospital for Therapeutic Purposes. 160p. 1961. pap. 16.50 (*0-87154-183-1*); Pt. 2. Improving Staff Motivation & Competence in the General Hospital. 194p. 1962. pap. 19.95 (*0-87154-184-X*); Pt. 3. Patients As People. 164p. 1965. pap. 14.95 (*0-87154-185-8*); 160p. pap. write for info. (*0-318-55563-8*) Russell Sage.

— Newer Dimensions of Patient Care, 3 vols., Set. Incl. Pt. 1. Use of the Physical & Social Environment of the General Hospital for Therapeutic Purposes. 160p. 1961. pap. 16.50 (*0-87154-183-1*); Pt. 2. Improving Staff Motivation & Competence in the General Hospital. 194p. 1962. pap. 19.95 (*0-87154-184-X*); Pt. 3. Patients As People. 164p. 1965. pap. 14.95 (*0-87154-185-8*); 160p. write for info. (*0-87154-182-3*) Russell Sage.

— Social Work As a Profession. 4th ed. LC 75-17207. (Social Problems & Social Policy Ser.). 1976. reprint ed. 20.95 (*0-405-07479-4*) Ayer.

***Brown, Etta.** Life's Real Moments. 1999. pap. write for info. (*1-58235-239-9*) Watermrk Pr.

Brown, Eugene, jt. auth. see Snow, Donald M.

Brown, Eugene, jt. ed. see Seefeldt, Vern.

Brown, Eugene, jt. ed. see Youth Sports Institute Staff.

Brown, Eulalia B. As I Think It. (Orig.). 1996. pap. 8.95 (*0-533-11783-6*) Vantage.

Brown, Eurnestine & Burgess, Norma J., eds. The African-American Woman: An Ecological Perspective. LC 99-30094. (MSU Series on Children, Youth & Families: No. 6). 212p. 1999. 55.00 (*0-8153-1591-0*) Garland.

Brown, Eva. My Parent's Keeper: Adult Children of the Emotionally Disturbed. 152p. (Orig.). 1989. pap. 11.95 (*0-934986-78-9*) New Harbinger.

Brown, Evelyn M. Kateri Tekakwitha: Mohawk Maid. LC 91-72271. (Vision Bks.). (Illus.). 178p. (J). (gr. 4-9). 1991. reprint ed. pap. 9.95 (*0-89870-380-8*) Ignatius Pr.

Brown, Evelyn W. & Sikes, Opal W. Wright: Descendants of Owen Wright & Letitia Dow Collins Wright, James Wright & Lydia E. Sorrels Wright & Anna L. Davenbrock Wright. (Illus.). 870p. 1994. reprint ed. pap. 89.50 (*0-8328-4044-0*); reprint ed. lib. bdg. 99.50 (*0-8328-4043-2*) Higginson Bk Co.

— Wright Book: Descendants of Owen & Letitia Dow (Collins) Wright; James & Lydia E. (Sorrels) Wright - Anna L. Dannenbrock Wright. 1000p. 1993. pap. 109.00 (*0-8328-2825-4*) Higginson Bk Co.

Brown, Evelyn W. & Wright, Alice G. Moran Family Pts. I & II: Descendants of Hezekiah, Robert Milton, Franklin Pierce Moran & Alice Grace Moran Wright; Services of George Brinton Mcclellan for the Preservation of the Union. (Illus.). 369p. 1997. pap. 45.00 (*0-8328-9475-3*); lib. bdg. 55.00 (*0-8328-9474-5*) Higginson Bk Co.

Brown, Evelyn W., et al. Moran: Descendants of Franklin Peirce Moran & Mary Adelaide Snyder Moran, with Family Tree of Early Moran Ancestors (From Hezekia of Montgomery Co., Md.) (Illus.). 373p. 1993. pap. 59.00 (*0-8328-2823-8*); lib. bdg. 69.00 (*0-8328-2822-X*) Higginson Bk Co.

Brown, Evelyne, tr. see Baines, John.

Brown, Everen T. Panoramic World: A Global Adventure in 80 Astounding Images. (Illus.). 88p. (Orig.). 1993. pap. 19.95 (*0-9636596-0-X*) E T Brown Spec.

Brown, Everett S. The Constitutional History of the Louisiana Purchase, 1803-1812. LC 68-55492. xi, 248p. 1972. reprint ed. 39.50 (*0-678-00742-X*) Kelley.

— Ratification of the 21st Amendment to the Constitution of the United States. LC 78-114757. (American Constitutional & Legal History Ser). 1970. reprint ed. 85.00 (*0-306-71928-2*) Da Capo.

Brown, F. Emile Zola: Critical Essays. 1999. pap. write for info. (*0-670-80463-0*) Viking Penguin.

— Fiber Plus Cookbook. 32p. 1999. pap. 4.95 (*0-9669535-1-7*) Amerigrain.

— Healthy Skin Cookbook. 56p. 1999. pap. 6.95 (*0-9669535-0-9*) Amerigrain.

— Rewriting the Good Fight: Critical Essays on the Literature of the Spanish Civil War. Brown, Frieda S. et al, eds. LC 88-43431. 266p. (C). 1989. text 26.00 (*0-87013-269-5*) Mich St U Pr.

Brown, F., ed. New Approaches to Stabilisation of Vaccines Potency: WHO Headquarters, May 1995. (Developments in Biological Standardization Ser.: Vol. 87). xii, 364p. 1996. pap. 278.25 (*3-8055-6309-4*) S Karger.

— Recombinant Vectors in Vaccine Development. (Developments in Biological Standardization Ser.: Vol. 82). (Illus.). viii, 272p. 1994. pap. 217.50 (*3-8055-5997-6*) S Karger.

— Transmissible Spongiform Enecephalopathies: Impact on Animal & Human Health. (Developments in Biological Standardization Ser.: Vol. 80). (Illus.). x, 234p. 1993. pap. 191.50 (*3-8055-5831-7*) S Karger.

B

— Virological Safety Aspects of Plasma Derivatives. (Developments in Biological Standardization Ser.: Vol. 81). (Illus.). x, 310p. 1994. pap. 235.00 (*3-8055-5879-1*) S Karger.

***Brown, F., et al, eds.** Alternatives to Animals in the Development & Control of Biological Products for Human & Veterinary Use: Congress, London, September 1998. (Developments in Biological Standardization Ser.: Vol. 101). (Illus.). xii, 340p. 1999. 274.00 (*3-8055-6953-X*) S Karger.

Brown, F., et al, eds. Animal Sera, Animal Sera Derivatives & Substitutes Used in the Manufacture of Pharmaceuticals: Viral Safety & Regulatory Aspects: Symposium, Strasbourg, May 1998. (Developments in Biological Standardization Ser.: Vol. 99). (Illus.). x, 216p. 1999. pap. 174.00 (*3-8055-6806-1*) S Karger.

***Brown, F., et al, eds.** A Celebration of 50 Years of Progress in Biological Standardization & Control of WHO: WHO Headquarters, Geneva, October 1998. (Illus.). VIII, 184p. 1999. pap. 148.00 (*3-8055-6952-1*) S Karger.

Brown, F., et al, eds. Continuous Cell Lines: An International Workshop on Current Issues Held in Bethesda, MD, March 1991. (Developments in Biological Standardization Ser.: Vol. 76). (Illus.). x, 354p. 1992. pap. 278.50 (*3-8055-5618-7*) S Karger.

***Brown, F., et al, eds.** Inactivated Influenza Vaccines Prepared in Cell Culture: Symposium National Institute for Biological Standards & Control Potters Bar 1997. (Developments in Biological Standardization Ser.: Vol. 98). (Illus.). x, 214p. 1999. pap. 174.00 (*3-8055-6896-7*) S Karger.

B

Brown, F., et al, eds. Replacement, Reduction & Refinement of Animal Experiments in the Development & Control of Biological Products. (Developments in Biological Standardization Ser.: Vol. 86, 1996). (Illus.). x, 374p. 1996. pap. 300.00 (*3-8055-6260-8*) S Karger.

Brown, F. & Lewis, B. P., eds. Poliovirus Attenuation: Molecular Mechanisms & Practical Aspects. (Developments in Biological Standardization Ser.: Vol. 78). (Illus.). viii, 192p. 1993. pap. 156.75 (*3-8055-5744-2*) S Karger.

Brown, F. & Mire-SLuis, T., eds. Biological Characterization & Assay of Cytokines & Growth Factors: Symposium at the National Institute for Biological Standards & Control, Potters Bar, September 1997. (Developments in Biological Standardization Ser.: Vol. 97). (Illus.). viii, 204p. 1999. pap. 161.00 (*3-8055-6895-9*) S Karger.

Brown, F. & Revillard, J. P., eds. Standardization of the Immunopharmacology of Natural & Synthetic Immunomodulators. (Developments in Biological Standardization Ser.: Vol. 77). (Illus.). x, 254p. 1992. pap. 182.75 (*3-8055-5619-5*) S Karger.

Brown, F. & Vannier, P., eds. The First Steps Towards an International Harmonization of Veterinary Biologicals: 1993 & Free Circulation of Vaccines Within the E.E.C. (Developments in Biological Standardization Ser.: Vol. 79). (Illus.). x, 238p. 1992. pap. 182.75 (*3-8055-5650-0*) S Karger.

***Brown, F. & Vyas, G., eds.** Advances in Transfusion Safety: Meeting, San Francisco, California, March 1999. (Developments in Biologicals Ser.: Vol. 102). (Illus.). xii, 252p. 2000. 208.75 (*3-8055-7043-0*) S Karger.

Brown, F., et al. The Brown-Driver-Briggs Hebrew & English Lexicon: Coded to Strong's Numbering System. 1184p. 1996. 34.95 (*1-56563-206-0*) Hendrickson MA.

Brown, F., jt. ed. see May, J. C.

Brown, F. B. Cornaceae & Allies in the Marquesas & Neighboring Islands. (BMB Ser.). 1972. reprint ed. pap. 25.00 (*0-527-02158-X*) Periodicals Srv.

— Flora of Southeastern Polynesia: Bayard Dominick Expedition Publication Nos. 20, 21, & 22, 3 vols. (BMB Ser.: No. 84). 1972. reprint ed. 25.00 (*0-527-02190-3*) Periodicals Srv.

— Flora of Southeastern Polynesia: Bayard Dominick Expedition Publication Nos. 20, 21, & 22, 3 vols, 89. (BMB Ser.: No. 84). 1972. reprint ed. 25.00 (*0-527-02195-4*) Periodicals Srv.

— Flora of Southeastern Polynesia: Bayard Dominick Expedition Publication Nos. 20, 21, & 22, 3 vols, 130. (BMB Ser.: No. 84). 1972. reprint ed. 55.00 (*0-527-02236-5*) Periodicals Srv.

Brown, F. C., et al. The 4th Marines & Soochow Creek: The Legend & the Medal. (World War II Monograph: Vol. 3). (Illus.). 28p. 1997. pap. 4.95 (*1-57638-103-X*, M3S) Merriam Pr.

Brown, F. D., jt. ed. see Camic, P. M.

Brown, F. E. & Oxenfeldt, A. R. Misperceptions of Economic Phenomena. LC 72-79606. 1977. 26.95 (*0-89197-851-8*) Irvington.

Brown, F. K. Last Hurdle. LC 87-29761. (Illus.). 202p. (J). (gr. 3-9). 1988. reprint ed. lib. bdg. 18.50 (*0-208-02212-0*, Linnet Bks) Shoe String.

Brown, F. K., jt. auth. see Frazier, Claude A.

Brown, F. Lee, jt. auth. see Kneese, Allen V.

***Brown, F. W.** Some of the Ancestors of Oliver Hazard Perry of Lowell, Mass. Pts. 1 & 2: Perry Ancestry; Moseley Ancestry. fac. ed. 60p. 1999. reprint ed. 22.00 (*0-7404-0020-7*) Higginson Bk Co.

Brown, Fahamisha P. Performing the Word: African American Poetry As Vernacular Culture. LC 98-46273. 225p. (C). 1999. pap. text 17.00 (*0-8135-2632-9*) Rutgers U Pr.

— Performing the Word: African American Poetry As Vernacular Culture. LC 98-46273. 225p. (C). 1999. text 48.00 (*0-8135-2631-0*) Rutgers U Pr.

***Brown, Fan & Brown, Elizabeth.** Ned's Journal. (Illus.). 65p. 2000. 15.95 (*0-9661847-4-2*, Pub. by Tatra Pr) Midpt Trade.

Brown, Faye. Chinch Bugs, Chinky Pins, & Chinie-Berry Beads. (Illus.). 191p. (Orig.). (J). 1990. pap. 9.95 (*0-943487-24-2*) Sevgo Pr.

***Brown, Faye.** ICD-9-CM Coding Handbook: Handbook with Answers. 1999. pap. write for info. (*1-55648-281-7*) AHPI.

— ICD-9-CM Coding Handbook: Handbook Without Answers. 1999. pap. 50.00 (*1-55648-282-5*) AHPI.

Brown, Faye. ICD-9-CM Coding Handbook: 1998 Edition. rev. ed. LC 99-161776. 1998. pap. 58.00 (*1-55648-238-8*) AHPI.

— ICD-9-CM Coding Handbook, Without Answers. 1998. pap. 48.00 (*1-55648-239-6*) AHPI.

— Pot Likker, Pulley Bones, & Pea Vine Hay. (Illus.). 226p. (Orig.). 1987. pap. 9.95 (*0-943487-02-1*) Sevgo Pr.

— Roas'nears, Rabbit Toback'r, 'n Rosebud Salve. (Illus.). 238p. (Orig.). 1992. pap. 9.95 (*0-943487-39-0*) Sevgo Pr.

Brown, Faye, ed. ICD-9-CM Coding Handbook, with Answers. 1997th rev. ed. LC 97-13109. 428p. 1997. pap. text 55.00 (*1-55648-202-7*, 148182) AHPI.

— ICD-9-CM Coding Handbook, Without Answers. 1997th rev. ed. LC 97-10675. 418p. 1997. pap. text 46.00 (*1-55648-203-5*, 148183) AHPI.

Brown, Faye, jt. auth. see Meads, Sue.

Brown, Faye C. Letters Home: The True Story of Lt. Harry Frank Hunt, Veterinary Reserve Corps, AEF, WWI. LC 98-160279. (Illus.). 108p. 1998. pap. 22.95 (*0-9661807-0-4*) Daphne Pub.

Brown, Felicia M. Indecorous Chain of Command: Chronicle of Sexual Harrassment in the Military. (Illus.). 125p. (Orig.). 1998. pap. 9.99 (*0-9662043-0-1*) R J Pubng.

Brown, Fern G. Daisy & the Girl Scouts: The Story of Juliette Gordon Low. (Illus.). 112p. (J). (gr. 3-6). 1996. lib. bdg. 14.95 (*0-8075-1440-3*) A Whitman.

— Franklin Pierce: Fourteenth President of the United States. Young, Richard G., ed. LC 88-30050. (Presidents of the United States Ser.). (Illus.). (J). (gr. 5-9). 1989. lib. bdg. 21.27 (*0-944483-25-9*) Garrett Ed Corp.

— Indians of North America. (J). 1995. pap. 10.98 (*0-8050-3250-9*) H Holt & Co.

— Indians of North America. LC 96-48802. (J). 1997. lib. bdg. 17.98 (*0-8050-3251-7*) H Holt & Co.

— James A. Garfield: Twentieth President of the United States. Young, Richard G., ed. LC 89-39953. (Presidents of the United States Ser.). (Illus.). 128p. (J). (gr. 5-9). 1990. lib. bdg. 21.27 (*0-944483-63-1*) Garrett Ed Corp.

— Owls. Perrotta, Mary, ed. LC 90-13093. (First Bks.). (Illus.). 64p. (J). (gr. 4-6). 1991. lib. bdg. 22.00 (*0-531-20008-6*) Watts.

— Special Olympics. Rich, Mary P., ed. LC 91-31661. (First Bks.). (Illus.). 64p. (J). (gr. 3-5). 1992. lib. bdg. 22.00 (*0-531-20062-0*) Watts.

Brown, Fiona, ed. see Constance, A.

Brown, Flora Rodriguez, jt. ed. see Shanahan, Timothy.

Brown, Florence M. & Hare, John W., eds. Diabetes Complicating Pregnancy: The Joslin Clinic Method. 2nd ed. LC 95-8383. 232p. 1995. 110.00 (*0-471-11031-0*) Wiley.

Brown, Floyd, jt. ed. see Wilbur, Kirby.

Brown, Floyd G. Slick Willie: Why America Cannot Trust Bill Clinton. (Illus.). 200p. 1992. pap. 8.95 (*0-9634397-0-7*) Annapolis-Wash Bk Pubs.

Brown, Floyd G., jt. auth. see Bossie, David N.

Brown, Forbes T., ed. see American Society of Mechanical Engineers Staff.

Brown, Forbes T., ed. see Fluidics Symposium Staff.

Brown, Fordyce M., et al, eds. Photographic Systems for Engineers. 2nd ed. LC 77-378304. (Illus.). 278p. reprint ed. pap. 86.20 (*0-8357-8648-X*, 203508900092) Bks Demand.

***Brown, Forman.** Better Angel: A Novel. 216p. 2000. reprint ed. pap. 11.95 (*1-55583-573-2*, Pub. by Alyson Pubns) Consort Bk Sales.

Brown, Forman. Better Angel: A Novel. 4th ed. LC 99-88591. (Illus.). 222p. 2000. pap. 11.95 (*1-55583-284-9*) Alyson Pubns.

Brown, Foster. Statistical Concepts: A Basic Program. 4th ed. (C). 1999. pap. text. write for info. (*0-8013-3123-4*) Longman.

Brown, Foster F., et al. Statistical Concepts: A Basic Program. 3rd ed. LC 94-35670. 160p. (C). 1997. pap. text 36.00 (*0-673-99440-6*) Addson-Wesley Educ.

Brown, Fran. Living Reiki: Takata's Teachings. 116p. 1992. pap. 12.95 (*0-940795-10-8*) LifeRhythm.

Brown, Frances. Tourism: Blight or Blessing? 1998. 45.95 (*0-7506-3989-X*) Buttrwrth-Heinemann.

***Brown, Frances.** Tourism Reassessed: Blight or Blessing? 160p. 2000. pap. 32.95 (*0-7506-4705-1*) Buttrwrth-Heinemann.

Brown, Francis. A History of the Roman Catholic Diocese of Steubenville, Ohio, Vol. I: The Mussio Years (1945-1977) LC 93-48794. 520p. 1994. text 119.95 (*0-7734-9110-4*) E Mellen.

Brown, Francis, ed. see Gesenius, William.

Brown, Francis, jt. tr. see Hitchcock, Roswell A.

Brown, Frank. Roman Architecture. pap. 15.95 (*0-8076-1472-6*, Pub. by Braziller) Norton.

Brown, Frank, ed. The Frame Problem in Artificial Intelligence: Proceedings of the 1987 Workshop. LC 87-4140. (Illus.). 360p. (Orig.). 1987. pap. text 23.95 (*0-934613-32-X*) Morgan Kaufmann.

Brown, Frank, jt. auth. see Lawless, Paul.

Brown, Frank B. Religious Aesthetics: A Theological Study of Making & Meaning. (Illus.). 242p. 1990. pap. text 17.95 (*0-691-02472-3*, Pub. by Princeton U Pr) Cal Prin Full Svc.

— Transfiguration: Poetic Metaphor & the Languages of Religious Belief. LC 82-24714. (Studies in Religion). x, 230p. 1983. 39.95 (*0-8078-1560-8*) U of NC Pr.

Brown, Frank C. The Frank C. Brown Collection of North Carolina Folklore, 7 vols. White, Newman I., ed. Incl. Vol. 2. Folk Ballads from North Carolina. LC 58-10967. 1964. text 45.95 (*0-8223-0254-3*); Vol. 3. Folk Songs from North Carolina. LC 58-10967. 1964. 32.50 (*0-8223-0255-1*); Vol. 4. Music of the Ballads. LC 58-10967. 1964. 32.50 (*0-8223-0256-X*); Vol. 5. Music of the Folk Songs. LC 58-10967. 1964. 32.50 (*0-8223-0257-8*); Vol. 7. Popular Beliefs & Superstitions from North Carolina, Pt. 2. LC 58-10967. 1964. 32.50 LC 58-10967. (Illus.). 1964. 175.00 (*0-8223-0260-8*) Duke.

Brown, Frank C., ed. see Miner, Robert G. & Early American Society Staff.

Brown, Frank E. Cosa: The Making of a Roman Town. (Illus.). 150p. 1980. text 44.50 (*0-472-04100-2*, 04100) U of Mich Pr.

Brown, Frank E. & Richardson, Emeline H., eds. Cosa III: The Buildings of the Forum:Colony, Municipium & Village. (Memoirs of the American Academy in Rome Ser.: Volume 37). (Illus.). 431p. (C). 1993. text 72.00 (*0-472-10609-0*, 10609) U of Mich Pr.

Brown, Frank E., et al. Cosa III: The Buildings of the Forum: Colony, Municipium, & Village. LC 92-20337. (Memoirs of the American Academy in Rome Ser.: Vol. XXXVII). (Illus.). 256p. 1993. 65.00 (*0-271-00825-3*) Pa St U Pr.

Brown, Frank M. Boolean Reasoning. (C). 1990. text 103.50 (*0-7923-9121-7*) Kluwer Academic.

Brown, Frank R., III, et al, eds. Diagnosis & Management of Learning Disabilities: An Interdisciplinary - Lifespan Approach. 3rd ed. (Illus.). 352p. (Orig.). 1996. pap. text 45.00 (*1-56593-420-2*, 1278) Thomson Learn.

Brown, Frank R. & Elksnin, Nick. An Introduction to Developmental Disabilities: A Neurodevelopmental Perspective. LC 94-7358. (Illus.). 232p. (Orig.). (C). 1994. pap. text 39.95 (*1-56593-103-3*, 0406) Thomson Learn.

Brown, Franklin L. Water & Poverty in the Southwest. Ingram, Helen M., ed. LC 87-19217. 237p. 1987. reprint ed. pap. 73.50 (*0-608-02349-3*, 206299000004) Bks Demand.

Brown, Franklin L. & Lebeck, A. O. Cars, Cans, & Dumps: Solutions for Rural Residuals. LC 75-24984. (Illus.). 222p. reprint ed. pap. 68.90 (*0-608-18386-5*, 203019100067) Bks Demand.

Brown, Fred. Best from Georgia Farms: A Cookbook & Tour Book. 1998. pap. text 18.95 (*1-58072-001-3*) C I Publ.

— Coker Creek: Cross Roads to History. 128p. 1991. pap. 9.95 (*0-9630962-0-6*) C C Ruritan.

— The Dillard House Cookbook & Mountain Guide. 2nd rev. exp. ed. LC 98-88549. (Illus.). 224p. 1998. pap. 15.95 (*1-56352-547-X*) Longstreet.

Brown, Fred. Making of a Modern Quaker: Roger Cowan Wilson 1906-1991. 1996. pap. 36.00 (*0-7162-0502-5*) Epworth Pr.

Brown, Fred. Riverkeeper's Guide to the Chattahoochee River: From Its Origin at Chattahoochee Gap to Apalachi. 1997. pap. text 18.95 (*1-58072-000-5*) C I Publ.

— Unofficial Guide to Atlanta, 1996. 476p. 1995. 14.95 (*0-02-860665-5*) Macmillan.

Brown, Fred, et al, eds. Characterization of Biotechnology Pharmaceutical Products: Symposium, Washington, D. C., December, 1995, No. 96. (Developments in Biological Standardization Ser.: Vol. 96). (Illus.). 212p. 1998. pap. 174.00 (*3-8055-6805-3*) S Karger.

— Pertussis Vaccine Trials: Symposium at the Istituto Superiore di Sanita, Rome, October/November 1995. LC 97-202571. (Developments in Biological Standardization Ser.: Vol. 89, 1997). (Illus.). xiv, 418p. 1997. pap. 339.25 (*3-8055-6481-3*) S Karger.

— Safety of Biological Products Prepared from Mammalian Cell Culture: Symposium Organized & Sponsored by the Marcel-Merieux Foundation & the International Association of Biological Standarization, Veyrier-du-Lac, Annecy, September-October 1996. LC 98-215112. (Developments in Biological Standardization Ser.: Vol. 93, 1998). (Illus.). viii, 248p. 1998. 200.00 (*3-8055-6732-4*) S Karger.

— Vaccines, '86: New Approaches to Immunization--Developing Vaccines Against Parasitic, Bacterial & Viral Diseases. LC 86-2589. 418p. (Orig.). 1986. pap. 75.00 (*0-87969-190-5*) Cold Spring Harbor.

— Vaccines, 1992: Modern Approaches to New Vaccines Including Prevention of AIDS. (Illus.). 400p. (C). 1992. text 100.00 (*0-87969-405-X*) Cold Spring Harbor.

— Vaccines, '90: Modern Approaches to New Vaccines Including Prevention of AIDS. (Illus.). 528p. 1990. pap. 100.00 (*0-87969-341-X*) Cold Spring Harbor.

— Vaccines, '97: Molecular Approaches to the Control of Infectious Diseases. (Illus.). 367p. (C). 1997. pap. text 100.00 (*0-87969-516-1*) Cold Spring Harbor.

— Vaccines, '96: Molecular Approaches to the Control of Infectious Diseases. (Illus.). 364p. (C). 1996. pap. text 100.00 (*0-87969-479-3*) Cold Spring Harbor.

Brown, Fred & Fernandez, James, eds. Development of Specifications for Biotechnology Pharmaceutical Products: Symposium at Hyatt Regency, San Francisco, Calif., May 1996. LC 98-100685. (Developments in Biological Standardization Ser.: Vol. 91, 1997). (Illus.). x, 122p. 1997. pap. 104.50 (*3-8055-6569-0*) S Karger.

Brown, Fred & Haaheim, Lars R., eds. Modulation of the Immune Response to Vaccine Antigens: Symposium, University of Bergen, June 1996. LC 98-134905. (Developments in Biological Standardization Ser.: Vol. 92, 1998). (Illus.). xii, 380p. 1998. 313.25 (*3-8055-6640-9*) S Karger.

Brown, Fred & Lewis, Andrew M., eds. Simian Virus 40 (SV40) - A Possible Human Polyomavirus: Workshop, Natcher Auditorium, National Institute of Health, Bethesda, MD, January 1997. (Illus.). xii, 412p. 1998. 330.50 (*3-8055-6733-2*) S Karger.

Brown, Fred & Lubiniecki, Anthony S., eds. Genetic Stability & Recombinant Product Consistency. (Developments in Biological Standardization Ser.: Vol. 83). (Illus.). viii, 204p. 1994. pap. 165.25 (*3-8055-5998-4*) S Karger.

— Viral Safety & Evaluation of Viral Clearance from Biopharmaceutical Products: National Institute of Health, Bethesda, Md., June 1995. (Developments in Biological Standardization Ser.: Vol. 88, 1996). (Illus.). x, 350p. 1996. pap. 274.00 (*3-8055-6391-4*) S Karger.

Brown, Fred, et al. Vaccine Design. LC 93-9132. (Molecular Medical Science Ser.). 136p. 1993. 120.00 (*0-471-93727-4*) Wiley.

Brown, Fred L. Vietnam War Diary of Fred Leo Brown. LC 98-94785. (Illus.). 520p. 1999. pap. 19.95 (*0-942551-15-X*) Combat Ready.

— Wall of Blood. 2nd rev. ed. LC 97-94706. (Illus.). 400p. (Orig.). 1998. pap. 19.95 (*0-942551-07-9*) Combat Ready.

***Brown, Fred Leo.** Lessons of War: The Play. LC 99-93476. 70p. 1999. write for info. (*0-942551-11-7*) Combat Ready.

Brown, Fred R., ed. Management: Concepts & Practice. LC 77-84858. 1977. 18.95 (*0-912338-15-6*); fiche 7.95 (*0-912338-16-4*) Lomond.

Brown, Fredda, jt. auth. see Snell, Martha E.

Brown, Fredda, jt. ed. see Lehr, Donna H.

Brown, Frederic J. Chemical Warfare: A Study in Restraints. LC 80-27993. 355p. 1981. reprint ed. lib. bdg. 45.50 (*0-313-22823-X*, BRCHW, Greenwood Pr) Greenwood.

— The U. S. Army in Transition Vol. II: Landpower in the Information Age. LC 92-12999. (Association of the U. S. Army Book Ser.). 224p. 1992. 25.00 (*0-02-881034-1*, 4154M) Brasseys.

Brown, Frederick. Biography of Gustave Flaubert. 2001. write for info. (*0-316-11878-8*) Little.

— From Tientsin to Peking with the Allied Forces. LC 73-111735. (American Imperialism Ser.). 126 p. 1970. reprint ed. 13.95 (*0-405-02004-X*) Arno Press.

— Zola: A Life. LC 94-33758. (Illus.). 888p. 1995. 37.50 (*0-374-29742-8*) FS&G.

— Zola: A Life. 888p. 1996. reprint ed. pap. 24.95 (*0-8018-5463-6*) Johns Hopkins.

Brown, Frederick G., et al, eds. Boylston, Mass. in the Civil War: The Letters Home of Pvt. John W. Partridge with Biographical Sketches of Other Boylston Soldiers. 183p. (Orig.). 1995. pap. text 16.50 (*0-7884-0225-0*) Heritage Bk.

***Brown, Frederick M.** America's Yesterday. (LC History-America-E). 319p. 1999. reprint ed. lib. bdg. 89.00 (*0-7812-4243-6*) Rprt Serv.

***Brown, Frederick M. & Griffiths, Pamela S.** P450Guide - Pocket Reference to Enzymatic Drug Metabolism: Year 2000 Edition. 36p. (C). 1999. pap. 4.95 (*0-9700084-0-6*) PFourFiveZeroguide.

Brown, Fredric. And the Gods Laughed. 1987. 19.00 (*0-932096-47-6*) Phantasia Pr.

— Murder Can Be Fun. 219p. 1989. pap. 3.95 (*0-88184-504-3*) Carroll & Graf.

— The Screaming Mimi. 166p. 1989. mass mkt. 3.50 (*0-88184-449-7*) Carroll & Graf.

— Space on My Hands. 1993. reprint ed. lib. bdg. 18.95 (*0-89968-332-0*, Lghtyr Pr) Buccaneer Bks.

— What Mad Universe? 1976. reprint ed. lib. bdg. 21.95 (*0-88411-892-4*) Amereon Ltd.

— What Mad Universe? 1993. reprint ed. lib. bdg. 18.95 (*0-89968-333-9*, Lghtyr Pr) Buccaneer Bks.

Brown, Fredrick M. & Conforti, Daniel A. Advanced Placement Comparative Government: A Practical Guide for Teachers. 76p. 1996. 29.95 (*1-930731-13-2*) DAC Ed Pubns.

— Advanced Placement European History: A Practical Curriculum Guide for Teachers. 87p. 1991. teacher ed. write for info. (*1-930731-04-3*) DAC Ed Pubns.

Brown, Fredrick M., jt. auth. see Conforti, Daniel A.

Brown, Freeda. Western Thunder. 1998. mass mkt. 5.99 (*1-55262-018-2*) SOV5.

Brown, Freeda, et al. Western Thunder. 464p. Date not set. mass mkt. 5.99 (*1-55197-027-9*) Picasso Publ.

Brown, Frieda S., jt. auth. see Tyrrell, William B.

Brown, Frieda S., ed. see Brown, F.

Brown, Friedl, tr. see Van Der Meer, Frederik.

Brown, G. Introduction to Inorganic Chemistry. 1985. pap. text. write for info. (*0-582-35459-5*, Pub. by Addison-Wesley) Longman.

Brown, G. & Opie, A. Chaos: Proceedings of the International Conference. 212p. 1993. text 81.00 (*981-02-1375-1*) World Scientific Pub.

Brown, G. & Wainwright, S. D., eds. The Pineal Gland & Its Endocrine Aspects: Proceedings of a Symposium with the 7th International Endocrinology Congress, Canada, April 1984. LC 85-9571. (Advances in the Biosciences Ser.: Vol. 53). (Illus.). 390p. 1985. 92.00 (*0-08-031992-0*, Pub. by Pergamon Repr) Franklin.

Brown, G., jt. auth. see Hughes, H. D.

Brown, G., jt. ed. see Leeser, M.

Brown, G. Baldwin, ed. see Vasari, Giorgio.

Brown, G. C., et al, eds. Deep-Marine Sedimentation: Depositional Models & Case Histories in Hydrocarbon Exploration & Development. (Illus.). 326p. (Orig.). 1990. pap. 23.00 (*1-878861-00-X*) Pac Section SEPM.

Brown, G. C. & Cooper, C. E., eds. Bioenergetics: A Practical Approach, No. 154. (Practical Approach Ser.: Vol. 154). (Illus.). 244p. 1995. text 110.00 (*0-19-963489-0*); pap. text 55.00 (*0-19-963488-2*) OUP.

An Asterisk (*) at the beginning of an entry indicates that the title is appearing for the first time.

Brown, G. E. George Orwell's Nineteen Eighty-Four. rev. ed. (Brodie's Notes Ser.). 80p. 1997. text 5.95 (*0-333-58158-X*, Pub. by Macmillan) Trans-Atl Phila.
— Selected Papers of T. H. R. Skyrme with Commentaries. (Series on Twentieth Century Physics). 456p. 1994. text 86.00 (*981-02-1646-7*) World Scientific Pub.
Brown, G. E., jt. auth. see Rho, Mannaque.
Brown, G. E., jt. ed. see Clark, J. R.
Brown, G. F. Robert Peers & the Department of Adult Education. 1981. pap. 22.00 (*0-902031-59-7*, Pub. by Univ Nottingham) St Mut.
— Robert Peers & the Department of Adult Education. (C). 1981. 30.00 (*0-902030-59-0*, Pub. by Univ Nottingham); text 30.00 (*0-7855-3177-7*, Pub. by Univ Nottingham) St Mut.
Brown, G. F., jt. auth. see Hughes, H. D.
Brown, G. I. The Big Bang: A History of Explosives. LC 98-230235. (Illus.). 272p. 2000. 35.00 (*0-7509-1878-0*, Pub. by Sutton Publng) Intl Pubs Mktg.
***Brown, G. I.** The Big Bang: A History of Explosives. (Illus.). 272p. 2000. pap. 16.95 (*0-7509-2361-X*) Sutton Publng.
Brown, G. I. Scientist, Soldier, Statesman, Spy; Count Rumford: The Extraordinary Life of a Scientific Genius. 2000. 21.95 (*0-7509-2184-6*) Sutton Pub Ltd.
Brown, G. K., jt. ed. see Agarwala, V. S.
Brown, G. M., et al, eds. Melatonin: Binding Sites in Endocrine & Immune Systems. (Journal: Biological Signals: Vol. 3, No. 2, 1994). (Illus.). 60p. 1994. pap. 30.50 (*3-8055-6007-9*) S Karger.
Brown, G. R. Property Investment & the Capital Markets. (Illus.). 350p. 1991. pap. 52.00 (*0-419-15530-9*) Thomson Learn.
Brown, G. S. & Le, Tony. Golfer's Gold. rev. ed. 250p. 1987. 28.00 (*0-940889-17-X*) Classics Golf.
Brown, G. Thompson. Presbyterians in World Mission: A Handbook for Congregations. 2nd rev. ed. (Illus.). 160p. 1995. pap. 11.95 (*1-885121-11-3*) CTS Press.
Brown, G. W. Understanding Business & Personal Law. 7th ed. 576p. 1983. text 24.28 (*0-07-053635-X*) McGraw.
— Understanding Business & Personal Law. 8th ed. 608p. 1987. pap. text 23.12 (*0-07-008433-5*) McGraw.
Brown, G. Z. Sun, Wind & Light: Architectural Design Strategies. LC 84-29117. 192p. (C). 1985. pap. 54.95 (*0-471-82063-6*) Wiley.
Brown, G. Z., et al. Insideout: Design Procedures for Passive Environmental Technologies. 2nd ed. LC 91-44625. 352p. 1992. pap. 69.95 (*0-471-55461-8*) Wiley.
Brown, Gail. Sensational Silk. LC 82-80827. (Illus.). 128p. (Orig.). 1982. pap. 6.95 (*0-935278-07-9*) Palmer-Pletsch.
Brown, Gail & Keeney, Bobbie. All-New Instant Interiors. LC 92-60757. (Illus.). 96p. 1992. pap. 14.95 (*0-932086-33-0*) Krause Pubns.
Brown, Gail & Young, Tammy. Innovative Serging. LC 89-42854. (Illus.). 192p. 1989. pap. 14.95 (*0-8019-7986-2*) Krause Pubns.
Brown, Gail, jt. auth. see Dillon, Karen.
Brown, Gail, jt. auth. see Phillips, Jeffery D.
***Brown, Gail J., ed.** Photodetectors Vol. 3287: Materials & Devices III. LC 98-172295. 368p. 1998. 89.00 (*0-8194-2726-8*) SPIE.
Brown, Gail J. & Razeghi, Manijeh, eds. Photodetectors Vol. 2999: Materials & Devices II. LC 97-193061. 458p. 1997. 89.00 (*0-8194-2410-2*) SPIE.
Brown, Gar, jt. auth. see Spence, Jim.
Brown, Gardner M., jt. auth. see Hammack, Judd.
Brown, Gareth. Scooter Boys. 128p. pap. 15.95 (*0-7119-6159-X*) Omnibus NY.
Brown, Gary. The Great Bear Almanac. (Illus.). 336p. 1993. 30.00 (*1-55821-210-8*) Lyons Pr.
— The Great Bear Almanac. (Illus.). 336p. 1996. pap. 19.95 (*1-55821-474-7*, 14747) Lyons Pr.
***Brown, Gary.** Hesitant Martyr in the Texas Revolution: James Walker Fannin. (Illus.). 275p. 2000. pap. 18.95 (*1-55622-778-7*, Rep of TX Pr) Wordware Pub.
— Mercenaries in the Texas Revolution: The New Orleans Greys. LC 98-31802. 336 p. 1999. pap. 18.95 (*1-55622-675-6*, Rep of TX Pr) Wordware Pub.
— Outwitting Bears. 2001. pap. 14.95 (*1-58574-160-4*) Lyons Pr.
Brown, Gary. Safe Travel in Bear Country. LC 95-40200. (Illus.). 152p. 1995. pap. 10.95 (*1-55821-349-X*) Lyons Pr.
— Sam's Mission Call. (Illus.). 24p. (J). 12.95 (*0-910523-13-4*) Grandin Bk Co.
Brown, Gary, ed. The NAFTA Business Guide. 250p. 1997. spiral bd. 185.00 (*1-893323-01-3*) WorldTrade Exec.
— Sourcing Manufactured Products in China. 600p. 1999. pap. 4.95 (*1-893323-14-5*) WorldTrade Exec.
— Technological Change in the Chavez Pass Region, North-Central Arizona. LC 90-84767. (Anthropological Research Papers: No. 41). (Illus.). xiv, 226p. 1990. pap. 20.00 (*0-936249-06-4*) AZ Univ ARP.
***Brown, Gary D.** Advanced COBOL for Structured & Object-Oriented Programming. 3rd ed. LC 98-38910. 640p. 1998. pap. 49.99 (*0-471-31481-1*) Wiley.
Brown, Gary D. System 390 Job Control Language. 4th ed. LC 97-53197. 480p. 1998. pap. 49.99 (*0-471-28309-6*) Wiley.
Brown, Gary D. & Smith, S. A. MVS - VSAM for the Application Programmer. 10th ed. 484p. 1993. pap. 49.95 (*0-471-56045-6*, GD423X) Wiley.
Brown, Gary E. How to Improve Your Grades & Live Happily Ever After: A Brief Guide to Academic Survival. 1973. pap. 4.95 (*0-87212-034-1*) Libra.
Brown, Gaye L., ed. The Dial: Arts & Letters in the 1920s. LC 80-54667. (Illus.). 160p. 1983. pap. 16.95 (*0-87023-407-2*) U of Mass Pr.
Brown, Gaye L. & Gibson, Anne P., eds. The Cookbook II. (Illus.). 184p. (Orig.). 1985. pap. 12.95 (*0-936042-40-0*) Worcest Art.
Brown, Gayle C. Signs by Gayle. 2nd ed. (Illus.). 60p. 1997. 10.95 (*1-57377-016-7*) Easl Pubns.
Brown, Gene. Anne Frank: Child of the Holocaust. LC 92-30735. (Library of Famous Women). (Illus.). 64p. (J). (gr. 4-7). 1991. lib. bdg. 17.95 (*1-56711-030-4*) Blackbirch.
— Anne Frank: Child of the Holocaust. 1993. 13.15 (*0-606-12589-2*, Pub. by Turtleback) Demco.
— Conflict in Europe & the Great Depression: World War I (1914-1940) LC 93-24998. (First Person America Ser.). (Illus.). 64p. (J). (gr. 5-8). 1995. lib. bdg. 18.90 (*0-8050-2585-5*) TFC Bks NY.
— Discovery & Settlement: Europe Meets the New World (1490-1700) LC 93-8537. (First Person America Ser.). (Illus.). 64p. (J). (gr. 5-8). 1995. lib. bdg. 18.90 (*0-8050-2574-X*) TFC Bks NY.
— H. Ross Perot: Texas Billionaire. LC 93-11998. (Made in America Ser.). 48p. (J). (gr. 4-8). 1993. lib. bdg. 21.60 (*0-86592-060-5*) Rourke Enter.
— Movie Time: A Chronology of Hollywood & the Movie Industry from Its Beginnings to the Present. LC 95-9091. (Illus.). 448p. 1995. 19.95 (*0-02-860429-6*, Pub. by Macmillan) S&S Trade.
— The Nation in Turmoil: Civil Rights & the Vietnam War (1960-1973) LC 93-24995. (First Person America Ser.). (Illus.). 64p. (J). (gr. 5-8). 1995. lib. bdg. 18.90 (*0-8050-2588-X*) TFC Bks NY.
— The Nineteen Ninety-Two Election. LC 92-19963. (Headliners Ser.). (Illus.). 64p. (J). (gr. 5-8). 1992. pap. 6.95 (*1-56294-806-7*); lib. bdg. 23.40 (*1-56294-080-5*) Millbrook Pr.
— Show Time: A Cronology of Broadway & the Theater from its Beginning to Present. LC 97-16529. (Illus.). 448p. 1997. 22.95 (*0-02-862072-0*) Macmillan.
— Showtime. LC 97-16529. (Illus.). 448p. 1997. 39.95 (*0-02-860830-5*) Macmillan.
— Sports of the Times: Great Moments in Sports History. Keylin, Arleen & Lundy, Daniel, eds. 1982. 18.95 (*0-405-14225-0*, 19816) Ayer.
— The Struggle to Grow: Expansionism & Industrialization (1880-1913) LC 93-24992. (First Person America Ser.). (Illus.). 64p. (J). (gr. 5-8). 1995. lib. bdg. 18.90 (*0-8050-2584-7*) TFC Bks NY.
— Violence on America's Streets. (YA). 1992. pap. 4.80 (*0-395-62469-X*) HM.
— Violence on America's Streets. LC 91-28929. (Headliners Ser.). (Illus.). 64p. (J). (gr. 5-8). 1992. pap. 6.95 (*1-878841-95-5*) Millbrook Pr.
Brown, Gene, ed. The Kennedys: A New York Times Profile. LC 80-10744. (Illus.). 256p. 1980. lib. bdg. 12.95 (*0-405-13142-9*) Ayer.
— The New York Times Encyclopedia of Film, 13 vols., Set. 1992. 495.00 (*0-8153-0349-1*) Garland.
Brown, Gene & Keylin, Arleen, eds. Sports: As Reported by the New York Times. LC 76-2450. (Illus.). 1976. 16.95 (*0-405-06689-9*) Ayer.
Brown, Gene, jt. auth. see Bruchey, Stuart.
Brown, Gene, jt. auth. see Hechinger, Fred M.
Brown, Gene, jt. auth. see Hovey, Graham.
Brown, Gene, jt. auth. see Lipsyte, Robert.
Brown, Gene, jt. auth. see McLanathan, Richard B.
Brown, Gene, jt. auth. see Middleton, Drew.
Brown, Gene, jt. auth. see Stein, Leon.
Brown, Gene, jt. auth. see Wade, Richard C.
Brown, Gene, jt. ed. see Keylin, Arleen.
Brown, Gene, jt. ed. see Shenton, James P.
Brown, Gene, jt. ed. see Teifer, Leonore.
Brown, Genevieve & Irby, Beverly J. The Principal Portfolio. LC 97-4757. (Illus.). 72p. 1997. 51.95 (*0-8039-6541-9*); pap. 22.95 (*0-8039-6542-7*) Corwin Pr.
— The Principal Portfolio. 72p. 1997. wbk. ed. 39.95 (*2-8106-6541-9*); pap., wbk. ed. 19.95 (*2-8106-6542-7*) NEA.
— Women & Leadership: Creating Balance in Your Life. LC 98-23872. 239p. 1998. 59.00 (*1-56072-571-0*) Nova Sci Pubs.
Brown, Geoff. James Brown: A Biography. (Illus.). 192p. 24.95 (*0-7119-2077-X*, OP45657) Omnibus NY.
— Music of Michael Jackson & Family. (Illus.). 152p. 1996. pap. 8.95 (*0-7119-5303-1*, OP47801) Omnibus NY.
— Prince. (Complete Guides to the Music Of...Ser.). (Illus.). 136p. (Orig.). (C). 1995. pap. 8.95 (*0-7119-4979-4*, OP 47773) Omnibus NY.
— Sabotage: A Study in Industrial Conflict. 402p. 1977. 42.50 (*0-85124-158-1*, Pub. by Spkesman) Coronet Bks.
Brown, Geoff, intro. The Industrial Syndicalist. (Documents on Socialist History Ser.: No. 3). 390p. 1974. 34.00 (*0-685-71537-X*, Pub. by Spkesman) Coronet Bks.
— The Syndicalist: Reproduced in Facsimile, 1912-1914. 104p. 1975. 57.50 (*0-685-71536-1*, Pub. by Spkesman) Coronet Bks.
Brown, Geoff & DeGooysr, Kemit. Mountain Bike Nova Scotia: A Guide to Off-Road Cycling in Nova Scotia. (Illus.). 96p. (Orig.). 1996. pap. 9.95 (*1-55109-155-0*) Nimbus Publ.
Brown, Geoffrey C. & Mussett, Alan E. The Inaccessible Earth. (Illus.). 272p. 1981. pap. text 34.95 (*0-04-550028-2*) Routledge.
— The Inaccessible Earth: An Integrated Approach to Geophysics & Geochemistry. 2nd ed. LC 93-13469. 288p. (gr. 13). 1993. pap. text 42.95 (*0-412-48160-X*) Chapman & Hall.
Brown, Geoffrey C., jt. auth. see Thorpe, Richard S.
Brown, Geoffrey W. The Marble Game, Vols. 1-4. 936p. (Orig.). 1986. pap. 19.95 (*0-936061-00-6*) Foothills.
Brown, George, Jr. Alien Presence. LC 99-93582. 2000. 8.95 (*0-533-09450-X*) Vantage.
Brown, George. George Brown, D. D. Pioneer-Missionary & Explorer, an Autobiography. LC 75-32802. (Illus.). 1976. reprint ed. 62.50 (*0-404-14104-8*) AMS Pr.
— Human Evolution. LC 94-71592. 288p. (C). 1995. text. write for info. (*0-697-24307-9*, WCB McGr Hill) McGrw-H Hghr Educ.
— Lecturing & Explaining. 1978. pap. 15.95 (*0-416-70920-6*, NO. 2009) Routledge.
— Melanesians & Polynesians. LC 71-174440. (Illus.). 465p. 1972. reprint ed. 19.95 (*0-405-08308-4*, Pub. by Blom Pubns) Ayer.
Brown, George & Atkins, Madeleine. Effective Teaching in Higher Education. 256p. 1988. pap. text 14.95 (*0-416-09082-6*) Routledge.
— Effective Teaching in Higher Education. 256p. (C). 1988. pap. 20.99 (*0-415-03675-5*) Routledge.
Brown, George & Lavigne, Michel. Canadian Wing Commanders of Fighter Command in W. W. Two. 324p. (C). 1987. 105.00 (*0-7855-2172-0*, Pub. by Picton) St Mut.
Brown, George, et al. Assessing Student Learning in Higher Education. LC 96-43134. 336p. (C). 1997. pap. 24.99 (*0-415-14460-4*) Routledge.
Brown, George, jt. auth. see Merry, Uri.
Brown, George, jt. auth. see Wyckoff, D. Campbell.
Brown, George A., ed. see American Society of Mechanical Engineers Staff.
Brown, George A., jt. ed. see Gupta, D. C.
Brown, George D. House with the Green Shutters. 59.00 (*0-403-00447-0*) Scholarly.
— The House with the Green Shutters. 310p. 1996. pap. 9.95 (*0-86241-549-7*, Pub. by Canongate Books) Interlink Pub.
— House with the Green Shutters. 1988. reprint ed. lib. bdg. 59.00 (*0-7812-0452-6*) Rprt Serv.
— Syllabification & Accent in the Paradise Lost. LC 73-39543. reprint ed. 29.50 (*0-404-01129-2*) AMS Pr.
Brown, George E. The Importance of Communication Within the Church. 77p. 1993. pap. 5.95 (*1-56794-050-1*, C-2328) Star Bible.
Brown, George E., et al. The Pruning of Trees, Shrubs & Conifers. LC 94-46985. (Illus.). 374p. 1995. 29.95 (*0-88192-319-2*) Timber.
Brown, George F., Sr. At the Rivers Edge. (Illus.). 30p. (Orig.). 1997. pap. 10.00 (*0-9645242-2-8*) Oceanfront Pub.
— Collective Works Vol. 1: Osprey, Vol. 1. 34p. 1993. 10.00 (*0-9645242-0-1*) OceanFront IA.
— More Works of George F. Brown, Sr., Vol. 2. 34p. 1995. lib. bdg. 10.00 (*0-9645242-1-X*) OceanFront IA.
— Musing in Rhyme. (Illus.). 46p. (Orig.). 1998. pap. 10.00 (*0-9663188-1-1*) Oceanfront Pub.
— The River's Edge. (Illus.). 1997. pap. text 10.00 (*0-614-31270-1*) OceanFront IA.
Brown, George F., Sr., et al. Poems from Pawleys. (Illus.). 32p. (Orig.). 1996. pap. text 12.00 (*0-9645242-3-6*) OceanFront IA.
Brown, George G. Brown on Divorce. (C). 1986. ring bd. 750.00 (*0-7219-1050-5*, Pub. by Scientific) St Mut.
— Brown on Separation. (C). 1981. pap. 125.00 (*0-7219-0840-3*, Pub. by Scientific) St Mut.
Brown, George H. And Part of Which I Was - Recollections of a Research Engineer. LC 82-72256. (Illus.). 342p. 1982. 30.00 (*0-9612524-0-5*) Angus Cupar.
— Bede the Venerable. (Twayne's English Authors Ser.). 144p. 1987. 22.95 (*0-8057-6940-4*, TEAS 443, Twyne) Mac Lib Ref.
— Doodles, Diddles, Puzzles, Quizzes & Fun Stuff for the Sports Fan, Vol. 3. Donaldson, Judith E., ed. & illus. by. Peters, Robert, illus. 144p. (Orig.). 1982. pap. 2.50 (*0-939942-02-X*) Larkspur.
— Travel Games Vol. 3: Sports. Donaldson, Judith E., ed. (Illus.). 36p. reprint ed. pap. text 1.50 (*0-939942-07-0*) Larkspur.
Brown, George H., jt. auth. see Donaldson, Judith E.
Brown, George H., ed. see Donaldson, Judith E.
Brown, George H., ed. see Greenfield, Stanley B.
Brown, George I., jt. auth. see Shiflett, John M.
Brown, George L. Elizabethtown Pleasant Valley: A History of Elizabethtown, Essex County. (Illus.). 480p. 1995. reprint ed. lib. bdg. 51.00 (*0-8328-5080-2*) Higginson Bk Co.
Brown, George M. Beside the Ocean of Time. large type ed. 240p. 1996. 21.95 (*1-85695-249-5*, Pub. by ISIS Lrg Prnt) Transaction Pubs.
— Following a Lark: Poems. 86p. 1996. pap. 14.95 (*0-7195-5620-1*, Pub. by John Murray) Trafalgar.
— For the Islands I Sing: An Autobiography. (Illus.) 192p. 1998. 35.00 (*0-7195-5628-7*, Pub. by John Murray) Trafalgar.
— For the Islands I Sing: An Autobiography. 192p. 1998. pap. 19.95 (*0-7195-5889-1*, Pub. by John Murray) Trafalgar.
— In the Margins of a Shakespeare. 1993. 450.00 (*0-907664-28-8*, Pub. by Old Stiles); boxed set 150.00 (*0-907664-24-5*, Pub. by Old Stiles) St Mut.
— The Island of the Women: And Other Stories. LC 99-176733. 320p. 1998. 27.00 (*0-7195-5869-7*, Pub. by John Murray) Trafalgar.
— Keepers of the House. (Illus.). 1993. 90.00 (*0-907664-08-3*, Pub. by Old Stiles) St Mut.
— Magnus. 1999. pap. 11.95 (*0-86241-814-3*, Pub. by Canongate Books) Interlink Pub.
— Prayer Power. 160p. (Orig.). 1992. pap. 8.95 (*0-940999-94-3*, C2264) Star Bible.
— Under Brinkie's Brae. 152p. (C). 1989. 39.00 (*0-903065-29-0*, Pub. by G Wright Pub) St Mut.
Brown, George M. Vinland. 232p. 1995. mass mkt. 11.95 (*0-00-654618-8*, Pub. by HarpC) Trafalgar.
— Winter Tales. 1996. pap. 13.95 (*0-00-655031-2*, Pub. by HarpC) Trafalgar.
Brown, George M. Winter Tales. large type ed. (Magna Large Print Ser.). 324p. 1997. 27.99 (*0-7505-1090-0*, Pub. by Mgna Lrg Print) Ulverscroft.
***Brown, George Mackay.** Northern Lights: A Poet's Sources. (Illus.). 336p. 2000. 29.95 (*0-7195-5949-9*, Pub. by John Murray) Trafalgar.
Brown, George R. The Leadership of Congress. LC 73-19135. (Politics & People Ser.). 318p. 1974. reprint ed. 23.95 (*0-405-05859-4*) Ayer.
Brown, George S. Yarmouth, Nova Scotia Genealogies: Transcribed from the Yarmouth Herald. Reamy, Martha & Reamy, William, eds. 956p. 1993. 60.00 (*0-8063-1372-2*, 705) Genealog Pub.
Brown, George T. Earthen Vessels & Transcendent Power: American Presbyterians in China 1837-1952. LC 97-38238. (American Society of Missiology Ser.: No. 25). (Illus.). 512p. 1997. 40.00 (*1-57075-150-1*) Orbis Bks.
Brown, George W. Reminiscences of Gov. R. J. Walker: With the True Story of the Rescue of Kansas from Slavery. LC 79-38010. (Black Heritage Library Collection). 1977. reprint ed. 21.95 (*0-8369-8978-3*) Ayer.
Brown, George W., ed. Canada. LC 71-134059. (Essay Index Reprint Ser.). 1977. 44.95 (*0-8369-2147-X*) Ayer.
Brown, George W. & Harris, Tirril O. Social Origins of Depression: A Study of Psychiatric Disorder in Women. LC 78-3209. 1978. 50.00 (*0-02-904890-7*) Free Pr.
***Brown, George W. & Harris, Tirril O.** Where Inner & Outer Worlds Meet: Psychosocial Research in the Tradition of George W. Brown. LC 00-42214. 2000. write for info. (*0-415-20268-X*) Routledge.
Brown, George W. & Harris, Tirril O., eds. Life Events & Illness. 496p. 1989. lib. bdg. 65.00 (*0-89862-723-0*) Guilford Pubns.
Brown, Georgina. Eye of the Storm. (Black Lace Ser.). 304p. (Orig.). 1996. mass mkt. 5.95 (*0-352-33044-9*, Pub. by Virgin Bks) London Brdge.
— Like Mother, Like Daughter. (Black Lace Ser.). 1999. mass mkt. 6.95 (*0-352-33422-3*) BLA4.
— Runners & Riders. (Black Lace Ser.). 300p. 1996. mass mkt. 5.95 (*0-352-33117-8*, Pub. by Virgin Bks) London Brdge.
— The Stallion. (Black Lace Ser.). 1995. mass mkt. 5.95 (*0-352-33005-8*, Pub. by Virgin Bks) London Brdge.
Brown, Gerald. I Was Drafted. (Illus.). 150p. pap. write for info. (*1-886364-11-7*) Rabeth Pub Co.
Brown, Gerda. Carismas de Dios. (SPA., Illus.). 589p. (Orig.). (C). 1983. pap. 8.95 (*0-939868-98-9*) Chr Intl Pubs.
Brown, Gerry & Morrison, Mike. The 2000 ESPN Information Please Sports Almanac. (Illus.). 959p. 1999. pap. 12.99 (*0-7868-8472-X*, Pub. by Hyperion) Time Warner.
Brown, Gerry, ed. see Morrison, Mike.
Brown, Gilbert T. Korean Pricing Policies & Economic Development in the 1960s. LC 73-8121. 336p. reprint ed. pap. 104.20 (*0-608-11890-7*, 202308600032) Bks Demand.
Brown, Gillian. Ancient Circle. 96p. (Orig.). (YA). (gr. 6-10). 1997. pap. 5.00 (*0-9657180-0-X*) Brown Bks.
***Brown, Gillian.** Consent of the Governed: The Lockean Legacy in Early American Culture. 256p. 2001. 49.95 (*0-674-00298-9*) HUP.
Brown, Gillian. Domestic Individualism: Imagining Self in Nineteenth-Century America. (New Historicism: Studies in Cultural Poetics: No. 14). (C). 1990. pap. 16.95 (*0-520-08099-8*, Pub. by U CA Pr) Cal Prin Full Svc.
— Held in Trust. large type ed. 1991. pap. 16.99 (*0-7089-6970-4*) Ulverscroft.
— Sleep Talk. large type ed. 1990. pap. 16.99 (*0-7089-6872-4*) Ulverscroft.
Brown, Gillian, et al, eds. Performance & Competence in Second Language Acquisition. (Illus.). 221p. (C). 1996. text 54.95 (*0-521-55193-5*); pap. text 21.95 (*0-521-55861-1*) Cambridge U Pr.
Brown, Gillian & Yule, George. Discourse Analysis. LC 82-23571. (Cambridge Textbooks in Linguistics Ser.). 304p. 1983. pap. text 23.95 (*0-521-28475-9*) Cambridge U Pr.
— Teaching the Spoken Language: An Approach Based on the Analysis of Conversational English. 162p. 1984. audio 19.95 (*0-521-25378-0*) Cambridge U Pr.
Brown, Gillian, jt. auth. see Howard, Ron.
Brown, Gilmor & Garwood, Alice. General Principles of Play Direction. 1936. 5.75 (*0-573-69010-3*) French.
Brown, Gina, et al, eds. 1997 Metroplex Wedding Directory. (Illus.). 101p. 1996. pap. 12.95 (*0-9635013-0-5*) JP Ink.
Brown, Gina & Brown, Jean, eds. 1998 Austin Wedding Directory. (Illus.). 116p. 1998. pap. 12.95 (*0-9635013-2-1*) JP Ink.
— 1998 Metroplex Wedding Directory. (Illus.). 118p. 1998. pap. 12.95 (*0-9635013-1-3*) JP Ink.
Brown, Ginger, jt. auth. see Brown, Ron.
Brown, Gita. Be I Whole. LC 95-18009. 267p. 1995. 16.95 (*1-878448-66-8*) MacMurray & Beck.
Brown, Glen. Yes, No, Maybe. Spelius, Carol, ed. (Illus.). 66p. (Orig.). 1995. pap. 9.95 (*0-941363-37-6*) Lake Shore Pub.
Brown, Glen, et al. Troika Vol. V: Don't Ask Why - File under Melancholy - Lithic Scatter. Fink, Eloise B., ed. LC 93-61783. 96p. 1994. pap. 5.95 (*0-939395-19-3*) Thorntree Pr.
Brown, Glen R. Intimate Immensity: Recent Works by Patti Warashina. 62p. 1996. pap. write for info. (*0-9650808-1-1*) Landmark Arts.
— Kradaad: Contemporary Thai Works on Paper. 35p. 1995. pap. write for info. (*0-9650808-0-3*) Landmark Arts.
Brown, Glenn. PalmPilot Resource Kit. (Illus.). 208p. 1998. spiral bd. 29.99 incl. cd-rom (*0-7645-3219-7*) IDG Bks.
— So There You Are: The Selected Prose of Glenn Brown.

B

Journalist. Ruffin, Paul D., ed. LC 98-11420. 272p. 1998. 30.00 (*1-881515-11-7*); pap. 20.00 (*1-881515-12-5*) TX Review Pr.

Brown, Gloria, ed. see Smith, Gerald H.

Brown, Godfrey N. & Hiskett, Mervyn. Conflict & Harmony in Education in Tropical Africa. 496p. 45.00 (*0-8386-1938-X*) Fairleigh Dickinson.

Brown, Goold. The Institutes of English Grammar. LC 81-18517. 376p. 1982. reprint ed. 50.00 (*0-8201-1372-7*) Schol Facsimiles.

Brown, Gordon. Administration of Wills, Trusts & Estates. 672p. 1997. write for info. (*0-8273-8284-7*) Delmar.

***Brown, Gordon.** Business Law with UCC Applications. 10th ed. 2000. 93.50 (*0-07-821041-0*) McGraw.

Brown, Gordon. Classic Spirits of the World. (Illus.). 264p. 1996. 35.00 (*0-7892-0165-8*) Abbeville Pr.

— Handbook of Fine Brandies. 1990. 24.95 (*0-02-517301-4*) Macmillan.

— The Whiskey Trails: A Traveller's Guide to Scotch Whisky. (Illus.). 224p. 1997. pap. 19.95 (*1-85375-227-4*) Prion.

Brown, Gordon, ed. High on the Walls: Mordant Tower Anthology. LC 90-80815. 128p. 1990. pap. 14.95 (*1-85224-148-9*, Pub. by Bloodaxe Bks) Dufour.

Brown, Gordon. Apples of Gold. 1962. boxed set 9.95 (*0-8378-1793-5*) Gibson.

— Wings of Silver. LC 67-21924. 1968. 9.95 (*0-8378-1773-0*) Gibson.

Brown, Gordon & Naughtie, James. John Smith: Life & Soul of the Party. (Illus.). 192p. 1996. 35.00 (*1-85158-692-X*, Pub. by Mainstream Pubng) Trafalgar.

Brown, Gordon & Wright, Tony, eds. Values Visions & Voices: An Anthology of Socialism. LC 96-145518. 224p. 1996. 35.00 (*1-85158-731-4*, Pub. by Mainstream Pubng) Trafalgar.

Brown, Gordon, jt. auth. see Drucker, Henry M.

Brown, Gordon, jt. ed. see Oaksford, Michael.

Brown, Gordon F., ed. see National Association of Retired Federal Employees.

Brown, Gordon S. Coalition, Coercion, & Compromise: Diplomacy of the Gulf Crisis, 1990-91. (Institute for the Study of Diplomacy Monograph Ser.). (Illus.). 104p. 1997. pap. 7.00 (*0-934742-93-6*) Geo U Inst Dplmcy.

Brown, Gordon W. Administration of Wills, Trusts & Estates. 90p. 1993. pap., teacher ed. 17.00 (*0-8273-5054-6*) Delmar.

— Administration of Wills, Trusts & Estates. LC 92-33816. 556p. 1993. text 47.25 (*0-8273-5053-8*) Delmar.

— Administration of Wills, Trusts & Estates. 2nd ed. LC 96-13114. (Paralegal Ser.). 640p. (C). 1997. mass mkt. 77.95 (*0-8273-7564-6*) Delmar.

***Brown, Gordon W.** Legal Terminology. LC 99-195589. 240p. (C). 1999. pap. text 15.00 (*0-536-02034-5*) Pearson Custom.

Brown, Gordon W. Legal Terminology. 3rd ed. LC 97-25589. 444p. 1997. pap. text 44.00 (*0-13-260373-X*) P-H.

— Massachusetts Student Pocket Part to Accompany Administration of Wills, Trusts, & Estates. 119p. 1993. 10.50 (*0-8273-6022-3*) Delmar.

Brown, Gordon W. & Rosenberg, R. Robert. Understanding Business & Personal Law: Performance Guide. 7th ed. (Illus.). 144p. 1983. pap. text 9.44 (*0-07-053636-8*) McGraw.

***Brown, Gordon W. & Sukys, Paul.** Business Law: With UCC Applications. 10th ed. LC 00-32129. (Illus.). 2000. write for info. (*0-07-821037-2*) McGraw.

Brown, Gordon W., et al. Business Law: With UCC Applications. 8th ed. LC 92-30558. 1992. 38.00 (*0-02-800653-4*) Glencoe.

— Business Law: With UCC Applications. 9th ed. LC 96-24988. 1996. write for info. (*0-02-802854-6*) Glencoe.

— Business Law: With UCC Applications. 9th ed. 800p. 1997. student ed. 48.59 (*0-02-802865-1*) Glencoe.

— Business Law: With UCC Applications. 9th annot. ed. 1997. teacher ed. 59.90 (*0-02-802859-7*) Glencoe.

— Business Law with UCC Applications. 7th ed. 704p. 1988. text 79.44 (*0-07-053919-7*) McGraw.

***Brown, Gordon W., et al.** Understanding Business & Personal Law: Teacher's Wraparound Edition. 1998. teacher ed. write for info. (*0-02-814637-9*) Glencoe.

Brown-Graham, Anita R. Creating Effective Partnerships for Community Economic Development. LC 98-204437. 39p. (C). 1997. pap. text 11.50 (*1-56011-314-6*, 97.11) Institute Government.

— A Practical Guide to Local Government Liability in North Carolina. (C). 1999. ring bd. 45.00 (*1-56011-347-2*, 99.05) Institute Government.

***Brown-Grant, Rosalind.** Christine de Pizan & the Moral Defence of Women: Reading Beyond Gender. (Cambridge Studies in Medieval Literature: No. 40). 240p. (C). 2000. 64.95 (*0-521-64194-2*) Cambridge U Pr.

Brown, Grayson W. Jesusgate: A Novel. LC 97-3917. (Crossroad Fiction Program Ser.). 228p. 1997. pap. 13.95 (*0-8245-1587-0*) Crossroad NY.

Brown, Greg, jt. auth. see Blair, Bonnie.

Brown, Greg, jt. auth. see Bledsoe, Drew.

Brown, Greg, jt. auth. see Elway, John.

Brown, Greg, jt. auth. see Marino, Dan.

Brown, Greg, jt. auth. see Martinez, Edgar.

Brown, Greg, jt. auth. see Pippen, Scottie.

Brown, Greg, jt. auth. see Ripken, Cal, Jr.

Brown, Greg, jt. auth. see Strug, Kerri.

Brown, Greg, jt. auth. see Swoopes, Sheryl.

Brown, Greg, jt. auth. see Vaughn, Mo.

Brown, Greg, jt. auth. see Young, Steve.

Brown, Gregory, jt. ed. see Ackerman, David.

Brown, Gregory, jt. ed. see Harvey, David.

Brown, Gregory D. The Song Prophet. 210p. (Orig.). (YA). 1996. pap. 10.99 (*1-57502-160-9*, PO758) Morris Pubng.

Brown, Gregory G., jt. ed. see Bornstein, Robert A.

Brown, Gregory M., et al, eds. Neuroendocrinology & Psychiatric Disorder. fac. ed. LC 84-4727. (Illus.). 446p. pap. 138.30 (*0-7837-7286-6*, 204702000005) Bks Demand.

Brown, Gregory N. Job Hunting for Pilots: Networking Your Way to a Flying Job. (Illus.). 166p. 1995. pap. 16.95 (*0-8138-2413-3*) Iowa St U Pr.

— The Savvy Flight Instructor: Secrets of the Successful CFI. LC 97-29694. (Illus.). 213p. 1997. pap. 19.95 (*1-56027-296-1*, ASA-SFI) ASA Inc.

Brown, Gregory N. & Holt, Mark J. The Turbine Pilot's Flight Manual. (Illus.). 208p. 1995. pap. 34.95 (*0-8138-2900-3*) Iowa St U Pr.

***Brown, Gregory N. & Holt, Mark J.** The Turbine Pilot's Flight Manual Set: Book & CD-ROM. 1998. pap. 74.95 incl. cd-rom (*0-8138-2901-1*) Iowa St U Pr.

Brown, Gregory N., jt. ed. see Duryea, Mary L.

Brown, Grey. Staying In. 24p. 1992. pap. 5.00 (*0-9624274-7-0*) NC Writers Network.

Brown-Guillory, Elizabeth. Alice Childress: The Writings of a Rebel Spirit. (Illus.). (C). text. write for info. (*0-472-10798-4*) U of Mich Pr.

Brown-Guillory, Elizabeth. Their Place on the Stage: Black Women Playwrights in America. LC 89-26672. 184p. 1990. pap. 14.95 (*0-275-93566-3*, B3566, Praeger Pubs) Greenwood.

— Their Place on the Stage: Black Women Playwrights in America, 117. LC 88-10237. (Contributions in Afro-American & African Studies: No. 117). 177p. 1988. 59.95 (*0-313-25985-2*, BGY/, Greenwood Pr) Greenwood.

Brown-Guillory, Elizabeth, compiled by. Wines in the Wilderness: Plays by African American Women from the Harlem Renaissance to the Present. LC 90-7120. (Contributions in Afro-American & African Studies: No. 135). 272p. 1990. pap. 16.95 (*0-275-93567-1*, B3537) Greenwood.

— Wines in the Wilderness: Plays by African American Women from the Harlem Renaissance to the Present, 135. LC 89-25857. (Contributions in Afro-American & African Studies: No. 135). 272p. 1990. 59.95 (*0-313-26509-7*) Greenwood.

Brown-Guillory, Elizabeth, ed. Women of Color: Mother-Daughter Relationships in Twentieth-Century Literature. LC 96-15697. 1997. 40.00 (*0-292-70846-7*); pap. 14.95 (*0-292-70847-5*) U of Tex Pr.

***Brown-Gutnik, Natalie.** The Complete Guide to Cross-Country Ski Preparation. LC 99-6249. 144p. 1999. pap. 18.95 (*0-89886-600-6*) Mountaineers.

***Brown, Guy.** The Energy of Life: The Science of What Makes Our Minds & Bodies Work. LC 99-86780. 288p. 2000. 25.00 (*0-684-86257-3*) Free Pr.

— Mitochondria & Cell Death. 1999. 75.00 (*0-691-05026-0*) Princeton U Pr.

***Brown, Guy Story.** Calhoun's Philosophy of Politics: A Study of "A Disfunctiion on Government" 512p. 2000. 45.00 (*0-86554-680-0*) Mercer Univ Pr.

***Brown, Gwen.** We Who Were Raised Poor. (JPN.). 1999. pap. 2.00 (*1-58429-061-7*) Rational Isl.

Brown, Gwen. We Who Were Raised Poor: Ending the Oppression of Classism. 1994. pap. 2.00 (*0-913937-90-8*) Rational Isl.

— Why Lead in RC. 25p. 1999. pap. 2.00 (*1-58429-038-2*) Rational Isl.

Brown, H. Rabelais in English Literature. 1972. 59.95 (*0-8490-0923-5*) Gordon Pr.

Brown, H., ed. Hypermedia-Hypertext & Object-Oriented Databases. (UNICOM Applied Information Technology Ser.: No. 8). (Illus.). 300p. 1991. write for info. (*0-412-39970-9*) Chapman & Hall.

Brown, H. & Berry, M., eds. Speak to the Hills: An Anthology of Twentieth Century British & Irish Mountain Poetry. (Illus.). 550p. 1985. text 29.00 (*0-08-030406-0*, Pub. by Aberdeen U Pr) Macmillan.

Brown, H. & Douglas, A. A Practical Guide to Language Learning: A Fifteen Week Program of Strategies for Success. (C). 1989. text 22.50 (*0-07-008208-1*) McGraw.

Brown, H. C. The Story of Old New York. 1977. lib. bdg. 59.95 (*0-8490-2683-0*) Gordon Pr.

Brown, H. Douglas. New Vistas, Bk. 1. 2nd ed. LC 98-14842. 144p. (C). 1998. pap. text 14.60 (*0-13-908195-X*) P-H.

— New Vistas, Getting Started. LC 97-44199. 128p. (C). 1998. pap. text 14.00 (*0-13-908351-0*) P-H.

— Principles of Language Learning & Teaching. 3rd ed. LC 93-26090. 352p. (C). 1993. pap. text 34.60 (*0-13-191966-0*) P-H.

***Brown, H. Douglas.** Principles of Language Learning & Teaching. 4th ed. LC 99-58205. 2000. write for info. (*0-13-017816-0*) P-H.

Brown, H. Douglas. Teaching by Principles: An Interactive Approach to Language Pedagogy. LC 93-29654. 480p. (Orig.). 1994. pap. text 37.33 (*0-13-328220-1*) P-H.

Brown, H. Douglas & Gonzo, Susan, eds. Readings on Second Language Acquisition. LC 93-42222. 500p. (C). 1994. pap. text 36.33 (*0-13-102260-1*) P-H.

Brown, H. G., jt. auth. see Wilson, J. I.

Brown, H. H., rev. Brown's Rule of the Road Manual. rev. ed. (Illus.). (C). 1987. 100.00 (*0-85174-405-2*) St Mut.

Brown, H. Jackson, Jr. The Complete Life's Little Instruction Book. deluxe ed. LC 97-5575. 224p. 1997. lthr. 19.95 (*1-55853-490-3*) Rutledge Hill Pr.

— The Complete Live & Learn & Pass It On. (Illus.). 333p. 1998. 19.95 (*1-55853-582-9*) Rutledge Hill Pr.

— A Father's Book of Wisdom. LC 89-3517. 160p. 1989. pap. 6.95 (*1-55853-018-5*) Rutledge Hill Pr.

— A Father's Book of Wisdom. 160p. 1999. lthr. 16.95 (*1-55853-754-6*) Rutledge Hill Pr.

— A Father's Book of Wisdom. LC 89-3517. 160p. 1991. reprint ed. 12.95 (*1-55853-107-6*) Rutledge Hill Pr.

— El Librito de Instrucciones para la Vida. LC 91-9800. (SPA.). 160p. (Orig.). 1994. pap. 6.95 (*1-55853-291-9*) Rutledge Hill Pr.

— Life's Little Instruction Book. LC 91-9800. 160p. 1991. pap. 6.95 (*1-55853-102-5*) Rutledge Hill Pr.

Brown, H. Jackson. Life's Little Instruction Book, Vol. I. LC 91-9800. 1992. 12.95 (*1-55853-121-1*) Rutledge Hill Pr.

Brown, H. Jackson, Jr. Life's Little Instruction Book, Vol. II. LC 91-9800. 160p. 1993. pap. 6.95 (*1-55853-216-1*) Rutledge Hill Pr.

— Life's Little Instruction Book, Vol. II. LC 91-9800. 160p. 1994. 12.95 (*1-55853-275-7*) Rutledge Hill Pr.

— Life's Little Instruction Book, Vol. 2. large type ed. 140p. 1994. lib. bdg. 16.95 (*0-8161-5957-2*, G K Hall Lrg Type) Mac Lib Ref.

— Life's Little Instruction Book, Vol. III. LC 91-9800. 160p. 1995. pap. 6.95 (*1-55853-353-2*) Rutledge Hill Pr.

Brown, H. Jackson. Life's Little Instruction Book, Vol. III. LC 91-9800. 160p. 1997. 12.95 (*1-55853-467-9*) Rutledge Hill Pr.

Brown, H. Jackson, Jr. Life's Little Instruction Book: 511 Reminders for a Happy & Rewarding Life. large type ed. LC 92-31115. (General Ser.). 160p. 1993. 17.95 (*0-8161-5644-1*, G K Hall Lrg Type) Mac Lib Ref.

— Life's Little Treasure Book of Christmas Memories. (Life's Little Treasure Bks. Ser.). (Illus.). 96p. 1998. 4.95 (*1-55853-687-6*) Rutledge Hill Pr.

— Life's Little Treasure Book on Friendship. LC 97-116080. (Life's Little Treasure Bks.). (Illus.). 96p. 1996. 4.95 (*1-55853-420-2*) Rutledge Hill Pr.

— Life's Little Treasure Book on Hope. (Life's Little Treasure Bks.). (Illus.). 96p. 1996. 4.95 (*1-55853-419-9*) Rutledge Hill Pr.

— Life's Little Treasure Book on Joy. 96p. 1994. 4.95 (*1-55853-278-1*) Rutledge Hill Pr.

— Life's Little Treasure Book on Love. (Illus.). 96p. 1995. 4.95 (*1-55853-329-X*) Rutledge Hill Pr.

— Life's Little Treasure Book on Marriage. (Illus.). 96p. 1994. 4.95 (*1-55853-277-3*) Rutledge Hill Pr.

— Life's Little Treasure Book on Mothers. LC 98-150064. (Illus.). 96p. 1998. 4.95 (*1-55853-609-4*) Rutledge Hill Pr.

— Life's Little Treasure Book on Parenting. (Illus.). 96p. 1995. 4.95 (*1-55853-330-3*) Rutledge Hill Pr.

— Life's Little Treasure Book on Success. (Illus.). 96p. 1994. 4.95 (*1-55853-280-3*) Rutledge Hill Pr.

— Life's Little Treasure Book on Wisdom. 96p. 1994. 4.95 (*1-55853-279-X*) Rutledge Hill Pr.

***Brown, H. Jackson, Jr.** Life's Little Treasures on Simple Pleasures, 1. LC 99-236736. (Life's Little Treasure Bks.). 1999. 4.95 (*1-55853-746-5*) Rutledge Hill Pr.

Brown, H. Jackson, Jr. Life's Little Treasures on Things That Really Matter, 1. (Life's Liffle Treasure Bks.). 1999. 4.95 (*1-55853-747-3*) Rutledge Hill Pr.

— Live & Learn & Pass It On. LC 91-32132. 1992. pap. 6.95 (*1-55853-156-4*) Rutledge Hill Pr.

— Live & Learn & Pass It On. LC 91-32132. (Illus.). 160p. 1993. 12.95 (*1-55853-149-1*) Rutledge Hill Pr.

Brown, H. Jackson. Live & Learn & Pass It On, Vol. 2. LC 91-32132. 160p. 1996. 12.95 (*1-55853-394-X*) Rutledge Hill Pr.

Brown, H. Jackson, Jr. Live & Learn & Pass It On, Vol. III. LC 91-32132. (Illus.). 160p. 1997. pap. 6.95 (*1-55853-472-5*) Rutledge Hill Pr.

— Live & Learn & Pass It On: People Ages 5 to 95 Share What They've Discovered about Life, Love, & Other Good Stuff, Vol. 2. (Live & Learn & Pass It on Ser.). 160p. 1995. pap. 5.95 (*1-55853-331-1*) Rutledge Hill Pr.

— P. S. I Love You. 160p. 1999. lthr. 16.95 (*1-55853-753-8*) Rutledge Hill Pr.

Brown, H. Jackson. P. S. I Love You. 2nd ed. LC 90-8309. (Illus.). 160p. 1990. reprint ed. pap. 6.95 (*1-55853-071-1*) Rutledge Hill Pr.

Brown, H. Jackson. P. S. I Love You. 2nd ed. LC 90-8309. 160p. 1991. reprint ed. 12.95 (*1-55853-108-4*) Rutledge Hill Pr.

Brown, H. Jackson, Jr. Le Petit Livre de la Vie: Manuel d'Instructions, Vol. 1. Ouellet, Denis, tr. LC 92-97170.Tr. of Life's Little Instruction Book. (ENG & FRE.). 1992. 8.95 (*2-920083-66-X*) Edns Roseau.

— Le Petit Livre de la Vie: Manuel d'Instructions, Vol. 2. Ouellet, Denis, tr. LC 92-97170.Tr. of Life's Little Instruction Book. (ENG & FRE.). 1993. 8.95 (*2-920083-74-0*) Edns Roseau.

— Le Petit Livre de la Vie: Manuel d'Instructions, Vol. 3. Ouellet, Denis, tr. LC 92-97170.Tr. of Life's Little Instruction Book. (ENG & FRE.). 1996. 8.95 (*2-89466-002-2*) Edns Roseau.

— Postcards from Life's Little Instruction Book. (Illus.). 30p. 1993. pap. 8.95 (*1-55853-233-1*) Rutledge Hill Pr.

— Postcards from Live & Learn & Pass It On. (Illus.). 30p. 1994. pap. 8.95 (*1-55853-285-4*) Rutledge Hill Pr.

— Postcards from P.S. I Love You. (Illus.). 1993. pap. 8.95 (*1-55853-232-3*) Rutledge Hill Pr.

— Toute la Sagesse du Monde, 2. 1995. 8.95 (*2-920083-94-5*) Edns Roseau.

— Toute la Sagesse du Monde: De 5 a 95 Ans. 160p. 1993. 8.95 (*2-920083-70-8*) Edns Roseau.

— When You Lick a Slug, Your Tongue Goes Numb. LC 95-2626. (Illus.). 150p. 1995. pap. 7.95 (*1-55853-326-5*) Rutledge Hill Pr.

Brown, H. Jackson. Wit & Wisdom from the Peanut Butter Gang: A Collection of Wise Words from Young Hearts. LC 94-7991. 150p. 1994. 14.95 (*1-55853-276-5*) Rutledge Hill Pr.

Brown, H. Jackson, Jr., compiled by. Kid's Little Treasure Book on Happy Families. LC 97-213061. (Kid's Little Treasure Bks.). (Illus.). 96p. 1997. 4.95 (*1-55853-554-3*) Rutledge Hill Pr.

— Kid's Little Treasure Book on What We've Learned So Far. (Kid's Little Treasure Bks.). (Illus.). 96p. (J). 1997. 4.95 (*1-55853-555-1*) Rutledge Hill Pr.

***Brown, H. Jackson, Jr. & Brown, Rosemary C.** Life's Little Instructions from the Bible. 2000. pap. 6.99 (*1-55853-831-3*) Rutledge Hill Pr.

***Brown, H. Jackson, Jr. & Shea, Kim.** Life's Little Instruction Book from Mothers to Daughters. 2000. pap. 6.99 (*1-55853-832-1*) Rutledge Hill Pr.

***Brown, H. Jackson, Jr. & Spizman, Robyn.** Life's Little Instruction Book for Incurable Romantics. 2000. pap. 6.99 (*1-55853-833-X*) Rutledge Hill Pr.

Brown, H. Jackson, et al. Life's Little Treasure Book of Christmas Traditions. (Illus.). 96p. 1996. 4.95 (*1-55853-418-0*) Rutledge Hill Pr.

Brown, H. Jackson, Jr., et al. The Little Book of Christmas Joys. 160p. 1994. pap. 4.95 (*1-55853-310-9*) Rutledge Hill Pr.

Brown, H. James, ed. Land Use & Taxation: Applying the Insights of Henry George. LC 97-20086. 106p. (Orig.). 1997. pap. 12.00 (*1-55844-124-7*) Lincoln Inst Land.

Brown, H. Larry. Lifetime Fitness. 4th ed. 145p. (Orig.). (C). 1995. pap. text 22.00 (*0-13-776618-1*) P-H.

Brown, H. P. An Elementary Manual on Indian Wood Technology. 121p. 1989. pap. 375.00 (*81-7089-116-7*, Pub. by Intl Bk Distr) St Mut.

— Manual of Indian Wood Technology. 121p. 1985. pap. 175.00 (*0-7855-0379-X*, Pub. by Intl Bks & Periodicals) St Mut.

Brown, H. T. Five Hundred Seven Mechanical Movements. 1984. reprint ed. pap. 7.95 (*0-917914-25-2*) Lindsay Pubns.

Brown, H. U. Telecommunications in Health Care. 112p. 1982. 69.00 (*0-8493-5588-5*, R118, CRC Reprint) Franklin.

Brown, H. W., tr. see Preyer, William.

Brown, H. Wesley. Topical Anesthesia: Perspectives on Medicine & Life. LC 99-93227. (Illus.). 96p. 1999. pap. 11.95 (*0-9671627-0-X*) Pantoum Pr.

Brown, Halina S., et al. Corporate Environmentalism in a Global Economy: Societal Values in International Technology Transfer. LC 92-19851. 264p. 1993. 57.95 (*0-89930-802-3*, Q802, Quorum Bks) Greenwood.

***Brown, Halina Szejnwald, et al.** Effective Environmental Regulation: Learning from Poland's Experience. LC 99-98179. 392p. 2000. 75.00 (*0-275-96971-1*, C6971, Praeger Pubs) Greenwood.

Brown, Hallie Q. Homespun Heroines & Other Women of Distinction. (Schomburg Library of Nineteenth-Century Black Women Writers). 350p. 1988. text 38.00 (*0-19-505237-4*) OUP.

— Homespun Heroines & Other Women of Distinction. (Schomburg Library of Nineteenth-Century Black Women Writers). (Illus.). 354p. 1992. pap. 10.95 (*0-19-507575-7*) OUP.

Brown, Hallie Q., ed. Homespun Heroines. LC 70-152917. (Black Heritage Library Collection). 1977. 27.95 (*0-8369-8761-6*) Ayer.

Brown, Hamilton. Survival Guide for Elected Leaders: Essential Skills & Resources for Small Town Officials. LC 93-45605. 1994. pap. 19.95 (*0-925532-10-X*) Natl Ctr Small Commun.

***Brown, Hamilton & Stark, Nancy.** Keys to Successful Funding: A Small Community Guide to Federal & Foundation Resources. Duff, Deborah, ed. (Illus.). 65p. 1999. pap. text 24.95 (*0-925532-11-8*) Natl Ctr Small Commun.

Brown, Hamish. Exploring the Edinburgh to Glasgow Canals: (The Union Canal, the Forth & Clyde Canal) (Illus.). 100p. 1997. pap. 18.00 (*0-11-495735-5*, Pub. by Statnry Office) Balogh.

— Fife. (Twenty-Five Walks Ser.). (Illus.). vii, 102p. 1995. pap. 18.00 (*0-11-495219-1*, Pub. by Statnry Office) Balogh.

— The Fife Coast. (Illus.). 224p. 1994. 29.95 (*1-85158-608-3*, Pub. by Mainstream Pubng) Trafalgar.

— Hamish Brown's Scotland: A Chapbook of Explorations. (Illus.). 224p. 1988. 25.00 (*0-08-036391-1*, Pergamon Pr) Elsevier.

— The Last Hundred. (Illus.). 191p. 1995. 34.95 (*1-85158-607-5*, Pub. by Mainstream Pubng) Trafalgar.

Brown, Handy N. Necromancer: or Voo-Doo Doctor. LC 77-39544. reprint ed. 29.50 (*0-404-00008-8*) AMS Pr.

Brown, Hank, ed. Afghanistan - Is There Hope for Peace? Hearings Before the Committee on Foreign Relations, U. S. Senate. 265p. (C). 1998. pap. text 40.00 (*0-7881-7066-X*) DIANE Pub.

— An Overview of Affirmative Action: Hearing Before the Committee on the Judiciary, U. S. Senate. 137p. (C). 1998. pap. text 35.00 (*0-7881-4956-3*) DIANE Pub.

Brown, Hank, ed. see Fury, David.

Brown, Harcourt. Science & the Human Comedy: Natural Philosophy in French Literature from Rabelais to Maupertuis. LC 74-84353. (University of Toronto Romance Ser.: No. 30). 244p. reprint ed. pap. 75.70 (*0-608-17015-1*, 202642700049) Bks Demand.

Brown, Hariet & Roth, Stephanie. The Babysitter's Handbook: The Care & Keeping of Kids. LC 99-13916. 1999. pap. text 7.95 (*1-56247-751-X*) Pleasant Co.

Brown, Harold. Franchising: Realities & Forms Volume. 1988. ring bd. 90.00 (*0-318-23688-5*) NY Law Pub.

— Franchising: Realities & Remedies. 1300p. 1981. ring bd. 110.00 (*0-317-05386-8*, 00569) NY Law Pub.

— Strategic Forces & Deterrence. (CISA Working Papers: No. 42). 48p. (Orig.). 1983. pap. 15.00 (*0-86682-054-X*) Ctr Intl Relations.

An Asterisk (*) at the beginning of an entry indicates that the title is appearing for the first time.

— U. S.- Japan Relations: Technology, Economics, & Security. 48p. 1987. 4.00 (*0-87641-228-2*) Carnegie Ethics & Intl Affairs.

Brown, Harold & Rudman, Warren B. Preparing for the 21st Century: An Appraisal of U. S. Intelligence. (Illus.). 200p. (Orig.). (C). 1996. pap. text 35.00 (*0-7881-3179-6*) DIANE Pub.

Brown, Harold, et al. Crystallographic Groups of Four-Dimensional Space. LC 77-9312. (Wiley Monographs in Crystallography). 459p. 1978. reprint ed. pap. 142.30 (*0-7837-3521-9*, 205785500008) Bks Demand.

Brown, Harold, jt. auth. see Haig, Alexander.

Brown, Harold, ed. see Van Opstal, Debra.

Brown, Harold I. Perception, Theory & Commitment: The New Philosophy of Science. LC 76-22991. (Illus.). 204p. 1979. pap. text 11.95 (*0-226-07618-0*, P812) U Ch Pr.

— Rationality: Problems of Philosophy. 224p. 1988. text 35.00 (*0-415-00181-1*) Routledge.

Brown, Harold M. Cambridge, Magdalen College, Pepys 1760. (Renaissance Music in Facsimile Ser.: Vol. 2). 200p. 1988. text 30.00 (*0-8240-1451-0*) Garland.

Brown, Harold O. Heresies: Heresy & Orthodoxy in the History of the Church. 486p. 1998. 24.95 (*1-56563-365-2*) Hendrickson MA.

— The Sensate Culture: Reversing America's Decline into Cultural Chaos. LC 96-24595. 272p. 17.99 (*0-8499-1313-6*) Word Pub.

Brown, Harper. Harper Brown: Poetry. Epstein, Leonard J., ed. 80p. 1992. pap. 8.95 (*1-877809-77-2*) Park Pl Pubns.

Brown, Harriet. The Good-Bye Window: A Year in the Life of a Day-Care Center. LC 98-17528. 248p. 1998. 22.95 (*0-299-15870-5*) U of Wis Pr.

— Learn a Little Sign Language. LC 99-207878. 1999. pap. text 1.95 (*1-56247-736-6*) Pleasant Co.

***Brown, Harriet, et al.** Imagine--Girls on Art. LC 00-23112. (Illus.). (YA). 2000. write for info. (*1-58485-208-9*) Pleasant Co.

Brown, Harriet, jt. auth. see Friedhoffer, Robert.

Brown, Harriet C. Grandmother Brown's Hundred Year. 1993. reprint ed. lib. bdg. 89.00 (*0-7812-5344-6*) Rprt Serv.

— Grandmother Brown's Hundred Years, 1827-1927. Baxter, Annette K., ed. LC 79-8778. (Signal Lives Ser.). (Illus.). 1980. reprint ed. lib. bdg. 33.95 (*0-405-12827-4*) Ayer.

Brown, Harrison, ed. China among the Nations of the Pacific. LC 81-14828. (Westview Special Studies on China & East Asia). 148p. (Orig.). reprint ed. pap. 45.90 (*0-7837-3977-X*, 204380700011) Bks Demand.

Brown, Harry. Measuring Man & Other Poems. Schultz, Patricia, ed. LC 89-33519. (Poetry Ser.: Vol. 3). 72p. 1989. pap. 14.95 (*0-88946-888-5*) E Mellen.

— Paint Lick Idyll & Other Poems. Schultz, Patricia, ed. LC 89-33520. (Poetry Ser.: Vol. 1). 72p. 1989. pap. 12.95 (*0-88946-886-9*) E Mellen.

— The Stars in Their Courses. 1995. reprint ed. lib. bdg. 24.95 (*1-56849-664-8*) Buccaneer Bks.

— A Walk in the Sun. 187p. 1985. mass mkt. 3.95 (*0-88184-117-X*) Carroll & Graf.

— A Walk in the Sun. LC 98-29019. 187p. 1998. pap. 12.00 (*0-8032-6148-9*, Bison Books) U of Nebr Pr.

— A Walk in the Sun. 192p. reprint ed. lib. bdg. 20.95 (*0-88411-075-3*) Amereon Ltd.

— A Walk in the Sun. 1993. reprint ed. lib. bdg. 25.95 (*1-56849-191-3*) Buccaneer Bks.

Brown, Harry & Hedman, Bruce. Energy Analysis of 108 Industrial. 314p. (C). 1996. 68.00 (*0-13-576992-2*) P-H.

Brown, Harry C. Sundays in August: A Novel. LC 97-25073. 196p. 1997. 26.95 (*0-86534-261-X*) Sunstone Pr.

Brown, Harry G. The Economics of Taxation. LC 79-10160. (Midway Reprint Ser.). 1979. pap. text 18.00 (*0-226-07620-2*) U Ch Pr.

— The Economics of Taxation. LC 79-10160. (Midway Reprint Ser.). (Illus.). 366p. reprint ed. pap. 113.50 (*0-608-09399-8*, 205414400004) Bks Demand.

— Selected Articles by Harry Gunnison Brown: The Case for Land Value Taxation. LC 80-25662. 245p. 1980. 6.00 (*0-911312-50-1*) Schalkenbach.

Brown, Harry H. Stories of Yesteryear: Horse & Buggy Days. LC 82-90882. (Illus.). 74p. 1982. 6.95 (*0-9610806-0-4*) Kemah Pr.

Brown, Harry L. Design & Maintenance of Accounting Manuals. 3rd ed. LC 98-13512. 576p. 1998. 145.00 (*0-471-25368-5*) Wiley.

***Brown, Harry L.** Design & Maintenance of Accounting Manuals: 1999 Supplement. 3rd ed. 112p. 1999. pap. 60.00 (*0-471-36126-7*) Wiley.

Brown, Harry L., et al. Energy Analysis of 108 Industrial Processes. LC 96-15741. 314p. 1996. 68.00 (*0-88173-247-8*) Fairmont Pr.

Brown, Harry W., tr. see Azevedo, Aluizio.

Brown, Harvey E. Zinc Chemicals: Applications. Carr, Dodd S., ed. 275p. (Orig.). 1989. pap. 10.00 (*0-932893-04-X*) Intl Lead Zinc.

Brown, Harvey E., ed. see U. S. Surgeon General's Office Staff.

Brown, Harvey R., Jr. When God Strikes the Match: Igniting Passion for Holiness & Renewal. LC 98-151048. 160p. 1997. pap. 11.99 (*0-7684-1000-2*, Revival Pr) Destiny Image.

Brown, Harvey R. & Harre, Rom, eds. Philosophical Foundations of Quantum Field Theory. (Illus.). 196p. 1990. reprint ed. pap. text 29.95 (*0-19-824289-1*) OUP.

Brown, Hayden & Dickins, Roberts. The Sombrero. LC 93-6633. (Voyages Ser.). (Illus.). (J). 1994. write for info. (*0-383-03714-X*) SRA McGraw.

Brown, Hayes. Carhood: A Southern Memoir. LC 99-94509. (Illus.). 61p. 1999. pap. 7.95 (*0-9671843-0-4*) Broken Watch.

Brown, Hazel & Cambourne, Brian. Read & Retell: A Strategy for the Whole Language/Natural Learning Classroom. 144p. (C). 1990. pap. text 21.00 (*0-435-08506-9*, 08506) Heinemann.

Brown, Hazel & Mathie, Vonne. Inside Whole Language: A Classroom View. LC 90-26936. 89p. (C). 1991. pap. text 16.00 (*0-435-08583-2*, 08583) Heinemann.

Brown, Hazel J. Christmas Bells & Blessings: All a Church Needs for the Advent/Christmas Season. (Resources for Christmas Drama Programs Ser.). 64p. 1996. 6.95 (*0-687-01774-2*) Abingdon.

— The Holy Bible Wholly. (Sharpen Your Sword Ser.). 88p. (Orig.). 1994. pap. 6.95 (*0-687-38333-1*) Abingdon.

Brown, Hazel P. American Speech Sounds & Rhythm: Advanced. 3rd ed. (Speechphone Ser.). 64p. (Orig.). 1981. pap. text 39.50 incl. audio (*0-88432-063-4*, S23709) Audio-Forum.

— American Speech Sounds & Rhythm: Intermediate. 2nd ed. (Speechphone Ser.). 64p. 1981. pap. text 39.50 incl. audio (*0-88432-062-6*, S23705) Audio-Forum.

— Speechphone Series: Elementary Course. (Speechphone Ser.). 64p. pap. text 39.50 incl. audio (*0-88432-061-8*, S23701) Audio-Forum.

— Speechphone Word List, Set 3. (Speechphone Ser.). 125p. pap. text 39.50 incl. audio (*0-88432-064-2*, S23713) Audio-Forum.

Brown, Helen. Literacy of Older Adults in America: Results from the National Adult Literacy Survey. 203p. (Orig.). 1996. pap. 18.00 (*0-16-048896-6*) USGPO.

Brown, Helen, et al. Literacy of Older Adults in America: Results from the National Adult Literacy Survey. (Illus.). 187p. (Orig.). (C). 1997. pap. text 40.00 (*0-7881-3998-3*) DIANE Pub.

Brown, Helen Gurley. Cosmopolitan's Love Book: A Guide to Ecstasy in Bed. 1978. pap. 7.00 (*0-87980-355-X*) Wilshire.

***Brown, Helen Gurley.** I'm Wild Again: Snippets from My Life & a Few Brazen Thoughts. LC 99-56096. (Illus.). 304p. 2000. text 24.95 (*0-312-25192-0*) St Martin.

Brown, Helen Gurley. The Late Show: A Practical, Semiwild Survival Guide for Every Woman in Her Prime or Approaching It. 400p. 1994. mass mkt. 5.99 (*0-380-77654-5*, Avon Bks) Morrow Avon.

— Sex & the Office. 1983. pap. 2.95 (*0-380-64048-1*, 64048-1, Avon Bks) Morrow Avon.

— Sex & the Single Girl. 1983. pap. 2.95 (*0-380-64030-9*, 64030-9, Avon Bks) Morrow Avon.

— The Writer's Rules: The Power of Positive Prose - How to Create It & Get It Published. LC 98-22368. 160p. 1998. 22.95 (*0-688-15906-0*, Wm Morrow) Morrow Avon.

***Brown, Helen T.** Honey in the Wind. Wilkey, Elmira S., ed. & illus. by. 66p. 1999. 5.95 (*0-9672960-0-5*); pap. 4.95 (*0-9672960-1-3*) Studio Sans.

Brown, Helene G. L' Effet Fantastique Ou la Mise-en-Jeu Du Sujet. (Stanford French & Italian Studies: Vol. 83). (FRE.). 250p. (Orig.). 1996. pap. 56.50 (*0-915838-49-4*) Anma Libri.

Brown, Henry. Sold. 92p. (C). 1989. text 32.00 (*0-902662-70-8*, Pub. by R K Pubns); pap. text 21.00 (*0-902662-71-6*, Pub. by R K Pubns) St Mut.

— Sonnets of Shakespeare Solved. LC 70-39545. reprint ed. 41.50 (*0-404-01135-7*) AMS Pr.

Brown, Henry, jt. auth. see D'Amato, Donald.

Brown, Henry, jt. auth. see Salt, Adrian.

Brown, Henry A. Salt Pork & Poor Bread & Whiskey. (Illus.). xxii, 92p. 1997. pap. 14.00 (*0-7884-0732-5*, B658) Heritage Bk.

Brown, Henry A. & Walton, Richard J. John Brown's Tract: Lost Adirondack Empire. LC 88-9962. xv, 366p. 1988. 20.00 (*0-914659-34-0*) Phoenix Pub.

Brown, Henry C. In the Golden Nineties. LC 71-133516. (Select Bibliographies Reprint Ser.). 1977. 35.95 (*0-8369-5548-X*) Ayer.

— My Life on Either Side of the Rockies. Greenlee, Carolyn W., ed. LC 98-35630. 167p. 1999. pap. 19.95 (*1-887400-20-6*) Earthen Vessel Prodns.

Brown, Henry F. Real Prison. A Life in Poetry: 54 Years of Pain & Survival. 93p. 1998. pap. 11.95 (*1-890622-42-7*) Leathers Pub.

Brown, Henry H. How to Control Fate Through Suggestion. 56p. 1996. reprint ed. spiral bd. 10.00 (*0-7873-0124-8*) Hlth Research.

— Self Healing. 61p. 1996. reprint ed. spiral bd. 11.00 (*0-7873-0122-1*) Hlth Research.

— The Six Steps in Mental Mastery. 105p. 1996. reprint ed. spiral bd. 12.50 (*0-7873-0123-X*) Hlth Research.

Brown, Henry L. EDP for Auditors. LC 68-22301. 207p. reprint ed. pap. 64.20 (*0-608-10771-9*, 200736900061) Bks Demand.

Brown, Henry T. 507 Mechanical Movements. LC 96-233419. (Illus.). 128p. 1995. pap. 13.95 (*1-879335-63-8*) Astragal Pr.

Brown, Herb. Basketball Box Offense. (Spalding Sports Library). (Illus.). 192p. (Orig.). 1995. pap. 12.95 (*1-57028-031-2*, 80312H, Mstrs Pr) NTC Contemp Pub Co.

Brown, Herb, ed. A Guide for Using the Internet. unabridged ed. LC 96-149426. (Illus.). 63p. (Orig.). (C). 1996. pap. text 12.00 (*1-881530-03-5*) Delta Pi Epsilon.

Brown, Herbert. Sentimental Novel in America, 1789-1860. (BCL1-PS American Literature Ser.). 407p. 1993. reprint ed. lib. bdg. 99.00 (*0-7812-6590-8*) Rprt Serv.

Brown, Herbert & Buskirk, Bruce. Readings & Cases in Direct Marketing. 352p. 1994. pap. 24.95 (*0-8442-3183-5*, NTC Business Bks) NTC Contemp Pub Co.

Brown, Herbert C. Explorations in the Nonclassical Ion Area. 1976. pap. 12.75 (*0-08-020488-0*, Pergamon Pr) Elsevier.

Brown, Herbert E., et al. Cases in Direct Marketing. 2nd rev. ed. LC 95-22871. 165p. 1995. pap. 24.95 (*0-8442-3321-8*) NTC Contemp Pub Co.

Brown, Herbert N., jt. ed. see Jacobs, Douglas G.

Brown, Herbert O. & Nitz, Dwight V. Fields of Glory: The Facts Book of the Battle of Gettysburg. (Illus.). 120p. 1990. pap. text 9.95 (*0-939631-28-8*) Thomas Publications.

Brown, Herbert O., tr. see Thomas, James E. & Thomas, Dean S.

Brown, Herbert R. Sentimental Novel in America, 1789-1860. LC 75-107685. (Essay Index Reprint Ser.). 1977. reprint ed. 24.95 (*0-8369-1490-2*) Ayer.

Brown, Hilary & Craft, Ann. Responding to the Sexual Abuse of Adults with Learning Disabilities. 200p. 1996. pap. 33.00 (*1-85302-204-7*, Pub. by Jessica Kingsley) Taylor & Francis.

Brown, Hilary, jt. ed. see Cambridge, Paul.

Brown, Hilary A. Reference Room: A Resource for Serious Writers. 200p. 1999. pap. 12.99 (*1-58365-015-6*) BT Pub.

Brown, Hilary F. & Kozlowski, Roland. Physiology & Pharmacology of the Heart. (Illus.). 126p. 1997. pap. text 30.95 (*0-86542-722-4*) Blackwell Sci.

Brown, Hilda M. Leitmotiv & Drama: Wagner, Brecht, & the Limits of "Epic" Theatre. (Illus.). 232p. 1991. 65.00 (*0-19-816227-8*) OUP.

Brown, Hilda Meldrum. Heinrich von Kleist: The Ambiguity of Art the Necessity of Form. (Illus.). 420p. 1998. text 90.00 (*0-19-815895-5*) OUP.

Brown, Hilton. Rudyard Kipling. LC 74-7017. (English Literature Ser.: No. 33). 1974. lib. bdg. 75.00 (*0-8383-1853-3*) M S G Haskell Hse.

Brown, Hobart & Wilson, John. Kinetic Sculpture Racing. (Orig.). 1991. pap. 19.95 (*1-879312-07-7*) Hi Heart Pub.

Brown, Homer E. Solution of Large Networks by Matrix Methods. 2nd ed. LC 85-5380. 336p. reprint ed. pap. 104.20 (*0-7837-2835-2*, 205763700006) Bks Demand.

Brown, Homer O. Institutions of the English Novel: From Defoe to Scott. LC 96-47118. 244p. 1996. text 29.95 (*0-8122-3383-2*) U of Pa Pr.

— Institutions of the Enlgish Novel: From Defoe to Scott. (Critical Authors & Issues Ser.). 256p. 1998. pap. 16.50 (*0-8122-1603-2*) U of Pa Pr.

Brown, Howard. The Organist's Picture Chords. (Illus.). 32p. 1977. pap. 8.95 (*0-86001-500-9*, AM20843) Music Sales.

Brown, Howard, ed. Nureyev. (Illus.). 208p. (C). 1993. text 49.95 (*0-7148-2966-8*, Pub. by Phaidon Press) Phaidon Pr.

— Nureyev. rev. ed. (Illus.). 208p. 1995. reprint ed. pap. 29.95 (*0-7148-3470-X*, Pub. by Phaidon Press) Phaidon Pr.

Brown, Howard, et al, eds. Milan, Biblioteca del Conservatorio Di Musica Giuseppe Verdi ("The Tarasconi Codex") LC 86-753537. (Renaissance Music in Facsimile Ser.: Vol. 11). 870115p. 1987. text 35.00 (*0-8240-1460-X*) Garland.

— Munich, Bayerische Staatsbibliothek, Mus. MS. 10. LC 86-751772. (Renaissance Music in Facsimile Ser.: Vol. 14). 460p. 1986. text 35.00 (*0-8240-1463-4*) Garland.

— Oxford, Bodleian Library, MSS Music School E 376-381. (Renaissance Music in Facsimile Ser.: Vol. 15). 1456p. 1986. text 70.00 (*0-8240-1464-2*) Garland.

— Siena, Biblioteca Comunale Degli Intronati, MS K. I. 2. (Renaissance Music in Facsimile Ser.: Vol. 17). 464p. 1986. text 35.00 (*0-8240-1466-9*) Garland.

Brown, Howard G. War, Revolution, & the Bureaucratic State: Politics & Army Administration in France, 1791-1799. (Oxford Historical Monographs). (Illus.). 370p. 1995. text 65.00 (*0-19-820542-2*) OUP.

Brown, Howard Mayer. Embellishing Sixteenth-Century Music. (Early Music Ser.). 94p. 1976. pap. 26.50 (*0-19-323175-1*) OUP.

— Instrumental Music Printed Before 1600: A Bibliography. LC 65-12783. (Illus.). 571p. 1965. 39.00 (*0-674-45610-6*) HUP.

Brown, Howard Mayer, ed. A Florentine Chansonnier from the Time of Lorenzo the Magnificent, Set, Vol. 1, text; Vol. 2, music. LC 81-16515. (Monuments of Renaissance Music Ser.). 996p. (C). 1983. lib. bdg. 180.00 (*0-226-07623-7*) U Ch Pr.

— Italian Opera Librettos, 1640-1770, Vol. 56. LC 76-20993. 1978. lib. bdg. 15.00 (*0-8240-2655-1*) Garland.

— Italian Opera Librettos, 1640-1770, Vol. 60. LC 76-20993. 1978. lib. bdg. 15.00 (*0-8240-2659-4*) Garland.

— London, British Library, MS Royal 8 G. VII. (Renaissance Music in Facsimile Ser.). 160p. 1987. text 30.00 (*0-8240-1458-8*) Garland.

— London, British Library, Royal 20. A. XVI. (Renaissance Music in Facsimile Ser.: Vol. 10). 96p. 1987. text 30.00 (*0-8240-1459-6*) Garland.

— Verona, Biblioteca Capitolare, Cod. DCCLVII. (Renaissance Music in Facsimile Ser.). 152p. 1987. text 30.00 (*0-8240-1473-1*) Garland.

Brown, Howard Mayer, et al, eds. Florence, Archivio Musicale Dell'Opera di Santa Maria del Fiore, MS11. (Renaissance Music in Facsimile Ser.). 330p. 1987. text 35.00 (*0-8240-1452-9*) Garland.

— Modena, Biblioteca Estense e Univesitaria, MS Alpha F.9.9. (Renaissance Music in Facsimile Ser.). 200p. 1987. text 30.00 (*0-8240-1462-6*) Garland.

— Turin, Biblioteca Nazionale Universitaria, MS Ris. Mus. I. 27 (Olim Qm III.59) LC 87-750231. (Renaissance Music in Facsimile Ser.: Vol. 18). 232p. 1987. text 30.00 (*0-8240-1467-7*) Garland.

— Uppsala, Universitetsbibliotheket, MS Vokalmusik i Handskrift 76a. (Renaissance Music in Facsimile Ser.). 192p. 1987. text 30.00 (*0-8240-1468-5*) Garland.

— Uppsala, Universitetsbibliotheket, MS Vokalmusik i Handskrift 76b. LC 86-753539. (Renaissance Music in Facsimile Ser.: Vol. 20). 352p. 1987. text 35.00 (*0-8240-1469-3*) Garland.

Brown, Howard Mayer & Lascelle, Joan. Musical Iconography: A Manual for Cataloguing Musical Subjects in Western Art Before 1800. LC 76-180151. (Illus.). 236p. 1972. 34.95 (*0-674-59220-4*) HUP.

Brown, Howard Mayer & Sadie, Stanley, eds. Performance Practice, 2 vols., I. (Grove Handbooks in Music Ser.). (Illus.). (C). 1990. 32.50 (*0-393-02807-0*) Norton.

— Performance Practice, 2 vols., II. (Grove Handbooks in Music Ser.). (Illus.). (C). 1990. 44.50 (*0-393-02808-9*) Norton.

Brown, Howard Mayer, ed. see Peri, Jacopo.

Brown, Howard P., jt. auth. see George, Rickey L.

***Brown, Hugh B.** An Abundant Life: The Memoirs of Hugh B. Brown. 2nd enl. ed. Firmage, Edwin B., ed. LC 99-24831. (Illus.). 200p. (Orig.). 1999. pap. 17.95 (*1-56085-123-6*) Signature Bks.

Brown, Hugh B. God Is the Gardener & Profile of a Prophet. LC 97-78183. (Classic Talk Ser.). 48 p. 1998. write for info. (*0-87579-974-4*) Deseret Bk.

Brown, Hume. Early Travellers in Scotland. 326p. (C). 1978. 80.00 (*0-901824-51-8*, Pub. by Mercat Pr Bks) St Mut.

Brown, Humphrey. Out of Season. LC 97-73439. 200p. 1997. 15.00 (*1-879418-83-5*) Audenreed Pr.

***Brown, Hunter.** William James on Radical Empiricism & Religion. 192p. 2000. 40.00 (*0-8020-4734-3*) U of Toronto Pr.

Brown, Hunter L., et al, eds. Images of the Human: The Philosophy of the Human Person in a Religious Context. LC 95-8782. 633p. (C). 1997. pap. 18.95 (*0-8294-0825-8*) Loyola Pr.

Brown, Huntington. Rabelais in English Literature. 254p. 1967. reprint ed. 35.00 (*0-7146-2051-3*, Pub. by F Cass Pubs) Intl Spec Bk.

Brown, Hy & Thomas, Nancy. Comic Character Timepieces: Seven Decades of Memories. LC 92-60629. (Illus.). 280p. 1992. text 79.95 (*0-88740-426-X*) Schiffer.

Brown, I. H. G. Wells. LC 75-30878. (H. G. Wells Ser.: No. 78). 1975. lib. bdg. 59.00 (*0-8383-2108-9*) M S G Haskell Hse.

Brown, I. D., et al, eds. Bond Index to the Determinations of Inorganic Crystal Structures: BIDICS-1981. 132p. 1982. pap. 40.00 (*0-686-45046-9*, 0318-126X) Polycrystal Bk Serv.

Brown, I. D. & Dolley, M. Bibliography of Coin Hoards of Great Britain & Ireland, Fifteen Hundred to Nineteen Sixty-Seven. 1977. 20.00 (*0-685-51521-4*) S J Durst.

Brown, I. D., et al. Vision in Vehicles 4: Selected-Edited Proceedings of the 4th International Conference, Leiden, the Netherlands, August 1991. Gale, A. G., ed. xiv,364p. 1993. 149.50 (*0-444-89362-8*) Elsevier.

Brown, I. D., jt. ed. see Janssen, W.

Brown, I. G. Building for Books: The Architectural Evolution of the Advocates' Library, 1680-1925. 1989. text 59.00 (*0-08-037968-0*, Pergamon Pr) Elsevier.

Brown, I. R., jt. ed. see Mayer, R. John.

Brown, I. W. & Fielder, D. R., eds. The Coconut Crab: Aspects of Birgus Latro Biology & Ecology in Vanuatu. 136p. 1991. pap. 120.00 (*1-86320-054-1*, Pub. by ACIAR) St Mut.

Brown, Iain Gordon. Scott's Interleaved Waverley Novels. 142p. 1989. 80.00 (*0-08-035082-8*, Pub. by Mercat Pr Bks) St Mut.

Brown, Iain Gordon & National Library of Scotland. Poet & Painter: Allan Ramsay, Father & Son, 1684-1784. LC 85-117162. 51 p. 1984. 0.00 (*0-902220-63-2*) Nat Lib Scot.

***Brown, Ian.** Cambodia. (Country Profiles Ser.: Vol. 22). (Illus.). 80p. 2000. pap. 9.95 (*0-85598-430-9*, Pub. by Oxfam Pub) Stylus Pub VA.

— Economic Change in South-East Asia, c. 1830-1980. LC 96-43168. (Illus.). 318p. (C). 1997. text 52.00 (*983-56-0014-7*) OUP.

— Sixty Questions Every Jehovah's Witness Should Be Asked. 95p. 1999. pap. 9.99 (*1-84030-063-9*) Emerald House Group Inc.

Brown, Ian, ed. The Economies of Africa & Asia During the Inter-War Depression. 256p. 1989. lib. bdg. 55.00 (*0-415-00377-6*) Routledge.

Brown, Ian & Chandler, Adrian. Law of Contract: Blackstone's Law Questions & Answers. 2nd ed. 307p. 1996. pap. 22.00 (*1-85431-494-7*, Pub. by Blackstone Pr) Gaunt.

— Q & A Law of Contract. (Q & A Ser.). 287p. 1994. pap. 20.00 (*1-85431-306-1*, Pub. by Blackstone Pr) Gaunt.

Brown, Ian & Fisher, Mark, eds. Made in Scotland: An Anthology of New Scottish Plays. LC 95-223551. (Methuen Anthologies Ser.). 256p. 1995. pap. 19.95 (*0-413-69180-2*, A0745) Heinemann.

Brown, Ian G., ed. The Physics & Technology of Ion Sources. LC 88-20507. 444p. 1989. 173.50 (*0-471-85708-4*) Wiley.

Brown, Ian L., jt. auth. see More, Ian A.

Brown, Ian M. British Logistics on the Western Front: 1914-1919. LC 97-21444. 280p. 1998. 65.00 (*0-275-95894-9*, Praeger Pubs) Greenwood.

Brown, Ian W. Natchez Indian Archaeology: Culture Change & Stability in the Lower Mississippi Valley. (Mississippi Department of Archives & History Archaeological Reports: No. 15). (Illus.). xiv, 304p. (Orig.). 1984. pap. 10.00 (*0-938896-42-3*) Mississippi Archives.

— The Southeastern Check Stamped Pottery Tradition: A View from Louisiana. LC 82-10101. (MCJA Special Paper: No. 4). (Illus.). 100p. reprint ed. pap. 31.00 (*0-7837-0502-6*, 204082600018) Bks Demand.

Brown, Ian W., jt. auth. see Burger, Hillel S.

Brown, Ida Lu, jt. auth. see Cuttler, Dona Lou.

B

An Asterisk (*) at the beginning of an entry indicates that the title is appearing for the first time.

Brown, Iem & Davis, Joan, eds. Di Serambi: On the Verandah: A Bilingual Anthology of Modern Indonesian Poetry. (Illus.). 160p. (C). 1995. pap. text 15.95 (*0-521-47714-X*) Cambridge U Pr.

— Di Serambi: On the Verandah: A Bilingual Anthology of Modern Indonesian Poetry. (Illus.). 160p. (C). 1995. text 54.95 (*0-521-47202-4*) Cambridge U Pr.

Brown, Imogene E. American Aristides: A Biography of George Wythe. LC 77-89776. 324p. 1978. 39.50 (*0-8386-2142-2*) Fairleigh Dickinson.

Brown, Ira V. Mary Grew: Abolitionist & Feminist, 1813-1896. LC 90-50769. 216p. 1991. 40.00 (*0-945636-20-2*) Susquehanna U Pr.

Brown, Irene B. The Plainswoman. large type ed. 508p. (Orig.). 1996. 21.95 (*0-7838-1599-9*, G K Hall Lrg Type) Mac Lib Ref.

***Brown, Irene Bennett.** The Morning Glory Afternoon. large type ed. (Thorndike Romance Ser.). (J). 1999. 24.95 (*0-7862-2253-0*) Thorndike Pr.

— The Plainswoman. LC 00-41715. 2000. write for info. (*0-7862-2775-3*) Five Star.

Brown, Irene K. New Millennium NASA: International Space Station & 21st Century Space Exploration. LC 98-65118. 116p. 1998. write for info. (*1-881547-26-4*) Pioneer Pubns.

Brown, Irving H. Nights & Days on the Gypsy Trail: Through Andalusia & Other Mediterranean Shores. LC 75-3452. (Illus.). reprint ed. 49.50 (*0-404-16885-X*) AMS Pr.

Brown, Isaac B., jt. auth. see Klein, Theodore B.

Brown, Isaac V. Biography of the Reverend Robert Finley. LC 73-82178. (Anti-Slavery Crusade in America Ser.). 1979. reprint ed. 24.95 (*0-405-00617-9*) Ayer.

Brown, Isabel Zakrzewski. Culture & Customs of the Dominican Republic. LC 99-27184. (Culture & Customs of Latin America & the Caribbean Ser.). 224p. 1999. 45.00 (*0-313-30314-2*, Greenwood Pr) Greenwood.

Brown, Isobel, et al. Doors Held Ajar. 192p. 1996. pap. 12.95 (*1-895387-76-0*) Creative Bk Pub.

Brown, Ivan, et al, eds. Ergonomics International '85. 900p. 1985. 143.00 (*0-85066-300-8*) Taylor & Francis.

Brown, Ivor, compiled by. Charles Dickens: 1812-1870. 39.00 (*1-56696-006-1*) Jackdaw.

Brown, Ivor, ed. see Observer Staff.

Brown, Ivor J. Dickens & His World. LC 70-540999. 48 p. 1970. write for info. (*0-7188-1425-8*) Lutterwrth.

— Ivor Brown's Books of Word, Comprising a Word in Your Ear & Just Another Word. LC 78-5328. 264p. 1978. reprint ed. lib. bdg. 59.50 (*0-313-20393-8*, BRWY, Greenwood Pr) Greenwood.

— Shaw in His Time. LC 79-17319. (Illus.). 212p. 1979. reprint ed. lib. bdg. 59.50 (*0-313-21999-0*, BRSW, Greenwood Pr) Greenwood.

Brown, Ivor J. The Women in Shakespeare's Life. LC 70-350091. 224 p. 1968. write for info. (*0-370-00463-9*, Pub. by Bodley Head) Trafalgar.

Brown, Ivor J. Words in Season. LC 74-4839. 159p. 1974. reprint ed. lib. bdg. 55.00 (*0-8371-7489-9*, BRWS, Greenwood Pr) Greenwood.

Brown, Ivor J. & Fearon, George. This Shakespeare Industry. LC 70-92951. (Studies in Shakespeare: No. 24). 1970. reprint ed. lib. bdg. 75.00 (*0-8383-1063-X*) M S G Haskell Hse.

— This Shakespeare Industry: Amazing Monument. LC 77-98824. 332p. 1970. reprint ed. lib. bdg. 65.00 (*0-8371-2850-1*, BRSI, Greenwood Pr) Greenwood.

Brown, Ivorine. Don't Cry: But Smile & Remember. (Illus.). 18p. (Orig.). (J). (ps-5). 1997. pap. 10.00 (*1-889732-03-6*, Key-A-Teese Prod) Word-For-Word.

Brown, J. Elements of Language Curriculum. (Teaching Methods Ser.). 240p. (J). 1994. mass mkt. 33.95 (*0-8384-5810-6*) Heinle & Heinle.

— Part of a Whole. 90p. 1999. pap. 11.95 (*0-7392-0198-0*, P3194) Morris Pubng.

Brown, J. Probabilistic Accident Consequence Uncertainty Analysis, Food Chain Uncertainty Assessment: Appendices. 347p. 1997. per. 29.00 (*0-16-054678-8*) USGPO.

— Probabilistic Accident Consequence Uncertainty Analysis, Food Chain Uncertainty Assessment: Main Report. 76p. 1997. pap. 7.00 (*0-16-054677-X*) USGPO.

Brown, J. Radar - How It All Began. LC 96-207920. (Illus.). 180p. 1996. pap. 15.95 (*1-85756-212-7*, Pub. by Janus Pubng) Paul & Co Pubs.

Brown, J. & Cullen, A. Electromagnetic Wave Theory, 2 vols., Set. LC 66-17928. 1967. reprint ed. 481.00 (*0-08-006532-5*, Pub. by Pergamon Repr) Franklin.

— Electromagnetic Wave Theory Pt. 2: Proceedings Symposium, Delft, Sept. 1965. LC 66-17928. (International Series of Monographs in Electromagnetic Waves: Vol. 11). 1967. 241.00 (*0-08-011922-0*, Pub. by Pergamon Repr) Franklin.

Brown, J. & Pawlowski, Mark. Casebook on the Law of Landlord & Tenant, Vol. 1. 1994. pap. text 48.00 (*0-421-50500-1*, Pub. by Sweet & Maxwll) Gaunt.

Brown, J., ed. see Cheldelin, Larry V.

Brown, J., jt. ed. see Davies, P. C.

Brown, J. A., ed. Television Critical Viewing Skills: A Survey & Evaluation of Major Media Literacy Projects in the U. S. & Selected Countries. (Communication Ser.). 392p. (C). 1991. pap. 39.95 (*0-8058-0974-0*); text 69.95 (*0-8058-0786-1*) L Erlbaum Assocs.

Brown, J. A., jt. auth. see Aitchison, John.

Brown, J. Aaron. Love Songs & Lullabyes for Daddy's Little Dreamer. (Illus.). 8p. (J). (gr. 3). 1995. 15.95 incl. audio compact disk (*0-927945-14-2*) Someday Baby.

— Love Songs & Lullabyes for Daddy's Little Dreamer. (Illus.). 8p. (J). (ps). 1995. 12.95 incl. audio (*0-927945-13-4*) Someday Baby.

Brown, J. Aaron, ed. Little Sleepy Eyes. (Illus.). 8p. (Orig.). (J). (ps). 1994. 12.95 incl. audio compact disk (*0-927945-08-8*) Someday Baby.

— Little Sleepy Eyes. (Illus.). 8p. (Orig.). (J). (ps). 1995. 15.95 incl. audio compact disk (*0-927945-12-6*) Someday Baby.

— Un Regalo de Arrullos Para Ninos. Pineda, Sysy, tr. (SPA., Illus.). 14p. (J). (ps). 1988. 12.95 incl. audio (*0-927945-02-9*) Someday Baby.

— Snuggle Up: A Gift of Songs for Sweet Dreams. (Illus.). 8p. (J). (ps). 1992. 12.95 incl. audio (*0-927945-06-1*) Someday Baby.

— Snuggle Up: A Gift of Songs for Sweet Dreams. (Illus.). 8p. (J). (ps). 1995. 15.95 incl. audio compact disk (*0-927945-11-8*) Someday Baby.

Brown, J. Aaron, jt. auth. see Ragland, Teresa.

Brown, J. Anne, et al, eds. New Insights in Vertebrate Kidney Function. (Society for Experimental Biology Seminar Ser.: No. 52). (Illus.). 403p. (C). 1993. text 130.00 (*0-521-38324-2*) Cambridge U Pr.

Brown, J Anthony. Players Rules: Time-Tested Secrets for Capturing Ms. Right Without Marrying Her! 1999. pap. text 7.95 (*1-890194-08-5*) Pines One.

***Brown, J. Anthony.** Rev. Adenoids' Church Announcements. (Illus.). 144p. 2000. pap. 8.00 (*0-9675935-0-6*) KKT Pub.

— Rev. Adenoids' Church Announcements. 2nd rev. ed. (Illus.). 144p. 2000. pap. 8.00 (*0-9675935-1-4*) KKT Pub.

Brown, J. B. Three P's in Recovery. 2nd ed. 24p. 1984. pap. write for info. (*0-318-58107-8*) H & H Pubs.

Brown, J. C., jt. auth. see Craig, I. J.

Brown, J. C., jt. auth. see Forrester, D. M.

Brown, J. Carter. Federal Buildings in Context: The Role of Design Review. 1995. 22.00 (*0-89468-209-1*) Natl Gallery Art.

Brown, J. Carter, ed. Federal Buildings in Context: The Role of Design Review. (Illus.). 1995. 25.00 (*0-300-07698-3*) Yale U Pr.

Brown, J. Coggin & Key, A. K. The Mineral & Nuclear Fuels of the Indian Subcontinent & Burma. 1976. 38.00 (*0-19-560172-6*) OUP.

Brown, J. D. Digging to China: Down & out in the Middle Kingdom. LC 91-7805. 230p. 1991. 18.95 (*0-939149-51-6*) Soho Press.

— Digging to China: Down & Out in the Middle Kingdom. LC 91-7805. 230p. 1993. pap. 10.00 (*0-939149-88-5*) Soho Press.

— Frommer's China: The 50 Most Memorable Trips. 384p. 1998. 21.95 (*0-02-861636-7*) Macmillan.

***Brown, J. D.** Frommer's China: The 50 Most Memorable Trips. 2nd ed. (Illus.). 592p. 2000. pap. 21.99 (*0-02-863673-2*) Mac Bks.

— Frommer's Shanghai. (Illus.). 2000. pap. 15.99 (*0-02-863672-4*) Macmillan Gen Ref.

Brown, J. D. Lower Dimensional Gravity. 164p. 1988. text 33.00 (*9971-5-0622-X*) World Scientific Pub.

Brown, J. D., ed. New Ways of Classroom Assessment. LC 97-61577. 397p. 1998. pap. 27.95 (*0-939791-72-2*) Tchrs Eng Spkrs.

Brown, J. D. & Pickett, Bob. A Boat Named Clancy: A Builder's Guide to a Superb Little Sailboat. rev. ed. Orig. Title: Build a Clancy. pap. 15.95 (*0-917436-04-0*) Tamal Vista.

Brown, J. Daniel. Logic Primer for Undergraduates. 165p. (C). 1991. pap. text. write for info. (*0-9629643-0-1*) J Daniel Brown.

— Logic Primer for Undergraduates Solutions to Exercises. 36p. (C). 1991. teacher ed. write for info. (*0-9629643-1-X*) J Daniel Brown.

— Masks of Mystery: Explorations in Christian Faith & Arts. LC 96-46098. 184p. 1996. 49.50 (*0-7618-0596-6*); pap. 27.50 (*0-7618-0597-4*) U Pr of Amer.

Brown, J. David, et al, eds. Proceedings of the Cornelius Lanczos International Centenary Conference. LC 94-22243. (Proceedings in Applied Mathematics Ser.: No. 73). lxv, 644p. 1994. pap. 89.00 (*0-89871-339-0*) Soc Indus-Appl Math.

Brown, J. E. Brown: Genealogy of the Brown Family of Prince William Co., VA & Allied Families Bland, Buckner, Byrne, Fairfax, Morgan, Tebbs, Watson, Zimms & Others. 2nd ed. (Illus.). 874p. 1991. reprint ed. pap. 117.50 (*0-8328-1716-3*); reprint ed. lib. bdg. 127.50 (*0-8328-1715-5*) Higginson Bk Co.

Brown, J. F. Eastern Europe & Communist Rule. LC 87-30572. xii, 564p. (C). 1988. text 62.95 (*0-8223-0810-X*) Duke.

— Hopes & Shadows: Eastern Europe after Communism. LC 93-47347. 320p. 1994. text 54.95 (*0-8223-1446-0*); pap. text 19.95 (*0-8223-1464-9*) Duke.

— Soviet-East European Relations: 1945 to the Present. 400p. (C). 1999. text. write for info. (*0-8133-0946-8*); pap. text. write for info. (*0-8133-0947-6*) Westview.

— Surge to Freedom: The End of Communist Rule in Eastern Europe. LC 90-44883. 350p. 1991. text 49.95 (*0-8223-1126-7*); pap. text 21.95 (*0-8223-1145-3*) Duke.

Brown, J. Francis, IV, intro. Take No As a Starter: The Life of Richard L. Graves, Set. 661p. 1980. lib. bdg. 84.50 (*1-56475-080-9*); fiche. write for info. (*1-56475-354-9*) U NV Oral Hist.

***Brown, J. Gregory.** Baldwin's Secret. LC 99-91044. (Illus.). 32p. 1999. lib. bdg. 15.00 (*0-9674484-0-9*) New Castle.

Brown, J. H. Footsteps in Science. 122p. (Orig.). (C). 1992. pap. text 19.50 (*0-8191-8694-5*); lib. bdg. 42.50 (*0-8191-8693-7*) U Pr of Amer.

— A Guide to Collecting Fine Prints. LC 89-34288. (Illus.). 192p. 1989. 29.00 (*0-8108-2228-8*) Scarecrow.

— The Health Care Dilemma. LC 78-3891. 183p. 1978. 32.95 (*0-87705-360-X*, Kluwer Acad Hman Sci) Kluwer Academic.

— The High Cost of Healing: Physicians & the Health Care System. 213p. 1985. 35.95 (*0-89885-222-6*, Kluwer Acad Hman Sci) Kluwer Academic.

— Management in Health Care Systems. 152p. 1984. 91.00 (*0-8493-5572-9*, RA393, CRC Reprint) Franklin.

Brown, J. H. & Comola, Jacqueline. Improving Productivity in Health Care. 208p. 1988. 132.00 (*0-8493-6911-8*, RA10, CRC Reprint) Franklin.

Brown, J. H. & Comolo, Jacqueline. Educating for Excellence: Improving Quality & Productivity in the 90's. LC 90-22298. 184p. 1991. 49.95 (*0-86569-030-8*, T030, Auburn Hse) Greenwood.

Brown, J. Jackson, Jr. Life's Little Treasure Book on Fathers. LC 98-150049. (Illus.). 96p. 1998. 4.95 (*1-55853-610-8*) Rutledge Hill Pr.

Brown, J. L. The Story of Kings County California. (Illus.). 123p. 1986. reprint ed. 8.75 (*0-9612298-1-0*) Forsan Bks.

***Brown, J. M., et al, eds.** Activation of Unreactive Bonds & Organic Synthesis. LC 99-14671. (Topics in Organometallic Chemistry Ser.: Vol. 3). (Illus.). x, 317p. 1999. 139.00 (*3-540-64862-3*) Spr-Verlag.

Brown, J. M., ed. see Kobayashi, S.

Brown, J. Marvin. A. U. A. Language Center Thai Course, 3 Bks., Bk. 1. 1991. pap. text 14.00 (*0-87727-506-8*) Cornell SE Asia.

— A. U. A. Language Center Thai Course, 3 Bks., Bk. 2. 1991. pap. text 14.00 (*0-87727-507-6*) Cornell SE Asia.

— A. U. A. Language Center Thai Course, 3 Bks., Bk. 3. 1991. pap. text 14.00 (*0-87727-508-4*) Cornell SE Asia.

Brown, J. Marvin, jt. auth. see Hsu Ying.

Brown, J. Marvin, jt. auth. see Ying, Hsu.

Brown, J. Newton. Baptist Church Manual. 38p. 1940. pap. 3.00 (*0-8170-0015-1*) Judson.

Brown, J. Paul. Counseling with Senior Citizens. LC 64-15217. (Successful Pastoral Counseling Ser.). 144p. reprint ed. pap. 44.70 (*0-608-16299-X*, 202717400054) Bks Demand.

Brown, J. R. How to Play Saxophone. 1990. 7.95 (*0-685-32222-X*, 8513) Hansen Ed Mus.

Brown, J. R., ed. Soil Testing: Sampling, Correlation, Calibration, & Interpretation. (Special Publications: No. 21). 144p. 1987. 12.00 (*0-89118-784-7*) Soil Sci Soc Am.

Brown, J. Robert. The Ministry of Finance: Bureaucratic Practices & the Transformation of the Japanese Economy. LC 98-23644. 288p. 1999. 65.00 (*1-56720-230-6*, Quorum Bks) Greenwood.

Brown, J. Robert, Jr. Raising Capital: Private Placement Forms & Techniques, 2 vols. 3rd ed. 1964p. 1993. ring bd. 195.00 (*0-13-109265-0*) Aspen Law.

— The Regulation of Corporate Disclosure. 716p. 1989. ring bd. 126.00 (*0-13-102294-6*) Aspen Law.

— The Regulation of Corporate Disclosure. LC 95-24566. 750p. 1995. 149.00 (*1-56706-160-5*) Panel Pubs.

Brown, J. Robert. The Regulation of Corporate Disclosure. 3rd ed. LC 98-48891. 1998. ring bd. 165.00 (*0-7355-0156-4*) Panel Pubs.

Brown, J. Robert, Jr., ed. Colorado Corporation Law & Practice. (National Corporation Law Ser.). 1992. ring bd. 126.00 (*0-13-179961-4*) Aspen Law.

Brown, J. Robert, Jr. & Macy, Jonathan R., eds. Contemporary Corporation Forms. expanded ed. 5330p. 1993. 395.00 (*0-13-296790-1*, 40149) Aspen Law.

Brown, J. Robert, Jr. & Max, Herbert B. Raising Capital: Private Placement Forms & Techniques, 2 vols. 3rd ed. 2282p. ring bd. 189.00 (*0-13-752817-5*, 75289) Aspen Law.

Brown, J. S. Minor Surgery: A Text & Atlas. 3rd ed. LC 96-84210. (Illus.). 448p. 1996. text 75.00 (*0-412-75060-0*, Pub. by E A) OUP.

Brown, J. S., jt. ed. see Sleeman, D.

Brown, J. T. The Deacon Problem Solved. LC 95-18848. 1995. write for info. (*0-910683-17-4*) Townsnd-Pr.

Brown, J. W. Self & Process: Brain States & the Conscious Present. (Illus.). xiii, 201p. 1991. 57.95 (*0-387-97514-4*) Spr-Verlag.

Brown, J. Wesley. Innovation for Excellence: The Paracollege Model. (Illus.). 132p. (Orig.). (C). 1989. pap. text 16.50 (*0-8191-7244-8*) U Pr of Amer.

Brown, Jack. WM Color Guide to Freight & Passenger Equipment. (Illus.). 128p. 1996. 49.95 (*1-878887-53-X*) Morning NJ.

Brown, Jack & Brown, Darlene. Flight to the Last Frontier. (Illus.). 143p. (Orig.). 1988. reprint ed. pap. 9.95 (*0-9617572-0-5*) Times Journal Pub.

Brown, Jack, jt. auth. see Brown, Darlene E.

Brown, Jack, ed. see Bowling, Evelyn.

Brown, Jack, ed. see Outdoor Writers Association of America Staff.

Brown, Jack P. Louis I. Kahn: A Bibliography. LC 86-25781. 112p. 1986. text 44.00 (*0-8240-9918-4*) Garland.

Brown, Jack R., jt. auth. see Hunt, Roger D.

Brown, Jackie. "Expecting" a New Cat Doesn't Cause Morning Sickness: And Other Reasons to Adopt a Cat. LC 99-94554. (Illus.). 144p. 1999. pap. 9.95 (*0-9672583-1-6*) JB Impressions.

***Brown, Jackum.** Thai Cooking. (Illus.). 2000. pap. 14.95 (*0-600-60094-7*) P HM.

— Vegetarian Thai. (Illus.). 128p. 1999. pap. 14.95 (*0-600-59955-8*, Pub. by Hamlyn Publishing Group Ltd) Sterling.

Brown, Jacob. Stop It Where It Starts: Dr. Brown's Home Drug-Abuse Program. 1996. pap. text 7.95 (*0-931761-58-1*) Beckham Pubns.

Brown, Jacqueline, et al. A Distinct Voice: Medieval Studies in Honor of Leonard E. Boyle, O. P. LC 97-5348. 704p. 1997. 70.00 (*0-268-00883-3*) U of Notre Dame Pr.

Brown, Jacqueline M. & Connelly, Dixie. 29 Stepping Stones: A Wisewoman Journal. 128p. 1996. pap. 9.95 (*0-9651782-0-X*) Upstream Pr.

Brown, James. Advanced Machining Technology Handbook. LC 97-39192. (Illus.). 740p. 1998. 79.95 (*0-07-008243-X*) McGraw-Hill Prof.

— History of the Origin & Progress of the Sikhs, ISPP Vol. II, No. 4. 74p. 1975. reprint ed. 2.00 (*0-88065-068-0*) Scholarly Pubns.

— Inner Healing in Marriage & Family. 108p. 1998. pap. 10.00 (*1-57502-750-X*) Morris Pubng.

— Introductory Solid Mechanics. LC 74-156805. 448p. reprint ed. pap. 138.90 (*0-608-30551-0*, 205122500093) Bks Demand.

— James Brown. 2nd ed. 1997. pap. text 13.95 (*1-56025-115-8*, Thunders Mouth) Avalon NY.

— James Brown: Black & Blue. (Illus.). 64p. 1991. pap. 25.00 (*2-903004-14-5*, Pub. by Galerie Isy Brachot) Dist Art Pubs.

— The Letter Book of James Brown of Providence, Merchant, 1735-1738. (American Biography Ser.). 66p. 1991. reprint ed. lib. bdg. 59.00 (*0-7812-8043-5*) Rprt Serv.

— Modern Manufacturing Processes. (Illus.). 256p. 1991. 24.95 (*0-8311-3034-2*) Indus Pr.

— Second Story Theatre & Two Encores. (Fiction Ser.). 181p. 1994. pap. 16.95 (*0-934257-49-3*) Story Line.

— Value Engineering: A Blueprint. 260p. 1992. 48.95 (*0-8311-3038-5*) Indus Pr.

Brown, James, ed. Arms Control in a Multi-Polar World. 300p. 1997. pap. 43.50 (*90-5383-499-0*, Pub. by VUB Univ Pr) Paul & Co Pubs.

— Challenges in Arms Control for the 1990s. 250p. 1993. pap. text 49.50 (*90-5383-154-1*, Pub. by VU Univ Pr) Paul & Co Pubs.

— Concerns, Opportunities & New Horizons in Arms Control & Verification. LC 94-242526. 250p. 1994. pap. 33.00 (*90-5383-281-5*, Pub. by VU Univ Pr) Paul & Co Pubs.

— Old Issues & New Strategies in Arms Control & Verification. 410p. 1996. 50.00 (*90-5383-421-4*, Pub. by VUB Univ Pr) Paul & Co Pubs.

Brown, James & Fishco, Vivian V. Efficient Reading. 8th ed. 530p. (C). 1997. pap. text 35.96 (*0-669-41593-6*) HM Trade Div.

Brown, James & Snyder, William P., eds. The Regionalization of Warfare: The Falkland Islands, Lebanon & the Iran-Iraq Conflict. (Illus.). 266p. (C). 1984. 39.95 (*0-88738-022-0*); pap. 24.95 (*0-87855-985-X*) Transaction Pubs.

Brown, James, et al. Apple Two at a Glance. (Illus.). 464p. 1988. pap. text 48.00 (*0-13-038670-7*) P-H.

Brown, James, jt. auth. see Pawlowski, Mark.

Brown, James, jt. ed. see Snyder, William P.

Brown, James A. Prehistoric Southern Ozark Marginality: A Myth Exposed. Wood, W. Raymond, ed. LC 83-63187. (Special Publications: No. 6). (Illus.). 85p. (Orig.). 1984. pap. 5.00 (*0-943414-18-0*) MO Arch Soc.

— The Spiro Ceremonial Center: The Archaeology of Arkansas Valley Caddoan Culture in Eastern Oklahoma. LC 95-36153. (Memoirs of the Museum of Anthropology, University of Michigan Ser.: No. 29). 1996. pap. 65.00 (*0-915703-39-4*) U Mich Mus Anthro.

Brown, James A. & O'Brien, Patricia J., eds. At the Edge of Prehistory: Huber Phase Archaeology in the Chicago Area. LC 90-20801. (Illus.). (Orig.). 1990. pap. 15.00 (*0-942118-30-8*) Ctr Amer Arche.

Brown, James A. & Quaal, Ward L. Radio-Television-Cable Management. 3rd ed. LC 97-70794. 640p. (C). 1997. text 48.50 (*0-697-13237-4*, WCB McGr Hill) McGrw-H Hghr Educ.

Brown, James A., et al. The Gentleman Farm Site, la Salle County, Illinois. (Reports of Investigations: No. 12). (Illus.). 48p. 1967. pap. 2.00 (*0-89792-032-5*) Ill St Museum.

Brown, James A., jt. auth. see Phillips, Philip.

Brown, James A., jt. auth. see Quaal, Ward L.

Brown, James A., ed. see Orr, Kenneth G., et al.

Brown, James B. Bible Truths with Shakespearian Parallels. 6th ed. LC 74-19106. reprint ed. 37.50 (*0-404-01136-5*) AMS Pr.

— Memoirs of Howard, Compiled from His Diary. LC 73-156007. reprint ed. 39.50 (*0-404-09107-5*) AMS Pr.

— Stoics & Saints. 296p. 1977. 20.95 (*0-8369-2936-5*) Ayer.

Brown, James B., jt. auth. see Zaydon, Thomas J.

Brown, James C. Brown & Comly Families Genealogy. Mougalian, Susan, ed. 185p. 1998. reprint ed. pap. 27.50 (*0-8328-9641-1*); reprint ed. lib. bdg. 37.50 (*0-8328-9640-3*) Higginson Bk Co.

— Loglan 1: A Logical Language. 4th ed. ("Loglan N" Ser.). 599p. (C). 1989. pap. 21.50 (*1-877665-00-2*) Loglan Inst.

— The Origin & Early History of the Office of Notary. 1976. lib. bdg. 59.95 (*0-8490-2383-1*) Gordon Pr.

Brown, James D. An American Philosophy of Social Security: Evolution & Issues. LC 71-39781. 254p. 1972. reprint ed. pap. 78.80 (*0-608-02873-8*, 206393700007) Bks Demand.

— Biographical Dictionary of Musicians. vii, 637p. 1970. reprint ed. 150.00 (*0-318-71889-8*) G Olms Pubs.

— Understanding Research in Second Language Learning. LC 85-30569. (New Directions in Language Teaching Ser.). (Illus.). 240p. 1988. pap. text 20.95 (*0-521-31551-4*) Cambridge U Pr.

Brown, James D. & Stratton, Stephen S. British Musical Biography: A Dictionary of Musical Artists, Authors & Composers Born in Britain & Its Colonies. LC 76-139197. (Music Ser.). 1971. reprint ed. lib. bdg. 55.00 (*0-306-70076-X*) Da Capo.

An Asterisk (*) at the beginning of an entry indicates that the title is appearing for the first time.

Brown, James Dean. Testing in Language Programs. 2nd ed. (Illus.). 544p. (C). 1995. pap. 29.75 (*0-13-124157-5*) P-H.

Brown, James E. Book of James: Messages in Simple Terms. 66p. (C). 1999. pap. text 12.00 (*0-536-02315-8*) S&S Trade.

— Old Freight Train Coloring Book. (ENG & SPA.). 24p. (Orig.). (J). 1992. pap. 0.50 (*0-9632358-0-X*) J E Brown.

— The Plan (Demon & Lesly) LC 97-91124. 1998. 14.95 (*0-533-12567-7*) Vantage.

Brown, James E. & Priiatkina, Alla F. Informational Types of Expressions: A Handbook of Conversational Themes & Notions with Associated Grammatical Structures for Teachers & Students of Russian. LC 96-5897. 358p. (C). 1996. pap. text 44.00 (*0-7618-0335-1*); lib. bdg. 64.00 (*0-7618-0334-3*) U Pr of Amer.

Brown, James F., Jr. Considering the Military? How Do You Rank? Vol. 1: From Experience, from One Who's Been There. 60p. (Orig.). 1996. 10.00 (*0-9661446-2-7*) J F Brown.

Brown, James F. Nationalism, Democracy & Security in the Balkans. 300p. 1992. 73.95 (*1-85521-316-8*, Pub. by Dartmth Pub) Ashgate Pub Co.

Brown, James G. Agroindustrial Investment & Operations. LC 93-3077. 318p. 1994. pap. 22.00 (*0-8213-2345-8*, 12345) World Bank.

Brown, James H. Macroecology. 284p. 1995. pap. text 15.95 (*0-226-07615-6*); lib. bdg. 42.50 (*0-226-07614-8*) U Ch Pr.

Brown, James H. & Lomolino, Mark V. Biogeography. 2nd ed. LC 98-20356. (C). 1998. text 69.95 (*0-87893-073-6*) Sinauer Assocs.

Brown, James H. & Real, Leslie A., eds. Foundations of Ecology: Classic Papers with Commentaries. 920p. 1991. pap. text 36.00 (*0-226-70594-3*) U Ch Pr.

— Foundations of Ecology: Classic Papers with Commentaries. 1000p. 1993. lib. bdg. 70.00 (*0-226-70593-5*) U Ch Pr.

***Brown, James H., et al.** Scaling in Biology. LC 99-42515. 368p. 2000. write for info. (*0-19-513141-X*); write for info. (*0-19-513142-8*) OUP.

Brown, James H., jt. auth. see Grant, Billie A.

Brown, James I. Efficient Reading Instructors Manual. 5th ed. 75p. 1982. reprint ed. pap. text 19.95 (*0-943000-07-6*) Telstar Inc.

— Reading Power. 3rd ed. LC 86-80504. 361p. (C). 1987. pap. text 17.00 (*0-318-40039-1*) HM Trade Div.

— Word Power Study Guide. (Illus.). 50p. (C). 1982. reprint ed. pap. text 4.95 (*0-943000-04-1*) Telstar Inc.

Brown, James I. & Fishco, Vivian V. Efficient Reading. 7th ed. 384p. (C). 1993. pap. text 35.96 (*0-669-29758-5*) HM Trade Div.

— Reading Power. 5th ed. LC 94-212298. 448p. (C). 1995. pap. text 36.76 (*0-669-34071-5*) HM Trade Div.

— Reading Power with "Newsweek" 5th ed. (C). 1995. text 43.56 (*0-669-39519-6*) HM Trade Div.

Brown, James I. & Pearsall, Thomas E. Better Spelling: Fourteen Steps to Spelling Improvement. 3rd ed. 132p. (C). 1990. pap. text 31.56 (*0-669-07653-8*) HM Trade Div.

— Better Spelling: Fourteen Steps to Spelling Improvement. 5th ed. 160p. (C). 1996. pap. text 30.76 (*0-669-35555-0*) HM Trade Div.

Brown, James I. & Prois, Karyn S. A Study Guide for Efficient Reading: Alternate Edition. Kemmerer, W. W., ed. 52p. (C). pap. text 4.95 (*0-943000-05-X*) Telstar Inc.

— A Study Guide for Efficient Reading: Form B. 52p. (C). 1982. reprint ed. pap. text 4.95 (*0-943000-06-8*) Telstar Inc.

***Brown, James J.** Judgment Enforcement. 2nd ed. LC 99-28129. 1999. boxed set 160.00 (*0-7355-0453-9*) Panel Pubs.

Brown, James J. Scientific Evidence & Experts Handbook. LC 99-34443. 627p. 1999. boxed set 160.00 (*0-7355-0676-0*) Panel Pubs.

— Yokley's Zoning Law & Practice: 1999 Cumulative Supplement, 8 vols. 1048p. 1999. suppl. ed. write for info. (*0-327-01291-9*, 6950518) LEXIS Pub.

— Yokley's Zoning Law & Practice Vol. 1: 1999 Cumulative Supplement. 4th ed. 1999. suppl. ed. write for info. (*0-327-01292-7*, 6947018) LEXIS Pub.

— Yokley's Zoning Law & Practice Vol. 2: 1999 Cumulative Supplement. 4th ed. 1999. suppl. ed. write for info. (*0-327-01293-5*, 6947118) LEXIS Pub.

— Yokley's Zoning Law & Practice Vol. 3: 1999 Cumulative Supplement. 4th ed. 1999. suppl. ed. write for info. (*0-327-01294-3*, 6947218) LEXIS Pub.

— Yokley's Zoning Law & Practice Vol. 4: 1999 Cumulative Supplement. 4th ed. 1999. suppl. ed. write for info. (*0-327-01295-1*, 6947318) LEXIS Pub.

— Yokley's Zoning Law & Practice Vol. 5: 1999 Cumulative Supplement. 4th ed. 1999. suppl. ed. write for info. (*0-327-01296-X*, 6947418) LEXIS Pub.

— Yokley's Zoning Law & Practice Vol. 6: 1999 Cumulative Supplement. 4th ed. 1999. suppl. ed. write for info. (*0-327-01297-8*, 6947518) LEXIS Pub.

— Yokley's Zoning Law & Practice Vol. 7: 1999 Cumulative Supplement. 1999. suppl. ed. write for info. (*0-327-01298-6*, 6947618) LEXIS Pub.

— Yokley's Zoning Law & Practice Vol. 8: 1999 Cumulative Supplement. 1999. suppl. ed. write for info. (*0-327-01299-4*, 6947718) LEXIS Pub.

Brown, James J., ed. State & Local Government Finance: A Selectively Annotated Bibliography, No. 783. 1975. 5.50 (*0-686-20351-8*, Sage Prdcls Pr) Sage.

Brown, James K., et al, eds. Proceedings: Symposium on Fire in Wilderness & Park Management. (Illus.). 283p. (Orig.). (C). 1996. pap. text 45.00 (*0-7881-3201-6*) DIANE Pub.

Brown, James K., jt. auth. see Bacon, Jeremy.

Brown, James L. Beowulf. (Illus.). 1974. 15.40 (*0-912314-06-0*) Academy Santa Clara.

— Dissension in Arcady: Bear Flag Revolution. 1978. 18.00 (*0-912314-15-X*) Academy Santa Clara.

— Fascicles in French Grammar Vols. I & II: The Article, The Demonstrative. 136p. 1998. pap. text 15.20 (*0-9612298-2-9*) Forsan Bks.

— History of the Thirty-Seventh Regiment, Massachusetts Volunteers in the Civil War of 1861-1865. (Illus.). li, 431p. 1998. reprint ed. lib. bdg. 52.00 (*0-8328-7027-7*) Higginson Bk Co.

— The Mussel Slough Tragedy. (Illus.). 153p. 1980. reprint ed. pap. 6.00 (*0-686-31567-7*) J L Brown.

— Treasures on Earth. 1979. pap. 7.80 (*0-685-00099-0*) Academy Santa Clara.

— Treasures on Earth. LC 79-54075. 282p. 1979. pap. 7.50 (*0-317-00106-X*) J L Brown.

Brown, James L., tr. see Valery, Paul.

Brown, James M. Brown: Handbook of Our Extended Family: an Account of Some of the American & European Ancestors of James M. Brown & Cheryl A. (Gustafson) Brown & the Descendants of Those Ancestors. (Illus.). 523p. 1992. pap. 59.00 (*0-8328-2431-3*); lib. bdg. 69.00 (*0-8328-2430-5*) Higginson Bk Co.

***Brown, James N. & Sant, Patricia M.** Indigeneity: Construction & Re-Presentation. LC 99-25733. 307p. 1999. 49.00 (*1-56072-674-1*) Nova Sci Pubs.

Brown, James-Paul. The Paintings of James-Paul Brown. LC 98-8804. 240p. 1998. 55.00 (*0-88496-434-5*) Capra Pr.

Brown, James R. Blackjack: Atlantic City Style. 100p. (Orig.). 1991. pap. 16.95 (*0-9628308-5-2*) M & H Dist.

— The Laboratory of the Mind: Thought Experiments in the Natural Sciences. (Philosophical Issues in Science Ser.). (Illus.). 208p. (C). 1993. pap. 22.99 (*0-415-09579-4*, B0292) Routledge.

***Brown, James R.** My Journey Through Life. LC 99-93732. 1999. 22.95 (*0-533-13134-0*) Vantage.

Brown, James R. Philosophy of Mathematics: Introduction to a World of Proofs & Pictures. LC 98-8014. (Philosophical Issues in Science Ser.). (Illus.). 224p. (C). 1999. 75.00 (*0-415-12274-0*); pap. 24.99 (*0-415-12275-9*) Routledge.

— Smoke & Mirrors: How Science Reflects Reality. LC 93-25307. (Philosophical Issues in Science Ser.). 224p. (C). 1994. pap. 22.99 (*0-415-09181-0*) Routledge.

Brown, James R., ed. Scientific Rationality: The Sociological Turn. (University of Western Ontario Series in Phylosophy of Science: No. 25). 337p. 1984. text 178.50 (*90-277-1812-1*) Kluwer Academic.

Brown, James R. & Mittelstrass, Juergen, eds. An Intimate Relation: Studies in the History & Philosophy of Science Presented to Robert E. Butts on His 60th Birthday. LC 96-32535. (Boston Studies in the Philosophy of Science: No. 116). 544p. 1989. lib. bdg. 271.50 (*0-7923-0169-2*, Pub. by Kluwer Academic) Kluwer Academic.

Brown, James R., jt. auth. see Ryser, Otto E.

Brown, James R., jt. ed. see Butts, Robert E.

Brown, James R., jt. ed. see Okruhlik, Kathleen.

Brown, James S. Beech Creek: A Study of a Kentucky Mountain Neighborhood. (Illus.). 320p. 1988. 20.00 (*0-938211-04-8*) Berea College Pr.

— Life of a Pioneer. LC 77-17574. reprint ed. 46.50 (*0-404-08432-X*) AMS Pr.

Brown, James S., Jr., ed. Up Before Daylight: Life Histories from the Alabama Writers' Project, 1938-1939. LC 81-21988. 280p. 1982. pap. text 19.95 (*0-8173-0099-6*) U of Ala Pr.

***Brown, James T.** Fly Reel: An Illustrated History. LC 99-34048. 1999. write for info. (*1-55821-948-X*) Lyon Press.

Brown, James T. & Kobbe, Gustav. 19th Century Whaling Tales: Stray Leaves from a Whaleman's Log; The Perils & Romance of Whaling. Jones, William R., ed. 40p. 1996. pap. 3.95 (*0-89646-089-4*) Vistabooks.

Brown, James W. Drawback Made Easy: Drawback Procedures. 2nd rev. ed. 215p. 2000. spiral bd. 49.00 (*1-891249-15-0*) Global Train Ctr.

— Fictional Meals & Their Function in the French Novel, 1789-1848. (Romance Ser.: No. 48). 232p. 1984. text 32.50 (*0-8020-5605-9*) U of Toronto Pr.

— Semiotics & Second Language Pedogogy. LC 90-13287. (American University Studies: Linguistics: Ser. XIII, Vol. 16). X, 232p. (C). 1991. text 43.95 (*0-8204-1233-3*) P Lang Pubng.

— Utah Publicity Source Book, 1995. 1995. lib. bdg. 115.00 (*1-884689-03-5*); ring bd. 130.00 (*1-884689-02-7*) Orton Grp.

Brown, James W. & Churchill, Ruel V. Complex Variables & Applications. 6th ed. LC 95-9898. (Churchill-Brown Ser.: International Series in Pure & Applied Mathematics). 1995. write for info. (*0-07-008496-3*) McGraw.

— Complex Variables & Applications (MacIntosh) 6th ed. LC 96-173968. 352p. (C). 1995. pap., student ed. 78.75 (*0-07-912146-2*); pap., student ed. 82.19 (*0-07-912147-0*) McGraw.

— Fourier Series & Boundary Value Problems. 5th ed. LC 92-12194. 320p. (C). 1993. 78.75 (*0-07-008202-2*) McGraw.

Brown, James W. & Stokes, Lawrence D., eds. Silence of the Sea: A Novel of French Resistance During the Second World War by "Vercors"Tr. of Silence de la Mer. 102p. (C). 1992. pap. 12.50 (*0-85496-378-2*, Pub. by Berg Pubs) NYU Pr.

Brown, James W., jt. auth. see Churchill, Ruel V.

Brown, James W., jt. auth. see Lloyd, Norma.

***Brown, James Ward & Churchill, Ruel Vance.** Fourier Series & Boundary Value Problems. 6th ed. LC 00-28168. 2000. write for info. (*0-07-232570-4*) McGraw.

Brown, Jamie. Freeholder: Poems by Jamie Brown. Baker, R. D., ed. (Poetry Chapbook Ser.). (Illus.). 28p. (Orig.). 1996. pap. 4.00 (*1-887641-13-0*) Argonne Hotel Pr.

— Superbike! 256p. (YA). (gr. 7-11). 1991. reprint ed. pap. 5.95 (*0-7736-7312-1*) Stoddart Publ.

Brown, Jamie Foster. Betty Shabazz: A Sisterfriends' Tribute in Words & Pictures. LC 98-7691. (Illus.). 160p. 1998. 22.50 (*0-684-85294-2*) S&S Trade.

Brown, Jamieson-Fausett. Comentario Exegetico y Explicativo de la Biblia, Vol. 2. Quarles, Jaime C. & Quarles, Lemuel C., trs. from ENG.Tr. of An American Commentary of the Old Testament. (SPA.). 382p. 1961. reprint ed. 29.99 (*0-311-03004-1*) Casa Bautista.

Brown, Jamieson-Fausett & Quarles, Jaime C. Comentario Exegetico y Explicativo de la Biblia, Vol. 1.Tr. of An American Commentary of the Old Testament. (SPA.). 982p. 1961. reprint ed. 29.99 (*0-311-03002-5*) Casa Bautista.

Brown, Jan. Strap-on Book: Penetrating Philosophies & Practicalities. 1999. pap. 11.95 (*1-890159-10-7*) Greenery Pr.

Brown, Jan & Kmetz, Yoko S. Exploring Tohoku: A Guide to Japan's Back Country. LC 82-17467. (Exploring Japan Ser.). (Illus.). 344p. (Orig.). 1983. pap. 19.95 (*0-8348-0177-9*) Weatherhill.

Brown, Jane. Beatrix. 1999. pap. 11.95 (*0-14-023457-8*) Viking Penguin.

— The English Garden in Our Time. (Illus.). 272p. 1986. 59.50 (*1-85149-012-4*) Antique Collect.

— English Garden Through the Twentieth Century. 1998. 49.50 (*1-870673-29-8*, Pub. by Garden Art Pr) Antique Collect.

***Brown, Jane.** Faces: The Creative Process Behind Great Portraits. (Illus.). 2000. 29.95 (*1-85585-789-8*, Pub. by Collins & Br) Sterling.

— The Modern Garden. (Illus.). 224p. 2000. 45.00 (*1-56898-238-0*) Princeton Arch.

Brown, Jane. Sissinghurst: Portrait of a Garden. (Illus.). 144p. 1998. pap. 22.95 (*0-7538-0437-9*, Pub. by Orion Pubng Grp) Trafalgar.

— Sissinghurst: Portrait of a Garden. (Illus.). 144p. 1994. pap. 19.95 (*0-297-83350-2*) Trafalgar.

Brown, Jane H. Coaching the Rider: Theory & Practice. LC 95-662. 1995. pap. 29.95 (*0-632-03931-0*) Blackwell Sci.

— Teaching Jumping. LC 97-471. (Illus.). 208p. (Orig.). 1997. pap. 36.95 (*0-632-04127-7*) Blackwell Sci.

Brown, Jane K. Faust: Theater of the World. (MWS Ser.). 170p. 1992. 25.95 (*0-8057-9407-7*) Macmillan.

Brown, Jane K., et al, eds. Interpreting Goethe's Faust Today. LC 93-32513. (GERM Ser.). xv, 277p. 1994. 60.00 (*1-879751-49-6*) Camden Hse.

Brown, Jane K., ed. see Atkins, Stuart.

Brown, Jane K., tr. see Goethe, Johann Wolfgang Von.

Brown, Jane L. Insurance Administration. LC 97-70687. 599p. text 61.95 (*0-939921-94-4*, Pub. by Life Office) PBD Inc.

Brown, Jane L., jt. auth. see Brown, Barbara F.

***Brown, Jane Lightcap.** Administracion de Seguros. Vallenilla, Ines, ed. (PFSL Programa of Formacion en Seguros Ser.: Vol. 3). (SPA.). 598p. (C). 1998. pap. text 105.00 (*1-57974-071-5*, Pub. by Life Office) PBD Inc.

— Administration de L'Assurance. Fonteneau, Fabien, ed. (FLMI Insurance Education Program Ser.). (FRE.). 598p. (C). 1998. pap. text 88.00 (*1-57974-014-6*) Life Office.

Brown, Jane Lightcap, jt. auth. see Herrod, Jennifer W.

Brown, Jane W., ed. see Lesser, Andrew J.

Brown, Janet. Taking Center Stage: Feminism in Contemporary U. S. Drama. LC 91-23952. 177p. 1991. 25.00 (*0-8108-2448-5*) Scarecrow.

Brown, Janet, jt. auth. see Roopnarine, Jaipaul L.

Brown, Janet Allison, jt. auth. see Pratt, Martin.

Brown, Janet H. & Shavelson, Richard J. Assessing Hands-On Science: A Teacher's Guide to Performance Assessment. 160p. 1996. pap., teacher ed. 29.95 (*0-8039-6443-9*) Corwin Pr.

Brown, Janet M. Thanksgiving at Obaachan's. LC 93-43933. (Illus.). (J). 1994. 14.95 (*1-879965-07-0*) Polychrome Pub.

Brown, Janet W., jt. auth. see Porter, Gareth.

***Brown, Janice.** The Seven Deadly Sins in the Work of Dorothy L. Sayers. LC 98-14366. 286p. 1999. text 35.00 (*0-87338-605-1*) Kent St U Pr.

Brown, Janice, tr. see Fumiko, Hayashi.

Brown, Janis F., jt. auth. see Hannigan, Gale G.

Brown, Jared. The Theatre in America During the Revolution. (Studies in American Theatre & Drama: No. 4). 239p. (C). 1995. text 64.95 (*0-521-49537-7*) Cambridge U Pr.

Brown, Jared & Miller, Anistatia R. What Logos Do: And How They Do It. (Illus.). 144p. 1998. 29.99 (*1-56496-382-9*) Rockport Pubs.

Brown, Jared, jt. auth. see Miller, Anistatia.

Brown, Jared, ed. see Spinrad, Leonard & Spinrad, Thelma.

Brown, Jared M., jt. auth. see Miller, Anastatia R.

Brown, Jared M., jt. auth. see Miller, Anistatia R.

Brown, Jarred, jt. auth. see Miller, Anastasia M.

Brown, Jason. Driving the Heart & Other Stories. LC 98-37725. 192p. 1999. 23.00 (*0-393-04721-0*) Norton.

***Brown, Jason Robert.** Parade. 104p. 2000. otabind 17.95 (*0-634-01175-8*) H Leonard.

Brown, Jason W. The Life of the Mind. (Comparative Cognition & Neuroscience Ser.). 440p. 1988. pap. text 45.00 (*0-8058-0422-6*) L Erlbaum Assocs.

— The Life of the Mind. (Comparative Cognition & Neuroscience Ser.). 440p. 1988. 99.95 (*0-8058-0236-3*) L Erlbaum Assocs.

***Brown, Jason W.** Self-Embodying Mind: Process, Brain Dynamics & the Conscious Present. 240p. 2000. pap. 22.95 (*1-58177-077-4*) Barrytown Ltd.

Brown, Jason W. Time, Will & Mental Process. (Cognition & Language Ser.). (Illus.). 276p. 1996. 45.00 (*0-306-45231-6*, Kluwer Plenum) Kluwer Academic.

Brown, Jason W., ed. Agnosia & Apraxia: Selected Papers of Liepman, Lange, & Potzl. (Institute for Research in Behavioral Neuroscience Ser.). 336p. 1988. 69.95 (*0-8058-0286-X*) L Erlbaum Assocs.

— Neuropsychology of Visual Perception. (Institute for Research in Behavioral Neuroscience Ser.). 280p. 1989. 59.95 (*0-8058-0284-3*) L Erlbaum Assocs.

Brown, Jay. The Complete Guide to Limited Edition Art Prints: How to Identify, Invest & Care for Your Collection. LC 98-87360. (Illus.). 160p. 1999. pap. 14.95 (*0-87341-704-6*, HTLT) Krause Pubns.

— Jay Brown Readers 1-9 & Travels with Ted, 4 vols. 2nd ed. (Wilson Reading System Ser.). 1998. reprint ed. pap. text 35.00 (*1-56778-112-8*) Wilson Lang Trning.

— Stories for Students 1-6: Plus Travels with Ted, 3 vols. 3rd rev. ed. 1998. pap. text 23.00 (*1-56778-114-4*) Wilson Lang Trning.

— Travels with Ted. 3rd rev. ed. 57p. 1994. pap. text 8.00 (*1-56778-043-1*) Wilson Lang Trning.

Brown, Jay C., jt. auth. see Volk, Wesley A.

Brown, Jay H. Truth in Government: Restoring Pride & Prosperity in America. LC 96-226567. 302p. 1996. pap. 12.95 (*0-9638152-3-7*) Freedom Pubng.

Brown, Jean. Traditional Metalworking in Kenya. (Oxbow Monographs in Archaeology; Cambridge Monographs in African Archaeology: Nos. 44 & 38). (Illus.). 192p. 1995. pap. 45.00 (*0-946897-99-9*, Pub. by Oxbow Bks) David Brown.

Brown, Jean, et al, eds. The Vision of Modern Dance: In the Words of Its Creators. 2nd ed. LC 97-28330. (Illus.). 230p. 1998. pap. 18.95 (*0-87127-205-9*) Princeton Bk Co.

Brown, Jean, jt. ed. see Brown, Gina.

Brown, Jean E., ed. Preserving Intellectual Freedom: Fighting Censorship in Our Schools. LC 94-19860. 252p. 1994. 19.95 (*0-8141-3671-0*) NCTE.

Brown, Jean E., et al, eds. Images from the Holocaust: A Literary Anthology. LC 96-2131. (Illus.). 600p. 1996. pap. 27.44 (*0-8442-5920-9*, 59209) NTC Contemp Pub Co.

Brown, Jean E. & Stephens, Elaine C. Exploring Diversity: Literature Themes & Activities for Grades 4-8. x, 220p. 1996. lib. bdg. 23.50 (*1-56308-322-1*) Teacher Ideas Pr.

— Teaching Young Adult Literature: Sharing the Connection. LC 94-35183. 320p. 1994. 38.95 (*0-534-19938-0*) Wadsworth Pub.

Brown, Jean E. & Stephens, Elaine C., eds. United in Diversity: Using Multicultural Young Adult Literature in the Classroom. (Classroom Practices in Teaching English Ser.: Vol. 29). 226p. 1998. pap. 22.95 (*0-8141-5571-5*, 55715-3050) NCTE.

Brown, Jean E., et al. Images from the Holocaust: A Literature Anthology. 600p. 1997. pap. text 42.66 (*0-8442-5911-X*) NTC Contemp Pub Co.

Brown, Jean E., et al. Toward Literacy: Theory & Applications for Teaching Writing in the Content Areas. LC 92-20370. 436p. (C). 1992. 27.50 (*0-534-17658-5*) Wadsworth Pub.

Brown, Jean E., jt. auth. see Stephens, Elaine C.

Brown, Jeanell W. Amy Beach & Her Chamber Music: Biography, Documents, Style. LC 94-9689. (Composers of North America Ser.: Vol. 16). (Illus.). 439p. 1994. 52.00 (*0-8108-2884-7*) Scarecrow.

Brown, Jeanette & Crombleholme, William. Handbook of Gynecology & Obstetrics. (Illus.). 626p. (C). 1996. pap. text 34.95 (*0-8385-3608-5*, A3608-5, Apple Lange Med) McGraw.

Brown, Jeannette A. & Pate, Robert H., Jr. Being a Counselor: Directions & Challenges. LC 82-20764. (Psychology Ser.). 450p. (C). 1983. text 43.95 (*0-534-01261-2*) Brooks-Cole.

Brown, Jeff. Alaskan Wildlife Maze & Puzzle Book. (ENG.). 40p. (J). 1997. pap. 6.00 (*1-57833-042-4*) Todd Commns.

Brown, Jeff. Clement Aplati. (Folio - Cadet Ser.). (FRE., Illus.). 79p. (J). 1989. pap. 10.95 (*2-07-031196-1*) Schoenhof.

— The Crayon Chronicles. 112p. (Orig.). 1998. pap. 9.95 (*1-890069-02-7*, 864, Brownflower Pr) Brownflower Creat.

— An Exciting Wonderful. 82p. (Orig.). 1996. pap. 9.95 (*1-890069-01-9*, 863, Brownflower Pr) Brownflower Creat.

— Flat Stanley. LC 63-17525. (Illus.). 48p. (J). (ps-3). 1964. lib. bdg. 15.89 (*0-06-020681-0*) HarpC Child Bks.

— Flat Stanley. LC 63-17525. (Trophy Bk.). (Illus.). 48p. (J). (gr. 2-5). 1989. pap. 4.95 (*0-06-440293-2*, HarpTrophy) HarpC Child Bks.

— Flat Stanley. LC 95-11369. (Trophy Chapter Bk.). (Illus.). 64p. (J). (gr. 4-7). 1996. pap. 4.25 (*0-06-442026-4*, HarpTrophy) HarpC Child Bks.

— Flat Stanley. LC 95-11369. 1996. 9.15 (*0-606-09285-4*, Pub. by Turtleback) Demco.

— Invisible Stanley. LC 96-52. (Trophy Chapter Bk.). (Illus.). 96p. (J). (gr. 1-5). 1996. pap. 4.25 (*0-06-442029-9*, HarpTrophy) HarpC Child Bks.

— Invisible Stanley. LC 96-52. 1996. 9.15 (*0-606-09475-X*, Pub. by Turtleback) Demco.

— A Lamp for the Lambchops. LC 82-48628. (Illus.). 96p. (J). (gr. 2-6). 1983. 11.95 (*0-06-020693-4*) HarpC Child Bks.

B

An Asterisk (*) at the beginning of an entry indicates that the title is appearing for the first time.

— Slow Christmas. 2nd ed. 77p. 1996. reprint ed. pap. 9.95 (*1-890069-00-0*, 862, Brownflower Pr) Brownflower Creat.

— Stanley & the Magic Lamp. LC 95-23158. (Trophy Chapter Bk.). (Illus.). 96p. (J). (gr. 4-7). 1996. pap. 4.25 (*0-06-442028-0*, HarpTrophy) HarpC Child Bks.

— Stanley & the Magic Lamp. 1996. 9.15 (*0-606-09889-5*, Pub. by Turtleback) Demco.

— We Like Kids! A Multicultural Storybook, Pre-Grade 3. (Illus.). 88p. (Orig.). 1994. pap. 13.95 incl. audio (*0-673-36167-5*, GoodYrBooks) Addson-Wesley Educ.

— We Like Kids! Letters & Numbers. (Illus.). 88p. (J). (ps-3). 1994. pap. 13.95 incl. audio (*0-673-36126-8*, GoodYrBooks) Addson-Wesley Educ.

Brown, Jeff & Pelzer, Chris, prods. Molly's Pilgrim. (Literature to Go Ser.). pap., teacher ed. Price not set. incl. VHS (*0-7919-2685-0*) Phoenix Films.

***Brown, Jeff, et al.** Design Methodology & Technology: A4, Version 4.07. Lane, Susan M., ed. (CIW Site Designer Track A4 Ser.). (Illus.). 1999. pap. write for info. (*1-58143-069-8*) Prosoft I-net.

— Design Methodology & Technology: Version 4.07. Lane, Susan M., ed. (CIW Site Designer Track Ser.). (Illus.). 1999. pap. write for info. (*1-58143-033-7*) Prosoft I-net.

Brown, Jeff, et al. We Like Kids! (Illus.). 88p. (J). (ps-3). 1992. pap. 13.95 incl. audio (*0-673-36038-5*, GoodYrBooks) Addson-Wesley Educ.

— We Like Kids! Songs for the Earth. (Illus.). 80p. (Orig.). (J). (ps-3). 1992. pap. 13.95 incl. audio (*0-673-36052-0*, GoodYrBooks) Addson-Wesley Educ.

***Brown, Jeffrey A.** Black Superheroes, Milestone Comics & Their Fans. LC 00-21978. (Studies in Popular Culture). (Illus.). 256p. 2001. pap. 45.00 (*1-57806-282-9*); lib. bdg. 45.00 (*1-57806-281-0*) U Pr of Miss.

Brown, Jeffrey C., ed. Professional Negligence & Insurance Law: A Lloyd's of London Press Industry Report. 96p. 1991. pap. 160.00 (*1-85044-348-3*) LLP.

Brown, Jeffrey C., ed. see Jones, Neil F., & Co. Staff.

Brown, Jeffrey J. & Higgins, Charles B. Pocket Atlas of Cardiac & Thoracic MRI. (Illus.). 72p. 1989. pap. text 16.95 (*0-88167-488-5*, 1961) Lppncott W & W.

Brown, Jeffrey J. & Wippold, Franz J., II. Practical MRI: A Teaching File. (Illus.). 592p. 1995. text 135.00 (*0-7817-0200-3*) Lppncott W & W.

Brown, Jeffrey J., jt. ed. see Heiken, Jay P.

Brown, Jeffrey L. Pediatric Telephone Medicine: Principles, Triage & Advice. 2nd ed. (Illus.). 275p. 1994. pap. text 35.00 (*0-397-51379-8*) Lppncott W & W.

— Pediatric Telephone Medicine: Principles, Triage & Advice. 3rd ed. 320p. 1998. spiral bd. 34.95 (*0-7817-1631-4*) Lppncott W & W.

Brown, Jeffrey L., ed. Sustaining the Future: Activities for Environmental Education in U. S. History. 270p. (Orig.). 1995. pap. 25.00 (*0-928630-03-X*) Global Learning.

Brown, Jeffrey L. & Gotsch, Paula, eds. A Sustainable Development Curriculum Framework for World History & Cultures. 1991. pap. 20.00 (*0-614-02992-9*) Amer Forum.

Brown, Jeffrey L., et al. A Sustainable Development Curriculum Framework for World History & Cultures: Lessons on the Environment Development & Equity. (Illus.). 300p. (Orig.). 1991. pap. 4.00 (*0-928630-00-5*) Global Learning.

Brown, Jeffrey L., ed. see Chen, Loris.

Brown, Jeffrey P. & Cayton, Andrew R., eds. The Pursuit of Public Power: Political Culture in Ohio, 1787-1861. LC 94-6142. 272p. 1994. pap. 22.00 (*0-87338-496-2*) Kent St U Pr.

Brown, Jennie. Medgar Evers: Civil Rights Activist. (Black American Ser.). (Illus.). 208p. (Orig.). (YA). 1994. mass mkt. 3.95 (*0-87067-594-X*, Melrose Sq) Holloway.

Brown, Jennifer, ed. Environmental Threats: Perception, Analysis & Management. (Belhaven Press Bk.). (Illus.). 200p. 1992. 51.95 (*1-85293-015-2*, Pub. by P P Pubs) CRC Pr.

Brown, Jennifer M. & Campbell, Elizabeth A. Stress & Policing: Sources & Strategies. 214p. 1994. 245.00 (*0-471-94138-7*) Wiley.

Brown, Jennifer Maze. Hooray! It's a Duck Day. (Illus.). 32p. (J). (ps-2). 1999. 6.99 (*0-570-05081-2*, 56-1905GJ) Concordia.

Brown, Jennifer S. Strangers in Blood: Fur Trade Company Families in Indian Country. LC 95-36771. (Illus.). 292p. 1996. pap. 17.95 (*0-8061-2813-5*) U of Okla Pr.

Brown, Jennifer S. & Brightman, Robert. The Orders of the Dreamed: George Nelson on Cree & Northern Ojibwa Religion & Myth, 1823. (Illus.). 226p. 1998. pap. 15.95 (*0-87351-370-3*) Minn Hist.

Brown, Jennifer S. & Hallowell, A. Irving. The Ojibwa of Berens River, Manitoba: Ethnography into History. (Illus.). 180p. (C). 1992. pap. text 18.50 (*0-03-055122-6*, Pub. by Harcourt Coll Pubs) Harcourt.

Brown, Jennifer S. & Vibert, Elizabeth, eds. Reading Beyond Words: The Contexts of Native History. 472p. 1996. pap. 27.95 (*1-55111-070-9*) Broadview Pr.

Brown, Jenny, jt. auth. see McNeilly, Rob.

***Brown, Jerald E.** The Years of the Life of Samuel Lane, 1718-1806: A New Hampshire Man & His World. Garvin, Donna-Belle, ed. & intro. by. LC 99-89809. (Illus.). 304p. 2000. pap. 19.95 (*1-58465-052-4*); text 50.00 (*1-58465-051-6*) U Pr of New Eng.

***Brown, Jeremy.** The Serpent & the Staff. 1999. mass mkt. 9.99 (*1-55279-012-6*) Picasso Publ.

Brown, Jeremy H., et al. Horse & Stable Management: Incorporating Horse Care. 3rd ed. LC 96-24285. 470p. (Orig.). 1996. pap. 36.95 (*0-632-04152-8*) Blackwell Sci.

Brown, Jeremy M. Explaining the Reagan Years in Central America: A World System Perspective. 312p. (Orig.). (C). 1995. pap. text 29.50 (*0-8191-9813-7*); lib. bdg. 54.00 (*0-8191-9812-9*) U Pr of Amer.

Brown, Jeri W., ed. Space Safety & Rescue 1979-1981 (with Abstracts 1976-1978), Proceedings of Symposia of the International Academy of Astronautics Held in Conjunction with the 30th, 31st, & 32nd International Astronautical Federation Congresses, Munich, Germany, 1979, Toky. (Science & Technology Ser.: Vol. 54). (Illus.). 456p. 1983. pap. 35.00 (*0-87703-178-9*, Am Astronaut Soc) Univelt Inc.

— Space Safety & Rescue 1979-1981 (with Abstracts 1976-1978), Proceedings of Symposia of the International Academy of Astronautics Held in Conjunction with the 30th, 31st, & 32nd International Astronautical Federation Congresses, Munich, Germany, 1979, Tokyo: 1979-1981. (Science & Technology Ser.: Vol. 54). (Illus.). 456p. 1983. 45.00 (*0-87703-177-0*, Am Astronaut Soc) Univelt Inc.

Brown, Jerilyn B. & Bedford, Nancy K. Gerontological Protocols for Nurse Practitioners. LC 99-24355. 512p. 1998. spiral bd. 38.95 (*0-7817-1567-9*) Lppncott W & W.

Brown, Jerold E. Where Eagles Land: Planning & Development of U. S. Army Airfields, 1910-1941. 94. LC 89-23256. (Contributions in Military Studies Ser.: No. 94). 232p. 1990. 62.95 (*0-313-26800-2*, BUF/, Greenwood Pr) Greenwood.

***Brown, Jerold E., ed.** Historical Dictionary of the U. S. Army. LC 00-22373. 608p. 2000. lib. bdg. 100.00 (*0-313-29322-8*, GR9322, Greenwood Pr) Greenwood.

Brown, Jerold E. & Reagan, Patrick D., eds. Voluntarism, Planning, & the State: The American Planning Experience, 1914-1946. 130. LC 88-15462. (Contributions in American History Ser.: No. 130). 188p. 1988. 49.95 (*0-313-26177-6*, BVM/) Greenwood.

Brown, Jerome C. Dinosaur Color & Pattern Book. (J). (gr. k-3). 1989. pap. 8.99 (*0-8224-2322-7*) Fearon Teacher Aids.

— Great Gifts for All Occasions That Kids Can Make for Practically Nothing. (J). (gr. 1-6). 1986. pap. 12.99 (*0-8224-3596-9*) Fearon Teacher Aids.

— Greeting Cards for All Occasions. 112p. (J). (gr. 1-6). 11.99 (*0-614-16786-8*, FE0881) Fearon Teacher Aids.

— Holiday Art Projects. (J). (gr. 3-12). 1984. pap. 4.99 (*0-8224-5190-5*) Fearon Teacher Aids.

— Holiday Crafts & Greeting Cards. (PaperCrafts & Literature Ser.). (J). (gr. 3-6). 1982. pap. 5.99 (*0-8224-5194-8*) Fearon Teacher Aids.

— Holiday Gifts & Decorations Kids Can Make for Practically Nothing. (J). (gr. 1-6). 1986. pap. 12.99 (*0-8224-3595-0*) Fearon Teacher Aids.

— Legends & Fables Papercrafts. 1991. 8.99 (*0-8224-4234-5*) Fearon Teacher Aids.

— Mother Goose PaperCrafts. (PaperCrafts & Literature Ser.). (J). (gr. k-5). 1989. pap. 7.99 (*0-8224-3154-8*) Fearon Teacher Aids.

— Paper Designs. (Lake's Paper Crafts Ser.). (J). (gr. 1-6). 1982. pap. 6.99 (*0-8224-5193-X*) Fearon Teacher Aids.

— Tales from Many Lands Papercrafts. 1991. 7.99 (*0-8224-3157-2*) Fearon Teacher Aids.

Brown, Jerram L. Helping & Communal Breeding in Birds: Ecology & Evolution. LC 86-18669. (Monographs in Behavior & Ecology). (Illus.). 373p. reprint ed. pap. 115.70 (*0-608-06297-9*, 206665900008) Bks Demand.

Brown, Jerrold G. & Cox, Clarice R. Report Writing for Criminal Justice Professionals. 2nd ed. LC 97-52768. 395p. (C). 1998. pap. 34.95 (*0-87084-204-8*) Anderson Pub Co.

***Brown, Jerry.** Commentaries. 2000. pap. 9.00 (*1-893163-19-9*) Berkeley Hills.

Brown, Jerry. Dialogues. LC 98-8389. 309p. 1998. pap. 14.95 (*0-9653774-9-0*) Berkeley Hills.

Brown, Jerry & Dudley, Denise. The Supervisor's Guide. viii, 68p. (Orig.). 1989. 12.95 (*1-878542-01-X*, 12-0001) SkillPath Pubns.

***Brown, Jerry & Tulumello, Mike.** Jason Kidd: Rising Sun. (SuperStar Series: Vol. 7). 96p. (J). 1999. pap. 4.95 (*1-58261-181-5*, Pub. by Sprts Pubng) Partners-West.

Brown, Jerry B. Profiles in Power: The Antinuclear Movement & the Dawn of the Solar Age. LC 97-26458. 1997. 33.00 (*0-8057-3879-7*) Macmillan.

Brown, Jerry E. Roy Blount, Jr. (Twayne's United States Authors Ser.: No. 567). 176p. 1990. 21.95 (*0-8057-7609-5*, Twyne) Mac Lib Ref.

Brown, Jerry E. & Whorton, J. C., Jr. Exchange of Futures for Physicals: New Market Opportunities for North America. 22p. 1993. pap. 10.00 (*0-918714-38-9*) Intl Res Ctr Energy.

Brown, Jerry E., jt. auth. see Southerland, Henry D., Jr.

Brown, Jesse & Willard, A. M. The Black Hills Trails: A History of the Struggles of the Pioneers... LC 75-83. (Mid-American Frontier Ser.). (Illus.). 1975. reprint ed. 48.95 (*0-405-06852-2*) Ayer.

Brown, Jesse B. Investing in the Dream: Personal Wealth-Building Strategies for African-Americans in Search of Financial Freedom. LC 99-22119. 304p. 2000. text 22.95 (*0-7868-6462-1*, Pub. by Hyperion) Time Warner.

— Pay Yourself First - A Guide to Financial Success. LC 97-93987. (Illus.). 152p. 1997. 29.95 (*0-9659384-0-9*) Krystal Pr Pub.

Brown, Jessica S. Sino-Conflict: A Historical Bibliography. (ABC-CLIO Research Guides). 1984. lib. bdg. 49.50 (*0-87436-382-9*) ABC-CLIO.

Brown, Jill S., et al. Bibliography of Published Studies Using the Child Behavior Checklist & Related Materials, 1999. rev. ed. 1999. disk 50.00 (*0-938565-38-9*) U of VT Psych.

Brown, Jill S., jt. auth. see Myers, Jane E.

***Brown, Jim.** Country Women in Music: Man I Feel Like a Woman. (Illus.). 272p. 1999. pap. 16.95 (*1-55082-247-0*, QP00795, Pub. by Quarry Pr) Music Sales.

Brown, Jim. Eternity Together-You & I. (Orig.). 1988. pap. text 2.95 (*0-9620659-0-0*) J Brown FL.

— From Ignorance to Blasphemy Within the Church: "Pentecostal Television Evangelists' Heresy Exposed" 64p. 1992. pap. 3.95 (*0-9620659-2-7*) J Brown FL.

— George Jones: Why Baby Why. (Illus.). 240p. 1999. pap. 16.95 (*1-55082-243-8*) Quarry Pr.

— Hubbard: The Forgotten Boeing Aviator. LC 96-69416. 132p. (Orig.). 1996. pap. 19.95 (*0-89716-651-5*, Peanut Btr Pubng) Elton-Wolf Pub.

— NAUI Course Director Guidelines. 2nd ed. 280p. 1992. ring bd. 45.00 (*0-916974-52-9*, 14501) NAUI.

— The Rapture - But When? Before or after the Tribulation? 80p. 1992. pap. 4.95 (*0-9620659-1-9*) J Brown FL.

— Tennis: Steps to Success. 2nd ed. LC 94-43319. (Steps to Success Activity Ser.). (Illus.). 160p. (Orig.). 1995. pap. 15.95 (*0-87322-555-4*, PBRO0555) Human Kinetics.

— A Treasury of Reels. (From the Collections of the American Museum of Fly Fishing). (Illus.). 1990. 50.00 (*0-685-30055-2*) Amer Mus Fly Fishing.

— Willie Nelson: My Life. (Illus.). 240p. 1999. pap. 16.95 (*1-55082-255-1*) LPC InBook.

Brown, Jim, ed. American Tapestry Today. (Illus.). 40p. (Orig.). 1990. pap. 12.95 (*0-945858-02-7*) Am Tapestry Alliance.

— World Tapestry Today. Trans-Laangg Co. Staff, tr. LC 88-70295. (ENG, FRE & GER., Illus.). 80p. (Orig.). 1988. per. 14.95 (*0-945858-01-9*) Am Tapestry Alliance.

Brown, Jim & Brown, Wes. Hunting Western Deer. (Illus.). 174p. 1991. pap. 14.95 (*0-912299-51-7*) Stoneydale Pr Pub.

Brown, Jim, jt. auth. see Howard, Clay.

***Brown, Jo.** Romantic Days & Nights in Seattle: Romantic Diversions in & Around the City. 2nd ed. LC 99-33565. (Illus.). 288p. 1999. pap. text 15.95 (*0-7627-0470-5*) Globe Pequot.

Brown, Jo, ed. see Litman, Todd & Kart, Suzanne.

Brown, Jo, ed. see Satterfield, Archie.

Brown, Jo-Anne Clark. Wild Strawberries & Cream. LC 99-24748. (Hearthside Ser.). (Illus.). 176p. 1999. pap. 16.95 (*1-58182-023-2*) Cumberland Hse.

Brown, Jo Langham, see Langham Brown, Jo.

Brown, Joan. Welcome the Word. 304p. 1990. pap. 29.95 (*0-225-66525-5*) Morehouse Pub.

Brown, Joan, et al, eds. Science in Schools. LC 86-16336. 416p. 1987. 133.00 (*0-335-15982-6*); pap. 39.95 (*0-335-15981-8*) OpUniv Pr.

Brown, Joan, jt. auth. see Claggett, Fran.

Brown, Joan, jt. auth. see Edwards, Gunvor.

Brown, Joan C. A Taxonomic Analysis of Avian Faunal Remains from Three Archaeological Sites in Marina Del Rey, Los Angeles County, California. (Archives of California Prehistory Ser.: Vol. 30). 72p. (Orig.). (C). 1989. pap. text 8.44 (*1-55567-068-7*) Coyote Press.

Brown, Joan Heller, ed. The Muscarinic Receptors. LC 89-15539. (Receptors Ser.). 496p. 1989. 125.00 (*0-89603-156-X*) Humana.

Brown, Joan L. Secrets from the Back Room: The Fiction of Carmen Martin Gaite. LC 86-14619. (Romance Monographs: No. 46). 206p. 1987. 33.00 (*84-599-1600-6*) Romance.

Brown, Joan L., ed. Women Writers of Contemporary Spain. LC 89-40296. 1991. 39.50 (*0-87413-386-6*) U Delaware Pr.

Brown, Joan L. & Gaite, Carmen M. Conversaciones Creadoras. (SPA.). pap. text, teacher ed. 32.37 (*0-669-17374-6*) HM Schl Div.

— Conversaciones Creadoras. (SPA.). 247p. (C). 1994. pap. text 36.76 (*0-669-17373-8*) HM Trade Div.

Brown, Joan S. Life in American Public Schools. 332p. 1991. pap. 13.95 (*0-9700118-0-6*) J&F Consult.

Brown, Joan W. Heaven in a Wild Flower. (Illus.). 64p. 1989. 8.95 (*0-8378-1841-9*) Gibson.

— The Shelter of His Wings. (Illus.). 64p. 1994. 8.95 (*0-8378-7688-5*) Gibson.

Brown, Joan W., compiled by. Day-by-Day with Billy Graham. 1991. pap. 6.95 (*0-89066-056-5*) World Wide Pubs.

— Dia-Tras-Dia con Billy Graham.Tr. of Day by Day by Billy Graham. (SPA.). 192p. 1978. reprint ed. 11.50 (*0-311-40039-6*, Edit Mundo) Casa Bautista.

Brown, Joanie & Brown, Bill. Tennis Camps, Clinics, & Resorts. 2nd ed. LC 97-28502. (Illus.). 340p. 1998. pap. 14.95 (*1-55921-217-9*) Moyer Bell.

Brown, Joanie S. & Thompson, Shirley A. Peterson's Tennis Camps & Clinics. LC 95-5038. 276p. 1995. pap. 13.95 (*1-56079-445-3*) Petersons.

Brown, JoAnne. The Definition of a Profession: The Authority of Metaphor in the History of Intelligence Testing, 1890-1930. 216p. 1992. text 45.00 (*0-691-08632-X*, Pub. by Princeton U Pr) Cal Prin Full Svc.

— Presenting Kathry Lasky. LC 98-35177. 173p. 1998. 28.00 (*0-8057-1677-7*, Twyne) Mac Lib Ref.

Brown, JoAnne & Van Keuren, David K., eds. The Estate of Social Knowledge. LC 90-39696. (Symposia in Comparative History Ser.). 272p. 1991. text 47.00 (*0-8018-4060-0*) Johns Hopkins.

Brown, Joanne C. & Bohn, Carole R., eds. Christianity, Patriarchy & Abuse: A Feminist Critique. LC 89-35505. 192p. (Orig.). (C). 1989. pap. 15.95 (*0-8298-0808-6*) Pilgrim OH.

***Brown, Joanne Nelson King.** I Swam with Piranhas. 2000. pap. 10.95 (*0-533-13552-4*) Vantage.

Brown, Jodi M., et al. Correctional Populations in the U. S., (1994) (Illus.). 181p. (Orig.). (C). 1996. pap. text 40.00 (*0-7881-3512-0*) DIANE Pub.

Brown, Joe E. Maryfield U. S. A. A Success Story. LC 97-70101. (Illus.). 168p. 1997. write for info. (*0-9656718-0-1*) Maryfield Nursing.

Brown, Joel H., ed. Advances in Confluent Education: In Preparation, Summer 1997, Vol. 2. 1999. 78.50 (*0-7623-0156-2*) Jai Pr.

— Advances in Confluent Education Vol. 1: Integrating Consciousness for Human Change. 175p. 1996. 78.50 (*0-7623-0080-9*) Jai Pr.

***Brown, Joel H., et al.** Resilience Education. LC 00-9565. 2000. write for info. (*0-7619-7626-4*) Sage.

***Brown, Joetta.** Chapters. 1999. pap. write for info. (*1-58235-380-8*) Watermrk Pr.

Brown, Joey C. Inspirations. (Orig.). 1997. pap. write for info. (*1-57553-427-4*) Watermrk Pr.

Brown, John. Brief Sketch of the First Settlement of the County of Schoharie by the Germans. 1981. reprint ed. pap. 5.00 (*0-910746-85-0*, BSO01) Hope Farm.

— Christ the Way, the Truth, & the Life. 319p. 1995. 24.95 (*1-57358-020-1*) Soli Deo Gloria.

— Discourses & Sayings of Our Lord. 528p. 1990. 74.99 (*0-85151-581-9*) Banner of Truth.

— Essays on the Characteristics of the Earl of Shaftesbury. (Anglistica & Americana Ser.: No. 15). viii, 408p. 1969. reprint ed. 105.00 (*0-685-66436-8*, 05102035) G Olms Pubs.

***Brown, John.** Foseco Iron Foundryman's Handbook. (Illus.). 300p. 2000. text 85.00 (*0-7506-4285-8*, Newnes) Buttrwrth-Heinemann.

— Foseco Steel Foundryman's Handbook. (Illus.). 300p. 2000. text 85.00 (*0-7506-4287-4*, Newnes) Buttrwrth-Heinemann.

Brown, John. Hebrews. (Geneva Commentaries Ser.). 329p. 1983. reprint ed. text 27.99 (*0-85151-099-X*) Banner of Truth.

— History & Battlefields of the Civil War. 1991. 29.98 (*1-55521-752-4*) Bk Sales Inc.

— John Bunyan. 1988. reprint ed. lib. bdg. 75.00 (*0-7812-0346-5*) Rprt Serv.

— Life, Trial & Execution of Captain John Brown, Known As "Old Brown of Ossawatomie" LC 69-18827. (Law, Politics & History Ser.). 1969. reprint ed. lib. bdg. 22.50 (*0-306-71250-4*) Da Capo.

— Morning Faces. (American Autobiography Ser.). 187p. 1995. reprint ed. lib. bdg. 69.00 (*0-7812-8466-X*) Rprt Serv.

— Provisional Constitution & Ordinances for the People of the United States. 32p. 1969. 15.00 (*0-87730-001-1*) M & S Pr.

— Rab & His Friends. LC 72-5910. (Short Story Index Reprint Ser.). 1977. reprint ed. 21.95 (*0-8369-4193-4*) Ayer.

— Rogue's Bluff: Murder in the Ohio River Valley. LC 98-75062. 270p. 1998. pap. 15.95 (*1-57860-068-5*) Guild Pr IN.

— Slave Life in Georgia. Chamerovzow, L. A., ed. LC 77-168512. (Black Heritage Library Collection). 1977. reprint ed. 27.95 (*0-8369-8865-5*) Ayer.

— Slave Life in Georgia: A Narrative of the Life, Sufferings, & Escape of John Brown, a Fugitive Slave. 218p. 1991. 25.00 (*0-88322-007-5*) Beehive GA.

— Welsh Stick Chairs: A Workshop Guide to the Windsor Chair. LC 93-28897. (Illus.). 93p. 1993. reprint ed. pap. 14.95 (*0-941936-28-7*) Linden Pub Fresno.

Brown, John, ed. Recall & Recognition. LC BF0371.R33. 285p. reprint ed. pap. 88.40 (*0-608-18757-7*, 205224000068) Bks Demand.

***Brown, John & DeRamus, Dorothy, eds.** The Heritage of Autauga County, Alabama. (Heritage of Alabama Ser.: Vol. 1). 320p. 2000. 59.95 (*1-891647-34-2*) Herit Pub Consult.

Brown, John, jt. auth. see Carr, Joseph.

Brown, John, jt. auth. see Dunster, Mark.

Brown, John, jt. ed. see Nolte, Carl.

Brown, John A. Handbook of Social Work Practice. 356p. 1992. pap. 43.95 (*0-398-06035-5*) C C Thomas.

— Handbook of Social Work Practice. 356p. (C). 1992. text 65.95 (*0-398-05799-0*) C C Thomas.

Brown, John A., jt. auth. see Ruby, Robert H.

Brown, John B. Sword & Firearm Collection of the Society of the Cincinnati in the Anderson House Museum. LC 65-25758. (Illus.). 120p. 1965. 10.00 (*0-318-16567-8*) Anderson Hse Mus.

Brown, John C. Beyond the Silence: The Role of Silence in Determining Authority. LC 99-62351. xiv, 168p. 1999. pap. 14.95 (*1-928736-00-9*, Candlewood Pr) Liberal Arts & Crafts.

— A Hundred Years of Merchant Banking. Wilkins, Mira, ed. LC 78-3900. (International Finance Ser.). (Illus.). 1979. reprint ed. lib. bdg. 42.95 (*0-405-11205-X*) Ayer.

Brown, John C., jt. ed. see Schmelz, Joan T.

Brown, John D. The Bley's Barn. LC PS3552.R683B. 31p. 1975. reprint ed. pap. 30.00 (*0-7837-9163-1*, 204986400003) Bks Demand.

— Two Kids & the Three Bears. LC 75-40538. (Lucky Heart Bk.). 32p. 1976. reprint ed. pap. 30.00 (*0-7837-9165-8*, 204986600003) Bks Demand.

Brown, John E. Memoirs of an American Gold Seeker. 34p. 1986. pap. 5.95 (*0-87770-368-X*) Ye Galleon.

Brown, John F. Engineering Report Writing. 3rd rev. ed. Laws, Lynda & Bowers, Carol, eds. LC 89-85350. Orig. Title: A Student Guide to Engineering Report Writing. (Illus.). 179p. (C). 1989. reprint ed. pap. text 19.95 (*0-9612488-5-8*) United Western Pr.

Brown, John F. & Obenski, Kenneth S. Forensic Engineering Reconstruction of Accidents. (Illus.). 270p. 1990. pap. 36.95 (*0-398-06605-1*) C C Thomas.

— Forensic Engineering Reconstruction of Accidents. (Illus.). 270p. (C). 1990. text 66.95 (*0-398-05624-2*) C C Thomas.

Brown, John G. Decorations in a Ruined Cemetery. large type ed. LC 94-6613. 352p. 1994. lib. bdg. 23.95 (*0-8161-7430-X*) Thorndike Pr.

— The Wrecked, Blessed Body of Shelton Lafleur. 1996. write for info. (*0-614-17410-4*) HM.

An Asterisk (*) at the beginning of an entry indicates that the title is appearing for the first time.

— The Wrecked, Blessed Body of Shelton Lafleur. 272p. 1997. pap. 12.00 (*0-380-72965-2*, Avon Bks) Morrow Avon.

— The Wrecked, Blessed Body of Shelton Lafleur. large type ed. LC 97-9267. (Paperback Ser.). 361p. 1997. pap. 21.95 (*0-7838-8198-3*, G K Hall Lrg Type) Mac Lib Ref.

Brown, John H. The Completely Revised How to Run Your Business So You Can Leave It in Style. 2nd rev. ed. Carroll, Kathryn B., ed. LC 96-80008. 299p. 1997. pap. 19.95 (*0-9655731-1-7*) Busn Ent Pr.

— Hippopotamus & Other Stories. LC 96-90443. (Illus.). 1998. 8.95 (*0-533-12057-8*) Vantage.

— History of Texas, 1685-1892, 2 vols., Set. 1993. reprint ed. lib. bdg. 180.00 (*0-7812-5869-3*) Rprt Serv.

— Indian Wars & Pioneers of Texas. LC 88-28254. (Illus.). 1166p. (C). 1988. reprint ed. 125.00 (*0-938349-33-3*) State House Pr.

— Indian Wars & Pioneers of Texas, 1685-1892. 1993. reprint ed. lib. bdg. 75.00 (*0-7812-5870-7*) Rprt Serv.

Brown, John H., jt. ed. see Pelltreau, William S.

Brown, John J. American Angler's Guide: or Complete Fisher's Manual for the U. S. (Illus.). 332p. 45.00 (*1-56416-132-3*) Derrydale Pr.

Brown, John K. The Baldwin Locomotive Works, 1831-1915: A Study in American Industrial Practice. LC 94-44850. (Studies in Industry & Society). (Illus.). 344p. 1995. text 35.95 (*0-8018-5047-9*) Johns Hopkins.

Brown, John L. Methodus Ad Facilem Historiarum Cognitionem of Jean Bodin: A Critical Study. LC 76-94167. (Catholic University of America. Studies in Romance Languages & Literatures: No. 18). reprint ed. 37.50 (*0-404-50318-7*) AMS Pr.

— Observing Dimensions of Learning in Classrooms & Schools. LC 95-32520. 143p. 1995. pap. 16.95 (*0-87120-255-7*, 195209) ASCD.

Brown, John L. & Moffett, Cerylle A. The Hero's Journey: How Educators Can Transform Schools & Improve Learning. LC 99-6342. 1999. pap. 20.95 (*0-87120-344-8*) ASCD.

Brown, John M. Broadway in Review. 1977. 18.95 (*0-8369-0007-3*) Ayer.

— Letters from Greenroom Ghosts. LC 67-23187. (Essay Index Reprint Ser.). 1977. reprint ed. 20.95 (*0-8369-0258-0*) Ayer.

— Maori & Polynesian, Their Origin, History & Culture. LC 75-35240. reprint ed. 41.50 (*0-404-14415-2*) AMS Pr.

— Molecular Spectroscopy. (Oxford Chemistry Primers Ser.: No. 55). (Illus.). 96p. (C). 1998. pap. text 12.95 (*0-19-855785-X*) OUP.

— Morning Faces: A Book of Children & Parents. LC 78-167317. (Essay Index Reprint Ser.). (Illus.). 1977. reprint ed. 20.95 (*0-8369-2755-9*) Ayer.

— Peoples & Problems of the Pacific, 2 vols., Set. LC 75-35176. reprint ed. 125.00 (*0-404-14250-8*) AMS Pr.

— The Portable Charles Lamb. LC 75-11488. 594p. 1975. reprint ed. lib. bdg. 38.50 (*0-8371-8202-6*, LAPCL, Greenwood Pr) Greenwood.

— The Riddle of the Pacific. (Atlantis Reprint Ser.). 460p. 1996. pap. 16.95 (*0-932813-29-1*) Adventures Unltd.

— The Riddle of the Pacific. LC 75-35177. reprint ed. 72.50 (*0-404-14205-2*) AMS Pr.

— Seeing Things. LC 75-138209. 341p. 1971. reprint ed. lib. bdg. 38.50 (*0-8371-5564-9*, BRST, Greenwood Pr) Greenwood.

— Through These Men: Some Aspects of Our Passing History. LC 71-167318. (Essay Index Reprint Ser.). 1977. reprint ed. 23.95 (*0-8369-2756-7*) Ayer.

***Brown, John M. & Hofmann, P., eds.** Organometallic Bonding & Reactivity: Fundamental Studies. LC 99-33293. (Topics in Organometallic Chemistry Ser.: Vol. 4). (Illus.). 220p. 1999. 125.00 (*3-540-64253-6*) Spr-Verlag.

Brown, John M., jt. auth. see Carr, Joseph J.

Brown, John P. Darvishes: or Oriental Spiritualism. Rose, Horace A., ed. (Illus.). 496p. 1968. 45.00 (*0-7146-1980-9*, Pub. by F Cass Pubs) Intl Spec Bk.

— Israel & Hellas, Vol. 231. LC 95-340223. (Beiheft zur Zeitschrift fuer die Alttestamentliche Wissenschaft Ser.: No. 231). xxii, 407p. (C). 1995. 136.95 (*3-11-014233-3*) De Gruyter.

— Lebanon & Phoenicia - Ancient Texts Illustrating Their Physical Geography & Native Industries Vol. 1: The Physical Setting & the Forest. 1969. pap. 29.95 (*0-8156-6090-1*, Pub. by Am U Beirut) Syracuse U Pr.

— Old Frontiers: The Story of the Cherokee Indians from the Earliest Times to the Date of Their Removal to the West, 1838. LC 74-146379. (First American Frontier Ser.). (Illus.). 1975. reprint ed. 74.95 (*0-405-02830-X*) Ayer.

Brown, John P., tr. see Barbe, Dominique.

***Brown, John Pairman.** Israel & Hellas II. 1999. 124.00 (*3-11-016434-5*) De Gruyter.

Brown, John R. Discovering Shakespeare: A New Guide to the Plays. 192p. 1986. pap. text 19.50 (*0-231-05359-2*) Col U Pr.

***Brown, John R.** Foseco Non-Ferrous Foundryman's Handbook. 11th ed. LC 99-34984. 296p. 1999. text 85.00 (*0-7506-4286-6*) Buttrwrth-Heinemann.

Brown, John R. Free Shakespeare. expanded ed. 144p. 1998. pap. text 12.95 (*1-55783-283-8*) Applause Theatre Bk Pubs.

— How to Play Saxophone. (Illus.). 80p. 1993. pap. 7.95 (*0-312-10477-4*) St Martin.

— New Sites for Shakespeare: Theatre, the Audience, & Asia. LC 98-29630. 18p. 1998. 65.00 (*0-415-19449-0*); pap. 21.99 (*0-415-19450-4*) Routledge.

— The Oxford Illustrated History of Theatre. LC 97-30250. (Oxford Illustrated Histories). (Illus.). 590p. 1997. reprint ed. pap. 25.00 (*0-19-288062-4*) OUP.

— Shakespeare's Dramatic Style: Romeo & Juliet, as You Like It, Julius Caesar, Twelfth Night, Macbeth. LC 72-21493. 191p. 1971. write for info. (*0-389-04064-9*) B&N Imports.

— Shakespeare's Plays in Performance. 256p. (Orig.). 1999. pap. 15.95 (*1-55783-136-X*) Applause Theatre Bk Pubs.

Brown, John R., ed. Focus on Macbeth. (Critical Essays Ser.). 224p. 1982. 25.00 (*0-7100-9015-3*, Routledge Thoemms) Routledge.

— The Oxford Illustrated History of Theatre. (Oxford Illustrated Histories Ser.). (Illus.). 616p. (YA). 1995. 55.00 (*0-19-212997-X*) OUP.

Brown, John R., jt. auth. see Webster, John.

Brown, John R., ed. see Master, Wakefield.

Brown, John R., ed. see Shakespeare, William.

Brown, John R., ed. see Webster, John.

Brown, John Randall. Countdown to Atlanta. 320p. mass mkt. 5.99 (*1-55197-291-3*) Picasso Publ.

***Brown, John Russell.** Shakespeare: The Tragedies. LC 00-41498. 2000. pap. write for info. (*0-333-58956-4*, Macmillan UK) S1 & J.

Brown, John Russell. What Is Theatre? An Introduction & Exploration. LC 96-41113. (Illus.). 320p. 1997. pap. 36.95 (*0-240-80232-2*, Focal) Buttrwrth-Heinemann.

Brown, John Russell, ed. see Shakespeare, William.

Brown, John S. Draftee Division: The 88th Infantry Division in World War II. 256p. 1998. pap. 15.95 (*0-89141-666-8*) Presidio Pr.

— Minor Surgery: A Text & Atlas. 2nd ed. (Illus.). 344p. (C). (gr. 13). 1992. mass mkt. 99.95 (*0-412-44910-2*, Chap & Hall NY) Chapman & Hall.

Brown, John S., ed. Genesis of Stratiform Lead, Zinc, Barite, Fluorite Deposits in Carbonate Rocks (The So-called Mississippi Valley Type Deposits) A Symposium. LC QE0078.7.G4. (Economic Geology, Monographs: No. 3). 453p. reprint ed. pap. 140.50 (*0-608-13058-3*, 201476500093) Bks Demand.

— Seeing Differently: Insights on Innovation. (Business Review Bks.). 288p. 1997. 29.95 (*0-87584-755-2*) Harvard Busn.

Brown, John S. & Alexander-Williams, John. Minor Surgery: A Text & Atlas. 2nd ed. LC 92-49983. 1992. write for info. (*0-442-31713-1*) Chapman & Hall.

***Brown, John Seely & Duguid, Paul.** The Social Life of Information. 304p. 2000. 25.95 (*0-87584-762-5*, HBS Pr) Harvard Busn.

Brown, John T. Among the Bantu Nomads. LC 77-79270. (Illus.). 272p. 1969. reprint ed. lib. bdg. 59.50 (*0-8371-1466-7*, BRB&) Greenwood.

Brown, John W. Death Rides a Carousel. LC 97-77238. 1998. pap. 15.95 (*1-57860-013-8*) Guild Pr IN.

***Brown, John W. & Powell, Jerry A.** Systematics of Anopina Obraztsov: Lepidopters, Tortricidae, Euliini. LC 99-86762. (Publications in Entomology: Vol. 120). 180p. 2000. pap. 32.00 (*0-520-09835-8*, Pub. by U CA Pr) Cal Prin Full Svc.

Brown, John W. & Powell, Jerry A. Systematics of the Chrysoxena Group of Genera: Lepidoptera, Tortricidae, Euliini. (Publications in Entomology: Vol. 111). (C). 1992. pap. 18.95 (*0-520-09765-3*, Pub. by U CA Pr) Cal Prin Full Svc.

Brown, John W. & Sherbert, Donald R. Methods of Finite Mathematics. LC 88-27605. 688p. 1989. text 84.95 (*0-471-63003-9*) Wiley.

Brown, John W., et al. Butterflies of Baja California: Faunal Survey, Natural History, Conservation Biology. LC 90-63964. (Illus.). 146p. (Orig.). (C). 1992. pap. text 25.00 (*0-9611464-3-5*) Lepidoptera.

***Brown-Johnson, Patricia.** Discipleship: A More Excellent Ministry. 128p. 1999. mass mkt. 8.00 (*0-927936-20-8*) Vincom Pubng Co.

— Warriors on Call: The Ministry of the Intercessor. 32p. 1999. mass mkt. 3.00 (*0-927936-21-6*) Vincom Pubng Co.

Brown, Jonald J. Humanitarian Operations in Northern Iraq, 1991: With Marines in Operation Provide Comfort. 135p. 1995. per. 15.00 (*0-16-061346-9*) USGPO.

Brown, Jonathan. Claude Debussy. (Classic FM Lifelines Ser.). 112p. 1997. 9.95 (*1-85793-972-7*, Pub. by Pavilion Bks Ltd) Trafalgar.

— The Golden Age of Painting in Spain. LC 90-12564. (Illus.). 339p. 1991. reprint ed. pap. 105.10 (*0-608-07881-6*, 205998800010) Bks Demand.

— History & Present Condition of St. Domingo, 2 vols. 1972. reprint ed. 75.00 (*0-7146-2704-6*, Pub. by F Cass Pubs) Intl Spec Bk.

— The Horse in Husbandry. (Illus.). 128p. 1991. 29.95 (*0-85236-217-X*, Pub. by Farming Pr) Diamond Farm Bk.

— Images & Ideas in Seventeenth Century Spanish Painting. LC 78-52485. (Essays in Literature Ser.). (Illus.). 201p. 1978. pap. text 21.95 (*0-691-00315-7*, Pub. by Princeton U Pr) Cal Prin Full Svc.

— Johannes Brahms. (Classic FM Lifelines Ser.). 112p. 1997. 9.95 (*1-85793-967-0*, Pub. by Pavilion Bks Ltd) Trafalgar.

— Kings & Connoisseurs: Collecting Art in Seventeenth-Century Europe. LC 95-10548. (A. W. Mellon Lectures in the Fine Arts, 1994: Vol. XXXV, No. 43). (Illus.). 264p. 1995. text 49.50 (*0-691-04497-X*, Pub. by Princeton U Pr) Cal Prin Full Svc.

— Kings & Connoisseurs: Collecting Art in Seventeenth-Century Europe. LC 95-15646. 1995. 49.50 (*0-300-06437-3*) Yale U Pr.

— Painting in Spain, 1500-1700. LC 98-23228. (Yale University Press Pelican History of Art Ser.). (Illus.). 342p. 1998. 75.00 (*0-300-06472-1*) Yale U Pr.

— Painting in Spain, 1500-1700. LC 98-23228. (Yale University Press Pelican History of Art Ser.). (Illus.). 342p. 1999. pap. 35.00 (*0-300-06474-8*) Yale U Pr.

***Brown, Jonathan.** Tristan und Isolde on Record: A Comprehensive Discography of Wagner's Music Drama with a Critical Introduction to the Recordings. LC 00-26440. (Discographies Ser.: Vol. 85). (Illus.). 296p. 2000. lib. bdg. 79.50 (*0-313-31489-6*, GR1489) Greenwood.

Brown, Jonathan. Valazquez: Painter & Courtier. LC 85-14234. 336p. (C). 1988. reprint ed. pap. 35.00 (*0-300-03894-1*) Yale U Pr.

— Zurbaran. (Illus.). 128p. 1991. 24.95 (*0-8109-3962-2*, Pub. by Abrams) Time Warner.

Brown, Jonathan, compiled by. Parsifal on Record: A Discography of Complete Recordings, Selections, & Excerpts of Wagner's Music Drama, 48. LC 92-12292. (Discographies Ser.: No. 48). 168p. 1992. lib. bdg. 52.95 (*0-313-28541-1*, BPR/, Greenwood Pr) Greenwood.

Brown, Jonathan, ed. Picasso & the Spanish Tradition. LC 96-60716. (Illus.). 224p. 1996. 45.00 (*0-300-06475-6*) Yale U Pr.

— The Word Made Image: Religion, Art, & Architecture in Spain & Spanish America, 1500-1600. (Fenway Court Ser.: Vol. 28). (Illus.). 128p. 1998. pap. 24.95 (*0-9648475-7-4*, Pub. by I S Gardner Mus) U Pr of New Eng.

Brown, Jonathan, et al. Velazquez: The Technique of Genius. LC 98-19941. (Illus.). 224p. 1998. 50.00 (*0-300-07293-7*) Yale U Pr.

Brown, Jonathan, jt. auth. see Enggass, Robert.

Brown, Jonathan, ed. see National Gallery of Art Staff.

Brown, Jonathan C. Oil & Revolution in Mexico. LC 92-25649. 460p. 1993. 50.00 (*0-520-07934-5*, Pub. by U CA Pr) Cal Prin Full Svc.

— A Socioeconomic History of Argentina, 1776-1860. LC 78-6800. (Cambridge Latin American Studies: No. 35). 318p. reprint ed. pap. 90.70 (*0-608-15696-5*, 2031623) Bks Demand.

Brown, Jonathan C., ed. Workers' Control in Latin America. LC 97-1880. 344p. 1997. pap. 19.95 (*0-8078-4566-X*); lib. bdg. 55.00 (*0-8078-2362-7*) U of NC Pr.

Brown, Jonathan C. & Knight, Alan, eds. The Mexican Petroleum Industry in the Twentieth Century. LC 92-30049. (Symposia on Latin America Ser.). 331p. 1992. text 35.00 (*0-292-76533-9*) U of Tex Pr.

Brown, Jonathan C., jt. auth. see Szuchman, Mark D.

Brown, Jonathan D. The Self. LC 97-1298. 368p. 1997. pap. 29.69 (*0-07-008306-1*) McGraw.

Brown, Jordan & Gibbs, Greg. Humorology: A Curriculum & Resource Guide. 1990. pap. 14.99 (*0-89824-503-6*) Trillium Pr.

Brown, Joseph. At Night. LC 97-197738. (YA). (gr. 6 up). 1997. pap. 9.99 (*0-88092-377-6*) Royal Fireworks.

Brown, Joseph A. A Retreat with Thea Bowman & Bede Abram: Leaning on the Lord. Hutchinson, Gloria, ed. 160p. (Orig.). 1997. pap. 9.95 (*0-86716-277-5*, B2775) St Anthony Mess Pr.

— To Stand on the Rock: Meditations on Black Catholic Theology. LC 97-38960. 180p. (Orig.). 1998. pap. 15.00 (*1-57075-172-2*) Orbis Bks.

Brown, Joseph E. Animals of the Soul: Sacred Animals of the Oglala Sioux. LC 97-17472. (Earth Quest Ser.). (Illus.). 160p. 1997. pap. 14.95 (*1-86204-137-7*, Pub. by Element MA) Penguin Putnam.

— Off-Season: A Guide to Visiting the Western National Parks Without the Crowds. 120p. 1988. pap. 14.95 (*0-15-667841-1*) Harcourt.

— Padre Island National Seashore. Priehs, T. J., ed. LC 90-60725. (Illus.). 64p. (Orig.). 1991. pap. 8.95 (*0-911408-90-8*) SW Pks Mnmts.

— The Spiritual Legacy of the American Indian. 160p. (Orig.). 1984. pap. 14.95 (*0-8245-0618-9*) Crossroad NY.

— The Spiritual Legacy of the American Indian. LC 64-17425. (Illus.). (Orig.). 1964. pap. 4.00 (*0-87574-135-5*) Pendle Hill.

Brown, Joseph E., ed. Lure of the Sea. deluxe ed. (Wilderness Experience Ser.). (Illus.). 100p. 1996. 30.00 (*1-887656-28-6*) Tehabi Bks.

Brown, Joseph E., ed. The Sacred Pipe: Black Elk's Account of the Seven Rites of the Oglala Sioux. LC 53-8810. (Civilization of the American Indian Ser.: No. 36). (Illus.). 176p. 1989. 28.95 (*0-8061-0272-1*); pap. 10.95 (*0-8061-2124-6*) U of Okla Pr.

Brown, Joseph E., et al, texts. The Sierra Club Guides to the National Parks of California, Hawaii, & American Samoa: California, Hawaii, & American Samoa. rev. ed. LC 95-11450. (Sierra Club Guides to the National Parks Ser.). (Illus.). 352p. 1995. pap. 24.95 (*0-679-76497-6*) Stewart Tabori & Chang.

Brown, Joseph E., jt. auth. see Curtis, Edward S.

Brown, Joseph Epes & Steltenkamp, Michael F. Sacred Pipe/Black Elk, Holy Man of the Oglala. (Illus.). 1996. 9.98 (*1-56731-088-5*, MJF Bks) Fine Comms.

Brown, Joseph F. Dark Things. 158p. (YA). (gr. 8-12). 1995. pap. 9.99 (*0-88092-110-2*) Royal Fireworks.

Brown, Joseph G., intro. If Elected... Presidential Campaign Memorabilia. LC 88-28090. (Western Reserve Historical Society Publication Ser.: No. 171). (Illus.). vi, 24p. (Orig.). 1988. pap. 9.95 (*0-911704-41-8*) Western Res.

Brown, Joseph H. & Brown, Carolyn S. Consulting with Parents & Teachers: A Case Approach. LC 81-10100. 224p. 1982. 21.00 (*0-910328-35-8*); pap. 16.00 (*0-910328-36-6*) Sulzburger & Graham Pub.

Brown, Joseph H. & Christensen, Dana N. Family Therapy: Theory & Practice. LC 85-24271. (Psychology-Counseling Ser.). 312p. (C). 1986. pap. 38.00 (*0-534-05580-X*) Brooks-Cole.

— Family Therapy: Theory & Practice. 2nd ed. LC 98-22364. (Counseling Ser.). 336p. 1998. pap. 54.95 (*0-534-34651-0*) Brooks-Cole.

Brown, Joseph H., jt. auth. see Hana, Suzanne M.

Brown, Joseph H., jt. auth. see Hanna, Suzanne M.

***Brown, Joseph M.** Fundamentals of Physics. (Illus.). 318p. 1999. pap. 39.95 (*0-9626768-1-0*) Basic Res Pr.

— Lectures on Physics. (Illus.). 1999. pap. text 19.95 (*0-9626768-2-9*) Basic Res Pr.

Brown, Joseph M. Principles of Science. 215p. 1991. 39.95 (*0-9626768-0-2*) Basic Res Pr.

Brown, Joseph W., jt. ed. see Barlow, Robin.

Brown, Josephine & Rollin, Frank A. Two Biographies by African-American Women. (Schomburg Library of Nineteenth-Century Black Women Writers). 512p. 1991. 32.50 (*0-685-47937-4*) OUP.

Brown, Joshua, et al, eds. History from South Africa: Alternative Visions & Practices. (Critical Perspectives on the Past Ser.). 600p. 1991. 59.95 (*0-87722-848-5*); pap. 19.95 (*0-87722-849-3*) Temple U Pr.

Brown, Joy. Dating for Dummies. LC 97-80878. (For Dummies Ser.). (Illus.). 432p. 1997. pap. 19.99 (*0-7645-5072-1*) IDG Bks.

Brown, Joy. Tastes of Montana, No. 1. 128p. 1994. pap. text 12.50 (*0-9644206-0-0*) Jaybee Pubns.

Brown, Joy S. The Joy of Knowing. 1994. pap. 3.95 (*1-55673-578-2*, 7977, Fairway Pr) CSS OH.

***Brown, Joyce.** Breaking New Ground. Arant, Bruce & Foresman, Paul, eds. 100p. 2000. pap. 4.95 (*1-892150-20-4*) Design Basics.

— Courageous Christians: Devotional Stories for Family Reading. 2000. pap. 12.99 (*0-8024-4348-6*) Moody.

— Impressions of Home: A Photo Essay of Homes & Places for Real People. Arant, Bruce, ed. 88p. 2000. 4.99 (*1-892150-19-0*) Design Basics.

Brown, Joyce, et al. Echoes of Hope. Gibbs, Wilma, ed. (Illus.). 100p. 1994. 20.00 (*0-9646863-0-9*) A Bixby Womens Ctr.

Brown, Joyce A. Joyce Ann Brown: Justice Denied. LC 90-61626. 192p. (Orig.). 1990. pap. 11.95 (*0-9622683-5-6*) Noble Pr.

Brown, Joyce G. Kathy's Connection. LC 98-90863. 1999. pap. 8.95 (*0-533-12954-0*) Vantage.

Brown, Joyce H. Heavenly Answers for Earthly Challenges: Near-Death Experience Reveals How to Make Certain You Enjoy the Other Side When You Get There. LC 97-1023. 208p. 1997. pap. 14.95 (*0-9658112-9-8*, Pub. by Jemstar Pr) Origin Bk Sales.

***Brown, Joyce H.** Heavenly Answers to Earthly Questions: Simple Lessons for a Life Worth Living. 272p. 2000. mass mkt. 6.99 (*0-451-19882-4*) NAL.

Brown, Joyce Leacy, ed. see Tucker, Norma Jacke.

Brown, Joyce V. Pearls for Parents. 40p. 1995. 8.95 (*0-8378-9860-9*) Gibson.

***Brown, Joyce V.** Snapshots of Heaven. (Illus.). 2000. pap. 9.99 (*0-8499-5654-4*) J Countryman.

***Brown Jr.** Life's Treasure Book of Christmas Memories. 1999. pap. text 7.95 (*1-55853-804-6*) Rutledge Hill Pr.

— Life's Treasure Book on Friendship. (Illus.). 96p. 2000. pap. text 7.95 (*1-55853-802-X*) Rutledge Hill Pr.

— Life's Treasure Book on Things That Really Matter. (Illus.). 96p. 2000. pap. text 7.95 (*1-55853-803-8*) Rutledge Hill Pr.

Brown, Judie. Evangelium Vitae - a Topical Guide: A Study Guide. (Evangelium Vitae Ser.). 106p. (Orig.). 1996. pap. 3.00 (*1-890712-05-1*, EV5) Amer Life League.

— The Facts about Abortion. (Life Guide Ser.: Vol. 3). (Illus.). 117p. 1998. pap. 2.95 (*1-890712-14-0*, LG03) Amer Life League.

— It Is I Who Have Chosen You: Autobiography of Judie Brown. 2nd rev. ed. (Illus.). 173p. 1997. pap. 5.95 (*1-890712-00-0*, B010) Amer Life League.

— Life Guide Series. Incl. Facts about Birth Control. (Illus.). 74p. 1997. pap. 5.00 (*1-890712-13-2*, LG02); Facts about Title X: The Six Billion Dollar Scam. Cavanaugh-O'Keefe, John. (Illus.). 84p. 1997. pap. 5.00 (*1-890712-11-6*, LG04); Facts of Life. (Illus.). 80p. 1998. pap. 2.95 (*1-890712-12-4*, LG01); pap. write for info. (*1-890712-23-X*) Amer Life League.

— Veritatis Splendor: The Splendor of Truth: A Study Guide for Pro-Life Americans. (Evangelium Vitae Ser.). 20p. (Orig.). 1996. pap. 2.00 (*1-890712-01-9*, EVI) Amer Life League.

Brown, Judie & O'Brien, Denis. Evangelium Vitae: Short Reflections for Personal Thought & Prayer: A Commuter Guide. (Evangelium Vitae Ser.). 162p. (Orig.). 1996. pap. 3.00 (*1-890712-04-3*, EV4) Amer Life League.

Brown, Judith. Gandhi: Prisoner of Hope. (Illus.). 452p. 1991. reprint ed. pap. 20.00 (*0-300-05125-5*) Yale U Pr.

— God's Spirit in Nature. 1998. write for info. (*0-87574-336-6*) Pendle Hill.

Brown, Judith C. Immodest Acts: The Life of a Lesbian Nun in Renaissance Italy. (Studies in the History of Sexuality). 222p. 1986. pap. text 13.95 (*0-19-504225-5*) OUP.

Brown, Judith C. & Davis, Robert C. Gender Society Renaissance Italy. LC 97-42981. (Women & Men in History Ser.). 272p. (C). 1998. 75.00 (*0-582-29325-1*) Longman.

Brown, Judith E. Everywoman's Guide to Nutrition. LC 89-20473. 382p. 1991. reprint ed. pap. 118.50 (*0-608-00787-0*, 205933600010) Bks Demand.

— Nutrition & Pregnancy: A Complete Guide from Preconception to Postdelivery. LC 97-38624. 240p. 1998. 25.00 (*1-56565-790-X*, 07909W, Pub. by Lowell Hse) NTC Contemp Pub Co.

— Nutrition & Pregnancy: A Complete Guide from Preconception to Postdelivery. LC 97-38624. (Illus.). 288p. 1998. reprint ed. pap. 16.00 (*0-7373-0018-3*, 00183W) NTC Contemp Pub Co.

— Nutrition Now. LC 94-42869. 712p. (C). 1995. 49.95 (*0-314-04447-7*) West Pub.

— The Science of Human Nutrition. 619p. (C). 1990. pap. text 34.00 (*0-15-578688-1*); trans. write for info. (*0-318-67033-X*) SCP.

B

Brown, Judith F. The Science of Human Nutrition. 2nd ed. 640p. (C). 1996. text. write for info. (0-03-005084-7) SCP.

Brown, Judith G. Bless All Creatures Here Below: A Celebration for the Blessings of the Animlas. (Illus.). 32p. (J). (ps-3). 1996. 15.95 (0-8192-1665-8) Morehouse Pub.

Brown, Judith K. & Kerns, Virginia, eds. In Her Prime: A New View of Middle-Aged Women. (Illus.). 240p. (C). 1985. 39.95 (0-89789-056-6, Bergin & Garvey) Greenwood.

Brown, Judith K., jt. ed. see Dickerson-Putman, Jeanette.

Brown, Judith K., jt. ed. see Kerns, Virginia.

Brown, Judith M. Modern India: The Origins of an Asian Democracy. 2nd ed. (Short Oxford History of the Modern World Ser.). (Illus.). 474p. (C). 1994. pap. text 27.95 (0-19-873113-2) OUP.

Brown, Judith M. & Foot, Rosemary, eds. Migration: The Asian Experience. LC 93-47025. 1994. text 75.00 (0-312-09723-9) St Martin.

Brown, Judith M. & Louis, Roger, eds. The Oxford History of the British Empire Vol. 4: The Twentieth Century. (Oxford History of the British Empire Ser.: Vol. IV). (Illus.). 800p. 1999. 45.00 (0-19-820564-3) OUP.

Brown, Judith M. & Prozesky, Martin, eds. Gandhi in South Africa: Principles & Politics. LC 96-11317. 208p. 1996. text 49.95 (0-312-16036-4) St Martin.

Brown, Judith R. Back to the Beanstalk: Enchantment & Reality for Couples. (Gestalt Institute of Cleveland Book Ser.). 172p. 1998. pap. 21.95 (0-88163-295-3) Analytic Pr.

— Back to the Beanstalk: Enchantment & Reality for Couples. LC 79-89476. (C). 1980. 9.95 (0-930626-03-6); pap. 6.95 (0-930626-04-4) Psych & Consul Assocs.

— Faranji: A Venture into Ethiopia. LC 93-11475. (Illus.). 224p. (Orig.). 1994. pap. 12.95 (1-56474-072-2) Fithian Pr.

— The I in Science: Training to Utilize Subjectivity in Research. 199p. 1996. 31.00 (82-00-22661-1) Scandnvan Univ Pr.

Brown, Judith R., et al. Visualization: Using Computer Graphics to Explore Data & Present Information. LC 95-15663. 320p. 1995. pap. 49.95 incl. cd-rom (0-471-12991-7) Wiley.

Brown, Judson S. Current Theory & Research in Motivation: A Symposium. LC 53-11655. 200p. reprint ed. pap. 62.00 (0-608-16529-8, 202733700055) Bks Demand.

Brown, Judy. The Choice: Seasons of Loss & Renewal after a Father's Decision to Die. 250p. 1995. pap. 12.95 (1-57324-021-4) Conari Press.

— Joke Soup: 1,000 of the Funniest Jokes from the Best Comedians. LC 98-27463. 288p. 1998. pap. 9.95 (0-8362-6754-0) Andrews & McMeel.

***Brown, Judy.** Joke Stew: 1,229 More Servings of Jokes from Today's Funniest Comedians. LC 00-36178. 2000. pap. 9.95 (0-7407-0992-5) Andrews & McMeel.

Brown, Judy. Judy Brown's Guide to Natural Foods Cooking. LC 89-552. (Illus.). 160p. (Orig.). 1989. pap. 10.95 (0-913990-62-0) Book Pub Co.

— Natural Lunchbox. LC 96-18107. 192p. 1996. pap. text 12.95 (1-57067-026-9) Book Pub Co.

Brown, Judy L. Women Ministers According to Scripture. 348p. (Orig.). 1997. pap. 15.95 (1-57502-449-7, PO1042B) Morris Pubng.

Brown, Jules. The Rough Guide to Hong Kong & Macau. 4th ed. (Illus.). 1999. 16.95 (1-85828-435-X, Pub. by Rough Guides) Penguin Putnam.

Brown, Jules D. American Painting: From Its Beginnings to the Armory Show, Vol. I. LC 70-80455. (Illus.). 134p. 1989. pap. 25.00 (0-8478-0841-6, Pub. by Rizzoli Intl) St Martin.

Brown, Juli. Taste of the Triangle: A Guide to the Finer Restaurants of Raleigh, Durham, Cary & Chapel Hill with Recipes. LC 97-66333. (Illus.). 224p. 1997. pap. 14.95 (1-878086-56-1, Pub. by Down Home NC) Blair.

Brown, Julia. After Mountains & Sea: Frankenthaler,1956-1959. (Illus.). 96p. 1998. 45.00 (0-8109-6911-4, Pub. by Abrams) Time Warner.

Brown, Julia, ed. see Ruppersberg, Allen.

Brown, Julia P. Cosmopolitan Criticism: Oscar Wilde's Philosophy of Art. LC 96-37986. 1997. 30.00 (0-8139-1728-X) U Pr of Va.

— Cosmopolitan Criticism: Oscar Wilde's Philosophy of Art. 157p. 1999. pap. text 14.50 (0-8139-1888-X) U Pr of Va.

— Jane Austen's Novels: Social Change & Literary Form. LC 78-16879. 197p. reprint ed. pap. 61.10 (0-7837-2229-X, 205731900004) Bks Demand.

***Brown, Julian.** Minds, Machines & the Multiverse: The Quest for the Quantum Computer. LC 99-56638. 464p. 2000. 27.00 (0-684-81481-1) S&S Trade.

Brown, Julie. Messy Tessie Has a Tea Party. (Illus.). 32p. (J). (gr. 1-3). 1997. 5.95 (1-885744-10-2) Otter Creek.

— Messy Tessie Takes a Bath. (Illus.). 32p. (Orig.). (J). (gr. 1-3). 1996. pap. 5.95 (1-885744-06-4) Otter Creek.

Brown, Julie, ed. American Women Short Story Writers Vol. 8: A Collection of Critical Essays. LC 94-8739. (Wellesley Studies in Critical Theory: Vol. 8). 400p. 1995. text 80.00 (0-8153-1338-1, H1737) Garland.

***Brown, Julie, ed.** American Women Short Story Writers Vol. 8: A Collection of Critical Essays. (Wellesley Studies in Critical Theory, Literary History & Culture: 8). 400p. 1999. 24.95 (0-8153-3587-3) Garland.

Brown, Julie & Brown, Robert, eds. Mahoning Valley Poetry. (Illus.). 150p. (Orig.). 1993. pap. 8.00 (0-9637849-3-5) Bacchae Pr.

Brown, Julie & Cain, William, eds. Ethnicity & the American Short Story. LC 97-25196. (Wellesley Studies in Critical Theory, Literary History & Culture: Vol. 16). 272p. 1997. text 60.00 (0-8153-2105-8, H1940) Garland.

Brown, Julie K. Contesting Images: Photography & the World's Columbian Exposition. LC 93-19891. (Illus.). 185p. (Orig.). 1994. pap. 28.50 (0-8165-1410-0); lib. bdg. 62.00 (0-8165-1382-1) U of Ariz Pr.

Brown, Julienne V. The Brown Adobe Sampler: For a Taste of New Mexico. LC 88-72067. (Illus.). 64p. (Orig.). 1988. pap. 5.95 (0-9621170-0-5) Wagner Gourmet.

Brown, Juliet. Heart Healthy. (Illus.). (Orig.). 1989. pap. write for info. (0-318-65731-7) Franklin-Belle.

***Brown, June.** Karen Brown's England: Charming Bed & Breakfasts. LC 00-37927. (Karen Brown's Country Inn Ser.). (Illus.). 2001. pap. write for info. (1-928901-02-6) K Browns Guides.

***Brown, June & Brown, Karen.** Karen Brown's Ireland: Charming Inns & Itineraries. LC 00-37931. (Karen Brown's Country Inn Ser.). (Illus.). 2001. pap. write for info. (1-928901-07-7) K Browns Guides.

Brown, June, jt. auth. see Brown, Karen.

Brown, June W. Inside American Paradise. Wilensky, Julius M., ed. LC 91-65345. (Illus.). 224p. (Orig.). 1991. pap. 12.95 (0-918752-14-0) Wescott Cove.

Brown, Justine. All Possible Worlds: Utopian Experiments in British Columbia. (Transmontanus Ser.: Vol. 5). (Illus.). 96p. 1995. pap. 12.00 (0-921586-46-9, Pub. by New Star Bks) Genl Dist Srvs.

Brown, K. From Meiji to Major. 320p. 1998. 79.95 (0-7190-5290-4, Pub. by Manchester Univ Pr) St Martin.

— From Meiji to Major. 320p. 1998. pap. 27.95 (0-7190-5291-2) St Martin.

Brown, K., jt. ed. see Sawhney, B. L.

Brown, K. C. Haunted Dreams. 152p. (Orig.). 1987. pap. 3.95 (0-940649-01-2) Parnell Pub.

— Sherlock's Veiled Secret: Based on a Story by K. C. Brown & Arne Zaslove. 1996. pap. 5.25 (0-8222-1492-X) Dramatists Play.

Brown, K. Dawson. I Just Bought a House in the Caribbean. (Illus.). 96p. 1996. pap. 12.00 (0-8059-3989-X) Dorrance.

Brown, K. J. & Lacey, A. A., eds. Reaction-Diffusion Equations. (Illus.). 234p. 1990. text 69.00 (0-19-853533-0) OUP.

Brown, K. S. Buildings. (Monographs in Mathematics). (Illus.). 225p. 1996. 46.95 (0-387-96876-8) Spr-Verlag.

— Buildings. (Monographs in Mathematics). (Illus.). 224p. 1998. 46.95 (0-387-98624-3) Spr-Verlag.

— Cohomology of Groups. (Graduate Texts in Mathematics Ser.: Vol. 87). (Illus.). 336p. 1996. 54.95 (0-387-90688-6) Spr-Verlag.

Brown, K. W. & Warner, A. R. Economics of Our Free Enterprise System. 1982. text 26.00 (0-07-067501-5) McGraw.

Brown, K. W., et al. Acute & Genetic Toxicity of Municipal Landfill Leachate. (Illus.). 91p. (C). 1998. pap. text 20.00 (0-7881-7237-9) DIANE Pub.

Brown, Kaori A., jt. auth. see Brown, Douglas E.

***Brown, Karen.** Austria Charming Inns & Itineraries 2000. LC 99-15260. (Karen Brown's Guides Ser.). 1999. pap. 18.95 (0-930328-84-1) K Browns Guides.

— California Charming Inns & Itineraries 2000. LC 99-15259. (Karen Brown's Guides Ser.). 1999. pap. 18.95 (0-930328-85-X) K Browns Guides.

Brown, Karen. Dinner Party Cookbook: Menus, Recipes, & Decorating Ideas for 21 Theme Parties. LC 99-17771. 150p. 1999. pap. 9.00 (0-671-31727-X, Pub. by Meadowbrook) S&S Trade.

***Brown, Karen.** England Charming Bed & Breakfasts 2000. LC 99-15258. (Karen Brown's Guides Ser.). 1999. pap. 17.95 (0-930328-86-8) K Browns Guides.

— England, Wales, Scottland Charming Hotels & Itineraries 2000. LC 99-15257. (Karen Brown's Guides Ser.). (Illus.). 1999. pap. 18.95 (0-930328-87-6) K Browns Guides.

— Fairy Kisses & Stork Bites: Amazing, Adorable Facts about Babies. LC 99-55085. 2000. 9.95 (0-7407-0468-0) Andrews & McMeel.

Brown, Karen. Fodor's Karen Brown's Italy. Date not set. pap. write for info. (0-679-00066-6) Fodors Travel.

***Brown, Karen.** France Charming Bed & Breakfasts 2000. LC 99-15256. (Karen Brown's Guides Ser.). (Illus.). 1999. pap. 17.95 (0-930328-88-4) K Browns Guides.

— France Charming Inns & Itineraries 2000. LC 99-15253. (Karen Brown's Guides Ser.). 1999. pap. 18.95 (0-930328-89-2) K Browns Guides.

— Germany Charming Inns & Itineraries 2000. LC 99-15254. (Karen Brown's Guides Ser.). (Illus.). 1999. pap. 18.95 (0-930328-90-6) K Browns Guides.

— Ireland Charming Inns & Itineraries 2000. LC 99-15249. (Guides Ser.). (Illus.). 1999. pap. 18.95 (0-930328-91-4) K Browns Guides.

— Italy Charming Bed & Breakfast 2000. LC 99-15247. (Guides Ser.). (Illus.). 1999. pap. 17.95 (0-930328-92-2) K Browns Guides.

— Italy Charming Inns & Itineraries 2000. LC 99-15255. (Karen Brown's Guides Ser.). (Illus.). 1999. pap. 18.95 (0-930328-93-0) K Browns Guides.

Brown, Karen. The Joy of Sisters. LC 97-16066. 1997. write for info. (0-88166-295-X) Meadowbrook.

— The Joy of Sisters. 110p. 1997. 7.00 (0-671-57681-X, Scribner Pap Fic) S&S Trade Pap.

***Brown, Karen.** Karen Brown's New England: Charming Inns & Itineraries. (Country Inn Ser.). (Illus.). 2000. pap. 19.95 (1-928901-12-3) K Browns Guides.

Brown, Karen. Kids Are Cookin' LC 96-29926. 112p. (Orig.). (J). (gr. 1 up). 1997. lib. bdg. 8.00 (0-671-57552-X) Meadowbrook.

— Mommy Meals. (Illus.). 107p. (Orig.). 1988. pap. 11.95 (0-9621948-0-8) Legacy Mktg.

***Brown, Karen.** Mommy's Little Helper Cookbook. LC 99-53515. (Illus.). 140p. (J). (ps-1). 2000. pap. 9.00 (0-689-83072-6) S&S Childrens.

— Portugal Charming Inns & Itineraries 2000. LC 99-15248. (Guides Ser.). 1999. pap. 18.95 (0-930328-94-9) K Browns Guides.

Brown, Karen. Real World Math. Celecia, Deneen, ed. (Illus.). 80p. 1994. pap., student ed. 8.95 (1-56472-172-8) Edupress Inc.

***Brown, Karen.** Spain Charming Inns & Itineraries 2000. LC 99-15246. (Guides Ser.). 1999. pap. 18.95 (0-930328-95-7) K Browns Guides.

— Switzerland Charming Inns & Itineraries 2000. LC 99-15245. (Guides Ser.). (Illus.). 1999. pap. 18.95 (0-930328-96-5) K Browns Guides.

***Brown, Karen & Brown, Clare.** Karen Brown's France: Charming Bed & Breakfasts. LC 00-37929. (Karen Brown's Country Inn Ser.). (Illus.). 2001. pap. write for info. (1-928901-04-2) K Browns Guides.

— Karen Brown's Switzerland: Charming Inns & Itineraries. LC 00-37937. (Karen Brown's Country Inn Ser.). (Illus.). 2001. pap. write for info. (1-928901-11-5) K Browns Guides.

***Brown, Karen & Brown, June.** Karen Brown's England, Wales & Scotland: Charming Hotels & Itineraries. LC 00-37926. (Karen Brown's Country Inn Ser.). (Illus.). 2001. pap. write for info. (1-928901-03-4) K Browns Guides.

Brown, Karen & Engel, Holly. Read & Respond: Colonial American Literature. Milliken, Linda, ed. (Illus.). 64p. (J). (gr. 3-6). 1994. pap., student ed. 7.95 (1-56472-028-4) Edupress Inc.

— Read & Respond: Frontier American Literature. Milliken, Linda, ed. (Illus.). 64p. (J). (gr. 3-6). 1994. pap., student ed. 7.95 (1-56472-027-6) Edupress Inc.

— Read & Respond: Native American Literature. Milliken, Linda, ed. (Illus.). 64p. (J). (gr. 3-6). 1994. pap., student ed. 7.95 (1-56472-029-2) Edupress Inc.

— Real World Reading. Celecia, Deneen, ed. (Illus.). 80p. 1994. pap., student ed. 8.95 (1-56472-044-6) Edupress Inc.

Brown, Karen & Stielstra, Diane. Aldus Persuasion for the Macintosh. LC 89-28521. 339p. 1990. pap. 26.95 (0-471-51412-8) Wiley.

***Brown, Karen, et al.** Karen Brown's California: Charming Inns & Itineraries. LC 00-37925. (Karen Brown's Country Inn Ser.). (Illus.). 2001. pap. write for info. (1-928901-01-8) K Browns Guides.

— Karen Brown's France: Charming Inns & Itineraries. LC 00-37928. (Karen Brown's Country Inn Ser.). (Illus.). 2001. pap. write for info. (1-928901-05-0) K Browns Guides.

— Karen Brown's Germany: Charming Inns & Itineraries. LC 00-37930. (Karen Brown's Country Inn Ser.). (Illus.). 2001. pap. write for info. (1-928901-06-9) K Browns Guides.

Brown, Karen, jt. auth. see Brown, Clare.

Brown, Karen, jt. auth. see Brown, June.

Brown, Karen, jt. auth. see Engel, Holly.

Brown, Karen, jt. auth. see Franchini, Nicole.

Brown, Karen, jt. auth. see Wolverton, Lynda.

Brown, Karen B. Karl Lueger, the Liberal Years: Democracy, Municipal Reform, & the Struggle for Power in the Vienna City Council, 1875-1882. (Modern European History Ser.). 376p. 1987. text 15.00 (0-8240-8046-7) Garland.

Brown, Karen B. & Fellows, Mary L., eds. Taxing America. (Critical America Ser.). 340p. (C). 1997. text 65.00 (0-8147-2648-8); pap. text 26.00 (0-8147-2661-5) NYU Pr.

Brown, Karen B., jt. auth. see Kole, Karen V.

Brown, Karen F., jt. ed. see Fry, Don.

Brown, Karen M. Mama Lola: A Vodou Priestess in Brooklyn. LC 90-40070. (Comparative Studies in Religion & Society: No. 4). (Illus.). 432p. 1991. 48.00 (0-520-07073-9, Pub. by U CA Pr) Cal Prin Full Svc.

— Mama Lola: A Vodou Priestess in Brooklyn. (Illus.). 1992. reprint ed. pap. 17.95 (0-520-07780-6, Pub. by U CA Pr) Cal Prin Full Svc.

Brown, Karen M. & Charles, Curtis B. Computers in the Professional Practice of Design. LC 94-25997. 227p. 1992. 32.00 (0-07-011075-1) McGraw.

Brown, Karen M., jt. auth. see Charles, Curtis B.

Brown, Karl & Haskell, Daniel C., eds. Shorthand Collection in the New York Public Library: A Catalogue of Books, Periodicals & Manuscripts. LC 77-137704. (New York Public Library Publications in Reprint). 1971. reprint ed. 51.95 (0-405-01746-4) Ayer.

Brown, Karl W., jt. auth. see Clem, Keith M.

Brown, Kate H., jt. ed. see Haddad, Amy M.

Brown, Kathan. Ink, Paper, Metal, Wood: How to Recognize Contemporary Artists' Prints. (Illus.). 61p. 1992. pap. 15.00 (1-891300-10-5) Crown Point Pr.

— Ink, Paper, Metal, Wood: Painters & Sculptors at Crown Point Press. LC 96-1603. (Illus.). 288p. 1996. 45.00 (0-8118-0469-0) Chronicle Bks.

— Voyage to the Cities of the Dawn. (Illus.). 143p. 1997. 15.00 (1-891300-07-5) Crown Point Pr.

***Brown, Kathan.** Why Draw a Landscape? (Illus.). 110p. 1999. 20.00 (1-891300-11-3) Crown Point Pr.

Brown, Kathan, et al. John Cage Etchings 1978-1982. (Illus.). 60p. 1982. pap. 15.00 (1-891300-08-3) Crown Point Pr.

Brown, Katharine R. Frankish Art in American Collections. (Illus.). 32p. 1984. pap. 1.95 (0-87099-403-4) Metro Mus Art.

— Guide to the Provincial Roman & Barbarian Metalwork & Jewelry in the Metropolitan Museum of Art. (Illus.). 28p. 1981. 2.95 (0-87099-262-7) Metro Mus Art.

Brown, Katherine. The Small One: A Good Samaritan. LC 98-84803. (J). 1998. write for info. (0-7868-0481-5) Hyperion.

Brown, Katherine, ed. see Mwalimu.

Brown, Katherine K., jt. auth. see Aston, Richard.

Brown, Katherine R. Migration Art: A. D. 300-800. LC 95-13786. (Illus.). 1995. pap. 9.95 (0-87099-750-5) Metro Mus Art.

Brown, Kathi A. Critical Connection: The Motorola Service Station Story. LC 91-73592. 250p. (C). 1992. pap. 10.00 (1-56946-003-5) Motorola Univ.

Brown, Kathi A., jt. auth. see Marriott, J. W., Jr.

Brown, Kathleen. Herbal Teas: 101 Nourishing Blends for Daily Health & Vitality. LC 99-18420. 1999. pap. 16.95 (1-58017-099-4, Storey Pub) Storey Bks.

— Management Guidelines for Women's Health Nurse Practitioners. LC 99-26449. (Illus.). 464p. (C). 1999. pap. text 38.95 (0-8036-0292-8) Davis Co.

***Brown, Kathleen.** Natural & Herbal Remedies for Indigestion. LC 00-32223. (Country Wisdom Bulletin Ser.). 2000. pap. write for info. (1-58017-320-9) Storey Bks.

Brown, Kathleen, jt. ed. see Vandivier, Elizabeth L.

***Brown, Kathleen L.** Chamomile. LC 00-36364. 2000. pap. write for info. (1-58017-299-7) Storey Bks.

— Lemon Balm. LC 00-30781. (Country Wisdom Bulletin Ser.). 2000. pap. write for info. (1-58017-319-5) Storey Bks.

Brown, Kathleen M. Good Wives, Nasty Wenches & Anxious Patriarchs: Gender, Race & Power in Colonial Virginia. LC 96-16502. (Illus.). 512p. (C). 1996. pap. 19.95 (0-8078-4623-6); lib. bdg. 59.95 (0-8078-2307-4) U of NC Pr.

Brown, Kathryn. Muledred. LC 89-11027. (Illus.). 32p. (J). (ps-3). 1990. 12.95 (0-15-256265-6) Harcourt.

Brown, Kathryn H. Beneath This Stone. LC 91-76735. 60p. (Orig.). 1991. pap. 8.95 (1-878149-08-3) Counterpoint Pub.

— Galli-Curci. unabridged ed. (Great Voices Ser.: No. 6). 1997. 38.00 (1-880909-51-0) Baskerville.

Brown, Kathy. The Edible Flower Garden: From Garden to Kitchen: Choosing, Growing & Cooking with Edible Flowers. (Illus.). 160p. 1999. 30.00 (1-85967-879-3) Anness Pub.

***Brown, Kathy.** Flower Power. (Illus.). 2000. 11.95 (0-7548-0478-X, Lorenz Bks) Anness Pub.

Brown, Kathy. Living Happily Ever Laughter: A Guide to Thinking Funny in a Fast Paced World. Adams, Milton E., ed. LC 99-60409. (Illus.). 128p. 1997. pap. 7.95 (1-890676-00-4) Beavers Pond.

Brown, Kathy & Sokol, Frank, eds. Issues in the Christian Initiation of Children: Catechesis & Liturgy. LC 89-14512. (Font & Table Ser.). 219p. 1989. pap. 7.95 (0-930467-97-3, CIKIDS) Liturgy Tr Pubns.

Brown, Kathy, ed. see Utility Data Institute Staff.

***Brown, Katie.** Katie Brown Entertains: 16 Menus 16 Occasions 16 Tables. (Illus.). 288p. 2000. 35.00 (0-06-271615-8, HarpRes) HarpInfo.

Brown, Katie. Life Is a Dance: You Should Only Know the Steps. Bacon, Sydney & Kashtan, Rose, trs. from YID. (Illus.). 87p. 1987. 20.00 (0-89304-060-6); pap. 10.00 (0-89304-061-4) Cross-Cultrl NY.

Brown, Katrina, et al. Economics & the Conservation of Global Biological Diversity. (Working Papers: No. 2). 75p. (Orig.). (C). 1993. pap. 6.95 (1-884122-01-9, 72019) Global Environ.

Brown, Katrina, jt. auth. see Adger, W. Neil.

Brown, Katrina, jt. auth. see Auty, R. M.

Brown, Katy. Stars: The Art of Making Stellar Gifts & Radiant Crafts. LC 93-23144. (Illus.). 128p. 1994. 23.00 (0-671-88436-0) S&S Trade.

Brown, Kay. The Art of Love. Young, Jacqueline C. & Massey, William, eds. 150p. (Orig.). 1995. mass mkt. 3.79 (0-9634431-3-5) C Y Pub Grp.

— Willy's Summer Dream. LC 88-21876. 144p. (YA). (gr. 7 up). 1989. 13.95 (0-15-200645-1, Gulliver Bks) Harcourt.

Brown, Keann, jt. auth. see Privett, Dave.

***Brown, Keith.** Distributed Security in Windows 2000. 352p. 2000. pap. 39.95 (0-201-60442-6) Addison-Wesley.

— The Interactive Marketplace. LC 00-41577. 268p. 2001. write for info. (0-07-136343-2) McGraw.

Brown, Keith. Life above the Rim. 184p. (Orig.). (YA). (gr. 6 up). 1994. pap. 8.95 (1-887002-10-3) Cross Trng.

— Sacred Bond: Black Men & Their Mothers. (Illus.). 272p. 2000. pap. 15.95 (0-316-10984-3) Little.

— Syntax Today. (Approaches to Linguistics Ser.). 256p. (C). 1992. pap. 14.95 (0-521-42452-6) Cambridge U Pr.

— Syntax Today. (Approaches to Linguistics Ser.). 256p. (C). 1994. write for info. (0-521-41401-6) Cambridge U Pr.

Brown, Keith, ed. Rethinking Lawrence. 256p. 1990. 123.00 (0-335-09387-6); pap. 34.95 (0-335-09388-4) OpUniv Pr.

Brown, Keith & Hoover, John W. Faith Promise & Beyond. 130p. (Orig.). 1996. pap. 6.95 (1-57502-101-3) Morris Pubng.

Brown, Keith & Miller, James V. Concise Encyclopedia of Syntactic Theories. LC 96-32931. 494p. 1996. 158.00 (0-08-042711-1, Pergamon Pr) Elsevier.

— Syntax: A Linguistics Introduction to Sentence Structure. 2nd ed. (Illus.). 384p. 1991. pap. 22.50 (0-04-445561-5, A8202) Routledge.

— Syntax: Linguistic Introduction to Sentence Structure. 2nd ed. (Illus.). 384p. (Orig.). (C). 1992. pap. 24.99 (0-415-08421-0) Routledge.

Brown, Keith C., ed. Regulation of the Natural Gas Producing Industry. LC 71-186502. (Resources for the Future Ser.). (Illus.). 271p. 1972. pap. 10.00 (0-8018-1383-2) Johns Hopkins.

Brown, Keith C. & Smith, Donald J. Interest Rate & Currency Swaps: A Tutorial. 138p. (Orig.). 1996. pap. text 30.00 (0-943205-32-8) RFICFA.

Brown, Keith C., jt. auth. see Reilly, Frank K.

An Asterisk (*) at the beginning of an entry indicates that the title is appearing for the first time.

Brown, Keith M. The Merry Mariner: A Travelogue. LC 98-61994. (Illus.). 148p. 1997. mass mkt. 5.95 (*1-56550-078-4*) Vis Bks Intl.

— Poor Little Neil. LC 98-61023. 176p. 1998. 5.95 (*1-56550-082-2*) Vis Bks Intl.

***Brown, Keith Michael.** Sacred Bond: Black Men & Their Mothers. LC 98-20757. (Illus.). 288p. (gr. 8). 1998. 25.00 (*0-316-10556-2*) Little.

Brown, Keith T. The Builders' Revolution: How the Information Revolution Will Bring Vast Opportunity to Builders, Subcontractors, Manufacturers & Suppliers, Bankers, & Homeowners Working in Today's Building Industry. Wagner, John D., ed. (Illus.). 256p. (Orig.). 1996. pap. text 14.95 (*0-9649339-0-X*) BuildNet Pub.

Brown, Kelli M., jt. auth. see Edlin, Gordon.

***Brown, Kelly R.** Florence Lawrence, the Biograph Girl: America's First Movie Star. LC 99-19661. (Illus.). 230p. 1999. lib. bdg. 39.95 (*0-7864-0627-5*) McFarland & Co.

Brown, Ken. Adam & Eve-olution. (Illus.). 104p. (Orig.). 1989. pap. 4.95 (*0-941104-45-1*) Real Comet.

— A Celebration of Love. (Thoughtful Moments Ser.: Vol. 1). (Illus.). 24p. 1996. pap. write for info. (*0-9630231-6-0*) K Brown Studio.

— Education, Culture & Critical Thinking. LC 98-73765. 9p. 1998. text 59.95 (*1-84014-324-X*, Pub. by Ashgate Pub) Ashgate Pub Co.

— The Ken Brown Calligraphy Handbook. (Illus.). 80p. 1991. 22.95 (*0-9630231-1-X*); pap. 14.95 (*0-9630231-0-1*) K Brown Studio.

— Mucky Pup. LC 97-220330. (Illus.). 32p. (J). (ps-4). 1997. 14.99 (*0-525-45886-7*) NAL.

— Mucky Pup's Christmas LC 98-47019. 1999. 16.99 (*0-525-46141-8*, Dutton Child) Peng Put Young Read.

— Nellie's Knot. LC 92-27910. (Illus.). 32p. (J). (ps-1). 1993. lib. bdg. 13.95 (*0-02-714930-7*, Four Winds Pr) S&S Childrens.

Brown, Ken, intro. Masterpieces of the English Short Novel. 896p. 1992. pap. 14.95 (*0-88184-848-4*) Carroll & Graf.

Brown, Ken, jt. auth. see Oram, Hiawyn.

Brown, Kendall. Between Two Worlds: The Life & Art of Lilian May Miller. LC 98-65619. (Illus.). 96p. 1998. pap. 25.00 (*1-877921-15-7*) Pacific Asia.

Brown, Kendall, et al. Light in Darkness: Women in Prints of Early Showa Japan, 1925-1941. Lenihan, Mary, ed. LC 95-61954. (Illus.). 96p. (Orig.). (C). 1996. pap. 20.00 (*0-945192-18-5*) USC Fisher Gallery.

Brown, Kendall H. The Politics of Reclusion: Painting & Power in Momoyama Japan. LC 96-39173. (Illus.). 224p. 1997. text 52.00 (*0-8248-1779-6*); pap. text 34.95 (*0-8248-1913-6*) UH Pr.

Brown, Kendall H. & Goodall-Cristante, Hollis. Shin-hanga: New Prints in Modern Japan. (Illus.). 120p. 1996. pap. 35.00 (*0-295-97517-2*) U of Wash Pr.

Brown, Kenneth. Barn House Book: Rhymes, Riddles, & Jokes. (Illus.). (J). 12.95 (*1-56743-046-5*, Amistad) HarperTrade.

— Como Pronunciar Ingles Correctamente. (How to Pronounce...Ser.). (SPA.). 64p. 1995. pap. 16.95 incl. audio (*0-8442-0837-X*, 0837X, Natl Textbk Co) NTC Contemp Pub Co.

Brown, Kenneth, compiled by. The Greenwood Annual Abstract of Legal Dissertations & Theses, 1985-1987. 404p. 1988. lib. bdg. 115.00 (*0-313-26486-4*, GLW88, Greenwood Pr) Greenwood.

Brown, Kenneth. Dollhouse Book: Color & Counting Concepts. (J). 1994. 12.95 (*1-56743-044-9*, Amistad) HarperTrade.

Brown, Kenneth, ed. see Burns, Robert.

Brown, Kenneth A. Four Corners: History, Land & People of the Desert Southwest. LC 95-40208. 400p. 1996. pap. 14.00 (*0-06-092759-3*) HarpC.

Brown, Kenneth D. The British Toy Business: A History since 1700. LC 95-49430. 1996. 55.00 (*1-85285-136-8*) Hambledon Press.

— A Social History of the Nonconformist Ministry in England & Wales, 1800-1930. (Illus.). 254p. 1988. text 58.00 (*0-19-822763-9*) OUP.

Brown, Kenneth D., jt. ed. see McKay, Ian A.

Brown, Kenneth H. You'd Never Know It from the Way I Talk: Lectures & Readings. LC 90-83801. (Writers-in-Residence Ser.). 88p. 1990. pap. 7.00 (*0-912592-29-X*) Ashland Poetry.

***Brown, Kenneth H., et al.** Debt Collection Practice in California: February 2000 Update. 2nd ed. Kronenberg, Hale, ed. LC 98-74729. 452p. 2000. 72.00 (*0-7626-0402-6*) Cont Ed Bar-CA.

***Brown, Kenneth N.** The Grand Scam: How to Make Grand Theft Legal. 220p. 2000. pap. write for info. (*1-878647-62-8*) APU Pub Grp.

Brown, Kenneth N. Strategics: The Logistics - Strategy Link. 75p. (Orig.). (C). 1995. pap. text 20.00 (*0-7881-2147-2*) DIANE Pub.

Brown, Kenneth T. & Flaming, Dale G. Advanced Micropipette Techniques for Cell Physiology. (IBRO Handbook Series: Methods in the Neurosciences). 306p. 1987. 450.00 (*0-471-90952-1*) Wiley.

Brown, Kenny L. The Italians in Oklahoma. LC 79-23342. (Newcomers to a New Land Ser.). 83p. reprint ed. pap. 30.00 (*0-608-15447-4*, 202929400059) Bks Demand.

Brown, Kent M. Cushing of Gettysburg: The Story of a Union Artillery Commander. LC 93-19602. (Illus.). 368p. 1993. 32.00 (*0-8131-1837-9*) U Pr of Ky.

— Cushing of Gettysburg: The Story of a Union Artillery Commander. (Illus.). 368p. 1998. reprint ed. pap. 18.00 (*0-8131-0953-1*) U Pr of Ky.

***Brown, Kent Masterson, ed.** The Civil War in Kentucky: Battle for the Bluegrass State. LC 99-67799. 312p. (C). 2000. 29.95 (*1-882810-47-3*) Savas Pub.

Brown, Kent R. Dancing the Box Step. 1994. pap. 5.50 (*0-87129-333-1*, D58) Dramatic Pub.

— Larry's Favorite Chocolate Cake. 85p. 1997. pap. 5.50 (*0-87129-649-7*, L14) Dramatic Pub.

— The Phoenix Dimension. 58p. 1996. pap. 5.50 (*0-87129-650-0*, P19) Dramatic Pub.

— The Screenwriter As Collaborator. Jowett, Garth S., ed. LC 79-6669. (Dissertations on Film, 1980 Ser.). 1980. lib. bdg. 20.95 (*0-405-12903-3*) Ayer.

— A Trick of the Light. 37p. 1996. pap. 3.50 (*0-87129-662-4*, TA3) Dramatic Pub.

— The View from Sunset Towers. 75p. 1996. pap. 5.50 (*0-87129-739-6*, V26) Dramatic Pub.

— Welcome to Four Way: The Town That Time Forgot. 1993. pap. 5.50 (*0-87129-303-X*, W75) Dramatic Pub.

***Brown, Kent R., ed.** Scenes & Monologues for Young Actors. 255p. 2000. pap. 14.95 (*0-87129-958-5*, SE3) Dramatic Pub.

Brown, Kent R., jt. ed. see McDonough, Ann.

***Brown, Kenyon.** Lotus Notes & Domino 5 Bible. Brown, Kevin & Brown, Kyle, eds. LC 99-37073. (Bible Ser.). 936p. 2000. pap. 39.99 (*0-7645-4590-6*) IDG Bks.

Brown, Kenyon. Mastering Lotus Notes Release 5. 3rd ed. LC 99-61234. (Mastering Ser.). 1168p. 1999. pap. text 39.99 (*0-7821-2185-3*) Sybex.

Brown, Kenyon, et al. Mastering Lotus Notes 4.5 & Domino. 2nd ed. LC 97-65366. 1152p. 1997. pap. text 49.99 incl. cd-rom (*0-7821-1996-4*) Sybex.

Brown, Kermit E. The Technology of Artificial Lift Methods, 6 vol. set. Incl. Vol. 1. 487p. 1977. 75.95 (*0-87814-031-X*); Vol. 2A. 736p. 1980. 75.95 (*0-87814-119-7*); Vol. 2B. 616p. 1980. 75.95 (*0-87814-133-2*); Vol. 3A. 1087p. 1980. 75.95 (*0-87814-137-5*, P4244); Vol. 3B. 1152p. 1980. 125.95 (*0-87814-138-3*, P4245); Vol. 4. 474p. 1984. 125.95 (*0-87814-252-5*, P4345); 400.00 (*0-685-06893-5*, P4378) PennWell Bks.

***Brown, Kerry.** Iner the Dreamer. LC 00-22664. (J). 2001. write for info. (*0-7614-5076-9*) Marshall Cavendish.

Brown, Kerry. Sikh Art & Literature: Splendors of the Punjab. LC 98-41124. (Illus.). 250p. 1999. pap. 30.00 (*0-415-20289-2*) Routledge.

Brown, Kerry, ed. Sikh Art & Literature: Splendors of the Punjab. LC 98-41124. (Illus.). 250p. 1999. 90.00 (*0-415-20288-4*) Routledge.

Brown, Kerry L., jt. auth. see Volhard, Wendy.

***Brown, Keven & Von Kitzing, Eberhard.** Evolution & Bahai Belief: Addul-Bahais Response to Nineteenth-Century Darwinism. 2000. pap. 29.95 (*1-890688-08-8*) Kalimat.

Brown, Keven, ed. see Cuevas, Lou.

Brown, Keven, ed. see Freeman, James A.

Brown, Keven, ed. see Moffet, Ruth.

Brown, Keven, ed. see Renfro, Elizabeth.

Brown, Kevin. Malcolm X: His Life & Legacy. LC 94-5381. (Illus.). 112p. (YA). (gr. 7 up). 1995. lib. bdg. 27.40 (*1-56294-500-9*) Millbrook Pr.

— Romare Bearden: Artist. Huggins, Nathan I., ed. (Black Americans of Achievement Ser.). (Illus.). 124p. (YA). (gr. 5 up). 1993. lib. bdg. 19.95 (*0-7910-1119-4*) Chelsea Hse.

Brown, Kevin, ed. see Brown, Kenyon.

***Brown, Kevin M.** Rhetorics of Welfare. LC 99-88130. 2000. text 69.95 (*0-312-23203-9*) St Martin.

Brown, Kevin R. & Baratta, Francis I., eds. Chevron-Notch Fracture Test Experience - Metals & Non-Metals. LC 92-24966. (Special Technical Publication Ser.: No. 1172). (Illus.). 210p. 1992. text 68.00 (*0-8031-1480-X*, STP1172) ASTM.

Brown, Kevin R. & Jacobson, Sheldon. Mastering Dysrhythmias. LC 87-15448. (Illus.). 295p. (C). 1987. pap. 20.00 (*0-8036-1251-6*) Delmar.

Brown, Kim A. Love Me, Thorn. 320p. (Orig.). 1996. pap. 5.50 (*0-9637762-5-8*) Binders Keepers.

Brown, Kim J., ed. Get a Clue: Guide to Cornell & Ithaca, NY. 288p. (C). 1992. pap. text 5.95 (*0-9633055-0-6*) Clue Pubns.

Brown, Kimberley, jt. auth. see Drake, Chris.

Brown, Kimberly R., ed. see Mullan, John.

Brown, Kimila S., jt. auth. see Chalker, Christopher S.

Brown, Kirk & Petersen, Daniel. Ready-to-Run Java 3D. LC 98-31971. (Illus.). 416p. 1999. pap. 44.99 incl. cd-rom (*0-471-31702-0*) Wiley.

Brown, Kristine & Hood, Susan. Writing Matters: Writing Skills & Strategies for Students of English. (Illus.). 160p. 1989. pap. text 15.95 (*0-521-34895-1*) Cambridge U Pr.

Brown, Kurt. Return of the Prodigals. LC 98-72336. (Stahlecker Ser.). 1999. pap. 12.95 (*1-884800-22-X*) Four Way Bks.

Brown, Kurt, ed. Drive, They Said: Poems about Americans & Their Cars. LC 93-33856. (Illus.). 328p. 1994. pap. 14.95 (*0-915943-90-5*) Milkweed Ed.

— Facing the Lion: Writers on Life & Craft. LC 95-47633. (Writers on Life & Craft Ser.). 208p. (Orig.). 1996. pap. 14.00 (*0-8070-6209-X*) Beacon Pr.

— Verse & Universe: Contemporary Poems about Science & Mathematics. LC 98-19340. 380p. 1998. pap. 15.95 (*1-57131-407-5*) Milkweed Ed.

— Writing It down for James: Writers on Life & Craft. LC 93-40635. 216p. (Orig.). 1995. pap. 12.00 (*0-8070-6349-5*) Beacon Pr.

Brown, Kurt & Bosselaar, Laure-Anne, eds. Night Out: Poems about Hotels, Motels, Restaurants & Bars. LC 96-47358. 384p. 1997. pap. 14.95 (*1-57131-405-9*) Milkweed Ed.

Brown, Kurt, ed. see Barrington, Hermester.

Brown, Kurt, tr. see Tadjeck, Sandor.

Brown, Kyle, jt. auth. see Dines, Nicholas T.

Brown, Kyle, ed. see Brown, Kenyon.

Brown, Kysha N., jt. ed. see Ya Salaam, Kalamu.

Brown, L. New Term at Lechlade College. mass mkt. 6.95 (*0-7472-5409-5*, Pub. by Headline Bk Pub) Trafalgar.

Brown, L. A Rusty Person Is Worse Than Rusty Iron: Adult Education & the Development of Africa. (Tolley Medal Ser.). 1975. pap. text 1.50 (*0-685-76692-6*, WPT 6) Syracuse U Cont Ed.

Brown, L., et al. Whatcom Writes! (Illus.). 92p. 1997. 5.95 (*0-9644683-5-2*, 100) Sunporch Prods.

Brown, L. B. Human Side of Prayer: The Psychology of Praying. 325p. 1994. pap. 27.95 (*0-89135-092-6*) Religious Educ.

— The Psychology of Religious Belief. 1988. text 00.00 (*0-12-136355-4*) Acad Pr.

Brown, L. B., ed. Religion, Personality & Mental Health. (Recent Research in Psychology Ser.). (Illus.). 225p. 1993. write for info. (*3-540-97773-2*) Spr-Verlag.

Brown, L. B., et al, eds. The Birds of Africa. LC 81-69594. 1982. text 157.00 (*0-12-137301-0*) Acad Pr.

Brown, L. B., jt. auth. see Huon, G. F.

Brown, L. B., ed. see Kiefer, J. C., et al.

***Brown, L. Carl.** Religion & State: The Muslim Approach to Politics. LC 00-22700. 2000. write for info. (*0-231-12039-7*) Col U Pr.

— Religion & State: The Muslim Approach to Politics. 2000. 27.50 (*0-231-12038-9*) Col U Pr.

Brown, L. Carl, ed. Centerstage: American Diplomacy since World War II. LC 89-24676. (Illus.). 483p. 1989. pap. 24.95 (*0-8419-1270-X*) Holmes & Meier.

— Centerstage: American Diplomacy since World War II. LC 89-24676. (Illus.). 483p. 1990. 49.95 (*0-8419-1265-3*) Holmes & Meier.

— From Madina to Metropolis: Heritage & Change in the Near Eastern City. LC 76-161054. (Illus.). 343p. (C). 1973. pap. text 19.95 (*0-87850-007-3*) Darwin Pr.

— The Imperial Legacy: The Ottoman Imprint on the Balkans & the Middle East. LC 95-15506. (Illus.). 320p. 1996. 55.00 (*0-231-10304-2*) Col U Pr.

Brown, L. Carl & Gordon, Matthew S., eds. Franco-Arab Encounters. 510p. 1997. text 29.95 (*0-8156-6095-2*) Syracuse U Pr.

Brown, L. Carl & Itzkowitz, Norman, eds. Psychological Dimensions of Near Eastern Studies. LC 75-43499. 382p. 1977. 9.95 (*0-87850-028-6*) Darwin Pr.

***BROWN, L .D.** Crossfire. 367p. 1999. pap. 14.95 (*1-58275-003-3*) Black Forest Pr.

Brown, L. D. Crossfire: Witness in the Clinton Investigation. 300p. 1999. pap. text 14.95 (*1-58275-002-5*) Black Forest Pr.

Brown, L. Dave. Managing Conflict at Organizational Interfaces. LC 82-6762. (Managing Human Resources Ser.). 250p. (C). 1983. pap. text 25.75 (*0-201-00884-X*) Addison-Wesley.

Brown, L. David, jt. ed. see Fox, Jonathan.

Brown, L. Dean. The Land of Palestine: West Bank Not East Bank. LC 83-107611. (Middle East Problem Paper Ser.: No. 23). 25p. reprint ed. pap. 30.00 (*0-608-12094-4*, 202413000035) Bks Demand.

Brown, L. F., Jr., ed. Proceedings, Fourth Forum on Geology of Industrial Minerals, Austin TX, March 1968. (Illus.). 174p. 1969. pap. 2.00 (*0-318-03314-3*) Bur Econ Geology.

Brown, L. F., Jr., et al. Natural Hazards of the Texas Coastal Zone, SR0002. (Illus.). 13p. 1974. pap. 3.00 (*0-317-05185-7*, SR0002) Bur Econ Geology.

— Pennsylvanian Depositional Systems in North-Central Texas, A Guide for Interpreting Terrigenous Clastic Facies in a Cratonic Basin. (Guidebook Ser.: GB 14). (Illus.). 122p. 1973. reprint ed. pap. 5.00 (*0-686-29322-3*) Bur Econ Geology.

— Regional Depositional Systems Tracts, Paleogeography, & Sequence Stratigraphy, Upper Pennsylvanian & Lower Permian Strata, North- & West-Central Texas. (Reports of Investigations: RI 197). (Illus.). 116p. 1990. pap. 25.00 (*0-317-03122-8*) Bur Econ Geology.

— Sequence Stratigraphy in Offshore South African Divergent Basins: An Atlas on Exploration for Cretaceous Lowstand Traps by Soekor (Pty.) Ltd. (AAPG Studies in Geology: No. 41). (Illus.). vii, 184p. 1995. spiral bd. 89.00 (*0-89181-049-8*, 533) AAPG.

Brown, L. F., Jr., jt. auth. see Fisher, W. L.

Brown, L. F., Jr., jt. auth. see Galloway, William E.

Brown, L. K. A Thesaurus of Spanish Idioms. (ENG & SPA.). 155p. 1980. pap. 5.15 (*0-8288-2325-1*, S14394) Fr & Eur.

Brown, L. M., ed. Renormalization: From Lorentz to Landau & Beyond. (Theoretical Physics, History of Science, Applied Mathematics Ser.). 192p. 1994. 34.95 (*0-387-94401-X*) Spr-Verlag.

Brown, L. M., ed. see Institute of Physics, Great Britain, Electron Micr.

Brown, L. M., tr. see Yukawa, Hideki.

Brown, L. Neville & Bell, John S. French Administrative Law. 5th ed. LC 98-11115. (Illus.). 388p. 1998. text 95.00 (*0-19-876513-4*) OUP.

Brown, L. Susan. The Politics of Individualism: Liberalism, Liberal Feminism & Anarchism. LC 93-72750. 212p. 1994. 48.99 (*1-895431-79-4*, Pub. by Black Rose); pap. 19.99 (*1-895431-78-6*, Pub. by Black Rose) Consort Bk Sales.

Brown, Lance. On the Road with Will Rogers. LC 97-70649. (Illus.). 312p. (Orig.). 1997. pap. 14.00 (*1-879418-25-8*) Biddle Pub.

Brown, Larine A. Tracks from the Junction: Historical Anecdotes of San Anselmo. 208p. 1992. pap. 18.95 (*0-9632390-0-7*) Marin Light.

Brown, Larissa V. Africans in the New World, 1493-1834. (Illus.). 64p. (Orig.). 1988. pap. 15.00 (*0-916617-31-9*, Pub. by J C Brown) Oak Knoll.

Brown, Larry. America's Most Charming Towns & Villages. 3rd ed. LC 97-76016. 504p. 1998. pap. text 16.95 (*1-883323-76-2*) Open Rd Pub.

— Big Bad Love. 240p. 1990. 17.95 (*0-945575-46-7*) Algonquin Bks.

— Big Bad Love. LC 91-50044. (Vintage Contemporaries Ser.). 240p. 1991. pap. 13.00 (*0-679-73491-0*) Vin Bks.

— Dirty Work. 252p. 1989. 16.95 (*0-945575-20-3*) Algonquin Bks.

— Dirty Work. LC 90-50262. (Vintage Contemporaries Ser.). 256p. 1990. pap. 12.00 (*0-679-73049-4*) Vin Bks.

— Facing the Music. (Front Porch PB Ser.). 184p. 1996. pap. 9.95 (*1-56512-125-2*) Algonquin Bks.

— Father & Son. LC 96-13270. 360p. 1996. 22.95 (*1-56512-014-0*) Algonquin Bks.

— Father & Son. LC 97-15382. 352p. 1997. 13.00 (*0-8050-5303-4*) H Holt & Co.

— Father & Son. large type ed. (Niagara Large Print Ser.). 422p. 1997. 29.50 (*0-7089-5867-2*) Ulverscroft.

***Brown, Larry.** Fay. LC 99-88594. 504p. 2000. 24.95 (*1-56512-168-6*, 72168) Algonquin Bks.

Brown, Larry. Frugal Yachting: Family Adventuring in Small Sailboats. 2nd ed. LC 93-40391. 1994. pap. 17.95 (*0-07-008247-2*) Intl Marine.

— Joe. 360p. 1991. 19.95 (*0-945575-61-0*) Algonquin Bks.

Brown, Larry. Joe. 368p. 1992. mass mkt. 10.99 (*0-446-39438-6*, Pub. by Warner Bks) Little.

Brown, Larry. On Fire. 192p. 1995. mass mkt. 12.99 (*0-446-67114-2*, Pub. by Warner Bks) Little.

— Wingshooter's Guide to Iowa. LC 98-16417. (Illus.). (Orig.). 1998. pap. 26.95 (*1-885106-45-9*) Wild Adven Pr.

— You Are Respectfully Invited to My Execution: Untold Stories of Men Legally Executed in Wyoming Territory. LC 97-2511. 1997. 24.95 (*0-931271-42-8*); pap. 11.95 (*0-931271-41-X*) Hi Plains Pr.

Brown, Larry, et al. Basketball Coaches Guide: Preparing for Special Situations. LC 97-7511. (Spalding Sports Library). (Illus.). 240p. (Orig.). 1996. pap. 12.95 (*1-57028-095-9*, 80959H, Mstrs Pr) NTC Contemp Pub Co.

Brown, Larry, jt. auth. see Hall, Marty.

Brown, Larry C., ed. Drainage in the 21st Century: Food Production & the Environment. LC 98-70344. (Illus.). 738p. 1998. pap. 82.25 (*0-929355-90-3*, 701P0298) Am Soc Ag Eng.

Brown, Larry K. The Hog Ranches of Wyoming: Liquor, Lust & Lies under Sagebrush Skies. (Illus.). 128p. 1995. pap. 9.95 (*0-931271-30-4*) Hi Plains Pr.

***Brown, Larry K.** Petticoat Prisoners of Old Wyoming. LC 00-33460. 2000. pap. write for info. (*0-931271-56-8*) High Plains.

Brown, Larry N. Dolphins & Whales, Including Other Sea Mammals & the Manatee. LC 90-71145. (Illus.). 64p. 1991. pap. 5.95 (*0-89317-039-9*) Windward Pub.

— A Guide to the Mammals of the Southeastern United States. LC 96-25272. 256p. 1997. 50.00 (*0-87049-965-3*); pap. 25.00 (*0-87049-966-1*) U of Tenn Pr.

— Mammals of Florida. (Illus.). 224p. 1997. pap. 22.95 (*0-89317-042-9*) Windward Pub.

Brown, Laura. Ends of Empire: Women & Ideology in Early Eighteenth-Century English Literature. LC 92-36853. 224p. 1993. pap. text 14.95 (*0-8014-8095-7*) Cornell U Pr.

— Media Relations in Your Spare Time: A Step-by-Step Guide for Anyone in Business. 65p. 1995. 37.50 (*0-9630335-2-2*) Natl Assoc Mfrs.

— Subversive Dialogues: Theory in Feminist Therapy. LC 94-18185. 288p. 1994. 42.00 (*0-465-08322-6*, Pub. by Basic) HarpC.

Brown, Laura, ed. Vermont Holistic Health Directory. 2nd rev. ed. LC 98-74454. 53p. 1998. pap. 20.00 (*1-893553-01-9*) AMRITA Pr.

Brown, Laura, jt. ed. see Nussbaum, Felicity.

***Brown, Laura Catherine.** Quickening: A Novel. LC 00-28094. 336p. 2000. 23.95 (*0-375-50373-0*) Random.

Brown, Laura F., ed. The International Arbitration Kit. LC 93-70838. 1993. pap. write for info. (*0-943001-52-8*) Am Arbitration.

Brown, Laura S. & Ballou, Mary, eds. Personality & Psychopathology: Feminist Reappraisals. LC 91-38466. 272p. 1994. pap. text 23.00 (*0-89862-500-9*, 2500) Guilford Pubns.

Brown, Laura S. & Root, Maria P., eds. Diversity & Complexity in Feminist Therapy. LC 90-31689. (Women & Therapy Ser.: Vol. 9, Nos. 1-2). 355p. 1995. pap. text 19.95 (*0-918393-74-4*, Harrington Park) Haworth Pr.

— Diversity & Complexity in Feminist Therapy: Women in Therapy, Vol. 9, Nos. 1-3. LC 90-31160. 355p. 1994. text 49.95 (*0-86656-997-9*) Haworth Pr.

Brown, Laura S. & Rothblum, Esther D., eds. Overcoming Fear of Fat. LC 89-19860. (Women & Therapy Ser.: Vol. 8, No. 3). 99p. 1994. pap. text 9.95 (*0-918393-71-X*, Harrington Park) Haworth Pr.

Brown, Laura S., jt. auth. see Pope, Kenneth S.

Brown, Laura S., jt. ed. see Rothblum, Esther D.

Brown, Laurel, ed. see Puckett, Ruby.

Brown, Lauren. Grasses: An Identification Guide. (Illus.). 256p. 1992. pap. 13.00 (*0-395-62881-4*) HM.

— Wildflowers & Winter Weeds. 252p. 1997. pap. 12.95 (*0-393-31678-5*) Norton.

Brown, Laurence, et al, eds. Modern Spiritualities: An Inquiry. LC 96-41522. (Westminster College - Oxford Ser.). 256p. 1997. 32.95 (*1-57392-112-2*) Prometheus Bks.

Brown, Laurence B., ed. Religion, Personality & Mental Health. LC 93-15258. (Recent Research in Psychology Ser.). 1994. 92.95 (*0-387-97773-2*) Spr-Verlag.

Brown, Laurene Krasny. The Bionic Bunny Show. (Reading Rainbow Ser.). (Illus.). 32p. (J). (gr. k-3). 1985. pap. 5.95 (*0-316-10992-4*, Joy St Bks) Little.

— Dinosaurs Alive & Well! A Guide to Good Health. 32p. (J). (ps-3). 1992. pap. 6.95 (*0-316-11009-4*, Joy St Bks) Little.

An Asterisk (*) at the beginning of an entry indicates that the title is appearing for the first time.

— Dinosaurs Divorce: A Guide for Changing Families. (Illus.). 32p. (J). (gr. k-3). 1986. 15.95 (0-316-11248-8) Little.

Brown, Laurene Krasny. Dinosaurs to the Rescue! A Guide to Protecting Our Planet. LC 91-27177. 1992. 12.15 (0-606-06326-9, Pub. by Turtleback) Demco.

Brown, Laurene Krasny. Dinosaurs to the Rescue! A Guide to Protecting Our Planet. 32p. (J). (gr. k-3). 1994. pap. 6.95 (0-316-11397-2) Little.

— Dinosaurs Travel: A Guide for Families on the Go. 32p. (J). (gr. k-3). 1991. pap. 5.95 (0-316-11253-4) Little.

— How to Be a Friend: A Guide to Making Friends & Keeping Them. LC 97-10179. 32p. (J). (gr. k-3). 1998. 14.95 (0-316-10913-4) Little.

— Rex & Lilly Family Time. LC 93-24162. (Illus.). 32p. (J). (gr. k-3). 1995. 12.95 (0-316-11385-9) Little.

— Rex & Lilly Family Time. (Dino Easy Reader Ser.). (Illus.). 32p. (J). (gr. k-3). 1997. pap. 3.95 (0-316-11109-0) Little.

— Rex & Lilly Family Time. (Dino Easy Reader Ser.). 1997. 9.15 (0-606-11793-8, Pub. by Turtleback) Demco.

— Rex & Lilly Playtime. LC 93-25877. (Illus.). 32p. (J). (gr. k-3). 1995. 12.95 (0-316-11386-7) Little.

— Rex & Lilly Playtime. (Dino Easy Reader Ser.). (Illus.). 32p. (J). (gr. k-3). 1997. pap. 3.95 (0-316-11110-4) Little.

— Rex & Lilly Playtime. (Dino Easy Reader Ser.). 1997. 9.15 (0-606-11794-6, Pub. by Turtleback) Demco.

— Rex & Lilly Schooltime. LC 95-2912. (Illus.). 32p. (J). (gr. k-3). 1997. 13.95 (0-316-10920-7, Pub. by Bulfinch Pr) Little.

— Rex & Lilly Schooltime. (Dino Easy Reader Ser.). (Illus.). (J). (ps-1). 1997. 12.95 (0-614-28841-X) Little.

— Taking Advantage of Media: A Manual for Parents & Teachers. (Illus.). 208p. 1986. 19.95 (0-7102-0402-7, Routledge Thoemms) Routledge.

— Visiting the Art Museum. 1992. pap. 6.99 (0-14-054820-3) NAL.

— What's the Big Secret? Talking about Sex with Girls & Boys. LC 96-15521. (Illus.). 32p. (J). (gr. k-3). 1997. 15.95 (0-316-10915-0) Little.

***Brown, Laurene Krasny.** What's the Big Secret? Talking about Sex with Girls & Boys. (Illus.). 32p. (J). (ps-3). 2000. pap. 5.95 (0-316-10183-4) Little.

Brown, Laurene Krasny. When Dinosaurs Die: A Guide to Understanding Death. (Illus.). 32p. (J). (gr. k-3). 1996. 14.95 (0-316-10917-7) Little.

Brown, Laurene Krasny & Brown, Marc Tolon. Dinosaurs Divorce: A Guide for Changing Families. (Illus.). 32p. (J). (ps-3). 1988. pap. 6.95 (0-316-10996-7) Little.

— Dinosaurs Divorce: A Guide for Changing Families. LC 87-3031. (J). 1986. 11.90 (0-606-03969-4, Pub. by Turtleback) Demco.

Brown, Laurene Krasny, et al. When Dinosaurs Die: A Guide to Understanding Death. Vol. 1. (Illus.). 32p. (J). (ps-3). 1998. pap. 5.95 (0-316-11955-5) Little.

***Brown, Laurie.** Recent Terrains: Terraforming the American West. LC 99-52972. (Creating the North American Landscape Ser.). (Illus.). 112p. 2000. 55.00 (0-8018-6399-6) Johns Hopkins.

***Brown, Laurie, et al.** Recent Terrains: Terraforming the American West. LC 99-52972. (Creating the North American Landscape Ser.). (Illus.). 112p. 2000. pap. 24.95 (0-8018-6400-3) Johns Hopkins.

Brown, Laurie, ed. see Smyth, Cactus.

Brown, Laurie M., ed. Renormalization: From Lorentz to Landau & Beyond. LC 92-32376. (Illus.). 192p. 1993. 75.95 (0-387-97933-6) Spr-Verlag.

Brown, Laurie M., et al, eds. Pions to Quarks: Particle Physics in the 1950's. (Illus.). 766p. (C). 1989. text 90.00 (0-521-30984-0) Cambridge U Pr.

— Twentieth Century Physics, 3 vols. Incl. Vol. 1. 1995. Not sold separately (0-7503-0353-0); Vol. 2. 1995. Not sold separately (0-7503-0354-9); Vol. 3. 1995. Not sold separately (0-7503-0355-7); (Illus.). 2576p. 1995. 400.00 (0-7503-0310-7) IOP Pub.

— Twentieth Century Physics, Vol. 1. LC 95-37751. 1995. write for info. (1-56396-047-8) Am Inst Physics.

— Twentieth Century Physics, Vol. 2. LC 95-37751. 1995. write for info. (1-56396-048-6) Am Inst Physics.

— Twentieth Century Physics, Vol. 3. LC 95-37751. 1995. write for info. (1-56396-049-4) Am Inst Physics.

Brown, Laurie M. & Rechenberg, Helmut. Origin of the Concept of Nuclear Forces. LC 96-31758. (Illus.). 384p. 1996. 87.00 (0-7503-0373-5) IOP Pub.

Brown, Laurie M. & Rigden, John S., eds. Most of the Good Stuff: Memories of Richard Feynman. LC 92-46471. 181p. 1993. text 39.95 (0-88318-870-8, AIP Pr) Spr-Verlag.

Brown, Laurie V. Applied Principles of Horticultural Science. LC 97-111506. 208p. 1996. pap. 32.95 (0-7506-2954-1) Buttrwrth-Heinemann.

Brown, LaVyrne H. I Am Glad I Have Had My Flight. (Illus.). 80p. (Orig.). 1983. pap. text 7.75 (0-930982-04-5) U of Evansville Pr.

Brown, Lawrence. Diffusion Processes & Location. (Bibliography Ser.: No. 4). 177p. 1968. 20.00 (1-55869-026-3) Regional Sci Res Inst.

— Might of the West. 1962. 27.95 (0-8392-1069-8) Astor-Honor.

— My Country Is Called Earth: A Mythology from the Twenty-First Century. LC 94-94555. 144p. (Orig.). 1994. pap. 12.95 (0-9642458-0-9) Gorilla Pr CA.

— Thinking about the World: Building Geography Foundations. (YA). 1993. pap. 16.00 (0-201-45546-3) Addison-Wesley.

Brown, Lawrence D. Fundamentals of Statistical Exponential Families. LC 87-80020. (IMS Lecture Notes - Monographs: Vol. 9). x, 286p. (C). 1987. pap. 25.00 (0-940600-10-2) Inst Math.

— New Policies, New Politics: Government's Response to Government's Growth. LC 82-45979. 71p. 1983. pap. 7.95 (0-8157-1165-4) Brookings.

— The Political Structure of the Federal Health Planning Program. LC 81-70468. 47p. 1982. pap. 7.95 (0-8157-1159-X) Brookings.

— Politics & Health Care Organization: HMO's As Federal Policy. LC 81-70466. 540p. 1983. 44.95 (0-8157-1158-1); pap. 19.95 (0-8157-1157-3) Brookings.

Brown, Lawrence D., ed. Health Policy & the Disadvantaged. LC 91-21831. 222p. 1991. text 39.95 (0-8223-1138-0); pap. text 17.95 (0-8223-1142-9) Duke.

— Health Policy in Transition: A Decade of Health Politics, Policy, & Law. LC 87-13714. viii, 176p. (C). 1987. pap. text 16.95 (0-8223-0790-1) Duke.

Brown, Lawrence D., et al. Accounting Research Directory: Database of Accounting Literature. 3rd ed. LC 93-21572. 700p. 1994. 69.95 (1-55876-068-7) Wiener Pubs Inc.

— The Changing Politics of Federal Grants. LC 84-45275. 169p. 1984. 32.95 (0-8157-1168-9); pap. 12.95 (0-8157-1167-0) Brookings.

Brown, Lawrence G. Immigration: Cultural Conflicts & Social Adjustments. LC 69-18761. (American Immigration Collection. Series 1). 1977. reprint ed. 25.95 (0-405-00509-1) Ayer.

***Brown, Lee, et al, eds.** Training for Speed, Agility & Quickness. LC 99-88413. (Illus.). 248p. 2000. pap. write for info. (0-7360-0239-1) Human Kinetics.

***Brown, Lee & Allen, Robert L.** Strong in the Struggle: My Life as a Militant Unionist. LC 00-31107. (Voices & Visions Ser.). 2001. write for info. (0-8476-9191-8) Rowman.

Brown, Lee, jt. auth. see Goldblatt, David.

Brown, Lee A. Polyverse. (New American Poetry Ser.: No. 31). 189p. (Orig.). 1999. pap. 11.95 (1-55713-290-9, Pub. by Sun & Moon CA) Consort Bk Sales.

***Brown, Lee E.** Isokinetics in Human Performance. LC 99-42887. 456p. 2000. 49.00 (0-7360-0005-4) Human Kinetics.

Brown, Lee P. Pulse Check: National Trends in Drug Abuse. (Illus.). 36p. (Orig.). (C). 1995. pap. text 20.00 (0-7881-1842-0) DIANE Pub.

Brown, Lee R. The Emerson Museum: Practical Romanticism & the Pursuit of the Whole. LC 96-44959. (Illus.). 304p. 1997. 41.50 (0-674-24883-X); pap. 19.95 (0-674-24884-8) HUP.

***Brown, LeMoyne.** Dawn of Religion: Introduction to the Nature of Religion. 300p. 2000. pap. 19.95 (1-883866-20-0) Clarion Pub.

Brown, LeMoyne. The Godhead by Subsistence: Featuring the Holy Spirit in the Family. 112p. 1999. pap. 11.00 (0-8059-4532-6) Dorrance.

Brown, Lena M., ed. see Brown, Lewis S.

Brown, Leon C. The Tunisia of Ahmed Bey, 1837-1855. LC 73-16770. (Princeton Studies on the Near East). 428p. 1974. reprint ed. pap. 132.70 (0-7837-9306-5, 206004600004) Bks Demand.

Brown, Leon C., tr. see al Funisi, khayr.

Brown, Leonard. The Genesis, Growth & Meaning of Endymion. LC 73-100733. 1970. reprint ed. pap. 39.95 (0-8383-0007-3) M S G Haskell Hse.

Brown, Leonard, jt. ed. see Kartman, Ben.

Brown, Leonard F. & Fisher, W. L. Seismic Stratigraphic Interpretation & Petroleum Exploration. LC TN0269.B76. (AAPG Continuing Education Course Note Ser.: No. 16). 192p. 1980. pap. 59.60 (0-608-05608-1, 206606600006) Bks Demand.

Brown, Leroy. Formula for Success. 192p. Date not set. pap. 12.95 (0-89896-410-5) Larksdale.

Brown, Les. Les Brown's Encyclopedia of Television. 3rd ed. 723p. 1992. 22.95 (0-8103-9420-0); 57.00 (0-8103-8871-5, 089165) Visible Ink Pr.

Brown, Les. Courage to Live Your Dreams Vol. 1: Brown & Les. abr. ed. (Courage to Live Your Dreams Ser.: Vol. 1). 1993. audio 12.00 (1-55994-790-X, CPN 1976) HarperAudio.

— Courage to Live Your Dreams Vol. 2: Brown & Les. abr. ed. (Courage to Live Your Dreams Ser.: Vol. 2). 1993. audio 11.00 (1-55994-842-6, CPN 10004) HarperAudio.

— Courage to Live Your Dreams Vol. 3: Brown & Les. abr. ed. (Courage to Live Your Dreams Ser.: Vol. 3). 1994. audio 12.00 (1-55994-873-6, CPN 1977) HarperAudio.

— Courage to Live Your Dreams Vol. 4: Brown & Les. abr. ed. (Courage to Live Your Dreams Ser.: Vol. 4). 1994. audio 12.00 (1-55994-874-4, CP 1998) HarperAudio.

— Courage to Live Your Dreams Vol. 5: Brown & Les. abr. ed. (Courage to Live Your Dreams Ser.: Vol. 5). 1995. audio 12.00 (1-55994-875-2, CPN 1999) HarperAudio.

— Courage to Live Your Dreams Vol. 6: Brown & Les. unabridged ed. (Courage to Live Your Dreams Ser.: Vol. 6). 1995. audio 12.00 (1-55994-876-0, CPN 10000) HarperAudio.

Brown, Les. God's Guidance System: Setting Your Course for Destiny. McDougal, Harold, ed. 210p. 1998. pap. 9.99 (1-884369-95-2) McDougal Pubng.

— It's Not over until You Win. LC 96-35856. 256p. 1997. 22.50 (0-684-81560-5) S&S Trade.

— It's Not over until You Win. 256p. 1998. per. 12.00 (0-684-83528-2, Fireside) S&S Trade Pap.

— Live Your Dreams. 272p. 1994. reprint ed. pap. 12.00 (0-380-72374-3, Avon Bks) Morrow Avon.

Brown, Les. Live Your Dreams: Brown,&Les, Set. abr. ed. 1993. audio 18.00 (1-55994-750-0, CPN 2361) HarperAudio.

***Brown, Les D.** There It Is: A Canadian in the Vietnam War. 256p. 2000. 25.95 (0-7710-1692-1) McCland & Stewart.

Brown, Lesley. Cassell Compact Dictionary. 1998. 23.95 incl. audio, cd-rom (0-304-35089-3, Pub. by Cassell) LPC InBook.

— Cassell Compact Dictionary. (Illus.). 1296p. 1998. 15.95 (0-304-35006-0) Continuum.

— Cassell Concise Dictionary. 1998. 19.95 (0-304-35003-6); 34.95 (0-304-35012-5) Continuum.

— Cassell Paperback Dictionary. 1998. pap. text 14.95 (0-304-35016-8) Continuum.

Brown, Lesley, ed. The New Shorter Oxford English Dictionary, 2 vols., Set. 3840p. (C). Date not set. pap., boxed set. write for info. (0-19-863142-1) OUP.

Brown, Lesley, ed. The New Shorter Oxford English Dictionary on Historical Principles, 2 vols. 4th ed. 3,836p. (C). 1993. 135.00 (0-19-861271-0, 6036) OUP.

Brown, Lesley A. Designing & Developing Electronic Performance Support Systems. (Illus.). 250p. 1996. pap. 36.95 (1-55558-139-0, Digital DEC) Buttrwrth-Heinemann.

Brown, Leslie, ed. Medee et Jason, Tragedie en Musique. LC 89-755086. (French Opera in the 17th & 18th Centuries Ser.: No. 6, Vol. XXVIII). (Illus.). 1991. lib. bdg. 86.00 (0-945193-15-7) Pendragon NY.

Brown, Leslie & Brown, Alan. Transitional Light: Facing Death with Dignity. LC 83-61016. (Illus.). 60p. 1983. pap. 8.00 (0-934306-04-4) Springfield.

Brown, Leslie E. & Craddock, Patricia B., eds. Studies in Eighteenth-Century Culture, Vol. 19. 452p. 1989. 35.00 (0-937191-14-0) Mich St U Pr.

— Studies in Eighteenth-Century Culture, Vol. 20. LC 75-648277. 353p. 1990. 35.00 (0-937191-24-8) Mich St U Pr.

Brown, Leslie E., jt. ed. see Yolton, John W.

Brown, Leslie K. The Registry of California Wineries: A Complete Guide to California Wines & Wineries. LC 88-71590. (Illus.). 346p. (Orig.). 1988. pap. text 22.00 (0-9621771-0-5) Colwyn Corp.

Brown, Lester. State of the World, 1999. 256p. 1998. 25.00 (0-393-04565-X) Norton.

Brown, Lester. State of the World 2001. write for info. (0-393-04866-7) Norton.

— The State of the World 2001. pap. 15.95 (0-393-32082-0) Norton.

Brown, Lester. 2000 States of the World. 256p. 2000. text 27.50 (0-393-04848-9) Norton.

— State of the World 2000. 256p. 2000. pap. 14.95 (0-393-31998-9) Norton.

Brown, Lester B., ed. Two Spirit People: American Indian Lesbian Women & Gay Men. LC 97-3475. (Journal of Gay & Lesbian Social Services Ser.: Vol. 6, No. 2). 120p. (C). 1997. pap. text 12.95 (1-56023-089-4, Harrington Park) Haworth Pr.

— Two Spirit People: American Indian Lesbian Women & Gay Men. LC 97-3475. (Journal of Gay & Lesbian Social Services Ser.: Vol. 6, No. 2). 120p. (C). 1997. 29.95 (0-7890-0003-2) Haworth Pr.

Brown, Lester B., et al. Gay Men & Aging. LC 97-13967. (Studies on the Elderly in America). (Illus.). 128p. 1997. text 36.00 (0-8153-2866-4) Garland.

Brown, Lester R. The Changing World Food Prospect: The Nineties & Beyond. 60p. (Orig.). (C). 1988. pap. 5.00 (0-916468-86-0) Worldwatch Inst.

— Facing the Challenge Food: Facing the Challenge of Food Scarcity. LC 96-231727. 159p. 1996. 19.95 (0-393-04048-8) Norton.

— Food or Fuel: New Competition for the World's Cropland. LC 80-50216. (Worldwatch Papers). 1980. pap. 5.00 (0-916468-34-8) Worldwatch Inst.

— The Global Economic Prospect: New Sources of Economic Stress. 1978. pap. write for info. (0-916468-19-4) Worldwatch Inst.

— In the Human Interest: A Strategy to Stabilize World Population. LC 74-6339. 190p. 1974. 6.95 (0-393-05526-4) Norton.

— In the Human Interest: A Strategy to Stabilize World Population. LC 74-6339. 190p. (C). 1974. pap. write for info. (0-393-09288-7) Norton.

— Increasing World Food Output. LC 75-26298. (World Food Supply Ser.). (Illus.). 1976. reprint ed. 17.95 (0-405-07770-X) Ayer.

— Man, Land & Food. LC 75-26299. (World Food Supply Ser.). (Illus.). 1976. reprint ed. 17.95 (0-405-07771-8) Ayer.

— The Politics & Responsibility of the North American Breadbasket. 1975. pap. write for info. (0-318-70405-6) Worldwatch Inst.

— Population Policies for a New Economic Era. 1983. pap. write for info. (0-916468-52-6) Worldwatch Inst.

— Redefining National Security. 1977. pap. write for info. (0-916468-13-5) Worldwatch Inst.

— Resource Trends & Population Policy: A Time for Reassessment. LC 79-64839. (Worldwatch Papers). 1979. pap. 5.00 (0-916468-28-3) Worldwatch Inst.

— Soil Erosion: Quiet Crisis in the World Economy. LC 84-62062. (Worldwatch Papers). 1984. pap. 5.00 (0-916468-60-7) Worldwatch Inst.

— Tough Choices: Facing the Challenge of Food Scarcity. 160p. 1996. pap. 11.00 (0-393-31573-8) Norton.

— U. S. & Soviet Agriculture: The Shifting Balance of Power. 1982. pap. write for info. (0-916468-51-8) Worldwatch Inst.

***Brown, Lester R.** Vital Signs: The Environmental Trends That Are Shaping Our Future 2000. 200p. 2000. pap. 13.00 (0-393-32022-7) Norton.

Brown, Lester R. Who Will Feed China? Wake-Up Call for a Small Planet. LC 95-237124. (Illus.). 160p. 1995. 19.95 (0-393-03897-1); pap. 8.95 (0-393-31409-X, Norton Paperbks) Norton.

— World Population Trends: Signs of Hope, Signs of Stress. 1976. pap. write for info. (0-916468-07-0) Worldwatch Inst.

— The Worldwide Loss of Cropland. 1978. pap. write for info. (0-318-70406-4) Worldwatch Inst.

***Brown, Lester R. & Ayres, Ed, eds.** The World Watch Reader: On Global Environmental Issues, 1998 Edition. LC 98-184369. (Illus.). 358p. 1998. pap. 14.95 (0-393-31753-6) Norton.

Brown, Lester R. & Jacobson, Jodi L. The Future of Urbanization: Facing the Ecological & Economic Constraints. LC 87-50550. (Worldwatch Papers). (Illus.). 56p. (Orig.). (C). 1987. pap. 5.00 (0-916468-78-X) Worldwatch Inst.

— Our Demographically Divided World. LC 86-51475. (Worldwatch Papers: No. 74). 64p. (Orig.). (C). 1986. pap. 5.00 (0-916468-75-5) Worldwatch Inst.

Brown, Lester R. & Shaw, Pamela. Six Steps to a Sustainable Society. 1982. pap. write for info. (0-916468-47-X) Worldwatch Inst.

Brown, Lester R. & Wolf, Edward C. Reversing Africa's Decline. LC 85-51311. (Worldwatch Papers). 1985. pap. 5.00 (0-916468-65-8) Worldwatch Inst.

Brown, Lester R., et al. Beyond Malthus: Nineteen Dimensions of the Population Challenge. (Worldwatch Environmental Alert Ser.). (Illus.). 256p. 1999. pap. 13.00 (0-393-31906-7) Norton.

***Brown, Lester R., et al.** Beyond Malthus: Sixteen Dimensions of the Population Problem, Vol. 143. Starke, Linda, ed. LC 98-61216. 80p. 1998. pap. 5.00 (1-878071-45-9) Worldwatch Inst.

Brown, Lester R., et al. Saving the Planet: How to Shape an Environmentally Sustainable Global Economy. LC 91-24623. (Illus.). 224p. 1991. pap. 8.95 (0-393-30823-5) Norton.

— State of The World, 1984. LC 83-25123. (Worldwatch Papers). 1984. 10.95 (0-393-01835-0) Worldwatch Inst.

***Brown, Lester R., et al.** State of the World, 1999: Millennium Edition. (Illus.). 256p. 1999. pap. 13.95 (0-393-31815-X, Norton Paperbks) Norton.

— State of the World 1996: A Worldwatch Institute Report on Progress Toward a Sustainable Society. (Illus.). 288p. 1996. 23.00 (0-393-03851-3) Norton.

Brown, Lester R., et al. State of the World, 1994: A Worldwatch Institute Report on Progress Toward a Sustainable Society. 256p. 1993. 19.95 (0-393-03439-9) Norton.

— Vital Signs 1998: The Environmental Trends That Are Shaping Our Future. (Illus.). 176p. 1998. pap. 12.00 (0-393-31762-5) Norton.

— Vital Signs 1997: The Trends That Are Shaping Our Future. 6th ed. (Illus.). 207p. (C). 1997. 24.95 (0-393-04067-4) Norton.

Brown, Lester R., jt. auth. see Kane, Hal.

***Brown, Lew G. & Rosenthal, David W.** Cases in Strategic Marketing. 610p. 2000. 72.00 (0-13-086359-9) P-H.

Brown, Lewis S. Yes, Helen, There Were Dinosaurs. (Illus.). 143p. (Orig.). (J). (ps-12). 1982. pap. 7.95 (0-9647505-0-3, 82144370-AC-R90) L Brown Pubng.

— Yes, Helen, There Were Dinosaurs. Brown, Lena M., ed. (Illus.). 152p. (Orig.). 1982. pap. 7.95 (0-9608542-0-7) L S Brown Pub.

Brown, Lewis S., ed. see Ellenberger, W., et al.

Brown, Lewis S., ed. see Muybridge, Eadweard.

Brown, Liane I. From Fear to Freedom: Sustained by Faith - an East German Family's Struggle for Survival. 250p. (Orig.). 1993. pap. 9.95 (0-9618730-2-7) FEA Ministries.

— Refuge. (Illus.). 211p. (Orig.). 1987. pap. 10.95 (0-89084-392-9, 032177) Bob Jones Univ.

Brown, Lightning. Untouchable Clouds. 56p. 1997. pap. 8.95 (1-879934-50-7) St Andrews NC.

Brown, Lillian. The Polished Politician: The Political Candidate's Personal Handbook. 87p. 1995. pap. 9.95 (0-9641061-0-8) LB-LTD Pr.

— Your Public Best: The Complete Guide to Making Successful Public Appearances on the Job, at Interviews, on the Platform & on TV. LC 89-30759. 240p. 1989. 19.95 (1-55704-042-7, Pub. by Newmarket) Norton.

— Your Public Best: The Complete Guide to Making Successful Public Appearances on the Job, at Interviews, on the Platform, & on TV. LC 89-30759. 240p. 1992. pap. 12.95 (1-55704-079-6, Pub. by Newmarket) Norton.

Brown, Linda. An Annotated Bibliography of the Literature on Livability: With an Introduction & an Analysis of the Literature, No. 853. 1975. 6.00 (0-686-20366-6, Sage Prdcls Pr) Sage.

Brown, Linda & Ciffolillo, Kathryn, eds. Invitation to Change 1994 Winners: Better Government Competition on Welfare Reform. (Invitation to Change Ser.). 200p. (Orig.). 1994. pap. 10.00 (0-929930-13-4) Pioneer Inst.

Brown, Linda B. Crossing over Jordan. 304p. 1996. pap. 11.00 (0-345-40231-6) One Wrld.

Brown, Linda C. Secret Waters. (Women's Poetry Ser.). (Illus.). 68p. (Orig.). 1997. pap. 10.00 (0-911287-24-8) Blue Begonia.

Brown, Linda G., ed. Marsha Norman: A Casebook. LC 95-52416. (Casebooks on Modern Dramatists Ser.: Vol. 19). 272p. 1996. text 60.00 (0-8153-1352-7, H1750) Garland.

Brown, Linda K. & Mussell, Kay, eds. Ethnic & Regional Foodways in the United States: The Performance of Group Identity. LC 83-16715. (Illus.). 284p. (C). 1984. pap. text 17.00 (0-87049-419-8) U of Tenn Pr.

Brown, Linda K., jt. ed. see Bennett, V. Ruth.

Brown, Linda N. Think Book: Reproducible Problem-Solving Activities. (Illus.). 240p. (Orig.). (J). (gr. 4-8). 1990. pap. text 16.95 (0-86530-087-9, IP 190-1) Incentive Pubns.

Brown, Linda P., jt. auth. see Gediman, Judith S.

Brown, Lindy. Easy Airbrush Projects for Crafters & Decorative Painters. LC 96-54738. (Illus.). 128p. 1997. pap. 23.99 (0-89134-746-1, North Lght Bks) F & W Pubns Inc.

Brown, Linfield C., jt. auth. see Berthouex, P. Mac.

Brown, Lisa. Ribbons: Over 20 Decorative Projects for the Home (Inspirations Ser.). 1999. 12.95 (*0-7548-0187-X*, Lorenz Bks) Anness Pub.

Brown, Lisa E. & Davis, David W. Jingle Bell Rock. LC 98-93347. (Illus.). 416p. 1998. pap. 9.95 (*1-892642-49-2*, B6-143) Aalida Pr.

— Lisa's down Home Tennessee Country Cookin' LC 98-93346. (Illus.). 200p. 1998. pap. 9.95 (*1-892642-48-4*, B6-947) Aalida Pr.

Brown, Lisa G. Sleeping at the Magnolia. 464p. 1997. mass mkt. 5.99 (*0-06-108214-7*) HarpC.

Brown, Lisa R. Preparing for Y2K: A Checklist for Families, Communities & Businesses. 16p. 1999. pap. write for info. (*1-889482-09-9*) Nat Congress CED.

Brown, Liza, ed. see Mothers' Aid Staff.

Brown, Llewellyn, tr. see Ouaknin, Marc-Alain.

Brown, Lloyd A. The Story of Maps. (Illus.). 464p. 1980. reprint ed. pap. 12.95 (*0-486-23873-3*) Dover.

Brown, Lloyd A. & Peckham, Howard H., eds. Revolutionary War Journals of Henry Dearborn, 1775-1783. (Illus.). 264p. 1994. pap. text 19.00 (*0-7884-0124-6*) Heritage Bk.

Brown, Lloyd A., ed. see Dearborn, Henry.

Brown, Lloyd L. Iron City. LC 94-17812. (Northeastern Library of Black Literature). 288p. 1994. text 45.00 (*1-55553-205-5*); pap. text 16.95 (*1-55553-206-3*) NE U Pr.

— The Young Paul Robeson: "On My Journey Now" LC 96-24715. (C). 1998. pap. text 18.00 (*0-8133-3177-3*, Pub. by Westview) HarpC.

Brown, Lloyd W. Women Writers in Black Africa, 21. LC 80-1710. (Contributions in Women's Studies: No. 21). 204p. 1981. 59.95 (*0-313-22540-0*, BRW/, Greenwood Pr) Greenwood.

Brown, Lois, ed. see Paul, Susan.

Brown, Lonnie T. & Szweda, Eric A., eds. Trade Related Aspects of Intellectual Property. LC 90-82986. vii, 398p. 1990. reprint ed. lib. bdg. 55.00 (*0-89941-747-7*, 306220) W S Hein.

Brown, Lonny. Self-Actuated Healing: The Alternative to Doctors & Drugs Is Within You. 176p. (Orig.). 1988. pap. 8.95 (*0-87961-185-5*) Naturegraph.

Brown, Loraine. Why Me? The Real-Life Guide to Infertility. 1998. pap. text 12.00 (*0-7318-0687-5*) Simon & Schuster.

***Brown, Loranne.** The Handless Maiden. LC 98-184377. 432p. 1998. 32.95 (*0-385-25702-3*) BDD Bks Young Read.

Brown, Loree R. How To's of Motivation & Good Behavior. 96p. (Orig.). 1993. pap. write for info. (*0-9638456-9-1*) Aloli Pubns.

Brown, Loren R. Point Loma Theosophical Society: A List of Publications, 1898 - 1942. LC 81-187499. (Illus.). 136p. (C). 1977. pap. 10.00 (*0-913510-46-7*) Wizards.

Brown, Loren Totch G. Totch: A Life in the Everglades. LC 93-4529. (Illus.). 320p. 1993. 29.95 (*0-8130-1227-9*); pap. 17.95 (*0-8130-1228-7*) U Press Fla.

Brown, Lorena, et al. Options for the Control of Influenza No. III: Proceedings of the 3rd International Conference on Options for the Control of Influenza, Cairns, Australia, 4-9 May, 1996. LC 96-47465. (International Congress Ser.: 1123). 880p. 1996. 273.00 (*0-444-82461-8*) Elsevier.

Brown, Lorene B. Subject Headings for African-American Materials. LC 95-10847. xvii, 118p. 1995. pap. text 31.00 (*1-56308-252-7*) Libs Unl.

Brown, Lori D. Assessing the Quality of Management Module 7: User's Guide. (Primary Health Care Management Advancement Programme (PHC MAP) Modules Ser.). 90p. 1993. pap. text. write for info. (*1-882839-05-6*) Aga Khan Fnd.

— Assessing the Quality of Services Module 6: User's Guide. (Primary Health Care Management Advancement Programme (PHC MAP) Modules Ser.). 190p. 1993. pap. text. write for info. (*1-882839-04-8*) Aga Khan Fnd.

Brown, Lorna, ed. Sex Education in the Eighties: The Challenge of Healthy Sexual Evolution. LC 81-15738. (Perspectives in Sexuality Ser.). 278p. (C). 1981. 49.50 (*0-306-40762-0*, Plenum Trade) Perseus Pubng.

Brown, Lorne. When Freedom Was Lost: The Unemployed, the Agitator & the State. (Illus.). 208p. 1986. 43.99 (*0-920057-75-6*, Pub. by Black Rose); pap. 14.99 (*0-920057-77-2*, Pub. by Black Rose) Consort Bk Sales.

Brown, Lorraine. In Search of Myself: A Celebration of Miracles. LC 97-93392. 320p. (Orig.). 1997. pap. 12.95 (*0-9657653-0-X*) Miracle Creat.

Brown, Lorraine, ed. Liberty Defenced & Other Living Newspapers of the 1930's. LC 88-21425. 327p. (C). 1989. 69.00 (*0-913969-20-6*) Univ Pub Assocs.

Brown, Lou, et al. Signos Para el Ingles Exacto: A Book for Spanish-Speaking Families of Deaf Children in Schools Using Signing Exact English. LC 82-61647. (Illus.). 160p. 1983. pap. 14.95 (*0-916708-06-3*) Modern Signs.

***Brown, Louis.** Technical & Military Imperatives. LC 99-38978. 580p. 2000. 38.00 (*0-7503-0659-9*) IOP Pub.

Brown, Louis, et al. Stop Domestic Violence. LC 96-40417. 1997. pap. 11.95 (*0-312-16611-7*) St Martin.

Brown, Louis J., jt. ed. see Haring, Norris G.

Brown, Louis M. Lawyering Through Life: The Origin of Preventive Law. LC 86-10078. xviii, 298p. 1986. reprint ed. 40.00 (*0-8377-0348-4*, Rothman) W S Hein.

— Preventive Law. LC 72-97326. 346p. 1970. reprint ed. lib. bdg. 75.00 (*0-8371-3077-8*, BRPL, Greenwood Pr) Greenwood.

***Brown, Louis R. & Payne, Brian, eds.** Rite of Death. LC 99-95121. (Illus.). 80p. 1999. pap. 14.95 (*0-9673090-0-X*, 1223-01) Teletrans.

Brown, Louise F. & Carson, George B. Men & Centuries of European Civilization. LC 76-134060. (Essay Index Reprint Ser.). 1977. 51.95 (*0-8369-2100-3*) Ayer.

Brown, Louise K. A Revolutionary Town. LC 74-30897. (Illus.). 336p. 1975. 15.00 (*0-914016-14-8*) Phoenix Pub.

Brown, Loulou. National Women's Directory. 384p. 1999. pap. 19.95 (*0-304-70192-0*) Continuum.

***Brown, Loulou.** Teach Yourself Alternative Medicine. (Teach Yourself Ser.). 224p. 1999. pap. 10.95 (*0-8442-0043-3*, 00433, Teach Yrslf) NTC Contemp Pub Co.

Brown, Loulou & Humm, Maggie. International Handbook of Women's Studies: W. I. S. H. 464p. (C). 1994. pap. text 61.00 (*0-13-302209-9*) P-H.

Brown, LoVerne. The Under Side of Snow. LC 96-60890. 60p. (Orig.). 1996. pap. 8.95 (*0-938711-41-5*) Tecolote Pubns.

Brown, LoVerne, ed. Living on Lassen. LC 90-71932. 152p. (Orig.). 1991. pap. 8.95 (*0-938711-09-1*) Tecolote Pubns.

Brown, Lowell. Sunday School Standards, No. 960270. Capps & Fulbright, eds. LC 81-51621. 1988. pap. 10.99 (*0-87148-189-8*) Pathway Pr.

Brown, Lowell S. Quantum Field Theory. (Illus.). 556p. (C). 1994. pap. text 49.95 (*0-521-46946-5*) Cambridge U Pr.

Brown, Lucy. This Is My Beloved: Psalms of Communion. LC 88-71798. (Illus.). 196p. (Orig.). (C). 1988. pap. 8.95 (*0-9620560-0-6*) Cedargarden.

Brown, Lucy M. & Christie, Ian R. Bibliography of British History, 1789-1851. 798p. 1977. text 125.00 (*0-19-822390-0*) OUP.

Brown, Luke S. Small Claims Court Guide for Florida: Win Your Case & Collect Your Money. (Legal Ser.). 240p. 1993. pap. 15.95 (*0-88908-780-6*) Self-Counsel Pr.

Brown, Luther P., jt. auth. see Walbridge, Mark R.

Brown, Lydia, ed. Aquaculture for Veterinarians: Fish Husbandry & Medicine. LC 92-41237. 1993. text 155.00 (*0-08-040835-4*, Pergamon Pr); pap. text 70.00 (*0-08-040836-2*, Pergamon Pr) Elsevier.

Brown, Lymnwood. Oracle Database Administration on UNIX Systems. LC 97-183203. 224p. (C). 1997. pap. text 39.95 incl. cd-rom (*0-13-244666-9*) P-H.

Brown, Lyn M. Raising Their Voices: The Politics of Girls' Anger. LC 98-15216. 288p. 1998. 24.95 (*0-674-83871-8*) HUP.

— Raising Their Voices: The Politics of Girls' Anger. 1999. pap. 14.95 (*0-674-74721-6*) HUP.

***Brown, Lyn M. & Gilligan, Carol.** Meeting at the Crossroads. 1999. pap. 12.50 (*0-345-91550-X*) Ballantine Pub Grp.

Brown, Lyn M. & Gilligan, Carol. Meeting at the Crossroads: Women's Psychology & Girls' Development. 258p. (C). 1998. text 20.00 (*0-7881-5290-4*) DIANE Pub.

— Meeting at the Crossroads: Women's Psychology & Girls' Development. LC 92-14312. 240p. 1992. text 19.95 (*0-674-56464-2*) HUP.

— Meeting at the Crossways: Woman's Psychology & Girls' Development. 272p. 1999. pap. 12.50 (*0-345-38295-1*) Ballantine Pub Grp.

Brown, Lynda. Gardeners' World Vegetables for Small Gardens. (Illus.). 128p. (Orig.). 1994. pap. 14.95 (*0-563-36466-1*, BBC-Parkwest) Parkwest Pubns.

***Brown, Lynda.** The Shopper's Guide to Organic Food. 1999. pap. 17.95 (*1-85702-840-6*, Pub. by Fourth Estate) Trafalgar.

Brown, Lynn. All about Me. (Illus.). 92p. (J). (ps-1). 1993. 14.95 (*0-9640001-0-5*) Jikani Pr.

— Fire & Firecrackers. 3rd ed. Walker, Granville, Jr., ed. (Fun & Safety Ser.). (Illus.). 14p. (Orig.). (J). (ps-6). 1982. pap. 2.97 (*0-9608466-1-1*) Fun Reading.

— Ms. Worm. 3rd ed. Walker, Granville, Jr., ed. (Fun & Safety Ser.). (Illus.). (Orig.). (J). (ps-6). 1982. pap. 2.95 (*0-9608466-0-3*) Fun Reading.

Brown, Lynn C. Golf Tournaments for Fun & Profit: How Anyone Can Easily Put on One Day Golf Tournaments. 139p. (Orig.). (C). 1994. pap. 12.95 (*1-882589-00-9*) Brockton Pubng.

***Brown, Lynne S.** Gulfport. (Images of America Ser.). (Illus.). 128p. 1999. pap. 18.99 (*0-7385-0215-4*) Arcadia Publng.

***Brown, Lynnwood.** The Complete Oracle DBA Training Course: Student Edition. (C). 1999. pap., student ed. 71.93 (*0-13-014620-X*) P-H.

Brown, Lynnwood. Oracle 8 Database Administration on Windows NT. LC 98-11705. 400p. 1998. pap. text 39.99 (*0-13-927443-X*) P-H.

Brown, M. Bridge to Heaven. 1994. pap. 7.95 (*1-880479-22-2*) Marian Comms.

Brown, M. Continuum Theory & Dynamical Systems. LC 91-11451. (Contemporary Mathematics Ser.: Vol. 117). 182p. 1991. pap. 66.00 (*0-8218-5123-3*, CONM/117) Am Math.

— Get the Job You Want! (C). 1991. pap. text 25.16 (*0-395-53975-7*) HM.

— Manager's Guide to Behavioural Sciences. (C). 1986. 50.00 (*0-7855-4095-4*, Pub. by Witherby & Co) St Mut.

Brown, M. Structure of Disadvantage. 1983. 48.95 (*0-435-82094-X*) Ashgate Pub Co.

Brown, M., jt. auth. see Ashworth, J. R.

Brown, M., jt. auth. see Butter, E.

Brown, M., jt. auth. see McDonald, D.

Brown, M. Christopher, ed. The Quest to Define Collegiate Desegregation: Black Colleges, Title VI Compliance & Post-Adams Litigation. LC 98-49934. 192p. 1999. 49.95 (*0-89789-608-4*, Bergin & Garvey) Greenwood.

***Brown, M. Christopher, II & Davis, James Earl, eds.** Black Sons to Mothers: Compliments, Critiques, & Challenges for Cultural Workers in Education. LC 99-13961. (Counterpoints: Vol. 107). 256p. 2000. pap. text 29.95 (*0-8204-4292-5*) P Lang Pubng.

Brown, M. H. Generations of the Dead. 1993. pap. 6.95 (*0-88145-105-3*) Broadway Play.

Brown, M. H., ed. Meat Microbiology. (Illus.). 528p. 1982. 88.25 (*0-85334-138-9*, I-305-82) Elsevier.

Brown, M. K., jt. auth. see Lay, Carol.

Brown, M. Leann. Developing Countries & Regional Economic Cooperation. LC 94-8314. 192p. 1994. 59.95 (*0-275-94960-5*, Praeger Pubs) Greenwood.

Brown, M. Ralph. Legal Psychology. (Historical Foundations of Forensic Psychiatry & Psychology Ser.). (Illus.). 346p. 1980. reprint ed. lib. bdg. 39.50 (*0-306-76065-7*) Da Capo.

Brown, M. T. Making Money with the Telephone: The Complete Handbook of Telephone Marketing. LC 77-89655. 1977. 12.95 (*0-930490-01-0*) Future Shop.

Brown, M. T., jt. auth. see Brown, W. L.

Brown, M. V. & Hacket, J. A. Western Australian Introduction to Law. 3rd ed. 1989. 36.00 (*0-409-30129-9*, AT, MICHIE) LEXIS Pub.

Brown, M. W., jt. ed. see Miller, K. J.

Brown, Mac H., ed. Quality Environments: Developmentally Appropriate Experiences for Young Children. 139p. (Orig.). (C). 1988. pap. text 6.80 (*0-87563-321-8*) Stipes.

Brown, Macalister & Zasloff, Joseph J. Cambodia Confounds the Peacemakers, 1979-1998. LC 98-7448. 272p. 1998. 39.95 (*0-8014-3536-6*) Cornell U Pr.

Brown, MacAlister & Zasloff, Joseph J. Settlement for Cambodia: The Khmer Rouge Dilemma. (Pew Case Studies in International Affairs). 50p. (C). 1993 pap. text 3.50 (*1-56927-356-1*) Geo U Inst Dplmcy.

Brown, Madeleine D. Texas in the Morning: The Love Story of Madeleine Duncan Brown & President Lyndon Baines-Johnson. LC 97-66180. (Harrison Edward Livingstone Bks.). (Illus.). 255p. 1997. 25.00 (*0-941401-06-5*) Conservatory.

Brown, MaeHill. Tracings. 1982. pap. text 6.00 (*0-88982-034-1*, Pub. by Oolichan Bks) Genl Dist Srvs.

Brown, Maggie. Working Together for Public Service: Report of the United States Secretary of Labor's Task Force on Excellence in State & Local Government Through Labor-Management Cooperation. 194p. 1996. per. 14.00 (*0-16-048655-6*) USGPO.

Brown, Maggie, ed. see Florio, James J. & Abramson, Jerry.

Brown, Maggie W. Making Decisions. Zanzig, Thomas, ed. (Discovering Program Ser.). (Illus.). 37p. (J). 1990. teacher ed. 6.00 (*0-88489-201-8*); text 3.00 (*0-88489-200-X*) St Marys.

Brown, Malcolm. The Healing Touch: An Introduction to Organismic Psychotherapy. (Illus.). 325p. 1990. reprint ed. pap. 16.95 (*0-940795-01-9*) LifeRhythm.

— Imperial War Museum Book of 1918: Year of Victory. (Illus.). 425p. 1998. 52.50 (*0-283-06307-6*) Trans-Atl Phila.

— The Imperial War Museum Book of the Somme. (Illus.). 416p. 1997. pap. 22.50 (*0-330-35220-2*, Pub. by Pan) Trans-Atl Phila.

— The Imperial War Museum Book of the Somme. (Illus.). 380p. 1996. 57.50 (*0-283-06249-5*, Pub. by S1 & J) Trans-Atl Phila.

— T. E. Lawrence: The Selected Letters. (Illus.). 564p. 1994. pap. 16.95 (*1-56924-995-4*) Marlowe & Co.

***Brown, Malcolm.** Tommy Goes to War. (Illus.). 192p. 1999. 32.50 (*0-7524-1772-X*, Pub. by Tempus Pubng) Arcadia Publng.

— Verdun, 1916. (Illus.). 192p. 1999. 29.99 (*0-7524-1774-6*, Pub. by Tempus Pubng) Arcadia Publng.

Brown, Malcolm, ed. The Imperial War Museum Book of the First World War. LC 92-50723. 1993. reprint ed. pap. 27.95 (*0-8061-2525-X*) U of Okla Pr.

***Brown, Malcolm & Seaton, Shirley.** Christmas Truce: The Western Front December 1914. rev. ed. (Grand Strategy Ser.). (Illus.). 278p. 1999. pap. 17.95 (*0-330-39065-1*, Pub. by Pan) Trans-Atl Phila.

Brown, Malcolm & Webb, John N. Seven Stranded Coal Towns: A Study of an American Depressed Area. LC 76-165680. (Research Monographs: Vol. 23). 1971. reprint ed. lib. bdg. 25.00 (*0-306-70355-6*) Da Capo.

Brown, Malcolm, jt. auth. see Wilson, Paul.

Brown, Malcolm, ed. see Nietzsche, Friedrich Wilhelm.

Brown, Malcolm, ed. see Plato.

Brown, Malcolm H., ed. Papers of the Yugoslav-American Seminar on Music. xii, 208p. 1970. pap. 9.95 (*0-89357-006-0*) Slavica.

— Russian & Soviet Music: Essays for Boris Schwarz. LC 84-50049. (Russian Music Studies: No. 11). (Illus.). 335p. reprint ed. pap. 103.90 (*0-8357-1545-0*, 207053400001) Bks Demand.

Brown, Malcolm H. & Wiley, Roland J., eds. Slavonic & Western Music: Essays for Gerald Abraham. LC 84-2625. (Russian Music Studies: No. 12). 331p. reprint ed. 102.70 (*0-8357-1594-9*, 207032900078) Bks Demand.

Brown, Malcolm H., ed. see Joseph, Charles M.

Brown, Malcom. Sir Samuel Ferguson. (Irish Writers Ser.). 101p. 1973. pap. 1.95 (*0-8387-1208-8*) Bucknell U Pr.

Brown, Mandy. Dangerous Illusion. large type ed. 1990. 27.99 (*0-7089-2149-3*) Ulverscroft.

— Just for You. large type ed. 336p. 1995. 27.99 (*0-7089-3408-0*) Ulverscroft.

— Signpost to Romance. large type ed. 288p. 1988. 27.99 (*0-7089-1861-1*) Ulverscroft.

Brown-Manrique, Gerardo. Ticino Guide. LC 89-3625. (Illus.). 192p. (Orig.). 1996. pap. 19.95 (*0-910413-46-0*) Princeton Arch.

— Words & Works: Writings & Projects. 80p. 1989. ring bd. 16.00 (*0-9630969-0-7*) Interalia Des.

Brown, Mara. Landing on Your Feet: An Inspirational Guide to Surviving, Coping, Prospering from Job Loss. 1995. pap. 14.95 (*0-07-551377-3*) McGraw.

***Brown, Marc.** Arthur & the Lost Diary. (Illus.). (J). 1999. pap. 11.05 (*0-613-11277-6*) Econo-Clad Bks.

— Arthur & the Popularity Test. (Illus.). (J). 1999. pap. 11.05 (*0-613-11278-4*) Econo-Clad Bks.

— Arthur Babysits. (Illus.). (J). 1999. pap. 13.35 (*0-7857-5838-0*) Econo-Clad Bks.

— Arthur, Clean Your Room. 24p. 1999. mass mkt. 3.99 (*0-375-80873-6*, Pub. by Random Bks Yng Read) Random.

— Arthur Rocks with Binky. (Illus.). (J). 1999. pap. 11.05 (*0-613-11281-4*) Econo-Clad Bks.

— Arthur's First Kiss. (J). 2001. 11.99 (*0-375-90602-9*) Random.

— Arthur's Teacher Moves In. (J). 2000. 15.95 (*0-316-11856-7*) Little.

— Buster Baxter Cat Saver. (J). 2000. pap. 3.95 (*0-316-11817-6*) Little.

— Marc Brown Arthur Chapter, Bks. 1-3. 208p. (J). 2000. 9.95 (*0-316-12096-0*, Pub. by Little) Time Warner.

***Brown, Marc A.** Locked In The Library. (Illus.). (J). 1999. pap. 11.05 (*0-613-07017-8*) Econo-Clad Bks.

Brown, Marc A., ed. The Literate Cat. (Illus.). 112p. 1995. 25.95 (*1-56313-740-2*) BrownTrout Pubs Inc.

Brown, Marc D., jt. auth. see Leffell, David J.

Brown, Marc Tolon. ABC Reach for the Stars. (Arthur Ser.). (Illus.). 24p. (J). (gr. 1-3). 1998. pap. 3.99 (*0-679-89284-2*, Pub. by Random Bks Yng Read) Random.

Brown, Marc Tolon. Arthur Accused! (Arthur Chapter Book Ser.: No. 5). 58p. (J). (gr. 3-6). pap. 3.95 (*0-8072-1299-7*) Listening Lib.

Brown, Marc Tolon. Arthur Accused! LC 97-75722. (Arthur Chapter Book Ser.: No. 5). (Illus.). 64p. (J). (gr. 2-4). 1998. pap. 3.95 (*0-316-11556-8*) Little.

— Arthur Accused! (Arthur Chapter Book Ser.: No. 5). (Illus.). 64p. (J). (gr. 3-6). 1998. 12.95 (*0-316-11554-1*) Little.

— Arthur Accused! (Arthur Chapter Book Ser.: No. 5). (J). (gr. 3-6). 1998. pap. 3.95 (*0-316-12150-9*) Little.

— Arthur Accused! unabridged ed. (Arthur Chapter Book Ser.: No. 5). (J). (gr. 3-6). 1998. pap. 15.98 (*0-8072-0385-8*, FTR191SP) Listening Lib.

— Arthur Adventures: Four Books in a Box, 4 bks. (Arthur Adventure Ser.). (Illus.). 32p. (J). (ps-3). 1996. boxed set 14.95 (*0-316-10953-3*) Little.

***Brown, Marc Tolon.** Arthur & the Big Blow-up. LC PZ7.K883Ap 2000. (Arthur Chapter Book Ser.: No. 20). (Illus.). 64p. (J). (gr. 3-6). 2000. 12.95 (*0-316-12129-0*); pap. 3.95 (*0-316-12203-3*) Little.

— Arthur & the Big Blow-Up. (J). 1999. pap. 3.95 (*0-316-12326-9*, Pub. by Little) Time Warner.

— Arthur & the Big Blow-Up. (Illus.). (J). 2000. 9.40 (*0-606-18251-9*) Turtleback.

Brown, Marc Tolon. Arthur & the Cootie Catcher. (Arthur Chapter Book Ser.: No. 15). (J). (gr. 3-6). 1999. pap. 3.95 (*0-316-12085-5*) Little.

— Arthur & the Cootie Catcher. LC 98-52061. (Arthur Chapter Book Ser.: No. 15). (Illus.). 64p. (J). (gr. 2-4). 1999. pap. 3.95 (*0-316-12266-1*) Little.

Brown, Marc Tolon. Arthur & the Crunch Cereal Contest. (Arthur Chapter Book Ser.: No. 4). 61p. (J). (gr. 3-6). pap. 3.95 (*0-8072-1298-9*) Listening Lib.

Brown, Marc Tolon. Arthur & the Crunch Cereal Contest. LC 97-76786. (Arthur Chapter Book Ser.: No. 4). (Illus.). 64p. (J). (gr. 2-4). 1998. 12.95 (*0-316-11552-5*) Little.

— Arthur & the Crunch Cereal Contest. LC 97-76786. (Arthur Chapter Book Ser.: No. 4). (Illus.). 64p. (J). (gr. 3-6). 1998. pap. 3.95 (*0-316-11553-3*) Little.

— Arthur & the Crunch Cereal Contest. (Arthur Chapter Book Ser.: No. 4). (J). (gr. 3-6). 1998. pap. 3.95 (*0-316-10546-5*) Little.

— Arthur & the Crunch Cereal Contest. (Arthur Chapter Book Ser.: No. 4). (J). (gr. 3-6). 1998. 9.15 (*0-606-13150-7*, Pub. by Turtleback) Demco.

Brown, Marc Tolon. Arthur & the Lost Diary. (Arthur Chapter Book Ser.: No. 9). 55p. (J). (gr. 3-6). pap. 3.95 (*0-8072-1305-5*) Listening Lib.

Brown, Marc Tolon. Arthur & the Lost Diary. LC PZ7.K883Ar 1998. (Arthur Chapter Book Ser.: No. 9). 64p. (J). (gr. 3-6). 1998. pap. 3.95 (*0-316-11537-1*); pap. 3.95 (*0-316-61004-6*) Little.

***Brown, Marc Tolon.** Arthur & the Lost Diary. unabridged ed. (Arthur Chapter Book Ser.). (J). (gr. 3-6). 1999. pap. 15.98 incl. audio (*0-8072-0404-8*, EFTR200SP) Listening Lib.

— Arthur & the Perfect Brother. (Arthur Chapter Book Ser.: No. 21). 64p. (J). (gr. 3-6). 2000. 13.95 (*0-316-12163-0*); pap. 3.95 (*0-316-12226-2*) Little.

— Arthur & the Perfect Brother. (Illus.). (J). 2000. 9.40 (*0-606-18252-7*) Turtleback.

— Arthur & the Poetry Contest. (J). 1999. pap. 3.95 (*0-316-12153-3*, Pub. by Little) Time Warner.

Brown, Marc Tolon. Arthur & the Poetry Contest. LC 99-35270. (Arthur Chapter Book Ser.: No. 18). (Illus.). 64p. (J). (gr. 2-4). 1999. pap. 3.95 (*0-316-12295-5*) Little.

***Brown, Marc Tolon.** Arthur & the Poetry Contest. LC 99-35270. (Arthur Chapter Book Ser.: No. 18). (Illus.). 64p. (J). (gr. 3-6). 1999. 12.95 (*0-316-12062-6*) Little.

— Arthur & the Popularity Test. (Arthur Chapter Book Ser.: No. 12). 58p. (J). (gr. 3-6). pap. 3.95 (*0-8072-1308-X*) Listening Lib.

Brown, Marc Tolon. Arthur & the Popularity Test. LC 98-66679. (Arthur Chapter Book Ser.: No. 12). (Illus.). 64p. (J). (gr. 2-4). 1998. 12.95 (*0-316-11544-4*); pap. 3.95 (*0-316-11545-2*) Little.

***Brown, Marc Tolon.** Arthur & the Popularity Test. (J). 1999. pap. 3.95 (*0-316-11999-7*, Pub. by Little) Time Warner.

— Arthur & the Scare-Your-Pants-Off Club. (Arthur Chapter Book Ser.: No. 1). 58p. (J). (gr. 3-6). pap. 3.95 (*0-8072-1296-2*) Listening Lib.

B

— Arthur & the Scare-Your-Pants-Off Club. (Arthur Chapter Book Ser.). (J). (gr. 3-6). 1998. pap. 15.98 incl. audio (*0-8072-0376-9*) Listening Lib.

Brown, Marc Tolon. Arthur & the Scare-Your-Pants-Off Club. LC 97-74908. (Arthur Chapter Book Ser.: No. 2). (Illus.). 64p. (J). (gr. 2-4). 1998. 12.95 (*0-316-11548-7*); pap. 3.95 (*0-316-11549-5*) Little.

— Arthur & the Scare-Your-Pants-Off Club. (Arthur Chapter Book Ser.: No. 2). (J). (gr. 3-6). 1998. pap. 3.95 (*0-316-10496-5*) Little.

— Arthur & the Scare-Your-Pants-Off Club. (Arthur Chapter Book Ser.). (J). (gr. 3-6). 1998. 9.15 (*0-606-13151-5*, Pub. by Turtleback) Demco.

— Arthur & the True Francine. LC 87-4136. (Arthur Adventure Ser.). (Illus.). 32p. (J). (ps-3). 1996. pap. 5.95 (*0-316-10949-5*) Little.

— Arthur & the True Francine. (Arthur Adventure Ser.). (Illus.). 32p. (J). (ps-3). 1998. pap. 9.95 incl. audio (*0-316-11946-6*) Little.

Brown, Marc Tolon. Arthur & the True Francine. (Arthur Adventure Ser.). (J). (gr. k-3). 7.98 incl. audio NewSound.

Brown, Marc Tolon. Arthur & the True Francine. LC 87-4136. (Arthur Adventure Ser.). (J). (gr. k-3). 1996. 11.15 (*0-606-09012-6*, Pub. by Turtleback) Demco.

— Arthur at Camp Grade 2 Reading Book. (Learn Along with Arthur Ser.). (Illus.). 32p. (J). (gr. 2-3). 1999. pap. text 2.25 (*1-56189-520-2*) Amer Educ Pub.

— Arthur at School Grade 1 Reading Book. (Learn Along with Arthur Ser.). (Illus.). 32p. (J). (gr. 1-2). 1999. pap. text 2.25 (*1-56189-519-9*) Amer Educ Pub.

— Arthur Babysits. (Arthur Adventure Ser.). 32p. (J). (gr. k-3). 1996. pap. 9.95 incl. audio (*0-316-11103-1*) Little.

— Arthur Babysits. LC 97-139967. (Arthur Adventure Ser.). (Illus.). 32p. (J). (gr. k-3). 1997. 5.95 (*0-316-11134-1*) Little.

— Arthur Babysits. LC 91-46516. (Arthur Adventure Ser.). (J). (gr. k-3). 1994. 10.90 (*0-606-06185-1*, Pub. by Turtleback) Demco.

— Arthur, Clean Your Room. (Step into Reading Ser.: A Step 1 Book). (J). (ps-3). 1999. lib. bdg. 11.99 (*0-679-98467-4*, Pub. by Random Bks Yng Read) Random.

*__Brown, Marc Tolon.__ Arthur Counts! LC 97-75806. (Arthur Ser.). (Illus.). 22p. (J). (ps-k). 1998. 3.99 (*0-679-88462-9*, Pub. by Random Bks Yng Read) Random.

Brown, Marc Tolon. Arthur Decks the Hall. LC 98-65593. (Arthur Ser.). (Illus.). 6p. (J). (ps-k). 1998. 7.99 (*0-679-88472-6*, Pub. by Random Bks Yng Read) Random.

— Arthur Goes Shopping Grade One Math Book. (Learn Along with Arthur Ser.). (Illus.). 32p. (J). (gr. 1-2). 1999. pap. text 2.25 (*1-56189-522-9*) Amer Educ Pub.

— Arthur Goes to Camp. (Arthur Adventure Ser.). (J). (gr. k-3). 1982. 11.15 (*0-606-03970-8*, Pub. by Turtleback) Demco.

— Arthur Goes to School. LC 95-68104. (Arthur Ser.). (Illus.). 10p. (J). (ps-3). 1995. 11.99 (*0-679-86734-1*) Random.

— Arthur in a Pickle. LC 98-43340. (Step into Reading Ser.: A Step 1 Book). (J). (ps-1). 1999. lib. bdg. 11.99 (*0-679-98469-0*) Random.

*__Brown, Marc Tolon.__ Arthur in a Pickle. LC 98-43340. (Step into Reading Ser.: A Step 1 Book). (Illus.). 24p. (J). (ps-3). 1998. pap. 7.99 (*0-679-88469-6*, Pub. by Random Bks Yng Read) Random.

Brown, Marc Tolon. Arthur Lost & Found. LC 97-46992. (Arthur Adventure Ser.). (Illus.). 32p. (J). (ps-3). 1998. 15.95 (*0-316-10912-6*) Little.

*__Brown, Marc Tolon.__ Arthur Lost & Found. (Arthur Adventure Ser.). 32p. (J). 2000. pap. 5.95 (*0-316-10824-3*) Little.

— Arthur Makes the Team. (Arthur Chapter Book Ser.: No. 3). 61p. (J). (gr. 3-6). pap. 3.95 (*0-8072-1297-0*) Listening Lib.

Brown, Marc Tolon. Arthur Makes the Team. LC 97-69736. (Arthur Chapter Book Ser.: No. 3). (Illus.). 64p. (J). (gr. 2-4). 1998. 12.95 (*0-316-11550-9*) Little.

— Arthur Makes the Team. LC 97-69736. (Arthur Chapter Book Ser.: No. 3). (Illus.). 64p. (J). (gr. 3-6). 1998. pap. 3.95 (*0-316-11551-7*) Little.

— Arthur Makes the Team. (Arthur Chapter Book Ser.: No. 3). (J). (gr. 3-6). 1998. pap. 3.95 (*0-316-10536-8*) Little.

— Arthur Makes the Team. (Arthur Chapter Book Ser.: No. 3). (J). (gr. 3-6). 1998. 9.15 (*0-606-13152-3*, Pub. by Turtleback) Demco.

— Arthur Meets the President. (Arthur Adventure Ser.). (J). (gr. k-3). 1920. pap. 71.40 (*0-316-10291-1*) Little.

— Arthur Meets the President. LC 90-13298. (Arthur Adventure Ser.). (Illus.). 32p. (J). (ps-3). 1992. pap. 5.95 (*0-316-11291-7*, Joy St Bks) Little.

— Arthur Meets the President. (Arthur Adventure Ser.). (J). (gr. k-3). 1998. pap. 5.95 (*0-316-10554-6*, Joy St Bks) Little.

— Arthur Meets the President. (Arthur Adventure Ser.). (J). (gr. k-3). 1991. 11.15 (*0-606-02222-8*, Pub. by Turtleback) Demco.

— Arthur on the Farm. (Arthur Ser.). (Illus.). 20p. (J). (ps-k). 1998. 3.99 (*0-679-88461-0*, Pub. by Random Bks Yng Read) Random.

Brown, Marc Tolon. Arthur Rocks with Binky. (Arthur Chapter Book Ser.: No. 11). 61p. (J). (gr. 3-6). pap. 3.95 (*0-8072-1307-1*) Listening Lib.

Brown, Marc Tolon. Arthur Rocks with Binky. LC 98-66440. (Arthur Chapter Book Ser.: No. 11). (Illus.). 64p. (J). (gr. 2-4). 1998. 12.95 (*0-316-11542-8*); pap. 3.95 (*0-316-11543-6*) Little.

*__Brown, Marc Tolon.__ Arthur Rocks with Binky Paper Special Scholastic Edition. (Arthur Chapter Book Ser.: No. 11). (J). (gr. 3-6). 1999. pap. 3.95 (*0-316-10422-1*) Little.

Brown, Marc Tolon. Arthur Tricks the Tooth Fairy. LC 97-25787. (Step into Reading Ser.: A Step 1 Book). (J). (gr. k-3). 1998. lib. bdg. 11.99 (*0-679-98464-X*, Pub. by Random Bks Yng Read) Random.

— Arthur Tricks the Tooth Fairy. LC 97-25787. (Step into Reading Ser.: A Step 1 Book). (Illus.). 24p. (J). (gr. k-3). 1998. pap. 3.99 (*0-679-88464-5*, Pub. by Random Bks Yng Read) Random.

— Arthur Writes a Story. LC 95-43201. (Arthur Adventure Ser.). (Illus.). 32p. (J). (gr. k-3). 1996. 15.95 (*0-316-10916-9*) Little.

— Arthur Writes a Story. (Arthur Adventure Ser.). (J). (gr. k-3). 1998. pap. 5.95 (*0-316-11973-3*) Little.

— Arthur Writes a Story. LC 95-43201. (Arthur Adventure Ser.). (Illus.). 32p. (J). (ps-3). 1998. pap. 5.95 (*0-316-11164-3*) Little.

— Arthur Writes a Story. (Arthur Adventure Ser.). (Illus.). 32p. (J). (ps-3). 1999. 9.95 incl. audio (*0-316-11976-8*) Little.

— Arthur Writes a Story. (Arthur Adventure Ser.). (J). (gr. k-3). 1998. 11.15 (*0-606-13153-1*, Pub. by Turtleback) Demco.

— Arthur's All Star Game Grade 3 Math Book. (Learn Along with Arthur Ser.). (Illus.). 32p. (J). (gr. 3-4). 1999. pap. text 2.25 (*1-56189-524-5*) Amer Educ Pub.

— Arthur's April Fool. (Arthur Adventure Ser.). (Illus.). 32p. (J). (ps-3). 1995. 9.95 incl. audio (*0-316-11181-3*) Little.

— Arthur's April Fool. (Arthur Adventure Ser.). (J). (gr. k-3). 1998. pap. 5.95 (*0-316-10555-4*, Joy St Bks) Little.

— Arthur's April Fool. (Arthur Adventure Ser.). (J). (gr. k-3). 1983. 11.15 (*0-606-03987-2*, Pub. by Turtleback) Demco.

— Arthur's B-Day. 1995. 39.95 (*1-57135-082-9*) Living Bks.

— Arthur's B-Day. 1995. lib. bdg. 119.95 (*1-57135-083-7*) Living Bks.

— Arthur's Baby. LC 87-3988. (Arthur Adventure Ser.). (Illus.). 32p. (J). (ps-3). 1990. pap. 5.95 (*0-316-11007-8*, Joy St Bks) Little.

— Arthur's Baby. (Arthur Adventure Ser.). (Illus.). 30p. (J). (gr. k-3). 1998. 5.95 (*0-316-11858-3*) Little.

— Arthur's Baby. (Arthur Adventure Ser.). (J). (gr. k-3). 1987. 11.15 (*0-606-03035-2*, Pub. by Turtleback) Demco.

— Arthur's Birthday. (Arthur Adventure Ser.). (Illus.). 30p. (J). (ps-k). 1998. 5.95 (*0-316-11857-5*) Little.

— Arthur's Birthday. (Arthur Adventure Ser.). (Illus.). 32p. (J). (ps-3). 1998. pap. 17.95 (*0-316-11588-6*) Little.

— Arthur's Birthday. (Arthur Adventure Ser.). (J). (gr. k-3). 1997. cd-rom 23.75 (*1-57135-301-1*) Living Bks.

— Arthur's Birthday. LC 88-25912. (Arthur Adventure Ser.). (J). (gr. k-3). 1989. 11.15 (*0-606-06186-X*, Pub. by Turtleback) Demco.

*__Brown, Marc Tolon.__ Arthur's Boo-Boo Book: With Peel-Off Stickers for First Aid Fun! LC 97-75906. (Arthur Ser.). (Illus.). 6p. (J). (ps-k). 1998. 7.99 (*0-679-88465-3*, Pub. by Random Bks Yng Read) Random.

Brown, Marc Tolon. Arthur's Chicken Pox. (Arthur Adventure Ser.). 32p. (J). (ps-3). 1998. pap. 9.95 incl. audio (*0-316-11947-4*) Little.

*__Brown, Marc Tolon.__ Arthur's Chicken Pox. (Arthur Adventure Ser.). (Illus.). 30p. (J). (ps-k). 1999. 5.95 (*0-316-11953-9*, Joy St Bks) Little.

Brown, Marc Tolon. Arthur's Chicken Pox. (Arthur Adventure Ser.). (J). (gr. k-3). 1994. 11.15 (*0-606-08691-9*, Pub. by Turtleback) Demco.

— Arthur's Christmas. (Arthur Adventure Ser.). (J). (gr. k-3). 1996. pap. 5.95 (*0-316-11536-3*) Little.

*__Brown, Marc Tolon.__ Arthur's Christmas. (Arthur Adventure Ser.). 32p. (J). (ps-3). 1999. pap. 9.95 incl. audio (*0-316-11964-4*) Little.

Brown, Marc Tolon. Arthur's Christmas. (Arthur Adventure Ser.). (J). (gr. k-3). 1984. 11.15 (*0-606-03988-0*, Pub. by Turtleback) Demco.

— Arthur's Computer Disaster. LC 96-42418. (Arthur Adventure Ser.). (Illus.). 32p. (J). (ps-3). 1997. 15.95 (*0-316-11016-7*) Little.

*__Brown, Marc Tolon.__ Arthur's Computer Disaster. (Arthur Adventure Ser.). (Illus.). 32p. (J). (gr. k-3). 1999. pap. 5.95 (*0-316-10534-1*) Little.

— Arthur's Computer Disaster. (J). 1999. pap. 5.95 (*0-316-12373-0*, Pub. by Little) Time Warner.

Brown, Marc Tolon. Arthur's Eyes. (Arthur Adventure Ser.). (Illus.). 32p. (J). (gr. k-3). 1986. pap. 5.95 (*0-316-11069-8*, Joy St Bks) Little.

— Arthur's Eyes. LC 79-11734. (Arthur Adventure Ser.). (J). (gr. k-3). 1979. 11.15 (*0-606-03716-0*, Pub. by Turtleback) Demco.

— Arthur's Family Treasury. LC 99-26215. (Illus.). 96p. (J). (ps-3). 1999. 18.95 (*0-316-12147-9*) Little.

— Arthur's Family Vacation. (Arthur Adventure Ser.). (Illus.). 32p. (J). (gr. k-3). 1995. pap. 5.95 (*0-316-10958-4*) Little.

— Arthur's Family Vacation. (Arthur Adventure Ser.). (Illus.). 32p. (J). (ps-3). 1996. pap. 9.95 incl. audio (*0-316-11043-4*) Little.

— Arthur's Family Vacation. (Arthur Adventure Ser.). (J). (gr. k-3). 1993. 11.15 (*0-606-07209-8*, Pub. by Turtleback) Demco.

*__Brown, Marc Tolon.__ Arthur's Fire Drill. LC 99-34964. (Step into Reading Ser.: Sticker Books). (Illus.). 24p. (J). (gr. k-3). 2000. lib. bdg. 11.99 (*0-679-98476-3*, Pub. by Random Bks Yng Read) Random.

— Arthur's First Kiss. LC 00-38714. (Step into Reading Ser.: Sticker Books). (Illus.). (J). 2001. pap. 3.99 (*0-375-80602-4*, Pub. by Knopf Bks Yng Read) Random.

Brown, Marc Tolon. Arthur's First Sleepover. LC 93-46113. (Arthur Adventure Ser.). 32p. (J). (gr. k-3). 1994. 15.95 (*0-316-11445-6*) Little.

— Arthur's First Sleepover. LC 99-192062. (Arthur Adventure Ser.). (Illus.). 32p. (J). (ps-3). 1996. pap. 5.95 (*0-316-11049-3*) Little.

— Arthur's First Sleepover. (Arthur Adventure Ser.). 32p. (J). (ps-3). 1998. pap. 9.95 incl. audio (*0-316-11948-2*) Little.

— Arthur's First Sleepover. (Arthur Adventure Ser.). (J). (gr. k-3). 1998. pap. 5.95 (*0-316-11974-1*) Little.

— Arthur's First Sleepover. (Arthur Adventure Ser.). (Illus.). 30p. (J). (ps-k). 1999. 5.95 (*0-316-10560-0*, Joy St Bks) Little.

— Arthur's First Sleepover. LC 93-46113. (Arthur Adventure Ser.). (J). (gr. k-3). 1994. 11.40 (*0-606-10128-4*) Turtleback.

— Arthur's Halloween. (Arthur Adventure Ser.). (J). (gr. k-3). 1989. pap. 71.40 (*0-316-11004-3*) Little.

— Arthur's Halloween. (Arthur Adventure Ser.). (J). (gr. k-3). 1996. pap. 5.95 (*0-316-11516-9*) Little.

— Arthur's Halloween. (Arthur Adventure Ser.). (Illus.). 32p. (J). (ps-3). 1996. pap. 9.95 incl. audio (*0-316-11105-8*) Little.

— Arthur's Halloween. (Arthur Adventure Ser.). (J). (gr. k-3). 1982. 11.15 (*0-606-03989-9*, Pub. by Turtleback) Demco.

— Arthur's Lost Puppy. LC 99-58251. (Step into Reading Ser.). (Illus.). 24p. (J). (gr. k-3). 2000. pap. 3.99 (*0-679-88466-1*, Pub. by Random Bks Yng Read) Random.

*__Brown, Marc Tolon.__ Arthur's Lost Puppy. (Step into Reading Ser.: Sticker Books). (Illus.). 24p. (J). (gr. k-3). 2000. lib. bdg. 11.99 (*0-679-98466-6*, Pub. by Random Bks Yng Read) Random.

Brown, Marc Tolon. Arthur's Magic Math Glasses Grade 2 Math Book. (Learn Along with Arthur Ser.). (Illus.). 32p. (J). (gr. 2-3). 1999. pap. text 2.25 (*1-56189-523-7*) Amer Educ Pub.

— Arthur's Messy Room. LC 98-43341. (J). 1999. 3.99 (*0-679-88467-X*) Random.

Brown, Marc Tolon. Arthur's Mystery Envelope. (Arthur Chapter Book Ser.: No. 1). 58p. (J). (gr. 3-6). pap. 3.95 (*0-8072-1295-4*) Listening Lib.

Brown, Marc Tolon. Arthur's Mystery Envelope. LC 97-74756. (Arthur Chapter Book Ser.: No. 1). (Illus.). 64p. (J). (gr. 2-4). 1998. pap. 3.95 (*0-316-11547-9*) Little.

— Arthur's Mystery Envelope. LC 97-74756. (Arthur Chapter Book Ser.: No. 1). (Illus.). 64p. (J). (gr. 3-6). 1998. 12.95 (*0-316-11546-0*) Little.

*__Brown, Marc Tolon.__ Arthur's Mystery Envelope. (Arthur Chapter Book Ser.: No. 1). (J). (gr. 3-6). 1998. pap. 3.95 (*0-316-10464-7*) Little.

— Arthur's Mystery Envelope. (Arthur Chapter Book Ser.). (J). (gr. 3-6). 12.78 incl. audio NewSound.

Brown, Marc Tolon. Arthur's Mystery Envelope. (Arthur Chapter Book Ser.: No. 1). (J). (gr. 3-6). 1998. 9.15 (*0-606-13154-X*, Pub. by Turtleback) Demco.

— Arthur's Mystery Envelope. unabridged ed. (Arthur Chapter Book Ser.). (J). (gr. 3-6). 1998. pap. 15.98 incl. audio (*0-8072-0372-6*, FTR187SP) Listening Lib.

— Arthur's Neighborhood. LC 96-68300. (Arthur Ser.). (Illus.). 10p. (J). (ps-3). 1996. 11.99 (*0-679-86737-6*) Random.

— Arthur's New Baby Book. LC 99-70231. (Arthur Ser.). (Illus.). 12p. (J). (ps-k). 1999. pap. 12.99 (*0-679-88463-7*, Pub. by Random Bks Yng Read) Random.

— Arthur's New Puppy. LC 92-46342. (Arthur Adventure Ser.). 32p. (J). (gr. k-3). 1993. 15.95 (*0-316-11355-7*, Joy St Bks) Little.

— Arthur's New Puppy. LC 92-46342. (Arthur Adventure Ser.). (Illus.). 32p. (J). (ps-3). 1995. pap. 5.95 (*0-316-10921-5*) Little.

— Arthur's New Puppy. LC 97-139977. (Arthur Adventure Ser.). (Illus.). 32p. (J). (ps-k). 1997. 5.95 (*0-316-11133-3*) Little.

— Arthur's New Puppy. (Arthur Adventure Ser.). (Illus.). 32p. (J). (ps-3). 1998. pap. 9.95 incl. audio (*0-316-11949-0*) Little.

Brown, Marc Tolon. Arthur's New Puppy. (Arthur Adventure Ser.). (J). (gr. k-3). 7.98 incl. audio NewSound.

Brown, Marc Tolon. Arthur's New Puppy. (Arthur Adventure Ser.). (J). (gr. k-3). 1993. 11.15 (*0-606-07210-1*, Pub. by Turtleback) Demco.

— Arthur's Nose. (Arthur Adventure Ser.). (J). (gr. k-3). 1976. 11.15 (*0-606-03971-6*, Pub. by Turtleback) Demco.

*__Brown, Marc Tolon.__ Arthur's Perfect Christmas. (Illus.). 40p. (J). (ps-3). 2000. 15.95 (*0-316-11968-7*, Pub. by Little) Time Warner.

Brown, Marc Tolon. Arthur's Pet Business. LC 89-26991. (Arthur Adventure Ser.). 32p. (J). (ps-3). 1990. 15.95 (*0-316-11262-3*, Joy St Bks) Little.

— Arthur's Pet Business. LC 89-26991. (Arthur Adventure Ser.). (Illus.). 32p. (J). (ps-3). 1993. pap. 5.95 (*0-316-11316-6*) Little.

Brown, Marc Tolon. Arthur's Pet Business. (Arthur Adventure Ser.). (J). (gr. k-3). 1990. 11.15 (*0-606-05126-0*, Pub. by Turtleback) Demco.

Brown, Marc Tolon. Arthur's Reading Race. (Step into Reading Ser.: Sticker Books). (J). (ps-3). 1996. lib. bdg. 11.99 (*0-679-96738-9*, Pub. by Random Bks Yng Read) Random.

— Arthur's Reading Race. LC 95-38987. (Step into Reading Ser.: Sticker Books). (Illus.). 24p. (J). (ps-3). 1996. pap. 3.99 (*0-679-86738-4*, Pub. by Random Bks Yng Read) Random.

— Arthur's Really Helpful Bedtime Stories. LC 98-3663. (Arthur Ser.). 44p. (J). (ps-3). 1998. 14.99 (*0-679-88468-8*, Pub. by Random Bks Yng Read); lib. bdg. 15.99 (*0-679-98468-2*, Pub. by Random Bks Yng Read) Random.

— Arthur's Really Helpful Word Book. LC 96-54227. (Arthur Ser.). (J). (ps-1). 1997. lib. bdg. 14.99 (*0-679-98735-5*, Pub. by Random Bks Yng Read) Random.

— Arthur's Really Helpful Word Book. LC 96-54227. (Arthur Ser.). (Illus.). 40p. (J). (ps-1). 1997. 12.99 (*0-679-88735-0*, Pub. by Random Bks Yng Read) Random.

— Arthur's Surprise Grade 3 Reading Book. (Learn Along with Arthur Ser.). (J). (gr. 2-4). 1999. pap. text 2.25 (*1-56189-521-0*) Amer Educ Pub.

*__Brown, Marc Tolon.__ Arthur's Teacher Moves In. LC 99-43720. (Arthur Adventure Ser.). 32p. (J). (ps-3). 2000. 15.95 (*0-316-11979-2*) Little.

Brown, Marc Tolon. Arthur's Teacher Trouble. (Arthur Adventure Ser.). (J). (gr. k-3). 1994. pap. 23.75 incl. cd-rom (*1-57135-017-9*) Living Bks.

— Arthur's Teacher Trouble, Class Set. (Arthur Adventure Ser.). (J). (gr. k-3). 1995. pap. 79.95 (*1-57135-018-7*); lib. bdg. 99.95 (*1-57135-019-5*) Living Bks.

— Arthur's Teacher Trouble. (Arthur Adventure Ser.). (J). (gr. k-3). 1986. 11.15 (*0-606-04161-3*, Pub. by Turtleback) Demco.

— Arthur's $10 Allowance. (Illus.). (J). 1996. write for info. (*0-316-11512-6*) Little.

— Arthur's Thanksgiving. (Arthur Adventure Ser.). (J). (gr. k-3). 1989. pap. 71.40 (*0-316-11005-1*) Little.

— Arthur's Thanksgiving. (Arthur Adventure Ser.). (J). (gr. k-3). 1996. pap. 5.95 (*0-316-11513-4*) Little.

— Arthur's Thanksgiving. LC 83-798. (Arthur Adventure Ser.). (J). (gr. k-3). 1984. 11.15 (*0-606-03990-2*, Pub. by Turtleback) Demco.

Brown, Marc Tolon. Arthur's Tooth. (Arthur Adventure Ser.). (J). (gr. k-3). 1985. 11.15 (*0-606-11058-5*, Pub. by Turtleback) Demco.

— Arthur's Truck Adventure. (Arthur Ser.). (Illus.). 12p. (J). (ps-k). 2000. bds. 7.99 (*0-679-88470-X*, Pub. by Random Bks Yng Read) Random.

— Arthur's TV Trouble. LC 94-48816. (Arthur Adventure Ser.). (Illus.). 32p. (J). (gr. k-3). 1995. 15.95 (*0-316-10919-3*) Little.

Brown, Marc Tolon. Arthur's TV Trouble. (Arthur Adventure Ser.). (Illus.). 32p. (J). (ps-3). 1999. 9.95 incl. audio (*0-316-11594-0*) Little.

— Arthur's TV Trouble. (Arthur Adventure Ser.). (J). (gr. k-3). 1997. 11.15 (*0-606-12620-1*, Pub. by Turtleback) Demco.

— Arthur's TV Trouble. LC 94-48816. (Arthur Adventure Ser.). (Illus.). 32p. (J). (ps-3). 1997. reprint ed. pap. 5.95 (*0-316-11047-7*) Little.

— Arthur's TV Trouble. rev. ed. (Arthur Adventure Ser.). (J). (gr. k-3). 1997. pap. 5.95 (*0-316-11959-8*) Little.

— Arthur's Underwear. LC 99-25702. (Arthur Adventure Ser.). 32p. (J). (gr. k-3). 1999. 15.95 (*0-316-11012-4*) Little.

— Arthur's Valentine. (Arthur Adventure Ser.). 32p. (J). (ps-3). 2000. pap. 9.95 incl. audio (*0-316-11866-4*) Little.

Brown, Marc Tolon. Arthur's Valentine. (Arthur Adventure Ser.). (J). (gr. k-3). 1980. 11.15 (*0-606-03717-9*, Pub. by Turtleback) Demco.

— Arthur's Valentine Countdown. LC 99-70230. (Arthur Ser.). (Illus.). 10p. (J). (ps-3). 1999. pap. 7.99 (*0-679-88475-0*, Pub. by Random Bks Yng Read) Random.

— Arturo y el Dia de Accion de Gracias. (SPA.). 2000. 6.95 (*1-880507-79-X*) Lectorum Pubns.

— Arturo y los Terribles Gemelos. LC 99-31982. (Arthur Adventure Ser.).Tr. of Arthur Babysits. (SPA., Illus.). (J). (gr. k-2). 2000. pap. 6.95 (*1-880507-65-X*) Lectorum Pubns.

Brown, Marc Tolon. Arturo y sus Problemas con el Profesor. (Arthur Adventure Ser.).Tr. of Arthur's Teacher Trouble. (SPA.). (J). (gr. k-3). 1986. 11.40 (*0-606-06188-6*) Turtleback.

— Baby Rhymes. 16p. (J). 1998. 7.99 (*0-525-45610-4*) NAL.

*__Brown, Marc Tolon.__ BINKY Rules. (Arthur Chapter Book Ser.: No. 24). (Illus.). 64p. (J). (gr. 2-4). 2000. 13.95 (*0-316-12193-2*, Pub. by Little); pap. 3.95 (*0-316-12333-1*, Pub. by Little) Time Warner.

Brown, Marc Tolon. The Bionic Bunny Show. (Reading Rainbow Ser.). (Illus.). 32p. (J). (ps-3). 1984. 14.95 (*0-316-11120-1*, Joy St Bks) Little.

— The Bionic Bunny Show. 1985. 11.95 (*0-606-02541-3*, Pub. by Turtleback) Demco.

— Buster Baxter, Cat Saver. LC 99-42427. (Arthur Chapter Book Ser.: No. 19). (Illus.). 64p. (J). (gr. 2-4). 2000. 12.95 (*0-316-12111-8*); pap. 3.95 (*0-316-12220-3*) Little.

*__Brown, Marc Tolon.__ Buster Baxter, Cat Saver. (Illus.). (J). 1999. 9.40 (*0-606-18250-0*) Turtleback.

Brown, Marc Tolon. Buster Makes the Grade. LC 99-18410. (Arthur Chapter Book Ser.: No. 16). (Illus.). 64p. (J). (gr. 2-4). 1999. pap. 3.95 (*0-316-12277-7*) Little.

*__Brown, Marc Tolon.__ Buster Makes the Grade. (J). 1999. pap. 3.95 (*0-316-12262-9*, Pub. by Little) Time Warner.

— Buster's Dino Dilemma. (Arthur Chapter Book Ser.: No. 7). 58p. (J). (gr. 3-6). pap. 3.95 (*0-8072-1303-9*) Listening Lib.

Brown, Marc Tolon. Buster's Dino Dilemma. (Arthur Chapter Book Ser.: No. 7). (Illus.). 64p. (J). (gr. 3-6). 1998. 12.95 (*0-316-11559-2*) Little.

— Buster's Dino Dilemma. LC 98-65023. (Arthur Chapter Book Ser.: Vol. 7). (Illus.). 64p. (J). (gr. 2-4). 1998. pap. 3.95 (*0-316-11560-6*) Little.

An Asterisk (*) at the beginning of an entry indicates that the title is appearing for the first time.

***Brown, Marc Tolon.** Buster's Dino Dilemma. unabridged ed. (Arthur Chapter Book Ser.). (J). (gr. 3-6). 1999. pap. 15.98 incl. audio (*0-8072-0397-1*, EFTR198SP) Listening Lib.

— Buster's New Friend. (Arthur Chapter Book Ser.: No. 23). (Illus.). 64p. (J). (gr. 2-4). 2000. 13.95 (*0-316-12212-2*) Little.

— Buster's New Friend. (Arthur Chapter Book Ser.: Vol. 23). (Illus.). 64p. (J). (gr. 2-4). 2000. pap. 3.95 (*0-316-12307-2*) Little.

— El Cachorrito de Arturo. LC 99-25104. (SPA., Illus.). (J). 1999. 6.95 (*1-880507-59-5*) Lectorum Pubns.

— El Cumpleanos de Arturo. (SPA.). 2000. 0.00 (*1-880507-78-1*) Lectorum Pubns.

Brown, Marc Tolon. D. W. All Wet. LC 87-15752. (D. W. Ser.). (Illus.). 32p. (J). (ps-3). 1988. 15.95 (*0-316-11077-9*, Joy St Bks) Little.

— D. W. All Wet. (D. W. Ser.). (Illus.). 24p. (J). (ps-k). 1997. 5.95 (*0-316-11172-4*) Little.

— D. W. All Wet. (D. W. Ser.). (J). (gr. k-2). 1991. 11.15 (*0-606-13299-6*, Pub. by Turtleback) Demco.

— D. W. Flips. (D. W. Ser.). (Illus.). 32p. (J). (gr. k-2). 1987. 15.95 (*0-316-11239-9*, Joy St Bks) Little.

— D. W. Flips. (D. W. Ser.). (J). (gr. k-2). 1991. write for info. (*0-318-68259-1*); pap. 5.95 (*0-316-11269-0*) Little.

— D. W. Flips. (D. W. Ser.). (Illus.). 24p. (J). (ps-k). 1997. 5.95 (*0-316-11523-1*) Little.

— D. W. Flips. (D. W. Ser.). (J). (gr. k-2). 1991. 11.15 (*0-606-13300-3*, Pub. by Turtleback) Demco.

— D. W., Go to Your Room! LC 98-42841. (D. W. Ser.). (Illus.). 32p. (J). (ps-3). 1999. 13.95 (*0-316-10905-3*) Little.

— D. W. Rides Again! (D. W. Ser.). (J). (gr. k-2). pap. 4.95 (*0-614-15673-4*) Little.

— D. W. Rides Again! LC 93-7192. (D. W. Ser.). (Illus.). 24p. (J). (ps-3). 1993. 14.95 (*0-316-11356-5*) Little.

— D. W. Rides Again! LC 98-164945. (D. W. Ser.). (Illus.). 52p. (J). (ps-k). 1998. 5.95 (*0-316-11128-7*) Little.

— D. W. Rides Again! (D. W. Ser.). (J). (gr. k-2). 1993. 11.15 (*0-606-08722-2*, Pub. by Turtleback) Demco.

— D. W. the Picky Eater. LC 94-25674. (D. W. Ser.). (Illus.). 32p. (J). (gr. k-2). 1995. 14.95 (*0-316-10957-6*) Little.

— D. W. the Picky Eater. (D. W. Ser.). (Illus.). (J). (gr. k-2). 1997. 4.95 (*0-614-28847-9*) Little.

— D. W. the Picky Eater. LC 94-25674. (D. W. Ser.). (Illus.). 32p. (J). (ps-3). 1997. pap. 5.95 (*0-316-11048-5*) Little.

— D. W. the Picky Eater. (D. W. Ser.). (J). (gr. k-2). 1997. pap. 5.95 (*0-316-10453-1*) Little.

— D. W. the Picky Eater. (D. W. Ser.). (J). (gr. k-2). 1997. 11.15 (*0-606-13301-1*, Pub. by Turtleback) Demco.

— D. W. Thinks Big. LC 98-164841. (D. W. Ser.). (Illus.). 52p. (J). (ps-k). 1998. 5.95 (*0-316-11112-0*) Little.

Brown, Marc Tolon. D. W. Thinks Big. (D. W. Ser.). (J). (gr. k-2). 1995. 11.15 (*0-606-13302-X*) Turtleback.

Brown, Marc Tolon. D. W. Thinks Big: With Plush Toy. (D. W. Ser.). (Illus.). 32p. (J). (ps-3). 1999. pap. 17.95 (*0-316-11966-0*) Little.

— D. W.'s Color Book. LC 97-67314. (D. W. Ser.). (J). (gr. k-2). 1997. pap. 3.99 (*0-679-88439-4*, Pub. by Random Bks Yng Read) Random.

— D. W.'s Lost Blankie. LC 97-6944. (D. W. Ser.). (Illus.). 32p. (J). (ps-3). 1998. 13.95 (*0-316-10914-2*) Little.

***Brown, Marc Tolon.** D. W.'S Lost Blankie. (D. W. Ser.). 24p. (J). (ps-1). 2000. pap. 5.95 (*0-316-11595-9*) Little.

Brown, Marc Tolon. Dinosaurs, Beware! A Safety Guide. (J). 1982. 12.90 (*0-606-03972-4*, Pub. by Turtleback) Demco.

— Favorite Hand Rhymes, 1 vol. (Illus.). 16p. (ps). 1999. bds. 7.99 (*0-525-45997-9*, Dutton Child) Peng Put Young Read.

***Brown, Marc Tolon.** La Fiesta de Arturo. (Arthur Adventure Ser.).Tr. of Arthur's First Sleepover. (SPA., Illus.). (J). (gr. k-3). 1999. pap. 6.95 (*1-880507-64-1*) Lectorum Pubns.

Brown, Marc Tolon. Finger Rhymes. LC 80-11492. (Illus.). 32p. (J). (ps-3). 1996. pap. 5.99 (*0-14-055815-2*, PuffinBks) Peng Put Young Read.

— Finger Rhymes. LC 80-11492. 1996. 10.19 (*0-606-09275-7*, Pub. by Turtleback) Demco.

— Francine, Believe it or Not. LC 98-75148. (Arthur Chapter Book Ser.: No. 14). (Illus.). 64p. (J). (gr. 2-4). 1999. 12.95 (*0-316-12011-1*) Little.

***Brown, Marc Tolon.** Francine, Believe It or Not. LC 98-75148. (Arthur Chapter Book Ser.: No. 14). (Illus.). 64p. (J). (gr. 3-6). 1999. pap. 3.95 (*0-316-12258-0*) Little.

— Francine, Believe It or Not: Special Scholastic Edition. (Frog Band Ser.). (J). 1999. pap. 3.95 (*0-316-10463-9*) Little.

— Francine the Superstar. (Arthur Chapter Book Ser.: No. 22). (Illus.). 64p. (J). (gr. 3-6). 2000. 13.95 (*0-316-12227-0*) Little.

— Francine the Superstar. Krensky, Stephen, tr. (Arthur Chapter Book Ser.: No. 22). (Illus.). 64p. (J). (gr. 3-6). 2000. pap. 3.95 (*0-316-12250-5*) Little.

— Francine the Superstar. (Illus.). (J). 2000. 13.40 (*0-606-18253-5*) Turtleback.

Brown, Marc Tolon. Glasses for D. W. (Step into Reading Ser.: Sticker Books). (J). (gr. k-2). 1996. lib. bdg. 11.99 (*0-679-96740-0*) McKay.

— Glasses for D. W. LC 95-25763. (Step into Reading Ser.: Sticker Books). (Illus.). 24p. (J). (ps-3). 1996. pap. 3.99 (*0-679-86740-6*) Random.

— Hand Rhymes. (Illus.). 32p. (J). (ps-1). 1993. pap. 5.99 (*0-14-054939-0*, PuffinBks) Peng Put Young Read.

— King Arthur. (Arthur Chapter Book Ser.: No. 13). (Illus.). 64p. (J). (gr. 3-6). 1999. 13.95 (*0-316-12178-9*); pap. 3.95 (*0-316-12241-6*) Little.

***Brown, Marc Tolon.** King Arthur. (J). 1999. pap. 3.95 (*0-316-10667-4*, Pub. by Little) Time Warner.

Brown, Marc Tolon. Kiss Hello, Kiss Good-Bye. LC 96-70075. (Arthur Ser.). (J). (ps). 1997. 4.99 (*0-679-86739-2*) Random.

Brown, Marc Tolon. Locked in the Library. (Arthur Chapter Book Ser.: No. 6). 58p. (J). (gr. 3-6). pap. 3.95 (*0-8072-1300-4*) Listening Lib.

Brown, Marc Tolon. Locked in the Library. LC 97-75973. (Arthur Chapter Book Ser.: No. 6). (Illus.). 64p. (J). (gr. 2-4). 1998. 12.95 (*0-316-11557-6*); pap. 3.95 (*0-316-11558-4*) Little.

— Locked in the Library. unabridged ed. (Arthur Chapter Book Ser.). (J). (gr. 3-6). 1998. pap. 15.98 incl. audio (*0-8072-0388-2*, FTR192SP) Listening Lib.

— Monster's Lunchbox. LC 94-26103. 8p. (J). (gr. k-3). 1995. 14.95 (*0-316-11313-1*) Little.

— Muffy's Secret Admirer. LC 99-35312. (Arthur Chapter Book Ser.: No. 17). (Illus.). 64p. (J). (gr. 2-4). 1999. pap. 3.95 (*0-316-12230-0*) Little.

— Muffy's Secret Admirer. LC 99-35312. (Arthur Chapter Book Ser.: No. 17). (Illus.). 64p. (J). (gr. 3-6). 1999. 12.95 (*0-316-12017-0*) Little.

Brown, Marc Tolon. The Mystery of the Stolen Bike. (Arthur Chapter Book Ser.: No. 8). 59p. (J). (gr. 3-6). pap. 3.95 (*0-8072-1304-7*) Listening Lib.

Brown, Marc Tolon. The Mystery of the Stolen Bike. LC 98-65411. (Arthur Chapter Book Ser.: No. 8). (Illus.). 64p. (J). (gr. 3-6). 1998. 12.95 (*0-316-11570-3*); pap. 3.95 (*0-316-11571-1*) Little.

***Brown, Marc Tolon.** The Mystery of the Stolen Bike. unabridged ed. (Arthur Chapter Book Ser.). (J). (gr. 3-6). 1999. pap. 15.98 incl. audio (*0-8072-0401-3*, EFTR199SP) Listening Lib.

Brown, Marc Tolon. 1, 2, 3 Monsters on Parade! (Arthur Ser.). 24p. (J). (ps-3). 1998. pap. 3.99 (*0-679-89283-4*, Pub. by Random Bks Yng Read) Random.

— Perfect Pigs: An Introduction to Manners. (J). 1983. 12.15 (*0-606-03991-0*, Pub. by Turtleback) Demco.

— Play Rhymes. (J). 1993. 9.94 (*0-606-05977-6*, Pub. by Turtleback) Demco.

— Reading & Math. (Learn Along with Arthur Ser.). (Illus.). 32p. (J). (gr. 1-4). 1999. pap. 10.95 (*1-56189-525-3*) Amer Educ Pub.

— Say the Magic Word. LC 96-70076. (Arthur Ser.). (J). (ps). 1997. 4.99 (*0-679-86736-8*, Pub. by Random Bks Yng Read) Random.

— Say the Magic Word. (Arthur Ser.). (Illus.). (J). (ps). 1997. 4.99 (*0-614-28921-1*) Random Bks Yng Read.

— Spooky Riddles. LC 83-6051. (Illus.). 48p. (J). (gr. k-3). 1983. 7.99 (*0-394-86093-4*) Beginner.

— Stop, Go, Listen. 1997. lib. bdg. 11.99 (*0-679-96735-4*) Random Bks Yng Read.

— The True Francine. (Illus.). 32p. (J). (ps-3). 1981. 15.95 (*0-316-11212-7*, Joy St Bks) Little.

***Brown, Marc Tolon.** Las Vacaciones de Arturo. LC 99-25122. (SPA., Illus.). (J). (ps-3). 1999. 6.95 (*1-880507-60-9*) Lectorum Pubns.

Brown, Marc Tolon. Where's Arthur's Gerbil? LC 97-67315. (Arthur Ser.). (J). (ps). 1997. 3.99 (*0-679-88460-2*, Pub. by Random Bks Yng Read) Random.

Brown, Marc Tolon. Who's in Love with Arthur? (Arthur Chapter Book Ser.: No. 10). 57p. (J). (gr. 3-6). pap. 3.95 (*0-8072-1306-3*) Listening Lib.

Brown, Marc Tolon. Who's in Love with Arthur? LC 98-66009. (Arthur Chapter Book Ser.: No. 10). (Illus.). 64p. (J). (gr. 2-4). 1998. 12.95 (*0-316-11539-8*); pap. 3.95 (*0-316-11540-1*) Little.

***Brown, Marc Tolon.** Who's in Love with Arthur? (J). 1999. pap. 3.95 (*0-316-10671-2*, Pub. by Little) Time Warner.

Brown, Marc Tolon. Wings & Things. LC 81-12095. (Bright & Early Bks.: No. 26). (Illus.). 36p. (J). (ps-1). 1982. 7.99 (*0-394-85130-7*, XBYR, Pub. by Random Bks Yng Read); lib. bdg. 11.99 (*0-394-95130-1*, Pub. by Random Bks Yng Read) Random.

— Witches Four. (Illus.). 42p. (J). (ps-3). 1993. lib. bdg. 19.93 (*0-8368-0893-2*) Gareth Stevens Inc.

— The Witch's Pocketbook. (J). 1997. write for info. (*0-316-11315-8*) Little.

— Your First Garden Book. (Illus.). (J). (gr. 1 up). 1981. 12.95 (*0-316-11217-8*); mass mkt. 6.95 (*0-316-11215-1*) Little.

Brown, Marc Tolon, ed. Hand Rhymes. LC 84-25918. 32p. (J). (ps-1). 1985. 15.99 (*0-525-44201-4*, Dutton Child) Peng Put Young Read.

Brown, Marc Tolon. The Family Read-Aloud Christmas Treasury. 144p. (J). (ps up). 1995. pap. 12.95 (*0-316-53284-3*) Little.

— Read-Aloud Rhymes for the Very Young. LC 86-7147. 112p. (J). (ps-3). 1986. 20.00 (*0-394-87218-5*, Pub. by Knopf Bks Yng Read) Random.

Brown, Marc Tolon. Scared Silly! A Book for the Brave. LC 93-13501. 64p. (J). (gr. k-3). 1994. 18.95 (*0-316-11360-3*) Little.

Brown, Marc Tolon, reader. Arthur's Eyes. (Arthur Adventure Ser.). (Illus.). (J). (ps-3). 1993. pap. 9.95 incl. audio (*0-316-11338-7*) Little.

— Arthur's Pet Business. (Arthur Adventure Ser.). (Illus.). 32p. (J). (ps-3). 1995. 9.95 incl. audio (*0-316-11182-1*) Little.

— Arthur's Teacher Trouble. (Arthur Adventure Ser.). (Illus.). (J). (gr. k-3). 1994. pap. 9.95 incl. audio (*0-316-11389-1*) Little.

— Arthur's Tooth. (Arthur Adventure Ser.). (Illus.). (J). (gr. k-3). 1993. pap. 9.95 incl. audio (*0-316-11339-5*) Little.

Brown, Marc Tolon & Krensky, Stephen. Dinosaurs, Beware! A Safety Guide. LC 82-15207. (Illus.). 32p. (J). (gr. k-3). 1984. pap. 7.95 (*0-316-11219-4*, Joy St Bks) Little.

— Perfect Pigs: An Introduction to Manners. LC 83-746. (Illus.). 32p. (J). (gr. k-3). 1983. pap. 6.95 (*0-316-11080-9*, Joy St Bks) Little.

Brown, Marc Tolon, et al. Arthur & the Cootie Catcher. LC 98-52061. (Arthur Chapter Book Ser.: No. 15). (Illus.). 64p. (J). (gr. 2-4). 1999. 12.95 (*0-316-11993-8*) Little.

— Arthur & the True Francine. LC 96-224803. (Arthur Adventure Ser.). (Illus.). 32p. (J). (ps-3). 1996. reprint ed. 15.95 (*0-316-11136-8*) Little.

— Arthur Babysits. LC 91-46516. (Arthur Adventure Ser.). (Illus.). 32p. (J). (ps-3). 1992. 15.95 (*0-316-11293-3*, Joy St Bks) Little.

— Arthur Babysits. (Arthur Adventure Ser.). (Illus.). (J). (ps-3). 1993. pap. 9.95 incl. audio (*0-316-11336-0*) Little.

— Arthur Babysits. LC 91-46516. (Arthur Adventure Ser.). (Illus.). 32p. (J). (ps-3). 1994. pap. 5.95 (*0-316-11442-1*) Little.

— Arthur Goes to Camp. LC 81-15588. (Arthur Adventure Ser.). (Illus.). 32p. (J). (ps-3). 1982. 15.95 (*0-316-11218-6*, Joy St Bks) Little.

— Arthur Goes to Camp. LC 81-15588. (Arthur Adventure Ser.). (Illus.). 32p. (J). (ps-3). 1984. pap. 5.95 (*0-316-11058-2*, Joy St Bks) Little.

— Arthur Meets the President. LC 90-13298. (Arthur Adventure Ser.). 32p. (J). (ps-3). 1991. 15.95 (*0-316-11265-8*) Little.

— Arthur Meets the President. (Arthur Adventure Ser.). 32p. (J). (ps-3). 1996. pap. 9.95 incl. audio (*0-316-11044-2*) Little.

— Arthur's April Fool. LC 82-20368. (Arthur Adventure Ser.). (Illus.). 32p. (J). (ps-3). 1983. 15.95 (*0-316-11196-1*, Joy St Bks) Little.

— Arthur's Baby. LC 87-3988. (Arthur Adventure Ser.: Vol. 1). 32p. (J). (ps-3). 1987. 15.95 (*0-316-11123-6*, Joy St Bks) Little.

— Arthur's Birthday. LC 88-25912. (Arthur Adventure Ser.). (Illus.). 32p. (J). (ps-3). 1989. 15.95 (*0-316-11073-6*, Joy St Bks) Little.

— Arthur's Birthday. LC 88-25912. (Arthur Adventure Ser.). (Illus.). 32p. (J). (ps-3). 1991. pap. 5.95 (*0-316-11074-4*) Little.

— Arthur's Birthday. (Arthur Adventure Ser.). (Illus.). (J). (ps-3). 1993. pap. 9.95 incl. audio (*0-316-11337-9*) Little.

— Arthur's Chicken Pox. LC 93-22996. (Arthur Adventure Ser.). 32p. (J). (ps-3). 1994. 15.95 (*0-316-11384-0*) Little.

— Arthur's Chicken Pox. LC 93-22996. (Arthur Adventure Ser.). (Illus.). 32p. (J). (ps-3). 1996. pap. 5.95 (*0-316-11050-7*) Little.

— Arthur's Christmas. LC 84-4373. (Arthur Adventure Ser.). (Illus.). 32p. (J). (ps-3). 1984. 15.95 (*0-316-11180-5*, Joy St Bks) Little.

— Arthur's Christmas. LC 84-4373. (Arthur Adventure Ser.). (Illus.). 30p. (J). (ps-3). 1985. pap. 5.95 (*0-316-10993-2*, Joy St Bks) Little.

— Arthur's Eyes. LC 79-11734. (Arthur Adventure Ser.). (Illus.). 32p. (J). (ps-3). 1979. 15.95 (*0-316-11063-9*, Joy St Bks) Little.

— Arthur's Family Vacation. LC 92-26650. (Arthur Adventure Ser.). 32p. (J). (ps-3). 1993. 15.95 (*0-316-11312-3*) Little.

— Arthur's Halloween. LC 82-14286. (Arthur Adventure Ser.). (Illus.). 32p. (J). (ps-3). 1982. 15.95 (*0-316-11116-3*, Joy St Bks) Little.

— Arthur's Halloween. LC 82-14286. (Arthur Adventure Ser.). (Illus.). 32p. (J). (ps-3). 1983. pap. 5.95 (*0-316-11059-0*, Joy St Bks) Little.

— Arthur's Nose. LC 75-30610. (Arthur Adventure Ser.). (Illus.). 32p. (J). (ps-3). 1976. 15.95 (*0-316-11193-7*, Joy St Bks) Little.

— Arthur's Nose. LC 75-30610. (Arthur Adventure Ser.). (Illus.). 32p. (J). (ps-3). 1986. pap. 5.95 (*0-316-11070-1*, Joy St Bks) Little.

— Arthur's Teacher Trouble. LC 95-189143. (Arthur Adventure Ser.). (Illus.). 32p. (J). (ps-3). 1987. 15.95 (*0-316-11244-5*, Joy St Bks) Little.

— Arthur's Teacher Trouble. LC 86-3539. (Arthur Adventure Ser.). (Illus.). 30p. (J). (ps-3). 1989. pap. 5.95 (*0-316-11186-4*, Joy St Bks) Little.

— Arthur's Thanksgiving. LC 83-798. (Arthur Adventure Ser.). (Illus.). 32p. (J). (ps-3). 1983. 15.95 (*0-316-11060-4*, Joy St Bks) Little.

— Arthur's Thanksgiving. LC 83-798. (Arthur Adventure Ser.). (Illus.). 30p. (J). (ps-3). 1984. pap. 5.95 (*0-316-11232-1*, Joy St Bks) Little.

— Arthur's Tooth. LC 87-3617. (Arthur Adventure Ser.). (Illus.). 32p. (J). (ps-3). 1985. 15.95 (*0-316-11245-3*, Joy St Bks) Little.

— Arthur's Tooth. LC 84-72092. (Arthur Adventure Ser.). (Illus.). 32p. (J). (ps-3). 1986. pap. 5.95 (*0-316-11246-1*) Little.

— Arthur's Valentine. LC 80-14001. (Arthur Adventure Ser.). 32p. (J). (ps-3). 1980. 15.95 (*0-316-11062-0*, Joy St Bks) Little.

— Arthur's Valentine. LC 80-14001. (Arthur Adventure Ser.). (Illus.). 32p. (J). (ps-3). 1988. pap. 5.95 (*0-316-11187-2*, Joy St Bks) Little.

— Buster Makes the Grade. LC 99-18410. (Arthur Chapter Book Ser.: No. 16). (Illus.). 64p. (J). (gr. 2-4). 1999. 12.95 (*0-316-11960-1*) Little.

— D. W. All Wet. LC 87-15752. (D. W. Ser.). (Illus.). (J). (ps-3). 1991. pap. 5.95 (*0-316-11268-2*) Little.

— D. W. Rides Again! LC 93-7192. (D. W. Ser.). (Illus.). 32p. (J). (ps-3). 1996. pap. 5.95 (*0-316-11052-3*) Little.

— D. W. Thinks Big. LC 92-19947. (D. W. Ser.). (Illus.). 32p. (J). (ps-3). 1993. 15.95 (*0-316-11305-0*, Joy St Bks) Little.

— D. W. Thinks Big. LC 92-19947. (D. W. Ser.). (Illus.). 32p. (J). (ps-3). 1995. pap. 5.95 (*0-316-10922-3*) Little.

— Happy Birthday Little Witch. LC 85-1796. (Step into Reading Ser.: A Step 2 Book). (Illus.). 48p. (J). (ps-3). 1985. pap. 3.99 (*0-394-87365-3*, Pub. by Random Bks Yng Read) Random.

— The Lost Diary. LC 98-66850. (Arthur Chapter Book Ser.: Vol. 9). (Illus.). 64p. (J). (gr. 2-4). 1998. 12.95 (*0-316-11573-8*) Little.

Brown, Marc Tolon, jt. auth. see Brown, Laurene Krasny.

Brown, Marcia. Backbone of the King. (Illus.). 180p. (J). (gr. 4-8). 1984. reprint ed. 9.95 (*0-8248-0963-7*, Kolowalu Bk) UH Pr.

— Dick Whittington & His Cat. Katcher, Ruth, ed. (J). (ps-3). 1997. per. 5.99 (*0-689-81525-5*) Aladdin.

— Dick Whittington & His Cat. LC 50-9157. (Illus.). 32p. (J). (gr. k-3). 1988. reprint ed. 16.00 (*0-684-18998-4*) Scribner.

— Dick Whittington's Cat. 1997. 11.19 (*0-606-13331-3*, Pub. by Turtleback) Demco.

— Once a Mouse... LC 61-14769. (Illus.). 32p. (J). (ps-3). 1972. lib. bdg. 16.00 (*0-684-12662-1*) Atheneum Yung Read.

— Sopa de Piedras. Mlawer, Teresa, tr.Tr. of Stone Soup. (Illus.). (J). (gr. 5-7). 1994. pap. 5.95 (*0-9625162-4-4*) Lectorum Pubns.

— Sopa de Piedras.Tr. of Stone Soup. 1991. 11.15 (*0-606-10510-7*, Pub. by Turtleback) Demco.

— Sopa de Piedras. unabridged ed.Tr. of Stone Soup. (SPA., Illus.). (J). (gr. k-3). 1992. 24.95 incl. audio (*0-87499-279-6*); pap. 15.95 incl. audio (*0-87499-278-8*) Live Oak Media.

— Sopa de Piedras, 4 bks., Set. unabridged ed.Tr. of Stone Soup. (SPA., Illus.). (J). (gr. k-3). 1992. pap., teacher ed. 33.95 incl. audio (*0-87499-280-X*) Live Oak Media.

— Sopa de Piedras (Stone Soup) Mlawer, Teresa, tr. from ENG. (Illus.). (J). (gr. k-2). 1991. lib. bdg. 12.95 (*0-9625162-1-X*) Lectorum Pubns.

— Stone Soup. LC 47-11630. (Illus.). 48p. (J). (ps-4). 1947. 16.00 (*0-684-92296-7*) Scribner.

— Stone Soup. unabridged ed. (Illus.). (J). (gr. k-4). 1987. 24.95 incl. audio (*0-87499-053-X*) Live Oak Media.

— Stone Soup. unabridged ed. (Illus.). (J). (gr. 1-4). 1987. pap. 15.95 incl. audio (*0-87499-052-1*) Live Oak Media.

— Stone Soup, 4 bks., Set. (Illus.). (J). (gr. k-4). 1987. pap., teacher ed. 33.95 incl. audio (*0-87499-054-8*) Live Oak Media.

Brown, Marcia. Stone Soup: An Old Tale. (J). 1986. 11.19 (*0-606-03331-9*, Pub. by Turtleback) Demco.

Brown, Marcia. Stone Soup: An Old Tale. LC 86-10964. (Aladdin Picture Bks. Ser.). (Illus.). 46p. (J). (ps-3). 1986. reprint ed. pap. 5.99 (*0-689-71103-4*) Aladdin.

***Brown, Marcia.** Stone Soup; Sopa De Piedras, 2 bks., Set. unabridged ed. Mlawer, Teresa, tr. (J). 1999. pap. 29.95 incl. audio (*0-87499-571-X*) Live Oak Media.

— Unsigned Beauties of Costume Jewelry: Identification & Values. (Illus.). 288p. 2000. 24.95 (*1-57432-182-X*) Collector Bks.

Brown, Marcia. Sing a Song of Popcorn: Every Child's Book of Poems. (J). (gr. 3-7). 1988. 16.89 (*0-590-40645-0*, 266909) Scholastic Inc.

Brown, Marcia & Perrault, Charles. Cinderella. LC 54-12897. (Illus.). 32p. (J). 1997. per. 5.99 (*0-689-81474-7*) Atheneum Yung Read.

— Cinderella. (Illus.). 32p. (J). (ps-4). 1971. 16.00 (*0-684-12676-1*) Scribner.

Brown, Marcia, tr. & illus. see Cendrars, Blaise.

Brown, Marcia H. The Setters: A Comprehensive Look at the English, Gordon, Irish & the Red & White Breeds. Anderson, Mark, ed. (Pure Breds Ser.). (Illus.). 320p. Date not set. 28.50 (*0-944875-55-6*) Doral Pub.

Brown, Marcus. What's Really Going On? 50p. (Orig.). 1995. pap. 8.95 (*0-9645118-0-0*) Consc Pub Co.

Brown, Margaret. AppleWorks (Version 3) Quick Reference Guide. (DDC Quick Reference Guides Ser.). (Orig.). 1990. spiral bd. 12.00 (*0-936862-94-7*, H-17) DDC Pub.

— Learning Desktop Publishing Basics with WorkPerfect 5.1. 260p. 1991. teacher ed. 5.00 (*1-56243-065-3*, WDB/TM); spiral bd. 27.00 (*1-56243-052-1*, WDB); trans. 130.00 (*1-56243-067-X*, WD-13); trans. 200.00 (*1-56243-068-8*, WD-26); trans. 200.00 (*1-56243-069-6*, WD-12); disk 65.00 (*1-56243-062-9*, DD-77); disk 12.50 (*1-56243-066-1*, DD-55) DDC Pub.

— Learning DOS & Windows. 1996. pap. text 27.00 (*1-56243-295-8*, Z-7) DDC Pub.

— Learning DOS Versions 5 & 6: For IBM & Compatibles. Berkemeyer, Kathy M., ed. (Fast-Teach Learning Ser.). (Illus.). 277p. (Orig.). 1993. spiral bd. 27.00 (*1-56243-120-X*, D-9) DDC Pub.

— Learning Microsoft Windows 95. LC 96-158357. 1995. spiral bd. 27.00 (*1-56243-233-8*, Z-3) DDC Pub.

— Learning Microsoft Windows 95. 1996. 29.00 (*1-56243-303-2*, Z-3HC) DDC Pub.

— Microsoft Windows 3.1: A Quick Study. 1992. teacher ed. 5.00 (*1-56243-082-3*, MW-TM); teacher ed. 5.00 (*1-56243-366-0*, MW-TM); spiral bd. 27.00 (*1-56243-081-5*, WQS-1) DDC Pub.

Brown, Margaret, et al. Boxes for the Protection of Books: Their Design & Construction. rev. ed. LC 93-1994. 1994. write for info. (*0-8444-0797-6*) Lib Congress.

***Brown, Margaret & Roberts, Doris Parker.** Growing Up with a Schizophrenic Mother. 200p. 2000. pap. 35.00 (*0-7864-0820-0*) McFarland & Co.

Brown, Margaret, jt. auth. see Brown, Rob.

Brown, Margaret, ed. see Dickens, Charles.

Brown, Margaret Carol, et al. Spanish for Life Textbook with Atajo CD-Rom. 432p. pap. 52.95 (*0-8384-0702-1*, Pub. by Heinle & Heinle) Thomson Learn.

Brown, Margaret D. Shepherdess of Elk River Valley. 2nd ed. (Illus.). 1967. 5.50 (*0-87315-037-6*) Golden Bell.

Brown, Margaret Gillies. Far from the Rowan Tree. LC 98-187724. 238 p. 1998. write for info. (*1-874640-69-6*) Argyll Pubng.

B

Brown, Margaret K. The Zimmerman Site: Further Excavations at the Grand Village of Kaskaskia. (Reports of Investigations: No. 32). (Illus.). 124p. 1975. pap. 3.00 (*0-89792-058-9*) Ill St Museum.

Brown, Margaret K. & Dean, Lawrie C. The French Colony in the Mid-Mississippi Valley. (Illus.). 36p. 1995. pap. 9.95 (*0-913415-09-X*) Am Kestrel Pr.

***Brown, Margaret L.** The Wild East: A Biography of the Great Smoky Mountains. LC 99-89346. (New Perspectives on the History of the South Ser.). (Illus.). 504p. 2000. 49.95 (*0-8130-1750-5*) U Press Fla.

***Brown, Margaret Phipps, et al.** The Role of Firearms in Domestic Violence: A Study of Victims, Police & Domestic Violence Shelter Workers in West Virginia. LC 99-51636. (Symposium Ser.: Vol. 59). 188p. 2000. 79.95 (*0-7734-7893-0*) E Mellen.

Brown, Margaret W. Diggers. (Illus.). 24p. (J). 1998. 5.95 (*0-7868-0424-6*, Pub. by Disney Pr) Time Warner.

***Brown, Margaret W.** The Golden Egg Book. (Little Golden Storybks.). (Illus.). (J). 1998. 3.99 (*0-307-16149-8*, 16149, Goldn Books) Gldn Bks Pub Co.

— Goodnight Moon. (J). 1994. 29.95 incl. audio (*0-317-07120-3*) Live Oak Media.

Brown, Margaret W. Home for a Bunny. (Little Golden Storybks.). (Illus.). (J). 1998. 3.99 (*0-307-16193-5*, 16193, Goldn Books) Gldn Bks Pub Co.

— Important Book. 1990. 11.15 (*0-606-04270-9*, Pub. by Turtleback) Demco.

— The Little Lost Lamb. 32p. (J). (ps-1). 2000. lib. bdg. 15.49 (*0-7868-2322-4*, Pub. by Hyprn Child) Little.

— The Little Lost Lamb. 32p. (J). (ps-1). Date not set. pap. 5.70 (*0-7868-1258-3*, Pub. by Hyprn Ppbks) Little.

— The Little Lost Lamb. 32p. (J). (ps-1). 2000. 14.95 (*0-7868-0372-X*) Hysolli Prod.

— The Little Scarecrow Boy. LC 97-32558. (Illus.). 40p. (J). (ps-2). 1998. 15.95 (*0-06-026284-2*); lib. bdg. 15.89 (*0-06-026290-7*) HarpC.

— Margaret Wise Brown's Pussy Willow. (Little Golden Storybks.). (J). 1997. 3.99 (*0-307-16069-6*, 16069, Goldn Books) Gldn Bks Pub Co.

— Nibble Nibble: Poems for Children. LC 84-43128. (Illus.). 64p. (J). (ps-3). 1998. 15.95 (*0-06-027997-4*) HarpC Child Bks.

— The Runaway Bunny. (J). 1977. 11.15 (*0-606-01112-9*, Pub. by Turtleback) Demco.

***Brown, Margaret W.** The Runaway Bunny Board Book & Tape. unabridged ed. (Illus.). 16p. (J). (ps up). 1998. bds. 9.95 incl. audio (*0-694-70095-9*) HarpC Child Bks.

Brown, Margaret W. The Runaway Bunny Book & Tape. LC 71-183168. (Illus.). 40p. (J). (ps-2). 1989. pap. 7.95 incl. audio (*0-89845-995-8*) HarperAudio.

— The Sailor Dog. (Little Golden Storybks.). (J). 1997. 3.99 (*0-307-16046-7*, 16046, Goldn Books) Gldn Bks Pub Co.

— Sleepy Bunnie. 32p. (J). (ps-1). Date not set. lib. bdg. 15.49 (*0-7868-2321-6*, Pub. by Hyprn Child) Little.

— Sleepy Bunnie: The Lost Lullabies of Margaret Wise Brown. 32p. (J). Date not set. 14.99 (*0-7868-0371-1*, Pub. by Hyprn Child) Little.

— Sleepy Bunnie: The Lost Lullabies of Margaret Wise Brown. 32p. (J). (ps-1). 2000. pap. 5.70 (*0-7868-1257-5*, Pub. by Hyprn Ppbks) Little.

— The Wonderful House. (Little Golden Treasures Ser.). 26p. (J). (ps). 1998. 5.99 (*0-307-20313-1*, 20313, Goldn Books) Gldn Bks Pub Co.

Brown, Margaret W. & Brown, Margaret Wise. Goodnight Moon. unabridged ed. (J). (gr. k-3). 1984. 24.95 incl. audio (*0-941078-30-2*); pap. 15.95 incl. audio (*0-941078-28-0*) Live Oak Media.

— Goodnight Moon, 4 bks., Set. unabridged ed. (J). (gr. k-3). 1984. pap. 33.95 incl. audio (*0-941078-29-9*) Live Oak Media.

Brown, Margaret Wise. Animals in the Snow. LC 94-8470. (Illus.). 32p. (J). (ps-k). 1995. 14.45 (*0-7868-0039-9*, Pub. by Hyprn Child); lib. bdg. 14.89 (*0-7868-2032-2*, Pub. by Hyprn Child) Little.

— Another Important Book. LC 98-7212. (Joanna Cotler Bks.). (Illus.). 32p. (J). (ps-3). 1999. 15.95 (*0-06-026282-6*) HarpC Child Bks.

***Brown, Margaret Wise.** Another Important Book. LC 98-7212. (Joanna Cotler Bks.). (Illus.). 32p. (J). (ps-3). 1999. lib. bdg. 15.89 (*0-06-026283-4*) HarpC Child Bks.

Brown, Margaret Wise. Big Red Barn. LC 84-43121. (Illus.). (J). 1965. 8.95 (*0-201-09115-1*) HarpC Child Bks.

Brown, Margaret Wise. Big Red Barn. (Illus.). 1989. write for info. (*0-694-00159-7*) HarpC Child Bks.

Brown, Margaret Wise. Big Red Barn. LC 85-45814. (Illus.). 32p. (J). (ps-1). 1996. pap. 5.95 (*0-06-443349-8*, HarpTrophy) HarpC Child Bks.

— Big Red Barn. rev. ed. LC 85-45814. (Illus.). 32p. (J). (ps-1). 1989. 15.95 (*0-06-020748-5*); lib. bdg. 15.89 (*0-06-020749-3*) HarpC Child Bks.

— Big Red Barn Big Book. LC 85-45814. (Big Bk.). (Illus.). 32p. (J). (ps-1). 1991. 21.95 (*0-06-020750-7*) HarpC Child Bks.

— Big Red Barn Board Book. LC 85-45814. (Illus.). 32p. (J). (ps up). 1994. 7.95 (*0-694-00624-6*, HarpFestival) HarpC Child Bks.

— Big Red Barn Board Book & Tape. (Share a Story Ser.). (Illus.). (J). (ps up). 1998. 9.95 incl. audio (*0-694-70097-5*) HarpC.

— Big Red Barn, The (Spanish edition) El gran granero rojo. Marcuse, Aida E., tr. from SPA. LC 95-1675. (SPA., Illus.). 32p. (J). (ps-3). 1996. 16.95 (*0-06-026225-7*, HpArco Iris) HarpC Child Bks.

Brown, Margaret Wise. Bonsoir Lune. 1997. pap. 12.95 (*2-211-07293-3*) Distribks Inc.

Brown, Margaret Wise. Buenos Noches, Luna. (J). 1995. 11.15 (*0-606-08503-3*, Pub. by Turtleback) Demco.

— Bunny's Noisy Book. LC 99-19024. (Illus.). 32p. (ps-2). 2000. lib. bdg. 15.49 (*0-7868-2428-X*, Pub. by Hyprn Child) Little.

***Brown, Margaret Wise.** Child Is Born: A Picturebook. (Illus.). 32p. (J). 2000. lib. bdg. 17.49 (*0-7868-2564-2*, Pub. by Disney Pr) Time Warner.

— Child Is Born, a Picturebook. (Illus.). 32p. (J). 2000. 16.99 (*0-7868-0673-7*, Pub. by Hyprn Child) Time Warner.

Brown, Margaret Wise. A Child's Good Morning Book. LC 94-719. (Illus.). 40p. (J). (ps-3). 1995. 10.00 (*0-06-024538-7*) HarpC.

— A Child's Good Morning Book. (Illus.). 32p. (J). (ps-3). 1996. 6.95 (*0-694-00882-6*, HarpFestival) HarpC Child Bks.

— A Child's Good Night Book. LC 91-45340. (Illus.). 32p. (J). (ps-2). 1992. 11.95 (*0-06-021028-1*) HarpC Child Bks.

— A Child's Good Night Book Board Book. LC 00-. (Illus.). 12p. (J). (ps-3). 1996. 7.95 (*0-694-00839-7*, HarpFestival) HarpC Child Bks.

Brown, Margaret Wise. Colors. 32p. (J). Date not set. 14.99 (*0-7868-0605-2*, Pub. by Hyprn Child) Time Warner.

— Colors. 32p. (J). 2000. lib. bdg. 15.49 (*0-7868-2519-7*, Pub. by Hyperion) Little.

Brown, Margaret Wise. El Conejito Andarin. 1995. 12.15 (*0-606-07473-2*, Pub. by Turtleback) Demco.

— David's Little Indian. (Illus.). 48p. (J). (gr. 2-5). 1989. reprint ed. 10.95 (*0-929077-02-4*); reprint ed. lib. bdg. 10.95 (*0-317-92547-4*) WaterMark Inc.

— The Day Before Now. Blos, Joan W., ed. LC 93-12814. (Illus.). 40p. (J). 1994. per. 15.00 (*0-671-79628-3*) S&S Bks Yung.

Brown, Margaret Wise. The Dead Bird. 32p. 15.95 (*0-06-028931-7*); pap. 5.95 (*0-06-443668-3*); lib. bdg. 15.89 (*0-06-028932-5*) HarpC.

Brown, Margaret Wise. The Dead Bird. LC 84-43124. (Illus.). 48p. (J). (ps-3). 1995. pap. 5.95 (*0-06-443326-9*, HarpTrophy) HarpC Child Bks.

— The Dead Bird. (J). 1985. 10.15 (*0-606-07421-X*, Pub. by Turtleback) Demco.

— Diggers. LC 94-7995. 1997. 10.15 (*0-606-11257-X*, Pub. by Turtleback) Demco.

— The Diggers. large type ed. LC 94-7995. (Illus.). 32p. (J). (ps-1). 1995. lib. bdg. 14.89 (*0-7868-2001-2*, Pub. by Hyprn Child) Little.

— The Diggers. large type ed. LC 94-7995. (Illus.). 32p. (J). (ps-3). 1995. 14.95 (*0-7868-0006-2*, Pub. by Hyprn Child) Time Warner.

— The Dream Book. (J). 2000. write for info. (*0-7868-0124-7*) Hyperion.

— The Dream Book. (J). (ps). 1990. 9.95 (*0-929077-12-1*) WaterMark Inc.

— Dream Book. (J). Date not set. write for info. (*0-7868-2097-7*) Hyprn Child.

— The Dream Book. LC 90-81630. (Illus.). 32p. (J). (ps-k). 1992. reprint ed. 10.45 (*1-56282-211-X*, Pub. by Hyprn Child) Time Warner.

— The Dream Book: First Comes the Dream. (Illus.). 32p. (J). (gr. 1-3). 1990. reprint ed. 9.95 (*0-685-45149-6*) WaterMark Inc.

— Four Fur Feet. LC 93-31523. (Illus.). 24p. (J). (ps-1). 1994. 12.95 (*0-7868-0002-X*, Pub. by Hyprn Child) Time Warner.

— Four Fur Feet. LC 93-31523. 1994. 10.15 (*0-606-09293-5*, Pub. by Turtleback) Demco.

— Four Fur Feet. (Illus.). 48p. (J). (gr. 1-3). 1989. reprint ed. 13.95 (*0-929077-03-2*); reprint ed. lib. bdg. 12.95 (*0-317-92548-2*) WaterMark Inc.

***Brown, Margaret Wise.** Good Little Bad Little Pig. 32p. (J). 2005. lib. bdg. 15.49 (*0-7868-2514-6*, Pub. by Hyperion) Little.

— Good Little Bad Little Pig. 32p. (J). Date not set. 14.99 (*0-7868-0600-1*, Pub. by Hyprn Child) Little.

Brown, Margaret Wise. Goodnight Moon. LC 47-30762. (Picture Bks.). (Illus.). 32p. (J). (ps up). 1977. pap. 5.95 (*0-06-443017-0*, HarpTrophy) HarpC Child Bks.

— Goodnight Moon. (J). 1989. pap. text 22.00 (*0-590-65236-2*) Scholastic Inc.

— Goodnight Moon. (J). 1975. 11.15 (*0-606-01149-8*, Pub. by Turtleback) Demco.

— Goodnight Moon. large type ed. (J). (ps-2). 1989. 19.95 (*0-590-73302-8*, HarpTrophy) HarpC Child Bks.

— Goodnight Moon. 50th anniversary ed. LC 47-30762. (Illus.). 32p. (J). (gr. k-3). 1947. 14.95 (*0-06-020705-1*) HarpC Child Bks.

— Goodnight Moon: A 50th Anniversary Retrospective. (Illus.). 64p. (J). (ps up). 1997. 19.95 (*0-06-027504-9*) HarpC Child Bks.

— Goodnight Moon: 50th Anniversary Edition. LC 67-174. (Illus.). 32p. (J). (ps-1). 1947. lib. bdg. 14.89 (*0-06-020706-X*) HarpC Child Bks.

Brown, Margaret Wise. Goodnight Moon, a Hallmark. (J). 1970. write for info. (*0-06-095382-9*) HarpC Child Bks.

Brown, Margaret Wise. Goodnight Moon Bedtime Box: 50th Anniversary. gif. ed. (Illus.). 32p. (J). (ps). 1997. 24.95 (*0-694-00979-2*, HarpFestival) HarpC Child Bks.

— Goodnight Moon Board Book. LC 47-30762. (Illus.). 17p. (J). (ps up). 1991. 7.95 (*0-694-00361-1*, HarpFestival) HarpC Child Bks.

— Goodnight Moon Board Book & Rattle. gif. ed. (Illus.). (J). (ps up). 1998. 17.95 (*0-694-01201-7*, HarpFestival) HarpC Child Bks.

— Goodnight Moon Board Book & Slippers. (Illus.). 32p. (J). (ps up). 1997. 19.95 (*0-694-01008-1*, HarpFestival) HarpC Child Bks.

***Brown, Margaret Wise.** Goodnight Moon Board Book, Comb, & Brush Set. (Illus.). 32p. (J). (ps up). 1999. 16.95 (*0-694-01274-2*, HarpFestival) HarpC Child Bks.

Brown, Margaret Wise. Goodnight Moon Book & Tape. LC 47-30762. (Illus.). 32p. (J). (ps-3). 1989. 7.95 incl. audio (*0-89845-988-5*) HarperAudio.

— Goodnight Moon Book & Tape (Spanish edition) Buenas noches, Luna. LC 47-30762. (SPA., Illus.). 32p. (J). (ps-3). 1996. 10.95 incl. audio (*0-694-70021-5*, HarpTrophy) HarpC Child Bks.

— Goodnight Moon Room Popup. LC 83-48169. (Illus.). 10p. (J). (ps-1). 1985. 12.95 (*0-694-00003-5*) HarpC Child Bks.

— Goodnight Moon (Spanish edition) Buenas Noches, Luna. Mlawer, Teresa, tr. LC 94-43633. (SPA., Illus.). 32p. (J). (ps-3). 1995. 15.95 (*0-06-026214-1*, HpArco Iris) HarpC Child Bks.

— Goodnight Moon (Spanish edition) Buenas noches, Luna. Mlawer, Teresa, tr. LC 94-43633. (Trophy Picture Bk.). (SPA., Illus.). 32p. (J). (ps-3). 1995. pap. 6.95 (*0-06-443416-8*, HpArco Iris) HarpC Child Bks.

***Brown, Margaret Wise.** I Like Bugs. LC 98-33796. (Road to Reading Ser.). (Illus.). (ps-3). 1999. 10.99 (*0-307-46107-6*, Goldn Books) Gldn Bks Pub Co.

Brown, Margaret Wise. I Like Stars. LC 98-12015. (Road to Reading Ser.). (Illus.). 32p. (J). (ps-3). 1998. pap. 3.99 (*0-307-26105-0*, 26105, Goldn Books) Gldn Bks Pub Co.

— The Important Book. LC 49-9133. (Illus.). 24p. (J). (ps-3). 1949. 14.95 (*0-06-020720-5*); lib. bdg. 14.89 (*0-06-020721-3*) HarpC Child Bks.

— The Important Book. LC 49-9133. (Trophy Picture Bk.). (Illus.). 24p. (J). (ps-3). 1990. pap. 5.95 (*0-06-443227-0*, HarpTrophy) HarpC Child Bks.

— The Indoor Noisy Book. LC 92-46879. (Illus.). 48p. (J). (ps-1). 1942. lib. bdg. 15.89 (*0-06-020821-X*) HarpC Child Bks.

— Little Chicken. LC 43-16942. (Illus.). 32p. (J). (ps-3). 1943. 13.00 (*0-06-020739-6*) HarpC Child Bks.

— Little Donkey Close Your Eyes. LC 94-16523. (Illus.). 32p. (J). (ps-3). 1995. 14.95 (*0-06-024482-8*); lib. bdg. 13.89 (*0-06-024483-6*) HarpC Child Bks.

— The Little Fir Tree. (Illus.). 32p. (J). (ps-1). Date not set. 15.95 (*0-06-028189-8*); pap. 5.95 (*0-06-443529-6*); lib. bdg. 15.89 (*0-06-028190-1*) HarpC.

— The Little Fir Tree. LC 54-5534. (Illus.). 24p. (J). (gr. k-3). 1979. lib. bdg. 14.89 (*0-690-04016-4*) HarpC Child Bks.

— LITTLE FIREMAN. LC 84-43127. (Illus.). 40p. (J). 1952. 11.95 (*0-201-09261-1*) HarpC Child Bks.

— Little Fur Family. LC 51-11657. (Illus.). 32p. (J). (ps-3). 1951. 15.95 (*0-06-020745-0*) HarpC Child Bks.

— Little Fur Family Fur Edition. LC 51-11657. (Illus.). 16p. (J). (ps-3). 1985. 7.95 (*0-694-00004-3*) HarpC Child Bks.

Brown, Margaret Wise. Little Island. (Dell Picture Yearling Ser.). (J). 1973. 11.19 (*0-606-05908-3*, Pub. by Turtleback) Demco.

Brown, Margaret Wise. Love Song of the Little Bear. (Illus.). 32p. 2000. 15.49 (*0-7868-2445-X*, Pub. by Hyprn Child) Little.

— Love Song of the Little Bear. (Illus.). 32p. Date not set. 4.99 (*0-7868-1361-X*, Pub. by Hyprn Ppbks) Little.

— Love Song of the Little Bear. (Illus.). 32p. 2000. pap. 14.99 (*0-7868-0509-9*, Pub. by Hyprn Ppbks) Little.

***Brown, Margaret Wise.** Mouse of My Heart: A Treasury of Sense & Nonsense. LC 99-87878. 192p. (J). 2000. 19.99 (*0-7868-0628-1*, Pub. by Hyprn Child) Time Warner.

Brown, Margaret Wise. On Christmas Eve. (Illus.). (J). 1985. lib. bdg. 12.89 (*0-06-020764-7*) HarpC Child Bks.

— On Christmas Eve. LC 93-43636. (Illus.). 32p. (J). (ps-3). 1996. 14.95 (*0-06-023648-5*) HarpC Child Bks.

***Brown, Margaret Wise.** On Christmas Eve. LC 93-43636. (Illus.). 32p. (J). (ps-3). 2000. pap. 5.95 (*0-06-443670-5*, HarpTrophy) HarpC Child Bks.

Brown, Margaret Wise. Once upon a Time in a Pigpen & Three Other Stories. LC 84-43130. (Illus.). (J). 1980. 12.95 (*0-201-00343-0*) HarpC Child Bks.

— A Pussycat's Christmas. LC 93-4424. (Illus.). 32p. (J). (gr. k-4). 1998. pap. 5.95 (*0-06-443466-4*) HarpC.

— A Pussycat's Christmas. LC 93-4424. (Illus.). 32p. (J). (ps-3). 1994. 15.95 (*0-06-023532-2*) HarpC Child Bks.

— Red Light, Green Light. 40p. (J). (ps-3). 1994. pap. 4.95 (*0-590-44559-6*) Scholastic Inc.

— Red Light, Green Light. LC 91-14569. (Blue Ribbon Bks.). 1992. 11.19 (*0-606-06692-6*, Pub. by Turtleback) Demco.

***Brown, Margaret Wise.** Robin's Room. 32p. (J). 2005. 14.99 (*0-7868-0602-8*, Pub. by Hyprn Child) Little.

— Robin's Room. 32p. (J). Date not set. lib. bdg. 15.49 (*0-7868-2516-2*, Pub. by Hyperion) Little.

Brown, Margaret Wise. The Runaway Bunny. LC 94-13860. (Illus.). 40p. (J). (ps-2). 1942. lib. bdg. 14.89 (*0-06-020766-3*) HarpC Child Bks.

— The Runaway Bunny. LC 94-13860. (Illus.). 48p. (J). (ps-2). 1942. 14.95 (*0-06-020765-5*) HarpC Child Bks.

— The Runaway Bunny. LC 94-13860. (Trophy Picture Bk.). (Illus.). 48p. (J). (ps-2). 1977. pap. 5.95 (*0-06-443018-9*, HarpTrophy) HarpC Child Bks.

— The Runaway Bunny. unabridged ed. LC 94-13860. (Illus.). (J). (gr. k-3). 1985. 24.95 incl. audio (*0-941078-78-7*); pap. 15.95 incl. audio (*0-941078-76-0*) Live Oak Media.

— The Runaway Bunny, 4 bks., Set. unabridged ed. LC 94-13860. (Illus.). (J). (gr. k-3). 1985. pap., teacher ed. 33.95 incl. audio (*0-941078-77-9*) Live Oak Media.

— The Runaway Bunny Board Book. LC 71-183168. (Illus.). 16p. (J). (ps-2). 1991. pap. 7.95 (*0-06-107429-2*) HarpC Child Bks.

— The Runaway Bunny Book & Tape (Spanish edition) El conejito andarin. Marcuse, Aida E. & Marcuse, Aida, trs. LC 94-13860. (Harper Arco Iris Ser.). (SPA., Illus.). 40p. (J). (ps-2). 1995. 10.95 incl. audio (*0-694-70024-X*, HpArco Iris) HarpC Child Bks.

— Runaway Bunny, The (Spanish edition) El conejito andarin. Marcuse, Aida E., tr. LC 94-13860. (SPA., Illus.). 48p. (J). (ps-2). 1995. pap. 6.95 (*0-06-443390-0*, HpArco Iris) HarpC Child Bks.

— Runaway Bunny, The (Spanish edition) El conejito andarin. Marcuse, Aida E., tr. LC 94-13860. (SPA., Illus.). 40p. (J). (ps-3). 1995. 15.95 (*0-06-025434-3*) HarpC Child Bks.

— The Sleepy Men. LC 94-41939. (Illus.). 32p. (J). (ps-2). 1996. 14.95 (*0-7868-0154-9*, Pub. by Hyprn Child); lib. bdg. 14.89 (*0-7868-2126-4*, Pub. by Hyprn Child) Little.

***Brown, Margaret Wise.** Sneakers: Seven Stories about a Cat. 32p. (J). (ps-3). 2001. lib. bdg. 15.89 (*0-06-028693-8*) HarpC Child Bks.

Brown, Margaret Wise. Three Orphan Kittens. LC 94-71790. (Illus.). 32p. (J). 1995. lib. bdg. 13.89 (*0-7868-5010-8*, Pub. by Disney Pr) Little.

— The Train to Timbuctoo. LC 98-84180. (Family Storytime Ser.: No. 4). (Illus.). 32p. (J). (ps-k). 1998. 9.95 (*0-307-10215-7*, 10215, Goldn Books) Gldn Bks Pub Co.

Brown, Margaret Wise. 2 LITTLE TRAINS. LC 84-43138. 40p. (J). 1986. lib. bdg. 12.89 (*0-06-020768-X*) HarpC Child Bks.

Brown, Margaret Wise. The Ugly Duckling. LC 93-73578. (Illus.). 32p. (J). 1994. 13.95 (*0-7868-3007-7*, Pub. by Disney Pr) Time Warner.

— Under the Sun & the Moon & Other Poems. LC 92-72031. (Illus.). 40p. (J). (ps-3). 1993. lib. bdg. 14.89 (*1-56282-355-8*, Pub. by Hyprn Child) Little.

— Under the Sun & the Moon & Other Poems. (J). 1995. 10.15 (*0-606-08335-9*, Pub. by Turtleback) Demco.

— Wait Till the Moon Is Full. LC 48-9278. (Illus.). 32p. (J). (ps-1). 1948. lib. bdg. 14.89 (*0-06-020801-5*) HarpC Child Bks.

— Wait Till the Moon Is Full. LC 48-9278. (Illus.). 32p. (J). (ps-1). 1948. 15.00 (*0-06-020800-7*) HarpC Child Bks.

— Wait Till the Moon Is Full. LC 48-9278. (Trophy Picture Bk.). (Illus.). 36p. (J). (ps-3). 1989. pap. 5.95 (*0-06-443222-X*, HarpTrophy) HarpC Child Bks.

— The Walt Disney's the Grasshopper & the Ants. LC 93-70938. (Illus.). 32p. (J). 1993. lib. bdg. 12.89 (*1-56282-535-6*, Pub. by Disney Pr) Little.

— Walt Disney's the Ugly Duckling. LC 93-73578. Orig. Title: Grimme aelling. (Illus.). 32p. (J). 1994. lib. bdg. 13.89 (*0-7868-5001-9*, Pub. by Disney Pr) Little.

— Wheel on the Chimney. LC 84-48379. (Illus.). 32p. (J). (ps-3). 1954. 14.00 (*0-397-30288-6*); lib. bdg. 13.89 (*0-397-30296-7*) HarpC Child Bks.

— Wheel on the Chimney. LC 93-29423. (Illus.). 32p. (J). (ps-3). 1996. 15.00 (*0-06-024247-7*) HarpC Child Bks.

— When the Wind Blew. LC 76-58734. (Illus.). 32p. (J). (ps-3). 1977. 11.95 (*0-06-020867-8*) HarpC Child Bks.

— Where Have You Been? 32p. (J). (ps-1). Date not set. lib. bdg. 15.89 (*0-06-028379-3*) HarpC Child Bks.

— Xmas in the Barn. (J). 1952. 14.00 (*0-690-19271-1*) HarpC Child Bks.

— Xmas in the Barn. LC 52-7858. (Illus.). 32p. (J). (gr. k-3). 1961. lib. bdg. 14.89 (*0-690-19272-X*) HarpC Child Bks.

— Xmas in the Barn. LC 85-42738. (Trophy Picture Bk.). (Illus.). 32p. (J). (ps-3). 1985. reprint ed. mass mkt. 5.95 (*0-06-443082-0*, HarpTrophy) HarpC Child Bks.

Brown, Margaret Wise, ed. Homes in the Wilderness: A Pilgrim's Journal of Plymouth Plantation in 1620, by William Bradford & Others of the Mayflower Company. LC 87-27321. (Illus.). 76p. (J). (gr. 5-12). 1988. reprint ed. pap. 12.50 (*0-208-02269-4*, Linnet Bks); reprint ed. lib. bdg. 17.50 (*0-208-02197-3*, Linnet Bks) Shoe String.

***Brown, Margaret Wise & Kahn, Si.** Goodnight Moon Board Book & Tape. unabridged ed. (Illus.). (J). (ps up). 1998. 9.95 incl. audio (*0-694-70094-0*) HarpC Child Bks.

***Brown, Margaret Wise & Provensen, Martin.** The Color Kittens. LC 99-43664. (Illus.). (J). 2000. 9.95 (*0-307-10234-3*, Goldn Books) Gldn Bks Pub Co.

***Brown, Margaret Wise & Salerno, Steven.** How the Animals Took a Bath. LC 00-31916. (Illus.). (J). 2001. write for info. (*1-890817-52-X*) Winslow Pr.

Brown, Margaret Wise, jt. auth. see Brown, Margaret W.

***Brown, Margeret Wise.** Big & Little. 32p. (J). 2002. lib. bdg. 16.49 (*0-7868-2544-8*, Pub. by Disney Pr) Time Warner.

— Big & Little. 32p. (J). 2002. 15.99 (*0-7868-0630-3*, Pub. by Hyperion); pap. 5.99 (*0-7868-1450-0*, Pub. by Hyperion) Time Warner.

— Mouse of My Heart: A Treasury of Sense & Nonsense. LC 99-87878. 192p. (J). 2000. lib. bdg. 20.49 (*0-7868-2546-4*) Hyprn Child.

— Songs from the Earth. 32p. (J). 2002. lib. bdg. 16.49 (*0-7868-2543-X*, Pub. by Disney Pr) Time Warner.

— Songs from the Earth. 32p. (J). 2002. 15.99 (*0-7868-0629-X*, Pub. by Hyperion); pap. 5.99 (*0-7868-1449-7*, Pub. by Hyperion) Time Warner.

Brown, Margery W. Afro-Bets: Book of Colors. LC 91-76334. (Illus.). 24p. (Orig.). (J). (ps-1). 1991. pap. 3.95 (*0-940975-28-9*) Just Us Bks.

— Afro-Bets: Book of Shapes. LC 91-76333. (Illus.). 24p. (Orig.). (J). (ps-1). 1991. pap. 3.95 (*0-940975-29-7*) Just Us Bks.

— Baby Jesus Like My Brother. LC 95-76530. (Illus.). 32p. (J). (gr. 1 up). 1995. 15.95 (*0-940975-53-X*); pap. 7.95 (*0-940975-54-8*) Just Us Bks.

— Baby Jesus Like My Brother. (J). 1995. 13.20 (*0-606-09028-2*, Pub. by Turtleback) Demco.

Brown, Margie. The Stick Stories. LC 82-60030. (Illus.). 64p. (Orig.). 1982. pap. 7.95 (*0-89390-035-4*) Resource Pubns.

Brown, Margie G. Genealogical Abstracts Revolutionary War Veterans: Scrip Act 1852. 463p. 1997. pap. 32.00 (*1-888265-12-4*) Willow Bend.

An Asterisk (*) at the beginning of an entry indicates that the title is appearing for the first time.

Brown, Marguerite. Born to Be Fit: Discover Your Natural Ability to Be Healthy, Happy & Fit. LC 95-61074. (Illus.). 288p. (Orig.). 1996. pap. 14.95 (*1-896560-08-3*) Tll Pubng.
— Magnificent Muslims. LC 81-80056. 98p. 1981. 8.00 (*0-911026-10-X*) New World Press NY.
Brown, Margueritte A. The Last Summer of Our Childhood: Imagery & Style Collection. Wiliams, Dewilda M., ed. 104p. 1996. pap. 12.00 (*1-886493-08-1*) NBC Study Pub.
Brown, Marianne G., jt. auth. see Tennant, Richard A.
Brown, Marianne P. & Froines, John, eds. Technological Change in the Workplace: Health Impacts for Workers. 1993. 18.50 (*0-89215-180-3*) U Cal LA Indus Rel.
Brown, Marice C. Amen, Brother Ben: A Mississippi Collection of Children's Rhymes. LC 78-32017. 111p. reprint ed. pap. 34.50 (*0-8357-5344-1*, 203200100077) Bks Demand.
Brown, Marie. Coloring the Dream. 1997. pap. write for info. (*0-345-37681-1*) Ballantine Pub Grp.
Brown, Marie A. & Powell-Cope, Gail M. Caring for a Loved One with AIDS: The Experiences of Families, Lovers, & Friends. LC 92-2695. (Illus.). 76p. 1992. pap. 5.95 (*0-295-97183-5*) U of Wash Pr.
Brown, Marietta, ed. see Gore, Elizabeth Griffin.
Brown, Marilyn. Statehood. 304p. 1995. pap. 9.95 (*1-56236-308-5*, Pub. by Aspen Bks) Origin Bk Sales.
Brown, Marilyn & Babcock, Eileen. The Art of Solving Problems. Date not set. teacher ed. 8.95 (*0-910857-69-5*, 069-5AP) Educ Impress.
Brown, Marilyn R. Degas & the Business of Art: A Cotton Office in New Orleans. LC 92-34466. (College Art Association Monographs on the Fine Arts: Vol. LI). (Illus.). 176p. 1993. 65.00 (*0-271-00944-6*) Pa St U Pr.
— French Paintings of Three Centuries from the New Orleans Museum of Art. LC 91-50764. (Illus.). 92p. 1991. 22.50 (*0-89494-035-X*) New Orleans Mus Art.
— Gypsies & Other Bohemians: The Myth of the Artist in Nineteenth-Century France. Foster, Stephen, ed. LC 85-8427. (Studies in the Fine Arts: The Avant-Garde: No. 51). 247p. reprint ed. 76.60 (*0-8357-1704-6*, 207043200089) Bks Demand.
Brown, Marion. Marion Brown's Southern Cook Book. rev. ed. LC 68-14365. ix, 489p. 1968. 34.95 (*0-8078-1065-7*); pap. 19.95 (*0-8078-4078-5*) U of NC Pr.
Brown, Marion A. The Second Bank of the United States & Ohio, 1803-1860: A Collision of Interests. LC 98-22821. (Studies in American History: Vol. 22). 296p. 1998. text 89.95 (*0-7734-8354-3*) E Mellen.
Brown, Marion M. Homeward the Arrow's Flight: The Story of Susan La Flesche (Dr. Susan La Flesche Picotte) rev. ed. Lukesh, Jean, ed. (Illus.). 185p. (J). (gr. 4-12). 1995. reprint ed. pap. 12.95 (*0-9647586-0-1*) Field Mouse Prodns.
Brown, Marion R. Putting Life Back Together. LC 85-51548. 106p. 1986. pap. 1.98 (*0-87159-132-4*) Unity Bks.
— Survival Power. 47p. 1989. 1.98 (*0-87159-149-9*) Unity Bks.
Brown, Marjorie. It's Me, Marva! 2001. 15.95 (*0-679-88993-0*) Random.
***Brown, Marjorie.** It's Me, Marva! 2001. lib. bdg. 17.99 (*0-679-98993-5*) Random.
Brown, Marjorie M. & Baldwin, Edith E. The Concept of Theory: A Philosophical Dialogue. 87p. 1995. 17.50 (*1-929083-02-5*) Kappa Omi Nu.
Brown, Mark. Deluxe Netscape Navigator Starter Kit. 500p. 1997. pap. text 39.99 incl. cd-rom (*0-7897-0981-3*) Que.
— Emergency!, Vol. 1. 1997. mass mkt. 6.50 (*0-312-96265-7*) St Martin.
— Emergency! True Stories from the Nation's ER. large type ed. LC 96-11709. 1996. reprint ed. write for info. (*0-7838-1731-2*) Thorndike Pr.
— Emergency! True Stories from the Nation's ERs. 1997. mass mkt. write for info. (*0-614-27783-3*) St Martin.
— Emergency Room. 1996. 22.00 (*0-614-15456-1*) Villard Books.
— Game Face. LC 91-36005. (Ben McMillen Hawaiian Mystery Ser.). 302p. 1992. 19.95 (*0-918024-92-7*) Ox Bow.
— Netscape Navigator 3 Starter Kit. LC 96-69457. 560p. 1996. pap. text 34.99 incl. cd-rom (*0-7897-0924-4*) Que.
— Netscape Navigator 3 Starter Kit for Macintosh. LC 96-77657. 544p. 1996. pap. text 34.99 incl. cd-rom (*1-56830-320-3*) Hayden.
— The Puna Kahuna: A Ben McMillen Hawaiian Mystery. LC 93-24262. 1993. 19.95 (*1-881987-02-7*) Ox Bow.
***Brown, Mark.** Shadowdragon No. SD4: Dr. Scorpio. 172p. 1999. pap. 13.95 (*0-7414-0138-X*) Buy Books.
Brown, Mark. Using Internet HTML: Special Edition. LC 96-69608. 1080p. 1996. pap. text 59.99 incl. cd-rom (*0-7897-0852-3*) Que.
— Using Netscape 3. 1997. pap. text 59.99 (*0-7897-1186-9*) Que.
— Yellowfin. LC 91-36801. (Ben McMillen Hawaiian Mystery Ser.). 256p. 1992. 19.95 (*0-918024-93-5*) Ox Bow.
Brown, Mark & Honeycutt, Jerry. Special Edition Using HTML 3.2: Version X. 3rd ed. 1000p. 1997. 49.99 (*0-7897-1097-8*) Que.
***Brown, Mark & Semelka, Richard C.** MRI: Principles & Applications. 2nd ed. LC 99-12462. 210p. (C). 1999. pap. 49.95 (*0-471-33062-0*) Wiley.
Brown, Mark, et al. Forever Lounge: A Laid-Back Price Guide to the Languid Sounds of Lounge Music. (Illus.). 304p. 1999. pap. 24.95 (*1-58221-004-7*, Antique Trader) Krause Pubns.
Brown, Mark A., ed. Liquid Chromatography - Mass Spectrometry: Applications in Agricultural, Pharmaceutical, & Environmental Chemistry. LC 89-18611. (ACS Symposium Ser.: No. 420). (Illus.). 280p. 1989. text 75.00 (*0-8412-1740-8*, Pub. by Am Chemical) OUP.
Brown, Mark A. & Carmo, Jose, eds. Deontic Logic, Agency, & Normative Systems: DEON '96: Third International Workshop on Deontic Logic in Computer Science, Lisbon, 11-13 January 1996. LC 95-46521. (Workshops in Computing Ser.). (Illus.). 233p. 1995. 69.00 (*3-540-76015-6*) Spr-Verlag.
Brown, Mark A., jt. auth. see Salibi, Nouha.
***Brown, Mark G.** Baldridge Award Winning Quality: How to Interpret the Baldridge Criteria for Performance Excellence. 9th ed. 1999. pap. 36.95 (*0-527-76349-7*) Productivity Inc.
Brown, Mark G. Baldrige Award Winning Quality. LC 91-2889. (Illus.). 400p. 1991. pap. text 29.95 (*0-527-91647-1*, 916471) Productivity Inc.
— Baldrige Award Winning Quality. 6th ed. 440p. 1996. pap. text 29.95 (*0-527-76318-7*) Productivity Inc.
— Baldrige Award Winning Quality: How to Interpret the Baldrige Criteria for Performance. 7th rev. ed. (Illus.). 276p. 1997. pap. 32.95 (*0-527-76330-6*, 763306) Productivity Inc.
— Baldrige Award Winning Quality: How to Interpret the Baldrige Criteria for Performance Exellence. 8th ed. (Illus.). 404p. 1998. pap. text 32.95 (*0-527-76348-9*, 763489) Productivity Inc.
— Baldrige Award Winning Quality: How to Interpret the Malcolm Baldrige Award Criteria. 2nd ed. LC 92-4133. (Illus.). 430p. 1992. pap. text 32.95 (*0-527-91658-7*, 916587) Productivity Inc.
— Baldrige Award Winning Quality: How to Interpret the Malcolm Baldrige Award Criteria. 3rd ed. LC 93-19996. (Illus.). 450p. 1993. pap. text 32.95 (*0-527-91722-2*, 917222) Productivity Inc.
— Baldrige Award Winning Quality: How to Interpret the Malcolm Baldrige Award Criteria. 4th ed. LC 94-2795. (Illus.). 400p. 1994. pap. text 29.95 (*0-527-76250-4*, 762504) Productivity Inc.
— Keeping Score: Using the Right Metrics to Drive World-Class Performance. 224p. 1996. 29.95 (*0-8144-0327-1*) AMACOM.
— Keeping Score: Using the Right Metrics to Drive World-Class Performance. LC 95-52139. 224p. 1996. 29.95 (*0-527-76312-8*) Productivity Inc.
— The Pocket Guide to the Baldrige Award Criteria. 66p. (Orig.). 1994. pap. text 4.50 (*0-527-76315-2*, 762466) Productivity Inc.
— The Pocket Guide to the Baldrige Award Criteria. 4th rev. ed. 66p. (Orig.). 1997. pap. 4.50 (*0-527-76331-4*, 763314) Productivity Inc.
— The Pocket Guide to the Baldrige Award Criteria. 5th ed. 64p. (Orig.). 1998. pap. 4.50 (*0-527-76347-0*, 763470) Productivity Inc.
— The Small Business Pocket Guide to the Baldrige Award Criteria. 60p. 1997. pap. 4.50 (*0-527-76329-2*) Productivity Inc.
Brown, Mark G., et al. Rx for Business: A Troubleshooting Guide for Building a High Performance Organization. LC 96-3990. (Illus.). 250p. 1996. text 24.95 (*0-7863-0477-4*, H0945) ASQ Qual Pr.
— Rx for Business: A Troubleshooting Guide for Building a High-Performance Organization. 1996. pap. 25.00 (*0-614-12582-0*, Irwn Prfssnl) McGraw-Hill Prof.
— Why TQM Fails & What to Do About It. 252p. 25.00 (*0-614-04831-1*, DJ20H) Assn Qual & Part.
— Why TQM Fails & What to Do About It. 276p. 1994. text 30.00 (*0-7863-0140-6*, Irwn Prfssnl) McGraw-Hill Prof.
***Brown, Mark Graham.** Baldrige Award Winning Quality: How to Interpret the Baldrige Criteria for Performance Excellence. 10th ed. 420p. 2000. pap. text 39.95 (*1-56327-232-6*) Productivity Inc.
— Pocket Guide to the Baldrige Award Criteria. 7th ed. 2000. pap. 5.25 (*1-56327-233-4*) Productivity Inc.
— Winning Score: How to Design & Implement Winning Scorecards. LC 00-34159. 2000. write for info. (*1-56327-223-7*) Productivity Inc.
Brown, Mark H. The Flight of the Nez Perce. LC 82-2717. (Illus.). 480p. 1982. reprint ed. pap. 15.00 (*0-8032-6069-5*, Bison Books) U of Nebr Pr.
— The Plainsmen of the Yellowstone: A History of the Yellowstone Basin. LC 60-5262. (Illus.). 480p. 1969. pap. 17.95 (*0-8032-5026-6*, Bison Books) U of Nebr Pr.
Brown, Mark J. Peripheral Nerve Disease. 1999. write for info. (*0-7506-9068-2*) Buttrwrth-Heinemann.
Brown, Mark K. The Perfect Husband. 78p. (Orig.). 1995. pap. 7.95 (*1-56245-197-9*) Great Quotations.
Brown, Mark N., ed. see Savile, George.
Brown, Mark R., ed. Order in the Offices: Essays Defining the Roles of Church Officers. LC 93-73703. 312p. 1993. pap. 11.95 (*0-9638961-0-5*) Classic Presby.
Brown, Mark R., jt. auth. see Honeycutt, Jerry.
Brown, Marlene B. Technotouch: The Journey to Twenty First Century Success. LC 92-90740. 112p. 1994. pap. text 14.95 (*1-56728-015-3*) Sunrise PI.
Brown, Marsha. Once a Mouse: A Fable Cut in Wood. (J). 1989. 9.15 (*0-606-00546-3*, Pub. by Turtleback) Demco.
Brown, Marsha, ed. see Grigsby, Rosemari.
Brown, Marsha H., jt. auth. see Mason, Bethny H.
Brown, Marshall. Eighteenth-Century Literary History: An MLQ Reader. LC 98-29562. 1999. 49.95 (*0-8223-2135-1*) Duke.
***Brown, Marshall.** Eighteenth-Century Literary History: An MLQ Reader. LC 98-29562. 1999. pap. 17.95 (*0-8223-2267-6*) Duke.
Brown, Marshall. Preromanticism. LC 90-21043. (Illus.). 516p. 1991. 55.00 (*0-8047-1561-0*) Stanford U Pr.
— Preromanticism. (Illus.). 516p. (C). 1993. pap. 19.95 (*0-8047-2211-0*) Stanford U Pr.
— Turning Points: Essays in the History of Cultural Expressions. 1997. pap. text 16.95 (*0-8047-2523-9*) Stanford U Pr.
— Turning Points: Essays in the History of Cultural Expressions. LC 96-21910. 1997. write for info. (*0-8047-2708-2*) Stanford U Pr.
— Wit & Humor of Bench & Bar. xv, 578p. 1986. reprint ed. 58.00 (*0-8377-1938-0*, Rothman) W S Hein.
***Brown, Marshall, ed.** The Cambridge History of Literary Criticism Vol. 5: Romanticism. (Cambridge History of Literary Criticism Ser.). 512p. 2000. 110.00 (*0-521-30010-X*) Cambridge U Pr.
Brown, Marshall, ed. Pierre Bourdieu & Literary History, Vol. 58, No. 4. 150p. 1997. pap. 10.00 (*0-8223-6457-3*) Duke.
— The Uses of Literary History. LC 95-42027. (Illus.). 290p. 1995. text 54.95 (*0-8223-1704-4*); pap. text 17.95 (*0-8223-1714-1*) Duke.
Brown, Marshall G. & Stein, Gordon. Freethought in the United States: A Descriptive Bibliography. LC 77-91103. 146p. 1978. lib. bdg. 79.50 (*0-313-20036-X*, BFT/, Greenwood Pr) Greenwood.
Brown, Martha I. Spiritual Depths. 104p. 1986. pap. 5.00 (*0-9618538-0-8*) Martha I Brown.
***Brown, Martin.** Active Perl Developer's Guide. (Application Development Ser.). 2000. pap. 59 99 (*0-07-212339-7*) Osborne-McGraw.
Brown, Martin. Core Porting to the Beos. 1997. 49.99 (*1-56276-548-5*, Ziff-Davis Pr) Que.
***Brown, Martin.** Debugging Perl: Troubleshooting for Programmers. (Debugging Ser.). (Illus.). 2000. pap. 39.99 (*0-07-212676-0*) Osborne-McGraw.
***Brown, Martin C.** Activeperl Application Development Tools. (Illus.). 2000. pap. 39.99 (*0-07-212304-4*) McGrw-H Intl.
Brown, Martin C. BeOS: Porting UNIX Applications. LC 98-33836. 500p. 1998. pap. 44.95 (*1-55860-532-0*) Morgan Kaufmann.
***Brown, Martin C.** iMac FYI. 240p. 2000. pap. 14.95 (*1-929685-06-8*, Pub. by Muska Lipman) IPG Chicago.
Brown, Martin C. Perl: Annotated Archives. LC 99-194897. 800p. 1998. pap. 49.99 incl. cd-rom (*0-07-882557-1*) McGraw.
— Perl: The Complete Reference. (Complete Reference Ser.). 1100p. 1999. pap. text 49.99 (*0-07-212000-2*) Osborne.
— Perl Programmer's Reference. 380p. 1999. pap. 15.99 (*0-07-212142-4*) McGraw.
***Brown, Martin C.** Python Annotated Archives. 722p. 1999. pap. 49.99 (*0-07-212104-1*) Osborne.
Brown, Marty. Power Supply Cookbook. 248p. 1997. pap. text 29.95 (*0-7506-7010-X*, Newnes) Buttrwrth-Heinemann.
— Practical Switching Power Supply Design. (Professional & Technical Ser.). 240p. 1990. text 48.00 (*0-12-137030-5*) Acad Pr.
***Brown, Martyn.** HACCP in the Meat Industry. 320p. 2000. text 170.00 (*1-85573-448-6*, Pub. by Woodhead Pubng) Am Educ Systs.
Brown, Marvin. House Calls: Memoirs of a Country Doctor. LC 88-4076. 214p. 1988. 27.95 (*0-87975-448-6*) Prometheus Bks.
— How to Buy Advertising Like the Pros...& Save 15 to 50 Percent: A Primer for Anyone in a Small- to Medium-Sized Business or Profession. LC 93-91390. (Illus.). 208p. 1995. 29.50 (*0-9639618-0-2*, Valmaran Bks) Marbro Guide.
Brown, Marvin, et al, eds. Stress: Neurobiology & Neuroendocrinology. (Illus.). 720p. 1990. text 250.00 (*0-8247-8325-5*) Dekker.
Brown, Marvin A. Greensboro: An Architectural Record: A Survey of the Historic & Architecturally Significant Structures of Greensboro, North Carolina. LC 95-34449. (Illus.). 464p. 1995. 34.95 (*0-9647647-0-9*) Preserv Greensboro.
Brown, Marvin L., Jr. The Wisdom of Christendom. 131p. 1982. pap. 5.95 (*0-317-00315-1*) Edenwood Hse.
Brown, Marvin T. Ethical Process: An Approach to Controversial Issues. 2nd ed. LC 98-35794. 83p. 1998. pap. text 16.20 (*0-13-977620-6*) P-H.
***Brown, Marvin T.** Working Ethics: Strategies for Decision Making & Organizational Responsibility. 219p. 2000. pap. 35.95 (*1-889059-55-2*) Regent Pr.
Brown, Mary. Coyote Plants a Peach Tree. (Books for Young Learners). (Illus.). 16p. (J). (gr. k-2). 1996. pap. text 5.00 (*1-57274-017-5*, A2732) R Owen Pubs.
— Coyote Siembra un Arbol de Durazno. Torres, Raquel, tr. (Books for Young Learners).Tr. of Coyote Plants a Peach Tree. (SPA., Illus.). 16p. (J). (gr. k-2). 1996. pap. text 5.00 (*1-57274-035-3*, A2842) R Owen Pubs.
— Dragonne's Eg. 1999. mass mkt. 6.99 (*0-671-57816-3*) Baen Bks.
— Global Change: How Humans & Nature Impact Our Planet. (Learning Packets - Science Ser.). (Illus.). 86p. 1998. ring bd. 18.00 (*1-56976-084-5*, 1438-F3) Zephyr Pr AZ.
— The Hurting Women Handbook. large type ed. (Illus.). 76p. 1997. pap. 21.95 (*1-891601-04-0*) Ladies Caliber.
— The Little Point Guard, the Greg Brown Story (a Mother's Perspective) (Illus.). 124p. (Orig.). 1994. 24.95 (*1-880047-20-9*); pap. text 12.95 (*1-880047-16-0*) Creative Des.
— Master of Many Treasures. 384p. 1995. mass mkt. 5.99 (*0-671-87693-7*) Baen Bks.
— Pigs Don't Fly. 336p. 1994. mass mkt. 6.99 (*0-671-87601-5*) Baen Bks.
— Strange Deliverance. 384p. 1997. per. 5.99 (*0-671-87795-X*) Baen Bks.
— The Unlikely Ones. 432p. 1987. mass mkt. 4.99 (*0-671-65361-X*) Baen Bks.
Brown, Mary & Dickinson, Rosemary. Meteorology: Observing, Understanding & Predicting Weather. (Learning Packets - Science Ser.). 72p. 1996. ring bd. 18.00 (*1-56976-031-4*, 1429-F3) Zephyr Pr AZ.
Brown, Mary, et al. Agricultural Education in a Technical Society: An Annotated Bibliography of Resources. LC 72-7501. 240p. reprint ed. pap. 74.40 (*0-8357-5270-4*, 202418900035) Bks Demand.
Brown, Mary, jt. auth. see Baen Bks. Staff.
Brown, Mary, jt. auth. see Rebeschi, Lisa.
Brown, Mary A. Speak. 42p. 1982. pap. 11.95 (*1-891601-03-2*) Ladies Caliber.
— Studying Is Fun, Vol. 2. 24p. 1993. pap. 12.95 (*1-891601-06-7*) Ladies Caliber.
— Studying Is Fun: Creative Ideas for Children. rev. ed. Gordon, Vickie, ed. 32p. (J). (gr. 3 up). 1980. pap. 12.95 (*1-891601-05-9*) Ladies Caliber.
Brown, Mary A., ed. Paul of Pergula: Logica & Tractatus de Sensu Composito et Diviso. xiv, 162p. 1961. pap. 11.00 (*1-57659-053-4*) Franciscan Inst.
Brown, Mary B., jt. auth. see Brown, Charles.
Brown, Mary B., jt. auth. see Brown, Charles R.
Brown, Mary Barrett. Wings along the Waterway. LC 91-18559. (Illus.). 80p. (J). (gr. 3-6). 1999. pap. 8.95 (*0-531-07114-6*) Orchard Bks Watts.
***Brown, Mary C.** Free to Believe: Liberating Images of God for Women. LC 00-34346. 2000. pap. write for info. (*0-8298-1394-2*) Pilgrim OH.
Brown, Mary C., ed. see Brown, Campbell, Jr.
Brown, Mary E. Churches, Communities, & Children: Italian Immigrants & the Archdiocese of New York, 1880-1950. (Migration & Ethnicity Ser.). (Illus.). 219p. (C). 1995. text 19.50 (*0-934733-56-2*); pap. text 14.50 (*0-934733-57-0*) CMS.
— From Italian Villages to Greenwich Village: Our Lady of Pompei, 1892-1992. LC 92-24247. (Illus.). 176p. (C). 1992. text 19.50 (*0-934733-69-4*); pap. text 14.50 (*0-934733-68-6*) CMS.
— Guide to Archives XII: United States Catholic Conference (USCC) Migration & Refugee Services 1921-1975. 230p. 1997. pap. 14.95 (*1-57703-001-X*) CMS.
— The Scalabrinians in North America (1887-1934) LC 95-37420. 420p. 1996. pap. 19.95 (*0-934733-88-0*) CMS.
— Soap Opera & Women's Talk: The Pleasure of Resistance. (Communication & Human Values Ser.: Vol. 14). 280p. (C). 1994. text 52.00 (*0-8039-4392-X*); pap. text 24.95 (*0-8039-4393-8*) Sage.
Brown, Mary E., ed. A Migrant Missionary Story: The Autobiography of Giacomo Gambera. Clarke, Serafina M. & Carlesimo, Thomas F., trs. LC 94-22750. 336p. 1994. 14.50 (*0-934733-85-6*) CMS.
— Television & Women's Culture: The Politics of the Popular. (Communication & Human Values Ser.: Vol. 7). (Illus.). 256p. (C). 1990. 52.00 (*0-8039-8228-3*); pap. 24.95 (*0-8039-8229-1*) Sage.
Brown, Mary E., jt. ed. see Rosenberg, Bruce A.
Brown, Mary Elizabeth. Shapers of the Great Debate on Immigration: A Biographical Dictionary, 1. LC 98-21664. (Shapers of the Great American Debates Ser.: Vol. 1). 352p. 1999. lib. bdg. 59.95 (*0-313-30339-8*, Greenwood Pr) Greenwood.
Brown, Mary F., jt. ed. see Kraft, Walter H.
Brown, Mary G., ed. Reflections. 154p. 1988. pap. 25.00 (*0-09-173185-2*) Dufour.
Brown, Mary H. & Dickinson, Rosemary. Earth Science: A Multifaceted Investigation of Soil. (Learning Packets - Science Ser.). (Illus.). 86p. 1994. ring bd. 18.00 (*0-913705-96-9*, 1423-F3) Zephyr Pr AZ.
Brown, Mary H. & Floyd, Cathy. Activities in Professional Communication. 2nd ed. 192p. 1995. spiral bd. 23.95 (*0-8403-8813-6*) Kendall-Hunt.
Brown, Mary H., et al. Standards of Oncology Nursing Practice. LC 86-11102. 622p. 1989. pap. text 39.95 (*0-8273-4212-8*) Delmar.
***Brown, Mary Jane.** Eradicating This Evil: Women in the American Anti-Lynching Movement, 1892-1940. LC 99-54623. (Studies in African American History & Culture). 2000. write for info. (*0-8153-3632-2*) Garland.
Brown, Mary Kay. Let's Go Swimming with Mr. Sillypants. (Reading Rainbow Bks.). (J). 1992. 11.19 (*0-606-01556-6*, Pub. by Turtleback) Demco.
Brown, Mary L., jt. auth. see Hall, Betty L.
Brown, Mary Martha. My Window. 1999. 24.00 (*1-891721-55-0*) McBrown S&S.
Brown, Mary T. & Hildebrand, Frederick L. Writing for Success. LC 96-75257. 559p. (Orig.). 1996. pap. text 35.95 (*0-943202-54-X*) H & H Pub.
Brown, Mary W. Tongues of Flame. LC 93-8608. (Library of Alabama Classics). 184p. (C). 1993. pap. 14.95 (*0-8173-0722-2*) U of Ala Pr.
Brown, Marzella. Newspaper Reporters. Coan, Sharon, ed. (Illus.). 48p. (J). (gr. 3-6). 1990. student ed. 7.95 (*1-55734-137-0*) Tchr Create Mat.
Brown, Matt, et al. Professional ADO & RDS Programming with ASP. 585p. 1999. pap. 49.99 (*1-86100-164-9*, Pub. by Wrox Press) Wrox Pr Inc.
Brown, Matthew. Complete Idiot's Guide to Microsoft FrontPage 97. 320p. 1997. 19.99 (*0-7897-1346-2*) Que.
***Brown, Matthew B.** The Gate of Heaven: Insights on the Doctrines & Symbols of the Temple. LC 99-45044. 1999. 24.95 (*1-57734-511-8*, 01114115) Covenant Comms.
Brown, Matthew B. & Smith, Paul T. Symbols in Stone: Symbolism on the Early Temples of the Restoration. LC 97-32097. 1997. 21.95 (*1-57734-134-1*, 01113054) Covenant Comms.
***Brown, Matthew D., et al.** Advising California Nonprofit Corporations: 6/99 Update, 2 vols. 2nd rev. ed. Brown, Wendy L., ed. LC 98-71190. 790p. 1999. ring bd. 72.00 (*0-7626-0337-2*, BU-32951) Cont Ed Bar-CA.

B

Brown, Matthew E. Using Web Mapper. 1997. pap. 19.99 (*0-7897-1335-7*) Macmillan.

Brown, Maureen & Masters, June. Leighton Buzzard & Linslade: With Heath & Reach, Eggington, Stanbridge & Billington. LC 97-130920. (Britain in Old Photographs Ser.). 126p. 1998. write for info. (*0-7509-0871-8*) Sutton Pub Ltd.

Brown, Maureen, jt. auth. see Wade, Sheila.

Brown, Maurice. Adam Smith's Economics: Its Place in the Development of Economic Thought. 208p. 1988. lib. bdg. 60.00 (*0-7099-5079-9*) Routledge.

Brown, Maurice & Korzenik, Diana. Art Making & Education. LC 92-35667. (Disciplines in Art Education Ser.). 240p. (C). 1993. text 39.95 (*0-252-02007-3*); pap. text 14.95 (*0-252-06312-0*) U of Ill Pr.

Brown, Maurice J. Chopin: An Index of His Works in Chronological Order. 2nd ed. LC 70-39498. (Music Ser.). 1972. reprint ed. 32.50 (*0-306-70500-1*) Da Capo.

— Essays on Schubert. LC 77-22216. (Music Reprint Ser.). (Illus.). 1978. reprint ed. lib. bdg. 39.50 (*0-306-77439-9*) Da Capo.

— New Grove Composer Biography Schubert. (New Grove Composer Biography Ser.). 1997. pap. 12.95 (*0-393-31586-X*) Norton.

Brown, Maxwell L. Farm Budgets: From Farm Income Analysis to Agricultural Project Analysis. LC 79-3704. (World Bank Staff Occasional Papers: Vol. 29). 155p. reprint ed. pap. 48.10 (*0-608-15867-4*, 203073900070) Bks Demand.

Brown, May W. Reel Life on Hollywood Movie Sets. LC 95-10391. (Biography, Autobiography, Memoirs Ser.). (Illus.). 225p. 1995. pap. 19.95 (*1-57241-016-7*) Ariadne CA.

Brown, Meg L. Donne & the Politics of Conscience in Early Modern England. (Studies in the History of Christian Thought). ix, 159p. 1994. 75.00 (*90-04-10157-8*) Brill Academic Pubs.

Brown, Megan. The Christmas Burbles. 32p. (YA). (gr. 3 up). 1996. 15.95 (*1-889279-02-1*) Best Small Pr.

Brown, Megan, ed. see Braunschweiger, Lois.

***Brown, Meggita.** Mirror of the Soul. 67p. 2000. 15.95 (*0-7541-1280-2*) Minerva Pr.

Brown, Melanie & Mikula-Toth, Agnes. Adult Conductive Education: A Practical Guide. 227p. 1997. 59.95 (*1-56593-338-9*, 0668) Singular Publishing.

Brown, Melissa, ed. Negotiating Ethnicities in China & Taiwan. (China Research Monographs: No. 46). (Illus.). 335p. (C). 1995. pap. 20.00 (*1-55729-048-2*) IEAS.

Brown, Melissa C., jt. auth. see Frolik, Lawrence A.

Brown, Meredith, ed. Global Offerings of Securities: Access to World Equity Capital Markets. (IBA Ser.). 208p. (C). 1994. lib. bdg. 87.50 (*1-85966-045-2*, Pub. by Graham & Trotman) Kluwer Academic.

***Brown, Meredith M.** International Mergers & Acquisitions. LC 99-30971. 1999. 75.00 (*90-411-9733-8*) Kluwer Law Intl.

Brown, Meredith M., ed. Mechanics of Global Equity Offerings: Structuring the Offering & Negotiating the Underwriting Agreement. LC 95-32860. 1995. write for info. (*90-411-0855-6*) Kluwer Law Intl.

— Privatisation - Focus, 1993. LC 97-32. (IBA Ser.). 224p. (C). 1997. lib. bdg. 76.00 (*1-85333-096-5*, Pub. by Graham & Trotman) Kluwer Academic.

Brown, Merle E. Kenneth Burke. LC 70-625286. (University of Minnesota Pamphlets on American Writers Ser.: No. 75). 48p. (Orig.). reprint ed. pap. 30.00 (*0-7837-2896-4*, 205755900006) Bks Demand.

— Neo-Idealistic Aesthetics: Croce-Gentile-Collingwood. LC 65-20757. 261p. reprint ed. pap. 81.00 (*0-7837-3682-7*, 204355600009) Bks Demand.

Brown, Meta & Mulholland, Joyce L. Drug Calculations: Process & Problems for Clinical Practice. 5th ed. LC 95-39518. (Illus.). 336p. (C). (gr. 13). 1995. pap. text 29.00 (*0-8151-0508-8*, 24413) Mosby Inc.

***Brown, Micah, et al.** Essential Perl 5 for Web Masters. LC 99-32974. (Essential Series for Web Professionals Ser.). (Illus.). 208p. 1999. pap. text 29.99 (*0-13-012653-5*) P-H.

Brown, Micah, jt. auth. see Livingston, Dan.

Brown, Michael. The Day Will Come: Answers to Your Questions about Mystics, Prophecies, & Miracles. 340p. 1996. pap. 12.99 (*0-89283-944-9*) Servant.

— The Hunt down Under. LC 97-94714. (Illus.). 160p. 1997. write for info. (*1-57579-100-5*) Pine Hill Pr.

— The Israeli-American Connection: Its Roots in the Yishuv, 1914-1945. LC 96-5939. (America-Holy Land Monographs Ser.). (Illus.). 374p. (C). 1996. 39.95 (*0-8143-2536-X*) Wayne St U Pr.

— The Jewish Gardening Cookbook: Growing Plants & Cooking for Holidays & Festivals. LC 98-10721. 224p. 1998. 21.95 (*1-58023-004-0*) Jewish Lights.

***Brown, Michael.** Kilimanjaro: Safari in Tanzania. (Illus.). 254p. 1999. write for info. (*1-57579-166-8*, Pub. by Pine Hill Pr) Penmarch Pub.

Brown, Michael. Last Secret. LC 97-42592. 1998. pap. text 14.99 (*1-56955-023-9*) Servant.

— Nurses: The Human Touch. 1992. mass mkt. 5.99 (*0-8041-0800-5*) Ivy Books.

***Brown, Michael.** Revolution! 2000. pap. 12.99 (*0-8307-2640-3*, Renew) Gospel Lght.

Brown, Michael. Streetwise Houston. (Illus.). 1998. 5.95 (*0-935039-89-9*) Stwise Maps.

— Swimming with Crocs: Safari in Zambia. LC 97-94715. (Illus.). 136p. 1997. write for info. (*1-57579-101-3*) Pine Hill Pr.

— Zulus & Gnomes: Safari in South Africa. LC 97-94713. (Illus.). 136p. 1997. write for info. (*1-57579-102-1*) Pine Hill Pr.

Brown, Michael, ed. Approaches to Antisemitism: Context & Curriculum. LC 94-33857. 1994. write for info. (*0-87495-106-2*) Am Jewish Comm.

Brown, Michael & Lightman, Bernard, eds. Creating the Jewish Future. LC 98-25340. 272p. (C). 1998. 62.00 (*0-7619-9032-1*); pap. 24.95 (*0-7619-9033-X*) AltaMira Pr.

Brown, Michael B. Africa's Choices: After Thirty Years of the World Bank. LC 96-49254. 456p. (C). 1997. pap. text 30.00 (*0-8133-3334-2*, Pub. by Westview) HarpC.

— Be All That You Can Be: 12 Sermons on Developing God-Given Potential. LC 94-38267. 92p. (Orig.). 1995. pap. 9.95 (*0-7880-0381-X*) CSS OH.

— European Union: Fortress of Democracy. 1990. 55.00 (*0-85124-520-X*, Pub. by Spkesman); pap. 21.00 (*0-85124-521-8*, Pub. by Spkesman) Dufour.

— It Works For Us! The Clergy's Church Growth Handbook. LC 92-39129. 1992. pap. 9.95 (*1-55673-509-X*, 9301) CSS OH.

Brown, Michael B., et al, eds. Full Employment. 144p. 1978. pap. 23.50 (*0-85124-218-9*, Pub. by Spkesman) Coronet Bks.

Brown, Michael B., ed. see Aganbegyan, Abel.

Brown, Michael B., jt. ed. see Coates, Ken.

Brown, Michael Barratt & Tiffen, Pauline M. Short Changed: Africa in World Trade. LC 92-34001. (Transnational Institute Ser.). 220p. (C). 54.95 (*0-7453-0694-2*, Pub. by Pluto GBR) Stylus Pub VA.

Brown, Michael D. God Created Poetry. LC 95-94616. 126p. (Orig.). 1995. pap. write for info. (*1-57502-023-8*, P00414) Morris Pubng.

— Views from Asian California: An Illustrated History, 1920-1965. (Illus.). 71p. (Orig.). 1992. pap. 25.00 (*0-9633968-0-3*) M Brown.

— Washington, D. C. Schieken, Julia, ed. (Illus.). 20p. 1995. pap. 7.95 (*1-887498-01-X*) Winterberry Pub.

Brown, Michael D. & Metzger, Philip W. Realistic Collage Step-by-Step. LC 97-35158. (Illus.). 128p. 1998. 27.99 (*0-89134-819-0*, North Lght Bks) F & W Pubns Inc.

***Brown, Michael E.** Artwise Boston. (Illus.). 1998. pap. 5.95 (*0-935039-12-0*) Stwise Maps.

— Artwise Chicago. (Illus.). 1998. 5.95 (*0-935039-50-3*) Stwise Maps.

— Artwise Florence. (Illus.). 1998. 5.95 (*0-935039-37-6*) Stwise Maps.

— Artwise London. (Illus.). 1998. 5.95 (*0-935039-40-6*) Stwise Maps.

— Artwise Los Angeles. (Illus.). 1998. 5.95 (*0-935039-13-9*) Stwise Maps.

— Artwise Manhattan. (Illus.). 1998. 5.95 (*0-935039-23-6*) Stwise Maps.

— Artwise Melbourne. (Illus.). 1998. 4.95 (*1-886705-02-X*) Stwise Maps.

— Artwise Paris. (Illus.). 1998. 5.95 (*0-935039-39-2*) Stwise Maps.

— Artwise Rome. (Illus.). 1998. 5.95 (*0-935039-14-7*) Stwise Maps.

— Artwise Sydney. (Illus.). 1998. 5.95 (*0-935039-93-7*) Stwise Maps.

— Artwise Venice. (Illus.). 1998. 5.95 (*0-935039-45-7*) Stwise Maps.

— Artwise Vienna. (Illus.). 1998. 5.95 (*0-935039-41-4*) Stwise Maps.

— Artwise Washington D. C. (Illus.). 1998. 5.95 (*0-935039-38-4*) Stwise Maps.

Brown, Michael E. Europe: Major Rail Routes. (Illus.). 1998. 5.95 (*1-886705-30-5*) Stwise Maps.

— European Security: The Defining Debates. LC 98-17399. (BCSIA Studies in International Security). (Illus.). 250p. 1999. pap. text 17.50 (*0-262-52253-5*) MIT Pr.

— Flying Blind: The Politics of the U. S. Strategic Bomber Program. LC 91-55064. (Cornell Studies in Security Affairs). (Illus.). 416p. 1992. text 52.50 (*0-8014-2285-X*) Cornell U Pr.

***Brown, Michael E.** Mini Metro Chicago. (Illus.). 1998. 1.95 (*0-935039-56-2*) Stwise Maps.

— Mini Metro London. (Illus.). 1998. 1.95 (*0-935039-33-3*) Stwise Maps.

— Mini Metro Los Angeles. (Illus.). 1998. 1.95 (*0-935039-11-2*) Stwise Maps.

— Mini Metro Manhattan Bus/Subway. (Illus.). 1998. 1.95 (*0-935039-00-7*) Stwise Maps.

— Mini Metro Paris. (Illus.). 1998. 1.95 (*0-935039-32-5*) Stwise Maps.

— Mini Metro San Francisco. (Illus.). 1998. 1.95 (*0-935039-18-X*) Stwise Maps.

— Mini Metro Washington D. C. (Illus.). 1998. 1.95 (*0-935039-34-1*) Stwise Maps.

— Pocketsize Central Boston & Rapid Transit. (Illus.). 1998. 2.95 (*0-935039-98-8*) Stwise Maps.

— Pocketsize Downtown Chicago & Transit. (Illus.). 1998. 2.95 (*0-935039-97-X*) Stwise Maps.

— Pocketsize Downtown Washington D. C. & Metrorail. (Illus.). 1998. 2.95 (*1-886705-00-3*) Stwise Maps.

— Pocketsize Manhattan Bus/Subway. (Illus.). 1998. 2.95 (*1-886705-01-1*) Stwise Maps.

Brown, Michael E. The Production of Society: A Marxian Foundation for Social Theory. 176p. (C). 1986. 58.00 (*0-8476-7472-X*) Rowman.

***Brown, Michael E.** Rational Choice & Security Studies: Stephen Walt & His Critics. (International Security Readers Ser.). 2000. pap. text 15.00 (*0-262-52275-6*) MIT Pr.

— Rise of China. (International Security Readers Ser.). 2000. pap. 20.00 (*0-262-52276-4*) MIT Pr.

— Streetwise Address Map. (Illus.). 1998. 1.95 (*0-935039-01-5*) Stwise Maps.

Brown, Michael E. Streetwise Amsterdam. (Illus.). 1998. 5.95 (*0-935039-82-1*) Stwise Maps.

***Brown, Michael E.** Streetwise Athens. (Illus.). 1998. 5.95 (*1-886705-34-8*) Stwise Maps.

— Streetwise Atlanta. (Illus.). 1998. 5.95 (*0-935039-64-3*); ring bd. 6.95 (*0-935039-85-6*) Stwise Maps.

— Streetwise Austin. (Illus.). 1998. 5.95 (*0-935039-90-2*) Stwise Maps.

— Streetwise Baltimore. (Illus.). 1998. 5.95 (*0-935039-60-0*) Stwise Maps.

Brown, Michael E. Streetwise Barcelona. 1998. 5.95 (*1-886705-11-9*) Stwise Maps.

***Brown, Michael E.** Streetwise Berlin. (Illus.). 1998. 6.95 (*1-886705-41-0*) Stwise Maps.

— Streetwise Boston. (Illus.). 1998. 5.95 (*0-935039-08-2*); ring bd. 6.95 (*0-935039-86-4*) Stwise Maps.

Brown, Michael E. Streetwise Budapest. (Illus.). 1998. 5.95 (*1-886705-22-4*) Stwise Maps.

— Streetwise California. (Illus.). 1998. 6.95 (*1-886705-29-1*) Stwise Maps.

***Brown, Michael E.** Streetwise Central Park. (Illus.). 1998. 1.95 (*0-935039-31-7*) Stwise Maps.

— Streetwise Chicago. (Illus.). 1998. 5.95 (*0-935039-24-4*); ring bd. 6.95 (*0-935039-96-1*) Stwise Maps.

— Streetwise Cote d'Azur: The French Riviera. (Illus.). 1998. 6.95 (*1-886705-43-7*) Stwise Maps.

— Streetwise Dallas. (Illus.). 1998. 5.95 (*0-935039-88-0*) Stwise Maps.

— Streetwise Denver. (Illus.). 1998. 5.95 (*0-935039-80-5*) Stwise Maps.

— Streetwise Downtown Chicago. (Illus.). 1998. 5.95 (*0-935039-54-6*) Stwise Maps.

— Streetwise Downtown Manhattan. (Illus.). 1998. 3.95 (*0-935039-48-1*) Stwise Maps.

Brown, Michael E. Streetwise Dublin. (Illus.). 1998. 5.95 (*1-886705-04-6*) Stwise Maps.

— Streetwise East Hampton. (Illus.). 1998. 5.95 (*0-935039-83-X*) Stwise Maps.

— Streetwise Florence. (Illus.). 1998. 5.95 (*0-935039-65-1*) Stwise Maps.

***Brown, Michael E.** Streetwise Florida. (Illus.). 1998. 5.95 (*1-886705-39-9*) Stwise Maps.

Brown, Michael E. Streetwise Greenwich Village, Chinatown, Little Italy, East Village, Soho, TriBeCa. (Illus.). 1998. 5.95 (*0-935039-28-7*) Stwise Maps.

— Streetwise Hawaii. (Illus.). 1998. 5.95 (*0-935039-79-1*) Stwise Maps.

— Streetwise Jerusalem. (Illus.). 1998. 5.95 (*1-886705-23-2*) Stwise Maps.

— Streetwise Las Vegas. (Illus.). 1998. 5.95 (*1-886705-07-0*) Stwise Maps.

***Brown, Michael E.** Streetwise London. (Illus.). 1998. 5.95 (*0-935039-27-9*); ring bd. 6.95 (*1-886705-24-0*) Stwise Maps.

— Streetwise London Underground. (Illus.). 1998. ring bd. 6.95 (*1-886705-25-9*) Stwise Maps.

— Streetwise Long Island. (Illus.). 1998. ring bd. 6.95 (*1-886705-06-2*) Stwise Maps.

— Streetwise Long Island Roads. (Illus.). 1998. 5.95 (*0-935039-99-6*) Stwise Maps.

Brown, Michael E. Streetwise Los Angeles. (Illus.). 1998. 5.95 (*0-935039-17-1*) Stwise Maps.

***Brown, Michael E.** Streetwise Los Angeles. (Illus.). 1998. ring bd. 6.95 (*0-935039-73-2*) Stwise Maps.

— Streetwise Madrid. (Illus.). 1998. 5.95 (*0-935039-63-5*) Stwise Maps.

Brown, Michael E. Streetwise Manhattan. (Illus.). 1998. 5.95 (*0-935039-03-1*) Stwise Maps.

***Brown, Michael E.** Streetwise Manhattan. (Illus.). 1998. ring bd. 6.95 (*0-935039-66-X*) Stwise Maps.

— Streetwise Maryland & the Virginias. (Illus.). 1998. 6.95 (*1-886705-36-4*) Stwise Maps.

— Streetwise Melbourne. (Illus.). 1998. 4.95 (*1-886705-03-8*) Stwise Maps.

Brown, Michael E. Streetwise Miami. (Illus.). 1998. 5.95 (*0-935039-51-1*) Stwise Maps.

***Brown, Michael E.** Streetwise Midtown Manhattan. (Illus.). 1998. 5.95 (*0-935039-04-X*) Stwise Maps.

— Streetwise Milan. (Illus.). 1998. 5.95 (*1-886705-33-X*) Stwise Maps.

Brown, Michael E. Streetwise Monterey. (Illus.). 1998. 5.95 (*1-886705-28-3*) Stwise Maps.

— Streetwise Montreal. (Illus.). 1998. 5.95 (*1-886705-09-7*) Stwise Maps.

***Brown, Michael E.** Streetwise Montreal. (Illus.). 1998. ring bd. 6.95 (*1-886705-15-1*) Stwise Maps.

— Streetwise Munich. (Illus.). 1998. 5.95 (*1-886705-05-4*) Stwise Maps.

— Streetwise New Jersey. (Illus.). 1998. 5.95 (*1-886705-37-2*) Stwise Maps.

Brown, Michael E. Streetwise New Orleans. (Illus.). 1997. 5.95 (*0-935039-10-4*) Stwise Maps.

***Brown, Michael E.** Streetwise New York Metro Commuter Rail Map. (Illus.). 1998. ring bd. 6.95 (*0-935039-84-8*) Stwise Maps.

Brown, Michael E. Streetwise New York, New Jersey. (Illus.). 1998. 5.95 (*1-886705-21-6*) Stwise Maps.

***Brown, Michael E.** Streetwise Orlando. (Illus.). 1998. 5.95 (*1-886705-40-2*) Stwise Maps.

— Streetwise Paris. (Illus.). 1998. 5.95 (*0-935039-25-2*); ring bd. 6.95 (*1-886705-12-7*) Stwise Maps.

— Streetwise Pennsylvania. (Illus.). 1998. 5.95 (*1-886705-38-0*) Stwise Maps.

Brown, Michael E. Streetwise Philadelphia. (Illus.). 1998. 5.95 (*0-935039-07-4*) Stwise Maps.

***Brown, Michael E.** Streetwise Philadelphia. (Illus.). 1998. ring bd. 6.95 (*0-935039-75-9*) Stwise Maps.

Brown, Michael E. Streetwise Phoenix. (Illus.). 1998. 5.95 (*0-935039-94-5*) Stwise Maps.

***Brown, Michael E.** Streetwise Prague. (Illus.). 1998. 5.95 (*1-886705-20-8*) Stwise Maps.

— Streetwise Provence. (Illus.). 1998. 6.95 (*1-886705-42-9*) Stwise Maps.

— Streetwise Rome. (Illus.). 1998. 5.95 (*0-935039-67-8*) Stwise Maps.

Brown, Michael E. Streetwise San Antonio. (Illus.). 1998. 4.95 (*0-935039-91-0*) Stwise Maps.

— Streetwise San Diego. (Illus.). 1998. 5.95 (*0-935039-53-8*) Stwise Maps.

— Streetwise San Francisco. (Illus.). 1998. 5.95 (*0-935039-20-1*) Stwise Maps.

***Brown, Michael E.** Streetwise San Francisco. (Illus.). 1998. ring bd. 6.95 (*0-935039-87-2*) Stwise Maps.

Brown, Michael E. Streetwise Seattle. (Illus.). 1998. 5.95 (*0-935039-55-4*) Stwise Maps.

— Streetwise Southampton. (Illus.). 1998. 5.95 (*1-886705-31-3*) Stwise Maps.

***Brown, Michael E.** Streetwise Southern New England. (Illus.). 1998. 6.95 (*1-886705-35-6*) Stwise Maps.

Brown, Michael E. Streetwise Sydney. (Illus.). 1998. 5.95 (*0-935039-92-9*) Stwise Maps.

— Streetwise Toronto. (Illus.). 1998. 5.95 (*1-886705-08-9*) Stwise Maps.

***Brown, Michael E.** Streetwise Toronto. (Illus.). 1998. ring bd. 6.95 (*1-886705-16-X*) Stwise Maps.

— Streetwise Tuscany. (Illus.). 1998. 6.95 (*1-886705-32-1*) Stwise Maps.

— Streetwise U. S. A. Area Code & Time Zones. (Illus.). 1998. ring bd. 6.95 (*0-935039-76-7*) Stwise Maps.

— Streetwise U. S. A. Interstate Highways. (Illus.). 1998. ring bd. 6.95 (*0-935039-77-5*) Stwise Maps.

Brown, Michael E. Streetwise Vancouver. (Illus.). 1998. 5.95 (*1-886705-10-0*) Stwise Maps.

***Brown, Michael E.** Streetwise Vancouver. (Illus.). 1998. ring bd. 6.95 (*1-886705-14-3*) Stwise Maps.

— Streetwise Venice. (Illus.). 1998. 5.95 (*0-935039-78-3*) Stwise Maps.

— Streetwise Vienna. (Illus.). 1998. 5.95 (*0-935039-81-3*) Stwise Maps.

Brown, Michael E. Streetwise Washington, D. C. (Illus.). 1998. 5.95 (*0-935039-06-6*) Stwise Maps.

***Brown, Michael E.** Streetwise Washington D. C. (Illus.). 1998. ring bd. 6.95 (*0-935039-74-0*) Stwise Maps.

— Transitwise. (Illus.). 1998. 5.95 (*0-935039-19-8*) Stwise Maps.

— U. S. A. Interstate Highways. (Illus.). 1998. 5.95 (*0-935039-68-6*) Stwise Maps.

Brown, Michael E. Welcome to New York. (Illus.). 1998. 7.95 (*0-935039-30-9*) Stwise Maps.

***Brown, Michael E.** Worldwise. (Illus.). 1998. 5.95 (*0-935039-29-5*); ring bd. 6.95 (*0-935039-16-3*) Stwise Maps.

Brown, Michael E., ed. Ethnic Conflict & International Security. LC 93-2175. 280p. 1993. text 49.50 (*0-691-03368-4*, Pub. by Princeton U Pr); pap. text 16.95 (*0-691-00068-9*, Pub. by Princeton U Pr) Cal Prin Full Svc.

— The International Dimensions of Internal Conflict. (CSIA Studies in International Security: No. 10). (Illus.). 671p. (C). 1996. pap. text 29.50 (*0-262-52209-8*) MIT Pr.

— The International Dimensions of Internal Conflict. (CSIA Studies in International Security: Vol. 10). (Illus.). 672p. 1996. 60.00 (*0-262-02397-0*) MIT Pr.

***Brown, Michael E., et al, eds.** America's Strategic Choices. rev. ed. LC 99-58455. (International Security Readers Ser.). 275p. 2000. pap. text 21.00 (*0-262-52274-8*) MIT Pr.

Brown, Michael E., et al, eds. Debating the Democratic Peace. (International Security Readers Ser.). (Illus.). 416p. 1996. pap. text 21.00 (*0-262-52213-6*) MIT Pr.

— East Asian Security. LC 96-6329. (IS Reader Ser.). (Illus.). 378p. 1996. pap. text 21.00 (*0-262-52220-9*) MIT Pr.

— Nationalism & Ethnic Conflict. LC 96-52337. (IS Reader Ser.). (Illus.). 452p. 1997. pap. text 20.00 (*0-262-52224-1*) MIT Pr.

— New Studies in the Politics & Culture of U. S. Communism. 384p. (C). 1993. text 38.00 (*0-85345-851-0*, Pub. by Monthly Rev); pap. text 18.00 (*0-85345-852-9*, Pub. by Monthly Rev) NYU Pr.

— The Perils of Anarchy: Contemporary Realism & International Security. LC 94-24041. (International Security Reader Ser.). 541p. 1995. pap. text 24.50 (*0-262-52202-0*) MIT Pr.

— Theories of War & Peace. LC 98-21051. (IS Readers Ser.). (Illus.). 570p. 1998. pap. text 27.50 (*0-262-52252-7*) MIT Pr.

Brown, Michael E. & Cote, Owen R., eds. America's Strategic Choices. LC 97-22496. (IS Readers Ser.). (Illus.). 360p. 1997. pap. text 19.50 (*0-262-52243-8*) MIT Pr.

Brown, Michael E. & Ganguly, Sumit, eds. Government Policies & Ethnic Relations in Asia & the Pacific. LC 97-25825. (CSIA Studies in International Security). (Illus.). 624p. (Orig.). 1997. pap. text 27.50 (*0-262-52245-4*) MIT Pr.

Brown, Michael E. & Rosecrance, Richard N., eds. The Costs of Conflict: Prevention & Cure in the Global Arena. LC 98-41030. (Carnegie Commission on Preventing Deadly Conflict Ser.: Vol. 118). 304p. 1999. 69.00 (*0-8476-8893-3*); pap. 28.95 (*0-8476-8894-1*) Rowman.

Brown, Michael E., jt. auth. see Galwey, A. K.

Brown, Michael F. The Channeling Zone: American Spirituality in an Anxious Age. LC 96-38375. 256p. 1997. 22.00 (*0-674-10882-5*) HUP.

— The Channeling Zone: American Spirituality in an Anxious Age. 1999. pap. text 14.00 (*0-674-10883-3*) HUP.

Brown, Michael F. Criminal Investigation: Law & Practice. 368p. Date not set. pap. 41.95 (*0-7506-7352-4*) Buttrwrth-Heinemann.

Brown, Michael F. Criminal Investigation, Law & Practice. LC 96-48004. 368p. 1997. 41.95 (*0-7506-9665-6*) Buttrwrth-Heinemann.

— Tsewa's Gift: Magic & Meaning in an Amazonian Society.

LC 85-40401. (Series in Ethnographic Inquiry). (Illus.). 220p. (C). 1993. reprint ed. pap. text 14.95 (*1-56098-306-X*) Smithsonian.

— War of Shadows: The Struggle for Utopia in the Peruvian Amazon. LC 90-26076. (C). 1993. pap. 17.95 (*0-520-07448-3*, Pub. by U CA Pr) Cal Prin Full Svc.

Brown, Michael F. & Fernandez, Eduardo. War of Shadows: The Struggle for Utopia in the Peruvian Amazon. LC 90-26076. (Illus.). 275p. 1991. 45.00 (*0-520-07435-1*, Pub. by U CA Pr) Cal Prin Full Svc.

Brown, Michael H. After Life: What It's Like in Heaven, Hell, & Purgatory. LC 97-77031. 120p. 1997. pap. 6.50 (*1-880033-25-9*) Queenship Pub.

— The Day the Bronx Died. 96p. 1996. pap. 6.95 (*1-55783-229-3*) Applause Theatre Bk Pubs.

— The Final Hour. LC 92-71997. (Illus.). 371p. (Orig.). 1992. pap. 12.50 (*1-880033-03-8*) Queenship Pub.

— PK: A Report on the Power of Psychokinesis, the Mental Energy to Move Matter. LC 76-21121. (Freedeeds Library). (Illus.). 320p. 1976. 15.95 (*0-8334-0716-3*, Freedeeds Libr) Garber Comm.

— Prayer of the Warrior. LC 93-72630. (Illus.). 248p. (Orig.). 1993. pap. 11.00 (*1-880033-10-0*) Queenship Pub.

— Secrets of the Eucharist. LC 96-85387. 96p. 1996. pap. 5.50 (*1-880033-23-2*) Queenship Pub.

— Seven Days with Mary. Riehle Foundation Staff, ed. & photos by by. LC 98-73954. (Illus.). 112p. 1998. pap. 6.50 (*1-880033-26-7*) Queenship Pub.

— The Trumpet of Gabriel. LC 94-61406. 365p. 1994. pap. 11.00 (*1-880033-16-X*) Queenship Pub.

***Brown, Michael H.** The Trumpet of Gabriel. 312p. 2000. pap. 10.00 (*1-57918-134-1*, 7714) Queenship Pub.

***Brown, Michael H. & Terelya, Josyp.** The Final Hour. (Illus.). 352p. (Orig.). 2000. pap. 12.50 (*1-57918-133-3*, 7716) Queenship Pub.

Brown, Michael H., jt. auth. see Terelya, Josyp.

Brown, Michael J. Baseball Techniques in Pictures. (Orig.). 1993. pap. 8.95 (*0-399-51798-7*, Perigee Bks) Berkley Pub.

— Basketball Rules in Pictures. (Illus.). 80p. 1993. pap. 8.95 (*0-399-51842-8*, Perigee Bks) Berkley Pub.

— Football Techniques in Pictures. (Sports Techniques in Pictures Ser.). (Illus.). 80p. (Orig.). 1992. pap. 8.95 (*0-399-51769-3*, Perigee Bks) Berkley Pub.

— Golf Techniques in Pictures: Easy-to-Follow Instruction for Mastering Your Game. (Sports Rules in Pictures Ser.). (Illus.). 80p. 1991. pap. 10.00 (*0-399-51664-6*, Perigee Bks) Berkley Pub.

— Soccer Techniques in Pictures. (Techniques in Pictures Ser.). (Illus.). 80p. (Orig.). (YA). 1991. pap. 8.95 (*0-399-51701-4*, Perigee Bks) Berkley Pub.

***Brown, Michael J.** What They Don't Tell You: A Survivor's Guide to Biblical Studies. 2000. pap. 10.95 (*0-664-22220-X*) Westminster John Knox.

Brown, Michael J., ed. see United States Golf Association Staff.

Brown, Michael K. Race, Money, & The American Welfare State LC 98-31999. 1999. 22.50 (*0-8014-8510-X*) Cornell U Pr.

— Race, Money & the American Welfare State. LC 98-31999. 1999. write for info. (*0-8014-3510-2*) Cornell U Pr.

— Working the Street: Police Discretion & the Dilemmas of Reform. LC 88-20951. 384p. 1988. pap. 16.95 (*0-87154-191-2*) Russell Sage.

***Brown, Michael L.** Answering Jewish Objections to Jesus: General & Historical Objections, 1. 304p. 2000. pap. 15.99 (*0-8010-6063-X*) Baker Bks.

— Answering Jewish Objections to Jesus: Theological Objections, 2. 336p. (gr. 13 up). 2000. pap. 15.99 (*0-8010-6334-5*) Baker Bks.

Brown, Michael L. The End of the American Gospel Enterprise. 112p. (Orig.). 1993. pap. 8.99 (*1-56043-002-8*) Destiny Image.

— From Holy Laughter to Holy Fire. LC 96-230394. 294p. (Orig.). 1996. pap. 10.99 (*1-56043-181-4*) Destiny Image.

***Brown, Michael L.** Go & Sin No More. LC 98-50206. 312p. 1999. pap. 17.99 (*0-8307-2389-7*, Regal Bks) Gospel Lght.

Brown, Michael L. Go & Sin No More: A Call to Holiness. LC 98-50206. 312p. 1999. 17.99 (*0-8307-2395-1*, Renew) Gospel Lght.

— How Saved Are We? 140p. 1990. pap. 9.99 (*1-56043-055-9*) Destiny Image.

— Israel's Divine Healer. LC 95-2139. (Studies in Old Testament Biblical Theology Ser.). 440p. 1995. pap. 19.99 (*0-310-20029-6*) Zondervan.

— It's Time to Rock the Boat. 210p. (Orig.). 1993. pap. 10.99 (*1-56043-106-7*) Destiny Image.

— Let No One Deceive You. LC 97-220120. 312p. 1997. pap. 13.99 (*1-56043-693-X*, Revival Pr) Destiny Image.

— Our Hands Are Stained with Blood. 266p. (Orig.). 1992. pap. 10.99 (*1-56043-068-0*) Destiny Image.

— Whatever Happened to the Power of God. 210p. (Orig.). 1991. pap. 10.99 (*1-56043-042-7*) Destiny Image.

Brown, Michael L., et al. Seminar on Intelligence, Command, & Control: Guest Presentations, Spring 1995. unabridged ed. (Illus.). 232p. (Orig.). 1996. pap. text. write for info. (*1-879716-29-1*, I-96-2) Ctr Info Policy.

***Brown, Michael P.** Closet Geographies: Geographies of Metaphor from the Body to the Globe. LC 00-27301. (Critical Geographies Ser.). 2000. pap. write for info. (*0-415-18765-6*) Routledge.

Brown, Michael P. New Jersey Parks, Forests, & Natural Areas: A Guide. rev. ed. (Illus.). 250p. 1997. pap. 16.00 (*0-8135-2481-4*) Rutgers U Pr.

— Replacing Citizenship: AIDS Activism & Radical Democracy. LC 96-52388. 222p. 1997. lib. bdg. 42.95 (*1-57230-210-0*) Guilford Pubns.

— RePlacing Citizenship: AIDS Activism & Radical Democracy. LC 96-52388. (Mappings). 222p. 1997. pap. text 19.95 (*1-57230-222-4*, 0222) Guilford Pubns.

***Brown, Michael P., et al.** Gex 3: Deep Cover Gecko - Prima's Official Strategy Guide. LC 99-70145. (Illus.). 156p. 1999. pap. 12.99 (*0-7615-2090-2*) Prima Pub.

***Brown, Michael Patrick.** BattleTanx - Global Assault: Prima's Official Strategy Guide. LC 00-10036. (Official Strategy Guides Ser.). (Illus.). 141p. (YA). 2000. pap. 14.99 (*0-7615-2787-7*) Prima Pub.

— Yahoo! Card Games. (Official Strategy Guides Ser.). 128p. 2000. pap. 9.99 (*0-7615-2715-X*) Prima Pub.

Brown, Michael R. Falling Wallendas. 96p. 1994. pap. 7.95 (*1-882688-02-3*) Tia Chucha Pr.

Brown, Michael R., ed. Resistance of Pseudomonas Aeruginosa. LC 74-30224. 342p. reprint ed. pap. 97.50 (*0-608-08656-8*, 2016181) Bks Demand.

Brown, Michael R. & Gilbert, Peter, eds. Microbiological Quality Assurance: A Guide Towards Relevance & Reproducibility of Inocula. LC 94-43936. 320p. 1995. boxed set 179.95 (*0-8493-4752-1*, 4752) CRC Pr.

***Brown, Michael R., et al.** Magnetic Helicity in Space & Laboratory Plasmas. LC 99-26374. (Geophysical Monograph Ser.: Vol. 111). 11p. 1999. 69.00 (*0-87590-094-1*) Am Geophysical.

Brown, Michael S. God's Gifts to Us All. 184p. 1997. 24.95 (*0-9661776-0-6*) Bluebird Mead.

Brown, Michael S. & Find/SVP (Firm) Staff. Consumer Health & Medical Information on the Internet. LC 98-207835. iv, 126p. 1996. write for info. (*1-56241-402-X*) FIND-SVP.

Brown, Michael S., jt. auth. see Nelkin, Dorothy.

Brown, Michael S., jt. ed. see Goldstein, Joseph L.

Brown, Michael Z., jt. auth. see Hambright, Robert.

Brown, Michele. Edward Bear ESQ. (Illus.). 112p. 1997. 14.95 (*1-55670-542-5*) Stewart Tabori & Chang.

— The Teddy Bear Hall of Fame: A Century of Historic Bears Presented by the Teddy Bear Museum. (Illus.). 144p. 1998. pap. 24.95 (*0-7472-7763-X*, Pub. by Headline Bk Pub) Trafalgar.

***Brown, Michele C. & Browne, Steven E.** The Accident Report: Questions to Be Asked When You're Involved in a Car Accident. ii, 62p. 2000. spiral bd. 7.95 (*0-914499-04-1*, Pub. by Wilton Place) Brodart.

Brown, Michele D., jt. auth. see Maikovich, Andrew J.

Brown, Michelle, jt. ed. see Webster, Leslie.

Brown, Michelle P. Anglo-Saxon Manuscripts. (Illus.). 80p. (Orig.). 1992. pap. 18.95 (*0-8020-7728-5*) U of Toronto Pr.

— The Book of Cerne: Prayer, Patronage, & Power in Ninth-Century England. (British Library Studies in Medieval Culture). (Illus.). 256p. 1996. text 85.00 (*0-8020-4113-2*) U of Toronto Pr.

— The British Library Guide to Writing & Scripts: History & Techniques. LC 98-192946. (British Library Guides Ser.). (Illus.). 92p. 1998. pap. 19.95 (*0-8020-8172-X*) U of Toronto Pr.

— A Guide to Western Historical Scripts from Antiquity to 1600. 136p. 1990. text 40.00 (*0-8020-5866-3*) U of Toronto Pr.

— A Guide to Western Historical Scripts from Antiquity to 1600. (Illus.). 149p. (C). 1994. pap. text 25.00 (*0-8020-7206-2*) U of Toronto Pr.

— Understanding Illuminated Manuscripts: A Guide to Technical Terms. LC 93-42239. (Looking at...Ser.). (Illus.). 112p. (Orig.). 1994. pap. 14.95 (*0-89236-217-0*, Pub. by J P Getty Trust) OUP.

Brown, Michelle P. & McKendrick, Scot, eds. Illuminating the Book: Makers & Interpreters. (British Library Studies in Medieval Culture). (Illus.). 320p. 1998. text 75.00 (*0-8020-4411-5*) U of Toronto Pr.

Brown, Mick. Performance Movie Guide. 208p. 1999. pap. 15.95 (*1-58234-043-9*) Bloomsbury Pubg.

— Richard Branson: The Authorized Biography. 2nd rev. ed. (Illus.). 544p. (Orig.). 1998. mass mkt. 13.95 (*0-7472-3216-4*, Pub. by Headline Bk Pub) Trafalgar.

— The Spiritual Tourist: A Personal Odyssey Through the Outer Reaches of Belief. 256p. 1998. 24.95 (*1-58234-001-3*) Bloomsbury Pubg.

— The Spiritual Tourist: A Personal Odyssey Through the Outer Reaches of Belief. 1999. pap. 13.95 (*1-58234-034-X*) Bloomsbury Pubg.

Brown, Mik. Crack-Ups: A Very Silly Joke Book. LC 93-28644. (Illus.). 64p. (Orig.). (J). (gr. 2-7). 1994. pap. 3.95 (*1-85697-930-X*) LKC.

***Brown, Mike.** The Design of Roundabouts: State-of-the-Art Review, 2 vols., Set. 278p. 2000. reprint ed. pap. 85.00 (*0-11-551741-3*, Pub. by Statnry Office) Balogh.

Brown, Mike. Escape from Outer Alcatraz Vol. 1: How to Manipulate Men. 189p. (Orig.). 1991. pap. 15.00 (*0-9629888-1-2*) L L Brown Pub.

Brown, Mike, jt. auth. see Michaels, Charlie.

Brown, Mike, ed. see Webb, Roy.

Brown, Mikhail, ed. see Steelman, Charles R. & Steelman, Sharon B.

Brown, Mildred L. & Rounsley, Chloe A. True Selves: Understanding Transsexualism: For Family, Friends, Coworkers & Helping Professionals. LC 96-10107. 1996. 24.50 (*0-7879-0271-3*) Jossey-Bass.

Brown, Millard F., jt. auth. see Green, William.

Brown, Milli. How to Interview a Sleeping Man: 50 Hilarious & Heart-Warming Hints to Help You Save Your Family Memories. Mackin, Karey, ed. (Illus.). 112p. 1998. pap. 14.95 (*0-9643885-9-6*) Personal Profiles.

Brown, Milton P., Jr. Authentic Writings of Ignatius: A Study of Linguistic Criteria. LC 63-19458. 175p. reprint ed. pap. 54.30 (*0-8357-9096-7*, 201788800010) Bks Demand.

Brown, Milton P. Biblical Prophets, Seers, & the New Apocalypticism: Rightly Explaining the Word of Truth. LC 95-11853. 100p. 1996. pap. 14.95 (*0-7734-2424-5*) E Mellen.

— To Hear the Word: Invitation to Serious Study of the Bible. LC 86-31082. 256p. 1987. 29.95 (*0-86554-251-1*, MUP H-216); pap. 14.95 (*0-86554-252-X*, MUP/P040) Mercer Univ Pr.

Brown, Milton W. American Painting from the Armory Show to the Depression. 256p. 1955. pap. text 24.95 (*0-691-00301-7*, Pub. by Princeton U Pr) Cal Prin Full Svc.

— American Painting, from the Armory Show to the Depression. LC 53-10147. 256p. reprint ed. pap. 79.40 (*0-608-09120-0*, 206975200006) Bks Demand.

Brown, Milton W., et al. American Art: Painting, Sculpture, Architecture, Decorative Arts, Photography. (Illus.). 616p. 1979. 60.00 (*0-8109-0658-9*, Pub. by Abrams) Time Warner.

Brown, Molly. Cracker: To Say I Love You. 1996. mass mkt. 5.99 (*0-312-95996-6*) St Martin.

— Invitation to a Funeral: A Tale of Restoration Intrigue. LC 98-12772. 288p. (YA). 1998. text 22.95 (*0-312-18598-7*) St Martin.

Brown, Molly Y. Growing Whole: Exploring the Wilderness Within. x, 113p. (Orig.). 1997. pap. 16.95 incl. audio (*0-9611444-2-4*) Psychosynth Pr.

— Growing Whole: Self-Realization on an Endangered Planet. LC 92-53254. x, 245p. (Orig.). 1997. pap. 12.00 (*0-9611444-1-6*) Psychosynth Pr.

— The Unfolding Self: Psychosynthesis & Counseling. LC 83-61449. (Illus.). 181p. (C). 1983. reprint ed. pap. 20.00 (*0-9611444-0-8*) Psychosynth Pr.

Brown, Molly Y., jt. auth. see Macy, Joanna R.

Brown, Montague. Integrated Health Care Delivery: Theory, Practice, Evaluation & Prognosis. LC 95-52251. (Health Care Management Review Ser.). 224p. 1996. pap. 43.00 (*0-8342-0814-8*, 20814) Aspen Pub.

— Managed Care: Strategies, Networks & Management. (HCMR Ser.). 272p. 1993. 41.00 (*0-8342-0504-1*, 20504) Aspen Pub.

— The Quest for Moral Foundations: An Introduction to Ethics. LC 95-42088. 192p. (C). 1996. pap. 14.95 (*0-87840-613-1*) Georgetown U Pr.

— The Romance of Reason: An Adventure in the Thought of Thomas Aquinas. 177p. (Orig.). 1993. pap. 18.95 (*0-932506-96-8*) St Bedes Pubns.

Brown, Montague, ed. Health Care Financial Management. (HCMR Ser.). 222p. 1992. 41.00 (*0-8342-0303-0*, 20303) Aspen Pub.

— Health Care Management: Strategy, Structure, & Process. (HCMR Ser.). 232p. 1992. 41.00 (*0-8342-0299-9*, 20299) Aspen Pub.

— Health Care Management Review Series, 7 vols., Set. 1992. 278.00 (*0-8342-0337-5*) Aspen Pub.

— Health Care Marketing Management. (HCMR Ser.). 224p. 1992. 41.00 (*0-8342-0302-2*, 20302) Aspen Pub.

— Human Resource Management in Health Care. (HCMR Ser.). 256p. 1992. pap. 41.00 (*0-8342-0340-5*, 20340) Aspen Pub.

— Nursing Management: Issues & Ideas. (Health Care Management Review Ser.). 220p. 1992. 41.00 (*0-8342-0301-4*, 20301) Aspen Pub.

— Physicians & Management in Health Care. (Health Care Management Review Ser.). 244p. 1992. 41.00 (*0-8342-0300-6*, 20300) Aspen Pub.

Brown, Monty. Where Giants Trod: The Saga of Kenya's Desert Lake. 1992. 35.00 (*1-870948-25-4*, Pub. by Quiller Pr) St Mut.

Brown, Morris & Brown, Eli M., eds. Comprehensive Postanesthesia Care. LC 96-14627. (Illus.). 573p. 1997. 89.95 (*0-683-01116-2*) Lppncott W & W.

Brown, Mort. So You Want to Own the Store. LC 97-6705. 272p. 1996. pap. 15.95 (*0-8092-3236-7*, 323670, Contemporary Bks) NTC Contemp Pub Co.

Brown, Muriel & Foudray, Rita S. Newbery & Caldecott Medalists & Honor Book Winners: Bibliographies & Resource Materials Through 1991. 2nd ed. Roginski, Jim, ed. 530p. 1992. 65.00 (*1-55570-118-3*) Neal-Schuman.

Brown, Murray, ed. The Theory & Empirical Analysis of Production. (Studies in Income & Wealth: No. 31). 525p. 1967. reprint ed. 136.50 (*0-87014-486-3*) Natl Bur Econ Res.

Brown, Murray M. Amsden. Some Descendants of Isaac Amsden of Cambridge, Mass. 116p. 1997. reprint ed. pap. 18.00 (*0-8328-7261-X*); reprint ed. lib. bdg. 28.00 (*0-8328-7260-1*) Higginson Bk Co.

Brown, Myrtle L., et al, eds. Present Knowledge in Nutrition. 6th ed. LC 90-82033. (Illus.). 532p. (C). 1990. pap. text 40.00 (*0-944398-05-7*) ILSI.

Brown, N. Russian: An Essential Grammar. (Grammars Ser.). (ENG & RUS.). 224p. (C). 1999. 55.00 (*0-415-13709-8*, D3921); pap. 22.99 (*0-415-13710-1*, D3925) Routledge.

Brown, Nacio J. Rag Theater: The Twenty-Four Hundred Block of Telegraph Avenue 1969-1973. LC 75-15320. (Illus.). 74p. 1979. pap. 10.95 (*0-915572-42-7*) Panjandrum.

Brown, Nadine. God's Armor. 200p. 1998. pap. 10.00 (*0-9664956-0-8*) Intercessors NE.

Brown, Nan M. The Patience to Wait Vol. I: Sermons by a Patient Black Woman. Brown, Arnethea H. & Kelley, Joan T., eds. (Illus.). 160p. (Orig.). (C). 1988. 9.95 (*0-317-91214-3*) N M Brown.

— The Patience to Wait Vol. II: Sermons for Special Days of the Church. Kelly, Joan A., ed. 160p. (Orig.). (C). 1992. pap. write for info. (*0-9620736-2-8*) N M Brown.

***Brown, Nancy.** Nude & Beauty Photography. LC 99-37076. (Kodak Pro Workshop Ser.). (Illus.). 2000. pap. write for info. (*0-87985-774-9*, Kodak) Saunders Photo.

Brown, Nancy & Krimbill, Jane C. Widowing: Surviving the First Year. rev. ed. LC 95-68228. 96p. 1995. reprint ed. pap., wbk. ed. 9.95 (*0-9652809-0-X*) Magoo Ltd.

Brown, Nancy, jt. auth. see Brown, Terri.

Brown, Nancy, jt. auth. see Saricks, Joyce G.

Brown, Nancy L., ed. National Speedway Directory, Vol. 18. rev. ed. 464p. 1997. pap. 8.00 (*0-931105-48-X*) Slideways Pubns.

Brown, Nancy L., jt. auth. see Brown, Allan E.

Brown, Nancy L., jt. ed. see Brown, Allan E.

Brown, Nancy P., ed. see Southwell, Robert.

Brown, Naomi C. Comprehensive Guide & Directory of Schools - Orleans Parish, 2 vols. LC 89-80766. 125p. (Orig.). 1989. pap. 10.00 (*0-9623619-1-7*); pap. 10.00 (*0-9623619-2-5*) Guide To Schls.

— Comprehensive Guide & Directory of Schools - Orleans Parish, 2 vols., Set. LC 89-80766. (Orig.). 1989. pap. 18.00 (*0-9623619-0-9*) Guide To Schls.

Brown, Naomi Y. Haiku Tapestry. LC 96-90858. (Illus.). 96p. (C). 1996. pap. 9.95 (*0-9624188-1-1*) Yucca Bks.

— Seasons' Enigma. LC 89-51412. (Illus.). 80p. (Orig.). (C). 1989. pap. 7.95 (*0-9624188-0-3*) Yucca Bks.

Brown, Nathan J. The Rule of Law in the Arab World: Courts in Egypt & the Gulf. (Middle East Studies: Vol. 6). 276p. (C). 1997. text 59.95 (*0-521-59026-4*) Cambridge U Pr.

Brown, Nathaniel. Sexuality & Feminism in Shelley. LC 79-4634. 298p. 1979. 37.95 (*0-674-80285-3*) HUP.

Brown, Nazarene. Smoking Barrel. (Illus.). 170p. (Orig.). 1998. pap. 15.95 (*0-9663712-0-8*) N Brown.

Brown, Nellie C., et al, eds. Battenberg & Point Lace Book. 2nd ed. 64p. 1987. pap. 8.00 (*0-916896-26-9*) Lacis Pubns.

Brown, Neville. French Administrative Law. 5th ed. 398p. 1998. pap. text (*0-19-826555-7*) OUP.

— The Future of Air Power. LC 86-14854. (C). 1986. 49.50 (*0-8419-1092-8*) Holmes & Meier.

— New Strategy Through Space. 352p. 1990. text 52.50 (*0-7185-1279-0*, Pub. by Leicester U Pr) Cassell & Continuum.

— The Strategic Revolution. 245p. 1992. 37.00 (*0-08-040721-8*, Pub. by Brasseys) Brasseys.

***Brown, Neville.** The Strategic Revolution: Thoughts for the Twenty-First Century. 248p. 1999. reprint ed. text 25.00 (*0-7881-6673-5*) DIANE Pub.

Brown, Neville, et al. French Administrative Law. 4th ed. LC 92-27365. 370p. 1993. text 48.00 (*0-19-825290-0*, Clarendon Pr) OUP.

Brown, Neville, jt. auth. see Issar, A.

Brown, Neville G. Challenge of Climatic Change. 288p. (C). 1999. write for info. (*0-415-01959-1*); pap. write for info. (*0-415-08826-7*) Routledge.

Brown, Newell, et al. Hockey Drills for Scoring. LC 97-13802. (Illus.). 216p. (Orig.). 1997. pap. 14.95 (*0-88011-736-2*, PBRO0736) Human Kinetics.

Brown, Nicholas. Governing Prosperity: Social Change & Social Analysis in Australia in the 1950s. (Studies in Australian History). (Illus.). 311p. (C). 1995. text 64.95 (*0-521-47160-5*) Cambridge U Pr.

***Brown, Nicholas & Szeman, Imre, eds.** Pierre Bourdieu: Fieldwork in Culture. LC 99-44609. 256p. 2000. pap. 24.95 (*0-8476-9389-9*); text 70.00 (*0-8476-9388-0*) Rowman.

Brown, Nicholas, jt. ed. see Decker, Jennifer E.

Brown, Nicholas J. New Penguin Russian Course: A Complete Course for Beginners. LC 96-232400. 528p. 1996. pap. 15.95 (*0-14-012041-6*, Penguin Bks) Viking Penguin.

— Russian. LC 98-7345. (RUS & ENG.). 1998. pap. 29.95 incl. audio (*0-7894-3586-1*) DK Pub Inc.

— Russian Learner's Dictionary. 440p. (C). 1996. pap. 25.99 (*0-415-13792-6*) Routledge.

Brown, Nicholas P. & Bron, Anthony J. Lens Disorders: A Clinical Manual of Cataract Diagnosis. LC 94-32580. (Illus.). 256p. 1996. text 125.00 (*0-7506-1482-X*) Buttrwrth-Heinemann.

Brown, Nicole, ed. see Yount, Lisa.

Brown, Nicole A. Devolution of Authority over the Management of Natural Resources: The Soufriere Marine Management Area, St. Lucia. (Illus.). 21p. 1997. pap. 7.00 (*1-890792-01-2*) Caribbean Nat Res.

***Brown, Nina W.** Creating High Performance Classroom Groups. LC 00-28336. (Reference Library of Social Science). 2000. write for info. (*0-8153-3690-X*) Garland.

Brown, Nina W. The Destructive Narcissistic Pattern. LC 97-27928. 200p. 1998. 55.00 (*0-275-96017-X*, Praeger Pubs) Greenwood.

— Expressive Processes in Group Counseling: Theory & Practice. LC 95-45417. 168p. 1996. 55.00 (*0-275-95509-5*, Praeger Pubs) Greenwood.

— Group Counseling for Elementary & Middle School Children. LC 93-5396. 168p. 1994. 52.95 (*0-275-94651-7*, Praeger Pubs) Greenwood.

— Psychoeducational Groups. LC 97-43840. 264p. 1998. pap. 24.95 (*1-56032-676-X*) Hemisp Pub.

— Teaching Group Dynamics: Process & Practices. LC 92-16144. 176p. 1992. 47.95 (*0-275-94380-1*, C4380, Praeger Pubs) Greenwood.

Brown, Nina W., jt. see Wetzel, Roberta.

Brown-Nixon, Candace & Nixon, Robert. First Responder in Action: A Practical Approach. (Illus.). 517p. 1985. pap. text 35.00 (*0-8359-2055-0*) P-H.

Brown, Norman D. Hood, Bonnet, & Little Brown Jug: Texas Politics, 1921-1928. LC 83-45099. (Southwestern Studies: No. 1). (Illus.). 584p. 1983. 19.95 (*0-89096-157-3*) Tex A&M Univ Pr.

Brown, Norman D., ed. Journey to Pleasant Hill: The Civil War Letters of Captain Elijah P. Petty, Walker's Texas Division, C.S.A. (Illus.). 471p. 1982. 17.50 (*0-933164-94-7*) U of Tex Inst Tex Culture.

B

Brown, Norman H. Profiting from IPOs & Small Cap Stocks. LC 98-17862. 256p. 1998. text 26.00 (0-7352-0029-7) PH Pr.

***Brown, Norman M. & Amatea, Ellen S.** Love & Intimate Relationships: Journeys of the Heart. LC 99-53202. 2000. 34.95 (0-87630-979-1) Brunner-Mazel.

Brown, Norman O. Apocalypse & or Metamorphosis. LC 90-47940. 250p. 1991. 40.00 (0-520-07298-7, Pub. by U CA Pr) Cal Prin Full Svc.

— Apocalypse & or Metamorphosis. 1996. pap. 15.95 (0-520-07828-4, Pub. by U CA Pr) Cal Prin Full Svc.

— Hermes the Thief. 192p. 1990. reprint ed. pap. 10.95 (0-940262-26-6, Lindisfarne) Anthroposophic.

— Life Against Death: The Psychoanalytical Meaning of History. 2nd ed. LC 85-17928. 387p. 1985. pap. 22.95 (0-8195-6144-4, Wesleyan Univ Pr) U Pr of New Eng.

— Love's Body. 285p. 1990. 48.00 (0-520-07105-0, Pub. by U CA Pr); pap. 15.95 (0-520-07106-9, Pub. by U CA Pr) Cal Prin Full Svc.

— Theogony: Hesiod. 96p. (C). 1953. pap. text 11.20 (0-02-315310-5, Macmillan Coll) P-H.

Brown, O., Jr. & Hendrick, H. W., eds. Human Factors in Organizational Design & Management, No. II. xx,696p. 1986. 187.50 (0-444-70076-5, North Holland) Elsevier.

— Human Factors in Organizational Design & Management: Proceedings of the Fifth International Symposium on Human Factors in Organizational Design & Management, Breckenridge, CO, U.S.A., July 31-August 3, 1996. 690p. 1996. text 152.50 (0-444-82468-5, North Holland) Elsevier.

Brown, O., jt. auth. see Hendrick, W., Jr.

Brown, O., Jr., jt. ed. see Noro, K.

Brown, O. Gilbert. Debunking the Myth: Stories of African-American University Students. 108p. 1994. pap. 10.00 (0-87367-469-3) Phi Delta Kappa.

Brown, O. Gilbert. Helping African-American Students Prepare for College. Walling, Donovan R., ed. LC 97-65151. (Fastback Ser.: Vol. 413). 41p. 1997. pap. 3.00 (0-87367-613-0) Phi Delta Kappa.

Brown, O. Michael, ed. see Horace.

Brown, O. Phelps. The Complete Herbalist. (Illus.). 504p. 1993. reprint ed. pap. 14.95 (0-87877-184-0) Newcastle Pub.

— The Complete Herbalist: The People Their Own Physicians. 504p. 1992. pap. 35.00 (0-89540-118-5, SB-118) Sun Pub.

— The Complete Herbalist: The People Their Own Physicians. 504p. 1996. reprint ed. pap. 30.00 (0-7873-0121-3) Hlth Research.

Brown-Oden, Marilyn. Manger & Mystery: An Advent Adventure. Collett, Rita, ed. LC 98-55298. 128p. 1999. pap. 10.00 (0-8358-0861-0) Upper Room Bks.

Brown, Ola M., ed. Tips at Your Fingertips: Teaching Strategies for Adult Literacy Tutors. LC 95-43785. 140p. 1996. pap. 21.95 (0-87207-141-3, 141-3) Intl Reading.

Brown, Oliver, photos by. Let's Switch: Poems. 40p. 1998. pap. 8.00 (0-9665390-0-1) Emerick Bell.

Brown, Oliver B., ed. Vital Records of Falmouth, Massachusetts to the Year 1850. LC 76-3955. 272p. 1993. reprint ed. 22.50 (0-89725-108-3, 1403) Picton Pr.

Brown, Oliver M. Gabriel Denver. LC 72-129368. reprint ed. 39.50 (0-404-01137-3) AMS Pr.

Brown, Olympia. Suffrage & Religious Principle: Speeches & Writings of Olympia Brown. Greene, Dana, ed. LC 83-20129. 192p. 1983. 24.00 (0-8108-1665-2) Scarecrow.

Brown, Opal H. Classroom Challengers - 5s to 50s. (Illus.). 160p. 1990. 16.95 (0-934188-33-5) Evans Pubns.

Brown, Opal Hartsell. Indomitable Oklahoma Women. (Oklahoma Horizons Ser.). (Illus.). 124p. 1994. 20.00 (0-86546-088-4) OK Heritage.

Brown, Oren L. Discover Your Voice: How to Develop Healthy Voice Habits. (Illus.). 300p. (Orig.). 1996. pap. 49.95 (1-56593-704-X, 1380) Thomson Learn.

Brown, Oscar J. Nature Rectitude & Divine Law in Aquinas. xiv, 210p. pap. text 20.57 (0-88844-055-3) Brill Academic Pubs.

Brown, Otis. One Day Celestial Navigation for Offshore Sailing. 2nd ed. 218p. 1994. pap. 12.95 (1-56790-021-6) C & O Research.

Brown, Otis S. One Day Celestial Navigation. LC 79-67243. (Illus.). 133p. 1988. pap. 9.95 (0-89709-132-9) Liberty Pub.

Brown, P., et al, eds. Microstructural Development During Hydration of Cement: (MRS Symposium Proceedings Ser.: Vol. 85). 1987. text 17.50 (0-931837-50-2) Materials Res.

Brown, P. & Stone, C., eds. Granite Reef: A Study in Desert Archaeology. (Anthropological Research Papers: No. 28). (Illus.). xvii, 443p. 1982. pap. 25.00 (0-685-73904-X) AZ Univ ARP.

Brown, P. Charles & Boeckner, Keith. Oxford English Computing. (Illus.). 212p. 1993. pap. text, student ed. 12.95 (0-19-457387-7) OUP.

— Oxford English for Computing: Answer Book. (Illus.). 64p. 1993. pap. text 6.95 (0-19-457388-5) OUP.

Brown, P. Clement. Art in Dress (1922) Shep, R. L., ed. LC 93-8795. (Illus.). 192p. 1993. pap. 17.95 (0-914046-19-5) R L Shep.

Brown, P. D. William of Cavendish, Memoranda. (Camden Fourth Ser.: No. 27). 27.00 (0-86193-097-5) David Brown.

Brown, P. Hume. Life of Goethe, 2 Vols, Set. LC 77-163114. (Studies in German Literature: No. 13). 1971. reprint ed. lib. bdg. 150.00 (0-8383-1307-8) M S G Haskell Hse.

— The Youth of Goethe. LC 77-133283. (Studies in German Literature: No. 13). 1970. reprint ed. lib. bdg. 75.00 (0-8383-1182-2) M S G Haskell Hse.

Brown, P. Hume, jt. auth. see Moore, Margaret F.

Brown, P. J. Measurement, Regression, & Calibration. (Oxford Statistical Science Ser.: No. 12). (Illus.). 210p. 1994. text 55.00 (0-19-852245-2) OUP.

***Brown, P. J.** Million Man March: Book of the American Dead. 2000. pap. 9.95 (0-533-13099-9) Vantage.

Brown, P. J., jt. auth. see Masser, Ian.

Brown, P. M. Lucretius: De Rerum Natura I. (Bristol Latin Texts Ser.). (LAT.). 292p. 1984. 29.95 (0-86292-076-0, Pub. by Brist Class Pr) Focus Pub-R Pullins.

Brown, P. Michael. Lucretius Bk. III: De Rerum Natura. (Classical Texts Ser.). 232p. 1997. 59.99 (0-85668-694-8); pap. 28.00 (0-85668-695-6) David Brown.

Brown, P. Michael, ed. see Horace.

Brown Packaging Books, Ltd. Staff, ed. see Crawford, Steve.

***Brown, Paige.** Climate, Biodiversity & Forests: Issues & Opportunities from the Kyoto Protocol. LC SD387.E58B76 1998. 80p. 1998. pap. 20.00 (1-56973-285-X) World Resources Inst.

Brown, Paige, et al. Carbon Counts: Estimating Climate Change Mitigation in Forestry Projects. 32p. 1997. pap. 20.00 (1-56973-229-9) World Resources Inst.

Brown, Pam. Happy Anniversary. Exley, Helen, ed. (To Give & to Keep Ser.). (Illus.). 28p. 1992. 7.00 (1-85015-263-2) Exley Giftbooks.

— Lean on Me: How to Help a Friend with a Problem. Nelson, Becky, ed. 32p. (Orig.). (YA). (gr. 7-12). 1993. pap. text 4.95 (1-56309-068-6, C936101, Wrld Changers Res) Womans Mission Union.

— Merry Christmas. Exley, Helen, ed. (To Give & to Keep Ser.). (Illus.). 28p. 1992. 6.00 (1-85015-322-1) Exley Giftbooks.

— Outback by Escort. 290p. 1994. pap. 16.95 (0-9641728-2-8) Custom Services.

***Brown, Pam.** Tackling Racism: One Day-Training Workshop. 160p. 2000. ring bd. 175.00 (0-7494-3036-2, Pub. by Kogan Page Ltd) Stylus Pub VA.

Brown, Pam. Thank You to a Very Special Dad. Exley, Helen, ed. (Illus.). 32p. 1998. 7.50 (1-86187-031-0) Exley Pubns Ltd.

— To a Special Couple on Your Wedding Day. Exley, Helen, ed. (To Give & to Keep Ser.). (Illus.). 28p. 1996. 7.00 (1-85015-708-1) Exley Giftbooks.

***Brown, Pam.** To a Very Special Aunt. Exley, Helen, ed. (To Give & to Keep Ser.). (Illus.). 32p. 1998. 7.00 (1-85015-930-0) Exley Giftbooks.

Brown, Pam. To a Very Special Brother. 1998. 7.00 (1-86187-098-1) Exley Giftbooks.

— To a Very Special Dad. Exley, Helen, ed. (To Give & to Keep Ser.). (Illus.). 28p. 1993. 7.00 (1-85015-396-5) Exley Giftbooks.

— To a Very Special Daughter. Exley, Helen, ed. (To Give & to Keep Ser.). (Illus.). 28p. 1992. reprint ed. 7.00 (1-85015-278-0) Exley Giftbooks.

— To a Very Special Friend. Exley, Helen, ed. (To Give & to Keep Ser.). (Illus.). 28p. 1992. 7.00 (1-85015-262-4) Exley Giftbooks.

— To a Very Special Granddaughter. Exley, Helen, ed. (To Give & to Keep Ser.). (Illus.). 28p. 1993. 7.00 (1-85015-437-6) Exley Giftbooks.

— To a Very Special Grandmother. Exley, Helen, ed. (To Give & to Keep Ser.). (Illus.). 28p. 1992. 7.00 (1-85015-265-9) Exley Giftbooks.

— To a Very Special Grandpa. Exley, Helen, ed. (To Give & to Keep Ser.). (Illus.). 28p. 1994. 7.00 (1-85015-497-X) Exley Giftbooks.

— To a Very Special Grandson. Exley, Helen, ed. (To Give & to Keep Ser.). (Illus.). 28p. 1996. 7.00 (1-85015-694-8) Exley Giftbooks.

— To a Very Special Husband. Exley, Helen, ed. (To Give & to Keep Ser.). (Illus.). 28p. 1992. 7.00 (1-85015-264-0) Exley Giftbooks.

— To a Very Special Mother. Exley, Helen, ed. (To Give & to Keep Ser.). (Illus.). 28p. 1992. 7.00 (1-85015-256-X) Exley Giftbooks.

— To a Very Special Mother-in-Law. Exley, Helen, ed. (To Give & to Keep Ser.). (Illus.). 32p. 1997. 7.00 (1-85015-933-5) Exley Giftbooks.

— To a Very Special Son. Exley, Helen, ed. (To Give & to Keep Ser.). (Illus.). 28p. 1993. 7.00 (1-85015-424-4) Exley Giftbooks.

— To a Very Special Teacher. Exley, Helen, ed. (To Give & to Keep Ser.). (Illus.). 28p. 1995. 7.00 (1-85015-648-4) Exley Giftbooks.

— Welcome to New Baby. Exley, Helen, ed. (To Give & to Keep Ser.). (Illus.). 28p. 1993. 7.00 (1-85015-436-8) Exley Giftbooks.

— Wishing You Happiness. Exley, Helen, ed. (To Give & to Keep Ser.). (Illus.). 28p. 1992. 7.00 (1-85015-323-X) Exley Giftbooks.

— With Love to a Special Dad. Exley, Helen, ed. (So-Much-More-Than-a-Card Ser.). (Illus.). 28p. (Orig.). 1995. pap. 2.99 (1-85015-660-3) Exley Giftbooks.

Brown, Pamela, jt. auth. see Walker, Dot.

Brown, Pamela N. Facing Cancer Together: How to Help Your Friend or Loved One. LC 99-14110. 96p. 1999. mass mkt. 6.99 (0-8066-3833-8, 9-3833, Augsburg) Augsburg Fortress.

Brown, Pamela R. Charleston: An Artist's Sketchbook. (Illus.). 40p. 1992. pap. 8.00 (1-884824-00-5) Tryon Pubng.

Brown, Pamela S. & Yirgu, Fassil, eds. One House: The Battle of Aowa 1896 - 100 Years. 1996. 37.00 (0-9642068-1-1) Nyala Pubng.

***Brown, Parry A.** Sexy Doesn't Have a Dress Size: Lessons in Love. 112p. 2000. pap. 9.95 (0-9666503-1-X) ShanKrys.

Brown, Parry A. Shirt off His Back. 1998. pap. text 14.95 (0-9666503-0-1) ShanKrys.

Brown, Pat. Locating & Preserving Your Church's Records. Deweese, Charles W., ed. (Resource Kit for Your Church's History Ser.). 8p. 1984. 0.60 (0-939804-15-8) Hist Comm S Baptist.

Brown, Pat, jt. auth. see Schulz, Jane.

Brown, Pat, ed. see Hale, Jim.

Brown, Patricia. Humanism in Education. 70p. 1981. pap. 2.00 (0-913098-39-6) Orion Society.

— The Mountain Dulcimer. LC 85-71923. (Illus.). 130p. 1985. pap. 12.95 (0-9614939-3-3) Backyard Music.

— 365 Meditations for Mothers of Young Children. 352p. 1993. pap. 12.00 (0-687-01246-5) Dimen for Liv.

— A War Story. LC 93-80596. 140p. (Orig.). 1994. pap. 8.00 (0-9625313-5-9) Mntn Pr MA.

Brown, Patricia & Goren, Paul D. Ability Grouping & Tracking: Current Issues & Concerns. Glass, Karen, ed. 42p. (Orig.). 1993. pap. text 15.00 (1-55877-213-8) Natl Governor.

***Brown, Patricia D.** From the Heart Journal: A Personal Prayer Journal for Women. LC 99-49342. 96p. 1999. spiral bd. 20.00 (0-687-07064-3) Dimen for Liv.

— Heart to Heart Guidebook: A Spiritual Journey for Women. LC 99-49343. 208p. 1999. pap. 15.00 (0-687-07044-9) Dimen for Liv.

Brown, Patricia D. Learning to Lead from Your Spiritual Center. 144p. (Orig.). 1996. pap. 9.95 (0-687-00612-0) Abingdon.

— Spirit Gifts: One Spirit, Many Gifts. 168p. (Orig.). 1996. pap., teacher ed. 19.95 (0-687-00857-3) Abingdon.

— Spirit Gifts: Participant's Workbook. 96p. (Orig.). 1996. pap., wbk. ed. 5.95 (0-687-00858-1) Abingdon.

— 365 Affirmations for Hopeful Living. LC 92-18261. 384p. 1992. pap. 10.00 (0-687-41889-5) Dimen for Liv.

Brown, Patricia E. & Rogge, A. E. Archaeological Investigations at AZ U, 6, 61 (ASU), a Prehistoric Limited Activity Site in South-Central Arizona. (Anthropological Research Papers: No. 21). (Illus.). viii, 83p. 1980. pap. 10.00 (0-685-19304-7) AZ Univ ARP.

Brown, Patricia F. Art & Life in Renaissance Venice. LC 96-49514. (Perspectives Ser.). (Illus.). 176p. 1997. 18.95 (0-8109-2747-0, Pub. by Abrams) Time Warner.

— Venetian Narrative Painting in the Age of Carpaccio. LC 87-10669. 320p. (C). 1988. 75.00 (0-300-04025-3) Yale U Pr.

— Venetian Narrative Painting in the Age of Carpaccio. 318p. (C). 1990. reprint ed. pap. 35.00 (0-300-04743-6) Yale U Pr.

— Venice & Antiquity: The Venetian Sense of the Past. LC 96-3196. (Illus.). 361p. 1996. 65.00 (0-300-06700-3) Yale U Pr.

Brown, Patricia Fortini. Art & Life in Renaissance Venice. LC 96-49514. (Perspectives Ser.). 1997. pap. text 16.40 (0-13-618455-3) P-H.

Brown, Patricia G. Preaching from the Pew. LC 97-47075. 176p. 1997. pap. 12.95 (0-664-50019-6) Geneva Press.

Brown, Patricia L., et al, eds. To Gwen with Love: A Tribute to Gwendolyn Brooks. LC 76-128546. (Illus.). 149p. (Orig.). 1971. pap. 1.95 (0-87485-044-4) Johnson Chicago.

Brown, Patricia M. Merchant Princes of Fremantle: The Rise & Decline of a Colonial Elite 1870-1900. LC 97-114775. (Illus.). 239p. 1996. pap. 24.95 (1-875560-76-9, Pub. by Univ of West Aust Pr) Intl Spec Bk.

Brown, Patrick B., jt. auth. see Grein, Randy Brown.

Brown, Patrick J. Bond Markets: Structures & Yield Calculations. 96p. 1998. 45.00 (1-888998-55-5) Glenlake Pub.

— Constructing & Calculating Bond Indices: A Guide to the Effas Standard Rules. 1994. text 65.00 (1-55738-814-8, Irwn Prfssnl) McGraw-Hill Prof.

Brown, Patty & Rice, Janett. Ready-to-Wear Apparel Analysis. 2nd ed. LC 97-8726. 370p. 1997. 65.00 (0-13-606591-0, Merrill Coll) P-H.

***Brown, Patty & Rice, Janett.** Ready-to-Wear Apparel Analysis. 3rd ed. LC 99-89104. (Illus.). 384p. 2000. 56.00 (0-13-025434-7) P-H.

Brown, Patty, jt. auth. see Barrett, Ron.

Brown, Paul. Energy & Resources. LC 97-34829. (Living for the Future Ser.). (J). (gr. 3-7). 1998. 18.50 (0-531-14483-6) Watts.

— Global Warming: Can Civilization Survive? LC 97-126948. (Illus.). 256p. 1997. pap. 19.95 (0-7137-2602-4, Pub. by Blandford Pr) Sterling.

— Greenpeace. LC 94-7476. (Organizations That Help the World Ser.). 64p. (J). 1999. text 22.00 (0-02-726336-3) Macmillan.

— Greenpeace. (Organizations That Help the World Ser.). (Illus.). 64p. (YA). (gr. 6 up). 1995. pap. 7.95 (0-382-24980-1, New Dscvry Bks) Silver Burdett Pr.

***Brown, Paul.** Object-Relational Database Development: A Plumber's Guide. 600p. 2000. pap. 49.99 (0-13-019460-3) P-H.

Brown, Paul. Paul Brown's Wild Visions. 128p. 1998. 39.95 (0-9642595-1-6) True Exposures.

— Wivenhoe & Brightlingsea Railway. (Illus.). 128p. (Orig.). 1991. pap. 20.00 (0-86025-889-0, Pub. by I Henry Pubns); pap. 12.00 (0-86025-456-9, Pub. by I Henry Pubns) Empire Pub Srvs.

Brown, Paul, jt. auth. see Ayers, Tess.

Brown, Paul, jt. auth. see Palmer, Helen.

Brown, Paul A. & Hoffman, Richard. Success of the Business Jungle: Secrets of an Entrepreneurial Animal. (Illus.). 344p. 1998. pap. 24.00 (0-8059-4336-6) Dorrance.

Brown, Paul B., jt. auth. see Sewell, Carl.

Brown, Paul D., jt. auth. see Klapthor, Margaret B.

Brown, Paul L. Managing Behavior on the Job: Performance Improvement. LC 81-23063. 208p. 1982. pap. 18.95 (0-471-86516-8) Wiley.

Brown, Paul M. Wild Orchids of the Northeastern United States: A Field Guide. LC 96-34508. (Comstock Bk.). (Illus.). 224p. 1996. pap. text 17.95 (0-8014-8341-7, Comstock Pub) Cornell U Pr.

Brown, Paul T. Wildlife of the South: The Photographs of Paul T. Brown. 1995. 39.95 (0-9642595-0-8) True Exposures.

Brown, Paul W., ed. Cements Research Progress, 1990. 283p. 1993. pap. 70.00 (0-944904-70-X, CRP90) Am Ceramic.

Brown, Paul W. & Constantz, Brent, eds. Hydroxyapatite & Related Materials. LC 93-47252. 368p. 1994. lib. bdg. 159.00 (0-8493-4750-5) CRC Pr.

Brown, Paul W., jt. auth. see Bender's Editors.

Brown, Paul W., ed. see Engineering Foundation (U.S.) Staff.

Brown, Paul W., jt. ed. see Oversby, V. M.

Brown, Paula. Beyond a Mountain Valley: The Simbu of Papua New Guinea. LC 95-19834. (Illus.). 320p. (C). 1995. text 36.00 (0-8248-1701-X) UH Pr.

— The Chimbu: A Study of Change in the New Guinea Highlands. LC 72-183948. (Illus.). 192p. 1972. pap. 13.95 (0-87073-757-0) Schenkman Bks Inc.

***Brown, Pauline.** The Creative Quilter: Techniques & Projects. (Illus.). 160p. 2000. pap. 19.95 (1-86108-138-3, Pub. by Guild Master) Sterling.

Brown, Pauline. The Embellished Embroidery Kit. 48p. 1998. text 24.95 (0-8230-1595-5) Watsn-Guptill.

— Encyclopedia of Embroidery Techniques. LC 93-61662. 176p. 1994. pap. 21.95 (0-14-023771-2, Viking Studio) Studio Bks.

Brown, Pean. Gifts of Silence. 84p. 1983. pap. 6.95 (0-942494-79-2) Coleman Pub.

Brown, Penelope & Levinson, Stephen C. Politeness: Some Universals in Language Usage. (Illus.). 352p. 1987. pap. text 22.95 (0-521-31355-4) Cambridge U Pr.

Brown, Percy. Indian Paintings under the Mughals. 201p. 1981. 85.00 (0-318-36338-0) Asia Bk Corp.

Brown, Percy. Picturesque Nepal. 1997. pap. 132.00 (0-7855-7617-7) St Mut.

***Brown, Peter.** Augustine of Hippo. 576p. 2000. 35.00 (0-520-22835-9); pap. 19.95 (0-520-22757-3) U CA Pr.

Brown, Peter. Augustine of Hippo: A Biography. 1967. reprint ed. pap. 18.95 (0-520-01411-1, Pub. by U CA Pr) Cal Prin Full Svc.

— Authority & the Sacred: Aspects of the Christianisation of the Roman World. (Canto Book Ser.). 106p. (C). 1997. pap. 10.95 (0-521-59557-6) Cambridge U Pr.

— The Body & Society: Men, Women & Sexual Renunciation in Early Christianity. (American Council of Learned Societies Lectures on the History of Religion: No. 13). 1990. text 77.50 (0-231-06100-5); pap. text 21.00 (0-231-06101-3) Col U Pr.

— Brunei Rainforest Adventure. (Illus.). 64p. (YA). 1993. 11.95 (0-563-36756-3, Pub. by BBC) Parkwest Pubns.

— Chaucer at Work. (C). 1995. pap. text 47.95 (0-582-23719-X) Addison-Wesley.

— Chaucer at Work: Making of Canterbury Tales. LC 93-39019. 224p. (C). 1994. pap. text 24.75 (0-685-72601-0, 76440) Longman.

— Chaucer Work. (C). 1995. pap. text 35.63 (0-582-01319-4) Addison-Wesley.

— The Cult of the Saints: Its Rise & Function in Latin Christianity. LC 80-11210. Vol. 2. xvi, 200p. 1982. pap. 11.00 (0-226-07622-9) U Ch Pr.

***Brown, Peter.** Ethics, Economics & International Relations. 176p. 2000. pap. text 24.00 (0-7486-0892-3) Col U Pr.

Brown, Peter. How to Buy a Horse: Without Being Taken for a Ride. (Illus.). 50p. (Orig.). 1997. pap. 4.95 (1-86054-047-3, Pub. by Ringpr Bks) Seven Hills Bk.

— The Hypnotic Brain: Hypnotherapy & Social Communication. 335p. 1991. 55.00 (0-300-05001-1); pap. 20.00 (0-300-05942-6) Yale U Pr.

— Into Music, 3 bks. (Illus.). 64p. 1984. pap., teacher ed. 11.95 (0-7175-1155-3) Dufour.

— Into Music, 3 bks., Bk. 1. (Illus.). 64p. 1983. pap. 11.95 (0-7175-1097-2) Dufour.

— Into Music, 3 bks., Bk. 2. (Illus.). 64p. 1983. pap. 11.95 (0-7175-1098-0) Dufour.

— Into Music, 3 bks., Bk. 3. (Illus.). 64p. 1983. pap. 11.95 (0-7175-1099-9) Dufour.

— Late Antiquity. LC 97-42973. 96p. 1998. pap. 10.00 (0-674-51170-0) Belknap Pr.

— The Making of Late Antiquity. (Jackson Lectures). 152p. (C). 1993. pap. 13.50 (0-674-54321-1) HUP.

***Brown, Peter.** On the Plains. LC 98-46999. (Illus.). 128p. 1999. 39.95 (0-393-04730-X) Norton.

Brown, Peter. Power & Persuasion in Late Antiquity: Towards a Christian Empire. LC 92-50245. (Curti Lectures: Vol. 1988). 192p. (C). 1992. pap. 15.95 (0-299-13344-3) U of Wis Pr.

— The Rise of Western Christendom: Triumph & Diversity Adzoo-1000. rev. ed. Le Goff, Jacques, ed. LC 95-11589. (Making of Europe Ser.). xii, 353p. 1997. pap. 26.95 (1-57718-092-5) Blackwell Pubs.

— Society & the Holy in Late Antiquity. LC 80-39862. 350p. 1982. pap. 16.95 (0-520-06800-9, Pub. by U CA Pr) Cal Prin Full Svc.

— World of Late Antiquity. (Library of World Civilization Ser.). (Illus.). 216p. (Orig.). (C). 1989. pap. text 16.75 (0-393-95803-5) Norton.

Brown, Peter, ed. Reading Dreams: The Interpretation of Dreams from Chaucer to Shakespeare. LC PR428.D74B76 1999. 204p. 1999. text 60.00 (0-19-818363-1) OUP.

Brown, Peter & Higgs, Elton D. The Index of Middle English Prose Handlist V: Manuscripts in the Additional Collection (10001-14000), British Library, London. (Index of Middle English Prose Ser.). 74p. 1988. 55.00 (0-85991-270-1) Boydell & Brewer.

An Asterisk (*) at the beginning of an entry indicates that the title is appearing for the first time.

Brown, Peter & Stratton, George, eds. World List of Scientific Periodicals Published in the Years 1900-1960, Vol. 1. 4th ed. LC 64-9729. 557p. 1963. reprint ed. pap. 172.70 (0-608-10406-X, 202575200001) Bks Demand.
— World List of Scientific Periodicals Published in the Years 1900-1960, Vol. 2. 4th ed. LC 64-9729. 674p. 1964. reprint ed. pap. 200.00 (0-608-10407-8, 202575200002) Bks Demand.
— World List of Scientific Periodicals Published in the Years 1900-1960, Vol. 3. 4th ed. LC 64-9729. 660p. 1965. reprint ed. pap. 200.00 (0-608-10408-6, 202575200003) Bks Demand.
Brown, Peter, jt. auth. see Bronze, Lewis.
Brown, Peter, jt. auth. see Raysman, Richard.
Brown, Peter, tr. see Van Der Meer, Frederik.
Brown, Peter A. Carlos d'Ordonez (1754-1786) LC 78-61024. (Detroit Studies in Music Bibliography: No.39). 234p. 1978. 25.00 (0-911772-89-8) Harmonie Park Pr.
Brown, Peter C. The Complete Guide to Money-Making Ventures for Nonprofit Organizations. 256p. (Orig.). 1986. pap. 50.00 (0-914977-30-X) Taft Group.
Brown, Peter D. Oskar Panizza: His Life & Works. LC 83-48749. (American University Studies: Germanic Languages & Literature: Ser. I, Vol. 27). 232p. (C). 1983. pap. text 24.65 (0-8204-0038-6) P Lang Pubng.
Brown, Peter D., ed. see Decker, Bernard H.
Brown, Peter D., ed. see Keiser, Brenda E.
Brown, Peter D., ed. see Walther, Ingeborg C.
Brown, Peter D., ed. see Warg, Isle-Rose.
Brown, Peter D., ed. see Warmbold, Joachim.
Brown, Peter D., ed. see Wolf, Ernest M.
Brown, Peter G., ed. Human Rights & U. S. Foreign Policy: Principles & Applications. 1979. pap. 15.00 (0-317-05208-X) IPPP.
Brown, Peter G., et al, eds. Income Support: Conceptual & Policy Issues. LC 80-26540. (Maryland Studies in Public Philosophy). 392p. 1981. 56.00 (0-8476-6969-6) Rowman.
Brown, Peter G. & Shue, Henry, eds. The Border That Joins: Mexican Migrants & U. S. Responsibility. LC 82-7526. (Maryland Studies in Public Philosophy). 264p. 1983. text 59.00 (0-8476-7072-4, R7072); pap. text 35.50 (0-8476-7206-9, R7206) Rowman.
— Boundaries: National Autonomy & Its Limits. 1981. 45.00 (0-317-05219-5) IPPP.
Brown, Peter G., jt. ed. see MacLean, Douglas.
Brown, Peter H. Down at the End of Lonely Street: The Life & Death of Elvis Presley. 1998. mass mkt. 7.99 (0-451-19094-7, Sig) NAL.
— History of Scotland, 3 vols. LC 74-181922. (BCL Ser. I). reprint ed. write for info. (0-404-09940-8) AMS Pr.
Brown, Peter H., ed. Scotland Before 1700: From Contemporary Documents. LC 77-87675. reprint ed. 65.00 (0-404-16467-6) AMS Pr.
Brown, Peter H. & Barham, Patte B. Marilyn: The Last Take. 23.00 (0-685-61645-2, Dutt) Dutton Plume.
***Brown, Peter Harry & Broeske, Pat H.** Howard Hughes: The Untold Story. (Illus.). 482p. 2000. 25.00 (0-7881-9407-0) DIANE Pub.
Brown, Peter J. Macro Processors & Techniques for Portable Software. LC 73-17597. (Wiley Series in Computing). 258p. reprint ed. pap. 80.00 (0-608-18442-X, 203265400080) Bks Demand.
— Understanding & Applying Medical Anthropology. LC 97-31050. xii, 451p. 1998. pap. text 43.95 (1-55934-723-6, 1726) Mayfield Pub.
Brown, Peter J., jt. auth. see Inhorn, Marcia C.
Brown, Peter J., jt. auth. see Podolefsky, Aaron.
Brown, Peter J., jt. ed. see Inhorn, Marcia C.
Brown, Peter M. The Art of Questioning: Thirty Maxims of Cross-Examination. 121p. 1988. pap. 6.95 (0-02-013090-2) Macmillan.
— Village: Where to Live & How to Live. unabridged ed. xii, 237p. 1997. 20.00 (0-915011-00-X) Benchmrk Pr.
Brown, Phil. Catskill Culture: A Mountain Rat's Memories of the Great Jewish Resort Area. LC 98-11996. (Illus.). 304p. 1998. text 34.95 (1-56639-642-5) Temple U Pr.
— The Transfer of Care: Psychiatric Deinstitutionalization & Its Aftermath. 292p. (C). 1988. pap. text 13.95 (0-415-00188-9) Routledge.
Brown, Phil, ed. Perspectives in Medical Sociology. 2nd rev. ed. LC 97-205600. (Illus.). 804p. (C). 1996. pap. text 32.95 (0-88133-903-2) Waveland Pr.
***Brown, Phil, ed.** Perspectives in Medical Sociology. 3rd ed. 673p. (C). 2000. pap. 31.95 (1-57766-134-6) Waveland Pr.
Brown, Phil & Mikkelsen, Edwin J. No Safe Place: Toxic Waste, Leukemia & Community Action. 284p. 1997. pap. text 17.95 (0-520-21248-7, Pub. by U CA Pr) Cal Prin Full Svc.
Brown, Philip. Field Guide to California Snakes. (Gulf's Field Guides Ser.). 216p. 1997. pap. 21.95 (0-87719-308-8, 9308) Gulf Pub.
— Longstreet Highroad Guide to the New York Adirondacks. LC 98-89176. (Illus.). 352p. 1999. pap. 18.95 (1-56352-505-4) Longstreet.
— Picture Making. 1989. pap. 39.00 (1-873812-00-0, Pub. by Icon Pr) St Mut.
— Uncle Whiskers. 1976. mass mkt. 2.95 (0-446-87108-7, Pub. by Warner Bks) Little.
— A Wife Unravelled. 1989. pap. 30.00 (1-873812-01-9, Pub. by Icon Pr) St Mut.
Brown, Philip, ed. Mental Health Care & Social Policy. 428p. 1985. pap. 19.95 (0-7102-0472-8, Routledge Thoemms) Routledge.
Brown, Philip & Scase, Richard, eds. Poor Work: Disadvantages & the Division of Labor. 176p. 1991. pap. 34.95 (0-335-09940-8) OpUniv Pr.
Brown, Philip, et al. Market Microstructure & Capital Market Information Content Research. (Studies in Accounting Research: No. 32). 183p. 1992. 15.00 (0-86539-078-9) Am Accounting.
— Security Analyst Multi-Year Earnings Forecasts & the Capital Market, Vol. 21. (Studies in Accounting Research). 172p. 1985. 12.00 (0-86539-049-5) Am Accounting.
— Should Pharmaceutical Prices Be Regulated? The Strengths & Weaknesses of the British Pharmaceutical Price Regulation Scheme. (IEA Health & Welfare Unit Choice in Welfare Ser.: No. 40). 132p. 1997. pap. 32.50 (0-255-36430-X, Pub. by Inst Economic Affairs) Coronet Bks.
Brown, Philip C. Central Authority & Local Autonomy in the Formation of Early Modern Japan: The Case of Kaga Domain. LC 93-10240. 332p. 1993. 47.50 (0-8047-2036-3) Stanford U Pr.
Brown, Philip K., jt. auth. see Chatterton, Clifford E.
Brown, Philip L. The Other Annapolis. (Illus.). 148p. 1994. 27.50 (1-884878-00-8) Annapol Pubng.
Brown, Philip M. & Shalett, John S., eds. Cross-Cultural Practice with Couples & Families. LC 97-760. (Journal of Family Social Work Monograph Ser.: Vol. 2, Nos. 1-2). 232p. (C). 1997. 49.95 (0-7890-0032-6); pap. text 19.95 (0-7890-0308-2) Haworth Pr.
Brown, Philip S., et al. Residential Care - Assisted Living Administrators Exam Study Guide. 150p. 1998. pap. 125.00 (0-9635064-4-7) Nat Assn Bds Exam.
Brown, Philippa, ed. Sibton Abbey Cartularies & Charters, Pt. II. (Suffolk Charters Ser.: No. VIII). 330p. 1987. 45.00 (0-85115-443-3) Boydell & Brewer.
— Sibton Abbey Cartularies & Charters, Pt. III. (Suffolk Records Society-Suffolk Charters Ser.: No. 9). 1987. 45.00 (0-85115-474-3) Boydell & Brewer.
— Sibton Abbey Cartularies & Charters, Pt. IV. (Suffolk Records Society-Suffolk Charters Ser.: No. 10). 180p. 1988. 45.00 (0-85115-499-9) Boydell & Brewer.
Brown, Phillip, ed. Beyond Thatcherism: Social Policy, Politics & Society. 192p. 1989. pap. 34.95 (0-335-09903-3) OpUniv Pr.
Brown, Phyllis R. HPLC in Nucleic Acid Research: Methods & Applications. (Chromatographic Science Ser.: Vol. 28). (Illus.). 424p. 1984. text 190.00 (0-8247-7236-9) Dekker.
Brown, Phyllis R., et al, eds. Modes of Interpretation in Old English Literature: Essays in Honour of Stanley B. Greenfield. 298p. 1986. text 40.00 (0-8020-5678-4) U of Toronto Pr.
Brown, Phyllis R. & Grushka, E. Advances in Chromatography. (Advances in Chromatography Ser.: Vol. 33). (Illus.). 296p. 1993. text 185.00 (0-8247-9064-2) Dekker.
Brown, Phyllis R. & Grushka, Eli, eds. Advances in Chromatography, Vol. 34. (Illus.). 456p. 1994. text 199.00 (0-8247-9087-1) Dekker.
— Advances in Chromatography, Vol. 36. (Illus.). 464p. 1995. text 195.00 (0-8247-9551-2) Dekker.
— Advances in Chromatography, Vol. 37. LC 65-27435. (Illus.). 544p. 1997. text 210.00 (0-8247-9804-X) Dekker.
— Advances in Chromatography, Vol. 38. (Illus.). 280p. 1998. text 175.00 (0-8247-9999-2) Dekker.
***Brown, Phyllis R. & Grushka, Eli, eds.** Advances in Chromatography, Vol. 40. 651p. 2000. 225.00 (0-8247-0018-X) Dekker.
Brown, Phyllis R. & Gruska, Eli, eds. Advances in Chromatography, Vol. 35. (Illus.). 448p. 1995. text 185.00 (0-8247-9361-7) Dekker.
Brown, Phyllis R. & Hartwick, Richard A., eds. High Performance Liquid Chromatography. LC 88-726. (Chemical Analysis Ser.). 688p. 1989. 215.00 (0-471-84506-X) Wiley.
Brown, Phyllis R., jt. ed. see Weston, Andrea.
Brown-Price, Aimee. Pierre Puvis de Chavannes. LC 94-65750. (Illus.). 272p. 1994. 60.00 (0-8478-1826-8, Pub. by Rizzoli Intl) St Martin.
Brown, Prince, jt. auth. see Ferrante, Joan.
Brown, Quentin & Gould, Phil. Dr. Sweet's Guide to Rude Health. 160p. 1988. 50.00 (1-85283-213-4, Pub. by Boxtree); pap. 30.00 (1-85283-219-3, Pub. by Boxtree) St Mut.
Brown, R. Advanced Math. 1993. text, student ed. 68.36 (0-395-42168-3) HM.
— The BEMS Book. 1990. pap. 40.00 (0-86022-244-6, Pub. by Build Servs Info Assn) St Mut.
Brown, R. I Don't Like It. 1992. mass mkt. write for info. (0-09-970240-1, Pub. by Random) Random House.
Brown, R. Prodromus Flora Novae-Hollandiae et Insulae Van Dieman (Now Australia & Tasmania) 1960. reprint ed. 120.00 (3-7682-0033-7) Lubrecht & Cramer.
Brown, R. Radiant Heating. 1996. pap. 120.00 (0-86022-426-0, Pub. by Build Servs Info Assn) St Mut.
Brown, R. & Lang, J., eds. Astrophysical & Laboratory Spectroscopy. (Scottish Universities Summer School in Physics, a NATO Advanced Study Institute Ser.: No. 33). (Illus.). 416p. 1987. 180.00 (0-905945-16-6) IOP Pub.
***Brown, R. & Ropert, M.** Guidance & the Standard Specification for Water Risk Assessment. 1999. pap. 100.00 (0-86022-518-6, Pub. by Build Servs Info Assn) St Mut.
Brown, R., jt. ed. see Jahanshahi, M.
Brown, R. A. Documentary Evidence in Australia. 2nd ed. LC 97-179780. 400p. 1996. 115.00 (0-455-21416-6, Pub. by Cameron May) Gaunt.
Brown, R. A. & Beck, J. Swanson. Medical Statistics on Microcomputers. 103p. 1990. pap. text 26.00 (0-7279-0290-3, Pub. by BMJ Pub) Login Brothers Bk Co.
Brown, R. A. & Beck, J. Swanson, eds. Medical Statistics on Personal Computers. 2nd ed. 160p. 1994. pap. text 21.00 (0-7279-0771-9, Pub. by BMJ Pub) Login Brothers Bk Co.
Brown, R. Allen. Anglo-Norman Studies IX Proceedings of the Battle Conference, 1986. (Illus.). 246p. 1987. 75.00 (0-85115-476-X) Boydell & Brewer.
Brown, R. Allen. The Norman Conquest. LC 84-142214. (Documents of Medieval History Ser.). xix, 181p. 1984. write for info. (0-7131-6406-9, Pub. by E A) Routldge.
Brown, R. Allen. The Normans. 2nd ed. (Illus.). 190p. (C). 1995. reprint ed. pap. 29.95 (0-85115-359-3, Boydell Pr) Boydell & Brewer.
— The Normans. 2nd ed. (Illus.). 190p. (C). 1997. reprint ed. text 29.95 (0-85115-358-5, Boydell Pr) Boydell & Brewer.
— The Normans & the Norman Conquest. 272p. (C). 1998. reprint ed. pap. 29.95 (0-85115-367-4, Boydell Pr) Boydell & Brewer.
— The Origins of Modern Europe: The Medieval Heritage of Western Civilization. LC 96-212595. 264p. 1996. pap. 24.95 (0-85115-665-7, Boydell Pr) Boydell & Brewer.
Brown, R. Allen, ed. Anglo-Norman Studies III Proceedings of the Battle Conference, 1980. 253p. (C). 1990. 75.00 (0-85115-141-8) Boydell & Brewer.
— Anglo-Norman Studies IV Proceedings of the Battle Conference, 1981. (Illus.). 247p. (C). 1990. 75.00 (0-85115-161-2) Boydell & Brewer.
— Anglo-Norman Studies II Proceedings of the Battle Conference, 1979. (Illus.). 224p. 1980. 75.00 (0-85115-126-4) Boydell & Brewer.
— Anglo-Norman Studies V Proceedings of the Battle Conference, 1982. (Illus.). 245p. 1990. reprint ed. 75.00 (0-85115-178-7) Boydell & Brewer.
— Anglo-Norman Studies VI Proceedings of the Battle Conference, 1983. (Illus.). 260p. (C). 1990. reprint ed. 75.00 (0-85115-197-3) Boydell & Brewer.
— Anglo-Norman Studies VII Proceedings of the Battle Conference, 1984. LC 84-29281. (Illus.). 255p. 1985. 75.00 (0-85115-416-6) Boydell & Brewer.
— Anglo-Norman Studies VIII Proceedings of the Battle Conference, 1985. (Illus.). 252p. 1986. 75.00 (0-85115-444-1) Boydell & Brewer.
— Anglo-Norman Studies X Proceedings of the Battle Conference, 1987. 301p. 1988. 75.00 (0-85115-502-2) Boydell & Brewer.
— Anglo-Norman Studies XI Proceedings of the Battle Conference, 1988. (Illus.). 305p. 1989. 75.00 (0-85115-526-X) Boydell & Brewer.
— Castles: A History & Guide. LC 81-140451. 1981. 19.95 (0-7137-1100-0) Blandford Pr.
Brown, R. C. Air Filtration: An Integrated Approach to the Theory & Applications of Fibrous Filters. LC 92-10258. 272p. 1993. 114.25 (0-08-041274-2, Pergamon Pr) Elsevier.
Brown, R. C., et al, eds. Mechanisms in Fibre Carcinogenesis. (NATO ASI Ser.: Vol. 223). (Illus.). 608p. (C). 1991. text 198.00 (0-306-44091-1, Kluwer Plenum) Kluwer Academic.
Brown, R. C., intro. The Future of the Public Library: March 1988 Conference, Dublin, Ohio. (Library, Information, & Computer Science Ser.: No. 8). 152p. (Orig.). 1988. pap. 13.50 (1-55653-050-1) OCLC Online Comp.
Brown, R. D. Lucretius on Love & Sex. 1987. 54.00 (90-04-08512-2, CSCT, 15) Brill Academic Pubs.
Brown, R. D., ed. The Biology of Deer. (Illus.). xxvii, 596p. 1991. 130.95 (0-387-97576-4) Spr-Verlag.
Brown, R. Douglas. East Anglia, 1939. 216p. 1990. 50.00 (0-86138-000-2, Pub. by T Dalton) St Mut.
— East Anglia, 1940. 176p. 1990. 39.00 (0-86138-008-8, Pub. by T Dalton) St Mut.
— East Anglia, 1941. 144p. 1990. 39.00 (0-86138-019-3, Pub. by T Dalton) St Mut.
— East Anglia, 1942. 224p. 1990. 55.00 (0-86138-056-8, Pub. by T Dalton) St Mut.
— East Anglia, 1943. 192p. 1990. 45.00 (0-86138-074-6, Pub. by T Dalton) St Mut.
— East Anglia, 1944. 188p. 1990. 48.00 (0-86138-076-2, Pub. by T Dalton) St Mut.
— East Anglia, 1945. 164p. 1990. 51.00 (0-86138-102-5, Pub. by T Dalton) St Mut.
— The Port of London. 212p. (C). 1988. 50.00 (0-900963-87-5, Pub. by T Dalton) St Mut.
Brown, R. E. Pamphlet for Spies: Invisible Inks, Codes & Ciphers. 1994. 10.00 (1-885293-12-7) Maldonado Pubng.
— Pamphlet for Spies: The Field. 1994. 15.00 (1-885293-13-5) Maldonado Pubng.
Brown, R. F. Biomedical Systems Analysis, Vol. 9. LC 89-9100. (Cybernetics & Systems Ser., Abacus Bks.). (Illus.). xii, 686p. 1989. text 277.00 (0-85626-433-4) Gordon & Breach.
— English-Spanish Dictionary. (ENG & SPA.). 35.95 (0-87557-077-1) Saphrograph.
— English-Spanish Dictionary. (ENG & SPA.). 35.95 (0-87559-172-8) Shalom.
— Fixed Point Theory & Its Applications. LC 88-10926. (Contemporary Mathematics Ser.: Vol. 72). 268p. 1988. reprint ed. pap. 36.00 (0-8218-5080-6, CONM/72) Am Math.
— Spanish-English Dictionary. (ENG & SPA.). 35.95 (0-87557-076-3) Saphrograph.
— A Topological Introduction to Nonlinear Analysis. 2nd ed. LC 93-3192. (Illus.). 146p. 1996. pap. 26.50 (0-8176-3706-0) Birkhauser.
Brown, R. F., ed. Spanish-English Dictionary. (ENG & SPA.). 35.95 (0-87559-033-0) Shalom.
Brown, R. G., et al. Report upon the Illegal Practices of the United States Department of Justice. LC 73-90206. (Mass Violence in America Ser.). 1979. reprint ed. 17.95 (0-405-01301-9) Ayer.
Brown, R. G., jt. auth. see Dicks, M. J.
Brown, R. G., jt. auth. see Teekaram, A. J. H.
Brown, R. H. The Institute Time Clauses Hulls, 1995: Analysis of Marine Insurance Clauses. 370p. 1996. pap. 195.00 (1-85609-116-3, Pub. by Witherby & Co) St Mut.
— The Insurance of Merchant Ships & Shipowners Interests, Bk. 3. 200p. 1990. 130.00 (1-85609-009-4, Pub. by Witherby & Co) St Mut.
Brown, R. H., ed. Handbook of Engineering in Agriculture, Vol. I. 272p. 1988. lib. bdg. 229.00 (0-8493-3861-1, S675) CRC Pr.
— Handbook of Engineering in Agriculture, Vol. II. 256p. 1988. lib. bdg. 229.00 (0-8493-3862-X, S675) CRC Pr.
— Handbook of Engineering in Agriculture, Vol. III. 320p. 1988. lib. bdg. 229.00 (0-8493-3863-8, S675) CRC Pr.
Brown, R. H., jt. ed. see Ducker, T. B.
Brown, R. Hanbury. Boffin: A Personal Story of the Early Days of Radar & Radio Astronomy & Quantum Optics. LC 91-3074. (Illus.). 192p. 1991. 43.00 (0-7503-0130-9) IOP Pub.
Brown, R. I. Quality of Life for People with Disabilities. 2nd ed. (Illus.). 384p. 1997. pap. 85.00 (1-56593-780-5, 1522) Singular Publishing.
Brown, R. J. The English Country Cottage. (Illus.). 272p. 1990. 25.00 (0-7091-7381-4, Pub. by R Hale Ltd) Antique Collect.
— English Country Cottage. 1988. pap. 11.95 (0-09-933620-0) Hutchinson UK.
— English Farmhouses. (Illus.). 304p. 1993. pap. 19.95 (0-7090-5250-2, Pub. by R Hale Ltd) Antique Collect.
— Timber Framed Buildings in England. 1997. pap. text 30.00 (0-7090-6092-0, Pub. by R Hale Ltd) Assoc Pubs Grp.
Brown, R. K. AIDS, Cancer & the Medical Establishment. (Illus.). 240p. 1986. 16.95 (0-8315-0196-0) Speller.
Brown, R. L. Elk Seasonal Ranges & Migrations in Arizona. (Arizona Game & Fish Department Technical Report: No. 15). (Illus.). 122p. 1994. pap. 5.00 (0-917563-20-4) AZ Game & Fish.
Brown, R. Lamon. Growing Spiritually with the Saints: Catherine of Genoa & William Law. LC 96-15753. (Reclaiming the Sacred Ser.). 112p. 1996. pap. 13.00 (1-57312-037-5) Smyth & Helwys.
Brown, R. Laurie. Walking in Indian Moccasins: The Native Policies of Tommy Douglas & the CCF. (Illus.). 288p. 1997. 24.95 (0-7748-0610-9) U of Wash Pr.
Brown, R. Malcolm, Jr., ed. Cellulose & Other Natural Polymer Systems: Biogenesis, Structure, & Degradation. LC 82-3796. 540p. 1982. 110.00 (0-306-40856-2, Plenum Trade) Perseus Pubng.
Brown, R. Philip. Authentic Individualism: A Guide for Reclaiming the Best of America's History. 264p. 1996. pap. text 32.00 (0-7618-0152-9); lib. bdg. 49.00 (0-7618-0151-0) U Pr of Amer.
Brown, R. S., Jr., ed. see Walpole, Horace.
Brown, R. Steven, et al. Resource Guide to the State Environmental Management. 2nd ed. 198p. 1990. pap. 40.00 (0-87292-097-6, C-184) Coun State Govts.
Brown, R. Steven, jt. auth. see Feazell, Larry M.
Brown, Rachel. The Weaving, Spinning & Dyeing Book. 2nd ed. (Illus.). 1983. pap. 40.00 (0-394-71595-0) Knopf.
Brown, Raj, ed. Chinese Business Enterprise, 4 vols., Set. 1688p. (C). 1996. 625.00 (0-415-13241-X) Routledge.
Brown, Rajeswary A. Capital & Entrepreneurship in South-East Asia. LC 93-40401. (Studies in the Economies of East & Southeast Asia). 1994. text 79.95 (0-312-12096-6) St Martin.
Brown, Rajeswary A. & Felstead, Alan. Franchising at Work: The Corporate Paradox. LC 93-9882. 256p. (C). 1993. pap. 29.95 (0-415-09984-6) Thomson Learn.
***Brown, Rajeswary Ampalavanar.** Chinese Big Business & the Wealth of Asian Nations. LC 00-33329. 2000. write for info. (0-312-23653-0) St Martin.
Brown, Ralf & Kyle, Jim. Network Interrupts: A Programmer's Reference to Network APIs. 736p. (C). 1994. pap. 32.95 (0-201-62644-6) Addison-Wesley.
Brown, Ralph, Jr. Loyalty & Security: Employment Tests in the United States. 1958. 89.50 (0-685-26658-3) Elliots Bks.
Brown, Ralph. Mathematical Difficulties of Students of Educational Statistics. LC 70-176599. (Columbia University. Teachers College. Contributions to Education Ser.: No. 569). reprint ed. 37.50 (0-404-55569-1) AMS Pr.
Brown, Ralph A. The Presidency of John Adams. LC 75-5526. (American Presidency Ser.). xii, 248p. 1975. 29.95 (0-7006-0134-1) U Pr of KS.
Brown, Ralph H. Mirror for Americans: Likeness of the Eastern Seaboard, 1810. LC 67-27449. (American Scene Ser.). 1968. reprint ed. 45.00 (0-306-70974-0) Da Capo.
Brown, Ralph H., tr. see Diderot, Denis.
Brown, Ralph S., Jr Loyalty & Security: Employment Tests in the United States. LC 79-151417. (Civil Liberties in American History Ser.). 522p. 1972. reprint ed. lib. bdg. 59.50 (0-306-70218-5) Da Capo.
Brown, Ralph S. & Danicola, Robert C. Cases on Copyright, Unfair Competition & Other Topics Bearing on the Protection of Literary Musical & Artistic Works. 7th ed. LC 98-14119. (University Casebook Ser.). 808p. 1998. text 39.75 (1-56662-607-2) Foundation Pr.
Brown, Ralph S. & Denicola, Robert C. Cases on Copyright, Unfair Competition & Other Topics Bearing on the Protection of Literary, Musical & Artistic Works. 6th ed. (University Casebook Ser.). 804p. 1994. text 44.50 (1-56662-192-5) Foundation Pr.

B

— Cases on Copyright, Unfair Competition & Other Topics Bearing on the Protection of Literary, Musical & Artistic Works: Statutory Supplement. 6th ed. (University Casebook Ser.). 285p. 1994. pap. text 12.95 (*1-56662-232-8*) Foundation Pr.
— Copyright, Unfair Competition, & Other Topics Bearing on the Protection of Literary, Musical, & Artistic Works, Fifth Edition, Cases On. 5th ed. (University Casebook Ser.). 754p. 1989. text 40.50 (*0-88277-744-0*) Foundation Pr.
— Copyright, Unfair Competition, & Other Topics Bearing on the Protection of Literary, Musical, & Artistic Works, 1993: Statutory & Case Supplement to Cases On. 5th ed. (University Casebook Ser.). 364p. 1993. pap. text. write for info. (*1-56662-072-4*) Foundation Pr.
— Copyright, Unfair Competition, & Other Topics Bearing on the Protection of Literary, Musical, & Artistic Works, 1996 Statutory & Case Supplement To. (University Casebook Ser.). 336p. 1996. pap. text. write for info. (*1-56662-371-5*) Foundation Pr.

Brown, Ramsey, jt. auth. see Brown, Roman.

***Brown, Randy.** Uncle Sam's Nieces & Nephews. 132p. 1999. pap. 11.00 (*1-56411-225-X*) Untd Bros & Sis.

Brown, Randy, et al. Graves & Sites on the Oregon & California Trails. LC 98-31429. 1998. 17.95 (*0-9635901-9-7*) OR-CA Trails.

Brown, Randy, ed. see Williams, Ronald A., et al.

Brown, Raphael. The Roots of St. Francis. 216p. 1982. 9.50 (*0-8199-0824-X*, Frncscn Herld) Franciscan Pr.
— Saints Who Saw Mary. LC 93-61596. Orig. Title: Mary Communes with the Saints. (Illus.). 145p. 1994. pap. 10.00 (*0-89555-506-9*) TAN Bks Pubs.

Brown, Raphael, compiled by. The Life of Mary As Seen by the Mystics. LC 90-71852. 264p. 1994. reprint ed. pap. 12.50 (*0-89555-436-4*) TAN Bks Pubs.

Brown, Raphael, tr. Little Flower of St. Francis. 368p. 1971. pap. 9.95 (*0-385-07544-8*, Image Bks) Doubleday.

Brown, Raphael, ed. see Duboin, Alain-Marie.

Brown, Raven M. As the World Is Seen Through the Eyes of the Raven - Hear Her Cry: A Book of Inspirational Poetry. Crawford, Lillian R. et al, eds. ixv, 41p. 1999. pap. 12.90 (*0-9670415-0-3*) R M B Pub.

Brown, Rawdon, tr. see Giustiniani, Sebastiano.

Brown, Ray. Broken Silence. LC 98-105843. 192p. 1996. mass mkt. 5.99 (*0-7860-0343-X*, Pinncle Kensgtn) Kensgtn Pub Corp.
— How to Experience the Inexhaustible Fullness of God. 1979. pap. 1.49 (*1-56632-006-2*) Revival Lit.
— Micro-Trains: A Color History. 140p. 1993. pap. 49.95 (*1-881341-04-6*) Two-Ten-Four.
— Micro-Trains: A Color History. 2nd ed. (Illus.). 130p. 1995. 59.95 (*1-881341-06-2*); pap. 49.95 (*1-881341-07-0*) Two-Ten-Four.
— Micro-Trains: A Color History, Vol. 1. (Illus.). 140p. 1993. 59.95 (*1-881341-03-8*) Two-Ten-Four.
— Shadows. 1997. pap. write for info. (*1-57553-665-X*) Watermrk Pr.

Brown, Ray & Angus, Raymond. A. K. A. Narc. 256p. (Orig.). 1991. mass mkt. 4.95 (*0-671-69261-5*) PB.

Brown, Ray & Lynch, S. Eighteen Wheels of Justice. Grad, Doug, ed. 256p. (Orig.). 1992. mass mkt. 4.99 (*0-671-70890-2*) PB.

Brown, Ray, jt. auth. see Baron, Wade.

Brown, Ray, jt. auth. see Tyson, Eric.

Brown, Ray B., jt. ed. see Fishwick, Marshall W.

Brown, Ray H. Robert Stewart Hyer, the Man I Knew. (Illus.). 1957. 10.00 (*0-685-05005-X*) A Jones.

Brown, Ray W., jt. ed. see Holzworth, Larry K.

Brown, Raymond. Christ in the Gospels of the Ordinary Sundays: Essays on the Gospel Readings of the Ordin. Sundays in the Three-Year Liturgical Cycle. LC 98-25613. 112p. 1998. pap. 5.95 (*0-8146-2542-8*) Liturgical Pr.

Brown, Raymond E. An Adult Christ at Christmas: Essays on the Three Biblical Christmas Stories - Matthew 2 & Luke 2. 50p. 1978. pap. 4.95 (*0-8146-0997-X*) Liturgical Pr.
— Bible Guide. 1993. pap. 8.00 (*0-00-470281-6*) Collins.
— The Birth of the Messiah: A Commentary on the Infancy Narratives in the Gospels of Matthew & Luke. 752p. 1999. pap. 19.95 (*0-385-49447-5*) Doubleday.
— The Birth of the Messiah: A Commentary on the Infancy Narratives of Matthew & Luke. rev. ed. LC 93-11256. (Anchor Bible Reference Library Ser.). 752p. 1993. 45.00 (*0-385-47202-1*) Doubleday.
— The Churches the Apostles Left Behind. 160p. (Orig.). (C). 1984. pap. 10.95 (*0-8091-2611-7*) Paulist Pr.
— A Coming Christ in Advent: Essays on the Gospel Narratives Preparing for the Birth of Jesus - Matthew 1 & Luke 1. 72p. 1988. pap. 4.95 (*0-8146-1587-2*) Liturgical Pr.
— The Community of the Beloved Disciple. LC 78-65894. 204p. 1979. pap. 12.95 (*0-8091-2174-3*) Paulist Pr.
— The Critical Meaning of the Bible. LC 81-82333. 160p. (Orig.). 1981. pap. 9.95 (*0-8091-2406-8*) Paulist Pr.
— A Crucified Christ in Holy Week: Essays on the Four Gospel Passion Narratives. 80p. 1986. pap. 4.95 (*0-8146-1444-2*) Liturgical Pr.
— Death of the Messiah. 752p. 1999. pap. 19.95 (*0-385-49449-1*) Doubleday.
— Death of the Messiah: From Gethsemane to the Grave, 2 Vols., Set. LC 93-9241. 1994. pap. text, boxed set 100.00 (*0-385-47177-7*) Doubleday.
— Death of the Messiah Vols. 1 & 2: From Gethsemane to the Grave: A Commentary on the Passion Narratives in the Four Gospels. LC 98-24248. (Anchor Bible Reference Library Ser.). 912p. 1999. pap. 19.95 (*0-385-49448-3*) Doubleday.
— The Death of the Messiah: from Gethsemane to the Grave: A Commentary on the Passion Narratives in the Four Gospels, 2. LC 93-9241. (Anchor Bible Reference Library Ser.). 752p. 1994. 37.50 (*0-385-19397-1*) Doubleday.
— The Death of the Messiah: from Gethsemane to the Grave: A Commentary on the Passion Narratives in the Four Gospels, Vol. 1. LC 93-9241. (Anchor Bible Reference Library Ser.). 912p. 1994. 37.50 (*0-385-19396-3*) Doubleday.
— The Epistles of John. LC 81-43380. (Anchor Bible Ser.: Vol. 30). 840p. 1982. 47.50 (*0-385-05686-9*) Doubleday.
— Giants of the Faith: Classic Christian Writings & the Men Behind Them. LC 97-39241. 1998. pap. 12.99 (*0-89107-987-4*) Crossway Bks.
— The Gospel & Epistles of John: A Concise Commentary. 4th ed. 129p. 1988. pap. 5.95 (*0-8146-1283-0*) Liturgical Pr.
— An Introduction to New Testament Christology. LC 94-14569. 240p. 1994. pap. 11.95 (*0-8091-3516-7*) Paulist Pr.
— An Introduction to the New Testament. LC 96-37742. (Illus.). 928p. 1997. 45.00 (*0-385-24767-2*, Anchor Bib) Doubleday.
— The Message of Nehemiah. LC 98-26065. (Bible Speaks Today Ser.). 256p. 1998. pap. 14.99 (*0-8308-1242-3*, 1242) InterVarsity.
— A Once-&-Coming Spirit at Pentecost: Essays on the Liturgical Readings between Easter & Pentecost, Taken from the Acts of the Apostles & from the Gospel According to John. LC 93-28726. 104p. (Orig.). 1994. pap. 4.95 (*0-8146-2154-6*) Liturgical Pr.

***Brown, Raymond E.** Priest & Bishop. 88p. 1999. pap. 12.00 (*1-57910-277-8*) Wipf & Stock.
— Raymond E. Brown, S. S., 6 vols. pap. 27.50 (*0-8146-2560-6*, Liturg Pr Bks) Liturgical Pr.

Brown, Raymond E. Reading the Gospels with the Church: From Christmas Through Easter. 96p. (Orig.). 1996. pap. 7.95 (*0-86716-268-6*, B2686) St Anthony Mess Pr.
— Recent Discoveries & the Biblical World. 103p. 1989. pap. 24.00 (*0-86217-181-4*, Pub. by Veritas Pubns) St Mut.
— Responses to One Hundred One Questions on the Bible. 160p. 1990. pap. 10.95 (*0-8091-3188-9*) Paulist Pr.
— A Retreat with John the Evangelist: That You May Have Life. LC 99-173685. 112p. 1998. pap. 7.95 (*0-86716-353-4*) St Anthony Mess Pr.
— A Risen Christ in Eastertime: Essays on the Gospel Narratives of the Resurrection. 96p. (Orig.). 1991. pap. 4.95 (*0-8146-2014-0*) Liturgical Pr.
— Timothy-James. (Bible Study Commentaries Ser.). 1983. pap. 4.95 (*0-87508-174-6*) Chr Lit.
— The Virginal Conception & Bodily Resurrection of Jesus. LC 72-97399. 1973. pap. 12.95 (*0-8091-1768-1*) Paulist Pr.

Brown, Raymond E., et al, eds. Jerome Biblical Commentary. 1986. 71.95 (*0-13-509612-X*) P-H.
— Mary in the New Testament. LC 78-8797. 336p. 1978. pap. 14.95 (*0-8091-2168-9*) Paulist Pr.
— The New Jerome Bible Handbook. LC 92-46508. 416p. 1993. 24.95 (*0-8146-2204-6*) Liturgical Pr.

Brown, Raymond E., tr. The Gospel According to John: Chapters I-XII. LC 66-12209. (Anchor Bible Ser.: Vol. 29). 688p. 1966. 45.00 (*0-385-01517-8*, Anchor NY) Doubleday.
— The Gospel According to John: Chapters XIII-XXI. LC 66-12209. (Anchor Bible Ser.: Vol. 29A). 688p. 1970. 45.00 (*0-385-03761-9*, Anchor NY) Doubleday.

Brown, Raymond R. Memories of Eden. (Illus.). 120p. (Orig.). 1996. pap. 14.95 (*0-9658238-0-6*) R R Brown.

Brown, Rebecca. Annie Oakley's Girl. LC 93-21777. 160p. (Orig.). 1993. pap. 8.95 (*0-87286-279-8*) City Lights.
— Becoming a Vessel of Honor. LC 98-22799. 304p. 1992. pap. 12.99 (*0-88368-322-9*) Whitaker Hse.
— Como Llegar a ser una Vasija para Honra.Tr. of Becoming a Vessel of Honor. (SPA.). 304p. 1993. pap. 11.99 (*0-88368-317-2*) Whitaker Hse.

***Brown, Rebecca.** The Dogs: A Modern Bestiary. LC 98-36228. 166p. 1998. pap. 10.95 (*0-87286-344-1*) City Lights.

Brown, Rebecca. The Gifts of the Body. 176p. 1995. pap. 12.00 (*0-06-092653-8*) HarpC.
— He Came to Set the Captives Free. LC 97-36658. 288p. 1992. pap. 12.99 (*0-88368-323-7*) Whitaker Hse.
— Prepare for War. LC 97-36659. 336p. 1992. pap. 12.99 (*0-88368-324-5*) Whitaker Hse.
— Preparemonos para la Guerra. LC 97-44282.Tr. of Prepare for War. (SPA.). 328p. 1992. pap. 11.99 (*0-88368-321-0*) Whitaker Hse.
— The Terrible Girls. 144p. (Orig.). 1992. pap. 8.95 (*0-87286-266-6*) City Lights.
— El Vino a dar Libertad a los Cautivos. LC 97-109.Tr. of He Came to Set the Captives Free. (SPA.). 288p. 1992. pap. 10.99 (*0-88368-320-2*) Whitaker Hse.

Brown, Rebecca & Yoder, Daniel. Maldiciones Sin Quebrantar. LC 97-7480.Tr. of Unbroken Curses. (SPA.). 175p. 1996. pap. 10.99 (*0-88368-399-7*) Whitaker Hse.
— Unbroken Curses: Hidden Source of Trouble in the Christian's Life. 175p. 1995. pap. 12.99 (*0-88368-372-5*) Whitaker Hse.

Brown, Rebecca H., ed. see Gatewood, James R.

Brown, Regina. Little Brother. (Illus.). (J). (gr. 3-7). 1962. 8.95 (*0-8392-3019-2*) Astor-Honor.
— Play at Your House. (Illus.). (J). (gr. 3-7). 1962. 8.95 (*0-8392-3027-3*) Astor-Honor.

Brown, Regina A., ed. see Geoscience Information Society Staff.

Brown, Reginald A. The Normans & the Norman Conquest. LC 77-366379. xvi, 292p. 1969. write for info. (*0-09-456260-1*, Pub. by Constable & Co) Trafalgar.

Brown-Reinsel, Beth. Knitting Ganseys. (Illus.). 160p. 1993. pap. 16.95 (*0-934026-85-8*) Interweave.

Brown, Rexford G. Schools of Thought: How the Politics of Literacy Shape Thinking in the Classroom. LC 90-19892. (Education-Higher Education Ser.). 320p. 1991. text 38.45 (*1-55542-314-0*) Jossey-Bass.

Brown, Rexford G. Schools of Thought: How the Politics of Literacy Shape Thinking in the Classroom. LC 90-19892. (Education-Higher Education Ser.). 320p. 1993. reprint ed. pap. 19.00 (*1-55542-558-5*) Jossey-Bass.

Brown, Richard. Chartism. (Perspectives in History Ser.). v, 138p. (C). 1998. pap. 11.95 (*0-521-58617-8*) Cambridge U Pr.
— Eighty-Three Years & No Longer Counting: An Informal History of Tracy-Locke Advertising 1913-1996. LC 98-132486. (Illus.). 74p. 1997. pap. text 15.00 (*0-9637402-4-5*) Brown Comm.
— James Joyce. Page, Norman, ed. LC 91-27199. (Modern Novelists Ser.). 152p. 1992. text 35.00 (*0-312-06887-5*) St Martin.
— Managing in the Single European Market. LC 94-166168. (Illus.). 198p. 1993. reprint ed. pap. 61.40 (*0-608-07425-X*, 206765200009) Bks Demand.
— Managing the Learning of History. (Quality in Secondary Schools & Colleges Ser.). 144p. 1995. pap. 24.95 (*1-85346-345-0*, Pub. by David Fulton) Taylor & Francis.
— Moments in Eden. (Illus.). 144p. 1996. pap. 22.95 (*0-395-77186-2*) HM.
— Moments in Eden, Vol. 1. 1989. 40.00 (*0-316-10999-1*) Little.
— 100 Words about Animals. LC 86-22774. (Illus.). 32p. (J). (ps). 1987. 5.95 (*0-15-200550-1*, Gulliver Bks) Harcourt.
— 100 Words about My House. (Illus.). (J). (gr. k-2). 1990. 22.95 incl. audio (*0-87499-153-6*) Live Oak Media.
— One Hundred Words about My House, 4 bks., Set. (Illus.). (J). (gr. k-2). 1990. pap. 29.95 incl. audio (*0-87499-154-4*) Live Oak Media.
— 100 Words about Transportation. LC 86-22781. (Illus.). 32p. (J). (ps). 1987. 5.95 (*0-15-200551-X*, Gulliver Bks) Harcourt.
— 100 Words about Transportation. (Illus.). (J). (gr. k-2). 1990. 22.95 incl. audio (*0-87499-186-2*) Live Oak Media.
— A Perfect Day for the Tajar. (Illus.). 56p. 1987. pap. 5.00 (*0-87603-101-7*) Am Camping.
— Restoring the Vow of Stability: The Keys to Pastoral Longevity. LC 93-70741. 250p. 1993. pap. 10.99 (*0-87509-532-1*) Chr Pubns.

***Brown, Richard.** Revolution, Radicalism, & Reform: English History 1780-1846. (Cambridge Perspectives in History Ser.). 160p. 2000. pap. write for info. (*0-521-56788-2*) Cambridge U Pr.

Brown, Richard. Richard Brown's New England. (Illus.). 144p. 1996. 40.00 (*1-55209-070-1*) Firefly Bks Ltd.
— Sleep & Disease & the Immune Response. Date not set. 89.95 (*0-8493-7698-X*) CRC Pr.

***Brown, Richard.** Stop Depression Now: Sam-E: The Breakthrough Supplement That Works as Well as Prescription Drugs. 2000. pap. 12.00 (*0-425-17643-6*) Berkley Pub.

Brown, Richard. Voyage of the Iceberg. (Illus.). 160p. 1995. 17.95 (*0-88862-656-8*) Formac Dist Ltd.
— Whisked Away: Poems for More Than One Voice. LC 93-17849. (C). 1992. pap. 9.50 (*0-521-44588-4*) Cambridge U Pr.

Brown, Richard, ed. Theology Vol. 3: Revisioning the Church. (Theology Colloquy Papers). 164p. (Orig.). 1995. pap. text 12.00 (*0-8309-0722-X*) Herald Pub Hse.

Brown, Richard. Gulliver's Travels: A Kid's Guide to Southern California. 135p. (J). (gr. 1 up). 1988. 6.95 (*0-318-33430-5*, Gulliver Bks) Harcourt.
— A Kid's Guide to Florida. (Gulliver Travels Travel Guide). 160p. (J). (gr. 1 up). 1989. pap. 6.95 (*0-15-200461-0*, Gulliver Bks) Harcourt.
— A Kid's Guide to National Parks. (Gulliver Travels Travel Guide). 160p. (J). (gr. 1 up). 1989. pap. 6.95 (*0-318-37140-5*, Gulliver Bks) Harcourt.
— A Kid's Guide to New York City. (Gulliver Travels Travel Guide). 160p. (J). (gr. 1 up). 1988. pap. 6.95 (*0-15-200458-0*, Gulliver Bks) Harcourt.
— Kids Guide to Washington, D. C. (Gulliver Travels Travel Guide). 160p. (J). (gr. 1 up). 1989. pap. 11.00 (*0-15-200459-9*, Gulliver Bks) Harcourt.
— Muchas Palabras Sobre Animales. LC 88-21364.Tr. of Hundred Words about Animals. (SPA.). 32p. (J). (ps-1). 1989. pap. 6.00 (*0-15-200531-5*) Harcourt.
— Muchas Palabras Sobre Mi Casa. LC 88-21363.Tr. of Hundred Words about My House. (SPA.). 32p. (J). (ps-1). 1989. pap. 6.00 (*0-15-200532-3*, Gulliver Bks) Harcourt.
— 100 Words about Animals. LC 86-22744. (One Hundred Words about Ser.). 32p. (J). (ps-1). 1989. pap. 4.95 (*0-15-200554-4*, Gulliver Bks) Harcourt.
— 100 Words about My House. LC 87-7574. (One Hundred Words about Ser.). 32p. (J). (ps-1). 1989. pap. 3.95 (*0-15-200556-0*, Gulliver Bks) Harcourt.
— 100 Words about Transportation. LC 86-22781. (One Hundred Words about Ser.). 32p. (J). (ps-3). 1989. pap. 3.95 (*0-15-200555-2*) Harcourt.
— 100 Words about Working. LC 87-8363. (One Hundred Words about Ser.). 32p. (J). (ps-1). 1989. pap. 3.95 (*0-15-200557-9*, Gulliver Bks) Harcourt.

Brown, Richard, photos by. Tasha Tudor's Garden. LC 94-7886. (Illus.). 160p. 1994. 35.00 (*0-395-43609-5*) HM.

Brown, Richard & Brett, Stanley. The London Bookshop, Pt. 2. (Illus.). 75p. 1977. 20.00 (*0-900002-23-9*, 1267, Pub. by Priv Lib Assn) Oak Knoll.

Brown, Richard, et al. Stop Depression Now: SAM-e, the Breakthrough Supplement that Works as Well as Prescription Drugs, in Half the Time. . . With No Side Effects. LC 99-27451. 208p. 1999. pap. 19.95 (*0-399-14530-3*, G P Putnam) Peng Put Young Read.

Brown, Richard, jt. auth. see Ziefert, Harriet.

Brown, Richard, ed. see Prymak, Gregory.

Brown, Richard, ed. see Towers, June.

Brown, Richard A. Short Sermons for Worship: One Hundred Fifty Bible-Based Themes, Vol. 2. 160p. 1990. pap. text 6.00 (*0-8309-0632-0*) Herald Pub Hse.
— Temple Foundations: Essays on an Emerging Concept. 150p. (Orig.). 1991. pap. 5.00 (*0-8309-0589-8*) Herald Pub Hse.

Brown, Richard A., ed. Theology Vol. 4: Justice or Just Us? 206p. (Orig.). 1997. pap. text 13.00 (*0-8309-0754-8*) Herald Pub Hse.

Brown, Richard A., et al. Practical Guide to On-Site in Situ Remedial Technology. Date not set. 69.95 (*0-87371-348-6*, L348) Lewis Pubs.

Brown, Richard A., jt. ed. see Miers, Earl S.

Brown, Richard C. Social Attitudes of American Generals, Eighteen Ninety-Eight to Nineteen Forty. Kohn, Richard H., ed. LC 78-22413. (American Military Experience Ser.). 1980. lib. bdg. 31.95 (*0-405-11887-2*) Ayer.

Brown, Richard C., jt. auth. see Nishiyama, Hidetaka.

Brown, Richard D. Knowledge Is Power: The Diffusion of Information in Early America, 1700-1865. (Illus.). 384p. 1991. reprint ed. pap. text 26.00 (*0-19-507265-0*) OUP.
— The New Poet: Novelty & Tradition in Spenser's "Complaints" LC 99-494968. 320p. 1998. 45.95 (*0-85323-803-0*, Pub. by Liverpool Univ Pr); pap. 23.95 (*0-85323-813-8*, Pub. by Liverpool Univ Pr) Intl Spec Bk.
— Revolutionary Politics in Massachusetts: The Boston Committee of Correspondence & the Towns, 1772-1774. LC 71-119072. (Illus.). 298p. 1970. 29.95 (*0-674-76781-0*) HUP.
— The Strength of a People: The Idea of an Informed Citizenry in America, 1650-1870. 272p. 1997. pap. 18.95 (*0-8078-4663-5*) U of NC Pr.
— The Strength of a People: The Idea of an Informed Citizenry in America, 1650-1870. LC 95-35013. (Illus.). 272p. (gr. 13). 1997. 39.95 (*0-8078-2261-2*) U of NC Pr.

Brown, Richard D., ed. Major Problems in the Era of the American Revolution, 1760-1791: Documents & Essays. (Major Problems in American History Ser.). 620p. (C). 1992. pap. text 29.16 (*0-669-19755-6*) HM Trade Div.

***Brown, Richard D. & Tager, Jack.** Massachusetts: A Concise History. (Illus.). 400p. 2000. 60.00 (*1-55849-248-8*); pap. 19.95 (*1-55849-249-6*) U of Mass Pr.

Brown, Richard D., et al. Farm Labor in Southern New England During the Agricultural-Industrial Transition. 113p. 1989. reprint ed. pap. 14.50 (*0-944026-11-7*) Am Antiquarian.

Brown, Richard D., jt. ed. see O'Brien, Robert.

***Brown, Richard Danson.** A Shakespearean Reader: Sources & Criticism. LC 99-48799. 340p. 2000. text 59.95 (*0-312-23039-7*) St Martin.

***Brown, Richard Danson & Johnson, David.** Shakespeare 1609: Cymbeline & the Sonnets. LC 99-55778. 2000. write for info. (*0-312-23037-0*); pap. write for info. (*0-312-23038-9*) St Martin.

Brown, Richard Danson, jt. auth. see Johnson, David.

Brown, Richard E. Chester's Last Stand. LC 88-10659. 200p. 1988. 20.00 (*0-87417-138-5*) U of Nev Pr.
— Fishing for Ghosts: Twelve Short Stories. LC 93-29446. 216p. 1994. 20.00 (*0-87417-229-2*) U of Nev Pr.
— The GAO: Untapped Source of Congressional Power. LC 78-111049. 140p. reprint ed. pap. 43.40 (*0-608-14402-9*, 202177300023) Bks Demand.
— An Introduction to Neuroendocrinology. (Illus.). 430p. (C). 1994. pap. text 42.95 (*0-521-42665-0*) Cambridge U Pr.
— The Planning Process on the Pine Ridge & Rosebud Indian Reservations. 1969. 1.00 (*1-55614-078-9*) U of SD Gov Res Bur.

Brown, Richard E., ed. Accounting & Accountability in Public Administration. (PAR Classics Ser.: No. VII). 200p. 1988. 17.95 (*0-936678-11-9*) Am Soc Pub Admin.
— The Effectiveness of Legislative Program Review. LC 78-66237. 150p. 1979. pap. text 21.95 (*0-87855-712-1*) Transaction Pubs.

Brown, Richard E. & Brown, Beverly A. The Rose Engagement. expanded ed. 205p. (Orig.). (C). 1996. pap. text 12.00 (*0-9654000-2-6*) Kent Info Srvcs.
— The Rose Engagement. unabridged ed. LC 98-153675. 203p. (Orig.). 1996. pap. 12.00 (*0-9654000-1-8*) Kent Info Srvcs.

Brown, Richard E. & MacDonald, David W., eds. Social Odours in Mammals, 2 vols., 1. (Illus.). 566p. (C). 1985. text 125.00 (*0-19-857546-7*) OUP.
— Social Odours in Mammals, 2 vols., 2. (Illus.). 340p. (C). 1985. text 89.00 (*0-19-857617-X*) OUP.

Brown, Richard G. Basic Algebra. 1989. text, student ed. 56.20 (*0-395-50112-1*) HM.

Brown, Richard H. I Am of Ireland. (Illus.). 157p. 1995. pap. 11.95 (*1-57098-014-4*) Roberts Rinehart.
— A Poetic for Sociology: Toward a Logic of Discovery for the Human Sciences. xvi, 320p. 1989. pap. text 17.95 (*0-226-07619-9*) U Ch Pr.
— Social Science As Civic Discourse: Essays on the Invention, Legitimation & Uses of Social Theory. 246p. 1989. 33.00 (*0-226-07624-5*) U Ch Pr.
— Society As Text: Essays on Rhetoric, Reason, & Reality. LC 86-30893. (Illus.). x, 264p. (C). 1987. 29.95 (*0-226-07616-4*) U Ch Pr.
— Society As Text: Essays on Rhetoric, Reason, & Reality. LC 86-30893. x, 262p. 1992. pap. text 16.95 (*0-226-07617-2*) U Ch Pr.

— Toward a Democratic Science: Scientific Narration & Civice Communication. LC 97-14234. 320p. 1998. 30.00 (*0-300-06707-0*) Yale U Pr.

Brown, Richard H., ed. Postmodern Representations: Truth, Power, & Minesis in the Human Sciences & Public Culture. LC 94-24083. 288p. 1995. text 49.95 (*0-252-02176-2*); pap. text 22.50 (*0-252-06465-8*) U of Ill Pr.

***Brown, Richard H. & Schubert, J. Daniel.** Knowledge & Power in Higher Education: A Reader. LC 99-44312. 216p. 1999. pap. text 26.95 (*0-8077-3905-7*) Tchrs Coll.

Brown, Richard Harvey, ed. Writing the Social Text: Poetics & Politics in Social Science Discourse. (Communication & Social Order Ser.). 240p. 1992. pap. text 26.95 (*0-202-30387-X*); lib. bdg. 49.95 (*0-202-30386-1*) Aldine de Gruyter.

***Brown, Richard Harvey & Schubert, J. Daniel, eds.** Knowledge & Power in Higher Education: A Reader. LC 99-44312. 216p. 1999. write for info. (*0-8077-3906-5*) Tchrs Coll.

Brown, Richard L. The L. E. A. P. Lifetime Exercise Adherence Plan. (Illus.). 368p. 1999. pap. 13.00 (*0-06-098733-2*) HarpC.

— Palace Gates: Under Seige in Hue City: TET January 1968. LC 95-67279. (Illus.). 240p. 1995. 24.95 (*0-88740-745-5*) Schiffer.

***Brown, Richard L.** The 10-Minute L. E. A. P. Lifetime Exercise Adherence Plan. (Illus.). 345p. 2000. reprint ed. 25.00 (*0-7881-9290-6*) DIANE Pub.

Brown, Richard L. & Henderson, Joe. Fitness Running. LC 93-27143. (Fitness Spectrum Ser.). (Illus.). 184p. 1994. pap. 15.95 (*0-87322-451-5*, PBRO0451) Human Kinetics.

Brown, Richard M. No Duty to Retreat: Violence & Values in American History & Society. 280p. 1992. 25.00 (*0-19-504510-6*) OUP.

— No Duty to Retreat: Violence & Values in American History & Society. LC 93-32549. 268p. 1994. reprint ed. pap. 13.95 (*0-8061-2618-3*) U of Okla Pr.

Brown, Richard M., jt. ed. see Gottesman, Ronald.

Brown, Richard M., ed. & intro. see Breakenridge, William M.

Brown, Richard W. My Kind of Garden. LC 97-22927. (Illus.). 160p. 1997. 40.00 (*0-395-79123-5*) HM.

Brown, Richard W., jt. auth. see Martin, Tovah.

Brown, Richmond F. Juan Fermin de Aycinena: Central American Colonial Entrepreneur, 1729-1796. LC 97-3818. (Illus.). xvii, 298p. 1997. 34.95 (*0-8061-2948-4*) U of Okla Pr.

Brown, Rick. Imago Relationship Therapy. LC 98-45981. 198p. 1999. 55.00 (*0-471-24289-6*) Wiley.

— Seventy-Five Picture Prompts for Young Writers. 88p. (gr. 1-3). 1993. pap. 10.95 (*0-590-49408-2*) Scholastic Inc.

Brown, Rick. The First Christmas Rubber Stamp Storybook. 16p. (J). (ps up). 1996. student ed. 9.99 (*0-7847-0536-4*, 03586) Standard Pub.

Brown, Rick, jt. auth. see Cundy, Dale R.

Brown, Risa W., jt. auth. see Stein, Barbara L.

Brown, Risa W., jt. auth. see Totten, Herman L.

Brown, Rita Mae. Bingo. 384p. 1989. mass mkt. 6.50 (*0-553-28220-4*) Bantam.

— Bingo. 288p. 1999. reprint ed. pap. 11.95 (*0-553-38040-0*) Bantam.

— Cat on the Scent. LC 99-31994. 1999. write for info. (*1-56895-749-1*) Wheeler Pub.

***Brown, Rita Mae.** Cat on the Scent. 336p. 2000. reprint ed. mass mkt. 6.99 (*0-553-57541-4*) Bantam.

Brown, Rita Mae. Dolley: A Novel of Dolley Madison in Love & War. 432p. 1995. mass mkt. 6.50 (*0-553-56949-X*) Bantam.

— High Hearts. 448p. 1987. mass mkt. 6.99 (*0-553-27888-6*) Bantam.

— In Her Day. 192p. 1988. mass mkt. 6.50 (*0-553-27573-9*) Bantam.

— Loose Lips. LC 98-56079. 384p. 1999. 24.95 (*0-553-09972-8*) Bantam.

***Brown, Rita Mae.** Loose Lips. 384p. 2000. pap. 13.95 (*0-553-38067-2*, Spectra) Bantam.

Brown, Rita Mae. Murder at Monticello, or, Old Sins. 320p. 1995. mass mkt. 6.99 (*0-553-57235-0*, Crimeline) Bantam.

— Murder on the Prowl. large type ed. LC 98-14023. 536p. 1998. 28.95 (*0-7862-1458-9*) Mac Lib Ref.

— Murder on the Prowl. 400p. 1999. reprint ed. mass mkt. 6.99 (*0-553-57540-6*) Bantam.

— Murder, She Meowed. (Mrs. Murphy Mystery Ser.). (Illus.). 300p. 1997. mass mkt. 6.99 (*0-553-57237-7*) Bantam.

***Brown, Rita Mae.** Outfoxed. LC 99-44243. 384p. 2000. 24.00 (*0-345-42818-8*) Ballantine Pub Grp.

— Outfoxed. large type ed. LC 99-86684. 2000. 26.95 (*1-56895-844-7*) Wheeler Pub.

Brown, Rita Mae. Pay Dirt. 288p. 1996. mass mkt. 6.99 (*0-553-57236-9*) Bantam.

— Rest in Pieces. LC 92-7257. 368p. 1993. mass mkt. 6.99 (*0-553-56239-8*) Bantam.

— Rest in Pieces. large type ed. LC 92-37866. 429p. 1993. reprint ed. lib. bdg. 20.95 (*1-56054-595-X*) Thorndike Pr.

— Riding Shotgun. 368p. 1997. mass mkt. 6.99 (*0-553-57224-5*) Bantam.

— Riding Shotgun. large type ed. LC 96-14352. (Large Print Bks.). 1996. pap. 23.95 (*1-56895-332-1*) Wheeler Pub.

— Rita Will: Memoir of a Literary Rabble-Rouser. 496p. 1999. pap. 13.95 (*0-553-37826-0*) Bantam.

— Rubyfruit Jungle. 256p. 1983. reprint ed. mass mkt. 6.99 (*0-553-27886-X*, Bantam Classics) Bantam.

— Six of One. 288p. 1999. reprint ed. pap. 11.95 (*0-553-38037-0*) Bantam.

— Sneaky Pie's Cookbook for Mystery Lovers. LC 99-12337. 64p. 1999. 15.95 (*0-553-10635-X*) Bantam.

— Southern Discomfort. 288p. 1983. mass mkt. 6.50 (*0-553-27446-5*, Bantam Classics) Bantam.

— Starting from Scratch: A Different Kind of Writers' Manual. 272p. 1996. pap. 13.95 (*0-553-34630-X*) Bantam.

— Sudden Death. 256p. 1984. mass mkt. 6.50 (*0-553-26930-5*, Bantam Classics) Bantam.

— Venus Envy. 400p. 1994. mass mkt. 6.99 (*0-553-56497-8*) Bantam.

— Wish You Were Here. 304p. 1991. mass mkt. 6.99 (*0-553-28753-2*) Bantam.

***Brown, Rita Mae & Brown, Sneaky Pie.** Pawing Through the Past. LC 99-86213. (Illus.). 368p. 2000. 24.95 (*0-553-10738-0*, Spectra) Bantam.

Brown, Riva, ed. see Fard Muhammad, Mahdi.

Brown, Rob. The Fairy Door; Only I Am. (Illus.). 48p. (J). (gr. k-3). 1995. 14.95 (*1-56313-744-5*) BrownTrout Pubs Inc.

— Skeena, BC. (River Journal Ser.: Vol. 3, No. 4). (Illus.). 48p. 1996. pap. 15.95 (*1-57188-032-1*) F Amato Pubns.

Brown, Rob & Brown, Margaret. Empowered: A Practical Guide to Leadership in the Liberated Organization. (People Skills for Professionals Ser.). (Illus.). 276p. (Orig.). 1996. pap. 19.95 (*1-85788-022-6*) Nicholas Brealey.

Brown, Robert. Analyzing Love. (Cambridge Studies in Philosophy). 144p. 1987. text 59.95 (*0-521-34038-1*) Cambridge U Pr.

— Basic Guitar, Stand Alone Tracks, Bk. 1. (Alfred's Handy Guide Ser.). 1995. pap. 12.95 incl. audio compact disk (*0-88284-660-4*) Alfred Pub.

— Basic Guitar, Stand Alone Tracks, Bk. 1. 1996. pap. 12.95 incl. audio compact disk (*0-88284-699-X*) Alfred Pub.

— Basingstoke Past & Present. (C). 1989. 50.00 (*1-85455-007-1*, Pub. by Ensign Pubns & Print) St Mut.

— Basix Jazz Guitar Concepts. 1997. pap. 7.95 (*0-88284-756-2*); pap. 9.95 incl. audio compact disk (*0-88284-757-0*) Alfred Pub.

***Brown, Robert.** Financing Start-Ups: How to Raise Money for Emerging Companies 2001. 400p. 2000. pap. 139.00 (*0-15-607191-6*) Harcourt.

Brown, Robert. First Journey of Exploration Across Vancouver Island. 36p. 1991. pap. 6.95 (*0-87770-416-3*) Ye Galleon.

— The Golfing Mind: Psychological Principles of Good Golf. LC 94-12731. 184p. 1994. pap. 14.95 (*1-58080-008-4*) Burford Bks.

— The Golfing Mind: The Psychological Principles of Good Golf. 184p. 1995. pap. 14.95 (*1-55821-439-9*) Lyons Pr.

— House of Magic. 112p. 1991. pap. 12.00 (*0-9629565-0-3*) Orioles Inc.

— House of Magic. rev. ed. 1991. pap. 14.95 (*0-9629565-1-1*) Orioles Inc.

— Illustrated Encyclopaedia of Peoples & Cultures of the World: A Graphic Account of the Characteristics, Customs, Languages, Religions & Folklore of the Human Family, 6 vols. 1952p. 1998. pap. 3600.00 (*81-7305-043-0*, Pub. by Print Hse) St Mut.

— In-House Training in Technical Communication: An STC Anthology. 237p. 1998. per. 50.00 (*1-891709-02-X*, 178-98) Soc Tech Comm.

— Introducing Jazz for the Rock Guitarist. (National Guitar Workshop Arts Ser.). 48p. 1995. pap. 7.95 (*0-88284-652-3*, 7100) Alfred Pub.

— Notes on Jonah. 24p. (Orig.). 1994. pap. 2.50 (*1-880573-06-7*) Bible Search Pubns.

— Rhythm Guitar Stand Alone Tracks. 1995. pap. 12.95 incl. audio compact disk (*0-88284-659-0*) Alfred Pub.

— Rock Keyboard for Beginners. (National Guitar Workshop Arts Ser.). 48p. 1998. pap. 7.50 (*0-88284-923-9*, 18411); pap. 17.50 incl. audio compact disk (*0-88284-924-7*, 18412) Alfred Pub.

— Science for You - One Hundred & Twelve Illustrated Experiments. 1988. 12.95 (*0-8306-0325-5*, 3025); pap. 7.95 (*0-8306-9325-4*) McGraw-Hill Prof.

— Semitic Influence in Hellenic Mythology. 1977. 25.95 (*0-405-10084-1*, 14709) Ayer.

— Sleepwalking with Mayakovsky. LC 93-35960. (Wick Poetry Chapbook Ser.: No. 2). 46p. (Orig.). 1994. pap. 4.75 (*0-87338-502-0*) Kent St U Pr.

— SONET Primer: A Course Workbook. LC 73-85629. (Specialized Ser.). (Illus.). 33p. (C). 1997. spiral bd. 16.95 (*1-56016-069-1*) ABC TeleTraining.

— Stand Alone Blues. (Alfred's Handy Guide Ser.). 1995. pap. 12.95 incl. audio compact disk (*0-88284-734-1*) Alfred Pub.

— Stand Alone Blues. (Alfred's Handy Guide). 32p. (YA). 1992. reprint ed. pap. 9.95 incl. audio (*0-88284-543-8*, 4428) Alfred Pub.

— Stand Alone Classic Rock. 1995. pap. 12.95 incl. audio compact disk (*0-88284-772-4*) Alfred Pub.

— Stand Alone Jazz. (National Guitar Workshop Arts Ser.). 1994. pap. 12.95 (*0-88284-641-8*, 11289) Alfred Pub.

— Stand Alone Jazz. (Alfred's Handy Guide Ser.). 1995. pap. 12.95 incl. audio compact disk (*0-88284-764-3*) Alfred Pub.

— Stand Alone Tracks Basic Guitar, Bk. 2. (Alfred's Handy Guide Ser.). 1997. pap. 13.95 incl. audio compact disk (*0-88284-782-1*) Alfred Pub.

— Stand Alone Tracks Funk: Handy Guide. (Alfred's Handy Guide Ser.). 1995. pap. 12.95 incl. audio compact disk (*0-88284-781-3*) Alfred Pub.

***Brown, Robert.** The Way of Golf: Reconnecting with the Spirit of the Game. 192p. 2000. 20.00 (*1-58080-081-5*) Burford Bks.

Brown, Robert, et al, eds. Salt in Our Veins: Poems & Stories from the Astoria Fisher Poets Gathering. (Illus.). 80p. 1999. pap. 8.00 (*1-890767-01-8*, South Jetty Bks) Bacchae Pr.

Brown, Robert & Barrow. Principles of Small Business. 224p. 1997. pap. 18.99 (*1-86152-189-8*) Thomson Learn.

Brown, Robert & Blonshine, Susan. Spirometry Quality: The Essentials. (Illus.). 180p. 1996. spiral bd. 29.95 (*0-932887-11-2*) Health Ed Pubns.

Brown, Robert & Boger-Brown, Uta. Cytotoxic Drug Resistance Mechanisms. LC 98-43528. (Methods in Molecular Medicine Ser.: Vol. 28). 248p. 1999. 89.50 (*0-89603-603-0*) Humana.

Brown, Robert & Gutterman, Alan S. Financing Start-Ups: How to Raise Money for Emerging Companies. 617p. 1999. pap. 139.00 incl. cd-rom (*0-15-606799-4*) Harcourt.

Brown, Robert & Reed, Peter. Marine Reinsurance 343p. 1987. 230.00 (*0-900886-61-7*, Pub. by Witherby & Co) St Mut.

Brown, Robert, ed. see American Outdoor Safety League Staff.

Brown, Robert, jt. ed. see Brown, Julie.

Brown, Robert, ed. see Harris, John W.

Brown, Robert, ed. see Mayes, Eric A., Jr.

Brown, Robert, ed. see Means, Evan.

Brown, Robert, jt. ed. see Priest, John M.

Brown, Robert, tr. see Janich, Peter.

Brown, Robert A. Fluid Mechanics of the Atmosphere. (International Geophysics Ser.: Vol. 47). 489p. (C). 1991. text 103.00 (*0-12-137040-2*) Acad Pr.

Brown, Robert A., ed. Endeavour Views the Earth: Astronauts' Photographs from Space Shuttle Mission STS-47. (Illus.). 91p. (C). 1996. pap. 11.95 (*0-521-57099-9*) Cambridge U Pr.

Brown, Robert A. & Davis, Stephen H., eds. Free Boundaries in Viscous Flows. LC 93-50711. (IMA Volumes in Mathematics & Its Applications Ser.: Vol. 61). 1994. 65.95 (*0-387-94253-X*) Spr-Verlag.

Brown, Robert D., ed. Antler Development in Cervidae. LC 82-74285. (Illus.). 400p. 1983. 15.00 (*0-912229-04-7*); pap. 10.00 (*0-912229-05-5*) CK Wildlife Res.

Brown, Robert D., ed. Livestock & Wildlife Management During Drought. (Illus.). 66p. (Orig.). 1986. pap. text 5.00 (*0-912229-11-X*) CK Wildlife Res.

Brown, Robert D. & Gillespie, Terry J. Microclimatic Landscape Design: Creating Thermal Comfort & Energy Efficiency. LC 95-10902. 208p. 1995. pap. 54.95 (*0-471-05667-7*) Wiley.

Brown, Robert D. & McKeown, Patrick G. Structured Programming with Microsoft BASIC. 350p. (C). 1992. teacher ed. write for info. incl. disk (*0-15-500561-8*); teacher ed. write for info. incl. disk (*0-15-500560-X*) Dryden Pr.

Brown, Robert D., jt. auth. see McKlown, Patrick.

Brown, Robert D., jt. auth. see Newman, Dianna L.

Brown, Robert D., jt. ed. see Canon, Harry J.

Brown, Robert E. Charles Beard & the Constitution: A Critical Analysis of "An Economic Interpretation of the Constitution" LC 78-14426. 219p. 1979. reprint ed. lib. bdg. 55.00 (*0-313-21048-9*, BRBC, Greenwood Pr) Greenwood.

— Family Doc: The Making of a Family Practitioner. LC 97-23974. 176p. 1997. pap. 17.95 (*1-85070-969-5*) Prthnon Pub.

— Feature-Based Definition of Bevel Gears. (Technical Papers: Vol. 95FTM11). (Illus.). 12p. 1995. pap. text 30.00 (*1-55589-660-X*) AGMA.

— Gathering the Light. 1976. pap. 2.50 (*0-88031-026-X*) Invisible-Red Hill.

— On Collecting, Collectors & Collections: The Collector's Paradise. (Illus.). 175p. (Orig.). 1999. pap. 19.95 (*0-9653701-0-0*) Brimfield Publns.

Brown, Robert E. & Mouser, G. W. Techniques for Teaching Conservation Education. LC 64-24115. 120p. reprint ed. 37.20 (*0-8357-9054-1*, 201332300086) Bks Demand.

Brown, Robert F. The Later Philosophy of Schelling: The Influence of Boehme on the Works of 1809-1815 LC 75-10138. 295p. 1976. 38.50 (*0-8387-1755-1*) Bucknell U Pr.

— Schelling's Treatise on "The Deities of Samothrace" A Translation & an Interpretation. LC 76-42239. (American Academy of Religion. Studies in Religion: No. 12). 75p. reprint ed. pap. 30.00 (*0-7837-5480-9*, 204524500005) Bks Demand.

Brown, Robert F. & Brown, Brenda. Essentials of Finite Mathematics. (Illus.). 454p. 1990. text 57.95 (*0-912675-78-0*) Ardsley.

Brown, Robert F. & Brown, Brenda W. Finite Mathematics. 614p. (C). 1992. text 59.95 (*0-912675-96-9*) Ardsley.

Brown, Robert F., ed. see Hegel, Georg Wilhelm Friedrich.

Brown, Robert G. Materials Management Systems. LC 83-19978. 448p. (C). 1984. reprint ed. lib. bdg. 46.50 (*0-89874-707-4*) Krieger.

Brown, Robert G. We Learned Together: Story of First Year Teacher. 94p. 1995. pap. 20.60 (*0-536-58773-6*) Fearson Custom.

Brown, Robert G. & Hwang, Patrick Y. Introduction to Random Signal Analysis & Kalman Filtering. 2nd ed. LC 91-21354. 512p. (C). 1991. text 90.95 (*0-471-52573-1*) Wiley.

— Introduction to Random Signal Analysis & Kalman Filtering. 2nd ed. 208p. (C). 1992. pap. text 18.59 (*0-471-52568-5*) Wiley.

— Introduction to Random Signal Analysis & Kalman Filtering: With Matlab Exercises & Solutions. 3rd ed. LC 96-25880. 484p. 1996. text 102.95 (*0-471-12839-2*) Wiley.

Brown, Robert G., et al. Lines, Waves, & Antennas: The Transmission of Electric Energy. 2nd ed. LC 92-15562. 486p. (C). 1992. reprint ed. lib. bdg. 72.50 (*0-89464-758-X*) Krieger.

Brown, Robert H. Analysis of Marine Insurance Clauses Bk. 1: The Institute Cargo Clauses. 59p. 1983. pap. 80.00 (*0-900886-84-6*, Pub. by Witherby & Co) St Mut.

— Analysis of Marine Insurance Clauses Bk. 2: The Institute Time Clauses Hulls. 50p. 1984. pap. 80.00 (*0-900886-89-7*, Pub. by Witherby & Co) St Mut.

— The Cargo Insurance Contract & the Institute Cargo Caluses (Training Notes for Brokers) 146p. 1995. pap. 45.00 (*1-85609-085-X*, Pub. by Witherby & Co) St Mut.

— Dictionary of Marine Insurance Terms. 395p. 1975. 150.00 (*0-900886-11-0*, Pub. by Witherby & Co) St Mut.

— Dictionary of Marine Insurance Terms & Clauses. 5th ed. 656p. (C). 1995. 295.00 (*0-948691-43-3*, Pub. by Witherby & Co) St Mut.

— The Insurance of Merchant Ships & Shipowners Interests, Bk. 1. 200p. 1990. 130.00 (*1-85609-007-8*, Pub. by Witherby & Co) St Mut.

— The Insurance of Merchant Ships & Shipowners Interests, Bk. 2. 200p. 1990. 130.00 (*1-85609-008-6*, Pub. by Witherby & Co) St Mut.

— Introduction to Marine Insurance (Training Notes for Brokers) 265p. 1995. pap. 44.00 (*1-85609-079-5*, Pub. by Witherby & Co) St Mut.

— Marine Insurance: Cargo Practice, Vol. 2. 4th ed. (C). 1985. 225.00 (*0-7855-6043-2*, Pub. by Witherby & Co) St Mut.

— Marine Insurance: Hull Practice, Vol. 3. 425p. 1975. 81.00 (*0-900886-13-7*, Pub. by Witherby & Co) St Mut.

— Marine Insurance: Principles & Basic Practice, Vol. 1. 5th ed. (C). 1986. write for info. (*0-7855-2604-8*, Pub. by Witherby & Co) St Mut.

— Marine Insurance Vol. 1: Principles & Basic Practice. 343p. (C). 1986. 155.00 (*0-948691-19-0*, Pub. by Witherby & Co) St Mut.

***Brown, Robert H.** Marine Insurance Vol. 1: Principles & Basic Practice. 408p. 1998. 140.00 (*1-85609-150-3*, Pub. by Witherby & Co) St Mut.

Brown, Robert H. Marine Insurance Vol. 2: Cargo Practice. 5th ed. 630p. 1998. 180.00 (*1-85609-132-5*, Pub. by Witherby & Co) St Mut.

— Marine Insurance Abbreviations. 91p. 1974. 60.00 (*0-900886-00-5*, Pub. by Witherby & Co) St Mut.

— Marine Insurance Abbreviations. (C). 1984. 100.00 (*0-7855-4090-3*, Pub. by Witherby & Co) St Mut.

— Marine Insurance & Reinsurance Abbreviations. 130p. (C). 1994. pap., per. 50.00 (*0-948691-63-8*, Pub. by Witherby & Co) St Mut.

— Marine Reinsurance Terms & Abbreviations. 32p. 1982. 85.00 (*0-900886-58-7*, Pub. by Witherby & Co) St Mut.

— Nature's Hidden Terror: Violent Nature Imagery in 18th-Century Literature. (GERM Ser.: Vol. 69). (Illus.). vii, 148p. 1992. 50.00 (*1-879751-06-2*) Camden Hse.

— Sedona: Arizona's Red Rock Community. (Illus.). (Orig.). 1993. pap. write for info. (*0-9639209-1-X*) Bronze Age.

— Stellar Theology & Masonic Astronomy. 117p. 1996. reprint ed. spiral bd. 18.00 (*0-7873-1222-3*) Hlth Research.

— Stellar Theology & Masonic Astronomy. 120p. 1993. reprint ed. pap. 16.95 (*1-56459-357-6*) Kessinger Pub.

— Training Notes for Brokers: Introduction to Marine Insurance. (C). 1987. 80.00 (*0-948691-26-3*, Pub. by Witherby & Co) St Mut.

— Wyoming: A Geography. (Geographies of the United States Ser.). (Illus.). 375p. 1980. text 50.50 (*0-89158-560-5*) Westview.

Brown, Robert H., ed. Marine Insurance: Hull Practice, Vol. 3. 1200p. (C). 1995. 395.00 (*0-948691-45-X*, Pub. by Witherby & Co) St Mut.

Brown, Robert H. & Novitt, J. J. Marine Insurance Vol. 2: Cargo Practice. 450p. (C). 1985. 200.00 (*0-900886-83-8*, Pub. by Witherby & Co) St Mut.

Brown, Robert H. & Reed, P. B. Marine Reinsurance. (C). 1981. 210.00 (*0-7855-4085-7*, Pub. by Witherby & Co) St Mut.

Brown, Robert H. & Wormell, John. Introduction to Working in the Lloyd's Market. 161p. (C). 1988. pap. 110.00 (*0-948691-38-7*, Pub. by Witherby & Co) St Mut.

— Lloyd's Market Practice. 110p. (C). 1992. 110.00 (*1-85609-023-X*, Pub. by Witherby & Co) St Mut.

Brown, Robert H., ed. & intro. see Brauner, Sigrid.

Brown, Robert J. Manipulating the Ether: The Power of Broadcast Radio in Thirties America. LC 97-43336. 324p. 1998. lib. bdg. 48.50 (*0-7864-0397-7*) McFarland & Co.

— Three Hundred Thirty-Three More Science Tricks & Experiments. 208p. 1984. pap. 10.95 (*0-07-156204-4*) McGraw.

— Three Hundred Thirty-Three More Science Tricks & Experiments. (Illus.). 208p. (J). (gr. 6-9). 1984. pap. 10.95 (*0-8306-1835-X*, 1835) McGraw-Hill Prof.

— Three Hundred Thirty-Three Science Tricks & Experiments. 240p. (Orig.). 1984. pap. 11.95 (*0-07-156080-7*) McGraw.

— Three Hundred Thirty-Three Science Tricks & Experiments. (Illus.). 208p. (Orig.). 1984. 15.95 (*0-8306-0825-7*) McGraw-Hill Prof.

— Three Hundred Thirty-Three Science Tricks & Experiments. (Illus.). 208p. (Orig.). (J). (gr. 6-9). 1986. pap. 9.95 (*0-8306-1825-2*, 1825) McGraw-Hill Prof.

— Two Hundred Illustrated Science Experiments for Children. 196p. (Orig.). 1987. pap. 12.95 (*0-07-157390-9*) McGraw.

— Two Hundred Illustrated Science Experiments for Children. (Illus.). 196p. (Orig.). 1987. pap. 9.95 (*0-8306-2825-8*) McGraw-Hill Prof.

B

Brown, Robert K. & Norton, Mark R., eds. The One Year Book of Hymns. LC 94-43726. 1502p. 1995. pap. 19.99 (*0-8423-5095-0*) Tyndale Hse.

Brown, Robert K., jt. auth. see Newman, Bob.

Brown, Robert K., ed. see Bayo, Alberto.

Brown, Robert K., jt. ed. see Jones, Michael P.

Brown, Robert K., ed. see Petersen, William J. & Petersen, Randy.

Brown, Robert K., tr. see Douglas, J. D., ed.

Brown, Robert L. Central City & Gilpin County: Then & Now. LC 94-15643. (Illus.). 217p. (Orig.). 1994. pap. 8.95 (*0-87004-363-3*) Caxton.

— Colorado Ghost Towns, Past & Present. LC 77-140121. (Illus.). 1972. pap. 14.95 (*0-87004-218-1*) Caxton.

— Colorado on Foot. LC 91-8054. (Illus.). 1991. pap. 10.95 (*0-87004-336-6*) Caxton.

— The Dvaravati Wheels of the Law & the Indianization of South East Asia. LC 95-41624. (Studies in Asian Art & Archaeology: Vol. 18). xxxii, 237p. 1995. 165.50 (*90-04-10435-6*) Brill Academic Pubs.

***Brown, Robert L.** Economic Security for an Aging Canadian Population. 1999. pap. text 35.00 (*0-938959-58-1*) Soc Actuaries.

Brown, Robert L. An Empire of Silver. rev. ed. Sundance Publications, Ltd. Staff, ed. (Illus.). 224p. 1984. 39.00 (*0-913582-36-0*) Sundance.

— Ghost Towns of the Colorado Rockies. LC 68-10099. (Illus.). 1968. pap. 17.95 (*0-87004-342-0*) Caxton.

— Introduction to Ratemaking & Loss Reserving for Property & Casualty Insurance. LC 93-20279. 157p. 1993. pap. text 42.50 (*0-936031-11-5*) Actex Pubns.

— Introduction to the Mathematics of Demography. 3rd rev. ed. (C). 1997. pap. text 52.50 (*1-56698-205-7*) Actex Pubns.

— Jeep Trails to Colorado Ghost Towns. LC 63-7443. (Illus.). 1963. pap. 10.95 (*0-87004-021-9*) Caxton.

***Brown, Robert L.** Mergers, Acquisitions & Divestitures: Business, Legal, Finance & Tax Aspects with CD-ROM. (Illus.). 500p. 2000. pap. 120.00 incl. cd-rom (*0-15-607104-5*) Harcourt Prof.

— Uphill Both Ways: Hiking Colorado's High Country. LC 73-83111. (Illus.). 1976. pap. 7.95 (*0-87004-249-1*) Caxton.

***Brown, Robert L., ed.** Art from Thailand. (Illus.). 112p. 1999. 60.00 (*81-85026-46-7*) Art Media Resources.

Brown, Robert L., ed. Ganesh: Studies of an Asian God. LC 90-46163. (SUNY Series in Tantric Studies). 352p. (C). 1991. text 21.50 (*0-7914-0656-3*) State U NY Pr.

Brown, Robert L., jt. auth. see Zima, Petr.

***Brown, Robert M.** America's Way in the World. 136p. 2000. pap. 24.50 (*0-7618-1693-3*) U Pr of Amer.

Brown, Robert M. The Bible Speaks to You. LC 84-19578. 324p. (C). 1985. pap. 19.95 (*0-664-24597-8*) Westminster John Knox.

— The Cocker Spaniel Owners' Medical Manual. LC 87-71369. 305p. (Orig.). 1988. pap. 18.00 (*0-938681-01-X*) Breed Manual Pubns.

— The Essential Reinhold Niebuhr. LC 85-22798. 288p. 1987. reprint ed. pap. 16.00 (*0-300-04001-6*, Y-663) Yale U Pr.

— Liberation Theology: An Introductory Guide. LC 92-30934. 160p. (Orig.). 1993. pap. 14.95 (*0-664-25424-1*) Westminster John Knox.

— Persuade Us to Rejoice: The Liberating Power of Fiction. 160p. (Orig.). 1992. pap. 14.95 (*0-664-25381-4*) Westminster John Knox.

— The Poodle Owners' Medical Manual. LC 87-71345. 288p. (Orig.). 1988. pap. 17.00 (*0-938681-02-8*) Breed Manual Pubns.

— Reclaiming the Bible: Words for the 90s. LC 94-8687. 160p. (Orig.). 1994. pap. 14.95 (*0-664-25553-1*) Westminster John Knox.

— Saying Yes & Saying No: On Rendering to God & Caesar. LC 85-29575. 144p. (Orig.). 1986. pap. 12.95 (*0-664-24695-8*) Westminster John Knox.

— Spirituality & Liberation: Overcoming the Great Fallacy. LC 87-29425. (Illus.). 160p. (Orig.). 1988. pap. 16.95 (*0-664-25002-5*) Westminster John Knox.

— Theology in a New Key: Responding to Liberation Themes. LC 78-6494. 212p. 1978. pap. 13.95 (*0-664-24204-9*) Westminster John Knox.

— Unexpected News: Reading the Bible with Third World Eyes. LC 84-2380. 166p. 1984. pap. 17.95 (*0-664-24552-8*) Westminster John Knox.

Brown, Robert M., contrib. by. Speaking of Christianity: Practical Compassion, Social Justice, & Other Wonders. LC 97-15534. 161p. 1997. pap. 14.00 (*0-664-25742-9*) Westminster John Knox.

Brown, Robert M., ed. Kairos: Three Prophetic Challenges to the Church. fac. ed. LC 91-161589. 116p. 1990. reprint ed. pap. 36.00 (*0-7837-7946-1*, 204770200008) Bks Demand.

Brown, Robert M., et al. How to Read Electronic Circuit Diagrams. 2nd ed. 224p. 1987. pap. 19.95 (*0-07-155463-7*) McGraw.

— How to Read Electronic Circuit Diagrams. 2nd ed. (Illus.). 224p. 1987. 20.95 (*0-8306-0480-4*, 2880); pap. 14.95 (*0-8306-2880-0*) McGraw-Hill Prof.

Brown, Robert McAfee. Dark the Night, Wild the Sea. large type ed. LC 99-16091. 1999. pap. 23.95 (*0-7862-2056-2*) Mac Lib Ref.

— Dark the Night, Wild the Sea: A Novel. LC 98-7944. 200p. 1998. 15.00 (*0-664-22128-9*) Westminster John Knox.

Brown, Robert N. & Legal Counsel for the Elderly Staff. The Rights of Older Persons: A Basic Guide to the Legal Rights of Older Persons under Current Law. LC 88-2030. 413p. 1988. pap. 9.95 (*0-8093-1432-0*) S Ill U Pr.

Brown, Robert R. And One Was a Soldier: The Spiritual Pilgrimage of Robert E. Lee. LC 98-34566. 125p. 1998. 19.95 (*1-57249-118-3*, Burd St Pr) White Mane Pub.

***Brown, Robert S.** My Alphabet Letter Books, AA to ZZ. (Illus.). (J). 2000. pap. 3.95 (*0-13-014808-3*) P-H.

Brown, Robert T. Immigrants to Liberia. (Liberian Research Working Papers: No. 7). 1980. 15.00 (*0-686-33172-9*) Arden Assocs.

— The Rise & Fall of the People's Colleges: The Westfield Normal School, 1839 to 1914. (Illus.). 170p. 1988. 10.00 (*0-685-44692-1*) WSC Inst MA Studies.

Brown, Robert T., jt. auth. see Cordor, Henry.

Brown, Robert T., jt. auth. see Strasburger, Victor C.

Brown, Robert T., jt. ed. see Reynolds, Cecil R.

Brown, Robert W. Foundation Behavior & Repair: Residential & Light Construction. 3rd ed. LC 96-35227. 352p. 1997. 74.95 (*0-07-008204-9*) McGraw.

— Practical Foundation Engineering Handbook. 1120p. 1995. 99.95 (*0-07-008194-8*) McGraw.

Brown, Robert W. & Jeffrey A., Kottler. Introduction to Therapeutic Counseling: Voices from the Field. 4th ed. LC 99-39354. 442p. 1999. pap. text 83.95 (*0-534-35878-0*) Brooks-Cole.

Brown, Robert W., jt. auth. see Haacke, E. Mark.

Brown, Robert W., jt. auth. see Kottler, Jeffrey A.

***Brown, Robert Wade.** Foundation Repair Manual. LC 98-32430. 1999. write for info. (*0-07-008244-8*) McGraw-Hill Prof.

— Practical Foundation Engineering Handbook. 2nd ed. (Illus.). 1104p. 2000. 115.00 (*0-07-135139-6*) McGraw.

Brown, Roberta. The Walking Trees & Other Scary Stories. 139p. (J). (gr. 4 up). 1991. pap. 7.95 (*0-87483-143-1*) August Hse.

Brown, Roberta S. Queen of the Cold-Blooded Tales. (American Storytelling Ser.). (Illus.). 176p. (YA). (gr. 6 up). 1995. pap. text 9.95 (*0-87483-408-2*) August Hse.

— Scared in School. LC 97-23602. (J). 1997. pap. 8.95 (*0-87483-496-1*) August Hse.

Brown, Roberta S. The Scariest Stories Ever. unabridged ed. (American Storytelling Ser.). (J). (gr. 7 up). 1992. 12.00 incl. audio (*0-87483-301-9*) August Hse.

— Scary Stories for All Ages. unabridged ed. (American Storytelling Ser.). 1992. 12.00 incl. audio (*0-87483-302-7*) August Hse.

Brown, Roberta S. & Carey, Susan. Hands-On Alphabet Activities for Young Children: A Whole Language Plus Phonics Approach to Reading. LC 94-45840. 346p. 1995. spiral bd. 28.95 (*0-87628-394-6*) Ctr Appl Res.

Brown, Roberta Seckler. Hands-On Alphabet Activities for Young Children: A Whole Language Plus Phonics Approach to Reading. 346p. (C). 1998. pap. 28.50 (*0-87628-390-3*) P-H.

Brown, Robin. Arms Control: Has the West Lost Its Way? (C). 1990. 60.00 (*0-907967-86-8*, Pub. by Inst Euro Def & Strat) St Mut.

— Milestones in Australian History. Appleton, Richard, ed. (Reference Books - Non-Fiction). (Illus.). 500p. (C). 1986. 40.00 (*0-8161-8820-3*, Hall Reference) Macmillan.

Brown, Robin, ed. Children in Crisis. LC 94-2779. (Reference Shelf Ser.: Vol. 66, No. 1). 1994. pap. 25.00 (*0-8242-0853-6*) Wilson.

— Women's Issues. LC 93-4940. (Reference Shelf Ser.). 154p. 1993. pap. 25.00 (*0-8242-0844-7*) Wilson.

Brown, Robin. Reflections: The Story of Redford Glass. 48p. 1979. pap. 8.95 (*1-890402-02-8*) Clinton Cnty Hist.

Brown, Robin C. Florida's First People: 12,000 Years of Human History. LC 93-40084. (Illus.). 262p. 1994. 34.95 (*1-56164-032-8*) Pineapple Pr.

— Florida's Fossils: Guide to Location, Indentification & Enjoyment. rev. ed. LC 96-22119. (Illus.). 208p. 1996. pap. 18.95 (*1-56164-114-6*) Pineapple Pr.

Brown, Robin L., jt. ed. see Foundyller, Charles M.

***Brown, Robyn S.** Carmine Gets Adopted! (Kitty Ser.). (Illus.). (ps-3). 2000. 9.99 (*1-56245-415-3*) Great Quotations.

— Carmine Meets Horatio! (Kitty Ser.). (Illus.). (ps-3). 2000. 9.99 (*1-56245-416-1*) Great Quotations.

— Carmine Takes a Nap! (Kitty Ser.). 2000. 9.99 (*1-56245-417-X*) Great Quotations.

— Carmine Wants to Play! (Kitty Ser.). (Illus.). (ps-3). 2000. 9.99 (*1-56245-418-8*) Great Quotations.

Brown, Rodger. Ghost Dancing on the Cracker Circuit: The Culture of Festivals in the American South. LC 96-17962. (Illus.). 224p. 1997. 47.50 (*0-87805-905-9*); pap. 17.00 (*0-87805-906-7*) U Pr of Miss.

Brown, Rodney. Noah's Great Adventure. (Illus.). 20p. (J). 1993. 15.95 (*1-883909-00-7*) Wisdom Tree.

Brown, Roger. Against My Better Judgment: An Intimate Memoir of an Eminent Gay Psychologist. LC 96-25488. 253p. 1996. pap. 17.95 (*1-56023-888-7*, Harrington Park) Haworth Pr.

— Against My Better Judgment: An Intimate Memoir of an Eminent Gay Psychologist. 253p. 1996. 29.95 (*0-7890-0087-3*) Haworth Pr.

— A First Language: The Early Stages. LC 72-95455. (Illus.). 449p. 1973. 38.00 (*0-674-30325-3*) HUP.

— A First Language: The Early Stages. LC 72-95455. (Illus.). 449p. 1976. pap. 19.50 (*0-674-30326-1*) HUP.

— Prescribed Usage. Date not set. 19.95 (*0-465-06271-7*, Pub. by Basic); pap. 18.00 (*0-465-06270-9*) Basic.

— Social Psychology. 2nd ed. 720p. (C). 1985. 35.00 (*0-02-908300-1*) Free Pr.

— Words & Things. LC 58-9395. 1968. pap. 13.95 (*0-02-904810-9*) Free Pr.

***Brown, Roger, ed.** Handbook of Physical Polymer Testing. LC 98-45735. (Plastics Engineering Ser.). (Illus.). 880p. 1999. text 225.00 (*0-8247-0171-2*) Dekker.

Brown, Roger, frwd. The Artworks of William Dawson. (Exhibition Catalog Ser.). (Illus.). 48p. 1990. pap. 15.00 (*0-938903-08-X*) Cty of Chicago.

Brown, Roger & Thie, Harry J. Future Career Management Systems for U. S. Military Officers. LC 94-30296. 1994. pap. text 15.00 (*0-8330-1572-9*, MR-470-OSD) Rand Corp.

Brown, Roger, jt. auth. see Mason, Linda.

Brown, Roger A., et al. Assessing the Potential for Using Reserves in Operations Other Than War. LC 97-49418. 96p. 1997. pap. text 13.00 (*0-8330-2473-6*, MR-796-OSD) Rand Corp.

— Assessing the State & Federal Missions of the National Guard. LC 95-33171. (Illus.). 123p. 1995. pap. text 9.00 (*0-8330-1668-7*, MR-557-OSD) Rand Corp.

Brown, Roger G. Fashoda Reconsidered: The Impact of Domestic Politics on French Policy in Africa, 1893-1898. LC 70-94393. (Johns Hopkins University Studies in Historical & Political Science: No. 88, 1). 169p. reprint ed. pap. 52.40 (*0-608-14679-X*, 202583900046) Bks Demand.

Brown, Roger H. Redeeming the Republic: Federalists, Taxation, & the Origins of the Constitution. LC 92-28958. 320p. 1993. text 38.50 (*0-8018-4497-5*) Johns Hopkins.

Brown, Roger J. Permafrost in Canada: Its Influence on Northern Development. LC 70-464841. (Canadian Building Ser.: No. 4). (Illus.). 250p. reprint ed. pap. 77.50 (*0-8357-8265-4*, 203398600088) Bks Demand.

Brown, Roger K. Making Taxes Pay You: The Practical Guide to Property Tax Sales. write for info. (*0-8187-0104-8*) Harlo Press.

Brown, Roger L. A History of the Fleet Prison, London: The Anatomy of the Fleet. LC 96-20614. (Studies in British History: Vol. 42). (Illus.). 372p. 1996. text 99.95 (*0-7734-8762-X*) E Mellen.

— Wilhelm von Humboldt's Conception of Linguistic Relativity. LC 67-30542. (Janua Linguarum, Ser. Minor: No. 65). (Orig.). 1967. pap. text 36.95 (*90-279-0593-2*) Mouton.

Brown, Roger S., ed. see DeGraf, Anna.

Brown, Roland. A-Z of Motorcycles: The Ultimate Photographic Guide. (Illustrated Encyclopedias Ser.). (Illus.). 1999. pap. 10.95 (*0-7548-0029-6*, Lorenz Bks) Anness Pub.

— The Classic Harley Davidson: A Celebration of America's Legendary Bikes. (Illus.). 64p. 1997. 12.95 (*1-85967-504-2*, Lorenz Bks) Anness Pub.

***Brown, Roland.** Encyclopedia of Motorcycles. 1998. 19.98 (*1-84038-000-4*) Anness Pub.

Brown, Roland. Superbikes. 1993. 15.98 (*1-55521-860-1*) Bk Sales Inc.

— Superbikes: Road Machines of the '60s, '70s, '80s & '90s. (Illus.). 112p. 1998. text 25.00 (*0-7881-5374-9*) DIANE Pub.

Brown, Roland W. Composition of Scientific Words. 882p. (C). 1985. reprint ed. text 40.00 (*0-87474-286-2*) Smithsonian.

Brown, Rollo W. The Firemakers. 1993. reprint ed. lib. bdg. 89.00 (*0-7812-5345-4*) Rprt Serv.

— Lonely Americans. LC 74-121452. (Essay Index Reprint Ser.). 1977. 23.95 (*0-8369-1699-9*) Ayer.

Brown, Roman & Brown, Ramsey. 101 Ways Kids Can Spoil Their Parents . . . Gift Book: And Increase Their Allowance. (Illus.). 128p. (J). (gr. k-10). 1998. 5.99 (*1-881830-92-6*) Garborgs.

Brown, Ron. Back Roads of Ontario. LC 97-178314. (Illus.). 256p. 1996. pap. 15.95 (*1-55046-166-4*) Boston Mills.

— Basketball Two Thousand: Coaching & Playing into the 21st Century. 165p. 1992. pap. text 16.95 (*0-9634459-0-1*) Bktball Two.

— 50 Even More Unusual Things to See in Ontario. (Illus.). 80p. 1996. pap. 14.50 (*1-55046-057-9*) Boston Mills.

— Fifty Unusual Things to See in Ontario. Hudson, Noel, ed. (Illus.). 80p. (Orig.). 1989. pap. 14.50 (*0-919783-87-2*, Pub. by Boston Mills) Genl Dist Srvs.

— How to Make Money. 256p. 1997. pap. 19.95 (*1-888024-13-5*) Ahead Desktop.

— The Mark of a Champion. 32p. 1996. pap. 2.95 (*1-887002-33-2*) Cross Trng.

— Ontario's Secret Landscape. (Illus.). 168p. 1999. pap. 13.95 (*1-55046-298-9*, Pub. by Boston Mills) Genl Dist Srvs.

***Brown, Ron.** Teamwork: Principles for Race Reconciliation. 90p. 1999. pap. 6.95 (*1-887002-60-X*) Cross Trng.

Brown, Ron. Unfinished Business. 126p. 1995. pap. 7.95 (*1-887002-22-7*) Cross Trng.

Brown, Ron & Brown, Ginger. Learning Guide the Infinite Geometric Progression Puzzles. (Illus.). 135p. (Orig.). 1994. pap. 16.00 (*0-9646339-0-6*) With You in Mind.

***Brown, Ron & Lindsay, Art.** I Can 2: If Coach Ron Brown Can. (Illus.). 288p. (J). 1999. pap. text 19.95 (*1-887002-93-6*) Cross Trng.

Brown, Ron & Thiessen, Gordon. Peak Performance: You Can Be a Winner. 1999. pap. 3.95 (*1-887002-59-6*) Cross Trng.

Brown, Ronald. From Selling to Managing: Guidelines for the First-Time Sales Manager. rev. ed. LC 90-55201. 192p. 1990. pap. 17.95 (*0-8144-7746-1*) AMACOM.

— The Practical Manager's Guide to Excellence in Management. LC 79-11883. 128p. reprint ed. pap. 39.70 (*0-608-12855-4*, 202358700033) Bks Demand.

— Sacred Fires: Berurya, a Daughter, a Wife, but First a Woman. 272p. 1995. pap. 24.95 (*965-229-126-9*, Pub. by Gefen Pub Hse) Gefen Bks.

***Brown, Ronald.** Three-Toes the Raccoon Visits the Farm. (J). 2000. pap. 6.95 (*0-533-13539-7*) Vantage.

Brown, Ronald. Topology. 352p. 1988. text 62.95 (*0-470-21217-9*) P-H.

Brown, Ronald & Oren, John W. Physical Distribution in Agribusiness: Activity Guide. Lee, Jasper S., ed. (Career Preparation for Agriculture-Agribusiness Ser.). 1980. text 19.96 (*0-07-008181-6*) McGraw.

Brown, Ronald B. Future Interests & Real Estates: A Programmed Learning Approach. 194p. 1989. pap. text 18.00 (*0-685-54303-X*, Chicago Law Bk) Cambridge Law.

Brown, Ronald C. Understanding Chinese Courts & Legal Process: Law with Chinese Characters. LC 97-25740. 448p. 1997. 135.00 (*90-411-0607-3*) Kluwer Law Intl.

Brown, Ronald C. & Nelson, David C. Up the Hill, down the Years: A Century in the Life of the College in San Marcos, Southwest Texas State University, 1899-1999 LC 99-17609. 1999. write for info. (*1-57864-065-2*) Donning Co.

Brown, Ronald H., jt. auth. see Gore, Al, Jr.

Brown, Ronald J. United States Marines in the Persian Gulf, 1990-1991: With Marine Forces Afloat in Desert Shield & Storm. LC 99-160438. (Illus.). 263p. 1998. pap. 25.00 (*0-16-049765-5*) USGPO.

***Brown, Ronald J., ed.** U. S. Marines in the Persian Gulf, 1990-1991: With Marine Forces Afloat in Desert Shield & Desert Storm. (Illus.). 253p. (C). 2000. reprint ed. pap. text 35.00 (*0-7881-8563-2*) DIANE Pub.

***Brown, Ronald K.** Book of Enoch. 2nd ed. 180p. 2000. 19.95 (*0-9675737-0-X*) Guadalupe.

Brown, Ronald L. Valuing Professional Practices & Licenses: A Guide for the Matrimonial Practitioner. LC 87-12620. write for info. (*0-13-940669-7*) P-H.

— Valuing Professional Practices & Licenses: A Guide for the Matrimonial Practitioner. 3rd ed. LC 98-37104. 1998. ring bd. 155.00 (*0-7355-0238-2*) Panel Pubs.

Brown, Ronald L., ed. Bankruptcy Issues in Matrimonial Cases: A Practical Guide. 638p. 1992. ring bd. 116.00 (*0-13-289075-5*) Aspen Law.

— Bankruptcy Issues in Matrimonial Cases: A Practical Guide. LC 92-17146. 1992. 100.00 (*0-13-068701-4*) P-H.

— Encyclopedia of Matrimonial Practice. 1744p. 1991. ring bd. 126.00 (*0-13-291063-2*) Aspen Law.

— Valuing Professional Practices & Licenses: A Guide for the Matrimonial Practitioner. 2nd ed. LC 93-11975. 1993. 85.00 (*0-13-102302-0*) Aspen Law.

Brown, Ronald L., jt. auth. see Foster, Henry H.

Brown, Ronald T. Pediatric Pain Pt. 2: A Special Issue of "Children's Health Care", Vol. 26, No. 1, 1997. 64p. 1997. pap. 20.00 (*0-8058-9877-8*) L Erlbaum Assocs.

***Brown, Ronald T., ed.** Cognitive Aspects of Chronic Illness in Children. LC 98-56207. 420p. 1999. lib. bdg. 44.00 (*1-57230-468-5*) Guilford Pubns.

Brown, Ronald T. & Sawyer, Michael G. Medications for School-Age Children: Effects on Learning & Behavior. LC 97-50080. (School Practitioner Ser.). 228p. 1998. lib. bdg. 30.00 (*1-57230-316-6*, C0316) Guilford Pubns.

Brown, Rose M. The PMS Zone. (Illus.). 80p. (Orig.). (YA). 1988. pap. 7.95 (*0-9622109-0-0*) Skeetoonies.

— The Wets & Drys of Springdale. (Illus.). 136p. (Orig.). 1987. pap. 9.95 (*0-940151-01-4*) Statesman-Exam.

Brown, Rosellen. The Autobiography of My Mother. 320p. 1998. pap. 11.95 (*0-385-33357-9*) Dell.

— Before & After. 368p. 1998. pap. 11.95 (*0-385-33326-9*) Dell.

— Before & After. LC 92-81571. 354p. 1992. text 21.00 (*0-374-10999-0*) FS&G.

— Before & After. 1999. 9.98 (*0-671-04406-0*) S&S Trade.

— Civil Wars. 512p. 1998. pap. 11.95 (*0-385-33292-0*) Dell.

— Cora Fry. 100p. 1989. reprint ed. pap. 14.95 (*0-87775-211-7*) Unicorn Pr.

— Cora Fry's Pillow Book. LC 94-14729. 124p. 1994. 15.00 (*0-374-14402-8*) FS&G.

— Cora Fry's Pillow Book. 179p. 1996. pap. 9.00 (*0-374-52443-2*) FS&G.

Brown, Rosellen. Half a Heart. text 24.00 (*0-374-16772-9*) FS&G.

— Half a Heart. LC 00-22926. 368p. 2000. 24.00 (*0-374-29987-0*) FS&G.

Brown, Rosellen. Mojo: Photographs by Keith Carter. Gladsky, Kristen, ed. Chimol, Carlos & Watt, Haydee, trs. (SPA., Illus.). 32p. (Orig.). 1995. pap. 1.50 (*1-882603-02-8*) Mid Am Arts.

— Tender Mercies. 288p. 1998. pap. 11.95 (*0-385-33332-3*) Dell.

Brown, Rosellen, ed. Ploughshares Fall, 1994: Intimate Exile. (Ploughshares Ser.). 251p. (Orig.). (C). 1994. pap. 8.95 (*0-933277-11-3*) Ploughshares.

Brown, Rosellen, et al, eds. The Whole Word Catalogue 1: A Handbook of Writing Ideas for Teachers. 72p. (Orig.). 1975. pap. 11.95 (*0-915924-02-1*) Tchrs & Writers Coll.

Brown, Rosellen, et al. Banquet: Five Short Stories. LC 78-56621. (Illus.). 1978. 15.00 (*0-915778-24-6*); pap. 8.00 (*0-915778-25-4*) Penmaen Pr.

Brown, Rosellen, jt. ed. see Abbott, Dorothy.

Brown, Rosemarie. The Cry God Answers: The Restoration Thru Intercession. LC 97-195542. 182p. 1997. pap. 10.99 (*1-56043-293-4*, Treasure Hse) Destiny Image.

***Brown, Rosemary.** Big Kitchen Instruction Book. (Illus.). 448p. 2000. 10.99 (*0-517-16221-0*) Random Hse Value.

Brown, Rosemary. Rosemary Brown's Big Kitchen Instruction Book. LC 98-6306. 448p. 1998. 19.95 (*0-8362-6755-9*) Andrews & McMeel.

Brown, Rosemary, ed. see Murry, Donald A., et al.

Brown, Rosemary C., jt. auth. see Brown, H. Jackson, Jr.

Brown, Ross & Jurasek, Lubo, eds. Hydrolysis of Cellulose: Mechanisms of Enzymatic & Acid Catalysis. LC 79-20842. (Advances in Chemistry Ser.: No. 181). 1979. 65.95 (*0-8412-0460-8*) Am Chemical.

Brown, Ross, jt. ed. see Raines, Philip.

Brown, Ross D. Afro-American World Almanac: What Do You Know about Your Race? (Illus.). 112p. 1998. reprint ed. pap. 15.95 (*1-58073-018-3*) BCP Bks.

An Asterisk (*) at the beginning of an entry indicates that the title is appearing for the first time.

Brown, Ross D., Jr. & Jurasek, Lubo, eds. Hydrolysis of Cellulose: Mechanisms of Enzymatic & Acid Catalysis. LC 79-20842. (Advances in Chemistry Ser.: Vol. 181). 410p. 1979. reprint ed. pap. 127.10 (*0-608-03854-7*, 206430100008) Bks Demand.

***Brown, Roxanna & Sjostrand, Sten.** Turiang: A Fourteenth Century Shipwreck in Southeast Asian Waters. (Museum Monographs: Vol. 2). (Illus.). 80p. 2000. pap. 25.00 (*1-877921-17-3*) Pacific Asia.

***Brown, Roxanna M.** The Ceramics of South-East Asia: Their Dating & Identification. 2nd ed. (Illus.). 272p. 2000. pap. 49.95 (*1-878529-70-6*) Art Media Resources.

***Brown, Roy.** Tracks & Signs of the Birds of Britain & Europe. 1999. pap. 26.95 (*0-7136-5208-X*) A & C Blk.

Brown, Roy B. Arqueologia y Paleocologia del Norcentro de Mexico. 123p. 1992. pap. 10.00 (*968-29-4513-5*, IN025) UPLAAP.

— Paleoecologia y Arqueologia en la Frontera Norte de Mesoamerica: Un Analisis. 134p. 1991. pap. 5.00 (*968-6487-61-1*, IN062) UPLAAP.

Brown, Roy C. Christian Dietrich Grabbe. LC 76-169639. (Twayne's World Authors Ser.). 176p. (C). text 20.95 (*0-8290-1733-X*) Irvington.

Brown, Roy C., ed. Quantity & Quality in Economic Research, Vol. 2. LC 85-26360. 212p. (Orig.). (C). 1988. pap. text 23.00 (*0-8191-6702-9*) U Pr of Amer.

Brown, Roy I., ed. Quality of Life for Handicapped People. (Rehabilitation Education Ser.: Vol. 3). 300p. 1988. lib. bdg. 59.50 (*0-7099-3992-2*, Pub. by C Helm) Routldge.

Brown, Roy I. & Chazan, Maurice, eds. Learning Difficulties & Emotional Problems. 239p. (Orig.). (C). 1989. pap. text 18.95 (*0-920490-89-1*) Temeron Bks.

Brown, Roy I. & Hughson, E. Anne. Behavioural & Social Rehabilitation & Training. fac. ed. LC 86-28952. (Illus.). 204p. pap. 63.30 (*0-7837-7366-8*, 204717500005) Bks Demand.

Brown, Roy I., jt. ed. see Mitchell, David.

Brown, Roy I., jt. ed. see Robertson, Sharon E.

Brown, Roy M. Public Poor Relief in North Carolina. LC 75-17208. (Social Problems & Social Policy Ser.). (Illus.). 1976. reprint ed. 19.95 (*0-405-07480-8*) Ayer.

Brown, Roy M., jt. auth. see Steiner, Jesse F.

Brown, Royal S. Overtones & Undertones: Reading Film Music. LC 93-46924. 1994. pap. 24.95 (*0-520-08544-2*, Pub. by U CA Pr) Cal Prin Full Svc.

Brown, Royce N. Compressors: Selection & Sizing. 2nd ed. LC 96-35816. 280p. 1997. 80.00 (*0-88415-164-6*, 5164) Gulf Pub.

— Compressors, Selection & Sizing. LC 85-17567. 512p. reprint ed. pap. 158.80 (*0-608-00825-7*, 206161400010) Bks Demand.

Brown, Royden. Royden Brown's Bee Hive Product Bible: Wonderous Products from One of Nature's Most Productive Creatures. LC 93-3222. 256p. pap. 9.95 (*0-89529-521-0*, Avery) Penguin Putnam.

Brown, Royston. Public Library Administration. LC Z 0678.B828. (Outlines of Modern Librarianship Ser.: Vol. 9). 95p. reprint ed. pap. 30.00 (*0-608-08887-0*, 206952400004) Bks Demand.

***Brown, Roz & Cornett, Linda.** The Insiders' Guide to Boulder & Rocky Mountain National Park. 5th ed. (Insiders' Guide Travel Ser.). (Illus.). 408p. 1999. pap. 16.95 (*1-57380-133-X*, The Insiders Guide) Falcon Pub Inc.

Brown, Ruben S. Hydro for the Eighties: Bringing Hydroelectric Power to Poor People. (Orig.). 1980. 15.00 (*0-936130-01-6*) Intl Sci Tech.

Brown, Ruby, ed. see Lars, Melvin.

Brown, Ruby M. Decorating Eggs. LC 98-101792. (Illus.). 104p. 1997. pap. text 12.95 (*1-86351-181-4*, Pub. by Sally Milner) Sterling.

— Good Food for Diabetes. 1998. pap. text 15.95 (*1-86351-216-0*, Pub. by Sally Milner) Sterling.

Brown, Rupert. Group Processes: Dynamics Within & Between Groups. (Illus.). 256p. 1988. pap. text 29.95 (*0-631-14439-0*) Blackwell Pubs.

***Brown, Rupert.** Group Processes: Dynamics Within & Between Groups. 2nd ed. 320p. 1999. 69.95 (*0-631-21852-1*); pap. text 32.95 (*0-631-18496-1*) Blackwell Pubs.

Brown, Rupert. Prejudice: Its Social Psychology. (Illus.). 272p. (C). 1995. pap. 28.95 (*0-631-18315-9*) Blackwell Pubs.

***Brown, Rupert & Gaertner, Samuel L., eds.** Intergroup Processes. 2001. 145.00 (*0-631-21062-8*) Blackwell Pubs.

Brown, Rus L. Going Barefoot on Mustang Creek. LC 92-90650. 256p. 17.00 (*0-9633230-0-8*) R L Brown Ent.

— Lingering Echoes, in the Land of the Cherokee. Smede, Marilee, ed. LC 94-70999. (Orig.). pap. 10.00 (*0-9633230-1-6*) R L Brown Ent.

Brown, Russell A. Sherlock Holmes & the Mysterious Friend of Oscar Wilde. (Stonewall Inn Mysteries Ser.). 192p. 1990. text 8.95 (*0-312-03932-8*) St Martin.

Brown, Russell K. Fallen in Battle: American General Officer Combat Fatalities from 1775. LC 88-5644. 269p. 1988. lib. bdg. 65.00 (*0-313-26242-X*, BGN/, Greenwood Pr) Greenwood.

— To the Manner Born: The Life of General William H. T. Walker. LC 93-9954. (Illus.). 392p. (C). 1994. 50.00 (*0-8203-1569-9*) U of Ga Pr.

Brown, Russell L. Preparing Your Business for Sale: Sell Your Business for the Most Money! LC 98-92392. (Illus.). 304p. 1998. 29.95 (*0-9657400-1-3*, Busn Bk Pr); 49.95 (*0-9657400-2-1*, Busn Bk Pr) RDS Assocs.

— Strategies for Successfully Buying or Selling a Business: Laws of the Jungle: Proven Techniques, Insiders Secrets & Fundamentals for Business Buyers & Sellers to Find Each Other & Successfully Close the Deal. LC 97-66714. (Illus.). 176p. 1997. pap. 29.95 (*0-9657400-0-5*, B101, Busn Bk Pr) RDS Assocs.

Brown, Rustie. The Mariner's Trivia Book. LC 85-73570. 280p. (Orig.). 1986. pap. 9.95 (*0-9605278-1-8*) Blue Harbor.

— The Titanic, the Psychic & the Sea. LC 80-70551. (Illus.). 176p. 1981. 14.95 (*0-9605278-0-X*) Blue Harbor.

Brown, Ruth. The Big Sneeze. (J). Date not set. pap. text. write for info. (*0-05-004391-9*) Addison-Wesley.

— The Big Sneeze. LC 84-23385. (Illus.). 32p. (ps up). 1997. mass mkt. 4.95 (*0-688-15282-1*, Wm Morrow) Morrow Avon.

— Big Sneeze. 1997. 10.15 (*0-606-11126-3*, Pub. by Turtleback) Demco.

— Copycat. 1999. pap. 4.99 (*0-14-055665-6*) Viking Penguin.

— Crazy Charlie. (Illus.). 32p. (J). 1998. pap. 9.95 (*0-86264-840-8*) Trafalgar.

— Cry Baby. LC 97-215790. 32p. (J). (ps-1). 1997. 15.99 (*0-525-45902-2*) NAL.

— A Dark Dark Tale. 1992. pap. 4.99 (*0-14-055716-4*) NAL.

— Destroying the Works of Witchcraft Through Fasting & Prayer. 57p. 1994. pap. 4.95 (*0-89228-110-3*) Impact Christian.

***Brown, Ruth.** Holly: The True Story of a Cat. LC 99-59561. (Illus.). 32p. (J). (ps-2). 2000. 14.95 (*0-8050-6500-8*) H Holt & Co.

Brown, Ruth. If at First You Do Not See. LC 82-15527. (Illus.). 48p. (J). (ps-2). 1995. 14.95 (*0-8050-1053-X*, Bks Young Read); pap. 5.95 (*0-8050-1031-9*, Bks Young Read) H Holt & Co.

— Ladybug, Ladybug. LC 88-14852. (Illus.). 32p. (J). (ps-1). 1992. pap. 5.99 (*0-14-054543-3*, PuffinBks) Peng Put Young Read.

Brown, Ruth. Ladybug, Ladybug. (Picture Puffin Ser.). (Illus.). (J). 1992. 10.19 (*0-606-01712-7*, Pub. by Turtleback) Demco.

— Mad Summer Night's Dream. LC 98-43734. (Illus.). 32p. (J). (ps-2). 1999. 15.99 (*0-525-46010-1*, Dutton Child) Peng Put Young Read.

Brown, Ruth. The Shy Little Angel. LC 98-19319. (Illus.). (J). (gr. k-2). 1998. 15.99 (*0-525-46079-9*, Dutton Child) Peng Put Young Read.

***Brown, Ruth.** Snail Trail. (Illus.). 24p. (J). (ps up). 2000. 9.95 (*0-375-80696-2*, Pub. by Knopf Bks Yng Read) Random.

Brown, Ruth. The Toad. LC 97-147747. (J). 1997. 15.99 (*0-525-45757-7*, Dutton Child) Peng Put Young Read.

***Brown, Ruth.** Toad. (ps-3). 1999. pap. 5.99 (*0-14-056550-7*, PuffinBks) Peng Put Young Read.

***Brown, Ruth & Yule, Andrew.** Miss Rhythm: The Autobiography of Ruth Brown, Rhythm & Blues Legend. (Illus.). 360p. (Orig.). 1999. reprint ed. text 24.00 (*0-7881-6331-0*) DIANE Pub.

Brown, Ruth & Yule, Andrew. Miss Rhythm: The Autobiography of Ruth Brown, Rhythm & Blues Legend. LC 98-31733. (Illus.). 368p. (Orig.). 1999. reprint ed. mass mkt. 15.95 (*0-306-80888-9*, Pub. by Da Capo) HarpC.

Brown, Ruth, ed. see Levine, Mel, et al.

Brown, Ruth A. S. Aureli Augustini - De Beata Vita: A Translation with an Introduction & Commentary, Vol. 72. (Patristic Studies). 211p. 1984. reprint ed. 30.00 (*0-939738-30-9*) Zubal Inc.

***Brown, Ruth A. & Connelly, Margaret D.** Simplified Phonics. 192p. 1999. pap. text 24.95 (*0-9671828-0-8*) Cottage Park.

Brown, Ruth B. Ruth Rosetta's Memories. 150p. 1993. pap. text 10.00 (*1-881908-06-2*) PanPress.

Brown, S. Only Way to Walk. Date not set. pap. 6.99 (*1-871676-43-6*, Pub. by Christian Focus) Spring Arbor Dist.

— Rough Diamond Bill Gilvear. 1994. pap. 11.99 (*1-871676-85-1*, Pub. by Christian Focus) Spring Arbor Dist.

Brown, S. A. Say It Right: (NLP Focused) VanHoozer, W. R., ed. (Illus.). 82p. 1996. ring bd. 15.95 (*1-889530-01-8*) McClure-Brown.

Brown, S. A., ed. Cell-Culture Test Methods - STP 810. LC 83-70421. 157p. 1983. text 30.00 (*0-8031-0249-6*, STP810) ASTM.

Brown, S. Azby. The Genius of Japanese Carpentry: An Account of a Temple's Construction. (Illus.). 140p. 1995. pap. 25.00 (*4-7700-1978-5*, Pub. by Kodansha Ltd) Kodansha.

Brown, S. B., et al, eds. Microelectromechanical Structures for Materials Research Vol. 518: Proceedings Materials Research Society Symposium. 248p. 1998. text 84.00 (*1-55899-424-6*) Materials Res.

Brown, S. C. & Mays, Wolfe, eds. Linguistic Analysis & Phenomenology. LC 70-165551. 307p. 1972. 36.50 (*0-8387-1025-5*) Bucknell U Pr.

Brown, S. J., ed. see American Society of Mechanical Engineers Staff.

Brown, S. J., ed. see National Congress on Pressure Vessels & Piping Sta.

Brown, S. Kent, et al, eds. Historical Atlas of Mormonism. LC 94-21912. (Illus.). 176p. 1995. 40.00 (*0-13-045147-9*) P-H.

Brown, S. Moira & MacLean, Alasdair R., eds. Herpes Simplex Virus Protocols. LC 97-35999. (Methods in Molecular Medicine Ser.: Vol. 10). (Illus.). 432p. 1997. 99.50 (*0-89603-347-3*) Humana.

Brown, S. R., ed. Materials Evaluation under Fretting Conditions - STP 780. 189p. 1982. 24.75 (*0-8031-0829-X*, STP780) ASTM.

Brown, S. S. & Davies, D. S. Organ-Directed Toxicity: Symposium on Chemical Indices & Mechanisms of Organ-Directed Toxicity, Barcelona, Spain, 4-7 March 1981. (IUPAC Symposium Ser.). (Illus.). 400p. 1981. 160.00 (*0-08-026197-3*, Pub. by Pergamon Repr) Franklin.

Brown, S. W. Secularization of American Education As Shown by State Legislation, State Constitutional Provisions & State Supreme Court Decisions. LC 70-176600. (Columbia University. Teachers College. Contributions to Education Ser.: No. 49). reprint ed. 37.50 (*0-404-55049-5*) AMS Pr.

Brown, Sallie A. & Miller, Douglas E. The Active Learner: Successful Study Strategies. 2nd rev. ed. LC 95-78958. (Illus.). 300p. (C). 1996. pap. text. write for info. (*0-935732-60-8*) Roxbury Pub Co.

***Brown, Sallie A. & Miller, Douglas E.** The Active Learner: Successful Study Strategies. 3rd ed. LC 98-46241. (Illus.). 410p. (C). 2000. pap. text. write for info. (*1-891487-18-3*) Roxbury Pub Co.

Brown, Sally. Assessment - A Changing Practice. 90p. 1989. pap. 26.00 (*0-7073-0515-2*, Pub. by Mercat Pr Bks) St Mut.

***Brown, Sally.** Where Journeys Begin: Tips for the Novice & Seasoned Traveler. Cook, Roger, ed. (Illus.). 130p. 2000. mass mkt. 12.00 (*1-889388-05-X*) Alistair Pr IN.

Brown, Sally & Horne, Heather. 500 Tips for School Improvement. (Five Hundred Tips Ser.). 160p. 1998. pap. 19.95 (*0-7494-2230-0*, Kogan Pg Educ) Stylus Pub VA.

Brown, Sally & Knight, Peter. Assessing Learners in Higher Education. LC 94-8558. (Teaching & Learning in Higher Education Ser.). 160p. 1994. pap. 29.95 (*0-7494-1113-9*, Kogan Pg Educ) Stylus Pub VA.

Brown, Sally & McIntyre, Donald. Making Sense of Teaching. LC 92-17382. (Developing Teachers & Teaching Ser.). 1993. pap. 34.95 (*0-335-15795-5*) OpUniv Pr.

Brown, Sally & Smith, Brenda, eds. Resource Based Learning. 192p. 1996. pap. 34.95 (*0-7494-1932-6*) Taylor & Francis.

Brown, Sally, et al. Beneficial Co-Utilization of Agricultural, Municipal & Industrial By-Products. LC 98-26193. 1998. 185.00 (*0-7923-5189-4*) Kluwer Academic.

***Brown, Sally, et al.** Computer Assisted Assessment of Students. 224p. 1999. pap. 29.95 (*0-7494-3035-4*, Kogan Pg Educ) Stylus Pub VA.

Brown, Sally, et al. 500 Tips for Academic Librarians. 192p. 1997. pap. 45.00 (*1-85604-228-6*, LAP2286, Pub. by Library Association) Bernan Associates.

***Brown, Sally, et al.** 500 Tips for Getting Published. 160p. 1998. pap. 24.95 (*0-7494-2637-3*, Kogan Pg Educ) Stylus Pub VA.

Brown, Sally, et al. 500 Tips for Quality Enhancement in Universities & Colleges. (Five Hundred Tips Ser.). 160p. 1997. pap. 16.95 (*0-7494-2223-8*, Kogan Pg Educ) Stylus Pub VA.

***Brown, Sally, et al.** 500 Tips for Teachers. 2nd ed. 192p. 1999. pap. 25.00 (*0-7494-2835-X*, Kogan Pg Educ) Stylus Pub VA.

Brown, Sally, et al. 500 Tips on Assessment. 160p. 1996. pap. 19.95 (*0-7494-1941-5*, Kogan Pg Educ) Stylus Pub VA.

Brown, Sally, jt. auth. see Race, Phil.

Brown, Sally, jt. auth. see Wisker, Gina.

Brown, Sally, jt. ed. see Knight, Peter.

Brown, Sally A. & Glasner, Angela. Assessment Matters in Higher Education. LC 98-20742. xi, 210p. 1998. pap. 34.95 (*0-335-20242-X*) Taylor & Francis.

— Assessment Matters in Higher Education: Choosing & Using Diverse Approaches. LC 98-20742. 1998. 115.00 (*0-335-20243-8*) Taylor & Francis.

Brown, Sally J. Where Journeys Begin. 128p. 1998. pap. 9.95 (*0-89730-202-8*, Travel Memories Pr) R J Berg.

Brown, Sam. The Big Lonely. 203p. 1993. 19.95 (*0-8027-1234-7*) Walker & Co.

— The Big Lonely. large type ed. LC 93-13779. 327p. 1993. lib. bdg. 18.95 (*1-56054-779-0*) Thorndike Pr.

— Crime of Coy Bell. 192p. 1992. 19.95 (*0-8027-4115-0*) Walker & Co.

Brown, Sam. Devil's Rim. LC 97-42304. 224p. 1997. 21.95 (*0-8027-4161-4*) Walker & Co.

Brown, Sam. The Long Drift. 192p. 1995. 20.95 (*0-8027-4146-0*) Walker & Co.

— The Long Drift. large type ed. LC 95-30258. 368p. 1995. 21.95 (*0-7838-1448-8*, G K Hall Lrg Type) Mac Lib Ref.

— The Long Season. 1987. 16.95 (*0-8027-4073-1*) Walker & Co.

— The Long Season. Grad, Doug, ed. 256p. 1994. reprint ed. mass mkt. 4.50 (*0-671-67186-3*) PB.

Brown, Sam. The Trail to Honk Ballard's Bones. 192p. 1990. 17.95 (*0-8027-4101-0*) Walker & Co.

Brown, Sam. The Trail to Honk Ballard's Bones. large type ed. LC 90-41904. 349p. 1990. reprint ed. lib. bdg. 15.95 (*1-56054-043-5*) Thorndike Pr.

Brown, Sam & Scott, Gini G. Private Eyes. 1990. pap. 12.95 (*0-8065-1182-6*, Citadel Pr) Carol Pub Group.

Brown, Sam E. Instant Math for Beginning Skills & Concepts: Hands-on Manipulative Activities. (Illus.). 142p. (Orig.). (J). (gr. k-3). 1991. pap. text 12.95 (*0-86530-206-5*, IP 192-8) Incentive Pubns.

— Instant Science: For Primary Grades. Lewis, Sherri Y., ed. (Illus.). 144p. (Orig.). (J). (gr. k-4). 1990. pap. text 12.95 (*0-86530-143-3*, IP 190-7) Incentive Pubns.

— One, Two, Buckle My Shoe: Math Activities for Young Children. (Illus.). 112p. (Orig.). (J). (ps). 1982. pap. 8.95 (*0-87659-103-9*) Gryphon Hse.

Brown, Samuel, tr. see Men, Alexander.

Brown, Samuel G. The Works of Rufus Choate: With a Memoir of His Wife, 2 vols. 1098p. 1998. reprint ed. 275.00 (*1-56169-406-1*, 15553) Gaunt.

Brown, Samuel G., ed. see Choate, Rufus.

Brown, Samuel R. Western Gazetteer: Or Emigrant's Directory. LC 79-146380. (First American Frontier Ser.). (Illus.). 1977. reprint ed. 35.95 (*0-405-02831-8*) Ayer.

Brown, Samuel R., compiled by. Finding the Source in Sociology & Anthropology: A Thesaurus-Index to the Reference Collection, 1. LC 86-31879. 284p. 1987. lib. bdg. 49.95 (*0-313-25263-7*, BFS/, Greenwood Pr) Greenwood.

Brown, Sanborn C. Basic Data of Plasma Physics: The Fundamental Data on Electrical Discharges in Gases. LC 93-27400. (American Vacuum Society Classics Ser.). (Illus.). 336p. 1994. pap. text 39.95 (*1-56396-273-X*, AIP Pr) Spr-Verlag.

— Count Rumford, Physicist Extraordinary. LC 78-25712. (Illus.). 178p. 1979. reprint ed. lib. bdg. 45.00 (*0-313-20772-0*, BRCR, Greenwood Pr) Greenwood.

— Wines & Beers of Old New England: A How-to-Do-It History. LC 77-72519. (Illus.). 185p. reprint ed. pap. 52.80 (*0-7837-2994-4*, 2042947) Bks Demand.

— Wines & Beers of Old New England: A How-to-Do-It History. LC 77-72519. (Illus.). 187p. 1998. reprint ed. pap. 12.95 (*0-87451-148-8*) U Pr of New Eng.

Brown, Sanborn C., jt. ed. see Oleson, Alexandra.

Brown, Sanborn C., ed. see Rumford, Benjamin T.

Brown, Sandford. Louis Armstrong: Swinging, Singing Satchmo. (Impact Biographies Ser.). (Illus.). 144p. (YA). (gr. 7-12). 1993. pap. 6.95 (*0-531-15680-X*) Watts.

Brown, Sandra. Above & Beyond. 1997. mass mkt. 6.99 (*1-55166-291-4*, 0-66291-6, Mira Bks) Harlequin Bks.

— Adam's Fall. 208p. 1994. mass mkt. 6.99 (*0-553-56768-3*) Bantam.

— Adam's Fall. large type ed. LC 94-6748. 1994. 23.95 (*1-56895-068-3*) Wheeler Pub.

— The Alibi. LC 99-31444. 448p. 1999. 25.95 (*0-446-51980-4*, Pub. by Warner Bks) Little.

***Brown, Sandra.** The Alibi. 592p. 2000. mass mkt. 7.99 (*0-446-60865-3*) Warner Bks.

— The Alibi. large type ed. LC 99-34288. 1999. 25.00 (*0-375-40860-6*) Wheeler Pub.

— The Alibi. large type ed. 2000. pap. 14.95 (*0-375-72792-2*) Random.

Brown, Sandra. Anhelos Ocultos. 1998. pap. 6.95 (*84-01-50553-4*) Lectorum Pubns.

— Another Dawn. 1993. 5.99 (*0-446-77698-X*) Warner Bks.

— Another Dawn. 448p. 1991. reprint ed. mass mkt. 7.50 (*0-446-35687-5*, Pub. by Warner Bks) Little.

— Another Dawn. 448p. 1997. reprint ed. mass mkt. 3.99 (*0-446-60565-4*, Pub. by Warner Bks) Little.

— Best Kept Secrets. 432p. 1989. reprint ed. mass mkt. 7.99 (*0-446-35393-0*, Pub. by Warner Bks) Little.

— Bittersweet Rain. 275p. 2000. mass mkt. 6.99 (*0-446-60309-0*, Pub. by Warner Bks) Little.

Brown, Sandra. Bittersweet Rain. large type ed. LC 99-57480. 1950. 28.95 (*0-7862-2286-7*) Thorndike Pr.

— Bittersweet Rain. large type ed. LC 99-57480. (Americana Series). 2000. 30.95 (*0-7862-2285-9*) Thorndike Pr.

Brown, Sandra. Breakfast in Bed. large type ed. LC 96-2295. (Large Print Bks.). 1996. 25.95 (*1-56895-307-0*) Wheeler Pub.

— Breakfast in Bed. rev. ed. 240p. 1996. mass mkt. 6.99 (*0-553-57158-3*) Bantam.

— Breath of Scandal. 464p. 1991. reprint ed. mass mkt. 7.99 (*0-446-35963-7*, Pub. by Warner Bks) Little.

— Charade. large type ed. LC 94-9233. 672p. 1994. lib. bdg. 24.95 (*0-7862-0228-9*) Thorndike Pr.

— Charade. large type ed. LC 94-9233. 579p. 1995. pap. 18.95 (*0-7862-0229-7*) Thorndike Pr.

— Charade. 496p. 1995. reprint ed. mass mkt. 7.99 (*0-446-60185-3*, Pub. by Warner Bks) Little.

— Coming in from the Rain. Ewen, David, ed. (Little Worthen Brown Ser.). (Illus.). 48p. (Orig.). (J). (gr. k-3). 1997. pap. 7.00 (*1-889436-01-1*) Ewen Prime.

B

— The Devil's Own. 256p. 1994. per. 4.99 (*1-55166-001-6*, 1-66001-8, Mira Bks) Harlequin Bks.

— The Devil's Own. (Mira Bks.). 1998. mass mkt. 5.99 (*1-55166-481-X*, 1-66481-2, Mira Bks) Harlequin Bks.

— Eloquent Silence. large type ed. (Americana Series). 1996. 23.95 (*0-7862-0647-0*) Thorndike Pr.

— Eloquent Silence. 272p. 1995. reprint ed. mass mkt. 6.99 (*0-446-36051-1*, Pub. by Warner Bks) Little.

— Exclusive. large type ed. LC 96-19301. 1996. 26.95 (*0-7862-0698-5*) Thorndike Pr.

— Exclusive. large type ed. LC 96-19301. 688p. 1997. pap. 24.95 (*0-7862-0701-9*) Thorndike Pr.

— Exclusive. 496p. 1997. reprint ed. mass mkt. 7.99 (*0-446-60423-2*, Pub. by Warner Bks) Little.

— Fanta C. 256p. 1997. mass mkt. 6.99 (*0-553-56274-6*) Bantam.

— Fat Tuesday. large type ed. LC 97-23290. (Wheeler Large Print Book Ser.). 1997. 26.95 (*1-56895-465-4*) Wheeler Pub.

— Fat Tuesday. 480p. 1998. reprint ed. mass mkt. 7.99 (*0-446-60558-1*, Pub. by Warner Bks) Little.

— French Silk. 512p. 1993. reprint ed. mass mkt. 7.99 (*0-446-36426-6*, Pub. by Warner Bks) Little.

— Hawk O'Toole's Hostage. 224p. 1997. mass mkt. 6.50 (*0-553-29751-1*) Bantam.

— Hawk O'Toole's Hostage. large type ed. LC 97-9699. Date not set. 25.95 (*1-56895-425-5*) Wheeler Pub.

Brown, Sandra. Heaven's Price. 240p. 1995. reprint ed. pap., mass mkt. 6.99 (*0-553-57157-5*, Fanfare) Bantam.

Brown, Sandra. Hidden Fires. 512p. 1994. reprint ed. mass mkt. 6.99 (*0-446-36415-0*, Pub. by Warner Bks) Little.

— Hidden Fires. 512p. 1997. reprint ed. mass mkt. 3.99 (*0-446-60569-7*, Pub. by Warner Bks) Little.

— Honor Bound. 251p. 1994. per. 4.99 (*1-55166-028-8*, 1-66028-1, Mira Bks) Harlequin Bks.

— Honor Bound. 1999. 5.99 (*1-55166-482-8*, 1-66482-0) Silhouette.

— In a Class by Itself. LC 99-46461. 208p. 1999. 18.95 (*0-553-10413-6*) Bantam.

***Brown, Sandra.** In a Class by Itself. LC 99-36461. 1999. 18.95 (*0-375-40867-3*) Random Hse Lrg Prnt.

— In a Class by Itself. 2000. pap. 11.95 (*0-375-70790-5*) Random.

— In Class by Itself. 2000. mass mkt. 6.99 (*0-553-57602-X*) Bantam.

Brown, Sandra. Un Largo Atardecer. 1998. pap. 6.95 (*84-01-50550-X*) Lectorum Pubns.

***Brown, Sandra.** Un Largo Atardecer. (SPA.). 432p. 2000. pap. 9.50 (*0-553-06125-9*) Bantam.

Brown, Sandra. Led Astray. 1995. per. 4.99 (*1-55166-041-5*, 1-66041-4, Mira Bks) Harlequin Bks.

— Led Astray. 1999. mass mkt. 6.99 (*1-55166-427-5*, 0-66427-6, Mira Bks) Harlequin Bks.

— Long Time Coming. 240p. 1997. mass mkt. 6.99 (*0-553-56278-9*, Fanfare) Bantam.

— Love Beyond Reason. 256p. 1994. reprint ed. mass mkt. 7.50 (*0-446-36070-8*, Pub. by Warner Bks) Little.

— Love Beyond Reason. 256p. 1997. reprint ed. mass mkt. 3.99 (*0-446-60568-9*, Pub. by Warner Bks) Little.

— Love's Encore. LC 98-24003. 228 p. 1998. 26.95 (*1-56895-566-9*) Wheeler Pub.

— Love's Encore. 256p. 1997. reprint ed. mass mkt. 6.50 (*0-446-36428-2*, Pub. by Warner Bks) Little.

— Mirror Image. 448p. 1990. reprint ed. mass mkt. 7.99 (*0-446-35395-7*, Pub. by Warner Bks) Little.

— Prime Time. 240p. 1995. reprint ed. mass mkt. 6.99 (*0-446-36429-0*, Pub. by Warner Bks) Little.

— Sandra Brown: Three Complete Novels. 784p. 1992. 13.99 (*0-517-07774-4*) Random Hse Value.

— A Secret Splendor. (Mira Bks.). 1996. per. 5.99 (*1-55166-095-4*, 1-66095-0, Mira Bks) Harlequin Bks.

***Brown, Sandra.** Seduction by Design. 2001. mass mkt. write for info. (*0-446-60310-4*) Warner Bks.

— Send No Flowers. LC 98-31409. 240p. 1999. 18.95 (*0-553-10404-7*) Bantam.

— Send No Flowers. 304p. 2000. mass mkt. 6.99 (*0-553-57601-1*) Bantam.

Brown, Sandra. Send No Flowers. large type ed. LC 99-19340. 1999. pap. write for info. (*1-56895-720-3*) Wheeler Pub.

***Brown, Sandra.** Send No Flowers. large type ed. 2000. pap. write for info. (*1-56895-974-5*) Wheeler Pub.

Brown, Sandra. Shadows of Yesterday. large type ed. LC 93-20593. 286p. 1993. lib. bdg. 19.95 (*1-56054-788-X*) Thorndike Pr.

— Shadows of Yesterday. 272p. 1992. reprint ed. mass mkt. 6.99 (*0-446-36071-6*, Pub. by Warner Bks) Little.

— Shadows of Yesterday. 272p. 1997. reprint ed. mass mkt. 3.99 (*0-446-60566-2*, Pub. by Warner Bks) Little.

— The Silken Web. large type ed. LC 92-43519. 522p. 1993. pap. 14.95 (*1-56054-886-X*) Thorndike Pr.

— The Silken Web. large type ed. LC 92-43519. 522p. 1993. reprint ed. lib. bdg. 21.95 (*1-56054-638-7*) Thorndike Pr.

— The Silken Web. 336p. 1993. reprint ed. mass mkt. 6.99 (*0-446-36479-7*, Pub. by Warner Bks) Little.

— Slow Heat in Heaven. large type ed. LC 94-20367. 680p. 1994. 22.95 (*1-56054-791-X*) Thorndike Pr.

— Slow Heat in Heaven. 464p. 1991. reprint ed. mass mkt. 7.99 (*0-446-36173-9*, Pub. by Warner Bks) Little.

***Brown, Sandra.** Standoff. large type ed. LC 00-21657. 352p. 2000. 19.95 (*0-375-43054-7*) Random Hse Lrg Prnt.

— Standoff: A Novel. LC 99-52374. 224p. 2000. 19.95 (*0-446-52701-7*, Pub. by Warner Bks) Little.

Brown, Sandra. Sun-Kissed Kitty Learns How to Say "No" Resisting Peer Pressure. LC 94-77203. 16p. (J). (gr. 1-4). 1991. 5.95 (*1-884063-25-X*) Mar Co Prods.

— Sunset Embrace. 368p. 1990. reprint ed. mass mkt. 6.50 (*0-446-35685-9*, Pub. by Warner Bks) Little.

— Sunset Embrace. 368p. 1997. reprint ed. mass mkt. 3.99 (*0-446-60564-6*, Pub. by Warner Bks) Little.

— Sweet Anger. 304p. 1999. mass mkt. 6.50 (*0-446-60308-2*, Pub. by Warner Bks) Little.

Brown, Sandra. Sweet Anger, Lp. LC 99-56055. 1950. 30.00 (*0-7862-2293-X*) Mac Lib Ref.

— Sweet Anger, Lp. LC 99-56055. 2000. 30.00 (*0-7862-2292-1*) Mac Lib Ref.

— Switch. 480p. 2000. 25.95 (*0-446-52703-3*) Warner Bks.

Brown, Sandra. Temperatures Rising. 256p. 1993. mass mkt. 6.99 (*0-553-56045-X*) Bantam.

***Brown, Sandra.** Tempest in Eden. large type ed. LC 99-88729. (Americana Series). 245p. 2000. 30.95 (*0-7862-2294-8*) Thorndike Pr.

— Tempest in Eden. large type ed. (Americana Series). 2001. 28.95 (*0-7862-2295-6*) Thorndike Pr.

Brown, Sandra. Tempest in Eden. 240p. 1996. reprint ed. mass mkt. 6.50 (*0-446-36431-2*, Pub. by Warner Bks) Little.

— Temptation's Kiss. large type ed. LC 98-24432. (Large Print Book Ser.). 1998. 26.95 (*1-56895-581-2*) Wheeler Pub.

— Temptation's Kiss. 240p. 1998. reprint ed. mass mkt. 5.99 (*0-446-36430-4*, Pub. by Warner Bks) Little.

— Testigo. 1999. 32.95 (*84-08-02714-X*) Planeta.

— Texas Chase. 352p. 1991. mass mkt. 6.99 (*0-553-28990-X*) Bantam.

— Texas Chase. large type ed. LC 91-35829. 382p. 1992. reprint ed. lib. bdg. 20.95 (*1-56054-296-9*) Thorndike Pr.

— Texas Lucky. 288p. 1991. mass mkt. 6.99 (*0-553-28951-9*) Bantam.

— Texas Lucky. large type ed. 382p. 1992. lib. bdg. 14.95 (*1-56054-942-4*) Thorndike Pr.

— Texas Lucky. large type ed. 382p. 1992. reprint ed. lib. bdg. 19.95 (*1-56054-295-0*) Thorndike Pr.

— Texas Sage. 352p. 1992. mass mkt. 6.99 (*0-553-29500-4*) Bantam.

— Texas Sage. large type ed. 380p. 1992. pap. 14.95 (*1-56054-940-8*) Thorndike Pr.

— Texas Sage. large type ed. 380p. 1992. reprint ed. lib. bdg. 19.95 (*1-56054-297-7*) Thorndike Pr.

— The Thrill of Victory. 1994. per. 4.99 (*0-373-48296-5*, 5-48296-3) Harlequin Bks.

— The Thrill of Victory. 250p. 1995. mass mkt. 4.99 (*1-55166-025-3*, 0-66025-8, Mira Bks) Harlequin Bks.

— The Thrill of Victory. 1998. per. 5.99 (*1-55166-483-6*, 0-66483-9, Mira Bks) Harlequin Bks.

— Tidings of Great Joy. 256p. 1999. mass mkt. 6.99 (*0-553-57600-3*) Bantam.

— Tiger Prince. 251p. 1994. per. 4.99 (*1-55166-023-7*, 1-66023-2, Mira Bks) Harlequin Bks.

***Brown, Sandra.** Tiger Prince. 1999. mass mkt. 6.99 (*1-55166-531-X*, 1-66531-4, Mira Bks) Harlequin Bks.

Brown, Sandra. Tiger Prince. 1994. mass mkt. 4.99 (*0-373-48295-7*, 5-48295-5) Silhouette.

— Tomorrow's Promise. LC 93-13696. (American Romance Ser.). 192p. 1993. mass mkt. 4.99 (*0-373-83282-6*) Harlequin Bks.

— Tomorrow's Promise. 301p. 1994. per. 4.99 (*1-55166-034-2*, 1-66034-9, Mira Bks) Harlequin Bks.

— Tomorrow's Promise. 1998. mass mkt. 5.99 (*1-55166-557-3*, Mira Bks) Harlequin Bks.

***Brown, Sandra.** Tomorrow's Promise. 2000. per. 6.99 (*1-55166-601-4*, 1-66601-5, Mira Bks) Harlequin Bks.

Brown, Sandra. A Treasure Worth Seeking. 288p. 1992. reprint ed. mass mkt. 6.99 (*0-446-36073-2*, Pub. by Warner Bks) Little.

— A Treasure Worth Seeking. 288p. 1997. reprint ed. mass mkt. 3.99 (*0-446-60567-0*, Pub. by Warner Bks) Little.

— Twenty-Two Indigo Place. 224p. (Orig.). 1991. mass mkt. 6.99 (*0-553-29085-1*) Bantam.

— Twenty-Two Indigo Place. large type ed. 234p. (Orig.). 1992. reprint ed. lib. bdg. 22.95 (*1-56054-406-6*) Thorndike Pr.

— Two Alone. (Mira Bks.). 249p. 1995. per. 4.99 (*1-55166-049-0*, 1-66049-7, Mira Bks) Harlequin Bks.

— Unspeakable. LC 98-13711. 448p. 1998. 25.00 (*0-446-51979-0*, Pub. by Warner Bks) Little.

— Unspeakable. 486p. 1999. mass mkt. 7.99 (*0-446-60719-3*, Pub. by Warner Bks) Little.

— Unspeakable. large type ed. LC 98-23617. 1998. 28.95 (*0-7862-1516-X*) Thorndike Pr.

— Unspeakable. large type ed. LC 98-23617. 1999. pap. 20.00 (*0-7862-1517-8*) Thorndike Pr.

— Where There's Smoke. large type ed. LC 93-23766. 1993. 22.95 (*1-56054-781-2*) Thorndike Pr.

— Where There's Smoke. large type ed. LC 93-23766. 1994. lib. bdg. 15.95 (*1-56054-782-0*) Thorndike Pr.

— Where There's Smoke. 512p. 1994. reprint ed. mass mkt. 7.50 (*0-446-60034-2*, Pub. by Warner Bks) Little.

— A Whole New Light. 304p. 1992. mass mkt. 6.99 (*0-553-29783-X*) Bantam.

— A Whole New Light. large type ed. 244p. 1993. reprint ed. lib. bdg. 21.95 (*1-56054-564-X*) Thorndike Pr.

— The Witness. 1996. pap. 6.99 (*0-614-98109-3*, Warner Vision) Warner Bks.

— The Witness. large type ed. LC 95-14159. 1996. pap. 22.95 (*0-7862-0477-X*) Thorndike Pr.

— The Witness. 448p. 1996. reprint ed. mass mkt. 7.99 (*0-446-60330-9*, Pub. by Warner Bks) Little.

Brown, Sandra & McGreevy, William J. Experiencing Reading. 352p. (C). 1994. pap. text 33.95 (*0-8403-9138-2*) Kendall-Hunt.

Brown, Sandy S. San Diego County. Miller, Kristine, ed. 375p. 1995. pap. 11.95 (*1-56413-184-X*) Auto Club.

Brown, Sandy S., et al. San Diego. Miller, Kristine, ed. (Like A Native Ser.). 1999. pap. 13.95 (*1-56413-479-2*) Auto Club.

Brown, Sandy S., jt. auth. see Lugenbuehl, Michael.

Brown, Sanford J. Getting into Medical School. 8th rev. ed. LC 96-35971. 256p. 1997. pap. 11.95 (*0-8120-9647-9*) Barron.

— You Can Get into Medical School: Letters from Premeds. LC 85-61493. (Illus.). 144p. (Orig.). 1986. pap. 7.95 (*0-9615167-0-4*) Mendocino Found Health.

Brown, Sanford M. Planning Environmental Health Programs. LC 86-21267. 250p. 1986. 59.95 (*0-275-92237-5*, C2237, Praeger Pubs) Greenwood.

Brown, Sanford M., et al. Environmental Health Field Practice. LC 82-19026. 288p. 1983. 29.95 (*0-275-91387-2*, C1387, Praeger Pubs) Greenwood.

Brown, Sanger. Sex Worship & Symbolism: An Interpretation. LC 72-9624. reprint ed. 36.50 (*0-404-57419-X*) AMS Pr.

Brown, Sanger, II. The Sex Worship & Symbolism of Primitive Races: An Interpretation. 2nd ed. 145p. 1998. reprint ed. spiral bd. 12.00 (*1-885395-30-2*) Book Tree.

Brown, Sara D. & Starkey, Chad. Laboratory Activities for Therapeutic Modalities. 2nd ed. (Illus.). 171p. 1998. pap. 23.95 (*0-8036-0353-3*) Davis Co.

Brown, Sara H. The Vegetarian Kitchen. 1995. mass mkt. 7.99 (*0-563-37037-8*, BBC-Parkwest) Parkwest Pubns.

Brown, Sarah. Quick & Easy Vegetarian Cookery. (Illus.). 136p. 1992. pap. 9.95 (*0-563-20695-0*, BBC-Parkwest) Parkwest Pubns.

— Sarah Brown's Fresh Vegetarian Cookery. (Illus.). 256p. 1996. 28.95 (*0-563-37055-6*) BBC.

— Stained Glass: Create Five Original Designs Inspired by Masterpieces from Around the World. 1999. 16.95 (*0-7624-0576-7*) Running Pr.

— Stained Glass at York Minister, 1. 1999. pap. text 12.95 (*1-85759-219-0*) Scala Books.

— Sumptuous & Richly Adorn'd: The Decoration of Salisbury Cathedral. xii, 218p. 1999. 90.00 (*0-11-300096-0*, Pub. by Statnry Office) Balogh.

***Brown, Sarah.** The Vegetarian Bible: The Complete Illustrated Guide to Vegetarian Food & Cooking. (Illus.). 2000. pap. 24.95 (*1-86204-788-X*) Element MA.

Brown, Sarah. Vegetarian Kitchen. (Illus.). 240p. 1993. pap. 13.95 (*0-563-21034-6*, BBC-Parkwest) Parkwest Pubns.

Brown, Sarah & MacDonald, Lindsay, eds. Life, Death & Art: The Medieval Stained Glass of Fairford Parish Church, a Multimedia Exploration. LC NK5344.F3L54 1997. (Illus.). 192p. 1997. 81.00 incl. cd-rom (*0-7509-1523-4*, Pub. by Sutton Pub Ltd) Intl Pubs Mktg.

Brown, Sarah & O'Connor, David. Glass-Painters. (Medieval Craftsmen Ser.). (Illus.). 72p. 1991. pap. text 19.95 (*0-8020-6917-7*) U of Toronto Pr.

***Brown, Sarah A.** The Metamorphosis of Ovid. LC 99-37998. 2000. text 55.00 (*0-312-22844-9*) St Martin.

Brown, Sarah H. Standing Against Dragons: Three Southern Lawyers in an Era of Fear. LC 98-24110. 302p. 1998. text 35.00 (*0-8071-2207-6*) La State U Pr.

***Brown, Sarah Hart.** Standing Against Dragons: Three Southern Lawyers in an Era of Fear. (Illus.). 308p. 2000. pap. 17.95 (*0-8071-2575-X*) La State U Pr.

Brown, Sarah J. Knowledge for Health Care Practice: A Guide to Using Research Evidence. Eoyang, Thomas, ed. LC 98-27551. 1999. pap. text. write for info. (*0-7216-7803-3*, W B Saunders Co) Harcrt Hlth Sci Grp.

Brown, Sarah Leigh. Genesis: Journey into Light. Parrish-Harra, Carol E. et al, eds. LC 94-74001. 100p. 1995. pap. 7.95 (*0-945027-12-5*, Pub. by Sparrow Hawk Pr) Distributors.

Brown, Sarah S., ed. see Institute of Medicine, Committee of Unintended Pre.

Brown, Saskia, jt. auth. see Keenoy, Ray.

Brown, Schuyler. The Origins of Christianity: A Historical Introduction to the New Testament. 2nd rev. ed. (Oxford Bible Ser.). 190p. (Orig.). (C). 1993. pap. text 16.95 (*0-19-826207-8*) OUP.

— Text & Psyche: Experiencing Scripture Today. LC 76-15660. 144p. 1998. 18.95 (*0-8264-1111-8*) Continuum.

Brown, Scott & Hilbert, Robert. A Case of Mistaken Identity: The Life & Music of James P. Johnson. LC 86-3830. (Studies in Jazz: No. 4). (Illus.). 522p. 1986. 50.00 (*0-8108-1887-6*) Scarecrow.

Brown, Scott, et al. Running for Their Lives: Physical & Sexual Abuse of Runaway Adolescents. LC 95-7515. (Children of Poverty Ser.). (Illus.). 120p. 1995. text 39.00 (*0-8153-2058-2*) Garland.

Brown, Scott, jt. auth. see Fisher, Roger.

Brown, Scott S. Bounds on Transfer Principles for Algebraically Closed & Complete Discretely Valued Fields. LC 78-9121. (Memoirs of the American Mathematical Society Ser.: Vol. 204). 92p. 1978. pap. 19.00 (*0-8218-2204-7*, MEMO/15/204C) Am Math.

Brown, Scott Wesley. Keeping the Gospel in Gospel Music. 1998. 10.00 (*0-9656749-6-7*) ACW Press.

Brown, Serena-Lynn & Van Praag, Herman M., eds. The Role of Serotonin in Psychiatric Disorders. LC 90-2285. (Einstein Clinical & Experimental Psychiatry Monograph Ser.: No. 4). (Illus.). 352p. 1991. text 51.95 (*0-87630-589-3*) Brunner-Mazel.

Brown, Seyom. Causes & Prevention of War. 2nd ed. 288p. 1994. text 49.95 (*0-312-10269-0*) St Martin.

— The Faces of Power: Constancy & Change in United States Foreign Policy from Truman to Reagan. 2nd ed. LC 83-1861. 672p. 1983. pap. text 29.00 (*0-231-04737-1*) Col U Pr.

— The Faces of Power: United States Foreign Policy from Truman to Clinton. LC 93-41945. 1994. 76.00 (*0-231-09668-2*); pap. 27.00 (*0-231-09669-0*) Col U Pr.

— International Relations in a Changing Global System: Toward a Theory of the World Polity. 190p. (C). 1992. pap. text 20.00 (*0-8133-0815-1*, Pub. by Westview) HarpC.

— New Forces in World Politics. LC 74-912. 236p. reprint ed. pap. 73.20 (*0-8357-8969-1*, 203358800086) Bks Demand.

— New Forces, Old Forces, & the Future of World Politics. (C). 1988. pap. text 22.00 (*0-673-39709-2*) Addson-Wesley Educ.

— New Forces, Old Forces, & the Future of World Politics. 2nd ed. LC 94-9128. 280p. (C). 1997. pap. text 45.00 (*0-673-52210-5*) Addson-Wesley Educ.

Brown, Seyom, et al. Regimes for the Ocean, Outer Space, & Weather. 257p. 1977. 26.95 (*0-8157-1156-5*); pap. 9.95 (*0-8157-1155-7*) Brookings.

Brown, Sharon, ed. Poetry of Our Times. LC 79-51956. (Granger Poetry Library). 1980. reprint ed. 40.00 (*0-89609-179-1*) Roth Pub Inc.

Brown, Sharon E., ed. see Alexander, Caitlind L.

Brown, Sharon E., ed. see Insurance Career Development Center Staff & Alexander, Caitlind L.

Brown, Sharon E., ed. see Insurance Career Development Center Staff, et al.

Brown, Sharon R. American Travel Narratives As a Literary Genre from 1542-1832: The Art of a Perpetual Journey. LC 93-19567. 152p. 1993. text 69.95 (*0-7734-9304-2*) E Mellen.

Brown, Sharon Y., ed. see Webb, Michael L. & Webb, Mitchell T.

Brown, Shaun, jt. auth. see Brzycki, Matt.

Brown, Shaun A., jt. auth. see Voutira, Eftihia.

Brown, Sheila. Magistrates at Work: Sentencing & Social Structure. 176p. 1991. 113.00 (*0-335-09651-4*); pap. 33.95 (*0-335-09650-6*) OpUniv Pr.

— Understanding Youth & Crime: Listening to Youth? LC 97-47447. (Crime & Justice Ser.). 160p. 1998. 25.95 (*0-335-19505-9*) OpUniv Pr.

Brown, Shelby. Late Carthaginian Child Sacrifice & Sacrificial Monuments in Their Mediterranean Context. (Journal for the Study of the Old Testament Supplement Monographs Ser.: Vol. 3). 335p. 1991. 85.00 (*1-85075-240-0*, Pub. by Sheffield Acad) CUP Services.

***Brown, Sheldon S.** Biotechnology Careers. rev. ed. (Opportunities in . . . Ser.). 2000. 14.95 (*0-658-00479-4*, VGM Career); pap. 11.95 (*0-658-00480-8*, VGM Career) NTC Contemp Pub Co.

Brown, Sheldon S. Opportunities in Biotechnology Careers. 1993. pap. 10.95 (*0-8442-8647-8*, VGM Career) NTC Contemp Pub Co.

— Opportunities in Biotechnology Careers. 1993. 13.95 (*0-8442-8645-1*, VGM Career) NTC Contemp Pub Co.

— Opportunities in Biotechnology Careers. Han, Julie, ed. LC 93-47487. (Opportunities in...Ser.). (Illus.). 160p. 1995. 14.95 (*0-8442-4125-3*, 41253, VGM Career) NTC Contemp Pub Co.

— Opportunities in Biotechnology Careers. 2nd ed. Han, Julie, ed. LC 93-47487. (Opportunities In . . . Ser.). (Illus.). 160p. pap. 11.95 (*0-8442-4126-1*, 41261, VGM Career) NTC Contemp Pub Co.

Brown, Sherrod. Congress from the Inside: Observations from the Majority & the Minority. LC 98-45317. (Illus.). 264p. 1999. text 28.00 (*0-87338-630-2*) Kent St U Pr.

***Brown, Sherrod.** Congress from the Inside: Observations from the Majority & the Minority. 2nd ed. LC 00-35217. 2000. pap. write for info. (*0-87338-676-0*) Kent St U Pr.

Brown, Shirley, ed. see Ornish, Dean.

Brown, Shona L. & Eisenhardt, Kathleen M. Competing on the Edge: Strategy As Structured Chaos. LC 97-41459. 320p. 1998. 27.95 (*0-87584-754-4*) Harvard Busn.

Brown, Sidney D. & Hirota, Akiko, eds. The Diary of Kido Takayoshi, Vol. 3. 380p. 1986. 99.50 (*0-86008-386-1*, Pub. by U of Tokyo) Col U Pr.

Brown, Sidney D., ed. see Takayoshi, Kido.

***Brown, Simon.** Essential Feng Shui: Your Practical Guide to Health, Wealth & Happiness. LC 99-494985. (Illus.). 96p. 1999. 9.95 (*0-7063-7854-7*, Pub. by WrLock) Sterling.

Brown, Simon. Practical Feng Shui: Arrange, Decorate & Accessorize Your Home to Promote Health, Wealth & Happiness. LC 98-128278. (Illus.). 160p. 1998. 19.95 (*0-7063-7634-X*, Pub. by WrLock) Sterling.

***Brown, Simon.** Practical Feng Shui Astrology: Using the Nine Ki System to Make Important Decisions in Your Life. (Illus.). 128p. 1999. pap. 17.95 (*0-7063-7825-3*, Pub. by WrLock) Sterling.

Brown, Simon. Practical Feng Shui for Business. LC 99-209806. 1999. pap. 19.95 (*0-7063-7768-0*, Pub. by WrLock) Sterling.

***Brown, Simon.** Practical Feng Shui Solutions: Easy-to-Follow Practical Advice on Making the Most of Modern Living. 2000. pap. 19.95 (*0-304-35476-7*, Pub. by Cassell) Sterling.

Brown, Simon, jt. auth. see Saunders, Steven.

Brown, Sneaky Pie, jt. auth. see Brown, Rita Mae.

Brown, Son & Ferguson Ltd. Staff. Bernard's Nautical Star Chart. (C). 1987. 50.00 (*0-85174-559-8*) St Mut.

— Brown's Completed Burdwood Azimuth Tables. (C). 1987. 30.00 (*0-85174-078-2*) St Mut.

— Brown's Nautical Almanac. (C). 1987. 165.00 (*0-85174-541-5*) St Mut.

— Brown's North Atlantic Track Chart. (C). 1987. 30.00 (*0-85174-133-9*) St Mut.

— Brown's Seamen's Wages Calculator from 1 Day to 12 Months, & from 1.00 Pound to 200.00 Pounds per Month. (C). 1987. 22.00 (*0-85174-182-7*) St Mut.

— Brown's Star Atlas. (C). 1987. 75.00 (*0-85174-271-8*) St Mut.

— Brown's Tidal Streams: In Twelve Charts, for Each Hour of the Tide at Dover. (C). 1987. 75.00 (*0-85174-170-3*) St Mut.

— Brown's Vick Morse Cards. (C). 1987. 30.00 (*0-85174-177-0*) St Mut.

An Asterisk (*) at the beginning of an entry indicates that the title is appearing for the first time.

— Brown's Vick Semaphore Cards. (C). 1987. 25.00 (*0-85174-178-9*) St Mut.

— The International Code of Signals. (C). 1987. 22.00 (*0-7855-2550-5*) St Mut.

— The Marq Brown Sight Book: Compiled by an Instructor in Navigation. (C). 1987. 60.00 (*0-85174-101-0*) St Mut.

— Mate, Master & Extra Master, Vol. 11. (C). 1987. 180.00 (*0-7855-6058-0*) St Mut.

— Napier's Curves: As Used in the Examinations. (C). 1987. 40.00 (*0-7855-6056-4*) St Mut.

— Ships & Their Cargoes. 60p. (C). 1987. 75.00 (*0-85174-073-1*) St Mut.

— Supplement to Cargo Work: Guide Lines to the Safe Handling of Roll on-Roll off Vessels. (C). 1987. 60.00 (*0-7855-6057-2*) St Mut.

— Tide, Distance & Speed Tables. (C). 1987. 50.00 (*0-85174-544-X*) St Mut.

— Watch-Keeping Certificate. (C). 1987. 45.00 (*0-7855-6055-6*) St Mut.

— The Weymouth Yacht Log Book. (C). 1987. 100.00 (*0-85174-180-0*) St Mut.

Brown, Son & Ferguson Ltd. Staff, ed. Brown's Nautical Diary & Days Work Book. (C). 1987. 47.00 (*0-7855-6059-9*) St Mut.

Brown-Spruill, Debra, jt. auth. see Hodge, Gail.

Brown, Stacy. The Errant Bride. (Scarlet Ser.). (Orig.). 1997. mass mkt. 3.99 (*1-85487-965-0*, Pub. by Scarlet Bks) London Brdge.

— Heaven Scent. 1998. mass mkt. 3.99 (*1-85487-569-8*, Pub. by Scarlet Bks) London Brdge.

Brown, Stanley. Introduction to Exercise Science. 500p. 40.00 (*0-683-30280-9*) Lppncott W & W.

— Total Quality Service. 1993. 21.95 (*0-13-923392-X*) P-H.

Brown, Stanley A. Breakthrough Customer Service: Best Practices Of Leaders In Customer Support. 416p. 1998. 45.00 (*0-471-64232-0*) Wiley.

— Customer Relationship Management: Linking People, Process & Technology. 384p. 2000. 29.95 (*0-471-64409-9*) Wiley.

— What Customers Value Most: How To Achieve Business Transformation By Focusing On Processes That Touch Your Customers. 288p. 1996. 39.95 (*0-471-64123-5*) Wiley.

Brown, Stanley A. & Lemons, Jack E., eds. Medical Applications of Titanium No. 1272: The Material & Biological Issues, Vol. 1272. LC 96-13656. (Special Technical Publication Ser.). (Illus.). 425p. 1996. text 79.00 (*0-8031-2010-9*, STP1272) ASTM.

Brown, Stanley B., et al, eds. Photochemotherapy: Photodynamic Therapy & Other Modalities II. (Europto Ser.: Vol. 2924). 342p. 1996. 94.00 (*0-8194-2326-2*) SPIE.

Brown, Stanley H., jt. auth. see Girard, Joe.

Brown, Stanley S. & Kodama, Yasushi, eds. Toxicology of Metals: Clinical & Experimental Research. 1987. text 89.95 (*0-470-20909-7*) P-H.

Brown, Stanley S. & Sunderman, F. William, Jr., eds. Nickel Toxicology. 1981. text 104.00 (*0-12-137680-X*) Acad Pr.

Brown, Stephanie. Allegory of the Supermarket. LC 98-25555. (Contemporary Poetry Ser). 104p. 1999. pap. 15.95 (*0-8203-2068-4*) U of Ga Pr.

— Preventing Computer Injury: The HAND Book with KeyMoves Software. 100p. 1993. pap. 49.95 incl. 3.5 hd (*1-884388-01-9*) Ergonome.

— Thea the Yellow Tomato. large type ed. (Illus.). 32p. (J). (gr. k-4). 1998. text 14.95 (*0-9638152-6-1*) Freedom Pubng.

— Treating Adult Children of Alcoholics: A Developmental Perspective. 333p. 1996. pap. 39.95 (*0-471-15559-4*) Wiley.

— Treating Alcoholism. LC 94-39887. 416p. 1995. pap. text 30.95 (*0-7879-3876-9*) Jossey-Bass.

— Treating the Alcoholic: A Developmental Model of Recovery. LC 85-3172. 376p. 1996. pap. 39.95 (*0-471-16163-2*) Wiley.

***Brown, Stephanie & Lewis, Virginia.** The Alcoholic Family in Recovery: A Developmental Model. LC 98-36077. 318p. 1998. 33.50 (*1-57230-402-2*) Guilford Pubns.

Brown, Stephanie, et al. Children of Alcoholics: Selected Readings. Abbott, Stephanie, ed. (Illus.). 189p. (Orig.). (YA). 1995. pap. 12.95 (*0-9645327-0-0*) Nat Asn Childrn.

— Children of Alcoholics: Selected Readings. rev. ed. Abbott, Stephanie, ed. (Illus.). 190p. (Orig.). 1996. pap. 12.95 (*0-9645327-1-9*) Nat Asn Childrn.

***Brown, Stephanie, et al.** The Family Recovery Guide: A Map for Healthy Growth. 280p. 2000. pap. 15.95 (*1-57224-218-3*, Pub. by New Harbinger) Publishers Group.

Brown, Stephanie, et al. Missing Voices: The Experience of Motherhood. (Illus.). 312p. 1995. pap. text 29.95 (*0-19-553378-X*) OUP.

Brown, Stephen. Postmodern Marketing. (Consumer Research & Policy Ser.). 208p. (C). 1995. pap. 28.95 (*0-415-10982-5*) Thomson Learn.

— Postmodern Marketing. LC 94-39939. (Consumer Research & Policy Ser.). 240p. (C). (gr. 13). 1995. pap. 71.95 (*0-415-10155-7*) Thomson Learn.

— Postmodern Marketing: Telling Tales. 2nd ed. LC 98-124021. 224p. 1998. pap. 22.00 (*1-86152-018-2*) Thomson Learn.

— Quando a Corde Se Rompe.Tr. of When Your Rope Breaks. (POR & SPA.). 156p. 1991. pap. 7.95 (*0-8297-1642-4*) Vida Pubs.

***Brown, Stephen.** Railroad Regulation: Changes in Railroad Rates & Service Quality Since 1990. (Illus.). 107p. (C). 2000. pap. text 30.00 (*0-7881-8493-8*) DIANE Pub.

Brown, Stephen. Retail Location: A Micro-Sale Perspective. 329p. 1992. 91.95 (*1-85628-049-7*, Pub. by Avebry) Ashgate Pub Co.

— Tlingit Totem Poles. (J). (gr. 1-9). 1992. pap. 5.95 (*0-88388-150-0*) Bellerophon Bks.

Brown, Stephen & Bell, Jim, eds. Marketing Apocalypse: Eschatology, Escapology, & the Illusion of the End. 314p. (C). 1997. 90.00 (*0-415-14822-7*) Routledge.

Brown, Stephen & Clarke, Desmond. Ireland in Fiction. 1985. pap. 50.00 (*0-946645-02-7*) Dufour.

Brown, Stephen & Turley, Darach. Consumer Research: Postcards from the Edge. LC 97-18705. (Illus.). 424p. (C). 1998. 100.00 (*0-415-15684-X*); pap. 32.99 (*0-415-17317-5*) Routledge.

Brown, Stephen & Walter, Marion, eds. Problem Posing: Reflections & Applications. 352p. 1993. pap. 34.50 (*0-8058-1065-X*) L Erlbaum Assocs.

— Problem Posing: Reflections & Applications, 2 vols., Set. 1993. 45.00 (*0-8058-1331-4*) L Erlbaum Assocs.

Brown, Stephen, et al. Marketing Apocalypse: Eschatology, Escapology, & the Illusion of the End. LC 97-16140. 312p. (C). 1998. pap. 29.99 (*0-415-17356-6*) Routledge.

— Romancing the Market. LC 98-4028. (Interpretive Marketing Research Ser.). (Illus.). 256p. (C). 1998. 100.00 (*0-415-18417-7*); pap. 36.99 (*0-415-18418-5*) Routledge.

Brown, Stephen, jt. auth. see Wistow, Gerald.

Brown, Stephen, tr. see Denmei Shudo.

Brown, Stephen, tr. see Masunaga, Shizuto.

Brown, Stephen A. Revolution at the Checkout Counter: The Explosion of the Bar Code. LC 97-2776. (Wertheim Publications in Industrial Relations). (Illus.). 320p. 1997. 29.95 (*0-674-76720-9*) HUP.

***Brown, Stephen D. & Vranesic, Zvonko G.** Fundamentals of Digital Logic with VHDL Design. LC 99-17056. (Illus.). 2000. write for info. (*0-07-012591-0*) McGraw.

Brown, Stephen D., et al. Field-Programmable Gate Arrays. LC 92-13785. (International Series in Engineering & Computer Science, VLSI, Computer Architecture, & Digital Screen Processing: Vol. SECS 180). 224p. (C). 1992. reprint ed. text 116.50 (*0-7923-9248-5*) Kluwer Academic.

Brown, Stephen E., et al. Criminology: Explaining Crime & Its Context. 3rd rev. ed. LC 98-24868. (Illus.). 602p. (C). 1998. pap., student ed. 48.95 (*0-87084-115-7*) Anderson Pub Co.

Brown, Stephen F. Christianity. (World Religions Ser.). (Illus.). 128p. (J). (gr. 4-9). 1991. 19.95 (*0-8160-2441-3*) Facts on File.

Brown, Stephen F., jt. auth. see Morrison, Martha.

Brown, Stephen F., ed. & intro. see Aquinas, Thomas, Saint.

Brown, Stephen G. & Disaia, Philip J. Cancer of the Cervix. (Oncologic Ser.: Vol. 14). (Illus.). 308p. 1981. pap. 135.00 (*0-08-027465-X*, Pergamon Pr) Elsevier.

Brown, Stephen Gilbert. The Bush Teacher: Critical Literacy in the Borderlands. LC 99-38732. (C). 2000. pap. text 17.95 (*0-7914-4406-6*) State U NY Pr.

— Bush Teacher, The: Critical Literacy in the Borderlands. LC 99-38732. 229p. (C). 2000. text 54.50 (*0-7914-4405-8*) State U NY Pr.

Brown, Stephen I. Some "Prime" Comparisons. LC 78-12339. (Illus.). 106p. 1978. pap. 10.95 (*0-87353-131-0*) NCTM.

Brown, Stephen I., et al, eds. Readings from Progressive Education, Vol. I: A Movement & Its Professional Journal, Vol. I. LC 88-5713. 366p. (Orig.). (C). 1988. pap. text 29.50 (*0-8191-6917-X*); lib. bdg. 50.00 (*0-8191-6916-1*) U Pr of Amer.

Brown, Stephen I. & Walter, Marion I. The Art of Problem Posing. 2nd ed. 160p. 1990. text 49.95 (*0-8058-0257-6*); pap. text 18.50 (*0-8058-0258-4*) L Erlbaum Assocs.

Brown, Stephen J. The World of Imagery: Metaphor & Kindred Imagery. LC 65-26462. 352p. (C). 1965. lib. bdg. 75.00 (*0-8383-0677-2*) M S G Haskell Hse.

***Brown, Stephen J. & Crocker, Liu H.** A Global Perspective on Real Estate Cycles. LC 00-25876. (New York University Salomon Center Series on Financial Markets & Institutions). 2000. write for info. (*0-7923-7808-3*, Kluwer Plenum) Kluwer Academic.

Brown, Stephen M. & Seidner, Constance J., eds. Evaluating Corporate Training: Models & Issues. LC 97-36963. (Evaluation in Education & Human Services Ser.: 6). 400p. 1998. 105.00 (*0-7923-8026-6*) Kluwer Academic.

Brown, Stephen P., jt. ed. see O'Driscoll, Gerald P., Jr.

Brown, Stephen W., et al, eds. Service Quality: Multidisciplinary & Multinational Perspectives. (Issues in Organization & Management Ser.). 49p. 1990. 51.00 (*0-669-21152-4*) Lxngtn Bks.

Brown, Stephen W. & Fisk, Raymond P., eds. Marketing Theory: Distinguished Contributions. LC 83-23452. (Theories in Marketing Ser.). (Illus.). 388p. reprint ed. pap. 120.30 (*0-7837-3503-0*, 205783600008) Bks Demand.

Brown, Stephen W., et al. Patient Satisfaction Pays: Quality Service for Practice Success. LC 93-20094. 432p. 1993. 67.00 (*0-8342-0394-4*) Aspen Pub.

Brown, Stephen W., jt. auth. see Rice, Otis K.

Brown, Sterling A. The Collected Poems of Sterling Brown. Harper, Michael S., ed. LC 95-53303. 267p. 1996. pap. 14.95 (*0-8101-5045-X*) Northwestern U Pr.

— First Lady of the Air: The Harriet Quimby Story. LC 97-23405. (Illus.). 64p. 1997. pap. 7.95 (*0-936389-53-2*) Tudor Pubs.

— The Last Ride of Wild Bill & 11 Narrative Poems. 53p. (YA). (gr. 12 up). 1975. pap. 5.00 (*0-910296-02-2*) Broadside Pr.

— Negro in American Fiction. 1969. reprint ed. 15.00 (*0-87266-002-8*) Argosy.

— Negro in American Fiction. LC 69-18582. 372p. 1972. reprint ed. 18.95 (*0-405-01851-7*) Ayer.

— A Son's Return: Selected Essays. Sanders, Mark A., ed. & intro. by. LC 96-1192. (Northeastern Library of Black Literature). 304p. 1996. text 45.00 (*1-55553-274-8*); pap. text 16.95 (*1-55553-275-6*) NE U Pr.

Brown, Sterling A., et al, eds. Negro Caravan. LC 69-18584. (American Negro: His History & Literature. Series 2). 1969. reprint ed. pap. 4.95 (*0-8434-6099-7*) Ayer.

— Negro Caravan. LC 69-18584. (American Negro: His History & Literature. Series 2). 1978. reprint ed. 71.95 (*0-405-01852-5*) Ayer.

Brown, Sterling A. Tailypo: A New Fangled Tall Tale. 32p. (J). (gr. k-3). 1996. lib. bdg. 15.95 (*0-8234-1249-0*) Holiday.

Brown, Sterling A., jt. auth. see Haynes, George E.

Brown, Steve. The ABCs of Visual Basic X. 1997. pap. text 24.99 (*0-7821-1995-6*) Sybex.

***Brown, Steve.** Black Fire. 284p. 2000. pap. 13.95 (*0-9670273-2-2*) Chick Springs.

Brown, Steve. Carving Pen Figures. 48p. 1998. pap. 12.95 (*0-7643-0609-X*) Schiffer.

***Brown, Steve.** Color Her Dead: A Generation X Mystery, Vol. 1. 259p. 1999. pap. 13.95 (*0-9670273-1-4*) Chick Springs.

Brown, Steve. Follow the Wind: Our Lord, the Holy Spirit. LC 99-41446. 192p. 1999. pap. 13.99 (*0-8010-5834-1*, Ravens Ridge) Baker Bks.

***Brown, Steve.** How to Talk So People Will Listen. 176p. 1999. pap. 10.99 (*0-8010-6144-X*) Baker Bks.

Brown, Steve. Jumping Hurdles: Illustrations of the Simple & Profound Ways God Delivers Hope. LC 96-40524. 254p. 1997. pap. 12.99 (*0-8010-5768-X*, Jumping Hurdles, Ravens Ridge) Baker Bks.

***Brown, Steve.** Manufacturing: Beyond Lean & World Class. (Illus.). 288p. 2000. 39.00 (*0-273-64322-3*, Pub. by F T P H) Trans-Atl Phila.

— Of Love & War. 260p. 1999. pap. 13.95 (*0-9670273-0-6*) Chick Springs.

Brown, Steve. Strategic Manufacturing for Competitive Advantage: Transforming Operations from Shop Floor to Strategy. 304p. 1996. pap. 55.00 (*0-13-184508-X*) P-H.

Brown, Steve. Streetwise to Sex-Wise: Sexuality Education for High-Risk Youth. 186p. 1993. 25.00 (*0-9609366-6-1*) Plan Parenthood.

— Stripped to Kill. (Susan Chase Mysteries Ser.). 2000. pap. 13.95 (*0-9670273-3-0*) Chick Springs.

— VB Developer's Guide to the Win32 API. 4th ed. 416p. 1999. 39.99 (*0-7821-2559-X*) Sybex.

Brown, Steve. Visual Basic 6 in Record Time. LC 98-86633. 688p. 1998. pap. 29.99 (*0-7821-2310-4*) Sybex.

— When Your Rope Breaks. LC 96-18304. 192p. (YA). (gr. 10). 1996. pap. 11.99 (*0-8010-5729-9*, Ravens Ridge) Baker Bks.

Brown, Steve, jt. auth. see White Wolf Publishing Staff, Wolf.

***Brown, Steve D. & Lent, Robert W., eds.** Handbook of Counseling Psychology. 3rd ed. LC 99-16054. 865p. 2000. 85.00 (*0-471-25458-4*) Wiley.

Brown, Steven. Chemistry 102A Laboratory Manual. 164p. (C). 1996. pap. text, spiral bd., lab manual ed. 12.95 (*0-7872-2704-8*) Kendall-Hunt.

— Chemistry 102B Laboratory Manual. 168p. (C). 1996. pap. text, spiral bd., lab manual ed. 15.95 (*0-7872-2705-6*, 41270501) Kendall-Hunt.

***Brown, Steven.** Implementing Virtual Private Networks. LC 99-14543. (Networking Ser.). (Illus.). 594p. 1999. pap. 55.00 (*0-07-135185-X*) McGraw.

Brown, Steven. Palanthas. 96p. 1998. 11.95 (*0-7869-1199-9*, Pub. by TSR Inc) Random.

Brown, Steven, ed. The Spirit Within. (Illus.). 312p. 1995. 75.00 (*0-8478-1847-0*, Pub. by Rizzoli Intl) St Martin.

***Brown, Steven & Attardo, Salvatore.** Understanding Language Structure, Interaction & Variation: An Introduction to Applied Linguistics & Sociolinguistics for Nonspecialists. (Illus.). 440p. (C). 2000. pap. text 24.95 (*0-472-08686-3*, 08686) U of Mich Pr.

Brown, Steven, et al. The Spirit Within: Northwest Coast Native Art from the John H. Hauberg Collection. Abbott, Helen, ed. (Illus.). 304p. (Orig.). 1995. pap. 35.00 (*0-932216-45-5*) Seattle Art.

Brown, Steven, jt. auth. see Adams, Carl R.

Brown, Steven, jt. auth. see Goncalves, Marcus.

Brown, Steven, jt. auth. see Helgesen, Marc.

Brown, Steven C. Native Visions: Evolution in Northwest Coast Art, from the 18th Through the 20th Century. LC 97-30413. (Illus.). 244p. 1998. 70.00 (*0-295-97657-8*) U of Wash Pr.

— Native Visions: Evolution in Northwest Coast Art, from the 18th Through the 20th Century. LC 97-30413 (Illus.). 228p. 1998. pap. 70.00 (*0-295-97658-6*) U of Wash Pr.

— Player's Guide to the Sabbat. (Vampire Ser.). (Illus.). 1994. per. 15.00 (*1-56504-042-2*, 2055) White Wolf.

— The Storytellers Handbook to the Sabbat. (Vampire Ser.). (Illus.). 1994. 15.00 (*1-56504-054-6*, 2225) White Wolf.

***Brown, Steven C., ed.** Spirits of the Water: Native Art Collected on Expeditions to Alaska & British Columbia, 1774-1910. (Illus.). 208p. 2000. pap. 45.00 (*0-295-97986-0*) U of Wash Pr.

***Brown, Steven C. & Averill, Lloyd J.** Sun Dogs & Eagle Down: The Indian Paintings of Bill Holm. LC 00-21618. (Illus.). 208p. 2000. 35.00 (*0-295-97947-X*) U of Wash Pr.

Brown, Steven C., jt. auth. see White Wolf Publishing Staff, Wolf.

Brown, Steven D. & Lent, Robert W. Handbook of Counseling Psychology. LC 91-30150. 880p. 1992. text 160.00 (*0-471-51254-0*) Wiley.

Brown, Steven F. Erotic Mask. LC 83-903. (Contemporary Poetry Ser.: No. 2). (Illus.). 48p. (Orig.). 1984. pap. 5.00 (*0-938136-01-1*) Lunchroom Pr.

Brown, Steven F., ed. Astonishing World: The Selected Poems of Angel Gonzalez, 1956 to 1986. Revuelta, Gutierrez, tr. LC 93-9273. (ENG & SPA.). 296p. 1993. pap. 14.95 (*0-915943-58-1*) Milkweed Ed.

Brown, Steven J., ed. see Spainhower, Steven D.

Brown, Steven K. The Sanctuary for Lent, 1995. 48p. (Orig.). 1995. pap. 0.40 (*0-687-01331-3*) Abingdon.

Brown, Steven R. & Brenner, Donald J., eds. Science, Psychology & Communication: Essays Honoring William Stephenson. LC 73-165607. (Foresight Books in Psychology). 493p. reprint ed. pap. 152.90 (*0-608-14967-5*, 202599600048) Bks Demand.

Brown, Steven R. & Marshall, Karen, eds. Advances in Genetic Information: A Guide for State Policy Makers: Employment Issues, Insurance, Criminal Justice, Health Care, Genetic Testing, Civil Liberties. LC 94-225447. 123p. 1995. pap. 10.00 (*0-87292-983-3*) Coun State Govts.

Brown, Steven R. & Melam, Lawrence E. Experimental Design & Analysis. (Quantitative Applications in the Social Sciences Ser.: Vol. 74). (Illus.). 96p. (C). 1990. pap. 10.95 (*0-8039-3854-3*) Sage.

Brown, Steven S. Cellular Travel Guide: How to Use Your Cellular Telephone Wherever You Travel in North America. 5th ed. (Illus.). 768p. 1999. pap. text 19.95 (*0-945592-11-6*) Telecom Pubng.

Brown, Steward, jt. auth. see Wilson, Susan.

Brown, Stewart. The Art of Derek Walcott. LC 90-3799. 220p. 1991. 35.00 (*0-8023-1290-X*) Dufour.

— The Art of Kamau Brathwaite. 288p. 1996. pap. 22.95 (*1-85411-127-2*, Pub. by Seren Bks) Dufour.

— Lugard's Bridge. LC 89-82060. 72p. (Orig.). 1990. pap. 14.95 (*1-85411-013-6*, Pub. by Seren Bks) Dufour.

***Brown, Stewart, ed.** All Are Involved: The Art of Martin Carter. 413p. 2000. pap. 25.95 (*1-900715-26-0*, Pub. by Peepal Tree Pr) Paul & Co Pubs.

Brown, Stewart, ed. The Art of Kamau Brathwaite. 288p. 1996. 50.00 (*1-85411-092-6*, Pub. by Seren Bks) Dufour.

— Caribbean New Wave: Contemporary Short Stories. (Caribbean Writers Ser.). 181p. (Orig.). (C). 1990. pap. 9.95 (*0-435-98814-X*, 98814) Heinemann.

Brown, Stewart & Wickham, John, eds. The Oxford Book of Caribbean Short Stories. LC 98-29731. 512p. 1999. pap. 18.95 (*0-19-283241-7*) OUP.

Brown, Stewart, jt. ed. see McDonald, Ian.

Brown, Stewart J. Thomas Chalmers & Godly Commonwealth in Scotland. (Illus.). 1983. 75.00 (*0-19-213114-1*) OUP.

Brown, Stewart J., ed. William Robertson & the Expansion of Empire. LC 96-31665. (Ideas in Context Ser.: No. 45). 291p. (C). 1997. text 59.95 (*0-521-57083-2*) Cambridge U Pr.

Brown, Stewart J. & Fry, Michael, eds. Scotland & the Age of the Disruption. (Illus.). 256p. 1993. pap. 35.00 (*0-7486-0433-2*, Pub. by Edinburgh U Pr) Col U Pr.

***Brown, Stewart J. & Miller, David W., eds.** Piety & Power in Ireland, 1760-1960: Essays in Honour of Emmet Larkin. 360p. 2000. 30.00 (*0-268-03863-5*, Pub. by U of Notre Dame Pr) Chicago Distribution Ctr.

Brown, Stewart L., jt. auth. see Errera, Steven.

Brown, Stuart. The Nearest in Affection: Towards a Christian Understanding of Islam. LC 95-6760. (Pathways Bk.). 136p. (Orig.). 1995. pap. 12.00 (*1-56338-114-1*) TPI PA.

***Brown, Stuart.** Philosophy of Religion: An Introduction with Readings. 184p. 2000. 65.00 (*0-415-21237-5*); pap. write for info. (*0-415-21238-3*) Routledge.

Brown, Stuart, ed. Routledge History of Philosophy Vol. 5: British Empiricism & the Enlightenment, Vol. 5. LC 95-15815. 440p. (C). (gr. 13). 1995. 90.00 (*0-415-05379-X*) Routledge.

Brown, Stuart B., ed. see International Conference on the Semi-Solid Process.

Brown, Stuart C., et al. One Hundred Twentieth-Century Philosophers. LC 97-30846. 256p. (C). 1998. pap. 19.99 (*0-415-17996-3*) Routledge.

Brown, Stuart C., et al. The Writer's Toolbox. LC 96-18561. 215p. 1996. pap. text 25.00 (*0-205-19563-6*) Allyn.

Brown, Stuart C., jt. ed. see Enos, Theresa.

Brown, Stuart C., jt. ed. see Herndl, Carl G.

Brown, Stuart E., Jr. Annals of Blackwater & the Land of Canaan, 1746-1880. LC 59-10184. (Illus.). 42p. 1959. reprint ed. pap. 3.00 (*0-685-05214-1*); reprint ed. write for info. (*0-685-65060-X*) VA Bk.

— Annals of Clarke County, Virginia: Old Homes, Families, Etcetera of the Southern (South of U. S. Route 50) Section, Vol. 1. (Illus.). 425p. 1983. 42.50 (*0-317-05706-5*) VA Bk.

Brown, Stuart E. The Challenge of the Scriptures: The Bible & the Quran. LC 89-8828. (Faith Meets Faith Ser.). 112p. 1989. reprint ed. pap. 34.80 (*0-7837-9842-3*, 206057100005) Bks Demand.

Brown, Stuart E., Jr. The Guns of Harpers Ferry. (Illus.). 158p. 1998. reprint ed. pap. 18.50 (*0-8063-4640-X*, 9116) Clearfield Co.

— Pocahontas. 34p. 1989. pap. 9.95 (*0-685-56616-1*) VA Bk.

— Pocahontas (In the Words of Her Contemporaries) (Illus.). 36p. 1998. pap. 9.95 (*0-8063-4605-1*) Clearfield Co.

— Reverend Thomas Barton (1728-1780) & Some of His Descendants & Some of Their In-Laws. 268p. 1988. 37.50 (*0-685-56618-8*); pap. 27.50 (*0-685-70054-2*) VA Bk.

— Virginia Baron: The Story of Thomas, Sixth Lord of Fairfax. LC 65-19262. (Illus.). 245p. 1965. 15.00 (*0-685-65062-6*) VA Bk.

B

— Virginia Genealogies: A Trial List of Printed Books & Pamphlets. LC 67-7956. 310p. 1967. 30.00 (0-685-65061-8) VA Bk.

Brown, Stuart E., Jr. & Myers, Lorraine F. Patsy Cline, Singing Girl from the Shenandoah Valley. (Illus.). 110p. 1996. 19.50 (0-911578-00-5) VA Bk.

Brown, Stuart E. & Myers, Lorraine F. Third Corrections & Additions to Pocahontas' Descendants. 3rd ed. 197p. 1997. 28.50 (0-8063-1542-3) Genealog Pub.

Brown, Stuart E., Jr., et al. Annals of Clarke County, Virginia, Vol. 2: Biographical & Genealogical Records of Persons Buried at Old Chapel. (Illus.). iv, 210p. 1987. 32.50 (0-685-34653-6) VA Bk.

— Gabriel Jones (1724-1806) & Some of His Descendants: Notes on "Bogota" & on "Vaucluse" 103p. 1990. pap. 24.50 (0-685-56617-X) VA Bk.

— Pocahontas' Descendants with Corrections & Additions. (Illus.). 715p. 1994. 50.00 (0-317-40516-0) VA Bk.

— Virginia Genealogies, Vol. 2. 351p. 1980. 30.00 (0-686-64384-4) VA Bk.

— Virginia Genealogies, Vol. III. 420p. 1989. 49.50 (0-685-34656-0) VA Bk.

Brown, Stuart G. Conscience in Politics: Adlai E. Stevenson in the 1950s. LC 61-13115. (Men & Movements Ser.). 343p. reprint ed. pap. 106.40 (0-608-15223-4, 202741700055) Bks Demand.

— The First Republicans: Political Philosophy & Public Policy in the Party of Jefferson & Madison. LC 76-48247. 186p. 1977. reprint ed. lib. bdg. 55.00 (0-8371-9339-7, BRFR, Greenwood Pr) Greenwood.

Brown, Stuart G., ed. Great Issues. LC 70-134061. (Essay Index Reprint Ser.). 1977. 34.95 (0-8369-2148-8) Ayer.

— Revolution, Confederation & Constitution. LC 78-151607. (Literature of History Ser.). (C). 1971. 32.50 (0-89197-384-2); pap. text 12.95 (0-89197-385-0) Irvington.

Brown, Stuart G., ed. see Royce, Josiah.

Brown, Stuart S., jt. auth. see Enos, Theresa.

Brown, Stuart S., jt. ed. see Enos, Theresa.

Brown, Sue. Indian Territory: A Cookbook of the Early Years. 189p. 20.00 (0-9674380-0-4) Three Sisters.

Brown, Sue. The Syntax of Negation in Russian: A Minimalist Approach. LC 99-18173. (Stanford Monographs in Linguistics: No. 3). 152p. (C). 1999. text 59.95 (1-57586-169-0, Pub. by CSLI); pap. text 18.95 (1-57586-168-2, Pub. by CSLI) Cambridge U Pr.

Brown, Sue H. & Pearson-Adams, Sandra. Your Career in Coaching: Study Guide for EFA/NCAS Level 1 (G) Accreditation. 240p. 1995. spiral bd. 59.95 (0-644-45215-3, Pub. by AGPS Pr) Intl Spec Bk.

Brown, Sue H., et al. My Neckline & the Collapse of Western Civilization. (Orig.). 1987. pap. 7.95 (0-9617736-0-X, 1) Smartweed Pr.

***Brown, Suellen.** Say It with Flowers: A Collection of David's Stories. Eid, Bonnie B., ed. (Illus.). 1999. pap. 12.95 (0-9644074-5-0) Hayter Hse Pubs.

Brown, Suellen, jt. auth. see Schreiner, Carol D.

***Brown, Susan.** Better Bones Better Body: Beyond Estrogen & Calcium. 400p. 2000. pap. 19.95 (0-658-00289-9, 002899, Keats Publng) NTC Contemp Pub Co.

Brown, Susan A. & Rosenthal, Karen, eds. Self-Assessment Color Review of Small Mammals. LC 97-164753. (Illus.). 192p. 1997. pap. 31.95 (0-8138-2092-8) Iowa St U Pr.

Brown, Susan B. & Simmons, Monica. 365 Strategies for Positive Single Parenting. LC 97-50024. 224p. 1998. pap. 16.00 (1-57312-177-0) Smyth & Helwys.

Brown, Susan C. Church History Activity Book. Muggli, Glorianne, ed. (Primary Activity Bks.). (Illus.). 80p. (Orig.). (J). 1996. pap. 6.95 (1-57665-024-3) Muggli Graphics.

Brown, Susan C. & Lucy, Jack A., eds. Dystrophin: Gene, Protein & Cell Biology. LC 96-37800. (Illus.). 356p. (C). 1997. text 95.00 (0-521-55033-5) Cambridge U Pr.

***Brown, Susan Cox.** Book of Mormon Activity Book. (Activity Bks.). (Illus.). 76p. (J). 1999. pap. 8.95 (1-57665-060-X) Muggli Graphics.

Brown, Susan E., ed. Maintenance of Roadway Pavement & Structures (TRR 1392) (Transportation Research Record Ser.). (Illus.). 160p. 1993. pap. text 31.00 (0-309-05464-8) Transport Res Bd.

Brown, Susan H. Head Games. (Illus.). 24p. (Orig.). 1993. pap. write for info. (0-9637244-0-1) S H Brown.

Brown, Susan M. You're Dead, David Borelli. 160p. (J). (gr. 3-6). 1995. 15.00 (0-689-31959-2) Atheneum Yung Read.

Brown, Susan M., ed. see Pessoa, Fernando.

Brown, Susan M., tr. see Pessoa, Fernando.

Brown, Susan S. Enjoy Watercolor & Acrylic, Vol. 31. (Illus.). (Orig.). 1997. pap. 11.95 (1-56770-399-2) S Scheewe Pubns.

— Introduction to Watercolor, Vol. 24. 107p. 1995. pap. 11.95 (1-56770-314-3) S Scheewe Pubns.

— Paint Box of Ideas, Vol. 34. (Illus.). 109p. 1998. pap. 12.95 (1-56770-430-1) S Scheewe Pubns.

— Scheewe Art Workshop - Watercolor & Acrylic, Vol. 30. (Illus.). 100p. (Orig.). 1997. pap. 11.95 (1-56770-398-4) S Scheewe Pubns.

— Watercolor - The Garden Scene T. V. Book. 94p. 1995. pap. 11.95 (1-56770-339-9) S Scheewe Pubns.

— Watercolor Garden Treasures. 1996. pap. 11.95 (1-56770-361-5) S Scheewe Pubns.

— Watercolor Landscapes T. V. Book. 1996. pap. 11.95 (1-56770-360-7) S Scheewe Pubns.

— Watercolors Anyone Can Paint, Vol. 25. 94p. 1995. pap. 11.95 (1-56770-325-9) S Scheewe Pubns.

Brown, Susan S., jt. auth. see Stempel, Charleen.

Brown, Susan T. A Pony Named Midnight. (Illus.). 24p. 1998. boxed set 9.99 (1-885101-94-5) Writers Pr ID.

— The Very Patient Pony. (Illus.). 24p. 1998. boxed set 9.99 (1-885101-95-3) Writers Pr ID.

Brown, Susan Taylor. Better Bones, Better Body. Herman, Phyllis, ed. 224p. 1996. pap. 19.95 (0-87983-700-4, Keats Publng) NTC Contemp Pub Co.

— Can I Pray with My Eyes Open? LC 98-51676. (Illus.). 32p. (J). (ps-3). 1999. lib. bdg. 16.49 (0-7868-2273-2, Pub. by Hyperion) Little.

— Can I Pray with My Eyes Open? LC 98-51676. (Illus.). 32p. (J). (ps-3). 1999. 15.99 (0-7868-0328-2, Pub. by Hyprn Child) Time Warner.

— Old Testament Activity Book. (Activity Book Ser.). (Illus.). 100p. 1997. pap. 7.95 (1-57665-035-9) Muggli Graphics.

Brown, Susan Taylor, ed. American Studio Ceramics, 1920-1950. LC 88-51175. (Illus.). 100p. (Orig.). 1988. pap. text 20.00 (0-938713-04-3) Univ MN Art Mus.

— Driver Performance: Measurement & Modeling, IVHS, Information Systems, & Simulation (TRR 1403) (Transportation Research Record Ser.). (Illus.). 106p. 1993. pap. text 25.00 (0-309-05551-2) Transport Res Bd.

— Durability of Geosynthetics (TRR 1439) (Transportation Research Record Ser.). (Illus.). 64p. 1994. pap. text 17.00 (0-309-05520-2, R1439) Transport Res Bd.

— Hydrology, Hydraulics, & Water Quality (TRR 1420) (Transportation Research Record Ser.). (Illus.). 92p. 1994. pap. text 25.00 (0-309-05568-7) Natl Res Coun.

— Innovations in Travel Survey Methods (TRR 1412) (Transportation Research Record Ser.). (Illus.). 100p. 1994. pap. text 24.00 (0-309-05559-8) Natl Res Coun.

— International Symposium on Motor Carrier Transportation (CP 3) LC 94-240649. (Conference Proceedings Ser.). (Illus.). 232p. 1994. pap. text 38.00 (0-309-05517-2, CP003) Transport Res Bd.

— Multimodal Priority Setting & Application of Geographic Information Systems (TRR 1429) (Transportation Research Record Ser.). (Illus.). 96p. 1994. pap. text 25.00 (0-309-05507-5, R1429) Transport Res Bd.

— Pavement Management Systems (TRR 1397) (Transportation Research Record Ser.). (Illus.). 128p. 1993. pap. text 28.00 (0-309-05468-0) Transport Res Bd.

— Pavement Monitoring & Evaluation (TRR 1410) large type ed. (Transportation Research Record Ser.). (Illus.). 128p. 1994. pap. text 28.00 (0-309-05557-1) Natl Res Coun.

— Pedestrian, Bicycle, & Older Driver Research (TRR 1405) (Transportation Research Record Ser.). (Illus.). 100p. 1993. pap. text 24.00 (0-309-05554-7) Transport Res Bd.

— Public Transit: Current Research in Planning, Marketing, Operations, & Technology (TRR 1402) (Transportation Research Record Ser.). (Illus.). 116p. 1993. pap. text 28.00 (0-309-05473-7) Transport Res Bd.

— Public Transportation: Bus, Rail, Ridesharing, Paratransit Services, & Transit Security (TRR 1433) (Transportation Research Record Ser.). (Illus.). 220p. 1994. pap. text 43.00 (0-309-05510-5, R1433) Transport Res Bd.

— Roadside Safety Features & Landscape & Environmental Design (TRR 1419) (Transportation Research Record Ser.). (Illus.). 140p. 1994. pap. text 29.00 (0-309-05567-9) Natl Res Coun.

— Segmental Concrete MSE Walls, Geogrid Reinforcements, & Soil Nailing (TRR 1414) (Transportation Research Record Ser.). (Illus.). 80p. 1994. pap. text 23.00 (0-309-05562-8) Natl Res Coun.

— Traffic Flow & Highway Capacity. LC 93-35536. (Transportation Research Record Ser.: No. 1398). (Illus.). 144p. 1993. pap. text 28.00 (0-309-05467-2) Transport Res Bd.

Brown, Susan Taylor, et al, eds. A Glass of Green Tea - with Honig. (Illus.). 415p. (Orig.). (C). 1994. pap. text 12.95 (0-9625518-7-2) AlephoeBooks.

Brown, Susan Taylor & Jedda, Barbara. Bow Wow House U. S. A. Invitational, 1993. LC 93-90295. (Illus.). 28p. (Orig.). 1993. 7.95 (0-9615072-0-9) Dog Museum.

Brown, Susan Taylor & Muggli, Glorianne. The Primary Help! Book: Book of Mormon. (Help! Bks.). (Illus.). 100p. (Orig.). 1995. pap. 7.95 (1-57665-009-X) Muggli Graphics.

— The Primary Help! Book: New Testament. (Help! Bks.). (Illus.). 80p. (Orig.). 1994. pap. 6.95 (1-57665-006-5) Muggli Graphics.

Brown, Susan Taylor, et al. Lassie: A Collie & Her Influence. LC 93-73130. (Illus.). 36p. (Orig.). 1993. 12.00 (0-9615072-2-5) Dog Museum.

Brown, Susan Taylor, jt. auth. see Simmons, Monica.

Brown, Susan Taylor, jt. auth. see Stephenson, Anne.

Brown, Susan Taylor, ed. see Donovan, Fiona I.

Brown, Susan Taylor, jt. ed. see Kassabian, Naomi.

Brown, Susan Taylor, ed. see Lewis, David.

Brown, Susan Taylor, ed. see Nelson, Marion J.

Brown, Susan Taylor, ed. see University of MN American Studies Seminar Students.

Brown, Susan Taylor, ed. see Wright, John S. & Smith, Tracy E.

Brown, Susan Taylor, tr. see Haug, Wolfgang F.

Brown, Susan W., ed. Contemporary Novelists. 6th ed. LC 95-36181. 1173p. 1995. 160.00 (1-55862-189-X) St James Pr.

Brown, Susie Connell, see Connell Brown, Susie.

Brown, Sydney. The Diary of Kido Takayoshi, Vol. 1. 1983. 74.50 (0-86008-328-4) Col U Pr.

***Brown, Sylvia.** Women's Writing in Stuart England: The Mother's Legacies of Elizabeth Joscelin, Elizabeth Richardson & Dorothy Leigh. 256p. 2000. pap. 27.95 (0-7509-1855-1) Sutton Publng.

Brown, Sylvia A. Larrymore, see Larrymore Brown, Sylvia A.

Brown, T., ed. GONG, 1992: Seismic Investigation of the Sun & Stars. (ASP Conference Series Proceedings: Vol. 42). 495p. 1993. 34.00 (0-937707-61-9) Astron Soc Pacific.

Brown, T., tr. see Trotter, Catherine.

***Brown, T. A.** Gene Cloning. 3rd ed. (Illus.). 348p. 1998. pap. 47.50 (0-7487-4070-8, Pub. by S Thornes Pubs) Trans-Atl Phila.

Brown, T. A., tr. see Piaget, Jean, ed.

Brown, T. C. & Fisk, G. C. Anaesthesia for Children. 2nd ed. (Illus.). 560p. 1992. 195.00 (0-632-03023-2) Blackwell Sci.

Brown, T. D., Jr. C for BASIC Programmers. 210p. (Orig.). (C). 1987. pap. 22.95 (0-9615336-1-7) Silicon Pr.

— C for FORTRAN Programmers. 220p. 1990. 22.95 (0-929306-01-5) Silicon Pr.

— C for Pascal Programmers. 215p. (C). 1987. pap. 22.95 (0-9615336-4-1) Silicon Pr.

Brown, T. D., jt. ed. see Cavanagh, D.

Brown, T. E. FO'C'S' Le Yarns: An Uncensored Edition of Four Manx Narratives in Verse. Sutton, Max K. et al, eds. LC 98-29733. 328p. 1998. 49.00 (0-7618-1215-6) U Pr of Amer.

Brown, T. H. & Irving, M. H., eds. Introduction to Minimal Access Surgery. 100p. (Orig.). 1996. pap. text 24.00 (0-7279-0885-5, Pub. by BMJ Pub) Login Brothers Bk Co.

Brown, T. Louise. The Challenge to Democracy in Nepal: A Political History. 1996. pap. 335.00 (0-7855-7370-4, Pub. by Ratna Pustak Bhandar) St Mut.

***Brown, T. Robins & Warmflash, Schuyler.** The Architecture of Bergen County, New Jersey: The Colonial Period to the Twentieth Century. LC 00-39034. (Illus.). 416p. (C). 2001. 35.00 (0-8135-2867-4) Rutgers U Pr.

Brown, T. S. Onesicritus: A Study In Hellenistic Historiography. 196p. 1981. pap. 20.00 (0-89005-384-7) Ares.

Brown, T. Sullivan, jt. auth. see Sperandeo, Victor.

Brown, Tami. Touched by Jesus: Character Studies from the Gospel of John. unabridged ed. 67p. 1996. pap. 6.00 (0-89137-338-1, 73381) Quality Pubns.

Brown, Tanya, ed. see Brown, Darrell.

Brown-Taylor, Barbara. God in Pain: Teaching Sermons on Suffering. Allen, Ronald J., ed. LC 97-44059. (Teaching Sermon Ser.). 96p. 1998. 9.95 (0-687-05887-2) Abingdon.

Brown Taylor, Barbara, see Taylor, Barbara Brown.

Brown, Tehane. Saturn's Garden. (Illus.). 16p. (J). (gr. 2). 1993. write for info. (0-9637099-0-9) T Brown.

Brown, Tena L. NAACP Never Ending Struggle Will Be Okay, We Can Still Come Out on Top. (Illus.). 30p. (YA). (gr. 5 up). 1997. pap. text 10.00 (1-890925-23-3) Stori Tyme.

Brown, Tena L. Tena, Joshua, & Friends, 22 vols. Incl. Always, Forever & Five Days Are 5 Big Words. (Illus.). 24p. (J). (ps-4). 1997. spiral bd. 5.00 (1-890925-13-6); Be Careful What You Do: Your Friends Are Always Watching You. (Illus.). 24p. (J). (ps-4). 1997. spiral bd. 5.00 (1-890925-07-1); Clean Your Room. (Illus.). 24p. (J). (ps-4). 1997. spiral bd. 5.00 (1-890925-19-5); Eat Your Veggies. (Illus.). 24p. (J). (ps-4). 1997. spiral bd. 5.00 (1-890925-20-9); Family Comes 1st Is What We Say: Family Comes 1st Each & Everyday. (Illus.). 24p. (J). (ps-4). 1997. spiral bd. 5.00 (1-890925-04-7); Follow Your Dreams to the Stars. (Illus.). 24p. (J). (ps-4). 1997. spiral bd. 5.00 (1-890925-14-4); I Am Me. (Illus.). 24p. (J). (ps-4). 1997. spiral bd. 5.00 (1-890925-15-2); It Is Okay to Be #1. (Illus.). 24p. (J). (ps-4). 1997. spiral bd. 5.00 (1-890925-18-7); It Is Okay to Like You & Everything That You Do: No One Is a Misfit. (Illus.). 24p. (J). (ps-4). 1997. spiral bd. 5.00 (1-890925-11-X); Just Say No & Turn & Walk Away. (Illus.). 24p. (J). (ps-4). 1997. spiral bd. 5.00 (1-890925-17-9); Learn Reading, Writing & Arithmetic: You Cannot Get over If You Think That You Are Slick. (Illus.). 24p. (J). (ps-4). 1997. spiral bd. 5.00 (1-890925-12-8); My A-B-Cs Say Be Kind to You & Me. (Illus.). 24p. (J). (ps-4). 1997. spiral bd. 5.00 (1-890925-09-8); My 1-2-3s Say Be Kind to You & Me. (Illus.). 24p. (J). (ps-4). 1997. spiral bd. 5.00 (1-890925-08-X); No One Is Perfect: Just Be the Best That You Can Be. (Illus.). 24p. (J). (ps-4). 1997. spiral bd. 5.00 (1-890925-06-3); Take Care of Your Body. (Illus.). 24p. (J). (ps-4). 1997. spiral bd. 5.00 (1-890925-10-1); Tena & Joshua Friends 'til the End. (Illus.). 24p. (J). (ps-4). 1997. spiral bd. 5.00 (1-890925-02-0); Tena Gets Help from Her Friend Joshua. (Illus.). 24p. (J). (ps-4). 1997. spiral bd. 5.00 (1-890925-01-2); Traffic Light Name Game. (Illus.). 24p. (Orig.). (J). 1997. spiral bd. 5.00 (1-890925-21-7); Trust, Honor & Loyalty - That Is What Friends Are Made Of. (Illus.). 24p. (J). (ps-4). 1997. spiral bd. 5.00 (1-890925-03-9); Use Your Brain for Your Present, Future & Past. (Illus.). 24p. (J). (ps-4). 1997. spiral bd. 5.00 (1-890925-16-0); We Are Growing up Too Fast. (Illus.). 24p. (J). (ps-4). 1997. spiral bd. 5.00 (1-890925-05-5); When Will I Be 1 Year Old. (Illus.). 24p. (J). (ps-4). 1997. spiral bd. 5.00 (1-890925-22-5); 125.00 (1-890925-00-4) Stori Tyme.

Brown, Terence. Ireland: A Social & Cultural History, 1922 to the Present. LC 85-47695. 296p. (C). 1985. pap. 16.95 (0-8014-9349-8) Cornell U Pr.

— Ireland's Literature: Essays in Historical Criticism. LC 88-16638. 240p. (C). 1988. text 53.50 (0-389-20802-7, N8360) B&N Imports.

***Brown, Terence.** The Life of W. B. Yeats: A Critical Biography. LC 99-28388. (Critical Biographies Ser.). 384p. (C). 1999. 39.95 (0-631-18298-5) Blackwell Pubs.

Brown, Terence & Grene, Nicholas, eds. Tradition & Influence in Anglo-Irish Poetry. LC 88-29243. 224p. (C). 1988. lib. bdg. 46.00 (0-389-20817-5, N8375) B&N Imports.

Brown, Terence A. Genetics: A Molecular Approach. 1990. pap. 29.50 (0-412-02621-X, Chap & Hall NY) Chapman & Hall.

Brown, Terence A., ed. Essential Molecular Biology: A Practical Approach, 2 vols., Set. (Practical Approach Ser.). (Illus.). 640p. 1992. pap. text 100.00 (0-19-963115-8) OUP.

— Essential Molecular Biology, Vol. One: A Practical Approach. (Practical Approach Ser.). (Illus.). 320p. 1991. pap. text 55.00 (0-19-963111-5) OUP.

— Essential Molecular Biology, Vol. Two: A Practical Approach. (Practical Approach Ser.). (Illus.). 320p. 1991. 95.00 (0-19-963112-3); pap. text 55.00 (0-19-963113-1) OUP.

Brown, Terence A., tr. see Piaget, Jean.

Brown, Terrance, tr. see Piaget, Jean, et al.

Brown, Terri & Brown, Nancy. Heritage Trails. 48p. 1987. pap. text 6.50 (1-56770-169-8) S Scheewe Pubns.

— Mini Mini More, Vol. 2. 48p. 1985. pap. text 6.50 (1-56770-151-5) S Scheewe Pubns.

Brown, Terry. The Ancient Heroes Devotional Bible. (Illus.). 1200p. (J). (gr. 1-4). 1997. 20.00 (1-891082-02-7) Youth Life Creats.

— English Martial Arts. LC 98-106174. (Illus.). 237p. 1998. 45.00 (1-898281-18-1, Pub. by Anglo-Saxon Bks) Paul & Co Pubs.

Brown, Terry. The Lifestyle Enhancement Program Survival Guide for the 90's. (Illus.). 120p. 1992. pap., student ed. 99.95 incl. audio, digital audio (0-9632607-1-5) TJs Body Cnslts.

Brown, Terry. Molecular Biology Labfax Vol. 2: Gene Analysis, Vol. 2. 2nd ed. (Labfax Ser.). (Illus.). 288p. 1998. 59.95 (0-12-136110-1) Acad Pr.

***Brown, Terry.** Portrait. LC 00-20021. (Todaysgirls.Com Ser.: Vol. 2). (Illus.). 128p. (J). (gr. 5-9). 2000. pap. 5.99 (0-8499-7561-1) Tommy Nelson.

***Brown, Terry, creator.** R U 4 Real? Vol. 4. 128p. (J). (gr. 5-9). 2000. pap. 5.99 (0-8499-7563-8) Tommy Nelson.

— Tangled Web. Vol. 3. 128p. (J). (gr. 5-9). 2000. pap. 5.99 (0-8499-7562-X) Tommy Nelson.

***Brown, Terry, ed.** Essential Molecular Biology: A Practical Approach, 1 vol., Vol. 1. (The Practical Approach Ser.: 234). (Illus.). 272p. 2000. text 110.00 (0-19-963643-5); pap. text 50.00 (0-19-963642-7) OUP.

Brown, Terry A., et al, eds. Molecular Biology Labfax Vol. I: Recombinant DNA, Vol. 1. 2nd ed. LC 97-45533. (Labfax Ser.). (Illus.). 408p. (C). 1998. text 59.95 (0-12-136055-5) Morgan Kaufmann.

***Brown, Tessa & Coulson, Sheila.** Stitch & Stencil: Over 40 Easy Fabric-Based Projects. LC 99-22293. (Illus.). 96p. 1999. pap. 21.95 (1-56477-274-8, PasTimes) Martingale & Co.

Brown, Thad A. Migration & Politics: The Impact of Population Mobility on American Voting Behavior. LC 87-16240. xxii, 198p. (C). 1988. 45.00 (0-8078-1765-1) U of NC Pr.

— Mitration & Politics: The Impact of Population Mobility on American Voting Behavior. LC 87-16240. (Illus.). 220p. reprint ed. pap. 68.20 (0-608-08605-3, 206912800003) Bks Demand.

***Brown, Thaddeus C. S., et al.** Behind the Guns: The History of Battery I, 2nd Regiment, Illinois Light Artillery. LC 00-29164. 2000. write for info. (0-8093-2342-7) S Ill U Pr.

Brown, Thelma, jt. auth. see Gilbert, Ed.

Brown, Theo. Deere & Company's Early Tractor Development. Cherry, Jack D., ed. (Illus.). 64p. Date not set. 12.95 (1-887446-04-4) Two-Cylinder.

Brown, Theodore. Stereoscopic Phenomena of Light & Sight: A Guide to the Practice of Steoscopic Photography & Its Relation to Binocular Vision. (Illus.). 144p. (C). 1994. reprint ed. pap. 14.95 (0-939617-01-3) Reel Three-D.

Brown, Theodore, Jr., jt. auth. see Ely, James W., Jr.

***Brown, Theodore L.** Chemistry. 8th ed. LC 99-25748. 1120p. 1999. 106.33 (0-13-010310-1) P-H.

Brown, Theodore L. & Bursten, Bruce E. Chemistry: The Central Science. 7th ed. LC 96-27480. 1039p. (C). 1996. student ed. 105.00 (0-13-533480-2) P-H.

Brown, Theodore L. & Cohen, I. Bernard, eds. The Mechanical Philosophy & the "Animal Oeconomy" LC 80-2085. (Development of Science Ser.). (Illus.). 1981. lib. bdg. 38.95 (0-405-13851-2) Ayer.

Brown, Theodore L., et al. Chemistry - Student Version: The Central Science. 6th ed. LC 93-35988. 1045p. (C). 1993. text 99.00 (0-13-336397-X) P-H.

Brown, Theodore M., jt. ed. see Fee, Elizabeth.

***Brown, Theophilus.** Paul Harris Sculpture: Fifty Years. LC 99-67355. (Illus.). 136p. 2000. pap. 35.00 (0-295-97928-3) U of Wash Pr.

Brown, Thomas. Account of the People Called Shakers. LC 77-17584. reprint ed. 49.50 (0-404-08459-1) AMS Pr.

— Inquiry into the Relation of Cause & Effect. 4th ed. LC 77-16224. 496p. 1977. reprint ed. lib. bdg. 75.00 (0-8201-1301-8) Schol Facsimiles.

— JFK, History of an Image. LC 87-45373. 160p. 1988. reprint ed. pap. 49.60 (0-608-01051-0, 205935900001) Bks Demand.

— The Narrative of Thomas Brown. 24p. 1995. pap. 6.95 (0-87770-552-6) Ye Galleon.

— Sketch of a System of the Philosophy of the Human Mind, 1. LC 77-72191. (Contributions to the History of Psychology Ser.: Pt. A, Orientations). 320p. 1977. reprint ed. lib. bdg. 69.50 (0-313-26925-4, U6925, Greenwood Pr) Greenwood.

Brown, Thomas A. The Aesthetics of Robert Schumann. LC 73-16607. (Illus.). 207p. 1975. reprint ed. lib. bdg. 59.50 (*0-8371-7184-9*, BRAS, Greenwood Pr) Greenwood.

— Afro-Latin Rhythm Dictionary. (Alfred Handy Guides Ser.). 48p. 1984. pap. text 5.50 (*0-88284-151-3*, 2427) Alfred Pub.

— The Celtic Roots of Camelot. LC 99-19. 280p. 1999. pap. 16.24 (*1-55212-250-6*) Trafford Pub.

— History of the American Stage. LC 72-81206. (Illus.). 421p. 1972. reprint ed. 31.95 (*0-405-08309-2*, Pub. by Blom Pubns) Ayer.

— A History of the New York Stage, 3 vols., Set. LC 64-14704. reprint ed. 139.95 (*0-405-08310-6*, Pub. by Blom Pubns) Ayer.

— History of the New York Stage, 3 vols., Vol. 1. LC 64-14704. 1972. reprint ed. 48.95 (*0-405-08311-4*, Pub. by Blom Pubns) Ayer.

— A History of the New York Stage, 3 vols., Vol. 2. LC 64-14704. 1972. reprint ed. 48.95 (*0-405-08312-2*, Pub. by Blom Pubns) Ayer.

— A History of the New York Stage, 3 vols., Vol. 3. LC 64-14704. 1972. reprint ed. 48.95 (*0-405-08313-0*, Pub. by Blom Pubns) Ayer.

***Brown, Thomas A.** Storm over Show Low. 216p. 2000. pap. 11.95 (*0-929408-28-4*) Amer Eagle Pubns Inc.

Brown, Thomas A. & Weinfield, Mark. Test Yourself Precalculus Mathematics. LC 98-54447. (Test Yourself Ser.). (Illus.). 192p. 1997. pap. 12.95 (*0-8442-2382-4*, 23824) NTC Contemp Pub Co.

Brown, Thomas A., et al. Kentucky Tax Law. 2nd ed. (Illus.). xvi, 264p. 1995. pap. 45.00 (*1-58757-005-X*, TM018) Univ of KY.

Brown, Thomas C., jt. auth. see Binkley, Dan.

Brown, Thomas C., jt. auth. see Gillilan, David M.

Brown, Thomas D. Journal of the Southern Indian Mission: Diary of Thomas D. Brown. LC 74-182832. (Western Text Society Ser.: No. 4). 195p. reprint ed. pap. 60.50 (*0-8357-7911-4*, 203633900002) Bks Demand.

***Brown, Thomas E., ed.** Attention-Deficit Disorders & Comorbidities in Children, Adolescents & Adults. 736p. 2000. 59.00 (*0-88048-711-9*) Am Psychiatric.

Brown, Thomas G. & Conseil Quebecois de la Recherche Sociale. Substance Abusers in Treatment: What About the Families? LC 96-123979. (ENG & FRE.). 1995. write for info. (*0-88947-225-4*) Cncordia U.

Brown, Thomas H. Langue et Litterature. 3rd ed. LC 83-81015. (FRE.). 380p. (C). 1984. text 48.36 (*0-669-06682-6*); teacher ed. 2.66 (*0-669-07406-3*); student ed. 28.76 (*0-669-06683-4*); audio 31.16 (*0-669-06685-0*) HM Trade Div.

— Langue et Litterature: A Second Course in French. 2nd ed. (Illus.). 448p. (C). 1974. text 24.95 (*0-07-008400-9*) McGraw.

— Pas a Pas French: Listening, Speaking, Reading, Writing. 544p. 1991. 84.95 (*0-471-61773-3*); pap., wbk. ed. 34.95 (*0-471-61774-1*) Wiley.

— Pas a Pas French: Listening, Speaking, Reading, Writing. 850p. 1993. text, wbk. ed. 51.00 (*0-471-03750-8*) Wiley.

— Themes et Discussions. (FRE.). 223p. (C). 1982. pap. text 33.56 (*0-669-02844-4*) HM Trade Div.

Brown, Thomas J. Dorothea Dix: New England Reformer, Vol. 127. LC 97-44207. 432p. 1998. 35.00 (*0-674-21488-9*) HUP.

— Parenting Behaviors That Promote School Success. LC 98-93068. 80p. 1998. pap. 9.95 (*1-891404-06-7*, BA016, B&A Pr) Brown & Assocs.

— Providing the Home Court Advantage in the Classroom. LC 98-92866. 64p. 1998. 6.50 (*1-891404-01-6*, BA009); pap. 8.50 (*1-891404-03-2*, BH009) Brown & Assocs.

— Quest for Equity & Excellence: A Staff Development Program for K-12 Teachers. 80p. 1999. pap., teacher ed., wbk. ed. 14.95 (*1-891404-08-3*, BA018, B&A Pr) Brown & Assocs.

— Teaching Minorities More Effectively: A Model for Educators. 82p. (Orig.). (C). 1987. lib. bdg. 33.00 (*0-8191-5662-0*) U Pr of Amer.

— Teaching The Poor & Children of Color: Public Education's Moral Dilemma. LC 98-93895. 96p. 1999. pap. text 11.95 (*1-891404-07-5*) Brown & Assocs.

— Ten Commandments for Success in Teaching. LC 98-92921. 80p. 1998. 7.95 (*1-891404-02-4*, BH015); pap. 9.95 (*1-891404-04-0*, BH015) Brown & Assocs.

— Toward a Rebirth of Common Sense in Education. LC 95-83913. 128p. (Orig.). 1996. pap. 11.95 (*1-56167-246-7*) Am Literary Pr.

Brown, Thomas J., ed. Civil War & Reconstruction (1850-1877), Vol. 7. LC 97-16011. (American Eras Ser.). 400p. 1997. 85.00 (*0-7876-1484-X*, GML00198-110849) Gale.

Brown, Thomas J. & Green, Kitty K. Lessons Learned from the Gullah Experience: Powerful Focus in Educating African-American Youth. LC 98-92835. 96p. 1998. pap. 12.95 (*1-891404-00-8*, BA001) Brown & Assocs.

Brown, Thomas K., tr. see Jorns, Auguste.

Brown, Thomas M., ed. Molecular Genetics & Evolution of Pesticide Resistance, Vol. 645. LC 96-29234. (ACS Symposium Ser.). (Illus.). 280p. 1996. text 105.00 (*0-8412-3453-1*, Pub. by Am Chemical) OUP.

Brown, Thomas M. & Stoudemire, Alan. Psychiatric Side Effects of Prescription & over-the-Counter Medications: Recognition & Management. LC 97-42717. 417p. 1998. text 79.00 (*0-88048-868-9*, 8868) Am Psychiatric.

Brown, Thomas M., jt. auth. see Scammell, Henry.

Brown, Thomas M., jt. auth. see Stine, Karen.

Brown, Thomas N. Irish-American Nationalism, 1870-1890. LC 80-11094. (Critical Periods of History Ser.). 206p. 1980. reprint ed. lib. bdg. 55.00 (*0-313-22204-5*, BRIA, Greenwood Pr) Greenwood.

Brown, Thomas R., pref. Handbook of Institutional Pharmacy Practice. 3rd ed. (C). 1992. text 60.00 (*1-879907-21-6*) Am Soc Hlth-Syst.

Brown, Thomas S. The Personal Relevance of Truth. LC 55-7711. (C). 1955. pap. 4.00 (*0-87574-081-2*) Pendle Hill.

Brown, Tim. Brothers in Blood. 1996. mass mkt. 4.99 (*1-85782-096-7*, Pub. by Blake Publng) Seven Hills Bk.

Brown, Tim, jt. auth. see Passmore, Jon.

Brown, Tim W. Deconstruction Acres. 192p. (Orig.). 1997. pap. 10.00 (*1-886625-03-4*) III Pub.

***Brown, Timothy.** Psalms & Compassions: A Jesuit's Journey Through Cancer. Hodges, Susan, ed. LC 00-103822. 2000. pap. write for info. (*0-9668716-4-2*) Resonant Pubg.

Brown, Timothy & Lee, Tony. Offical Guide to Role Playing Games. 1998. pap. 17.00 (*0-676-60144-8*) Ballantine Pub Grp.

Brown, Timothy A. & Barlow, David H. Casebook in Abnormal Psychology: An Integrative Approach. LC 96-28116. (Psychology Ser.). 248p. (C). 1996. mass mkt. 25.95 (*0-534-34247-7*) Brooks-Cole.

— Casebook in Abnormal Psychology: An Integrative Approach. 1997. teacher ed. write for info. (*0-534-34631-6*) Brooks-Cole.

Brown, Timothy B. Wizard's Challenge II. (Advanced Dungeons & Dragons, 2nd Edition: One-on-One Adventures Ser.). 1994. 6.95 (*1-56076-889-4*) TSR Inc.

Brown, Timothy B. & Sullivan, Patricia A. Setting Hearts on Fire: A Spirituality for Leaders. LC 96-50064. 144p. (Orig.). 1997. pap. 12.95 (*0-8189-0771-1*) Alba.

Brown, Timothy C. The Causes of Continuing Conflict in Nicaragua: A View from the Radical Middle. LC 95-11396. (Essays in Public Policy Ser.: No. 59). 1995. pap. 5.00 (*0-8179-5642-5*) Hoover Inst Pr.

***Brown, Timothy C.** When the AK-47s Fall Silent: Revolutionaries, Guerillas & the Dangers of Peace. LC 00-23505. 2000. write for info. (*0-8179-9842-X*) Hoover Inst Pr.

***Brown, Timothy J. & Mielke, Paul W.** Statistical Mining & Data Visualization in Atmospheric Sciences. LC 00-22048. (Illus.). 2000. write for info. (*0-7923-7816-4*) Kluwer Academic.

***Brown, Timothy N., et al.** California Real Property Sales Transactions: December 1999 Update. 3rd ed. Blanchette, Janis L., ed. 564p. 1999. 64.00 (*0-7626-0380-1*, RE-32992) Cont Ed Bar-CA.

***Brown, Timothy Tatton.** Lambeth Palace: A History of the Archbishops of Canterbury & Their Houses. 2000. 35.00 (*0-281-05347-2*, Pub. by Society Prom Christ Know) Intl Pubs Mktg.

***Brown, Titus & Hadley, Jack.** African-American Life on the Southern Hunting Plantation. (Voices of America Ser.). (Illus.). 128p. 2000. pap. write for info. (*0-7385-0555-2*) Arcadia Publng.

Brown, Todd D. Entries from a Hot Pink Notebook. Rubenstein, Julie, ed. 320p. 1995. pap. 10.00 (*0-671-89084-0*) PB.

Brown, Tom, Jr. Awakening Spirits. LC 94-162087. 224p. (Orig.). 1994. pap. 12.95 (*0-425-14140-3*) Berkley Pub.

— Grandfather. 208p. (Orig.). 1993. pap. 12.00 (*0-425-13804-6*) Berkley Pub.

— Grandfather. 240p. (Orig.). 1996. mass mkt. 6.50 (*0-425-15593-5*) Berkley Pub.

Brown, Tom. The Heaven's Gate Suicide: Unlocking the Answer to Why It Happened. LC 98-122053. 128p. (Orig.). 1997. pap. 9.99 (*0-9658305-0-0*) T Brown Minist.

Brown, Tom, Jr. The Journey. 256p. (Orig.). 1992. pap. 12.95 (*0-425-13364-8*) Berkley Pub.

Brown, Tom. The Quest. 1991. pap. 12.95 (*0-425-12660-9*) Berkley Pub.

Brown, Tom, Jr. The Science & Art of Tracking: Nature's Path to Spiritual Discovery. LC 99-174161. 240p. 1999. pap. 12.95 (*0-425-15772-5*) Berkley Pub.

— Tom Brown's Field Guide to Nature & Survival for Children. (Tom Brown's Field Guide Ser.: No. 7). (J). 1989. pap. 12.95 (*0-425-11106-7*) Berkley Pub.

— Tom Brown's Guide to Wild Edible & Medicinal Plants. 288p. 1986. pap. 12.95 (*0-425-10063-4*) Berkley Pub.

— The Vision. 256p. (Orig.). 1991. pap. 6.99 (*0-425-12911-X*) Berkley Pub.

Brown, Tom. Vision: The Dramatic True Story of One Man's Search For. 1988. pap. 12.95 (*0-425-10703-5*) Berkley Pub.

Brown, Tom, Jr. The Way of the Scout. 288p. (Orig.). 1995. pap. 12.95 (*0-425-14779-7*) Berkley Pub.

— The Way of the Scout. 288p. (Orig.). 1997. mass mkt. 6.99 (*0-425-15910-8*) Berkley Pub.

Brown, Tom. You Can Predict Your Future. 192p. 1996. mass mkt. 5.99 (*0-88368-386-5*) Whitaker Hse.

Brown, Tom, compiled by. The Lakhovsky Multiple Wave Oscillator Handbook. (Illus.). 160p. 1988. student ed. 19.95 (*0-945685-03-3*) Borderland Sciences.

Brown, Tom, Jr. & Morgan, Brandt. Tom Brown's Field Guide to City & Suburban Survival, Vol. 3. 288p. (Orig.). 1986. pap. 12.00 (*0-425-09172-4*) Berkley Pub.

— Tom Brown's Field Guide to Living with the Earth. (Illus.). 288p. 1986. pap. 12.95 (*0-425-09147-3*) Berkley Pub.

— Tom Brown's Field Guide to Nature Observation & Tracking. 256p. 1986. pap. 12.95 (*0-425-09966-0*) Berkley Pub.

— Tom Brown's Guide to Wilderness Survival. (Illus.). 240p. (Orig.). 1987. pap. 12.95 (*0-425-10572-5*) Berkley Pub.

Brown, Tom, Jr. & Owen, William. The Search. 1986. pap. 12.95 (*0-425-10251-3*) Berkley Pub.

Brown, Tom, ed. see Davidson, Alison.

Brown, Tom, ed. see Haroldine.

Brown, Tom, tr. see Scarron, Paul.

Brown, Toni A., ed. see Izumi, Alan N.

Brown, Toni L. Awakenings: A Jewish Woman's Search for Truth. 200p. (Orig.). 1993. pap. 12.95 (*1-884052-06-1*) Kochav.

Brown, Toni S. Family Portraits for the 21st Century. (Illus.). 124p. 1997. pap. 29.97 (*0-918368-23-5*) Studio Pr PA.

— Happy Mother's Day...Wake Me When It's Over. Sealander, Evelyn, ed. LC 96-68196. 150p. (Orig.). 1996. pap. 6.95 (*1-57636-014-8*) SunRise Pbl.

— The Story Only You Can Tell: Creating Your Family History with Ease & Expertise. LC 95-72365. (Illus.). 150p. (Orig.). 1995. pap. text 13.95 (*1-57636-006-7*) SunRise Pbl.

— Story-Telling Portraits of Children. 2nd ed. (Illus.). 72p. 1993. reprint ed. pap. 29.50 (*0-934420-16-5*) Studio Pr NE.

— Tis the Season . . . To Go Crazy! LC 96-71674. 110p. 1996. pap. text 6.95 (*1-57636-030-X*) SunRise Pbl.

***Brown, Toni Sorenson.** Check Lost & Found My Mind is Missi. 128p. 1999. reprint ed. mass mkt. 3.99 (*0-312-97090-0*) St Martin.

— In My Quest for Personal Growth, the Rest Grew with Me Too. 144p. 2000. mass mkt. 3.99 (*0-312-97078-1*, St Martins Paperbacks) St Martin.

Brown, Toni Sorenson. Validate Me Quick, I'm Double Parked. 128p. 2000. mass mkt. 3.99 (*0-312-97005-6*, St Martins Paperbacks) St Martin.

— Validate Me Quick, I'm Double Parked. LC 95-71763. 100p. 1995. pap. text 6.95 (*0-9644552-9-3*) SunRise Pbl.

Brown, Tony. Alluvial Geoarchaeology: Floodplain Archaeology & Environmental Change. LC 96-2413. (Cambridge Manuals in Archaeology Ser.). (Illus.). 400p. (C). 1997. text 74.95 (*0-521-56097-7*); pap. text 29.95 (*0-521-56820-X*) Cambridge U Pr.

— Black Lies, White Lies: The Truth According to Tony Brown. LC 95-13315. 368p. 1995. 23.00 (*0-688-13270-7*, Wm Morrow) Morrow Avon.

— Black Lies, White Lies: The Truth According to Tony Brown. 400p. 1997. reprint ed. pap. 14.00 (*0-688-15131-0*, Quil) HarperTrade.

— The Collected Stories of Gwyn Jones. 448p. 1998. pap. 19.95 (*0-7083-1457-0*, Pub. by Univ Wales Pr) Paul & Co Pubs.

***Brown, Tony.** Complete Book of the British Charts. (Illus.). 512p. 2000. pap. text 24.95 (*0-7119-7670-8*) Omnibus NY.

Brown, Tony. Coordinating Maths Across the Primary School. (Subject Leaders Handbks.). 236p. 1998. pap. 23.95 (*0-7507-0687-2*, Falmer Pr) Taylor & Francis.

***Brown, Tony.** Empower the People: A 7-Step Plan to Overthrow the Conspiracy That Is Stealing Your Money & Freedom. LC 97-36579. 352p. 1998. 24.00 (*0-688-15762-9*, Wm Morrow) Morrow Avon.

Brown, Tony. Empower the People: Overthrow the Conspiracy That Is Stealing Your Money & Your Freedom. 400p. 1999. reprint ed. pap. 15.00 (*0-688-16974-0*, Quil) HarperTrade.

***Brown, Tony.** Jimi Hendrix: Concert File. (Illus.). 1999. pap. 29.95 (*0-7119-7510-8*) Music Sales.

Brown, Tony. Jimi Hendrix: In His Own Words. LC 95-1850. (In Their Own Words Ser.). (Illus.). 96p. 1995. pap. 15.95 (*0-7119-4248-X*, OP 47719) Omnibus NY.

— Jimi Hendrix: The Final Days. (Illus.). 192p. 1997. pap. 19.95 (*0-7119-5238-8*) Omnibus NY.

— Jimi Hendrix: Visual Documentary. (Illus.). 123p. pap. 24.95 (*0-7119-2761-8*, OP 46580) Omnibus NY.

— Mathematics Education & Language: Interpreting Hermeneutics & Post-Structuralism. LC 97-11134. (Mathematics Education Library). 1997. lib. bdg. 113.50 (*0-7923-4554-1*) Kluwer Academic.

— Understanding BS5750 & Other Quality Systems. LC 93-36860. 180p. 1993. pap. 25.95 (*0-566-07455-9*, Pub. by Gower) Ashgate Pub Co.

— World Snowboard Guide. 3rd ed. 1998. pap. text. write for info. (*1-900916-05-3*, Pub. by ICE Publ) Seven Hills Bk.

— World Snowboard Guide, 2000. 4th ed. (Illus.). 366p. 2000. pap. 18.95 (*1-900916-08-8*, Pub. by ICE Publ) Trans-Atl Phila.

Brown, Tony, ed. Edward Carpenter & Late Victorian Radicalism. 238p. 1990. text 25.00 (*0-7146-3400-X*, Pub. by F Cass Pubs) Intl Spec Bk.

Brown, Tony, jt. ed. see Harper, David.

Brown, Towana J. Leave, Retard, Leave! (Illus.). 127p. (Orig.). (YA). (gr. 8-12). 1988. pap. 3.50 (*0-9622060-0-8*) T J Brown.

— Raglagger. LC 89-90647. (Illus.). 168p. (Orig.). (J). (gr. 5-7). 1989. pap. 3.50 (*0-9622060-2-4*) T J Brown.

— Scottie. LC 88-93029. (One Ser.). (Illus.). 150p. (Orig.). (J). (gr. 5-6). 1989. pap. 3.50 (*0-9622060-1-6*) T J Brown.

Brown, Townsend, 2nd. A Very Rich School. 184p. (Orig.). 1996. pap. text. write for info. (*0-9639999-3-2*) Jay St Pubs.

Brown, Tracey L. The Life & Times of Ron Brown: A Memoir by His Daughter. LC 97-32016. (Illus.). 256p. 1998. 26.00 (*0-688-15320-8*, Wm Morrow) Morrow Avon.

Brown, Tracy, jt. auth. see Puryear, Kay.

Brown, Travis. Historical First Patents: The First United States Patents for Many Everyday Things. LC 94-14814. 224p. 1994. 41.50 (*0-8108-2898-7*) Scarecrow.

***Brown, Travis.** Popular Patents: America's First Inventions from the Airplane to the Zipper. (Illus.). 224p. 2000. pap. 18.95 (*1-57886-010-5*, Pub. by Scarecrow) Natl Bk Netwk.

Brown, Tricia. Alaskan Wilderness LC 99-27645. (Discovery Travel Adventures Ser.). 1999. pap. 19.95 (*1-56331-837-7*) Discovery.

— L' Chaim: The Story of a Russian Emigre Boy. LC 93-44853. (J). 1995. write for info. (*0-8050-2354-2*) H Holt & Co.

— Children of the Midnight Sun: Voices of Alaska's Native Children. LC 97-41534. (Illus.). 48p. (J). (gr. 3-7). 1998. 16.95 (*0-88240-500-4*, Alaska NW Bks) Gr Arts Ctr Pub.

— Chinese New Year. LC 87-8532. (Illus.). 88p. (J). (ps-2). 1995. 14.95 (*0-8050-0497-1*, Bks Young Read) H Holt & Co.

— Chinese New Year. (J). 1997. 12.15 (*0-606-13269-4*, Pub. by Turtleback) Demco.

— Chinese New Year. (Illus.). (J). (gr. k-4). 1997. reprint ed. pap. text 6.95 (*0-8050-5544-4*) H Holt & Co.

— Hello, Amigos! LC 86-9882. (Illus.). 48p. (J). (ps-2). 1995. 15.95 (*0-8050-0090-9*, Owlet BYR); pap. 5.95 (*0-8050-1891-3*, Owlet BYR) H Holt & Co.

— Iditarod Country: Exploring the Route of the Last Great Race. Ummel, Christine, ed. LC 97-77237. (Illus.). 64p. (gr. 5 up). 1998. 16.95 (*0-945397-66-6*) Epicenter Pr.

— Konnichiwa. (J). (gr. 3-5). 1995. 15.95 (*0-8050-2353-4*) H Holt & Co.

***Brown, Tricia.** Konnichiwa: I am a Japanese-american Girl. 1999. pap. 7.95 (*0-8050-6266-1*) St Martin.

Brown, Tricia. Someone Special, Just Like You. LC 83-18377. (Illus.). 64p. (J). (ps-2). 1995. 15.95 (*0-8050-0481-5*, Bks Young Read) H Holt & Co.

— Someone Special, Just Like You. LC 83-18377. (Illus.). 64p. (J). (ps-3). 1995. pap. 5.95 (*0-8050-4268-7*, Owlet BYR) H Holt & Co.

— Someone Special, Just Like You. 1995. 11.15 (*0-606-09871-2*, Pub. by Turtleback) Demco.

***Brown, Tricia.** The World Famous Alaska Highway: A Guide to the ALCAN & Other Wilderness Roads of the North. (Illus.). 304p. 2000. pap. 21.95 (*1-55591-446-2*) Fulcrum Pub.

Brown, Tricia, ed. Lessons My Sled Dog Taught Me: Humor & Heartwarming Tails from Alaska's Mushers. (Illus.). 160p. 1998. 9.95 (*0-945397-69-0*) Epicenter Pr.

***Brown, Tricia & Corral, Roy.** Fairbanks: Alaska's Heart of Gold: A Traveler's Guide. LC 99-54835. (Illus.). 96p. 2000. 12.95 (*0-88240-528-4*, Alaska NW Bks) Gr Arts Ctr Pub.

Brown, Tricia & Junior League of San Francisco Staff. The City by the Bay: A Magical Journey Around San Francisco. LC 92-32104. (Illus.). 32p. (J). 1993. 14.95 (*0-8118-0233-7*) Chronicle Bks.

— The City by the Bay: A Magical Journey Around San Francisco. (Illus.). 32p. (J). (ps up). 1998. pap. 6.95 (*0-8118-2012-2*) Chronicle Bks.

— The City by the Bay: A Magical Journey Around San Francisco. Shigaki, Michiko, tr. (JPN., Illus.). 32p. (J). (ps up). 1998. 15.95 (*0-8118-2101-3*) Chronicle Bks.

Brown, Tricia, ed. see Freedman, Lew.

Brown, Tricia, ed. see Hahn, Otis & Vollmar, Alice.

Brown, Tricia, ed. see Hudson, Ray.

Brown, Tricia, ed. see Kneece, Judy C.

Brown, Tricia, ed. see O'Donoghue, Brian.

Brown, Trillie. Granny's Teacakes, Grab'led 'Taters & a Gillion Twice-Told Tales. 240p. (Orig.). 1994. pap., per. 9.95 (*0-614-17681-6*) Sevgo Pr.

Brown, Trisha, et al, contrib. by. Robert Rauschenberg: A Retrospective. (Guggenheim Museum Publication Ser.). (Illus.). 544p. 1997. 75.00 (*0-8109-6903-3*, Pub. by Abrams) Time Warner.

Brown-Turrell, Julia. Playspaces: Architecture for Children. LC 89-50429. (Illus.). 59p. (Orig.). 1989. pap., spiral bd. 25.00 (*0-9614615-7-8*) Edmundson.

Brown University, Bell Gallery Staff. Flying Tigers: Painting & Sculpture in New York, 1939-1946. LC 85-70817. (Illus.). 143p. (Orig.). 1985. pap. text 20.00 (*0-933519-00-1*) D W Bell Gallery.

Brown University, Department of Art Staff. All the Banners Wave: Art & War in the Romantic Era, 1792-1851. LC 81-71834. (Illus.). 125p. (Orig.). 1982. pap. text 20.00 (*0-933519-04-4*) D W Bell Gallery.

— Children of Mercury: The Education of Artists in the Sixteenth & Seventeenth Centuries. LC 84-70128. (Illus.). 143p. (Orig.). 1984. pap. text 20.00 (*0-933519-03-6*) D W Bell Gallery.

— The Classical Spirit in American Portraiture. LC 76-380. (Illus.). 120p. (Orig.). 1976. pap. text 20.00 (*0-933519-09-5*) D W Bell Gallery.

— Definitive Statements: American Art, 1964-66. LC 86-70127. (Illus.). 180p. (Orig.). 1986. pap. text 20.00 (*0-933519-01-X*) D W Bell Gallery.

— Festivities: Ceremonies & Celebrations in Western Europe 1500-1790. LC 79-83684. (Illus.). 112p. (Orig.). 1979. pap. text 20.00 (*0-933519-06-0*) D W Bell Gallery.

— Ladies of Shalott: A Victorian Masterpiece in Its Contexts. LC 84-73113. (Illus.). 184p. (Orig.). 1985. pap. text 20.00 (*0-933519-02-8*) D W Bell Gallery.

— Origins of the Italian Veduta. LC 78-52897. (Illus.). 105p. (Orig.). 1978. pap. text 20.00 (*0-933519-07-9*) D W Bell Gallery.

— Ornament & Architecture: Renaissance Drawings, Prints, & Books. (Illus.). 175p. (Orig.). 1980. pap. 20.00 (*0-933519-05-2*) D W Bell Gallery.

— The Survival of the Gods: Classical Mythology in Medieval Art. LC 86-72762. (Illus.). 226p. (Orig.). 1986. pap. text 20.00 (*0-933519-10-9*) D W Bell Gallery.

— Transformations of the Court Style: Gothic Art in Europe, 1270-1330. LC 77-70260. (Illus.). 163p. (Orig.). 1977. pap. text 20.00 (*0-933519-08-7*) D W Bell Gallery.

Brown University, John Carter Brown Library Staff. Bibliotheca Americana, Books to 1674, 3 Vols, Set. 3rd ed. 1972. reprint ed. 200.00 (*0-527-46200-4*) Periodicals Srv.

Brown University, John Hay Library Staff. Catalog of Broadsides of American Verse in the Harris Collection of American Poetry & Plays, 5 reels. (Library Reference Ser.). (C). 1986. 825.00 (*0-8161-1469-2*, G K Hall & Co) Mac Lib Ref.

B

Brown University Library Staff. A Contribution to a Union Catalogue of Sixteenth Century Imprints in Certain New England Libraries. LC 54-1641. 475p. reprint ed. pap. 147.30 (*0-608-14779-6*, 202564400045) Bks Demand.

— Hessian Documents of the American Revolution, 1776-1783: Transcripts & Translations from the Lidgerwood Collection at Morristown National Historical Park, Morristown, NJ. (Microcats Ser.). 362p. 1989. 1890.00 (*0-8161-1748-9*, G K Hall & Co) Mac Lib Ref.

— The Life & Works of John Hay, 1838-1905: A Commemorative Catalogue of the Exhibition Shown at the John Jay Library of Brown University in Honor of the Centennial of His Graduation at the Commencement of 1858. LC 61-3289. 69p. reprint ed. pap. 30.00 (*0-608-15235-8*, 202750100055) Bks Demand.

Brown University Staff. Coming to Terms: Feminism - Theory - Politics. Weed, Elizabeth, ed. 320p. 1989. 42.50 (*0-415-90067-0*) Routledge.

— Dictionary Catalog of the Harris Collection of American Poetry & Plays. 1975. 1935.00 (*0-8161-1497-8*, G K Hall & Co) Mac Lib Ref.

Brown University Staff & Malamat, Abraham. Exodus: The Egyptian Evidence. Frerichs, Ernest S. & Lesko, Leonard H., eds. LC 97-2703. 112p. 1997. 24.95 (*1-57506-025-6*) Eisenbrauns.

Brown University Staff & Stockbridge, John C. The Anthony Memorial: Catalogue of the Harris Collection of American Poetry with Biographical & Bibliographical Notes. LC 77-20882. xxii, 320 p. 1978. write for info. (*0-89341-200-7*, Longwood Academic) Hollowbrook.

Brown University Staff, jt. auth. see Harrington, Peter.

***Brown, Ursula M.** The Interracial Experience: Growing Up Black/White Racially Mixed in the United States. LC 00-39148. 176p. 2000. write for info. (*0-275-97046-9*, Praeger Pubs) Greenwood.

Brown, Uzee. O Redeemed. Foss, Scott, ed. 46p. (C). 1994. pap. 9.95 (*0-89328-128-X*, 30/1067); pap. text 9.95 (*0-89328-129-8*, 30/1072) Lorenz Corp.

Brown, V. A., et al. Our Daily Fix: Drugs in Australia. (Illus.). 320p. 1986. pap. text 18.50 (*0-08-033044-4*, Pub. by Aberdeen U Pr) Macmillan.

Brown, Valerie, et al. Risks & Opportunities. 354p. 1995. pap. 34.00 (*1-85383-236-7*, Pub. by Escan Pubns) Island Pr.

Brown, Valerie, ed. see Greenwood, Marcia.

Brown, Valerie, jt. ed. see Thompson, Mike.

Brown, Valerie A. Psychiatric Assessment: Pre & Post Admission. LC 97-222449. (Forensic Focus Ser.: Vol. 8). 48p. 1997. pap. 36.95 (*1-85302-575-5*, Pub. by Jessica Kingsley) Taylor & Francis.

Brown, Valerie S. The Elderly in Poor Urban Neighborhoods. rev. ed. LC 96-46552. (Studies on the Elderly in America). (Illus.). 149p. 1997. text 51.00 (*0-8153-2540-1*) Garland.

Brown, Vandella. Celebrating the Family: Steps to Planning a Family Reunion. LC 90-1182. (Illus.). 64p. 1991. pap. 9.95 (*0-916489-46-9*) Ancestry.

Brown-VanHoozer, S. A. Say It Right (NLP Focused) 2nd rev. ed. VanHoozer, W. R., ed. & illus. by. 178p. 1997. 15.95 (*1-889530-04-2*) McClure-Brown.

Brown, Vera. Vera Brown's Natural Beauty Book. 1983. 15.95 (*0-02-499870-2*, Macmillan Coll) P-H.

Brown, Vera & Culligan, Pat. Vera Brown's Natural Beauty Book. 220p. 1983. 15.95 (*0-89037-265-9*) Anderson World.

***Brown, Vernon H., Jr.** Mount Up! We're Moving Out! A World War II Memoir of D Troop, 94th Cavalry Reconnaissance Squadron (Mechanized) of the 14th Armored Division. (World War II Memoir Ser.: Vol. 59). (Illus.). 98p. 1999. 34.95 (*1-57638-180-3*, M59-H); pap. 19.95 (*1-57638-179-X*, M59-S) Merriam Pr.

Brown, Vernon K. Acute & Sub-Acute Toxicology. (Illus.). 135p. (C). 1992. pap. text 24.95 (*0-521-42757-6*) Cambridge U Pr.

— Acute Toxicity in Theory & Practice: With Special Reference to the Toxicology of Pesticides. LC 79-42905. (Monographs in Toxicology: Environmental & Safety Aspects). (Illus.). 169p. reprint ed. pap. 52.40 (*0-8357-5091-4*, 203040600069) Bks Demand.

Brown, Vicki. MacPerl: Power & Ease. 1998. pap. text 40.00 (*1-881957-32-2*) PT Freeware.

Brown, Vicki, jt. auth. see Fram, Eugene H.

Brown, Vicki K. Youth on Mission Vol. 3: Come, Go with Me. (Illus.). 128p. (YA). (gr. 7). 1997. pap. text 15.95 (*1-56309-201-8*, W976104) Womans Mission Union.

Brown, Victor L., Jr. Human Intimacy. 1997. pap. 8.95 (*1-57008-309-6*) Bookcraft Inc.

Brown, Victoria. Before & after You Fall in Love Vol. 1. 1995. mass mkt. 5.99 (*0-312-95390-9*) St Martin.

— Feltwork. (New Crafts Ser.). (Illus.). 96p. 1996. 14.95 (*1-85967-297-3*, Lorenz Bks) Anness Pub.

Brown, Victoria, jt. auth. see Pleydell, Sarah.

Brown, Victoria A. Complete Guide to Silk Ribbon Embroidery. (Illus.). 144p. 1996. 24.95 (*0-8230-0795-2*) Watsn-Guptill.

— New Ribbon Embroidery: Innovative, Easy Techniques for Embellishing Ribbon Embroidery with Creativity. LC 97-19403. (Illus.). 144p. 1997. pap. text 24.95 (*0-8230-3171-3*) Watsn-Guptill.

Brown, Vinson. The Californian Wildlife Region. 3rd rev. ed. LC 99-14521. (Illus.). 302p. 1999. pap. 14.95 (*0-87961-201-0*) Naturegraph.

— Crazy Horse, Hoka Hey: It is a Good Time to Die! LC 74-13458. 192p. 1987. pap. 9.95 (*0-87961-173-1*) Naturegraph.

— Exploring Pacific Coast Tide Pools. enl. rev. ed. LC 96-6085. (Illus.). 128p. 1996. pap. 9.95 (*0-87961-217-7*) Naturegraph.

— How to Make a Miniature Zoo. 3rd ed. (Illus.). 256p. 1989. 16.95 (*0-8306-9206-1*); pap. 7.95 (*0-8306-3206-9*) McGraw-Hill Prof.

— The Incredible Paradox: La Nekredeble Paradokso. rev. ed. Evans, Darlene, tr. from ESP. LC 90-46214. (ESP.). 62p. 1992. reprint ed. pap. 6.95 (*0-87961-225-8*) Naturegraph.

— Investigating Nature Through Outdoor Projects: 36 Strategies for Turning the Natural Environment into Your Own Laboratory. LC 82-19660. 256p. (C). 1983. pap. 14.95 (*0-8117-2213-9*) Stackpole.

— Native Americans of the Pacific Coast. LC 76-30677. (Illus.). 272p. 1985. pap. 9.95 (*0-87961-135-9*) Naturegraph.

— Pomo Indians of California & Their Neighbors. Elsasser, Albert B., ed. LC 78-13946. (American Indian Map Book: Vol. 1). (Illus.). 64p. (Orig.). 1969. pap. 8.95 (*0-911010-30-0*) Naturegraph.

— Reptiles & Amphibians of the West. LC 74-3204. (Illus.). 79p. 1974. pap. text 7.95 (*0-87961-028-X*) Naturegraph.

— Return of the Indian Spirit. Johnson, Phyllis, ed. LC 81-65887. (Illus.). 64p. (YA). (gr. 5 up). 1995. pap. 6.95 (*0-89087-401-8*) Celestial Arts.

— The Sierra Nevadan Wildlife Region. 4th rev. ed. LC 95-42041. (Illus.). 144p. 1996. pap. 8.95 (*0-87961-227-4*) Naturegraph.

— Tracking the Glorious Lord: Vital Scientific Proofs of the Existence of God. LC 87-1689. (Paperback Ser.). (Illus.). 128p. (Orig.). 1987. pap. 8.95 (*0-8022-2519-5*) Naturegraph.

— Voices of Earth & Sky: The Vision Life of the Native Americans. LC 76-41761. (Illus.). 177p. (C). 1976. pap. 8.95 (*0-87961-060-3*) Naturegraph.

Brown, Vinson & Weston, Henry, Jr. Handbook of California Birds. 3rd rev. ed. LC 73-6826. (Illus.). 224p. (C). 1986. pap. 12.95 (*0-911010-16-5*) Naturegraph.

Brown, Vinson & Willoya, William. A New Economic Initiative for the Former Soviet Republics: A Policy Statement by the NPA Board of Trustees. 16p. (Orig.). 1992. pap. text 2.45 (*0-614-03253-9*, NPA 258) Natl Planning.

Brown, Vinson, et al. Rocks & Minerals of California. 3rd rev. ed. LC 72-13423. (Illus.). 200p. 1987. pap. 9.95 (*0-911010-58-0*) Naturegraph.

Brown, Vinson, jt. auth. see Allan, David.

Brown, Vinson, jt. auth. see Willoya, William.

Brown, Vinson, ed. see Allen, Elsie.

Brown, Virginia. Highland Hearts. 320p. 1997. mass mkt. 5.50 (*0-8217-5749-0*, Zebra Kensgtn) Kensgtn Pub Corp.

— Legacy of Shadows. 1987. mass mkt. 3.95 (*0-446-32954-1*, Pub. by Warner Bks) Little.

— Reckless. 320p. 1998. pap. 5.99 (*0-8217-5923-X*, Zebra Kensgtn) Kensgtn Pub Corp.

Brown, Virginia, et al, eds. Catalogus Translationum et Commentariorum Vol. VII: Medieval & Renaissance Latin Translations & Commentaries. LC 60-4006. 356p. 1992. text 66.95 (*0-8132-0713-4*) Cath U Pr.

Brown, Virginia & Stayman, Susan. Macrobiotic Miracle: A Woman Cures Herself of Cancer. (Illus.). 240p. 1985. pap. 15.00 (*0-87040-573-X*) Japan Pubns USA.

Brown, Virginia, et al. In Love with an Angel. (Orig.). 1996. mass mkt. write for info. (*0-446-60266-3*) Warner Bks.

Brown, Virginia, jt. auth. see Brown, David.

Brown, Virginia, jt. ed. see Cranz, F. Edward.

Brown, Virginia, ed. see Danforth, Carol.

Brown, Virginia P. Cochula's Journey. 160p. (J). (gr. 5-8). 1996. 18.00 (*1-881320-40-5*, Black Belt) Black Belt Communs.

Brown, Virginia P. & Owens, Laurella. Toting the Lead Row: Ruby Pickens Tartt, Alabama Folklorist. fac. ed. LC 81-4902. (Illus.). 192p. 1981. pap. 59.60 (*0-7837-8106-7*, 205917500009) Bks Demand.

— World of the Southern Indians. LC 83-6376. (Illus.). 176p. (YA). (gr. 6-9). 1997. reprint ed. pap. 15.95 (*0-912221-06-2*) Beechwood.

Brown, Virginia P. & Owens, Laurella, eds. Southern Indian Myths & Legends. (Illus.). 160p. (J). (gr. 6-9). 1994. reprint ed. pap. 12.95 (*0-912221-05-4*) Beechwood.

Brown, Virginia P., jt. auth. see Garmon, Katherine P.

Brown, Virginia P., ed. see Stiggins, George.

Brown, Virginia S., ed. Grundy County Illinois Landmarks Vol. 1: A Guide to Places of Historic Interest. 2nd rev. ed. (Illus.). 93p. 1997. pap. 10.00 (*0-9660474-1-9*) Grundy Cty Hist.

Brown, Vivian B., jt. ed. see Pruett, Harold L.

Brown, Vivien, ed. Eye Priory Cartulary & Charters, Pt. 2. (Suffolk Charters Ser.: Vol. XIII). (Illus.). 212p. (C). 1994. 45.00 (*0-85115-347-X*) Boydell & Brewer.

— Eye Priory Cartulary & Charters I, 2 vols., Pt. 1. (Suffolk Charters Ser.: No. XII). 272p. (C). 1992. 55.00 (*0-85115-322-4*, Boydell Pr) Boydell & Brewer.

Brown, W. D., et al, eds. Dielectric Material Integration for Microelectronics. LC 99-159837. (Proceedings Ser.: Vol. 98-3). (Illus.). 366p. 1998. 70.00 (*1-56677-197-8*) Electrochem Soc.

Brown, W. D., jt. ed. see Kapoor, V. J.

Brown, W. Dale. Of Fiction & Faith: Twelve American Writers Talk about Their Vision & Work. LC 97-17558. (Illus.). 278p. 1997. pap. 20.00 (*0-8028-4313-1*) Eerdmans.

Brown, W. Dean. The Handwritten Will Book. (Illus.). 96p. (Orig.). 1998. pap. 12.95 (*1-879760-39-8*) Consumer TN.

***Brown, W. Dean.** How to Form a Corporation, LLC or Partnership in Alabama. (Illus.). 138p. 1999. pap. 24.95 (*1-930617-00-3*) Corporate Pub.

— How to Form a Corporation, LLC or Partnership in Arizona. (Illus.). 140p. 2000. pap. 24.95 (*1-930617-01-1*) Corporate Pub.

— How to Form a Corporation, LLC or Partnership in Arkansas. (Illus.). 136p. 2000. pap. 24.95 (*1-930617-02-X*) Corporate Pub.

— How to Form a Corporation, LLC or Partnership in California, 1. LC 98-26066. (Illus.). 138p. 2000. per. 24.95 (*1-930617-03-8*) Corporate Pub.

— How to Form a Corporation, LLC or Partnership in Colorado. 138p. 2000. per. 24.95 (*1-930617-04-6*) Corporate Pub.

— How to Form a Corporation, LLC or Partnership in Florida. (Illus.). 138p. 2000. per. 24.95 (*1-930617-05-4*) Corporate Pub.

— How to Form a Corporation, LLC or Partnership in Georgia. LC 98-50097. (Illus.). 138p. 2000. 24.95 (*1-930617-06-2*) Corporate Pub.

— How to Form a Corporation, LLC or Partnership in Illinois. (Illus.). 138p. 2000. per. 24.95 (*1-930617-07-0*) Corporate Pub.

— How to Form a Corporation, LLC or Partnership in Indiana. (Illus.). 146p. 2000. per. 24.95 (*1-930617-08-9*) Corporate Pub.

— How to Form a Corporation, LLC or Partnership in Kansas. (Illus.). 138p. 2000. pap. 24.95 (*1-930617-09-7*) Corporate Pub.

— How to Form a Corporation, LLC or Partnership in Kentucky. (Illus.). 138p. 2000. pap. 24.95 (*1-930617-10-0*) Corporate Pub.

— How to Form a Corporation, LLC or Partnership in Maryland. (Illus.). 138p. 2000. pap. 24.95 (*1-930617-11-9*) Corporate Pub.

— How to Form a Corporation, LLC or Partnership in Massachusetts. (Illus.). 125p. 2000. pap. 24.95 (*1-930617-12-7*) Corporate Pub.

— How to Form a Corporation, LLC or Partnership in Michigan. (Illus.). 138p. 2000. per. 24.95 (*1-930617-13-5*) Corporate Pub.

Brown, W. Dean. How to Form a Corporation, LLC or Partnership in Mississippi. (Illus.). 140p. (Orig.). 1999. pap. 24.95 (*1-879760-67-3*) Consumer TN.

***Brown, W. Dean.** How to Form a Corporation, LLC or Partnership in Missouri. (Illus.). 139p. 2000. pap. 24.95 (*1-930617-14-3*) Corporate Pub.

— How to Form a Corporation, LLC or Partnership in Nevada. (Illus.). 138p. 2000. per. 24.95 (*1-930617-15-1*) Corporate Pub.

— How to Form a Corporation, LLC or Partnership in New Jersey. LC 98-50095. (Illus.). 138p. 2000. per. 24.95 (*1-930617-16-X*) Corporate Pub.

— How to Form a Corporation, LLC or Partnership in New York. (Illus.). 140p. 2000. per. 24.95 (*1-930617-17-8*) Corporate Pub.

— How to Form a Corporation, LLC or Partnership in North Carolina. (Illus.). 138p. 2000. per. 24.95 (*1-930617-18-6*) Corporate Pub.

— How to Form a Corporation, LLC or Partnership in Ohio. (Illus.). 138p. 2000. per. 24.95 (*1-930617-19-4*) Corporate Pub.

— How to Form a Corporation, LLC or Partnership in Oklahoma. (Illus.). 139p. 2000. pap. 24.95 (*1-930617-20-8*) Corporate Pub.

— How to Form a Corporation, LLC or Partnership in Oregon. (Illus.). 138p. 2000. per. 24.95 (*1-930617-21-6*) Corporate Pub.

— How to Form a Corporation, LLC or Partnership in Pennsylvania. (Illus.). 138p. 2000. per. 24.95 (*1-930617-22-4*) Corporate Pub.

— How to Form a Corporation, LLC or Partnership in Tennessee. LC 98-50098. (Illus.). 138p. 2000. per. 24.95 (*1-930617-23-2*) Corporate Pub.

— How to Form a Corporation, LLC or Partnership in Texas. LC 98-50094. (Illus.). 138p. 2000. per. 24.95 (*1-930617-24-0*) Corporate Pub.

— How to Form a Corporation, LLC or Partnership in Virginia. LC 98-50096. (Illus.). 138p. 2000. per. 24.95 (*1-930617-25-9*) Corporate Pub.

— How to Form a Corporation, LLC or Partnership in Washington. (Illus.). 139p. 2000. per. 24.95 (*1-930617-26-7*) Corporate Pub.

— How to Form a Corporation, LLC or Partnership in Wisconsin. 140p. 2000. per. 24.95 (*1-930617-27-5*) Corporate Pub.

Brown, W Dean. How to Incorporate in Any State: With Free Forms on Disk & Free Help by Phone. 2000. pap. 24.95 (*1-879760-85-1*, Pub. by Consumer TN) IPG Chicago.

Brown, W. Dean. How to Incorporate Tax Free. (Illus.). 216p. (Orig.). 1997. pap. 19.95 (*1-879760-37-1*) Consumer TN.

Brown, W. F. & Kaufman, J. G., eds. Developments in Fracture Mechanics Test Methods Standardization - STP 632. 290p. 1977. 24.75 (*0-8031-0321-2*, STP632) ASTM.

Brown, W. G. Basement Involved Tectonics Foreland Areas. LC QE0601.2.B76. (Continuing Education Course Notes Ser.: Vol. 26). 95p. 1984. reprint ed. pap. 30.00 (*0-608-03024-4*, 206347400006) Bks Demand.

— The Lower South in American History. LC 68-24973. (American History & Americana Ser.: No. 47). 1969. reprint ed. lib. bdg. 75.00 (*0-8383-0919-4*) M S G Haskell Hse.

— On the Enumeration of Non-Planar Maps. LC 52-42839. (Memoirs of the American Mathematical Society Ser.: No. 65). 42p. 1966. pap. 16.00 (*0-8218-1265-3*, MEMO/1/65C) Am Math.

Brown, W. Gregory. Lonely Planet Diving & Snorkeling Guide to Fiji Islands. LC 92-45216. (Pisces Diving & Snorkeling Guides Ser.). 96p. 1993. pap. 14.95 (*1-55992-063-7*, Pisces Books) Lonely Planet.

Brown, W. Jethro. Austinian Theory of Law: Being an Edition of Lectures I, V & VI of Austin's "Jurisprudence", & of Austin's "Essay on the Uses of the Study of Jurisprudence" with Critical Notes & Excursus. LC 83-22935. xv, 383p. 1983. reprint ed. 45.00 (*0-8377-0342-5*, Rothman) W S Hein.

Brown, W. L., et al, eds. Conservation of Crop Germplasm - An International Perspective. (Special Publication Ser.: Vol. 8). 67p. 1983. 11.00 (*0-89118-518-6*) Crop Sci Soc Am.

Brown, W. L. & Brown, M. T. Brown. Ancestors of Florence Julia Brown & Some of Their Descendants. (Illus.). 341p. 1995. reprint ed. pap. 52.00 (*0-8328-4752-6*); reprint ed. lib. bdg. 62.00 (*0-8328-4751-8*) Higginson Bk Co.

Brown, W. L., jt. auth. see Smith, J. V.

Brown, W. Norman. India & Indology. Rocher, Rosane, ed. 1979. 52.00 (*0-8364-0362-2*) S Asia.

— The Mahimnastavae: or Mahimna Stotra. 1983. reprint ed. 20.00 (*0-8364-1001-7*, Pub. by Motilal Bnarsidass) S Asia.

— The United States & India, Pakistan, Bangladesh. 3rd ed. LC 72-81270. (American Foreign Policy Library). Orig. Title: The United States & India & Pakistan. (Illus.). 462p. 1972. 46.50 (*0-674-92446-0*) HUP.

Brown, W. Norman, ed. The Vasanta Vilasa. (American Oriental Ser.: Vol. 46). (Illus.). 1962. 20.00 (*0-940490-46-3*) Am Orient Soc.

Brown, W. P., jt. auth. see Graham, M. P.

Brown, W. Penman. Offshore Financial Services Handbook. 2nd ed. 304p. 1999. 155.00 (*1-85573-413-3*) Am Educ Systs.

***Brown, W. S.** Human Performance in Radiological Survey Scanning. 58p. 1998. pap. 5.00 (*0-16-062896-2*) USGPO.

Brown, W. S. & Priest, Josiah. Bible Defence of Slavery. 1988. reprint ed. lib. bdg. 89.00 (*0-7812-0387-2*) Rprt Serv.

Brown, W. S., jt. auth. see Priest, Josiah.

Brown, W. Steven. 13 Fatal Errors Managers Make: And How You Can Avoid Them. 200p. 1987. mass mkt. 5.99 (*0-425-09644-0*) Berkley Pub.

— 13 Fatal Errors Managers Make: And How You Can Avoid Them. LC 85-8245. 160p. (gr. 13). 1989. 17.99 (*0-8007-1423-7*) Revell.

Brown, W. Virgil & Braunwald, Eugene, eds. Atlas of Heart Disease Vol. 10: Atherosclerosis: Risk Factors & Treatment. LC 95-50019. (Illus.). 248p. 1996. text 134.00 (*1-878132-31-8*) Current Med.

Brown, W. Virgil, jt. auth. see Fischer, Lynn.

Brown, Wade E. Wade E. Brown: Recollections & Reflections. LC 97-18450. (Illus.). 150p. 1997. 20.00 (*1-887905-06-5*) Pkway Pubs.

Brown-Walker, Sheila M., jt. auth. see Burke, Debra D.

Brown, Wallace C. The Triumph of Form. LC 73-13452. 212p. 1974. reprint ed. lib. bdg. 35.00 (*0-8371-7135-0*, BRTF, Greenwood Pr) Greenwood.

Brown, Waln K. The Other Side of Delinquency. LC 82-23162. (Crime, Law, & Deviance Ser.). 204p. 1983. reprint ed. pap. 63.30 (*0-7837-5658-5*, 205908400005) Bks Demand.

Brown, Waln K., jt. ed. see Jenkins, Richard L.

Brown, Waln K., jt. ed. see Rhodes, Warren A.

Brown, Walt. In the Beginning: Compelling Evidence for Creation & the Flood. rev. ed. (Illus.). 208p. 1996. 24.95 (*1-878026-06-2*); pap. 17.95 (*1-878026-05-4*) Ctr Sci Creation.

— In the Beginning: Compelling Evidence for Creation & the Flood. 6th rev. ed. (Illus.). 240p. 1995. pap. 17.95 (*1-878026-01-1*) Ctr Sci Creation.

— John Adams & the American Press: Politics & Journalism at the Birth of the Republic. LC 94-41569. 223p. 1995. lib. bdg. 38.50 (*0-89950-998-3*) McFarland & Co.

— The People vs. Lee Harvey Oswald. (Illus.). 656p. 1994. pap. 15.95 (*0-7867-0081-5*) Carroll & Graf.

— Referenced Index Guide to the Warren Commission. 304p. 1995. 30.00 (*1-887934-00-6*) Delmax.

Brown, Walt, Jr., ed. see Genet, Edmond C.

Brown, Walter, jt. auth. see Martin, Ruth.

Brown, Walter A. Psychological Care During Pregnancy & the Postpartum Period. fac. ed. LC 78-64644. 171p. pap. 53.10 (*0-7837-7505-9*, 204700100005) Bks Demand.

Brown, Walter C. Basic Mathematics. 133p. 1998. 15.96 (*1-56637-377-8*) Goodheart.

— Drafting for Industry. rev. ed. (Illus.). 704p. 1995. text 50.64 (*1-56637-048-5*) Goodheart.

— Lizards of the Genus Emoia (Scincidae) with Observations on Their Evolution & Biogeography. Iwamoto, Tomio, ed. (Memoirs of the California Academy of Sciences Ser.: No. 15). 94p. 1990. 25.00 (*0-940228-24-6*) Calif Acad Sci.

— Print Reading for Construction: Residential & Commercial. LC 96-47086. (Illus.). 276p. 1997. text 39.96 (*1-56637-355-7*) Goodheart.

— Print Reading for Industry. LC 94-17774. (Illus.). 404p. 1995. spiral bd. 38.64 (*1-56637-062-0*) Goodheart.

Brown, Walter C. & Walker, Ernest L. A Study of the Holy Ghost. 160p. (Orig.). 1996. pap. 5.95 (*1-56794-123-0*, C-2445) Star Bible.

Brown, Walter C., ed. see Gerrish, Howard H. & Dugger, William E., Jr.

Brown, Walter L. A Life of Albert Pike. LC 97-19116. (Illus.). 800p. 1997. 48.00 (*1-55728-469-5*) U of Ark Pr.

***Brown, Walter L. & Jackson, Phyllis S.** From the Heart. McKnight, Donna & Lee, Melinda, eds. LC 99-96984. (Illus.). 100p. 2000. pap. 9.95 (*0-9656473-2-3*) Brown Bear Pub.

Brown, Walter L., jt. auth. see Jackson, Phyllis S.

Brown, Walter R. Sea Disasters. LC 84-40788. (Illus.). 112p. (J). 1981. 11.95 (*0-201-09154-2*) HarpC Child Bks.

Brown, Walton J. Home at Last. 96p. pap. 7.99 (*0-8280-0887-6*) Review & Herald.

Brown, Walton J. & Woolsey, Raymond H. Angels. 177p. (Orig.). 1987. pap. 7.99 (*0-8280-0409-9*) Review & Herald.

An Asterisk (*) at the beginning of an entry indicates that the title is appearing for the first time.

Brown, Walton L. Democracy & Race in Brazil, Britain & the United States: Reaching for Higher Ground. LC 96-37776. 300p. 1997. text 89.95 (*0-7734-8729-8*) E Mellen.

Brown, Wanta L., jt. auth. see Goldin, Phyllis R.

Brown, Warren. Colin Powell: Military Leader. Huggins, Nathan I., ed. (Black Americans of Achievement Ser.). (Illus.). 124p. (YA). (gr. 5 up). 1992. lib. bdg. 19.95 (*0-7910-1647-1*) Chelsea Hse.

— Colin Powell: Military Leader. Huggins, Nathan I., ed. (Black Americans of Achievement Ser.). (Illus.). 124p. (YA). (gr. 5 up). 1992. pap. 8.95 (*0-7910-1648-X*) Chelsea Hse.

— Hampten Falls, NH. (Illus.). 637p. 1993. reprint ed. lib. bdg. 65.00 (*0-8328-3204-9*) Higginson Bk Co.

— Robert E. Lee. (World Leaders Past & Present Ser.). (Illus.). 120p. (YA). (gr. 5 up). 1982. pap. 8.95 (*0-7910-0698-0*) Chelsea Hse.

— Robert E. Lee. (World Leaders Past & Present Ser.). (Illus.). 120p. (YA). (gr. 5 up). 1992. lib. bdg. 19.95 (*1-55546-814-4*) Chelsea Hse.

— Robert E. Lee. (World Leaders Past & Present Ser.). 1992. 13.15 (*0-606-08078-3*) Turtleback.

***Brown, Warren, Jr., ed.** A Journey Towards Wisdom: The Source & Science of Spiritual Principles. (Laws of Life Symposia Ser.: No. 3). 372p. 1999. 22.95 (*1-890151-31-9*); pap. 14.95 (*1-890151-30-0*) Templeton Fnd.

***Brown, Warren H.** It's Fun to Remember: A King's Pine Autobiography. (Illus.). 98p. 1999. pap. write for info. (*0-9676957-0-8*) W H Brown.

Brown, Warren S., et al, eds. Whatever Happened to the Soul? Scientific & Theological Portraits of Human Nature. LC 98-37943. 272p. 1998. pap. 19.00 (*0-8006-3141-2*, 1-3141) Augsburg Fortress.

Brown-Watson, Abby V. Still Kicking: Restorative Groups for Frail Older Adults. LC 98-36865. (Illus.). 304p. 1998. 36.95 (*1-878812-48-3*) Hlth Prof Pr.

Brown, Wayne. Prophetic Significance of the Different Church Doctrines: The Prophecies of Jesus, Peter & Paul. LC 97-40894. 203p. 2000. pap. 27.00 (*1-56072-480-3*, Nova Troitsa Bks) Nova Sci Pubs.

Brown, Wayne, ed. see Gallagher, Kathy.

Brown, Wells, & Jacobs Staff. Toy Story: A Pop-Up Book. LC 95-74735. 10p. (J). 1995. 13.95 (*0-7868-3084-0*, Pub. by Disney Pr) Time Warner.

Brown, Wendi-Starr, jt. auth. see Northern, Tamara.

Brown, Wendy. States of Injury: Power & Freedom in Late Modernity. LC 94-24068. 219p. 1995. text 45.00 (*0-691-02990-3*, Pub. by Princeton U Pr); pap. text 13.95 (*0-691-02989-X*, Pub. by Princeton U Pr) Cal Prin Full Svc.

Brown, Wendy, ed. see Browne, Allan, et al.

Brown, Wendy, ed. see Foster, Twila L. & Tufts, Robert R.

Brown, Wendy L. Manhood & Politics: A Feminist Reading in Political Thought. LC 87-12850. (New Feminist Perspectives Ser.). 248p. 1988. 66.00 (*0-8476-7576-9*); pap. 23.00 (*0-8476-7577-7*) Rowman.

Brown, Wendy L., ed. see Adler, Betsy B., et al.

Brown, Wendy L., ed. see Allen, Jamerson C.

Brown, Wendy L., ed. see Bradus, Gary L., et al.

Brown, Wendy L., ed. see Brennan, Lynne, et al.

Brown, Wendy L., ed. see Brown, Matthew D., et al.

Brown, Wendy L., ed. see Burgess, David C., et al.

Brown, Wendy L., ed. see Schug, Charles.

Brown, Wendy L., ed. see Tufts, Robert R.

Brown, Wes, jt. auth. see Brown, Jim.

Brown, Wesley. Darktown Strutters. LC 93-72463. 225p. (Orig.). (C). 1994. pap. text 11.95 (*0-943433-11-8*) Cane Hill Pr.

***Brown, Wesley.** Darktown Strutters: A Novel. 2000. pap. 16.95 (*1-55849-270-4*) U of Mass Pr.

Brown, Wesley. Early Intervention Regulation: Annotation & Analysis. expanded rev. ed. LC 93-47535. 306p. 1994. ring bd. 51.00 (*0-934753-98-9*) LRP Pubns.

Brown, Wesley, ed. The Teachers & Writers Guide to Frederick Douglass. (Illus.). 128p. (Orig.). 1995. pap. 12.95 (*0-915924-46-3*) Tchrs & Writers Coll.

Brown, Wesley & Ling, Amy, eds. Imagining America: Stories from the Promised Land. LC 91-26828. 384p. 1991. pap. 11.95 (*0-89255-167-4*) Persea Bks.

— Visions of America: Personal Narratives from the Promised Land. LC 92-11725. 384p. 1992. 29.95 (*0-89255-173-9*); pap. 11.95 (*0-89255-174-7*) Persea Bks.

Brown, Wesley A. Coker: A Mountain Man's Story. LC 97-66574. 288p. 1997. 17.95 (*0-9636845-8-2*) Senior Pr.

Brown Widdison. Electronic Image Bank-General Psychology. 2nd ed. 1995. (*0-697-29647-4*, WCB McGr Hill) McGrw-H Hghr Educ.

Brown, Wilkes. Images of Family Life in Magazine Advertising: 1920-1978. LC 81-14366. 131p. 1981. 45.00 (*0-275-90587-X*, C0587, Praeger Pubs) Greenwood.

Brown, Will C. Caprock Rebel. large type ed. (Sagebrush Large Print Westerns Ser.). 192p. 1996. lib. bdg. 17.95 (*1-57490-013-7*) T T Beeler.

— The Kelly Man. LC 96-6550. (Sagebrush Large Print Westerns Ser.). 1997. lib. bdg. 17.95 (*1-57490-110-9*) T T Beeler.

***Brown, Will C.** Nameless Breed. 2000. mass mkt. 5.99 (*0-425-17399-2*) Berkley Pub.

Brown, Will C. The Nameless Breed. large type ed. LC 98-29044. 1998. 30.00 (*0-7838-0337-0*) Thorndike Pr.

***Brown, Will C.** Think Fast Ranger. 1999. pap. 19.00 (*0-7540-8061-7*) Chivers N Amer.

Brown, Will C. Think Fast, Ranger! large type ed. LC 97-44871. (Nightingale Ser.). 274p. 1998. pap. 18.95 (*0-7838-8378-1*, G K Hall & Co) Mac Lib Ref.

***Brown, Will C.** Trouble on the Brazos. large type ed. LC 99-55722. (G. K. Hall Nightingale Ser.). 2000. pap. 20.95 (*0-7838-8850-3*, G K Hall & Co) Mac Lib Ref.

Brown, Will K., jt. auth. see Watt, John R.

Brown, Willard J. The Signal Corps, U. S. A. in the War of the Rebellion. LC 74-4670. (Telecommunications Ser.). (Illus.). 916p. 1974. reprint ed. 89.95 (*0-405-06036-X*) Ayer.

Brown, William. Baseballs' Fabulous Montreal Royals. (Illus.). 224p. 1996. pap. text 14.99 (*1-895854-64-4*) Genl Dist Srvs.

— The Conversion & Seasoning of Wood. LC 89-32562. (Illus.). 222p. 1989. reprint ed. pap. 16.95 (*0-941936-14-7*) Linden Pub Fresno.

— Petroleum Prices: Past, Present & Prospective. 135p. 1987. pap. text 10.00 (*1-55813-003-9*) Hudson Instit IN.

— The Tabernacle: Its Priests & Its Services. rev. ed. 220p. 1996. 19.95 (*1-56563-195-1*) Hendrickson MA.

— The Tabernacle: Its Priests & Its Services. rev. ed. 220p. 1996. pap. 12.95 (*1-56563-229-X*) Hendrickson MA.

Brown, William A. Christian Theology in Outline. LC 75-41044. (BCL Ser. II). reprint ed. 51.50 (*0-404-14648-1*) AMS Pr.

Brown, William A., Jr. England & the New Gold Standard: 1919-1926. Wilkins, Mira, ed. LC 78-3901. (International Finance Ser.). (Illus.). 1979. reprint ed. lib. bdg. 31.95 (*0-405-11206-8*) Ayer.

— The International Gold Standard Reinterpreted, 1914-1934, 2 vols. reprint ed. 110.00 (*0-404-04645-2*) AMS Pr.

— The International Gold Standard Reinterpreted, 1914-1934, 2 vols., 1. (General Ser.: No. 37). 1940. reprint ed. mic. film 80.00 (*0-685-61203-1*) Natl Bur Econ Res.

— The International Gold Standard Reinterpreted, 1914-1934, 2 vols., 2. (General Ser.: No. 37). 1940. reprint ed. mic. film 80.00 (*0-685-61204-X*) Natl Bur Econ Res.

— The International Gold Standard Reinterpreted, 1914-1934, 2 vols., Vol. 1. (General Ser.: No. 37). 776p. 1940. reprint ed. 160.00 (*0-87014-036-1*) Natl Bur Econ Res.

Brown, William B. Fenton: Family History of Jeremiah Fenton (1764-1841), of Adams Co., Ohio, & His Descendants. (Illus.). 206p. 1997. reprint ed. pap. 31.50 (*0-8328-8548-7*); reprint ed. lib. bdg. 41.50 (*0-8328-8547-9*) Higginson Bk Co.

***Brown, William C.** The Evolutionary Science of Extraterrestrial Life. 150p. 2000. pap. text 20.00 (*1-55605-306-1*) Wyndham Hall.

Brown, William C. The Literary Primer. 97p. (Orig.). 1994. pap. 9.95 (*0-9642156-0-8*) QCorp.

— Matrices & Vector Spaces. (Pure & Applied Mathematics Ser.: Vol. 145). (Illus.). 328p. 1991. text 69.75 (*0-8247-8419-7*) Dekker.

— Matrices over Commutative Rings. LC 92-29098. (Pure & Applied Mathematics Ser.: Vol. 169). (Illus.). 296p. 1992. text 155.00 (*0-8247-8755-2*) Dekker.

Brown, William C., Jr. & Abraham, Amy. Ready, Aim . . . Retire! 50p. (Orig.). 1993. pap. 19.95 incl. VHS (*0-9638898-0-X*) C Brown.

Brown, William C., et al. Mary Moses' Statement. (Illus.). 70p. 1990. 17.95 (*0-87770-453-8*) Ye Galleon.

Brown, William D. Advanced Electronic Packaging: With Emphasis on Multichip Modules. LC 98-33575. (Microelectronic Systems Ser.). 1998. 110.95 (*0-7803-4700-5*) IEEE Comp Soc.

— The Way to the Uncle Sam Hotel. (Orig.). 1966. pap. 2.75 (*0-940556-00-6*) Coyote.

Brown, William D. & Brewer, Joe E., eds. Nonvolatile Semiconductor Memory Technology: A Comprehensive Guide to Understanding & Using NVSM Devices. LC 97-19691. (IEEE Press on Microelectronic Systems Ser.). 616p. 1997. 99.95 (*0-7803-1173-6*, PC5644) Inst Electrical.

Brown, William E. Alaska National Parklands: This Last Treasure. LC 82-71677. (Illus.). 128p. 1982. 7.95 (*0-685-05859-X*) Alaska Natural.

— Denali, Symbol of the Alaskan Wild: An Illustrated History of the Denali-Mount McKinley Region, Alaska. LC 93-569. (Illus.). 1993. write for info. (*0-89865-860-8*) Donning Co.

— A History of Russian Literature of the Romantic Period, 4 vols., I. 1700p. 1986. write for info. (*0-88233-939-7*) Ardis Pubs.

— A History of Russian Literature of the Romantic Period, 4 vols., II. 1700p. 1986. write for info. (*0-88233-940-0*) Ardis Pubs.

— A History of Russian Literature of the Romantic Period, 4 vols., III. 1700p. 1986. write for info. (*0-88233-941-9*) Ardis Pubs.

— A History of Russian Literature of the Romantic Period, 4 vols., IV. 1700p. 1986. write for info. (*0-88233-942-7*) Ardis Pubs.

— A History of Russian Literature of the Romantic Period, 4 vols., Set. 1700p. 1986. 40.00 (*0-88233-938-9*) Ardis Pubs.

— Islands of Hope: Parks & Recreation in Environmental Crisis. LC 76-168481. 196p. reprint ed. pap. 60.80 (*0-7837-1549-8*, 204183700024) Bks Demand.

Brown, William E., ed. Plastics in Food Packaging: Properties, Design & Fabrication. (Packaging & Converting Technology Ser.: Vol. 5). (Illus.). 544p. 1992. text 199.00 (*0-8247-8685-8*) Dekker.

Brown, William E. & Heinze, Ruth-Inge. Denali, Symbol of the Alaskan Wild: An Illustrated History of the Denali-Mount McKinley Region, Alaska. LC 93-569. (Illus.). 223p. 1993. pap. 29.95 (*0-89865-861-6*) Donning Co.

Brown, William E. & Lamperti, Giovanni B. Vocal Wisdom. Strongin, Lillian, ed. (Illus.). 1957. pap. 9.95 (*0-8008-8023-4*, Crescendo) Taplinger.

Brown, William E., jt. auth. see Howard, Gary C.

Brown, William E., jt. auth. see Phillips, W. Gary.

***Brown, William F.** ERISA Fiduciary Answer Book: Special Supplement, Forms & Worksheets LC 99-186262. (Panel Answer Book Ser.). 1999. write for info. (*0-7355-0261-7*) Panel Pubs.

Brown, William F. Helping Hands Across the Galaxy. LC 92-93886. (Illus.). 110p. 1994. pap. 15.00 (*1-881936-17-1*) WFB Ent.

— Love Merry-Go-Round. 116p. 1999. pap. 25.00 (*1-881936-13-9*) WFB Ent.

Brown, William F., Jr. Micromagnetics. LC 78-2342. 154p. 1979. reprint ed. lib. bdg. 18.50 (*0-88275-665-6*) Krieger.

Brown, William F. Rattlesnake Tales: Fact & Fiction about Texas Diamondback Rattlers. (Illus.). 134p. 1999. pap. 15.00 (*1-881936-22-8*) WFB Ent.

— True Texas Tales. LC 92-93887. (Illus.). 64p. (Orig.). (YA). (gr. 4 up). 1992. per. 8.75 (*1-881936-14-7*) WFB Ent.

— True Texas Tales Teacher's Guide to Student Activities. 24p. 1995. pap. text, teacher ed. 3.50 (*1-881936-21-X*) WFB Ent.

Brown, William F. & Bolton, Charles F. Clinical Electromyography. 2nd ed. (Illus.). 810p. 1993. text 170.00 (*0-7506-9204-9*) Buttrwrth-Heinemann.

Brown, William F. & Gadzella, Bernadette. Study Skills Test. 28p. (Orig.). (YA). 1987. pap. text 3.50 (*1-881936-15-5*) WFB Ent.

Brown, William F. & Holtzman, Wayne H. A Guide to College Survival. (Illus.). 85p. 1987. pap. text 8.00 (*0-937734-12-8*) ACT.

Brown, William F. & Wait, Gregory D. ERISA Fiduciary Answer Book: Forms & Worksheets. annuals 500p. pap. 96.00 (*1-56706-812-X*, 6812X) Panel Pubs.

Brown, William F., et al. CAI Study Skills Notebook. 30p. (Orig.). (C). 1992. pap. text 5.00 (*1-881936-16-3*) WFB Ent.

— Computer-Assisted Study Skills Improvement Program Manual of Directions. rev. ed. 24p. 1995. pap. text 3.50 (*1-881936-19-8*) WFB Ent.

Brown, William G. History of Nicholas County, West Virginia. 425p. 1994. reprint ed. lib. bdg. 42.50 (*0-8328-4152-8*) Higginson Bk Co.

— The Lower South in American History. LC 69-13843. 271p. 1969. reprint ed. lib. bdg. 35.00 (*0-8371-0925-6*, BRO&, Greenwood Pr) Greenwood.

— The Lower South in American History. (BCL1 - United States Local History Ser.). 271p. 1991. reprint ed. text 79.00 (*0-7812-6283-6*) Rprt Serv.

— The Lower South in American History. LC 71-108464. 1970. reprint ed. 15.00 (*0-403-00446-2*) Scholarly.

— On the Enumeration of Non-Planar Maps. LC 52-42839. (American Mathematical Society Ser.: No. 65). (Illus.). 44p. pap. 30.00 (*0-608-05168-3*, 205258900001) Bks Demand.

Brown, William G., ed. Reviews in Graph Theory (1940-78), 4 vols., Set. LC 80-17817. 2035p. 1980. pap. 401.00 (*0-8218-0214-3*, REVGRAPH) Am Math.

— Reviews in Graph Theory, (1940-78), 4 vols., Vol. 1. LC 80-17817. 588p. 1980. pap. 135.00 (*0-8218-0210-0*, REVGRA/1) Am Math.

— Reviews in Graph Theory, (1940-78), 4 vols., Vol. 2. LC 80-17817. 546p. 1980. pap. 135.00 (*0-8218-0211-9*, REVGRA/2) Am Math.

— Reviews in Graph Theory, (1940-78), 4 vols., Vol. 3. LC 80-17817. 574p. 1980. pap. 135.00 (*0-8218-0212-7*, REVGRA/3) Am Math.

— Reviews in Graph Theory, (1940-78), 4 vols., Vol. 4. LC 80-17817. 327p. 1980. pap. 82.00 (*0-8218-0213-5*, REVGRA/4) Am Math.

***Brown, William H.** Deadly Deceit: A Holly Slade Novel. 348p. 1999. pap. 10.95 (*0-9675439-0-8*) Vicki Brown.

Brown, William H. How to Stop the Corporate Polluters. (Illus.). 1972. pap. 1.50 (*0-88388-020-2*) Bellerophon Bks.

— Introduction to Organic & Biochemistry. 2nd ed. 1979. 18.25 (*0-87150-719-6*, WG 4191); 5.25 (*0-87150-720-X*, WG 4196) PWS Pubs.

***Brown, William H.** Introduction to Organic Chemistry. 2nd ed. LC 99-62547. 1999. text 96.00 (*0-03-025988-6*) HarBrace.

— Introduction to Organic Chemistry. 2nd ed. LC 99-62547. 672p. 1999. 65.00 (*0-03-031161-6*, Pub. by SCP) Harcourt.

Brown, William H. Ira & Isabella: or The Natural Children. LC 78-64067. reprint ed. 37.50 (*0-404-17393-4*) AMS Pr.

***Brown, William H.** The Kinetics of Solvolysis of 2-Chloro-2-Methylpropane. Jeffers, Joe, ed. (Modular Laboratory in Chemistry Ser.). 8p. (C). 1999. pap. text 1.75 (*0-87540-733-1*, KINE 733-1) Chem Educ Res.

Brown, William H. The Power of Sympathy. (Masterworks of Literature Ser.). 1970. write for info. (*0-8084-0345-1*); pap. 15.95 (*0-8084-0346-X*) NCUP.

— Selected Poems & Verse Fables, Seventeen Eighty-Four to Seventeen Ninety-Two. Walser, Richard, ed. LC 82-2660. 94p. 1982. 23.50 (*0-87413-223-1*) U Delaware Pr.

***Brown, William H.** Student Solutions Guide to Accompany Introduction to Organic Chemistry. 2nd ed. 312p. (C). 1999. pap. text, student ed. 30.00 (*0-03-026009-4*) SCP.

Brown, William H. Studying the Kinetics of the Solvolysis of 2-Chloro-2-Methylpropane. Neidig, H. Anthony, ed. (Modular Laboratory Program in Chemistry Ser.). 12p. (C). 1993. pap. text 1.50 (*0-87540-429-4*, KINE 429-4) Chem Educ Res.

— Test Bank to Accompany Introduction to Organic Chemistry. 2nd ed. 200p. (C). 1999. pap. text 44.50 (*0-03-026011-6*) Harcourt Coll Pubs.

Brown, William H., ed. History of Warren County. (Illus.). 302p. 1997. reprint ed. lib. bdg. 37.50 (*0-8328-6267-3*) Higginson Bk Co.

Brown, William H. & Conroy, Maureen A., eds. Inclusion of Preschool Children with Developmental Delays in Early Childhood Programs. unabridged ed. (Illus.). 125p. 1997. pap. text 12.00 (*0-942388-22-4*) So Early Chldhood Assn.

Brown, William H. & Foster, Hannah W. The Power of Sympathy & the Coquette. Mulford, Carla, ed. & intro. by. LC 96-5347. (Penguin Classics Ser.). 384p. 1996. pap. 13.95 (*0-14-043468-2*, Penguin Bks) Viking Penguin.

Brown, William H., III, et al. Issues & Answers in Vascular Surgery, Vol. 1. (Orig.). 1985. pap. 47.50 (*0-935717-00-5*) Mercury Pub.

— Issues & Answers in Vascular Surgery, Vol. II. 200p. (Orig.). 1986. pap. 47.50 (*0-935717-01-3*) Mercury Pub.

Brown, William H., et al. Issues & Answers in Vascular Surgery, Vol. III. 240p. (Orig.). 1988. pap. 52.50 (*0-935717-02-1*) Mercury Pub.

Brown, William H., jt. auth. see Dziegielewska, K. M.

Brown, William Houston. Bankruptcy Exemption Manual. LC 98-128457. (West's Bankruptcy Ser.). 555 p. 1997. write for info. (*0-314-22922-1*) West Pub.

Brown, William J. Basic Corporate Shareholder Taxation. LC 96-22718. (Casebook Ser.). 1996. 50.00 (*0-8205-2491-3*) Bender.

— The Life of William J. Brown, of Providence, R. I. With Personal Recollections of Incidents in Rhode Island. LC 78-164382. (Black Heritage Library Collection). 1977. reprint ed. 22.95 (*0-8369-8841-8*) Ayer.

— Understanding Corporate-Shareholder Taxation. LC 88-62368. 155p. 1989. pap. 20.00 (*0-916081-16-8*) J Marshall Pub Co.

Brown, William J., et al. Antipatterns: Refactoriy Software Architectures & Projects in Crisis. LC 97-39023. 336p. 1998. 39.99 (*0-471-19713-0*) Wiley.

— AntiPatterns & Patterns in Software Configuration Management. LC 99-10822. 336p. 1999. 44.99 (*0-471-32929-0*) Wiley.

***Brown, William J., et al.** AntiPatterns in Project Management. 416p. 2000. 49.99 (*0-471-36366-9*) Wiley.

Brown, William J., et al. Syphilis & Other Venereal Diseases. LC 77-88803. 263p. reprint ed. pap. 81.60 (*0-608-15241-2*, 202917000059) Bks Demand.

Brown, William L., III. The Army Called It Home: Military Interiors of the 19th Century. (Illus.). 232p. (C). 1992. text 29.95 (*0-939631-42-3*) Thomas Publications.

Brown, William L. Mysticism: The Common Foundation of World Religion. unabridged ed. 52p. (Orig.). 1997. pap. 13.00 (*0-9657531-0-7*) Strange As Angels.

***Brown, William L., III.** Thoughts on Men's Shirts in America, 1750-1900. (Illus.). 128p. (C). 1999. pap. 20.00 (*1-57747-048-6*) Thomas Publications.

Brown, William L., ed. Feldspars & Feldspathoids: Structures, Properties & Occurences. 1984. text 252.50 (*90-277-1826-1*) Kluwer Academic.

Brown, William L., jt. auth. see Hilty, Steven L.

Brown, William M. Communism & Christianism. 252p. pap. 10.00 (*0-88286-045-3*) C H Kerr.

Brown, William M., III, et al, eds. The Directory of the World Landslide Inventory. (Illus.). 239p. (Orig.). 1993. pap. text 50.00 (*1-56806-402-0*) DIANE Pub.

Brown, William N. The Indian & Christian Miracles of Walking on the Water. LC 78-72381. reprint ed. 37.50 (*0-404-17243-1*) AMS Pr.

Brown, William N., ed. Resources for South Asian Language Studies in the United States: Report of a Conference Convened by the University of Pennsylvania for the United States Office of Education, January 15-16, 1960. LC 60-15611. 103p. reprint ed. pap. 32.00 (*0-608-11626-2*, 200289800015) Bks Demand.

Brown, William O. Daddy Must Die: True Story of Patricide. 192p. 1993. mass mkt. 3.95 (*0-87067-374-2*) Holloway.

Brown, William P. Character in Crisis: A Fresh Approach to the Wisdom Literature of the Old Testament. LC 95-50895. 190p. 1996. pap. 17.00 (*0-8028-4135-X*) Eerdmans.

***Brown, William P.** Ecclesiastes. LC 99-53620. (Interpretation Ser.). 112p. 2000. 21.95 (*0-8042-3146-X*, Pub. by Westminster John Knox) Presbyterian Pub.

Brown, William P. The Ethos of the Cosmos: The Genesis of Moral Imagination in the Bible. LC 98-50871. (Illus.). 458p. 1999. pap. 35.00 (*0-8028-4539-8*) Eerdmans.

***Brown, William P.** God Who Creates: Essays in Honor of W. Sibley Towner. 2000. pap. text 24.00 (*0-8028-4626-2*) Eerdmans.

Brown, William P. Obadiah Through Malachi. LC 96-17773. (Westminster Bible Companion Ser.). 200p. 1996. pap. 17.00 (*0-664-25520-5*) Westminster John Knox.

Brown, William P. & Sederberg, Kathryn. The Complete Dictionary of Media Times. 156p. 1986. pap. 14.95 (*0-913247-01-4*) CCH INC.

Brown, William R. The Horse of the Desert. (Documenta Hippologica Ser.). (Illus.). xxviii, 218p. 1977. reprint ed. 80.00 (*3-487-08142-3*) G Olms Pubs.

Brown, William R. & Warda, Mark. How to Start a Business in Texas. 2nd ed. LC 99-13348. (Legal Survival Guides Ser.). 144p. 1999. pap. 16.95 (*1-57071-365-0*) Sourcebks.

— How to Win in Small Claims Court in Texas. 2nd ed. LC 99-59255. (Legal Survival Guides Ser.). 176p. 2000. pap. 14.95 (*1-57248-111-0*, Sphinx Pubng) Sourcebks.

— Landlords' Rights & Duties in Texas. 2nd ed. LC 99-53002. (Legal Survival Guides Ser.). 208p. 2000. pap. 19.95 (*1-57248-110-2*, Sphinx Pubng) Sourcebks.

Brown, William R., jt. auth. see Bowen, B. A.

Brown, William S. Principles of Economics. LC 94-16366. 1104p. (C). 1994. mass mkt. 97.95 (*0-314-04229-6*) West Pub.

B

Brown, William S. Principles Of Macroeconomics. LC 94-16368. (SWC-Economics). 688p. (C). 1995. mass mkt. 72.95 (*0-314-04230-X*) West Pub.

Brown, William S. Principles of Microeconomics. LC 94-16367. 768p. (C). 1995. mass mkt. 72.95 (*0-314-04231-8*) West Pub.

Brown, William S., et al, eds. Organic Voice Disorders: Assessment & Treatment. LC 96-23807. (Illus.). 398p. (C). 1996. 55.00 (*1-56593-268-4*, 0590) Thomson Learn.

Brown, William T., ed. Atlas of Thoracoscopic Surgery. LC 93-36925. 1994. text 167.00 (*0-7216-3793-0*, W B Saunders Co) Harcrt Hlth Sci Grp.

Brown, William W. The Black Man: His Antecedents, His Genius, & His Achievements. 4th ed. LC 76-79018. 314p. 1977. reprint ed. 32.95 (*0-8369-8516-8*) Ayer.

— Black Man, His Antecedents, His Genius, & His Achievements. LC 77-82179. (Anti-Slavery Crusade in America Ser.). 1975. reprint ed. 18.95 (*0-405-00618-7*) Ayer.

— Clotel: Or, The President's Daughter. 1989. pap. 10.95 (*0-8216-0180-6*, Univ Books) Carol Pub Group.

— Clotel, or the President's Daughter. LC 75-75852. (American Negro: His History & Literature. Series 2). 1969. reprint ed. 27.95 (*0-405-01853-3*) Ayer.

— Clotel; or The President's Daughter: A Narrative of Slave Life in the United States. LC 96-762. (American History Through Literature Ser.). 216p. (C). (gr. 13). 1996. pap. 21.95 (*1-56324-804-2*) M E Sharpe.

— Clotelle: Or, the Colored Heroine. LC 71-81108. (Black Heritage Library Collection). 1977. 10.95 (*0-8369-8517-6*) Ayer.

— Estate Planning: A Practice Guide. LC 91-61219. 1992. ring bd. 135.00 (*0-685-59862-4*); disk 75.00 (*0-685-59861-6*) West Group.

— My Southern Home: The South & Its People. LC 70-78570. (Muckrakers Ser.). (Illus.). 260p. reprint ed. lib. bdg. 32.95 (*0-8398-0177-7*) Irvington.

— Narrative of William W. Brown. (American Biography Ser.). 98p. 1991. reprint ed. lib. bdg. 59.00 (*0-7812-8044-3*) Rprt Serv.

— Negro in the American Rebellion: His Heroism & His Fidelity. LC 78-79021. (Black Heritage Library Collection). 1977. 32.95 (*0-8369-8518-4*) Ayer.

— Negro in the American Rebellion: His Heroism & His Fidelity. 1971. pap. 3.95 (*0-8065-0238-X*, Citadel Pr) Carol Pub Group.

— The President's Daughter. (X Press Black Classics Ser.). 178p. 1996. pap. 9.95 (*1-874509-25-5*, Pub. by X Pr) LPC InBook.

— Rising Son: The Antecedents & Advancement of the Colored Race. LC 79-79008. (Black Heritage Library Collection). 1977. 41.95 (*0-8369-8519-2*) Ayer.

— Sketches of Places & People Abroad. LC 71-133149. (Black Heritage Library Collection). 1977. 28.95 (*0-8369-8705-5*) Ayer.

— The Travels of W. W. Brown: Narratives of William Wells Brown, & the American Fugitive in Europe, Sketches of Places & People Abroad. Jefferson, Paul, ed. LC 91-8667. (Illus.). 292p. (C). 1991. pap. text 14.95 (*1-55876-043-1*) Wiener Pubs Inc.

— Works of William Wells Brown, 3 vols. in 1. (B. E. Ser.: No. 73). 1858. 45.00 (*0-8115-3024-8*) Periodicals Srv.

Brown, William Walter, et al. Principles of Economics. 2nd aut. ed. (C). 1997. pap. text 37.00 (*0-201-34308-8*) Addison-Wesley.

***Brown, William Wells.** Clotel, or The President's Daughter. (Library Classics). 2000. pap. 10.95 (*0-679-78323-7*) Modern Lib NY.

Brown, William Wells. Clotel; or, The President's Daughter: A Narrative of Slave Life in the United States. LC 96-762. (American History Through Literature Ser.). 216p. (C). (gr. 13). 1996. 68.95 (*1-56324-803-4*) M E Sharpe.

***Brown, William Wells.** The Escape: or A Leap for Freedom. (Americana Series). 45p. 2000. reprint ed. pap. 4.95 (*0-937657-53-0*) Feedbk Theabks & Prospero.

***Brown, William Wells & Ernest, John.** The Escape: or A Leap for Freedom: A Drama in Five Acts. LC 00-9484. 2000. pap. write for info. (*1-57233-106-2*) U of Tenn Pr.

Brown, Willie C. Reaching Your Full Potential: Success in College & Life. LC 98-16690. 432p. (C). 1998. pap. text 31.60 (*0-13-956814-X*) P-H.

Brown, Wilmott G. The Significance of Lourdes, Fatima, & Medjugorje As Explained in Scripture. LC 95-94530. (Illus.). 72p. (Orig.). 1995. pap. 1.50 (*0-9647294-0-7*) W G Brown.

Brown, Wilson H., jt. auth. see Hogendorn, Jan S.

Brown, Woodlief. A Long Narrow Strip of Land. (Illus.). 97p. 1998. lib. bdg. 24.95 (*0-9670760-0-5*) H V Chapman.

Brown, Wyn, ed. Light Scattering: Principles & Development. LC 95-45401. (Monographs on the Physics & Chemistry of Materials). (Illus.). 544p. (C). 1996. text 175.00 (*0-19-851783-1*, Clarendon Pr) OUP.

***Brown, Wyn & Mortensen, Kell, eds.** Scattering in Polymeric & Colloidal Systems. 496p. 2000. text 140.00 (*90-5699-260-0*, G & B Science) Gordon & Breach.

Brown, Yelanda M., ed. see Williams, Shirley.

***Brown, Zahn.** Mcse Testprep Software: Elective Exams. 48p. 1998. pap. text 49.99 (*1-56205-900-9*) Pearson Educ.

***Brownback, Sam, ed.** Are Military Adultery Standards Changing? What Are the Implications? Congressional Hearing. (Illus.). 102p. (C). 2000. reprint ed. pap. text 25.00 (*0-7881-8684-1*) DIANE Pub.

Brownbridge, Martin, et al. Banking in Africa: The Impact of Financial Sector Reform since Independence. LC 98-22728. 1998. 79.95 (*0-86543-692-4*); pap. 21.95 (*0-86543-693-2*) Africa World.

Brownd, Elizabeth K. Cattitudes: From A to Z. LC 98-156048. 64p. 1998. pap. 8.95 (*0-14-026874-X*) Viking Penguin.

— Decorative Prints for Children's Rooms: A Portfolio of Six Self-Matted Full Color Prints. (Illus.). (J). (gr. k-3). 1993. pap. 3.95 (*0-486-27711-9*) Dover.

— My Teddy Bear Diary. (Illus.). (J). (gr. k-3). 1992. pap. 1.00 (*0-486-27206-0*) Dover.

Brownd, Elizabeth King. Panda-Sticker Paper Doll. (Illus.). (J). 1991. pap. text 1.00 (*0-486-26614-1*) Dover.

Browne. Handbook of Early Prediction & Prevention of Child Abuse. text. write for info. (*0-471-49122-5*) Wiley.

Browne. Recombinant Cell Surface Receptors. 223p. 1997. 74.00 (*0-12-137765-2*) Acad Pr.

Browne, ed. Sortes Astrampsychi Vol. I: Ecdosis. (GRE.). 1983. 24.95 (*3-322-00143-1*, T1002, Pub. by B G Teubner) U of Mich Pr.

***Browne & Crist.** Confined Space Rescue. 2nd ed. (Fire Science Ser.). 256p. (C). 1999. pap. 34.95 (*0-8273-8559-5*) Delmar.

Browne, et al. Beyond the Crystal Cave. 1983. 5.50 (*0-394-53004-7*) Random.

— Production Management Systems: An Integrated Perspective. 2nd ed. LC 95-26032. 425p. (C). 1996. 72.95 (*0-201-42297-2*) Addison-Wesley.

Browne, jt. auth. see Gordon Staff.

Browne, A. Gorila. 1995. 12.99 (*968-16-3650-3*) Lectorum Pubns.

Browne, A. & Norton-Wayne, L. Vision & Information Processing for Automation. (Illus.). 498p. (C). 1986. 115.00 (*0-306-42245-X*, Plenum Trade) Perseus Pubng.

Browne, A. G. Recent Advances in Chemistry of B-Lactam Antibiotics, No. 52. 3rd ed. 1988. 122.00 (*0-85186-955-6*) CRC Pr.

Browne, Alix, ed. see Gan, Stephen.

Browne, Allan. Competitive Business Practices. 2nd ed. Giacomini, Edward D., ed. LC 91-70523. Orig. Title: Attorney's Guide to Competitive Business Practices. 829p. 1991. text 115.00 (*0-88124-359-0*, BU-31650) Cont Ed Bar-CA.

***Browne, Allan, et al.** Competitive Business Practices - 12/99 Update. 2nd ed. Brown, Wendy, ed. LC 91-70523. 382p. 1999. pap. text 84.00 (*0-7626-0384-4*, BU-31658) Cont Ed Bar-CA.

Browne, Angela. When Battered Women Kill. 240p. 1989. pap. 12.95 (*0-02-903881-2*) Free Pr.

Browne, Anita. The One Hundred Best Books by American Women, 1833-1933. 1985. 250.00 (*0-8490-0767-4*) Gordon Pr.

Browne, Ann. Teaching Writing: Key Stage 1 & Before. (Stanley Thornes Teaching Primary English Ser.). (Illus.). 224p. 1999. pap. 29.50 (*0-7487-4041-4*) S Thornes Pubs.

Browne, Anne. Developing Language & Literacy 3-8. LC 96-215971. (One-Off Ser.). (Illus.). 296p. 1996. pap. (*1-85396-282-1*) Corwin Pr.

— Helping Children to Write. 176p. 1993. pap. 25.00 (*1-85396-224-4*, Pub. by P Chapman) Taylor & Francis.

Browne, Anthony. Cambios.Tr. of Changes. (SPA., Illus.). 28p. 1995. 12.99 (*968-16-4270-8*, Pub. by Fondo) Continental Bk.

— Cosas Que Me Gustan. Esteva, Carmen, tr. (Illus.). 20p. 1995. 12.99 (*968-16-3779-8*) Fondo.

— Un Cuento de Oso. Esteva, Carmen, tr.Tr. of Bear-y Tale. (SPA., Illus.). 24p. 1995. 6.99 (*968-16-4528-6*) Fondo.

— Gorila. (Illus.). 32p. Date not set. 12.99 (*968-16-3651-1*, Pub. by Fondo) Continental Bk.

— I Like Books. LC 88-8471. (Illus.). 24p. (Orig.). (J). (ps-1). 1989. pap. 5.99 (*0-394-84186-7*, Pub. by Knopf Bks Yng Read); lib. bdg. 13.99 (*0-394-94186-1*, Pub. by Knopf Bks Yng Read) Random.

— Me Gusta los Libros. Esteva, Carmen, tr. (SPA., Illus.). 20p. 1995. 12.99 (*968-16-3780-1*, Pub. by Fondo) Continental Bk.

— El Libro de los Cerdos.Tr. of Piggybook. (Illus.). 32p. 1995. 12.99 (*958-9093-33-7*, Pub. by Fondo) Continental Bk.

— El Libro del Osito. Esteva, Carmen, tr.Tr. of Little Bear Book. (SPA., Illus.). 24p. 1995. 6.99 (*968-16-4529-4*, Pub. by Fondo) Continental Bk.

— The Little Bear Book. (Illus.). 24p. (J). (ps). 1989. 4.95 (*0-385-26006-7*) Doubleday.

***Browne, Anthony.** My Dad. LC 99-47083. (J). 2000. write for info. (*0-7894-2681-1*) DK Pub Inc.

— My Dad. LC 00-37951. (Illus.). (J). 2001. write for info. (*0-374-35101-5*) FS&G.

Browne, Anthony. Piggybook. (J). 1986. 13.19 (*0-606-04771-9*, Pub. by Turtleback) Demco.

— Things I Like. LC 88-26632. (Illus.). 24p. (Orig.). (J). (ps-1). 1989. pap. 5.99 (*0-394-84192-1*, Pub. by Knopf Bks Yng Read) Random.

— El Tunel. (Illus.). 27p. 1996. 12.99 (*968-16-3971-5*, Pub. by Fondo) Continental Bk.

— Voices in the Park. LC 97-48730. 32p. (J). (gr. 2-5). 1998. 15.95 (*0-7894-2522-X*) DK Pub Inc.

— Willy & Hugh. LC 90-4938. (J). 1996. 12.19 (*0-606-10073-3*, Pub. by Turtleback) Demco.

— Willy el Campeon.Tr. of Willy the Champ. (SPA.). 32p. 1995. 12.99 (*968-16-3909-X*) Fondo.

— Willy el Mago (Willy the Wizzard) (SPA.). 28p. (J). (gr. 1-3). 1995. 12.99 (*968-16-5022-0*, Pub. by Fondo) Continental Bk.

— Willy el Sonador (Willy the Dreamer) (SPA.). 24p. (J). (gr. 1-3). 1997. 12.99 (*968-16-5277-0*, Pub. by Fondo) Continental Bk.

— Willy el Timido. (SPA., Illus.). 36p. (ps-3). 1995. 12.99 (*968-16-3653-8*, Pub. by Fondo) Continental Bk.

— Willy the Champ. 1995. 12.19 (*0-606-08386-3*, Pub. by Turtleback) Demco.

— Willy the Dreamer. (J). 1998. 16.99 (*0-7636-0617-0*) Candlewick Pr.

— Willy the Dreamer. LC 97-2135. (Illus.). 32p. (J). (ps-3). 1998. 16.99 (*0-7636-0378-3*) Candlewick Pr.

***Browne, Anthony.** Willy the Wizard. (J). 1998. 12.19 (*0-606-13919-2*, Pub. by Turtleback) Demco.

Browne, Anthony. Willy y Hugo.Tr. of Willy & Hugh. (SPA., Illus.). 32p. (ps-3). 1995. 12.99 (*968-16-4271-6*, Pub. by Fondo) Continental Bk.

***Browne, Anthony.** Willy's Pictures. LC 98-47804. (Illus.). 32p. (YA). (ps up). 1999. 16.99 (*0-7636-0962-5*) Candlewick Pr.

— Willy's Pictures. (Illus.). (J). 2000. 16.99 (*0-7636-1323-1*) Candlewick Pr.

Browne, Anthony. Zoologico.Tr. of Zoo. (SPA., Illus.). 28p. 1995. 12.99 (*968-16-4272-4*) Fondo.

Browne, Anthony, ed. Current Perspectives in Neural Computing. LC 97-31333. 1997. text 63.00 (*0-7503-0455-3*) IOP Pub.

Browne, Anthony M. Long Sunset. 400p. 1997. pap. 24.95 (*0-575-40040-4*, Pub. by V Gollancz) Trafalgar.

— Long Sunset: Memoirs of Winston Churchill's Last Private Secretary. LC 95-174752. 400p. 1997. 50.00 (*0-304-34478-8*, Pub. by V Gollancz) Trafalgar.

Browne, Antony, ed. Neural Network Analysis, Architectures & Applications. LC 97-31332. 263p. 1997. 63.00 (*0-7503-0499-5*) IOP Pub.

Browne, Arthur. A Compendious View of the Civil Law & of the Law of the Admirality: Being the Substance of a Course of Lectures Read in the University of Dublin, 1840. LC 99-18284. 2000. 175.00 (*1-886363-88-9*) Lawbk Exchange.

Browne, Barbara C. & Communication Skill Builders & VORT Corporation Editors. Developmental Play Group Guide. LC 95-161299. 286p. 1995. write for info. (*0-88450-171-X*) Commun Skill.

Browne, Barbara Cole, jt. auth. see Steeves, Kathleen Anderson.

Browne, Bernie. America Online & Best Web Sites: See the Best of Cyberspace & Get There with the Click of a Mouse. 4th rev. ed. Browne, Carolyn, ed. LC 98-92709. (Illus.). 480p. 1999. pap. 19.95 (*0-9634182-3-8*, Pub. by Byte Masters) Distributors.

— America Online & Best Web Sites Version 3: Featuring over 1000 Sites with Easy "Click & Go" Quick Access. LC 96-96854. (Illus.). 416p. (Orig.). 1997. pap. 19.95 (*0-9634182-7-0*) Byte Masters.

— Office Power with Personal Computers: Complete Highly Illustrated User's Guides & Smart Indexes for DOS BASICS, Windows 3.1, WordPerfect 5.1 (DOS), & Lotus 1-2-3 for Windows Plus Office Power Applications. LC 92-97506. (Illus.). 768p. (Orig.). 1993. pap. 19.95 (*0-9634182-0-3*) Byte Masters.

Browne, C., et al, eds. Northeastern Accelerator Personnel: Proceedings of the 20th Symposium. 560p. 1987. text 131.00 (*9971-5-0325-5*) World Scientific Pub.

Browne, C. A. Story of Our National Ballads. rev. ed. Heaps, Willard A., ed. LC 60-15255. (J). (gr. 5 up). 1960. 13.95 (*0-690-77707-8*) HarpC Child Bks.

Browne, C. A. & Luff, R. MCQs in Physiology. 176p. 1996. text 11.50 (*0-412-75640-4*, Pub. by E A) OUP.

***Browne, Cameron.** Hex Strategy: Making the Right Connections. LC 00-29334. (Illus.). 384p. 2000. pap. 38.50 (*1-56881-117-9*) AK Peters.

Browne, Carolyn, ed. see Browne, Bernie.

Browne, Caryl. The World Game: What It Is: The Rules for Playing. (Illus.). 118p. (Orig.). 1994. pap. text 6.50 (*0-9644390-0-X*) Software World.

Browne, Causten. A Treatise on the Construction of the Statute of Frauds: As in Force in England & the United States. 5th ed. cxxv, 687p. 1997. reprint ed. 195.00 (*1-56169-311-1*) Gaunt.

Browne, Chalres F., see Ward, Artemus, pseud.

Browne, Charles A. A Source Book of Agricultural Chemistry. Egerton, Frank N., 3rd, ed. LC 77-74205. (History of Ecology Ser.). 1978. reprint ed. lib. bdg. 25.95 (*0-405-10375-1*) Ayer.

Browne, Charles F. Artemus Ward: His Book. (Works of Charles Farrar Browne). 1989. reprint ed. lib. bdg. 79.00 (*0-7812-2091-2*) Rprt Serv.

— Artemus Ward: His Travels. (Works of Charles Farrar Browne). 1989. reprint ed. lib. bdg. 79.00 (*0-7812-2092-0*) Rprt Serv.

— Artemus Ward in London. (Works of Charles Farrar Browne). 1989. reprint ed. lib. bdg. 79.00 (*0-7812-2093-9*) Rprt Serv.

— Artemus Ward's Panorama. (Works of Charles Farrar Browne). 1989. reprint ed. lib. bdg. 79.00 (*0-7812-2096-3*) Rprt Serv.

— Complete Works of Artemus Ward. 1993. reprint ed. lib. bdg. 89.00 (*0-7812-5346-2*) Rprt Serv.

— Letters. (Works of Charles Farrar Browne). 1989. reprint ed. lib. bdg. 79.00 (*0-7812-2097-1*) Rprt Serv.

— The Mormans. (Works of Charles Farrar Browne). 1989. reprint ed. lib. bdg. 79.00 (*0-7812-2094-7*) Rprt Serv.

— Sandwiches by Artemus Ward. (Works of Charles Farrar Browne). 1989. reprint ed. lib. bdg. 79.00 (*0-7812-2095-5*) Rprt Serv.

Browne, Charles F., jt. auth. see Ward, Artemus, pseud.

Browne, Christopher. The Journalist's Handbook. unabridged ed. 192p. 1999. pap. 15.95 (*0-7136-4949-6*) A & C Blk.

— The Prying Game: The Sex, Sleaze, & Scandals of Fleet Street & the Media Mafia. (Illus.). 160p. 1996. 25.95 (*0-86051-927-9*, Robson-Parkwest) Parkwest Pubns.

Browne, Christopher & Bascand, Geoffrey M. Indonesia: Maintaining the Development Momentum, Vol. 155. LC 97-35060. (Occasional Paper/International Monetary Fund Ser.). 1997. write for info. (*1-55775-692-9*) Intl Monetary.

Browne, Christopher & Scott, Douglas A. Economic Development in Seven Pacific Island Countries. viii, 220p. 1989. pap. 18.00 (*1-55775-035-1*) Intl Monetary.

— Economic Development in Seven Pacific Island Countries. LC 88-29660. 230p. reprint ed. pap. 71.30 (*0-7837-1258-8*, 204139500020) Bks Demand.

Browne, Clare, ed. Silk Designs of the Eighteenth Century: From the Victoria & Albert Museum, London. LC 95-62053. (Illus.). 112p. 1996. pap. 19.95 (*0-500-27880-6*, Pub. by Thames Hudson) Norton.

Browne, Colin. Abraham. 1987. pap. 9.95 (*0-919626-33-5*, Pub. by Brick Bks) Genl Dist Srvs.

Browne, Collette V. Women, Feminism, & Aging: A New Look at Theory & Practice. LC 98-10304. (Focus on Women Ser.). 360p. 1998. 49.95 (*0-8261-1200-5*) Springer Pub.

Browne, Corinne, jt. auth. see Bodie, Scott.

Browne, Courtney. Tojo: The Last Banzai. LC 97-29822. (Illus.). 288p. 1998. reprint ed. pap. 14.95 (*0-306-80844-7*) Da Capo.

Browne, D., et al, eds. Treatment of Radiation Injuries. LC 90-14216. (Illus.). 260p. 1990. 79.50 (*0-306-43729-5*, Plenum Trade) Perseus Pubng.

Browne, D. A., et al, eds. High Performance Computing & Its Applications in the Physical Sciences: Proceedings of the Mardi Gras Symposium, 1993. 272p. 1994. text 86.00 (*981-02-1740-4*) World Scientific Pub.

Browne, D. Anne. You Can Get There from Here: Life Lessons on Growth & Self Discovery for the Black Woman. LC 95-77774. 204p. (Orig.). 1995. pap. 12.95 (*0-9638672-6-1*) Bryant & Dillon.

Browne, D. J. & Turnbull, D. Danger at Dunwater. 1982. 5.50 (*0-394-53003-9*) Random.

Browne, David. Teach Yourself . . . Pagemaker 5.0 for Windows. 89p. 1995. pap. 21.95 (*1-55828-245-9*, MIS Pr) IDG Bks.

— Teach Yourself . . . Pagemaker 5.0 for the MAC. 89p. 1995. pap. 21.95 (*1-55828-246-7*, MIS Pr) IDG Bks.

— Welcome to Desktop Publishing. 1995. pap. 19.95 (*1-55828-295-5*, MIS Pr) IDG Bks.

***Browne, David G.** A Millennium of Praise. 171p. 1999. pap. 9.99 (*1-84030-062-0*) Emerald House Group Inc.

Browne, David M. Roman Cambridgeshire. (Cambridge Town, Gown & County Ser.: Vol. 13). (Illus.). 1977. pap. 5.95 (*0-900891-09-2*) Oleander Pr.

Browne, Dennis J. M. 238p. 1992. 19.95 (*0-9614382-0-7*) Filmbook Pr.

Browne, Dik. The Best of Hagar. LC 85-72413. (Illus.). 240p. pap. 10.95 (*0-03-005599-7*) Comicana.

— Hagar: Again & Again. 128p. 1991. pap. 3.50 (*0-8125-1507-2*, Pub. by Tor Bks) St Martin.

— Hagar: Hear No Evil. (Illus.). 128p. 1992. pap. 3.50 (*0-8125-2043-2*, Pub. by Tor Bks) St Martin.

— Hagar: Motley Crew. 128p. 1992. pap. 3.50 (*0-8125-1544-7*, Pub. by Tor Bks) St Martin.

— Hagar: Pillage Idiot. 1989. pap. 2.95 (*0-8125-0605-7*, Pub. by Tor Bks) St Martin.

— Hagar: Room for One More. 128p. 1995. 3.50 (*0-8125-1437-8*, Pub. by Tor Bks) St Martin.

— Hagar: Sacking Paris on a Budget. 1990. pap. 2.95 (*0-8125-1022-4*, Pub. by Tor Bks) St Martin.

— Hagar & the Golden Maiden. 1989. pap. 2.95 (*0-8125-0560-3*, Pub. by Tor Bks) St Martin.

— Hagar the Horrible: Gangway. 1989. pap. 2.95 (*0-8125-0072-5*, Pub. by Tor Bks) St Martin.

— Hagar the Horrible: I See London, I See France... (Illus.). (Orig.). 1991. pap. 3.50 (*0-8125-1802-0*, Pub. by Tor Bks) St Martin.

— Hagar the Horrible: Pillage Idiot. 128p. (Orig.). (J). 1986. pap. 1.95 (*0-8125-6788-9*, Pub. by Tor Bks) St Martin.

— Hagar the Horrible: Special Delivery. 1992. pap. 3.50 (*0-8125-1543-9*, Pub. by Tor Bks) St Martin.

— Hagar the Horrible: Things That Go Bump. (Illus.). 128p. 1992. pap. 3.50 (*0-8125-1545-5*, Pub. by Tor Bks) St Martin.

— Hagar the Horrible's Very Nearly Complete Viking Handbook. LC 84-40314. (Illus.). 96p. (Orig.). 1985. pap. 5.95 (*0-89480-937-7*, 937) Workman Pub.

Browne, Dik & Walker, Mort. Hi & Lois: Mom, Where's My Homework? 288p. (Orig.). 1984. pap. 2.50 (*0-8125-6290-9*) Tor Bks.

Browne, Dik, jt. auth. see Walker, Mort.

Browne, Donald R. Electronic Media & Industrialized Nations: A Comparative Study. LC 98-55110. (Illus.). 576p. 1999. text 54.95 (*0-8138-0422-1*) Iowa St U Pr.

— International Radio Broadcasting: The Limits of the Limitless Medium. LC 81-22707. 369p. 1982. 89.50 (*0-275-90767-8*, C0767, Praeger Pubs) Greenwood.

Browne, Douglas G. Too Many Cousins. (Detective Stories Ser.). 192p. 1984. reprint ed. pap. 3.95 (*0-486-24774-0*) Dover.

Browne, E. English-Italian: Odd Pairs & False Friends: Dictionary of False Analogies & Ambiguous Affinities Between English & Italian. 267p. 1987. 57.75 (*88-08-02946-8*, Pub. by Zanichelli) IBD Ltd.

Browne, E. G. A Literary History of Persia, 4 vols., Set. (Illus.). 2268p. 1996. reprint ed. boxed set 395.00 (*0-7007-0406-X*, Pub. by Curzon Pr Ltd) Paul & Co Pubs.

— A Literary History of Persia: From the Earliest Times until Firdawsi; From Firdawsi to Sad'i; The Tartar Dominion (1265-1502); Modern Times, 4 vols. (C). 1997. 175.00 (*81-215-0753-7*, Pub. by M Manoharial) Coronet Bks.

Browne, E. Martin. Beginnings in Drama. LC 98-45635. 32p. (Orig.). 1994. pap. 5.00 (*0-88734-909-9*) Empire Pub Srvs.

Browne, E. Martin, ed. Religious Drama Vol. 2: 21 Medieval Mystery & Morality Plays. 1990. 18.00 (*0-8446-2793-3*) Peter Smith.

Browne, Edgar. Phiz & Dickens. LC 72-39035. (Studies in Dickens: No. 52). 320p. 1972. reprint ed. lib. bdg. 75.00 (*0-8383-1391-4*) M S G Haskell Hse.

An Asterisk (*) at the beginning of an entry indicates that the title is appearing for the first time.

Browne, Edgardo & Firestone, Richard B. Table of Radioactive Isotopes. LC 86-9069. 1056p. 1986. 350.00 (*0-471-84909-X*) Wiley.
Browne, Edmond C. The Coming of the Great Queen: A Narrative of the Acquisition of Burma. LC 77-87009. reprint ed. 38.50 (*0-404-16798-5*) AMS Pr.
Browne, Edna S. & Smith, Nelson A. Haven. 500p. 1994. 19.95 (*0-910523-19-3*) Grandin Bk Co.
Browne, Edward. A Book Named Hope: A Collection of Short Stories. v, 55p. 1997. 11.99 (*0-9659605-0-1*) Browne Books.
Browne, Edward G. A Literary History of Persia, 4 vols., Set. LC 96-44208. (Classics of Iranian Studies: No. 1). (Illus.). 2324p. 1996. lib. bdg. 275.00 (*0-936347-66-X*) IBEX.
— A Literary History of Persia Vol. I: From the Earliest Times until Firdawsi. LC 96-44208. (Classics of Iranian Studies: No. 1). (Illus.). 536p. 1996. lib. bdg. 75.00 (*0-936347-62-7*) IBEX.
— A Literary History of Persia Vol. II: From Firdawsi to Saadi. LC 96-44208. (Classics of Iranian Studies). (Illus.). 584p. 1996. lib. bdg. 75.00 (*0-936347-63-5*) IBEX.
— A Literary History of Persia Vol. III: The Tartar Dominion (1265-1502) LC 96-44208. (Classics of Iranian Studies: No. 1). (Illus.). 626p. 1996. lib. bdg. 75.00 (*0-936347-64-3*) IBEX.
— A Literary History of Persia Vol. IV: Modern Times (1500-1924) LC 96-44208. (Classics of Iranian Studies: No. 1). (Illus.). 578p. 1995. lib. bdg. 75.00 (*0-936347-65-1*) IBEX.
— The Persian Revolution of 1905-1909. LC 95-9633. (Illus.). 640p. 1995. reprint ed. 39.95 (*0-934211-45-0*) Mage Pubs Inc.
— The Press & Poetry of Modern Persia. (Illus.). xi, 357p. 1983. reprint ed. 35.00 (*0-933770-39-1*) Kalimat.
— A Year Amongst the Persians: Impressions As to the Life, Character, & Thought of the People of Persia. 3rd ed. LC 83-45722. reprint ed. 61.50 (*0-404-20046-X*) AMS Pr.
Browne, Edward G., tr. see Abdu'l-Baha.
Browne, Edward T., Jr. & Athey, Raymond. Vascular Plants of Kentucky: An Annotated Checklist. LC 91-2499. 200p. 1992. text 22.50 (*0-8131-1675-9*) U Pr of Ky.
Browne, Eileen. Handa's Surprise: Level Four, Green. LC 98-88069. (Reading Together Ser.). (Illus.). 32p. (J). 1999. pap. write for info. (*0-7636-0863-7*) Candlewick Pr.
— No Problem. LC 92-53134. (Illus.). 40p. (J). (ps up). 1993. 14.99 (*1-56402-200-5*) Candlewick Pr.
— La Sorpresa de Nandi (Nandi's Surprise) (SPA., Illus.). 28p. (J). (ps-1). pap. 6.95 (*980-257-196-2*, Pub. by Ediciones Ekare) Kane-Miller Bk.
— Tick-Tock. LC 93-927. (Illus.). 32p. (J). (ps up). 1994. 14.95 (*1-56402-300-1*) Candlewick Pr.
— Tick-Tock. LC 93-927. 1996. 11.19 (*0-606-09968-9*, Pub. by Turtleback) Demco.
— Tick-Tock. LC 93-927. (Illus.). 32p. (J). (ps-3). 1996. reprint ed. pap. 5.99 (*1-56402-608-6*) Candlewick Pr.
Browne, Elizabeth. The Disabled Disciple: Ministering in a Church Without Barriers. LC 96-78936. 144p. (Orig.). 1997. pap. 12.95 (*0-7648-0045-0*) Liguori Pubns.
Browne, Francis. Granny's Wonderful Chair. (Illus.). 24.95p. 1999. 24.95 (*1-85149-706-4*) Antique Collect.
Browne, Francis F. The Everyday Life of Abraham Lincoln. LC 94-45451. (Illus.). iv, 747p. 1995. pap. 20.00 (*0-8032-6115-2*, Bison Books) U of Nebr Pr.
Browne, Francis F., ed. Bugle Echoes. LC 75-116394. (Granger Index Reprint Ser.). 1977. 20.95 (*0-8369-6135-8*) Ayer.
— Golden Poems: By British & American Authors. LC 73-152146. (Granger Index Reprint Ser.). 1977. reprint ed. 29.95 (*0-8369-6249-4*) Ayer.
Browne, G. Lathom. Nelson: The Public & Private Life of Horatio Viscount Nelson. 762p. 1999. 24.95 (*1-888777-67-2*) Trident Pr Intl.
Browne, G. Orde. African Labourer. 240p. 1967. reprint ed. 35.00 (*0-7146-1706-7*, Pub. by F Cass Pubs) Intl Spec Bk.
Browne, Gary F., jt. auth. see Bee, Roger.
Browne, Gary L. Baltimore in the Nation, 1789-1861. LC 79-13180. 363p. reprint ed. pap. 112.60 (*0-7837-0311-2*, 204063300018) Bks Demand.
Browne, George H. Notes on Shakespeare's Versification. 4th ed. LC 78-39547. reprint ed. 20.00 (*0-404-01138-1*) AMS Pr.
Browne, George W. The Amoskeag Manufacturing County of Manchester: A History. (Illus.). 288p. 1996. reprint ed. lib. bdg. 39.00 (*0-8328-5057-8*) Higginson Bk Co.
— History of Hillsborough, 1735-1921, 2 vols. 1262p. 1997. reprint ed. lib. bdg. 129.00 (*0-8328-5995-8*) Higginson Bk Co.
Browne, George W., ed. Vital Records of Londonderry: Full & Accurate Transcript of Births, Marriages & Deaths...from the Earliest Date to 1910. (Illus.). 330p. 1998. reprint ed. lib. bdg. 39.50 (*0-8328-9721-3*) Higginson Bk Co.
Browne, George W., ed. see Webster, Kimball.
Browne, Gerald A. The Arousers. 208p. 1989. pap. 3.95 (*0-380-70417-X*, Avon Bks) Morrow Avon.
— 11 Harrowhouse. 320p. 1995. mass mkt. 5.99 (*0-446-60114-4*) Warner Bks.
— Hot Siberian. 432p. 1989. mass mkt. 4.95 (*0-380-70332-7*, Avon Bks) Morrow Avon.
— It's All Zoo. 224p. 1990. pap. 3.95 (*0-380-70419-6*, Avon Bks) Morrow Avon.
— Eighteen mm Blues. 384p. 1994. mass mkt. 5.99 (*0-446-36577-7*, Pub. by Warner Bks) Little.
— 19 Purchase Street. 480p. 1995. mass mkt. 6.50 (*0-446-36540-8*) Warner Bks.
— The Ravishers. 272p. 1990. mass mkt. 4.50 (*0-380-70418-8*, Avon Bks) Morrow Avon.
— Rush 929. 1998. pap. 23.95 (*1-55611-509-1*, Pub. by D I Fine) Penguin Putnam.
Browne, Glenn J., jt. auth. see Browne, Ray B.
Browne, Gordon. Beginnings & Beyond. 5th ed. LC 99-21476. 570p. (C). 1999. pap. text 67.95 (*0-8273-8420-3*) Delmar.
Browne, Gretta Curran. Tread Softly on my Dreams: Robert Emmet's Story. 704p. 1998. pap. 11.95 (*0-86327-648-2*, Pub. by Wolfhound Press) Irish Amer Bk.
Browne-Gutnik, Natalie, jt. auth. see Gutnik, Martin J.
Browne, H. Joseph Chamberlain. (Seminar Studies in History). 164p. (C). 1974. pap. text 7.50 (*0-582-35214-2*) Longman.
Browne, Harry. Cross Border Links Environmental Directory. 67p. 1997. pap. 5.95 (*0-911213-63-5*) Interhemisp Res Ctr.
— Cross Border Links Labor Directory, 1997: Citizen Diplomats Shaping Globalization. 3rd rev. ed. 60p. 1997. pap. 5.95 (*0-911213-59-7*) Interhemisp Res Ctr.
— Fail-Safe Investing: 30 Minutes to Lifelong Financial Security. LC 99-15902. 128p. 1999. text 15.95 (*0-312-24703-6*) St Martin.
— For Richer, for Poorer: Shaping U. S.-Mexican Integration. 128p. 1994. pap. 9.95 (*0-911213-47-3*) Interhemisp Res Ctr.
***Browne, Harry.** Great Libertarian Offer. 2000. pap. text 14.95 (*0-9656036-9-5*) LiamWorks.
— Great Libetarian Promise. text. write for info. (*0-312-25504-7*) St Martin.
Browne, Harry. How I Found Freedom in an Unfree World. 408p. 1976. mass mkt. 4.95 (*0-380-00423-2*, Avon Bks) Morrow Avon.
— How I Found Freedom in an Unfree World: A Handbook for Personal Liberty. 25th anniversary ed. 1998. 24.95 (*0-9656036-7-9*) LiamWorks.
— Spain's Civil War. 2nd ed. LC 96-16745. (Seminar Studies in History). (C). 1996. pap. text 14.06 (*0-582-28988-2*, Pub. by Addison-Wesley) Longman.
— Suez & Sinai. LC 72-101536. (Flashpoints Ser.). 136p. reprint ed. pap. 42.20 (*0-608-30139-6*, 200492000047) Bks Demand.
— Why Government Doesn't Work: How Reducing Government Will Bring Us Safer Cities, Better Schools, Lower Taxes, More Freedom, & Prosperity for All. LC 95-20251. 245p. 1995. 19.95 (*0-9656036-0-1*, 0965603601) LiamWorks.
Browne, Harry & Sims, Beth. Runaway America: U. S. Jobs & Factories on the Move. 149p. 1993. 11.95 (*0-911213-43-0*) Interhemisp Res Ctr.
Browne, Henry J. The Catholic Church & the Knights of Labor. LC 76-6326. (Irish Americans Ser.). (Illus.). 1976. reprint ed. 35.95 (*0-405-09323-3*) Ayer.
Browne, Howard. Halo in Brass. 223p. 1988. pap. 7.95 (*0-89366-278-X*) Ultramarine Pub.
— The Taste of Ashes. 221p. 1988. pap. 7.95 (*0-89366-277-1*) Ultramarine Pub.
***Browne, Irene, ed.** African American & Latina Women at Work: Race, Gender & Economic Inequality. LC 98-19536. (Illus.). 356p. (C). 1998. 39.95 (*0-87154-147-5*) Russell Sage.
Browne, Irving. Elements of the Law of Domestic Relations & of Employer & Employed. xxi, 162p. 1981. reprint ed. 32.50 (*0-8377-0321-2*, Rothman) W S Hein.
— Elements of the Law of Domestic Relations & of Employer & Employed. xxi, 162p. 1981. reprint ed. lib. bdg. 22.50 (*0-685-04376-2*) W S Hein.
— Humorous Phases of the Law. (Legal Recreations Ser.: Vol. 1). 1982. reprint ed. 32.50 (*0-8377-0323-9*, Rothman) W S Hein.
— Judicial Interpretation of Common Words & Phrases. LC 97-81140. vii, 538p. 1998. reprint ed. 78.00 (*1-57588-426-7*, 311690) W S Hein.
— Law & Lawyers in Literature. LC 82-82459. xv, 413p. 1982. reprint ed. 85.00 (*0-912004-22-3*) Gaunt.
— Law & Lawyers in Literature. xv, 413p. 1982. reprint ed. 42.50 (*0-8377-0329-8*, Rothman) W S Hein.
— Short Studies of Great Lawyers. iv, 382p. 1982. reprint ed. 42.50 (*0-8377-0330-1*, Rothman) W S Hein.
— Treatise on the Admissibility of Parol Evidence in Respect to Written Instruments. xlviii, 510p. 1982. reprint ed. 75.00 (*0-8377-0325-5*, Rothman) W S Hein.
Browne, J., et al, eds. It & Manufacturing Partnerships. LC 96-78116. (Advances in Design & Manufacturing Ser.: Vol. 7). 450p. (gr. 12). 1996. 112.00 (*90-5199-296-3*, 296-3) IOS Press.
Browne, J. Jason. A Holy Experiment II: The Resurrection of the Spirit of America. LC 94-96339. 256p. 1994. 21.95 (*0-9642667-1-7*) Visionary Pr.
— Miracle Moments. (Illus.). 176p. (Orig.). 1994. pap. 11.95 (*0-9642667-0-9*) Visionary Pr.
Browne, J. Orde. The Vanishing Tribes of Kenya: A Description of the Manners & Customs of the Primitive & Interesting Tribes Dwelling on the Vast Southern Slopes of Mount Kenya & Their Fast Disappearing Native Methods of Life. (B. E. Ser.: No. 148). 1925. 35.00 (*0-8115-3069-8*) Periodicals Srv.
Browne, J. Patrick, ed. Ohio Civil Rules Handbook, 1992. (Baldwin's Deskset Ser.). 699p. (Orig.). 1991. pap. 49.00 (*0-8322-0410-2*) Banks-Baldwin.
Browne, J. Ross. A Peep at Washoe: Sketches of Virginia City, N. T. (Illus.). 48p. 1986. 4.95 (*0-913814-77-6*) Nevada Pubns.
— A Trip to Bodie Bluff & the Dead Sea of the West in 1863. (Illus.). 1978. reprint ed. pap. 2.95 (*0-89646-076-2*) Vistabooks.
Browne, James. The Letter Book of James Brown of Providence, Merchant, 1735-1738. LC 75-164613. (Select Bibliographies Reprint Ser.). 1977. reprint ed. 15.95 (*0-8369-5897-7*) Ayer.
Browne, Jane, jt. auth. see Tomlinson, Theresa.
Browne, Jane J. The Food Lover's Handbook to the Southwest: Where to Find the Very Best Restaurants, Gourmet Shops, Outdoor Markets, Food Fiestas. (Illus.). 304p. 1992. pap. 16.95 (*1-55958-171-9*) Prima Pub.
Browne, Janet. Charles Darwin: Voyaging. LC 95-53319. 622p. (C). 1996. pap. text 18.95 (*0-691-02606-8*, Pub. by Princeton U Pr) Cal Prin Full Svc.
— The Secular Ark: Studies in the History of Biogeography. LC 82-17497. (Illus.). 273p. 1983. 50.00 (*0-300-02460-6*) Yale U Pr.
Browne, Janet, ed. see Darwin, Charles.
Browne, Jefferson B. Key West: The Old & the New. LC 72-14327. (Bicentennial Floridiana Facsimile & Reprint Ser.). (Illus.). 266p. 1973. reprint ed. 17.95 (*0-8130-0367-9*) U Press Fla.
***Browne, Jill C.** God Save Sweet Potato Queens. 2001. pap. 14.00 (*0-609-80619-X*, Pub. by Crown Pub Group) Random House.
Browne, Jill C. The Sweet Potato Queens' Book of Love. LC 98-41879. 224p. 1999. pap. 12.00 (*0-609-80413-8*, Crown) Crown Pub Group.
Browne, Jill Conner. Sweet Potato Queens' Book of Love. 224p. 1999. 18.00 (*0-609-60381-7*) Random Hse Value.
Browne, Jimmie, jt. auth. see McMahon, Chris.
Browne, John. The Marchants Aviso, 1589. McGrath, Patrick, ed. (Kress Library of Business & Economics Publication: No. 11). xxxvi, 64p. 1957. pap. 9.95 (*0-678-09906-5*) Kelley.
Browne, John H. South Africa: A Glance at Current Conditions. LC 70-76494. 238p. 1969. reprint ed. lib. bdg. 35.00 (*0-8371-1091-2*, BRS&, Greenwood Pr) Greenwood.
Browne, John R. Adventures in the Apache Country: A Tour Through Arizona & Sonora, with Notes on the Silver Regions of Nevada. LC 72-9430. (Far Western Frontier Ser.). (Illus.). 540p. 1973. reprint ed. 39.95 (*0-405-04961-7*) Ayer.
— Adventures in the Apache Country: A Tour through Arizona & Sonora, 1864. LC 74-83332. 313p. reprint ed. pap. 97.10 (*0-8357-5202-X*, 202555100044) Bks Demand.
— Report of the Debates in the Convention of California on the Formation of the State Constitution, in Sept. & Oct., 1849. LC 72-9431. (Far Western Frontier Ser.). 532p. 1973. reprint ed. 40.95 (*0-405-04962-5*) Ayer.
— Yusef: The Journey of the Frangi; a Crusade in the East. Davis, Moshe, ed. LC 77-70686. (America & the Holy Land Ser.). (Illus.). 1977. reprint ed. lib. bdg. 35.95 (*0-405-10232-1*) Ayer.
— Yusef: or The Journey of the Frangi: A Crusade in the East. (American Biography Ser.). 421p. 1991. reprint ed. lib. bdg. 89.00 (*0-7812-8045-1*) Rprt Serv.
Browne, Joseph. The Moon-Calf: or Accurate Reflections on the Consolidator. LC 93-36533. (Augustan Reprints Ser.: No. 269 (1991)). 1993. reprint ed. 14.50 (*0-404-70269-4*) AMS Pr.
Browne, Josephine. The Juridification of the Employment Relationship: A Study of the Impact of the Unfair Dismissals Acts 1977 & the Unfair Dismissals (Amendment) Act 1993. 376p. 1994. 72.95 (*1-85628-688-6*, Pub. by Avebry) Ashgate Pub Co.
***Browne, Joy.** Dating for Dummies: Browne,&Joy. 1999. audio 12.00 (*0-694-52073-X*) HarperAudio.
Browne, Joy. Dating for Dummies: Mini Edition. 1999. 4.95 (*0-7624-0631-3*) Running Pr.
***Browne, Joy.** It's a Jungle Out There, Jane: How to Understand the Male Animal in Your Life. 272p. 2000. reprint ed. pap. 13.00 (*0-609-80521-5*, Three Riv Pr) Crown Pub Group.
Browne, Joy. It's a Jungle Out There, Jane: Understanding the Male Animal. LC 99-36230. 272p. 1999. 23.00 (*0-609-60357-4*, Crown) Crown.
— The Nine Fantasies That Will Ruin Your Life & the Eight Realities That Will Save You. abr. ed. LC 98-36245. 272p. 1998. 23.00 incl. audio (*0-609-60354-X*, Three Riv Pr) Crown Pub Group.
***Browne, Joy.** Nine Fantasies That Will Ruin Your Life & the Eight Realities That Will Save You, Vol. 1. 1999. pap. 13.00 (*0-609-80473-1*) Crown.
Browne, Juanita. African American Lifestyles. 1998. 30.00 (*0-9638296-0-2*) Imani Kuumba.
— African American Literature. 30.00 (*0-9638296-3-7*) Imani Kuumba.
— African American Roots. 1997. 28.00 (*0-9638296-1-0*) Imani Kuumba.
— Black Woman. 1995. 13.00 (*0-9638296-5-3*) Imani Kuumba.
— I Thought I Heard My People Cry. 1996. 10.00 (*0-9638296-4-5*) Imani Kuumba.
Browne, Juanita K. Nuggets of Nevada County History. LC 83-23781. (Illus.). xii, 143p. (Orig.). 1983. pap. 10.50 (*0-915641-00-3*) Nevada County Hist Society.
— Sketches of Yesterday & Today in Nevada County. LC 88-22584. (Illus.). xii, 92p. (Orig.). 1988. pap. 17.50 (*0-915641-02-X*) Nevada County Hist Society.
— A Tale of Two Cities & a Train: History of the Nevada County Narrow Gauge Railroad 1874-1942. LC 87-60181. (Illus.). viii, 216p. 1990. pap. 14.50 (*0-915641-03-8*) Nevada County Hist Society.
— Thomasina & the Tommyknocker. LC 93-13732. (Illus.). viii, 85p. (Orig.). (J). (gr. 4-7). 1993. pap. 8.75 (*0-9636621-0-4*) Browne Bks.
Browne, Junius H. Four Years in Secessia. LC 72-125681. (American Journalists Ser.). 1971. reprint ed. 24.95 (*0-405-01656-5*) Ayer.
— The Great Metropolis: A Mirror of New York... LC 75-1833. (Leisure Class in America Ser.). (Illus.). 1975. reprint ed. 51.95 (*0-405-06902-2*) Ayer.
Browne, Kathryn W., jt. auth. see Gordon, Ann.
Browne, Kathryn W., jt. auth. see Gordon, Ann M.
Browne, Kathryn Williams, jt. auth. see Gordon, Ann M.
Browne, Kevin & Herbert, Martin. Preventing Family Violence. LC 96-28875. (Series in Family Psychology). 402p. 1997. 119.95 (*0-471-92771-6*) Wiley.
— Preventing Family Violence. LC 96-28875. (Series in Family Psychology). 250p. 1999. pap. text 35.00 (*0-471-94140-9*) Wiley.
Browne, Kevin, jt. ed. see Archer, John.
Browne, Kevin D. & Archer, John, eds. Human Aggression: Naturalistic Approaches. 240p. 1989. pap. 16.95 (*0-415-03037-4*); lib. bdg. 49.95 (*0-415-03036-6*) Routledge.
***Browne, Kingsley.** Divided Labours: An Evolutionary View of Women at Work. LC 99-28269. 80p. 1999. pap. text 9.95 (*0-300-08026-3*) Yale U Pr.
Browne, L. In the Track of the Bookworm. 1976. lib. bdg. 59.95 (*0-8490-2046-8*) Gordon Pr.
***Browne, L. Virginia, et al.** Letters from Cleo & Tyrone: A Feline Perspective on Love, Life & Litter. LC 00-40515. (Illus.). 2000. write for info. (*0-312-26706-1*, St Martin Griffin) St Martin.
Browne, Laynie. Rebecca Letters. Dienstfrey, Patricia, ed. LC 97-9462. 80p. 1997. per. 10.00 (*0-932716-43-1*) Kelsey St Pr.
Browne, Laynie & Carefoot, George M. The Agency of Wind. (National Poetry Ser.). 125p. 1999. pap. 12.00 (*1-880713-12-8*, Pub. by AVEC Bks) SPD-Small Pr Dist.
Browne, Leslie M., et al. Office Leasing: Drafting & Negotiating the Lease, 2 vols. rev. ed. Millner, Dianne, ed. LC 96-83539. 626p. 1997. ring bd. 90.00 (*0-7626-0078-0*, RE-30891) Cont Ed Bar-CA.
***Browne, Lionel.** Bridges. 1998. pap. 10.95 (*1-880908-62-X*) Todtri Prods.
Browne-Iles, Warthell. Imagery: Its Affect on Black Male-Female Relations. LC 91-70645. 6.95 (*0-938818-70-8*) ECA Assoc.
Browne, Lois A. Humanitarianism in Today's World: Index of World Activities. 147p. 1997. 47.50 (*0-7883-1540-4*); pap. 44.50 (*0-7883-1541-2*) ABBE Pubs Assn.
Browne, Lydia. Autumn Fires. 1996. mass mkt. 5.99 (*0-515-11928-8*, Jove) Berkley Pub.
— Snowflake Wishes. 336p. 1997. mass mkt. 5.99 (*0-515-12181-9*, Jove) Berkley Pub.
— Spring Dreams. (Homespun Ser.). 320p. 1997. mass mkt. 5.99 (*0-515-12068-5*, Jove) Berkley Pub.
— Summer Lightning. 320p. (Orig.). 1995. mass mkt. 4.99 (*0-515-11657-2*, Jove) Berkley Pub.
Browne, M. & Thurlby, P., eds. Genomes, Molecular Biology & Drug Discovery. (Illus.). 270p. 1996. text 72.00 (*0-12-137790-3*) Acad Pr.
***Browne, M. N. & Keeley, Stuart.** Asking the Right Questions: A Guide to Critical Thinking. 6th ed. 240p. 2000. pap. 20.00 (*0-13-089134-7*) P-H.
Browne, M. Neil & Haas, Paul. Modern Economics: Principles, Goals & Trade-Offs. (Illus.). 432p. (C). 1987. pap. text 40.00 (*0-13-587940-X*) P-H.
Browne, M. Neil & Keeley, Stuart. Asking the Right Questions: A Guide to Critical Thinking. 5th ed. LC 97-25524. (Illus.). 179p. (C). 1997. pap. text 27.00 (*0-13-758186-6*) P-H.
Browne, M. Neil & Keeley, Stuart M. Striving for Excellence in College. LC 96-31843. 121p. (C). 1996. pap. text 16.80 (*0-13-458878-9*) P-H.
***Browne, M. Neil & Keeley, Stuart M.** Striving for Excellence in College: Tips for Active Learning. 2nd ed. LC 99-48529. 128p. 2000. pap. 20.00 (*0-13-022058-2*) P-H.
Browne, Mairead. Organizational Decision Making & Information. LC 92-42684. 272p. 1993. pap. 39.50 (*1-56750-017-X*); text 73.25 (*0-89391-870-9*) Ablx Pub.
Browne, Marmaduke E., tr. see Mozart, Wolfgang Amadeus.
Browne, Martha G. Autobiography of a Female Slave. LC 71-92745. 401p. 1970. reprint ed. lib. bdg. 45.00 (*0-8371-2194-9*, GRS&) Greenwood.
— Autobiography of a Female Slave. (American Biography Ser.). 401p. 1991. reprint ed. lib. bdg. 89.00 (*0-7812-8046-X*) Rprt Serv.
Browne, Mary T. Life after Death. 1995. mass mkt. 5.99 (*0-8041-1386-6*) Ivy Books.
Browne, Matthew, pseud. Chaucer's England, 2 vols. LC 74-113566. 1970. reprint ed. 84.50 (*0-404-01139-X*) AMS Pr.
Browne, Max. The Romantic Art of Theodor von Holst, 1810-44. (Illus.). 112p. (C). 1994. pap. 32.50 (*0-85331-661-9*, Pub. by Lund Humphries) Antique Collect.
Browne, Michael. Physics for Engineering & Science. LC 98-35391. (Schaum's Outline Ser.). (Illus.). 452p. 1999. pap. 15.95 (*0-07-008498-X*) McGraw.
Browne, Michael, jt. auth. see Forster, John.
Browne, Michael D. Selected Poems, 1965-1995. LC 96-83421. 128p. 1997. 20.95 (*0-88748-243-0*); pap. 11.95 (*0-88748-244-9*) Carnegie-Mellon.
— Smoke from the Fires. LC 84-72533. (Poetry Ser.). 80p. 1985. 20.95 (*0-88748-006-3*); pap. 11.95 (*0-88748-007-1*) Carnegie-Mellon.
— You Won't Remember This. LC 91-72052. (Poetry Ser.). 88p. 1992. pap. 11.95 (*0-88748-135-3*) Carnegie-Mellon.
Browne-Miller, A. Working Dazed: Why Drugs Pervade the Workplace & What Can Be Done about It. LC 91-7247. (Illus.). 346p. (C). 1991. 26.95 (*0-306-43765-1*, Plen Insight) Perseus Pubng.

B

An Asterisk (*) at the beginning of an entry indicates that the title is appearing for the first time.

Browne-Miller, Angela. Adventures in Death: Riding Your Apocalypses into Power Freedom. (Illus.). 160p. (Orig.). 1995. pap. 16.00 (*0-9645472-4-4*) Metaterra Pubns.

— Gestalting Addiction: The Addiction-Focused Group Therapy of Dr. Richard Louis Miller. LC 93-12291. (Frontiers in Psychotherapy Ser.). 142p. 1993. pap. 39.50 (*0-89391-905-5*); text 73.25 (*0-89391-904-7*) Ablx Pub.

— How to Die & Survive: The Interdimensional Travel Manual. rev. ed. LC 97-72279. (Illus.). 318p. 1999. pap. 24.95 (*0-939040-06-9*, B302) Truth Seeker.

Browne-Miller, Angela. Intelligence Policy: Its Impact on College Admissions & Other Social Policies. (Illus.). 276p. (C). 1995. 42.50 (*0-306-44745-2*, Plenum Trade) Perseus Pubng.

Browne-Miller, Angela. Shameful Admissions: The Losing Battle to Serve Everyone in Our Universities. LC 95-32120. (Jossey-Bass Higher & Adult Education Ser.). 304p. 1996. mass mkt. 32.95 (*0-7879-0182-2*) Jossey-Bass.

— Transcending Addiction & Other Afflictions: Lifehealing. LC 93-2901. (Frontiers in Psychotherapy Ser.). 1993. pap. 39.50 (*0-89391-903-9*); text 73.25 (*0-89391-900-4*) Ablx Pub.

Browne-Miller, Angela & Klotsche, Charles. Omega Point: An Apocalyptic Parable of Spiritual Transcendence for the New Millennium. (Illus.). 400p. (Orig.). 1995. pap. 18.50 (*0-9645472-0-1*) Metaterra Pubns.

Browne, Murray, jt. auth. see Berry, Michael W.

Browne, Naima. Young Children's Literacy Development & the Role of Televisual Texts. 150p. 1999. 79.00 (*0-7507-0855-7*, Falmer Pr); pap. 23.95 (*0-7507-0856-5*, Falmer Pr) Taylor & Francis.

Browne, Naima, ed. Science & Technology in the Early Years: An Equal Opportunities Approach. (Gender & Education Ser.). 160p. 1990. 31.95 (*0-335-09229-2*) OpUniv Pr.

Browne, Nick, ed. American Television: New Directions in History & Theory, Vol. 2. 296p. 1994. pap. text 20.00 (*3-7186-0563-5*) Gordon & Breach.

— Cahiers du Cinema, 1969-1972: The Politics of Representation. (Harvard Film Studies). 384p. 1989. 43.50 (*0-674-09063-2*) HUP.

***Browne, Nick, ed.** Francis Ford Coppola's "The Godfather" Trilogy. LC 99-17674. (Cambridge Film Handbooks Ser.). (Illus.). 208p. (C). 1999. 49.95 (*0-521-55084-X*); pap. 16.95 (*0-521-55950-2*) Cambridge U Pr.

Browne, Nick, ed. Refiguring American Film Genres: History & Theory. LC 97-42091. (Illus.). 370p. 1997. pap. text 19.95 (*0-520-20731-9*, Pub. by U CA Pr) Cal Prin Full Svc.

— Refiguring American Film Genres: History & Theory. LC 97-42091. (Illus.). 370p. 1998. 50.00 (*0-520-20730-0*, Pub. by U CA Pr) Cal Prin Full Svc.

Browne, P. W. Construction Estimating: An Analytical Approach. (Illus.). 96p. 1997. pap. 22.95 (*0-86840-241-9*, Pub. by New South Wales Univ Pr) Intl Spec Bk.

Browne, Pat, ed. Heroines of Popular Culture. LC 87-72240. (Illus.). 192p. 1987. 32.95 (*0-87972-408-0*); pap. 16.95 (*0-87972-409-9*) Bowling Green Univ Popular Press.

Browne, Pat & Browne, Ray B. Encyclopedia of American Popular Culture. 600p. Date not set. text 90.00 (*0-8153-1346-2*) Garland.

Browne, Pat, jt. ed. see Browne, Ray B.

Browne, Pat, jt. ed. see Motz, Marilyn F.

Browne, Patricia Harrigan. Quincy: A Past Carved in Stone. LC 96-209867. (Images of America Ser.). 128p. 1996. pap. 16.99 (*0-7524-0299-4*) Arcadia Publng.

Browne, Patrick. Civil & Natural History of Jamaica. LC 71-141130. (Research Library of Colonial Americana). (Illus.). 1972. reprint ed. 72.95 (*0-405-03276-5*) Ayer.

Browne, Patrick S. Basic Facts in Orthopaedics. 2nd ed. (Illus.). 288p. (gr. 13). 1985. 23.95 (*0-86793-184-1*, B-0870-8) Mosby Inc.

Browne, Paul L., tr. see Heinich, Nathalie.

Browne, Philippa-Alys. Elephants & Emus: And Other Animal Rhymes. LC 96-52708. (Illus.). 32p. (J). (gr. k-5). 1997. 14.95 (*0-88106-698-2*, Talewinds) Charlesbridge Pub.

— A Gaggle of Geese & Other Animal Groups. (Illus.). 32p. (J). (ps-1). 1996. 15.00 (*0-689-80761-9*) S&S Childrens.

— Kangaroos Have Joeys. (Animal Families Ser.). (J). 1996. write for info. (*0-614-96370-2*) Atheneum Yung Read.

— Kangaroos Have Joeys. (Illus.). 32p. (J). (ps-2). 1996. 15.00 (*0-689-81040-7*) S&S Childrens.

Browne, Phyllis. Thanks for the Tea, Mrs Browne: My Life with Noel. LC 98-229555. 168p. 1998. 18.95 (*1-874597-85-5*) New Island Books.

Browne, Ray B. Against Academia: The History of the Popular Culture Association - American Culture Association & the Popular Culture Movement 1967-1988. (Illus.). 195p. 1989. 34.95 (*0-87972-451-X*); pap. 17.95 (*0-87972-452-8*) Bowling Green Univ Popular Press.

— Heroes & Humanities: Detective Fiction & Culture. LC 86-72643. 141p. (C). 1987. 20.95 (*0-87972-370-X*); pap. 9.95 (*0-87972-371-8*) Bowling Green Univ Popular Press.

— The Many Tongues of Literacy. LC 92-71958. 201p. (C). 1992. 40.95 (*0-87972-559-1*); pap. 20.95 (*0-87972-560-5*) Bowling Green Univ Popular Press.

— The Spirit of Australia: The Crime Fiction of Arthur W. Upfield. LC 87-71998. (Illus.). 292p. (C). 1988. 31.95 (*0-87972-402-1*); pap. 16.95 (*0-87972-403-X*) Bowling Green Univ Popular Press.

Browne, Ray B., ed. The Alabama Folk Lyric: A Study in Origins & Media of Dissemination. LC 78-61076. 1979. 26.00 (*0-87972-129-4*) Bowling Green Univ Popular Press.

— Contemporary Heroes & Heroines Bk. 1: A Biographical Guide to Heroic Figures of the Twentieth Century. (Illus.). 451p. 1989. 63.00 (*0-8103-4860-8*, GML00198-004878) Gale.

— Forbidden Fruits: Taboos & Tabooism in Culture. LC 84-71938. 192p. 1984. 22.95 (*0-87972-255-X*) Bowling Green Univ Popular Press.

— Lincoln-Lore: Lincoln in the Popular Mind. LC 96-29461. (Illus.). 344p. 1996. 49.95 (*0-87972-719-5*); pap. 19.95 (*0-87972-720-9*) Bowling Green Univ Popular Press.

— A Night with the Hants & Other Alabama Folk Experiences. LC 76-43449. 1976. 17.95 (*0-87972-075-1*); pap. 11.95 (*0-87972-167-7*) Bowling Green Univ Popular Press.

— Objects of Special Devotion: Fetishes & Fetishism in Popular Culture. LC 81-85521. 1982. 22.95 (*0-87972-191-X*) Bowling Green Univ Popular Press.

— Rituals & Ceremonies in Popular Culture. LC 80-83188. 1981. 22.95 (*0-87972-160-X*); pap. 14.95 (*0-87972-161-8*) Bowling Green Univ Popular Press.

Browne, Ray B., et al, eds. Celtic Cross. LC 78-121453. (Essay Index Reprint Ser.). 1980. 23.95 (*0-8369-1744-8*) Ayer.

— Dominant Symbols in Popular Culture. LC 89-82333. 249p. (C). 1990. 40.95 (*0-87972-481-1*) Bowling Green Univ Popular Press.

Browne, Ray B. & Ambrosetti, Ronald J., eds. Continuities in Popular Culture: The Present in the Past & the Past in the Present & Future. LC 93-70931. 268p. 1993. 39.95 (*0-87972-592-3*); pap. 14.95 (*0-87972-593-1*) Bowling Green Univ Popular Press.

Browne, Ray B. & Browne, Glenn J. Laws of Our Fathers: Popular Culture & the U. S. Constitution. LC 86-70852. 298p. 1986. 25.95 (*0-87972-337-8*); pap. 13.95 (*0-87972-338-6*) Bowling Green Univ Popular Press.

Browne, Ray B. & Browne, Pat, eds. Defining Concise Guide to United States Popular Culture. (Illus.). 1000p. write for info. (*0-87972-821-3*); pap. write for info. (*0-87972-822-1*) Bowling Green Univ Popular Press.

Browne, Ray B. & Browne, Pat, eds. Digging into Popular Culture. (Illus.). 186p. (C). 1991. 34.95 (*0-87972-521-4*); pap. 17.95 (*0-87972-522-2*) Bowling Green Univ Popular Press.

***Browne, Ray B. & Fishwick, Marshall W.** The Global Village: Dead or Alive? LC 98-27831. 1998. 49.95 (*0-87972-771-3*); 24.95 (*0-87972-772-1*) Bowling Green Univ Popular Press.

Browne, Ray B. & Fishwick, Marshall W., eds. The Hero in Transition. LC 83-71003. 1983. 23.95 (*0-87972-237-1*) Bowling Green Univ Popular Press.

— Preview 2001+ Popular Culture Studies in the Future. LC 95-46247. 222p. 1996. 35.95 (*0-87972-689-X*); pap. 15.95 (*0-87972-690-3*) Bowling Green Univ Popular Press.

— Rejuvenating the Humanities. LC 91-77025. (Illus.). 220p. (C). 1992. 39.95 (*0-87972-545-1*); pap. 19.95 (*0-87972-546-X*) Bowling Green Univ Popular Press.

— Symbiosis: Popular Culture & Other Fields. LC 88-71361. 224p. (C). 1988. 31.95 (*0-87972-439-0*); pap. 15.95 (*0-87972-440-4*) Bowling Green Univ Popular Press.

Browne, Ray B. & Geist, Christopher D., eds. Popular Abstracts. 1978. 13.95 (*0-87972-166-9*); pap. 7.95 (*0-87972-165-0*) Bowling Green Univ Popular Press.

Browne, Ray B. & Marsden, Michael T. Pioneers in Popular Culture Studies. LC 98-30244. 221p. 1998. 49.95 (*0-87972-775-6*); pap. 24.95 (*0-87972-776-4*) Bowling Green Univ Popular Press.

Browne, Ray B. & Marsden, Michael T., eds. The Cultures of Celebrations. LC 93-74428. (Outdoor Entertainment Ser.). (Illus.). 244p. (C). 1994. 35.95 (*0-87972-651-2*); text 15.95 (*0-87972-652-0*) Bowling Green Univ Popular Press.

Browne, Ray B., jt. auth. see Browne, Pat.

Browne, Ray B., jt. ed. see Fishwick, Marshall W.

Browne, Ray B., jt. ed. see Hoppenstand, Gary.

Browne, Ray B., ed. see Twain, Mark, pseud.

***Browne, Ray Broadus & Kreiser, Lawrence A.** The Detective as Historian: History & Art in Historical Crime Fiction. LC 00-29245. (Illus.). 2000. pap. 29.95 (*0-87972-816-7*) Bowling Green Univ Popular Press.

Browne, Ray Broadus & Kreser, Lawrence A., Jr., eds. The Detective as Historian: History & Art in Historical Crime Fiction. 59.95 (*0-87972-815-9*) Bowling Green Univ Popular Press.

Browne, Renni & King, Dave. Self Edit Fiction Wr. LC 92-11229. (Illus.). 240p. 1994. pap. 13.00 (*0-06-272046-5*, Harper Ref) HarpC.

***Browne, Rick & Bettridge, Jack.** Barbecue America: A Pilgrimage in Search of America's Best Barbecue. LC 98-54427. (Illus.). 224p. (YA). (gr. 11). 1999. 24.95 (*0-7370-0021-X*) T-L Custom Pub.

Browne, Robert, et al. Artemia Biology. (Illus.). 352p. 1990. lib. bdg. 259.00 (*0-8493-6729-8*, QL444) CRC Pr.

Browne, Robert S., ed. Political Morality of the International Monetary Fund. (Ethics in Foreign Policy Ser.: Vol. 3). 164p. 1987. text 39.95 (*0-88738-143-X*) Transaction Pubs.

Browne, Roger M., ed. Investigative Pathology of the Odontogenic Cysts. 264p. 1990. lib. bdg. 195.00 (*0-8493-5038-7*, RK307) CRC Pr.

Browne, Roland A. The Holy Jerusalem Voyage of Ogier VIII, Seigneur d'Anglure. LC 75-4773. (Illus.). 173p. reprint ed. pap. 53.70 (*0-7837-5104-4*, 204480300004) Bks Demand.

Browne, Rollo. An Aboriginal Family. LC 84-19447. (Families the World Over Ser.). (Illus.). 32p. (J). (gr. 2-5). 1985. lib. bdg. 13.95 (*0-8225-1655-1*, Lerner Publctns) Lerner Pub.

Browne, Scribner. Tidal Swings of the Stock Market. LC 92-74294. 120p. (C). 1992. reprint ed. pap. 12.00 (*0-87034-106-5*) Fraser Pub Co.

Browne, Sheila & Miller, John. Qualifications for a Director of Music Ministries: A Statement & Bibliography. 21p. 1995. reprint ed. pap. text 3.50 (*1-888360-00-3*) NPM Pubns.

***Browne, Stephen.** Beyond Aid: From Patronage to Partnership. 200p. 1999. text 61.95 (*0-7546-1133-7*, Pub. by Ashgate Pub) Ashgate Pub Co.

Browne, Stephen B. & Schlesinger, Stephen L., intros. Byron Browne: Ten Paintings of the 1950's. (Illus.). (Orig.). 1986. pap. 5.00 (*0-9614661-1-1*) Gallery Schlesinger Boisante.

***Browne, Stephen H.** Angelina Grimke: Rhetoric, Identity & the Radical Imagination. LC 99-6955. (Rhetoric & Public Affairs Ser.). 224p. 1999. pap. 24.95 (*0-87013-542-2*) Mich St U Pr.

— Angelina Grimke: Rhetoric, Identity & the Radical Imagination. LC 99-6955. (Rhetoric & Public Affairs Ser.). 224p. 2000. 50.00 (*0-87013-530-9*) Mich St U Pr.

Browne, Stephen H. Edmund Burke & the Discourse of Virtue. LC 92-46656. (Studies in Rhetoric & Communication). 160p. 1993. text 34.95 (*0-8173-0676-5*) U of Ala Pr.

Browne, Stephen H., jt. auth. see Morris, Charles E., III.

Browne, Steve. Internet via Mosaic & World-Wide Web. LC 94-234135. (Illus.). 176p. (Orig.). 1994. pap. 24.95 (*1-56276-259-1*, Ziff-Davis Pr) Que.

Browne, Steven. Film-Video Terms & Concepts: A Focal Handbook. (Illus.). 192p. 1992. pap. 31.95 (*0-240-80111-3*, Focal) Buttrwrth-Heinemann.

Browne, Steven E. Nonlinear Editing Basics: A Primer on Electronic Film & Video Editing. LC 98-9166. 224p. 1998. pap. 29.95 (*0-240-80282-9*, Focal) Buttrwrth-Heinemann.

— Protecting the Source. 242p. 1996. pap. 14.95 (*0-914499-03-3*) Wilton Place.

— Videotape Editing: A Post-Production Primer. 3rd ed. (Illus.). 326p. 1996. pap. 37.95 (*0-240-80269-1*, Focal) Buttrwrth-Heinemann.

Browne, Steven E., jt. auth. see Brown, Michele C.

***Browne, Sylvia.** Adventures of a Psychic: The Fascinating & Inspiring True-Life Story of One of America's Most Successful Clairvoyants. (SPA.). 2001. pap. 13.95 (*1-56170-800-3*) Hay House.

— Astrology Through a Psychic's Eyes. LC 00-39622. 128p. 2000. pap. 7.00 (*1-56170-720-1*, 5029) Hay House.

— Conversations with the Other Side. 256p. 2001. pap. 13.95 (*1-56170-718-X*, 5030) Hay House.

— God, Creation & Tools for Life. LC 99-52804. (Journey of the Soul Ser.: Vol. 1). 256p. 2000. pap. 13.95 (*1-56170-722-8*, 5024) Hay House.

— Meditations. LC 99-87364. (Illus.). 128p. 2001. 9.95 (*1-56170-719-8*, 5026) Hay House.

— The Nature of Good & Evil. (Journey of the Soul Ser.: Vol. 3). 256p. 2001. pap. 13.95 (*1-56170-724-4*, 5027) Hay House.

— The Other Side & Back: A Psychic's Guide to Our World & Beyond. 2000. mass mkt. 7.50 (*0-451-19863-8*, Sig) NAL.

— The Other Side & Back: A Psychic's Guide to Our World & Beyond. large type ed. (Core Ser.). 343p. 2000. 29.95 (*0-7838-9018-4*, G K Hall Lrg Type) Mac Lib Ref.

— Soul's Perfection. (Journey of the Soul Ser.: Vol. 2). 256p. 2000. pap. 13.95 (*1-56170-723-6*, 5025) Hay House.

— Women's Writing in Stuart England: The Mother's Legacies of Elizabeth Joscelin, Elizabeth Richardson & Dorothy Leigh. 256p. 2000. 72.00 (*0-7509-1854-3*, Pub. by Sutton Publng) Bks Intl VA.

***Browne, Sylvia & Harrison, Lindsay.** Blessings from the Other Side: Wisdom & Comfort from the Afterlife for This Life. 224p. 2000. 17.95 (*0-525-94574-1*) NAL.

— Life on the Other Side: A Psychic's Tour of the Afterlife. 304p. 2000. 23.95 (*0-525-94539-3*, Dutt) Dutton Plume.

Browne, Sylvia & Harrison, Lindsay. The Other Side & Back: A Psychic's Guide to Our World & Beyond. LC 99-18283. 304p. 1999. 23.95 (*0-525-94504-0*) NAL.

Browne, Sylvia & May, Antoinette. Adventures of a Psychic: The Fascinating & Inspiring True-Life Story of One of America's Most Successful Clairvoyants. 2nd rev. ed. LC 98-35785. (Illus.). 272p. 1998. pap. 12.95 (*1-56170-621-3*, 589) Hay House.

Browne, Sylvia, jt. auth. see Parrett, Sherii.

Browne, T. R., ed. Stable Isotopes in Pharmaceutical Research. (Pharmacochemistry Library: Vol. 26). 464p. 1997. 284.50 (*0-444-81941-X*, North Holland) Elsevier.

Browne, Thomas. Browne's Religio Medici & Digby's Observations. (BCL1-PR English Literature Ser.). 183p. 1992. reprint ed. lib. bdg. 69.00 (*0-7812-7324-2*) Rprt Serv.

— Hydriotaphia (Urn Burial) & the Garden of Cyrus. Huntley, Frank L., ed. (Crofts Classics Ser.). 136p. 1966. pap. text 4.95 (*0-88295-017-7*) Harlan Davidson.

— Hydriotaphia, Urne-Buriall, or, a Discourse of the Sepulchrall Urnes Lately Found in Norfolk. Together with the Garden of Cyrus, or the Quincunciall Lozenge, or Network Plantations of the Ancients, Artificially, Naturally Mystically Considered. Kastenbaum, Robert J., ed. LC 76-19562. (Death & Dying Ser.). 1977. reprint ed. lib. bdg. 19.95 (*0-405-09558-9*) Ayer.

— The Major Works. Patrides, C. A., ed. & intro. by. 560p. 1977. pap. 15.95 (*0-14-043109-8*, Penguin Classics) Viking Penguin.

— Religio Medici, Hydriotaphia & the Garden of Cyrus. Robbins, R. H., ed. (Illus.). 224p. 1972. pap. text 19.95 (*0-19-871064-X*) OUP.

— Religio Medici, Letter to a Friend, & Christian Morals. enl. ed. Greenhill, W. A., ed. 450p. 1990. reprint ed. pap. 16.95 (*0-89385-034-9*) Sugden.

— Selected Writings of Sir Thomas Browne. Keynes, Geoffrey L., ed. LC 68-55536. (Illus.). 1970. pap. text 3.25 (*0-226-07636-9*, P347) U Ch Pr.

— Works, 6 vols., Set. Keynes, Geoffrey L., ed. (BCL1-PR English Literature Ser.). 1992. reprint ed. lib. bdg. 540.00 (*0-7812-7323-4*) Rprt Serv.

— Works & Life of Thomas Browne, 4 vols. Wilkin, Simon, ed. LC 68-57225. reprint ed. 365.00 (*0-404-01150-0*) AMS Pr.

Browne, Thomas E., Jr. Circuit Interruption: Theory & Techniques. (Electrical Engineering & Electronics Ser.: Vol. 21). (Illus.). 720p. 1984. text 185.00 (*0-8247-7177-X*) Dekker.

Browne, Thomas P., ed. see Mayo, Patrick.

Browne, Thomas R. & Feldman, Robert G., eds. Epilepsy: Diagnosis & Management. 376p. 1983. 75.00 (*0-316-11114-7*, Little Brwn Med Div) Lppncott W & W.

Browne, Thomas R. & Holmes, Gregory L. Handbook of Epilepsy. LC 97-10478. 300p. 1997. pap. text 34.95 (*0-316-11053-1*) Lppncott W & W.

***Browne, Thomas R. & Holmes, Gregory L.** Handbook of Epilepsy. 2nd ed. LC 99-40669. 1999. write for info. (*0-7817-2407-4*) Lppncott W & W.

Browne, Tom & Manocchi, Vincent. International Truck Color History: International Pickups, Panels, Metros, Metroettes, Travelalls, Scouts, Semit-Trucks & More. LC 97-38057. (Illus.). 128p. 1997. pap. 21.95 (*0-7603-0361-4*) MBI Pubg.

Browne, Turner. Louisiana Cajuns - Cajuns de la Louisiane. Spohrer, James & Spohrer, Elisabeth, trs. LC 77-24171. (ENG & FRE.). 118p. 1977. pap. 36.60 (*0-7837-8454-6*, 20492590001 0) Bks Demand.

Browne, Vee. Animal Lore & Legend: Owl. 1995. 10.15 (*0-606-07195-4*, Pub. by Turtleback) Demco.

Browne, Vee. Maria Tallchief, Prima Ballerina. (Illus.). (J). (gr. 1-4). 1995. pap. 4.99 (*0-8136-5767-9*); lib. bdg. 10.60 (*0-8136-6081-5*) Modern Curr.

— Monster Birds: A Navajo Folktale. LC 92-82139. (Illus.). 32p. (J). 1993. lib. bdg. 14.95 (*0-87358-558-5*, Rising Moon Bks) Northland AZ.

Browne, Vincent B. Big Business & Other Plays. Irish, J. A., ed. 120p. (Orig.). 1991. pap. text 10.00 (*1-878433-09-1*) Caribbean Diaspora Pr.

Browne, Virginia. Odd Pairs & False Friends Dizionario di False Analogie e Ambigue Affinta Fra Inglese e Italiano. (ENG & ITA.). 272p. 1987. lib. bdg. 75.00 (*0-8288-3333-8*, F120170) Fr & Eur.

Browne, W. A. What Asylums Were, Are, & Ought to Be: Being the Substance of Five Lectures Delivered Before the Managers of the Montrose Royal Lunatic Asylum. LC 75-16691. (Classics in Psychiatry Ser.). 1976. reprint ed. 21.95 (*0-405-07421-2*) Ayer.

***Browne, Walden.** Sahagbun & the Transition to Modernity. LC 99-47301. (Project for Discourse & Theory Ser.). 272p. 2000. 34.95 (*0-8061-3233-7*) U of Okla Pr.

Browne, Waldo R., ed. Joys of the Road. LC 79-107686. (Essay Index Reprint Ser.). 1977. 17.95 (*0-8369-1491-0*) Ayer.

Browne, Waldo R., ed. see Barnum, Phineas T.

Browne, Wayles M., et al, eds. Formal Approaches to Slavic Linguistics: The Cornell Meeting, 1995. LC 97-15476. (Michigan Slavic Materials Ser.: No. 39). 1997. pap. 18.00 (*0-930042-79-4*) Mich Slavic Pubns.

Browne, William. Poems, 2 vols. 1988. reprint ed. lib. bdg. 99.00 (*0-317-90892-8*) Rprt Serv.

— The Whole Works, 2 vols. in 1. Hazlitt, W. Carew, ed. (Anglistica & Americana Ser.: No. 66). xxxix, 579p. 1970. reprint ed. 130.00 (*0-685-66437-6*, 05102767) G Olms Pubs.

Browne, William & Hadwiger, Don F., eds. Rural Policy. (Orig.). (C). 1982. pap. 15.00 (*0-918592-55-0*) Pol Studies.

Browne, William, jt. ed. see Hadwiger, Don F.

Browne, William B. The Babbitt Family History 1643-1900. (Illus.). 761p. 1988. reprint ed. pap. 109.00 (*0-8328-0149-6*); reprint ed. lib. bdg. 119.00 (*0-8328-0148-8*) Higginson Bk Co.

Browne, William F. Two Kinds of Courage: Frederick Douglass & John Brown - a Look at Their Relationship. (Illus.). 49p. (Orig.). (YA). (gr. 9-12). 1996. pap. text 7.95 (*0-9647239-2-1*) Spiritual Nerve.

Browne, William H. Maryland, the History of a Palatinate. enl. rev. ed. LC 72-3758. (American Commonwealths Ser.: No. 3). reprint ed. 39.50 (*0-404-57203-0*) AMS Pr.

— Witty Sayings by Witty People. LC 74-15727. (Popular Culture in America Ser.). 304p. 1975. reprint ed. 28.95 (*0-405-06363-6*) Ayer.

Browne, William H., jt. auth. see Johnston, Richard M.

Browne, William P. Cultivating Congress: Constituents, Issues, & Interests in Agricultural Policymaking. (Studies in Government & Public Policy). 216p. 1995. 29.95 (*0-7006-0700-5*); pap. 15.95 (*0-7006-0701-3*) U Pr of KS.

— Groups, Interests, & U. S. Public Policy. LC 97-41520. 276p. 1998. 49.95 (*0-87840-681-6*); pap. 15.95 (*0-87840-682-4*) Georgetown U Pr.

— Private Interests, Public Policy, & American Agriculture. LC 87-23131. (Studies in Government & Public Policy). xviii, 294p. (C). 1988. pap. 15.95 (*0-7006-0335-2*) U Pr of KS.

Browne, William P. & Cigler, Allan J., eds. U. S. Agricultural Groups: Institutional Profiles. LC 89-25786. 312p. 1990. lib. bdg. 75.00 (*0-313-25088-X*, CGR/, Greenwood Pr) Greenwood.

Browne, William P. & Olson, Laura K., eds. Aging & Public Policy: The Politics of Growing Old in America, 83. LC 82-6138. (Contributions in Political Science Ser.: No. 83). (Illus.). 266p. 1983. 57.95 (*0-313-22855-8*, BAG/, Greenwood Pr) Greenwood.

Browne, William P. & VerBurg, Kenneth. Michigan Politics & Government: Facing Change in a Complex State. LC 94-18928. (Politics & Governments of the American States Ser.). (Illus.). xxxiv, 409p. 1995. text 55.00 (*0-8032-1209-7*) U of Nebr Pr.

An Asterisk (*) at the beginning of an entry indicates that the title is appearing for the first time.

Browne, William T. Poems, 2 vols., Set. 1971. reprint ed. 69.00 (*0-403-00846-8*) Scholarly.

***Browne, Yolanda.** Daytime Stories & Prayers. (Sleepytime Board Bks.). (Illus.). 8p. (J). 2000. bds. 5.99 (*1-57584-664-0*) Rdrs Digest.

— A Family Christmas. (Advent Calendar Ser.). (Illus.). 32p. (J). (ps). 2000. pap. 12.99 (*1-57584-666-7*, Pub. by Rdrs Digest) S&S Trade.

— Sleepytime Stories & Prayers. (Sleepytime Board Bks.). (Illus.). 8p. (J). (ps). 2000. bds. 5.99 (*1-57584-665-9*) Rdrs Digest.

Brownell. Desktop Publishing Using Pagemaker. (DF - Computer Applications Ser.). 1990. mass mkt. 30.95 (*0-538-60355-0*) S-W Pub.

— PC for the Teacher. LC 98-48105. 1998. pap. 56.95 (*0-534-53862-2*) Brooks-Cole.

— Social Development. 2000. pap. 55.00 (*0-8133-3089-0*); pap. 21.00 (*0-8133-3090-4*) HarpC.

Brownell, Baker. Art Is Action. LC 73-90616. (Essay Index Reprint Ser.). 1977. 18.95 (*0-8369-1250-0*) Ayer.

Brownell, Barbara. Spin's Really Wild U. S. A. Tour. LC 95-44643. (Illus.). 32p. (J). (gr. k-4). 1996. pap. 7.95 (*0-7922-3422-7*) Natl Geog.

Brownell, Blaine A. The Urban Ethos in the South, 1920 to 1930. LC 74-82003. 262p. reprint ed. pap. 81.30 (*0-608-13705-7*, 205529900013) Bks Demand.

— Using Microcomputers: A Guidebook for Writers, Teachers, & Researchers in the Social Sciences. LC 84-27668. 320p. reprint ed. pap. 99.20 (*0-7837-1120-4*, 204165000022) Bks Demand.

Brownell, C. L. Scale for Measuring the Antero-Posterior Posture of Ninth Grade Boys. LC 74-176601. (Columbia University. Teachers College. Contributions to Education Ser.: No. 325). reprint ed. 37.50 (*0-404-55325-7*) AMS Pr.

***Brownell, Charles D.** The Indian Races of North & South America. (LC History-America-E). 708p. 1999. reprint ed. lib. bdg. 169.00 (*0-7812-4244-4*) Rprt Serv.

Brownell, Charles E., et al. The Making of Virginia Architecture. Rumsey, Monica S., ed. (Illus.). 472p. (Orig.). (C). 1992. 50.00 (*0-917046-34-X*); pap. 24.95 (*0-917046-33-1*) Va Mus Arts.

Brownell, Charles E., jt. auth. see Cohen, Jeffrey A.

Brownell, Dave. Hemmings Vintage Auto Almanac. 9th ed. (Illus.). 350p. 1991. pap. 9.95 (*0-917808-05-3*) Hemmings.

Brownell, David. The Automobile Collection: Heritage Plantation of Sandwich. Melber, G., ed. LC 86-81676. (Illus.). 72p. (Orig.). 1986. pap. 8.00 (*0-939059-00-2*) Herit Plant Sandwich.

— Great Composers Bk. I: Bach to Bevlioz. (Illus.). (J). (gr. 7 up). 1978. pap. 4.95 (*0-88388-058-X*) Bellerophon Bks.

— Great Composers Bk. II: Chopin to Tchaikovsky. (J). (gr. 1-9). 1992. pap. 4.95 (*0-88388-046-6*) Bellerophon Bks.

— Great Composers Bk. III: Mahler to Stravinsky. (J). (gr. 1-9). 1992. pap. 4.95 (*0-88388-134-9*) Bellerophon Bks.

— Great Lawyers. (Illus.). 48p. (Orig.). (J). (gr. 8). 1988. pap. 3.95 (*0-88388-133-0*) Bellerophon Bks.

— Hemmings Vintage Auto Almanac. 10th ed. 1993. pap. 9.95 (*0-917808-12-6*) Hemmings.

— Hemmings' Vintage Auto Almanac. 11th ed. (Illus.). 464p. 1995. pap. 9.95 (*0-917808-15-0*) Hemmings.

— Heroes of the American Revolution. (J). (gr. 1-9). 1992. pap. 4.95 (*0-88388-050-4*) Bellerophon Bks.

— Ludwig Van Beethoven. (Illus.). 64p. 1980. pap. 3.95 (*0-88388-057-1*) Bellerophon Bks.

— Nutcracker. (J). (gr. 1-9). 1992. pap. 4.95 (*0-88388-052-0*) Bellerophon Bks.

— Peter & the Wolf. (J). (gr. 1-9). 1992. pap. 4.95 (*0-88388-093-8*) Bellerophon Bks.

Brownell, David, ed. Hemmings Vintage Auto Almanac. 7th ed. LC 76-649715. 320p. 1986. pap. 9.95 (*0-917808-08-8*) Hemmings.

— Hemmings' Vintage Auto Almanac. 8th ed. 350p. 1989. pap. 9.95 (*0-917808-09-6*) Hemmings.

Brownell, David & Knill, Harry, eds. Kings & Queens of England. (Illus.). 1978. pap. 4.95 (*0-88388-053-9*) Bellerophon Bks.

Brownell, David L., jt. auth. see Guyer, Eric C.

***Brownell, Eleanor Elliott.** About Face: A Daughter Looks Back at a Soldier & the Great War. LC 99-91644. 2000. pap. 10.95 (*0-9679784-0-8*) World War One.

Brownell, Elijah E., compiled by. Bennington County Genealogical Gleanings. (Illus.). 207p. 1997. reprint ed. pap. 24.50 (*0-8328-6498-6*) Higginson Bk Co.

Brownell, Elizabeth R. They Lived in Tubac. LC 85-51587. (Illus.). 290p. 1987. 26.95 (*0-87026-061-8*) Westernlore.

Brownell, F. William, et al. Clean Air Handbook. 3rd rev. ed. LC 98-155016. 332p. 1998. pap. text 95.00 (*0-86587-616-9*, 616) Gov Insts.

Brownell, Gary, ed. see Diehl, Dennis R.

Brownell, George A. The Origin & Development of the National Security Agency. 98p. 1981. pap. 20.80 (*0-89412-054-9*) Aegean Park Pr.

Brownell, George B. Prophecies of Great World Changes. 53p. 1989. pap. 4.00 (*0-89540-176-2*, SB-176) Sun Pub.

— Reincarnation. 153p. 1981. pap. 14.00 (*0-89540-107-X*, SB-107) Sun Pub.

Brownell, George C. Travel Agency Management. LC 75-15476. 1975. pap. 12.50 (*0-87651-206-6*) Southern U Pr.

Brownell, Gertrude. The Wagnerian Romances. 414p. 1990. reprint ed. lib. bdg. 89.00 (*0-7812-9096-1*) Rprt Serv.

Brownell, Gregg. A Mac for the Teacher: ClarisWorks Version. 2nd ed. LC 96-19129. 350p. 1996. pap. 44.95 (*0-314-20057-6*) West Pub.

Brownell, Gregg, et al. A Mac for the Teacher: ClarisWorks Version. Baxter, ed. LC 93-41588. 450p. (C). 1994. mass mkt. 27.25 (*0-314-02505-7*) West Pub.

Brownell, H., jt. ed. see Joanette, Yves.

Brownell, Henry H. War-Lyrics & Other Poems. LC 72-4953. (Romantic Tradition in American Literature Ser.). 256p. 1972. 21.95 (*0-405-04625-1*) Ayer.

Brownell, Herbert & Burke, John P. Advising Ike: The Memoirs of Attorney General Herbert Brownell. LC 92-37584. (Illus.). 426p. 1993. 29.95 (*0-7006-0590-8*) U Pr of KS.

Brownell, Hiram H. & Joanette, Yves, eds. Narrative Discourse in Normal Aging & Neurologically-Impaired Adults. LC 93-15128. (Illus.). 354p. (Orig.). (C). 1993. pap. text 65.00 (*1-56593-083-5*, 0388) Thomson Learn.

Brownell, Joseph W. & Enos, Patricia W. Adirondack Tragedy: The Gillette Murder Case of 1906. rev. ed. LC 98-96286. (Illus.). ix, 212p. (Orig.). 1998. pap. 14.95 (*0-9665129-0-1*) J Brownell.

Brownell, Judi. Listening. LC 95-23519. 353p. 1995. pap. text 52.00 (*0-13-146937-1*) P-H.

Brownell, Kelly D. The LEARN Program for Weight Control: Meal Replacement Edition. 356p. 1998. pap. 24.95 (*1-878513-17-6*) Am Hlth Pub.

***Brownell, Kelly D.** The LEARN Program for Weight Control: Special Medication Edition. rev. ed. (Illus.). 356p. 1999. pap. 24.95 (*1-81751-319-2*) Am Hlth Pub.

— The LEARN Program for Weight Management: Meal Replacement Edition. rev. ed. (Illus.). 400p. pap. write for info. (*1-81751-317-6*) Am Hlth Pub.

— The LEARN Program for Weight Management: Meal Replacement Edition - Module 1. rev. ed. (Illus.). 144p. pap. write for info. (*1-81751-321-4*) Am Hlth Pub.

— The LEARN Program for Weight Management: Meal Replacement Edition - Module 2. rev. ed. (Illus.). 128p. pap. write for info. (*1-81751-322-2*) Am Hlth Pub.

— The LEARN Program for Weight Management: Meal Replacement Edition - Module 3. rev. ed. (Illus.). 128p. pap. write for info. (*1-81751-323-0*) Am Hlth Pub.

— The LEARN Program for Weight Management 2000. rev. ed. (Illus.). 320p. 2000. pap. 27.95 (*1-81751-324-9*) Am Hlth Pub.

***Brownell, Kelly D., ed.** Behavioral Medicine & Women: A Comprehensive Handbook. 876p. 1999. pap. text 39.95 (*1-57230-522-3*, CO522) Guilford Pubns.

Brownell, Kelly D. & Fairburn, Chrisopher G., eds. Eating Disorders & Obesity: A Comprehensive Handbook. 583p. 1998. pap. text 33.50 (*1-57230-380-8*) Guilford Pubns.

Brownell, Kelly D. & Fairburn, Christopher G., eds. Eating Disorders & Obesity: A Comprehensive Handbook. 583p. 1995. lib. bdg. 60.00 (*0-89862-850-4*) Guilford Pubns.

Brownell, Kelly D. & Foreyt, John P., eds. Handbook of Eating Disorders: Physiology, Psychology, & Treatment. LC 85-48021. 528p. 1986. pap. 55.00 (*0-465-02862-4*, Pub. by Basic) HarpC.

Brownell, Kelly D. & Wadden, Thomas A. The LEARN Program for Weight Control: Special Medication Edition. rev. ed. (Illus.). 356p. 1998. pap. text 24.95 (*1-878513-16-8*) Am Hlth Pub.

Brownell, Kelly D. & Wadden, Thomas A. The LEARN Program for Weight Control: Special Medication Edition - Module 1. (POR., Illus.). 52p. write for info. (*1-81751-325-7*) Am Hlth Pub.

— The LEARN Program for Weight Control: Special Medication Edition - Module 10. (POR., Illus.). 16p. pap. write for info. (*1-81751-334-6*) Am Hlth Pub.

— The LEARN Program for Weight Control: Special Medication Edition - Module 11. (POR., Illus.). 16p. pap. write for info. (*1-81751-335-4*) Am Hlth Pub.

— The LEARN Program for Weight Control: Special Medication Edition - Module 12. (POR., Illus.). 16p. pap. write for info. (*1-81751-336-2*) Am Hlth Pub.

— The Learn Program for Weight Control: Special Medication Edition - Module 2. (POR., Illus.). 40p. pap. write for info. (*1-81751-326-5*) Am Hlth Pub.

— The LEARN Program for Weight Control: Special Medication Edition - Module 3. (POR.). 44p. pap. write for info. (*1-81751-327-3*) Am Hlth Pub.

— The Learn Program for Weight Control: Special Medication Edition - Module 4. (POR., Illus.). 44p. pap. write for info. (*1-81751-328-1*) Am Hlth Pub.

— The LEARN Program for Weight Control: Special Medication Edition - Module 5. (POR., Illus.). 16p. pap. write for info. (*1-81751-329-X*) Am Hlth Pub.

— The LEARN Program for Weight Control: Special Medication Edition - Module 6. (POR., Illus.). 16p. pap. write for info. (*1-81751-330-3*) Am Hlth Pub.

— The LEARN Program for Weight Control: Special Medication Edition - Module 7. (POR., Illus.). 16p. pap. write for info. (*1-81751-331-1*) Am Hlth Pub.

— The LEARN Program for Weight Control: Special Medication Edition - Module 8. (POR., Illus.). 16p. pap. write for info. (*1-81751-332-X*) Am Hlth Pub.

— The LEARN Program for Weight Control: Special Medication Edition - Module 9. (POR., Illus.). 16p. pap. write for info. (*1-81751-333-8*) Am Hlth Pub.

Brownell, Kelly D., et al. Eating, Body Weight, & Performance in Athletes: Disorders of Modern Society. (Illus.). 363p. 1992. pap. text 32.95 (*0-8121-1474-4*) Lppncott W & W.

— The Health & Fitness Club Leader's Guide: Administering a Weight Management Program. 224p. (Orig.). 1992. pap. 29.95 (*1-878513-06-0*) Am Hlth Pub.

Brownell, Kelly D., jt. ed. see Blechman, Elaine A.

Brownell, Lloyd E. & Young, Edwin H. Process Equipment Design: Vessel Design. 420p. 1959. 235.00 (*0-471-11319-0*) Wiley.

Brownell, Louise B. Life Abundant for You (1928) 248p. 1998. reprint ed. pap. 19.95 (*0-7661-0324-2*) Kessinger Pub.

— Your Destiny in the Zodiac & Its Mastery. 1991. lib. bdg. 79.95 (*0-8490-4935-0*) Gordon Pr.

— Your Destiny in the Zodiac & Its Mastery. 106p. 1996. reprint ed. spiral bd. 13.50 (*0-7873-0125-6*) Hlth Research.

Brownell, M. Barbara. Mammals. LC 93-19467. (Nature Library). (J). (gr. 1-3). 1994. 10.50 (*0-87044-890-0*) Natl Geog.

Brownell, Morris R. Samuel Johnson's Attitudes to the Arts. (Illus.). 240p. 1989. 65.00 (*0-19-812956-4*) OUP.

Brownell, Patricia J. Family Crimes Against the Elderly: Elderly Abuse & the Criminal Justice System. LC 98-39287. (Studies on the Elderly in America). 1998. 50.00 (*0-8153-3209-2*) Garland.

— Rejection & Betrayal Gave Me the Strength to Succeed. LC 98-92421. (Illus.). 76p. 1998. pap. 5.95 (*0-9662544-1-4*) Gismondi Publ.

Brownell, Philip & Polis, Gary A. Scorpion Biology & Research. (Illus.). 400p. 2000. text 95.00 (*0-19-508434-9*) OUP.

Brownell, Rick. Receptive One-Word Picture Vocabulary Test-Upper Extension. (ENG & SPA.). 29p. 1987. 10.00 (*0-87879-591-X*); 17.00 (*0-685-31204-6*); student ed., vinyl bd. 70.00 (*0-87879-588-X*); 30.00 (*0-87879-589-8*); 10.00 (*0-685-44985-8*); lp 20.00 (*0-87879-590-1*) Acad Therapy.

— Trixie. LC 93-169. (Illus.). (J). 1994. write for info. (*0-383-03670-4*) SRA McGraw.

***Brownell, Rick, ed.** Expressive One-Word Picture Vocabulary Test: 2000 Edition Manual. 3rd rev ed. 128p. 1999. pap. text 38.00 (*1-57128-135-5*, 8135-5) Acad Therapy.

— Receptive One-Word Picture Vocabulary Test: 2000 Edition Manual. 2nd rev. ed. 112p. 1999. pap. text 38.00 (*1-57128-139-8*, 8139-8) Acad Therapy.

Brownell, Rick, ed. see Grill, J. Jeffrey & Kirwin, Margaret M.

Brownell, Rick, ed. see Richards, Regina G.

Brownell, Rick, ed. see Sims, Matt.

Brownell, Rick, ed. see Stemach, Jerry & Williams, William B.

Brownell, Sara, ed. see Piper, Christina.

Brownell, Susan. Training the Body for China: Sports in the Moral Order of the People's Republic. LC 94-49561. 406p. 1995. pap. text 18.95 (*0-226-07647-4*) U Ch Pr.

— Training the Body for China: Sports in the Moral Order of the People's Republic. LC 94-49561. 360p. 1995. lib. bdg. 49.95 (*0-226-07646-6*) U Ch Pr.

***Brownell, Thomas.** Do-It-Yourself Guide to Custom Painting. (Illus.). 128p. 2000. pap. 18.95 (*1-884089-49-6*, Pub. by CarTech) Voyageur Pr.

Brownell, Tom. How to Restore Chevrolet Pickup. (Illus.). 224p. 1991. pap. 24.95 (*0-87938-500-6*) MBI Pubg.

— How to Restore Your Collector Car. LC 99-31697. (Illus.). 288p. 1999. pap. 24.95 (*0-7603-0592-7*) MBI Pubg.

— How to Restore Your Ford Pick-Up. (MBI Ser.). (Illus.). 224p. 1993. pap. 24.95 (*0-87938-726-2*) MBI Pubg.

— Illustrated Buyers Guide International Pickup & Scout. LC 93-24188. (Illustrated Buyer's Guide Ser.). (Illus.). 128p. 1993. pap. 17.95 (*0-87938-777-7*) MBI Pubg.

— Illustrated Chevrolet Pickup Buyer's Guide. 2nd ed. LC 97-50153. (Illustrated Buyer's Guide Ser.). 176p. 1998. pap. 17.95 (*0-7603-0540-4*) MBI Pubg.

Brownell, Tom & Bunn, Don. Dodge Pickups: History & Restoration Guide, 1918-1971. (Illus.). 224p. 1991. pap. 21.95 (*0-87938-491-3*) MBI Pubg.

Brownell, Tom & Mueller, Mike. Chevrolet Pickup Color History. (Illus.). 128p. 1994. pap. 21.95 (*0-87938-876-5*) MBI Pubg.

— Ford Pickup Color History. (Illus.). 128p. 1994. pap. 21.95 (*0-87938-913-3*) MBI Pubg.

Brownell, W. E. Structural Clay Products. LC 76-40216. (Applied Mineralogy Ser: Vol. 9). 1977. 91.95 (*0-387-81382-9*) Spr-Verlag.

Brownell, William A. Arithmetical Abstractions: The Movement Toward Conceptual Maturity under Differing Systems of Instructions. LC 67-65751. (University of California Publications in Social Welfare: Vol. 17). 232p. reprint ed. pap. 72.00 (*0-8357-5738-2*, 202135900021) Bks Demand.

Brownell, William C. Standards. (BCL1-PS American Literature Ser.). 151p. 1992. reprint ed. lib. bdg. 69.00 (*0-7812-6680-7*) Rprt Serv.

— Victorian Prose Masters. 1972. 59.95 (*0-8490-1260-0*) Gordon Pr.

— Victorian Prose Masters. (BCL1-PR English Literature Ser.). 289p. 1992. reprint ed. lib. bdg. 79.00 (*0-7812-7112-6*) Rprt Serv.

— Victorian Prose Masters: Thackeray-Carlyle-George Eliot-Matthew Arnold-Ruskin-George Meredith. LC 72-108771. (BCL Ser. I). reprint ed. 52.50 (*0-404-01142-X*) AMS Pr.

Browner, Bruce D. Skeletal Trauma. 1999. text. write for info. (*0-7216-5993-4*, W B Saunders Co) Harcrt Hlth Sci Grp.

— Skeletal Trauma, 3 vols. 2nd ed. 1997. text 395.00 (*0-7216-7526-3*, W B Saunders Co) Harcrt Hlth Sci Grp.

Browner, Bruce D., ed. The Science & Practice of Intramedullary Nailing. 2nd ed. LC 95-14195. (Illus.). 374p. 1996. 135.00 (*0-683-01123-5*) Lppncott W & W.

Browner, Bruce D. & Edwards, Charles C. The Science & Practice of Intramedullary Nailing. LC 86-15292. 383p. reprint ed. pap. 118.80 (*0-7837-2693-7*, 204307100006) Bks Demand.

Browner, Bruce D., et al. Skeletal Trauma: Fractures, Dislocations, Ligmaentous Injuries, 2 vols., Set. 2nd ed. Lampert, Richard, ed. LC 96-50086. (Illus.). 2400p. 1997. text 295.00 (*0-7216-6884-4*, W B Saunders Co) Harcrt Hlth Sci Grp.

Browner, Carol M., ed. EPA Strategic Plan. (Illus.). 108p. 1998. pap. text 20.00 (*0-7881-2707-1*) DIANE Pub.

***Browner, Carol M., ed.** Profile of the Aerospace Industry: EPA Office of Compliance Sector Notebook Project. (Illus.). 122p. (C). 2000. reprint ed. pap. text 30.00 (*0-7567-0068-X*) Branden Bks.

***Browner, Stephanie, et al.** Literature & the Internet: A Guide for Students, Teachers, & Scholars. LC 99-27760. (Wellesley Studies in Critical Theory, Literary History & Culture). 300p. 1999. pap. 24.95 (*0-8153-3453-2*) Garland.

Browner, Warren S. Publishing & Presenting Clinical Research. LC 98-36024. 206p. 1998. pap. 34.95 (*0-683-30745-2*) Lppncott W & W.

Brownfield, William H. How to Adjust Operating Expenses for Occupancy Changes in Office Buildings: The "Gross-up" Process. 37p. (Orig.). 1990. pap. 45.00 (*0-943130-12-3*) Build Own & Man.

Brownfoot, Andrew. High Fashion in Shakespeare's Time: A Study of the Period Costume with Pull-Up Scenes. 1993. pap. 8.95 (*0-906212-82-0*, Pub. by Tarquin Pubns) Parkwest Pubns.

— High Fashion in Stuart Times: A Study of Period Costume with Pull-Up Scenes. (Illus.). 32p. (YA). (gr. 3 up). 1997. pap. 8.95 (*1-899618-08-2*, Pub. by Tarquin Pubns) Parkwest Pubns.

— High Fashion in Victorian Times. (Illus.). (J). 1996. pap. 8.95 (*0-906212-83-9*, Pub. by Tarquin Pubns) Parkwest Pubns.

— Shakespeare on Stage: Including Pull-Up Scenes to Make Yourself. 1999. pap. 10.95 (*1-899618-19-8*, Pub. by Tarquin Pubns) Parkwest Pubns.

Brownhill, Geo H. Illustrated Guide to Geelong Issued by the Committee of the Geelong Progress Association 1908 (Facsimile No. 1) 232p. (C). 1990. 75.00 (*0-7855-6745-3*, Pub. by Deakin Univ) St Mut.

Brownhill, George H. Illustrated Guide to Geelong: Issued by the Committee of the Geelong Progress Association 1908. (Facsimile Ser.: No. 1). (Illus.). 232p. 1990. pap. 75.00 (*0-7300-9811-7*, Pub. by Deakin Univ) St Mut.

Brownie. Biochemistry. LC 99-38214. (C). 1998. pap. text 24.95 (*0-443-05693-5*) Church.

Browning. Otoscopy. write for info. (*0-340-61376-9*, Pub. by E A) Routldge.

— Writing Skills for the Health Care Professional. (Allied Health Ser.). (C). 2000. pap. 29.95 (*0-7668-1259-6*) Delmar.

Browning, A. W. The Early Quarter Dollars of the United States, 1796-1838. rev. ed. (Illus.). 182p. 1998. reprint ed. pap. 22.00 (*0-943161-40-1*) S J Durst.

— The Early Quarter Dollars of the United States, 1796-1838. rev. ed. (Illus.). 182p. 1992. text 29.95 (*0-943161-44-4*) Bowers & Merena.

Browning, Amanda. Amants et Ennemis. (Azur Ser.). (FRE.). 1997. pap. 3.50 (*0-373-34656-5*, 1-34656-8) Harlequin Bks.

— Amor Robado: A Husband for the Taking. (Bianca Ser.: Vol. 457).Tr. of Stolen Love. (SPA.). 1998. per. 3.50 (*0-373-33457-5*, 1-33457-2) Harlequin Bks.

— Angel's Baby: New Arrivals. 1995. pap. 3.50 (*0-373-16600-1*) Harlequin Bks.

***Browning, Amanda.** Arriesgando el Corazon (To Risk One's Heart) The Seduction Bid. (Bianca Ser.: No. 195). (SPA.). 2000. per. 3.50 (*0-373-33545-8*, 1-33546-2) Silhouette.

Browning, Amanda. The Bitter Price of Love. LC 95-22370. (Presents Ser.). 189p. 1996. per. 3.25 (*0-373-11789-2*, 1-11789-4) Harlequin Bks.

— The Bitter Price of Love. large type ed. 288p. 1996. 23.99 (*0-263-14382-1*, Pub. by Mills & Boon) Ulverscroft.

***Browning, Amanda.** A Christmas Seduction. large type ed. 1999. 25.99 (*0-263-15954-X*, Pub. by Mills & Boon) Ulverscroft.

Browning, Amanda. Enemy Within. LC 95-13566. (Presents Ser.). 188p. 1995. per. 3.25 (*0-373-11750-7*, 1-11750-6) Harlequin Bks.

— An Old Enchantment. (Presents Ser.). 1994. per. 2.99 (*0-373-11677-2*, 1-11677-1) Harlequin Bks.

— A Promise to Repay. (Presents Ser.: No. 432). 1992. pap. 2.79 (*0-373-11432-X*, 1-11432-1) Harlequin Bks.

— Prueba de Amor (Test of Love) (SPA.). 1997. per. 3.50 (*0-373-33418-4*, 1-33418-4) Harlequin Bks.

— Savage Destiny: (Too Hot to Handle) (Presents Ser.). 1995. per. 3.25 (*0-373-11724-8*, 1-11724-1) Harlequin Bks.

— A Time for Love. (Presents Ser.). 1993. per. 2.99 (*0-373-11566-0*, 1-11566-6) Harlequin Bks.

— A Time for Love. large type ed. 1992. reprint ed. 18.95 (*0-263-13088-6*) Mac Lib Ref.

— Trail of Love. LC 95-7048. (Presents Ser.). 189p. 1995. per. 3.25 (*0-373-11742-6*, 1-11742-3) Harlequin Bks.

Browning, Andrew, ed. English Historical Documents, 1660-1714, Vol. 6. (Illus.). 998p. (C). 1996. 265.00 (*0-415-14371-3*, D2255) Routledge.

Browning, Andrew, et al, eds. The Memoirs of Sir John Reresby: The Complete Text & a Selection from His Letters. 2nd ed. (Camden Fourth Ser.). 669p. (C). reprint ed. 53.00 (*0-86193-128-9*) David Brown.

Browning, Anne. Anne's Back Door Cookbook: With Helpful Hints for the Hypersensitive. (Illus.). vii, 70p. (Orig.). 1985. pap. 6.99 (*0-933145-00-4*) Stoneground Pub.

Browning, Barb. Arizona Glimpses. LC 88-92218. (Illus.). 36p. (Orig.). 1988. 6.50 (*0-9622076-0-8*); pap. 3.50 (*0-9622076-1-6*) Bobarb Pr.

Browning, Barbara. Infectious Rhythm: Metaphors of Contagion & the Spread of African Culture. LC 97-39528. 256p. 1998. pap. 19.99 (*0-415-91981-9*) Routledge.

— Infectious Rhythm: Metaphors of Contagion & the Spread of African Culture. LC 97-39528. 256p. (C). 1998. 75.00 (*0-415-91980-0*) Routledge.

— Samba: The Body Articulate. LC 94-38586. (Arts & Politics of the Everyday Ser.). (Illus.). 192p. 1995. pap. 14.95 (0-253-20956-0) Ind U Pr.

Browning, Bertie L. Methods of Wood Chemistry, 2 vols., 1. LC 66-28537. (Illus.). 406p. reprint ed. pap. 125.90 (0-608-11506-1, 200634600058) Bks Demand.

— Methods of Wood Chemistry, 2 vols., 2. LC 66-28537. (Illus.). 521p. reprint ed. pap. 161.60 (0-608-11507-X, 200634600059) Bks Demand.

Browning, Bertiel L., ed. The Chemistry of Wood. LC 74-23593. 700p. 1975. reprint ed. 76.00 (0-88275-245-6) Krieger.

Browning, Beverley J., jt. auth. see Browning, Charles H.

***Browning, Beverly A.** Getting Grants Funded in Your Community: A Workbook for Grantseekers. large type ed. Max's Word Services Staff, ed. 200p. 1999. wbk. ed. 149.00 (0-9671073-0-X) B Browning Assocs.

— How to Become a Grantwriting Consultant. large type ed. Max's Word Services Staff, ed. 50p. 1999. 79.00 (0-9671073-1-8) B Browning Assocs.

Browning, Bonnie. Flowering Dogwood Patterns LC 98-223373. 31 p. :p. 1998. write for info. (1-57432-717-8) Collector Bks.

— Ribbons & Threads: Baltimore Style. LC 96-49792. 1996. 14.95 (0-89145-897-2, Am Quilters Soc) Collector Bks.

Browning, Bonnie, ed. A Quilted Christmas. 112p. 1995. 18.95 (0-89145-863-8, 4542, Am Quilters Soc) Collector Bks.

Browning, Bonnie K. Borders & Finishing Touches. LC 98-4751. 128p. 1997. pap. 16.95 (0-89145-899-9, 4898, Am Quilters Soc) Collector Bks.

***Browning, Bonnie K. & Miller, Phyllis D.** Play with Triangles: Patchwork Designs & Projects. Pyron, Cherry, ed. 32p. 2000. pap. 15.95 (1-57432-753-4, Am Quilters Soc) Collector Bks.

Browning, Bonnie K., ed. see Buckingham, Michael.

***Browning, Bonnie Kay.** Anybody Can Learn to Quilt. (Illus.). 128p. 2000. pap. 22.95 (1-57432-746-1, Am Quilters Soc) Collector Bks.

Browning, Brian, ed. see Drake, Barbara.

Browning, Brian, ed. see Shaw, William.

Browning, Brian, ed. see Thomas, F. R.

Browning, C. E., ed. Compositve Materials: Quality Assurance & Processing - STP 797. LC 82-72889. 173p. 1983. 29.00 (0-8031-0234-8, STP797) ASTM.

Browning, Charles H. Americans of Royal Descent: Genealogies Showing the Lineal Descent from Kings of Some American Families. (Illus.). 575p. 1998. pap. 42.50 (0-8063-0054-X, 720) Clearfield Co.

— The Magna Carta Barons & Their American Descendants: Together with the Pedigrees of the Founders of the Order of Runnedmede Deduced from the Sureties for the Enforcement of the Statues of the Magna Carta of King John. 463p. 1998. reprint ed. lib. bdg. 45.00 (0-8328-7009-9) Higginson Bk Co.

— The Magna Charta Barons & Their American Descendants (1898) Together with the Pedigrees of the Founders of the Order of Runnemede. LC 73-77634. (Illus.). 463p. 2000. reprint ed. 18.50 (0-8063-0055-8) Genealog Pub.

— Some "Colonial Dames" of Royal Descent: Pedigrees Showing the Lineal Descent from Kings of Some Members of the National Society of the Colonial Dames of America & of the Order of the Crown. LC 76-81187. 360p. 1997. reprint ed. 32.50 (0-8063-0057-4) Clearfield Co.

— Welsh Settlement of Pennsylvania. (Illus.). 633p. 1999. reprint ed. pap. 42.00 (0-7884-1063-6, B644) Heritage Bk.

Browning, Charles H. & Browning, Beverley J. Browning Outcomes Survey Scale: For Brief Therapy, 3 vols. (Illus.). (Orig.). 1996. pap. text, wbk. ed. 75.00 (0-911663-11-8) Duncliffs Intl.

— How to Partner with Managed Care. 358p. (Orig.). 1995. pap. text 29.95 (0-8309-0714-9) Herald Pub Hse.

— How to Partner with Managed Care: A Do-It-Yourself-Kit for Building Working Relationships & Getting Steady Referrals. expanded ed. LC 93-23447. 366p. (Orig.). 1997. pap. 34.95 (0-911663-84-3) Duncliffs Intl.

— How to Partner with Managed Care: "A Do-It-Yourself Kit" for Building Working Relationships & Getting Steady Referrals. expanded ed. LC 96-7717. 366p. 1996. 59.95 (0-471-15751-1) Wiley.

— Private Practice Handbook: The Tools, Tactics & Techniques for Successful Practice Development. 4th ed. 310p. 1994. pap. 29.95 (0-911663-77-0) Duncliffs Intl.

Browning, Christopher R. Fateful Months: Essays on the Emergence of the Final Solution, 1941-1942. LC 84-9089. 288p. (C). 1986. 24.95 (0-8419-0967-9) Holmes & Meier.

— Fateful Months: Essays on the Emergence of the Final Solution, 1941-1942. rev. ed. LC 84-9089. 288p. (C). 1991. pap. 15.00 (0-8419-1266-1) Holmes & Meier.

***Browning, Christopher R.** Nazi Policy, Jewish Workers, German Killers. (Illus.). 208p. 2000. 49.95 (0-521-77299-0); pap. 15.95 (0-521-77490-X) Cambridge U Pr.

Browning, Christopher R. Ordinary Men RI. LC 91-50471. (Illus.). 304p. 1998. pap. 14.00 (0-06-099506-8, Perennial) HarperTrade.

— The Path to Genocide: Essays on Launching the Final Solution. 207p. (C). 1992. text 52.95 (0-521-41701-5) Cambridge U Pr.

— The Path to Genocide: Essays on Launching the Final Solution. (Canto Book Ser.). 207p. (C). 1995. pap. 12.95 (0-521-55878-6) Cambridge U Pr.

Browning, Christopher S. The Apple Pie Savings System. (Illus.). 96p. (Orig.). 1991. pap. 8.95 (0-9626640-0-6) Apple GA.

***Browning, Dave.** Marvin Measures Up. LC 99-38026. (Illus.). 12p. (YA). (ps-3). 2000. pap. 6.95 (0-688-17734-4, Wm Morrow) Morrow Avon.

— Marvin Weighs In. LC 99-38022. (Illus.). 12p. (YA). (ps-3). 2000. pap. 6.95 (0-688-17735-2, Wm Morrow) Morrow Avon.

Browning, David. El Salvador: Landscape & Society. LC 71-855356. xx, 329 p. 1971. write for info. (0-19-823208-X) OUP.

Browning, David R. Physical Sciences, Level I. LC 77-27083. (Longman Technician Ser.). 249p. reprint ed. pap. 77.20 (0-608-11600-9, 20196070013) Bks Demand.

Browning, David R. & McKenzie-Smith, I. Engineering Science for Techniques, Level I. LC 77-30749. (Longman Tehnician Series in Mathematics & Sciences). 185p. reprint ed. pap. 57.40 (0-608-13151-2, 202523600043) Bks Demand.

Browning, Dixie. Al Modo Tradicional/The Baby Notion. Vol. 197. (Silhouette Deseo - Silhouette Desire Ser.). (SPA.). 1997. per. 3.50 (0-373-35197-6, Harlequin) Harlequin Bks.

— Alex & the Angel: Tall, Dark, & Handsome - Man of the Month. (Silhouette Desire Ser.: No. 949). 1995. pap., mass mkt., per. 3.25 (0-373-05949-3) Harlequin Bks.

— Atrapado en Ti - Trapped in You. (SPA.). 1997. per. 3.50 (0-373-35205-0, 1-35205-3) Harlequin Bks.

— The Baby Notion. (Desire Ser.: No. 1011). 1996. mass mkt. 3.50 (0-373-76011-6, 1-76011-5) Silhouette.

— The Beauty, the Beast & the Baby (Man of the Month, Tall, Dark & Handsome) LC 96-7335. (Desire Ser.). 185p. 1996. per. 3.50 (0-373-05985-X, 1-05985-6) Silhouette.

— Best Man for the Job. (Desire Ser.: No. 720). 1992. pap. 2.89 (0-373-05720-2, 5-05720-3) Harlequin Bks.

***Browning, Dixie.** Bride for Jackson Powers. (Desire Ser.: Vol. 127). 2000. mass mkt. 3.99 (0-373-76273-9) Silhouette.

Browning, Dixie. The Bride-in-Law. (Desire Ser.: No. 1251). 1999. mass mkt. 3.75 (0-373-76251-8, 1-76251-7) Silhouette.

***Browning, Dixie.** Cinderella's Midnight Kiss. (Romance Ser.: Bk. 1450). 2000. per. 3.50 (0-373-19450-1, 1-19450-5) Silhouette.

Browning, Dixie. Contra el Viento: Stryker's Wife. (Deseo Ser.).Tr. of Against the Wind. (SPA.). 1997. per. 3.50 (0-373-35207-7, 1-35207-9) Harlequin Bks.

— Encuentro Casual: The Beauty, the Beast, & the Baby. (Deseo Ser.). (SPA.). 1996. per. 3.50 (0-373-35155-0, 1-351550) Harlequin Bks.

— First Things Last. (Born in the U. S. A. Ser.). 1998. per. 4.50 (0-373-47196-3, 1-47196-0) Harlequin Bks.

— Gus & the Nice Lady. (Desire Ser.: No. 691). 1992. pap. 2.79 (0-373-05691-5, 5-05691-6) Harlequin Bks.

— His Business, Her Baby. (World's Most Eligible Bachelors Ser.: No. 3). 256p. 1998. per. 4.50 (0-373-65020-5, 1-65020-9) Harlequin Bks.

***Browning, Dixie.** Just Desserts. 2000. mass mkt. 4.50 (0-373-82238-3, 1-82338-6) Harlequin Bks.

Browning, Dixie. Kane's Way. (Desire Ser.). 1993. per. 2.99 (0-373-05801-2, 5-05801-1) Silhouette.

— Keegan's Hunt: Outer Banks. (Desire Ser.). 1993. per. 2.99 (0-373-05820-9, 5-05820-1) Silhouette.

— A Knight in Rusty Armor: Man of the Month Anniversary. 1999. per. 3.75 (0-373-76195-3, Harlequin) Harlequin Bks.

— Look What the Stork Brought: Man of the Month. (Desire Ser.: No. 1111). 1997. per. 3.50 (0-373-76111-2, 1-76111-3) Harlequin Bks.

— The Love Thing. 1994. per. 3.59 (0-373-45170-9) Silhouette.

— Lucy & the Stone. 1994. per. 2.99 (0-373-05853-5) Silhouette.

— The Passionate G-Man. (Silhouette Desire Ser.). 184p. 1998. per. 3.75 (0-373-76141-4, 0-76141-1) Silhouette.

***Browning, Dixie.** Piege pour un Solitaire. 1999. mass mkt. 3.99 (0-373-37536-0) Silhouette.

Browning, Dixie. The Security Man. 1995. per. 3.99 (0-373-45183-0, 1-45183-0) Harlequin Bks.

— Single Female (Reluctantly) Seeks... 1995. per. 3.50 (0-373-52007-1, 1-52007-1) Silhouette.

— Spring Fancy '94. 1994. mass mkt. 4.99 (0-373-48266-3, 5-48266-6) Silhouette.

— Stryker's Wife. 1996. per. 3.50 (0-373-76033-7, 1-76033-9) Silhouette.

— Stryker's Wife. 1999. 21.95 (0-373-59604-9) Silhouette.

— Texas Millionaire. (Desire Ser.: No. 1232). 1999. per. 3.75 (0-373-76232-1, 1-76232-7) Silhouette.

***Browning, Dixie.** Todo un Caballero. (Deseo Ser.: No. 183).Tr. of Gentleman. (SPA.). 1999. per. 3.50 (0-373-35313-8, 1-35313-5) Harlequin Bks.

Browning, Dixie. Two Hearts, Slightly Used. 1994. per. 2.99 (0-373-05890-X, 1-05890-8) Harlequin Bks.

— Two Hearts, Slightly Used. large type ed. (Silhouette Romance Ser.). 1996. 18.95 (0-373-59662-6) Harlequin Bks.

— Unreasonable Summer. 1980. pap. 1.50 (0-373-58013-4) Harlequin Bks.

***Browning, Dixie.** The Virgin & the Vengeful Groom. (Desire Ser.: Bk. 1331). 2000. mass mkt. 3.99 (0-373-76331-X, 1-76331-7) Silhouette.

Browning, Dixie & Major, Ann. Bad Boys. 1993. per. 5.50 (0-373-20094-3, 1-20094-8) Harlequin Bks.

Browning, Don, jt. auth. see Armour, Michael C.

Browning, Don S. A Fundamental Practical Theology. 336p. 1996. pap. 21.00 (0-8006-2973-6, 1-2973) Augsburg Fortress.

— Pluralism & Personality: William James & Some Contemporary Cultures of Psychology. LC 78-75196. 280p. 1970. 38.50 (0-8387-2265-2) Bucknell U Pr.

— Religious Thought & the Modern Psychologies: A Critical Conversation in the Theology of Culture. LC 86-45205. 272p. 1988. pap. 21.00 (0-8006-2322-3, 1-2322, Fortress Pr) Augsburg Fortress.

Browning, Don S., et al, eds. The Education of the Practical Theologian: Responses to Joseph Hough & John Cobb's Christian Identity & Theological Education. 125p. 1989. pap. write for info. (1-55540-347-6) Assn of Theol Schls.

— Religious & Ethical Factors in Psychiatric Practice. 313p. 1990. text 36.95 (0-8304-1225-5) Burnham Inc.

Browning, Don S. & Evison, Ian S., eds. Does Psychiatry Need a Public Philosophy? 131p. (Orig.). 1991. text 36.95 (0-8304-1244-1) Burnham Inc.

***Browning, Don S. & Stackhouse, Max L., eds.** God & Globalization Vol. 2: The Spirit & the Modern Authorities. 240p. 2001. 35.00 (1-56338-330-6) TPI PA.

Browning, Don S., et al. From Culture Wars to Common Ground: Religion & the American Family Debate. LC 97-20801. (Family, Religion, & Culture Ser.). 416p. 1997. pap. 19.00 (0-664-25651-1) Westminster John Knox.

Browning, Don S., ed. see Campbell, Alastair V.

Browning, Douglas. Ontology & the Practical Arena. LC 89-8369. 180p. 1990. lib. bdg. 35.00 (0-271-00677-3) Pa St U Pr.

Browning, Douglas & Myers, William T., eds. Philosophers of Progress. 2nd ed. LC 98-25568. xlv, 449p. 1998. 35.00 (0-8232-1878-3); pap. 19.95 (0-8232-1879-1) Fordham.

***Browning, Earl.** 1997 Coach of the Year Clinics Football Manual. (Illus.). 264p. 1999. pap. 22.95 (1-57167-376-8) Coaches Choice.

***Browning, Earl, ed.** Coach of the Year Clinics 1996 Football Manual. (Illus.). 254p. 1998. pap. 22.95 (1-57167-323-7) Coaches Choice.

Browning, Earl, ed. Coach of the Year Clinics 1998 Football Manual. (Illus.). 286p. 1998. pap. 22.95 (1-57167-265-6) Coaches Choice.

***Browning, Earl, ed.** Coaching the Defensive Line: By the Experts. (Illus.). 160p. 1999. pap. 16.95 (1-57167-432-2) Coaches Choice.

— Coaching the Offensive Line: By the Experts. (Illus.). 160p. 1999. pap. 16.95 (1-57167-425-X) Coaches Choice.

— The 4 - 3 Defense: By the Experts. LC 98-87456. (Coaching by the Experts Ser.). (Illus.). 214p. 1998. pap. 16.95 (1-57167-324-5) Coaches Choice.

— 1990 Coach of the Year Clinics Football Manual. (Illus.). 256p. 2000. pap. 22.95 (1-57167-402-0) Coaches Choice.

Browning, Earl, ed. 1995 Coach of the Year Clinics Football Manual. (Illus.). 256p. 1999. pap. 22.95 (1-57167-406-3) Coaches Choice.

***Browning, Earl, ed.** 1994 Coach of the Year Clinics Football Manual. (Illus.). 256p. 1999. pap. 22.95 (1-57167-405-5) Coaches Choice.

Browning, Earl, ed. 1999 Coach of the Year Clinics Football Manual. (Illus.). 256p. 1999. pap. 22.95 (1-57167-401-2) Coaches Choice.

***Browning, Earl, ed.** 1991 Coach of the Year Clinics Football Manual. (Illus.). 256p. 2000. pap. 22.95 (1-57167-403-9) Coaches Choice.

— 1993 Coach of the Year Clinics Football Manual. (Illus.). 280p. 1999. pap. 22.95 (1-57167-396-2) Coaches Choice.

— 1992 Coach of the Year Clinics Football Manual. (Illus.). 256p. 2000. pap. 22.95 (1-57167-404-7) Coaches Choice.

***Browning, Edgar K.** Microeconomic Theory & Applications Study Guide. 6th ed. 384p. 1999. pap. 31.95 (0-471-36443-6) Wiley.

— Microeconomic Theory & Applications/Microeconomic Cases & Applications. 4th ed. 1992. 87.00 (0-673-52264-4) Addison-Wesley.

— Microeconomics Theory & Applications 6th ed. (Economics Ser.). 608p. 1999. text 96.95 (0-471-36442-8) Wiley.

Browning, Edgar K. & Browning, Jacquelene M. Public Finance & the Price System. 4th ed. LC 93-34339. (Illus.). 566p. (C). 1994. 101.27 (0-02-315671-6, Macmillan Coll) P-H.

Browning, Edgar K. & Zupan, Mark A. Microeconomic Theory & Applications. 6th ed. LC 97-47610. (C). 1999. text 78.75 (0-321-00933-9) Addison-Wesley.

Browning, Edmond. Year of Days with the Book of Common Prayer. LC 97-21593. 384p. 1997. pap. 12.95 (0-345-41682-1) Ballantine Pub Grp.

Browning, Edmond L. No Outcasts: The Public Witness of Edmond L. Browning XXIVth Presiding Bishop of the Episcopal Church. Grieves, Brian J., ed. 228p. (Orig.). 1997. pap. 8.95 (0-88028-177-4, 1405) Forward Movement.

Browning, Edward F. Genealogy of the Brownings in America from 1621 to 1908. 982p. 1989. reprint ed. pap. 147.00 (0-8328-0335-9); reprint ed. lib. bdg. 155.00 (0-8328-0334-0) Higginson Bk Co.

Browning, Elizabeth Barrett. Aurora Leigh. 351p. 1992. pap. 12.00 (0-915864-85-1) Academy Chi Pubs.

— Aurora Leigh. Reynolds, Margaret, ed. LC 94-4511. (Critical Editions Ser.). (C). 1995. pap. text 14.75 (0-393-96298-9) Norton.

— Aurora Leigh. 408p. 1998. pap. 11.95 (0-19-283653-6) OUP.

— Aurora Leigh. Reynolds, Margaret, ed. LC 90-47489. (Illus.). 706p. 1992. text 69.95 (0-8214-0956-5) Ohio U Pr.

— Aurora Leigh. Bolton, John R. & Halloway, Julia B., eds. 544p. 1996. pap. 11.95 (0-14-043412-7) Penguin Putnam.

— The Brownings' Correspondence Vol. 11: Letters 1982-2177. Lewis, Scott, ed. LC 84-5287. (Illus.). xvi, 422p. 1993. 85.00 (0-911459-22-7) Wedgestone Pr.

— Burning Passion. 1999. 19.95 (1-86019-303-X) Brockhampton Pr Ltd.

— Complete Poems. 1992. reprint ed. lib. bdg. 45.95 (0-89968-287-1, Lghtyr Pr) Buccaneer Bks.

— Complete Poetical Works. (BCL1-PR English Literature Ser.). 548p. 1992. reprint ed. lib. bdg. 99.00 (0-7812-7455-9); reprint ed. lib. bdg. 119.00 (0-7812-7458-3) Rprt Serv.

— The Complete Poetical Works of Elizabeth Barrett Browning. 560p. 1991. reprint ed. pap. text 79.00 (1-878592-32-7); reprint ed. lib. bdg. 95.00 (1-878592-31-9) Native Amer Bk Pubs.

— The Complete Poetical Works of Elizabeth Barrett Browning. Harriet Waters, Preston, ed. LC 75-14491. (Illus.). xviii, 548p. 1972. reprint ed. 95.00 (0-403-00848-4) Scholarly.

— The Complete Works of Elizabeth Barrett Browning, 6 vols. Porter, Charlotte & Clarke, Helen A., eds. LC 74-148759. reprint ed. 545.00 (0-404-08840-6) AMS Pr.

— Elizabeth Barrett Browning: Letters to Her Sister, 1846-1859. (BCL1-PR English Literature Ser.). 344p. 1992. reprint ed. lib. bdg. 89.00 (0-7812-7456-7) Rprt Serv.

— Elizabeth Barrett Browning: Selected Poems. (Bloomsbury Poetry Classics Ser.). 1993. text 9.95 (0-312-09751-4) St Martin.

— Elizabeth Barrett Browning, 1806-1861: Selected Poems. Hicks, Malcolm, ed. 1983. pap. 7.50 (0-85635-412-0, Pub. by Carcanet Pr) Paul & Co Pubs.

— Essays on the Greek Christian Poets & the English Poets. LC 72-7041. (Essay Index Reprint Ser.). 1977. reprint ed. 21.95 (0-8369-7273-2) Ayer.

— Letters of the Brownings to George Barrett. Landis, Paul & Freeman, Ronald E., eds. LC 57-6950. (Illus.). 402p. reprint ed. pap. 124.70 (0-608-17988-4, 201503500098) Bks Demand.

— Sonnets From The Portugese. Markus, Julia & Peterson, William S., eds. LC 95-43253. (Illus.). 128p. 1996. 22.00 (0-88001-451-2) HarpC.

— Sonnets From The Portugese. Peterson, William S. & Markus, Julia, eds. LC 95-43253. (Illus.). 128p. 1998. pap. 14.00 (0-88001-510-1) HarpC.

— Sonnets from the Portuguese. 1998. lib. bdg. 24.95 (1-56723-025-3) Yestermorrow.

— Sonnets from the Portuguese: A Celebration of Love. 7th ed. 64p. 1986. text 9.95 (0-312-74501-X) St Martin.

— Sonnets from the Portuguese & Other Love Poems. (Illus.). 112p. 1990. 14.95 (0-385-41618-0) Doubleday.

— Sonnets from the Portuguese & Other Poems. (Thrift Editions Ser.). 64p. (Orig.). 1992. pap. 1.00 (0-486-27052-1) Dover.

— The Works of Elizabeth Barrett Browning. (Poetry Library). 624p. 1998. pap. 7.95 (1-85326-424-5, 4245WW, Pub. by Wrdsworth Edits) NTC Contemp Pub Co.

Browning, Elizabeth Barrett, et al, contrib. by. A Little Book of Love Poems. (Illus.). 60p. 1998. 9.95 (0-86281-454-5, Pub. by Appletree Pr) Irish Bks Media.

Browning, Elizabeth Barrett & Browning, Robert. The Brownings' Correspondence Vol. 14: September 1846 - December 1847, Letters 2616-2716. Kelley, Philip & Lewis, Scott, eds. LC 84-5287. (Illus.). xvi, 434p. 1998. lib. bdg. 85.00 (0-911459-25-1) Wedgestone Pr.

Browning, Elizabeth Barrett, et al. Twenty-Two Unpublished Letters of Elizabeth Barrett Browning & Robert Browning Addressed to Henrietta & Arabella Moulton-Barrett. LC 75-163206. (Studies in Browning: No. 4). 1971. reprint ed. lib. bdg. 75.00 (0-8383-1313-2) M S G Haskell Hse.

Browning, Elizabeth Barrett, jt. auth. see Browning, Robert.

Browning, Elizabeth Barrett, tr. see Aeschylus.

Browning, Ellen. Teaching Students with Severe Emotional & Learning Impairments. 331p. 1983. text 37.95 (0-205-07677-7, H76771) Allyn.

***Browning, Frank.** Apple Harvest: Apple Recipes & Orchard Lore. LC 99-29344. (Illus.). 144p. 1999. 17.95 (1-58008-104-5) Ten Speed Pr.

Browning, Frank. Apples. LC 98-27252. (Illus.). 256p. 1998. 24.00 (0-86547-537-7) N Point Pr.

— Apples: The Story of the Fruit of Temptation. (Illus.). 256p. 1999. pap. 13.00 (0-86547-579-2) N Point Pr.

— The Culture of Desire: Paradox & Perversity in Gay Lives Today. 1994. pap. 12.00 (0-679-75030-4) Vin Bks.

— A Queer Geography: Journeys Toward a Sexual Self. LC 97-36600. 256p. 1998. pap. text 13.00 (0-374-52542-0, Noonday) FS&G.

— Steam Plant Errors. (Shorey Lost Arts Ser.). 90p. reprint ed. pap. 10.00 (0-8466-6010-5, U10) Shoreys Bkstore.

— The Vanishing Land: The Corporate Theft of America. 1990. 16.00 (0-8446-5166-4) Peter Smith.

Browning, G. G. Clinical Otology & Audiology. 2nd ed. LC 98-20406. (Illus.). 224p. 1998. text 75.00 (0-7506-3373-5) Buttrwrth-Heinemann.

Browning, G. G., jt. auth. see McGarry, G. W.

Browning, G. G., jt. auth. see Wormald, P. J.

Browning, Gary. Boris Pilnyak: Scythian at a Typewriter. 200p. 1985. 32.50 (0-88233-888-9) Ardis Pubs.

***Browning, Gary.** Lyotard & the End of Grand Narratives. 192p. 2000. 49.95 (0-7083-1507-0, Pub. by U Wales Pr); pap. 27.50 (0-7083-1479-1, Pub. by U Wales Pr) Paul & Co Pubs.

Browning, Gary. Russia & the Restored Gospel. LC 96-37332. xxi, 377p. 1997. 21.95 (1-57345-202-5) Deseret Bk.

Browning, Gary, jt. auth. see Axford, Barry.

Browning, Gary K., ed. Hegel's Phenomenology of Spirit: A Reappraisal. LC 97-7796. (International Archives of the History of Ideas Ser.). 1997. lib. bdg. 130.50 (0-7923-4480-4) Kluwer Academic.

Browning, Gary L. Workbook to Russian Root List. 85p. (Orig.). 1985. pap. text 8.95 (0-89357-114-8) Slavica.

B

An Asterisk (*) at the beginning of an entry indicates that the title is appearing for the first time.

Browning, Grace. Rural Public Welfare: Selected Records. LC 75-17209. (Social Problems & Social Policy Ser.). 1976. reprint ed. 47.95 (*0-405-07481-6*) Ayer.

Browning, H. W., et al. Florida Citrus Diagnostic Guide. LC 95-60087. (Illus.). 244p. (C). 1995. text 80.00 (*0-944961-01-0*) FL Sci Source.

***Browning, Henry & Van Velsor, Ellen.** Three Keys to Development: Using Assessment, Challenge & Support to Drive Your Leadership. (Illus.). 30p. 2000. pap. text 6.95 (*1-882197-40-2*) Ctr Creat Leader.

Browning, Hugh C. Principles of Architectural Drafting: A Sourcebook of Techniques & Graphic Standards. (Illus.). 256p. 1996. pap. text 35.00 (*0-8230-4288-X*) Watsn-Guptill.

Browning, Iben & Garriss, Evelyn M. Past & Future History: A Planner's Guide. LC 81-69751. 392p. 1981. pap. 21.00 (*0-87034-063-8*) Fraser Pub Co.

Browning, Iben, jt. auth. see Winkless, Nels, III.

Browning, Jacquelene M., jt. auth. see Browning, Edgar K.

Browning, James. Read the Label Carefully: Separating New Age & Christianity. Nelson, Becky, ed. (Illus.). 22p. (Orig.). (YA). (gr. 7-12). 1992. pap. text 1.95 (*1-56309-062-7*, C926111, Wrld Changers Res) Womans Mission Union.

Browning, James A., compiled by. The Western Reader's Guide: A Selected Bibliography of Nonfiction Magazines, 1953-91. LC 92-35419. 360p. 1993. 29.95 (*0-935269-09-6*, Barbed Wire Pr) Western Pubns.

***Browning, James A. & McCravey, Janice B.** A Complete Guide to Hunter's Frontier Times. LC 99-12726. 2000. pap. 18.95 (*1-57168-299-6*, Eakin Pr) Sunbelt Media.

Browning, James A., Jr., jt. auth. see Flynn, Dan.

Browning, Jane, jt. auth. see Baker, T. Harri.

Browning, Jeannine B. Appetizers & Punch...with Love. 1994. pap. write for info. (*0-9627729-3-3*) J B Browning.

— Beef...with Love. 1994. pap. write for info. (*0-9627729-9-2*) J B Browning.

— Chicken...with Love. 1994. pap. write for info. (*0-9627729-8-4*) J B Browning.

— Chocolate, Chocolate, Chocolate...with Love. 1994. pap. write for info. (*0-9627729-7-6*) J B Browning.

— Cookies & Bars...with Love. 1994. pap. write for info. (*0-9627729-5-X*) J B Browning.

— Florida Fixin's. 1992. text 12.95 (*0-9627729-1-7*) J B Browning.

— Kids at Work. (Illus.). 174p. (J). (ps-9). 1993. 9.95 (*0-9627729-2-5*) J B Browning.

— Pound Cakes . . . with Love. 1994. pap. write for info. (*0-9627729-6-8*) J B Browning.

— Sand in My Shoes. 1990. 14.95 (*0-9627729-0-9*) J B Browning.

— Soups & Salads... With Love. 1994. pap. write for info. (*0-9627729-4-1*) J B Browning.

Browning, John. Tarantulas. (Illus.). 44p. 1989. 9.95 (*0-86622-833-0*, KW-075) TFH Pubns.

Browning, John & Minelli, Fiorigio, trs. Tirso de Molina: The Bashful Man at Court; Don Gil of the Breeches Green; The Doubter Damned. 374p. 1990. 28.00 (*0-919473-98-9*, DH61, Pub. by Dovehouse); pap. 14.00 (*0-919473-80-6*, DH61P, Pub. by Dovehouse) Sterling.

Browning, John G. An Artist at War: The Journal of John Gaitha Browning. Toliver, Oleta S., ed. LC 94-20152. (War & the Southwest Ser.: No. 3). (Illus.). 331p. 1994. 29.95 (*0-929398-76-9*) UNTX Pr.

Browning, Judith H. New York City, Yesterday & Today: Thirty Timeless Walking Adventures. Bacon, Midge, ed. LC 90-81118. (Illus.). 414p. (Orig.). 1990. pap. 21.95 (*0-9626067-0-7*) Corsair Pubns.

Browning, K. A. & Gurney, Robert J., eds. Global Energy & Water Cycles. LC 98-4546. (Illus.). 448p. (C). 1999. 95.00 (*0-521-56057-8*) Cambridge U Pr.

Browning, Kathleen, ed. see Deitz, J. Dennis.

***Browning, Larry D. & Shetler, Judy C.** Sematech: Saving the U. S. Semiconductor Industry. LC 99-57068. 320p. 2000. 44.95 (*0-89096-937-X*) Tex A&M Univ Pr.

Browning, Larry M., jt. auth. see Graetzer, Hans G.

***Browning-Larsen, Eric.** Lucky at Love: Stories & Essays from Asia. 336p. 1999. pap. 12.00 (*0-9673413-0-2*) Pacific Path Inc.

Browning, Lyle E., jt. ed. see Wittkofski, J. Mark.

***Browning, M.** HLA & MHC: Genes, Molecules & Function. 438p. 1999. 120.00 (*0-12-220438-7*) Acad Pr.

Browning, M. & McMichael, A. HLA & MHC: Genes, Molecules & Function. (Human Molecular Genetics Ser.). (Illus.). 256p. 1996. text 150.00 (*1-85996-115-0*, Pub. by Bios Sci) Bks Intl VA.

Browning, M. J., jt. ed. see Dalgleish, A. G.

Browning, Margaret, selected by. Poems of Love. 64p. 1992. text 8.95 (*0-312-07065-9*) St Martin.

***Browning, Marie.** Hand Decorating Paper. 2000. 21.95 (*0-8069-2753-4*) Sterling.

— Handcrafted Journals, Albums, Scrapbooks & More. LC 99-20751. 128p. 1999. 27.95 (*0-8069-3935-4*) Sterling.

Browning, Marie. Making Glorious Gifts from Your Garden. (Illus.). 128p. 1999. 27.95 (*0-8069-2479-9*) Sterling.

***Browning, Marie.** Memory Gifts. LC 99-54257. 2000. 24.95 (*0-8069-3933-8*) Sterling.

— Natural Soapmaking. (Illus.). 128p. 1999. pap. 14.95 (*0-8069-6289-5*) Sterling.

Browning, Mark. Haunted by Waters: Fly Fishing in North American Literature. LC 97-35279. 224p. 1998. pap. 16.95 (*0-8214-1219-1*); text 34.95 (*0-8214-1218-3*) Ohio U Pr.

Browning, Meshach. Forty-Four Years of the Life of a Hunter. (American Biography Ser.). 400p. 1991. reprint ed. lib. bdg. 79.00 (*0-7812-8047-8*) Rprt Serv.

Browning, Michael, jt. auth. see Maples, William R.

Browning Miller, Elise, jt. auth. see Blackman, Carol.

Browning, Myron E., jt. ed. see Rice, Rip G.

Browning, N. & Ogg, R. He Saw a Hummingbird. 143p. 1984. reprint ed. 12.50 (*0-87359-043-0*) Northwood Univ.

Browning, Nancy P., jt. auth. see Thomas, Helen M.

***Browning, Nigel & Pennycook, Stephen, eds.** Characterization of High-TC Materials & Devices by Electron Microscopy. LC 99-18754. (Illus.). 330p. (C). 1999. 69.95 (*0-521-55490-X*) Cambridge U Pr.

Browning, Oscar. Dante: His Life & Writings. LC 72-3093. (Studies in Dante: No. 9). (C). 1972. reprint ed. lib. bdg. 75.00 (*0-8383-1520-8*) M S G Haskell Hse.

— Goethe: His Life & Writings. LC 72-2126. (Studies in German Literature: No. 13). 1972. reprint ed. lib. bdg. 75.00 (*0-8383-1493-7*) M S G Haskell Hse.

Browning, P. Works Big Healeys. (Illus.). 200p. Date not set. 39.95 (*0-85429-966-1*, Pub. by GT Foulis) Haynes Manuals.

***Browning, Pamela.** Baby Christmas. (American Romance Ser.). 2000. mass mkt. 4.25 (*0-373-16854-3*, 1168541) Harlequin Bks.

— Feathers in the Wind. 2000. mass mkt. 4.50 (*0-373-82242-1*, 1-82242-8) Harlequin Bks.

Browning, Pamela. Lover's Leap. (American Romance Ser.). 1996. per. 3.75 (*0-373-16632-X*, 1-16632-1) Harlequin Bks.

— Merry Christmas, Baby. (American Romance Ser.). 1993. per. 3.50 (*0-373-16516-1*, 1-16516-6) Harlequin Bks.

— RSVP... Baby: The Wedding Party. 1999. per. 3.99 (*0-373-16786-5*, 1-16786-5) Harlequin Bks.

— Sunshine & Shadows. (American Romance Ser.: No. 439). 1992. mass mkt. 3.39 (*0-373-16439-4*, 1-16439-1) Harlequin Bks.

***Browning, Pamela.** That's Our Baby! (American Romance Ser.: Vol. 818). 2000. per. 4.25 (*0-373-16818-7*) Harlequin Bks.

Browning, Pamela. The World's Last Bachelor. (American Romance Ser.). 1995. per. 3.50 (*0-373-16565-X*, 1-16565-3) Harlequin Bks.

Browning, Pamela & Winters, Rebecca. A Daddy for Christmas, 3 bks. in 1. 1998. per. 5.99 (*0-373-20154-0*, 1-20154-0) Harlequin Bks.

Browning, Paul L. Welcome to DOS: Mastering the Basics. 112p. (Orig.). (C). 1991. pap. text 12.95 (*0-929915-05-4*) Headline Bks.

Browning, Peter. Day Trips: Roaming the Backroads of Northern California. rev. ed. LC 96-35086. (Illus.). 208p. 1997. pap. 12.95 (*0-8118-1423-8*) Chronicle Bks.

— John Muir, in His Own Words: A Book of Quotations. LC 87-83325. 112p. (Orig.). (C). 1988. pap. 9.95 (*0-944220-02-9*) Great West Bks.

— Outline History of an Expedition to California: Containing the Fate of the Get All You Can Mining Association. LC 99-19022. (Illus.). 48p. 1999. reprint ed. 8.95 (*0-944220-09-6*) Great West Bks.

— Place Names of the Sierra Nevada. 2nd ed. LC 84-52655. 264p. 1991. 16.95 (*0-89997-072-9*) Wilderness Pr.

***Browning, Peter.** Revolution & Nationalities: Europe 1825-1890. (Cambridge Perspectives in History Ser.). 160p. 2000. pap. write for info. (*0-521-78607-X*) Cambridge U Pr.

Browning, Peter. San Francisco/Yerba Buena: From the Beginning to the Gold Rush. LC 98-10155. (Illus.). 192p. 1998. pap. 17.95 (*0-944220-08-8*) Great West Bks.

— To the Golden Shore. LC 95-35819. (Illus.). 432p. (Orig.). (C). 1995. pap. 22.95 (*0-944220-07-X*) Great West Bks.

— The Works Minis: The International History of Competition Minis. (Illus.). 224p. 1996. 44.95 (*0-85429-967-X*, Pub. by J H Haynes & Co) Motorbooks Intl.

— Yosemite Place Names. LC 87-29793. (Illus.). 256p. (Orig.). (C). 1988. pap. 12.95 (*0-944220-00-2*) Great West Bks.

Browning, Peter, jt. auth. see Allison, Mike.

Browning, Peter, ed. see Lekisch, Barbara.

Browning, Peter, ed. see Narell, Irena.

Browning, Peter, ed. see Sargent, Shirley.

Browning, R. L. The Loss Rate Concept in Safety Engineering. LC 80-22339. (Occupational Safety & Health Ser.: Vol. 6). (Illus.). 174p. reprint ed. pap. 54.00 (*0-608-08915-X*, 206955000005) Bks Demand.

Browning, Ray, jt. auth. see Sleamaker, Rob.

***Browning, Rebecca.** You Have Looked, My Love. 88p. 2000. 9.95 (*0-9679383-0-9*) Rebfer.

***Browning, Reed.** Cy Young: A Baseball Life. LC 99-88275. (Illus.). 304p. 2000. 26.95 (*1-55849-262-3*) U of Mass Pr.

Browning, Reed. Political & Constitutional Ideas of the Court Whigs. LC 81-19372. 295p. 1982. pap. 91.50 (*0-7837-8529-1*, 204933800011) Bks Demand.

— The War of the Austrian Succession. LC 93-12439. 445p. 1993. text 45.00 (*0-312-09483-3*) St Martin.

— The War of the Austrian Succession. 480p. 1995. pap. 18.00 (*0-312-12561-5*) St Martin.

Browning, Robert. Browning's Essay on Chatterton. Smalley, Donald, ed. LC 79-100145. 194p. 1970. reprint ed. lib. bdg. 55.00 (*0-8371-3257-6*, BRCH, Greenwood Pr) Greenwood.

— The Byzantine Empire. rev. ed. LC 91-25402. 310p. 1992. pap. text 24.95 (*0-8132-0754-1*) Cath U Pr.

— Complete Poems. 1992. reprint ed. lib. bdg. 41.95 (*0-89968-288-X*, Lghtyr Pr) Buccaneer Bks.

***Browning, Robert.** The Complete Works of Robert Browning, Vol. XII. Turner, Paul & Patteson, Rita, eds. 350p. (C). 2000. text 65.00 (*0-8214-1359-7*) Ohio U Pr.

Browning, Robert. The Complete Works of Robert Browning with Variant Readings & Annotations, Vol. V. King, Roma A., Jr. et al, eds. LC 68-18389. (Illus.). xxiv, 395p. 1981. 65.00 (*0-8214-0220-X*, 82-82261) Ohio U Pr.

— The Complete Works of Robert Browning with Variant Readings & Annotations, Vol. VI. Berkey, John C. et al, eds. LC 68-18389. (Illus.). 499p. (C). 1996. text 65.00 (*0-8214-1137-3*) Ohio U Pr.

— The Complete Works of Robert Browning with Variant Readings & Annotations, Vol. XIII. Crowder, Ashby B., ed. LC 68-18389. (Illus.). 418p. (C). 1995. text 65.00 (*0-8214-1111-X*) Ohio U Pr.

— The Complete Works of Robert Browning with Variant Readings & Annotations Vol. 1, Vol. 1. King, Roma A., Jr. et al, eds. LC 68-18389. xx, 306p. 1969. 65.00 (*0-8214-0049-5*) Ohio U Pr.

— The Complete Works of Robert Browning, with Variant Readings & Annotations Vol. 2, Vol. 2. King, Roma A., Jr. et al, eds. LC 68-18389. xx, 422p. 1971. 65.00 (*0-8214-0074-6*) Ohio U Pr.

— The Complete Works of Robert Browning, with Variant Readings & Annotations Vol. 3, Vol. 3. King, Roma A., Jr. et al, eds. LC 68-18389. xxviii, 397p. 1972. 65.00 (*0-8214-0084-3*) Ohio U Pr.

— The Complete Works of Robert Browning with Variant Readings & Annotations, Vol. IX: The Ring & the Book, Books 9-12. King, Roma A., Jr. & Crowl, Susan, eds. LC 68-18389. (Complete Works of Robert Browning). 384p. 1990. lib. bdg. 65.00 (*0-8214-0381-8*) Ohio U Pr.

— Dearest Isa: Robert Browning's Letters to Isabella Blagden. McAleer, Edward C., ed. LC PR4231.A33. 440p. reprint ed. pap. 136.40 (*0-8357-7712-X*, 203606900002) Bks Demand.

— An Essay on Percy Bysshe Shelley. Harden, W. Tyas, ed. LC 74-30276. (Shelley Society, Fourth Ser.: No. 8). reprint ed. 22.50 (*0-404-11518-7*) AMS Pr.

— Essential Poets: Browning, Set. 1992. 6.98 (*0-88365-802-X*) Galahad Bks.

***Browning, Robert.** Greek World: Classical, Byzantine & Modern. 2000. pap. 34.95 (*0-500-28162-9*, Pub. by Thames Hudson) Norton.

Browning, Robert. History, Language & Literacy in the Byzantine World. (Collected Studies: No. CS299). (Illus.). 276p. (C). 1989. reprint ed. text 101.95 (*0-86078-247-6*, Pub. by Variorum) Ashgate Pub Co.

— A History of Golf. rev. ed. (Classics of Golf Ser.). (Illus.). 236p. 1985. 28.00 (*0-940889-05-6*) Classics Golf.

— Learned Lady: Letters from Robert Browning to Mrs. Thomas FitzGerald, 1876-1889. McAleer, E. C., ed. LC 66-11358. (Illus.). 244p. 1966. text 31.50 (*0-674-51900-0*) HUP.

— Men & Women: And Other Poems. Harper, J. W., ed. 256p. 1993. pap. 6.95 (*0-460-87328-8*, Everyman's Classic Lib) Tuttle Pubng.

— My Last Duchess, & Other Poems. LC 93-22035. (Thrift Editions Ser.). 128p. (Orig.). 1993. reprint ed. pap. 1.00 (*0-486-27783-6*) Dover.

— The Pied Piper of Hamelin. (J). 1993. 12.95 (*0-679-42812-7*) Everymns Lib.

Browning, Robert. Poems of Robert Browning, 001. Smalley, Donald, ed. LC 56-3004. (YA). (gr. 9 up). 1956. pap. 13.96 (*0-395-05103-7*, RivEd) HM.

Browning, Robert. The Poetical Works of Robert Browning Books I-IV: The Ring & the Book, Vol. VII. Hawlin, Stefan & Burnett, T. A. J., eds. (Oxford English Texts Ser.). 398p. 1998. text 120.00 (*0-19-812356-6*) OUP.

— The Poetical Works of Robert Browning Vol. 1: Pauline & Paracelsus, Vol. 1. Jack, Ian & Smith, Margaret, eds. (Oxford English Texts Ser.). 570p. (C). 1983. text 125.00 (*0-19-811893-7*) OUP.

— The Poetical Works of Robert Browning Vol. 2: Strafford, Sordello, Vol. 2. Ian, Jack & Smith, Margaret, eds. (Oxford English Texts Ser.). 536p. 1984. text 115.00 (*0-19-812317-5*) OUP.

— The Poetical Works of Robert Browning Vol. 3: Bells & Pomegranates I-VI (Including Pippa Passes & Dramatic Lyrics) Jack, Ian & Fowler, Rowena, eds. (Oxford English Texts Ser.). 560p. 1988. text 140.00 (*0-19-812762-6*) OUP.

— The Poetical Works of Robert Browning Vol. 4: Bells & Pomegranates VII. Jack, Ian et al, eds. (Oxford English Texts Ser.). (Illus.). 478p. (C). 1991. text 150.00 (*0-19-812789-8*) OUP.

— The Poetical Works of Robert Browning Vol. 5: Men & Women, Vol. 5. Jack, Ian & Inglesfield, Robert, eds. (Oxford English Texts Ser.). (Illus.). 556p. (C). 1996. text 130.00 (*0-19-812790-1*) OUP.

— The Ring & the Book, 4 vols. (BCL1-PR English Literature Ser.). 1992. reprint ed. lib. bdg. 300.00 (*0-7812-7460-5*) Rprt Serv.

— Robert Browning. Roberts, Adam, ed. LC 96-22017. (The Oxford Authors). 860p. 1997. pap. 19.95 (*0-19-282372-8*); text 65.00 (*0-19-254203-6*) OUP.

— Robert Browning: The Poems, 2 vols., Vol. 1. Pettigrew, John, ed. LC 80-53976. (English Poets Ser.). 1225p. 1981. reprint ed. pap. 200.00 (*0-7837-3541-3*, 205772000001) Bks Demand.

— Robert Browning: The Poems, 2 vols., Vol. 2. Pettigrew, John, ed. LC 80-53976. (English Poets Ser.). 1205p. 1981. reprint ed. pap. 200.00 (*0-7837-3542-1*, 205772000002) Bks Demand.

— Robert Browning's Poetry. Loucks, James M., ed. (Critical Editions Ser.). (C). 1979. pap. text 20.25 (*0-393-09092-2*) Norton.

— Selected Poems. DeVane, William C., ed. (Crofts Classics Ser.). 128p. 1949. pap. text 4.95 (*0-88295-019-3*) Harlan Davidson.

— Selected Poems. Karlin, Daniel, ed. & intro. by. LC 90-166503. 352p. 1990. pap. 16.99 (*0-14-058615-6*, Penguin Bks) Viking Penguin.

— The Works of Robert Browning, 10 vols., Set. (BCL1-PR English Literature Ser.). 1992. reprint ed. lib. bdg. 900.00 (*0-7812-7457-5*) Rprt Serv.

Browning, Robert & Browning, Elizabeth Barrett. The Brownings' Correspondence: Letters 2178-2383, Vol. 12. Kelley, Philip & Lewis, Scott, eds. LC 84-5287. (Illus.). xiv, 426p. 1994. 85.00 (*0-911459-23-5*) Wedgestone Pr.

— The Brownings' Correspondence: Letters 2384-2615, Vol. 13. Kelley, Philip & Lewis, Scott, eds. LC 84-5287. (Illus.). xvi, 424p. 1995. 85.00 (*0-911459-24-3*) Wedgestone Pr.

— The Brownings' Correspondence, 1841-1842, Vol. 5. Kelley, Philip & Hudson, Ronald, eds. LC 84-5287. (Illus.). xiv, 428p. 1987. 85.00 (*0-911459-16-2*) Wedgestone Pr.

— The Brownings' Correspondence, 1842-1843, Vol. 6. Kelley, Philip & Hudson, Ronald, eds. LC 84-5287. (Illus.). xiv, 425p. 1988. 85.00 (*0-911459-17-0*) Wedgestone Pr.

— The Brownings' Correspondence, 1843, Vol. 7: Letters 1174-1406. Kelley, Philip & Hudson, Ronald, eds. LC 84-5287. (Illus.). xiv, 429p. 1989. 85.00 (*0-911459-18-9*) Wedgestone Pr.

— The Brownings' Correspondence, 1843-1844 Vol. 8: Letters 1407-1617. Kelley, Philip & Hudson, Ronald, eds. LC 84-5287. (Illus.). xiv, 447p. 1990. 85.00 (*0-911459-19-7*) Wedgestone Pr.

— The Brownings' Correspondence, 1844 Vol. 9: Letters 1618-1798. Kelley, Philip & Lewis, Scott, eds. LC 84-5287. (Illus.). xvi, 423p. 1991. 85.00 (*0-911459-20-0*) Wedgestone Pr.

— The Brownings' Correspondence, 1845, Vol. 10: Letters 1799-1981. Kelley, Philip & Lewis, Scott, eds. LC 84-5287. (Illus.). xiv, 422p. 1992. 85.00 (*0-911459-21-9*) Wedgestone Pr.

— New Poems. (BCL1-PR English Literature Ser.). 186p. 1992. reprint ed. lib. bdg. 69.00 (*0-7812-7459-1*) Rprt Serv.

— Robert & Elizabeth Browning. (Poets Ser.). 146p. 1993. 5.95 (*0-7117-0442-2*, Pub. by JARR UK) Seven Hills Bk.

Browning, Robert & Lewis, Scott. The Brownings' Correspondence: 1809-1826, Vol. 1. Kelley, Philip & Hudson, Ronald, eds. LC 84-5287. (Illus.). xlviii, 383p. 1984. 85.00 (*0-911459-09-X*) Wedgestone Pr.

***Browning, Robert & Peen, Bud.** The Pied Piper of Hamelin: Poem. LC 98-43395. (Illus.). 32p. 1999. 14.95 (*0-8109-4351-4*, Pub. by Abrams) Time Warner.

Browning, Robert, jt. auth. see Browning, Elizabeth Barrett.

Browning, Robert, jt. auth. see Greenaway, Kate.

Browning, Robert, jt. ed. see Ryder, Frank G.

Browning, Robert L., ed. The Pastor As Religious Educator. 277p. (Orig.). 1989. pap. 25.95 (*0-89135-066-7*) Religious Educ.

Browning, Robert L. & Reed, Roy A. Models of Confirmation & Baptismal Affirmation: Educational & Liturgical Designs. 266p. (Orig.). 1995. pap. 24.95 (*0-89135-097-7*) Religious Educ.

— The Sacraments in Religious Education & Liturgy: An Ecumenical Model. LC 84-27536. 313p. (Orig.). 1985. pap. 24.95 (*0-89135-044-6*) Religious Educ.

Browning, Robert M. Eyes & Ears of the Convoy: Development of the Helicopter as an Anti-Submarine Weapon. 16p. 1993. pap. 2.00 (*0-16-062467-3*) USGPO.

Browning, Robert M., Jr. From Cape Charles to Cape Fear: The North Atlantic Blockading Squadron During the Civil War. LC 92-38697. 472p. 1993. text 39.95 (*0-8173-0679-X*) U of Ala Pr.

Browning, Robert M. German Poetry in the Age of the Enlightenment: From Brockes to Klopstock. LC 77-26832. (Studies in German Literature). 1978. text 40.00 (*0-271-00541-6*) Pa St U Pr.

Browning, Robert M., Jr. U. S. Merchant Vessel War Casualties of World II. LC 95-10711. (Illus.). 600p. 1996. 49.95 (*1-55750-087-8*) Naval Inst Pr.

Browning, Robert M. & Kerth, Thomas, eds. German Novellen: From Goethe to Schnitzler - An Annotated Anthology. (Illus.). 543p. (C). 1998. pap. 24.96 (*1-881089-49-5*) Brandywine Press.

— German Poetry: A Critical Anthology. (GER., Illus.). 496p. 1995. pap. text 24.96 (*1-881089-40-1*) Brandywine Press.

***Browning, Robert M. & Kerth, Thomas A., eds.** German Drama: Lessing - Goethe - Lenz - Schiller - Kleist. (GER., Illus.). 592p. 2000. pap. 24.96 (*1-881089-85-1*) Brandywine Press.

— German Drama: The Nineteenth Century. (GER., Illus.). 576p. (Orig.). (C). 2000. pap. text. write for info. (*1-881089-84-3*) Brandywine Press.

Browning, Robert M., ed. see Von Kleist, Heinrich & Paul, Jean.

Browning, Robert M., ed. & tr. see Goethe, Johann Wolfgang Von.

Browning, Robert M., tr. see Goethe, Johann Wolfgang Von, et al.

Browning, Robert S., 3rd. Two If by Sea: The Development of American Coastal Defense Policy, 33. LC 83-1638. (Contributions in Military History Ser.: No. 33). (Illus.). 210p. 1983. 49.95 (*0-313-23688-7*, BRT/, Greenwood Pr) Greenwood.

Browning, Robert X. Politics & Social Welfare Policy in the United States. LC 85-17837. 220p. (C). 1986. pap. text 20.00 (*0-87049-714-6*) U of Tenn Pr.

Browning, Rufus P. Racial Politics in American Cities. 2nd ed. LC 96-30443. 313p. (C). 1995. pap. 47.00 (*0-8013-1535-2*) Addison-Wesley.

— Racial Politics in American Cities. 2nd ed. 336p. (C). 1997. pap. text. write for info. (*0-8013-1691-X*) Addison-Wesley.

Browning, Rufus P., et al. Protest Is Not Enough: The Struggle of Blacks & Hispanics for Equality in Urban Politics. LC 83-15552. (Illus.). 311p. 1984. pap. 16.95 (*0-520-05730-9*, Pub. by U CA Pr) Cal Prin Full Svc.

B

Browning, Sally. Originial Alice. (Illus.). 64p. 1997. pap. text 9.95 (*0-7123-4533-7*) U of Toronto Pr.
Browning, Sandra, jt. auth. see Miller, A. Robin.
***Browning, Sherri.** Once Wicked. 2000. mass mkt. 5.99 (*0-440-23528-6*) Bantam Dell.
Browning, Sherri. The Scoundrel's Vow. 384p. 1999. mass mkt. 5.99 (*0-440-23527-8*) Dell.
Browning, Sinclair. The Last Song Dogs. 288p. 1999. mass mkt. 5.50 (*0-553-57940-1*) Bantam.
***Browning, Sinclair.** Sporting Club. (Trade Ellis Mysteries Ser.). 304p. 2000. mass mkt. 5.50 (*0-553-57943-6*) Bantam.
Browning, Tatiana, jt. auth. see Fitzlyon, Kyril.
Browning, Ted. Tales from Turtle Creek. (Illus.). 156p. 1991. 19.95 (*0-940540-04-5*) Brandywine Conserv.
Browning, W. R. F. A Dictionary of the Bible. LC 97-23686. (Oxford Paperback Reference). (Illus.). 428p. 1998. reprint ed. pap. 15.95 (*0-19-280060-4*) OUP.
Browning, Will, tr. see Ducharme, Rejean.
Browning, William D., jt. auth. see Barnett, Dianna L.
Browning, William G. Memory Power for Exams. (Cliffs Test Preparation Ser.). 1983. pap. 6.95 (*0-8220-2059-9*, Cliff) IDG Bks.
— Memory Power for Exams. (Cliffs Test Preparation Ser.). (Illus.). 113p. (C). 1983. pap. text 5.95 (*0-8220-2020-3*, Cliff) IDG Bks.
Browning, William S. The History of the Huguenots During the Sixteenth Century, 2 vols., Set. LC 83-45604. reprint ed. 87.50 (*0-404-19871-6*) AMS Pr.
Browning, Wilt. Deadly Goals. 1997. mass mkt. 5.99 (*0-614-27792-2*) St Martin.
— Deadly Goals, Vol. 1. 1997. mass mkt. 5.99 (*0-312-96220-7*) St Martin.
— Deadly Goals: The True Story of an All-American Football Hero Who Stalked & Murdered. Bledsoe, Jerry, ed. (Illus.). 240p. 1996. 21.95 (*1-878086-55-3*, Pub. by Down Home NC) Blair.
— The Rocks: The True Story of the Worst Team in Baseball History. Jackson, Dot, ed. LC 92-72178. (Illus.). 139p. 1992. 19.95 (*1-878086-14-6*, Pub. by Down Home NC) Blair.
Browning, Zupan. Micro Theory & Applications. 6th ed. (C). 1999. pap. text, student ed. 22.50 (*0-321-03345-0*) Addson-Wesley Educ.
Brownjohn, Alan. Lions' Mouths. LC 67-28704. 1967. 15.95 (*0-8023-1132-6*) Dufour.
— Sandgrains on a Tray: Poems. LC 69-19125. 1969. 15.95 (*0-8023-1212-8*) Dufour.
Brownjohn, Alan, jt. auth. see Basevski, Dimitar.
Brownjohn, Alan, jt. auth. see Corneille, Pierre.
Brownjohn, Alan, tr. see Goethe, Johann Wolfgang Von.
Brownjohn, J. Maxwell, tr. see Herlin, Hans.
Brownjohn, J. Maxwell, tr. see Lapouge, Gilles.
Brownjohn, J. Maxwell, tr. see Wodin, Natascha.
Brownjohn, John, tr. Pierre Lalande: Special Agent: The Wartime Memoirs of Guido Zembsch-Schreve. (Illus.). 207p. 1996. 31.95 (*0-85052-533-0*, Pub. by Leo Cooper) Trans-Atl Phila.
Brownjohn, John, tr. see Beyer, Marcel.
Brownjohn, John, tr. see Boeser, Knut.
Brownjohn, John, tr. see Brussig, Thomas.
Brownjohn, John, tr. see Glavinic, Thomas.
Brownjohn, John, tr. see Herlin, Hans.
Brownjohn, John, tr. see Poirier, Jacques R.
Brownjohn, John, tr. see Schneider, Peter.
Brownjohn, John, tr. see Sole, Robert.
Brownjohn, John, tr. see Ziegler, Jean.
Brownjohn, Sandy. The Ability to Name Cats: Teaching Children to Write Poetry. 90p. 1989. pap. text 9.95 (*0-340-50339-4*, Pub. by Hodder & Stought Ltd) Lubrecht & Cramer.
— What Rhymes with "Secret"? 104p. (Orig.). 1990. pap. text 15.00 (*0-340-28271-1*, Pub. by Hodder & Stought Ltd) Lubrecht & Cramer.
Brownlee, A. Fomento de la Investigacion Sobre Sistemas de Salud Como Instrumento de Gestion. 1995. pap. 17.50 (*0-88936-741-8*, Pub. by IDRC Bks) Stylus Pub VA.
Brownlee, David B. Building the City Beautiful: The Benjamin Franklin Parkway & the Philadelphia Museum of Art. LC 89-22806. (Illus.). 136p. (Orig.). 1989. pap. 22.95 (*0-87633-081-2*) Phila Mus Art.
— The Law Courts: The Architecture of George Edmund Street. LC 83-25625. (Architectural History Foundation-MIT Press Ser.: Vol. 8). 432p. 1984. 60.00 (*0-262-02199-4*) MIT Pr.
— Louis I. Kahn. (Illus.). 240p. 1997. pap. 25.00 (*0-7893-0099-0*, Pub. by Universe) St Martin.
— Making a Modern Classic: The Architecture of the Philadelphia Museum of Art. LC 97-7682. (Illus.). 126p. 1997. 32.00 (*0-87633-112-6*); pap. 22.00 (*0-87633-111-8*) Phila Mus Art.
Brownlee, David B. & DeLong, David G. Louis I. Kahn: In the Realm of Architecture. LC 91-9760. (Illus.). 448p. 1991. pap. 42.50 (*0-8478-1330-4*, Pub. by Rizzoli Intl) St Martin.
Brownlee, David B., jt. auth. see Thomas, George E.
Brownlee, Donald, jt. auth. see Ward, Peter D.
***Brownlee, E. Richard, et al.** Corporate Financial Reporting. 4th ed. LC 00-36960. 2000. write for info. (*0-07-231636-5*) McGraw-Hill Prof.
Brownlee, E. Richard, et al. Corporate Financial Reporting: Text & Cases. 3rd ed. LC 97-2601. 1997. write for info. (*0-256-16622-6*, Irwn Prfssnl) McGraw-Hill Prof.
Brownlee, Ian. Community Punishment: A Critical Introduction. LC 98-174982. (Criminology Ser.). vii, 221p. 1998. write for info. (*0-582-29772-9*) Longman.
Brownlee, Jack. Excuse Me, Did You Know Him? Eight Sermons & Orders of Service for Lent. LC 93-30821. 72p. 1993. pap. 8.75 (*1-55673-705-X*) CSS OH.
Brownlee, John S. Japanese Historians & the National Myths, 1600-1945: The Age of the Gods & Emperor Jinmu. 267p. 1999. pap. text 29.95 (*0-7748-0645-1*, Pub. by UBC Pr) U of Wash Pr.
— Political Thought in Japanese Historical Writing: From Kojiki (712) to Tokushi Yoron (1712) 168p. (C). 1991. text 35.00 (*0-88920-997-9*) W Laurier U Pr.
Brownlee, Juanita. Tangram Geometry in Metric. Laycock, Mary, ed. (Illus.). 64p. (Orig.). (J). (gr. 5-10). 1975. pap. 8.50 (*0-918932-43-2*, AA-1407) Activity Resources.
Brownlee, K. A. Statistical Theory & Methodology: In Science & Engineering. 2nd ed. LC 84-3941. 608p. (C). 1984. reprint ed. lib. bdg. 66.50 (*0-89874-748-1*) Krieger.
Brownlee, Keith, jt. auth. see Craig, Adam.
Brownlee, Ken. Valley of the Gray Moon: A Trilogy. 627p. 1994. pap. 22.00 (*0-9644894-0-6*) Valley Enter.
Brownlee, Ken, jt. auth. see Magarick, Pat.
Brownlee, Kevin. Poetic Identity in Guillaume de Machaut. LC 83-14498. 279p. 1984. reprint ed. pap. 86.50 (*0-608-07460-8*, 206768700009) Bks Demand.
Brownlee, Kevin & Brownlee, Marina S., eds. Romance: Generic Transformation from Chretien de Troyes to Cervantes. LC 84-40581. 303p. 1985. reprint ed. pap. 94.00 (*0-608-02304-3*, 206294500004) Bks Demand.
Brownlee, Kevin & Huot, Sylvia, eds. Rethinking the Romance of the Rose: Text, Image, Reception. (Middle Ages Ser.). (Illus.). 400p. (Orig.). (C). 1992. text 46.95 (*0-8122-3115-5*); pap. text 19.95 (*0-8122-1395-5*) U of Pa Pr.
Brownlee, Kevin & Stephens, Walter, eds. Discourses of Authority in Medieval & Renaissance Literature. LC 88-40346. 309p. 1989. reprint ed. pap. 95.80 (*0-608-02303-5*, 206294400004) Bks Demand.
Brownlee, L. M. Intellectual Property Due Diligence in Corporate Transactions: Investment, Risk Assessment, Management. LC 98-179777. 1998. write for info. (*0-8366-1248-5*) West Group.
***Brownlee, Marina S.** The Cultural Labyrinth of Marbia de Zayas. LC 99-54377. 2000. 38.50 (*0-8122-3537-1*) U of Pa Pr.
Brownlee, Marina S. The Status of the Reading Subject n the Libro de Buen Amor. LC 85-2903. (North Carolina Studies in the Romance Languages & Literatures: No. 224). 142p. reprint ed. pap. 44.10 (*0-608-20064-6*, 207133600011) Bks Demand.
Brownlee, Marina S., et al, eds. The New Medievalism. LC 91-2927. (Parallax: Re-Visions of Culture & Society Ser.). (Illus.). 312p. 1991. text 50.00 (*0-8018-4171-2*); pap. text 18.95 (*0-8018-4172-0*) Johns Hopkins.
Brownlee, Marina S. & Gumbrecht, Hans U., eds. Cultural Authority in Golden Age Spain. LC 94-35505. (Parallax). 264p. 1995. text 45.00 (*0-8018-4936-5*); pap. text 18.95 (*0-8018-4937-3*) Johns Hopkins.
Brownlee, Marina S., jt. ed. see Brownlee, Kevin.
Brownlee, Mary M., jt. auth. see Brownlee, W. Elliot.
***Brownlee, Michael, ed.** Just in Case: Dispatches from the Front Lines of the Y2K Crisis. LC 99-30082. 199p. 1999. pap. 16.95 (*1-57983-004-8*, Pub. by Origin Pr CA) SCB Distributors.
Brownlee, Richard. CPS Corporate Financial Reporting Select Text & Cases. 2nd ed. 196p. (C). 1995. text 25.95 (*0-256-21383-6*, Irwn McGrw-H) McGrw-H Hghr Educ.
— CPS Corporate Social Challenge Select Cases. 5th ed. 196p. (C). 1995. text 12.95 (*0-256-21382-8*, Irwn McGrw-H) McGrw-H Hghr Educ.
Brownlee, Richard S. Gray Ghosts of the Confederacy: Guerrilla Warfare in the West, 1861-1865. LC 83-19634. (Illus.). xi, 274p. 1984. pap. 19.95 (*0-8071-1162-7*) La State U Pr.
Brownlee, W. Elliot. Federal Taxation in America: A Short History. (Woodrow Wilson Center Press Ser.). 200p. (C). 1996. text 49.95 (*0-521-56265-1*); pap. text 14.95 (*0-521-56586-3*) Cambridge U Pr.
Brownlee, W. Elliot, ed. Funding the Modern American State, 1941-1995: The Rise & Fall of the Era of Easy Finance. (Woodrow Wilson Center Press Ser.). 479p. (C). 1996. text 69.95 (*0-521-55240-0*) Cambridge U Pr.
Brownlee, W. Elliot & Brownlee, Mary M. Women in the American Economy: A Documentary History, 1675 to 1929. LC 75-18168. (Yale Paperbound Ser.: No. Y-289). 358p. 1995. reprint ed. pap. 111.00 (*0-8357-8773-7*, 203368300087) Bks Demand.
Brownlee, William H. The Midrash Pesher of Habakkuk. LC 76-30560. (Society of Biblical Literatur, Ser.: No. 24). 230p. reprint ed. pap. 71.30 (*0-7837-5446-9*, 204521100005) Bks Demand.
Brownleigh, Eleanora. Memento. 512p. 1987. mass mkt. 3.95 (*0-8217-2037-6*, Zebra Kensgtn) Kensgtn Pub Corp.
— That Certain Style. (Lucky in Love Ser.: No. 23). 320p. 1993. mass mkt. 3.50 (*0-8217-4082-2*, Zebra Kensgtn) Kensgtn Pub Corp.
Brownley, Margaret. Body Language: Hero for Hire. 1998. per. 3.75 (*0-373-25805-4*, 1-25805-2) Harlequin Bks.
— Gay Youth: A Positive Approach for Parents & Siblings. 30p. (Orig.). 1988. pap. 3.95 (*0-945485-06-9*) Comm Intervention.
— A Parents' Guide to Teenage Pregnancy. 36p. (Orig.). 1988. pap. 3.95 (*0-945485-05-0*) Comm Intervention.
— A Youths' Guide to Job Hunting. 28p. (Orig.). (YA). (gr. 8-12). 1988. pap. 3.95 (*0-945485-02-6*) Comm Intervention.
Brownley, Margaret, et al. Chocolate Kisses. 1997. mass mkt. 5.99 (*0-312-96111-1*) St Martin.
***Brownley, Martine Watson.** Deferrals of Domain: Contemporary Women Novelists & the State. LC 99-43175. 2000. text 45.00 (*0-312-22811-2*) St Martin.
Brownley, Martine Watson & Kimmich, Allison B., eds. Women & Autobiography. LC 99-10956. (Worlds of Women Ser.). 229p. 1999. pap. 18.95 (*0-8420-2702-5*) Scholarly Res Inc.
— Women & Autobiography, Vol. 5. LC 99-10956. (Worlds of Women Ser.: No. 5). 229p. 1999. 55.00 (*0-8420-2701-7*) Scholarly Res Inc.
Brownley, Martine Watson, jt. ed. see Perry, Ruth.
Brownley, Megan. Cry of the Seagull. (Superromance Ser.: No. 501). 1992. per. 3.39 (*0-373-70501-8*, 1-70501-1) Harlequin Bks.
Brownley, Nancie, jt. ed. see McGiffin, Heather.
***Brownlie, Alison.** Charities: Do They Work? LC 98-33206. (Talking Points Ser.). 64p. (J). 1999. 27.12 (*0-8172-5319-X*) Raintree Steck-V.
Brownlie, Alison. Crime & Punishment: Changing Attitudes 1900-2000. LC 99-26777. 64p. 1999. 27.12 (*0-8172-5573-7*) Raintree Steck-V.
— Jamaica. LC 97-5823. (Country Insights Ser.). (J). 1998. lib. bdg. 25.69 (*0-8172-4792-0*) Raintree Steck-V.
— Senegal. LC 95-26778. (Worldfocus Ser.). (J). 1998. 18.50 (*1-57572-076-0*) Heinemann Lib.
***Brownlie, Alison.** We Come from Jamaica. LC 98-52970. (Country Insights Ser.). 1999. 22.83 (*0-8172-5511-7*) Raintree Steck-V.
— We Come from Nigeria. LC 99-23157. (We Come from Ser.). 2000. 22.83 (*0-8172-5513-3*) Raintree Steck-V.
— We Come from South Africa. LC 99-14211. (We Come from... Ser.). (J). 2000. 22.83 (*0-8172-5221-5*) Raintree Steck-V.
— West Africa. LC 98-25102. (Food & Festivals Ser.). (Illus.). 32p. (J). (ps-3). 1999. lib. bdg. 22.83 (*0-8172-5552-4*) Raintree Steck-V.
Brownlie, Christine L., jt. auth. see Boysen, Claudia L.
Brownlie, Faye, et al. Tomorrow's Classroom Today: Strategies for Creating Active Readers, Writers, & Thinkers. Hughes, Art, ed. LC 90-43250. (Illus.). 160p. (Orig.). (C). 1990. pap. text 21.00 (*0-435-08550-6*, 08550) Heinemann.
Brownlie, G. The Pteridophyte Flora of Fiji. (Beiheft zur Nova Hedwigia Ser.: No. 55). 1977. lib. bdg. 170.00 (*3-7682-5455-0*) Lubrecht & Cramer.
Brownlie, Ian. The British Year Book of International Law 1982, Vol. 53. Bowett, Derek W., ed. 1985. text 85.00 (*0-19-825491-1*) OUP.
— The British Yearbook of International Law 1985, Vol. 56. Bowett, Derek W., ed. (Illus.). 564p. 1987. text 119.00 (*0-19-825547-0*) OUP.
— The British Yearbook of International Law 1986, Vol. 57. Bowett, Derek W., ed. 680p. 1988. text 135.00 (*0-19-825604-3*) OUP.
— The British Yearbook of International Law 1987, Vol. 58. Bowett, Derek W., ed. 680p. 1988. text 140.00 (*0-19-825619-1*) OUP.
— International Law & the Use of Force by the States. 560p. 1991. text 125.00 (*0-19-825158-0*) OUP.
— Principles of Public International Law. 5th ed. LC 98-38843. 792p. 1999. text 110.00 (*0-19-876298-4*); pap. text 49.95 (*0-19-876299-2*) OUP.
— The Rule of Law in International Affairs: International Law at the Fiftieth Anniversary of the United Nations. LC 98-34678. 1998. 84.00 (*90-411-1068-2*, Pub. by M Nijhoff) Kluwer Academic.
— System of the Law of Nations Pt. 1: State Responsibility. 320p. 1983. text 78.00 (*0-19-825452-0*) OUP.
— Treaties & Indigenous Peoples. Brookfield, F. M., ed. 118p. 1992. text 49.95 (*0-19-825716-3*) OUP.
Brownlie, Ian, ed. Basic Documents in International Law. 4th ed. 484p. 1995. pap. text 28.00 (*0-19-876381-6*) OUP.
— Basic Documents on Human Rights. 3rd ed. 642p. 1993. pap. text 39.95 (*0-19-825712-0*) OUP.
Brownlie, Ian & Bowet, Derek W., eds. The British Year Book of International Law 1992, Vol. 62. 754p. 1993. text 175.00 (*0-19-825445-8*) OUP.
Brownlie, Ian & Bowett, Derek, eds. The British Year Book of International Law 1993, Vol. 64. 790p. 1995. text 145.00 (*0-19-825447-4*) OUP.
Brownlie, Ian & Bowett, Derek W. The British Yearbook of International Law 1983, Vol. 54. 586p. 1985. text 125.00 (*0-19-825508-X*) OUP.
— The British Yearbook of International Law 1983, Vol. 54. 577p. 1986. text 115.00 (*0-19-825520-9*) OUP.
Brownlie, Ian & Bowett, Derek W., eds. The British Year Book of International Law 1989: Sixtieth Year of Issue, Vol. 60. (Illus.). 740p. 1991. text 175.00 (*0-19-825431-8*) OUP.
— The British Year Book of International Law 1990, Vol. 61. (Illus.). 678p. 1992. text 170.00 (*0-19-825726-0*) OUP.
— The British Year Book of International Law 1992, Vol. 63. 896p. (C). 1994. text 150.00 (*0-19-825446-6*, 8191) OUP.
***Brownlie, Ian & Crawford, James, eds.** British Year Book of International Law 1998: Sixty-Ninth Year of Issue, Vol. 69. 664p. 2000. text 190.00 (*0-19-826900-5*) OUP.
Brownlie, Ian & Crawford, James, eds. British Year Book of International Law, Vol. 67. (Illus.). 896p. 1998. text 185.00 (*0-19-825883-6*) OUP.
— The British Year Book of International Law 1994: Sixty-Fifth Year of Issue, Vol. 65. 750p. 1996. text 165.00 (*0-19-825881-X*) OUP.
— The British Yearbook of International Law 1995 Vol. 66: Sixty-Sixth Year of Issue, Vol. 66. (Illus.). 794p. 1997. text 185.00 (*0-19-825882-8*) OUP.
Brownlie, Ian, jt. auth. see Jennings, R. Y.
Brownlie, Ian, jt. ed. see Bos, Maarten.
Brownlie, Ian, ed. see Bowett, Derek W.
Brownlie, Ian, jt. ed. see Jennings, R. Y.
Brownlie, Lisa. How to Baby-Proof Your Home. (Illus.). 240p. 1998. pap. 17.95 (*1-85158-934-1*, Pub. by Mainstream Pubng) Trafalgar.
Brownlie, Noreen. That Outlaw Attitude. 1994. per. 3.50 (*0-373-09888-X*) Silhouette.
***Brownlie, William D.** Life Insurance Boot Camp 2000: The Buyer's Guide with Respect to Life Insurance & Other Financial Issues. 2nd ed. 2000. spiral bd. 44.95 (*0-9662791-3-1*) LIBC.
— Life Insurance Boot Camp 2000: The Buyer's Guide with Respect to Life Insurance & Other Financial Issues. 2nd abr. ed. 330p. 2000. disk 14.95 (*0-9662791-1-5*) LIBC.
Brownlow. Catch of the Day. LC 99-237348. 1999. pap. text 5.99 (*1-57051-270-1*) Brownlow Pub Co.
— Christmas Memories Victorian Journal: Christmas Skating. 96p. 1995. 9.99 (*1-57051-073-3*) Brownlow Pub Co.
— From the Heart of a Friend: 101 Words to Share With a Friend. (Easelette Miniatures Ser.). (Illus.). 101p. 1995. spiral bd. 5.99 (*1-57051-009-1*) Brownlow Pub Co.
— Gardens of Love. LC 99-236523. 1999. 5.99 (*1-57051-259-0*) Brownlow Pub Co.
— Gifts of Love Wire Journal. 1999. 9.99 (*1-57051-252-3*) Brownlow Pub Co.
— Happiness is Homemade. LC 99-237357. 1999. pap. text 5.99 (*1-57051-265-5*) Brownlow Pub Co.
— Hearts at Home. LC 99-237220. 1999. pap. text 8.99 (*1-57051-268-X*) Brownlow Pub Co.
— Home is Where Love Abides. 1999. 9.99 (*1-57051-266-3*) Brownlow Pub Co.
— Homespun Wisdom. LC 99-236540. 1999. 5.99 (*1-57051-267-1*) Brownlow Pub Co.
— Little Book of Love: Mini Book. LC 99-237089. 1999. pap. text 5.99 (*1-57051-251-5*) Brownlow Pub Co.
— Side Yard Sutton, England. 1999. 9.99 (*1-57051-260-4*) Brownlow Pub Co.
— Sister Dear. LC 99-231882. 1999. 9.99 (*1-57051-170-5*) Brownlow Pub Co.
— Words of Friendship: 101 Words to Share with a Friend. (Easelette Miniatures Ser.). (Illus.). 101p. 1995. spiral bd. 5.99 (*1-877719-75-7*) Brownlow Pub Co.
Brownlow & Reid. Communications. (Spotlight Australia Ser.). 1996. pap. write for info. (*0-08-020937-8*, Pergamon Pr) Elsevier.
— Urban Australia. (Spotlight Australia Ser.). 1996. pap. write for info. (*0-08-020938-6*, Pergamon Pr) Elsevier.
Brownlow, Art. The Last Trumpet: A History of the English Slide Trumpet. LC 96-28052. (Bucina Ser.: No. 1). 277p. 1996. 54.00 (*0-945193-81-5*) Pendragon NY.
Brownlow, Arthur H. Geochemistry. 2nd ed. LC 95-37089. (Illus.). 580p. (C). 1995. 93.33 (*0-13-398272-6*) P-H.
Brownlow, Arthur H., jt. ed. see Lyons, Paul C.
Brownlow, Cecelia F. & Wilner, Leslie S. White Cloud - Lakota Spirit: Legends. LC 92-16827. 1992. 10.95 (*0-86534-166-4*) Sunstone Pr.
Brownlow, Donald G. Checkmate at Ruweisat: Auchinleck's Finest Hour. LC 77-78440. (Illus.). 1977. 12.95 (*0-8158-0356-7*) Chris Mass.
— The Life & Times of Horst Wessel. LC 94-68121. 1996. 22.95 (*0-8158-0507-1*) Chris Mass.
Brownlow, F. W. Robert Southwell. (Twayne's English Authors Ser.: No. 516). 1996. 32.00 (*0-8057-7806-3*, Twayne) Mac Lib Ref.
Brownlow, Frank W. Shakespeare, Harsnett, & the Devils of Denham. LC 90-51010. (Illus.). 440p. 1993. 49.50 (*0-87413-436-6*) U Delaware Pr.
Brownlow, Frank W., ed. see Skelton, John.
Brownlow, Jeanne P., ed. see Boudreau, H. L.
Brownlow, Kevin. Behind the Mask of Innocence: Sex, Violence, Crime: Films of Social Conscience in the Silent. 1992. pap. 30.00 (*0-520-07626-5*, Pub. by U CA Pr) Cal Prin Full Svc.
— David Lean. (Illus.). 832p. 1997. pap. 24.95 (*0-312-16810-1*) St Martin.
— The Parade's Gone By. LC 75-17302. 1976. reprint ed. pap. 27.50 (*0-520-03068-0*, Pub. by U CA Pr) Cal Prin Full Svc.
Brownlow, Kevin & Cushman, Robert. Mary Pickford Rediscovered: Rare Pictures of a Hollywood Legend. LC 98-41302. (Illus.). 256p. 1999. 39.95 (*0-8109-4374-3*, Pub. by Abrams) Time Warner.
Brownlow, Leroy. Cheerful Hearts - Are Better Than Medicine. deluxe ed. 96p. 1967. 9.99 (*0-915720-07-8*) Brownlow Pub Co.
— Flowers for You: Reflections on the Beauty of Living. (Illus.). 96p. 1963. 9.99 (*0-915720-01-9*) Brownlow Pub Co.
— Flowers That Never Fade: Words of Hope & Inspiration with Everlasting Value. (Illus.). 96p. 1959. 9.99 (*0-915720-00-0*) Brownlow Pub Co.
— Jesus Wept: Trusting the Good Shepherd When You Lose a Loved One. deluxe ed. 63p. 1969. 9.99 (*0-915720-12-4*) Brownlow Pub Co.
— A Psalm in My Heart: Daily Devotionals from the Book of Psalms. deluxe ed. (Devotions for Today Ser.). 365p. 1989. 14.99 (*0-915720-32-9*) Brownlow Pub Co.
***Brownlow, Mike.** Little Robots. 32p. (J). 2000. 12.95 (*1-929927-05-3*) Ragged Bears NY.
— Way Out West... With a Baby! (Illus.). 32p. (J). (gr. 2). 2000. 13.95 (*1-929927-04-5*) Ragged Bears NY.
Brownlow, Paul. Baseball's Heritage & Heroes. 126p. 1997. spiral bd. 9.99 (*1-57051-154-3*) Brownlow Pub Co.
— Golf at St. Andrews. 126p. 1997. spiral bd. 9.99 (*1-57051-148-9*) Brownlow Pub Co.
— Strength for a Man's Heart. LC 99-231759. 48p. 1997. 9.99 (*1-57051-140-3*) Brownlow Pub Co.
Brownlow, Paul C. Angels of Mercy, Whispers of Love. (Illus.). 63p. 1994. 9.99 (*1-57051-002-4*) Brownlow Pub Co.
— Dear Teacher. (Little Treasures Ser.). (Illus.). 88p. 1993. 4.99 (*1-877719-60-9*) Brownlow Pub Co.
— Friendship Warms the Heart. (Little Ribbons of Love Ser.). (Illus.). 90p. 1996. pap. 5.99 (*1-57051-133-0*) Brownlow Pub Co.
— Leaves of Gold: An Inspirational Classic for Our Time. (Cherished Moments Ser.). (Illus.). 120p. 1996. 12.99 (*1-57051-128-4*) Brownlow Pub Co.

B

An Asterisk (*) at the beginning of an entry indicates that the title is appearing for the first time.

— Shepherd's Heart: Blank Wiro Journal. 1997. 9.99 (*1-57051-158-6*) Brownlow Pub Co.

— Shepherd's Heart: Drawing Near to the Heart of God. 48p. 1997. 14.99 (*1-57051-156-X*) Brownlow Pub Co.

Brownlow, Paul C., ed. A Celebration of Christmas. LC 99-232449. (Cherished Moments Ser.). 48p. 1998. 12.99 (*1-57051-178-0*, 1780) Brownlow Pub Co.

— Golf & Other Essentials of Life. LC 99-232661. (Cherished Moments Ser.). 48p. 1998. 14.99 (*1-57051-093-8*, 0938) Brownlow Pub Co.

Brownlow Pub Staff, ed. China & Chintz. 1997. 9.99 (*1-57051-152-7*) Brownlow Pub Co.

Brownlow Publishing Co. Staff. A+ Teacher. 7.99 (*1-57051-102-0*) Brownlow Pub Co.

Brownlow Publishing Co. Staff. God's Promises for Everyday Spiral. 236p. 1996. 8.99 (*1-57051-124-1*) Brownlow Pub Co.

***Brownlow Publishing Co. Staff.** Love Is, Ribbon Book. LC 99-235832. 1999. pap. 8.99 (*1-57051-250-7*) Brownlow Pub Co.

Brownlow Publishing Co. Staff. Reflections for Each Day: From Leaves of Gold. deluxe ed. (Daily Reflections). (Illus.). 365p. 1990. spiral bd. 7.99 (*1-877719-15-3*) Brownlow Pub Co.

Brownlow Publishing Company, Creative Department S, compiled by. Baby's First Book: Prayers & Lullabies, Blue. (Little Treasures Ser.). 88p. 1998. 4.99 (*1-57051-173-X*, 173X) Brownlow Pub Co.

— Baby's First Book: Prayers & Lullabies, Yellow. (Little Treasures Ser.). 88p. 1998. pap. 4.99 (*1-57051-174-8*, 1748) Brownlow Pub Co.

— Blessings for Today: 101 Blessings from the Heart. LC 99-236534. (Easelette Miniatures Ser.). 101p. 1998. spiral bd. 5.99 (*1-57051-142-X*, 0997) Brownlow Pub Co.

— Dear Daughter: Loving Reflections Just for You. LC 99-237009. (Little Treasures Ser.). 64p. 1998. 5.99 (*1-57051-127-6*, 1276) Brownlow Pub Co.

— Dear Teacher: 101 Words of Encouragement. (Easelette Miniatures Ser.). 101p. 1997. spiral bd. 5.99 (*1-57051-203-5*, 2035) Brownlow Pub Co.

— Garden Gatherings: 101 Thoughts from the Garden. LC 99-236673. (Easelette Miniatures Ser.). 101p. 1998. spiral bd. 5.99 (*1-57051-099-7*, 0997) Brownlow Pub Co.

— The Lord Is My Shepherd: 101 Thoughts of Encouragement. LC 99-236649. (Easelette Miniatures Ser.). 101p. 1998. spiral bd. 5.99 (*1-57051-187-X*, 187X) Brownlow Pub Co.

— Merry Christmas: Season of Peace & Goodwill. LC 99-236724. (Little Treasures Ser.). 64p. 1998. 5.99 (*1-57051-180-2*, 595) Brownlow Pub Co.

— Quiet Moments of Inspiration. LC 99-237377. (Little Treasures Ser.). 64p. 1997. 5.99 (*1-57051-168-3*, 1683) Brownlow Pub Co.

— Reading the Greens: 101 Thoughts on Golf & Life. LC 99-236664. (Easelette Miniatures Ser.). 101p. 1998. spiral bd. 5.99 (*1-57051-094-6*, 0946) Brownlow Pub Co.

— Seasons of Friendship. LC 99-237370. (Little Treasures Ser.). 64p. 1998. 5.99 (*1-57051-141-1*, 1411) Brownlow Pub Co.

— They Call It Golf. LC 99-237231. (Little Treasures Ser.). 64p. 1998. 5.99 (*1-57051-143-8*, 1438) Brownlow Pub Co.

Brownlow Publishing Company, Inc. Staff. Beside Still Waters: Miniature Book. LC 99-237032. 64p. 1997. 5.99 (*1-57051-157-8*) Brownlow Pub Co.

Brownlow Publishing Company Staff. Heavenly Angels. 140p. 1997. 7.99 (*1-57051-053-9*) Brownlow Pub Co.

— Thoughts from the Garden Gate. (Ribbons of Love Ser.). 90p. 1997. pap. 8.99 (*1-57051-130-6*) Brownlow Pub Co.

***Brownlow Publishing Company Staff.** With All My Heart. 1999. 9.99 (*1-57051-418-6*) Brownlow Pub Co.

Brownlow, Tim. Climbing Croagh Patrick. LC 99-200501. 96p. 1998. pap. 14.95 (*0-88982-172-0*, Pub. by Oolichan Bks) Genl Dist Srvs.

Brownlow, Timothy. John Clare & Picturesque Landscape. (Illus.). 170p. 1983. 70.00 (*0-19-812808-8*) OUP.

Brownlow, William G. A Political Register, Setting Forth the Principles of the Whig & Locofoco Parties in the United States, with the Life & Public Services of Henry Clay. LC 73-23063. 348p. 1974. reprint ed. 27.50 (*0-87152-153-9*) Reprint.

Brownlow, William G. & Pryne, Abram. Ought American Slavery to Be Perpetuated. LC 79-83959. (Black Heritage Library Collection). 1977. 22.95 (*0-8369-8520-6*) Ayer.

Brownmiller, Sara & Dickstein, Ruth. An Index to Women's Studies Anthologies: Research across the Disciplines, 1980-1984. 1994. 160.00 (*0-8161-0589-8*, G K Hall & Co) Mac Lib Ref.

Brownmiller, Sara, jt. auth. see Dickstein, Ruth.

Brownmiller, Susan. Against Our Will: Men, Women & Rape. 480p. 1993. pap. 12.50 (*0-449-90820-8*, Columbine) Fawcett.

— Femininity. 1985. pap. 11.00 (*0-449-90142-4*, Columbine) Fawcett.

***Brownmiller, Susan.** In Our Time. 2000. pap. 14.95 (*0-385-31831-6*, Dial Pr) Dell.

Brownmiller, Susan. In Our Time: Memoir of a Revolution. LC 99-39344. 343p. 1999. 24.95 (*0-385-31486-8*) Delacorte.

Brownridge, Dennis R. Metric in Minutes: The Comprehensive Resource for Learning the Metric System (SI) (Illus.). 100p. (Orig.). 1994. pap. 19.95 (*0-912045-71-X*) Prof Pubns CA.

***Brownridge, Douglas A. & Halli, Shivalingappa S.** Explaining Violence Against Women: The Role of Marital Status. LC 00-42434. 288p. 2000. 65.00 (*0-7391-0166-8*) Lxngtn Bks.

Brownridge, Eleanor. I'm Hungry: Your Guide to Nutritious & Task. rev. ed. 1993. 12.33 (*0-394-22347-0*) Beginner.

Brownridge, Eleanor, ed. Membership Directory. rev. ed. 224p. 5.00 (*0-614-05244-0*, MEM0694) ASFE.

Brownridge, William R. The Final Game. (Illus.). 32p. (J). (gr. k-3). 1998. pap. 6.95 (*1-55143-102-5*) Orca Bk Pubs.

— The Moccasin Goalie. (Illus.). 32p. (J). (ps-3). 1996. reprint ed. pap. 6.95 (*1-55143-054-1*) Orca Bk Pubs.

Brownrigg. I'm An Artist. (J). Date not set. mass mkt. 16.00 (*0-689-80250-1*) Aladdin.

Brownrigg, Elisabeth. Falling to Earth: A Novel. LC 98-33588. 176p. 1998. pap. 12.95 (*1-56341-100-8*) Firebrand Bks.

Brownrigg, Elizabeth. Falling to Earth: A Novel. LC 98-33588. 176p. 1998. 26.95 (*1-56341-101-6*) Firebrand Bks.

Brownrigg, Henry. Betel Cutters: From the Samuel Eilenberg Collection. LC 89-50633. (Illus.). 160p. 1992. 35.00 (*0-500-97376-8*, Pub. by Thames Hudson) Norton.

Brownrigg, Linda L., ed. Making the Medieval Book: Techniques of Production. (Proceedings of the Seminar in the History of the Book to 1500 Ser.). (Illus.). xvi, 248p. (C). 1995. 98.00 (*0-9626372-2-X*) Anderson-Lovelace Pubs.

— Making the Medieval Book: Techniques of Production. (Proceedings of the Seminar in the History of the Book to 1500 Ser.). (Illus.). xvi, 248p. (C). 1995. pap. 55.00 (*0-9626372-3-8*) Anderson-Lovelace Pubs.

Brownrigg, Ronald. Who's Who in the New Testament. (Who's Who Ser.). 304p. (C). 1993. pap. 17.95 (*0-19-521031-X*, 3952) OUP.

Brownrigg, Ronald & Comay, Joan. Who's Who in the Bible, 2 vols. in 1. (Illus.). 864p. 1993. 19.99 (*0-517-32170-X*) Random Hse Value.

Brownrigg, Sheri. All Tutus Should Be Pink. LC 90-40325. (Illus.). 32p. (J). (ps-3). 1992. pap. 3.50 (*0-590-43904-9*, Cartwheel) Scholastic Inc.

Brownrigg, Sheri. All Tutus Should Be Pink. (Hello, Reader! Ser.). (J). 1992. 8.70 (*0-606-01776-3*, Pub. by Turtleback) Demco.

Brownrigg, Sheri. Best Friends Wear Pink Tutus. LC 92-27569. (Hello Reader! Ser.). (Illus.). 32p. (J). (ps-3). 1993. 3.50 (*0-590-46437-X*) Scholastic Inc.

— Heart & Crafts. LC 95-12079. (Illus.). 96p. (J). (gr. 2 up). 1995. pap. 9.95 (*1-883672-28-7*) Tricycle Pr.

***Brownrigg, Sylvia.** The Metaphysical Touch. LC 98-48755. 400p. 1999. text 23.00 (*0-374-19965-5*) FS&G.

— The Metaphysical Touch. LC 00-36721. 400p. 2000. pap. 15.00 (*0-312-26357-0*) St Martin.

— Ten Women Who Shook the World: Stories. LC 99-55341. 160p. 2000. 20.00 (*0-374-27289-1*) FS&G.

Browns, Ken. An Introduction to Sociology. 2nd ed. LC 98-6187. 480p. 1998. 64.95 (*0-7456-2020-5*) Blackwell Pubs.

— An Introduction to Sociology. 2nd ed. LC 98-6187. 480p. 1998. pap. 34.95 (*0-7456-2021-3*) Blackwell Pubs.

Brownsberger, Kenneth R., jt. auth. see Snow, Theodore P.

Brownsberger, Susan, tr. see Bitov, Andrei.

Brownsell, V. Basic Science for Food Studies. 1985. pap. text. write for info. (*0-582-41328-1*, Pub. by Addison-Wesley) Longman.

Brownsell, V. L., et al. Basic Science for Food Studies. LC 85-65. (Longman Hotelwork & Catering Ser.). (Illus.). 251p. reprint ed. pap. 77.90 (*0-7837-5182-6*, 204491200004) Bks Demand.

Brownsell, Vivian L. Applied Science Food. 1987. pap. text. write for info. (*0-582-41367-2*, Pub. by Addison-Wesley) Longman.

Brownsey, K. Lorne, ed. Canada-Japan: Policy Issues for the Future. 222p. 1989. 23.95 (*0-88645-086-1*, Pub. by Inst Res Pub) Ashgate Pub Co.

Brownsey, K. Lorne, jt. auth. see Langford, John W.

Brownsey, Keith. The Provencial State: Politics in Canada's Provinces & Territories. (C). 1992. pap. text 33.95 (*0-7730-5192-9*) Addison-Wesley.

***Brownsey, Ken.** The Essence of Data Structures Using C++ LC 00-25355. (Essence of Computing Ser.). 2000. write for info. (*0-13-948886-3*) P-H.

***Brownsey, Lois & Lantz, Marti.** The Big Yellow Schoolbus: Plus 19 Other Splendiferous Songs for Autumn & Winter. 48p. 1999. pap. 39.95 incl. audio compact disk (*0-7390-0333-X*, 18742) Alfred Pub.

— The Big Yellow Schoolbus Activity Sheets: Plus 19 Other Splendiferous Songs for Autumn & Winter. 20p. 1991. pap. 9.95 (*0-7390-0335-6*, 3565) Alfred Pub.

— The Big Yellow Schoolbus Songbook: Plus 19 Other Splendiferous Songs for Autumn & Winter. 48p. 1991. pap. 9.95 (*0-7390-0334-8*, 3564) Alfred Pub.

Brownsey, Lois, jt. auth. see Lunn, Marti.

Brownson, Anna L., ed. Congressional Staff Directory Advance Locator, 1989: With Biographical Material on Members. 27th ed. LC 59-13987. 488p. 1989. pap. 15.00 (*0-87289-077-5*) C Q Staff.

— Congressional Staff Directory Advance Locator, 1990: With Biographical Material on Members. 28th ed. LC 59-13987. 536p. 1990. pap. 15.00 (*0-87289-083-X*) C Q Staff.

— Congressional Staff Directory Advance Locator, 1991: With Biographical Material on Members. 29th ed. LC 59-13987. 480p. 1991. pap. 20.00 (*0-87289-089-9*) C Q Staff.

— Congressional Staff Directory Advance Locator, 1992: With Biographical Material on Members. 30th ed. LC 59-13987. 560p. 1992. pap. 20.00 (*0-87289-095-3*) C Q Staff.

— Congressional Staff Directory Advance Locator, 1993: With Biographical Material on Members. 31st ed. LC 59-13987. 504p. 1993. pap. 25.00 (*0-87289-101-1*) C Q Staff.

— Congressional Staff Directory Advance Locator, 1994: With Biographical Material on Members. 32nd ed. LC 59-13987. 500p. 1994. pap. 25.00 (*0-87289-105-2*) C Q Staff.

— Congressional Staff Directory Advance Locator, 1995: With Biographical Material on Members. 33rd ed. 1995. pap. 30.00 (*0-87289-112-7*) C Q Staff.

— Congressional Staff Directory, 1989-1: With Biographical Information on Members & Key Congressional Staff. 31st ed. LC 59-13987. 992p. 1989. 50.00 (*0-87289-078-3*) C Q Staff.

— Congressional Staff Directory, 1989-2: With Biographical Information on Members & Key Congressional Staff. 32nd ed. LC 59-13987. 1024p. 1989. pap. 50.00 (*0-87289-080-5*) C Q Staff.

— Congressional Staff Directory, 1990-1: With Biographical Information on Members & Key Congressional Staff. 33rd ed. LC 59-13987. 1160p. 1990. 50.00 (*0-87289-084-8*) C Q Staff.

— Congressional Staff Directory, 1990-2: With Biographical Information on Members & Key Congressional Staff. 34th ed. LC 59-13987. 1168p. 1990. pap. 50.00 (*0-87289-086-4*) C Q Staff.

— Congressional Staff Directory, 1991-1: With Biographical Information on Members & Key Congressional Staff. 35th ed. LC 59-13987. 1184p. 1991. 59.00 (*0-87289-090-2*) C Q Staff.

— Congressional Staff Directory, 1991-2: With Biographical Information on Members & Key Congressional Staff. 36th ed. LC 59-13987. 1200p. 1991. pap. 59.00 (*0-87289-092-9*) C Q Staff.

— Congressional Staff Directory, 1992-1: With Biographical Information on Members & Key Congressional Staff. 37th ed. LC 59-13987. 1184p. 1992. 59.00 (*0-87289-096-1*) C Q Staff.

— Congressional Staff Directory, 1992-2: With Biographical Information on Members & Key Congressional Staff. 38th ed. LC 59-13987. 1214p. 1992. pap. 59.00 (*0-87289-098-8*) C Q Staff.

— Congressional Staff Directory, 1994 No. 1: With Biographical Information on Members & Key Congressional Staff. 41st ed. LC 59-13987. 1200p. 1994. 69.00 (*0-87289-108-9*) C Q Staff.

— Congressional Staff Directory, 1994-2: With Biographical Material on Members & Key Congressional Staff. 42nd ed. 1994. pap. 69.00 (*0-87289-110-0*) C Q Staff.

— Congressional Staff Directory, 1995-1: With Biographical Material on Members & Key Congressional Staff. 43rd ed. 1995. 79.00 (*0-87289-115-1*) C Q Staff.

— Election Index to Redistricted States, 1966. LC 59-13987. 250p. 1966. pap. 5.00 (*0-87289-011-2*) C Q Staff.

— Election Index to Redistricted States, 1968. LC 59-13987. 256p. 1968. pap. 5.00 (*0-87289-016-3*) C Q Staff.

— Election Index to Redistricted States, 1970. LC 59-13987. 276p. 1970. pap. 5.00 (*0-87289-021-X*) C Q Staff.

— Election Index to Redistricted States, 1972. LC 59-13987. 284p. 1972. pap. 5.00 (*0-87289-026-0*) C Q Staff.

— Election Index to Redistricted States, 1974. LC 59-13987. 272p. 1974. pap. 5.00 (*0-87289-031-7*) C Q Staff.

— Election Index to Redistricted States, 1976. LC 59-13987. 276p. 1976. pap. 7.00 (*0-87289-036-8*) C Q Staff.

— Election Index to Redistricted States, 1978. LC 59-13987. 276p. 1978. pap. 8.00 (*0-87289-041-4*, 87289) C Q Staff.

— Election Index to Redistricted States, 1980. LC 59-13987. 277p. 1980. reprint ed. pap. 8.00 (*0-87289-046-5*, 87289) C Q Staff.

— Federal Staff Directory, 1989-1: With Biographical Information on Executive Staff Personnel. 8th ed. LC 59-13987. 1374p. 1989. 50.00 (*0-87289-076-7*) C Q Staff.

— Federal Staff Directory, 1989-2: With Biographical Information on Executive Staff Personnel. 9th ed. LC 59-13987. 1384p. 1989. pap. 50.00 (*0-87289-079-1*) C Q Staff.

— Federal Staff Directory, 1990-1: With Biographical Information on Executive Staff Personnel. 10th ed. LC 59-13987. 1406p. 1990. 50.00 (*0-87289-082-1*) C Q Staff.

— Federal Staff Directory, 1990-2: With Biographical Information on Executive Staff Personnel. 11th ed. LC 59-13987. 1464p. 1990. pap. 50.00 (*0-87289-085-6*) C Q Staff.

— Federal Staff Directory, 1991-1: With Biographical Information on Executive Staff Personnel. 12th ed. LC 59-13987. 1464p. 1991. 59.00 (*0-87289-088-0*) C Q Staff.

— Federal Staff Directory, 1991-2: With Biographical Information on Executive Staff Personnel. 13th ed. LC 59-13987. 1472p. 1991. pap. 59.00 (*0-87289-091-0*) C Q Staff.

— Federal Staff Directory, 1992-1: With Biographical Information on Executive Staff Personnel. 14th ed. LC 59-13987. 1588p. 1992. 59.00 (*0-87289-094-5*) C Q Staff.

— Federal Staff Directory, 1992-2: With Biographical Information on Executive Staff Personnel. 15th ed. LC 59-13987. 1608p. 1992. pap. 59.00 (*0-87289-097-X*) C Q Staff.

— Federal Staff Directory, 1994 No. 1: With Biographical Information on Executive Staff Personnel. 18th ed. LC 59-13987. 1500p. 1994. 69.00 (*0-87289-107-0*) C Q Staff.

— Federal Staff Directory, 1994 No. 2: With Biographical Information on Executive Staff Personnel. 19th ed. LC 59-13987. 1564p. 1994. pap. 69.00 (*0-87289-109-7*) C Q Staff.

— Federal Staff Directory, 1995-1: With Biographical Information on Executive Staff Personnel. 20th ed. 1995. 79.00 (*0-87289-113-5*) C Q Staff.

— Federal Staff Directory, 1995-2: With Biographical Information on Executive Staff Personnel. 21st ed. LC 59-13987. 1995. pap. 79.00 (*0-87289-116-X*) C Q Staff.

— Federal Staff Directory, 1996-Spring: With Biographical Information on Executive Staff Personnel. 22nd ed. LC 59-13987. 1996. 79.00 (*0-87289-119-4*) C Q Staff.

— Judicial Staff Directory 1989: With Biographical Information on Judges & Key Court Staff. 3rd ed. LC 59-13987. 912p. 1988. 50.00 (*0-87289-075-9*) C Q Staff.

— Judicial Staff Directory 1990: With Biographical Information on Judges & Key Court Staff. 4th ed. LC 59-13987. 912p. 1989. 50.00 (*0-87289-081-3*) C Q Staff.

— Judicial Staff Directory 1991: With Biographical Information on Judges & Key Court Staff. 5th ed. LC 59-13987. 944p. 1990. 59.00 (*0-87289-087-2*) C Q Staff.

— Judicial Staff Directory 1992: With Biographical Information on Judges & Key Court Staff. 6th ed. LC 59-13987. 946p. 1991. 59.00 (*0-87289-093-7*) C Q Staff.

— Judicial Staff Directory 1993: With Biographical Information on Judges & Key Court Staff. 7th ed. LC 59-13987. 970p. 1992. 69.00 (*0-87289-099-6*) C Q Staff.

— Judicial Staff Directory 1994: With Biographical Information on Judges & Key Court Staff. 8th ed. LC 59-13987. 900p. 1993. 69.00 (*0-87289-105-4*) C Q Staff.

— Judicial Staff Directory 1995: With Biographical Information on Judges & Key Court Staff. 9th ed. 1994. 79.00 (*0-87289-111-9*) C Q Staff.

— Judicial Staff Directory, 1996: With Biographical Information on Judges & Key Court Staff. LC 59-13987. 1996. write for info. (*0-87289-117-8*) C Q Staff.

Brownson, Anna L., jt. auth. see Brownson, C. B.

Brownson, Anna L., jt. ed. see Brownson, C. B.

Brownson, C. B., ed. Advance Locator for Capitol Hill, 1963: With Biographical Material on Members. LC 59-13987. 196p. 1963. pap. 2.50 (*0-685-58881-5*) C Q Staff.

— Advance Locator for Capitol Hill, 1964: With Biographical Material on Members. 2nd ed. LC 59-13987. 196p. 1964. pap. 2.50 (*0-87289-005-8*) C Q Staff.

— Advance Locator for Capitol Hill, 1965: With Biographical Material on Members. 3rd ed. LC 59-13987. 196p. 1965. pap. 2.50 (*0-87289-007-4*) C Q Staff.

— Advance Locator for Capitol Hill, 1966: With Biographical Material on Members. 4th ed. LC 59-13987. 196p. 1966. pap. 1.50 (*0-87289-009-0*) C Q Staff.

— Advance Locator for Capitol Hill, 1967: With Biographical Material on Members. 5th ed. LC 59-13987. 196p. 1967. pap. 2.00 (*0-87289-012-0*) C Q Staff.

— Advance Locator for Capitol Hill, 1968: With Biographical Material on Members. 6th ed. LC 59-13987. 196p. 1968. pap. 2.50 (*0-87289-014-7*) C Q Staff.

— Advance Locator for Capitol Hill, 1969: With Biographical Material on Members. 7th ed. LC 59-13987. 196p. 1969. pap. 2.50 (*0-87289-017-1*) C Q Staff.

— Advance Locator for Capitol Hill, 1970: With Biographical Material on Members. 8th ed. LC 59-13987. 193p. 1970. pap. 2.50 (*0-87289-019-8*) C Q Staff.

— Advance Locator for Capitol Hill, 1971: With Biographical Material on Members. 9th ed. LC 59-13987. 196p. 1971. pap. 3.50 (*0-87289-022-8*) C Q Staff.

— Advance Locator for Capitol Hill, 1972: With Biographical Material on Members. 10th ed. LC 59-13987. 196p. 1972. pap. 3.50 (*0-87289-024-4*) C Q Staff.

— Advance Locator for Capitol Hill, 1973: With Biographical Material on Members. 11th ed. LC 59-13987. 200p. 1973. pap. 3.50 (*0-87289-027-9*) C Q Staff.

— Congressional Staff Directory Advance Locator for Capitol Hill, 1978: With Biographical Material on Members. 16th ed. LC 59-13987. 480p. 1978. pap. 7.00 (*0-87289-039-2*) C Q Staff.

— Congressional Staff Directory Advance Locator, 1974: With Biographical Material on Members. 12th ed. LC 59-13987. 198p. 1974. pap. 3.50 (*0-87289-029-5*) C Q Staff.

— Congressional Staff Directory Advance Locator, 1975: With Biographical Material on Members. 13th ed. LC 59-13987. 240p. 1975. pap. 5.00 (*0-87289-032-5*) C Q Staff.

— Congressional Staff Directory Advance Locator, 1976: With Biographical Material on Members. 14th ed. LC 59-13987. 276p. 1976. pap. 5.00 (*0-87289-034-1*) C Q Staff.

— Congressional Staff Directory Advance Locator, 1977: With Biographical Material on Members. 15th ed. LC 59-13987. 300p. 1977. pap. 5.50 (*0-87289-037-6*) C Q Staff.

— Congressional Staff Directory Advance Locator, 1979: With Biographical Material on Members. 17th ed. LC 59-13987. 500p. 1979. pap. 8.00 (*0-87289-042-2*) C Q Staff.

— Congressional Staff Directory Advance Locator, 1980: With Biographical Material on Members. 18th ed. LC 59-13987. 520p. 1980. pap. 8.00 (*0-87289-044-9*) C Q Staff.

— Congressional Staff Directory Advance Locator, 1981: With Biographical Material on Members. 19th ed. LC 59-13987. 520p. 1981. reprint ed. pap. 9.00 (*0-87289-047-3*) C Q Staff.

— Congressional Staff Directory Advance Locator, 1982: With Biographical Material on Members. 20th ed. LC 59-13987. 520p. 1982. pap. 10.00 (*0-87289-050-3*) C Q Staff.

— Congressional Staff Directory Advance Locator, 1983: With Biographical Material on Members. 21st ed. LC 59-13987. 520p. 1983. pap. 10.00 (*0-87289-054-6*) C Q Staff.

— Congressional Staff Directory Advance Locator, 1984: With Biographical Material on Members. 22nd ed. LC 59-13987. 440p. 1984. pap. 10.00 (*0-87289-057-0*) C Q Staff.

— Congressional Staff Directory Advance Locator, 1985: With Biographical Material on Members. 23rd ed. LC 59-13987. 464p. 1985. pap. 12.00 (*0-87289-060-0*) C Q Staff.

— Congressional Staff Directory Advance Locator, 1986: With Biographical Material on Members. 24th ed. LC 59-13987. 464p. 1986. pap. 12.00 (*0-87289-063-5*) C Q Staff.

— Congressional Staff Directory Advance Locator, 1987: With Biographical Material on Members. 25th ed. LC 59-13987. 464p. 1987. pap. 12.00 (*0-87289-067-8*) C Q Staff.

— Congressional Staff Directory Advance Locator, 1988: With Biographical Material on Members. 26th ed. LC 59-13987. 476p. 1988. pap. 12.00 (*0-87289-072-4*) C Q Staff.

— Congressional Staff Directory, 1959: With Biographical Material on Members & Congressional Staff. LC 59-13987. 464p. 1959. 7.50 (*0-87289-000-7*) C Q Staff.

— Congressional Staff Directory, 1960: With Biographical Material on Members & Key Congressional Staff. 2nd ed. LC 59-13987. 512p. 1960. 7.50 (*0-87289-001-5*) C Q Staff.

— Congressional Staff Directory, 1961: With Biographical Material on Members & Congressional Staff. 3rd ed. LC 59-13987. 512p. 1961. 7.95 (*0-87289-002-3*) C Q Staff.

— Congressional Staff Directory, 1962: With Biographical Material on Members & Congressional Staff. 4th ed. LC 59-13987. 528p. 1962. 7.95 (*0-87289-003-1*) C Q Staff.

— Congressional Staff Directory, 1963: With Biographical Material on Members & Key Congressional Staff. 5th ed. LC 59-13987. 560p. 1963. 7.95 (*0-87289-004-X*) C Q Staff.

— Congressional Staff Directory, 1964: With Biographical Material on Members & Key Congressional Staff. 6th ed. LC 59-13987. 560p. 1964. 8.95 (*0-87289-006-6*) C Q Staff.

— Congressional Staff Directory, 1965: With Biographical Material on Members & Key Congressional Staff. 7th ed. LC 59-13987. 566p. 1965. 10.00 (*0-87289-008-2*) C Q Staff.

— Congressional Staff Directory, 1966: With Biographical Material on Members & Key Congressional Staff. 8th ed. LC 59-13987. 566p. 1966. 10.00 (*0-87289-010-4*) C Q Staff.

— Congressional Staff Directory, 1967: With Biographical Material on Members & Key Congressional Staff. 9th ed. LC 59-13987. 644p. 1967. 10.00 (*0-87289-013-9*) C Q Staff.

— Congressional Staff Directory, 1968: With Biographical Material on Member & Key Congressional Staff. 10th ed. LC 59-13987. 672p. 1968. 10.00 (*0-87289-015-5*) C Q Staff.

— Congressional Staff Directory, 1969: With Biographical Material on Members & Key Congressional Staff. 11th ed. LC 59-13987. 672p. 1969. 12.50 (*0-87289-018-X*) C Q Staff.

— Congressional Staff Directory, 1970: With Biographical Material on Members & Key Congressional Staff. 12th ed. LC 59-13987. 710p. 1970. 12.50 (*0-87289-020-1*) C Q Staff.

— Congressional Staff Directory, 1971: With Biographical Materials on Members & Key Congressional Staff. 13th ed. LC 59-13987. 780p. 1971. 13.50 (*0-87289-023-6*) C Q Staff.

— Congressional Staff Directory, 1972: With Biographical Materials on Members & Key Congressional Staff. 14th ed. LC 59-13987. 800p. 1972. 13.50 (*0-87289-025-2*) C Q Staff.

— Congressional Staff Directory, 1973: With Biographical Material on Members & Key Congressional Staff. 15th ed. 820p. 1973. 15.00 (*0-87289-028-7*) C Q Staff.

— Congressional Staff Directory, 1974: With Biographical Materials on Members & Key Congressional Staff. 16th ed. LC 59-13987. 850p. 1974. 15.00 (*0-87289-030-9*) C Q Staff.

— Congressional Staff Directory, 1975: With Biographical Material on Members & Key Congressional Staff. 17th ed. LC 59-13987. 850p. 1975. 18.00 (*0-87289-033-3*) C Q Staff.

— Congressional Staff Directory, 1976: With Biographical Materials on Members & Key Congressional Staff. 18th ed. LC 59-13987. 850p. 1976. 18.00 (*0-87289-035-X*) C Q Staff.

— Congressional Staff Directory, 1977: With Biographical Materials on Members & Key Congressional Staff. 19th ed. LC 59-13987. 870p. 1977. 19.50 (*0-87289-038-4*) C Q Staff.

— Congressional Staff Directory, 1978: With Biographical Materials on Members & Key Congressional Staff. 20th ed. LC 59-13987. 980p. 1978. 19.50 (*0-87289-040-6*) C Q Staff.

— Congressional Staff Directory, 1979: With Biographical Material on Members & Key Congressional Staff. 21st ed. LC 59-13987. 1000p. 1979. 22.00 (*0-87289-043-0*) C Q Staff.

— Congressional Staff Directory, 1980: With Biographical Material on Members & Key Congressional Staff. 22nd ed. LC 59-13987. 1096p. 1980. 24.00 (*0-87289-045-7*) C Q Staff.

— Congressional Staff Directory, 1981: With Biographical Information on Members & Key Congressional Staff. 23rd ed. LC 59-13987. 1086p. 1981. 25.00 (*0-87289-048-1*) C Q Staff.

— Congressional Staff Directory, 1982: With Biographical Material on Members & Key Congressional Staff. 24th ed. LC 59-13987. 1198p. 1982. 30.00 (*0-87289-051-1*) C Q Staff.

— Congressional Staff Directory, 1983: With Biographical Material on Members & Key Congressional Staff. 25th ed. LC 59-13987. 1176p. 1983. 30.00 (*0-87289-055-4*) C Q Staff.

— Congressional Staff Directory, 1984: With Biographical Material on Members & Key Congressional Staff. 26th ed. LC 59-13987. 1210p. 1984. 35.00 (*0-87289-058-9*) C Q Staff.

— Congressional Staff Directory, 1985: With Biographical Material on Members & Key Congressional Staff. 27th ed. LC 59-13987. 1232p. 1985. 40.00 (*0-87289-061-9*) C Q Staff.

— Congressional Staff Directory, 1986: With Biographical Information on Members & Key Congressional Staff. 28th ed. LC 59-13987. 1220p. 1986. 45.00 (*0-87289-064-3*) C Q Staff.

— Congressional Staff Directory, 1987: With Biographical Information on Members & Key Congressional Staff. 29th ed. LC 59-13987. 1092p. 1987. 45.00 (*0-87289-068-6*) C Q Staff.

— Congressional Staff Directory, 1988: With Biographical Information on Members & Key Congressional Staff. 30th ed. LC 59-13987. 1000p. 1988. 45.00 (*0-87289-073-2*) C Q Staff.

— Federal Staff Directory, 1982: With Biographical Material on Executive Staff Personnel. LC 59-13987. 1160p. 1982. 30.00 (*0-87289-049-X*) C Q Staff.

— Federal Staff Directory, 1982-83: With Biographical Information on Executive Staff Personnel. 2nd ed. LC 59-13987. 1270p. 1983. 30.00 (*0-87289-053-8*) C Q Staff.

Brownson, C. B. & Brownson, Anna L. Federal Staff Directory, 1984: With Biographical Material on Executive Staff Personnel. 3rd ed. LC 82-647381. 1330p. 1984. 35.00 (*0-87289-056-2*) C Q Staff.

Brownson, C. B. & Brownson, Anna L., eds. Federal Staff Directory, 1985: With Biographical Material on Executive Staff Personnel. 4th ed. LC 59-13987. 1344p. 1985. 40.00 (*0-87289-059-7*) C Q Staff.

— Federal Staff Directory, 1986: With Biographical Information on Executive Staff Personnel. 5th ed. LC 59-13987. 1380p. 1986. 45.00 (*0-87289-062-7*) C Q Staff.

— Federal Staff Directory, 1987: With Biographical Information on Executive Staff Personnel. 6th ed. LC 59-13987. 1466p. 1987. 45.00 (*0-87289-066-X*) C Q Staff.

— Federal Staff Directory, 1988: With Biographical Information on Executive Staff Personnel. 7th ed. LC 59-13987. 1340p. 1988. 45.00 (*0-87289-071-6*) C Q Staff.

— Judicial Staff Directory 1987: With Biographical Information on Judges & Key Court Staff. LC 59-13987. 752p. 1986. 45.00 (*0-87289-065-1*) C Q Staff.

— Judicial Staff Directory 1988: With Biographical Information on Judges & Key Court Staff. 2nd ed. LC 59-13987. 864p. 1987. 45.00 (*0-87289-070-8*) C Q Staff.

Brownson, C. L. Hellenica, & Anabasis, 3 vols., Vol. 2, Bks. 5-7: Hellenica. (Loeb Classical Library: No. 88-90). 366p. 1921. 18.95 (*0-674-99099-4*) HUP.

Brownson, C. L., tr. Hellenica, & Anabasis, 3 vols., Vol. 1, Bks. 1-4: Hellenica. (Loeb Classical Library: No. 88-90). 396p. 1918. 18.95 (*0-674-99098-6*) HUP.

— Hellenica, & Anabasis, 3 vols., Vol. 3, Bks. 1-7: Anabasis. (Loeb Classical Library: No. 88-90). 652p. 1922. 18.95 (*0-674-99100-1*) HUP.

***Brownson, Carleton L.** Xenophon. LC 99-218930. (Loeb Classical Library). 1999. 19.95 (*0-674-99101-X*) HUP.

Brownson, Henry F., ed. see Brownson, Orestes A.

Brownson, J. Jamil. In Cold Margins: Sustainable Development in Northern Bioregions. rev. ed. LC 94-3141. (Studies on Sustainable Development in Northern Rim Bioregions). 254p. (Orig.). 1995. pap. text 17.95 (*0-9640086-7-X*) Northern Rim.

***Brownson, James V.** Speaking the Truth in Love: New Testament Resources for a Missional Hermeneuti. LC 97-32870. (Christian Mission & Modern Culture Ser.). 96p. 1998. 9.00 (*1-56338-239-3*) TPI PA.

Brownson, M. Dictionary of Assamese & English. (ASM & ENG.). 614p. 1991. 49.95 (*0-7859-9828-4*) Fr & Eur.

Brownson, Orestes A. The American Republic. Lapati, Americo D., ed. (Masterworks of Literature Ser.). 1972. 17.95 (*0-8084-0012-6*); pap. 14.95 (*0-8084-0013-4*) NCUP.

— The American Republic: Its Constitution, Tendencies, & Destiny. (Works of Orestes Augustus Brownson). 1989. reprint ed. lib. bdg. 79.00 (*0-7812-2111-0*) Rprt Serv.

— The Brownson Reader. 1978. 34.95 (*0-405-10848-6*, 11851) Ayer.

— Charles Elwood: or The Infidel Converted. (Works of Orestes Augustus Brownson). 1989. reprint ed. lib. bdg. 79.00 (*0-7812-2106-4*) Rprt Serv.

— Conversation on the Liberalism & the Church. (Works of Orestes Augustus Brownson). 1989. reprint ed. lib. bdg. 90.00 (*0-7812-2112-9*) Rprt Serv.

— The Convert: or Leaves from My Experience. (Works of Orestes Augustus Brownson). 1989. reprint ed. lib. bdg. 79.00 (*0-7812-2110-2*) Rprt Serv.

— Essays & Reviews. (Works of Orestes Augustus Brownson). 1989. reprint ed. lib. bdg. 90.00 (*0-7812-2108-0*) Rprt Serv.

— Essays & Reviews Chiefly on Theology, Politics & Socialism. LC 72-4954. (Romantic Tradition in American Literature Ser.). 538p. 1980. reprint ed. 51.95 (*0-405-04626-X*) Ayer.

— The Laboring Classes. LC 78-17952. 144p. 1978. reprint ed. 50.00 (*0-8201-1314-X*) Schol Facsimiles.

— The Mediatorial Life of Jesus. (Works of Orestes Augustus Brownson). 1989. reprint ed. lib. bdg. 79.00 (*0-7812-2107-2*) Rprt Serv.

— New Views of Christianity, Society, & the Church: The Works of Orestes Augustus Brownson. 1989. reprint ed. lib. bdg. 79.00 (*0-7812-2105-6*) Rprt Serv.

— The Spirit-Rapper: An Autobiography. (Works of Orestes Augustus Brownson). 1989. reprint ed. lib. bdg. 79.00 (*0-7812-2109-9*) Rprt Serv.

— Works of Orestes A. Brownson, 20 vols. Brownson, Henry F., ed. LC 12-30124. reprint ed. 1530.00 (*0-404-01180-2*) AMS Pr.

— The Works of Orestes Augustus Brownson. 1989. reprint ed. lib. bdg. 63.00 (*0-685-74132-X*) Rprt Serv.

***Brownson, Orestes A. & Carey, Patrick W.** The Early Works of Orestes A. Brownson. LC 99-50779. (Studies in Theology). 2000. pap. write for info. (*0-87462-647-1*) Marquette.

Brownson, Roger. Beef Producers Guidebook. rev. ed. (Illus.). 188p. (C). 1996. pap. text 40.00 (*0-7881-2712-8*) DIANE Pub.

Brownson, Ross C., et al, eds. Chronic Disease Epidemiology & Control. 358p. 1993. pap. 35.00 (*0-87553-214-4*, 072) Am Pub Health.

— Chronic Disease Epidemiology & Control. 2nd ed. LC 98-74062. 358p. 1998. pap. 45.00 (*0-87553-237-3*) Am Pub Health.

Brownson, Ross C. & Petitti, Diana B., eds. Applied Epidemiology: Theory to Practice. (Monographs in Epidemiology & Biostatistics). (Illus.). 416p. 1998. text 52.50 (*0-19-511190-7*) OUP.

Brownson, Ross C., et al. Community-Based Prevention: Programs That Work. LC 98-43313. 320p. 1998. pap. 32.00 (*0-8342-1241-2*, 12412) Aspen Pub.

Brownstead, Frank & McCollam, Pat. The Volunteer Choir. 1987. 7.95 (*0-912405-37-6*, Pastoral Press) OR Catholic.

Brownstein, jt. auth. see Palkovits, Miklos.

Brownstein, Aaron J., et al, eds. Progress in Behavioral Studies, Vol. I. 144p. 1989. 29.95 (*0-89859-511-8*) L Erlbaum Assocs.

Brownstein, Art. Healing Back Pain Naturally: The Mind-Body Program Proven to Work. LC 98-50021. (Illus.). 288p. 2000. 19.95 (*0-936197-39-0*, Pub. by Harbor Pr) Natl Bk Netwk.

Brownstein, Bernard H., jt. ed. see Nelson, David L.

***Brownstein, Bill.** Sex Carnival: Travels in the World of Porn. (Illus.). 2000. pap. 18.95 (*1-55022-415-8*) ECW.

Brownstein, Bruce & Bronner, Shaw. Functional Evaluation & Outcomes in Sports & Orthopedic Physical Therapy: Evaluation, Treatment & Outcomes. LC 96-36811. 1996. text 59.95 (*0-443-07530-1*) Church.

Brownstein, David. The Miracle of Natural Hormones. 2nd rev. ed. (Illus.). 204p. 1999. pap. 14.95 (*0-9660882-0-4*) Med Alternat.

Brownstein, Dena, jt. ed. see Henderson, Deborah.

***Brownstein, Elizabeth Smith.** If This House Could Talk: Historic Homes Extraordinary Americans. LC 99-19626. 288p. 1999. 40.00 (*0-684-83931-8*) S&S Trade.

Brownstein, Henry H. The Rise & Fall of a Violent Crime Wave: Crack Cocaine & the Social Construction of a Crime Problem. (C). 1996. pap. text 19.90 (*0-911577-36-X*, Criminal Justice) Willow Tree NY.

***Brownstein, Henry H.** Social Reality of Violence & Violent Crime. LC 99-26300. 224p. (C). 1999. pap. 26.00 (*0-205-28807-3*) Allyn.

Brownstein, Larry. Talcott Parsons' General Action Scheme. 310p. 1982. text 22.95 (*0-87073-097-5*) Schenkman Bks Inc.

Brownstein, Michael. Country Cousins. (New American Fiction Ser.: No. 9). 349p. 1986. pap. 11.95 (*0-940650-74-6*) Sun & Moon CA.

— Music from the Evening of the World. (New American Fiction Ser.: No. 17). 104p. 1987. pap. 10.95 (*1-55713-038-8*) Sun & Moon CA.

— Music from the Evening of the World. (New American Fiction Ser.: No. 17). 104p. 1989. 15.95 (*1-55713-036-1*) Sun & Moon CA.

— Self-Reliance. LC 93-23690. 280p. (Orig.). 1994. pap. 12.95 (*1-56689-018-7*) Coffee Hse.

— Strange Days Ahead. LC 75-26450. (Illus.). 98p. (Orig.). 1976. pap. 5.00 (*0-915990-01-6*) Z Pr.

— The Touch. 122p. Date not set. 7.00 (*0-936756-80-2*) Autonomedia.

Brownstein, Michael H. Poems from the Body Bag. (Offset Offshoot Ser.: No. 11). 21p. 1989. pap. 4.00 (*0-941240-14-2*) Ommation Pr.

Brownstein, Oscar L. Strategies of Drama: The Experience of Form. 39. LC 91-10431. (Contributions in Drama & Theatre Studies: No. 39). 216p. 1991. 55.00 (*0-313-27754-0*, BEY, Greenwood Pr) Greenwood.

Brownstein, Oscar L. & Daubert, Darlene M. Analytical Sourcebook of Concepts in Dramatic Theory. LC 80-1200. 560p. 1981. lib. bdg. 85.00 (*0-313-21309-7*, BRN/, Greenwood Pr) Greenwood.

Brownstein, Rachel M. Becoming a Heroine: Reading about Women in Novels. 1994. pap. 19.00 (*0-231-10000-0*) Col U Pr.

— Tragic Muse: Rachel of the Comedie-Francaise. LC 94-30101. (Illus.). 344p. 1995. pap. text 18.95 (*0-8223-1571-8*) Duke.

Brownstein, Rita Milos. Jewish Holiday Style: A Beautiful Guide to Celebrating the Jewish Rituals in Style. LC 99-20723. (Illus.). 144p. (J). 1999. 27.50 (*0-684-84959-3*) Simon & Schuster.

Brownstein, Ronald. Reagan's Ruling Class: Portraits of the President's Top 100 Officials. Easton, Nina, ed. LC 82-60917. (Illus.). 759p. 1983. 24.50 (*0-936486-03-1*) Presidential Acct.

Brownstein, Ronald, jt. auth. see Balz, Dan.

Brownstein, Ronald, ed. see Easton, Nina.

***Brownstein, Samuel, et al.** How to Prepare for the GRE: Graduate Record Exam. 13th ed. LC 99-20234. (Illus.). 662p. 1999. pap. 29.95 incl. cd-rom (*0-7641-7238-7*) Barron.

— How to Prepare for the GRE - Graduate Record Exam. 13th ed. LC 99-20234. (Illus.). 662p. 1999. pap. 13.95 (*0-7641-0779-8*) Barron.

Brownstein, Samuel C. Pass Key to the PSAT/NMSQT. 1995. pap., student ed. 7.95 (*0-8120-9022-5*) Barron.

Brownstein, Samuel C. & Green, Sharon W. Pass Key to the GRE. 2nd ed. LC 97-30086. 420p. 1997. pap. text 7.95 (*0-8120-9742-4*) Barron.

Brownstein, Samuel C., et al. Basic Word List. 3rd ed. LC 96-47038. 1997. pap. 6.95 (*0-8120-9649-5*) Barron.

— Fourteen Days to Higher SAT Scores, 2 cassettes. 3rd ed. 64p. 1994. 16.95 incl. audio (*0-8120-8164-1*) Barron.

— How to Prepare for the GED: Canadian Edition. 3rd rev. ed. Shukyn, Murray, ed. LC 98-29929. 832p. 1998. pap. 18.95 (*0-7641-0324-5*) Barron.

— A Pocket Guide to Vocabulary. 3rd ed. LC 97-117. 256p. 1997. pap. 6.95 (*0-8120-9818-8*) Barron.

— SAT I Computer Study Program, Macintosh. 3rd ed. 1994. 24.95 incl. disk (*0-8120-8158-7*) Barron.

— SAT I Computer Study Program, Windows. 3rd ed. 1994. 24.95 incl. disk (*0-8120-8157-9*) Barron.

Brownstein, Ted, ed. Weiss Ratings' Guide to Life, Health & Annuity Insurers Vol. 34: A Quarterly Compilation of Insurance Company Ratings & Analysis. 396p. 1998. reprint ed. pap. 219.00 (*1-889499-45-5*) Weiss Ratings.

Brownstone & Franck. Yankee Ingenuity. 1994. pap. 18.00 (*0-671-85037-7*) S&S Trade.

Brownstone, Arni. War Paint: Blackfoot & Sarcee Painted Buffalo Robes in the Royal Ontario Museum. (Illus.). 96p. 1993. pap. write for info. (*0-88854-408-1*) Royal Ontario.

Brownstone, David & Franck. People in the News. 7th ed. 1997. 85.00 (*0-02-864711-4*) Mac Lib Ref.

Brownstone, David & Franck, Irene. People in the News, 1997. 1997. 85.00 (*0-02-864779-3*) S&S Trade.

— Sports People in the News, 1996. 253p. 1996. 85.00 (*0-02-864525-1*, Hall Reference) Macmillan.

— Timelines of the Twentieth Century: A Chronology of 7,500 People That Shaped the Century. 512p. 1997. pap. 19.95 (*0-316-11501-0*) Little.

— Timelines of War: Chronology of Warfare from the Earliest Times to the Present. LC 94-203. 1994. pap. 19.95 (*0-685-71375-X*) Little.

Brownstone, David & Franck, Irene M. People in the News. 2nd ed. 403p. 1992. 85.00 (*0-02-897074-8*) Macmillan.

Brownstone, David, jt. auth. see Franck, Irene M.

Brownstone, David M. The Chinese-American Heritage. (America's Ethnic Heritage Ser.). (Illus.). 144p. (YA). (gr. 7 up). 1988. 19.95 (*0-8160-1627-5*) Facts on File.

— Complete Self-Publishing Handbook. LC 98-50134. 224p. 1999. pap. 13.95 (*0-452-28073-7*) NAL.

Brownstone, David M. & Frack, I. M. The VNR Investor's Dictionary. 326p. 1981. 29.95 (*0-8288-4682-0*, M9374) Fr & Eur.

Brownstone, David M. & Franck, Irene M. Parenting A to Z: Mom & Dad's Guide to Everything from Conception to College. 2nd rev. ed. LC 96-6311. Orig. Title: The Parent's Desk Reference. 736p. 1996. 32.50 (*0-06-271598-4*) HarpC.

Brownstone, David M. & Franck, Irene M., eds. The Wilson Chronology of Asia & the Pacific. LC 99-29402. 500p. 1999. 60.00 (*0-8242-0950-8*) Wilson.

Brownstone, David M. & Hawes, Gene R. The College Money Book: How to Get A High-Quality Education at the Lowest Possible Cost. LC 83-15582. 256p. 1984. pap. write for info. (*0-672-52772-3*) Macmillan.

Brownstone, David M., et al. The VNR Dictionary of Business & Finance. 288p. 1980. 35.00 (*0-8288-4715-0*, M9376) Fr & Eur.

Brownstone, David M., jt. auth. see Franck, Irene M.

Brownstone, Douglass L. A Field Guide to America's History. LC 82-7434. (Illus.). 335p. reprint ed. pap. 103.90 (*0-8357-5599-1*, 203523800093) Bks Demand.

Brownstone, Douglass L., jt. auth. see Hawes, Gene R.

Brownstone, Franck. Women's Desk Reference. 1999. pap. 11.95 (*0-14-017046-4*) Viking Penguin.

Brownstone, Meyer & Plunkett, T. J. Metropolitan Winnipeg: Politics & Reform of Local Government. LC 81-19658. (Publication of the Franklin K. Lane Memorial Fund, Institute of Governmental Studies, University of California, Berkeley). (Illus.). 262p. reprint ed. pap. 81.30 (*0-608-20127-8*, 207139900011) Bks Demand.

Brownsville Junior Service League Staff. Beneath the Palms. 1996. 18.95 (*0-9653293-0-5*) Brownsville Jr.

Brownsword, Alan W. It Takes All Types! 2nd rev. ed. 163p. (Orig.). 1998. pap. 18.00 (*0-944393-02-0*) HRM.

— Psychological Type: An Introduction. 46p. (Orig.). (C). 1988. pap. text 8.00 (*0-944393-01-2*) Baytree Pubn.

Brownsword, Roger, et al, eds. Law & Genetics: Regulating a Revolution. 224p. 1998. pap. 27.00 (*1-84113-006-0*, Pub. by Hart Pub) Intl Spec Bk.

— Welfarism in Contract Law. 360p. 1994. 82.95 (*1-85521-246-3*, Pub. by Dartmth Pub) Ashgate Pub Co.

BrownTrout Publishers Incorporated, Staff. Beagles Postcard Book. 1997. pap. text 7.95 (*1-56313-911-1*) BrownTrout Pubs Inc.

— Chicago: A Book of 30 Postcards. 1995. pap. text 8.95 (*1-56313-778-X*) BrownTrout Pubs Inc.

An Asterisk (*) at the beginning of an entry indicates that the title is appearing for the first time.

BrownTrout Publishers Incorporated, Staff. Dakotas: Postcard Book. (Illus.). 1996. pap. 7.95 (*1-56313-815-8*) BrownTrout Pubs Inc.
— Outhouses: Postcard Book. (Illus.). 1997. pap. 7.95 (*1-56313-932-4*) BrownTrout Pubs Inc.
— South Carolina: Postcard Book. (Illus.). 1997. pap. 7.95 (*1-56313-940-5*) BrownTrout Pubs Inc.
Browntrout Publishers Staff. Labrador Retrievers. (Illus.). 1997. pap. text 7.95 (*1-56313-919-7*) BrownTrout Pubs Inc.
— Postcard-Wyoming. 1996. pap. 7.95 (*1-56313-859-X*) BrownTrout Pubs Inc.
BrownTrout Publishing Company Staff. Postcard-Chesapeake Bay. (Illus.). 1996. pap. 7.95 (*1-56313-808-5*) BrownTrout Pubs Inc.
— Postcard-Washington. (Illus.). 1996. pap. 7.95 (*1-56313-857-3*) BrownTrout Pubs Inc.
BrownTrout Publishing Company Staff, ed. Alabama: Postcard Book. (Illus.). 1997. pap. 7.95 (*1-56313-934-0*) BrownTrout Pubs Inc.
— Barns: Postcard Book. (Illus.). 1997. pap. 7.95 (*1-56313-923-5*) BrownTrout Pubs Inc.
— Boxers: Postcard Book. (Illus.). 1997. pap. 7.95 (*1-56313-914-6*) BrownTrout Pubs Inc.
— Dachshunds: Postcard Book. (Illus.). 1997. pap. 7.95 (*1-56313-915-4*) BrownTrout Pubs Inc.
— Golden Retrievers: Postcard Book. (Illus.). 1997. pap. 7.95 (*1-56313-918-9*) BrownTrout Pubs Inc.
— Kitten: Postcard Book. (Illus.). 1997. pap. 7.95 (*1-56313-862-X*) BrownTrout Pubs Inc.
— Loons: Postcard Book. (Illus.). 1997. pap. 7.95 (*1-56313-881-6*) BrownTrout Pubs Inc.
— Michigan: A Book of 30 Postcards. (Illus.). 1995. pap. 7.95 (*1-56313-775-5*) BrownTrout Pubs Inc.
— New England Lighthouses: Postcard Book. (Illus.). 1997. pap. 7.95 (*1-56313-930-8*) BrownTrout Pubs Inc.
— Pacific Coast Lighthouses: Postcard Book. (Illus.). 1997. pap. 7.95 (*1-56313-931-6*) BrownTrout Pubs Inc.
— Route 66: Postcard Book. (Illus.). 1996. pap. 7.95 (*1-56313-788-7*) BrownTrout Pubs Inc.
***Brownworth, Victoria.** Coming Out of Cancer: Writings from the Lesbian Cancer Epidemic. 2000. pap. 14.95 (*1-58005-044-1*) Seal Pr WA.
Brownworth, Victoria A. Night Bites: Vampire Stories by Women. LC 95-43877. 280p. (Orig.). 1996. pap. text 12.95 (*1-878067-71-0*) Seal Pr WA.
— Too Queer: Essays from a Radical Life. LC 96-2701. 256p. 1996. pap. 13.95 (*1-56341-074-5*); lib. bdg. 26.95 (*1-56341-075-3*) Firebrand Bks.
Brownworth, Victoria A. & Raffo, Susan, eds. Restricted Access: Lesbians on Disability. LC 99-38054. 320p. 1999. pap. 15.95 (*1-58005-028-X*, Pub. by Seal Pr WA) Publishers Group.
***Brownworth, Victoria A. & Redding, Judith M., eds.** Night Shade: Gothic Tales by Women. LC 99-13306. 288p. 1999. pap. 14.95 (*1-58005-024-7*) Seal Pr WA.
Brownworth, Victoria A., jt. auth. see Redding, Judith M.
***Browse, Lillian.** Duchess of Cork Street: The Autobiography of an Art Dealer. (Illus.). 188p. 2000. pap. 29.95 (*1-900357-14-3*, Pub. by Giles Mare Pubs) Trafalgar.
Browse, Norman. Diseases of the Veins. 2nd ed. LC 99-177290. (Illus.). 800p. 1998. text 195.00 (*0-340-58894-2*) OUP.
Browse, Norman L. Diseases of the Veins. 704p. text. write for info. (*0-7131-4523-4*, Pub. by E A) Routldge.
— An Introduction to the Symptoms & Signs of Surgical Disease. 3rd ed. LC 96-49623. (Arnold Publication). (Illus.). 464p. 1997. pap. text 39.95 (*0-340-66211-5*) OUP.
Browse, Norman L., et al. Carotid Endarterectomy: A Practical Guide. LC 97-206421. 144p. 1997. text 110.00 (*0-7506-0530-8*) Buttrwrth-Heinemann.
Browston, Lee, et al. Programming Expert Systems in OPS5: An Introduction to Rule-Based Programming. (Artificial Intellegence Ser.). (C). 1985. text 49.50 (*0-201-10647-7*) Addison-Wesley.
Brox, Andrea. All about Outlets: The Guide to Factory & Off-Price Shopping in New England. 2nd ed. (Illus.). pap. 12.95 (*0-924771-30-5*) Brick Hse Pub.
— Brox's Ultimate Outlet Guide to New England: An Insider's Guide to the Region's Best Factory Outlet & Off-Price Shopping. Wood, Beverly J., ed. LC 94-27142. (Illus.). 338p. (Orig.). 1994. pap., per. 12.95 (*0-9636123-1-X*) Pleasant St Pr.
— Romantic New England Getaways. Wood, Beverly J., ed. LC 93-5825. (Illus.). 348p. 1993. pap. 15.95 (*0-9636123-0-1*) Pleasant St Pr.
— Romantic New England Getaways. 2nd ed. LC 98-10991. 1998. pap. 15.95 (*0-9636123-4-4*) Pleasant St Pr.
— The Student Guide to Boston. pap. 9.95 (*0-924771-21-6*) Brick Hse Pub.
Brox, Andrea, ed. see Ruggles, Ellen.
Brox, Jane. Five Thousand Days Like This One: An American Family History. LC 98-35051. (Concord Library). 208p. 1999. 23.00 (*0-8070-2106-7*) Beacon Pr.
***Brox, Jane.** Five Thousand Days Like This One: An American Family History. 2000. pap. 13.00 (*0-8070-2107-5*) Beacon Pr.
Brox, Jane. Five Thousand Days Like This One: An American Family History, Vol. 1. LC 99-26430. 1999. 27.95 (*0-7838-8642-X*) Thorndike Pr.
— Here & Nowhere Else: Late Seasons of a Farm & Its Family. 160p. 1996. pap. 12.95 (*0-8070-6201-4*) Beacon Pr.
***Brox, Jane.** Here & Nowhere Else: Late Seasons of a Farm & Its Family. large type ed. LC 99-52493. 1999. 21.95 (*0-7838-8816-3*) Mac Lib Ref.
Brox, Jane, et al, eds. The Four Way Reader #1, No. 1. LC 94-71640. 220p. 1996. pap. 14.95 (*1-884800-00-9*) Four Way Bks.
Brox, Norbert. A Concise History of the Early Church. 192p. 1995. 19.95 (*0-8264-0792-7*) Continuum.
Broxmeyer, Hal E., ed. Cellular Characteristics of Cord Blood & Cord Blood Transplantation. LC 98-9427. 227p. 1998. text 149.00 (*1-56395-084-7*) Am Assn Blood.
Broy, M., et al, eds. Formal Systems Verification Vol. XXIII: The RPC-Memory Specification Case Study. LC 97-119744. (Lecture Notes in Computer Science: Vol. 1169). 541p. 1996. pap. 87.00 (*3-540-61984-4*) Spr-Verlag.
Broy, Manfred. Programming & Mathematical Method. LC 92-26379. (NATO ASI Series F: Computer & Systems Sciences, Special Programme AET: Vol. 88). viii, 428p. 1992. 124.00 (*0-387-55558-7*) Spr-Verlag.
Broy, Manfred, ed. Constructive Methods in Computing Science. (NATO Asi Series F: Vol. 55). (Illus.). viii, 478p. 1989. 123.95 (*0-387-51369-8*, 3249) Spr-Verlag.
— Control Flow & Data Flow: Concepts of Distributed Programming. (NATO Asi Series F: Vol. 14). viii, 525p. 1985. 122.95 (*0-387-13919-2*) Spr-Verlag.
— Control Flow & Data Flow: Concepts of Distributed Programming. (Springer Study Edition Ser.). viii, 525p. 1986. 52.95 (*0-387-17082-0*) Spr-Verlag.
— Deductive Program Design. LC 96-10788. (NATO ASI Series F: Computer & Systems Science: Vol. 152). 467p. 1996. 139.50 (*3-540-60947-4*) Spr-Verlag.
— Logic of Programming & Calculi of Discrete Design. (NATO Asi Series F: Vol. 36). vii, 415p. 1987. 107.95 (*0-387-18003-6*) Spr-Verlag.
— Program Design Calculi. LC 93-34001. (NATO ASI Series F: Computer & Systems Sciences, Special Programme AET: Vol. 118). viii, 409p. 1993. 107.95 (*0-387-56943-X*) Spr-Verlag.
Broy, Manfred, et al, eds. Methods of Programming: Selected Papers on the CIP-Project. (Lecture Notes in Computer Science Ser.: Vol. 544). xiv, 268p. 1991. 32.95 (*0-387-54576-X*) Spr-Verlag.
Broy, Manfred & Jahnichen, S. KORSO: Methods, Languages, & Tools for the Construction of Correct Software, Final Report. LC 95-45669. (Lecture Notes in Computer Science Ser.: No. 1009). 449p. 1995. 75.00 (*3-540-60589-4*) Spr-Verlag.
Broy, Manfred & Schmidt, G., eds. Theoretical Foundations of Programming Methodology. 1982. pap. text 126.50 (*90-277-1462-2*); lib. bdg. 211.50 (*90-277-1460-6*) Kluwer Academic.
Broy, Manfred, jt. ed. see Bauer, F. L.
Broyard, Anatole. Kafka Was the Rage. 1997. pap. 11.00 (*0-679-78126-9*) Vin Bks.
— That Time & Place: A Greenwich Village Memoir. LC 93-7830. 1993. 18.00 (*0-685-65374-9*, Crown) Crown Pub Group.
***Broyard, Bliss.** My Father, Dancing. LC 00-35066. (Harvest Bks.). 208p. 2000. pap. text 13.00 (*0-15-601396-7*) Harcourt.
Broyard, Bliss. My Father, Dancing. LC 99-31090. 224p. 1999. 22.00 (*0-375-40060-5*) Knopf.
Broyde. Marriage Abandoned Wife Jewish Law. write for info. (*0-88125-678-1*); pap. write for info. (*0-88125-679-X*) Ktav.
Broyde, Michael & Witte, John. Human Rights in Judaism: Cultural Religions & Political Perspectives. LC 97-27141. 1998. pap. 30.00 (*0-7657-9977-4*) Aronson.
Broyde, Michael J. The Pursuit of Justice & Jewish Law: Halakhic Perspectives on the Legal Profession. LC 96-22594. 1996. 29.50 (*0-88125-559-9*) Ktav.
Broyde, Steven. Osip Mandelstam & His Age. LC 74-16801. (Slavic Monographs: No. 1). 264p. 1975. 34.95 (*0-674-64492-1*) HUP.
Broydo, S., ed. see International Symposium on Very Large Scale Integr.
Broydrick, Stephen C. How May I Help You: Providing Personal Service in an Impersonal World. LC 93-13572. 176p. 1993. 22.50 (*1-55623-989-0*, Irwn Prfssnl) McGraw-Hill Prof.
— The 7 Universal Laws of Customer Value: How to Win Customers & Influence Markets. 160p. 1996. text 24.95 (*0-7863-0732-3*, Irwn Prfssnl) McGraw-Hill Prof.
Broyer, John A. & Minor, William S., eds. Creative Interchange. LC 81-18538. 566p. 1982. 31.95 (*0-8093-1032-5*) S Ill U Pr.
Broyle. Strategic Financial Management. 1969. pap. text. write for info. (*0-471-89934-8*) Wiley.
Broyle, Bonnie, ed. see Thomas, R. Roosevelt, Jr., et al.
Broyles, Anne. Growing Together in Love. 1998. 9.95 (*0-687-60422-2*) Abingdon.
— Growing Together in Love. LC 93-60484. 176p. 1993. pap. 10.00 (*0-8358-0687-1*) Upper Room Bks.
— Journaling: A Spirit Journey. rev. ed. Williams, Karen F., ed. LC 98-37057. 144p. 1999. pap. 11.00 (*0-8358-0866-1*) Upper Room Bks.
— Meeting God Through Worship. (Vital Signs Ser.). 96p. (Orig.). 1992. pap. 1.49 (*0-687-24655-5*) Abingdon.
***Broyles, Anne.** Shy Mama's Halloween. (Illus.). 40p. (J). (gr. 3-6). 2000. 16.95 (*0-88448-218-9*) Tilbury Hse.
Broyles, Bill. Organ Pipe Cactus National Monument: Where Edges Meet. LC 96-42360. 64p. 1996. pap. 9.95 (*1-877856-69-X*) SW Pks Mnmts.
Broyles, Bill, et al. Texas in Transition. Gillette, Michael L., ed. (Symposia Ser.). (Illus.). 254p. 1986. pap. 7.00 (*0-89940-419-7*) LBJ Sch Pub Aff.
Broyles, C. Adhesives & Sealants. 375p. 1998. 1195.00 (*0-318-00507-7*) Busn Trend.
— Automotive Chemical Suppliers, Distributors & Consumer Markets. 200p. 1999. 1995.00 (*0-945235-17-8*) Lead Edge Reports.
— Household Cleaning Chemicals. 640p. 1999. 1295.00 (*0-685-72787-4*) Busn Trend.
— Lubricating Oils & Greases. 385p. 1998. 1195.00 (*0-318-04168-5*) Busn Trend.
— The Market for Industrial & Institutional Cleaners. 450p. 1999. pap. 1995.00 (*0-685-43869-4*) Lead Edge Reports.
— Market Trends for Advanced Paints & Coatings. 470p. 1998. 1495.00 (*0-945235-33-X*) Busn Trend.
— The Paints & Coatings Industry. 450p. 1995. pap. 1495.00 (*0-318-04170-7*) Busn Trend.
— Printing Ink. 200p. 2000. 1995.00 (*0-614-06125-3*, LE406) Lead Edge Reports.
— The U. S. Adhesives & Sealants Industry. 375p. 1998. 1195.00 (*0-685-10301-3*) Busn Trend.
— The U. S. Agricultural Chemicals Industry. (Illus.). 170p. 1999. spiral bd. 1995.00 (*0-685-21990-9*) Lead Edge Reports.
— The U. S. Market for Animal Health Products: Fast Performance, Current Trends & Strategies for the Future. 280p. 2000. 1995.00 (*0-317-55211-2*) Lead Edge Reports.
Broyles, Craig. Psalms. LC 99-40849. (New International Biblical Commentary Ser.: Vol. 11). 560p. 1999. pap. 11.95 (*1-56563-220-6*) Hendrickson MA.
Broyles, Craig C. The Conflict of Faith & Experience in the Psalms: A Form-Critical & Theological Study. (JSOT Supplement Ser.: No. 52). 272p. 1989. 75.00 (*1-85075-052-1*, Pub. by Sheffield Acad); pap. 24.50 (*1-85075-053-X*, Pub. by Sheffield Acad) CUP Services.
Broyles, Craig C. & Evans, Craig A. Writing & Reading the Scroll of Isaiah: Studies of an Interpretive Tradition. LC 97-44787. (Supplements to Vetus Testamentum Ser.). 1997. 172.00 (*90-04-11027-5*) Brill Academic Pubs.
Broyles, Craig C., jt. auth. see Evans, Craig A.
Broyles-Gonzalez, Yolanda. El Teatro Campesino: Theater in the Chicano Movement. LC 94-935. (Illus.). 304p. (C). 1994. pap. 17.95 (*0-292-70801-7*); text 37.50 (*0-292-72082-3*) U of Tex Pr.
Broyles, India L., ed. Bound to Be Teachers. 72p. (Orig.). 1992. pap. text. write for info. (*0-939561-12-3*) Univ South ME.
Broyles, John R. Another Little Horn. 176p. 1995. pap. 9.95 (*0-9645494-3-3*) Alpha Om Pr.
Broyles, Michael. Beethoven: The Emergence & Evolution of Beethoven's Heroic Style. LC 87-30473. 310p. 1994. text 39.00 (*0-935016-74-0*, Pub. by Zinn Pub Grp) Empire Pub Srvs.
— Music of the Highest Class: Elitism & Populism in Antebellum Boston. LC 92-12422. (Illus.). 384p. (C). 1992. 45.00 (*0-300-05495-5*) Yale U Pr.
Broyles, Michael, ed. A Yankee Musician in Europe No. 110: The 1837 Journals of Lowell Mason. LC 89-20256. 214p. 1991. 50.00 (*0-8357-2002-0*) Univ Rochester Pr.
Broyles, Robert W. & Rosko, Michael D. Planning & Internal Control under Prospective Payment. 1986. 90.00 (*0-87189-266-9*) Aspen Pub.
Broyles, Robert W., jt. auth. see Rosko, Michael D.
Broyles, William, Jr. Brothers in Arms: A Journey from War to Peace. 288p. (Orig.). 1987. mass mkt. 4.50 (*0-380-70355-6*, Avon Bks) Morrow Avon.
— Brothers in Arms: A Journey from War to Peace. 304p. (Orig.). 1996. pap. 18.95 (*0-292-70849-1*) U of Tex Pr.
Broz, Alfred L., jt. ed. see Rempt, Raymond D.
Broz, J. Lawrence. The International Origins of the Federal Reserve System. LC 97-11932. (Illus.). 280p. 1997. text 35.00 (*0-8014-3332-0*) Cornell U Pr.
Broze, Guy. Handbook of Detergents. LC 99-14708. (Surfactant Science Ser). (Illus.). 816p. 1999. text 225.00 (*0-8247-1417-2*) Dekker.
Broze, Laurence. Reduced Forms of Rational Expectations Models, Vol. 42. (Fundamentals of Pure & Applied Economics Ser.). x, 199p. 1991. text 55.00 (*3-7186-5031-2*, Harwood Acad Pubs) Gordon & Breach.
Broze, Matt, jt. auth. see Gronseth, George.
Brozeit, A., et al, eds. Selected Papers on Single Mode Optical Fibers: Characteristics & Applications of Standard Birefringent Fibers, MS 101. LC 94-28411. (Milestone Ser.). 1994. pap. text 50.00 (*0-8194-1693-2*) SPIE.
***Brozek, Joan Bartlett.** Hiram & the Rattales. (Illus.). 84p. 1999. reprint ed. pap. 7.95 (*0-913507-39-3*, Pub. by New Forums) Booksource.
Brozek, Josef & Slobin, Dan I., eds. Psychology in the U. S. S. R. An Historical Perspective. LC 72-12930. 312p. reprint ed. pap. 96.80 (*0-608-30672-X*, 2021853000023) Bks Demand.
Brozek, Josef, ed. see Watson, Robert.
Brozek, Josef M., ed. Explorations in the History of Psychology in America. LC 81-72024. (Illus.). 336p. 1984. 45.00 (*0-8387-5039-7*) Bucknell U Pr.
Brozel, M. & Stirland, D. J., eds. Defect Recognition in Semiconductors Before & after Processing: Proceedings of the 4th International Conference Held 18-22 March 1991. (Illus.). 326p. 1992. 154.00 (*0-7503-0188-0*) IOP Pub.
Brozel, M.R. & Stillman, G. E., eds. Properties of Gallium Arsenide. (EMIS Datareviews Ser.: No. 16). 1000p. 1996. 395.00 (*0-85296-885-X*, EM016) INSPEC Inc.
Brozen, Yale. Mergers in Perspective. LC 82-3937. (AEI Studies: No. 353). (Illus.). 96p. reprint ed. pap. 30.00 (*0-8357-4505-8*, 203736200008) Bks Demand.
Brozenec, Sally A. Coping with Multisystem Complications. LC 97-30022. 448p. 1998. pap. text 39.95 (*1-55664-484-1*) Mosby Inc.
Brozenec, Sally A., jt. auth. see Lauer, Kathy.
Brozic, Joe, jt. auth. see Spiegel, Jill.
Brozinsky, Patricia-Bravata, jt. auth. see Gibson, James Aloysius.
Brozman, Bob. The History & Art of National Resonator Instruments. LC 93-70855. (Illus.). 296p. 1993. 48.00 (*0-931759-65-X*, 00000153) H Leonard.
— The History & Artistry of National Resonator Instruments. (Illus.). 293p. 1993. 35.00 (*0-931759-70-6*, 00000154) Centerstream Pub.
Brozo, William G. & Simpson, Michele L. Readers, Teachers, Learners: Expanding Literacy Across the Content Areas. 3rd ed. LC 97-50270. 484p. (C). 1998. 72.00 (*0-13-647272-9*, Merrill Coll) P-H.
Brozovic, Blanka. Croatian-English--English-Croatian Pocket Dictionary. (CRO & ENG.). 428p. 1992. pap. 16.00 (*0-7859-8832-7*) Fr & Eur.
— Croatian-English, English-Croatian Pocket Dictionary. (CRO & ENG.). 428p. 1992. pap. 15.95 (*0-7859-7471-7*, 860300725X) Fr & Eur.
Brozozowski, Janusz A. & Seger, Carl-Johan H. Asynchronous Circuits. LC 94-42873. (Monographs in Computer Science). (Illus.). xvi, 404p. 1995. 48.95 (*0-387-94420-6*) Spr-Verlag.
Brozyma, Andrea E. Labour, Love & Prayer: Female Piety in Ulster Religious Literature, 1850-1914. LC 99-492149. 360p. 1998. 65.00 (*0-7735-1757-X*) McG-Queens Univ Pr.
Brozzo, P., jt. ed. see Abbruzzese, G.
Brtis, John S., jt. auth. see Cleff, William C.
***Bru, Eduard.** Coming from the South. 2000. pap. 30.00 (*84-95273-03-9*) Actar.
Bru, Eduard. Three on the Site. 1997. pap. 22.00 (*84-89698-16-3*) Dist Art Pubs.
Bru, Eduard, compiled by. New Landscapes, New Territories. 209p. 1998. pap. 34.00 (*84-89698-40-6*, 810741, Pub. by Actar) Dist Art Pubs.
Bru, Hedin. Old Man & His Sons. West, John F., tr. (Illus.). 1970. 15.95 (*0-8397-8412-0*) Eriksson.
Bru, Jutta. Acid Rain & Ozone Depletion: International Law & Regulation. 315p. (C). 1988. lib. bdg. 45.00 (*0-941320-51-0*) Transnatl Pubs.
Bruacher & Riegert. Introduction to Commercial Transactions. 1977. text 29.00 (*0-88277-427-1*) Foundation Pr.
Brualdi, Richard A. Introductory Combinatorics. 2nd ed. 374p. 1991. 42.75 (*0-7204-8610-6*) P-H.
— Introductory Combinatorics. 3rd ed. LC 98-46880. 614p. (C). 1998. 92.00 (*0-13-181488-5*) P-H.
Brualdi, Richard A., et al, eds. Combinatorial & Graph-Theoretical Problems in Linear Algebra. LC 93-2099. (IMA Volumes in Mathematics & Its Applications Ser.: Vol. 50). 1993. 69.95 (*0-387-94086-3*) Spr-Verlag.
— Combinatorial & Graph-Theoretical Problems in Linear Algebra. (IMA Volumes in Mathematics & Its Applications Ser.: Vol. 50). (Illus.). 280p. 1993. write for info. (*3-540-94086-3*) Spr-Verlag.
— Linear Algebra & Its Role in Systems Theory. LC 85-18620. (Contemporary Mathematics Ser.: Vol. 47). 506p. 1985. pap. 46.00 (*0-8218-5041-5*, CONM/47) Am Math.
— Linear Algebra & Its Role in Systems Theory: Proceedings of the AMS-IMS-SIAM Joint Summer Research Conference Held on July 29-August 4, 1984, with Support from the National Science Foundation. LC 85-18620. (Contemporary Mathematics Ser.: No. 47). (Illus.). 520p. 1985. reprint ed. pap. 161.20 (*0-608-07823-9*, 205266800010) Bks Demand.
Brualdi, Richard A. & Ryser, Herbert J. Combinatorial Matrix Theory. (Encyclopedia of Mathematics & Its Applications Ser.: No. 39). 377p. (C). 1991. text 69.95 (*0-521-32265-0*) Cambridge U Pr.
Brualdi, Richard A. & Shader, Brian L. Matrices of Sign-Solvable Linear Systems. (Tracts in Mathematics Ser.: No. 116). (Illus.). 312p. (C). 1995. text 54.95 (*0-521-48296-8*) Cambridge U Pr.
Bruan, Hans. Helpflanzen-Lexikon fur Arzte und Apotheker: Lexicon for Doctors & Pharmacists. 5th ed. (GER.). 315p. 1987. 85.00 (*0-7859-8361-9*, 3437110713) Fr & Eur.
Bruant, Aristide. L' Argot Au XXe Siecle: Dictionnaire Francais-Argot. (FRE.). 458p. 1990. pap. 115.00 (*0-7859-8244-2*, 2908266040) Fr & Eur.
Bruaset, A. M. A Survey of Preconditioned Iterative Methods. LC 95-6872. (Pitman Research Notes in Mathematics Ser.). 1995. write for info. (*0-614-32282-0*) Longman.
***Brubach, Holly.** A Dedicated Follower of Fashion. 224p. 1999. 29.95 (*0-7148-3887-X*) Phaidon Pr.
Brubacher, G. B., ed. Diet & Health in Europe - the Evidence. (Journal: Annals of Nutrition & Metabolism: Vol. 35, Suppl. 1, 1991). (Illus.). iv, 120p. 1991. pap. 38.50 (*3-8055-5400-1*) S Karger.
Brubacher, G. B., et al, eds. Elevated Dosages of Vitamins: Benefits & Hazards. LC 88-13601. (International Journal for Vitamin & Nutrition Research, Supplement Ser.: No. 30). 250p. (C). 1989. text 52.00 (*0-920887-29-5*) Hogrefe & Huber Pubs.
Brubacher, John S. The Courts & Higher Education. LC 74-138458. (Jossey-Bass Higher Education Ser.). 166p. reprint ed. pap. 51.50 (*0-608-30910-9*, 201394400087) Bks Demand.
— The Law & Higher Education: A Casebook, 2 vols., 1. LC 70-150238. 701p. 1975. 45.00 (*0-8386-7897-1*) Fairleigh Dickinson.
— The Law & Higher Education: A Casebook, 2 vols., 2. LC 70-150238. 701p. 1975. 45.00 (*0-8386-7947-1*) Fairleigh Dickinson.
— The Law & Higher Education: A Casebook, 2 vols., Set. LC 70-150238. 701p. 1975. 60.00 (*0-685-02293-5*) Fairleigh Dickinson.
Brubacher, John S. & Rudy, Willis. Higher Education in Transition: A History of American Colleges & Universities. 4th ed. LC 96-53075. (Foundations of Higher Education Ser.). 566p. 1997. pap. text 24.95 (*1-56000-917-9*) Transaction Pubs.
Brubacher, John W., et al. Becoming a Reflective Educator: How to Build a Culture of Inquiry in the Schools. LC 93-27065. 160p. 1993. pap. text 22.95 (*0-8039-6095-6*) Corwin Pr.

B

— Becoming a Reflective Educator: How to Build a Culture of Inquiry in the Schools. LC 93-27065. 160p. 1993. text 51.95 (*0-8039-6094-8*) Corwin Pr.

Brubaker, Beryl, jt. ed. see Miller, Roman.

Brubaker, Bill. Stewards of the House: The Detective Fiction of Jonathan Latimer. LC 92-75452. 128p. (C). 1993. 21.95 (*0-87972-610-5*); pap. 8.95 (*0-87972-611-3*) Bowling Green Univ Popular Press.

Brubaker, C. William. Planning & Designing Schools. LC 97-35484. (Illus.). 240p. 1997. 59.95 (*0-07-049405-3*) McGraw-Hill Prof.

Brubaker, Dale L. Creative Curriculum Leadership. LC 93-45689. 152p. 1994. 49.95 (*0-8039-6140-5*); pap. 21.95 (*0-8039-6141-3*) Corwin Pr.

Brubaker, Dale L. & Coble, Larry D. Staying on Track: An Educational Leader's Guide to Preventing Derailment & Ensuring Personal & Organizational Success. (Illus.). 160p. 1996. 51.95 (*0-8039-6537-0*); pap. 22.95 (*0-8039-6538-9*) Corwin Pr.

Brubaker, Dale L. & Simon, Lawrence H. Teacher As Decision Maker: Real-Life Cases to Hone Your People Skills. LC 93-13917. 200p. 1993. 55.95 (*0-8039-6081-6*); pap. 24.95 (*0-8039-6082-4*) Corwin Pr.

Brubaker, Dale L., jt. auth. see Thomas, R. Murray.

Brubaker, Daniel B., jt. ed. see Kurtz, Sanford R.

Brubaker, Daniel B., jt. ed. see Simpson, Marcus B., Jr.

Brubaker, Donald. Absent from the Body: One Man's Clinical Death - A Journey Through Heaven & Hell. Penney, Mary B., ed. & photos by by. LC 95-68236. (Illus.). 192p. 1995. pap. 12.95 (*0-9645438-0-X*) Peninsla Pub.

Brubaker, Douglas. Marine Pollution & International Law: Principles & Practices. 420p. 1993. 79.95 (*0-85293-273-1*, BH3273) CRC Pr.

— Marine Pollution & International Law: Principles & Practices. 485p. 1994. 79.95 (*1-85293-273-2*) Halsted Pr.

Brubaker, Earl R. Public Expenditure Decisions Vol. 5: Behavior, Institutions, Procedures & Performance. Breit, William & Elzinga, Kenneth G., eds. LC 89-1891. (Political Economy & Public Policy Ser.: Vol. 5). 179p. 1989. 78.50 (*0-89232-835-5*) Jai Pr.

Brubaker, Ed. Portable Lowlife. (Illus.). 48p. (Orig.). 1994. pap. 4.95 (*1-883847-16-8*) MU Press.

***Brubaker, Ed.** Scene of the Crime: A Little Piece of Goodnight. (Illus.). 112p. (J). 2000. pap. text 12.95 (*1-56389-670-2*, Pub. by DC Comics) Time Warner.

Brubaker, Edward & Brubaker, Mary. Golden Fire: The Anniversary Book of the Oregon Shakespearean Festival. LC 85-2905. (Illus.). 141p. 1985. 22.95 (*0-9614515-0-5*) Or Shakespearean.

Brubaker, Edward S. Shakespeare Aloud: A Guide to His Verse on Stage. LC 76-52176. 1977. pap. 6.25 (*0-9613496-0-3*) Brubaker.

Brubaker, J. Lester. God's Servant Leader in the Christian School. 1987. pap. text 8.99 (*0-88469-207-8*) BMH Bks.

— Personnel Administration in the Christian School. 168p. (Orig.). 1980. pap. 9.99 (*0-88469-130-6*) BMH Bks.

Brubaker, Jean, ed. see Denton, Betty.

Brubaker, Jean, ed. see Hopper, Beebe.

Brubaker, John H., 3rd. The Last Capital: Danville, Virginia, & the Final Days of the Confederacy. LC 79-109027. (Illus.). 76p. 1996. 19.95 (*0-9651635-0-4*) Danville Mus.

Brubaker, John K., jt. auth. see Slaff, James I.

Brubaker, Leslie. Vision & Meaning in Ninth-Century Byzantium: Image as Exegesis in the Homilies of Gregory of Nazianzus. LC 97-43385. (Cambridge Studies in Palaeography & Codicology: No. 6). (Illus.). xxiii, 489 p. 1999. 95.00 (*0-521-62153-4*) Cambridge U Pr.

Brubaker, Leslie, ed. Dead or Alive? Byzantium in the Ninth Century: Papers from the 30th Spring Symposium of Byzantine Studies, Birmingham, March, 1996. LC 97-52737. (Society for the Promotion of Byzantine Studies: No. 6). 271p. 1998. text 78.95 (*0-86078-686-2*, DF553.S68, Pub. by Ashgate Pub) Ashgate Pub Co.

Brubaker, Leslie, jt. ed. see Ousterhout, Robert G.

Brubaker, Linda T., et al, eds. The Female Pelvic Floor: Disorders of Function & Support. (Illus.). 309p. (C). 1996. text 89.00 (*0-8036-0075-5*) Davis Co.

Brubaker, Louis, jt. ed. see Best, Katherine.

Brubaker, Mary, jt. auth. see Brubaker, Edward.

Brubaker, Pamela K. Women Don't Count: The Challenge of Women's Poverty to Christian Ethics. LC 94-2380. 288p. 1994. pap. 19.95 (*1-55540-958-X*, 010187) OUP.

— Women Don't Count: The Challenge of Women's Poverty to Christian Ethics. LC 94-2380. (AAR Academy Ser.: Vol. 87). 288p. 1994. 29.95 (*1-55540-957-1*, 010187) OUP.

Brubaker, Pamela K. & Rhoades, Ruby, frwds. She Hath Done What She Could: A History of Women's Participation in the Church of the Brethren. LC 85-6622. (Illus.). 240p. reprint ed. pap. 74.40 (*0-8357-5590-8*, 203522200093) Bks Demand.

***Brubaker, Paul E.** The Cuban Missile Crisis in American History. LC 00-9663. (In American History Ser.). 2001. write for info. (*0-7660-1414-2*) Enslow Pubs.

Brubaker, Rogers. Citizenship & Nationhood in France & Germany. 352p. 1992. 39.95 (*0-674-13177-0*) HUP.

— Citizenship & Nationhood in France & Germany. (Illus.). 288p. 1994. pap. text 19.95 (*0-674-13178-9*, BRUCIX) HUP.

— The Limits of Rationality: An Essay on the Social & Moral Thought of Max Weber. LC 83-15152. (Controversies in Sociology Ser.: No. 16). 119p. 1984. text 34.95 (*0-04-301172-1*); pap. text 16.95 (*0-04-301173-X*) Routledge.

— Nationalism Reframed: Nationhood & the National Question in the New Europe. 213p. (C). 1996. pap. text 17.95 (*0-521-57649-0*) Cambridge U Pr.

Brubaker, Roy. Learn Novell Netware Software in a Day: For Versions 3.11-4.0. 3rd ed. (Popular Applications Ser.). (Illus.). 128p. (Orig.). 1993. pap. 15.95 incl. disk (*1-55622-306-4*) Wordware Pub.

Brubaker, Sterling. In Command of Tomorrow: Resource & Environmental Strategies for Americans. LC 74-24401. (Resources for the Future Study). 192p. reprint ed. pap. 59.60 (*0-7837-3037-3*, 202378900034) Bks Demand.

— In Command of Tomorrow: Resources & Environmental Strategies for Americans. (Resources for the Future Ser.). 192p. 1977. pap. 9.95 (*0-8018-1957-1*) Johns Hopkins.

— To Live on Earth: Man & His Environment in Perspective. LC 75-185514. 202p. 1972. pap. 18.50 (*0-8018-1378-6*) Resources Future.

— Trends in the World Aluminum Industry. LC 67-16035. 274p. reprint ed. pap. 85.00 (*0-608-12236-X*, 202379000034) Bks Demand.

Brubaker, Sterling, ed. Rethinking the Federal Lands. LC 83-43261. 306p. (C). 1984. pap. 16.95 (*0-915707-01-2*); lib. bdg. 39.00 (*0-915707-00-4*) Resources Future.

Brubaker, Sterling, jt. auth. see Crosson, Pierre R.

Brubaker, Susan H. Basic Level Workbook for Aphasia. (William Beaumont Hospital Speech & Language Pathology Ser.). 352p. (C). 1996. 40.00 (*0-8143-2620-X*) Wayne St U Pr.

— Sourcebook for Aphasia: A Guide to Family Activities & Community Resources. LC 81-23099. 205p. 1981. reprint ed. pap. 63.60 (*0-608-10632-1*, 207125400009) Bks Demand.

— Sourcebook for Speech, Language & Cognition: Stimulus Materials for Rehabilitation, Bk. 1. LC 92-13721. (William Beaumont Hospital Speech & Language Pathology Ser.: Bks. 1-2). 200p. 1992. 48.00 (*0-8143-2411-8*) Wayne St U Pr.

— Sourcebook for Speech, Language & Cognition: Stimulus Materials for Rehabilitation, Bk. 2. LC 92-13721. (William Beaumont Hospital Speech & Language Pathology Ser.: Bks. 1-2). 194p. 1992. 48.00 (*0-8143-2412-6*) Wayne St U Pr.

— Sourcebook for Speech, Language & Cognition Bk. 3: Stimulus Materials for Rehabilitation. LC 92-13721. 208p. 1994. text 48.00 (*0-8143-2501-7*) Wayne St U Pr.

— Workbook for Aphasia: Exercises for the Redevelopment of Higher Level Language Functioning. rev. ed. LC 85-91276. (William Beaumont Hospital Speech & Language Pathology Ser.). 376p. 1985. reprint ed. spiral bd. 40.00 (*0-8143-1803-7*) Wayne St U Pr.

— Workbook for Cognitive Skills: Exercises for Thought Processing & Word Retrieval. LC 87-7352. (William Beaumont Hospital Speech & Language Pathology Ser.). 292p. 1987. spiral bd. 40.00 (*0-8143-1903-3*) Wayne St U Pr.

— Workbook for Language Skills: Exercises for Written & Verbal Expression. LC 84-11893. (William Beaumont Hospital Speech & Language Pathology Ser.). 288p. 1984. spiral bd. 40.00 (*0-8143-1778-2*) Wayne St U Pr.

— Workbook for Reasoning Skills: Exercises for Cognitive Facilitation. LC 83-50961. (William Beaumont Hospital Speech & Language Pathology Ser.). 300p. 1983. spiral bd. 40.00 (*0-8143-1760-X*) Wayne St U Pr.

Brubaker, Timothy H. Family Relations: Challenges for the Future. (Current Issues in the Family Ser.: Vol. 1). (Illus.). 320p. (C). 1992. 56.00 (*0-8039-3945-0*); pap. 25.00 (*0-8039-3946-9*) Sage.

— Later Life Families. (Family Studies Text Ser.: Vol. 1). 1985. 42.00 (*0-8039-2293-0*); pap. 18.95 (*0-8039-2294-9*) Sage.

Brubaker, Timothy H., ed. Aging, Health, & Family: Long-Term Care. LC 86-17749. (Sage Focus Editions Ser.: No. 85). 288p. 1987. reprint ed. pap. 89.30 (*0-608-01087-1*, 205939600001) Bks Demand.

— Family Relationships in Later Life. 2nd ed. (Focus Editions Ser.: Vol. 64). (Illus.). 320p. (C). 1990. text 59.95 (*0-8039-3321-5*); pap. text 26.00 (*0-8039-3322-3*) Sage.

Brubaker, Timothy H. & Price, Sharon J., eds. Families & Aging. (Vision 2010 Ser.: Vol. 4, No. 1). 44p. (Orig.). (C). 1996. pap. 20.95 (*0-916174-53-0*) Natl Coun Family.

Brubaker, Timothy H., jt. auth. see Springer, Dianne.

Brubaker, William R., ed. Immigration & the Politics of Citizenship in Europe & North America. 196p. (C). 1989. lib. bdg. 38.50 (*0-8191-7428-9*) U Pr of Amer.

Brubeck, Dave. Earth Is Our Mother. Dingley, Bob, ed. 80p. (C). 1997. pap. text 8.95 (*0-7692-1625-0*, OCT02613) Wrner Bros.

— The Genius Continues. 1986. pap. 11.95 (*0-89898-492-0*, TPF0137) Wrner Bros.

Brucan, Silviu. Pluralism & Social Conflict: A Social Analysis of the Communist World. LC 89-48745. 216p. 1990. 55.00 (*0-275-93475-6*, C3475, Greenwood Pr) Greenwood.

— The Post-Brezhnev Era. LC 83-16158. 144p. 1983. 47.95 (*0-275-90953-0*, C0953, Praeger Pubs) Greenwood.

— Social Change in Russia & Eastern Europe: From Party Hacks to Nouveaux Riches. LC 98-14925. 136p. 1998. 49.95 (*0-275-96322-5*, Praeger Pubs) Greenwood.

— World Socialism at the Crossroads: An Insider's View. LC 87-11704. 201p. 1987. 55.00 (*0-275-92782-2*, C2782, Praeger Pubs) Greenwood.

Brucar, Wayne E., jt. auth. see Rich, Malcolm C.

Brucato, John. A Sicilian in America. 448p. 1992. 18.95 (*0-9635292-0-X*) Green Hills.

Brucato, John M., jt. auth. see Gainey, Donald D.

Brucato, Laurel, jt. auth. see Abascal, Juan.

Brucato, Phil. Book of Mirrors: Mage Storytellers Guide. (Mage Ser.). 1997. pap. 18.00 (*1-56504-403-7*, 4302) White Wolf.

***Brucato, Phil.** Infernalism: The Path of Screams. (Mage Ser.). (Illus.). 128p. 1999. pap. 18.00 (*1-56504-495-9*, 4806) White Wolf.

— Technocracy Assembled, Vol. 2. 2000. pap. 14.95 (*1-56504-419-3*) White Wolf.

Brucato, Phil & Campbell, Brian. Mage: The Sorcerer's Crusade. (Mage Ser.). (Illus.). 1998. 28.00 (*1-56504-489-4*, 4800) White Wolf.

Brucato, Phil & Hite, Kenneth. Crusade Lore: The Storyteller Screen & Book. (Mage Ser.). (Illus.). 1998. pap. 15.00 (*1-56504-490-8*, 4801) White Wolf.

Brucato, Phil & Rosenberg, Aaron. Tales of Magick: Dark Adventure. (Illus.). 96p. 1999. pap. 14.95 (*1-56504-404-5*, 4021) White Wolf.

Brucato, Phil & Skemp, Ethan. Bastet: Changing Breeds Book. (Werewolf Ser.). (Illus.). 160p. (Orig.). 1997. pap. 18.00 (*1-56504-335-9*, 3075) White Wolf.

Brucato, Phil, et al. Book of Shadows: The Mage Players Guide. (Mage Ser.). 250p. 1994. pap., per. 18.00 (*1-56504-119-4*, 4050) White Wolf.

***Brucato, Phil, et al.** Guide to the Technocracy. (Mage Ser.). (Illus.). 224p. 1999. pap. 25.95 (*1-56504-417-7*, 4014) White Wolf.

Brucato, Phil, et al. Hidden Lore: Storytellers Screen & Book. 2nd ed. (Mage Ser.). 1996. pap. 15.00 (*1-56504-402-9*, 4301) White Wolf.

— Horizon: Stronghold of Hope. (Mage Ser.). (Illus.). 112p. (Orig.). 1996. pap. 15.00 (*1-56504-425-8*, 4012) White Wolf.

— Mage: The Ascension. 2nd ed. (Mage). 1995. 28.00 (*1-56504-400-2*, 4300) White Wolf.

— Mage Chronicles, Vol. I. (Mage Ser.). (Illus.). 200p. 1997. pap. 22.00 (*1-56504-415-0*, 4013) White Wolf.

Brucato, Phil, jt. auth. see Ryan, Kathleen.

Brucato, Phil, jt. auth. see Skemp, Ethan.

Bruccoli, Mary. Concise Dictionary of American Literary Biography: The Twenties, 1917-1929. 326p. 1993. 80.00 (*0-8103-1824-5*) Gale.

— Concise Dictionary of American Literary Biography Vol. V: The Age of Maturity, 1929-1941. 426p. 1993. 80.00 (*0-8103-1820-2*) Gale.

Bruccoli, Mary. Dictionary of Literary Biography. (Documentary Ser.: Vol. 2). (Illus.). 480p. 1982. text 146.00 (*0-8103-1114-3*) Gale.

— Dictionary of Literary Biography No. 85: Austrian Writers after 1914, Vol. 85. 400p. 1989. text 155.00 (*0-8103-4563-3*) Gale.

— Dictionary of Literary Biography No. 86: American Short-Story Writers, 1910-1945, First Series, Vol. 86. 400p. 1989. text 155.00 (*0-8103-4564-1*) Gale.

— Dictionary of Literary Biography Vol. 80: Restoration Dramatists & 18th Century Dramatists, First Series, Vol. 80. 400p. 1989. text 155.00 (*0-8103-4558-7*) Gale.

— Dictionary of Literary Biography Vol. 81: Austrian Fiction Writers, 1875-1913, Vol. 81. 400p. 1989. text 155.00 (*0-8103-4559-5*) Gale.

— Dictionary of Literary Biography Vol. 82: Chicano Writers, First Series, Vol. 82. Shirley, Carl R., ed. 350p. 1989. text 155.00 (*0-8103-4560-9*) Gale.

— Dictionary of Literary Biography Vol. 84: Restoration & 18th Century Dramatists, Vol. 84. (Second Ser.). 350p. 1989. text 155.00 (*0-8103-4562-5*) Gale.

— Dictionary of Literary Biography Vol. 88: French Novelists since 1960, Vol. 83. 400p. 1989. text 155.00 (*0-8103-4561-7*) Gale.

— Dictionary of Literary Biography Yearbook, 1988. 88th ed. 400p. 1989. text 155.00 (*0-8103-1836-9*) Gale.

Bruccoli, Mary, ed. Dictionary of Literary Biography Vol. 88: Canadian Writers, 1920-1959, Second Series, Vol. 88. (Second Ser.). 400p. 1989. text 146.00 (*0-8103-4566-8*) Gale.

— Dictionary of Literary Biography Documentary Series: An Illustrated Chronicle, Vol. 3. 416p. 1983. text 155.00 (*0-8103-1115-1*) Gale.

Bruccoli, Mary, et al, eds. Dictionary of Literary Biography: Modern American Poets: James Dickey, Robert Frost, & Marianne Moore. (Documentary Ser.: Vol. 7). (Illus.). 400p. 1989. text 146.00 (*0-8103-2782-1*) Gale.

— Dictionary of Literary Biography Vol. 89: Restoration & 18th Century Dramatists, Vol. 89. (Third Ser.). 400p. 1989. text 155.00 (*0-8103-4567-6*) Gale.

— Dictionary of Literary Biography Vol. 90: German Writers in the Age of Goethe, 1789-1832, Vol. 90. 400p. 1989. text 155.00 (*0-8103-4568-4*) Gale.

Bruccoli, Mary & Layman, Richard, eds. Concise Dictionary of American Literary Biography, 6 vols., Set. 1987. 435.00 (*0-8103-1818-0*) Gale.

Bruccoli, Mary, et al. American Bibliographers & Bibliophiles. LC 94-7047. (Dictionary of Literary Biography Ser.: Vol. 140). 400p. 1994. text 155.00 (*0-8103-5399-7*, 007475) Gale.

— Dictionary of Literary Biography, Vol. 135. 400p. 1993. text 155.00 (*0-8103-5394-6*, 007470) Gale.

— Dictionary of Literary Biography, Vol. 137. 400p. 1994. text 155.00 (*0-8103-5396-2*, 007472) Gale.

— Dictionary of Literary Biography, Vol. 138. 400p. 1994. text 155.00 (*0-8103-5397-0*, 007473) Gale.

— Dictionary of Literary Biography, Vol. 139. 400p. 1994. text 155.00 (*0-8103-5398-9*, 007474) Gale.

— Dictionary of Literary Biography, Vol. 141. 400p. 1994. text 155.00 (*0-8103-5555-8*, 007476) Gale.

— Dictionary of Literary Biography, Vol. 142. 400p. 1994. text 155.00 (*0-8103-5556-6*, 007477) Gale.

— Dictionary of Literary Biography, Vol. 143. 400p. 1994. text 155.00 (*0-8103-5557-4*, 007478) Gale.

— Dictionary of Literary Biography, Vol. 144. 400p. 1994. text 155.00 (*0-8103-5558-2*, 007479) Gale.

— Dictionary of Literary Biography, Vol. 145. 400p. 1994. text 155.00 (*0-8103-5559-0*, 007480) Gale.

— DLB Documentary Series, Vol. 12. 400p. 1994. text 146.00 (*0-8103-5561-2*, 006486) Gale.

— DLB Yearbook, 1993. 93rd ed. 400p. 1994. text 155.00 (*0-8103-5560-4*, 006463) Gale.

Bruccoli, Mathew J. F. Scott Fitzgerald: A Descriptive Bibliography. LC 77-181395. (Pittsburg Series in Bibliography). 393p. reprint ed. pap. 121.90 (*0-608-11169-4*, 202061800018) Bks Demand.

Bruccoli, Mathew J., jt. auth. see Schnee, Charles.

Bruccoli, Matthew, ed. Conversations with Ernest Hemingway. LC 86-11140. (Literary Conversations Ser.). 220p. 1986. pap. 15.95 (*0-87805-273-9*) U Pr of Miss.

Bruccoli, Matthew, ed. see Dickey, James.

Bruccoli, Matthew J. F. Scott Fitzgerald: A Descriptive Bibliography. rev. ed. LC 87-40220. (Poetry Series in Bibliography). (Illus.). 504p. 1988. 100.00 (*0-8229-3560-0*) U of Pittsburgh Pr.

— F. Scott Fitzgerald 24 September 1896-24 September 1996: Centenary Exhibition Catalog. LC 96-10075. (Matthew J. & Arlyn Bruccoli Collection). (Illus.). 176p. 1996. pap. text 19.95 (*1-57003-150-9*) U of SC Pr.

— Fitzgerald & Hemingway: A Dangerous Friendship. (Illus.). 224p. 1995. pap. 11.95 (*0-7867-0261-3*) Carroll & Graf.

— Fortunes of Mitchell Kennerley, Bookman. (Illus.). 432p. 1986. 24.95 (*0-15-132671-1*) Harcourt.

— James Gould Cozzenz: A Descriptive Bibliography. LC 80-53553. (Series in Bibliography). (Illus.). 208p. 1981. 100.00 (*0-8229-3435-3*) U of Pittsburgh Pr.

— John O'Hara: A Descriptive Bibliography. LC 77-15737. (Series in Bibliography). (Illus.). 344p. 1978. 100.00 (*0-8229-3349-7*) U of Pittsburgh Pr.

— Modern Women Writers. Baughman, Judith S., ed. LC 93-8642. (Essential Bibliography of American Fiction Ser.). 112p. 1994. 19.95 (*0-8160-3000-6*) Facts on File.

— Nelson Algren: A Descriptive Bibliography. LC 85-1180. (Series in Bibliography). (Illus.). 200p. 1985. text 100.00 (*0-8229-3517-1*) U of Pittsburgh Pr.

— The O'Hara Concern: A Biography of John O'Hara. LC 95-10698. 488p. 1995. pap. 24.95 (*0-8229-5559-8*) U of Pittsburgh Pr.

— The Professions of Authorship: Essays in Honor of Matthew J. Bruccoli. Layman, Richard & Myerson, Joel, eds. LC 96-10095. 258p. 1996. text 34.95 (*1-57003-144-4*) U of SC Pr.

— Raymond Chandler: A Checklist. LC 68-16892. (Serif Series: Bibliograhies & Checklists: No. 2). 45p. reprint ed. pap. 30.00 (*0-8357-9373-7*, 201538300093) Bks Demand.

— Raymond Chandler: A Descriptive Bibliography. LC 78-4280. (Series in Bibliography). 168p. 1979. 100.00 (*0-8229-3382-9*) U of Pittsburgh Pr.

— Ross MacDonald. LC 83-293. 176p. 1984. pap. 7.95 (*0-15-679082-3*, Harvest Bks) Harcourt.

— Ross MacDonald-Kenneth Millar: A Descriptive Bibliography. LC 83-1398. (Series in Bibliography). (Illus.). 280p. 1983. text 100.00 (*0-8229-3482-5*) U of Pittsburgh Pr.

— Some Sort of Epic Grandeur. LC 80-8740. 656p. 1983. pap. 12.95 (*0-15-683803-6*, Harvest Bks) Harcourt.

— Some Sort of Epic Grandeur: The Life of F. Scott Fitzgerald. (Illus.). 768p. 1993. pap. 16.95 (*0-88184-907-3*) Carroll & Graf.

— Some Sort of Epic Grandeur: The Life of F. Scott Fitzgerald. LC 80-8740. 640p. 1981. 25.00 (*0-15-183242-0*) Harcourt.

Bruccoli, Matthew J., ed. Conversations with Ernest Hemingway. LC 86-11140. (Literary Conversations Ser.). 220p. 1986. text 39.50 (*0-87805-272-0*) U Pr of Miss.

***Bruccoli, Matthew J., ed.** Great Gatsby: A Documentary. LC 99-56682. 400p. 1999. text 151.00 (*0-7876-3128-0*) Gale.

Bruccoli, Matthew J., ed. Concise Dictionary of American Literary Biography: The New Consciousness, 1941-1968. (Concise Dictionary of American Literary Biography Ser.). 539p. 1987. 80.00 (*0-8103-1822-9*) Gale.

— New Essays on "The Great Gatsby" (American Novel Ser.). 128p. 1985. pap. text 14.95 (*0-521-31963-3*) Cambridge U Pr.

— The Sun Also Rises, 2 vols., Set, Vols. I & 2. (Archive of Literary Documents Ser.: Vol. II). 1990. lib. bdg. 285.00 (*1-55888-267-7*) Omnigraphics Inc.

Bruccoli, Matthew J., et al, eds. A Dark Night's Dreaming: Contemporary American Horror Fiction. LC 95-38981. (Understanding Contemporary American Literature Ser.). 190p. (C). 1996. 24.95 (*1-57003-070-7*) U of SC Pr.

— Dictionary of Literary Biography. (Documentary Ser.: Vol. 17). 400p. 1998. 146.00 (*0-7876-1932-9*, GML00198-111368) Visible Ink Pr.

***Bruccoli, Matthew J., et al, eds.** Dictionary of Literary Biography, Vol. 19. LC 82-1105. (Documentary Ser.). 400p. 1999. text 155.00 (*0-7876-2523-X*, GML00299-112047, Gale Res Intl) Gale.

Bruccoli, Matthew J., et al, eds. Dictionary of Literary Biography, Vol. 191. LC 97-52103. (Dictionary of Literary Biography Ser.). 400p. 1998. 146.00 (*0-7876-1846-2*, GML00198-111266) Visible Ink Pr.

***Bruccoli, Matthew J., et al, eds.** Dictionary of Literary Biography, Vol. 206. LC 99-13127. 400p. 1999. text 155.00 (*0-7876-3100-0*, GML00299-112695, Gale Res Intl) Gale.

— Dictionary of Literary Biography, Vol. 207. LC 99-14525. 400p. 1999. text 155.00 (*0-7876-3101-9*, GML00299-112696, Gale Res Intl) Gale.

Bruccoli, Matthew J., et al, eds. Dictionary of Literary Biography: American Expatriate Writers. (Dictionary of Literary Biography Ser.: Vol. 16). (Illus.). 400p. 1997. 146.00 (*0-7876-1931-0*, GML00198-111367) Visible Ink Pr.

— Dictionary of Literary Biography: French Dramatists, 1789-1914, Vol. 192. LC 98-16251. 400p. 1998. 146.00 (*0-7876-1847-0*, GML00198-111267) Visible Ink Pr.

Bruccoli, Matthew J., et al, eds. Dictionary of Literary Biography Vol. 179: Modern Japanese Writers. LC 97-11573. 400p. 1997. text 155.00 (*0-7876-1068-2*, GML00197-110417) Gale.

— Dictionary of Literary Biography Vol. 180: German Renaissance, 1280-1580. LC 97-2716. 400p. 1997. text 155.00 (*0-7876-1069-0*, GML00197-110418) Gale.

Bruccoli, Matthew J., et al, eds. Dictionary of Literary Biography Vol. 193: American Women Prose Writers to 1920. LC 98-3658. 400p. 1998. 146.00 (*0-7876-1848-9*, GML00198-111268) Visible Ink Pr.

— Dictionary of Literary Biography Vol. 194: 20th Century British Book Collectors & Bibliographers. LC 98-7839. 400p. 1998. 146.00 (*0-7876-1849-7*, GML00198-111269) Visible Ink Pr.

— Dictionary of Literary Biography Vol. 195: British Travel Writers, 1910-1939. LC 98-21847. xxi, 465p. 1998. 146.00 (*0-7876-1850-0*, GML00198-111270) Visible Ink Pr.

***Bruccoli, Matthew J., et al, eds.** Dictionary of Literary Biography Yearbook, 1998. 400p. 1999. text 155.00 (*0-7876-2520-5*, GML00299-112044, Gale Res Intl) Gale.

— Russian Literature in the Age of Pushkin & Gogol. LC 98-53956. (Dictionary of Literary Biography Ser.: Vol. 205). 400p. 1999. text 155.00 (*0-7876-3099-3*, GML00299-112694, Gale Res Intl) Gale.

Bruccoli, Matthew J. & Baughman, Judith S. Modern African American Writers. LC 93-8643. (Essential Bibliography of American Fiction Ser.). 96p. 1994. pap. 9.95 (*0-8160-2999-7*) Facts on File.

— Modern Classic Writers. LC 93-8641. (Essential Bibliography of American Fiction Ser.). 112p. 1993. pap. 9.95 (*0-8160-3003-0*) Facts on File.

— Modern Women Writers. LC 93-8642. (Essential Bibliography of American Fiction Ser.). 112p. 1994. lib. bdg. 9.95 (*0-8160-3001-4*) Facts on File.

— Reader's Companion to F. Scott Fitzgerald's Tender Is the Night. LC 95-4408. (Illus.). 274p. 1995. 29.95 (*1-57003-078-2*) U of SC Pr.

— Reader's Companion to F. Scott Fitzgerald's Tender Is the Night. LC 95-4408. (Illus.). 274p. 1997. pap. 14.95 (*1-57003-223-8*) U of SC Pr.

Bruccoli, Matthew J. & Baughman, Judith S., eds. Modern African American Writers. LC 93-8643. (Essential Bibliography of American Fiction Ser.). 112p. 1994. 19.95 (*0-8160-2998-9*) Facts on File.

Bruccoli, Matthew J. & Bauhman, Judith S., eds. Modern Classic Writers. LC 93-8641. (Essential Bibliography of American Fiction Ser.). 112p. 1994. 19.95 (*0-8160-3002-2*) Facts on File.

***Bruccoli, Matthew J. & Bucker, Park, eds.** To Loot My Life Clean: The Thomas Wolfe-Maxwell Perkins Correspondence. (Illus.). 512p. 2000. 39.95 (*1-57003-355-2*) U of SC Pr.

Bruccoli, Matthew J. & Clark, C. E., Jr., eds. Fitzgerald-Hemingway Annual 1969. 1969. 25.00 (*0-910972-54-0*) Bruccoli.

Bruccoli, Matthew J. & Clark, C. E., eds. Fitzgerald-Hemingway Annual 1970. 1970. 25.00 (*0-910972-03-6*) Bruccoli.

Bruccoli, Matthew J. & Clark, C. E., Jr., eds. Fitzgerald-Hemingway Annual 1971. 1973. 25.00 (*0-910972-12-5*) Bruccoli.

— Fitzgerald-Hemingway Annual 1972. 1973. 25.00 (*0-910972-34-6*) Bruccoli.

— Fitzgerald-Hemingway Annual 1973. 1974. 25.00 (*0-910972-38-9*) Bruccoli.

Bruccoli, Matthew J. & Layman, Richard. American Decades, 1960-1969, Vol. 3. 7th ed. (American Decades 1900-2000 Ser.). 500p. 1994. 90.00 (*0-8103-8883-9*, 021002) Gale.

— Concise Dictionary of American Literary Biography: Realism, Naturalism, & Local Color, 1865-1917. (Dictionary of Literary Biography Ser.). 392p. 1988. 80.00 (*0-8103-1821-0*) Gale.

— Ring W. Lardner: A Descriptive Bibliography. LC 75-9126. (Series in Bibliography). (Illus.). 488p. 1976. 100.00 (*0-8229-3306-3*) U of Pittsburgh Pr.

Bruccoli, Matthew J. & Layman, Richard, eds. American Decades, 1980-1989. 9th ed. 500p. 1995. 90.00 (*0-8103-8881-2*, 021000) Gale.

— American Decades, 1970-1979, Vol. 2. 8th ed. (American Decades 1900-2000 Ser.). 500p. 1995. 90.00 (*0-8103-8882-0*, 021001) Gale.

— Concise Dictionary of American Literary Biography: Broadening Views, 1968-1988. LC 86-33657. (Illus.). 408p. 1989. 80.00 (*0-8103-1823-7*, 007182) Gale.

— Fitzgerald-Hemingway Annual. Incl. 1977-78 Annual., 2 Vols. 77th ed. LC 75-83781. 1978. 70.00 (*0-8103-0909-2*); 1978 Annual. 78th ed. LC 75-83781. 1979. 70.00 (*0-8103-0910-6*); LC 75-83781. (Illus.). 1975. write for info. (*0-318-52359-0*) Gale.

Bruccoli, Matthew J. & Trogdon, Robert W., eds. Dear Ernest, Dear Max: The Ernest Hemingway/Maxwell Perkins Correspondence. 367p. 1996. 34.50 (*0-684-81562-1*, Scribners Ref) Mac Lib Ref.

Bruccoli, Matthew J., jt. auth. see Schnee, Charles.

Bruccoli, Matthew J., jt. auth. see Tate, Mary J.

Bruccoli, Matthew J., ed. see Baughman, Judith S.

Bruccoli, Matthew J., ed. see Bryer, Jackson R.

Bruccoli, Matthew J., ed. see Clareson, Thomas D.

Bruccoli, Matthew J., ed. see Cozzens, James G.

Bruccoli, Matthew J., ed. see Cummins, Elizabeth.

Bruccoli, Matthew J., ed. see Diedrick, James.

Bruccoli, Matthew J., ed. see Fitzgerald, F. Scott.

Bruccoli, Matthew J., ed. see Fitzgerald, Zelda.

Bruccoli, Matthew J., ed. see Foster, Edward H.

Bruccoli, Matthew J., ed. see Fowler, Douglas.

Bruccoli, Matthew J., ed. see Friedman, Lawrence S.

Bruccoli, Matthew J., ed. see Hanson, Gillian M.

Bruccoli, Matthew J., ed. see Hemingway, Ernest.

Bruccoli, Matthew J., ed. see James, Henry.

Bruccoli, Matthew J., jt. ed. see Nabokov, Dmitri.

Bruccoli, Matthew J., ed. see O'Hara, John.

Bruccoli, Matthew J., ed. see Spikes, Michael P.

Bruccoli, Matthew J., ed. see Wald, Malvin & Maltz, Albert.

Bruccoli, Matthew J., ed. & anno. see Fitzgerald, F. Scott.

Bruccoli, Matthew S., ed. see Fitzgerald, F. Scott.

Bruce. Assessment of Personal Injury Damages. 2nd ed. 328p. 1992. text 82.00 (*0-409-89768-X*, MICHIE) LEXIS Pub.

— Business Review Book. 1992. pap. text. write for info. (*0-582-06449-X*, Pub. by Addison-Wesley) Longman.

— Inorganic Materials. 2nd ed. 610p. 1997. pap. 84.95 (*0-471-96036-5*) Wiley.

— Nursing in Gastroenterology. 1997. text 33.00 (*0-443-05484-3*, W B Saunders Co) Harcrt Hlth Sci Grp.

— Oliver's Numbers. (J). 1997. 14.95 (*0-689-80544-6*) S&S Childrens.

— Orondo los Unos por los Otros. (Serie Discipulado - Discipleship Ser.).Tr. of Praying for One Another. (SPA.). 26p. 1996. write for info. (*0-614-27089-8*) Editorial Unilit.

Bruce, et al. Visual Perception: Physiology, Psychology, & Ecology. 3rd ed. 1997. 59.95 (*0-86377-450-4*) L Erlbaum Assocs.

Bruce, jt. auth. see Lincoln.

Bruce, A. & Gao, H. Y. Applied Wavelet Analysis with S-PLUS. LC 96-12971. 338p. 1996. pap. 49.95 (*0-387-94714-0*) Spr-Verlag.

***Bruce, A. B.** Training of the Twelve. 2000. pap. 17.99 (*0-8254-2088-1*) Kregel.

Bruce, A. J. A Synopsis of the Indo-West Pacific Genera of the Pontoniinae (Crustacea: Decapoda: Palaemonidae) (Theses Zoologicae Ser.: Vol. 25). (Illus.). 172p. 1994. 79.50 (*3-87429-373-4*, Pub. by Koeltz Sci Bks) Lubrecht & Cramer.

Bruce, A. J., jt. auth. see Chace, Fenner A.

Bruce, A. J., jt. ed. see Potter, B. G., Jr.

Bruce, A. M., ed. Anaerobic Digestion of Sewage Sludge & Organic Agricultural Wastes. 164p. 1986. pap. 60.50 (*0-85334-431-0*) Thomson Learn.

Bruce, A. M., et al, eds. Disinfection of Sewage Sludge: Technical, Economic & Microbiological Aspects. 1982. text 112.50 (*90-277-1502-5*) Kluwer Academic.

Bruce, A. M. & Connor, E. S., eds. Stabilisation, Disinfection & Odour Control in Sewage Sludge Treatment: An Annotated Bibliography Covering the Period 1950-1983. 200p. 1984. text 76.95 (*0-470-20033-2*) P-H.

Bruce, A. Wayne. Basic Quality Assurance & Quality Control in the Clinical Laboratory. 179p. 1984. 29.95 (*0-316-11252-6*, Little Brwn Med Div) Lppncott W & W.

Bruce, Alan & Hill, Sandra. Managing Doctors. LC 96-187337. 64p. 1996. pap. 17.00 (*0-7486-0728-5*, Pub. by Edinburgh U Pr) Col U Pr.

Bruce, Alan & Palfreyman, John W., eds. Forest Products Biotechnology. LC 98-120468. 326p. 1997. 75.00 (*0-7484-0415-5*, Pub. by Tay Francis Ltd) Taylor & Francis.

Bruce, Alastair. Keepers of the Kingdom: The Ancient Offices of Britain. LC 99-28167. 1999. text 40.00 (*0-86565-202-3*) Vendome.

***Bruce, Alex.** Open & Free: Dean Bennett of Chester. (Liverpool Historical Studies: No. 17). 240p. 1999. pap. 19.95 (*0-85323-924-X*, Pub. by Liverpool Univ Pr) Intl Spec Bk.

Bruce, Alexander B. The Moral Order of the World in Ancient & Modern Thought. LC 77-527224. (Gifford Lectures: 1898). reprint ed. 49.50 (*0-404-60456-0*) AMS Pr.

— The Moral Order of the World in Ancient & Modern Thought (1899) 425p. 1998. reprint ed. pap. 29.95 (*0-7661-0165-7*) Kessinger Pub.

— The Providential Order of the World. LC 77-27225. (Gifford Lectures: 1897). 1978. reprint ed. 47.50 (*0-404-60455-2*) AMS Pr.

— The Training of the Twelve. LC 73-129738. 576p. 1979. pap. 17.99 (*0-8254-2236-1*, Kregel Class) Kregel.

Bruce, Alexandra. The Philadelphia Experiment Murder. Moon, Peter, ed. 260p. 1999. pap. 19.95 (*0-9631889-5-X*) Sky Bks NY.

Bruce, Alfred & Sandbank, Harold. The History of Prefabrication. LC 72-5038. (Technology & Society Ser.). (Illus.). 80p. 1977. reprint ed. 23.95 (*0-405-04691-X*) Ayer.

Bruce, Allan & Jonsson, Ernest. Competition in the Provision of Health Care. LC 96-85813. 212p. 1996. text 59.95 (*1-85742-305-4*, Pub. by Arena) Ashgate Pub Co.

Bruce, Allan J. & Hiremath, Basavaraj V., eds. Solid-State Optical Materials. LC 92-27701. (Ceramic Transactions Ser.: Vol. 28). 724p. 1992. 74.00 (*0-944904-52-1*, CT028) Am Ceramic.

Bruce, Alma. Fly Soul, Free As a Bird. 48p. 2000. pap. 8.00 (*0-8059-4723-X*) Dorrance.

Bruce, Andasia K. Uncle Tom's Cabin of To-Day. LC 72-6488. (Black Heritage Library Collection). 1977. reprint ed. 18.95 (*0-8369-9161-3*) Ayer.

Bruce, Andrew. Criminal Procedure - Trial on Indictment. 1996. write for info. (*0-409-99830-3*, MICHIE) LEXIS Pub.

Bruce, Andrew & McCoy, Gerard. Criminal Evidence in Hong Kong. 2nd ed. 530p. 1992. boxed set 151.00 (*0-409-99609-2*, MICHIE) LEXIS Pub.

Bruce, Andrew, jt. auth. see Langdon, Ken.

Bruce, Andrew A., et al. Workings of the Indeterminate-Sentence Law & the Parole System in Illinois. LC 68-19466. (Criminology, Law Enforcement, & Social Problems Ser.: No. 5). 1968. reprint ed. 26.00 (*0-87585-005-7*) Patterson Smith.

***Bruce, Andy.** Project Management. (Illus.). 72p. 2000. pap. 6.95 (*0-7894-5971-X*) DK Pub Inc.

— Strategic Thinking. (Essential Managers Ser.). (Illus.). 72p. 2000. pap. write for info. (*0-7894-5972-8* Pub. by DK Pub Inc) Pub Resources Inc.

Bruce, Anne & Pepitone, James S. Motivating Employees. LC 98-41554. (Briefcase Books Ser.). (Illus.). 192p. 1998. pap. 14.95 (*0-07-071868-7*) McGraw.

Bruce, Annette J. Tellable Cracker Tales. LC 95-41668. (Illus.). 104p. 1996. 14.95 (*1-56164-100-6*); pap. 8.95 (*1-56164-094-8*) Pineapple Pr.

***Bruce, Annie. Cat Be Good: A Commonsense Approach to Training Your Cat. LC 99-94833. (Illus.). 208p. 2000. pap. write for info. (*0-9674062-0-X*, Pub. by Good Cats) Bookpeople.**

Litter box problems? Aggressive cat? Cat owner consultant, Annie Bruce, reveals new information on how to: train your cat to come when called; solve peeing, pooping or hairball problems; deal with aggression, chewing, crying and much, much more. Bruce explains why to never declaw a cat. She offers dozens of helpful & unique suggestions on modifying behaviors from shyness to scratching, from spraying to straying. Bruce shows how through gentle commands, proper diet, exercise, & rewards, nearly any cat can turn into a well-behaved housemate. Sally Rosenthal in the March 2000 issue of "Cats" magazine says, "Bruce gives readers the scoop on all things feline-adoption, diet, wellness, safety, behavior, etc." Rene Knapp, host of TV show, "Pet Talk" in Connecticut wrote, "From the first sentence dealing with bringing the kitten home to the last chapter on how to say goodbye, CAT BE GOOD had this veteran cat owner's full attention & approval." Amy Hubbard in the May 2000 issue of "The Whole Cat Journal" says, CAT BE GOOD is a great guide or gift for anyone who is thinking about sharing life with a feline friend." For more information, check out Annie's delightful web site at www.goodcatswearblack.com. *Publisher Paid Annotation.*

Bruce, Anthony. Shakespeare Country. 1999. pap 14.95 (*0-7181-3243-2*) Viking Penguin.

***Bruce, Anthony, ed.** An Encyclopedia of Naval History. 400p. 1998. pap. text 55.00 (*1-57958-109-9*) Fitzroy Dearborn.

Bruce, Anthony & Cogar, William. An Encyclopedia of Naval History. (Illus.). 448p. 1999. pap. 24.95 (*0-8160-4068-0*, Checkmark) Facts on File.

Bruce, Anthony & Cogar, William B. An Encyclopedia of Naval History. LC 97-7243. (Illus.). 448p. 1998. 50.00 (*0-8160-2697-1*, Checkmark) Facts on File.

Bruce, Arden. Witch, Witch Come to My Party. (GRE.). (J). 1991. pap. 6.99 (*0-85953-822-2*) Childs Play.

— Witch, Witch Come to My Party. (SPA.). (J). 1996. pap. 6.99 (*0-85953-975-X*) Childs Play.

***Bruce, Barbara.** 7 Ways of Teaching the Bible to Adults: Using Our Multiple Intelligences to Build Faith. LC 00-33192. 2000. write for info. (*0-687-09084-9*) Abingdon.

Bruce, Barbara, jt. auth. see Kishpaugh, Charles R.

Bruce, Bertram, et al, eds. Network-Based Classrooms: Promises & Realities. LC 92-31680. (Illus.). 314p. (C). 1993. text 64.95 (*0-521-41636-1*); pap. text 20.95 (*0-521-45702-5*) Cambridge U Pr.

Bruce, Bertrum & Rubin, Andee. Electronic Quills: A Situated Evaluation of Using Computers to Teach Writing in Classrooms. (Technology & Education Ser.). 248p. 1992. pap. 29.95 (*0-8058-1168-0*) L Erlbaum Assocs.

— Electronic Quills: A Situated Evaluation of Using Computers to Teach Writing in Classrooms. (Technology & Education Ser.). 248p. 1993. text 59.95 (*0-8058-0985-6*) L Erlbaum Assocs.

***Bruce, Bonnie.** Calcium: Nature's Bone Builder. LC 00-35544. 192p. 2000. pap. 12.95 (*1-58333-058-5*, Avery) Penguin Putnam.

Bruce, Brian, ed. Investment Guides for Plan Sponsors Vol. 1: Enhanced Index Strategies for the Multi-Manager Portfolio. (Illus.). 128p. 1998. pap. 75.00 (*0-9619446-6-8*) Institutional Investor.

Bruce, Brian R. Corporate Earnings Estimates: Superior Investment Decisions Using Forecasts & Predictive Measures. 1997. 60.00 (*0-7863-1222-X*, Irwn Prfssnl) McGraw-Hill Prof.

— Quantitative International Investing: A Handbook of Analytical & Modeling Techniques &... (Guide to World Markets Ser.). 1990. 69.95 (*1-55738-121-6*, Irwn Prfssnl) McGraw-Hill Prof.

Bruce-Briggs, B., ed. The New Class? LC 78-62999. 225p. 1979. 39.95 (*0-87855-306-1*) Transaction Pubs.

Bruce, Britta, ed. see Bruce, Robert D.

Bruce, C., ed. Assessing Excellence: A Guide for Studying the Middle Level School. (Orig.). 1988. pap. 7.00 (*0-88210-218-4*) Natl Assn Principals.

Bruce, C., ed. see Reum, Earl.

Bruce, Calvin E. & Jones, William R., eds. Black Theology II: Essays on the Formation & Outreach of Contemporary Black Theology. LC 75-39113. 285p. 1978. 35.00 (*0-8387-1893-0*) Bucknell U Pr.

***Bruce, Cara, ed.** Viscera. 204p. 2000. pap. 12.95 (*0-9673638-0-2*, 2000) Venus Vixen.

Bruce, Carla, ed. see Mulvaney, Maureen G.

Bruce, Carol, ed. The Best of the NASSP Bulletin Vol. II: Leadership in the Small School. 272p. (Orig.). (C). 1987. pap. text 12.00 (*0-88210-284-2*) Natl Assn Principals.

Bruce, Catherine F., ed. see Isaac, Mia.

Bruce, Charles. The Broad Stone of Empire: Problems of Crown Colony Administration, 2 vols, Set. LC 70-179507. (Select Bibliographies Reprint Ser.). 1977. reprint ed. 75.95 (*0-8369-6636-8*) Ayer.

— The Channel Shore. 398p. (Orig.). 1954. pap. 12.95 (*0-88780-065-3*, Pub. by Formac Publ Co) Formac Dist Ltd.

***Bruce, Charles M.** United States Taxation of Foreign Trusts. LC 99-86143. 2000. write for info. (*90-411-9382-9*) Kluwer Law Intl.

Bruce, Chris & Andrews, Richard. James Turrell: Sensing Space. LC 92-21768. (Illus.). 64p. (Orig.). 1992. pap. 25.00 (*0-935558-31-4*) Henry Art.

Bruce, Chris & Sarkis, Robert. William Ivey: Three Decades of Painting. LC 89-15649. (Illus.). 60p. 1989. pap. 20.00 (*0-935558-26-8*) Henry Art.

Bruce, Chris & Shields, Kathleen. Withinsight: Visual Territories of Thirty Artists. Elrick, Krista, ed. & frwd. by. Neal, Barbara et al, frwds. LC 94-61356. (Illus.). 94p. (Orig.). 1995. pap. 18.00 (*0-9611710-0-6*) Western States.

Bruce, Chris, jt. auth. see Leavens, Ileana B.

Bruce, Chris, jt. auth. see West, Harvey.

Bruce, Chris, jt. auth. see Yau, John.

Bruce, Christopher & Kneebone, Ronald, eds. A Government Reinvented: A Study of Alberta's Deficit Elimination Program. LC 97-201823. (Illus.). 500p. (Orig.). 1997. pap. text 32.00 (*0-19-541269-9*) OUP.

***Bruce, Christopher W.** The Arthurian Name Dictionary. 542p. (YA). (gr. 9 up). 1999. 120.00 (*0-8153-2865-6*, H2063) Garland.

Bruce-Chwatt, Leonard J. Bruce-Chwatt's Essential Malariology. 3rd ed. Gilles, Herbert M. & Warrell, David A., eds. 360p. 1993. text 98.50 (*0-340-57190-X*, Pub. by E A) OUP.

Bruce, Claudia, ed. Profiles in Business & Management: An International Directory of Scholars & Their Research Version 2.0, 2 vols., Set. 2720p. 1996. 495.00 (*0-87584-517-7*) Harvard Busn.

Bruce, Colin. The Einstein Paradox: And Other Science Mysteries Solved by Sherlock Holmes. LC 98-87055. 272p. 1998. reprint ed. pap. text 12.00 (*0-7382-0023-9*, Helix Bks) Perseus Pubng.

***Bruce, Colin.** Invaders: British & American Experience of Seaborne Landings, 1939-1945. (Illus.). 288p. 1999. 34.95 (*1-55750-395-8*) Naval Inst Pr.

Bruce, Colin, 2nd, ed. see Krause, Chester L. & Mishler, Clifford.

Bruce, Colin J., jt. auth. see Smithies, Edward.

***Bruce, Colin R.** Standard Catalog of World Paper Money: Modern Issues, Vol. III. 6th ed. Shafer, Neil, ed. 864p. 2000. pap. 39.95 (*0-87341-879-4*) Krause Pubns.

— Standard Catalog of World Paper Money, General Issues, Vol. 2. 9th rev. ed. (Illus.). 1,144p. 2000. 65.00 (*0-87341-931-6*, PM09) Krause Pubns.

Bruce, Colin R., II, ed. Standard Catalog of World Crowns & Talers: From 1601 to 1992. LC 92-71448. (Illus.). 1360p. 1993. pap. 75.00 (*0-87341-211-7*, CW01) Krause Pubns.

Bruce, Colin R., II, ed. see Krause, Chester L. & Mishler, Clifford.

Bruce, Colin R., 2nd, ed. see Nicol, N. Douglas.

Bruce, Colin R., 2nd, ed. see Pick, Albert.

Bruce, D. W. & O'Hare, D. Inorganic Materials. 2nd ed. LC 97-138823. 610p. 1996. 210.00 (*0-471-96035-7*) Wiley.

Bruce, Dan W. The Thru-Hikers Handbook, 1998: No. 1 Guide for Long-Distance Hikes on the Appalachian Trail. (Illus.). 204p. 1997. pap. 10.95 (*0-9636342-7-5*) Ctr AT Studies.

— The Thru-Hiker's Planning Guide (Workbook Edition) A Detailed Manual for Planning End-to-End Appalachian Trail Hikes. LC 94-70565. (Illus.). 125p. (Orig.). 1994. pap. 11.95 (*0-9636342-3-2*) Ctr AT Studies.

Bruce, Daniel. Life & Times of Buck Hooey. 1999. pap. 12.50 (*0-88739-195-8*) Creat Arts Bk.

Bruce, David. Bird of Jove. LC 93-21439. (Louise Lindsey Merrick Natural Environment Ser.: No. 17). (Illus.). 288p. 1994. reprint ed. pap. 13.95 (*0-89096-604-4*) Tex A&M Univ Pr.

***Bruce, David.** Klaus & Max. LC 99-63264. 200p. 2000. pap. 13.95 (*0-88739-283-0*) Creat Arts Bk.

— Scotland: The Movie. 320p. 1996. pap. 19.95 (*0-7486-6209-X*, Pub. by Polygon) Subterranean Co.

Bruce, Debra. Dissolves: Poems. deluxe ed. (Burning Deck Poetry Ser.). 1977. pap. 15.00 (*0-930900-14-6*) Burning Deck.

— What Wind Will Do. LC 96-29068. (Poetry Ser.). 1997. 19.95 (*1-881163-18-0*); pap. 11.95 (*1-881163-19-9*) Miami Univ Pr.

Bruce, Debra, jt. auth. see Bruce, Robert.

Bruce, Debra, jt. auth. see Bruce, Robert G.

Bruce, Debra, jt. auth. see McIlwain, Harris.

Bruce, Debra F. Making Memories That Count: Nurturing Your Child in Christian Values. 176p. (Orig.). 1994. pap. 7.99 (*0-88243-345-8*, 02-0345) Gospel Pub.

B

Bruce, Debra F. & Bruce, Robert. The ABCs of Christian Marriage: Twenty-Six Ways to Love & Nurture Your Spouse Today & Every Day. LC 98-29173. (ABCs of Christian Life Ser.). 48p. 1999. 5.99 (*0-570-05351-X*, 12-3399GJ) Concordia.

Bruce, Debra F. & McIlwain, Harris H. The Unofficial Guide to Impotence. 400p. 1998. pap. 15.95 (*0-02-862870-5*, Pub. by Macmillan) S&S Trade.

***Bruce, Debra F. & Oldacre, Ellen.** Celebrate the Journey. LC 99-59018. 171p. 1999. 19.99 (*0-570-05244-0*) Concordia.

Bruce, Debra F., et al. Winning with Heart Attack: A Complete Program for Health & Well-Being. LC 94-25409. (Illus.). 189p. (C). 1994. 27.95 (*0-87975-914-3*); pap. 17.95 (*0-87975-915-1*) Prometheus Bks.

Bruce, Debra F., jt. auth. see McIlwain, Harris H.

***Bruce, Debra Fulghum & Thatcher, Samuel.** Making a Baby: Everything You Need to Know to Get Pregnant. 416p. (Orig.). 2000. pap. 14.00 (*0-345-43543-5*) Ballantine Pub Grp.

Bruce, Debra Fulghum, jt. auth. see McIlwain, Harris.

Bruce, Denice, et al. Staff Training & Recognition Program: Cross-Selling (S120) 3rd ed. LC 99-184067. vii, 120 p. 1995. write for info. (*0-7872-2107-4*) Kendall-Hunt.

Bruce, Dickson D., Jr. And They All Sang Hallelujah: Plain-Folk Camp-Meeting Religion, 1800-1845. LC 74-11344. (Illus.). 168p. 1974. pap. 15.00 (*0-87049-310-8*) U of Tenn Pr.

Bruce, Dickson D., Jr. Archibald Grimke: Portrait of a Black Independent. LC 92-42703. (Southern Biography Ser.). (Illus.). 312p. (C). 1993. text 42.50 (*0-8071-1796-X*) La State U Pr.

— Black American Writing from the Nadir: The Evolution of a Literary Tradition, 1877-1915. LC 88-22039. (Illus.). 272p. (C). 1989. pap. text 17.95 (*0-8071-1806-0*) La State U Pr.

Bruce, Dickson D. The Rhetoric of Conservatism: The Virginia Convention of 1829-30 & the Conservative Tradition in the South. LC 82-9224. (Illus.). 240p. reprint ed. pap. 74.40 (*0-7837-6681-5*, 204629700011) Bks Demand.

Bruce, Dix. Backup Trax: Swing & Jazz for Alto Sax Book-CD Set. 24p. 1992. 17.95 (*0-7866-2504-X*, 94342BCD) Mel Bay.

— Backup Trax/Old Time & Fiddle Tune for Guitar & Banjo: Beginning Level. 56p. 1996. pap. 17.95 incl. audio compact disk (*0-7866-2345-4*, 94338BCD) Mel Bay.

— Backup Trax/Old Time & Fiddle Tunes for Fiddle & Mandolin. 32p. 1995. pap. 17.95 incl. audio compact disk (*1-56222-394-1*, 94339BCD) Mel Bay.

— Backup Trax/Swing & Jazz for Guitar, Violin, Mandolin, Banjo, Flute & C Instruments: Beginning Level. 48p. 1996. pap. 17.95 incl. audio compact disk (*0-7866-2344-6*, 94344BCD) Mel Bay.

— Backup Trax/Swing & Jazz for Trombone & Other Bass Clef. 24p. 1992. pap. 17.95 incl. audio compact disk (*0-7866-2505-8*, 94343BCD) Mel Bay.

— Backup Trax/Swing & Jazz for Trumpet, TNR Sax, Clarinet. 24p. 1992. pap. 17.95 incl. audio compact disk (*0-7866-2507-4*, 94345BCD) Mel Bay.

— Backup Trax/Traditional Jazz & Dixieland for Alto Sax. 32p. 1996. pap. 17.95 incl. cd-rom (*0-7866-2510-4*, 94579BCD) Mel Bay.

— Backup Trax/Traditional Jazz & Dixieland for Trombone & Bass Clef. 32p. 1996. pap. 17.95 incl. cd-rom (*0-7866-2511-2*, 94580BCD) Mel Bay.

— Backup Trax/Traditional Jazz & Dixieland for Trumpet, Clarinet & TN. 32p. 1996. pap. 17.95 incl. cd-rom (*0-7866-2508-2*, 94577BCD) Mel Bay.

— Backup Trax/Traditional Jazz & Dixieland for Violin, Guitar & Banjo. 40p. 1996. pap. 17.95 incl. cd-rom (*0-7866-2509-0*, 94578BCD) Mel Bay.

— Beginning Country Guitar Handbook. 104p. 1998. pap. 19.95 (*0-7866-3396-4*, 94330BCD) Mel Bay.

— Doc Watson & Clarence Ashley - Org Flkwys Rec '60-62. 152p. 1999. pap. 19.95 (*0-7866-4498-2*, 97056) Mel Bay.

— Early JZ & HT Tunes Trombone, Bass, Tuba & Bass Instruments - Backup Trax. 40p. 1995. pap. 17.95 incl. audio compact disk (*0-7866-1428-5*, 95644BCD) Mel Bay.

— Early U&H Tunes for Clarinet, Tenor Sax & B Flat Instruments - Backup Trax. 40p. 1995. pap. 17.95 incl. audio compact disk (*0-7866-1427-7*, 95643BCD) Mel Bay.

— Great Mandolin Pickin Tunes. 32p. 2000. pap. 5.95 (*0-7866-4985-2*, 98420BCD) Mel Bay.

— Green Grass Grew All Around. 40p. 1998. pap. 22.95 incl. audio compact disk (*0-7866-4383-8*, 96706CDP) Mel Bay.

— String Band Classics for Guitar. 72p. 1998. pap. 19.95 (*0-7866-3545-2*, 96687BCD) Mel Bay.

— String Band Classics for Mandolin. 64p. 1999. pap. 19.95 (*0-7866-3544-4*, 96686BCD) Mel Bay.

Bruce, Dix. You Can Teach Yourself Country Guitar. 1993. 38.95 incl. VHS (*0-7866-0614-2*, 94818VPX); 24.95 incl. audio compact disk (*0-7866-1121-9*, 94818CDP); 18.95 incl. audio (*0-7866-1122-7*, 94818P); audio 9.98 (*1-56222-457-3*, 94818); audio compact disk 15.98 (*0-7866-0387-9*, 94818CD) Mel Bay.

— You Can Teach Yourself Country Guitar. 96p. 1993. pap. 9.95 (*1-56222-456-5*, 94818) Mel Bay.

— You Can Teach Yourself Country Guitar. 1995. VHS 29.95 (*0-7866-0613-4*, 94818VX) Mel Bay.

— You Can Teach Yourself Mandolin. LC 94-774000. 104p. 1993. pap. 9.95 (*1-56222-447-6*, 94331); pap. 18.95 incl. audio (*1-56222-524-3*, 94331P); audio 9.98 (*1-56222-171-X*, 94331C); audio compact disk 15.98 (*0-7866-0378-X*, 94331CD) Mel Bay.

— You Can Teach Yourself Mandolin. 1996. VHS 29.95 (*0-7866-0615-0*, 94331VX) Mel Bay.

***Bruce, Dix.** You Can Teach Yourself Mandolin. 104p. 1998. pap. 17.95 incl. audio compact disk (*0-7866-4710-8*, 94331BCD) Mel Bay.

Bruce, Dix, tr. see Rosenthal, Phil.

Bruce, Douglas & Kopel, Jerry. Amendment 12, Pro & Con: Douglas Bruce vs. Jerry Kopel. (Issue Paper #9-94 Ser.). 18p. 1994. pap. text 8.00 (*1-57655-137-7*); pap. text 8.00 (*1-57655-106-7*) Independ Inst.

Bruce, Duncan A. Mark of the Scots: Their Astonishing Contributions to History, Science, Democracy, Literature, LC 98-29039. (Illus.). 368p. 1998. pap. 18.95 (*0-8065-2060-4*, Citadel Pr) Carol Pub Group.

— The Mark of the Scots: Their Astonishing Contributions to History, Science, Democracy, Literature & the Arts. LC 95-50374. (Illus.). 320p. 1996. 21.95 (*1-55972-356-4*, Birch Ln Pr) Carol Pub Group.

— The Mark of the Scots: Their Astonishing Contributions to History, Science, Democracy, Literature & the Arts. 1998. pap. 24.95 (*0-8065-1754-9*, Citadel Pr) Carol Pub Group.

***Bruce, Duncan A.** The Scottish 100: Portraits of History's Most Influential Scot. (Illus.). 416p. 2000. 26.00 (*0-7867-0770-4*, Pub. by Carroll & Graf) Publishers Group.

Bruce, Dwight H. Memorial History of Syracuse, from Its Settlement to the Present Time. With Biographical Sketches. (Illus.). 849p. 1997. reprint ed. lib. bdg. 85.00 (*0-8328-6259-2*) Higginson Bk Co.

— Onondaga's Centennial: Gleanings of a Century. (Illus.). 1657p. 1997. reprint ed. lib. bdg. 164.00 (*0-8328-6191-X*) Higginson Bk Co.

***Bruce, Earl.** Buckeye Wisdom: Insight & Inspiration from Earle Bruce. 112p. 1999. pap. 14.95 (*1-57243-376-0*) Triumph Bks.

***Bruce, Earle, et al.** Earle: A Coach's Life. 184p. 2000. pap. 19.95 (*1-882203-62-3*, Pub. by Orange Frazer) Partners Pubs Grp.

Bruce, Edith. Keys to the Kingdom. 1996. pap. 14.95 (*0-929385-94-2*) Light Tech Pubng.

Bruce, Eileen D. Holmes. Our Holmes Ancestors (of New Jersey) (Illus.). 90p. 1997. reprint ed. pap. 17.50 (*0-8328-9194-0*); reprint ed. lib. bdg. 27.50 (*0-8328-9193-2*) Higginson Bk Co.

Bruce, Erroll. Deep Sea Sailing. (Illus.). 1978. pap. 5.95 (*0-679-50853-8*) McKay.

***Bruce, Eugene N.** Biomedical Signal Processing & Signal Modeling. 596p. (C). 2001. 125.00 (*0-471-34540-7*) Wiley.

Bruce, Evangeline. Napoleon & Josephine. 576p. 1996. pap. 16.00 (*1-57566-056-3*, Knsington) Kensgtn Pub Corp.

— Napoleon & Josephine: An Improbable Marriage. 1995. 32.00 (*0-02-517810-5*) S&S Trade.

Bruce, F. F. The Book of Acts. rev. ed. Fee, Gordon D., ed. (New International Commentary on the New Testament Ser.). 564p. 1988. 38.00 (*0-8028-2505-2*) Eerdmans.

— The Canon of Scripture. LC 88-29206. 349p. (C). 1988. reprint ed. 24.99 (*0-8308-1258-X*, 1258) InterVarsity.

— Colossians, Philemon & Ephesians. (New International Commentary on the Old Testament Ser.). 470p. 1984. 35.00 (*0-8028-2510-9*) Eerdmans.

— En Los Pasos de Nuestro Senor. 64p. 1997. 24.99 (*0-8254-1075-4*) Kregel.

— En los Pasos del Apostol Pablo (Full-Color Edition) (SPA., Illus.). 64p. 1995. 24.99 (*0-8254-1074-6*, Edit Portavoz) Kregel.

— The Epistle to the Hebrews. rev. ed. (New International Commentary on the New Testament Ser.). 448p. 1990. 32.00 (*0-8028-2514-1*) Eerdmans.

— I & II Thessalonians. (Biblical Commentary Ser.: Vol. 45). 29.99 (*0-8499-0244-4*) Word Pub.

— The Gospel of John. 440p. 1994. pap. 18.00 (*0-8028-0883-2*) Eerdmans.

— The Hard Sayings of Jesus. LC 83-10793. (Hard Sayings Ser.). 266p. (C). 1983. pap. 12.99 (*0-87784-927-7*, 927) InterVarsity.

— History of the Bible in English. 3rd ed. 288p. 1978. pap. 12.95 (*0-19-520088-8*) OUP.

— In the Steps of Our Lord. LC 97-7913. 64p. 1997. 29.99 (*0-8254-2335-X*) Kregel.

— In the Steps of the Apostle Paul. LC 95-9694. (Illus.). 64p. 1995. 29.99 (*0-8254-2254-X*) Kregel.

— Israel & the Nations. 258p. 1997. reprint ed. pap. 14.99 (*0-85364-762-3*, Pub. by Paternoster Pub) OM Literature.

— Israel y las Naciones. Orig. Title: Israel & the Nations. (SPA.). 320p. 1979. pap. 9.99 (*0-8254-1076-2*, Edit Portavoz) Kregel.

— Jesus: Lord & Savior. Green, Michael, ed. LC 86-7157. (Jesus Library). 228p. 1986. pap. 12.99 (*0-87784-932-3*, 932) InterVarsity.

— Jesus Past, Present & Future: The Work of Christ. LC 98-23785. 144p. 1998. reprint ed. pap. 11.99 (*0-8308-1928-2*, 1928) InterVarsity.

— Men & Movements in the Primitive Church: Studies in Early Non-Pauline Christianity. (Biblical Classics Library: Vol. 13). 159p. 1995. reprint ed. mass mkt. 5.99 (*0-85364-705-4*, Pub. by Paternoster Pub) OM Literature.

— The Message of the New Testament. 120p. 1973. pap. 8.00 (*0-8028-1525-1*) Eerdmans.

— New International Commentary on the New Testament, 16 vols. 1984. 617.00 (*0-8028-2445-5*) Eerdmans.

— New Testament Documents: Are They Reliable? 120p. (Orig.). 1967. pap. 5.99 (*0-87784-691-X*, 691) InterVarsity.

— New Testament History. LC 78-144253. 480p. 1983. pap. 16.95 (*0-385-02533-5*, Anchor NY) Doubleday.

— Orando los Unos por los Otros - Praying for One Another. (Serie Discipulado Ser.). (SPA.). 26p. 1996. write for info. (*0-614-24383-1*) Editorial Unilit.

— Orando por los Hijos de los Misioneros. (Serie Discipulado - Discipleship Ser.).Tr. of Praying for Missionary Kids. (SPA.). 20p. 1996. 1.99 (*1-56063-895-8*, 498249) Editorial Unilit.

— Paternoster Bible History Atlas. 96p. 1982. 19.50 (*0-85364-312-1*, Pub. by Paternoster Pub) McClelland & Stewart.

— Paul: Apostle of the Heart Set Free. LC 77-26127. 1978. 30.00 (*0-8028-3501-5*) Eerdmans.

— The Pauline Circle. (Biblical Classics Library: Vol. 14). 106p. (Orig.). 1995. reprint ed. mass mkt. 5.99 (*0-85364-706-2*, Pub. by Paternoster Pub) OM Literature.

— Philippians. (New International Biblical Commentary Ser.). 184p. 1989. pap. 11.95 (*0-943575-15-X*) Hendrickson MA.

— Por Que Orar por los Misioneros y Como Hacerlo. (Serie Discipulado Ser.).Tr. of Why & How to Pray for Missionaries. (SPA.). 24p. 1996. 1.99 (*1-56063-894-X*, 498248) Editorial Unilit.

— Romans. rev. ed. Morris, Leon, ed. (Tyndale New Testament Commentaries Ser.). 288p. 1985. pap. 13.00 (*0-8028-0062-9*) Eerdmans.

Bruce, F. F., ed. New Testament Documents: Are They Reliable? (Orig.). 1960. pap. 8.00 (*0-8028-1025-X*) Eerdmans.

Bruce, F. F. & Marshall, I. Howard. Galatians. Gasque, W. Ward, ed. (New International Greek Testament Commentary Ser.). 305p. 1982. 33.00 (*0-8028-2387-4*) Eerdmans.

Bruce, F. F. & Payne, David F. Israel & the Nations: The History of Israel from the Exodus to the Fall of the Second Temple. rev. ed. LC 98-22122. 270p. 1998. reprint ed. pap. 19.99 (*0-8308-1510-4*, 1510) InterVarsity.

Bruce, F. F., et al. History, Criticism & Faith. 234p. 1995. reprint ed. ring bd. 19.95 (*1-57383-037-2*) Regent College.

Bruce, F. F., jt. auth. see CARTA Staff.

Bruce, F. F., jt. ed. see Boadt, Lawrence.

Bruce, F. F., jt. ed. see Youngblood, Ronald F.

Bruce, Gail C., jt. auth. see Harper, Frederick D.

Bruce, Geoff. The Colorado Brew Guide. 1996. write for info. (*0-9647569-0-0*) Simm-Bennett.

Bruce, George. Perspectives: Collected Poems, 1970-1986. 90p. 1987. pap. text 13.90 (*0-08-035062-3*, Pub. by Aberdeen U Pr) Macmillan.

— To Foster & Enrich: The First Fifty Years of the Saltire Society. 84p. 1986. 30.00 (*0-85411-006-2*, Pub. by Saltire Soc) St Mut.

Bruce, George & Rennie, Frank, eds. The Land Out There: A Scottish Land Anthology. (Illus.). 248p. 1991. pap. 25.90 (*0-08-040907-5*, Pub. by Aberdeen U Pr) Macmillan.

Bruce, George A. Civil War Infantry, the 20th Regiment of Massachusetts Volunteer Infantry, 1861-1865. (Illus.). 519p. 1995. reprint ed. lib. bdg. 57.00 (*0-8328-4629-5*) Higginson Bk Co.

Bruce, Glen, jt. auth. see Dempsey, Rob.

Bruce, Graham D. Bernard Herrmann: Film Music & Narrative. Kirkpatrick, Diane, ed. LC 85-16336. (Studies in Cinema: No. 38). 256p. 1985. reprint ed. pap. 79.40 (*0-8357-1966-9*, 207066600016) Bks Demand.

Bruce, Gregg, ed. see Tomovic, Mileta.

Bruce, Gustav M. Luther As an Educator. LC 77-114482. (Illus.). 318p. 1979. reprint ed. lib. bdg. 65.00 (*0-8371-4771-9*, BRLD, Greenwood Pr) Greenwood.

***Bruce, Guy S.** Instructional Design Made Easy: A Workbook for Designing Accelerated Learning Programs. 2nd ed. 737p. 1999. pap. 135.00 (*0-937100-05-6*) Perf Manage.

Bruce, H. Addington. Sleep & Sleeplessness (1915) 232p. 1998. reprint ed. pap. 17.95 (*0-7661-0584-9*) Kessinger Pub.

Bruce, H. C. The New Man: Twenty-Nine Years a Slave, Twenty-Nine Years a Free Man, Recollections of H. C. Bruce. LC 96-9626. (Blacks in the American West Ser.). (Illus.). xxvii, 165p. 1996. pap. 10.00 (*0-8032-6132-2*, Bison Books) U of Nebr Pr.

Bruce, Hal. How to Grow Wildflowers & Wild Shrubs & Trees in Your Own Garden. LC 97-41010. (Horticulture Garden Classics Ser.). 336p. 1998. reprint ed. pap. 16.95 (*1-55821-656-1*) Lyons Pr.

Bruce, Hank. Dangerous Plants in Florida Vol. 2: Pocket Library of Florida Gardening. Lampert, Erv, ed. (Illus.). 48p. 1998. pap. 4.95 (*0-932855-52-0*) Winner Enter.

— Easy Plants for Your Florida Landscape. Lampert, Erv, ed. (Pocket Library of Florida Gardening: No. 1). (Illus.). 48p. 1997. pap. 4.95 (*0-932855-51-2*) Winner Enter.

— Florida Gardening for Seniors. Lampert, Erv, ed. (Pocket Library of Florida Gardening: Vol. 3). (Illus.). 48p. 1998. pap. 4.95 (*0-932855-53-9*) Winner Enter.

— Uncommon Scents: Growing Herbs & Spices in Florida. Lampert, Erv, ed. (Illus.). 224p. (Orig.). 1996. pap. 13.95 (*0-932855-50-4*) Winner Enter.

***Bruce, Hank.** Where do Snowmen Go When They Melt? Lampert, Erv, ed. (Winner Coloring Bks.). (J). (gr. k-3). 1999. pap. text 4.95 (*0-932855-58-X*) Winner Enter.

Bruce, Hank & Bruce, Marlene. Yankee's Guide to Florida Gardening. Lampert, Erv, ed. (Illus.). 168p. 1995. pap. 12.95 (*0-932855-45-8*) Winner Enter.

***Bruce, Hank, et al.** Gardens for the Senses: Gardening As Therapy. Lampert, Erv, ed. (Illus.). 120p. 1999. pap. 14.95 (*0-932855-57-1*) Winner Enter.

Bruce, Harold. Winterthur in Bloom: Winter, Spring, Summer, Autumn. LC 68-15483. (Illus.). 196p. 1967. reprint ed. pap. 15.00 (*0-912724-01-3*) Winterthur.

Bruce, Harold L. William Blake in This World. 1977. 18.95 (*0-8369-6924-3*, 7805) Ayer.

— William Blake in This World. LC 73-18085. (Studies in Blake: No. 3). 1974. reprint ed. lib. bdg. 75.00 (*0-8383-1732-4*) M S G Haskell Hse.

Bruce, Harry. Corporate Navigator: The Life of Frank Manning Covert. (Illus.). ix, 294p. 1995. 32.99 (*0-7710-1709-X*) McCland & Stewart.

— The Short, Happy Walks of Max MacPherson LC 78-303445. 167p. 1976. write for info. (*0-00-211621-9*) Collins SF.

Bruce, Harry, et al. A Short Guide to Business Writing. LC 94-11834. 208p. 1994. pap. text 32.20 (*0-13-124728-X*) P-H.

Bruce, Harry J., jt. auth. see Cadotte, Ernest R.

Bruce, Henry C. The New Man: 29 Years a Slave, 29 Years a Free Man. LC 72-89421. (Black Heritage Library Collection). 1977. 18.95 (*0-8369-8526-5*) Ayer.

Bruce, Herbert A. Our Heritage, & Other Addresses. LC 68-54334. (Essay Index Reprint Ser.). 1977. reprint ed. 23.95 (*0-8369-0259-9*) Ayer.

Bruce, Howard C., jt. auth. see Denny, Bill.

***Bruce, Ian.** Eclipse: An Introduction to Total & Partial Eclipses of the Sun & Moon. 144p. 1999. pap. 17.95 (*1-873668-63-5*, Pub. by Take That Bks) Trafalgar.

Bruce, Ian. Plan Your Home with Feng Shui. 1998. pap. 14.95 (*0-572-02395-2*, Pub. by W Foulsham) Trans-Atl Phila.

— Successful Mail Order Marketing: How to Build a Really Cost Effective Operation from Scratch. (Business Basics Ser.). 110p. 1996. pap. 19.95 (*1-85703-334-5*, Pub. by How To Bks) Trans-Atl Phila.

***Bruce, Ian.** Understand Shares in a Day. 128p. 1999. pap. 11.95 (*1-873668-73-2*, Pub. by Take That Bks) Trafalgar.

— Understanding Bonds & Gilts in a Day. 1999. pap. 11.95 (*1-873668-72-4*, Pub. by Take That Bks) Trafalgar.

Bruce, Isabel & Eickhoff, Edith. The Michigan Poor Law: Its Development & Administration with Special Reference to State Provision for Medical Care of the Indigent. LC 75-17210. (Social Problems & Social Policy Ser.). 1976. reprint ed. 25.95 (*0-405-07482-4*) Ayer.

Bruce, J. Campbell. Escape from Alcatraz. rev. ed. 218p. 1976. reprint ed. pap. 6.95 (*0-89174-003-1*) Comstock Edns.

Bruce, J. Douglas, ed. Mort Artu: An Old French Prose Romance of the Thirteenth Century. LC 75-178546. reprint ed. 54.50 (*0-404-56649-9*) AMS Pr.

— Le Morte Arthur, a Romance in Stanzas of Eight Lines. LC 75-41201. reprint ed. 21.50 (*0-404-14793-3*) AMS Pr.

— Le Morte D'Arthur. (EETS, ES Ser.: No. 88). 1974. reprint ed. 40.00 (*0-527-00293-3*) Periodicals Srv.

Bruce, J. Percy, tr. see Chu Hsi.

Bruce, J. W. & Giblin, P. J. Curves & Singularities. 2nd ed. (Illus.). 339p. (C). 1993. text 80.00 (*0-521-41985-9*) Cambridge U Pr.

***Bruce, J. W. & Tari, F.** Real & Complex Singularities LC 99-37308. (Research Notes in Mathematics Ser.). 288p. 1999. per. 59.95 (*1-58488-142-9*, Chap & Hall CRC) CRC Pr.

Bruce, J. W., et al. Microcomputers & Mathematics. (Illus.). 441p. (C). 1990. pap. text 44.95 (*0-521-31238-8*) Cambridge U Pr.

Bruce, James, tr. see Bloch, Iwan.

Bruce, James G., jt. auth. see Snyder, Lloyd H., Jr.

Bruce, James G., jt. auth. see Weatherbee, Ellen E.

Bruce, James P., et al, eds. Climate Change 1995 - Economic & Social Dimensions of Climate Change: Contribution of Working Group III to the Second Assessment Report of the Intergovernmental Panel on Climate Change. (Illus.). 458p. (C). 1996. pap. text 35.95 (*0-521-56854-4*) Cambridge U Pr.

— Climate Change 1995 - Economic & Social Dimensions of Climate Change: Contribution of Working Group III to the Second Assessment Report of the Intergovernmental Panel on Climate Change. LC 96-34912. (Illus.). 458p. (C). 1996. text 85.00 (*0-521-56051-9*) Cambridge U Pr.

Bruce, James S. The Intuitive Pragmatists: Conversations with Chief Executive Officers. (Special Reports: No. 310G). 42p. pap. 12.00 (*0-912879-59-9*) Ctr Creat Leader.

Bruce, James T., III, jt. auth. see Waller, Douglas C.

Bruce, Janet. The Kansas City Monarchs: Champions of Black Baseball. LC 85-8535. (Illus.). x, 182p. 1985. pap. 12.95 (*0-7006-0343-3*) U Pr of KS.

Bruce, Jean, ed. Arizona Revised Statutes, 1998 Edition, Vol. 1. rev. ed. 1345p. 1998. pap. write for info. (*0-327-06061-1*, 40522-16) LEXIS Pub.

— Arizona Revised Statutes, 1998 Edition, Vol. 2. rev. ed. 1158p. 1998. pap. write for info. (*0-327-06062-X*, 40523-16) LEXIS Pub.

— Arizona Revised Statutes, 1998 Edition, Vol. 3. rev. ed. 1574p. 1998. pap. write for info. (*0-327-06063-8*, 40524-16) LEXIS Pub.

— Arizona Revised Statutes, 1998 Edition, Vol. 4. rev. ed. 1485p. 1998. pap. write for info. (*0-327-06064-6*, 40525-16) LEXIS Pub.

Bruce, Jerome. Studies in Black & White. 1977. 21.95 (*0-8369-9160-5*, 9035) Ayer.

***Bruce, Jerome E.** Proclaiming the Scandal: Reflections on Post-Modern Ministry. 96p. 2000. pap. 12.00 (*1-56338-332-2*) TPI PA.

Bruce, Jill B. Anzac Day: Australia's Forces in War & Peace. (Illus.). 32p. (J). 1998. pap. 10.95 (*0-86417-838-7*, Pub. by Kangaroo Pr) Seven Hills Bk.

— Aussie Jokes & Riddles. (Illus.). 48p. (J). (ps-5). 1997. pap. 5.95 (*0-86417-770-4*, Pub. by Kangaroo Pr) Seven Hills Bk.

An Asterisk (*) at the beginning of an entry indicates that the title is appearing for the first time.

— The Australian Seashore. (Illus.). 40p. (Orig.). (J). (gr. 5-8). 1995. pap. 7.95 (*0-86417-663-5*, Pub. by Kangaroo Pr) Seven Hills Bk.
— Austranimals. (Illus.). 32p. (J). (gr. k-4). 1994. 12.95 (*0-86417-569-8*, Pub. by Kangaroo Pr) Seven Hills Bk.
— Mixed up Monsters. (Illus.). 32p. (J). 1997. 14.95 (*0-86417-834-4*, Pub. by Kangaroo Pr) Seven Hills Bk.
— Surf Lifesavers of Australia. (Illus.). 64p. 1993. 12.95 (*0-86417-480-2*, Pub. by Kangaroo Pr) Seven Hills Bk.
— Who Did That? (Illus.). 48p. (J). (gr. 2-6). 1994. pap. text 7.95 (*0-86417-575-2*, Pub. by Kangaroo Pr) Seven Hills Bk.
— Whose Chick Is That? (Illus.). 48p. (Orig.). (J). (gr. 3-7). 1995. pap. 7.95 (*0-86417-576-0*, Pub. by Kangaroo Pr) Seven Hills Bk.
Bruce, Jill B. & Wade, Jan. Flags & Emblems of Australia. (Illus.). 32p. reprint ed. 6.95 (*0-86417-396-2*, Pub. by Kangaroo Pr) Seven Hills Bk.
— Money of Australia. (Illus.). 40p. (Orig.). 1993. pap. 7.95 (*0-86417-464-0*, Pub. by Kangaroo Pr) Seven Hills Bk.
Bruce, Joe. Fly Fishing for Panfish. LC 97-13391. 96p. 1997. pap. text 11.95 (*0-9637161-3-1*) K&D Ltd.
— Fly Fishing for Small Mouth Bass. LC 97-41329. 96p. 1997. pap. text 11.95 (*0-9637161-4-X*) K&D Ltd.
— Fly Fishing for Striped Bass. LC 97-11155. (Illus.). 96p. (Orig.). 1997. pap. 11.95 (*0-9637161-2-3*) K&D Ltd.
Bruce, John. Synthetic Functional Fluids & Lubricants, No. YC-179. (Illus.). 152p. 1994. 2650.00 (*1-56965-006-3*) BCC.
Bruce, John, ed. Historie of the Arrivall of Edward Fourth in England & the Finall Recoverye of His Kingdomes from Henry Sixth, A. D. 1471. LC 77-164757. (Camden Society, London. Publications, First Ser.: No. 1). reprint ed. 19.50 (*0-404-50101-X*) AMS Pr.
Bruce, John, ed. see Borough, John.
Bruce, John, jt. ed. see Crosby, Allan J.
Bruce, John, ed. see H. R. M. Charles I.
Bruce, John, ed. see H. R. M. Queen Elizabeth I & H. R. M. King James VI.
Bruce, John, ed. see Hayward, John.
Bruce, John, ed. see James First King of England.
Bruce, John, ed. see Leicester, Robert D.
Bruce, John, ed. see Manningham, John.
Bruce, John, jt. ed. see Nichols, John G.
Bruce, John, ed. see Verney Family Staff.
Bruce, John, ed. see Verney, Ralph.
Bruce, John, ed. see Whitelocke, James.
Bruce, John, jt. ed. see Wilcox, Clyde.
Bruce, John E. The Awakening of Hezekiah Jones. LC 73-18567. reprint ed. 37.50 (*0-404-11381-8*) AMS Pr.
— The Select Writings of John Edward Bruce: Militant Black Journalist. 182p. 1971. 11.95 (*0-405-01982-3*) Arno Press.
Bruce, John W., ed. Country Profiles of Land Tenure: Africa, 1996. (Research Paper Ser.: Vol. 130). vi, 282p. (C). 1998. pap. 15.00 (*0-934519-79-X*, RP130) U of Wis Land.
Bruce, John W. & Ely, James W., Jr. Law of Easements & Licences in Land. 600p. 1994. suppl. ed. 145.00 (*0-88712-905-6*); suppl. ed. 72.00 (*0-7913-1186-4*) Warren Gorham & Lamont.
Bruce, John W. & Fortmann, Louise. Agroforestry: Tenure & Incentives. (LTC Paper Ser.: Vol. 135). v, 46p. (C). 1989. pap. 4.00 (*0-934519-51-X*, LTC135) U of Wis Land.
Bruce, John W. & Harrell, Paula. Land Tenure Reform in the People's Republic of China, 1978-1988. (Research Papers: No. 100). 70p. (Orig.). 1989. pap. 7.00 (*0-934519-10-2*, RP 100) U of Wis Land.
Bruce, John W., et al. Land Tenure Issues in Project Design & Strategies for Agricultural Development in Sub-Saharan Africa. (LTC Paper Ser.: Vol. 128). xxvii, 190p. (C). 1986. pap. 12.00 (*0-934519-43-9*, LTC128) U of Wis Land.
Bruce, John W., jt. auth. see Roth, Michael R.
***Bruce, Jon W.** Cases & Materials on Modern Property Law. 4th ed. LC 99-219149. (C). 1999. 45.00 (*0-314-22760-1*) West Pubns Serv.
Bruce, Jon W. Real Estate Finance in a Nutshell. 3rd ed. (Nutshell Ser.). 287p. 1991. reprint ed. pap. text 15.50 (*0-314-87477-1*) West Pub.
— REAL ESTATE FINANCE IN A NUTSHELL 4E. 4th ed. LC 97-9347. (Paralegal). 264p. (C). 1997. pap. text 15.00 (*0-314-21161-6*) West Pub.
Bruce, Jon W., ed. Land Use Anthology. LC 98-142800. 368p. 1997. pap. 29.95 (*0-87084-023-1*) Anderson Pub Co.
Bruce, Jon W. & Ely, James W., Jr. Cases & Materials on Modern Property Law. 3rd ed. (American Casebook Ser.). 945p. (C). 1994. text. write for info. (*0-314-03493-5*) West Pub.
— Modern Property Law, Teacher's Manual to Accompany Cases & Materials on Modern Property Law. 3rd ed. (American Casebook Ser.). 179p. pap. text. write for info. (*0-314-04144-3*) West Pub.
Bruce, Joseph P. Chu Hsi & His Masters: An Introduction to Chu Hsi & the Sung School of Chinese Philosophy. 1973. lib. bdg. 250.00 (*0-87968-078-4*) Krishna Pr.
— Chu Hsi & His Masters, An Introduction to Chu Hsi & the Sung School of Chinese Philosophy. LC 78-38050. (China Classic & Contemporary Works in Reprint Ser.). reprint ed. 42.50 (*0-404-56904-8*) AMS Pr.
Bruce, Joseph T., Jr., ed. Sandlapper Cookbook. LC 73-88594. (Illus.). 241p. 1982. pap. 12.95 (*0-87844-020-8*) Sandlapper Pub Co.
Bruce, Judith, et al. Families in Focus: New Perspectives on Mothers, Fathers, & Children. LC 95-3862. 115p. 1995. pap. 12.50 (*0-87834-084-X*) Population Coun.
Bruce, Judith, jt. ed. see Dwyer, Daisy H.
Bruce, Judith O. Colored Pencil Craze. (Art Start Kits Ser.). 24p. (J). (ps up). 1997. pap. 9.95 (*1-56010-350-7*, AS02) W Foster Pub.
Bruce, Julia. The New Planning System in Victoria. xxxii, 390p. 1988. pap. 74.50 (*0-455-20792-5*, Pub. by LawBk Co) Gaunt.
Bruce, J.W. & Mond, D., eds. Singularity Theory. LC 99-19678. (London Mathematical Society Lecture Note Ser.: No. 263). 350p. (C). 1999. pap. text 49.95 (*0-521-65888-8*) Cambridge U Pr.
Bruce, Kathy & Robbins, Mari L. The Golden Goblet: Literature Unit. (Literature Units Ser.). 48p. 1995. pap. text, wbk. ed. 7.95 (*1-55734-442-6*) Tchr Create Mat.
Bruce, Kirk W. Into Your Hands: A Maundy Thursday Service. LC 98-170012. 16p. 1997. pap. 3.95 (*0-7880-1129-4*) CSS OH.
Bruce, Lennart. The Broker. 80p. 1984. pap. 5.00 (*0-915572-75-3*) Panjandrum.
— Subpoemas. 68p. 1974. pap. 6.00 (*0-915572-06-0*) Panjandrum.
Bruce, Lennart & Bruce, Sonja, eds. Speak to Me: Swedish-language Women Poets. LC 88-15874. (Contemporary Anthology Ser.: No. 7). (ENG & SWE., Illus.). 224p. 1989. pap. 8.75 (*0-930370-36-8*) Spirit That Moves.
— Speak to Me: Swedish-language Women Poets. LC 88-15874. (Contemporary Anthology & Ethnic Diversity Ser.: No. 7, Vol. 4). (ENG & SWE., Illus.). 224p. 1989. 14.75 (*0-930370-35-X*) Spirit That Moves.
— Speak to Me: Swedish-language Women Poets, Signed A-Z. limited ed. LC 88-15874. (Contemporary Anthology Ser.: No. 7). (ENG & SWE., Illus.). 224p. 1989. 30.00 (*0-930370-37-6*) Spirit That Moves.
Bruce, Lennart, tr. see Andersson, Claes.
Bruce, Lenny. How to Talk Dirty & Influence People. 22.95 (*0-8488-0924-6*) Amereon Ltd.
— How to Talk Dirty & Influence People: An Autobiography. (Illus.). 208p. 1992. per. 11.00 (*0-671-75108-5*) S&S Trade.
Bruce, Leo. Case for Sergeant Beef. large type ed. 320p. 1982. 27.99 (*0-7089-0842-X*) Ulverscroft.
— Case for Three Detectives. 240p. 1985. pap. 10.95 (*0-89733-033-1*) Academy Chi Pubs.
— Case for Three Detectives. 248p. 1995. 19.50 (*0-7451-8661-0*, Black Dagger) Chivers N Amer.
— Cold Blood. large type ed. 320p. 1983. 11.50 (*0-7089-0968-X*) Ulverscroft.
— Dead Man's Shoes. (Carolus Deene Mystery Ser.). 216p. 1987. pap. 5.95 (*0-89733-271-7*) Academy Chi Pubs.
— Death at St Asprey's School. (Carolus Deene Mystery Ser.). 221p. 1984. pap. 5.95 (*0-89733-094-3*) Academy Chi Pubs.
— Death in Albert Park. (Carolus Deene Mystery Ser.). 239p. 1983. reprint ed. pap. 5.95 (*0-89733-073-0*) Academy Chi Pubs.
— Death of a Commuter. (Carolus Deene Mystery Ser.). 192p. 1988. pap. 5.95 (*0-89733-326-8*) Academy Chi Pubs.
— Death on Allhallowe'en. (Carolus Deene Mystery Ser.). 176p. 1988. pap. 5.95 (*0-89733-292-X*) Academy Chi Pubs.
— Death with Blue Ribbon. 176p. 1994. pap. 5.95 (*0-89733-345-4*) Academy Chi Pubs.
— Die All, Die Merrily. (Carolus Deene Mystery Ser.). 192p. 1987. pap. 5.95 (*0-89733-253-9*) Academy Chi Pubs.
— Furious Old Women. (Carolus Deene Mystery Ser.). 191p. 1983. reprint ed. pap. 5.95 (*0-89733-084-6*) Academy Chi Pubs.
— Jack on the Gallows Tree. (Carolus Deene Mystery Ser.). 189p. 1983. 15.00 (*0-89733-071-4*); pap. 5.95 (*0-89733-072-2*) Academy Chi Pubs.
— Murder in Miniature: The Uncollected Stories of Leo Bruce. 208p. 1993. 20.00 (*0-89733-367-5*) Academy Chi Pubs.
— Neck & Neck. large type ed. 368p. 1983. 11.50 (*0-7089-0898-5*) Ulverscroft.
— Nothing Like Blood. (Carolus Deene Mystery Ser.). 192p. 1985. 15.00 (*0-89733-128-1*) Academy Chi Pubs.
— Our Jubilee Is Death. (Carolus Deene Mystery Ser.). 189p. 1986. pap. 5.95 (*0-89733-229-6*) Academy Chi Pubs.
— Such Is Death. (Carolus Deene Mystery Ser.). 192p. 1985. pap. 5.95 (*0-89733-160-5*) Academy Chi Pubs.
— Such Is Death. (Carolus Deene Mystery Ser.). 192p. 1986. 15.00 (*0-89733-159-1*) Academy Chi Pubs.
Bruce, Linda. Al Phillip Bettle. (Illus.). (J). (gr. k-3). 1965. 8.95 (*0-8392-3050-8*) Astor-Honor.
Bruce, Lindell. Paragraphs. 80p. (C). 1994. pap. text 13.95 (*0-8403-9700-3*, 40970001) Kendall-Hunt.
— Punctuation. 60p. (C). 1994. pap. text 13.95 (*0-8403-9697-X*, 40969701) Kendall-Hunt.
— Sentence Structure. 80p. (C). 1994. 10.95 (*0-8403-9699-6*) Kendall-Hunt.
— Sentence Style. 84p. (C). 1994. 10.95 (*0-8403-9698-8*) Kendall-Hunt.
Bruce, Lisa. Oliver's Alphabets. LC 92-39471. (Illus.). 24p. (J). (ps-1). 1993. text 13.95 (*0-02-735996-4*, Bradbury S&S) S&S Childrens.
***Bruce, M. C.** Ungiven Eulogies Vol. 1: A Poem Cycle. 16p. 1999. pap. 4.00 (*1-893297-02-0*) Swan Duck Pr.
Bruce, M., Corporation Staff. Zzaap! Taming ESD, RFI, & EMI. 236p. 1990. text 54.00 (*0-12-189930-6*) Acad Pr.
Bruce, M. E. Bruce: Family Record of the Bruces & the Cumyns, with an History Introduction & Appendix. (Illus.). 692p. 1991. reprint ed. pap. 99.00 (*0-8328-1761-9*); reprint ed. lib. bdg. 109.00 (*0-8328-1760-0*) Higginson Bk Co.
Bruce, Marcy, ed. see Hall, Marilyn.
***Bruce, Margaret.** Getting the Most Out of Design. 225p. 2000. 65.00 (*0-471-97475-7*) Wiley.
Bruce, Margaret & Biemans, Wim G., eds. Product Development: Meeting the Challenge of the Design-Marketing Interface. LC 94-41380. 362p. 1995. 115.00 (*0-471-95353-9*) Wiley.
Bruce, Margaret & Cooper, Rachel. Marketing & Design Management. 256p. 1996. pap. 59.00 (*0-415-12008-X*) Thomson Learn.
— Marketing & Design Management. 256p. 1997. pap. 19.99 (*1-86152-173-1*) Thomson Learn.
Bruce, Margaret & Jevnaker, Birgit. Management of Design Alliances. LC 97-12957. 310p. 1998. 82.95 (*0-471-97476-5*) Wiley.
Bruce, Marie L. Anne Boleyn. LC 72-146093. 380p. 1972. write for info. (*0-698-10480-3*, Coward) Putnam Pub Group.
Bruce, Mark C. Clients & Other Poems. 54p. 1998. pap. 5.00 (*1-893297-00-4*) Swan Duck Pr.
Bruce, Marlene, jt. auth. see Bruce, Hank.
Bruce, Martha. South Texas Wildflowers. 71p. 1984. pap. 5.95 (*0-916983-00-5*) Tex A&I Conner Mus.
***Bruce, Martha I.** How Do You Eat Your Foo-Foo? (J). 2000. pap. 5.95 (*0-533-13376-9*) Vantage.
Bruce, Martin M. A Guide to Human Relations in Business & Industry. LC 73-6907. 1969. pap. 20.35 (*0-935198-00-8*) M M Bruce.
Bruce, Mary A. & Borg, Barbara. Psychosocial Occupational Therapy: Frames of Reference for Intervention. 2nd ed. LC 91-52849. (Illus.). 450p. (C). 1993. pap. 37.00 (*1-55642-203-2*) SLACK Inc.
Bruce, Mary A., jt. auth. see Borg, Barbara.
***Bruce, Mary Ann & Borg, Barbara.** Psychosocial Occupational Therapy: Frames of Reference Intervention. (C). 2001. pap. text 37.00 (*1-55642-494-9*) SLACK Inc.
Bruce, Maureen L., jt. auth. see Arneson, D. J.
***Bruce, Maxwell.** Ending War: The Force of Reason. LC 99-26118. 179p. 1999. text 59.95 (*0-312-22570-9*) St Martin.
***Bruce, Michael & James, Billy.** No More Mr. Nice Guy: The Inside Story of the Original Alice Cooper Group. (Illus.). 2000. pap. 17.95 (*0-946719-17-9*, Pub. by SAF Pub) Interlink Pub.
Bruce-Mitford, Miranda. The Illustrated Book of Signs & Symbols. 1996. 24.95 (*0-614-20407-0*) DK Pub Inc.
— The Illustrated Book of Signs & Symbols: Thousands of Signs & Symbols from Around the World. LC 96-14202. (Illus.). 128p. (J). 1996. 24.95 (*0-7894-1000-1*) DK Pub Inc.
Bruce-Mitford, R. The Sutton Hoo Viking Ship Burial. 1999. pap. 21.00 (*0-900657-46-4*, Pub. by W Sessions) St Mut.
Bruce, Muriel. Mukara. Reginald, R. & Melville, Douglas, eds. LC 77-84204. (Lost Race & Adult Fantasy Ser.). 1978. reprint ed. lib. bdg. 26.95 (*0-405-10960-1*) Ayer.
***Bruce, Neil.** Public Finance. (C). 1998. text. write for info. (*0-321-01771-4*) Addison-Wesley.
— Public Finance & the American Economy. LC 97-30044. 691p. (C). 1997. 98.00 (*0-321-01167-8*) Addison-Wesley Educ.
Bruce, Neil. Public Finance & the American Economy. 160p. (C). 1997. text 24.00 (*0-321-01770-6*) Addison-Wesley Educ.
Bruce, Nigel. Teamwork for Preventive Care. LC 80-41095. (Social Policy Research Monographs: No. 1). 261p. reprint ed. pap. 81.00 (*0-8357-7047-8*, 203333000085) Bks Demand.
Bruce-Novoa, Juan. Chicano Authors: Inquiry by Interview. LC 79-28327. 304p. reprint ed. pap. 94.30 (*0-608-17842-X*, 203260400080) Bks Demand.
— Only the Good Times. LC 95-9770. 286p. 1995. pap. 9.95 (*1-55885-078-3*) Arte Publico.
— RetroSpace: Collected Essays on Chicano Literature. LC 89-18371. 190p. (Orig.). 1990. pap. 11.00 (*1-55885-013-9*) Arte Publico.
Bruce-Novoa, Juan, tr. see Garcia Ponce, Juan.
Bruce, Paul. Nemesis File: The True Story of an SAS Execution Squad. 300p. 1996. 22.95 (*1-85782-135-1*, Pub. by Blake Publng) Seven Hills Bk.
***Bruce, Peter.** Adlard Coles' Heavy Weather Sailing. LC 99-461844. 288p. 1999. 39.95 (*0-07-135325-2*) McGraw.
Bruce, Peter G., ed. Solid State Electrochemistry. (Chemistry of Solid State Materials Ser.: No. 5). (Illus.). 360p. 1997. pap. text 39.95 (*0-521-59949-0*) Cambridge U Pr.
Bruce, Philip A. Institutional History of Virginia in the Seventeenth Century, Vols. 1 & 2. 1964. 35.00 (*0-8446-1090-9*) Peter Smith.
Bruce-Phipps, Terrisa, ed. Little Book of Love Tips, Vol. II. 40p. 1997. pap. 5.95 (*1-889237-10-8*) Options Now.
Bruce-Phipps, Terrisa, ed. see Beveridge, Martha B.
Bruce, R. Teach Yourself Cantonese. (Teach Yourself Ser.). 1992. 15.95 (*0-8288-8306-8*) Fr & Eur.
— Teach Yourself Cantonese: A Complete Course for Beginners. 240p. 1994. pap. 12.95 (*0-8442-3756-6*, Teach Yrslf) NTC Contemp Pub Co.
Bruce, R., jt. ed. see Hopkins, J. D.
Bruce, Randall R., jt. auth. see Pyrczak, Fred.
***Bruce, Ransom G.** Stop Sexual Harassment: The Clean & Simple Guide to Reasonable Behavior in Today's Workplace. 40p. 1998. 2.49 (*0-9645093-7-7*) Ransom & Benjamin.
— Taking Family & Medical Leave: Your Rights & Responsibilities under the FMLA. 60p. 1999. 2.49 (*0-9645093-9-3*) Ransom & Benjamin.
Bruce, Ray, jt. auth. see Chisholm, Margo.
Bruce, Raymon R. & Wyman, Sherman M. Changing Organizations: Using Action Training & Research. LC 97-33907. 1998. write for info. (*0-7619-1005-0*); pap. write for info. (*0-7619-1006-9*) Sage.
Bruce, Richard. Farm Safety: Specialty Safety Training. (ENG & SPA.). 1996. 29.95 (*0-913702-59-5*) Thomson Pubns.
— Orchard Safety: Specialty Safety Training. (ENG & SPA.). 1996. 29.95 (*0-913702-60-9*) Thomson Pubns.
Bruce, Rita. Vision of Sai, Bk. 1. LC 95-1937. Vol. 1. (Illus.). 320p. (Orig.). 1995. pap. 12.95 (*0-87728-833-X*) Weiser.
***Bruce, Robert.** Astral Dynamics: A New Approach to Out-of-Body Experiences. LC 99-71614. (Illus.). 560p. 1999. pap. 16.95 (*1-57174-143-7*) Hampton Roads Pub Co.
Bruce, Robert. German Automatic Weapons of World War II. (Illus.). 128p. 1997. 29.95 (*1-85915-043-8*, Pub. by W & G) Motorbooks Intl.
— German Automatic Weapons World War II. (Illus.). 128p. 1998. pap. 44.95 (*1-86126-269-8*) Crolwood.
— Machine Guns of World War I: Live Firing Classic Military Weapons in Color Photographs. (Illus.). 128p. 1997. 29.95 (*1-85915-078-0*, Pub. by W & G) Motorbooks Intl.
— U. S. Automatic Weapons of World War II - Live Firing Classic Military Weapons in Color Photographs. (Illus.). 128p. 1998. 39.95 (*1-85915-155-8*, Pub. by Windrow & Green) Motorbooks Intl.
Bruce, Robert, ed. The M-1 Does My Talking! The U. S. M-1 Garand Rifle in Pictures, World War II & Korea, Vol. 1. 2nd rev. ed. (Weapons in Action Ser.). (Illus.). 80p. (Orig.). 1993. pap. 12.95 (*0-9631495-1-2*) R Bruce Photo.
Bruce, Robert, et al, eds. Handbook of Australian Corporate Finance. 2nd ed. LC 85-52134. 478p. reprint ed. pap. 148.20 (*0-7837-1306-1*, 204145400020) Bks Demand.
— Handbook of Australian Corporate Finance. 4th ed. 368p. 1992. pap. 69.00 (*0-409-30398-4*, AT, MICHIE) LEXIS Pub.
Bruce, Robert & Bruce, Debra. Reclaiming Intimacy in Your Marriage: Plan for Facing Life's Ebb & Flow...Together. LC 96-25293. 24p. 1996. pap. 9.99 (*1-55661-807-7*) Bethany Hse.
***Bruce, Robert, et al.** Standing up Against the Odds. LC 99-43447. 191p. 1999. pap. 10.99 (*0-570-05377-3*) Concordia.
Bruce, Robert, et al. Worldwide Restrictions on Advertising: An Outline of Principles, Problems & Solutions. 65p. 1986. 70.00 (*0-317-01165-0*) Intl Advertising Assn.
Bruce, Robert, jt. auth. see American Automobile Manufacturers Association, Inc.
Bruce, Robert, jt. auth. see Bruce, Debra F.
Bruce, Robert, jt. ed. see Cheeseman, Graeme.
Bruce, Robert C. Executive Job Search Strategies: The Guide to Career Transitions. Kennedy, Sarah, ed. LC 93-47508. (Illus.). 240p. (Orig.). 1994. pap. 16.95 (*0-8442-4375-2*, VGM Career) NTC Contemp Pub Co.
***Bruce, Robert D.** Petey Putt-Putt & His Friends. Bruce, Britta, ed. (Illus.). 20p. 1999. 5.95 (*0-9664248-9-1*) Sloane Prtlnd ME.
Bruce, Robert D., jt. auth. see Perera, Victor.
Bruce, Robert G. & Bruce, Debra. The ABCs of Christian Grandparenting. (ABCs of Christian Life Ser.). 48p. 1999. 6.00 (*0-570-05350-1*, 12-3398GJ) Concordia.
— The ABCs of Christian Mothers & Daughters. (ABCs of Christian Life Ser.). 48p. 1999. 6.00 (*0-570-05352-8*, 12-3400GJ) Concordia.
— The ABCs of Christian Parenting. (ABCs of Christian Life Ser.). 48p. 1999. 6.00 (*0-570-05349-8*, 12-3397GJ) Concordia.
Bruce, Robert G., et al. The Christian Parent's Guide to Guilt-Free Parenting. LC 97-19480. 216p. 1997. pap. 12.00 (*0-687-05994-1*) Dimen for Liv.
Bruce, Robert M. Checklist of Sports & Recreation. (Illus.). 46p. (Orig.). 1973. pap. 4.00 (*0-614-25046-3*) Am Topical Assn.
Bruce, Robert V. Bell: Alexander Graham Bell & the Conquest of Solitude. LC 89-22951. (Illus.). 576p. 1990. 49.95 (*0-8014-2419-4*); pap. text 19.95 (*0-8014-9691-8*) Cornell U Pr.
— Eighteen Seventy-Seven: Year of Violence. 384p. 1989. reprint ed. pap. text 9.95 (*0-929587-05-7*, Elephant Paperbacks) I R Dee.
— Lincoln & the Tools of War. (Illus.). 400p. (Orig.). 1989. text 32.50 (*0-252-01665-3*); pap. text 15.95 (*0-252-06090-3*) U of Ill Pr.
Bruce, Roger R., ed. see Collins, Douglas & Bedi, Joyce.
Bruce, Roy W. & Leonard, Charles R. Crommelin's Thunderbirds: Air Group 12 Strikes the Heart of Japan. LC 94-16277. (Illus.). 230p. 1994. 33.95 (*1-55750-509-8*) Naval Inst Pr.
Bruce, Scott. Cereal Box Bonanza - The Nineteen Fifties: Identification & Value Guide. LC 95-211945. 216p. 1995. pap. 19.95 (*0-89145-634-1*, 3959) Collector Bks.
— Cereal Boxes & Prizes, 1960s: A Tribute & Price Guide. (Illus.). 250p. (Orig.). 1998. pap. 29.95 (*0-9662123-0-4*) Flake Wrld Publng.
Bruce, Shelley. Tomorrow Is Today. 1983. 15.95 (*0-02-517800-8*) Macmillan.
— Tomorrow Is Today. LC 83-3797. (Illus.). 224p. 1983. 15.95 (*0-672-52756-1*) Macmillan.
Bruce, Sonja, jt. ed. see Bruce, Lennart.
Bruce, Sonja, tr. see Andersson, Claes.
Bruce, Stephen, ed. Best Practices for HR Managers. LC 98-110749. 133p. 1997. 39.95 (*0-9645093-3-4*) Ransom & Benjamin.
— Best Practices for HR Managers. 490p. 1998. 99.95 (*0-9645093-5-0*) Ransom & Benjamin.
Bruce, Stephen D. The BLR Encyclopedia of Personnel Forms: Employment & Termination, 2 vols., Set. rev. ed. 760p. 1986. ring bd. 99.95 (*1-55645-548-8*, 548) Busn Legal Reports.

B

— The BLR Encyclopedia of Prewritten Job Descriptions, 2 vols., Set. rev. ed. 1040p. 1986. ring bd. 159.95 (*1-55645-550-X*, 31500300) Busn Legal Reports.

— Every Manager's Guide to Better Appraisal & Discipline Interviews. 144p. 1989. per. 25.46 (*1-55645-524-0*, 524) Busn Legal Reports.

— Face to Face: Every Manager's Guide to Better Interviewing. 1984. ring bd. 24.95 (*1-55645-517-8*, 517) Busn Legal Reports.

— How to Meet OSHA's Safety & Health Guidelines. 1990. ring bd. 129.95 (*1-55645-596-8*, 596) Busn Legal Reports.

— How to Review Resumes. (BLR Career Ideas Ser.). 1986. per. 21.20 (*1-55645-530-5*, 530) Busn Legal Reports.

— Personnel Manager's Handbook of College Recruiting. rev. ed. 90p. 1983. per. 33.95 (*1-55645-507-0*, 507) Busn Legal Reports.

— Quickstep Hiring: The Step-by-Step Guide to Every Manager's Most Important Responsibility. 76p. 1997. 14.95 (*0-9645093-4-2*) Ransom & Benjamin.

— Quik Step Firing: Step by Step Through Management's Most Difficult Task. 78p. 1998. 14.95 (*0-9645093-6-9*) Ransom & Benjamin.

***Bruce, Stephen D.** QuikStep Discipline: The Step-by-Step Guide to Every Manager's Least-Liked Responsibility. 74p. 1999. 14.95 (*0-9645093-8-5*) Ransom & Benjamin.

Bruce, Stephen D., ed. Business Writing Made Simple: A Manager's Handbook. 182p. 1986. ring bd. 25.46 (*1-55645-421-X*, 421) Busn Legal Reports.

— How to Write Your Employee Handbook. 524p. 1986. ring bd. 139.95 (*1-55645-504-6*, 504) Busn Legal Reports.

***Bruce, Stephen D., ed.** HR Manager's Legal Encyclopedia: The Comprehensive Quick-Reference Desktop Advisor. 425p. 2000. spiral bd. 249.95 (*1-930262-00-0*) Ransom & Benjamin.

Bruce, Stephen D., ed. Planning for a Satisfying Retirement: Program Workbook. 72p. 1989. 9.95 (*1-55645-426-0*) Busn Legal Reports.

Bruce, Stephen D., ed. see Cagney, J. Kenneth.

Bruce, Stephen D., ed. see Gallup, David A. & Beauchemin, Katherine V.

Bruce, Stephen D., ed. see Whiteman, Gilbert L.

Bruce, Stephen E., ed. see Micolo, Anthony M.

Bruce, Stephen R. Pension Claims: Rights & Obligations. 2nd ed. LC 92-42811. 883p. 1993. 145.00 (*0-87179-743-7*, 0743) BNA Books.

***Bruce, Steve.** Choice & Religion: A Critique of Rational Choice Theory. LC 99-33114. 264p. 2000. write for info. (*0-19-829584-7*) OUP.

Bruce, Steve. Conservative Protestant Politics. 246p. 1998. text 55.00 (*0-19-829392-5*) OUP.

— The Edge of the Union: The Ulster Loyalist Political Vision. (Illus.). 188p. (C). 1994. pap. (*0-19-827976-0*) OUP.

***Bruce, Steve.** Fundamentalism. 2000. 59.95 (*0-7456-2365-4*, Pub. by Polity Pr); pap. 24.95 (*0-7456-2366-2*, Pub. by Polity Pr) Blackwell Pubs.

Bruce, Steve. A House Divided: Protestantism, Schism & Secularization. LC 89-32960. 265p. reprint ed. pap. 82.20 (*0-608-20323-8*, 207157600002) Bks Demand.

— Religion in the Modern World: From Cathedrals to Cults. (Illus.). 266p. 1996. text 65.00 (*0-19-878152-0*) OUP.

— Religion in the Modern World: From Cathedrals to Cults. (Illus.). 266p. 1996. pap. text 17.95 (*0-19-878151-2*) OUP.

— The Rise & Fall of the New Christian Right: Conservative Protestant Politics in America, 1978-1988. 224p. 1990. reprint ed. pap. 24.00 (*0-19-827861-6*) OUP.

— Sociology: A Very Short Introduction. (Very Short Introductions Ser.). (Illus.). 144p. 1999. pap. 8.95 (*0-19-285347-3*) OUP.

Bruce, Steve, ed. Religion & Modernization: Sociologists & Historians Debate the Secularization Thesis. LC 92-15171. (Illus.). 236p. 1992. text 49.95 (*0-19-827369-X*, Clarendon Pr) OUP.

— The Sociology of Religion, 2 vols., Set. (International Library of Critical Writings in Sociology: No. 3). 1240p. 1995. 440.00 (*1-85278-899-2*) E Elgar.

Bruce, Steve, et al, eds. The Rapture of Politics: The Christian Right As the United States Approaches the Year 2000. LC 94-28321. 196p. (C). 1994. pap. 21.95 (*1-56000-802-4*) Transaction Pubs.

Bruce, Susan. William Shakespeare, King Lear. LC 98-39508. (Critical Guides Ser.). 192p. 1998. 39.50 (*0-231-11528-8*); pap. 14.50 (*0-231-11529-6*) Col U Pr.

Bruce, Susan, ed. see More, Thomas, et al.

Bruce, Thomas. Southwest Virginia & Shenandoah Valley. x, 266p. 1997. reprint ed. pap. 17.50 (*0-7884-0765-1*, B682) Heritage Bk.

Bruce, Thomas A. Designing Quality Databases with IDEF1X Information Models. LC 91-18092. (Illus.). 584p. (C). 1992. text 57.95 (*0-932633-18-8*) Dorset Hse Pub Co.

Bruce, Thomas R., jt. ed. see Schaffer, Ellen.

Bruce, Timothy J. & Sanderson, William C. Specific Phobias: Clinical Applications of Evidence-Based Psychotherapy. LC 97-42371. (Illus.). 280p. 1998. 40.00 (*1-56821-883-4*) Aronson.

Bruce, Tina, et al. Recurring Themes in Education. (One-Off Ser.). 160p. 1995. pap. (*1-85396-264-3*) Corwin Pr.

Bruce, Todd. Jiggers. 1997. pap. 7.95 (*0-88801-175-X*, Pub. by Turnstone Pr) Genl Dist Srvs.

— Rhapsody in D. LC 97-205069. 96p. 1997. pap. 8.95 (*0-88801-211-X*, Pub. by Turnstone Pr) Genl Dist Srvs.

Bruce, V., et al, eds. Processing the Facial Image: Proceedings of a Royal Society Discussion Meeting Held on 9-10 July 1991. (Illus.). 138p. 1992. text 85.00 (*0-19-852261-4*) OUP.

Bruce, Vicki, et al, eds. Processing Images of Faces. (Tutorial Monographs in Cognitive Science: Vol. 2). 272p. (C). 1992. text 73.25 (*0-89391-684-6*) Ablx Pub.

Bruce, Vicki & Burton, Mike. Processing Images of Faces. Shadbolt, Nigel, ed. (Tutorial Monographs in Cognitive Science: Vol. 2). 272p. (C). 1992. pap. 39.50 (*0-89391-771-0*) Ablx Pub.

Bruce, Vicki & Young, Andrew. In the Eye of the Beholder: The Science of Face Perception. LC 99-165890. (Illus.). 352p. 1998. text 39.95 (*0-19-852440-4*) OUP.

Bruce, Vicki, et al. Visual Perception: Physiology, Psychology, & Ecology. 3rd ed. 448p. 1997. pap. 26.00 (*0-86377-451-2*) L Erlbaum Assocs.

Bruce, Vicki, jt. auth. see Roth, Ilona.

Bruce, Victoria. Windmills in Time. 368p. 1998. mass mkt. 5.50 (*0-505-52280-2*, Love Spell) Dorchester Pub Co.

Bruce, Virginia. Amy's Book of Poems. 1997. pap. write for info. (*1-57553-712-5*) Watermrk Pr.

***Bruce, Virginia.** Children's Book of Poems. 2000. pap. write for info. (*1-58235-370-0*) Watermrk Pr.

Bruce, W. Robert. Orando los Unos por los Otros. (Serie Discipulo - Discipleship Ser.).Tr. of Praying for One Another. (SPA.). 1.79 (*1-56063-896-6*, 498250) Editorial Unilit.

Bruce, W. Robert, et al, eds. Gastrointestinal Cancer: Endogenous Factors. LC 80-28016. (Banbury Report: No. 7). 482p. reprint ed. pap. 149.50 (*0-7837-1995-7*, 204226900002) Bks Demand.

Bruce, Walter & Schroth, J. Que's Using Enable. 2nd ed. (Illus.). 800p. 1993. 29.95 (*1-56529-217-0*) Que.

***Bruce, Wendy.** Grandfather's Ship, The S. S. "United States" 50p. (J). (gr. 3-5). 2000. write for info. (*0-9701870-0-9*) E B Fletcher.

Bruce, Wendy R. Arthritis: 277 Things Everyone Should Know. Date not set. write for info. (*1-891985-00-0*) Live Oak LA.

Bruce, Willa M. Problem Employee Management: Proactive Strategies for Human Resource Managers. LC 89-24330. 224p. 1990. 57.95 (*0-89930-501-6*, BJE/, Quorum Bks) Greenwood.

Bruce, Willa M. & Blackburn, J. Walton. Balancing Job Satisfaction & Performance: A Guide for Human Resource Professionals. LC 92-15989. 256p. 1992. 59.95 (*0-89930-658-6*, BBX, Quorum Bks) Greenwood.

Bruce, Willa M. & Reed, Christine M. Dual Career Couples in the Public Sector: A Management Guide for Human Resource Professionals. LC 90-22121. 184p. 1991. 59.95 (*0-89930-552-0*, BDB, Quorum Bks) Greenwood.

Bruce, Willa M., jt. auth. see Blackburn, J. Walton.

Bruce, William B. Letters Home. Murray, Joan, ed. 254p. 1982. 24.95 (*0-920806-36-8*, Pub. by Penumbra Pr) U of Toronto Pr.

Bruce, William C. John Randolph of Roanoke, 1773-1833: A Biography Based Largly on New Material, 2 vols., Set. (BCL1 - U. S. History Ser.). 1992. reprint ed. lib. bdg. 150.00 (*0-7812-6129-5*) Rprt Serv.

Bruce, William G., ed. History of Milwaukee: City & County, 3 vols. (Illus.). 2528p. 1997. reprint ed. lib. bdg. 229.50 (*0-8328-6975-9*) Higginson Bk Co.

Bruce, William H. How I Became A Millionaire Buying, Renting & Selling Real Estate. 104p. (Orig.). 1995. per. 14.95 (*0-9644967-0-4*) Bruce Intl.

— The Other Side of Hope. 245p. (Orig.). 1995. per. 14.95 (*0-9644967-2-0*) Bruce Intl.

— Secret Messengers: How Governments Correspond. 312p. (Orig.). 1995. pap. 14.95 (*0-9644967-1-2*) Bruce Intl.

Bruce, William S. The Log of the "Scotia" Speak, Peter, ed. 256p. 1992. text 145.00 (*0-7486-0293-3*, Pub. by Edinburgh U Pr) Col U Pr.

— The Railways of Fife. 248p. (C). 1989. 52.00 (*0-906664-03-9*, Pub. by Mercat Pr Bks) St Mut.

Bruce Woodcock's Business Network Writers Staff. The Great Universal Business Network: And How It Grew. large type ed. Fisher, Suzanne, ed. (WeWrite Kids! Ser.: Vol. 43). (Illus.). 45p. (J). (gr. 3-8). 1999. pap. 3.95 (*1-57635-051-7*) WeWrite.

Bruce-Young, Doris M. Cash for College: An ABC Guide for High School Students & Parents. 1997. pap. 10.95 (*0-9639490-2-0*) Young Ent Intl Inc.

Brucer, Marshall. A Chronology of Nuclear Medicine. Buntaine, Robert R., ed. (Illus.). 514p. (C). 1990. lib. bdg. 55.00 (*0-9625674-0-X*) Heritage MO.

Bruce's Son & Company Staff. Victorian Frames, Borders & Cuts. LC 76-3052. (Pictorial Archive Ser.). (Illus.). 128p. (Orig.). 1976. pap. 8.95 (*0-486-23320-0*) Dover.

Bruch, Carl, jt. ed. see Austin, Jay.

Bruch, E. The Boundary Element Method for Groundwater Flow. Brebbia, Carlos A. & Orszag, S. A., eds. (Lecture Notes in Engineering Ser.: Vol. 70). (Illus.). 120p. 1991. 32.95 (*0-387-54407-0*) Spr-Verlag.

Bruch, Hilde. Conversations with Anorexics: A Compassionate & Hopeful Journey through the Therapeutic Process. LC 94-70808. 238p. 1994. pap. 30.00 (*1-56821-261-5*) Aronson.

— Eating Disorders: Obesity, Anorexia Nervosa, & the Person Within. LC 72-89189. 400p. 1979. pap. 25.00 (*0-465-01782-7*, Pub. by Basic) HarpC.

— The Golden Cage: The Enigma of Anorexia Nervosa. 168p. 1978. text 24.95 (*0-674-35650-0*) HUP.

— The Golden Cage: The Enigma of Anorexia Nervosa. LC 78-11185. 159p. 1979. pap. 9.00 (*0-394-72688-X*) Vin Bks.

— Learning Psychotherapy: Rationale & Ground Rules. LC 74-83848. 166p. 1980. pap. 15.95 (*0-674-52026-2*) HUP.

Bruch, Joanne H. Unlocking the Golden Cage: An Intimate Biography of Hilde Bruch, M. D. LC 96-75699. (Illus.). 336p. 1996. 29.95 (*0-936077-16-6*, HIL) Gurze Bks.

Bruch, Johanna. Making Places in the Prehistoric World. 1999. pap. text 29.95 (*1-85728-753-3*) UCL Pr Ltd.

Bruch, L. W., et al. Physical Adsorption: Forces & Phenomena. LC 97-164754. (International Series of Monotraphs on Chemistry: No. 33). (Illus.). 352p. 1997. text 85.00 (*0-19-855638-1*) OUP.

Bruch, M. Scotch Phantasy Opus 46: Violin & Piano. 36p. 1986. pap. 7.95 (*0-7935-5132-3*) H Leonard.

Bruch, Marilyn. Phonics Art Projects. (J). (gr. 1-3). 1985. pap. 8.99 (*0-8224-5541-2*) Fearon Teacher Aids.

Bruch, Martha D. NMR Spectroscopy Techniques. 2nd ed. (Pratical Spectroscopy Ser.: Vol. 21). (Illus.). 632p. 1996. text 215.00 (*0-8247-9450-8*) Dekker.

Bruch, Max. First Violin Concerto & Scottish Fantasy in Full Score. 240p. 1994. pap. 13.95 (*0-486-28295-3*) Dover.

Bruch, Max & Bloch, Ernst. Bruch's "Kol Nidrei" & Bloch's "Schelomo" for Cello & Orchestra in Full Score. 112p. 1996. pap. 9.95 (*0-486-29039-5*) Dover.

***Bruch, Michael & Bond, Frank W.** Beyond Diagnosis: Case Formulation Approaches in CBT. LC 98-2989. (Series in Clinical Psychology). 238p. 1999. pap. 38.50 (*0-471-98222-9*) Wiley.

Bruch, Vicki L. U. S. Government Overviews of International Electric Vehicle Activities: Part A: Advanced Battery Systems R & D Program Plan; Part B: Fuel Cells in Transportation, National Program Plan (Executive Summary); Part C: Electric & Hybrid Vehicles Research & Development Program Plan; Part D: Hydrogen Program Plan; Part E: Ultracapacitor Program Plan; Part F: Partnership for a New Generation of Vehicles Program Plan. (Electric Vehicle Information Ser.: Vol. 4, Pts. A-C). (Illus.). 172p. 1996. lib. bdg. 135.00 (*0-89934-248-5*, BT931) Bus Tech Bks.

— U. S. Government Overviews of International Electric Vehicle Activities: Part A: An Assessment of Research & Development Leadership in Advanced Batteries for EVs; Part B: Electric Vehicles: Likely Consquences of U. S. & Other Nations Programs & Policies. (Electric Vehicle Information Ser.: Vol. 4, Pts. A-B). (Illus.). 172p. 1996. pap. 85.00 (*0-89934-247-7*, BT031) Bus Tech Bks.

Bruchac. Survival This Way: Interviews with American Indian Poets. LC 87-16224. (Sun Tracks Ser.: Vol. 15). 363p. 1990. reprint ed. pap. 19.95 (*0-8165-1178-0*) U of Ariz Pr.

Bruchac, Carol, et al, eds. The Stories We Hold Secret: Tales of Women's Spiritual Development. LC 85-70536. 316p. (Orig.). 1987. pap. 12.95 (*0-912678-66-6*, Greenfld Rev Pr) Greenfld Rev Lit.

Bruchac, Carol, jt. ed. see Watanabe, Sylvia.

***Bruchac, James & Bruchac, Joseph.** Native American Games. (Illus.). 64p. (J). 2000. pap. 12.95 (*1-55591-979-0*) Fulcrum Pub.

Bruchac, James & Bruchac, Joseph. When the Chenoo Howls: Native American Tales of Horror. LC 97-48715. (Illus.). 128p. (J). (gr. 3-7). 1999. lib. bdg. 17.85 (*0-8027-8639-1*) Walker & Co.

— When the Chenoo Howls: Native American Tales of Terror. LC 97-48715. (Illus.). 136p. (J). (gr. 3-7). 1999. 16.95 (*0-8027-8638-3*); pap. 8.95 (*0-8027-7576-4*) Walker & Co.

Bruchac, James, jt. ed. see Francis, Lee.

Bruchac, Joe, jt. reader see Bruchac, Joseph.

Bruchac, Joseph. Adirondack Tall Tales: Hoop Snakes, Hide Behinds & Side Hill Winders. (Illus.). 115p. pap. write for info. (*0-925168-73-4*) North Country.

— The Arrow over the Door. LC 96-36701. (Illus.). 89p. (J). (gr. 2-4). 1998. 15.99 (*0-8037-2078-5*, Dial Yng Read) Peng Put Young Read.

— Between Earth & Sky: Legends of Native American Sacred Places. LC 95-10862. (Illus.). 32p. (J). (gr. 3-6). 1996. 16.00 (*0-15-200042-9*) Harcourt.

— Between Earth & Sky: Legends of Native American Sacred Places. LC 95-10862. (Illus.). 32p. 1999. pap. 7.00 (*0-15-202062-4*) Harcourt.

— A Boy Called Slow: The True Story of Sitting Bull. LC 93-21233. (Illus.). 32p. (J). (ps-3). 1995. 15.95 (*0-399-22692-3*, Philomel) Peng Put Young Read.

— A Boy Called Slow: The True Story of Sitting Bull. (Illus.). 32p. (J). (ps-3). 1998. pap. 5.99 (*0-698-11616-X*, PapStar) Peng Put Young Read.

***Bruchac, Joseph.** A Boy Called Slow: The True Story of Sitting Bull. 1998. 11.19 (*0-606-13223-6*, Pub. by Turtleback) Demco.

Bruchac, Joseph. Children of the Longhouse. LC 95-11344. (Illus.). 160p. (J). (gr. 3-6). 1996. 14.99 (*0-8037-1793-8*, Dial Yng Read) Peng Put Young Read.

— Children of the Longhouse. 1998. 10.09 (*0-606-13268-6*, Pub. by Turtleback) Demco.

— The Circle of Thanks. LC 95-41175. (Illus.). 32p. (J). (ps-3). 1996. 15.95 (*0-8167-4012-7*) BridgeWater.

***Bruchac, Joseph.** Crazy Horse's Vision. LC 99-47451. (Illus.). 40p. (J). 2000. 16.95 (*1-880000-94-6*) Lee & Low Bks.

Bruchac, Joseph. Dawn Land. LC 92-54767. 336p. 1993. 19.95 (*1-55591-134-X*) Fulcrum Pub.

— Dawn Land. 336p. 1995. pap. 12.95 (*1-55591-215-X*) Fulcrum Pub.

— Dawn Land. 1995. 18.05 (*0-606-12673-2*, Pub. by Turtleback) Demco.

— Dog People: Native Dog Stories. LC 95-9804. (Fulcrum Kids Ser.). (Illus.). 64p. (J). (gr. 3-6). 1995. 14.95 (*1-55591-228-1*) Fulcrum Pub.

— The Earth under Sky Bear's Feet: Native American Poems of the Land. (Illus.). 32p. (J). (gr. k up). 1998. pap. 5.99 (*0-698-11647-X*, PapStar) Peng Put Young Read.

— The Faithful Hunter: Abenaki Stories. (Bowman Bks.). (Illus.). 74p. (Orig.). 1989. pap. 9.95 (*0-912678-75-5*) Greenfld Rev Lit.

— First Strawberries: A Cherokee Story. (Picture Puffin Ser.). (Illus.). 32p. (J). 1998. pap. 5.99 (*0-14-056409-8*, PuffinBks) Peng Put Young Read.

— First Strawberries: A Cherokee Story. (Picture Puffin Ser.). 1998. 11.19 (*0-606-13388-7*, Pub. by Turtleback) Demco.

— Flying with the Eagle, Racing the Great Bear: Stories from Native North America. (J). 1993. 11.05 (*0-606-07526-7*) Turtleback.

— Fox Song. 1997. 11.15 (*0-606-11349-5*, Pub. by Turtleback) Demco.

— The Girl Who Married the Moon, Tales from Native North America. (J). 1994. 11.15 (*0-606-08751-6*, Pub. by Turtleback) Demco.

— The Good Message of Handsome Lake. LC 79-973335. (Keepsake Ser.: Vol. 9). 1979. 17.50 (*0-87775-112-9*) Unicorn Pr.

— The Great Ball Game: A Muskogee Story. LC 93-6269. (Illus.). (J). (ps-3). 1994. 16.99 (*0-8037-1539-0*, Dial Yng Read) Peng Put Young Read.

— The Heart of a Chief. LC 97-49248. 176p. (J). (gr. 4-7). 1998. 15.99 (*0-8037-2276-1*, Dial Yng Read) Peng Put Young Read.

— Heroes & Heroines, Monsters & Magic: Native American Legends & Folktales. (Illus.). 198p. (J). (gr. 3-7). reprint ed. pap. 12.95 (*0-89594-995-4*) Crossing Pr.

***Bruchac, Joseph.** How Chipmunk Got His Stripes. LC 99-16793. (J). 2001. 15.99 (*0-8037-2404-7*, Dial Yng Read) Peng Put Young Read.

Bruchac, Joseph. Lasting Echoes. LC 97-11884. (Illus.). 176p. (J). (gr. 5). 1997. 16.00 (*0-15-201327-X*) Harcourt.

— Lasting Echoes: An Oral History of Native American People. 176p. 1999. mass mkt. 5.99 (*0-380-73184-3*, Avon Bks) Morrow Avon.

— Long River: A Novel. 320p. 1995. 19.95 (*1-55591-213-3*) Fulcrum Pub.

— The Man Who Loved Buffalo. LC 95-35358. (Illus.). (J). 1998. 16.00 (*0-15-200044-5*) Harcourt.

— Many Nations: An Alphabet of Native America. LC 97-12271. (Illus.). 32p. (J). (ps-2). 1997. 15.95 (*0-8167-4389-4*) BrdgeWater.

— Many Nations: An Alphabet of Native America. (Illus.). 32p. (J). (ps-2). 1998. pap. 5.95 (*0-8167-4460-2*) Troll Communs.

— Native American Animal Stories. LC 92-53040. (Illus.). 140p. 1992. pap. 12.95 (*1-55591-127-7*) Fulcrum Pub.

Bruchac, Joseph. Native American Animal Stories. LC 92-53040. 1992. 18.05 (*0-606-06610-1*, Pub. by Turtleback) Demco.

Bruchac, Joseph. Native American Stories. LC 90-85267. (Illus.). 160p. 1991. pap. 12.95 (*1-55591-094-7*) Fulcrum Pub.

— Native American Stories. LC 90-85267. 1991. 18.05 (*0-606-06611-X*, Pub. by Turtleback) Demco.

— The Native American Sweat Lodge: History & Legends. (Illus.). 146p. 1993. pap. 12.95 (*0-89594-636-X*) Crossing Pr.

— Native Plant Stories. 1995. 18.05 (*0-606-12780-1*, Pub. by Turtleback) Demco.

— No Borders: Poems. LC 99-10867. 96p. 1999. pap. 12.95 (*0-930100-84-0*, Pub. by Holy Cow) Consort Bk Sales.

— Pushing up the Sky: Seven Native American Plays for Children. LC 98-20483. (Illus.). 96p. (J). (gr. 1-5). 2000. 17.99 (*0-8037-2168-4*, Dial Yng Read) Peng Put Young Read.

— The Return of the Sun: Native American Tales from the Northeast Woodlands. (Illus.). 210p. 1989. pap. 12.95 (*0-89594-343-3*) Crossing Pr.

— Roots of Survival: Native American Storytelling & the Sacred. 272p. 1996. 24.95 (*1-55591-145-5*) Fulcrum Pub.

***Bruchac, Joseph.** Sacajawea. LC PZ7.B82816Sac 2000. 208p. (J). 2000. 17.00 (*0-15-202234-1*) Harcourt.

— Seeing the Circle. LC 99-25330. (Meet the Author Ser.). (Illus.). 32p. (J). (gr. 2-5). 1999. 14.95 (*1-57274-327-1*, 724) R Owen Pubs.

— Skeleton Man. 144p. 14.95 (*0-06-029075-7*) HarpC.

— Skeleton Man. 144p. (gr. 5 up). lib. bdg. 14.89 (*0-06-029076-5*); mass mkt. 4.95 (*0-06-440888-4*) HarpC.

— Squanto's Journey: The Story of the First Thanksgiving. (Illus.). 2000. 28.54 (*0-7398-3072-4*) Raintree Steck-V.

— Squanto's Story: The Story of the First Thanksgiving. LC 99-12012. (Illus.). 32p. (J). (ps-3). 2000. 16.00 (*0-15-201817-4*, Harcourt Child Bks) Harcourt.

Bruchac, Joseph. Tell Me a Tale: A Book about Storytelling. LC 96-21697. 144p. (J). 1997. 16.00 (*0-15-201221-4*) Harcourt.

— Tell Me a Tale: A Book about Storytelling. (YA). (gr. 5 up). 1997. 16.00 (*0-614-28819-3*) Harcourt.

— Telling Tales: A Book about Story & Storytelling. LC 96-21697. (J). 1996. pap. write for info. (*0-15-201268-0*) Harcourt.

— There Are No Trees in the Prison. 1978. pap. 2.50 (*0-942396-24-3*) Blackberry ME.

— 13 Moons on Turtle's Back: A Native American Year of Moons. 1997. 11.15 (*0-606-12824-7*, Pub. by Turtleback) Demco.

— The Trail of Tears. LC 98-36199. (Step into Reading Ser.: A Step 4 Book). (Illus.). 48p. (J). (gr. 2-4). 1999. pap. 3.99 (*0-679-89052-1*, Pub. by Random Bks Yng Read); lib. bdg. 11.99 (*0-679-99052-6*, Pub. by Random Bks Yng Read) Random.

— Translator's Son. Barkan, Stanley H., ed. (Cross-Cultural Review Chapbook Ser.: No. 10: Native American Abenaki Poetry 1). (Illus.). 40p. 1980. 15.00 (*0-89304-833-X*, CCC135); pap. 5.00 (*0-89304-809-7*); audio 10.00 (*0-685-01277-8*) Cross-Cultrl NY.

— Turtle Meat & Other Stories. LC 92-54182. 119p. (Orig.). 1992. pap. 12.95 (*0-930100-49-2*) Holy Cow.

***Bruchac, Joseph.** Waters Between: A Novel of Dawn Land. LC 98-6225. (Hardscrabble Bks.). 310p. 1998. pap. 14.95 (*1-58465-015-X*) U Pr of New Eng.

Bruchac, Joseph. The Waters Between: A Novel of the Dawn Land. LC 98-6225. (Hardscrabble Bks.). 310p. 1998. 22.95 (*0-87451-881-4*) U Pr of New Eng.

— The Wind Eagle & Other Abenaki Folk Stories. (Bowman Bks.). (Illus.). 48p. (Orig.). 1985. pap. 5.95 (*0-912678-64-X*, Greenfld Rev Pr) Greenfld Rev Lit.

Bruchac, Joseph, as told by. Flying with the Eagle, Racing the Great Bear: Stories from Native North America. LC 93-21966. (Illus.). 144p. (YA). (gr. 5-8). 1997. 13.95 (*0-8167-3026-1*) BrdgeWater.

— Flying with the Eagle, Racing the Great Bear: Stories from Native North America. LC 93-21966. (Illus.). 144p. (J). (gr. 5-8). 1995. pap. 5.95 (*0-8167-3027-X*, Troll Medallion) Troll Communs.

Bruchac, Joseph, ed. Aniyunwiya, Real Human Beings: Contemporary Cherokee Indian Fiction. 1995. pap. 14.95 (*0-912678-92-5*) Greenfld Rev Lit.

— The Last Stop. 1974. per. 3.00 (*0-912678-10-0*, Greenfld Rev Pr) Greenfld Rev Lit.

— The Light from Another Country: Poetry from American Prisons. LC 83-788. 350p. (Orig.). 1984. pap. 9.95 (*0-912678-60-7*, Greenfld Rev Pr) Greenfld Rev Lit.

— Native Wisdom. LC 94-29472. 112p. 1994. pap. 11.00 (*0-06-251172-6*, Pub. by Harper SF) HarpC.

— New Voices from the Longhouse: An Anthology of Modern Iroquois Literature. 1988. 12.95 (*0-912678-68-2*, Greenfld Rev Pr) Greenfld Rev Lit.

— Raven Tells Stories: An Anthology of Alaska Native Writing. LC 90-85173. 232p. (Orig.). (C). 1991. pap. 12.95 (*0-912678-80-1*) Greenfld Rev Lit.

Bruchac, Joseph, et al, eds. North Country: Writing from the Upper Hudson Valley & the Adirondacks. LC 85-70358. 472p. (Orig.). 1986. pap. 12.95 (*0-912678-65-8*, Greenfld Rev Pr) Greenfld Rev Lit.

Bruchac, Joseph, intro. Breaking Silence: An Anthology of Contemporary Asian American Poets. LC 83-80759. 300p. (Orig.). 1984. pap. 9.95 (*0-912678-59-3*, Greenfld Rev Pr) Greenfld Rev Lit.

— Songs from This Earth on Turtle's Back: An Anthology of Poetry by American Indian Writers. LC 82-82420. 300p. (Orig.). 1983. pap. 10.95 (*0-912678-58-5*, Greenfld Rev Pr) Greenfld Rev Lit.

Bruchac, Joseph & Association for the Study of American Indian Liter, eds. Returning the Gift: Poetry & Prose from the First North American Native Writers Festival. LC 94-4845. (Sun Tracks Ser.: Vol. 29). 369p. 1994. pap. 19.95 (*0-8165-1486-0*) U of Ariz Pr.

Bruchac, Joseph & Bruchac, Joe, readers. Animal Tales. (Wonder Ser.). (J). (gr. k-7). 9.95 incl. audio (*1-57098-054-3*, Pub. by Roberts Rinehart) Publishers Group.

Bruchac, Joseph & London, Jonathan. Thirteen Moons on Turtle's Back: A Native American Year of Moons. LC 91-3961. (Illus.). 32p. (J). (ps up). 1997. pap. 5.99 (*0-698-11584-8*, PapStar) Peng Put Young Read.

Bruchac, Joseph & Ross, Gayle. The Girl Who Married the Moon: Tales from Native North America. LC 93-43824. (Illus.). 128p. (J). (gr. 5-8). 1996. 13.95 (*0-8167-3480-1*) BrdgeWater.

— The Girl Who Married the Moon: Tales from Native North America. LC 93-43824. (Illus.). 128p. (J). (gr. 5-8). 1997. pap. 5.95 (*0-8167-3481-X*, Troll Medallion) Troll Communs.

— The Story of the Milky Way: A Cherokee Tale. LC 94-20926. (Illus.). 32p. (J). (ps-3). 1995. 15.99 (*0-8037-1737-7*, Dial Yng Read) Peng Put Young Read.

Bruchac, Joseph, et al. Talking Book Box B: Multiethnic (Native American, African Interest, Latin American) Poetry. Barkan, Stanley H., ed. Alcalay, Ammiel, tr. (Talking Bks.). (Illus.). 92p. 1989. 50.00 incl. audio (*0-89304-676-0*) Cross-Cultrl NY.

Bruchac, Joseph, jt. auth. see Bruchac, James.

Bruchac, Joseph, jt. auth. see Caduto, Michael J.

Bruchac, Joseph, jt. auth. see Fawcett, Melissa J.

Bruchac, Joseph, jt. ed. see Barkan, Stanley H.

Bruchalski, Ted, ed. see Flynn, Ted & Flynn, Maureen.

Brucher, H. Useful Plants of Neotropical Origin. (Illus.). 335p. 1989. 196.95 (*0-387-18743-X*) Spr-Verlag.

Brucher, Horst. Bone Marrow Diagnosis in Clinical Practice. Kucera, Emil, tr. LC 88-45402. (Johns Hopkins Series in Contemporary Medicine & Public Health). (Illus.). 276p. 1989. reprint ed. pap. 85.60 (*0-608-05930-7*, 206626600008) Bks Demand.

Bruchev, Stuart & Carosso, Vincent P., eds. Companies & Men: Business Enterprise in America, 38 bks. 1976. 1537.00 (*0-405-08062-X*, 413) Ayer.

Bruchey, Eleanor. Business Elite in Baltimore, Eighteen Eighty to Nineteen Fourteen. LC 75-43406. (Companies & Men: Business Enterprises in America Ser.). (Illus.). 1976. 34.95 (*0-405-08103-0*) Ayer.

Bruchey, Eleanor, ed. see Abrahams, Paul P.

Bruchey, Eleanor, ed. see Adams, Frederick U.

Bruchey, Eleanor, ed. see Arnold, Dean A.

Bruchey, Eleanor, ed. see Bain, Foster H. & Read, Thomas T.

Bruchey, Eleanor, ed. see Brewster, Kingman, Jr.

Bruchey, Eleanor, jt. ed. see Bruchey, Stuart.

Bruchey, Eleanor, ed. see Callis, Helmut G.

Bruchey, Eleanor, ed. see Crowther, Samuel.

Bruchey, Eleanor, ed. see David, Jules.

Bruchey, Eleanor, ed. see Davies, Robert B.

Bruchey, Eleanor, ed. see De La Torre, Jose, Jr.

Bruchey, Eleanor, ed. see Dunning, John H.

Bruchey, Eleanor, ed. see Edelberg, Guillermo S.

Bruchey, Eleanor, ed. see Edwards, Corwin D. & Bruchey, Stuart.

Bruchey, Eleanor, ed. see Elliott, William Y., et al.

Bruchey, Eleanor, ed. see Eysenbach, Mary L.

Bruchey, Eleanor, ed. see Gates, Theodore R. & Linden, Fabian.

Bruchey, Eleanor, ed. see Hufbauer, G. & Adler, F. W.

Bruchey, Eleanor, ed. see Lewis, Cleona & Schlotterbeck, Karl T.

Bruchey, Eleanor, ed. see McKenzie, Fred A.

Bruchey, Eleanor, ed. see Moore, John R.

Bruchey, Eleanor, ed. see National Planning Association Staff.

Bruchey, Eleanor, ed. see Nordyke, James W.

Bruchey, Eleanor, ed. see O'Connor, Harvey.

Bruchey, Eleanor, ed. see Overlach, Theodore W.

Bruchey, Eleanor, ed. see Phelps, William C.

Bruchey, Eleanor, ed. see Porter, Robert P.

Bruchey, Eleanor, ed. see Queen, George S.

Bruchey, Eleanor, ed. see Rippy, J. Fred.

Bruchey, Eleanor, ed. see Southard, Frank A., Jr.

Bruchey, Eleanor, ed. see Staley, Eugene.

Bruchey, Eleanor, ed. see Stern, Siegfried.

Bruchey, Eleanor, ed. see Thwaite, et al.

Bruchey, Eleanor, ed. see U. S. Congress, House of Representatives Staff.

Bruchey, Eleanor, ed. see U. S. Congress, Senate Staff.

Bruchey, Eleanor, ed. see U. S. Department of Commerce & Labor Staff.

Bruchey, Eleanor, ed. see U. S. Department of Commerce Staff.

Bruchey, Eleanor, ed. see U. S. Federal Trade Commission Staff.

Bruchey, Eleanor, ed. see Vanderlip, Frank A.

Bruchey, Eleanor, ed. see Winkler, Max.

Bruchey, Eleanor, ed. see Yeoman, Wayne A.

Bruchey, Eleanor, ed. see Yudin, Elinor B.

Bruchey, Stuart. Enterprise: The Dynamic Economy of a Free People. 656p. 1990. pap. 28.00 (*0-674-25746-4*) HUP.

— The Modernization of the American Stock Exchange, 1971-1989. LC 91-35983. 236p. 1991. text 15.00 (*0-8153-0722-5*) Garland.

— Robert Oliver: Merchant of Baltimore, 1783-1819. Carosso, Vincent P., ed. LC 78-18954. (Small Business Enterprise in America Ser.). 1979. reprint ed. lib. bdg. 35.95 (*0-405-11458-3*) Ayer.

— Robert Oliver & Mercantile Bookkeeping in the Early Nineteenth Century. LC 75-18460. (History of Accounting Ser.). 1979. 17.95 (*0-405-07544-8*) Ayer.

— A Type Study of American Banking. Stevenson, Russell A., ed. LC 80-1169. (Rise of Commercial Banking Ser.). (Illus.). 1981. reprint ed. lib. bdg. 24.95 (*0-405-13679-X*) Ayer.

Bruchey, Stuart, ed. Development of Public Land Law in the U. S. Series, 29 bks., Set. 1979. lib. bdg. 1070.00 (*0-405-11363-3*) Ayer.

— Dissertation in European Economic History Series, 30 bks., Set. (Illus.). 1977. lib. bdg. 643.00 (*0-405-10773-0*) Ayer.

— Dissertations in American Economic History, 29 vols. 7894p. 1975. 2914.00 (*0-405-07252-X*) Ayer.

— Dissertations in American Economic History: 1977, 34 pts. (Continuing Series for American Dissertations). (Illus.). 1977. reprint ed. lib. bdg. 734.00 (*0-405-11024-3*) Ayer.

— Dissertations in European Economic History II Series, 39 vols., Set. 1981. lib. bdg. 2492.50 (*0-405-13975-6*) Ayer.

— Energy in the American Economy, Set, Vols. 1[00ad]28. (Illus.). 1979. lib. bdg. 1202.00 (*0-405-11957-7*) Ayer.

— Entrepreneurship in Maine: Essays in Business Enterprise. LC 95-21430. (Studies in Entrepreneurship). (Illus.). 208p. 1995. text 15.00 (*0-8153-1960-6*) Garland.

— Garland Studies in Historical Demography, 29 vols., Set. 747.00 (*0-8153-0269-X*) Garland.

— Garland Studies on the Elderly in America, 24 vols., Set. 1992. 1763.00 (*0-8153-0505-2*) Garland.

— The History of the Chemical Bank, Eighteen Twenty-Three to Nineteen Thirteen. LC 80-1185. (Rise of Commercial Banking Ser.). (Illus.). 1981. reprint ed. lib. bdg. 18.95 (*0-405-13654-4*) Ayer.

— Land, Water, & Settlement in Kern County, California, 1850-1890. LC 78-56723. (Management of Public Lands in the U. S. Ser.). 1979. lib. bdg. 31.95 (*0-405-11328-5*) Ayer.

— The Management of Public Lands in the U. S. Series, 43 bks., Set. 1979. lib. bdg. 1123.50 (*0-405-11315-3*) Ayer.

— Memoirs of Three Railroad Pioneers. LC 80-1293. 1981. lib. bdg. 18.95 (*0-405-13763-X*) Ayer.

— Multinational Corporations Series, 35 bks., Set. 1980. lib. bdg. 1048.00 (*0-405-13350-2*) Ayer.

— The Railroads Series, 65 vols. 1981. lib. bdg. 1781.00 (*0-405-13750-8*) Ayer.

— Sixty-Five Years of Progress & a Record of New York City Banks. LC 80-1189. (Rise of Commercial Banking Ser.). (Illus.). 1981. reprint ed. lib. bdg. 15.95 (*0-405-13674-9*) Ayer.

Bruchey, Stuart & Brown, Gene. Energy & Environment. (Great Contemporary Issues Ser.). 1978. 27.95 (*0-405-11195-9*) Ayer.

Bruchey, Stuart & Bruchey, Eleanor, eds. American Business Abroad Series, 50 vols. 1976. reprint ed. 1451.50 (*0-405-09261-X*) Ayer.

— Estimates of United States Direct Foreign Investment, 1929-1943 & 1947: An Original Anthology. LC 76-5008. (American Business Abroad Ser.). (Illus.). 1976. reprint ed. 33.95 (*0-405-09277-6*) Ayer.

— Use & Abuse of America's Natural Resources, 41 bks. 1972. 1506.50 (*0-405-04500-X*) Ayer.

Bruchey, Stuart & Carosso, Vincent P., eds. The Rise of Commercial Banking Series, 60 bks. 1981. lib. bdg. 794.00 (*0-405-13626-9*) Ayer.

— Small Business Enterprise in America Series, 42 bks. (Illus.). 1979. lib. bdg. 1049.50 (*0-405-11457-5*) Ayer.

Bruchey, Stuart, jt. auth. see Edwards, Corwin D.

Bruchey, Stuart, jt. auth. see Hall, Billy R., Jr.

Bruchey, Stuart, ed. see Abdel-Barr, Hussein A.

Bruchey, Stuart, ed. see Abrahams, Paul P.

Bruchey, Stuart, ed. see Abrams, Charles.

Bruchey, Stuart, ed. see Adams, Charles F., Jr.

Bruchey, Stuart, ed. see Adams, Frederick U.

Bruchey, Stuart, ed. see Aggarwal, Raj K.

Bruchey, Stuart, ed. see Ahrari, Mohammed E.

Bruchey, Stuart, ed. see Alcorn, Edgar G.

Bruchey, Stuart, ed. see Alhadeff, David A.

Bruchey, Stuart, ed. see Allain, Louis J.

Bruchey, Stuart, ed. see Andersen, Theodore A.

Bruchey, Stuart, ed. see Andrew, A. Piatt & Kent, Frederick I.

Bruchey, Stuart, ed. see Ankli, Robert E.

Bruchey, Stuart, ed. see Armstrong, Leroy & Denny, J. O.

Bruchey, Stuart, ed. see Arnold, Dean A.

Bruchey, Stuart, ed. see Atkin, John M.

Bruchey, Stuart, ed. see Atkins, Edwin F.

Bruchey, Stuart, ed. see Attles, Henrietta S.

Bruchey, Stuart, ed. see Ayarslan, Solmaz D.

Bruchey, Stuart, ed. see Bain, Foster H. & Read, Thomas T.

Bruchey, Stuart, ed. see Bakerman, Theodore.

Bruchey, Stuart, ed. see Barnes, William C.

Bruchey, Stuart, ed. see Barnett, Harold J.

Bruchey, Stuart, ed. see Bartley, Ernest R.

Bruchey, Stuart, ed. see Bassiry, Reza.

Bruchey, Stuart, ed. see Bayard, Charles J.

Bruchey, Stuart, ed. see Becker, Clarence F.

Bruchey, Stuart, ed. see Bensidoun, Sylvain.

Bruchey, Stuart, ed. see Bentley, Jerome T.

Bruchey, Stuart, ed. see Blair, William A. & Clark, W. A.

Bruchey, Stuart, ed. see Bledsoe, Samuel T.

Bruchey, Stuart, ed. see Bogen, Jules I. & Nadler, Marcus.

Bruchey, Stuart, ed. see Bogue, Margaret B.

Bruchey, Stuart, ed. see Bolles, Albert S.

Bruchey, Stuart, ed. see Bouhabib, Abdallah R.

Bruchey, Stuart, ed. see Boyd, William H.

Bruchey, Stuart, ed. see Brayer, Herbert O.

Bruchey, Stuart, ed. see Brewster, Kingman, Jr.

Bruchey, Stuart, ed. see Brooks, John G.

Bruchey, Stuart, ed. see Brosselin, Arlette.

Bruchey, Stuart, ed. see Brumont, Francis.

Bruchey, Stuart, ed. see Bunn, Verne A.

Bruchey, Stuart, ed. see Bunzel, John A.

Bruchey, Stuart, ed. see Burgess, Eugene W. & Harbison, Frederick H.

Bruchey, Stuart, ed. see Caldwell, Stephen A.

Bruchey, Stuart, ed. see Calef, Wesley.

Bruchey, Stuart, ed. see Callis, Helmut G.

Bruchey, Stuart, ed. see Cannon, James G.

Bruchey, Stuart, ed. see Carlson, Rodger D.

Bruchey, Stuart, ed. see Carlson, Theodore L.

Bruchey, Stuart, jt. ed. see Carosso, Vincent P.

Bruchey, Stuart, ed. see Carpenter, Walter H., Jr. & Handler, Edward.

Bruchey, Stuart, ed. see Carr, Hobart C.

Bruchey, Stuart, ed. see Carstensen, Vernon.

Bruchey, Stuart, ed. see Cartinhour, Gaines T. & Westerfield, Ray B.

Bruchey, Stuart, ed. see Cary, John W.

Bruchey, Stuart, ed. see Casey, Joan D.

Bruchey, Stuart, ed. see Cecchi, Anna.

Bruchey, Stuart, ed. see Cederberg, Herbert.

Bruchey, Stuart, ed. see Challa, Krishna.

Bruchey, Stuart, ed. see Chandler, Alfred D., Jr.

Bruchey, Stuart, jt. ed. see Chandler, Alfred D., Jr.

Bruchey, Stuart, ed. see Chandler, Alfred N.

Bruchey, Stuart, ed. see Chandler, David L.

Bruchey, Stuart, ed. see Chapman, Berlin B.

Bruchey, Stuart, ed. see Chapman, John M. & Westerfield, Ray B.

Bruchey, Stuart, ed. see Cherington, Charles R.

Bruchey, Stuart, ed. see Christensen, Roland C.

Bruchey, Stuart, ed. see Clawson, Marion.

Bruchey, Stuart, ed. see Cleaveland, John & Hutchinson, G. S.

Bruchey, Stuart, ed. see Cleveland, Frederick A. & Powell, Fred W.

Bruchey, Stuart, ed. see Cleveland, Harlan, et al.

Bruchey, Stuart, ed. see Cohen, Jon S.

Bruchey, Stuart, ed. see Coles, Harry L.

Bruchey, Stuart, jt. ed. see Colton, Joel.

Bruchey, Stuart, ed. see Commerce Clearing House, Inc.

Bruchey, Stuart, ed. see Conway, Thomas, Jr. & Patterson, Ernest M.

Bruchey, Stuart, ed. see Cookenboo, Leslie, Jr.

Bruchey, Stuart, ed. see Copp, Henry N.

Bruchey, Stuart, ed. see Cotroneo, Ross R.

Bruchey, Stuart, ed. see Crippen, Waldo.

Bruchey, Stuart, ed. see Crowther, Samuel.

Bruchey, Stuart, ed. see Daggett, Stuart.

Bruchey, Stuart, ed. see Dagneau, Jacques.

Bruchey, Stuart, ed. see Dale, Alfred G.

Bruchey, Stuart, ed. see Dalgaard, Bruce R.

Bruchey, Stuart, ed. see Dana, Samuel T. & Krueger, Myron.

Bruchey, Stuart, jt. ed. see Daniel, James.

Bruchey, Stuart, ed. see Daughters, Charles G.

Bruchey, Stuart, ed. see David, Jules.

Bruchey, Stuart, ed. see Davies, Robert B.

Bruchey, Stuart, ed. see Davis, A. M.

Bruchey, Stuart, ed. see Davis, John A.

Bruchey, Stuart, ed. see Davison, Stanley S.

Bruchey, Stuart, ed. see Dawes, Charles G.

Bruchey, Stuart, ed. see Daynes, Gary.

Bruchey, Stuart, ed. see De Bodinat, Henri.

Bruchey, Stuart, ed. see De Brabander, Guido L.

Bruchey, Stuart, ed. see De La Torre, Jose, Jr.

Bruchey, Stuart, ed. see Deal, Zack J., III.

Bruchey, Stuart, ed. see Deegan, James F.

Bruchey, Stuart, ed. see Dente, Leonard A.

Bruchey, Stuart, ed. see Desert, Gabriel.

Bruchey, Stuart, ed. see Dewey, Davis & Shugrue, Martin.

Bruchey, Stuart, ed. see Dickey, George E.

Bruchey, Stuart, ed. see Diller, Robert.

Bruchey, Stuart, ed. see Dillon, Robert J.

Bruchey, Stuart, ed. see Dixon, Frank H.

Bruchey, Stuart, ed. see Douty, Christopher M.

Bruchey, Stuart, ed. see Dubin, Michael.

Bruchey, Stuart, ed. see DuBoff, Richard B.

Bruchey, Stuart, ed. see Dufwa, Thamar E.

Bruchey, Stuart, ed. see Duke, Basil W.

Bruchey, Stuart, ed. see Dunbar, Charles F.

Bruchey, Stuart, ed. see Dunning, John H.

Bruchey, Stuart, ed. see Eckenrode, Hamilton J. & Edmunds, Pocahontas W.

Bruchey, Stuart, ed. see Edelberg, Guillermo S.

Bruchey, Stuart, ed. see Eichner, Donald O.

Bruchey, Stuart, ed. see Elliott, William Y., et al.

Bruchey, Stuart, ed. see Ellis, Joyce.

Bruchey, Stuart, ed. see Ellis, Theodore J.

Bruchey, Stuart, ed. see Engberg, Holger L.

Bruchey, Stuart, ed. see Ephraim, Asher.

Bruchey, Stuart, ed. see Epstein, Ralph C.

Bruchey, Stuart, ed. see Erickson, Edward W.

Bruchey, Stuart, ed. see Ernst, Joseph W.

Bruchey, Stuart, ed. see Eysenbach, Mary L.

Bruchey, Stuart, ed. see Fenichel, Allen H.

Bruchey, Stuart, ed. see Fierain, Jacques.

Bruchey, Stuart, ed. see Finney, Katherine.

Bruchey, Stuart, ed. see Finnie, David H.

Bruchey, Stuart, ed. see Fisher, John S.

Bruchey, Stuart, ed. see Fiske, Amos K.

Bruchey, Stuart, ed. see Flink, Salomon J.

Bruchey, Stuart, ed. see Foster, Abram J.

Bruchey, Stuart, ed. see Foulke, Roy A.

Bruchey, Stuart, ed. see Fournier, Leslie T.

Bruchey, Stuart, ed. see Fulda, Michael.

Bruchey, Stuart, ed. see Galloway, J. D.

Bruchey, Stuart, ed. see Gates, Paul W.

Bruchey, Stuart, ed. see Gates, Paul W. & Swenson, Robert W.

Bruchey, Stuart, jt. ed. see Gates, Paul W.

Bruchey, Stuart, ed. see Gates, Theodore R. & Linden, Fabian.

Bruchey, Stuart, ed. see George, Peter J.

Bruchey, Stuart, ed. see Gessford, John E.

Bruchey, Stuart, ed. see Gilbreth, Terry J.

Bruchey, Stuart, ed. see Glover, John D.

Bruchey, Stuart, ed. see Gordon, Wendell C.

Bruchey, Stuart, ed. see Goreux, Louis-Marie.

Bruchey, Stuart, ed. see Gould, Clarence P.

Bruchey, Stuart, ed. see Granger, J. T.

Bruchey, Stuart, ed. see Grayson, C. Jackson.

Bruchey, Stuart, ed. see Greever, William S.

Bruchey, Stuart, ed. see Grodinsky, Julius.

Bruchey, Stuart, ed. see Guignet, Philippe.

Bruchey, Stuart, ed. see Haas, Harold M.

Bruchey, Stuart, ed. see Haines, Michael R.

Bruchey, Stuart, ed. see Hall, Harry S.

Bruchey, Stuart, ed. see Hamburg, James F.

Bruchey, Stuart, ed. see Hammond, Charles.

Bruchey, Stuart, ed. see Harder, Klaus P.

Bruchey, Stuart, ed. see Harnsberger, John L.

Bruchey, Stuart, ed. see Harper, Ann K.

Bruchey, Stuart, ed. see Harrington, Fred H.

Bruchey, Stuart, ed. see Harrison, Fairfax.

Bruchey, Stuart, ed. see Hausman, William J.

Bruchey, Stuart, ed. see Heap, Gwinn H.

Bruchey, Stuart, ed. see Helderman, Leonard C.

Bruchey, Stuart, ed. see Heller, Kenneth H.

Bruchey, Stuart, ed. see Hernandez, Pedro M.

Bruchey, Stuart, ed. see Herring, James M.

Bruchey, Stuart, ed. see Heyn, Udo.

Bruchey, Stuart, ed. see Hinchman, T. H.

Bruchey, Stuart, ed. see Hoffman, Elizabeth.

Bruchey, Stuart, ed. see Hohorst, Gerd.

Bruchey, Stuart, ed. see Holbrook, Stewart H.

Bruchey, Stuart, ed. see Hollander, Edward, et al.

Bruchey, Stuart, ed. see Holt, Charles F.

Bruchey, Stuart, ed. see Howard, Marshall C.

Bruchey, Stuart, ed. see Hubert, Philip G., Jr.

Bruchey, Stuart, ed. see Huertas, Thomas F.

Bruchey, Stuart, ed. see Hufbauer, G. & Adler, F. W.

Bruchey, Stuart, jt. ed. see Hull, Walter.

Bruchey, Stuart, ed. see Hunt, Pearson.

Bruchey, Stuart, ed. see Hutchinson, William T.

Bruchey, Stuart, ed. see Inoki, Takenori.

Bruchey, Stuart, ed. see Ise, John.

Bruchey, Stuart, ed. see Ishii, Osamu.

Bruchey, Stuart, ed. see Jacoby, Henry D.

Bruchey, Stuart, ed. see Jacoby, Neil H. & Saulnier, Raymond J.

Bruchey, Stuart, ed. see Jadwani, Hassanand T.

Bruchey, Stuart, ed. see Jankowski, Manfred.

Bruchey, Stuart, ed. see Jeannet, Jean-Pierre.

Bruchey, Stuart, ed. see Jefferys, James B.

Bruchey, Stuart, ed. see Johnson, Charles J.

Bruchey, Stuart, ed. see Johnson-Hillery, Julie.

Bruchey, Stuart, ed. see Johnson, James P.

Bruchey, Stuart, ed. see Johnson, V. Webster & Barlowe, Raleigh.

Bruchey, Stuart, ed. see Kane, Thomas P. & Corosso, Vincent.

B

Bruchey, Stuart, ed. see Kaplan, Abraham D.
Bruchey, Stuart, ed. see Katz, Harold.
Bruchey, Stuart, ed. see Keating, William T.
Bruchey, Stuart, ed. see Kemmerer, Edwin W.
Bruchey, Stuart, ed. see Kennan, George F.
Bruchey, Stuart, ed. see Kennis, Kenneth G.
Bruchey, Stuart, ed. see Kijakazi, Kilolo.
Bruchey, Stuart, ed. see Kilfoil, Jack F.
Bruchey, Stuart, ed. see Kirchhain, Gunter.
Bruchey, Stuart, ed. see Kniffin, William H., Jr.
Bruchey, Stuart, ed. see Kolb, Jeffrey A.
Bruchey, Stuart, ed. see Konopa, Leonard J.
Bruchey, Stuart, ed. see Konz, Leo E.
Bruchey, Stuart, ed. see Kossler, Armin.
Bruchey, Stuart, ed. see Krueger, Leonard B.
Bruchey, Stuart, ed. see La Potin, Armand S.
Bruchey, Stuart, ed. see Lampen, Dorothy.
Bruchey, Stuart, ed. see Lang, Aldon S.
Bruchey, Stuart, ed. see Langston, L. H.
Bruchey, Stuart, jt. ed. see Laughlin, J. Laurence, Jr.
Bruchey, Stuart, ed. see Lawrence, Anthony G.
Bruchey, Stuart, ed. see Lee, Lawrence B.
Bruchey, Stuart, ed. see Lee, Susan P.
Bruchey, Stuart, ed. see Lee, W. R.
Bruchey, Stuart, ed. see Legler, John B.
Bruchey, Stuart, ed. see Lehman, Edward R.
Bruchey, Stuart, ed. see LeVeen, E. Phillip.
Bruchey, Stuart, ed. see Lewis, Cleona & Schlotterbeck, Karl T.
Bruchey, Stuart, ed. see Lewis, Oscar.
Bruchey, Stuart, ed. see Lightner, David L.
Bruchey, Stuart, ed. see Logar, Cyril M.
Bruchey, Stuart, ed. see Longley, Ronald S.
Bruchey, Stuart, ed. see Lopata, Edwin L.
Bruchey, Stuart, ed. see Lovett, H. A.
Bruchey, Stuart, ed. see Lubrano, Annteresa.
Bruchey, Stuart, ed. see Lumer, Wilfred.
Bruchey, Stuart, ed. see Lyons, Beverly P.
Bruchey, Stuart, ed. see Macaluso, Donald G.
Bruchey, Stuart, ed. see Macaulay, Frederick R.
Bruchey, Stuart, ed. see MacMurray, Robert R.
Bruchey, Stuart, ed. see Macveagh, Rogers.
Bruchey, Stuart, ed. see Malone, Joseph J.
Bruchey, Stuart, ed. see Manes, Rene P.
Bruchey, Stuart, ed. see Marcus, Kenneth K.
Bruchey, Stuart, ed. see Marker, Gordon A.
Bruchey, Stuart, ed. see Martz, Clyde O.
Bruchey, Stuart, ed. see Mascarenhas, Oswald A.
Bruchey, Stuart, ed. see McAlpine, R. W.
Bruchey, Stuart, ed. see McDonald, Philip R.
Bruchey, Stuart, ed. see McGee, John S.
Bruchey, Stuart, ed. see McKenzie, Fred A.
Bruchey, Stuart, ed. see McKitrick, Reuben.
Bruchey, Stuart, ed. see Melby, Eric D.
Bruchey, Stuart, ed. see Meloe, Torleif.
Bruchey, Stuart, ed. see Mendels, Franklin F.
Bruchey, Stuart, ed. see Merwin, Charles L.
Bruchey, Stuart, ed. see Metzer, Jacob.
Bruchey, Stuart, ed. see Million, John W.
Bruchey, Stuart, ed. see Minneman, Paul G.
Bruchey, Stuart, ed. see Mitchell, Waldo F.
Bruchey, Stuart, ed. see Moe, Thorvald.
Bruchey, Stuart, ed. see Montgomery, Mary & Clawson, Marion.
Bruchey, Stuart, ed. see Moore, Elwood S.
Bruchey, Stuart, ed. see Moore, John R.
Bruchey, Stuart, ed. see Moore, Russell M.
Bruchey, Stuart, ed. see Morris, Bruce R.
Bruchey, Stuart, ed. see Morris, Keith.
Bruchey, Stuart, ed. see Mosk, Sanford A.
Bruchey, Stuart, ed. see Mueller, Reinhold C.
Bruchey, Stuart, ed. see Mullin, John.
Bruchey, Stuart, ed. see Nash, Gerald D.
Bruchey, Stuart, ed. see National Industrial Conference Board Staff.
Bruchey, Stuart, ed. see National Planning Association Staff.
Bruchey, Stuart, ed. see Neifeld, Morris R.
Bruchey, Stuart, ed. see Netschert, Bruce C.
Bruchey, Stuart, ed. see Neuburger, Hugh M.
Bruchey, Stuart, ed. see Newcomb, H. T.
Bruchey, Stuart, ed. see Newell, William H.
Bruchey, Stuart, ed. see Nipp, Luitgard.
Bruchey, Stuart, ed. see Nordyke, James W.
Bruchey, Stuart, ed. see Nowill, Paul H.
Bruchey, Stuart, ed. see Noyes, Alexander D.
Bruchey, Stuart, ed. see O'Callaghan, Jerry A.
Bruchey, Stuart, ed. see O'Connor, Harvey.
Bruchey, Stuart, ed. see O'Connor, Walter F.
Bruchey, Stuart, ed. see Odell, Marcia L.
Bruchey, Stuart, ed. see Ogilvie, John S.
Bruchey, Stuart, ed. see Ohlin, Per G.
Bruchey, Stuart, ed. see Okada, Yasue.
Bruchey, Stuart, ed. see O'Reilly, Evelyn M.
Bruchey, Stuart, ed. see Otenasek, Mildred B.
Bruchey, Stuart, ed. see Ottoson, Howard W., et al.
Bruchey, Stuart, ed. see Overlach, Theodore W.
Bruchey, Stuart, ed. see Paas, Martha W.
Bruchey, Stuart, ed. see Pagoulatos, Angelos.
Bruchey, Stuart, ed. see Pallanti, Giuseppe.
Bruchey, Stuart, ed. see Papendieck, Henner.
Bruchey, Stuart, ed. see Parks, Robert J.
Bruchey, Stuart, ed. see Parsons, Burke A.
Bruchey, Stuart, ed. see Patten, Claudius B.
Bruchey, Stuart, ed. see Pattison, William D.
Bruchey, Stuart, ed. see Pendergrass, Bonnie B.
Bruchey, Stuart, ed. see Pepper, Roger S.
Bruchey, Stuart, ed. see Perkins, J. R.
Bruchey, Stuart, ed. see Persaud, Thakoor.
Bruchey, Stuart, ed. see Peters, William E.
Bruchey, Stuart, ed. see Petrowski, William R.
Bruchey, Stuart, ed. see Phelps, William C.
Bruchey, Stuart, ed. see Phillips, Chester A.
Bruchey, Stuart, ed. see Phillips, David G.
Bruchey, Stuart, ed. see Porter, Robert P.
Bruchey, Stuart, ed. see Powlison, Keith.
Bruchey, Stuart, ed. see Preston, Howard H.
Bruchey, Stuart, ed. see Primack, Martin L.
Bruchey, Stuart, ed. see Pris, Claude.
Bruchey, Stuart, ed. see Pritchett, Bruce M.
Bruchey, Stuart, ed. see Prochnow, Peter-Michael.
Bruchey, Stuart, ed. see Prosper, Peter A., Jr.
Bruchey, Stuart, ed. see Proxmire, William.
Bruchey, Stuart, ed. see Przeworski, Joanne F.
Bruchey, Stuart, ed. see Queen, George S.
Bruchey, Stuart, ed. see Rakestraw, Lawrence.
Bruchey, Stuart, ed. see Raveed, Sion.
Bruchey, Stuart, ed. see Reed, Clyde G.
Bruchey, Stuart, ed. see Reed, S. G.
Bruchey, Stuart, ed. see Reeder, Clarence A., Jr.
Bruchey, Stuart, ed. see Renforth, William & Raveed, Sion.
Bruchey, Stuart, ed. see Rettig, Rudi.
Bruchey, Stuart, ed. see Richards, Max D.
Bruchey, Stuart, ed. see Ripley, William Z.
Bruchey, Stuart, ed. see Rippy, J. Fred.
Bruchey, Stuart, ed. see Robinson, John R.
Bruchey, Stuart, ed. see Robinson, William W.
Bruchey, Stuart, ed. see Rollins, George W.
Bruchey, Stuart, ed. see Rostow, Walt W.
Bruchey, Stuart, ed. see Russell, Robert R.
Bruchey, Stuart, ed. see Saly, Pierre.
Bruchey, Stuart, ed. see Sanborn, John B.
Bruchey, Stuart, ed. see Schachter, Joseph.
Bruchey, Stuart, ed. see Schaefer, Donald F.
Bruchey, Stuart, ed. see Schmitz, Mark.
Bruchey, Stuart, ed. see Schor, Stanley S.
Bruchey, Stuart, ed. see Schramm, Gunter.
Bruchey, Stuart, ed. see Scott, William A.
Bruchey, Stuart, ed. see Secretan, J. H.
Bruchey, Stuart, ed. see Shambaugh, Benjamin F.
Bruchey, Stuart, ed. see Sharpless, John B.
Bruchey, Stuart, ed. see Sheridan, George J., Jr.
Bruchey, Stuart, ed. see Shields, Roger E.
Bruchey, Stuart, ed. see Shrimpton, Colin.
Bruchey, Stuart, ed. see Siddiqi, Shahid.
Bruchey, Stuart, ed. see Simon, Simon M.
Bruchey, Stuart, ed. see Smathers, George H.
Bruchey, Stuart, ed. see Smith, David B.
Bruchey, Stuart, ed. see Smith, Philip R.
Bruchey, Stuart, ed. see Sorey, Gordon K.
Bruchey, Stuart, ed. see Southard, Frank A., Jr.
Bruchey, Stuart, ed. see Spann, Robert M.
Bruchey, Stuart, ed. see Spooner, Robert D.
Bruchey, Stuart, ed. see Stafford, Marshall P.
Bruchey, Stuart, ed. see Staley, Eugene.
Bruchey, Stuart, ed. see Stanford Research Institute Staff.
Bruchey, Stuart, ed. see Starr, John W., Jr.
Bruchey, Stuart, ed. see Steele, Henry B.
Bruchey, Stuart, ed. see Stern, Siegfried.
Bruchey, Stuart, ed. see Stettler, Henry L.
Bruchey, Stuart, ed. see Stewart, Lowell O.
Bruchey, Stuart, ed. see Stigum, Marcia L.
Bruchey, Stuart, ed. see Still, Jack W.
Bruchey, Stuart, ed. see Stopford, John M.
Bruchey, Stuart, ed. see Strausberg, Stephen.
Bruchey, Stuart, ed. see Striner, Herbert E.
Bruchey, Stuart, ed. see Strout, Alan M.
Bruchey, Stuart, ed. see Sturm, James L.
Bruchey, Stuart, ed. see Sutton, Robert M.
Bruchey, Stuart, ed. see Talbot, Frederick A.
Bruchey, Stuart, ed. see Tatter, Henry W.
Bruchey, Stuart, ed. see Taylor, George & Neu, Irene D.
Bruchey, Stuart, ed. see Taylor, Paul S.
Bruchey, Stuart, ed. see Teele, Ray P.
Bruchey, Stuart, ed. see Tenebaum, Marcel.
Bruchey, Stuart, ed. see Thbaut, Louis.
Bruchey, Stuart, ed. see Thomas, Robert P.
Bruchey, Stuart, ed. see Thomas, Rollin G.
Bruchey, Stuart, ed. see Thorp, Rosemary & Bertram, Geoffrey.
Bruchey, Stuart, ed. see Thwaite, et al.
Bruchey, Stuart, ed. see Tortella, Gabriel C.
Bruchey, Stuart, ed. see Tosiello, Rosario J.
Bruchey, Stuart, ed. see Toyne, Brian.
Bruchey, Stuart, ed. see Trent, Logan D.
Bruchey, Stuart, ed. see Tsurumi, Yoshihiro.
Bruchey, Stuart, ed. see U. S. Comptroller of the Currency Staff.
Bruchey, Stuart, ed. see U. S. Congress, House of Representatives Staff.
Bruchey, Stuart, ed. see U. S. Congress, Senate Staff.
Bruchey, Stuart, ed. see U. S. Department of Commerce & Labor Staff.
Bruchey, Stuart, ed. see U. S. Department of Commerce Staff.
Bruchey, Stuart, ed. see U. S. Federal Trade Commission Staff.
Bruchey, Stuart, ed. see U. S. House of Representative Subcommittee No. 2 o.
Bruchey, Stuart, ed. see U. S. House of Representatives Select Committee on.
Bruchey, Stuart, ed. see U. S. House of Representatives Staff.
Bruchey, Stuart, ed. see U. S. Senate Committee on Banking & Currency.
Bruchey, Stuart, ed. see U. S. Senate Select Committee on Small Business, S.
Bruchey, Stuart, ed. see U. S. Senate Staff.
Bruchey, Stuart, ed. see University of Pittsburgh, Bureau of Business Resea.
Bruchey, Stuart, ed. see Van Name, Willard G.
Bruchey, Stuart, ed. see Van Young, James.
Bruchey, Stuart, ed. see Vanderlip, Frank A.
Bruchey, Stuart, ed. see Vatter, Harold G.
Bruchey, Stuart, ed. see Vatter, Paul A.
Bruchey, Stuart, ed. see Viallon, Jean-Baptiste.
Bruchey, Stuart, ed. see Vickery, William E.
Bruchey, Stuart, ed. see Villard, Henry.
Bruchey, Stuart, ed. see Villiers, Patrick.
Bruchey, Stuart, ed. see Von Laer, Hermann.
Bruchey, Stuart, ed. see Wade, William W.
Bruchey, Stuart, ed. see Walters, R. H.
Bruchey, Stuart, ed. see Waltrip, John R.
Bruchey, Stuart, ed. see Waters, Joseph P.
Bruchey, Stuart, ed. see Watkins, Leonard L.
Bruchey, Stuart, ed. see Wedemeyer, Karl E.
Bruchey, Stuart, ed. see Weissman, Rudolph L.
Bruchey, Stuart, ed. see Wells, Louis T., Jr.
Bruchey, Stuart, ed. see Wendt, Lloyd & Kogan, Herman.
Bruchey, Stuart, ed. see Westerfield, Ray B.
Bruchey, Stuart, ed. see Whartenby, Franklee G.
Bruchey, Stuart, ed. see Wheelwright, William B.
Bruchey, Stuart, ed. see Whiflier, Austin.
Bruchey, Stuart, jt. ed. see Whyman, John.
Bruchey, Stuart, ed. see Wiel, Samuel C.
Bruchey, Stuart, ed. see Wilkinson, Norman R.
Bruchey, Stuart, ed. see Willis, Henry P.
Bruchey, Stuart, ed. see Winkler, Donald R.
Bruchey, Stuart, ed. see Winkler, Max.
Bruchey, Stuart, ed. see Winter, Charles E.
Bruchey, Stuart, ed. see Wirth, Fremont P.
Bruchey, Stuart, ed. see Wright, Benjamin C.
Bruchey, Stuart, ed. see Wright, Ivan.
Bruchey, Stuart, ed. see Yeoman, Wayne A.
Bruchey, Stuart, ed. see Yudin, Elinor B.
Bruchey, Stuart, ed. see Zeigler, Harmon.
Bruchey, Stuart R., et al. Money & Banking in Maryland. LC 96-558. 1996. 65.00 (*0-938420-52-6*) MD Hist.
Bruchey, Stuart Weems, jt. ed. see Coclanis, Peter A.
Bruchez, Dardo, tr. see McDowell, Josh.
Bruchez, Dardo, tr. see Tozer, A. W.
Bruchez, Dardo L. La Doncella de Galilea.Tr. of Maiden of Galilee. (SPA.). 70p. 1993. pap. 4.50 (*1-56063-542-8*, 498585) Editorial Unilit.
Bruchhof, Georg. Britischer Ruckzug Aus Asien - Etappensieg der Asiaten? Die Indo-Britischen Wirtschaftsbeziehungen, 1939-1950: Politische und Wirtschaftliche Aspekte des "Transfer of Power" und die Wandlung der Direkten Herrschaft in Die Indirekte Einflussnahme Mittels Finanzoekonomischer Vormachtstellung des Westens. (Europaische Hochschulschriften Ser.: Reihe 3, Band 777). (GER.). XII, 335p. 1998. pap. 51.95 (*3-631-32855-9*) P Lang Pubng.
Bruchhof, Georg. Asians Ahead after the First Round? Indo-British Economic Relations from 1939 to 1950 Political & Economic Aspects of the "Transfer of Power" & the Change from Direct Rule to Indirect Influence Through Western Financial & Economic Supremacy. LC 98-33943. (European University Studies: Series 3, Vol. 780). 146p. 1998. pap. 31.95 (*0-8204-3591-0*) P Lang Pubng.
— Asians Ahead after the First Round? Indo-British Economic Relations from 1939 to 1950 Political & Economic Aspects of the "Transfer of Power" & the Change from Direct Rule to Indirect Influence Through Western Financial & Economic Supremacy. LC 98-33943. (European University Studies: Series 3, Vol. 780). 146p. 1998. pap. 31.95 (*3-631-33280-7*) P Lang Pubng.
Bruchi, Phil. Mind Aerobics: The Fundamentals of Memory Fitness. Levinson, Robin, ed. LC 97-210287. (Illus.). x, 102p. (Orig.). 1997. pap. 14.95 (*0-9656555-0-4*) Mind Aerobics.
Bruchis, Michael. Nations, Nationalities Peoples: A Study of the Nationality Policies of the Communist Party in Soviet Moldavia. 230p. 1984. text 55.50 (*0-88033-057-0*, Pub. by East Eur Monographs) Col U Pr.
— One Step Back, Two Steps Forward: On the Language Policy of the Communist Party of the Soviet Union in the National Republics. (East European Monographs: No. 109). 371p. 1982. text 64.50 (*0-88033-002-3*, Pub. by East Eur Monographs) Col U Pr.
Bruchis, Michael. Republic of Moldavia: From the Collapse of the Soviet Empire to the Restoration of the Russian Empire. LC 97-60359. 225p. 1997. lib. bdg. 31.50 (*0-88033-373-1*, 476, Pub. by East Eur Monographs) Col U Pr.
Bruchis, Michael. U. S. S. R. Languages & Realities: Nations, Leaders, & Scholars. (East European Monographs: No. 250). 393p. 1988. text 96.50 (*0-88033-147-X*, Pub. by East Eur Monographs) Col U Pr.
Bruchovsky, Nicholas & Goldine, James H., eds. Drug & Hormone Resistance in Neoplasia: Basic Concepts, Vol. I. LC 96-2084. (Illus.). 208p. 1983. 118.00 (*0-8493-6516-3*, RC271, CRC Reprint) Franklin.
— Drug & Hormone Resistance in Neoplasia: Clinical Concepts, Vol. II. (Illus.). 184p. 1983. 105.00 (*0-8493-6517-1*, RC271, CRC Reprint) Franklin.
Brucia, Margaret A. & Henry, Madeline M. Horace Satire 1.9: The Boor. 1998. pap., teacher ed. 3.00 (*0-86516-429-0*) Bolchazy-Carducci.
Brucia, Margaret A., ed. see Horace, et al.
Brucie, Thomas. Residential Construction Costs, 1990. 9th ed. Felber, Paul, ed. (Illus.). 193p. (Orig.). 1990. pap. 49.95 (*0-931708-22-2*) Saylor.
Bruck, Arthur Moeller Van Den, see Moeller Van Den Bruck, Arthur.
Bruck, Bill. The Essential Book for Microsoft Office: The Get-It-Done Tutorial for Professionals. 1996. pap. text 27.99 (*0-7615-0430-3*) Prima Pub.
— The Essential Office 2000 Book. LC 98-67709. 800p. 1999. pap. 29.99 (*0-7615-1886-X*, Prima Tech) Prima Pub.
— The Essential Office 97 Book. LC 96-72126. (Essential Book Ser.). 600p. 1997. per. 27.99 (*0-7615-0969-0*) Prima Pub.
— Using Novell GroupWise. LC 94-69625. (Illus.). 450p. (Orig.). 1994. 24.99 (*0-7897-0086-7*) Que.
— Using Novell Groupwise XTD, Special Edition. 600p. 1998. 39.99 (*0-7897-0690-3*) Que.
Bruck, Bill, et al. Using Perfect Office: Special Edition. (Illus.). 804p. (Orig.). 1995. 34.99 (*0-7897-0089-1*) Que.
Bruck, Connie. The Predators' Ball: The Inside Story of Drexel Burnham & the Rise of the Junk Bond Raiders. 384p. 1989. pap. 13.95 (*0-14-012090-4*, Penguin Bks) Viking Penguin.
Bruck, David. Plant Biology. 1998. pap., lab manual ed. 25.95 (*0-7872-5268-9*) Kendall-Hunt.
— Plant Biology Laboratory Manual for Biology I. 156p. (C). 1996. pap. text, spiral bd. 19.95 (*0-7872-2809-5*) Kendall-Hunt.
*Bruck, Edith. Who Loves You Like This. 2nd ed. Kelso, Thomas, tr. 120p. 2000. pap. 14.95 (*0-9664913-7-8*, Pub. by Paul Dry Bks) IPG Chicago.
Bruck, Eva D., jt. auth. see Crawford, Tad.
Bruck, G., ed. Laser Materials Processing. (Illus.). 375p. 1989. 214.95 (*0-387-51537-2*) Spr-Verlag.
Bruck, H. A. The Story of Astronomy in Education: From Its Beginnings until 1975. 151p. 1984. 25.00 (*0-85224-480-0*, Pub. by Edinburgh U Pr) Col U Pr.
Bruck, Julie. The Woman Downstairs. 64p. 1993. pap. 11.95 (*0-919626-66-1*, Pub. by Brick Bks) Genl Dist Srvs.
Bruck, M. T. Exercises in Practical Astronomy: Using Photographs. (Illus.). 124p. (C). 1990. 26.00 (*0-7503-0061-2*) IOP Pub.
Bruck, Maggie, jt. auth. see Ceci, Stephen J.
Bruck, Michael Von, see Von Bruck, Michael.
Bruck, Nicholas, ed. Capital Markets under Inflation. LC 82-16623. 435p. 1982. 45.00 (*0-275-90768-6*, C0768, Praeger Pubs) Greenwood.
Bruck, Nicole S. Government Home Foreclosures & Affordable Financing. 2nd rev. ed. Shemwell, Chris D., ed. (Government Ser.: Vol. II). (Illus.). 132p. 1996. pap. 12.95 (*1-889976-00-8*) Natl Info.
— Government Loans & Assistance Small Business Directory. Shemwell, Chris D., ed. (Government Ser.: No. III). (Illus.). 136p. 1997. pap. 44.99 (*1-889976-01-6*) Natl Info.
Bruck, Peter. Von der "Store Front Church" Zum "American Dream" James Baldwin und der Amerikanische Rassenkonflikt. (Bochumer Anglistische Studien: No. 2). (GER., Illus.). viii, 147p. 1975. pap. 24.00 (*90-6032-056-5*, Pub. by B R Gruner) Humanities.
Bruck, Peter, ed. The Black American Short Story in the Twentieth Century: A Collection of Critical Essays. viii, 209p. 1977. pap. 26.00 (*90-6032-085-9*, Pub. by B R Gruner) Humanities.
Bruck, Peter A., jt. ed. see Raboy, Marc.
Bruck, Stephen D. Properties of Biomaterials in the Physiological Environment. 160p. 1980. 110.00 (*0-8493-5685-7*, R857, CRC Reprint) Franklin.
Bruck, Stephen D., ed. Controlled Drug Delivery, 2 vols. LC 82-12921. 528p. 1983. 116.00 (*0-8493-5181-2*, RS201, CRC Reprint); 153.00 (*0-8493-5182-0*, RS201, CRC Reprint) Franklin.
Bruckberger, R. L. God & Politics. LC 78-190754. (Howard Greenfield Bk.). 1971. 9.95 (*0-87955-302-2*) O'Hara.
Bruckdorfer, K. R. & Rice-Evans, Catherine A., eds. Oxidative Stress, Lipoproteins & Cardiovascular Dysfunction. (Portland Press Research Monographs: Vol. 6). 184p. (C). 1995. text 102.00 (*1-85578-045-3*, Pub. by Portland Pr Ltd) Ashgate Pub Co.
*Bruckenstein, Shmuel. Time to Refrain. 92p. 1998. 12.95 (*0-87306-917-X*) Feldheim.
Brucker, Alexander J., jt. auth. see Bloom, Steven M.
Brucker, Betty, jt. auth. see Brucker, Jeff.
Brucker, Gene. Florence: The Golden Age, 1138-1737. 278p. 1998. pap. 32.50 (*0-520-21522-2*, Pub. by U CA Pr) Cal Prin Full Svc.
Brucker, Gene A. The Civic World of Early Renaissance Florence. LC 76-45891. 539p. reprint ed. pap. 167.10 (*0-8357-2612-6*, 203993200014) Bks Demand.
— Giovanni & Lusanna: Love & Marriage in Renaissance Florence. LC 85-16556. (Illus.). 100p. 1986. pap. 14.95 (*0-520-06328-7*, Pub. by U CA Pr) Cal Prin Full Svc.
— Renaissance Florence. LC 82-40097. (Illus.). 320p. 1983. pap. 16.95 (*0-520-04695-1*, Pub. by U CA Pr) Cal Prin Full Svc.
— Renaissance Florence. LC 74-10921. 320p. 1975. reprint ed. lib. bdg. 24.50 (*0-88275-184-0*) Krieger.
Brucker, Gene A., ed. Two Memoirs of Renaissance Florence: The Diaries of Buonaccorso Pitti & Gregorio Dati. Martines, Julia, tr. from ITA. 141p. (C). 1991. reprint ed. pap. text 9.95 (*0-88133-622-X*) Waveland Pr.
Brucker, Gene A., et al. History at Berkeley: A Dialog in Three Parts. LC 97-49679. (Chapters in the History of the University of California Ser.: No. 7). (Illus.). 54p. 1998. pap. 10.00 (*0-87772-377-X*) UCB IGS.

B

An Asterisk (*) at the beginning of an entry indicates that the title is appearing for the first time.

Brucker, Herbert. Freedom of Information. LC 81-1711. 307p. 1981. reprint ed. lib. bdg. 65.00 (*0-313-22956-2*, BRFRI, Greenwood Pr) Greenwood.
— Privatization in Eastern Germany: A Neo-Institutional Analysis. LC 96-39063. (German Development Institute Book Ser.: Vol. 8). 304p. (Orig.). (C). 1997. pap. text 37.50 (*0-7146-4335-1*, Pub. by F Cass Pubs) Intl Spec Bk.
Brucker, Janet M. & Wallin, Kelly D., eds. Manual of Pediatric Nursing. LC 95-52479. (Peds Fact Finder Ser.). 450p. 1996. spiral bd. 29.95 (*0-316-11451-0*) Lppncott W & W.
Brucker, Jeff & Brucker, Betty. Preparation & Presentation of the Show Dog: The Complete Handling Guide. 3rd ed. LC 95-44723. (Illus.). 96p. 1995. reprint ed. pap. 12.95 (*0-931866-80-4*) Alpine Pubns.
Brucker, Johann J. Historia Critica Philosophiae a Mundi Incunabulis ad Nostram Usque Aetatem Deducta, Bd. 6. (Historia Philosophiae Ser.: No. 4). (GER.). 176p. 1975. reprint ed. write for info. (*3-487-05807-3*) G Olms Pubs.
Brucker, Meredith B. Close to the Stars. large type ed. (Dales Romance Ser.). 299p. 1993. pap. 18.99 (*1-85389-370-6*) Ulverscroft.
— One Love Forever. large type ed. (Linford Romance Library). 368p. 1993. pap. 16.99 (*0-7089-7399-X*, Linford) Ulverscroft.
Brucker, Peter. Scheduling Algorithms. 2nd enl. rev. ed. LC 98-16264. (Illus.). xii, 342p. 1998. 89.95 (*3-540-64105-X*) Spr-Verlag.
— Scheduling Algorithms, Vol. X. (Illus.). 326p. 1995. 98.00 (*3-540-60087-6*) Spr-Verlag.
Brucker, Roger W. & Watson, Richard A. The Longest Cave. LC 86-15537. 360p. 1987. pap. 17.95 (*0-8093-1322-7*) S Ill U Pr.
Brucker, Roger W., jt. auth. see Borden, James D.
Brucker, Roger W., jt. auth. see Lawrence, Joe, Jr.
Brucker, Roger W., jt. auth. see Murray, Robert K.
Brucker, Roger W., ed. see Crowther, Patricia P., et al.
Bruckerhoff, Charles E. Between Classes: Faculty Life at Truman High. 160p. (C). 1991. pap. text 17.95 (*0-8077-3075-0*) Tchrs Coll.
Bruckheim, Allan H. Answers from the Family Doctor: Three Hundred Fifty Questions Patients Ask Most. LC 93-37715. 384p. 1994. pap. 12.95 (*1-56943-006-3*) NTC Contemp Pub Co.
Bruckheim, Allan H., jt. ed. see Bollet, Alfred J.
Bruckheimer, Linda. Dreaming Southern. LC 98-35761. 263p. 1999. 23.95 (*0-525-94453-2*, Dutt) Dutton Plume.
***Bruckheimer, Linda.** Dreaming Southern. 2000. pap. 12.95 (*0-452-28036-2*, Plume) Dutton Plume.
Bruckman, Clyde. Dizzy Pilots. LC 92-11180. 1992. lib. bdg. 12.94 (*1-56239-166-6*) ABDO Pub Co.
— I Can Hardly Wait. LC 92-11184. 1992. lib. bdg. 12.94 (*1-56239-165-8*) ABDO Pub Co.
Bruckmann, Patricia C. A Manner of Correspondence: A Study of the Scriblerus Club. LC 96-103948. 200p. 1997. 55.00 (*0-7735-1546-1*, Pub. by McG-Queens Univ Pr) CUP Services.
Bruckner, ed. see Mann, Richard A. & Roberts, Barry S.
Bruckner, Andrew. Differentiation of Real Functions. 2nd ed. LC 94-6314. (CRM Monographs: Vol. 5). 195p. 1994. text 53.00 (*0-8218-6990-6*, CRMM/5) Am Math.
Bruckner, Andrew & Bruckner, Judith. Real Analysis. LC 96-22123. 736p. (C). 1996. 90.67 (*0-13-458886-X*) P-H.
Bruckner, Anton & Haas, Robert, eds. Symphonies Nos. 4 & 7 in Full Score. 288p. 1990. pap. 15.95 (*0-486-26262-6*) Dover.
Bruckner, Bernhard, jt. ed. see Shewfelt, Robert L.
Bruckner, D. J., ed. Politics & Language: Spanish & English in the United States. (Orig.). 1980. pap. 4.00 (*0-686-28732-0*) U Chi Ctr Policy.
Bruckner, D. J., et al. Art Against War: Four Hundred Years of Protest Art. LC 83-6342. (Illus.). 128p. 1984. pap. 22.50 (*0-89659-389-4*) Abbeville Pr.
Bruckner, D. J., jt. ed. see Murphy, William M.
Bruckner, David A., jt. auth. see Garcia, Lynne S.
Bruckner, Geza, ed. Application of Gnotobiotics to Transplantation & Microbial Translocation. 1992. 49.95 (*0-915340-18-6*) PJD Pubns.
Bruckner, Hannah, jt. auth. see Bearman, Peter S.
Bruckner, Heidrun, et al, eds. Flags of Fame: Studies in South Asian Folk Culture. (C). 1993. text 44.00 (*81-7304-049-4*, Pub. by Manohar) S Asia.
Bruckner, J. A Bibliographical Catalogue of Seventeenth-Century German Books Published in Holland. (Anglica Germanica Ser.: No. 13). 1971. text 124.60 (*90-279-1706-X*) Mouton.
Bruckner, Jan. The Gait Workbook: A Practical Guide to Clinical Gait Analysis. (Illus.). 208p. (Orig.). 1997. pap. text 30.00 (*1-55642-344-6*, 43446) SLACK Inc.
Bruckner, Jan. People Walking: Pathological Patterns & Normal Changes over the Life Span. LC 98-125405. 1997. VHS 39.95 (*1-55642-350-0*, 43500) SLACK Inc.
Bruckner, Jan, jt. auth. see Edelstein, Joan E.
Bruckner, Judith, jt. auth. see Bruckner, Andrew.
***Bruckner, Markus.** Sprache ALS Schlachtfeld: Narrative Strategien in der Auseinandersetzung Mit Dem Vietnamkrieg. viii, 242p. 1999. 46.00 (*3-631-33898-8*) P Lang Pubng.
Bruckner, Matilda T. Narrative Invention in 12th-Century French Romance: The Convention of Hospitality (1160-1200) LC 79-53400. (Edward C. Armstrong Monographs on Medieval Literature: No. 17). 230p. (Orig.). 1980. pap. 13.95 (*0-917058-16-X*) French Forum.
— Shaping Romance: Interpretation, Truth, & Closure in Twelfth-Century French Fictions. LC 93-2069. (Middle Ages Ser.). 304p. (C). 1993. text 39.95 (*0-8122-3169-4*) U of Pa Pr.
Bruckner, Matilda T., et al, eds. Songs of the Women Troubadours. LC 95-2961. (Library of Medieval Literature: Vol. 97A). 194p. 1995. text 54.00 (*0-8153-0817-5*) Garland.
Bruckner, Pascal. Allez Jouer Ailleurs. (FRE.). 256p. 1989. pap. 12.95 (*0-7859-2109-5*, 2070381072) Fr & Eur.
— Monsieur Tac. (FRE.). 310p. 1986. pap. 12.95 (*0-7859-2055-2*, 2070377873) Fr & Eur.
***Bruckner, Pascal.** The Temptation of Innocence: Living in the Age of Entitlement. 300p. 2000. pap. 19.95 (*1-892941-56-2*, Pub. by Algora Pubng) Midpt Trade.
***Bruckner, Peter.** A Fondness of Learning, Vol. I. (Illus.). 30p. 1999. 16.00 (*1-891211-06-4*) Gazelle Books.
***Bruckner, Reinhard.** Advanced Organic Chemistry. 1999. 74.95 (*0-12-138110-2*) Morgan Kaufmann.
Bruckner, S. & Kingman, L. The Letter B. (Consonant Easy Readers Ser.). 8p. (J). (ps-1). 1997. pap. 1.99 (*1-57690-289-7*) Tchr Create Mat.
— The Letter C: Consonant Easy Readers. (Consonant Easy Readers Ser.). 8p. (J). (ps-1). 1997. pap. 1.99 (*1-57690-290-0*) Tchr Create Mat.
— The Letter D. (Easy Readers Ser.). 8p. (J). (ps-1). 1997. pap. 1.99 (*1-57690-291-9*) Tchr Create Mat.
— The Letter F. (Easy Readers Ser.). 8p. (J). (ps-1). 1997. pap. 1.99 (*1-57690-292-7*) Tchr Create Mat.
— The Letter G: Consonant Easy Readers. (Easy Readers Ser.). 8p. (J). (ps-1). 1997. pap. 1.99 (*1-57690-293-5*) Tchr Create Mat.
— The Letter H: Consonant Easy Readers. (Easy Readers Ser.). 8p. (J). (ps-1). 1997. pap. 1.99 (*1-57690-294-3*) Tchr Create Mat.
— The Letter J. (Easy Readers Ser.). 8p. (J). (ps-1). 1997. pap. 1.99 (*1-57690-295-1*) Tchr Create Mat.
— The Letter K: Consonant Easy Readers. (Easy Readers Ser.). 8p. (J). (ps-1). 1997. pap. 1.99 (*1-57690-296-X*) Tchr Create Mat.
— The Letter L: Consonant Easy Readers. (Easy Readers Ser.). 8p. (J). (ps-1). 1997. pap. 1.99 (*1-57690-297-8*) Tchr Create Mat.
— The Letter M. (Easy Readers Ser.). 8p. (J). (ps-1). 1997. pap. 1.99 (*1-57690-298-6*) Tchr Create Mat.
— The Letter N: Consonant Easy Readers. (Easy Readers Ser.). 8p. (J). (ps-1). 1997. pap. 1.99 (*1-57690-299-4*) Tchr Create Mat.
— The Letter P: Consonant Easy Readers. 8p. (J). (ps-1). 1997. pap. 1.99 (*1-57690-300-1*) Tchr Create Mat.
— The Letter Q: Consonant Easy Readers. (Easy Readers Ser.). 8p. (J). (ps-1). 1997. pap. 1.99 (*1-57690-301-X*) Tchr Create Mat.
— The Letter R: Consonant Easy Readers. (Easy Readers Ser.). 8p. (J). (ps-1). 1997. pap. 1.99 (*1-57690-302-8*) Tchr Create Mat.
— The Letter S. (Easy Readers Ser.). 8p. (J). (ps-1). 1997. pap. 1.99 (*1-57690-303-6*) Tchr Create Mat.
— The Letter T: Consonant Easy Readers. (Easy Readers Ser.). 8p. (J). (ps-1). 1997. pap. 1.99 (*1-57690-304-4*) Tchr Create Mat.
— The Letter V: Consonant Easy Readers. (Easy Readers Ser.). 8p. (J). (ps-1). 1997. pap. 1.99 (*1-57690-305-2*) Tchr Create Mat.
— The Letter W. (Easy Readers Ser.). 8p. (J). (ps-1). 1997. pap. 1.99 (*1-57690-306-0*) Tchr Create Mat.
— The Letter X: Consonant Easy Readers. (Easy Readers Ser.). 8p. (J). (ps-1). 1997. pap. 1.99 (*1-57690-307-9*) Tchr Create Mat.
— The Letter Y: Consonant Easy Readers. (Easy Readers Ser.). 8p. (J). (ps-1). 1997. pap. 1.99 (*1-57690-308-7*) Tchr Create Mat.
— The Letter Z: Consonant Easy Readers. (Easy Readers Ser.). 8p. (J). (ps-1). 1997. pap. 1.99 (*1-57690-309-5*) Tchr Create Mat.
***Bruckner, Sharon, comment.** Oakland Cemetery: St. Paul Minnesota, 1 Aug. 1885-31 December 1889. 90p. 1999. pap. 15.00 (*0-915709-73-2*) Pk Geneal Bk.
Bruckner, Sharon, compiled by. Oakland Cemetery, St. Paul Minnesota Vol. 4: Interment Records from 1 June 1878 to 30 July 1885. (Illus.). 80p. 1997. pap. 15.00 (*0-915709-33-3*) Pk Geneal Bk.
Bruckner, Steven, jt. auth. see Bergman, Samuel.
Brucks, Merrie & MacInnis, Debbie, eds. Advances in Consumer Research Vol. 24: Proceedings of the 1996 Conference. 1997. 59.00 (*0-915552-37-X*) Assn Consumer Res.
Bruckstein, A., jt. auth. see Dori, D.
Brudenell, J. M., et al. Diabetic Pregnancy. (Current Reviews in Obstetrics & Gynaecology Ser.). (Illus.). 147p. 1989. pap. text 44.95 (*0-443-02792-7*) Church.
Bruder. Consultation Programming for Young Children. 1998. 27.50 (*1-56593-095-9*) Thomson Learn.
Bruder, Carl H. Tamieion Ton Tes Kaines Diathekes Lexeon. lii, 885p. 1975. reprint ed. 230.00 (*3-487-05894-4*) G Olms Pubs.
Bruder, Gerry. Heroes of the Horizon: Flying Adventures of Alaska's Legendary Bush Pilots. LC 91-14326. (Illus.). 280p. 1995. pap. 14.95 (*0-88240-363-X*, Alaska NW Bks) Gr Arts Ctr Pub.
Bruder, Kenneth, jt. auth. see Moore, Brooke N.
Bruder, Kenneth, jt. auth. see Moore, Brooke Noel.
Bruder, Mary. Much Ado about a Lot: How to Mind Your Manners in Print & in Person. LC 99-35897. 288p. 2000. 22.95 (*0-7868-6517-2*, Pub. by Hyperion) Time Warner.
Bruder, Mary N., jt. ed. see Tillitt, Bruce.
Bruder-Mattson, Robert J. Finding the Right Corporate Dollars for Your Charity. LC 92-37156. 168p. 1993. text 10.00 (*0-8153-0947-3*) Garland.
Bruder, Melissa. Practical Handbook for the Actor. 1986. pap. 9.00 (*0-394-74412-8*) Random.
Bruder, Noel, jt. auth. see Barton, Hugh.
Bruder, Reinhold. Die Germanische Frau im Lichte der Runeninschriften & der antiken Historiographie. LC 73-75482. (Quellen und Forschungen zur Sprach und Kulturgeschichte der Germanischen Voelker: NF 57 181). 192p. (C). 1974. 108.50 (*3-11-004152-9*, De Gruyter.
Bruderhof, ed. see Arnold, Eberhard & Merton, Thomas.
Bruderhof Communities Staff. Discipleship: Living for Christ in the Daily Grind, Leader's Guide. 121p. 1997. pap., teacher ed. 4.50 (*0-87486-089-X*) Plough.
— Discipleship: Living for Christ in the Daily Grind, Study Guide. 90p. 1997. pap., student ed. 3.50 (*0-87486-088-1*) Plough.
Bruderhof Communities Staff, ed. Behold That Star: A Christmas Anthology. 2nd ed. LC 96-43565. 364p. 2000. pap. 15.00 (*0-87486-084-9*) Plough.
Bruderhof Communities Staff, ed. see Dostoyevsky, Fyodor.
Bruderhof Staff, ed. Sing Through the Seasons: Ninety-Nine Songs for Children. LC 70-164916. (Illus.). 139p. (J). (gr. k-6). 1972. 20.00 incl. audio compact disk (*0-87486-006-7*) Plough.
Bruderhof Staff, ed. see Arnold, Eberhard.
Bruderhof Staff, ed. see Arnold, J. Heinrich.
Bruderle, Elizabeth R., jt. auth. see Valiga, Theresa M.
Bruderlin, B. & Roller, D., eds. Geometric Constraint Solving & Applications. 310p. 1997. 79.95 (*3-540-64416-4*) Spr-Verlag.
***Bruderlin, Markus.** Renzo Piano - Fondation Beyeler: A Home for Art. enl. ed. (GER., Illus.). 156p. 2000. 45.00 (*3-7643-6274-X*, Pub. by Birkhauser); 45.00 (*3-7643-6275-8*, Pub. by Birkhauser); 45.00 (*3-7643-6276-6*, Pub. by Birkhauser); 45.00 (*3-7643-6277-4*, Pub. by Birkhauser) Princeton Arch.
***Brudet, Julie & McAlister, Renee, contrib. by.** Discovering God's Love, Guide: A Faith Development Program for Five Year Olds. (Discovering God Ser.). (Illus.). 212p. 1999. teacher ed., spiral bd. 24.99 (*0-8215-2471-2*) Sadlier.
— Discovering God's World, Guide: A Faith Development Program for Four Year Olds. rev. ed. (Discovering God Ser.). (Illus.). 212p. 1999. teacher ed., spiral bd. 24.99 (*0-8215-2461-5*) Sadlier.
Brudick, Emily M. Blacks & Jews in Literary Conversation. LC 98-3676. (Cambridge Studies in American Literature & Culture Ser.: No. 120). 272p. (C). 1998. text 54.95 (*0-521-63194-7*); pap. text 17.95 (*0-521-63575-6*) Cambridge U Pr.
Brudner, Alan. The Unity of the Common Law: Studies in Hegelian Jurisprudence. LC 94-37053. (Philosophy, Social Theory & the Rule of Law Ser.: Vol. 2). 368p. 1995. 50.00 (*0-520-08596-5*, Pub. by U CA Pr) Cal Prin Full Svc.
Brudney, Daniel. Marx's Attempt to Leave Philosophy. LC 97-38497. 480p. 1999. 45.00 (*0-674-55133-8*) HUP.
Brudney, David. Life Is Not a Rehearsal: A Memoir. LC 97-42972. 300p. 1998. pap. 15.95 (*0-571-19933-X*) Faber & Faber.
Brudney, Jeffrey L. Fostering Volunteer Programs in the Public Sector: Planning, Initiating & Managing Voluntary Activities. LC 90-4226. (Public Administration, Nonprofit Sector Ser.). 282p. 1990. 36.95 (*1-55542-242-X*) Jossey-Bass.
***Brudney, Jeffrey L., et al, eds.** Advancing Public Management: New Developments in Theory, Methods & Practice. LC 99-38857. (Illus.). 272p. 2000. text 65.00 (*0-87840-760-X*) Georgetown U Pr.
Brudney, Jeffrey L., jt. auth. see Meier, Kenneth J.
Brudney, Kent M. & Culver, John H. Critical Thinking & American Government. 192p. (C). 1997. pap. text 24.00 (*0-15-505323-X*, Pub. by Harcourt Coll Pubs) Harcourt.
Brudney, Victor & Bratton, William W. Corporate Finance: 1997 Supplement to Cases & Materials. (University Casebook Ser.). (C). Date not set. pap. text. write for info. (*1-56662-573-4*) Foundation Pr.
— Corporate Finance: Cases & Materials, 1994 Supplement. 4th ed. (University Casebook Ser.). 118p. 1994. 8.50 (*1-56662-200-X*) Foundation Pr.
— 1996 Supplement to Cases & Materials on Corporate Finance. 4th ed. (University Casebook Ser.). 227p. 1996. pap. text, suppl. ed. write for info. (*1-56662-433-9*) Foundation Pr.
Brudney, Victor, et al. Corporate Finance, Cases & Materials On. 4th ed. (University Casebook Ser.). 1200p. (C). 1993. text. write for info. (*1-56662-055-7*) Foundation Pr.
Brudno, A. L., et al. Eighteen Papers on Algebra. (Translations Ser.: Series 2, Vol. 27). 304p. 1963. reprint ed. 36.00 (*0-8218-1727-2*, TRANS2/27) Am Math.
Brudno, Barbara E. Poverty, Inequality & the Law: Cases, Commentary & Analyses. 934p. 1976. write for info. (*0-318-57525-6*) West Pub.
Brudny, Yitzhak M. Reinventing Russia: Russian Nationalism & the Soviet State, 1953-1991. LC 98-23969. (Russian Research Center Studies). x, 352 p. 1998. 45.00 (*0-674-75408-5*) HUP.
Brudnyi, Y. A. & Krugljak, N. Y. Interpolation Functors & Interpolation Spaces, Vol. 1. (North-Holland Mathematical Library: No. 47). xvi,718p. 1991. 207.50 (*0-444-88001-1*, North Holland) Elsevier.
Brudon-Jakobowicz, P., et al. Indicators for Monitoring National Drug Policies: A Practical Manual. (FRE.). iii, 216p. (C). 1994. pap. text 22.50 (*0-614-08060-6*, 1930060) World Health.
Brudvik, James S. Advanced Removable Partial Dentures. LC 99-21231. 23p. 1999. write for info. (*0-86715-351-2*) Quint Pub Co.
Brue, Boyd. Lodging for Travelers: Upper Midwest. (Orig.). 1993. pap. 11.95 (*0-927290-01-4*) Lodging Unlimited.
Brue, Deborah F., jt. ed. see Orem, Sue D.
Brue, L. Jane, jt. auth. see Carroll, Mary.
Brue, S. L., jt. auth. see McConnell, Campbell R.
***Brue, Stanley L.** Evolution of Economic Thought. 6th ed. (C). 1999. text 94.50 (*0-03-025998-3*, Pub. by Harcourt Coll Pubs) Harcourt.
Brue, Stanley L. & Wentworth, Donald R. Economic Scenes: Theory in Today's World. 5th ed. 304p. (C). 1991. pap. text 62.00 (*0-13-223934-5*) P-H.
Brue, Stanley L., jt. auth. see McConnell, Campbell R.
Brue, Susan. Minnesota Lodging Directory: Directory of Motels, Hotels, & Bed & Breakfasts in Minnesota 1989. (Orig.). 1988. pap. 1.95 (*0-927290-00-6*) Lodging Unlimited.
Bruechert, Anna M., jt. auth. see Reichenfeld, Robert.
Brueck, Katherine T. The Redemption of Tragedy: The Literary Vision of Simone Weil. LC 94-9152. (SUNY Series, Simone Weil Studies). 185p. (C). 1994. pap. text 16.95 (*0-7914-2282-8*) State U NY Pr.
— The Redemption of Tragedy: The Literary Vision of Simone Weil. LC 94-9152. (SUNY Series, Simone Weil Studies). 185p. (C). 1995. text 49.50 (*0-7914-2281-X*) State U NY Pr.
Brueckman, Henry & Moreau, Jeffrey. Forty Four Forty Nine: The Queen of Steam. LC 83-72151. 64p. 1984. 23.00 (*0-934406-01-4*) Carbarn Press.
Brueckmann, F. Robert. The Art of Effective Fracture Fixation with Rush Pins. (Illus.). 144p. 1989. text 72.00 (*0-86577-323-8*) Thieme Med Pubs.
Brueckmann, Robin. When Two Are One: The True Story of a Remarkable Relationship Between Horse & Rider. LC 98-65926. (Illus.). 280p. 1998. pap. 19.95 (*0-9664043-0-0*) Namaste.
Brueckner, G. E. & Somov, Boris V., eds. Magnetic Energy Conversion: Proceedings of Symposium 13 of the COSPAR 27th Plenary Meeting Held in Espoo, Finland, 18-29 July, 1988. (Advances in Space Research Ser.: Vol. 10). (Illus.). 208p. 1990. pap. 97.00 (*0-08-040169-4*, Pergamon Pr) Elsevier.
Brueckner, Keith A. & Sinanoglu, Oktay. Three Approaches to Electron Correlation in Atoms. LC 76-89666. (Yale Series in the Sciences). (Illus.). 398p. reprint ed. pap. 123.40 (*0-608-30005-5*, 202203900024) Bks Demand.
Brueckner, Keith A., et al. Inertial Confinement Fusion. 256p. 1992. 120.00 (*0-88318-925-9*) Am Inst Physics.
Bruegel, Peter. Graphic Worlds. Klein, ed. (Illus.). 1990. 16.75 (*0-8446-1755-5*) Peter Smith.
— Graphic Worlds of Peter Bruegel the Elder: Reproducing Sixty-Four Engravings & a Woodcut After Designs by Peter Bruegel the Elder. Klein, H. Arthur, ed. (Illus.). 176p. (Orig.). 1963. pap. 13.95 (*0-486-21132-0*) Dover.
***Bruegge.** Object Oriented Software Engineering: Conquering Complex & Changing Systems. LC 99-42746. 553p. 1999. 50.00 (*0-13-489725-0*) P-H.
Brueggeman, Brenda J. Lend Me Your Ear: Rhetorical Constructions of Deafness. LC 99-20807. xii, 290p. 1999. 49.95 (*1-56368-079-3*) Gallaudet Univ Pr.
Brueggeman, Laura J., jt. auth. see Klecan-Aker, Joan S.
Brueggeman, William B. & Fisher, Jeffrey. Real Estate Finance & Investments. 10th ed. LC 96-23787. 880p. (C). 1996. text 68.25 (*0-256-15254-3*, Irwn McGrw-H) McGrw-H Hghr Educ.
Brueggemann. Georgia Corporations, Partnerships & Associations Law: 1993 Edition. annot. ed. 35.00 (*0-614-05827-9*, MICHIE) LEXIS Pub.
***Brueggemann.** Macro Social Work Practice. 2nd ed. (Social Work Ser.). 2000. 44.50 (*0-534-57322-3*) Wadsworth Pub.
Brueggemann, Aminia. Chronotopos Amerika Bei Max Frisch, Peter Handke, Gunter Kunert, und Martin Walser. (Studies in Modern German Literature: Vol. 70). (GER.). VIII, 244p. (C). 1996. text 47.95 (*0-8204-2554-0*) P Lang Pubng.
Brueggemann, W. & Hemberger, K. Testfragen Wirtschaftsdeutsch: Testbuch. (GER.). 104p. (C). 1993. pap. text 11.75 (*3-12-675230-6*, Pub. by Klett Edition) Intl Bk Import.
Brueggemann, Walter. Abiding Astonishment: Psalms, Modernity, & the Making of History. (Literary Currents in Biblical Interpretation Ser.). 96p. (Orig.). 1991. pap. 12.95 (*0-664-25134-X*) Westminster John Knox.
— The Bible Makes Sense. LC 76-29883. 1985. pap. 13.00 (*0-8042-0063-7*) Westminster John Knox.
— The Bible Makes Sense. 2nd rev. ed. LC 76-29883. 128p. 1997. pap. 9.95 (*0-88489-356-1*) St Marys.
— Biblical Perspectives on Evangelism: Living in a Three-Storied Universe. 160p. (C). 1993. pap. 13.95 (*0-687-41233-1*) Abingdon.
— Cadences of Home: Preaching among Exiles. LC 97-18835. 176p. 1997. pap. 16.00 (*0-664-25749-6*) Westminster John Knox.
— The Covenanted Self: Explorations in Law & Covenant. Miller, Patrick, ed. LC 99-30511. 1999. pap. 18.00 (*0-8006-3176-5*, Fortress Pr) Augsburg Fortress.
— The Creative Word: Canon As a Model for Biblical Education. LC 81-71387. 176p. 1982. pap. 17.00 (*0-8006-1626-X*, 1-1626, Fortress Pr) Augsburg Fortress.
— David's Truth in Israel's Imagination & Memory. LC 85-47717. 132p. 1985. pap. 14.00 (*0-8006-1865-3*, 1-1865, Fortress Pr) Augsburg Fortress.
— Finally Comes the Poet: Daring Speech for Proclamation. LC 89-37524. 184p. (Orig.). 1989. pap. 17.00 (*0-8006-2394-0*, 1-2394) Augsburg Fortress.
— First & Second Samuel. (Interpretation: A Bible Commentary for Teaching & Preaching Ser.). 420p. 1990. 28.00 (*0-8042-3108-7*) Westminster John Knox.
— Gathering the Church in the Spirit: Reflections on Exile & the Inscrutable Wind of God. 64p. 1995. pap. 5.00 (*1-885121-16-4*) CTS Press.
— Genesis. LC 81-82355. (Interpretation: A Bible Commentary for Teaching & Preaching Ser.). 432p. (C). 1986. 31.00 (*0-8042-3101-X*) Westminster John Knox.

B

— Hopeful Imagination: Prophetic Voices in Exile. LC 86-45207. 160p. 1986. pap. 16.00 (*0-8006-1925-0*, 1-1925, Fortress Pr) Augsburg Fortress.

— Interpretation & Obedience: From Faithful Reading to Faithful Living. LC 90-19231. 336p. 1991. pap. 21.00 (*0-8006-2478-5*, 1-2478) Augsburg Fortress.

— Isaiah, 40-66, Vol. 2. LC 98-16400. (Bible Companion Ser.). 280p. 1998. pap. 18.00 (*0-664-25791-7*) Westminster John Knox.

— Isaiah, 1-39. LC 98-16400. (Bible Companion Ser.). 312p. 1999. pap. 20.00 (*0-664-25524-8*) Westminster John Knox.

— Israel's Praise: Doxology Against Idolatry & Ideology. LC 86-46419. 208p. 1988. pap. 18.00 (*0-8006-2044-5*, 1-2044, Fortress Pr) Augsburg Fortress.

— The Land: Place As Gift, Promise & Challenge in Biblical Faith. Donahue, John R., ed. LC 76-15883. (Overtures to Biblical Theology Ser.: No. 1). 224p. 1977. pap. 17.00 (*0-8006-1526-3*, 1-1526, Fortress Pr) Augsburg Fortress.

— Living Toward a Vision: Biblical Reflections on Shalom. LC 76-22172. 208p. 1982. pap. 11.95 (*0-8298-0613-X*) Pilgrim OH.

— The Message of the Psalms: A Theological Commentary. LC 84-21734. (Augsburg Old Testament Studies). 208p. (Orig.). 1984. pap. 15.99 (*0-8066-2120-6*, 10-4370, Augsburg) Augsburg Fortress.

— Old Testament Theology: Essays on Structure, Theme, & Text. Miller, Patrick D., ed. LC 91-37202. 336p. 1992. pap. 24.00 (*0-8006-2537-4*, 1-2537) Augsburg Fortress.

— Power, Providence, & Personality: Biblical Insight into Life & Ministry. 120p. (Orig.). 1990. pap. 14.95 (*0-664-25138-2*) Westminster John Knox.

— The Prophetic Imagination. LC 78-54546. 128p. 1978. pap. 14.00 (*0-8006-1337-6*, 1-1337, Fortress Pr) Augsburg Fortress.

— The Psalms & the Life of Faith. Miller, Patrick D., ed. LC 95-21448. 240p. 1995. pap. 20.00 (*0-8006-2733-4*, Fortress Pr) Augsburg Fortress.

— Revelation & Violence: A Study in Contextualization. LC 86-60473. (Pere Marquette Lectures). 72p. 1986. 15.00 (*0-87462-541-6*) Marquette.

— A Social Reading of the Old Testament: Prophetic Approaches to Israel's Communal Life. Miller, Patrick D., ed. LC 93-34115. 336p. 1994. pap. 23.00 (*0-8006-2734-2*, 1-2734, Fortress Pr) Augsburg Fortress.

— Texts under Negotiation: The Bible & Postmodern Imagination. LC 93-18154. 128p. 1993. pap. 14.00 (*0-8006-2736-9*, 1-2736, Fortress Pr) Augsburg Fortress.

— Theology of the Old Testament: Testimony, Dispute, Advocacy. LC 97-21888. 800p. 1997. 48.00 (*0-8006-3087-4*, 1-3087, Fortress Pr) Augsburg Fortress.

— The Threat of Life: Sermons on Pain, Power & Weakness. Campbell, Charles, ed. 160p. 1996. pap. 16.00 (*0-8006-2975-2*, 1-2975, Fortress Pr) Augsburg Fortress.

— Using God's Resources Wisely: Isaiah & Urban Possibility. LC 93-3260. 96p. (Orig.). 1993. pap. 13.95 (*0-664-25460-8*) Westminster John Knox.

***Brueggemann, Walter & Miller, Patrick D.** Deep Memory, Exuberant Hope: Contested Truth in a Post-Christian World. LC 00-24752. 2000. write for info. (*0-8006-3237-0*, Fortress Pr) Augsburg Fortress.

— Texts That Linger, Words That Explode. LC 99-47465. 2000. pap. 16.00 (*0-8006-3231-1*, Fortress Press) Pub Hse ELCA.

Brueggemann, Walter, et al. Texts for Preaching: A Lectionary Commentary Based on the NRSV Year A. 608p. 1995. 33.00 (*0-664-21927-6*) Westminster John Knox.

— To Act Justly, Love Tenderly, Walk Humbly: An Agenda for Ministers. 70p. 1997. pap. 7.00 (*1-57910-064-3*) Wipf & Stock.

Brueggemann, Walter, ed. see Fretheim, Terence E.

Brueggemann, Walter, ed. see Guthrie, Shirley C.

Brueggemann, William G. The Practice of Macro Social Work. LC 95-30670. (Illus.). 1996. text 61.95 (*0-8304-1368-5*) Thomson Learn.

Brueghel, Jan. Where's the Bear? A Look-&-Find Book. LC 96-39856. (J. Paul Getty Museum Staff). (Illus.). 52p. (J). (ps-3). 1997. 16.95 (*0-89236-378-9*, Pub. by J P Getty Trust) OUP.

***Brueghel, Pieter.** Masters of Dutch Art. (Illus.). 140p. 1999. 19.95 (*3-8290-2579-3*) Konemann.

Bruegman, Joanne M., ed. see Bruegman, William R., III.

Bruegman, Randy R., jt. auth. see OnGuard Inc. Staff.

Bruegman, William R., III. Aurora History & Price Guide: A Pictorial Price Guide. 3rd ed. (Illus.). 220p. 1996. pap. 19.95 (*0-9632637-6-5*) Toy Scouts.

— Cartoon Friends of the Baby Boom Era: A Pictorial Price Guide. Bruegman, Joanne M., ed. (Illus.). 180p. 1993. pap. 19.95 (*0-9632637-3-0*) Toy Scouts.

— Toys of the 60s: A Pictorial Price Guide. 4th ed. Bruegman, Joanne M., ed. (Illus.). 206p. 1996. reprint ed. pap. 19.95 (*0-9632637-7-3*) Toy Scouts.

Bruegmann, Robert. The Architects & the City: Holabird & Roche of Chicago, 1880-1918. LC 96-22151. 1997. 65.00 (*0-226-07695-4*) U Ch Pr.

Bruegmann, Robert. Benicia, Portrait of an Early California Town. 2nd ed. (Illus.). 160p. 1997. pap. 24.95 (*1-885852-09-6*) J D Stevenson.

Bruegmann, Robert, ed. Holabird & Roche & Root: An Illustrated Catalogue of Works, 1880-1940, 3 vols. LC 90-19652. (Illus.). 1300p. 1991. text 275.00 (*0-8240-3974-2*) Garland.

— Modernism at Mid-Century: The Architecture of the U. S. Air Force Academy. (Illus.). 200p. 1994. 70.00 (*0-226-07693-8*) U Ch Pr.

— Modernism at Mid-Century: The Architecture of the United States Air Force Academy. (Illus.). 200p. 1994. pap. text 45.00 (*0-226-07694-6*) U Ch Pr.

Bruehl, Bill. The Technique of Inner Action: The Soul of a Performer's Work. LC 95-16495. 97p. 1995. pap. 14.95 (*0-435-08687-1*, 08687) Heinemann.

Bruehl, Charles P. The Pope's Plan for Social Reconstruction. 10.00 (*0-8159-6507-9*) Devin.

Bruehl, Elisabeth Y. Vigil; A Novel. LC 82-17160. 175p. 1983. reprint ed. pap. 54.30 (*0-608-00875-3*, 206166900010) Bks Demand.

Bruehl, Elizabeth Y. Anna Freud: A Biography. 1994. pap. 14.95 (*0-393-31157-0*) Norton.

Bruel, Andree. Emerson et Thoreau. (BCL1-PS American Literature Ser.). 215p. 1992. reprint ed. lib. bdg. 79.00 (*0-7812-6706-4*) Rprt Serv.

Bruelheide, Helge. Die Gruenlandgesellschaften Des Harzes und Ihre Standortsbedingungen: Mit Einem Beitrag Zum Gliederungsprinzip Auf der Basis Von Statistisch Ermittelten Artengruppen. (Dissertationes Botanicae Ser.: Band 244). (Illus.). x, 338p. 1995. pap. 71.00 (*3-443-64156-3*, Pub. by Gebruder Borntraeger) Balogh.

***Bruell, Christopher.** On the Socratic Education: An Introduction to the Shorter Platonic Dialogues. LC 99-13993. 240p. 1999. 35.00 (*0-8476-9401-1*) Rowman.

Bruell, Clifford J., jt. auth. see Inyang, Hilary I.

Bruemmer, Alice, et al, eds. Library Management in Review, Vol. 1. LC 81-13562. 112p. pap. 34.80 (*0-7837-0266-3*, 204057500001) Bks Demand.

Bruemmer, Fred. Arctic Memories: Living with the Inuit. (Illus.). 160p. 1993. 24.95 (*1-55013-461-2*, Pub. by Key Porter) Firefly Bks Ltd.

— The Narwhal: Unicorn of the Sea. 1993. 24.95 (*1-55013-187-7*) U of Toronto Pr.

— Seals in the Wild. LC 98-7001. (Illus.). 256p. 1998. 19.99 (*1-57145-622-8*, Laurel Glen Pub) Advantage Pubs.

Bruemmer, Fred, jt. auth. see Mangelsen, Thomas D.

***Bruemmer, Paul J.** #1 Search Engine Primer. xvii, 82p. 1999. pap. 95.00 (*0-9677579-0-8*) Web Ignite Corp.

Bruemmer, S. M., ed. see Parkins Symposium on Fundamental Aspects of Stress.

Bruen, Alexander J., et al. Federal Income Taxation of Oil & Gas Investments. 2nd ed. 1989. 195.00 (*0-7913-0111-7*) Warren Gorham & Lamont.

Bruen, Bernie. Keep Your Head Down: A Falklands Farewell. (Illus.). 211p. 1998. 42.50 (*1-85776-262-2*, Pub. by Book Guild Ltd) Trans-Atl Phila.

***Bruen, Ella Jane & Fitzgibbons, Brian M., eds.** Through Ordinary Eyes: The Civil War Correspondence of Rufus Robbins, Private, 7th Regiment, Massachusetts Volunteers. LC 99-86222. 240p. 2000. 40.00 (*0-275-96589-9*, C6589, Praeger Pubs) Greenwood.

Bruen, Frank. Forrer: Christian Forrer the Clockmaker & His Descendants. (Illus.). 294p. 1997. reprint ed. pap. 39.00 (*0-8328-8612-2*); reprint ed. lib. bdg. 49.00 (*0-8328-8611-4*) Higginson Bk Co.

Bruen, Ken. The Hackman Blues. LC 98-135107. (Bloodlines Ser.). 156p. 1998. pap. 15.95 (*1-899344-22-5*, Pub. by Do-Not Pr) Dufour.

— Her Last Call to Louis MacNeice. LC 97-61914. (Mask Noir Ser.). 128p. 1998. pap. 11.99 (*1-85242-585-7*) Serpents Tail.

— Rilke on Black. LC 95-72964. (Mask Noir Ser.). 144p. (Orig.). 1997. pap. text 12.99 (*1-85242-511-3*, Mask Noir) Serpents Tail.

***Bruen, Ken.** Taming the Alien. 2000. pap. 15.95 (*1-899344-49-7*, Pub. by Do-Not Pr) Dufour.

Bruen, Ken. White Arrest, 1. 1999. pap. text 14.95 (*1-899344-41-1*) Do-Not Pr.

Bruen, Patricia E., jt. auth. see Knab, Raymond W.

Bruenchenhein, Eugene Von, see Cubbs, Joanne & Von Bruenchenhein, Eugene, contrib. by.

Bruenig, E. F. Conservation & Management of Tropical Rainforests: An Integrated Approach to Sustainability. LC 96-215130. (CAB International Publication Ser.). 362p. 1996. text 105.00 (*0-85198-994-2*) OUP.

Bruening, George, et al, eds. Tailoring Genes for Crop Improvements: An Agricultural Perspective. (Basic Life Sciences Ser.: Vol. 41). (Illus.). 223p. 1987. 65.00 (*0-306-42579-3*, Plenum Trade) Perseus Pubng.

Bruening, Jeff, ed. see Turpoff, Glen.

Bruening, Mary A., jt. auth. see Hulme, Gilbert N.

***Bruening, Sandra.** Candlestick Characters. (Illus.). 18p. 1999. write for info. (*1-58050-083-8*, 40-6211) Provo Craft.

Bruening, Thomas M., jt. auth. see Holt, James S.

Bruening, William. Ethics Theory & Practice. 2nd ed. 272p. (C). 1995. pap. text, per. 38.95 (*0-7872-1200-8*, 41120001) Kendall-Hunt.

***Bruer, John T.** Carving Our Destiny: Scientific Research Faces a New Millennium. 2000. 44.95 (*0-309-06848-7*, Joseph Henry Pr) Natl Acad Pr.

Bruer, John T. The Myth of the First Three Years: A New Understanding of Early Brain Development & Lifelong Learning. LC 99-34934. 256p. 1999. pap. text 24.50 (*0-684-85184-9*) Free Pr.

— Schools for Thought: A Science of Learning in the Classroom. (Illus.). 398p. 1993. 38.50 (*0-262-02352-0*, Bradford Bks) MIT Pr.

— Schools for Thought: A Science of Learning in the Classroom. 336p. 1994. pap. text 19.50 (*0-262-52196-2*, Bradford Bks) MIT Pr.

Bruera, Eduardo & Higginson, Irene, eds. Cachexia-Anorexia in Cancer Patients. (Illus.). 208p. (C). 1996. text 69.50 (*0-19-262540-3*) OUP.

Bruera, Eduardo & Portenoy, Russell K., eds. Topics in Palliative Care, Vol. 2. (Topics in Palliative Care Ser.). (Illus.). 368p. 1998. text 55.00 (*0-19-510245-2*) OUP.

Bruera, Eduardo, jt. ed. see Portenoy, Russell K.

Bruera, Eduardo, jt. ed. see Portenoy, Russell.

Bruerd, Bonnie, jt. auth. see Entwistle, Beverly.

Brues, Austin M. & Sacher, George A., eds. Aging & Levels of Biological Organization. LC 65-17281. 365p. reprint ed. pap. 113.20 (*0-8357-5258-5*, 201995700015) Bks Demand.

Brues, Charles T. Insects' Food & Ecology. Orig. Title: Insect Dietary. (Illus.). 1990. 13.00 (*0-8446-4521-4*) Peter Smith.

Bruesch, P. Phonons: Theory & Experiments II, Experiments & Interpretation of Experimental Results. (Solid-State Sciences Ser.: Vol. 65). (Illus.). 350p. 1986. 71.95 (*0-387-16623-8*) Spr-Verlag.

— Phonons: Theory & Experiments III, Phenomena Related with Phonons. (Solid-State Sciences Ser.: Vol. 66). (Illus.). 270p. 1987. 70.95 (*0-387-17223-8*) Spr-Verlag.

Brueschke, Jason D., jt. auth. see Brower, Charles N.

Bruess & Richards. Healthy Decisions. 1993. 10.62 (*0-697-20878-8*, WCB McGr Hill) McGrw-H Hghr Educ.

Bruess & Richardson. Decisions for Health. 4th ed. 1995. teacher ed. 16.56 (*0-697-15228-6*); teacher ed. 25.00 (*0-697-15225-1*) McGraw.

— Decisions for Health. 4th ed. 1995. pap. text, teacher ed. 42.18 (*0-697-15226-X*) McGraw.

— Testwell Decision Health. 4th ed. 1995. wbk. ed. 39.00 (*0-697-25961-7*, WCB McGr Hill) McGrw-H Hghr Educ.

Bruess, Clint E. & Greenberg, Jerrold S. Sexuality Education: Theory & Practice. 3rd ed. 352p. (C). 1993. text. write for info. (*0-697-17124-8*) Brown & Benchmark.

Bruess, Clint E. & Laing, Susan. Decisions for Health. 4th ed. 608p. (C). 1995. text, student ed. 15.62 (*0-697-15227-8*) Brown & Benchmark.

Bruess, Clint E. & Richardson, Glenn. Decisions for Health: Family Life Education (Central State University) 4th ed. 146p. (C). 1995. per. write for info. (*0-697-33076-1*) Brown & Benchmark.

— Healthy Decisions. 96p. (C). 1993. text, student ed. write for info. (*0-697-17043-8*) Brown & Benchmark.

— Healthy Decisions. 432p. (C). 1993. text. write for info. (*0-697-21449-4*) Brown & Benchmark.

— Healthy Decisions. 96p. (C). 1994. text, student ed. 10.00 (*0-697-25867-X*) Brown & Benchmark.

Bruess, R. J. RISC - the MIPS-R3000 Family: Architecture, System Components, Compilers, Tools, Applications. (Illus.). 340p. 1991. 68.00 (*3-8009-4103-1*, Wiley-VCH) Wiley.

Bruess-Richards. Healthy Decisions. 1993. teacher ed. 23.75 (*0-697-17044-6*, WCB McGr Hill) McGrw-H Hghr Educ.

Bruess-Richardson. Complete Problem Solving for Decisions for Health. 1989. 20.50 (*0-697-11409-0*) McGraw.

Bruess/Richardson. Text with Decision for Health. 4th ed. 1995. 48.25 (*0-697-25964-1*, WCB McGr Hill) McGrw-H Hghr Educ.

Bruessard, Edward E. The Age of Homo Sapiens Sapiens. LC 91-92987. (Illus.). 300p. (Orig.). (C). 1999. pap. 27.95 (*0-9630815-9-4*) Bruessards Ent.

Bruestle, Beaumont. The Wonderful Tang. (J). (gr. 1-7). 1952. 6.00 (*0-87602-222-0*) Anchorage.

***Brueton, Diana.** Discovering Meditation: How to Practice Meditation Techniques to Find Inner Calm & Resolution. (Illus.). 144p. (Orig.). 1999. pap. 19.95 (*1-85703-447-3*, Pub. by How To Bks) Trans-Atl Phila.

Brueton, Diana. Many Moons. 1992. per. 16.00 (*0-13-553355-4*) P-H.

— Many Moons. (Illus.). 256p. 1992. pap. 14.00 (*0-671-76801-8*, Fireside) S&S Trade Pap.

Brueton, Diana, jt. auth. see Chetan, Anand.

Bruetsch, Anne. Multiple Intelligences Lesson Plan Book. 192p. 1995. ring bd. 37.00 (*1-56976-019-5*) Zephyr Pr AZ.

Bruette, William A. & Donnelly, Kerry V. The Complete Dog Buyer's Guide. rev. ed. (Illus.). 608p. (Orig.). 1983. 19.95 (*0-86622-026-7*, H-1061) TFH Pubns.

Bruey, Alfred J. Practicing Insanity. 21p. 1982. pap. 7.95 (*0-944754-02-3*) Pudding Hse Pubns.

— Visual Basic for Beginners: A Project Approach to Object-Oriented Programming. LC 95-94248. 128p. (C). 1995. pap. text 12.95 (*0-9646968-0-0*) Comp Systs Consult.

Bruff, Harold H., jt. auth. see Shane, Peter M.

Bruffee, Kenneth A. Collaborative Learning: Higher Education, Interdependence, & the Authority of Knowledge. 256p. 1995. reprint ed. pap. text 16.95 (*0-8018-5232-3*) Johns Hopkins.

— Collaborative Learning: Higher Education, Interdependence, & the Authority of Knowledge. 2nd ed. LC 98-75126. 288p. 1998. 38.00 (*0-8018-5973-5*) Johns Hopkins.

— Collaborative Learning: Higher Education, Interdependence, & the Authority of Knowledge. 2nd ed. LC 98-75126. xxiv, 319 p. 1999. pap. text 16.95 (*0-8018-5974-3*) Johns Hopkins.

— Short Course Writing. 4th ed. LC 92-1644. 380p. (C). 1997. pap. text 50.00 (*0-673-52190-7*) Addson-Wesley Educ.

Bruffy, Madison D. Dickess Vol. 1: Prisoner of the Past. LC 97-91028. 1998. pap. 12.95 (*0-533-12541-3*) Vantage.

Bruford, A., ed. The Green Man of Knowledge: And Other Scots Traditional Tales. (Illus.). 128p. 1982. text 21.00 (*0-08-025757-7*, Pergamon Pr); pap. text 15.90 (*0-08-025758-5*, Pergamon Pr) Elsevier.

Bruford, A. J. & MacDonald, D. A., eds. Scottish Traditional Tales. 1994. pap. 26.00 (*0-7486-6150-6*, Pub. by Polygon) Subterranean Co.

Bruford, B. When in Doubt, Roll. 136p. 1988. pap. 13.95 (*0-7935-3529-8*, 06630298) H Leonard.

Bruford, Walter H. The German Tradition of Self-Cultivation: Bildung from Humboldt to Thomas Mann. LC 74-79143. 300p. reprint ed. pap. 85.50 (*0-608-13308-6*, 2025578) Bks Demand.

— Theatre, Drama, & Audience in Goethe's Germany. LC 73-10579. 388p. 1974. reprint ed. lib. bdg. 69.50 (*0-8371-7016-8*, BRTD, Greenwood Pr) Greenwood.

Brufsky, Allen D., jt. auth. see Kramer, Barry.

Brug, John F. A Bible Study on Man & Woman in God's World. 55p. (Orig.). 1992. pap. 5.00 (*0-8100-0450-X*, 22N0845) Northwest Pub.

— Biblical Prophecy. 32p. (Orig.). 1980. pap. 4.00 (*0-8100-0112-8*, 22N0782) Northwest Pub.

— Catholicism Today. 36p. (Orig.). 1991. pap., teacher ed. 7.50 (*0-8100-0393-7*, 22N0821); pap., student ed. 5.00 (*0-8100-0392-9*, 22N0820) Northwest Pub.

— Ezra, Nehemiah, Ester. LC 85-60722. (People's Bible Ser.). 201p. (Orig.). 1985. pap. 9.99 (*0-8100-0209-4*, 15N0422) Northwest Pub.

— Ezra, Nehemiah, Esther. LC 96-224245. (People's Bible Commentary Ser.). 208p. 1994. pap. 9.99 (*0-570-04663-7*, 12-8028) Concordia.

— Ezra, Nehemiah, Esther. (The People's Bible Ser.). 60p. 1985. pap., student ed. 5.00 (*0-938272-53-5*, 22-2178) WELS Board.

— Justified by Faith. 60p. (Orig.). 1985. pap. 5.00 (*0-8100-0124-1*, 22N0784) Northwest Pub.

— Psalms, Vol. 1. LC 88-62293. (People's Bible Ser.). 292p. 1988. pap. 11.99 (*0-8100-0299-X*, 15N0457) Northwest Pub.

— Psalms, Vol. 1. (The People's Bible Ser.). 64p. 1989. pap. text, student ed. 5.00 (*0-938272-61-6*, 22-2204) WELS Board.

— Psalms, Vol. 1, Pts. 1-72. LC 88-62293. (People's Bible Ser.). 56p. 1989. student ed. 5.00 (*0-938272-62-4*, 22-2203) Northwest Pub.

— Psalms, Vol. 2. LC 88-62293. (People's Bible Ser.). 285p. 1989. pap. 11.99 (*0-8100-0309-0*, 15N0468) Northwest Pub.

— Psalms 1. (People's Bible Commentary Ser.). 292p. (Orig.). 1992. pap. 10.99 (*0-570-04584-3*, 12-8002) Concordia.

— Psalms 2. (People's Bible Commentary Ser.). 285p. (Orig.). 1992. pap. 10.99 (*0-570-04590-8*, 12-8008) Concordia.

— The Revelation of Jesus Christ. 40p. (Orig.). 1985. pap. 4.00 (*0-8100-0088-1*, 22N0767) Northwest Pub.

Brug, Jos Van Der, see Locher, Kees & Van Der Brug, Jos.

Brugaletta, John J. Tilling the Land: Poems. LC 92-22418. (Illus.). 68p. 1992. pap. 14.95 (*0-7734-0022-2*, Mellen Poetry Pr) E Mellen.

Brugel, Werner. Handbook of NMR Spectral Parameters, 3 vols., 1. LC 81-206159. 290p. reprint ed. pap. 89.90 (*0-8357-8615-3*, 203504000001) Bks Demand.

— Handbook of NMR Spectral Parameters, 3 vols., 2. LC 81-206159. 392p. reprint ed. pap. 121.60 (*0-8357-8616-1*, 203504000002) Bks Demand.

— Handbook of NMR Spectral Parameters, 3 vols., 3. LC 81-206159. 271p. reprint ed. pap. 84.10 (*0-8357-8617-X*, 203504000003) Bks Demand.

Brugemann, Hans, ed. Bioresonance & Multiresonance Therapy (BRT) New, Forward-Looking Forms of Therapy with Ultrafine Body Energies & Environmental Signals. Williams, Robert E., tr. from GER. (Illus.). 277p. 1993. text 49.95 (*2-8043-4010-4*, Pub. by Edits Haug Intl) Medicina Bio.

Brugerolles, Emmanuelle & Guillet, David. The Renaissance in France: Drawings from the Ecole des Beaux-Arts, Paris. Schub, Judith, tr. from FRE. (Illus.). 346p. 1995. pap. 30.00 (*0-916724-86-7*, Pub. by Harvard Art Mus) U of Wash Pr.

Brugge, David M. Hubbell Trading Post National Historic Site. Foreman, Ronald J., ed. LC 92-62158. (Illus.). 80p. (Orig.). 1993. pap. 9.95 (*1-877856-18-5*) SW Pks Mnmts.

— The Navajo-Hopi Land Dispute: An American Tragedy. (Illus.). 320p. 1999. pap. 18.95 (*0-8263-2156-9*) U of NM Pr.

Brugge, Doug, et al. Memories Come to Us in the Rain & the Wind: Oral Histories & Photographs of Navajo Uranium Miners & Their Families. 2nd ed. Austm-Garrison, Martha & Fasthorse-Begay, Lydia, trs. from NAV. (Illus.). 62p. 1997. reprint ed. pap. 15.00 (*0-9660050-1-5*) Navajo Uranium.

Brugge, Joan, et al, eds. Origins of Human Cancer: A Comprehensive Review. fac. ed. LC 91-13383. (Illus.). 922p. 1991. reprint ed. pap. 200.00 (*0-7837-8112-1*, 204791900008) Bks Demand.

Brugge, John F., jt. ed. see Poon, Paul W.

Bruggeling, A. S. Structural Concrete: Theory & Its Application. (Illus.). 504p. (C). 1991. text 155.00 (*90-6191-182-6*, Pub. by A A Balkema) Ashgate Pub Co.

Bruggeling, A. S. & Huyghe, G. F. Prefabrication with Concrete. (Illus.). 397p. (C). 1991. text 155.00 (*90-6191-183-4*, Pub. by A A Balkema) Ashgate Pub Co.

***Bruggeman, C. A., et al, eds.** Novel Immunological Aspects of CMV-Related Diseases: Pathogenesis, Diagnosis & Therapy. (Intervirology Ser.: Vol. 42, Nos. 5-6). (Illus.). 158p. 2000. pap. 39.25 (*3-8055-7049-X*) S Karger.

Bruggeman, G. A. Analytical Solutions of Geohydrological Problems. LC 99-20172. (Developments in Water Ser.). 970p. 1999. 236.00 (*0-444-81829-4*) Elsevier.

Bruggeman, Hedwig. Pastoral Associations in Chad: Oxfam Research Discussion Papers. (Oxfam Research Discussions Papers). 40p. (C). 1993. pap. 15.95 (*0-85598-214-4*, Pub. by Oxfam Pub) Stylus Pub VA.

Bruggeman, Linda S., et al. Contract Costs. Bova, Regina M., ed. (National Contract Management Association National Education Seminar Ser.). 408p. (Orig.). 1995. pap. 59.95 (*0-940343-67-3*, NES10) Natl Contract Mgmt.

Bruggeman, Roelof W. Families of Automorphic Forms. LC 94-22198. (Monographs in Mathematics: 88). 328p. 1994. 115.00 (*0-8176-5046-6*) Birkhauser.

Bruggemann, Aminia & Rast, Hubert. Assoziationen: Deutsch fur die Mittlestufe. (C). 1991. pap., wbk. ed., lab manual ed. 35.94 (*0-07-557368-7*) McGraw.

Bruggemann, Diethelm. Drei Mystifikationen Heinrich von Kleists: Kleists Wurzburger Reise-Kleists Lust-Spiel mit Goethe-Aloysius, Marquis von Montferrat. (Germanic Studies in America: Vol. 51). (GER.). 222p. 1985. text 20.00 (*0-8204-0228-1*) P Lang Pubng.

***Bruggemann, Diethelm.** Makarie und Mercurius: Goethes Wilhelm Meisters Wanderjahre Als Hermetischer Roman. Mommsen, Katharina, ed. (Germanic Studies in America). 158p. 1999. 30.95 (*3-906763-44-7*, Pub. by P Lang) P Lang Pubng.

Bruggemann, Jurgen K., et al. Zempoala: El Estudio de una Ciudad Prehispanica. 400p. 1991. pap. 20.00 (*968-6487-88-3*, IN016) UPLAAP.

Bruggemann, Walter. Praying the Psalms. rev. ed. LC 94-154133. 72p. 1993. pap. 5.95 (*0-88489-322-7*) St Marys.

Bruggen, A. C., et al, eds. Biodiversity & Conservation of the Mollusca: Proceedings of the Alan Solem Memorial Symposium on the Biodiversity & Conservation of the Mollusca, 11th International Malacological Congress, Siena, Italy, 1992. (Illus.). 240p. 1995. pap. 45.00 (*90-73348-47-1*, Pub. by Backhuys Pubs) Balogh.

Bruggen, Bill & Wade, Tom. Carve Your Own Carousel Horse. LC 89-85082. (Illus.). 96p. (Orig.). (YA). 1989. pap. 14.95 (*0-929758-04-8*) Beeman Jorgensen.

Bruggen, Bill, jt. auth. see Machan, Wayne.

Bruggen, Coosje Van, see Van Bruggen, Coosje.

Bruggen, Coosje Van, see Oldenburg, Claes & Van Bruggen, Coosje.

Bruggen, Coosje Van, see Van Bruggen, Coosje.

Bruggen, J. Van, see Van Bruggen, J.

Bruggen, Peter. Who Cares? True Stories of the NHS Reforms. LC 98-175073. 720p. 1998. pap. 24.95 (*1-897766-32-7*, Pub. by Jon Carpenter) Paul & Co Pubs.

Bruggen, Theodore Van, see Van Bruggen, Theodore.

Bruggencate, Ten K. Dutch-English Dictionary. 19th ed. (DUT & ENG.). 1990. 58.00 (*0-7859-8950-1*) Fr & Eur.

— English-Dutch Dictionary. (DUT & ENG.). 1048p. 1980. 59.95 (*0-8288-0451-6*, M9747) Fr & Eur.

— English-Dutch Dictionary. 20th ed. (DUT & ENG.). 1990. 58.00 (*0-7859-8953-6*) Fr & Eur.

Brugger. Beginners Guide Program Basic. 1998. pap. 11.74 (*0-07-234607-8*) McGraw.

— Republican Theory Political. LC 98-43284. 1999. text 59.95 (*0-312-22053-7*) St Martin.

Brugger, Bill. China: Liberation & Transformation, 1942-1962. LC 81-102749. 1981. 44.00 (*0-389-20086-7*, N6859) B&N Imports.

— China: Radicalism to Revisionism 1962-1979. LC 81-102749. 1981. 44.00 (*0-389-20087-5*, N6860) B&N Imports.

Brugger, Bill, ed. Chinese Marxism in Flux, 1978-1984: Essays on Epistemology, Ideology, & Political Economy. LC 84-26680. 230p. 1985. reprint ed. pap. 71.30 (*0-7837-9943-8*, 206067000006) Bks Demand.

— Chinese Marxism in Flux, 1978-84. LC 84-26680. 226p. (gr. 13). 1985. pap. text 43.95 (*0-87332-323-8*) M E Sharpe.

Brugger, Bill & Kelly, David. Chinese Marxism in the Post-Mao Era. LC 89-26310. 237p. 1990. 37.50 (*0-8047-1782-6*) Stanford U Pr.

Brugger, Bill & Reglar, Stephen. Politics, Economy, & Society in Contemporary China. 376p. (C). 1994. 47.50 (*0-8047-2349-4*) Stanford U Pr.

— Politics, Economy, & Society in Contemporary China. viii, 367p. 1994. pap. 17.95 (*0-8047-2350-8*) Stanford U Pr.

Brugger, E. & Stuckey, B. Self Reliant Development in Europe. 300p. 1986. text 77.95 (*0-566-05095-1*, Pub. by Dartmth Pub) Ashgate Pub Co.

Brugger, Ernst A. & Rajapatirana, Sarath, eds. New Perspectives on Financing Small Business in Developing Countries. LC 95-9273. 194p. 1995. pap. 19.95 (*1-55815-341-1*) ICS Pr.

Brugger, Kathleen J., jt. auth. see Hancock, Arthur B.

Brugger, Robert J. Beverley Tucker: Heart over Head in the Old South. LC 77-16294. (Johns Hopkins University Studies in Historical & Political Science: Ser. 96, No. 2). 322p. reprint ed. pap. 99.90 (*0-8357-7153-9*, 202583400046) Bks Demand.

— Maryland: A Middle Temperament, 1634-1980. (Maryland Paperback Bookshelf Ser.). (Illus.). 864p. 1996. reprint ed. pap. 25.95 (*0-8018-5465-2*) Johns Hopkins.

Brugger, Robert J., ed. see Madison, James, et al.

Brugger, Suzanne. Australians & Egypt: 1914-1919. (Illus.). 188p. 1980. 29.95 (*0-522-84175-9*, Pub. by Melbourne Univ Pr) Paul & Co Pubs.

Brugger, Walter. Diccionario de Filosofia. (FRE & SPA.). 736p. 1988. 75.00 (*0-7859-3345-X*, 8425401461) Fr & Eur.

— Dictionary of Philosophy. 21st ed. (ENG & GER.). 592p. 1992. 75.00 (*0-8288-2277-8*, M7587) Fr & Eur.

***Bruggermann, A.** Privatisierung und Restrukturierung in Mittle und Osteuropa: Die Rolle Schlechter Schulden und der Einfluß der sozialen Absicherung. (Internationale Wirtschaftspolitik (International Economic Policy): Vol. 5).Tr. of Privatisation & Restructuring in Central & Eastern Europe: The Role of "Bad Debts" & the Impact of Social Security. (GER.). 260p. 1999. text 54.00 (*90-5708-057-5*, Verlag Fakultas) Gordon & Breach.

Bruggink, Darrell. Ultra Narrow Row Corn: Squeezing the Most Out of Your Crop. (Illus.). 48p. (Orig.). 1996. pap. 7.95 (*0-944079-26-1*) Lessiter Pubns.

Bruggink, Donald J., ed. see Boersma, Jeanette.

Bruggink, Donald J., ed. see Brouwer, Arie R.

Bruggink, Donald J., ed. see Gasero, Russell L.

Bruggman, Maximilien, jt. auth. see Acatos, Sylvio.

Bruggmoser, G., ed. see Wannenmacher, M.

Brugh, Anne, jt. auth. see Beede, Benjamin R.

Brugha, T. S., ed. Social Support & Psychiatric Disorder: Research Findings & Guidelines for Clinical Practice. (Studies in Social & Community Psychiatry). (Illus.). 361p. (C). 1995. text 95.00 (*0-521-44238-9*) Cambridge U Pr.

Brughere, C. F. The Children of Dipsea. 86p. (Orig.). 1997. pap. 9.95 (*1-880710-02-1*) Monterey Pacific.

Brughton. Pyramids. (C). 1999. teacher ed. write for info. (*0-321-40643-5*) Addison-Wesley.

Brugioni, Dino A. Photo Fakery: The History & Techniques of Photographic Deception & Manipulation. LC 99-36376. (Illus.). 227p. 1999. 32.95 (*1-57488-166-3*) Brasseys.

Brugiroux, Andre. One People, One Planet: Adventures of a World Citizen. 288p. (Orig.). 1994. pap. 13.95 (*1-85168-029-2*, Pub. by Onewrld Pubns) Penguin Putnam.

Brugman, Claudia M. Communication in Context: A Guide to Issues in the Interactional & Transactional Uses of Language. LC 96-154795. 125p. (C). 1995. pap. 24.95 (*0-908569-96-3*, Pub. by Univ Otago Pr) Intl Spec Bk.

Brugman, Karl, jt. auth. see Osthoff, Hermann.

Brugmann, Karl. Kurze Vergleichende Grammatik der Indogermanischen Sprachen. (C). 1969. reprint ed. 215.40 (*3-11-000179-9*) De Gruyter.

Brugmann, Karl & Delbrueck, Berthold. Grundriss der Vergleichenden Grammatik der Indogermanischen Sprachen, 5 vols. (GER.). (C). 1967. reprint ed. 1461.55 (*3-11-000180-2*) De Gruyter.

Brugmann, Karl, jt. ed. see Curtius, Georg.

Brugnano, L. & Trigiante, D. Solving Differential Equations by Multistep Initial & Boundary Value Methods. (Stability & Control). 412p. 1998. text 65.00 (*90-5699-107-8*) Gordon & Breach.

Brugnaro, Ferruccio. Fist of Sun. Hirschman, Jack, tr. from ITA. LC 97-22945. 120p. 1997. pap. 10.95 (*1-880684-52-7*) Curbstone.

Brugnola, Orlanda. King of Thornbushes. 1972. pap. 2.00 (*0-685-36813-0*) Oyez.

Brugsch-Bey, Heinrich. Egypt under the Pharoahs. (Illus.). 469p. 1998. reprint ed. pap. text 19.00 (*0-7881-5813-9*) DIANE Pub.

Brugsch, Emile, jt. auth. see Maspero, Gaston C.

Brugsch, Heinrich K. Dictionnaire Geographique De l'Ancienne Egypte. (FRE.). 1420p. 1974. reprint ed. 480.00 (*3-487-05312-8*) G Olms Pubs.

— Recueil des Monuments Egyptiens. 196p. 1981. reprint ed. 375.00 (*3-487-06979-2*) G Olms Pubs.

Bruguera Grane, Francisco. Diccionario Ingles-Espanol, Espanol-Ingles. 3rd ed. (ENG & SPA.). 680p. 1979. pap. 6.95 (*0-8288-4770-3*, S50345) Fr & Eur.

Brugues, Jean-Louis. Dictionnaire de la Morale Catholique. (FRE.). 473p. 1991. 105.00 (*0-7859-8093-8*, 2854432193) Fr & Eur.

Bruguier, Leonard R., ed. see Sansom-Flood, Renee & Bernie, Shirley A.

Bruhacs, J. The Law of Non-Navigational Uses of International Watercourses. Zehery, M., tr. LC 92-18240. 1993. lib. bdg. 121.00 (*0-7923-1822-6*) Kluwer Academic.

Bruhat, Maurice A., ed. Endometriosis. (Contributions to Gynecology & Obstetrics Ser.: Vol. 16). (Illus.). xiv, 394p. 1987. 200.00 (*3-8055-4627-0*) S Karger.

— The Management of Adnexal Cysts: Proceedings of the First European Congress of the Raoul Palmer Club of Gynecologic Endoscopy, Clermont-Ferrand, 10-11 September, 1992. LC 93-26992. (Illus.). 264p. 1994. 125.00 (*0-632-03794-6*) Blackwell Sci.

Bruhi, P. A. A Century of New & Rare Indian Plants. (C). 1988. 80.00 (*0-7855-3231-5*, Pub. by Scientific) St Mut.

Bruhl, Carlrichard. Aus Mittelalter und Diplomatik. (GER.). xxiv, 852p. 1989. 238.00 (*3-615-00052-8*, Pub. by Weidmann) Lubrecht & Cramer.

— Aus Mittelalter und Diplomatik Bd. 3: Studien zur Verfassungsgeschichte und Diplomatik (1984, 1988-1996) (GER.). x, 272p. 1997. write for info. (*3-615-00182-6*) G Olms Pubs.

— Geschichte der Philatelie. (GER.). 1200p. 1985. write for info. (*3-487-07618-7*) G Olms Pubs.

Bruhl, Christine Grafin von, see von Bruhl, Christine Grafin.

Bruhl, P. A. A Census of Indian Mosses. (C). 1988. 95.00 (*0-7855-3255-2*, Pub. by Scientific) St Mut.

— A Guide to the Orchids of Sikkim. 208p. (C). 1978. 50.00 (*0-7855-3290-0*, Pub. by Scientific) St Mut.

Bruhlmann, W., jt. ed. see Buchmann, P.

Bruhm, Steven. Gothic Bodies: The Politics of Pain in Romantic Fiction. 208p. (C). 1994. text 32.50 (*0-8122-3291-7*) U of Pa Pr.

Bruhn, Arnold R. Earliest Childhood Memories: Theory & Application to Clinical Practice, Vol. 1. LC 90-7079. 192p. 1990. 45.00 (*0-275-92699-0*, C2699, Praeger Pubs) Greenwood.

Bruhn, Arthur F. Exploring Southern Utah's Land of Color. 2nd rev. ed. (Illus.). 96p. 1993. pap. 6.48 (*0-915630-32-X*) Zion.

Bruhn, David D., et al. Ready to Answer All Bells: A Blueprint for Successful Naval Engineering. LC 97-11970. (Illus.). 208p. 1997. 22.95 (*1-55750-227-7*) Naval Inst Pr.

Bruhn, E. F. Analysis & Design of Flight Vehicle Structures. (Illus.). 1973. write for info. (*0-9615234-0-9*) Jacobs Pub.

Bruhn, Gert. Das Selbstzitat Bei Thomas Mann: Untersuchungen Zum Verhaltnis von Fiktion und Autobiographie in Seinem Werk. LC 92-21920. (American University Studies: Germanic Languages & Literature: Ser. I, Vol. 98). XVI, 203p. (C). 1992. text 39.95 (*0-8204-1810-2*) P Lang Pubng.

Bruhn, J. G. & Rebach, H. M. Clinical Sociology: An Agenda for Action. LC 96-38679. (Clinical Sociology Ser.). (Illus.). 260p. (C). 1996. 47.00 (*0-306-45448-3*, Kluwer Plenum) Kluwer Academic.

Bruhn, J. G., jt. auth. see Rebach, H. M.

Bruhn-Jade, Christa. Small Secretary's Lexicon: Kleines Sekretaerinnenlexikon. (GER.). 517p. 1986. 75.00 (*0-8288-1276-4*, M7086) Fr & Eur.

Bruhn, John B., et al. Social Support & Health: An Annotated Bibliography. LC 87-17796. (Library of Sociology: Vol. 13). 528p. 1987. text 40.00 (*0-8240-8348-2*, SS412) Garland.

Bruhn, John G. Angles to Grow By. (Illus.). 107p. 1981. pap. 6.00 (*0-9616570-1-4*) J G Bruhn.

— Being Me Is Being Human. (Illus.). 64p. 1980. pap. 6.00 (*0-9616570-0-6*) J G Bruhn.

— Border Health: Challenges for the United States & Mexico. LC 97-1984. (Illus.). 240p. 1997. text write for info. (*0-8153-1386-1*, SS909) Garland.

— Life Is an Inside Job. (Illus.). 87p. (Orig.). 1995. pap. 6.00 (*0-9616570-3-0*) J G Bruhn.

***Bruhn, John G.** Voices of the Soul. 96p. 1999. pap. 11.00 (*0-9616570-4-9*) J G Bruhn.

Bruhn, John G., jt. auth. see Wolf, Stewart G.

Bruhn, John G., ed. see Sylvester, Judith L.

Bruhn, Jutta-Annetta. Coins & Costume in Late Antiquity. LC 93-30777. (Byzantine Collection Publications: No. 9). (Illus.). 68p. 1993. pap. 12.00 (*0-88402-219-6*) Dumbarton Oaks.

Bruhn, Jutta-Annette. Designs in Miniature: The Story of Mosaic Glass, 1995. LC 94-74823. (Illus.). 48p. (Orig.). 1995. pap. 9.95 (*0-87290-136-X*) Corning.

***Bruhn, Karl, ed.** Fly Fishing British Columbia. (Illus.). 207p. 1999. pap. 29.95 (*1-895811-67-8*, Pub. by Heritage Hse) F Amato Pubns.

Bruhn, Kathleen. Taking on Goliath: Party Formation, Party System Change, & Democratization in Mexico. LC 95-47061. (C). 1996. pap. 22.50 (*0-271-01587-X*); text 60.00 (*0-271-01586-1*) Pa St U Pr.

Bruhn, Klaus, et al, eds. Ludwig Alsdorf & Indian Studies. (C). 1990. 23.50 (*81-208-0681-6*, Pub. by Motilal Bnarsidass) S Asia.

Bruhn, Sheila. Diary of a Girl in Changi 1941-45. (Illus.). 144p. (Orig.). 1994. pap. 14.95 (*0-86417-619-8*, Pub. by Kangaroo Pr) Seven Hills Bk.

Bruhn, Sigland. The Temptation of Paul Hindemith: Mathis der Mahler As a Spiritual Testimony. 1998. text 46.00 (*1-57647-013-X*) Pendragon NY.

Bruhn, Siglind. Images & Ideas in Modern French Piano Music. LC 97-40215. (Aesthetics in Music Ser.: Vol. 6). 1998. text 46.00 (*0-945193-95-5*) Pendragon NY.

Bruhn, Siglind, ed. Encrypted Messages in Alban Berg's Music. LC 97-9719. (Border Crossings Ser.: Vol. 1). (Illus.). 323p. 1998. text 60.00 (*0-8153-2480-4*, H2020) Garland.

Bruhn, Siglind & Auner, Joseph, eds. Messiaen's Language of Mystical Love. LC 98-12602. (Twentieth-Century Music Ser.: Vol. 1). 271p. 1998. 45.00 (*0-8153-2747-1*) Garland.

Bruhn, Thomas. Defining Ourselves: Photography & Drawings from the Sandra & David Bakalar Collection. (Illus.). 16p. (Orig.). Date not set. pap. 5.00 (*0-918386-45-4*) W Benton Mus.

— Defining Ourselves: Photography & Drawings from the Sandra & David Bakalar Collection. (Illus.). 16p. (Orig.). 1995. 5.00 (*0-614-10435-1*) W Benton Mus.

Bruhn, Thomas & Steinway, Kate. The American Print: Originality & Experimentation 1790-1890. (Illus.). 128p. (Orig.). 1993. 14.95 (*0-614-10432-7*) W Benton Mus.

Bruhn, Thomas P. The Art of Al Frueh. (Illus.). 16p. 2.00 (*0-918386-35-7*) W Benton Mus.

— Harold Hugo (1910-1985) Museum Patron. (Illus.). 24p. 1989. 3.00 (*0-918386-41-1*) W Benton Mus.

— The Landscape Etchings of Robert C. Minor. (Illus.). 8p. Date not set. 3.00 (*0-614-10425-4*) W Benton Mus.

Bruhn, Thomas P. & Berlind, Robert, contrib. by. Li-Lan: Stationary Images. (Illus.). 12p. 1990. 4.50 (*0-918386-42-X*) W Benton Mus.

Bruhn, Thomas P. & Sternway, Kate. The American Print: Originality & Experimentation 1790-1890. (Illus.). 128p. (Orig.). Date not set. pap. 14.95 (*0-918386-44-6*) W Benton Mus.

Bruhn, Thomas P., jt. auth. see Terenzio, Stephanie.

Bruhn, Wolfgang & Tilke, Max. A Pictorial History of Costume. (Illus.). 200p. 1992. 60.00 (*3-8030-5008-1*, Pub. by E J Wasmuth) Empire Pub Srvs.

— A Pictorial History of Costume: A Survey of Costume of All Periods & Peoples from Antiquity to Modern Times Including National Costume in Europe & Non-European Countries. LC 95-19731. (Illus.). 200p. 1995. 60.00 (*0-88734-920-X*) Empire Pub Srvs.

Bruhn, Wolfgang, jt. auth. see Tilke, Max.

Bruhns, E. Maxine. Nationality Rooms Book. 4th ed. 60p. 1994. pap. 6.50 (*0-9634096-0-3*) U Pitt Nat Rms & IEP.

Bruhns, Karen O. Ancient South America. (World Archaeology Ser.). (Illus.). 448p. (C). 1994. pap. text 25.95 (*0-521-27761-2*) Cambridge U Pr.

— Cihuatan: An Early Postclassic Town of El Salvador: the 1977-78 Excavations. Feldman, Lawrence, ed. (Monographs in Anthropology: No. 5). (Illus.). vii, 171p. 1980. pap. 9.00 (*0-913134-82-1*) Mus Anthro MO.

***Bruhns, Karen O. & Stothert, Karen E.** Women in Ancient America. 352p. 1999. 34.95 (*0-8061-3169-1*) U of Okla Pr.

***Bruhns, Nina.** Catch Me If You Can. (Intimate Moments Ser.: Vol. 990). 2000. mass mkt. 4.50 (*0-373-07990-7*) Silhouette.

Bruhns, O. T. & Stein, Erwin. IUTAM Symposium on Micro & Macrostructural Aspects of Thermoplasticity: Proceedings of the IUTAM Symposium Held in Bochum, Germany, 25-29 August, 1997. LC 98-34746. (Solid Mechanics & Its Applications Ser.). 1998. 214.00 (*0-7923-5265-3*) Kluwer Academic.

Bruice. Organic Chemistry. 2nd ed. LC 97-29107. 1362p. 1997. 112.00 (*0-13-841925-6*) P-H.

***Bruigom, B. L.** Dolphin Tales: True Stories of Atlantic Spotted Dolphins. (Illus.). 50p. 1999. 12.00 (*0-9676074-0-X*) W S Smith.

Bruijn, De, see De Bruijn.

Bruijn, Frans J. De, see Akkermans, A. D.

Bruijn, Gerald. Distribution, Vol. II-4. (Single Market Review Ser.). 1998. 80.00 (*0-7494-2316-1*) Kogan Page Ltd.

Bruijn, J. T. De, see De Bruijn, J. T.

Bruijn, Jaap R. The Dutch Navy of the Seventeenth & Eighteenth Centuries. LC 93-18700. (Studies in Maritime History). (Illus.). 273p. (C). 1993. text 34.95 (*0-87249-875-1*) U of SC Pr.

Bruijn, Jeanne De, see De Bruijn, Jeanne, ed.

Bruijn, N. G. De, see De Bruijn, N. G.

Bruijn, Norbert P. De, see De Bruijn, Norbert P., ed.

Bruijne, G. A. De, see Baud, I. S. A. & De Bruijne, G. A., eds.

Bruijnzeel & Proctor. Tropical Forest Ecosystems. (Physical Environment Ser.). 352p. (C). 1999. pap. 25.00 (*0-415-11168-4*) Routledge.

Bruijnzeel-Koomen, C. A. & Hoefsmit, F. C., eds. Immunopharmacology of Macrophages & Other Antigen-Presenting Cells. (Handbook of Immunopharmacology Ser.). (Illus.). 208p. 1994. text 79.00 (*0-12-137800-4*) Acad Pr.

***Bruijnzeel-Koomen, C. A. & Knol, E., eds.** Immunology & Drug Therapy of Allergic Skin Diseases. (Progress in Drug Research Ser.). 260p. 2000. 129.00 (*3-7643-5970-6*) Birkhauser.

Bruin, A. De, see De Bruin, A.

Bruin, E. J. De, see Mulder, C. L., ed.

Bruin, E. J. De, see Mulder, C. L. & De Bruin, E. J., eds.

Bruin, Frans & Vonjidis, Alexander, trs. from GRE. The Books of Autolykos: On a Moving Sphere & on Risings & Settings. (Illus.). 83p. (C). 1971. text 12.00 (*0-8156-6034-0*, Pub. by Am U Beirut) Syracuse U Pr.

Bruin, G., et al. Marine Fishery Resources of Sri Lanka. LC 96-146477. (FAO Species Identification Guide for Fishery Purpose Ser.). 425p. 1994. pap. 75.00 (*92-5-103293-9*) Food & Agri Org UN.

***Bruin, J., et al.** Ecology & Evolution of the Acari. LC 99-18970. (Series Entomologica). 1999. write for info. (*0-7923-5658-6*) Kluwer Academic.

Bruin, Jacqualyn De, see De Bruin, Jacqualyn.

Bruin, Ronald De, see De Bruin, Ronald.

Bruington, Finis M. It's All True: An Autobiography. LC 86-90923. (Illus.). 366p. 1986. text 9.95 (*0-9616838-0-5*) F M Bruington.

— The Rest of the Story. LC 87-71127. (Illus.). 381p. 1987. 9.95 (*0-9616838-1-3*) F M Bruington.

Bruington-Rudeseal, Pat. Get It in Writing. 512p. (C). 1990. teacher ed. write for info. (*0-03-026607-6*) Harcourt Coll Pubs.

Bruininks, Robert H., et al, eds. Deinstitutionalization & Community Adjustment of Mentally Retarded People. LC 80-70191. (Monographs of the American Association on Mental Retardation: No. 4). 412p. 1981. text 7.00 (*0-940898-10-1*) Am Assn Mental.

Bruininks, Robert H., jt. auth. see Werder, Judy K.

Bruins, C., tr. see Van Mierop, L. H. & Opperheimer-Dekker, A., eds.

Bruins, Elton J. The Americanization of a Congregation. 2nd ed. (Historical Series of the Reformed Church in America: Vol. 26). 260p. 1996. pap. 15.00 (*0-8028-4144-9*) Eerdmans.

Bruins, Hendrik J. & Lithwick, Harvey, eds. The Arid Frontier: Interactive Management of Environment & Development. LC 97-42019. (Geojournal Library: No. 41). 396p. 1997. 187.00 (*0-7923-4227-5*) Kluwer Academic.

Bruins, Paul F. Basic Principles of Rotational Molding. x, 286p. 1971. text 274.00 (*0-677-14980-8*) Gordon & Breach.

— Unsaturated Polyester Technology. LC 74-12774. x, 438p. 1976. text 295.00 (*0-677-21160-0*) Gordon & Breach.

Bruins, Paul F., ed. Packaging with Plastics. LC 72-78922. x, 212p. 1974. text 249.00 (*0-677-12200-4*) Gordon & Breach.

— Polyurethane Technology. LC 68-54598. (Polymar Engineering & Technology Ser.). 299p. reprint ed. pap. 92.70 (*0-608-13424-4*, 205576300037) Bks Demand.

Bruinsma, Frank R., jt. auth. see Rietveld, Piet.

Bruinsma, R., jt. auth. see Rabin, Y.

Bruinsma, Reinder. It's Time to Stop Rehearsing What We Believe & Start Looking at What Difference It Makes. LC 97-22394. 1998. pap. 9.99 (*0-8163-1401-2*) Pacific Pr Pub Assn.

***Bruinsma, Reinder.** Our Awesome God: The God Many Christians Claim to Know Is Not the God of the Bible. Holt, B. Russell, ed. LC 99-87385. 159p. 2000. pap. 11.99 (*0-8163-1781-X*) Pacific Pr Pub Assn.

B

Bruinsma, Reinder. Seventh-Day Adventist Attitudes Toward Roman Catholicism, 1844-1965. LC 94-72955. 390p. 1994. pap. 19.99 (*1-883925-04-5*) Andrews Univ Pr.

Bruinsma, Sheryl. New Object Lessons: For Children of All Ages. (Object Lessons Ser.). 128p. (YA). (gr. 10). 1980. pap. 6.99 (*0-8010-0775-5*) Baker Bks.

— Object Lessons for Family Devotions. LC 97-1659. (Object Lessons Ser.). 80p. (Orig.). (gr. 10 up). 1997. pap. 7.99 (*0-8010-5762-0*) Baker Bks.

— Object Lessons for Very Young Children. (Object Lesson Ser.). 128p. (YA). (gr. 11). 1988. pap. 7.99 (*0-8010-0956-1*) Baker Bks.

— Object Lessons from Paper Projects. LC 97-28456. (Object Lessons Ser.). 96p. (gr. 10). 1997. pap. 7.99 (*0-8010-5776-0*) Baker Bks.

Bruinsma, Ted. Foresight Capacity. LC 95-77641. 325p. (Orig.). 1995. pap. 12.95 (*0-9647561-0-2*) Libris Bks.

Bruinvels, J., jt. ed. see Gershon, Samuel.

Brujo, Elizardo. Rainbow Lightning & the Santa Fe Trail. 256p. 1993. pap. write for info. (*0-9639582-0-8*) ELMAC Press.

Brukner, Ira B. Questions, Short Poems, Water & Air. LC 98-65855. 78p. (Orig.). pap. 11.00 (*1-881523-08-X*) Junction CA.

***Brukner, Peter.** Clinical Sports Medicine. 2nd ed. (Hazelden Chronic Illness Ser.). (Illus.). 820p. 2000. 89.95 (*0-07-470651-9*) McGraw-Hill Prof.

Brukner, Peter & Miran-Khan, Karim, eds. Clinical Sports Medicine. 624p. 1993. text 79.00 (*0-07-008607-9*) McGraw-Hill HPD.

Brukoff, Barry, photos by. Morocco. LC 93-20181. (Illus.). 128p. 1993. 49.50 (*0-8109-3631-3*) Abrams.

Bruland, Kristine, ed. Technology Transfer: Scandinavian Industrialization & Economic Growth. 424p. 1992. 19.50 (*0-85496-605-6*) Berg Pubs.

Bruland, Kristine & O'Brian, Patrick, eds. From Family Firms to Corporate Capitalism: Essays in Business & Industrial History in Honour of Peter Mathias. (Illus.). 388p. (C). 1998. text 85.00 (*0-19-829046-2*) OUP.

Bruland, Kristine, jt. ed. see Berg, Maxine.

Bruleigh, Dianne L. New England Church Supper Favorites. (Illus.). 48p. (Orig.). 1989. pap. 3.95 (*0-933050-71-2*) New Eng Pr VT.

Bruley. Women In Britain Since 1900 LC 99-18545. 1999. text 59.95 (*0-312-22375-7*) St Martin.

Bruley, Duane F., jt. ed. see Erdmann, W.

Bruley, Duane F., jt. ed. see Hudetz, A. G.

Brulhart, Marius & Hine, R. C. Intra-Industry Trade & Adjustment: The European Experience. LC 98-16157. 1999. text 69.95 (*0-312-21568-1*) St Martin.

Brulin, O. & Hsieh, R. K., eds. Mechanics of Micropolar Media. 484p. 1982. text 66.00 (*9971-950-02-2*) World Scientific Pub.

Brull, Dieter. Waldorf Schools & Threefold Structure. Mitchell, David, ed. 96p. 1997. pap. 7.50 (*1-888365-05-6*) Assn Waldorf Schls.

Brull, Sorin & Cunningham, Anthony. Anesthesia & Critical Care Manual. 3rd ed. 400p. 39.00 (*0-683-30607-3*) Lppncott W & W.

Brull, Sorin J., jt. auth. see Greene, Nicholas M.

***Brulle, Robert J.** Agency, Democracy & Nature. LC 00-28264. (Illus.). 715p. 2000. 62.00 (*0-262-02480-2*); pap. 25.00 (*0-262-52281-0*) MIT Pr.

***Brulle, Robert V.** Angels Zero: P-47 Close Air Support in Europe. LC 00-26765. 2000. 29.95 (*1-56098-374-4*) Smithsonian.

Bruller, O., et al. Advances in Continuum Mechanics. (Illus.). 528p. 1991. 122.95 (*0-387-53988-3*) Spr-Verlag.

Brulotte, Gaetan. The Secret Voice. 96p. 1990. pap. write for info. (*0-88984-097-0*) Porcup Quill.

Brum. Biology Exploring Life Study Guide. 2nd ed. 1997. text 24.00 (*0-471-31398-X*) Wiley.

Brum, Gil, et al. Biology: Exploring Life. 2nd ed. 264p. 1993. pap. text, teacher ed. 14.95 (*0-471-59591-8*) Wiley.

Brum, Gil, et al. Biology: Exploring Life: Unit 1: Cell Bio & Genetics, Unit 3: Form & Function of Animal Life, Unit 4: Evolution Set. 2nd ed. 920p. 1996. pap. text 96.85 (*0-471-16898-X*) Wiley.

Brum, Gil, et al. Biology: Exploring Life: Unit 1, Unit 4, Unit 5 & Unit 6 Set. 2nd ed. 915p. 1994. pap. text 103.80 (*0-471-10657-7*) Wiley.

— Biology Chaps. 1-17: Exploring Life, Cell Biology & Genetics, vol. 1. 2nd ed. 444p. 1994. pap. 50.95 (*0-471-01827-9*) Wiley.

— Biology Chaps. 18-21: Exploring Life, Form & Function of Plant Life, vol. 2. 2nd ed. 114p. 1993. pap. 20.95 (*0-471-01831-7*) Wiley.

— Biology Chaps. 22-32: Exploring Life, Form & Function of Animal Life, vol. 3. 2nd ed. 320p. 1993. pap. 27.95 (*0-471-01830-9*) Wiley.

— Biology Chaps. 33-35: Exploring Life, Evolution, vol. 4. 2nd ed. 156p. 1993. pap. 20.95 (*0-471-01829-5*) Wiley.

— Biology Chaps. 36-39: Exploring Life, Diversity & Classification, vol. 5. 2nd ed. 168p. 1993. pap. 20.95 (*0-471-01828-7*) Wiley.

— Biology Chaps. 40-44: Exploring Life, Ecology & Animal Behavior, vol. 6. 2nd ed. 183p. 1993. pap. 20.95 (*0-471-01832-5*) Wiley.

— Biology Vols. 1, 2, & 4-6: Exploring Life Set. 2nd ed. 1029p. 1994. pap. text 40.50 (*0-471-11025-6*) Wiley.

— Biology Vols. 1, 3, & 6: Exploring Life Set. 2nd ed. 409p. 1994. pap. text 39.50 (*0-471-11076-0*) Wiley.

— Biology Vols. 1, 4, & 5: Exploring Life Set. 2nd ed. 732p. 1994. pap. text 34.50 (*0-471-11140-6*) Wiley.

— Biology Vols. 1, 4, & 6: Exploring Life Set. 2nd ed. 732p. 1994. pap. text 34.50 (*0-471-11232-1*) Wiley.

— Biology Vols. 1-6: Exploring Life Set. 2nd ed. 1378p. 1994. text, student ed. 54.50 (*0-471-10958-4*) Wiley.

— Biology Vols. 1 & 6: Exploring Life Set. 2nd ed. 409p. 1994. pap. text 30.00 (*0-471-11192-9*) Wiley.

— Biology Fundamentals. 688p. 1995. pap. 77.95 (*0-471-59401-6*) Wiley.

Brum, Gil, et al. Biology Fundamentals & Caplan's Moral Matters: Ethical Issues in Medicine & the Life Science Set. 822p. 1995. pap. text 90.90 (*0-471-15464-4*) Wiley.

Brum, Gil, et al. Biology Fundamentals & Study Guide Biology Fundamentals Set. 843p. 1995. text 104.90 (*0-471-13462-7*) Wiley.

— Biology Study Guide for Biology Second Edition & Moral Matters Set, set. 2nd ed. 1704p. 1995. text, student ed. 131.85 (*0-471-13453-8*) Wiley.

— Biology 2 Units 1 4 6 & SG S, Units 1, 4 & 6. 2nd ed. 1115p. 1995. text, student ed. 115.80 (*0-471-14042-2*) Wiley.

Brum, Gil D. Biology: Exploring Life. 2nd ed. 368p. 1993. pap., student ed. 34.95 (*0-471-59585-3*) Wiley.

— Biology Fundamentals. 237p. 1995. pap., student ed. 33.95 (*0-471-07623-6*) Wiley.

Brum, Gil D. & McKane, Larry K. Biology: Exploring Life. 2nd ed. LC 93-23383. 1120p. 1993. text 99.95 (*0-471-54408-6*) Wiley.

— Biology: Exploring Life. 2nd ed. 532p. 1994. pap., lab manual ed. 39.95 (*0-471-59806-2*) Wiley.

Brum, L. J. How to Beat the Car Dealer at His Own Game: Buying a New or Used Car. LC 82-70174. (Illus.). 134p. 1982. pap. 5.95 (*0-942662-00-8*) BM Consumer Pubns.

Brumagin, Leslie, ed. see Spangler, Randal & Davis, Bonnie.

Brumagin, Wayne, jt. auth. see Tucker, Bettie E.

Brumagin, Wayne, ed. see Young, Philip G.

***Bruman, Henry J.** Alcohol in Ancient Mexico. LC 99-50946. (Illus.). 224p. 2000. 30.00 (*0-87480-658-5*) U of Utah Pr.

Brumana, Fernando G. & Martinez, E. G. Spirits from the Margin: Umbana in Sao Paulo: A Study in Popular Religion & Social Experience. (Uppsala Studies in Cultural Anthropology: No. 12). 308p. (Orig.). 1989. pap. 49.50 (*91-554-2498-8*) Coronet Bks.

Brumbach. Electronic Variable Speed Drives. (Electronics Technology Ser.). 32p. 1996. teacher ed. 15.00 (*0-8273-6938-7*) Delmar.

Brumbach, Hetty J. & Jarvenpa, Robert. Ethnoarchaeological & Cultural Frontiers: Athapaskan, Algonquian & European Adaptations in the Central Subarctic. (American University Studies: Anthropology & Sociology: Ser. XI, Vol. 20). XII, 325p. (C). 1989. text 46.50 (*0-8204-0684-8*) P Lang Pubng.

Brumbach, Michael E. Electronic Variable Speed Drives. abr. ed. LC 95-22748. (Electronics Technology Ser.). 208p. 1995. pap. 43.95 (*0-8273-6937-9*) Delmar.

Brumback, Carl. What Meaneth This? 352p. 1947. pap. 4.95 (*0-88243-624-4*, 02-0624) Gospel Pub.

Brumback, Dorothy, jt. auth. see Rainbolt, Jo.

Brumback, Roger A. Neurology & Clinical Neuroscience. LC 92-48938. (Oklahoma Notes Ser.). 220p. 1993. 16.95 (*0-387-97959-X*) Spr-Verlag.

— Neurology & Clinical Neuroscience. 2nd ed. Claudet, Rita R., ed. LC 96-13784. (Oklahoma Notes Ser.). 186p. 1996. pap. 17.95 (*0-387-94635-7*) Spr-Verlag.

Brumback, Roger A. & Leech, Richard W., eds. Neuropathology & Basic Neuroscience. LC 94-42193. (Oklahoma Notes Ser.). 289p. 1995. 17.95 (*0-387-94389-7*) Spr-Verlag.

Brumback, Roger A., jt. auth. see Coffey, C. Edward.

Brumback, Roger A., jt. ed. see Herndon, Robert M.

Brumbaugh. Secondary Mathematics. 1995. pap. write for info. (*0-312-13303-0*) St Martin.

Brumbaugh, Alex. Transformation & Recovery: A Guide for the Design & Development of Acupuncture-Based Chemical Dependency Treatment Programs. 650p. 1994. pap. 39.00 (*0-9639791-0-8*) Stillpoint Pr.

Brumbaugh, Allyne. Big Magic Number Puzzles. 1992. pap. 10.95 (*0-590-49275-6*) Scholastic Inc.

— Do-It-Yourself Math Stories. 1992. pap. 12.95 (*0-590-49155-5*) Scholastic Inc.

Brumbaugh, Brenda & Thompson-Trenta, Nan. Listening for Articulation All Year Round: A Language Based Articulation Program. 208p. 1993. spiral bd. 37.95 (*1-55999-262-X*) LinguiSystems.

— Listening for Basic Concepts All Year 'Round: An Active Listening Program for Teaching Basic Concepts. 186p. 1990. spiral bd. 37.95 (*1-55999-108-9*) LinguiSystems.

— Listening for Language All Year 'Round: An Active Listening Program for Teaching Semantics. 187p. (gr. 2-6). 1993. spiral bd. 37.95 (*1-55999-250-6*) LinguiSystems.

— Listening for Vocabulary All Year 'Round: An Active Listening Program for Teaching Vocabulary. 196p. 1992. spiral bd. 37.95 (*1-55999-225-5*) LinguiSystems.

***Brumbaugh-Cayford, Cheryl.** Such a Time as This: Faith & Risk-Taking in the Book of Esther. (Good Ground Ser.: Vol. 1:7). 48p. 1999. pap. 5.95 (*0-87303-357-4*) Faith & Life.

Brumbaugh, Dan & Sauerhaft, Daniel E. Thrifts under Siege: Restoring Order to American Banking. 240p. 1988. text 39.95 (*0-88730-141-X*, HarpBusn) HarpInfo.

Brumbaugh, David. Earthquakes. LC 98-30046. 251p. 1998. pap. text 36.20 (*0-13-523847-1*) P-H.

Brumbaugh, Douglas. Scratch Your Brain Where It Itches C1: Math Games, Tricks & Quick Activities. 42p. (Orig.). (YA). (gr. 6-8). 1994. pap. 9.95 (*0-89455-524-3*) Crit Think Bks.

— Scratch Your Brain Where It Itches D1-Algebra: Math Games, Tricks & Quick Activities. 62p. (Orig.). (YA). (gr. 8-12). 1994. pap. 10.95 (*0-89455-525-1*) Crit Think Bks.

— Scratch Your Brain where It Itches E1-Geometry: Math Games, Tricks & Quick Activities. 54p. (Orig.). (YA). (gr. 8-12). 1994. pap. 10.95 (*0-89455-526-X*) Crit Think Bks.

Brumbaugh, Douglas & Rock, David. Activities for the FX-7400 G Mini Graph Calculator. unabridged ed. 46p. 1997. pap. text 10.95 (*0-9659710-0-7*) Paragon Publns.

— Problem of the Week Contest Manual. unabridged ed. (Problem of the Week Ser.: Vol. 1). 46p. 1997. pap. text 10.95 (*0-9659710-1-5*) Paragon Publns.

Brumbaugh, Douglas, jt. auth. see Rock, David.

***Brumbaugh, Douglas K.** Learning Activities Package. 270p. 2000. write for info. (*1-58692-007-3*) Copyright Mgmt.

— Mathematics Activities Handbook. 208p. 2000. write for info. (*1-58692-006-5*) Copyright Mgmt.

Brumbaugh, Douglas K., et al. Secondary Mathematics Methods. 500p. 1996. text 100.00 (*0-8058-8036-4*); pap. text 37.00 (*0-8058-8037-2*) L Erlbaum Assocs.

Brumbaugh, Eldon, jt. auth. see Erb, David.

***Brumbaugh, Frank.** Basic Boat Maintenance. O'Connor, John P., Jr., ed. (Illus.). 184p. 2000. spiral bd. 24.95 (*1-892216-23-X*) Bristol Fash.

— Marine Weather Forecasting. O'Connor, John P., Jr., ed. (Illus.). 96p. 2000. spiral bd. 15.95 (*1-892216-22-1*) Bristol Fash.

Brumbaugh, Gaius M. Maryland Records: Colonial, Revolutionary, County & Church from Original Sources, 2 vols., Set. (Illus.). 1201p. 1993. 75.00 (*0-8063-0059-0*, 750) Genealog Pub.

— Revolutionary War Records: Virginia. LC 67-28613. (Illus.). 707p. 1995. reprint ed. 45.00 (*0-8063-0060-4*) Genealog Pub.

Brumbaugh, Harley. Riverside Reflections: Poetic Moods from "The Valley of the Moon" LC 97-90715. ix, 119p. 1997. pap. 9.95 (*0-9659362-0-1*) Tusko Pr.

Brumbaugh, J. Frank. Mail Order Made Easy. 1982. pap. 20.00 (*0-87980-394-0*) Wilshire.

Brumbaugh, James E. Heating, Ventilating, & Air Conditioning, 3 vols., Set. 2nd ed. 1983. 76.95 (*0-672-23388-6*, Bobbs) Macmillan.

— Heating, Ventilating, & Air Conditioning Library, 3 vols. 2nd ed. LC 83-7064. (Illus.). 1984. 53.95 (*0-672-23227-8*) Macmillan.

— Heating, Ventilating, & Air Conditioning Library: Heating Fundamentals, Vol. 1. 2nd ed. LC 83-7064. (Illus.). 656p. 1983. 27.95 (*0-672-23389-4*, 23248, Aude IN) IDG Bks.

— Roofing & Reroofing: Installation, Repair, & Maintenance. 256p. Date not set. pap. 18.95 (*0-471-30498-0*) Wiley.

— Wood Furniture: Finishing, Refinishing, Repairing. 3rd ed. (Illus.). 384p. 1992. 30.00 (*0-02-517871-0*) Macmillan.

Brumbaugh, James E., ed. Truck Guide, Set. Incl. Vol. 2. Transmissions, Steering & Brakes. 304p. 1984. 16.95 (*0-672-23357-6*); 1984. Set text 50.95 (*0-672-23392-4*) Macmillan.

Brumbaugh, John M. Criminal Law & Approaches to the Study of Law, Cases & Materials. 2nd ed. (University Casebook Ser.). 1002p. 1991. text 43.50 (*0-88277-866-8*) Foundation Pr.

— Criminal Law & Approaches to the Study of Law, Manual for Teachers to Accompany Cases & Materials On. 2nd ed. (University Casebook Ser.). 175p. 1991. pap. text. write for info. (*0-88277-894-3*) Foundation Pr.

— Criminal Law & Approaches to the Study of Law, 1996 Supplement to Cases & Materials On. 2nd ed. (University Casebook Ser.). 159p. 1996. pap. text. write for info. (*1-56662-405-3*) Foundation Pr.

Brumbaugh, Judith A. Answers to Questions - Deuteronomy 24:4; Jeremiah 3:1; Matthew 5:32 & 19:9: Returning to an Original Mate; Marriage to an Unsaved Mate Followed by a Subsequent Marriage to a Christian; The "Exception Clause" rev. ed. 18p. pap. write for info. (*0-9624603-4-6*) Comt Restoration Fam.

— It's a Matter of Life or Death: Wrong Thinking about Marriage Leads to Destruction! (Illus.). 198p. (Orig.). 1989. pap. 7.00 (*0-9624603-1-1*) Comt Restoration Fam.

— Marriage from God's Perspective: Love Your Mate! (Illus.). 44p. (Orig.). 1993. student ed. 9.00 (*0-9624603-5-4*) Comt Restoration Fam.

— The Miracle of Marriage. (Illus.). 250p. (Orig.). 1996. pap. 13.00 (*0-9624603-8-9*) Comt Restoration Fam.

Brumbaugh, Linda. Scratch Your Brain Where It Itches A1: Math Games, Tricks & Quick Activities. 46p. (Orig.). (J). (gr. 1-3). 1994. pap. 9.95 (*0-89455-522-7*) Crit Think Bks.

— Scratch Your Brain Where it Itches B1: Math Games, Tricks & Quick Activities. 52p. (Orig.). (J). (gr. 3-6). 1994. pap. 9.95 (*0-89455-523-5*) Crit Think Bks.

Brumbaugh, Martin G. Christopher Dock. 1993. reprint ed. lib. bdg. 89.00 (*0-7812-5437-X*) Rprt Serv.

— A History of the German Baptist Brethren in Europe & America. LC 73-134377. (Communal Societies in America Ser.). (Illus.). reprint ed. 51.50 (*0-404-08425-7*) AMS Pr.

— Life & Works of Christoper Dock. LC 70-89154. (American Education: Its Men, Institutions, & Ideas. Series 1). 1977. reprint ed. 23.95 (*0-405-01392-2*) Ayer.

Brumbaugh, Robert S. The Philosophers of Greece. LC 81-9120. (Illus.). 274p. (C). 1981. reprint ed. pap. text 16.95 (*0-87395-551-X*) State U NY Pr.

— Plato for the Modern Age. (Illus.). 256p. (C). 1991. reprint ed. pap. text 24.50 (*0-8191-8356-3*) U Pr of Amer.

— Platonic Studies of Greek Philosophy: Form, Arts, Gadgets, & Hemlock. LC 88-8578. (SUNY Series in Philosophy). 296p. (C). 1989. text 24.50 (*0-88706-897-9*) State U NY Pr.

— Unreality & Time. LC 83-5084. (SUNY Series in Philosophy). 164p. (C). 1984. pap. text 24.95 (*0-87395-798-9*) State U NY Pr.

— Western Philosophic Systems & Their Cyclic Transformations. LC 91-28604. (Philosophical Explorations Ser.). 192p. (C). 1992. 31.95 (*0-8093-1771-0*) S Ill U Pr.

— Whitehead, Process Philosophy, & Education. 154p. (C). 1992. pap. text 22.50 (*0-8191-8484-5*) U Pr of Amer.

Brumbaugh, Thomas B. & Ladis, Andrew. The Art of Gerald Brockhurst. Phagan, Patricia Elaine, ed. LC 92-39990. (Illus.). 156p. 1993. pap. 20.00 (*0-915977-11-7*) Georgia Museum of Art.

Brumbaum, Ava J., et al. The Subject of Our Lives: Thirteen San Francisco Women Tell Their Stories. Thacher, Jean-Louise, ed. LC 98-4486. 240p. (Orig.). 1999. pap. 15.00 (*1-56474-270-9*) Fithian Pr.

***Brumbeau, Jeff.** The Quiltmaker's Gift. LC 99-6547. (Illus.). 48p. (J). (ps-3). 1999. 17.95 (*1-57025-199-1*) Pfeifer-Hamilton.

Brumberg, Bruce & Axelrod, Karen. Watch It Made in the U. S. A. A Visitor's Guide to the Companies That Make Your Favorite Products. 2nd rev. ed. LC 97-11093. (Illus.). 400p. 1997. pap. 17.95 (*1-56261-337-5*) Avalon Travel.

Brumberg, Bruce & Kaplan, Eve. The Best in M & A: The Full Text of Insightful Articles to Help You Get the Deal Done. Koffman, Susan, ed. 202p. 1996. pap. 99.00 (*1-886100-01-2*) Bowne Pubng.

Brumberg, Bruce S., ed. see Friedman, Howard M.

Brumberg, Elaine. Ageless. 1997. 22.00 (*0-614-27868-6*, Harper Ref) HarpC.

— Ageless: What Every Woman Needs to Know to Look Good & Feel Great. LC 96-52182. 368p. 1997. 24.00 (*0-06-270159-2*) HarpC.

— Save Your Money, Save Your Face: What Every Cosmetics Buyer Needs to Know. LC 84-4134. 368p. reprint ed. pap. 114.10 (*0-8357-4247-4*, 203703600007) Bks Demand.

Brumberg, Eugene V., jt. auth. see Brumberg, Victor A.

Brumberg, Joan Jacobs. The Body Project: An Intimate History of American Girls. LC 98-8098. (Illus.). 336p. 1998. pap. 13.00 (*0-679-73529-1*) Vin Bks.

***Brumberg, Joan Jacobs.** Body Project: An Intimate History of American Girls. (Illus.). (J). 1998. 18.35 (*0-606-18736-7*) Turtleback.

Brumberg, Joan Jacobs. Fasting Girls: The Emergence of Anorexia Nervosa As a Modern Disease. LC 87-25092. (Illus.). 376p. 1988. 38.50 (*0-674-29501-3*) HUP.

***Brumberg, Joan Jacobs.** Fasting Girls: The History of Anorexia Nervosa. (Illus.). 384p. 2000. pap. 14.00 (*0-375-72448-6*) Knopf.

— Fasting Girls: The History of Anorexia Nervosa. LC 00-28210. 2000. write for info. (*0-375-72453-2*) Vin Bks.

Brumberg, Joan Jacobs. Fasting Girls: The Surprising History of Anorexia Nervosa. 1989. pap. 14.95 (*0-452-26327-1*, Plume) Dutton Plume.

Brumberg, Stephan F. Going to America Going to School: The Jewish Immigrant Public School Encounter in Turn-of-the-Century New York City. LC 85-16791. 282p. 1986. 55.00 (*0-275-92030-5*, C2030, Praeger Pubs) Greenwood.

Brumberg, V. A. & Kovalevsky, Jean, eds. Relativity in Celestial Mechanics & Astrometry. (Publications of The International Astronomical Union-Proceedings of Symposia Ser.). (Orig.). 1986. lib. bdg. 154.50 (*90-277-2189-0*) Kluwer Academic.

Brumberg, Victor A. Analytical Techniques of Celestial Mechanics. LC 94-43966. (Astronomy & Astrophysics Library). 1995. 83.95 (*3-540-58782-9*) Spr-Verlag.

— Essential Relativistic Celestial Mechanics. LC 91-9865. 280p. 1991. 147.00 (*0-7503-0062-0*) IOP Pub.

***Brumberg, Victor A. & Brumberg, Eugene V.** Celestial Dynamics at High Eccentricities. (Advances in Astronomy & Astrophysics Ser.). 220p. 1999. text 95.00 (*90-5699-212-0*) Gordon & Breach.

Brumberg, Victor A., jt. ed. see Kovalevsky, J.

Brumberger, H., ed. see NATO Advanced Study Institute on Modern Aspects of.

Brumble, H. David, III. An Annotated Bibliography of American Indian & Eskimo Autobiographies. LC 80-23449. xii, 170p. 1981. text 40.00 (*0-8032-1175-9*) U of Nebr Pr.

Brumble, H. David. Classical Myths & Legends in the Middle Ages & Renaissance: A Dictionary of Allegorical Meanings. LC 96-53527. 480p. 1998. lib. bdg. 95.00 (*0-313-29451-8*, Greenwood Pr) Greenwood.

Brumble, H. David, III, tr. G. A. Bredero, the Spanish Brabanter: A Seventeenth-Century Dutch Social Satire in Five Acts. LC 81-19004. (Medieval & Renaissance Texts & Studies: Vol. 11). (Illus.). 160p. 1982. 20.00 (*0-86698-018-0*, MR11) MRTS.

***Brumby, Steven P., ed.** Small Missions for Energetic Astrophysics: Ultraviolet to Gamma-Ray. (AIP Conference Proceeding Ser.: Vol. 499). (Illus.). 176p. 1999. 80.00 (*1-56396-912-2*) Am Inst Physics.

Brumer, Leah R. Investing Natural Resource Revenues: Options for the States. LC HJ4169.B78. (Western Natural Resources Policy Ser.: No. 101). 50p. reprint ed. pap. 30.00 (*0-7837-2160-9*, 204246400004) Bks Demand.

Brumet, Robert. Al Encontrarte en Transicion: Usando los Cambios de la Vida para el Despertar Espiritual. (SPA.). 175p. Date not set. pap. 11.95 (*0-87159-245-2*, 267, Unity Hse) Unity Bks.

Brumet, Robert. Finding Yourself in Transition: Using Life's Changes for Spiritual Awakening. LC 94-17226. 167p. 1994. pap. 9.95 (*0-87159-012-3*) Unity Bks.

***Brumett, Jonas O.** The Dove Story: The Weavus Family. large type ed. (Illus.). 26p. (J). (gr. k-2). 1999. pap. 7.95 (*1-892812-54-1*) Critters Kids.

— The Dove Story: The Weavus Family. large type ed. (Illus.). 26p. (J). (ps-2). 1999. pap. 9.95 incl. audio (*1-892812-58-4*) Critters Kids.

An Asterisk (*) at the beginning of an entry indicates that the title is appearing for the first time.

— The Legend of Kittyfish: The Weavus Family. large type ed. (Illus.). 26p. (J). (gr. k-2). 1999. pap. 7.95 (*1-892812-52-5*) Critters Kids.

— The Legend of Kittyfish: The Weavus Family. large type ed. (Illus.). 26p. (J). (ps-2). 1999. pap. 9.95 incl. audio (*1-892812-57-6*) Critters Kids.

— A Real Fishing Experience: The Weavus Family. large type ed. (Illus.). 24p. (J). (gr. k-2). 1999. pap. 7.95 (*1-892812-51-7*) Critters Kids.

— A Real Fishing Experience: The Weavus Family. large type ed. (Illus.). 24p. (J). (ps-2). 1999. pap. 9.95 incl. audio (*1-892812-56-8*) Critters Kids.

— The Weavus Family Storybook: The Weavus Family. large type ed. (Illus.). 64p. (J). (gr. k-2). 1999. pap. 7.95 (*1-892812-50-9*) Critters Kids.

— The Weavus Family Storybook: The Weavus Family. large type ed. (Illus.). 64p. (J). (ps-2). 1999. pap. 16.95 incl. audio compact disk (*1-892812-55-X*) Critters Kids.

Brumfiel, Elizabeth M. & Fox, John W., eds. Factional Competition & Political Development in the New World. LC 92-32371. (New Directions in Archaeology Ser.). (Illus.). 246p. (C). 1994. text 54.95 (*0-521-38400-1*) Cambridge U Pr.

Brumfiel, Gregory W. Partially Ordered Rings & Semi-Algebraic Geometry. LC 80-469087. (London Mathematical Society Lecture Note Ser.: No. 37). (Illus.). 288p. reprint ed. pap. 82.10 (*0-608-17518-8*, 2030604) Bks Demand.

Brumfiel, Gregory W. & Hilden, H. M. SL(2) Representations of Finitely Presented Groups. LC 95-15002. (Contemporary Mathematics Ser.: Vol. 187). 196p. 1995. 49.00 (*0-8218-0416-2*, CONM/187) Am Math.

Brumfield, Allaire C. The Attic Festivals of Demeter & Their Relation to the Agricultural Year. Connor, W. R., ed. LC 80-2643. (Monographs in Classical Studies). 1981. lib. bdg. 29.00 (*0-405-14031-2*) Ayer.

Brumfield, Allaire C. The Attic Festivals of Demeter & Their Relation to the Agricultural Year. 1981. 35.95 (*0-88143-030-7*) Ayer.

Brumfield, Blackman O., jt. auth. see Brumfield, Ray C.

Brumfield, Gordon. Searching for Truth in the Rearview Mirror: Conversations with a Chicago Cabbie. iv, 561p. 1998. pap. text 14.00 (*0-9666482-3-4*); pap. text 14.00 (*0-9666482-2-6*) Gordon R Brumfield.

Brumfield, J. C. Comfort for Troubled Christians. (Acorn Ser.). 1975. pap. text 15.00 (*0-8024-1400-1*) Moody.

***Brumfield, J. C.** Comfort for Troubled Christians. 2000. pap. 6.99 (*0-8024-1426-5*) Moody.

***Brumfield, James M.** Tourist in the Yucatan. 2000. pap. write for info. (*1-928781-31-4*) Hollis Bks.

Brumfield, Kirby. This Was Wheat Farming. LC 68-22356. (Illus.). 192p. (YA). (gr. 10 up). 1996. pap. 19.95 (*0-7643-0188-8*) Schiffer.

Brumfield, Ray C. & Brumfield, Blackman O. Brumfield: Descendants of Thomas Brumfield of Berks County, Pennsylvania: Genealogy & Family History, 1720-1960. 493p. 1992. reprint ed. pap. 76.00 (*0-8328-2405-4*); reprint ed. lib. bdg. 86.00 (*0-8328-2404-6*) Higginson Bk Co.

Brumfield, William C. A History of Russian Architecture. LC 92-29554. (Illus.). 656p. (C). 1993. text 125.00 (*0-521-40333-2*) Cambridge U Pr.

— A History of Russian Architecture. (Illus.). 656p. 1997. pap. 49.95 (*0-521-59724-2*) Cambridge U Pr.

— Landmarks of Russian Architecture: A Photographic Survey, Vol. 5. (Documenting the Image Ser.). 256p. 1997. text 49.00 (*90-5699-536-7*); pap. text 23.00 (*90-5699-537-5*) Gordon & Breach.

— Lost Russia: Photographing the Ruins of Russian Architecture. LC 94-23065. (Illus.). 144p. 1995. 64.95 (*0-8223-1557-2*); pap. 27.95 (*0-8223-1568-8*) Duke.

— The Origins of Modernism in Russian Architecture. LC 90-34093. (Illus.). 400p. 1991. 95.00 (*0-520-06929-3*, Pub. by U CA Pr) Cal Prin Full Svc.

Brumfield, William C., ed. Reshaping Russian Architecture: Western Technology, Utopian Dreams. (Woodrow Wilson Center Ser.). (Illus.). 240p. (C). 1990. text 80.00 (*0-521-39418-X*) Cambridge U Pr.

Brumfield, William C. & Ruble, Blair A., eds. Russian Housing in the Modern Age: Design & Social History. (Woodrow Wilson Center Ser.). (Illus.). 336p. (C). 1993. text 110.00 (*0-521-43197-2*) Cambridge U Pr.

Brumfit, Christopher J. & Carter, Ronald A. Literature & Language Teaching. (Illus.). 304p. 1987. pap. text 15.95 (*0-19-437082-8*) OUP.

Brumfit, Christopher J. & Johnson, K., eds. The Communicative Approach to Language Teaching. (Illus.). 254p. 1980. pap. text 17.95 (*0-19-437078-X*) OUP.

Brumfit, Christopher J. & Stubbs, Michael, eds. Language Education in the National Curriculum. (Language in Education Ser.). 224p. 1995. pap. 28.95 (*0-631-18901-7*) Blackwell Pubs.

Brumfit, Christopher J., jt. auth. see Byram, Michael.

Brumfit, Christopher J., jt. auth. see Finocchiaro, Mary.

Brumfitt. Urinary Tract Infections. 512p. 1999. text 115.00 (*0-412-63050-8*, Pub. by E A) OUP.

Brumfitt, J. H. The French Enlightenment. LC 72-91535. (Philosophers in Perspective Ser.). 176p. 1973. reprint ed. pap. 54.60 (*0-608-05330-9*, 206503500012) Bks Demand.

— Voltaire, Historian. LC 84-29037. 178p. 1985. reprint ed. lib. bdg. 41.50 (*0-313-24734-X*, BRVO, Greenwood Pr) Greenwood.

Brumfitt, J. H. & Davis, M. I., eds. Voltaire: L'Ingenu & Histoire de Jenni. (Bristol French Texts Ser.). (FRE.). 207p. 1992. pap. 20.95 (*1-85399-286-0*, Pub. by Brist Class Pr) Focus Pub-R Pullins.

Brumfitt, J. H., ed. see Rousseau, Jean-Jacques.

Brumfitt, J. H., ed. see Voltaire.

***Brumfitt, Shelagh.** Social Psychology of Communication Impairments. 1. 1999. pap. text 29.95 (*1-86156-095-8*) Whurr Pub.

Brumfitt, William, ed. New Perspectives in Clinical Microbiology. 1978. text 99.50 (*90-247-2074-5*) Kluwer Academic.

Brumfitt, William, et al, eds. Combined Antimicrobial Therapy. (New Perspectives in Clinical Microbiology Ser.: No. 3). 1980. text 141.50 (*90-247-2280-2*) Kluwer Academic.

Brumfitt, William, jt. ed. see Asscher, A. W.

Brumfitt, William, ed. see International Symposium on Pyelonephritis Staff.

Brumgardt, John R. Civil War Nurse: The Diary & Letters of Hannah Ropes. LC 79-28372. (C). 1992. pap. 13.95 (*0-87049-790-1*) U of Tenn Pr.

Brumi, D. Going to Mass. (J). 1996. bds. 3.95 (*0-88271-450-3*) Regina Pr.

— Noah & the Ark. (J). 1996. bds. 3.95 (*0-88271-452-X*) Regina Pr.

— Praying to God. (J). 1996. bds. 3.95 (*0-88271-451-1*) Regina Pr.

— The Story of Christmas. (J). (ps-3). 1995. bds. 3.95 (*0-88271-453-8*) Regina Pr.

Brumley, Charles. Guides of the Adirondacks: A History. LC 94-10561. (Illus.). 384p. 1994. 35.00 (*0-925168-32-7*); pap. 22.50 (*0-925168-36-X*) North Country.

***Brumley, Doug & Mizell, Leslie.** Microsoft Devil's Own: Inside Moves. 1998. pap. 16.99 (*1-57231-714-0*) Microsoft.

Brumley, Linda, jt. ed. see Jones, Sheila.

***Brumlik.** Framework Molecular Model Student Kit. 1998. pap. text 42.00 (*0-13-330076-5*) P-H.

Brumlik. Universal Molecular Models. 1995. pap. text 52.00 (*0-13-931700-7*) P-H.

Brumlik, Joel. The Messenger That I Sent. unabridged ed. 580p. 1998. pap. 36.95 (*1-892896-90-7*) Buy Books.

Brumm, Anne-Marie. Come Drink Coffee with Me: Husband Hunting in Israel. 388p. 1995. pap. 12.00 (*0-9648809-0-3*) Widener & Lewis.

Brumm, Don, jt. auth. see Brumm, Penn.

Brumm, Eugenia K. Managing Records for ISO 9000 Compliance. LC 94-46885. 437p. 1995. 50.00 (*0-87389-312-3*, H0870) ASQ Qual Pr.

Brumm, Penn. The Micro-to-Mainframe Connection. (Illus.). 210p. 1986. pap. 15.95 (*0-8306-2637-9*, NO. 2637) McGraw-Hill Prof.

Brumm, Penn & Brumm, Don. Assembly Language 80386 (MS DOS) 1991. 29.95 (*0-8306-6665-6*) McGraw-Hill Prof.

— Assembly Language 80386 (OS-2) 1991. 29.95 (*0-8306-6666-4*) McGraw-Hill Prof.

— Eighty Thousand Three Hundred Eighty-Six Assembly Language: A Complete Tutorial & Subroutine Library. (Illus.). 336p. 1988. pap. 24.95 (*0-8306-9347-5*, 3047) McGraw-Hill Prof.

— Eighty Three Eighty-Six Assembly Language: A Complete Tutorial & Subroutine Library, MS-DOS. 1988. pap. 29.95 (*0-07-155992-2*) McGraw.

— Macro Assembler & Toolkit 80386. (Illus.). 608p. (Orig.). 1989. 35.95 (*0-8306-0247-X*) McGraw-Hill Prof.

— A Programming & Design Handbook-80386. (Illus.). 448p. 1987. pap. 19.95 (*0-8306-2937-8*) McGraw-Hill Prof.

Brumm, Penn, et al. Programming 80486. 1991. 29.95 incl. disk (*0-8306-3543-2*) McGraw-Hill Prof.

Brummel, George H. Bible Medicine with Healing Verses. LC 83-91263. 172p. (Orig.). 1984. pap. 9.95 (*0-9613041-0-3*) G Brummel Pub.

***Brummel, Klazien, ed.** West 8. (Library of Architecture). 212p. 2000. pap. 19.95 (*88-8118-659-4*, Pub. by Skira IT) Abbeville Pr.

Brummel, Steven W., jt. ed. see Newman, Sally.

Brummelen, Harro W. Van, see Van Brummelen, Harro W.

Brummelhuis, Han Ten, see Ten Brummelhuis, Han, ed.

Brummell, George B. Male & Female Costume. Parker, Eleanor, ed. LC 71-177521. (Illus.). 334p. 1978. reprint ed. 27.95 (*0-405-08314-9*, Pub. by Blom Pubns) Ayer.

Brummer, Alex & Cowe, Roger. Hanson: The Rise & Rise of Britain's Most Buccaneering Businessman. (Illus.). 352p. 1996. pap. 19.95 (*1-85702-351-X*) Trafalgar.

Brummer, G., ed. Gas Extraction: An Introduction to Fundamentals of Supercritical Fluids & the Application to Separation Processes. (Topics in Physical Chemistry Ser.: Vol. 4). 400p. 1995. 49.00 (*0-387-91477-3*) Spr-Verlag.

Brummer, James J. Corporate Responsibility & Legitimacy: An Interdisciplinary Analysis, 47. LC 90-25223. (Contributions in Philosophy Ser.: No. 47). 344p. 1991. 75.00 (*0-313-24726-9*, BCR/, Greenwood Pr) Greenwood.

Brummer, Richard, ed. Static & Dynamic Considerations in Rock Engineering: Proceedings of the ISRM International Symposium, Swaziland, 10-12 September 1990. (Illus.). 410p. (C). 1990. text 162.00 (*90-6191-153-2*, Pub. by A A Balkema) Ashgate Pub Co.

Brummer, Sidney D. Political History of New York State During the Period of the Civil War. LC 11-19977. (Columbia University. Studies in the Social Sciences: No. 103). reprint ed. 37.50 (*0-404-51103-1*) AMS Pr.

Brummer, Vincent. The Model of Love: A Study in Philosophical Theology. LC 92-42300. 261p. (C). 1993. text 64.95 (*0-521-44463-2*); pap. text 18.95 (*0-521-44909-X*) Cambridge U Pr.

— Speaking of a Personal God. 170p. (C). 1992. text 59.95 (*0-521-43052-6*); pap. text 17.95 (*0-521-43632-X*) Cambridge U Pr.

Brummet, Ed, jt. auth. see Claycomb, William B.

Brummett, Barry. Civilization Past & Present: Everything You Need To Know About It. 9th ed. 16p. (C). 1999. pap. text, student ed. 7.00 (*0-321-06629-4*) Addson-Wesley Educ.

— Contemporary Apocalyptic Rhetoric. LC 91-18921. (Praeger Series in Political Communication). 208p. 1991. 55.00 (*0-275-94082-9*, C4082, Praeger Pubs) Greenwood.

— Reading Rhetorical Theory. 1999. 88.50 (*0-15-508304-X*, Pub. by Harcourt Coll Pubs) Harcourt.

— Rhetoric of Machine Aesthetics. LC 99-18012. 160p. 1999. 55.00 (*0-275-96644-5*) Greenwood.

— Rhetorical Dimensions of Popular Culture. LC 90-35565. 284p. 1991. text 34.95 (*0-8173-0516-5*) U of Ala Pr.

Brummett, Barry, ed. Landmark Essays on Kenneth Burke. (Landmark Essays Ser.: Vol. 2). 304p. (C). 1993. pap. text 27.50 (*1-880393-05-0*, Hermagoras) L Erlbaum Assocs.

Brummett, Curt. My Dog's a Democrat. (Illus.). 96p. reprint ed. pap. 6.95 (*1-879894-01-7*) Saratoga Pub.

— Roping Can be Hazardous to Your Health: More Stories by Curt Brummett. 96p. 1991. pap. 6.95 (*0-87483-146-6*) August Hse.

Brummett, John. Highwire: From the Back Roads to the Beltway - the Education of Bill Clinton. 304p. (J). 1995. pap. 14.45 (*0-7868-8123-2*, Pub. by Hyperion) Time Warner.

***Brummett, Nancy Parker.** It Takes a Home: And Other Lessons from the Heart. LC 00-32993. 2000. write for info. (*0-7814-3385-1*) Cook Communs Minist.

— Journey of Elisa: From Switzerland to America. LC 99-41981. (Immigrants Chronicles Ser.). 132p. (J). 2000. pap. 5.99 (*0-7814-3286-3*) Chariot Victor.

Brummett, Nancy Parker. Simply the Savior. LC 98-23393. 1998. 9.99 (*1-56476-752-3*, Victor Bks) Chariot Victor.

Brummett, Palmira. Image & Imperialism in the Ottoman Revolutionary Press. LC 99-56265. (C). 2000. text 86.50 (*0-7914-4463-5*); pap. text 29.95 (*0-7914-4464-3*) State U NY Pr.

— Ottoman Seapower & Levantine Diplomacy in the Age of Discovery. LC 92-44704. (SUNY Series in the Social & Economic History of the Middle East). 285p. (C). 1993. text 64.50 (*0-7914-1701-8*); pap. text 21.95 (*0-7914-1702-6*) State U NY Pr.

Brummett, R., ed. Aquaculture Policy Options for Integrated Resource Management in SubSaharan Africa: Extended Abstracts & Discussions. (ICLARM Conference Proceedings Ser.: No. 46). 38p. 1994. write for info. (*971-8709-58-4*, Pub. by ICLARM) Intl Spec Bk.

Brummett, R. E., jt. auth. see Noble, R.

Brummett, William J. The Essence of Home: Design Solutions for Assisted-Living Housing. (Architecture Ser.). 160p. 1996. text 49.95 (*0-442-02241-7*, VNR) Wiley.

Brummett, William J. The Essence of Home: Design Solutions for Assisted Living Housing. 160p. 1996. 59.95 (*0-471-28755-5*, VNR) Wiley.

Brummitt, David, jt. auth. see Choksy, Lois.

Brummitt, R. K., compiled by. Vascular Plant Families & Genera: A Listing of the Genera of Vascular Plants of the World According to Their Families...with an Analysis of Relationships of the Flowering Plant Families According to Eight Systems of Classification. viii, 804p. 1992. 48.00 (*0-947643-43-5*, Pub. by Royal Botnic Grdns) Balogh.

Brummitt, R. K. & Powell, C. E., eds. Authors of Plant Names: A List of Authors of Scientific Names of Plants with Recommended Standard Forms of Their Names, Including Abbreviations. iv, 732p. 1992. 48.00 (*0-947643-44-3*, Pub. by Royal Botnic Grdns) Balogh.

Brummitt, R. K., jt. auth. see Hollis, S.

Brummitt, R. K., jt. auth. see Kent, D. H.

Brummitt, R. K., jt. auth. see Pope, G. V.

Brumont, Francis. La Burebs l'Epoque de Philippe II. Bruchey, Stuart, ed. LC 77-81824. (Dissertations in European Economic History Ser.). (FRE., Illus.). 1978. lib. bdg. 29.95 (*0-405-10776-5*) Ayer.

Brumpton, Karen B. Freeman Earns a Bike. LC 84-60947. (Illus.). 32p. (J). (ps-4). 1984. 10.95 (*0-917487-00-1*) McVie Pub.

Brumsted, Harlan B., et al. Voices from Connecticut Hill: Recollections of Cornell Wildlife Students, 1930-1942. LC 94-72544. 132p. 1994. 30.00 (*0-9605314-7-5*) NY St Coll Ag.

Brumter, Christian. The North Atlantic Assembly. 1986. lib. bdg. 96.00 (*90-247-3318-9*) Kluwer Academic.

Brun, A., jt. auth. see Gustafson, L.

***Brun-Abdelnour, Christine.** Big Ideas for Small Spaces. 144p. 2000. pap. 29.99 (*1-56496-607-0*) Rockport Pubs.

Brun, Annie Le, see Le Brun, Annie.

Brun, Birgitte, et al. Symbols of the Soul: Therapy & Guidance Through Fairy Tales. 128p. 1993. 29.95 (*1-85302-107-5*) Taylor & Francis.

Brun, Christian F., jt. auth. see Wheat, James C.

Brun, Ellen & Hersh, Jacques. Socialist Korea: A Case Study in the Strategy of Economic Development. LC 76-1651. (Illus.). 432p. 1977. 16.50 (*0-85345-386-1*, Pub. by Monthly Rev) NYU Pr.

***Brun, Friederike.** Briefe aus Rom. Keith-Smith, Brian & Moens, Herman, trs. LC 99-58584. (German Woman Writers Ser.: Vol. 12). 106p. 2000. text 59.95 (*0-7734-7861-2*) E Mellen.

— Wahrheit aus Morgentraumen. Keith-Smith, Brian, tr. LC 99-58588. (German Woman Writers Ser.: Vol. 11). 120p. 2000. text 59.95 (*0-7734-7857-4*) E Mellen.

Brun, Fritze, tr. see Slavkin, Viktor.

Brun, Herbert & Gaburo, Kenneth. Collaboration One. 24p. 1976. pap. 15.00 (*0-939044-10-2*) Lingua Pr.

Brun, Laura, jt. auth. see Currie, Jennie.

Brun, Marlene Le, see Le Brun, Marlene.

Brun, Michel. Incident at Sakhalin: The True Mission of KAL Flight 007. LC 95-21661. (Illus.). 326p. 1996. 24.95 (*1-56858-054-1*) FWEW.

Brun, M.J. Le, see Lauchland, K. A. & Le Brun, M. J.

Brun, P. & Waegell, B. Reactivite des Hypobromites. 1976. pap. 12.75 (*0-08-021014-7*, Pergamon Pr) Elsevier.

Brun, R., et al, eds. Data Structures for Particle Physics Experiments: Evolution or Revolution? Proceedings of the 14th Workshop on the INFN Eloisatron Project, Erice, Trapani, Sicily, 11-18 November 1990. 400p. (C). 1991. text 104.00 (*981-02-0641-0*) World Scientific Pub.

Brun, R. & Dumitrescu, L., eds. Shock Waves at Marseille: Proceedings of the 19th International Symposium on Shock Waves Held at Marseille, France, 26-30 July 1993, 4 vols., Set. 1995. 412.95 (*0-387-57713-0*) Spr-Verlag.

— Shock Waves at Marseille Vol. 1: Proceedings of the 19th International Symposium on Shock Waves Held at Marseille, France, 26-30 July 1993: Hypersonics, Shock Tube & Shock Tunnel Flow. LC 96-183552. (Illus.). 504p. 1995. 132.95 (*0-387-57710-6*) Spr-Verlag.

— Shock Waves at Marseille Vol. 2: Proceedings of the 19th International Symposium on Shock Waves Held at Marseille, France, 26-30 July 1993: Physico-Chemical Processes & Nonequilibrium Flow. LC 95-13593. (Illus.). 464p. 1995. 132.95 (*0-387-57711-4*) Spr-Verlag.

— Shock Waves at Marseille Vol. 3: Proceedings of the 19th International Symposium on Shock Waves Held at Marseille, France, 26-30 July 1993: Shock Waves in Condensed Matter & Heterogenous Media. LC 95-13594. (Illus.). 504p. 1995. 132.95 (*0-387-57712-2*) Spr-Verlag.

— Shock Waves at Marseille Vol. 4: Proceedings of the 19th International Symposium on Shock Waves Held at Marseille, France, 26-30 July 1993: Shock Structure & Kinematics, Blast Waves & Detonation. LC 95-13595. (Shock Waves at Marseilles Ser.: Vol. 4). 544p. 1995. 132.95 (*3-540-58862-0*) Spr-Verlag.

Brun, R. & Dumitrescu, L. Z., eds. Physico-Chemical Processes & Nonequilibrium Flow: Proceedings of the 19th International Symposium on Shock Waves, Held at Marseille, France, July 1993. LC 95-14593. (Shock Waves at Marseilles Ser.: No. 2). 1995. write for info. (*3-540-57711-4*) Spr-Verlag.

— Shock Waves in Condensed Matter & Heterogeneous Media: Proceedings of the 19th International Symposium on Shock Waves, Held at Marseille, France, July 1993. LC 95-13594. (Shock Waves at Marseilles Ser.: Vol. 3). 1995. write for info. (*3-540-57712-2*) Spr-Verlag.

Brun, R., ed. see International Symposium on Shock Waves Staff.

Brun, Rudolf. Christianity, Science & Art: Towards an Updated Christian Doctrine of Creation. large type ed. (Illus.). 1999. 14.99 (*0-9667579-0-4*) Rudolf Brun.

Brun, Samuel J. Tales of Languedoc: From the South of France. LC 98-27817. (Library of Folklore). (Illus.). 248p. (YA). (gr. 4 up). 1999. 14.95 (*0-7818-0715-8*) Hippocrene Bks.

Brun, Sheva G. Thinking about Judaism: Philosophical Reflections on Jewish Thought. LC 98-38765. 216p. 1998. 30.00 (*0-7657-6037-1*) Aronson.

***Brun, Yves V. & Skimkets, Lawrence J., eds.** Prokaryotic Development. LC 99-44864. (Illus.). 475p. 2000. 89.95 (*1-55581-158-2*) ASM Pr.

***Bruna, Dick.** Auntie Alice's Party: A Miffy Storybook. (Illus.). 28p. (J). (ps-k). 2000. 14.00 (*1-56836-304-4*) Kodansha.

Bruna, Dick. Good Morning, Miffy. (Illus.). 12p. (J). (ps-k). 1998. 4.95 (*1-56836-264-1*) Kodansha.

— Miffy. Noma, Chikako, ed. LC 95-48495. (Illus.). 28p. (J). (ps-k). 1996. bds. 4.95 (*1-56836-151-3*) Kodansha.

***Bruna, Dick.** Miffy & Melanie. (Illus.). 28p. (J). (ps-k). 2000. 4.95 (*1-56836-305-2*) Kodansha.

Bruna, Dick. Miffy at Play: A Flip Book. LC 97-76169. (Illus.). 16p. (J). (ps-k). 1998. bds. 5.95 (*1-56836-223-4*) Kodansha.

— Miffy at School. (Miffy Ser.). (Illus.). 32p. (J). (ps-1). 1997. bds. 4.95 (*1-56836-176-9*) Kodansha.

— Miffy at the Museum. (Illus.). 28p. (J). (ps-k). 1998. 4.95 (*1-56836-270-6*) Kodansha.

— Miffy at the Playground. Noma, Chikako, ed. LC 96-11539.Tr. of Usako-Chan to Yuenchi. (Illus.). 28p. (J). (ps-k). 1996. 4.95 (*1-56836-159-9*) Kodansha.

— Miffy at the Zoo. (Miffy Ser.). (Illus.). 32p. (J). (ps-1). 1997. bds. 4.95 (*1-56836-175-0*) Kodansha.

— Miffy Goes Flying. (Illus.). 28p. (J). (ps-k). 1998. pap. 4.95 (*1-56836-221-8*) Kodansha.

— Miffy Goes for a Walk. (J). (ps). 1998. 8.95 (*1-56836-269-2*) Kodansha.

— Miffy Goes Outside. LC 97-73066. (Miffy Ser.). (Illus.). 14p. (J). (ps-3). 1997. bds. 5.95 (*1-56836-193-9*) Kodansha.

— Miffy Helps at Home. (J). (ps). 1998. 4.95 (*1-56836-265-X*) Kodansha.

— Miffy in the Hospital: A Storybook. (Illus.). 28p. (J). (ps-k). 1999. pap. 4.95 (*1-56836-297-8*) Kodansha.

— Miffy in the Snow: A Storybook. (Illus.). 28p. (J). (ps-k). 1999. pap. 4.95 (*1-56836-296-X*) Kodansha.

— Miffy in the Tent. 28p. (J). (ps-k). 1998. pap. 4.95 (*1-56836-218-8*) Kodansha.

— Miffy Is Crying. (Illus.). 28p. (J). (ps-k). 1998. 4.95 (*1-56836-263-3*) Kodansha.

Bruna, Dick. Miffy Likes to... LC 97-73065. (Miffy Ser.). (Illus.). 14p. (J). (ps-1). 1997. bds. 5.95 (*1-56836-194-7*) Kodansha.

Bruna, Dick. Miffy Likes to Ride. (J). (ps). 1998. 8.95 (*1-56836-268-4*) Kodansha.

***Bruna, Dick.** Miffy Rides a Bike. (Miffy Ser.). (Illus.). 28p. (ps-k). 1999. 4.95 (*1-56836-280-3*) Kodansha.

Bruna, Dick. Miffy Tours the Zoo. (J). (ps). 1998. 4.95 (1-56836-266-8) Kodansha.

— Miffy Visits the Zoo. (J). (ps). 1998. 8.95 (1-56836-267-6) Kodansha.

— Miffy's Birthday. LC 97-71722. (Miffy Ser.). (Illus.). 28p. (J). (ps-k). 1997. bds. 4.95 (1-56836-192-0) Kodansha.

— Miffy's Busy Morning: A Flip Book. (Miffy Ser.). (Illus.). 16p. (ps-k). 1999. 5.95 (1-56836-288-9) Kodansha.

***Bruna, Dick.** Miffy's Counting Book. (Miffy Ser.). (Illus.). 20p. (ps-k). 1999. bds. 7.95 (1-56836-281-1) Kodansha.

Bruna, Dick. Miffy's First Sleepover. (Miffy Ser.). (Illus.). 28p. (ps-k). 1999. 4.95 (1-56836-279-X) Kodansha.

***Bruna, Dick.** My Miffy. (Illus.). (J). 2000. pap. 10.95 (1-56836-307-9) Kodansha.

Bruna, Dick. Peek-a-Boo, Miffy! A Flip Book. LC 97-76168. (Illus.). 16p. (J). (ps-k). 1998. bds. 5.95 (1-56836-222-6) Kodansha.

***Bruna, Dick.** What Time is It, Miffy? (Miffy Ser.). (Illus.). 20p. (ps-k). 1999. bds. 7.95 (1-56836-282-X) Kodansha.

Brunacci, G., jt. auth. see Cusatelli, G.

Brunacini, Alan V. Essentials of Fire Department Customer Service. Smith, Carol S., ed. (Illus.). 136p. 1996. pap. text 25.00 (0-87939-127-8) IFSTA.

Brunais, Andrea. Night of the Litani. 254p. 1996. pap. 18.50 (0-931541-55-7) Mancorp Pub.

Brunak, S. & Lautrup, B. Neural Networks: Computers with Intuition. 200p. (C). 1990. text 39.00 (9971-5-0938-5); pap. text 18.00 (9971-5-0939-3) World Scientific Pub.

Brunak, Soren, jt. auth. see Baldi, Pierre.

Brunak, Soren, jt. auth. see Bohr, H.

Brunak, Soren, jt. ed. see Bohr, Henrik.

Brunal-Perry, ed. see Ibanez, Aniceto & Resano, Francisco.

Brunal-Perry, Omaira. A Question of Sovereignty: What Legitimate Right Did Spain Have to Its Territorial Expansion? Driver, Marjorie G., tr. (Educational Ser.: No. 15). (Illus.). 52p. 1993. 3.50 (1-878453-15-7) Univ Guam MAR Ctr.

Brunal-Perry, Omaira, tr. see McGrath, Thomas B., ed.

Brunanburh. The Battle of Brunanburh. Campbell, Alistair, ed. 184p. reprint ed. lib. bdg. 39.00 (0-403-03315-2) Scholarly.

Brunas, Michael, et al. Universal Horrors: The Studio's Classic Films, 1931-1946. LC 89-42706. (Illus.). 624p. 1990. lib. bdg. 55.00 (0-89950-369-1) McFarland & Co.

Brunas-Wagstaff, Jo. Personality: A Cognitive Approach. LC 97-39541. (Psychology Focus Ser.). 184p. (C). 1998. 50.00 (0-415-16304-8); pap. 14.99 (0-415-16305-6) Routledge.

***Brunchhauser, Axel.** Cantilever Chair. 1999. 35.00 (3-88375-351-3) Walther Konig.

Brunck, Arthur E., jt. auth. see Flitner, Arthur L.

Bruncken, Ernest & Register, Layton B., trs. Science of Legal Method: Select Essays. (Modern Legal Philosophy Ser.: Vol. 9). lxxxvi, 593p. 1969. reprint ed. 58.00 (0-8377-2600-X, Rothman) W S Hein.

— The Science of Legal Method: Select Essays by Various Authors. LC 68-54756. (Modern Legal Philosophy Ser.: Vol. 9). lxxxvi, 593p. 1969. reprint ed. 57.50 (0-678-04520-8) Kelley.

***Brunckhorst, D. J.** Bioregional Planning: Resource Management Beyond the New Millennium. 200p. 2000. text 28.00 (90-5823-046-5, Harwood Acad Pubs) Gordon & Breach.

Brunckhorst, Friedl U. Architektur im Bild. (Studien Zur Kunstgeschichte: Bd. 106). (Illus.). 272p. 1997. 55.00 (3-487-10245-5) G Olms Pubs.

Bruncko, D., et al, eds. Multiparticle Dynamics: Proceedings of the XXV International Symposium, Stara Lesna, Slovakia 12 - 16 September 1995. 600p. 1996. text 128.00 (981-02-2478-8, Ph-P2949) World Scientific Pub.

Brundage, Anthony. England's "Prussian Minister" Edwin Chadwick & the Politics of Government Growth. (Illus.). 208p. 1988. lib. bdg. 32.50 (0-271-00629-3) Pa St U Pr.

— Going to the Sources: A Guide to Historical Research & Writing. 2nd ed. LC 96-45502. 115p. 1997. pap. text 7.95 (0-88295-936-0) Harlan Davidson.

— The Making of the New Poor Law: The Politics of Inquiry, Enactment, & Implementation, 1832-1839. LC 77-20881. 219p. reprint ed. pap. 67.90 (0-7837-5895-2, 205908300006) Bks Demand.

— The People's Historian: John Richard Green & the Writing of History in Victorian England, 2. LC 93-10379. (Studies in Historiography: No. 2). 200p. 1993. 62.95 (0-313-27954-3, BGK/, Greenwood Pr) Greenwood.

Brundage, Barbara, jt. auth. see Sax, Alan.

Brundage, Burr C. Empire of the Inca. LC 63-18070. (Civilization of the American Indian Ser.: Vol. 69). 414p. (Orig.). 1985. pap. 18.95 (0-8061-1924-1) U of Okla Pr.

— The Jade Steps: A Ritual Life of the Aztecs. LC 85-13358. (Illus.). 296p. reprint ed. pap. 91.80 (0-7837-5545-7, 204532000005) Bks Demand.

***Brundage, Buz.** Be a Better Hitter: Baseball Basics. LC 99-87961. 2000. 17.95 (0-8069-2461-6) Sterling.

Brundage, David. The Making of Western Labor Radicalism: Denver's Organized Workers, 1878-1905. LC 93-34180. (Working Class in American History Ser.). (Illus.). 224p. 1994. text 26.95 (0-252-02075-8) U of Ill Pr.

Brundage, Dorothy. Renal Disorders. (Illus.). 256p. (C). (gr. 13). 1991. text 32.95 (0-8016-1685-9, 01685) Mosby Inc.

Brundage, George. Daily Prayers. (Illus.). 16p. (J). (ps-3). 1996. bds. 2.75 (0-89942-842-8, 842/22) Catholic Bk Pub.

— Gifts of God. (Illus.). 16p. (J). 1995. bds. 2.75 (0-89942-843-6, 843/22) Catholic Bk Pub.

— Our Blessed Mother. (Illus.). 16p. (J). 1993. bds. 2.75 (0-89942-846-0, 846/22) Catholic Bk Pub.

— Our Friends the Saints. (Illus.). 16p. (J). (ps-3). 1994. bds. 2.75 (0-89942-844-4, 844/22) Catholic Bk Pub.

— Our Guardian Angel. (Illus.). 16p. (J). 1994. bds. 2.75 (0-89942-845-2, 845/22) Catholic Bk Pub.

— We Go to Mass. (Illus.). 16p. (J). (ps-3). 1994. bds. 2.75 (0-89942-841-X, 841/22) Catholic Bk Pub.

Brundage, James A. The Crusades: A Documentary Survey. LC 62-12897. (Illus.). 332p. 1962. reprint ed. pap. 103.00 (0-608-04191-2, 206492600011) Bks Demand.

— The Crusades, Holy War & Canon Law. (Collected Studies: No. CS338). 320p. 1991. text 103.95 (0-86078-291-3, Pub. by Variorum) Ashgate Pub Co.

— Law, Sex & Christian Society in Medieval Europe. LC 87-10759. xxvi, 646p. 1987. 45.00 (0-226-07783-7) U Ch Pr.

— Law, Sex & Christian Society in Medieval Europe. LC 87-10759. xxvi, 398p. 1990. pap. text 32.50 (0-226-07784-5) U Ch Pr.

— Medieval Canon Law. LC 94-33506. (Medieval World Ser.). 264p. (C). 1996. text 51.95 (0-582-09357-0) Addison-Wesley.

— Medieval Canon Law. LC 94-33506. (Medieval World Ser.). 272p. (C). 1995. pap. 40.06 (0-582-09356-2) Longman.

— Sex, Law & Marriage in the Middle Ages. (Collected Studies: Vol. 397). 300p. 1993. 104.95 (0-86078-367-7, Pub. by Variorum) Ashgate Pub Co.

Brundage, James A., jt. ed. see Bullough, Vern L.

Brundage, James A., jt. ed. see Bullough, Vern.

Brundage, Jane B. The Baroness, the Scribe & the Camel-Driver. LC 95-92624. (Illus.). 192p. (Orig.). 1995. pap. 14.95 (0-9649017-0-6) RYSE.

Brundage, Kip, photos by. Middlebury College. (First Edition Ser.). (Illus.). 112p. 1988. 39.00 (0-916509-44-3) Harmony Hse Pub.

Brundage, Paul D., jt. auth. see Starchild, Adam.

Brundage, Percival F. Changing Concepts of Business Income. LC 75-21163. 1975. reprint ed. text 30.00 (0-914348-18-3) Scholars Bk.

Brundage, Slim. From Bughouse Square to the Beat Generation: Selected Ravings of Slim Brundage. Rosemont, Franklin, ed. LC 97-42588. (Bughouse Square Ser.: Vol. 1). (Illus.). 320p. 1997. pap. 14.00 (0-88286-232-4) C H Kerr.

Brundage, W. Fitzhugh. Lynching in the New South: Georgia & Virginia, 1880-1930. LC 92-26034. (Blacks in the New World Ser.). (Illus.). 432p. 1993. 14.95 (0-252-06345-7); text 39.95 (0-252-01987-3) U of Ill Pr.

— A Socialist Utopia in the New South: The Ruskin Colonies in Tennessee & Georgia, 1894-1901. 288p. (C). 1996. text 38.95 (0-252-02244-0); pap. text 16.95 (0-252-06548-4) U of Ill Pr.

— Under Sentence of Death: Lynching in the South. LC 96-30204. 400p. (C). (gr. 13). 1997. 55.00 (0-8078-2326-0); pap. 18.95 (0-8078-4636-8) U of NC Pr.

***Brundage, W. Fitzhugh, ed.** Where These Memories Grow: History, Memory, & Southern Identity. LC 00-26211. (Illus.). 360p. 2000. pap. 19.95 (0-8078-4886-7); lib. bdg. 49.95 (0-8078-2572-7) U of NC Pr.

Brundell, Harry. Pierre Gassendi: From Aristotelianism to a New Natural Philosophy. (Synthese Historical Library: No. 30). 268p. 1987. text 144.00 (90-277-2428-8) Kluwer Academic.

Brunden, Marshall N., et al, eds. Drug Interaction & Lethality Analysis. LC 87-30917. 192p. 1988. 100.00 (0-8493-5743-8, RM302, CRC Reprint) Franklin.

Brundick, William. A Disciple's Legacy: The Eternal Quest for Spiritual Power. LC 96-80193. 352p. 1997. 24.95 (0-9655893-0-7) Gauntlett Pr.

Brundige, Don & Brundige, Sharron. Outdoor Recreation Checklists. LC 96-95421. (Illus.). 422p. 1998. pap. 14.95 (0-9619151-9-6) BD Enterprises.

Brundige, Donald G. & Brundige, Sharron L. Bicycle Rides: Inland Empire. LC 89-91606. (Illus.). 154p. (Orig.). 1993. pap. 8.95 (0-9619151-4-5) BD Enterprises.

— Bicycle Rides: Orange County. LC 88-71407. (Illus.). 168p. (Orig.). 1993. pap. 9.95 (0-9619151-2-9) BD Enterprises.

— Bicycle Rides: San Diego & Imperial Counties. LC 90-93234. (Illus.). 218p. (Orig.). 1992. pap. 11.95 (0-9619151-5-3) BD Enterprises.

— Bicycle Rides: Santa Barbara & Ventura Counties. LC 94-94025. (Illus.). 280p. (Orig.). 1994. pap. 10.95 (0-9619151-6-1) BD Enterprises.

— Mountain Biking L. A. County: Southern Section. LC 95-94085. (Illus.). 218p. 1996. pap. 11.95 (0-9619151-7-X) BD Enterprises.

Brundige, Dononald G. & Brundige, Sharron L. Bicycle Rides: Los Angeles County. LC 88-72328. (Illus.). 218p. (Orig.). 1991. pap. 10.95 (0-9619151-3-7) BD Enterprises.

Brundige, Patricia. Traveling with Aunt Patty: Aunt Patty Visits London. Wright, Cindy, ed. (Illus.). (J). (gr. 1-4). Date not set. text 12.95 (0-9659668-0-1) Aunt Pattys.

Brundige, Sharron, jt. auth. see Brundige, Don.

Brundige, Sharron L., jt. auth. see Brundige, Donald G.

Brundige, Sharron L., jt. auth. see Brundige, Dononald G.

Brundle, C. R. Materials Characterization Series. 1993. 683.00 (0-7506-9452-1) Buttrwrth-Heinemann.

Brundle, C. R., et al, eds. Encyclopedia of Materials Characterization: Surfaces, Interfaces & Thin Films. (Surface Materials Characterization Ser.). 800p. 1992. 125.00 (0-7506-9168-9) Buttrwrth-Heinemann.

Brundle, C. R. & Baker, A. D., eds. Electron Spectroscopy: Theory, Techniques, & Applications, Vol. 1. 1977. text 192.00 (0-12-137801-2) Acad Pr.

Brundrett, Charles. Family Chronicle. 1986. 40.00 (0-86332-029-5) St Mut.

Brundrett, Geoffrey W. Legionella & Building Services. LC 91-36049. (Illus.). 426p. 1992. reprint ed. pap. 132.10 (0-608-07926-X, 206790000012) Bks Demand.

Brundtland, Arne O. & Snider, Don M. Nordic-Baltic Security from an International Perspective. (CSIS Panel Reports). 132p. (Orig.). (C). 1994. pap. 16.95 (0-89206-256-8) CSIS.

***Brundtland, Gro Harlem.** The World Health Report, 1999: Making a Difference. 122p. 1999. pap. 20.00 (92-4-156194-7, Pub. by Statnry Office) Balogh.

Brundy, Clyde M. The Maverick Touch. 224p. 1988. pap. 3.95 (0-380-89600-1, Avon Bks) Morrow Avon.

***Brundy, Yitzhak M.** Reinventing Russia: Russian Nationalism & the Soviet State, 1953-1991. 368p. 2000. pap. 19.95 (0-674-00438-8) HUP.

Brune, D. The Global Environment: Science, Technology & Management, 2 Vols. LC 98-108257. 1330p. 1997. 733.00 (3-527-28771-X) Wiley.

Brune, Dag, et al, eds. Surface Characterization: A User's Sourcebook. 716p. 1997. 325.00 (3-527-28843-0, Wiley-VCH) Wiley.

Brune, Dag K. & Edling, Christer, eds. Occupational Hazards in the Health Professions. 416p. 1989. lib. bdg. 143.00 (0-8493-6931-2, RC965) CRC Pr.

Brune, David E. & Tomasso, Joseph R., eds. Aquaculture & Water Quality. (Advances in World Aquaculture Ser.: Vol. 3). (Illus.). 606p. (C). 1991. text 48.00 (0-9624529-2-0) World Aquaculture.

Brune, Gunnar. Springs of Texas, Vol. 1. LC 80-71016. (Illus.). 584p. 1981. 35.00 (0-9604766-0-1); write for info. (0-318-52335-3) G Brune.

Brune, Iris. Laparo-Endoscopic Surgery. 2nd ed. (Illus.). 400p. 1996. 135.00 (0-86542-900-6) Blackwell Sci.

Brune, Kay. New Pharmacological & Epidemiological Data in Analgesics Research. 60p. 1990. 22.50 (0-8176-2452-X) Birkhauser.

Brune, Kay, ed. Dipyrone: Recent Investigations on Its Mode of Action, Pharmacokinetics, & Clinical Use, Berlin, October 24, 1991. LC 92-49454. vii, 45p. 1992. write for info. (3-7643-2804-5, Pub. by Birkhauser); 29.00 (0-8176-2804-5, Pub. by Birkhauser) Princeton Arch.

— One Hundred Years of Pyrazolone Drugs. (Agents & Actions Supplements Ser.: Vol. 19). 356p. 1986. 77.00 (0-8176-1814-7, Pub. by Birkhauser) Princeton Arch.

Brune, Kay, ed. see World Conference on Clinical Pharmacology & Therap.

Brune, Lester H. America & the Iraqi Crisis, 1990-1992: Origins & Aftermath. LC 93-20611. (Guides to Contemporary Issues Ser.: Vol. 8). 1993. 29.95 (0-941690-53-9); pap. 13.95 (0-941690-54-7) Regina Bks.

— Chronological History of U. S. Foreign Relations Vol. III: The Reagan Years. LC 91-21076. 300p. 1991. text 25.00 (0-8240-5690-6, 586) Garland.

— Chronological History of United States Foreign Relations, 1766-January 20, 1981. LC 83-48210. 1328p. 1985. text 50.00 (0-8240-9056-X) Garland.

— The Cuba-Caribbean Missile Crisis of October 1962. rev. ed. (Guides to Historical Issues Ser.: No. 6). Orig. Title: The Missile Crisis of October 1962. (Illus.). 160p. 1996. pap. text 12.95 (0-941690-70-9); lib. bdg. 21.95 (0-941690-69-5) Regina Bks.

— Origins of American National Security Policy: Sea Power, Air Power & Foreign Policy, 1900-1941. 348p. 1981. pap. text 36.95 (0-89126-075-7) MA-AH Pub.

Brune, Lester H. The United States & Post-Cold War Interventions: Bush & Clinton in Somalia, Haiti & Bosnia, 1992-1998. LC 98-52432. (Guides to Contemporary Issues Ser.). 1999. pap. 14.95 (0-941690-90-3) Regina Bks.

***Brune, Lester H.** The United States & Post-Cold War Interventions: Bush & Clinton in Somalia, Haiti & Bosnia, 1992-1998. LC 98-52432. (Guides to Contemporary Issues Ser.: No. 11). 177p. 1999. 29.95 (0-941690-86-5) Regina Bks.

Brune, Lester H., ed. The Korean War: Handbook of the Literature & Research. LC 95-35710. 472p. 1996. lib. bdg. 85.00 (0-313-28969-7, Greenwood Pr) Greenwood.

Brune, Lester H. & Burns, Richard D., eds. America & the Indochina Wars, 1945-1990: A Bibliographical Guide. (New War - Peace Bibliographical Ser.). 350p. 1991. lib. bdg. 39.95 (0-941690-43-1) Regina Bks.

***Bruneau, Bonnie.** Discovering Me. 101p. 2000. 19.95 (0-7541-1240-3, Pub. by Minerva Pr) Unity Dist.

Bruneau, Carol. Depth Rapture. 304p. 1998. pap. 15.95 (1-896951-07-4) Cormor Bks.

***Bruneau, Charles-Henri E.** The Sixteenth International Conference on Numerical Methods in Fluid Dynamics: Proceedings of the Conference Held in Arcachon,France, July 6-10, 1998, Vol. 515. LC 98-48707. (Lecture Notes in Physics Ser.). 1998. 119.00 (3-540-65153-5) Spr-Verlag.

Bruneau, Edmond A. Prescription for Advertising: A Common Sense Guide for Understanding the Complex & Confusing World of Advertising. unabridged ed. 176p. 1986. pap. 29.95 incl. audio (0-9616683-2-6); pap. 19.95 incl. audio (0-9616683-3-4) Boston Bks.

Bruneau, Edmond A. Prescription for Advertising: A Common Sense Guide for Understanding the Complex & Confusing World of Advertising. unabridged ed. 176p. 1986. 37.95 incl. audio (0-9616683-1-8) Boston Bks.

Bruneau, Jean, ed. see Flaubert, Gustave.

Bruneau, Louis O. Uncommon Sense. 272p. 1995. pap. 11.95 (1-57087-169-8) Prof Pr NC.

Bruneau, Marie-Florine. Women Mystics Confront the Modern World: Marie de l'Incarnation (1599-1672) & Madame Guyon (1648-1717) LC 97-19144. (SUNY Series in Western Esoteric Traditions). 256p. (C). 1998. text 59.50 (0-7914-3661-6); pap. text 19.95 (0-7914-3662-4) State U NY Pr.

Bruneau, Michel, et al. Ductile Design of Steel Structures. (Illus.). 485p. 1997. 74.95 (0-07-008580-3) McGraw.

Bruneau, Philippe, et al. Sculpture Vol. I: From Antiquity to the Middle Ages. (Jumbo Ser.). (Illus.). 544p. 1999. 49.99 (3-8228-7059-5) Taschen Amer.

Bruneau, Thomas C. The Church in Brazil: The Politics of Religion. LC 81-16391. (University of Texas at Austin, Institute of Latin American Studies-Latin American Monographs: No. 56). 253p. reprint ed. pap. 78.50 (0-608-16461-5, 202656400050) Bks Demand.

— The Political Transformation of the Brazilian Catholic Church. LC 73-79318. (Perspective on Development Ser.: Vol. 2). 284p. (J). (gr. 4-7). reprint ed. pap. 81.00 (0-608-13317-5, 2025579) Bks Demand.

Brunee, Jutta & Hey, Ellen, eds. Yearbook of International Environmental Law, Vol. 8. 736p. 1999. text 175.00 (0-19-826799-1) OUP.

Bruneel, Herwig & Kim, Dyung G. Discrete-Time Models for Communication Systems Including ATM. LC 92-33773. (International Series in Engineering & Computer Science, VLSI, Computer Architecture, & Digital Screen Processing). 224p. (C). 1992. text 113.00 (0-7923-9292-2) Kluwer Academic.

Brunel & Deschamps. Dictionnaire des Eglises de Paris. (FRE.). 440p. 1995. 295.00 (0-7859-9046-1) Fr & Eur.

Brunel, Bernard. Bunny Brunel's Bass Secrets. 240p. 1995. pap. 24.95 (0-7866-0429-8, 95448) Mel Bay.

Brunel, Bunny. The Complete Book of Bass Essentials: For 4 & 5 String Bass. (Complete Book). 256p. 1992. pap. 22.95 (1-56222-367-4, 94740) Mel Bay.

— The Complete Book of Bass Tech. 252p. 1993. pap. 22.95 (1-56222-646-0, 94523) Mel Bay.

***Brunel, Bunny.** J. S. Bach Pt. 1: 15 Two-Part Inventions for Two Basses. 96p. 1999. pap. 22.95 incl. audio compact disk (0-7866-3224-0, 96978BCD) Mel Bay.

Brunel, Isambard. The Life of Isambard Kingdom Brunel: Civil Engineer (1870) LC 72-850. (Illus.). 568p. 1972. 80.00 (0-8386-1201-6) Fairleigh Dickinson.

Brunel, Philippe. An Intimate Portrait of the Tour de France: Masters & Slaves of the Road. Lovett, Lois, tr. (Illus.). 156p. (C). 1996. text 39.95 (0-9649835-0-8) Buonpane.

Brunel, Pierre. Dictionnaire de Mythes Litteraires. (FRE.). 1436p. 1988. 275.00 (0-7859-7878-X, 2268007146) Fr & Eur.

— Dictionnaire des Sequences D'Encheres. (FRE.). 1998. 55.00 (0-320-00219-5) Fr & Eur.

— Histoire de la Litterature Francaise 19-20th Century. (FRE.). 770p. 1986. 29.95 (0-8288-7446-8) Fr & Eur.

Brunel, Pierre, et al. Catalogue of the Marine Invertebrates of the Estuary & Gulf of Saint Lawrence: Critical Catalogue of the Marine Invertebrates of the Estuary & Gulf of Saint Lawrence, Vol. 126. 405p. 1998. pap. 81.50 (0-660-60366-7) NRC Res Pr.

Brunel, Sigrid. Flight from Chador. LC 99-25698. 200p. 1999. pap. 10.95 (1-892281-06-6) New Victoria Pubs.

— Woman with Red Hair. LC 90-24051. 200p. (Orig.). 1991. pap. 8.95 (0-934678-30-8) New Victoria Pubs.

Brunell, Valerie & Swain, Ralph. Wilderness Ranger Cookbook. (Illus.). 112p. 1990. reprint ed. pap. 9.95 (1-56044-038-4) Falcon Pub Inc.

Brunelle, Daniel J. Ring-Opening Polymerization: Mechanism, Catalysis, Structure, Utility. 361p. 1992. 125.00 (1-56990-009-4) Hanser-Gardner.

Brunelle, Francis, et al. Liver Disease in Children: An Atlas of Angiography & Cholangiography. (Illus.). 290p. 1994. 165.00 (3-540-19674-9) Spr-Verlag.

— Liver Disease in Children: An Atlas of Angiography & Cholangiography. LC 93-33451. (Illus.). 290p. 1994. 181.00 (0-387-19674-9) Spr-Verlag.

Brunelle, Gayle K. The New World Merchants of Rouen, 1559-1630. (Sixteenth Century Essays & Studies: Vol. 16). (Illus.). 190p. 1991. 40.00 (0-940474-17-4, SCJP) Truman St Univ.

Brunelle, Jim. The Best of New England Humor...Or Pretty Darn Close. 256p. 1990. pap. 12.95 (0-89909-226-8, 80-550-3) Yankee Bks.

Brunelle, Lynn. Elmo's Movie Star Diary. LC 99-10795. (J). 1999. 7.99 (0-375-80132-4, Pub. by Random Bks Yng Read) Random.

***Brunelle, Lynn.** I Go Places: A Fun Sticker Book. (Illus.). 20p. (J). 1999. reprint ed. 7.95 (1-892374-23-4) Weldon Owen.

— My Blue Zoo. (Gymboree Colorblock Ser.). (Illus.). 20p. (J). 1999. reprint ed. 4.95 (1-892374-13-7) Weldon Owen.

— Nursery Rhymes: Music & Dance. (Illus.). 20p. (J). 1999. 5.95 (1-892374-25-0) Weldon Owen.

— Red on the Go: A Counting Book of Red. (Illus.). 20p. (J). 1999. reprint ed. 4.95 (1-892374-12-9) Weldon Owen.

Brunelle, Lynn, jt. auth. see McGuire, Leslie.

Brunelle, Mark. Fray Junipero Serra. 90p. (Orig.). 1987. pap. 4.95 (0-931887-00-3) Dobronte Pubns.

Brunelle, Michael Anthony. The Cocktail Handbook: Entertaining with Drink & Food. 7th rev. ed. LC 98-71417. 1998. write for info. (0-9664834-0-5) B Cortabarria.

Brunelle, Richard L. & Reed, Robert W. Forensic Examination of Ink & Paper. (Illus.). 302p. 1984. 78.95 (0-398-04935-1); pap. 47.95 (0-398-06039-8) C C Thomas.

Brunelle, Wallace & O'Neill, Robert. Constructional Geometry: Student Syllabus. 2nd ed. Gray, Allan W., ed. 1972. pap. text 11.95 (0-89420-229-4, 350299); audio 108.05 (0-89420-201-4, 350300) Natl Book.

Brunelli, B. & Knoepfel, Heinz, eds. Safety, Environmental Impact & Economic Prospects of Nuclear Fusion. (Ettore Majorana International Science Series, Life Sciences: Vol. 48). (Illus.). 360p. 1990. 105.00 (0-306-43524-1, Plenum Trade) Perseus Pubng.

An Asterisk (*) at the beginning of an entry indicates that the title is appearing for the first time.

Brunelli, B. & Leotta, G. G., eds. Muon-Catalyzed Fusion & Fusion with Polarized Nuclei. LC 87-29171. (Ettore Majorana International Science Series, Life Sciences: Vol. 33). (Illus.). 302p. 1988. 79.50 (*0-306-42784-2*, Plenum Trade) Perseus Pubng.
Brunelli, G. & Saffar, P. Wrist Imaging. (Illus.). 220p. 1993. 286.00 (*0-387-59561-9*) Spr-Verlag.
Brunelli, Jean, jt. auth. see Lindsay, Jeanne W.
Brunelli, Roberto. A Family Treasury of Bible Stories: One for Each Week of the Year. Jenkens, Lawrence, tr. from ITA. LC 96-54800. (Illus.). 126p. (J). 1997. 24.95 (*0-8109-1248-1*, Pub. by Abrams) Time Warner.
***Brunelli, Roberto & Fiodorov, Michael.** A World Treasury of Myths, Legends & Folktales. LC 99-42602. (Illus.). 128p. (J). (gr. 3-7). 2000. 24.95 (*0-8109-4554-1*, Pub. by Abrams) Time Warner.
Brunello, N., et al, eds. Critical Issues in the Treatment of Affective Disorders. (International Academy for Biomedical & Drug Research Ser.: Vol. 9). (Illus.). viii, 198p. 1995. 195.00 (*3-8055-6032-X*) S Karger.
Brunello, N., et al. New Generation of Antipsychotic Drugs: Novel Mechanisms of Action. Racagni, G. et al, eds. (International Academy for Biomedical & Drug Research Ser.: Vol. 4). (Illus.). vi, 150p. 1993. 146.25 (*3-8055-5654-3*) S Karger.
Brunello, Nicoletta, et al, eds. Mental Disorders in the Elderly: New Therapeutic Approaches - Rome, April, 1997. LC 97-52828. (International Academy for Biomedical & Drug Research Ser.: Vol. 13, 1997). (Illus.). vi, 192p. 1998. 189.75 (*3-8055-6536-4*) S Karger.
Brunemeister, S. L., jt. auth. see Fotheringham, Nick.
Bruneni, Joseph L. Looking Back: An Illustrated History of the American Ophthalmic Industry. LC 94-68862. (Illus.). 232p. (C). 1994. 68.00 (*1-886308-00-4*) Optical Lab.
Bruneni, Joseph L., ed. Making Managed Care Work for You. (Illus.). 1997. 48.00 (*1-886308-01-2*) Optical Lab.
Bruner, A. Crustacea, Copepoda, Calanoida und Cyclopoida. Zwick, Schwoerbel & Zwick, P., eds. (Suesswasserfauna von Mitteleuropa Ser.: Vol. 8/4-1). (Illus.). 209p. 1993. pap. 160.00 (*3-447-30631-9*, Pub. by Gustav Fischer) Balogh.
Bruner, Brodie, jt. auth. see Mason, Mike.
Bruner, Charles & Carter, Judy L. Family Support & Education: A Holistic Approach to School Readiness. 50p. 1991. pap. text 10.00 (*1-55516-327-0*, 3118) Natl Conf State Legis.
Bruner, Charles & Perrin, James M. More Than Health Insurance: State Initiatives to Improve Infant & Child Health. (Illus.). 44p. (Orig.). 1995. pap. write for info. (*1-887748-00-8*) Milbank Memorial.
Bruner, Charlotte. Unwinding Threads: Writing by Women in Africa. (African Writers Ser.). 224p. 1994. pap. 10.95 (*0-435-90989-4*, 90989) Heinemann.
Bruner, Charlotte, ed. The Heinemann Book of African Women's Writing. 224p. (C). 1993. pap. 10.95 (*0-435-90673-9*, 90673) Heinemann.
Bruner, Charlotte H., ed. Unwinding Threads: Writing by Women in Africa. LC 83-17175. (African Writers Ser.). 208p. (C). 1984. pap. 8.95 (*0-435-90256-3*, 90256) Heinemann.
Bruner, David, tr. see Accad, Evelyn.
Bruner, Donald & Bruner, Marilyn. The Legend of Wappato: Chief Cassino of the Multnomah. LC 99-53593. (Illus.). 224p. 2000. pap. 16.95 (*1-58151-039-X*, Pub. by BookPartners) Midpt Trade.
Bruner, Dorothy. Readings in Non Western Cultures. 296p. (C). 1995. text 42.00 (*0-536-58900-3*) Pearson Custom.
Bruner, Dorothy. A Study Guide for Contemporary Non-Western Cultures. 150p. (C). 1996. pap. text 14.95 (*0-7872-2775-7*) Kendall-Hunt.
— A Study Guide for Contemporary Non-Western Cultures. 2nd ed. 154p. (C). 1998. spiral bd. 17.95 (*0-7872-5173-9*) Kendall-Hunt.
Bruner, Edward M. Text, Play, & Story: The Construction & Reconstruction of Self & Society. (Illus.). 364p. (C). 1988. reprint ed. pap. text 18.95 (*0-88133-365-4*) Waveland Pr.
Bruner, Edward M., jt. ed. see Turner, Victor W.
Bruner, Fabrizio. Gas Chromatographic Environmental Analysis: Principles, Techniques, Instrumentation. LC 93-4959. 1993. 65.00 (*1-56081-011-4*, Wiley-VCH) Wiley.
Bruner, Fabrizio. Gas Chromatographic Environmental Analysis: Principles, Techniques, Instrumentation. 233p. 1993. 99.95 (*0-471-18778-X*, Wiley-VCH) Wiley.
Bruner, Frederick Dale. A Theology of the Holy Spirit: The Pentecostal Experience & the New Testament Witness. 390p. 1997. pap. 30.00 (*1-57910-094-5*) Wipf & Stock.
Bruner, Gordon C. & Hensel, Paul J. Marketing Scales Handbook: A Compilation of Multi-Item Measures. LC 92-18858. 1320p. 1992. 149.95 (*0-87757-226-7*) Am Mktg.
Bruner, Gordon C. & Hensel, Paul J. Marketing Scales Handbook: A Compilation of Multi-Item Measures. 1320p. 1994. pap. 89.95 (*0-87757-251-8*) Am Mktg.
— Marketing Scales Handbook: A Compilation of Multi-Item Measures. 1068p. 1996. 149.95 (*0-87757-261-5*) Am Mktg.
Bruner, James M., ed. see Watson, K. Rhydell.
Bruner, Jerome S. Acts of Meaning. (Jerusalem Lectures). 208p. 1992. pap. text 13.50 (*0-674-00361-6*) HUP.
— Acts of Meaning: Four Lectures on Mind & Culture. LC 90-40485. 160p. 1990. text 25.00 (*0-674-00360-8*) HUP.
— Actual Minds, Possible Words. LC 85-27297. 215p. 1986. pap. text 15.00 (*0-674-00366-7*) HUP.
— Actual Minds, Possible Worlds. (Jerusalem Lectures). 215p. 1990. 29.95 (*0-674-00365-9*) HUP.
— Child's Talk: Learning to Use Language. LC 83-42676. (Illus.). (C). 1985. pap. text 12.00 (*0-393-95345-9*) Norton.
— Contemporary Approaches to Cognition. LC 57-12963. (Illus.). 220p. reprint ed. pap. 68.20 (*0-608-30598-7*, 201673400005) Bks Demand.
— The Culture of Education. LC 95-46844. 240p. (C). 1996. 24.95 (*0-674-17952-8*) HUP.
— Culture of Education. 240p. 1997. pap. text 14.95 (*0-674-17953-6*) HUP.
— On Knowing: Essays for the Left Hand. LC 62-13264. (Illus.). 201p. 1979. 27.50 (*0-674-63475-6*); pap. text 10.95 (*0-674-63525-6*) Belknap Pr.
— Process of Education. LC 60-15235. 113p. 1976. pap. 12.95 (*0-674-71001-0*) HUP.
— Processes of Cognitive Growth: Infancy. LC 68-27831. (Heinz Werner Lectures: No. 3). 1968. 9.00 (*0-8271-6810-1*) Clark U Pr.
— Toward a Theory of Instruction. LC 66-13179. (Illus.). 186p. 1974. pap. 13.00 (*0-674-89701-3*) Belknap Pr.
Bruner, Jerome S. & Haste, Helen, eds. Making Sense. 260p. 1988. 65.00 (*0-416-38240-1*); pap. 15.95 (*0-416-92490-5*) Routledge.
Bruner, Jerome S., et al. A Study of Thinking. (Social Science Classics Ser.). 352p. 1986. reprint ed. pap. 21.95 (*0-88738-656-3*) Transaction Pubs.
Bruner, Jerome S., jt. auth. see Amsterdam, Anthony G.
Bruner, Jerome S., jt. ed. see Bornstein, M. H.
Bruner, Jerome S., ed. see Goodnow, Jacqueline.
Bruner, Jerome S., ed. see Stern, Daniel N.
Bruner, Jim, jt. auth. see Buckely, Clem.
Bruner, Johnny, ed. see King, Todd.
Bruner, Katherine, jt. auth. see Wolff, Robert L.
Bruner, Katherine, ed. see Wolff, Robert L.
Bruner, Katherine F., et al, eds. Entering China's Service: Robert Hart's Journals, 1854-1863. (East Asian Monographs: No. 125). 400p. 1987. 35.00 (*0-674-25735-9*) HUP.
Bruner, Katherine F., ed. see Hart, Robert.
Bruner, Kathy R., jt. auth. see Smosna, Richard.
Bruner, Kurt. Family Compass. LC 99-15577. (Heritage Builders Ser.). 1999. pap. 10.99 (*1-56476-781-7*, Victor Bks) Chariot Victor.
Bruner, Kurt, jt. auth. see Ledbetter, J. Otis.
***Bruner, Kurt D. & Ledbetter, J. Otis.** Your Heritage: How to Be Intentional about the Legacy You Leave. LC 99-44171. (Heritage Builders Ser.). 276p. 2000. pap. 10.99 (*0-7814-3374-6*) Chariot Victor.
Bruner, Leon. Validation Approaches for Alternative Methods. 100p. 1997. pap. text 36.00 (*90-5699-617-7*) Gordon & Breach.
Bruner, Marilyn, jt. auth. see Bruner, Donald.
Bruner, Mary L. Binford Family Genealogy. 375p. 1994. reprint ed. pap. 57.00 (*0-8328-4038-6*); reprint ed. lib. bdg. 67.00 (*0-8328-4037-8*) Higginson Bk Co.
— Binford Genealogy Supplement. 126p. 1994. reprint ed. pap. 19.50 (*0-8328-4198-6*); reprint ed. lib. bdg. 29.50 (*0-8328-4197-8*) Higginson Bk Co.
Bruner, Michael. Advertising Clocks: America's Timeless Heritage with Price Guide. LC 95-6994. (Collectors Bks.). (Illus.). 128p. (Orig.). 1995. pap. 29.95 (*0-88740-790-0*) Schiffer.
— Encyclopedia of Porcelain Enamel Advertising. 2nd rev. ed. LC 99-60439. (Illus.). 176p. (Orig.). 1999. pap. 29.95 (*0-7643-0816-5*) Schiffer.
— Encyclopedia of Porcelain Enamel Advertising Signs. LC 94-65626. (Illus.). 17662p. (Orig.). 1994. pap. 29.95 (*0-88740-605-X*) Schiffer.
— Gasoline Treasurers. LC 96-4676. (Illus.). 160p. (YA). (gr. 10-13). 1996. pap. write for info. (*0-7643-0050-4*) Schiffer.
— More Porcelain Enamel Advertising. LC 97-19062. 160p. 1997. pap. 29.95 (*0-7643-0373-2*) Schiffer.
Bruner, Michael & Polack, Lisa. Stop, Look, & Listen! A Holistic Guide to More Effective Listening. 130p. (Orig.). 1997. pap. 9.95 (*0-9656937-0-8*) Sagebrush Srvs.
Bruner, Pat A. How to Own & Operate a Retail Cart. 70p. 1995. 15.95 (*0-9649340-0-0*) Trump Properties.
Bruner, Philip L., jt. auth. see Kauffman, Caryn A.
Bruner, R. R., et al. Hoo Ring Spectra & Their Applications. (Lecture Notes in Mathematics Ser.: Vol. 1176). vii, 388p. 1986. 52.95 (*0-387-16434-0*) Spr-Verlag.
Bruner, Robert F. Case Studies in Finance: Managing for Corporate Value Creation. 2nd ed. 1993. pap. text 69.00 (*0-256-09465-9*) McGraw.
— Case Studies in Finance: Managing for Corporate Value Creation. 2nd ed. LC 93-8383. (Finance Ser.). 896p. (C). 1993. text 71.75 (*0-256-09464-0*, Irwn McGrw-H) McGrw-H Hghr Educ.
— Case Studies in Finance: Managing for Corporate Value Creation. 2nd ed. LC 98-23633. 1998. write for info. (*0-256-16698-6*, Irwn Prfssnl) McGraw-Hill Prof.
— CPS - Case Studies in Finance Select Cases. 2nd ed. 80p. (C). 1995. text 15.95 (*0-256-20411-X*, Irwn McGrw-H) McGrw-H Hghr Educ.
— The Poison Pill Anti-Takeover Defense: The Price of Strategic Deterrence. (Orig.). 1991. pap. text 20.00 (*0-943205-11-5*) RFICFA.
Bruner, Robert F., et al. The Essential Portable MBA. 2nd ed. LC 97-17566. 368p. 1997. 34.95 (*0-471-18093-9*) Wiley.
Bruner, Ross P. Analytical Approaches to Stock Selection. 275p. 1997. 65.00 (*1-888998-31-8*) Glenlake Pub.
— Global Equity Selection Strategies. (Illus.). 232p. 1998. 65.00 (*0-8144-0446-4*) AMACOM.
— Global Equity Selection Strategies. 1997. 65.00 (*1-888998-39-3*) Glenlake Pub.
Bruner, Ross P., ed. Analytical Approaches to Stock Selection. (Glenlake Business Monographs). 275p. 1998. 65.00 (*1-884964-76-1*) Fitzroy Dearborn.
— Global Equity Selection Strategies. (Glenlake Business Monographs). 240p. 1999. 65.00 (*1-57958-006-8*) Fitzroy Dearborn.
Bruner, Tom. Basic Concepts of Arranging & Orchestrating Music. 172p. 1988. pap. 17.95 (*0-87166-514-X*, 93970) Mel Bay.
Bruner, William E., et al, eds. Manual of Corneal Surgery. LC 86-23280. (Illus.). 149p. reprint ed. pap. 46.20 (*0-7837-6251-8*, 204596300010) Bks Demand
Brunet, Edward & Craver, Charles B. Alternate Dispute Resolution: Advocates Perspective. LC 97-71239. (Illus.). 724p. 1997. text 52.00 (*1-55834-479-9*, 10652-10, MICHIE) LEXIS Pub.
Brunet, Edward J., et al. Summary Judgment: Federal Law & Practice. 450p. 1996. text. write for info. (*0-7620-0102-X*) West Group.
— Summary Judgment: Federal Law & Practice 1996 Supplement. Davis, Russ, ed. 76p. 1996. pap. text, suppl. ed. write for info. (*0-7620-0057-0*) West Group.
Brunet, F. Bilingual Dictionary of Today's Slang French-English/English-French. 2nd ed. Orig. Title: Dictionnaire bilingue de L'argot d'Aujourd'hui. (ENG & FRE.). 688p. 1996. pap. 20.00 (*2-266-02591-6*, Pub. by Presses Pocket) IBD Ltd.
Brunet, Francoise. Dictionnaire Bilingue de l'Argot d'Aujour'dhui, Anglais-Francais-Francais-Anglais. (ENG & FRE.). 692p. 1996. 29.95 (*0-7859-9320-7*) Fr & Eur.
Brunet, Frantz. Dictionnaire du Parler Bourbonnais. (FRE.). 258p. 1993. 75.00 (*0-7859-8245-0*, 2908592177) Fr & Eur.
Brunet, J. P. American-French - French-American Dictionary of Police Force & Underworld Language. (ENG & FRE., Illus.). 1000p. 1990. 120.00 (*2-85608-037-5*) IBD Ltd.
— French & American English Dictionary of Police & Criminal Language. (ENG & FRE.). 1000p. 1990. 110.00 (*0-8288-7242-2*, 2856080375) Fr & Eur.
— Manuel du Libraire et de l'Amateur des Livres. 7449p. 1990. 1200.00 (*0-7859-5218-7*) Fr & Eur.
— Manuel du Libraire et de l'Amateur des Livres, 7 tomes, Set. 995.00 (*0-685-11350-7*) Fr & Eur.
— Supplement aux Supercheries Litteraires. 99.95 (*0-685-35982-4*) Fr & Eur.
***Brunet, Julie & McAlister, Renee, contrib. by.** Discovering God's Child, Pattern Book: A Faith Development Program for Three Year Olds, Vol. 3. 32p. (J). 2000. 7.95 (*0-8215-2452-6*) Sadlier.
— Discovering God's Child, Song Book: A Faith Development Program for Three Year Olds, Vol. 3. (Discovering God Ser.). 64p. (J). 2000. 7.95 (*0-8215-2458-5*) Sadlier.
— Discovering God's Love, Pattern Book: A Faith Development Program for Five Year Olds. (Discovering God Ser.). 32p. (J). (gr. 6). 2000. 7.95 (*0-8215-2472-0*) Sadlier.
— Discovering God's Love, Song Book: A Faith Development Program for Five Year Olds, Vol. 3, set 64p. (J). (gr. 6). 2000. 7.95 (*0-8215-2478-X*) Sadlier.
— Discovering God's World, Pattern Book: A Faith Development Program for Four Year Olds, Vol. 3, set (Discovering God Ser.). 32p. (J). 2000. 7.95 (*0-8215-2462-3*) Sadlier.
— Discovering God's World, Song Book: A Faith Development Program for Four Year Olds, Vol. 3, set 64p. (J). (gr. 6). 2000. 7.95 (*0-8215-2468-2*) Sadlier.
Brunet, M., ed. see Frick.
***Brunet, P., et al, eds.** CAD for Product Design: Tools & Algorithms. LC 99-45238. 380p. 2000. 89.95 (*3-540-66204-9*) Spr-Verlag.
Brunet, P., et al, eds. Photorealistic Rendering in Computer Science: Proceedings of the 2nd Eurographics Workshop on Rendering. (Focus on Computer Graphics Ser.). x, 281p. 1994. 107.95 (*0-387-56449-7*) Spr-Verlag.
Brunet-Perrault, Nicole & Doss, Cheryl R. Women Professionals in the Agricultural Sector: Cote d'Ivoire Case Study. Bryant, Denise F., ed. (Development Studies). 23p. (Orig.). 1992. pap. 6.00 (*0-933595-14-X*) Winrock Intl.
Brunetaud, Jean M., jt. ed. see Jensen, Dennis M.
Brunetiere, F. Manual of French Literature. LC 71-127998. (Studies in French Literature: No. 45). 1970. reprint ed. lib. bdg. 75.00 (*0-8383-1149-0*) M S G Haskel. Hse.
***Bruneton, J.** Pharmacognosy: Phytochemistry, Medicinal Plant. 2nd ed. (Illus.). 1136p. 1999. 218.00 (*1-898298-63-7*, Pub. by Intercept UK) Spr-Verlag.
— Toxic Plants: Dangerous to Human & Animals. (Illus.). 560p. 1999. 163.00 (*1-898298-62-9*, Pub. by Intercept UK) Spr-Verlag.
Bruneton, J. N., et al. Ultrasonography of the Spleen. (Illus.). 120p. 1988. 86.95 (*0-387-18595-X*) Spr-Verlag.
Bruneton, Jean. Pharmacognosy, Phytochemistry, Medicinal Plants. 196.50 (*1-898298-13-0*) Spr-Verlag.
Brunette, Donald M. Critical Thinking: Understanding & Evaluating Dental Research. LC 95-26777. (Illus.). 248p. 1996. pap. text 38.00 (*0-86715-301-6*) Quint Pub Co.
Brunette, Joan. Michael's Story: The Story of a Burn Victim. 105p. (Orig.). (YA). (gr. 7-12). 1995. pap. 6.95 (*1-57515-085-9*) PPI Pubng.
Brunette, Mary J. Fallen Star. 226p. (Orig.). 1992. pap. text 12.95 (*0-930401-48-4*) Artex Pub.
Brunette, Peter. The Films of Michelangelo Antonioni. LC 97-51311. (Cambridge Film Classics). (Illus.). 232p. (C). 1998. text 54.95 (*0-521-38085-5*); pap. text 16.95 (*0-521-38992-5*) Cambridge U Pr.
— Roberto Rossellini. LC 95-10239. (Illus.). 425p. (C). 1996. pap. 18.95 (*0-520-20053-5*, Pub. by U CA Pr) Cal Prin Full Svc.
Brunette, Peter, ed. Martin Scorsese: Interviews. LC 98-28414. (Interviews with Filmmakers Ser.). (Illus.). 256p. 1999. pap. 18.00 (*1-57806-072-9*); text 45.00 (*1-57806-071-0*) U Pr of Miss.
Brunette, Peter & Wills, David. Screen Play: Derrida & Film Theory. LC 89-33404. 222p. (Orig.). reprint ed. pap. 68.90 (*0-608-07661-9*, 205998300010) Bks Demand.
Brunette, Peter & Wills, David, eds. Deconstruction & the Visual Arts: Art, Media, Architecture. LC 92-44388. (Cambridge Studies in New Art History & Criticism). (Illus.). 328p. (C). 1993. pap. text 22.95 (*0-521-44781-X*) Cambridge U Pr.
Brunette, Peter, jt. ed. see Movshovitz, Howie.
Brunette, Peter, jt. ed. see Sterritt, David.
Brunette, Peter, ed. see Truffaut, Francois.
Brunette, Pierre. Francis of Assisi & His Conversions. Lachance, Paul & Krug, Kathryn, trs. from FRE. LC 97-6549. 1997. pap. 8.95 (*0-8199-0978-5*) Franciscan Pr.
Brunette, William K. Mortgage Handbook. LC 96-41436. 1997. pap. 12.95 (*0-452-27710-8*, Plume) Dutton Plume.
Brunetti, Argentina, jt. auth. see Reynolds, Althea C.
Brunetti, Aymo. Politics & Economic Growth: A Cross-Country Data Perspective. LC 98-121829. 160p. 1998. pap. 23.00 (*92-64-16017-5*, 41-98-02-1, Pub. by Org for Econ) OECD.
Brunetti, Aymo, et al. How Businesses See Government: Responses from Private Sector Surveys in 69 Countries. LC 97-50467. (Discussion Paper Ser.: No. 33). 76p. 1998. pap. 22.00 (*0-8213-4174-X*, 14174) World Bank.
Brunetti, E. Diptera: Brachycera, Vol. II. (Fauna of British India Ser.). (Illus.). x, 410p. 1977. reprint ed. 30.00 (*0-88065-071-0*) Scholarly Pubns.
— Diptera: Nematocera (Excluding Chironomidae & Culcidae), Vol. 1. (Fauna of British India Ser.). (Illus.). xxviii, 610p. 1977. reprint ed. 30.00 (*0-685-04535-8*) Scholarly Pubns.
— Diptera: Pipunculidae, Syrphidae, Conopidae, Ostridae, Vol. III. (Fauna of British India Ser.). (Illus.). xii, 436p. 1977. reprint ed. 30.00 (*0-88065-072-9*) Scholarly Pubns.
Brunetti, F., jt. auth. see Schenkel, F.
Brunetti, John. Brigitta Riesebrodt: Ruins, Recollections, Revelations. (Illus.). 32p. 1998. 10.00 (*0-9652065-3-X*) Fassbender Gallery.
***Brunetti, John.** Out of Line: Drawings by Illinois Artists. (Illus.). 32p. 2000. pap. 15.00 (*0-938903-29-2*) Cty of Chicago.
Brunetti, P., et al, eds. Artificial Systems for Insulin Delivery. LC 82-47688. (Serono Symposia Publications from Raven Press: No. 6). (Illus.). 639p. 1983. reprint ed. pap. 198.10 (*0-7837-9545-9*, 206029400005) Bks Demand.
Brunetti, Wayne H. Achieving Total Quality: Integrating Business Strategy & Customer Needs. LC 93-7276. 242p. 1993. text 28.95 (*0-527-91724-9*) Productivity Inc.
Brunetto, Carolyn. Math Art Activities. 1997. pap. 12.95 (*0-590-96371-6*) Scholastic Inc.
***Brunetto, Carolyn Ford.** All Gone! (Shaped Little Nugget Book Ser.). 18p. 1999. 3.99 (*0-307-14529-8*) Gldn Bks Pub Co.
Brunetto, Carolyn Ford. Baby A-B-C. (Shaped Little Nugget Bks.). 18p. (J). 1998. 3.99 (*0-307-13058-4*, 13058, Goldn Books) Gldn Bks Pub Co.
***Brungardt, Curtis.** Social Change Leadership Inventory: Self-Assessment & Analysis. 2nd ed. 51p. 1999. wbk. ed. 10.95 (*1-929149-00-X*, 1104) Rocky Mt Inst.
***Brungardt, Curtis & Crawford, Chris.** Risk Leadership: The Courage to Confront & Challenge. 216p. 1999. pap. 19.95 (*1-929149-01-8*, 1105) Rocky Mt Inst.
***Brungardt, Curtis L.** Social Change Leadership Inventory. 2nd ed. 4p. 1999. 2.95 (*1-929149-02-6*, 1103) Rocky Mt Inst.
Brungardt, Helen. Beyond Liberation. LC 84-23407. (Illus.). 64p. (Orig.). 1984. pap. 5.25 (*0-941992-04-7*) Los Arboles Pub.
— The Mystical Meaning of Jesus the Christ: Significant Episodes in the Life of the Master. 2nd ed. (Illus.). 64p. 1983. pap. 5.25 (*0-941992-03-9*) Los Arboles Pub.
Brungardt, Kurt. The Complete Book of Abs: Revised & Expanded Edition. expanded rev. ed. 256p. 1998. pap. 20.00 (*0-375-75143-2*) Villard Books.
— The Complete Book of Shoulders & Arms. 1997. pap. 20.00 (*0-614-27353-6*, Perennial) HarperTrade.
— The Complete Book of Shoulders & Arms: The Definitive Resource for Shaping & Strengthening the Shoulders & Arms. (Illus.). 320p. (Orig.). 1997. pap. 21.00 (*0-06-095166-4*, Perennial) HarperTrade.
— 3-Minute Abs: Achieving the Look You've Always Wanted in Only 3 Minutes a Day. LC 97-51851. 96p. 1998. pap. 12.00 (*0-06-095270-9*) HarpC.
Brungardt, Kurt, et al. The Complete Book of Butt & Legs. LC 94-29524. 1995. pap. 20.00 (*0-679-75481-4*) Villard Books.
Brunger, Axel T. X-PLOR Version 3.1: A System for X-ray Crystallography & NMR. LC 93-183161. (Illus.). 405p. (C). 1993. 40.00 (*0-300-05402-5*) Yale U Pr.
***Brunger, Bruce A & Reimers, Cathy L.** Buzz & Pixie Activity Coloring Book: An Entertaining Way to Help Young Children Understand Their Behavior. (Illus.). 109p. (J). (ps-2). 1999. pap. 9.95 (*1-886941-33-5*, Pub. by Spec Pr FL) Partners Pubs Grp.
Brunger, Scott. A Trade in Death: An Economics Mystery. LC 93-23202. 192p. (Orig.). 1993. pap. 7.95 (*0-377-00265-8*) Friendship Pr.
Brunger, Scott & Kim, Young-Bae, eds. Effects of Japanese Investment in a Small Community: A Case Study of Autoparts in East Tennessee. LC 97-41657. (Illus.). 110p. 1997. lib. bdg. 39.00 (*1-56072-454-4*) Nova Sci Pubs.
Brungers, Bruce A., jt. auth. see REIMERS, CATHY L.
Brungess, James R. Setting the Context: Suppression of Enemy Air Defenses & Joint War Fighting in an Uncertain World. LC 94-19404. (Illus.). 244p. 1994. pap. 15.00 (*1-58566-051-5*) Air Univ.

B

Brungs, Robert & Postiglione, Marianne, eds. Beauty in Faith, Science & Technology. (Illus.). 304p. (Orig.). 1994. pap. text 15.95 (*0-9625431-8-7*) ITEST Faith.
— Creation & Evolution. LC 98-181079. (Illus.). 270p. 1998. pap. text 15.95 (*1-885583-06-0*) ITEST Faith.
— The Family of the Future/The Future of the Family. (Illus.). 228p. 1999. pap. 15.95 (*1-885583-07-9*) ITEST Faith.
***Brungs, Robert & Postiglione, Marianne, eds.** The Genome: Plant, Animal, Human. 240p. 2000. pap. 15.95 (*1-885583-08-7*) ITEST Faith.
Brungs, Robert A., frwd. The Inner Environment: Clinical Research, Health Care Delivery, Economics. 172p. (Orig.). 1990. pap. 15.95 (*0-9625431-2-8*) ITEST Faith.
— Science-Technology Education in Church-Related Colleges & Universities. (Illus.). 271p. (Orig.). 1990. pap. 15.95 (*0-9625431-0-1*) ITEST Faith.
Brungs, Robert A. & Postiglione, Marianne, eds. Christianity & the Environmental Ethos. LC 96-222430. (Illus.). 213p. (Orig.). 1996. pap. 15.95 (*1-885583-04-4*) ITEST Faith.
Brungs, Robert A., jt. ed. see Postiglione, Marianne.
Brunhammer, Yvonne. Jewels of Lalique: Yvonne Brunhammer. LC 97-48532. (Illus.). 224p. 1998. 50.00 (*2-08-013632-1*, Pub. by Flammarion) Abbeville Pr.
Brunhammer, Yvonne, intro. Baccarat the Perfume Bottles: A Collector's Guide. 2nd rev. ed. LC 86-216083. (Illus.). 232p. 1994. reprint ed. 70.00 (*2-906309-05-2*) Addor.
Brunhammer, Yvonne, et al. Art Nouveau Belgium-France. LC 76-1649. 1976. 45.00 (*0-914412-11-6*, Inst Arts Catalogues) Menil Found.
Brunhes Delamarre, Mariel J., et al. Geographie Regionale, 2 vols., 2. write for info. (*0-318-52012-5*) Fr & Eur.
Brunhes, Jean. Human Geography, an Attempt at a Positive Classification: Principles & Examples. LC 75-41040. (Illus.). reprint ed. 67.50 (*0-404-14724-0*) AMS Pr.
Brunhoff, Jean de, see de Brunhoff, Jean.
Brunhoff, Laurent de, see de Brunhoff, Laurent.
Brunhoff, Laurent de, see de Brunhoff, Jean & de Brunhoff, Laurent.
Brunhoff, Laurent de, see de Brunhoff, Laurent.
Brunhoff, Laurent de, see de Brunhoff, Jean & de Brunhoff, Laurent.
Brunhoff, Laurent de, see de Brunhoff, Laurent.
Brunhoff, Laurent de, see de Brunhoff, Jean & de Brunhoff, Laurent.
Brunhoff, Laurent de, see de Brunhoff, Laurent.
Brunhoff, Laurent de, see de Brunhoff, Jean & de Brunhoff, Laurent.
Brunhoff, Laurent de, see de Brunhoff, Laurent.
Brunhouse, Barbara, jt. auth. see Laird, Ellen.
Brunhouse, Jay. The Maverick Guide to Berlin. 2nd ed. (Maverick Guides Ser.). 400p. 1993. pap. text 15.95 (*1-56554-314-9*) Pelican.
— Traveling Europe's Trains. 4th ed. LC 96-45611. (Illus.). 544p. 1997. pap. 15.95 (*1-56554-261-4*) Pelican.
Brunhouse, Robert L. En Busca de los Mayas (In Search of the Mayas) (SPA.). 222p. 1989. pap. 11.99 (*968-16-3303-2*, Pub. by Fondo) Continental Bk.
Brunhuber, Ernst. Giesserei-Lexikon: Foundry Dictionary in German. (GER.). 960p. 1978. 135.00 (*0-8288-5440-8*, M7425) Fr & Eur.
— Multilingual Dictionary of Foundry Terms: English, French, German, Italian. 4th ed. (ENG, FRE, GER & ITA.). 1158p. 1988. 295.00 (*0-8288-0604-7*, M7424) Fr & Eur.
Bruni, Antonio B. Antonio Bartolomeo Bruni: Caprices & Airs Varies & Cinquante Etudes. Stolba, K. Marie, ed. (Recent Researches in Music of the Classic Era Ser.: Vol. RRC14). (Illus.). xix, 102p. 1982. pap. 45.00 (*0-89579-163-3*) A-R Eds.
Bruni, C., ed. Systems Theory in Immunology. (Lecture Notes in Biomathematics Ser.: Vol. 32). 273p. 1980. 36.95 (*0-387-09728-7*) Spr-Verlag.
Bruni, Franco, et al, eds. Risk Management in Volatile Financial Markets. LC 96-16268. (Financial & Monetary Policy Studies: Vol. 32). xii, 371p. 1996. lib. bdg. 157.50 (*0-7923-4053-1*) Kluwer Academic.
Bruni, Giancarlo. Rejoice, Mary: Lectio Divina of the Hail Mary. 96p. (C). 1996. pap. 40.00 (*0-85439-278-5*, Pub. by St Paul Pubns) St Mut.
Bruni, J. Edward, jt. auth. see Montemurro, Donald G.
Bruni, Joseph, jt. auth. see Guberman, Alan H.
Bruni, Mary-Ann S. Elif: Child of Turkey. (Middle Eastern Magic Ser.: Vol. 1). (Illus.). 48p. (J). (gr. k-8). 1988. 12.95 (*0-935857-13-3*); pap. text. write for info. (*0-935857-14-1*) Texart.
— Journey Through Kurdistan. (Illus.). 211p. (YA). 1996. pap. 24.95 (*0-941671-01-1*) U of Tex Pr.
— Rosita's Christmas Wish. LC 85-52040. (Texas Ser.). (Illus.). 48p. (J). (gr. k-8). 1985. 13.95 (*0-935857-00-1*); write for info. (*0-935857-09-5*); pap. write for info. (*0-935857-01-X*); pap. write for info. (*0-935857-10-9*) Texart.
— Rosita's Christmas Wish. limited ed. LC 85-52040. (Texas Ser.). (Illus.). 48p. (J). (gr. k-8). 1985. 125.00 (*0-935857-03-6*) Texart.
— El Sueno de Rosita. De Castro, Rogelio, tr. from ENG. (Texas Ser.: Vol. 1).Tr. of Rosita's Christmas Wish. (SPA., Illus.). 48p. (J). (gr. k-8). 1987. 13.95 (*0-935857-02-8*); pap. write for info. (*0-935857-04-4*); write for info. (*0-935857-11-7*); write for info. (*0-935857-12-5*) Texart.
Bruni, Mary-Ann S., photos by. Viva la Virgen de Guadalupe! (Illus.). 64p. 1989. 24.95 (*0-935857-18-4*); pap. 14.95 (*0-935857-19-2*) Texart.
Bruni, Mary-Ann S., jt. auth. see De Luca, L.
Bruni, Mary-Ann S., ed. see Cormier, Larry.
Bruni, Maryanne. Fine Motor Skills in Children with Down Syndrome: A Guide for Parents & Professionals. LC 98-34362. (Topics in Down Syndrome Ser.). (Illus.). 350p. 1998. pap. 16.95 (*1-890627-03-8*) Woodbine House.
Brunicardi, Victor A., jt. auth. see Griffin, Anthony.
Brunier, Dominique P. & Nahler, Gerhard R., eds. International Clinical Trails: A Guide Book & Compendium of National Drug Laws. LC 99-22061. 500p. 1999. 229.00 (*1-57491-094-9*) Interpharm.
***Brunier, Serge.** Majestic Universe: Views from Here to Infinity... Dunlop, Storm, tr. (Illus.). 216p. 2000. 39.95 (*0-521-66307-5*) Cambridge U Pr.
***Brunier, Serge & Luminet, Jean-Pierre.** Glorious Eclipses: Their Past, Present & Future. (Illus.). 190p. 2000. text 39.95 (*0-521-79148-0*) Cambridge U Pr.
Bruning, E., jt. auth. see Blanchard, P.
Bruning, J., ed. see Guillemin, V. W. & Sternberg, S.
Bruning, James L. & Guillemin, Victor W., eds. Mathematics Past & Present: Fourier Integral Operators. LC 93-38405. 300p. 1994. 86.95 (*0-387-56741-0*) Spr-Verlag.
Bruning, James L. & Kintz, B. L. Computational Handbook of Statistics. 4th ed. LC 96-30391. 352p. (C). 1997. pap. text 57.00 (*0-673-99085-0*) Longman.
Bruning, John R. Crimson Sky: The Air Battle for Korea. LC 98-43110. (Illus.). 224p. 1999. 24.95 (*1-57488-158-2*) Brasseys.
***Bruning, John R.** Crimson Sky: The Air Battle for Korea. 2000. reprint ed. pap. 18.95 (*1-57488-296-1*) Brasseys.
Bruning, Nancy Pauline. Breast Implants: Everything You Need to Know. 2nd ed. LC 94-46995. (Illus.). 224p. 1995. 21.95 (*0-89793-176-9*); pap. 12.95 (*0-89793-175-0*) Hunter Hse.
— Natural Medicine for Colds & Flu. LC 98-179265. (Natural Medicine Library). 240p. 1998. mass mkt. 5.99 (*0-440-22523-X*) Dell.
Bruning, Nancy Pauline, jt. auth. see Katz, Jane.
Bruning, Nancy Pauline, jt. auth. see Lieberman, Shari.
Bruning, P. F. & Tchekmedyian, N. S., eds. Recent Advances in Hormonal Therapy in Cancer: Supplement 2, 1992. (Journal: Oncology: Vol. 49). (Illus.). iv, 56p. 1992. pap. 17.50 (*3-8055-5710-8*) S Karger.
Bruning, Richard, ed. see Baron, Mike & Rude, Steve.
Bruning, Richard, ed. see Barr, M. & Bolland, B.
Bruning, Richard, ed. see DeMatteis, J. M. & Giffen, Keith.
Bruning, Richard, ed. see Miller, Frank.
Bruning, Richard, ed. see Motter, D. & Askwith, M.
Bruning, Richard, ed. see Siegel, Jerry.
Bruning, Roger H., et al. Cognitive Psychology & Instruction. 3rd ed. LC 98-7091. 433p. 1998. pap. text 51.00 (*0-13-716606-0*, Merrill Coll) P-H.
Bruning, Roger H., jt. auth. see Calfee, Robert.
Bruning, Stephen D., jt. ed. see Ledingham, John A.
***Bruning, Ted.** Historic Pubs of London. 256p. 2000. 24.95 (*0-658-00502-2*, 005022) NTC Contemp Pub Co.
Bruning, Ted. Historic Pubs of London. LC 99-214819. (Illus.). 192p. 1998. 19.95 (*1-85375-262-2*, Pub. by Prion) Trafalgar.
Brunini, John G., ed. From One Word: Selected Poems. 124p. 1950. 9.95 (*0-8159-5511-1*) Devin.
Brunious, Loretta J. How Black Disadvantaged Adolescents Socially Construct Reality: Listen, Do You Hear What I Hear? rev. ed. LC 98-27138. (Children of Poverty Ser.). (Illus.). 250p. 1998. 52.00 (*0-8153-3235-1*) Garland.
Brunk, Chip. PhotoStory. 1998. 24.95 (*0-9636796-7-8*, PS) Chimeric.
Brunk, Conrad G., et al. Value Assumptions in Risk Assessment: A Case Study of the Alachlor Controversy. 168p. (C). 1991. pap. 19.95 (*0-88920-266-4*); text 29.95 (*0-88920-200-1*) W Laurier U Pr.
Brunk, Gregory C. Identifying Coins, Medals & Tokens - Late Antiquity to Modern Times: A Bibliographical Survey of Useful Articles. 145p. (Orig.). 1991. pap. 35.00 (*1-878420-04-6*) Laurion Pub.
— Merchant Countermarks on World Coins. (Illus.). 160p. 1989. 39.95 (*0-912317-12-4*); pap. 29.95 (*0-912317-11-6*) World Exo.
Brunk, Gregory G., ed. Theories of Political Processes: A Bibliographic Guide to the Journal Literature, 1965-1995, 27. LC 96-52498. (Bibliographies & Indexes in Law & Political Science Ser.: Vol. 27). 280p. 1997. lib. bdg. 82.95 (*0-313-30259-6*, Greenwood Pr) Greenwood.
— World Countermarks on Medieval & Modern Coins. LC 75-39496. (Gleanings from the Numismatist Ser.: Vol. 8). (Illus.). 1976. 35.00 (*0-88000-074-0*) Quarterman.
Brunk, Gregory G., et al. Understanding Attitudes about War: Modeling Moral Judgments. LC 95-53043. (Pitt Series in Policy & Institutional Studies). 237p. (C). 1996. pap. 19.95 (*0-8229-5585-7*); text 45.00 (*0-8229-3926-6*) U of Pittsburgh Pr.
Brunk, Juanita. Brief Landing on the Earth's Surface. LC 96-15118. (Brittingham Prize in Poetry Ser.). 64p. (Orig.). 1996. pap. 11.95 (*0-299-15204-9*) U of Wis Pr.
— Brief Landing on the Earth's Surface. LC 96-15118. (Brittingham Prize in Poetry Ser.). 64p. (Orig.). 1996. 18.95 (*0-299-15200-6*) U of Wis Pr.
Brunk, Menno J. Fulfilled Prophecies. 160p. 1971. pap. 5.75 (*0-7399-0222-9*, 2245) Rod & Staff.
***Brunk, Raymond.** Proverbs for Today: 2001 Original Sayings. 256p. 2000. 4.97 (*1-57748-798-2*) Barbour Pub.
Brunk, Raymond P. Originals: One Thousand One Proverbs for Today. LC 92-73780. 128p. (Orig.). 1992. pap. 4.25 (*0-9634038-2-6*) Anthony Pubs.
Brunk, Robert S., ed. May We All Remember Well: A Journal of the History & Cultures of Western North Carolina. (Illus.). 288p. (Orig.). 1997. pap. 40.00 (*0-9656461-0-6*) R S Brunk.
Brunk, Samuel. Emiliano Zapata! Revolution & Betrayal in Mexico. (Illus.). 360p. 1995. pap. 24.95 (*0-8263-1620-4*) U of NM Pr.
Brunk, Terence, ed. see Smith, Ken.
Brunk, Teresa. Sewing for Conservative Men. LC 94-228424. 1994. spiral bd. 8.95 (*0-87813-555-3*) Christian Light.
Brunke, Ernst-Joachim, ed. Progress in Essential Oil Research: Proceedings of the International Symposium on Essential Oils, Holzminden-Neuhaus, Federal Republic of Germany, September 18-21, 1985. (Illus.). xvi, 668p. 1986. 211.55 (*3-11-010614-0*) De Gruyter.
Brunke, Ottillie S. Chapter Ceremonies & Poems. iv, 60p. 1985. reprint ed. pap. text 4.00 (*0-88053-305-6*, S-192) Macoy Pub.
— O. E. S. Floor Work. 16p. 1993. reprint ed. pap. 3.00 (*0-88053-331-5*, S-241) Macoy Pub.
Brunke, Ottillies S. Deputy Addresses. 1990. pap. 3.00 (*0-88053-353-6*, S180) Macoy Pub.
— Star Point Series & Ceremonies. enl. rev. ed. 96p. 1996. pap. 6.50 (*0-88053-362-5*, S-307) Macoy Pub.
***Brunken, Patricia Krout.** Tough... No Matter What: The Legacy of Leisa. LC 99-97763. 2000. pap. 14.95 (*0-533-13480-3*) Vantage.
Brunker, Dick. Steel Buffalo. 328p. 1999. per. 12.95 (*0-89992-121-3*) Coun India Ed.
***Brunkhorst, Hauke.** Adorno & Critical Theory. 192p. 1999. (*0-7083-1529-1*, Pub. by Univ Wales Pr); pap. (*0-7083-1528-3*, Pub. by Univ Wales Pr) Paul & Co Pubs.
Brunkhorst, Martin. Shakespeares Coriolanus in deutscher Bearbeitung: Sieben Beispiele zum literaturaesthetischen Problem der Umsetzung und Vermittlung Shakespeares. (Komparatistische Studien: Vol. 3). (C). 1973. 95.40 (*3-11-003997-4*) De Gruyter.
Brunkus, Denise, jt. auth. see Levy, Elizabeth.
Brunkus, Denise, jt. illus. see Bottner, Barbara.
Brunkus, Denise, jt. illus. see Korman, Justine.
Brunler, Oscar. Rays & Radiation Phenomena. 45p. 1996. reprint ed. pap. 10.00 (*0-7873-1177-4*) Hlth Research.
Brunn. Cities of the World. 3rd ed. (C). 2000. pap. text. write for info. (*0-321-04876-8*) Addison-Wesley.
Brunn, ed. see Stromayr, Caspar.
Brunn, Daniel. The Cave Dwellers of Southern Tunisia. 352p. 1984. 250.00 (*1-85077-064-6*, Pub. by Darf Pubs Ltd) St Mut.
Brunn, Emilie Z. Le Dilemme de l'Etre et du Neant Chez Saint Augustin: Des Premiers Dialogues aux "Confessions" (Bochumer Studien zur Philosophie Ser.: Vol. 4). (FRE.). iv, 102p. 1984. 29.00 (*90-6032-234-7*, Pub. by B R Gruner) Humanities.
— St. Augustine: Being & Nothingness. LC 86-22642. 129p. 1987. 22.95 (*0-913729-17-5*) Paragon Hse.
Brunn, Emilie Z. & Epiney-Burgard, Georgette. Women Mystics in Medieval Europe. Hughes, Sheila, tr. (Illus.). 233p. 1989. pap. 16.95 (*1-55778-196-6*) Paragon Hse.
Brunn, Erik. Good-Sense Guide: Household Hints & Formulas. 368p. pap. 12.98 (*1-884822-19-3*) Blck Dog & Leventhal.
Brunn, George. California Judges Benchbook: Search & Seizure 1991, 4 vols., Set. LC 90-86111. 455p. 1991. pap. text 65.00 (*0-88124-366-3*, CR-31791) Cont Ed Bar-CA.
Brunn, S. & Leinbach, T. Collapsing Space & Time: Geographic Aspects of Communications & Information. 384p. (C). 1991. text 89.95 (*0-04-910119-6*) Routledge.
Brunn, Stanley D. Urbanization in Developing Countries: An International Bibliography. LC 79-172535. (Latin American Studies Center Research Report: No. 8). 711p. reprint ed. pap. 200.00 (*0-8357-4336-5*, 203713700007) Bks Demand.
Brunn, Stanley D. & Williams, Jack F. Cities of the World: World Regional Urban Development. 2nd ed. 512p. (C). 1997. 80.00 (*0-06-041028-0*) Addson-Wesley Educ.
Brunn, Stanley D., ed. see Elkins, T. H., et al.
Brunner, Albert. Reports of Cases: The Circuit Courts of the United States. xi, 742p. 1968. reprint ed. 40.00 (*0-89941-592-X*, 502100) W S Hein.
Brunner, Borgna. Information Please Almanac. 1024p. 1997. pap. 10.95 (*0-395-88276-1*) HM.
Brunner, Borgna, ed. Information Please Almanac. 1024p. 1997. 24.95 (*0-395-88275-3*) HM.
***Brunner, C. Cryss.** Principles of Power: Women Superintendents & the Riddle of the Heart. LC 99-47840. (C). 2000. text 57.50 (*0-7914-4569-0*); pap. text 18.95 (*0-7914-4570-4*) State U NY Pr.
Brunner, C. Cryss, ed. Sacred Dreams: Women & the Superintendency. LC 98-36545. (SUNY Series in Women in Education). 288p. (C). 1999. text 57.50 (*0-7914-4159-8*); pap. text 18.95 (*0-7914-4160-1*) State U NY Pr.
Brunner, C. Elijah. How to Find God. (Illus.). 144p. 1995. pap. 9.95 (*0-9631075-5-0*) Cent Systs.
Brunner, C. F. & Waber, B. G. Special Techniques in Internal Fixation. (Illus.). 198p. 1981. 155.00 (*0-387-11056-9*) Spr-Verlag.
Brunner, Calvin R. Incineration Systems Handbook. (Illus.). 530p. 1996. text 150.00 (*0-9621774-0-7*) Incinerat Consults.
— Medical Waste Disposal. LC 95-95256. (Illus.). 560p. (C). 1996. text 150.00 (*0-9621774-1-5*) Incinerat Consults.
Brunner, Charles R., compiled by. Game Graphics: The Best New Video & Board Game Design. (Illus.). 160p. 1995. 34.99 (*1-56496-079-X*) Rockport Pubs.
Brunner, Christopher J. Sasanian Stamp Seals in the Metropolitan Museum of Art. (Illus.). 152p. 1979. 35.00 (*0-87099-176-0*) Metro Mus Art.
Brunner, Constantin. Tyranny of Hate: The Roots of Antisemitism. abr. ed. Harrison, Graham, tr. LC 92-13724. 208p. 1992. lib. bdg. 89.95 (*0-7734-9562-2*) E Mellen.
Brunner, Cornelia & Talley, William. The Media Literacy Handbook: An Educator's Guide to Bringing New Media into the Classroom. LC 99-11339. 240p. 1999. pap. 14.00 (*0-385-49614-1*, Anchor NY) Doubleday.
Brunner, D., jt. ed. see Jokl, E.
Brunner, Diane D. Between the Masks. LC 98-23717. 180p. 1998. pap. 19.95 (*0-8476-8896-8*) Rowman.
— Between the Masks: Resisting the Politics of Essentialism. LC 98-23717. 180p. 1998. 60.00 (*0-8476-8895-X*) Rowman.
— Inquiry & Reflection: Framing Narrative Practice in Education. LC 93-17270. (SUNY Series, Teacher Empowerment & School Reform). 290p. (C). 1994. pap. text 21.95 (*0-7914-1870-7*) State U NY Pr.
— Inquiry & Reflection: Framing Narrative Practice in Education. LC 93-17270. (SUNY Series, Teacher Empowerment & School Reform). 290p. (C). 1994. text 64.50 (*0-7914-1869-3*) State U NY Pr.
Brunner, Doris & Mellitzer, Jurgen. Sunrise Uber Osterreichs Betrieben: Die Adoption Thermischer Solaranlagen in Unternehmen des Gewerbe Und des Tourismus In Osterreich Eine Empirische Bestandsanalyse. (Illus.). XIX, 334p. 1998. 56.95 (*3-631-33393-5*) P Lang Pubng.
Brunner, E. & Denker, M., eds. Research Developments in Probability & Statistics. (Illus.). 464p. 1996. 220.00 (*90-6764-209-6*, Pub. by VSP) Coronet Bks.
Brunner, Edmund D. Rural Australia & New Zealand: Some Observations of Current Trends. LC 75-30123. (Institute of Pacific Relations Ser.). reprint ed. 34.50 (*0-404-59513-8*) AMS Pr.
— Working with Rural Youth. LC 74-1669. (Children & Youth Ser.). 132p. 1974. reprint ed. 17.95 (*0-405-05949-3*) Ayer.
Brunner, Edmund D., et al, eds. Farmers of the World. LC 73-134062. (Essay Index Reprint Ser.). 1977. 18.95 (*0-8369-2182-8*) Ayer.
Brunner, Edmund D. & Lorge, Irving. Rural Trends in Depression Years: A Survey of Village-Centered Agricultural Communities, 1930-1936. LC 75-137157. (Poverty U. S. A. Historical Record Ser.). 1977. reprint ed. 29.95 (*0-405-03095-9*) Ayer.
Brunner, Edmund D., jt. auth. see Wayland, Sloan.
Brunner, Edmund de S. & Kolb, John H. Rural Social Trends. LC 70-98825. 386p. 1970. reprint ed. lib. bdg. 35.00 (*0-8371-2889-7*, BRRS, Greenwood Pr) Greenwood.
Brunner, Edmund de S., jt. auth. see Chase, Stuart.
***Brunner, Edward.** Cold War Poetry. LC 00-8405. 312p. 2000. text 29.95 (*0-252-02592-X*) U of Ill Pr.
Brunner, Edward J. Poetry As Labor & Privilege: The Writings of W. S. Merwin. (Illus.). 352p. 1991. text 44.95 (*0-252-01775-7*) U of Ill Pr.
— Splendid Failure: Hart Crane & the Making of the Bridge. LC 84-2690. 296p. 1985. text 29.95 (*0-252-01094-9*) U of Ill Pr.
Brunner, Emil. The Divine-Human Encounter. LC 80-12399. 207p. 1980. reprint ed. lib. bdg. 35.00 (*0-313-22398-X*, BRDH, Greenwood Pr) Greenwood.
Brunner, Emma B. Bits of Background in One-Act Plays. LC 77-94334. (One-Act Plays in Reprint Ser.). 1978. reprint ed. 20.00 (*0-8486-2034-8*) Roth Pub Inc.
Brunner, F. K., ed. Advances in Positioning & Reference Frames: International Symposium No. 118: Rio De Janeiro, Brazil, September 3-9, 1997. LC 98-25812. 396p. 1998. 139.00 (*3-540-64604-3*) Spr-Verlag.
— Geodetic Refraction. (Illus.). 230p. 1984. 56.95 (*0-387-13830-7*) Spr-Verlag.
Brunner, F. K. & Rizos, C. Developments in Four-Dimensional Geodesy. (Lecture Notes in Earth Sciences Ser.: Vol. 29). (Illus.). x, 264p. 1990. 50.95 (*0-387-52332-4*) Spr-Verlag.
Brunner, Fernand. Metaphysique d'Ibn Gabirol et de la Tradition Platonicienne. Schulthess, Daniel, ed. LC 97-26921. (Variorum Collected Studies Ser.: Vol. 589). 384p. 1997. text 115.95 (*0-86078-654-4*, Pub. by Ashgate Pub) Ashgate Pub Co.
Brunner, Francis A., tr. see Fellerer, Karl G.
Brunner, Francis A., tr. see Jungmann, Josef A.
Brunner, G., ed. see Schmidt, F. W.
Brunner, Georg, jt. ed. see Solyom, Laszlo.
Brunner, Georg, jt. ed. see Weilemann, Peter R.
Brunner, Gerhard. Aquarium Plants. Vevers, Gwynne, tr. from GER. 244p. 1973. 35.95 (*0-87666-455-9*, H-966) TFH Pubns.
Brunner, Gisbert & Pfeiffer-Belli, Christian. Swiss Wristwatches: Chronology of Worldwide Success. LC 90-63793. (Illus.). 248p. 1991. 69.95 (*0-88740-301-8*) Schiffer.
Brunner, Gisbert, jt. auth. see Viola, Gerald.
Brunner, Gisbert L. Mastering Time. 1997. 100.00 (*2-908228-82-3*, Pub. by Assouline) Rizzoli Intl.
***Brunner, Gisbert L. & Pfeiffer-Belli, Christian.** Wristwatches. 3rd rev. ed. (Illus.). 192p. 2000. pap. 19.95 (*0-7643-1000-3*) Schiffer.
Brunner, Gisbert L. & Pfeiffer-Belli, Christian. Wristwatches: A Handbook & Price Guide. rev. ed. 166p. 1997. pap. 19.95 (*0-7643-0381-3*) Schiffer.
Brunner, Hans-Peter. Closing the Technology Gap: Change in India's Computer Industry. LC 95-13140. 200p. 1995. 28.00 (*0-8039-9251-3*) Sage.
Brunner, Hans R. Imidazoline Receptors Linking the Brain & the Cardiovascular System. 1997. text. write for info. (*0-397-51818-8*) Lppncott W & W.
Brunner, Hans R., ed. ACE-Inhibition: State of the Art. (Journal: Cardiology: Vol. 76, Suppl. 2, 1989). (Illus.). iv, 68p. 1989. pap. 22.75 (*3-8055-5062-6*) S Karger.
— Aging Process: Implications for ACE Inhibition: Proceedings of a Symposium Held in Montreux, March 1987. (Journal: Gerontology: Vol. 33, Suppl. 1). (Illus.). x, 56p. 1988. pap. 18.50 (*3-8055-4729-3*) S Karger.

Brunner, Hans R. & Gavras, Haralambos, eds. Clinical Hypertension & Hypotension. LC 81-19430. (Illus.). 521p. reprint ed. pap. 161.60 (0-7837-0910-2, 204121500019) Bks Demand.

Brunner, Hans R. & Waeber, Bernard, eds. Ambulatory Blood Pressure Recording. LC 91-43057. (Illus.). 206p. 1992. reprint ed. pap. 63.90 (0-608-07247-8, 206747200009) Bks Demand.

Brunner, Harald & Thaler, Heribert, eds. Hepatology: A Festschrift for Hans Popper. LC 84-18381. (Illus.). 402p. 1985. reprint ed. pap. 124.70 (0-608-00651-3, 206123900007) Bks Demand.

Brunner, Heinrich E. Christianity & Civilisation, 2 vols. LC 77-27182. (Gifford Lectures: 1947-48). reprint ed. 55.00 (0-404-60530-3) AMS Pr.

Brunner, Helen M. & Russell, Don. Money to Work II: Funding for Visual Artists. rev. ed. Samuelsen, Grant, ed. 312p. 1992. pap. 15.20 (0-685-65202-5) Art Resources Intl.

Brunner, Hellmut. Das Horende Herz: Kleine Schriften zur Religions- und Geistesgeschichte Agyptens. Rollig, Wolfgang, ed. (Orbis Biblicus et Orientalis Ser.: Vol. 80). (GER.). 427p. 1988. text 75.75 (3-7278-0567-6, Pub. by Presses Univ Fribourg) Eisenbrauns.

Brunner, Ingrid & Mathes, John. Technician As Writer: Preparing Technical Reports. 160p. (C). 1980. 9.00 (0-02-315960-X, Macmillan Coll) P-H.

Brunner, J. & Wolff, G. Pulmonary Function Indices in Critical Care Patients. 180p. 1988. 77.95 (0-387-18432-5) Spr-Verlag.

Brunner, Jake, et al. Logging Burma's Frontier Forests: Resources & the Regime. LC 98-86983. (Illus.). 56p. 1998. pap. 20.00 (1-56973-266-3) World Resources Inst.

Brunner, James. Encountering Christ Today: A Catechism of the Catholic Church. Srouji, Jacqueline, ed. LC 97-210523. (Illus.). 914p. (Orig.). 1997. pap. text 30.00 (0-9656546-0-5) Didache Pub.

*Brunner, James R. Wildlands Workers' Handbook. 2000. pap. 20.00 (0-615-11532-2) Wildlands Workers.

Brunner, John. A New Settlement of Old Scores. LC 83-62071. (Illus.). 68p. 1983. pap. 8.00 (0-915368-22-6); ring bd. 8.00 (0-915368-26-9) New Eng SF Assoc.

— The Shockwave Rider. 288p. 1984. mass mkt. 5.99 (0-345-32431-5, Del Rey) Ballantine Pub Grp.

— The Squares of the City. 320p. 1992. reprint ed. pap. 5.95 (0-02-017511-6) Macmillan.

— Stand on Zanzibar. LC 79-19062. 1979. reprint ed. lib. bdg. 30.00 (0-8376-0438-9) Bentley Pubs.

— The Tides of Time. 240p. 1984. mass mkt. 2.95 (0-345-31838-2, Ballantine) Ballantine Pub Grp.

— Tomorrow May Be Even Worse. limited ed. (Illus.). 64p. 1978. pap. 4.00 (0-915368-15-3) New Eng SF Assoc.

Brunner, John, ed. see Kipling, Rudyard.

Brunner, John, ed. see Mason, Peter.

Brunner, John W. The OSS Crossbows. (Illus.). 162p. 1991. 14.95 (0-932572-15-4) Phillips Pubns.

*Brunner, Jose. Freud & the Politics of Psychoanalysis. 238p. 2000. pap. 24.95 (0-7658-0672-X) Transaction Pubs.

Brunner, K. W., et al, eds. Biophosphonates & Tumor-Osteolysis. (Recent Results in Cancer Research Ser.: Vol. 116). (Illus.). 95p. 1989. 43.00 (0-387-50560-1) Spr-Verlag.

Brunner, Karl. Economic Analysis & Political Ideology: The Selected Essays of Karl Brunner, Vol. 1. Lys, Thomas, ed. LC 95-42417. (Economists of the Twentieth Century Ser.). 360p. 1996. 100.00 (1-85898-025-9) E Elgar.

— Monetary Theory & Monetary Policy Vol. 2: The Selected Essays of Karl Brunner. Lys, Thomas, ed. LC 96-48955. 328p. 1997. 100.00 (1-85898-026-7) E Elgar.

Brunner, Karl, ed. The First World & the Third World: Essays on the New International Economic Order. LC 78-62660. 1978. 9.95 (0-932468-00-4); pap. 3.95 (0-932468-01-2) U of Rchstr BPRC.

Brunner, Karl & Meltzer, Allan H. Money & the Economy: Issues in Monetary Analysis. 411p. 1997. pap. text 23.95 (0-521-59974-1) Cambridge U Pr.

*Brunner, Lance W., ed. Early Medieval Chants from Nonantola Pt. IV: Sequences. (Recent Researches in Music of the Middle Ages & Early Renaissance Ser.: No. RRM33). (Illus.). 78p. 1999. pap. 55.00 (0-89579-425-X) A-R Eds.

Brunner, Larry. Tragic Victory: The Doctrine of Subjective Salvation in the Poetry of W. B. Yeats. LC 86-50163. viii, 184p. 1987. 39.50 (0-87875-315-X) Whitston Pub.

Brunner, Laurel. Introducing the Internet. LC 97-60740. 176p. (YA). (gr. 9 up). 1997. pap. text 10.95 incl. cd-rom (1-874166-84-6, Pub. by Totem Bks) Natl Bk Netwk.

Brunner, Lawrence P. United States Productivity Growth: Who Benefited? LC 83-9108. (Research in Business Economics & Public Policy Ser.: No. 3). 160p. reprint ed. pap. 49.60 (0-8357-1442-X, 207036400088) Bks Demand.

Brunner, Lillian S. The Lippincott Manual of Nursing Practice. 6th ed. (Illus.). 1,552p. 1996. text 56.95 (0-397-55163-0) Lppncott W & W.

— Tratado de Enfermeria Medico Quirurgica. 6th ed. 1989. text 79.95 (0-07-104007-2) McGraw.

*Brunner, Lillian Sholtis, et al. Brunner & Suddarth's Textbook of Medical-Surgical Nursing. 9th ed. LC 99-16398. 1999. write for info. (0-7817-1575-X) Lppncott W & W.

Brunner, M., et al. Major Timber Trees of Guyana: A Lens Key. (Tropenbos Technical Ser.: No. 10). (Illus.). 184p. 1994. pap. 65.00 incl. disk (90-5113-022-8, Pub. by Backhuys Pubs) Balogh.

Brunner, Maria E. Der Deserteur und Erzahler Alfred Andersch: Dab Nichts Dunkel Gesagt Werden Darf, Was Auch Klar Gesagt Werden Kann. 491p. 1997. 76.95 (3-631-31892-8) P Lang Pubng.

*Brunner, Michael D., et al. Final FRCA: Multiple Choice Questions. 304p. 2000. pap. text 32.00 (0-7506-4214-9) Buttrwrth-Heinemann.

Brunner, Michael S. Retarding America: The Imprisonment of Potential. LC 93-5889. 1993. 14.95 (0-89420-292-8, Halcyon) Natl Book.

Brunner, Otto. Land & Lordship: Structures of Governance in Medieval Austria. Kaminsky, Howard & Melton, James V., trs. from GER. LC 91-31649. (Middle Ages Ser.). 498p. (C). 1992. text 55.00 (0-8122-8183-7) U of Pa Pr.

Brunner, P. H., jt. auth. see Baccini, P.

Brunner, Pat, ed. see Luoy, Mark.

Brunner, Peter, jt. auth. see Salzedo, Simon.

Brunner, Robert F., et al. Listen to Your Mother. (Illus.). 70p. (Orig.). (J). (ps-3). 1991. teacher ed. write for info. (0-318-68317-2); lib. bdg. write for info. (1-879209-00-4) Saundras Story Bks.

Brunner, Rudolf & Dolling, Dieter. Jugendgerichtsgesetz: Kommentar. rev. ed. xx, 817p. 1996. write for info. (3-11-015117-0) De Gruyter.

Brunner, S., ed. Radiology in Oto-Rhino-Laryngology. (Advances in OtoRhinoLaryngology Ser.: Vol. 21). (Illus.). 162p. 1974. 80.00 (3-8055-1632-0) S Karger.

Brunner, S., et al, eds. Advances in Breast Cancer Detection. (Recent Results in Cancer Research Ser.: Vol. 119). 208p. 1990. 106.00 (0-387-52089-9) Spr-Verlag.

Brunner, Scott R. Due South. LC 98-49559. 1999. 19.95 (0-375-50255-6) Villard Books.

Brunner, Sharon H. Perfect Vision: A Mother's Experience with Childhood Cancer. LC 96-69281. 128p. (Orig.). 1996. pap. 10.00 (1-884570-49-6) Research Triangle.

Brunner, T. & Kundert, M. Gerustprothetik. 2nd rev. ed. (Illus.). x, 82p. 1988. pap. 34.00 (3-8055-4553-3) S Karger.

Brunner, Theodore F., ed. Oedipus Tyrannus. (Critical Editions Ser.). (Orig.). (C). 1970. pap. 12.50 (0-393-09874-5) Norton.

Brunner, Theodore F., jt. ed. see Berkowitz, Luci.

Brunner, Theodore F., ed. see Persius.

Brunner, Theodore F., tr. see Sophocles.

Brunner, Thomas W., et al. The Legal Assistant's Handbook. 2nd ed. 248p. 1988. trans. 44.00 (0-87179-590-6, 0590) BNA Books.

Brunner, Virginia. Tahlequah. LC 94-60011. (Illus.). 1994. 35.00 (0-936029-34-X) Western Bk Journ.

Brunner, Virginia R. Kaleidoscope: A Book of Adventures. LC 97-60415. (Illus.). 424p. 1997. 49.95 (0-936029-44-7) Western Bk Journ.

*Brunnermeier, Smita & Martin, Shelia A. Interoperability Cost Analysis of the U. S. Automotive: Supply Chain: Final Report. (Illus.). 82p. (C). 2000. pap. text 25.00 (0-7881-8409-1) DIANE Pub.

Brunnert, H. S. & Hagelstrom, V. V. Present-Day Political Organization of China. 288p. 1998. text 60.00 (0-7007-1018-3, Pub. by Curzon Pr Ltd) UH Pr.

Brunning & McKenna. Tumors of the Bone Marrow. (AFIP Atlas of Tumor Pathology Ser.: Vol. 9). (Illus.). 496p. 1994. pap. text 65.00 (1-881041-09-3) Am Registry Path.

Brunning, Bob. Fleetwood Mac: The First 30 Years. (Illus.). 197p. 1998. pap. 19.95 (0-7119-6907-8, OP48069) Omnibus NY.

— Heavy Metal. LC 99-27832. (Sound Trackers Ser.). 32p. (J). 1999. 15.95 (0-87226-580-3, 65803B, P Bedrick Books) NTC Contemp Pub Co.

— 1980's Pop. LC 99-27664. (Sound Trackers Ser.). 32p. (YA). 1999. 15.95 (0-87226-579-X, 6579XB, P Bedrick Books) NTC Contemp Pub Co.

— 1970s Pop. LC 98-45753. (Sound Trackers Ser.). 32p. (YA). (gr. 5-9). 1999. 15.95 (0-87226-578-1, 65781B, P Bedrick Books) NTC Contemp Pub Co.

— 1960s Pop. LC 98-41697. (Sound Trackers Ser.). 32p. (YA). (gr. 5-9). 1999. 15.95 (0-87226-576-5, 65765B, P Bedrick Books) NTC Contemp Pub Co.

— Reggae. LC 98-41695. (Sound Trackers Ser.). 32p. (YA). (gr. 5-9). 1999. 15.95 (0-87226-577-3, 65773B, P Bedrick Books) NTC Contemp Pub Co.

— Rock 'n Roll. LC 98-41696. (Sound Trackers Ser.). 32p. (YA). (gr. 5-9). 1999. 15.95 (0-87226-575-7, 65757B, P Bedrick Books) NTC Contemp Pub Co.

Brunning, Halina, jt. ed. see Huffington, Clare.

Brunning, Jacqueline & Forster, Paul, eds. The Rule of Reason: The Philosophy of C. S. Peirce. (Toronto Studies in Philosophy). 352p. 1996. text 80.00 (0-8020-0829-1) U of Toronto Pr.

— The Rule of Reason: The Philosophy of C. S. Peirce. (Toronto Studies in Philosophy). 352p. 1997. pap. text 24.95 (0-8020-7819-2) U of Toronto Pr.

Brunnow, Rudolf E. & Domaszewski, Alfred V. Provincia Arabia, 3 vols., Vol. I. (Illus.). 532p. reprint ed. write for info. (0-318-71491-4) G Olms Pubs.

Brunnsaker, Sture, ed. Opuscula Atheniensia X. (Acta Instituti Atheniensis Regni Sueciae Ser.: Vol. XVIII). (Illus.). 90p. 1971. pap. 33.50 (91-85086-01-0, Pub. by P Astroms) Coronet Bks.

Brunnschweiler, D. & Hearle, John W., eds. Polyester: Fifty Years of Achievement, Tomorrow's Ideas & Profit. (C). 1993. 135.00 (1-870812-50-6, Pub. by Textile Inst) St Mut.

*Bruno. Hot Fudge. (Illus.). 288p. (J). 2000. 23.95 (0-312-86651-8) Forge NYC.

Bruno, jt. auth. see Lewin, B.

*Bruno, Gmunder Verlag. Bel Ami Perfect Couples. 1999. pap. 39.95 (3-86187-144-0) B Gmunder.

— Euros 14: Bel Ami, Photos of Ion. (Illus.). 1998. 16.95 (3-86187-128-9) B Gmunder.

Bruno, Gmunder Verlag. Frisky Memories. 1999. 42.95 (3-86187-136-X) B Gmunder.

— Hamburg & Hannover. 1998. pap. 14.95 (3-86187-113-0) Bookazine Co Inc.

*Bruno, Gmunder Verlag. Sauno Guide International. 1999. pap. 17.95 (3-86187-155-6) B Gmunder.

— Spartacus. 29th ed. 2000. pap. text 39.95 (3-86187-162-9) B Gmunder.

Bruno, Gmunder Verlag. Spartacus: International Gay Guide, 1999-2000. 28th ed. 1999. pap. text 32.95 (3-86187-134-3, Pub. by B Gmunder) Bookazine Co Inc.

Bruno, A. & Mouilleron-Becar, Claude. Maritime Thematic Dictionary English & French. 2nd ed. (ENG & FRE.). 472p. 1994. pap. 225.00 (0-7859-8895-5) Fr & Eur.

Bruno, A. & Mouilloron-Becar. English-French Thematic Maritime Vocabulary. (ENG & FRE.). 448p. 195.00 (0-8288-7366-6, 2225820988) Fr & Eur.

Bruno, A. D. Local Methods in Nonlinear Differential Equations. (Illus.). 370p. 1989. 158.95 (0-387-18926-2) Spr-Verlag.

Bruno, Agnes M. Toward a Quantitative Methodology for Stylistic Analyses. LC 73-80835. (University of California Publications in Social Welfare: Vol. 109). 90p. reprint ed. pap. 30.00 (0-608-14166-6, 202125900021) Bks Demand.

Bruno, Albert V., jt. auth. see Cleland, Alan S.

Bruno, Aleksandr D. The Restricted Three-Body Problem: Plane Periodic Orbits. Erdi, Balin, tr. LC 94-27982. (Expositions in Mathematics Ser.: No. 17).Tr. of Ogranichennaia Zadacha Trekh Tel. (RUS.). 1994. 149.95 (3-11-013703-8) De Gruyter.

Bruno, Anthony. Devil's Food. 1996. 21.95 (0-312-85990-2) Forge NYC.

— Devil's Food. 1998. mass mkt. 5.99 (0-8125-4437-9, Pub. by Forge NYC) St Martin.

— Double Espresso. LC 98-13570. 256p. 1998. text 21.95 (0-312-86650-X) St Martin.

*Bruno, Anthony. Double Expresso. 256p. 1999. mass mkt. 6.99 (0-8125-4166-9, Pub. by Forge NYC) St Martin.

— Hot Fudge. 2000. pap. write for info. (0-312-87590-8) St Martin.

Bruno, Anthony. Mission Impossible: The Tokyo Mandate. 1996. mass mkt. 5.99 (0-671-00231-7) PB.

— Seven: Penguin Readers Level 4. 64p. 1998. pap. 7.00 (0-14-081638-0) Viking Penguin.

Bruno, Barbara A. Worth Your Weight. 192p. 1996. pap. 12.95 (1-887750-32-0) Rutledge Bks.

Bruno, Bob. Serious Surveillance for the Private Investigator. (Illus.). 96p. 1992. pap. 20.00 (0-87364-665-7) Paladin Pr.

Bruno, Bonnie. Close to Home. LC 93-22187. 128p. 1993. pap. 9.99 (0-7814-0925-X, Chariot Bks) Chariot Victor.

— Mourning: The Prelude to Laughter. (Beatitudes Ser.). 1993. mass mkt. 5.99 (0-310-59613-0) Zondervan.

Bruno, Bonnie & Comm, Joel. Internet Family Fun: The Parent's Guide to Safe Surfing. LC 97-9756. (Illus.). 168p. 1997. pap. text 14.95 (1-886411-19-0) No Starch Pr.

Bruno, Bonnie & Reinsma, Carol. The Young Reader's Bible. rev. ed. Holder, Greg, ed. (Illus.). 448p. (J). (gr. k-3). 1998. 12.88 (0-7847-0505-4, 24-23945) Standard Pub.

Bruno, C., et al, trs. For Love of Nature: Brazilian Flora & Fauna in Watercolor by Etienne, Rosalia & Yvonne Demonte. (ENG & POR., Illus.). 46p. 1985. pap. 5.00 (0-913196-48-7) Hunt Inst Botanical.

Bruno, Carole A. Paralegal's Litigation Handbook. LC 79-19960. 544p. 1980. 45.00 (0-87624-425-8, Inst Busn Plan) P-H.

— Paralegal's Litigation Handbook. 2nd ed. Hannan, ed. LC 92-40067. 600p. (C). 1993. mass mkt. 43.00 (0-314-01177-3) West Pub.

Bruno, Clara E., see Charley, Aunt, pseud.

Bruno, David M. Bosnia Peace Operation: Pace of Implementing Dayton Accelerated As International Involvement Increased. (Illus.). 202p. 1999. text 35.00 (0-7881-7921-7) DIANE Pub.

Bruno, David W. & Poppe, Trygve T., eds. A Colour Atlas of Salmonid Diseases. (Illus.). 208p. 1996. text 120.00 (0-12-137810-1) Acad Pr.

Bruno, E. J., ed. High-Velocity Forming of Metals. LC 68-23024. (American Society of Tool & Manufacturing Engineers Manufacturing Data Ser.). (Illus.). 239p. reprint ed. pap. 74.10 (0-608-11670-X, 201600400097) Bks Demand.

Bruno, E. J., ed. see Weyher, Douglas F.

Bruno, Emmy. The Newfoundland. Luther, Luana & Young, Ellen, eds. Palmisano, Louis, tr. from ITA. LC 97-65308. (Pure Breds Ser.). (Illus.). 168p. 1997. 34.95 (0-944875-47-5) Doral Pub.

Bruno, Frank. Going Back to School. 2nd ed. LC 97-81088. 192p. 1998. 12.95 (0-02-862514-5, Arc) IDG Bks.

Bruno, Frank & Giller, Norman. Frank Bruno: From Zero to Hero. (Illus.). 224p. 1996. 35.00 (0-233-99007-0, Pub. by Andre Deutsch) Trafalgar.

Bruno, Frank J. Adjustment & Personal Growth: Seven Pathways. 2nd ed. 480p. 1983. text 65.95 (0-471-09296-7) Wiley.

— College after 25. LC 94-30033. 1995. 12.95 (0-671-88765-3, Arco) Macmillan Gen Ref.

— Defeat Depression. LC 96-85333. (Life's Little Keys Ser.). 144p. 1997. pap. 10.95 (0-02-861305-8, Arc) IDG Bks.

— Dictionary of Key Words in Psychology. 274p. 1988. pap. 14.95 (0-7102-1394-8, A3116, Routledge Thoemms) Routledge.

— The Family Mental Health Encyclopedia. LC 88-33968. 422p. 1989. 32.50 (0-471-63573-1) Wiley.

— Get a Good Night's Sleep. LC 96-85341. (Life's Little Keys Ser.). 144p. 1997. 10.95 (0-02-861306-6, Arc) IDG Bks.

— Going Back to School: College Survival Strategies for Adult Students. 192p. 1995. 175.00 (0-02-860320-6) Macmillan.

— Psychological Symptoms. LC 92-28510. 288p. 1994. pap. 24.95 (0-471-01610-1) Wiley.

— Trends in Social Work, 1874-1956: A History Based on the Proceedings of the National Conference of Social Work. 2nd ed. LC 80-19210. 462p. 1980. reprint ed. lib. bdg. 79.50 (0-313-22665-2, BRTI) Greenwood.

Bruno, G. & Bala. Model Based Software Engineering. (ITCP-UK Computer Science Ser.). (C). 1994. mass mkt. 42.95 (0-412-48670-9) Chapman & Hall.

Bruno, Gerard. The Process Analysis Workbook for Government: How to Achieve More with Less. LC 94-19797. 219p. 1995. pap. 35.00 (0-87389-259-3, H0814) ASQ Qual Pr.

Bruno, Giordano. The Ash Wednesday Supper. Jaki, Stanley L., tr.Tr. of La/Cena de Le Ceneri. (Illus.). 174p. 1975. text 37.70 (90-279-7581-7) Mouton.

— The Ash Wednesday Supper. Gosselin, Edward A. & Lerner, Lawrence S., eds. & trs. by. (Renaissance Society of America Reprints for Text Ser.),Tr. of La/Cena de Le Ceneri. 238p. 1995. pap. text 19.95 (0-8020-7469-3) U of Toronto Pr.

— Cause, Principle & Unity: Five Dialogues. Lindsay, Jack, tr. LC 76-28448. 177p. 1976. reprint ed. lib. bdg. 59.75 (0-8371-9040-1, BRCP, Greenwood Pr) Greenwood.

— The Expulsion of the Triumphant Beast. Imerti, Arthur D., tr. from ITA. LC 91-43914. xii, 324p. 1992. reprint ed. pap. 12.95 (0-8032-6104-7, Bison Books) U of Nebr Pr.

*Bruno, Giordano. Giordano Bruno: "Cause, Principle & Unity": And Essays on Magic. Blackwell, Richard J. et al, eds. De Lucca, Robert, tr. LC 98-15503. (Cambridge Texts in the History of Philosophy Ser.). (Illus.). 222p. (C). 1998. text 54.95 (0-521-59359-X); pap. text 19.95 (0-521-59658-0) Cambridge U Pr.

Bruno, Giovanni, et al, eds. Plasma Deposition of Amorphous Silicon-Based Materials. (Plasma-Materials Interactions Ser.). (Illus.). 368p. 1995. text 90.00 (0-12-137940-X) Acad Pr.

Bruno, Giovanni C., ed. A Repertory of Decisions of the International Court of Justice, 1947-1992. LC 94-25721.Tr. of Repertoire de la Jurisprudence de la Cour Internationale de Justice, 1947-1992. 1994. lib. bdg. 471.50 (0-7923-2993-7, Pub. by M Nijhoff) Kluwer Academic.

*Bruno, Giuliana. Atlas of Emotion: Journeys in Art, Architecture & Film. (Illus.). 384p. (C). 2000. 39.00 (1-85984-802-8, Pub. by Verso) Norton.

Bruno, Giuliana. Streetwalking on a Ruined Map: Cultural Theory & the City Films of Elvira Notari. (Illus.). 424p. 1993. text 70.00 (0-691-08628-1, Pub. by Princeton U Pr); pap. text 24.95 (0-691-02533-9, Pub. by Princeton U Pr) Cal Prin Full Svc.

Bruno, Giuliana & Nadotti, Maria, eds. Off Screen: Women & Film in Italy. 160p. 1988. text 37.50 (0-415-00856-5); pap. text 16.95 (0-415-00857-3) Routledge.

— Off Screen: Women & Film in Italy. LC 87-30778. (Illus.). 214p. reprint ed. pap. 66.40 (0-608-20365-3, 207161800002) Bks Demand.

Bruno Gmunder Publishers Staff. Amsterdam City Guide. 1997. pap. text 14.95 (3-86187-096-7) LPC InBook.

*Bruno Gmunder Publishers Staff. Bel Ami Summertime. 2000. 42.95 (3-86187-164-5) B Gmunder.

— Best of Bel Ami Summertime. 2000. pap. 8.95 (3-86187-171-8) B Gmunder.

Bruno Gmunder Publishers Staff. Sauna Guide Europe. 2nd ed. 1997. pap. text 16.95 (3-86187-097-5) LPC InBook.

Bruno-Hardy. Two-over-One Game Force: An Introduction. 9.95 (0-939460-01-7, 4750) Devyn Pr.

Bruno, J., jt. ed. see Leclercq, D.

Bruno, J. A., Jr., jt. auth. see Keane, John D.

Bruno, James E. It's about Time: Leading School Reform in an Era of Time Scarcity. LC 97-21136. 184p. 1997. 55.95 (0-8039-6504-4); pap. 24.95 (0-8039-6505-2) Corwin Pr.

Bruno, James F. Beyond Fighter Escort. LC 95-70702. (Illus.). 252p. 1995. 24.50 (0-9648032-1-6) J F Bruno.

Bruno, Jane, ed. see Holliman, Linda.

Bruno, Jane A. The Expat's Guide to U. S. Taxes: Hands on Help for Americans Overseas. 3rd rev. ed. 178p. 1998. pap. 19.95 (0-9662869-0-1) Bruno Expat.

Bruno, Janet, ed. Addition & Subtraction, Vol. 2656. (Child-Centered Math Ser.: Vol. 6). (Illus.). 80p. 1997. pap. text 4.98 (1-57471-239-X, 2656) Creat Teach Pr.

— Estimation, Vol. 2651. (Child-Centered Math Ser.). (Illus.). 80p. 1997. pap. 4.98 (1-57471-234-9, 2651) Creat Teach Pr.

— Fractions, Vol. 2659. (Child-Centered Math Ser.: Vol. 9). (Illus.). 80p. 1997. pap. 4.98 (1-57471-242-X, 2659) Creat Teach Pr.

— Geometry, Vol. 2662. (Child-Centered Math Ser.: Vol. 12). (Illus.). 80p. 1997. pap. 4.98 (1-57471-245-4, 2662) Creat Teach Pr.

— Graphing, Vol. 2652. (Child-Centered Math Ser.: Vol. 2). (Illus.). 80p. 1997. pap. 4.98 (1-57471-235-7, 2652) Creat Teach Pr.

— Measurement, Vol. 2653. (Child-Centered Math Ser.: Vol. 3). (Illus.). 80p. 1997. pap. 4.98 (1-57471-236-5, 2653) Creat Teach Pr.

— Multiplication & Division, Vol. 2657. (Child-Centered Math Ser.: Vol. 7). (Illus.). 80p. 1997. pap. 4.98 (1-57471-240-3, 2657) Creat Teach Pr.

— Numbersense & Place Value, Vol. 2655. (Child-Centered Math Ser.: Vol. 5). (Illus.). 80p. 1997. pap. 4.98 (1-57471-238-1, 2655) Creat Teach Pr.

— Patterns, Vol. 2658. (Child-Centered Math Ser.: Vol. 8). (Illus.). 80p. 1997. pap. 4.98 (1-57471-241-1, 2658) Creat Teach Pr.

— Probability & Logical Reasoning, Vol. 2661. (Child-Centered Math Ser.: Vol. 11). (Illus.). 80p. 1997. pap. 4.98 (1-57471-244-6, 2661) Creat Teach Pr.

B

— Sorting & Classifying, Vol. 2654. (Child-Centered Math Ser.: Vol. 4). (Illus.). 80p. 1997. pap. 4.98 (*1-57471-237-3*, 2654) Creat Teach Pr.
— Time & Money, Vol. 2660. (Child-Centered Math Ser.: Vol. 10). (Illus.). 80p. 1997. pap. 4.98 (*1-57471-243-8*, 2660) Creat Teach Pr.
Bruno, Janet & Dakan, Peggy. Cooking in the Classroom. 1974. pap. 8.99 (*0-8224-1610-7*) Fearon Teacher Aids.
***Bruno, Janet, et al.** Instant Math Centers 2-3. Simon, Ruth B., ed. (Illus.). 128p. 2000. pap. text 12.98 (*1-57471-690-5*) Creat Teach Pr.
— Seasons, Vol. 2597. Wolkoff, Stacey, ed. (Primary Theme Ser.: Vol. 2458). (Illus.). 32p. (J). (gr. 1-3). 2000. pap. 6.98 (*1-57471-684-0*) Creat Teach Pr.
Bruno, Janet, ed. see Allen, Margaret.
***Bruno, Jimmy.** Jimmy Bruno - Jazz Guitar Virtuoso. 120p. 1999. spiral bd. 19.95 (*0-7866-4749-3*, 97116) Mel Bay.
Bruno-Jofre, Rosa Del C., ed. Issues in the History of Education in Manitoba: From the Construction of the Common School to the Politics of Voices. LC 93-4629. (Illus.). 676p. 1993. text 129.95 (*0-7734-9330-1*) E Mellen.
Bruno, Joseph A., Jr., jt. auth. see Appleman, Bernard R.
Bruno, Joseph A., Jr., jt. auth. see Keane, John D.
Bruno, Josh. Put Money in Your Pockets: How to Retire Your Mortgage on Your Own Terms at a Fraction of the Cost. LC 94-94531. (Illus.). 384p. 1995. write for info. (*0-9641964-1-7*) Capital Search.

B

-Put Money in Your Pockets: How to Retire Your Mortgage on Your Own Terms at a Fraction of the Cost. LC 94-84531. (Illus.). 384p. 1995. pap. 29.95 (*0-9641964-2-5*) Capital Search.
The book shows how the total cost of a mortgage can actually reach OVER THREE TIMES the original amount during the course of the term. It exposes five dire consequences that may occur when a buyer allows the cost build-up. The author reveals in clear, step-by-step illustrated details how a homeowner can: * Reduce the massive interest cost on a mortgage & produce substantial money savings * Tap six little known sources of extra cash to help pay off the mortgage early * Correctly & easily apply a POWERFUL KEY technique that will eliminate ALL debts at a DAZZLING pace * Use four different techniques alone or in combination to prepay the mortgage & eliminate a big burden before retirement * Determine exactly when the mortgage will be paid off & how much interest cost will be eliminated for any fixed prepayment amount * Determine exactly how much to prepay in order to eliminate the mortgage within a precise number of years * Activate, automatically & virtually COST-FREE, two forms of bi-weekly mortgage payment handling to disintegrate YEARS off the term & painlessly SAVE a major portion of the interest cost * Determine when it's better to invest available money rather than use it for prepayments. To order contact: Capital Search Systems, 84 Surrey Lane, Hempstead, NY 11550. *Publisher Paid Annotation.*

Bruno, Kenny, jt. auth. see Greer, Jed.
Bruno, L., jt. auth. see White, J. J.
Bruno, L. B., jt. auth. see White, J. J.
Bruno, Leonard C. Landmarks of Science: From the Collections of the Library of Congress. LC 89-33579. 362p. 1989. reprint ed. pap. 112.30 (*0-608-02856-8*, 206392000007) Bks Demand.
***Bruno, Leonard C.** Math & Mathematicians: The History of Math Discoveries Around the World, 2 vols. Baker, Lawrence W., ed. LC 99-32424. 420p. (J). (gr. 6-10). 1999. text 63.00 (*0-7876-3812-9*) Gale.
Bruno, Leonard C. Science & Technology Breakthroughs: From the Wheel to the World Wide Web. LC 97-34039. 1997. write for info. (*0-7876-1928-0*, UXL) Gale.
— Science & Technology Breakthroughs: From the Wheel to the World Wide Web. LC 97-34039. (J). 1997. write for info. (*0-7876-1929-9*, UXL) Gale.
Bruno, Leonard C. Science & Technology Breakthroughs: From the Wheel to the World Wide Web, 2 vols. LC 97-34039. (Illus.). 416p. (J). 1997. text 63.00 (*0-7876-1927-2*, GML06197-111363, UXL) Gale.
Bruno, Leonard C. Science & Technology Firsts. LC 96-43595. 636p. 1996. 70.00 (*0-7876-0256-6*) Gale.
— The Tradition of Science: Landmarks of Western Science in the Collections of the Library of Congress. LC 86-600088. 351p. 1987. 30.00 (*0-8444-0528-0*, 030-000-00183-4) Lib Congress.
— The Tradition of Technology: Landmarks of Western Technology in the Collections of the Library of Congress. (Illus.). 356p. 1998. text 29.00 (*0-8444-0888-3*) Johns Hopkins.
— The Tradition of Technology: Landmarks of Western Technology in the Collections of the Library of Congress. LC 93-16406. 1993. write for info. (*0-8444-0781-X*) Lib Congress.
Bruno, Leonard C. Tradition of Technology: Landmarks of Western Technology in the Collections of the Library of Congress. 368p. 1995. boxed set 28.00 (*0-16-061800-2*, Library of Cong) USGPO.
Bruno, Leonard C., ed. On the Move: A Chronology of Advances in Transportation. (Illus.). 423p. 1998. text 30.00 (*0-7881-5615-2*) DIANE Pub.
***Bruno, Leonard C. & Baker, Lawrence W.** Math & Mathematicians: The History of Math Discoveries Around the World LC 99-32424. 1999. write for info. (*0-7876-3814-5*) Visible Ink Pr.
Bruno, M. Christianity in Power. 1994. pap. 10.95 (*0-936369-70-1*) Son-Rise Pubns.
Bruno, Marilyn, ed. see Glozman, Alex.
Bruno, Michael. Crisis, Stabilization, & Economic Reform: Therapy by Consensus. LC 93-16300. (Illus.). 320p. 1993. text 45.00 (*0-19-828663-5*, Clarendon Pr) OUP.
— Deep Crises & Reform: What Have We Learned? LC 96-26892. (Directions in Development Ser.). 40p. 1996. pap. 22.00 (*0-8213-3697-5*, 13697) World Bank.
— High Inflation & the Nominal Anchors of an Open Economy. Riccardi, Margaret B., ed. LC 91-23185. (Essays in International Finance Ser.: No. 183). 34p. 1991. pap. text 10.00 (*0-88165-090-0*) Princeton U Int Finan Econ.
Bruno, Michael, et al, eds. Inflation Stabilization: The Experience of Israel, Argentina, Brazil, Bolivia, & Mexico. 466p. 1988. 38.50 (*0-262-02279-6*) MIT Pr.
— Lessons of Economic Stabilization & Its Aftermath. (Illus.). 436p. 1991. 46.00 (*0-262-02324-5*) MIT Pr.
Bruno, Michael & Pleskovic, Boris, eds. Annual Conference on Development Economics 1998. 360p. 1997. pap. 30.00 (*0-8213-3786-6*) World Bank.
Bruno, Michael & Pleskovic, Boris, eds. Annual World Bank Conference on Development Economics 1995. 392p. 1996. pap. 25.00 (*0-8213-3280-5*, 13280) World Bank.
— Proceedings of the World Bank Annual Conference on Development Economics 1993. 496p. 1994. pap. 22.00 (*0-8213-2558-2*, 12558) World Bank.
Bruno, Michael & Sachs, Jeffrey D. Economics of Worldwide Stagflation. (Illus.). 336p. 1985. 46.50 (*0-674-23475-8*) HUP.
Bruno, Michael H. Principles of Color Proofing: A Manual on the Measurement & Control of Tone & Color Reproduction. 395p. 65.00 (*0-614-25601-1*, 00DC44105) Print Indus Am.
Bruno, Michael H., ed. Pocket Pal Spanish Edition: Manual de Artes Graficas. 15th rev. ed. (SPA., Illus.). 264p. 1993. pap. text 20.00 (*0-88362-255-6*, OODC44482) GATFPress.
Bruno Natlis, Elena. Estudio Comparativo de Vocabularios Tobas y Pilagas. (SPA.). 107p. 1965. pap. 55.00 (*0-8288-6747-X*, S33083) Fr & Eur.
Bruno, Nicola, tr. see Garau, Augusto.
Bruno, Pasquale, Jr. The Great Chicago-Style Pizza Cookbook. (Illus.). 144p. 1983. pap. 12.95 (*0-8092-5730-0*, 573000, Contemporary Bks) NTC Contemp Pub Co.
— Italian Light & Easy. LC 92-46326. (Illus.). 208p. 1993. pap. 14.95 (*0-8092-3858-6*, 385860, Contemporary Bks) NTC Contemp Pub Co.
— Pasta Tecnica. (Illus.). 128p. 1982. pap. 15.95 (*0-8092-5894-3*, 58943) NTC Contemp Pub Co.
— The Ultimate Pasta Cookbook. LC 96-33493. (Illus.). 176p. 1997. pap. 14.95 (*0-8092-3169-7*, 316970, Contemporary Bks) NTC Contemp Pub Co.
— The Ultimate Pizza. LC 95-31565. (Illus.). 176p. 1995. pap. 12.95 (*0-8092-3349-5*, 334950, Contemporary Bks) NTC Contemp Pub Co.
Bruno, Richard D. InfoQuick Guide to Infomercials. rev. ed. LC 95-115145. 250p. 1994. pap. 14.95 (*1-882862-01-5*) Hawksbill.
Bruno, Robert. Steelworker Alley: How Class Works in Youngstown. LC 98-52184. 224p. 1999. pap. 16.95 (*0-8014-8600-9*) Cornell U Pr.
***Bruno, Robert.** Steelworker Alley: How Class Works in Youngstown. LC 98-52184. 224p. 1999. 45.00 (*0-8014-3439-4*) Cornell U Pr.
***Bruno, Susan.** Insiders' Guide to Williamsburg. 10th ed. 436p. 2000. pap. text 16.95 (*1-57380-159-3*) IPBI.
Bruno, Susan, jt. auth. see Cease, Cheryl.
***Bruno, Theresa.** For Such a Time As This. 250p. 1999. pap. 15.00 (*0-9653700-4-6*) B L Pubng.
Bruno, Thomas J. Handbook of Analysis & Identification of Alternative Refrigerants. 672p. 1994. boxed set 190.00 (*0-8493-3926-X*) CRC Pr.
Bruno, Thomas J. & Ely, James F. Supercritical Fluid Technology. (Illus.). 608p. 1991. boxed set 225.00 (*0-8493-6847-2*, TP156) CRC Pr.
Bruno, Thomas J. & Svoronos, Paris D. Handbook of Basic Tables for Chemical Analysis. 528p. 1989. boxed set 187.95 (*0-8493-3935-9*, QD78) CRC Pr.
Bruno, V. J. Hellenistic Painting Techniques: The Evidence of the Delos Fragments. 1985. 19.00 (*90-04-07159-8*, CSCT, 11) Brill Academic Pubs.
Bruno, Vincent J. The Parthenon. rev. ed. (Illus.). 352p. 1996. pap. 18.95 (*0-393-31440-5*, Norton Paperbks) Norton.
Bruno, Vincent J. & Scott, Russell T., eds. Cosa IV: The Houses. (Memoirs of the American Academy in Rome Ser.: Volume 38). (Illus.). 230p. (C). 1993. text 62.00 (*0-472-10610-4*, 10610) U of Mich Pr.
Brunold, Paul. Francois Couperin. 75p. 1993. reprint ed. lib. bdg. 59.00 (*0-7812-9591-2*) Rprt Serv.
Brunold, Paul, ed. see Chambonnieres, Jacques C.
Brunon, Danielle, tr. see Chalem, Denise.
Brunori, David. The Future of State Taxation. LC 98-16507. 260p. 1998. lib. bdg. 66.50 (*0-87766-680-6*) Urban Inst.
— The Future of State Taxation. LC 98-16507. 260p. 1998. pap. 24.95 (*0-87766-681-4*) Urban Inst.
Brunot, Ferdinand. Histoire de la Langue Francaise des Origines a nos Jours, 13 tomes. Incl. Set. Dix-Huitieme Siecle., 4 pts. 118.95 Set. Formation de la Langue Classique., 2 pts. 59.95 Set. Francais hors de France au XVIIIe Siecle., 3 pts. en 2 pts. 59.95 Set. Langue Classique dans la Tourmente., 2 pts. 59.95 Set. Langue Classique, 1660-1715., 2 pts. 59.95 Set. Revolution et l'Empire., 2 pts. 59.95 Tome I. De l'Epoque Latine a la Renaissance. 29.95 Tome II. Seizieme Siecle. 25.50 Tome V. Francais en France et Hors de France au XVIIe Siecle. 29.95 Tome VII. Propagation du Francais en France Jusqu'a la Fin de l'Ancien Regime. 29.95 Tome XI. Francais au-dehors sous la Revolution, le Consulat et l'Empire. 29.95 Tome XII. Epoque Romantique. Bruneau, Jean. (FRE.). 29.95 Tome XIII. Epoque Realiste. Bruneau, Jean. (FRE.). 59.95 write for info. (*0-318-52018-4*) Fr & Eur.
— Histoire de la Langue Francaise des Origines a Nose Jours, Vol. 10, Pt. 2. (FRE.). 392p. 1968. 65.00 (*0-7859-4415-X*, 2200360932) Fr & Eur.
Brunotte, Leonard. Construction Profit Management: The Secrets to Successful Contracting. 320p. 1987. text 49.95 (*0-13-168980-0*) P-H.
Brunquell, Philip. Fly-Fishing with Children: A Guide for Parents. (Illus.). 200p. 1995. reprint ed. pap. 13.00 (*0-88150-350-9*, Foul Play) Norton.
Bruns, et al. Cohen-Macaulay Rings. 2nd ed. (Studies in Advanced Mathematics: Vol. 39). 415p. 1993. pap. text 34.95 (*0-521-56674-6*) Cambridge U Pr.
Bruns, Bill, jt. auth. see Braden, Vic.
Bruns, Cheryl L., jt. auth. see Rutkosky, Nita H.
Bruns, Friedrich, ed. Lese der Deutschen Lyrik: Von Klopstock bis Rilke. (GER.). (Orig.). 1961. pap. text 22.95 (*0-89197-274-9*) Irvington.
***Bruns, Gabriele.** Die Japanische Demokratie: Das Politische System Zwischen Stagnation und Aufbruch. (GER., Illus.). 329p. 1999. 51.95 (*3-631-34859-2*) P Lang Pubng.
Bruns, Gerald L. Heidegger's Estrangements: Language, Truth, & Poetry in the Later Heidegger. LC 88-26148. 272p. (C). 1989. 37.50 (*0-300-04420-8*) Yale U Pr.
— Hermeneutics Ancient & Modern. LC 92-14839. 384p. (C). 1992. 45.00 (*0-300-05450-5*) Yale U Pr.
— Hermeneutics Ancient & Modern. 1995. pap. 20.00 (*0-300-06303-2*) Yale U Pr.
— Maurice Blanchot: The Refusal of Philosophy. LC 96-34860. 384p. 1997. text 39.95 (*0-8018-5471-7*) Johns Hopkins.
— Tragic Thoughts at the End of Philosophy: Language, Literature, & Ethical Theory. LC 99-21879. (Rethinking Theory Ser.). 1999. pap. text 19.95 (*0-8101-1675-8*) Northwestern U Pr.
— Tragic Thoughts at the End of Philosophy: Language, Literature & Ethical Theory. LC 99-21879. 280p. 1999. 79.95 (*0-8101-1674-X*) Northwestern U Pr.
Bruns, Glenn. Distributing System Analysis. LC 96-32684. 200p. 1996. pap. 63.00 (*0-13-398389-7*) P-H.
***Bruns, Heike.** Akteure der Umweltpolitik: Die Organisation der Statlichen Umweltadministration Auf Bundeseene Als Rechtsproblem. 496p. 1999. 73.95 (*3-631-34811-8*) P Lang Pubng.
Bruns, Ivo. Das Literarische Portrat der Griechen Im Funften und Vierten Jahrhundert v. Chr. - Die Personlichkeit in der Geschichtsschreibung der Alten, 2 vols. in 1. 715p. 1985. reprint ed. 135.00 (*3-487-00082-2*) G Olms Pubs.
Bruns, James. Turk Bird: The High-Flying Life & Times of Eddie Gardner. (Illus.). 105p. 1998. pap. write for info. (*1-891568-03-5*) Natl Postal Mus.
Bruns, James H. Great American Post Office. LC 97-12050. 288p. 1997. pap. 24.95 (*0-471-14388-X*) Wiley.
— Horse Drawn Mail Vehicles. Harris, Marion & Plachno, Larry, eds. LC 96-34191. (Illus.). 72p. 1997. pap. 21.00 (*0-933449-28-3*) Transport Trails.
— Mail on the Move. LC 92-22587. (Illus.). 224p. 1992. pap. 37.00 (*0-933449-15-1*) Transport Trails.
Bruns, James H. & Krause Publications Staff. Motorized Mail. LC 97-73776. (Illus.). 272p. 1997. pap. 19.95 (*0-87341-485-3*, MOTM) Krause Pubns.
Bruns, Jean R. Abstracts of the Wills & Inventions of Bath County, Virginia, 1791-1842: Will Books 1-4. LC 95-125126. 282p. 2000. reprint ed. pap. 26.50 (*0-8063-4519-5*, Pub. by Clearfield Co) ACCESS Pubs Network.
Bruns, Jerome H. They Can but They Don't: Helping Students Overcome Work Inhibition. 240p. 1993. pap. 12.95 (*0-14-015229-6*, Penguin Bks) Viking Penguin.
***Bruns, P. & Hass, H. C., eds.** On the Determination of Sediment Accumulation Rates. (GeoResearch Forum Ser.: Vol. 5). (Illus.). 256p. (C). 1999. pap. 96.00 (*0-87849-837-0*, Pub. by Trans T Pub) Enfield Pubs NH.
Bruns, Roger. Abraham Lincoln. (World Leaders Past & Present Ser.). (Illus.). 120p. (YA). (gr. 5 up). 1986. pap. 8.95 (*0-7910-0649-2*); lib. bdg. 19.95 (*0-87754-597-9*) Chelsea Hse.
***Bruns, Roger.** Almost History: Close Calls, Plan B's & Twist of Fate in America's Past. (Illus.). 224p. 2000. 23.95 (*0-7868-6663-2*, Pub. by Hyperion) Time Warner.
— Billy the Kid: Outlaw of the Wild West. LC 99-16689. (Historical American Biographies Ser.). (Illus.). 128p. (gr. 6 up). 2000. lib. bdg. 20.95 (*0-7660-1091-0*) Enslow Pubs.
Bruns, Roger. George Washington. (World Leaders Past & Present Ser.). (Illus.). 120p. (YA). (gr. 5 up). 1987. lib. bdg. 19.95 (*0-87754-584-7*) Chelsea Hse.
— Julius Caesar. (World Leaders Past & Present Ser.). (Illus.). 120p. (YA). (gr. 5 up). 1987. lib. bdg. 19.95 (*0-87754-514-6*) Chelsea Hse.
— Thomas Jefferson. (World Leaders Past & Present Ser.). (Illus.). 120p. (YA). (gr. 5 up). 1986. pap. 8.95 (*0-7910-0644-1*) Chelsea Hse.
— Thomas Jefferson. (World Leaders Past & Present Ser.). (Illus.). 120p. (YA). (gr. 5 up). 1987. lib. bdg. 19.95 (*0-87754-583-9*) Chelsea Hse.
***Bruns, Roger A.** Desert Honkytonk: The Story of Tombstone's Bird Cage Theatre. (Illus.). 2000. pap. 17.95 (*1-55591-416-0*) Fulcrum Pub.
Bruns, Roger A. Jesse James: Legendary Outlaw. LC 97-24615. (Historical American Biographies Ser.). (Illus.). 128p. (YA). (gr. 6 up). 1998. lib. bdg. 20.95 (*0-7660-1055-4*) Enslow Pubs.
— John Wesley Powell: Explorer of the Grand Canyon. LC 96-32600. (Historical American Biographies Ser.). (Illus.). 128p. (YA). (gr. 6 up). 1997. lib. bdg. 20.95 (*0-89490-783-2*) Enslow Pubs.
Bruns, W., et al, eds. Commutative Algebra: Proceedings of a Workshop Held in Salvador, Brazil, August 8-17, 1988. (Lecture Notes in Mathematics Ser.: Vol. 1430). v, 160p. 1990. 34.95 (*0-387-52745-1*) Spr-Verlag.
Bruns, William J., Jr. Accounting for Managers: Text & Cases. LC 93-8521. (C). 1993. pap. 80.95 (*0-538-83310-6*, AS65AA) S-W Pub.
Bruns, William J. Accounting for Managers: Text & Cases. 2nd ed. LC 98-2670. 1998. mass mkt. 102.95 (*0-538-88777-X*) S-W Pub.
Bruns, William J., Jr., ed. Performance Measurement, Evaluation & Incentives. 400p. 1992. 39.95 (*0-07-103375-0*) McGraw.
Bruns, William J., Jr., jt. auth. see McKinnon, Sharon M.
Bruns, William R. Cenacle Sessions: A Modern Mystagogy. 1991. pap. 6.95 (*0-8091-3249-4*) Paulist Pr.
— Easter Bread: Reflections on the Gospels of the Easter Season for Neophytes & Their Companions. 1991. pap. 6.95 (*0-8091-3247-8*) Paulist Pr.
— Guiding Your Parish Through the Christian Initiation Process: A Handbook for Leaders. 152p. 1993. pap. 7.95 (*0-86716-188-4*) St Anthony Mess Pr.
Bruns, Winifrid & Herzog, Jurgen. Cohen-Macaulay Rings. LC 93-16069. (Cambridge Studies in Advanced Mathematics: No. 39). 415p. (C). 1993. text 95.00 (*0-521-41068-1*) Cambridge U Pr.
Brunschvicg, Leon, jt. auth. see Pascal, Blaise.
Brunschvig, Robert. Etudes Sur l'Islam Classique et l'Afrique du Nord. Turki, Abdel-Magid, ed. (Collected Studies: No. CS243). (FRE., Illus.). 324p. (C). 1986. reprint ed. lib. bdg. 124.95 (*0-86078-191-7*, Pub. by Variorum) Ashgate Pub Co.
Brunschwig, C., et al. One Hundred Years of French Song: Cent Ans de Chanson Francaise. (FRE.). 447p. 1981. pap. 14.95 (*0-8288-4427-5*, M12411) Fr & Eur.
Brunschwig, Henri. Enlightenment & Romanticism in Eighteenth-Century Prussia. Jellinek, Frank, tr. LC 73-87299. 333p. Date not set. reprint ed. pap. 103.30 (*0-608-20612-1*, 205458000003) Bks Demand.
Brunschwig, Jacques. Papers in Hellenistic Philosophy. (Illus.). 291p. (C). 1994. text 80.00 (*0-521-41712-0*) Cambridge U Pr.
Brunschwig, Jacques, ed. see Pellegrin, Pierre.
Brunsdale, Mitzi M. Dorothy L. Sayers: Solving the Mystery of Wickedness. LC 89-18454. (Women's Ser.). 247p. 1990. 16.50 (*0-85496-249-2*) Berg Pubs.
— James Herriot. LC 96-43137. 1997. 32.00 (*0-8057-7835-7*, Hall Reference) Macmillan.
— James Herriot. 1997. text 22.95 (*0-8057-4505-X*) Macmillan.
— James Joyce: A Study of the Short Fiction. LC 92-39802. (Twayne's Studies in Short Fiction). 288p. 1993. 29.00 (*0-8057-0854-5*) Macmillan.
***Brunsdale, Mitzi M.** Student Companion to George Orwell. LC 99-49690. (Student Companions to Classic Writers Ser.). 192p. 2000. 29.95 (*0-313-30637-0*) Greenwood.
Brunsden, Denys & Prior, David B., eds. Slope Instability. LC 83-16923. (Landscape Systems Ser.). (Illus.). 646p. reprint ed. pap. 200.00 (*0-7837-6161-9*, 204588300009) Bks Demand.
Brunsden, Denys, jt. auth. see Goudie, Andrew.
***Brunsdon, Charlotte.** The Feminist, the Housewife & the Soap Opera. (Oxford Television Studies). (Illus.). 272p. 2000. pap. 24.95 (*0-19-815981-1*); text 45.00 (*0-19-815980-3*) OUP.
Brunsdon, Charlotte. Screen Tastes: From Soap Opera to Satellite Dishes. LC 96-35327. (Illus.). 192p. (C). 1997. pap. 18.99 (*0-415-12155-8*) Routledge.
— Screen Tastes: From Soap Opera to Satellite Dishes. LC 96-35327. (Illus.). 256p. (C). 1997. 75.00 (*0-415-12154-X*) Routledge.
Brunsdon, Charlotte, ed. Films for Women. LC 86-187284. (Illus.). 236p. 1986. pap. 13.95 (*0-85170-155-8*, Pub. by British Film Inst) Ind U Pr.
Brunsdon, Charlotte, et al, eds. Feminist Television Criticism: A Reader. (Oxford Television Studies). (Illus.). 398p. 1997. text 95.00 (*0-19-871152-2*); pap. text 19.95 (*0-19-871153-0*) OUP.
Brunsdon, Charlotte, jt. auth. see Morley, David.
Brunser, Oscar, et al, eds. Clinical Nutrition of the Young Child. LC 91-114. (Illus.). 335p. 1991. reprint ed. pap. 103.90 (*0-608-07212-5*, 206743700009) Bks Demand.
Brunsick, David J., ed. Methods for Genetic Risk Assessment. LC 93-5520. 272p. 1994. lib. bdg. 120.00 (*1-56670-039-6*, L1039) Lewis Pubs.
Brunsken, E., jt. ed. see Register, Layton B.
Brunskill. Traditional Buildings of Britain: Introduction to Vernacular Architecture. 1994. pap. 24.95 (*0-575-05299-6*, Pub. by V Gollancz) Trafalgar.
Brunskill, Bill. Learning to Write. 2nd ed. 180p. (C). 1991. pap. text 23.22 (*1-56226-059-6*) CAT Pub.
Brunskill, David. Gifts for Disciples. (C). 1988. 35.00 (*0-7223-2195-3*, Pub. by A H S Ltd) St Mut.
Brunskill, David & Turner, John. Understanding Algorithms & Data Structures. LC 96-8874. 1996. write for info. (*0-07-709141-8*) McGraw.
***Brunskill, R. W.** Timber Building in Britain. 246p. 1999. pap. 40.00 (*0-575-06735-7*, Pub. by V Gollancz) Trafalgar.
Brunskill, Ronald W. Brick Buildings in Britain. (Illus.). 208p. 1998. pap. 35.00 (*0-575-06535-4*, Pub. by V Gollancz) Trafalgar.

An Asterisk (*) at the beginning of an entry indicates that the title is appearing for the first time.

— Houses & Cottages of Britain: Origins & Development of Traditional Buildings. 1996. 55.00 (0-575-06321-1, Pub. by V Gollancz) Trafalgar.
— Timber Building in Britain. 2nd ed. (Illus.). 256p. 1985. 55.00 (0-575-05611-8, Pub. by V Gollancz) Trafalgar.
Brunsma, David L., jt. ed. see Dasilva, Fabio.
Brunsman, Deborah. Red & Yellow, Black & White . . . 184p. 1991. 12.99 (0-89900-385-0) College Pr Pub.
Brunsman, Laura & Askey, Ruth. Modernism & Beyond: Women Artists of the Pacific Northwest. LC 92-62399. (Regional Women Artists Ser.). (Illus.). 192p. (Orig.). 1993. pap. text 15.00 (1-877675-13-X) Midmarch Arts.
Brunsman, Philippa, ed. see MacColl, E. Kimbark & Stein, Harry H.
Brunsmann, F. & von Gizycki, R. Retinitis Pigmentosa: Proceedings of the 4th Congress of the International Retinitis Pigmentosa Association, Bad Nauheim 1986, FRG, Pt. 2. (Advances in the Biosciences Ser.: Vol. 63). 322p. 1988. 116.00 (0-08-035725-3, North Holland) Elsevier.
Brunsmann, Sandra M. Mary Elizabeth Ryder - Grand Dame: Matriarch of Women. 1997. pap. 14.95 (0-9632178-1-X) S M Brunsmann.
— Plan-B, Personal Budget Planner Vol. 1: A Simple Blueprint for Success. 23p. 1986. pap. text. write for info. (0-9632178-2-8) S M Brunsmann.
Brunson, Alfred. A Western Pioneer: Or, Incidents of the Life & Times of Rev. Alfred Brunson..., 2 Vols. LC 75-89. (Mid-American Frontier Ser.). 1975. reprint ed. 66.95 (0-405-06856-5) Ayer.
Brunson, B. R. The Adventures of Samuel Swartwout in the Age of Jefferson & Jackson. LC 88-13702. (Studies in American History: Vol. 2). 275p. 1989. lib. bdg. 89.95 (0-88946-097-3) E Mellen.
Brunson, Chris, ed. see Keyarts, Eugene.
***Brunson, Dorothy & Bolton, Barbara.** God Gives Us Helpers. Levering, Marcy, ed. 40p. 2000. pap. text 10.99 (0-7847-1144-5, 42110) Standard Pub.
— God Helps Me Grow. Levering, Marcy, ed. (Easy-to-Teach Bible Picture Lessons Ser.). (Illus.). 40p. 2000. 10.99 (0-7847-1196-8, 42120) Standard Pub.
***Brunson, Dorothy & DaHarb, Peggy.** God Is Good to Me. Levering, Marcy, ed. (Illus.). 40p. 2000. pap. text 10.99 (0-7847-1143-7, 42019) Standard Pub.
— God's Promises for Me. Levering, Marcy, ed. (Easy-to-Teach Bible Picture Lessons Ser.). (Illus.). 40p. 2000. 10.99 (0-7847-1195-X, 42119) Standard Pub.
Brunson, Harold E. Homosexuality & the New Testament: What Does Christian Scripture Really Teach. LC 97-10290. 102p. 1998. 74.95 (1-57309-172-3); pap. 54.95 (1-57309-171-5) Intl Scholars.
Brunson, Howard & Klahn, Barney. I Remember Logging, 1923-1997. Watkins, Marjorie M., ed. LC 97-94756. (Illus.). 126p. 1998. per. 29.95 (0-9661667-0-1) Fir Tree Pr.
Brunson, Jamie. Jamie Brunson: Traveler. (Illus.). 40p. 1998. per. 15.00 (0-9662319-0-2) J Brunson Studio.
Brunson, Kenneth W., ed. Local Invasion & Spread of Cancer. (Cancer Growth & Progression Ser.). (C). 1989. text 207.50 (0-89838-996-8) Kluwer Academic.
Brunson, Laura, ed. see Kulchak, Craig.
Brunson, Madelon. Dying, Death & Grief. 1978. pap. 1.00 (0-8309-0223-6) Herald Pub Hse.
Brunson, Mark W., et al, eds. Defining Social Acceptability in Ecosystem Management: A Workshop Proceeding. (Illus.). 142p. (C). 1997. pap. text 35.00 (0-7881-4675-0) DIANE Pub.
— Defining Social Acceptability in Ecosystem Management: A Workshop Proceedings. (Illus.). 152p. 1997. reprint ed. 21.00 (0-89904-559-6, Bear Meadows Resrch Grp); reprint ed. pap. 16.00 (0-89904-560-X, Bear Meadows Resrch Grp) Crumb Elbow Pub.
***Brunson, Ross & Greggory, Bernadette.** UNIX to NT Administration Survival Guide. Schmidt, Susan, ed. (Illus.). 200p. 1999. pap. text. write for info. (1-893596-06-0) Specialized Solns.
Brunsson, Nils. The Organization of Hypocrisy: Talk, Decisions & Actions in Organizations. Adler, Nancy, tr. LC 89-14785. 250p. 1989. reprint ed. pap. 77.50 (0-608-03997-7, 206473400011) Bks Demand.
***Brunsson, Nils.** Organizing Organizations. 1999. 42.00 (87-16-13427-3) Mksgaard.
***Brunsson, Nils & Jacobsson, Bengt.** A World of Standards. 220p. 2000. text 60.00 (0-19-829693-2) OUP.
Brunsson, Nils & Olsen, Johann. The Reforming Organization? Making Sense of Administrative Change. LC 93-18708. 240p. (C). 1993. pap. 24.95 (0-415-08288-9) Thomson Learn.
Brunst, John C. Practice of Neural Science. LC 99-43399. (C). 1999. pap. text 29.95 (0-8385-8117-X, A-8117-2) Appleton & Lange.
Brunstein, Ingrid, ed. Human Resource Management in Western Europe. (De Gruyter Studies in Organization: No. 68). xvi, 342p. (C). 1995. pap. text 29.95 (3-11-014275-9); lib. bdg. 64.95 (3-11-014274-0) De Gruyter.
Brunstetter, Max R. Business Management in School Systems of Different Sizes. LC 76-176607. (Columbia University. Teachers College. Contributions to Education Ser.: No. 455). reprint ed. 37.50 (0-404-55455-5) AMS Pr.
Brunstetter, Richard W. Adolescents in Psychiatric Hospitals: A Psychodynamic Approach to Evaluation & Treatment. LC 98-10206. 208p. 1998. text 45.95 (0-398-06860-7); pap. text 32.95 (0-398-06861-5) C C Thomas.
***Brunsting, Bernard.** Ultimate Guide to Good Clean Humor: Your Resource for Good, Clean Fun. 448p. 2000. pap. 4.97 (1-57748-730-3) Barbour Pub.
Brunsvold, Brian G., et al. Drafting Patent License Agreements. 4th ed. LC 98-27883. 374p. 1998. 125.00 (1-57018-129-2, 1129) BNA Books.
Brunswick, G. The Haunted House Three-D Coloring Book. 32p. (Orig.). (J). (gr. 4-7). 1988. pap. 3.95 (0-942025-57-1) Kidsbks.
— Wild Wheels Three-D Coloring Book. 32p. (Orig.). (J). (gr. 4-7). 1988. pap. 3.95 (0-942025-60-1) Kidsbks.
Brunswick Pro Staff, jt. auth. see Bohn, Parker, III.
***Brunswick, Richard.** UFO: Richard Brunswick Photocollection. (Illus.). 320p. 2000. pap. 27.95 (3-9805876-3-0, Pub. by Goliath) SCB Distributors.
Brunswig, Heinrich. Explosives: A Synoptic & Critical Treatment of the Literature of the Subject As Gathered from Various Sources. Monroe, Charles E. & Kibler, Alton L., trs. 1980. lib. bdg. 300.00 (0-8490-3153-2) Gordon Pr.
Brunt. Market Research in Travel & Tourism. 200p. 1997. pap. 39.95 (0-7506-3082-5) Buttrwrth-Heinemann.
Brunt, Alan A., et al. Viruses of Plants, 2 vols. (CABI Publishing Ser.). 1488p. 1996. text 175.00 (0-85198-794-X) OUP.
Brunt, Barry. Western Europe: Economic & Social Studies: Ireland. 256p. (C). 1988. pap. 35.00 (1-85396-019-5) St Mut.
***Brunt, Deborah.** Things Fail, People Fall. 1999. pap. 7.99 (1-56309-768-0) Womans Mission Union.
Brunt, Deborah Van, see Stigleman, Michelle & Van Brunt, Deborah.
Brunt, Denis, jt. auth. see Van Deusen, Julia.
Brunt, Elyse. Peacemaking Skills for Little Kids: Grade 2. Burke, James A., II et al, eds. (Illus.). 128p. 1997. pap. text, teacher ed. 23.95 (1-878227-41-6) Peace Educ.
Brunt, H. L. Van, see Van Brunt, H. L.
Brunt, James W., jt. auth. see Michener, William K.
Brunt, John C. Good News for Troubled Times. LC 93-8814. 1993. pap. 1.99 (0-8280-0696-2) Review & Herald.
Brunt, John C. & Clark, Douglas R., eds. Introducing the Bible Vol. II: The New Testament. 392p. 1997. 67.50 (0-7618-0631-8); pap. 39.50 (0-7618-0632-6) U Pr of Amer.
Brunt, John C., jt. ed. see Clark, Douglas R.
Brunt, Lloyd Van, see Van Brunt, Lloyd.
Brunt, M. A., ed. The Cayman Islands: Natural History & Biogeography. LC 93-27017. (Monographiae Biologicae: Vol. 71). 576p. (C). 1995. text 468.00 (0-7923-2462-5) Kluwer Academic.
Brunt, Madge A. Christian Verses. (C). 1989. pap. 29.00 (0-7223-2375-1, Pub. by A H S Ltd) St Mut.
Brunt, P. A. The Fall of the Roman Republic & Related Essays. 560p. 1988. text 150.00 (0-19-814849-6) OUP.
— Italian Manpower, 225 B. C.-A. D. 14. 776p. 1987. text 145.00 (0-19-814283-8) OUP.
— Roman Imperial Themes. 558p. 1990. text 129.00 (0-19-814476-8) OUP.
— Studies in Greek History & Thought. LC 92-11118. 320p. (C). 1993. 79.00 (0-19-814783-X) OUP.
— Studies in Greek History & Thought. 420p. 1998. reprint ed. pap. text 49.95 (0-19-815242-6) OUP.
Brunt, P. A., tr. Anabisis of Alexander, Indica, 2 vols. (Loeb Classical Library: No. 236, 269). 15.50 (0-674-99260-1) HUP.
— Anabisis of Alexander, Indica, 2 vols., Vol. 1. (Loeb Classical Library: No. 236, 269). 634p. 1976. 18.95 (0-674-99297-0) HUP.
Brunt, P. A., jt. ed. see Moore, J. M.
Brunt, Samuel, et al. Gulliveriana, No. 4. LC 70-18975. 416p. 1974. 60.00 (0-8201-1122-8) Schol Facsimiles.
Brunt, Stephen. Hockey: The Season: A Year in the Life of the NHL. (Illus.). 196p. 1999. 22.95 (0-7710-1711-1) McCland & Stewart.
Bruntjen, Carol R., jt. compiled by see Bruntjen, Scott.
Bruntjen, Scott, ed. A Checklist of American Imprints for 1840: Items 40-1 - 40-7198. LC 64-11784. 566p. 1990. 70.50 (0-8108-2376-4) Scarecrow.
— A Checklist of American Imprints for 1841: Items 41-1 - 41-5692. LC 64-11784. 471p. 1990. 63.00 (0-8108-2377-2) Scarecrow.
Bruntjen, Scott & Bruntjen, Carol R., compiled by. A Checklist of American Imprints for 1833: Items 17208-22795. LC 64-11784. (Checklist of American Imprints Ser.: Vol. 1833). 482p. 1979. lib. bdg. 55.00 (0-8108-1191-X) Scarecrow.
Bruntjen, Scott, jt. auth. see Rinderknecht, Carol.
Bruntjen, Scott, jt. ed. see Rinderknecht, Carol.
***Brunton, Alan, et al, eds.** Big Smoke: New Zealand Poems, 1960-75. (Illus.). 320p. 2000. pap. 39.95 (1-86940-230-8, Pub. by Auckland Univ) Paul & Co Pubs.
Brunton, Guy. British Museum Expedition to Middle Egypt. LC 77-86429. reprint ed. 45.00 (0-404-16626-1) AMS Pr.
Brunton, Guy & Caton-Thompson, Gertrude. The Badarian Civilisation & Predynastic Remains Near Badari. LC 77-86424. (British School of Archaeology in Egypt & Egyptian Research Account. 30th Yr., 1924. Publication Ser.: No. 46). reprint ed. 42.50 (0-404-16625-3) AMS Pr.
Brunton, Jerry, jt. ed. see Mehlman, Myron A.
Brunton, Jolee, ed. see McPeak, Ronald H., et al.
Brunton, Lauri. Sanctuary: Gardening for the Soul. LC 99-26666. 1999. text 35.00 (1-56799-791-0, Friedman-Fairfax) M Friedman Pub Grp Inc.
Brunton, Mary. Discipline: A Novel, 3 vols., 1 bk. LC 79-8241. reprint ed. 44.50 (0-404-61797-2) AMS Pr.
***Brunton, Mary.** Self-Control: A Novel. 2nd unabridged ed. LC 99-75957. (Jane Austen Library). 352p. 1999. reprint ed. 29.95 (0-9654299-3-8, Pub. by Revive) Baker & Taylor.
Brunton, Paul. Advanced Contemplation - The Peace Within You: The Notebooks of Paul Brunton, Vol. 15. Smith, Timothy, ed. (Illus.). 352p. 1988. 29.95 (0-943914-42-6); pap. 16.95 (0-943914-43-4) Larson Pubns.
— Discover Yourself. rev. ed. LC 83-60832. 320p. 1972. reprint ed. pap. 14.95 (0-87728-592-6) Weiser.
— Enlightened Mind - Divine Mind Vol. 16: The Notebooks of Paul Brunton. Smith, Timothy, ed. (Illus.). 480p. 1988. 29.95 (0-943914-44-2); pap. 16.95 (0-943914-46-9) Larson Pubns.
— The Hidden Teaching Beyond Yoga. rev. ed. LC 83-60830. 366p. 1972. pap. 16.95 (0-87728-590-X) Weiser.
— Inspiration & the Overself: The Notebooks of Paul Brunton, Vol. 14. Smith, Timothy, ed. (Illus.). 270p. (YA). (gr. 7 up). 1988. 25.00 (0-943914-40-X); pap. 14.95 (0-943914-41-8) Larson Pubns.
***Brunton, Paul.** Market Research in Travel & Tourism, Vol. 1. 1998. pap. 34.95 (0-7506-4347-1) Buttrwrth-Heinemann.
Brunton, Paul. Meditations for People in Crisis. Cohen, Sam, ed. & selected by by. 112p. (Orig.). 1996. pap. 10.95 (0-943914-77-9) Larson Pubns.
— The Notebooks of Paul Brunton: Pt. 1, Human Experience; Pt. 2, The Arts in Culture, Vol. 9. LC 87-81537. (Notebooks of Paul Brunton Ser.). (Illus.). 400p. 1987. 29.95 (0-943914-30-2); pap. 16.95 (0-943914-31-0) Larson Pubns.
— The Notebooks of Paul Brunton: The Orient - Its Legacy to the West, Vol. 10. (Notebooks of Paul Brunton Ser.). (Illus.). 272p. 1987. 25.00 (0-943914-32-9); pap. 14.95 (0-943914-33-7) Larson Pubns.
— The Notebooks of Paul Brunton: The Sensitives-Dynamics & Dangers of Mysticism, Vol. 11. (Notebooks of Paul Brunton Ser.). (Illus.). 352p. 1987. 29.95 (0-943914-35-3); pap. 16.95 (0-943914-34-5) Larson Pubns.
— The Notebooks of Paul Brunton Vol. 1: Perspectives (Posthumous) Cash, Paul et al, eds. LC 84-47752. 408p. 1984. 25.00 (0-943914-09-4); pap. 16.95 (0-943914-12-4) Larson Pubns.
— The Notebooks of Paul Brunton Vol. 1: Perspectives (Posthumous) limited ed. Cash, Paul et al, eds. LC 84-47752. 408p. 1984. 30.00 (0-943914-10-8) Larson Pubns.
— The Notebooks of Paul Brunton, Vol. 2: The Quest. Cash, Paul & Smith, Timothy, eds. LC 85-81507. (Illus.). 384p. 1986. 29.95 (0-943914-13-2); pap. 16.95 (0-943914-14-0) Larson Pubns.
— The Notebooks of Paul Brunton, Vol. 3: Part 1, Practices for the Quest; Part 2, Relax & Retreat. Cash, Paul & Smith, Timothy, eds. LC 86-81030. 392p. 1986. 29.95 (0-943914-15-9); pap. 16.95 (0-943914-16-7) Larson Pubns.
— The Notebooks of Paul Brunton, Vol. 4: Pt. 1 - Meditation; Pt. 2 - The Body. Cash, Paul & Smith, Timothy, eds. LC 86-81949. 432p. 1986. 29.95 (0-943914-18-3) Larson Pubns.
— The Notebooks of Paul Brunton, Vol. 4: Pt. 1 - Meditation; Pt. 2 - The Body, Pt. 1: Meditation. Cash, Paul & Smith, Timothy, eds. LC 86-81949. 272p. 1986. pap. 14.95 (0-943914-19-1) Larson Pubns.
— The Notebooks of Paul Brunton, Vol. 4: Pt. 1 - Meditation; Pt. 2 - The Body, Pt. 2: The Body. Cash, Paul & Smith, Timothy, eds. LC 86-81949. 160p. 1986. pap. 12.50 (0-943914-20-5) Larson Pubns.
— The Notebooks of Paul Brunton, Vol. 5: Pt. 1 - Emotions & Ethics; Pt. 2 - The Intellect. Cash, Paul & Smith, Timothy, eds. LC 86-82480. (Illus.). 432p. 1986. 29.95 (0-943914-21-3); pap. 16.95 (0-943914-22-1) Larson Pubns.
— The Notebooks of Paul Brunton, Vol. 6: Pt. 1 - The Ego; Pt. 2 - From Birth to Rebirth. Cash, Paul & Smith, Timothy, eds. LC 86-82481. (Illus.). 320p. 1987. 29.95 (0-943914-24-8); pap. 16.95 (0-943914-25-6) Larson Pubns.
— The Notebooks of Paul Brunton, Vol. 7: Healing of the Self; Pt. 2 the Negatives, Pt. 1. Cash, Paul & Smith, Timothy, eds. LC 87-80403. (Illus.). 320p. 1987. 29.95 (0-943914-26-4); pap. 16.95 (0-943914-27-2) Larson Pubns.
— The Notebooks of Paul Brunton, Vol. 8: Reflections on My Life & Writings. Smith, Timothy, ed. LC 87-80402. (Illus.). 272p. 1987. 25.00 (0-943914-28-0); pap. 14.95 (0-943914-29-9) Larson Pubns.
— The Quest of the Overself. rev. ed. LC 83-159508. 240p. (Orig.). 1972. pap. 14.95 (0-87728-594-2) Weiser.
— Relativity, Philosophy & Mind: The Notebooks of Paul Brunton, Vol. 13. Cash, Paul & Smith, Timothy, eds. (Illus.). 550p. 1988. 29.95 (0-943914-38-8); pap. 19.95 (0-943914-39-6) Larson Pubns.
— The Religious Urge-Reverential Life: The Notebooks of Paul Brunton, Vol. 12. 384p. 1988. 29.95 (0-943914-36-1); pap. 16.95 (0-943914-37-X) Larson Pubns.
— Search in Secret Egypt. rev. ed. LC 83-50399. 304p. 1973. reprint ed. pap. 16.95 (0-87728-603-5) Weiser.
— Search in Secret India. LC 83-50400. (Illus.). 336p. 1984. reprint ed. pap. 14.95 (0-87728-602-7) Weiser.
— The Secret Path. LC 85-50917. 128p. 1985. reprint ed. pap. 9.95 (0-87728-652-3) Weiser.
— What Is Karma? 128p. 1998. pap. 10.95 (0-943914-87-6) Larson Pubns.
— Wisdom of the Overself. rev. ed. LC 83-60833. 464p. (Orig.). 1972. pap. 22.95 (0-87728-591-8) Weiser.
Brunton, Paul, et al. Meditations for People in Charge: A Handbook for Men & Women Whose Decisions Affect the World. Cash, Paul, ed. & pref. by. 112p. (Orig.). 1995. pap. 10.95 (0-943914-72-8) Larson Pubns.
Brunton, Richard H. Building Japan, 1868-1876. (Illus.). 240p. (C). 1996. text 42.00 (1-873410-05-0, Pub. by Curzon Pr Ltd) UH Pr.
Brunton, Richard H. & Beauchamp, Edward R., eds. Schoolmaster to an Empire: Richard Henry Brunton in Meiji Japan, 1868-1876. 1. LC 90-19931. (Contributions in Asian Studies: No. 1). 200p. 1991. 62.95 (0-313-27795-8, BHW/, Greenwood Pr) Greenwood.
Bruntrup, Michael. Agricultural Price Policy & Its Impact on Production, Income, Employment & the Adoption of Innovations: A Farming Systems Based Analysis of Cotton Policy in Northern Benin. Heidhues, Franz, ed. (Development Economics & Policy Ser.: Vol. 9). (Illus.). xxviii, 517p. 1997. pap. 95.95 (3-631-31877-4) P Lang Pubng.
— Agricultural Price Policy & Its Impact on Production, Income, Employment & the Adoption of Innovations: A Farming Systems Based Analysis of Cotton Policy in Northern Benin. Heidhues, Franz, ed. LC 97-20669. (Development Economics & Policy Ser.: Vol. 9). (Illus.). XXVIII, 517p. 1997. pap. 95.95 (0-8204-3284-9) P Lang Pubng.
Bruntz, George G. Allied Propaganda & the Collapse of the German Empire in 1918. LC 72-4658. (International Propaganda & Communications Ser.). (Illus.). 246p. 1977. reprint ed. 19.95 (0-405-04741-X) Ayer.
Bruntz, Nelle L. Contemporary Psalms. (Illus.). 64p. 1984. pap. 3.99 (0-938462-13-X) Green Leaf CA.
Brunvand, Jan. Study of American Folklore: An Introduction. 4th ed. LC 97-26188. (C). 1998. text 51.50 (0-393-97223-2) Norton.
Brunvand, Jan H. The Baby Train: And Other Lusty Urban Legends. 1994. pap. 11.95 (0-393-31208-9, Norton Paperbks) Norton.
— The Choking Doberman & Other "New" Urban Legends. LC 83-22031. (Illus.). 1986. reprint ed. pap. 11.95 (0-393-30321-7) Norton.
— Curses! Broiled Again! 1990. pap. 12.95 (0-393-30711-5) Norton.
— The Mexican Pet: More "New" Urban Legends & Some Old Favorites. 1988. pap. 11.95 (0-393-30542-2) Norton.
— Readings in American Folklore. (Illus.). 466p. (C). 1979. pap. text 25.00 (0-393-95029-8) Norton.
— The Taming of the Shrew: A Comparative Study of Oral & Literary Versions. LC 90-39612. (Folklore Library: Vol. 5). 298p. 1991. text 15.00 (0-8240-7149-2, 1289) Garland.
— The Vanishing Hitchhiker: American Urban Legends & Their Meanings. (Orig.). (C). 1989. pap. 12.95 (0-393-95169-3) Norton.
Brunvand, Jan H., ed. American Folklore: An Encyclopedia. LC 95-53734. (Reference Library of the Humanities: Vol. 1551). (Illus.). 816p. 1996. text 125.00 (0-8153-0751-9, H1551) Garland.
— American Folklore: An Encyclopedia. LC 98-38863. 794p. 1998. pap. 34.95 (0-8153-3350-1) Garland.
***Brunvand, Jan Harold.** Encyclopedia of Urban Legends. 2001. lib. bdg. 70.00 (1-57607-076-X) ABC-CLIO.
Brunvand, Jan Harold. Too Good to Be True: The Colossal Book of Urban Legends. LC 99-17562. 480p. 1999. text 29.95 (0-393-04734-2) Norton.
— The Truth Never Stands in the Way of a Good Story. LC 99-6465. (Illus.). 232p. 2000. 22.95 (0-252-02424-9) U of Ill Pr.
Brunzel, Nancy A. Fundamentals of Urine & Body Fluid Analysis. LC 92-48472. (Illus.). 544p. 1994. pap. text 41.00 (0-7216-3976-3, W B Saunders Co) Harcrt Hlth Sci Grp.
Brus, Eric, jt. auth. see Golob, Richard.
Brus, Gunther. Pictionary Fictionary: Selected Writings of Gunther Brus. Spampinato, Denise, ed. 150p. 2000. pap. 25.00 (1-889195-34-0) Smart Art Pr.
Brus, Marcel, ed. The United Nations Decade of International Law: Reflections on International Dispute Settlement. 168p. (C). 1991. lib. bdg. 101.00 (0-7923-1220-1) Kluwer Academic.
Brus, Wlodzimierz & Laski, Kazimiera. From Marx to Market: Socialism in Search of an Economic System. (Illus.). 184p. 1991. reprint ed. pap. text 21.00 (0-19-828399-7, 7661) OUP.
Brusa, Betty W. Salinan Indians of California & Their Neighbors. LC 74-13249. (American Indian Map Book: Vol. 2). (Illus.). 96p. (C). 1975. pap. 8.95 (0-87961-022-0) Naturegraph.
Brusati, Celeste. Artifice & Illusion: The Art & Writing of Samuel van Hoogstraten. LC 94-30354. 428p. 1995. 75.00 (0-226-07785-3) U Ch Pr.
Brusatin, Manlio, et al. The Baroque in Central Europe: Places, Architecture, & Art. 320p. 1993. 60.00 (1-56886-000-5) Marsilio Pubs.
Brusatin, Manlio, jt. auth. see Ferrari, Claudia G.
Brusatti, Otto, jt. ed. see Hilmar, Ernst.
Brusaw. The Business Writers Companion 2. LC 98-84416. 1999. pap. text 26.95 (0-312-18334-8) St Martin.
— Business Writing Handbook. 6th ed. 2000. pap. text 32.95 (0-312-19805-1) St Martin.
— Concise Handbook on Technical Writing, Vol. 1. LC 98-84417. 1999. pap. 26.95 (0-312-18335-6) St Martin.
***Brusaw.** Handbook of Technical Writing. 6th ed. 2000. pap. text 32.95 (0-312-19804-3) St Martin.
Brusaw, Charles T. The Business Writers. 5th ed. 1997. pap. text, wbk. ed. 5.00 (0-312-15286-8) St Martin.
— The Business Writers Handbook. 5th ed. 832p. 1997. pap. text 32.95 (0-312-13751-6); pap. text 29.95 (0-312-16691-5) St Martin.
— The Concise Handbook of Technical Writing. 432p. 1996. pap. text 26.95 (0-312-13315-4) St Martin.
— Handbook Technical Writing 5. 832p. 1997. pap. text 32.95 (0-312-13289-1) St Martin.
— Technical Writing. 5th ed. 1997. pap. text, wbk. ed. 5.00 (0-312-15288-4) St Martin.

B

An Asterisk (*) at the beginning of an entry indicates that the title is appearing for the first time.

Brusaw, Charles T., et al. The Business Writer's Companion. LC 95-44466. 400p. 1996. pap. 24.95 (*0-312-13789-3*, St Martin Griffin) St Martin.
— Business Writer's Handbook. 5th ed. (Illus.). 720p. 1997. text 27.95 (*0-312-16689-3*) St Martin.
— Handbook of Technical Writing. 4th ed. 1992. pap. text, teacher ed. 0.41 (*0-312-08940-6*) St Martin.
— Handbook of Technical Writing. 5th ed. 832p. 1997. text 29.95 (*0-312-16690-7*) St Martin.
Brusaw, Ted, jt. auth. see Knappe, Siegfried.
Brusawet. Business Writing Handbook. 4th ed. 1992. pap. text, teacher ed. 0.41 (*0-312-08941-4*) St Martin.
Brusberg, Dieter & Volker, Brigitte. Ernst (Max) The Graphic Work - with an Original Lithograph. (GER., Illus.). 158p. 1972. pap. 140.00 (*1-55660-096-8*) A Wofsy Fine Arts.
***Brusberg-Kiermeier, Stefani.** Korper-Inszenierungen in Shakespeares Historien. (Beitrage Zur Anglo-Amerikanischen Literatur Ser.). 173p. 1999. 35.95 (*3-631-35003-1*) P Lang Pubng.
Brusca, Gary J., jt. auth. see Brusca, Richard C.
Brusca, Maria C. My Mama's Little Ranch on the Pampas. LC 93-28113. (J). 1995. 15.95 (*0-8050-2782-3*) H Holt & Co.
— On the Pampas. LC 90-40938. (Illus.). 40p. (J). (ps-2). 1995. pap. 5.95 (*0-8050-2919-2*, Bks Young Read) H Holt & Co.
— When Jaguars Ate the Moon: And Other Stories about Animals & Plants of the Americas. LC 93-50197. (Illus.). (J). (ps-3). 1995. 16.95 (*0-8050-2797-1*) H Holt & Co.
Brusca, Maria C. Pedro Fools the Gringo: And Other Tales of a Latin American Trickster. LC 95-9984. (Redfeather Bks.). 55p. (J). (gr. 3-6). 1995. 14.95 (*0-8050-3827-2*) H Holt & Co.
Brusca, Maria C. & Wilson, Tona. Three Friends/Tres Amigos: A Counting Book/Un Cuento Para Contar. LC 94-44648.Tr. of Tres Amigos: Un Cuento para Contar. (ENG & SPA., Illus.). 32p. (J). (ps-3). 1995. 14.95 (*0-8050-3707-1*) H Holt & Co.
Brusca, Maria Cristina. On the Pampas. (Owlet Bks.). 1993. 11.15 (*0-606-05960-1*, Pub. by Turtleback) Demco.
Brusca, Maria Cristina. Tres Amigos. pap. (*0-8050-6310-2*) H Holt & Co.
Brusca, Richard C. & Brusca, Gary J. Invertebrates. LC 90-30061. (Illus.). 922p. (C). 1990. text 77.95 (*0-87893-098-1*) Sinauer Assocs.
Brusca, Richard C. & Hendrickx, Michel E., eds. Benthic Macro-Crustacians of the Eastern Tropical Pacific - Macro-Crustaceos Bentonicos del Pacifico Este Tropical. (Illus.). 150p. 1992. pap. 24.00 (*0-918969-03-4*) San Diego Soc Nat Hist.
Brusch, John L., jt. ed. see Weinstein, Louis.
Bruschi, G. & Borghetti, A., eds. Cellular Aspects of Hypertension. (Illus.). 264p. 1991. 93.95 (*0-387-53987-5*) Spr-Verlag.
Bruschi, R., et al, eds. Proceedings of the 16th International Conference on Offshore Mechanics & Arctic Engineering, Yokohama, Japan, April 13-17, 1997 Vol. V: Pipeline Technology. 256p. 1997. 120.00 (*0-7918-1803-9*, H01084) ASME Pr.
Bruschke, A. V., ed. Lipid Lowering Therapy & Progression of Coronary Atherosclerosis. (Developments in Cardiovascular Medicine Ser.). 240p. (C). 1996. text 129.00 (*0-7923-3807-3*) Kluwer Academic.
Bruscia, Kenneth, ed. The Dynamics of Music Psychotherapy. LC 99-163029. 584p. (C). 1998. pap. text 45.00 (*1-891278-05-3*) Barcelona Pubs.
Bruscia, Kenneth E. Defining Music Therapy. 2nd ed. LC 99-167032. 320p. (Orig.). 1998. pap. text 26.00 (*1-891278-07-X*) Barcelona Pubs.
— Improvisational Models of Music Therapy. (Illus.). 606p. 1987. pap. 62.95 (*0-398-06040-1*) C C Thomas.
— Improvisational Models of Music Therapy. (Illus.). 606p. (C). 1987. text 97.95 (*0-398-05272-7*) C C Thomas.
Bruscia, Kenneth E., ed. Case Studies in Music Therapy. 656p. (C). 1991. pap. text 40.00 (*0-9624080-1-8*) Barcelona Pubs.
Brusco, Elizabeth E. The Reformation of Machismo: Evangelical Conversion & Gender in Colombia. LC 94-21340. (Illus.). 224p. (C). 1995. text 35.00 (*0-292-70820-3*) U of Tex Pr.
Brusendorff, Aage. The Chaucer Tradition. (BCL1-PR English Literature Ser.). 510p. 1992. reprint ed. lib. bdg. 129.00 (*0-7812-7171-1*) Rprt Serv.
Bruser, Madekine. The Art of Practicing: A Guide to Making Music from the Heart. 288p. 1999. pap. 14.00 (*0-609-80177-5*) Bell T.
***Bruser, Peter & Gilbert, Alain, eds.** Finger Bone & Joint Injuries. 383p. 1999. 115.00 (*1-85317-690-7*) Martin Dunitz.
Bruseth, Nels. Indian Stories & Legends of the Stillaguamish, Sauks & Allied Tribes. 36p. 1977. reprint ed. pap. 9.95 (*0-87770-078-8*) Ye Galleon.
Brush, Barbara L. Nurses of All Nations: A History of the International Council of Nurses, 1899-1999. LC 98-37564. 1999. write for info. (*0-7817-1904-6*) Lppncott W & W.
Brush, C. B. Montaigne & Bayle: Variations on the Theme of Skepticism. (International Archives of the History of Ideas Ser.: No. 14). 361p. 1966. lib. bdg. 99.50 (*90-247-0190-2*, Pub. by M Nijhoff) Kluwer Academic.
Brush, Candida G. International Entrepreneurship: The Effect of Firm Age on Motives for Internationalization. rev. ed. LC 94-43144. (Garland Studies in Entrepreneurship). (Illus.). 256p. 1995. text 20.00 (*0-8153-1978-9*) Garland.
Brush, Christine. Colonel's Opera Cloak. LC 78-137723. (American Fiction Reprint Ser.). 1977. reprint ed. 19.95 (*0-8369-7022-5*) Ayer.
Brush, Craig B. From the Perspective of the Self: Montaigne's Self-Portrait. 321p. 1994. 32.50 (*0-8232-1550-4*) Fordham.
Brush, Daniel & Kuspit, Donald B. Gold Without Boundaries. LC 97-51377. (Illus.). 276p. 1998. 65.00 (*0-8109-4018-3*, Pub. by Abrams) Time Warner.
Brush, Daniel H. Growing up with Southern Illinois: Pioneer Memoirs of Daniel H. Brush. Quaife, Milo M., ed. 380p. 1992. reprint ed. 24.95 (*0-9623990-7-8*); reprint ed. pap. 12.95 (*0-9623990-6-X*) Crossfire Pr.
Brush, Edward H. Iroquois Past & Present. LC 74-7944. reprint ed. 32.50 (*0-404-11831-3*) AMS Pr.
Brush, Elizabeth P. Guizot in the Early Years of the Orleanist Monarchy. LC 74-2319. (University of Illinois Studies in the Social Sciences). 236p. 1975. reprint ed. 39.50 (*0-86527-090-2*) Fertig.
Brush, Gary G. How to Choose the Proper Sample Size. (Basic "How to" Ser.: Vol. 12). (Illus.). 115p. (Orig.). 1988. pap. 31.00 (*0-87389-050-7*, T3512) ASQ Qual Pr.
***Brush, Jack & Miller, William.** Candy Novelties & Containers: Identification & Value Guide. (Illus.). 144p. 2000. pap. 19.95 (*1-57432-186-2*) Collector Bks.
***Brush, Jennifer A. & Camp, Cameron J.** A Therapy Technique for Improving Memory: Spaced Retrieval. 84p. 1998. pap. 42.95 (*0-9676343-0-X*) Myers Resear Inst.
Brush, John E. & Gauthier, Howard L. Service Centers & Consumer Trips: Studies on the Philadelphia Metropolitan Fringe. LC 67-25274. (University of Chicago, Department of Geography, Research Paper Ser.: No. 113). 195p. reprint ed. pap. 60.50 (*0-7837-0393-7*, 204071400018) Bks Demand.
Brush, Karen A. The Demon Pig. 256p. (Orig.). 1991. mass mkt. 4.50 (*0-380-75760-5*, Avon Bks) Morrow Avon.
— Pig, the Prince & the Unicorn. 224p. 1987. pap. 2.95 (*0-380-75062-7*, Avon Bks) Morrow Avon.
Brush, Katharine. Don't Ever Leave Me. 1993. reprint ed. lib. bdg. 89.00 (*0-7812-5438-8*) Rprt Serv.
— Red-Headed Woman. 1993. reprint ed. lib. bdg. 89.00 (*0-7812-5347-0*) Rprt Serv.
Brush, Kathleen Nixon, jt. auth. see Nixon, Joan Lowery.
Brush, Kathryn. The Shaping of Art History: Wilhelm Voge, Adolph Goldschmidt & the Study of Medieval Art. LC 97-6531. (Illus.). 276p. (C). 1996. text 74.95 (*0-521-47541-4*) Cambridge U Pr.
Brush, Lorelei R., et al. Encouraging Girls in Mathematics: The Problem & the Solution. (Illus.). 180p. 1984. reprint ed. lib. bdg. 39.00 (*0-8191-4109-7*) U Pr of Amer.
Brush, Lucien M., et al, eds. Taming the Yellow River - Silt & Floods: Proceedings of a Bilateral Seminar on Problems in the Lower Reaches of the Yellow River, China. x, 690 p. (C). 1989. text 420.50 (*0-7923-0416-0*) Kluwer Academic.
Brush, M. G. & Goudsmit, E. M., eds. Functional Disorders of the Menstrual Cycle. LC 87-27371. (Wiley Medical Publications). 313p. 1988. reprint ed. pap. 97.10 (*0-7837-8869-X*, 204958000001) Bks Demand.
Brush, Mary M., jt. auth. see Burt, Richard K.
Brush, Michael. Lessons from the Front Line: Market Tools & Investing Tactics from the Pros. LC 99-32876. (Investments Ser.). 272p. 1999. 29.95 (*0-471-35017-6*) Wiley.
Brush, Richard E. Wells Construction. (C). 1988. text 250.00 (*0-7855-5995-7*, Pub. by Scientific) St Mut.
Brush, Robert & Overmier, Bruce J. Affect, Conditioning & Cognition: Essays on the Determinants of Behavior. LC 85-15862. 400p. (C). 1985. text 79.95 (*0-89859-586-X*) L Erlbaum Assocs.
Brush, Robert L., jt. ed. see Reasoner, Victor P.
Brush, S. G. The Kind of Motion We Call Heat: A History of the Kinetic Theory of Gases in the 19th Century, 2 bks., Bk. 1. (North-Holland Personal Library: 1). xl, 300p. 1994. reprint ed. pap. 69.00 (*0-444-87008-3*, North Holland) Elsevier.
— The Kind of Motion We Call Heat: A History of the Kinetic Theory of Gases in the 19th Century, 2 bks., Bk. 2. (North-Holland Personal Library: Vol. 6). xi, 470p. 1986. reprint ed. pap. 69.00 (*0-444-87009-1*, North Holland) Elsevier.
Brush, Stanley E. Farewell the Winterline: Memories of a Boyhood in India. LC 97-94779. (Illus.). ix, 231p. 1998. pap. write for info. (*0-9661084-0-X*) S E Brush.
Brush, Stephanie. Men: An Owner's Manual. 1985. pap. 11.00 (*0-671-60413-9*) S&S Trade.
***Brush, Stephen B.** Genes in the Field. 300p. 2000. pap. text 25.00 (*0-88936-884-8*, Pub. by IDRC Bks) Stylus Pub VA.
— Genes in the Field: On-Farm Conservation of Crop Diversity. LC 99-44933. (Illus.). 304p. 1999. per. 29.95 (*1-56670-405-7*) Lewis Pubs.
Brush, Stephen B. Mountain, Field & Family: The Economy & Human Ecology of an Andean Valley. LC 77-24364. 223p. reprint ed. pap. 69.20 (*0-8357-3320-3*, 203954400013) Bks Demand.
Brush, Stephen B. & Stabinsky, Doreen, eds. Valuing Local Knowledge: Indigenous Peoples & Intellectual Property Rights. 351p. 1996. text 55.00 (*1-55963-378-6*); pap. text 32.00 (*1-55963-379-4*) Island Pr.
Brush, Stephen B., jt. ed. see Turner, B. L., II.
Brush, Stephen G. A History of Modern Planetary Physics, Set, Vols. 1-3. (C). 1997. text 145.00 (*0-521-55215-X*) Cambridge U Pr.
— A History of Modern Planetary Physics Vol. 1: Nebulous Earth: The Origin of the Solar System & the Core of the Earth from Laplace to Jeffreys. (Illus.). 324p. (C). 1996. text 54.95 (*0-521-44171-4*) Cambridge U Pr.
— A History of Modern Planetary Physics Vol. 2: Transmuted Past: The Age of the Earth & the Evolution of the Elements from Lyall to Patterson. (Illus.). 144p. (C). 1996. text 44.95 (*0-521-55213-3*) Cambridge U Pr.
— A History of Modern Planetary Physics Vol. 3: Fruitful Encounters: The Origin of the Solar System & of the Moon from Chamberlin to Apollo. (Illus.). 366p. (C). 1996. text 54.95 (*0-521-55214-1*) Cambridge U Pr.
— The History of Modern Science: A Guide to the Second Scientific Revolution, 1800-1950. LC 87-26177. (History of Technology & Science Ser.: Vol. 2). 560p. (C). 1988. text 59.95 (*0-8138-0883-9*) Iowa St U Pr.
— Kinetic Theory, 3 vols. Incl. Vol. 2. Irreversible Processes. 1966. write for info. (*0-318-55170-5*, Pub. by Pergamon Repr) Franklin.
— Statistical Physics & the Atomic Theory of Matter: From Boyle & Newton to Landau & Onsager. LC 82-61357. (Princeton Series in Physics). 367p. reprint ed. pap. 104.60 (*0-7837-0247-7*, 2040556) Bks Demand.
Brush, Stephen G., ed. History of Physics: Selected Reprints. (Reprint Bks.). (Illus.). 235p. (Orig.). (C). 1988. per. 28.00 (*0-917853-29-6*, RB-50) Am Assn Physics.
— Resources for the History of Physics: Guide to Books & Audiovisual Materials, Guide to Original Works of Historical Importance & Their Translations into Other Languages. LC 70-186306. 192p. reprint ed. pap. 59.60 (*0-608-11355-7*, 202232400026) Bks Demand.
Brush, Stephen G. & Levin, A. E. The Origin of the Solar System: Soviet Research, 1925-1991. (Illus.). 400p. 1994. text 69.95 (*1-56396-281-0*, AIP Pr) Spr-Verlag.
Brush, Stephen G., ed. see International Working Seminar on the Role of the H.
Brush, Stephen G., tr. see Boltzmann, Ludwig.
Brush, Thomas. Opening Night. 104p. 1981. pap. 12.00 (*0-937669-05-9*) Owl Creek Pr.
Brush, Warren D., jt. auth. see Collingwood, G. H.
Brushtein, A. I. & Temkin, S. I. Spectroscopy of Molecular Rotation in Gases & Liquids. (Illus.). 308p. (C). 1994. text 74.95 (*0-521-45465-4*) Cambridge U Pr.
Brushwood, Carolyn, tr. see Aguilera-Malta, Demetrio.
Brushwood, Carolyn, tr. see Galindo, Sergio.
Brushwood, Carolyn, tr. see Solares, Ignacio, et al.
Brushwood, David B. Medical Malpractice: Pharmacy Law. 1986. text 125.00 (*0-07-008576-5*) Shepards.
***Brushwood, David B.** Pharmacy Malpractice: Law & Regulations. 1. 2nd ed. LC 98-158259. 408p. 1998. boxed set 160.00 (*1-56706-848-0*) Panel Pubs.
Brushwood, David B., jt. auth. see Abood, Richard R.
Brushwood, John S. Enrique Gonzalez Martinez. LC 71-75878. (Twayne's World Authors Ser.). 1969. lib. bdg. 20.95 (*0-8057-2592-X*) Irvington.
— Genteel Barbarism: Experiments in Analysis of Nineteenth-Century Spanish-American Novels. LC 80-27722. 255p. 1981. reprint ed. pap. 79.10 (*0-608-07996-0*, 206796100012) Bks Demand.
— Narrative Innovation & Political Change in Mexico. (University of Texas Studies in Contemporary Spanish-American Fiction: Vol. 4). XII, 131p. (C). 1989. text 32.50 (*0-8204-0966-9*) P Lang Pubng.
Brushwood, John S., tr. see Aguilera-Malta, Demetrio.
Brushwood, John S., tr. see Galindo, Sergio.
Brushwood, John S., tr. see Solares, Ignacio, et al.
Brusic. Mission 21: Level III Sampler. (Tech & Industrial Education Ser.). 1991. pap. write for info. (*0-8273-4896-7*) Delmar.
Brusic, Lucy M. Amidst Cultivated & Pleasant Fields: A Bicentennial History of North Haven, Connecticut. LC 86-18721. (Illus.). 352p. 1986. 10.00 (*0-914659-20-0*) Phoenix Pub.
Brusic, Lucy M., ed. Sherlock Holmes: The Detective & the Collector: Essays on the John Bennett Shaw Collection. (Illus.). 204p. 1995. 35.00 (*0-9632976-1-9*) A Givens Sr Collect.
Brusic, Sharon A. Kids & Technology - Mission 21: Student Handbooks, Level 2. (Illus.). 32p. 1991. pap., student ed. 9.95 (*0-8273-4107-5*); text, student ed. 174.95 (*0-8273-4098-2*) S-W Pub.
— Kids & Technology - Mission 21: Student Handbooks, Level 3. (Illus.). 32p. 1991. pap., student ed. 9.95 (*0-8273-4100-8*); pap., student ed. 9.95 (*0-8273-4101-6*); pap., student ed. 9.95 (*0-8273-4103-2*); text, student ed. 174.95 (*0-8273-4099-0*) S-W Pub.
— Launching Science & Technology Across the Curriculum Design. (Kids & Technology - Mission Twenty-One Ser.). 1993. pap. 9.95 (*0-8273-4950-5*) S-W Pub.
— Launching Science & Technology Across the Curriculum Explore. (Kids & Technology - Mission Twenty-One Ser.). 1993. pap. 9.95 (*0-8273-4951-3*) S-W Pub.
— Launching Science & Technology Across the Curriculum Space. (Kids & Technology - Mission Twenty-One Ser.). 1993. pap. 9.95 (*0-8273-4948-3*) S-W Pub.
— Launching Science & Technology Across the Curriculum Transportation. (Kids & Technology - Mission Twenty-One Ser.). 1993. pap. 9.95 (*0-8273-4949-1*) S-W Pub.
— Space Colonization, Level 3. (Kids & Technology - Mission Twenty-One Ser.). (Illus.). 32p. 1991. pap., student ed. 9.95 (*0-8273-4102-4*) S-W Pub.
Brusic, Sharon A. & Wells, John G. Kids & Technology: Mission Twenty-One, 4 bks., Level 1. (J). 1991. text, teacher ed. 174.95 (*0-8273-4952-1*) S-W Pub.
— Kids & Technology: Mission Twenty-One, 4 bks., Set. (J). 1993. pap. 31.95 (*0-8273-5997-7*) S-W Pub.
Brusick, D. Principles of Genetic Toxicology. 2nd ed. LC 87-17169. (Illus.). 302p. (C). 1987. text 54.50 (*0-306-42532-7*, Kluwer Plenum) Kluwer Academic.
Brusilov, Aleksiei A. A Soldier's Note-Book, 1914-1918. LC 75-84265. 340p. 1971. reprint ed. lib. bdg. 45.00 (*0-8371-5003-5*, BRSN, Greenwood Pr) Greenwood.
Brusilovsky, Peter, et al, eds. Adaptive Hypertext & Hypermedia. LC 97-49840. 252p. 1998. lib. bdg. 175.00 (*0-7923-4843-5*) Kluwer Academic.
Brusilovsky, Peter, et al. Multimedia, Hypermedia, & Virtual Reality: Models, Systems, & Applications, Vol. 107. LC 96-283. (Lecture Notes in Computer Science Ser.). 1996. pap. 56.00 (*3-540-61282-3*) Spr-Verlag.
Brusius, Beth L. Directory of Community, Junior, & Technical College with Home Economics & Related Program. LC TX0173.B78. 133p. reprint ed. pap. 41.30 (*0-7837-1919-1*, 204212300001) Bks Demand.
Bruskewitz, Fabian. Bishop Bruskewitz: A Shepherd Speaks. LC 96-78017. 1997. pap. text 14.95 (*0-89870-626-2*) Ignatius Pr.
Bruskin, David N., ed. Behind the Three Stooges: The White Brothers: Conversations with David N. Bruskin. rev. ed. LC 93-72187. (Oral History Ser.). 395p. 1993. pap. 16.95 (*1-882766-00-8*) Dirs Guild Am.
Bruskin, David N., ed. see White, Jack, et al.
Bruskin, Deborah M., jt. ed. see Blackstone, Sarah W.
***Brusko, Mike.** Writing Rules! Teaching Kids to Write for Life, Grades K-8. LC 99-26109. (Beeline Ser.). (Illus.). 96p. 1999. pap. 10.95 (*0-325-00157-X*) Heinemann.
***Brusniak, John.** Brusniak's Texas Property Tax Digest. 1999. write for info. (*1-58012-042-3*) James Pub Santa Ana.
Brusotti, Marco. Die Leidenschaft der Erkenntnis: Philosophie und Aesthetische Lebensgestaltung Bei Nietzsche Von "Morgenroethe" Bis "Also Sprach Zarathustra" (Monographien und Texte Zur Nietzsche-Forschung Ser.: Vol. 37). (GER.). xiii, 702p. (C). 1997. lib. bdg. 236.00 (*3-11-014563-4*) De Gruyter.
Bruss, Elizabeth W. Autobiographical Acts: The Changing Situation of a Literary Genre. LC 76-13460. 192p. reprint ed. pap. 59.60 (*0-8357-5905-9*, 202970300063) Bks Demand.
— Beautiful Theories: The Spectacle of Discourse in Contemporary Criticism. LC 81-48178. 528p. 1982. reprint ed. pap. 163.70 (*0-608-06714-8*, 206691100009) Bks Demand.
Bruss, F. Thomas, et al. Strategies for Sequential Search & Selection in Real Time. LC 91-38281. (Contemporary Mathematics Ser.: Vol. 125). 248p. 1992. pap. 47.00 (*0-8218-5133-0*, CONM/125) Am Math.
Bruss, Glenn M. Profiles in Medical History, Vol. I. (Illus.). 120p. 1997. pap. 12.00 (*0-8059-4215-7*) Dorrance.
***Bruss, Jon S.** Ancillary Exercises for "From Alpha to Omega" (Classical Texts Ser.). 142p. (C). 1999. pap. text 8.95 (*0-941051-61-7*) Focus Pub-R Pullins.
Bruss, Michael, jt. ed. see Woodard, James C.
Bruss, Paul. Conrad's Early Sea Fiction: The Novelist As Navigator. LC 77-74402. 185p. 1979. 29.50 (*0-8387-2133-8*) Bucknell U Pr.
— Victims: Textual Strategies in Recent American Fiction. LC 80-67319. 259p. 1981. 36.50 (*0-8387-5006-0*) Bucknell U Pr.
Bruss, Robert, jt. auth. see Pivar, William H.
Bruss, Robert J., jt. auth. see Pivar, William H.
Brussaard, L. & Ferrara-Cerrato, Ronald. Soil Ecology in Sustainable Agricultural Systems. LC 96-30093. 176p. 1997. lib. bdg. 69.95 (*1-56670-277-1*) Lewis Pubs.
Brussaard, L. & Kooistra, M. J., eds. Soil Structure - Soil Biota Interrelationships: Proceedings of the International Workshop on Methods of Research on Soil Structure Soil Biota Interrelationships, Wageningen, the Netherlands, November, 1991. 846p. 1993. 344.00 (*0-444-81490-6*) Elsevier.
Brussaard, Wim & Grossman, Margaret R., eds. Agrarian Land Law in the Western World. (Illus.). 296p. 1992. text 105.00 (*0-85198-727-3*) OUP.
Brussard, P. J. & Koch, J. H., eds. New Vistas in Nuclear Dynamics. (NATO ASI Series B, Physics: Vol. 139). 410p. 1986. 105.00 (*0-306-42371-5*, Plenum Trade) Perseus Pubng.
Brussard, Peter F., ed. Ecological Genetics: The Interface. LC 78-27196. (Proceedings in Life Sciences Ser.). (Illus.). 1979. 114.00 (*0-387-90378-X*) Spr-Verlag.
***Brussat, Frederic.** Spiritual Literacy: Reading the Sacred in Everyday Life. 1998. audio 18.00 (*0-671-57903-7*) S&S Audio.
Brussat, Frederic & Brussat, Mary A. 100 More Ways To Keep Your Soul Alive. LC 97-2617. 128p. 1997. pap. 10.00 (*0-06-251521-7*, Pub. by Harper SF) HarpC.
Brussat, Frederic & Brussat, Mary A. Spiritual Literacy: Reading the Sacred in Everyday Life. 608p. 1996. pap. 16.00 (*0-684-81533-8*, Touchstone) S&S Trade Pap.
— Spiritual Rx: Prescriptions for Living a Meaningful Life. LC 99-22001. 352p. 2000. 23.95 (*0-7868-6450-8*, Pub. by Hyperion) Time Warner.
Brussat, Frederic & Brussat, Mary Ann. 100 Ways to Keep Your Soul Alive: Living Deeply & Fully Every Day. LC 93-46210. 128p. 1994. pap. 10.00 (*0-06-251050-9*, Pub. by Harper SF) HarpC.
Brussat, Frederic & Brussat, Mary Ann. Spiritual Literacy: Reading the Sacred in Everyday Life. 608p. 1998. pap. 15.00 (*0-684-83534-7*, Touchstone) S&S Trade Pap.
Brussat, Mary A., jt. auth. see Brussat, Frederic.
Brussat, Mary Ann, jt. auth. see Brussat, Frederic.
Brusse, Janet, jt. auth. see Freestone, Julie.
Brusse, Wendy A. Tariffs, Trade & European Integration, 1947-57: From Study Group to Common Market. LC 96-39531. 250p. 1997. text 49.95 (*0-312-16518-8*) St Martin.
Brusseau, James. Isolated Experiences: Gilles Deleuze & the Solitudes of Reversed Platonism. LC 97-12980. (SUNY Series in Contemporary Continental Philosophy). 224p. (C). 1998. text 59.50 (*0-7914-3671-3*); pap. text 19.95 (*0-7914-3672-1*) State U NY Pr.
***Brusseau, Mark L., et al, eds.** Innovative Subsurface Remediation: Field Testing of Physical, Chemical & Characterization Technologies. LC 99-12285. (ACS Symposium Ser.: No. 725). 304p. 1999. text 110.00 (*0-8412-3596-1*, Pub. by Am Chemical) OUP.
Brusseau, Peggy & Cox, Peter. Lifepoints. LC 97-13141. 1997. pap. 6.99 (*0-684-83373-5*) S&S Trade.

An Asterisk (*) at the beginning of an entry indicates that the title is appearing for the first time.

Brusseau, Peggy, jt. auth. see Cox, Peter.
Brussel, Gabrielle S. The Cuban Missile Crisis: U. S. Deliberations & Negotiations at the Edge of the Precipice. (Pew Case Studies in International Affairs). 50p. (C). 1992. pap. text 3.50 (*1-56927-334-0*) Geo U Inst Dplmcy.
Brussel, James A. & Cantzlaar, George L. Diccionario de Psiquiatria. (SPA.). 306p. pap. 49.50 (*0-7859-0781-5*, S50209) Fr & Eur.
Brussel, Nicolas & Bisson, Thomas N. Nouvel Examen de l'usage General des Fiefs en France Pendant le XIe, le XIIe, le XIIIe & le XIVe Siecle, 2 vols., Set. LC 79-8359. reprint ed. 175.00 (*0-404-18337-9*) AMS Pr.
Brussell, David E. Potions, Poisons, & Panaceas: An Ethnobotanical Study of Montserrat. LC 90-25873. (Illus.). 208p. (C). 1997. 69.95 (*0-8093-1552-1*) S Ill U Pr.
Brussell, Eugene E. Webster's New World Dictionary of Quotable Definitions 688p. (C). 1996. pap. 6.98 (*0-13-619057-X*) P-H.
Brusselmans, Christiane & Matthews, Edward. Sunday: Handbook for Those Who Share the Word with Children. (Illus.). 36p. (Orig.). 1989. pap. text 7.95 (*0-929496-06-X*) Treehaus Comns.
Brusselmans, Christiane, et al. Sunday: A Leaders Weekly Guidebook Year A. 192p. 1992. text 49.95 (*0-929496-93-0*) Treehaus Comns.
— Sunday: Book of Readings Adapted for Children Year A, Year A. 176p. (J). (ps-7). 1989. text 49.95 (*0-929496-38-8*) Treehaus Comns.
— Sunday: Book of Readings Adapted for Children, Year B, Year B. 176p. (J). (ps-8). 1990. text 49.95 (*0-929496-57-4*) Treehaus Comns.
— Sunday: Book of Readings Adapted for Children Year C, Year C. 176p. (J). text 49.95 (*0-929496-91-4*) Treehaus Comns.
— Sunday: Leaders Weekly Guidebook, Year B. 160p. (J). (ps-8). 1990. text 49.95 (*0-929496-58-2*) Treehaus Comns.
— Sunday: Leaders Weekly Guidebook, Year C. 160p. (J). text 49.95 (*0-929496-92-2*) Treehaus Comns.
Brusselmans-Dehairs, Christiane, et al. Gender Differences in Learning Achievement: Evidence from Cross-National Surveys. LC 98-178255. (Educational Studies & Documents: No. 65). 86p. 1997. pap. 15.00 (*92-3-103346-8*, U3346, Pub. by UNESCO) Bernan Associates.
Brussig, Thomas. Heroes Like Us. Brownjohn, John, tr. from GER. LC 97-16652. 288p. 1997. 23.00 (*0-374-16983-7*) FS&G.
Brusso, Clifton. Tales from the U. P.'s Copper Country. (Illus.). 123p. (Orig.). 1992. pap. 4.95 (*0-9633548-0-9*, TXU 433 567) Iroquois Pr.
— Tales from the U. S. Mid West. 123p. (Orig.). 1992. pap. 4.95 (*0-9633548-1-7*) Iroquois Pr.
Brussow, Herbert L., jt. ed. see Kohls, L. Robert.
Brusstar, James H. & Jones, Ellen. The Russian Military's Role in Politics. 62p. (Orig.). (C). 1996. pap. text 25.00 (*0-7881-3233-4*) DIANE Pub.
Brust. Dads & Babies: Easy Animal Reader. (Illus.). 16p. (J). (ps-1). 1996. pap. 2.49 (*1-57690-052-5*) Tchr Create Mat.
— What Am I? Easy Animal Reader. (Easy Readers Ser.). (Illus.). 16p. (J). (ps-1). 1997. pap. 2.49 (*1-57690-054-1*) Tchr Create Mat.
— Who Made This Nest? Easy Animal Reader. (Illus.). 16p. (J). (ps-1). 1996. pap. 2.49 (*1-57690-053-3*) Tchr Create Mat.
Brust, Andrew & Eidahl, Loren. Using Visual Basic 5: Platinum Edition. LC 97-68766. 1462p. 1997. 60.00 (*0-7897-1412-4*) Que.
Brust, Beth. Dolphins & Porpoises. (Zoobooks Ser.). (Illus.). 24p. (J). (gr. 1-6). 1997. 13.95 (*1-888153-49-0*) Wildlife Educ.
Brust, Beth W. The Amazing Paper Cuttings of Hans Christian Andersen. LC 93-24532. 80p. (J). (gr. 2-4). 1994. 17.00 (*0-395-66787-9*) Ticknor & Flds Bks Yng Read.
— The Great Molasses Flood: Level 3. LC 98-173820. (Planet Reader Picture Bks.). (Illus.). 48p. (J). (gr. 1-4). 1998. pap. 2.95 (*0-8167-4523-4*) Troll Communs.
Brust, Beth W., jt. auth. see Wildlife Education, Ltd. Staff.
Brust, Bill. Defending Principles: The Political Legacy of Bill Brust. Brust, Jean, ed. (Illus.). 268p. 1993. pap. 16.95 (*0-929087-66-6*) Mehring Bks.
Brust, Bill, tr. see Weber, Wolfgang.
Brust, Donna J. & Foster, Joyce A. From Nursing Assistant to Patient Care Technician: New Roles, New Knowledge, New Skills. Biello, Lisa, ed. 432p. 1996. pap. text 41.95 (*0-7216-6046-0*, W B Saunders Co) Harcrt Hlth Sci Grp.
— From Nursing Assistant to Patient Care Technician: New Roles, New Knowledge, New Skills. (Illus.). 1997. pap., teacher ed. write for info. (*0-7216-7087-3*, W B Saunders Co) Harcrt Hlth Sci Grp.
Brust, Frederick W., jt. ed. see Atluri, Satya N.
Brust, Jean, ed. see Brust, Bill.
Brust, John C. Neurological Aspects of Substance Abuse. (Illus.). 289p. 1993. text 99.95 (*0-7506-9005-4*) Buttrwrth-Heinemann.
— Neurotoxic Side Effects of Prescription Drugs. LC 96-23662. 435p. 1996. pap. text 49.50 (*0-7506-9663-X*) Buttrwrth-Heinemann.
Brust, Steven. Agyar. 256p. 1994. mass mkt. 4.99 (*0-8125-1521-8*, Pub. by Tor Bks) St Martin.
— Athyra. 256p. (Orig.). 1993. mass mkt. 5.99 (*0-441-03342-3*) Ace Bks.
— The Book of Jhereg. (Orig.). 1999. pap. 13.00 (*0-441-00615-9*) Ace Bks.
— Brokendown Palace. 288p. 1987. mass mkt. 5.99 (*0-441-07182-1*) Ace Bks.
— Dragon. LC 98-23558. 288p. 1998. 22.95 (*0-312-86692-5*, Pub. by Tor Bks) St Martin.
***Brust, Steven.** Dragon. 288p. 1999. mass mkt. 6.99 (*0-8125-8916-5*, Pub. by Tor Bks) St Martin.
Brust, Steven. Five Hundred Years After. 576p. 1995. 5.99 (*0-8125-1522-6*, Pub. by Tor Bks) St Martin.
***Brust, Steven.** Issola. 2000. text 23.95 (*0-312-85927-9*) St Martin.
Brust, Steven. Jhereg. 256p. 1987. mass mkt. 5.99 (*0-441-38554-0*) Ace Bks.
— Orca. 304p. (Orig.). 1996. mass mkt. 5.99 (*0-441-00196-3*) Ace Bks.
— The Paths of the Dead. 1996. write for info. (*0-312-85579-6*) Tor Bks.
— Phoenix. 1990. mass mkt. 4.99 (*0-441-66225-0*) Ace Bks.
— The Phoenix Guards. 512p. 1995. 4.99 (*0-8125-0689-8*, Pub. by Tor Bks) St Martin.
— The Sun, the Moon & the Stars. 224p. 1996. pap. 11.95 (*0-312-86039-0*) Orb NYC.
— Taltos. 1988. mass mkt. 5.99 (*0-441-18200-3*) Ace Bks.
— Teckla. 224p. 1987. mass mkt. 5.99 (*0-441-79977-9*) Ace Bks.
***Brust, Steven.** To Reign in Hell. 288p. 2000. pap. 14.95 (*0-312-87049-3*, Pub. by Tor Bks) St Martin.
Brust, Steven. Yendi. 224p. 1987. pap. 2.95 (*0-441-94459-0*, DiamondBks) Berkley Pub.
Brust, Steven & Bull, Emma. Freedom & Necessity. LC 96-27428. 1997. 25.95 (*0-312-85974-0*, Pub. by Tor Bks) St Martin.
— Freedom & Necessity. 1997. mass mkt. 9.75 (*0-8125-6261-5*, Pub. by Tor Bks) St Martin.
Brust, Steven & Lindholm, Megan. The Gypsy. 352p. 1993. mass mkt. 4.99 (*0-8125-2498-5*, Pub. by Tor Bks) St Martin.
Brustad, Kristen. Textbook for Beginning Arabic. 224p. 1996. pap. 35.00 (*0-614-21657-5*, 1386) Kazi Pubns.
Brustad, Kristen, et al. Al-Kitaab Fii Ta allum Al-Arabiyya: A Textbook for Arabic, Pt. 2. LC 97-2858. (ARA & ENG.). 432p. (Orig.). 1997. pap. 42.50 (*0-87840-350-7*) Georgetown U Pr.
***Brustad, Kristen E.** The Syntax of Spoken Arabic: A Comparative Study of Moroccan, Egyptian, Syrian & Kuwaiti Dialects. 456p. 2000. pap. text 39.95 (*0-87840-789-8*) Georgetown U Pr.
Brustad, Tor, et al, eds. Radiation & Cancer Risk. (Cancer Ser.). 300p. 1989. 94.95 (*0-89116-978-4*) Hemisp Pub.
Brustein, Michael, et al. Manual on Civil Rights in Vocational Education. 1984. write for info. (*0-318-57735-6*) NYS Ed Dept.
Brustein, Robert. Cultural Calisthenics: Writings on Race, Politics & Theatre. LC 98-29317. 288p. 1998. 26.00 (*1-56663-220-X*, Pub. by I R Dee) Natl Bk Netwk.
— Cultural Calisthenics: Writings on Race, Politics & Theatre. LC 99-32037. 304p. 1999. pap. 14.95 (*1-56663-266-8*, Pub. by I R Dee) Natl Bk Netwk.
— Dumbocracy in America: Studies in the Theatre of Guilt, 1987-1994. LC 94-17515. 288p. 1994. text 26.00 (*1-56663-060-6*, Pub. by I R Dee) Natl Bk Netwk.
— Dumbocracy in America: Studies in the Theatre of Guilt, 1987-1994. 288p. 1995. pap. 12.95 (*1-56663-098-3*, Pub. by I R Dee) Natl Bk Netwk.
— Reimagining American Theatre. 324p. 1992. reprint ed. pap. 12.95 (*0-929587-99-5*, Pub. by I R Dee) Natl Bk Netwk.
— Revolution As Theatre: Essays on Radical Style. 1970. pap. 1.95 (*0-87140-238-6*, Pub. by Liveright) Norton.
— The Theatre of Revolt: Studies in Modern Drama from Ibsen to Genet. 456p. 1991. reprint ed. pap. text 18.95 (*0-929587-53-7*, Pub. by I R Dee) Natl Bk Netwk.
Brustein, William. The Logic of Evil: The Social Origins of the Nazi Party, 1925 to 1933. LC 95-47263. (Illus.). 256p. 1996. 35.00 (*0-300-06533-7*) Yale U Pr.
— The Logic of Evil: The Social Origins of the Nazi Party, 1925-1933. 256p. 1998. pap. 16.00 (*0-300-07432-8*) Yale U Pr.
***Bruster, Douglas.** Quoting Shakespeare: Form & Culture in Early Modern Drama. LC 00-24202. 288p. 2000. text 50.00 (*0-8032-1303-4*) U of Nebr Pr.
Brustowicz, Robert M., jt. auth. see Krauss, Baruch.
Bruszt, Laszlo, jt. auth. see Stark, David.
Bruteau, Beatrice. Easter Mysteries. 180p. 1995. pap. 14.95 (*0-8245-1493-9*) Crossroad NY.
— God's Ecstasy: The Creation of a Self-Creating World. LC 97-15611. 204p. 1997. pap. 19.95 (*0-8245-1683-4*) Crossroad NY.
— The Other Half of My Soul: Bede Griffiths & the Hindu-Christian Dialogue. (Illus.). 300p. 1996. pap. 16.00 (*0-8356-0717-8*, Quest) Theos Pub Hse.
— Radical Optimism: Rooting Ourselves in Reality. 112p. (Orig.). 1993. pap. 11.95 (*0-8245-1264-2*) Crossroad NY.
— What We Can Learn from the East. LC 94-46868. 132p. (Orig.). 1995. pap. 11.95 (*0-8245-1457-2*) Crossroad NY.
— Worthy Is the World: The Hindu Philosophy of Sri Aurobindo. LC 73-144091. (Illus.). 288p. 1975. 25.00 (*0-8386-7872-6*) Fairleigh Dickinson.
Bruter, C. P., et al, eds. Bifurcation Theory, Mechanics & Physics. 1983. text 206.50 (*90-277-1631-5*) Kluwer Academic.
Bruthiaux, Paul. The Discourse of Classified Advertising: Exploring the Nature of Linguistic Simplicity. (Oxford Studies in Sociolinguistics). (Illus.). 224p. 1996. text 55.00 (*0-19-510032-8*) OUP.
Bruton, C. J. The Neuropathology of Temporal Lobe Epilepsy. (Maudsley Monographs: No. 31). (Illus.). 176p. 1988. 52.50 (*0-19-712155-1*) OUP.
Bruton, Charles. Handbook of Federal Judicial Practices Eastern District of Pennsylvania. 400p. 1996. pap. text 29.00 (*0-314-20082-7*) West Pub.
Bruton, Eric. Hallmarks & Date Letters on Silver, Gold & Platinum. (Illus.). 40p. 1977. pap. 7.50 (*0-7198-0072-2*, Pub. by NAG Press) Antique Collect.
— The Wetherfield Collection of Clocks: A Guide to Dating English Antique Clocks. (Illus.). 264p. 1981. 49.50 (*0-7198-0150-8*, Pub. by NAG Press) Antique Collect.
Bruton, Heather, jt. auth. see Huff, Tanya.
Bruton, Henry J. On the Search for Well-Being. LC 96-40106. 240p. (C). 1997. text 49.50 (*0-472-10791-7*, 10791) U of Mich Pr.
— The Promise of Peace: Economic Cooperation Between Egypt & Israel. 1981. pap. 6.95 (*0-8157-1125-5*) Brookings.
Bruton, Henry J. & Hill, Cathrine B. The Evaluation of Public Expenditure in Africa. LC 96-25632. (EDI Learning Resource Ser.). 180p. 1997. pap. 22.00 (*0-8213-3680-0*, 13680) World Bank.
Bruton, Julie B., jt. auth. see Tracy, Carol V.
Bruton, Kevin. The Business Culture in Spain. 288p. 1994. pap. text 32.95 (*0-7506-1831-0*) Buttrwrth-Heinemann.
— The Business Culture in Spain. LC 94-241063. 173p. reprint ed. pap. 53.70 (*0-608-07969-3*, 206794100012) Bks Demand.
Bruton, Lynn, ed. see Baxter, John.
Bruton, Michael N., ed. Alternative Life: History Styles of Animals. (Perspectives in Vertebrate Science Ser.). (C). 1989. lib. bdg. 353.00 (*90-6193-662-4*) Kluwer Academic.
— Alternative Life-History Styles of Fishes. (C). 1990. lib. bdg. 236.00 (*0-7923-0801-8*) Kluwer Academic.
Bruton, Noel. How to Manage the IT Help Desk. LC 97-219671. 240p. 1997. pap. 29.95 (*0-7506-3811-7*) Buttrwrth-Heinemann.
Bruton, Robert H. Exploring Washington on Foot: Twelve Hikes Between Metro Stops. (Illus.). 232p. (Orig.). 1995. pap. 12.95 (*0-9647813-0-1*) Rockrose Pubns.
Bruton-Simmonds, Ian. Mend Your English: What You Should Have Been Taught at Primary School. 150p. (C). 1990. 80.00 (*0-7855-6630-9*, Pub. by Ivy Pub) St Mut.
Brutsaert, Wilfred H. Evaporation into the Atmosphere: Theory, History & Applications. 308p. 1982. text 147.00 (*90-277-1247-6*) Kluwer Academic.
Brutsaert, Wilfred H. & Jirka, Gerhard H., eds. Gas Transfer at Water Surfaces. 1983. text 274.00 (*90-277-1697-8*) Kluwer Academic.
***Brutschy, Jennifer & Smith, Cat Bowman.** Just One More Story. LC 99-58610. (J). 2000. lib. bdg. write for info. (*0-531-30296-2*) Orchard Bks Watts.
Brutti, Ray. Fat Tire Tales & Trails by Cosmic Ray: Arizona Montain Bike Guide. 11th rev. ed. (Illus.). 123p. 1998. pap. 9.95 (*0-9664769-0-5*) Cos Ray Publ.
— Flagstaff & Sedona Favorite Hikes. 4th rev. ed. (Illus.). 96p. 1998. pap. 7.95 (*0-9664769-1-3*) Cos Ray Publ.
Bruttig, Dana E. The Days of Wine & Software: Building a Business by Following the Principals of Nature. Strand, Laurel, ed. LC 98-74121. 1999. pap. 14.95 (*0-944958-39-7*) Elfin Cove Pr.
***Brutting, Richard & Sacco, Sergio.** Dissens und Dialog Dissenso e Dialogo: Italien, Deutschland und Ru & Beta; Land im Interkulturellen Vergleich Ergebnisse des 4. Internationalen Seminars 1997 Italia, Germania, Russia: Confronto Interculturale Atti Del Iv Seminario Internazionale, 1997. (Italien In Geschichte und Gegenwart Ser.). (GER.). 271p. 1999. 42.95 (*3-631-33756-6*) P Lang Pubng.
Bruttini, Alberto. Dictionnaire de Sylviculture: French, German, English, Spanish, Italian. (ENG, FRE, GER, ITA & SPA.). 384p. 1930. pap. 95.00 (*0-7859-7963-8*, 2720501670) Fr & Eur.
Brutto, Oscar H., et al. Neurocysticercosis: A Clinical Handbook. LC 98-11617. 1998. 88.00 (*90-265-1513-8*) Swets.
Brutton, Philip. A Captain's Mandate: Palestine 1946-1948. LC 96-214628. (Illus.). 219p. 1996. 31.95 (*0-85052-497-0*, Pub. by Leo Cooper) Trans-Atl Phila.
Brutus, Dennis. Airs. 1989. 1.50 (*0-685-25947-1*) Whirlwind Pr.
— Airs & Tributes. Ott, Gil, ed. (Illus.). 32p. (Orig.). 1989. pap. 10.00 (*0-922827-00-1*) Whirlwind Pr.
— A Simple Lust: Collected Poems of South African Jail & Exile. (African Writers Ser.). 176p. (C). 1973. pap. 11.95 (*0-435-90115-X*, 90115) Heinemann.
— A Stubborn Hope: Selected Poems of South Africa & a Wider World. LC 91-9327. (African Writers Ser.). 98p. (C). 1991. pap. 9.95 (*0-435-90208-3*, 90208) Heinemann.
Brutus, Stephane, jt. auth. see McCawley, Cynthia D.
Brutvan, Cheryl A. The Paintings of Sylvia Plimack Mangold. LC 93-41205. 1994. 35.00 (*0-914782-90-8*) Buffalo Fine-Albrght-Knox.
Brutvan, Cheryl A. & Mayer, Marc. In Western New York 1995. LC 95-76522. (Illus.). 1995. write for info. (*0-914782-93-2*) Buffalo Fine-Albrght-Knox.
Brutvan, Cheryl A., et al. Masterworks on Paper from the Albright-Knox Art Gallery. LC 87-3619. (Illus.). 176p. 1987. 50.00 (*0-933920-89-X*); pap. 30.00 (*0-933920-90-3*) Buffalo Fine-Albrght-Knox.
***Brutvan, Cheryl A., et al.** Susan Rothenberg: Paintings from the Nineties. LC 99-45615. (Illus.). 80p. 1999. text 27.50 (*0-8478-2267-2*, Pub. by Rizzoli Intl) St Martin.
Bruu, Dina A., ed. see Buckles, G. Matthew.
Bruun. Science Values & Politics in Max Webbers. 1993. 43.95 (*0-7512-0162-6*) Ashgate Pub Co.
Bruun, Bertel, jt. auth. see Bruun, Ruth D.
Bruun, Eric & Keith, Buzzy. Heavy Equipment: Giant Machines That Crush, Cut, Dig, Dredge, Drill, Excavate, Grade, Haul & Mill. LC 97-28292. (Illus.). 128p. 1997. 24.98 (*1-884822-72-X*) Blck Dog & Leventhal.
***Bruun, Eric A. & Crosby, Jay.** Our Nation's Archive: The History of the United States in Documents. LC 99-29451. 1999. 29.98 (*1-57912-067-9*) Blck Dog & Leventhal.
***Bruun, Erik.** The Kids' Book of Giant Machines: That Crush, Cut, Dig, Dredge, Drill, Excavate, Grade, Haul, Pave, Pulverize, Pump, Push, Roll, Stack, Thresh & Transport Big Things. LC 99-40458. (Illus.). 64p. (J). (gr. 4-7). 1999. 12.98 (*1-57912-071-7*, Pub. by Blck Dog & Leventhal) Workman Pub.
— State Smarts: California. LC 00-24687. (Illus.). 48p. (J). (gr. 3-7). 2000. 7.98 (*1-57912-100-4*, 81100) Blck Dog & Leventhal.
— State Smarts: Illinois. LC 00-24686. (Illus.). 48p. (J). (gr. 3-7). 2000. 7.98 (*1-57912-101-2*, 81101) Blck Dog & Leventhal.
— State Smarts: Texas. LC 00-24671. (Illus.). 48p. (J). (gr. 3-7). 2000. 7.98 (*1-57912-102-0*, 81102) Blck Dog & Leventhal.
— State Smarts: Virginia. LC 00-24670. (Illus.). 48p. (J). (gr. 3-7). 2000. 7.98 (*1-57912-103-9*, 81103) Blck Dog & Leventhal.
Bruun, Erik, jt. ed. see Getzen, Robin.
Bruun, G. La Europa del Siglo XIX (1815-1914) (Breviarios Ser.). (SPA.). pap. 8.99 (*968-16-0299-4*, Pub. by Fondo) Continental Bk.
Bruun, Geoffrey. A Survey of European Civilization, 004. 4th ed. Incl. Complete. Ferguson, Wallace K. 1972. text. Ferguson, Wallace K. 1972. (C). 1972. Set text 48.76 (*0-395-04425-1*) HM.
Bruun, H. H. Hot-Wire Anemometry: Principles & Signal Analysis. (Illus.). 532p. 1995. text 120.00 (*0-19-856342-6*) OUP.
Bruun, Kettil & Hauge, Ragnar. Drinking Habits Among Northern Youth: A Cross-National Study in the Scandinavian Capitals. (Finnish Foundation for Alcohol Studies: Vol. 12). 1963. 4.00 (*951-9192-04-2*) Rutgers Ctr Alcohol.
Bruun, Kettil, et al. Alcohol Control Policies in Public Health Perspective. (Finnish Foundation for Alcohol Studies). (Illus.). 1975. 8.00 (*951-9191-29-1*) Rutgers Ctr Alcohol.
— The Gentlemen's Club: International Control of Drugs & Alchol. LC 74-21343. (Studies in Crime & Justice). 352p. Date not set. reprint ed. pap. 109.20 (*0-608-20613-X*, 205458100003) Bks Demand.
— The Gentlemen's Club: International Control of Drugs & Alcohol. LC 74-21343. (Studies in Crime & Justice). xiv, 338p. 1975. lib. bdg. 20.00 (*0-226-07777-2*) U Ch Pr.
— The Gentlemen's Club: International Control of Drugs & Alcohol. LC 74-21343. (Studies in Crime & Justice). xiv, 338p. 1978. pap. text 5.95 (*0-226-07778-0*) U Ch Pr.
Bruun, Niklas, et al. The Nordic Labour Relations Model. 250p. 1992. 78.95 (*1-85521-239-0*, Pub. by Dartmth Pub) Ashgate Pub Co.
Bruun, Ole. Business & Bureaucracy in a Chinese City: An Ethnography of Private Business Households in Contemporary China. LC 93-31927. (China Research Monographs: No. 43). 1993. pap. 20.00 (*1-55729-042-3*) IEAS.
Bruun, Ole & Kalland, Arne, eds. Asian Perceptions of Nature: A Critical Approach. LC 96-106413. (NIAS Studies in Asian Topics: No. 18). 260p. (C). 1996. text 45.00 (*0-7007-0301-2*, Pub. by Curzon Pr Ltd) UH Pr.
— Asian Perceptions of Nature: A Critical Approach. LC 96-106413. (NIAS Studies in Asian Topics: No. 18). 260p. (C). 1996. pap. text 24.95 (*0-7007-0290-3*, Pub. by Curzon Pr Ltd) UH Pr.
Bruun, Ole & Odgaard, Ole, eds. Mongolia in Transition: Old Patterns, New Challenges. (NIAS Studies in Asian Topics: No. 22). 260p. (C). 1996. text 48.00 (*0-7007-0418-3*, Pub. by Curzon Pr Ltd); pap. text 24.95 (*0-7007-0441-8*, Pub. by Curzon Pr Ltd) UH Pr.
Bruun, Per. Port Engineering Vol. 1: Harbor Planning, Breakwaters & Marine Terminals. 4th ed. 1464p. 1989. 195.00 (*0-87201-843-1*, 1843) Gulf Pub.
Bruun, Ruth D. & Bruun, Bertel. The Human Body. LC 82-5210. (Library of Knowledge). (Illus.). 96p. (J). (gr. 3-8). 1982. lib. bdg. 15.99 (*0-394-94424-0*, Pub. by Random Bks Yng Read) Random.
— The Human Body. LC 82-5210. (Library of Knowledge). (Illus.). 96p. (YA). (gr. 5 up). 1998. pap. 14.00 (*0-394-84424-6*, Pub. by Random Bks Yng Read) Random.
— A Mind of Its Own: Tourette's Syndrome, a Story & a Guide. (Illus.). 192p. (C). 1994. 32.50 (*0-19-506587-5*) OUP.
Bruvelaitis, Lisa. Nearly Noodles. (Annikins Ser.: Vol. 10). (Illus.). 32p. (Orig.). (J). (ps-2). 1990. pap. 0.99 (*1-55037-128-2*, Pub. by Annick) Firefly Bks Ltd.
Bruwelheide, Janis H. The Copyright Primer for Librarians & Educators. 160p. Date not set. pap. 22.00 (*0-614-30869-0*) NEA.
— The Copyright Primer for Librarians & Educators. 2nd ed. LC 95-17840. 160p. 1995. pap. 25.00 (*0-8389-0642-7*, 0642-7-2045) ALA.
Brux. Economic Issues: Theory & Policy. (Introduction to Economics Ser.). 1998. pap., student ed. 14.95 (*0-538-84797-2*) S-W Pub.
— Economic Issues & Policy. LC 98-7412. (Introductory Economics Ser.). 1998. pap. 62.95 (*0-538-84796-4*) S-W Pub.
Bruxvoort, Barbara, jt. ed. see Ingalls, Lee.
Bruya, Brian, tr. from CHI. Confucius Speaks: Words to Live By. LC 95-45157. (Illus.). 176p. 1996. pap. 12.95 (*0-385-48034-2*, Anchor NY) Doubleday.
— Sunzi Speaks: The Art of War. LC 93-40994. (CHI & ENG., Illus.). 144p. 1994. pap. 12.95 (*0-385-47258-7*, Anchor NY) Doubleday.

B

An Asterisk (*) at the beginning of an entry indicates that the title is appearing for the first time.

— Tao Speaks. LC 94-33828. (CHI., Illus.). 112p. 1995. pap. 12.95 (*0-385-47259-5*, Anchor NY) Doubleday.

— Zen Speaks: Shouts of Nothingness. (Illus.). 160p. 1994. pap. 12.95 (*0-385-47257-9*, Anchor NY) Doubleday.

— Zhuangzi Speaks: The Music of Nature. 160p. 1992. pap. 14.95 (*0-691-00882-5*, Pub. by Princeton U Pr) Cal Prin Full Svc.

— Zhuangzi Speaks II: More Music of Nature. LC 96-40071. (Illus.). 144p. 1997. pap. 11.95 (*0-385-48742-8*, Anchor NY) Doubleday.

Bruya, Brian, tr. see Chung, Tsai Chih.

Bruya, Lawrence D., ed. Play Spaces for Children: A New Beginning, Vol. II. (Illus.). 243p. (Orig.). 1988. pap. text 9.50 (*0-88314-391-7*, A3917) AAHPERD.

Bruya, Lawrence D. & Langerdorfer, Stephen J., eds. Where Our Children Play Vol. 1: Elementary School Playground Equipment. (Illus.). 261p. (Orig.). 1988. pap. text 9.50 (*0-88314-390-9*, A3909) AAHPERD.

Bruya, Lawrence D., jt. auth. see Langendorfer, Stephen J.

Bruya, Margaret A., jt. auth. see Lishner, Kris M.

Bruyas, Jacques. Radical Words of the Mohawk Language, with Their Derivatives. LC 10-30198. (Library of American Linguistics: Vol. 10). reprint ed. 42.75 (*0-404-50990-8*) AMS Pr.

Bruyer, Raymond. The Neuropsychology of Face Perception & Facial Expression. 344p. (C). 1986. text 89.95 (*0-89859-602-5*) L Erlbaum Assocs.

Bruyere, Carol. Romantic Michigan: A Guidebook for Couples Seeking Unique Romantic Experiences. (Illus.). v, 326p. 1998. pap. 15.95 (*0-9661313-0-4*) EFP.

Bruyere, Christian, jt. auth. see Inwood, Robert.

Bruyere, La, see La Bruyere.

Bruyere, Rosalyn L. Wheels of Light: Chakras, Auras, & the Healing Energy of the Body. Farrens, Jeanne, ed. 288p. 1994. pap. 14.00 (*0-671-79624-0*, Fireside) S&S Trade Pap.

Bruyere, Susan M. & Golden, Thomas P., eds. The Job Developer's Guide to the Americans with Disabilities Act: Using the ADA to Promote Job Opportunities for People with Disabilities. LC 96-3230. 102p. (Orig.). 1996. pap. 29.00 (*1-883302-05-6*) Trning Res.

Bruyere, Susanne M. & O'Keefe, Janet, eds. Implications of the Americans with Disabilities Act for Psychology. LC 93-39427. 256p. 1994. pap. text 33.95 (*0-8261-8450-2*) Springer Pub.

Bruyn, C. V., tr. see Carling, Finn & Haecker, Theodor.

Bruyn, Clive De, see De Bruyn, Clive.

Bruyn, G. W., jt. auth. see Poser, Charles M.

Bruyn, George W. & Moser, Hugo W. Neurodystrophies & Neurolipidoses. LC 96-51995. (Handbook of Clinical Neurology Ser.). 790p. 1996. 306.25 (*0-444-81285-7*) Elsevier.

Bruyn, George W., jt. auth. see Vinken, Pierre J.

Bruyn, Gerd De, see De Bruyn, Gerd.

Bruyn, J. A Corpus of Rembrandt Paintings, Vol. 1. 1982. lib. bdg. 807.00 (*90-247-2614-X*) Kluwer Academic.

Bruyn, J., et al. Dawn of the Golden Age: Northern Netherlandish Art, 1580-1620. (Illus.). 658p. 1994. 95.00 (*0-300-06016-5*) Yale U Pr.

Bruyn Kops, C. De, see Van Thiel, Pieter J. & Kops, C. De Bruyn.

Bruyn, Lieven Le, see Le Bruyn, Lieven.

Bruyn, Lieven Le, see Van Oystaeyen, Freddy & Le Bruyn, Lieven, eds.

Bruyn, Lucy De, see De Bruyn, Lucy.

Bruyn, Maria De, see De Bruyn, Maria.

Bruyn, Severyn. Quaker Testimonies & Economic Alternatives. LC 80-80915. 35p. 1980. pap. 1.00 (*0-87574-231-9*) Pendle Hill.

Bruyn, Severyn T. Civil Economy: Transforming the Marketplace in the Twenty-First Century. LC 99-46137. (Evolving Values for a Capitalist World Ser.). 328p. 2000. text 65.00 (*0-472-09706-7*, 09706); pap. text 21.95 (*0-472-06706-0*, 06706) U of Mich Pr.

Bruyn, Severyn T., Jr. Communities in Action: A Comparative Study. 1963. pap. 16.95 (*0-8084-0086-X*) NCUP.

Bruyn, Severyn T. The Field of Social Investment. (American Sociological Assn. Rose Monographs). (Illus.). 316p. (C). 1991. pap. text 19.95 (*0-521-40776-1*) Cambridge U Pr.

— A Future for the American Economy: The Social Market. 440p. 1991. 49.50 (*0-8047-1872-5*) Stanford U Pr.

Bruyn, Severyn T. & Meehan, James. Beyond the Market & the State: New Direction. LC 86-30065. (Labor & Social Change Ser.). 272p. 1987. 37.95 (*0-87722-484-6*) Temple U Pr.

Bruyn, Severyn T. & Rayman, Paula, eds. Nonviolent Action & Social Change. 320p. 1980. pap. text 15.95 (*0-8290-0271-5*) Irvington.

Bruyn, Severyn T., jt. auth. see Nicolaou-Smokoviti, Litsa.

Bruyn, Susan. Drawing Out the Dragon. 2nd ed. (Illus.). 30p. 1993. reprint ed. pap. 12.00 (*1-891817-01-9*) Light Works Pr.

— The Light Baby Book: A Little Bit of Me. (Illus.). 12p. 1992. reprint ed. pap. 7.50 (*1-891817-03-5*) Light Works Pr.

— The Reason for Pain: Blues Are Part of the Rainbow. 2nd ed. (Illus.). 32p. 1993. reprint ed. pap. 12.00 (*1-891817-00-0*) Light Works Pr.

— The T. L. C. Manual - For Light Babies. (Illus.). 36p. 1997. reprint ed. spiral bd. 12.00 (*1-891817-02-7*) Light Works Pr.

Bruyne, Bernard De, see Pijls, Nico H.

Bruyne, Bernard De, see Pijls, Nico H. & De Bruyne, Bernard.

Bruyne, Bernard De, see Pijls, Nico H. J. & De Bruyne, Bernard.

Bruyne, Jacques De, see De Bruyne, Jacques.

Bruyne, R. H., et al. Nederlandse Naamlijst Van de Weekdieren (Mollusca) Van Nederland en Belgie. (Illus.). 149p. 1994. pap. 27.00 (*90-73348-33-1*, Pub. by Backhuys Pubs) Balogh.

Bruyne, R. H. De, see De Boer, T. W. & De Bruyne, R. H.

Bruyninckx, Jozef. Phototypography & Graphic Art. LC 74-115394. (Illus.). 155p. reprint ed. 29.50 (*0-911126-03-1*) Perfect Graphic.

Bruynooghe, Maurice & Penjam, Jaan, eds. Programming Language Implementation & Logic Programming: Fifth International Symposium, PLILP '93, Tallinn, Estonia, August 1993, Proceedings. LC 93-11822. (Lecture Notes in Computer Science Ser.: Vol. 714). 1993. 60.00 (*0-387-57186-8*) Spr-Verlag.

Bruynooghe, Maurice & Wirsing, M., eds. Programming Language Implementation & Logic Programming: 4th International Symposium, PLILP '92, Leuven, Belgium, August 26-28, 1-92: Proceedings. LC 92-26380. (Lecture Notes in Computer Science Ser.: Vol. 631). xi, 492p. 1992. 76.95 (*0-387-55844-6*) Spr-Verlag.

Bruzek, Anton & Durrant, Christopher J., eds. Illustrated Glossary for Solar & Solar-Terrestrial Physics. (Astrophysics & Space Science Library: No. 69). 1977. text 112.50 (*90-277-0825-8*) Kluwer Academic.

Bruzelius, Anders & Thelin, Krister, eds. Swedish Code of Judicial Procedure. rev. ed. LC 79-14151. (American Series of Foreign Penal Codes: Vol. 24). xvii, 253p. 1979. 32.50 (*0-8377-0044-2*, Rothman) W S Hein.

Bruzelius, Anders, et al. Concise English-Swedish Glossary of Legal Terms. (ENG & SWE.). 200p. 1980. 89.95 (*0-8288-0408-7*, M9477) Fr & Eur.

Bruzelius, Caroline & Meredith, Jill, eds. The Brummer Collection of Medieval Art: Duke University Museum of Art. LC 90-3300. (Illus.). 318p. 1991. text 74.95 (*0-8223-1055-4*) Duke.

Bruzelius, Caroline, et al. American Art in Private Italian Collections. Blanchard, Paul, tr. (American-Italian Contemporary Art Ser.). (ENG & ITA., Illus.). 100p. (Orig.). 1994. pap. 15.00 (*1-879549-01-8*) Am Acad Rome.

Bruzewicz, Andrew J., jt. auth. see Berry, Brian J. L.

Bruzik, K. S. Phosphoinositides: Chemistry, Biochemistry, & Biomedical Applications, Vol. 718. LC 98-38729. (ASC Symposium Ser.). (Illus.). 312p. 1998. text 115.00 (*0-8412-3628-3*, Pub. by Am Chemical) OUP.

Bruzina, Ronald. Logos & Eidos: The Concept in Phenomenology. LC 70-129299. (Janua Linguarum, Ser. Minor: No. 93). (Orig.). 1971. pap. text 60.00 (*90-279-1542-3*) Mouton.

Bruzina, Ronald, tr. see Fink, Eugen.

Bruzos, Socorro Calvo, see Calvo Bruzos, Socorro.

Bruzzese, Anita. Take This Job & Thrive: 60 Ways to Make Life More Rewarding in Today's New Workplace. LC 99-41897. 160p. 1999. pap. 14.95 (*1-57023-122-2*, Pub. by Impact VA) Natl Bk Netwk.

***Bruzzese, J. Peter.** MCSE Windows 2000 Directory Services Design Exam Prep. LC 00-29490. (Exam Prep Ser.). 700p. 2000. pap. write for info. (*1-57610-668-3*) Coriolis Grp.

***Bruzzi, Stella.** Contemporary Documentary: A Critical Introduction. LC 00-36637. 2000. write for info. (*0-415-18296-4*) Routledge.

Bruzzi, Stella. Undressing Cinema: Clothing & Identity in the Movies. LC 97-7260. (Illus.). 248p. 1997. pap. 19.99 (*0-415-13957-0*) Routledge.

— Undressing Cinema: Clothing & Identity in the Movies. LC 97-7260. (Illus.). 248p. (C). 1997. 75.00 (*0-415-13956-2*) Routledge.

Bruzzi, Zara, jt. auth. see Bromham, A. A.

Bruzzi, Zara A., jt. auth. see Bromham, A. A.

Bruzzo, Maria, tr. see Thomas, Pamela.

Bruzzone. Ingles para Ninos: Learner's Book. (ENG & SPA., Illus.). 80p. (J). 1994. pap. 16.89 (*0-8442-0783-7*) NTC Contemp Pub Co.

***Bruzzone, Agostino G., et al, eds.** 1999 International Conference on Web-Based Modeling & Simulation. (Simulation Ser.: Vol. 31, No. 3). 256p. 1999. 100.00 (*1-56555-156-7*) Soc Computer Sim.

Bruzzone, Catherine. Christmas Activity Book. (Illus.). 24p. (J). (gr. k-5). 1993. pap. 4.95 (*0-8120-1745-5*) Barron.

— French for Children. 80p. (J). (gr. 1-6). 1995. pap. 15.95 (*0-8442-9175-7*, Natl Textbk Co) NTC Contemp Pub Co.

— French for Children. (FRE., Illus.). 80p. (J). (gr. 1-6). 1995. pap. text 29.95 incl. audio (*0-8442-9179-X*, Natl Textbk Co) NTC Contemp Pub Co.

— French Fun: Games, Puzzles, Crosswords, Dot to Dot Wordsearch. (Language Fun Books for Kids Ser.). (FRE., Illus.). 16p. 1995. pap. 5.95 (*0-8442-1376-4*, 13764, Passprt Bks) NTC Contemp Pub Co.

— A Friendship in French & English. (Pen Pals Ser.). (Illus.). 28p. (J). 1998. 14.95 (*0-8442-1375-6*, 13756, Passprt Bks) NTC Contemp Pub Co.

— German for Children. 80p. (J). (gr. 1-6). 1993. pap. 15.95 (*0-8442-9281-8*, Natl Textbk Co) NTC Contemp Pub Co.

— German for Children. (GER., Illus.). 80p. (J). (gr. 1-6). 1995. pap. 29.95 incl. audio (*0-8442-9280-X*, Natl Textbk Co) NTC Contemp Pub Co.

— German Fun: Games, Puzzles, Crosswords, Dot to Dot Wordsearch. (Language Fun Books for Kids Ser.). (GER., Illus.). 16p. (J). 1995. pap. 5.95 (*0-8442-2186-4*, 21864, Passprt Bks) NTC Contemp Pub Co.

— Italian for Children. (ITA.). 64p. (J). (gr. 1-6). 1994. pap. 15.95 (*0-8442-9285-0*, Natl Textbk Co) NTC Contemp Pub Co.

— Italian for Children. (ITA., Illus.). 80p. (J). (gr. 1-6). 1995. teacher ed., student ed. 29.95 incl. audio (*0-8442-9313-X*, Natl Textbk Co) NTC Contemp Pub Co.

— Italian Fun: Games, Puzzles, Crossword, Connect the Dots, Wordsearch. (Illus.). 16p. 1997. pap. 5.95 (*0-8442-8079-8*, 80798) NTC Contemp Pub Co.

— My First Family Tree Book. (Illus.). 24p. (J). (gr. k-3). 1992. pap., per. 3.95 (*0-8249-8546-X*, Ideals Child) Hambleton-Hill.

— Sp-Ingles for Children. (ENG & SPA., Illus.). 80p. (J). 1995. pap. 29.95 incl. audio (*0-8442-0787-X*, 0787X) NTC Contemp Pub Co.

— A Spanish & English Friendship. (Pen Pals Ser.). (Illus.). 28p. (J). (gr. 4-7). 1998. 14.95 (*0-8442-7501-8*, 75018) NTC Contemp Pub Co.

— Spanish for Children. (SPA., Illus.). 129p. (J). 1995. pap. 29.95 incl. audio (*0-8442-9165-X*, Natl Textbk Co) NTC Contemp Pub Co.

— Spanish for Children: For Young Learners. (SPA.). 80p. (J). 1995. pap. 15.95 (*0-8442-9166-8*, Natl Textbk Co) NTC Contemp Pub Co.

— Spanish Fun: Games & Puzzles, Cutting, Sticking & Colouring. (SPA., Illus.). 16p. 1995. pap. 5.95 (*0-8442-7644-8*, 76448, Passprt Bks) NTC Contemp Pub Co.

***Bruzzone, Catherine & Beaton, Clare.** Action French! A Lively Activity Starter Pack for Adults & Children. LC 00-37456. (Illus.). 20p. (ps-7). 2000. pap. 14.95 incl. audio (*0-658-00448-4*, 004484) NTC Contemp Pub Co.

— Action Spanish! A Lively Activity Starter Pack for Adults & Children. LC 00-37352. (ENG & SPA., Illus.). 20p. (ps-7). 2000. pap. 14.95 incl. audio (*0-658-00443-3*, 004433) NTC Contemp Pub Co.

Bruzzone, Catherine & Morton, Lone. My Friends. (Illus.). 24p. (Orig.). (J). (gr. k-3). 1994. pap., per. 3.95 (*0-8249-8650-4*, Ideals Child) Hambleton-Hill.

***Bruzzone, Roberto & Giaume, Christian, eds.** Connexin Methods & Protocols. LC 99-87338. (Methods in Molecular Biology Ser.: Vol. 154). (Illus.). 453p. 2000. 125.00 (*0-89603-658-8*) Humana.

Brwon, F., jt. ed. see Horaud, F.

Bry, Brenna Hafer, jt. auth. see Boyd-Franklin, Nancy.

Bry, Doris, jt. ed. see Callaway, Nicholas.

Bry, Francois, et al, eds. Deductive & Object-Oriented Databases: Proceedings, 5th International Conference, DOOD'97, Montreux, Switzerland, December 8-11, 1997, Vol. 134. LC 97-39142. (Lecture Notes in Computer Science Ser.: Vol. 1341). xiv, 430p. 1997. pap. 67.00 (*3-540-63792-3*) Spr-Verlag.

Bry, Gerhard. The Average Workweek As an Economic Indicator. 6.00 (*0-405-18756-4*, 16470) Ayer.

— The Average Workweek As an Economic Indicator. (Occasional Papers: No. 69). 127p. 1959. reprint ed. 33.10 (*0-87014-383-2*) Natl Bur Econ Res.

Bry, Gerhard & Boschan, Charlotte. Cyclical Analysis of Time Series: Selected Procedures & Computer Programs. LC 70-123122. 230p. reprint ed. pap. 71.30 (*0-8357-7569-0*, 205689000096) Bks Demand.

— Cyclical Anaylsis of Time Series: Selected Procedures & Computer Programs. (Technical Papers: No. 20). (Illus.). 230p. 1971. text 59.80 (*0-87014-223-2*) Natl Bur Econ Res.

— Wages in Germany, 1871-1945. (General Ser.: No. 68). 512p. 1975. reprint ed. 133.20 (*0-87014-067-1*) Ayer.

Bryan. Canada in the New Global Economy: Problems & Policies. 3rd ed. 360p. (C). 1993. pap. write for info. (*0-471-64096-4*) Wiley.

— The History of Health & Medicine. (Science Discovery Ser.). 48p. (J). (gr. 6-7). 1996. lib. bdg. 24.26 (*0-8172-4559-6*) Raintree Steck-V.

— Skeletal Anatomy. 3rd ed. 1996. pap. text 44.00 (*0-443-05150-X*, B2220) Church.

Bryan & Potter, eds. Effect of Load Variables on Fatigue Crack Initiation & Propagation - STP 714. 242p. 1980. 27.00 (*0-8031-0720-X*, STP714) ASTM.

Bryan & Tocci. Digital Systems. 238p. 1997. pap. text 16.96 (*0-536-00702-0*) Pearson Custom.

Bryan, Alan L. & Gruhn, Ruth. Brazilian Studies. 168p. 1993. pap. 33.00 (*0-912933-10-0*) Ctr Study First Am.

Bryan, Alex, et al. The Ride of Your Life: Being a Young Adventist Isn't for the Faint of Heart. LC 96-46654. (YA). 1997. 10.99 (*0-8280-1066-8*) Review & Herald.

Bryan, Anthony T., ed. The Caribbean: New Dynamics in Trade & Political Economy. LC 94-47502. 264p. (C). 1995. pap. 25.95 (*1-56000-751-6*, Pub. by U Miami N-S Ctr) L Rienner.

Bryan, Anthony T. & Serbin, Andres, eds. Distant Cousins: The Caribbean-Latin American Relationship. LC 96-28718. 133p. (C). 1996. pap. 23.95 (*1-57454-003-3*, Pub. by U Miami N-S Ctr) L Rienner.

Bryan, Ashley. All Night, All Day: A Child's First Book of African-American Spirituals. LC 90-753145. (Illus.). 48p. (J). (ps-4). 1991. text, lib. bdg. 16.00 (*0-689-31662-3*) Atheneum Yung Read.

— Ashley Bryan Folktale Anthology. LC 97-77743. 208p. (YA). (gr. 4). 1998. 22.00 (*0-689-82076-3*) S&S Childrens.

— Beat the Story-Drum, Pum-Pum. LC 86-20598. (Illus.). 80p. (J). (gr. 4-6). 1987. reprint ed. mass mkt. 8.95 (*0-689-71107-7*) Aladdin.

— The Cat's Purr. LC 84-21534. (Illus.). 48p. (J). (ps-3). 1985. 14.00 (*0-689-31086-2*) Atheneum Yung Read.

— Lion & the Ostrich Chicks. (Illus.). 96p. (J). (gr. 2-6). 1996. mass mkt. 6.95 (*0-689-80713-9*) S&S Childrens.

— The Lion & the Ostrich Chicks & Other African Folk Tales. LC 86-3349. 1996. 12.05 (*0-606-09557-8*, Pub. by Turtleback) Demco.

— The Night Has Ears: African Proverbs. LC 98-48772. (Illus.). 32p. (J). (gr. 2-4). 1999. 16.00 (*0-689-82427-0*) Atheneum Yung Read.

— The Ox of the Wonderful Horns: And Other African Folktales. LC 75-154749. (Illus.). 48p. (J). (gr. k-4). 1993. 14.95 (*0-689-31799-9*) Atheneum Yung Read.

— Sing to the Sun. LC 91-38359. (Trophy Picture Bk.). (Illus.). 32p. (J). (gr. 2 up). 1996. pap. 6.95 (*0-06-443437-0*, HarpTrophy) HarpC Child Bks.

Bryan, Ashley. Sing to the Sun. 1992. 10.15 (*0-606-08606-4*, Pub. by Turtleback) Demco.

Bryan, Ashley. The Story of Lightning & Thunder. LC 92-40509. (Illus.). 32p. (J). (ps-3). 1993. 15.00 (*0-689-31836-7*) Atheneum Yung Read.

— The Story of Lightning & Thunder. (Illus.). 32p. (J). 1999. pap. 5.99 (*0-689-82450-5*) S&S Childrens.

— Turtle Knows Your Name. LC 89-2. (Illus.). 32p. (J). (ps-2). 1989. 14.95 (*0-689-31578-3*) Atheneum Yung Read.

— Turtle Knows Your Name. (J). 1993. 10.15 (*0-606-05673-4*, Pub. by Turtleback) Demco.

Bryan, Ashley, ed. Ashley Bryan's ABC of African American Poetry. LC 96-25148. 32p. (J). 1997. 16.00 (*0-689-81209-4*) S&S Childrens.

***Bryan, Ashley.** Salting the Ocean: 100 Poems by Young Poets. LC 99-30590. 128p. (YA). 2000. 16.95 (*0-688-16193-6*, Grenwillow Bks) HarpC Child Bks.

Bryan, Ashley. What a Morning! The Christmas Story in Black Spirituals. LC 87-750130. 32p. (J). 1987. 14.95 (*0-689-50422-5*) McElderry Bks.

Bryan, Ashley. Lion & the Ostrich Chicks & Other African Folk Tales. large type ed. 1993. 25.00 (*0-614-09836-X*, L-34117-00) Am Printing Hse.

— Turtle Knows Your Name. LC 92-33553. 32p. (J). (ps-3). 1993. reprint ed. mass mkt. 4.95 (*0-689-71728-8*) Aladdin.

Bryan, Ashley & Langstaff, John M. Climbing Jacob's Ladder: Heroes of the Bible in African-American Spirituals. LC 90-27297. (Illus.). 32p. (J). 1991. 14.95 (*0-689-50494-2*) McElderry Bks.

Bryan, Ashley, ed. see Dunbar, Paul Laurence.

Bryan, Barbara. From Collards to Caviar: The Alabama Cookbook. 342p. 1992. spiral bd. 20.50 (*0-926291-03-3*) Greenberry Pub.

Bryan, Betsy M. The Reign of Thutmose IV. LC 90-27688. 416p. 1991. pap. 129.00 (*0-7837-7459-1*, 204918100010) Bks Demand.

Bryan, Betsy M. & Cohen, Judith. Tu Puedes Ser una Egiptologa. Yanez, Juan, tr. from ENG. (SPA., Illus.). 40p. (J). (gr. 4-7). 1993. pap. 7.00 (*1-880599-11-2*) Cascade Pass.

— You Can Be a Woman Egyptologist. rev. ed. LC 99-51887. (Illus.). 40p. (J). (gr. 3-6). 1993. reprint ed. pap. 7.00 (*1-880599-10-4*) Cascade Pass.

***Bryan, Betsy M. & Cohen, Judith Love.** You Can Be a Woman Egyptologist. rev. ed. Martin, Janice, ed. LC 99-51887. (Illus.). 40p. (J). (gr. 3-6). 1999. reprint ed. 13.95 (*1-880599-45-7*) Cascade Pass.

Bryan, Bill, jt. auth. see Towns, Elmer L.

Bryan, Brooks A. Line upon Line. LC 98-94863. 1999. write for info. (*0-7392-0058-5*) Morris Pubng.

Bryan-Brown, Christopher W. & Ayres, Stephen M., eds. New Horizons II: Oxygen Transport & Utilization. 1987. write for info. (*0-318-61520-7*) SCCM Fullerton.

Bryan, Bruce. Archeological Explorations on San Nicolas Island. (Illus.). 160p. 1970. 12.50 (*0-916561-07-0*) Southwest Mus.

Bryan, C. D. Close Encounters of the Fourth Kind: A Reporter's Notebook on Alien Abduction, UFOs & the Conference at MIT. 496p. 1996. pap. 13.95 (*0-14-019527-0*, Penguin Bks) Viking Penguin.

— The National Air & Space Museum. 2nd rev. ed. (Illus.). 1988. 75.00 (*0-8109-1380-1*) Abrams.

— The National Geographic Society: 100 Years of Adventure & Discovery. (Illus.). 480p. 1990. 55.00 (*0-8109-1376-3*) Abrams.

— The National Geographic Society: 100 Years of Adventure & Discovery. rev. enl. ed. LC 97-10714. (Illus.). 528p. 1997. 49.50 (*0-8109-3696-8*, Pub. by Abrams) Time Warner.

Bryan, Charles S. A Most Satisfactory Man: The Story of Theodore Brevard Hayne, Last Martyr of Yellow Fever. LC 95-50693. (Illus.). 220p. 1996. text 19.95 (*1-57003-123-1*) U of SC Pr.

— Osler: Inspirations from a Great Physician. LC 96-30172. (Illus.). 280p. (C). 1997. 39.95 (*0-19-511251-2*) OUP.

Bryan, Christopher. A Preface to Mark: Notes on the Gospel in Its Literary & Cultural Settings. 232p. 1997. reprint ed. pap. text 18.95 (*0-19-511567-8*) OUP.

Bryan, Clarice. Driving to Nirvana: A Woman's Path for Drivers Without Cellular Phones. LC 97-7259. (Illus.). 96p. 1997. pap. 9.95 (*0-89254-037-0*) Nicolas-Hays.

***Bryan, Clarice.** Expect Nothing: A Zen Guide. 2001. pap. 16.95 (*1-58290-039-6*, Pub. by Jrny Editions) Tuttle Pubng.

Bryan, Clark W. The Book of Berkshire: Describing & Illustrating Its Hills & Homes. LC 93-85392. (Great American Guidebook Ser.). (Illus.). 304p. 1993. reprint ed. pap. 24.95 (*1-884022-00-6*) Past Perfect.

Bryan, Claude G., jt. auth. see Parker, Gilbert.

Bryan, Coleman J., et al, eds. Alternatives to Chlorofluorocarbon Fluids in the Cleaning of Oxygen & Aerospace Systems & Components, STP 1181: STP 1181. LC 93-5755. (Illus.). 160p. 1993. text 43.00 (*0-8031-1496-6*, STP1181) ASTM.

Bryan, Colgan. Prime Cuts Classic Rock Guitar: Easy Tab Deluxe. (Prime Cuts Ser.). 128p. (Orig.). 1997. pap. 16.95 (*1-57623-904-7*, 0025B) Wrner Bros.

Bryan, Colgan, ed. Doobie Brothers: The Guitar Collection. 88p. (Orig.). 1996. pap. text 19.95 (*0-89724-830-9*, PG9551) Wrner Bros.

— Eagles Vol. 1: Acoustic Classics. 168p. (Orig.). (YA). 1996. pap. text 19.95 (*1-57623-367-7*, PG9615) Wrner Bros.

— Eagles Vol. 2: Acoustic Classics. 168p. (Orig.). (YA). 1996. pap. text 19.95 (*1-57623-366-9*, PG9616) Wrner Bros.

An Asterisk (*) at the beginning of an entry indicates that the title is appearing for the first time.

— The Essential Industrial Guitar. (Essential Ser.). 112p. (Orig.). 1997. pap. text 14.95 (*1-57623-964-0*, 0003B) Wrner Bros.
— The Essential Progressive Rock Guitar. 144p. (Orig.). (YA). 1996. pap. text 14.95 (*1-57623-472-X*, GF9608) Wrner Bros.
— The Essential Southern Rock Guitar. 176p. 1997. pap. 14.95 (*0-7692-0059-1*, GF9707) Wrner Bros.
— John Petrucci: Rock Discipline. 84p. (Orig.). 1996. pap. text 24.95 (*1-57623-474-6*, REHBK010CD) Wrner Bros.
— Neil Young: Acoustic Classics. 120p. (Orig.). (YA). 1996. pap. text 19.95 (*1-57623-673-0*, PG9618) Wrner Bros.
— The New Best of Collective Soul for Guitar. 64p. (Orig.). 1996. pap. text 12.95 (*1-57623-551-3*, PG9640) Wrner Bros.
— The New Best of Gin Blossoms. 64p. (Orig.). (YA). 1996. pap. text 12.95 (*1-57623-526-2*, PG9639) Wrner Bros.
— The New Best of James Taylor for Guitar. (New Best of...Ser.). 64p. (Orig.). 1997. pap. text 12.95 (*0-7692-0007-9*) Wrner Bros.
— The New Best of Neil Young for Guitar. (Best of...Ser.). 40p. (Orig.). 1996. pap. 12.95 (*1-57623-447-9*, PG9620) Wrner Bros.
— The New Best of Parteet for Guitars: Guitar Personality Book. (New Best of Ser.). 84p. (Orig.). 1997. pap. 12.95 (*1-57623-960-8*, 0052B) Wrner Bros.
— New York Underground. 112p. (Orig.). 1997. pap. text 19.95 (*1-57623-926-8*) Wrner Bros.
— Prime Cuts Acoustic Rock Guitar EZ: Easy Tab Deluxe. (Prime Cuts Ser.). 128p. (Orig.). 1997. pap. 16.95 (*1-57623-905-5*, 0026B) Wrner Bros.
— Prime Cuts Alternative Rock Gtr. Easy Tab Deluxe. (Prime Cuts Ser.). 128p. (Orig.). 1997. pap. 16.95 (*1-57623-906-3*, 0027B) Wrner Bros.
— Van Halen, Vols. I & II. 158p. (Orig.). 1996. pap. 21.95 (*1-57623-430-4*, PG9629) Wrner Bros.
— Van Halen: 5150 & OU812. 188p. (Orig.). (YA). 1996. pap. text 24.95 (*1-57623-706-0*, PG9668) Wrner Bros.
— Vince Gill. (Guitar Anthology Ser.). 124p. (Orig.). 1996. pap. text 22.95 (*1-57623-588-2*, PG9646) Wrner Bros.
Bryan, Colgan & Stan, Aaron, eds. The New Best of Smashing Pumpkins. LC 97-3. (New Best of Ser.). 72p. (Orig.). 1997. pap. text 12.95 (*1-57623-756-7*, PG9703) Wrner Bros.
Bryan, Colgan & Stang, Aaron, eds. Dream Theater: Awake. 160p. (Orig.). (YA). 1995. pap. text 24.95 (*0-89724-608-X*, PG9505) Wrner Bros.
— The Herb Ellis Jazz Guitar Method: All the Shapes You Are. 48p. (Orig.). 1996. pap. text 19.95 (*1-57623-342-1*, EL9531CD) Wrner Bros.
— The Herb Ellis Jazz Guitar Method: Rhythm Shapes. 48p. (Orig.). 1996. pap. text 19.95 (*1-57623-341-3*, EL9530CD) Wrner Bros.
Bryan, Colgan, jt. ed. see Delisa, Jeannette.
Bryan, Colgan, jt. ed. see DeLisa, Jeannette.
Bryan, Colgan, ed. see Gross, David.
Bryan, Colgan, jt. ed. see Lefferts, Michael.
Bryan, Colgan, jt. ed. see Stang, Aaron.
Bryan, Cyril. Ancient Egyptian Medicine: The Papyrus Ebers. 208p. 1991. pap. 25.00 (*0-89005-004-X*) Ares.
— The Ebers Papyrus: Oldest Medical Book in the World. (African Studies). reprint ed. 25.00 (*0-938818-27-9*) ECA Assoc.
Bryan, David. Cosmos, Chaos & the Kosher Mentality. LC 96-143258. (Journal for the Study of the Pseudepigrapha Supplement Ser.: No. 12). 343p. 1995. 85.00 (*1-85075-536-1*, Pub. by Sheffield Acad) CUP Services.
***Bryan-Day, Lisa.** Sketches II of Carmel by the Sea Vol. 2: A Literary Map in a Book. (Sketches Collection). (Illus.). 16p. 2000. pap. 30.00 (*0-9655874-1-X*) Sketches-Wildreach.
Bryan-Day, Lisa & Day, Ashley M. Sketches of Carmel by the Sea: An Artistic Souvenir Guide with Maps & Personal Journal. Livingstone, John, ed. (Sketches Collection: Vol. SKI). (Illus.). 26p. 1997. 27.00 (*0-9655874-0-1*) Sketches-Wildreach.
Bryan, Denver, photos by. 101 Uses for a Golden. LC 99-10839. ("Just Pets" Ser.). (Illus.). 112p. 1999. 14.95 (*1-57223-211-0*, 2110) Willow Creek Pr.
***Bryan, Denver & Thomas, E. Donnall, Jr.** Labs Afield. (Illus.). 160p. 2000. 29.50 (*1-57223-389-3*) Willow Creek Pr.
***Bryan, Dick & Rafferty, Michael.** The Global Economy in Australia: Global Integration & National Economic Policy. LC 99-180756. 304p. 1999. pap. 35.00 (*1-86448-745-3*, Pub. by Allen & Unwin Pty) Paul & Co Pubs.
***Bryan, Dominic.** Orange Parades: The Politics of Ritual, Tradition & Control. (Anthropology, Culture & Society Ser.). 2000. pap. 22.50 (*0-7453-1413-9*) Pluto GBR.
— Orange Parades: The Politics of Ritual, Tradition & Control. LC 00-8816. (Anthropology, Culture & Society Ser.). 2000. write for info. (*0-7453-1418-X*, Pub. by Pluto GBR) Stylus Pub VA.
Bryan, E. A., jt. auth. see Bryan, L. A.
Bryan, Edwin H., Jr. Stars over Hawaii. (Illus.). 1977. reprint ed. pap. 7.95 (*0-912180-30-7*) Petroglyph.
Bryan, Edwin H., Jr., et al. Insects of Hawaii, Johnston Island, & Wake Island. (BMB Ser.: No. 31). 1969. reprint ed. 25.00 (*0-527-02134-2*) Periodicals Srv.
Bryan, Elizabeth. Twins, Triplets, & More: From Pre-Birth Through High School - What Every Parent Needs to Know When Raising Two or More. 160p. 1992. text 19.95 (*0-312-07876-5*) St Martin.
Bryan, Elizabeth J. Collaborative Meaning in Medieval Scribal Culture: The Otho Lazamon. LC 99-27014. (Editorial Theory & Literary Criticism Ser.). (Illus.). 264p. 1999. text 49.50 (*0-472-10949-9*, 10949) U of Mich Pr.
Bryan, Eric A., jt. auth. see Bryan, Luis A.
Bryan, Eugene L. The Best Possible Sawmill: Guidebook for the High-Tech Journey Ahead. (Illus.). 232p. 1996. 45.00 (*0-87930-466-9*, 454) Miller Freeman.
Bryan, Ferald J. Henry Grady or Tom Watson? The Rhetorical Struggle for the New South, 1880-1890. LC 94-25517. 167p. 1994. pap. text 14.00 (*0-86554-439-5*, MUP-H350) Mercer Univ Pr.
Bryan, Ford R. Beyond the Model T: The Other Ventures of Henry Ford. LC 89-27663. (Illus.). 205p. reprint ed. pap. 63.60 (*0-608-06274-X*, 206660300008) Bks Demand.
— Beyond the Model T: The Other Ventures of Henry Ford. rev. ed. LC 96-47199. (Great Lakes Bks.). (Illus.). 248p. 1997. pap. 25.95 (*0-8143-2682-X*); text 39.95 (*0-8143-2704-4*) Wayne St U Pr.
— The Fords of Dearborn: An Illustrated History. LC 87-81816. (Illus.). 286p. 1989. 21.95 (*0-8187-0102-1*) Wayne St U Pr.
— Henry's Attic: Some Fascinating Gifts to Henry Ford & His Museum. LC 95-40243. (Illus.). 432p. 1995. pap. 24.95 (*0-8143-2642-0*) Wayne St U Pr.
— Henry's Lieutenants. LC 92-31789. (Great Lakes Bks.). (Illus.). 324p. (C). 1993. 26.95 (*0-8143-2428-2*, Great Lks Bks) Wayne St U Pr.
Bryan, Frank & Mares, Bill. Out! The Vermont Secession Book. LC 87-62288. (Illus.). 176p. (Orig.). 1987. pap. 8.95 (*0-933050-52-6*) New Eng Pr VT.
— Real Vermonters Address Book. (Illus.). 112p. 1984. spiral bd. 6.95 (*0-933050-24-0*) New Eng Pr VT.
Bryan, Frank & McLaughry, John. The Vermont Papers: Recreating Democracy on a Human Scale. LC 89-569. 308p. 1990. reprint ed. pap. 12.95 (*0-930031-31-8*) Chelsea Green Pub.
Bryan, Frank, jt. auth. see Mares, Bill.
Bryan, Frank L., jt. ed. see Riemann, Hans.
Bryan, Frank M. Politics in States America: People, Parties, & Policy. (Special Studies). 320p. (Orig.). (C). 1981. text 41.50 (*0-89158-561-3*); pap. text 14.90 (*0-89158-984-8*) Westview.
— Yankee Politics in Rural Vermont. LC 73-78913. 334p. reprint ed. pap. 103.60 (*0-7837-0372-4*, 204069200018) Bks Demand.
Bryan, G. McLeod. Dissenter in the Baptist Southland: Fifty Years in the Career of William Wallace Finlator. LC 85-13752. (Illus.). xi, 198p. 1985. text 19.95 (*0-86554-176-0*, MUP-H166) Mercer Univ Pr.
Bryan, Gayle, jt. auth. see Reeves, Diane Lindsey.
Bryan, Geoffrey, jt. auth. see Bryan, Martha.
Bryan, George. The Great American Myth: The True Story of Lincoln's Murder. (Illus.). xxxii, 436p. 1995. reprint ed. pap. 20.00 (*0-9625290-3-6*) Abraham Lincoln.
— Law of Petroleum & Natural Gas with Forms. xvi, 522p. 1983. reprint ed. 55.00 (*0-8377-0335-2*, Rothman) W S Hein.
Bryan, George, jt. ed. see Mieder, Wolfgang.
Bryan, George B. American Theatrical Regulation, 1607-1900: Conspectus & Texts. LC 93-42485. 447p. 1993. 55.00 (*0-8108-2825-1*) Scarecrow.
— Ethel Merman: A Bio-Bibliography, 27. LC 92-6428. (Bio-Bibliographies in the Performing Arts Ser.: No. 27). 320p. 1992. lib. bdg. 55.00 (*0-313-27975-6*, BEX, Greenwood Pr) Greenwood.
— A Historical Who's Who of Vermont Theatre. (Occasional Papers: No. 13). 77p. (Orig.). 1991. pap. text 7.50 (*0-944277-21-7*, B79) U VT Ctr Rsch VT.
— An Ibsen Companion: A Dictionary-Guide to the Life, Works & Critical Reception of Henrik Ibsen. LC 83-18551. 437p. 1984. lib. bdg. 75.00 (*0-313-23506-6*, BIB/, Greenwood Pr) Greenwood.
— The Light of Other Days: The First Twenty Years of the Center for Research on Vermont. (Occasional Papers: No. 18). (Illus.). 108p. 1995. pap. text 8.50 (*0-944277-33-0*) U VT Ctr Rsch VT.
— Stage Deaths: A Biographical Guide to International Theatrical Obituaries, 1850-1990, Vol. 1. LC 91-10304. (Bibliographies & Indexes in the Performing Arts Ser.: Vol. 9). 704p. 1991. lib. bdg. 195.00 (*0-313-28037-1*, Greenwood Pr) Greenwood.
— Stage Deaths: A Biographical Guide to International Theatrical Obituaries, 1850-1990, Vol. 2. LC 91-10304. (Bibliographies & Indexes in the Performing Arts Ser.: Vol. 9). 688p. 1991. lib. bdg. 195.00 (*0-313-28038-X*, Greenwood Pr) Greenwood.
— Stage Lives: A Bibliography & an Index to Theatrical Biographies in English, 2. LC 84-19833. (Bibliographies & Indexes in the Performing Arts Ser.: No. 2). 368p. 1985. lib. bdg. 79.50 (*0-313-24577-0*, BSV/, Greenwood Pr) Greenwood.
Bryan, George B., compiled by. Stage Deaths: A Biographical Guide to International Theatrical Obituaries, 1850 to 1990, 9. LC 91-10304. (Bibliographies & Indexes in the Performing Arts Ser.: No. 9). 1376p. 1991. lib. bdg. 195.00 (*0-313-27593-9*, BDH/, Greenwood Pr) Greenwood.
Bryan, George B., ed. Focus: Vermont, 1975. 24p. 1975. pap. text 5.00 (*0-944277-00-4*) U VT Ctr Rsch VT.
Bryan, George B. & Mieder, Wolfgang, compiled by. The Proverbial Eugene O'Neill: An Index to Proverbs in the Works of Eugene Gladstone O'Neill, 21. LC 95-36073. (Bibliographies & Indexes in American Literature Ser.: No. 21). 376p. 1995. lib. bdg. 79.50 (*0-313-29794-0*, Greenwood Pr) Greenwood.
Bryan, George B. & Mieder, Wolfgang, eds. The Proverbial Bernard Shaw: An Index to the Proverbs in the Works of George Bernard Shaw, 41. LC 93-41215. (Bibliographies & Indexes in World Literature Ser.: No. 41). 304p. 1994. lib. bdg. 75.00 (*0-313-29218-3*, Greenwood Pr) Greenwood.
Bryan, George B., jt. ed. see Mieder, Wolfgang.
Bryan, George M. & Heirtzler, James R. Ocean Margin Drilling Program Atlases, Vol. 5. (Regional Atlas Ser.). 1984. pap. 295.00 (*0-86720-255-6*) Jones & Bartlett.
Bryan, George S. The Great American Myth: The True Story of Lincoln's Murder. (Illus.). xxxii, 436p. 1990. reprint ed. 40.00 (*0-9625290-0-1*) Abraham Lincoln.
Bryan, George T., ed. Nitrofurans: Chemistry, Metabolism, Mutagenesis, & Carcinogenesis. fac. ed. LC 77-72824. (Carcinogenesis - A Comprehensive Survey Ser.: No. 4). 248p. pap. 76.90 (*0-7837-7171-1*, 204712600005) Bks Demand.
Bryan, George T. & Cohen, Samuel M., eds. The Pathology of Bladder Cancer, 2 Vols., Vol. I. 248p. 1983. 118.00 (*0-8493-6225-3*, RD755, CRC Reprint) Franklin.
— The Pathology of Bladder Cancer, 2 Vols., Vol. II. 256p. 1983. 141.00 (*0-8493-6226-1*, CRC Reprint) Franklin.
Bryan, George T., jt. ed. see Anderson, M. Brownwell.
Bryan, Glenda J. Diagnostic Radiography: A Concise Practical Manual. 4th ed. LC 87-8072. (Illus.) 500p. 1987. pap. text 46.00 (*0-443-02992-X*) Church.
— Johnson & Kennedy Radiographic Skeletal Anatomy. 2nd ed. LC 82-12971. (Illus.). 302p. 1992. text 59.95 (*0-443-01627-5*) Church.
Bryan, Gordon, compiled by. Scottish Nationalism & Cultural Identity in the Twentieth Century: An Annotated Bibliography of Secondary Sources, 1. LC 84-4667. (Bibliographies & Indexes in Law & Political Science Ser.: No. 1). (Illus.). 180p. 1984. lib. bdg. 55.00 (*0-313-23998-3*, BNA/) Greenwood.
Bryan, Helen. Planning Applications & Appeals. LC 96-32860. 192p. 1997. pap. text 42.95 (*0-7506-2792-1*) Buttrwrth-Heinemann.
Bryan, Howard. The Incredible Elfego Baca. LC 93-5332. (Illus.). 112p. 1993. 22.95 (*0-940666-34-0*); pap. 12.95 (*0-940666-37-5*) Clear Light.
— Robbers, Rogues & Ruffians: True Tales of the Wild West. LC 91-72481. (Illus.). 332p. 1991. 22.95 (*0-940666-04-9*); pap. 14.95 (*0-940666-23-5*) Clear Light.
— Tours for All Seasons. (Illus.). 128p. (Orig.). 1986. reprint ed. pap. 4.95 (*0-910467-04-8*) Heritage Assocs.
— True Tales of the American Southwest. LC 96-30706. (Illus.). 286p. 1996. 24.95 (*0-940666-95-2*); pap. 14.95 (*0-940666-96-0*) Clear Light.
— Wildest of the Wild West: True Tales of a Frontier Town on the Santa Fe Trail. LC 91-72480. (Illus.). 288p. 1991. reprint ed. pap. 14.95 (*0-940666-13-8*) Clear Light.
— Wildest of the Wild West: True Tales of New Mexico on the Old Santa Fe Trail. LC 91-71799. 288p. 1991. 24.95 (*0-940666-08-1*) Clear Light.
Bryan, Ian. Interrogation & Confession: A Study of Progress, Process & Practice. LC 97-19616. (Illus.). 352p. 1997. text 87.95 (*1-85521-875-5*, Pub. by Dartmth Pub) Ashgate Pub Co.
Bryan, J., jt. auth. see Halsey, William.
Bryan, J. W. The Development of the English Law of Conspiracy. LC 72-77737. (Law, Politics & History Ser.). 1970. reprint ed. lib. bdg. 25.00 (*0-306-71375-6*) Da Capo.
Bryan, James. The Fine Art of Seduction: A Step-By-Step Guide to Attract, Meet, & Make Love with More Women. LC 86-80826. (Illus.). 138p. (Orig.). 1986. pap. 14.95 (*0-9616219-5-8*) Gallant Pub CA.
***Bryan, James H.** Emra Guide to Antibiotic Use in the Emergency Department 2000. 6th ed. (Illus.). 94p. 1999. pap. text 15.95 (*0-07-136067-0*) McGraw-Hill Prof.
Bryan, James H. The Great Composers Fakebook. (Library Of...). 96p. 1996. pap. 12.95 (*0-8256-1434-1*, AM 92229) Music Sales.
Bryan, James P. & Hanak, Walter K. Texas in Maps. (Illus.). 40p. 1961. pap. 10.00 (*0-87959-126-9*) U of Tex H Ransom Ctr.
Bryan, James T., Jr., jt. auth. see Thompson, Gregg D.
***Bryan, James Wallace.** The Development of the English Law of Conspiracy. 161p. 1999. reprint ed. 50.00 (*1-56169-556-4*) Gaunt.
Bryan, Jane. Wales in the 21st Century. text 45.00 (*0-312-23306-X*) St Martin.
Bryan, Janine, jt. auth. see Griffiths, John.
***Bryan, Jenny.** Adolescence. LC 99-17026. (Health & Fitness Ser.). 48p. (J). 2000. lib. bdg. 25.69 (*0-7398-1346-3*) Raintree Steck-V.
Bryan, Jenny. Breathing: The Respiratory System. LC 92-36353. (Body Talk Ser.). (Illus.). 48p. (YA). (gr. 5 up). 1993. lib. bdg. 13.95 (*0-87518-563-0*, Dillon Silver Burdett) Silver Burdett Pr.
— Digestion: The Digestive System. LC 92-35052. (Body Talk Ser.). (Illus.). 48p. (YA). (gr. 5 up). 1993. lib. bdg. 13.95 (*0-87518-564-9*, Dillon Silver Burdett) Silver Burdett Pr.
***Bryan, Jenny.** Eating Disorders. LC 99-23147. (Talking Points Ser.). 64p. 1999. 27.12 (*0-8172-5321-7*) Raintree Steck-V.
Bryan, Jenny. Genetic Engineering. (Global Issues Ser.). (Illus.). 64p. (J). (gr. 7-9). 1995. lib. bdg. 24.26 (*1-56847-268-4*) Raintree Steck-V.
— Genetic Engineering. (Global Issues Ser.). (Illus.). 64p. (J). (gr. 6-7). 1997. lib. bdg. 25.69 (*0-8172-4860-9*) Raintree Steck-V.
***Bryan, Jenny.** Living with Diabetes. LC 98-20105. (Living with... Ser.). (Illus.). 32p. (J). (gr. 1-5). 1999. lib. bdg. 22.83 (*0-8172-5575-3*) Raintree Steck-V.
Bryan, Jenny. Living with Down Syndrome. LC 98-29145. 32 p. 1999. write for info. (*0-8172-5569-9*) Raintree Steck-V.
***Bryan, Jenny.** Living with Down Syndrome. (Living with... Ser.). 32p. (J). 1999. lib. bdg. 22.83 (*0-8172-5577-X*) Raintree Steck-V.
Bryan, Jenny. Mind & Matter. LC 93-71714. (Body Talk Ser.). (Illus.). 48p. (YA). (gr. 5 up). 1993. lib. bdg. 13.95 (*0-87518-588-6*, Dillon Silver Burdett) Silver Burdett Pr.
— Movement: The Muscular & Skeletal System. LC 92-35092. (Body Talk Ser.). (Illus.). 48p. (YA). (gr. 5 up). 1993. lib. bdg. 13.95 (*0-87518-565-7*, Dillon Silver Burdett) Silver Burdett Pr.
— The Pulse of Life: The Circulatory System. LC 92-36410. (Body Talk Ser.). (Illus.). 48p. (J). (gr. 5 up). 1993. lib. bdg. 13.95 (*0-87518-566-5*, Dillon Silver Burdett) Silver Burdett Pr.
— Reproduction. LC 93-2038. (Body Talk Ser.). (Illus.). 48p. (YA). (gr. 5 up). 1993. lib. bdg. 13.95 (*0-87518-589-4*, Dillon Silver Burdett) Silver Burdett Pr.
— Smell, Taste & Touch. (Body Talk Ser.). (Illus.). 48p. (J). (gr. 5). 1994. lib. bdg. 13.95 (*0-87518-590-8*, Dillon Silver Burdett) Silver Burdett Pr.
— Sound & Vision. LC 93-37306. (Body Talk Ser.). (Illus.). 48p. (J). (gr. 5). 1994. lib. bdg. 13.95 (*0-87518-591-6*, Dillon Silver Burdett) Silver Burdett Pr.
— What's Wrong with Me? (Illus.). 32p. (J). 1994. lib. bdg. 5.00 (*1-56847-199-8*) Raintree Steck-V.
Bryan, John. I Bought My First Sixpack When I Was Thirty-Five. LC 89-36836. 146p. (Orig.). 1989. pap. 10.00 (*0-910309-54-X*, 5029) Am Atheist.
Bryan, John & Griffiths, Mark, eds. Manual of Bulbs. (Illus.). 446p. 1995. 49.95 (*0-88192-339-7*) Timber.
Bryan, John L. Automatic Sprinkler & Standpipe Systems. 3rd ed. Linville, Jim L., ed. LC 97-68315. 1997. 67.00 (*0-87765-424-7*, AUTO-97) Natl Fire Prot.
— Fire Suppression & Detection Systems. 3rd ed. LC 92-33532. (Fire Science Ser.). (Illus.). 608p. (C). 1993. text 60.80 (*0-02-315990-1*, Macmillan Coll) P-H.
Bryan, John M. Biltmore Estate: The Most Distinct Private Place. LC 94-14245. 160p. 1994. 45.00 (*0-8478-1811-X*, Pub. by Rizzoli Intl) St Martin.
— Creating the South Carolina State House. LC 98-40220. (Illus.). 320p. 1999. 39.95 (*1-57003-291-2*) U of SC Pr.
***Bryan, John M.** Duke University. (Campus Guide Ser.). (Illus.). 168p. 2000. pap. 24.95 (*1-56898-228-3*) Princeton Arch.
— The South Carolina State Museum: A History & Highlights of the Collection. (Illus.). 132p. Date not set. write for info. (*0-9701267-0-0*); pap. write for info. (*0-9701267-1-9*) Alt Lee.
Bryan, Joseph, jt. auth. see Halsey, William F.
***Bryan, Josephine.** Nature Lab: The Ultimate Nature Pack. (Science Lab Ser.). (Illus.). 32p. (J). (ps-3). 2000. 19.95 (*1-57145-407-1*, Silver Dolph) Advantage Pubs.
Bryan, Joyce & Edson, Thomas F. Caring Hands: Planning & Implementing a Caregiver Retreat. 63p. (Orig.). 1995. pap. 25.00 (*0-9644874-0-3*) Orange Caregiver.
Bryan, Joyce, et al. Talk about It! An Integrated Approach to Bold, Dynamic Topics. 112p. (Orig.). 1997. pap. text 16.95 (*0-472-08395-3*, 08395) U of Mich Pr.
— Talk about It! An Integrated Approach to Bold, Dynamic Topics. 112p. (Orig.). 1997. pap., teacher ed. 18.95 (*0-472-08396-1*, 08396) U of Mich Pr.
Bryan, Karen & Maxim, Jane, eds. Communication Disability & the Psychiatry of Old Age. (Illus.). 348p. (Orig.). 1996. pap. text 45.00 (*1-56593-747-3*, 1450) Thomson Learn.
Bryan, Karen, jt. auth. see Maxim, Jane.
***Bryan, Kate.** Murder on the Barbary Coast, 1 vol. (Maggie Maguire Mysteries Ser.). 1999. mass mkt. 5.99 (*0-425-16933-2*) Berkley Pub.
Bryan, Kate. A Record of Death. 213p. 1998. mass mkt. 5.99 (*0-425-16537-X*) Berkley Pub.
Bryan, Katherine A. Baltzly-Balsley-Polsley Family: With Other Variations of the Name; Also, a Sketch of Maj. Wm. Haymond. 373p. 1995. reprint ed. pap. 57.00 (*0-8328-4898-0*); reprint ed. lib. bdg. 67.00 (*0-8328-4897-2*) Higginson Bk Co.
Bryan, Kay. Look! I Can Cook! A Simplified Guide to Cooking & Household Skills. LC 79-89358. 269p. 1979. pap. 15.98 (*0-88290-130-3*) Horizon Utah.
Bryan, Kimberli, jt. auth. see Blake, Stephen.
Bryan, L. A., et al, eds. Installation, Start-Up, Maintenance, & Troubleshooting of the Micrologix 1000. (Illus.). 126p. 1998. pap. text 32.00 (*0-944107-37-0*, 424) Indust Text.
— Understanding & Programming the Micrologix 1000. (Illus.). 143p. 1998. pap. text 32.00 (*0-944107-34-6*, 414) Indust Text.
Bryan, L. A. & Bryan, E. A. AC Motor Controls & Troubleshooting No. 647: Video Booklet/Workbook. Thompson, L. B., ed. (Illus.). 60p. 1995. pap. 32.00 (*0-944107-17-6*, 647) Indust Text.
— DC Motor Controls & Troubleshooting No. 649: Video Booklet/Workbook. Thompson, L. B., ed. (Illus.). 40p. 1995. pap. 32.00 (*0-944107-18-4*, 649) Indust Text.
— Electrical Switching, Timing & Control Devices No. 605: Video Booklet/Workbook. Thompson, L. B., ed. (Illus.). 52p. 1995. pap., wbk. ed. 32.00 (*0-944107-11-7*, 605) Indust Text.
— Instrumentation - Discrete & Sensory No. 607: Video Booklet/Workbook. unabridged ed. Thompson, L. B., ed. (Illus.). 48p. 1995. pap. 32.00 (*0-944107-12-5*, 607) Indust Text.
— Introduction to Motor Control Operations & Protection No. 633: Video Booklet/Workbook. Thompson, L. B., ed. (Illus.). 56p. 1995. pap. 32.00 (*0-944107-15-X*, 633) Indust Text.
— Preventive Maintenance & Troubleshooting Control Circuits No. 612: Video Booklet/Workbook. Thompson, L. B., ed. (Illus.). 40p. 1995. pap. 32.00 (*0-944107-14-1*, 612) Indust Text.
— Programmable Controllers: Theory & Implementation. 2nd ed. Phillipo, Stephanie, ed. LC 96-49350. (Illus.). 1050p. 1997. pap. 88.00 incl. VHS (*0-944107-32-X*, 206) Indust Text.

B

— Programmable Logic Controllers: Video Guide & Workbook. unabridged ed. Thompson, L. B., ed. (Illus.). 417p. 1992. pap. text 57.00 incl. VHS (*0-944107-02-8*, 561) Indust Text.

— Sizing the Protection of Motors & Control Circuits No. 637: Video Booklet/Workbook. Thompson, L. B., ed. (Illus.). 28p. 1995. pap. 32.00 (*0-944107-16-8*, 637) Indust Text.

— Understanding & Applying PLCs in Electrical Controls No. 677: Video Booklet/Workbook. Thompson, L. B., ed. (Illus.). 52p. 1995. pap. 32.00 (*0-944107-19-2*, 677) Indust Text.

— Understanding Electrical Diagrams & Control Circuits No. 611: Video Booklet/Workbook. Thompson, L. B., ed. (Illus.). 48p. (Orig.). 1995. pap. 32.00 (*0-944107-13-3*, 611) Indust Text.

— Understanding 30 Power & Plant Distribution No. 602: Video Booklet/Workbook. unabridged ed. Thompson, L. B., ed. (Illus.). 48p. 1995. pap. 32.00 (*0-944107-10-9*, 602) Indust Text.

Bryan, L. E., ed. Microbial Resistance to Drugs. (Handbook of Experimental Pharmacology Ser.: Vol. 91). (Illus.). 510p. 1989. 322.00 (*0-387-50318-8*) Spr-Verlag.

Bryan, Lowell L. Bankrupt: Why the Financial System Is Collapsing & How to Rescue It. 250p. 1991. 22.95 (*0-88730-511-3*, HarpBusn) HarpInfo.

Bryan, Lowell L. & Farrell, Diana. Market Unbound: Unleashing Global Capitalism. LC 95-50490. 268p. 1996. 27.95 (*0-471-14446-0*) Wiley.

Bryan, Lowell L., et al. Race for the World: Strategies to Build a Great Global Firm. LC 99-18401. (Illus.). 364p. 1999. 29.95 (*0-87584-846-X*, HBS Pr) Harvard Busn.

Bryan, Luis A. & Bryan, Eric A. PLC Selected Applications, Vol. 1. 2nd ed. Phillipo, Stephanie & Dupree, Lisa, eds. (Selected Application Ser.). (Illus.). 435p. (Orig.). 1997. pap. text 45.95 (*0-944107-25-7*, 106) Indust Text.

— PLC Workbook & Study Guide. 2nd ed. Phillipo, Stephanie, ed. (Illus.). 327p. 1997. pap. text, student ed., wbk. ed. 25.00 incl. VHS (*0-944107-33-8*, 224) Indust Text.

— Troubleshooting & Understanding Electrical & Motor Controls: Video Guide & Workbook. Thompson, Lou, ed. (Illus.). 417p. (C). 1995. pap. text 54.00 incl. VHS (*0-944107-07-9*, 661) Indust Text.

Bryan, M. A., jt. auth. see Tucker, Archibald N.

Bryan, M. A., jt. auth. see Westermann, Diedrich.

Bryan, M. B., jt. auth. see Bryan, William J.

Bryan, Margaret A. The Bantu Languages of Africa. LC 60-1171. (Handbook of African Languages Ser.: Pt. 4). 195p. 1959. reprint ed. pap. 60.50 (*0-8357-3211-8*, 205708200011) Bks Demand.

***Bryan, Mark.** Codes of Love: How to Rethink Your Family, Remake Your Life. LC 99-46336. 275p. 1999. 23.00 (*0-671-03662-9*, PB Hardcover) PB.

Bryan, Mark & Cameron, Julia. Money Drunk/Money Sober: 90 Days to Financial Freedom. 225p. 1999. pap. 10.00 (*0-345-43265-7*) Ball Well.

Bryan, Mark, et al. The Artist's Way at Work: Riding the Dragon. LC 98-10310. (Illus.). 224p. 1998. 26.00 (*0-688-15788-2*, Wm Morrow) Morrow Avon.

— The Artist's Way at Work: Riding the Dragon. LC 98-10310. (Illus.). 304p. 1999. reprint ed. pap. 15.95 (*0-688-16635-0*, Quil) HarperTrade.

Bryan, Mark, jt. auth. see Cameron, Julia.

Bryan, Mark A. The Prodigal Father: Reuniting Fathers & Their Children. LC 98-13497. 278p. 1998. pap. 14.00 (*0-609-80203-8*, Three Riv Pr) Crown Pub Group.

Bryan, Martha & Bryan, Geoffrey. Print Pizzazz: Desktop Publishing for the Rest of Us. (Illus.). 181p. 1997. pap. 19.95 (*0-9658513-3-8*) Gldn Dragon.

Bryan, Martin. SGML & HTML Explained. 2nd ed. LC 97-187288. 256p. 1997. pap. text 39.95 (*0-201-40394-3*) Addison-Wesley.

Bryan, Marvin. Digital Typography Sourcebook. LC 96-13161. 384p. 1996. pap., pap. text 39.95 incl. cd-rom (*0-471-14811-3*) Wiley.

Bryan, Mary. Forrest Reid. Bowman, Sylvia E., ed. LC 76-48210. (Twayne's English Authors Ser.). 173p. (C). 1976. text 18.95 (*0-8057-6661-8*) Irvington.

— Sonnets & Metrical Tales, 1815. LC 94-44532. (Revolution & Romanticism, 1789-1834 Ser.). 1995. 48.00 (*1-85477-178-7*) Continuum.

Bryan, Mary E. Manch. (Works of Mary (Edwards) Bryan). 1989. reprint ed. lib. bdg. 79.00 (*0-7812-2121-8*) Rprt Serv.

— Wild Work. (Works of Mary (Edwards) Bryan). 1989. reprint ed. lib. bdg. 90.00 (*0-7812-2122-6*) Rprt Serv.

— The Works of Mary (Edwards) Bryan, Set. 1989. reprint ed. lib. bdg. 63.00 (*0-685-74125-7*) Rprt Serv.

Bryan, Mary G. Passports Issued by Governors of Georgia, 1785 to 1809. 58p. 1959. pap. 8.00 (*0-915156-21-0*, 21) Natl Genealogical.

Bryan, Mary G., jt. auth. see Dumont, William.

Bryan, Mary L. & Davis, Allen F., eds. One Hundred Years at Hull-House. LC 88-46032. (Illus.). 351p. 1991. 20.95 (*0-253-31621-9*); pap. 10.95 (*0-253-20579-4*, MB 579) Ind U Pr.

Bryan, McLeod G., ed. see Moltmann, Jurgen, et al.

Bryan, Mike. Baseball Forever. 1999. text 22.95 (*0-670-86526-5*) Viking Penguin.

— Dogleg Madness. LC 87-28947. 228p. 1990. pap. 8.95 (*0-87113-330-X*, Atlntc Mnthly) Grove-Atltic.

— Uneasy Rider. 1998. pap. 13.00 (*0-679-74265-4*) Vin Bks.

— Uneasy Rider: The Interstate Way of Knowledge. LC 96-38901. 1997. 3.99 (*0-679-41671-4*) Random.

Bryan, Mike, jt. auth. see Ripken, Cal, Jr.

Bryan, Mollie C., ed. Unsilenced: The Spirit of Women. LC 97-3126. (Illus.). 256p. (Orig.). 1997. pap. 14.95 (*1-881394-11-5*) Commune-A-Key.

Bryan, Nonobah G. & Young, Stella. Navajo Native Dyes. (Wild & Woolly West Ser.: No. 34). (Illus.). 76p. 1978. reprint ed. pap. 5.00 (*0-910584-57-5*) Filter.

Bryan, Nora Sherwood, jt. ed. see Bamberger, William J.

Bryan, Patty, jt. auth. see Sweet, O. Robin.

Bryan, Paul. Johann Van Hal, Viennese Symphonist: His Life & His Musical Environment. (Thematic Catalogue Ser.: Vol. 23). 1997. text 86.00 (*0-945193-63-7*) Pendragon NY.

Bryan, Paul, ed. see Vanhal, Johann.

Bryan, Peter, jt. auth. see Parker, Hohn.

Bryan, Pryor. Computers: Community Access. 1995. 40.00 (*1-885522-02-9*) Telecommunity Pr.

Bryan, Robert A., jt. auth. see Tucker, Allan.

Bryan, Samuel. The Letters of Centinel. Hope, Warren, ed. LC 98-74072. 160p. 1998. reprint ed. pap. 21.99 (*1-892355-01-9*) Fifth Season.

Bryan, Sandra "Johnsie". Coffee with Barbie Doll. LC 97-80172. 160p. 1998. pap. 19.95 (*0-7643-0412-7*) Schiffer.

***Bryan, Sandra L.** Teaching Aesthetics. (Fastback Ser.: No. 443). 54p. 1999. pap. 3.00 (*0-87367-643-2*, FB# 443) Phi Delta Kappa.

***Bryan, Sarah Jane.** Robots Everywhere! (All-Star Readers Ser.). (Illus.). 48p. (J). (gr. 2-3). 2001. 3.99 (*1-57584-726-4*, Pub. by Rdrs Digest) S&S Trade.

Bryan, Sharon. Flying Blind: Poems. LC 96-86. 72p. 1996. 20.95 (*0-9641151-6-6*); pap. 12.95 (*0-9641151-7-4*, Pub. by Sarabande Bks) Consort Bk Sales.

— Tabitha Bible Class Teachers Manual, Vol. 1. (Illus.). 44p. 1981. pap., teacher ed. 5.45 (*0-89137-819-7*) Quality Pubns.

Bryan, Sharon. Tabitha Bible Class Teachers Manual, Vol. 3. unabridged ed. (Illus.). 75p. 1994. pap., teacher ed. 6.35 (*0-89137-834-0*, 78340) Quality Pubns.

Bryan, Sharon. Tabitha Bible Class Workbook, Vol. 1. 33p. 1981. pap., student ed., wbk. ed. 6.35 (*0-89137-818-9*) Quality Pubns.

Bryan, Sharon. Tabitha Bible Class Workbook, Vol. 3. unabridged ed. 34p. 1994. pap. 5.45 (*0-89137-833-2*, 78332) Quality Pubns.

Bryan-Smith, Lissa & Smith, Richard. Holiday Collectibles: Vintage Flea Market Treasures. LC 98-84092. (Illus.). 128p. 1998. pap. 16.95 (*0-87069-769-2*, FMHC) Krause Pubns.

Bryan, T. Avril. Censorship & Social Conflict in the Spanish Theatre: The Case of Alfonso Sastre. LC 82-17445. 156p. (Orig.). (C). 1983. lib. bdg. 46.00 (*0-8191-2829-5*) U Pr of Amer.

Bryan, T. Scott. Geysers: What They Are & How They Work. (Illus.). 32p. (Orig.). (J). 1990. pap. 5.95 (*0-911797-74-2*) Roberts Rinehart.

— The Geysers of Yellowstone. 3rd ed. (Illus.). 464p. 1995. pap. 19.95 (*0-87081-365-X*) Univ Pr Colo.

Bryan, T. Scott & Tucker-Bryan, Betty. The Explorer's Guide to Death Valley National Park. (Illus.). 416p. 1995. pap. 22.50 (*0-87081-409-5*) Univ Pr Colo.

Bryan, Timothy. Bible People Prophets. pap. 5.95 (*0-687-07405-3*) Abingdon.

— Prophets. (Bible People Ser.). 1996. pap. 5.95 (*0-687-07415-0*) Abingdon.

Bryan, Vernanne. Laura Keene: A British Actress on the American Stage, 1826-1873. LC 96-37417. (Illus.). 232p. 1997. lib. bdg. 38.50 (*0-7864-0075-7*) McFarland & Co.

Bryan, Violet H. The Myth of New Orleans in Literature: Dialogues of Race & Gender. LC 92-42846. 248p. (C). 1993. text 33.00 (*0-87049-789-8*) U of Tenn Pr.

Bryan, Virginia, et al. Rivers Curriculum Guide - Chemistry. Anderson, Catherine & Freeman, Christine, eds. (Rivers Curriculum Project Ser.). (Illus.). 238p. (Orig.). (YA). (gr. 9-12). 1996. pap. 23.95 (*0-201-49367-5*, 30617) Seymour Pubns.

Bryan, W. J. & Beck, J. V., eds. Proceedings of the 1995 National Heat Transfer Conference: August 6-9, 1995, Portland, Oregon, Vol. 1. 196p. 1995. 100.00 (*0-7918-1711-3*, H00993) ASME.

Bryan, W. S. & Rose, Robert. History of the Pioneer Families of Missouri, with Numerous Sketches, Anecdotes, Adventures, Etc., Related to Early Days in Missouri. (Illus.). 569p. 1992. reprint ed. lib. bdg. 39.50 (*0-8328-2373-2*) Higginson Bk Co.

Bryan, Walter R. Italic Hut Urns & Hut Urn Cemeteries: A Study in the Early Iron Age of Latium & Etruria. LC 25-20377. (American Academy in Rome. Papers & Monographs: Vol. 4). 237p. reprint ed. pap. 73.50 (*0-608-16459-3*, 202671900051) Bks Demand.

Bryan, William A. Administrative Psychiatry. LC 58-14143. 1958. reprint ed. 46.00 (*0-8154-0034-9*) Cooper Sq.

— Key to the Birds of the Hawaiian Group. (BMB Ser.). 1979. reprint ed. 30.00 (*0-527-01628-4*) Periodicals Srv.

Bryan, William A., et al, eds. Using Professional Standards in Student Affairs. LC 85-644751. (New Directions for Student Services Ser.: No. SS 53). 1991. 22.00 (*1-55542-797-9*) Jossey-Bass.

Bryan, William A. & Mullendore, Richard H., eds. Rights, Freedoms, & Responsibilities of Students. LC 85-644751. (New Directions for Student Services Ser.: No. 59). 115p. (Orig.). 1992. pap. 19.00 (*0-614-03602-X*) Jossey-Bass.

Bryan, William J. Bryan on Imperialism. LC 71-111701. (American Imperialism: Viewpoints of United States Foreign Policy, 1898-1941 Ser.). 1976. reprint ed. 18.95 (*0-405-02005-8*) Ayer.

— The Chosen Ones: The Art of Jury Selection. 2nd ed. (Illus.). 438p. 1985. 37.50 (*0-930298-24-1*) Westwood Pub Co.

— The Cross of Gold: Speech Delivered Before the National Democratic Convention at Chicago, July 9, 1896. LC 96-8597. iv, 28p. 1996. pap. 5.00 (*0-8032-6131-4*) U of Nebr Pr.

— In His Image. LC 73-156618. (Essay Index Reprint Ser.). 1977. reprint ed. 20.95 (*0-8369-2270-0*) Ayer.

— Memoirs of William Jennings Bryan: By Himself & His Wife, 2 vols., Set. (American Biography Ser.). 1991. reprint ed. lib. bdg. 148.00 (*0-7812-8048-6*) Rprt Serv.

Bryan, William J., Jr. The Religious Aspects of Hypnosis. 2nd ed. Hauser, Joe, ed. (Illus.). 80p. Date not set. reprint ed. pap. 12.95 (*0-9615140-5-1*) Relaxed Bks.

Bryan, William J. & Bryan, M. B. Memoirs of William Jennings Bryan. LC 72-130261. (American Biography Ser.: No. 32). 1970. reprint ed. lib. bdg. 75.00 (*0-8383-1165-2*) M S G Haskell Hse.

Bryan, William L. Montana's Indians: Yesterday & Today. 2nd ed. (Illus.). 144p. (Orig.). 1996. pap. 24.95 (*1-56037-064-5*) Am Wrld Geog.

— Software Product Assurance. (C). 1987. text 65.20 (*0-13-500505-1*) P-H.

Bryan, William L., jt. auth. see Book, William F.

Bryan, William S. & Rose, Robert. A History of the Pioneer Families of Missouri. (Illus.). 586p. 1996. reprint ed. pap. 45.00 (*0-8063-0753-6*, 770) Clearfield Co.

— A History of the Pioneer Families of Missouri. 586p. 1991. reprint ed. lib. bdg. 39.50 (*0-8328-2249-3*) Higginson Bk Co.

Bryan, Willie V. In Search of Freedom: How Persons with Disabilities Have Been Disenfranchised from the Mainstream of American Society. LC 95-44875. 214p. 1996. text 50.95 (*0-398-06563-2*) C C Thomas.

— In Search of Freedom: How Persons with Disabilities Have Been Disenfranchized from the Mainstream of American Society. 214p. 1996. pap. text 31.95 (*0-398-06564-0*) C C Thomas.

***Bryan, Willie V.** Multicultural Aspects of Disabilities: A Guide to Understanding & Assisting Minorities in the Rehabilitation Process. LC 98-52829. 300p. 1999. text 57.95 (*0-398-06941-7*); pap. text 45.95 (*0-398-06942-5*) C C Thomas.

Bryan, Willie V., jt. auth. see Henderson, George.

Bryans. Business Solutions for Budget Managers. 144p. 1994. pap. 41.95 (*0-582-25532-5*) Ashgate Pub Co.

Bryans, et al. American Passages: A U. S. History Reader. 2nd ed. 318p. (C). 1997. per. 28.95 (*0-7872-3739-6*) Kendall-Hunt.

Bryans, J. Lonsdale. The Curve of Fate: From Man-Ape to the Man-God. 1977. lib. bdg. 59.95 (*0-8490-1696-7*) Gordon Pr.

Bryans, J. T., ed. see International Conference on Equine Infectious Dise.

Bryans, John V. Calderon de la Barca: Imagery, Drama & Rhetoric. (Monografias A Ser.: Vol. LXIV). 207p. (C). 1977. 51.00 (*0-7293-0047-1*, Pub. by Tamesis Bks Ltd) Boydell & Brewer.

Bryans, Nena. Full Circle: A Proposal to the Church for an Arts Ministry. Sanders, Vernon, ed. 81p. (Orig.). (C). 1988. pap. text 9.95 (*0-944230-00-8*) Schuyler Inst Worship.

Bryanskaya, Faina. The Key to Music Making: Piano Method for Beginners, Pt. I. LC 88-50726. (Illus.). 48p. (J). (gr. 1-5). 1988. pap. 8.00 (*0-929571-00-2*) White Lilac Pr.

— The Key to Music Making: Piano Method for Beginners, Pt. II. LC 88-50726. (Illus.). 56p. 1989. pap. 9.95 (*0-929571-01-0*) White Lilac Pr.

— The Key to Music Making: Piano Method for Beginners, Pt. III. LC 88-50726. (Illus.). 56p. 1989. pap. 9.95 (*0-929571-02-9*) White Lilac Pr.

Bryant. Anne Abrams: Engineering Drafter. (J). 1995. 0.85 (*0-8050-2037-3*) H Holt & Co.

— Margaret Murie. (J). 1995. 14.95 (*0-8050-2125-6*) H Holt & Co.

— Practice Data Analysis, Vol. 3. 2nd ed. 128p. 1998. pap. 13.75 (*0-07-365488-4*) McGraw.

***Bryant.** Refrigeration: An Introduction. 1998. pap. write for info. (*0-419-21710-X*) Thomson Learn.

Bryant, ed. Mineral Deposits & Geology of Central Colorado. (IGC Field Trip Guidebooks Ser.). 80p. 1989. 21.00 (*0-87590-645-1*, T129) Am Geophysical.

Bryant, jt. auth. see Otto et al.

Bryant, jt. auth. see Willis.

Bryant, Beauford & Krause, Mark. John. LC 98-33931. (NIV Commentary Ser.). 415p. 1998. 21.99 (*0-89900-631-0*) College Pr Pub.

Bryant, Robert P. Georgia Llc/llp Handbook: A Practitioner's Guide to Limited Liability Companies & Limited Liability Partnerships in Georgia. LC 98-223790. 340p. 1995. write for info. (*1-879590-95-6*) Amer Law Media.

Bryant, A. C. Refrigeration Equipment: A Servicing & Installation Handbook. 2nd ed. LC 98-229124. (Illus.). 224p. 1998. pap. text 39.95 (*0-7506-3688-2*, Newnes) Buttrwrth-Heinemann.

Bryant, Adam. Canada, Good Neighbor to the World. 2nd ed. LC 96-2555. (Discovering Our Heritage Ser.). (Illus.). (J). 1996. lib. bdg. 14.95 (*0-382-39498-4*) Silver Burdett Pr.

***Bryant, Al.** Climbing the Heights. 2000. pap. 14.99 (*0-8254-2068-7*) Kregel.

Bryant, Al. Climbing the Heights. LC 91-24339. 384p. 1991. reprint ed. pap. 12.99 (*0-8254-2286-8*) Kregel.

— More Sermon Outlines for Special Occasions. LC 95-7832. (Sermon Outlines Ser.). 64p. 1995. pap. 4.99 (*0-8254-2268-X*) Kregel.

— More Sermon Outlines on Prayer. (Sermon Outline Ser.). 64p. 1995. pap. 4.99 (*0-8254-2190-X*) Kregel.

— Revival Sermon Outlines. LC 91-41882. 64p. 1992. pap. 4.99 (*0-8254-2193-4*) Kregel.

— Sermon Outlines for Evangelistic Occasions. LC 91-21641. 64p. 1992. pap. 4.99 (*0-8254-2295-7*) Kregel.

***Bryant, Al.** Sermon Outlines for Evangelistic Occasions. 64p. 2000. pap. 4.99 (*0-8254-2054-7*) Kregel.

Bryant, Al. Sermon Outlines for Lay Leaders. LC 95-7843. 64p. 1995. pap. 4.99 (*0-8254-2271-X*) Kregel.

— Sermon Outlines for Special Occasions. LC 91-39389. 64p. 1992. pap. 4.99 (*0-8254-2195-0*) Kregel.

— Sermon Outlines for Worship Services. LC 91-21653. 64p. 1992. pap. 4.99 (*0-8254-2298-1*) Kregel.

— Sermon Outlines from Romans & Other New Testament Passages. LC 97-28878. 64p. 1997. 4.99 (*0-8254-2160-8*) Kregel.

— Sermon Outlines from the Psalms. LC 97-30133. 64p. 1997. 4.99 (*0-8254-2159-4*) Kregel.

— Sermon Outlines on Bible Characters (New Testament) LC 91-21655. 64p. 1992. pap. 4.99 (*0-8254-2297-3*) Kregel.

— Sermon Outlines on Bible Characters (Old Testament) LC 91-21654. 64p. 1992. pap. 4.99 (*0-8254-2296-5*) Kregel.

— Sermon Outlines on Faith, Hope, & Love. LC 96-10317. 64p. 1996. pap. 4.99 (*0-8254-2154-3*) Kregel.

Bryant, Al. Sermon Outlines on Faith, Hope & Love. 1996. pap. 4.99 (*0-8254-2055-5*) Kregel.

Bryant, Al. Sermon Outlines on Family & Home. 64p. 1996. pap. 4.99 (*0-8254-2153-5*) Kregel.

— Sermon Outlines on Prayer. LC 91-39390. 64p. 1992. pap. 4.99 (*0-8254-2194-2*) Kregel.

— Sermon Outlines on the Death, Resurrection & Return of Christ. LC 98-16988. (Sermon Outline Ser.). 64p. 1998. pap. text 4.99 (*0-8254-2078-4*) Kregel.

— Sermon Outlines on the Deeper Life. LC 91-39391. 64p. 1992. pap. 4.99 (*0-8254-2196-9*) Kregel.

— Sermon Outlines on the Fruit of the Spirit. LC 96-30472. 64p. 1996. pap. 4.99 (*0-8254-2155-1*) Kregel.

— Sermon Outlines on the Grace of God. LC 96-30470. 64p. 1996. pap. 4.99 (*0-8254-2156-X*) Kregel.

***Bryant, Al.** Sermon Outlines on the Holy Spirit. 2000. pap. 4.99 (*0-8254-2057-1*) Kregel.

Bryant, Al. Sermon Outlines on the Holy Spirit & Spiritual Life. LC 98-17622. (Sermon Outline Ser.). 64p. 1998. pap. text 4.99 (*0-8254-2077-6*) Kregel.

— Sourcebook of Poetry. LC 92-16102. 768p. 1992. reprint ed. pap. 26.99 (*0-8254-2192-6*) Kregel.

Bryant, Al, compiled by. New Every Morning: Meditations from Your Favorite Christian Writers. LC 92-16143. 288p. 1992. reprint ed. pap. 12.99 (*0-8254-2282-5*) Kregel.

— Sermon Outlines on Prophetic Themes. LC 92-23982. 64p. 1993. pap. 4.99 (*0-8254-2191-8*) Kregel.

— Sermon Outlines on the Attributes of God. LC 92-23980. 64p. 1993. 4.99 (*0-8254-2188-8*) Kregel.

— Sermon Outlines on the Cross of Christ. LC 92-23981. 64p. 1993. 4.99 (*0-8254-2189-6*) Kregel.

— Sermon Outlines on the Life of Christ. LC 92-26143. 64p. 1993. 4.99 (*0-8254-2186-1*) Kregel.

Bryant, Al, ed. Songs of My Soul: Devotional Thoughts from the Writings of W. Phillip Keller. 272p. 1998. 9.99 (*0-88486-226-7*, Inspirational Pr) Arrowood Pr.

Bryant, Al, jt. auth. see Murray, Andrew.

Bryant, Alan D. Creating Successful Bulletin Board Systems. 416p. 1994. pap. text 39.95 (*0-201-62668-3*) Addison-Wesley.

Bryant, Alan D. Growing & Maintaining a Successful BBS: The Sysop's Handbook. 352p. (C). 1995. pap. 39.95 incl. cd-rom (*0-201-48380-7*) Addison-Wesley.

Bryant, Alden. Broken Planet - Broken Systems Vol. 1: A 15-Year Climate Stabilization Program for Humanity. 110p. 1998. pap. 20.00 (*0-9602410-3-5*) Earth Regnrtn.

Bryant, Alden & Wood, Fred B., eds. Whose World to Lose? Ours. (Illus.). 102p. (Orig.). 1992. 18.00 (*0-9602410-2-7*); pap. 5.00 (*0-9602410-0-0*); spiral bd. 8.00 (*0-9602410-1-9*) Earth Regnrtn.

Bryant, Alfred T. Zulu People As They Were Before the White Man Came. LC 75-100282. 769p. 1970. reprint ed. lib. bdg. 35.00 (*0-8371-2933-8*, Greenwood Pr) Greenwood.

Bryant, Alice & Seebach, Linda. Opening to the Infinite: Human Multidimensional Potential. Demmon, Amy O., ed. LC 97-27079. 276p. 1997. per. 15.00 (*0-926524-43-7*) Granite Pub.

Bryant, Andy. The Baldness Cure: The Unique Regrowth Programme That Really Works. (Illus.). 116p. 1995. 13.95 (*0-09-178242-2*, Pub. by Random) Trafalgar.

Bryant, Anne & Bernfeld, Ellen. The Adventures of the Mirror Kids: The First & the Bravest. 10p. (J). (ps-2). 1996. mass mkt. 10.95 incl. audio (*0-9648762-3-X*, EV/Kids1) Gloryvision.

— Songs for Cats (& the People Who Love Them) (Songs for...Ser.: Vol. 2). (Illus.). 48p. (Orig.). 1997. mass mkt., boxed set 18.95 incl. cd-rom (*0-9648762-1-3*, Cats/CD); mass mkt., boxed set 16.95 incl. audio (*0-9648762-0-5*, Cats/Cass) Gloryvision.

— Songs for Dogs (& the People Who Love Them), Vol. 3. 2nd rev. ed. (Songs for...Ser.). (Illus.). 48p. (Orig.). 1995. mass mkt., boxed set 18.95 incl. cd-rom (*0-9648762-8-0*, Dogs/CD) Gloryvision.

Bryant, Anne, jt. auth. see Bernfeld, Ellen.

Bryant, Anthony J. Early Samurai 200-1500. (Elite Ser.: No. 35). (Illus.). 64p. pap. 12.95 (*1-85532-131-9*, 9450, Pub. by Ospry) Stackpole.

— Sekigahara, 1600. (Campaign Ser.). (Illus.). 96p. 1995. pap. 14.95 (*1-85532-395-8*, Pub. by Ospry) Stackpole.

— Sengoku: Chanbara Roleplaying in Period of Warring States. Arsenault, Mark, ed.Tr. of Period of Warring States. (Illus.). 256p. 1998. pap. 25.00 (*1-890305-10-3*) Gold Rush.

Bryant, Antony, ed. see British Computer Society Staff, et al.

***Bryant, Arlene.** A Hidden Past: An Exploration of Eastside History. 104p. 2000. reprint ed. pap. 5.95 (*0-944912-07-9*) Seattle Times.

Bryant, Arthur. American Ideal. LC 77-90617. (Essay Index Reprint Ser.). 1977. 21.95 (*0-8369-1251-9*) Ayer.

An Asterisk (*) at the beginning of an entry indicates that the title is appearing for the first time.

— The England of Charles II. LC 78-37873. (Select Bibliographies Reprint Ser.). 1977. reprint ed. 233.10 (*0-8369-6710-0*) Ayer.

— Pepys, 1683-1689 Vol. III: The Saviour of the Navy. 367p. 1985. pap. 10.00 (*0-586-06472-9*) Academy Chi Pubs.

— Pepys, 1669-1683 Vol. II: The Years of Peril. 365p. 1985. pap. 10.00 (*0-586-06471-0*) Academy Chi Pubs.

— Pepys, 1633-1669 Vol. I: The Man in the Making. 334p. 1985. pap. 10.00 (*0-586-06470-2*) Academy Chi Pubs.

— Postman's Horn. LC 77-119927. (Select Bibliographies Reprint Ser.). 1977. 24.95 (*0-8369-5370-3*) Ayer.

— Triumph in the West. LC 73-22634. (Illus.). 438p. (C). 1974. reprint ed. lib. bdg. 72.50 (*0-8371-7344-2*, BRTR, Greenwood Pr) Greenwood.

Bryant, B. & Bryant, R. Change & Conflict: A Study of Community Work in Glasgow. 250p. 1983. text 26.00 (*0-08-028475-2*, Pergamon Pr); pap. text 14.95 (*0-08-028480-9*, Pergamon Pr) Elsevier.

Bryant, B., jt. auth. see Reed, T.

Bryant, Barbara & Anderson, G. Twyford Down: Roads, Campaigning & Environmental Law. LC 95-71098. (Illus.). 352p. (Orig.). (C). 1995. pap. 26.99 (*0-419-20270-6*, E & FN Spon) Routledge.

Bryant, Barbara E. & Dunn, William. Moving Power & Money: The Politics of Census Taking. 234p. 1995. 24.95 (*0-9628092-7-6*) New Strategist.

***Bryant, Barbara S. & Simon, Woward A.** Bring & Defending a Sexual Harassment Action Pts. 1 & 2: Winter 2000 Action Guide, 2 vols., Set. Johnson, Elizabeth M., ed. 176p. 2000. pap. 58.00 (*0-7626-0417-4*) Cont Ed Bar-CA.

Bryant, Barry. Cancer & Consciousness. 277p. 1990. pap. 18.95 (*0-938434-74-8*) Sigo Pr.

***Bryant, Barry.** 101+ Ways to Steal by a Clerk: How to Analyze, Entrap & Eject a Thief. 110p. 2000. pap. 12.95 (*0-9676916-0-5*) W Davis Corp.

***Bryant-Bertail, Sarah.** Space & Time on Stage in Epic Theater. LC 99-58828. (Illus.). 200p. 2000. 59.00 (*1-57113-186-8*) Camden Hse.

Bryant, Betty. Here Comes the Showboat! LC 93-47998. (Ohio River Valley Ser.). 216p. (C). 1994. 24.95 (*0-8131-1862-X*) U Pr of Ky.

— Leaning into the Wind: The Wilderness of Widowhood. LC 75-13031. 96p. reprint ed. pap. 30.00 (*0-608-16807-6*, 202693000053) Bks Demand.

Bryant, Betty, jt. auth. see Taylor, Louise.

Bryant, Betty R. Sweeping up the Heart. 60p. (Orig.). 1993. pap. 12.50 (*0-914125-04-4*) Serif Pr.

Bryant, Beverley. In Search of Wings: A Journey Back from Traumatic Brain Injury. 256p. 1992. pap. 14.95 (*1-882332-00-8*) Wings Pub.

Bryant, Beverley A. To Wherever Oceans Go. 300p. (Orig.). 1996. pap. 15.00 (*1-882332-01-6*) Wings Pub.

Bryant, Bonnie. Autumn Trail. (Saddle Club Ser.: No. 30). (J). (gr. 4-6). 1993. 9.09 (*0-606-08102-X*) Turtleback.

— Autumn Trail, No. 30. (Saddle Club Ser.: No. 30). 160p. (J). (gr. 4-7). 1993. pap. 3.99 (*0-553-48077-4*) Bantam.

***Bryant, Bonnie.** Back in the Saddle. (Pine Hollow Ser.: No. 12). 256p. (YA). (gr. 7-12). 2000. mass mkt. 4.50 (*0-553-49302-7*) BDD Bks Young Read.

Bryant, Bonnie. Beach Ride. (Saddle Club Ser.: No. 26). (J). (gr. 4-6). 1993. 9.09 (*0-606-08097-X*, Pub. by Turtleback) Demco.

— Before They Rode Horses. (Saddle Club Super Edition Ser.: No. 5). 224p. (J). (gr. 4-7). 1997. pap. 4.50 (*0-553-48376-5*, Skylark BDD) BDD Bks Young Read.

— Broken Horse. (Saddle Club Ser.: No. 61). (J). (gr. 4-6). 1996. 9.09 (*0-606-10917-X*, Pub. by Turtleback) Demco.

— Carole. (Saddle Club Ser.). 288p. (J). (gr. 4-6). 1999. pap. 4.50 (*0-553-48678-0*) Bantam.

— Changing Leads. (Pine Hollow Ser.: No. 4). 192p. (YA). (gr. 7-12). 1999. mass mkt. 4.50 (*0-553-49245-4*) BDD Bks Young Read.

— Chocolate Horse. LC Skylark. (Saddle Club Ser.: No. 32). 160p. (J). (gr. 5-7). 1996. pap. 3.99 (*0-553-48405-2*) Bantam.

— Chocolate Horse. (Saddle Club Ser.: No. 32). (J). (gr. 4-6). 1994. 9.34 (*0-606-08104-6*) Turtleback.

— Christmas Treasure. (Saddle Club Super Edition Ser.: No. 7). 224p. (J). (gr. 4-7). 1998. pap. 4.50 (*0-553-48636-5*) BDD Bks Young Read.

— Conformation Faults. (Pine Hollow Ser.: No. 5). 192p. (YA). (gr. 7-12). 1999. mass mkt. 4.50 (*0-553-49246-2*) BDD Bks Young Read.

— Corey & the Spooky Pony. (Pony Tails Ser.: No. 9). (Illus.). 96p. (J). (gr. 3-5). 1996. pap. 3.50 (*0-553-48382-X*, Skylark BDD) BDD Bks Young Read.

— Corey & the Spooky Pony. (Pony Tails Ser.: No. 9). (Illus.). 96p. (J). (gr. 3-5). 1996. 8.60 (*0-606-09760-0*, Pub. by Turtleback) Demco.

— Corey in the Saddle. (Pony Tails Ser.: No. 6). (Illus.). 96p. (J). (gr. 3-5). 1996. pap. 3.50 (*0-553-48378-1*, Skylark BDD) BDD Bks Young Read.

— Corey in the Saddle. (Pony Tails Ser.: No. 6). (Illus.). 96p. (J). (gr. 3-5). 1996. 8.60 (*0-606-09757-0*, Pub. by Turtleback) Demco.

— Corey's Christmas Wish. (Pony Tails Ser.: No. 15). (Illus.). 96p. (Orig.). (J). (gr. 2-5). 1997. pap. 3.99 (*0-553-48485-0*) BDD Bks Young Read.

— Corey's Pony Is Missing. (Pony Tails Ser.: No. 3). (Illus.). (J). (gr. 3-5). 1995. pap. 4.75 (*0-553-54208-7*) BDD Bks Young Read.

— Corey's Pony is Missing. (Pony Tails Ser.: No. 3). (Illus.). (J). (gr. 3-5). 1995. 8.60 (*0-606-08586-6*, Pub. by Turtleback) Demco.

— Corey's Secret Friend. (Pony Tails Ser.: No. 12). (Illus.). 112p. (J). (gr. 2-5). 1997. pap. 3.99 (*0-553-48482-6*, Skylark BDD) BDD Bks Young Read.

— Course of Action. (Pine Hollow Ser.: No. 8). 224p. (YA). (gr. 7 up). 1999. mass mkt. 4.50 (*0-553-49286-1*) Bantam.

***Bryant, Bonnie.** Cross-Ties. (Pine Hollow Ser.: No. 11). (YA). (gr. 7-12). 2000. mass mkt. 4.50 (*0-553-49301-9*) BDD Bks Young Read.

Bryant, Bonnie. Cutting Horse. (Saddle Club Ser.: No. 56). 144p. (J). (gr. 4-6). 1996. pap. 3.99 (*0-553-48368-4*, Skylark BDD) BDD Bks Young Read.

— Cutting Horse. (Saddle Club Ser.: No. 56). (J). (gr. 4-6). 1996. 9.09 (*0-606-09810-0*, Pub. by Turtleback) Demco.

— Dream Horse. (Saddle Club Super Edition Ser.: No. 4). 208p. (J). (gr. 4-7). 1996. pap. 4.99 (*0-553-48367-6*, Skylark BDD) BDD Bks Young Read.

— Dream Horse. (Saddle Club Super Edition Ser.: No. 4). (J). (gr. 4-6). 1996. 9.60 (*0-606-09813-5*, Pub. by Turtleback) Demco.

***Bryant, Bonnie.** Driving Team. (Saddle Club Ser.: No. 90). 160p. (J). (gr. 4-7). 2000. pap. 4.50 (*0-553-48677-2*) BDD Bks Young Read.

Bryant, Bonnie. Dude Ranch. (Saddle Club Ser.: No. 6). 144p. (J). (gr. 4-6). 1989. pap. 3.99 (*0-553-15728-0*) Bantam.

— Dude Ranch. (Saddle Club Ser.: No. 6). (J). (gr. 4-6). 1989. 9.09 (*0-606-08120-8*) Turtleback.

— Endurance Ride. (Saddle Club Ser.: No. 69). 144p. (J). (gr. 4-7). 1997. pap. 3.99 (*0-553-48424-9*) BDD Bks Young Read.

— English Horse. (Saddle Club Ser.: No. 79). 192p. (J). (gr. 4-7). 1998. pap. 3.99 (*0-553-48629-2*, Skylark BDD) BDD Bks Young Read.

— English Rider. (Saddle Club Ser.: No. 80). 192p. (J). (gr. 4-7). 1998. pap. 3.99 (*0-553-48630-6*, Skylark BDD) BDD Bks Young Read.

— Flying Horse. (Saddle Club Ser.: No. 46). (J). (gr. 4-6). 1995. 9.09 (*0-606-08119-4*) Turtleback.

— Fox Hunt. (Saddle Club Ser.: No. 22). (J). (gr. 4-6). 1992. 8.60 (*0-606-08093-7*) Turtleback.

— Ghost Rider. (Saddle Club Ser.: No. 24). 144p. (J). (gr. 4-7). 1992. pap. 4.50 (*0-553-48067-7*) Bantam.

— Ghost Rider. (Saddle Club Ser.: No. 24). (J). (gr. 4-6). 1992. 9.34 (*0-606-08095-3*) Turtleback.

— Gift Horse. (Saddle Club Ser.: No. 40). (J). (gr. 6). 1994. pap. 4.50 (*0-553-54186-2*) Bantam.

— Gift Horse. (Saddle Club Ser.: No. 40). (J). (gr. 4-6). 1994. 9.09 (*0-606-08113-5*) Turtleback.

— Gold Medal Horse. (Saddle Club Ser.: No. 55). 144p. (J). (gr. 4-7). 1996. pap. 4.50 (*0-553-48366-8*) Bantam.

— Gold Medal Horse. (Saddle Club Ser.: No. 55). (J). (gr. 4-6). 1996. 9.09 (*0-606-09809-7*, Pub. by Turtleback) Demco.

— Gold Medal Rider. (Saddle Club Ser.: no. 54). (J). (gr. 4-6). 1996. 9.09 (*0-606-09808-9*, Pub. by Turtleback) Demco.

***Bryant, Bonnie.** Ground Training. (Pine Hollow Ser.: No. 10). 256p. (YA). (gr. 7-12). 2000. mass mkt. 4.50 (*0-553-49300-0*) BDD Bks Young Read.

Bryant, Bonnie. Hay Fever. (Saddle Club Ser.: No. 34). (J). (gr. 4-6). 1994. 8.60 (*0-606-08106-2*) Turtleback.

— Hayride. (Saddle Club Ser.: No. 31). 160p. (J). (gr. 4-6). 1993. pap. 3.99 (*0-553-48145-2*) Bantam.

— Hayride. (Saddle Club Ser.: No. 31). (J). (gr. 4-6). 1993. 9.09 (*0-606-08103-8*) Turtleback.

***Bryant, Bonnie.** Headstrong. (Pine Hollow Ser.: Vol. 14). (Illus.). 2000. mass mkt. 4.50 (*0-553-49304-3*) Bantam.

Bryant, Bonnie. High Horse. (Saddle Club Ser.: No. 33). (J). (gr. 4-6). 1994. 8.60 (*0-606-08105-4*) Turtleback.

***Bryant, Bonnie.** High Stakes. (Pine Hollow Ser.: No. 13). (YA). (gr. 7 up). 2000. mass mkt. 4.50 (*0-553-49303-5*) BDD Bks Young Read.

Bryant, Bonnie. Hobbyhorse. (Saddle Club Ser.: No. 60). 144p. (J). (gr. 4-6). 1996. pap. 3.99 (*0-553-48374-9*) BDD Bks Young Read.

— Hobbyhorse. (Saddle Club Ser.: No. 60). (J). (gr. 4-6). 1996. 9.09 (*0-606-10916-1*, Pub. by Turtleback) Demco.

— Holiday Horse. (Saddle Club Ser.: No. 72). 160p. (Orig.). (J). (gr. 4-7). 1997. pap. 4.50 (*0-553-48427-3*) BDD Bks Young Read.

— Hoof Beat. (Saddle Club Ser.: No. 9). (J). (gr. 4-6). 1990. 9.09 (*0-606-08123-2*) Turtleback.

— Horse Blues. LC 49-244090. (Saddle Club Ser.: No. 62). 160p. (J). (gr. 5-7). 1996. pap. 3.99 (*0-553-48417-6*) BDD Bks Young Read.

— Horse Blues. (Saddle Club Ser.: No. 62). (J). (gr. 4-6). 1997. 9.09 (*0-606-10918-8*, Pub. by Turtleback) Demco.

— Horse Capades. (Saddle Club Ser.: No. 64). 144p. (J). (gr. 4-7). 1997. pap. 3.99 (*0-553-48419-2*, Skylark BDD) BDD Bks Young Read.

— Horse Care. (Saddle Club Ser.: No. 76). 144p. (J). (gr. 4-7). 1998. pap. 3.99 (*0-553-48626-8*, Skylark BDD) BDD Bks Young Read.

— Horse Crazy. (Saddle Club Ser.: No. 1). 160p. (J). (gr. 5-7). 1996. pap. 4.50 (*0-553-48402-8*) Bantam.

— Horse Crazy. Demco Staff, ed. (Saddle Club Ser.: No. 1). (J). (gr. 4-6). 1996. 9.09 (*0-606-08088-0*, Pub. by Turtleback) Demco.

— Horse Fever. (Saddle Club Ser.: No. 85). (J). (gr. 4-7). 1998. pap. 3.99 (*0-553-48635-7*) BDD Bks Young Read.

— Horse Guest. (Saddle Club Ser.: No. 73). 144p. (Orig.). (J). (gr. 4-7). 1997. pap. 3.99 (*0-553-48623-3*) BDD Bks Young Read.

***Bryant, Bonnie.** Horse Love. (Saddle Club Ser.: No. 93). (Illus.). (J). (gr. 4-6). 2000. pap. 4.50 (*0-553-48697-7*, Skylark BDD) BDD Bks Young Read.

Bryant, Bonnie. Horse Magic. (Saddle Club Ser.: No. 47). 144p. (J). (gr. 4-7). 1995. pap. 3.99 (*0-553-48265-3*, Skylark BDD) BDD Bks Young Read.

— Horse Magic. (Saddle Club Ser.: No. 47). (J). (gr. 4-6). 1995. 8.60 (*0-606-08594-7*, Pub. by Turtleback) Demco.

— Horse Play. (Saddle Club Ser.: No. 7). 144p. (J). (gr. 4-6). 1989. pap. 3.99 (*0-553-15754-X*) Bantam.

— Horse Play. (Saddle Club Ser.: No. 7). (J). (gr. 4-6). 1989. 9.09 (*0-606-08121-6*) Turtleback.

— Horse Power. (Saddle Club Ser.: No. 4). (J). (gr. 4-6). 1989. 9.09 (*0-606-08112-7*) Turtleback.

— Horse Race. (Saddle Club Ser.: No. 70). 160p. (J). (gr. 4-7). 1997. pap. 3.99 (*0-553-48425-7*) BDD Bks Young Read.

— Horse Sense. (Saddle Club Ser.: No. 3). 144p. (J). (gr. 4-6). 1996. pap. 3.99 (*0-553-48404-4*) Bantam.

— Horse Sense. (Saddle Club Ser.: No. 3). (J). (gr. 4-6). 1989. 9.09 (*0-606-08101-1*) Turtleback.

— Horse Show. LC 90-103750. (Saddle Club Ser.: No. 8). 144p. (J). (gr. 4-7). 1989. pap. 3.99 (*0-553-15769-8*) Bantam.

— Horse Show. (Saddle Club Ser.: No. 8). (J). (gr. 4-6). 1989. 9.09 (*0-606-08122-4*) Turtleback.

— Horse Shy. (Saddle Club Ser.: No. 2). 160p. (J). (gr. 5-7). 1996. pap. 4.50 (*0-553-48403-6*) Bantam.

— Horse Shy. (Saddle Club Ser.: No. 2). (J). (gr. 4-6). 1996. 9.09 (*0-606-08091-0*) Turtleback.

— Horse-Sitters. (Saddle Club Ser.: No. 53). 144p. (J). (gr. 4-7). 1996. pap. 3.99 (*0-553-48363-3*) Bantam

— Horse-Sitters. (Saddle Club Ser.: No. 53). (J). (gr. 4-6). 1996. 9.09 (*0-606-09807-0*, Pub. by Turtleback) Demco.

***Bryant, Bonnie.** Horse Spy. (Saddle Club Ser.: Vol. 94). (Illus.). (J). 2000. pap. 4.50 (*0-553-48698-5*, Skylark BDD) BDD Bks Young Read.

Bryant, Bonnie. Horse Tale. (Saddle Club Ser.: No. 35). 144p. (J). (gr. 4-7). 1994. pap. 3.99 (*0-553-48150-9*) Bantam.

— Horse Tale. (Saddle Club Ser.: No. 35). (J). (gr. 4-6). 1994. 9.34 (*0-606-08107-0*) Turtleback.

— Horse Talk. (Saddle Club Ser.: No. 71). 144p. (Orig.). (J). (gr. 4-7). 1997. pap. 3.99 (*0-553-48426-5*) BDD Bks Young Read.

— Horse Thief. (Saddle Club Ser.: No. 83). 160p. (J). (gr. 4-7). 1998. pap. 3.99 (*0-553-48633-0*) Bantam.

— Horse Trade. (Saddle Club Ser.: No. 38). (J). (gr. 4-6). 1994. 9.34 (*0-606-08110-0*) Turtleback.

— Horse Trouble. (Saddle Club Ser.: No. 23). (J). (gr. 4-6). 1992. 8.60 (*0-606-08094-5*) Turtleback.

— Horse Whispers. (Saddle Club Ser.: No. 74). 144p. (J). (gr. 4-6). 1998. pap. 4.50 (*0-553-48624-1*, Skylark BDD) BDD Bks Young Read.

— Horse Wise. (Saddle Club Ser.: No. 11). (J). (gr. 4-6). 1990. 9.09 (*0-606-03650-4*, Pub. by Turtleback) Demco.

— Horseflies. (Saddle Club Ser.: No. 78). 144p. (J). (gr. 4-7). 1998. pap. 3.99 (*0-553-48628-4*, Skylark BDD) BDD Bks Young Read.

— Horsenapped. (Saddle Club Ser.: No. 17). (J). (gr. 4-6). 1991. 9.09 (*0-606-04935-5*, Pub. by Turtleback) Demco.

— Horseshoe. (Saddle Club Ser.: No. 44). 144p. (J). (gr. 4-7). 1995. pap. 3.99 (*0-553-48262-9*) Bantam.

— Horseshoe. (Saddle Club Ser.: No. 44). (J). (gr. 4-6). 1995. 8.60 (*0-606-08117-8*) Turtleback.

— Jasmine & the Jumping Pony. (Pony Tails Ser.: No. 16). (Illus.). 112p. (J). (gr. 2-5). 1998. pap. 3.99 (*0-553-48590-3*, Skylark BDD) BDD Bks Young Read.

— Jasmine Trots Ahead. (Pony Tails Ser.: No. 7). (Illus.). 96p. (J). (gr. 3-5). 1996. 8.60 (*0-606-09758-9*, Pub. by Turtleback) Demco.

— Jasmine's Christmas Ride. (Pony Tails Ser.: No. 4). (Illus.). (J). (gr. 3-5). 1995. pap. 4.75 (*0-553-54209-5*) BDD Bks Young Read.

— Jasmine's Christmas Ride. (Pony Tails Ser.: No. 4). (Illus.). 96p. (J). (gr. 3-5). 1995. pap. 3.50 (*0-553-48258-0*, Skylark BDD) BDD Bks Young Read.

— Jasmine's Christmas Ride. (Pony Tails Ser.: No. 4). (Illus.). (J). (gr. 3-5). 1995. 8.60 (*0-606-08587-4*, Pub. by Turtleback) Demco.

— Lisa. (Saddle Club Ser.). 304p. (J). (gr. 4-6). 1999. pap. 4.50 (*0-553-48676-4*) BDD Bks Young Read.

— The Long Ride. (Pine Hollow Ser.: No. 1). 192p. (YA). (gr. 5-9). 1998. mass mkt. 4.50 (*0-553-49242-X*) BDD Bks Young Read.

— Lucky Horse. (Saddle Club Ser.: No. 89). 160p. (J). (gr. 4-6). 1999. pap. 3.99 (*0-553-48675-6*) BDD Bks Young Read.

— May Goes to England. (Pony Tails Ser.: No. 11). (Illus.). 112p. (J). (gr. 3-5). 1997. pap. 3.50 (*0-553-48481-8*, Skylark BDD) BDD Bks Young Read.

— May Rides A New Pony. (Pony Tails Ser.: No. 8). (Illus.). 96p. (J). (gr. 4-7). 1996. pap. 3.50 (*0-553-48380-3*, Skylark BDD) BDD Bks Young Read.

— May Rides a New Pony. (Pony Tails Ser.: No. 8). (Illus.). 96p. (J). (gr. 3-5). 1996. 8.60 (*0-606-09759-7*, Pub. by Turtleback) Demco.

— May Takes the Lead. (Pony Tails Ser.: No. 5). (Illus.). 96p. (J). (gr. 3-5). 1995. pap. 3.50 (*0-553-48360-9*, Skylark BDD) BDD Bks Young Read.

— May Takes the Lead. (Pony Tails Ser.: No. 5). (Illus.). 96p. (J). (gr. 3-5). 1996. pap. 4.75 (*0-553-54248-6*) BDD Bks Young Read.

— May Takes the Lead. (Pony Tails Ser.: No. 5). (Illus.). 96p. (J). (gr. 3-5). 1996. 8.60 (*0-606-08588-2*, Pub. by Turtleback) Demco.

— May's Riding Lesson. (Pony Tails Ser.: No. 2). (Illus.). (J). (gr. 3-5). 1995. pap. 4.50 (*0-553-54207-9*) BDD Bks Young Read.

— May's Riding Lesson. (Pony Tails Ser.: No. 2). (Illus.). (J). (gr. 3-5). 1995. 8.60 (*0-606-08030-9*) Turtleback.

***Bryant, Bonnie.** Million-Dollar Horse. (Saddle Club Ser.: No. 92). (Illus.). 160p. (J). (gr. 4-6). 2000. pap. 4.50 (*0-553-48696-9*, Skylark BDD) BDD Bks Young Read.

Bryant, Bonnie. Mystery Ride. (Saddle Club Ser.: No. 48). 144p. (J). (gr. 4-7). 1995. pap. 3.99 (*0-553-48266-1*, Skylark BDD) BDD Bks Young Read.

— Mystery Ride. (Saddle Club Ser.: No. 48). (J). (gr. 4-6). 1995. 8.60 (*0-606-08595-5*, Pub. by Turtleback) Demco.

— Nightmare. (Saddle Club Super Edition Ser.: No. 6). 208p. (Orig.). (J). (gr. 4-7). 1997. pap. 4.99 (*0-553-48428-1*) BDD Bks Young Read.

— Pack Trip. (Saddle Club Ser.: No. 18). 144p. (J). (gr. 4-7). 1991. pap. 3.99 (*0-553-15928-3*) Bantam.

— Pack Trip. (Saddle Club Ser.: No. 18). (J). (gr. 4-6). 1991. 9.09 (*0-606-00683-4*, Pub. by Turtleback) Demco.

— Painted Horse. (Saddle Club Ser.: No. 75). 144p. (J). (gr. 4-6). 1998. pap. 3.99 (*0-553-48625-X*, Skylark BDD) BDD Bks Young Read.

— Penalty Points. (Pine Hollow Ser.: No. 7). 224p. (YA). (gr. 7-12). 1999. mass mkt. 4.50 (*0-553-49285-3*) Bantam.

— Phantom Horse. (Saddle Club Ser.: No. 59). (J). (gr. 4-6). 1997. 9.09 (*0-606-10915-3*, Pub. by Turtleback) Demco.

— Photo Finish. (Saddle Club Ser.: No. 43). (J). (gr. 4-6). 1995. 8.60 (*0-606-08116-X*) Turtleback.

— Pleasure Horse. (Saddle Club Ser.: No. 51). (J). (gr. 4-6). 1996. 9.09 (*0-606-09805-4*, Pub. by Turtleback) Demco.

— Pony Crazy. (Pony Tails Ser.: No. 1). (Illus.). (J). (gr. 3-5). 1995. pap. 4.50 (*0-553-54206-0*) BDD Bks Young Read.

— Pony Crazy. (Pony Tails Ser.: No. 1). (Illus.). (J). (gr. 3-5). 1998. 9.09 (*0-606-08029-5*, Pub. by Turtleback) Demco.

— Purebred. (Saddle Club Ser.: No. 39). (J). (gr. 4-6). 1994. 9.09 (*0-606-08111-9*) Turtleback.

— Quarter Horse. (Saddle Club Ser.: No. 82). 144p. (J). (gr. 4-7). 1998. pap. 3.99 (*0-553-48632-2*, Skylark BDD) BDD Bks Young Read.

— Racehorse. (Saddle Club Ser.: No. 21). (J). (gr. 4-6). 1992. 9.09 (*0-606-08092-9*) Turtleback.

— Ranch Hands. (Saddle Club Ser.: No. 29). (J). (gr. 4-6). 1993. 9.34 (*0-606-08100-3*) Turtleback.

— Reining In. (Pine Hollow Ser.: No. 3). (YA). (gr. 7-12). 1998. mass mkt. 4.50 (*0-553-49244-6*) Bantam.

— Riding Camp. (Saddle Club Ser.: No. 10). 144p. (J). (gr. 4-7). 1990. pap. 3.99 (*0-553-15790-6*) Bantam.

— Riding Camp. (Saddle Club Ser.: No. 10). (J). (gr. 4-6). 1990. 9.09 (*0-606-04526-0*, Pub. by Turtleback) Demco.

— Riding Class. (Saddle Club Ser.: No. 52). 144p. (J). (gr. 4-6). 1996. pap. 3.99 (*0-553-48362-5*) Bantam.

— Riding Class. (Saddle Club Ser.: No. 52). (J). (gr. 4-6). 1996. 9.09 (*0-606-09806-2*, Pub. by Turtleback) Demco.

— Riding Lesson. (Saddle Club Ser.: No. 36). (J). (gr. 4-6). 1994. 9.09 (*0-606-08108-9*) Turtleback.

— Riding To Win. (Pine Hollow Ser.: No. 9). 272p. (YA). (gr. 4-7). 1999. mass mkt. 4.50 (*0-553-49287-X*) Bantam.

— Rocking Horse. (Saddle Club Ser.: No. 77). 144p. (J). (gr. 4-6). 1998. pap. 3.99 (*0-553-48627-6*, Skylark BDD) BDD Bks Young Read.

— Rodeo Rider. (Saddle Club Ser.: No. 12). 144p. (J). (gr. 4-6). 1990. pap. 3.99 (*0-553-15821-X*) Bantam.

— Rodeo Rider. (Saddle Club Ser.: No. 12). (J). (gr. 4-6). 1990. 9.09 (*0-606-04528-7*, Pub. by Turtleback) Demco.

— Saddle Club Boxed Set, 6 vols. (Saddle Club Ser.). (J). (gr. 4-6). lib. bdg. 95.58 (*0-8368-1279-4*) Gareth Stevens Inc.

— Saddle Club Boxed Set, 11 bks. enl. large type ed. Incl. Hoof Beat. large type ed. 144p. (J). (gr. 4-6). 1996. lib. bdg. 19.93 (*0-8368-1531-9*); Horse Play. large type ed. 144p. (J). (gr. 4-6). 1996. lib. bdg. 21.27 (*0-8368-1529-7*); Horse Show. large type ed. 144p. (J). (gr. 4-6). 1996. lib. bdg. 21.27 (*0-8368-1530-0*); (Saddle Club Ser.). (Illus.). (J). (gr. 4-6). 1996. Set lib. bdg., boxed set 239.20 (*0-8368-1554-8*) Gareth Stevens Inc.

— Saddle Club Boxed Set, 6 bks., Set. enl. ed. (Saddle Club Ser.). 864p. (J). (gr. 4-6). 1995. lib. bdg. 71.70 (*0-8368-1528-9*) Gareth Stevens Inc.

— Saddle Sore. (Saddle Club Ser.: No. 66). 160p. (J). (gr. 4-7). 1997. pap. 3.99 (*0-553-48421-4*) BDD Bks Young Read.

— Saddlebags. (Saddle Club Ser.: No. 42). (J). (gr. 4-6). 1995. 8.60 (*0-606-08115-1*) Turtleback.

— Schooling Horse. 553rd ed. (Saddle Club Ser.: No. 84). (J). (gr. 4-7). 1998. pap. 3.99 (*0-553-48634-9*) BDD Bks Young Read.

— Sea Horse. (Saddle Club Ser.: No. 14). 144p. (J). (gr. 4-7). 1990. pap. 3.99 (*0-553-15847-3*) Bantam.

— Sea Horse. (Saddle Club Ser.: No. 14). (J). (gr. 4-6). 1990. 9.09 (*0-606-08089-9*) Turtleback.

— Secret Horse. (Saddle Club Ser.: No. 86). 160p. (J). (gr. 4-6). 1999. pap. 3.99 (*0-553-48671-3*) BDD Bks Young Read.

— The Secret of the Stallion. (Saddle Club Super Edition Ser.: No. 2). 208p. (J). (gr. 4-7). 1995. pap. 4.99 (*0-553-48152-5*) Bantam.

— The Secret of the Stallion. (Saddle Club Super Edition Ser.: No. 2). (J). (gr. 4-6). 1995. 9.85 (*0-606-08125-9*) Turtleback.

***Bryant, Bonnie.** Setting the Pace. (Pine Hollow Ser.: Vol. 15). (Illus.). (J). 2000. mass mkt. 4.50 (*0-553-49305-1*) Bantam.

Bryant, Bonnie. Show Horse. (Saddle Club Ser.: No. 25). (J). (gr. 4-6). 1992. 9.09 (*0-606-08096-1*) Turtleback.

***Bryant, Bonnie.** Show Judge. (Saddle Club Ser.: Vol. 95). (Illus.). (J). 2000. pap. 4.50 (*0-553-48699-3*, Skylark BDD) BDD Bks Young Read.

Bryant, Bonnie. Show Jumper. (Saddle Club Ser.: No. 87). 160p. (J). (gr. 4-6). 1999. pap. 3.99 (*0-553-48672-1*) BDD Bks Young Read.

— Shying at Trouble. (Pine Hollow Ser.: No. 6). (YA). (gr. 7 up). 1999. mass mkt. 4.50 (*0-553-49247-0*) Bantam.

— Sidesaddle. (Saddle Club Ser.: No. 88). 144p. (J). (gr. 4-6). 1999. pap. 3.99 (*0-553-48673-X*) BDD Bks Young Read.

— Snow Ride. (Saddle Club Ser.: No. 20). 144p. (J). (gr. 4-7). 1992. pap. 3.99 (*0-553-15907-0*) Bantam.

— Snow Ride. (Saddle Club Ser.: No. 20). (J). (gr. 4-6). 1992. 9.09 (*0-606-00759-8*, Pub. by Turtleback) Demco.

— Stable Farewell. (Saddle Club Ser.: No. 49). 144p. (J). (gr. 4-7). 1995. pap. 3.50 (*0-553-48267-X*, Skylark BDD) BDD Bks Young Read.

— Stable Farewell. (Saddle Club Ser.: No. 49). (J). (gr. 4-6). 1995. 8.60 (*0-606-08596-3*, Pub. by Turtleback) Demco.

B

— Stable Groom. (Saddle Club Ser.: No. 45). 144p. (J). (gr. 4-7). 1995. pap. 3.99 (*0-553-48263-7*) Bantam.
— Stable Groom. (Saddle Club Ser.: No. 45). (J). (gr. 4-6). 1995. 8.60 (*0-606-08118-6*) Turtleback.
— Stable Manners. (Saddle Club Ser.: No. 28). (J). (gr. 4-6). 1993. 9.09 (*0-606-08099-6*) Turtleback.
— Stable Witch. (Saddle Club Ser.: No. 41). 144p. (J). (gr. 4-6). 1995. pap. 3.99 (*0-553-48259-9*) Bantam.
— Stable Witch. (Saddle Club Ser.: No. 41). (J). (gr. 4-6). 1995. 9.09 (*0-606-08114-3*) Turtleback.
— Stage Coach. (Saddle Club Ser.: No. 37). (J). (gr. 4-6). 1994. 9.34 (*0-606-08109-7*) Turtleback.
— Star Rider. (Saddle Club Ser.: No. 19). 144p. (J). (gr. 4-7). 1991. pap. 3.99 (*0-553-15938-0*) Bantam.
— Star Rider. (Saddle Club Ser.: No. 19). (J). (gr. 4-6). 1991. 9.09 (*0-606-00772-5*, Pub. by Turtleback) Demco.
— Starlight Christmas. (Saddle Club Ser.: No. 13). 144p. (J). (gr. 4-7). 1990. pap. 3.99 (*0-553-15832-5*) Bantam.
— Starlight Christmas. (Saddle Club Ser.: No. 13). (J). (gr. 4-6). 1990. 9.09 (*0-606-04807-3*, Pub. by Turtleback) Demco.
***Bryant, Bonnie.** Starting Gate. (Saddle Club Ser.: Vol. 91). (J). (gr. 4-7). 2000. pap. 4.50 (*0-553-48695-0*) BDD Bks Young Read.
Bryant, Bonnie. Stevie. (Saddle Club Ser.). 304p. (J). (gr. 4-6). 1999. pap. 4.50 (*0-553-48674-8*) BDD Bks Young Read.
— Summer Horse. (Saddle Club Ser.: No. 67). 144p. (J). (gr. 4-7). 1997. pap. 3.99 (*0-553-48422-2*) Bantam.
— Summer Rider. (Saddle Club Ser.: No. 68). 160p. (J). (gr. 4-7). 1997. pap. 3.99 (*0-553-48423-0*) BDD Bks Young Read.
— A Summer Without Horses. (Saddle Club Super Edition Ser.: No. 1). 208p. (J). (gr. 4-7). 1994. pap. 4.99 (*0-553-48149-5*) Bantam.
— A Summer Without Horses. (Saddle Club Super Edition Ser.: No. 1). (J). (gr. 4-6). 1994. 9.85 (*0-606-08124-0*) Turtleback.
— Team Play. (Saddle Club Ser.: No. 15). 144p. (J). (gr. 4-7). 1991. pap. 3.99 (*0-553-15862-7*) Bantam.
— Team Play. (Saddle Club Ser.: No. 15). (J). (gr. 4-6). 1991. 9.09 (*0-606-08090-2*) Turtleback.
— Tight Rein. (Saddle Club Ser.: No. 57). 144p. (J). (gr. 4-7). 1996. pap. 3.99 (*0-553-48370-6*, Skylark BDD) BDD Bks Young Read.
— Tight Rein. (Saddle Club Ser.: No. 57). (J). (gr. 4-6). 1996. 9.09 (*0-606-09811-9*, Pub. by Turtleback) Demco.
— The Trail Home. (Pine Hollow Ser.: No. 2). (YA). (gr. 7 up). 1998. mass mkt. 4.50 (*0-553-49243-8*) Bantam.
— Trail Mates. (Saddle Club Ser.: No. 5). 144p. (J). (gr. 4-7). 1989. pap. 4.50 (*0-553-15703-5*) Bantam.
— Trail Mates. (Saddle Club Ser.: No. 5). (J). (gr. 4-6). 1989. 9.09 (*0-606-04563-5*, Pub. by Turtleback) Demco.
— Wagon Trail. (Saddle Club Ser.: No. 81). 144p. (J). (gr. 4-7). 1998. pap. 3.99 (*0-553-48631-4*, Skylark BDD) BDD Bks Young Read.
— Western Star. (Saddle Club Super Edition Ser.: No. 3). 208p. (J). (gr. 4-7). 1995. pap. 4.99 (*0-553-48270-X*, Skylark BDD) BDD Bks Young Read.
— Western Star. (Saddle Club Super Edition Ser.: No. 3). (J). (gr. 4-6). 1995. 9.60 (*0-606-08598-X*, Pub. by Turtleback) Demco.
— Wild Horses. (Saddle Club Ser.: No. 58). (J). (gr. 4-6). 1996. pap. 4.99 (*0-553-54267-2*) BDD Bks Young Read.
— Wild Horses. (Saddle Club Ser.: No. 58). 144p. (J). (gr. 4-7). 1996. pap. 4.50 (*0-553-48371-4*, Skylark BDD) BDD Bks Young Read.
— Wild Horses. (Saddle Club Ser.: No. 58). (J). (gr. 4-6). 1996. 9.09 (*0-606-09812-7*, Pub. by Turtleback) Demco.
— Yankee Swap. (Saddle Club Ser.: No. 50). 144p. (J). (gr. 4-7). 1995. pap. 3.99 (*0-553-48268-8*, Skylark BDD) BDD Bks Young Read.
— Yankee Swap. (Saddle Club Ser.: No. 50). (J). (gr. 4-6). 1996. 9.09 (*0-606-08597-1*, Pub. by Turtleback) Demco.
Bryant, Bonnie & Leppard, Louis Gladys. Who's Mandie? (Mantlemass Ser.: No. 1). 128p. (J). 1999. pap. 4.50 (*0-553-48659-4*) BDD Bks Young Read.
Bryant, Bonnie, jt. auth. see Hiller, B. B.
Bryant, Brenda K., compiled by. Counseling for Racial Understanding. LC 93-36424. 123p. 1994. pap. text 23.95 (*1-55620-126-5*, 72111) Am Coun Assn.
Bryant, Brenda K., jt. ed. see Boll, Thomas J.
Bryant, Brenda K., jt. ed. see VandenBos, Gary R.
Bryant, Bunyan, ed. Environmental Justice: Issues, Policies & Solutions. 300p. 1995. text 48.00 (*1-55963-416-2*) Island Pr.
— Environmental Justice: Issues, Policies & Solutions. 300p. (C). 1995. pap. text 25.00 (*1-55963-417-0*) Island Pr.
Bryant, Bunyan & Jones, Alan H. Seeking Effective Schools for African American Children. LC 92-73154. 88p. (Orig.). 1993. pap. 11.95 (*1-880192-01-2*) Caddo Gap Pr.
Bryant, C. Stafford Cripps. 1997. text 50.00 (*0-340-67892-5*, Pub. by Hodder & Stought Ltd) Trafalgar.
Bryant, C. & Behm, Carol. Biochemical Adaptation in Parasites. 250p. 1988. text 79.95 (*0-318-32871-2*, Pub. by C Helm) Routldge.
Bryant, C. & Johnson, T. Agriculture in the City's Countryside. 256p. 1989. 39.00 (*1-85293-027-6*) St Martin.
Bryant, C. R. & Johnston, T. R. Agriculture in the City's Countryside. 256p. 1992. text 45.00 (*0-8020-2842-X*); pap. text 18.95 (*0-8020-7723-4*) U of Toronto Pr.
Bryant, Carl L., et al. Travel Selling Skills. 112p. 1992. pap., teacher ed. write for info. (*0-538-70752-6*) S-W Pub.
— Travel Selling Skills. 112p. 1992. pap. 22.95 (*0-538-70553-1*) S-W Pub.
Bryant, Carol A., et al. The Cultural Feast: An Introduction to Food Society & Change. (Illus.). 481p. 1985. 43.75 (*0-314-85222-0*) West Pub.
Bryant, Carolyn H., jt. auth. see Peck, Carole.
Bryant, Carolyn H., ed. see Shanley, Mary K.
Bryant, Cecelia. I Dance with God: A Cojourney in Prayer. LC 97-196110. 185p. 1995. pap. 21.00 (*1-888077-01-8*) Akosua Visions.
***Bryant, Cedric X., et al.** 101 Frequently Asked Questions about "Health & Wellness" & "Nutrition" (Illus.). 160p. 2000. pap. 16.95 (*1-57167-452-7*) Coaches Choice.
Bryant, Cedric X., jt. auth. see Sandusky, Jerry.
Bryant, Cedric X., jt. ed. see Peterson, James A.
Bryant, Charles S. History of Fillmore County, Minnesota. 626p. 1993. reprint ed. lib. bdg. 65.00 (*0-8328-3612-5*) Higginson Bk Co.
Bryant, Charles S., jt. auth. see Neill, Edward D.
Bryant, Charles V. Rediscovering Our Spirit. 1991. pap. 9.95 (*0-687-60971-2*) Abingdon.
— Rediscovering Our Spiritual Gifts. LC 90-71865. 187p. 1991. pap. 11.00 (*0-8358-0633-2*) Upper Room Bks.
Bryant, Charles V. Your Spiritual Gifts Inventory. LC 97-11416. 1997. pap. text 20.00 (*0-8358-0819-X*) Upper Room Bks.
Bryant, Charray, jt. auth. see Bryant, John.
***Bryant, Choice L. & Goff, Clyde O.** Justification, Imputed Righteousness, Assurance-Unity & Diversitry. 1999. pap. 9.95 (*1-56794-188-5*) Star Bible.
***Bryant, Chris.** CCNP Foundation of Routing & Switching Cheat Sheets. (Illus.). 600p. 2000. pap. 29.99 (*0-7897-2363-8*) Que.
Bryant, Chris, jt. auth. see Gilchrist, Paige.
Bryant, Christopher. The Heart in Pilgrimage: Christian Guidelines for the Human Journey. 208p. 1984. 9.95 (*0-8164-0457-7*) Harper SF.
— A Preface to Romans: Notes on the Epistle in Its Literary & Cultural Setting. LC 99-10412. 336p. 2000. text 60.00 (*0-19-513023-5*) OUP.
Bryant, Christopher G. Practical Sociology: Postempiricism & the Reconstruction of Theory & Application. (Illus.). 186p. (C). 1996. 70.95 (*0-7456-1492-2*); pap. 30.95 (*0-7456-1493-0*) Blackwell Pubs.
Bryant, Christopher G. & Jary, David, eds. Anthony Giddens: Critical Assessments, Set. LC 96-1120. 1808p. (C). 1996. 700.00 (*0-415-11688-0*) Routledge.
Bryant, Christopher G. & Mokrzycki, Edmund, eds. The New Great Transformation? Change & Continuity in East-Central Europe. LC 93-20938. (Illus.). 240p. (C). 1994. pap. 27.99 (*0-415-09250-7*) Routledge.
Bryant, Claire. Alpine Flowers Iron-On Transfer Patterns. (Illus.). 48p. 1999. pap. 3.95 (*0-486-40290-8*) Dover.
— American Wildflower Iron-On Transfer Patterns. (Illus.). 1988. pap. 3.95 (*0-486-25624-3*) Dover.
— Candlewicking: Twenty-Four Iron-on Transfer Patterns & Complete Instructions. (Crafts Ser.). 56p. (Orig.). 1984. pap. 4.95 (*0-486-24572-1*) Dover.
— Garden Flowers Iron-On Transfer Patterns. (Illus.). 48p. 1989. pap. 3.95 (*0-486-25985-4*) Dover.
— Make Your Own Old Fashioned Cl. 80p. 1990. pap. 5.95 (*0-486-26361-4*) Dover.
— Make Your Own Southern Belle Cloth Doll & Her Wardrobe. LC 99-23441. (Illus.). 80p. 1999. pap. text 6.95 (*0-486-40483-8*) Dover.
— Redoute Flowers Iron-On Transfers. (Illus.). 48p. 1998. pap., spiral bd. 3.95 (*0-486-29990-2*) Dover.
— Victorian Floral Iron-On Transfer Patterns. (Transfer Patterns Ser.). (Illus.). 48p. (Orig.). 1991. pap. 3.95 (*0-486-26665-6*) Dover.
***Bryant, Clifton D.** Encyclopedia of Criminology & Deviant Behavior, 4 vols. (Illus.). 2000. 325.00 (*1-56032-772-3*) Taylor & Francis.
Bryant, Clifton D. Sexual Deviancy & Social Proscription: The Social Context of Carnal Behavior. LC 81-6216. 432p. 1982. 52.00 (*0-89885-024-X*, Kluwer Acad Hman Sci); pap. 24.95 (*0-89885-094-0*, Kluwer Acad Hman Sci) Kluwer Academic.
Bryant, Clifton D., ed. Deviant Behavior: Readings in the Sociology of Norm Violations. 250p. 1989. 59.95 (*0-89116-696-3*); pap. 45.95 (*0-89116-779-X*) Hemisp Pub.
Bryant, Clifton D., et al. The Rural Workforce: Non-Agricultural Occupations in America. LC 84-28410. 288p. (C). 1985. 49.95 (*0-89789-076-0*, Bergin & Garvey) Greenwood.
Bryant, Clora, et al, eds. Central Avenue Sounds: Jazz in Los Angeles. LC 97-2560. 250p. 1999. pap. 18.95 (*0-520-22098-6*, Pub. by U CA Pr) Cal Prin Full Svc.
Bryant, Clora, jt. auth. see Isoardi, Steven L.
Bryant, Clyde T. Reaching for God's Highest. 240p. (Orig.). 1987. pap. write for info. (*0-9618387-0-1*) Clyde T Bryant.
Bryant College Staff & Guay, E. Joseph. Programming in VAX-BASIC. LC 84-14602. 288p. (C). 1986. write for info. (*0-201-11568-9*) Addison-Wesley.
— VAX BASIC Programming. LC 84-14602. 288p. (C). 1986. pap. text, student ed. 8.00 (*0-201-11567-0*) Addison-Wesley.
Bryant, Coralie, ed. Poverty, Policy, & Food Security in Southern Africa. LC 87-32243. 280p. 1988. lib. bdg. 40.00 (*1-55587-092-9*) L Rienner.
***Bryant, Cottrell.** Gimp for Linux. LC 99-51486. (Bible Ser.). 768p. 2000. 39.99 (*0-7645-3398-3*) IDG Bks.
Bryant, D. A. Accleration of Electrons in the Aurora & Beyond. LC 98-43372. 311p. 1998. write for info. (*0-7503-0533-9*) IOP Pub.
Bryant, D. C., et al. An Historical Anthology of Select British Speeches. LC 67-21676. 558p. reprint ed. 173.00 (*0-8357-9904-2*, 201247100081) Bks Demand.
Bryant, Dana. Song of the Siren: Tales of Rhythm & Revolution. LC 96-127101. 128p. (Orig.). 1995. pap. 8.00 (*1-57297-004-9*) Blvd Books.
Bryant, Daniel, tr. see Zhang Kangkang.
Bryant, Darrol M., ed. Proceedings of the Virgin Islands' Seminar on Unification Theology. LC 80-52594. (Conference Ser.: No. 6). (Illus.). xv, 323p. (Orig.). 1980. pap. text 9.95 (*0-932894-06-2*) Unif Theol Seminary.
Bryant, David. Conciertos de Oracion.Tr. of Concerts of Prayer. (SPA.). 188p. 1990. pap. 4.99 (*1-56063-030-2*, 498456) Editorial Unilit.
— En la Brecha.Tr. of In the Gap. (SPA.). 1990. pap. write for info. (*0-614-27037-5*) Editorial Unilit.
— En la Brecha (In the Gap) (SPA.). 1990. 4.99 (*1-56063-016-7*, 498457) Editorial Unilit.
— The Rhetoric of Pessimism & Strategies of Containment in the Short Stories of Guy de Maupassant. LC 93-27111. (Studies in French Literature: Vol. 7). 200p. 1993. text 79.95 (*0-7734-9344-1*) E Mellen.
— Short Fiction & the Press in France, 1829-1841: Followed by a Selection of Short Fiction from the Periodical & Daily Press. LC 95-3920. (Studies in French Literature: Vol. 24). 396p. 1995. text 99.95 (*0-7734-8956-8*) E Mellen.
— Wooden Clock Cases. LC 94-46442. (Illus.). 160p. 1995. pap. 17.95 (*0-8117-2597-9*) Stackpole.
Bryant, David J. Faith & the Play of Imagination: On the Role of Imagination in Religion. LC 88-37108. (Studies in American Biblical Hermeneutics: No. 5). xi, 130p. (C). 1989. pap. text 16.95 (*0-86554-349-6*, MUP/P078) Mercer Univ Pr.
Bryant, Deborah & Driscoll, Mark J. Exploring Classroom Assessment in Mathematics: A Guide for Professional Development. LC 97-43839. (Illus.). 59p. 1998. pap. 13.95 (*0-87353-438-7*) NCTM.
Bryant, Deborah, ed. see National Research Council Staff.
Bryant, Delmar. The Art of Alchemy, or The Generation of Gold, Pt. II, Lessons 4-6. 1990. pap. 5.95 (*1-55818-170-9*) Holmes Pub.
— The Art of Alchemy, or The Generation of Gold, Pt. III, Lessons 7-9. 1990. pap. 5.95 (*1-55818-171-7*) Holmes Pub.
— The Art of Alchemy, or The Generation of Gold, Pt. IV, Lessons 10-12. 1990. pap. 5.95 (*1-55818-172-5*) Holmes Pub.
— The Art of Alchemy, or The Generation of Gold, Pt. I, Lessons 1-3: A Course of Practical Lessons in Metallic Transmutation. 1990. pap. 5.95 (*1-55818-169-5*) Holmes Pub.
Bryant, Delmar D. The Light of Life: The Mastery of Death. 165p. 1996. reprint ed. spiral bd. 13.50 (*0-7873-0126-4*) Hlth Research.
— The Light of Life or the Mastery of Death (1911) 170p. 1996. reprint ed. pap. 12.95 (*1-56459-921-3*) Kessinger Pub.
Bryant, Denise Clayton. Opening the Door. 1997. 12.95 (*1-55630-877-9*) Brentwood Comm.
Bryant, Denise F., ed. see Brunet-Perrault, Nicole & Doss, Cheryl R.
***Bryant, Diane Pedrotty, et al.** Step-by-Step Guide for Including Students with Disabilities in State & District-Wide Assessment. LC 00-39050. 2001. write for info. (*0-89079-855-9*) PRO-ED.
Bryant, Dirk, et al. The Last Frontier Forests: Ecosystems & Economies on the Edge. (FRE.). 44p. 1997. pap. 20.00 (*1-56973-221-3*); pap. 20.00 (*1-56973-223-X*) World Resources Inst.
— The Last Frontier Forests: Ecosystems & Economies on the Edge. 44p. 1997. pap. 20.00 (*1-56973-198-5*) World Resources Inst.
Bryant, Dirk, et al. Reefs at Risk: A Map-Based Indicator of Threats to the World's Coral Reefs. LC 98-86375. (Illus.). 56p. 1998. pap. 20.00 (*1-56973-257-4*) World Resources Inst.
Bryant, Donald A., ed. The Molecular Biology of Cyanobacteria. (Advances in Photosynthesis Ser.: Vol. 1). 1995. lib. bdg. 355.00 (*0-7923-3222-9*) Kluwer Academic.
Bryant, Donald A., jt. ed. see Stevens, S. Edward, Jr.
Bryant, Donna M. & Graham, Mimi A., eds. Implementing Early Intervention: From Research to Effective Practice. LC 93-30813. 358p. 1993. lib. bdg. 44.00 (*0-89862-247-6*) Guilford Pubns.
Bryant, Doris & Kessler, Judy. Beyond Integration: One Multiple's Journey. 176p. 1995. 23.00 (*0-393-70206-5*) Norton.
Bryant, Doris, et al. The Family Inside: Working with the Multiple. 320p. (C). 1992. 32.95 (*0-393-70142-5*) Norton.
Bryant, Dorothy. Anita, Anita. LC 93-72365. 300p. 1994. 25.00 (*0-931688-17-5*); pap. 12.95 (*0-931688-18-3*) Ata Bks.
— Confessions of Madame Psyche. LC 97-42178. (Illus.). 400p. (Orig.). 1998. reprint ed. pap. 18.95 (*1-55861-186-X*) Feminist Pr.
— Day in San Francisco. LC 82-73209. 144p. 1982. 20.00 (*0-931688-09-4*); pap. 9.95 (*0-931688-10-8*) Ata Bks.
— Ella Price's Journal. LC 75-39758. 225p. 1982. reprint ed. pap. text 9.95 (*0-931688-08-6*) Feminist Pr.
— Ella Price's Journal. LC 75-39758. 256p. 1997. reprint ed. lib. bdg. 35.00 (*1-55861-181-9*) Feminist Pr.
— Ella Price's Journal. LC 75-39758. 265p. 1998. reprint ed. pap. 14.95 (*1-55861-175-4*) Feminist Pr.
— Killing Wonder. LC 81-66995. 180p. 1981. 20.00 (*0-931688-06-X*); pap. 9.95 (*0-931688-07-8*) Ata Bks.
— The Kin of Ata Are Waiting for You. 1997. pap. 11.95 (*0-679-77843-8*) Random.
— Miss Giardino. LC 78-54280. 160p. 1978. pap. 9.95 (*0-931688-01-9*) Feminist Pr.
— Miss Giardino. LC 78-54280. 192p. 1997. reprint ed. pap. 11.95 (*1-55861-174-6*); reprint ed. lib. bdg. 32.00 (*1-55861-180-0*) Feminist Pr.
— Myths to Lie By. LC 83-51600. 192p. 1984. 20.00 (*0-931688-11-6*); pap. 9.95 (*0-931688-12-4*) Ata Bks.
— Prisoners. LC 79-55170. 178p. (Orig.). 1980. 20.00 (*0-931688-04-3*); pap. 9.95 (*0-931688-05-1*) Ata Bks.
— The Test. LC 91-72556. 146p. 1991. 20.00 (*0-931688-15-9*); pap. 9.95 (*0-931688-16-7*) Ata Bks.
— Writing a Novel. LC 78-69766. 120p. 1978. pap. 9.95 (*0-931688-02-7*) Ata Bks.
Bryant, Edward. Climate Process & Change. (Illus.). 225p. (C). 1997. text 59.95 (*0-521-48189-9*); pap. text 22.95 (*0-521-48440-5*) Cambridge U Pr.
— Models & Moments: Paintings & Drawings by John Koch. (Illus.). 52p. 1977. pap. 5.00 (*0-911209-11-5*) Palmer Mus Art.
— Natural Hazards: Threat, Disaster, Effect Response. (Illus.). 312p. (C). 1991. text 85.00 (*0-521-37295-X*); pap. text 30.95 (*0-521-37889-3*) Cambridge U Pr.
Bryant, Edward, jt. auth. see Pennell, Joseph.
Bryant, Edward A., et al. Disinfection Alternatives for Safe Drinking Water. (Environmental Engineering Ser.). 518p. 1992. 110.00 (*0-471-29068-8*, VNR) Wiley.
***Bryant, Edwin.** The Indo-Aryan Migration Debate: In Quest of the Origins of Vedic Culture. LC 99-86274. (Illus.). 416p. 2001. text 45.00 (*0-19-513777-9*) OUP.
Bryant, Edwin. What I Saw in California. LC 84-28003. xxi, 455p. 1985. reprint ed. pap. 18.00 (*0-8032-6070-9*, Bison Books) U of Nebr Pr.
— What I Saw in California: Journal of a Tour. 1967. reprint ed. 20.00 (*0-87018-004-5*) Ross.
Bryant, Edwin E. Constitution of the U. S. A. With Notes of Decisions of the Supreme Court Thereon, from the Organization of the Court till October, 1900. xlii, 422p. 1986. reprint ed. lib. bdg. 47.50 (*0-89941-477-X*, 304050) W S Hein.
— History of the Third Regiment of Wisconsin Veteran Volunteer Infantry, 1861-1865. (Illus.). 445p. 1995. reprint ed. lib. bdg. 48.00 (*0-8328-5138-8*) Higginson Bk Co.
— Outlines of Law. vi, 415p. 1987. reprint ed. 45.00 (*0-8377-1945-3*, Rothman) W S Hein.
Bryant, Elizabeth & Tietjen, Alfred. GROAN in Washington & Other Strange Things That Go Bump in the Daytime: The Nearly Complete Works of Fusion Studios. (Illus.). 112p. (Orig.). 1986. pap. 6.95 (*0-9618537-0-0*) Fusion Studios.
Bryant, Elizabeth, ed. see Virgil, James.
Bryant, Eric H. Arrest Me Not: The Common Sense Survival Guide for Teens (& Adults) When Stopped by Police. 41p. (J). (gr. 7 up). 1994. pap. 5.95 (*0-9640336-0-7*) Arrest Me Not Pub.
— Arrest Me Not 2: Your Complete Pullover Survival Guide When Stopped by Police. 2nd rev. ed. LC 96-94910. (Illus.). 40p. 1996. pap. 6.00 (*0-9640336-2-3*) Arrest Me Not Pub.
— No Me Arrestes. Gurney, Karen, tr. (SPA., Illus.). 50p. (Orig.). 1996. pap. text 6.00 (*0-9640336-1-5*, NMA9601) Arrest Me Not Pub.
Bryant, Eric T. Collecting Gramophone Records. LC 77-28263. (Illus.). 153p. 1978. reprint ed. lib. bdg. 38.50 (*0-313-20258-3*, BRCGR, Greenwood Pr) Greenwood.
— Music Librarianship: A Practical Guide. 503p. 1990. reprint ed. lib. bdg. 99.00 (*0-7812-9269-7*) Rprt Serv.
Bryant, Eric T. & Marco, Guy A. Music Librarianship: A Practical Guide. 2nd ed. LC 84-27731. (Illus.). 473p. 1985. 47.50 (*0-8108-1785-3*) Scarecrow.
Bryant, Ernie. Garage Building: Complete Step-by-Step Plans. (Illus.). 272p. 1989. 24.95 (*0-8306-9214-2*); pap. 14.95 (*0-8306-3314-6*) McGraw-Hill Prof.
— Making Space: Remodeling for More Living Area. 240p. 1992. 22.95 (*0-8306-3932-2*, 2803); pap. 12.60 (*0-8306-3931-4*, 2803) McGraw-Hill Prof.
Bryant, Estrella S., et al, eds. Bibliography of Asian Studies, Nineteen Seventy-seven. LC Z 3001.B49. 732p. reprint ed. pap. 200.00 (*0-8357-7177-6*, 201478600096) Bks Demand.
Bryant, Eunice. Run with the Torch: The Church of the Nazarene in El Salvador. 96p. 1995. pap. 6.25 (*0-8341-1532-8*) Nazarene.
Bryant, F. B., et al. Methodological Issues in Applied Social Psychology. (Social Psychological Applications to Social Issues Ser.: Vol. 2). (Illus.). 328p. (C). 1992. 57.50 (*0-306-44173-X*, Plenum Trade) Perseus Pubng.
Bryant, Franklin H. Black Smiles: Or, the Sunny Side of Sable Life. LC 72-178469. (Black Heritage Library Collection). 1977. reprint ed. 15.95 (*0-8369-8917-1*) Ayer.
Bryant, Fred C., jt. auth. see Payne, Neil F.
Bryant, G. C. Clark: Deacon George Clark(e) 258p. 1991. reprint ed. pap. 41.00 (*0-8328-2114-4*); reprint ed. lib. bdg. 51.00 (*0-8328-2113-6*) Higginson Bk Co.
Bryant, G. F. & Yeung, L. F. Multivariate Control System Design Techniques: Dominance & Direct Methods. LC 95-52281. 238p. 1996. 135.00 (*0-471-95866-2*) Wiley.
Bryant, G. H. Principles of Microwave Measurements. (Electrical Measurement Ser.: No. 5). 373p. 1993. reprint ed. pap. 49.00 (*0-86341-296-3*, EL005z) INSPEC Inc.
***Bryant, Gail A., et al.** Orthopaedic Nursing Care Competencies: Adult Acute Care. Smith, Susan, ed. 102p. 1999. pap. 45.00 (*1-892665-04-2*) Natl Assn Ortho Nurse.
Bryant, Gary. The Seventh Spirit of the Sun: The Seventh Sojourn. Hilton, Charles & Laffie, Lynn, eds. 639p. (Orig.). 1994. pap. 13.95 (*0-9640780-9-0*) Futuristic Pub.
Bryant, Gay D. Introduction to WordPerfect 6.0 for DOS. LC 94-72574. 352p. (C). 1994. text 32.95 (*0-697-22709-X*) Bus & Educ Tech.
Bryant, Geoff. Propagation Handbook: Basic Techniques for Gardeners. LC 94-37457. 1995. 12.95 (*0-8117-3065-4*) Stackpole.
Bryant, Grady L. Roswell One. 232p. 1999. pap. 5.99 (*0-9671506-0-4*, Pub. by Red River Pr TX) Herveys Bklink.

Bryant, Hallman. A Separate Peace: The War Within. (Twayne's Masterworks Ser.: No. 50). 152p. (C). 1990. 23.95 (*0-8057-8087-4*) Macmillan.

Bryant, Hannah, tr. see Brahms, Johannes.

Bryant, Harold S. History of Coos Turnpike (New Hampshire) (Orig.). 1985. pap. 4.00 (*0-9607906-6-7*) ACETO Bookmen.

Bryant, Helen. Fixin' to Be Texan. LC 98-37934. 1998. pap. text 18.95 (*1-55622-648-9*, Rep of TX Pr) Wordware Pub.

Bryant, Henry. Simplemente Religioso o Cristiano de Verdad? (SPA.). 80p. 1990. pap. 2.99 (*0-8254-1080-0*, Edit Portavoz) Kregel.

Bryant, Henry E. Tar Heel Tales. LC 72-6511. (Black Heritage Library Collection). 1977. reprint ed. 23.95 (*0-8369-9162-1*) Ayer.

Bryant, I. D., jt. auth. see Flint, S. S.

Bryant, Ian, jt. auth. see Usher, Robin.

Bryant, J., jt. auth. see Bankowski, Z.

Bryant, J., ed. see Labbe, Armand J. & Apodaca, Paul.

Bryant, J. A., Jr. Shakespeare & the Uses of Comedy. LC 86-7770. 280p. 1986. 32.50 (*0-8131-1595-7*) U Pr of Ky.

— Twentieth Century Southern Literature. LC 97-10495. (New Perspectives on the South Ser.). 288p. (C). 1997. pap. 18.00 (*0-8131-0937-X*) U Pr of Ky.

Bryant, J. A. & Chiatante, Donato. Plant Cell Proliferation & Its Regulation in Growth & Development. LC 97-14886. 224p. 1998. 137.95 (*0-471-97267-3*) Wiley.

Bryant, J. A. & Dunham, V. L. DNA Replication in Plants. 208p. 1988. 119.00 (*0-8493-6770-0*, QK898, CRC Reprint) Franklin.

Bryant, J. A., jt. ed. see Jennings, Bryant.

Bryant, J. D., ed. Aluminum & Magnesium for Automotive Applications. (Illus.). 225p. 1996. 20.00 (*0-87339-332-5*) Minerals Metals.

Bryant, J. H., jt. ed. see Bankowski, Z.

Bryant, J. M. Silent Chain, Its Application to the Drive Problems of Industry. (Technical Papers: Vol. P175). (Illus.). 31p. 1938. pap. text 30.00 (*1-55589-445-3*) AGMA.

Bryant, J.A., jt. ed. see Jennings, Bryant.

Bryant, J.A., ed. see Shakespeare, William.

Bryant, Jacqueline, ed. see Moure, Nancy D.

Bryant, Jacqueline K. The Foremother Figure in Early Black Women's Literature: Clothed in My Right Mind. rev. ed. LC 99-13134. (Studies in African American History & Culture). 176p. 1999. 45.00 (*0-8153-3380-3*) Garland.

Bryant, Jacquelyn. The Power Tower: Prayer Is the Tower to Power. 95p. (Orig.). 1995. pap. 8.99 (*0-9634306-4-5*) End-Time Wave.

Bryant, Jamal, frwd. How Shall We Live? Morehouse Men Speak Out. 111p. (Orig.). 1996. pap. 10.95 (*0-9652568-0-4*) Genesis Publns.

Bryant, James, jt. ed. see Kester, Walt.

Bryant, James C. A Gift for Giving: The Story of Lamar Rich Plunkett. LC 93-36176. (C). 1993. 39.99 (*0-86554-430-1*, MUP-H343) Mercer Univ Pr.

— Mountain Island in Owen County, KY: The Settlers & Their Churches. 488p. (Orig.). (C). 1986. pap. text 19.00 (*0-9617100-0-4*) Owen Cnty Hist.

Bryant, James W. Problem Management: A Guide for Producers & Players. LC 89-9050. (Illus.). 352p. 1989. pap. 109.20 (*0-608-05260-4*, 206579800001) Bks Demand.

***Bryant, Jane Quincy, ed.** Association of Management/ International Association of Management (AOM/IAOM) Vol. 17, No. 1: Project 2001 Proceedings, Pages 1-75. 146p. 1999. pap. text 24.95 (*0-9668650-9-X*) Maximilian Pr.

— Association of Management/International Association of Management (AOM/IAOM) Vol. 17, No. 2: Proceedings: Health Care Management, Human Resources, Business, Education Administration. 134p. 1999. pap. text 24.95 (*0-9668650-8-1*) Maximilian Pr.

Bryant, Jean. Anybody Can Write: A Playful Approach; Ideas for Aspiring Writers, the Beginning Writer, the Blocked Writer. 2nd rev. ed. LC 98-42425. 175p. 1999. pap. 12.95 (*1-57731-056-X*) New Wrld Lib.

Bryant, Jean R. & Bryant, John D. Mexico Living & Travel. 3rd rev. ed. LC 94-228235. (Illus.). 290p. 1999. pap. text 29.95 (*1-878061-01-1*) M R T A.

Bryant-Jefferies, Richard, jt. auth. see Frances, Lynne.

Bryant, Jennifer. Anne Abrams: Engineering Drafter. (Working Moms: A Portrait of Their Lives Ser.). (Illus.). 89p. (J). (gr. 2-4). 1995. lib. bdg. 15.95 (*0-941477-51-7*) H Holt & Co.

— Jane Sayler: Veterinarian. (J). 1991. 21.27 (*0-516-07378-8*) Childrens.

— Jane Sayler: Veterinarian. (Working Moms: A Portrait of Their Lives Ser.). (Illus.). 40p. (J). (gr. 2-4). 1995. lib. bdg. 15.95 (*0-941477-55-X*) TFC Bks NY.

— Margaret Murie's Wilderness Life. (J). 1993. 19.93 (*0-516-07398-2*) Childrens.

Bryant, Jennifer F. Louis Braille: Inventor. (Great Achievers Ser.). (Illus.). 120p. (YA). (gr. 5 up). 1994. lib. bdg. 19.95 (*0-7910-2077-0*, Chelsea Juniors) Chelsea Hse.

— Thomas Merton: Poet, Prophet, Priest. LC 96-2783. (Illus.). 215p. (YA). (gr. 7 up). 1997. 15.00 (*0-8028-5109-6*, Eerdmans Bks) Eerdmans.

— Thomas Merton: Poet, Prophet, Priest. LC 96-2783. (Illus.). 150p. (YA). (gr. 7 up). 1997. pap. 8.00 (*0-8028-5140-1*, Eerdmans Bks) Eerdmans.

***Bryant, Jennifer O.** Olympic Equestrian: The Sport & the Stories from Stockholm to Sydney. 2000. pap. 29.95 (*1-58150-044-0*) Blood-Horse.

Bryant, Jennings, ed. Television & the American Family. (Communication Ser.). 392p. (C). 1990. text 89.95 (*0-8058-0116-2*) L Erlbaum Assocs.

Bryant, Jennings, et al, eds. Public Relations Theory. 368p. 1989. pap. 39.95 (*0-8058-0692-X*) L Erlbaum Assocs.

Bryant, Jennings & Zillmann, Dolf, eds. Media Effects: Advances in Theory & Research. (LEA's Communication Ser.). 504p. 1994. pap. 39.95 (*0-8058-0918-X*); text 99.95 (*0-8058-0917-1*) L Erlbaum Assocs.

— Perspectives on Media Effects. 374p. 1989. pap. text 36.00 (*0-8058-0721-7*) L Erlbaum Assocs.

— Responding to the Screen: Reception & Reaction Processes. (Communication Ser.). 416p. (C). 1991. pap. 39.95 (*0-8058-1044-7*); text 79.95 (*0-8058-0033-6*) L Erlbaum Assocs.

Bryant, Jennings, jt. auth. see Black, J. Jay.

Bryant, Jennings, jt. auth. see Heath, Robert L.

Bryant, Jennings, ed. see Moore.

Bryant, Jennings, jt. ed. see Salvaggio, J. L.

Bryant, Jennings, jt. ed. see Zillmann, Dolf.

Bryant, Jerold M. Single Man Screaming. 1997. 24.95 (*0-9669595-0-7*) S M S Co.

Bryant, Jerry H. Victims & Heroes: Racial Violence in the African American Novel. LC 96-48656. (Illus.). 392p. 1997. pap. 19.95 (*1-55849-095-7*) U of Mass Pr.

Bryant, Jill. Sew Your Own Bean Bag Bears. (Illus.). 40p. (YA). (gr. 3 up). 1999. pap. 12.99 (*1-58184-019-5*) Somerville Hse.

— Sew Your Own Bean Bag Friends. (Illus.). 40p. (YA). (gr. 3 up). 1998. pap. 12.99 (*1-58184-000-4*, Pub. by S1omerville Hse) Penguin Putnam.

***Bryant, Jill.** Sew Your Own Bean Bag Friends. (Illus.). 40p. (J). (gr. 3 up). 1998. pap. 12.99 (*1-894042-20-4*) Somerville Hse.

***Bryant, Jill & McTaggart, Bonnie.** Wilderness Cookbook: A Guide to Good Food on the Trail. (Illus.). 168p. 1999. pap. 12.95 (*1-896764-18-5*, Pub. by Sec Story Pr) LPC InBook.

Bryant, Jimmy R. Man of the River: Memoir of a Brown Water Sailor in Vietnam, 1968-1969. Seagrave, Pia S., ed. LC 98-25602. (Illus.). 160p. 1998. pap. 6.95 (*1-887901-23-X*) Sergeant Kirk.

***Bryant, Joel.** Journey Toward Greatness. 1998. pap. 13.95 (*0-9663405-0-7*) Word Season.

Bryant, John. Barryations: John Bryant Kicks Butt on Dave Barry's Turf. 39p. (Orig.). 1997. pap. 3.95 (*1-886739-38-2*) Socratic Pr.

— Better Than Shakespeare: A Modern Author Demonstrates Shakespearian Incompetence & the Establishment's Corruption by Rewriting the Shakespearian Sonnets & the Poetry of Other Major Authors. 117p. (Orig.). 1996. pap. 9.95 (*1-886739-34-X*) Socratic Pr.

— Bryant's Law & Other Broadsides: Recent Controversial Writings of John Bryant. 1990. pap. 16.95 (*0-9617444-2-1*) Socratic Pr.

— Everything You Always Wanted to Know about Blacks: But Were Afraid to Ask Because You Thought You'd Be Called "Racist" 133p. (Orig.). 1995. pap. 9.95 (*1-886739-01-3*) Socratic Pr.

— Everything You Always Wanted to Know about Eating, Drinking, & Merriment: But Were Afraid to Ask Because You Were Too Full, Too Drunk & Too Depressed. 91p. (Orig.). 1995. pap. 7.95 (*1-886739-12-9*) Socratic Pr.

— Everything You Always Wanted to Know about Economics & Finance: But Were Afraid to Ask Because You Thought No One Would Give You Any Credit. 95p. (Orig.). 1995. pap. 8.95 (*1-886739-17-X*) Socratic Pr.

— Everything You Always Wanted to Know about Government & Politics: But Were Afraid to Ask Because You Thought It Was Treasonous. 157p. (Orig.). 1995. pap. 10.95 (*1-886739-16-1*) Socratic Pr.

— Everything You Always Wanted to Know about Health, Disease & Medicine & Youth, Aging, Life & Death: But Were Afraid to Ask Because You Couldn't Reach Your Bedpan. 69p. (Orig.). 1995. pap. 6.95 (*1-886739-13-7*) Socratic Pr.

— Everything You Always Wanted to Know about Human Behavior & Misbehavior: But Were Afraid to Ask Because You Thought You'd Be Misbehaving. 59p. (Orig.). 1995. pap. 5.95 (*1-886739-10-2*) Socratic Pr.

— Everything You Always Wanted to Know about Indians, Homosexuals, the Handicapped & Other Groups: But Were Afraid to Ask Because You Thought You'd End up in a Wheelchair with an AIDS-Infected Tomahawk in Your Skull. 67p. (Orig.). 1995. pap. 6.95 (*1-886739-06-4*) Socratic Pr.

— Everything You Always Wanted to Know about Interpersonal Relations: But Were Afraid to Ask Because You Thought You'd Lose All Your Friends. 43p. (Orig.). 1995. pap. 4.95 (*1-886739-08-0*) Socratic Pr.

— Everything You Always Wanted to Know about Jews: But Were Afraid to Ask Because You Thought You'd Be Called "Antisemitic" 121p. (Orig.). 1995. pap. 9.95 (*1-886739-02-1*) Socratic Pr.

— Everything You Always Wanted to Know about Language & Communication: But Were Afraid to Ask Because You Were Tongue-Tied. 95p. (Orig.). 1995. pap. 8.95 (*1-886739-21-8*) Socratic Pr.

— Everything You Always Wanted to Know about Law & Justice: But Were Afraid to Ask Because You Thought You'd Be Arrested. 81p. (Orig.). 1995. pap. 7.95 (*1-886739-15-3*) Socratic Pr.

— Everything You Always Wanted to Know about Liberals, Conservatives, & the Philosophy of Race & Groups: But Were Afraid to Ask Because You Thought You'd Be Called a Racist Sexist Ageist Homophobic Lookist, 2 vols. 224p. (Orig.). 1995. pap. 16.95 (*1-886739-03-X*) Socratic Pr.

— Everything You Always Wanted to Know about Living & the Quality of Life: But Were Afraid to Ask Because You Thought Your Quality of Life Might Be Adversely Affected. 77p. (Orig.). 1995. pap. 6.95 (*1-886739-11-0*) Socratic Pr.

— Everything You Always Wanted to Know about Men, Women, Children & Feminism: But Were Afraid to Ask Because You Thought You'd Be Called "Sexist" 169p. (Orig.). 1995. pap. 10.95 (*1-886739-00-5*) Socratic Pr.

— Everything You Always Wanted to Know about People, Places, & Things: But Were Afraid to Ask Because You Thought That People Would Throw Things at Your Place. 81p. (Orig.). 1995. pap. 6.95 (*1-886739-14-5*) Socratic Pr.

— Everything You Always Wanted to Know about Philosophy & Philosophers: But Were Afraid to Ask Because You Thought You Should Be Philosophical about It. 117p. (Orig.). 1995. pap. 8.95 (*1-886739-20-X*) Socratic Pr.

— Everything You Always Wanted to Know about Religion, Science & Superstition: But Were Afraid to Ask Because You Thought You'd Be Excommunicated, Cursed & Denied Your Research Grant. 143p. (Orig.). 1995. pap. 10.95 (*1-886739-19-6*) Socratic Pr.

— Everything You Always Wanted to Know about Sex & Other Filth: But Were Afraid to Ask Because You Thought You'd Be Called a "Pervert" 77p. (Orig.). 1995. pap. 6.95 (*1-886739-07-2*) Socratic Pr.

— Everything You Always Wanted to Know about Socialism & Communism: But Were Afraid to Ask Because You Thought You'd Be Called a Capitalist Tool. 63p. (Orig.). 1995. pap. 5.95 (*1-886739-18-8*) Socratic Pr.

— Everything You Always Wanted to Know about the Mind's Construction: But Were Afraid to Ask Because You Thought the Answers Might Change Yours. 59p. (Orig.). 1995. pap. 5.95 (*1-886739-09-9*) Socratic Pr.

— Explosive Revolutionary Ideas That Can Change Your Life - & the World, 2 vols., Set. 306p. (Orig.). 1995. pap. 19.95 (*1-886739-31-5*) Socratic Pr.

— Handbook of the Coming American Revolution: Vital Secrets of Nonviolent National & Personal Liberation the Establishment Doesn't Want You to Know. (Illus.). 140p. 1998. pap. 10.95 (*1-886739-39-0*) Socratic Pr.

— Information, Free Speech, Censorship, & Truth. 99p. 1995. pap. 8.95 (*1-886739-30-7*) Socratic Pr.

— The John Bryant Sampler: Explosive Excerpts from 25 Books of the World's Most Controversial Author. 145p. (Orig.). 1995. pap. 10.95 (*1-886739-25-0*) Socratic Pr.

— Leaves of Grass: A Legal High of Humorous & Serious Poetry. 91p. (Orig.). 1996. pap. 8.95 (*1-886739-35-8*) Socratic Pr.

— Logical Alternatives: Studies in the Philosophy of Logic & Existence. write for info. (*0-9617444-6-4*) Socratic Pr.

— Melville & Repose: The Rhetoric of Humor in the American Renaissance. LC 92-46150. 336p. (C). 1993. text 65.00 (*0-19-507782-2*) OUP.

— Melville Dissertations, 1924-1980: An Annotated Bibliography & Subject Index. LC 83-5683. 156p. 1983. lib. bdg. 59.95 (*0-313-23811-1*, BMD/, Greenwood Pr) Greenwood.

— The Mortal Words Birds Politically-Incorrect Scientifically-Unsupported Treasonous Government-Bashing Libertarian Cartoon Book. (Illus.). 126p. (Orig.). 1997. pap. 12.95 (*1-886739-36-5*) Socratic Pr.

— The Mortal Words of J. B. R. Yant & Other Irritations. (Illus.). 1987. 16.95 (*0-9617444-0-5*); pap. 12.95 (*0-9617444-1-3*) Socratic Pr.

— The Most Powerful Idea Ever Discovered. 1987. pap. 7.95 (*0-9617444-5-6*) Socratic Pr.

— Nasty Letter-Bombs: 150 Politically-Incorrect Unfit-to-Print Explosive Guided Missives That Shook the St. Petersburg Times. 280p. (Orig.). 1995. pap. 19.95 (*1-886739-26-9*) Socratic Pr.

— Nasty Letter-Bombs: 150 Politically-Incorrect Unfit-to-Print Explosive Guided Missives That Shook the St. Petersburg Times, Vol. 1: 1992 & 1993. 133p. (Orig.). 1995. pap. 9.95 (*1-886739-27-7*) Socratic Pr.

— Nasty Letter-Bombs: 150 Politically-Incorrect Unfit-to-Print Explosive Guided Missives That Shook the St. Petersburg Times, Vol. 2: 1994. 145p. (Orig.). 1995. pap. 9.95 (*1-886739-28-5*) Socratic Pr.

— Political Correctness, Censorship & Liberal-Jewish Strongarm Tactics in High-IQ/Low-Morals Mensa: A Case Study. 60p. (Orig.). 1997. pap. 4.95 (*1-886739-37-4*) Socratic Pr.

***Bryant, John.** Should Liberals Be Lynched? The World's Most Controversial Author's Four Years. 108p. 1999. pap. 9.95 (*1-886739-41-2*) Socratic Pr.

Bryant, John. Success in Marriage-Guaranteed!!! The Secret of Making Friends & Keeping them. (Orig.). 1987. pap. 4.95 (*0-9617444-4-8*) Socratic Pr.

— Systems Theory & Scientific Philosophy: An Application of the Cybernetics of W. Ross Ashby to Personal & Social Philosophy, the Philosophy of Mind, & the Problems of Artificial Intelligence. 288p. (C). 1991. pap. text 28.50 (*0-8191-8304-0*); lib. bdg. 56.50 (*0-8191-8303-2*) U Pr of Amer.

— The Wayword Dictionary: JBR Yant's Definitions from Hell. 125p. (Orig.). 1995. pap. 10.95 (*1-886739-22-6*) Socratic Pr.

— What the Establishment Doesn't Want You to Know about Government & Politics. 95p. (Orig.). 1995. pap. 9.95 (*1-886739-23-4*) Socratic Pr.

— Words As Smoking Guns: What Vocabulary Teaches Us That the Establishment Doesn't Want Us to Know. 75p. (Orig.). 1995. pap. 9.95 (*1-886739-24-2*) Socratic Pr.

Bryant, John, ed. A Companion to Melville Studies. LC 86-361. 934p. 1986. lib. bdg. 135.00 (*0-313-23874-X*, BMV/, Greenwood Pr) Greenwood.

Bryant, John & Bryant, Charray. Authentic Vegetarian Cookery. (Illus.). 406p. (C). 1989. ring bd. 39.95 (*0-9622778-1-9*) Wild Thyme.

Bryant, John & Cones, Harold. The Zenith Trans-Oceanic: The Royalty of Radios. LC 94-46624. (Illus.). 128p. (Orig.). 1995. pap. 24.95 (*0-88740-708-0*) Schiffer.

Bryant, John & Milder, Robert, eds. Melville's Evermoving Dawn: Centennial Essays. LC 96-42483. 1997. 45.00 (*0-87338-562-4*) Kent St U Pr.

Bryant, John, jt. auth. see Cones, Harold N.

Bryant, John D., jt. auth. see Bryant, Jean R.

Bryant, John E. Sounds Good to Me: Phonological Awareness Fun. LC 98-38154. 1998. pap. 37.00 (*1-888222-29-8*) Thinking Pubns.

***Bryant, John H. & Cones, Harold N.** Dangerous Crossings: The First Modern Polar Expedition, 1925. LC 00-26344. (Illus.). 224p. 2000. 27.95 (*1-55750-187-4*) Naval Inst Pr.

Bryant, Jonathan M. How Curious a Land: Conflict & Change in Greene County, Georgia, 1850-1885. LC 95-23506. (Fred W. Morrison Series in Southern Studies). (Illus.). 288p. (C). 1996. text 19.95 (*0-8078-2257-4*) U of NC Pr.

Bryant, Joseph A. Eudora Welty. LC 68-63651. (University of Minnesota Pamphlets on American Writers Ser.: No. 66). 48p. (Orig.). reprint ed. pap. 30.00 (*0-7837-2895-6*, 205756000006) Bks Demand.

Bryant, Joseph M. Moral Codes & Social Structure in Ancient Greece: A Sociology of Greek Ethics from Homer to the Epicureans & Stoics. LC 95-40573. (SUNY Series in the Sociology of Culture). 592p. (C). 1996. text 81.50 (*0-7914-3041-3*); pap. text 27.95 (*0-7914-3042-1*) State U NY Pr.

Bryant, Joy L. Protecting Your Ideas: The Inventor's Guide to Patents. LC 98-86601. (Illus.). 222p. (C). 1998. pap. 25.00 (*0-12-138410-1*) Acad Pr.

Bryant, Julius. London's Country House Collections. (Illus.). 144p. 1993. 30.00 (*1-85759-013-9*) Scala Books.

— London's Country House Collections: Kenwood, Chiswick, Marble Hill, Ranger's House. (Illus.). 144p. 1997. pap. 30.00 (*1-85759-012-0*) Scala Books.

Bryant, Katherine. Thawing. LC 98-67019. (Illus.). 80p. 1998. pap. 12.95 (*0-9620115-9-2*) Post Oak Pubns.

Bryant, Kathleen M., ed. see Cady, Roslynn W.

Bryant, Keith L. Arthur E. Stilwell: Promoter with a Hunch. LC 78-170282. 272p. 1971. reprint ed. pap. 84.40 (*0-7837-9887-3*, 206061300006) Bks Demand.

***Bryant, Keith L., Jr.** Culture in the American Southwest: The Earth, the Sky, the People. (Tarleton State University Southwestern Studies in the Humanities: Vol. 12). (Illus.). 448p. 2001. 34.95 (*0-89096-945-5*) Tex A&M Univ Pr.

Bryant, Keith L., Jr. History of the Atchison, Topeka & Santa Fe Railway. LC 81-16024. (Illus.). xx, 400p. 1982. pap. 21.00 (*0-8032-6066-0*, Bison Books) U of Nebr Pr.

Bryant, Keith L., ed. Railroads in the Age of Regulation, 1900-1980. (Encyclopedia of American Business History & Biography Ser.). (Illus.). 560p. 1988. lib. bdg. 99.00 (*0-8160-1371-3*) Facts on File.

Bryant, Keith L., Jr., jt. auth. see Dethloff, Henry C.

Bryant, Kendall J., et al, eds. The Science of Prevention: Methodological Advances from Alcohol & Substance Abuse Research. LC 97-14910. (Illus.). 458p. 1997. text 49.95 (*1-55798-439-5*) Am Psychol.

Bryant, Kim & Meloan, Becky. Prematurely Yours: The Baby Book Designed Exclusively for the Premature Infant. 3rd ed. (Illus.). 40p. (J). Date not set. reprint ed. 21.95 (*0-9614786-0-8*) Premature Yours.

Bryant, L. P., jt. compiled by see Kneeland, F. N.

Bryant, LaRee. Azure Nights. 384p. 1998. pap. 4.99 (*0-8217-5685-0*, Zebra Kensgtn) Kensgtn Pub Corp.

Bryant, Laree. Forever My Love. 384p. 1995. mass mkt. 4.99 (*0-8217-5073-9*, Zebra Kensgtn) Kensgtn Pub Corp.

Bryant, LaRee, ed. see Pavlyak, Michele M.

Bryant, Larkin. Larkin's Dulcimer Book. LC 82-84550. (Illus.). 103p. 1998. spiral bd. 10.98 (*0-9667520-0-7*) Riverlark Music.

Bryant, Larre. Learn to Country & Western Dance. (Illus.). Date not set. pap. text 10.95 (*0-9665370-0-9*) Ruby Moon Pr.

Bryant, Laurie J. Non-Dinosaurian Lower Vertebrates Across the Cretaceous-Tertiary Boundary in Northeastern Montana. 1990. pap. 20.00 (*0-520-09735-1*, Pub. by U CA Pr) Cal Prin Full Svc.

Bryant, Laurie J., ed. see Parker, Albert.

Bryant, Lawrence C. Autobiography of Lawrence C. Bryant. 230p. 1971. 15.00 (*0-686-01113-9*); pap. 10.00 (*0-686-01114-7*) L C Bryant.

— Bills & Resolutions Proposed by Negro Legislators in South Carolina. 1967. pap. 5.00 (*0-686-05557-8*) L C Bryant.

— A Guidance Handbook of Junior & Senior Colleges in Mississippi. 1957. pap. 5.00 (*0-686-05555-1*) L C Bryant.

— A Historical & Genealogical Record of Fanny Sills & Related Lines of Nash County, North Carolina. 1968. pap. 10.00 (*0-686-05560-8*) L C Bryant.

— A Historical & Genealogical Record of Lawrence Bryant & Pattie Sessoms' Five Other Sons. 1968. 15.00 (*0-686-05561-6*); pap. 10.00 (*0-686-05562-4*) L C Bryant.

— A Historical & Genealogical Record of Lee Clay & Related Families. 1972. 15.00 (*0-686-05820-8*); pap. 10.00 (*0-686-05821-6*) L C Bryant.

— Negro Lawmakers in the South Carolina Legislature, 1868-1902. 1968. pap. 10.00 (*0-686-05563-2*) L C Bryant.

— Negro Legislators in South Carolina, 1865-1894. 1966. 15.00 (*0-686-05568-3*); pap. 10.00 (*0-686-05569-1*) L C Bryant.

— Negro Legislators in South Carolina, 1868-1902. 1967. 15.00 (*0-686-05564-0*); pap. 10.00 (*0-686-05565-9*) L C Bryant.

— Negro Senators & Representatives in the South Carolina Legislature. 1968. 15.00 (*0-686-05566-7*); pap. 10.00 (*0-686-05567-5*) L C Bryant.

B

— Record of Achievement of Dr. Lawrence C. Bryant. 1966. 5.00 (*0-686-05556-X*) L C Bryant.

— South Carolina Negro Legislators: A Glorious Success. 1974. 15.00 (*0-686-05553-5*); pap. 10.00 (*0-686-05554-3*) L C Bryant.

Bryant, Lawrence E. & McIntire, Paul, eds. ASNT Nondestructive Testing Handbook, Vol. 3: Radiography & Radiation Testing. 2nd ed. (Illus.). 925p. 1984. 121.25 (*0-931403-00-6*, 128) Am Soc Nondestructive.

Bryant, Linda G., et al, contrib. by. Bad Girls. LC 93-87805. (Illus.). 144p. (Orig.). 1994. pap. 19.95 (*0-262-70053-0*) New Mus Contemp Art.

***Bryant-Logan, William.** The Tool Book. rev. ed. (Illus.). 320p. 2000. pap. 19.95 (*0-7611-2136-6*) Workman Pub.

Bryant, Louella. The Black Bonnet. LC 96-31672. (YA). (gr. 5 up). 1996. pap. 12.95 (*1-881535-22-3*) New Eng Pr VT.

— Father by Blood. LC 99-10953. (Illus.). 160p. (YA). (gr. 6-8). 1999. pap. 12.95 (*1-881535-33-9*) New Eng Pr VT.

Bryant, Louise. Six Red Months in Russia: An Observer's Account of Russia Before & During the Proletarian Dictatorship. LC 70-115578. (Russia Observed, Series I). 1978. reprint ed. 29.95 (*0-405-03006-1*) Ayer.

Bryant, Lucind L. & Hooker, Tracey A. Testing Sex Offenders for HIV. (State Legislative Reports: Vol. 16, No. 7). 12p. 1991. pap. text 15.00 (*1-55516-306-8*, 7302-1607) Natl Conf State Legis.

Bryant, Lucinda L., jt. auth. see Craig, Rebecca T.

Bryant, Lyle. MCSD Training Guide: Visual Basic 5. LC 98-84019. (MCSD Training Guides). 750p. 1998. 49.99 (*1-56205-850-9*) New Riders Pub.

***Bryant, Lyle A.** MCSD Fast Track: 4-in-1 Set. (Fast Tracks Ser.). 1500p. 1999. pap. text 119.95 (*0-7357-0913-0*) New Riders Pub.

Bryant, Lyle A., jt. auth. see Sharkey, Kent.

Bryant, Lynn R. Americans with Disabilities Act: A Sourcebook for Business, Baltimore - Washington Edition. (Illus.). 224p. (Orig.). 1993. pap. 34.95 (*0-9635859-0-8*) RehabTech.

— Training Programs in Assistive Technology: 1992 Guide. 87p. 1992. pap. 15.00 (*0-9635859-1-6*) RehabTech.

Bryant, Lynwood, jt. auth. see Hunter, Louis C.

Bryant, M. Church Cats & Clerical Cats in Stories. (Illus.). (J). 1997. mass mkt. 15.95 (*0-340-69424-6*, Pub. by Hodder & Stought Ltd) Trafalgar.

— Ghosts in the Cloisters. (Illus.). (J). text 15.95 (*0-340-71376-3*, Pub. by Hodder & Stought Ltd) Trafalgar.

Bryant, M., tr. see Goncharov, Ivan A.

Bryant, M. D., et al. Application of A Hierarchical Habitat Unit Classification System: Stream Habitat Unit Classification System: Stream Habitat & Salmonid Distribution in Ward Creek, Southeast Alaska. (Illus.). 24p. 1997. reprint ed. pap. 3.40 (*0-89904-620-7*, Bear Meadows Resrch Grp) Crumb Elbow Pub.

Bryant, M. Darrol. Jonathan Edwards' Grammar of Time, Self, & Society: A Critique of the Heimert Thesis. LC 93-38455. (Studies in American Religion: Vol. 60). 256p. 1993. text 89.95 (*0-7734-9389-1*) E Mellen.

***Bryant, M. Darrol.** Woven on the Loom of Time: Many Faiths & One Divine Purpose. vi, 145p. 1999. 15.00 (*81-86921-06-0*, Pub. by Decent Bks) Nataraj Bks.

Bryant, M. Darrol, ed. The Future of Anglican Theology. LC 84-8983. (Toronto Studies in Theology: Vol. 17). 208p. 1984. lib. bdg. 89.95 (*0-88946-763-3*) E Mellen.

— Huston Smith: Essays on World Religion. 290p. 1992. 14.95 (*1-55778-447-7*); pap. text 14.95 (*1-55778-722-0*) Paragon Hse.

Bryant, M. Darrol & Ali, Syed A., eds. The Muslim-Christian Dialogue: Promise & Problems. LC 98-26383. 275p. 1998. pap. 14.95 (*1-55778-764-6*) Paragon Hse.

Bryant, M. Darrol & Flinn, Frank, eds. Interreligious Dialogue: Voices from a New Frontier. 250p. 1989. 24.95 (*0-89226-067-X*) Paragon Hse.

Bryant, M. Darrol & Huessy, Hans R., eds. Eugen Rosenstock-Huessy: Studies in His Life & Thought. LC 86-28469. (Toronto Studies in Theology: Vol. 28). 280p. 1986. lib. bdg. 28.95 (*0-88946-772-2*) E Mellen.

Bryant, M. Darrol & Richardson, Herbert W. A Time for Consideration: A Scholarly Appraisal of the Unification Church. 2nd ed. LC 78-61364. (Symposium Ser.: Vol. 3). xi, 332p. 1978. lib. bdg. 99.95 (*0-88946-954-7*) E Mellen.

Bryant, M. Darrol, et al. Religion & Political Society. LC 73-18424. (Symposium Ser.: Vol. 1). xi, 209p. 1976. reprint ed. 89.95 (*0-88946-953-9*) E Mellen.

Bryant, M. Darrol, jt. ed. see Lamb, Christopher.

Bryant, M. Darrol, jt. ed. see Sontag, Frederick.

Bryant, M. Kevin. Annual Tax Planning Guide for Individuals & Business. (Orig.). 1996. pap. 75.00 (*1-886035-07-5*) Pro Tax & Business.

— Annual Tax Planning Guide for S Corporations, Partnerships & LLCs. 500p. 1996. ring bd. 85.00 (*1-886035-00-8*) Pro Tax & Business.

Bryant, M. Kevin. Bender's Tax Return Manual. text 69.00 (*0-8205-4033-1*) Bender.

Bryant, M. Kevin. Bender's Tax Return Manual. annuals 1973. write for info. (*0-8205-1121-8*) Bender.

— S Corporations: Complete Tax Practice & Planning Guide. 1000p. 1996. ring bd. 135.00 (*1-886035-01-6*) Pro Tax & Business.

Bryant, M. Kevin, jt. auth. see Benesh, Bruce K.

Bryant, M. Kevin, jt. auth. see Benish, Bruce K.

Bryant, M. Kevin, jt. auth. see Brody, Evelyn.

Bryant, Marcella. Ancient Child: Poetry about Incest. 72p. 1990. pap. 10.00 (*0-911051-47-3*) Plain View.

Bryant, Margaret E. The London Experience of Secondary Education. LC 85-22987. (Illus.). 540p. (C). 1986. text 39.95 (*0-485-11302-3*, Pub. by Athlone Pr) Humanities.

Bryant, Margaret M. Proverbs & How to Collect Them. (Publications of the American Dialect Society: No. 4). 25p. 1945. pap. 2.50 (*0-8173-0604-8*) U of Ala Pr.

Bryant, Margaret M., et al. Maple Sugar Language in Vermont; Comments on PADS 5 & 6; Supplementing Word-Lists. (Publications of the American Dialect Society: No. 8). 41p. 1947. pap. 4.50 (*0-8173-0608-0*) U of Ala Pr.

— A Selected List of Compounds from Present-Day Reading; On the Interpretation of Occasional Spellings; The Stressed Vowels of Yiddish-American English. (Publications of the American Dialect Society Ser.: No. 48). 59p. 1969. pap. text 5.90 (*0-8173-0648-X*) U of Ala Pr.

Bryant, Mark. The Cat Name Companion: Facts & Fables to Help You Name Your Feline. (Illus.). 224p. 1995. pap. 8.95 (*0-8065-1671-2*, Citadel Pr) Carol Pub Group.

***Bryant, Mark.** Dictionary of 20th Century British Cartoonists & Caricaturists. LC 99-45326. (Illus.). 224p. 2000. text 61.95 (*1-84014-286-3*, Pub. by Ashgate Pub) Ashgate Pub Co.

Bryant, Mark. Hidden Assets: An Adventure to Find Inner Resources. 350p. 1998. pap. 16.95 (*1-886710-03-1*, Pub. by New Leaders) Natl Bk Netwk.

Bryant, Mark, ed. The Mammoth Book of Cats. (Mammoth Book Ser.). 512p. 1999. pap. text 10.95 (*0-7867-0651-1*) Carroll & Graf.

— Thin Blue Lines: Cartoons for the United Nations: A Light-Hearted Look at Peace, Human Rights, the Environment & Poverty to Mark the 50th Anniversary of the U. N. (Illus.). 82p. (Orig.). 1995. pap. 9.95 (*0-85052-466-0*, Pub. by Leo Cooper) Trans-Atl Phila.

Bryant, Mark & Heneage, Simon. Dictionary of British Cartoonists & Caricaturists. LC 93-21363. 270p. 1994. 51.95 (*0-85967-976-4*, Pub. by Scolar Pr) Ashgate Pub Co.

Bryant, Marsha. Auden & Documentary in the 1930s. 208p. 1997. text 35.00 (*0-8139-1756-5*) U Pr of Va.

Bryant, Marsha, ed. Photo-Textualities: Reading Photographs & Literature. LC 95-44280. 168p. 1996. 45.00 (*0-87413-551-6*) U Delaware Pr.

Bryant, Martha F. Sacajawea: A Native American Heroine. Gilliland, Hap, ed. & illus. by. Sargent, Heather, illus. (Indian Culture Ser.). 256p. (Orig.). (J). 1989. 21.95 (*0-89992-320-8*); pap. 15.95 (*0-89992-120-5*) Coun India Ed.

Bryant, Mary H. Integrating Technology into the Curriculum (Intermediate) (Illus.). 144p. 1996. pap., teacher ed. 14.95 (*1-55734-934-7*, TCM934) Tchr Create Mat.

Bryant, Mary K. My Ego. (Illus.). 64p. (Orig.). 1986. 6.95 (*0-934391-06-8*) Quotidian.

Bryant-Mason, Mary. The After-School Academy: A "How-to" Guide for School-Age Care Professionals, 2 vols., Set. (Illus.). 250p. 1996. ring bd. 49.95 (*0-9652916-0-X*) Dotson & Jacklin.

— The After-School Academy Vol. 1: A "How-to" Guide for School-Age Care Professionals. (Illus.). 1996. ring bd. 24.95 (*0-9652916-1-8*) Dotson & Jacklin.

***Bryant, Matthew.** America Online 4.0. LC 99-64500. (Fast & Easy Ser.). 1999. pap. 16.99 (*0-7615-2309-X*) Prima Pub.

***Bryant, Michael.** Creating Spreadsheets with Excel 2000. (Illus.). 128p. 2000. pap. 8.99 (*0-7645-8627-0*, CPG Pr) IDG Bks.

Bryant, Michael, jt. auth. see Fionda, Julia.

Bryant, Michael, jt. auth. see Grimes, Nikki.

Bryant, Michel J. The Legal Edge for Homeowners, Buyers & Renters. (Illus.). 200p. 1999. pap. 16.95 (*1-58063-066-9*, Pub. by Renaissance) St Martin.

Bryant, Mildred C. Sister. LC 99-62004. 1999. pap. write for info. (*0-9652973-1-4*) BenchMark Ent.

Bryant, Miles T., et al, eds. Nebraska Policy Choices, 1989: Education. (Illus.). 155p. (Orig.). (C). 1989. pap. 9.95 (*1-55719-182-4*) U NE CPAR.

Bryant, Miles T., ed. see Michael, et al.

Bryant, Miles T., ed. see Wendel, Frederick C. & Sybouts, Ward.

***Bryant-Mole, K., ed.** Color. rev. ed. (First Learning Ser.). (Illus.). 24p. (J). (ps-3). 2000. pap. 4.95 (*0-7460-3800-3*, Pub. by Usbrne Pbng UK) EDC.

— Sizes. rev. ed. (First Learning Ser.). (Illus.). 24p. (J). (ps-3). 2000. pap. 4.95 (*0-7460-3585-3*, Pub. by Usbrne Pbng UK) EDC.

— Time. rev. ed. (First Learning Ser.). (Illus.). 24p. (J). (ps-3). 2000. pap. 4.95 (*0-7460-3806-2*, Pub. by Usbrne Pbng UK) EDC.

Bryant-Mole, K., jt. auth. see Gee, R.

***Bryant-Mole, Karen.** Alimentos. LC 99-10791. (Picture This! Ser.).Tr. of Food. (SPA., Illus.). 24p. (J). (ps-1). 1999. lib. bdg. 12.95 (*1-57572-915-6*) Heinemann Lib.

Bryant-Mole, Karen. Amarillo. (Images Ser.).Tr. of Yellow. (SPA., Illus.). 24p. 1996. pap. text 4.95 (*0-382-39581-6*) Silver Burdett Pr.

— Amarillo. (Imagenes Ser.).Tr. of Yellow. 1996. 10.15 (*0-606-10375-9*, Pub. by Turtleback) Demco.

— At the Seashore. LC 99-10783. (Picture This! Ser.). 1999. write for info. (*1-57572-898-2*) Heinemann Lib.

— Autumn. LC 97-406. (Picture This! Ser.). (J). 1998. (*1-57572-148-1*) Heinemann Lib.

— Azul. (Images Ser.).Tr. of Blue. (SPA., Illus.). 24p. 1996. pap. text 4.95 (*0-382-39574-3*) Silver Burdett Pr.

— Azul. (Imagenes Ser.).Tr. of Blue. 1996. 10.15 (*0-606-10379-1*, Pub. by Turtleback) Demco.

— Blue. (Images Ser.). (Illus.). 24p. (J). 1996. pap. 4.95 (*0-382-39626-X*) Silver Burdett Pr.

— Blue. LC 95-51089. (Images Ser.). (Illus.). 24p. (J). 1996. reprint ed. lib. bdg. 10.95 (*0-382-39590-5*, Silver Pr NJ) Silver Burdett Pr.

— Chart & Graph Puzzles. LC 95-11617. (Math Skills Ser.). (Illus.). 32p. (J). (gr. 2-6). 1994. pap. 6.95 (*0-7460-1724-3*, Usborne) EDC.

— Clothes. LC 96-37244. (Picture This! Ser.). (J). 1998. 18.50 (*1-57572-149-X*) Heinemann Lib.

— Colors. (First Learning Ser.). (Illus.). 24p. (J). (ps up). 1990. pap. 3.95 (*0-7460-0594-6*, Usborne) EDC.

— Counting Sticker Book. (First Learning Ser.). (Illus.). 16p. (J). (ps-3). 1996. pap. 6.95 (*0-7460-2428-2*, Usborne) EDC.

— Dot-to-Dot Dinosaurs. (Dot to Dot Ser.). (Illus.). 24p. (J). (ps-2). 1993. pap. 3.95 (*0-7460-1374-4*, Usborne) EDC.

— Dot to Dot Nature. (Dot to Dot Ser.). (Illus.). 24p. (J). (ps-2). 1993. pap. 3.95 (*0-7460-1375-2*, Usborne) EDC.

— Dot-to-Dot Space. (Dot to Dot Ser.). (Illus.). 24p. (J). (ps-2). 1993. pap. 3.95 (*0-7460-1373-6*, Usborne) EDC.

***Bryant-Mole, Karen.** Drugs. LC 98-42284. (Talking about Ser.). 32p. (J). 1999. lib. bdg. 22.83 (*0-8172-5887-6*) Raintree Steck-V.

Bryant-Mole, Karen. Electricity. LC 96-22977. (Science All Around Me Ser.). 1998. 11.95 (*1-57572-109-0*) Heinemann Lib.

— En el Campo. LC 99-10799. (Picture This! Ser.).Tr. of In the Country. (SPA., Illus.). 24p. (J). (gr. k-2). 1999. lib. bdg. 12.95 (*1-57572-905-9*) Heinemann Lib.

***Bryant-Mole, Karen.** En la Ciudad. (Picture This! Ser.).Tr. of In the City. (SPA., Illus.). 24p. (J). (gr. k-2). 1999. lib. bdg. 12.95 (*1-57572-906-7*) Heinemann Lib.

Bryant-Mole, Karen. En la Granja. LC 99-10866. (Picture This! Ser.).Tr. of On the Farm. (Illus.). 24p. (J). (gr. k-2). 1999. lib. bdg. 12.95 (*1-57572-907-5*) Heinemann Lib.

— En la Playa. (Picture This! Ser.).Tr. of At the Beach. (SPA., Illus.). 24p. (J). (gr. k-2). 1999. lib. bdg. 12.95 (*1-57572-904-0*) Heinemann Lib.

— Floating & Sinking. LC 97-41946. (Science All Around Me Ser.). (Illus.). 24p. (J). 1998. write for info. (*1-57572-627-0*) Heinemann Lib.

— Flowers. LC 95-31132. (See for Yourself Ser.). (Illus.). 30p. (J). (ps-4). 1996. lib. bdg. 21.40 (*0-8172-4211-2*) Raintree Steck-V.

— Food. LC 96-48156. (Picture This Ser.). (J). 1998. 18.50 (*1-57572-150-3*) Heinemann Lib.

— Forces. (J). 1998. 11.95 (*1-57572-108-2*) Heinemann Lib.

— Fractions & Decimals. (Math Skills Ser.). (Illus.). 32p. (J). (gr. 2-6). 1994. pap. 6.95 (*0-7460-1683-2*, Usborne) EDC.

— Games. LC 96-47755. (Picture This! Ser.). (J). 1998. 18.50 (*1-57572-151-1*) Heinemann Lib.

— Grammar Puzzles. (English Skills Ser.). (Illus.). 32p. (J). (gr. 2-6). 1994. pap. 6.95 (*0-7460-1682-4*, Usborne) EDC.

— Green. (Illus.). 24p. (J). 1996. pap. 4.95 (*0-382-39625-1*, Silver Pr NJ); lib. bdg. 10.95 (*0-382-39589-1*) Silver Burdett Pr.

— Las Herramientas. (Images Ser.).Tr. of Tools. (SPA., Illus.). 24p. (J). 1996. pap. text 4.95 (*0-382-39580-8*) Silver Burdett Pr.

— Las Herramientas. (Imagenes Ser.).Tr. of Tools. (J). 1997. 10.15 (*0-606-10472-0*, Pub. by Turtleback) Demco.

***Bryant-Mole, Karen.** Hot & Cold. LC 97-41947. (Science All Around Me Ser.). (Illus.). 24p. (J). 1998. 19.92 (*1-57572-628-9*) Heinemann Lib.

Bryant-Mole, Karen. In the Town. LC 99-11184. (Picture This Ser.). 1999. write for info. (*1-57572-900-8*) Heinemann Lib.

— Insects. LC 95-33272. (See for Yourself Ser.). (Illus.). 30p. (J). (ps-4). 1996. lib. bdg. 21.40 (*0-8172-4210-4*) Raintree Steck-V.

***Bryant-Mole, Karen.** Invierno. (Picture This! Ser.).Tr. of Winter. (SPA., Illus.). 24p. (J). (gr. k-2). 1999. lib. bdg. 12.95 (*1-57572-912-1*) Heinemann Lib.

— Juegos.Tr. of Games. (SPA., Illus.). 24p. (J). (gr. k-2). 1999. lib. bdg. 12.95 (*1-57572-916-4*) Heinemann Lib.

— Juegutes. (Picture This! Ser.).Tr. of Toys. (SPA., Illus.). 24p. (J). (gr. k-2). 1999. lib. bdg. 12.95 (*1-57572-917-2*) Heinemann Lib.

Bryant-Mole, Karen. Letters Sticker Book. (First Learning Ser.). (Illus.). 16p. (J). (ps-3). 1996. pap. 6.95 (*0-7460-2429-0*, Usborne) EDC.

— Los Materiales. (Imagenes Ser.). 1997. 10.15 (*0-606-10474-7*, Pub. by Turtleback) Demco.

— Machines. LC 95-48064. (Illus.). 24p. (J). 1996. pap. 4.95 (*0-382-39624-3*); lib. bdg. 10.95 (*0-382-39588-3*) Silver Burdett Pr.

***Bryant-Mole, Karen.** Magnets. LC 97-41943. (Science All Around Me Ser.). (Illus.). 24p. (J). (gr. k-2). 1998. 12.95 (*1-57572-629-7*) Heinemann Lib.

Bryant-Mole, Karen. Las Maquinarias. (Images Ser.). (SPA., Illus.). 24p. 1996. pap. text 4.95 (*0-382-39576-X*) Silver Burdett Pr.

— Las Maquinarias. (Imagenes Ser.). 1997. 10.15 (*0-606-10473-9*, Pub. by Turtleback) Demco.

— Los Materiales. (Images Ser.).Tr. of Materials. (SPA., Illus.). 24p. 1996. pap. text 4.95 (*0-382-39577-8*) Silver Burdett Pr.

— Materials. LC 95-51186. (Illus.). 24p. (J). 1996. pap. 4.95 (*0-382-39623-5*, Silver Pr NJ); lib. bdg. 10.95 (*0-382-39587-5*) Silver Burdett Pr.

— Matter. (Science All Around Me Ser.). 1998. 11.95 (*1-57572-110-4*) Heinemann Lib.

***Bryant-Mole, Karen.** Mortimer's Fun with Words, 6 bks. Incl. Beginning Letters. Mukhida, Zul. 24p. (J). (ps up). 2000. lib. bdg. 19.93 (*0-8368-2746-5*); Ending Letters. Mukhida, Zul, photos by. (Illus.). 24p. (J). (ps up). 2000. lib. bdg. 19.93 (*0-8368-2747-3*); Letters Make Words. Mukhida, Zul, photos by. (Illus.). 24p. (J). (ps up). 2000. lib. bdg. 19.93 (*0-8368-2748-1*); Mortimer Plays I-Spy. Mukhida, Zul. 24p. (J). (ps up). 2000. lib. bdg. 19.93 (*0-8368-2749-X*); Mortimer's ABC's. Mukhida, Zul. 24p. (J). (ps up). 2000. lib. bdg. 19.93 (*0-8368-2750-3*); Rhyming Words. Mukhida, Zul. 24p. (J). (ps up). 2000. lib. bdg. 19.93 (*0-8368-2751-1*); 24p. (J). (ps up). 2000. Set lib. bdg. 119.58 (*0-8368-2745-7*) Gareth Stevens Inc.

— Mortimer's Math, 6 bks. Incl. Counting. LC 99-54603. (Illus.). 24p. (J). (ps up). 1999. lib. bdg. 19.93 (*0-8368-2617-5*); Patterns. LC 99-56188. (Illus.). 24p. (J). (ps up). 1999. lib. bdg. 19.93 (*0-8368-2618-3*); Shapes. LC 99-55987. (Illus.). 24p. (J). (ps up). 1999. lib. bdg. 19.93 (*0-8368-2619-1*); Size. LC 99-55989. (Illus.). 24p. (J). (ps up). 1999. lib. bdg. 19.93 (*0-8368-2620-5*); Sorting. LC 99-55988. (Illus.). 24p. (J). (ps up). 1999. lib. bdg. 19.93 (*0-8368-2621-3*); Where Is Mortimer? LC 99-54602. (Illus.). 24p. (J). (ps up). 1999. lib. bdg. 19.93 (*0-8368-2622-1*); (Illus.). (J). (ps up). 1999. Set lib. bdg. 119.58 (*0-8368-2616-7*) Gareth Stevens Inc.

Bryant-Mole, Karen. Moving. LC 97-41944. (Science All Around Me Ser.). (Illus.). 24p. (J). (gr. k-2). 1998. 18.50 (*1-57572-630-0*) Heinemann Lib.

— Numbers. (First Learning Ser.). (Illus.). 24p. (J). (ps-3). 1992. pap. 4.50 (*0-7460-1042-7*) EDC.

***Bryant-Mole, Karen.** Numbers. (First Learning Ser.). (Illus.). 24p. (YA). (ps up). 2000. pap. 4.95 (*0-7460-3802-X*, Usborne) EDC.

Bryant-Mole, Karen. On the Farm. LC 99-10866. (Picture This Ser.). (Illus.). (J). 1999. write for info. (*1-57572-901-6*) Heinemann Lib.

***Bryant-Mole, Karen.** Otono. (Picture This! Ser.).Tr. of Fall. (SPA., Illus.). 24p. (J). (gr. k-2). 1999. lib. bdg. 12.95 (*1-57572-909-1*) Heinemann Lib.

— Primavera. (Picture This! Ser.).Tr. of Spring. (SPA., Illus.). 24p. 1999. lib. bdg. 12.95 (*1-57572-910-5*) Heinemann Lib.

Bryant-Mole, Karen. Red. LC 95-51092. (Images Ser.). (Illus.). 24p. (J). 1996. pap. 4.95 (*0-382-39622-7*, Silver Pr NJ) Silver Burdett Pr.

— Red. LC 95-51092. (Images Ser.). (Illus.). 24p. (J). 1996. reprint ed. lib. bdg. 10.95 (*0-382-39586-7*, Silver Pr NJ) Silver Burdett Pr.

— Rojo. (Images Ser.).Tr. of Red. (SPA., Illus.). 24p. (J). 1996. pap. text 4.95 (*0-382-39578-6*) Silver Burdett Pr.

— Rojo. (Imagenes Ser.).Tr. of Red. (J). 1996. 10.15 (*0-606-10498-4*, Pub. by Turtleback) Demco.

***Bryant-Mole, Karen.** Ropa. LC 99-10796. (Picture This! Ser.).Tr. of Clothes. (SPA., Illus.). 24p. (J). (ps-1). 1999. lib. bdg. 12.95 (*1-57572-914-8*) Heinemann Lib.

Bryant-Mole, Karen. 2nd Big Dot to Dot. 2nd ed. (Dot to Dot Ser.). (Illus.). 96p. (J). (ps-2). 1993. pap. 11.95 (*0-7460-1377-9*, Usborne) EDC.

— Shapes. (First Learning Ser.). (Illus.). 24p. (J). (ps-3). 1991. pap. 3.95 (*0-7460-0593-8*, Usborne) EDC.

— Sound & Light. LC 96-22976. (Science All Around Me Ser.). (Illus.). 24p. (J). 1998. 11.95 (*1-57572-111-2*) Heinemann Lib.

— Spring. LC 97-396. (Picture This! Ser.). (J). 1998. (*1-57572-055-8*) Heinemann Lib.

— Summer. LC 97-393. (Picture This! Ser.). (J). 1998. (*1-57572-056-6*) Heinemann Lib.

— Textura. (Imagenes Ser.). 1997. 10.15 (*0-606-10475-5*, Pub. by Turtleback) Demco.

— Las Textura. (Images Ser.).Tr. of Texture. (SPA., Illus.). 24p. 1996. pap. text 4.95 (*0-382-39579-4*) Silver Burdett Pr.

— Texture. LC 95-48063. (Illus.). 24p. (J). 1996. pap. 4.95 (*0-382-39621-9*, Silver Pr NJ); lib. bdg. 10.95 (*0-382-39585-9*) Silver Burdett Pr.

— Tools. LC 95-51187. (Illus.). 24p. (J). 1996. pap. 4.95 (*0-382-39620-0*, Silver Pr NJ); lib. bdg. 10.95 (*0-382-39584-0*) Silver Burdett Pr.

— Toys. LC 96-37243. (Picture This! Ser.). (J). 1998. 18.50 (*1-57572-057-4*) Heinemann Lib.

— Trees. LC 95-31131. (See for Yourself Ser.). (Illus.). 30p. (J). (ps-4). 1996. lib. bdg. 21.40 (*0-8172-4212-0*) Raintree Steck-V.

— Usborne Dot to Dot at the Seaside. (Usborne Kid Kits Ser.). (Illus.). (J). (ps-2). 1998. 9.95 (*1-58086-142-3*, Usborne) EDC.

— Usborne Dot to Dot Dinosaurs. (Usborne Kid Kits Ser.). (Illus.). (J). (ps-2). 1998. 9.95 (*1-58086-139-3*, Usborne) EDC.

— Usborne Dot to Dot Nature. (Usborne Kid Kits Ser.). (Illus.). (J). (ps-2). 1998. 9.95 (*1-58086-140-7*, Usborne) EDC.

***Bryant-Mole, Karen.** Verano. (Picture This! Ser.).Tr. of Summer. (SPA., Illus.). 24p. (J). (gr. k-2). 1999. lib. bdg. 12.95 (*1-57572-911-3*) Heinemann Lib.

Bryant-Mole, Karen. Verde. (Images Ser.). Orig. Title: Green. (SPA., Illus.). 24p. 1996. pap. text 4.95 (*0-382-39575-1*) Silver Burdett Pr.

— Verde. (Imagenes Ser.). Orig. Title: Green. 1996. 10.15 (*0-606-10535-2*, Pub. by Turtleback) Demco.

— Winter. LC 97-392. (Picture This! Ser.). (J). 1998. (*1-57572-058-2*) Heinemann Lib.

— Yellow. (Images Ser.). (Illus.). 24p. (J). 1996. pap. 4.95 (*0-382-39619-7*, Silver Pr NJ); lib. bdg. 10.95 (*0-382-39583-2*, Silver Pr NJ) Silver Burdett Pr.

— You're a Community Helper. LC 97-20058. 1998. (*1-57572-184-8*) Heinemann.

— You're a Grownup. LC 97-16971. (Pretend Ser.). (J). 1998. (*1-57572-185-6*) Heinemann Lib.

— You're a Sports Pro. LC 97-20057. (Pretend Ser.). (J). 1998. (*1-57572-187-2*) Heinemann Lib.

— You're a Star. LC 97-20059. (Pretend Ser.). (J). 1998. (*1-57572-186-4*) Heinemann Lib.

Bryant-Mole, Karen & Gee, Robyn. Multiplying & Dividing Puzzles. (Math Skills Ser.). (Illus.). 32p. (J). (gr. 2-6). 1993. pap. 6.95 (*0-7460-1073-7*, Usborne) EDC.

Bryant-Mole, Karen, jt. auth. see Tyler, J.

Bryant, Nancy, jt. auth. see Burns, Leslie.

Bryant, Nancy O., jt. auth. see Burns, Leslie D.

Bryant, Napoleon A. African American Scientists. 95th ed. LC 97-108393. (J). (gr. 1-6). 1995. text 9.70 (*0-15-306858-2*) Harcourt.

Bryant, Nerisa B. Decimals & Percent. (Mathematics in Daily Living Ser.). 1997. pap., student ed. 10.32 (*0-8114-1514-7*) Raintree Steck-V.

— Measurement & Geometry. (Mathematics in Daily Living Ser.). 1997. pap., student ed. 10.32 (*0-8114-1515-5*) Raintree Steck-V.

Bryant, Neville J. An Introduction to Immunohematology. 3rd ed. LC 93-36574. 1994. text 47.00 (*0-7216-3883-X*, W B Saunders Co) Harcrt Hlth Sci Grp.

— Laboratory Immunology & Serology. 3rd ed. 1992. pap. text 47.00 (*0-7216-4212-8*, W B Saunders Co) Harcrt Hlth Sci Grp.

Bryant, Nigel. The High Book of the Grail: A Translation of the Thirteenth Century Romance of Perlesvaus. LC 96-224817. 271p. 1996. pap. 29.95 (*0-85991-510-7*) Boydell & Brewer.

Bryant, Nigel, tr. see De Troyes, Chretien.

***Bryant, Niobia.** Admission of Love. 2000. mass mkt. 5.99 (*1-58314-164-2*) BET Bks.

Bryant, Page. Awakening Arthur! His Return in Our Time. 208p. 1993. pap. 15.00 (*1-85538-071-4*, Pub. by Aqrn Pr) Harper SF.

— Crystals & Their Use: A Study of At-One-Ment with the Mineral Kingdom. 64p. 1984. pap. 7.50 (*0-89540-151-7*, SB-151) Sun Pub.

— Earth Changes Now! 62p. 1989. pap. 7.00 (*0-89540-171-1*, SB-171) Sun Pub.

— The Earth Changes Survival Handbook. (Illus.). 440p. 1983. pap. 27.00 (*0-89540-150-9*, SB-150) Sun Pub.

— The Magic of Minerals. 64p. 1987. pap. 7.50 (*0-89540-162-2*, SB-162) Sun Pub.

— Sedona Vortex Guide Book. 232p. (Orig.). 1991. pap. 14.95 (*0-929385-25-X*) Light Tech Pubng.

— The Spiritual Re-Awakening of the Great Smoky Mountains. LC 95-104306. (Illus.). 264p. (Orig.). 1994. pap. 16.00 (*0-9641390-0-6*) P Bryant.

— Starwalking: Shamanic Practices for Traveling into the Night Sky. LC 97-13044. (Illus.). 408p. (Orig.). 1997. pap. 18.95 (*1-879181-36-3*) Bear & Co.

Bryant, Pat, ed. Mark of the Beast. (Southern Exposure Ser.). (Illus.). 112p. (Orig.). 1980. pap. 3.00 (*0-943810-09-4*) Inst Southern Studies.

Bryant, Paul. Backyard Fish Farming. (Illus.). 128p. (Orig.). (C). 1980. pap. text 9.95 (*0-904727-24-6*, Pub. by Prism Pr) Assoc Pubs Grp.

— Bear Bryant on Winning Football. 240p. 1983. 18.95 (*0-13-071274-4*); pap. 7.95 (*0-13-071266-3*) P-H.

Bryant, Paula. Tinker's Journey Home. (J). 11.95 (*0-671-75182-4*) S&S Bks Yung.

Bryant, Peter, jt. auth. see Bradley, Lynette.

Bryant, Peter, jt. auth. see Nunes, Terezhina.

Bryant, Peter, jt. auth. see Nunes, Terezinha.

Bryant, Peter, jt. ed. see Butterworth, George.

Bryant, Peter, ed. see Cox, Maureen V.

Bryant, Peter, ed. see Smith, Leslie.

Bryant, Peter G. & Smith, Marlene A. CPS Practical Data Analysis: Case Studies in Business Statistics Select Material, Set, Vols. 1 & 2. 72p. (C). 1995. text 6.00 (*0-256-21240-6*, Irwn McGrw-H) McGrw-H Hghr Educ.

— Practical Data Analysis: Case Studies in Business Statistics. LC 94-21385. 96p. (C). 1994. text 26.75 (*0-256-15827-4*, Irwn McGrw-H) McGrw-H Hghr Educ.

— Practical Data Analysis: Case Studies in Business Statistics, Vol. 2. 112p. (C). 1994. text 26.75 (*0-256-15828-2*, Irwn McGrw-H) McGrw-H Hghr Educ.

Bryant, Philip. Blue Island. 38p. (Orig.). 1997. pap. 6.00 (*1-889460-00-1*) CrossplusRds.

— Sermon on a Perfect Spring Day: Poems. LC 97-69734. (Minnesota Voices Project Ser.: Vol. 85). 88p. 1998. pap. 12.95 (*0-89823-185-X*) New Rivers Pr.

Bryant, Philip J. & Johnsen, Kjell. The Principles of Circular Accelerators & Storage Rings. (Illus.). 383p. (C). 1993. text 110.00 (*0-521-35578-8*) Cambridge U Pr.

Bryant, R., jt. auth. see Bryant, B.

Bryant, R. B., et al, eds. Quantitative Modeling of Soil Forming Process. LC 94-31647. (Special Publications: Vol. 39). 185p. 1994. pap. 24.00 (*0-89118-814-2*) Soil Sci Soc Am.

Bryant, Ralph C. Controlling Money: The Federal Reserve & Its Critics. LC 82-45983. 155p. 1983. pap. 10.95 (*0-8157-1135-2*) Brookings.

— Financial Interdependence & Variability in Exchange Rates. LC 80-24883. 26p. 1980. pap. 7.95 (*0-8157-1127-1*) Brookings.

— International Coordination of National Stabilization Policies. (Integrating National Economies: Promise & Pitfalls Ser.). 163p. 1995. 34.95 (*0-8157-1256-1*); pap. 14.95 (*0-8157-1255-3*) Brookings.

— International Financial Intermediation. LC 87-10358. (Studies in International Economics). 181p. 1987. 34.95 (*0-8157-1138-7*); pap. 14.95 (*0-8157-1137-9*) Brookings.

— Money & Monetary Policy in Interdependent Nations. LC 80-19225. 584p. 1980. 44.95 (*0-8157-1130-1*); pap. 19.95 (*0-8157-1129-8*) Brookings.

Bryant, Ralph C., et al, eds. Empirical Macroeconomics for Interdependent Economies, 2 vols, Set. LC 87-34156. 720p. 1988. text 49.95 (*0-8157-1140-9*) Brookings.

— Evaluating Policy Regimes: New Research in Empirical Macroeconomics. 880p. (C). 1993. 59.95 (*0-8157-1150-6*); pap. 29.95 (*0-8157-1149-2*) Brookings.

— External Deficits & the Dollar: The Pit & the Pendulum. LC 87-27214. 147p. 1988. pap. 14.95 (*0-8157-1145-X*); text 34.95 (*0-8157-1146-8*) Brookings.

— Macroeconomic Policies in an Interdependent World. vi, 420p. 1989. pap. 17.50 (*1-55775-111-0*) Intl Monetary.

Bryant, Ralph G. Be King of the Mountain. 1987. pap. 5.25 (*0-89137-820-0*) Quality Pubns.

Bryant, Randall E. Switch Level VLSI. (C). 1996. text. write for info. (*0-201-07404-4*) Addison-Wesley.

Bryant, Ray & Knighton, Raymond. Introduction to Soils. (C). 2001. 84.00 (*0-13-260829-4*, Macmillan Coll) P-H.

Bryant, Raymond L. The Political Ecology of Forestry in Burma, 1824-1994. LC 96-30877. 1997. text 39.00 (*0-8248-1909-8*) UH Pr.

Bryant, Raymond L. & Bailey, Sinead. Third World Political Ecology: An Introduction. LC 96-43170. (Illus.). 256p. (C). 1997. 75.00 (*0-415-12743-2*) Routledge.

— Third World Political Ecology: An Introduction. LC 96-43170. (Illus.). 256p. (C). 1997. pap. 24.99 (*0-415-12744-0*) Routledge.

Bryant, Raymond L. & Parnwell, Michael J., eds. Environmental Change in South-East Asia: People, Politics & Sustainable Development. LC 95-26276. (Global Environmental Change Ser.). 400p. (C). 1996. 85.00 (*0-415-12932-X*); pap. 25.99 (*0-415-12933-8*) Routledge.

Bryant, Raymond L., jt. auth. see Wilson, Geoff A.

***Bryant, Rebecca.** Discovery & Decision: Exploring the Metaphysics & Epistemology of Scientific Classification. LC 00-37169. 2000. pap. write for info. (*0-8386-3876-7*) Fairleigh Dickinson.

***Bryant, Rees.** Baptism, Why Wait? Faith's Response in Conversion. LC 99-46669. 1999. write for info. (*0-89900-858-5*) College Pr Pub.

Bryant, Richard. Non-U. S. Worldwide Telecommunications: Asia-Oceania, Vol. 4. LC 95-231952. (Illus.). 471p. 1994. 1500.00 (*1-56965-053-5*, HG-148D) BCC.

— Non-U. S. Worldwide Telecommunications: Europe, Vol. 1. LC 95-231952. (Illus.). 410p. 1994. 1500.00 (*1-56965-055-1*, G-148A) BCC.

— Non-U. S. Worldwide Telecommunications: Latin America, Vol. 3. LC 95-231952. (Illus.). 346p. 1993. 1500.00 (*1-56965-052-7*, G-148C) BCC.

— Non-U. S. Worldwide Telecommunications Vol. 2: Africa-Middle East. LC 95-231952. (Illus.). 208p. 1994. 1500.00 (*1-56965-054-3*, G-148B) BCC.

— We Overcame: History of the Civil Rites of the Disabled. 350p. (C). 1993. pap. text 17.95 (*0-9631345-2-3*) Regal Direct.

***Bryant, Richard, photos by.** Carlo Scarpa, Gipsoteca Canoviana, Possagno. (Opus Ser.: Vol. 22). (ITA & ENG., Illus.). 60p. 2001. 42.00 (*3-930698-22-6*) Edition A Menges.

— Sir John Soane's Museum, London. (Opus Ser.: Vol. 14). (Illus.). 64p. write for info. (*3-8030-2714-4*) Edition A Menges.

***Bryant, Richard A. & Harvey, Allison G.** Acute Stress Disorder: A Handbook of Theory, Assessment & Treatment. LC 99-44989. 251p. 2000. text 39.95 (*1-55798-612-6*, 431737A) Am Psychol.

***Bryant, Rita.** Last Blue Promise. 60p. 1998. pap. 6.00 (*0-935931-97-X*, Gray Matter Pubg) Iberian Pub.

Bryant, Robert L., et al, eds. Integral Geometry. LC 86-28902. (Contemporary Mathematics Ser.: Vol. 63). 350p. 1987. pap. 42.00 (*0-8218-5071-7*, CONM/63) Am Math.

Bryant, Roger. Accountancy. Kettell, Brian, ed. (Banking & Finance Ser.: Vol. 2). 350p. 1985. pap. text 36.00 (*0-86010-567-9*); lib. bdg. 50.00 (*0-86010-584-9*) G & T Inc.

***Bryant, Ron D.** Kentucky History: An Annotated Bibliography, 9. LC 99-45451. (Bibliographies of the States of the United States Ser.). 592p. 2000. lib. bdg. write for info. (*0-313-28239-0*) Greenwood.

Bryant, Roy. Manual on Demonology: Diary of an Exorcist. 1997. 19.95 (*0-89228-123-5*) Impact Christian.

Bryant, Ruth, ed. Management of Acute & Chronic Wounds: Nursing Management. (Illus.). 368p. (C). (gr. 13). 1992. text 45.00 (*0-8016-0896-1*, 00896) Mosby Inc.

***Bryant, Ruth & Doughty, Dorothy.** Acute & Chronic Wound: Nursing Management. 2nd ed. (C). 1998. write for info. (*1-55664-410-8*) Mosby Inc.

Bryant, Sally S. Here's Juggins. LC 96-47308. (Illus.). 176p. (J). (gr. 4-7). 1996. 19.95 (*0-945980-62-0*) Nrth Country Pr.

Bryant, Sandy N. Mountian Air: The Life of Gordon Stuart, Mountain Man of the North Cascades. 1991. pap. 15.95 (*1-879992-02-7*) Directed Media.

Bryant, Sara C. Epaminondas & His Auntie. (Illus.). 16p. 1986. reprint ed. pap. 8.95 (*0-89966-556-X*) Buccaneer Bks.

— How to Tell Stories to Children. 1980. lib. bdg. 59.95 (*0-8490-3176-1*) Gordon Pr.

— How to Tell Stories to Children. 1979. reprint ed. 40.00 (*1-55888-994-9*) Omnigraphics Inc.

Bryant, Smith. Practical Data Analysis I. 2nd ed. 112p. (C). 1998. pap. 13.75 (*0-256-23871-5*) McGraw.

— Practical Data Analysis II. 2nd ed. 128p. (C). 1998. pap. 13.75 (*0-256-23872-3*) McGraw.

Bryant, Stephanie Cottrell. Teach Yourself Html 4. (Teach Yourself Ser.). 512p. 1999. pap. 29.99 (*0-7645-7512-0*) IDG Bks.

***Bryant, Stephen L.** It's Mom-and-Pop, Stupid. 2000. pap. 12.95 (*0-533-13490-0*) Vantage.

Bryant, Steven A., jt. auth. see Burden, Gail.

***Bryant, Steven W., et al.** The JCAHO Troubleshooter: Best Policies, Practices, & Model Documents for Survey Success. (Illus.). 280p. 2000. pap. text 147.00 (*1-57839-073-7*) Opus Communs.

Bryant, Steven W., jt. ed. see Coburn, Jay.

***Bryant, Sue.** Barcelona. 2nd ed. (Globetrotter Travel Guide Ser.). (Illus.). 128p. 2000. pap. 10.95 (*1-85974-067-7*) New5 Holland.

— Costa del Sol. 2nd ed. (Globetrotter Travel Guides Ser.). (Illus.). 2000. pap. 10.95 (*1-85974-069-3*) New5 Holland.

Bryant, Sue. Globetrotter Travel Guide to Ibiza. (Globetrotter Travel Guide Ser.). 128p. 1998. pap. text 10.95 (*1-85368-442-2*, Pub. by New5 Holland) Globe Pequot.

***Bryant, Sue.** Ibiza & Formentera. 2nd ed. (Globetrotter Travel Guides Ser.). (Illus.). 128p. 2000. pap. 10.95 (*1-85974-360-9*) New5 Holland.

— Istanbul. (Globetrotter Travel Guides Ser.). (Illus.). 128p. 2000. pap. 10.95 (*1-85974-295-5*) New5 Holland.

Bryant, Sue. Travel Guide Israel. (Globetrotter Travel Guide Ser.). (Illus.). 128p. 1998. pap. 10.95 (*1-85368-571-2*) Globe Pequot.

Bryant, Sue L. Personal Professional Development & the Solo Librarian: Library Training Guide. 88p. 1995. pap. text 40.00 (*1-85604-141-7*, LAP1417, Pub. by Library Association) Bernan Associates.

Bryant, Susan. The Seagram Museum. (Illus.). 46p. (Orig.). 1992. pap. 9.95 (*1-55046-068-4*, Pub. by Boston Mills) Genl Dist Srvs.

Bryant, T. Alton, ed. Zondervan Compact Bible Dictionary. 1967. 14.99 (*0-310-22080-7*, 6726) Zondervan.

— Zondervan Compact Bible Dictionary. 640p. 1972. pap. 9.99 (*0-310-22082-3*, 6726P) Zondervan.

— Zondervan Compact Bible Dictionary. 640p. 1993. 14.99 (*0-310-48981-4*) Zondervan.

Bryant, T. L., et al. The Law of Evidence in Canada. 1120p. 1992. pap., student ed. 95.00 (*0-409-90639-5*, MICHIE) LEXIS Pub.

Bryant, T. L., jt. auth. see Eccles, D.

Bryant, Tamera. Phonics Flipper. 39p. (J). (gr. 3 up). 1997. 6.95 (*1-878383-35-3*) C Lee Pubns.

— Spelling Flipper. 39p. (J). (gr. 3 up). 1997. 6.95 (*1-878383-38-8*) C Lee Pubns.

Bryant, Tannetje, jt. auth. see Eccles, Des.

***Bryant, Terry L.** Building Healthy Marriages. (Spiritual Discovery Ser.). 112p. 1999. pap., teacher ed. 9.95 (*0-88243-229-X*, 02-0229) Gospel Pub.

— Building Healthy Marriages. (Spiritual Discovery Ser.). 126p. 1999. pap., student ed. 4.95 (*0-88243-129-3*, 02-0129) Gospel Pub.

Bryant, Thema S. The Birthing of a Lioness: A Collection of Poems & Prophecies. 112p. Date not set. pap. write for info. (*1-888077-04-2*) Akosua Visions.

Bryant, Theodore. Self-Discipline in 10 Days: How to Go from Thinking to Doing. LC 98-75039. (Illus.). 165p. 1999. pap. 19.95 (*1-880115-02-6*, 410) HUB Pub.

Bryant, Thomas A. Rodeo, America's Number One Sport. 2nd ed. (Illus.). 64p. (J). (gr. 3-5). 1986. reprint ed. pap. 4.00 (*0-941875-00-8*) Wolverine Distrib.

Bryant, Tom. Taste of Texas Ranching. (Illus.). 228p. 1994. pap. 15.95 (*1-884374-05-0*) Border Bks.

Bryant, Tom & Bernstein, Joel. A Taste of Texas Ranching: Recipe Postcards. (Illus.). 30p. (Orig.). 1996. pap. 9.95 (*0-89672-367-4*) Tex Tech Univ Pr.

Bryant, Tom, jt. auth. see Bernstein, Joel.

Bryant, Tony. Methods, Standards & Maturity: Developing the Standard for SSADM. LC 95-1440. (International Series in Software Engineering). 1995. 29.95 (*0-07-709115-9*) McGraw.

— Samurai, 1550-1600. (Warrior Ser.). (Illus.). 64p. 1994. pap. 12.95 (*1-85532-345-1*, 9606, Pub. by Ospry) Stackpole.

Bryant, Tracey L. & Pennock, Jonathan R., eds. The Delaware Estuary: Rediscovering a Forgotten Resource. 2nd ed. (Illus.). 144p. 1991. reprint ed. pap. 25.00 (*0-9619792-1-6*) U of Del Sea Grant.

Bryant, Vaughn M., Jr. & Holloway, Richard G., eds. Pollen Records of Late-Quaternary North American Sediments. LC 85-71610. (Illus.). 440p. (C). 1985. 35.00 (*0-931871-01-8*) Am Assn Strat.

Bryant, Vaughn M., jt. auth. see Carlson, David L.

Bryant, Victor W. Aspects of Combinatorics: A Wide-Ranging Introduction. (Illus.). 274p. (C). 1993. text 80.00 (*0-521-41974-3*) Cambridge U Pr.

— Yet Another Introduction to Analysis. (Illus.). 298p. (C). 1990. text 69.95 (*0-521-38166-5*); pap. text 25.95 (*0-521-38835-X*) Cambridge U Pr.

Bryant, W. Keith. The Economic Organization of the Household. (Illus.). 304p. (C). 1991. pap. text 27.95 (*0-521-39840-1*) Cambridge U Pr.

— The Economic Organization of the Household. (Illus.). 304p. (C). 1991. text 89.95 (*0-521-39187-3*) Cambridge U Pr.

Bryant, Wayne M. Bisexual Characters in Film: From Anais to Zee. LC 96-25868. 187p. 1997. pap. 17.95 (*1-56023-894-1*) Haworth Pr.

— Bisexual Characters in Film: From Anais to Zee. LC 96-25868. 187p. 1997. 24.95 (*0-7890-0142-X*) Haworth Pr.

Bryant, William. The Veiled Pulse of Time: An Introduction to Biographical Cycles & Destiny. LC 96-27832. (Spirituality & Social Renewal Ser.). 1996. pap. 16.95 (*0-940262-80-0*, Lindisfarne) Anthroposophic.

Bryant, William C. A Border Tradition. Drew, Bernard A., ed. (Illus.). 48p. 1988. pap. 6.50 (*0-941583-13-9*) Attic Rev Pr.

— A Discourse on the Life & Genius of James Fenimore Cooper. (Works of William Cullen Bryant). 1989. reprint ed. lib. bdg. 79.00 (*0-7812-2138-2*) Rprt Serv.

— A Discourse on the Life, Character & Genius of Washington Irving. (Works of William Cullen Bryant). 1989. reprint ed. lib. bdg. 79.00 (*0-7812-2139-9*) Rprt Serv.

— A Discourse on the Life Character & Work of Gulian Crommelin Verplanck. (Works of William Cullen Bryant). 1989. reprint ed. lib. bdg. 79.00 (*0-7812-2142-0*) Rprt Serv.

— The Embargo. (Works of William Cullen Bryant). 1989. reprint ed. lib. bdg. 79.00 (*0-7812-2125-0*) Rprt Serv.

— The Flood of Years. (Works of William Cullen Bryant). 1989. reprint ed. lib. bdg. 79.00 (*0-7812-2135-8*) Rprt Serv.

— A Forest Hymn. (Works of William Cullen Bryant). 1989. reprint ed. lib. bdg. 90.00 (*0-7812-2130-7*) Rprt Serv.

— The Fountain & Other Poems. (Works of William Cullen Bryant). 1989. reprint ed. lib. bdg. 79.00 (*0-7812-2128-5*) Rprt Serv.

— The Iliad of Homer Translated into English Blank Verse. (Works of William Cullen Bryant). 1989. reprint ed. lib. bdg. 79.00 (*0-7812-2133-1*) Rprt Serv.

— Letters from the East. (Works of William Cullen Bryant). 1989. reprint ed. lib. bdg. 79.00 (*0-685-44808-8*) Rprt Serv.

— Letters of a Traveller. (Works of William Cullen Bryant). 1989. reprint ed. lib. bdg. 79.00 (*0-7812-2137-4*) Rprt Serv.

— Library of World Poetry. LC 94-39050. (Illus.). 912p. 1995. 12.99 (*0-517-11892-0*) Gramrcy Bks.

— Poems. (Works of William Cullen Bryant). 1989. reprint ed. lib. bdg. 79.00 (*0-685-27995-2*) Rprt Serv.

— Poetical Works. (BCL1-PS American Literature Ser.). 130p. 1992. reprint ed. lib. bdg. 69.00 (*0-7812-6681-5*) Rprt Serv.

— Poetical Works of William Cullen Bryant. Date not set. lib. bdg. 26.95 (*0-8488-1895-4*) Amereon Ltd.

— Poetical Works of William Cullen Bryant. LC 79-85192. 1969. reprint ed. 42.50 (*0-404-01143-8*) AMS Pr.

— Some Notices on the Life & Writings of Fitz Greene Halleck. (Works of William Cullen Bryant). 1989. reprint ed. lib. bdg. 79.00 (*0-7812-2141-2*) Rprt Serv.

— Tales of the Glauber Spa. (Works of William Cullen Bryant). 1989. reprint ed. lib. bdg. 79.00 (*0-7812-2136-6*) Rprt Serv.

— Thirty Poems. (Works of William Cullen Bryant). 1989. reprint ed. lib. bdg. 79.00 (*0-7812-2131-5*) Rprt Serv.

— Voices of Nature. (Works of William Cullen Bryant). 1989. reprint ed. lib. bdg. 79.00 (*0-7812-2132-3*) Rprt Serv.

— The White Footed Doe & Other Poems. (Works of William Cullen Bryant). 1989. reprint ed. lib. bdg. 79.00 (*0-7812-2129-3*) Rprt Serv.

— The Works of William Cullen Bryant. 1989. reprint ed. lib. bdg. 63.00 (*0-685-74131-1*) Rprt Serv.

Bryant, William C., ed. The Letters of William Cullen Bryant, 1849-1857, Vol. 3. LC 74-27169. (Illus.). 564p. 1981. 65.00 (*0-8232-0993-8*) Fordham.

— The Library of Poetry & Song: Revised & Enlarged with Recent Authors & Dictionary of Poetical Quotations, 3 Vols., Set. LC 72-3178. (Granger Index Reprint Ser.). 1977. reprint ed. 82.95 (*0-8369-8238-X*) Ayer.

— Power for Sanity: Selected Editorials of William Cullen Bryant, 1829-1861. LC 93-44266. (Illus.). 321p. (C). 1994. 30.00 (*0-8232-1543-1*); pap. 20.00 (*0-8232-1544-X*) Fordham.

— Tales of Glauber-Spa, 2 vols., 1. 1972. reprint ed. lib. bdg. 29.00 (*0-8422-8012-X*) Irvington.

— Tales of Glauber-Spa, 2 vols., 2. 1972. reprint ed. lib. bdg. 29.00 (*0-8422-8013-8*) Irvington.

Bryant, William C. & Voss, Thomas G., eds. The Letters of William Cullen Bryant, 6 vols., Set, Vols. 1-6. (Illus.). 1993. 300.00 (*0-8232-0997-0*) Fordham.

— The Letters of William Cullen Bryant, 6 vols., Vol. VI: 1872-1878. (Illus.). 474p. 1993. 65.00 (*0-8232-0996-2*) Fordham.

— The Letters of William Cullen Bryant, 1809-1836, Vol. 1. LC 74-27169. (Illus.). viii, 501p. 1975. 65.00 (*0-8232-0991-1*) Fordham.

— The Letters of William Cullen Bryant, 1836-1849, Vol. 2. LC 74-27169. (Illus.). viii, 567p. 1977. 65.00 (*0-8232-0992-X*) Fordham.

— The Letters of William Cullen Bryant, 1858-1864, Vol. 4. LC 74-27169. (Illus.). 450p. 1984. 65.00 (*0-8232-0994-6*) Fordham.

— The Letters of William Cullen Bryant, 1865-1871, 6 vols., Vol. 5. LC 74-27169. (Illus.). 462p. 1993. 65.00 (*0-8232-0995-4*) Fordham.

Bryant, William C., ed. see Leonard, Irving A.

Bryant, William M. Hegel's Educational Ideas. LC 72-136415. reprint ed. 29.50 (*0-404-01144-6*) AMS Pr.

Bryant, William M., tr. see Hegel, Georg Wilhelm Friedrich.

Bryant, William O. Cahaba Prison & the Sultana Disaster. LC 90-18013. 192p. 1990. pap. 59.60 (*0-608-05125-X*, 206568400005) Bks Demand.

Bryant, Winifred, jt. auth. see Hackworth, Julie K.

Bryar, Rosamund & Blytheway, Bill. Changing Primary Health Care: The Teamcare Valleys Experience. (Illus.). 256p. (Orig.). 1996. pap. text 34.95 (*0-632-03938-8*) Blackwell Sci.

Bryc, Wlodzimierz. The Normal Distribution: Characterizations with Applications. LC 95-12920. (Lecture Notes in Statistics Ser.: Vol. 100). (Illus.). 140p. 1995. 48.95 (*0-387-97990-5*) Spr-Verlag.

Bryce, Alexander. Minty Mixtures. 1997. pap. write for info. (*1-57553-651-X*) Watermrk Pr.

Bryce, Betty K. American Printmakers, 1946-1996: An Index to Reproductions & Biocritical Information. LC 98-43773. 570p. 1999. 65.00 (*0-8108-3586-X*) Scarecrow.

Bryce, Debbie. Edge of Darkness. (Intimate Moments Ser.). 1993. per. 3.50 (*0-373-07504-9*, 5-07504-9) Silhouette.

Bryce, Derek. Celtic Legends of the Beyond: A Celtic Book of the Dead. LC 98-49114.Tr. of Legende de la Mort en Basse-Bretagne. (Illus.). 144p. 1999. pap. 9.95 (*1-57863-122-X*) Weiser.

— The Mystical Way & the Arthurian Quest. LC 96-3309. 160p. 1996. pap. 9.95 (*0-87728-863-1*) Weiser.

B

An Asterisk (*) at the beginning of an entry indicates that the title is appearing for the first time.

— Symbolism of the Celtic Cross. LC 95-19403. (Illus.). 128p. (Orig.). 1995. pap. 9.95 (*0-87728-850-X*) Weiser.

Bryce, Derek, tr. see Lao-Tzu.

Bryce, Douglas M. Plastic Injection Molding: Manufacturing Process Fundamentals. LC 96-67394. (Illus.). 277p. 1996. 76.00 (*0-87263-472-8*, 2457) SME.

***Bryce, Douglas M.** Plastic Injection Molding: Manufacturing Startup & Management. LC 98-61657. 208p. 1999. 76.00 (*0-87263-503-1*) SME.

Bryce, Douglas M. Plastic Injection Molding: Material Selection & Product Design Fundamentals. LC 97-68807. (Illus.). 380p. 1997. 76.00 (*0-87263-488-4*, 2599) SME.

— Plastic Injection Molding: Mold Design & Construction Fundamentals. LC 98-60567. (Illus.). 193p. 1998. 76.00 (*0-87263-495-7*, 2673) SME.

Bryce Echenique, A. Antologia Personal de Bryce Echenique. (SPA.). 496p. 1995. pap. 19.95 (*0-8477-0216-2*) U of PR Pr.

— A World for Julius: A Novel. Gerdes, Dick, tr. from SPA. LC 91-45310. (Texas Pan American Ser.). 444p. 1992. pap. 19.95 (*0-292-79071-6*); text 45.00 (*0-292-79046-5*) U of Tex Pr.

Bryce, Ellen. Once Upon a Holy Night: A Musical Christmas Story Based on Luke 2:1-20 & Matthew 2:1-2. 72p. pap. 17.95 (*0-687-09850-5*) Abingdon.

— Once upon a Holy Night: Listening Tape. (J). (gr. 2-5). 12.00 (*0-687-09870-X*) Abingdon.

— Once upon a Holy Night: Singer's Edition. (J). (gr. 2-5). 4.00 (*0-687-09860-2*) Abingdon.

— Once upon a Holy Night: Value Pak. (J). (gr. 2-5). 25.00 (*0-687-09900-5*) Abingdon.

Bryce, George. The Scotsman in Canada Vol. 2: Western Canada, Including Manitoba, Saskatchewan, Alberta, British Columbia & Portions of Old Rupert's Land & Indian Territories, 2. (Illus.). 439p. 1998. reprint ed. pap. 60.00 (*1-58211-068-9*, 097640) Quintin Pub RI.

Bryce, Glendon E. A Legacy of Wisdom: The Egyptian Contribution to the Wisdom of Israel. LC 74-4984. 336p. 1979. 38.50 (*0-8387-1576-1*) Bucknell U Pr.

Bryce, Herb, ed. see Barlee, N. L.

Bryce, Herb, ed. see Harbo, Rick.

Bryce, Herb, ed. see Moore, Terry.

Bryce, Herb, ed. see Norton, D.

Bryce, Herb, ed. see Waite, Don.

Bryce, Herrington J. The Financial & Strategic Management for Non-Profit Organizations. 528p. (C). 1992. 57.00 (*0-13-377573-9*) P-H.

Bryce, Ian B. A Chronology of the Castles of Scotland, 1100-1685. 108p. 1990. pap. 30.00 (*1-898218-88-9*) St Mut.

Bryce, Iris. Canals Are My Home. 142p. 1987. 50.00 (*0-7855-3043-6*, Pub. by K Mason Pubns Ltd) St Mut.

— Canals Are My Home. large type ed. (Illus.). 1991. 27.99 (*0-7089-2511-1*) Ulverscroft.

— Canals Are My Life. 104p. 1987. 50.00 (*0-85937-277-4*, Pub. by K Mason Pubns Ltd) St Mut.

— Canals Are My World. large type ed. (Large Print Ser.). (Illus.). 336p. 1996. 27.99 (*0-7089-3608-3*) Ulverscroft.

Bryce, Ivar. You Only Live Once: Memories of Ian Fleming. (Foreign Intelligence Book Ser.). 142p. 1975. reprint ed. lib. bdg. 45.00 (*0-313-26999-8*, U6999, Greenwood Pr) Greenwood.

Bryce, J. C., ed. see Smith, Adam.

Bryce, Jackson. Letters from England. 1998. 20.00 (*0-939394-06-5*) Blck Willw Pr.

Bryce, James. Constitutions. xvii, 341p. 1997. reprint ed. 98.00 (*1-56169-339-1*) Gaunt.

— Reflections on the American Institutions: Selections from the American Commonwealth. 1990. 16.50 (*0-8446-0517-4*) Peter Smith.

— South America: Observations & Impressions. (Latin America in the 20th Century Ser.). 1977. reprint ed. lib. bdg. 69.50 (*0-306-70835-3*) Da Capo.

— Special Edition Using ISDN: Special Edition. deluxe ed. (Illus.). 500p. (Orig.). 1995. 29.99 (*0-7897-0405-6*) Que.

— Studies in History & Jurisprudence, 2 vols. 1096p. 1997. reprint ed. 238.00 (*1-56169-320-0*) Gaunt.

Bryce, James, et al. The Power Basics of Baseball. LC 84-22839. 109p. (C). 1984. pap. text 5.95 (*0-13-688292-7*, Busn) P-H.

Bryce, James, jt. auth. see Morris, Peter.

Bryce, James B. American Commonwealth, 3 vols. LC 73-39551. reprint ed. 345.00 (*0-404-03770-4*) AMS Pr.

— The American Commonwealth, 2 vols., Set. LC 95-11187. 1995. 35.00 (*0-86597-116-1*); pap. 16.50 (*0-86597-117-X*) Liberty Fund.

— Essays & Addresses in War Time. LC 68-16914. (Essay Index Reprint Ser.). 1977. 23.95 (*0-8369-0260-2*) Ayer.

— Hindrances to Good Citizenship. 160p. (C). 1992. pap. 29.95 (*1-56000-648-X*) Transaction Pubs.

— The Holy Roman Empire. enl. rev. ed. LC 75-41045. (BCL Ser. II). reprint ed. 49.50 (*0-404-14516-7*) AMS Pr.

— Impressions of South Africa. LC 73-76495. (Illus.). 499p. 1970. reprint ed. lib. bdg. 69.50 (*0-8371-1315-6*, BSA&) Greenwood.

— The Predictions of Hamilton & de Tocqueville. LC 78-63775. (Johns Hopkins University. Studies in the Social Sciences. Thirtieth Ser. 1912: 9). reprint ed. 11.50 (*0-404-61041-2*) AMS Pr.

— Studies in Contemporary Biography. LC 77-156619. (Essay Index Reprint Ser.). 1977. reprint ed. 28.95 (*0-8369-2271-9*) Ayer.

— Studies in History & Jurisprudence, 2 Vols, Set. LC 68-8444. (Essay Index Reprint Ser.). 1977. reprint ed. 48.95 (*0-8369-0261-0*) Ayer.

— The Study of American History. LC 72-136056. 1971. reprint ed. lib. bdg. 59.75 (*0-8371-5206-2*, BRAH, Greenwood Pr) Greenwood.

— The Study of American History: Being the Inaugural Lecture of Literature, & Institutions; with an Appendix Relating to the Foundation. (BCL1 - U. S. History Ser.). 118p. 1991. reprint ed. lib. bdg. 69.00 (*0-7812-6036-1*) Rprt Serv.

— Transcaucasia & Ararat Being Notes of a Vacation Tour in the Autumn of 1876. LC 73-115509. (Russia Observed, Series I). 1970. reprint ed. 29.95 (*0-405-03007-X*) Ayer.

— University & Historical Addresses. LC 68-55842. (Essay Index Reprint Ser.). 1977. 23.95 (*0-8369-0262-9*) Ayer.

Bryce, James R. Basic Finance, an Introduction to Financial Theory, Practices & Institutions. 158p. 1980. pap. text 13.95 (*0-89641-038-2*) American Pr.

— First Principles of Accounting. (Illus.). 197p. (Orig.). (C). 1983. pap. text 13.95 (*0-89641-115-X*) American Pr.

Bryce, James Y. Special Edition Using ISDN. 2nd ed. LC 96-69605. 627p. 1996. 39.99 (*0-7897-0843-4*) Que.

Bryce, Judith. Harrap's Italian Grammar. 1991. pap. 5.00 (*0-13-382664-3*) P-H.

Bryce, Judith & Thompson, Doug. Moving in Measure: Essays in Honour of Brian Moloney. 242p. 1989. 45.00 (*0-85958-475-5*) Denali Press.

Bryce-Laporte, Roy S., ed. Sourcebook on New Immigration, Vol. II. 302p. 1980. pap. text 29.95 (*0-87855-796-2*) Transaction Pubs.

Bryce, Margaret. Physical Therapy after Amputation: The Treatment of the Unilateral Lower-Extremity Amputee. LC 54-6930. (Illus.). 103p. reprint ed. pap. 32.00 (*0-8357-6799-X*, 203547800095) Bks Demand.

Bryce, Mike. Turtle Teasers: Puzzles. 128p. (J). (gr. k up). 1991. pap. 4.95 (*0-924771-34-8*, Covered Brdge Pr) Douglas Charles Ltd.

Bryce, Milt & Bryce, Tim. The IRM Revolution: Blueprint for the 21st Century. LC 88-92571. (Illus.). 265p. (Orig.). (C). 1988. 50.00 (*0-9621189-0-7*) M Bryce Assocs.

Bryce, Rick. Peace Officers' Guide to California's Dangerous Weapons Laws. LC 96-85775. (Illus.). 128p. (C). 1998. pap. 9.95 (*0-9653621-1-6*) Copperhouse.

Bryce, Robert. A Question of Time. large type ed. 274p. (Orig.). 1995. mass mkt. 6.99 (*1-881542-17-3*) Blue Star Prodns.

Bryce, Robert B. Maturing in Hard Times: Canada's Department of Finance through the Great Depression. (Canadian Public Administration Ser.). 320p. 1986. 65.00 (*0-7735-0555-5*, Pub. by McG-Queens Univ Pr) CUP Services.

Bryce, Robert M. Cook & Peary: The Polar Controversy, Resolved. LC 96-38215. (Illus.). 1152p. 1997. 50.00 (*0-8117-0317-7*) Stackpole.

Bryce, Sheridan. Joy Riding the Universe: Shapshots of the Journey, Vol. 1. LC 93-78950. (Illus.). 504p. (Orig.). 1993. pap. 24.00 (*0-9636636-0-7*) Homewords Pub.

Bryce-Smith, D. Heavy Metals as Contaminants of the Human Environment. (C). 1989. pap. text 24.00 (*0-85186-979-3*) CRC Pr.

— Photochemistry, Vol. 11. 1989. 274.00 (*0-85186-095-8*) CRC Pr.

— Photochemistry, Vol. 12. 1989. 274.00 (*0-85186-105-9*) CRC Pr.

— Photochemistry, Vol. 13. 1989. 296.00 (*0-85186-115-6*) CRC Pr.

— Photochemistry, Vol. 14. 1988. 286.00 (*0-85186-125-3*) CRC Pr.

— Photochemistry, Vol. 15. 1988. 330.00 (*0-85186-135-0*) CRC Pr.

— Photochemistry, Vol. 16. 1988. 362.00 (*0-85186-145-8*) CRC Pr.

— Photochemistry, Vol. 19. 1988. 296.00 (*0-85186-175-X*) CRC Pr.

— Photochemistry, Vol. 20. 1989. 330.00 (*0-85186-185-7*) CRC Pr.

— Photochemistry, Vols. 1-10. LC 73-17909. write for info. (*0-318-50480-4*) Am Chemical.

Bryce-Smith, D., ed. Photochemistry, Vol. 25. (Specialist Periodical Reports). 620p. 1994. 293.00 (*0-85186-481-3*, R6481) CRC Pr.

Bryce-Smith, D. & Gilbert, A. The Organic Photochemistry of Benezene-1. 18p. 1976. pap. 15.50 (*0-08-020464-3*, Pergamon Pr) Elsevier.

— Photochemistry, Vol. 21. 1990. 318.00 (*0-85186-195-4*) CRC Pr.

— Photochemistry, Vol. 22. 1991. 325.00 (*0-85186-205-5*) CRC Pr.

Bryce-Smith, D. & Gilbert, A., eds. Photochemistry, Vol. 24. 560p. 1993. 294.00 (*0-85186-225-X*, Q) CRC Pr.

Bryce, Tim, jt. auth. see Bryce, Milt.

***Bryce, Tom G. & Humes, Walter.** Scottish Education. 704p. 1999. 118.00 (*0-7486-1095-2*, Pub. by Edinburgh U Pr); pap. 36.00 (*0-7486-0980-6*, Pub. by Edinburgh U Pr) Col U Pr.

Bryce, Trevor. The Kingdom of the Hittites. (Illus.). 482p. 1999. pap. text 35.00 (*0-19-924010-8*) OUP.

***Bryceland, Conny.** Accidental Rewards. 2000. pap. 19.95 (*1-893162-51-6*) Erica Hse.

Brycelea, Clifford. Moon & Otter & Frog. LC 93-39879. 32p. (J). (gr. 1-4). 1995. lib. bdg. 14.89 (*0-7868-2022-5*, Pub. by Hyprn Child) Little.

— Moon & Otter & Frog. LC 93-39879. 32p. (J). (ps-3). 1995. 14.95 (*0-7868-0027-5*, Pub. by Hyprn Child) Time Warner.

Bryceson. Liberalizing Tanzania's Food Trade: The Public & Private Faces of Urban Marketing Policy, 1939-88. 306p. (C). 1993. text 65.00 (*0-435-08077-6*, 08077) Heinemann.

Bryceson, David, compiled by. The Titanic Disaster: As Reported in the British National Press April-July 1912. LC 96-48325. (Illus.). 320p. (C). 1997. 35.00 (*0-393-04108-5*) Norton.

Bryceson, Deborah F., et al, eds. Women Wielding the Hoe: Lessons from Rural Africa for Feminist Theory & Development Practice. (Cross-Cultural Perspectives on Women Ser.). 288p. 1995. 49.50 (*1-85973-068-X*, Pub. by Berg Pubs); pap. 19.50 (*1-85973-073-6*, Pub. by Berg Pubs) NYU Pr.

Bryceson, Deborah F. & Jamal, Vali, eds. Farewell to Farms: De-Agrarianisation & Employment in Africa. (African Studies Centre Leiden Ser.). 265p. 1997. pap. 29.95 (*1-84014-193-X*, Pub. by Ashgate Pub) Ashgate Pub Co.

Bryceson, Jamal. Beyond the Farm. 38.95 (*1-85972-577-5*) Ashgate Pub Co.

Brycha, M. Automatic Transmissions. 2nd ed. 1982. pap. text 41.00 (*0-13-054577-5*) P-H.

Brychkov, Yu A., et al, eds. Multidimensional Integral Transformations. LC 91-41471. xiii, 379p. 1992. text 191.00 (*2-88124-839-X*, QA432) Gordon & Breach.

Brychkov, Yu A. & Prudnikov, A. P. Integral Transforms of Generalized Functions. xii, 344p. 1989. text 261.00 (*2-88124-705-9*) Gordon & Breach.

Brychta, Alex. The Arrow. (A Cat on the Mat Bk.). (Illus.). 16p. (J). (ps-k). 1987. pap. 4.25 (*0-19-272166-6*) OUP.

Brychta, Ivan. The Girard Case. 110p. 1994. pap. 29.50 (*0-930329-60-0*) Kabel Pubs.

— The Girard Case. 110p. (C). 1994. 24.50 (*0-930329-98-8*) Kabel Pubs.

— Interpreting the Welfare Clause - Authenticity & Fiction. (Illus.). 202p. (Orig.). (C). 1994. pap. 29.50 (*0-930329-58-9*) Kabel Pubs.

***Bryd, Vernon B., Jr.** Passing Gas - the History of Inflight Refueling. rev. ed. Kenedi, Aaron, ed. 288p. 1999. 39.95 (*0-9639977-2-6*) Byrd Pubng.

***Brydels, Faye & Jenkins, Donna.** Froggy Bottom. 288p. 1999. spiral bd. 11.95 (*0-935545-19-0*) Land & Land.

Bryden. Reinventing King Arthur. 75.95 (*1-84014-619-2*) Ashgate Pub Co.

Bryden-Brook, Simon. Take, Bless, Break, Share: Agapes, Table Blessings & Other Liturgies. LC 98-181139. 1998. pap. 13.95 (*1-85311-214-3*, 5975, Pub. by Canterbury Press Norwich) Morehouse Pub.

Bryden, Diana F., et al. Beds & Shotguns: An Anthology. LC 95-189176. 96p. pap. 13.99 (*1-895837-28-6*) Insomniac.

Bryden, H. Anderson. Gun & Camera in Southern Africa. 1988. 37.00 (*0-935632-73-5*) Wolfe Pub Co.

Bryden, Ian. Current Acoustic Research in Subsea Technology. 1989. 150.00 (*90-6314-591-8*, Pub. by Lorne & MacLean Marine) St Mut.

— Current Acoustic Research in Subsea Technology. (C). 1989. 110.00 (*0-89771-738-4*, Pub. by Lorne & MacLean Marine) St Mut.

Bryden, Inga. The Pre-Raphaelites: Writings & Sources, 4 vols. LC 98-14090. (Illus.). 1160p. (C). 1998. reprint ed. 655.00 (*0-415-16908-9*) Routledge.

Bryden, Inga & Floyd, Janet, eds. Domestic Space: Reading the Nineteenth-Century Interior. (Illus.). 220p. 1999. 69.95 (*0-7190-5450-8*, Pub. by Manchester Univ Pr) St Martin.

Bryden, John. Deadly Allies: Canada's Secret War, 1937-1947. 316p. 1998. pap. text 10.00 (*0-7881-5760-4*) DIANE Pub.

Bryden, John M. Tourism & Development: A Case Study of the Commonwealth Caribbean. LC 73-77260. 248p. reprint ed. pap. 70.70 (*0-608-12297-1*, 2024415) Bks Demand.

Bryden, John R. & Hughes, David G. An Index of Gregorian Chant, Vol. 1: Alphabetical Index. LC 71-91626. 476p. reprint ed. pap. 147.60 (*0-7837-3079-9*, 205746300001) Bks Demand.

— An Index of Gregorian Chant, Vol. 2: Thematic Index. LC 71-91626. 363p. reprint ed. pap. 112.60 (*0-7837-3080-2*, 205746300002) Bks Demand.

Bryden, Kenneth. Old Age Pensions & Policy Making in Canada. (Canadian Public Administration Ser.). 288p. 1974. 49.95 (*0-7735-0206-8*, Pub. by McG-Queens Univ Pr); pap. 24.95 (*0-7735-0221-1*, Pub. by McG-Queens Univ Pr) CUP Services.

— Old Age Pensions & Policy-Making in Canada. LC 74-75972. (Canadian Public Administration Ser.). 274p. reprint ed. pap. 85.00 (*0-7837-6931-8*, 204676000003) Bks Demand.

Bryden, Mary. Women in Samuel Beckett's Prose & Drama: Her Own Other. LC 92-39389. 256p. (C). 1993. lib. bdg. 54.50 (*0-389-21005-6*) B&N Imports.

Bryden, Mary, ed. Samuel Beckett & Music. LC 97-33497. (Illus.). 288p. 1998. text 75.00 (*0-19-818427-1*) OUP.

Bryden, Michael & Carwardine, Mark, eds. Whales, Dolphins, & Porpoises. 2nd ed. LC 99-461832. (Illus.). 240p. 1999. 39.95 (*0-8160-3991-7*, Checkmark) Facts on File.

***Bryden, Michael, et al.** Dugongs, Whales, Dolphins & Seals: A Guide to the Sea Mammals of Australasia. (Illus.). 176p. 1999. pap. 24.95 (*1-86448-656-2*, Pub. by Allen & Unwin Pty) Paul & Co Pubs.

Bryden, Michael, jt. ed. see Harrison, Richard.

Bryden, P. E. Planners & Politicians: Liberal Politics & Social Policy, 1957-1968. 256p. 1997. text 60.00 (*0-7735-1650-6*, Pub. by McG-Queens Univ Pr) CUP Services.

Bryden, Penny. Planners & Politicians: Liberal Politics & Social Policy, 1957-1968. 1998. pap. 22.95 (*0-7735-1651-4*) McG-Queens Univ Pr.

Bryden, Philip, et al, eds. The Charter: Ten Years after Essays on the Charter's Place in Canada's Political, Legal, & Intellectual Life. 272p. 1993. text 45.00 (*0-8020-2902-7*); pap. text 18.95 (*0-8020-7410-3*) U of Toronto Pr.

***Bryden, Sydney.** View from the Mountain: A Twentieth-Century Memoir. (Illus.). 240p. 1999. 19.95 (*0-9648754-1-1*) Two Pillars.

Bryden', John, jt. ed. see Bollman, Ray D.

Bryder, Linda. Below the Magic Mountain: A Social History of Tuberculosis in Twentieth Century Britain. (Oxford Historical Monographs). (Illus.). 320p. 1988. pap. 75.00 (*0-19-822947-X*) OUP.

Bryder, Linda, jt. ed. see Austoker, Joan.

Brydges, Egerton, ed. see Milton, John.

Brydges, Grey. Horae Subsecivae: Observations & Discourses. LC 70-26258. (English Experience Ser.: No. 232). 542p. 1970. reprint ed. 75.00 (*90-221-0232-7*) Walter J Johnson.

Brydges, Harford J. The Dynasty of the Kajars. LC 73-6272. (Middle East Ser.). 1978. reprint ed. 51.95 (*0-405-05327-4*) Ayer.

Brydges, Samuel E. British Bibliographer, 4 vols. LC 03-25390. reprint ed. 306.00 (*0-404-01200-0*) AMS Pr.

— Censura Literaria, 10 vols. in 5. LC 03-25387. reprint ed. 675.00 (*0-404-01210-8*) AMS Pr.

Brydlova, Bozena. Io Unveiled: The Brydlovan Theory of the Origin of Numbers. 90p. 1993. reprint ed. pap. 14.95 (*1-56459-393-2*) Kessinger Pub.

Brydon, Anne & Niessen, Sandra, eds. Consuming Fashion: Adorning the Transnational Body. LC 98-230628. (Dress, Body, Culture Ser.). (Illus.). 224p. 1998. 55.00 (*1-85973-964-4*, Pub. by Berg Pubs); pap. 19.50 (*1-85973-969-5*, Pub. by Berg Pubs) NYU Pr.

Brydon, Diana. Christina Stead. LC 86-22307. (Women Writers Ser.). 250p. (C). 1987. 44.00 (*0-389-20689-X*, N8247); pap. 13.00 (*0-389-20690-3*, N8248) B&N Imports.

— Timothy Findley. LC 98-29217. (Twayne's World Authors Ser.). 159p. 1998. 32.00 (*0-8057-1666-1*, Twyne) Mac Lib Ref.

— Writing on Trial No. 32: Timothy Findley's Famous Last Words. LC 96-109870. (Canadian Fiction Studies). 150p. 1995. pap. 14.95 (*1-55022-181-7*, Pub. by ECW) Genl Dist Srvs.

Brydon, Lynne. Adjusting Society: The World Bank, the IMF & Ghana. LC 95-61523. 256p. 1996. text 65.00 (*1-86064-000-1*) St Martin.

Brydon, Lynne & Chant, Sylvia. Women in the Third World: Gender Issues in Rural & Urban Areas. 336p. 1989. pap. 25.00 (*1-85278-190-4*) E Elgar.

— Women in the Third World: Gender Issues in Rural & Urban Areas. LC 89-6119. 336p. (C). 1989. text 45.00 (*0-8135-1470-3*); pap. text 17.95 (*0-8135-1471-1*) Rutgers U Pr.

Brydon-Miller, Mary, jt. auth. see Williams, Brownyn T.

Brydon, Ruth V. Westwood, California, a Company Town in Comparative Perspective, 1900-1930. 59p. 1995. 8.00 (*0-614-15361-1*) Assn NC Research.

Brydon, Steven R. & Scott, Michael D. Between One & Many: The Art & Science of Public Speaking. 3rd ed. LC 99-29042. xxvii, 463p. 1999. pap. text 39.95 (*0-7674-0817-9*) Mayfield Pub.

Brydon, Steven R., jt. auth. see Scott, Michael D.

Brydson, J. A. Flow Properties of Polymer Melts. 2nd ed. LC 81-148705. (Illus.). 238p. reprint ed. pap. 73.80 (*0-8357-2972-9*, 203923400011) Bks Demand.

— Plastics Materials. 6th ed. LC 94-44833. (Illus.). 896p. 1995. text 175.00 (*0-7506-1864-7*) Buttrwrth-Heinemann.

***Brydson, J. A.** Plastics Materials. 7th ed. LC 99-30623. 920p. 1999. text 175.00 (*0-7506-4132-0*) Buttrwrth-Heinemann.

***Bryen, David.** The Man Loves the Wine She Serves Through Her Body: An Erotic Encounter with the Divine Feminine. (Illus.). 100p. 1999. pap. 21.95 (*0-9674947-0-2*) West Hills.

Bryennios, Philotheos, ed. The Didache: The Teaching of the Twelve Apostles. (GRE.). 1989. pap. text 2.50 (*0-89981-204-X*) Eastern Orthodox.

Bryer, Anthony. Peoples & Settlement in Anatolia & the Caucasus, 800-1900. (Collected Studies: No. CS274). (Illus.). 336p. (C). 1988. reprint ed. lib. bdg. 115.95 (*0-86078-222-0*, Pub. by Variorum) Ashgate Pub Co.

Bryer, Anthony & Cunningham, Mary, eds. Mount Athos & Byzantine Monasticism: Papers from the 28th Spring Symposium of Byzantine Studies, University of Birmingham, March 1994. LC 96-902. (Society for the Promotion of Byzantine Studies: Vol. 4). 304p. 1996. 78.95 (*0-86078-551-3*, Pub. by Variorum) Ashgate Pub Co.

Bryer, Anthony & Winfield, David. The Byzantine Monuments & Topography of the Pontos, 2 vols., Set. LC 84-1661. (Dumbarton Oaks Studies: Vol. 20). (Illus.). 752p. 1985. 80.00 (*0-88402-122-X*) Dumbarton Oaks.

Bryer, David, tr. see Corneille, et al.

***Bryer, Jackson R.** F. Scott Fitzgerald: New Perspectives. LC 99-88355. 2000. 45.00 (*0-8203-2187-7*) U of Ga Pr.

Bryer, Jackson R. F. Scott Fitzgerald in His Own Time: A Miscellany. Bruccoli, Matthew J., ed. LC 76-126919. 503p. 156.00 (*0-8357-9365-6*, 203018000017) Bks Demand.

Bryer, Jackson R., ed. Conversations with Lillian Hellman. LC 85-31473. (Literary Conversations Ser.). 298p. 1986. text 39.50 (*0-87805-293-3*) U Pr of Miss.

***Bryer, Jackson R., ed.** F. Scott Fitzgerald: Novels & Other Stories 1920-1922. LC 00-24287. Vol. 117. 2000. 35.00 (*1-883011-84-1*, Pub. by Library of America) Penguin Putnam.

Bryer, Jackson R., ed. The Heath Bibliography of American Literature. 2nd ed. 28p. (C). 1994. pap. text 2.66 (*0-669-35346-9*) HM Trade Div.

— New Essays on F. Scott Fitzgerald's Neglected Stories. 384p. (C). 1996. 49.95 (*0-8262-1039-2*) U of Mo Pr.

— The Playwright's Art: Conversations with Contemporary American Dramatists. LC 94-14070. (Illus.). 359p. (C). 1995. pap. 18.00 (*0-8135-2129-7*) Rutgers U Pr.

— Sixteen Modern American Authors: A Survey of Research & Criticism. LC 73-97454. xx, 673p. 1973. text 54.95 (*0-8223-0297-7*) Duke.

An Asterisk (*) at the beginning of an entry indicates that the title is appearing for the first time.

— Sixteen Modern American Authors, Vol. 2: A Survey of Research & Criticism since 1972. LC 89-11789. 810p. (C). 1989. text 69.95 (*0-8223-0976-9*); pap. text 29.95 (*0-8223-1018-X*) Duke.

***Bryer, Jackson R. & Davison, Richard A., eds.** The Actor's Art: Conversations with Contemporary American Stage Performers. LC 00-39035. (Illus.). 288p. (C). 2001. pap. 20.00 (*0-8135-2873-9*); text 50.00 (*0-8135-2872-0*) Rutgers U Pr.

Bryer, Jackson R. & Harding, Eugene, compiled by. Hamlin Garland & the Critics: An Annotated Bibliography. LC 75-183300. viii, 282p. 1973. 45.00 (*0-87875-020-7*) Whitston Pub.

Bryer, Jackson R., ed. see Fitzgerald, F. Scott.

Bryer, Jackson R., jt. ed. see Kennedy, J. Gerald.

Bryer, Jackson R., ed. see O'Neill, Eugene.

Bryer, Jackson R., ed. see Wilder, Thornton.

Bryer, James. Guitar AdLib: Three Techniques in One Book: Improvising, Lead Solos, & Chords. (Illus.). 48p. (Orig.). pap. 8.95 (*0-9622499-1-2*); pap. 14.95 (*0-685-27813-1*) Soundbox Pubns.

— Guitar Forms. Stang, Aaron, ed. 40p. (Orig.). (C). 1995. pap. text 8.95 (*0-7692-1349-9*, GF0363) Wrner Bros.

— Guitar Forms: Thirty Improvising Techniques. (Illus.). 36p. (Orig.). pap. 8.95 (*0-9622499-2-0*); pap. 14.95 (*0-685-27814-X*) Soundbox Pubns.

— Reading Skills Songbook Vol. 1: Read, Rapp, & Rock to the Skills of Reading. (Illus.). 48p. (Orig.). (J). (gr. 2-6). 1989. pap. 14.95 incl. audio (*0-9622499-0-4*) Soundbox Pubns.

Bryer, M., ed. Planning in Child Care. (C). 1989. 80.00 (*0-903534-76-2*, Pub. by Brit Ag for Adopt & Fost) St Mut.

***Bryer, Michelle.** Harry Potter & the Sorcerer's Stone: Intermediate. 48p. 2000. pap. 7.95 (*1-57690-638-8*) Tchr Create Mat.

***Bryer, Robin.** Hair: Fashion & Fantasy down the Ages. (Illus.). 160p. 2000. 39.95 (*0-85667-506-7*, Pub. by P Wilson) Antique Collect.

***Bryers, James D., ed.** Biofilms II: Analysis, Process & Applications. LC 99-55613. 416p. 2000. text 139.95 (*0-471-29656-2*) Wiley.

Bryers, Paul. In a Pig's Ear. LC 96-19667. 288p. 1996. 23.00 (*0-374-17564-0*) FS&G.

Bryers, Paul. The Prayer of the Bone. 288p. 1999. 23.95 (*1-58234-022-6*) Bloomsbury Pubg.

***Bryers, Paul.** The Prayer of the Bone. 2000. pap. 13.95 (*1-58234-075-7*) Bloomsbury Pubg.

Bryers, Richard W., ed. Ash Deposits & Corrosion Due to Impurities in Combustion Gases: Proceedings of the Symposium, June 26-July 1, 1977, New England College, Henniker, New Hampshire. LC 78-7001. (Illus.). 691p. 1978. text 205.00 (*0-89116-074-4*) Hemisp Pub.

— Fouling & Slagging Resulting from Impurities in Combustion Gases. LC 83-80600. 550p. 1983. text 50.00 (*0-939204-18-5*, 81-18) Eng Found.

— Fouling of Heat Exchanger Surfaces. LC 83-82098. 826p. 1983. text 50.00 (*0-939204-20-7*, 83-01) Eng Found.

— Incinerating Municipal & Industrial Waste: Fireside Problems & Prospects for Improvement. 400p. 1990. 104.00 (*1-56032-145-8*) Hemisp Pub.

Bryers, Richard W. & Harding, N. S., eds. Coal-Blending & Switching of Low-Sulfur Western Coals. LC 93-74945. 476p. 1994. pap. 75.00 (*0-7918-1200-6*, I00363) ASME.

Bryett. An Introduction to Policing: Policing in the Community, Vol. 3. 1993. pap. 35.00 (*0-409-30725-4*, Austral, MICHIE) LEXIS Pub.

— An Introduction to Policing: The Role & Functions of Police in Australia, Vol. 2. 1993. pap. 35.00 (*0-409-30724-6*, Austral, MICHIE) LEXIS Pub.

Bryett, Keith & Lewis, Colleen, eds. Un-Peeling Tradition: Contemporary Policing. 224p. 1995. pap. 39.95 (*0-7329-2786-2*, Pub. by Macmill Educ) Paul & Co Pubs.

***Bryher, Winifred.** Bryher: Two Novels. LC 99-43638. (Living Out Ser.). 2000. pap. 19.95 (*0-299-16774-7*) U of Wis Pr.

Bryher, Winifred. The days of Mars: A memoir, 1940-1946. LC 73-163586. 1972. write for info. (*0-7145-0942-6*) M Boyars Pubs.

Bryher, Winifred, jt. ed. see MacPherson, Kenneth.

***Bryjak & Soroka.** Sociology: Study Guide: Changing Societies in a Diverse World. 4th ed. 2000. pap. 19.00 (*0-205-32361-8*) Allyn.

Bryjak, jt. auth. see Soroka.

Bryjak, George J. & Soroka, Michael P. Sociology. 3rd ed. 320p. 1996. pap. text, student ed. 20.00 (*0-205-26241-4*) Allyn.

— Sociology: Cultural Diversity in a Changing World. 3rd ed. 574p. 1996. pap. text 53.00 (*0-205-19155-X*) Allyn.

— Sociology: Cultural Diversity in a Changing World. 3rd ed. 384p. (C). 1996. teacher ed. write for info. (*0-205-27056-5*, T7056-9) Allyn.

— Sociology: Cultural Diversity in a Changing World, Examination Copy. 3rd ed. 592p. (C). 1996. write for info. (*0-205-26435-2*, T6435-6) Allyn.

Bryk, Anthony S. Charting Chicago School Reform. 1999. 27.00 (*0-8133-6625-9*) HarpC.

Bryk, Anthony S. & Raudenbush, Stephen W. Hierarchical Linear Models: Applications & Data Analysis Methods. (Advanced Quantitative Techniques in the Social Sciences Ser.: Vol. 1). (Illus.). 288p. 1992. 48.00 (*0-8039-4627-9*) Sage.

Bryk, Anthony S., et al. Catholic Schools & the Common Good. (Illus.). 432p. (C). 1993. 46.50 (*0-674-10310-6*) HUP.

— Catholic Schools & the Common Good. (Illus.). 416p. 1995. pap. text 18.50 (*0-674-10311-4*, BRYCAX) HUP.

Bryk, Felix. Circumcision in Man & Woman: Its History, Psychology & Ethnology. LC 72-9625. reprint ed. 37.50 (*0-404-57420-3*) AMS Pr.

— Dark Rapture: The Sex Life of the African Negro. Norton, Arthur J., tr. LC 72-9712. reprint ed. 39.50 (*0-404-57421-1*) AMS Pr.

Bryk, Nancy V. American Dress Pattern Catalogs, 1873-1909: Four Complete Reprints. (Illus.). 160p. 1988. reprint ed. pap. 9.95 (*0-486-25654-5*) Dover.

Brykczynska, Gosia M., ed. Caring: Compassion & Wisdom. 224p. 1996. pap. 38.25 (*1-56593-769-4*, 1496) Thomson Learn.

Brykczynska, Gosia M. & Jolley, Moya, eds. Caring. LC 97-122198. 1997. write for info. (*0-340-66196-8*, Pub. by E A) Routldge.

Brykczynski, Terry. Armchair Angler. 416p. 1994. 9.98 (*0-88365-876-3*) Galahad Bks.

Brykczynski, Terry, et al, eds. The Armchair Angler. (Illus.). 404p. 1999. text 27.00 (*0-7881-6029-X*) DIANE Pub.

Brylawski, E. Fulton & Goldman, Abe, eds. Legislative History of the 1909 Copyright Act, 6 vols., Set. 1976. text 325.00 (*0-8377-0806-0*, Rothman) W S Hein.

Brylawski-Miller, Laura. The Snow on Lake Como. LC 90-25997. (Series Fifteen). 72p. (Orig.). 1991. pap. 9.00 (*0-931846-38-2*) Wash Writers Pub.

Bryld, Claus, et al. Fremad og Aldrig Glemme: Ti Aars Forskning i Arbejderbevaegelsens Historie. Callesen, Gerd et al, eds. LC 82-110941. (DAN., Illus.). 328p. (Orig.). 1981. pap. 19.50 (*87-87739-14-3*) Kent Popular.

Bryld, Mette & Kulavig, Erik, eds. Soviet Civilization Between Past & Present. 193p. 1998. pap. 29.00 (*87-7838-330-7*, Pub. by Odense Univ) Intl Spec Bk.

***Bryld, Mette & Lykke, Nina.** Cosmo-Dolphins: Feminist Cultural Studies of Technology, Animals & the Sacred. LC 99-52387. (Illus.). 2000. pap. 25.00 (*1-85649-816-6*) Zed Books.

— Cosmodolphins: Feminist Cultural Studies of Technology, Animals & the Sacred. LC 99-52387. 69.95 (*1-85649-815-8*, Pub. by Zed Books) St Martin.

Brylinski, J. L., et al. Advances in Geometry & Mathematical Physics. LC 98-43464. (Progress in Mathematics Ser.: 172). 400p. 1998. 59.50 (*0-8176-4044-4*) Birkhauser.

Brylinski, J. L. Advances in Geometry & Mathematical Physics. LC 98-43464. (Progress in Mathematics Ser.). 1998. write for info. (*3-7643-4044-4*) Birkhauser.

Brylinski, Jean-Luc. Loop Spaces, Characteristic Classes, & Geometric Quantization. LC 92-34421. (Progress in Mathematics Ser.: Vol. 107). xvi, 300p. 1994. 54.50 (*0-8176-3644-7*) Birkhauser.

Brylinski, Jean-Luc, et al, eds. Lie Theory & Geometry: In Honor of Bertram Kostant. LC 94-32297. (Progress in Mathematics Ser.: Vol. 123). xliii, 596p. 1994. 72.50 (*0-8176-3761-3*) Birkhauser.

Brylinski, Jean-Luc & MacPherson, R. D. Nilpotent Orbits: Primitive Ideals & Characteristic Classes. (Progress in Mathematics Ser.: No. 78). 144p. 1989. 45.00 (*0-8176-3473-8*) Birkhauser.

Brylinski, Jean-Luc, et al. Lie Theory & Geometry: In Honor of Bertram Kostant. LC 94-32297. 123. 1994. write for info. (*3-7643-3761-3*) Birkhauser.

Brylowski, Walter. Faulkner's Olympian Laugh: Myth in the Novels. LC 68-11137. 237p. reprint ed. pap. 73.50 (*0-7837-3786-6*, 204360600010) Bks Demand.

***Brylske, Alex.** Beating the Bends: The Diver's Guide to Avoiding Decompression Sickness. (Illus.). 121p. 1999. pap. 14.95 (*0-941332-80-2*, BO749) Best Pub Co.

Brylske, Alex. PADI Divemaster Manual. 2nd ed. Palazzi, Tonya & Beveridge, Mary E., eds. (Illus.). 224p. (C). 1990. reprint ed. pap. text 19.75 (*1-878663-07-0*) PADI.

Brylske, Alex, et al. The Encyclopedia of Recreational Diving. (Illus.). 565p. 1988. reprint ed. text 42.15 (*1-878663-01-1*); reprint ed. pap. text 26.35 (*1-878663-02-X*) PADI.

— Rescue Diver Manual. rev. ed. Hurrell, Mary E. & Palazzi, Tonya, eds. (Illus.). 170p. (C). 1991. reprint ed. pap. 23.95 (*1-878663-09-7*) PADI.

Brym. Why Sociology? (C). Date not set. text. write for info. (*0-15-507212-9*); pap. text, student ed. write for info. (*0-15-507213-7*) Harcourt Coll Pubs.

Brym, Robert J., et al, eds. The Jews in Canada. 452p. (C). 1993. pap. text 32.00 (*0-19-540829-2*) OUP.

Brym, Robert J & Fox, Bonnie J. From Culture To Power: The Sociology Of English Canada. 224p. 1989. pap. text 14.95 (*0-19-540689-3*) OUP.

Brym, Robert J. & Ryvkina, Rozalina. The Jews of Moscow, Kiev, & Minsk: Identity, Antisemitism, Emigration. LC 94-9893. (Illus.). 142p. (C). 1994. text 50.00 (*0-8147-1226-6*) NYU Pr.

— The Jews of Moscow, Kiev, & Minsk: Identity, Antisemitism, Emigration. (Illus.). 142p. (C). 1994. pap. text 19.50 (*0-8147-1230-4*) NYU Pr.

Bryman, Alan. Charisma & Leadership in Organizations. 224p. (C). 1992. 49.95 (*0-8039-8317-4*); pap. 17.95 (*0-8039-8318-2*) Sage.

— Disney & His Worlds. LC 94-42064. 232p. (C). 1995. pap. 24.99 (*0-415-10376-2*) Routledge.

— Quantitative Data Analysis with SPSS Release 8 for Windows: For Social Scientists. LC 98-44332. 1999. 90.00 (*0-415-20696-0*) Routledge.

— Quantity & Quality in Social Research. 208p. (C). 1988. pap. 22.99 (*0-415-07898-9*) Routledge.

— Research Methods & Organization Studies. (Contemporary Social Research Ser.: No. 20). 224p. 1989. pap. 19.95 (*0-04-445213-6*) Routledge.

Bryman, Alan, ed. Doing Research in Organisations. 268p. 1988. lib. bdg. 55.00 (*0-415-00257-5*) Routledge.

Bryman, Alan & Burgess, Robert G., eds. Analyzing Qualitative Data. LC 93-3471. 288p. (C). 1994. pap. 24.99 (*0-415-06063-X*) Routledge.

— Analyzing Qualitative Data. LC 93-3471. 288p. (C). (gr. 13). 1994. text 65.00 (*0-415-06062-1*) Routledge.

Bryman, Alan & Cramer, Duncan. Quantitative Data Analysis with Minitab: A Guide to Social Scientists. LC 95-44812. (Illus.). 304p. (C). 1996. 80.00 (*0-415-12323-2*); pap. 25.99 (*0-415-12324-0*) Routledge.

— Quantitative Data Analysis with SPSS for Windows: A Guide for Social Scientists. LC 96-7866. (Illus.). 332p. (C). 1997. 85.00 (*0-415-14719-0*); pap. 27.99 (*0-415-14720-4*) Routledge.

— Quantitative Data Analysis with SPSS Release 8 for Windows: For Social Scientists. LC 98-44332. 303p. 1999. pap. 27.99 (*0-415-20697-9*) Routledge.

Bryman, D., et al. Rare Decay: Symposium. 520p. (C). 1989. text 151.00 (*9971-5-0838-9*) World Scientific Pub.

***Brymer, Robert A.** Hospitality & Tourism: An Introduction to the Industry. 9th ed. 460p. (C). 1999. per. 48.95 (*0-7872-5857-1*) Kendall-Hunt.

— Hospitality & Tourism: An Introduction to the Industry. 9th ed. 272p. (C). 1999. pap. text. write for info. (*0-7872-6524-1*) Kendall-Hunt.

Brymer, Robert A. Hospitality Management: An Introduction to the Industry. 7th ed. 480p. (C). 1996. per. write for info. (*0-8403-8436-X*) Kendall-Hunt.

Brymer, Robert A. & Lefever, Michael. Hospitality Management (Text) & Workbook to Accompany Hospitality Management (Video) Value Pack. 680p. (C). 1996. 40.95 (*0-8403-9606-6*) Kendall-Hunt.

Brynat-Mole, Karen. In the Country. LC 99-10799. (Picture This Ser.). 1999. write for info. (*1-57572-899-0*) Heinemann Lib.

Bryndle, Daniel C. A Fly on the Wall in the NHL. 80p. (Orig.). (YA). (gr. 7-12). 1994. mass mkt. 3.00 (*0-9644974-0-9*) Cliffstar Assocs.

Bryndzia, L. T., jt. ed. see Spry, P. G.

Bryne, R. M. How to Make Liqueurs. (Illus.). 80p. 1993. reprint ed. 12.95 (*0-86417-384-9*, Pub. by Kangaroo Pr) Seven Hills Bk.

Bryne, Richard. The Complete Art of Breaking. Lee, Mike, ed. (Specialties Ser.). 128p. 1984. pap. 12.95 (*0-89750-099-7*, 434) Ohara Pubns.

***Brynen, Rex.** A Very Political Economy: Peacebuilding & Foreign Aid in the West Bank & Gaza. (Illus.). 296p. 2000. pap. 19.95 (*1-929223-04-8*) US Inst Peace.

Brynen, Rex, et al, eds. Political Liberalization & Democratization in the Arab World Vol. 1: Theoretical Perspectives. 350p. 1995. lib. bdg. 58.00 (*1-55587-559-9*) L Rienner.

Bryner, Andy, jt. auth. see Markova, Dawna.

Bryner, Cloyd. Bugle Echoes: The Story of Illinois 47th Infantry. (Illus.). 262p. 1995. reprint ed. lib. bdg. 35.00 (*0-8328-4994-4*) Higginson Bk Co.

Bryner, Gary. From Promises to Performance: Achieving Global Environmental Goals. LC 97-33694. 400p. (C). 1997. pap. text 16.75 (*0-393-97172-4*) Norton.

Bryner, Gary. Politics & Public Morality: The Great Welfare Reform Debate. LC 97-33693. (Illus.). 300p. (C). 1998. pap. 16.75 (*0-393-97173-2*) Norton.

Bryner, Gary C. Blue Skies, Green Politics: The Clean Air Act of 1990 & Its Implementation. 2nd rev. ed. LC 95-38400. 280p. (YA). (gr. 11). 1996. pap. text 24.95 (*1-56802-134-8*) Congr Quarterly.

— Bureaucratic Discretion: Law & Policy in Federal Regulatory Agencies. (Government & Politics Ser.). 240p. 1987. 50.00 (*0-08-034494-1*, Pergamon Pr); pap. 18.95 (*0-08-034493-3*, Pergamon Pr) Elsevier.

— U. S. Land & Natural Resources Policy: A Public Issues Handbook. LC 97-16716. 312p. 1998. lib. bdg. 95.00 (*0-313-29688-X*, Greenwood Pr) Greenwood.

Bryner, Gary C. & Sorensen, A. Don, eds. The Bill of Rights: A Bicentennial Assessment. LC 94-1729. 280p. (C). 1994. text 39.50 (*0-7914-2225-9*) State U NY Pr.

Bryner, Gary C. & Thompson, Dennis L., eds. The Constitution & the Regulation of Society. LC 88-457. 258p. (C). 1988. text 21.50 (*0-88706-851-0*) State U NY Pr.

Bryner, Gary C., jt. auth. see Vetterli, Richard.

***Bryner, Jeanne.** Blind Horse: Poems. (Working Lives Ser.). 98p. 1999. pap. 9.95 (*0-933087-57-8*, Pub. by Bottom Dog Pr) SPD-Small Pr Dist.

Bryner, Jeanne. Breathless. LC 95-5599. (Wick Poetry Chapbook Ser.: No. 7). 36p. (Orig.). 1995. pap. 4.75 (*0-87338-533-0*) Kent St U Pr.

Bryner, Michael, jt. auth. see Spilsbury, Ariel.

Brynie, Faith. Six Minute Science Experiments, No. 2. LC 98-40851. 80 p. (J). 1999. 17.95 (*0-8069-9827-X*) Sterling.

Brynie, Faith, ed. My Mama Always Said . . . Advice - Good & Bad - from Mothers Everywhere. (Illus.). 112p. 1998. pap. 9.95 (*0-9660944-0-9*) Verity West.

Brynie, Faith H. AIDS: Facts, Issues, Choices. 125p. (Orig.). (YA). (gr. 7-12). 1997. pap. 7.95 (*1-57515-089-1*) PPI Pubng.

— Genetics & Human Health: A Journey Within. (Illus.). 128p. (YA). (gr. 7 up). 1995. lib. bdg. 23.90 (*1-56294-545-9*) Millbrook Pr.

***Brynie, Faith H.** 101 Questions about Your Immune System You Felt Defenseless to Answer... until Now. LC 99-33368. 176p. (J). (gr. 7). 2000. lib. bdg. 25.90 (*0-7613-1569-1*) TFC Bks NY.

Brynie, Faith H. 101 Questions Your Brain Has Asked about Itself. LC 98-9797. 176p. (J). (gr. 7 up). 1998. 23.90 (*0-7613-0400-2*, Copper Beech Bks) Millbrook Pr.

— 101 Questions Your Skin Has Always Wanted to Ask Itself. LC 98-50695. 128p. (YA). (gr. 7 up). 1999. 23.90 (*0-7613-1259-5*, Copper Beech Bks) Millbrook Pr.

— Six-Minute Science Experiments. LC 95-24478. (Illus.). 80p. (J). 1996. 17.95 (*0-8069-0624-3*) Sterling.

— Six-Minute Science Experiments. (Illus.). 80p. (J). 1997. pap. 9.95 (*0-8069-0623-5*) Sterling.

— Six-Minute Science Experiments Book & Kit. (Illus.). 80p. 1997. pap. 19.95 (*0-8069-9588-2*) Sterling.

Brynie, Faith Hickman, see Hickman Brynie, Faith.

Brynildsen, Ken. Reflections of a Cape Cod Washashore. 72p. (Orig.). 1997. pap. 7.95 (*0-9659205-1-8*) Inklngs MA.

Brynildson, Inga, ed. Birds in Art: The Masters, Nineteen Seventy-Six to Nineteen Ninety. LC 90-43625. (Illus.). 128p. 1991. 14.95 (*0-945529-05-8*) Le Yawkey.

Brynin, John. Pressure on Education. 240p. 1993. 66.95 (*1-85628-339-9*, Pub. by Avebry) Ashgate Pub Co.

Brynin, Robert. Stop Smoking for Good: With the NHA Stop-Smoking Program. 210p. 1996. pap. 8.95 (*0-340-63240-2*, Pub. by Hodder & Stought Ltd) Trafalgar.

Bryninckx, John, ed. see Loski, Diana.

Brynjolfsson, et al. Icelandic-German Dictionary: Islaendisch-Deutsches Woerterbuch. (GER & ICE.). 1985. write for info. (*0-8288-1102-4*, F39627) Fr & Eur.

***Brynjolfsson, Erik & Kahin, Brian, eds.** Understanding the Digital Economy: Data, Tools & Research. (Illus.). 375p. 1999. 35.00 (*0-262-02474-8*) MIT Pr.

Brynjolfsson, John B. Inflation Protection Bonds. LC 99-219980. (Illus.). 96p. 1997. pap. 42.00 (*1-883249-22-8*) F J Fabozzi.

Brynjolfsson, John B. & Fabozzi, Frank J., eds. Handbook of Inflation Linked Bonds. (Illus.). 1999. 60.00 (*1-883249-48-1*) F J Fabozzi.

***Brynjolson, Rhian.** Art & Illustration for the Classroom: A Guide for Teachers & Parents. 1999. pap. 22.00 (*1-895411-90-4*) Peguis Pubs Ltd.

Brynjuifson, Larry. Tending the Fire Within: How to Protect Male Potency. (Illus.). 128p. (Orig.). 1994. pap. text 17.95 (*0-9640877-0-7*) Hid Treas Pub.

Brynmill Press Ltd. Staff, ed. Chaucer's Prosody. 263p. (C). 1989. 125.00 (*0-907839-28-2*, Pub. by Brynmill Pr Ltd) St Mut.

— The Dislocation of Everyday Life. (C). 1989. 35.00 (*0-907839-33-9*, Pub. by Brynmill Pr Ltd) St Mut.

— Druid Madonna. (C). 1989. 70.00 (*0-907839-07-X*, Pub. by Brynmill Pr Ltd) St Mut.

— The Gross Anatomy Lab. (C). 1989. 60.00 (*0-907839-18-5*, Pub. by Brynmill Pr Ltd) St Mut.

— Interpretation As Heresy. (C). 1989. 30.00 (*0-907839-14-2*, Pub. by Brynmill Pr Ltd) St Mut.

— Language. (C). 1989. 60.00 (*0-907839-00-2*, Pub. by Brynmill Pr Ltd) St Mut.

— The New Grammarians Funeral. 203p. (C). 1989. 110.00 (*0-907839-30-4*, Pub. by Brynmill Pr Ltd) St Mut.

— Nothing Larger Than Life: A Novel. 240p. (C). 1989. 85.00 (*0-907839-46-0*, Pub. by Brynmill Pr Ltd) St Mut.

— Politics Needs Literature. (C). 1989. 40.00 (*0-907839-13-4*, Pub. by Brynmill Pr Ltd) St Mut.

— Prayers for the New Babel: A Criticism of the Alternative Service Book, 1980. 106p. (C). 1989. 45.00 (*0-907839-04-5*, Pub. by Brynmill Pr Ltd); pap. 30.00 (*0-907839-31-2*, Pub. by Brynmill Pr Ltd) St Mut.

— Psalms from the Suburbs. (C). 1989. 40.00 (*0-907839-27-4*, Pub. by Brynmill Pr Ltd) St Mut.

— Richard II & Woodstock. (C). 1989. 50.00 (*0-907839-35-5*, Pub. by Brynmill Pr Ltd) St Mut.

— The Store's Outing: A Tale of the 1960's. 112p. (C). 1989. 70.00 (*0-9502723-5-3*, Pub. by Brynmill Pr Ltd) St Mut.

— The Story of the Prussian Officer: Revisions: Littlewood among the Lawrence Scholars. (C). 1989. 50.00 (*0-907839-15-0*, Pub. by Brynmill Pr Ltd) St Mut.

— Swift: Madness & Art. (C). 1989. 40.00 (*0-907839-12-6*, Pub. by Brynmill Pr Ltd) St Mut.

— Tragedy Against Psychology. (C). 1989. 60.00 (*0-907839-11-8*, Pub. by Brynmill Pr Ltd) St Mut.

Brynner, Rock. The Doomsday Report: A Novel. LC 97-36568. 272p. 1998. 23.00 (*0-688-15919-2*, Wm Morrow) Morrow Avon.

— Yul: The Man Who Would Be King. large type ed. LC 90-10935. 475p. 1990. reprint ed. lib. bdg. 18.95 (*1-56054-017-6*) Thorndike Pr.

Brynner, Victoria, ed. The Yul Brynner, Photographer. LC 95-47200. (Illus.). 210p. 1996. 39.95 (*0-8109-3144-3*, Pub. by Abrams) Time Warner.

Brynteg Comprehensive School Pupils & Hawthorn, Susan M., eds. Island Farm. 88p. (C). 1989. 39.00 (*0-9515395-0-7*, Pub. by D Brown & Sons Ltd) St Mut.

Brys, Aurel & Pulickal, Joseph, compiled by. We Heard the Bird Sing: Interacting with Anthony de Mello, S.J. LC 95-24093. 122p. (C). 1995. pap. 12.95 (*0-8294-0866-5*) Loyola Pr.

Brysac, Shareen, jt. auth. see Meyer, Karl.

Brysac, Shareen Blair, jt. auth. see Meyer, Karl.

Brysch, O. P. & Ball, W. E. Expansion Behavior of Coal During Carbonization: A Literature Study. iv, 60p. 1951. pap. 25.00 (*1-58222-020-4*) Inst Gas Tech.

***Brysk, Alison.** From Tribal Village to Global Village: Indian Rights & International Relations in Latin America. LC 99-52771. 400p. 2000. pap. 24.95 (*0-8047-3459-3*) Stanford U Pr.

Brysk, Alison. The Politics of Human Rights in Argentina: Protest, Change, & Democratization. LC 93-34802. xvi, 291p. 1994. 45.00 (*0-8047-2275-7*) Stanford U Pr.

Bryskett, Lodowick. A Discourse of Civil Life: Containing the Ethike Part of Morall Philosophie. LC 70-38162. (English Experience Ser.: No. 358). 288p. 1971. reprint ed. 55.00 (*90-221-0358-7*) Walter J Johnson.

Bryski, Bruce G., jt. auth. see Elmes, Robert J.

Bryskier, A. Macrolides, Chemistry, Pharmacology & Clinical Uses. (Illus.). 714p. 1993. 225.00 (*2-7184-0589-9*) Blackwell Sci.

Bryskin, B. D., ed. Rhenium & Rhenium Alloys. LC 97-71551. (Illus.). 826p. 1997. 166.00 (*0-87339-365-1*, 3651) Minerals Metals.

***Bryson.** Effective Library & Information Management 2nd Edition. LC 99-176517. 448p. 1999. pap. 42.95 (*0-566-07691-8*) Ashgate Pub Co.

Bryson. Police Dog Tactics. (C). 1995. pap. text 47.50 (*0-07-008649-4*) McGraw.

B

An Asterisk (*) at the beginning of an entry indicates that the title is appearing for the first time.

***Bryson.** Strategic Management. LC 98-52082. (Best of Long Range Planning Ser.). 240p. 1999. text 65.00 (*0-08-043440-1*, Pergamon Pr) Elsevier.

Bryson, A. & Marsh, A. Leaving Family Credit. (DSS Research Report Ser.). 1996. write for info. (*0-11-762411-X*, Pub. by Statnry Office) Bernan Associates.

Bryson, A. E. & Ho, Y. C. Applied Optimal Control: Optimization, Estimation, & Control. rev. ed. LC 75-16114. (Illus.). 481p. 1975. reprint ed. pap. text 44.95 (*0-89116-228-3*) Hemisp Pub.

***Bryson, Alan.** Light after Death. 2nd ed. 2000. pap. 8.50 (*81-207-2072-5*, Pub. by Sterling Pubs) S Asia.

— Seeing the Light of World Faith: Passages from the Scriptures of Hinduism, Judaism, Buddhism, Christianity, Islam, Baha'I. 1998. pap. 7.00 (*81-207-2083-0*, Pub. by Sterling Pubs) S Asia.

Bryson, Ann, tr. see Vopekna, Martin.

Bryson, Anna. From Courtesy to Civility: Changing Codes of Conduct in Early Modern England. LC 97-32460. (Oxford Studies in Social History). 322p. 1998. text 75.00 (*0-19-821765-X*) OUP.

Bryson, Anna, tr. see Vopenka, Martin.

Bryson, Anthony. The Waters of Egypt. (C). 1990. 150.00 (*1-898162-45-X*, Pub. by IMMEL Pubng); pap. 125.00 (*0-7855-7118-3*, Pub. by IMMEL Pubng) St Mut.

Bryson, Arthur, compiled by. U. S. Military Vehicles, 1941 to 1945. 100p. 1987. pap. 16.95 (*0-938242-16-4*) Portrayal.

Bryson, Arthur E., Jr. Control of Spacecraft & Aircraft. LC 92-29102. (Illus.). 408p. (C). 1993. text 69.50 (*0-691-08782-2*, Pub. by Princeton U Pr) Cal Prin Full Svc.

— Dynamic Optimization. LC 98-35556. 448p. 1999. 85.95 (*0-201-59790-X*) Addison-Wesley.

— Dynamic Optimization. LC 98-35556. 550p. 1998. 95.00 (*0-201-36187-6*, Prentice Hall) P-H.

***Bryson, Bill.** I'm a Stranger Here Myself. 304p. 2000. pap. 14.00 (*0-7679-0382-X*) Broadway BDD.

Bryson, Bill. I'm a Stranger Here Myself: Notes on Returning to America after Twenty Years Away. LC 99-18074. (Illus.). 288p. 1999. 25.00 (*0-7679-0381-1*) Broadway BDD.

— I'm a Stranger Here Myself: Notes on Returning to America after Twenty Years Away. large type ed. LC 99-27388. 1999. pap. 30.00 (*0-7862-2003-1*) Mac Lib Ref.

— I'm a Stranger Here Myself: Notes on Returning to America after Twenty Years Away. large type ed. LC 99-27388. 1999. 29.95 (*0-7862-2002-3*) Thorndike Pr.

***Bryson, Bill.** In a Sunburned Country. LC 00-25566. 304p. 2000. 25.00 (*0-7679-0385-4*) Broadway BDD.

— In a Sunburned Country. large type ed. LC 00-21858. 480p. 2000. 25.00 (*0-375-43056-3*) Random Hse Lrg Prnt.

Bryson, Bill. The Lost Continent: Travels in Small Town America. LC 89-45027. 320p. 1990. reprint ed. pap. 13.50 (*0-06-092008-4*, Perennial) HarperTrade.

— Made in America: An Informal History of the English Language in the United States. 432p. 1996. pap. 12.50 (*0-380-71381-0*, Avon Bks) Morrow Avon.

— Mother Tongue. LC 89-77521. 272p. 1991. reprint ed. pap. 13.50 (*0-380-71543-0*, Avon Bks) Morrow Avon.

***Bryson, Bill.** Neither Here nor There: Travels in Europe. LC 99-59457. (Illus.). 2000. 25.95 (*1-56895-831-5*, Compass) Wheeler Pub.

— Neither Here Nor There: Travels in Europe. 256p. 1999. pap. 13.50 (*0-380-71380-2*, Avon Bks) Morrow Avon.

Bryson, Bill. Notes from a Small Island. LC 95-43437. 324p. 1996. 25.00 (*0-688-14725-9*, Wm Morrow) Morrow Avon.

— Notes from a Small Island. LC 95-43437. 324p. 1997. reprint ed. pap. 13.50 (*0-380-72750-1*, Avon Bks) Morrow Avon.

— A Walk in the Woods: Rediscovering America on the Appalachian Trail. LC 97-32627. 288p. 1998. 25.00 (*0-7679-0251-3*) Broadway BDD.

— A Walk in the Woods: Rediscovering America on the Appalachian Trail. 274p. 1998. 32.95 (*0-385-25715-5*) Doubleday.

— A Walk in the Woods: Rediscovering America on the Appalachian Trail. 320p. 1998. pap. 13.00 (*0-385-25713-9*) Doubleday.

— A Walk in the Woods: Rediscovering America on the Appalachian Trail. large type ed. LC 98-21552. 469p. 1998. 28.95 (*0-7862-1513-5*) Thorndike Pr.

— A Walk in the Woods: Rediscovering America on the Appalachian Trail. 284p. 1999. reprint ed. pap. 13.95 (*0-7679-0252-1*) Broadway BDD.

***Bryson, Bill & Wilson, Jason, eds.** The Best American Travel Writing 2000. (Best American Ser.). 320p. 2000. 27.50 (*0-618-07466-X*); pap. 13.00 (*0-618-07467-8*) HM.

Bryson, Breeze. My Teacher Is a Song: Based on the Album among Friends. Conn, Aimee et al, eds. (Illus.). 56p. (Orig.). 1988. pap. 6.00 (*0-9621411-0-0*) New Breeze Prodns.

Bryson, C. & Austin, N. Educating Employers. (DSS Research Report Ser.). 1994. write for info. (*0-11-762249-4*, Pub. by Statnry Office) Bernan Associates.

Bryson, C. & Smith, N. The Take-Up of Second Adult Rebate. (DSS Research Report Ser.). 1996. write for info. (*0-11-762390-3*, Pub. by Statnry Office) Bernan Associates.

Bryson, Carlton W. & Gray, Allan W. Numerical Trigonometry: Syllabus. 1973. pap. text 10.95 (*0-89420-050-X*, 355110); audio 70.70 (*0-89420-164-6*, 355000) Natl Book.

Bryson, Charles H., ed. see L'Abate, Luciano.

***Bryson, David.** Queen Jeanne & the Promised Land. LC 99-16388. (Studies in Intellectual History). 400p. 1999. 117.50 (*90-04-11378-9*) Brill Academic Pubs.

Bryson, Gene. Dover Downs NASCAR: The Monster Mile, Three Decades of Speed. Fleming, Kevin, ed. (Illus.). 160p. 1998. 39.95 (*0-9662423-0-0*) Portfolio Bks.

Bryson, George. The Five Points of Calvinism. 117p. 1996. pap. 4.99 (*0-936728-67-1*) Word for Today.

Bryson, Hamilton, ed. Virginia Circuit Court Opinions, No. 43. 656p. 1998. write for info. (*0-327-05034-9*, 49296-10) LEXIS Pub.

Bryson, Harold T. Expository Preaching: The Art of Preaching Through a Bible Book. 1999. pap. text 19.99 (*0-8054-1891-1*) Broadman.

Bryson, J. M. & Taylor, B. Strategic Planning for Public Service & Non-Profit Organizations, Vol. 12. LC 92-35238. (Best of Long Range Planning Ser.). 1993. 72.00 (*0-08-040672-6*, Pub. by Pergamon Repr) Franklin.

Bryson, J. R. & Daniels, P. W. Service Industries in the Global Economy, 2 vols. LC 98-27692. (International Library of Critical Writings in Economics). 1472p. 1998. 500.00 (*1-85898-718-0*) E Elgar.

Bryson, Jamie. First Time Around. Wilensky, Julius M., ed. LC 95-62056. (Illus.). 192p. 1996. pap. 24.95 (*0-918752-21-3*) Wescott Cove.

Bryson, Jo. Managing Information Services: An Integrated Approach. 2nd ed. LC 96-52110. 448p. 1997. text 78.95 (*0-566-07690-X*, Pub. by Gower) Ashgate Pub Co.

Bryson, John. The Private World of Katharine Hepburn. 176p. 1992. pap. 24.95 (*0-316-11333-6*) Little.

Bryson, John & Troxell, Janet C., eds. Dante Gabriel Rossetti & Janey Morris: Their Correspondence. (Illus.). 242p. 1976. text 19.95 (*0-19-812464-3*) OUP.

Bryson, John M. Strategic Planning for Public & Nonprofit Organizations: A Guide to Strengthening & Sustaining Organizational Achievement. 2nd rev. ed. LC 95-22313. (Public Administration, Nonprofit Sector Ser.). 348p. 1995. 32.95 (*0-7879-0141-5*) Jossey-Bass.

Bryson, John M., ed. Strategic Planning for Public Service & Non-Profit Organizations. LC 92-35238. (Best of Long Range Planning Ser.: No. 12). 1993. 77.00 (*0-685-62558-3*, Pergamon Pr) Elsevier.

Bryson, John M. & Alston, Farnum K. Creating & Implementing Your Strategic Plan. (Public Administration Ser.). 139p. 1995. wbk. ed. 25.95 (*0-7879-0142-3*) Jossey-Bass.

Bryson, John M. & Crosby, Barbara C. Leadership for the Common Good: Tackling Public Problems in a Shared-Power World. LC 92-19032. (Public Administration & Nonprofit Sector Ser.). 464p. 1992. 35.95 (*1-55542-480-5*) Jossey-Bass.

Bryson, John M. & Einsweiler, Robert C. Shared Power: What Is It? How Does It Work? How Can We Make It Work Better? (Readings for Leaders Ser.: Vol. IV). 420p. (Orig.). (C). 1992. pap. text 43.50 (*0-8191-8458-6*); lib. bdg. 71.00 (*0-8191-8457-8*) U Pr of Amer.

Bryson, John M. & Einsweiler, Robert C., eds. Strategic Planning: Threats & Opportunities for Planners. LC 87-73537. (Illus.). 230p. (Orig.). 1988. pap. 31.95 (*0-918286-54-9*, Planners Press) Am Plan Assn.

Bryson, John R., et al. The Economic Geography Reader: Producing & Consuming Global Capitalism. (Illus.). 481p. 1999. 110.00 (*0-471-98527-9*); pap. 34.95 (*0-471-98528-7*) Wiley.

Bryson, Joseph. Handbook on Virginia Civil Procedure: 1990 Supplement. 2nd ed. 1990. write for info. (*0-87473-716-8*, 60653-10, MICHIE) LEXIS Pub.

Bryson, Judy, ed. Baptist Dishes Worth Blessing. LC 78-631. (Illus.). 192p. 1978. pap. 12.95 (*1-56554-668-7*) Pelican.

Bryson, L., ed. see Conference On Science - Philosophy And Religion -.

Bryson, Lawrence. The Travel Health Clinic Pocket Guide to Healthy Travel. 175p. (Orig.). 1994. pap. 13.95 (*0-9624945-4-2*) Silvercat Pubns.

Bryson, Lew. Pennsylvania Breweries. LC 98-12060. (Illus.). 256p. 1998. 16.95 (*0-8117-2879-X*) Stackpole.

***Bryson, Lew.** Pennsylvania Breweries. 2nd ed. LC 00-35787. (Illus.). 2000. write for info. (*0-8117-2898-6*) Stackpole.

Bryson, Lois & Winter, Ian. Social Change, Suburban Lives: An Australian Newtown, 1960s-1990s. (Studies in Society Ser.). 208p. 1998. pap. 29.95 (*1-86448-699-6*, Pub. by Allen & Unwin Pty) Paul & Co Pubs.

Bryson, Lyman, ed. Science & Freedom. LC 71-156620. (Essay Index Reprint Ser.). 1977. reprint ed. 20.95 (*0-8369-2385-5*) Ayer.

Bryson, Mary, jt. ed. see De Castell, Suzanne.

Bryson, Maureen, jt. auth. see Inkster, Ian.

Bryson, Maureen S. Extracts of Wills in the Archdeaconry of Colchester for All Persons Listed As Being from Coggeshall, Great & Little, 1782-1857. i, 39p. 1998. 15.00 (*0-9664088-4-5*) M S Bryson.

Bryson, Maureen S. & Bate, Kerry W. The Lives & Letters of the Sylvesters & Nicholsons. (Illus.). vii, 710p. 1997. 50.00 (*0-9664088-0-2*) M S Bryson.

Bryson, Maureen S., jt. auth. see Bate, Kerry W.

Bryson, McDowell & Ziminski, Adele. The Concierge: Key to Hospitality. LC 92-2561. 256p. 1992. pap. 44.95 (*0-471-52893-5*) Wiley.

Bryson, Michael G., Sr., ed. The Babe Didn't Point: And Other Stories about Iowans & Sports. LC 88-9103. 255p. 1989. reprint ed. pap. 79.10 (*0-608-06846-2*, 206705200009) Bks Demand.

Bryson, Norman. Looking at the Overlooked: Four Essays on Still-Life Painting. (Illus.). 192p. 1990. 32.50 (*0-674-53905-2*) HUP.

— Looking at the Overlooked: Four Essays on Still-Life Painting. 192p. (C). 1991. pap. text 22.50 (*0-674-53906-0*) HUP.

— Vision & Painting: The Logic of the Gaze. LC 82-10901. (Illus.). 208p. 1983. 42.50 (*0-300-02855-5*) Yale U Pr.

— Vision & Painting: The Logic of the Gaze. LC 82-10901. (Illus.). 208p. 1986. pap. 15.00 (*0-300-03583-7*, Y-556) Yale U Pr.

— Word & Image: French Painting of the Ancient Regime. LC 81-10124. 304p. 1983. pap. text 28.95 (*0-521-27654-3*) Cambridge U Pr.

Bryson, Norman, et al, eds. Visual Culture: Images & Interpretations. LC 93-13614. (Illus.). 461p. 1994. pap. 24.95 (*0-8195-6267-X*, Wesleyan Univ Pr) U Pr of New Eng.

Bryson, Norman, jt. auth. see Krauss, Rosiland.

Bryson, Norman, jt. ed. see Minglu, Gau.

Bryson, Peter D. Comprehensive Review in Toxicology for Emergency Clinicians. 3rd ed. LC 96-9209. 960p. 1996. 125.00 (*1-56032-612-3*) Hemisp Pub.

— Comprehensive Review in Toxicology for Emergency Clinicians. 3rd ed. LC 95-25465. 1996. write for info. (*0-614-95880-6*) Lppncott W & W.

Bryson, Phillip J. The Consumer under Socialist Planning: The East German Case. LC 84-8270. 207p. 1984. 57.95 (*0-275-91135-7*, C1135, Praeger Pubs) Greenwood.

— The Reluctant Retreat: The Soviet & East German Departure from Central Planning. (Illus.). 420p. 1995. text 79.95 (*1-85521-523-3*, Pub. by Dartmth Pub) Ashgate Pub Co.

Bryson, R. L., ed. Contracting in All 50 States: Who to Contact & General Licensing Requirements for Every State. LC 98-22680. 416p. 1998. pap. 36.00 (*1-57218-070-6*) Craftsman.

Bryson, Reid A. & Murray, Thomas J. Climates of Hunger: Mankind & the World's Changing Weather. LC 76-53649. (Illus.). 190p. 1979. pap. 14.95 (*0-299-07374-2*) U of Wis Pr.

Bryson, Sandy. Search Dog Training. (Illus.). 359p. (Orig.). 1984. pap. 12.95 (*0-910286-94-9*) Boxwood.

Bryson, Scott S. The Chastised Stage: Bourgeois Drama & the Exercise of Power. (Stanford French & Italian Studies: No. 70). 128p. 1991. pap. 56.50 (*0-915838-86-9*) Anma Libri.

Bryson, Stephen T. Implementing Virtual Reality. (C). 1997. text. write for info. (*0-201-52551-8*) Addison-Wesley.

Bryson, T. S. & Metger, C. A. Individual Tooth Site Failure Analysis for Surface Fatigue Testing. (1985 Fall Technical Meeting Ser.: Vol. 85FTM16). (Illus.). 11p. 1985. pap. text 30.00 (*1-55589-109-8*) AGMA.

Bryson, Thomas A. United States-Middle East Diplomatic Relations, 1784-1978: An Annotated Bibliography. LC 78-26754. 219p. 1979. lib. bdg. 31.00 (*0-8108-1197-9*) Scarecrow.

— Walter George Smith. LC 77-9967. 239p. reprint ed. pap. 74.10 (*0-608-18721-6*, 202950000061) Bks Demand.

Bryson, Valerie. Feminist Debates Issues of Theory & Political Practice. LC 98-49775. 1999. text 55.00 (*0-8147-1347-5*) NYU Pr.

— Feminist Political Theory. 304p. 1994. pap. 16.95 (*1-56924-973-3*) Marlowe & Co.

Bryson, Valerie & Campling, Jo. Feminist Debates: Issues of Theory & Political Practice. LC 98-49775. 267p. 1999. pap. text 19.00 (*0-8147-1348-3*) NYU Pr.

Bryson, W. H. The Equity Side of the Exchequer. LC 85-48165. (Cambridge Studies in English Legal History). 228p. 1986. reprint ed. 60.00 (*0-912004-36-3*) Gaunt.

Bryson, W. Hamilton. Bryson on Virginia Civil Procedure: 1998 Supplement. 3rd ed. 1998. suppl. ed. 35.00 (*0-327-00211-5*, 60650-15) LEXIS Pub.

***Bryson, W. Hamilton.** Bryson on Virginia Civil Procedure, 1999 Cumulative Supplement. 210p. 1999. write for info. (*0-327-01488-1*, 6065016) LEXIS Pub.

— Samuel Dodd's Reports 1678-1713 & Miscellaneous Exchequer Cases 1671-1713. 2000. pap. write for info. (*0-89089-695-X*) Carolina Acad Pr.

Bryson, W. Hamilton. Virginia Circuit Court Opinions, 40 vols., Set. 1993. 1150.00 (*1-56257-338-1*, 49250-10, MICHIE) LEXIS Pub.

Bryson, W. Hamilton, ed. Essays on Legal Education in 19th Century Virginia. LC 98-18443. 211p. 1998. 65.00 (*1-57588-446-1*, 311780) W S Hein.

Bryson, W. Hamilton, ed. see Randolph, John.

Bryson, William C., jt. auth. see Beale, Sara S.

***Bryson, William E.** Cryogenics. LC 99-23530. 210p. 1999. 36.95 (*1-56990-274-7*) Hanser-Gardner.

Bryson, William E. Heat Treatment, Selection, & Application of Tool Steels. LC 97-18613. 198p. 1997. 34.95 (*1-56990-238-0*) Hanser-Gardner.

Bryson, William H. A Bibliography of Virgina Legal History Before 1900. 2nd ed. LC 97-38503. 292p. 1997. 50.00 (*1-57588-407-0*, 311520) W S Hein.

— Dictionary of Sigla & Abbreviations to & in Law Books Before 1607. 2nd ed. LC 96-32076. xiii, 184p. 1996. 55.00 (*1-57588-126-8*, 310730) W S Hein.

Brysz, Simon. Das Ding an Sich und die Empirische Anschauung in Kants Philosophie. (Abhandlungen zur Philosophie und Ihrer Geschichte Ser.: Vol. 41). (GER.). 111p. 1981. write for info. (*3-487-06791-9*) G Olms Pubs.

Bryszewski, Kristina. Step by Step Knitting Stitch Patterns. (Illus.). 104p. (Orig.). 1989. pap. 9.95 (*0-88925-833-3*) Gordon Soules Bk.

Bryteson, Paul. Essentials of Physical Activity. rev. ed. 224p. 1996. pap. text 16.95 (*0-945483-67-8*) E Bowers Pub.

Bryzcki, Matt. Youth Strength & Conditioning. (Spalding Youth Ser.). (Illus.). 208p. (Orig.). (J). (gr. 1-5). 1996. pap. 12.95 (*1-57028-041-X*, 8041XH, Mstrs Pr) NTC Contemp Pub Co.

Brzeczek, Marietta, jt. auth. see Defrank, Carol.

Brzezenski, Jan, tr. see Goswami, Rupa.

Brzezinski. Struggle for Constitutionalism. LC 97-15100. 276p. 1997. text 49.95 (*0-312-17612-0*) St Martin.

***Brzezinski, Mark.** The Struggle for Constitutionalism in Poland. 2000. pap. 22.95 (*0-312-23196-2*) St Martin.

Brzezinski, Mary Jo, ed. Employee Benefit Issues Vol. 36: The Multiemployer Perspective, 1994. 578p. 1995. 20.00 (*0-89154-480-1*) Intl Found Employ.

Brzezinski, Mary Jo, ed. see Black, Ann.

Brzezinski, Mary Jo, ed. see Bloss, Julie L.

Brzezinski, Mary Jo, ed. see Brislin, Joseph A.

Brzezinski, Mary Jo, ed. see Burroughs, Eugene B.

Brzezinski, Mary Jo, ed. see Glazer, William M. & Bell, Nancy N.

Brzezinski, Mary Jo, ed. see Johnson, Richard E.

Brzezinski, Mary Jo, ed. see Nielson, Norma L., et al.

Brzezinski, Mary Jo, ed. see Siebold, Dennis P.

Brzezinski, Richard. The Army of Gustavus Adolphus Vol. 1, Infantry. (Men-at-Arms Ser.: No. 235). (Illus.). 48p. 1991. pap. 11.95 (*0-85045-997-4*, 9193, Pub. by Osprey) Stackpole.

— The Army of Gustavus Adolphus Vol. 2, Cavalry. (Men-at-Arms Ser.). (Illus.). 48p. 1993. pap. 11.95 (*1-85532-350-8*, 9233, Pub. by Osprey) Stackpole.

***Brzezinski, Richard.** Lutzen 1632. (Campaign Ser.: Vol. 68). 2000. pap. 17.95 (*1-85532-552-7*) Osprey.

Brzezinski, Richard. Polish Armies, 1569-1696, Vol. 2. (Men-at-Arms Ser.: No. 188). (Illus.). 48p. pap. 11.95 (*0-85045-744-0*, 9121, Pub. by Osprey) Stackpole.

— The Polish Army, 1569-1696, Vol. 1. (Men-at-Arms Ser.: No. 184). (Illus.). 48p. pap. 11.95 (*0-85045-736-X*, 9116, Pub. by Osprey) Stackpole.

Brzezinski, Z., jt. auth. see Abelin, T.

Brzezinski, Zbigniew. The Grand Chessboard: American Primacy & Its Geostrategic Imperatives. 240p. 1998. pap. 15.00 (*0-465-02726-1*, Pub. by Basic) HarpC.

Brzezinski, Zbigniew & Sullivan, Paige, eds. Russia & the Commonwealth of Independent States: Documents, Data, & Analysis. LC 96-18164. (Illus.). 888p. (C). (gr. 13). 1996. text 261.95 (*1-56324-637-6*) M E Sharpe.

Brzezinski, Zbigniew K. Between Two Ages: America's Role in the Technetronic Era. LC 82-15867. 334p. 1982. reprint ed. lib. bdg. 45.00 (*0-313-23498-1*, BRZB, Greenwood Pr) Greenwood.

— Ideology & Power in Soviet Politics. LC 76-6571. 180p. 1976. reprint ed. lib. bdg. 55.00 (*0-8371-8880-6*, BRIP, Greenwood Pr) Greenwood.

— New Dimensions of Human Rights. 22p. (Orig.). 1995. pap. 5.00 (*0-87641-145-6*) Carnegie Ethics & Intl Affairs.

— Out of Control: Global Turmoil on the Eve of the Twenty-First Century. Stewart, Robert, ed. 240p. 1993. text 21.00 (*0-684-19630-1*, Scribners Ref) Mac Lib Ref.

— Soviet Bloc: Unity & Conflict. enl. rev. ed. LC 67-12531. (Center for International Affairs Ser.: No. 37). 599p. 1967. pap. 24.95 (*0-674-82548-9*) HUP.

— The Soviet Political System: Transformation or Degeneration. (Reprint Series in Political Science). (C). 1993. reprint ed. pap. text 5.00 (*0-8290-3572-9*, PS-438) Irvington.

***Brzezinski, Zbigniew K.** U. S. Policy Toward Northeastern Europe: Report of an Independent Task Force. 1999. pap. 7.00 (*0-87609-259-8*) Brookings.

Brzezinski, Zbigniew K. & Huntington, Samuel P. Political Power: U. S. A. - U. S. S. R. LC 82-9178. 461p. 1982. reprint ed. lib. bdg. 79.50 (*0-313-23497-3*, BRZP, Greenwood Pr) Greenwood.

Brzezinski, Zbigniew K., et al. American Security in an Interdependent World. 108p. (Orig.). (C). 1988. pap. text 15.00 (*0-8191-7085-2*) Atl Coun US.

Brzezniak, Zdzisaw & Zastawniak, Tomasz. Basic Stochastic Processes: A Course Through Exercises. LC 98-7021. (Undergraduate Mathematics Ser.). 1998. 29.95 (*3-540-76175-6*) Spr-Verlag.

Brzin, M., et al, eds. Cholinesterases: Fundamental & Applied Aspects. LC 84-12062. xiv, 527p. 1984. 152.35 (*3-11-009873-3*) De Gruyter.

***Brzinski, Joanne B., et al, eds.** Compounded Representation in West European Federations. LC 99-34551. (West European Politics Ser.). 200p. 1999. 54.50 (*0-7146-4997-X*, Pub. by F Cass Pubs); pap. 24.50 (*0-7146-8058-3*, Pub. by F Cass Pubs) Intl Spec Bk.

Brzoska, David W., jt. auth. see Graves, Robert C.

Brzoska, Michael & Pearson, Frederic S. Arms & Warfare: Escalation, De-Escalation & Negotiation. LC 93-46038. 329p. (C). 1994. text 39.95 (*0-87249-982-0*) U of SC Pr.

Brzostek, T. Thrombolysis & Acute Myocardial Infarction: Early & Late Effects on Clinical Status, Left Ventricular Function & Exercise Capacity. No. 39. 134p. (Orig.). 1991. pap. 32.50 (*90-6186-441-0*, Pub. by Leuven Univ) Coronet Bks.

Brzovic, Kathy. Bonaventura's Nachtwachen: A Satirical Novel. LC 89-48409. (Studies in Modern German Literature: Vol. 36). 169p. (C). 1990. text 41.95 (*0-8204-1225-2*) P Lang Pubng.

Brzozowska-Krajka, Anna. Polish Traditional Folklore: The Magic of Time. 224p. 1998. 31.00 (*0-88033-395-2*, 498, Pub. by East Eur Monographs) Col U Pr.

Brzuzy, Stephanie, jt. auth. see Segal, Elizabeth A.

Brzycki, Matt. Maximize Your Training: Insights from Top Strength & Fitness Professionals. LC 99-13968. (Illus.). 464p. 1999. 19.95 (*0-8442-8317-7*, 83177, Mstrs Pr) NTC Contemp Pub Co.

— Practical Approach to Strength Training. 3rd rev. ed. (Illus.). 256p. 1995. pap. 17.95 (*1-57028-018-5*, 80185H, Mstrs Pr) NTC Contemp Pub Co.

Brzycki, Matt & Brown, Shaun. Conditioning for Basketball. (Illus.). 192p. (Orig.). 1993. pap. 14.95 (*0-940279-56-8*, 79568H, Mstrs Pr) NTC Contemp Pub Co.

Brzycki, Matt, ed. see Castellano, Rocco.

An Asterisk (*) at the beginning of an entry indicates that the title is appearing for the first time.

BS Poetry Society Staff, jt. auth. see Hunter-Dixon, Christie.

BSC Staff. Saloman Henning's Chronicle of Courland & Livonia. 268p. 1992. per. 30.00 (*0-8403-7763-0*) Kendall-Hunt.

BSCS Staff. Basic Genetics. 7th ed. 144p. 1994. per. 18.90 (*0-8403-5705-2*) Kendall-Hunt.

— Biological Perspectives. 624p. 1998. 62.95 (*0-7872-3743-4*) Kendall-Hunt.

— Biological Perspectives Laboratory Manual: Thinking Biologically. 132p. 1998. spiral bd., lab manual ed. 19.95 (*0-7872-4607-7*) Kendall-Hunt.

***BSCS Staff.** Biological Science: A Molecular Approach. 8th ed. 2000. pap. 57.30 (*0-538-69039-9*) Sth-Wstrn College.

BSCS Staff. Biological Science: Red Patterns & Processes. 3rd ed. 816p. 1995. teacher ed., boxed set 44.90 (*0-8403-5864-4*) Kendall-Hunt.

— Developing Biology Literacy. 152p. (C). 1994. pap. text, per. 16.95 (*0-7872-0193-6*) Kendall-Hunt.

— Making Healthy Decisions. (Injury Prevention Ser.: Vol. 1). 80p. 1996. ring bd. 7.90 (*0-7872-1218-0*) Kendall-Hunt.

— Making Healthy Decisions, No. 1. (Injury Prevention Ser.: Vol. 1). 176p. 1996. teacher ed., ring bd. 22.90 (*0-7872-1219-9*) Kendall-Hunt.

— Making Healthy Decisions Fitness, No. 1. 172p. 1996. teacher ed., spiral bd. 22.90 (*0-7872-1223-7*) Kendall-Hunt.

— Making Healthy Decisions Fitness, No. 2. 166p. 1996. teacher ed., spiral bd. 22.90 (*0-7872-1225-3*) Kendall-Hunt.

— Making Healthy Decisions Fitness, Unit 1. 86p. 1996. spiral bd. 7.90 (*0-7872-1222-9*) Kendall-Hunt.

— Making Healthy Decisions Fitness, Unit 2. 82p. 1996. spiral bd. 7.90 (*0-7872-1224-5*) Kendall-Hunt.

— Making Healthy Decisions Nutrition, Unit 1. 200p. 1996. teacher ed., spiral bd. 22.90 (*0-7872-1207-5*) Kendall-Hunt.

— Middle School Science & Technology: Investigating Diversity & Limits, Level B. 448p. 1993. pap. text, teacher ed. 79.90 (*0-8403-6679-5*) Kendall-Hunt.

— Middle School Science & Technology: Investigating Diversity & Limits, Level B. 368p. 1995. boxed set 42.90 (*0-8403-6678-7*) Kendall-Hunt.

— Middle School Science & Technology: Investigating Diversity & Limits Level B Teachers Guide & Resource Book. 336p. 1993. pap. text 66.90 (*0-8403-7497-6*) Kendall-Hunt.

— Middle School Science & Technology: Investigating Patterns of Change Level A. 384p. 1995. boxed set 42.90 (*0-8403-6676-0*) Kendall-Hunt.

— Middle School Science & Technology: Investigating Patterns of Change Level A Teacher's Edition. 338p. 1993. pap. text 66.90 (*0-8403-7496-8*); pap. text, teacher ed. 79.90 (*0-8403-6677-9*) Kendall-Hunt.

— Middle School Science & Technology: Investigating Systems & Change, Level C. 528p. 1993. pap. text, teacher ed. 79.90 (*0-8403-6681-7*) Kendall-Hunt.

— Middle School Science & Technology: Investigating Systems & Change, Level C. 496p. 1995. boxed set 42.90 (*0-8403-6680-9*) Kendall-Hunt.

— Middle School Science & Technology Level C: Investigating Systems & Change. 464p. 1993. pap. text, teacher ed. 66.90 (*0-8403-7498-4*) Kendall-Hunt.

***BSCS Staff.** A Molecular Approach to Bscs Biology Science. 8th ed. 2000. pap. 2.95 (*0-538-69406-8*) Thomson Learn.

BSCS Staff. Science for Life & Living: Integrating Science, Technology & Health. 7th ed. 368p. (J). (gr. 5). 1991. boxed set 29.90 (*0-8403-5998-5*) Kendall-Hunt.

— Science for Life & Living: Integrating Science, Technology & Health. 7th ed. 560p. 1991. teacher ed., ring bd. 64.90 (*0-8403-5999-3*) Kendall-Hunt.

— Science for Life & Living: Integrating Science, Technology & Health Grade 2. 7th ed. 240p. 1991. 29.90 (*0-8403-5992-6*); ring bd. 64.90 (*0-8403-5991-8*) Kendall-Hunt.

— Science for Life & Living: Integrating Science, Technology & Health Grade 2. 7th ed. 208p. 1995. per. 12.90 (*0-8403-5990-X*) Kendall-Hunt.

— Science for Life & Living: Integrating Science, Technology, & Health, Grade 3. 7th ed. 320p. 1991. boxed set 29.90 (*0-8403-5996-9*) Kendall-Hunt.

— Science for Life & Living: Integrating Science, Technology, & Health, Grade 3. 7th ed. 368p. 1991. boxed set 29.90 (*0-8403-5994-2*) Kendall-Hunt.

— Science for Life & Living: Integrating Science, Technology, & Health, Grade 3. 7th ed. 464p. (J). (gr. 2). 1991. teacher ed., ring bd. 64.90 (*0-8403-5993-4*) Kendall-Hunt.

— Science for Life & Living: Integrating Science, Technology, & Health, Grade 3. 7th ed. 480p. 1991. teacher ed., ring bd. 64.90 (*0-8403-5995-0*); teacher ed., ring bd. 64.90 (*0-8403-5997-7*) Kendall-Hunt.

— Science for Life & Living Grade 6. 7th ed. 352p. 1991. 29.90 (*0-8403-6000-2*) Kendall-Hunt.

— Science for Life & Living Teachers Edition: Grade 6. 7th ed. 416p. 1991. teacher ed., ring bd. 64.90 (*0-8403-6001-0*) Kendall-Hunt.

— Teaching Edition for Student Study Guide for Biological Science: An Ecological Approach. 7th ed. 208p. 1994. teacher ed., per. 34.90 (*0-8403-5867-9*) Kendall-Hunt.

BSCS Staff & Pyper-Smith, Diane. National Standards & the Science Curriculum. LC 97-127280. 184p. (C). 1996. pap. text, per. 17.90 (*0-7872-2589-4*) Kendall-Hunt.

***BSCS Staff & Videodiscovery, Inc. Staff.** Cell Biology & Cancer. (Illus.). 200p. 1999. teacher ed. write for info. (*1-929614-01-2*) Biological Sciences.

— Emerging & Re-Emerging Infectious Diseases. (Illus.). 200p. 1999. teacher ed. write for info. (*1-929614-02-0*) Biological Sciences.

— Human Genetic Variation. (Illus.). 200p. 1999. teacher ed. write for info. (*1-929614-00-4*) Biological Sciences.

BSCS Staff, jt. auth. see SSEC Staff.

BSI Staff. Records of Botanical Survey of India, 11 vols. (C). 1988. text 800.00 (*0-7855-3168-8*) St Mut.

***Bsliwibnski, Antoni, et al.** Acousto-Optics & Applications III: 18-22 May 1998, Gdabnsk-Jurata, Poland. LC 99-192664. (Proceedings Ser.). xx, 414p. 1998. write for info. (*0-8194-3048-X*) SPIE.

BSM Consulting Group Staff. Guidebook to Medical Practice Finances Reporting. (Illus.). 65p. 1997. pap. write for info. (*1-929196-04-0*) Am Opthlmc Admin.

BSRIA Staff. Air Curtains, LB 1-87. (C). 1987. 60.00 (*0-86022-159-8*, Pub. by Build Servs Info Assn) St Mut.

— Air Leakage in Office Buildings. Potter, I. N. et al, eds. 1993. pap. 60.00 (*0-86022-402-3*, Pub. by Build Servs Info Assn) St Mut.

— BEMS Interactive Training Technology Overview. (C). 1989. 630.00 (*0-7855-4403-8*, Pub. by Build Servs Info Assn) St Mut.

— Building Services Equipment-7. (C). 1988. 1050.00 (*0-7855-4402-X*, Pub. by Build Servs Info Assn) St Mut.

— The Building Services Industry: The Single European Market & 1992. 2nd ed. (C). 1988. 150.00 (*0-86022-219-5*, Pub. by Build Servs Info Assn) St Mut.

— A Client's Guide to Greener Construction. 1995. pap. 85.00 (*0-86017-423-9*, Pub. by Build Servs Info Assn) St Mut.

— Commissioning of VAV systems in Buildings. 1991. pap. 100.00 (*0-86022-270-5*, Pub. by Build Servs Info Assn) St Mut.

— Condensing Boilers Pt. 2: Selection Procedure. 1990. pap. 120.00 (*0-86022-303-5*, Pub. by Build Servs Info Assn) St Mut.

— Condition Based Maintenance for Building Services. 1995. pap. 60.00 (*0-86022-396-5*, Pub. by Build Servs Info Assn) St Mut.

— Control of Natural Ventilation. 91p. 1995. pap. 75.00 (*0-86022-406-6*, Pub. by Build Servs Info Assn) St Mut.

— Domestic Boiler Market. (C). 1984. 350.00 (*0-7855-4400-3*, Pub. by Build Servs Info Assn) St Mut.

BSRIA Staff. Environmental Code of Practice for Buildings & Their Services: Case Studies. 1996. pap. 100.00 (*0-86022-430-9*, Pub. by Build Servs Info Assn) St Mut.

BSRIA Staff. Environmental Conditions at VDU's LB 14-86. (C). 1986. 70.00 (*0-86022-153-9*, Pub. by Build Servs Info Assn) St Mut.

— Free Cooling Systems. 1997. pap. 675.00 (*0-86022-453-8*, Pub. by Build Servs Info Assn) St Mut.

— Guide to BEMS Centre Standard Specification, Vol. 1. 1990. pap. 80.00 (*0-86022-259-4*, Pub. by Build Servs Info Assn) St Mut.

— Heat Rejection Systems: Some Methods & Their Operating Costs. 1993. pap. 40.00 (*0-86022-337-X*, Pub. by Build Servs Info Assn) St Mut.

— Indoor Air Quality Sensors. 1997. pap. 120.00 (*0-86022-403-1*, Pub. by Build Servs Info Assn) St Mut.

— Infrared Condition Based Maintenance for Building Services. 1995. pap. 60.00 (*0-86022-397-3*, Pub. by Build Servs Info Assn) St Mut.

— Life Cycle & Failure Data, LB 11-82. (C). 1982. 70.00 (*0-86022-165-2*, Pub. by Build Servs Info Assn) St Mut.

— Lifts, LB Two to Eighty-Seven. (C). 1987. 60.00 (*0-86022-169-5*, Pub. by Build Servs Info Assn) St Mut.

— Manual for Regulating Air Conditioning Installations (Including Set of Forms) (C). 1975. 60.00 (*0-86022-009-5*, Pub. by Build Servs Info Assn) St Mut.

— Manual for Regulating Water Systems. (C). 1979. 75.00 (*0-86022-069-9*, Pub. by Build Servs Info Assn) St Mut.

— The Ozone Layer Chlorofluorocarbons & Building Services. 1988. 35.00 incl. audio (*0-86022-225-X*, Pub. by Build Servs Info Assn) St Mut.

— Quality Assurance in Building Services: A One-Day Conference. (C). 1989. 175.00 (*0-7855-4405-4*, Pub. by Build Servs Info Assn) St Mut.

— Radiators & Other Heat Emitters-3. (C). 1988. 1750.00 (*0-7855-4401-1*, Pub. by Build Servs Info Assn) St Mut.

— Refrigeration & the Environment: Typical Applications for Air Conditioning. (C). 1994. pap. 25.00 (*0-86022-365-5*, Pub. by Build Servs Info Assn) St Mut.

— The Replacement Cost Is the Basis. (C). 1985. 90.00 (*0-7855-4406-2*, Pub. by Build Servs Info Assn) St Mut.

— Standard Specifications for BEMS, Vol. 2, Version 3.1. 1990. pap. 120.00 (*0-86022-260-8*, Pub. by Build Servs Info Assn) St Mut.

— Static Electricity in Building, LB 9-87. (C). 1987. 80.00 (*0-86022-184-9*, Pub. by Build Servs Info Assn) St Mut.

— Supermarkets & Department Stores, LB 21-86. (C). 1986. 75.00 (*0-86022-173-3*, Pub. by Build Servs Info Assn) St Mut.

— Value Engineering. 1997. pap. 125.00 (*0-86022-450-3*, Pub. by Build Servs Info Assn) St Mut.

BSRIA Staff, ed. Laboratoreis, LB 13-85. (C). 1985. 85.00 (*0-86022-132-6*, Pub. by Build Servs Info Assn) St Mut.

BSRIA Staff & Alamdari, F. Air Curtains: Commercial Applications. aup. 1997. pap. 120.00 (*0-86022-439-2*, Pub. by Build Servs Info Assn) St Mut.

BSRIA Staff & deSaules, T. Handover Information for Building Services. 1995. pap. 60.00 (*0-86022-416-3*, Pub. by Build Servs Info Assn) St Mut.

BSRIA Staff & Halliday, S. P. Environmental Code of Practice for Buildings & Their Services. 130p. 1994. pap. 100.00 (*0-86022-367-1*, Pub. by Build Servs Info Assn) St Mut.

BSRIA Staff & Johansson, M. Contingency Planning. 1997. pap. 80.00 (*0-86022-447-3*, Pub. by Build Servs Info Assn) St Mut.

BSRIA Staff & Loyd, S. Ventilation System Hygiene: A Review. 8th ed. 60p. 1996. pap. 80.00 (*0-86022-452-X*, Pub. by Build Servs Info Assn) St Mut.

BSRIA Staff & Nanayakkara, R. The CDM Regulations & Health & Safety File. 95p. 1997. pap. 35.00 (*0-86022-459-7*, Pub. by Build Servs Info Assn) St Mut.

BSRIA Staff & Parsloe, C. J. Overengineering in Building Services: An International Comparison of Design & Installation Methods. 82p. 1995. pap. 120.00 (*0-86022-423-6*, Pub. by Build Servs Info Assn) St Mut.

BSRIA Staff & Pike, P. G. Air Filters. 1997. pap. 140.00 (*0-86022-460-0*, Pub. by Build Servs Info Assn) St Mut.

BSRIA Staff, et al. Advanced Air Filtration. 132p. 1996. pap. 1200.00 (*0-86022-441-4*, Pub. by Build Servs Info Assn) St Mut.

— BEMS As Condition Based Maintenance Tools. 1995. pap. 60.00 (*0-86022-399-X*, Pub. by Build Servs Info Assn) St Mut.

— Rules & Regulations for Building Services Contractors in France. 1995. pap. 300.00 (*0-86022-427-9*, Pub. by Build Servs Info Assn) St Mut.

— Rules & Regulations for Building Services Contractors in Germany. 1995. pap. 300.00 (*0-86022-428-7*, Pub. by Build Servs Info Assn) St Mut.

BSRIA Staff, ed. see Barnard, N. & Starr, A.

Bsullak, Nicole, jt. auth. see McCreight, Tim.

BSW Consulting, Inc. Staff. The Millenium Strategies Workbook: Preparing for the Future. 63p. 1998. pap., wbk. ed. 79.95 (*1-56829-094-2*) Med Group Mgmt.

Bt Abdullah, Maisom. Transfer of Industrial Technology to the Manufacturing Sector: The Case of Malaysia. (Studies in Technology & Social Change: No. 1). 86p. (Orig.). (C). 1988. pap. 8.00 (*0-945271-01-8*) ISU-CIKARD.

BTA Staff. Camping & Caravan Parks in Britain 1997. (Illus.). 180p. (Orig.). 1997. pap. 10.95 (*0-7095-6625-5*, Pub. by JARR UK) Seven Hills Bk.

B.Treacy, Gerald. Washington Guardianship Law: Administration & Litigation. 3rd ed. 105.00 (*0-327-12496-2*) LEXIS Pub.

Bu, Peter. New Mime in Europe. Leabhart, Thomas, ed. (Mime Journal Ser.). (Illus.). 179p. (Orig.). 1983. pap. 12.00 (*0-9611066-7-0*) Mime Jour.

Bua & Barnes, eds. Actors Almanac: Original Scene Book. LC 83-18995. (Actors Almanac Ser.: Vol. 1). 1984. pap. 4.95 (*0-913290-54-8*) Camaro Pub.

BUA German Chemical Society Staff. Existing Chemicals of Environmental Relevance: Criteria & List of Chemicals I. LC 89-5480. 218p. 1989. pap. 80.00 (*3-527-27878-8*, Wiley-VCH) Wiley.

— Existing Chemicals of Environmental Relevance: Criteria & List of Chemicals II. LC 89-37418. 76p. 1989. pap. text 45.00 (*3-527-27998-9*, Wiley-VCH) Wiley.

Bua, Robert N. The Inside Guide to America's Nursing Homes: Rankings & Ratings for Every Nursing Home in the U. S., 1998-1999 Edition. LC 97-11197. 1344p. (Orig.). 1997. mass mkt. 24.99 (*0-446-67308-0*, Pub. by Warner Bks) Little.

Buan, Carolyn. A Changing Mission: The Story of a Pioneer Church. (Illus.). 176p. 1995. 45.00 (*0-9646549-1-1*); pap. text 35.00 (*0-9646549-0-3*) Untd Church Christ.

Buan, Carolyn M. This Far-Off Sunset Land: A Pictorial History of Washington County, Oregon. LC 98-26219. 192p. 1998. write for info. (*1-57864-037-7*) Donning Co.

Buan, Carolyn M., jt. ed. see Gamboa, Erasmo.

Buar, Ruprecht S., et al. Superlearning und Suggestopadie: Grundlagen-Andwendung-Kritik-Perspektiven. 135p. 1990. 30.50 (*3-468-49449-1*) Langenscheidt.

Buasai, Somsong & Smyth, David. Conversational Thai in Seven Days. (THA., Illus.). 96p. 1993. pap. 8.95 (*0-8442-4551-8*, 45518, Natl Textbk Co) NTC Contemp Pub Co.

— Conversational Thai in Seven Days. 96p. 1995. boxed set 12.95 incl. audio (*0-8442-4550-X*, Natl Textbk Co) NTC Contemp Pub Co.

Buasai, Somsong, et al. Conversational Thai in Seven Days. (Language in 7 Days Ser.). (THA.). 96p. 1995. pap. 14.95 incl. audio (*0-8442-9142-0*, Natl Textbk Co) NTC Contemp Pub Co.

Buat-Menard, Patrick, ed. The Role of Air-Sea Exchange in Geochemical Cycling. 1986. text 247.50 (*90-277-2318-4*) Kluwer Academic.

Buazzi, Mahmoud M. Guide for Studying in America. (ARA.). 112p. (Orig.). 1990. pap. 35.00 (*0-9625643-0-3*) Amer Res & Pub Hse.

***Bub, Andrew S.** Toy Commander. LC 99-68769. (Official Strategy Guides Ser.). (Illus.). 79p. (YA). 2000. pap. 12.99 (*0-7615-2733-8*) Prima Pub.

Bub, Hans. Bird Trapping & Bird Banding: A Handbook for Trapping Methods All over the World. Hamerstrom, Frances & Wuertz-Schaefer, Karin, trs. (Illus.). 448p. 1995. pap. text 35.00 (*0-8014-8312-3*) Cornell U Pr.

Bub, Jeffrey. Interpreting the Quantum World. (Illus.). 312p. (C). 1997. text 52.95 (*0-521-56082-9*) Cambridge U Pr.

— Interpreting the Quantum World. (Illus.). 312p. (C). 1999. pap. text 27.95 (*0-521-65386-X*) Cambridge U Pr.

Buback, Michael & Vogel, Hans P. FT-NIR Atlas. (A/SpecBook by Chemical Concepts: 0942-9735). 1085p. 1993. 925.00 (*3-527-28567-9*, Wiley-VCH) Wiley.

Bubacz, Bruce. St. Augustine's Theory of Knowledge: A Contemporary Analysis. LC 81-18754. (Texts & Studies in Religion: Vol. 11). 234p. (C). 1981. lib. bdg. 89.95 (*0-88946-959-8*) E Mellen.

Bubak, Jozef. Ksiega Naszych Imion. (POL.). 360p. 1993. 16.00 (*0-614-02650-4*) Szwede Slavic.

Bubak, Marian, et al, eds. Recent Advances in Parallel Virtual Machine & Message Passing Interface: Proceedings, 4th European PVM-MPI Users' Group Meeting Cracow, Poland, November 3-5, 1997. LC 97-45489. (Lecture Notes in Computer Science Ser.: Vol. 1332). xv, 518p. 1997. pap. 75.00 (*3-540-63697-8*) Spr-Verlag.

Buban, et al. Electricity & Electronics Technology. 7th ed. 1999. teacher ed. 35.00 (*0-02-683428-6*) Glencoe.

— Electricity & Electronics Technology. 7th ed. (Illus.). (YA). (gr. 6-12). 1999. student ed. 35.99 (*0-02-683427-8*); student ed., wbk. ed. 6.99 (*0-02-683429-4*) Glencoe.

Buban, Peter, Sr. & Schmitt, Marshall L. Understanding Electricity & Electronics. 3rd ed. (J). 1974. text 28.32 (*0-07-008675-3*) McGraw.

Buban, Peter, Sr., et al. Understanding Electricity & Electronics Technology. 5th ed. 544p. (J). 1987. text 19.96 (*0-07-008646-X*) McGraw.

Bubani, Pietro. Flora Virgiliana. (Illus.). 135p. 1974. reprint ed. 55.00 (*3-87429-075-1*, 022480, Pub. by Koeltz Sci Bks) Lubrecht & Cramer.

Bubar, Benjamin, Sr. The Devil Let Loose in Maine, Vol. 1. Bubar, David N., ed. (Illus.). 1996. pap. 9.95 (*1-885273-05-3*) First Century.

Bubar, David N. Play Today the Bubar Way. 130p. 1996. 29.95 incl. VHS (*1-885273-00-2*) First Century.

— Play Today the Bubar Way, Vol. 1, Church ed. 130p. 1996. 29.95 incl. VHS (*1-885273-01-0*) First Century.

Bubar, David N., ed. see Bubar, Benjamin, Sr.

Bube, Richard H. Electrons in Solids: An Introductory Survey. 3rd ed. (Illus.). 329p. 1992. text 77.00 (*0-12-138553-1*) Acad Pr.

— Photoelectronic Properties of Semiconductors. (Illus.). 336p. (C). 1992. pap. text 42.95 (*0-521-40681-1*) Cambridge U Pr.

— Photovoltaic Materials. LC 97-36334. 300p. 1997. text 46.00 (*1-86094-065-X*) World Scientific Pub.

— Putting It All Together: Seven Patterns for Relating Science & the Christian Faith. 224p. (Orig.). (C). 1995. lib. bdg. 49.00 (*0-8191-9755-6*) U Pr of Amer.

Bube, Richard H., jt. auth. see Redfield, David.

Bubeck, Diemut. Care, Gender, & Justice. 290p. 1995. text 49.95 (*0-19-827990-6*) OUP.

Bubeck, Mark. Preparing for Battle: A Spiritual Warfare Workbook. 1999. pap. 12.99 (*0-8024-9082-4*) Moody.

— Winning Spiritual Victories: Preparing for Battles with the Enemy. (Believer's Life System Ser.). 48p. 1997. ring bd. 5.99 (*0-8024-2682-4*) Moody.

Bubeck, Mark I. El Adversario. Orig. Title: The Adversary. (SPA.). 160p. 1988. pap. 6.99 (*0-8254-1093-2*, Edit Portavoz) Kregel.

— The Adversary. pap. 10.99 (*0-8024-0143-0*, 74) Moody.

— Overcoming the Adversary. pap. 9.99 (*0-8024-0333-6*, 241) Moody.

— Raising Lambs among Wolves: How to Protect Your Children from Evil. LC 97-200788. 256p. 1997. pap. 11.99 (*0-8024-7194-3*, 262) Moody.

— The Rise of Fallen Angels: Victory over the Adversary Through Spiritual Renewal. LC 96-207805. pap. 11.99 (*0-8024-7189-7*, 273) Moody.

— Spiritual Warfare Prayers. 18p. 1997. pap. 12.50 (*0-8024-7132-3*, 365) Moody.

— Venciendo al Adversario. Orig. Title: Overcoming the Adversary. (SPA.). 160p. 1992. pap. 6.99 (*0-8254-1094-0*, Edit Portavoz) Kregel.

Bubel, Andreas. Microstructure & Function of Cells: Electron Micrographs of Cell Ultrastructure. 280p. 1989. text 69.95 (*0-470-21176-8*) P-H.

Bubel, Frank. Herodot-Bibliographie, 1980-1988. (Altertumswissenschaftliche Texte und Studien: Bd. 20). (GER.). vi, 64p. 1991. 20.00 (*3-487-09507-6*) G Olms Pubs.

Bubel, Mike & Bubel, Nancy. Root Cellaring: Natural Cold Storage of Fruits & Vegetables. 2nd ed. Art, Pam, ed. LC 91-55012. (Illus.). 320p. 1991. pap. 14.95 (*0-88266-703-3*, Garden Way Pub) Storey Bks.

— Root Cellaring: Natural Cold Storage of Fruits & Vegetables. 2nd ed. Art, Pam, ed. LC 91-55012. (Illus.). 320p. 1991. 21.95 (*0-88266-740-8*, Garden Way Pub) Storey Bks.

Bubel, N. Braided Rugs. 1983. pap. 2.95 (*0-88266-177-9*, Storey Pub) Storey Bks.

— Grow Super Salad Greens. 1983. pap. 2.95 (*0-88266-285-6*, Storey Pub) Storey Bks.

Bubel, Nancy. Fifty-Two Weekend Garden Projects. (Illus.). 368p. (Orig.). 1992. 25.95 (*0-87857-963-X*, 01-140-0) Rodale Pr Inc.

— The New Seed Starter's Handbook. LC 87-27698. 416p. 1988. pap. 15.95 (*0-87857-752-1*) Rodale Pr Inc.

Bubel, Nancy, jt. auth. see Allen, Oliver E.

Bubel, Nancy, jt. auth. see Bubel, Mike.

Bubenheimer, Glen, jt. auth. see Durbal, Bryan.

Bubenheimer, Ulrich. Thomas Muntzer: Herkunft und Bildung. LC 89-31185. (Studies in Medieval & Reformation Thought: Vol. XLVI). (GER.). xx, 359p. 1989. 110.50 (*90-04-08850-4*) Brill Academic Pubs.

Bubenik, A. B., jt. ed. see Bubenik, G. A.

Bubenik, G. A. & Bubenik, A. B., eds. Horns, Pronghorns, & Antlers: Evolution, Morphology, Physiology, & Social Significance. (Illus.). 552p. 1990. 175.95 (*0-387-97176-9*) Spr-Verlag.

Bubenik, Vit. Hellenistic & Roman Greece As a Sociolinguistic Area. LC 88-7598. (Current Issues in Linguistic Theory Ser.: Vol. 57). xvi, 331p. (C). 1989. 94.00 (*90-272-3551-1*) J Benjamins Pubng Co.

— Structure & Development of Middle Indo-Aryan Dialects. (C). 1996. 23.00 (*81-208-1317-0*, Pub. by Motilal Bnarsidass) S Asia.

Bubenik, Vit, jt. auth. see Hewson, John.

Bubenik, Vit, jt. auth. see Ratcliffe, Robert R.

B

B

Bubenzer, Donald & West, John. Counseling Couples. (Counselling in Action Ser.: Vol. 8). 160p. (C). 1993. text 49.95 (0-8039-8420-0); pap. text 21.50 (0-8039-8421-9) Sage.

Buber. Que es el Hombre? (Breviarios Ser.). (SPA.). pap. 6.99 (968-16-0246-3, Pub. by Fondo) Continental Bk.

Buber, Edward J., jt. auth. see Karch, Robert R.

Buber, Martin. A Believing Humanism: My Testament, 1902-1965. 2nd ed. LC 90-32330. 264p. (C). 1990. pap. 15.00 (0-391-03654-8) Humanities.

— Between Man & Man. 2nd ed. Smith, Ronald G., tr. LC 85-6702. 229p. 1985. pap. 12.00 (0-02-084210-4) Macmillan.

— Chinese Tales: Zhuangzi: Sayings & Parables & Chinese Ghost & Love Stories. Page, Alex, tr. from GER. LC 90-20517. 240p. (C). 1991. pap. 15.00 (0-391-03699-8) Humanities.

***Buber, Martin.** Chinese Tales: Zhuangzi: Sayings & Parables & Chinese Ghost & Love Stories. LC 98-53301. 1998. write for info. (1-57392-612-4); pap. write for info. (1-57392-615-9) Prometheus Bks.

Buber, Martin. Eclipse de Dios. (Breviarios Ser.). (SPA.). pap. 7.99 (968-16-4611-8, Pub. by Fondo) Continental Bk.

***Buber, Martin.** Eclipse of God: Studies in the Relation Between Religion & Philosophy. LC 98-54409. 148p. 1998. 16.95 (1-57392-401-6, Humanity Bks) Prometheus Bks.

Buber, Martin. Eclipse of God: Studies in the Relation Between Religion & Philosophy. LC 87-19594. 168p. (C). 1988. reprint ed. pap. 15.00 (0-391-03533-9) Humanities.

— First Buber: Youthful Zionist Writings of Martin Buber. Schmidt, Gilya G., ed. & tr. by. from GER. LC 99-20625. 256p. 1999. pap. text 19.95 (0-8156-0595-1) Syracuse U Pr.

— Gog & Magog: A Novel. LC 98-51564. 320p. 1999. pap. 17.95 (0-8156-0589-7) Syracuse U Pr.

— Good & Evil. 143p. (C). 1980. pap. text 13.40 (0-02-316280-5, Macmillan Coll) P-H.

— Hasidism & Modern Man. LC 87-22907. 264p. (C). 1988. reprint ed. pap. 19.95 (0-391-03550-9) Humanities.

***Buber, Martin.** I & Thou. (Illus.). 128p. 2000. 21.50 (0-7432-0133-7) Free Pr.

Buber, Martin. I & Thou. Smith, Ronald G., tr. 182p. 1998. pap. 19.95 (0-567-22060-5, Pub. by T & T Clark) Bks Intl VA.

— Israel & the World: Essays in a Time of Crisis. LC 97-15822. 266p. 1997. pap. 16.95 (0-8156-0481-5) Syracuse U Pr.

— Kingship of God. 2nd ed. Scheimann, Richard, tr. from GER. LC 90-32309. 228p. (C). 1990. pap. 15.00 (0-391-03658-0) Humanities.

— The Knowledge of Man: Selected Essays. LC 88-12825. (Illus.). 192p. (Orig.). (C). 1988. pap. 15.00 (0-391-03546-0) Humanities.

— A Land of Two Peoples. Mendes-Flohr, Paul R., ed. & comment by. 1994. 28.50 (0-8446-6722-6) Peter Smith.

— The Legend of the Baal-Shem. Friedman, Maurice, tr. LC 94-42486. (Mythos Ser.). 223p. 1995. pap. text 13.95 (0-691-04389-2, Pub. by Princeton U Pr) Cal Prin Full Svc.

— Martin Buber's Ten Rungs: Collected Hasidic Sayings. 126p. 1995. pap. 6.95 (0-8065-1593-7, Citadel Pr) Carol Pub Group.

— Moses: The Revelation & the Covenant. LC 87-26169. 232p. (C). 1988. reprint ed. pap. 17.50 (0-391-03547-9) Humanities.

— On Intersubjectivity & Cultural Creativity. LC 91-47187. (Heritage of Sociology Ser.). 272p. 1992. lib. bdg. 44.00 (0-226-07805-1) U Ch Pr.

— On Intersubjectivity & Cultural Creativity. LC 91-47187. (Heritage of Sociology Ser.). 272p. 1992. pap. text 25.00 (0-226-07807-8) U Ch Pr.

***Buber, Martin.** On the Bible: Eighteen Studies. (Martin Buber Library). 224p. 2000. pap. 22.95 (0-8156-2840-4) Syracuse U Pr.

Buber, Martin. On Zion. 194p. 1993. pap. 19.95 (0-567-29129-4, Pub. by T & T Clark) Bks Intl VA.

— On Zion: The History of an Idea. Godman, Stanley, tr. LC 97-15823. xxii, 165p. 1997. pap. 16.95 (0-8156-0482-3) Syracuse U Pr.

— The Origin & Meaning of Hasidism. LC 87-26192. 264p. (C). 1988. reprint ed. pap. 19.95 (0-391-03549-5) Humanities.

— Paths in Utopia. Hull, R. F. C., tr. LC 96-32897. (Martin Buber Library). 152p. 1996. reprint ed. pap. 15.95 (0-8156-0421-1, BUBUP) Syracuse U Pr.

— Pointing the Way. LC 77-134063. (Essay Index Reprint Ser.). 1977. 18.95 (0-8369-2149-6) Ayer.

— Pointing the Way: Collected Essays. 2nd ed. LC 90-32310. 264p. (C). 1990. pap. 15.95 (0-391-03655-6) Humanities.

— The Tales of Rabbi Nachman. LC 87-22906. (C). 1988. reprint ed. pap. 17.50 (0-391-03548-7) Humanities.

— Tales of the Hasidim. LC 90-52921. 736p. 1991. pap. 20.00 (0-8052-0995-6) Pantheon.

— The Way of Man: According to the Teaching of Hasidism. 44p. 1995. pap. 5.95 (0-8065-0024-7, Citadel Pr) Carol Pub Group.

— The Way of Man, 1959. 1960. 4.00 (0-87574-106-1) Pendle Hill.

Buber, Martin, ed. On Judaism. 272p. 1996. pap. 13.00 (0-8052-1050-4) Schocken.

Buber, Martin & Agassi, Judith B. Martin Buber on Psychology & Psychotherapy: Essays, Letters, & Dialogue. LC 98-37835. 1998. 45.00 (0-8156-0582-X) Syracuse U Pr.

***Buber, Martin & Schmidt, Gilya G.** The First Buber: Youthful Zionist Writings of Martin Buber. LC 99-20625. (Martin Buber Library). 256p. 1999. 45.00 (0-8156-0575-7) Syracuse U Pr.

Buber, Martin, et al. I & Thou. Kaufman, Walter & Smith, S. G., trs. LC 72-123845. (Hudson River Editions Ser.). 188p. 1978. 35.00 (0-684-15575-3, Scribners Ref) Mac Lib Ref.

— I & Thou. Kaufman, Walter & Smith, S. G., trs. LC 72-123845. 192p. 1971. pap. 10.00 (0-684-71725-5, Hudson Rvr Edtn) S&S Trade.

Buber-Neumann, Margarete. Milena. Manheim, Ralph, tr. LC 87-28718. (GER.). 213p. 1988. 18.95 (0-8050-0748-2) Seaver Bks.

— Milena: The Tragic Story of Kafka's Great Love. Manheim, Ralph, tr. from GER. LC 97-26760. 213p. 1997. pap. 12.45 (1-55970-390-3, Pub. by Arcade Pub Inc) Time Warner.

Buber, Rafael. Knowledge of Man. (Illus.). 1988. pap. 16.95 (1-57392-442-3) Prometheus Bks.

Bubic, S. Dictionary of Economic Terms. (CRO, ENG & SER.). 1048p. 1975. 95.00 (0-8288-5838-1, M9699) Fr & Eur.

Bubien, Rosemary S., jt. auth. see Kay, G. Neal.

Bubik, Roland. Geschichte der Marketing - Theorie: Historische Einfuhrung in die Marketing - Lehre. (Europaische Hochschulschriften: Reihe 5: Bd. 1889). (GER., Illus.). 231p. 1996. pap. 44.95 (3-631-50036-X) P Lang Pubng.

Bubis, Gerald B., ed. Serving the Jewish Family. 35.00 (0-87068-439-6) Ktav.

***Bubka, Bob.** Ryder Cup: Golf's Greatest Event. 1999. pap. 13.00 (0-609-80562-2, Crown) Crown Pub Group.

Bubka, Bob & Clavin, Tom. The Ryder Cup. LC 99-12131. 256p. 1999. 24.00 (0-609-60404-X) Random Hse Value.

***Bubley, Russ.** Randomized Algorithms: Approximation, Generation & Counting. LC 00-34426. (Distinguished Dissertations Ser.). 2000. write for info. (1-85233-325-1) Spr-Verlag.

Bublitz. Intermediate Accounting. 5th ed. (C). 1997. text. write for info. (0-03-097001-6) Harcourt Coll Pubs.

Bublitz, Ruth M. One-Drous Light. 128p. (Orig.). 1985. pap. 5.95 (0-87516-556-7) DeVorss.

Bublitz, Siv, ed. see Pilcher, Rosamunde.

Bublitz, Wolfram. Supportive Fellow Speakers & Cooperative Conversations: Discourse Topics & Topical Actions, Participant Roles & 'Recipientaction' in a Particular Type of Everyday Conversation. LC 88-10119. xii, 308p. (C). 1988. 83.00 (1-55619-047-6) J Benjamins Pubng Co.

Bublitz, Wolfram, et al, eds. Coherence in Spoken & Written Discourse: How to Create It & How to Describe It. Selected Papers From the International Workshop on Coherence, Augsburg, 24-27 April 1997. LC 99-28183. (Pragmatics & Beyond New Ser.: Vol. 63). xiv, 300p. 1999. lib. bdg. 79.00 (1-55619-941-4) J Benjamins Pubng Co.

Bubmann, Klaus. Sculpture Projects in Munster, 1997. 2nd ed. 540p. 1997. 65.00 (3-7757-0667-4, Pub. by Gerd Hatje) Dist Art Pubs.

Bubna, Paul F. Second Corinthians: Ministry: God's Work in Me for the Good of Others. LC 93-72165. (Deeper Life Pulpit Commentary Ser.). 237p. (Orig.). 1993. pap. 10.99 (0-87509-538-0) Chr Pubns.

Bubna, Paul F. & Bailey, Keith M. Christ & the Crisis. (Christian Living Ser.). 1995. pap. 1.59 (0-87509-622-0) Chr Pubns.

Bubnack, Sue & Hyde, Joyce L., eds. Only in California: Recipes Which Capture the Spirit & Lifestyles Which Make California Unique. (Illus.). 272p. 1989. 17.95 (0-317-93905-X) CHSC.

Bubner, Rudiger, ed. German Idealist Philosophy. LC 97-217930. 432p. 1997. reprint ed. pap. 13.95 (0-14-044660-5) Viking Penguin.

Bubnis, Michelle, jt. auth. see Valentine, Lynn.

Bubniuk, Irena. Preliminary Piano Work for the Student of Music, Set. (Illus.). (J). (gr. k up). 1992. student ed. 75.00 (1-882596-00-5) BML.

— Preliminary Piano Work for the Student of Music, Vol. 1. (Illus.). 159p. (J). (gr. k up). 1992. student ed. write for info. (1-882596-01-3); student ed., spiral bd. write for info. (1-882596-02-1) BML.

Bubnov, A. D., jt. auth. see Golovin, Nikolai N.

Bubnov, V. A. Convective Heat & Mass Transfer in an Insulated Trailing Swirl (Theory & Design of Vortex Equipment) Shakhlevich, Kirill, tr. LC 98-9167. 247p. 1998. 99.00 (1-56700-102-5) Begell Hse.

Bubnov, Yu N., jt. auth. see Mikhailov, B. M.

Bubnova, Nina C. & Way, Lucan A. Trends in Financing Regional Expenditures in Transition Economies: The Case of Ukraine. LC 97-37548. (Discussion Paper Ser.: No. 378). 64p. 1998. pap. 22.00 (0-8213-4064-6, 14064) World Bank.

Buboltz-Bodle, Debbie. Philip Simon Miller: Butcher, Banker & Benefactor: His Life & Legacy in Douglas County, Colorado. LC 98-46446. 1998. write for info. (0-929526-84-8) Double B Pubns.

Bubolz, George C. Father Julius & Mother Emilie: A Personal Biography of Midwestern Pioneers. LC 75-329401. (Exposition-Lochinvar Book Ser.). (Illus.). 196p. reprint ed. pap. 60.80 (0-608-30143-4, 201073500071) Bks Demand.

Bubolz, Gordon A. The Land of the Fox: Saga of Outagamie County, Wisconsin. (Illus.). 302p. 1994. reprint ed. lib. bdg. 32.50 (0-8328-3866-7) Higginson Bk Co.

Bubolz, Margaret M. & Sontag, M. Suzanne. Families on Small Farms: Case Studies in Human Ecology. 375p. 1996. 45.00 (0-87013-409-4) Mich St U Pr.

Bubriski, Kevin, photos by. Power Places of Kathmandu: Hindu & Buddhist Holy Sites in the Sacred Valley of Nepal. (Illus.). 144p. 1995. 39.95 (0-89281-540-X) Inner Tradit.

Bubser, Reinhold K. First Year German. (C). 1996. text. write for info. (0-03-004757-9) Harcourt Coll Pubs.

Bubulka, Grace. Beyond This Reality: A Personal Account of the Near Death Experience. 114p. (Orig.). 1995. pap. 11.95 (1-884995-03-9) Word Dancer.

Buby, Bertrand. Mary of Galilee: The Marian Heritage of the Early Church. (Trilogy of Marian Studies: Vol. 3). 346p. (Orig.). 1996. pap. 19.95 (0-8189-0698-7) Alba.

— Mary of Galilee Vol. 1: Mary in the New Testament. LC 94-10788. (Mary of Galilee Ser.). 193p. 1994. pap. 11.95 (0-8189-0692-8) Alba.

— Mary of Galilee Vol. 2: Woman of Israel Daughter of Zion. 318p. 1995. 17.95 (0-8189-0697-9) Alba.

— Mary of Galilee Vol. 3: The Marian Heritage of the Early Church. 346p. 1997. 39.95 (0-8189-0699-5) Alba.

Buby, Bertrand, tr. see De la Potterie, Ignace.

***Buby, Bertrand A.** A Journey Through Revelation: A Message for the Millennium. LC 99-55451. 176p. 2000. pap. 14.95 (0-8189-0832-7) Alba.

Bucaille, Maurice. The Bible, the Quran & Science. 1989. pap. 14.50 (0-935782-49-4) Kazi Pubns.

— The Bible the Qur'an & Science. 1990. 12.00 (0-685-66736-7, 9) Tahrike Tarsile Quran.

— What Is the Origin of Man? 1992. pap. 14.50 (0-933511-89-2) Kazi Pubns.

***Bucar, Liz.** Caution - Catholic Health Restrictions May Be Hazardous to Your Health: Merger Trends 2. LC 99-490004. 58p. 1999. pap. 7.00 (0-915365-34-0) Cath Free Choice.

— When Catholic & Non-Catholic Hospitals Merge: Reproductive Health Compromised. 68p. 1998. 10.00 (0-915365-33-2) Cath Free Choice.

Bucarelli, Mauro, ed. see Rossini, Gioachino.

Bucaro, Frank C., jt. auth. see O'Connor, Kevin E.

Buccellati, Giorgio & Kelly-Buccellati, Marilyn. Mozan One: The Soundings of the First Two Seasons. LC 87-50698. (Bibliotheca Mesopotamica Ser.: Vol. 20). (Illus.). 164p. 1988. text 31.00 (0-89003-195-9); pap. text 22.00 (0-89003-194-0) Undena Pubns.

Buccellati, Giorgio & Knudstad, J. Terqa Preliminary Reports No. 10: The Fourth Season, Introduction & the Stratigraphic Record. (Bibliotheca Mesopotamica Ser.: Vol. 10). (Illus.). 130p. 1979. 45.00 (0-89003-042-1) Undena Pubns.

Buccellati, Giorgio & Knudstad, J. Terqa Preliminary Reports No. 10: The Fourth Season, Introduction & the Stratigraphic Record. (Bibliotheca Mesopotamica Ser.: Vol. 10). (Illus.). 130p. 1979. pap. 32.00 (0-89003-043-X) Undena Pubns.

Buccellati, Giorgio, jt. auth. see Rouault, Oliver.

Buccellato, Steve, ed. see Simonson, Walter & Simonson, Louise.

Buccheri, R., et al. The Many Faces of Neutron Stars. LC 98-28190. (NATO ASI Ser.). 608p. 1998. 80.00 (0-7923-5194-0) Kluwer Academic.

Buccheri, R., jt. ed. see Morfill, G. E.

***Bucchi, Kenneth C.** Inside Job: Deep Undercover As a Corporate Spy. LC 99-44302. 336p. 1999. 23.95 (1-883955-28-9, Pub. by Penmarin Bks) ACCESS Pubs Network.

— Operation Pseudo Miranda: A Veteran of the CIA Drug Wars Tells All. 350p. 2000. 23.95 (1-883955-17-3, Pub. by Penmarin Bks) Midpt Trade.

Bucchi, Massimiano. Science & the Media: Alternative Routes in Scientific Communication. LC 98-9973. (Studies in Science, Technology, & Society). xii, 195 p. (C). 1998. 85.00 (0-415-18952-7) Routledge.

Bucchianeri, Virgil A. St. Mary's in the Mountains. (Illus.). 52p. 1984. pap. 5.95 (0-940936-01-1) Gold Hill.

Bucchioni, Eugene, jt. auth. see Cordasco, Francesco.

Bucci, jt. ed. see Hudak, Jr.

Bucci, Al. A Perfect War. LC 97-185708. 320p. 1997. pap. 20.00 (1-886094-65-9) Chicago Spectrum.

Bucci, Federico. Albert Kahn: Architect of Ford. LC 93-36693. (Illus.). 186p. 1994. 24.95 (1-878271-84-9) Princeton Arch.

— Small Objects: Rassegna 71. (Rassegna Ser.: Vol. 71). 1999. pap. 35.00 (88-85322-29-8, Pub. by CIPIA) Princeton Arch.

Bucci, Federico, ed. Company Towns. (Rassegna Ser.: No. 70). (Illus.). 110p. 1997. pap. 39.95 (88-85322-28-X) Spr-Verlag.

Bucci, Luke. Healing Arthritis the Natural Way: The Breakthrough Program for Reversing Arthritis Using Nutrition & Supplements. LC 97-21101. 288p. (Orig.). 1997. pap. 16.99 (1-56530-277-X, Pub. by Summit TX) BookWorld.

— Pain Free: The Definitive Guide to Healing Arthritis, Low-Back Pain, & Sports Injuries Through Nutrition & Supplements. LC 94-47120. 276p. 1995. 24.95 (1-56530-161-7) Summit TX.

Bucci, Luke R. Nutrients As Ergogenic Aids for Sports & Exercise. 192p. 1993. boxed set 104.95 (0-8493-4223-6, QP176) CRC Pr.

— Nutrients as Ergogenic Aids for Sports & Exercise. 2nd ed. (Nutrition in Exercise & Sport Ser.). 1999. 89.95 (0-8493-7922-9) CRC Pr.

— Nutrition Applied to Injury Rehabilitation & Sports Medicine. 304p. 1994. boxed set 131.95 (0-8493-7913-X, 7913) CRC Pr.

Bucci, M. G. Glaucoma: Decision Making in Therapy. LC 96-25619. 350p. 1996. pap. 169.50 (3-540-75021-5) Spr-Verlag.

Bucci, Wilma. Psychoanalysis & Cognitive Science: A Multiple Code Theory. LC 96-52825. (Illus.). 362p. 1997. lib. bdg. 44.00 (1-57230-213-5, 0213) Guilford Pubns.

Buccianti, G., ed. Risk Profiles in Clinical Nephrology. (Contributions to Nephrology Ser.: Vol. 37). (Illus.). x, 202p. 1984. pap. 29.75 (3-8055-3739-5) S Karger.

Bucciarelli, Elizabeth R., jt. ed. see Shirato, Linda.

Bucciarelli, John. Leaders Are Made: A Building Block Approach to Effective Leadership. LC 97-71735. (Illus.). 432p. (C). 1997. 43.00 (1-878398-17-2) Blue Note Pubns.

Bucciarelli, Louis L. Designing Engineers. (Inside Technology Ser.). (Illus.). 230p. 1996. reprint ed. pap. text 12.50 (0-262-52212-8) MIT Pr.

Buccilli, Joseph C. Wise Stuff about Relationships: Spiritual Reflections & Recovery Journal. 1997. pap. text 13.95 (0-9615995-4-5) Recover Comns.

Buccini, Eugene P. & Mullaney, Charles P. Personnel Policies & Procedures for Health Care Facilities: A Manager's Deskbook & Guide. LC 88-36491. 311p. 1989. 89.50 (0-89930-425-7, BPQ, Quorum Bks) Greenwood.

Buccini, Stefania. The Americas in Italian Literature & Culture, 1700-1825. LC 95-8913. 1996. 59.25 (0-271-01418-0) Pa St U Pr.

— The Americas in Italian Literature in the Eighteenth & Early Nineteenth Centuries. Giammanco, Rosanna M., tr. from ITA. LC 95-8913.Tr. of Dilemma Della Grande Atlantide. 1996. 42.50 (0-271-01513-6) Pa St U Pr.

Buccino, Anthony. A Father's Place. LC 91-72299. 154p. 1991. pap. 7.95 (0-9629824-0-7) Cherry Blossom.

— Sister Dressed Me Funny. LC 95-92578. 64p. 1996. pap. 14.95 (0-9629824-1-5) Cherry Blossom.

Buccino, Sharon, et al. Reclaiming Our Heritage: What We Need to Do to Preserve America's National Parks. (Illus.). 100p. 1997. pap. 10.50 (1-893340-06-6) Natl Resources Defense Coun.

Buccione, Andrew, ed. Geriatric Physical Therapy: Principles & Practices. LC 92-49977. 1992. write for info. (0-8016-1960-2) Mosby Inc.

Bucco, Gloria & Hobbs, Ron. Arthritis: Everything You Need to Know about. LC 98-50705. (Natural Pharmacist Ser.). (Illus.). 180p. 2000. pap. 6.99 (0-7615-1556-9) Prima Pub.

Bucco, Martin. An American Tragedy Notes. (Cliffs Notes Ser.). 80p. (Orig.). (C). 1974. pap. text 4.95 (0-8220-0169-1, Cliff) IDG Bks.

— E. W. Howe. LC 77-76322. (Western Writers Ser.: No. 26). 48p. 1977. pap. 4.95 (0-88430-050-1) Boise St U W Writ Ser.

— Main Street: The Revolt of Carol Kennicott. LC 93-7659. (Twayne's Masterwork Studies). 160p. 1993. 23.95 (0-8057-8373-3, Twyne); pap. 13.95 (0-8057-8377-6, Twyne) Mac Lib Ref.

— Western American Literary Criticism. LC 84-70250. (Western Writers Ser.: No. 62). 57p. (Orig.). 1984. pap. 4.95 (0-88430-036-6) Boise St U W Writ Ser.

— Wilbur Daniel Steele. Bowman, Sylvia E., ed. LC 77-161826. (Twayne's United States Authors Ser.). 181p. (C). 1972. 20.95 (0-8290-1708-9) Irvington.

Bucer, Martin. A Briefe Treatise Concerning the Burnynge of Bucer & Phagius at Cambridge. LC 76-57362. (English Experience Ser.: No. 780). 1977. reprint ed. lib. bdg. 30.00 (90-221-0780-9) Walter J Johnson.

— Correspondance Vol. IV: 1527-1529, Publie Par C. Krieger et J. Rott. (Studies in Medieval & Reformation Thought: No.56). (FRE.). xxxvi, 444p. 1995. 161.50 (90-04-10369-4) Brill Academic Pubs.

— A Treatise How by the Worde of God, Christian Mens Almose Oght to Be Distributed. LC 76-57360. (English Experience Ser.). 1977. reprint ed. lib. bdg. 10.00 (90-221-0779-5) Walter J Johnson.

Bucerra, Patricia. Colors. (Water Babies Ser.). 1999. 6.99 (0-439-04774-9) Scholastic Inc.

— The Complete Guide to Alabama Weather. (Illus.). 112p. 1998. pap. 10.95 (1-878561-59-6) Seacoast AL.

— Counting. (Water Babies Ser.). (J). 1999. 6.99 (0-439-04775-7) Scholastic Inc.

Bucerzan, D., tr. see Ogden, Thomas H.

Buch, A. Fatigue Strength Calculation. 478p. 1988. text 108.00 (0-87849-536-3, Pub. by Trans T Pub) Enfield Pubs NH.

***Buch, A.** Pure Metals Properties: A Scientific & Technical Handbook. 306p. 1999. 85.00 (0-87170-637-7, 06815G) ASM.

Buch, A., ed. Fatigue Data Handbook. (Illus.). 352p. (C). 1998. text 99.50 (0-87849-803-6, Pub. by Trans T Pub) Enfield Pubs NH.

Buch, Benjamin H. Gerhard Richter. Marian Goodman Gallery Staff, ed. (Illus.). (Orig.). 1993. pap. text. write for info. (0-944219-11-X) M Goodman Gallery.

Buch, Claudia M. Creating Efficient Banking Systems: Theory & Evidence from Western Europe. 260p. (C). 1996. text 86.50 (0-472-10830-1, 10830) U of Mich Pr.

— Foreign Capital & Economic Transformation: Risks & Benefits of Free Capital Flows. 1999. 72.50 (3-16-147132-6) JCB Mohr.

Buch, David. Dance Music from the Ballets De Cour, 1575-1651: Historical Commentary, Source Study, & Transcriptions from the Philidor Manuscripts. (Dance & Music Ser.: No. 7). 1994. lib. bdg. 54.00 (0-945193-33-5) Pendragon NY.

Buch, David J., ed. see Gaultier, Denis.

Buch, Hans C. The Wedding at Port-Au-Prince. Manheim, Ralph, tr. 304p. 1986. 17.95 (0-15-195598-0) Harcourt.

Buch, Jane. Complete Testing Program for Fitness & Nutrition: The Winning Combination. 3rd ed. Bard, Tate, ed. LC 84-51951. (Illus.). 60p. (YA). (gr. 7-12). 1993. teacher ed. 6.66 incl. disk (0-914127-48-9) Univ Class.

— Fitness & Nutrition: The Winning Combination. 3rd ed. Bard, Tate, ed. LC 84-51951. (My School Ser.). (Illus.). 160p. (YA). (gr. 7-12). 1993. pap., student ed. 7.60 (0-914127-46-2) Univ Class.

— Teacher's Planning Guide for Fitness & Nutrition: The Winning Combination. 3rd rev. ed. Bard, Tate, ed. LC 84-51951. (Illus.). 160p. 1994. 18.27 (0-914127-18-7) Univ Class.

An Asterisk (*) at the beginning of an entry indicates that the title is appearing for the first time.

***Buch, Linda & Snider-Copley, Beth Anne.** Commercial Break: The Complete Couch Potato's Guide to Fitness. large type ed. (Illus.). 162p. 1999. pap. 21.95 (*0-9677136-0-9*) Balance Fitness Bks.
Buch, M., jt. ed. see Siebert, W.
Buchachenko, Anatoly L. Stable Radicals. Turton, C. Nigel & Turton, Tatiana I., trs. from RUS. LC 65-900. (Illus.). 188p. reprint ed. pap. 58.30 (*0-608-30037-3*, 202067000018) Bks Demand.
Buchachenko, Anatoly L. & Frankevich, E. L. Chemical Generation & Reception of Radio & Microwaves. 180p. 1993. 99.95 (*0-471-18859-X*) Wiley.
Buchachenko, Anatoly L. & Frankevich, Eugene L. Chemical Generation & Reception of Radio & Microwaves. LC 93-28335. 1993. 65.00 (*1-56081-630-9*, Wiley-VCH) Wiley.
Buchachenko, Anatoly L., jt. auth. see Emanuel, N. M.
Buchal, James L. The Great Salmon Hoax: An Eyewitness Account of the Collapse of Science & Law & the Triumph of Politics in Salmon Recovery. unabridged ed. LC 97-94732. (Illus.). 382p. 1997. pap. 14.95 (*0-9661951-0-8*) Iconoclast Pub.
***Buchan.** Perfect Love. 1999. mass mkt. write for info. (*0-312-97152-4*) St Martin.
Buchan. Three Great Thrillers. 1994. 12.00 (*0-19-521094-8*) OUP.
Buchan, Alastair, ed. A World of Nuclear Power? LC 66-29073. 1966. 3.95 (*0-317-02972-X*, 95875); pap. 1.95 (*0-317-02973-8*, 96874) Am Assembly.
Buchan, Alex. Conditional Surrender. LC 96-25918. 44p. (Orig.). 1996. pap. 5.00 (*0-88734-390-2*) Players Pr.
Buchan, Bette A. & Vanzandt, Zark. Lessons for Life: A Complete Career Development Curriculum for Busy Educators. LC 97-28088. (Illus.). 244p. 1997. pap. text 28.95 (*0-87628-514-0*) Ctr Appl Res.
Buchan, Carole, ed. The Catch: Prize-Winning Stories by Women. LC 96-72580. 183p. 1998. pap. 14.99 (*1-85242-573-3*) Serpents Tail.
Buchan, David. Europe: The Strange Superpower. 189p. 1993. 72.95 (*1-85521-441-5*, Pub. by Dartmth Pub); pap. 35.95 (*1-85521-439-3*, Pub. by Dartmth Pub) Ashgate Pub Co.
Buchan, Elizabeth. Beatrix Potter: The Story of the Creator of Peter Rabbit. 80p. (J). (gr. 3 up). 1998. 12.99 (*0-7232-4427-8*, F Warne) Peng Put Young Read.
— Daughters of the Storm. large type ed. 700p. 1997. pap. 22.95 (*0-7862-1063-X*) Thorndike Pr.
Buchan, Elizabeth. Perfect Love. LC 99-25323. 1999. text 24.95 (*0-312-20568-6*) St Martin.
***Buchan, Elizabeth.** Perfect Love. 448p. 2000. mass mkt. 6.99 (*0-312-97426-4*) St Martin.
Buchan, Glenn C. U. S. Nuclear Strategy for the Post-Cold War Era. LC 94-11713. 1994. pap. 15.00 (*0-8330-1531-1*, MR-420-RC) Rand Corp.
Buchan, Greg, jt. auth. see Ray, Blaine.
Buchan, Jack. Step-by-Step Art School: Landscape. 1993. 14.98 (*1-55521-828-8*) Bk Sales Inc.
Buchan, James. Davy Chadwick. large type ed. 1990. 27.99 (*0-7089-2150-7*) Ulverscroft.
— Frozen Desire: The Psychology of Money. LC 97-16107. 256p. 1997. text 25.00 (*0-374-15909-2*) FS&G.
— The Golden Plough: A Novel. LC 94-24630. 240p. 1995. text 21.00 (*0-374-16873-3*) FS&G.
— High Latitudes: A Romance. LC 96-17250. 192p. 1996. text 22.00 (*0-374-16999-3*) FS&G.
— Jeddah Old & New. (Illus.). 1980. 45.00 (*0-86685-517-3*) Intl Bk Ctr.
— A Parish of Rich Women. LC 98-27440. 192p. 1998. pap. 13.95 (*1-56924-692-0*) Marlowe & Co.
***Buchan, James.** The Persian Bride: A Novel. (Illus.). 352p. 2000. 23.00 (*0-618-06740-X*) HM.
Buchan, James, et al, eds. Nurses Work: An Analysis of the U. K. Nursing Labour Market. LC 98-771462. (Developments in Nursing & Health Care Ser.). 160p. 1998. text 55.95 (*1-84014-386-X*, Pub. by Ashgate Pub) Ashgate Pub Co.
Buchan, James, et al. Jeddah Old & New. 3rd ed. (Illus.). 144p. 1982. boxed set 49.95 (*0-905743-64-4*, Pub. by Stacey Intl) Intl Bk Ctr.
Buchan, John. The Blanket of the Dark. 264p. 1994. pap. 13.95 (*1-873631-41-3*, Pub. by B&W Pub) Firebird Dist.
— Canadian Occasions. LC 70-90618. (Essay Index Reprint Ser.). 1977. 21.95 (*0-8369-1275-6*) Ayer.
— Castle Gay. LC 93-28809. 1993. pap. 7.00 (*0-7509-0483-6*, Pub. by Sutton Pub Ltd) Intl Pubs Mktg.
— Comments & Characters. LC 79-104999. (Essay Index Reprint Ser.). 1977. 30.95 (*0-8369-1453-8*) Ayer.
— The Courts of the Morning. 256p. 1993. pap. 16.95 (*1-873631-20-0*, Pub. by B&W Pub) Firebird Dist.
— The Dancing Floor. Deegan, Marilyn, ed. LC 96-31079. (World's Classics Ser.). (Illus.). 268p. 1997. pap. write for info. (*0-19-283287-5*) OUP.
— The Far Islands. (Illus.). 1984. 17.00 (*0-937986-68-2*) D M Grant.
— The Four Adventures of Richard Hannay: The Thirty-Nine Steps; Greenmantle; Mr. Standfast; the Three Hostages. 688p. 1988. pap. 20.95 (*0-87923-871-2*) Godine.
— The Free Fishers. 263p. 1994. pap. 13.95 (*1-873631-32-4*, Pub. by B&W Pub) Firebird Dist.
— The Gap in the Curtain. 256p. 1992. pap. 16.95 (*1-873631-09-X*, Pub. by B&W Pub) Firebird Dist.
— Greenmantle. lib. bdg. 20.95 (*0-8488-0925-4*) Amereon Ltd.
— Greenmantle. Macdonald, Kate, ed. 320p. 1999. pap. 8.95 (*0-19-283684-6*) OUP.
— Greenmantle. (Classics Library). 225p. 1998. pap. 3.95 (*1-85326-204-8*, 2048WW, Pub. by Wrdsworth Edits) NTC Contemp Pub Co.
— A History of the Great War, 4 vols. 176.95 (*0-405-13279-4*) Ayer.
— The History of the South African Forces in France. (Great War Ser.: No. 21). (Illus.). 404p. reprint ed. 39.95 (*0-89839-178-4*) Battery Pr.
— Homilies & Recreations. LC 73-86737. (Essay Index Reprint Ser.). 1977. 21.95 (*0-8369-1172-5*) Ayer.
— Huntingtower. 199p. 1993. pap. 11.95 (*1-873631-19-7*, Pub. by B&W Pub) Firebird Dist.
— Huntingtower. Stonehouse, Ann F., ed. (The World's Classics Ser.). (Illus.). 272p. 1997. pap. 8.95 (*0-19-283229-8*) OUP.
— Huntingtower. Stonehouse, Ann F., ed. & intro. by. (Oxford World's Classics Ser.). (Illus.). 260p. 2000. pap. 9.95 (*0-19-283721-4*) OUP.
— Huntingtower. LC 93-20802. 1993. 7.00 (*0-7509-0484-4*, Pub. by Sutton Pub Ltd) Intl Pubs Mktg.
— Huntingtower. 316p. reprint ed. lib. bdg. 23.95 (*0-89190-244-9*, Rivercity Pr) Amereon Ltd.
— The Island of Sheep. 22.95 (*0-8488-0926-2*) Amereon Ltd.
— The Island of Sheep. Duncan, Ian, ed. LC 97-2941. (World's Classics Ser.). (Illus.). 268p. 1997. pap. write for info. (*0-19-282433-3*) OUP.
— John Burnet of Barns. 293p. 1994. pap. 13.95 (*1-873631-31-6*, Pub. by B&W Pub) Firebird Dist.
***Buchan, John.** John Burnet of Barns. 252p. 2000. pap. 9.95 (*0-594-01332-1*) Eighth Hundrd.
Buchan, John. John Burnet of Barns: A Romance. (BCL1-PR English Literature Ser.). 317p. 1992. reprint ed. lib. bdg. 89.00 (*0-7812-7467-2*) Rprt Serv.
— John Macnab. 22.95 (*0-8488-0434-1*) Amereon Ltd.
— John Macnab. 248p. 1989. mass mkt. 3.95 (*0-88184-497-7*) Carroll & Graf.
— John Macnab. Daniell, David, ed. & intro. by. (Illus.). 276p. (C). 1994. pap. (*0-19-282935-1*) OUP.
— John MacNab. (Classics Library). 208p. 1998. pap. 3.95 (*1-85326-296-X*, 296XWW, Pub. by Wrdsworth Edits) NTC Contemp Pub Co.
***Buchan, John.** The Leithen Stories: The Power House - John Macnab - Dancing Floor - Sick Heart River. 2000. pap. 16.00 (*0-86241-995-6*, Pub. by Canongate Books) Interlink Pub.
Buchan, John. A Lost Lady of Old Years. 213p. 1995. pap. 13.95 (*1-873631-42-1*, Pub. by B&W Pub) Firebird Dist.
— The Marquis of Montrose: Prion Lost Treasures. 325p. 1997. pap. 14.95 (*1-85375-224-X*) Trafalgar.
***Buchan, John.** The Massacre of Glencoe. 176p. 1999. pap. 40.00 (*1-86227-062-7*, Pub. by Spellmnt Pubs) St Mut.
Buchan, John. Men & Deeds. LC 69-17567. (Essay Index Reprint Ser.). 1977. 20.95 (*0-8369-0065-0*) Ayer.
— Midwinter. 1988. reprint ed. lib. bdg. 49.00 (*0-7812-0467-4*) Rprt Serv.
— Midwinter. 1971. reprint ed. 59.00 (*0-403-00878-6*) Scholarly.
— Mr. Standfast. 19.95 (*0-8488-0927-0*) Amereon Ltd.
— Mr. Standfast. (Classics Library). 400p. 1998. pap. 3.95 (*1-85326-225-0*, 2250WW, Pub. by Wrdsworth Edits) NTC Contemp Pub Co.
— Mr. Standfast. LC 77-144916. 374p. 1928. reprint ed. 69.00 (*0-403-00879-4*) Scholarly.
— Mister Standfast. 1988. reprint ed. lib. bdg. 69.00 (*0-7812-0165-9*) Rprt Serv.
— Pilgrim's Way. (Illus.). 352p. 1984. pap. 10.95 (*0-88184-107-2*) Carroll & Graf.
— Pilgrim's Way: An Essay in Recollection. LC 76-6591. (BCL Ser. II). reprint ed. 41.50 (*0-404-15278-3*) AMS Pr.
— Prester John. LC 75-131650. (Illus.). 1970. 65.00 (*0-403-00537-X*) Scholarly.
— Prester John. 1988. reprint ed. lib. bdg. 49.00 (*0-7812-0160-8*) Rprt Serv.
— A Prince of the Captivity. 236p. 1996. pap. 16.95 (*1-873631-68-5*, Pub. by B&W Pub) Firebird Dist.
— The Runagates Club. (Pocket Classics Ser.). 192p. 1996. pap. 10.95 (*0-7509-1159-X*, Pub. by Sutton Pub Ltd) Intl Pubs Mktg.
***Buchan, John.** Salute to Adventurers. 252p. 2000. pap. 9.95 (*0-594-01498-0*) Eighth Hundrd.
Buchan, John. Sick Heart River. Daniell, David, ed. & intro. by. 254p. (C). 1994. pap. (*0-19-282937-8*) OUP.
— Supernatural Tales. Greig, James C., ed. & intro. by. 356p. 1997. pap. 16.95 (*1-873631-78-2*, Pub. by B&W Pub) Firebird Dist.
— The Thirty-Nine Steps. 1967. pap. text. write for info. (*0-582-53752-5*, Pub. by Addison-Wesley) Longman.
— The Thirty-Nine Steps. (Twelve-Point Ser.). 250p. 1999. lib. bdg. write for info. (*1-58287-102-7*) North Bks.
— The Thirty-Nine Steps. Hedge, Tricia, ed. (Illus.). 80p. 1995. pap. text 5.95 (*0-19-421677-2*) OUP.
***Buchan, John.** The Thirty-Nine Steps. Harvie, Christopher, ed. (Oxford World's Classics Ser.). 160p. 1999. pap. 6.95 (*0-19-283931-4*) OUP.
Buchan, John. The Thirty-Nine Steps. LC 93-26287. (Pocket Classics Ser.). 1993. pap. 4.95 (*0-7509-0482-8*, Pub. by Sutton Pub Ltd) Intl Pubs Mktg.
— The Thirty-Nine Steps. 128p. 1991. pap. 6.95 (*0-14-001130-7*, Penguin Bks) Viking Penguin.
— The Thirty-Nine Steps. (Classics Library). 100p. 1998. pap. 3.95 (*1-85326-080-0*, 0800WW, Pub. by Wrdsworth Edits) NTC Contemp Pub Co.
***Buchan, John.** The Thirty-Nine Steps. large type ed. 400p. 1999. lib. bdg. 24.00 (*0-939495-95-3*) North Bks.
Buchan, John. The Thirty-Nine Steps. large type ed. LC 99-25493. 323p. 1999. 27.95 (*1-56000-497-5*) Transaction Pubs.
— The Thirty-Nine Steps. 1976. reprint ed. lib. bdg. 19.95 (*0-89190-243-0*, Rivercity Pr) Amereon Ltd.
— The Thirty-Nine Steps. 1990. reprint ed. lib. bdg. 21.95 (*0-89968-487-4*) Buccaneer Bks.
— The Thirty-Nine Steps. unabridged ed. (Illus.). 96p. 1994. pap. text 1.50 (*0-486-28201-5*) Dover.
— Three Hostages. (Classics Library). 1998. pap. 3.95 (*1-85326-252-8*, 2528WW, Pub. by Wrdsworth Edits) NTC Contemp Pub Co.
— The Three Hostages. 284p. reprint ed. lib. bdg. 23.95 (*0-89190-245-7*, Rivercity Pr) Amereon Ltd.
— Watcher by the Threshold. 1988. reprint ed. lib. bdg. 59.00 (*0-7812-0013-X*) Rprt Serv.
— Watcher by the Threshold. 1971. reprint ed. 39.00 (*0-403-00880-8*) Scholarly.
— The Watcher by the Threshold & Other Stories: Shorter Scottish Fiction. 544p. 1997. pap. 14.95 (*0-86241-682-5*, Pub. by Canongate Books) Interlink Pub.
— Witch Wood. (Classics Ser.). 306p. 1996. pap. 9.95 (*0-86241-202-1*, Pub. by Canongate Books) Interlink Pub.
— Witch Wood. 289p. 1989. mass mkt. 3.95 (*0-88184-496-9*) Carroll & Graf.
Buchan, John, ed. The Kirk in Scotland. (C). 1990. pap. text 30.00 (*0-85305-275-1*, Pub. by Arthur James) St Mut.
Buchan, John, pref. The Poetry of Neil Munro. 88p. 1989. 12.95 (*0-907590-24-1*, Pub. by SPA Bks Ltd) Seven Hills Bk.
***Buchan, John & Roberts, Dafydd Lloyd.** Pocket Guide to Malignant Melanoma. LC 99-53650. (Illus.). 72p. 2000. pap. 29.95 (*0-632-05421-2*) Blackwell Sci.
Buchan, John, jt. auth. see Stout, Rex.
Buchan, Morag. Women in Plato's Political Theory. LC 99-191553. 224p. (C). (gr. 13). 1998. 70.00 (*0-415-92183-X*) Routledge.
— Women in Plato's Political Theory. Bach, Alice, ed. LC 99-191553. 224p. (C). (gr. 13). 1998. pap. 19.99 (*0-415-92184-8*, D5994) Routledge.
Buchan, P. Bruce, jt. auth. see Daub, Mervin.
Buchan, R. D., et al. Estimating for Builders & Quantity Surveyors. (Illus.). 256p. 1991. pap. 49.95 (*0-7506-0041-1*) Buttrwrth-Heinemann.
Buchan, Ursula. Gardening for Pleasure: A Practical Guide to the Essential Skills. LC 96-45716. (Illus.). 192p. 1997. 35.00 (*0-7892-0279-4*) Abbeville Pr.
— Gardening for Pleasure: A Pratical Guide to the Essential Skills. (Illus.). 192p. 1999. 17.98 (*0-89660-110-2*, Artabras) Abbeville Pr.
— Plants for All Seasons: Beautiful & Versatile Plants That Change Through the Year. 1999. 29.95 (*1-84000-051-1*, Pub. by Mitchell Beazley) Trafalgar.
Buchan, Vivian. Make Presentations with Confidence. 2nd rev. ed. LC 97-10352. (Barron's Business Success Ser.). (Orig.). 1997. pap. text 6.95 (*0-8120-9892-7*) Barron.
Buchan, William & Holt, L. Emmett, Jr. The Physician & Child-Rearing: Two Guides, 1809-1894. 1974. 18.95 (*0-405-03965-4*, 15717) Ayer.
Buchanah & Edmund. Art Attack. 1995. mass mkt. 11.95 (*0-340-58372-X*, Pub. by Hodder & Stought Ltd) Trafalgar.
Buchanan. Cases & Readings in Market Ethics,1998-9. 9. 5th ed. 502p. 1998. pap. text 43.75 (*0-536-01370-5*) Pearson Custom.
— Epilepsy: A Handbook. 1995. pap. text 25.00 (*0-7020-2014-1*, W B Saunders Co) Harcrt Hlth Sci Grp.
Buchanan. Jackson's Way: Andrew Jackson & the People of the Western Waters. 400p. Date not set. 30.00 (*0-471-28253-7*) Wiley.
Buchanan. Just Plain English. (C). 1998. pap. text 26.50 (*0-15-503863-X*, Pub. by Harcourt Coll Pubs) Harcourt.
— Just Plain English. (C). 1998. pap. text 60.50 (*0-15-503864-8*) Harcourt Coll Pubs.
— Limits. 1990. pap., teacher ed. 24.72 (*0-395-43045-3*) HM.
***Buchanan.** Professional Responsibility. 6th ed. 526p. 1999. pap. text 44.00 (*0-536-02763-3*) Pearson Custom.
Buchanan & Chauvin. Expanding Horizons Quikeprint. 626p. 1998. pap. text 40.00 (*0-536-01811-1*) Pearson Custom.
Buchanan, Michaelson. SAPscript. LC 98-55122. 272p. 1999. pap. 59.99 incl. cd-rom (*0-07-134618-X*) McGraw.
Buchanan, A., et al. Organizational Behaviour & Introductory Text. 488p. (C). 1985. 170.00 (*0-7855-5690-7*, Pub. by Inst Pur & Supply) St Mut.
Buchanan, A. W. The Buchanan Book: The Life of Alexander Buchanan. (Illus.). 501p. 1989. reprint ed. pap. 78.00 (*0-8328-0337-5*); reprint ed. lib. bdg. 88.00 (*0-8328-0336-7*) Higginson Bk Co.
***Buchanan, Aimee W., et al.** All That We Are: An Arts & Worship Workbook LC 98-55770. vii, 88 p. 1999. write for info. (*1-57895-025-2*) Bridge Resources.
Buchanan, Allen. Ethics, Efficiency & the Market. LC 84-27525. (Texts in Philosophy Ser.). 152p. (C). 1985. 58.00 (*0-8476-7395-2*); pap. 26.95 (*0-8476-7396-0*) Rowman.
Buchanan, Allen & Brock, Dan W. Deciding for Others: The Ethics of Surrogate Decisionmaking. LC 89-33209. (Studies in Philosophy & Health Policy). 440p. (C). 1990. pap. text 28.95 (*0-521-31196-9*) Cambridge U Pr.
***Buchanan, Allen, et al.** From Chance to Choice: Genetics & Justice. LC 99-24025. (Illus.). 408p. 2000. 29.95 (*0-521-66001-7*) Cambridge U Pr.
Buchanan, Allen, jt. ed. see Coleman, Jules L.
***Buchanan, Andrew S.** Peace with Justice: A History of the Israeli-Palestinian Declaration. 2000. text 65.00 (*0-312-22953-4*) St Martin.
Buchanan, Angus. Three Years of War in East Africa. LC 72-90108. 247p. 1970. reprint ed. lib. bdg. 35.00 (*0-8371-2026-8*, BUY&, Greenwood Pr) Greenwood.
Buchanan, Ann. Cycles of Child Maltreatment: Facts, Fallacies, & Interventions. LC 96-18899. (Wiley Series in Child Care & Protection). 328p. 1996. pap. 45.00 (*0-471-95889-1*) Wiley.
— Partnership in Practice: The Children Act of 1989. 140p. 1994. 63.95 (*1-85628-561-8*, Pub. by Avebry) Ashgate Pub Co.
Buchanan, Ann & Clayden, Graham. Children Who Soil: Assessment & Treatment. LC 92-15864. 278p. (Orig.). 1996. pap. 99.95 (*0-471-93479-8*) Wiley.
Buchanan, Ann & Hudson, Barbara, eds. Parenting, Schooling & Children's Behaviour: Interdisciplinary Approaches. LC 98-73508. 218p. 1998. text 59.95 (*1-84014-556-0*, Pub. by Ashgate Pub) Ashgate Pub Co.
***Buchanan, Ann & Hudson, Barbara, eds.** Promoting the Emotional Well-Being of Children. (Illus.). 272p. 2001. pap. text 45.00 (*0-19-263174-8*) OUP.
***Buchanan, Anne & Klingsporn, Debra K.** 100 Voices: Words That Shaped Our Souls & Wisdom to Guide Our Future. 176p. 1999. 12.99 (*1-58375-478-4*) Garborgs.
Buchanan, Anne, jt. auth. see Barnes, Emilie.
Buchanan, Anne C. Simpler Times. (Illus.). 96p. (Orig.). 1996. 24.99 (*1-56507-416-5*) Harvest Hse.
Buchanan, Anne C. & Klingsporn, Debra K. The Quickening Heart: A Journal of Discovery for Expectant Mothers. (Illus.). 160p. 1996. boxed set 18.00 (*0-8358-0776-2*) Upper Room Bks.
Buchanan, Anne C., jt. auth. see Barnes, Emilie.
Buchanan, Anne C., ed. see Barnes, Emilie.
Buchanan, Anne Christian, jt. auth. see Barnes, Emilie.
Buchanan, Anne Christian, ed. see Klingsporn, Debra.
Buchanan, Anne L. R3 = Ratios, Ratings, & Reference. (RUSA Occasional Papers: No. 20). 78p. 1996. pap. 20.00 (*0-8389-7874-6*) ALA.
Buchanan, Anne L. & Herubel, Jean-Pierre V., compiled by. The Doctor of Philosophy Degree: A Selective, Annotated Bibliography, 15. LC 95-21268. (Bibliographies & Indexes in Education Ser.: Vol. 15). 144p. 1995. lib. bdg. 65.00 (*0-313-29539-5*, Greenwood Pr) Greenwood.
Buchanan, B., et al. Organizational Behaviour: An Introductory Text. 488p. (C). 1989. 220.00 (*0-7855-4621-9*, Pub. by Inst Pur & Supply) St Mut.
Buchanan, Barbara N. & Yarnevich, Anne E. What Do Children Need? (Illus.). 32p. 1993. pap. 10.00 (*1-891330-02-0*) Health Ed Consults.
— What's on Your Mind? Answers to Your Questions about Childhood Mental Wellness. 120p. 1997. pap. 20.00 (*1-891330-03-9*) Health Ed Consults.
— When Being a Good Parent or Teacher Is Not Enough: Recognizing, Understanding, & Dealing with Difficult or Disturbed Children. 3rd rev. ed. (Illus.). 236p. 1997. ring bd. 39.95 (*1-891330-00-4*) Health Ed Consults.
Buchanan, Barbara N., et al. What to Do When Kids Say, "No!" 2nd rev. ed. 64p. (C). 1997. pap. 20.00 (*1-891330-01-2*) Health Ed Consults.
Buchanan, Barbara N., jt. auth. see Yarnevich, Anne E.
Buchanan, Barry, jt. auth. see Smith, William, Jr.
Buchanan, Bay. Bay. 1998. 24.00 (*0-684-83034-5*) S&S Trade.
Buchanan, Beki, jt. ed. see Knott, Mendy.
***Buchanan, Bill.** Clearwater. 2000. mass mkt. 6.99 (*0-425-17364-X*) Berkley Pub.
Buchanan, Bill. Handbook of Data Communications & Networks. LC 98-45183. 983p. 1999. 240.00 (*0-412-84060-X*) Kluwer Academic.
— Virus: A Novel. 432p. 1997. mass mkt. 6.50 (*0-515-12011-1*, Jove) Berkley Pub.
— Virus: A Novel. 415p. 1998. pap. text 6.50 (*0-7881-5789-2*) DIANE Pub.
***Buchanan, Bob B., et al, eds.** Biochemistry & Molecular Biology of Plants. 1200p. 2000. pap. text 99.95 (*0-943088-39-9*) Am Soc of Plan.
— Biochemistry & Molecular Biology of Plants. 1200p. 2000. text 149.95 (*0-943088-37-2*) Am Soc of Plan.
Buchanan, Bobbie. In the Tracks of Old Bluey: The Life Story of N. Buchanan. (Illus.). xiv, 188p. 1997. pap. 24.95 (*1-875998-19-5*, Pub. by Central Queensland) Accents Pubns.
Buchanan, Brenda J., ed. Gunpowder: The History of an International Technology. 1996. 75.00 (*0-86197-124-8*, Pub. by Bath Univ Pr) Intl Spec Bk.
Buchanan, Brian. Bibliothekarische Klassifikationstheorie. Reimer-Bohner, Ute, tr. (GER.). 150p. 1989. lib. bdg. 28.00 (*3-598-10788-9*) K G Saur Verlag.
Buchanan, Briggs. Early Near Eastern Seals in the Yale Babylonian Collection. Kasten, Ulla, ed. LC 75-43309. (Illus.). 522p. 1981. reprint ed. pap. 161.90 (*0-608-07882-4*, 205998900010) Bks Demand.
Buchanan, Briggs & Moorey, Peter R. Catalogue of Ancient Near Eastern Seals in the Ashmolean Museum Vol. III: The Iron Age Stamp Seals c. 1200-350 B. C., Vol. 3. 140p. 1988. 130.00 (*0-19-813404-5*) OUP.
Buchanan-Brown, John, jt. compiled by see Kogan Page, Ltd. Staff.
Buchanan-Brown, John, ed. see Aubrey, John.
Buchanan, Bruce. Electing a President: The Markle Commission Research on Campaign '88. 252p. 1991. 27.95 (*0-292-72077-7*) U of Tex Pr.
— Renewing Presidential Politics: Campaigns, Media & the Public Interest. LC 96-23925. 232p. 1996. 60.50 (*0-8476-8311-7*); pap. 20.95 (*0-8476-8312-5*) Rowman.
Buchanan, Bruce G. & Wilikins, David C., eds. Readings in Knowledge Acquisition & Learning: Automating the Construction & Improvement of Expert Systems. 906p. 1993. pap. text 54.95 (*1-55860-163-5*) Morgan Kaufmann.
Buchanan, C. D. Substantivized Adjectives in Old Norse. (LD Ser.: No. 15). 1974. reprint ed. pap. 25.00 (*0-527-00761-7*) Periodicals Srv.
— Teaching the Short Story Curriculum Guide. (Classic Short Stories Ser.). 64p. 1994. pap. 19.95 (*0-7854-0618-2*, 40101) Am Guidance.
Buchanan, C. D., ed. Charles W. Chesnutt: Great American Short Stories I. LC 94-75021. (Classic Short Stories Ser.). (Illus.). 80p. 1994. pap. 5.95 (*0-7854-0621-2*, 40010) Am Guidance.

B

Buchanan, C. D., et al, eds. Observable Standard Model Physics at the SSC: Monte Carlo Simulation & Detector Capabilities - University of California, Los Angeles, January 15-24, 1986. 420p. 1986. text 59.00 (*9971-5-0125-2*) World Scientific Pub.

Buchanan, Carl J. Ripper! LC 98-58088. (James Dickey Contemporary Poetry Ser.). 90p. 1998. 15.95 (*1-57003-297-1*); pap. 9.95 (*1-57003-298-X*) U of SC Pr.

Buchanan, Carol. Brother Crow, Sister Corn. LC 96-32204. 136p. 1997. pap. 11.95 (*0-89815-850-8*) Ten Speed Pr.

— The Wildlife Sanctuary Garden. LC 98-49793. (Illus.). 192p. 1999. pap. 11.95 (*1-58008-002-2*) Ten Speed Pr.

***Buchanan, Cathy.** Gardening with Bulbs: A Practical Guide. (Gardening Ser.). (Illus.). 96p. 1999. pap. 15.95 (*0-7078-0320-9*, Pub. by Natl Trust) Trafalgar.

— Gardening with Herbs: A Practical Guide. (Gardening Ser.). (Illus.). 96p. 1999. pap. 15.95 (*0-7078-0325-X*, Pub. by Natl Trust) Trafalgar.

Buchanan, Celia. Tie Dying. 1995. 7.98 (*0-7858-0315-7*) Bk Sales Inc.

***Buchanan, Christopher.** Street Poison. 208p. 2000. pap. 12.95 (*1-881524-72-8*) Milligan Bks.

***Buchanan, Christy M.** Adolescents after Divorce. 2000. pap. text 19.95 (*0-674-00170-2*) HUP.

Buchanan, Christy M., et al. Adolescents after Divorce. (Illus.). 352p. 1996. 42.50 (*0-674-00517-1*) HUP.

Buchanan, Clive. Herbal Knowledge. 1996. 14.95 (*1-885670-05-2*) Woodland UT.

— Herbal Knowledge: A Layman's Introduction to the Herbal World. 401p. (Orig.). 1999. reprint ed. pap. 14.95 (*1-890261-01-7*) Missions Pub.

Buchanan, Clive J. & Bandley, Michale J. Walking with Lions. LC 98-213910. (Illus.). (Orig.). 1996. pap. 14.95 (*1-890261-00-9*) Missions Pub.

Buchanan, Constance H. Choosing to Lead: Women & the Crisis of American Values. LC 95-43515. 288p. 1997. pap. 15.00 (*0-8070-2003-6*) Beacon Pr.

Buchanan, Constance Packer, ed. see Kobza, Kim P.

Buchanan, Courtney, et al. The Salsa Book. O'Mahony, Kieran, ed. (Illus.). 475p. (Orig.). 1996. pap. 19.95 (*1-889548-00-6*) Wall Data WA.

***Buchanan, Cynthia.** Maiden: A Novel. LC 99-26438. 224p. 1999. reprint ed. pap. 12.00 (*0-688-16789-6*, Wm Morrow) Morrow Avon.

***Buchanan, D. Douglas.** Stanly County, North Carolina. (Images of America Ser.). (Illus.). 128p. 1999. pap. 18.99 (*0-7385-0275-8*) Arcadia Publng.

Buchanan, D. Kirk. The IRA Explanation: A User's Guide to the Individual Retirement Account. 144p. (Orig.). 1994. pap. 9.95 (*0-9630879-1-6*) Buchanan Res.

— The IRA Explanation: A User's Guide to the Individual Retirement Account. 2nd rev. ed. (Illus.). 144p. (Orig.). 1996. mass mkt. 9.95 (*0-9654078-0-2*) Intl Legal Pubng.

— The IRA Explanation: A User's Guide to the Individual Retirement Account. 3rd ed. 145p. (Orig.). 1997. pap. 9.95 (*0-9654078-2-9*) Intl Legal Pubng.

— 100Deductible: Retirement Plans for Small Business. Davis, Lon L., ed. 239p. (C). 1997. 14.95 (*0-9654078-3-7*) Intl Legal Pubng.

— 100Deductible: Tax Advantaged Pension & Retirement Plans for Small Business. (Illus.). 225p. 1996. 19.95 (*0-9630879-2-4*) Buchanan Res.

— Understanding IRAs: An Amiable Approach. 110p. 1990. pap. 7.95 (*0-9630879-0-8*) Buchanan Res.

Buchanan, D. V., et al, eds. Native Trout Project, 1994. (Illus.). 44p. 1997. reprint ed. pap. 5.40 (*0-89904-645-2*, Cascade Geog Soc) Crumb Elbow Pub.

Buchanan, D. V., et al. Native Trout Project, 1991. (Illus.). 52p. 1998. reprint ed. 11.20 (*0-89904-864-1*, Cascade Geog Soc); reprint ed. pap. 6.20 (*0-89904-865-X*, Cascade Geog Soc) Crumb Elbow Pub.

Buchanan, Dana, ed. & tr. see De Betanzos, Juan.

Buchanan, Daniel C., ed. Japanese Proverbs & Sayings. LC 65-24192. 296p. (Orig.). 1987. pap. 15.95 (*0-8061-1082-1*) U of Okla Pr.

Buchanan, Daniel H. Development of Capitalistic Enterprise in India. 489p. 1966. reprint ed. 35.00 (*0-7146-1998-1*, Pub. by F Cass Pubs) Intl Spec Bk.

Buchanan, David. Davidis Buchanani De Scriptoribus Scotis. Irving, David, ed. LC 74-39554. (Bannatyne Club, Edinburgh. Publications: No. 55). reprint ed. 37.50 (*0-404-52765-5*) AMS Pr.

— Observations on the Subjects Treated of in Dr. Smith's Inquiry into the Nature & Causes of the Wealth of Nations. 2nd ed. LC 65-26360. (Reprints of Economic Classics Ser.). xvi, 318p. 1966. reprint ed. 49.50 (*0-678-00191-X*) Kelley.

Buchanan, David. Organizational Behaviour: Integrated Readings. 1997. pap. 28.00 (*0-13-234345-2*) P-H.

Buchanan, David & Cernada, George, eds. Progress in Preventing AIDS? Dogma, Dissent & Innovation - Global Perspectives. LC 97-1804. (Health Services Ser.). 360p. 1998. pap. text 46.95 (*0-89503-176-0*) Baywood Pub.

Buchanan, David A. The Development of Job Design Theories & Techniques. LC 79-83808. 179p. 1979. 57.95 (*0-275-90335-4*, C0335, Praeger Pubs) Greenwood.

— Greek Athletics. McLeish, Kenneth & McLeish, Valerie, eds. (Aspects of Greek Life Ser.). (Illus.). 48p. (YA). (gr. 7-12). 1976. reprint ed. pap. text 9.00 (*0-582-20059-8*, 70659) Longman.

— Roman Sport & Entertainment. Hodge, Peter, ed. (Aspects of Roman Life Ser.). (Illus.). 64p. (Orig.). (gr. 7-12). 1976. pap. text 9.00 (*0-582-31415-1*, 71975) Longman.

Buchanan, David A. & Huczynski, Andrzej A. Organisational Behaviour: An Introductory Text. 2nd ed. 637p. (C). 1991. pap. 120.00 (*0-13-639899-5*, Pub. by IPM Hse) St Mut.

Buchanan, David A. & McCalman, James. High Performance Work Systems: The Digital Experience. 176p. 1988. lib. bdg. 49.95 (*0-415-00101-3*) Routledge.

***Buchanan, David R.** An Ethic for Health Promotion: Rethinking the Sources of Human Well-Being. LC 99-23897. (Illus.). 232p. 2000. text 39.95 (*0-19-513057-X*) OUP.

Buchanan, Dawna L. The Falcon's Wing. 128p. (J). (gr. 4). 1993. pap. 3.50 (*0-380-72102-3*, Avon Bks) Morrow Avon.

— The Falcon's Wing. LC 91-22545. 144p. (YA). (gr. 4-7). 1992. 15.95 (*0-531-05986-3*); lib. bdg. 16.99 (*0-531-08586-4*) Orchard Bks Watts.

Buchanan, Debby, jt. auth. see Buchanan, Ken.

Buchanan, Devon. Surfacing. LC 98-85384. 325p. 1998. 25.00 (*0-9663501-4-6*); pap. 15.00 (*0-7388-0026-0*) Xlibris Corp.

Buchanan, Doug. Air & Space. (Female Firsts in Their Field Ser.). (Illus.). 64p. (YA). (gr. 3 up). 1999. 16.95 (*0-7910-5141-2*) Chelsea Hse.

Buchanan, Dougal. Gaelic English, English Gaelic Practical Dictionary. 252p. 1999. pap. 12.95 (*0-7818-0789-1*) Hippocrene Bks.

Buchanan, E. Clyde, et al. Principles of Sterile Product Preparation. (Illus.). 192p. (Orig.). (C). 1995. pap. text 50.00 (*1-879907-57-7*) Am Soc Hlth-Syst.

***Buchanan, Edna.** A Britt Montero Novel. 320p. 2000. mass mkt. 6.99 (*0-380-79841-7*, Avon Bks) Morrow Avon.

Buchanan, Edna R. Act of Betrayal. 320p. 1996. 21.95 (*0-7868-6098-7*, Pub. by Hyperion) Time Warner.

— Act of Betrayal. 448p. 1997. mass mkt. 5.99 (*0-7868-8923-3*, Pub. by Hyperion) Time Warner.

— Act of Betrayal. large type ed. LC 96-22224. (Cloak & Dagger Ser.). 492p. 1996. 23.95 (*0-7862-0811-2*) Thorndike Pr.

— Contents under Pressure. LC 92-15949. 304p. (YA). 1992. 21.95 (*1-56282-932-7*, Pub. by Hyperion) Time Warner.

— Contents under Pressure. large type ed. 497p. 1992. reprint ed. lib. bdg. 22.95 (*1-56054-544-5*) Thorndike Pr.

***Buchanan, Edna R.** Contents Under Pressure: A Britt Montero Novel. (Britt Montero Mystery Ser.). 368p. 1999. mass mkt. 6.99 (*0-380-72260-7*, Avon Bks) Morrow Avon.

Buchanan, Edna R. The Corpse Had a Familiar Face. 1991. mass mkt. 6.99 (*0-425-12994-2*) Berkley Pub.

***Buchanan, Edna R.** Garden of Evil: A Britt Montero Mystery. LC 99-36111. 336p. 1999. 24.00 (*0-380-97654-4*, Avon Bks) Morrow Avon.

— Garden of Evil: A Britt Montero Mystery. large type ed. LC 99-55920. (Mystery Ser.). 439p. 2000. 29.95 (*0-7862-2331-6*) Thorndike Pr.

— Margin of Error. large type ed. 488p. 2000. write for info. (*0-7089-4189-3*) Ulverscroft.

Buchanan, Edna R. Margin of Error. large type ed. LC 98-6707. 1998. pap. 23.95 (*1-56895-563-4*, Wheeler) Wheeler Pub.

— Margin of Error. 384p. 1998. reprint ed. mass mkt. 5.99 (*0-7868-8931-4*, Pub. by Hyperion) Time Warner.

— Miami, It's Murder. large type ed. LC 93-28628. 1994. lib. bdg. 24.95 (*0-7862-0033-2*) Thorndike Pr.

— Miami, It's Murder. large type ed. LC 93-28628. 409p. 1994. pap. 15.95 (*0-7862-0034-0*) Thorndike Pr.

— Miami, It's Murder: A Britt Montero Novel. 320p. 1995. mass mkt. 6.99 (*0-380-72261-5*, Avon Bks) Morrow Avon.

— Never Let Them See You Cry. 336p. 1993. mass mkt. 5.99 (*0-425-13824-0*) Berkley Pub.

— Nobody Lives Forever. 1992. mass mkt. 5.99 (*0-8217-3712-0*, Zebra Kensgtn) Kensgtn Pub Corp.

— Nobody Lives Forever. 400p. 1997. mass mkt. 5.99 (*1-57566-123-3*, Knsington) Kensgtn Pub Corp.

— Pulse. LC 97-32292. 336p. 1999. mass mkt. 6.99 (*0-380-72833-8*, Avon Bks) Morrow Avon.

— Pulse. large type ed. LC 98-27979. 1998. 26.95 (*0-7862-1622-0*) Thorndike Pr.

— Pulse: A Novel. LC 97-32292. 336p. 1998. mass mkt. 23.00 (*0-380-97331-6*, Avon Bks) Morrow Avon.

— Suitable for Framing. 256p. 1995. 21.45 (*0-7868-6047-2*, Pub. by Hyperion) Time Warner.

— Suitable for Framing. 368p. 1996. mass mkt. 4.99 (*0-7868-8901-2*, Pub. by Hyperion) Time Warner.

— Suitable for Framing. large type ed. LC 95-5402. 1995. 25.95 (*1-56895-210-4*) Wheeler Pub.

***Buchanan, Edna R.** You Only Die Twice: A Britt Montero Mystery. 2001. write for info. (*0-380-97655-2*, Wm Morrow) Morrow Avon.

Buchanan, Edward A., jt. auth. see Johnson, L. T.

Buchanan, Elizabeth S. My Day. 32p. (J). 1997. pap. 9.95 (*0-385-48264-7*, Main St Bks) Doubleday.

***Buchanan, Eugene, ed.** The Best of Paddler Magazine: Stories from the World's Premier Canoeing, Kayaking & Rafting Magazine. LC 00-39445. 2000. pap. 14.95 (*0-89732-330-0*) Menasha Ridge.

Buchanan, Forest W. The Breeding Birds of Carroll & Northern Jefferson Counties, Ohio, with Notes on Selected Vascular Plant Species. (Biological Notes Ser.: No. 12). 1980. pap. text 5.00 (*0-86727-086-1*) Ohio Bio Survey.

Buchanan, Francis. A Journey from Madras Through the Countries of Mysore, Canara, & Malabar, for the Express Purpose of Investigating the State of Agriculture, Arts & Commerce, the Religion, Manners, & Customs: The History, Natural & Civil & Antiquities, 3 vols., Set. (C). 1988. reprint ed. 168.50 (*81-206-0386-9*, Pub. by Asian Educ Servs) S Asia.

Buchanan, Frederick S. Culture Clash & Accommodation: Public Schooling in Salt Lake City, 1890-1994. LC 95-40863. (Illus.). 312p. 1996. 24.95 (*1-56085-082-5*, Smith Res) Signature Bks.

Buchanan, G. Sidney. Morality, Sex & the Constitution: A Christian Perspective on the Power of Government to Regulate Private Sexual Conduct Between Consenting Adults. LC 85-3249. 242p. (Orig.). 1985. pap. text 22.50 (*0-8191-4603-X*); lib. bdg. 50.00 (*0-8191-4602-1*) U Pr of Amer.

Buchanan, George. The Boat Repair Manual. LC 92-33040. (Illus.). 312p. 1992. 24.95 (*1-55992-070-X*, 2070) Gulf Pub.

— Country Furniture: The Kitchen. (Illus.). 160p. 1998. pap. 19.95 (*0-304-34243-2*, Pub. by Cassell) Sterling.

— Green Seacoast. LC 68-24548. 108p. 1969. 4.95 (*0-87376-008-5*); pap. 3.00 (*0-87376-009-3*) Red Dust.

— Living Room Country Furniture for the Home: Timeless Traditional Woodworking Projects. 1999. pap. text 19.95 (*0-304-34244-0*) Continuum.

— Making Country Furniture. LC 97-34430. 1998. 22.95 (*1-56158-262-X*) Taunton.

— My Mission to Russia & Other Diplomatic Memories. LC 78-115510. (Russia Observed, Series I). 1970. reprint ed. 28.95 (*0-405-03008-8*) Ayer.

— The Tragedy of Mesopotamia. LC 71-180324. (Mid-East Studies). reprint ed. 39.50 (*0-404-56218-3*) AMS Pr.

— The Tyrannous Reign of Mary Stewart, 10--10. Gatherer, W. A., tr. from LAT. LC 78-3556. (Edinburgh University Publication: History, Philosophy, & Economics: No. 10). 228p. 1978. reprint ed. lib. bdg. 59.75 (*0-313-20343-1*, BUTR) Greenwood.

Buchanan, George R. Schaum's Outline of Finite Element Analysis. (Schaum's Outline Ser.). 264p. (C). 1995. pap. 14.95 (*0-07-008714-8*) McGraw.

Buchanan, George W. Biblical & Theological Insights from Ancient & Modern Civil Law. LC 92-27602. (Studies in Religion & Society: Vol. 29). 180p. 1992. text 79.95 (*0-7734-9601-7*) E Mellen.

***Buchanan, George W.** The Book of Daniel LC 99-27735. (Mellen Biblical Commentary Ser.). 1999. write for info. (*0-7734-7948-1*) E Mellen.

Buchanan, George W. The Book of Revelation: Its Introduction & Prophecy. LC 93-36776. (Biblical Commentary, New Testament Ser.: Vol. 27). (Illus.). 732p. 1993. text 139.95 (*0-7734-2365-6*, Mellen Biblical Pr) E Mellen.

— Introduction to Intertextuality. LC 94-28482. (Biblical Press Ser.: Vol. 26). 104p. 1994. text 59.95 (*0-7734-2387-7*, Mellen Biblical Pr) E Mellen.

— Jesus: The King & His Kingdom. LC 83-24939. xx, 348p. 1984. text 21.95 (*0-86554-072-1*, MUP/H066) Mercer Univ Pr.

— New Testament Eschatology: Historical & Cultural Background. LC 93-28572. (Biblical Press Ser.: Vol. 15). 316p. 1993. text 99.95 (*0-7734-2378-8*, Mellen Biblical Pr) E Mellen.

— Revelation & Redemption: Jewish Documents of Deliverance from the Fall of Jerusalem to the Death of Nahmanides. vi, 632p. 1978. text 29.50 (*0-915948-04-4*) Eisenbrauns.

Buchanan, George W., ed. The Mellen Intertextual Bible Commentary, Vol. 1, Bk. 1. LC 96-31591. (New Testament Ser.). (Illus.). 600p. 1997. text 119.95 (*0-7734-2373-7*) E Mellen.

— The Mellen Intertextual Bible Commentary, Vol. 1, Bk. 2. LC 96-31591. (New Testament Ser.). (Illus.). 536p. 1997. text 119.95 (*0-7734-2421-0*) E Mellen.

Buchanan, George W., tr. To the Hebrews. LC 72-76127. (Anchor Bible Ser.: Vol. 36). 312p. 1972. 29.00 (*0-385-02995-0*, Anchor NY) Doubleday.

***Buchanan, George Wesley, ed.** The Mellen Biblical Commentary: Intertextual. LC 99-27735. 544p. 1999. text 119.95 (*0-7734-2470-9*) E Mellen.

Buchanan, Ginjer. Highlander: White Silence. 240p. 1999. mass mkt. 5.99 (*0-446-60634-0*, Pub. by Warner Bks) Little.

Buchanan, Gregory & Seligman, Martin E., eds. Explanatory Style. 312p. 1995. pap. 36.00 (*0-8058-1789-1*); text 69.95 (*0-8058-0924-4*) L Erlbaum Assocs.

Buchanan, Hayle. Wildflowers of Southwest Utah: Field Guide to Bryce Canyon Cedar Breaks. LC 92-70128. (Illus.). 119p. 1992. pap. 7.95 (*1-56044-074-0*) Falcon Pub Inc.

Buchanan, Heather S. George & Matilda Mouse & the Floating School. LC 89-22036. (Illus.). 40p. (J). (ps-3). 1990. pap. 13.95 (*0-671-70613-6*) S&S Trade.

— George & Matilda Mouse & the Moon Rocket. LC 91-24318. (Illus.). 40p. (J). (ps-3). 1992. pap. 14.00 (*0-671-75864-0*) S&S Bks Yung.

— This Little Piggy. LC 92-11895. (J). 1993. pap. 14.00 (*0-671-79351-9*) S&S Bks Yung.

Buchanan, Henry. And the Goat Cried: Southern Tales & Other Chance Meetings. LC 97-66001. (Illus.). 184p. 1998. pap. 14.50 (*0-88739-115-X*) Creat Arts Bk.

Buchanan, Ian. A Deleuzian Century? LC 99-13955. 272p. 1999. 54.95 (*0-8223-2359-1*); pap. text 18.95 (*0-8223-2392-3*) Duke.

***Buchanan, Ian.** Deleuzism: A Metacommentary. LC 99-56849. (Post-Contemporary Interventions Ser.). 269p. 2000. pap. 17.95 (*0-8223-2548-9*) Duke.

— Michel de Certeau in the Plural. 290p. 2000. pap. 12.00 (*0-8223-6473-5*) Duke.

***Buchanan, Ian & Colebrook, Claire, eds.** Deleuze & Feminist Theory. 256p. 2000. text 65.00 (*0-7486-1119-3*) Col U Pr.

— Deleuze & Feminist Theory. 256p. 2000. pap. text 25.00 (*0-7486-1120-7*) Col U Pr.

Buchanan, Ian & Mallon, Bill. Historical Dictionary of the Olympic Movement. LC 95-22858. (Religions, Philosophies, & Movements Ser.: No. 7). 340p. 1995. 47.00 (*0-8108-3062-0*) Scarecrow.

Buchanan, Ian, jt. auth. see Mallon, Bill.

Buchanan, Ian, jt. ed. see Barcan, Ruth.

Buchanan Ingersoll Staff. How to Hire Right, Fire Right: Managing Within the Law. LC 98-206791. 338p. 1998. ring bd. 167.00 (*0-925773-41-7*) M Lee Smith.

Buchanan, J. G. & Buchanan, P. G., eds. Basin Inversion. (Geological Society Special Publication Ser.: No. 88). (Illus.). 600p. 1995. 117.00 (*1-897799-29-2*, 251, Pub. by Geol Soc Pub Hse) AAPG.

Buchanan, James. The Doctrine of Justification. 514p. 1997. reprint ed. 39.99 (*0-85151-440-5*) Banner of Truth.

— Indian Affairs in Oregon & Washington Territories. 23p. 1988. pap. 4.95 (*0-87770-440-6*) Ye Galleon.

— James Buchanan's Mission to Russia, 1831-1833: His Speeches, State Papers & Private Correspondence. Moore, John B., ed. LC 71-115511. (Russia Observed Ser.: No. 1). 1970. reprint ed. 17.95 (*0-405-03009-6*) Ayer.

— Mr. Buchanan's Administration on the Eve of the Rebellion. (American Biography Ser.). 296p. 1991. reprint ed. lib. bdg. 69.00 (*0-7812-8049-4*) Rprt Serv.

— Mister Buchanan's Administration on the Eve of the Rebellion. LC 70-107795. (Select Bibliographies Reprint Ser.). 1977. 27.95 (*0-8369-5212-X*) Ayer.

***Buchanan, James.** Mr. Buchanan's Administration: On the Eve of the Rebellion. x, 296p. 2000. write for info. (*1-58218-180-2*); pap. write for info. (*1-58218-179-9*) Digital Scanning.

Buchanan, James. Not Guilty. 1990. pap. 4.99 (*0-946462-22-4*, Pub. by Evangelical Pr) P & R Pubng.

— The Political Economy of the Welfare State. 32p. (Orig.). 1988. pap. 17.50 (*91-7204-296-6*, Pub. by Industriens) Coronet Bks.

— What Should Economists Do? LC 79-19511. 1979. 14.00 (*0-913966-64-9*); pap. 7.00 (*0-913966-65-7*) Liberty Fund.

Buchanan, James H. Patient Encounters: The Experience of Disease. LC 88-19803. 366p. 1989. reprint ed. pap. 113.50 (*0-7837-8574-7*, 204938900011) Bks Demand.

Buchanan, James L. & Turner, Peter R. Numerical Methods & Analysis. 640p. (C). 1992. 70.31 (*0-07-008717-2*) McGraw.

Buchanan, James M. Better Than Plowing & Other Personal Essays. LC 91-44417. (Illus.). 194p. 1999. 24.95 (*0-226-07816-7*) U Ch Pr.

— Calculus of Consent: Logical Foundations of Constitutional Democracy. LC 98-45532. (Collected Works of James M. Buchanan : Vol. 3). 1999. 20.00 (*0-86597-217-6*); pap. 12.00 (*0-86597-218-4*) Liberty Fund.

***Buchanan, James M.** Choice, Contract & Constitutions. LC 99-41421. (Collected Works of James M. Buchanan : Vol. 16). 2000. 20.00 (*0-86597-243-5*); pap. 12.00 (*0-86597-244-3*) Liberty Fund.

Buchanan, James M. Cost & Choice: An Inquiry in Economic Theory. LC 98-32143. (Collected Works of James M. Buchanan : Vol. 6). 1999. pap. 12.00 (*0-86597-224-9*) Liberty Fund.

***Buchanan, James M.** Cost & Choice: An Inquiry in Economic Theory. LC 98-32143. (Collected Works of James M. Buchanan : Vol. 6). 1999. 20.00 (*0-86597-223-0*) Liberty Fund.

Buchanan, James M. Cost & Choice: An Inquiry in Economic Theory. LC 78-70150. (Midway Reprint Ser.). 120p. 1979. pap. text 12.95 (*0-226-07818-3*) U Ch Pr.

***Buchanan, James M.** Debt & Taxes. LC 99-41677. (Collected Works of James M. Buchanan : Vol. 14). (Illus.). 2000. pap. 12.00 (*0-86597-240-0*) Liberty Fund.

— Demand & Supply of Public Goods. LC 98-43536. (Collected Works of James M. Buchanan : Vol. 5). 1999. 20.00 (*0-86597-221-4*) Liberty Fund.

Buchanan, James M. The Demand & Supply of Public Goods. LC 98-43536. (Collected Works of James M. Buchanan : Vol. 5). 1999. 12.00 (*0-86597-222-2*) Liberty Fund.

***Buchanan, James M.** Economic Inquiry & Its Logic. LC 99-42838. (Collected Works of James M. Buchanan : Vol. 12). 2000. 20.00 (*0-86597-235-4*); pap. 12.00 (*0-86597-236-2*) Liberty Fund.

Buchanan, James M. Economics: Between Predictive Science & Moral Philosophy. LC 87-18096. (Economics Ser.: No. 7). (Illus.). 432p. 1988. 49.95 (*0-89096-350-9*) Tex A&M Univ Pr.

— The Economics & the Ethics of Constitutional Order. 272p. (C). 1991. text 57.50 (*0-472-10222-2*, 10222) U of Mich Pr.

— Ethics & Economic Progress. LC 93-31846. (Illus.). 168p. 1996. pap. 12.95 (*0-8061-2935-2*) U of Okla Pr.

***Buchanan, James M.** Externalities & Public Expenditure Theory. LC 99-41678. (Collected Works of James M. Buchanan : Vol. 15). 2000. 20.00 (*0-86597-241-9*) Liberty Fund.

— Externalities & Public Expenditure Theory. LC 99-41678. (Collected Works of James M. Buchanan : Vol. 15). 2000. pap. 12.00 (*0-86597-242-7*) Liberty Fund.

— Federalism, Liberty & the Law. LC 99-42628. (Collected Works of James M. Buchanan : Vol. 18). 2000. pap. 12.00 (*0-86597-248-6*) Liberty Fund.

— Federalism, Liberty & the Law. LC 99-42628. (Collected Works of James M. Buchanan : Vol. 18). 2001. 20.00 (*0-86597-247-8*) Liberty Fund.

— Ideas, Persons & Events. LC 99-42600. (Collected Works of James M. Buchanan : Vol. 19). 2000. pap. 12.00 (*0-86597-250-8*) Liberty Fund.

— The Limits of Liberty: Between Anarchy & Leviathan. LC 99-24059. (Collected Works of James M. Buchanan : Vol. 7). 2000. 20.00 (*0-86597-225-7*) Liberty Fund.

Buchanan, James M. The Limits of Liberty: Between Anarchy & Leviathan. LC 74-11616. 222p. 1977. reprint ed. pap. text 16.95 (*0-226-07820-5*, P714) U Ch Pr.

***Buchanan, James M.** The Limits of Liberty Vol. 7: Between Anarchy & Leviathan. LC 99-24059. (Collected Works of James M. Buchanan). 2000. pap. 12.00 (*0-86597-226-5*) Liberty Fund.

— The Logical Foundations of Constitutional Liberty. LC 98-45534. (Collected Works of James M. Buchanan : Vol. I). 1999. 20.00 (*0-86597-213-3*); pap. 12.00 (*0-86597-214-1*) Liberty Fund.

— Moral Science & Moral Order. LC 99-42627. (Collected Works of James M. Buchanan : Vol. 17). 2000. pap. 12.00 (*0-86597-246-X*) Liberty Fund.

— Moral Science & Moral Order. LC 99-42627. (Collected Works of James M. Buchanan : Vol. 17). 2001. 20.00 (*0-86597-245-1*) Liberty Fund.

— Politics as Public Choice. LC 99-41676. (Collected Works of James M. Buchanan : Vol. 13). 2000. 20.00 (*0-86597-237-0*); pap. 12.00 (*0-86597-238-9*) Liberty Fund.

Buchanan, James M. Post-Socialist Political Economy: Selected Essays. LC 97-25019. 296p. 1997. 85.00 (*1-85898-534-X*) E Elgar.

— Property As a Guarantor of Liberty. (Shaftesbury Papers: Vol. 1). 72p. 1993. pap. 13.00 (*1-85278-733-3*) E Elgar.

— Public Finance in Democratic Process: Fiscal Institutions & Individual Choice. LC 98-43535. (Collected Works of James M. Buchanan : Vol. 4). 1999. 12.00 (*0-86597-220-6*) Liberty Fund.

***Buchanan, James M.** Public Finance in Democratic Process: Fiscal Institutions & Individual Choice. LC 98-43535. (Collected Works of James M. Buchanan : Vol. 4). 1999. 20.00 (*0-86597-219-2*) Liberty Fund.

— Public Principles of Public Debt. LC 98-45533. (Collected Works of James M. Buchanan : Vol. 2). 1999. 20.00 (*0-86597-215-X*); pap. 12.00 (*0-86597-216-8*) Liberty Fund.

Buchanan, James M., contrib. by. Ethics of Capitalism & Critique of Sociobiology: Two Essays. LC 96-16078. 142p. 1996. 79.95 (*3-540-61035-9*) Spr-Verlag.

Buchanan, James M. & Congleton, Roger D. Politics by Principle, Not Interest: Towards Nondiscriminatory Democracy. LC 97-40983. (Illus.). 186p. (C). 1998. text 44.95 (*0-521-62187-9*) Cambridge U Pr.

Buchanan, James M. & Musgrave, Richard A. Public Finance & Public Choice: Two Contrasting Visions of the State. LC 99-15446. (Illus.). 264p. 1999. 27.50 (*0-262-02462-4*) MIT Pr.

Buchanan, James M. & Tollison, Robert D. The Theory of Public Choice, II. 464p. (C). 1984. pap. text 32.50 (*0-472-08041-5*, 08041) U of Mich Pr.

Buchanan, James M. & Tullock, Gordon. Calculus of Consent: Logical Foundations of Constitutional Democracy. 384p. 1962. pap. text 20.95 (*0-472-06100-3*, 06100, Ann Arbor Bks) U of Mich Pr.

Buchanan, James M. & Wagner, Richard E. Democracy in Deficit: The Political Legacy of Lord Keynes. 1977. text 64.95 (*0-12-138850-6*) Acad Pr.

***Buchanan, James M. & Wagner, Richard E.** Democracy in Deficit: The Political Legacy of Lord Keynes. LC 99-24064. (Collected Works of James M. Buchanan : Vol. 8). 2000. 20.00 (*0-86597-227-3*); pap. 12.00 (*0-86597-228-1*) Liberty Fund.

Buchanan, James M. & Wagner, Richard E. Fiscal Responsibility in Constitutional Democracy. (Studies in Public Choice: Vol. 1). 1978. lib. bdg. 22.50 (*90-207-0743-4*) Kluwer Academic.

Buchanan, James M. & Yoon, Yong J., eds. The Return to Increasing Returns. 392p. (C). 1994. text 75.00 (*0-472-10432-2*, 10432) U of Mich Pr.

Buchanan, James M., jt. auth. see Brennan, G.

Buchanan, James M., jt. auth. see Brennan, Geoffrey.

Buchanan, James P., jt. ed. see Becker, Gerhold K.

Buchanan, James R. Viewing the Earth from Space: The Complete Guide to Public Domain Radio-Based Imagery & Weather Services. Buchanan, Pamela, ed. (Illus.). 152p. (Orig.). 1996. pap. 24.00 (*0-9655390-0-8*) Woodhse Commun.

Buchanan, Jan. Flexible Access Library Media Programs. xii, 171p. 1991. lib. bdg. 26.00 (*0-87287-834-1*) Libs Unl.

Buchanan, Jane. Gratefully Yours. LC 96-54712. 128p. (J). (gr. 3-7). 1997. 15.00 (*0-374-32775-0*) FS&G.

— Gratefully Yours. LC 98-28616. 128p. (J). (gr. 3-7). 1999. pap. 4.99 (*0-14-130315-8*, PuffinBks) Peng Put Young Read.

***Buchanan, Jane.** Three Kinds of Touches. (Illus.). 82p. (J). (ps-5). 1999. 15.95 (*0-615-11183-1*) Penn Coaltn.

— Three Kinds of Touches. braille ed. 11p. (J). (ps-5). 1999. 15.95 (*0-615-11184-X*) Penn Coaltn.

— Tres Formas de Tocar. Sepulveda, Luis, tr. (SPA., Illus.). 82p. (J). (ps-5). 1999. 15.95 (*0-615-11182-3*) Penn Coaltn.

— Tres Formas de Tocar. braille ed. (SPA.). 11p. (J). (ps-5). 1999. 15.95 (*0-615-11185-8*) Penn Coaltn.

Buchanan, Jane G. Early Inns & Taverns of East Tennessee: A Photoessay. LC 96-84077. (Illus.). 81p. 1996. pap. 9.95 (*0-9647748-1-X*) J G Buchanan.

Buchanan, Jane G., photos by. Early Inns & Taverns of East Tennessee: A Photoessay. LC 96-84077. (Illus.). 96p. 1996. pap. 9.95 (*0-9647748-2-8*) J G Buchanan.

Buchanan, Jerry. The Alternating Currents of Love & Friendship. LC 85-73609. 1986. pap. 6.95 (*0-930668-02-2*) Towers Club.

— The Ego Trip: Your Ego is Your Rudder. 32p. 1993. pap. 4.95 (*0-930668-10-3*) Towers Club.

— How to Sell Gov't Publications for Personal Profit. 1984. pap. 29.95 (*0-930668-06-5*) Towers Club.

— Profitable Self-Publishing: The Entrepreneur's Guide to Gathering & Selling How-to Information. 93p. 1993. lib. bdg. 14.95 (*0-930668-08-1*) Towers Club.

— The Three Phases of Ease. 1993. pap. 4.95 (*0-930668-09-X*) Towers Club.

— Twenty-Two Mistakes the Beginner Always Makes in Mail Order. 32p. (Orig.). 1984. pap. 12.95 (*0-930668-01-4*) Towers Club.

— Writer's Utopia Formula Report. rev. ed. 1977. 12.00 (*0-930668-05-7*) Towers Club.

Buchanan, Jerry, ed. see Sackheim, Maxwell.

Buchanan, Jim. A Consumer's Guide to Mobile Home Ownership: Y-2000 Edition. 2nd ed. 24p. 2000. pap. 3.95 (*0-918734-32-0*) Reymont.

***Buchanan, Jim.** How to Have a Smooth Move! A Practical Handbook for Making Your Relocations Move a Pleasant. 40p. 1999. 8.00 (*1-929097-02-6*) Windmill Pubns.

— How to Successfully Market Your Book Overseas. 40p. 1999. 8.00 (*1-929097-01-8*) Windmill Pubns.

— So, You Want to Be a Best-Selling Author? 48p. 1999. 8.00 (*1-929097-00-X*) Windmill Pubns.

— Walking the Leadership Highway without Becoming Roadkill. LC 00-41027. 2000. write for info. (*1-57312-327-7*) Smyth & Helwys.

Buchanan, Joan. The Nana Rescue. LC 93-20803. (Illus.). (J). 1994. 4.25 (*0-383-03740-9*) SRA McGraw.

Buchanan, John. Road to Guilford Courthouse: The American Revolution in the Carolinas. 452p. 1999. pap. 17.95 (*0-471-32716-6*) Wiley.

Buchanan, John C. & Bos, Carole D. How to Use Video in Litigation: A Guide to Technology, Strategies, & Techniques. LC 85-9461. 1986. text 75.00 (*0-13-437070-8*) P-H.

Buchanan, John L. & MacLean, Alasdair. Travels in the Western Hebrides from 1782 to 1790. (Illus.). 124p. pap. 21.00 (*1-899272-04-6*, Pub. by Maclean Pr) Dufour.

Buchanan, John M. Being Church, Becoming Community. LC 96-20252. 144p. (Orig.). 1996. pap. 14.95 (*0-664-25669-4*) Westminster John Knox.

Buchanan, John M., jt. auth. see Davies, Elam.

Buchanan, John N. Marginal Scotland, Set. (American University Studies: History: Ser. IX, Vols. 64 & 65). (Illus.). 361 + 348p. 1990. text 103.50 (*0-8204-0900-6*) P Lang Pubng.

Buchanan, Joni. The Lewis Land Struggle: Na Gaisgich. LC 98-189059. 209 p. 1996. write for info. (*0-86152-166-8*) Acair Ltd.

Buchanan, Joseph. The Philosophy of Human Nature. Adams, James F., ed. 368p. 1970. 25.00 (*0-87730-005-4*) M & S Pr.

— The Philosophy of Human Nature. LC 71-90941. (History of Psychology Ser.). (Illus.). 360p. 1969. reprint ed. 50.00 (*0-8201-1064-7*) Schol Facsimiles.

Buchanan, Joseph R. Periodicity. 3rd ed. 138p. 1996. reprint ed. spiral bd. 12.00 (*0-7873-0129-9*) Hlth Research.

— The Story of a Labor Agitator. LC 75-148873. (Select Bibliographies Reprint Ser.). 1977. reprint ed. 29.95 (*0-8369-5644-3*) Ayer.

— The Story of a Labor Agitator. (American Biography Ser.). 460p. 1991. reprint ed. lib. bdg. 89.00 (*0-7812-8050-8*) Rprt Serv.

— Therapeutic Sarcogomy. 269p. 1993. reprint ed. spiral bd. 28.00 (*0-7873-0128-0*) Hlth Research.

Buchanan, Joyce. Bark Carving: Wood Spirits, Faces, Expressions. (Illus.). 44p. (Orig.). 1996. pap. 12.95 (*1-56523-065-5*) Fox Chapel Pub.

***Buchanan, Joyce.** Carving Wood Spirits in Tree Bark: Capturing Unique Faces & Expressions in Wood. 2nd ed. Orig. Title: Bark Carving. 48p. 2000. pap. 12.95 (*1-56523-132-5*, Pub. by Fox Chapel Pub) IPG Chicago.

Buchanan, Kay, jt. auth. see Tilton, Richard C.

***Buchanan, Keith.** Complete Guide to Stock Car Racing. LC 99-37743. 144p. 2000. pap. 14.95 (*1-57427-088-5*) Howell Pr VA.

Buchanan, Ken. This House Is Made of Mud (Esta Casa Esta Hecha de Lodo) LC 93-45711. (ENG & SPA., Illus.). 32p. (J). 1994. lib. bdg. 14.95 (*0-87358-593-3*, Rising Moon Bks) Northland AZ.

— This House Is Made of Mud (Esta Casa Esta Hecha de Lodo) LC 93-45711. (ENG & SPA., Illus.). 32p. (J). (ps-1). 1994. pap. 6.95 (*0-87358-580-1*, Rising Moon Bks) Northland AZ.

Buchanan, Ken & Buchanan, Debby. It Rained on the Desert Today. LC 93-44813. (Illus.). 32p. (J). (ps-3). 1994. lib. bdg. 14.95 (*0-87358-575-5*, Rising Moon Bks) Northland AZ.

— It Rained on the Desert Today. (J). 1999. write for info. (*0-87358-749-9*, Rising Moon Bks) Northland AZ.

Buchanan, Kimberly M. Apache Women Warriors. 2nd ed. LC 92-62469. (Southwestern Studies Ser.: No. 79). (Illus.). 60p. 1996. pap. 13.00 (*0-87404-154-6*) Tex Western.

Buchanan, Kina, tr. see Sauriol, Paul.

Buchanan, Larry. It Came from Hunger! Tales of a Cinema Schlockmeister. LC 96-18684. (Illus.). 233p. 1996. lib. bdg. 42.50 (*0-7864-0194-X*) McFarland & Co.

Buchanan, Lauretta. Smart Game Booklet: Alcohol & Other Drugs: Self-Motivational & Recreational Teaching Strategies. 64p. (J). (gr. 1-6). 1998. pap. text, teacher ed. 29.00 (*1-57035-163-5*, 72AD) Sopris.

— Smarts Game Booklet: Elementary Language Arts & Grammar: Self-Motivational & Recreational Teaching Strategies. 80p. 1998. pap. text, teacher ed. 29.00 (*1-57035-153-8*, 72ELA) Sopris.

— Smarts Game Booklet: Elementary Math: Self-Motivational & Recreational Teaching Strategies. 104p. 1998. pap. text, teacher ed. 29.00 (*1-57035-151-1*, 72EM) Sopris.

— Smarts Game Booklet: Elementary Writing Skills & Reading Comprehension: Self-Motivational & Recreational Teaching Strategies. 56p. (J). (gr. 1). 1998. pap. text, teacher ed. 29.00 (*1-57035-155-4*) Sopris.

— Smarts Game Booklet: Health 'n Me! Grade 4: Self-Motivational & Recreational Teaching Strategies. 92p. (J). (gr. 1-6). 1998. pap. text, teacher ed. 29.00 (*1-57035-193-7*, 90QUESTION) Sopris.

— Smarts Game Booklet: Health 'n Me! Grade 5: Self-Motivational & Recreational Teaching Strategies. 112p. (J). (gr. 1-6). 1998. pap. text, teacher ed. 29.00 (*1-57035-194-5*, 72QUESTION) Sopris.

— Smarts Game Booklet: Health 'n Me! Grade 6: Self-Motivational & Recreational Teaching Strategies. 96p. (J). (gr. 1-6). 1998. pap. text, teacher ed. 29.00 (*1-57035-195-3*, 72QUESTIONS) Sopris.

— Smarts Game Booklet: Secondary Math: Self-Motivational & Recreational Teaching Strategies. 120p. 1998. pap. text, teacher ed. 29.00 (*1-57035-154-6*, 725M) Sopris.

— Smarts Game Instructional Manual: Self-Motivational & Recreational Teaching Strategies. 12p. 1998. pap. text, teacher ed. 29.00 (*1-57035-152-X*, 72GAME) Sopris.

Buchanan, Lee, jt. auth. see Schaefer, Steven M.

Buchanan, Lorraine. Comprehensive Management of Spinal Cord Injury. 288p. 1987. 45.00 (*0-683-01128-6*) Lppncott W & W.

Buchanan, Marcellus, jt. auth. see Terrell, Bob.

Buchanan, Margaret G. DuVal, DuVals of Kentucky, from Va., 1794-1935, Descendants & Allied Families. (Illus.). 265p. 1993. reprint ed. pap. 41.00 (*0-8328-3593-5*); reprint ed. lib. bdg. 51.00 (*0-8328-3592-7*) Higginson Bk Co.

***Buchanan, Mark.** Beyond Conditional Surrender: Getting More of God by Giving up More of Yourself. 2001. 12.99 (*1-57673-774-8*) Multnomah Pubs.

Buchanan, Mary. Special Education Desk Reference. Weller, Carol & Buchanan, Michelle, eds. LC 96-32706. (Illus.). 324p. 1997. pap. 55.00 (*1-56593-800-3*, 1556) Thomson Learn.

Buchanan, Mary, jt. auth. see Weller, Carol.

Buchanan, Meg. Shuttered Heart. (Rainbow Romances Ser.). 160p. 1994. 14.95 (*0-7090-5005-4*, 910) Parkwest Pubns.

— Shuttered Heart. large type ed. (Linford Romance Library). 288p. 1995. pap. 16.99 (*0-7089-7778-2*, Linford) Ulverscroft.

Buchanan, Melisa. Teach a Beginning Reader with Common Sense & a Cookie Sheet: A Guide for Parents. (Illus.). 96p. (Orig.). 1990. pap. write for info. (*1-879129-00-0*) Oak Plantation.

Buchanan, Melisa, jt. auth. see Cain, Ann.

Buchanan, Meriel. Dissolution of an Empire. LC 75-115512. (Russia Observed Ser.). (Illus.). 1971. reprint ed. 19.95 (*0-405-03078-9*) Ayer.

Buchanan, Michael R. Commercial Real Estate Finance. (Illus.). 400p. (C). 1993. pap. text 45.00 (*0-89982-320-3*) Am Bankers.

— Introduction to Mortgage Lending. (Illus.). 400p. (C). 1993. pap. text 45.00 (*0-89982-319-X*) Am Bankers.

Buchanan, Michael R., et al, eds. Thrombin: Its Key Role in Thrombogenesis-Implications for Its Inhibition. LC 94-26483. 230p. 1994. boxed set 169.00 (*0-8493-7649-1*, 7649) CRC Pr.

Buchanan, Michael R. & Johnson, Ronald D. Real Estate Finance. 2nd ed. (Illus.). 522p. (C). 1988. text 49.00 (*0-89982-351-3*, 050020) Am Bankers.

Buchanan, Michelle, ed. see Buchanan, Mary.

Buchanan, Michelle V., ed. Fourier Transform Mass Spectrometry: Evolution, Innovation & Applications. LC 87-26107. (Symposium Ser.: No. 359). (Illus.). x, 216p. 1987. 49.95 (*0-8412-1441-7*) Am Chemical.

— Fourier Transform Mass Spectrometry: Evolution, Innovation & Applications. LC 87-26107. (ACS Symposium Ser.: Vol. 359). 216p. 1987. reprint ed. pap. 67.00 (*0-608-03882-2*, 206432900008) Bks Demand.

Buchanan, Mike & Slottje, Daniel, eds. Advances in the Economics of Sports, Supp. 1. LC 98-123213. 187p. 1997. 78.50 (*0-7623-0184-8*) Jai Pr.

Buchanan, Neil. Art Attack. LC 97-35376. (Illus.). 64p. (J). (gr. k-6). 1998. pap. 9.95 (*0-7894-2906-3*) DK Pub Inc.

— Art Attack. (Illus.). 64p. (J). (gr. k-6). 1998. 12.95 (*0-7894-2893-8*) DK Pub Inc.

Buchanan, Neil & Cooper, Peter. Childhood Asthma: What It Is & What You Can Do. LC 95-31279. (Illus.). 96p. 1995. pap. 8.95 (*1-883672-36-8*) Tricycle Pr.

Buchanan, Neil, tr. see Harnack, Adolph.

Buchanan, Nina K. & Feldhusen, John F., eds. Conducting Research & Evaluation in Gifted Education: A Handbook of Methods & Applications. (Education & Psychology of the Gifted Ser.: No. 6). 360p. (C). 1991. text 50.00 (*0-8077-3083-1*); pap. text 25.95 (*0-8077-3082-3*) Tchrs Coll.

Buchanan, P. G. & Nieuwland, D. A., eds. Modern Developments in Structural Interpretation, Validation & Modelling. (Geological Society Special Publication Ser.: No. 99). 376p. 1995. 117.00 (*1-897799-43-8*, 342, Pub. by Geol Soc Pub Hse) AAPG.

Buchanan, P. G., jt. ed. see Buchanan, J. G.

Buchanan, P. K. Mycological Papers No. 156: A Reappraisal of Ascochytula & Ascochytella (Coelomycetes) 83p. (C). 1987. pap. text 31.50 (*0-85198-579-3*) C A B Intl.

Buchanan, Pamela, ed. see Buchanan, James R.

Buchanan, Pat. Deng-Xiao Ping is a Chain Smoking Communist Dwarf: The Sayings of Pat Buchanan. LC 96-209697. 96p. 1996. pap. 5.00 (*0-345-40783-0*) Ballantine Pub Grp.

— Memoir on Nixon. 14.00 (*0-06-098823-1*) HarpC.

Buchanan, Patrick J. The Great Betrayal: How American Sovereignty & Social Justice Are Being Sacrificed to the Gods of the Global Economy. LC 97-38818. (Illus.). 384p. (gr. 8). 1998. 22.95 (*0-316-11518-5*) Little.

***Buchanan, Patrick J.** A Republic, Not an Empire: Reclaiming America's Destiny. LC 99-32102. 300p. 1999. 29.95 (*0-89526-272-X*, Pub. by Regnery Pub) Natl Bk Netwk.

Buchanan, Patrick J. Right from the Beginning. LC 87-35354. 1988. 18.95 (*0-316-11408-1*) Little.

— Right from the Beginning. LC 90-43500. (Illus.). 400p. 1990. pap. 12.95 (*0-89526-745-4*) Regnery Pub.

Buchanan, Paul. Battle of the Bands. LC 97-42127. (Misadventures of Willie Plummet Ser.). (gr. 3-7). 1998. pap. text 5.99 (*0-570-05046-4*, 56-1870) Concordia.

***Buchanan, Paul.** Brain Freeze, 1, 15. LC 99-47326. (Misadventures of Willie Plummett Ser.: Vol. 15). 127p. (J). (gr. 3-7). 1999. pap. text 5.99 (*0-570-07004-X*) Concordia.

— Dances with Werewolves, Vol. 8. LC 99-48294. (Heebie Jeebies Ser.: Vol. 6). 144p. (J). (gr. 3-7). 2000. pap. 5.99 (*0-8054-1982-9*) Broadman.

— Dog Days, 1, 14. 1999. pap. text 6.00 (*0-570-07054-6*) Concordia.

Buchanan, Paul. Gold Flakes for Breakfast. LC 97-42218. (Misadventures of Willie Plummet Ser.). 128p. (J). (gr. 3-7). 1998. pap. text 5.99 (*0-570-05045-6*, 56-1869) Concordia.

— Hail to the Chump. LC 98-19605. (Misadventures of Willie Plummet Ser.). 128p. (J). (gr. 1-5). 1998. pap. 5.99 (*0-570-05088-X*) Concordia.

— The Rat That Ate Poodles. LC 98-13937. (Heebie Jeebies Ser.: Vol. 1). 144p. (J). (gr. 1-6). 1998. pap. 5.99 (*0-8054-0170-9*) Broadman.

— The Return of the Eagle. Parker, Liz, ed. (Take Ten Bks.). (Illus.). 45p. (J). (gr. 6-12). 1992. pap. text 3.95 (*1-56254-052-1*) Saddleback Pubns.

***Buchanan, Paul.** The Return of the Eagle. rev. ed. (Take Ten Ser.). (Illus.). 54p. (YA). (gr. 4-12). 1999. pap. 3.95 (*1-58659-002-2*) Artesian.

— Stuck on You, 1, 13. 1999. pap. text 6.00 (*0-570-07052-X*) Concordia.

Buchanan, Paul. Tidal Wave. LC 98-19609. (Misadventures of Willie Plummet Ser.). 128p. (J). (gr. 1-5). 1998. pap. 5.99 (*0-570-05086-3*) Concordia.

— Uncle from Another Planet. LC 98-37533. (Heebie Jeebies Ser.: Vol. 4). 144p. (YA). 1999. pap. 5.99 (*0-8054-1650-1*) Broadman.

***Buchanan, Paul.** Wild Ride on Bigfoot Mountain, Vol. 6. LC 99-22417. (Heebie Jeebies Ser.: No. 6). 144p. (YA). (gr. 8-12). 1999. pap. 5.99 (*0-8054-1975-6*) Broadman.

Buchanan, Paul & Randall, Rod. Anything You Can Do I Can Do Better. LC 97-35026. (Misadventures of Willie Plummet Ser.). (J). (gr. 3-7). 1998. 5.99 (*0-570-05043-X*, 56-1867) Concordia.

***Buchanan, Paul & Randall, Rod.** Ask Willie. LC 98-50569. (Misadventures of Willie Plummet Ser.: Bk. 12). 128p. (J). (gr. 3-7). 1999. pap. 5.99 (*0-570-05478-8*, 56-1941GJ) Concordia.

Buchanan, Paul & Randall, Rod. Ballistic Bugs. LC 97-34970. (Misadventures of Willie Plummet Ser.). (J). (gr. 3-7). 1998. 5.99 (*0-570-05044-8*, 56-1868) Concordia.

***Buchanan, Paul & Randall, Rod.** Heads I Win, Tails You Lose. LC 98-32125. (Misadventures of Willie Plummet Ser.: Bk. 11). 128p. (J). (gr. 3-7). 1999. pap. 5.99 (*0-570-05477-X*, 56-1940GJ) Concordia.

Buchanan, Paul & Randall, Rod. Invasion from Planet X. LC 97-33078. (Misadventures of Willie Plummet Ser.). (J). (gr. 3-7). 1998. write for info. (*0-570-05041-3*, 56-1865) Concordia.

***Buchanan, Paul & Randall, Rod.** The Monopoly. LC 98-7206. (Misadventures of Willie Plummet Ser.). 128p. (J). (gr. 3-7). 1998. 5.99 (*0-570-05089-8*) Concordia.

Buchanan, Paul & Randall, Rod. Shooting Stars. LC 98-7205. (Misadventures of Willie Plummet Ser.). 128p. (J). (gr. 1-5). 1998. 5.99 (*0-570-05087-1*) Concordia.

— Submarine Sandwiched. LC 97-33070. (Misadventures of Willie Plummet Ser.). (J). (gr. 3-7). 1997. write for info. (*0-570-05042-1*, 56-1866) Concordia.

Buchanan, Paul & Sammarco, Anthony. Milton. (Images of America Ser.). 128p. 1996. pap. 16.99 (*0-7524-0286-2*) Arcadia Publng.

Buchanan, Paul, ed. see Aros, Robert & Ternan, Rob.

Buchanan, Paul D. Famous Animals of the States: True-to-Life Tales of the Most Unusual Beasts of the 50 States, Puerto Rico, & the District of Columbia. LC 96-18685. (Illus.). 150p. 1996. pap. 30.00 (*0-7864-0146-X*) McFarland & Co.

— Historic Places of Worship: Stories of 51 Extraordinary American Religious Sites since 1300. LC 99-18282. (Illus.). 240p. 1999. boxed set 39.95 (*0-7864-0588-0*) McFarland & Co.

Buchanan, Paul G. State, Labor, Capital: Democratizing Class Relations in the Southern Cone. (Latin American Ser.). 328p. (C). 1996. text 49.95 (*0-8229-3910-X*) U of Pittsburgh Pr.

Buchanan, Peggy & Schwartz, Linda. Movin & Groovin. LC 98-156084. (Illus.). 136p. (J). (gr. 1-6). 1997. pap. 12.95 (*0-88160-279-5*, LW349) Learning Wks.

Buchanan, Peneope. Looking Together: Introducing Young Children to the Cleveland Museum of Art. LC 96-47689. 1996. write for info. (*0-940717-38-7*) Cleveland Mus Art.

Buchanan, Peter. Renzo Piano Building Workshop, Vol. 1. (Renzo Piano Building Workshop Ser.). 240p. 1999. pap. 29.95 (*0-7148-3898-5*) Phaidon Pr.

— Renzo Piano Building Workshop, Vol. 1. LC 96-184067. (Illus.). 240p. (C). 1993. text 75.00 (*0-7148-2809-2*, Pub. by Phaidon Press) Phaidon Pr.

***Buchanan, Peter.** Renzo Piano Building Workshop, Vol. 2. (Renzo Piano Building Workshop Ser.). 240p. 1999. 29.95 (*0-7148-3899-3*) Phaidon Pr.

Buchanan, Peter. Renzo Piano Building Workshop Vol. 2: Complete Works. LC 96-184067. (Illus.). 240p. (C). 1995. text 75.00 (*0-7148-2859-9*, Pub. by Phaidon Press) Phaidon Pr.

— Renzo Piano Building Workshop Vol. 3: Complete Works. LC 96-184067. (Illus.). 240p. 1997. 75.00 (*0-7148-3543-9*, Pub. by Phaidon Press) Phaidon Pr.

***Buchanan, Peter.** Renzo Piano Building Workshop Complete Works, Vol. 3. Vol. 3. (Illus.). 240p. 2000. pap. 29.95 (*0-7148-3933-7*) Phaidon Pr.

— Renzo Piano Building Workshop Complete Works, Vol. 4. 2000. 75.00 (*0-7148-3931-0*) Phaidon Pr.

Buchanan, Peter. UIA Barcelona 96 Competitions. 1997. pap. 31.00 (*84-89698-04-X*, Pub. by Actar) Dist Art Pubs.

Buchanan, Peter, et al. The Architecture of Enric Miralles & Carme Pinos. (Illus.). 96p. (Orig.). 1990. pap. 20.00 (*0-930829-14-X*) Lumen Inc.

— Spain, 1920-1999. (Architectural Guides Ser.). (Illus.). 416p. 1998. 40.00 (*3-7643-5748-7*, Pub. by Birkhauser) Princeton Arch.

Buchanan, Polly W. Quantity Food Preparation: Standardizing Recipes & Controlling Ingredients. 3rd ed. LC 93-6122. 1993. write for info. (*0-88091-150-6*) Am Dietetic Assn.

Buchanan, R. A., ed. Engineers & Engineering: A Collection of Essays on the History of Technology. LC 96-144307. 1995. 69.95 (*0-86197-118-3*, Pub. by Bath Univ Pr) Intl Spec Bk.

Buchanan, Ray, ed. Gleanings: Hunger Meditations for Lent. rev. ed. 112p. pap. 5.50 (*0-939485-02-8*) St Andrew Pr.

Buchanan, Relva, ed. Ceramic Materials for Electronics, Processing, Properties & Applications: Processing, Properties & Applications. 2nd expanded rev. ed. (Electrical Engineering & Electronics Ser.: Vol. 72). (Illus.). 560p. 1991. text 195.00 (*0-8247-8194-5*) Dekker.

B

Buchanan, Relva C. & Park, Taeun. Materials Crystal Chemistry. LC 97-18615. (Illus.). 472p. 1997. text 185.00 (*0-8247-9798-1*) Dekker.

Buchanan, Rex, ed. Kansas Geology: An Introduction to Landscapes, Rocks, Minerals, & Fossils. LC 83-23546. xii, 228p. 1984. pap. 17.95 (*0-7006-0240-2*) U Pr of KS.

Buchanan, Rex & McCauley, James R. Roadside Kansas: A Traveler's Guide to Its Geology & Landmarks. LC 87-2013. (Illus.). xiv, 370p. 1987. 25.00 (*0-7006-0323-9*); pap. 12.95 (*0-7006-0322-0*) U Pr of KS.

Buchanan, Rex C., jt. auth. see Baars, Donald L.

Buchanan, Rex C., jt. auth. see Rossbacher, Lisa A.

Buchanan, Richard. The Enemy Within: Actions That Self-Destruct Companies & Customer Service. (Illus.). 248p. 1996. pap. 14.95 (*0-07-470324-2*) McGraw.

Buchanan, Richard & Margolin, Victor, eds. Discovering Design: Explorations in Design Studies. LC 94-27479. 283p. 1995. pap. text 14.95 (*0-226-07815-9*) U Ch Pr.

— Discovering Design: Explorations in Design Studies. LC 94-27479. 283p. 1995. lib. bdg. 37.50 (*0-226-07814-0*) U Ch Pr.

Buchanan, Richard, jt. ed. see Garver, Eugene.

Buchanan, Richard, jt. ed. see Margolin, Victor.

Buchanan, Richard R. Men of the 704: The Illustrated & Pictorial History of the 704th Tank Destroyer Battalion in World War II. Wissocik, Richard D. et al, eds. LC 98-38703. (Joe & Henny Heisel Ser.: Vol. 6). (Illus.). 114p. 1998. 30.00 (*1-885851-12-X*) St Vincent Coll.

Buchanan, Rita. A Dyer's Garden: From Plant to Pot; Growing Dyes for Natural Fibers. (Illus.). 112p. 1995. pap. 9.95 (*1-883010-07-1*) Interweave.

— Plants for Winter Beauty. LC 97-10466. (Taylor's Weekend Gardening Guides Ser.). (Illus.). 128p. 1997. pap. 12.95 (*0-395-82750-7*) HM.

— The Shaker Herb & Garden Book. LC 96-11239. (Illus.). 160p. 1996. 27.95 (*0-395-73325-1*) HM.

— The Shaker Herb & Garden Book. (Illus.). 160p. 1999. reprint ed. text 28.00 (*0-7881-6101-6*) DIANE Pub.

*__Buchanan, Rita.__ Taylor's Master Guide to Landscaping. LC 99-54110. (Illus.). 384p. 2000. 45.00 (*0-618-05590-8*) HM.

Buchanan, Rita. A Weaver's Garden. LC 86-83425. (Illus.). 230p. 1987. 16.95 (*0-934026-28-9*) Interweave.

— Weaver's Garden: Growing Plants for Natural Dyes & Fibers. LC 99-39858. 240p. 1999. pap. text 8.95 (*0-486-40712-8*) Dover.

— The Winter Garden. 1998. 24.00 (*0-8446-6933-4*) Peter Smith.

Buchanan, Rita & Buchanan, Steve. Making a Garden: Reliable Techniques, Outstanding Plants & Honest Advice. LC 98-28215. (Illus.). 160p. 1998. 35.00 (*0-395-89753-X*) HM.

Buchanan, Rita & Tenenbaum, Frances, eds. Taylor's Guide to Gardening in the South. (Taylor's Regional Guides to Gardening Ser.). (Illus.). 450p. 1992. pap. 21.00 (*0-395-59681-5*) HM.

— Taylor's Guide to Herbs. LC 94-44241. (Taylor's Guides to Gardening Ser.). (Illus.). 464p. 1995. pap. 19.95 (*0-395-68081-6*) HM.

Buchanan, Rita, jt. auth. see Holmes, Roger.

Buchanan, Rita, ed. see Jensen, Elizabeth.

Buchanan, Roberdeau. Shippen. Genealogy of the Descendants of Dr. William Shippen, the Elder, of Philadelphia, Member of the Continental Congress. 16p. 1996. lib. bdg. 15.00 (*0-8328-6579-6*) Higginson Bk Co.

Buchanan, Robert. Illusions of Equality: Deaf Americans in School & Factory, 1850-1950. LC 99-40421. 224p. 1999. 39.95 (*1-56368-084-X*) Gallaudet Univ Pr.

Buchanan, Robert J. Medicaid Cost Containment: Long-Term Care Reimbursement. LC 85-45028. 200p. 1987. 36.50 (*0-8386-3271-8*) Fairleigh Dickinson.

Buchanan, Robert L. Structured Programming in dBASE IV. 426p. (C). 1991. pap. 43.95 (*0-534-14400-4*) Course Tech.

Buchanan, Robert S., ed. see Maxwell, H. James & Sullivan, Bob.

Buchanan, Robert W. Art of Testing Network Systems. LC 95-45445. 592p. 1996. text 69.99 incl. cd-rom (*0-471-13223-3*) Wiley.

— The Complete Poetical Works of Robert Buchanan, 2 vols., Set. LC 79-148760. reprint ed. 145.00 (*0-404-08734-5*) AMS Pr.

— The Fleshly School of Poetry & Other Phenomena of the Day: Reprint of 1872 Edition. LC 72-148343. 34.50 (*0-404-08821-X*) AMS Pr.

Buchanan, Robert W. & Lukaszewski, Charles. Measuring the Impact of Your Web Site. LC 96-47396. 316p. 1997. pap. 29.95 (*0-471-17249-9*) Wiley.

Buchanan, Rodney J. We Are Not Alone: Studies in the Covenant of God. 95p. 1994. pap. 7.95 (*0-917851-98-6*) Bristol Hse.

Buchanan, Roger B., jt. auth. see Williams, Christopher J.

Buchanan, Sara A., jt. auth. see Hemenway, Michele.

Buchanan, Scott. The Doctrine of Signatures: A Defense of Theory in Medicine. 2nd ed. 248p. 1990. text 34.95 (*0-252-01782-X*); pap. text 13.95 (*0-252-06150-0*) U of Ill Pr.

— Poetry & Mathematics. (Midway Reprint Ser.). 156p. 1975. reprint ed. pap. text 9.95 (*0-226-07821-3*) U Ch Pr.

Buchanan, Scott, ed. see Plato.

Buchanan, Scott M. Possibility. LC 74-22904. 204p. reprint ed. pap. 63.30 (*0-8357-8993-4*, 205679100085) Bks Demand.

Buchanan-Smith, Hannah M., jt. ed. see Box, Hilary O.

Buchanan-Smith, Margaret & Davies, Susanna. Famine Early Warning & Response: The Missing Link. 240p. (Orig.). 1995. pap. 25.00 (*1-85339-291-X*, Pub. by Intermed Tech) Stylus Pub VA.

Buchanan, Steve, jt. auth. see Buchanan, Rita.

Buchanan, Sue. Duh-Votions: Words of Wisdom for the Spiritually Challenged. LC 99-32616. 160p. 2000. pap. 9.99 (*0-310-22865-4*) Zondervan.

— Girls Gatta Have Fun. LC 99-30108. 2000. 14.99 (*0-310-22885-9*) Zondervan.

— I'm Alive & the Doctor's Dead: Surviving Cancer with Your Sense of Humor & Your Sexuality Intact. LC 98-15530. 224p. 1998. pap. 12.99 (*0-310-22455-1*) Zondervan.

Buchanan, Susan & Gaylinn, Seymour. Commodity Year Book, 1989 Edition. 1989. 49.95 (*0-910418-22-5*) Commodity Res.

Buchanan, Susan & Gaylinn, Seymour, eds. Commodity Year Book, 1990. rev. ed. (Illus.). 320p. 1990. 49.95 (*0-910418-24-1*) Commodity Res.

Buchanan, Terry. William Hayes, 1871 to 1940: York Photographic Artist. 82p. 1986. 43.00 (*0-907033-39-3*) St Mut.

Buchanan, Thomas M., jt. auth. see Robison, Henry W.

Buchanan, Timm, et al. Teach Yourself Access 97 in 24 Hours. LC 96-71493. 384p. 1997. 19.99 (*0-672-31027-9*) Sams.

Buchanan, Timothy & Eddy, Craig. Teach Yourself Access 2000 in 24 Hours. (Teach Yourself Ser.). (Illus.). 403p. 1999. 19.99 (*0-672-31289-1*) Sams.

Buchanan, Todd, photos by. Bradley University: A Centennial Portrait. LC 96-78620. (Illus.). 112p. 1997. 39.95 (*1-56469-031-8*) Harmony Hse Pub.

— Lafayette College - Then & Now. (Illus.). 112p. 1993. 39.95 (*1-56469-006-7*) Harmony Hse Pub.

Buchanan, Tom. Britain & the Spanish Civil War. (Illus.). 256p. (C). 1997. text 64.95 (*0-521-45500-6*); pap. text 24.95 (*0-521-45569-3*) Cambridge U Pr.

Buchanan, Tom & Conway, Martin, eds. Political Catholicism in Europe, 1918-1965. LC 95-25450. (Illus.). 322p. (C). 1996. text 85.00 (*0-19-820319-5*, Clarendon Pr) OUP.

Buchanan, W. Microelectronic Systems: Design, Modelling & Testing. 314p. 1997. pap. 44.95 (*0-471-19142-6*) Wiley.

Buchanan, W. T. Powerful Perceptions. (Illus.). 280p. 1994. 24.00 (*0-9640175-0-4*) Value Concepts.

Buchanan, W. Watson, et al. Clinical Examination of the Musculoskeletal System. 2nd ed. LC 96-7787. (Illus.). 240p. 1997. pap. 29.95 (*0-683-01127-8*) Lppncott W & W.

Buchanan, William. Advanced PC Interfacing Graphics & Interrupts. LC 98-29435. 688p. (C). 1999. pap. text 44.95 (*0-201-17818-4*) Addison-Wesley.

— Computer Architecture & Networks. LC 97-105640. 400p. (C). 1996. pap. 39.95 (*0-201-87728-7*) Addison-Wesley.

*__Buchanan, William.__ Computer Busses Design & Application. (C). 2000. ring bd. 74.95 (*0-8493-0825-9*) CRC Pr.

Buchanan, William. Execution Eve. 1993. pap. 16.95 (*0-88282-176-8*) New Horizon NJ.

— An Inquiry into the Genealogy & Present State of Ancient Scottish Surnames: With the Origins & Descent of the Highland Clans & Family of Buchanan. 344p. (Orig.). 1994. pap. text 24.00 (*1-55613-997-7*) Heritage Bk.

— A Shining Season: The True Story of John Baker. LC 87-19072. (Illus.). 369p. 1987. reprint ed. pap. 15.95 (*0-8263-1016-8*) U of NM Pr.

— Treatise on the Law of Scotland on the Subject of Teinds or Tithes. LC 99-61967. x, 520p. 1999. reprint ed. 160.00 (*1-56169-506-8*) Gaunt.

— Understanding Political Variables. 4th ed. 395p. (C). 1988. pap. text 75.00 (*0-02-316360-7*, Macmillan Coll) P-H.

Buchanan, William, ed. J. Craig Annan: Selected Texts & Bibliography. LC 93-37065. (World Photographers Reference Ser.: No. 6). (Illus.). 212p. 1994. 95.00 (*0-8161-0617-7*, G K Hall & Co) Mac Lib Ref.

Buchanan, William, et al. Mackintosh's Masterwork: Charles Rennie Mackintosh & the Glasgow School of Art. (Illus.). 224p. 1989. 40.00 (*0-87701-663-1*) Chronicle Bks.

— Mackintosh's Masterwork: Charles Rennie Mackintosh & the Glasgow School of Art. (Illus.). 224p. 1995. reprint ed. pap. 22.95 (*0-8118-0932-3*) Chronicle Bks.

Buchanan, William J. One Last Time. 128p. (Orig.). (YA). 1992. pap. 2.99 (*0-380-76152-1*, Avon Bks) Morrow Avon.

Buchanan, William J. Software Development for Engineers with C, Pascal, C++, Assembly Language, Visual Basic, HTML, JavaScript & Java. 624p. 1997. 93.50 (*0-471-25266-2*) Wiley.

Buchanan, William T., Jr., jt. auth. see Maccord, Howard A., Sr.

Buchannan, Susan & Gaylinn, Seymour, eds. Commodity Year Book, 1988. LC 39-11418. 1988. 49.95 (*0-910418-21-7*) Commodity Res.

Buchanon, Nancy & Hassett, Jacquelyn, eds. The Blue Book: Program Development Guidelines for Nurse-Directed Health Services. rev. ed. 28p. 1994. pap. 30.00 (*0-614-30636-1*) Am Coll Hlth.

Buchar, Z., et al. Mechanical Behavior of Metals at Extremely High Strain Rates. (Materials Science Surveys Ser.: Vol. 4). (Illus.). 250p. (C). 1986. text 96.00 (*0-87849-528-2*, Pub. by Trans T Pub) Enfield Pubs NH.

Buchart & Associates, Inc. Staff. Indianapolis Guide Book for Kids. 36p. (J). (ps-5). 1993. pap. 2.75 (*1-883900-01-8*) Buchart & Assocs.

— Knoxville Guide Book for Kids. 28p. (J). (ps-5). 1993. pap. 1.50 (*1-883900-03-4*) Buchart & Assocs.

— Louisville Guide Book for Kids. 36p. (J). (ps-5). 1993. pap. 2.75 (*1-883900-02-6*) Buchart & Assocs.

Buchart, Greta, jt. auth. see Eaton, Deborah.

Buchberg, Wendy. Quilting a Thematic Unit: Easy Cross-Curricular Projects & Activities for the Classroom. 64p. 1997. pap. 10.95 (*0-590-96558-1*) Scholastic Inc.

Buchberger, B., ed. see Wang, D.

Buchberger, Bruno. EUROCAL '85: Proceedings Vol. 1: Invited Lectures. (Lecture Notes in Computer Science Ser.: Vol. 203). vi, 233p. 1985. 30.00 (*0-387-15983-5*) Spr-Verlag.

Buchberger, Bruno, et al, eds. Computer Algebra. (Illus.). 283p. 1985. 64.95 (*0-387-81776-X*) Spr-Verlag.

Buchberger, Bruno & Winkler, Franz, eds. Grobner Bases & Applications. LC 97-44181. (London Mathematical Society Lecture Note Ser.: No. 251). (Illus.). 545p. (C). 1998. pap. text 49.95 (*0-521-63298-6*) Cambridge U Pr.

Buchberger, Bruno, ed. see Joint Conference on Vector & Parallel Processing.

Buchberger, Bruno, ed. see Joint International Conference on Vector & Paralle.

Buchbinder, David. Basic Bankruptcy Law for Paralegals, Forms Manual, Vol. 1. 2nd ed. LC 94-75843. 1994. pap. text 17.95 (*0-316-10251-2*, Aspen Law & Bus) Aspen Pub.

— Fundamental Banking, Set. 1992. 125.00 (*0-316-11418-9*) Little.

— Fundamentals of Bankruptcy. 1991. 125.00 (*0-316-11414-6*, Aspen Law & Bus) Aspen Pub.

— Masculinites & Identities. LC 94-189135. (Interpretations Ser.). 160p. 1994. pap. 19.95 (*0-522-84545-2*, Pub. by Melbourne Univ Pr) Paul & Co Pubs.

— Performance Anxieties: Re-Producing Masculinity. (Illus.). 224p. 1998. pap. 24.95 (*1-86448-425-X*, Pub. by Allen & Unwin Pty) Paul & Co Pubs.

Buchbinder, David L. Basic Bankruptcy Law for Paralegals, Incl. instr's. manual. 3rd ed. 512p. 1997. pap. text 38.00 (*1-56706-507-4*, 65074) Panel Pubs.

— Basic Bankruptcy Law for Paralegals: Forms Manual, Incl. instr's. manual. 3rd ed. LC 96-79007. 288p. 1997. pap. text, teacher ed. 22.95 (*1-56706-512-0*, 65120) Panel Pubs.

Buchbinder, Eli, jt. auth. see Eisikovitz, Zvi.

Buchbinder, I. L. & Kuzenko, S. M. Ideas & Methods of Supersymmetry & Supergravity: Or a Walk Through Superspace. (Illus.). 640p. 1995. 326.00 (*0-7503-0258-5*) IOP Pub.

— Ideas & Methods of Supersymmetry & Supergravity: or A Walk Through Superspace. LC 99-179340. (Illus.). 640p. 1998. pap. 60.00 (*0-7503-0506-1*) IOP Pub.

Buchbinder, I. L., et al. Effective Action in Quantum Gravity. 424p. 1992. 130.00 (*0-7503-0122-8*) IOP Pub.

Buchbinder, Ligaya H. Skin Care: Clear & Simple. Orloff, Erica, ed. LC 96-93067. 192p. (Orig.). 1997. pap. 12.95 (*1-885843-05-4*) Saturn Press.

Buchdahl, Gerd. Fine Structure History of Science: Lessons for Methodology. 1981. pap. 16.25 (*0-08-028930-4*, Pergamon Pr) Elsevier.

Buchdahl, Gerd, ed. Changing Views about the Principles of Scientific Theory Evaluation. 90p. 1981. pap. 20.00 (*0-08-027408-0*, Pergamon Pr) Elsevier.

Buchdahl, Hans A. The Concepts of Classicals Thermodynamics. LC 66-70356. (Cambridge Monographs on Physics). 236p. reprint ed. pap. 67.30 (*0-608-10017-X*, 2022438) Bks Demand.

— An Introduction to Hamiltonian Optics. LC 93-4557. (Illus.). xv, 360p. 1993. reprint ed. pap. 10.95 (*0-486-67597-1*) Dover.

— Seventeen Simple Lectures on General Relativity Theory. LC 81-11376. 190p. 1981. 32.95 (*0-471-09684-9*) Krieger.

Bucheister, Pat. Near the Edge. 1995. mass mkt. 2.95 (*0-553-55035-7*) Bantam.

*__Bucheister, Patt.__ Below the Salt: A Gentlewoman's Commonplace Book. fac. ed. (Illus.). iii, 110p. 1999. 39.95 (*0-9676506-0-7*) Shady Hollow.

Bucheister, Patt. Instant Family. (Special Edition Ser.). 1995. per. 3.75 (*0-373-09953-3*, 1-09953-0) Silhouette.

— Unpredictable. 1994. per. 3.50 (*0-373-09899-5*, 1-09899-5) Harlequin Bks.

Bucheit, Kelly S., ed. see Jones, Mike & Mooney, Chuck, III.

*__Buchel, Bettina S., et al.__ International Joint Venture Management: Learning to Cooperate & Cooperating to Learn. LC 98-8257. 300p. 1998. 45.00 (*0-471-82894-7*) Wiley.

Buchel-Loder, Patrick, tr. see Goossen, Irvy W.

Buchele, Bonnie J., jt. auth. see Ganzarain, Ramon C.

Buchele, Robert, jt. auth. see Aldrich, Mark.

Buchele, Wesley F., jt. auth. see Quick, Graeme R.

Bucheler, Markus. Acute Pancreatitis. 1998. 54.95 (*3-89412-376-1*) Blackwell Sci.

Buchen, Irving H. & Fertman, Carl I. Creating a Culture of Service: Effective Service Learning: Facilitators Program Manual, Facilitators Guide, Student Manuals for Books I-VI. 32p. 1994. teacher ed. write for info. (*1-884063-29-2*) Mar Co Prods.

— Creating a Culture of Service: Effective Service Learning: Facilitators Program Manual, Facilitators Guide, Student Manuals for Books I-VI, Bklt. I. 16p. 1994. student ed. write for info. (*1-884063-38-1*) Mar Co Prods.

— Creating a Culture of Service: Effective Service Learning: Facilitators Program Manual, Facilitators Guide, Student Manuals for Books I-VI, Bklt. II. 16p. 1994. student ed. write for info. (*1-884063-39-X*) Mar Co Prods.

— Creating a Culture of Service: Effective Service Learning: Facilitators Program Manual, Facilitators Guide, Student Manuals for Books I-VI, Bklt. III. 16p. 1994. student ed. write for info. (*1-884063-40-3*) Mar Co Prods.

— Creating a Culture of Service: Effective Service Learning: Facilitators Program Manual, Facilitators Guide, Student Manuals for Books I-VI, Bklt. IV. 16p. 1994. student ed. write for info. (*1-884063-41-1*) Mar Co Prods.

— Creating a Culture of Service: Effective Service Learning: Facilitators Program Manual, Facilitators Guide, Student Manuals for Books I-VI, Bklt. V. 16p. 1994. student ed. write for info. (*1-884063-42-X*) Mar Co Prods.

— Creating a Culture of Service: Effective Service Learning: Facilitators Program Manual, Facilitators Guide, Student Manuals for Books I-VI, Bklt. VI. 16p. 1994. student ed. write for info. (*1-884063-43-8*) Mar Co Prods.

— Creating a Culture of Service: Effective Service Learning: Facilitators Program Manual, Facilitators Guide, Student Manuals for Books I-VI, Facilitator Guide I. 16p. 1994. write for info. (*1-884063-30-6*) Mar Co Prods.

— Creating a Culture of Service: Effective Service Learning: Facilitators Program Manual, Facilitators Guide, Student Manuals for Books I-VI, Facilitator Guide II. 16p. 1994. write for info. (*1-884063-31-4*) Mar Co Prods.

— Creating a Culture of Service: Effective Service Learning: Facilitators Program Manual, Facilitators Guide, Student Manuals for Books I-VI, Facilitator Guide III. 16p. 1994. write for info. (*1-884063-32-2*) Mar Co Prods.

— Creating a Culture of Service: Effective Service Learning: Facilitators Program Manual, Facilitators Guide, Student Manuals for Books I-VI, Facilitator Guide IV. 16p. 1994. write for info. (*1-884063-33-0*) Mar Co Prods.

— Creating a Culture of Service: Effective Service Learning: Facilitators Program Manual, Facilitators Guide, Student Manuals for Books I-VI, Facilitator Guide V. 16p. 1994. write for info. (*1-884063-34-9*) Mar Co Prods.

— Creating a Culture of Service: Effective Service Learning: Facilitators Program Manual, Facilitators Guide, Student Manuals for Books I-VI, Facilitator Guide VI. 16p. 1994. write for info. (*1-884063-35-7*) Mar Co Prods.

— Creating a Culture of Service: Effective Service Learning: Facilitators Program Manual, Facilitators Guide, Student Manuals for Books I-VI, Set. LC 94-77208. (YA). (gr. 6-12). 1994. 179.95 (*1-884063-26-8*) Mar Co Prods.

Buchen, Kathryn. Rainmaker. 153p. (Orig.). (J). 1995. pap. 7.50 (*0-9645405-0-9*) K Beson.

Buchenau, Jurgen. In the Shadow of the Giant: The Making of Mexico's Central America Policy, 1876-1930. LC 95-49581. 312p. (C). 1996. pap. text 32.95 (*0-8173-0829-6*) U of Ala Pr.

Buchenholz, Gretchen. Teach Your Child with Games. Tingue, Manon, ed. 128p. 1984. pap. 8.95 (*0-685-08792-1*, Fireside) S&S Trade Pap.

Buchenrieder, Klaus. Hardware - Software Co-Design: An Annotated Bibliography. LC 94-43365. (Microsystems Engineering Ser.: Vol. 203). 1995. pap. 39.95 (*0-9639887-7-8*) IT Press.

Buchenrieder, Klaus & Sedlmeier, Alexander, eds. Consyse '97: International Workshop on Conjoint Systems Engineering. (Applied Computer Science & Technology Ser.). (Illus.). 120p. 1998. pap. 69.80 (*0-9639887-0-0*) IT Press.

Buchenrieder, Klaus, et al. Hardware-Software Codesign. (Informationstechnik und Technische Informatik Ser.). (Illus.). 110p. 1998. pap. 39.80 (*3-929814-08-0*) IT Press.

Buchenrieder, Klaus, jt. ed. see Rozenblit, Jerzy.

Buchenroth, Michael L. Insanity an Anthology. LC 98-96283. 150p. 1998. pap. 19.95 (*0-9664914-0-8*, SAN 299-6022) Buchenroth Publ.

Bucher. Diversity Consciousness: Open Our Minds to People, Cultures & Opportunities. LC 99-42489. 233p. 1999. pap. text 17.00 (*0-13-080338-3*) P-H.

Bucher, Bernadette. Icon & Conquest: A Structural Analysis of the Illustrations of de Bry's Great Voyages. Gulati, Basia M., tr. LC 81-3415. (Chicago Original Paperback Ser.). (Illus.). 296p. (C). 1981. pap. text 20.00 (*0-226-07832-9*) U Ch Pr.

Bucher, Bernadette. Icon & Conquest: A Structural Analysis of the Illustrations of de Bry's Great Voyages. Gulati, Anastasia M., tr. LC 81-3415. (Illus.). 258p. reprint ed. pap. 80.00 (*0-608-09400-5*, 205414500004) Bks Demand.

— Icon & Conquest: A Structural Analysis of the Illustrations of de Bry's Great Voyages. Gulati, Basia M., tr. LC 81-3415. (Illus.). 257p. Date not set. reprint ed. pap. 79.70 (*0-608-20614-8*, 205458200003) Bks Demand.

Bucher, Charles A., et al. Foundations of Health. LC 67-10700. (Illus.). 1967. 19.95 (*0-8290-2398-4*) Irvington.

Bucher, Charles Augustus & Krotee, March L. Management of Physical Education & Sport. 466p. 1992. 39.95 (*0-8016-7442-5*) Mosby Inc.

Bucher, Charles Augustus, jt. auth. see Wuest, Deborah A.

An Asterisk (*) at the beginning of an entry indicates that the title is appearing for the first time.

Bucher, Christina. Biblical Imagery for God. LC 95-77971. 95p. 1995. pap. 5.95 (*0-87178-093-3*, 8933) Brethren.
— The Prophecy of Amos & Hosea. LC 97-19277. (Covenant Bible Studies). (Orig.). 1997. pap. 5.95 (*0-87178-008-9*) Brethren.
Bucher, Dorothy, tr. see Bailey, Keith M.
Bucher, Dorothy, tr. see Simpson, A. B.
Bucher, E. H., et al. An Initial Environmental Examination for the Hidrovia Waterway in the Paraquay-Parana River Basin. 100p. 1993. pap. text 25.00 (*1-883861-01-2*) Wetlnds Amer.
Bucher, Hubert. Spirits & Power: An Analysis of Shona Cosmology. (Illus.). 232p. 1981. text 29.95 (*0-19-570176-3*) OUP.
Bucher, J. Kannada-English Dictionary. 584p. 1983. 39.95 (*0-8288-1767-7*, F29632) Fr & Eur.
Bucher, J. & Watsa, C. A Kannada English Dictionary. 584p. 1986. reprint ed. 12.50 (*0-8364-1698-8*, Pub. by Usha) S Asia.
Bucher, Joe. Joe Bucher's Crankbait Secrets. LC 98-87361. (Illus.). 256p. 1999. pap. 19.95 (*0-87341-729-1*, JBCS) Krause Pubns.
Bucher, Joe & Smith, Otis. Hunting Trophy Muskies & Northerns. LC 92-80358. (Complete Angler's Library). 234p. 1992. write for info. (*0-914697-45-5*) N Amer Outdoor Grp.
Bucher-Jones, Simon. Ghost Devices. (Orig.). 1997. mass mkt. 5.95 (*0-426-20514-6*, Pub. by Virgin Bks) London Brdge.
***Bucher-Jones, Simon & Clapham, Mark.** The Taking of Planet 5. (Doctor Who Ser.). 288p. 2000. mass mkt. 6.95 (*0-563-55585-8*, Pub. by BBC Bks) Genl Dist Srvs.
Bucher, Julia A., ed. The Application of Problem-Solving Therapy to Psychosocial Oncology Care. LC 99-28083. (Journal of Psychosocial Oncology Ser.: Vol.1, Nos. 3 & 4). 122p. (C). 1999. 49.95 (*0-7890-0759-2*, Hawrth Medical) Haworth Pr.
Bucher, K. & Frey, M. Petrogenesis of Metamorphic Rocks. 6th ed. (Illus.). 320p. 1994. 47.95 (*0-387-57567-7*) Spr-Verlag.
Bucher, Katherine T. Information Technology for Schools. 2nd rev. ed. (Professional Growth Ser.). 400p. 1998. pap. 39.95 (*0-938865-65-X*) Linworth Pub.
Bucher, Linda & Melander, Sheila. Critical Care Nursing. Carter, Robin et al, eds. LC 98-7040. (Illus.). 1230p. (C). 1999. text. write for info. (*0-7216-6917-4*, W B Saunders Co) Harcrt Hlth Sci Grp.
***Bucher, Linda & Melander, Sheila.** Critical Care Nursing. Carter, Robin, ed. (Illus.). 285p. 1999. text, teacher ed. write for info. (*0-7216-6918-2*, W B Saunders Co) Harcrt Hlth Sci Grp.
Bucher, Linda & Melander, Sheila. Text Manual to Accompany Critical Care Nursing. 115p. write for info. (*0-7216-8323-1*, W B Saunders Co) Harcrt Hlth Sci Grp.
Bucher, Linda, jt. auth. see Melander, Sheila.
Bucher, Mary, ed. see Battelle Memorial Institute Staff.
Bucher, Rainer. Nietzsches Mensch und Nietzsches Gott: Das Spatwerk Als Philosophisch-Theologisches Programm. 2nd ed. (Wurzburger Studien Zur Fundamentaltheologie Ser.: Bd. 1). (GER.). XIX, 434p. 1993. 59.80 (*3-631-46374-X*) P Lang Pubng.
Bucher, Theodor. Einfuhrung in die Angewandte Logik: Auflage, Vol. 2. 448p. 1998. 21.00 (*3-11-015279-7*) De Gruyter.
Bucher, Timothy S. Stick & Tissue Modeler's Album: Construction Projects for Free Flight Aeromodelers. LC 98-92008. (Illus.). 80p. 1998. pap. 14.95 (*0-9666521-0-X*) Meteor Publishing.
— Stick & Tissue Modelers Album Vol. 2: Construction Projects for Free Flight Aeromodelers. (Illus.). 64p. 1999. pap. 14.95 (*0-9666521-1-8*) Meteor Publishing.
Bucher, Urs. Vocabulary of Modern Chinese. (CHI & ENG.). 815p. 1986. 49.95 (*0-8288-1603-4*, M4200) Fr & Eur.
— Vocabulary of Modern Chinese: English Translation of Illustrative Sentences. (CHI & ENG.). 250p. 1986. 49.95 (*0-8288-1604-2*, M4240) Fr & Eur.
— Vocabulary of Modern Standard Arabic. (ARA & ENG.). 458p. 1984. 49.95 (*0-8288-1584-4*, M3515) Fr & Eur.
Bucher, Ward, ed. Dictionary of Building Preservation. LC 96-19947. 560p. 1996. 49.95 (*0-471-14413-4*) Wiley.
Bucheri, Carol. My Homework Ate My Dog: The Best Cartoons from the Phi Delta Kappan, 1991-1996. 130p. 1996. pap. 18.00 (*0-87367-803-6*) Phi Delta Kappa.
Buchert, Lene. Education in the Development of Tanzania, 1919-1990. LC 93-50745. (Eastern African Studies). (Illus.). 208p. (C). 1994. text 39.95 (*0-8214-1083-0*); pap. text 19.95 (*0-8214-1084-9*) Ohio U Pr.
***Buchert, Lene & UNESCO Staff.** Education Reform in the South in the 1990s. LC 99-181958. (Education on the Move Ser.). 415 p. 1998. 35.00 (*92-3-103471-5*, Pub. by UNESCO) Bernan Associates.
***Buchert, Ulf.** Denkmalpflege im antiken Griechenland: Mafsnahmen zur Bewahrung historischer Bausubstanz. 2000. 48.95 (*3-631-34853-3*) P Lang Pubng.
Buchet, Christiane, tr. see Rinpoche, Bokar.
Buchet, Christiane, tr. see Rinpoche, Kalu.
Buchet, Christiane, tr. & intro. see Rinpoche, Bokar.
Buchet, Martine. The Taste of Provence: The Columbe D'Or at Saint Paul de Vence. (Illus.). 146p. 1996. text 40.00 (*2-908228-47-5*) St Martin.
Buchet, Philippe, jt. auth. see Morvan, Jean-David.
Bucheton, Dominique. Ecriture - Reecritures: Recits d'Adolescents. (Exploration Ser.). (FRE.). 320p. 1995. 47.95 (*3-906754-24-3*, Pub. by P Lang) P Lang Pubng.
Buchheia, Lother. The Boat. 1988. mass mkt. write for info. (*0-440-21020-8*) Doubleday.
***Buchheim, Christoph & Garside, Redvers, eds.** After the Slump: Industry & Politics in 1930s Britain & Germany. ix, 235p. (Orig.). 2000. pap. 37.95 (*0-8204-4343-3*) P Lang Pubng.
Buchheim, Durwood L. The Power of Darkness. 1985. 7.30 (*0-89536-746-7*, 5852, Fairway Pr) CSS OH.
— The Power to Change: Sermon for Lent-Easter: Cycle B, First Lesson Texts. LC 93-18008. 1993. pap. 11.50 (*1-55673-612-6*, 9337) CSS OH.
Buchheim, Durwood L., jt. auth. see Mills, Charles M.
Buchheit, jt. ed. see Radermacher.
Buchheit, Lee C. Secession: The Legitimacy of Self-Determination. LC 77-20687. (Illus.). 272p. reprint ed. pap. 84.40 (*0-8357-3741-1*, 203646700003) Bks Demand.
Buchheit, William A. & Truex, Raymond C., Jr., eds. Surgery of the Posterior Fossa. LC 78-73554. (Seminars in Neurological Surgery Ser.). 197p. 1979. reprint ed. pap. 61.10 (*0-608-00315-8*, 206103200007) Bks Demand.
Buchholdt, H. Structural Dynamics for Engineers. 316p. 1997. 112.00 (*0-7277-2559-9*) Am Soc Civil Eng.
Buchholtz, jt. auth. see Carroll.
Buchholtz, Curt W. Rocky Mountain National Park: A History. 1983. pap. 19.95 (*0-87081-146-0*) Univ Pr Colo.
Buchholz. Child Analytic. (Principles of Psychology Ser.: Vol. 11, No. 3). 1994. 20.00 (*0-8058-9963-4*) L Erlbaum Assocs.
— Mysteries from the Finger Lakes, 2 vols., Set. 1991. pap. 8.95 (*0-9624738-4-7*) Six Lakes Arts.
— What Makes Winning Brands Different: The Hidden Method Behind the World's Most Successful Brands. 238p. 2000. 34.95 (*0-471-72025-9*) Wiley.
Buchholz, jt. auth. see Fiedler.
Buchholz, Barbara & Skolnik, Lisa. French Country. LC 95-53858. (Architecture & Design Library Ser.: No. 1). (Illus.). 1996. 17.95 (*1-56799-254-4*, Friedman-Fairfax) M Friedman Pub Grp Inc.
***Buchholz, Barbara B. & Crane, Margaret.** Apartment Living Book: New Design for Urban Living. (Illus.). 2000. 35.00 (*1-56496-670-4*) Rockport Pubs.
Buchholz, Barbara B., et al. Minding Your Own Business: Arthur Andersen Answers the 101 Toughest Questions about Family Business. LC 99-34102. 256p. 1999. text 24.00 (*0-7352-0038-6*) PH Pr.
Buchholz, Barbara Ballinger & Skolnik, Lisa. Porch Perfect. LC 99-18741. 1999. write for info. (*1-56799-772-4*) M Friedman Pub Grp Inc.
Buchholz, Christopher. Franzosischer Staatskult, 1792-1813 Im Linksrheinischen Deutschland: Mit Vergleichen Zu Den Nachbardepartementen der Habsburgischen Niederlande. (Europaische Hochschulschriften Ser.: Reihe 3, Bd. 749). (GER.). 402p. 1997. 63.95 (*3-631-31904-5*) P Lang Pubng.
Buchholz, Daniel & Magnani, Gregorio, eds. International Index of Multiples. (Illus.). 396p. 1992. 75.00 (*3-88375-173-1*, Pub. by Walther Konig) Dist Art Pubs.
Buchholz, Ester S. & Mishne, Judith M., eds. Group Interventions with Children, Adolescents, & Parents: An Ego & Self Psychological Approach. LC 94-70251. 286p. 1994. pap. 50.00 (*1-56821-243-7*) Aronson.
Buchholz, Ester Schaler. The Call of Solitude: Alonetime in a World of Attachment. LC 97-20698. 1997. 23.50 (*0-684-81874-4*) S&S Trade.
Buchholz, Fredric L. & Graham, Andrew T. Modern Superabsorbent Polymer Technology. LC 97-12782. 304p. 1997. 105.00 (*0-471-19411-5*) Wiley.
Buchholz, Fredric L. & Peppas, Nicholas A., eds. Superabsorbent Polymers: Science & Technology. LC 94-34669. (Symposium Ser.: No. 573). (Illus.). 160p. 1994. text 55.00 (*0-8412-3039-0*, Pub. by Am Chemical) OUP.
Buchholz, Hans-Gunter. Ugarit, Zypern und Agaiis: Kulturbezienungen Im Zweiten Jahrtausend v. Chr. (Alter Orient und Altes Testament Ser.: Band 261). (GER.). xiii, 812p. 1999. text 118.00 (*3-927120-38-3*, Pub. by Ugarit-Verlag) Eisenbrauns.
Buchholz, Heinrich E. Fads & Fallacies in Present-Day Education. LC 75-156621. (Essay Index Reprint Ser.). 1977. reprint ed. 19.95 (*0-8369-2272-7*) Ayer.
***Buchholz, Jeannie.** A Tale of Two Cities. 90p. (YA). (gr. 9-12). 1999. student ed., ring bd. 14.99 (*1-58609-168-9*) Progeny Pr WI.
***Buchholz, Margaret T., ed.** Shore Chronicles: Diaries & Traveler's Tales from the Jersey Shore, 1764-1955. LC 99-13119. (Illus.). 368p. 1999. 26.95 (*0-945582-58-7*) Down the Shore Pub.
Buchholz, Margaret T., jt. auth. see Savadore, Larry.
Buchholz, Peter, ed. Bibliographie Zur alteuropaeischen Religionsgeschichte, Vol. 1: 1954 bis 1964 Literatur zu den antiken Rand-und Nachfolgekulturen im aussermediterranen Europa unter besonderer Beruecksichtigung der nichtchristlichen Religionen. (Arbeitem zur Fruhmittelalterforschung Ser.: Vol. 2). (C). 1967. 60.80 (*3-11-000373-2*) De Gruyter.
Buchholz, Quinn. Sleep Well, Little Bear. Neumeyer, Peter F., tr. (Illus.). 32p. (J). (ps). 1994. 15.00 (*0-374-37026-5*) FS&G.
Buchholz, Quint. The Collector of Moments. Neumeyer, Peter F., tr. from GER. LC 99-10202. (Illus.). 48p. (J). 1999. 18.00 (*0-374-31520-5*) FS&G.
Buchholz, Richard, jt. ed. see Clemmons, Janine R.
Buchholz, Richard H. Cultivating Character: A K-12 Curriculum for the Parent-Teacher Partnership. (Illus.). 32p. (YA). (gr. 9). 1997. pap., teacher ed. 19.95 (*0-89390-407-4*) Resource Pubns.
— Cultivating Character: A K-12 Curriculum for the Parent-Teacher Partnership. (Illus.). 32p. (YA). (gr. 10). 1997. pap., teacher ed. 19.95 (*0-89390-406-6*) Resource Pubns.
— Cultivating Character: A K-12 Curriculum for the Parent-Teacher Partnership. (Illus.). 32p. (YA). (gr. 11). 1997. pap., teacher ed. 19.95 (*0-89390-405-8*) Resource Pubns.
— Cultivating Character: Month-by-Month Resources for Parents & Teachers. (Illus.). 32p. (YA). (gr. 12). 1997. pap., teacher ed. 19.95 (*0-89390-404-X*) Resource Pubns.
— Cultivating Character: Month-by-Month Resources for Parents & Teachers. 32p. (YA). (gr. 8). 1998. pap. 19.95 (*0-89390-437-6*) Resource Pubns.
— Cultivating Character Grade 7: A K-12 Curriculum for the Parent-Teacher Partnership. (Illus.). 32p. 1999. pap., teacher ed. 19.95 (*0-89390-436-8*) Resource Pubns.
***Buchholz, Richard H.** Cultivating Character (Grade 6) Month-by-Month Resources for Parents & Teachers. 1999. pap. 19.95 (*0-89390-459-7*) Resource Pubns.
Buchholz, Rogene A. Business Environment & Public Policy: Implications for Management. 5th ed. LC 94-18070. 672p. 1994. 56.20 (*0-13-311085-0*) P-H.
— Management Responses to Public Issues. 3rd ed. LC 93-19558. 370p. (C). 1993. pap. text 51.00 (*0-13-554072-0*, Pub. by P-H) S&S Trade.
— Principles of Environmental Management: The Greening of Business. 2nd ed. LC 97-32583. 448p. (C). 1998. pap. text 57.00 (*0-13-684895-8*) P-H.
— Public Policy Issues for Management. (Illus.). 400p. (C). 1988. pap. text 14.25 (*0-13-738840-3*) P-H.
— Public Policy Issues for Management. 2nd ed. 352p. (C). 1991. pap. text 31.60 (*0-13-678087-3*, 140703) P-H.
Buchholz, Rogene A. & Rosenthal, Sandra B. Business Ethics: The Pragmatic Path Beyond Principles to Process. LC 97-13237. 544p. 1997. pap. text 50.00 (*0-13-350786-6*) P-H.
Buchholz, Rogene A., et al. Managing Environmental Issues: A Casebook. 304p. (C). 1991. pap. text 24.60 (*0-13-563891-7*) P-H.
Buchholz, Rogene A., jt. auth. see Rosenthal, Sandra B.
Buchholz, Todd. From Here to Economy. 1996. pap. 12.95 (*0-452-27482-6*, Plume) Dutton Plume.
— Market Shock: 9 Economic & Social Upheavals That Will Shake Your Financial Future - And What to Do about Them. LC HD30.27.B83 1999. 297p. 2000. 26.00 (*0-88730-949-6*, HarpBusn) HarpInfo.
Buchholz, Todd G. From Here to Economy: A Shortcut to Economic Literacy. 288p. 1996. pap. 11.95 (*0-614-12595-2*) NAL.
***Buchholz, Todd G.** Market Shock. 320p. 2000. pap. 15.00 (*0-88730-950-X*, HarpBusn) HarpInfo.
— New Ideas from Dead Economists: An Introduction to Modern Economic Thought. rev. ed. LC 99-222760. 332p. 1999. pap. 14.95 (*0-452-28052-4*) NAL.
Buchhorn, Gottfried H. & Willert, Hans-Georg, eds. Technical Principles, Design, & Safety of Joint Implants. LC 92-1425. (Illus.). 432p. 1994. 159.00 (*0-88937-090-7*) Hogrefe & Huber Pubs.
Buchignani, Norman. Fijian Indians in Canada: The Structural Determinants of a New Community. LC 91-3600. (Immigrant Communities & Ethnic Minorities in the U. S. & Canada Ser.: No. 82). 1992. 69.50 (*0-404-19492-3*) AMS Pr.
Buchignani, Walter. Tell No One Who You Are: The Hidden Childhood of Regine Miller. 1994. 15.05 (*0-606-09956-5*, Pub. by Turtleback) Demco.
— Tell No One Who You Are: The Hidden Childhood of Regine Miller. LC 92-80412. (Illus.). 185p. (YA). (gr. 7 up). 1996. reprint ed. pap. 9.95 (*0-88776-303-0*) Tundra Bks.
Buchin, Su. Affine Differential Geometry. viii, 248p. (C). 1983. text 274.00 (*0-677-31060-9*) Gordon & Breach.
— Lectures on Differential Geometry. 149p. 1981. text 24.00 (*9971-83-003-5*); pap. text 17.00 (*9971-83-004-3*) World Scientific Pub.
— Selected Mathematical Papers. xviii, 412p. 1983. text 274.00 (*0-677-31300-4*) Gordon & Breach.
Buchinger, Barbara. Die Fruhmittelalterlichen Grabfunde Von Wiesbaden. (Illus.). 559p. 1997. 88.95 (*3-631-31447-7*) P Lang Pubng.
Buchinger, Kurt, et al. Gruppe und Bildung. (GER.). 236p. (C). 1975. pap. 33.85 (*3-11-004546-X*) De Gruyter.
Buchino, J. J. Cytopathology in Pediatrics. (Monographs in Clinical Cytology Ser.: Vol. 13). (Illus.). x, 156p. 1991. 174.00 (*3-8055-5299-8*) S Karger.
Buchko, Aaron A., jt. auth. see Gundry, Lisa K.
Buchla. Experiments in Basic Circuits. 3rd ed. (C). 1997. write for info. (*0-13-505231-9*, Macmillan Coll) P-H.
— Experiments in Electronic Fundamentals. 4th ed. (C). 1997. pap. text, lab manual ed. 36.80 (*0-13-737164-0*) P-H.
— Fundamental Linear. 2nd ed. 272p. 1998. pap. text, lab manual ed. 36.80 (*0-13-743584-3*) P-H.
Buchla, David. Electronic Instrumentation & Measurement. (C). 1991. text 55.51 (*0-675-21162-X*, Merrill Coll) P-H.
***Buchla, David.** Principles of Electric Circuits. 6th ed. 1999. 37.33 (*0-13-021958-4*) P-H.
Buchler, Adolf. Die Tobiaden und die Oniaden. 396p. 1975. reprint ed. write for info. (*3-487-05582-1*) G Olms Pubs.
Buchler, Adolf, jt. auth. see Abrahams, Israel.
Buchler, Alexandra, ed. Allskin & Other Tales by Contemporary Czech Women. LC 97-48891. 220p. 1998. pap. 14.95 (*1-879679-11-6*) Women Translation.
— This Side of Reality: Modern Czech Short Stories. (Contemporary European Short Stories Ser.). 4p. (Orig.). 1996. pap. 14.99 (*1-85242-378-1*) Serpents Tail.
Buchler, Alexandra, tr. see Svacha, Rostislav & Dluhosch, Eric.
Buchler, Ira R. & Maddock, Kenneth, eds. The Rainbow Serpent: A Chromatic Piece. (World Anthropology Ser.). (Illus.). x, 228p. 1978. 43.10 (*90-279-7680-5*) Mouton.
Buchler, J. Robert, ed. The Numerical Modelling of Nonlinear Stellar Pulsations: Problems & Prospects: Proceedings of the NATO Advanced Research Workshop Held in Les Arcs, France, March 20-24, 1989. (C). 1990. text 201.00 (*0-7923-0598-1*) Kluwer Academic.
Buchler, J. Robert, et al, eds. Long-Range Correlations in Astrophysical Systems Vol. 848: Annals of the New York Academy of Sciences. LC 98-13137. 143p. 1998. 80.00 (*1-57331-112-X*); pap. 80.00 (*1-57331-113-8*) NY Acad Sci.
Buchler, J. Robert & Kandrup, Henry E. Nonlinear Signal & Image Analysis. LC 96-29561. (Annals of the New York Academy of Sciences Ser.). 1997. 80.00 (*1-57331-044-1*) NY Acad Sci.
— Nonlinear Signal & Image Analysis. LC 96-29561. (Annals of The New York Academy of Sciences Ser.: Vol. 808). 1997. pap. 80.00 (*1-57331-045-X*) NY Acad Sci.
Buchler, J. Robert & Kandrup, Henry E., eds. Stochastic Processes in Astrophysics. LC 93-41277. (Annals Ser.: Vol. 706). 203p. 1993. pap. 65.00 (*0-89766-801-4*) NY Acad Sci.
Buchler, J. Robert, et al. Chaos in Astrophysics. 1985. text 180.50 (*90-277-2125-4*) Kluwer Academic.
Buchler, J. Robert, ed. see Kontopoulos, Georgios I.
Buchler, J. Robert, jt. ed. see Takeuti, M.
Buchler, J. W. Metal Complexes with Tetrapyrrole Ligands I. (Structure & Bonding Ser.: Vol. 64). (Illus.). 290p. 1987. 158.95 (*0-387-17531-8*) Spr-Verlag.
Buchler, J. W., ed. Structure & Bonding Vol. 74: Metal Complexes with Tetrapyrrole Ligands II. (Illus.). 160p. 1991. 103.95 (*0-387-52899-7*) Spr-Verlag.
Buchler, J. W., ed. Structure & Bonding Vol. 84: Metal Complexes with Tetrapyrrole Ligands III. (Illus.). 215p. 1995. 174.95 (*3-540-59281-4*) Spr-Verlag.
Buchler, Justus. The Concept of Method. 188p. 1985. reprint ed. pap. text 19.50 (*0-8191-4671-4*) U Pr of Amer.
— Metaphysics of Natural Complexes. expanded ed. Wallace, Kathleen et al, eds. LC 89-4416. 308p. (C). 1989. pap. text 21.95 (*0-7914-0183-9*) State U NY Pr.
Buchler, Justus, ed. see Peirce, Charles Sanders.
***Buchler, M. W., ed.** Acute Pancreatitis: Novel Concepts in Biology & Therapy. 497p. 1999. 69.95 (*0-632-05339-9*) Blackwell Sci.
Buchler, M. W. & Baer, H. U., eds. European Society for Surgical Research (ESSR) 34th Congress of the European Society for Surgical Research, Bern, April 1999: Abstracts. (European Surgical Research Ser.: Vol. 31, Suppl. 1 (1999)). xxxii, 244p. 1999. pap. 47.00 (*3-8055-6892-4*) S Karger.
Buchler, M. W. & Krahenbuhl, L., eds. Laparoscopic Colorectal Surgery. (Journal Ser.: Vol. 12, No. 5, 1995). (Illus.). 42p. 1996. pap. 50.50 (*3-8055-6282-9*) S Karger.
Buchler, M. W., jt. ed. see Beglinger, C.
Buchler, M. W., jt. ed. see Krahenbuhl, L.
***Buchler, Pavel.** Ghost Stories: Stray Thoughts on Photography & Film. 1999. pap. text. write for info. (*1-901540-07-3*) Proboscis.
Buchler, Ueli, et al. Wrist Instability. 232p. 1997. write for info. (*1-85317-320-7*) Martin Dunitz.
Buchli, Victor. An Archaeology of Socialism. (Materializing Culture Ser.). (Illus.). 256p. 1998. 65.00 (*1-85973-212-7*, Pub. by Berg Pubs) NYU Pr.
***Buchli, Victor.** An Archaeology of Socialism. (Materializing Culture Ser.). (Illus.). 256p. 2000. pap. 22.50 (*1-85973-426-X*, Pub. by Berg Pubs) NYU Pr.
***Buchli, Victor, et al.** Archaeologies of the Contemporary Past. LC 00-44651. 2001. pap. write for info. (*0-415-23279-1*) Routledge.
Buchlin, J. M., jt. ed. see Bear, Jacob.
Buchloch, Benjamin, et al. A Reader. (Illus.). 352p. 1998. pap. 24.95 (*0-87633-120-7*) Phila Mus Art.
***Buchloh, B. H. D., et al.** Gabriel Orozco. LC 00-25662. (Illus.). 2000. write for info. (*0-914357-75-1*) Los Angeles Mus Contemp.
Buchloh, Benjamin H. Allan Sekula: Fish Story. (Illus.). 186p. 1995. 65.00 (*3-928762-28-1*) Dist Art Pubs.
— Neo-Avantgarde & Culture Industry: Essays on European & American Art from 1965-1975. LC 99-59406. (Illus.). 500p. 1999. 50.00 (*0-262-02454-3*) MIT Pr.
Buchloh, Benjamin H., ed. Broodthaers: Writings, Interviews, Photographs. (October Bks.). 211p. (Orig.). 1988. 30.00 (*0-262-02281-8*) MIT Pr.
— The Museum of Modern Art, Department of Eagles, Section Publicite. (Illus.). (Orig.). 1995. pap. write for info. (*0-944219-12-8*) M Goodman Gallery.
Buchloh, Benjamin H. & Fisher, Jean. James Coleman: Projected Images, 1972-94. LC 95-67932. (Illus.). 108p. (Orig.). 1995. pap. 24.95 (*0-944521-31-2*) Dia Ctr Arts.
Buchloh, Benjamin H., et al. Art & Ideology. LC 83-43254. (Illus.). 71p. 1984. pap. 10.50 (*0-915557-39-8*) New Mus Contemp Art.
— Cahier 1: Mutti-Vati Kultur. (Cahiers Ser.). 196p. 1994. pap. 29.95 (*90-73362-27-X*) Dist Art Pubs.
Buchloh, Benjamin H., jt. auth. see Feldman, Melissa.
***Buchloh, Benjamin H. D.** Experiments in the Everyday: Allan Kaprow & Robert Watts--Events, Objects, Documents. (Illus.). 172p. 2000. pap. 30.00 (*1-884919-07-3*) Wallach Art Gallery.
Buchloh, Benjamin H. D. Premises: Invested Spaces in Visual Arts & Architecture from France, 1958-98. (Illus.). 500p. 1998. 85.00 (*0-8109-6915-7*, Pub. by Abrams) Time Warner.
Buchman, Alan L. Handbook of Nutritional Support. LC 97-5928. (Illus.). 150p. 1997. pap. 19.95 (*0-683-30238-8*) Lppncott W & W.
***Buchman, Alex.** A Night in the Barracks: Authentic Accounts of Sex in the Armed Forces. 2000. 12.95 (*1-56023-988-3*); 39.95 (*1-56023-987-5*) Haworth Pr.
Buchman, Christopher, jt. auth. see Schneider, Rex.
Buchman, David, tr. The Niche of Lights. LC 98-25466. (slamic Translations Ser.). 300p. 1998. 24.95 (*0-8425-2353-7*, Pub. by Brigham) U Ch Pr.
Buchman, Dian D. Ancient Healing Secrets. 192p. 1996. 9.99 (*0-517-15991-0*) Random Hse Value.

B

— The Complete Book of Water Healing. Orig. Title: The Complete Book of Water Therapy. (Illus.). 268p. 1995. reprint ed. pap. 29.98 (*0-941683-33-8*) Instant Improve.

— The Complete Guide to Natural Sleep. 235p. (Orig.). 1999. reprint ed. pap. text 15.00 (*0-7881-6152-0*) DIANE Pub.

— Herbal Medicine. rev. ed. LC 97-161693. 352p. 1996. 9.99 (*0-517-14767-X*) Random Hse Value.

— Herbal Medicine: The Natural Way to Get Well & Stay Well. (Illus.). 1979. pap. 10.95 (*0-679-51081-8*) McKay.

— Medical Mysteries: Six Deadly Cases. 112p. (J). (gr. 4-7). 1993. pap. 2.75 (*0-590-43468-3*) Scholastic Inc.

Buchman, Dian D. & Groves, Seli. The Writer's Digest Guide to Manuscript Formats. 200p. 1988. 19.99 (*0-89879-293-2*, Wrtrs Digest Bks) F & W Pubns Inc.

Buchman, Dian Dincin. An ABC of Natural Beauty Recipes. Hirsch, Cheryl, ed. (Good Health Guides Ser.). 48p. 1996. pap. 3.95 (*0-87983-680-6*, 36806K, Keats Publng) NTC Contemp Pub Co.

— The Complete Book of Water Therapy. rev. ed. LC 93-47004. (Illus.). 264p. 1994. pap. 11.95 (*0-87983-613-X*, 3613XK, Keats Publng) NTC Contemp Pub Co.

— The Complete Guide to Natural Sleep. Bensen, Don R., ed. LC 97-12029. 240p. (Orig.). 1997. pap. 14.95 (*0-87983-686-5*, 36865K, Keats Publng) NTC Contemp Pub Co.

***Buchman, Dian Dincin.** The Herbal Way to Natural Health & Beauty. LC 99-46514. 2000. 7.99 (*0-517-20711-7*) Random Hse Value.

Buchman, Joseph, jt. auth. see Warner, Charles H.

Buchman, Marion. In His Pavilion. LC 86-80422. 120p. 1986. lib. bdg. 14.95 (*0-8383-2217-4*) M S G Haskell Hse.

Buchman, Matthew L. Cookbook from Hell. Goodfellow, Pamela R., ed. 384p. 1997. pap. 12.99 (*0-9639882-8-X*) Goodfellow Pr.

***Buchman, Matthew L.** The Dalari Accord. (Illus.). 2000. 19.99 (*1-891761-04-8*) Goodfellow Pr.

Buchman, Mel. Santa Carries 2 Spares in the Trunk. LC 97-75095. (Illus.). 44p. (J). (gr. k-7). 1997. pap. 10.95 (*1-56167-395-1*, SSE) Am Literary Pr.

Buchman, Norman. Slightly Out of Focus. (Illus.). 104p. 1998. pap. 10.00 (*0-8059-4323-4*) Dorrance.

***Buchman, Norman.** Still Slightly Fuzzy. LC 98-91088. 1999. pap. 8.95 (*0-533-13045-X*) Vantage.

Buchman, Rachel. Jewish Holiday Songs for Children. (ENG, HEB & YID.). 104p. 1997. pap. 14.95 (*0-7866-1346-7*, MB95623) Mel Bay.

Buchman, Rachel. Jewish Holiday Songs for Children. 104p. 1997. pap. 24.95 incl. audio (*0-7866-1350-5*, 95623P) Mel Bay.

— Jewish Holiday Songs for Children. 104p. 1997. pap. 29.95 incl. audio compact disk (*0-7866-1349-1*, 95623CDP) Mel Bay.

Buchmann, Christina & Spiegel, Celina, eds. Out of the Garden: Women Writers on the Bible. 368p. 1995. pap. 12.95 (*0-449-91017-2*) Fawcett.

***Buchmann, J., et al, eds.** Coding Theory, Cryptography & Related Areas. LC 99-54503. 266p. 1999. pap. 76.00 (*3-540-66248-0*) Spr-Verlag.

***Buchmann, Johannes.** Introduction to Cryptography. LC 00-30465. (Undergraduate Texts in Mathematics Ser.). 2000. write for info. (*0-387-95034-6*) Spr-Verlag.

Buchmann, Margret, et al. Detachment & Concern: Essays in the Philosophy of Teaching & Teacher Education. LC 93-1171. (Advances in Contemporary Educational Thought Ser.: No. 11). 312p. 1993. pap. 19.95 (*0-8077-3273-7*); text 42.00 (*0-8077-3274-5*) Tchrs Coll.

Buchmann, Marlis. The Script of Life in Modern Society: Entry into Adulthood in a Changing World. LC 88-23928. (Illus.). 264p. 1989. 33.00 (*0-226-07835-3*) U Ch Pr.

***Buchmann-Moller, Frank.** Is This to Be My Souvenir? Jazz Photos from the Timme Rosenkrantz Collection, 1918-1969. (Illus.). 200p. 2000. 34.99 (*87-7838-465-6*, Pub. by Odense Univ) Intl Spec Bk.

Buchmann-Moller, Frank. You Got to Be Original, Man! The Music of Lester Young, 33. LC 89-11986. (Discographies Ser.: No. 33). 539p. 1990. lib. bdg. 59.95 (*0-313-26514-3*, BLY/, Greenwood Pr) Greenwood.

— You Just Fight for Your Life: The Story of Lester Young. LC 89-3786. 298p. 1990. 39.95 (*0-275-93265-6*, C3265, Praeger Pubs) Greenwood.

Buchmann, P. & Bruhlmann, W., eds. Investigation of Anorectal Functional Disorders: With Special Emphasis on Defaecography. LC 92-26472. 1993. 220.00 (*0-387-55326-6*) Spr-Verlag.

Buchmann, Stephen L. & Nabhan, Gary P. The Forgotten Pollinators. (Illus.). 292p. (C). 1996. text 25.00 (*1-55963-352-2*) Island Pr.

— Forgotten Pollinators. (Illus.). 320p. 1997. pap. 16.95 (*1-55963-353-0*) Island Pr.

Buchner, jt. auth. see Morel.

Buchner, Alex. The German Infantry Handbook, 1939-1945. LC 90-62983. (Illus.). 288p. 1991. 29.95 (*0-88740-284-4*) Schiffer.

Buchner, Alex & Johnston, David. Weapons & Equipment of the German Fallschirmtruppe, 1941-1945. LC 96-192060.Tr. of Waffen und Ausrustung der Deutschen Fallschirm. (Illus.). 48p. 1996. pap. 9.95 (*0-88740-964-4*) Schiffer.

Buchner, Alex G., jt. auth. see Anand, Sarabot S.

Buchner, Alexander. Mechanical Muscial Instruments. LC 78-5429. (Illus.). 174p. 1978. reprint ed. lib. bdg. 95.00 (*0-313-20440-3*, BUMM, Greenwood Pr) Greenwood.

Buchner, Edward F., ed. see Kant, Immanuel.

Buchner, Georg. The Complete Plays. Patterson, Michael, ed. Brenton, Howard et al, trs. LC 87-149303. (Methuen World Dramatists Ser.). 306p. (C). 1987. pap. write for info. (*0-413-14090-3*, A0041, Methuen Drama) Methn.

Buchner, Georg. Complete Plays, Lenz & Other Writings. 1995. 21.50 (*0-8446-6850-8*) Peter Smith.

— Complete Plays, Lenz & Other Writings. Reddick, John, tr. & intro. by. 368p. 1994. pap. 12.95 (*0-14-044586-2*, Penguin Classics) Viking Penguin.

— Complete Works & Letters. Schmidt, Henry J., ed. & tr. by. Hinderer, Walter, ed. (German Library: Vol. 28). 320p. 1986. 39.50 (*0-8264-0300-X*) Continuum.

— Danton's Death. Brenton, Howard, tr. 72p. (Orig.). (C). 1983. pap. write for info. (*0-413-51260-6*, A0069, Methuen Drama) Methn.

— Danton's Death. Rappolt, Hedwig, tr. from GER. LC 82-51254. 96p. (Orig.). (C). 1983. pap. text 6.00 (*0-939858-02-9*) T S L Pr.

— Danton's Death, Leonce & Lena, Woyzeck. 2nd ed. Price, Victor, tr. & intro. by. (Oxford World's Classics Ser.). 176p. 1999. pap. 8.95 (*0-19-283650-1*) OUP.

— Georg Buchner: Complete Plays & Prose - Danton's Death, Leonce & Lena, Woyzeck. Mueller, Carl R., tr. (Mermaid Dramabook Ser.). 224p. 1963. pap. 12.00 (*0-8090-0727-4*) Hill & Wang.

— Lenz. Rappolt, Hedwig, tr. from GER. 96p. (C). 1983. pap. text 6.00 (*0-939858-04-5*) T S L Pr.

— Leonce & Lena: A Comedy. Rappolt, Hedwig, tr. from GER. LC 83-70614. 96p. (C). 1983. pap. text 6.00 (*0-939858-03-7*) T S L Pr.

— Leonce & Lena, Lenz, Woyzeck. Hamburger, Michael, tr. from GER. & intro. by. LC 78-184507. (German Literary Classics in Translation Ser.). 120p. 1972. lib. bdg. 9.00 (*0-226-07841-8*) U Ch Pr.

— Leonce & Lena, Lenz, Woyzeck. Hamburger, Michael, tr. & intro. by. LC 78-184507. (German Literary Classics in Translation Ser.). 115p. Date not set. reprint ed. pap. 35.70 (*0-608-20669-5*, 207210600003) Bks Demand.

— Woyzeck. Mackendrick, John, tr. 39p. (Orig.). (C). 1988. pap. 9.95 (*0-413-38820-4*, A0322) Heinemann.

— Woyzeck. Motton, Gregory, tr. from GER. (Drama Classics Ser.). 128p. (Orig.). 1997. pap. 6.95 (*1-85459-183-5*, Pub. by N Hern Bks) Theatre Comm.

— Woyzeck & Lenz. Rappolt, Hedwig, tr. from GER. & intro. by. 77p. (Orig.). 1988. pap. text 6.00 (*0-939858-06-1*) T S L Pr.

— Woyzeck/Leonce und Lena. (GER.). (C). 1985. 3.95 (*0-8442-2945-8*, X2945-8) NTC Contemp Pub Co.

***Buchner, J.** Plasma Astrophysics & Space Physics. LC 99-50108. 1999. write for info. (*0-7923-6002-8*) Kluwer Academic.

Buchner, J., ed. The Three-Dimensional Magnetosphere: Proceedings of the D3.1 Symposium of COSPAR Scientific Commission D. (Advances in Space Research Ser.: Vol. 18). 326p. 1996. pap. text 94.50 (*0-08-042674-3*, Pergamon Pr) Elsevier.

Buchner, J. H. The Moravians in Jamaica. LC 77-178470. (Black Heritage Library Collection). 1977. reprint ed. 24.95 (*0-8369-8918-X*) Ayer.

Buchner, Jack. The St. Monica Ministry: Spiritual Exercises to Help with Loved One's Faith Crisis. LC 98-71690. 76p. 1998. pap. 12.00 (*1-885938-13-6*) Cathdrl Fndtn Pr.

Buchner, Joachim R., tr. see Skobel'tsyn, D. V., ed.

Buchner, Karl. Wieland und die Weidmannsche Buchhandlung. viii, 168p. reprint ed. write for info. (*0-318-71748-4*) G Olms Pubs.

Buchner, Ludwig. Force & Matter: Principles of the Natural Order of the Universe. unabridged ed. (Classic Reprint Ser.). 400p. 1997. reprint ed. 40.00 (*0-936128-53-4*) De Young Pr.

Buchner, Luise. Women & Their Vocation: A Nineteenth-Century View by Luise Buchner. Piepke, Susan L., tr. from GER. (Women in German Literature Ser.: Vol. 5). (Illus.). 127p. (C). 1999. text 39.95 (*0-8204-4142-2*, 41422) P Lang Pubng.

Buchner, T., et al, eds. Acute Leukemias VI: Prognostic Factors & Treatment Strategies - Haematology & Blood Transfusion (Hamatologie und Bluttransfusion), Suppl. 38. LC 97-120581. (Illus.). 748p. 1996. 236.00 (*3-540-60763-3*) Spr-Verlag.

***Buchner, T., et al, eds.** Transplantation in Hematology & Oncology: Symposium of the New Bone Marrow Transplant Unit. LC 99-35457. (Illus.). 330p. 1999. 175.00 (*3-540-64898-4*) Spr-Verlag.

Buchner, T., et al, eds. Tumor Aneuploidy. LC 85-9897. (Illus.). 140p. 1985. 42.95 (*0-387-15376-4*) Spr-Verlag.

Buchner, T., et al. Acute Leukemias 4: Prognostic Factors & Treatment Strategies. LC 93-27989. (Haematology & Blood Transfusion Ser.: No. 36). 1993. 225.00 (*0-387-56951-0*) Spr-Verlag.

Buchner, W., et al. Industrial Inorganic Chemistry. LC 88-37860. 615p. 1989. 195.00 (*3-527-26629-1*, Wiley-VCH) Wiley.

Bucholtz, Alan H., jt. auth. see Jacobson, Ethan A.

Bucholtz, Frank, ed. Environmental Monitoring & Instrumentation. LC 96-72441. (Trends in Optics & Photonics Ser.: Vol. 8). (Illus.). 162p. 1997. pap. 55.00 (*1-55752-482-3*) Optical Soc.

Bucholtz, Mary, et al, eds. Reinventing Identities: The Gendered Self in Discourse. LC 98-50041. (Studies in Language & Gender). (Illus.). 448p. 1999. pap. 35.00 (*0-19-512630-0*); text 65.00 (*0-19-512629-7*) OUP.

Bucholtz, Mary, jt. ed. see Hall, Kira.

Bucholz, Ann, ed. see Wagemaker, Herbert.

Bucholz, Arden. Moltke, Schlieffen & Prussian War Planning. 363p. 1993. pap. 16.50 (*0-85496-889-X*) Berg Pubs.

Bucholz, Arden, ed. & tr. see Delbruck, Hans.

***Bucholz, Barbara B.** Porch Style. 2000. 35.00 (*0-8478-2238-9*, Pub. by Rizzoli Intl) St Martin.

Bucholz, Barbara B. & Crane, Margaret. Corporate Bloodlines: The Future of the Family Firm. Richardson, Stewart, ed. 288p. 1989. 20.00 (*0-8184-0507-4*) Carol Pub Group.

— Successful Homebuilding & Remodeling: Real-Life Advice for Getting the House You Want Without the Roof (or Sky) Falling In. LC 98-34007. 368p. 1999. pap. 22.95 (*0-7931-2883-8*, 56808301, G&C Learning) Dearborn.

Bucholz, O. Woerterbuch Albanisch-Deutsch. 6th ed. (ALB & GER.). 739p. 1993. 79.95 (*0-7859-7444-X*, 3324002508) Fr & Eur.

Bucholz, R. O. The Augustan Court: Queen Anne & the Decline of Court Culture. LC 92-440. (Illus.). 356p. (C). 1993. 49.50 (*0-8047-2080-0*) Stanford U Pr.

Bucholz, Robert W. Orthopaedic Decision Making. 2nd ed. (Illus.). 480p. (C). (gr. 13). 1996. text 92.95 (*0-8016-7356-9*, 07356) Mosby Inc.

Bucholz, Robert W., jt. auth. see Heckman, James D.

Bucholz, Sandra, jt. auth. see Maxfield, Kathryn E.

Bucholz, Stephanie, ed. see Hagerty, Donald J.

***Buchring, Michelle.** The Talking Edge: Co-operAvtivities in EASY Communication. Ashkenas, Joan, ed. (Illus.). 80p. 1999. pap. text 12.95 (*0-943327-23-7*) JAG Pubns.

Buchsbaum, Bill. The Little Book of Big Profits. LC 96-70374. (Illus.). 128p. 1996. 12.95 (*0-02-861283-3*) Macmillan.

Buchsbaum, Frank, et al. Design & Application of Small Standardized Components Data Book 757, Vol. 2. LC 83-60226. (Illus.). 784p. 1983. 12.95 (*0-9609878-1-9*) Stock Drive.

Buchsbaum, Herbert J., ed. The Menopause. (Clinical Perspectives in Obstetrics & Gynecology Ser.). (Illus.). 225p. 1983. 90.00 (*0-387-90825-0*) Spr-Verlag.

Buchsbaum, Herbert J. & Schmidt, Joseph D. Gynecologic & Obstetric Urology. 3rd ed. (Illus.). 752p. 1992. text 156.00 (*0-7216-3051-0*, W B Saunders Co) Harcrt Hlth Sci Grp.

Buchsbaum, Herbert J. & Walton, L. A., eds. Strategies in Gynecologic Surgery. (Clinical Perspectives in Obstetrics & Gynecology Ser.). (Illus.). 256p. 1986. 135.00 (*0-387-96278-6*) Spr-Verlag.

Buchsbaum, Herbert J., jt. auth. see Szulman, A. E.

Buchsbaum, Herbert J., jt. ed. see Collins, R. L.

Buchsbaum, Herbert J., ed. see Loose Leaf Reference Services Staff, et al.

Buchsbaum, Joel & Pro Football Weekly Editors. Pro Football Weekly Draft Preview, 1998. (Illus.). 184p. (Orig.). 1998. pap. 19.95 (*1-888924-01-2*) Pro Football.

— Pro Football Weekly Pro Prospects Preview, 1997-98. (Illus.). 136p. (Orig.). 1997. pap. 15.95 (*1-888924-02-0*) Pro Football.

Buchsbaum, Joel, jt. auth. see Pro Football Weekly Editors.

Buchsbaum, Jonathan. Cinema Engage: Film in the Popular Front. LC 87-19034. 320p. 1988. text 29.95 (*0-252-01485-5*) U of Ill Pr.

Buchsbaum, Mildred, et al. Living Invertebrates. LC 86-10790. (Illus.). 848p. (C). 1987. text 54.95 (*0-86542-312-1*) Boxwood.

Buchsbaum, Ralph. Animals Without Backbones. 2nd rev. ed. LC 48-9508. (Illus.). 405p. 1972. pap. text 15.00 (*0-226-07870-1*) U Ch Pr.

— Animals Without Backbones: An Introduction to the Invertebrates. rev. ed. LC 48-9508. (Illus.). (J). (gr. 9 up). 1948. lib. bdg. 22.00 (*0-226-07869-8*) U Ch Pr.

— Basic Ecology. 1957. pap. 6.95 (*0-910286-05-1*) Boxwood.

Buchsbaum, Ralph, et al. Animals Without Backbones. 3rd ed. LC 86-7046. (Illus.). x, 584p. (C). 1987. pap. text 29.00 (*0-226-07874-4*); lib. bdg. 37.00 (*0-226-07873-6*) U Ch Pr.

Buchsbaum, Robert. Nature Hikes in the White Mountains. LC 94-42245. (Nature Walks Guides Ser.). (Illus.). 400p. 1995. pap. text 12.95 (*1-878239-37-6*) AMC Books.

***Buchsbaum, Robert.** Nature Hikes in the White Mountains. 2nd ed. (Illus.). 2000. pap. 12.95 (*1-878239-72-4*) AMC Books.

Buchsbaum, Walter H. Buchsbaum's Complete Handbook of Practical Electronics Reference Data. 3rd ed. Genn, Robert C., Jr., ed. 672p. 1987. 16.95 (*0-13-084641-4*, Busn) P-H.

— Encyclopedia of Integrated Circuits: A Handbook of Essential Reference Data. LC 80-21596. 384p. 1981. text 34.95 (*0-13-275875-X*) P-H.

— Interface IC Vestpocket Handbook. write for info. (*0-318-58221-X*) P-H.

Buchsbaum, William. Blue Chip Stocks. 1997. 14.95 (*0-02-861494-1*) Macmillan.

***Buchsel, Patricia & Kapustay, Pamela M., eds.** Stem Cell Transplantation: A Clinical Textbook. 304p. 2000. ring bd. 52.00 (*1-890504-15-7*) Oncology Nursing.

Buchsel, Patricia C. & Whedon, Marie B. Bone Marrow Transplant: Administrative Strat Clinic. (Nursing-Health Science Ser.). 528p. (C). 1995. text 64.95 (*0-86720-691-8*) Jones & Bartlett.

Buchsel, Patricia C. & Yarbro, Connie H. Oncology Nursing Ambulatory Setting. 275p. 1993. 64.95 (*0-86720-637-3*) Jones & Bartlett.

Buchsenschutz, B. & Blumner, Hugo. Die Hauptstatten des Gewerbfleisses im Klassischen Alterthume & die Gewerbliche Thatigkeit der Volker des Klassischen Alterthums, 2 vols. Finley, Moses, ed. LC 79-4964. (Ancient Economic History Ser.). (GER.). 1979. reprint ed. lib. bdg. 25.95 (*0-405-12353-1*) Ayer.

Buchsenschutz, Olivier, jt. auth. see Audouze, Francoise.

Buchstaber, V. M. & Novikov, S. P., eds. Solitons, Geometry & Topology: On the Crossroad. Sossinsky, A. B., tr. from RUS. LC 91-640741. (American Mathematical Society Translations Ser.: Vol. 179). 189p. 1997. text 89.00 (*0-8218-0666-1*) Am Math.

Buchsteiner, Thomas & Honnef, Klaus. Photography Paintings: Werner Pawlok. 72p. 1995. 40.00 (*3-7231-0014-7*) Dist Art Pubs.

Buchtal, Hugo. Historia Troiana: Studies in the History of Mediaeval Secular Illustration. (Warburg Institute Studies: Vol. 32). 1969. reprint ed. pap. 40.00 (*0-8115-1396-3*) Periodicals Srv.

Buchtal, Rebecca, et al. Eating Well. 36p. (Orig.). 1986. pap. 3.25 (*0-940844-26-5*) Wellspring.

Buchtel, Henry A., tr. see Mazzarello, Paolo.

Buchter, Carol & Quigley, Elaine. Developing Basic Writing Skills, Bk. 1. (J). (gr. 3-4). 1983. student ed. 4.95 (*0-89525-391-7*) Ed Activities.

— Developing Basic Writing Skills, Bk. 2. (J). (gr. 5-6). 1983. student ed. 4.95 (*0-89525-392-5*) Ed Activities.

Buchter, Jonathan F., et al, eds. Baldwin's Ohio School Law, 3 vols. annuals 4678p. 1993. suppl. ed. 230.00 (*0-8322-0010-7*) Banks-Baldwin.

Buchwach, Kenneth A. & Konior, Raymond J. Contemporary Hair Transplant Surgery. LC 96-44701. (Illus.). 176p. 1997. text 59.00 (*0-86577-577-X*) Thieme Med Pubs.

Buchwald. Scientific Credibility. 1997. lib. bdg. 39.00 (*0-7923-4762-5*) Kluwer Academic.

Buchwald, Ann, jt. auth. see Stewart, Marjabelle Y.

Buchwald, Ann, jt. auth. see Young, Marjabelle Y.

Buchwald, Art. I'll Always Have Paris: A Memoir. (Illus.). 256p. 1997. pap. 12.00 (*0-449-91233-7*) Fawcett.

— I'll Always Have Paris: A Memoir. large type ed. LC 96-9844. (Illus.). 1996. 26.95 (*0-7862-0842-2*) Thorndike Pr.

— Leaving Home: A Memoir. large type ed. LC 93-44664. 350p. 1994. lib. bdg. 24.95 (*0-7862-0158-4*) Thorndike Pr.

— Lighten up, George. large type ed. LC 92-36472. (General Ser.). 447p. 1993. 21.95 (*0-8161-5675-1*, G K Hall Lrg Type) Mac Lib Ref.

***Buchwald, Art.** Stella in Heaven: Almost a Novel. LC 99-462233. 192p. 2000. 23.95 (*0-399-14642-3*) Putnam Pub Group.

Buchwald, Claire. The Puppet Book: How to Make & Operate Puppets. LC 90-38080. (Illus.). 134p. (Orig.). (YA). 1990. pap. 13.95 (*0-8238-0293-0*) Kalmbach.

Buchwald, Emilie. Gildaen: The Heroic Adventures of a Most Unusual Rabbit. LC 93-16255. (Illus.). 192p. (J). 1992. pap. 6.95 (*0-915943-75-1*) Milkweed Ed.

Buchwald, Emilie, et al, eds. Transforming a Rape Culture. LC 93-5693. 484p. 1993. 23.95 (*0-915943-06-9*) Milkweed Ed.

— Transforming a Rape Culture. 484p. 1995. pap. 18.95 (*1-57131-204-8*) Milkweed Ed.

Buchwald, Emilie & Roston, Ruth, eds. Mixed Voices: Contemporary Poems about Music. LC 91-15082. (Illus.). 190p. 1991. 14.95 (*0-915943-82-4*) Milkweed Ed.

— This Sporting Life: Contemporary American Poems about Sports & Games. (Illus.). 176p. (Orig.). 1998. pap. 14.95 (*1-57131-404-0*) Milkweed Ed.

Buchwald, Emilie, jt. ed. see Dorris, Michael.

Buchwald, Hans. Form, Style & Meaning in Byzantine Church Architecture. LC 99-23712. (Variorum Collected Studies: Vol. CS644). 352p. 1999. 138.95 (*0-86078-779-6*, Pub. by Ashgate Pub) Ashgate Pub Co.

Buchwald, J. Z., ed. see Dale, Andrew I.

Buchwald, Jed Z. From Maxwell to Microphysics: Aspects of Electromagnetic Theory in the Last Quarter of the Nineteenth-Century. LC 85-1191. (Illus.). xvi, 340p. 1985. 75.00 (*0-226-07882-5*) U Ch Pr.

— From Maxwell to Microphysics: Aspects of Electromagnetic Theory in the Last Quarter of the Nineteenth-Century. LC 85-1191. (Illus.). 356p. 1998. pap. text 24.95 (*0-226-07883-3*) U Ch Pr.

— The Rise of the Wave Theory of Light. LC 88-18647. (Illus.). 498p. 1989. lib. bdg. 90.00 (*0-226-07884-1*) U Ch Pr.

— The Rise of the Wave Theory of Light. LC 88-18647. (Illus.). 504p. 1989. pap. text 29.95 (*0-226-07886-8*) U Ch Pr.

Buchwald, Jed Z., ed. Scientific Credibility & Technical Standards. (Archimedes New Studies in the History & Philosophy of Science & Technology: No. 1). 192p. (C). 1996. lib. bdg. 113.50 (*0-7923-4241-0*) Kluwer Academic.

— Scientific Practice: Theories & Stories of Doing Physics. LC 94-49715. 412p. 1995. pap. text 24.95 (*0-226-07890-6*); lib. bdg. 65.00 (*0-226-07889-2*) U Ch Pr.

***Buchwald, Jed Z. & Cohen, I. Bernard, eds.** Isaac Newton's Natural Philosophy. LC 99-42985. (Dibner Institute Studies in the History of Science & Technology). (Illus.). 400p. 2000. 45.00 (*0-262-02477-2*) MIT Pr.

Buchwald, Robert P., contrib. by. Clinical Laboratory Safety: Approved Guideline (1996) 1996. 95.00 (*1-56238-300-0*, GP17-A) NCCLS.

Buchwald, Wolfgang. Dictionnaire des Auteurs Grecs et Latins de l'Antiquite et du Moyen Age. (FRE.). 897p. 1992. 135.00 (*0-7859-7901-8*, 2503500161) Fr & Eur.

Buchwalter, Andrew, tr. see Habermas, Jurgen, ed.

Buchwalter, Marianne. Memories of a Berlin Childhood. LC 95-67040. (Illus.). 192p. 1995. 17.95 (*0-9633818-4-9*) Premiere Edits.

Buchweitz, Ragnar-Olaf & Millson, John J. Cr-Geometry & Deformations of Isolated Singularities. LC 96-44758. (Memoirs of the American Mathematical Society Ser.). 96p. 1997. pap. 37.00 (*0-8218-0541-X*) Am Math.

Buci-Glucksmann, Christine & Turner, Bryan S. Baroque Reason: The Aesthetics of Modernity. (Theory, Culture & Society Ser.: Vol. 28). 192p. (C). 1994. text 65.00 (*0-8039-8975-X*); pap. text 19.95 (*0-8039-8976-8*) Sage.

Buci, Moreno. Drawings for the Stage: Italian Set Designs 1790-1850. 1984. pap. write for info. (*0-917105-01-X*) W Whitney.

An Asterisk (*) at the beginning of an entry indicates that the title is appearing for the first time.

Bucilla Design Group Staff. Inspirational Cross-Stitch. LC 95-40527. (Sterling/Chapelle Bks.). (Illus.). 128p. 1996. 24.95 (*0-8069-4279-7*) Sterling.
— Inspirational Cross-Stitch. (Illus.). 128p. 1997. pap. text 14.95 (*0-8069-4280-0*, Chapelle) Sterling.

Bucinell, Ronald B., ed. Composite Materials: Fatigue & Fracture, Vol. 7. (STP Ser.: No. 1330). (Illus.). 320p. 1998. text 123.00 (*0-8031-2609-3*, STP1330) ASTM.

Buck. Advanced Calculus. 3rd ed. 1978. student ed. 26.87 (*0-07-008729-6*) McGraw.
— Emotions. (C). 1999. pap. text 57.33 (*0-205-28247-4*, Macmillan Coll) P-H.
— Flying Know How. 1983. pap. 12.95 (*0-02-518210-2*) Macmillan.

***Buck.** Stick & Rudder Classic, 3 vols., Set. 1999. 59.95 (*0-07-135784-X*) McGraw.

Buck. Visual BASIC. 1994. write for info. (*0-201-41866-5*) Addison-Wesley.

Buck, et al. Voices at Serendipity. 35p. (Orig.). 1986. pap. 2.00 (*0-9618011-0-7*) Daisy Pr.

Buck, A. A., ed. Onchocerciasis: Symptomatology, Pathology, Diagnosis. 1974. pap. text 12.00 (*92-4-156041-X*, 1150123) World Health.

Buck, A. Colin, jt. ed. see Wickham, J. E.

Buck, Adriaan De, see De Buck, Adriaan.

Buck, Albert H. The Dawn of Modern Medicine. LC 75-23687. reprint ed. 49.50 (*0-404-13240-5*) AMS Pr.
— The Growth of Medicine from the Earliest Times to About 1800. LC 75-23688. reprint ed. 67.50 (*0-404-13241-3*) AMS Pr.
— A Treatise on Hygiene & Public Health, 2 vols. Rosenkrantz, Barbara G., ed. LC 76-25654. (Public Health in America Ser.). 1977. reprint ed. lib. bdg. 116.95 (*0-405-09810-3*) Ayer.
— A Treatise on Hygiene & Public Health, 2 vols., Vol. 1. Rosenkrantz, Barbara G., ed. LC 76-25654. (Public Health in America Ser.). 1977. reprint ed. lib. bdg. 58.95 (*0-405-09811-1*); reprint ed. lib. bdg. 58.95 (*0-405-09812-X*) Ayer.

Buck, Alex & Vogt, Matthias, eds. Garouste & Bonetti. (Designer Monographs: No. 7). (ENG & GER., Illus.). 144p. 1996. 65.00 (*3-931317-03-X*, Pub. by Art Bks Intl) Partners Pubs Grp.
— Matteo Thun. (Designer Monographs: No. 2). (Illus.). 160p. 1994. 35.00 (*1-85490-902-9*) Academy Ed UK.
— Michael Graves. (Designer Monographs Ser.: No. 3). (Illus.). 1995. 35.00 (*1-85490-903-7*) Academy Ed UK.
— Michele de Lucchi. (Designer Monographs: No. 1). (Illus.). 160p. 1994. 35.00 (*1-85490-901-0*) Academy Ed UK.
— Peter Maly. (Designer Monographs: No. 5). (ENG & GER., Illus.). 136p. 1995. 65.00 (*3-931317-01-3*, Pub. by Art Bks Intl) Partners Pubs Grp.
— Rolf Heide. (Designer Monographs: No. 6). (GER., Illus.). 120p. 1996. 65.00 (*3-931317-05-6*, Pub. by Art Bks Intl) Partners Pubs Grp.

Buck, Alfred A., intro. The Conference on Malaria in Africa - Proceedings: Practical Considerations on Malaria Vaccines & Clinical Trials. 328p. (Orig.). 1988. pap. write for info. (*0-936829-02-8*) Am Inst Bio Sci.

Buck, Alfred A., et al. Health & Disease in Four Peruvian Villages: Contrasts in Epidemiology. LC 68-15455. (Johns Hopkins Monograph in International Health Ser.). 160p. reprint ed. pap. 49.60 (*0-608-13622-0*, 202073900018) Bks Demand.

Buck, Angela E. Angels Walk with Me. 2nd rev. ed. (Illus.). 211p. 1997. pap. 10.95 (*0-9661767-1-5*) Hebron Bks.

Buck, Anita. Behind Barbed Wire: German Prisoner of War Camps in Minnesota. LC 98-19434. (Illus.). 144p. 1998. pap. 14.95 (*0-87839-113-4*) North Star.

Buck, Anita A. Steamboats on the St. Croix. LC 90-7915. (Illus.). 170p. 1990. pap. 19.95 (*0-87839-060-X*) North Star.

Buck, Anne. Clothes & the Child: A Handbook of Children's Dress in England 1500-1900. (Illus.). 272p. 1996. pap. 30.00 (*0-8419-1371-4*); text 50.00 (*0-8419-1370-6*) Holmes & Meier.
— Thomas Lester: His Lace & the East Midlands Industry. 1981. 15.00 (*0-903585-09-X*) Robin & Russ.
— Victorian Costume & Costume Accessories. 2nd rev. ed. (Illus.). 224p. 1997. pap. 24.95 (*0-89676-220-3*, Costume & Fashion Pr) QSMG Ltd.

Buck, Audrey. Audrey's Cookie Cookbook: Two Hundred Cookie & Bar Recipes. (Illus.). 219p. 1992. pap., spiral bd. 12.95 (*0-9632507-0-1*) Bayberry MO.

Buck, Brian & Macaulay, Vincent A., eds. Maximum Entropy in Action: A Collection of Expository Essays. (Illus.). 248p. 1991. pap. text 39.95 (*0-19-853963-0*) OUP.

Buck, Bunny. Through the Eyes of a Victim. large type ed. (Illus.). 203p. 1998. pap. 12.00 (*0-9664014-0-9*) B Buck.

Buck, C. An Employee's Perspective on Injury or Ill-Health Arising from Work. 1996. pap. 129.00 (*1-85953-060-5*, Pub. by Tech Comm) St Mut.

Buck, C., et al, eds. ATCC Animal Viruses & Antisera, Chlamydiae, & Rickettsiae. 7th ed. 256p. 1996. pap. text. write for info. (*0-930009-58-4*) ATCC.

Buck, C. & Llopis, A. The Challenge of Epidemiology: Issues & Selected Readings. (PAHO Scientific Publication Ser.: No. 505). 1003p. 1988. text 60.00 (*92-75-11505-2*) World Health.

Buck, Caitlin E., et al. Bayesian Approach to Intrepreting Archaeological Data. LC 96-194204. 402p. 1996. 125.00 (*0-471-96197-3*) Wiley.

Buck, Carl D. Comparative Grammar of Greek & Latin. LC 33-11254. 1933. lib. bdg. 34.00 (*0-226-07931-7*) U Ch Pr.
— A Dictionary of Selected Synonyms in the Principal Indo-European Languages. 416p. 1988. pap. text 36.00 (*0-226-07937-6*) U Ch Pr.
— A Grammar of Oscan & Umbrian: With a Collection of Inscriptions & a Glossary. 2nd ed. (Illus.). 371p. 1995. reprint ed. lib. bdg. 105.00 (*3-487-05362-4*) G Olms Pubs.
— Greek Dialects. 3rd ed. LC 55-5115. (Midway Reprint Ser.). 1973. pap. text 27.50 (*0-226-07934-1*) U Ch Pr.

Buck, Carl D. The Greek Dialects: Grammar, Selected Inscriptions, Glossary. LC PA0502.B8. (Midway Reprint Ser.). 392p. Date not set. reprint ed. pap. 121.60 (*0-608-20615-6*, 205458300003) Bks Demand.

Buck, Carl D. & Petersen, W. A Reverse Index of Greek Nouns & Adjectives Arranged by Terminations with Brief Historical Introduction. xvii, 765p. 1983. reprint ed. 160.00 (*3-487-03203-1*) G Olms Pubs.

Buck, Carl D., jt. auth. see Hale, William G.

Buck, Carol J. Comprehensive Medical Codes. Williams, Adrianne, ed. LC 98-38028. (Illus.). 1275p. 1999. text. write for info. (*0-7216-7787-8*, W B Saunders Co) Harcrt Hlth Sci Grp.
— Step-by-Step Medical Coding. 2nd ed. (Illus.). 555p. 1998. pap. write for info. (*0-7216-7537-9*, W B Saunders Co) Harcrt Hlth Sci Grp.
— Step-by-Step Medical Coding. 2nd ed. Biblis, Margaret, ed. LC 97-20508. (Illus.). 560p. (C). 1998. pap. text 36.95 (*0-7216-7536-0*, W B Saunders Co) Harcrt Hlth Sci Grp.

***Buck, Carol J.** Step-by-Step Medical Coding. 3rd ed. LC 99-49761. (Illus.). 510p. 2000. pap. text 39.95 (*0-7216-8458-0*, W B Saunders Co) Harcrt Hlth Sci Grp.

Buck, Carol J., ed. Step-by-Step Medical Coding. (Illus.). 1996. pap., teacher ed. write for info. (*0-7216-5345-6*, W B Saunders Co) Harcrt Hlth Sci Grp.

Buck, Carole. Annie Says I Do. (Desire Ser.). 1995. per. 3.25 (*0-373-05934-5*, 1-05934-4) Silhouette.
— A Bride for Saint Nick. 1996. per. 3.99 (*0-373-07752-1*, 1-07752-8) Silhouette.
— Buscando Marido - Zoe & the Best Man. (Deseo Ser.). (SPA.). 1997. per. 3.50 (*0-373-35174-7*, 1-351741) Harlequin Bks.
— Dark Intentions. (Desire Ser.). 1994. per. 2.99 (*0-373-05899-3*, 1-05899-9) Silhouette.
— Un Favor Entre Amigos. (SPA.). 1996. per. 3.50 (*0-373-35160-7*, 1-35160-0) Harlequin Bks.
— Knight & Day. (Desire Ser.: No. 699). 1992. per. 2.89 (*0-373-05699-0*, 5-05699-9) Harlequin Bks.
— Nous Nous Sommes Tant Aimes . . . (Rouge Passion Ser.: Vol. 471). 1998. mass mkt. 3.50 (*0-373-37471-2*, 1-37471-9) Harlequin Bks.
— Peachy's Proposal. (Desire Ser.). 1996. per. 3.25 (*0-373-05976-0*, 1-05976-5) Silhouette.
— Resolved to (Re) Marry. 1997. per. 3.50 (*0-373-76049-3*, 1-76049-5) Silhouette.
— Sparks. (Desire Ser.). 1993. per. 2.99 (*0-373-05808-X*, 5-05808-6) Silhouette.
— Three-Alarm Love. (Desire Ser.: No. 1127). 1998. per. 3.75 (*0-373-76127-9*, 1-76127-9) Silhouette.
— Zoe & the Best Man (Wedding Belles) LC 96-7346. (Desire Ser.). 185p. 1996. per. 3.50 (*0-373-05989-2*, 1-05989-8) Silhouette.

Buck, Carole, jt. auth. see Lovelace, Merline.

Buck, Christopher. Paradise & Paradigm: Key Symbols in Persian Christianity & the Baha'I Faith. LC 98-45882. 1p. (C). 1999. text 81.50 (*0-7914-4061-3*); pap. text 27.95 (*0-7914-4062-1*) State U NY Pr.
— Studies in the Babi & Baha'i Religions: Symbol & Secret: Qur'an Commentary in Baha'u'llah's Kitab-i Iqan, Vol. 7. LC 62-18891. 1995. pap. 32.50 (*0-933770-80-4*) Kalimat.

Buck, Claudia, jt. ed. see Block, A. G.

Buck, Clifford M. Dutchess County, N. Y. Tax Lists 1718-1787: With Rombout Precinct by William Willis Reese. LC 92-167108. 305p. 1991. lib. bdg. 55.00 (*1-56012-110-6*, 103) Kinship Rhinebeck.

Buck, Colin. Prostate Cancer: Questions & Answers. (Illus.). 120p. 1995. pap. 10.95 (*1-873413-85-8*) Merit Pub Intl.

Buck, Craig, jt. auth. see Forward, Susan.

Buck, Craig, jt. auth. see Foward, Susan.

Buck, David. Secrets to Meeting & Getting Dates with All the Desirable Women You Want. 20p. 1998. pap. 8.95 (*0-935540-20-2*) Plymouth Pr.

Buck, David D. Recent Chinese Studies of the Boxer Movement. LC 87-12910. 224p. (gr. 13). 1987. pap. text 41.95 (*0-87332-441-2*) M E Sharpe.
— Urban Change in China: Politics & Development in Tsinan, Shantung, 1890-1949. LC 76-11309. 313p. 1978. reprint ed. pap. 97.10 (*0-608-01907-0*, 206255900003) Bks Demand.

***Buck, David N.** Responding to Chaos: Tradition, Technology, Society & Order in Japanese Design. LC 00-24566. 2000. write for info. (*0-419-25110-3*, E & FN Spon) Routledge.

Buck, Debra J., jt. auth. see Fett, Dennis M.

Buck, Dennis. Car Songs. (J). (ps-5). 1990. 10.95 incl. audio (*0-937124-42-7*, KIM 9119C) Kimbo Educ.

***Buck, Dennis S.** Deaf Peddler: Confessions of an Inside Man. 2000. pap. 15.95 (*1-56368-096-3*) Gallaudet Univ Pr.

Buck, Diane M. & Palmer, Virginia A. Outdoor Sculpture in Milwaukee: A Cultural & Historical Guidebook. LC 94-39585. (Illus.). 240p. 1995. pap. 20.00 (*0-87020-276-6*, OUSC) State Hist Soc Wis.

Buck, Donald C., ed. see Salvo y Vela, Juan.

Buck, Dudley. Choir Accompaniment. 177p. 1992. pap. 33.00 (*1-881162-01-X*) W Leupold Edits.
— Illustrations in Choir Accompaniment. LC 79-137316. reprint ed. 36.50 (*0-404-01145-4*) AMS Pr.
— Musical Pronouncing Dictionary. 1976. reprint ed. lib. bdg. 39.00 (*0-403-03787-5*) Scholarly.
— Pronouncing Musical Dictionary. 1988. reprint ed. lib. bdg. 49.00 (*0-7812-0257-4*) Rprt Serv.

Buck, Edward R. Introduction to Data Security & Controls. LC 82-62128. (Illus.). 255p. (Orig.). reprint ed. pap. 79.10 (*0-8357-7516-X*, 203601100097) Bks Demand.
— Introduction to Data Security & Controls. 2nd ed. LC 91-12351. 264p. (Orig.). reprint ed. pap. 81.90 (*0-7837-5890-1*, 204561300006) Bks Demand.

Buck, Elizabeth. Paradise Remade: The Politics of Culture & History in Hawai'i. (Illus.). 256p. (C). 1994. pap. 22.95 (*1-56639-200-4*) Temple U Pr.

Buck, Elizabeth H., jt. auth. see Buck, Solon J.

***Buck-Emden, Rudiger.** SAP R/3 System: An Introduction to Enterprise Resource Planning. 2nd ed. 288p. (C). 1999. 39.95 (*0-201-59617-2*) Addison-Wesley.

Buck-Emden, Rudiger & Galimow, Jurgen. SAP R/3 System: A Client/Server Technology. LC 96-221721. 272p. (C). 1996. 29.95 (*0-201-40350-1*) Addison-Wesley.

Buck Engineering Staff. AC 1 Fundamentals. Buck Engineering Tech. Writers Staff, ed. (F. A. C. E. T. Ser.: Vol. 3). (Illus.). 60p. 1988. pap. text, teacher ed. 11.00 (*0-86657-013-6*); ring bd. 13.00 (*0-86657-012-8*) Lab-Volt.
— AC 2 Fundamentals. Buck Engineering Tech. Writers Staff, ed. (F. A. C. E. T. Ser.: Vol. 4). (Illus.). 56p. 1988. pap. text, teacher ed. 11.00 (*0-86657-015-2*); ring bd. 12.00 (*0-86657-014-4*) Lab-Volt.
— DC Fundamentals. Buck Engineering Tech. Writers Staff, ed. (F. A. C. E. T. Ser.: Vol. 1). (Illus.). 64p. 1988. pap. text, teacher ed. 11.00 (*0-86657-009-8*); ring bd. 17.00 (*0-86657-008-X*) Lab-Volt.
— DC Network Theorems. Buck Engineering Tech. Writers Staff, ed. (F. A. C. E. T. Ser.: Vol. 2). (Illus.). 92p. 1989. pap. text, teacher ed. 11.00 (*0-86657-011-X*); ring bd. 12.00 (*0-86657-010-1*) Lab-Volt.
— Digital Circuit Fundamentals No. 1. Buck Engineering Tech. Writers Staff, ed. (F. A. C. E. T. Ser.: Vol. 15). (Illus.). 216p. 1990. ring bd. 12.00 (*0-86657-036-5*) Lab-Volt.
— Digital Circuit Fundamentals No. 1: Instructor's Guide. Buck Engineering Tech Writers Staff, ed. (F. A. C. E. T. Ser.: Vol. 15). (Illus.). 80p. 1991. pap. text 11.00 (*0-86657-037-3*) Lab-Volt.
— Digital Circuit Fundamentals II. Buck Engineering Tech. Writers Staff, ed. (F. A. C. E. T. Ser.: Vol. 16). (Illus.). 216p. 1990. ring bd. 12.00 (*0-86657-038-1*) Lab-Volt.
— Digital Logic Fundamentals. Buck Engineering Tech. Writers Staff, ed. (F. A. C. E. T. Ser.: Vol. 14). (Illus.). 242p. 1989. ring bd. 13.00 (*0-86657-034-9*) Lab-Volt.
— Digital Logic Fundamentals. Buck Engineering Tech. Writers Staff, ed. (F. A. C. E. T. Ser.: Vol. 14). (Illus.). 92p. 1990. pap. text, teacher ed. 11.00 (*0-86657-035-7*) Lab-Volt.
— F.A.C.E.T. Computer Based Laboratory: User's Guide. Buck Engineering Tech Writers Staff, ed. (F. A. C. E. T. Ser.). (Illus.). 92p. 1990. pap. text 3.30 (*0-86657-040-3*) Lab-Volt.
— FET Fundamentals. Buck Engineering Tech. Writers Staff, ed. (F. A. C. E. T. Ser.: Vol. 10). (Illus.). 96p. 1988. pap. text, teacher ed. 11.00 (*0-86657-027-6*); ring bd. 13.00 (*0-86657-026-8*) Lab-Volt.
— Operational Amplifier Applications. Buck Engineering Tech. Writers Staff, ed. (F. A. C. E. T. Ser.: Vol. 13). (Illus.). 60p. 1989. pap. text, teacher ed. 11.00 (*0-86657-033-0*); ring bd. 12.00 (*0-86657-032-2*) Lab-Volt.
— Operational Amplifiers Fundamentals. Buck Engineering Tech. Writers Staff, ed. (F. A. C. E. T. Ser.: Vol. 12). (Illus.). 68p. 1988. pap. text, teacher ed. 11.00 (*0-86657-031-4*); ring bd. 13.00 (*0-86657-030-6*) Lab-Volt.
— Power Supply Regulators. Buck Engineering Tech. Writers Staff, ed. (F. A. C. E. T. Ser.: Vol. 9). (Illus.). 100p. 1989. pap. text, teacher ed. 11.00 (*0-86657-025-X*); ring bd. 13.00 (*0-86657-024-1*) Lab-Volt.
— Semiconductor Fundamentals. Buck Engineering Tech. Writers Staff, ed. (F. A. C. E. T. Ser.: Vol. 5). (Illus.). 60p. 1988. pap. text, teacher ed. 11.00 (*0-86657-017-9*); ring bd. 13.00 (*0-86657-016-0*) Lab-Volt.
— Thyristor & Phase Control Circuits. Buck Engineering Tech. Writers Staff, ed. (F. A. C. E. T. Ser.: Vol. 11). (Illus.). 100p. 1989. pap. text, teacher ed. 11.00 (*0-86657-029-2*); ring bd. 13.00 (*0-86657-028-4*) Lab-Volt.
— Transistor Amplifier Circuits. Buck Engineering Tech. Writers Staff, ed. (F. A. C. E. T. Ser.: Vol. 6). (Illus.). 108p. 1989. pap. text, teacher ed. 11.00 (*0-86657-019-5*); ring bd. 13.00 (*0-86657-018-7*) Lab-Volt.
— Transistor Feedback Circuits. Buck Engineering Tech. Writers Staff, ed. (F. A. C. E. T. Ser.: Vol. 8). (Illus.). 88p. 1989. pap. text, teacher ed. 11.00 (*0-86657-023-3*); ring bd. 13.00 (*0-86657-022-5*) Lab-Volt.
— Transistor Power Amplifiers. Buck Engineering Tech. Writers Staff, ed. (F. A. C. E. T. Ser.: Vol. 7). (Illus.). 152p. 1989. ring bd. 12.00 (*0-86657-020-9*) Lab-Volt.
— Transistor Power Amplifiers. Buck Engineering Tech. Writers Staff, ed. (F. A. C. E. T. Ser.: Vol. 7). (Illus.). 76p. 1990. pap. text, teacher ed. 11.00 (*0-86657-021-7*) Lab-Volt.

Buck Engineering Tech. Writers Staff, ed. see Buck Engineering Staff.

***Buck, Frank.** Vanishing Sunsets. 72p. 1999. pap. 10.50 (*0-7392-0100-X*, PO2964) Morris Pub.

***Buck, Frank & Lehrer, Steven.** Bring 'em Back Alive: The Best of Frank Buck. LC 99-86898. (Illus.). 256p. 2000. 28.95 (*0-89672-430-1*) Tex Tech Univ Pr.

Buck, Franziska & Munderloh, Andre. German Language Survival Kit. (Illus.). 256p. 1997. pap. 5.95 (*0-86442-451-5*) Lonely Planet.

Buck, Fraser, jt. auth. see Thompon, George.

Buck, Frederick H. Glossary of Mongolian Technical Terms. LC 58-59834. (American Council of Learned Societies Publications). (MON.). 79p. (Orig.). 1958. pap. 3.00 (*0-87950-257-6*) Spoken Lang Serv.

***Buck, Gayle.** Cassandra's Deception. (Regency Romance Ser.). 224p. 2000. mass mkt. 4.99 (*0-451-20037-3*, Sig) NAL.

Buck, Gayle. Chester Charade. 1999. mass mkt. 4.99 (*0-451-19543-4*) NAL.
— How to Write & Market the Regency Romance. 1991. pap. 12.95 (*0-9629423-0-8*) Regency Pr TX.
— Tempting Sarah. 224p. 1998. mass mkt. 4.99 (*0-451-19466-7*, Sig) NAL.

Buck, George. Preparing for Terrorism: An Emergency Services Guide. LC 97-24209. 288p. 1997. mass mkt. 55.95 (*0-8273-8397-5*) Delmar.

Buck, George C., jt. auth. see Meillet, Antoine.

Buck, George H. From Summit to Sea: An Illustrated History of Railroads in B. C. & Alberta. (Illus.). 192p. 1999. text 19.95 (*1-895618-94-0*) Fifth Hse Publ.

Buck, Gisela & Buck, Siegfried. Real Baby Animals, 7 bks. Incl. Billy & Bonnie the Goats. LC 97-11319. (Illus.). 24p. (J). (gr. 1 up). 1997. lib. bdg. 19.93 (*0-8368-1508-4*); Dora the Donkey. LC 97-11316. (Illus.). 24p. (J). (gr. 1 up). 1997. lib. bdg. 19.93 (*0-8368-1505-X*); Fuzzy the Duckling. Baumli, Othmar, photos by. LC 95-43696. (Illus.). 24p. (J). (gr. 1 up). 1996. lib. bdg. 19.93 (*0-8368-1502-5*); Gertie & Gus & the Guinea Pigs. LC 97-11318. (Illus.). 24p. (J). (gr. 1 up). 1997. lib. bdg. 18.60 (*0-8368-1507-6*); Goldie the Fox. LC 97-11317. (Illus.). 24p. (J). (gr. 1 up). 1997. lib. bdg. 19.93 (*0-8368-1506-8*); Sadie the Shrew. Huhn, Jurgen, photos by. LC 95-43695. (Illus.). 24p. (J). (gr. 1 up). 1996. lib. bdg. 19.93 (*0-8368-1504-1*); (Illus.). (J). Set lib. bdg. 139.53 (*0-8368-1960-8*) Gareth Stevens Inc.
— Real Baby Animals New Releases, 4 bks. lib. bdg. 69.08 (*0-8368-1959-4*) Gareth Stevens Inc.

Buck, Gordon H. Drafting Association Rules: Drafting Association Rules, No. 7. rev. ed. (GAP Reports: Vol. 7). 16p. (C). 1993. pap. 17.50 (*0-944715-25-7*) CAI.

Buck, Gordon S. Handbook of Machinery Alignment Tables. 1984. 45.00 (*0-88415-049-6*, 5049) Gulf Pub.

Buck-Gramcko, D. Congenital Malformations of the Hand & Upper Extremity. (Illus.). 704p. 1997. write for info. (*0-443-03560-1*) Church.

Buck, Gurdon H. Condominium Development: Forms with Commentary, 2 vols. (Real Property-Zoning Ser.). 1990. ring bd. 225.00 incl. disk (*0-685-34492-4*) West Group.

Buck, Heather. At the Window. 52p. 1982. pap. 13.95 (*0-85646-071-0*, Pub. by Anvil Press) Dufour.
— Psyche Unbound. LC 95-189497. 64p. 1995. pap. 14.95 (*0-85646-260-8*, Pub. by Anvil Press) Dufour.
— Waiting for the Ferry, 1. 1999. pap. text 17.95 (*0-85646-308-6*) Anvil Pub.

Buck, Helmut. Elternbilder Und Abwehrmechanismen: Eine Empirische Untersuchung Anhand des Giessen-tests Und des Abwehr-computer-Tests. (Illus.). 215p. 1999. 37.95 (*3-631-34324-8*) P Lang Pubng.

Buck, Henry W., jt. auth. see Task Force on Human Papillomavirus Disease, Americ.

Buck, Howard S. A Study in Smollett Chiefly "Peregrine Pickle" 228p. reprint ed. 12.50 (*0-911858-09-1*) Appel.
— Tempering. LC 70-144708. (Yale Series of Younger Poets: No. 1). reprint ed. 18.00 (*0-404-53801-0*) AMS Pr.

Buck, Irving A. Cleburne & His Command: And Pat Cleburne, Stonewall Jackson of the West. Hay, Thomas R., ed. (Illus.). 378p. 1991. reprint ed. 35.00 (*0-916107-20-5*) Broadfoot.

Buck, J. D. Constructive Psychology, or the Building of Character by Personal Effort. 207p. 1992. reprint ed. pap. 16.95 (*1-56459-206-5*) Kessinger Pub.
— The Genius of Freemasonry & the Twentieth Century Crusade. 339p. 1992. reprint ed. pap. 24.95 (*1-56459-205-7*) Kessinger Pub.
— Holy Roman Empire. 50p. 1992. reprint ed. pap. 5.00 (*1-56459-207-3*) Kessinger Pub.
— The Lost Word Found. 50p. 1992. reprint ed. pap. 7.00 (*0-922802-14-9*) Kessinger Pub.
— Mystic Masonry or the Symbols of Freemasonry & the Greater Mysteries of Antiquity. 239p. 1990. reprint ed. pap. 16.95 (*1-56459-271-5*) Kessinger Pub.
— A Study of Man & the Way to Health. 260p. 1994. reprint ed. pap. 17.95 (*1-56459-421-1*) Kessinger Pub.
— The Thirty-Third & Last Degree: Masonry or Politics? 50p. 1992. reprint ed. pap. 7.00 (*1-56459-208-1*) Kessinger Pub.

Buck, J. Orton, Jr. & Beard, Timothy F. Pedigrees of Some of the Emperor Charlemagne's Descendants, Vol. III. 309p. 1996. reprint ed. 30.00 (*0-8063-1211-4*, 775) Genealog Pub.

Buck, J. W. Description of Multimedia Environmental Pollutant Assessment System: Version 3.2 Modification for the Nuclear Regulatory Commission. 102p. 1997. per. 9.00 (*0-16-062868-7*) USGPO.

Buck, Jack. Jack Buck: That's a Winner! (Illus.). 1999. pap. 14.95 (*1-58261-135-1*) Sprts Pubng.

Buck, Jack, et al. Jack Buck: That's a Winner! 1997. 24.95 (*1-57167-111-0*) Sports Pub.

Buck, Jacqueline N., et al. WPS Career Planning Program: Leader's Handbook. 53p. (Orig.). 1985. pap. text 15.00 (*0-87424-201-0*, W-200B) Western Psych.
— WPS Career Planning Program: Student Handbook. 109p. 1986. pap. text 22.50 (*0-87424-200-2*, W-200A) Western Psych.

***Buck, James E.** The New York Stock Exchange: Another Century. 2nd rev. ed. LC 98-49162. (Illus.). 264p. 1998. write for info. (*0-944641-34-2*) Greenwich Pub Group.

Buck, James E., ed. The New York Stock Exchange: The First 200 Years. LC 92-10465. (Illus.). 264p. 1992. write for info. (*0-944641-02-4*) Greenwich Pub Group.

B

Buck, James R. Economic Risk Decisions in Engineering & Management. LC 88-13150. (Illus.). 468p. 1989. reprint ed. pap. 145.10 (*0-608-00163-5*, 206094400006) Bks Demand.

Buck, James S. Pioneer History of Milwaukee. (Illus.). 292p. 1994. reprint ed. lib. bdg. 32.00 (*0-8328-3877-2*) Higginson Bk Co.

— Pioneer History of Milwaukee, Wisconsin, 4 vols. (Illus.). 1709p. 1997. reprint ed. lib. bdg. 159.00 (*0-8328-7186-9*) Higginson Bk Co.

Buck, Janet, jt. auth. see Constantine, Brendan.

Buck, Janie, jt. auth. see Goebel, Wales.

Buck, Janie B., ed. see Buck, William P.

Buck, Jerry. Wheeler's Choice. LC 89-17228. (Novel of the West Ser.). 192p. 1989. 14.95 (*0-87131-597-1*) M Evans.

Buck, Jirah D. The New Avatar & the Destiny of the Soul: The Findings of Natural Science Reduced to Practical Studies in Psychology. 236p. 1992. reprint ed. pap. 17.00 (*1-56459-196-4*) Kessinger Pub.

— Symbolism of Freemasonry. 17.00 (*0-911164-31-6*) Powner.

Buck, John A. Fundamentals of Optical Fibers. LC 94-27481. (Pure & Applied Optics Ser.). 280p. 1995. 84.95 (*0-471-30818-8*) Wiley.

Buck, John L. Land Utilization in China: An Extremely Detailed Study of 16,786 Farms, 3 vols., Set. (Illus.). 1986. reprint ed. 290.00 (*0-89986-377-9*) Oriental Bk Store.

Buck, John N. House-Tree-Person Projective Drawing Technique: Manual & Interpretive Guide. rev. ed. 165p. (C). 1992. 65.00 (*0-87424-306-8*, W-306) Western Psych.

Buck, John R., et al. Computer Explorations in Signals & Systems Using Matlab. LC 96-223878. 216p. (C). 1996. pap. 23.20 (*0-13-732868-0*) P-H.

Buck, Joyce & Alterbaum, Irene. Listen Speak: Pathways to Better Speech. 2nd ed. 512p. 1996. pap. text 35.95 (*0-8403-8016-X*) Kendall-Hunt.

Buck, Kathryn & Greenquist, Bradley W. German Verbs Skill Builder, Set. (GER & ENG.). 1999. pap. 29.95 incl. audio (*0-609-60442-2*) Liv Lang.

Buck, Kathryn & Greenquist, Bradley W. German Verbs Skill Builder Manual. 1999. pap. 6.95 (*0-609-80431-6*) Liv Lang.

Buck, Kenneth W. Fungal Virology. 336p. 1986. 178.00 (*0-8493-6228-8*, QR343, CRC Reprint) Franklin.

Buck, Louisa. Moving Targets: An Inside Guide to British Art Now. LC 98-157311. (Illus.). 192p. 1997. pap. 25.00 (*1-85437-223-8*, Pub. by Tate Gallery) U of Wash Pr.

***Buck, Louisa.** Moving Targets 2: A User's Guide to British Art Now. (Illus.). 256p. 2000. pap. 25.95 (*1-85437-316-1*, Pub. by Tate Gallery) U of Wash Pr.

Buck, Louise E. & Lassoie, James P. Agroforestry in Sustainable Agricultural Systems. (Advances in Agroecology Ser.). 432p. 1998. boxed set 74.95 (*1-56670-294-1*) Lewis Pubs.

Buck, Lucy. Sad Earth, Sweet Heaven. 1995. 21.95 (*0-934530-07-6*) Buck Pub.

Buck, Lynn. Autumn Fires. 64p. 1989. pap. 9.00 (*0-9621850-1-9*) Red Creek Pr.

— Two Minus One. (C). 1994. pap. text 5.00 (*1-878173-40-5*) Birnham Wood.

Buck, M. Laurel, et al. Stream of Memory: Reflections of Megantic County. (Illus.). 96p. 1994. pap. 14.95 (*0-9695180-9-9*) Sh1oreline.

***Buck, Madison G.** Homes: A Critical Eye Comparing Construction Quality. 2nd deluxe ed. (Illus.). 150p. 1998. pap. 14.95 (*0-9674598-0-X*) Critical Eye.

Buck, Marcia L. & Hendrick, Anne. Pediatric Medication Education Text. Babel Communications Staff, tr. from SPA.Tr. of Texto Educativo de Medicamentos Pediatricos. 200p. (Orig.). 1997. pap. 35.00 (*1-880401-89-4*) Amer Coll of Clin.

Buck, Margaret W. The Face: What It Means. LC 78-56844. 1980. 7.95 (*0-87212-138-0*); pap. 4.95 (*0-87212-106-2*) Libra.

Buck, Martin, jt. auth. see Inman, Sally.

Buck, Michael G., et al. The Multiresource Forest Inventory for Oahu, Hawaii. (Illus.). 44p. 1997. reprint ed. 10.40 (*0-89904-929-X*, Ecosytems Resrch); reprint ed. pap. 5.40 (*0-89904-930-3*, Ecosytems Resrch) Crumb Elbow Pub.

Buck, Mitchell S. The Life of Casanova. LC 76-51406. (Studies in Italian Literature: No. 46). 1977. lib. bdg. 75.00 (*0-8383-2120-8*) M S G Haskell Hse.

Buck, Mitchell S., jt. auth. see Machen, Arthur.

Buck-Morss, Susan. The Dialectics of Seeing: Walter Benjamin & the Arcades Project. (Studies in Contemporary German Social Thought). (Illus.). 504p. 1989. 35.00 (*0-262-02268-0*) MIT Pr.

— The Dialectics of Seeing: Walter Benjamin & the Arcades Project. (Illus.). 508p. 1991. pap. text 24.50 (*0-262-52164-4*) MIT Pr.

***Buck-Morss, Susan.** Dreamworld & Catastrophe: The Passing of Mass Utopia in East & West. LC 99-45165. (Illus.). 432p. 2000. 45.00 (*0-262-02464-0*) MIT Pr.

Buck-Murray, Marian. Kids Make Pizza: 40 Fun & Easy Recipes. (Illus.). 89p. (J). 1998. pap. text 12.00 (*0-7881-5297-1*) DIANE Pub.

— The Mash & Smash Cookbook: Fun & Yummy Recipes Every Kid Can Make. LC 97-10746. 124p. (J). 1997. pap. 12.95 (*0-471-17969-8*) Wiley.

Buck-Murray, Marion. Kids Make Pizza: 40 Recipes Full of Fun for Kids Ages 5 to 12. LC 94-32640. (Illus.). 96p. 1995. pap. 12.95 (*1-55958-649-4*) Prima Pub.

Buck, Nick, et al. The London Employment Problem. (Inner City in Context Ser.). (Illus.). 214p. 1986. pap. 19.95 (*0-19-823263-2*) OUP.

Buck, Nola. Central Park Serenade. LC 99-30279. 32p. (J). (ps). 2001. 14.95 (*0-06-025891-8*); lib. bdg. 14.89 (*0-06-025892-6*) HarpC Child Bks.

— Christmas in the Manger: A Pat-and-Peek Book. (Pat-&-Peek Bk.). (Illus.). 16p. (J). (ps up). 1995. 9.95 (*0-694-00836-2*, HarpFestival) HarpC Child Bks.

— Christmas in the Manger Board Book. (Illus.). 16p. (J). (ps-k). 1998. 6.95 (*0-694-01227-0*) HarpC.

— Creepy Crawly Critters & Other Halloween Tongue Twisters. LC 94-15405. (I Can Read Bks.). (Illus.). 32p. (J). (ps-3). 1995. 14.95 (*0-06-024808-4*) HarpC Child Bks.

— Creepy Crawly Critters & Other Halloween Tongue Twisters. LC 94-15405. (I Can Read Bks.). (Illus.). 32p. (J). (ps-3). 1996. pap. 3.95 (*0-06-444222-5*, HarpTrophy) HarpC Child Bks.

Buck, Nola. Creepy Crawly Critters & Other Halloween Tongue Twisters. (I Can Read Bks.). (J). (ps-1). 1996. 8.95 (*0-606-09172-6*, Pub. by Turtleback) Demco.

— Forest. (I Can Read Bks.). 48p. (J). (gr. 1-3). 2000. pap. 3.95 (*0-06-444275-6*) HarpC Child Bks.

Buck, Nola. Hey, Little Baby! LC 97-78011. (Illus.). 24p. (J). (ps-3). 1999. 9.95 (*0-694-01200-9*, HarpFestival) HarpC Child Bks.

— How a Baby Grows. LC 97-74638. (Illus.). 14p. (J). (ps up). 1998. 5.95 (*0-694-00873-7*) HarpC.

— Oh, Cats! (My First I Can Read Bks.). (Illus.). 32p. (J). (ps-k). 1997. 12.95 (*0-06-025373-8*); lib. bdg. 12.89 (*0-06-025374-6*) HarpC Child Bks.

— Oh, Cats! LC 95-10129. (My First I Can Read Bks.). (Illus.). 32p. (J). (ps-k). 1998. pap. 3.95 (*0-06-444240-3*, HarpTrophy) HarpC Child Bks.

— Oh, Cats! (My First I Can Read Bks.). (J). (ps-k). 1998. 8.95 (*0-606-13005-5*, Pub. by Turtleback) Demco.

— Santa's Short Suit Shrunk: And Other Christmas Tongue Twisters. LC 96-29077. (I Can Read Bks.). (Illus.). 32p. (J). (ps-1). 1998. pap. 3.75 (*0-06-444247-0*) HarpC.

— Santa's Short Suit Shrunk: And Other Christmas Tongue Twisters. LC PN6371.5.B84 1997. (I Can Read Bks.). (Illus.). 32p. (J). (ps-1). 1997. lib. bdg. 14.89 (*0-06-026663-5*) HarpC Child Bks.

— Santa's Short Suit Shrunk: And Other Christmas Tongue Twisters. LC 96-29077. (I Can Read Bks.). (Illus.). 32p. (J). (ps-3). 1997. 14.95 (*0-06-026649-X*) HarpC Child Bks.

— Sid & Sam. LC 94-36711. (My First I Can Read Bks.). (Illus.). 32p. (J). (ps-k). 1996. 12.95 (*0-06-025371-1*); lib. bdg. 14.89 (*0-06-025372-X*) HarpC Child Bks.

— Sid & Sam. (My First I Can Read Bks.). (J). (ps-k). 1997. 8.95 (*0-606-11841-1*, Pub. by Turtleback) Demco.

— Sid & Sam. LC 94-36711. (My First I Can Read Bks.). (Illus.). 32p. (J). (ps-k). 1997. reprint ed. pap. 3.95 (*0-06-444211-X*, HarpTrophy) HarpC Child Bks.

Buck, Otto & Mitchell, M. R., eds. Cyclic Deformation, Fracture, & Nondestructive Evaluation of Advanced Materials, Vol. 2, STP 1184. LC 94-32123. (Special Technical Publication Ser.: Vol. 1184). (Illus.). 400p. 1994. text 115.00 (*0-8031-1989-5*, STP1184) ASTM.

Buck, Otto & Wolf, Stanley M., eds. Nondestructive Evaluation: Application to Materials Processing: Proceedings of a Symposium - Sponsored by the Energy & Resources Activity of the ASM at the TMS Fall Meeting, Philadelphia, PA, October 3-4, 1983. LC 84-71516. (Illus.). 223p. reprint ed. pap. 69.20 (*0-8357-4099-4*, 203686500005) Bks Demand.

Buck, Otto, ed. see Metallurgical Society of AIME Staff.

Buck, Otto, jt. ed. see Mitchell, M. R.

Buck, P. H., jt. auth. see Shapiro, H. L.

Buck, Pat Ringling. The Great Zacchinis: History in Pictures. Zacchini, Olympia, ed. & photos by by. (Illus.). 32p. (Orig.). 1996. pap. 19.95 (*0-9659099-0-5*) Casa Di Zacchini.

Buck, Patricia R. The John & Mabel Ringling Museum of Art. (Illus.). 48p. 1989. pap. 9.95 (*0-917859-33-2*) Sunrise SBCA.

Buck, Paul. Libraries & Universities: Addresses & Reports. Williams, E. E., ed. LC 64-25053. 191p. 1964. 26.95 (*0-674-53050-0*) Belknap Pr.

— No Title. 64p. (Orig.). 1991. pap. 8.00 (*0-937013-38-2*) Potes Poets.

Buck, Paul, tr. see Noel, Bernard.

Buck, Paul H., ed. see Church, Robert L., et al.

Buck, Paula Closson, see Closson Buck, Paula.

Buck, Pearl Synderstricker. American Unity & Asia. LC 72-107687. (Essay Index Reprint Ser.). 1977. 19.95 (*0-8369-1550-X*) Ayer.

— The Big Wave. LC 48-244. (Illus.). 80p. (J). (gr. 2-6). 1973. lib. bdg. 16.89 (*0-381-99923-8*) HarpC Child Bks.

— The Big Wave. LC 85-45402. (Trophy Bk.). (Illus.). 64p. (J). (gr. 3-7). 1986. pap. 4.95 (*0-06-440171-5*, HarpTrophy) HarpC Child Bks.

— Big Wave. 1986. 9.70 (*0-606-00834-9*, Pub. by Turtleback) Demco.

— Child Who Never Grew. 24.95 (*0-8488-1250-6*) Amereon Ltd.

— The Child Who Never Grew. 2nd ed. LC 92-34844. 128p. (C). 1992. pap. 14.95 (*0-933149-49-2*) Woodbine House.

— The Chinese Novel. LC 73-20425. (Studies in Asiatic Literature: No. 57). (C). 1974. lib. bdg. 75.00 (*0-8383-1766-9*) M S G Haskell Hse.

— Death in the Castle. 20.95 (*0-8488-0435-X*) Amereon Ltd.

— Dragon Seed. 1993. reprint ed. lib. bdg. 19.95 (*1-56849-133-6*) Buccaneer Bks.

— Dragon Seed. (Oriental Novels of Pearl S. Buck Ser.). 378p. 1992. reprint ed. pap. 12.95 (*1-55921-033-8*) Moyer Bell.

— East Wind - West Wind. LC 93-13214. Vol. 8. 272p. 1993. reprint ed. pap. 11.95 (*1-55921-086-9*) Moyer Bell.

— The Good Earth. 17.95 (*0-8488-1251-4*) Amereon Ltd.

— The Good Earth. (Barron's Book Notes Ser.). 1985. pap. 2.95 (*0-8120-3517-8*) Barron.

— The Good Earth. 1990. per. 5.99 (*0-671-72989-6*) PB.

— The Good Earth. 416p. 1994. per. 6.99 (*0-671-51012-6*, WSP) PB.

— The Good Earth. (YA). (gr. 8-12). 1999. pap. write for info. (*0-671-50086-4*, WSP) PB.

— The Good Earth. 1958. 11.09 (*0-606-00173-5*, Pub. by Turtleback) Demco.

***Buck, Pearl Synderstricker.** Good Earth. 1999. pap. 14.65 (*0-88103-224-7*) Econo-Clad Bks.

Buck, Pearl Synderstricker. Good Earth. 1994. 12.09 (*0-606-12947-2*, Pub. by Turtleback) Demco.

— The Good Earth. large type ed. LC 93-3322. 441p. 1993. lib. bdg. 22.95 (*0-8161-5691-3*, G K Hall Lrg Type) Mac Lib Ref.

— The Good Earth. 421p. 1981. reprint ed. lib. bdg. 35.95 (*0-89966-299-4*) Buccaneer Bks.

***Buck, Pearl Synderstricker.** The Good Earth, 1. (Contemporary Classics Ser.). 256p. 1999. reprint ed. per. 12.00 (*0-671-03577-0*) PB.

Buck, Pearl Synderstricker. A House Divided. LC 93-31157. 360p. 1994. reprint ed. pap. 8.95 (*1-55921-034-6*) Moyer Bell.

— The House of Earth: The Good Earth Trilogy Including the Good Earth, Sons, & a House Divided. 900p. 1995. reprint ed. 28.95 (*1-55921-147-4*) Moyer Bell.

— Imperial Woman. (Oriental Novels of Pearl S. Buck Ser.). 384p. 1996. reprint ed. pap. 11.95 (*1-55921-035-4*) Moyer Bell.

— Kinfolk. LC 95-41364. 418p. 1996. reprint ed. pap. 11.95 (*1-55921-156-3*) Moyer Bell.

— The Living Reed. 478p. 1990. pap. 14.95 (*1-55921-022-2*) Moyer Bell.

— Mandala: A Novel of India. 384p. 1995. pap. 9.95 (*1-55921-037-0*) Moyer Bell.

— The Mother. (Good Earth Trilogy Ser.: Vol. 3). 302p. (Orig.). 1993. reprint ed. pap. 8.95 (*1-55921-091-5*) Moyer Bell.

— My Several Worlds. 1992. reprint ed. lib. bdg. 27.95 (*0-89966-987-5*) Buccaneer Bks.

— Pavilion of Women. 316p. 1994. pap. 11.95 (*1-55921-024-9*) Moyer Bell.

***Buck, Pearl Synderstricker.** Pavilion of Women. 316p. 2000. reprint ed. pap. 11.95 (*1-55921-287-X*) Moyer Bell.

Buck, Pearl Synderstricker. Peony. 338p. 1990. pap. 11.95 (*0-8197-0593-4*) Bloch.

— Peony. LC 95-44446. (Illus.). 338p. 1996. reprint ed. lib. bdg. 24.95 (*0-8197-0617-5*) Bloch.

— Peony. LC 95-44446. 320p. 1996. reprint ed. pap. 11.95 (*1-55921-168-7*) Moyer Bell.

— Portrait of a Marriage. 21.95 (*0-8488-0791-X*) Amereon Ltd.

— The Promise. LC 97-6889. 248p. (Orig.). 1997. pap. 9.95 (*1-55921-209-8*) Moyer Bell.

— Sons. LC 92-14988. 314p. 1992. pap. 11.95 (*1-55921-039-7*) Moyer Bell.

— Tell the People: Talks with James Yen About the Mass Education Movement. 141p. 1984. reprint ed. pap. 5.00 (*0-318-14582-0*) Intl Inst Rural.

— The Three Daughters of Madam Liang. (Oriental Novels of Pearl S. Buck Ser.). 316p. 1991. reprint ed. pap. 8.95 (*1-55921-040-0*) Moyer Bell.

— To My Daughters, with Love. 1992. reprint ed. lib. bdg. 23.95 (*0-89966-989-1*) Buccaneer Bks.

— What America Means to Me. LC 79-156622. (Essay Index Reprint Ser.). 1977. reprint ed. 18.95 (*0-8369-2387-1*) Ayer.

— A Woman Who Changed & Other Stories. 19.95 (*0-8488-0436-8*) Amereon Ltd.

Buck, Pearl Synderstricker & Center for Learning Network Staff. The Good Earth: Curriculum Unit. (Novel Ser.). 100p. (YA). (gr. 9-12). 1990. spiral bd. 18.95 (*1-56077-342-1*) Ctr Learning.

Buck, Percy C. Scope of Music. LC 70-93321. (Essay Index Reprint Ser.). 1977. 17.95 (*0-8369-1276-4*) Ayer.

Buck, Peter H. Ethnology of Mangareva. (BMB Ser.: No. 157). 1972. reprint ed. 70.00 (*0-527-02265-9*) Periodicals Srv.

— Ethnology of Manihiki & Rakahanga. (BMB Ser.: No. 99). 1972. reprint ed. 45.00 (*0-527-02205-5*) Periodicals Srv.

— Ethnology of Tongareva. (BMB Ser.). 1972. reprint ed. 45.00 (*0-527-02198-9*) Periodicals Srv.

— Explorers of the Pacific: European & American Discoveries in Polynesia. LC 54-4097. (Bernice P. Bishop Museum Special Publications: No. 43). (Illus.). 133p. reprint ed. pap. 41.30 (*0-608-17287-1*, 203032300068) Bks Demand.

— Material Culture of Kapingamarangi: Coordinated Investigation of Micronesian Anthropology. (BMB Ser.: No. 200). 1969. reprint ed. 45.00 (*0-527-02308-6*) Periodicals Srv.

— The Material Culture of the Cook Islands (Aitutaki) LC 75-35178. reprint ed. 59.50 (*0-404-14206-0*) AMS Pr.

— Report of the Director for 1950. pap. 18.00 (*0-527-02313-2*, B205K) Periodicals Srv.

— Report of the Director for 1940. pap. 18.00 (*0-527-02279-9*, B171K) Periodicals Srv.

— Report of the Director for 1941. pap. 18.00 (*0-527-02283-7*, B175K) Periodicals Srv.

— Report of the Director for 1942. pap. 18.00 (*0-527-02288-8*, B180K) Periodicals Srv.

— Report of the Director for 1943. pap. 18.00 (*0-527-02290-X*, B182K) Periodicals Srv.

— Report of the Director for 1944. pap. 18.00 (*0-527-02294-2*, B186K) Periodicals Srv.

— Report of the Director for 1945. pap. 18.00 (*0-527-02296-9*, B188K) Periodicals Srv.

— Report of the Director for 1946. pap. 18.00 (*0-527-02300-0*, B192K) Periodicals Srv.

— Report of the Director for 1947. pap. 18.00 (*0-527-02302-7*, B194K) Periodicals Srv.

— Report of the Director for 1948. pap. 18.00 (*0-527-02305-1*, B197K) Periodicals Srv.

— Report of the Director for 1949. pap. 18.00 (*0-527-02307-8*, B199K) Periodicals Srv.

— Report of the Director for 1936. pap. 18.00 (*0-527-02257-8*, B149K) Periodicals Srv.

— Report of the Director for 1937. pap. 18.00 (*0-527-02263-2*, B155K) Periodicals Srv.

— Report of the Director for 1938. pap. 18.00 (*0-527-02272-1*, B164K) Periodicals Srv.

— Samoan Material Culture. (BMB Ser.). 1974. reprint ed. 105.00 (*0-527-02181-4*) Periodicals Srv.

Buck, Peter H. & Hiroa, Te Rangi. Arts & Crafts of Hawaii: Canoes. (Special Publications: No. 45 (6)). (Illus.). 41p. 1957. pap. 8.95 (*0-910240-39-6*) Bishop Mus.

— Arts & Crafts of Hawaii: Clothing. (Special Publications: No. 45 (5)). (Illus.). 97p. 1957. pap. 8.95 (*0-910240-38-8*) Bishop Mus.

— Arts & Crafts of Hawaii: Death & Burial. (Special Publications: No. 45 (13)). (Illus.). 26p. 1957. pap. 8.95 (*0-910240-46-9*) Bishop Mus.

— Arts & Crafts of Hawaii: Fishing. (Special Publications: No. 45 (7)). (Illus.). 78p. 1957. pap. 8.95 (*0-910240-40-X*) Bishop Mus.

— Arts & Crafts of Hawaii: Food. (Special Publications: No. 45 (1)). (Illus.). 83p. 1957. pap. 8.95 (*0-910240-34-5*) Bishop Mus.

— Arts & Crafts of Hawaii: Games & Recreation. (Special Publications: No. 45 (8)). (Illus.). 32p. 1957. pap. 8.95 (*0-910240-41-8*) Bishop Mus.

— Arts & Crafts of Hawaii: Houses. (Special Publications: No. 45 (2)). (Illus.). 52p. 1957. pap. 8.95 (*0-910240-35-3*) Bishop Mus.

— Arts & Crafts of Hawaii: Index. (Special Publications: No. 45 (14)). 19p. 1957. pap. 4.95 (*0-910240-47-7*) Bishop Mus.

— Arts & Crafts of Hawaii: Musical Instruments. (Special Publications: No. 45 (9)). 39p. 1957. pap. 8.95 (*0-910240-42-6*) Bishop Mus.

— Arts & Crafts of Hawaii: Ornaments & Personal Adornment. (Special Publications: No. 45 (12)). (Illus.). 40p. 1957. pap. 8.95 (*0-910240-45-0*) Bishop Mus.

— Arts & Crafts of Hawaii: Plaiting. (Special Publications: No. 45 (3)). (Illus.). 39p. 1957. pap. 8.95 (*0-910240-36-1*) Bishop Mus.

— Arts & Crafts of Hawaii: Religion. (Special Publications: No. 45 (11)). (Illus.). 77p. 1957. pap. 8.95 (*0-910240-44-2*) Bishop Mus.

— Arts & Crafts of Hawaii: Twined Baskets. (Special Publications: No. 45 (4)). (Illus.). 33p. 1957. pap. 8.95 (*0-910240-37-X*) Bishop Mus.

— Arts & Crafts of Hawaii: War & Weapons. (Special Publications: No. 45 (10)). (Illus.). 57p. 1957. pap. 8.95 (*0-910240-43-4*) Bishop Mus.

Buck, Philip W. Amateurs & Professionals in British Politics, 1918-59. LC 63-13073. 155p. reprint ed. pap. 48.10 (*0-8357-5339-5*, 201575100002) Bks Demand.

Buck, Philo M. Directions in Contemporary Literature. LC 75-58254. (Essay Index in Reprint Ser.). 1978. reprint ed. 35.00 (*0-8486-3016-5*) Roth Pub Inc.

Buck, Polly S. Adopted Son of Salem. 1971. 15.95 (*0-87233-020-6*) Bauhan.

Buck, R. Creighton. Advanced Calculus. 3rd ed. LC 77-2859. (McGraw-Hill International Series in Pure & Applied Mathematics). (Illus.). 640p. (C). 1978. 90.94 (*0-07-008728-8*) McGraw.

Buck, R. Creighton, ed. see Philosophy of Science Association Staff.

Buck, Rebecca A. & Gilmore, Jean A., eds. The New Museum Registration Methods. LC 98-16006. 427p. 1998. pap. 55.00 (*0-931201-31-4*) Am Assn Mus.

Buck, Richard. Silver Swimmer: The Struggle for Survival of the Wild Atlantic Salmon. 320p. 1993. 35.00 (*1-55821-251-5*) Lyons Pr.

Buck, Richard, jt. auth. see Merriman, Paul A.

Buck, Richard P., et al. Biosensor Technology: Fundamentals & Applications. (Illus.). 408p. 1990. text 155.00 (*0-8247-8414-6*) Dekker.

Buck, Richard P., ed. see Symposium on Ion Exchange: Transport & Interfacial.

Buck, Rinker. Flight of Passage. LC 96-27745. (Illus.). 368p. (J). 1997. 23.45 (*0-7868-6100-2*, Pub. by Hyperion) Time Warner.

— Flight of Passage: A True Story. LC 96-27745. (Illus.). 368p. (J). 1998. reprint ed. pap. 12.45 (*0-7868-8315-4*, Pub. by Hyperion) Time Warner.

— If We Had Wings. 2001. write for info. (*0-609-60553-4*) Crown.

Buck, Robert J., jt. auth. see Small, Alastair M.

Buck, Robert N. The Art of Flying. LC 91-46647. (Illus.). 186p. 1992. 24.95 (*1-56566-005-6*) Thomasson-Grant.

***Buck, Robert N.** The Pilot's Burden: Flight Safety & the Roots of Pilot Error. (Illus.). 252p. 2000. pap. 32.95 (*0-8138-2815-5*) Iowa St U Pr.

Buck, Robert N. Weather Flying. 4th ed. LC 97-35732. 304p. 1997. 29.95 (*0-07-008761-X*); text 29.95 (*0-07-008716-4*) McGraw.

Buck, Robert T., frwd. Installation Art at the Brooklyn Museum: A Decade of Grand Lobby Projects. 1995. write for info. (*0-87273-133-2*) Bklyn Mus.

Buck, Robert T., Jr., pref. The Armand Hammer Collection: Four Centuries of Masterpieces. LC 99-58789. 1978. 10.00 (*0-914782-95-9*) Buffalo Fine-Albrght-Knox.

Buck, Robert T., et al. Fernand Leger. (Illus.). 160p. 1995. 29.95 (*0-89659-256-1*) Abbeville Pr.

Buck, Robert T., et al. Fernand Leger. (Illus.). 160p. 1995. pap. 19.95 (*0-89659-254-5*) Abbeville Pr.

Buck, Robert T., jt. auth. see Hess, Thomas B., Jr.

***Buck, Roland, et al.** Angels on Assignment. 200p. 2000. pap. 11.99 (*0-88368-605-8*) Whitaker Hse.

An Asterisk (*) at the beginning of an entry indicates that the title is appearing for the first time.

B

Buckingham, John B. Dictionary of Organic Compounds. 6th ed. 1997. ring bd. 624.95 (*0-412-54120-3*, Chap & Hall CRC) CRC Pr.
— Dictionary of Organic Compounds: First Supplement. 6th ed. (C). 1996. ring bd. 624.95 (*0-412-54110-6*, Chap & Hall CRC) CRC Pr.
— Dictionary of Organic Compounds: Second Supplement. 5th ed. 700p. (gr. 13). 1984. text 595.00 (*0-412-17020-5*, NO. 6800, Chap & Hall CRC) CRC Pr.
Buckingham, John B., ed. Dictionary of Natural Products, Vol. 8. (Illus.). 480p. 1997. ring bd., suppl. ed. 624.95 (*0-412-57780-1*, Chap & Hall CRC) CRC Pr.
— Dictionary of Natural Products, Vol. 9. (Illus.). 480p. 1995. ring bd., suppl. ed. 624.95 (*0-412-60420-5*, Chap & Hall CRC) CRC Pr.
— Dictionary of Organic Compounds: Fourth Supplement. 5th ed. 800p. (gr. 13). 1989. text 495.00 (*0-412-17040-X*, 9935, Chap & Hall CRC) CRC Pr.
— Dictionary of Organic Compounds: Ninth Supplement. 720p. (C). (gr. 13). 1997. ring bd. write for info. (*0-412-17090-6*, A6859, Chap & Hall CRC) CRC Pr.
— Dictionary of Organic Compounds: The Eighth Supplement. 5th ed. 704p. (gr. 13). 1990. ring bd. write for info. (*0-412-17080-9*, A5185, Chap & Hall CRC) CRC Pr.
— Dictionary of Organic Compounds: The Fifth Supplement. 5th ed. 1300p. (gr. 13). 1987. ring bd. write for info. (*0-412-17050-7*, Chap & Hall CRC) CRC Pr.
— Dictionary of Organic Compounds: The Seventh Supplement. 740p. 1989. 499.00 (*0-412-17070-1*, A3817, Chap & Hall CRC) CRC Pr.
— Dictionary of Organic Compounds: The Sixth Supplement. 5th ed. (Illus.). 750p. (gr. 13). 1988. text 495.00 (*0-412-17060-4*, Chap & Hall CRC) CRC Pr.
— Dictionary of Organic Compounds: Third Supplement. 5th ed. 800p. (gr. 13). 1985. text 625.00 (*0-412-17030-2*, 9553, Chap & Hall CRC) CRC Pr.
Buckingham, John B., et al, eds. Dictionary of Organic Compounds, 7 vols., Set. 5th ed. 1982. ring bd. write for info. (*0-412-17000-0*, NO.6611, Chap & Hall CRC) CRC Pr.
— Dictionary of Organometallic Compounds, 3 vols., Set. 3000p. 1984. ring bd. write for info. (*0-412-24710-0*, NO. 9075, Chap & Hall CRC) CRC Pr.
— Dictionary of Organometallic Compounds: First Supplement. 400p. (gr. 13). 1985. ring bd. write for info. (*0-412-26320-3*, NO. 9076, Chap & Hall CRC) CRC Pr.
Buckingham, John B. & MacDonald, Finlay J., eds. Dictionary of Organic Compounds. 6th ed. (Illus.). 9000p. 1995. ring bd. write for info. (*0-412-54090-8*, Chap & Hall CRC) CRC Pr.
Buckingham, John B., jt. auth. see Klyne, W.
Buckingham, Joseph T. Personal Memoirs & Recollections of Editorial Life. LC 76-125682. (American Journalists Ser.). 1971. reprint ed. 26.95 (*0-405-01657-3*) Ayer.
— Personal Memoirs & Recollections of Editorial Life, 2 vols., Vols. 1 - 2. (American Biography Ser.). 1991. reprint ed. lib. bdg. 148.00 (*0-7812-8051-6*) Rprt Serv.
— Specimens of Newspaper Literature, 2 vols, Set. LC 79-146853. (Select Bibliographies Reprint Ser.). 1977. reprint ed. 48.95 (*0-8369-5620-6*) Ayer.
***Buckingham, Linda.** Finishing Touches for the Boat: Over 50 Projects to Personalize Your Boat. (Illus.). 192p. 2000. pap. 24.95 (*0-88179-192-X*, Pub. by Hartley & Marks) Publishers Group.
Buckingham, Linda & Bird, Leslie. Projection Stenciling. LC 99-43780. (Illus.). 224p. 1999. pap. 24.95 (*0-88179-180-6*, Pub. by Hartley & Marks) Andrews & McMeel.
Buckingham, M. J. & Potter, J. R. Sea Surface Sound, '94. 600p. 1996. text 118.00 (*981-02-1891-5*) World Scientific Pub.
Buckingham, M. J., jt. auth. see Blair, D. G.
Buckingham, Maggie A. Drops of Gold. 2nd rev. ed. Caffey, Jacquelyn S. & Watley, Gwendolyn S., eds. LC 95-62286. (Illus.). 100p. (Orig.). 1995. pap. 10.00 (*1-888587-00-8*) Write to Teach.
***Buckingham, Marcus & Coffman, Curt.** First, Break All the Rules: What the World's Greatest Managers Do Differently. LC 99-19452. 272p. 1999. 24.50 (*0-684-85286-1*) S&S Trade.
Buckingham, Margaret E. Biochemistry of Cellular Regulation Vol. III: Development & Differentiation. 272p. 1981. 151.00 (*0-8493-5456-0*, QH607, CRC Reprint) Franklin.
Buckingham, Martin, jt. ed. see Bennett, Richard.
***Buckingham, Michael.** Presidential Redwork: A Stitch in Time. Squire, Helen & Browning, Bonnie K., eds. (Illus.). 80p. 2000. pap. 16.95 (*1-57432-744-5*, Am Quilters Soc) Collector Bks.
Buckingham, Michael J. Noise in Electronic Devices & Systems. (Electrical & Electronic Engineering Ser.). 372p. 1985. pap. text 54.95 (*0-470-20164-9*) P-H.
***Buckingham, Mike.** Cwmikaze. 192p. 1999. pap. 13.95 (*0-575-60326-7*, Pub. by Vista) Trafalgar.
***Buckingham, Mike & Frame, Richard.** Alexander Cordell: Valient for Truth. 216p. 1999. pap. 16.95 (*0-7083-1488-0*, Pub. by Univ Wales Pr) Paul & Co Pubs.
Buckingham, Nancy. Call of Glengarron. large type ed. 1991. 27.99 (*0-7089-2425-5*) Ulverscroft.
— Cloud over Malverton. large type ed. 1990. 27.99 (*0-7089-2278-3*) Ulverscroft.
— The Dark Summer. large type ed. 1990. 27.99 (*0-7089-2199-X*) Ulverscroft.
— Kiss of Hot Sun. large type ed. 1991. 27.99 (*0-7089-2495-6*) Ulverscroft.
Buckingham, Nash. De Shootinest Gent'Man. 336p. 1992. reprint ed. lib. bdg. 32.95 (*0-89968-310-X*, Lghtyr Pr) Buccaneer Bks.
— De Shootinest Gent'man: And Other Tales. LC 97-32926. (Illus.). 200p. 1997. 35.00 (*1-885106-52-1*) Wild Adven Pr.
— De Shootinest Gent'man: And Other Tales. 4th ed. (Affordable Classics: Vol. 1). 240p. 1997. reprint ed. pap. 14.95 (*1-56416-164-1*) Derrydale Pr.
— Ole Miss. 2nd ed. (Fifty Greatest Bks.). (Illus.). 243p. 1992. reprint ed. 50.00 (*1-56416-034-3*) Derrydale Pr.
Buckingham, Peter H. America Sees Red - Anti-Communism in America, 1890s to 1980s: A Guide to Issues & References. 240p. 1987. 29.95 (*0-941690-23-7*); pap. 13.95 (*0-941690-22-9*) Regina Bks.
— Rebel Against Injustice: The Life of Frank P. O'Hare. Foley, William E., ed. (Missouri Biography Ser.). (Illus.). 296p. (C). 1995. 39.95 (*0-8262-1055-4*) U of Mo Pr.
— Woodrow Wilson: A Bibliography of His Times & Presidency. LC 89-10966. (Twentieth-Century Presidential Bibliography Ser.). (Illus.). 370p. 1990. 85.00 (*0-8420-2291-0*) Scholarly Res Inc.
Buckingham, Peter H., intro. International Normalcy, 1921-29: The Open Door Policy with the Former Central Powers, 1921-29. LC 83-18935. 206p. 1984. lib. bdg. 45.00 (*0-8420-2215-5*) Scholarly Res Inc.
Buckingham, Richard A., et al. Imaging of the Head & Neck. 2nd ed. (Illus.). 620p. 1994. 209.00 (*0-86577-549-4*) Thieme Med Pubs.
***Buckingham, Robert J.** Buckingham Family, Bk. II. 179p. 1999. lib. bdg. 37.00 (*0-8328-9915-1*) Higginson Bk Co.
— Buckingham Family Bk. II. 179p. 1999. pap. 27.00 (*0-8328-9916-X*) Higginson Bk Co.
Buckingham, Robert W. Among Friends: Hospice Care for the Person with AIDS. LC 91-45568. 191p. (C). 1992. 25.95 (*0-87975-720-5*); pap. 15.95 (*0-87975-759-0*) Prometheus Bks.
— The Handbook of Hospice Care. LC 96-11357. (Illus.). 262p. 1996. pap. 16.95 (*1-57392-060-6*) Prometheus Bks.
— International Health. (C). 1999. pap. text 42.67 (*0-205-19809-0*, Macmillan Coll) P-H.
— When Living Alone Means Living at Risk: A Guide for Caregivers & Families. LC 93-33990. (Golden Age Books - Perspectives on Aging Ser.). 167p. (Orig.). 1994. 26.95 (*0-87975-844-9*); pap. 17.95 (*0-87975-873-2*) Prometheus Bks.
Buckingham, Robert W. & Derby, Mary P. I'm Pregnant, Now What Do I Do? LC 96-48344. (Illus.). 228p. (Orig.). (YA). 1997. pap. 12.95 (*1-57392-117-3*) Prometheus Bks.
Buckingham, Sandra. Stencil It! (Illus.). 64p. (J). 1993. lib. bdg. 17.95 (*0-921820-75-5*) Firefly Bks Ltd.
— Stencil It! Kids Projects. (Illus.). 64p. (J). 1993. pap. 9.95 (*0-921820-73-9*) Firefly Bks Ltd.
— Stencilling: A Harrowsmith Guide. Mohr, Merilyn S., ed. (Illus.). 152p. 1989. pap. 19.95 (*0-920656-09-9*) Firefly Bks Ltd.
Buckingham, Sandra. Stencilling on a Grand Scale: Using Simple Stencils to Create Visual Magic. (Illus.). 156p. 1997. text 35.00 (*1-55209-143-0*) Firefly Bks Ltd.
— Stencilling on a Grand Scale: Using Simple Stencils to Create Visual Magic. (Illus.). 156p. 2000. pap. 24.95 (*1-55209-486-3*) Firefly Bks Ltd.
Buckingham, Simon. Alec & His Flying Bed LC 93-184997. (J). 1990. write for info. (*0-333-53690-8*, Pub. by S1 & J) Trafalgar.
— Data on GPRS. (Illus.). 253p. 1999. ring bd. 250.00 (*1-929105-06-1*) Mobile Lifestrms.
— Data on SMS. 1999. ring bd. write for info. (*1-929105-00-2*) Mobile Lifestrms.
— Data on WAP. (Illus.). 86p. 1999. ring bd. 150.00 (*1-929105-08-8*) Mobile Lifestrms.
— Data on WAP: An Introduction to the Wireless Application Protocol. 1999. ring bd. write for info. (*1-929105-09-6*) Mobile Lifestrms.
— YES to GPRS: An Introduction to the General Packet Radio Service. 1999. ring bd. write for info. (*1-929105-07-X*) Mobile Lifestrms.
— YES 2 SMS. (Illus.). 306p. 1999. ring bd. 150.00 (*1-929105-04-5*) Mobile Lifestrms.
— YES 2 SMS: An Introduction to the Short Message Service. 1999. ring bd. write for info. (*1-929105-05-3*) Mobile Lifestrms.
Buckingham, Stephan L., jt. ed. see Van Gorp, Wilfred G.
Buckingham, T. Nash. Mr. Buck: The Autobiography of Nash Buckingham. Smith, Steven R., ed. LC 90-81090. (Illus.). 288p. 1990. 40.00 (*0-924357-15-0*, 61200-A) Countrysport Pr.
— Mr. Buck: The Autobiography of Nash Buckingham. deluxe limited ed. Smith, Steven R., ed. LC 90-81090. (Illus.). 288p. 1990. lthr. 70.00 (*0-924357-16-9*, 61200-B); lthr. 100.00 (*0-924357-17-7*, 61205-B) Countrysport Pr.
Buckingham, W. & Ross, G. W. Honorable Alexander Mackenzie, His Life & Times. LC 68-25225. (English Biography Ser.: No. 31). 1969. reprint ed. lib. bdg. 75.00 (*0-8383-0920-8*) M S G Haskell Hse.
Buckingham, William. The Honourable Alexander Mackenzie, His Life & Times. (BCL1 - History - Canada Ser.). 678p. 1991. reprint ed. lib. bdg. 109.00 (*0-7812-6362-X*) Rprt Serv.
Buckingham, Willis J. Emily Dickinson's Reception in the 1890s: A Documentary History. LC 88-19816. 639p. pap. 198.10 (*0-608-05091-1*, 206564500005) Bks Demand.
Buckingham, Willis J., ed. Emily Dickinson, An Annotated Bibliography: Writings, Scholarship, Criticism & Ana 1850-1968. LC 75-108205. 336p. reprint ed. pap. 104.20 (*0-608-11487-1*, 205003900059) Bks Demand.
Buckinghamshire Federation of Women's Institutes. The Buckinghamshire Village Book. 192p. 1987. 30.00 (*0-905392-80-9*) St Mut.
Buckius, Richard O., jt. auth. see Howell, Jack R.
Buckland. Dance in the Field. LC 99-21778. 223p. 1999. text 65.00 (*0-312-22378-1*) St Martin.
Buckland & Oglesby. Guide to Salmon Flies. 45.00 (*1-85223-246-3*, Pub. by Crolwood) Trafalgar.
Buckland & Wood. Aspects of British Calender Customs. 190p. (C). 1991. 17.95 (*1-85075-243-5*, Pub. by Sheffield Acad) CUP Services.
Buckland, jt. auth. see Chimenes.
Buckland, A. R. Diccionario Biblico Universal. Orig. Title: Buckland Bible Dictionary. (SPA., Illus.). 456p. 1981. pap. 15.95 (*0-8297-0836-7*) Vida Pubs.
Buckland, Barry C., ed. Cell Culture Engineering. 4th ed. LC 94-48293. (Current Applications of Cell Culture Engineering Ser.: Vol. 1). 1995. text 209.50 (*0-7923-3353-5*) Kluwer Academic.
***Buckland, C. E.** Dictionary of Indian Biography, 2 vols. 1999. 72.00 (*81-7020-897-1*, Pub. by Cosmo Pubn) S Asia.
Buckland, C. E. Dictionary of Indian Biography. LC 68-26350. (Reference Ser.: No. 44). 1969. reprint ed. lib. bdg. 85.00 (*0-8383-0277-7*) M S G Haskell Hse.
Buckland, Dean. Parson Packs a Peacemaker. (Illus.). 64p. 1997. pap. 7.95 (*0-9658776-0-4*) Cntrl Coast Pr.
Buckland, Gail. The White House in Miniature: Based on the White House Replica by John & Jan Zweifel. LC 94-4193. (Illus.). 1994. 29.95 (*0-393-03663-4*) Norton.
Buckland, John. North American Game Fishing: A Compendium of Tips, Techniques, Habitats, Species & Conservation Information for Today's Fisherman. 256p. 19.99 (*1-57215-242-7*, JG2427) World Pubns.
Buckland, John A., ed. Total Quality Management in Information Services. 56p. 1993. pap. 64.99 (*0-471-56046-4*) Wiley.
Buckland, Michael, jt. auth. see Henken, John.
Buckland, Michael K. Information & Information Systems. LC 90-47541. 248p. 1991. pap. 19.95 (*0-275-93851-4*, B3851, Praeger Pubs) Greenwood.
— Information & Information Systems: New Directions in Information Management, 25. LC 90-47327. 248p. 1991. 59.95 (*0-313-27463-0*, BII/, Greenwood Pr) Greenwood.
— Library Services in Theory & Context. 250p. 1983. text 39.00 (*0-08-030134-7*, Pergamon Pr); pap. text 15.75 (*0-08-030133-9*, Pergamon Pr) Elsevier.
— Library Services in Theory & Context. 2nd ed. LC 88-17864. (Illus.). 268p. 1988. pap. text 22.00 (*0-08-035754-7*, Pergamon Pr) Elsevier.
— Redesigning Library Services: A Manifesto. LC 92-10546. 130p. (C). 1992. pap. text 23.00 (*0-8389-0590-0*) ALA.
Buckland, Michael K., jt. ed. see Hahn, Trudi B.
Buckland, Michael K., jt. ed. see Stone, Susan.
***Buckland, Nicholl.** Around the World with Wendy & Barb: More Tasting, Low-Fat Recipes. 2000. pap. 24.95 (*0-00-638548-6*) HarpC.
Buckland, Patrick. A History of Northern Ireland. (Illus.). 195p. 1981. pap. 21.95 (*0-7171-1069-9*, Pub. by Gill & MacMill) Irish Bks Media.
Buckland, Ray. Ray Buckland's Magic Cauldron: A Potpourri of Matters Metaphysical. LC 95-12527. (Illus.). 208p. 1995. pap. 12.95 (*1-880090-13-9*) Galde Pr.
Buckland, Raymond. Advanced Candle Magick: More Spells & Rituals for Every Purpose. LC 95-49693. (Illus.). 288p. 1996. pap. 12.95 (*1-56718-103-1*) Llewellyn Pubns.
— Book of African Divination: Interpreting the Forces of Destiny with Techniques from the Venda... 144p. 1992. pap. text 26.00 (*0-89281-364-4*) Inner Tradit.
— Buckland Gypsies' Domino Divination Deck. (Illus.). 32p. 1995. boxed set 12.95 (*1-56718-094-9*) Llewellyn Pubns.
— Buckland's Complete Book of Witchcraft. LC 85-45280. (Practical Magick Ser.). (Illus.). 272p. (Orig.). (C). 1999. pap. 14.95 (*0-87542-050-8*) Llewellyn Pubns.
— Cardinal's Sin: Psychic Defenders Uncover Evil in the Vatican. LC 95-4811. 336p. 1999. mass mkt. 5.99 (*1-56718-102-3*) Llewellyn Pubns.
***Buckland, Raymond.** Coin Divination: Pocket Fortuneteller. LC 99-88433. (Illus.). 216p. 2000. pap. 9.95 (*1-56718-089-2*) Llewellyn Pubns.
Buckland, Raymond. Doors to Other Worlds: A Practical Guide to Communicating with Spirits. LC 93-940. (Illus.). 272p. (Orig.). 1999. pap. 10.00 (*0-87542-061-3*) Llewellyn Pubns.
— Gypsy Dream Dictionary. 2nd expanded rev. ed. LC 98-31529. (Illus.). 240p. 1999. 4.99 (*1-56718-090-6*, K090) Llewellyn Pubns.
— Gypsy Fortune Telling & Tarot Reading. 2nd ed. LC 98-12173. 1998. pap. write for info. (*1-56718-092-2*) Llewellyn Pubns.
— Gypsy Fortune Telling Tarot Kit. (Illus.). 240p. 1999. 19.95 (*1-56718-091-4*) Llewellyn Pubns.
***Buckland, Raymond.** Gypsy Witchcraft & Magic. LC 98-22354. (Illus.). 192p. 1999. pap. 17.95 (*1-56718-097-3*, K097) Llewellyn Pubns.
Buckland, Raymond. Magic of Chant-O-Matics. 232p. (C). 1982. pap. text 9.95 (*0-13-545079-9*) P-H.
— Practical Candleburning Rituals. 3rd ed. LC 86-20915. (Practical Magick Ser.). (Illus.). 210p. 1982. pap. 7.95 (*0-87542-048-6*) Llewellyn Pubns.
— Practical Color Magick. LC 83-80173. (Practical Magick Ser.). (Illus.). 160p. 1983. pap. 6.95 (*0-87542-047-8*) Llewellyn Pubns.
— Rituales Practico con Velas. Rojas, Edgar, ed. & tr. by. from ENG. LC 97-37669. (SPA., Illus.). 192p. (Orig.). 1999. pap. 6.95 (*1-56718-096-5*) Llewellyn Pubns.
— Scottish Witchcraft: The History & Magick of the Picts. LC 91-32832. (Illus.). 256p. 1999. pap. 11.95 (*0-87542-057-5*) Llewellyn Pubns.
— Secrets of Gypsy Dream Reading. LC 90-39288. (New Age Ser.). (Illus.). 224p. (Orig.). 1990. mass mkt. 3.95 (*0-87542-086-9*) Llewellyn Pubns.
— Secrets of Gypsy Fortunetelling. LC 88-45196. (New Age Ser.). (Illus.). 240p. 1999. mass mkt. 4.99 (*0-87542-051-6*) Llewellyn Pubns.
— Secrets of Gypsy Love Magick. LC 89-77239. (New Age Ser.). (Illus.). 176p. (Orig.). 1990. mass mkt. 4.99 (*0-87542-053-2*) Llewellyn Pubns.
— The Tree: The Complete Book of Saxon Witchcraft. LC 74-79397. (Illus.). 168p. 1974. pap. 9.95 (*0-87728-258-7*) Weiser.
— The Truth about Spirit Communication. LC 95-161335. (Truth About Ser.). (Illus.). 64p. 1995. mass mkt. 1.99 (*1-56718-095-7*) Llewellyn Pubns.
— La Verdad Sobre la Communicacion con los Espiritus (The Truth about Spirit Communication) (Truth About Ser.). (SPA.). 64p. 1999. mass mkt. 1.99 (*1-56718-879-6*) Llewellyn Pubns.
— Witchcraft from the Inside: Origins of the Fastest Growing Religious Movement in America. 3rd rev. enl. ed. LC 94-44804. (Illus.). 240p. 1999. pap. 12.95 (*1-56718-101-5*) Llewellyn Pubns.
Buckland, Raymond, et al, contrib. by. Llewellyn's 2000 Magical Almanac. annuals (Illus.). 384p. 1999. pap. 6.95 (*1-56718-950-4*) Llewellyn Pubns.
Buckland, Raymond & Carrington, Hereward. Amazing Secrets of the Psychic World. 1976. pap. 4.95 (*0-686-96839-5*, Reward) P-H.
Buckland, Raymond, ed. see Holzer, Hans.
Buckland, Roger & Davis, Edward W., eds. Finance for Growing Enterprises. LC 94-44949. 288p. (C). (gr. 13). 1995. pap. 55.00 (*0-415-08233-1*) Thomson Learn.
Buckland, S. T., et al. Distance Sampling: Estimating Abundance of Biological Populations. 400p. 1993. 85.00 (*0-412-42660-9*, A9788) Chapman & Hall.
Buckland, Sidney. Francis Poulenc: Echo & Source Selected Correspondence 1915-1963. (Illus.). 448p. 1992. 65.00 (*0-575-05093-4*, Pub. by V Gollancz) Trafalgar.
Buckland, Sidney & Chimenes, Myriam, eds. Francis Pouleric: Music, Art & Literature. LC 99-31632. (Illus.). 320p. 1999. text 83.95 (*1-85928-407-8*, Pub. by Ashgate Pub) Ashgate Pub Co.
Buckland, Susan, ed. The Maverick Guide to New Zealand. 10th rev. ed. (Maverick Guides Ser.). (Illus.). 368p. 1999. pap. 17.95 (*1-56554-140-5*) Pelican.
Buckland, Tara. How to Make an Easy Charm to Attract Love into Your Life. LC 90-6018. (How-to Ser.). (Illus.). 112p. 1990. pap. 3.95 (*0-87542-087-7*) Llewellyn Pubns.
Buckland, W. W. Equity in Roman Law: Lectures Delivered in the University of London, at the Request of the Faculty of Laws. vii, 136p. 1983. reprint ed. 32.50 (*0-8377-0339-5*, Rothman) W S Hein.
***Buckland, W. W.** The Roman Law of Slavery: The Condition of the Slave in Private Law from Augustus to Justinian. fac. ed. LC 99-56922. 2000. write for info. (*1-58477-068-6*) Lawbk Exchange.
***Buckland, Warren.** The Cognitive Semiotics of Film. (Illus.). 192p. (C). 2000. 54.95 (*0-521-78005-5*) Cambridge U Pr.
Buckland, Warren. Film Studies. LC 98-65811. (Teach Yourself Ser.). (Illus.). 264p. 1998. pap. 12.95 (*0-8442-0230-4*, 02304, Teach Yrslf) NTC Contemp Pub Co.
Buckland, Warren, ed. The Film Spectator: From Sign to Mind. 200p. (C). 1995. pap. 24.95 (*90-5356-131-5*, Pub. by Amsterdam U Pr); text 54.50 (*90-5356-170-6*, Pub. by Amsterdam U Pr) U of Mich Pr.
Buckland, Wendy & Nicoll, Barb. Spread Yourself Thin: More Than 140 Delicious, Low-Fat, Easy Recipes for Every Occasion. LC 98-22289. 240p. 1998. pap. 16.95 (*0-7615-1566-6*) Prima Pub.
Buckland, William. Geology & Mineralogy Considered with Reference to Natural Theology, 2 vols., Set. Gould, Stephen Jay, ed. LC 79-8326. (History of Paleontology Ser.). (Illus.). 1980. reprint ed. lib. bdg. 75.95 (*0-405-12706-5*) Ayer.
— Geology & Mineralogy Considered with Reference to Natural Theology, 2 vols., Vol. 1. Gould, Stephen Jay, ed. LC 79-8326. (History of Paleontology Ser.). (Illus.). 1980. reprint ed. lib. bdg. 37.95 (*0-405-12707-3*) Ayer.
— Geology & Mineralogy Considered with Reference to Natural Theology, 2 vols., Vol. 2. Gould, Stephen Jay, ed. LC 79-8326. (History of Paleontology Ser.). (Illus.). 1980. reprint ed. lib. bdg. 37.95 (*0-405-12708-1*) Ayer.
— Reliquiae Diluvianae: Observations on the Organic Remains Contained in Caves Fissures, & Diluvial Gravel. Albritton, Claude C., Jr., ed. LC 77-6510. (History of Geology Ser.). (Illus.). 1978. reprint ed. lib. bdg. 33.95 (*0-405-10433-2*) Ayer.
Buckland, William W. Elementary Principles of the Roman Private Law. LC 93-79707. 430p. 1994. reprint ed. 110.00 (*1-56169-065-1*, 18164) Gaunt.
— The Main Institutions of Roman Private Law. LC 93-79708. 434p. 1994. reprint ed. 115.00 (*1-56169-066-X*) Gaunt.
— A Manual of Roman Private Law. 2nd ed. LC 94-75667. xxx, 434p. 1994. reprint ed. 105.00 (*1-56169-092-9*) Gaunt.
— The Roman Law of Slavery. LC 70-94318. (BCL Ser. I). reprint ed. 41.50 (*0-404-00140-8*) AMS Pr.
— The Roman Law of Slavery: The Condition of the Slave in Private Law from Augustus to Justinian. 749p. reprint ed. pap. 180.00 (*0-608-12282-3*, 2024426) Bks Demand.
— The Roman Law of Slavery: The Condition of the Slave in Private Law from Augustus to Justinian. 752p. 1994. reprint ed. 120.00 (*1-56169-098-8*) Gaunt.

An Asterisk (*) at the beginning of an entry indicates that the title is appearing for the first time.

— Text-Book of Roman Law from Augustus to Justinian. LC 90-55180. xiv, 756p. 1990. reprint ed. lib. bdg. 110.00 (*0-912004-82-7*) Gaunt.

Buckland, William W. & McNair, Arnold D. Roman Law & Common Law: A Comparison in Outline. LC 93-79709. 376p. 1994. reprint ed. 95.00 (*1-56169-067-8*) Gaunt.

Buckland-Wright, John. Etching & Engraving. (Illus.). 240p. 1973. pap. 8.95 (*0-486-22888-6*) Dover.

Buckle. Weather & Climate in Africa. 1996. pap. text. write for info. (*0-582-09333-3*, Pub. by Addison-Wesley) Longman.

Buckle, A. P. & Smith, R., eds. Rodent Pests & Their Control. (Illus.). 416p. 1994. text 100.00 (*0-85198-820-2*) OUP.

Buckle, D., et al. Aspects of Family Mental Health in Europe. (Public Health Papers: No. 28). 123p. 1965. pap. text 5.00 (*92-4-130028-0*, 1110028) World Health.

Buckle, E. Dams of National Hunt Winners, 1963-1964. 1990. pap. 25.00 (*0-85131-077-X*, Pub. by J A Allen) St Mut.

— Dams of National Hunt Winners, 1966-1973. 1990. pap. 25.00 (*0-85131-237-3*, Pub. by J A Allen) St Mut.

— Dams of National Hunt Winners, 1973-1975. 1990. pap. 25.00 (*0-85131-340-X*, Pub. by J A Allen) St Mut.

— Dams of National Hunt Winners, 1975-19777. 1990. pap. 21.00 (*0-85131-342-6*, Pub. by J A Allen) St Mut.

Buckle, E., compiled by. Dams of National Hunt Winners, 1977-1978. 1990. pap. 30.00 (*0-85131-347-7*, Pub. by J A Allen) St Mut.

Buckle, Gerard F. Mind & the Film: A Treatise on the Psychological Factors in the Film. LC 70-112573. (Literature of Cinema, Ser. 1). 1978. reprint ed. 11.95 (*0-405-01604-2*) Ayer.

Buckle, Glynis, jt. auth. see Gallen, Derek.

Buckle, Henry T. On Scotland & the Scotch Intellect. Hanham, Henry J., ed. 414p. (C). 1986. 45.00 (*0-7855-2152-6*) St Mut.

— On Scotland & the Scotch Intellect. Hanham, Henry J., ed. LC 78-114958. (Classics of British Historical Literature Ser.). 1972. pap. text 3.45 (*0-226-07977-5*, P383) U Ch Pr.

— On Scotland & the Scotch Intellect. LC 78-114958. (Classics of British Historical Literature Ser.). 452p. Date not set. reprint ed. pap. 140.20 (*0-608-20670-9*, 207210700003) Bks Demand.

Buckle, Ian G., jt. ed. see Shiff, Anshel J.

Buckle, Jane. Clinical Aromatherapy in Nursing. LC 97-205859. (Illus.). 304p. 1997. pap. 39.95 (*1-56593-876-3*, 1716) Singular Publishing.

— How to Massage Your Dog. LC 95-16893. (Illus.). 88p. 1995. 9.95 (*0-87605-645-1*) Howell Bks.

Buckle, Keith & Love, David. British Locomotive Builders' Plates. (Illus.). 80p. 1995. 25.00 (*1-85780-018-4*) Pincushion Pr.

Buckle, Linda, ed. see Shakespeare, William.

Buckle, M. J. U. K. Financial System. 2nd ed. 1995. text 89.95 (*0-7190-4815-X*, Pub. by Manchester Univ Pr) St Martin.

Buckle, M. J. & Thompson, J. L. The United Kingdom Financial System: Theory & Practice. 2nd ed. 336p. 1996. text 29.95 (*0-7190-4816-8*) Manchester Univ Pr.

Buckle, Malcolm, jt. ed. see Travers, Andrew.

Buckle, Mariette. All Dressed Up. LC 92-21447. (Voyages Ser.). (Illus.). (J). 1993. 3.75 (*0-383-03613-5*) SRA McGraw.

Buckle, Stephen. Natural Law & the Theory of Property: Grotius to Hume. 340p. (C). 1993. pap. text 24.95 (*0-19-824094-5*) OUP.

Buckleitner, Warren, et al. The Complete Sourcebook on Children's Software, 1999, Vol. 7. 592p. 1999. pap. 69.95 incl. cd-rom (*1-891983-03-2*) Child Sftware.

Buckleitner, Warren, jt. auth. see Hohmann, C.

Buckleitner, Warren W., et al, eds. Complete Sourcebook on Children's Software Vol. 6: Summer, 1998. 6th rev. ed. (Illus.). 650p. 1998. spiral bd. 85.00 (*1-891983-02-4*) Child Sftware.

Buckler, Alan J. & Houseman, David E. Methods of Genome Analysis: A Gene Hunter's Guide. (Illus.). 250p. Date not set. pap. 39.95 (*0-19-509341-0*) OUP.

Buckler, Carol A., jt. auth. see Weisberg, Anne C.

Buckler, Ernest. Mountain & the Valley. 304p. 1996. pap. 7.95 (*0-7710-9952-5*) McCland & Stewart.

Buckler, Francis W. Harunu'l-Rashid & Charles the Great. LC 75-41041. (BCL Ser. II). reprint ed. 29.50 (*0-404-14761-5*) AMS Pr.

Buckler, J. M. A Longitudinal Study of Adolescent Growth. (Illus.). 448p. 1990. 288.00 (*0-387-19569-6*) Spr-Verlag.

Buckler, John. Philip the Second & the Sacred War. (Supplements to Mnemosyne Ser.: No. 109). (Illus.). xvi, 224p. (Orig.). 1989. pap. text 75.50 (*90-04-09095-9*) Brill Academic Pubs.

— The Theban Hegemony, 371-362 B. C. (Historical Studies: No. 98). (Illus.). 355p. 1980. 25.00 (*0-674-87645-8*) HUP.

Buckler, John M. A Reference Manual for Growth & Development. 2nd ed. LC 96-30415. (Illus.). 128p. 1997. pap. text 36.95 (*0-86542-680-5*) Blackwell Sci.

***Buckler, Julie A.** Literary Lorgnette: Attending Opera in Imperial Russia. LC 99-86375. (Illus.). 322p. 2000. 45.00 (*0-8047-3247-7*) Stanford U Pr.

Buckler, S., jt. auth. see Lassman, P.

Buckler, W. W. Origin & History of Contract in Roman Law down to the End of the Republican Period: Being the York Prize Essay for the Year 1893. xi, 228p. 1983. reprint ed. 35.00 (*0-8377-0341-7*, Rothman) W S Hein.

Buckler, William E. Matthew Arnold's Prose: Three Essays in Literary Enlargement. LC 83-45276. (Studies in the Nineteenth Century: No. 3). 116p. 1984. 29.50 (*0-404-61481-7*) AMS Pr.

Buckler, William E., ed. The Major Victorian Poets, 001. LC 72-5645. 650p. (Orig.). (C). 1973. pap. 13.96 (*0-395-14024-2*, RivEd) HM.

— Prose of the Victorian Period, 001. (YA). (gr. 9 up). 1958. pap. 13.96 (*0-395-05128-2*, RivEd) HM.

Buckler, William E., jt. auth. see Anderson, George K.

Buckler, William E., ed. see Hardy, Thomas.

***Buckles.** Introduction to the Law. (Paralegal Ser.). (C). 2001. pap. 41.00 (*0-7668-0759-2*) Delmar.

— Principles of Economics. 2002. pap. text. write for info. (*1-57259-974-X*) Worth.

Buckles, Bill P. & Petry, Frederick E. Genetic Algorithms. LC 92-16233. 112p. 1992. pap. 35.00 (*0-8186-2935-5*) IEEE Comp Soc.

***Buckles, Bradley A., ed.** Commerce in Firearms in the United States. (Illus.). 85p. (C). 2000. pap. text 20.00 (*0-7881-8977-8*) DIANE Pub.

***Buckles, Daniel & International Bank for Reconstruction & Development Staff.** Cultivating Peace: Conflict & Collaboration in Natural Resource Management. 300p. 2000. pap. 24.95 (*0-88936-899-6*, Pub. by IDRC Bks) Stylus Pub VA.

***Buckles, Daniel, et al.** Cover Crops in Hillside Agriculture: Farmer Innovation with Mucuna. 230p. 1998. pap. 19.95 (*0-88936-841-4*, Pub. by IDRC Bks) Stylus Pub VA.

— Cover Crops in West Africa. (ENG & FRE.). 318p. 1998. pap. 19.95 (*0-88936-852-X*, Pub. by IDRC Bks) Stylus Pub VA.

Buckles, G. Matthew. Building Architectural & Interior Design Models Fast! An Easy to Follow Step-by-Step Guide to Constructing Design Studio Models. Bruu, Dina A., ed. (Illus.). 224p. (C). 1992. pap., student ed. 25.00 (*0-9629294-4-1*) Belpine Pub.

Buckles, Guy. The Dive Sites of Indonesia. (Dive Sites of . . . Ser.). (Illus.). 176p. 1997. pap. 24.95 (*0-8442-4856-8*, 48568, Natl Textbk Co) NTC Contemp Pub Co.

— Dive Sites of the Red Sea. LC 97-184752. (Dive Sites of . . . Ser.). (Illus.). 176p. 1997. pap. 24.95 (*0-8442-4865-7*, 48657, Natl Textbk Co) NTC Contemp Pub Co.

Buckles, Luke, jt. auth. see Toropov, Brandon.

Buckles, Mary P. The Flowers Around Us: A Photographic Essay on Their Reproductive Structures. LC 82-24815. (Illus.). 128p. 1985. 29.95 (*0-8262-0402-3*) U of Mo Pr.

— Margins: A Naturalist Meets Long Island Sound. LC 96-47946. 288p. 1997. 23.00 (*0-86547-516-4*) N Point Pr.

— Margins: A Naturalist Meets Long Island Sound. (Illus.). 286p. 1998. pap. text 13.00 (*0-86547-532-6*) N Point Pr.

Buckless, Andrea. Class Picture Day. LC 98-18725. (Hello Reader! Ser.: Level 2). (Illus.). 32p. (J). (gr. k-2). 1999. pap. 3.50 (*0-590-37975-5*, Pub. by Scholastic Inc) Penguin Putnam.

***Buckless, Andrea.** Too Many Cooks! LC 99-87654. (Hello Reader! Math Ser.). (Illus.). 2000. write for info. (*0-439-16966-6*) Scholastic Inc.

Buckley. Catholic University As Promise & Project. LC 98-16019. 1998. 55.00 (*0-87840-711-1*) Georgetown U Pr.

***Buckley.** Conservatism at the Millennium. 2001. write for info. (*0-15-100517-6*) Harcourt.

Buckley. Economics of Change in East & Central Europe. 1998. pap. 32.95 (*1-86152-426-9*) Thomson Learn.

Buckley. International Business. 135.95 (*1-85521-974-3*) Ashgate Pub Co.

Buckley. International Business: Economics & Anthropology, Theory & Method. LC 97-34977. 272p. 1998. text 69.95 (*0-312-21184-8*) St Martin.

— Joys of National Review, 1955-1980. 1995. 25.00 (*0-9627841-4-1*) Natl Review.

— Legal Structures. 1996. text 184.95 (*0-471-96631-2*) Wiley.

— Survey of Paralegalism. (Paralegal Ser.). 1995. text 41.95 (*0-8273-6206-4*) Delmar.

— Survey of Paralegalism. (Paralegal Ser.). 1995. teacher ed. 14.00 (*0-8273-6207-2*) Delmar.

Buckley & Gimple. Cases in Cardiology. 1997. 99.00 (*0-7872-4549-6*) Kendall-Hunt.

Buckley & Okrent, Cathy J. Torts & Personal Injury Law. 2nd ed. (Paralegal Ser.). 1998. teacher ed. 15.00 (*0-8273-7573-5*) Delmar.

Buckley, William F. Airborne: A Sentimental Journey. 1984. reprint ed. pap. 11.95 (*0-316-11439-1*) Little.

— A Very Private Plot: A Blackford Oakes Novel. large type ed. LC 94-7063. 328p. 1994. lib. bdg. 24.95 (*0-8161-7431-8*) Thorndike Pr.

— A Very Private Plot: A Blackford Oakes Novel. LC 97-47692. 256p. 1998. reprint ed. pap. 10.95 (*1-888952-74-1*) Cumberland Hse.

Buckley, William F., jt. auth. see Chambers, Whittaker.

Buckley, A., ed. U. K. Commodities Yearbook. 1990. 175.00 (*0-85941-050-1*) St Mut.

Buckley, Adrian. The Essence of International Money. 2nd ed. LC 95-40960. (Essence of Management Ser.). 182p. (C). 1996. pap. text 19.95 (*0-13-356494-0*) P-H.

— International Investment: Value Creation & Appraisal. 1999. 48.00 (*87-16-13388-9*) Mksgaard.

***Buckley, Adrian.** Multinational Finance. 4th ed. LC 99-41172. 1999. write for info. (*0-13-013166-0*) P-H.

***Buckley, Andrew.** The Bostoner. (Illus.). 441p. 1999. 25.00 (*0-9676082-0-1*) Stage Harbor.

Buckley, Andrew. Buying Electricity & Gas in the Competitive Marketplace. LC 98-208221. 150p. 1998. 74.95 (*0-566-08121-0*, Pub. by Gower) Ashgate Pub Co.

Buckley, Andrew, jt. ed. see Swain, Christopher.

Buckley, Ann, tr. see Baker, Theodore.

Buckley, Anthony D. Yoruba Medicine. 2nd unabridged ed. (Illus.). 280p. 1997. reprint ed. mass mkt. 24.95 (*1-890157-01-5*) Athelia-Henrietta.

Buckley, Anthony D. & Kenney, Mary C. Negotiating Identity: Rhetoric, Metaphor & Social Drama in Northern Ireland. LC 94-47184. 288p. 1995. text 44.50 (*1-56098-520-8*) Smithsonian.

Buckley, Arthur H. Card Control: Practical Methods & Forty Original Card Experiments. (Illus.). 224p. 1993. reprint ed. pap. text 8.95 (*0-486-27757-7*) Dover.

Buckley, B. J. Artifacts: Poems by B. J. Buckley. (Illus.). 80p. (Orig.). 1987. pap. 8.95 (*0-939635-02-X*) Willow Bee Pub.

Buckley, Barbara E., jt. auth. see Abel, Ernest L.

Buckley, Belle. A Child's Blessings. 1997. pap. write for info. (*1-57553-634-X*) Watermrk Pr.

— More Than a Sparrow. 1997. pap. write for info (*1-57553-633-1*) Watermrk Pr.

— A Ripe Harvest. 1997. pap. write for info. (*1-57553-752-4*) Watermrk Pr.

— A Special Child. 1997. pap. write for info. (*1-57553-598-X*) Watermrk Pr.

Buckley, Beth & Buckley, Dave. At Home in the Wilderness, Bk. 1: Tactics for Camp & Portage. LC 94-94369. (Illus.). 102p. 1994. pap. text 9.95 (*1-885376-00-6*) Ashford Outdoor.

***Buckley, Bill.** Dogs Are Stupid: After All, They're Man's Best Friend!, 1. (Illus.). 112p. 2000. 14.95 (*1-57223-395-8*) Willow Creek Pr.

Buckley, Bill. Waterfowler's World. LC 99-39864. (Illus.). 192p. 1999. 37.50 (*1-57223-281-1*, 2881) Willow Creek Pr.

Buckley, Bill & Grisamore, Ed. Once upon a Whoopee: A Town, a Team, a Song, a Dream. LC 98-3804 . 1998. 22.95 (*0-86554-625-8*, H468) Mercer Univ Pr.

Buckley, C., Jr. Life's Little Health Book. 160p. 1993. pap. 5.95 (*0-9635231-4-7*) CTA Resrch Corp.

— Life's Little Health Book for Women. 160p. (Orig.). 1993. pap. 5.95 (*0-9635231-5-5*) CTA Resrch Corp.

Buckley, C., jt. ed. see Michette, Alan G.

Buckley, C. A., jt. auth. see Hart, O. O.

Buckley, C. H. & Fox, H. Biopsy Pathology of the Endometrium. LC RG0316.. (Biopsy Pathology Ser.). (Illus.). 300p. reprint ed. pap. 93.00 (*0-608-09538-5*, 205441400001) Bks Demand.

Buckley, Carol. At the Still Point: A Memoir. LC 95-35910. (Illus.). 242p. 1996. 23.00 (*0-684-80217-1*) S&S Trade.

Buckley, Charles B. An Anecdotal History of Old Times in Singapore, 1819 to 1867. (Illus.). 824p. 1984. reprint ed. text 74.00 (*0-19-582602-7*) OUP.

Buckley, Charles E. Wallace Herndon Smith: Rediscovered. 64p. 1992. pap. 17.95 (*0-9632870-1-X*) D A Hanks.

***Buckley, Charlie.** Nameless. (Illus.). 96p. 2000. pap. 9.95 (*1-886028-04-4*) Savage Pr.

Buckley, Cheryl, ed. Potters & Paintresses: Women Designers in the Pottery Industry 1870-1955. 35.00 (*0-7043-4211-1*, Pub. by Womens Press) Trafalgar.

Buckley, Christopher. Blossoms & Bones: On the Life & Work of Georgia O'Keeffe. LC 88-20691. (Illus.). 50p. (Orig.). 1988. pap. 10.95 (*0-8265-1232-1*) Vanderbilt U Pr.

— Blue Autumn. LC 89-77314. 71p. (Orig.). 1990. pap. 9.95 (*0-914278-53-3*) Copper Beech.

— Camino Cielo. LC 96-19976. 80p. 1997. 21.95 (*0-914061-58-5*); pap. 12.95 (*0-914061-59-3*) Orchises Pr.

— Cruising State: Growing Up in Southern California. LC 94-4857. (Western Literature Ser.). 224p. 1994. 21.95 (*0-87417-247-0*) U of Nev Pr.

— Dark Matter. LC 93-4138. 64p. (Orig.). 1993. pap. 9.95 (*0-914278-62-2*) Copper Beech.

— Dust Light, Leaves: Poems. LC 86-4081. 80p. 1986. pap. 10.95 (*0-8265-1219-4*) Vanderbilt U Pr.

— Fall from Grace. LC 98-22107. 96p. 1998. pap. 11.95 (*1-886157-18-9*) BkMk.

— Last Rites. LC 80-12937. 92p. 1980. 4.50 (*0-87886-109-2*, Greenfld Rev Pr) Greenfld Rev Lit.

— Little Green Men. LC 98-36418. 300p. 1999. 24.95 (*0-679-45293-1*) Random.

***Buckley, Christopher.** Little Green Men: A Novel. LC 99-55682. 320p. 2000. pap. 13.00 (*0-06-095557-0*, Perennial) HarperTrade.

Buckley, Christopher. Other Lives. LC 85-5545. 75p. (Orig.). 1985. pap. 6.00 (*0-87886-125-4*, Greenfld Rev Pr) Greenfld Rev Lit.

— Thank You for Smoking: A Novel. LC 95-10356. 288p. 1995. pap. 13.00 (*0-06-097662-4*, Perennial) HarperTrade.

— The White House Mess. 1995. pap. 12.95 (*0-14-024928-1*, Penguin Bks) Viking Penguin.

— Wry Martinis. LC 97-42167. 320p. 1998. pap. 14.00 (*0-06-097742-6*, Perennial) HarperTrade.

Buckley, Christopher, ed. On the Poetry of Philip Levine: Stranger to Nothing. 376p. 1990. pap. 18.95 (*0-472-06392-8*, 06392); text 44.50 (*0-472-09392-4*, 09392) U of Mich Pr.

***Buckley, Christopher, et al, eds.** How Much Earth: An Anthology of Fresno Poets. (California Poetry Ser.). 2001. pap. 16.95 (*0-9666691-7-7*) Heyday Bks.

Buckley, Christopher & MacGuire, James. Campion. LC 89-83262. 174p. (Orig.). 1990. pap. 9.95 (*0-89870-285-2*) Ignatius Pr.

Buckley, Christopher & Young, Gary, eds. The Geography of Home: California's Poetry of Place. LC 99-19043. 464p. 1999. pap. 16.95 (*1-890771-19-8*) Heyday Bks.

Buckley, Cicely, ed. & illus. see Tsu, Lao, et al.

Buckley, Cicely, ed. & tr. see Eluard, Paul.

Buckley, Cornelius, tr. see Ravier, Andre.

***Buckley, Cornelius M.** When Jesuits Were Giants: Louis-Marie Ruellan, S.J., 1846-1885 & His Contemporaries. LC 98-75526. (Illus.). 1999. write for info. (*0-89870-703-X*) Ignatius Pr.

Buckley, Cornelius M., tr. see De Dalmases, Candido.

Buckley, Cornelius M., tr. see Ravier, Andre.

Buckley, Cornelius M., tr. & pref. see Idigoras, J. Ignacio.

Buckley, Cristie M. A Love Foundation. 32p. (Orig.). 1989. pap. 0.75 (*0-88144-140-6*) Christian Pub.

— A Love Foundation. (Orig.). 1987. pap. 0.75 (*0-9618333-0-0*) Renais Pub.

Buckley, D. No Mercy. text 35.00 (*0-340-68062-8*, Pub. by Hodder & Stought Ltd); mass mkt. 15.95 (*0-340-68065-2*, Pub. by Hodder & Stought Ltd) Trafalgar.

Buckley, D. N., et al, eds. Proceedings of the State-of-the-Art Program on Compound Semiconductor & the Symposium on Materials & Processing Issues for Large Scale Integrated Electronic & Photonic Arrays, 16th. LC 92-61520. (Proceedings Ser.: Vol. 92-20). 312p. 1992. 40.00 (*1-56677-019-X*) Electrochem Soc.

— Proceedings of the Symposium on Logic & Functional Devices for Photonics & the State-of-the-Art Program on Compound Semiconductors, 17th. LC 92-74537. (Proceedings Ser.: Vol. 93-10). 312p. 1993. 40.00 (*1-56677-054-8*) Electrochem Soc.

***Buckley, D. N., et al, eds.** State-of-the-Art Program on Compound Semiconductors (SOTAPOCS XXXI) Proceedings of the Thirty-first Symposium. LC 99-66094. 248p. 1999. 65.00 (*1-56677-240-0*, PV 99-17) Electrochem Soc.

Buckley, D. N., et al, eds. State-of-the-Art Program on Compound Semiconductors XXVI. LC 97-197094. (Proceedings Ser.: Vol. 97-1). (Illus.). 332p. 1997. 55.00 (*1-56677-128-5*) Electrochem Soc.

Buckley, Dave, jt. auth. see Buckley, Beth.

Buckley, David. Music of David Bowie. (Illus.). 160p. (Orig.). 1996. pap. 8.95 (*0-7119-5301-5*, OP4799) Omnibus NY.

Buckley, Dunford. Rough Med Europe. 1999. pap. 17.95 (*1-85828-085-0*) NAL.

Buckley, E. F., tr. see Recouly, Raymond.

Buckley, Ellen & Rout, Nancy E., eds. The Soap Opera Book: Who's Who in Daytime Drama. 320p. 1993. pap. 20.00 (*0-915344-23-8*) Todd Pubns.

***Buckley, Ellen & Rout, Nancy E., eds.** The Soap Opera Book: Who's Who in Daytime Drama. 2nd ed. 320p. 2000. 25.00 (*0-915344-91-2*) Todd Pubns.

Buckley, Eugene. Theoretical Aspects of Kashaya Phonology & Morphology. LC 93-8886. (Dissertations in Linguistics Ser.). 1995. 54.95 (*1-881526-03-8*); pap. 23.95 (*1-881526-02-X*) CSLI.

Buckley, Eugene K., et al. Missouri Evidentiary Foundations, 1999 Cumulative Supplement Vol. 1: Pocketpart. 150p. write for info. (*0-327-01655-8*, 6535614) LEXIS Pub.

***Buckley, F. H.** The Fall & Rise of Freedom of Contract. LC 99-13956. 520p. 1999. 65.95 (*0-8223-2333-8*) Duke.

***Buckley, Fiona.** Doublet Affair. 416p. 1999. per. 6.99 (*0-671-01532-X*, Pocket Books) PB.

— The Doublet Affair. large type ed. 408p. 2000. 31.99 (*0-7089-4180-X*) Ulverscroft.

Buckley, Fiona. The Doublet Affair: An Ursula Blanchard Mystery at Queen Elizabeth I's Court. LC 98-43016. 288p. 1998. 21.00 (*0-684-83842-7*) Scribner.

***Buckley, Fiona.** Queen's Ransom: A Mystery at Queen Elizabeth I's Court Featuring Ursula Blanchard. LC 99-36455. 352p. 2000. 22.50 (*0-684-86267-0*) Scribner.

Buckley, Fiona. The Robsart Mystery. large type ed. 480p. 1998. 29.99 (*0-7089-4009-9*) Ulverscroft.

— To Sheild the Queen. 1998. per. 6.50 (*0-671-01531-1*) S&S Trade.

— To Shield the Queen: A Mystery at Queen Elizabeth I's Court. LC 97-15684. (Illus.). 288p. 1997. 20.50 (*0-684-83841-9*) Simon & Schuster.

***Buckley, Francis J.** The Church in Dialogue: Culture & Traditions. 304p. 2000. pap. 47.50 (*0-7618-1675-5*) U Pr of Amer.

— Growing in the Church: From Birth to Death. 288p. 2000. pap. 42.50 (*0-7618-1680-1*) U Pr of Amer.

***Buckley, Francis J.** Team Teaching: What, Why, & How? 1998. write for info. (*0-7619-0743-2*) Sage.

Buckley, Francis J. Team Teaching: What, Why, & How? LC 98-40297. 1999. 19.95 (*0-7619-0744-0*) Sage Pub.

Buckley, Frankie. Meet Me for Coffee: Cup of Fast & Furious Energizing Espresso. LC 97-8312. (Illus.). 48p. (Orig.). 1998. 10.99 (*1-56507-661-3*) Harvest Hse.

Buckley, Fred & Harary, Frank. Distance in Graphs. (Illus.). 352p. (C). 1990. 44.95 (*0-201-09591-2*) Addison-Wesley.

Buckley, Fred, jt. auth. see Molluzzo, John C.

Buckley, G. P., ed. Biological Habitat Reconstruction. LC 89-7035. 224p. 1994. text 140.00 (*0-471-94500-5*) Wiley.

Buckley, Gary. Airbrush Rendering. (How to Draw & Paint Ser.). (Illus.). 32p. (Orig.). 1989. pap. 6.95 (*1-56010-025-7*, HT212) W Foster Pub.

Buckley, Harold. Squadron 95. LC 78-169409. (Literature & History of Aviation Ser.). 1972. reprint ed. 25.95 (*0-405-03754-6*) Ayer.

Buckley, Helen. From Wooden Ploughs to Welfare: Why Indian Policy Failed in the Prairie Provinces. 224p. 1993. pap. 22.95 (*0-7735-1155-5*, Pub. by McG-Queens Univ Pr) CUP Services.

Buckley, Helen E. Grandfather & I. LC 93-22936. (Illus.). (J). 1994. 16.00 (*0-688-12533-6*); lib. bdg. 15.93 (*0-688-12534-4*) Lothrop.

***Buckley, Helen E.** Grandfather & I. LC 93-22936. (Illus.). 24p. (J). (ps-3). 2000. pap. 5.95 (*0-688-17526-0*, Wm Morrow) Morrow Avon.

Buckley, Helen E. Grandmother & I. LC 93-22937. (Illus.). (J). (gr. 3 up). 1994. 16.00 (*0-688-12531-X*) Lothrop.

— Grandmother & I. rev. ed. LC 93-22937. (Illus.). 24p. (J). (gr. 3 up). 1994. lib. bdg. 15.93 (*0-688-12532-8*) Lothrop.

— Moonlight Kite. LC 91-34285. (Illus.). 32p. (J). (ps up). 1997. 16.00 (*0-688-10931-4*); lib. bdg. 15.93 (*0-688-10932-2*) Lothrop.

***Buckley, Helen E.** Where Did Josie Go. LC 98-21307. (J). 1999. lib. bdg. 15.89 (*0-688-16508-7*) Morrow Avon.

— Where Did Josie Go. LC 98-21307. (Illus.). 32p. (J). (ps-k). 1999. 16.00 (*0-688-16507-9*) Morrow Avon.

***Buckley, Henlen E.** Grandmother & I. LC 93-22937. (Illus.). 24p. (J). (ps-3). 2000. pap. 5.95 (*0-688-17525-2*, Wm Morrow) Morrow Avon.

***Buckley, Holland.** The Scottish Terrier. LC 98-3883. (Dog Breeds Ser.). (Illus.). 80p. 1998. 9.98 (*0-7651-0812-7*) Smithmark.

— The West Highland Terrier. LC 98-3902. (Dog Breeds Ser.). (Illus.). 64p. 1998. 9.98 (*0-7651-0811-9*) Smithmark.

Buckley-Holland, Susan J. & Knapf-MacDonald, Jane. Intermediate Algebra. 528p. (C). 1995. pap. write for info. (*0-697-26568-4*, WCB McGr Hill) McGrw-H Hghr Educ.

— Introductory Algebra. 624p. (C). 1995. pap. write for info. (*0-697-26567-6*, WCB McGr Hill) McGrw-H Hghr Educ.

Buckley-Holland, Susan J., jt. auth. see Knapf-MacDonald, Jane.

Buckley, I. Thomas. Penikese - Island of Hope: One of the Elizabeths, a Massachusetts Historical Site. Springer, Meg B., ed. (Illus.). ix, 140p. 1997. 24.95 (*1-887086-07-2*); pap. 15.95 (*1-887086-06-4*) Stony Brook Pr.

* **Buckley IV, John F.** Multistate Payroll Guide. 944p. 1999. pap. text 145.00 (*0-7355-0662-0*) Panel Pubs.

Buckley, J. A. Customs & Superstitions. (C). 1990. pap. 50.00 (*0-85025-328-4*, Pub. by Tor Mark Pr) St Mut.

— Mining Underground. (C). 1989. pap. text 35.00 (*0-85025-316-0*, Pub. by Tor Mark Pr) St Mut.

— Tudor Tin Bounds: West Penwith. (C). 1989. 40.00 (*1-85022-028-X*, Pub. by Dyllansow Truran) St Mut.

Buckley, J. F. Desire, the Self, the Social Critic: The Rise of Queer Performance Within the Demise of Transcendentalism. LC 96-29380. 152p. 1997. 31.50 (*1-57591-001-2*) Susquehanna U Pr.

Buckley, J. M. Two Weeks in the Yosemite & Vicinity. (Illus.). 36p. reprint ed. pap. 10.00 (*0-8466-0153-2*, S153) Shoreys Bkstore.

Buckley, James. America's Greatest Game: The Real Story of Football & the National Football League. LC 97-47744. (Illus.). 64p. (YA). (gr. 3-7). 1998. 16.95 (*0-7868-0433-5*, Pub. by Hyprn Child) Time Warner.

***Buckley, James.** Baseball. LC 99-44318. (Eyewitness Books). (Illus.). 64p. (J). (gr. 4-7). 2000. 15.95 (*0-7894-5241-3*, D K Ink) DK Pub Inc.

Buckley, James. Buckley's New Banjo Book. Ayers, Joseph W., ed. LC 92-61250. (Illus.). 84p. (Orig.). 1996. pap. 20.00 (*0-9633593-1-2*) Tuckahoe Music.

***Buckley, James.** Hurricane & Tornado. LC 99-44160. (Eyewitness Books). (Illus.). 64p. (J). (gr. 4-7). 2000. 15.95 (*0-7894-5242-1*, D K Ink) DK Pub Inc.

Buckley, James, Jr. Lost Cowboy Ghost. (Nfl Adventures Ser.). 1996. 9.09 (*0-606-10893-9*, Pub. by Turtleback) Demco.

Buckley, James. NFL Adventures. 1996. mass mkt. 3.99 (*0-590-16211-X*) Scholastic Inc.

***Buckley, James.** NFL's Greatest Upsets. LC 00-24795. (Illus.). (gr. 4-7). 2000. pap. 3.95 (*0-7894-6756-9*) DK Pub Inc.

— NFL's Greatest Upsets. LC 00-24795. (gr. 4-7). 2000. 12.95 (*0-7894-6379-2*) DK Pub Inc.

— Soccer. LC 99-52770. (Eyewitness Books). (Illus.). 64p. (J). (gr. 4-7). 2000. 15.95 (*0-7894-5245-6*, D K Ink) DK Pub Inc.

Buckley, James. Street Railways of St. Petersburg, Florida. (Illus.). 48p. (Orig.). 1983. pap. 8.00 (*0-911940-37-5*) Cox.

***Buckley, James.** Super Bowl. LC 00-20652. (Eyewitness Books). (Illus.). 64p. (J). (gr. 4-7). 2000. 15.95 (*0-7894-6300-8*) DK Pub Inc.

— Super Bowl Heroes. LC 00-24793. (Illus.). (gr. 4-7). 2000. pap. 3.95 (*0-7894-6757-7*) DK Pub Inc.

— Super Bowl Heroes. LC 00-24793. (gr. 4-7). 2000. 12.95 (*0-7894-6378-4*) DK Pub Inc.

— Troy Aikman. LC 00-24794. (NFL Readers Ser.). (Illus.). (gr. 4-7). 2000. pap. 3.95 (*0-7894-6759-3*) DK Pub Inc.

— Troy Aikman. LC 00-24794. (NFL Readers Ser.). (gr. 4-7). 2000. 12.95 (*0-7894-6376-8*) DK Pub Inc.

— The Visual Dictionary of Baseball. LC 00-31833. (Illus.). 2001. write for info. (*0-7894-6725-9*) DK Pub Inc.

Buckley, James. Where in the World Is Carmen Sandiego? Sticker Book. 1997. pap. 3.95 (*0-8167-4223-5*) Troll Communs.

***Buckley, James.** X-Men Readers Creating the X-Men: How Comic Books Come to Life. (Readers Ser.). (Illus.). (gr. 4-7). 2000. pap. 12.95 (*0-7894-6694-5*); pap. 3.95 (*0-7894-6695-3*) DK Pub Inc.

Buckley, James, Jr. & Teitelbaum, Michael. Where Is Carmen Sandiego? U. S. Sticker Book. (Illus.). 64p. (Orig.). (J). (gr. 5-7). 1996. pap. 3.95 (*0-8167-4134-4*) Troll Communs.

Buckley, James A. Large Deviation Techniques in Decision, Simulation & Estimation. LC 89-77144. 270p. 1990. 149.95 (*0-471-61856-X*) Wiley.

Buckley, James J. Fuzzy & Neural Interactions & Applications. LC 98-53205. (Studies in International Economics & Institutions). 1999. write for info. (*3-7908-1170-X*) Spr-Verlag.

— Gary Railways: Bulletin No. 84. (Illus.). 36p. 1975. pap. 4.00 (*0-915348-84-5*) Central Electric.

***Buckley, James J. & Kendall, Lane C.** Business of Shipping. 7th ed. 480p. 2000. text 50.00 (*0-87033-526-X*) Cornell Maritime.

Buckley, James J., jt. auth. see Jones, L. Gregory.

Buckley, James M. Travels in 3 Continents, Europe, Africa, Asia. LC 72-5586. (Black Heritage Library Collection). 1977. reprint ed. 60.95 (*0-8369-9136-2*) Ayer.

***Buckley, Jean, ed.** Annual Statement Instructions: Fraternal. rev. ed. 410p. 1999. ring bd. 150.00 (*0-89382-514-X*, ASI-FU99) Nat Assn Insurance.

— Annual Statement Instructions: Fraternal for 2001. 443p. 2000. ring bd. 200.00 (*0-89382-682-0*, ASI-FU00) Nat Assn Insurance.

— Annual Statement Instructions: Health for 2001. 322p. 2000. ring bd. 175.00 (*0-89382-679-0*, ASI-HEA00) Nat Assn Insurance.

— Annual Statement Instructions: Health Maintenance Organizations. 210p. 1998. pap. 150.00 (*0-89382-553-0*, ASI-HU98) Nat Assn Insurance.

— Annual Statement Instructions: Hospital, Medical, Dental & Indemnity Corporations. rev. ed. 256p. 1998. ring bd. 150.00 (*0-89382-554-9*, ASI-MU98) Nat Assn Insurance.

— Annual Statement Instructions: Hospital, Medical, Dental & Indemnity Corporations. rev. ed. 256p. 1999. ring bd. 150.00 (*0-89382-622-7*, ASI-MU99) Nat Assn Insurance.

— Annual Statement Instructions: Life. 464p. 1998. ring bd. 150.00 (*0-89382-550-6*, ASI-LU98) Nat Assn Insurance.

— Annual Statement Instructions: Life. rev. ed. 468p. 1999. ring bd. 150.00 (*0-89382-513-1*, ASI-LU99) Nat Assn Insurance.

— Annual Statement Instructions: Life for 2001. 472p. 2000. ring bd. 225.00 (*0-89382-681-2*, ASI-LU00) Nat Assn Insurance.

— Annual Statement Instructions: Limited Health Services Organization. rev. ed. 184p. 1998. ring bd. 150.00 (*0-89382-552-2*, ASI-SU98) Nat Assn Insurance.

— Annual Statement Instructions: Property & Casualty. rev. ed. 388p. 1999. ring bd. 150.00 (*0-89382-512-3*, ASI-PU99) Nat Assn Insurance.

— Annual Statement Instructions: Property & Casualty for 2001. 430p. 2000. ring bd. 225.00 (*0-89382-680-4*, ASI-PU00) Nat Assn Insurance.

— Annual Statement Instructions: Title. rev. ed. 260p. 1998. ring bd. 150.00 (*0-89382-555-7*, ASI-TU98) Nat Assn Insurance.

— Annual Statement Instructions: Title. rev. ed. 1999. ring bd. 150.00 (*0-89382-623-5*, ASI-TU99) Nat Assn Insurance.

— Annual Statement Instructions: Title for 2001. 341p. 2000. ring bd. 200.00 (*0-89382-683-9*, ASI-TU00) Nat Assn Insurance.

— Annual Statement of Instructions: Fraternal. 410p. 1998. ring bd. 150.00 (*0-89382-551-4*, ASI-FU98) Nat Assn Insurance.

— Annual Statements Instructions: Limited Health Services Organizations. rev. ed. 184p. 1999. ring bd. 150.00 (*0-89382-624-3*, ASI-SU99) Nat Assn Insurance.

Buckley, Jean, ed. Listing of Companies. 20th rev. ed. 590p. (C). 1996. ring bd. 190.00 (*0-89382-435-6*, LOC-ZS) Nat Assn Insurance.

— Listing of Companies. 21st rev. ed. 806p. 1997. pap. 190.00 (*0-89382-465-8*, LOC-ZS) Nat Assn Insurance.

Buckley, Jerome H. Season of Youth: The Bildungsroman from Dickens to Golding. LC 73-85887. 352p. 1974. 43.00 (*0-674-79640-3*) HUP.

— Tennyson: The Growth of a Poet. LC 60-13298. 312p. reprint ed. pap. 96.80 (*0-7837-4453-6*, 205798300012) Bks Demand.

— The Triumph of Time: A Study of the Victorian Concepts of Time, History, Progress, & Decadence. LC 66-21333. 198p. reprint ed. pap. 61.40 (*0-7837-4452-8*, 205798200012) Bks Demand.

— The Turning Key: Autobiography & the Subjective Impulse Since 1800. 208p. 1984. 27.50 (*0-674-91330-2*) HUP.

— Victorian Poets & Prose Writers. 2nd ed. LC 76-5212. (Goldentree Bibliographies Series in Language & Literature). (C). 1977. pap. text 14.95 (*0-88295-560-8*) Harlan Davidson.

— Victorian Temper: A Study in Literary Culture. (Illus.). 282p. 1966. 35.00 (*0-7146-2052-1*, Pub. by F Cass Pubs) Intl Spec Bk.

— The Victorian Temper: A Study in Literary Culture. LC 74-89967. (Illus.). 306p. reprint ed. pap. 94.90 (*0-7837-3855-2*, 204367700010) Bks Demand.

Buckley, Jerome H., ed. The Pre-Raphaelites: An Anthology. 503p. 1987. reprint ed. pap. 12.00 (*0-89733-237-7*) Academy Chi Pubs.

— The Worlds of Victorian Fiction. LC 75-5549. (English Studies: No. 6). 439p. 1975. 34.95 (*0-674-96205-2*); pap. 10.95 (*0-674-96207-9*) HUP.

Buckley, Jerome H. & Woods, George B. Poetry of the Victorian Period. 3rd ed. 1097p. (C). 1997. 77.00 (*0-673-05630-9*) Addson-Wesley Educ.

Buckley, Jerome H., ed. see Dickens, Charles.

Buckley, Jim. NFL Magic: Bloopers, Pranks, Upsets, & Touchdowns. LC 97-80387. (NFL/ABC Monday Night Football Club Ser.: No. 5). (Illus.). 96p. (J). (gr. 3-7). 1998. pap. 3.95 (*0-7868-1271-0*, Pub. by Hyprn Ppbks) Little.

***Buckley, Jim.** NFL Rules! 96p. (J). 1999. pap. 3.95 (*0-7868-1412-8*, Pub. by Disney Pr) Little.

Buckley, Jim. The Silent Knight. LC 76-28107. (Illus.). 79p. (J). 1976. 4.95 (*0-9649167-0-3*) P Plough.

Buckley, Joan N., ed. see Rosendahl, Peter J.

Buckley, John. Air Power in the Age of Total War. LC 98-48197. 1999. pap. 19.95 (*0-253-21324-X*); text 49.95 (*0-253-33557-4*) Ind U Pr.

— Going for Growth: Increasing Shareholder Value Through R&D. LC 97-37292. 160p. 1998. 27.95 (*0-07-008781-4*) McGraw.

— Guide to World Commodity Markets. 6th ed. 576p. 1990. pap. 144.00 (*0-8464-1361-2*) Beekman Pubs.

— Guide to World Commondity Markets. 7th ed. 1997. pap. text 85.00 (*0-7494-2003-0*) Kogan Page Ltd.

— Training of Secondary School Heads in Europe. (C). 1985. pap. text 20.00 (*0-7005-0691-8*) Routledge.

Buckley, John, et al. Exercise on Prescription: Cardiovascular Activity for Health. LC 98-28353. 248p. 1998. pap. text 32.50 (*0-7506-3288-7*) Buttrwrth-Heinemann.

— Mastering the Net with Netscape Communicator. McKenna, Jill, ed. (Illus.). 370p. 1997. pap. 29.95 (*1-58143-000-0*) Prosoft I-net.

Buckley, John D. & Edie, D. D., eds. Carbon-Carbon Materials & Composites. LC 92-35012. (Illus.). 218p. 1993. 98.00 (*0-8155-1324-0*) Noyes.

Buckley, John F., IV. Equal Employment Opportunity 1999 Compliance Guide, 1. 840p. 1999. pap. 145.00 (*0-7355-0336-2*) Panel Pubs.

— Multistate Guide to Benefits Law LC 98-106671. 1998. write for info. (*1-56706-378-0*) Panel Pubs.

***Buckley, John F., IV.** Multistate Guide to Benefits Law, 1. 800p. 1999. pap. text 145.00 (*0-7355-0664-7*) Panel Pubs.

Buckley, John F., IV. Multistate Payroll Guide. 600p. 1996. 145.00 (*1-56706-309-8*) Aspen Pub.

Buckley, John F., IV, ed. see Green, Ronald M., et al.

Buckley, John P. The New York Irish: Their View of American Foreign Policy, 1914-1921. LC 76-6327. (Irish Americans Ser.). 1976. 34.95 (*0-405-09324-1*) Ayer.

Buckley, John W. & Buckley, Marlene H. The Accounting Profession. LC 74-8880. (Melville Series on Management, Accounting, & Information Systems). (Illus.). 231p. reprint ed. pap. 71.70 (*0-8357-5070-1*, 201517400092) Bks Demand.

Buckley, Jonathan. Europe: 1999 Edition. (Rough Guide Ser.). (Illus.). 1232p. 1998. pap. text 19.95 (*1-85828-348-5*, Pub. by Rough Guides) Penguin Putnam.

Buckley, Jonathan & Robinson, Hilary. Venice. 4th ed. (Rough Guide Ser.). (Illus.). 448p. 1999. pap. 16.95 (*1-85828-380-9*, Pub. by Rough Guides) Penguin Putnam.

— Venice, No. 3. 3rd ed. (Rough Guides Ser.). (Illus.). 432p. 1996. pap. 14.95 (*1-85828-170-9*, Penguin Bks) Viking Penguin.

Buckley, Jonathan, jt. auth. see Raven, Sarah.

Buckley, Jorunn J. Female Fault & Fulfilment in Gnosticism. LC 85-29020. (Studies in Religion). 196p. 1986. reprint ed. pap. 60.80 (*0-7837-7078-2*, 204689000004) Bks Demand.

Buckley, Jorunn J., tr. The Scroll of Exalted Kingship: Diwan Malkuta 'Laita. (American Oriental Society Translation Ser.: Vol. 3). xix, 110p. 1993. 22.00 (*0-940490-83-8*) Am Orient Soc.

Buckley, Joseph P., et al, eds. Central Nervous System Mechanisms in Hypertension. LC 80-5660. (Perspectives in Cardiovascular Research Ser.: No. 6). (Illus.). 434p. 1981. reprint ed. pap. 134.60 (*0-608-00666-1*, 206125300007) Bks Demand.

Buckley, Joseph P. & Ferrario, Carlos M., eds. Brain Peptides & Catecholamines in Cardiovascular Regulation. LC 86-26304. 447p. 1987. reprint ed. pap. 138.60 (*0-608-03392-8*, 206408900008) Bks Demand.

Buckley, Julian G., Jr. & Loll, Leo M. The Over-the-Counter Securities Markets. 4th ed. (Illus.). 480p. 1986. 33.95 (*0-13-647172-2*) P-H.

***Buckley, K. D.** False Paradise: Australian Capitalism Revisited, 1915-1955. LC 99-458574. 1998. write for info. (*0-19-553571-5*) OUP.

Buckley, Karen K. Above & Beyond: A Medley of Quilted Memories. LC 96-27192. 144p. 1997. pap. 18.95 (*0-89145-866-2*, 4595, Am Quilters Soc) Collector Bks.

— Love to Quilt Bears Bears Bears. LC 96-37102. (Love to Quilt Ser.). 48p. 1997. pap. 14.95 (*0-89145-881-6*, 4815, Am Quilters Soc) Collector Bks.

Buckley, Karen Kay. Applique Basics: Flower Wreaths. Squire, Helen, ed. LC 99-48652. (Illus.). 144p. 2000. pap. 21.95 (*1-57432-730-5*, Am Quilters Soc) Collector Bks.

Buckley, Kathleen A. Handbook of Maternal Newborn Nursing. 2nd ed. (Nursing Education Ser.). 1989. 29.95 (*0-8273-4214-4*) Delmar.

Buckley, Kerry W. Mechanical Man: John B. Watson & the Beginnings of Behaviorism. LC 88-24081. 233p. 1989. lib. bdg. 26.95 (*0-89862-744-3*) Guilford Pubns.

***Buckley, Laurence, intro.** American Masterpieces: New Britain Museum of Art. LC 98-54933. (Illus.). 192p. 1999. 65.00 (*3-7913-2087-4*, Pub. by Prestel) te Neues.

Buckley, Laurene, et al. Joseph DeCamp: Master Painter of the Boston School. (Illus.). 160p. 1995. 65.00 (*3-7913-1604-4*, Pub. by Prestel) te Neues.

***Buckley, Linda.** Builder of the Past, Architect of the Future: The History of the REA - RUS Telephone Program. (Illus.). 96p. 1999. pap. 30.00 (*0-9674251-0-7*) Fnd Rural Service.

Buckley, Mark. Practical Chess Analysis. 3rd ed. (Illus.). 200p. 1998. pap. text 19.95 (*0-938650-88-2*) Thinkers Pr.

Buckley, Marlene H., jt. auth. see Buckley, John W.

***Buckley, Martin.** A-Z of Cars: The Century's Classic Automobiles. 1999. 30.00 (*1-85868-638-5*, Pub. by Carlton Bks Ltd) Natl Bk Netwk.

— Classic Cars: Illustrated Encyclopedia. (Illus.). 192p. 2000. 12.95 (*0-7548-0563-8*) Anness Pub.

— Classic Cars: The Golden Years. 64p. 1998. 9.98 (*1-84038-151-5*) Anness Pub.

— Encyclopedia of Classic Cars: A Celebration of the Motor Car from 1945 to 1975. (Illus.). 1999. 27.50 (*0-7548-0176-4*, Lorenz Bks) Anness Pub.

Buckley, Martin. Essential Fiat 124 Spider & Coupes: The Cars & Their Stories. (Essential Ser.). (Illus.). 80p. 1997. pap. 15.95 (*1-870979-99-0*, Bay View Bks) MBI Pubg.

— Jaguar. LC 98-71571. (Classic Makes Ser.). (Illus.). 176p. 1998. 34.95 (*1-85960-415-3*, Pub. by J H Haynes & Co) Motorbooks Intl.

Buckley, Mary. Women & Ideology in the Soviet Union. 266p. 1990. pap. text 18.95 (*0-472-06410-X*, 06410) U of Mich Pr.

Buckley, Mary, ed. Post-Soviet Women: From the Baltic to Central Asia. 333p. (C). 1997. text 59.95 (*0-521-56320-8*); pap. text 22.95 (*0-521-56530-8*) Cambridge U Pr.

Buckley, Mary, jt. ed. see David, Irene R.

***Buckley, Michael.** Catholic Morning Prayers. 154p. 2000. 9.99 (*1-56955-184-7*, Charis) Servant.

Buckley, Michael. Cycling to Xian & Other Excursions: Travels by Bicycle Through China & Tibet. (Illus.). 256p. (Orig.). 1988. pap. 14.95 (*0-9693370-0-0*) Gordon Soules Bk.

— Let Peace Disturb You. 128p. (C). 1991. 39.00 (*0-85439-410-9*, Pub. by St Paul Pubns) St Mut.

— Moon Handbooks: Vietnam, Cambodia & Laos. 2nd rev. ed. Vol. 2. (Illus.). 760p. 1998. pap. 18.95 (*1-56691-131-1*, Moon Handbks) Avalon Travel.

***Buckley, Michael.** A Prayer Book for Today's Catholic. LC 99-86139. 154p. 2000. pap. 9.99 (*1-56955-183-9*, Charis) Servant.

Buckley, Michael. Tibet Travel Adventure Guide. 1999. pap. text 24.95 (*1-895907-98-5*) ITMP Pub.

Buckley, Michael J. At the Origins of Modern Atheism. 253p. (C). 1990. reprint ed. pap. 19.00 (*0-300-04897-1*) Yale U Pr.

— The Catholic University As Promise & Project: Reflections in a Jesuit Idiom. LC 98-16019. 272p. 1998. pap. 22.95 (*0-87840-710-3*) Georgetown U Pr.

— Motion & Motion's God: Thematic Variations in Aristotle, Cicero, Newton, & Hegel. LC 73-132234. 295p. reprint ed. pap. 91.50 (*0-8357-3307-6*, 203953000013) Bks Demand.

— Papal Primacy & the Episcopate: Towards a Relational Understanding. LC 97-45932. 172p. 1998. pap. 12.95 (*0-8245-1745-8*, Herdr & Herdr) Crossroad NY.

Buckley, Michael J., tr. see Smirenskaia, Zhanna D.

Buckley, P. A., et al, eds. Neotropical Ornithology. (Ornithological Monographs: No. 36). (Illus.). 1041p. 1985. 40.00 (*0-943610-44-3*) Am Ornithologists

Buckley, P. A., jt. ed. see Cooke, F.

Buckley, Page S. Process Control Strategy & Profitability. LC 92-4130. 107p. 1992. pap. 28.00 (*1-55617-371-7*, TP155) ISA.

Buckley, Pat. A Thorn in the Side. 240p. 1997. pap. 13.95 (*0-86278-364-X*, Pub. by OBrien Pr) Irish Amer Bk.

Buckley, Patricia, jt. auth. see Maffei, Anthony C.

Buckley, Paul & Peat, David F., eds. Glimpsing Reality: Ideas in Physics & the Link to Biology. 2nd rev. ed. LC 96-137733. 296p. 1996. text 55.00 (*0-8020-0575-6*) U of Toronto Pr.

— Glimpsing Reality: Ideas in Physics & the Link to Biology. 2nd rev. ed. 296p. 1996. pap. text 19.95 (*0-8020-6994-0*) U of Toronto Pr.

Buckley, Paul & Peat, F. David. A Question of Physics: Conversations in Physics & Biology. LC 78-8096. 169p. reprint ed. pap. 52.40 (*0-8357-4134-6*, 203690600006) Bks Demand.

Buckley, Peter. Biological Habitat Reconstruction. 224p. 1992. 64.95 (*1-85293-058-6*, Pub. by P P Pubs) CRC Pr.

Buckley, Peter, ed. Essential Papers on Object Relations. (Essential Papers in Psychoanalysis). 512p. (C). 1986. pap. text 27.50 (*0-8147-1080-8*) NYU Pr.

— Essential Papers on Psychosis. (Essential Papers in Psychoanalysis). 384p. (C). 1988. text 75.00 (*0-8147-1096-4*); pap. text 27.50 (*0-8147-1097-2*) NYU Pr.

Buckley, Peter & Michie, Jonathan, eds. Firms, Organizations & Contracts: A Reader in Industrial Organization. LC 97-100009. (Oxford Management Readers Ser.). (Illus.). 488p. 1996. pap. text 24.95 (*0-19-877436-2*) OUP.

— Firms, Organizations & Contracts: A Reader in Industrial Organization. LC 97-100009. (Oxford Management Readers Ser.). (Illus.). 488p. (C). 1996. text 82.00 (*0-19-877435-4*) OUP.

***Buckley, Peter F., ed.** Sexuality & Serious Mental Illness. (Chronic Mental Illness Ser.). 335p. 1999. text 40.00 (*90-5702-598-1*, Harwood Acad Pubs) Gordon & Breach.

***Buckley, Peter F. & Waddington, John L.** Schizophrenia & Mood Disorders: The New Drug Therapies in Clinical Practice. (Illus.). 368p. 2000. pap. 60.00 (*0-7506-4096-0*) Buttrwrth-Heinemann.

Buckley, Peter F., jt. auth. see Waddington, John.

Buckley, Peter F., ed. see Harrison, Glynn & Bird, J. M.

Buckley, Peter J. International Strategic Management & Government Policy. LC 98-11551. 240p. 1998. text. write for info. (*0-312-21440-5*) St Martin.

***Buckley, Peter J.** Multinational Firms, Cooperation & Competition in the World Economy. LC 99-54659. 240p. 1999. text 69.95 (*0-312-22900-3*) St Martin.

— The Theory of the Multinational Enterprise. (Studia Oeconomiae Negotiorum: No. 26). 64p. (Orig.). 1987. pap. 33.50 (*91-554-2025-7*, Pub. by Uppsala Univ Acta Univ Uppsaliensis) Coronet Bks.

Buckley, Peter J., ed. International Investment. (International Library of Critical Writings in Economics: Vol. 1). 388p. 1990. 185.00 (*1-85278-152-1*) E Elgar.

Buckley, Peter J. & Casson, Mark, eds. Multinational Enterprises in the World Economy: Essays in Honour of John Dunning. (New Horizons in International Business Ser.). 304p. 1992. 95.00 (*1-85278-393-1*) E Elgar.

***Buckley, Peter J. & Ghauri, Pervez N.** The Global Challenge for Multinational Enterprises: Managing Increasing Interdependence. LC 99-32546. (International Business & Management Ser.). 525p. 1999. write for info. (*0-08-043584-X*, Pergamon Pr) Elsevier.

An Asterisk (*) at the beginning of an entry indicates that the title is appearing for the first time.

Buckley, Peter J. & Ghaurj, Pervez N., eds. The Economics of Change in East & Central Europe: Its Impact of International Business. (Illus.). 448p. 1994. pap. text 34.95 (0-12-139165-5) Acad Pr.

Buckley, Peter J. & Mucchielli, Jean-Louis, eds. Multinational Firms & International Relocation. LC 95-25263. (New Horizons in International Business Ser.). (Illus.). 272p. 1997. 90.00 (1-85898-302-9) E Elgar.

Buckley, R. Ant-Plant Interactions in Australia. 1982. text 176.50 (90-6193-684-5) Kluwer Academic.

— Oscillations & Waves. (Student Monographs in Physics). (Illus.). 64p. 1985. pap. 15.00 (0-85274-793-4) IOP Pub.

— Perspectives in Environmental Management. xi, 276p. 1991. 76.95 (0-387-53815-1) Spr-Verlag.

Buckley, R. A. The Law of Nuisance. 2nd ed. 242p. 1996. write for info. (0-406-02675-0, MICHIE) LEXIS Pub.

— The Modern Law of Negligence. (C). 1988. 420.00 (0-7855-4075-X, Pub. by Witherby & Co) St Mut.

Buckley, R. Philip. Husserl, Heidegger & the Crisis of Philosophical Responsibility. (Phaenomenologica Ser.). 328p. (C). 1992. lib. bdg. 185.00 (0-7923-1633-9, Pub. by Kluwer Academic) Kluwer Academic.

Buckley, R. V. Campos Electromagneticos. (SPA.). 208p. (C). 1993. pap. text 13.33 (0-201-60148-6) Addison-Wesley.

Buckley, Ramon, tr. see Dahl, Roald.

Buckley, Ray. The Give-Away: A Christmas Story in the Native American Tradition. (Illus.). 32p. 1999. 12.95 (0-687-07186-0) Abingdon.

— God's Love Is Like . . . (Illus.). 32p. (J). (gr. 1-3). 1998. 12.95 (0-687-05626-8) Abingdon.

Buckley, Raymond M., jt. auth. see Haw, Frank.

Buckley, Reid. Strictly Speaking: Reid Buckley's Indispensable Handbook on Public Speaking. LC 99-21413. 336p. 1999. 18.95 (0-07-134610-4) McGraw.

Buckley, Richard. The Foolish Tortoise. LC 93-20123. (Pixies Ser.: Vol. 25). (Illus.). (J). (gr. 1-8). 1993. pap. 4.95 (0-88708-323-4, Picture Book Studio) S&S Childrens.

***Buckley, Richard.** The Foolish Tortoise. (Illus.). 24p. (J). (ps-k). 1998. 5.99 (0-689-82058-5) S&S Childrens.

— The Greedy Python. (Illus.). 24p. (J). (ps-k). 1998. 5.99 (0-689-82059-3) S&S Childrens.

Buckley, Richard. The Greedy Python & the Foolish Tortoise. LC 86-25468. (Illus.). 48p. (J). (ps). 1991. pap. 13.00 (0-88708-039-1, Picture Book Studio) S&S Childrens.

Buckley, Robert. 1998 Annual Review of Development Effectiveness. (Operations Evaluation Department Ser.). 80p. 1999. pap. 22.00 (0-8213-4474-9, 14474) World Bank.

Buckley, Robert, jt. auth. see Gross, Elsie.

Buckley, Robert M. Housing Finance in Developing Countries. LC 96-26644. 220p. 1997. text 69.95 (0-312-16160-3) St Martin.

Buckley, Roger. Japan Today. 3rd ed. LC 98-38448. (Illus.). 248p. (C). 1999. text 49.95 (0-521-64373-2) Cambridge U Pr.

— Japan Today. 3rd ed. LC 98-38448. (Studies in Chinese History, Literature & Institutions). (Illus.). 150p. (C). 1999. pap. text 17.95 (0-521-64375-9) Cambridge U Pr.

— U. S.-Japan Alliance Diplomacy, 1945-1990. (Studies in International Relations: No. 21). (Illus.). 239p. (C). 1995. pap. text 19.95 (0-521-55865-4) Cambridge U Pr.

Buckley, Roger & Caple, Jim. One to One Training & Coaching Skills. 2nd ed. 144p. 1997. pap. 25.00 (0-7494-2065-0, Kogan Pg Educ) Stylus Pub VA.

Buckley, Roger N. The British Army in the West Indies: Society & the Military in the Revolutionary Age. LC 98-13516. 464p. 1998. 55.00 (0-8130-1604-5) U Press Fla.

— Congo Jack: A Novel. LC 97-65343. 312p. 1997. 22.95 (0-9632476-5-4) Pinto Pr.

Buckley, Roger N., ed. & intro. see Howard, Thomas P.

Buckley, Ron, tr. see Abdul-Aziz, Moudi M.

***Buckley, Ronald Paul.** The Book of the Islamic Market Inspector. (Journal of Semitic Studies Supplement: No. 9). 200p. 2000. text 65.00 (0-19-922434-X) OUP.

Buckley, Rosemary. Delivering Quality in Midwifery. 1997. pap. text. write for info. (0-7020-2134-2) Bailliere Tindall.

***Buckley, Ross P.** Emerging Markets Debt: An Analysis of the Secondary Market. LC 99-32404. 1999. 117.00 (90-411-9716-8) Kluwer Law Intl.

Buckley, Ruby. The Heart Binder: For the Wounded. Gems of Grace Ministry Staff, ed. 133p. (Orig.). 1995. pap. 10.99 (0-9648189-0-6) Gems of Grace.

Buckley, Sandra, ed. Broken Silence: Voices of Japanese Feminism. (Illus.). 324p. 1996. 45.00 (0-520-08513-2, Pub. by U CA Pr); pap. 17.95 (0-520-08514-0, Pub. by U CA Pr) Cal Prin Full Svc.

Buckley, Sarah. Watercolor. LC 99-199285. (Introduction to Art Ser.). (Illus.). 128p. 1998. pap. 12.95 (0-8069-3781-5) Sterling.

Buckley, Sarah Masters. Mystery of the Smuggler's Treasure. LC 98-47808. 1999. pap. text 4.76 (1-56247-757-9) Pleasant Co.

Buckley, Sheryl, jt. auth. see Donley, Carol C.

Buckley, Sheryl, jt. ed. see Donley, Carol.

Buckley, Steve. Sports Buddies: Superstar Athletes & Their Best Friends. Sieck, Margaret, ed. 32p. (J). (gr. 1-9). 1999. pap. 3.99 (1-886749-56-6) SI For Kids.

Buckley, Steve, jt. auth. see Rose, Ed.

***Buckley, Susan.** 15 Easy-To-Read Biography Mini-Books: Famous Americans. 48p. 2000. pap. 9.95 (0-590-96718-5) Scholastic Inc.

***Buckley, Susan L.** Teachings on Usury in Judaism, Christianity & Islam. LC 00-55434. (Texts & Studies in Religion Ser.). 2000. write for info. (0-7734-7656-3) E Mellen.

Buckley, Teresa A., ed. see Brewer, Floyd I.

Buckley, Terry. Aspects of Greek History 750-323 BC: A Source-Based Approach. LC 95-20497. (Illus.). 560p. (C). 1996. 85.00 (0-415-09957-9); pap. 25.99 (0-415-09958-7) Routledge.

Buckley, Theodore, tr. see Aristotle.

Buckley, Thomas & Gottlieb, Alma, eds. Blood Magic: The Anthropology of Menstruation. 1988. pap. 18.95 (0-520-06350-3, Pub. by U CA Pr) Cal Prin Full Svc.

Buckley, Thomas, tr. see Crevel, Rene.

Buckley, Thomas, tr. see de La Grange, Clementine.

Buckley, Thomas, tr. see Vircondelet, Alain.

Buckley, Thomas E. Church & State in Revolutionary Virginia, 1776-1787. LC 77-4283. 213p. reprint ed. pap. 66.10 (0-7837-1078-X, 204160800021) Bks Demand.

Buckley, Thomas H. The United States & the Washington Conference, 1921-1922. LC 79-100409. 236p. reprint ed. pap. 73.20 (0-608-11956-3, 202316600032) Bks Demand.

Buckley, Thomas H. & Strong, Edwin B., Jr. American Foreign & National Security Policies, 1914-1945. LC 87-10905. (Illus.). 224p. (C). 1988. pap. text 17.00 (0-87049-540-2) U of Tenn Pr.

Buckley, Thomas L. Nature, Science, Realism: A Re-Examination of Programmatic Realism & the Works of Adalbert Stifter & Gottfried Keller. LC 92-30111. (Literature & the Sciences of Man Ser.: Vol. 4). VIII, 209p. (C). 1995. text 48.95 (0-8204-1958-3) P Lang Pubng.

***Buckley, Thomas S. J., Jr., ed.** If You Love That Lady, Don't Marry Her: The Courtship Letters of Sally McDowell & John Miller, 1854-1856. 920p. 1999. 34.95 (0-8262-1278-6) U of Mo Pr.

Buckley, Timothy J. What Binds Marriage? Roman Catholic Theology in Practice. 1997. pap. 19.95 (0-225-66845-9) Continuum.

Buckley, Tony, ed. Symbols in Northern Ireland. LC 98-173326. (Illus.). 208p. 1998. pap. 17.95 (0-85389-692-5, Pub. by Inst Irish Studies) Irish Bks Media.

Buckley, Vincent. Essays in Poetry. LC 77-86738. (Essay Index Reprint Ser.). 1977. 20.95 (0-8369-1174-1) Ayer.

— Late Winter Child. 38p. 1980. pap. 7.00 (0-85105-358-0, Pub. by Smyth) Dufour.

— The Pattern. 64p. 1979. pap. 8.50 (0-85105-357-2, Pub. by Smyth) Dufour.

Buckley, W. K. 81 Mygrations. LC 97-39854. 80p. 1998. pap. 10.00 (1-56474-241-5) Fithian Pr.

Buckley, Walter. Society - A Complex Adaptive System: Essays in Social Theory. (International Studies in Global Change: Vol. 9). 256p. 1998. text 36.00 (90-5700-537-9, ECU52, Harwood Acad Pubs) Gordon & Breach.

Buckley, Wava, ed. see Larson, Al.

Buckley, William F., Jr. Brothers No More. large type ed. LC 95-46651. 1996. pap. 22.95 (1-56895-283-X) Wheeler Pub.

— God & Man at Yale: The Superstitions of "Academic Freedom" 304p. 1977. 12.95 (0-89526-697-0); pap. 12.95 (0-89526-692-X) Regnery Pub.

— High Jinx. LC 97-29703. 320p. 1997. reprint ed. pap. 10.95 (1-888952-52-0) Cumberland Hse.

— Lady Chatterley's Lover: Loss & Hope. LC 93-7658. (Twayne's Masterworks Ser.). 160p. 1993. pap. 18.00 (0-8057-8599-X) Macmillan.

— Lady Chatterley's Lover: Loss & Hope. LC 93-7658. (Twayne's Masterworks Ser.: Vol. 123). 160p. 1993. 25.95 (0-8057-9432-8) Macmillan.

***Buckley, William F., Jr** Let Us Talk of Many Things: The Collected Speeches. 608p. 2000. 30.00 (0-7615-2551-3) Prima Pub.

Buckley, William F., Jr The Lexicon: A Cornucopia of Wonderful Words for the Inquisitive Word Lover. (Illus.). 176p. (C). 1998. pap. 9.00 (0-15-600616-2, Harvest Bks) Harcourt.

— Marco Polo, If You Can. 1983. pap. 3.95 (0-380-61424-3, Avon Bks) Morrow Avon.

— Marco Polo, If You Can. LC 96-21123. 288p. 1996. reprint ed. pap. 10.95 (1-888952-11-3) Cumberland Hse.

— Mongoose R. I. P. A Blackford Oakes Novel. LC 97-47693. 376p. 1998. reprint ed. pap. 12.95 (1-888952-72-5) Cumberland Hse.

— Nearer, My God: An Autobiography of Faith. LC 98-16194. 368p. (C). 1998. pap. 14.00 (0-15-600618-9, Harvest Bks) Harcourt.

— The Red Hunter: A Novel Based on the Life of Senator Joe McCarthy. LC 98-31255. (Operation Babysitter Ser.: No. 2). 432p. (YA). (gr. 8). 1999. 25.00 (0-316-11589-4) Little.

— The Right Word. Vaughan, Samuel S., ed. LC 98-14828. 544p. (C). 1998. pap. 15.00 (0-15-600569-7) Harcourt.

— Saving the Queen. 288p. 1981. pap. 3.95 (0-380-55111-X, Avon Bks) Morrow Avon.

— Saving the Queen. LC 96-51926. 320p. 1997. reprint ed. pap. 10.95 (1-888952-27-X) Cumberland Hse.

— See You Later, Alligator. LC 97-13298. 320p. 1997. reprint ed. pap. 10.95 (1-888952-51-2) Cumberland Hse.

— Selected Works of J. S. Bach. 80p. 1991. pap. 12.98 (0-943748-49-6, PF0739) Ekay Music.

— Speed Learning W. A. - Mozart. 104p. (YA). 1991. pap. 12.98 (0-943748-54-2, PF0781) Ekay Music.

***Buckley, William F., Jr** Spytime: The Undoing of James Jesus Angelton. LC 99-54977. 320p. 2000. 25.00 (0-15-100513-3) Harcourt.

Buckley, William F., Jr. Stained Glass. 352p. 1981. pap. 3.95 (0-380-54791-0, Avon Bks) Morrow Avon.

— Stained Glass. LC 97-14254. 320p. 1997. reprint ed. pap. 10.95 (1-888952-29-6) Cumberland Hse.

— The Story of Henri Tod. LC 96-32827. 320p. 1996. reprint ed. pap. 10.95 (1-888952-12-1) Cumberland Hse.

— Torts & Personal Injury Law. LC 92-23761. 451p. 1993. text 40.95 (0-8273-5056-2) Delmar.

— Tucker's Last Stand: A Blackford Oakes Novel. LC 97-47691. 320p. 1998. reprint ed. pap. 10.95 (1-888952-73-3) Cumberland Hse.

— Who's on First? LC 96-51933. 320p. 1997. reprint ed. pap. 10.95 (1-888952-28-8) Cumberland Hse.

Buckley, William F., Jr., jt. auth. see Hodges, Candace.

Buckley, William F., Jr., jt. auth. see Murchison, William.

Buckley, William F., Jr., ed. & notes see Chambers, Whittaker & Buckley, William F.

***Buckley, William J., ed.** Kosovo: Contending Voices on Balkan Interventions. LC 99-59275. (Illus.). 473p. 2000. 30.00 (0-8028-3889-8) Eerdmans.

Buckley, William K. Senses' Tender: Recovering the Novel for the Reader. 165p. (C). 1989. text 41.50 (0-8204-0724-0) P Lang Pubng.

Buckley, William K., ed. Critical Essays on Louis-Ferdinand Celine. (Critical Essays on World Literature Ser.). 272p. 1988. 49.00 (0-8161-8841-6, G K Hall & Co) Mac Lib Ref.

Buckley, William K. & Seaton, James, eds. Beyond Cheering & Bashing: New Perspectives on The Closing of the American Mind. LC 91-75582. 200p. (C). 1992. 39.95 (0-87972-547-8); pap. 19.95 (0-87972-548-6) Bowling Green Univ Popular Press.

Buckley, William R. Torts & Personal Injury Law. 92p. 1993. pap., teacher ed. 13.00 (0-8273-5057-0) Delmar.

Buckley, William R. & Okrent, Cathy J. Torts & Personal Injury Law. 2nd ed. LC 96-20067. (Paralegal Ser.). 480p. (C). 1997. mass mkt. 66.95 (0-8273-7572-7) Delmar.

Bucklin, Linda & Keil, Mary. Come Rain or Come Shine. LC 99-15773. 256p. 1999. pap. 9.95 (1-58062-211-9) Adams Media.

Bucklin, Louis P. Productivity in Marketing. LC 78-24445. 130p. reprint ed. pap. 40.30 (0-608-14408-8, 202152100022) Bks Demand.

***Bucklin, Steven J.** Realism & American Foreign Policy: Wilsonians & The Kennan-Morgenthau Thesis. 2000. write for info. (0-275-96737-9, Praeger Pubs) Greenwood.

Bucklow & Russell. Russia: Why Revolution? 1976. pap. text. write for info. (0-582-68238-X, Pub. by Addison-Wesley) Longman.

— Russia: Why Revolution? 1991. pap. text. write for info. (0-582-87039-9, Pub. by Addison-Wesley) Longman.

Bucklow, Christopher, jt. auth. see Mellor, David A.

Bucklow, Eric. Coronation Wings: The Men & Machines of the Royal Air Force Coronation Review at Odiham, IS, July 1953. Ketley, Barry, ed. (Illus.). 96p. 1999. pap. 24.95 (0-9519899-6-0, Pub. by Hikoki Pubns) Howell Pr VA.

Bucklow, I. A., ed. see Welding Institute Staff, et al.

Buckman, A. Bruce. Guided-Wave Photonics. (Illus.). 384p. (C). 1995. text 77.95 (0-03-033354-7); student ed. write for info. (0-03-075909-9) OUP.

Buckman, Bruce. Computer Based Electronic Measurement Simulation. LC 99-49913. 300p. (C). 2000. pap. 35.40 (0-201-36182-5, Prentice Hall) P-H.

***Buckman, Carole Duncan.** Neighbors & Traitors. LC 99-50724. (Starmaker Books Ser.). 96p. (J). (gr. 6-9). 2000. pap. 5.50 (0-88489-548-3) St Marys.

Buckman, Carole Duncan. Signs & Wonders from Our Journals. Wilt, Michael, ed. LC 98-208093. 120p. (J). (gr. 4-7). 1998. pap. 6.95 (0-88489-532-7) St Marys.

Buckman, David L. Old Steamboat Days on the Hudson River. (Illus.). 136p. 1990. pap. 18.50 (0-941567-05-2) J C & A L Fawcett.

Buckman, Elcha S., ed. The Handbook of Humor: Clinical Applications in Psychotherapy. LC 92-17508. 206p. (C). 1994. 25.50 (0-89464-369-X) Krieger.

Buckman, Erik L. The Prankster's Ultimate Handbook. (Illus.). 103p. 1996. pap. 13.95 (0-9656356-0-0) E L Buckman.

— The Prankster's Ultimate Handbook. (Illus.). 140p. 1996. pap. 13.95 (0-9656356-1-9) E L Buckman.

Buckman, Gertrude, ed. Compliments: A Treasury of Tributes to Friends & Lovers, Relatives, & Rivals. LC 80-678. (Illus.). 88p. 1980. 9.95 (0-672-52650-6, Bobbs) Macmillan.

Buckman, Irene Graybill. Keepsake Recipes & Fascinating Food Facts. LC 99-71704. 178p. 1999. pap. 14.95 (1-883697-11-5, 1-883697) Hara Pub.

Buckman, Jerome-Allan, tr. see Ryssel, Heiner & Ruge, Ingolf.

Buckman, Mary. The Alphabet Cookbook. (One in a Series of Cook & Learn Books). (Illus.). (J). (gr. k-2). 1988. pap. text 9.95 (1-879414-03-1) Mary Bee Creat.

— The Alphagator. (Illus.). 32p. (J). (ps). 1992. pap. 8.95 (1-879414-10-4) Mary Bee Creat.

— The Animal Cookbook. (One in a Series of Cook & Learn Books). (Illus.). (J). (gr. k-2). 1982. pap. text 9.95 (1-879414-01-5) Mary Bee Creat.

— Ben. (Illus.). 32p. (J). (gr. k-5). 1992. pap. 8.95 (1-879414-09-0) Mary Bee Creat.

— The Count & Cook Book. (One in a Series of Cook & Learn Books). (Illus.). (J). (gr. k-2). 1982. pap. text 9.95 (1-879414-00-7) Mary Bee Creat.

— Leap Frog. LC 89-63379. (One in a Series of Predictable Readers). (Illus.). (Orig.). (J). (gr. k-2). 1989. pap. text 12.95 (1-879414-05-8) Mary Bee Creat.

— Magical Muriel. LC 90-60453. (One in a Series of Predictable Books). (Illus.). (Orig.). (J). (gr. k-2). 1991. pap. text 12.95 (1-879414-07-4) Mary Bee Creat.

— The Shape & Cook Book. (One in a Series of Cook & Learn Books). (Illus.). (J). (gr. k-2). 1982. pap. text 9.95 (1-879414-02-3) Mary Bee Creat.

— Wiggle Worm. LC 89-63502. (One in a Series of Predictable Books). (Illus.). (Orig.). (J). (gr. k-2). 1989. pap. text 12.95 (1-879414-06-6) Mary Bee Creat.

Buckman, Repha. Repha. Lawson, Robert, ed. & intro. by. (Illus.). 68p. (Orig.). 1986. 15.99 (0-940559-03-X); pap. 5.00 (0-940559-00-5); lp 6.95 (0-940559-02-1) Tri Crown Pr.

Buckman, Robert. How to Break Bad News: A Guide for Health Care Professionals. LC 92-10298. 208p. 1992. pap. text 15.95 (0-8018-4491-6) Johns Hopkins.

— I Don't Know What to Say: How to Help & Support Someone Who Is Dying. 1992. pap. 13.00 (0-679-73202-0) Vin Bks.

***Buckman, Robert.** Skin: An Owner's Manual: What Your Skin Does for You & What You Need to Do for It. 128p. 1999. pap. 11.00 (1-57500-082-2, Pub. by TV Bks) HarpC.

Buckman, Robert. What You Really Need to Know about Cancer: A Comprehensive Guide for Patients & Their Families. LC 97-5203. (Illus.). 384p. 1997. pap. 19.95 (0-8018-5593-4); text 39.95 (0-8018-5594-2) Johns Hopkins.

***Buckman, Robert.** What You Really Need to Know about Caring for a Child with Asthma. LC 99-43769. (Illus.). 80p. 2000. pap. 9.95 (0-86730-797-8) Lebhar Friedman.

— What You Really Need to Know about Diabetes. LC 99-44593. (Illus.). 80p. 2000. pap. 9.95 (0-86730-796-X) Lebhar Friedman.

— What You Really Need to Know about High Blood Pressure. LC 99-43768. (Illus.). 80p. 2000. pap. 9.95 (0-86730-795-1) Lebhar Friedman.

— What You Really Need to Know about Hormone Replacement Therapy. LC 99-43764. (Illus.). 80p. 2000. pap. 9.95 (0-86730-798-6) Lebhar Friedman.

***Buckman, Robert & Cleese, John.** What You Really Need to Know about Breast Cancer. (What You Really Need to Know Ser.). 80p. 2000. pap. 9.95 (0-86730-826-5) Lebhar Friedman.

— What You Really Need to Know about Caring for Someone after a Stroke. (What You Really Need to Know Ser.). (Illus.). 80p. 2000. pap. 9.95 (0-86730-828-1) Lebhar Friedman.

— What You Really Need to Know about Irritable Bowel Syndrome. (What You Really Need to Know Ser.). 80p. 2000. pap. 9.95 (0-86730-827-3) Lebhar Friedman.

— What You Really Need to Know about Living with Depression. 80p. 2000. pap. 9.95 (0-86730-825-7) Lebhar Friedman.

Buckman, Robert & Kason, Yvonne. How to Break Bad News: A Guide for Health Care Professionals. 1992. pap. text 17.95 (0-8020-6790-5) U of Toronto Pr.

Buckman, Robert & Sabbagh, Karl. Magic or Medicine? An Investigation of Healing & Healers. LC 94-42853. 261p. 1995. 27.95 (0-87975-948-8) Prometheus Bks.

Buckman, Robert, jt. auth. see Ezzo, Gary.

Buckman, Robert T. Latin America 1998. 32nd ed. (World Today Ser.). 1998. pap. 11.50 (1-887985-13-1) Stryker-Post.

***Buckman, Robert T.** Latin America, 1999. 33rd ed. 1999. pap. 11.50 (1-887985-20-4) Stryker-Post.

Buckman, Roy. Urine: Your Body's Secret Elixer of Health. 1999. pap. write for info. (0-8464-4954-4) Beekman Pubs.

Buckmaster, Charles. Charles Buckmaster Collected Poems. MacDonald, Simon, ed. 150p. (Orig.). 1989. pap. text 19.95 (0-7022-2242-9, Pub. by Univ Queensland Pr) Intl Spec Bk.

Buckmaster, H. Paul: A Man Who Changed the World. 1989. pap. 8.95 (0-933062-27-3) R H Sommer.

Buckmaster, Henrietta. Let My People Go: The Story of the Underground Railroad & the Growth of the Abolitionist Movement. Sproat, John G., ed. LC 92-16843. (Southern Classics Ser.). 424p. (C). 1992. reprint ed. pap. 16.95 (0-87249-865-4) U of SC Pr.

Buckmaster, John D., ed. The Mathematics of Combustion. LC 85-50339. (Frontiers in Applied Mathematics Ser.: No. 2). xii, 254p. 1985. 48.00 (0-89871-053-7) Soc Indus-Appl Math.

Buckmaster, John D., et al, eds. Combustion in High-Speed Flows. LC 94-7974. (ICASE-LaRC Interdisciplinary Series in Science & Engineering: Vol. 1). 656p. (C). 1994. lib. bdg. 278.50 (0-7923-2806-X) Kluwer Academic.

Buckmaster, John D. & Ludford, G. S. Lectures on Mathematical Combustion. LC 83-61375. (CBMS-NSF Regional Conference Series in Applied Mathematics: No. 43). viii, 126p. 1983. pap. text 28.50 (0-89871-186-X) Soc Indus-Appl Math.

Buckmaster, John D. & Takeno, Tadao, eds. Modeling in Combustion Science: Proceedings of the U. S.-Japan Seminar Held in Kapaa, Kuai, Hawaii, 24-29 July 1994. LC 95-15163. (Lecture Notes in Physics Ser.: Vol. 449). 369p. 1995. 92.95 (3-540-59224-5) Spr-Verlag.

Buckmaster, John D. & Takeno, Tadeo, eds. Mathematical Modeling in Combustion Science. (Lecture Notes in Physics Ser.: Vol. 299). vi, 168p. 1988. 34.95 (0-387-19181-X) Spr-Verlag.

Buckmaster, Lawrence W., jt. auth. see Lytel, Allan H.

Buckminster Staff. Synergetic Stew: Explorations in Dymaxion Dining. (Illus.). 120p. (Orig.). 1982. 6.95 (0-911573-00-3) Buckminster Fuller.

Bucknall, Barbara J. Marcel Proust Revisited. LC 92-12879. (Twayne's World Authors Ser.: No. 830). 160p. 1992. 32.00 (0-8057-8274-5, Twyne) Mac Lib Ref.

— Marie Cardinal. 1999. 22.95 (0-8057-4559-9, Twyne) Mac Lib Ref.

— The Religion of Art in Proust. LC 78-83546. (Illinois Studies in Language & Literature: No. 60). 224p. reprint ed. pap. 69.50 (0-8357-3515-X, 203442900090) Bks Demand.

Bucknall, Barbara J., ed. Marcel Proust. LC 87-19. (Critical Essays Ser.). 224p. 1987. 49.00 (0-8161-8833-5, Hall Reference) Macmillan.

B

Bucknall, Geoffrey, ed. The Bright Stream of Memory: The Golden Years of the "Fishing Gazette" LC 97-122648. (Illus.). 184p. 1998. 39.95 (*1-85310-767-0*, Pub. by Swan Hill Pr) Voyageur Pr.

Bucknall, John B. The Heyday of Steam: West Midlands. 80p. 28.95 (*0-7110-2450-2*) Spec Mkting Intl.

***Bucknall, Julia.** Poland: Complying with EU Environmental Legislation. LC 99-47657. (Technical Paper Ser.: No. 454). 1999. 22.00 (*0-8213-4595-8*, 14595) World Bank.

***Bucknall, Julian.** Tomes of Delphi: Algorithms & Data Structures. 2000. pap. text 59.95 (*1-55622-736-1*) Wordware Pub.

Bucknall, Kevin. Studying at University: How to Make a Success of Your Academic Course. (Student Handbks.). 135p. 1996. pap. 19.95 (*1-85703-219-5*, Pub. by How To Bks) Trans-Atl Phila.

Bucknall, Paul. Polymer Blends Set: Formulation & Performance. LC 99-36533. 1189p. 1999. 300.00 (*0-471-24825-8*) Wiley.

***Bucknam, Kevin P., et al.** Kentucky Administrative Law. Overstreet, Mark R., ed. 541p. 1999. 87.00 (*1-58757-028-9*) Univ of KY.

Bucknan, Robert. I Don't Know What to Say. large type ed. 260p. 1989. reprint ed. 19.95 (*1-85089-335-7*, Pub. by ISIS Lrg Prnt) Transaction Pubs.

Bucknell, Howard. Energy & the National Defense. LC 79-57566. (Essays for the Third Century Ser.). 255p. reprint ed. pap. 79.10 (*0-7837-5791-3*, 204545700006) Bks Demand.

Bucknell, Katherine, ed. see Auden, W. H.

Bucknell, Katherine, ed. & intro. see Isherwood, Christopher.

Bucknell, P. Misuse of Drugs & the Law. (Library of Criminal Law Ser.). 352p. 1986. 54.00 (*0-08-039203-2*, Pergamon Pr) Elsevier.

Bucknell, P. & Ghodse, H. Misuse of Drugs, Suppl. 1. (Criminal Law Library). 128p. 1986. pap. 8.25 (*0-08-033081-9*) Macmillan.

— Misuse of Drugs, Supplement 2. (Criminal Law Library). 192p. 1988. pap. 18.00 (*0-08-033107-6*) Macmillan.

— Misuse of Drugs, Supplement No. 3. (Criminal Law Library). 192p. 1989. pap. 30.00 (*0-08-036914-6*) Macmillan.

— Misuse of Drugs & Supplement 3: Combined Set, WCLL 2. (Criminal Law Library). 632p. 1989. 100.00 (*0-08-036915-4*, Pergamon Pr) Elsevier.

Bucknell, Peter A., jt. auth. see Hill, Margot H.

Bucknell, R. S. & Stuart-Fox, Martin. The Twilight Language: Explorations in Buddhist Meditation & Symbolism. 248p. (C). 1996. pap. text 19.00 (*0-7007-0234-2*, Pub. by Curzon Pr Ltd) UH Pr.

Bucknell, Robert C. Embrace the Truth: Prophecy Revealed Through Current Event. 290p. (Orig.). 1996. pap. 14.95 (*1-57502-133-1*) Morris Pubng.

Bucknell, Roderick S. Sanskrit Manual. (C). 1994. text 20.00 (*81-208-1188-7*, Pub. by Motilal Bnarsidass); pap. text 14.00 (*81-208-1189-5*, Pub. by Motilal Bnarsidass) S Asia.

Bucknell, Roderick S. & Kang, Chris. The Meditative Way: Readings in the Theory & Practice of Buddhist Meditation. LC 97-186644. 288p. (C). 1997. text 48.00 (*0-7007-0677-1*, Pub. by Curzon Pr Ltd); pap. text 24.95 (*0-7007-0678-X*, Pub. by Curzon Pr Ltd) UH Pr.

Buckner. Infants & Toddlers. (Early Childhood Education Ser.). (C). 2002. mass mkt. 29.25 (*0-7668-0251-5*) Delmar.

Buckner, Allen Z. Medical & Health Costs of Care, Illness & Disability: Index of New Information with References. rev. ed. 182p. 1997. 47.50 (*0-7883-1582-X*) ABBE Pubs Assn.

— Sports Encyclopedia: Index & Reference Books of New Information Vol. 2: Male & Female Athletes, Vol. 2. Bartone, John C., ed. 150p. 1996. 44.50 (*0-7883-1080-1*); pap. 39.50 (*0-7883-1081-X*) ABBE Pubs Assn.

Buckner, Allen Z. & De Leo, Vincent Z. Medical & Health Costs of Care, Illness & Disability: Index of New Information with References. rev. ed. 182p. 1997. pap. 44.50 (*0-7883-1583-8*) ABBE Pubs Assn.

Buckner, Arlene. Elphina. LC 98-25165. (Illus.). 32p. (J). (gr. k-2). 1998. 17.95 (*1-890309-56-7*) Tern Bk Co.

Buckner, C. Dale. Two Hundred Forty-Six Solved Structural Engineering Problems. (Engineering Reference Manual Ser.). (Illus.). 440p. 1991. pap. 62.95 (*0-912045-32-9*) Prof Pubns CA.

Buckner, C. Dale & Shahrooz, Bahram M., eds. Composite Construction in Steel & Concrete III: Proceedings of an Engineering Foundation, Irsee, Germany, June 9-14. LC 97-14840. 952p. 1996. 69.00 (*0-7844-0256-6*) Am Soc Civil Eng.

Buckner, C. Dale & Viest, Ivan M., eds. Composite Construction in Steel & Concrete. 832p. 1988. 66.00 (*0-87262-654-7*) Am Soc Civil Eng.

Buckner, C. Dean, ed. Technical & Biological Components of Marrow Transplantation. LC 95-1584. (Cancer Treatment & Research Ser.: Vol. 76). 400p. (C). 1995. text 260.00 (*0-7923-3394-2*) Kluwer Academic.

Buckner, Carl, et al. The University of Wisconsin School of Pharmacy: It's First Century, Vol. 1. (Illus.). 240p. 1997. 24.00 (*0-9658834-0-X*, U Pubns) U Wis-Madison.

Buckner, Leroy M. Customer Services. 2nd ed. (Occupational Manuals & Projects in Marketing Ser.). (Illus.). 1978. text, student ed. 12.28 (*0-07-008823-3*) McGraw.

Buckner, Marilyn, jt. auth. see Slavenski, Lynn.

Buckner, Phillip A. The Transition to Responsible Government: British Policy in British North America 1815-1850, 17. LC 84-12811. (Contributions in Comparative Colonial Studies: No. 17). 358p. 1985. 65.00 (*0-313-24630-0*, BTV/) Greenwood.

Buckner, Phillip A. & Reid, John C., eds. The Atlantic Region to Confederation: A History. (Illus.). 600p. (C). 1994. pap. 29.95 (*0-8020-6977-0*); text 60.00 (*0-8020-0553-5*) U of Toronto Pr.

Buckner, Phillip A., ed. see Joint Atlantic Canada-Western Canadian Studies Con.

Buckner, R. B. Astronomic & Grid Azimuth. (Illus.). 255p. 1989. pap. text 40.00 (*0-910845-22-0*, 955) Landmark Ent.

— Land Survey Review Manual. 2nd ed. 437p. (Orig.). 1993. pap. 48.00 (*0-910845-49-2*) Landmark Ent.

— Land Surveying Computations. 108p. 1991. pap. 30.00 (*0-910845-56-5*, 571) Landmark Ent.

— Surveying Measurements & Their Analysis. (Illus.). 288p. (C). 1983. text 48.00 (*0-910845-11-5*, 480) Landmark Ent.

Buckner, Reginald T. & Weiland, Steven, eds. Jazz in Mind: Essays on the History & Meanings of Jazz. LC 91-10851. (Jazz History, Culture & Criticism Ser.). 186p. (C). 1991. text 29.95 (*0-8143-2168-2*) Wayne St U Pr.

Buckner, Richard. Joy of Jesus. (Illus.). 126p. 1994. pap. 7.95 (*1-85311-067-1*, 843, Pub. by Canterbury Press Norwich) Morehouse Pub.

Buckner, Sally. Strawberry Harvest. 84p. (Orig.). 1986. pap. 10.00 (*0-932662-61-7*) St Andrews NC.

Buckner, Sally, ed. Our Words - Our Ways: Reading & Writing in North Carolina. 2nd ed. LC 95-68954. (Illus.). 748p. (J). (gr. 8). 1995. boxed set 40.00 (*0-89089-696-8*) Carolina Acad Pr.

***Buckner, Sally, ed.** Word & Witness: One Hundred Years of North Carolina Poetry. LC 99-65880. 336p. 1999. 28.00 (*0-89089-686-0*); pap. 17.95 (*0-89089-687-9*) Carolina Acad Pr.

***Buckner, Sharry.** Dallas - Ft. Worth. (City Smart Ser.). (Illus.). 224p. 2000. pap. 15.95 (*1-56261-433-9*, Pub. by Avalon Travel) Publishers Group.

Buckner, Sharry. Exploring Texas with Children. LC 98-33194. 1998. pap. text 18.95 (*1-55622-624-1*, Rep of TX Pr) Wordware Pub.

— Great Stay of Texas: The Official Guide to Texas' Finest Historic Bed & Breakfasts & Country Inns. LC 97-78284. 1998. pap. text 9.95 (*0-9654752-1-2*) Hist Accommod TX.

Buckner, Sharry, ed. see Historic Accommodations of Texas Staff.

Buckner, Steve, jt. auth. see Niedens, Lyle.

Buckney, T. A. Scipio Africanus: The Conqueror of Hannibal, Selections from Livy, Bks. XXIV-XXX. (ENG & LAT., Illus.). 112p. 1987. reprint ed. pap. 11.00 (*0-86516-208-5*) Bolchazy-Carducci.

Bucknill, John C. Medical Knowledge of Shakespeare. LC 72-155634. reprint ed. 29.50 (*0-404-01146-2*) AMS Pr.

— Notes on Asylums for the Insane in America. LC 73-2391. (Mental Illness & Social Policy; the American Experience Ser.). 1973. reprint ed. 14.95 (*0-405-05199-9*) Ayer.

— Psychology of Shakespeare. LC 72-131514. reprint ed. 39.50 (*0-404-01147-0*) AMS Pr.

Bucko, Bill, tr. see Champagne, Maurice.

Bucko, Raymond A. The Lakota Ritual of the Sweat Lodge: History & Contemporary Practice. LC 97-47504. (Studies in the Anthropology of North American Indians). (Illus.). 340p. 1999. text 40.00 (*0-8032-1272-0*, Bison Books) U of Nebr Pr.

***Bucko, Raymond A.** The Lakota Ritual of the Sweat Lodge: History & Contemporary Practice. LC 97-47504. (Studies in the Anthropology of North American Indians). (Illus.). 340p. 1999. pap. 14.95 (*0-8032-6165-9*, Bison Books) U of Nebr Pr.

***Buckrich, Judith R.** The Monte Homes: A History of the Melbourne Jewish Philanthropic Society & the Montefiore Homes. 224p. 1999. pap. (*0-522-84845-1*, Pub. by Melbourne Univ Pr) Paul & Co Pubs.

Buckridge, Patrick. The Scandalous Penton: A Biography of Brian Penton. LC 94-226034. 350p. 1994. pap. 29.95 (*0-7022-2602-5*, Pub. by Univ Queensland Pr) Intl Spec Bk.

Buckrop, Jacquelyn. Fundamentals of Public Communication. (C). 1993. student ed. 10.00 (*1-881592-06-5*) Hayden-McNeil.

Buckroyd, Allen, ed. Computer Integrated Testing. LC 89-30990. 394p. 1989. 175.00 (*0-471-50486-6*) Wiley.

Buckroyd, Julia. Element Guide to Anorexia/Bulimia. LC 95-47431. (Guide Ser.). 144p. 1996. pap. 9.95 (*1-85230-776-5*, Pub. by Element MA) Penguin Putnam.

Bucks, Christa & Sygall, Susan. A World of Options: A Guide to International Educational Exchange, Community Service & Travel. 3rd rev. ed. 658p. 1997. pap. 40.00 (*1-880034-24-7*) Mobility Intl.

***Bucks, Christine & Organic Gardening Magazine Staff, eds.** Rodale Organic Gardening Basics: Compost. (Illus.). 2000. pap. 14.95 (*0-87596-856-2*, Rodale Org Garden) Rodale Pr Inc.

— Rodale Organic Gardening Basics: Herbs. LC 00-9597. (Illus.). 2000. pap. 14.95 (*0-87596-854-6*, Rodale Org Garden) Rodale Pr Inc.

— Rodale Organic Gardening Basics: Perennials. LC 00-9601. (Illus.). 2000. pap. 14.95 (*0-87596-855-4*, Rodale Org Garden) Rodale Pr Inc.

— Rodale Organic Gardening Basics: Pests. LC 00-9602. (Illus.). 2000. pap. 14.95 (*0-87596-853-8*, Rodale Org Garden) Rodale Pr Inc.

Bucks County Schools Intermediate Unit No. 22 Staf. Restructuring the Science Curriculum for a Changing World: A Renewal Process. Seif, Elliot, ed. 179p. (Orig.). 1994. pap. 29.95 (*1-56602-057-3*) Research Better.

Bucks, D. A., jt. auth. see Nakayama, F. S.

Bucksch, H. Dictionary Dental Medicine: German/English/German. (GER.). 800p. 1997. 350.00 (*0-320-00442-2*) Fr & Eur.

— Dictionary Geotechnical Engineering (Wurterbuch Geotechnik) 5p. 1999. pap. 275.00 incl. cd-rom (*3-540-14758-6*) Spr-Verlag.

— English-German Dictionary of Wood & Woodworking. 531p. 1986. 110.00 (*3-7625-2412-2*) IBD Ltd.

— German-English - English-German Dictionary of Civil Engineering, Construction, Machinery & Equipment. 3rd ed. 930p. 1987. pap. 57.00 (*3-7625-2553-6*) IBD Ltd.

— German-English Dictionary of Architecture, Building & Construction. 2nd ed. 942p. 1987. 220.00 (*3-7625-2576-5*) IBD Ltd.

— German-English Dictionary of Wood & Woodworking. 2nd ed. 461p. 1986. 110.00 (*3-7625-2411-4*) IBD Ltd.

Bucksch, Hector. Diccionario para Obras Publica, Edificacion y Maquinaria en Obra. (GER & SPA.). 1116p. 1976. 150.00 (*0-8288-5617-6*, S50187) Fr & Eur.

— Dictionary of Geotechnical Engineering: English-German, German-English. (ENG & GER.). 281p. 1995. 395.00 (*0-7859-9997-3*) Fr & Eur.

— Dictionary of Public Works, Building & Construction Equipment: Dictionnaire pour les Travaux Publics, le Batiment et l'Equipement des Chantiers de Construction. 7th ed. (ENG & FRE.). 420p. 1979. 195.00 (*0-8288-4726-6*, M6922) Fr & Eur.

— Dictionnaire pour l'Architecture, le Batiment et les Materiaux de Construction, 2 vols., Band I. (FRE & GER.). 820p. 1977. 350.00 (*0-8288-5392-4*, M7095) Fr & Eur.

— Dictionnaire pour l'Architecture, le Batiment et les Materiaux de Construction, 2 vols., Band II. (FRE & GER.). 688p. 1979. 350.00 (*0-8288-4725-8*, M7096) Fr & Eur.

— Dictionnaire pour les Travaux Publics et l'Equipement des Chartiers de Construction, 2 vols., Band I. deluxe ed. (FRE & GER.). 875p. 1976. 195.00 (*3-7625-0379-6*) Fr & Eur.

— Dictionnaire pour les Travaux Publics et l'Equipement des Chartiers de Construction, 2 vols., Band II. deluxe ed. (FRE & GER.). 911p. 1978. 195.00 (*0-8288-5200-6*, M7098) Fr & Eur.

— Dictionnaire pour les Travaux Publics, le Batiment et l'Equipement des Chantiers en Construction Vol. 2: French-English. (ENG & FRE.). 550p. 1985. 165.00 (*0-7859-7774-0*, 2212010869) Fr & Eur.

— Dictionnaire pour les Travaux Publics, le Batiment et l'Equipement des Chantiers en Construction Vol. 3: German-French. 3rd ed. (FRE & GER.). 878p. 1972. 350.00 (*0-7859-8627-8*, 221201080x) Fr & Eur.

— Dictionnaire pour les Travaux Publics, le Batiment et l'Equipement des Chantiers en Construction Vol. 4: French-German. 4th ed. (FRE & GER.). 912p. 1978. pap. 350.00 (*0-7859-7773-2*, 2212010818) Fr & Eur.

Bucksch, Herbert. Construction Materials Dictionary, English-German. (ENG & GER.). 600p. 1996. 295.00 (*0-7859-9521-8*) Fr & Eur.

— Construction Materials Dictionary, German-English. (ENG & GER.). 600p. 1996. 295.00 (*0-7859-9520-X*) Fr & Eur.

— Dictionary Geological Engineering: Worterbuch GoeTechnik. LC 95-14636. (ENG & GER.). 1995. 235.00 (*0-387-58164-2*) Spr-Verlag.

— Dictionary of Architecture, Building Construction & Materials, Vol. 1. 2nd ed. (ENG & GER.). 942p. 1980. 295.00 (*0-8288-0199-1*, M7131) Fr & Eur.

— Dictionary of Architecture, Building Construction & Materials, Vol. 2. 2nd ed. (ENG & GER.). 1137p. 1983. 295.00 (*0-8288-0198-3*, M7130) Fr & Eur.

— Dictionary of Building Service Engineering, German/English-English/German. (ENG & GER.). 400p. 1997. pap. 95.00 (*0-7859-9512-9*) Fr & Eur.

— Dictionary of Civil Engineering: Woerterbuch fuer Bautechnik und Baumaschinen. 5th rev. ed. (FRE & GER.). 875p. 1982. pap. 195.00 (*0-8288-4425-9*, M15075) Fr & Eur.

— Dictionary of Civil Engineering Vol. 1: Woerterbuch Fuer Bautechnik und Baumaschinen. 8th rev. ed. (ENG & GER.). 1982. 225.00 (*0-8288-0202-5*, M7121) Fr & Eur.

— Dictionary of Civil Engineering Vol. 2: Woerterbuch Fuer Bautechnik und Baumaschinen. 8th rev. ed. (ENG & GER.). 1219p. 1982. 225.00 (*0-8288-0203-3*, M7122) Fr & Eur.

— Dictionary of Civil Engineering & Construction Machinery & Equipment, Vol. 1. 5th ed. (ENG & FRE.). 420p. 1976. 125.00 (*0-8288-5629-X*, M4647) Fr & Eur.

— Dictionary of Civil Engineering & Construction Machinery & Equipment, Vol. 2. 5th ed. (ENG & FRE.). 548p. 1976. 150.00 (*0-8288-5630-3*, M6050) Fr & Eur.

— Dictionary of Construction Equipment & Building Material Machines Vol. 3: German - English. (ENG & GER.). 1100p. 1987. 350.00 (*0-8288-0200-9*, F23350) Fr & Eur.

— Dictionary of Construction Equipment & Building Material Machines Vol. 4: English - German. (ENG & GER.). 1100p. 1987. 350.00 (*0-8288-0201-7*, F23360) Fr & Eur.

— Dictionary of Construction Law, Land Law & Regional Policy, Vol. 1. (ENG & GER.). 1052p. 1986. 450.00 (*0-8288-0388-9*, F830) Fr & Eur.

— Dictionary of Construction Law, Land Law & Regional Policy, Vol. 2. (ENG & GER.). 1140p. 1986. 450.00 (*0-8288-0389-7*, M15056) Fr & Eur.

— Dictionary of Geological Engineering: English-German. (ENG & GER.). 1000p. 1995. 395.00 (*0-7859-9978-7*) Fr & Eur.

— Dictionary of Geological Engineering: German-English. (ENG & GER.). 1000p. 1995. 395.00 (*0-7859-9979-5*) Fr & Eur.

— Dictionary of Geotechnical Engineering, English-German. (ENG & GER.). 688p. 1997. 395.00 (*0-7859-9513-7*) Fr & Eur.

— Dictionary of Mechanisms: German-English, English-German. deluxe ed. (ENG & GER.). 286p. 1976. 195.00 (*0-8288-5633-8*, M7111) Fr & Eur.

— Dictionary of Wood & Woodworking Practice Vol. 1: Holz-Woerterbuch. 2nd ed. (ENG & GER.). 461p. 1986. 150.00 (*0-8288-0330-7*, M7465) Fr & Eur.

— Dictionary of Wood & Woodworking Practice Vol. 2: Holz-Woerterbuch. (ENG & GER.). 536p. 1986. 175.00 (*0-8288-0329-3*, M7466) Fr & Eur.

— Woerterbuch Architektur Hochbau Vol. 1: German-English. 2nd ed. (ENG & GER.). 942p. 1987. 295.00 (*0-7859-7445-8*, 3762525765) Fr & Eur.

Bucksch, Herbert & Altmeyer, A. P. Pipeline Dictionary. (ENG, FRE & GER.). 288p. 1969. 150.00 (*0-8288-6612-0*, M7588) Fr & Eur.

Bucksch, Herbert & Galan e Hildalgo, Arturo. Diccionario Frances-Espanol de la Construccion y Obras Publicas. (FRE & SPA.). 564p. 1975. 56.95 (*0-8288-5822-5*, S50133) Fr & Eur.

Buckschl, H. Worterbuch GeoTechnik Dictionary Vol. 1: Geological Engineering. (ENG & GER.). 1000p. 1996. 235.00 (*0-387-58163-4*) Spr-Verlag.

Buckser, Andrew S. Communities of Faith: Sectarianism, Identity & Social Change on a Danish Island. LC 96-25652. (New Directions in Anthropology Ser.: Vol. 5). (Illus.). 288p. 1996. 59.95 (*1-57181-042-0*) Berghahn Bks.

Buckstaff, Kathryn. No One Dies in Branson. 1995. mass mkt. 4.99 (*0-312-95425-5*, Pub. by Tor Bks) St Martin.

Buckton, jt. auth. see Fonda.

Buckton, Graham. Interfacial Phenomena in Drug Delivery & Targeting. (Drug Targeting & Delivery Ser.). 304p. 1995. text 105.00 (*3-7186-5633-7*, Harwood Acad Pubs) Gordon & Breach.

Buckton, Graham K., jt. ed. see Evans, David F.

***Buckton, Henry.** Artists & Authors at War. 1999. write for info. (*0-85052-676-0*) Pen & Sword Bks Ltd.

Buckton, Henry. By Royal Command: An Account of Their Service by Members of the Royal Command. LC 98-131862. (Illus.). 192p. 1998. 29.95 (*0-7206-1025-7*, Pub. by P Owen Ltd) Dufour.

Buckton, K. E. & Evans, Harold J. Methods for the Analysis of Human Chromosome Aberrations. 1973. pap. text 12.00 (*92-4-154031-1*, 1150105) World Health.

Buckton, Keith, jt. auth. see Fonda, Nikki.

Buckton, Oliver S. Secret Selves: Confession & Same-Sex Desire in Victorian Autobiography. LC 97-30007. 288p. 1998. pap. 18.95 (*0-8078-4702-X*); lib. bdg. 49.95 (*0-8078-2435-6*) U of NC Pr.

Buckton, R., jt. auth. see Danes, E.

Buckvar, Felice. Dangerous Dream. Kemnitz, Myrna, ed. LC 98-226282. 123p. (J). 1998. pap. 9.99 (*0-88092-277-X*, 277X) Royal Fireworks.

Buckwald, Aaron & Martin, Kenneth W. Integrated Fiber-Optic Receivers. LC 94-45250. (International Series in Engineering & Computer Science). 488p. (C). 1995. text 151.50 (*0-7923-9549-2*) Kluwer Academic.

Buckwald, Jed Z. The Creation of Scientific Effects: Heinrich Hertz & Electric Waves. LC 93-41783. 496p. 1994. pap. text 32.95 (*0-226-07888-4*); lib. bdg. 75.00 (*0-226-07887-6*) U Ch Pr.

Buckwalter & Chandler Staff. Avionics Marketing, Airline Edition. 200p. 1993. pap. 115.00 (*1-885544-04-9*) Avionics Comm.

Buckwalter, H. Douglas. The Character & Purpose of Luke's Christology. (Society for New Testament Studies Monographs: No. 89). 364p. (C). 1996. text 64.95 (*0-521-56180-9*) Cambridge U Pr.

Buckwalter, H. Douglas & Shoaff, Mary K. Guide to Reference Systems for the Works of Flavius Josephus, Vol. 3. (ETS Monograph Ser.). 1995. pap. text 8.00 (*0-932055-01-X*) Evang Theolog Soc.

Buckwalter, Jane R., ed. International Perspectives on Organized Crime. 136p. (Orig.). (C). 1990. pap. 12.95 (*0-942511-41-7*) OICJ.

***Buckwalter, Jeff T., contrib. by.** Frame Relay: Technology & Practice. LC 99-51438. 448p. 1999. 39.95 (*0-201-48524-9*) Addison-Wesley.

Buckwalter, Joseph A., et al, eds. Musculoskeletal Soft-Tissue Aging: Impact on Mobility. LC 93-41652. 423p. 1994. 105.00 (*0-89203-086-0*) Amer Acad Ortho Surg.

— Skeletal Growth & Development: Clinical Issues & Basic Science Advances. LC 98-26059. (Symposium Ser.). (Illus.). 668p. 1998. 85.00 (*0-89203-183-2*) Amer Acad Ortho Surg.

Buckwalter, Joseph A., jt. ed. see Weinstein, Stuart L.

Buckwalter, Joseph A., jt. ed. see Woo, Savio L-Y.

Buckwalter, Len & Helfrick, Albert. Avionics Test Equipment Handbook & Directory. (Illus.). 209p. 1997. pap. 95.00 (*1-885544-08-1*, TEHB-1) Avionics Comm.

Buckwalter, Leoda A. The Chief's Son. LC 89-84625. xvi, 136p. (Orig.). 1989. pap. 7.95 (*0-916035-32-8*) Evangel Indiana.

— Conquest & Glory: True Tales from the Land of the Taj. LC 92-74955. (Illus.). 171p. 1992. pap. 7.95 (*0-916035-56-5*) Evangel Indiana.

— A Hybrid in America. LC 98-72639. (Illus.). 160p. 1998. pap. 9.95 (*0-916035-86-7*) Evangel Indiana.

— Manorma. LC 91-71664. 176p. 1991. pap. 7.95 (*0-916035-46-8*) Evangel Indiana.

— The Road to Chumba. LC 94-71563. 187p. (YA). 1994. pap. 7.95 (*0-916035-60-3*) Evangel Indiana.

Buckwell, A., jt. auth. see Yu, Chen L.

***Bucky, Steven F., et al.** Comprehensive Textbook of Ethics & Law in the Practice of Psychology. LC 00-22848. (Issues in the Practice of Psychology Ser.). 2000. write for info. (*0-306-46236-2*, Kluwer Plenum) Kluwer Academic.

***Buclet, Nicolas & Godard, Olivier.** Municipal Waste Management in Europe: A Comparative Study in Building Regimes LC 99-36539. (Environment & Management Ser.). 1999. write for info. (*0-7923-5885-6*) Kluwer Academic.

Bucman, Lamond, jt. auth. see Rickard, Joan.

Bucqueroux, Bonnie, jt. auth. see Trojanowicz, Robert.

Bucsis, Gerry. Guide to Training Your Pet Ferret. LC 97-14721. 96p. 1997. pap. 8.95 (*0-7641-0093-9*) Barron.

Bucur, Ionel. Selected Topics in Algebra. LC 83-24609. 1984. text 248.50 (*90-277-1671-4*) Kluwer Academic.

***Bucur, Maria.** Philanthropy, Nationalism & the Growth of Civil Society in Romania. (Working Papers of the Johns Hopkins Comparative Nonprofit Sector Project: Vol. 31). (Illus.). 32p. 1998. pap. text 6.00 (*1-886333-36-X*) JH Univ Inst Pol Studies.

Bucur, Mike, jt. auth. see Molyneux, Lynn.

Bucur, Voichita. The Acoustics of Wood. 298p. 1995. boxed set 264.95 (*0-8493-4801-3*) CRC Pr.

Bucurescu, D., et al, eds. Nuclear Collective Dynamics: Proceedings of the 1982 International Summer School of Nuclear Physics, Poiana Brasov, Romania, Aug. 26-Sept. 7, 1983. 522p. 1983. 91.00 (*9971-950-69-3*); pap. 41.00 (*9971-950-73-1*) World Scientific Pub.

— Recent Advances in Nuclear Structure. 528p. (C). 1991. text 147.00 (*981-02-0533-3*) World Scientific Pub.

Bucuvalas, Michael J., jt. auth. see Weis, Carol H.

Bucuvalas, Tina, et al. South Florida Folklife. LC 93-29928. (Folklife in the South Ser.). (Illus.). 224p. 1994. pap. 16.95 (*0-87805-660-2*); text 37.50 (*0-87805-659-9*) U Pr of Miss.

Bucy, Bill, ed. see Gallagher, Jane.

Bucy, David E. The Guide to Cape Perpetua. (Illus.). 74p. 1987. pap. write for info. (*0-9617967-0-7*) NW Natureworks.

Bucy, Douglas R. Help Yourself! Problem Solving for the Disabled. LC 96-16206. 208p. 1996. pap. 14.95 (*0-02-861059-8*) Macmillan.

Bucy, Pamela H. White Collar Crime: Cases & Materials. (American Casebook Ser.). 688p. (C). 1992. pap. text 48.50 (*0-314-00658-3*) West Pub.

— White Collar Crime: Cases & Materials. 2nd ed. LC 98-184387. (Paralegal). xxvii, 1190 p. 1998. 63.25 (*0-314-21114-4*) West Pub.

— White Collar Crime, Cases & Materials: Teacher's Manual to Accompany. (American Casebook Ser.). 217p. (C). 1992. pap. text. write for info. (*0-314-01146-3*) West Pub.

— White Collar Crime, Cases & Materials: 1994 Supplement. (American Casebook Ser.). 127p. 1994. pap. text 10.00 (*0-314-04389-6*) West Pub.

Bucy, Richard S. Lectures on Discrete Time Filtering. LC 93-43310. (Signal Processing & Digital Filtering Ser.). (Illus.). 176p. 1994. 54.95 (*0-387-94198-3*) Spr-Verlag.

Bucy, Richard S. & Joseph, Peter D. Filtering for Stochastic Processes, with Applications to Guidance. 2nd rev. ed. LC 86-70881. xviii, 206p. 1987. text 19.95 (*0-8284-0326-0*) Chelsea Pub.

Bucy, Richard S. & Moura, Jose M., eds. Nonlinear Stochastic Problems. 1983. text 257.50 (*90-277-1590-4*) Kluwer Academic.

***Buczacki, Stefan.** Beginner's Guide to Gardening. (Illus.). 2000. pap. 19.95 (*1-84091-153-0*) Conran Octopus.

Buczacki, Stefan. The Garden Book: Gardening & More. LC 96-44735. (Illus.). 256p. 1996. 24.98 (*1-57145-112-9*, Thunder Bay) Advantage Pubs.

***Buczacki, Stefan.** Gardening Dictionary: Garden Techniques, Guide to Cultivation & Planting, Comprehensive Glossary. (Illus.). 256p. 2000. pap. 24.95 (*0-600-60065-3*) Hamlyn Publishing Group Ltd.

— Stefan Buczacki's Gardening Dictionary: Gardening Techniques, Guide to Cultivation & Planting, Comprehensive Glossary. (Illus.). 256p. 1999. 39.95 (*0-600-59377-0*, Pub. by P HM) Trafalgar.

— Stefan Buczacki's Plant Dictionary: A-Z of 6,000 Plant Types - A-Z of 1,000 Common Names - A-Z of Plant Families. (Illus.). 2000. pap. 19.95 (*0-600-60066-1*, Pub. by Hamlyn Publishing Group Ltd) Sterling.

***Buczacki, Stefan & Harris, Keith.** Collins Photoguide Pests, Diseases & Disorders of Garden Plants. (Illus.). 512p. 1998. 35.00 (*0-00-220063-5*, Pub. by HarpC) Trafalgar.

Buczacki, Stefan T. A Garden for All Seasons. (Illus.). 160p. 1992. 24.95 (*1-55859-411-6*) Abbeville Pr.

— Stefan Buczacki's Plant Dictionary: A-Z of 6,000 Plant Types - A-Z of 1,000 Common Names - A-Z of Plan Families. (Illus.). 320p. 1999. 39.95 (*0-600-59378-9*, Pub. by Hamlyn Publishing Group Ltd) Sterling.

Buczacki, Stefan T., jt. auth. see National Gardening Association Staff.

Buczacki, Stefan T., jt. auth. see Wilkinson, J.

Buczala, George S. & Cassady, Michael J., eds. Buried Plastic Pipe Technology, STP 1093. LC 90-14395. (Special Technical Publication Ser.). (Illus.). 419p. 1990. text 55.00 (*0-8031-1395-1*, STP1093) ASTM.

***Buczek, Greg.** ASP Developer's Guide. LC 99-57026. (Application Development Reference Ser.). (Illus.). 2000. pap. 49.99 (*0-07-212294-3*) McGrw-H Intl.

— Instant ASP Components. 2000. 49.99 (*0-07-212552-7*) Osborne-McGraw.

Buczkowska, Iwona. Iwona Buczkowska: Breathing Spaces, 1. 1999. pap. text 25.00 (*88-7838-047-4*) L'Arca IT.

Buczkowske, Leo. Understanding Algebraic Concepts & Conics. (Illus.). 63p. 1992. pap. 14.99 (*0-88092-015-7*, 0157, Kav Bks) Royal Fireworks.

— Unique Approaches to Problem Solving. (Illus.). 81p. 1994. pap. 14.99 (*0-88092-084-X*, 084X, Kav Bks) Royal Fireworks.

Bud-Frierman, Lisa, ed. Information Acumen: The Understanding & Use of Knowledge in Modern Business. LC 93-10558. (Comparative & International Business: Modern Histories Ser.). 240p. (C). 1994. pap. 77.95 (*0-415-07788-5*) Thomson Learn.

Bud, Peggy. The Path to Popularity Through Friends & Self-Confidence. 1986. pap. 9.99 (*0-89824-147-2*) Trillium Pr.

***Bud, Robert, et al, eds.** Manifesting Medicine: Bodies & Machines. 174p. 1999. text 46.00 (*90-5702-408-X*, Harwood Acad Pubs); pap. text 24.00 (*90-5702-430-6*, Harwood Acad Pubs) Gordon & Breach.

***Bud, Robert & Gummett, Phillip, eds.** Cold War, Hot Science: Applied Research in Britain's Defence Laboratories 1945-1990. (Studies in the History of Science, Technology & Medicine Ser.: Vol. 7). 444p. 1999. text 68.00 (*90-5702-481-0*, Harwood Acad Pubs) Gordon & Breach.

Bud, Robert, ed. see Smithsonian Institution Staff & NMSI Trading Ltd. Staff.

Bud, Robert F. & Cozzens, Susan, eds. Invisible Connections: Instruments, Institutions, & Science. (Institute Ser.: Vol. IS09). 380p. 1992. 30.00 (*0-8194-0767-4*); pap. 30.00 (*0-8194-0768-2*) SPIE.

Bud, Robert F., et al. Chemistry in America, Eighteen Seventy-Six to Nineteen Seventy-Six. 1985. lib. bdg. 206.50 (*90-277-1720-6*) Kluwer Academic.

Buda, Andrew J. & Delp, Edward J., eds. Digital Cardiac Imaging. 1985. text 208.00 (*0-89838-697-7*) Kluwer Academic.

Buda, Francis B. Holistic Sleep: Beating Insomnia with Commonsense, Medical, & New Age Techniques. LC 99-18417. (Illus.). 256p. 1999. pap. 14.95 (*0-8065-2105-8*, Citadel Pr) Carol Pub Group.

Buda, M. Medieval History & Discourse: Toward a Topography of Textuality. LC 89-13309. (American University Studies: Comparative Literature: Ser. III, Vol. 28). 123p. (C). 1991. text 27.95 (*0-8204-1130-2*) P Lang Pubng.

Buda, Michael, ed. see Kuhl, Raymond G.

Budach, L., et al, eds. Fundamentals of Computation Theory. (Lecture Notes in Computer Science Ser.: Vol. 278). 505p. 1987. 44.00 (*0-387-18740-5*) Spr-Verlag.

— Fundamentals of Computation Theory: 8th International Conference, FCT '91 Gosen, Germany, September 9-13, 1991 Proceedings. (Lecture Notes in Computer Science Ser.: Vol. 529). xii, 426p. 1991. 44.95 (*0-387-54458-5*) Spr-Verlag.

Budahn, P. J. Careers: The Military Guide. LC 95-78663. 128p. 1995. pap. 16.95 (*0-9647942-0-9*) Army Times Pubng.

— Military Money Guide. 144p. 1996. pap. 10.95 (*0-8117-2557-X*) Stackpole.

— Reservist's Money Guide. LC 97-22437. 232p. 1997. pap. 11.95 (*0-8117-2917-6*) Stackpole.

— Veteran's Guide to Benefits. 272p. 1994. pap. 13.95 (*0-8117-2596-0*) Stackpole.

— Veteran's Guide to Benefits. 2nd ed. LC 97-17038. (Illus.). 272p. 1997. pap. 14.95 (*0-8117-2975-3*) Stackpole.

***Budahn, P. J.** What to Expect in the Military: A Practical Guide for Young People, Parents & Counselors. LC 00-25678. 222p. 2000. 40.00 (*0-313-31003-3*, GR1003, Greenwood Pr) Greenwood.

Budak, Ali C. Making Foreign People Pay. LC 98-16967. (Studies in Modern Law & Policy: Vol. 5). (Illus.). 8p. 1998. text 74.95 (*1-84014-436-X*, K1370.B83, Pub. by Ashgate Pub) Ashgate Pub Co.

Budak, Ali C., jt. auth. see Gessner, Volkmar.

Budak, Ali C., jt. ed. see Gessner, Volkmar.

Budak, Aram. Passive & Active Network Analysis & Synthesis. (Illus.). 733p. (C). 1991. reprint ed. text 56.95 (*0-88133-625-4*) Waveland Pr.

Budak, B. M. Collection of Problems in Math. 770p. 1988. pap. 19.95 (*0-486-65806-6*) Dover.

Budak, Michael K. Grand Mound. LC 94-45633. (Minnesota Historic Sites Pamphlet Ser.: No. 23). (Illus.). 32p. 1995. pap. 7.50 (*0-87351-308-8*) Minn Hist.

***Budak, Susan Weiss.** Guide to Nonprofit Contributions. LC 99-174152. 1998. write for info. (*0-7646-0489-9*) Prctnrs Pub Co.

***Budak, Susan Weiss & Practitioners Publishing Company Staff.** Guide to Nonprofit Expenses LC 99-177294. 1998. write for info. (*0-7646-0475-9*) Prctnrs Pub Co.

Budano, Rob & Kerr, Richard. Tomy AF-X. Kevin, Timothy, ed. (Collector's Quick Reference Ser.: Vol. 4). 100p. (Orig.). pap. text 14.95 (*0-88379-608-2*) What It Is.

Budano, Robert. The Complete Guide to Collecting Tomy HO Scale Slot Cars, Vol. 1. (Illus.). 100p. 1997. pap. 19.95 (*0-9660174-0-4*) Buds HO.

Budapest, Z. Summoning the Fates: A Woman's Guide to Destiny. 256p. 1999. pap. 12.00 (*0-609-80277-1*) Harmony Bks.

Budapest, Zsuzsanna E. The Goddess in the Bedroom: A Passionate Woman's Guide to Celebrating Sexuality Every Night of the Week. LC 94-38248. 176p. 1995. pap. 13.00 (*0-06-251186-6*, Pub. by Harper SF) HarpC.

— The Goddess in the Office: A Personal Energy Guide for the Spiritual Warrior At Work. LC 91-58920. 160p. 1993. 13.00 (*0-06-250087-2*, Pub. by Harper SF) HarpC.

— Grandmother Moon: Lunar Magic in Our Lives - Spells, Rituals, Goddesses, Legends, & Emotions under the Moon. LC 90-56443. (Illus.). 304p. (Orig.). 1991. pap. 19.00 (*0-06-250114-3*, Pub. by Harper SF) HarpC.

— The Grandmother of Time: A Women's Book of Celebrations, Spells, & Sacred Objects for Every Month of the Year. 288p. 1989. pap. 18.00 (*0-06-250109-7*, Pub. by Harper SF) HarpC.

— The Holy Book of Women's Mysteries. 332p. (Orig.). 1989. pap. 17.95 (*0-914728-67-9*) Wingbow Pr.

Budar, Valjeanne, ed. Ke Ahiahi Mamua O Kalikimaka Vol. II: 'Twas the Night Before Christmas in Hawaii. Roy, Lynette A., tr. LC 94-77954. (Illus.). 48p. (J). (gr. k-6). 1994. 12.95 (*1-880188-92-9*) Bess Pr.

Budaragin, Vladimir, jt. auth. see Smith, Abby.

Budarjowa, Ludmila. Woerterbuch Obersorbisch-Deutsch. 319p. 1990. 24.95 (*0-7859-8451-8*, 374200419) Fr & Eur.

Budavari, Susan, et al, eds. The Merck Index: An Encyclopedia of Drugs, Chemicals & Biologicals. 12th ed. LC 96-171642. (Illus.). 2500p. 1996. ring bd. 45.00 (*0-911910-12-3*) Merck.

Budavari, Susan, et al. The Merck Index: An Encyclopedia of Drugs, Chemicals, & Biologicals, Windows. 1996. 280.00 incl. cd-rom (*0-412-75990-X*) Chapman & Hall.

Buday. The Art of Computer Animation. (CAD/CAM Ser.). 1997. teacher ed. 15.00 (*0-8273-7345-7*) Delmar.

— Art of Computer Animation Video. (ID - CAD/CAM Ser.). 1997. 24.95 (*0-8273-7346-5*) Delmar.

Buday, George. The History of the Christmas Card LC 89-49428. (Illus.). 304p. 1992. reprint ed. lib. bdg. 42.00 (*1-55888-909-4*) Omnigraphics Inc.

Buday, Grant. Golden Goa. 200p. Date not set. pap. 17.95 (*1-55022-412-3*, Pub. by ECW) LPC InBook.

Buday, Grant. Under Glass. 144p. 1994. pap. text 10.95 (*0-88982-134-8*, Pub. by Oolichan Bks) Genl Dist Srvs.

— The Venetian. 1987. pap. text 8.95 (*0-88982-075-9*, Pub. by Oolichan Bks) Genl Dist Srvs.

Buday, Tibor, jt. ed. see Mahel, Michal.

Budberg, Moura, tr. see Gorki, Maxim.

Budberg, Moura, tr. see Simenon, Georges.

Budbill, David. Bones on Black Spruce Mountain. (J). 1994. 9.09 (*0-606-05762-5*, Pub. by Turtleback) Demco.

— Judevine. 5th rev. ed. LC 98-53059. 320p. 1999. pap. 17.95 (*1-890132-22-5*) Chelsea Green Pub.

— Moment to Moment: Poems of a Mountain Recluse. 132p. 1999. pap. 14.00 (*1-55659-133-0*, Pub. by Copper Canyon) Consort Bk Sales.

— Why I Came to Judevine. 70p. 1987. 7.00 (*0-934834-14-8*) White Pine.

Budbill, David, ed. see Robinson, Rowland E.

Budd. Data Structure in C++ Using STL World Student Series Version. 2nd ed. (C). 1998. pap. text. write for info. (*0-201-19838-X*) Addison-Wesley.

Budd, Alan. The Politics of Economic Planning LC 78-324079. (Political Issues of Modern Britain Ser.). 172p. 1978. write for info. (*0-7190-0708-9*) Manchester Univ Pr.

Budd, Alan, et al, eds. Unemployment & the Economists. LC 96-4213. (Illus.). 176p. (C). 1996. text 85.00 (*1-85898-351-7*) E Elgar.

Budd, Ann F. Bulletins of American Paleontology Vol. 101: Neogene Paleontology in the Northern Dominican Republic: 11. The Family Faviidae (Anthozoa: Scleractinia), Vol. 338, Pt. 1. 83p. 1991. 45.00 (*0-87710-422-0*) Paleo Res.

Budd, Bob. Send Fresh Horses. (Illus.). 128p. 1987. 12.95 (*0-943255-00-7*); pap. 8.95 (*0-943255-01-5*) Portfolio Pub.

— A Wide Spot in the Road. (Illus.). 280p. 1990. 14.95 (*0-943255-28-7*); pap. 9.95 (*0-943255-29-5*) Saratoga Pub.

Budd, Dale & Wilson, Randall. Melbourne's Marvellous Trams. (Illus.). 96p. 1997. pap. 29.95 (*0-86840-504-3*, Pub. by New South Wales Univ Pr) Intl Spec Bk.

Budd, David A., et al, eds. Unconformities & Porosity in Carbonate Strata. (AAPG Memoir Ser.: No. 63). (Illus.). xii, 313p. 1995. 119.00 (*0-89181-342-X*, 558) AAPG.

Budd, David A. & Harris, Paul M., compiled by. Carbonate-Siliciclastic Mixtures: Selected Papers Reprinted from Journal of Sedimentary Petrology, Geology, AAPG Bulletin, Sedimentary Geology, GSA Bulletin, the Persian Gulf. LC QE0471.15.C3. (SEPM Reprint Ser.: No. 14). (Illus.). 280p. reprint ed. pap. 86.80 (*0-608-04108-4*, 206484000011) Bks Demand.

Budd, Declan & Hinds, Ross. The Hist: And Edmund Burke's Club. LC 97-225148. 436p. 1997. 59.95 (*1-901866-00-9*); 199.95 (*1-901866-01-7*) Dufour.

Budd, Dona, et al. Thoughts from Walden Pond: By Henry David Thoreau. LC 97-44955. (Illus.). 96p. 1998. pap. 19.98 (*0-7649-0617-8*) Pomegranate Calif.

Budd, E. M. A Seal upon My Heart. LC 95-79070. 485p. 1996. pap. 12.95 (*1-885487-18-5*) Brownell & Carroll.

***Budd, E. S.** Fire Engines. LC 99-28598. (Illus.). 24p. (J). 1999. lib. bdg. 19.93 (*1-56766-656-6*) Childs World.

— Street Cleaners. LC 99-89471. (Illus.). (J). 2000. lib. bdg. write for info. (*1-56766-757-0*) Childs World.

Budd, Edward C., ed. Inequality & Poverty. (Problems of Modern Economy Ser.). 217p. (C). 1967. pap. text 4.95 (*0-393-09502-9*) Norton.

Budd, Elaine R., ed. see Budd, John F., Jr.

***Budd, Elizabeth.** Glad. LC 99-28177. (Thoughts & Feelings Ser.). (Illus.). 32p. (J). (ps-1). 1999. lib. bdg. 12.95 (*1-56766-669-8*) Childs World.

Budd, Eric M. Scottish Tartan Weddings: A Practical Guidebook. (Illus.). 180p. 1999. 22.50 (*0-7818-0754-9*) Hippocrene Bks.

Budd, Graham. Racing Art & Memorabilia: A Celebration of the Turf. (Illus.). 192p. 1997. 65.00 (*0-85667-485-0*, Pub. by P Wilson) Antique Collect.

***Budd, Graham.** Soccer Memorabilia. (Illus.). 128p. 2000. boxed set 29.95 (*0-85667-504-0*, Pub. by P Wilson) Antique Collect.

Budd, Hahotta M. Pali-English Dictionary. (ENG & PLI.). 43.95 (*0-87557-056-9*) Saphrograph.

Budd, J. Appreciating Fine Wines. 160p. 1996. 15.98 (*0-7858-0709-8*) Bk Sales Inc.

***Budd, Jackie.** A-Z of Horse Behavior & Training. (Illus.). 256p. 2000. 24.95 (*0-7645-6111-1*) IDG Bks.

Budd, Jackie. The Best Book of Ponies. LC 98-40276. 32p. (gr. k-3). 1999. teacher ed. 12.95 (*0-7534-5172-7*) LKC.

Budd, Jackie. The Complete Guides to Horses & Ponies, 6 bks. Incl. Horse & Pony Breeds. LC 97-31767. (Illus.). 64p. (J). (gr. 4 up). 1998. lib. bdg. 25.27 (*0-8368-2046-0*); Horse & Pony Care. LC 97-35496. (Illus.). 64p. (J). (gr. 4 up). 1998. lib. bdg. 25.27 (*0-8368-2047-9*); Horse & Pony Jumping. LC 99-20468. (Illus.). 64p. (J). (gr. 4 up). 1999. lib. bdg. 25.27 (*0-8368-2446-6*); Horse & Pony Tack. LC 99-20472. (Illus.). 64p. (J). (gr. 4 up). 1999. lib. bdg. 25.27 (*0-8368-2447-4*); Learning to Ride Horses & Ponies. LC 97-31772. (Illus.). 64p. (J). (gr. 4 up). 1998. lib. bdg. 25.27 (*0-8368-2045-2*); Understanding Horses & Ponies. LC 99-20471. (Illus.). 64p. (J). (gr. 4 up). 1999. lib. bdg. 25.27 (*0-8368-2448-2*); (Illus.). (J). Set lib. bdg. 151.60 (*0-8368-2470-9*) Gareth Stevens Inc.

— The Complete Guides to Horses & Ponies: Incl. Horse & Pony Jumping; Horse & Pony Tack; Understanding Horses & Ponies, 3 bks. (Illus.). (J). (gr. 4 up). 2000. lib. bdg. 75.80 (*0-8368-2445-8*) Gareth Stevens Inc.

Budd, Jackie. Horses: History, Behavior, Breeds, Riding, Jumping. LC 94-46478. (Illus.). 64p. (J). (gr. 2-6). 1995. 16.95 (*1-85697-566-5*) LKC.

— Reading the Horse's Mind. 1996. 25.95 (*0-87605-744-X*) Howell Bks.

Budd, James L., jt. auth. see Mick, Martin D.

Budd, John F., Jr. CEO Credibility: The Management of Reputation. Budd, Elaine R., ed. (Illus.). 80p. (Orig.). 1993. pap. 10.00 (*0-9633947-1-1*) Turtle Pub.

— How to Get along with the Press...& Why: A Street Savvy Guide for Legislators. (Orig.). 1995. pap. write for info. (*0-9633947-2-X*) Turtle Pub.

— Street Smart Public Relations: A Top Pro Tells How to Get Things Done. 218p. 1992. pap. 19.95 (*0-9633947-0-3*) Turtle Pub.

Budd, John M. The Academic Library: Its Context, Its Purposes & Its Operation. LC 97-35962. (Library & Information Science Text Ser.). 372p. 1998. 65.00 (*1-56308-614-X*); pap. 45.00 (*1-56308-457-0*) Libs Unl.

— The Library & Its Users: The Communication Process, 71. LC 91-42732. (Contributions in Librarianship & Information Science Ser.: No. 71). 216p. 1992. 57.95 (*0-313-28153-X*, BLX/, Greenwood Pr) Greenwood.

Budd, John M., compiled by. Eight Scandinavian Novelists: Criticism & Reviews in English. LC 80-24895. 180p. 1981. lib. bdg. 99.50 (*0-313-22869-8*, BSN/, Greenwood Pr) Greenwood.

— Henry James: A Bibliography of Criticism, 1975-1981. LC 82-24163. 190p. 1983. lib. bdg. 55.00 (*0-313-23515-5*, BHJ/, Greenwood Pr) Greenwood.

Budd, Karen S., jt. auth. see Kedesdy, Jurgen H.

Budd, Keith, jt. ed. see Simpson, Karen.

Budd, Ken, ed. Community Associations & the Environment. LC 93-16916. (Illus.). (Orig.). (C). 1993. pap. 5.99 (*0-941301-21-4*) CAI.

Budd, Kenneth. Be Reasonable! How Community Associations Can Enforce Rules Without Antagonizing Residents, Going to Court or Starting World War III. LC 97-48826. 72p. (C). 1998. pap. 14.95 (*0-941301-40-0*, 4084) CAI.

Budd, Larry, jt. auth. see Griffith, Fred.

Budd, Leonard H. New Creations in the Neighborhood LC 98-192230. 65 p. 1998. write for info. (*0-7880-0972-9*, Fairway Pr) CSS OH.

— The Spirit's Tether: Sermon for Pentecost Gospel, Cycle B. LC 93-2757. 1993. pap. 9.75 (*1-55673-608-8*, 9333) CSS OH.

Budd, Leonard H. & Talbott, Roger G. Resurrection Promises. Sherer, Michael L., ed. LC 86-28314. (Orig.). 1987. pap. 7.95 (*0-89536-850-1*, 7809) CSS OH.

Budd, Leonard H., et al. Homiletic Meditations, Cycle B, Vol. 3: Pentecost Through the Feast of Christ the King, Gospel Texts. LC 93-44100. 1994. pap. 19.95 (*1-55673-639-8*) CSS OH.

Budd, Leslie & Whimster, Sam. Global Finance & Urban Living. (International Library of Sociology Ser.). (Illus.). 272p. (C). 1992. pap. 27.99 (*0-415-03198-2*, A5924) Routledge.

Budd, Lillian. Land of Strangers. 1993. reprint ed. lib. bdg. 21.95 (*1-56849-165-4*) Buccaneer Bks.

Budd, Linda S. Living with the Active Alert Child: Groundbreaking Strategies for Parents. rev. ed. LC 93-83146. 272p. 1993. reprint ed. pap. 12.95 (*0-943990-88-2*) Parenting Pr.

Budd, Louis J. Critical Essays on Mark Twain, 1910-1980. (Critical Essays on American Literature Ser.). 256p. 1983. 49.00 (*0-8161-8652-9*, G K Hall & Co) Mac Lib Ref.

— Mark Twain: The Ecstasy of Humor. (Quarry Farm Papers: Vol. 6). 28p. 1995. pap. 5.00 (*1-880817-08-X*) EC Ctr Mark T Stu.

***Budd, Louis J., ed.** Mark Twain: The Contemporary Reviews. LC 98-38097. (American Critical Archives Ser.: No. 11). 850p. (C). 1999. 125.00 (*0-521-39024-9*) Cambridge U Pr.

Budd, Louis J. & Cady, Edwin, eds. On Whitman: The Best from American Literature. LC 87-8997. x, 298p. 1987. text 49.95 (*0-8223-0752-9*) Duke.

Budd, Louis J. & Cady, Edwin H., eds. On Faulkner: The Best from American Literature. LC 89-30913. 288p. (C). 1989. text 49.95 (*0-8223-0960-2*) Duke.

— On Henry James: The Best from American Literature. LC 90-37352. 328p. (C). 1990. text 49.95 (*0-8223-1064-3*) Duke.

— On Humor: The Best from American Literature. LC 91-4113. 288p. 1992. text 49.95 (*0-8223-1173-9*) Duke.

— On Melville. LC 88-18897. (Best from American Literature Ser.). x, 300p. (C). 1988. text 49.95 (*0-8223-0867-3*) Duke.

— On Poe. LC 92-28839. (Best from American Literature Ser.). 288p. 1993. text 49.95 (*0-8223-1311-1*) Duke.

Budd, Louis J., jt. ed. see Cady, Edwin H.

Budd, Louis J., ed. see Twain, Mark, pseud.

B

B

Budd, M. A. Low Blood Sugar. 224p. 1998. pap. 11.00 (*0-7225-3119-2*, 902624Q) Thorsons PA.

— Migraine. 1998. mass mkt. 7.00 (*0-7225-3326-8*, 902696Q) Thorsons PA.

Budd, Malcolm. Music & the Emotions: The Philosophical Theories. (International Library of Philosophy). 224p. 1985. 29.95 (*0-7102-0520-1*, Routledge Thoemms) Routledge.

— Music & the Emotions: The Philosophical Theories. (International Library of Philosophy). 224p. (C). 1992. pap. 25.99 (*0-415-08779-1*, A9610) Routledge.

Budd, Marjorie L., et al. Getting Results Through Learning. (Illus.). 63p. (C). 1998. pap. text 25.00 (*0-7881-4880-X*) DIANE Pub.

***Budd, Martin.** Why Am I So Tired? Is Your Thyroid Making You Ill? 2000. pap. 15.00 (*0-7225-3942-8*, Pub. by Thorsons PA) HarpC.

Budd, Martin L. Low Blood Sugar (Hypoglysemia) The Twentieth Century Epidemic? LC 83-5053. 128 sp. (Orig.). 1983. pap. 9.95 (*0-8069-7792-2*) Sterling.

Budd, Matthew & Rothstein, Larry. You Are What You Say: The Six-Week Proven Program That Teaches You How to Use the Power of Language to Conquer Emotional & Physical Stress. LC 99-56084. 288p. 2000. 24.00 (*0-8129-2961-6*, Times Bks) Crown Pub Group.

Budd, Mavis. Fit for a Duchess. large type ed. 1989. 12.00 (*0-685-29766-7*) Ulverscroft.

***Budd, Michael.** Digital Media Illustrator Training Course. 2000. pap. text 89.99 (*0-13-021912-6*) P-H.

Budd, Michael A. The Sculpture Machine. 218p. (C). 1997. pap. text 19.00 (*0-8147-1267-3*) NYU Pr.

— The Sculpture Machine: Physical Culture & Body Politics in the Age of Empire. (Illus.). 218p. (C). 1997. text 45.00 (*0-8147-1266-5*) NYU Pr.

Budd, Mike, et al. Consuming Environments: Television & Commercial Culture. LC 98-22954. (Communications, Media, & Culture Ser.). (Illus.). 280p. (C). 1999. 50.00 (*0-8135-2591-8*); pap. 22.00 (*0-8135-2592-6*) Rutgers U Pr.

Budd, Nicholas. Credit Enhancement in International Trade Transactions. 572p. 1992. 115.00 (*1-85044-457-9*) LLP.

Budd, Paul, et al, eds. Archaeological Sciences 1989. (Illus.). 408p. 1991. pap. 65.00 (*0-946897-29-8*, Pub. by Oxbow Bks) David Brown.

Budd, Philip J. Leviticus. (New Century Bible Ser.). 395p. 1996. pap. 19.95 (*0-551-02834-3*, Pub. by Sheffield Acad) CUP Services.

Budd, Philip J. Numbers. (Biblical Commentary Ser.: Vol. 5). 29.99 (*0-8499-0204-5*) Word Pub.

Budd, R., et al, eds. European Dimension in Pre- & In-Service Language: The Teacher Development. 1994. pap. 17.95 (*1-85359-242-0*, Pub. by Multilingual Matters) Taylor & Francis.

Budd, Richard W. & Ruben, Brent D., eds. Beyond Media: New Approaches to Mass Communication. rev. ed. 320p. (C). 1988. pap. 21.95 (*0-88738-698-9*) Transaction Pubs.

Budd, Richard W., jt. ed. see Ruben, Brent D.

Budd, Rosemary. Journey of Prayer. 1990. pap. 8.95 (*0-687-60588-1*) Abingdon.

Budd, Stanley, jt. auth. see McCarthy, Elmarie.

Budd, Susan, jt. auth. see Sharma, Ursala.

Budd, T. H., jt. ed. see Carlson, J. E.

Budd, Thomas, jt. auth. see Brock, Claude L.

***Budd, Timothy.** C++ for Java Programmers. LC 99-77280. (Illus.). 290p. (C). 1999. pap. 35.66 (*0-201-61246-1*) Addison-Wesley.

Budd, Timothy. Data Structures in C++ Using Standard Template Library. LC 97-8477. 576p. (C). 1997. 76.00 (*0-201-30879-7*); text. write for info. (*0-201-31659-5*) Addison-Wesley.

***Budd, Timothy.** Data Structures in Java: A Visual & Explorational Approach. LC 00-22798. 2000. write for info. (*0-201-70002-6*) Addison-Wesley.

Budd, Timothy. Introduccion a la Programacion a Objects. (SPA.). 432p. (C). 1993. pap. text 24.00 (*0-201-60103-6*) Addison-Wesley.

***Budd, Timothy.** Understanding Object-Oriented Programming with Java. 2nd ed. LC 99-32136. 420p. (C). 1999. pap. text 63.00 (*0-201-61273-9*) Addison-Wesley.

Budd, Timothy A. An APL Compiler. (Illus.). 170p. 1988. pap. 31.00 (*0-387-96643-9*) Spr-Verlag.

— An Introduction to Object Oriented Programming. 2nd ed. LC 96-23738. 432p. (C). 1996. 57.00 (*0-201-82419-1*) Addison-Wesley.

— Multiparadigm Programming in LEDA. (Illus.). 480p. (C). 1994. 47.81 (*0-201-82080-3*) Addison-Wesley.

Budd, Virginia. Fathers. large type ed. (General Ser.). 496p. 1993. 27.99 (*0-7089-2817-X*) Ulverscroft.

Budd, Warren, jt. auth. see Ames, Lee J.

Budd, William. Typhoid Fever: Its Nature, Mode of Spreading & Prevention. Rosenkrantz, Barbara G., ed. LC 76-25656. (Public Health in America Ser.). (Illus.). 1977. reprint ed. lib. bdg. 21.95 (*0-405-09809-X*) Ayer.

Budd, William C. Behavior Modification: The Scientific Way to Self Control. LC 73-79774. 1973. 10.95 (*0-87212-027-9*) Libra.

Budde, Barbara, jt. ed. see Baker, J. Robert.

Budde, James F. Measuring Performance in Human Service Systems: Planning, Organization, & Control. LC 79-19551. 221p. reprint ed. pap. 63.00 (*0-608-12832-5*, 2023557) Bks Demand.

***Budde, Michael.** Magic Kingdom of God: Christianity & Global Culture Industries. 192p. 1998. pap. text 22.00 (*0-8133-3076-9*, Pub. by Westview) HarpC.

Budde, Michael L. The Two Churches: Catholicism & Capitalism in the World System. LC 91-42023. 182p. 1992. text 37.95 (*0-8223-1229-8*) Duke.

***Budde, Michael L. & Brimlow, Robert W., eds.** The Church as Counterculture. LC 99-43439. (C). 2000. text 59.50 (*0-7914-4607-7*) State U NY Pr.

— The Church As Counterculture. LC 99-43439. 2000. pap. 19.95 (*0-7914-4608-5*) State U NY Pr.

Budde, Monika. Theoretical Linguistics & Grammatical Description: Papers in Honour of Hans-Heinrich Lieb. Sackmann, Robin, ed. LC 96-27962. (Current Issues in Linguistics Theory Ser.: No. 138). x, 375p. 1996. lib. bdg. 79.00 (*1-55619-593-1*) J Benjamins Pubng Co.

Budde, R., et al. Prototyping: An Approach to Evolutionary System Development. (Illus.). xi, 205p. 1992. 58.95 (*0-387-54352-X*) Spr-Verlag.

Budde, Rainer, intro. Wallraf-Richartz Museum, Cologne. (Illus.). 128p. 1991. 30.00 (*1-870248-76-7*) Scala Books.

Budde, Ray. Strengthen School-Based Management by Chartering All Schools. 130p. (Orig.). (C). 1995. pap. text. write for info. (*1-878234-09-9*) Reg Lab Educ IOT NE Isls.

Budde, Robert. Catch As Catch. 126p. 1997. pap. 7.95 (*0-88801-185-7*, Pub. by Turnstone Pr) Genl Dist Srvs.

— Misshapen. LC 98-136744. 216p. 1997. pap. 13.95 (*1-896300-22-7*) NeWest Pubs.

***Budde, William L.** Analytical Mass Spectrometry: Strategies for Environmental & Related Applications. LC 00-36186. 2000. write for info. (*0-8412-3664-X*) Am Chemical.

Buddecke, Eckhart. Pathobiochemie: Ein Lehrbuch fur Studierende und Aerzte. 2nd ed. (Illus.). 477p. 1983. 52.30 (*3-11-009658-7*) De Gruyter.

Buddemeyer-Porter, Mary. Will I See Fido in Heaven? Scripturally Revealing God's Eternal Plan for His Lesser Creatures. 107p. 1995. mass mkt. 6.95 (*1-56043-553-4*) Eden Pubns Inc.

***Buddemeyer-Porter, Mary.** Will I See My Pet (Fido) in Heaven? Scripturally Revealing God's Eternal Plan for His Lesser Creatures, Set. 1998. pap. 17.95 incl. audio Eden Pubns.

***Budden, Albert.** Psychic Close Encounters. (UFO Files Ser.). 2000. pap. 9.95 (*0-7137-2799-3*) Blandford Pr.

Budden, Albert. UFOs Psychic Close Encounters: The Electromagnetic Indictment. (Illus.). 264p. 1995. pap. 12.95 (*0-7137-2421-8*, Pub. by Blandford Pr) Sterling.

Budden, Henry. Bulbous Flowers. (Illus.). 1980. 15.95 (*0-19-558055-9*) OUP.

***Budden, John.** The Boss. 1999. text 35.00 (*1-84018-090-0*, Pub. by Mainstream Pubng) Trafalgar.

Budden, Julian. The Operas of Verdi: From Oberto to Rigoletto, Vol. 1. 2nd rev. ed. (Illus.). 538p. 1992. pap. 22.50 (*0-19-816261-8*) OUP.

— The Operas of Verdi Vol. 2: From Il Trovatore to La Forza del Destino, Vol. 2. 2nd rev. ed. (Illus.). 542p. 1992. pap. 22.50 (*0-19-816262-6*) OUP.

***Budden, Julian.** Verdi. (Illus.). 404p. 2000. reprint ed. 30.00 (*0-7881-9325-2*) DIANE Pub.

Budden, K. G. Lectures on Magnetoionic Theory. (Documents on Modern Physics Ser.). xiv, 82p. 1964. text 176.00 (*0-677-00100-2*) Gordon & Breach.

— Radio Waves in the Ionosphere: The Mathematical Theory of the Reflection of Radio Waves from Stratified Ionized Layers. 566p. reprint ed. pap. 161.40 (*0-608-13257-8*, 2055781) Bks Demand.

Budden, Mary & Baize, Nancy. Unwrapping Little Gifts: Making the Gospel Come Alive for Children. LC 94-32839. (Healing Presence Ser.). 216p. 1994. pap., teacher ed. 19.95 (*0-89390-290-X*) Resource Pubns.

Budden, Michael C. Protecting Trade Secrets under the Uniform Trade Secrets Act: Practical Advice for Executives. LC 96-3622. 192p. 1996. 57.95 (*1-56720-016-8*, Quorum Bks) Greenwood.

Budden, Michael Craig. Preventing Shoplifting Without Getting Sued: Practical Advice for Retail Executives. LC 98-6020. 176p. 1999. 55.00 (*1-56720-119-9*, Quorum Bks) Greenwood.

***Budden, Paul.** Looking at a Far Mountain: A Study of Kendo Kata. (Illus.). 2000. pap. 19.95 (*0-8048-3245-5*) Tuttle Pubng.

Buddenbaum, Judith. Reporting the News about Religion: An Introduction for Journalists. LC 98-3005. 240p. 1998. pap. text 29.95 (*0-8138-2977-1*) Iowa St U Pr.

Buddenbaum, Judith, jt. auth. see Stout, Daniel A.

Buddenbaum, Judith M. & Mason, Debra, eds. Readings on Religion as News. LC 99-47158. 546p. 1999. 36.95 (*0-8138-2926-7*) Iowa St U Pr.

Buddenbaum, Judith M., jt. auth. see Stout, Daniel A.

Buddensieg, Tilmann, et al. Berlin, 1900 to 1933: Architecture & Design. Aakre, Nancy, ed. LC 87-6766. (Exhibition Catalogue Ser.). (Illus.). 187p. (Orig.). 1987. pap. text 22.50 (*0-910503-55-9*) Cooper-Hewitt Museum.

Buddensiek, Friedemann. Die Modallogik des Aristoteles in den Analytica Priora A: Zur Modernen Deutung Der Aristotelischen Logik. (Zur Modernen Deutung der Aristotelischen Logic Ser.: Bd. 6). (GER.). xii, 144p. 1994. write for info. (*3-487-09888-1*) G Olms Pubs.

Buddensiek, V. Sukkulente Euphorbien (Succulent Euphorbias) (ENG & GER., Illus.). 176p. 1998. 58.00 (*3-8001-6634-8*, Pub. by Eugen Ulmer) Balogh.

Buddery, J. H., jt. auth. see Darwin, George E.

***Buddha.** The Buddha. 1999. pap. write for info. (*0-375-70553-8*) Knopf.

Buddha. Dhammapada. 3rd ed. 24p. 1973. pap. 3.50 (*0-942401-03-4*) Am Vegan Soc.

Buddha, G. Dhammapada: The Progress of the Invariable on the Wings of the Law. LC 95-95157. (Illus.). 113p. (Orig.). 1996. pap. 12.00 (*0-9649043-2-2*) Avian Story.

Buddha, Gautama. The Discourse on the All-Embracing Net of Views: The Brahmajala Sutta & Its Commentaries. Bodhi, Bhikkhu, tr. from PLI. 350p. (Orig.). (C). 1992. 18.00 (*955-24-0052-X*, Pub. by Buddhist Pub Soc) Vipassana Res Pubns.

Buddha, Guatama. The Dhammapada. Babbitt, Irving, tr. LC 64-23655. 1965. pap. 8.95 (*0-8112-0004-3*, NDP188, Pub. by New Directions) Norton.

Buddha Sakyamuni. The Dhammapada. Dharma Publishing Staff, ed. & tr. by. from PLI. Choephel, Gedun, tr. from PLI. LC 85-15969. (Tibetan Translation Ser.: Vol. 12). (Illus.). 381p. (Orig.). 1985. pap. 19.95 (*0-913546-98-4*) Dharma Pub.

Buddhadatta, A. P. Concise Pali-English Dictionary. (ENG & PLI.). 294p. 1992. 16.95 (*0-7859-7473-3*, 8120806042) Fr & Eur.

— English-Pali Dictionary. (ENG & PLI.). 1989. 33.00 (*0-7859-8972-2*) Fr & Eur.

— English-Pali Dictionary. (ENG & PLI.). 588p. 1992. 31.95 (*0-7859-7472-5*, 8120806069) Fr & Eur.

Buddhadatta, A. P. English-Pali Dictionary. (C). 1955. 23.00 (*0-86013-060-6*) Wisdom MA.

Buddhaghosa. The Atthasalini, Buddhaghosa's Commentary on the Dhammasangani. Muller, Edward, ed. LC 78-72383. reprint ed. 39.50 (*0-404-17245-8*) AMS Pr.

— Buddhaghosa's Parables. Rogers, T., tr. from BUR. LC 78-72384. reprint ed. 37.50 (*0-404-17246-6*) AMS Pr.

— Expositor--Atthasalini, 2 vols. in 1. rev. ed. Maung Tin, tr. LC 78-72385. reprint ed. 49.50 (*0-404-17247-4*) AMS Pr.

— The Padyacudamani of Buddhaghosacarya. LC 78-72387. reprint ed. 32.50 (*0-404-17248-2*) AMS Pr.

— Papancasudani Majjhimanikayatthakatha of Buddhaghosacariya, 5 vols. in 4. LC 78-72388. (Indian Life & Customs Ser.). reprint ed. write for info. (*0-404-17560-0*) AMS Pr.

— The Path of Purity, 3 vols. Pe Maung Tin, tr. LC 78-72389. reprint ed. write for info. (*0-404-17570-8*) AMS Pr.

Buddhaghosa, Acaeiya. The Path of Purification: Visuddhimagga. Nanamoli, Bhikkhu, tr. from PLI. 950p. (C). 1991. 48.00 (*955-24-0023-6*, Pub. by Buddhist Pub Soc) Vipassana Res Pubns.

***Buddhaghosa, Bhadantacariya.** Path of Purification: Visuddhimagga. Nanamoli, Bhikkha, tr. LC 99-90839. 960p. 2000. reprint ed. 50.00 (*1-928706-00-2*, POP, BPS Pariyatti) Vipassana Res Pubns.

— Path of Purification: Visuddhimagga. Nanamoli, Bhikkha, tr. LC 99-90839. 960p. 2000. reprint ed. per. 38.00 (*1-928706-01-0*, POP, BPS Pariyatti) Vipassana Res Pubns.

Buddharakkhita, Acharya. Metta: The Philosophy & Practice of Universal Love. 56p. 1989. 3.00 (*955-24-0036-8*, Pub. by Buddhist Pub Soc) Vipassana Res Pubns.

Buddharakkhita, Acharya, tr. The Dhammapada: Buddha's Path of Wisdom. 176p. 1996. 7.80 (*955-24-0131-3*, Pub. by Buddhist Pub Soc) Vipassana Res Pubns.

Buddhavamsa. The Buddhavamsa & the Carilya-Pitaka, Pt. 1. Morris, Richard, ed. LC 78-72391. reprint ed. 17.00 (*0-404-17249-0*) AMS Pr.

Buddhist Association of the United States, tr. see Chang, Garma C. C., ed.

Buddhist Bliss Culture Center Staff, ed. An Introduction to Jen Chen Buddhist Meditation. LC 98-74804. 28p. 1999. pap. text 6.00 (*1-886925-02-X*, Buddhist Bliss) Buddhist Ch.

Buddhist Books International, tr. see Yamaguchi, Susumu.

Buddhist Church of Diamond Springs Staff, tr. from CHI. The Sutra of Maitreya's Attaining Buddahood. 110p. (Orig.). 1996. pap. text. write for info. (*1-886925-00-3*, Buddhist Bliss) Buddhist Ch.

Buddhist Text Transaltion Society Staff, tr. see Master Hsuan Hua, Venerable.

Buddhist Text Translation Society, jt. ed. see Buddhist Text Translation Society Staff.

Buddhist Text Translation Society Staff. Cherishing Life, Vol. I. (Illus.). 134p. (J). (gr. 3 up). 1983. pap. 4.00 (*0-88139-004-6*) Buddhist Text.

— Cherishing Life, Vol. II. (Illus.). 149p. (J). (gr. 3 up). 1983. pap. 4.00 (*0-88139-015-1*) Buddhist Text.

— Filiality, the Human Source, Vol. 1. 117p. (J). (gr. 3 up). 1983. pap. 4.00 (*0-88139-006-2*) Buddhist Text.

— Filiality, the Human Source, Vol. 2. 109p. (J). (gr. 3 up). 1983. pap. 4.00 (*0-88139-020-8*) Buddhist Text.

Buddhist Text Translation Society Staff, ed. The Shurangama Sutra: The Fifty Skandha-Demon States. LC 96-13666. Orig. Title: Leng Yen Ching Wu Shih Yin Mo Chien Shih. (CHI & ENG.). 653p. 1996. 25.00 (*0-88139-400-9*) Buddhist Text.

***Buddhist Text Translation Society Staff, et al, eds.** Sutra of the Past Vows of Earth Store Bodhisattva. LC 00-23319. 2000. write for info. (*0-88139-312-6*) Buddhist Text.

Buddhist Text Translation Society Staff, tr. Flower Adornment (Avatamsaka) Sutra, 22 vols. Incl. Flower Adornment (Avantamsaka) Sutra: Chapter 26, The Ten Grounds, Pt. II. Tripitaka Master Hua, comment. (Illus.). 185p. 1981. pap. Not sold separately (*0-917512-74-X*); Flower Adornment (Avantamsaka) Sutra: Chapter 39, Entering the Dharma Realm, Part IV. Tripitaka Master Hua, comment. (Illus.). 159p. 1981. pap. Not sold separately (*0-917512-76-6*); Flower Adornment (Avatamsaka) Sutra: Chapter 11, Pure Conduct. Tripitaka Master Hua, comment. (Illus.). 249p. 1983. pap. Not sold separately (*0-917512-37-5*); Flower Adornment (Avatamsaka) Sutra: Chapter 15, The Ten Dwellings. Tripitaka Master Hua, comment. (Illus.). 163p. 1981. pap. Not sold separately (*0-917512-77-4*); Flower Adornment (Avatamsaka) Sutra: Chapter 17, Merit & Virtue from First Bringing Forth the Mind. Tripitaka Master Hua, comment. (Illus.). 176p. 1982. pap. Not sold separately (*0-917512-83-9*); Flower Adornment (Avatamsaka) Sutra: Chapter 22, The Ten Inexhaustible Treasuries. Hua, comment. (Illus.). 156p. 1982. pap. Not sold separately (*0-917512-38-3*); Flower Adornment (Avatamsaka) Sutra: Chapter 24, Praises in the Tushita Heaven. Tripitaka Master Hua, comment. (Illus.). 123p. 1982. pap. Not sold separately (*0-917512-39-1*); Flower Adornment (Avatamsaka) Sutra: Chapter 36, Universal Worthy's Conduct. Hua, Tripitaka M., comment. (Illus.). 78p. 1983. pap. Not sold separately (*0-88139-011-9*); Flower Adornment (Avatamsaka) Sutra: Chapter 39, Entering the Dharma Realm, Pt. I. Master Hua, Tripitaka, comment. (Illus.). 213p. 1980. pap. Not sold separately (*0-917512-68-5*); Flower Adornment (Avatamsaka) Sutra: Chapter 39, Entering the Dharma Realm, Pt. II. Master Hua, Tripitaka, comment. (Illus.). 267p. 1980. pap. Not sold separately (*0-917512-70-7*); Flower Adornment (Avatamsaka) Sutra: Chapter 39, Entering the Dharma Realm, Pt. V. Tripitaka Master Hua, comment. (Illus.). 283p. 1981. pap. Not sold separately (*0-917512-81-2*); Flower Adornment (Avatamsaka) Sutra: Chapter 39, Entering the Dharma Realm, Pt. VI. Hua, Tripitaka M., comment. (Illus.). 281p. 1982. pap. Not sold separately (*0-917512-48-0*); Flower Adornment (Avatamsaka) Sutra: Chapter 39, Entering the Dharma Realm, Pt. VIII. Hua, Tripitaka M., comment. 224p. 1984. pap. Not sold separately (*0-88139-055-0*); Flower Adornment (Avatamsaka) Sutra: Chapter 40, Universal Worthy's Conduct & Vows. Tripitaka Master Hua, comment. (Illus.). 246p. 1982. pap. Not sold separately (*0-917512-84-7*); Flower Adornment (Avatamsaka) Sutra: Chapter 5, Flower Store Adorned Sea of Worlds, Pt. I & Pt. II. Tripitaka Master Hua, comment. (Illus.). 194p. 1983. pap. Not sold separately (*0-917512-54-5*); Flower Adornment (Avatamsaka) Sutra: Chapter 5, Flower Store Adorned Sea of Worlds, Pt. III, & Chapter 6, Vairocana. Tripitaka Master Hua, comment. (Illus.). 191p. 1985. pap. Not sold separately (*0-88139-114-X*); Flower Adornment (Avatamsaka) Sutra: Chapter 9, Light Enlightenment. Tripitaka Master Hua, comment. (Illus.). 192p. 1983. pap. text Not sold separately (*0-88139-005-4*); Fower Adornment (Avantamsaka) Sutra: Chapter, 16, Brahma Conduct. Tripitaka Master Hua, comment. (Illus.). 55p. 1981. pap. Not sold separately (*0-917512-80-4*); Chapters 7 & 8. Flower Adornment (Avatamsaka) Sutra: Names of Thus Come Ones & the Four Holy Truths, Chapters 7 & 8. Tripitaka Master Hua, comment. 77p. 1983. pap. Not sold separately (*0-88139-014-3*); Pt. VII. Flower Adornment (Avatamsaka) Sutra: Chapter 39: Entering the Dharma Realm. Hua, Tripitaka M., comment. 156p. 1983. pap. Not sold separately (*0-88139-050-X*); Pt. One. Flower Adornment (Avatamsaka) Sutra: Chapter 26, The Ten Grounds. Master Hua, Tripitaka, comment. (Illus.). 133p. 1980. pap. Not sold separately (*0-917512-87-1*); Set pap. 174.50 (*0-917512-35-9*) Buddhist Text.

— A General Explanation of the Buddha Speaks of Amitabha Sutra. 152p. 1974. reprint ed. pap. 8.00 (*0-917512-01-4*) Buddhist Text.

***Buddhist Text Translation Society Staff, tr.** The Giant Turtle. LC 99-88878. (Yu Liang Ts'ung Shu Ser.). (CHI & ENG.). 2000. pap. write for info. (*0-88139-850-0*) Buddhist Text.

Buddhist Text Translation Society Staff, tr. The Shurangama Sutra, 7 vols. Incl. Vol. 1. Shurangama Sutra. Tripitaka Master Hua, comment. (Illus.). 207p. 1977. pap. Not sold separately (*0-917512-17-0*); Vol. 2. Shurangama Sutra. Tripitaka Master Hua, comment. (Illus.). 172p. 1979. pap. Not sold separately (*0-917512-25-1*); Vol. 3. Shurangama Sutra. Master Hua, Tripitaka, comment. (Illus.). 209p. 1980. pap. Not sold separately (*0-917512-94-4*); Vol. 4. Shurangama Sutra. Master Hua, Tripitaka, comment. (Illus.). 264p. 1980. pap. Not sold separately (*0-917512-95-2*); Vol. 5. Shurangama Sutra. Master Hua, Tripitaka, comment. (Illus.). 234p. 1981. pap. Not sold separately (*0-917512-91-X*); Vol. 6. Shurangama Sutra. Tripitaka Master Hua, comment. (Illus.). 180p. 1981. pap. Not sold separately (*0-917512-97-9*); Vol. 7. Shurangama Sutra. Hua, Tripitaka M., comment. (Illus.). 249p. 1982. pap. Not sold separately (*0-917512-93-6*); 1977. Set pap. 59.50 (*0-917512-41-3*) Buddhist Text.

— The Sixth Patriarch's Sutra: Great Master Hui Neng. (Illus.). 317p. (Orig.). 1977. 15.00 (*0-917512-33-2*); pap. 10.00 (*0-917512-19-7*) Buddhist Text.

Buddhist Text Translation Society Staff, tr. from CHI. The Sutra in Forty-Two Sections. (Illus.). 87p. (Orig.). 1977. pap. 5.00 (*0-917512-15-4*) Buddhist Text.

— Sutra of the Past Vows of Earth Store Bodhisattva. LC 74-18135. (Illus.). 227p. 1982. 16.00 (*0-917512-09-X*) Buddhist Text.

— Sutra of the Past Vows of Earth Store Bodhisattva. LC 74-18135. (Illus.). 93p. 1982. pap. 5.00 (*0-88139-502-1*) Buddhist Text.

Buddhist Text Translation Society Staff, tr. from CHI. The Wonderful Dharma Lotus Flower Sutra Vol. II, Chapter 1: Introduction. (Illus.). 291p. 1978. pap. Not sold separately (*0-917512-22-7*) Buddhist Text.

***Buddhist Text Translation Society Staff, tr. from CHI.** The Wonderful Dharma Lotus Flower Sutra Vol. 13, Chapters 17-19: Discrimination of Merit & Virtue; Rejoicing in Accord with Merit & Virtue; The Merit & Virtue of a Dharma Master. LC 77-87782. (Illus.). 224p. 1998. 10.00 (*0-88139-445-9*) Buddhist Text.

Buddhist Text Translation Society Staff & Buddhist Text Translation Society, eds. The Sutra in Forty-Two Sections Spoken by the Buddha, Bilingual Edition: A Simple Explanation by the Venerable Master Hsuan Hua. 347p. 1995. 12.00 (*0-88139-184-0*) Buddhist Text.

Buddhist Text Translation Society Staff, jt. auth. see Hua, Hsuan.

Buddhist Text Translation Society Staff, ed. see Hua, Hsuan.

Buddhist Text Translation Society Staff, ed. & tr. see Dharma Realm Buddhist Association Members.

Buddhist Text Translation Society Staff, ed. & tr. see Hsuan Hua.

Buddhist Text Translation Society Staff, ed. & tr. see Hua, Hsuan.

Buddhist Text Translation Society Staff, tr. see Ch'an Master Yung Chia.

Buddhist Text Translation Society Staff, tr. see Ch'Ing Liang.

Buddhist Text Translation Society Staff, tr. see De Tripitaka Hua, Maestro.

Buddhist Text Translation Society Staff, tr. see Hsuan Hua.

Buddhist Text Translation Society Staff, tr. see Hua, Hsuan.

Buddhist Text Translation Society Staff, tr. see Hua, Tripitaka M.

Buddhist Text Translation Society Staff, tr. see Master Hsuan Hua, Venerable.

Buddhist Text Translation Society Staff, jt. tr. see Master Hsuan Hua, Venerable.

Buddhist Text Translation Society Staff, tr. see Master Hua, Tripitaka.

Buddhist Text Translation Society Staff, tr. see Tripitaka Master Hua.

Buddhist Text Translation Society Staff, tr. see Vasubhandu, Bodhisattva.

Buddin, Richard & Grissmer, David. Skill Qualification & Turbulence in the Army National Guard & Army Reserve. LC 93-25652. 1994. pap. 15.00 (*0-8330-1422-6*, MR-289-RA) Rand Corp.

Buddin, Richard & Kirby, Sheila N. Enlisted Personnel Trends in the Selected Reserve, 1986-1994. LC 96-21941. (Illus.). 142p. 1996. pap. 15.00 (*0-8330-2366-7*, MR-681/2-OSD) Rand Corp.

— Enlisted Personnel Trends in the Selected Reserve, 1986-1994: An Executive Summary. LC 96-21938. (Illus.). 43p. (Orig.). 1996. pap. 7.50 (*0-8330-2365-9*, MR-681/1-OSD) Rand Corp.

— GED Accessions in the Selected Reserve: How Long Do They Serve? (Illus.). 34p. 1997. pap. 6.00 (*0-8330-2531-7*, DB-218-OSD) Rand Corp.

Buddin, Richard & Kirin, Stephen J. Army Reserve Component Accessions from Personnel Completing Their First Active-Duty Enlistment. LC 93-25903. 1994. pap. text 13.00 (*0-8330-1419-6*, MR-258-A) Rand Corp.

Buddin, Richard & Roan, Carole E. Assessment of Combined Active/Reserve Recruiting Programs. LC 95-126991. 47p. (Orig.). 1995. pap. text 7.50 (*0-8330-1604-0*, MR-504-A) Rand Corp.

Buddin, Richard, et al. An Evaluation of Housing Options for Military Families. LC 99-24937. 165p. 1999. pap. 15.00 (*0-8330-2729-8*, MR-1020-OSD) Rand Corp.

Buddin, Richard J. Building a Personnel Support Agenda: Goals, Analysis Framework & Data Requirements. LC 98-27533. (Illus.). 113p. 1998. pap. 15.00 (*0-8330-2639-9*, MR-916-OSD) Rand Corp.

Buddine, Laura. The Cornerstone Book: Twenty Blueprints for Applications. write for info. (*0-318-60211-3*) Addison-Wesley.

Budding, E., jt. ed. see Kitamura, M.

Budding, Edwin. Introduction to Astronomical Photometry. (Illus.). 286p. (C). 1993. text 49.95 (*0-521-41867-4*) Cambridge U Pr.

Budding, Karin E. & Bugden, Miriam H. Annotated Geothermal Bibliography of Utah. (Bulletin of the Utah Geological Survey Ser.: No. 121). (Illus.). 82p. (Orig.). 1986. pap. 5.00 (*1-55791-088-X*, B-121) Utah Geological Survey.

Budding, Karin E., jt. auth. see Mabey, Don R.

Buddle, Thomas. The Maori King Movement in New Zealand. LC 75-35241. reprint ed. 32.50 (*0-404-14416-0*) AMS Pr.

Budds, Michael & Ohman, Marian M. Rock & Roll Recall. 328p. (C). 1993. pap. text 44.00 (*0-536-58337-4*) Pearson Custom.

Buddy. How to Play Winning Darts. LC 92-85007. 1998. write for info. (*0-9633750-0-8*) Strad Darts.

Buddy, Cynthia M., ed. see Griggs, John D.

Buddy, Lee. What I've Learned from Life's Little Giants. 114p. 1994. pap. write for info. (*0-9643230-0-1*) Achieve Unltd.

Budeit, Janice L., jt. compiled by see Cox, Susan M.

Budeit, Janice L., jt. ed. see Research Publications, Inc. Staff.

Budel, Burkhard. Zur Biologie und Systematik der Flechtengattungen Heppia und Peltula Im Sudlichen Afrika. Wirth, Volkmar et al, eds. (Bibliotheca Lichenologica: Vol. 23). (GER., Illus.). 150p. 1987. 59.00 (*3-443-58002-5*, Pub. by Gebruder Borntraeger) Balogh.

Budel, Julius. Climatic Geomorphology. LC 81-47909. 468p. 1982. reprint ed. pap. 145.10 (*0-7837-9307-3*, 206004700004) Bks Demand.

Buden, David, jt. auth. see Angelo, Joseph A., Jr.

Budenz. Atlas of Visual Fields. LC 96-47934. 256p. 1997. text 98.00 (*0-397-51741-6*) Lppncott W & W.

Budenz, Jozsef. Comparative Dictionary of the Finno-Ugric Elements in the Hungarian Vocabulary. LC 66-64927. (Uralic & Altaic Ser.: Vol. 78). (FIN & HUN.). viii, 987p. 1966. pap. text 22.00 (*0-87750-029-0*) Res Inst Inner Asian Studies.

Budenz, Louis F. The Techniques of Communism. LC 76-46068. (Anti-Movements in America Ser.). 1977. reprint ed. lib. bdg. 27.95 (*0-405-09942-8*) Ayer.

Buder, Marianne, et al, eds. Grundlagen der Praktischen Information und Dokumentation - Ein Handbuch zur Einfuhrung in die Fachliche Informationsarbeit: Begrundet von Klaus Laisiepen, Ernst Lutterbeck und Karl-Heinz Meyer-Uhlenried. (GER.). 1991. lib. bdg. 67.00 (*3-598-21253-4*) K G Saur Verlag.

Buder, Marianne, et al. Grundlagen der Praktischen Information und Dokumentation - Ein Handbuch zur Einfuhrung in die Fachliche Informationsarbeit: Begrundet von Klaus Laisiepen, Ernst Lutterbeck und Karl-Heinz Meyer-Uhlenried. 4th ed. 1069p. 1996. write for info. (*3-598-11309-9*) K G Saur Verlag.

Buder, Stanley. Pullman: An Experiment in Industrial Order & Community Planning, 1880-1930. (Urban Life in America Ser.). (Illus.). 282p. 1970. pap. text 20.95 (*0-19-500838-3*) OUP.

Buderi, Charles L., jt. auth. see Caron, David D.

***Buderi, Robert.** Engines of Tomorrow: How the World's Best Companies Are Using Their Research Labs to Win the Future. LC 99-59910. 448p. 2000. 27.50 (*0-684-83900-8*) S&S Trade.

Buderi, Robert. The Invention That Changed the World: How a Small Group of Radar Pioneers Launched a Revolution. 576p. 1996. 29.50 (*0-684-81021-2*) S&S Trade.

— Invention That Changed the World: How a Small Group of Radar Pioneers Won the Second World War. 576p. 1998. pap. 16.00 (*0-684-83529-0*, Touchstone) S&S Trade Pap.

Budescu, David V., et al, eds. Games & Human Behavior. 335p. 1998. write for info. (*0-8058-2658-0*); pap. write for info. (*0-8058-2659-9*) L Erlbaum Assocs.

Budetti, P. P., jt. ed. see Solloway, M. R.

Budevski, Evgeni B., et al. Electrochemical Phase Formation & Growth: An Introduction to the Initial Stages of Metal Deposition. LC 96-28628. (Illus.). 410p. 1996. 210.00 (*3-527-29422-8*, Wiley-VCH) Wiley.

Budge. The New British Politics. 656p. (C). 1998. pap. 33.53 (*0-582-28925-4*) Longman.

Budge, Belinda, ed. Lesbian Looks: Postcards from the Edge. (Illus.). 88p. 1994. pap. 14.95 (*1-85727-096-7*, Pub. by Scarlet Pr) LPC InBook.

Budge, Belinda, jt. ed. see Hamer, Diane.

Budge, E. A. Wallis. Alexander Book in Ethiopia. LC 73-18834. (Illus.). reprint ed. 37.50 (*0-404-11307-9*) AMS Pr.

***Budge, E. A. Wallis.** Amulets & Magic: The Evil Eye in Western Asia, Egypt, Nubia & Ethiopia. 584p. 2000. text 144.50 (*0-7103-0713-6*) Col U Pr.

Budge, E. A. Wallis. Amulets & Superstitions: The original texts with translations & descriptions of a long series of Egyptian, Sumerian, Assyrian, Hebrew, Christian, Gnostic & Muslim amulets & talismans & magical figures, with chapters on the evil eye, the origin of the amulet, the pentagon, the swastika, the cross (pagan & Christian), the properties of stones, rings, divination, numbers, the Kabbalah, ancient as trology, etc. LC 77-86708. (Illus.). 543p. 1978. reprint ed. pap. 12.95 (*0-486-23573-4*) Dover.

— Ancient Egyptian Theology. 1985. pap. 7.95 (*0-916411-91-5*) Holmes Pub.

— Apophthegmata Patrum. 150p. 1975. pap. 6.95 (*0-89981-008-X*) Eastern Orthodox.

— Babylonian Life & History. LC 73-18836. (Illus.). reprint ed. 45.00 (*0-404-11308-7*) AMS Pr.

— The Babylonian Story of the Deluge & the Epic of Gilgamesh with an Account of the Royal Libraries of Nineveh. (Illus.). 57p. 1996. reprint ed. pap. 12.00 (*1-56459-572-2*) Kessinger Pub.

— The Book of Opening the Mouth: The Egyptian Texts with English Translations, 2 vols., 1 bk. LC 72-80498. (Illus.). 1980. reprint ed. 36.95 (*0-405-08315-7*, Pub. by Blom Pubns) Ayer.

— Book of the Dead. (Illus.). 1960. 25.00 (*0-8216-0021-4*) Carol Pub Group.

— The Book of the Kings of Egypt, 2 vols., Set. LC 73-18837. reprint ed. 64.50 (*0-404-11309-5*) AMS Pr.

— Book of the Mysteries of the Heavens & the Earth. 1972. 75.00 (*0-87968-772-X*) Gordon Pr.

— The Book of the Saints of the Ethiopian Church: A Translation of the Ethiopic Synaxarium, 4 vols. in 2, Set. 1400p. 1976. reprint ed. 400.00 (*3-487-05876-6*) G Olms Pubs.

— By Nile & Tigris, 2 vols., Set. LC 75-28120. (Illus.). reprint ed. 145.00 (*0-404-11312-5*) AMS Pr.

— Cleopatra Needles & Other Egyptian Obelisks: A series of descriptions of all the important inscribed obelisks, with hieroglyphic texts, translations, etc. (Illus.). 352p. 1990. pap. 8.95 (*0-486-26347-9*) Dover.

— Cleopatra's Needles & Other Egyptian Obelisks. LC 73-18841. (Illus.). reprint ed. 27.50 (*0-404-11315-X*) AMS Pr.

— Cleopatra's Needles & Other Egyptian Obelisks. LC 73-18841. 308p. 1979. reprint ed. 35.00 (*0-89005-278-6*) Ares.

— Coptic Texts Edited with Introductions & English Translations, 5 vols., Set. reprint ed. 452.00 (*0-404-11550-0*) AMS Pr.

— Decrees of Memphis & Canopus, 3 vols., Set. Incl. 1. Rosetta Stone. LC 73-18842. (*0-404-11323-0*); 2. Rosetta Stone. LC 73-18842. (*0-404-11324-9*); Vol. 3. Decree of Canopus. LC 73-18842. (*0-404-11325-7*); LC 73-18842. 1904. reprint ed. 115.00 (*0-404-11322-2*) AMS Pr.

— The Divine Origin of the Craft of the Herbalist. 108p. 1996. reprint ed. pap. 16.95 (*1-56459-600-1*) Kessinger Pub.

— The Divine Origin of the Craft of the Herbalist. unabridged ed. LC 95-49175. (Illus.). 112p. 1996. reprint ed. pap. text 4.95 (*0-486-29169-3*) Dover.

— The Dwellers on the Nile. LC 72-80141. (Illus.). 358p. 1972. reprint ed. 19.95 (*0-405-08316-5*, Pub. by Blom Pubns) Ayer.

— Egyptian Book of the Dead: The Papyrus of Ani. 1990. 25.00 (*0-8446-1764-4*) Peter Smith.

— Egyptian Book of the Dead: The Papyrus of Ani in the British Museum. 533p. 1967. pap. 10.95 (*0-486-21866-X*) Dover.

— The Egyptian Book of the Dead & the Papyrus of Ani. LC 99-40771. (Illus.). 534p. 1999. reprint ed. pap. 9.95 (*1-881316-99-8*) A&B Bks.

— The Egyptian Heaven & Hell. (Illus.). 218p. 1974. pap. 14.95 (*0-87548-298-8*) Open Court.

— Egyptian Heaven & Hell. 1980. lib. bdg. 59.95 (*0-8490-3203-2*) Gordon Pr.

— The Egyptian Heaven & Hell. unabridged ed. (Illus.). 864p. 1996. reprint ed. pap. text 18.95 (*0-486-29368-8*) Dover.

— The Egyptian Heaven & Hell, 3 vols., Set. LC 73-18844. (Illus.). reprint ed. 115.00 (*0-404-11326-5*) AMS Pr.

— Egyptian Hieroglyphic Dictionary Vols. 1 & 2, 1. LC 77-86708. 1978. pap. 18.95 (*0-486-23615-3*) Dover.

— Egyptian Hieroglyphic Dictionary Vols. 1 & 2, 2. LC 77-86708. 1978. pap. 19.95 (*0-486-23616-1*) Dover.

— An Egyptian Hieroglyphic Reading Book for Beginners. Orig. Title: An Egyptian Reading Book for Beginners. liv, 593p. 1993. reprint ed. pap. 12.95 (*0-486-27486-1*) Dover.

— Egyptian Ideas of the Afterlife. LC 94-39651. (Illus.). 208p. 1995. pap. text 6.95 (*0-486-28464-6*) Dover.

— Egyptian Ideas of the Future Life. LC 73-18839. reprint ed. 37.50 (*0-404-11330-3*) AMS Pr.

— Egyptian Language. x, 246p. 1975. pap. 20.00 (*0-89005-095-3*) Ares.

— Egyptian Language: Easy Lessons in Egyptian Hieroglyphics with Sign List. 8th ed. 246p. 1977. pap. 6.95 (*0-486-21394-3*) Dover.

— Egyptian Language: Easy Lessons in Hieroglyphics. 1991. lib. bdg. 75.00 (*0-8490-4611-4*) Gordon Pr.

— Egyptian Magic. 234p. 1971. reprint ed. pap. 6.95 (*0-486-22681-6*) Dover.

— An Egyptian Reading Book for Beginners. LC 73-18845. reprint ed. 49.50 (*0-404-11331-1*) AMS Pr.

— The Egyptian Sudan, Vol. 1. 1990. 140.00 (*1-85077-077-8*, Pub. by Darf Pubs Ltd) St Mut.

— The Egyptian Sudan, 2 vols., Vol. 2. 674p. (C). 1990. 140.00 (*1-85077-076-X*, Pub. by Darf Pubs Ltd) St Mut.

— The Egyptian Sudan: Its History & Monuments, 2 vols. LC 73-18840. (Illus.). reprint ed. 115.00 (*0-404-11332-X*) AMS Pr.

— First Steps in Egyptian: A Book for Beginners. 321p. 1996. reprint ed. spiral bd. 23.00 (*0-7873-0131-0*) Hlth Research.

— First Steps in Egyptian: A Book for Beginners (1895) 331p. 1996. reprint ed. pap. 22.95 (*1-56459-933-3*) Kessinger Pub.

— From Fetish to God in Ancient Egypt. (Illus.). 545p. 1988. pap. 11.95 (*0-486-25803-3*) Dover.

— From Fetish to God in Ancient Egypt. LC 72-82206. (Illus.). 1972. reprint ed. 41.95 (*0-405-08317-3*, Pub. by Blom Pubns) Ayer.

— The Gods of the Egyptians: Studies in Egyptian Mythology, 2 vols., Vol. 1. LC 67-28633. (Illus.). (C). 1969. reprint ed. pap. 12.95 (*0-486-22055-9*) Dover.

— The Gods of the Egyptians: Studies in Egyptian Mythology, 2 vols., Vol. 2. LC 67-28633. (Illus.). (C). 1969. reprint ed. pap. 12.95 (*0-486-22056-7*) Dover.

— Gods of the Egyptians or Studies in Egyptian Mythology, 2 Vols. (Illus.). 1990. 5.75 (*0-8446-0520-4*) Peter Smith.

— Herb-Doctors & Physicians in the Ancient World: The Divine Origin of the Craft of the Herbalist. xii, 96p. 1978. pap. 10.00 (*0-89005-252-2*) Ares.

— Hieroglyphic Vocabulary to the Book of the Dead. 528p. 1991. pap. 12.95 (*0-486-26724-5*) Dover.

— A Hieroglyphic Vocabulary to the Theban Recension of the Book of the Dead. LC 73-18846. reprint ed. 34.50 (*0-404-11335-4*) AMS Pr.

— The Histories of Rabban Hormizd the Persian & Rabban Bar-'Idta, 3 pts. in 2 vols. LC 73-18847. (Luzac's Semitic Text & Translation Ser.: Nos. 9, 10, 11). reprint ed. 62.50 (*0-404-11336-2*) AMS Pr.

— A History of Ethiopia, Nubia & Abyssina. (African Studies). 722p. reprint ed. 75.00 (*0-938818-91-0*) ECA Assoc.

— An Introduction to Ancient Egyptian Literature. LC 96-43172. (Illus.). 272p. 1997. reprint ed. pap. text 8.95 (*0-486-29502-8*) Dover.

— The Judgement of the Dead & the Weighing of the Heart Before Osiris. (Illus.). 1990. pap. 6.95 (*1-55818-151-2*) Holmes Pub.

— Legends of the Egyptian Gods: Hieroglyphic Texts & Translations. LC 93-49097. Orig. Title: Egyptian Literature, Vol. I: Legends of the Gods, the Egyptian Texts, Edited with Translations. (Illus.). 352p. 1994. reprint ed. pap. 8.95 (*0-486-28022-5*) Dover.

— Life & Exploits of Alexander the Great, 2 vols., Set. LC 68-56521. (Illus.). 1972. reprint ed. 72.95 (*0-405-08318-1*, Pub. by Blom Pubns) Ayer.

— Life & Exploits of Alexander the Great, 2 vols., Vol. 1. LC 68-56521. (Illus.). 1972. reprint ed. 36.95 (*0-405-08319-X*, Pub. by Blom Pubns) Ayer.

— Life & Exploits of Alexander the Great, 2 vols., Vol. 2. LC 68-56521. (Illus.). 1972. reprint ed. 36.95 (*0-405-08320-3*, Pub. by Blom Pubns) Ayer.

— The Liturgy of Funerary Offerings: The Egyptian Texts with English Translations. LC 72-83744. (Illus.) 1972. reprint ed. 24.95 (*0-405-08322-X*, Pub. by Blom Pubns) Ayer.

— The Liturgy of Funerary Offerings: The Egyptian Texts with English Translations. LC 94-17824. (Illus.) 288p. 1994. reprint ed. pap. text 9.95 (*0-486-28335-6*) Dover.

— The Magic of Egypt: The Foundation of the Egyptian Religions; with the Magical Rituals & Spells Described. 1995. pap. 6.95 (*1-55818-313-2*) Holmes Pub.

— The Monks of Kublai Khan, Emperor of China. LC 71-38051. reprint ed. 55.00 (*0-404-56905-6*) AMS Pr.

— Mummy. 2nd ed. LC 64-13391. (Illus.). 1994. pap. 25.00 (*0-8196-0139-X*) Biblo.

— The Mummy: A Handbook of Egyptian Funerary Archaeology. 576p. 1989. pap. 10.95 (*0-486-25928-5*) Dover.

— The Mummy: Chapters on Egyptian Funeral Archaeology. (Illus.). 404p. 1998. reprint ed. pap. 42.00 (*1-58073-005-1*) BCP Bks.

— The Mummy: Chapters on Egyptian Funeral Archaeology. (Illus.). 404p. 1998. reprint ed. pap. 42.00 (*0-933121-69-5*) Black Classic.

— The Nile: Notes for Travelers in Egypt (1901) 700p. 1998. reprint ed. pap. 49.95 (*0-7661-0360-9*) Kessinger Pub.

— Osiris & the Egyptian Resurrection, 2 vols., Vol. 1. LC 72-81534. (Illus.). 906p. 1973. reprint ed. pap. 10.95 (*0-486-22780-4*) Dover.

— Osiris & the Egyptian Resurrection, 2 vols., Vol. 2. 2nd ed. LC 72-81534. (Illus.). 906p. 1973. reprint ed. pap. 9.95 (*0-486-22781-2*) Dover.

— The Queen of Sheba & Her Only Son Menyelek, Vol. II. Obaba, Al I., ed. (Illus.). 214p. 1922. pap. text 27.00 (*0-916157-60-1*) African Islam Miss Pubns.

— The Rise & Progress of Assyriology. LC 73-18849. (Illus.). reprint ed. 37.50 (*0-404-11340-0*) AMS Pr.

— The Rosetta Stone. 352p. 1989. pap. 8.95 (*0-486-26163-8*) Dover.

— The Rosetta Stone in the British Museum. LC 73-16549. (Illus.). reprint ed. 32.50 (*0-404-11362-1*) AMS Pr.

— Sayings of the Fathers. 1975. pap. 6.95 (*0-89981-089-6*) Eastern Orthodox.

— Tutankhamen. 165p. 1995. pap. 18.00 (*0-8196-2484-5*) Biblo.

— Tutankhamen: Amenism, Atenism & Egyptian Monotheism. LC 79-160615. (Illus.). 1972. reprint ed. 23.95 (*0-405-08323-8*, Pub. by Blom Pubns) Ayer.

— Tutankhamen: Amenism, Atenism & Egyptian monotheism : with hieroglyphic texts of hymns to Amen & Aten. (Amenism, Atenism & Egyptian Monotheism - with Hieroglyphic Texts of Hymns to Amen & Aten Ser.). (Illus.). 192p. 1992. reprint ed. pap. 6.95 (*0-486-26950-7*) Dover.

Budge, E. A. Wallis, ed. Baralam & Yewasef - Baralaam & Joasaph, 3 pts. in 2 vols., Set. LC 73-18832. (Illus.). reprint ed. 78.50 (*0-404-11300-1*) AMS Pr.

— The Book of the Dead: The hieroglyphic transcript & translation into English of the Papyrus of Ani. LC 94-39049. (Illus.). 704p. 1995. 9.99 (*0-517-12283-9*) Random Hse Value.

— Coptic Apocrypha in the Dialect of Upper Egypt. LC 77-3589. (Coptic Texts Ser.: Vol. 3). (Illus.). reprint ed. 76.50 (*0-404-11553-5*) AMS Pr.

— Coptic Biblical Texts in the Dialect of Upper Egypt. LC 77-3590. (Coptic Texts Ser.: Vol. 2). (Illus.). 1977. reprint ed. 72.50 (*0-404-11552-7*) AMS Pr.

— Coptic Homilies in the Dialect of Upper Egypt. LC 77-3585. (Coptic Texts Ser.: Vol. 1). (Illus.). reprint ed. 76.50 (*0-404-11551-9*) AMS Pr.

— Coptic Martyrdoms, Etc. in the Dialect of Upper Egypt. LC 77-3588. (Coptic Texts Ser.: Vol. 4). (Illus.). reprint ed. 76.50 (*0-404-11554-3*) AMS Pr.

— The Egyptian Sudan, 2 vols., Vol. 2. 626p. (C). 1989. 105.00 (*0-7855-7069-1*, Pub. by Darf Pubs Ltd) St Mut.

— The Egyptian Sudan, 2 vols., Vols. 1-2. (C). 1989. 105.00 (*0-7855-7068-3*, Pub. by Darf Pubs Ltd) St Mut.

— The Laughable Stories Collected by Mar Gregory John Bar-Hebraeus. LC 72-173158. 1972. reprint ed. 24.95 (*0-405-08321-1*, Pub. by Blom Pubns) Ayer.

— Miscellaneous Coptic Texts in the Dialect of Upper Egypt, 2 vols. LC 77-3587. (Coptic Texts Ser.: Vol. 5). (Illus.). reprint ed. 150.00 (*0-404-11555-1*) AMS Pr.

Budge, E. A. Wallis, intro. The Book of the Dead. (Illus.). 736p. 1984. reprint ed. pap. 17.95 (*0-8065-0591-5*, Citadel Pr) Carol Pub Group.

Budge, E. A. Wallis, tr. The Bandlet of Righteousness: An Ethiopian Book of the Dead. (COP.). 1984. pap. 7.95 (*0-916411-23-0*, Near Eastern) Holmes Pub.

***Budge, E. A. Wallis, tr.** The Book of Medicines: Ancient Syrian Anatomy, Pathology & Therapeutics. 680p. 2000. text 110.00 (*0-7103-0707-1*) Col U Pr.

Budge, E. A. Wallis, tr. The Book of the Dead According to the Theban Recension. 398p. 1996. reprint ed. spiral bd. 23.00 (*0-7873-0130-2*) Hlth Research.

***Budge, E. A. Wallis, tr.** An Ethiopian Book of the Dead: The Bandlet of Righteousness. 166p. 2000. text 110.00 (*0-7103-0706-3*) Col U Pr.

Budge, E. A. Wallis, tr. George of Lydda, the Patron Saint of England. LC 77-87668. (Luzac's Semitic Text & Translation Ser.: No. 20). (ENG & ETH., Illus.). reprint ed. 75.00 (*0-404-11348-6*) AMS Pr.

— The History of the Blessed Virgin Mary & the History of the Likeness of Christ Which the Jews of Tiberius Made to Mock At, 2 vols., Set. LC 73-18848. (Luzac's Semitic Text & Translation Ser.: Nos. 4-5). reprint ed. 84.50 (*0-404-11341-9*) AMS Pr.

— Lausiac History: Palladius. 1977. pap. 6.95 (*0-89981-039-X*) Eastern Orthodox.

***Budge, E. A. Wallis, tr.** The Queen of Sheba & Her Son Menyelek: The Kebra Nagast. 350p. 2000. text 110.00 (*0-7103-0712-8*) Col U Pr.

Budge, E. A. Wallis, tr. The Wit & Wisdom of the Christian Fathers of Egypt: The Syrian Version of the Apophthegmata Patrum. LC 80-2354. reprint ed. 53.50 (*0-404-18900-8*) AMS Pr.

***Budge, E. A. Wallis, et al.** A Plague on Your Houses: How New York Was Burned down & National Public Health Crumbled. 2000. pap. 20.00 (*1-85984-253-4*, Pub. by Verso) Norton.

Budge, E. A. Wallis, jt. auth. see Prince, J. Dyneley.

Budge, E. A. Wallis, tr. see Bar Hebraeus.

Budge, E. A. Wallis, tr. see Dorson, Richard M., ed.

Budge, E. A. Wallis, tr. see Isho, Anan.

Budge, E. A. Wallis, tr. see Lefafa Sedek.

Budge, E. A. Wallis, tr. see Pachomius.

Budge, Helen. Study of Chord Frequencies Based on the Music of the Eighteenth & Nineteenth Centuries. LC 75-176604. (Columbia University. Teachers College. Contributions to Education Ser.: No. 882). reprint ed. 37.00 (*0-404-55882-8*) AMS Pr.

Budge, Ian. The New Challenge of Direct Democracy. LC 96-28104. (Orig.). 1996. pap. 25.95 (*0-7456-1765-4*, Pub. by Polity Pr) Blackwell Pubs.

— Politics of New Europe. LC 96-47848. (C). 1997. pap. text 26.25 (*0-582-23434-4*, Pub. by Addison-Wesley) Longman.

Budge, Ian, et al, eds. Ideology, Strategy & Party Change: A Spatial Analysis of Post-War Election Programmes in Nineteen Democracies. (Illus.). 312p. 1987. text 80.00 (*0-521-30648-5*) Cambridge U Pr.

— Party Identification & Beyond: Representations of Voting & Party Competition. LC 75-35615. 403p. reprint ed. pap. 125.00 (*0-608-16338-4*, 202668100051) Bks Demand.

Budge, Ian & Keman, Hans. Parties & Democracy: Coalition Formation & Government Functioning in Twenty States. (Comparative Politics Ser.). (Illus.). 256p. (C). 1993. reprint ed. pap. text 22.00 (*0-19-827925-6*) OUP.

Budge, Ian & McKay, David, eds. Developing Democracy. 352p. (C). 1994. text 65.00 (*0-8039-8842-7*); pap. text 22.95 (*0-8039-8883-4*) Sage.

Budge, Wallis E. Amulets & Talismans. (Illus.). 588p. 1992. pap. 14.95 (*0-8065-1323-3*, Citadel Pr) Carol Pub Group.

— The Dwellers on the Nile: The Life, History, Religion, & Literature of the Ancient Egyptians. (Illus.). 358p. 1978. reprint ed. pap. 9.95 (*0-486-23501-7*) Dover.

— Egyptian Magic. 252p. 1997. pap. 12.00 (*0-8065-0629-6*) Carol Pub Group.

— Egyptian Religion. (Illus.). 228p. 1997. pap. 12.00 (*0-8065-1229-6*, Citadel Pr) Carol Pub Group.

— The Rosetta Stone. 27p. 1986. pap. 7.50 (*0-89005-331-6*) Ares.

Budgell, Eustace, tr. see Theophrastus of Eresus.

Budgen, David. Software Design. 370p. (C). 1994. pap. text 49.00 (*0-201-54403-2*) Addison-Wesley.

Budgen, David, tr. see Pushkin, Aleksandr.

Budgen, Dennis, jt. auth. see Royal Tyrrell Museum of Palaeontology Staff.

Budgen, June. The Book of Appetizers. (Book of...Ser.). (Illus.). 128p. (Orig.). 1988. pap. 12.00 (*0-89586-482-7*, HP Books) Berkley Pub.

— The Book of Garnishes. LC 86-81041. (Illus.). 128p. 1988. pap. 12.00 (*0-89586-480-0*, Price Stern) Peng Put Young Read.

Budgen, Sebastian, ed. Mapping Social Theory. 320p. 1999. 60.00 (*1-85984-700-5*, Pub. by Verso); pap. 20.00 (*1-85984-227-5*, Pub. by Verso) Norton.

Budgen, Victor. Charismatics & the Word of God. 1985. pap. 13.99 (*0-85234-264-0*, Pub. by Evangelical Pr) P & R Pubng.

Budget Staff. Book of Days. 1994. 19.98 (*0-88365-880-1*) Galahad Bks.

Budgett-Meakin. Make the Future Work: Appropriate Technology Guide. 1993. pap. text. write for info. (*0-582-08838-0*, Pub. by Addison-Wesley) Longman.

Budgor, A. B., et al, eds. Tunable Solid-State Lasers II. (Optical Sciences Ser.: Vol. 52). (Illus.). 380p. 1987. 72.95 (*0-387-17320-X*) Spr-Verlag.

Budhananda. Joy of the Illumined. 96p. 1987. pap. 2.00 (*0-87481-541-X*, Pub. by Advaita Ashrama) Vedanta Pr.

— The Saving Challenge of Religion. 272p. (Orig.). 1982. pap. 4.95 (*0-87481-567-3*) Vedanta Pr.

Budhananda, S. Story of Mira's Love. 52p. (Orig.). 1987. pap. 2.00 (*0-87481-546-0*, Pub. by Ramakrishna Mission) Vedanta Pr.

Budhananda, Swami. Can One Be Scientific & Yet Spiritual? 114p. 1973. pap. 1.95 (*0-87481-145-7*, Pub. by Advaita Ashrama) Vedanta Pr.

— The Mind & Its Control. 112p. (Orig.). 1972. pap. 1.95 (*81-7505-034-9*, Pub. by Advaita Ashrama) Vedanta Pr.

Budhoo, Davison L. Enough Is Enough: Dear Mr. Camdessus...Open Letter of Resignation to the Managing Director of the International Monetary Fund. 128p. (Orig.). 1990. pap. 12.50 (*0-945257-28-7*) Apex Pr.

Budhos, Marina. Father's Tale. 28p. (Orig.). 1989. pap. 4.00 (*0-945926-09-X*) Paradigm RI.

— The Professor of Light. LC 98-33904. 254p. 1999. 23.95 (*0-399-14473-0*, G P Putnam) Peng Put Young Read.

— Remix: Conversations with Immigrant Teenagers. LC 99-25266. (Illus.). 165p. (YA). (gr. 9-12). 2000. 16.95 (*0-8050-5113-9*, Bks Young Read) H Holt & Co.

Budhos, Marina T. House of Waiting. LC 94-79269. 220p. 1995. pap. 12.00 (*0-9641292-2-1*) Global Cty Pr.

Budhos, Shirley. The Theme of Enclosure in Selected Works of Doris Lessing. LC 86-50290. x, 123p. 1987. 45.00 (*0-87875-314-1*) Whitston Pub.

***Budhu, M.** Soil Mechanics & Foundations. LC 99-50184. (Illus.). 616p. 1999. 108.95 incl. cd-rom (*0-471-25231-X*) Wiley.

Budiansky. The Horse Observed. 1997. 25.00 (*0-02-874127-7*) Free Pr.

Budiansky, B., ed. see International Union of Theoretical & Applied Mecha.

***Budiansky, Stephen.** Battle of Wits: The Complete Story of Codebreaking in World War II. 2000. 27.50 (*0-684-85932-7*) Free Pr.

Budiansky, Stephen. The Covenant of the Wild: Why Animals Chose Domestication. LC 99-17290. 212p. 1999. pap. 14.95 (*0-300-07993-1*) Yale U Pr.

— The Covenant of the Wild: Why Animals Chose Domestication. 192p. 1995. reprint ed. pap. 14.00 (*0-9648750-0-4*) Terrapin VA.

— If a Lion Could Talk: Animal Intelligence & the Evolution of Consciousness. LC 98-28211. 256p. 1998. 25.00 (*0-684-83710-2*) Free Pr.

— The Nature of Horses: Exploring Equine Evolution, Intelligence, & Behavior. LC 96-47004. (Illus.). 240p. 1997. 29.50 (*0-684-82768-9*) Free Pr.

— Nature's Keepers: The New Science of Nature Management. (Illus.). 310p. 1995. 25.00 (*0-02-904915-6*) Free Pr.

***Budiansky, Stephen.** The Truth about Dogs: An Inquiry Into the Ancestory, Social Conventions, Mental Habits & Moral Fiber. (Illus.). 320p. 2000. 24.95 (*0-670-89272-6*, Viking) Viking Penguin.

— The World According to Horses: How They Run, See & Think. LC 99-31778. (Illus.). 128p. (ps-1). 2000. 16.95 (*0-8050-6054-5*) H Holt & Co.

Budiardjo, Carmel. Surviving Indonesia's Gulag. LC 96-163484. 1996. pap. 21.95 (*0-304-33562-2*, Pub. by Cassell) LPC InBook.

Budick, E. Miller. Emily Dickinson & the Life of Language: A Study in Symbolic Poetics. LC 85-9609. 247p. 1985. pap. 76.60 (*0-7837-8528-3*, 204933700011) Bks Demand.

Budick, Emily M. American Romance Fiction: The 19th Century. 1996. 33.00 (*0-8057-0960-6*, Twyne) Mac Lib Ref.

— Engendering Romance: Women Writers & the Hawthorne Tradition, 1850-1990. LC 93-37419. 320p. 1994. 37.50 (*0-300-05557-9*) Yale U Pr.

Budick, Emily Miller, ed. see Shaked, Gershon.

Budick, Sanford. The Dividing Muse: Images of Sacred Disjunction in Milton's Poetry. LC 84-17270. 223p. reprint ed. pap. 69.20 (*0-7837-3286-4*, 205768800006) Bks Demand.

— Poetry of Civilization: Mythopoeic Displacement in the Verse of Milton, Dryden, Pope, & Johnson. LC 73-86887. 195p. reprint ed. pap. 60.50 (*0-608-14189-5*, 202198400024) Bks Demand.

***Budick, Sanford.** The Western Theory of Tradition: Terms & Paradigms of the Cultural Sublime. LC 99-86678. (Illus.). 352p. 2000. 40.00 (*0-300-08151-0*) Yale U Pr.

Budick, Sanford & Iser, Wolfgang, eds. Language of the Unsayable: The Play of Negativity in Literature & Literary Theory. (Irvine Studies in the Humanities). (Illus.). 418p. pap. 17.95 (*0-8047-2483-0*) Stanford Univ Committee on Linguistics.

— Languages of the Unsayable: The Play of Negativity in Literature & Literary Theory. 416p. 1989. text 49.00 (*0-231-06866-2*) Col U Pr.

— The Translatability of Cultures: Figurations of the Space Between. LC 95-13052. (Irvine Studies in the Humanities). (Illus.). xiv, 348 p. 1996. pap. 18.95 (*0-8047-2561-6*) Stanford U Pr.

— The Translatability of Cultures: Figurations of the Space Between. LC 95-13052. (Irvine Studies in the Humanities). (Illus.). 362p. (C). 1996. 47.50 (*0-8047-2484-9*) Stanford U Pr.

Budig, Gene A. Higher Education: Surviving the 1980's. LC 81-50932. 90p. 1981. pap. 7.50 (*0-937058-01-7*) West Va U Pr.

Budig, Gene A., ed. Higher Education Map for the Nineties. (ACE-Oryx Series on Higher Education). 128p. 1992. 29.95 (*0-02-897076-4*) Oryx Pr.

— Perceptions in Public Higher Education. LC 71-105647. 177p. reprint ed. pap. 54.90 (*0-7837-1393-2*, 204157400021) Bks Demand.

Budig-Markin, Valerie & Gaasch, James. Diversite: La Nouvelle Francophone. (FRE.). 254p. (C). 1994. pap. text 39.56 (*0-395-69866-9*) HM.

Budig, P. Dictionary Electrical Engineering Electronics Vol. 1: English to German. 6th ed. (ENG & GER.). 780p. 1997. 295.00 (*0-320-00456-2*) Fr & Eur.

— Dictionary Electrical Engineering Electronics Vol. 2: German to English. 5th ed. (ENG & GER.). 750p. 1998. 295.00 (*0-320-00395-7*) Fr & Eur.

Budig, Peter-Klaus. Dictionary of Electrical Engineering & Electronics vOL. 1: English - German. 5th ed. (ENG & GER.). 800p. 1992. 250.00 (*0-8288-0288-2*, M7394) Fr & Eur.

— Dictionary of Electrical Engineering & Electronics vOL. 2: German - English. 5th ed. (ENG & GER.). 704p. 1992. 250.00 (*0-685-63364-0*, F45830) Fr & Eur.

— Dictionary of Electrical Engineering & Electronics Vol. 2: German-English. 4th ed. (ENG & GER.). 700p. 1985. 250.00 (*0-8288-0287-4*, F45830) Fr & Eur.

— Fachworterbuch Electrotechnik: Elektronik. 3rd ed. (ENG & GER.). 700p. 1989. lib. bdg. 195.00 (*0-8288-3604-3*) Fr & Eur.

— Routledge Langenscheidt German Dictionary of Electrical Engineering, Vol. 1. 6th ed. LC 98-18535. (Routledge Bilingual Specialist Dictionaries Ser.). (GER.). 702p. (C). 1998. 110.00 (*0-415-17132-6*) Routledge.

— Routledge Langenscheidt German Dictionary of Electrical Engineering, Vol. 2. 5th ed. LC 98-18535. (Routledge Bilingual Specialist Dictionaries Ser.). (GER.). 744p. (C). (gr. 13). 1998. 110.00 (*0-415-17131-8*) Routledge.

Budig, Peter-Klaus, ed. German-English Electrotechnology & Electronics Dictionary. 700p. (C). 1982. 375.00 (*0-7855-5060-7*, Pub. by Collets) St Mut.

Budilovsky, Joan. The Complete Idiot's Guide to Massage. LC 98-87303. (Complete Idiot's Guides Ser.). 352p. 1998. pap. 18.95 (*0-02-862708-3*) Macmillan Gen Ref.

Budilovsky, Joan & Adamson, Eve. Complete Idiot's Guide to Yoga. LC 97-73163. 304p. 1997. 17.95 (*0-02-861949-8*, Pub. by Macmillan Gen Ref) S&S Trade.

***Budiman, Arief, ed.** State & Civil Society in Indonesia. 538p. 1999. reprint ed. pap. 39.95 (*0-7326-0233-5*, Pub. by Monash Asia Inst) Intl Spec Bk.

***Budiman, Arief, et al, eds.** Reformasi: Crisis & Change in Indonesia. 1999. pap. 24.95 (*0-7326-1179-2*, Pub. by Monash Asia Inst) Intl Spec Bk.

***Budimir, Djuradj.** EPFIL, Waveguide E-Plane Filter Design Software & User's Manual. (Illus.). 1999. 250.00 (*1-58053-083-4*) Artech Hse.

Budimir, Djuradj. Generalized Filter Design by Computer Optimization. LC 97-39465. 246p. 1998. 93.00 (*0-89006-579-9*) Artech Hse.

Budin, Gerhard, jt. compiled by see Wright, Sue E.

Budin, Howard, et al. Using Computers in the Social Studies. LC 85-27779. (Computers in the Curriculum Ser.). (Illus.). 128p. (Orig.). 1986. pap. 39.70 (*0-608-05094-6*, 206565000005) Bks Demand.

— Using Computers in the Social Studies. (Computers & the Curriculum Ser.). 118p. (Orig.). 1986. pap. text 14.95 (*0-8077-2781-4*) Tchrs Coll.

Budin, Wendy C., jt. auth. see Hott, Jacqueline R.

Budine, Phillip, et al. The New A. L. P. O. Jupiter Handbook. (Illus.). 181p. (Orig.). (YA). 1990. pap. text 15.00 (*0-9626527-0-9*) Cechoni Prodns.

Budingen, Hans J. Von, see Von Reutern, Gerhard-Michael & Von Budingen, Hans J.

Budinger, F. C., jt. auth. see Bender, Jo A.

Budinger, Thomas F., et al, eds. Noninvasive Techniques for Assessment of Atherosclerosis in Peripheral, Carotid, & Coronary Arteries. fac. ed. LC 82-20437. (Illus.). 269p. pap. 83.40 (*0-7837-7207-6*, 204709200005) Bks Demand.

Budinich, M., ed. Impact of Digital Microelectronics & Microprocessor on Particle Physics. 348p. (C). 1988. text 99.00 (*9971-5-0742-0*) World Scientific Pub.

Budinich, P. & Trautman, Andrzej. The Spinorial Chessboard. (Trieste Notes in Physics Ser.). 130p. 1988. 34.95 (*0-387-19078-3*) Spr-Verlag.

Budinski, Budinski. Engineering Materials: Properties & Selections. 6th ed. 719p. 1998. 100.00 (*0-13-904715-8*) P-H.

Budish, Armond D. All New Avoiding the Medicaid Trap: How to Beat the Catastrophic Costs of Nursing Home Care. 3rd ed. 1995. 30.00 (*0-8050-3426-9*) H Holt & Co.

— Avoiding Medicaid (New) 3rd rev. ed. 368p. 1996. reprint ed. pap. 15.00 (*0-380-72771-4*, Avon Bks) Morrow Avon.

— Avoiding the Medicaid Trap. 240p. 1991. pap. 15.00 (*0-380-71403-5*, Avon Bks) Morrow Avon.

— Golden Opportunities. 1995. pap. 19.95 (*0-8050-2956-7*) H Holt & Co.

Budjanu, M. S., et al. Nine Papers on Analysis. LC 77-11203. (Translations Ser.: Series 2, Vol. 110). 188p. 1977. 62.00 (*0-8218-3060-0*, TRANS2/110) Am Math.

— Ten Papers in Analysis. LC 73-16013. (Translations Ser.: Series 2, Vol. 102). 252p. 1973. 58.00 (*0-8218-3052-X*, TRANS2/102) Am Math.

Budka, Herbert, ed. see Garcia, Julio H.

Budke, Wesley E. Trends & Issues in Vocational Education, 1988. (Information Ser.: No. 334). 32p. 1988. 4.75 (*0-318-42051-1*) Ctr Educ Trng Employ.

Budkin, Alberto, jt. auth. see Lindsay, Alan E.

Budleigh, J. K. Trench Excavation & Support. 80p. 1989. pap. text 22.00 (*0-7277-1347-7*, Pub. by T Telford) RCH.

***Budlender, D., et al.** How to Do a Gender-Sensitive Budget Analysis. 82p. 2000. pap. 14.95 (*0-85092-615-7*, Pub. by Comm Sec) Stylus Pub VA.

Budler, Bob, ed. You Can Do It. LC 92-60702. (Illus.). 314p. 1994. pap. 10.00 (*0-937539-19-8*) Executive Bks.

***Budlong, Mo.** Cobol in 21 Days. 3rd ed. (Teach Yourself... in 24 Hours Ser.). 1100p. 1999. pap. 39.99 (*0-672-31788-5*) Sams.

Budlong, Mo. Sams Teach Yourself COBOL in 21 Days. 2nd ed. LC 97-67492. 1104p. 1997. 39.99 (*0-672-31137-2*) Sams.

Budlong, Morrison J. The Cobol Cook Book. (Illus.). 111p. 1992. ring bd. 49.95 (*1-892856-00-X*, 1) King Computer.

— The Cobol Cook Book. (Illus.). 111p. 1998. pap. 49.95 (*1-892856-01-8*, 2) King Computer.

— Cobol, Dates & the Year 2000. (Illus.). 348p. 1996. 30.00 incl. disk (*1-892856-06-9*, 7); pap. 124.95 incl. disk (*1-892856-07-7*, 8); ring bd. 99.95 (*1-892856-02-6*, 3); ring bd. 124.95 incl. disk (*1-892856-09-3*, 10) King Computer.

— Cobol, Dates & the Year 2000. (Illus.). 348p. 1998. pap. 99.95 (*1-892856-03-4*, 4) King Computer.

Budlong, Morrison J. Cobol Just in Time: Cobol Crash Course Study Guide. (Illus.). 87p. 1997. ring bd., wbk. ed. 60.00 (*1-892856-05-0*, 6) King Computer.

Budlong, Morrison J. Moving from Cobol to C. 2nd ed. (Illus.). 516p. 1993. pap. 64.95 incl. disk (*1-892856-10-7*, 11) King Computer.

— Moving from Cobol to C. 2nd ed. (Illus.). 516p. 1998. pap. 49.95 (*1-892856-04-2*, 5) King Computer.

— Teach Yourself COBOL in 21 Days. 1150p. 1994. pap. text 34.95 (*0-672-30469-4*) Sams.

Budlong, Tom & Brooks, Joan. The Desert Magazine Subject Index. LC 97-69623. 541p. 1997. 65.00 (*0-87062-281-1*) A H Clark.

Budman, Matthew, jt. auth. see Stevenson, Jay.

Budman, Simon H., ed. Forms of Brief Therapy. LC 81-2779. 482p. 1983. pap. text 30.00 (*0-89862-900-4*) Guilford Pubns.

Budman, Simon H., et al, eds. The First Session in Brief Therapy. LC 92-1533. 370p. 1992. lib. bdg. 40.00 (*0-89862-138-0*) Guilford Pubns.

Budman, Simon H. & Gurman, Alan S. Theory & Practice of Brief Therapy. LC 87-24847. 402p. 1988. lib. bdg. 47.00 (*0-89862-716-8*) Guilford Pubns.

Budman, Simon H. & Steenbarger, Brett N. The Essential Guide to Group Practice in Mental Health: Clinical, Legal & Financial Fundamentals. LC 97-20098. (Clinician's Toolbox Ser.). 318p. 1997. lib. bdg. 50.00 (*1-57230-254-2*) Guilford Pubns.

***Budney, Alan J.** Community Reinforcement Plus Vouchers Approach: Treating Cocaine Addiction. 158p. 1998. per. 14.00 (*0-16-049512-1*) USGPO.

Budney, Victor & Bratton, William W. Corporate Finance 1995 Supplement to Cases & Materials On. 4th ed. (University Casebook Ser.). 207p. (C). 1995. pap. text 9.95 (*1-56662-294-8*) Foundation Pr.

Budniakiewicz, Therese. Fundamentals of Story Logic: Introduction to Greimassian Semiotics. LC 92-22978. (Semiotic Crossroads Ser.: No. 5). xv, 230p. 1992. 65.00 (*1-55619-339-4*) J Benjamins Pubng Co.

Budnick, Dan, photos by. California Poly-Technic State University. (Illus.). 112p. 1987. 37.50 (*0-916509-25-7*) Harmony Hse Pub.

Budnick, Dean. "Jam Bands" North America's Hottest Live Groups, Plus How to Tape & Trade Their Shows. (Illus.). 300p. 1998. pap. 19.95 (*1-55022-353-4*, Pub. by ECW) Genl Dist Srvs.

— The Phishing Manual: A Compendium to the Music of Phish. 208p. (J). 1996. pap. 9.70 (*0-7868-8203-4*, Pub. by Hyperion) Time Warner.

Budnick, E. K., et al. Techniques of Quantitative Fire Hazard Analysis: Proceedings, Annual Symposium, 1985. 140p. 1986. 45.00 (*0-318-22359-7*) Society Fire Protect.

Budnick, Ernest J. Effectively Leveraging Business Technology: The Management of Business Technology to Affect Competitiveness & the Cost of Doing Business. (Illus.). 200p. (C). 1994. 39.95 (*1-56992-018-4*) Exper Exec Pr.

Budnick, Frank S. Applied Mathematics for Business, Economics, & the Social Sciences. 4th ed. LC 92-30009. (C). 1993. text 65.25 (*0-07-008902-7*) McGraw.

— Applied Mathematics for Business, Economics, & the Social Sciences. 4th ed. (C). 1993. pap. text, student ed. 30.00 (*0-07-008904-3*) McGraw.

Budnick, Herbert N. Heart to Heart: A Guide to the Psychological Aspects of Heart Disease. (Illus.). 117p. 1995. reprint ed. pap. 8.95 (*0-929173-15-5*) Health Press.

Budnick, Rich. How to Get the Job You Want in Hawaii. LC 98-93432. (Illus.). 192p. (C). 1998. 14.95 (*0-944081-03-7*) Aloha HI.

— Stolen Kingdom: An American Conspiracy. LC 92-72203. 204p. (Orig.). 1992. pap. 11.95 (*0-944081-02-9*) Aloha HI.

Budnick, Rich & Holt-Padilla, Hokulani. Maui Street Names: The Hawaiian Dictionary & History of Maui Street Names. LC 90-84607. (Illus.). 142p. (Orig.). 1991. pap. 10.95 (*0-944081-01-0*) Aloha HI.

Budnick, Rich & Wise, Duke K. Hawaiian Street Names: The Complete Guide O'ahu Street Names. LC 87-82281. (Illus.). 170p. (Orig.). 1993. pap. 11.95 (*0-944081-00-2*) Aloha HI.

Budnick, Steven D. Handbook of Pediatric Oral Pathology. LC 81-10505. (Illus.). 324p. reprint ed. pap. 100.50 (*0-8357-7677-8*, 205700500001) Bks Demand.

Budnik, Iv, ed. Arkhiv Vneshnei Politiki Rossiiskoi Imperii: Putevoditel. (RUS.). 453p. 1996. 59.95 (*1-879944-36-7*) East View Pubns.

***Budnik, Mary Ann.** Looking for Peace? Try Confession. 2nd ed. LC 00-190498. 184p. 1998. pap. 9.95 (*0-9700021-2-2*) R B Media.

— You Can Become a Saint! LC 89-63418. 303p. 1998. pap. 12.95 (*0-9700021-0-6*) R B Media.

— You Can Become a Saint! Workbook. 1999. 16.95 (*0-9700021-1-4*) R B Media.

Budnik, Vivian, et al, eds. International Review of Neurobiology: Neuromuscular Junctions in Drosophila, Vol. 43. (Illus.). 289p. 1999. 99.95 (*0-12-366843-3*) Acad Pr.

***Budnik, Vivian, et al, eds.** International Review of Neurobiology: Neuromuscular Junctions in Drosophila, Vol. 43. (Illus.). 289p. 1999. pap. 59.95 (*0-12-139370-4*) Acad Pr.

Budnitz, Judy. Flying Leap: Stories. LC 97-36088. 244p. 1997. text 20.00 (*0-312-18097-7*, Picador USA) St Martin.

— Flying Leap: Stories. LC 98-51204. 256p. 1998. pap. 12.00 (*0-312-19884-1*) St Martin.

***Budnitz, Judy.** If I Told You Once. LC 99-22249. 304p. 1999. text 24.00 (*0-312-20285-7*) St Martin.

— If I Told You Once. 2000. pap. 13.00 (*0-312-26751-7*, Picador USA) St Martin.

***Budnitz, R. J.** Methodology for Analyzing Precursors to Earthquake Initiated & Fire Initiated Accident Sequences. 172p. 1998. per. 15.00 (*0-16-062911-X*) USGPO.

Budny, Mildred, jt. auth. see Corpus Christi College (University of Cambridge) S.

Budoff, Nathan, tr. see Abad, Hector.

Budoff, Nathan, tr. see Febres, Mayra S.

Budoff, Nathan, tr. see Ospina, William.

Budoff, Nathon, tr. see Ortega, Antonia L.

Budoff, Penny W. No More Hot Flashes & Other Good News. 376p. 1989. mass mkt. 5.99 (*0-446-35879-7*, Pub. by Warner Bks) Little.

— No More Hot Flashes...and Even More Good News. (Illus.). 650p. 1999. mass mkt. 7.50 (*0-446-60780-0*, Pub. by Warner Bks) Little.

Budowle, Bruce, jt. auth. see Allen, Robert C.

Budowle, Bruce, ed. see Allen, Robert.

Budra, Paul & Schellenberg, Betty A., eds. Part Two: Reflections on the Sequel. LC 99-217365. (Theory - Culture Ser.). (Illus.). 272p. 1998. text 55.00 (*0-8020-0915-8*); pap. text 19.95 (*0-8020-7895-8*) U of Toronto Pr.

Budras & Fricke. Anatomy of the Dog. 1994. text 115.00 (*0-7234-1920-5*) Mosby Inc.

Budras & Rock, N. P. Anatomy of the Horse. 1994. text 115.00 (*0-7234-1921-3*) Mosby Inc.

Budreck, Frank. Goodbye Old Friend: A Pictorial Essay on the Final Season at Old Comiskey Park. Regnier, John, ed. LC 91-73448. (Illus.). 168p. 1991. 24.95 (*0-9630204-0-4*) ALAND Corp.

Budrewicz, Olgierd. Introduction to Poland. rev. ed. LC 84-73027. (Illus.). 216p. 1985. 15.00 (*1-881284-06-9*); pap. 15.00 (*1-881284-13-1*) Am Inst Polish.

Budris, Bill, jt. auth. see Solis, Ken M.

Budrock, Helen. Summary Guide to the Terms of the Watershed Agreement. 52p. (Orig.). Date not set. pap. write for info. (*0-9616712-7-0*) Catskill Ctr.

***Budryk, Peter.** Trout & Salmon Lakes of Connecticut: And How to Fish Them. (Illus.). 240p. (C). 1999. pap. 24.95 (*1-58066-056-8*, Covered Brdge Pr) Douglas Charles Ltd.

Budrys, Algis. Benchmarks: Galaxy Bookshelf. LC 84-10518. 380p. 1985. 21.95 (*0-8093-1187-9*) S Ill U Pr.

***Budrys, Algis.** Death Machine. 140p. 2000. pap. 12.00 (*1-58776-024-X*) Vivisphere.

Budrys, Algis. Entertainment. Katze, Rick & Lewis, Anthony, eds. LC 97-68910. (Illus.). 1997. pap. 12.00 (*1-886778-05-1*) New Eng SF Assoc.

***Budrys, Algis.** Falling Torch. 140p. 2000. pap. 12.00 (*1-58776-011-8*) Vivisphere.

Budrys, Algis. Nonliterary Influences on Science Fiction: An Essay. (Booklet Ser.: No. 9). 24p. (Orig.). 1983. pap. 1.25 (*0-936055-06-5*) C Drumm Bks.

— Rogue Moon. 1993. reprint ed. lib. bdg. 18.95 (*0-89968-334-7*, Lghtyr Pr) Buccaneer Bks.

***Budrys, Algis.** Some Will Not Die. 140p. 2000. pap. 12.00 (*1-58776-029-0*) Vivisphere.

— Unexplained. 140p. 2000. pap. 12.00 (*1-58776-023-1*) Vivisphere.

— Who? 140p. 2000. pap. 12.00 (*1-58776-010-X*, UniFont Bks) Vivisphere.

Budrys, Algis. Who? 224p. 1987. mass mkt. 3.50 (*0-445-20314-5*, Pub. by Warner Bks) Little.

— Writing to the Point. 64p. 1994. pap. text 10.50 (*1-886211-00-0*) Unifont.

Budrys, Algis, ed. L. Ron Hubbard Presents Writers of the Future, Vol. I. 1985. pap. 3.95 (*0-88404-170-0*) Bridge Pubns Inc.

— L. Ron Hubbard Presents Writers of the Future, Vol. II. (C). 1986. pap. 3.95 (*0-88404-254-5*) Bridge Pubns Inc.

— L. Ron Hubbard Presents Writers of the Future, Vol. III. (Writers of the Future Ser.). 1987. pap. 4.50 (*0-88404-245-6*) Bridge Pubns Inc.

— L. Ron Hubbard Presents Writers of the Future, Vol. IV. 430p. 1988. mass mkt. 4.95 (*0-88404-314-2*) Bridge Pubns Inc.

— L. Ron Hubbard Presents Writers of the Future, Vol. V. 1989. pap. 4.95 (*0-88404-379-7*) Bridge Pubns Inc.

— L. Ron Hubbard Presents Writers of the Future, Vol. VI. 1990. pap. 4.95 (*0-88404-504-8*) Bridge Pubns Inc.

— L. Ron Hubbard Presents Writers of the Future, Vol. VII. 1991. mass mkt. 5.95 (*0-88404-641-9*) Bridge Pubns Inc.

Budrys, Algis, ed. see Hubbard, L. Ron.

Budrys, Gladys. When Doctors Join Unions. LC 96-32596. (IRL Press Book). (Illus.). 224p. 1996. text 35.00 (*0-8014-3277-4*) Cornell U Pr.

— When Doctors Join Unions. (IRL Press Book). (Illus.). 224p. 1996. pap. text 14.95 (*0-8014-8354-9*) Cornell U Pr.

Budrys, Grace. Planning for the Nation's Health: A Study of 20th-Century Developments in the United States, 19. LC 86-12142. (Contributions in Medical Studies: No. 19). 168p. 1987. 45.00 (*0-313-25348-X*, BYP/, Greenwood Pr) Greenwood.

Budrys, Milda. Amerikos Lietuviai Gydytojai: Lithuanian American Physicians (1884-1984) LC 92-73123. Orig. Title: Amerikos Lietuviai Gydytojai. (LIT., Illus.). 194p. 1992. 10.00 (*0-929700-07-4*) Lith Res & Studies.

— Amerikos Lietuviu Gydytoju Vardynas: Lithuanian-American Medical Directory (1884-1984) LC 90-64053. 139p. 1991. 15.00 (*0-929700-06-6*) Lith Res & Studies.

— Lietuviai Gydytojai Sesiuose Kontinentuose. unabridged ed. Miglinas, Skirmante, ed. LC 96-77016.Tr. of Lithuanian Physicians Across Six Continents. (LIT., Illus.). 283p. 1996. 25.95 (*0-929700-15-5*) Lith Res & Studies.

Budson, R. D., jt. ed. see Barofsky, I.

***Budtz-Jergensen, Ejvind.** Prosthodontics for the Elderly: Diagnosis & Treatment. (Illus.). 255p. 2000. 120.00 (*4-87417-607-0*, Pub. by QPC) Quint Pub Co.

***Budtz-Jorgensen, Ejvind.** Prosthodontics for the Elderly: Diagnosis & Treatment. LC 99-38079. 266p. 1999. 89.00 (*0-86715-368-7*) Quint Pub Co.

Budvari-Barany, ZsuZsanna, jt. auth. see Szasz, Gyorgy.

Budwey, James, ed. Inter Comm 97, Global Communications Congress & Exhibition: Proceedings of the Global Communications Congress & Exhibition, Vancouver, B. C., 1997. LC 97-2072. (Communications Management Ser.). 612p. 1997. 131.00 (*0-89006-938-7*) Artech Hse.

Budwig, Nancy. A Developmental-Functionalist Approach to Child Language. 232p. 1995. text 45.00 (*0-8058-0520-6*) L Erlbaum Assocs.

Budwig, Nancy, et al. Communication: An Arena of Development. LC 99-29560. (Advances in Applied Developmental Psychology Ser.). 1999. write for info. (*1-56750-457-4*) Ablx Pub.

Budwig, R. S., et al, eds. Instructional Fluid Dynamics - 1995. LC 95-78760. (1995 ASME/JSME Fluids Engineering Conference Ser.: FED-Vol. 220). 104p. 1995. 72.00 (*0-7918-1475-0*, G00970) ASME.

— Instructional Fluid Dynamics Experiments, 1993. LC 93-71639. (FED Ser.: Vol. 152). 63p. 1993. pap. 25.00 (*0-7918-0960-9*, H00792) ASME.

Budwig, Robert. Vegetable Market Cookbook. (Illus.). 192p. 1994. pap. 16.95 (*0-89815-616-5*) Ten Speed Pr.

Budwig, Robert, jt. auth. see Coles, Janet.

Budwine, Greg, jt. auth. see Sommer, Carl.

Budworth, D. W. Finance & Innovation. (Innovation & Technology Management Ser.). 224p. 1996. pap. 59.00 (*0-415-13257-6*) Thomson Learn.

— Finance & Innovation. (Innovation & Technology Management Ser.). 224p. 1996. pap. 19.99 (*0-415-13258-4*) Thomson Learn.

Budworth, Geoffrey. The Complete Book of Decorative Knots. (Illus.). 160p. 1999. pap. 18.95 (*1-55821-791-6*) Lyons Pr.

— Complete Book of Fishing Knots. 160p. 1999. pap. text 18.95 (*1-55821-907-2*) Lyons Pr.

— The Complete Book of Knots. LC 97-16468. Orig. Title: The Hamlyn Book of Knots. (Illus.). 240p. 1997. pap. 16.95 (*1-55821-632-4*, 16324) Lyons Pr.

***Budworth, Geoffrey.** Complete Book of Sailing Knots. (Illus.). 2000. pap. 18.95 (*1-58574-067-5*) Lyons Pr.

— Illustrated Encyclopedia of Knots. (Illus.). 2000. 29.95 (*1-58574-073-X*) Lyons Pr.

Budworth, Geoffrey. The Knot Book. LC 84-26843. (Illus.). 160p. (J). (gr. 7 up). 1985. pap. 9.95 (*0-8069-7944-5*) Sterling.

***Budworth, Geoffrey.** Simple Knots & Basic Ropework. 128p. 2000. 17.95 (*1-84215-066-9*) Anness Pub.

— Tough & Versatile Knots. 128p. 2000. 17.95 (*1-84215-108-8*) Anness Pub.

Budworth, Geoffrey. Ultimate Encyclopedia of Knots & Ropework: Knots & Ropes for All Pursuits from Sailing & Fishing. 1999. 32.50 (*1-85967-911-0*, Lorenz Bks) Anness Pub.

Budy, Andrea H. House Without a Dreamer. 75p. 1993. pap. 11.95 (*0-934257-83-3*) Story Line.

— Living on the Cusp. Hettich, M. & Ahern, Colleen, eds. 35p. 1980. 3.00 (*0-686-38059-2*) MoonsQuilt Pr.

***Budy, Andrea Hollander.** The Other Life. 64p. 2001. pap. 12.95 (*1-885266-98-7*, Pub. by Story Line) Consort Bk Sales.

Budy, Danny. Pachyderms. 176p. mass mkt. 4.99 (*1-55197-130-5*) Picasso Publ.

Budy, Elizabeth E., jt. ed. see Elston, Robert G.

Budy, Jerry D., jt. auth. see Young, James A.

Budyko, M. I. Climatic Changes. Zolina, R., tr. from RUS. (Illus.). 261p. 1977. 24.00 (*0-87590-206-5*) Am Geophysical.

— The Evolution of the Biosphere. 1986. text 237.50 (*90-277-2140-8*) Kluwer Academic.

Budyko, M. I. & Golitsyn, G. S. Global Climatic Catastrophes. (Illus.). 110p. 1988. 38.95 (*0-387-18647-6*) Spr-Verlag.

Budyko, M. I. & Izrael, Yu A. Anthropogenic Climatic Change. LC 91-3722. 485p. 1990. 66.00 (*0-8165-1122-5*) U of Ariz Pr.

Budyko, M. I., et al. History of the Earth's Atmosphere. (Illus.). 150p. 1987. 76.95 (*0-387-17235-1*) Spr-Verlag.

Budynas, Richard G. Advanced Strength & Applied Stress Analysis. (Illus.). (C). 1977. text 82.50 (*0-07-008828-4*) McGraw.

— Advanced Strength & Applied Stress Analysis. 2nd ed. LC 98-29448. 960p. (C). 1998. 105.31 (*0-07-008985-X*) McGraw.

Budzik, Janet K., jt. auth. see Budzik, Richard S.

Budzik, Richard S. Fittings Used Today That Require Triangulation Including the Theory of Triangulation. 4th ed. LC 75-182389. (Illus.). (C). 1987. 29.95 (*0-912914-69-6*) Practical Pubns.

— Opportunities in Heating, Ventilation, Air-Conditioning, & Refrigeration Careers. LC 95-648. (Opportunities In . . . Ser.). (Illus.). 160p. pap. 11.95 (*0-8442-4590-9*, 45909, Natl Textbk Co) NTC Contemp Pub Co.

— Opportunities in Heating, Ventilation, Air-Conditioning, & Refrigeration Careers. LC 95-648. (Opportunities in... Ser.). (Illus.). 160p. 1995. 14.95 (*0-8442-4589-5*, 45895, Natl Textbk Co) NTC Contemp Pub Co.

— Opportunities in Refrigeration & Air Conditioning Careers. 1994. pap. 10.95 (*0-8442-8653-2*, VGM Career) NTC Contemp Pub Co.

— Practical Guide for Improving Your Metal Fabricating Shop Layout with Easy to Use Suggestions & Aids. 1988. 84.95 (*0-912914-23-8*) Practical Pubns.

— Practical Sheet Metal Projects-130 Graded Projects with Drawings, Forming Information & Sequences. 2nd ed. LC 79-93132. (Illus.). (gr. 7-12). 1986. 29.95 (*0-912914-28-9*) Practical Pubns.

— Precision Sheet Metal Blueprint Reading. LC 75-86373. 1969. 5.50 (*0-672-20687-0*, Bobbs); teacher ed. 5.00 (*0-672-20689-7*, Bobbs); student ed. 4.55 (*0-672-20688-9*, Bobbs) Macmillan.

— Precision Sheet Metal Blueprint Reading: Instructor Guide. 3rd ed. LC 75-86373. (Illus.). 127p. 1988. teacher ed. 29.95 (*0-912914-13-0*) Practical Pubns.

— Precision Sheet Metal Blueprint Reading: Student Workbook. 3rd ed. LC 75-86373. (Illus.). 127p. 1988. student ed. 24.95 (*0-912914-12-2*) Practical Pubns.

— Precision Sheet Metal Blueprint Reading: Textbook. 3rd ed. LC 75-86373. (Illus.). 127p. text 24.95 (*0-912914-40-8*) Practical Pubns.

— Precision Sheet Metal Mathematics. LC 71-83129. 1969. 9.70 (*0-672-97591-2*, Bobbs); teacher ed. 6.67 (*0-672-97593-9*, Bobbs); student ed. 4.80 (*0-672-97592-0*, Bobbs) Macmillan.

Budzik, Richard S. Precision Sheet Metal Mathematics. (Precision Sheet Metal Series). (Illus.). 349p. 1988. pap. text 24.95 (*0-912914-49-1*) Practical Pubns.

Budzik, Richard S. Precision Sheet Metal Mathematics: Instructor Guide. 2nd ed. LC 71-83129. (Illus.). 349p. 1988. teacher ed. 29.95 (*0-912914-16-5*) Practical Pubns.

— Precision Sheet Metal Mathematics: Student Workbook. 2nd ed. LC 71-83129. (Illus.). 349p. 1988. student ed. 24.95 (*0-912914-15-7*) Practical Pubns.

— Precision Sheet Metal Shop Practice. LC 78-97566. 1969. 4.55 (*0-672-97594-7*, Bobbs); teacher ed. 6.67 (*0-672-97596-3*, Bobbs); student ed. 4.80 (*0-672-97595-5*, Bobbs) Macmillan.

— Precision Sheet Metal Shop Practice: Instructor Guide. LC 78-97566. (Illus.). 96p. 1969. teacher ed. 29.95 (*0-912914-19-X*) Practical Pubns.

— Precision Sheet Metal Shop Practice: Student Workbook. LC 78-97566. (Illus.). 96p. 1969. student ed. 24.95 (*0-912914-18-1*) Practical Pubns.

— Precision Sheet Metal Shop Practice: Textbook. LC 78-97566. (Illus.). 96p. 1969. 24.95 (*0-912914-17-3*) Practical Pubns.

— Precision Sheet Metal Shop Theory. LC 79-77566. 1969. teacher ed. 5.00 (*0-672-20681-1*, Bobbs); pap. 9.20 (*0-672-20679-X*, Bobbs); student ed. 4.80 (*0-672-20680-3*, Bobbs) Macmillan.

— Precision Sheet Metal Shop Theory: Instructor Guide. 2nd ed. LC 79-77566. (Illus.). 450p. 1988. teacher ed. 29.95 (*0-912914-10-6*) Practical Pubns.

— Precision Sheet Metal Shop Theory: Student Workbook. 2nd ed. LC 79-77566. (Illus.). 450p. 1988. student ed. 24.95 (*0-912914-09-2*) Practical Pubns.

— Precision Sheet Metal Shop Theory: Textbook. 2nd ed. LC 79-77566. (Illus.). 450p. 1988. 24.95 (*0-912914-25-4*) Practical Pubns.

— Round Fittings Used Today Including Methods & Techniques of Fabricating Round Work. 4th ed. LC 71-182388. (Illus.). (C). 1988. 29.95 (*0-912914-68-8*) Practical Pubns.

— Sheet Metal Shop Fabrication Projects Including Over Three Hundred Fifty Graded Parts. LC 80-84009. (Illus.). (gr. 7-12). 1980. 29.95 (*0-912914-07-6*) Practical Pubns.

— Sheet Metal Technology. 2nd ed. 1981. 19.96 (*0-672-97360-X*, Bobbs); teacher ed. 3.67 (*0-672-97361-8*, Bobbs); student ed. 10.28 (*0-672-97362-6*, Bobbs) Macmillan.

— Sheet Metal Technology. 4th ed. 44.95 (*0-912914-64-5*) Practical Pubns.

— Specialty Items Used Today (Sheet Metal) Including Methods of Design & Fabrication & Important Trade Topics. 4th ed. LC 74-79537. (Illus.). (C). 1987. 64.95 (*0-912914-54-8*) Practical Pubns.

— Today's Forty Most Frequently Used Fittings: Including Supplemental Section of Other Fittings & Items, Vol. 1. 6th ed. 346p. 1988. 39.95 (*0-912914-67-X*) Practical Pubns.

— Today's Forty Most Frequently-Used Fittings: With Over 400 Pages of Shop & Field Information, Vol. 2. 5th ed. LC 73-188876. (Illus.). 402p. 1989. 39.95 (*0-912914-42-4*) Practical Pubns.

Budzik, Richard S. & Budzik, Janet K. One Minute Thoughts That Bring Wisdom, Harmony & Fulfillment. 1990. mass mkt. 4.95 (*0-446-36019-8*) Warner Bks.

— Today's Practical Guide to Increasing Profits for Contractors with Easy-to-Use Suggestions & Aids. LC 74-79535. (Illus.). (C). 1974. 59.95 (*0-912914-03-3*) Practical Pubns.

Budzik, Richard S. & Kuprianczyk, George. Everything You Want to Know about Bend Allowance: Including Flat Pattern Development. (Illus.). 423p. (Orig.). 1995. pap. 84.95 (*0-912914-58-0*) Practical Pubns.

— Practical Cost Estimating for Metal Fabrication. 1988. 84.95 (*0-912914-70-X*) Practical Pubns.

Budzikiewicz, Herbert & Djerassi, Carl. Interpretation of Mass Spectra of Organic Compounds. LC 64-14625. (Holden-Day Series in Physical Techniques in Chemistry). 288p. reprint ed. pap. 89.30 (*0-608-30704-1*, 205104000074) Bks Demand.

Budzilovich, G. N., tr. see Pashkov, P.

Budzine, Leona. Glances at Life: The Poetry of Leona Budzine. 110p. pap. 5.00 (*0-942698-12-6*) Trends & Events.

Budziszews. Case Studies, We the People. 1989. pap. text 10.00 (*0-03-023553-7*) Holt R&W.

— History Documents, We the People. 1989. pap. text 16.75 (*0-03-023549-9*) Holt R&W.

— We the People. 1989. text 74.00 (*0-03-022888-3*); pap. text, teacher ed., wbk. ed. 17.50 (*0-03-023558-8*); pap. text, wbk. ed. 14.50 (*0-03-023557-X*) Holt R&W.

— We the People: Testbook. 1989. pap. text 14.50 (*0-03-023559-6*) Holt R&W.

— We the People, '89. 1989. 51.75 (*0-03-022887-5*) Harcourt Schl Pubs.

Budziszews, jt. auth. see Konesky.

Budziszewski, J. How to Stay Christian in College: An Interactive Guide to Keeping the Faith. LC 98-49095. 143p. 1999. pap. 8.00 (*1-57683-061-6*) NavPress.

— The Resurrection of Nature: Political Theory & the Human Character. LC 86-6283. 224p. 1986. 37.50 (*0-8014-1900-X*) Cornell U Pr.

— The Resurrection of Nature: Political Theory & the Human Character. LC 86-6283. 219p. reprint ed. pap. 67.90 (*0-608-20878-7*, 207197700003) Bks Demand.

— The Revenge of Conscience: Politics & the Fall of Man. LC 99-23511. xx, 164p. 1999. 22.95 (*1-890626-16-3*) Spence Pub.

***Budziszewski, J.** The Revenge of Conscience: Politics & the Fall of Man. LC 99-23511. xx, 164p. 2000. pap. 12.95 (*1-890626-27-9*) Spence Pub.

Budziszewski, J. True Tolerance: Liberalism & the Necessity of Judgment. 240p. (C). 1992. 39.95 (*1-56000-026-0*) Transaction Pubs.

— True Tolerance: Liberalism & the Necessity of Judgment. 240p. 1999. pap. 24.95 (*0-7658-0666-5*) Transaction Pubs.

— Written on the Heart: The Case for Natural Law. LC 96-29818. 240p. (Orig.). 1997. pap. 14.99 (*0-8308-1891-X*, 1891) InterVarsity.

Budziszewski, J., jt. ed. see Muncy, Mitchell S.

Budzynski, A. Z., jt. ed. see Takada, Akikazy.

Budzynski, G. & Sliwinski, A. S., eds. Prospects in Modern Acoustics: Education & Development. 472p. (C). 1987. text 144.00 (*9971-5-0379-4*) World Scientific Pub.

Bue, Erberto Lo, see Ricca, Franco & Lo Bue, Erberto.

Bue, Henri, tr. see Carroll, Lewis, pseud.

Buech, Monte, jt. auth. see Brauer, Denny.

Bueche. Principles of Physics. 6th ed. 1994. pap., student ed. 86.88 (*0-07-008986-8*) McGraw.

— Technical Physics: Instructor's Free Copy. 4th ed. 1994. text 64.95 (*0-471-31159-6*) Wiley.

Bueche, F. Technical Physics. 4th ed. 704p. 1994. text 87.95 (*0-471-52462-X*) Wiley.

Bueche, Frederick J. College Physics. 1999. pap. text 8.95 (*0-07-052711-3*) McGraw-Hill Pubng.

— Introduction to Physics for Scientists & Engineers. 4th ed. 976p. (C). 1986. text 72.50 (*0-07-008871-3*) McGraw.

— Physical Science. LC 73-182927. (Illus.). 1972. text 54.95 (*0-87901-019-3*) Worth.

Bueche, Frederick J. & Hecht, Eugene. Schaum's Outline of College Physics. 9th ed. (Illus.). 416p. (C). 1997. pap. 15.95 (*0-07-008941-8*) McGraw.

Buechel, David J. The Used Car Buyer's Manual: How to Find the Best Buy on a Used Car. LC 95-70448. (Illus.). 174p. (Orig.). 1995. pap. 9.95 (*0-9647780-0-9*) Consumer Pubng.

— The Used Car Buyer's Manual II: How to Get the Best Buy on a Private-Party Sale. LC 96-92359. (Illus.). 123p. (Orig.). 1996. pap. 7.95 (*0-9647780-1-7*) Consumer Pubng.

B

Buechel, Eugene & Manhart, Paul. Lakota Tales & Texts in Translation, 2 vols., Set. 850p. 1998. 39.95 (*1-877976-22-9*) Tipi Pr.

LAKOTA TALES & TEXTS IN TRANSLATION has a remarkable history of its own. The original Lakota manuscript was rescued from destruction during the violent occupation of the village of Wounded Knee, South Dakota, during the late winter of 1973. In 1970, Paul Manhart, a Catholic priest of the Society of Jesus & at the time a pastor in that village, had published Eugene Buechel, S.J.'s monumental Lakota-English Dictionary, with the late Louis & Daisy Whirlwind Horse assisting. Louis had been a tribal interpreter & Daisy was a highly perceptive translator. Father Manhart had an office in the Sacred Heart of Jesus Church overlooking the mass grave of Lakota visitor victims of the 1890 massacre. At the time of occupation, he had borrowed the original manuscript of Buechel's "Lakota Tales & Texts" from the Holy Rosary Mission archives. He was planning soon to publish it. So he kept it on a lower shelf in the far corner of his small library. Early during the occupation, he & two local men, Benjamin White Butterfly & Ruben Mesteth, took a box & went to the office, only to find it in shambles & the room & library shelves stripped of books - all except the Tales & Texts manuscript in the corner, a dingy home-made book in Lakota long-hand, untouched. All else was gone. In June of 1978 then, "Lakota Tales & Texts" was published in St. Louis. Father Manhart prepared this translation to answer many requests from teachers of history, social sciences, & language; & to lay a groundwork for preparing a series of Lakota language texts for systematically teaching the language in a two or four-year high school course. In Louis & Daisy Whirlwind Horse's words: "Our children will lose some real & conscious contact with their roots unless we continues to record & study Lakota." ***Publisher Paid Annotation.***

Buechel, F., jt. auth. see Kober, R.

Buechel, Jenifer. Miniature Baltimore Album Quilts: 28 Embroidered & Embellished Block Designs. Lowe, Melissa, ed. LC 96-30983. (Illus.). 96p. (Orig.). 1997. pap. 17.95 (*1-56477-176-8*, B290) Martingale & Co.

— A Silk-Ribbon Album: More Than 30 Miniature Quilt Blocks. LC 98-20265. (Illus.). 112p. 1998. pap. 21.95 (*1-56477-229-2*, B346, That Patchwrk Pl) Martingale & Co.

Buecheler, Franz, ed. see Petronius.

Buecher, T., et al, eds. Biological Chemistry of Organelle Formation: Proceedings. (Colloquium Mosbach Ser.: Vol. 31). (Illus.). 254p. 1981. 60.95 (*0-387-10458-5*) Spr-Verlag.

Buechler, A. F. & Barr, R. J., eds. History of Hall County: Narrative of the Past with Special Emphasis upon the Pioneer Period, & Chronological Presentation of Its Social...& Civic Development from the Early Days to (1920)... (Illus.). 965p. 1997. reprint ed. lib. bdg. 97.00 (*0-8328-6868-X*) Higginson Bk Co.

Buechler, Hans & Buechler, Judith-Maria. The World of Sofia Velasquez: Autobiography of a Bolivian Market Vendor. LC 95-50815. (Illus.). 256p. (C). 1996. pap. 18.50 (*0-231-10467-7*) Col U Pr.

Buechler, Hans C. The Masked Media: Aymara Fiestas & Social Interaction in the Bolivian Highlands. (Approaches to Semiotics Ser.: No. 59). 400p. 1980. 69.25 (*90-279-7777-1*) Mouton.

Buechler, Hans C. & Buechler, Judith-Maria. Carmen: The Autobiography of a Spanish Galician Woman. LC 80-15487. 242p. 1981. pap. text 15.95 (*0-87073-846-1*) Schenkman Bks Inc.

Buechler, Hans C. & Buechler, Judith-Maria, eds. Migrants in Europe: The Role of the Family, Labor, & Politics, 12. LC 86-25722. (Contributions in Family Studies: No. 12). 327p. 1987. 85.00 (*0-313-23236-9*, BUM/, Greenwood Pr) Greenwood.

Buechler, Judith-Maria, jt. auth. see Buechler, Hans.

Buechler, Judith-Maria, jt. auth. see Buechler, Hans C.

Buechler, Judith-Maria, jt. ed. see Buechler, Hans C.

Buechler, M. W., et al, eds. Five Years of Laparoscopic Cholecystectomy: A Reappraisal. (Progress in Surgery Ser.: Vol. 22, 1996). (Illus.). viii, 216p. 1996. 159.25 (*3-8055-6271-3*) S Karger.

— Gastroesophageal Reflux Disease (GERD): Back to Surgery? International Meeting, Bern, May 1996. LC 97-7704. (Progress in Surgery Ser.: Vol. 23, 1997). (Illus.). viii, 248p. 1997. 184.50 (*3-8055-6476-7*) S Karger.

— Laparoscopic Hernia Repair: A New Standard? (Progress in Surgery Ser.: Vol. 21). (Illus.). viii, 194p. 1995. 139.25 (*3-8055-6047-8*) S Karger.

— Pancreatic Diseases: New Horizons. (Journal Ser.: Vol. 11, No. 3-6, 1994). (Illus.). vi, 342p. 1995. pap. 146.25 (*3-8055-6191-1*) S Karger.

— The Role of Somatostatin & Octreotide in Pancreatic Disease: Proceedings of a Symposium During the EPC Meeting, Ulm, October 1992. (Journal: Digestion: Vol. 55, Suppl. 1, 1994). (Illus.). vi, 52p. 1993. pap. 25.25 (*3-8055-5950-X*) S Karger.

Buechler, M. W., et al. Pankreaserkrankungen. (Illus.). x, 186p. 1996. 68.00 (*3-8055-6141-5*) S Karger.

Buechler, M. W., jt. ed. see Beger, H. G.

Buechler, Phil. In the World, Not of It! Jackson, Cecilia, ed. LC 95-78806. 196p. (Orig.). 1997. pap. 16.00 (*0-9639644-3-7*) Four Craftsmen.

Buechler, Ralph W. Science, Satire & Wit: The Essays of Georg Christoph Lichtenberg. LC 90-36002. (Studies in Modern German Literature: Vol. 41). 311p. (C). 1991. text 52.95 (*0-8204-1367-4*) P Lang Pubng.

Buechler, S. Essentials Stability Theory. LC 96-26226. (Perspectives in Mathematical Logic Ser.). 345p. 1996. 119.50 (*3-540-61011-1*) Spr-Verlag.

Buechler, Sandra. Sesquicentennial of Effingham County. (Illus.). 808p. 1982. 75.00 (*0-9609598-0-7*) Banbury Pub Co.

Buechler, Steven M. Social Movements in Advanced Capitalism: The Political Economy & Cultural Construction of Social Activism. LC 98-42230. 256p. (C). 1999. text 41.95 (*0-19-512603-3*); pap. text 22.95 (*0-19-512604-1*) OUP.

— Women's Movements in the United States: Woman Suffrage, Equal Rights & Beyond. LC 89-49083. 272p. (C). 1990. text 40.00 (*0-8135-1558-0*); pap. text 17.00 (*0-8135-1559-9*) Rutgers U Pr.

Buechler, Steven M. & Cylke, F. Kurt, Jr. Social Movements: Perspectives & Issues. LC 96-7995. 578p. (Orig.). (C). 1996. pap. text 42.95 (*1-55934-569-1*, 1569) Mayfield Pub.

Buechner, Alan & Shull, Bill, eds. Thirty Fiddle Tunes from the Manuscript Collection of William Sidney Mount. (Orig.). 1995. pap. 16.95 (*0-9637812-3-5*) MO St Old Time.

Buechner, Frederick. The Alphabet of Grace. LC 84-48765. 128p. 1989. pap. 12.00 (*0-06-061179-0*, Pub. by Harper SF) HarpC.

— Brendan: A Novel. LC 88-45128. 256p. 2000. reprint ed. pap. 13.00 (*0-06-061178-2*, Pub. by Harper SF) HarpC.

***Buechner, Frederick.** Eyes of the Heart: A Memoir of the Lost & Found. LC 99-23089. 192p. 1999. 18.00 (*0-06-251638-8*) HarpC.

— The Eyes of the Heart: A Memoir of the Lost & Found. LC 99-23089. 176p. 2000. reprint ed. pap. 13.00 (*0-06-251639-6*) Harper SF.

Buechner, Frederick. Godric: A Novel. LC 83-47717. 192p. 2000. reprint ed. pap. 14.00 (*0-06-061162-6*, CN 4078, Pub. by Harper SF) HarpC.

— The Hungering Dark. LC 84-48763. 128p. 1985. pap. 13.00 (*0-06-061175-8*, Pub. by Harper SF) HarpC.

— Listening to Your Life: Meditations with Frederick Buechner. 384p. 1992. pap. 14.00 (*0-06-069864-0*, Pub. by Harper SF) HarpC.

— The Longing for Home: Recollections & Reflections. LC 96-1008. 192p. 1996. 21.00 (*0-06-061191-X*, Pub. by Harper SF) HarpC.

— The Magnificent Defeat. LC 84-48764. 144p. 1985. pap. 11.00 (*0-06-061174-X*, Pub. by Harper SF) HarpC.

— Now & Then: A Memoir of Vocation. LC 91-55091. 128p. 1991. reprint ed. pap. 12.00 (*0-06-061182-0*, Pub. by Harper SF) HarpC.

— On the Road With Archangel. LC 97-4099. 160p. 1997. 17.00 (*0-06-061125-1*, Pub. by Harper SF) HarpC.

— On the Road with the Archangel. large type ed. LC 98-12005. (Inspirational Ser.). 152p. 1998. 22.95 (*0-7838-0129-7*, G K Hall & Co) Mac Lib Ref.

— Peculiar Treasures: A Biblical Who's Who. LC 92-54775. 224p. 1993. pap. 12.00 (*0-06-061141-3*, Pub. by Harper SF) HarpC.

— A Room Called Remember: Uncollected Pieces. 208p. 1992. reprint ed. pap. 13.00 (*0-06-061185-5*, Pub. by Harper SF) HarpC.

— The Sacred Journey: A Memoir of Early Days. LC 91-55089. 128p. 1991. reprint ed. pap. 13.00 (*0-06-061183-9*, Pub. by Harper SF) HarpC.

— The Son of Laughter: A Novel. LC 92-53899. 288p. 1994. reprint ed. pap. 15.00 (*0-06-250117-8*, Pub. by Harper SF) HarpC.

— The Storm. LC 98-7377. 2001. pap. 13.00 (*0-06-061145-6*) Harper SF.

— The Storm. large type ed. LC 99-20141. 203p. 1999. 24.95 (*0-7838-8605-5*) Mac Lib Ref.

— The Storm: A Novel. LC 98-7377. 208p. 1998. 18.00 (*0-06-061144-8*, Pub. by Harper SF) HarpC.

— Telling Secrets. LC 90-41770. 128p. 1992. reprint ed. pap. 13.00 (*0-06-060936-2*, Pub. by Harper SF) HarpC.

Buechner, Frederick. Telling the Truth: The Gospel As Tragedy, Comedy & Fairy Tale. LC 77-7839. 112p. 1977. 18.00 (*0-06-061156-1*, Pub. by Harper SF) HarpC.

Buechner, Frederick. Whistling in the Dark: An ABC Theologized. LC 87-45690. 144p. 1993. reprint ed. pap. 12.00 (*0-06-061140-5*, Pub. by Harper SF) HarpC.

— Wishful Thinking: A Seeker's ABC. rev. ed. LC 92-54776. 144p. 1993. pap. 13.00 (*0-06-061139-1*, Pub. by Harper SF) HarpC.

— Wizard's Tide. large type ed. (General Ser.). 156p. 1991. lib. bdg. 20.95 (*0-8161-5142-3*, G K Hall Lrg Type) Mac Lib Ref.

Buechner, Robert. The Eight Pathways to Financial Success. 1987. pap. 14.95 (*0-938067-11-7*) Jason Pub OH.

***Buechner, Robert.** The 8 Pathways to Financial Success. LC 99-205170. (Illus.). 1998. write for info. (*0-938067-56-7*) Jason Pub OH.

Buechner, T., ed. see Wormann, B., et al.

***Buechner, Thomas S.** How I Paint: Secrets of a Sunday Painter. LC 99-38327. 128p. 2000. 29.95 (*0-8109-4153-8*, Pub. by Abrams) Time Warner.

Buechner, Thomas S. Lino Tagliapietra. 1998. 75.00 (*1-902535-01-4*) Antique Collect.

— Norman Rockwell: Artist & Illustrator. (Illus.). 328p. 1996. pap. 49.98 (*0-8109-8150-5*, Pub. by Abrams) Time Warner.

Buechner, Thomas S., et al. Stanislav Libensky & Jaroslava Brychtova: A 40-Year Collaboration in Glass. LC 92-83742. (Illus.). 224p. 1994. 99.95 (*3-7913-1252-9*, Pub. by Prestel) te Neues.

Buechtemann, Christoph F., ed. Employment Security & Labor Market Behavior: Interdisciplinary Approaches & International Evidence. LC 92-11308. (Cornell International Industrial & Labor Relations Reports: No. 23). 528p. 1994. pap. text 29.95 (*0-87546-337-1*, ILR Press) Cornell U Pr.

Buecken, F. J. Vocabulario Tecnico: Portuguese-English-French-German. 5th ed. (FRE, GER & POR.). 600p. 1976. 105.00 (*0-7859-7144-0*) Fr & Eur.

Buecker, Bernard, jt. auth. see Tremml, Bernd.

***Buecker, Brad.** Fundamentals of Steam Generation Chemistry: A Guide for Operators, Engineers & Engineering Students. LC 00-23790. 2000. write for info. (*0-87814-750-0*) PennWell Bks.

Buecker, Brad. Power Plant Chemistry: A Practical Guide. LC 97-36403. 1997. 89.95 (*0-87814-619-9*) PennWell Bks.

Buecker, Thomas R. Fort Robinson & the American West, 1874-1899. LC 98-68787. (Illus.). 265p. 1999. 40.00 (*0-933307-26-8*) Nebraska Hist.

Buecker, Thomas R. & Paul, R. Eli, eds. The Crazy Horse Surrender Ledger. LC 94-65396. (Illus.). 208p. 1994. lib. bdg. 44.95 (*0-933307-01-2*) Nebraska Hist.

***Buede, Dennis M.** The Engineering Design of Systems: Models & Methods. LC 99-10823. (Series in Systems Engineering). 462p. 1999. 79.95 (*0-471-28225-1*) Wiley.

Buede, Dennis M., jt. auth. see Watson, Stephen R.

Buedel, J. Klima-Geomorphologie 2. (Boden in Niedersachsen Ser.). (DUT., Illus.). viii, 304p. 1981. 58.00 (*3-443-01017-2*, Pub. by Gebruder Borntraeger) Balogh.

Buedel, Julie. Studien zur Tropischen Reliefbildung. (Relief, Boden, Palaeoklima Ser.: Band 4). (GER., Illus.). viii, 225p. 1986. pap. 70.00 (*3-443-09004-4*, Pub. by Gebruder Borntraeger) Balogh.

***Bueford, Timothy W. & McBride, Stephanie G.** The Division: Defending Little Rock, August 25th-September 10th, 1863. (Illus.). xix, 250p. 1999. pap. 29.95 (*0-9673291-1-6*) WireStorm.

***Buegal, Dale.** Homeopathic Remedies: For Health Professionals & Laypeople. rev. ed. (Illus.). 250p. 2000. pap. 15.95 (*0-89389-177-0*) Himalayan Inst.

Buege, Bob. The Milwaukee Braves: A Baseball Eulogy. LC 88-70552. (Illus.). 415p. 1988. 19.95 (*1-882134-34-6*); pap. 12.95 (*1-882134-26-5*) Douglas Amer Sports Pubns.

Buege, Bob, jt. auth. see Mathews, Eddie.

Buege, Carol, jt. auth. see Stewig, John W.

Buege, Sandy. Recipes from Missouri: With Love. 190p. 1986. spiral bd. 13.95 (*0-913703-13-3*) Strawberry Pt.

Buehl, Doug. Classroom Strategies for Interactive Learning. 139p. 1995. pap. text 10.00 (*1-888714-00-X*) Wiscon St Rding.

Buehl, Olivia B. Tiles. LC 97-108602. 1996. 40.00 (*0-517-79976-6*) C Potter.

Buehler, contrib. by. A Walk with Peter & Paul. pap. 9.95 incl. VHS (*0-87162-518-0*) Warner Pr.

Buehler, Arthur F. Sufi Heirs of the Prophet: The Indian Naqshbandiyya & the Rise of the Mediating Sufi Shaykh. LC 97-40145. (Illus.). 240p. 1998. 39.95 (*1-57003-201-7*) U of SC Pr.

Buehler, Bruce A., jt. auth. see Anderson, Rebecca R.

Buehler, Dan Y., jt. auth. see Stewart, J. David.

Buehler, F. R., ed. Circadian Variation in Cardiovascular Disease: The Need for Compliance - Journal: Cardiology, Vol. 80, Suppl. 1, 1992. (Illus.). iv, 60p. 1992. pap. 20.00 (*3-8055-5613-6*) S Karger.

Buehler, George. Buehler's Backyard Boatbuilding. (Illus.). 256p. 1990. pap. text 24.95 (*0-87742-257-5*) Intl Marine.

— The Laws of Manu. LC 73-149682. (BCL Ser. II). reprint ed. 34.50 (*0-404-01148-9*) AMS Pr.

— The Troller Yacht Book: A Powerboater's Guide to Crossing Oceans Without Getting Wet or Going Broke. LC 98-48052. (Illus.). 192p. 1999. 25.95 (*0-393-04709-1*) Norton.

Buehler, Hans-Peter. Jaeger, Kosaken und Polnische Reiter. Josef Brandt, Alfred von Wierusz-Kowalski, Franz Roubaud und der MuenchnerPolen-Kreis. (GER., Illus.). 156p. 1993. 105.00 (*3-487-09655-2*) G Olms Pubs.

Buehler, J. L. Some Special Problems of Aircraft Gear Manufacture. (Technical Papers: Vol. P217). (Illus.). 18p. 1941. pap. text 30.00 (*1-55589-454-2*) AGMA.

Buehler, Janice A. Nurses & Physicians in Transition. Kalisch, Philip & Kalisch, Beatrice, eds. LC 82-10940. (Studies in Nursing Management: No. 10). 163p. 1982. reprint ed. pap. 50.60 (*0-8357-1379-2*, 207007100063) Bks Demand.

Buehler, Kathleen D. They Answered God's Call. Harman, Dan, ed. (Illus.). 1996. pap. 9.95 (*0-87162-690-X*) Warner Pr.

— A Walk with Jesus. 1992. 9.95 incl. VHS (*0-87162-619-5*, D4300) Warner Pr.

— A Walk with Old Testament Heroes. Harman, Dan, ed. (Illus.). 100p. (Orig.). (J). (gr. 5-7). 1996. pap. 9.95 incl. VHS (*0-87162-680-2*) Warner Pr.

Buehler, Lukas K., jt. auth. see Rashidi, Hooman H.

Buehler, Mary F., jt. auth. see Van Buren, Robert.

Buehler, Paula. Who's on Second Beach? (Geronimo Pack Ser.). 8p. (J). (gr. k-2). 1993. pap. write for info. (*1-882563-07-7*) Lamont Bks.

Buehler, Philip G. The Middle English Genesis & Exodus: A Running Commentary on the Text of the Poem. LC 73-79277. (De Proprietatibus Litterarum, Ser. Practica: No. 74). 85p. 1974. pap. text 33.10 (*90-279-3082-1*) Mouton.

Buehler, Randy. Official Guide: Magic Gathering. 1999. pap. 16.99 (*0-7869-1375-4*, Pub. by TSR Inc) Random.

Buehler, Robert C. Building on the Rock: Practical Advice from Jesus! 178p. 1998. pap. 19.50 (*1-55212-205-0*, No. 98-0001) Trafford Pub.

***Buehler, Stephanie & Kremer, Kelly Dos Santos.** Elections: Primary. (Illus.). 48p. 2000. pap., teacher ed. 7.95 (*1-57690-618-3*, TCM 2618) Tchr Create Mat.

Buehler, Stephanie J., ed. see Breyer, Michelle.

Buehler, Stephanie J., ed. see Clark, Sarah Kartchner.

Buehler, Stephanie J., ed. see Prior, Jennifer Overend.

Buehler, Vernon M., jt. ed. see Shetty, Y. Krishna.

Buehler, William & Seabrook, W. B. Magic Island. (Illus.). 336p. 1994. pap. 10.95 (*1-56924-949-0*) Marlowe & Co.

Buehlman, Barbara, ed. see Zajac, Victor W.

Buehlmann. Applications Cost Accounting. 9th ed. 1997. pap. text 30.00 (*0-13-567744-0*) P-H.

***Buehlmann, David.** Strategic & Operational Planning & Control. 176p. 2000. write for info. (*1-58692-034-0*) Copyright Mgmt.

Buehner, Caralyn. Escape of Marvin the Ape. (Illus.). 32p. (ps-3). 1999. pap. 5.99 (*0-14-056503-5*, PuffinBks) Peng Put Young Read.

— Fanny's Dream. LC 94-31910. (Illus.). 40p. (J). (ps-3). 1996. 15.99 (*0-8037-1496-3*, Dial Yng Read); 14.89 (*0-8037-1497-1*, Dial Yng Read) Peng Put Young Read.

— I Did It, I'm Sorry. LC 97-10216. (Illus.). 32p. (J). (gr. k-3). 1998. 15.99 (*0-8037-2010-6*, Dial Yng Read) Peng Put Young Read.

***Buehner, Caralyn.** I Did It, I'm Sorry. (Picture Puffin Ser.). (Illus.). 40p. (J). (ps-3). 2000. pap. 5.99 (*0-14-056722-4*, PuffinBks) Peng Put Young Read.

— I Did It, I'm Sorry. (Illus.). (J). 2000. 11.44 (*0-606-18838-X*) Turtleback.

Buehner, Caralyn. It's a Spoon Not a Shovel. LC 93-36293. (Illus.). (YA). (gr. 5 up). 1995. 14.99 (*0-8037-1494-7*, Dial Yng Read) Peng Put Young Read.

— It's a Spoon, Not a Shovel. 40p. (J). (gr. k-3). 1998. pap. 5.99 (*0-14-056427-6*, PuffinBks) Peng Put Young Read.

Buehner, Caralyn & Buehner, Mark. The Escape of Marvin the Ape. LC 91-10795. (Illus.). 32p. (J). (ps-3). 1992. 14.99 (*0-8037-1123-9*, Dial Yng Read) Peng Put Young Read.

***Buehner, Mark.** Wordless Christmas Picture Book. (J). 1999. 15.99 (*0-8037-2132-3*, Dial Yng Read) Peng Put Young Read.

Buehner, Mark, jt. auth. see Buehner, Caralyn.

Buehrens, Adam. Hi, I'm Adam: A Child's Book of Tourette Syndrome. LC 90-47552. (Illus.). 35p. (Orig.). (J). (gr. k-8). 1991. pap. 4.95 (*1-878267-29-9*) Hope Pr CA.

Buehrens, Adam & Buehrens, Carol. Adam & the Magic Marble: A Magical Adventure. LC 90-23906. (Illus.). 108p. (Orig.). (J). (gr. k-10). 1991. pap. 6.95 (*1-878267-30-2*) Hope Pr CA.

Buehrens, Carol. DataCAD for Architects & Designers. LC 95-3073. 1995. pap. 39.95 (*0-07-008914-0*) McGraw.

— DataCAD for the Architect. 2nd ed. 1990. pap. 27.95 (*0-8306-3746-X*) McGraw-Hill Prof.

— VersaCAD on the Mac. (Illus.). 496p. 1990. 34.95 (*0-8306-9514-1*, 3514); pap. 24.60 (*0-8306-3514-9*) McGraw-Hill Prof.

— VersaCAD Tutorial: A Practical Approach to Computer-Aided Design. (Illus.). 352p. 1988. 28.95 (*0-8306-0303-4*, 3003); pap. 19.95 (*0-8306-9303-3*) McGraw-Hill Prof.

Buehrens, Carol & Neubert, Kevin. DataCAD for the Architect. (Computer Graphics Technology & Management Ser.). (Illus.). 296p. 1989. 34.95 (*0-8306-9175-8*, 3075) McGraw-Hill Prof.

Buehrens, Carol, jt. auth. see Buehrens, Adam.

Buehrens, John A. Heaven, Hell & in Between: A Course on Good, Evil & Moral Ambiguity. 30p. (Orig.). 1989. pap. 6.00 (*0-9622111-3-3*) Unitarian Ch All Souls.

— Religious Liberals Read the Bible. 64p. (Orig.). 1989. pap. 8.00 (*0-9622111-4-1*) Unitarian Ch All Souls.

Buehrens, John A. & Church, F. Forrester. A Chosen Faith: An Introduction to Unitarian Universalism. LC 97-51479. 240p. 1998. pap. 14.00 (*0-8070-1617-9*) Beacon Pr.

Buehrens, John A. & Church, Forrest. A Chosen Faith: An Introduction to Unitarian Universalism. LC 97-51479. 240p. 1998. 25.00 (*0-8070-1616-0*) Beacon Pr.

— La Fe Que Hemos Escogido: Una Introduccion al Unitario Universalismo. Barrios, Ervin, tr.Tr. of Our Chosen Faith. (SPA.). 224p. 1998. pap. 12.95 (*1-55896-368-5*, Skinner Hse Bks) Unitarian Univ.

Buehrens, John A., ed. & intro. see Trapp, Jacob.

Buehrer, Beverly B. Boris Korloff: A Bio-Bibliography, 39. LC 93-9587. (Bio-Bibliographies in the Performing Arts Ser.: No. 39). 312p. 1993. lib. bdg. 59.95 (*0-313-27715-X*, BBN) Greenwood.

— Cary Grant: A Bio-Bibliography, 12. LC 90-31764. (Biliographies & Indexes in the Performing Arts Ser.: No. 12). 216p. 1990. lib. bdg. 45.00 (*0-313-26443-0*, BUG, Greenwood Pr) Greenwood.

Buehrer, Eric. Creating a Positive Public School Experience. 1994. pap. 12.99 (*0-7852-8156-8*) Nelson.

— The Public Orphanage. 1995. pap. 14.99 (*0-8499-3532-6*) Word Pub.

Buehrig, Edward H. The U. N. & the Palestinian Refugees: A Study in Nonterritorial Administration. LC 71-160124. (Indiana University International Development Research Center Studies in Development: No. 3). 231p. reprint ed. pap. 71.70 (*0-608-10184-2*, 205523500011) Bks Demand.

— Wilson's Foreign Policy in Perspective. 1990. 16.50 (*0-8446-0521-2*) Peter Smith.

— Woodrow Wilson & the Balance of Power. 1990. 16.50 (*0-8446-0522-0*) Peter Smith.

Buehring, Michelle. A Different Angle: Co-OperActivities in Communication. Ashkenas, Joan, ed. LC 98-65319. (Illus.). 112p. 1998. pap. text 12.95 (*0-943327-19-9*) JAG Pubns.

— A Different Angle: Co-OperActivities in Communication Teacher's Manual. Ashkenas, Joan, ed. 1998. pap. text 2.00 (*0-943327-20-2*) JAG Pubns.

Buekenhout, F. Handbook of Incidence Geometry: Buildings & Foundations. LC 94-20334. 1432p. 1994. 247.50 (*0-444-88355-X*, North Holland) Elsevier.

Buekens, A. G. & Dragalov, V. V., eds. Environmentally Devastated Areas in River Basins in Eastern Europe. LC 98-36220. (NATO ASI Ser.: Vol. 45). (Illus.). x, 386p. 1998. 159.00 (*3-540-64751-1*) Spr-Verlag.

Buekens, P., et al, eds. Perinatal Epidemiology & Health Care Organisation: The Case of Belgium. (Journal: Biology of the Neonate: Vol. 55, No. 1,1989). (Illus.). iv, 72p. 1989. pap. 51.50 (*3-8055-4978-4*) S Karger.

Buel, J. W. The Life & Wonderful Adventures of Wild Bill (J. B. Hicock) Jones, William R., ed. (Illus.). 1977. reprint ed. pap. 2.00 (*0-89646-013-4*) Vistabooks.

Buel, James W. Heroes of the Dark Continent. LC 73-138333. (Black Heritage Library Collection). 1977. 60.95 (*0-8369-8725-X*) Ayer.

— The Magic City. LC 74-15728. (Popular Culture in America Ser.). (Illus.). 294p. 1975. reprint ed. 87.95 (*0-405-06364-4*) Ayer.

Buel, Jesse. The Farmer's Companion: Or Essays on the Principles & Practice of American Husbandry. LC 72-89092. (Rural America Ser.). 1973. reprint ed. 30.00 (*0-8420-1478-0*) Scholarly Res Inc.

Buel, Joy D., jt. auth. see Buel, Richard, Jr.

Buel, Richard, Jr. In Irons: Britain's Naval Supremacy & the American Revolutionary Economy. LC 98-21281. 400p. 1998. 35.00 (*0-300-07388-7*) Yale U Pr.

Buel, Richard, Jr. & Buel, Joy D. The Way of Duty: A Woman & Her Family in Revolutionary America. 336p. 1995. pap. 12.95 (*0-393-31210-0*, Norton Paperbks) Norton.

***Buelens, Frans, ed.** Globalisation & the Nation-State. LC 99-39496. 208p. 2000. 80.00 (*1-84064-202-5*) E Elgar.

Buelens, Gert, ed. Deferring a Dream: Literary Sub-Versions of the American Columbiad. LC 94-6566. (International Cooper Series in English Language & Literature). 1994. 35.00 (*0-8176-5022-9*) Birkhauser.

— Enacting History in Henry James: Narrative, Power, & Ethics. 232p. (C). 1997. text 54.95 (*0-521-57089-1*) Cambridge U Pr.

Bueler, Gladys. Colorado's Colorful Characters. LC 74-25452. (Illus.). 115p. 1981. pap. 9.95 (*0-87108-595-X*) Pruett.

Bueler, Lois E. Clarissa's Plots. (Illus.). 184p. 1994. 33.50 (*0-87413-496-X*) U Delaware Pr.

Bueler, William M. Agenda for Sustainability: Fairness in a World of Limits. LC 97-71383. 150p. (Orig.). 1997. pap. 15.95 (*0-940121-42-5*, P308) Cross Cultural Pubns.

***Bueler, William M.** Roof of the Rockies: A History of Colorado Mountaineering. 3rd ed. (Illus.). 2000. pap. 16.95 (*0-9671466-1-5*) Colorado Mt.

Bueler, William M. U. S. China Policy & the Problem of Taiwan. LC 79-25371. 143p. 1980. reprint ed. lib. bdg. 49.75 (*0-313-22153-7*, BUUS, Greenwood Pr) Greenwood.

Buell. China's Caucasian Mummies. 1998. pap. 16.98 (*0-8050-5184-8*) H Holt & Co.

— Greenland Mummies. LC 97-15231. 1998. pap. 16.98 (*0-8050-5183-X*) H Holt & Co.

Buell, Arthur M. Griswold, Ancestors & Descendants of Edward Griswold of New York. 82p. 1996. reprint ed. pap. 16.50 (*0-8328-5306-2*); reprint ed. lib. bdg. 26.50 (*0-8328-5305-4*) Higginson Bk Co.

Buell, Augustus C. Paul Jones: Founder of the American Navy, 2 Vols. LC 70-157326. (Select Bibliographies Reprint Ser.). 1977. reprint ed. 49.95 (*0-8369-5786-5*) Ayer.

An Asterisk (*) at the beginning of an entry indicates that the title is appearing for the first time.

***Buell, Clarence C. & Johnson, Robert U., eds.** Battles & Leaders of the Civil War, 8 vols. unabridged ed. (Illus.). 3193p. 1999. reprint ed. 200.00 (*0-9650926-9-0*) J Kallmann.

Buell, D. A. Binary Quadratic Forms. 255p. 1989. 59.95 (*0-387-97037-1*, 2985) Spr-Verlag.

Buell, D. A. & Teitelbaum, J. T., eds. Computational Perspectives on Number Theory: Proceedings of a Conference in Honor of A. O. L. Atkin. (C). 1998. 42.00 (*1-57146-077-2*) Intl Pr Boston.

Buell, Denise Kimber, see Kimber Buell, Denise.

Buell, Duncan A., et al. Computational Perspectives on Number Theory. LC 97-45482. (Studies in Advanced Mathematics). 232p. 1997. pap. 59.00 (*0-8218-0880-X*) Am Math.

— Splash 2: FPGAs in a Custom Computing Machine. LC 95-47397. 224p. 1996. 40.00 (*0-8186-7413-X*, BPO7413) IEEE Comp Soc.

Buell, Ellen L. A Family Treasury of Little Golden Books. LC PZ5.F2146 1998. (Golden Classics Ser.). 192p. (J). 1998. 19.95 (*0-307-16850-6*, 16850, Goldn Books) Gldn Bks Pub Co.

Buell, Emmett H., Jr. & Sigelman, Lee, eds. Nominating the President. LC 90-43212. 320p. 1991. 42.95 (*0-87049-686-7*); pap. text 18.95 (*0-87049-687-5*) U of Tenn Pr.

Buell, Frederick. National Culture & New Global System. LC 94-2076. (Parallax). 384p. 1994. text 48.50 (*0-8018-4833-4*); pap. text 17.95 (*0-8018-4834-2*) Johns Hopkins.

***Buell, Hal.** Moments: The Pulitzer Prize Photographs: a Visual Chronicle of Our Time. LC 99-39193. (Illus.). 255p. 1999. 29.98 (*1-57912-078-4*, Pub. by Blck Dog & Leventhal) Workman Pub.

— Photo Oops: 101 Photo Opportunities Gone Horribly Awry. (Illus.). 96p. 2000. pap. 9.95 (*1-57912-155-1*) Blck Dog & Leventhal.

Buell, Janet. Ancient Horsemen of Siberia. LC 98-9909. (Time Travelers Ser.). 64p. (J). (gr. 6-9). 1998. lib. bdg. 23.40 (*0-7613-3005-4*) Millbrook Pr.

Buell, Janet. Bog Bodies. LC 97-5449. (Time Travelers Ser.). 64p. (YA). (gr. 5 up). 1997. 20.40 (*0-8050-5164-3*) TFC Bks NY.

— Burnout: How to Put Excitement Back into Your Life. rev. ed. (C). 1999. pap. 24.95 (*1-929830-03-3*) Innovat Pr CA.

— Choices in the Hereafter. 2nd ed. 110p. (C). 1999. pap. 9.95 (*1-929830-00-9*) Innovat Pr CA.

— Choices in the Hereafter. 2nd rev. ed. 130p. 1999. 16.95 (*1-929830-05-X*) Innovat Pr CA.

Buell, Janet. Greenland Mummies. LC 97-15231. (Time Travelers Ser.). 64p. (J). (gr. 5-8). 1998. lib. bdg. 23.40 incl. 5.25 hd (*0-7613-3004-6*) TFC Bks NY.

***Buell, Janet.** The Guardian. rev. ed. 1999. pap. 12.95 (*1-929830-04-1*) Innovat Pr CA.

Buell, Janet. Ice Maidens of the Andes. LC 97-23372. (Time Travelers Ser.). 64p. (YA). (gr. 5 up). 1997. 20.40 (*0-8050-5185-6*) TFC Bks NY.

***Buell, Janet.** The Learning Disabled: How You Can Help Them Regain Their Self Confidence. rev. ed. 130p. 1999. pap. 19.95 incl. cd-rom (*1-929830-01-7*) Innovat Pr CA.

— Your Mind & Body Are a Corporation & You Are the CEO. rev. ed. (C). 1999. pap. 24.95 (*1-929830-02-5*) Innovat Pr CA.

Buell, Jesse H. The Prediction of Growth in Uneven-Aged Timber Stands on the Basis of Diameter Distributions. LC SD0555.B9. (Duke University, School of Forestry Bulletin Ser.: No. 11). (Illus.). 70p. reprint ed. pap. 30.00 (*0-7837-6049-3*, 204586200008) Bks Demand.

Buell, John. Democracy by Other Means: The Politics of Work, Leisure & Environment. LC 94-45940. 178p. 1995. text 34.95 (*0-252-02181-9*); pap. text 14.95 (*0-252-06471-2*) U of Ill Pr.

— A Lot to Make up For. 201p. 1990. 18.95 (*0-374-19177-8*) FS&G.

Buell, John & DeLuca, Thomas S., Jr. Sustainable Democracy: Individuality & the Politics of Growth. LC 96-9976. 192p. 1996. 42.00 (*0-7619-0221-X*); pap. 18.95 (*0-7619-0222-8*) Sage.

Buell, John, jt. auth. see Kravolec, Etta.

Buell, Jon, ed. see Johnson, Phillip E.

Buell, Lawrence. The Environmental Imagination: Thoreau, Nature Writing, & the Formation of American Culture. LC 94-31321. 599p. 1995. text 39.50 (*0-674-25861-4*) Belknap Pr.

— The Environmental Imagination: Thoreau, Nature Writing, & the Formation of American Culture. (Illus.). 608p. 1996. pap. 16.95 (*0-674-25862-2*) Belknap Pr.

— New England Literary Culture: From Revolution Through Renaissance. (Cambridge Studies in American Literature & Culture: No. 15). 528p. (C). 1989. pap. text 25.95 (*0-521-37801-X*) Cambridge U Pr.

— The Rise & "Fall" of the Great American Novel. (12th James Russell Wiggins Lecture in the History of the Book in American Culture Ser.). 23p. 1995. pap. 6.00 (*0-944026-62-1*) Am Antiquarian.

Buell, Lawrence, ed. Ralph Waldo Emerson: A Collection of Critical Essays. LC 92-17658. (New Century Views Ser.). 256p. (C). 1992. pap. text 9.80 (*0-13-276783-X*) P-H.

Buell, Lawrence, ed. see Stoddard, Elizabeth.

Buell, Lawrence, ed. see Whitman, Walt.

Buell, Lawrence, ed. & intro. see Longfellow, Henry Wadsworth.

Buell, Linda M. Simplify Your Life, Set. (C). 1997. pap., wbk. ed. 29.95 incl. audio (*1-928607-03-9*, 9901) Simplify Life.

***Buell, Linda Manassee.** Simplify Your Life. 101 Ways to Create the Life You'll Love. iii, 17p. 1998. pap. 5.00 (*1-928607-00-4*) Simplify Life.

— Simplify Your Life Workbook: A Journey of Personal Discovery. viii, 70p. 1998. pap. 19.95 (*1-928607-01-2*) Simplify Life.

Buell, Maureen, jt. auth. see Cumming, Georgia.

Buell, Murray F., jt. auth. see Robichaud, Beryl.

Buell, Paul. Soup for the Qan: A Translation & Study. 200p. 1997. 225.00 (*0-7103-0583-4*, Pub. by Kegan Paul Intl) Col U Pr.

Buell, Raymond L. Liberia: A Century of Survival, 1847-1947. (African Handbooks Ser.: Vol. 7). (Illus.). viii, 140p. 1947. pap. 10.00 (*0-686-24090-1*) U Museum Pubns.

Buell, Thomas. The Warrior Generals. 528p. 1998. pap. 16.00 (*0-609-80173-2*, Crown) Crown Pub Group.

Buell, Thomas B. Master of Seapower: A Biography of Fleet Admiral Ernest J. King. (Classics of Naval Literature Ser.). (Illus.). 638p. 1995. 32.95 (*1-55750-092-4*) Naval Inst Pr.

— The Quiet Warrior. LC 87-15177. (Classics of Naval Literature Ser.). 544p. 1987. reprint ed. 32.95 (*0-87021-562-0*) Naval Inst Pr.

Buell, William A. Hamlets of the Theater. (Illus.). 1965. 27.95 (*0-8392-1158-9*) Astor-Honor.

Bueller, Bob. In the Beginning: Lessons from the Dawn of Time. Eichenberger, Jim, ed. (Solid Foundation Bible Studies: Vol. 1). 64p. 1999. 9.99 (*0-7847-0901-7*, 41101) Standard Pub.

Bueller, H. R., jt. ed. see Agnelli, G.

Buelow, Barry. BBS Sysop Guide. 54p. 1996. pap. 9.00 (*0-9644707-1-3*) Tucson Amat Pack Rad.

Buelow, Bernhard H. Von, see Von Buelow, Bernhard H.

Buelow, Carol J. Bed & Breakfast Favorites. LC 94-235934. (Illus.). 176p. (Orig.). 1994. pap. 11.95 (*0-9619607-3-6*) CJB Enterprises.

Buelow, Edeltraud & Schmitter, Peter, eds. Integrale Linguistik: Festschrift fur Helmut Gipper. (Illus.). xiii, 817p. 1979. 130.00 (*90-272-2001-8*) J Benjamins Pubng Co.

Buelow, George & Hebert, Suzanne. Counselor's Resource on Psychiatric Medications: Issues of Treatment & Referral. LC 94-16311. 130p. 1994. mass mkt. 18.25 (*0-534-24960-4*) Brooks-Cole.

Buelow, George, jt. auth. see Buelow, Sidne.

Buelow, George, ed. see Berger, Karol.

Buelow, George, ed. see Caluori, Eleanor.

Buelow, George, ed. see Cusick, Suzanne G.

Buelow, George, ed. see Gustafson, Bruce.

Buelow, George, ed. see Hanning, Barbara R.

Buelow, George, ed. see Holoman, D. Kern.

Buelow, George, ed. see Hyde, Martha M.

Buelow, George, ed. see Mead, Rita.

Buelow, George, ed. see Millner, Fredrick L.

Buelow, George, ed. see Pendle, Karin.

Buelow, George, ed. see Petty, Fred C.

Buelow, George, ed. see Schmidt, John C.

Buelow, George, ed. see Vollen, Gene E.

Buelow, George J. Thorough-Bass Accompaniment According to Johann David Heinichen. rev. ed. LC 92-16780. (Illus.). xviii, 462p. 1992. pap. text 30.00 (*0-8032-6106-3*) U of Nebr Pr.

Buelow, George J. & Marx, Hans J., eds. New Mattheson Studies. LC 83-5157. 512p. 1984. text 95.00 (*0-521-25115-X*) Cambridge U Pr.

Buelow, George J., jt. auth. see Daviau, Donald G.

Buelow, George J., ed. see Cunningham, Walker E.

Buelow, George J., ed. see Friedland, Bea.

Buelow, George J., ed. see Teplow, Deborah A.

Buelow, George J., ed. see White, Pamela C.

Buelow, George J., ed. see Whitesitt, Linda.

Buelow, Hebert. Psychotherapist's Resource on Psychiatric Medications. 2nd ed. LC 99-33331. 183p. 1999. 43.95 (*0-534-35703-2*) Thomson Learn.

Buelow, Sidne & Buelow, George. Psychotherapy in Chemical Dependence Treatment: A Practical & Integrative Approach. LC 97-23147. (Counseling Ser.). 200p. 1997. mass mkt. 23.95 (*0-534-26118-3*) Brooks-Cole.

Buelteman, Robert. The Unseen Peninsula. McDonald, Robert, ed. LC 94-26284. 1994. 65.00 (*1-881529-02-9*) Custom & Limited.

— The Unseen Peninsula. limited ed. McDonald, Robert, ed. LC 94-26284. 1994. 350.00 (*1-881529-03-7*) Custom & Limited.

Buen, Berta Gamboa de, see Fetter, Helga & Gamboa de Buen, Berta.

Buendia, Hernando G. The Elusive Miracle: Latin America in the 1990's. LC 98-112543. 84p. 1997. pap. 12.00 (*952-9520-37-9*) UN.

— The Elusive Miracle: Latin America in the 1990s. 76p. (C). 1999. reprint ed. pap. text 20.00 (*0-7881-7402-9*) DIANE Pub.

Buendia, Jose R., et al. Paintings of the Prado. (Illus.). 656p. 1995. 135.00 (*0-8212-2235-X*, Pub. by Bulfinch Pr) Little.

Buendia Julbez, Jose M., et al. The Life & Work of Luis Barragan. LC 97-67800. (Illus.). 248p. 1997. text 50.00 (*0-8478-2057-2*) St Martin.

***Buendia Sierra, Jose Luis.** Exclusive Rights & State Monopolies under EC Law: Article 86 (former Article 90) of the EC Treaty. LC 99-39678. 512p. 2000. text 165.00 (*0-19-829820-X*) OUP.

Buenfeld. Permeability of Concrete. (Illus.). 224p. 1997. text 55.00 (*0-419-16980-6*, E & FN Spon) Routledge.

Buenger, Barbara C., jt. auth. see Beckmann, Max.

Buenger, Barbara C., ed. see Beckmann, Max.

Buenger, H. J., jt. ed. see Werner, H. W.

Buenger, Victoria & Buenger, Walter L. Texas Merchant: Marvin Leonard & Fort Worth. LC 98-27607 (Kenneth E. Montague Series in Oil & Business History: No. 11). (Illus.). 288p. 1999. 36.95 (*0-89096-844-6*) Tex A&M Univ Pr.

Buenger, Walter L., ed. Texas History. 2nd ed. (Texas History Ser.). (Illus.). 546p. 1983. pap. text 24.95 (*0-89641-138-9*) American Pr.

Buenger, Walter L. & Calvert, Robert A., eds. Texas Through Time: Evolving Interpretations. LC 90-43716. 408p. 1991. 35.00 (*0-89096-490-4*) Tex A&M Univ Pr.

Buenger, Walter L., jt. auth. see Buenger, Victoria.

Buening, Charles R., II. Communicating on the Job: A Practical Guide for Supervisors. 100p. 1974. pap. 16.95 (*0-201-00855-6*) Addison-Wesley.

Buening, K. R. Pollen Rain, Vegetation & Climate in Lowland East Java, Indonesia. Bartstra, G. J. & Caspari, W. A., eds. (Modern Quarternary Research in Southeast Asia Ser.: Vol. 14). 112p. (C). 1996. text 76.00 (*90-5410-629-8*, Pub. by A A Balkema) Ashgate Pub Co.

Buenker, John D. The History of Wisconsin Vol. IV: The Progressive Era, 1893-1914. LC 72-12941. (Illus.). 830p. 1998. 40.00 (*0-87020-303-7*) State Hist Soc Wis.

Buenker, John D. & Kantowicz, Edward R., eds. Historical Dictionary of the Progressive Era, 1890-1920. LC 88-10241. 608p. 1988. lib. bdg. 135.00 (*0-313-24309-3*, BUH/, Greenwood Pr) Greenwood.

Buenker, John D. & Ratner, Lorman A., eds. Multiculturalism in the United States: A Comparative Guide to Acculturation & Ethnicity. LC 91-35116. 280p. 1992. lib. bdg. 57.95 (*0-313-25374-9*, BUC/, Greenwood Pr) Greenwood.

Buenker, John D., et al. Invention City: The Sesquicentennial History of Racine, Wisconsin (Illus.). viii, 132p. 1998. pap. 24.95 (*0-9665667-0-X*) Racine Hertge Mus.

Buenker, John D., jt. auth. see Greenfield, Gerald Michael.

***Bueno, Anibal A. & Ellis, Ralph D.** The Craft of Thinking: Logic, Scientific Method, & the Pursuit of Truth. LC 99-75806. (Illus.). 220p. (C). 1999. pap. text 18.95 (*0-9668555-2-3*) Clark Atl Univ.

Bueno Bueno, Carmen, tr. see Suzanne, Jamie.

***Bueno de Mesquita, Bruce.** Political Instability as a Source of Growth. LC 00-23814. (Essays in Public Policy Ser.: 99). 18p. 2000. pap. 5.00 (*0-8179-4342-0*) Hoover Inst Pr.

— Principles of International Politics: People's Power, Preferences & Perceptions. LC 99-47472. 588p. 1999. pap. 48.95 (*1-56802-423-1*) CQ Pr.

Bueno de Mesquita, Bruce. Strategy, Risk, & Personality in Coalition Politics: The Case of India. LC 75-3853. 208p. reprint ed. pap. 59.30 (*0-608-12204-1*, 2024439) Bks Demand.

— The War Trap. LC 80-24631. (Illus.). 238p. (C). 1981. 52.50 (*0-300-02558-0*); pap. 16.00 (*0-300-03092-6*, Y-469) Yale U Pr.

Bueno de Mesquita, Bruce & Lalman, David. War & Reason: Domestic & International Imperatives. 336p. (C). 1992. 50.00 (*0-300-05202-2*); pap. 20.00 (*0-300-05922-1*) Yale U Pr.

Bueno de Mesquita, Bruce & Mo, Jongryn. North Korean Economic Reform & Political Stability. (Essays in Public Policy Ser.: Vol. 70). 20p. 1996. pap. 5.00 (*0-8179-5752-9*) Hoover Inst Pr.

***Bueno de Mesquita, Bruce & Root, Hilton L.** Governing for Prosperity. LC 99-57676. (Illus.). 272p. 2000. 35.00 (*0-300-08017-4*); pap. 18.00 (*0-300-08018-2*) Yale U Pr.

Bueno de Mesquita, Bruce, et al. Red Flag over Hong Kong. LC 95-50248. 208p. (C). 1996. 30.00 (*1-56643-041-0*, Chatham House Pub); pap. text 22.95 (*1-56643-040-2*, Chatham House Pub) Seven Bridges.

Bueno, Eva & Caesar, Terry, eds. Imagination Beyond Nation: Latin American Popular Culture. LC PS3552.L36533C58 199. (Pitt Latin American Ser.). (Illus.). 332p. 1999. pap. 22.95 (*0-8229-5686-1*); text 50.00 (*0-8229-4085-X*) U of Pittsburgh Pr.

Bueno, Eva P. Resisting Boundaries: The Subject of Naturalism in Brazil. LC 95-3923. (Latin American Studies: Vol. 6). 208p. 1995. text 15.00 (*0-8153-1789-1*) Garland.

***Bueno, Eva P., et al, eds.** Naming the Father: Legacies, Genealogies & Explorations of Fatherhood in Modern & Contemporary Literature. LC 99-48890. 352p. 2000. 75.00 (*0-7391-0091-2*); pap. 25.95 (*0-7391-0092-0*) Lxngtn Bks.

Bueno, Julian A. La Sotana de Juan Ruiz-Elementos Eclesiasticos en el Libro de Buen Amor. LC 81-84295. 166p. 1983. 17.00 (*0-938972-02-2*) Spanish Lit Pubns.

Bueno, Lee. Ayumo, Fuente de Salud.Tr. of Fast Your Way to Health. (SPA.). 1995. pap. 10.99 (*0-8297-1948-2*) Vida Pubs.

— Fast Your Way to Health. LC 91-199860. 272p. 1991. mass mkt. 5.99 (*0-88368-219-2*) Whitaker Hse.

***Bueno, Maria de Los Reyes Castillo.** Reyita: The Life of a Black Cuban Woman in the Twentieth Century. LC 99-87007. 168p. 2000. lib. bdg. 45.95 (*0-8223-2579-9*) Duke.

***Bueno, Maria de Los Reyes Castillo & Castillo, Daisy.** Reyita: The Life of a Black Cuban Woman in the Twentieth Century (1902-1997) McLean, Anne, tr. LC 99-87007. 168p. 2000. pap. 16.95 (*0-8223-2593-4*) Duke.

Bueno, Martha. Elena Varela. LC 95-61916. (Coleccion Caniqui). (SPA.). 228p. (Orig.). 1995. pap. 16.00 (*0-89729-748-2*) Ediciones.

— Lina. LC 95-83322. (Coleccion Caniqui). (SPA.). 175p. (Orig.). 1996. pap. 15.00 (*0-89729-781-4*) Ediciones.

Bueno, Raul & Schmidt, Friedhlem. Asedios a la Heterogeneidad Cultural No. 1: Libro de Homenaje a Antonio Cornejo Polar. unabridged ed. Mazzotti, Jose A. & Aguilar, U. Juan, eds. (SPA., Illus.). 528p. (Orig.). 1996. pap. 25.00 (*0-9655345-0-2*) Asoc Inter De Peruanistas.

Buenos Aires, Universidad Nacional, Facultad de De. Catalogo Metodico de la Biblioteca de la Facultad de Derecho y Ciencias Sociales de Buenos Aires Seguido de una Tabla Alfabetica de Autores. (SPA.). 1976. lib. bdg. 134.95 (*0-8490-1584-7*) Gordon Pr.

***Buenting, Ruth.** Gloria: Letters from Hymnwriters. LC 99-37621. 122p. 1999. pap. 11.50 (*0-7880-1526-5*) CSS OH.

***Buenting, Ruth, et al.** A Musical Offering: Hymnfest for the Church Year. 40p. 1999. pap. 5.75 (*0-7880-1527-3*) CSS OH.

Buenzle, Fred J. & Day, A. Grove. Bluejacket: A Biography. LC 86-8528. (Classics of Naval Literature Ser.). (Illus.). 346p. 1986. reprint ed. 32.95 (*0-87021-190-0*) Naval Inst Pr.

Bueren, E. Lammerts Van, see Wirz, J. Ional & Van Bueren, E. Lammerts.

Bueren, E. M. Lammerts Van, see Lammerts Van Bueren, E. M.

Bueren, Thad Van, see Hylkema, Mark.

Buerge, David M. & Grover, Stuart R. Seattle in the 1880's. (Illus.). 128p. (Orig.). 1986. pap. 11.95 (*0-939806-06-1*) Hist Soc Seattle.

Buerge, David M. & Rochester, Junius. Roots & Branches: The Religious Heritage of Washington State. (Illus.). 280p. (Orig.). 1988. pap. 12.95 (*0-9619863-0-1*) CCGS.

Buergelt, Claus D. Color Atlas of Reproductive Pathology of Domestic Animals. (Illus.). 240p. (C). (gr. 13). 1996. text 110.00 (*0-8151-1305-6*, 28149) Mosby Inc.

Buergenthal, T., jt. tr. see Mueller, G. O.

Buergenthal, Thomas. International Human Rights in a Nutshell. (Nutshell Ser.). 283p. 1988. pap. text 17.00 (*0-314-43046-6*) West Pub.

— International Human Rights in a Nutshell. 2nd ed. LC 95-32611. (Nutshell Ser.). 358p. (C). 1995. pap. 21.00 (*0-314-06532-6*) West Pub.

— Law-Making in the International Civil Aviation Organization, Vol. 7. LC 72-80016. (Procedural Aspects of International Law Ser.). xiii, 247p. 1969. 42.00 (*0-8156-2139-6*, 306520) W S Hein.

Buergenthal, Thomas & Maier, Harold G. Public International Law in a Nutshell. 2nd ed. (Nutshell Ser.). 275p. (C). 1989. reprint ed. pap. 21.00 (*0-314-66371-1*) West Pub.

Buerger, David J. The Mysteries of Godliness: A History of Mormon Temple Worship. LC 94-37828. (Illus.). 244p. 1994. 24.95 (*1-56085-042-6*, Smith Res) Signature Bks.

Buerger, E. Woerterbuch Datenerfassung-Programmierung. (ENG, FRE, GER & RUS.). 1976. 95.00 (*0-8288-5767-9*, M6967) Fr & Eur.

Buerger, Jane & Davis, Jennie. The Child's World of Helping. LC 96-48273. (Child's World of Values Ser.). (Illus.). 24p. (J). (ps-2). 1997. lib. bdg. 18.50 (*1-56766-391-5*) Childs World.

Buerger, Janet E. The Era of the French Calotype. LC 82-82296. (Illus.). 64p. (Orig.). 1982. pap. 15.00 (*0-935398-07-4*) G Eastman Hse.

— French Daguerreotypes. LC 88-14334. (Illus.). 278p. 1989. 59.95 (*0-226-07985-6*) U Ch Pr.

— The Last Decade: The Emergence of Art Photography in the 1890s. (Illus.). 40p. (Orig.). 1984. pap. 10.00 (*0-935398-09-0*) G Eastman Hse.

Buerger, Martin J. Numerical Structure Factor Tables. LC QD0908.B8. (Geological Society of America, Special Paper: No. 33). 127p. reprint ed. pap. 39.40 (*0-7837-0356-2*, 204067600018) Bks Demand.

— Vector Space & Its Application in Crystal-Structure Investigation. LC 59-6760. 365p. reprint ed. pap. 113.20 (*0-608-30432-8*, 201196400080) Bks Demand.

Buerk, jt. auth. see Van Way, Charles W.

Buerk, Donald. Biosensors: Theory & Applications. LC 92-61490. 220p. 1992. text 59.95 (*0-87762-975-7*) Technomic.

Buerk, Dorothy, ed. Empowering Students by Promoting Active Learning in Mathematics: Teachers Speak to Teachers. LC 94-39425. (Illus.). 48p. 1994. pap. 7.95 (*0-87353-415-8*) NCTM.

Buerk, Mike. Easy Solos for Beginning Saxophone: Level 1. (Building Excellence Ser.). 48p. 1992. pap. 5.95 (*1-56222-389-5*, 94719) Mel Bay.

— Melodic Etudes for Beginning Saxophone, Level 1. (Building Excellence Ser.). 24p. 1991. pap. 5.95 (*1-56222-215-5*, 94589) Mel Bay.

Buerke, Patricia. Children & Scissors. 3rd ed. (Children &... Ser.). (Illus.). 180p. 1994. pap. 14.95 (*0-9616511-7-2*); spiral bd. 14.95 (*0-9616511-6-4*) Hampton Mae.

Buerkel-Rothfuss & Gray. Communication: Competencies & Contexts. 4th ed. LC 97-209939. 448p. (C). 1997. per. 54.95 (*0-7872-2796-X*, 41279601) Kendall-Hunt.

Buerkel-Rothfuss, Nancy L. & Gray, Pamela L. Communication: Competencies & Contexts. 3rd ed. 544p. (C). 1993. per. 27.95 (*0-8403-6035-5*) Kendall-Hunt.

Buerkert, B., et al, eds. Wind Erosion in Niger: Implications & Control Measures in a Millet-Based Farming System. (ENG & FRE.). 280p. (C). 1996. text 102.50 (*0-7923-3885-5*) Kluwer Academic.

Buerki, F. A. Stagecraft for Nonprofessionals. rev. ed. LC 83-1244. 192p. 1983. reprint ed. pap. 59.60 (*0-608-01923-2*, 206257800003) Bks Demand.

***Buerki, Robert A., ed.** Teaching the History of Pharmacy Today. 90p. (C). 1999. pap. 10.00 (*0-931292-35-2*) Am Inst Hist Pharm.

B

Buerki, Robert A. & Vottero, Louis D. Companion Manual to Ethical Practices in Pharmacy: A Guidebook for Pharmacy Technicians. 28p. 1997. pap. text, teacher ed. 5.00 (*0-931292-29-8*) Am Inst Hist Pharm.
— Ethical Practices in Pharmacy: A Guidebook for Pharmacy Technicians. 55p. 1997. pap. text 9.50 (*0-931292-28-X*) Am Inst Hist Pharm.
— Ethical Responsibility in Pharmacy Practice. 194p. (Orig.). (C). 1994. pap. text 15.00 (*0-931292-25-5*) Am Inst Hist Pharm.
— Instructor's Guide to Ethical Responsibility in Pharmacy Practice. 261p. (Orig.). (C). 1997. pap. text, teacher ed. 25.00 (*0-931292-30-1*) Am Inst Hist Pharm.
Buerki, Robert A., jt. ed. see Haddad, Amy M.
Buerkle, Randall G. The Conqueror: A Hero Battles Downsizing. 175p. (Orig.). (C). 1995. pap. 6.99 (*1-885397-01-1*) Flagship Pubns.
— The Grand Design: A Manic Depressive's True Story. 225p. (Orig.). (C). pap. 10.95 (*1-885397-02-X*) Flagship Pubns.
— How to Make a Total Flop of an Organization: Parables for the Workplace. LC 94-237137. (Illus.). 110p. (Orig.). (C). 1994. pap. 9.95 (*1-885397-00-3*) Flagship Pubns.
Buerlein, Robert A. Allied Military Fighting Knives & the Men Who Made Them Famous. 2nd ed. LC 85-70203. (Illus.). 194p. (Orig.). 1985. 34.95 (*0-933489-00-5*); pap. 19.95 (*0-933489-01-3*) Amer Hist Found.
— Allied Military Fighting Knives & the Men Who Made Them Famous. 2nd limited ed. LC 85-70203. (Illus.). 194p. (Orig.). 1985. write for info. (*0-933489-02-1*) Amer Hist Found.
Buerlen, Wolfgang, tr. see Schubring, Walther.
Buermann, Howard. Quiet, Please. 1946. pap. 3.25 (*0-8222-0927-6*) Dramatists Play.
Buero-Vallejo, Antonio. The Music Window (Musica Cercana) Halsey, Martha T., ed. Holt, Marion P., tr. from SPA. LC 93-74274. (Contemporary Spanish Plays Ser.: Vol. 5). xiv, 66p. 1994. pap. 6.00 (*0-9631212-4-3*) Estreno.
***Buero-Vallejo, Antonio.** The Sleep of Reason. Halsey, Martha T., ed. Holt, Marion P., tr. from SPA. LC 98-70409. (Contemporary Spanish Plays Ser.: Vol. 14).Tr. of Sueno de la Razon. (Illus.). xii, 67p. 1998. pap. 8.00 (*1-888463-04-X*) Estreno.
Buesa, Jose A. Horacio del Viento. (SPA.). 1971. pap. 6.95 (*0-89729-062-3*) Ediciones.
Buesch, Otto, ed. Handbuch der Preussischen Geschichte, Vol. 2: Das 19. Jahrhundert & Grosse Themen der Geschichte Preussens. (GER.). xxxii, 868p. (C). 1992. lib. bdg. 175.40 (*3-11-008322-1*) De Gruyter.
Buesch, Otto, et al. Industrialisierung und "Europaeische Wirtschaft" Im 19. Jahrhundert: Ein Tagungsbericht. (Veroeffentlichungen der Historischen Kommission zu Berlin, Band 67, Beitraege zu Inflation und Wiederaufbau in Deutschland und Europa 1914-1924: Vol. 46). (C). 1976. 69.25 (*3-11-006521-5*) De Gruyter.
Bueschel, Richard M. Arcade One: Illustrated Historical Guide to Arcade Machines. (Illus.). 304p. (Orig.). 1993. pap. 36.95 (*0-86667-051-3*) Coin Slot Bks.
— Arcade Sport Games. LC 96-72235. (Coin-Op Collector's Ser.). (Illus.). 270p. (Orig.). 1996. pap., spiral bd. 39.95 (*1-885160-03-8*) Coin-Op Classics.
— Big Head Lollipop Scales. (Coin-Op Classics Collector's Ser.). (Illus.). 250p. (Orig.). 1995. pap. 39.95 (*1-885160-02-X*) Coin-Op Classics.
— Bueschel's Saloon Series: B. A. Stevens - Billiard & Bar Goods. (Illus.). 264p. (Orig.). (C). 1990. pap. 29.95 (*0-86667-049-1*) Coin Slot Bks.
— Collector's Guide to Vintage Coin Machines. 2nd rev. ed. 192p. 1998. 39.95 (*0-7643-0579-4*) Schiffer.
— Collector's Guide to Vintage Trade Stimulators & Counter Games: With Price Guide. LC 97-21756. 196p. 1997. 34.95 (*0-7643-0119-5*) Schiffer.
— Encyclopedia of Pinball, 6 vols. Incl. Encyclopedia of Pinball Vol. 1: Whiffle to Rocket, 1930-1933. LC 96-71081. (Illus.). 253p. 1996. 49.95 (*1-889933-01-5*, EP-1); LC 96-71081. write for info. (*1-889933-00-7*) Silverball Amusements.
— Jennings Slot Machines, 1906-1990 Pts. 1-2: Illustrated Historical, Maintenance & Repair Guide to Jennings Mechanical & Electromechanical 3-Reel Machines. (Illus.). 800p. (Orig.). 1992. pap. 79.95 (*0-685-60286-9*); text 125.00 (*0-86667-050-5*) Coin Slot Bks.
— Kawasaki Ki-61 Hien in Japanese Army Air Force Service. LC 96-67281. (Illus.). 64p. 1996. pap. 14.95 (*0-7643-0069-5*) Schiffer.
— Lemons, Cherries & Bell-Fruit-Gum: Illustrated History of Automatic Payout Slot Machines. (Illus.). 352p. 1995. text 39.95 (*0-9647836-0-6*) Royal Bell Bks.
— Mills Consoles. (Coin-Op Collector's Ser.). (Illus.). 110p. (Orig.). 1994. spiral bd. 24.95 (*1-885160-00-3*) Coin-Op Classics.
— Mitsubishi A6M-1/2/-2N Zero-Sen of the Japanese Naval Air Service. rev. ed. LC 95-67278. (Illus.). 80p. 1995. pap. 14.95 (*0-88740-754-4*) Schiffer.
— Mitsubishi Ki-67/Ki-109 HIRYU in Japanese Army Air Force Service. LC 97-66914. 48p. 1997. pap. 14.95 (*0-7643-0350-3*) Schiffer.
— Mitsubishi/Nakajima G3M1/2/3 96 Rikko L3Y1/2 in Japanese Naval Air Service. LC 96-70489. (Illus.). 64p. 1997. pap. 14.95 (*0-7643-0148-9*) Schiffer.
— Nakajima KI-84 a/b Hayate in Japanese Army Air Force Service. LC 96-70490. (Illus.). 64p. 1997. pap. 14.95 (*0-7643-0149-7*) Schiffer.
— Nakajima KI-49 Donryu in Japanese Army Air Force Service. LC 97-66912. 64p. 1997. pap. 14.95 (*0-7643-0344-9*) Schiffer.
— Nakajima KI-43 Hayabusa in Japanese Army Air Force RATF-CAF-IP. LC 95-67623. (Illus.). 80p. (Orig.). 1995. pap. 14.95 (*0-88740-804-4*) Schiffer.
— Payout Dice Machines. (Coin-Op Collector's Ser.). (Illus.). 103p. (Orig.). 1994. spiral bd. 24.95 (*1-885160-01-1*) Coin-Op Classics.
— Pinball 1: Illustrated Historical Guide to Pinball Machines, Vol. 1. (Illus.). 256p. (Orig.). (C). 1988. pap. text 29.95 (*0-86667-047-5*) Coin Slot Bks.
Buescher, Gabriel. The Eucharistic Teaching of William Ockham. (Theology Ser.). xxviii, 157p. 1974. pap. 10.00 (*1-57659-031-3*) Franciscan Inst.
Buescher, Walter M. Religious Humor: 409 Bits of Humor for Preachers, Teachers & Public Speakers. LC 95-25439. 56p. (Orig.). 1996. pap. 11.50 (*0-7880-0707-6*) CSS OH.
Buescu, Helena C., jt. ed. see Tamen, Miguel.
Buescu, J. Exotic Attractors: From Liapunov Stability to Riddled Basins. LC 97-35733. (Progress in Mathematics Ser.: Vol. 153). (Illus.). 148p. 1997. 52.00 (*3-7643-5793-2*) Birkhauser.
Buescu, Jorge. Exotic Attractors: From Liapunov Stability to Riddled Basins. LC 97-35733. (Progress in Mathematics Ser.). 1997. write for info. (*0-8176-5793-2*) Birkhauser.
Buescu, Victor. Problemes de Critique et d'Histoire Textuelle. (Avienus, Ciceron, Dioscoride, Latin, Germanicus Cesar, Tibulle, Varron de l'Atax Ser.). xviii, 237p. 1973. reprint ed. 55.00 (*3-487-04670-9*) G Olms Pubs.
Bueso, Alberto T., jt. auth. see Conner, Dennis J.
Bueso, Alberto T., jt. auth. see O'Connor, Dennis J.
Bueso, J. L., et al. Compatibility, Stability & Sheaves. LC 94-32079. (Pure & Applied Mathematics Ser.: Vol. 185). (Illus.). 288p. 1994. text 145.00 (*0-8247-9589-X*) Dekker.
Buess, Bob. Deliverance from the Bondage of Fear. 1972. reprint ed. pap. 2.50 (*0-934244-03-0*) Sweeter Than Honey.
— Favor the Road to Success. 104p. 1992. mass mkt. 4.99 (*0-88368-251-6*) Whitaker Hse.
— Favor the Road to Success. 1982. reprint ed. pap. 5.00 (*0-934244-17-0*) Sweeter Than Honey.
— High Flight. 143p. 1980. 2.50 (*0-934244-10-3*) Sweeter Than Honey.
— Implanted Word. 1978. pap. 2.50 (*0-685-04831-4*) Sweeter Than Honey.
— King David & I. 1980. pap. 2.50 (*0-934244-09-X*) Sweeter Than Honey.
— King-Priest. 157p. 1992. pap. 4.00 (*0-934244-18-9*) Sweeter Than Honey.
— The Pendulum Swings. 92p. (Orig.). 1974. pap. 2.50 (*0-934244-12-X*, TX 391-560) Sweeter Than Honey.
— The Race Horse. 1978. pap. 2.50 (*0-934244-08-1*) Sweeter Than Honey.
— Setting the Captives Free. LC 42-1127. 1975. reprint ed. pap. 4.00 (*0-934244-02-2*) Sweeter Than Honey.
— Victory over Fear. 87p. 1997. pap. 5.99 (*0-88368-069-6*) Whitaker Hse.
— You Can Receive the Holy Ghost Today. 1967. pap. 2.50 (*0-934244-14-6*) Sweeter Than Honey.
Buess, G. F. & Cuschieki, A. Operative Manual of Endoscopic Surgery, Vol. 2. 280p. 1994. 198.00 (*0-387-56810-7*) Spr-Verlag.
Buess, G. F., ed. see Perissat, J.
Buess, Lynn M. Children of Light, Children of Denial. 150p. (Orig.). 1989. pap. 8.95 (*0-929385-15-2*) Light Tech Pubng.
— Numerology: Nuances in Relationships. rev. ed. 310p. (Orig.). 1997. pap. 13.75 (*0-929385-23-3*) Light Tech Pubng.
— Numerology for the New Age. 262p. 1991. pap. 11.00 (*0-929385-31-4*) Light Tech Pubng.
— Synergy Session. LC 80-67932. (Illus.). 113p. (Orig.). 1980. pap. 4.95 (*0-87516-427-7*) DeVorss.
— The Tarot & Transformation. LC 73-77608. (Illus.). 1977. reprint ed. pap. 8.95 (*0-87516-238-X*) DeVorss.
Buessing, Arndt, et al, eds. Misteltherapie & Immunologische Forschung: Arbeitstagung, Hercecke, Mai, 1996. (Journal Ser.: Vol. 3, Supplement 1, 1996). (GER., Illus.). iv, 20p. 1996. pap. 40.00 (*3-8055-6445-7*) S Karger.
Buethe, Cactus C. Wanna Be a Cowboy. (Illus.). 80p. (Orig.). 1995. pap. 10.00 (*0-944551-10-6*) Sundance Pr TX.
Buetow, Dennis E., ed. Biology of Euglena, 3 vols. 1968. write for info. (*0-318-50236-4*) Acad Pr.
Buetow, Harold A. All Things Made New: Homily Reflections for Sundays & Holy Days Cycle B. LC 95-20679. 283p. (Orig.). 1996. pap. 14.95 (*0-8189-0728-2*) Alba.
— God Still Speaks, Listen: Homilies for Sundays & Holy Days (Cycle A) LC 95-20679. 258p. (Orig.). 1995. pap. 14.95 (*0-8189-0727-4*) Alba.
— A History of Catholic Schooling in the United States. 89p. 1986. 3.00 (*0-318-20561-0*) Natl Cath Educ.
— Ode to Joy: Homilies for Sundays & Holy Days (Cycle C) (Orig.). 1997. pap. 14.95 (*0-8189-0729-0*) Alba.
— Pastoral Talks for Special Occasion. LC 94-23339. 238p. (Orig.). 1994. pap. 12.95 (*0-8189-0700-2*) Alba.
— Religion in Personal Development: An Analysis & a Prescription. LC 91-21225. (American University Studies: Theology & Religion: Ser. VII, Vol. 108). 446p. (C). 1992. text 65.95 (*0-8204-1580-4*) P Lang Pubng.
Buetow, Harold A., rev. Buetow 3 Volume Set. write for info. (*0-8189-0730-4*) Alba.
Buetter, Barbara M. Simple Puppets from Everyday Materials. LC 96-15475. (Illus.). 80p. (J). 1996. 19.95 (*1-895569-05-2*, Pub. by Tamos Bks) Sterling.
Buetter, Nancy. Simple Puppets from Everyday Materials. (Illus.). 80p. 1998. 12.95 (*1-895569-35-4*, Pub. by Tamos Bks) Sterling.
Buettgenbach, Stephan, ed. Chemical Microsensors & Applications, Vol. 3539. 1999. 69.00 (*0-8194-3000-5*) SPIE.
Buettner. Boccaccio's Des Cleres Femmes' Systems of Signification in an Illuminated Manuscript. LC 95-47407. (College Art Association Monograph on Fine Arts Ser.: Vol. LIII). (Illus.). 208p. (C). 1996. 45.00 (*0-295-97520-2*) U of Wash Pr.
Buettner, Dan. Africatrek. LC 96-3954. (Illus.). 112p. (J). (gr. 5-9). 1996. lib. bdg. 23.93 (*0-8225-2951-3*, Lerner Publctns) Lerner Pub.
— Sovietrek: A Journey by Bicycle across Russia. LC 94-5449. (Illus.). 104p. (YA). (gr. 5 up). 1994. lib. bdg. 23.93 (*0-8225-2950-5*, Lerner Publctns) Lerner Pub.
Buettner, Debi. Discover Bottlenose Dolphins Vol. 3: The Dangers of Dolphin Life. (Illus.). 24p. (J). (gr. k-5). 1998. write for info. (*1-890716-06-5*) K & M Intl.
— Discover Killer Whales Vol. 2: The Long Journey North. (Illus.). 24p. (J). (gr. k-5). 1998. write for info. (*1-890716-05-7*) K & M Intl.
— Discover Siberian Tigers Vol. 1: Cubs First Hunt. (Illus.). 24p. (J). (gr. k-5). 1998. write for info. (*1-890716-04-9*) K & M Intl.
Buettner, Donald R. & Becker, Roger J. Guide Specification for Precast, Prestressed Hollow Core Slabs. 2nd ed. LC 98-161946. 120p. 1998. 50.00 (*0-937040-57-6*, MNL-126-98) P-PCI.
Buettner-Janusch, John. Origins of Man: Physical Anthropology. LC 66-14128. 701p. reprint ed. pap. 200.00 (*0-608-13614-X*, 205513800008) Bks Demand.
Buettner, Johann C. Narrative of Johann Carl Buettner in the American Revolution. LC 75-180037. 70p. 1972. reprint ed. 18.95 (*0-405-08324-6*, Pub. by Blom Pubns) Ayer.
Buettner, Linda & Martin, Shelley. Therapeutic Recreation in the Nursing Home. LC 95-60609. (Illus.). 211p. (C). 1995. pap. text 29.95 (*0-910251-76-2*, TRN78) Venture Pub PA.
Buettner, Peter. Variabilitaet und Pathogenitaet bei Botrytis Cinerea. (Bibliotheca Mycologica: Band 177). (Illus.). 161p. 1999. 65.00 (*3-443-59079-9*, Pub. by Gebruder Borntraeger) Balogh.
Buettner, Shirley. Thorns. (Juniper Book Ser.: No. 61). 34p. (Orig.). 1995. pap. 8.00 (*0-614-03104-4*) Juniper Pr.
Buettner, Stewart. American Art Theory, 1945-1970. LC 81-1812. (Studies in the Fine Arts - Art Theory: No. 1). (Illus.). 225p. reprint ed. pap. 69.80 (*0-8357-1178-1*, 207068000017) Bks Demand.
***Bufalino, Gesualdo.** Night's Lies. Creagh, Patrick, tr. 160p. 2000. pap. text 13.00 (*1-86046-110-7*) Harvill Press.
Bufalino, Gesualdo. The Plague-Sower. Sartarelli, Stephen, tr. from ITA. LC 88-80810. 186p. 1988. pap. 13.00 (*0-941419-13-4*, Eridanos Library) Marsilio Pubs.
***Bufalino, Gesualdo.** Tommaso & the Blind Photographer. Creagh, Patrick, tr. 192p. 2000. pap. text 15.00 (*1-86046-568-4*) Harvill Press.
Bufe, Charles. Exercises for Individual & Group Development. 80p. 1998. pap. text 8.95 (*1-884365-15-9*) See Sharp Pr.
Bufe, Charles Q. Alcoholics Anonymous: Cult or Cure? 2nd expanded rev. ed. 208p. 1997. pap. 11.95 (*1-884365-12-4*) See Sharp Pr.
— An Understandable Guide to Music Theory: The Most Useful Aspects of Theory for Rock, Jazz & Blues Musicians. 3rd ed. (Illus.). 80p. 1994. reprint ed. pap. 9.95 (*1-884365-00-0*) See Sharp Pr.
Bufe, Charles Q., ed. The Heretic's Handbook of Quotations: Cutting Comments on Burning Issues. rev. ed. (Illus.). 256p. 1992. pap. 14.95 (*0-9613289-4-0*) See Sharp Pr.
Bufe, Charles Q., jt. auth. see Bierce, Ambrose.
Buff, Barbara B., et al. The Artists of Bronxville, 1890-1930. (Illus.). 28p. (Orig.). 1989. pap. 5.25 (*0-943651-22-0*) Hudson Riv.
Buff, Bradley. Where Do I Belong? A Kids' Guide to Stepfamilies. LC 84-40797, (Illus.). 112p. (J). 1982. pap. 7.95 (*0-201-10178-5*) HarpC Child Bks.
***Buff, Joe.** Deep Sound Channel. LC 00-24535. 353p. 2000. 23.95 (*0-553-80133-3*, Spectra) Bantam.
Buff, Sheila. Bears. LC 97-153202. (Nature's Window Ser.). 48p. 1997. 6.95 (*0-8362-2782-4*) Andrews & McMeel.
— The Birder's Sourcebook. 208p. 1994. pap. 13.95 (*1-55821-278-7*) Lyons Pr.
— The Birdfeeder's Handbook. (Illus.). 160p. 1991. pap. 10.95 (*1-55821-123-3*) Lyons Pr.
— Birding for Beginners. (Illus.). 192p. 1993. pap. 16.95 (*1-55821-209-4*) Lyons Pr.
***Buff, Sheila.** Birding for Beginners. (Illus.). 192p. 2000. 8.99 (*0-517-16189-3*) Random Hse Value.
Buff, Sheila. Butterflies. LC 98-214047. (Nature's Window Ser.). 1998. 6.95 (*0-8362-5299-3*) Andrews & McMeel.
— Corn Cookery. 232p. 1993. pap. 13.95 (*1-55821-245-0*) Lyons Pr.
***Buff, Sheila.** Custom Made: A Catalogue of Personalized & Handcrafted Items. (Illus.). 181p. 2000. 30.00 (*0-7881-9366-X*) DIANE Pub.
Buff, Sheila. Custom Made: A Catalogue of Personalized & Handcrafted Items. 191p. 1990. text 29.95 (*0-02-605960-6*) Macmillan.
— Dolphins: Nature's Window. LC 97-153225. (Nature's Window Ser.). 48p. 1997. 6.95 (*0-8362-2783-2*) Andrews & McMeel.
— Elephants. LC 98-214038. (Nature's Window Ser.). 1998. 6.95 (*0-8362-5327-2*) Andrews & McMeel.
— Frogs. LC 98-214058. (Nature's Window Ser.). 1998. 6.95 (*0-8362-5300-0*) Andrews & McMeel.
— The Gardener's Sourcebook. LC 96-22959. 320p. 1996. 30.00 (*1-55821-515-8*) Lyons Pr.
— The Great Tomato Book. LC 98-46916. (Illus.). 192p. 1999. pap. 16.95 (*1-58080-030-0*) Burford Bks.
— Love Your Dog. 93p. 1994. write for info. (*1-57215-005-X*) World Pubns.
— Nature Walks in & Around New York City: Discover Great Parks & Preserves Throughout the Tri-State... LC 96-9738. (AMC Nature Walks Guides Ser.). (Illus.). 368p. 1996. pap. 12.95 (*1-878239-53-8*) AMC Books.
***Buff, Sheila.** Old Farmer's Encyclepedia: A Practical Compendium of Traditional American Wisdom & Know-How. 2000. pap. 19.95 (*1-58574-155-8*) Lyon Press.
Buff, Sheila. Penguins: Nature's Window. LC 97-153218. (Nature's Window Ser.). 48p. 1997. 6.95 (*0-8362-2784-0*) Andrews & McMeel.
— Resumes for Freelancers. 1996. pap. 5.50 (*1-880407-18-3*) Edit Freelancers.
— Wolves: Nature's Window. LC 97-153214. (Nature's Window Ser.). 48p. 1997. 6.95 (*0-8362-2785-9*) Andrews & McMeel.
Buff, Sheila, ed. Good Dogs. (Illus.). 1999. 5.98 (*1-56731-348-5*, MJF Bks) Fine Comms.
Buff, Sheila & Olstein, Judi. Smoothies: Low-Alcohol & Nonalcoholic Drinks. 160p. 12.99 (*1-57215-240-0*, JG2400) World Pubns.
Buff, Sheila, jt. auth. see Atkins, Robert C.
Buff, Sheila, jt. auth. see Kessler, David.
Buff, Sheila, jt. auth. see Pressman, Alan.
Buff, Sheila, jt. auth. see Pressman, Alan H.
Buff, Shelia. The Complete Idiot's Guide to Birdwatching. (Complete Idiot's Guide Ser.). (Illus.). 409p. 1999. pap. 18.95 (*0-02-863106-4*, Alpha Ref) Macmillan Gen Ref.
— The Gardener's Sourcebook. LC 96-22959. 320p. 1996. pap. 18.95 (*1-55821-464-X*) Lyons Pr.
Buff, Wolfram & Von der Dunk, Klaus. Giftpflanzen in Natur und Garten. Bestimmungsmerkmale und Biologie. Anwendung in Medizin, Volksheilkunde und Homoeopathie. Symptomatik und Therapie Bei Vergiftungen (Poisonous Plants in the Wild & in the Garden) 2nd rev. ed. (Illus.). 352p. 1989. pap. 25.00 (*3-8263-2952-X*, Pub. by Blckwell Wissenschafts) Balogh.
Buffa, Anthony J., jt. auth. see Wilson, Jerry D.
Buffa, D. W. The Defense. 1998. mass mkt. 6.99 (*0-449-00399-X*, Crest) Fawcett.
— The Defense. LC 97-12861. 224p. 1997. 20.00 (*0-8050-5307-7*) H Holt & Co.
Buffa, Dudley, jt. auth. see Winograd, Morley.
Buffa, Dudley W. The Prosecution: A Legal Thriller. LC 99-13417. 256p. 1999. 25.00 (*0-8050-6107-X*, J Macrae Bks) H Holt & Co.
Buffa, Dudley W. Union Power & American Democracy. (Illus.). 280p. (C). 1984. text 42.50 (*0-472-10042-4*, 10042) U of Mich Pr.
Buffa, Dudley W. Union Power & American Democracy: The UAW & the Democratic Party, 1972-83. 304p. 1984. text 42.50 (*0-472-10053-X*, 10053) U of Mich Pr.
Buffa, Elwood S. Basic Production Management. 2nd ed. LC 74-28396. (Illus.). 697p. reprint ed. pap. 200.00 (*0-8357-5987-3*, 201783600009) Bks Demand.
Buffa, Elwood S. & Sarin, Rakesh K. Modern Production-Operations Management. 8th ed. (Production-Operations Management Ser.). 834p. 1987. text 83.95 (*0-471-81905-0*) Wiley.
Buffa, Liz. Cracking the SSAT & ISEE: 2000 Edition. 2000th ed. 572p. 1999. pap. 18.00 (*0-375-75412-1*) Random.
— Cracking the TOEFL '99 International. (Princeton Review Ser.). 1998. pap. 20.00 incl. cd-rom (*0-375-75210-2*) Villard Books.
— Grammar Smart Junior: Good Grammar Made Easy. (Princeton Review Ser.). (J). (gr. 6-8). 1995. pap. 12.00 (*0-679-76212-4*) Villard Books.
— Research Paper Smart: Where to Find It, How to Write It, How to Cite It. LC 98-172792. 192p. 1997. pap. 10.00 (*0-679-78382-2*) Random.
— Your Guide to an Informed Mind: What You Should Know at Each Grade Level. (Princeton Review Culturescope Ser.). 1995. pap. 18.00 (*0-679-75365-6*) Random.
Buffa, Sebastian, ed. The Illustrated Bartsch Vol. 34: Italian Artists of the Sixteenth Century. 1982. lib. bdg. 149.00 (*0-89835-034-4*) Abaris Bks.
— The Illustrated Bartsch Vol. 35: Italian Artists of the Sixteenth Century. 1984. lib. bdg. 149.00 (*0-89835-035-2*) Abaris Bks.
— The Illustrated Bartsch Vol. 36: Italian Artists of the Sixteenth Century. 348p. 1983. lib. bdg. 149.00 (*0-89835-036-0*) Abaris Bks.
— The Illustrated Bartsch Vol. 37: Italian Artists of the Sixteenth Century. 1984. lib. bdg. 149.00 (*0-89835-037-9*) Abaris Bks.
— The Illustrated Bartsch Vol. 38: Italian Artists of the Sixteenth Century. 1983. lib. bdg. 149.00 (*0-89835-038-7*) Abaris Bks.
Buffalo. Songs of the Wild West. (J). 1998. 20.00 incl. audio (*0-671-87175-7*) S&S Bks Yung.
Buffalo Bill Historical Center Staff. Buffalo Bill Museum. (Illus.). 72p. 1996. pap. 250.00 (*0-931618-57-6*) Buffalo Bill Hist Ctr.
— Treasures from Our West. (Illus.). 60p. 1992. pap. 5.00 (*0-931618-37-1*) Buffalo Bill Hist Ctr.
***Buffalo Bills Staff.** Buffalo Bills. CWC Sports Inc., ed. (NFL Team Yearbooks Ser.). (J). (gr. 1-12). 1998. pap. 9.99 (*1-891613-12-X*) Everett Sports.
Buffalo Bill, pseud. Buffalo Bill's True Tales. (Illus.). 24p. 1977. reprint ed. pap. 2.00 (*0-89646-022-3*) Vistabooks.
Buffalo Symposium on Modernist Interpretation of A. Ancient Logic & Its Modern Interpretations: Proceedings of the Buffalo Symposium on Modernist Interpretation of Ancient Logic, April 21 & 22, 1972. Corcoran, J., ed. LC 73-88589. (Synthese Historical Library: No. 9). 224p. 1974. text 141.50 (*90-277-0395-7*, D Reidel) Kluwer Academic.

An Asterisk (*) at the beginning of an entry indicates that the title is appearing for the first time.

Buffalohead, Priscilla. Cherish the Children: Parenting Skills for Indian Mothers with Young Children. 154p. 1988. lib. bdg., teacher ed. 85.00 (*1-881949-03-6*) MN Ind Wom Res.

Buffamanti, Deborah M., jt. ed. see Pautler, Albert J.

Buffard, A., jt. auth. see Jalil, Wolfgang.

Buffard-O'Shea, Nicole. Le Monde de Boris Vian et le Grotesque Litteraire. (American University Studies: Romance, Languages & Literature: Ser. 2, Vol. 185). 152p. 1993. 39.95 (*0-8204-1709-2*) P Lang Pubng.

Buffart, H. F., jt. ed. see Leeuwenberg, E. L.

Buffat, Marc. Les Mains Sales de Sartre. (FRE.). 247p. 1991. pap. 14.95 (*0-7859-2182-6*, 2070384411) Fr & Eur.

Bufferd, Lauren, et al. Performing Arts Resources Vol. 19: Exhibitions & Collections. LC 75-646287. (Illus.). 96p. 1995. 25.00 (*0-932610-16-1*) Theatre Lib.

Buffet, Cyril & Heuser, Beatrice, eds. Haunted by History: Myths in International Relations. LC 97-38353. 272p. 1998. 49.95 (*1-57181-940-1*) Berghahn Bks.

***Buffet, Guy.** Chef Waiter. 2000. 10.95 (*0-7407-0621-7*) Andrews & McMeel.

— Martini. 2000. 10.95 (*0-7407-0597-0*) Andrews & McMeel.

Buffet, Guy. The World of Guy Buffet. 253p. 1995. pap. 35.00 (*0-918684-76-5*) Cameron & Co.

Buffet, Guy & Ronck, Ron. Guy Buffet's Hawaii Fair Nights & Sunny Days. (Guy Buffet's Hawaii Ser.). 96p. (Orig.). 1987. pap. 14.95 (*0-918684-31-5*) Cameron & Co.

Buffet, Jimmy, et al. The Jolly Monster. unabridged ed. Van Doren, Liz, ed. (Bks. & Musical Cassettes). (J). (ps). 1990. audio 8.00 (*0-15-240533-X*) HarBrace.

Buffet, Savannah J., ed. see Buffett, Jimmy.

Buffet, Warren E., jt. auth. see Graham, Benjamin.

Buffetaut, Eric. A Short History of Vertebrate Palaeontology. (Illus.). 256p. 1987. 65.00 (*0-7099-3962-0*, Pub. by C Helm) Routldge.

Buffetaut, Eric, ed. Rare Events, Mass Extinction & Evolution, Vol. 2, No. 1. (Historical Biology Ser.). 104p. 1989. text 142.00 (*3-7186-4895-4*) Gordon & Breach.

Buffeteaut, jt. auth. see Restyn.

Buffett, Jimmy. Daybreak on the Equator. large type ed. LC 96-48622. 1997. pap. 19.00 (*0-679-77426-2*) Random.

— Jimmy Buffett Songs You Know by Heart. 76p. (Orig.). (YA). 1986. pap. text 15.95 (*0-89898-473-4*, PQ723SMX) Wrner Bros.

— The Jolly Mon. Buffet, Savannah J., ed. LC 87-8573. (Illus.). 32p. (J). (ps-3). 1988. 16.00 (*0-15-240530-5*) Harcourt.

— Jolly Mon. (J). 1988. 11.20 (*0-606-05894-X*, Pub. by Turtleback) Demco.

***Buffett, Jimmy.** A Pirate Looks at Fifty. 2000. pap. 14.00 (*0-449-00586-0*) Ballantine Pub Grp.

— A Pirate Looks at Fifty. 420p. 1999. mass mkt. 7.99 (*0-449-22334-5*, Crest) Fawcett.

Buffett, Jimmy. A Pirate Looks at Fifty. LC 98-10853. 385p. 1998. 24.95 (*0-679-43527-1*) Random.

— A Pirate Looks at Fifty. large type ed. LC 97-51827. 1998. pap. 24.95 (*0-375-70288-1*) Random.

— Tales from Margaritaville. 1999. pap. 5.99 (*0-449-45859-8*, Crest) Fawcett.

— Tales from Margaritaville: Fictional Facts & Factional Fictions. 240p. 1993. mass mkt. 5.99 (*0-449-22248-9*, Crest) Fawcett.

— Tales from Margaritaville: Fictional Facts & Factual Fictions. 1990. pap. 12.00 (*0-449-90542-X*, Columbine) Fawcett.

— Tales from Margaritaville: Fictional Facts & Factual Fictions. 256p. 1989. 16.95 (*0-15-187983-4*) Harcourt.

— Trouble Dolls. LC 89-34683. (Illus.). 32p. (J). 1997. pap. 6.00 (*0-15-201501-9*) Harcourt.

— Trouble Dolls. (J). 1997. 11.20 (*0-606-12012-2*, Pub. by Turtleback) Demco.

— Where Is Joe Merchant? 1992. 19.95 (*0-15-196299-5*) Harcourt.

— Where Is Joe Merchant. 416p. 1993. mass mkt. 6.99 (*0-380-72118-X*, Avon Bks) Morrow Avon.

— Where Is Joe Merchant? A Novel Tale. 1992. 75.00 (*0-15-196297-9*) Harcourt.

— Where Is Joe Merchant? A Novel Tale. (C). 1992. 25.00 (*0-15-196296-0*) Harcourt.

Buffett, Jimmy & Buffett, Savannah J. The Jolly Mon. LC 87-8573. (Illus.). 32p. (J). (gr. 4 up). 1993. pap. 6.00 (*0-15-240538-0*, Harcourt Child Bks) Harcourt.

— Trouble Dolls. LC 89-34683. (Illus.). 32p. (J). (gr. 1 up). 1991. 16.00 (*0-15-290790-4*) Harcourt.

***Buffett, Mary.** Buffettology: The Previously Unexplained Techniques That Have Made Warren Buffett Americans Most Famous Investor. 1998. 17.00 (*0-671-58219-4*) S&S Trade.

Buffett, Mary & Clark, David. Buffettology: The Previously Unexplained Techniques That Have Made Warren Buffet the World's Most Famous Investor. (Illus.). 320p. 1999. per. 14.00 (*0-684-84821-X*) S&S Trade Pap.

— Buffettology: The Previously Unexplained Techniques That Have Made Warren Buffet the World's Most Famous Investor. LC 97-36498. 320p. 1997. 30.00 (*0-684-83713-7*) Scribner.

***Buffett, Mary & Clark, David.** Buffettology Workbook: Value Investing the Buffett Way. 2001. pap., wbk. ed. 13.00 (*0-684-87171-8*, Fireside) S&S Trade Pap.

Buffett, Savannah J., jt. auth. see Buffett, Jimmy.

Buffett, Warren & Reynolds, Simon. Thoughts of Chairman Buffett: Thirty Years of Unconventional Wisdom from the Sage of Omaha. LC 97-41278. 112p. 1998. 12.00 (*0-88730-890-2*, HarpBusn) HarpInfo.

Buffett, Warren E., jt. auth. see Cunningham, Lawrence A.

Buffham, B. A., jt. auth. see Nauman, E. Bruce.

***Buffie, Edward F.** Trade Policy in Developing Countries. (Illus.). 384p. (C). 2001. write for info. (*0-521-78223-6*) Cambridge U Pr.

***Buffie, Margaret.** Angels Turn Their Backs. (J). 1998. pap. 6.95 (*1-55074-417-8*) Kids Can Pr.

Buffie, Margaret. Angels Turn Their Backs. 240p. (YA). (gr. 6 up). 1998. 16.95 (*1-55074-415-1*, Pub. by Kids Can Pr) Genl Dist Srvs.

Buffie, Margaret. The Dark Garden. 248p. (J). 1995. pap. 4.95 (*1-55074-344-9*) Kids Can Pr.

Buffie, Margaret. The Dark Garden. unabridged ed. 240p. (YA). (gr. 6-10). 1997. 16.95 (*1-55074-288-4*, Pub. by Kids Can Pr) Genl Dist Srvs.

— The Haunting of Frances Rain. 208p. (J). (gr. 7-9). 1989. pap. 12.95 (*0-590-42834-9*) Scholastic Inc.

Buffie, Margaret. My Mother's Ghost. 224p. (J). 1992. mass mkt. 4.95 (*1-55074-091-1*) Kids Can Pr.

Buffie, Margaret. Warnings. LC 90-40566. 256p. (YA). (gr. 7 up). 1994. pap. 3.25 (*0-590-43666-X*) Scholastic Inc.

Buffie, Margaret. Warnings. 1989. 8.35 (*0-606-06859-7*, Pub. by Turtleback) Demco.

— The Warnings. 248p. (J). 1989. mass mkt. 4.95 (*1-55074-251-5*) Kids Can Pr.

— Watcher. (Illus.). 264p. (YA). (gr. 7-12). 2000. 16.95 (*1-55074-829-7*, Pub. by Kids Can Press) Genl Dist Srvs.

— Who is Frances Rain? 192p. (J). 1987. pap. 4.95 (*0-919964-83-4*) Kids Can Pr.

Buffill, Elio A. Cubanos de Dos Siglos: Ensayistas y Criticos. LC 98-86348. (Coleccion Cuba y Sus Jueces Ser.). (SPA.). 223p. 1999. pap. 15.00 (*0-89729-876-4*) Ediciones.

Buffinghon, Charles, jt. auth. see Graham, Frank.

Buffington, Adriene. Hand-Dyed Fabric Made Easy. Lowe, Melissa, ed. LC 96-12989. (Illus.). 56p. (Orig.). 1996. pap. 12.95 (*1-56477-148-2*, B263) Martingale & Co.

Buffington, Albert F. Pennsylvania German Secular Folk Songs. LC 74-78062. (Pennsylvania German Folklore Ser.: Vol. 8). 1974. 15.00 (*0-911122-30-3*) Penn German Soc.

Buffington, Albert F., ed. The Reichard Collection of Early Pennsylvania German Dialogues & Plays. (Pennsylvania German Folklore Ser.: Vol. 61). 1962. 20.00 (*0-911122-15-X*) Penn German Soc.

***Buffington, G. N.** Virgin Spring: A Southwest Adventure Romance. 336p. (YA). 2000. pap. write for info. (*0-9700717-0-1*) Pony-Up Pr.

Buffington, Nancy, et al. Living Languages: Contexts for Reading & Writing. LC 96-45326. 462p. (C). 1997. pap. text 37.80 (*0-13-668963-9*) P-H.

Buffington, Perry W. Cheap Psychological Tricks: What to Do When Hard Work, Honesty, & Perseverance Fail. (Illus.). 1996. pap. 9.95 (*1-56145-130-4*) Peachtree Pubs.

***Buffington, Perry W.** Cheap Psychological Tricks for Lovers. (Illus.). 160p. 2000. pap. 9.95 (*1-56145-218-1*) Peachtree Pubs.

Buffington, Perry W. Right Time, Right Place, Right Move, Right Now! 1992. pap. 14.95 (*0-9632379-0-X*) GoBuff Ent.

— Your Behavior Is Showing: Over Forty Prescriptions for Understanding & Liking Yourself. 224p. 1988. pap. 9.95 (*0-929893-00-X*) Hillbrook Hse.

Buffington, Perry W. & Underwood, Kim. Archival Atlanta: Electric Street Dummies, the Great Stonehenge Explosion, Nerve Tonics, & Bovine Laws: Forgotten Facts & Well-Kept Secrets from Our City's Past. LC 95-52208. 160p. (Orig.). 1996. pap. 8.95 (*1-56145-105-3*) Peachtree Pubs.

Buffington, Robert. Criminal & Citizen in Modern Mexico. LC 99-38716. (Illus.). 272p. 2000. text 45.00 (*0-8032-1302-6*); pap. text 19.95 (*0-8032-6159-4*) U of Nebr Pr.

— The Equilibrist: A Study of John Crowe Ransom's Poems, 1916-1963. LC 67-27550. 172p. reprint ed. pap. 53.40 (*0-7837-6196-1*, 204591800009) Bks Demand.

Buffington, Rod, ed. see Hallmark, Donald P.

Buffington, Sherry. Who's Got the Compass? I Think I'm Lost: A Guide to Finding Your Ideal Self. 288p. 1998. pap. 14.95 (*1-885221-68-1*) BookPartners.

Buffinton, Arthur H. The Second Hundred Years War, 1689 to 1815. LC 75-14080. 114p. 1975. reprint ed. lib. bdg. 45.00 (*0-8371-8204-2*, BUSYW, Greenwood Pr) Greenwood.

***Buffle, Jacques.** Analytical Techniques. LC 99-89123. 2000. text. write for info. (*0-471-48979-4*) Wiley.

Buffle, Jacques. Chemical & Biological Regulation of Aquatic Systems. 40p. 1993. lib. bdg. 95.00 (*0-87371-448-2*, L448) Lewis Pubs.

— Complexation Reactions in Aquatic Systems: An Analytical Approach. Chalmers, R. A., tr. (Analytical Chemistry Ser.). 760p. 1988. text 152.00 (*0-470-20830-9*) P-H.

— Environmental Particles, Vol. 1. (Analytical Chemistry Ser.). 576p. 1992. lib. bdg. 119.00 (*0-87371-589-6*, L589) Lewis Pubs.

— Environmental Particles, Vol. 2. 448p. 1993. lib. bdg. 119.00 (*0-87371-895-X*, L895) Lewis Pubs.

Buffler, Richard T. Ocean Margin Drilling Program Atlases, Vol. 6. (Regional Atlas Ser.). 1984. pap. 295.00 (*0-86720-256-4*) Jones & Bartlett.

Buffler, Richard T., jt. auth. see Ladd, John W.

***Buffo, Alberto.** Ouranos Theorema: The Ancient Search for the Confines of the Universe. LC 99-75570. (Illus.). 346p. 2000. 32.95 (*0-9675538-0-6*) Bovolo.

Buffon. Histoire Naturelle. (Folio Ser.: No. 1569). (FRE.). 343p. 1984. pap. 12.95 (*2-07-037569-2*) Schoenhof.

— 368 Animal Illustrations from Buffon's "Natural History" LC 93-3708. (Pictorial Archive Ser.). (Illus.). 192p. pap. 11.95 (*0-486-27703-8*) Dover.

Buffon, Georges L. The History of Singing Birds Containing an Exact Description of Their Habits & Customs... Sterling, Keir B., ed. LC 77-81118. (Biologists & Their World Ser.). (Illus.). 1978. reprint ed. lib. bdg. 24.95 (*0-405-10709-9*) Ayer.

— The Natural History of Oviparous Quadrupeds & Serpents: Arranged & Published from the Papers & Collections of the Count De Buffon, 4 vols., Set. Sterling, Keir B., ed. Kerr, Robert, tr. LC 77-81119. (Biologists & Their World Ser.). (Illus.). 1978. reprint ed. lib. bdg. 145.95 (*0-405-10710-2*) Ayer.

— The Natural History of Oviparous Quadrupeds & Serpents: Arranged & Published from the Papers & Collections of the Count De Buffon, 4 vols., Vol. 1. Sterling, Keir B., ed. Kerr, Robert, tr. LC 77-81119. (Biologists & Their World Ser.). (Illus.). 1978. reprint ed. lib. bdg. 72.95 (*0-405-10711-0*) Ayer.

— The Natural History of Oviparous Quadrupeds & Serpents: Arranged & Published from the Papers & Collections of the Count De Buffon, 4 vols., Vol. 2. Sterling, Keir B., ed. Kerr, Robert, tr. LC 77-81119. (Biologists & Their World Ser.). (Illus.). 1978. reprint ed. lib. bdg. 72.95 (*0-405-10712-9*) Ayer.

Buffon, Georges-Louis De, see De Buffon, Georges-Louis.

Buffong, Jean. Snowflakes in the Sun. 180p. 1997. pap. 13.95 (*0-7043-4423-8*, Pub. by Womens Press) Trafalgar.

— Under the Silk Cotton Tree. LC 93-1663. (Emerging Voices: New International Fiction Ser.). 144p. 1993. 22.95 (*1-56656-126-4*); pap. 9.95 (*1-56656-122-1*) Interlink Pub.

***Bufford, Ben.** The Day God Slept. LC 99-67766. 250p. 2000. pap. 6.99 (*1-893181-32-4*) Le Gesse Stevens.

Bufford, Kathleen. Slivers of Light. 1994. pap. 7.95 (*1-55673-800-5*, Fairway Pr) CSS OH.

— Slivers of Light: Meditations on the Advent of Christ. LC 93-73940. 120 P. ;p. 1994. write for info. (*1-55673-835-8*, Fairway Pr) CSS OH.

Bufford, Rodger. Counseling & the Demonic. (Resources for Christian Counseling Ser.). pap. 10.99 (*0-8499-3616-0*) Word Pub.

Buffton, Barbara. Taking Control of Your Own Career: Using NLP & Other Techniques to Get the Working Life You Want. (Jobs & Careers). (Illus.). 144p. 1999. pap. 19.95 (*1-85703-395-7*, Pub. by How To Bks) Trans-Atl Phila.

***Buffton, Barbara.** Working for the Environment: How to Make a Career of Caring for the World We Live In. (Illus.). 144p. (Orig.). 1999. pap. 19.95 (*1-85703-366-3*, Pub. by How To Bks) Trans-Atl Phila.

Buffum, Francis H. A Memorial of the Great Rebellion Being a History of the Fourteenth Regiment New Hampshire Volunteers. large type unabridged ed. LC 96-44052. (Illus.). xii, 443p. (C). 1996. reprint ed. 38.95 (*1-889881-04-X*) Old Bks Pub.

Buffum, Imbrie. Agrippa d'Aubigne's "Les Tragiques" A Study of the Baroque Style in Poetry. LC 75-41042. reprint ed. 21.50 (*0-404-14804-2*) AMS Pr.

Buffum, Marjie, jt. auth. see Hatton, Henry.

Buffum, Richard. Keep the Wheels Turning Vol. 1 The Carl Owen Book. Behnke, Leo, ed. (Illus.). 303p. 1974. write for info. (*0-930110-05-6*) Owen Magic.

Bufkin, Don, jt. auth. see Walker, Henry P.

Bufkova-Hankelova, Karla, jt. auth. see Absolon, Karel B.

Bufkova-Wankelova, Karla. Moravian Tales: Legends & Myths. rev. ed. (Illus.). 209p. (J). 1992. pap. 19.50 (*0-685-71137-4*) Kabel Pubs.

Buford, Bill. Among the Thugs: The Experience & the Seduction of Crowd Violence. LC 92-50650. 1993. pap. 13.00 (*0-679-74535-1*) Vin Bks.

Buford, Bill, ed. The Granta Book of the Family. 2nd ed. 400p. 1999. pap. 14.95 (*0-9645611-4-X*) Granta.

— Granta Christmas. (Illus.). 256p. 1991. pap. 8.95 (*0-14-013860-9*, Penguin Bks) Viking Penguin.

— Granta 36. 256p. (Orig.). 1991. pap. 8.95 (*0-14-015208-3*, Penguin Bks) Viking Penguin.

— Granta 24: Letters. 256p. 1988. pap. 7.95 (*0-14-008606-4*, Penguin Bks) Viking Penguin.

— Granta 29: The Soviet Union. 256p. 1990. pap. 7.95 (*0-14-012863-8*, Penguin Bks) Viking Penguin.

— Granta 17: Graham Greene-While Waiting for a War. 254p. 1986. pap. 6.95 (*0-14-008594-7*, Penguin Bks) Viking Penguin.

— Granta 27: Death. 1989. pap. 7.95 (*0-14-012358-X*, Penguin Bks) Viking Penguin.

— Granta 28: The Anniversary Issue. 256p. 1989. pap. 7.95 (*0-14-012360-1*, Penguin Bks) Viking Penguin.

— Granta 30: The Soviet Union. 256p. 1990. pap. 8.95 (*0-14-013299-6*, Penguin Bks) Viking Penguin.

— Granta 31. 256p. 1990. pap. 8.95 (*0-14-013431-X*, Penguin Bks) Viking Penguin.

— Granta 32. 256p. 1990. pap. 8.95 (*0-14-013856-0*, Penguin Bks) Viking Penguin.

— Granta 33. 256p. 1990. pap. 8.95 (*0-14-013858-7*) Viking Penguin.

— Granta 35. 256p. 1991. pap. 8.95 (*0-14-014846-9*) Viking Penguin.

— Granta 38. 256p. (Orig.). 1992. pap. 9.95 (*0-14-015211-3*, Penguin Bks) Viking Penguin.

— Granta 39: The Body. (Illus.). 1992. pap. 9.95 (*0-14-014050-6*) Viking Penguin.

— Granta 42: Krauts! (Illus.). (Orig.). 1993. pap. 9.95 (*0-14-014053-0*) Viking Penguin.

— Granta 44. (Illus.). 256p. 1993. pap. 10.95 (*0-14-014063-8*, Penguin Bks) Viking Penguin.

— Granta 45. (Illus.). 256p. (Orig.). 1993. pap. 10.95 (*0-14-014065-4*, Penguin Bks) Viking Penguin.

— Granta 46. (Illus.). 256p. 1994. pap. 10.95 (*0-14-014067-0*, Penguin Bks) Viking Penguin.

— Granta 47. (Illus.). 256p. 1994. pap. 10.95 (*0-14-014083-2*, Penguin Bks) Viking Penguin.

— Granta 48: The Leaders We Trust. 256p. (Orig.). 1994. pap. 11.95 (*0-14-014084-0*, Penguin Bks) Viking Penguin.

— Granta 49. 256p. (Orig.). 1995. pap. 11.95 (*0-14-014085-9*, Penguin Bks) Viking Penguin.

— Granta 50. 256p. (Orig.). 1995. pap. 11.95 (*0-14-014104-9*, Penguin Bks) Viking Penguin.

— Granta 51. 256p. (Orig.). 1995. pap. 11.95 (*0-14-014108-1*, Penguin Bks) Viking Penguin.

— Granta 7: Best of Young British Novelists, Vol. 1. (Illus.). 256p. 1993. pap. 9.95 (*0-14-006833-3*, Penguin Bks) Viking Penguin.

— The Snap Revolution--James Fenton in the Philippines: Granta Eighteen. (Illus.). 1986. pap. 6.95 (*0-14-008596-3*, Penguin Bks) Viking Penguin.

Buford, Bob. The Game Plan. 2000. pap. 12.99 (*0-310-22908-1*) Zondervan.

— Game Plan: Winning Strategies for the Second Half of Your Life. LC 96-51875. 176p. 1997. 16.99 (*0-310-21205-7*) Zondervan.

— Half Time: Changing Your Game Plan from Success to Significance. 192p. 1997. pap. 10.99 (*0-310-21532-3*) Zondervan.

— Halftime. 1997. pap. 10.99 (*0-614-27654-3*) Zondervan.

***Buford, Bob.** Halftime: Changing Your Life Plan from Success to Significance. 2000. pap. 79.99 (*0-310-23275-9*) Zondervan.

Buford, Bob. Halftime Discussion Guide. 16p. 1995. pap. 3.99 (*0-310-20597-2*) Zondervan.

Buford, Brian, et al, eds. Preparing Tomorrow's Teachers: Integrating Alcohol & Other Drug Prevention into Preservice Training Proceedings. (Illus.). 59p. (C). 1996. reprint ed. pap. text 20.00 (*0-7881-2803-5*) DIANE Pub.

Buford, G. Dan. My Baby's Father: A Politics of Black Love Novel. LC 95-83300. 1996. pap. 12.00 (*0-9647635-1-6*) La Caille-Nous.

Buford, J. F., jt. auth. see Rutledge, L.

***Buford, James A.** Best of Times: And Other Clues of the Meaning of Life. 136p. 2000. 18.00 (*1-880216-93-0*) Black Belt Communs.

— Best of Times: More Clues to the Meaning of Life. 136p. 2000. 18.00 (*1-880216-66-3*, Elliott Clark) Black Belt Communs.

Buford, James A., Jr. The Kindness of Strangers: And Other Clues to the Meaning of Life. LC 95-20803. 128p. 1995. 18.00 (*1-881320-64-2*, Black Belt) Black Belt Communs.

***Buford, James A., Jr.** When the Lights Came on: A History of Pioneer Rural Electric Cooperative. 112p. 2000. 23.95 (*1-880216-90-6*) Black Belt Communs.

Buford, James A., Jr., et al. Management in Extension. 3rd ed. 380p. 1995. text 12.00 (*0-9648547-0-8*) OSU Extension.

***Buford, James Ansel.** When the Lights Came On. LC 99-47475. 2000. 15.95 (*1-880216-91-4*) Black Belt Communs.

Buford, Janine, ed. see DuBose, Sybil.

***Buford, Kate.** Burt Lancaster: An American Life. LC 99-37351. (Illus.). 448p. 2000. 27.50 (*0-679-44603-6*) Knopf.

— Burt Lancaster: An American Life. LC 00-37693. 2000. write for info. (*0-7862-2625-0*) Thorndike Pr.

Buford, P. D., jt. ed. see Davis, R. M.

Buford, Thomas O. In Search of a Calling: The College's Role in Shaping Identity. LC 94-39187. 1994. pap. text 16.95 (*0-86554-466-2*, MUP-P127) Mercer Univ Pr.

— Philosophy for Adults. LC 80-5524. 639p. 1980. pap. text 36.00 (*0-8191-1118-X*) U Pr of Amer.

Buford, Thomas O., ed. Ambushed on the Road to Glory: Finding the Way Through Jesus' Parables. 144p. 1991. pap. 12.00 (*0-9628455-6-6*) Smyth & Helwys.

— Essays on Other Minds. LC 73-122911. 432p. reprint ed. pap. 134.00 (*0-608-30007-1*, 201901100010) Bks Demand.

Buforn, E., jt. ed. see Udias, A.

Bugajski, Janusz. Czechoslovakia: Charter 77's Decade of Dissent, 125. LC 87-2435. (Washington Papers: No. 125). 136p. 1987. 45.00 (*0-275-92769-5*, C2769, Praeger Pubs); pap. 12.95 (*0-275-92770-9*, B2770, Praeger Pubs) Greenwood.

— Ethnic Politics in Eastern Europe: A Guide to Nationality Policies, Organizations, & Parties. LC 93-37732. 520p. (C). (gr. 13). 1994. text 101.95 (*1-56324-282-6*) M E Sharpe.

— Ethnic Politics in Eastern Europe: A Guide to Nationality Policies, Organizations, & Parties. LC 93-37732. 493p. (C). (gr. 13). 1995. pap. text 42.95 (*1-56324-283-4*) M E Sharpe.

— Sandinista Communism & Rural Nicaragua, 143. LC 89-71093. (Washington Papers: No. 143). 144p. 1990. 49.95 (*0-275-93535-3*, C3535); pap. 16.95 (*0-275-93536-1*) Greenwood.

Bugarin, Alicia. California's Job Training Programs: Financial & Outcome Data. 27p. 1996. pap. write for info. (*1-58703-048-9*) CA St Libry.

— Flattening Organizations: Practices & Standards. 54p. 1997. pap. write for info. (*1-58703-061-6*) CA St Libry.

— Linking Welfare Recipients to Jobs: The Role of Temporary Help Agencies. 39p. 1998. pap. write for info. (*1-58703-096-9*, CRB-98-017) CA St Libry.

— Restructuring Workforce Preparation Policy. 52p. 1995. pap. write for info. (*1-58703-038-1*, CRB-95-004) CA St Libry.

***Bugarin, Alicia & Lopez, Elias.** Farmworkers in California. 79p. 1998. pap. write for info. (*1-58703-085-3*, CRB-98-007) CA St Libry.

Bugarin, Alicia, jt. auth. see Simmons, Charlene Wear.

Bugarski, Ranko & Hawkesworth, Celia, eds. Language Planning in Yugoslavia. 233p. (Orig.). 1992. pap. 18.95 (*0-89357-232-2*) Slavica.

Bugat, Paul, jt. auth. see Healy, Bruce.

B

Bugaut, M., jt. ed. see Latruffe, N.

Bugay, David E. & Findlay, W. Paul. Pharmaceutical Excipients: Characterization by IR & NMR Spectroscopy. LC 98-56652. (Drugs & the Pharmaceutical Sciences Ser.). (Illus.). 680p. 1999. text 250.00 (*0-8247-9373-0*) Dekker.

Bugayevskiy, Lev M. & Snyder, John P. Map Projections: A Reference Manual. LC 94-45668. 1995. 95.00 (*0-7484-0303-5*, Pub. by Tay Francis Ltd); pap. 45.00 (*0-7484-0304-3*, Pub. by Tay Francis Ltd) Taylor & Francis.

Bugbee, Bruce L. What You Do Best: In the Body of Christ. Orig. Title: Your Perfect Fit. 176p. 1995. pap. 10.99 (*0-310-49431-1*) Zondervan.

Bugbee, Edward E. A Textbook of Fire Assaying. 3rd ed. Raese, Jon W., ed. LC 81-17021. (Illus.). 314p. (C). 1981. reprint ed. text 21.00 (*0-918062-47-0*) Colo Sch Mines.

— A Textbook of Fire Assaying. 4th rev. ed. LC 81-17021. (Illus.). 235p. 1991. pap. 17.95 (*0-9653923-2-5*) Western Tales.

Bugbee, Gordon P. Domino's Mansion: Thomas Monaghan, Gunnar Birkerts & the Spirit of Frank Lloyd Wright. LC 88-62139. (Illus.). 184p. 1988. 40.00 (*0-9621045-0-7*) PROBE Troy.

— Domino's Mansion: Thomas Monaghan, Gunnar Birkerts & the Spirit of Frank Lloyd Wright. Chu Lin, Paul, ed. LC 88-62139. 184p. 1988. 39.95 (*0-8093-9990-3*) S Ill U Pr.

Bugbee, Helen. Their Revolution or Ours. 140p. 1990. pap. 8.95 (*0-89697-263-1*) Intl Univ Pr.

Bugbee, Henry G. The Inward Morning: A Philosophical Exploration in Journal Form. LC 98-4177. 1999. pap. 14.95 (*0-8203-2071-4*) U of Ga Pr.

Bugbee, Louise A. Confessions of a Difficult Dame. 184p. (Orig.). 1990. pap. 10.00 (*0-9628140-0-8*) Gadfly Pr MA.

Bugbee, Percy & Cote, A. E. Principles of Fire Protection. 1988. text 67.00 (*0-87765-345-3*, ST-1) Natl Fire Prot.

Bugbey, Doris M., tr. see Steiner, Rudolf.

Bugday, M. Celalettin. Dizionario Italiano-Turco, Turco-Italiano. (ITA & TUR.). 410p. 1979. 9.95 (*0-8288-4734-7*, M9178) Fr & Eur.

Bugden, Miriam H. Geologic Resources of Washington County, Utah. (Public Information Ser.: Vol. 20). (Illus.). 26p. 1993. mass mkt. 2.00 (*1-55791-353-6*, PI-20) Utah Geological Survey.

— Geology & Scenery of the Central Wasatch Range, Salt Lake & Summit Counties, Utah. (Public Information Ser.: Vol. 9). (Illus.). 17p. 1991. pap. 3.00 (*1-55791-342-0*, PI-9) Utah Geological Survey.

— The Geology of Snow Canyon State Park, Washington County, Utah. (Public Information Ser.: Vol. 13). (Illus.). 16p. 1992. mass mkt. 1.75 (*1-55791-346-3*, PI-13) Utah Geological Survey.

Bugden, Miriam H. & Wilkerson, Christine M. Geological Resources of Summit County, Utah. (Public Information Ser.: Vol. 7). (Illus.). 23p. 1990. pap. 3.50 (*1-55791-340-4*, PI-7) Utah Geological Survey.

Bugden, Miriam H., jt. auth. see Budding, Karin E.

Bugeja, Michael. Talk. LC 97-15753. 1997. 20.00 (*1-55728-471-7*) U of Ark Pr.

— Talk. LC 97-15753. 72 p. 1997. pap. 14.00 (*1-55728-472-5*) U of Ark Pr.

Bugeja, Michael J. Academic Socialism. LC 94-3932. 176p. 1994. 22.95 (*0-914061-42-9*) Orchises Pr.

— After Oz. LC 92-32274. 80p. (Orig.). 1993. pap. 11.95 (*0-914061-32-1*) Orchises Pr.

— The Art & Craft of Poetry. 352p. 1994. 19.99 (*0-89879-633-4*, Wrtrs Digest Bks) F & W Pubns Inc.

Bugeja, Michael J. Culture's Sleeping Beauty: Essays on Poetry, Prejudice & Belief. LC 91-67974. x, 134p. 1992. 38.50 (*0-87875-425-3*); pap. 24.00 (*0-87875-429-6*) Whitston Pub.

Bugeja, Michael J. Family Values. LC 96-70656. 300p. 1997. 25.95 (*0-9651213-4-8*) Sligo Pr.

— Flight from Valhalla. 74p. (Orig.). 1993. 21.95 (*0-942979-13-3*); pap. 9.95 (*0-942979-12-5*) Livingston U Pr.

— Guide to Writing Magazine Nonfiction. LC 97-7212. 328p. 1997. pap. text 31.00 (*0-205-26113-2*) P-H.

— Little Dragons. 175p. 1996. pap. text 12.95 (*0-942544-21-8*) Negative Capability Pr.

— Living Ethics: Developing Values in Mass Communication. (C). 1995. pap. text, teacher ed. write for info. (*0-205-18436-7*, H8436-1) Allyn.

— Living Ethics: Developing Values in Mass Communication. LC 95-11987. 503p. 1995. pap. text 41.00 (*0-205-17323-3*) Allyn.

***Bugeja, Michael J.** Millennium's End: Poems. LC 99-41809. 120p. 2000. 20.00 (*0-9662299-3-2*, Pub. by Archer Books) Midpt Trade.

Bugeja, Michael J. Platonic Love. LC 90-19734. 80p. (Orig.). 1991. pap. 10.00 (*0-914061-21-6*) Orchises Pr.

— Poet's Guide: How to Publish & Perform Your Work. (SLP Writer's Guides Ser.). 152p. (Orig.). 1995. pap. 12.95 (*1-885266-00-6*) Story Line.

— The Visionary. rev. ed. LC 94-42460. 64p. 1995. reprint ed. pap. 10.00 (*0-914061-50-X*) Orchises Pr.

— What We Do for Music. (Amelia Chapbooks Ser.). 48p. (Orig.). 1991. pap. 10.95 (*0-936545-17-8*) Amelia.

Bugelski, B. R. An Introduction to the Principles of Psychology. 2nd ed. LC 73-323. 640p. (C). 1973. pap. text. write for info. (*0-672-61266-6*, Bobbs); write for info. (*0-672-61344-1*, Bobbs) Macmillan.

— Psychology in the Common Cause. LC 88-17838. 228p. 1989. 59.95 (*0-275-93034-3*, C3034, Praeger Pubs) Greenwood.

Bugenhagen, Jim, ed. Credit Life & Accident & Health Experience by State: 1992-1994. 5th rev. ed. 125p. (Orig.). 1996. pap. 40.00 (*0-89382-362-7*, CRE-LO) Nat Assn Insurance.

— Insurers' Distribution of Assets. annuals 7th ed. 120p. (C). 1998. ring bd. 125.00 (*0-89382-487-9*, IDA-BM97) Nat Assn Insurance.

— Insurers' Long-Term Mortgage Loan & Real Estate Investments. annuals 7th ed. 124p. (C). 1998. ring bd. 125.00 (*0-89382-489-5*, MRT-PB97) Nat Assn Insurance.

— Insurers' Medium & Lower Quality Bond Holdings. annuals 7th ed. 122p. (C). 1998. ring bd. 150.00 (*0-89382-488-7*, IML-ZM97) Nat Assn Insurance.

— Long-Term Care Experience Report for 1997. 6th rev. ed. 70p. (C). 1999. pap. 45.00i (*0-89382-594-8*, LTC-LR97) Nat Assn Insurance.

***Bugenhagen, Jim, ed.** Long-Term Care Experience Report for 1998. 6th rev. ed. 70p. 2000. pap. 45.00 (*0-89382-663-4*) Nat Assn Insurance.

Bugenhagen, Jim, ed. Long-Term Care Insurance Experience Report for 1995. 2nd rev. ed. 84p. (C). 1997. pap. 25.00 (*0-89382-457-7*, LTC-LR) Nat Assn Insurance.

— Long-Term Care Insurance Experience Reports for 1994. 76p. (Orig.). 1996. pap. 25.00 (*0-89382-385-6*, LTC-LR94) Nat Assn Insurance.

— Medicare Supplement Loss Ratios in 1998. 7th rev. ed. 122p. 1998. reprint ed. pap. 100.00i (*0-89382-531-X*, MED-BB97) Nat Assn Insurance.

— Medicare Supplement Loss Ratios Report. rev. ed. 140p. (C). 1995. ring bd. 100.00 (*0-89382-364-3*, MED-BB) Nat Assn Insurance.

— Profitability by Line by State in 1997. rev. ed. 376p. 1998. ring bd. 150.00i (*0-89382-593-X*, PBL-PB) Nat Assn Insurance.

— Profitability by Line by State Report for 1996. rev. ed. 375p. (C). 1997. ring bd. 150.00i (*0-89382-505-0*, PBL-PB97) Nat Assn Insurance.

— Report on Profitability by Line by State. rev. ed. (C). 1995. ring bd. 125.00 (*0-89382-368-6*, PBL-PB) Nat Assn Insurance.

Bugental, James F. The Art of the Psychotherapist. 336p. 1992. pap. 13.95 (*0-393-30911-8*) Norton.

— Psychotherapy & Process: The Fundamentals of an Existential-Humanistic Approach. 163p. (C). 1978. pap. text 28.25 (*0-07-554827-5*) McGraw.

— Psychotherapy Isn't What You Think: Bringing the Psychotherapeutic Engagement into the Living Moment. LC 98-41823. 1999. 38.95 (*1-891944-13-4*) Zeig Tucker.

— The Search for Authenticity: An Existential-Analytic Approach to Psychotheraphy. enl. ed. 477p. 1989. reprint ed. text 49.50 (*0-8290-0108-5*) Irvington.

— The Search for Authenticity: An Existential-Analytic Approach to Psychotheraphy. enl. ed. 477p. 1997. reprint ed. pap. text 19.95 (*0-8290-1298-2*) Irvington.

— The Search for Existential Identity: Patient-Therapist Dialogues in Humanistic Psychotherapy. LC 75-44882. (Social & Behavioral Science Ser.). 349p. 1976. 55.00 (*0-87589-273-6*) Jossey-Bass.

Bugere, Gerard, jt. auth. see Dietiker, Simone R.

Bugert, Bill & Wiley, Randy. The Complete Guide to Liberty Seated Half Dollars. (Illus.). 250p. 1993. 69.95 (*1-880731-17-7*) DLRC Pr.

Bugg, C. E. & Ealick, S. E., eds. Crystallographic & Modeling Methods in Molecular Design. (Illus.). 296p. 1990. 117.00 (*0-387-97210-2*) Spr-Verlag.

Bugg, Carol D. Divine Design: Decorating Den's 25th Anniversary Collection of Rooms. Hughes, Kathleen, ed. (Illus.). 216p. 1994. 35.00 (*0-9639596-1-1*) Judd Pubng.

— Smart & Simple Decorating: Creative Ideas & Solutions from the Experts at Decorating Den Interiors. LC 98-48802. (Illus.). 208p. (YA). (gr. 11). 1999. 22.95 (*0-7370-0038-4*) T-L Custom Pub.

Bugg, Charles. Learning to Dream Again: From Grief to Gratitude. 96p. 1993. pap. 8.00 (*1-880837-44-7*) Smyth & Helwys.

Bugg, Charles B. A Faith to Meet Our Fears. LC 96-38537. 96p. 1997. pap. 11.00 (*1-57312-093-6*) Smyth & Helwys.

***Bugg, Charles B.** Preaching & Intimacy. LC 99-14807. 160p. 1999. pap. 15.00 (*1-57312-263-7*) Smyth & Helwys.

***Bugg, Charles B., ed.** The Abingdon Preaching Annual. (Illus.). 464p. 2000. pap. 20.00 (*0-687-08197-1*) Abingdon.

Bugg, D. E., et al. Burglary Protection & Insurance Surveys. (C). 1985. 165.00 (*0-7855-4312-0*, Pub. by Witherby & Co) St Mut.

Bugg, D. V. Electronics: Circuits, Amplifiers & Gates. (Illus.). 392p. 1991. 171.00 (*0-7503-0109-0*); pap. 41.00 (*0-7503-0110-4*) IOP Pub.

— Hadron Spectroscopy & the Confinement Problem: Proceedings of a NATO ASI Held in London, England & Swansea, Wales, June 27-July 8, 1995. LC 96-17036. (NATO ASI Ser.: Vol. 353). (Illus.). 389p. (C). 1996. text 144.00 (*0-306-45303-7*) Plenum.

Bugg, James L., Jr. & Stewart, Peter c. Jacksonian Democracy. 2nd ed. 174p. (C). 1986. reprint ed. pap. text 19.00 (*0-8191-5404-0*) U Pr of Amer.

Bugg, Judy. Death by Chocolate. 1995. 5.98 (*0-7858-0419-6*) Bk Sales Inc.

— Italian Farmhouse Cooking. 64p. 1995. 5.98 (*0-7858-0421-8*) Bk Sales Inc.

Bugg, Keith. Building Better Interfaces with Microsoft Foundation Classes. LC 99-11440. (Illus.). 368p. 1999. pap. 39.99 (*0-471-33181-3*) Wiley.

— Debugging Visual C++ Windows. (Illus.). 220p. 1998. pap. 29.95 incl. disk (*0-87930-545-2*) C M P Books.

Bugg, Keith E. Building Windows Help Files. 280p. 1996. 29.95 incl. disk (*0-87930-439-1*) C M P Books.

Bugg, Keith E., jt. auth. see Tackett, Jack, Jr.

Bugg, Leila H. The People of Our Parish. 1978. 23.95 (*0-405-10811-7*) Ayer.

Bugg, Timothy D. Introduction to Enzyme & Coenzyme Chemistry. LC 96-26495. (Illus.). 320p. 1997. pap. text 59.95 (*0-86542-793-3*) Blackwell Sci.

Bugge, Anna, et al. Women's Work & Wages: A Selection of Papers from the 15th Arne Ryde Symposium on Economics of Gender & Family in Honor of Anna Bugge & Knut Wicksell. LC 97-20424. 272p. (C). 1998. write for info. (*0-415-14903-7*) Routledge.

***Bugge, Carole.** Haunting of Torre Abbey. LC 99-53751. 240p. 2000. text 22.95 (*0-312-24557-2*) St Martin.

— Treason. 36p. 1996. pap. 10.00 (*0-929741-14-5*) Playsmith.

— Who Killed Blanche Dubois? 1999. mass mkt. 5.99 (*0-425-17195-7*, Prime Crime) Berkley Pub.

— Who Killed Dorian Gray? 2000. mass mkt. 5.99 (*0-425-17553-7*) Berkley Pub.

Bugge, Henriette. Mission & Tamil Society: Social & Religious Change in South India 1840-1900. LC 95-114743. (SIAS Monographs: No. 65). 220p. (C). 1996. pap. text 38.00 (*0-7007-0292-X*, Pub. by Curzon Pr Ltd) UH Pr.

Bugge, Henriette & Rubies, Joan, eds. Shifting Cultures: Interaction & Discourse in the Expansion of Europe. LC 97-127039. 232p. 1995. pap. text 45.95 (*3-8258-2614-7*) Transaction Pubs.

Bugge, J. The Cephalic Arterial System in Insectivores, Primates, Rodents, & Lagomorphs, with Special Reference to the Systematic Classification. (Journal Ser.: Suppl. 62-1, Vol. 87). 160p. 1974. pap. 31.50 (*3-8055-1750-5*) S Karger.

Bugge, Sophus. Home of the Eddic Poems. Schofield, William H., tr. LC 74-144524. (Grimm Library: No. 11). reprint ed. 45.00 (*0-404-53554-2*) AMS Pr.

Buggett, Byrd. Taking Charge: 236 Proven Principles of Effective Leadership. LC 95-39699. 128p. 1995. 12.95 (*1-55853-358-3*) Rutledge Hill Pr.

Buggey, J. The Energy Crisis: What Are Our Choices? 1976. pap. text 11.84 (*0-13-277301-5*) P-H.

Buggs, George. Music from the Middle Passage. pap. 1.50 (*0-918476-02-X*) Cornerstone Pr.

Buggs, Michael A. Tabard. (Illus.). 64p. (Orig.). (J). (gr. 2-6). pap. 15.00 (*0-9657723-0-6*) Buggs Bks.

Buggy, M. & Hampshire, S., eds. Materials for Advanced Technology Applications. 704p. 1992. text 275.00 (*0-87849-646-7*, Pub. by Trans T Pub) Enfield Pubs NH.

Buggy, Tom. Golf's Lady of the Hudson: A Centennial History of Dutchess Golf & Country Club. LC 98-86503. (Illus.). 116p. 1998. 50.00 (*0-9651818-3-9*) Treewolf.

Bugh, Glenn R. The Horsemen of Athens. LC 88-3210. 289p. 1988. reprint ed. pap. 89.60 (*0-608-03294-8*, 206381200007) Bks Demand.

Bughes, Dean. Back-up Star. LC 94-15128. (J). (gr. 1 up). 1995. lib. bdg. 4.99 (*0-679-95442-2*, Bullseye Bks) Random Bks Yng Read.

***Bughgeim, A. L.** Volterra Equations & Inverse Problems. (Inverse & Ill-Posed Problems Ser.). 214p. 1999. 147.50 (*90-6764-302-5*, Pub. by VSP) Coronet Bks.

Bugialli, Giuliano. Best of Bugialli. LC 94-11153. (Illus.). 128p. 1994. 22.50 (*1-55670-384-8*) Stewart Tabori & Chang.

— Bugialli on Pasta. (Illus.). 352p. 1988. 27.50 (*0-671-62024-X*) S&S Trade.

— Bugialli on Southern Italy. 1924. write for info. (*0-688-16555-9*, Hearst) Hearst Commns.

***Bugialli, Giuliano.** Bugialli's Italy: Traditional Recipes from the Regions of Italy. Hoenig, Pam, ed. LC 98-5670. (Illus.). 320p. 1998. 28.00 (*0-688-15864-1*, Wm Morrow) Morrow Avon.

Bugialli, Giuliano. Fine Art of Italian Cooking. (Illus.). 1990. 30.00 (*0-8129-1838-X*, Times Bks) Crown Pub Group.

— The Foods of Sicily & Sardinia & the Smaller Islandss. (Illus.). 288p. 1996. 50.00 (*0-8478-1924-8*, Pub. by Rizzoli Intl) St Martin.

— Giuliano Bugialli's Foods of Italy. LC 84-2543. (Illus.). 304p. 1984. 50.00 (*0-941434-52-4*); pap. 24.95 (*1-55670-370-8*) Stewart Tabori & Chang.

— Giuliano Bugialli's Foods of Tuscany. (Illus.). 304p. 1992. pap. 24.95 (*1-55670-513-1*) Stewart Tabori & Chang.

— Giuliano Bugialli's Foods of Tuscany. LC 92-9783. (Illus.). 304p. 1992. 50.00 (*1-55670-200-0*) Stewart Tabori & Chang.

Bugl, Paul. Differential Equations. 1995. pap. text, student ed. 25.00 (*0-13-362864-7*) P-H.

— Differential Equations: Matrices & Models. LC 94-31812. 864p. 1994. text 63.00 (*0-02-316540-5*, Macmillan Coll) P-H.

***Buglear, John.** Stats to Go: A Handbook for Hospitality, Leisure & Tourism Studies. 224p. 2000. pap. 32.95 (*0-7506-4556-3*) Buttrwrth-Heinemann.

Bugliani, Ann. The Instruction of Philosophy & Psychoanalysis by Tragedy: Jacques Lacan & Gabriel Marcel Read Paul Claudel. LC 98-30393. 224p. 1998. 75.00 (*1-57309-308-4*); pap. 54.95 (*1-57309-307-6*) Intl Scholars.

Bugliani, Ann, ed. Chairing the Foreign Language & Literature Department. 128p. (Orig.). 1994. pap. 15.00 (*0-87352-564-7*, W405P) Modern Lang.

Bugliarello, G., ed. Intellectual Property Utilization & Global Markets: East-West Dialogue. LC 97-75192. (NATO-4 Science Ser.). 243p. 1998. 97.00 (*90-5199-371-4*) IOS Press.

Bugliarello, George. Physical & Information Sciences & Engineering: Report of the Project 2061 Phase I Physical & Info Sciences & Engineering Panel. 42p. 1989. 8.00 (*0-87168-345-8*, 89-04S) AAAS.

Bugliarello, George, et al, eds. East-West Technology Transfer - New Perspectives & Human Resources: Proceedings of the NATO Advanced Research Workshop on Human Resources & Leadership for Technology Transfer Between NATO Countries & Cooperation Partner Countries, Ankara, Turkey, July 18-21, 1994. LC 95-45695. (NATO ASI Series: Partnership Sub-Series 2: Environment: No. 3). 300p. (C). 1995. lib. bdg. 158.50 (*0-7923-3829-4*) Kluwer Academic.

Bugliarello, George & Simon, H. A., eds. Technology, the University, & the Community. 1976. 230.00 (*0-08-017872-3*, Pub. by Pergamon Repr) Franklin.

Bugliarello, George, et al. Ethics, Values, & the Promise of Science: Sigma Xi Forum Proceedings February 25-26, 1993. (Illus.). 260p. (Orig.). 1993. pap. 18.50 (*0-914446-04-5*) Sigma Xi.

Buglio, Rudecinda L., ed. see Garate, Donald T.

***Bugliosi, John.** The Art of Prosecution: Trial Advocacy Fundamentals from Case Preparation Through Summation. LC 00-42327. 2000. pap. write for info. (*1-889031-34-8*) Looseleaf Law.

Bugliosi, Vincent. Final Verdict: The True Account of the Murder of John F. Kennedy. (Illus.). 992p. 1998. 35.00 (*0-393-04525-0*) Norton.

— Helter Skelter: The True Story of the Manson Murders. 1975. 12.09 (*0-606-00598-6*, Pub. by Turtleback) Demco.

— No Island of Sanity: Paula Jones vs. Bill Clinton : The Supreme Court on Trial. LC 97-50261. 147p. 1998. pap. 9.95 (*0-345-42487-5*) Ballantine Pub Grp.

Bugliosi, Vincent T. And the Sea Will Tell. 1992. mass mkt. write for info. (*0-312-92716-9*) St Martin.

— Outrage: The Five Reasons Why O. J. Simpson Got Away. 528p. 1997. mass mkt. 7.50 (*0-440-22382-2*, Island Bks) Dell.

— Outrage: The Five Reasons Why O.J. Simpson Got Away with Murder. 320p. 1996. 25.00 (*0-393-04050-X*) Norton.

Bugliosi, Vincent T. & Gentry, Curt. Helter Skelter. (Illus.). 1995. reprint ed. lib. bdg. 39.95 (*1-56849-647-8*) Buccaneer Bks.

— Helter Skelter. rev. ed. 736p. 1995. mass mkt. 7.99 (*0-553-57435-3*) Bantam.

— Helter Skelter: The True Story of the Manson Murders. (Illus.). 502p. 1994. 25.00 (*0-393-08700-X*) Norton.

Bugliosi, Vincent T. & Henderson, Bruce B. And the Sea Will Tell. 1992. mass mkt. 5.99 (*0-8041-0917-6*) Ivy Books.

***Bugman, Shifty.** Basement Bugger's Bible: The Professional's Guide to Creating, Building, & Planting Custom Bugs & Wiretaps. 320p. 1999. pap. 48.00 (*1-58160-022-4*) Paladin Pr.

Bugni, Alice. Moose Racks, Bear Tracks & Other Alaska Kidsnacks: Cooking with Kids Has Never Been So Easy! LC 99-14003. (Illus.). 32p. (J). (gr. k-5). 1999. pap. 8.95 (*1-57061-214-5*) Sasquatch Bks.

Bugnini, Annibale. The Reform of the Liturgy, 1948-1975. O'Connell, Matthew J., tr. from ITA.Tr. of La Riforma Liturgica, 1948-1975. 1008p. 1990. 59.50 (*0-8146-1571-6*) Liturgical Pr.

Bugos, Alan R. XDSL, Digital Subscriber Line Technology. 2004. 48.00 (*0-13-081292-7*) P-H.

Bugos, Glenn E. Engineering the F-4 Phantom II: Parts into Systems. LC 95-47176. (Illus.). 264p. 1996. 31.95 (*1-55750-089-4*) Naval Inst Pr.

Bugosh Simko, C. Wired for Sound: An Advanced Student Workbook on Hearing & Hearing Aids. (Illus.). 156p. (YA). (gr. 8-12). 1986. pap. text, student ed. 7.95 (*0-930323-16-5*, Pub. by K Green Pubns) Gallaudet Univ Pr.

Bugra, Ayse. State & Business in Modern Turkey: A Comparative Study. LC 93-18517. (SUNY Series in Social & Economic History of the Middle East). 328p. (C). 1994. text 64.50 (*0-7914-1787-5*); pap. text 21.95 (*0-7914-1788-3*) State U NY Pr.

Bugra, Ayse & Usdiken, Behlul, eds. State, Market, & Organizational Form. LC 97-20076. (Studies in Organization: Vol. 80). xii, 323p. (C). 1997. text 64.95 (*3-11-015468-4*) De Gruyter.

Bugrov, Andrei, jt. auth. see Obminsky, Ernest.

Buhagiar, Marion, ed. The Book of Secrets. LC 86-31050. 416p. 1996. 59.00 (*0-88723-150-0*) Boardroom.

Buhagiar, Marion, jt. auth. see Edelston, Martin.

Buhalis, D., et al, eds. Information & Communication Technologies in Tourism, 1998: Proceedings of the International Conference in Istanbul, Turkey, 1998. (Illus.). xii, 344p. 1998. pap. 64.95 (*3-211-83088-X*) Spr-Verlag.

— Information & Communication Technologies in Tourism, 1999: Proceedings of the International Conference in Innsbruck, Austria, 1999. xii, 407p. 1999. pap. 79.95 (*3-211-83258-0*) Spr-Verlag.

Buhart, Jacques, ed. Joint Ventures in East Asia: Legal Issues. LC 92-9680. (International Association Ser.). 1992. lib. bdg. 114.00 (*1-85333-739-0*, Pub. by Graham & Trotman) Kluwer Academic.

— Joint Ventures in East Asia: Legal Issues. 192p. (C). 1992. lib. bdg. 95.00 (*1-85333-743-9*, Pub. by Graham & Trotman) Kluwer Academic.

Buheiry, Marwan R. The Formation & Perception of the Modern Arab World: Studies by Marwan R. Buheiry. Conrad, Lawrence I. et al, eds. LC 89-11608. (Illus.). 624p. 1989. 29.95 (*0-87850-064-2*) Darwin Pr.

Buheiry, Marwan R., ed. Intellectual Life in the Arab East, 1890 to 1930. (Middle East Bks.). 206p. (C). 1981. pap. 14.95 (*0-8156-6086-3*) Syracuse U Pr.

Buheler, George. Buheler's Backyard Boatbuilding. 320p. 1990. pap. 25.95 (*0-07-158380-7*) McGraw.

Buhite, Russell D. Decisions at Yalta: An Appraisal of Summit Diplomacy. LC 86-13779. 176p. (C). 1986. 45.00 (*0-8420-2256-2*); pap. text 12.95 (*0-8420-2268-6*) Scholarly Res Inc.

An Asterisk (*) at the beginning of an entry indicates that the title is appearing for the first time.

— Lives at Risk: Hostages & Victims in American Foreign Policy. LC 95-5688. (Illus.). 268p. 1995. 45.00 (*0-8420-2552-9*); pap. 17.95 (*0-8420-2553-7*) Scholarly Res Inc.

— Major Crises in Contemporary American Foreign Policy: A Documentary History. LC 96-32415. (Primary Documents in American History & Contemporary Issues Ser.). 520p. 1997. 65.00 (*0-313-29468-2*) Greenwood.

Buhite, Russell D. & Levy, David W., eds. FDR's Fireside Chats. LC 91-50299. 352p. (C). 1992. 24.95 (*0-8061-2370-2*) U of Okla Pr.

Buhl, H. U. A Neo-Classical Theory of Distribution & Wealth. (Lecture Notes in Economics & Mathematical Systems Ser.: Vol. 262). v, 146p. 1986. 25.95 (*0-387-16062-0*) Spr-Verlag.

Buhl, Hermann. Nanga Parbat Pilgrimage: The Lonely Challenge. LC 99-201697. (Illus.). 384p. 1998. pap. 16.95 (*0-89886-610-3*) Mountaineers.

Buhl, Horst. Advanced Aerospace Materials. LC 92-30704. x, 373p. 1992. 125.00 (*3-540-55888-8*); 153.95 (*0-387-55888-8*) Spr-Verlag.

Buhl, Marie-Louise & Holm-Nielsen, Svend. Shiloh. The Pre-Hellenistic Remains: The Danish Excavations at Tall Sailun, Palestine in 1926, 1929, 1932, & 1963. (Publications of the National Museum, Archaeological-Historical Ser.: No. 1, 12). (Illus.). 120p. (C). 1963. pap. 25.00 (*0-614-11378-4*, Pub. by Aarhus Univ Pr) David Brown.

Buhl, Tom. How to Start, Operate & Enjoy a Successful Typesetting Business. 2nd ed. (Illus.). 136p. 1981. pap. 15.95 (*0-939374-00-5*) Homefront Graphics.

Buhle, jt. auth. see Faragher, John Mack.

Buhle, Mari J. Women & American Socialism, 1870-1920. LC 81-719. (Working Class in American History Ser.). (Illus.). 370p. 1981. text 34.95 (*0-252-00873-1*) U of Ill Pr.

— Women & American Socialism, 1870-1920. fac. ed. LC 81-719. (Working Class in American History Ser.). 371p. 1981. pap. 115.10 (*0-7837-7609-8*, 204736100007) Bks Demand.

Buhle, Mari J., et al, eds. The American Radical. LC 93-41221. 400p. (C). (gr. 13). 1994. pap. 22.99 (*0-415-90804-3*) Routledge.

— Encyclopedia of the American Left. LC 90-30202. (Illus.). 962p. 1990. text 35.00 (*0-8240-4781-8*, SS502) Garland.

— Encyclopedia of the American Left. (Illus.). 976p. 1992. 29.95 (*0-252-06250-7*) U of Ill Pr.

— Encyclopedia of the American Left. 2nd ed. LC 98-30423. (Illus.). 1024p. 1998. reprint ed. text 125.00 (*0-19-512088-4*) OUP.

Buhle, Mari J., ed. see Stanton, Elizabeth C., et al.

Buhle, Mari Jo. Feminism & Its Discontents: A Century of Struggle with Psychoanalysis. LC 97-32397. 432p. 1999. 35.00 (*0-674-29868-3*) HUP.

Buhle, Mari Jo, jt. auth. see Faragher, John M.

***Buhle, Mary Jo.** Feminism & Its Discontents: A Century of Struggle with Psychoanalysis. 448p. 2000. pap. 18.95 (*0-674-00403-5*) HUP.

Buhle, Paul. From the Knights of Labor to the New World Order: Essays on Labor & Culture. LC 96-26916. (Labor in America Ser.: Vol. 3). (Illus.). 276p. 1997. text 54.00 (*0-8153-2225-9*) Garland.

— Marxism in the United States: Remapping the History of the American Left. rev. ed. (Haymarket Ser.). 300p. (C). 1991. pap. 20.00 (*0-86091-547-6*, A5356, Pub. by Verso) Norton.

— Taking Care of Business: Samuel Gompers, George Meany, Lane Kirkland & the Tragedy of America. LC 98-47888. 315p. 1999. pap. text 18.00 (*1-58367-003-3*, Pub. by Monthly Rev) NYU Pr.

— Taking Care of Business: Samuel Gompers, George Meany, Lane Kirkland & the Tragedy of American Labor. LC 98-47888. (Illus.). 224p. 1999. 40.00 (*1-58367-004-1*, Pub. by Monthly Rev) NYU Pr.

Buhle, Paul, ed. History & the New Left: Madison, Wisconsin, 1950-1970. (Critical Perspectives on the Past Ser.). 457p. 1991. pap. 22.95 (*0-87722-836-1*) Temple U Pr.

Buhle, Paul, ed. Labor's Joke Book. LC 84-82508. (Illus.). 64p. (Orig.). (C). 1985. pap. 3.95 (*0-9614272-0-5*) WD Pr.

Buhle, Paul, intro. Life & Deeds of Uncle Sam: A Satirical Look at U. S. History. 80p. pap. 10.00 (*0-88286-064-X*) C H Kerr.

Buhle, Paul & Dawley, Alan, eds. Working for Democracy: American Workers from the Revolution to the Present. LC 85-5845. (Illus.). 168p. 1985. text 24.95 (*0-252-01220-8*); pap. text 9.95 (*0-252-01221-6*) U of Ill Pr.

Buhle, Paul & Georgakas, Dan, eds. The Immigrant Left in the United States. LC 95-19955. (SUNY Series in American Labor History). 349p. (C). 1996. text 69.50 (*0-7914-2883-4*); pap. text 23.95 (*0-7914-2884-2*) State U NY Pr.

Buhle, Paul & Rice-Maximin, Edward. William Appleman Williams: The Tragedy of Empire. (American Radicals Ser.). 306p. (C). 1995. pap. 20.99 (*0-415-91131-1*, B4907) Routledge.

Buhle, Paul & Sullivan, Edmund B. Images of American Radicalism. LC 94-69075. (Illus.). 462p. 1998. 60.00 (*0-8158-0509-8*) Chris Mass.

***Buhle, Paul & Sullivan, Edmund B.** Images of American Radicalism. LC 94-69075. (Illus.). 462p. 1999. pap. 39.95 (*0-8158-0544-6*) Chris Mass.

***Buhle, Paul & Wagner, David.** A Very Dangerous Citizen: Abraham Lincoln Polonsky & the Hollywood Left. LC 00-28692. 2001. write for info. (*0-520-22383-7*) U CA Pr.

Buhle, Paul, jt. auth. see McGilligan, Patrick.

Buhle, Paul, jt. ed. see Henry, Paget.

Buhle, Paul, ed. see Stanton, Elizabeth C., et al.

Buhle, Paul M. A Dreamer's Paradise Lost: Louis C. Fraina & Lewis Corey & the Decline of Radicalism in the United States, 1910-1950. LC 94-6037. 308p. (C). 1995. pap. 18.50 (*0-391-03849-4*); text 49.95 (*0-391-03850-8*) Humanities.

Buhler, C. F., ed. The Epistle of Othea Translated from the French Text of Christine de Pisan by Stephen Scrope. (EETS Original Ser.: Vol. 264). 1970. 30.00 (*0-19-722263-3*, Pub. by EETS) Boydell & Brewer.

Buhler, Charlotte M. The First Year of Life. Greenberg, Pearl & Ripin, Rowena, trs. LC 74-21402. (Classics in Child Development Ser.). 296p. 1975. reprint ed. 24.95 (*0-405-06455-1*) Ayer.

Buhler, Curt F. Standards of Bibliographical Description. LC 73-1431. 120p. 1973. reprint ed. lib. bdg. 49.75 (*0-8371-6796-5*, BUBD, Greenwood Pr) Greenwood.

Buhler, Douglas D., ed. Expanding the Context of Weed Management. LC 98-53514. 300p. 1998. 79.95 (*1-56022-062-7*) Haworth Jrnl Co-Edits.

Buhler, G. The Laws of Manu. 1972. lib. bdg. 250.00 (*0-87968-492-5*) Krishna Pr.

Buhler, J. P. Icosahedral Galois Representations. (Lecture Notes in Mathematics Ser.: Vol. 654). 1978. 19.95 (*0-387-08844-X*) Spr-Verlag.

***Buhler, James, et al, eds.** Music & Cinema. LC 00-23696. (Music Culture Ser.). (Illus.). 384p. 2000. pap. 24.95 (*0-8195-6411-7*, Wesleyan Univ Pr) U Pr of New Eng.

— Music & Cinema. LC 00-23696. (Music Culture Ser.). (Illus.). 384p. 2000. text 70.00 (*0-8195-6410-9*, Wesleyan Univ Pr) U Pr of New Eng.

Buhler, Joe, ed. Algorithmic Number Theory: Third International Symposium, ANTS - III, Portland, Oregon, U. S. A., June 21-25, 1998. Proceedings, Vol. 142. LC 98-24670. (Lecture Notes in Computer Science Ser.: Vol. 1423). x, 640p. 1998. pap. 89.00 (*3-540-64657-4*) Spr-Verlag.

Buhler, Karl. The Mental Development of the Child: Summary of Modern Psychological Theory. Oeser, Oscar, tr. from GRE. LC 74-21403. (Classics in Child Development Ser.). 190p. 1978. reprint ed. 28.95 (*0-405-06456-X*) Ayer.

— Theory of Language: The Representational Function of Language. Goodwin, Donald F., tr. from GER. LC 90-20219. (Foundations of Semiotics Ser.: Vol. 25). lxii, 508p. 1990. 148.00 (*1-55619-200-2*) J Benjamins Pubng Co.

***Buhler-Lynes, Barbara.** Georgia O'Keeffe: Catalogue Raisonne, 2 vols. (Illus.). 1200p. 1999. 195.00 (*0-300-08176-6*) Yale U Pr.

Buhler, Phillip A. The Oder-Neisse Line: A Reappraisal under International Law. (East European Monographs). 160p. 1990. text 44.50 (*0-88033-174-7*, Pub. by East Eur Monographs) Col U Pr.

Buhler, W., et al, eds. Empirical Research on the German Capital Market. LC 99-13100. (Contributions to Management Science Ser.). (Illus.). viii, 322p. 1999. pap. 61.00 (*3-7908-1193-9*) Spr-Verlag.

Buhler, W. K., et al, eds. Operations Research Proceedings DGOR, 1990: Papers of the 19th Annual Meeting. (Illus.). xiv, 642p. 1992. 154.00 (*0-387-55081-X*) Spr-Verlag.

Buhler, W. K., tr. see Scharlau, Winfried & Opolka, H.

Buhler, Walther. Living with Your Body. Maloney, L., tr. from GER.Tr. of Der/Leib als Instrument der Seele. 117p. (Orig.). 1979. pap. 10.95 (*0-85440-345-0*, Pub. by R Steiner Pr) Anthroposophic.

Buhler, William, jt. auth. see Morse, Stephen.

Buhlman, William L. Adventures Beyond the Body: How to Experience Out-of-Body Travel. LC 95-25921. (Illus.). 304p. 1996. pap. 15.00 (*0-06-251371-0*, Pub. by Harper SF) HarpC.

***Buhlmann, Elisabeth.** La Ligne Siemens. (Illus.). xxxii, 165p. 1999. 32.95 (*3-906763-52-8*, Pub. by P Lang) P Lang Pubng.

Buhlmann, H. Mathematical Methods in Risk Theory. 2nd ed. Berger, M. et al, eds. (Grundlehren der Mathematischen Wissenschaften Ser.: Vol. 172). xii, 210p. 1996. pap. 69.95 (*3-540-61703-5*) Spr-Verlag.

Buhlmann, Rosemarie & Fearns, Anneliese. Handbuch des Fachsprachenunterrichts. 400p. 42.95 (*3-468-49435-1*) Langenscheidt.

Buhlmann, Rosemarie, et al. Wirtschaftsdeutsch Von A-Z: Kommunication und Fachwortschatz In der Wirtschaft. (GER.). 192p. 1996. 24.50 (*3-468-49849-7*) Langenscheidt.

***Buhlmann, Urs.** Malteserkreuz und Preu & Beta; Endadler: Ein Beitrag Zur Grundungsgeschichte der Genossenschaft der Rheinisch-westfalischen Malteser-Devotionsritter. (Beitrage zur Kirchen- und Kulturgeschichte Ser.). 298p. 1999. 48.95 (*3-631-35575-0*) P Lang Pubng.

Buhlmann, Walbert. All Have the Same God. (C). 1988. 39.00 (*0-7855-3223-4*, Pub. by St Paul Pubns) St Mut.

— The Chosen Peoples. (C). 1988. 39.00 (*0-85439-200-9*, Pub. by St Paul Pubns) St Mut.

— The Church of the Future: A Model for the Year 2001. LC 86-178053.Tr. of Weltkirche-Neue Dimensionen-Model fur das Jahr 2001. 221p. (Orig.). reprint ed. pap. 68.60 (*0-7837-5526-0*, 204529600005) Bks Demand.

— The Coming of the Third Church: An Analysis of the Present & Future of the Church. LC 76-23237. 431p. reprint ed. pap. 133.70 (*0-8357-8540-8*, 203484700091) Bks Demand.

— Forward, Church! (C). 1988. 60.00 (*0-85439-134-7*, Pub. by St Paul Pubns) St Mut.

— With Eyes to See: Church & World in the Third Millennium. 176p. (C). 1990. text 49.00 (*0-85439-342-0*, Pub. by St Paul Pubns) St Mut.

Buhmann, Martin D. & Iserles, Arieh, eds. Approximation Theory & Optimization. LC 97-15714. 234p. (C). 1997. text 52.95 (*0-521-58190-7*) Cambridge U Pr.

Buhner, Stephen H. One Spirit, Many Peoples: A Manifesto for Earth Spirituality. 288p. 1997. 24.95 (*1-57098-120-5*) Roberts Rinehart.

— Sacred & Herbal Healing Beers: The Secrets of Ancient Fermentation. LC 98-17064. (Illus.). 600p. 1998. pap. 19.95 (*0-937381-66-7*, Siris Bks) Brewers Pubns.

— Sacred Plant Medicine: Explorations in Indigenous Herbalism. LC 96-67085. (Illus.). 240p. 1996 pap. text 18.95 (*1-57098-091-8*) Roberts Rinehart.

— Sacred Plant Medicine: Explorations in the Practice of Indigenous Herbalism. (Illus.). 240p. 1996. 30.00 (*1-57098-085-3*) Roberts Rinehart.

Buhner, Stephen Harrod. Herbal Antibiotics. LC 99-33056. 144p. 1999. pap. 12.95 (*1-58017-148-6*) Storey Bks.

***Buhner, Stephen Harrod.** Herbs for Hepatitis C & the Liver. (Medicinal Herb Guide Ser.). 128p. 2000. pap. 12.95 (*1-58017-255-5*) Storey Bks.

Buholzer, Theres. Life of the Snail. Simon, Noel, tr. from GER. (Nature Watch Bks.).Tr. of Schneckenleben. (Illus.). 48p. (J). (gr. 2-5). 1987. lib. bdg. 19.95 (*0-87614-246-3*, Carolrhoda) Lerner Pub.

Buhr, Deborah E. I Cant Believe No Sugar Cookbook. rev. ed. LC 96-54846. 1997. pap. 12.95 (*0-312-15551-4*) St Martin.

— I Can't Believe This Has No Sugar. 1990. pap. 9.95 (*0-312-04330-9*) St Martin.

Buhr, M. Kleines Woerterbuch der Marxistisch-Leninistischen Philosophie: Small Dictionary of Marxist-Leninist Philosophy. 4th ed. (GER.). 385p. 1980. 19.95 (*0-8288-2278-6*, M15577) Fr & Eur.

Buhr, M., jt. auth. see Klaus, G.

Buhr, Raymond J. A. & Bailey, D. L. Introduction to Real Time Systems: From Design to Multitasking with C/C++ LC 98-25878. (Illus.). 350p. 1998. 62.00 (*0-13-606070-6*) P-H.

Buhren, Ralf Van, see Van Buhren, Ralf.

Buhrer, Emil M., jt. auth. see Isenbart, Hans-Heinrich.

Buhrer, Peter. Christmas Cooking in New York. (GER., Illus.). 72p. 1997. 40.00 (*3-87287-442-X*, Pub. by Buchverlage L M H) J Szoke Edns.

Buhrer, Peter, jt. ed. see Verlag, Mary H.

Buhrig, Marga. Woman Invisible: A Personal Odyssey in Christian Feminism. 160p. 1994. pap. 35.00 (*0-86012-202-6*, Pub. by Srch Pr) St Mut.

Buhring, Anne & Rather, Petra. Cooking to Suit Your Body's Needs Ayurveda Cookbook. LC 97-11641. (Illus.). 96p. 1997. pap. text 14.95 (*0-7641-0026-2*) Barron.

Buhringer, Gerhard & Platt, Jerome J., eds. Drug Addiction Treatment Research: German & American Perspectives. 550p. (C). 1992. lib. bdg. 94.50 (*0-89464-628-1*) Krieger.

Buhrke, Robin. Matter of Justice. 320p. (Orig.). (C). 1996. pap. 20.99 (*0-415-91469-8*) Routledge.

Buhrke, Robin A. Matter of Justice. 320p. (C). 1996. 70.00 (*0-415-91468-X*) Routledge.

Buhrke, Victor E., et al, eds. A Practical Guide for the Preparation of Specimens for X-Ray Fluorescence & X-Ray Diffraction Analysis. LC 97-16687. 360p. 1997. 89.95 (*0-471-19458-1*) Wiley.

Buhrow, B. J. House Fire: A Collection of Poems. LC 91-61254. (Minnesota Voices Project Ser.). 80p. (Orig.). 1992. pap. 6.50 (*0-89823-129-9*) New Rivers Pr.

Bui, Dang H., ed. The Future of Health & Health Care Systems in the Industrialized Societies. LC 87-7292. 304p. 1988. 69.50 (*0-275-92491-2*, C2491, Praeger Pubs) Greenwood.

Bui, H. D. Inverse Problems in the Mechanics of Materials: An Introduction. LC 94-1851. 224p. 1994. boxed set 105.00 (*0-8493-8471-0*) CRC Pr.

Bui, H. D. & Tanaka, M., eds. Inverse Problems in Engineering Mechanics: Proceedings of the 2nd International Symposium, Paris, France, 2-4 November 1994. (Illus.). 480p. (C). 1994. text 142.00 (*90-5410-517-8*, Pub. by A A Balkema) Ashgate Pub Co.

Bui, H. D., jt. ed. see Tanaka, Masataka.

Bui, Linda T., jt. auth. see White, Kenneth J.

***Bui, Phiet.** My Life Planner: 400 Years Calendar/Virtual Calendar. (Illus.). 68p. 1999. pap. 8.99 (*0-9671141-0-1*) Suhasian.

Bui, T. H., jt. ed. see Jaffe, R.

Bui, T. X. Co-op: A Group Decision Support System for Cooperative Multiple Criteria Group Decision Making. (Lecture Notes in Computer Science Ser.: Vol. 290). 250p. 1987. 36.00 (*0-387-18753-7*) Spr-Verlag.

***Bui, Tin.** Following Ho Chi Minh: Memoirs of a North Vietnamese Colonel. Van, Do, tr. from VIE. LC 94-10878. (Illus.). 202p. 1999. pap. 20.00 (*0-8248-2233-1*) UH Pr.

Buialov, N. I., et al. Quantitative Evaluation of Predicted Reserves of Oil & Gas (Authorized Translation from the Russian) LC 64-7759. 73p. reprint ed. pap. 30.00 (*0-608-11386-7*, 200335900021) Bks Demand.

Buiatti, E. Intervention Trials of Cancer Prevention: Results & New Research Programmes. (IARC Technical Reports: No. 18). v, 52p. 1994. pap. text 30.00 (*92-832-1432-3*, 1770018) World Health.

Buice, Christopher. A Bucketful of Dreams: Contemporary Parables for All Ages. 72p. (J). 1995. pap. 10.00 (*1-55896-288-3*, Skinner Hse Bks) Unitarian Univ.

Buick, Peter. Live Sound: PA for Performing Musicians. (Illus.). 200p. 1997. pap. 18.95 (*1-870775-44-9*, XC8028, Pub. by PC Pubg) Cimino Pub Grp.

Buick, Peter & Lennard, Vic. Music Technology Reference Book. (Illus.). 160p. 1995. pap. 15.95 (*1-870775-34-1*, Pub. by PC Pubg) Cimino Pub Grp.

Buick, T. Lindsay. Treaty of Waitangi. LC 72-1294. (Select Bibliographies Reprint Ser.). 1977. reprint ed. 31.95 (*0-8369-6822-0*) Ayer.

Buick, Thomas L. The Moa-Hunters of New Zealand: Sportsmen of the Stone Age. LC 75-35242. reprint ed. 39.50 (*0-404-14417-9*) AMS Pr.

Buickerood, James G., intro. A Philosophick Essay Concerning Ideas According to Dr. Sherlock's Principles. (Augustan Reprints Ser.: No. 270 (1991)). reprint ed. 14.50 (*0-404-70270-8*) AMS Pr.

Buidottis, Flavio. Luigi Snozzi - Monte Carasso. (Illus.). 128p. 1995. 45.00 (*3-7643-5596-4*, Pub. by Birkhauser) Princeton Arch.

Buie-Bryant, Carrie. From Hard to Heart. LC 98-91112. 250p. 1999. 23.95 (*1-889448-53-2*) NBN Publishers Group.

Buiel, Eric. Design & Evaluation of a Human-Machine Interface for a Teleoperated Space Manipulator. (Illus.). 280p. 1998. pap. 55.00 (*90-407-1687-0*, Pub. by Delft U Pr) Coronet Bks.

***Buigues, Pierre, et al, eds.** Competitiveness & the Value of Intangible Assets. LC 99-45192. 360p. 2000. 100.00 (*1-84064-391-9*) E Elgar.

Buigues, Pierre, et al, eds. European Policies on Competition, Trade & Industry: Conflict & Complementarities. LC 95-19501. 400p. 1995. 100.00 (*1-85898-315-0*) E Elgar.

Buijnsters, P. J., ed. Poems of Jacobus Bellamy. (Illus.). 64p. (C). 1994. pap. text 12.95 (*90-5356-107-2*, Pub. by Amsterdam U Pr) U of Mich Pr.

Buijs, A. & Erne, F. C., eds. Photon '97: Proceedings of the Conference on the Structure & Interactions of the Photon Egmond Aan Zee, The Netherlands 10-15 May, 1997. LC 97-52725. 500p. 1998. 96.00 (*981-02-3244-6*) World Scientific Pub.

Buijs, Gina, ed. Migrant Women: Crossing Boundaries & Changing Identities. LC 92-15999. (Cross-Cultural Perspectives on Women Ser.). 256p. 1993. 49.50 (*0-85496-729-X*); pap. 19.50 (*0-85496-869-5*, Pub. by Berg Pubs) NYU Pr.

Buijs, Joseph A., ed. Christian Marriage Today: Growth or Breakdown? LC 85-10466. (Symposium Ser.: Vol. 16). 168p. 1984. 79.95 (*0-88946-707-2*) E Mellen.

— Maimonides: A Collection of Critical Essays. LC 87-40617. 336p. (C). 1990. pap. text 17.50 (*0-268-01368-3*) U of Notre Dame Pr.

Buijs, R. M., jt. auth. see Nederlands Instituut Voor Hersenonderzoek Staff.

Buijsen, P. F. Electron Beam Induced Cationic Polymerization with Onium Salts. (Illus.). 151p. (Orig.). 1996. pap. 87.50 (*90-407-1228-X*, Pub. by Delft U Pr) Coronet Bks.

Buijtenen, J. P. Van, see Van Buijtenen, J. P.

Buijtenen, P. M. Van, see Van Buijtenen, P. M.

Buijtenhuijs, Robert. Le Frohnat et les Revoltes Populares du Tchad, 1965-1976. (Change & Continuity in Africa Ser.). 1978. pap. 42.35 (*90-279-7657-0*) Mouton.

Buikema, Jr. & Cairns, Jr., eds. Aquatic Invertebrate Bioassays- STP 715. 218p. 1980. 24.00 (*0-8031-0802-8*, STP715) ASTM.

Buikema, Arthur L. & Ward, Brian A. Plain Talk about Using the Web. 5th ed. 96p. (C). 1998. pap. text, teacher ed. 15.00 (*0-03-022112-9*) SCP.

Buikema, Rosemarie & Smelik, Anneke, eds. Women's Studies & Culture: A Feminist Introduction. LC 95-21716. 256p. (C). 1995. text 59.95 (*1-85649-311-3*, Pub. by Zed Books); text 22.50 (*1-85649-312-1*, Pub. by Zed Books) St Martin.

Buikhuisen, Wouter & Megnik, Sarnoff A., eds. Explaining Criminal Behaviour: Interdisciplinary Approaches. LC 87-20847. viii, 260p. (Orig.). 1988. pap. 41.00 (*90-04-08514-9*) Brill Academic Pubs.

Buikstra, Jane E. Hopewell in the Lower Illinois Valley. LC 82-101780. (Scientific Papers Ser.: No. 2). (Illus.). 104p. 1976. 7.50 (*0-942118-02-2*); pap. 4.50 (*0-942118-03-0*) Ctr Amer Arche.

Buikstra, Jane E., ed. A Life in Science: Papers in Honor of J. Lawrence Angel. LC 90-48080. (Scientific Papers: No. 6). (Illus.). 218p. (Orig.). 1990. pap. 12.50 (*0-942118-31-6*) Ctr Amer Arche.

— Prehistoric Tuberculosis in the Americas. LC 80-28660. (Scientific Papers Ser.: No. 5). (Illus.). 194p. (Orig.). 1981. pap. 7.25 (*0-942118-10-3*) Ctr Amer Arche.

Buikstra, Jane E. & Goldstein, Lynne G. The Perrins Ledge Crematory. (Reports of Investigations Ser.: No. 28). (Illus.). 40p. 1973. pap. 2.00 (*0-89792-052-X*) Ill St Museum.

Buikstra, Jane E. & Milner, George R. The Dickson Mounds Site: An Annotated Bibliography. (Reports of Investigations: No. 44). (Illus.). v, 77p. (Orig.). (C). 1989. pap. 5.00 (*0-89792-119-4*) Ill St Museum.

Buikstra, Jane E., et al. Staging Ritual: Hopewell Ceremonialism at the Mound House Site, Greene County, Illinois. LC 97-47776. (Kampsville Studies in Archeology & History: No. 1). (Illus.). 216p. 1998. pap. 20.00 (*0-942118-38-3*) Ctr Amer Arche.

Buikstra, Jane E., ed. see Haas, Jonathan.

Buikstra, Jane E., jt. ed. see Rathbun, Ted A.

Buil. CCD Astronomy. 1991. 24.95 (*0-943396-29-8*) Willmann-Bell.

Builder, Carl H. The Icarus Syndrome: The Role of Air Power in the Evolution & Fate of the U. S. Air Force. LC 93-31554. 300p. (C). 1994. 44.95 (*1-56000-141-0*) Transaction Pubs.

— The Masks of War: American Military Styles in Strategy & Analysis. LC 88-13517. 240p. 1989. pap. 15.95 (*0-8018-3776-6*) Johns Hopkins.

— Measuring the Leverage: Assessing Military Contributions to Drug Interdiction. LC 93-7134. 1993. pap. 13.00 (*0-8330-1338-6*, MR-158-A/AF) Rand Corp.

— Military Planning Today: Calculus or Charade? LC 93-28129. 1993. pap. 15.00 (*0-8330-1425-0*, MR-293-AF) Rand Corp.

B

Builder, Carl H. & Karasik, Theodore W. Organizing, Training, & Equipping the Air Force for Crises & Lesser Conflicts. 115p. 1995. pap. text 15.00 (*0-8330-2320-9*, MR-626-AF) Rand Corp.

Builder, Carl H., et al. Report of a Workshop on Expanding U. S. Air Force Noncombat Mission Capabilities. LC 93-4946. 1993. pap. 13.00 (*0-8330-1402-1*, MR-246-AF) Rand Corp.

Builder, Carl H., jt. auth. see Dewar, James A.

Builder, Carl H., jt. auth. see Nichiporuk, Brian.

Builder Magazine Editors. Building Products Buyers Guide: 12,000 Products - 2,500 Manufacturers. (Illus.). 256p. 1997. pap. 24.95 (*1-881955-39-7*) Home Planners.

Builder, Philip. Exploring Reading. (C). 1990. 80.00 (*0-86431-079-X*, Pub. by Aust Council Educ Res) St Mut.

Builders' Publishing Company Staff. Business Management Guide for Arizona Contractors. 5th rev. ed. 284p. 1993. reprint ed. spiral bd. 29.95 (*0-941385-03-5*) Builders AZ.

— Business Management Guide for Arizona Contractors. 6th rev. ed. (Illus.). 284p. 1995. pap., spiral bd. 29.95 (*0-941385-04-3*) Builders AZ.

Builders' Publishing Company Staff, ed. Business Management Guide for Arizona Contractors. 247p. 1986. 23.95 (*0-941385-00-0*) Builders AZ.

Building. European Directory of Property. 1997. 219.95 (*0-419-18270-5*, E & FN Spon) Routledge.

Building Council Staff. Uniform Mechanical Code, 1997. 1997. pap. text 46.75 (*1-884590-77-2*) Intl Conf Bldg Off.

Building Design Partnership Staff, jt. auth. see RICS Staff.

Building Employers Confederation Staff, jt. auth. see RICS Staff.

Building Owners & Managers Association Internation. ADA Compliance Guidebook: A Checklist for Your Building. 1991. pap. text 50.00 (*0-943130-00-X*) Build Own & Man.

— The Commercial Real Estate Compendium: Five Years of Insight & Analysis. 140p. (Orig.). 1993. pap. 155.00 (*0-943130-06-9*) Build Own & Man.

— Emergency Planning Guidebook: A Blueprint for Preparing Your Building's Response. 85p. (Orig.). 1994. pap. 140.00 (*0-943130-07-7*) Build Own & Man.

— Opening Doors: Your Guide for Accommodating Persons with Disabilities. 10 bks., Set. 15p. (Orig.). 1991. pap. 50.00 (*0-943130-02-6*) Build Own & Man.

— The Refrigerant Manual: Managing the Phase-Out of CFCs. 136p. (Orig.). 1993. pap. text 85.00 (*0-943130-05-0*) Build Own & Man.

Building Research Establishment Staff. Housing Defects Reference Manual: The Complete BRE Defect Action Sheets. 304p. 1991. write for info. (*0-419-16720-X*, E & FN Spon) Routledge.

Building Services Research & Development Associati. Building Services Materials Handbook: Heating, Sanitation & Fire Protection. 704p. 1987. text 110.00 (*0-419-14310-6*, E & FN Spon) Routledge.

Building Systems Institute Staff. Metal Building Systems. 2nd ed. (Illus.). 230p. (C). 1990. write for info. (*0-9626582-0-0*) Bldg Systs Inst.

Builta, Howard C., et al. Fundamentals of Real Property Administration. (Illus.). 610p. 1993. teacher ed., ring bd. write for info. (*1-928594-40-9*); student ed., ring bd. write for info. (*1-928594-39-5*) BOMI Inst.

Builta, Jeanine, ed. The Campaign Manuals. (Illus.). 388p. 1985. ring bd. 295.00 (*0-939120-05-4*) Third Sector.

Builtjes, P., jt. auth. see Borrell, Peter.

Buira, Ariel. Reflections on the International Monetary System. LC 95-1091. (Essays in International Finance Ser.: No. 195). 46p. 1995. pap. 10.00 (*0-88165-102-8*) Princeton U Int Finan Econ.

Buis, Lela E., et al. Worthy Foes: Differently Abled Heroes. Bowen, Gary, ed. (Orig.). 1996. pap. 6.00 (*1-887666-12-5*) Obelesk Bks.

Buis, Willem, photos by. Body Painting. LC 97-4126. (Illus.). 97p. 1997. 49.95 (*0-945456-48-4*) PT Pubns.

Buisine, A. Dictionnaire des Amoureux, Savant Couleurs de Venise. (FRE.). 1998. 49.95 (*0-320-00265-9*) Fr & Eur.

Buisseret, David. Envisioning the City: Six Studies in Urban Cartography. LC 97-37158. (Kenneth Nebenzahl, Jr., Lectures in the History of Cartography). 216p. 1998. 50.00 (*0-226-07993-7*) U Ch Pr.

— Henry IV. LC 83-22464. (French Monarche Ser.). (Illus.). 256p. 1989. pap. 19.95 (*0-04-445635-2*); text 65.00 (*0-04-944012-8*) Routledge.

— Historic Illinois from the Air. LC 89-20648. (Illus.). 250p. 1990. 39.95 (*0-226-07989-9*) U Ch Pr.

— Historic Jamaica from the Air. (Illus.). 160p. 1997. 35.00 (*976-8100-64-8*, Pub. by Ian Randle) Paul & Co Pubs.

— Rural Images: The Estate Plan in the Old & New Worlds. (Illus.). 37p. 1988. pap. 5.00 (*0-911028-40-4*) Newberry.

— Tools of Empire: Ships & Maps in the Process of Westward Expansion. (Illus.). 44p. 1986. pap. 5.00 (*0-911028-33-1*) Newberry.

Buisseret, David, ed. From Sea Charts to Satellite Images: Interpreting North American History Through Maps. LC 89-128. (Illus.). 340p. 1990. lib. bdg. 90.00 (*0-226-07991-0*) U Ch Pr.

— From Sea Charts to Satellite Images: Interpreting North American History Through Maps. LC 89-128. (Illus.). 338p. 1999. pap. text 29.95 (*0-226-07992-9*) U Ch Pr.

— Monarchs, Ministers, & Maps: The Emergence of Cartography As a Tool of Government in Early Modern Europe. LC 91-36088. (Kenneth Nebenzahl, Jr., Lectures in the History of Cartography). (Illus.). 202p. 1992. 49.95 (*0-226-07987-2*) U Ch Pr.

— Rural Images: Estate Maps in the Old & New Worlds. LC 95-30609. (Kenneth Nebenzahl, Jr., Lectures in the History of Cartography Ser.). 208p. 1996. 55.00 (*0-226-07990-2*) U Ch Pr.

***Buisseret, David & Reinhardt, Steven G., eds.** Creolization in the Americas. (Walter Prescott Webb Memorial Lectures: Vol. 32). (Illus.). 160p. (C). 2000. 29.95 (*0-89096-949-3*) Tex A&M Univ Pr.

— Creolization in the Americas. LC 00-29934. (Walter Prescott Webb Memorial Lectures: Vol. 32). (Illus.). 160p. (C). 2000. pap. 16.95 (*1-58544-101-5*) Texas A&M Univ.

Buisseret, Laurent. Teach Yourself WordPerfect 5.0 Module I & II. 158p. 1989. ring bd. 69.95 incl. disk (*0-929533-13-5*) Tutorland.

Buisson, Claudia, jt. auth. see Green, Katharine.

Buisson, Dominique, jt. auth. see Buisson, Sylvie.

Buisson, Sylvie & Buisson, Dominique. Foujita's Life & Work. (FRE., Illus.). 582p. 1987. 295.00 (*1-55660-072-0*) A Wofsy Fine Arts.

Buist, A. H. Information Extraction from Multiple Transmission Electron Microscopy Images. (Illus.). 149p. (Orig.). 1995. pap. 59.50 (*90-407-1117-8*, Pub. by Delft U Pr) Coronet Bks.

Buist, Robert. Food Chemical Sensitivity. 248p. pap. 9.95 (*0-89529-399-4*, Avery) Penguin Putnam.

Buist, Sonia. Hikes & Walks on Mt. Hood: Government Camp & Timberline Lodge Area. (Illus.). 120p. 1994. pap. 11.95 (*0-9643836-0-8*) Lolits Pr.

— Round Mt. Hood in Easy Stages. (Illus.). 120p. (Orig.). 1997. pap. 9.95 (*0-9643836-1-6*) Lolits Pr.

Buitelaar, Marjo. Fasting & Feasting in Morocco: Women's Participation in Ramadan. 256p. 1994. 30.00 (*0-85496-321-9*) Berg Pubs.

Buiten, Henk J. & Clevers, Jan G., eds. Land Observation by Remote Sensing: Theory & Applications. LC 93-25271. (Current Topics in Remote Sensing Ser.: Vol. 3).Tr. of Remote Sensing Theorie en Toepassingen van Landobservatie. xvi, 642p. 1994. text 182.00 (*2-88124-939-6*); pap. text 47.00 (*2-88124-940-X*) Gordon & Breach.

Buiten, J., ed. Shipboard Acoustics. (C). 1987. text 389.50 (*90-247-3420-7*) Kluwer Academic.

Buitendam, Arend, jt. ed. see Pennings, Johannes M.

Buitenen, A. Van, see Bilderbeek, A. S. & Van Buitenen, A., eds.

Buitenhuis, H. & Clason, A. T., eds. Archaeozoology of the Near East: Proceedings of the First International Symposium on the Archaeozoology of Southwestern Asia & Adjacent Areas. (Illus.). 130p. 1993. pap. 45.00 (*90-73348-25-0*, Pub. by Backhuys Pubs) Balogh.

Buitenhuis, H. & Uerpmann, H. P., eds. Archaeozoology of the Near East II: Proceedings of the 2nd International Symposium on the Archaeozoology of Southwestern Asia & Adjacent Areas. (Illus.). 155p. 1995. pap. 51.00 (*90-73348-49-8*, Pub. by Backhuys Pubs) Balogh.

Buitenhuis, Peter. The Grasping Imagination: The American Writings of Henry James. LC 79-149323. (Illus.). 304p. reprint ed. pap. 94.30 (*0-8357-6375-7*, 203572900096) Bks Demand.

— The House of the Seven Gables: Severing Family & Colonial Ties. (Twayne's Masterworks Ser.: No. 66). 128p. 1991. pap. 18.00 (*0-8057-8146-3*) Macmillan.

Buitenkamp, M., et al, eds. Action Plan Sustainable: Netherlands. 186p. 1994. pap. 60.00 (*90-6224-982-5*) LPC InBook.

Buiter, Willem H. International Macroeconomics. (Illus.). 360p. 1990. 75.00 (*0-19-828693-7*) OUP.

— Macroeconomic Theory & Stabilization Policy. LC 89-5010. 384p. 1989. text 65.00 (*0-472-10138-2*, 10138) U of Mich Pr.

— Principles of Budgetary & Financial Policy. 474p. 1990. 52.50 (*0-262-02303-2*) MIT Pr.

Buiter, Willem H. & Marston, Richard C., eds. International Economic Policy Coordination. LC 84-29246. 402p. reprint ed. pap. 124.70 (*0-7837-4094-8*, 205791500011) Bks Demand.

Buiter, Willem H., et al. Financial Markets & European Monetary Cooperation: The Lessons of the 1992-93 Exchange Rate Mechanism Crisis. LC 97-1241. (Japan-U. S. Center Monographs on International Financial Markets: Vol. 2). (Illus.). 236p. (C). 1998. text 49.95 (*0-521-49547-4*) Cambridge U Pr.

***Buiter, Willem H., et al.** Financial Markets & European Monetary Cooperation: The Lessons of the 1992-93 Exchange Rate Mechanism Crisis. (Japan-US Center Sanwa Monographs on International Financial Markets: No. 2). 237p. (C). 2000. pap. text. write for info. (*0-521-79440-4*) Cambridge U Pr.

Buiter, Willem H., et al. Interpreting the Erm Crisis: Country-Specific & Systemic Issues. LC 98-11535. (Studies in International Finance: No. 84). 1998. 13.50 (*0-88165-256-3*) Princeton U Int Finan Econ.

Buitrago, Alerto. De Viaje, Level 2. (Leer en Espanol Ser.). (SPA.). (C). 1998. pap. 5.95 (*84-294-4230-8*) Santillana.

Buitrago, J., et al, eds. Relativistic Astrophysics & Cosmology: LaLaguna, Tenerife, Spain, 4-7 September 1995. LC 98-120463. 270p. 1997. 58.00 (*981-02-3189-X*) World Scientific Pub.

Buitrago Jimenez, A. Dictionary of Modern Expressions & Phrases. (SPA.). 515p. 1996. pap. 26.50 (*84-239-9227-6*, Pub. by Espasa Calpe) IBD Ltd.

Buitrago, Orellano. Y Cristo Me Liberto.Tr. of And Jesus Set Me Free. (SPA.). 1992. 4.99 (*1-56063-214-3*, 497708) Editorial Unilit.

Buitrago Ortiz, Carlos. Esperanza: An Ethnographic Study of a Peasant Community in Puerto Rico. LC 73-90915. (Viking Fund Publications in Anthropology: No. 50). (Illus.). 229p. reprint ed. pap. 71.00 (*0-8357-6805-8*, 203548800095) Bks Demand.

Buitron-Oliver, Diana. The Greek Miracle: Classical Sculpture from the Dawn of Democracy: The Fifth Century B. C. (Illus.). 168p. 1993. 49.50 (*0-8109-3371-3*, Pub. by Abrams) Time Warner.

— New Perspectives in Early Greek Art. 1992. 60.00 (*0-89468-177-X*) Natl Gallery Art.

— The Sanctuary of Apollo Hylates at Kourion: Excavations in the Archaic Precinct. (Studies in Mediterranean Archaeology: Vol. CIX). (Illus.). 260p. (Orig.). 1996. pap. 136.50 (*91-7081-094-X*, Pub. by P Astroms) Coronet Bks.

Buitron-Oliver, Diana, ed. The Interpretation of Architectural Sculpture in Greece & Rome. LC 72-600309. (Studies in the History of Art Ser.: Vol. 49). (Illus.). 233p. 1997. 35.00 (*0-89468-202-4*) Natl Gallery Art.

— The Interpretation of Architectural Sculpture in Greece & Rome. (Illus.). 1996. 40.00 (*0-300-07700-9*) Yale U Pr.

— New Perspectives in Early Greek Art. 1996. 60.00 (*0-300-07699-1*) Yale U Pr.

Buium, A. Differential Algebraic Groups of Finite Dimension. (Lecture Notes in Mathematics Ser.: Vol. 1506). xv, 145p. 1992. 37.95 (*0-387-55181-6*) Spr-Verlag.

— Differential Function Fields & Moduli of Algebraic Varieties. (Lecture Notes in Mathematics Ser.: Vol. 1226). ix, 146p. 1987. pap. 30.00 (*0-387-17194-0*) Spr-Verlag.

***Bujack, Betty.** Ikandoo's Blue Ribbon Adventure: A Christmas Adventure Story. (Ikandoo Holiday Adventure Storybook Ser.). (Illus.). 32p. (J). (ps-3). 2000. 16.95 (*0-615-11228-5*) Bujack Enter.

Bujak, Adam. John Paul II. LC 92-71934. (Illus.). 112p. 1992. 19.95 (*0-89870-424-3*); pap. 14.95 (*0-89870-421-9*) Ignatius Pr.

Bujalance, E., et al. Automorphism Groups of Compact Bordered Klein Surfaces: A Combinatorial Approach. Dold, A. et al, eds. (Lecture Notes in Mathematics Ser.: Vol. 1439). (Illus.). xiii, 201p. 1990. 38.95 (*0-387-52941-1*) Spr-Verlag.

Bujas, Zeljko. Serbocroatian-English Encyclopedic Dictionary: Hrvatsko Ili Srpsko-Engleski Enciclopedijski Rjecnik, 2 vols. (ENG & SER.). 1983. 95.00 (*0-8288-0500-8*, F78460) Fr & Eur.

***Bujdoso, Balint.** Szent Magyarsag Versei. (HUN.). 256p. 1998. pap. 7.00 (*0-9651859-2-3*) St Stephens Magyar.

Bujdoso, E., jt. auth. see Braun, T.

***Bujea, Eleanor.** ARFORA - 60 Years, 1938-1998. (Illus.). 304p. 1998. 25.00 (*1-929200-08-0*) Roman Ortho Episco.

Bujese, Arlene, ed. see Namuth, Hans.

Bujo, Benezet. African Theology in Its Social Context. (Faith & Cultures Ser.). 1992. 18.00 (*0-88344-805-X*) Orbis Bks.

Bujold, Edward J. The Odyssey of Primary Care Research: Historical Perspectives. McGowen, Thomas, ed. LC 96-69743. 140p. 1997. pap. 24.95 (*0-9654202-0-5*) Speck Pub.

Bujold, Lois McMaster. Barrayar. 400p. 1991. per. 5.99 (*0-671-72083-X*) Baen Bks.

— Borders of Infinity. 1991. per. 5.99 (*0-671-72093-7*) Baen Bks.

— Borders of Infinity. 320p. 1999. per. 1.99 (*0-671-57829-4*) S&S Trade.

— Brothers in Arms. 352p. 1989. mass mkt. 5.99 (*0-671-69799-4*) Baen Bks.

— Cetaganda. LC 95-33243. 320p. 1996. 21.00 (*0-671-87701-1*) Baen Bks.

— Cetaganda. 352p. 1996. per. 6.99 (*0-671-87744-5*) Baen Bks.

***Bujold, Lois McMaster.** A Civil Campaign: A Vorkosigan Adventure. 2000. mass mkt. 7.99 (*0-671-57885-5*) Baen Bks.

Bujold, Lois McMaster. A Civil Campaign: A Vorkosigan Adventure. LC 99-16807. 416p. 1999. 24.00 (*0-671-57827-8*) S&S Trade.

— Cordelia's Honor. LC 96-24819. 496p. 1996. pap. 15.00 (*0-671-87749-6*) Baen Bks.

— Cordelia's Honor. 608p. 1999. per. 7.99 (*0-671-57828-6*) S&S Trade.

— Dreamweaver's Dilemma. Lewis, Suford, ed. LC 95-72735. (Illus.). xiv, 250p. 1997. pap. 12.00 (*0-915368-53-6*) New Eng SF Assoc.

— Ethan of Athos. 256p. 1986. mass mkt. 5.99 (*0-671-65604-X*) Baen Bks.

— Falling Free. 320p. 1988. pap. 4.99 (*0-671-65398-9*) Baen Bks.

— Falling Free. 1999. mass mkt. 6.99 (*0-671-57812-X*) S&S Trade.

— Komarr: A Miles Vorkosigan Adventure. LC 98-14345. (Vorkosigan Adventure Ser.). 320p. 1998. 22.00 (*0-671-87877-8*, Pocket Books) PB.

— Komarr: A Miles Vorkosigan Adventure. LC 98-14345. 366p. 2000. reprint ed. mass mkt. 6.99 (*0-671-57808-1*) PB.

— Memory. 480p. 1996. 22.00 (*0-671-87743-7*) Baen Bks.

— Memory. 480p. 1997. per. 6.99 (*0-671-87845-X*) Baen Bks.

— Mirror Dance. 592p. 1995. per. 6.99 (*0-671-87646-5*) Baen Bks.

— Shards of Honor. 1991. per. 5.99 (*0-671-72087-2*) Baen Bks.

— The Spirit Ring. 384p. 1992. 17.00 (*0-671-72142-9*) Baen Bks.

— The Spirit Ring. 384p. 1993. per. 5.99 (*0-671-72188-7*) Baen Bks.

***Bujold, Lois McMaster.** The Spirit Ring. 384p. 2000. reprint ed. per. 6.99 (*0-671-57870-7*) PB.

Bujold, Lois McMaster. The Vor Game. 352p. 1990. mass mkt. 6.99 (*0-671-72014-7*) Baen Bks.

— The Warrior's Apprentice. 320p. 1991. reprint ed. per. 5.99 (*0-671-72066-X*) Baen Bks.

— Women at War. 1997. pap. text 10.99 (*0-8125-4458-7*, Pub. by Tor Bks) St Martin.

— Young Miles. LC 97-2168. 544p. 1997. 22.00 (*0-671-87787-9*); per. 15.00 (*0-671-87782-8*) Baen Bks.

Buk, Askold. The Advanced Guitar Case Chord Book. (Illus.). 68p. 1992. pap. 5.95 (*0-8256-1243-8*, AM80227) Music Sales.

— Practical Pentatonics: An Introduction to Pentatonic Patterns, Theory, & Usage. 1996. pap. 5.95 (*0-8256-1495-3*, AM931326) Music Sales.

Buka, Agnes. Modern Topics in Liquid Crystals - From Neutron Scattering Ferroelectricity. 352p. 1993. text 109.00 (*981-02-1539-8*) World Scientific Pub.

Buka, Agnes & Kramer, Lorenz, eds. Pattern Formation in Liquid Crystals. LC 95-39607. (Partially Ordered Systems Ser.). 344p. 1996. 69.95 (*0-387-94604-7*) Spr-Verlag.

Bukacek, R. F. Equilibrium Moisture Content of Natural Gases. (Research Bulletin Ser.: No. 8). iv, 19p. 1959. pap. 30.00 (*1-58222-019-0*); suppl. ed. 10.00 (*1-58222-056-5*) Inst Gas Tech.

Bukantz, Samuel C., jt. auth. see Lockey, Richard F.

Bukar, Nat. How to Photograph Paintings. LC 96-79971. (Illus.). 104p. 1997. pap. 9.95 (*0-88108-105-1*) Art Dir.

— Running a Successful Graphic Design Business. LC 91-72286. 116p. (Orig.). 1991. text 16.95 (*0-88108-091-8*); pap. text 12.50 (*0-88108-092-6*) Art Dir.

Bukata, Robert P., et al. Optical Properties & Remote Sensing of Inland & Coastal Waters. LC 95-15157. (Illus.). 384p. 1995. boxed set 99.95 (*0-8493-4754-8*, 4754) CRC Pr.

Bukatko, Danuta. Child Development, 3 Vols. (C). Date not set. pap. 11.96 (*0-395-86829-7*) HM.

— Child Development, 2 vols. 2nd ed. (C). Date not set. pap. text, student ed. 19.56 (*0-395-71874-0*) HM.

— Child Development, 2 vols. 2nd ed. LC 94-76492. (C). 1994. text 64.76 (*0-395-69752-2*) HM.

— Child Development. 3rd ed. (C). 1997. pap. text 11.96 (*0-395-89156-6*) HM.

— Human Growth & Development. (C). 1995. pap. 35.16 (*0-395-72178-4*) HM.

Bukatko, Danuta & Daehler, Marvin W. Child Development: A Thematic Approach, 2 vols. 2nd ed. (C). 1995. text, teacher ed. 11.96 (*0-395-69913-4*) HM.

Bukatko, Danuta, jt. auth. see Daehler, Marvin W.

Bukatman, Scott. Blade Runner. (Modern Classics Ser.). (Illus.). 96p. 1998. pap. 10.95 (*0-85170-623-1*, Pub. by British Film Inst) Ind U Pr.

— Terminal Identity: The Virtual Subject in Postmodern Science Fiction. LC 92-39981. (Illus.). 420p. (C). 1993. text 59.95 (*0-8223-1332-4*); pap. text 19.95 (*0-8223-1340-5*) Duke.

***Bukau, Bernd, ed.** Molecular Chaperones & Folding Catalysts: Regulation, Cellular Functions & Mechanisms. (Illus.). 680p. 1998. text 175.00 (*90-5702-370-9*, Harwood Acad Pubs) Gordon & Breach.

Bukauskas, Feliksas, ed. Intercellular Communication. (Proceedings in Nonlinear Science Ser.). 244p. 1992. 440.00 (*0-471-93506-9*) Wiley.

Bukauskas, Paul. Professional Powerbuilder 4.O Programming. LC 96-35304. 512p. (C). 1997. pap. 39.95 (*0-13-508145-9*) P-H.

Bukenya, Gilbert, et al. Manual of District Health Management for Uganda. LC 97-37032. 128p. 1997. pap. 20.00 (*1-56474-251-2*) Fithian Pr.

Buker, Eloise. Talking Feminist Politics: Conversations on Law, Science & the Postmodern. LC 99-26313. 240p. 1999. pap. 24.95 (*0-8476-9617-0*); text 60.00 (*0-8476-9616-2*) Rowman.

Buker, Eloise A. Politics Through a Looking-Glass: Understanding Political Cultures Through a Structuralist Interpretation of Narratives, 184. LC 87-8671. (Contributions in Political Science Ser.: No. 184). 264p. 1987. 59.95 (*0-313-25662-4*, BPK/) Greenwood.

Buker, Eloise A., ed. see Bona, Mary J., et al.

Buker, George E. Blockaders, Refugees, & Contrabands: Civil War on Florida's Gulf Coast, 1861-1865. LC 92-46425. 248p. (C). 1993. text 29.95 (*0-8173-0682-X*) U of Ala Pr.

— Swamp Sailors: Riverine Warfare in the Everglades, 1835-1842. LC 74-186326. (Illus.). 152p. 1975. 16.95 (*0-8130-0352-0*) U Press Fla.

— Swamp Sailors in the Second Seminole War. LC 96-36994. (Florida Sand Dollar Bks.). (Illus.). 148p. 1997. reprint ed. pap. 16.95 (*0-8130-1514-6*) U Press Fla.

Buker, George E., et al. The Oldest City: St. Augustine, Saga of Survival. Waterbury, Jean P., ed. LC 83-50479. (Illus.). 274p. (Orig.). 1983. 25.00 (*0-9612744-1-7*); pap. 14.95 (*0-9612744-0-9*) St Augustine Hist.

Buker, George E., ed. see Simmons, William H.

Buker, Suzanne, jt. auth. see Weissburg, Robert.

Bukett, Larry. Financial Parenting. 1997. pap. 10.99 (*1-56476-709-4*, Victor Bks) Chariot Victor.

Bukey, Evan B. Hitler's Hometown: Linz, Austria, 1908-1945. LC 85-45762. (Illus.). 304p. 1986. reprint ed. pap. 94.30 (*0-608-01052-9*, 205936000001) Bks Demand.

Bukey, Evan Burr. Hitler's Austria: Popular Sentiment in the Nazi Era, 1938-1945. LC 99-21475. (Illus.). 368p. 2000. 39.95 (*0-8078-2516-6*) U of NC Pr.

Bukh, Jette. The Village Woman in Ghana. (Centre for Development Research Publications: No. 1). 118p. 1979. 18.95 (*91-7106-152-5*, Pub. by Nordic Africa) Transaction Pubs.

Bukharaev. Islam in Russia: The Four Seasons. 288p. 1999. text 59.95 (*0-312-21522-3*) St Martin.

An Asterisk (*) at the beginning of an entry indicates that the title is appearing for the first time.

*Bukharaev, Ravil. The Model of Tatarstan. LC 99-37895. 251p. 1999. text 39.95 (0-312-22829-5) St Martin.

Bukharaev, Ravil, jt. tr. see Matthews, David.

Bukhardt, Linda L. Can't to Can - A Book of Comprehensive & Sequential Phonics. rev. ed. (Illus.). 1989. reprint ed. pap. text 17.95 (0-685-29800-0) Reading Ctr.

Bukhari, A. I., ed. see DNA Insertion Meeting Staff, et al.

Bukhari, Emir. Napoleon's Cuirassiers & Carabiniers. (Men-at-Arms Ser.: No. 64). (Illus.). 48p. pap. 12.95 (0-85045-096-9, 9012, Pub. by Osprey) Stackpole.

— Napoleon's Dragoons & Lancers. (Men-at-Arms Ser.: No. 55). (Illus.). 48p. pap. 12.95 (0-85045-088-8, 9008, Pub. by Osprey) Stackpole.

— Napoleon's Guard Cavalry. (Men-at-Arms Ser.: No. 83). (Illus.). 48p. pap. 11.95 (0-85045-288-0, 9022, Pub. by Osprey) Stackpole.

— Napoleon's Hussars. (Men-at-Arms Ser.: No. 76). (Illus.). 48p. pap. 12.95 (0-85045-246-5, 9019, Pub. by Osprey) Stackpole.

— Napoleon's Line Chasseurs. (Men-at-Arms Ser.: No. 68). (Illus.). 48p. pap. 11.95 (0-85045-269-4, 9014, Pub. by Osprey) Stackpole.

— Napoleon's Marshals. (Men-at-Arms Ser.: No. 87). (Illus.). 48p. pap. 12.95 (0-85045-305-4, 9025, Pub. by Osprey) Stackpole.

Bukhari, Imam. Sahih Al-Bukhari Vols. I-IX: Foreign Edition, Set. Khan, M. Muhsin, tr. 1800p. (C). 1993. pap. 120.00 (1-56744-496-2) Kazi Pubns.

Bukhari, Muhammad. Imam Bukhari's Book of Muslim Morals & Manners. Delorenzo, Yusuf T., tr. from ARA. LC 97-5269. (ARA.). 1997. write for info. (1-881963-62-4) Al-Saadawi Pubns.

Bukhari, Muhammad I. Sahih Al-Bukhari, Vol. 1. Khan, Muhammad, tr. 1979. 29.95 (1-56744-587-X) Kazi Pubns.

— Sahih Al-Bukhari, Vol. 3. Khan, Muhammad, tr. from ARA. 1979. 29.95 (1-56744-589-6) Kazi Pubns.

— Sahih Al-Bukhari, Vol. 4. Khan, Muhammad, tr. from ARA. 1979. 29.95 (1-56744-590-X) Kazi Pubns.

— Sahih Al-Bukhari, Vol. 5. Khan, Muhammad, tr. from ARA. 1979. 29.95 (1-56744-591-8) Kazi Pubns.

— Sahih Al-Bukhari, Vol. 6. Khan, Muhammad, tr. from ARA. 1979. 29.95 (1-56744-592-6) Kazi Pubns.

— Sahih Al-Bukhari, Vol. 8. Khan, Muhammad, tr. from ARA. 1979. 29.95 (1-56744-594-2) Kazi Pubns.

— Sahih Al-Bukhari, Vol. 9. Khan, Muhammad, tr. from ARA. 1979. 29.95 (1-56744-595-0) Kazi Pubns.

Bukhari, Sohail, tr. Abuzar. 200p. 1985. pap. 9.00 (0-941724-35-2) Islamic Seminary.

*Bukharin, Nikola I. The Times. Shriver, George, tr. from RUS. LC 97-38428. (Illus.). 345p. 1998. 29.00 (0-231-10730-7) Col U Pr.

Bukharin, Nikolai. How It All Began: The Prison Novel. (Illus.). 400p. 1999. pap. 16.95 (0-231-10731-5) Col U Pr.

Bukharin, Nikolai I. The Economic Theory of the Leisure Class. LC 71-120560. reprint ed. 20.00 (0-404-01149-7) AMS Pr.

— The Economic Theory of the Leisure Class. LC 72-81775. (Modern Reader Ser.: No. PB-261). 227p. reprint ed. pap. 70.40 (0-7837-3903-6, 204375000010) Bks Demand.

— Imperialism & World Economy. LC 72-93461. (Illus.). 176p. 1973. reprint ed. pap. 10.00 (0-85345-290-3, PB-2903, Pub. by Monthly Rev) NYU Pr.

— Selected Writings on the State & the Transition to Socialism. Day, Richard B., ed. & tr. by. from RUS. LC 82-851. 412p. (gr. 13). 1982. text 87.95 (0-87332-190-1) M E Sharpe.

Bukharin, Nikolai I., jt. auth. see Luxemburg, Rosa.

Bukhees, E. O. & Choudhary, A. N., eds. 11th International Conference on Parallel & Distributed Computing Systems Proceedings: POCS-98, September 2, 1998, Chicago, IL, U. S. A. 297p. (C). 1998. 100.00 (1-880843-25-0) Int Soc Comp App.

*Bukhgeim, A. L. Introduction to the Tehory of Inverse Problems. (Inverse & Ill-Posed Problems). (Illus.). 238p. 2000. 152.50 (90-6764-319-X, Pub. by Uppsala Universitet) Coronet Bks.

Bukhsbaum, Genrikh. The Soviet Construction Materials Industry. Tamberg, Andreas, ed. 102p. (Orig.). 1987. pap. text 75.00 (1-55831-004-5) Delphic Associates.

Bukhsh, Salahuddin K. A History of the Islamic People. 176p. 1985. 185.00 (1-85077-070-0, Pub. by Darf Pubs Ltd) St Mut.

— The Renaissance of Islam. 1981. 29.00 (0-933511-39-6) Kazi Pubns.

Bukhsl, Salahuddin K., tr. see Mez, Adam.

Bukics, Rose Marie. Financial Statement Analysis: The Basics & Beyond. (Investor's Quick Reference Ser.). 150p. 1991. pap. 14.95 (1-55738-183-6, Irwn Prfssnl) McGraw-Hill Prof.

Bukics, Rose Marie & Chambers, Donald R. Medical Practice Accounting & Finance: A Practical Guide for Physicians, Dentists & Other Medical Practitioners. LC 95-223119. 200p. (C). 1995. text 45.00 (1-55738-617-X, Irwn Prfssnl) McGraw-Hill Prof.

Bukiet, Melvin J. After. 400p. 1997. pap. 14.00 (0-312-16760-1) St Martin.

— Signs & Wonders. LC 98-47800. 384p. 1999. text 26.00 (0-312-20009-9) St Martin.

*Bukiet, Melvin J. Signs & Wonders: Novel. 384p. 2000. pap. 14.00 (0-312-20433-7, Picador USA) St Martin.

Bukiet, Melvin J. While the Messiah Tarries. LC 97-25580. (Library of Modern Jewish Literature). 197p. 1997. pap. 16.95 (0-8156-0497-1) Syracuse U Pr.

— While the Messiah Tarries: Stories. LC 94-38038. 1995. 20.00 (0-15-100083-2) Harcourt.

*Bukiet, Melvin J., ed. Neurotica: Jewish Writers on Sex. 368p. 2000. pap. 14.95 (0-7679-0650-0) Broadway BDD.

Bukiet, Melvin Jules, ed. Neurotica: Jewish Writers on Sex. LC 99-27452. 352p. 1999. 26.95 (0-393-04808-X) Norton.

Bukkvoll, Tor. Ukraine & European Security. (Chatham House Papers). 128p. 1997. 44.95 (1-85567-464-5) Bks Intl VA.

Bukofzer, Manfred F. Check-List of Instrumental Ensemble Music Before Haydn. 1993. reprint ed. lib. bdg. 89.00 (0-7812-9694-3) Rprt Serv.

— List of Editions of Baroque Music: In His Music in the Baroque Era. 1993. reprint ed. lib. bdg. 89.00 (0-7812-9695-1) Rprt Serv.

— Music in the Baroque Era. (Illus.). (C). 1947. text 35.50 (0-393-09745-5) Norton.

Bukofzer, Manfred F., et al, eds. The Place of Musicology in American Institutions of Higher Learning, 2 vols. in 1. Incl. Some Aspects of Musicology. LC 77-4226. 1977. lib. bdg. LC 77-4226. (Music Reprint Ser.). 1977. reprint ed. Set lib. bdg. 27.50 (0-306-77407-0) Da Capo.

Bukold, Steffen. Kombinierter Verkehr Schiene - Strabe in Europa: Eine Vergleichende Studie zur Transformation von Gutertransportsystemen. (Illus.). 349p. 1996. 61.95 (3-631-49401-7) P Lang Pubng.

Bukoski, Anthony. Children of Strangers: Stories. LC 93-24483. 200p. (Orig.). 1993. 22.50 (0-87074-350-3); pap. 10.95 (0-87074-364-3) SMU Press.

— Polonaise: Stories. LC 98-26101. 192p. 1998. 19.95 (0-87074-434-8) SMU Press.

Bukoski, William J. Meta Analysis of Drug Abuse Prevention Programs. 267p. 1997. per. 17.00 (0-16-061518-6) USGPO.

Bukoski, William J., ed. Meta-Analysis of Drug Abuse Prevention Programs. (Illus.). 263p. (C). 1998. pap. text 45.00 (0-7881-7215-8) DIANE Pub.

Bukovskaia, M. Dictionary of English Proverbs in Modern Use. 232p. (C). 1985. 45.00 (0-7855-4230-2, Pub. by Collets) St Mut.

Bukovskaia, M., ed. Dictionary of English Proverbs in Modern Use. 232p. (C). 1985. 50.00 (0-7855-6428-4, Pub. by Collets) St Mut.

Bukowczyk, John J. Polish Americans & Their History: Community, Culture & Politics. LC 96-10071. 278p. 1996. text 49.95 (0-8229-3953-3) U of Pittsburgh Pr.

Bukowczyk, John J., et al, eds. Detroit Images: Photographs of the Renaissance City. LC 88-27950. (Great Lakes Bks.). (Illus.). 278p. (C). 1989. 49.95 (0-8143-1965-3) Wayne St U Pr.

Bukowicz, John, ed. see O'Connor, Shaun & Chwalek, Kazimierz.

Bukowiecki, Angeline. Leader's Evangelization Training Guide: Be an Evangelizer? Me? (Evangelizer's Handbook, Evangelistic Series Sisters of the New Convenant). 304p. (C). 1986. text 100.00 (0-924333-00-6) Sisters New Covenant.

— Parish Small Group System. (Evangelizer's Handbook, Evangelistic Series Sisters of the New Convenant). (Illus.). 14p. (Orig.). (C). 1989. pap. text 5.00 (0-924333-19-7) Sisters New Covenant.

— Parish Small Group System: A Long Term Goal for Evangelization. (Evangelizer's Handbook, Coordinators & Pastoral Leaders Evangelistic Series, Catholic Evangelization Training Center). (Illus.). 38p. (Orig.). (C). 1988. pap. text 19.00 (0-317-92540-7) Sisters New Covenant.

— Parish Small Group System, Policy Manual: A Long Term Goal for Evangelization. rev. ed. (Evangelizer's Handbook, Coordinators & Pastoral Leaders Evangelistic Series, Catholic Evangelization Training Center). (Illus.). 40p. (Orig.). (C). pap. text 19.00 (0-924333-11-1) Sisters New Covenant.

Bukowiecki, Angeline & Meierotto, Brigid. And You Shall Be My Witnesses! An Introduction to a Life in the Spirit. (Evangelizer's Handbook, Evangelistic Series Sisters of the New Convenant). 98p. (Orig.). (C). 1981. pap. text 10.00 (0-317-92539-3) Sisters New Covenant.

— Christian Spirituality & Discipleship. (Evangelizer's Handbook, Evangelistic Series Sisters of the New Convenant). (Illus.). 215p. (Orig.). (C). 1985. pap. text 20.00 (0-924333-15-4) Sisters New Covenant.

— Evangelization Outreach Guide. (Evangelizer's Handbook, Evangelistic Series Sisters of the New Convenant). 36p. (Orig.). (C). 1987. pap. text 5.00 (0-317-92533-4) Sisters New Covenant.

— Evangelization Outreach Guide: Evangelizer's Handbook. rev. ed. (Evangelizer's Handbook, Evangelistic Series Sisters of the New Convenant). 50p. (Orig.). (C). 1987. pap. text 5.00 (0-924333-10-3) Sisters New Covenant.

— Evangelized Anew Weekend. (Evangelizer's Handbook, Evangelistic Series Sisters of the New Convenant). 59p. (Orig.). (C). 1987. pap. text 15.00 (0-317-92532-6) Sisters New Covenant.

— Evangelized Anew Weekend: Evangelizer's Handbook. (Evangelizer's Handbook, Evangelistic Series Sisters of the New Convenant). 59p. (Orig.). (C). 1987. pap. text 15.00 (0-924333-04-9) Sisters New Covenant.

— Leader's Evangelization Training Guide: Evangelii Nuntiandi Weekend. (Evangelizer's Handbook, Evangelistic Series Sisters of the New Convenant). 77p. (Orig.). (C). 1987. pap. text 25.00 (0-924333-02-2) Sisters New Covenant.

— Leader's Evangelization Training Guide: Evangelization Outreach. (Evangelizer's Handbook, Evangelistic Series Sisters of the New Convenant). 48p. (C). 1987. pap. text 10.00 (0-685-37396-7) Sisters New Covenant.

— Leader's Evangelization Training Guide: Evangelization Outreach. rev. ed. (Evangelizer's Handbook, Evangelistic Series Sisters of the New Convenant). 64p. (C). 1987. pap. text 10.00 (0-924333-09-X) Sisters New Covenant.

— Leader's Evangelization Training Guide: Evangelized Anew Weekend. (Evangelizer's Handbook, Evangelistic Series Sisters of the New Convenant). 73p. (Orig.). (C). 1987. pap. text 25.00 (0-924333-03-0) Sisters New Covenant.

— Leader's Evangelization Training Guide: Pastoral Leader's Weekend. (Evangelizer's Handbook, Evangelistic Series Sisters of the New Convenant). 52p. (Orig.). (C). 1987. pap. text 25.00 (0-924333-05-7) Sisters New Covenant.

— Leader's Evangelization Training Guide: Scripture Handbook. (Evangelizer's Handbook, Evangelistic Series Sisters of the New Convenant). 173p. (Orig.). (C). 1987. pap. text 35.00 (0-924333-07-3) Sisters New Covenant.

— Leader's Evanglization Training Guide: Evangelized Anew Weekend. (Evangelizer's Handbook, Evangelistic Series Sisters of the New Convenant). 73p. (Orig.). (C). 1987. pap. text 25.00 (0-317-92541-5) Sisters New Covenant.

— Pastoral Leader's Handbook. (Evangelizer's Handbook, Evangelistic Series Sisters of the New Convenant). 28p. (Orig.). (C). 1987. pap. text 10.00 (0-924333-06-5) Sisters New Covenant.

— Scripture One: An Introduction to the Scriptures. (Evangelizer's Handbook, Evangelistic Series Sisters of the New Convenant). 112p. (Orig.). (C). 1984. pap. text 11.00 (0-924333-08-1) Sisters New Covenant.

— Scripture Two: The Formation & Exile of God's People. (Evangelizer's Handbook, Evangelistic Series Sisters of the New Convenant). 153p. (Orig.). (C). 1987. pap. text 25.00 (0-924333-16-2) Sisters New Covenant.

Bukowiecki, Angeline, et al. Be an Evangelizer? Me? Evangelizer's Handbook. (Evangelizer's Handbook, Evangelistic Series Sisters of the New Convenant). (Illus.). (Orig.). (C). 1984. pap. text 20.00 (0-317-92537-7) Sisters New Covenant.

— Be an Evangelizer? Me? Evangelizer's Handbook. rev. ed. (Evangelizer's Handbook, Evangelistic Series Sisters of the New Convenant). (Illus.). 280p. (Orig.). (C). 1984. pap. text 20.00 (0-924333-01-4) Sisters New Covenant.

*Bukowitz, Wendi & Williams, Ruth. Knowlege Management Fieldbook. (Illus.). 320p. 1999. 29.95 (0-273-63882-3, Pub. by F T P-H) Natl Bk Netwk.

Bukowkski, Charles. Run With the Hunted: Charles Bukowski Reader, A. Martin, John, ed. LC 92-53353. 512p. 1994. reprint ed. pap. 16.00 (0-06-092458-6, Perennial) HarperTrade.

Bukowski, Charles. Betting on the Muse: Poems & Stories. LC 96-14678. 402p. (C). 1998. reprint ed. 27.50 (1-57423-002-6); reprint ed. pap. 16.00 (1-57423-001-8) Black Sparrow.

— Bone Palace Ballet: New Poems. LC 97-12731. 363p. 1998. 27.50 (1-57423-029-8); pap. 16.00 (1-57423-028-X) Black Sparrow.

— Bring Me Your Love. LC 83-5023. (Illus.). 14p. 1998. reprint ed. 14.00 (0-87685-608-3); reprint ed. pap. 6.00 (0-87685-606-7) Black Sparrow.

— Burning in Water, Drowning in Flame: Selected Poems 1955-1973. LC 74-8125. 236p. 1998. reprint ed. 25.00 (0-87685-192-8); reprint ed. pap. 15.00 (0-87685-191-X) Black Sparrow.

— The Captain Is Out to Lunch & the Sailors Have Taken over the Ship. LC 98-4623. (Illus.). 145p. 1998. 27.50 (1-57423-059-X); pap. 14.00 (1-57423-058-1) Black Sparrow.

Bukowski, Charles. The Captain Is Out to Lunch & the Sailors Have Taken over the Ship. limited ed. (Illus.). 124p. 1997. 650.00 (0-9644115-2-0) Blck Sparrow.

Bukowski, Charles. Charles Bukowski: A Sure Bet. LC 96-149416. 100p. 1995. 25.00 (0-934953-43-0) Water Row Pr.

— Dangling in the Tournefortia. LC 81-10145. 286p. (C). 1998. reprint ed. pap. 16.00 (0-87685-525-7) Black Sparrow.

*Bukowski, Charles. Dangling in the Tournefortia. LC 81-10145. 286p. (C). 1998. reprint ed. 25.00 (0-87685-526-5) Black Sparrow.

Bukowski, Charles. Days Run Away Like Wild Horses over the Hills. LC 00-1538. 204p. 1998. reprint ed. 25.00 (0-87685-006-9); reprint ed. pap. 14.00 (0-87685-005-0) Black Sparrow.

— Factotum. LC 75-34231. 212p. 1998. reprint ed. 25.00 (0-87685-264-9); reprint ed. pap. 15.00 (0-87685-263-0) Black Sparrow.

— Ham on Rye. LC 82-9631. 288p. 1998. reprint ed. 25.00 (0-87685-558-3); reprint ed. pap. 15.00 (0-87685-557-5) Black Sparrow.

— Heat Wave, Signed ed. LC 94-48078. (Illus.). 100p. 1995. 1250.00 (0-9644115-0-4) Blck Sparrow.

— Heat Wave, Signed ed. deluxe ed. LC 94-48078. (Illus.). 100p. 1995. 3500.00 (0-9644115-1-2) Blck Sparrow.

— Hollywood. LC 89-836. 244p. 1998. reprint ed. 25.00 (0-87685-764-0); reprint ed. pap. 15.00 (0-87685-763-2) Black Sparrow.

— Hot Water Music. LC 83-15391. 226p. 1998. reprint ed. 25.00 (0-87685-597-4); reprint ed. pap. 15.00 (0-87685-596-6) Black Sparrow.

— The Last Night of the Earth Poems. LC 91-45022. 405p. 1998. reprint ed. 25.00 (0-87685-864-7); reprint ed. pap. 16.00 (0-87685-863-9) Black Sparrow.

— Living on Luck: Selected Letters 1960's-1970's, Vol. 2. LC 95-39244. (Illus.). 283p. (C). 1998. pap. 16.00 (0-87685-981-3) Black Sparrow.

— Living on Luck Vol. 2: Selected Letters 1960's-1970's, Vol. 2. LC 95-39244. (Illus.). 283p. (Orig.). (C). 1998. 25.00 (0-87685-982-1) Black Sparrow.

— Love Is a Dog from Hell: Poems, 1974-1977. LC 77-10501. 312p. 1998. reprint ed. 25.00 (0-87685-363-7); reprint ed. pap. 15.00 (0-87685-362-9) Black Sparrow.

— Mockingbird Wish Me Luck. 160p. 1998. reprint ed. 20.00 (0-87685-139-1); reprint ed. pap. 14.00 (0-87685-138-3) Black Sparrow.

— The Most Beautiful Woman in Town. 1983. reprint ed. pap. 12.95 (0-87286-156-2) City Lights.

— The Movie "Barfly" An Orginal Screenplay. LC 87-18237. (Illus.). 180p. (C). 1998. reprint ed. 25.00 (0-87685-708-X); reprint ed. pap. 14.00 (0-87685-707-1) Black Sparrow.

— Notes of a Dirty Old Man. 2nd ed. LC 73-84226. 1973. pap. 12.95 (0-87286-074-4) City Lights.

*Bukowski, Charles. Open All Night: New Poems. 375p. 2000. 30.00 (1-57423-136-7) Black Sparrow.

— Open All Night: New Poems. deluxe ed. 375p. 2000. 50.00 (1-57423-137-5) Black Sparrow.

Bukowski, Charles. Play the Piano Drunk Like a Percussion Instrument until the Fingers Begin to Bleed a Bit. LC 79-20429. 128p. 1998. reprint ed. 25.00 (0-87685-438-2); reprint ed. pap. 14.00 (0-87685-437-4) Black Sparrow.

— Post Office. 196p. 1998. reprint ed. 25.00 (0-87685-087-5); reprint ed. pap. 14.00 (0-87685-086-7) Black Sparrow.

— Pulp. LC 94-4352. 202p. 1998. reprint ed. 25.00 (0-87685-927-9); reprint ed. pap. 14.00 (0-87685-926-0) Black Sparrow.

*Bukowski, Charles. Reach for the Sun: Selected Letters, 1978-1994, Vol. 3. Cooney, Seamus, ed. LC 99-226703. 250p. 1999. 30.00 (1-57423-089-1) Black Sparrow.

Bukowski, Charles. Reach for the Sun: Selected Letters, 1978-1994, Vol. 3. deluxe ed. Cooney, Seamus, ed. 250p. 1999. 50.00 (1-57423-090-5) Black Sparrow.

— Reach for the Sun Vol. 3: Selected Letters, 1978-1994. Cooney, Seamus, ed. LC 99-226703. 309p. 1999. pap. 17.50 (1-57423-088-3, Pub. by Black Sparrow) SPD-Small Pr Dist.

— The Roominghouse Madrigals: Early Selected Poems 1946-1966. LC 88-10426. 260p. 1998. reprint ed. 25.00 (0-87685-733-0); reprint ed. pap. 15.00 (0-87685-732-2) Black Sparrow.

Bukowski, Charles. Run with the Hunted: Bukowkski,&Charles. abr. ed. Martin, John, ed. 1993. audio 12.00 (1-55994-769-1, CPN 2372) HarperAudio.

Bukowski, Charles. Screams from the Balcony: Selected Letters 1960-1970. LC 93-36411. 372p. 1998. reprint ed. 25.00 (0-87685-915-5); reprint ed. pap. 16.00 (0-87685-914-7) Black Sparrow.

— Septuagenarian Stew: Stories & Poems. LC 90-316. 380p. 1998. reprint ed. 25.00 (0-87685-795-0); reprint ed. pap. 16.00 (0-87685-794-2) Black Sparrow.

— Shakespeare Never Did This. (Illus.). 150p. (C). 1998. reprint ed. 25.00 (0-87685-969-4); reprint ed. pap. 17.00 (0-87685-968-6) Black Sparrow.

— South of No North. LC 73-19672. 192p. 1998. reprint ed. 25.00 (0-87685-190-1); reprint ed. pap. 15.00 (0-87685-189-8) Black Sparrow.

— Tales of Ordinary Madness. 1983. reprint ed. pap. 12.95 (0-87286-155-4) City Lights.

— There's No Business. LC 84-2977. (Illus.). 17p. 1998. reprint ed. 14.00 (0-87685-623-7); reprint ed. pap. 6.00 (0-87685-622-9) Black Sparrow.

— War All the Time: Poems 1981-1984. LC 84-20390. 280p. 1998. reprint ed. 25.00 (0-87685-638-5); reprint ed. pap. 15.00 (0-87685-637-7) Black Sparrow.

*Bukowski, Charles. What Matters Most Is How Well You Walk Through The Fire: New Verse. LC 99-47459. 416p. 1999. 30.00 (1-57423-106-5); pap. 16.00 (1-57423-105-7) Black Sparrow.

Bukowski, Charles. Women. LC 78-21998. 296p. 1998. reprint ed. 25.00 (0-87685-391-2); reprint ed. pap. 15.00 (0-87685-390-4) Black Sparrow.

— You Get So Alone at Times: That It Just Makes Sense. LC 86-13662. 318p. 1998. reprint ed. pap. 16.00 (0-87685-683-0) Black Sparrow.

— You Get So Alone at Times That It Just Makes Sense. LC 86-13662. 318p. 1998. reprint ed. 25.00 (0-87685-684-9) Black Sparrow.

Bukowski, Charles, et al. First Person Intense: A Prose Anthology. Newborn, Sasha, ed. LC 77-642342. (Rockbottom Magazine Ser.: Vols. 7 & 8). (Illus.). 188p. (C). 1978. pap. text 5.00 (0-930012-14-3) Bandanna Bks.

— Six Poets. 1979. 10.00 (0-912824-21-2) Vagabond Pr.

Bukowski, Charles J. & Cichock, Mark A., eds. Prospects for Change in Socialist Systems: Challenges & Responses. LC 86-30614. 157p. 1987. 49.95 (0-275-92434-3, C2434, Praeger Pubs) Greenwood.

*Bukowski, Charles J. & Racz, Barnabas, eds. The Return of the Left in Post-Communist States. LC 99-30950. 169p. 1999. 70.00 (1-85898-815-2) E Elgar.

Bukowski, Charles J. & Walsh, J. Richard, eds. Glasnost, Perestroika & the Socialist Community. LC 89-23050. 187p. 1990. 52.95 (0-275-93130-7, C3130, Praeger Pubs) Greenwood.

*Bukowski, Douglas. American History: A Concise Documents Collection , 2 vols. LC 98-89220. 1998. pap. text 10.95 (0-312-19668-7) St Martin.

— American History: A Concise Documents Collection. 1999. 8.00 (0-312-19667-9) Forge NYC.

Bukowski, Douglas. The Baseball Palace of the World: The Last Year of Comiskey Park. LC 91-40533. (Illus.). 256p. 1992. 30.00 (0-925065-45-5) Lyceum IL.

— Big Bill Thompson, Chicago & the Politics of Image. LC 97-4803. 304p. 1998. 21.95 (0-252-06668-5); text 49.95 (0-252-02365-X) U of Ill Pr.

— Navy Pier. (Illus.). 96p. 1996. text 19.95 (1-56663-139-4, Pub. by I R Dee) Natl Bk Netwk.

— Navy Pier: A Chicago Landmark. (Illus.). 96p. 1996. pap. 12.95 (1-56663-115-7, Pub. by I R Dee) Natl Bk Netwk.

B

***Bukowski, Elaine.** Muscular Analysis of Everyday Activities. 300p. (C). 2000. pap. text 32.00 (*1-55642-462-0*) SLACK Inc.

***Bukowski, Jeanie J. & Rajagopalan, Swarna, eds.** Re-Distribution of Authority: A Cross-Regional Perspective. LC 99-59848. 216p. 2000. 55.00 (*0-275-96377-2*, Praeger Pubs) Greenwood.

***Bukowski, Piotr.** Ordnungsschwund Ordnungswandel: Par Lagerkvist und der deutsche Expressionismus. 2000. 37.95 (*3-631-35508-4*) P Lang Pubng.

Bukowski, Richard W. & O'Laughlin, Robert J. Fire Alarm Signaling Systems. 3rd ed. (Illus.). 450p. 1994. 81.00 (*0-87765-399-2*, FASS-94) Natl Fire Prot.

***Bukowski, Ronald M. & Novick, Andrew, eds.** Renal Cell Carcinoma: Molecular Biology, Immunology & Clinical Management. LC 99-53889. (Current Clinical Oncology Ser.). 448p. 2000. 145.00 (*0-89603-781-9*) Humana.

Bukowski, William M., et al, eds. The Company They Keep: Friendships in Childhood & Adolescence. LC 97-4059. (Studies in Social & Emotional Development). (Illus.). 436p. (C). 1996. text 64.95 (*0-521-45198-1*) Cambridge U Pr.

— The Company They Keep: Friendships in Childhood & Adolescence. (Studies in Social & Emotional Development). (Illus.). 400p. (C). 1998. reprint ed. pap. text 24.95 (*0-521-62725-7*) Cambridge U Pr.

B

Bukrinskaya, A. G., ed. Implications of Gag Proteins for the Life Cycle of the Immunodeficiency Virus. (Soviet Medical Reviews Series, Section E: Virology Review: Vol. 5, Pt. 4). 140p. 1996. pap. text 41.00 (*3-7186-5759-7*, Harwood Acad Pubs) Gordon & Breach.

Buksbazen, Lydia. The Looked for a City. LC 58-17705. 1955. pap. 8.95 (*0-915540-15-0*) Frnds Israel.

— They Looked for a City. 1976. pap. 8.95 (*0-87508-041-3*) Chr Lit.

Buksbazen, Victor. The Gospel in the Feasts of Israel. (Illus.). 102p. (Orig.). 1954. mass mkt. 5.95 (*0-87508-043-X*) Chr Lit.

— The Gospel in the Feasts of Israel. (Orig.). 1997. mass mkt. 3.75 (*0-87508-430-3*) Chr Lit.

Bukstein, Oscar G. Adolescent Substance Abuse: Assessment, Prevention & Treatment. LC 94-40264. (Series on Personality Processes). 260p. 1995. 75.00 (*0-471-55080-9*) Wiley.

Buku Antar Bangsa (Firm) Staff & Grolier International Inc. Staff. Indonesian Heritage. LC 96-945825. 1996. write for info. (*981-3018-58-5*) Arch Pr.

Bukuku, Enos S. The Tanzanian Economy: Income Distribution & Economic Growth. LC 90-24562. 240p. 1992. 62.95 (*0-275-93812-3*, C3812, Praeger Pubs) Greenwood.

Bukva, V., jt. ed. see Dusabek, F.

Bul, A. Alexander, intro. Leasing Retail Space. LC 89-83354. (Illus.). 300p. (C). 1990. text 62.95 (*0-944298-41-9*) Inst Real Estate.

Bula, G., jt. auth. see Schnetter, R.

Bulaev, V. E., ed. Methods of Fertilizer Application. 1984. 28.00 (*0-8364-2558-8*, Pub. by Oxford IBH) S Asia.

Bulag, Uradyn E. Nationalism & Hybridity in Mongolia. LC 97-39268. (Oxford Studies in Social & Cultural Anthropology). (Illus.). 318p. 1998. text 75.00 (*0-19-823357-4*) OUP.

BuLa'ia, Keefah. Ask Bu. 112p. (Orig.). 1995. pap. 11.95 (*0-9647370-0-0*) Keefah Prodns.

Bulajic, Milan. Principles of International Development Law: Progressive Development of the Principles of International Law Relating to the New International Economic Order. 2nd rev. ed. LC 92-31349. (C). 1993. lib. bdg. 200.00 (*0-7923-1971-0*) Kluwer Academic.

Buland, Mable. The Presentation of Time in the Elizabethan Drama. 354p. (C). 1966. reprint ed. lib. bdg. 75.00 (*0-8383-0517-2*) M S G Haskell Hse.

Buland, Roberta, ed. see Jud, Brian.

Buland, Roberta J., ed. see Rosenberg, Ron.

Buland, Roberta J., ed. see Schultz, Jack.

Bulanda, Susan. Boston Terriers. (Barron's Pet Owner's Manuals Ser.). 64p. 1994. pap. 6.95 (*0-8120-1696-3*) Barron.

— On the Wind: Scent Work for Hunting Dogs. Anderson, Mark, ed. (Illus.). 104p. Date not set. pap. write for info. (*0-944875-52-1*) Doral Pub.

— Ready! A Step-By-Step Guide for Training the Search & Rescue Dog. Luther, Luana, ed. LC 93-74002. (Illus.). 170p. 1995. pap. 26.50 (*0-944875-41-6*) Doral Pub.

— Ready to Serve, Ready to Save: Strategies of Real-Life Search & Rescue Missions. (Illus.). 237p. 1999. pap. 21.95 (*0-944875-63-7*) Doral Pub.

Bulanti, Billy. Thanks for Everything: A Gift for Parents. LC 97-32345. 1998. write for info. (*0-8362-5304-3*) Andrews & McMeel.

Bulard-Cordeau, Brigitte. Kittens. LC 97-14722. (Illus.). 240p. (J). 1997. 18.95 (*0-8120-6630-8*) Barron.

— Puppies. LC 97-8732. (Illus.). 240p. 1997. 24.95 (*0-8120-6631-6*) Barron.

Bulas, Kazimierz. Kosciuszko Foundation English-Polish, Polish-English Dictionary, 2 vols. (Poland's Millennium Ser.). (ENG & POL.). 1986. reprint ed. text 27.50 (*0-917004-00-0*); reprint ed. text 27.50 (*0-917004-16-7*) Kosciuszko.

Bulas, Kazimierz, contrib. by. Corpus Vasorum Antiqvorum - Pologne Fascicule 1: Goluchow Musee Czartorysk. (FRE., Illus.). 44p. 1931. 80.00 (*0-614-25048-X*) Szwede Slavic.

Bulat, Thomas J., photos by. Hidden Orchids: A Photographic Discovery of the Disappearing Native Orchids of the United States & Canada. LC 95-16909. (Illus.). 128p. 1995. pap. 32.95 (*0-945213-19-0*) Rudi Pub.

Bulatao, Elizabeth Q., jt. ed. see VandenBos, Gary R.

Bulatao, Rodolfo A. Key Indicators for Family Planning Projects. (World Bank Technical Papers: Vol. 297). 40p. 1995. pap. 22.00 (*0-8213-3372-0*, 13372) World Bank.

— The Value of Family Planning Programs in Developing Countries. LC 98-8108. (Illus.). 79p. 1998. pap. 15.00 (*0-8330-2633-X*, MR-978-WFHF/RF) Rand Corp.

Bulatao, Rudolfo A. Effective Family Planning Programs. LC 92-45644. 112p. 1993. pap. 22.00 (*0-8213-2305-9*, 12305) World Bank.

Bulatov, A. I. Russian-English Dictionary on Oil & Gas. (RUS.). 424p. 1998. 49.95 (*0-8285-5492-7*) Firebird NY.

Bulatov, V. V. & Sridhar, S., eds. Geomechanics of Deep-Seated Deposits. (Russian Translation Ser.: Vol. 102). (Illus.). 260p. (C). 1994. text 123.00 (*90-5410-216-0*, Pub. by A A Balkema) Ashgate Pub Co.

Bulatova, N. S., jt. auth. see Orlov, Vladimir N.

***Bulatovich, A. K. & Seltzer, Richard.** Ethiopia Through Russian Eyes: Country in Transition, 1896-1898. LC 99-462347. (Illus.). 2000. pap. write for info. (*1-56902-117-1*) Red Sea Pr.

Bulau, Judith M. Quality Assurance Policies & Procedures for Ambulatory Health Care. 368p. 1990. 150.00 (*0-8342-0138-0*, 20138) Aspen Pub.

Bulback, Fred. Parallel Port Programming in Windows 95. 375p. 1998. 49.95 incl. cd-rom (*0-07-913662-1*) McGraw.

— Parallel Port Programming Through Windows 95. 1998. pap. text 39.95 (*0-07-913661-3*) McGraw.

Bulbeck, Chilla. Australian Women in Papua New Guinea: Colonial Passages 1920-1960. (Illus.). 339p. (C). 1992. text 74.95 (*0-521-41285-4*) Cambridge U Pr.

— Living Feminism: The Impact of the Women's Movement on Three Generations of Australian Women. LC 97-26347. (Reshaping Australian Institutions Ser.: Vol. 5). 284p. 1997. pap. text 24.95 (*0-521-46596-6*) Cambridge U Pr.

— Living Feminism: The Impact of the Women's Movement on Three Generations of Australian Women. LC 97-26347. (Reshaping Australian Institutions Ser.: Vol. 5). (Illus.). 303p. (C). 1997. text 69.95 (*0-521-46042-5*) Cambridge U Pr.

— Re-Orienting Western Feminisms: Women's Diversity in a Postcolonial World. LC 97-25836. (Illus.). 288p. (C). 1997. text 59.95 (*0-521-58030-7*); pap. text 19.95 (*0-521-58975-4*) Cambridge U Pr.

***Bulbeck, F. David.** Ancient Chinese & Southeast Asian Bronze Age Cultures, 2 vols. LC 00-272534. (Illus.). 1462p. 2000. 175.00 (*957-638-484-2*) SMC Pub.

Bulbring, Edith & Shuba, M. F., eds. Physiology of Smooth Muscle. fac. ed. LC 75-14566. (Illus.). 448p. pap. 138.90 (*0-7837-7539-3*, 204696500005) Bks Demand.

Bulbrook, Lee. The Curious Quantum. (Illus.). (J). 1996. pap. 8.95 (*0-906212-91-X*, Pub. by Tarquin Pubns) Parkwest Pubns.

Bulbrook, Mary Jo. Development of Therapeutic Skills. 1980. text 14.95 (*0-316-11472-3*, Little Brwn Med Div) Lppncott W & W.

***Bulbrook, Mary Jo.** Energetic Healing. 239p. 2000. pap. text 35.00 (*1-889293-06-7*) NC Ctr Healing.

— Healing Stories: Giving, Receiving, Teaching, Learning Energy-Based Therapy. 2000. pap. text 25.00 (*1-889293-09-1*) NC Ctr Healing.

— Holistic Approaches to Stress Relief & Pain Management. 1991. pap. text 22.00 (*1-889293-00-8*) NC Ctr Healing.

Bulbrook, Mary Jo, jt. auth. see Mentgen, Janet.

Bulbulian, Silvia. La Radiactividad. (Ciencia para Todos Ser.). (SPA.). pap. 6.99 (*968-16-2651-6*, Pub. by Fondo) Continental Bk.

Bulcha, Mekuria. Flight & Integration: Causes of Mass Exodus from Ethiopia & Problems of Integration in Sudan. (Illus.). 256p. (Orig.). 1988. pap. 53.00 (*91-7106-279-3*, Pub. by Nordisk Afrikainstitutet) Coronet Bks.

Bulcke, Kamil. English-Hindi Dictionary. (ENG & HIN.). 1987. 49.95 (*0-8288-1131-8*, M14242) Fr & Eur.

Bulcroft, Kris. Romancing the Honeymoon: Consummating Marriage in Modern Society. LC 98-58142. 1998. pap. write for info. (*0-7619-0804-8*) Sage.

***Bulcroft, Kris.** Romancing the Honeymoon: Consummating Marriage in Modern Society. LC 98-58142. 1998. write for info. (*0-7619-0803-X*) Sage.

***Buldygin, V. V. & Kharazishvili, A. B.** Geometric Aspects in Probability Theory & Mathematical Statistics. LC 00-33086. (Mathematics & Its Applications Ser.). 2000. write for info. (*0-7923-6413-9*) Kluwer Academic.

***Buldygin, V. V. & Kozachenko, Yu. V.** Metric Characterization of Random Variables & Random Processes. LC 99-87766. (MMONO Ser.: Vol. 188). 264p. 2000. 95.00 (*0-8218-0533-9*) Am Math.

Buldyrev, V. S., jt. auth. see Babic, V. M.

Bulechek, Gloria M. Nursing Interventions. 2nd ed. (Illus.). 641p. 1992. text 61.50 (*0-7216-3802-3*, W B Saunders Co) Harcrt Hlth Sci Grp.

Bulechek, Gloria M. & McCloskey, Joanne C. Nursing Interventions: Effective Nursing Treatments. 3rd ed. Eoyang, Thomas, ed. LC 98-43443. (Illus.). 685p. 1999. text. write for info. (*0-7216-7724-X*, W B Saunders Co) Harcrt Hlth Sci Grp.

Bulechek, Gloria M., ed. see McCloskey, Joanne C., et al.

Bulembat, Jean-Bosco M. Noyau et Enjeux de l'Eschatologie Paulinienne: De l'Apocalyptique Juive et de l'Eschatologie Hellenistique dans Quelques Argumentations de l'Apotre Paul. xx, 338p. 1997. 118.00 (*3-11-015387-4*) De Gruyter.

***Buler, Karl-Dietrich.** The Scandinavian Garden. (Illus.). 168p. 1999. 50.00 (*0-7112-1506-5*, Pub. by F Lincoln) Antique Collect.

Bulette, Greg P. SMS 1.2 MCSE Study Guide. LC 97-77804. 768p. 1998. student ed. 59.99 (*0-7645-3163-8*) IDG Bks.

— TCP/IP MCSE Study Guide. (MCSE Certification Ser.). 688p. 1998. student ed. 49.99 (*0-7645-3112-3*) IDG Bks.

Buletza, George F. Marriage of the Mind: Processes of Insight & Integration. LC 97-66324. (Illus.). 250p. 1997. pap. 11.95 (*0-912057-94-7*, 510813) GLELJ AMORC.

***Buley-Meissner, Mary-Louise, et al, eds.** The Academy & the Possibility of Belief: Essays on Intellectual & Spiritual Life. LC 99-47996. (Critical Education & Ethics Ser.). 288p. 1999. pap. 21.95 (*1-57273-221-0*) Hampton Pr NJ.

— The Academy & the Possibility of Belief: Essays on Intellectual & Spiritual Life. LC 99-47996. (Critical Education & Ethics Ser.). 288p. (C). 1999. 45.00 (*1-57273-220-2*) Hampton Pr NJ.

Buleza, Carole A. Faith of the Mountain: High School Series. Sabo, Sandra R., ed. (Religion, Theology, Non-Christian Religions Ser.: Bk. 1). (Illus.). 141p. (Orig.). 1993. teacher ed. 14.95 (*1-885589-03-4*); pap. text 6.95 (*1-885589-02-6*) St Maron Pubns.

— Faith of the Mountain: High School Series. Sabo, Sandra R., ed. (Religion, Theology, Non-Christian Religions Ser.: Bk. 2). (Illus.). 170p. (Orig.). 1994. teacher ed. 14.95 (*1-885589-01-8*); pap. text 6.95 (*1-885589-00-X*) St Maron Pubns.

Bulfield, Anthony, ed. The Icknield Way: A Journey Through the History & Country of England, from Hunstanton to Marlborough. 168p. (C). 1988. 35.00 (*0-900963-43-3*, Pub. by T Dalton) St Mut.

Bulfin, Robert, jt. auth. see Sipper, Daniel.

Bulfinch, Charles. The Life & Letters of Charles Bulfinch, Architect. (American Biography Ser.). 323p. 1991. reprint ed. lib. bdg. 79.00 (*0-7812-8052-4*) Rprt Serv.

Bulfinch, Ellen S., ed. The Life & Letters of Charles Bulfinch, Architect, with Other Family Papers. (Illus.). 323p. 1995. reprint ed. lib. bdg. 42.50 (*0-8328-4504-3*) Higginson Bk Co.

Bulfinch Press Staff. One Hundred Saints: Their Lives & Likenesses Drawn from Butler's "Lives of the Saints" & Great Works of Western Art. LC 93-4416. (Illus.). 288p. 1994. 40.00 (*0-8212-2009-8*, Pub. by Bulfinch Pr) Little.

Bulfinch, Thomas. The Age of Chivalry. 1971. 250.00 (*0-87968-585-9*) Gordon Pr.

— The Age of Chivalry. LC 97-16730. (The Illustrated Bulfinch's Mythology Ser.). (Illus.). 224p. 1997. pap. text 19.95 (*0-02-861478-X*) Macmillan.

— The Age of Chivalry. (Works of Thomas Bulfinch). 1989. reprint ed. lib. bdg. 79.00 (*0-7812-2163-3*) Rprt Serv.

***Bulfinch, Thomas.** The Age of Chivalry: The Illustrated Bulfinch's Mythology. (Illus.). 224p. 2000. reprint ed. pap. text 20.00 (*0-7881-9251-5*) DIANE Pub.

Bulfinch, Thomas. The Age of Fable. (Works of Thomas Bulfinch). 1989. reprint ed. lib. bdg. 79.00 (*0-7812-2162-5*) Rprt Serv.

***Bulfinch, Thomas.** The Age of Fable: The Illustrated Bulfinch's Mythology. (Illus.). 256p. 2000. reprint ed. pap. text 21.00 (*0-7881-9252-3*) DIANE Pub.

Bulfinch, Thomas. The Boy Inventor. (Works of Thomas Bulfinch). 1989. reprint ed. lib. bdg. 79.00 (*0-7812-2164-1*) Rprt Serv.

***Bulfinch, Thomas.** Bulfinch's Greek & Roman Mythology: The Age of Fable. LC 99-88473. (Thrift Editions Ser.). 320p. 2000. pap. 2.50 (*0-486-41107-9*) Dover.

Bulfinch, Thomas. Bulfinch's Mythology. LC 92-35376. 960p. 1993. 22.00 (*0-679-60046-9*) Modern Lib NY.

— Bulfinch's Mythology. LC 98-24149. 1998. pap. 16.95 (*0-375-75147-5*) Modern Lib NY.

— Bulfinch's Mythology. 1040p. 1988. 13.99 (*0-517-27415-9*) Random Hse Value.

— Bulfinch's Mythology. abr. ed. Fuller, Edmund, ed. 448p. 1959. mass mkt. 6.99 (*0-440-30845-3*, LE) Dell.

— Bulfinch's Mythology: The Age of Chivalry & the Legends of Charlemagne, Vol. 2. 1995. pap. 15.95 (*0-452-01153-1*, Mer) NAL.

Bulfinch, Thomas. Bulfinch's Mythology: The Age of Fable, the Age of Chivalry, Legends of Charlemagne. 40.00 (*0-8196-2810-7*) Biblo.

Bulfinch, Thomas. Bulfinch's Mythology: The Illustrated Age of Fable. LC 98-17191. 208p. 1998. 40.00 (*1-55670-825-4*) Stewart Tabori & Chang.

— Cupid & Psyche & Other Fables. 1996. pap. 1.99 (*0-679-77096-8*) Modern Lib NY.

— The Golden Age of Myth & Legend. (Illus.). 496p. 1999. reprint ed. text 25.00 (*0-7881-6370-1*) DIANE Pub.

— Hebrew Lyrical History. (Works of Thomas Bulfinch). 1989. reprint ed. lib. bdg. 79.00 (*0-7812-2161-7*) Rprt Serv.

— Illustrated Bulfinch's Myth, 1. LC 97-16776. (Illus.). 256p. 1997. 20.95 (*0-02-861475-5*) Macmillan.

— Illustrated Bulfinch's Myth, 3. LC 97-16778. (Illus.). 160p. 1997. 18.95 (*0-02-861477-1*) Macmillan.

— Illustrated Bulfinch's Mythology Boxed Set, 3 vols. (The Illustrated Bulfinch's Mythology Ser.). (Illus.). 640p. 1997. pap. text 59.85 (*0-02-862063-1*) Macmillan.

— Legends of Charlemagne. (Works of Thomas Bulfinch). 1989. reprint ed. lib. bdg. 79.00 (*0-7812-2165-X*) Rprt Serv.

— Mythology. (Laurel Classic Ser.). 1959. 12.09 (*0-606-00434-3*, Pub. by Turtleback) Demco.

— Oregon & El Dorado. (Works of Thomas Bulfinch). 1989. reprint ed. lib. bdg. 79.00 (*0-7812-2168-4*) Rprt Serv.

— Poetry of the Age of Fable. 1972. 250.00 (*0-8490-0864-6*) Gordon Pr.

— Poetry of the Age of Fable. (Works of Thomas Bulfinch). 1989. reprint ed. lib. bdg. 79.00 (*0-7812-2166-8*) Rprt Serv.

— Shakespeare Adapted for Reading Classes. (Works of Thomas Bulfinch). 1989. reprint ed. lib. bdg. 79.00 (*0-7812-2167-6*) Rprt Serv.

— The Works of Thomas Bulfinch. 1989. reprint ed. lib. bdg. 63.00 (*0-685-74130-3*) Rprt Serv.

***Bulgak, Hayder & Zenger, C.** Error Control & Adaptivity in Scientific Computing LC 99-15698. (NATO ASI Ser.). 1999. write for info. (*0-7923-5808-2*) Kluwer Academic.

Bulgakov, A. A., jt. auth. see Bass, F. G.

Bulgakov, Mikhail. Master & Margarita: A Critical Companion. Weeks, Laura D., ed. (AATSEEL/ Northwestern Critical Companions to Russian Literature Ser.). 160p. (C). 1995. pap. text, student ed. 16.95 (*0-8101-1212-4*) Northwestern U Pr.

Bulgakov, Mikhail Afanasevich. Belaia Gvardiia. Proffer, Ellendea C., ed. (Sobranie Sochineii Ser.: Vol. 4). (RUS.). 280p. 1989. lib. bdg. 25.00 (*0-88233-992-3*) Ardis Pubs.

— Diaboliad & Other Stories. 1993. pap. 13.00 (*0-679-74892-X*) Vin Bks.

— The Early Plays of Mikhail Bulgakov. 2nd ed. Proffer, Ellendea C. & Proffer, Carl R., trs. from RUS. 418p. 1997. reprint ed. pap. 15.95 (*0-87501-091-1*) Ardis Pubs.

Bulgakov, Mikhail Afanasevich. Flight & Bliss. Ginsburg, Mirra, tr. LC 84-29445. Orig. Title: Rus.. 192p. 1985. reprint ed. pap. 11.95 (*0-8112-0941-5*, NDP593, Pub. by New Directions) Norton.

Bulgakov, Mikhail Afanasevich. Flight & Bliss: Two Plays. Ginsburg, Mirra, tr. LC 84-29445. Orig. Title: Rus.. 192p. 1985. reprint ed. 10.95 (*0-8112-0940-7*, Pub. by New Directions) Norton.

— Heart of a Dog. 1988. pap. 5.25 (*0-8222-0507-6*) Dramatists Play.

— Heart of a Dog. Ginsburg, Mirra, tr. from RUS. LC 87-8545. 128p. 1989. pap. 11.00 (*0-8021-5059-4*, Grove) Grove-Atltic.

— The Heart of a Dog. Glenay, Michael, tr. 128p. 1997. pap. 13.00 (*1-86046-083-6*) Harvill Press.

Bulgakov, Mikhail Afanasevich. The Life of Monsieur de Moliere. Ginsburg, Mirra, tr. from RUS. LC 70-93921. (New Directions Classics Ser.). 272p. 1986. reprint ed. pap. 12.95 (*0-8112-0956-3*, NDP601, Pub. by New Directions) Norton.

Bulgakov, Mikhail Afanasevich. The Master & Margarita. Burgin, Diana & O'Connor, Katherine T., trs. from RUS. 367p. 1995. 35.00 (*0-87501-067-9*) Ardis Pubs.

— The Master & Margarita. Ginsburg, Mirra, tr. from RUS. LC 87-297. 416p. 1987. pap. 11.95 (*0-8021-3011-9*, Grove) Grove-Atltic.

— The Master & Margarita. 1992. 17.00 (*0-679-41046-5*) McKay.

— The Master & Margarita. 1974. pap. 12.95 (*0-452-00899-9*, Mer) NAL.

— The Master & Margarita. Burgin, Diana & O'Connor, Katherine, trs. LC 95-45873. 1996. pap. 13.00 (*0-679-76080-6*) Vin Bks.

— The Master & Margarita. 480p. 1999. reprint ed. pap. 12.95 (*0-14-118014-5*, Penguin Bks) Viking Penguin.

***Bulgakov, Mikhail Afanasevich.** Master & Margarita. 10th ed. 1999. pap. 9.95 (*5-7684-0317-5*) Distribks Inc.

Bulgakov, Mikhail Afanasevich. The Master & Margarita: or The Devil Comes to Moscow. Van Itallie, Jean-Claude, ed. & tr. by. 1995. pap. 5.25 (*0-8222-1412-1*) Dramatists Play.

— Master i Margarita. Proffer, Ellendea C., ed. (Sobranie Sochineii Ser.: Vol. 8). (RUS., Illus.). 425p. 1988. 25.00 (*0-88233-345-3*) Ardis Pubs.

— Povesti. (Sobranie Sochineii Ser.: Vol. 3). (RUS.). 248p. 1983. 25.00 (*0-88233-698-3*) Ardis Pubs.

— Ranniaia Proza, Tom 1. Ranniaia, Tom I., tr. (Sobranie Sochineii Ser.: Vol. 1). (RUS.). 421p. 1982. 25.00 (*0-88233-506-5*) Ardis Pubs.

— The White Guard. Gleeny, Michael, tr. from RUS. 319p. 2000. reprint ed. pap. 16.95 (*0-89733-246-6*) Academy Chi Pubs.

— Zoyka's Apartment: A tragic farce in three acts. Saunders, Nicholas & Dwyer, Frank, trs. (Great Translations for Actors Ser.). 128p. 1996. pap. 11.95 (*1-880399-93-8*) Smith & Kraus.

***Bulgakov, Mikhail Afanasevich & Hutchinson, Ron.** Flight. (Nick Hern Books). 96p. 1998. pap. 14.95 (*1-85459-389-7*, Pub. by N Hern Bks) Theatre Comm.

***Bulgakov, Sergefi Nikolaevich & Evtuhov, Catherine.** Philosophy of Economy. LC 99-55454. (Russian Literature & Thought Ser.). 300p. 2000. 35.00 (*0-300-07990-7*) Yale U Pr.

Bulgakov, Sergei. Holy Grail & the Eucharist. Jakim, Boris, tr. LC 97-1810. (Esalen-Lindisfaren Library of Russian Philosophy). (RUS.). 156p. 1997. pap. 14.95 (*0-940262-81-9*, Lindisfarne) Anthroposophic.

— Sophia - The Wisdom of God: An Outline of Sophiology. rev. ed. (Esalen Institute - Library of Russian Philosophy). 224p. 1993. reprint ed. pap. 17.95 (*0-940262-60-6*, Lindisfarne) Anthroposophic.

Bulgakov, Sergius. The Orthodox Church. rev. ed. Kesich, Lydia W., tr. from RUS. LC 88-1851.Tr. of Pravoslavie. 200p. (Orig.). 1988. pap. 11.95 (*0-88141-051-9*) St Vladimirs.

Bulgakov, Sergius. Orthodoxy & Modern Society. Bird, Robert, ed. & tr. by. (Readings in Russian Philosophy Ser.: Vol. 4). 62p. 1995. pap. 3.50 (*1-929829-03-5*) Variable Pr.

Bulgakov, Sergius & Reitlinger, Joanna. Sergius Bulgakov: Apocatastasis & Transfiguration. Jakim, Boris, ed. & tr. by. from RUS. (Readings in Russian Philosophy Ser.; Vol. 2). 53p. 1995. pap. 4.00 (*1-929829-01-9*) Variable Pr.

Bulgarian Academy of Sciences Staff, ed. F.E.C.S International Conference on Circular Dichroism. 442p. 1987. text 90.00 (*3-527-26648-8*, Wiley-VCH) Wiley.

Bulgarian National Statistical Institute Staff, jt. auth. see OECD Staff.

Bulger, Anthony. French with Ease. (With Ease Ser.). (FRE., Illus.). 428p. 1982. 24.95 (*2-7005-0095-4*, Pub. by Assimil) Distribks Inc.

An Asterisk (*) at the beginning of an entry indicates that the title is appearing for the first time.

— French with Ease, Level 1, Incl. 3 60-min. cassettes. (With Ease Ser.). (ENG & FRE.). pap. 59.95 incl. audio (*2-7005-1309-6*, Pub. by Assimil) Distribks Inc.

— Ingles Perfeccionamiento. Instituto Vikingo Staff, tr. from FRE. (ENG & SPA., Illus.). 457p. 1997. 24.95 (*2-7005-0154-3*, Pub. by Assimil) Distribks Inc.

— New French with Ease. 1999. pap. text 29.95 (*2-7005-0229-9*) Assimil USA.

— El Nuevo Ingles Sin Esfuerzo. Vasquez, Jose G., tr. from FRE. (Sin Esfuerzo Ser.). (Illus.). 585p. 1991. 24.95 (*2-7005-0099-7*, Pub. by Assimil) Distribks Inc.

— Using French. (With Ease Ser.). (FRE., Illus.). 357p. 1985. 24.95 (*2-7005-0109-8*, Pub. by Assimil) Distribks Inc.

Bulger, Anthony & Cherel, Jean L. El Nuevo Frances Sin Esfuerzo. Martinez, Felix J., tr. (Sin Esfuerzo Ser.). (Illus.). 436p. 1983. 24.95 (*2-7005-0103-9*, Pub. by Assimil) Distribks Inc.

— El Nuevo Frances Sin Esfuerzo, 3 cass., Set. Martinez, Felix J., tr. (Sin Esfuerzo Ser.). 1983. 75.00 incl. audio (*2-7005-1146-8*, Pub. by Assimil) Distribks Inc.

Bulger, Dorothy. All about Breeding Cockatiels. (Illus.). 96p. 1989. 11.95 (*0-86622-746-6*, PS-801) TFH Pubns.

Bulger, Elizabeth, et al. Adobe Photoshop 5.0 Certification Guide. LC 98-86223. (Illus.). 575p. 1999. pap. 45.00 incl. cd-rom (*1-56830-473-0*) Adobe Pr.

***Bulger, Jean.** New French with Ease. 1999. audio 69.95 (*2-7005-2013-0*) Assimil.

Bulger, Leonaye & Dierkheising, Judy. The Worst Days: A Journal from a Young Cancer Patient for Health-Care Professionals. LC 96-41962. 1996. 4.95 (*1-56123-098-7*) Centering Corp.

Bulger, Raymonde A., ed. Lettres a Julie Victoire Dauble (1824-1874) La Premiere Bacheliere de France et son Temps. LC 91-3695. (Writing about Women: Feminist Literary Studies: Vol. 2). (FRE., Illus.). 329p. (C). 1992. text 55.95 (*0-8204-1621-5*) P Lang Pubng.

Bulger, Roger J. The Quest for Mercy: The Forgotten Ingredient in Health Care Reform. 120p. 1997. pap. text 10.00 (*1-891524-01-1*) Carden Jennings.

— Technology, Bureaucracy, & Healing in America: A Postmodern Paradigm. LC 88-20597. 141p. 1988. text 19.95 (*0-87745-219-9*) U of Iowa Pr.

Bulger, Roger J., ed. In Search of the Modern Hippocrates. LC 86-24950. 268p. 1987. text 33.95 (*0-87745-160-5*) U of Iowa Pr.

Bulger, Roger J., et al, eds. Mission Management Vol. 1: A New Synthesis. 25.00 (*1-879694-13-1*) AAH Ctrs.

Bulger, Ruth E., et al, eds. The Ethical Dimensions of the Biological Sciences. LC 92-26258. 308p. (C). 1993. pap. text 29.95 (*0-521-43599-4*) Cambridge U Pr.

Bulger, Ruth E. & Reiser, Stanley J., eds. Integrity in Health Care Institutions: Humane Environments for Teaching, Inquiry, & Healing. LC 90-11189. 188p. 1990. text 29.95 (*0-87745-300-4*) U of Iowa Pr.

Bulger, Thomas F. The Historical Changes & Exchanges As Depicted by Spenser in The Faerie Queene. LC 93-29919. 216p. 1993. text 89.95 (*0-7734-9342-5*) E Mellen.

Bulger, William M. While the Music Lasts: My Life in Politics. LC 98-102179. (Illus.). 328p. 1997. pap. 14.95 (*0-571-19927-5*) Faber & Faber.

Bulgin, Kathleen. The Making of an Artist: Gautier's Voyage en Espagne. LC 88-61673. (ENG & FRE.). 113p. 1988. lib. bdg. 18.95 (*0-917786-64-5*) Summa Pubns.

Bulgin, Sally, ed. Art in Nature: Inspiration from the Natural World. (Illus.). 64p. (Orig.). 1996. pap. 19.95 (*0-85532-817-7*, 8177, Pub. by Srch Pr) A Schwartz & Co.

Bulgin, Sally, jt. auth. see Willis, Lucy.

Bulgren, W. G., et al. Vol. 2. Institute of Mathematical Statistics, ed. 388p. 1974. 42.00 (*0-8218-1902-X*, TABLES-2) Am Math.

Bulgren, William G., jt. auth. see Wetzel, Gregory F.

Bulhan, H. A. Frantz Fanon & the Psychology of Oppression. LC 85-19101. (PATH in Psychology Ser.). (Illus.). 314p. (C). 1985. text 71.00 (*0-306-41950-5*, Kluwer Plenum) Kluwer Academic.

Bulhof. Nijhoff, Van Ostaijen, "De Stijl" 1976. pap. text 82.00 (*90-247-1857-0*) Kluwer Academic.

Bulhof, Ilse N. The Language of Science: A Study of the Relationship Between Literature & Science in the Perspective of a Hermeneutical Ontology, with a Case Study of Darwin's "The Origin of Species" LC 92-26529. (Brill's Studies in Intellectual History: Vol. 34). 207p. 1992. 74.50 (*90-04-09644-2*) Brill Academic Pubs.

— Wilhelm Dilthey: A Hermeneutic Approach to the Study of History & Culture. (Martinus Nijhoff Philosophy Library: No. 2). 244p. 1980. lib. bdg. 112.50 (*90-247-2360-4*, Pub. by M Nijhoff) Kluwer Academic.

***Bulhof, Ilse N. & Laurens, Kate.** Flight of the Gods: Philosophical Perspectives on Negative Theology. (Perspectives in Continental Philosophy Ser.: Vol. 11). (C). 2000. 39.95 (*0-8232-2034-6*); pap. text 19.95 (*0-8232-2035-4*) Fordham.

Bulin. Supervision. (C). 1995. text 56.36 (*0-395-59138-4*) HM.

— Supervision. (C). 1995. pap., teacher ed. 11.96 (*0-395-59140-6*); pap. text, student ed. 20.36 (*0-395-59139-2*) HM.

Bulirsch, R., ed. Computational Optimal Control. LC 94-2473. (International Series of Numerical Mathematics: Vol. 115). 1994. 99.50 (*0-8176-5015-6*, Pub. by Birkhauser) Princeton Arch.

Bulirsch, R., et al. Optimal Control: Calculus of Variations, Optimal Control Theory, & Numerical Methods. LC 93-1951. (International Series of Numerical Mathematics). 360p. 1993. 110.00 (*0-8176-2887-8*) Birkhauser.

Bulirsch, R., jt. auth. see Golubitsky, Martin.

Bulirsch, R., jt. auth. see Stoer, J.

Bulirsch, R., ed. see Stoer, J.

Bulis, Christopher. A Device of Death. (Dr. Who Missing Adventures Ser.). 256p. (Orig.). 1997. mass mkt. 5.95 (*0-426-20501-4*, Pub. by Virgin Bks) London Brdge.

***Bulis, Christopher.** Imperial Moon. (Doctor Who Ser.). 288p. 2000. mass mkt. 6.95 (*0-563-53801-5*, Pub. by BBC Bks) Genl Dist Srvs.

Bulis, Christopher. Tempest. (New Adventures Ser.). 1998. pap. 5.95 (*0-426-20523-5*, Pub. by Virgin Bks) London Brdge.

— Vanderdeken's Children. 1998. pap. 5.95 (*0-563-40590-2*) BBC.

Bulitta, Erich & Bulitta, Hildegard. Dictionary of Synonyms & Antonyms: Woerterbuch der Synonyme und Antonyme. (ENG & GER.). 795p. 1983. 85.00 (*0-8288-1972-6*, F50310) Fr & Eur.

— Woerterbuch der Synonyme und Antonyme: 18000 Stichwoerter mit 200000 Worterklaerungen. 8th ed. (GER.). 800p. 1997. pap. 22.50 (*3-596-10224-3*, Pub. by Fischer Tasch) Intl Bk Import.

Bulitta, Hildegard, jt. auth. see Bulitta, Erich.

***Buljevich, Esteban C. & Park, Yoon S.** Project Financing & the International Financial Markets LC 99-31824. 1999. write for info. (*0-7923-8524-1*) Kluwer Academic.

***Bulka, Dov.** Efficient C++ Performance Programming Techniques. LC 99-39175. (Illus.). 320p. 1999. pap. text 34.95 (*0-201-37950-3*) Addison-Wesley.

— Java Performance & Scalability, Server-side Programming Techniques. 1. 272p. 2000. pap. text 34.95 (*0-201-70429-3*) Addison-Wesley.

Bulka, Michael, et al. The Art of Joseph Kinnebrew. Connell, Jane, ed. (Illus.). 68p. 1997. pap. text 25.00 (*0-942159-21-7*) Grnd Rpds Art Mus.

Bulka, Reuven P. The Coming Cataclysm: The Orthodox Reform Rift & the Future of the Jewish People. 128p. 1994. reprint ed. pap. 9.95 (*0-88962-275-2*) Mosaic.

— Critical Psychological Issues: Judaic Perspectives. 162p. (Orig.). (C). 1992. pap. text 21.50 (*0-8191-8477-2*); lib. bdg. 44.50 (*0-8191-8476-4*) U Pr of Amer.

— Individual - Family - Community: Judeo-Psychological Perspectives. 160p. 1995. 19.95 (*0-88962-377-5*); pap. 12.95 (*0-88962-378-3*) Mosaic.

Bulka, Reuven P. The Jewish Pleasure Principle. (Illus.). 152p. 1989. pap. 17.00 (*0-89885-474-1*, Kluwer Acad Hman Sci); text 27.95 (*0-89885-328-1*, Kluwer Acad Hman Sci) Kluwer Academic.

Bulka, Reuven P. Judaism on Illness & Suffering. 304p. 1998. 35.00 (*0-7657-5986-1*) Aronson.

— Judaism on Pleasure. LC 94-18409. 224p. 1995. 30.00 (*1-56821-308-5*) Aronson.

— More of What You Thought You Knew about Judaism: 354 Common Misconceptions about Jewish Life. LC 92-44591. 464p. 1996. pap. 35.00 (*1-56821-015-9*) Aronson.

— More Torah Therapy: Further Reflections on the Weekly Sedra & Special Occasions. LC 93-13931. 1993. 20.00 (*0-88125-464-9*) Ktav.

— What You Thought You Knew about Judaism: 341 Common Misconceptions about Jewish Life. LC 89-171. 448p. 1995. reprint ed. pap. 30.00 (*1-56821-407-3*) Aronson.

— Work, Love, Suffering, & Death: A Jewish - Psychological Perspective Through Logotherapy. 240p. 1998. pap. 30.00 (*0-7657-9996-0*) Aronson.

Bulka, Reuven P., ed. Holocaust Aftermath: Continuing Impact on the Generations: A Special Issue of Journal of Psychology & Judaism. LC 81-84341. 76p. 1982. pap. 16.95 (*0-89885-127-0*, Kluwer Acad Hman Sci) Kluwer Academic.

— Mystics & Medics: A Comparison of Mystical & Psychotherapeutic Encounters. LC 79-87593. 120p. 1979. pap. 16.95 (*0-87705-377-4*, Kluwer Acad Hman Sci) Kluwer Academic.

Bulke, K. An English - Hindi Dictionary. (HIN.). 900p. 1986. 15.00 (*0-317-52461-5*, Pub. by Promilla) S Asia.

Bulkeley, Alice T. Historic Litchfield, 1721-1907, Being a Short Account of the History of the Old Houses of Litchfield, Connecticut. 2nd ed. (Illus.). 37p. 1997. reprint ed. pap. 10.00 (*0-8328-5659-2*) Higginson Bk Co.

Bulkeley, Kelly. An Introduction to the Psychology of Dreaming. LC 96-53613. 144p. 1997. 52.95 (*0-275-95889-2*, Praeger Pubs) Greenwood.

Bulkeley, Kelly. An Introduction to the Psychology of Dreaming. LC 96-53613. 144p. 1997. pap. 17.95 (*0-275-95890-6*, Praeger Pubs) Greenwood.

Bulkeley, Kelly. Spiritual Dreaming: A Cross-Cultural & Historical Journey. LC 95-22278. 288p. (Orig.). 1995. pap. 16.95 (*0-8091-3592-2*) Paulist Pr.

***Bulkeley, Kelly.** Transforming Dreams: Learning Spiritual Lessons from the Dreams That Change Your Life. LC 99-32356. 236p. 2000. pap. 14.95 (*0-471-34961-5*) Wiley.

Bulkeley, Kelly. Visions of the Night: Dreams, Religion & Psychology. LC 98-53601. (SUNY Series in Dream Studies). 256p. (C). 1999. text 59.50 (*0-7914-4283-7*, Suny Pr); pap. text 19.95 (*0-7914-4284-5*, Suny Pr) State U NY Pr.

— The Wilderness of Dreams: Exploring the Religious Meanings of Dreams in Modern Western Culture. LC 93-9484. (SUNY Series in Dream Studies). 309p. (C). 1994. text 59.50 (*0-7914-1745-X*); pap. text 19.95 (*0-7914-1746-8*) State U NY Pr.

Bulkeley, Kelly, ed. Among All These Dreamers: Essays on Dreaming & Modern Society. LC 95-46090. (SUNY Series in Dream Studies). 259p. (C). 1996. text 57.50 (*0-7914-2929-6*); pap. text 18.95 (*0-7914-2930-X*) State U NY Pr.

Bulkeley, Rip & Spinardi, Graham. Space Weapons: Deterrence or Delusion. LC 86-10880. (Illus.). 352p. 1986. 59.50 (*0-389-20640-7*, N8197); pap. 23.00 (*0-389-20641-5*, N8198) B&N Imports.

***Bulkely, Morgan.** Post-Shopping Wink. (Illus.). 2000. pap. 19.95 (*1-889097-38-1*) Hard Pr MA.

Bulkin, Bernard J., jt. auth. see Grasselli, Jeannette G.

Bulkin, Elly, et al. Yours in Struggle: Three Feminist Perspectives on Anti-Semitism & Racism. LC 88-24411. 232p. 1984. pap. 11.95 (*0-932379-53-2*) Firebrand Bks.

Bulkin, Rena. Frommer's Atlanta, 1995-1996. 1995. pap. 13.00 (*0-671-88474-3*) S&S Trade.

— Frommer's Comprehensive Travel Guide Atlanta 96. 1996. per. 12.95 (*0-671-52010-5*) S&S Trade.

— Frommer's Comprehensive Travel Guide Las Vegas 96. 1996. per. 12.95 (*0-671-52012-1*) S&S Trade.

— Frommer's Comprehensive Travel Guide Orlando, 1996. 1995. pap. 13.00 (*0-671-51887-9*) S&S Trade.

— Frommer's Comprehensive Travel Guide Virginia, 1996-1997. 1996. pap. 14.00 (*0-671-51765-1*) S&S Trade.

— Frommer's Las Vegas. 1997. 13.95 (*0-02-860917-4*) Macmillan.

— Frommer's Las Vegas, 1995-1996. 1995. pap. 13.00 (*0-671-88490-5*) S&S Trade.

— Frommer's Walking Tours New York. LC 93-16491. (Illus.). 176p. 1993. pap. 12.00 (*0-671-79762-X*, P-H Travel) Prntice Hall Bks.

— Frommer's Walt Disney World & Orlando. 272p. 1996. 14.95 (*0-02-860910-7*) Macmillan.

— Frommer's Washington D. C. from $50.00. (Frommer's Travel Guides Ser.). 1997. 16.95 (*0-02-860922-0*, P-H Travel) Prntice Hall Bks.

— Frommer's Washington, D. C. on $ a Day, 1996-1997. 1995. pap. 17.00 (*0-671-51704-X*) S&S Trade.

— Frommer's Washington, D. C., 1996. 1995. pap. 13.00 (*0-671-51703-1*) S&S Trade.

— Frommer's Washington D. C., 1997. (Frommer's Travel Guides Ser.). 1996. 14.95 (*0-02-860918-2*, P-H Travel) Prntice Hall Bks.

Bulkin, Rena, jt. auth. see Dupre, Cindy.

Bulkin, Wilma, et al, eds. The Physician & Hospice Care: Roles, Attitudes, & Issues. LC 92-49811. (Loss, Grief & Care Ser.: Vol. 6, Nos. 2 & 3). (Illus.). 200p. 1993. lib. bdg. 39.95 (*1-56024-320-1*) Haworth Pr.

Bulkley, A. I. Browne: Chad Browne Memorial. (Illus.). 173p. 1990. reprint ed. pap. 25.50 (*0-8328-1447-4*); reprint ed. lib. bdg. 35.50 (*0-8328-1446-6*) Higginson Bk Co.

Bulkley, Dwight H. Psycles: Using Your Circadian Rhythms to Control Accidents, Illness, & Psychological Problems. LC 80-692. 224p. 1981. 10.95 (*0-672-52651-4*, Bobbs) Macmillan.

Bulkley, Ed. Why Christians Can't Trust Psychology. LC 93-31617. 1994. pap. 11.99 (*1-56507-026-7*) Harvest Hse.

Bulkley, Mildred E. Bibliographical Survey of Contemporary Sources for the Economic & Social History of the World War. 1922. 200.00 (*0-686-83490-9*) Elliots Bks.

Bulkoski, William J. & Evans, Richard I. Cost-Benefit/Cost-Effectiveness Research of Drug Abuse Prevention: Implications for Programming & Policy. (DHHS Publication Ser.: Vol. 98-4021). (Illus.). 237p. 1998. pap. 12.00 (*0-16-049687-X*) USGPO.

Bulkowski, Thomas N. Encyclopedia of Chart Patterns. LC 99-15789. (Illus.). 672p. 2000. 79.95 (*0-471-29525-6*) Wiley.

Bull. Color Atlas of ENT Diagnosis. 1989. 175.00 (*0-7234-1506-4*) Wolfe Pub.

— Diagnostic Picture Tests in ENT. (C). (gr. 13). 1990. 16.00 (*0-8151-1310-2*, 22500) Mosby Inc.

— The Economics of Travel & Tourism. 2nd ed. 1995. pap. text. write for info. (*0-582-80731-X*, Pub. by Addison-Wesley) Longman.

Bull. Ephemeral Channels in the Media. text. write for info. (*0-471-49123-3*) Wiley.

Bull. Michel Angelo. 1998. pap. 17.95 (*0-312-18746-7*) St Martin.

— Seeing Things Hidden 2000. 60.00 (*1-85984-742-0*) Norton.

— Vanbrugh & Farquhar. LC 97-32202. 160p. 1998. text 45.00 (*0-312-21268-2*) St Martin.

***Bull, Adrian.** The International Tourism Trade. (International Trade Ser.). 256p. 2000. text 225.00 (*1-85573-509-1*, Pub. by Woodhead Pubng) Am Educ Systs.

Bull, Alan T., et al, eds. Companion to Biochemistry: Selected Topics for Further Study, Vol. 1. LC 73-89489. 710p. reprint ed. pap. 200.00 (*0-608-17109-3*, 202771100056) Bks Demand.

Bull, Alan T. & Meadow, Pauline M., eds. Companion to Microbiology: Selected Topics for Further Study. LC 77-13967. (Illus.). 515p. reprint ed. pap. 159.70 (*0-8357-6065-0*, 203451300090) Bks Demand.

Bull, Alvin F., jt. auth. see Runkel, Sylvan T.

***Bull, Angela.** Flying Ace: The Story of Amelia Earhart. LC 99-42513. (Eyewitness Readers). 48p. (J). (gr. 2-4). 2000. 12.95 (*0-7894-5436-X*, D K Ink); pap. text 3.95 (*0-7894-5435-1*, D K Ink) DK Pub Inc.

— Free at Last! The Story of Martin Luther King, Jr. (Dorling Kindersley Readers). (Illus.). (J). (gr. 2-4). 1999. 12.95 (*0-7894-5716-4*, D K Ink); pap. 3.95 (*0-7894-5717-2*, D K Ink) DK Pub Inc.

— Joan of Arc. (Dorling Kindersley Readers). (Illus.). (J). (gr. 2-4). 1999. 12.95 (*0-7894-5718-0*, D K Ink) DK Pub Inc.

— Joan of Arc. (Dorling Kindersley Readers). (Illus.) (J). (gr. 2-4). 2000. pap. 3.95 (*0-7894-5719-9*, D K Ink) DK Pub Inc.

— Robin Hood. LC 99-47013. (Classic Readers Ser.). 32p. (J). (gr. k-5). 2000. 12.95 (*0-7894-5701-6*, D K Ink) DK Pub Inc.

— Robin Hood. LC 99-47013. (Illus.). 32p. (J). (gr. k-5). 2000. pap. 3.95 (*0-7894-5391-6*, D K Ink) DK Pub Inc.

— Time Traveler: Surfing the Centuries. LC 99-25596. (Eyewitness Readers). (Illus.). 48p. (J). (gr. 2-3). 1999. 12.95 (*0-7894-4763-0*); pap. text 3.95 (*0-7894-4762-2*) DK Pub Inc.

***Bull, Anna.** Social Identities & Political Cultures in Italy: Catholic, Communist & Leghist Communities Between Civicness & Localism. LC 99-86562. 2000. write for info. (*1-57181-944-4*) Berghahn Bks.

Bull, Anna & Corner, Paul. From Peasant to Entrepreneur: The Survival of the Family Economy in Italy. LC 92-25571. 192p. 1993. 30.00 (*0-85496-309-X*) Berg Pubs.

Bull, Anna, et al. Entrepreneurial Textile Communities: A Comparative Study of Small Textile & Clothing Firms. LC 92-38134. 1993. mass mkt. 74.95 (*0-412-42720-6*) Chapman & Hall.

Bull, Anthony, tr. see Ricciotti, Abbot G.

Bull, Arthur. 25 Scores. 25p. (Orig.). 1994. pap. 3.00 (*1-57141-006-6*) Runaway Spoon.

Bull, Arthur & Bull, Ruth. Hawthorn. 1994. pap. text 3.75 (*0-921411-24-3*) Genl Dist Srvs.

Bull, Barry L., et al. The Ethics of Multicultural & Bilingual Education. (Professional Ethics in Education Ser.). 224p. (C). 1992. pap. text 18.95 (*0-8077-3187-0*) Tchrs Coll.

***Bull, Bartle.** Around the Sacred Sea. (Illus.). 2000. 30.00 (*0-86241-846-1*, Pub. by Canongate Books) Interlink Pub.

Bull, Bartle. A Cafe on the Nile. LC 99-192206. 465p. 1998. 26.00 (*0-7867-0556-6*) Carroll & Graf.

— A Cafe on the Nile. (Illus.). 480p. 1999. 13.95 (*0-7867-0675-9*) Carroll & Graf.

— Radleigh's Choice. 1999. pap. 19.95 (*0-670-85368-2*); pap. 11.95 (*0-14-023458-6*) Viking Penguin.

— Safari: A Chronicle of Adventure. (Illus.). 383p. 1992. pap. 29.95 (*0-14-016885-0*, Penguin Bks) Viking Penguin.

***Bull, Bartle.** The White Rhino Hotel. 416p. 2000. reprint ed. pap. 14.00 (*0-7867-0798-4*, Pub. by Carroll & Graf) Publishers Group.

Bull, Bonnie K. Stamford. (Images of America Ser.). 1997. pap. 16.99 (*0-7524-0859-3*) Arcadia Publng.

Bull, C. Neil. Aging in Rural America. (Focus Editions Ser.: Vol. 162). (Illus.). 296p. (C). 1993. text 59.95 (*0-8039-4885-9*); pap. text 26.00 (*0-8039-4886-7*) Sage.

Bull, C. Neil, jt. ed. see Johannis, Theodore B.

Bull, Charles S., contrib. by. A Cultural Resource Survey of the Offense Area of the Live Fire Maneuver Range, Ft. Irwin, California. fac. ed. (Fort Irwin, Miscellaneous Reports). (Illus.). 36p. (C). 1981. reprint ed. pap. text 4.06 (*1-55567-519-0*) Coyote Press.

Bull, Chris, ed. Witness to Revolution: The Advocate Reports on Gay & Lesbian Politics, 1967-98. LC 99-19724. 1999. pap. 16.95 (*1-55583-465-5*, Pub. by Alyson Pubns) Consort Bk Sales.

Bull, Chris, jt. auth. see Gingrich, Candace.

Bull, Christopher & Gallagher, John. Perfect Enemies: The Religious Right, the Gay Movement, & the Politics of the 1990s. 1997. pap. 14.00 (*0-614-28099-0*) Crown Pub Group.

Bull, Christopher, jt. auth. see Hazeltine, Barrett.

Bull, Colin, ed. see Wright, Charles S.

Bull, Dave. What Every Girl Should Know: An A to Z of Health - From Allergies to Zits & Everything in Between. 160p. (YA). (gr. 4 up). 1999. pap. 5.95 (*1-902618-18-1*, Pub. by Element Childrns) Penguin Putnam.

***Bull, David.** Cool & Celibate? Sex & No Sex. LC 98-34601. 143p. (YA). (gr. 7 up). 1998. pap. 4.95 (*1-901881-17-2*, Pub. by Element MA) Penguin Putnam.

Bull, David & Plesters, Joyce. The Feast of the Gods: Conservation, Examination & Interpretation. LC 89-13828. (Studies in the History of Art: Vol. 40, No. II). (Illus.). 105p. reprint ed. pap. 32.60 (*0-608-10441-8*, 207107500040) Bks Demand.

Bull, David & Wilding, Paul. Thatcherism & the Poor. LC 84-242277. (Poverty Pamphlet Ser.). iv, 92 p. 1983. write for info. (*0-903963-57-4*) CPAG.

Bull, David, ed. see Satter, Ellyn.

Bull, David C., ed. see McGinn, Kerry A.

Bull, David R. Insights into Mobile Multimedia Communication. LC 99-212904. 682p. 1998. 75.00 (*0-12-140310-6*) Morgan Kaufmann.

Bull, Debby. Blue Jelly: Love Lost & the Lessons of Canning. LC 96-3019. (Illus.). 176p. (J). 1997. 18.45 (*0-7868-6255-6*, Pub. by Hyperion) Time Warner.

— Blue Jelly: Love Lost & the Lessons of Canning. 176p. (J). 1998. pap. 10.45 (*0-7868-8320-0*, Pub. by Hyperion) Time Warner.

***Bull, Debby.** Hillbilly Hollywood. 128p. 2000. text 39.95 (*0-8478-2278-8*) Rizzoli Intl.

***Bull, Deborah.** Dancing Away: A Covent Garden Diary. (Illus.). 272p. 2000. pap. 10.95 (*0-413-73490-7*) Methn.

Bull, Deborah C. & Eike, Torje. Totally Fit. LC 97-38636. 96p. (gr. 5 up). 1998. pap. 11.95 (*0-7894-2990-X*) DK Pub Inc.

Bull, Donald. Bull's Pocket Guide to Corkscrews LC 98-52983. (Illus.). 192p. 1999. pap. 19.95 (*0-7643-0793-2*) Schiffer.

— The Ultimate Corkscrew Book. LC 98-38891. 320p. 1999. 89.95 (*0-7643-0701-0*) Schiffer.

Bull, Donald & Stanley, John R. Just For Openers: A Guide To Beer, Soda & Other Openers. LC 99-17657. (Illus.). 160p. 1999. pap. 29.95 (*0-7643-0846-7*) Schiffer.

***Bull, Donald A.** Beer Advertising: Knives, Letter Openers, Ice Picks, Cigar Cutters. (Illus.). 176p. 2000. pap. 29.95 (*0-7643-1168-9*) Schiffer.

Bull, Donald A. The Ultimate Corkscrew Book. LC 98-87845. (Illus.). 160p. 1999. 89.95 (*0-7643-0702-9*) Schiffer.

B

***Bull, Donald A. & Stanley, John R.** Soda Advertising Openers. (Illus.). 160p. 2000. pap. 29.95 (*0-7643-1056-9*) Schiffer.

Bull, Emma. Falcon. 1989. mass mkt. 5.99 (*0-441-22569-1*) Ace Bks.

— Finder. 1996. pap. 14.95 (*0-312-86291-1*) St Martin.

— Finder. 317p. 1994. 21.95 (*0-312-85418-8*) Tor Bks.

— Finder. 320p. 1995. 4.99 (*0-8125-2296-6*, Pub. by Tor Bks) St Martin.

— The Princess & the Lord of Night. LC 93-19151. (Illus.). 32p. (J). (ps-5). 1994. 14.95 (*0-15-263543-2*, Harcourt Child Bks) Harcourt.

— War for the Oaks. 320p. 1996. mass mkt. 5.99 (*0-614-96135-1*) Ace Bks.

Bull, Emma & Shetterly, Will. Double Feature. 264p. 1999. reprint ed. pap. 13.00 (*1-886778-11-6*, NESFA Pr) New Eng SF Assoc.

Bull, Emma, jt. auth. see Brust, Steven.

Bull, Evelyn L. & Carter, Bernie E. Tailed Frogs: Distribution, Ecology, & Association with Timber Harvest in Northeastern Oregon. (Illus.). 20p. 1997. reprint ed. pap. 3.00 (*0-89904-580-4*, Wildlife Resrch Grp) Crumb Elbow Pub.

Bull, Evelyn L., et al. Resource Partitioning among Woodpeckers in Northeastern Oregon. (Illus.). 24p. 1997. reprint ed. pap. 4.00 (*0-89904-706-8*, Wildlife Resrch Grp) Crumb Elbow Pub.

— Trees & Logs Important to Wildlife in the Interior Columbia River Basin. (Illus.). 55p. (C). 1998. pap. text 20.00 (*0-7881-7493-2*) DIANE Pub.

— Trees & Logs Important to Wildlife in the Interior Columbia River Basin. (Illus.). 70p. 1998. reprint ed. 15.00 (*0-89904-772-6*, Cascade Geog Soc); reprint ed. pap. 10.00 (*0-89904-773-4*, Cascade Geog Soc) Crumb Elbow Pub.

Bull Family Staff. Fifty Years of the Bull Family Picnic, 1922-1972. 4.95 (*0-686-14963-7*) T E Henderson.

Bull, Fred, jt. auth. see Bull, Shirley.

Bull, George. Harmony on Justification, Defense of the Nicene Creed, Judgement of the Catholic Church, 5 vols. LC 71-39556. (Library of Anglo-Catholic Theology: No. 4). reprint ed. write for info. (*0-404-52070-7*) AMS Pr.

— Industrial Relations: The Boardroom Viewpoint. 208p. 1972. 12.00 (*0-370-01387-5*) Transatl Arts.

Bull, George, ed. & tr. see Vasari, Giorgio.

Bull, George, tr. see Castiglione, Baldassare.

Bull, George, tr. see Machiavelli, Niccolo.

Bull, George, tr. & intro. see Cellini, Benvenuto.

Bull, George, tr. & intro. see Machiavelli, Niccolo.

Bull, George A. Michelangelo: A Biography. LC 96-9923. 1996. text 29.95 (*0-312-15172-1*) St Martin.

Bull, George A., tr. see Vasari, Giorgio.

Bull, Gordon M., et al. Information Technology: Issues for Higher Education Management. LC 93-47586. (Higher Education Policy Ser.: No. 26). 250p. 1994. 55.00 (*1-85302-542-9*) Taylor & Francis.

***Bull, Graham R.** Decorative Woodcarving: The Complete Course. LC 99-43498. 2000. 19.95 (*0-8069-9587-4*) Sterling.

Bull, H. D. Bull: The Family of Stephen Bull of Kinghurst Hall, County Warwick, England & Ashley Hall, South Carolina, 1600-1960. 161p. 1994. reprint ed. pap. 25.00 (*0-8328-4146-3*); reprint ed. lib. bdg. 35.00 (*0-8328-4145-5*) Higginson Bk Co.

Bull, Hedley. The Anarchical Society: A Study of Order in World Politics. LC 76-21786. 335p. 1979. pap. text 21.00 (*0-231-04133-0*) Col U Pr.

— The Anarchical Society: A Study of Order in World Politics. 2nd ed. LC 94-23613. 1995. pap. 21.00 (*0-231-10297-6*) Col U Pr.

Bull, Hedley, ed. The Challenge of the Third Reich. (Adam von Trott Memorial Lectures). 174p. 1986. text 49.95 (*0-19-821962-8*) OUP.

Bull, Hedley, et al, eds. Hugo Grotius & International Relations. (Illus.). 346p. 1992. pap. text 32.00 (*0-19-827771-7*) OUP.

Bull, Hedley, jt. ed. see Louis, William R.

Bull, Hedley, ed. see Wight, Martin.

Bull, Henry D. All Saints Church, Waccamaw, 1739-1968 with Updates to Which Have Been Added Additional Text, Parish Register Updates, Appendixes, & Index 1948. LC 94-42749. (Illus.). 380p. 1995. 37.50 (*0-87152-488-0*) Reprint.

Bull, Ivan, et al, eds. Entrepreneurship: Perspectives on Theory Building. (Technology, Innovation, Entrepreneurship, & Competitive Strategy Ser.). 192p. 1995. text 69.00 (*0-08-042413-9*, Pergamon Pr) Elsevier.

Bull, J. W., ed. Computational Modelling of Masonry, Brickwork & Blockwork Structures. 350p. 1998. 300.00 (*1-874672-04-0*, Pub. by Civil-Comp) St Mut.

— Finite Element Applications to Thin-Walled Structures. 308p. 1990. mass mkt. 138.95 (*1-85166-373-8*) Elsevier.

— An Introduction to Safety at Sea. (C). 1987. 30.00 (*0-85174-392-7*) St Mut.

Bull, James C. Out of Time. (Illus.). 83p. 1999. pap. 15.00 (*0-9669299-0-X*) Wolff Pub Works.

Bull, James H. Record of the Descendants of John & Elizabeth Bull, Early Settlers in Pennsylvania. (Illus.). 387p. 1993. reprint ed. pap. 60.00 (*0-8328-3018-6*); reprint ed. lib. bdg. 70.00 (*0-8328-3017-8*) Higginson Bk Co.

Bull, John. Birds of New York State: Including the 1976 Supplement. LC 85-17415. (Illus.). 720p. (C). 1986. reprint ed. 59.95 (*0-8014-1897-6*); reprint ed. pap. text 29.95 (*0-8014-9314-5*) Cornell U Pr.

— Chromatic Hexachord Fantasy: Ut, Re, Mi, Fa, Sol, La for Four Viols. Cunningham, Walker, ed. (Viol Consort Ser.: No. 4). iii, 17p. 1990. pap. text 10.00 (*1-56571-025-8*) PRB Prods.

— Simon & Schuster's Guide to Birds. 1981. pap. 15.00 (*0-671-42235-9*, Fireside) S&S Trade Pap.

— Stage Right: Crisis & Recovery in British Contemporary Mainstream Theatre. LC 93-36479. 1994. pap. 18.95 (*0-312-12029-X*) St Martin.

— Vanbrugh & Farquhar LC 97-32202. (English Dramatists Ser.). xviii, 158 p. 1998. write for info. (*0-333-46233-5*) Macmillan.

Bull, John & Farrand, John, Jr. The National Audubon Society Field Guide to North American Birds: Eastern Region. LC 94-7768. (Illus.). 800p. 1994. 19.00 (*0-679-42852-6*) Knopf.

Bull, John, et al. Birds of North America: Eastern Region. (Quick Reference Field Guide Ser.). (Illus.). 160p. 1985. pap. 13.95 (*0-02-079660-9*) Macmillan.

Bull, John L., et al. Bull's Birds of New York State. LC 98-10626. 622p. 1998. 39.95 (*0-8014-3404-1*) Cornell U Pr.

Bull, John W. The Practical Design of Structural Elements in Aluminium. 201p. 1994. 78.95 (*0-291-39798-0*, Pub. by Avebury Technical) Ashgate Pub Co.

— The Practical Design of Structural Elements in Timber. 2nd ed. LC 94-7967. 1994. 78.95 (*0-291-39802-2*) Ashgate Pub Co.

— Precast Concrete Raft Units. 180p. 1991. mass mkt. 157.95 (*0-442-30296-7*, Osprey Bks) Chapman & Hall.

Bull, John W., ed. Life Cycle Costing for Construction. (Illus.). 169p. 1993. text 144.95 (*0-7514-0056-4*, Pub. by B Acad & Prof) Routldge.

— The Numerical Analysis & Modelling of Soil Structure Interaction. 1993. write for info. (*1-85861-014-1*) Elsevier.

Bull, Joseph W. Lakota Warrior: A Personal Narrative. Howard, James H., ed. & tr. by. LC 98-39666. (ENG & NAI., Illus.). 1998. pap. 15.00 (*0-8032-9806-4*, Bison Books) U of Nebr Pr.

Bull, Josiah. But Now I See. 370p. 1998. pap. 7.99 (*0-85151-742-0*) Banner of Truth.

Bull, Julie. Implementing the Children Act for Children under 8. 92p. 1995. pap. 25.00 (*0-11-701971-2*, HM19712, Pub. by Statnry Office) Bernan Associates.

Bull, Klaus-Michael. Gemeinde Zwischen Integration und Abgrenzung: Ein Beitrag zur Frage Nach Dem Ort der Joh Gemeinde(n) in der Geschichte des Urchristentums. (Beitrage zur Biblischen Exegese und Theologie Ser.: Bd. 24). (GER.). XVI, 257p. 1992. 51.80 (*3-631-44135-5*) P Lang Pubng.

Bull, Leonard S. Nutritional Energetics. 1999. 60.00 (*0-8493-8750-7*) CRC Pr.

Bull, M. Access: The Pick Enquiry Language. (Illus.). 350p. 1991. pap. 49.95 (*0-442-31319-5*) Chapman & Hall.

— Systems Development Using Structured Tec. (ITCP-UK Computer Science). 368p. 1989. mass mkt. 42.95 (*0-412-31020-1*) Chapman & Hall.

— Systems Development Using Structured Techniques. 368p. 1989. mass mkt. 89.95 (*0-412-31010-4*, A3691) Chapman & Hall.

Bull, M. J. Surg. Procedures in Primary Care. (Illus.). 128p. 1995. pap. text 69.50 (*0-19-262458-X*) OUP.

Bull, Malcolm. The Pick Programming Language: BASIC. LC 93-673. (Computing Ser.). 456p. 1994. mass mkt. 64.95 (*0-412-46660-0*) Chapman & Hall.

***Bull, Malcolm.** Seeing Things Hidden: Apocalypse, Vision & Totality. 1999. pap. 22.00 (*1-85984-263-1*, Pub. by Verso) Norton.

***Bull, Marcus.** The Miracles of Our Lady of Rocamadour: Analysis & Translation. LC 99-37959. 256p. 1999. 75.00 (*0-85115-765-3*, Suffolk Records Soc) Boydell & Brewer.

Bull, Marcus G. Knightly Piety & the Lay Response to the First Crusade: The Limousin & Gascony, 970-C. 1130. LC 92-21403. (Illus.). 342p. 1993. text 75.00 (*0-19-820354-3*, Clarendon Pr) OUP.

Bull, Martin J. Contemporary Italy: A Research Guide, 43. LC 95-39488. (Bibliographies & Indexes in World History Ser.: No. 43). 160p. 1996. lib. bdg. 65.00 (*0-313-29137-3*, Greenwood Pr) Greenwood.

Bull, Martin J. & Heywood, Paul, eds. West European Communist Parties after the Revolutions of 1989. LC 94-14211. 1994. text 69.95 (*0-312-12268-3*) St Martin.

Bull, Martin J. & Ingham, Mike. Reform of the Socialist System in Central & Eastern Europe. LC 97-22992. 208p. 1998. text 59.95 (*0-312-17732-1*) St Martin.

Bull, Martin J., jt. auth. see Rhodes, Martin.

Bull, Mary, jt. ed. see Smith, Alison.

Bull, Mary A. Hunter. Record of Hunter of Hunterson, Ayrshire, Scotland. 95p. 1997. reprint ed. pap. 18.00 (*0-8328-9273-4*); reprint ed. lib. bdg. 28.00 (*0-8328-9272-6*) Higginson Bk Co.

***Bull, Michael.** Sounding Out the City: Personal Stereos & the Management of Everyday Life. (Materializing Culture Ser.). 192p. 2000. 65.00 (*1-85973-337-9*, Pub. by Berg Pubs); pap. 19.50 (*1-85973-342-5*, Pub. by Berg Pubs) NYU Pr.

Bull, Mike. Restructuring the Electric Industry. 62p. 1998. reprint ed. pap. text 20.00 (*0-7881-4305-0*) DIANE Pub.

Bull, Molly N. Brides & Blessings. 1999. mass mkt. 4.50 (*0-373-87054-X*) Harlequin Bks.

— For Always. (Serenade Serenata Ser.: No. 36). 1986. pap. 1.49 (*0-310-47352-7*, 15581P) Zondervan.

Bull, Norman. Church of Jesus Grows. (Bible Story & Its Background Ser.: Vol. 8). 156p. (J). (gr. 2-7). 1979. 10.95 (*0-7175-0454-9*) Dufour.

— Church of the Jews. (Bible Story & Its Background Ser.: Vol. 4). 162p. (J). (gr. 2-7). 1975. 10.95 (*0-7175-0450-6*) Dufour.

— Founders of the Jews. (Bible Story & Its Background Ser.: Vol. 1). 138p. (J). (gr. 2-7). 1985. pap. 10.95 (*0-7175-0977-X*) Dufour.

— Jesus the Nazarene. (Bible Story & Its Background Ser.: Vol. 5). 190p. (J). (gr. 2-7). 1984. pap. 10.95 (*0-7175-0981-8*) Dufour.

— Prophets of the Jews. (Bible Story & Its Background Ser.: Vol. 3). 204p. (J). (gr. 2-7). 1984. pap. 12.95 (*0-7175-0979-6*) Dufour.

Bull, Peter & Roger, Derek, eds. Conversation: An Interdisciplinary Approach. 1988. 99.00 (*0-905028-87-2*, Pub. by Multilingual Matters); pap. 39.95 (*0-905028-86-4*, Pub. by Multilingual Matters) Taylor & Francis.

Bull, Peter D. Lecture Notes on Diseases of the Ear, Nose & Throat. 8th ed. (Illus.). 113p. 1996. pap. 29.95 (*0-86542-634-1*) Blackwell Sci.

Bull, Philip. Land, Politics & Nationalism: A Study of the Irish Land Question. LC 96-28749. 288p. 1996. text 45.00 (*0-312-16442-4*) St Martin.

Bull, R. & Rumsey, N. The Social Psychology of Facial Appearance. (Social Psychology Ser.). 400p. 1988. 137.00 (*0-387-96607-2*) Spr-Verlag.

Bull, R. Charles. Handbook of Sports Injuries. LC 98-36208. (Illus.). 865p. 1999. pap. text 32.00 (*0-07-008993-0*) McGraw-Hill HPD.

Bull, R. J., et al. Accounting in Business. 6th ed. 550p. 1990. pap. 34.00 (*0-406-50056-8*, UK, MICHIE) LEXIS Pub.

Bull, Ray & Carson, David, eds. Handbook of Psychology in Legal Contexts. LC 94-35582. 694p. 1995. 241.50 (*0-471-94182-4*) Wiley.

***Bull, Ray & Carson, David, eds.** Handbook of Psychology in Legal Contexts. 696p. 2000. pap. 125.00 (*0-471-49242-6*) Wiley.

Bull, Rene. The Arabian Knights. (J). (gr. 2-6). 1986. 8.98 (*0-685-16864-6*, 619342) Random Hse Value.

Bull, Richard J. & Stauber, Anja J. Mechanisms of Carcinogenesis by Dichloroacetate (DCA) & Trichloroacetate (TCA) LC 98-8262. 1998. write for info. (*0-89867-962-1*) Am Water Wks Assn.

Bull, Robert J., ed. The Joint Expedition to Caesarea Maritima: Preliminary Reports in Microfiche. 1987. 35.00 (*0-910885-00-1*) Drew Institute for Archaeological Research.

Bull, Ruah, jt. auth. see Loughran, Joni.

Bull, Ruth, ed. Housing for People with Disabilities. LC 98-189578. 280p. 1997. pap. 29.95 (*1-85302-454-6*, Pub. by Jessica Kingsley) Taylor & Francis.

Bull, Ruth, jt. auth. see Bull, Arthur.

***Bull, S. J., ed.** Adherence Issues in Sport & Exercise. LC 98-54171. (Illus.). 328p. 1999. write for info. (*0-471-98848-0*) Wiley.

Bull, Sara C. Ole Bull: A Memoir. LC 81-1508. (Music Ser.). (Illus.). iv, 417p. 1981. reprint ed. lib. bdg. 39.50 (*0-306-76120-3*) Da Capo.

Bull, Schuyler. Along the Luangwa: A Story of an African Floodplain. LC 99-25917. (Habitat Ser.: No. 13). (Illus.). 36p. (J). (gr. 1-4). 1999. 15.95 (*1-56899-776-0*); pap. 5.95 (*1-56899-777-9*) Soundprints.

***Bull, Schuyler.** Along the Luangwa: A Story of an African Floodplain. LC 99-25917. (Habitat Ser.: Vol. 13). (Illus.). 36p. (J). (gr. 1-4). 1999. 19.95 incl. audio (*1-56899-778-7*, BC7013) Soundprints.

Bull, Schuyler. Along the Luangwa: A Story of an African Floodplain, Includes plush toy. (Habitat Ser.: Vol. 13). (Illus.). 36p. (J). (gr. 1-4). 1999. 26.95 (*1-56899-780-9*); pap. 16.95 (*1-56899-781-7*) Soundprints.

— Through Tsavo: A Story of an East African Savanna. LC 97-47611. (Habitat Ser.). (Illus.). 36p. (J). (gr. 1-4). 1998. 15.95 (*1-56899-552-0*); 19.95 incl. audio (*1-56899-554-7*, BC7008) Soundprints.

— Through Tsavo: A Story of an East African Savanna, Incl. toy. (Habitat Ser.). (Illus.). 36p. (J). (gr. 1-4). 1998. 26.95 (*1-56899-556-3*); pap. 16.95 (*1-56899-557-1*) Soundprints.

— Through Tsavo: A Story of an East African Savannah. LC 97-47611. (Illus.). 36p. (J). (gr. 1-4). 1998. pap. 5.95 (*1-56899-553-9*) Soundprints.

***Bull, Shirley & Bull, Fred.** Paddling Cape Cod: A Coastal Explorer's Guide. LC 99-87152. 2000. pap. 16.95 (*0-88150-441-6*, Pub. by Countryman) Norton.

Bull, Shirley & Solity, Jonathan. Classroom Management. (Principles of Practice Ser.). 208p. 1987. lib. bdg. 55.00 (*0-7099-1415-6*, Pub. by C Helm) Routldge.

Bull, Shirley, jt. auth. see Solity, Jonathan.

Bull, Stephen. European Swords. (Album Ser.: No. 298). (Illus.). 32p. 1999. pap. 4.75 (*0-7478-0234-3*, Pub. by Shire Pubns) Parkwest Pubns.

— An Historical Guide to Arms & Armor. North, Tony, ed. (Illus.). 224p. 1991. 35.00 (*0-8160-2620-3*) Facts on File.

***Bull, Stephen.** SAS: Special Forces in Action. (Illus.). 2000. 34.95 (*1-903040-05-1*, Pub. by Military Illustrated) Combined Pub.

Bull, Stephen. 20th Century Arms & Armor. LC 95-12020. (Illus.). 224p. 1995. 35.00 (*0-8160-3349-8*) Facts on File.

— Vietnam. (Guidebook Ser.). (Illus.). 1991. pap. 9.95 (*962-217-120-6*) L A Michaux.

Bull, Stephen B. World War One: British Army. Newark, Tim, ed. LC 98-6551. (Brassey's History of Uniforms Ser.). (Illus.). 144p. 1998. 32.95 (*1-85753-270-8*, Pub. by Brasseys) Brasseys.

— World War I: German Army. Newark, Tim, ed. (Brassey's History of Uniforms Ser.). (Illus.). 144p. 2000. 32.95 (*1-85753-271-6*, Pub. by B T B) Bks Intl VA.

Bull, Stephen J. Sports Psychology: A Self Help Guide. (Illus.). 1992. 29.95 (*1-85223-568-3*, Pub. by Crowood) Trafalgar.

Bull, Stephen J., et al. The Mental Game Plan. 216p. 1996. pap. 16.95 (*0-9519543-2-6*, Pub. by Sports Dynamics) Fit Info Tech.

Bull, Stephen R. Dances with Blackflies: Funny Stories about Life in Maine & Life in General. 150p. 1994. pap. text 9.95 (*0-9644753-0-8*) Mt Blue Pub.

— Waiter! There's a Blackfly in My Chowder! More Funny Stories about Life in Maine & Life in General. (Illus.). 150p. (Orig.). 1996. pap. 9.95 (*0-9644753-1-6*, W001) Mt Blue Pub.

Bull, Storm. Index to Biographies of Contemporary Composers, Vol. III. LC 64-11781. 878p. 1987. 75.00 (*0-8108-1930-9*) Scarecrow.

Bull, T. R. A Color Atlas of Ear, Nose, & Throat Diagnosis. 2nd ed. (Illus.). 368p. (C). (gr. 13). 1987. 53.00 (*0-8151-1317-X*, 09834) Mosby Inc.

— Color Atlas of ENT Diagnosis. 3rd ed. 1995. pap. text 29.95 (*0-7234-2271-0*, Pub. by Wolfe Pub) Mosby Inc.

Bull, Thuh. Only the Dog Knows for Sure: The Best of Thuh Bull. LC 96-79803. (Illus.). 128p. (Orig.). 1997. pap. 9.95 (*1-56352-391-4*) Longstreet.

Bull, William B. Landscape Change Vol. 1: Geomorphic Responses to Climactic Change. (Illus.). 352p. 1991. text 90.00 (*0-19-505570-5*) OUP.

Bull, William E. Spanish for Communication. 1972. 35.96 (*0-685-39915-X*) HM.

— Spanish for Communication, Level 2. (C). 1976. student ed. 6.60 (*0-685-02312-5*); text 20.40 (*0-685-02311-7*); teacher ed. 26.76 (*0-685-02313-3*) HM.

Bull, William E., et al. Spanish for Communication, Level 1. (C). 1975. write for info. (*0-318-53418-5*) HM.

Bulla, Ben F. Textiles & Politics: The Life of B. Everett Jordan - From Saxapahaw to the United States Senate. LC 91-76747. (Illus.). 402p. 1992. 24.95 (*0-89089-486-8*) Carolina Acad Pr.

Bulla, Clyde R. The Beast of Lor. LC 77-6751. (Illus.). (J). (gr. 3-7). 1977. 12.95 (*0-690-01377-9*) HarpC Child Bks.

— The Chalk Box Kid. LC 87-4683. (Stepping Stone Bks). (Illus.). 64p. (J). (gr. 1-4). 1987. lib. bdg. 11.99 (*0-394-99102-8*, Pub. by Random Bks Yng Read) Random.

— The Chalk Box Kid. 10th annot. ed. LC 87-4683. (Stepping Stone Bks). (Illus.). 59p. (J). (gr. 2-4). 1987. pap. 3.99 (*0-394-89102-3*, Pub. by Random Bks Yng Read) Random.

— Charlie's House. (J). (gr. 4 up). 1983. 12.95 (*0-690-04259-0*) HarpC Child Bks.

— Daniel's Duck. LC 77-25647. (I Can Read Bks.). (Illus.). 64p. (J). (gr. 2-4). 1979. 11.95 (*0-06-020908-9*) HarpC Child Bks.

— Daniel's Duck. LC 77-25647. (I Can Read Bks.). (Illus.). 64p. (J). (ps-3). 1979. lib. bdg. 15.89 (*0-06-020909-7*) HarpC Child Bks.

— Daniel's Duck. LC 78-22156. (I Can Read Bks.). (Illus.). 64p. (J). (ps-3). 1982. pap. 3.95 (*0-06-444031-1*, HarpTrophy) HarpC Child Bks.

— Daniel's Duck. (I Can Read Bks.). (J). (gr. 2-4). 1980. 8.95 (*0-606-00422-X*, Pub. by Turtleback) Demco.

— Eagle Feather. LC 94-6582. (Illus.). 96p. (J). (gr. 3-7). 1994. pap. 4.99 (*0-14-036730-6*, PuffinBks) Peng Put Young Read.

— Ghost of Windy Hill. LC 68-11059. (Illus.). (J). (gr. 3-7). 1968. lib. bdg. 14.89 (*0-690-32764-1*) HarpC Child Bks.

— A Lion to Guard Us. LC 80-2455. (Illus.). 128p. (J). (gr. 2-5). 1981. lib. bdg. 14.89 (*0-690-04097-0*) HarpC Child Bks.

— A Lion to Guard Us. (J). 1989. 10.05 (*0-606-04267-9*, Pub. by Turtleback) Demco.

— My Friend the Monster. LC 79-7826. (Trophy Bk.). (Illus.). 96p. (J). (gr. 2-5). 1990. pap. 3.50 (*0-06-440378-5*, HarpTrophy) HarpC Child Bks.

— Pirate's Promise. LC 58-8209. (Illus.). 96p. (J). (gr. 2-5). 1994. pap. 4.95 (*0-06-440457-9*, HarpTrophy) HarpC Child Bks.

— Pirate's Promise. 1995. 19.00 (*0-8446-6813-3*) Peter Smith.

— Pocahontas & the Strangers. LC 77-139094. (Illus.). 176p. (J). (ps-3). 1987. pap. 3.50 (*0-590-43481-0*) Scholastic Inc.

— Poor Boy, Rich Boy. LC 79-2685. (I Can Read Bks.). (Illus.). 64p. (J). (ps-3). 1982. 9.95 (*0-06-020896-1*) HarpC Child Bks.

— The Poppy Seeds. (Illus.). 48p. (J). (gr. 2-5). 1994. pap. 3.99 (*0-14-036731-4*, PuffinBks) Peng Put Young Read.

***Bulla, Clyde R.** The Poppy Seeds, Class Set. unabridged ed. (J). 1998. boxed set 70.70 incl. audio (*0-7887-2534-3*, 46704) Recorded Bks.

— The Poppy Seeds, Homework. unabridged ed. (J). (gr. 2). 1998. boxed set 22.24 incl. audio (*0-7887-2229-8*, 40713) Recorded Bks.

Bulla, Clyde R. Secret Valley. LC 49-10917. (Trophy Bk.). (Illus.). 112p. (J). (gr. 2-5). 1993. pap. 4.50 (*0-06-440456-0*, HarpTrophy) HarpC Child Bks.

***Bulla, Clyde R.** The Secret Valley. (gr. 1-4). 1999. 19.00 (*0-8446-6997-0*) Peter Smith.

Bulla, Clyde R. Shoeshine Girl. LC 75-8516. (Illus.). 80p. (J). (gr. 3 up). 1975. 12.95 (*0-690-00758-2*) HarpC Child Bks.

— Shoeshine Girl. LC 75-8516. (Illus.). 96p. (J). (gr. 3-5). 1989. lib. bdg. 15.89 (*0-690-04830-0*) HarpC Child Bks.

Bulla, Clyde R. Shoeshine Girl. (J). 1975. 9.70 (*0-606-04030-7*, Pub. by Turtleback) Demco.

— Squanto, Friend of the Pilgrims. (J). 1954. 9.09 (*0-606-02537-5*, Pub. by Turtleback) Demco.

Bulla, Clyde R. The Story of Valentine's Day. LC 97-37195. (Illus.). 40p. (J). (gr. 2-5). 1999. 14.95 (*0-06-027883-8*); lib. bdg. 14.89 (*0-06-027884-6*) HarpC Child Bks.

***Bulla, Clyde R.** The Story of Valentine's Day. LC 97-37195. (Illus.). 40p. (J). (gr. 2-5). 2000. pap. 5.95 (*0-06-443626-8*) HarpC Child Bks.

Bulla, Clyde R. The Stubborn Old Woman. LC 78-22506. (Illus.). 48p. (J). (gr. 1-4). 1980. 11.95 (*0-690-03945-X*); lib. bdg. 11.89 (*0-690-03946-8*) HarpC Child Bks.

An Asterisk (*) at the beginning of an entry indicates that the title is appearing for the first time.

— Surprise for a Cowboy. LC 50-8508. (Illus.). (J). (gr. 2-5). 1950. 11.74 (*0-690-79837-7*) HarpC Child Bks.
— The Sword in the Tree. LC 56-5699. (Illus.). (J). (gr. 2-5). 1956. 12.95 (*0-690-79908-X*) HarpC Child Bks.
— The Sword in the Tree. LC 56-5699. (Illus.). 128p. (J). (gr. 4-7). 1962. lib. bdg. 15.89 (*0-690-79909-8*) HarpC Child Bks.
— Three-Dollar Mule. LC 94-18508. (Illus.). 96p. (J). (gr. 1-3). 1995. pap. 2.50 (*0-8167-3598-0*) Troll Communs.
— Three-Dollar Mule. (Illus.). (J). (gr. 1-4). 1995. lib. bdg. 15.35 (*0-8167-3711-8*, Little Rainbow) Troll Communs.
— Tree Is a Plant. LC 60-11540. (Let's-Read-&-Find-Out Science Bks.). (Illus.). (J). (gr. k-3). 1973. pap. 4.95 (*0-690-00201-7*) HarpC Child Bks.
***Bulla, Clyde R.** A Tree Is a Plant. (Let's-Read-&-Find-Out Science Bks.). 40p. (J). (ps-1). 2001. 15.95 (*0-06-028171-5*); pap. 4.95 (*0-06-445196-8*) HarpC Child Bks.
Bulla, Clyde R. The Valentine Cat. LC 94-18353. (Illus.). 64p. (J). (gr. k-3). 1995. pap. 4.95 (*0-8167-3599-9*) Troll Communs.
— What Makes a Shadow? LC 62-11001. (Let's-Read-&-Find-Out Science Bks.). (Illus.). (J). (gr. k-3). 1962. lib. bdg. 11.89 (*0-690-87648-3*) HarpC Child Bks.
Bulla, Clyde R. What Makes a Shadow. LC 92-36350. (Illus.). 32p. (J). (ps-1). 1996. pap. 7.95 incl. audio (*0-694-70081-9*) HarpC.
Bulla, Clyde R. What Makes a Shadow. rev. ed. LC 92-36350. (Let's-Read-&-Find-Out Science Bks.: Stage 1). (Illus.). 32p. (J). (ps-1). 1994. lib. bdg. 15.89 (*0-06-022916-0*) HarpC Child Bks.
— White Bird. LC 89-70231. (Stepping Stone Bks). (Illus.). 64p. (J). (ps-3). 1990. pap. 3.99 (*0-679-80662-8*, Pub. by Random Bks Yng Read) Random.
Bulla, Clyde R. & Burke, Jim. Shoeshine Girl. LC 99-20063. (Trophy Bk.). (Illus.). 96p. (J). (gr. 2-5). 1989. reprint ed. pap. 4.50 (*0-06-440228-2*, HarpTrophy) HarpC Child Bks.
Bulla, Clyde R. & Syson, Michael. Conquista! LC 77-26585. (Illus.). (J). (gr. 2-5). 1978. lib. bdg. 12.89 (*0-690-03871-2*) HarpC Child Bks.
Bulla, Clyde Robert. The Chalk Box Kid. (Stepping Stone Bks.). (J). 1987. 9.19 (*0-606-01193-5*, Pub. by Turtleback) Demco.
Bulla, Clyde Robert. Eagle Feather. LC 94-6582. 1994. 9.09 (*0-606-06343-9*, Pub. by Turtleback) Demco.
Bulla, Clyde Robert. Ghost Town Treasure. 1994. 9.09 (*0-606-06987-9*, Pub. by Turtleback) Demco.
— Last Look. (J). 1995. 9.19 (*0-606-07774-X*, Pub. by Turtleback) Demco.
— A Lion to Guard Us. LC 80-2455. (Trophy Bk.). (Illus.). 128p. (J). (gr. 2-5). 1989. pap. 4.95 (*0-06-440333-5*, HarpTrophy) HarpC Child Bks.
— My Friend the Monster. (J). 1980. 12.95 (*0-690-04031-8*) HarpC Child Bks.
Bulla, Clyde Robert. Pirate's Promise. LC 58-8209. (Trophy Chapter Bks.). 1994. 9.70 (*0-606-06670-5*, Pub. by Turtleback) Demco.
Bulla, Clyde Robert. Pocahontas & the Strangers. (J). 1971. 9.09 (*0-606-03892-2*, Pub. by Turtleback) Demco.
— Singing Sam. LC 88-19758. (Step into Reading Ser.: A Step 3 Book). (Illus.). 48p. (J). (gr. 2-3). 1989. pap. 3.99 (*0-394-81977-2*, Pub. by Random Bks Yng Read); lib. bdg. 11.99 (*0-394-91977-7*, Pub. by Random Bks Yng Read) Random.
Bulla, Clyde Robert. Singing Sam. (Step into Reading Ser.: A Step 3 Book). (J). (gr. 2-3). 1989. 9.19 (*0-606-12517-5*, Pub. by Turtleback) Demco.
Bulla, Clyde Robert. Squanto: Friend of the Pilgrims. (Illus.). 112p. (J). (gr. 2-5). 1990. pap. 3.50 (*0-590-44055-1*) Scholastic Inc.
***Bulla, Clyde Robert.** The Sword in the Tree. LC 99-47119. (Trophy Chapter Bk.). (Illus.). 112p. (J). (gr. 2-5). 2000. pap. 4.25 (*0-06-442132-5*, HarpTrophy) HarpC Child Bks.
Bulla, Clyde Robert. Three-Dollar Mule. (J). 1994. 7.60 (*0-606-08300-6*, Pub. by Turtleback) Demco.
— A Tree Is a Plant. rev. ed. (Illus.). 40p. (J). (ps-1). lib. bdg. 15.89 (*0-06-028172-3*) HarpC Child Bks.
— Valentine Cat. 1994. 10.15 (*0-606-08342-1*, Pub. by Turtleback) Demco.
Bulla, D. R. Roughnecks. 327p. (Orig.). 1994. 8.95 (*0-9643895-0-9*) DRB-ROUGHNECK.
Bulla, Dale. Loops for Learning: Memory Boosters Across the Curriculum, Grades 4-10. LC 95-13799. 1995. pap. 29.00 (*1-56976-027-6*) Zephyr Pr AZ.
— The Magic Box. (Illus.). 24p. (J). (gr. 2-6). 1993. 14.95 (*1-884197-00-0*) N Horizon Educ.
— The Magic Box. (Illus.). 24p. (J). (gr. 2-6). 1994. pap. 6.95 (*1-884197-04-3*) N Horizon Educ.
— My Brother's a Pain in the Back Seat. LC 95-92283. (Illus.). 28p. (J). (gr. 2-6). 1995. 14.95 (*1-884197-05-1*); pap. 6.95 (*1-884197-06-X*) N Horizon Educ.
***Bulla, Gisela.** Fancy Rats. LC 99-10570. (Complete Pet Owner's Manual Ser.). (Illus.). 104p. 1999. pap. 6.95 (*0-7641-0940-5*) Barron.
Bulla, Gisela. Natural Healing with Aromatherapy. LC 99-20262. (Healthful Alternatives Ser.). (Illus.). 96p. 1999. pap. 14.95 (*0-8069-4221-5*) Sterling.
Bulla, Robert C. The Paint Brush Kid. LC 97-51153. 1998. lib. bdg. 11.99 (*0-679-99282-0*, Pub. by Random Bks Yng Read) Random.
— The Paint Brush Kid. (J). 1998. pap. 3.99 (*0-679-89282-6*, Pub. by Random Bks Yng Read) Random.
Bulla, W., et al. Algebro-Geometric Quasi-Periodic Finite-Gap Solutions of the Toda & Kac-van Moerbeke Hierarchies. LC 98-25199. (Memoirs of the American Mathematical Society Ser.: Vol. 135, No. 641). 79p. 1998. pap. 38.00 (*0-8218-0808-7*) Am Math.
Bullamore, Henry W. Louisiana: A Geography. (Westview Geographies of the United States Ser.). (C). 1996. text 35.00 (*0-86531-310-5*); pap. text 20.00 (*0-86531-472-1*) Westview.
Bullan, Bob. Perfect Partners? 176p. 1988. 45.00 (*1-85283-209-6*, Pub. by Boxtree); pap. 30.00 (*1-85283-214-2*, Pub. by Boxtree) St Mut.
Bullard. Land Consolidation & Rural. 55.95 (*1-84014-937-X*) Ashgate Pub Co.
Bullard, et al. Science Probe Ten. 155.00 (*0-471-79536-4*) Thomson Learn.
Bullard, Anne, jt. auth. see Engstrand, Iris.
Bullard, Arthur. Comrade Yetta. LC 68-57516. (Muckrakers Ser.). 454p. (C). 1986. reprint ed. pap. text 9.95 (*0-8290-1911-1*); reprint ed. lib. bdg. 21.00 (*0-8398-0178-5*) Irvington.
Bullard, Barbara & Carroll, Kat. Communicating... Inside Out. 202p. (C). 1999. per. 20.95 (*0-7872-5708-7*, 41570803) Kendall-Hunt.
Bullard, Bethany, jt. auth. see Kearns, Elizabeth.
Bullard, C. & Wameldorff, P., eds. Trends in Electric Utility Research: Proceedings of the Electric Utility Research Conference, Chicago, April 1984. 500p. 1984. pap. 170.00 (*0-08-030982-8*) Elsevier.
Bullard, CeCe. Goochland: Yesterday & Today. LC 94-30183. (Illus.). 1994. write for info. (*0-89865-911-6*) Donning Co.
***Bullard, Chloe.** Qualified Teachers for All California Students: Current Issues in Recruitment, Retention, Preparation, & Professional Development. 67p. 1998. pap. write for info. (*1-58703-091-8*, CRB-98-012) CA St Libry.
— Taxing the Internet: An Update on State Policies. 11p. 1998. pap. write for info. (*1-58703-078-0*, CRB Note 5) CA St Libry.
Bullard, Dexter M., ed. see Fromm-Reichmann, Frieda.
Bullard, E. John. Mary Cassatt Oils & Pastels. (Great Artists Ser.). (Illus.). 88p. 1984. pap. 16.95 (*0-8230-0570-4*) Watsn-Guptill.
— New Art for a New Building. LC 93-83952. (Illus.). 44p. 1993. pap. 12.95 (*0-89494-042-2*) New Orleans Mus Art.
Bullard, E. John, et al. Handbook of the Collection. LC 95-69921. (Illus.). 304p. 1995. pap. 15.95 (*0-89494-051-1*) New Orleans Mus Art.
Bullard, E. John, jt. auth. see Vine, Richard.
***Bullard, Florence, et al.** Catalog of the Library at the Bullard Colonial Farm, Holliston, Massachusetts. LC 99-41397. .p. 1999. write for info. (*0-9612610-8-0*) Bullbrier Pr.
Bullard, Foncie, et al. Mobile: A Gulf Coast Treasure. Turner, James E. & Gilreath, Lenita, eds. LC 94-30172. (Illus.). 240p. 1994. pap. 24.95 (*1-885352-01-8*) Community Comm.
Bullard, Frederick L. Famous War Correspondents. (American Newspapermen 1790-1933 Ser.). (Illus.). xii, 437p. 1974. reprint ed. 34.95 (*0-8464-0029-4*) Beekman Pubs.
Bullard, J. M. Rotch: The Rotches (Biography & Genealogy of the Rotch Family of Nantucket & New Bedford, Mass.) (Illus.). 583p. 1991. reprint ed. pap. 89.00 (*0-8328-1887-9*); reprint ed. lib. bdg. 99.00 (*0-8328-1886-0*) Higginson Bk Co.
Bullard, J. W., et al, eds. Computational & Mathematical Models of Microstructural Evolution Vol. 529: Proceedings Materials Research Society Symposium. 183p. 1998. text 81.00 (*1-55899-435-1*) Materials Res.
Bullard, Jean. How I Spent My Christmas Vacation Vol. IV. Bocknek, Jonathan, ed. LC 99-177132. (Illus.). 41p. (J). (gr. 1 up). 1997. pap. 10.00 (*0-9658044-9-6*) Bufflehead Pub.
Bullard, Jean, jt. auth. see Oborne, Louise.
Bullard, Jean, ed. see Trimble, Stephen A.
Bullard, Jean V., jt. auth. see Spohr, Betty B.
Bullard, Jean V., ed. see Dercum, Edna S.
***Bullard, John R.** Bach for the Banjo. 72p. 1999. pap. 12.95 (*0-7866-4096-0*, 97163) Mel Bay.
Bullard-Johnson, Mary, jt. auth. see Johnson, Ben.
Bullard, L. G. Solid Modeling with AutoCAD's AME. (Illus.). 87p. 1992. pap. text 14.80 (*0-87563-402-8*) Stipes.
Bullard, Lacy, jt. auth. see Gephardt, Dennis.
Bullard, Linda M. Shades of Justice. 1999. reprint ed. mass mkt. 6.99 (*0-451-19768-2*, Sig) NAL.
***Bullard, Lisa.** Not Enough Beds! LC 98-30518. (Picture Bks.). (Illus.). 32p. (J). (gr. k-3). 1999. 15.95 (*1-57505-356-X*) Lerner Pub.
Bullard, Lucy & Sollitt, Kenneth. A Family History. LC 92-96987. (Ann of the Prairie Ser.: Vol. 5). 233p. 1992. pap. 7.95 (*0-940652-10-2*) Inhtce Pubns.
***Bullard, Mary.** Always Present. 1999. pap. write for info. (*1-58235-255-0*) Watermrk Pr.
Bullard, Mary R. Robert Stafford of Cumberland Island: Growth of a Planter. LC 95-15470. 368p. (C). 1995. pap. 19.95 (*0-8203-1738-1*) U of Ga Pr.
Bullard, Mary R., jt. auth. see Wood, Virginia S.
Bullard, Mike. Open Book: Little Thoughts from a Big Head. 231p. 1999. text 29.95 (*0-385-25886-0*) Doubleday.
Bullard, Monte. The Soldier & the Citizen: The Role of the Military in Taiwan's Development. LC 96-38663. (Taiwan in the Modern World Ser.). 238p. (C). 1997. 74.95 (*1-56324-978-2*, East Gate Bk) M E Sharpe.
— The Soldier & the Citizen: The Role of the Military in Taiwan's Development. LC 96-38663. (Taiwan in the Modern World Ser.). (Illus.). 238p. (C). 1997. pap. 27.95 (*1-56324-979-0*, East Gate Bk) M E Sharpe.
Bullard, Oral. Konapee's Eden: Historic & Scenic Handbook: The Columbia River Gorge. Worcester, Thomas K., ed. (Illus.). 93p. 1985. pap. 5.95 (*0-911518-69-X*) F Amato Pubns.
Bullard, Pamela & Taylor, Barbara O. Keepers of the Dream: The Triumph of Effective Schools. LC 92-13428. Orig. Title: Making School Reform Happen. 444p. (C). reprint ed. 24.95 (*0-9640729-3-9*) Excelsior Fnd.
Bullard, Pamela, jt. auth. see Taylor, Barbara O.
Bullard, R. K. & Dixon-Gough, R. W. Britain from Space: An Atlas of Landsat Images. (Illus.). 128p. 1984. 59.95 (*0-85066-277-X*) Taylor & Francis.
Bullard, Reader. Letters from Tehran: An Ambassador in World War II Persia. Hodgkin, E. C., ed. 300p. 1991. 49.50 (*0-685-38701-1*, Pub. by I B T) St Martin.
Bullard, Rebecca, et al. The Occasional Trainer's Handbook. LC 93-36515. 264p. 1994. 39.95 (*0-87778-270-9*) Educ Tech Pubns.
Bullard, Richard D. Tellin' It Like It Is: An African-Centered Christian Interpretation of Black Life & Issues. (Illus.). 160p. (Orig.). 1995. pap. 10.00 (*0-9652135-0-1*) Vision Impact.
Bullard, Robert, et al. We Speak for Ourselves: Social Justice, Race, & Environment. Alston, Dana et al, eds. (Illus.). 50p. (Orig.). 1990. pap. write for info. (*1-879358-01-8*) Panos Inst.
Bullard, Robert D. Dumping in Dixie: Race, Class & Environmental Quality. 2nd ed. LC 93-41558. 216p. (C). 1994. pap. text 25.00 (*0-8133-1963-3*, Pub. by Westview) HarpC.
***Bullard, Robert D.** Dumping in Dixie: Race, Class & Environmental Quality. 3rd ed. LC 99-53168. 1999. pap. 23.00 (*0-8133-6792-1*) Westview.
Bullard, Robert D. Unequal Protection: Environmental Justice & Communities of Color. (Illus.). 416p. 1996. pap. 16.00 (*0-87156-380-0*, Pub. by Sierra) Random.
Bullard, Robert D., ed. Confronting Environmental Racism: Voices from the Grassroots. 262p. 1993. 40.00 (*0-89608-447-7*); pap. 16.00 (*0-89608-446-9*) South End Pr.
— Unequal Protection: Environmental Justice & Communities of Color. LC 93-20942. (Sierra Club Guides Ser.). 400p. 1994. 25.00 (*0-87156-450-5*, Pub. by Sierra) Random.
***Bullard, Robert D., et al, eds.** Sprawl City: Race, Politics & Planning in Atlanta. 230p. 2000. pap. 30.00 (*1-55963-790-0*) Island Pr.
Bullard, Robert D. & Johnson, Glenn S., eds. Just Transportation: Dismantling Race & Class Barriers to Mobility. LC 98-106741. 208p. 1997. pap. 15.95 (*0-86571-357-X*) New Soc Pubs.
Bullard, Robert D., et al. Residential Apartheid: The American Legacy. (Urban Policies Ser.: Vol. 2). 250p. 1994. pap. text 18.95 (*0-934934-43-6*) CAAS Pubns.
Bullard, Robert L. Personalities & Reminiscences of the War. 1977. 18.95 (*0-8369-6967-7*, 7848) Ayer.
Bullard, Roger A., ed. The Hypostasis of the Archons: The Coptic Text with Translation & Commentary. (Patristische Texte und Studien: Vol. 10). (C). 1970. 52.30 (*3-11-006356-5*) De Gruyter.
Bullard, Roger W., ed. Flavor Chemistry of Animal Foods. LC 77-27295. (ACS Symposium Ser.: No. 67). 1978. 21.95 (*0-8412-0404-7*) Am Chemical.
— Flavor Chemistry of Animal Foods. LC 77-27295. (ACS Symposium Ser.: Vol. 67). 183p. 1978. reprint ed. pap. 56.80 (*0-608-03927-6*, 206437400009) Bks Demand.
Bullard, Roger W., jt. ed. see Shumake, Stephen A.
Bullard, Roland K., III & Yasinski, Cynthia P. Managing Risk in Transactional Products. LC 85-14753. 32p. 1984. pap. text 13.00 (*0-936742-18-6*) Robt Morris Assocs.
Bullard, Ruth K. Annual Buyer's Guide. (Library Acquisitions, Practice & Theory). 1982. pap. 30.00 (*0-08-028805-7*, Pergamon Pr) Elsevier.
— ATM Security. 1999. text 49.68 (*0-13-080421-5*) P-H.
Bullard, Ruth K., et al. Science Probe 10. (UK - Science Ser.). 1992. text 57.95 (*0-471-79534-8*) S-W Pub.
Bullard, Ruth K., jt. auth. see O'Tuel, Frances S.
Bullard, Sara. Free at Last: A History of the Civil Rights Movement & Those Who Died in the Struggle. LC 92-38174. (Illus.). 112p. (YA). (gr. 5 up). 1993. text 25.00 (*0-19-508381-4*) OUP.
— Free at Last: A History of the Civil Rights Movement & Those Who Died in the Struggle. (Illus.). 112p. (YA). (gr. 5 up). 1994. pap. text 12.95 (*0-19-509450-6*) OUP.
— Teaching Tolerance. 256p. 1997. pap. 11.95 (*0-385-47265-X*) Doubleday.
Bullard, Sara, ed. The Ku Klux Klan: A History of Racism & Violence. 4th ed. (Illus.). 64p. 1998. reprint ed. pap. text 15.00 (*0-7881-7031-7*) DIANE Pub.
Bullard, Scott R., ed. Library Acquisitions Special Reports. 115p. 1981. pap. 31.00 (*0-08-026112-4*, Pergamon Pr) Elsevier.
Bullard, Steven H. & Straka, Thomas J. Introduction to Forest Valuation & Investment Analysis. (Illus.). 69p. (C). 1994. student ed. 20.00 (*0-9641291-0-8*) GTR Prnt & Pubng.
Bullard, Thomas R. Street, Interurban & Rapid Transit Railways of the United States: A Selective Historical Bibliography. (Illus.). 96p. (Orig.). 1984. pap. 11.00 (*0-911940-38-3*) Cox.
Bullas, Will. A Fool & His Bunny: The Art of Will Bullas. LC 98-147779. (Illus.). 64p. 1993. pap. 14.95 (*0-86713-019-9*, 88073) Greenwich Wrkshop.
Bullaty, Sonja. America, America. LC 99-14181. 216p. 1999. 45.00 (*0-7892-0530-0*) Abbeville Pr.
Bullaty, Sonja & Lomeo, Angelo, photos by. Tuscany. (Illus.). 180p. 1995. 45.00 (*1-55859-895-2*) Abbeville Pr.
Bullchild, Percy. American Indian Genesis: The Story of Creation. LC 98-30543. (Illus.). 112p. 1998. reprint ed. 17.00 (*1-56975-156-0*) Ulysses Pr.
Bulle, O. & Rigutini, Guiseppe. Italian-German - German-Italian Dictionary. (GER & ITA.). 1992. reprint ed. 195.00 (*0-8288-9425-6*) Fr & Eur.
Bulle, Oscar, jt. auth. see Rigutini, Giuseppe.
Bulleid, Ann, et al. Food Preparation & Cooking: Core Units. 2nd ed. (Catering & Hospitality Ser.). (Illus.). 113p. 1993. pap., student ed. 32.50 (*0-7487-2567-9*, Pub. by S Thornes Pubs) Trans-Atl Phila.
— Reception. 2nd rev. ed. (Catering & Hospitality Ser.). (Illus.). 199p. 1996. pap. 36.50 (*0-7487-2593-8*, Pub. by S Thornes Pubs) Trans-Atl Phila.
— Serving Food & Drink in the Bar. 2nd rev. ed. (Catering & Hospitality Ser.). (Illus.). 276p. 1996. pap. 37.50 (*0-7487-2592-X*, Pub. by S Thornes Pubs) Trans-Atl Phila.
Bulleid, H. A. Cylinder Musical Box Design & Repair. LC 87-1779. (Illus.). 228p. (Orig.). 1987. pap. 14.95 (*0-930256-16-6*, Vestal Pr) Madison Bks UPA.
— Cylinder Musical Box Technology: Including Makers, Types, Dating, & Music. LC 93-46171. (Illus.). 280p. 1994. pap. 21.95 (*0-930256-22-0*, Vestal Pr) Madison Bks UPA.
Bulleid, Peter. The Environment & the Planning System: Business Implications. (Business & the Environment Practitioner Ser.). 96p. (C). 1993. pap. 39.95 (*0-946655-79-0*, Pub. by SRIS) L Erlbaum Assocs.
Bullein, William. Bulleins Bulwarke of Defence Againste All Sickness, Sorness & Woundes. LC 73-37139. (English Experience Ser.: No. 350). (Illus.). 488p. 1971. reprint ed. 125.00 (*90-221-0350-1*) Walter J Johnson.
Bullen. Dictionary of Inequalities. 1998. write for info. (*0-582-32748-2*) Longman.
— Managing With Infomation Technology. 1995. text, teacher ed. 23.00 (*0-07-008913-2*) McGraw.
Bullen, jt. auth. see Lawrence.
Bullen, A. H., ed. see Bullen, Mark W.
Bullen, Andrew H. & Davis, Charles H. Database Techniques for Librarians: A Primer Using Turbo Pascal. LC 92-33524. 256p. 1993. 40.00 (*0-8161-1967-8*, G K Hall & Co); 30.00 (*0-8161-1968-6*, G K Hall & Co) Mac Lib Ref.
Bullen, Anthony. Fifty Prayers for Young People. (Illus.). (C). 1988. 40.00 (*0-85439-132-0*, Pub. by St Paul Pubns) St Mut.
— My Book about Confession. (Illus.). (C). 1996. pap. 39.95 (*0-85439-248-3*, Pub. by St Paul Pubns) St Mut.
— My Book about the Mass. (Illus.). (C). 1996. pap. 39.95 (*0-85439-249-1*, Pub. by St Paul Pubns) St Mut.
Bullen, Arthur H. Elizabethans. LC 78-58255. (Essay Index in Reprint Ser.). 1978. reprint ed. 25.00 (*0-8486-3017-3*) Roth Pub Inc.
— Some Shorter Elizabethan Poems. LC 64-16746. (Arber's an English Garner Ser.). 1964. reprint ed. 41.00 (*0-8154-0041-1*) Cooper Sq.
Bullen, Arthur H., ed. Collection of Old English Plays, 7 vols., 4 bks., Set. LC 64-14699. reprint ed. 184.95 (*0-405-08325-4*, Pub. by Blom Pubns) Ayer.
— Collection of Old English Plays, 7 vols., 4 bks., Vol. 1. LC 64-14699. 1972. reprint ed. 44.95 (*0-405-08326-2*, Pub. by Blom Pubns) Ayer.
— Collection of Old English Plays, 7 vols., 4 bks., Vol. 2. LC 64-14699. 1972. reprint ed. 44.95 (*0-405-08327-0*, Pub. by Blom Pubns) Ayer.
— Collection of Old English Plays, 7 vols., 4 bks., Vol. 3. LC 64-14699. 1972. reprint ed. 48.95 (*0-405-08328-9*, Pub. by Blom Pubns) Ayer.
— Collection of Old English Plays, 7 vols., 4 bks., Vol. 4. LC 64-14699. 1972. reprint ed. 48.95 (*0-405-08329-7*, Pub. by Blom Pubns) Ayer.
— Collections of Lyrics & Poems: Sixteenth & Seventeenth Centuries, 6 vols., Set. Incl. Lyrics from the Dramatists of the Elizabethan Age. LC 70-164695. reprint ed. 34.50 (*0-404-01223-X*); Lyrics from the Song-Books of the Elizabethan Age. LC 70-164695. reprint ed. 34.50 (*0-404-01221-3*); More Lyrics from the Song-Books of the Elizabethan Age. LC 70-164695. reprint ed. 34.50 (*0-404-01222-1*); Musa Proterva: Love Poems of the Restoration. LC 70-164695. reprint ed. 34.50 (*0-404-01224-8*); Poems, Chiefly Lyrical, from Romances & Prose-Tracts of the Elizabethan Age: With Chosen Poems of Nicholas Breton. LC 70-164695. reprint ed. 34.50 (*0-404-01226-4*); Speculum Amantis: Love Poems from Rare Song-Books & Miscellanies of the Seventeenth Century. LC 70-164695. reprint ed. 34.50 (*0-404-01225-6*); LC 70-164695. 1970. reprint ed. 207.00 (*0-404-01220-5*) AMS Pr.
— England's Helicon: A Collection of Lyrical & Pastoral Poems, Published in 1600. LC 75-119956. (Select Bibliographies Reprint Ser.). 1977. reprint ed. 23.95 (*0-8369-5399-1*) Ayer.
— Lyrics from the Dramatists of the Elizabethan Age. LC 72-38342. (Select Bibliographies Reprint Ser.). 1977. reprint ed. 23.95 (*0-8369-6759-3*) Ayer.
Bullen, Arthur H., ed. see Beaumont, Francis.
Bullen, Arthur H., ed. see Davenport, Robert.
Bullen, Arthur H., ed. see Middleton, Thomas.
Bullen, Arthur H., ed. see Nabbes, Thomas.
Bullen, D. J. & Griffiths, E., eds. Iron & Infection. 2nd ed. LC 98-37166. 526p. 1999. 245.00 (*0-471-93940-4*) Wiley.
Bullen, Fiona. From Pillar to Post. large type ed. (Ulverscroft Large Print Ser.). 464p. 1997. 27.99 (*0-7089-3805-1*) Ulverscroft.
— A Worthy Man. large type ed. 576p. 1995. 27.99 (*0-7089-3388-2*) Ulverscroft.
Bullen, Frank T. Creatures of the Sea: Sea Birds, Beasts, & Fishes. 1977. lib. bdg. 69.95 (*0-8490-1682-7*) Gordon Pr.
— The Cruise of the Cachalot. (Illus.). 1980. pap. 4.95 (*0-918172-06-3*) Leetes Isl.
— Deep-Sea Plunderings. LC 75-106251. (Short Story Index Reprint Ser.). 1977. 23.95 (*0-8369-3288-9*) Ayer.
— Idylls of the Sea. LC 71-98564. (Short Story Index Reprint Ser.). 1977. 20.95 (*0-8369-3138-6*) Ayer.

B

Bullen, J. B. The Expressive Eye: Fiction & Perception in the Work of Thomas Hardy. (Illus.). 294p. 1986. text 69.00 (*0-19-812858-4*) OUP.

— The Myth of the Renaissance in Nineteenth-Century Writing. LC 93-5373. (Illus.). 348p. 1994. text 75.00 (*0-19-812888-6*, Clarendon Pr) OUP.

— The Pre-Raphaelite Body: Fear & Desire in Painting, Poetry & Criticism. (Illus.). 256p. (C). 1998. text 65.00 (*0-19-818257-0*) OUP.

— Writing & Victorianism. LC 96-41669. (Crosscurrents Ser.). (C). 1997. text 57.25 (*0-582-28917-3*); pap. text 28.13 (*0-582-28916-5*) Longman.

Bullen, J. B., ed. Post-Impressionism in England. 288p. 1989. text 75.00 (*0-415-00216-8*) Routledge.

— The Sun Is God: Painting, Literature, & Mythology in the Nineteenth Century. (Illus.). 248p. 1989. 64.00 (*0-19-812884-3*) OUP.

Bullen, Keith & Cromer, John, eds. Salamander. LC 79-103084. (Granger Index Reprint Ser.). 1977. 19.95 (*0-8369-6099-8*) Ayer.

Bullen, Mark W. Bullein's Dialogue Against the Fever Pestilence. Bullen, A. H., ed. (EETS, ES Ser.: No. 52). 1972. reprint ed. 40.00 (*0-527-00258-5*) Periodicals Srv.

***Bullen, Martha M.** Tales from the Homefront. 1999. pap. 12.95 (*0-9670359-1-0*) Spencer & Waters.

Bullen, Martha M., jt. auth. see Sanders, Darcie.

***Bullen, P. S.** Dictionary of Inequalities. 1999. 86.95 (*0-8493-0634-5*) CRC Pr.

Bullen, P. S., et al, eds. New Integrals. (Lecture Notes in Mathematics Ser.: Vol. 1419). v, 202p. 1990. pap. 34.80 (*0-387-52322-7*) Spr-Verlag.

Bullen, R. Excavations in Northeastern Massachusetts, Vol. 1, No. 3. LC 49-48491. 1949. pap. 10.00 (*0-939312-02-6*) Peabody Found.

Bullen, Ripley P. Six Sites Near the Chattahoochee River in the Jim Woodruff Reservoir Area, Florida, Paper No. 14. fac. ed. (Smithsonian Institution, Bureau of American Ethnology Ser.: Bulletin 169). (Illus.). 61p. (C). 1958. reprint ed. pap. text 7.75 (*1-55567-687-1*) Coyote Press.

Bullen, Roger. The Foreign Office: Seventeen Eighty-Two to Nineteen Eighty-Two. LC 84-19482. 141p. 1984. lib. bdg. 49.50 (*0-313-27089-9*, U7089, Greenwood Pr) Greenwood.

Bullen, Roger. The London Conferences: Anglo-American Relations & Cold War Strategy, January-June 1950. (Documents on British Policy Overseas Ser.: Vol. 2). xxxiii, 406p. 1987. 90.00 (*0-11-591693-8*, Pub. by Statnry Office) Balogh.

Bullen, Roger & Yasamee, H. J. The Schumann Plan, the Council of Europe & Western European Integration, May 1950-December 1952. 1023p. 1986. pap. 175.00 (*0-11-591692-X*, Pub. by Statnry Office) Balogh.

Bullen, Roger, et al. The Great Powers & the European States System: 1815-1914. LC 79-41567. (Illus.). 208p. (Orig.). (C). 1989. pap. text 35.80 (*0-582-49135-5*, 73495) Longman.

***Bullen, Stephen.** Professional Excel 2000 Programming. 600p. 2000. pap. 49.99 (*1-86100-336-6*) Wrox Pr Inc.

Bullen, Susan. The Alps & Their People. LC 93-42277. (People & Places Ser.). (Illus.). 48p. (J). (gr. 5-8). 1994. lib. bdg. 24.26 (*1-56847-165-3*) Raintree Steck-V.

— The Arctic & Its People. LC 93-27125. (People & Places Ser.). (Illus.). 48p. (J). (gr. 5-6). 1994. 24.26 (*1-56847-153-X*) Raintree Steck-V.

Bullen, Victor, jt. auth. see Weeks, Nora.

***Bullene, Emma F.** The Psychic History of the Cliff Dwellers, Their Origin & Destruction. (LC History-America-E). 256p. 1999. reprint ed. lib. bdg. 89.00 (*0-7812-4314-9*) Rprt Serv.

Buller. Statistical Account of the Parish of St. Just-in-Penwith. (C). 1989. 80.00 (*0-907566-61-8*, Pub. by Dyllansow Truran) St Mut.

Buller, A. J., et al, eds. Molecular Genetics of Muscle Disease: Duchenne & Other Dystrophies. (Illus.). 222p. 1989. text. write for info. (*0-443-04199-7*) Church.

Buller, A. T., et al, eds. North Sea Oil & Gas Reservoirs II. (C). 1990. lib. bdg. 407.50 (*1-85333-283-6*, Pub. by Graham & Trotman) Kluwer Academic.

Buller, Bob. All-Star Games from All-Star Youth Leaders. LC 97-37805. 112p. (Orig.). 1998. per. 14.99 (*0-7644-2020-8*) Group Pub.

— Family Friendly Ideas Your Church Can Do. LC 97-32379. 96p. 1998. per. 14.99 (*0-7644-2035-6*) Group Pub.

***Buller, Bob.** Living in God's Household: Lessons for a Healthy Church. Eichenberger, Jim, ed. (Solid Foundation Bible Studies: Vol. 8). 64p. 2000. pap. 9.99 (*0-7847-1178-X*, 41108) Standard Pub.

— Surviving Prosperity: Lessons from Solomon's Reign. Eichenberger, Jim, ed. (Solid Foundation Bible Studies Ser.). 64p. 2000. pap. 9.99 (*0-7847-1200-X*, 41109) Standard Pub.

Buller, Bob. Wrestling with Life: Lessons from the Story of Jacob. Eichenberger, Jim, ed. (Bible Studies: Vol. 3). 64p. 1999. 9.99 (*0-7847-0943-2*, 41103) Standard Pub.

Buller, Bob & Thornton, Dave, eds. Awesome Worship Services for Youth: 12 Powerful, Faith-Building Worship Services. LC 98-13277. (Illus.). 96p. (YA). 1998. per. 16.99 (*0-7644-2057-7*, Vital Ministry) Group Pub.

Buller, Bob, ed. see Crabtree, Jack.

Buller, Bob, ed. see Dockrey, Karen.

Buller, Bob, ed. see Freudenburg, Ben & Lawrence, Rick.

Buller, Bob, ed. see Hunt, Josh.

Buller, Bob, ed. see Lingo, Susan L.

Buller, Bob, ed. see Schultz, Joani.

Buller, Bob, ed. see Warden, Michael.

***Buller, Carlton J.** Stolen Innocence: The Autobiography of a Lost Soul. xvi, 304p. 2000. pap. 13.95 (*0-9701238-0-9*, FairWeather Pubns) Buller Enter.

Buller, Cornelius A. The Unity of Nature & History in Pannenberg's Theology. 224p. (C). 1996. pap. text 22.95 (*0-8226-3055-9*); lib. bdg. 57.50 (*0-8226-3054-0*) Rowman.

Buller, David B., et al. Nonverbal Communication: The Unspoken Dialogue. (Illus.). 545p. (C). 1994. pap. text 21.95 (*1-57074-093-3*) Greyden Pr.

Buller, David J., ed. Function, Selection & Design. LC 98-47343. (SUNY Series in Philosophy & Biology). 325p. (C). 1999. pap. text 21.95 (*0-7914-4212-8*) State U NY Pr.

— Function, Selection & Design. LC 98-47343. (SUNY Series in Philosophy & Biology). 288p. (C). 1999. text 65.50 (*0-7914-4211-X*) State U NY Pr.

Buller, H. & Hoggart, Keith. Nondecision-Making & Community Power: Residential Development Control in Rural Areas. (Progress in Planning Ser.: Vol. 25). (Illus.). 74p. 1986. pap. 22.00 (*0-08-034277-9*, Pub. by PPL) Elsevier.

Buller, Henry. Citizen Action & Urban Renewal: A Case Study. (C). 1985. 29.00 (*0-7855-3834-8*, Pub. by Oxford Polytechnic) St Mut.

***Buller, Henry, et al, eds.** Agri-Environmental Policy in the European Union. (Perspectives on Europe Ser.). 310p. 2000. text 74.95 (*1-84014-504-8*, Pub. by Ashgate Pub) Ashgate Pub Co.

Buller, Henry & Hoggart, Keith. International Counterurbanization: British Migrants to Rural France. (Illus.). 154p. 1994. 56.95 (*1-85628-508-1*, Pub. by Avebry) Ashgate Pub Co.

Buller, Henry & Wright, Susan, eds. Rural Development: Problems & Practices. (Illus.). 258p. 1990. text 85.95 (*0-566-07018-9*, Pub. by Avebry) Ashgate Pub Co.

Buller, Jeffrey L. Historical Films in the Latin Classroom. 57p. 1992. spiral bd. 8.25 (*0-939507-39-0*, B303) Amer Classical.

***Buller, Jim.** National Statecraft & European Integration, 1979-1997: The Conservative Government & the European Union. LC 00-21790. 208p. 2000. write for info. (*1-85567-588-9*, Pub. by P P Pubs) Continuum.

Buller, Jon. Buller's Professional Course in Bartending for Home Study. LC 82-23309. (Illus.). 160p. 1983. pap. 8.95 (*0-916782-33-6*) Harvard Common Pr.

— Draw Your Own Superheroes Now. (Books & Stuff Ser.). (Illus.). 32p. (J). (gr. 1-6). 1996. pap. text 8.95 (*0-448-41259-4*, G & D) Peng Put Young Read.

— I Love You Good Night. LC 88-6484. (Illus.). 32p. (J). (ps up). 1990. pap. 3.25 (*0-671-70297-1*) Litle Simon.

— Mike & the Magic Cookies. (J). 1992. 9.15 (*0-606-12423-3*, Pub. by Turtleback) Demco.

Buller, Jon. 20,000 Baseball Cards under the Sea. (Step into Reading Ser.: A Step 3 Book). (J). (gr. 2-3). 1991. 9.19 (*0-606-12553-1*, Pub. by Turtleback) Demco.

Buller, Jon & Schade, Susan. Felix & the Four Hundred Frogs. (J). 1996. pap. 3.99 (*0-679-86745-7*) Random.

Buller, Jon & Schade, Susan. Felix & the 400 Frogs. LC 95-52061. (Step into Reading Ser.: A Step 3 Book). (J). (ps-3). 1996. lib. bdg. 11.99 (*0-679-96745-1*) Random.

— Felix & the 400 Frogs. (Step into Reading Ser.: A Step 3 Book). (J). (gr. 2-3). 1996. 9.19 (*0-606-11322-3*, Pub. by Turtleback) Demco.

Buller, Jon & Schade, Susan. No Tooth, No Quarter! LC 89-30250. (Step into Reading Ser.: A Step 3 Book). (Illus.). 48p. (J). (gr. 2-3). 1989. lib. bdg. 11.99 (*0-394-94956-0*, Pub. by Random Bks Yng Read) Random.

— No Tooth, No Quarter! LC 89-30250. (Step into Reading Ser.: A Step 3 Book). (Illus.). 48p. (J). (ps-3). 1989. pap. 3.99 (*0-394-84956-6*, Pub. by Random Bks Yng Read) Random.

Buller, Jon & Schade, Susan. No Tooth, No Quarter! (Step into Reading Ser.: A Step 3 Book). (J). (gr. 2-3). 1989. 9.19 (*0-606-04284-9*, Pub. by Turtleback) Demco.

Buller, Jon & Schade, Susan. Pig at Play: Level 1. (Planet Reader Picture Bks.). (Illus.). 32p. (J). (ps-1). 1998. pap. 2.95 (*0-8167-4375-4*) Troll Communs.

— Pig at Work: Level 1. (Planet Reader Picture Bks.). (Illus.). 32p. (J). (ps-1). 1998. pap. 2.95 (*0-8167-4374-6*) Troll Communs.

— Snow Bugs. (Illus.). 1996. 7.99 (*0-679-87913-7*) Random.

— Snow Bugs, Go Bugs. (Illus.). 1996. lib. bdg. 11.99 (*0-679-97913-1*) Random.

— Space Mall. LC 96-25564. (Illus.). (J). 1997. pap. 3.99 (*0-679-87919-6*, Pub. by Random Bks Yng Read) Random.

— Space Mall. LC 96-25564. (Illus.). (J). 1997. lib. bdg. 11.99 (*0-679-97919-0*, Pub. by Random Bks Yng Read) Random.

— Sweet Dreams. (All by Myself Bks.). (Illus.). 16p. (J). 1999. 6.95 (*1-58260-010-4*, Pub. by Infnty Plus One) Assoc Pubs Grp.

— Toad on the Road. LC 91-4246. (Step into Reading Ser.: A Step 1 Book). (Illus.). 32p. (J). (ps-3). 1992. pap. 3.99 (*0-679-82689-0*, Pub. by Random Bks Yng Read) Random.

— Toad on the Road. (Step into Reading Ser.: A Step 1 Book). (J). (ps-1). 1992. 9.19 (*0-606-01495-0*, Pub. by Turtleback) Demco.

— Toad Takes Off. LC 96-8773. (Step into Reading Ser.: A Step 1 Book). 32p. (J). (ps-1). 1997. pap. 3.99 (*0-679-86935-2*) Random.

— Toad Takes Off. LC 96-8773. (Step into Reading Ser.: A Step 1 Book). (J). (ps-1). 1997. lib. bdg. 11.99 (*0-679-96935-7*) Random.

Buller, Jon & Schade, Susan. Toad Takes Off. LC 96-8773. (Step into Reading Ser.: A Step 1 Book). (J). (ps-1). 1997. 9.19 (*0-606-11993-0*, Pub. by Turtleback) Demco.

— 20,000 Baseball Cards under the Sea. LC 90-40704. (Step into Reading Ser.: A Step 3 Book). (Illus.). 48p. (J). (ps-3). 1991. pap. 3.99 (*0-679-81569-4*, Pub. by Random Bks Yng Read) Random.

Buller, Jon, jt. auth. see Schade, Susan.

***Buller, Kate.** Ultimate Knitter's Guide: Patterns & Techniques. (Illus.). 2000. 39.95 (*1-56477-337-X*) Ferguson.

Buller, M. & Sanders, D. Part-Time Profits from Home: 111 Creative & Pratical Home-Based Money-Making Opportunities. 1997. pap. 9.00 (*0-517-88721-5*) Random Hse Value.

Buller, Michael. The Cooking of Paul Bocuse. 336p. 1999. text 25.00 (*0-02-861009-1*, Pub. by Macmillan) S&S Trade.

***Buller, Paul F. & Schuler, Randall S.** Managing Organizations & People: Cases in Management, Organizational Behavior & Human Resource Management. 6th ed. LC 99-15313. 377p. 1999. pap. 46.95 (*0-324-00713-2*) Thomson Learn.

Bullerdiek, J. & Bartnitzke, S., eds. Chromosome 12 Aberrations in Human Solid Tumors: Cytogenetics & Molecular Genetics. LC 94-20576. 1994. 86.00 (*0-387-55759-8*) Spr-Verlag.

Bullert, B. J. Public Television: Politics & the Battle over Documentary Film. LC 97-17633. (Communications, Media, & Culture Ser.). (Illus.). 224p. 1997. pap. text 20.00 (*0-8135-2470-9*); lib. bdg. 49.00 (*0-8135-2469-5*) Rutgers U Pr.

Bullert, Gary. The Politics of John Dewey. LC 83-62872. 223p. 1983. 37.95 (*0-87975-208-4*) Prometheus Bks.

Bullesbach, Erika E., jt. auth. see Schwabe, Christian.

Bullet, B. T. Tales from over the Edge: A Madcap Collection of Memoirs from Marin County California's Sunday Morning Ride. (Illus.). 530p. 1999. pap. 82.95 (*0-9668924-0-2*) Bullet Pr.

Bulletin of Concerned Asian Scholars Staff. China from Mao to Deng: The Politics & Economics of Socialist Development. LC 82-19668. 99p. reprint ed. pap. 30.70 (*0-608-15772-4*, 203098600073) Bks Demand.

***Bulletin of Labour Statistics Staff.** 1998 Yearbook of Labour Statistics. (FRE, SPA & ENG., Illus.). 1339p. 1999. 239.50 (*92-2-007357-9*, Pub. by Statnry Office) Balogh.

Bulletin of the Chinese Academy of Sciences Editor. Science & Technology in China: Selections from the Bulletin of the Chinese Academy of Sciences, Vol. 1. 570p. 1996. 68.00 (*7-03-000280-6*, Pub. by Sci Pr) Lubrecht & Cramer.

— Science & Technology in China: Selections from the Bulletin of the Chinese Academy of Sciences, Vol. 2. 670p. 1996. 65.00 (*7-80003-032-6*, Pub. by Sci Pr) Lubrecht & Cramer.

— Science & Technology in China: Selections from the Bulletin of the Chinese Academy of Sciences, Vol. 3. 600p. 1996. 75.00 (*7-03-001488-X*, Pub. by Sci Pr) Lubrecht & Cramer.

— Science & Technology in China: Selections from the Bulletin of the Chinese Academy of Sciences, Vol. 4, Nos. 1 & 2. 1996. 90.00 (*7-03-002083-9*, Pub. by Sci Pr) Lubrecht & Cramer.

— Science & Technology in China: Selections from the Bulletin of the Chinese Academy of Sciences, Vol. 5. 550p. 1996. 89.95 (*7-03-002625-X*, Pub. by Sci Pr) Lubrecht & Cramer.

— Science & Technology in China: Selections from the Bulletin of the Chinese Academy of Sciences, Vol. 6. 530p. 1996. 89.95 (*7-03-003202-0*, Pub. by Sci Pr) Lubrecht & Cramer.

— Science & Technology in China: Selections from the Bulletin of the Chinese Academy of Sciences, Vol. 7. 545p. 1996. 89.95 (*7-03-003928-9*, Pub. by Sci Pr) Lubrecht & Cramer.

Bullett, Gerald, ed. see Keats, John.

Bullett, Gerald W. Baker's Cart, & Other Tales. LC 77-125208. (Short Story Index Reprint Ser.). 1977. 20.95 (*0-8369-3575-6*) Ayer.

— George Eliot: Her Life & Books. LC 76-156178. 273p. 1971. reprint ed. lib. bdg. 65.00 (*0-8371-6121-5*, BUGE, Greenwood Pr) Greenwood.

— Street of the Eye, & Nine Other Tales. LC 77-167444. (Short Story Index Reprint Ser.). 1977. reprint ed. 20.95 (*0-8369-3970-0*) Ayer.

— Sydney Smith: A Biography & a Selection. LC 77-138578. (Illus.). 1971. reprint ed. lib. bdg. 69.50 (*0-8371-5777-3*, BUSS, Greenwood Pr) Greenwood.

Bullett, Gerald W., ed. The English Galaxy of Shorter Poems. LC 72-3002. (Granger Index Reprint Ser.). 1977. reprint ed. 21.95 (*0-8369-8239-8*) Ayer.

Bulletti, Carlo, et al, eds. The Human Endometrium. LC 94-28726. (Annals Ser.: Vol. 734). (Illus.). 500p. 1994. pap. 155.00 (*0-89766-871-5*) NY Acad Sci.

— The Uterus: Endometrium & Myometrium. LC 97-18287. (Annals of the New York Academy of Sciences Ser.: No. 828). 368p. 1997. 110.00 (*1-57331-104-9*) NY Acad Sci.

— The Uterus: Endometrium & Myometrium. LC 97-18287. (Annals of the New York Academy of Sciences Ser.). 1997. pap. 110.00 (*1-57331-105-7*) NY Acad Sci.

Bulley, Bishop. Glimpses of the Divine: A Spiritual Anthology for Use on Every Day of the Year. 2nd ed. 400p. 1994. pap. 24.95 (*1-898595-05-4*, Pub. by Alpha Pr Ltd) Intl Spec Bk.

Bulley, Cyril. Glass of Time. 2nd ed. 1994. pap. 19.95 (*1-898595-06-2*, Pub. by Alpha Pr Ltd) Intl Spec Bk.

***Bullfinch, Thomas.** Legends of Charlemagne: The Illustrated Bullfinch's Mythology. (Illus.). 160p. (YA). (gr. 9-12). 2000. reprint ed. 20.00 (*0-7881-6913-0*) DIANE Pub.

Bulli, John. Guitar History Vol. 2: Gibson SG. (Illus.). 46p. 1989. pap. 14.95 (*0-933224-20-6*, T017) Bold Strummer Ltd.

Bullians, Andrew M. Health, Wealth & Wisdom: Christian Principles for Prosperous Living. 1996. pap. 10.95 (*0-7880-0618-5*, Fairway Pr) CSS OH.

Bulliet, Richard W. The Camel & the Wheel. (Morningside Bk.). (Illus.). 352p. 1990. text 57.50 (*0-231-07234-1*); pap. text 19.00 (*0-231-07235-X*) Col U Pr.

— The Camel & the Wheel. LC 75-571. (Illus.). 341p. reprint ed. pap. 105.80 (*0-7837-1677-X*, 205720900024) Bks Demand.

— Conversion to Islam in the Medieval Period: An Essay in Quantitative History. LC 79-14411. (Illus.). 170p. reprint ed. pap. 52.70 (*0-7837-1676-1*, 205720800024) Bks Demand.

— Islam: The View from the Edge. 236p. 1994. 40.50 (*0-231-08218-5*) Col U Pr.

— Islam: The View from the Edge. 236p. 1995. pap. 18.00 (*0-231-08219-3*) Col U Pr.

— The Patricians of Nishapur: A Study in Medieval Islamic Social History. LC 70-173413. (Harvard Middle Eastern Studies: No. 16). (Illus.). 305p. 1972. reprint ed. pap. 94.60 (*0-7837-4454-4*, 205798400012) Bks Demand.

Bulliet, Richard W., et al. The Earth & Its Peoples: A Global History. (C). 1997. text, teacher ed. 11.96 (*0-395-81536-3*) HM.

— The Earth & Its Peoples: A Global History, 5 vols., Vols. I-II, A-C. 1056p. (C). 1997. text 64.76 (*0-395-52757-0*) HM.

— The Earth & Its Peoples Vol. I: A Global History: To 1500. 480p. (C). 1997. pap. text 46.76 (*0-395-53492-5*) HM.

— The Earth & Its Peoples Vol. II: A Global History: Since 1500. 560p. (C). 1997. pap. text 46.76 (*0-395-53493-3*) HM.

— The Earth & Its Peoples Vol. C: A Global History: Since 1750. 400p. (C). 1997. pap. text 39.16 (*0-395-81535-5*) HM.

— The Earth & Its Peoples Vol. A: A Global History: To 1200. 368p. (C). 1997. pap. text 39.16 (*0-395-81533-9*) HM.

— The Earth & Its Peoples Vol. B: A Global History: From 1200 to 1870. 448p. (C). 1997. pap. text 39.16 (*0-395-81534-7*) HM.

***Bulliett, Richard W.** Arab-Syrian Gentleman & Warrior in the Period of the Crusades: Memoirs of Usamah Ibn-Munqidh. 2000. 45.00 (*0-231-12124-5*); pap. text 16.50 (*0-231-12125-3*) Col U Pr.

— Columbia History of the 20th Century. 2000. pap. text 25.00 (*0-231-07629-0*) Col U Pr.

Bulliett, Richard W., ed. The Columbia History of the Twentieth Century. LC 97-39426. 620p. 1998. 52.50 (*0-231-07628-2*) Col U Pr.

Bullimore. Study Skills. (C). 1998. pap. text 9.95 (*0-7020-2287-X*, Pub. by W B Saunders) Saunders.

Bullimore, Tom. Baker Street Puzzles. LC 94-17217. (Illus.). 128p. 1994. pap. 5.95 (*0-8069-0856-4*) Sterling.

Bullinaria, John A., et al, eds. 4th Neural Computation & Psychology Workshop, London, 9-11 April 1997: Connectionist Representation. LC 97-33526. (Perspectives in Neural Computing Ser.). xiv, 343p. 1997. pap. 89.95 (*3-540-76208-6*) Spr-Verlag.

***Bulling, A., et al.** Body Explorer 2.0: An Interactive Multilingual Program on the Cross-Sectional Anatomy of the Visible Human - English, German, French, Spanish, Italian, PC Version. 2nd ed. (ENG, FRE & GER.). 20p. 1999. pap. 39.95 incl. cd-rom (*3-540-14793-4*) Spr-Verlag.

— BodyExplorer 2.0: An Interactive Multilingual Program on the Cross-Sectional Anatomy of the Visible Human - English, German, French, Spanish, Italian - Multi User Version. 2nd ed. 20p. 1999. pap. 259.00 incl. cd-rom (*3-540-14792-6*) Spr-Verlag.

Bullinger, E. W. The Church Epistles: Romans to Thessalonians - Their Importance, Order, Inter-Relation, Structure, Scope & Interpretation. 261p. 1997. reprint ed. 16.95 (*1-883228-17-4*) Invictus MI.

***Bullinger, E. W.** Companion Bible. large type ed. 2176p. 1999. 62.99 (*0-8254-2099-7*) Kregel.

— A Critical Lexicon & Concordance to the English & Greek New Testament. 1040p. 1999. 49.99 (*0-8254-2096-2*) Kregel.

Bullinger, E. W. Figures of Speech Used in the Bible. 1160p. 1968. reprint ed. 44.99 (*0-8010-0559-0*) Baker Bks.

— The Name of Jehovah in the Book of Esther. 24p. 1999. reprint ed. pap. 3.00 (*1-880573-76-8*) Bible Search Pubns.

***Bullinger, E. W.** The Spirits in Prison. 2nd ed. 36p. 2000. reprint ed. pap. 4.00 (*1-880573-58-X*) Bible Search Pubns.

Bullinger, Ethelbert W. The Book of Job. LC 90-36536. 224p. 1990. reprint ed. pap. 11.99 (*0-8254-2291-4*, Kregel Class) Kregel.

— Commentary on Revelation. LC 83-24917. 768p. 1990. pap. 25.99 (*0-8254-2289-2*, Kregel Class) Kregel.

— The Companion Bible. deluxe ed. 2176p. 1993. bond lthr. 84.99 (*0-8254-2179-9*, Kregel Class) Kregel.

— The Foundations of Dispensational Truth. 288p. 1993. reprint ed. 16.95 (*1-883228-02-6*) Invictus MI.

— Great Cloud of Witnesses in Hebrews Eleven. LC 79-14425. 472p. 1986. pap. 15.99 (*0-8254-2247-7*, Kregel Class) Kregel.

— How to Enjoy the Bible: A Guide to Better Understanding & Greater Enjoyment of God's Word. LC 89-77694. 464p. 1990. reprint ed. pap. 15.99 (*0-8254-2213-2*, Kregel Class) Kregel.

— The Names & Order of the Books of the Old Testament. 40p. 1996. reprint ed. pap. 3.00 (*1-880573-30-X*) Bible Search Pubns.

— Number in Scripture. LC 67-26498. 320p. 1980. pap. 12.99 (*0-8254-2238-8*, Kregel Class) Kregel.

— The Rich Man & Lazarus: The Intermediate State. LC 91-44383. 60p. 1992. pap. text 3.50 (*1-880573-01-6*) Bible Search Pubns.

— Ten Sermons on the Second Advent. LC 95-24908. 144p. 1996. pap. 9.99 (*0-8254-2162-4*, Kregel Class) Kregel.

— The Witness of the Stars. LC 68-16762. 296p. 1984. pap. 14.99 (*0-8254-2245-0*, Kregel Class) Kregel.

An Asterisk (*) at the beginning of an entry indicates that the title is appearing for the first time.

— The Witness of the Stars. 204p. 1996. reprint ed. pap. 16.50 (*0-7873-0132-9*) Hlth Research.

— Word Studies on the Holy Spirit. LC 85-7631. 232p. 1985. pap. 12.99 (*0-8254-2246-9*, Kregel Class) Kregel.

Bullinger, Ethelbert W., notes. The Companion Bible. 2176p. 1990. 54.99 (*0-8254-2203-5*, Kregel Class) Kregel.

— The Companion Bible. 2176p. 1993. 59.99 (*0-8254-2180-2*, Kregel Class) Kregel.

— The Companion Bible. deluxe ed. 2176p. 1990. bond lthr. 79.99 (*0-8254-2288-4*, Kregel Class) Kregel.

— The Companion Bible. deluxe ed. 2176p. 1994. bond lthr. 79.99 (*0-8254-2177-2*, Kregel Class) Kregel.

— The Companion Bible. deluxe ed. 2176p. 1994. bond lthr. 84.99 (*0-8254-2178-0*, Kregel Class) Kregel.

— The Companion Bible. deluxe ed. 2176p. 1995. lthr. 89.99 (*0-8254-2237-X*, Kregel Class) Kregel.

— The Companion Bible. deluxe ed. 2176p. 1995. lthr. 95.99 (*0-8254-2240-X*, Kregel Class) Kregel.

Bullinger, H. J., ed. Human Aspects in Computing: Proceedings of the 44th International Conference on Human-Computer Interaction, Stuttgart, Germany, Sept. 1-6, 1991, 2 vols., Set. (Advances in Human Factors-Ergonomics Ser.: Vol. 18). lx,1368p. 1991. 411.00 (*0-444-88775-X*) Elsevier.

— Human Aspects in Computing: Proceedings of the 44th International Conference on Human-Computer Interaction, Stuttgart, Germany, Sept. 1-6, 1991, Vol. 18A Design & Use of Interactive Systs & Work. 1402p. 1991. write for info. (*0-318-68818-2*) Elsevier.

— Human Aspects in Computing: Proceedings of the 44th International Conference on Human-Computer Interaction, Stuttgart, Germany, Sept. 1-6, 1991, Vol. 18B: Design & Use of Interactive Systs & Info. 1402p. 1991. write for info. (*0-318-68819-0*) Elsevier.

Bullinger, H. J. & Shackel, B. Human-Computer Interaction - Interact '87. xlii,1138p. 1987. 269.00 (*0-444-70304-7*) Elsevier.

Bullinger, H. J. & Warschat, Joachim, eds. Concurrent Simultaneous Engineering Systems: The Way to Successful Product Development. (Illus.). 394p. 1995. 87.95 (*3-540-76003-2*) Spr-Verlag.

Bullinger, Hans-Joerg. Software Ergonomics: Advocations & Applications for the Human Computer Interface. 1988. text 51.95 (*0-470-21177-6*) P-H.

***Bullinger, Hans-Jorg & Ziegler, Jurgen.** Human-Computer Interaction: Ergonomics & User Interfaces, Two, Set, one. 1384p. 1999. 395.00 (*0-8058-3391-9*) L Erlbaum Assocs.

— Human-Computer Interaction Vol. 2: Communication, Cooperation & Application Design. (Series in Human Factors). 1384p. 1999. 395.00 (*0-8058-3392-7*) L Erlbaum Assocs.

***Bullinger, Hans-Jorg & Ziegler, Jurgen, eds.** Human-Computer Interaction: Ergonomics & User Interfaces, 2, Set, one. (A Volume in LEA's Series in Human Factors). 1384p. 1999. 595.00 (*0-8058-3646-2*) L Erlbaum Assocs.

Bullinger, Heinrich. The Christian State of Matrimonye. Coverdale, Myles, tr. LC 74-80167. (English Experience Ser.: No. 646). 168p. 1974. reprint ed. 30.00 (*90-221-0646-2*) Walter J Johnson.

Bullington, Jeffery, et al, eds. Head in the Clouds, Feet on the Ground: Serials Vision & Common Sense. LC 99-25066. (Serials Librarian Ser.: Vol. 36, Nos. 1-4). 568p. 1999. text 75.00 (*0-7890-0768-1*) Haworth Pr.

***Bullington, Jennifer.** The Mysterious Life of the Body: A New Look at Psychosomatics. (Linkoping Studies in Arts & Science). (Illus.). 336p. 1999. pap. 52.50 (*91-22-01844-1*, Pub. by Almqvist) Coronet Bks.

Bullington, John J., jt. ed. see Ross, Robert W.

Bullington, Meade, ed. see Hermit.

Bullington, Rachel. The Alexis in the Saint Albans Psalter: A Look into the Heart of the Matter. LC 91-22717. (Studies in Medieval Literature: Vol. 4). 296p. 1991. text 15.00 (*0-8240-4038-4*, H1229) Garland.

Bullington, Ruth. Stars in My Eyes. (Illus.). 191p. 1998. pap. 25.00 (*1-880308-09-6*) Suntop.

Bullion, Alan J. India, Sri Lanka & the Tamil Crisis, 1976-1994: An International Perspective. 160p. 1995. 89.50 (*1-85567-374-6*) Bks Intl VA.

Bullions, Peter. The Principles of English Grammar. LC 82-10418. (American Linguistics Ser.). 264p. 1983. 50.00 (*0-8201-1386-7*) Schol Facsimiles.

Bullis, Don. The Old West Trivia Book. Shepherd, Robin, ed. LC 92-75447. (Illus.). 160p. (Orig.). 1992. pap. 10.95 (*0-935182-62-4*) Gem Guides Bk.

Bullis, Douglas. Culture Shock! Succeed in Business: Sri Lanka. LC 97-70776. (Culture Shock Ser.). 1997. pap. 12.95 (*1-55868-320-8*) Gr Arts Ctr Pub.

— Doing Business in Today's India. LC 97-1705. 344p. 1998. 69.50 (*1-56720-136-9*, Quorum Bks) Greenwood.

***Bullis, Douglas.** Fashion Asia. LC 00-101550. 208p. 2000. pap. 29.95 (*0-500-28238-2*, Pub. by Thames Hudson) Norton.

Bullis, Douglas. Preparing for Electronic Commerce in Asia. LC 98-7576. 288p. 1999. 69.50 (*1-56720-206-3*, Quorum Bks) Greenwood.

— Selling to India's Consumer Market. LC 97-1704. 312p. 1997. 69.50 (*1-56720-105-9*, Quorum Bks) Greenwood.

Bullis, Douglas & Mahanama. The Mahavamsa: The Great Chronicle of Sri Lanka. LC 98-12597. 480p. 1999. 70.00 (*0-89581-943-0*) Asian Humanities.

Bullis, Howard C. & Bullis, Rosemary A. Bullis Family Genealogy & Associated Families. LC 95-79658. 3700p. 1996. write for info. (*0-9645654-0-4*) R A Bullis.

Bullis, Janis. Braids & Bows for Kids. (Arts-Crafts-Cooking-Drawing Books for Children Ser.). (Illus.). 64p. (J). (ps up). 1995. lib. bdg. 17.95 (*1-56674-098-3*) Forest Hse.

— No-Sew, Low-Sew Interior Decor: Instant Style Using Easy Techniques: Gluing, Stapling, Fusing, Draping, Gathering. 128p. 1996. pap. 19.95 (*0-8019-8747-4*) Krause Pubns.

— Snazaroo Zoo: Great Faces & Easy Costumes to Bring Out the Animal in You. LC 96-38024. 96p. 1997. pap. 12.95 (*0-8019-8940-X*) Krause Pubns.

Bullis, Jerald. Orion. LC 76-40995. (Orig.). 1976. pap. 5.00 (*0-917492-03-X*) Jackpine Pr.

— Orion. deluxe limited num. ed. LC 76-40995. (Orig.). 1976. 10.00 (*0-917492-02-1*) Jackpine Pr.

Bullis, Michael & Davis, Cheryl. Functional Assessment in Transition & Rehabilitation for Adolescents & Adults with Learning Disorders. LC 98-30835. 1999. write for info. (*0-89079-803-6*) PRO-ED.

Bullis, Ronald K. Clinical Social Worker Misconduct: Law, Ethics & Interpersonal Dynamics. LC 94-43290. 1995. pap. text 29.95 (*0-8304-1327-8*) Thomson Learn.

— Law & Management of a Counseling Agency or Private Practice. Remley, Theodore P., Jr., ed. LC 92-20722. (ACA Legal Ser.: Vol. 3). 75p. (C). 1992. pap. text 18.95 (*1-55620-101-X*, 72303) Am Coun Assn.

— Spirituality in Social Work Practice. 200p. 1996. 59.95 (*1-56032-407-4*); pap. 24.95 (*1-56032-406-6*) Hemisp Pub.

— Spirituality in Social Work Practice. LC 96-7063. 1996. pap. write for info. (*1-56303-240-6*) Taylor & Francis.

Bullis, Ronald K. & Mazur, Cynthia S. Legal Issues & Religious Counseling. 112p. (Orig.). 1993. pap. 15.95 (*0-664-25386-5*) Westminster John Knox.

Bullis, Ronald K., jt. auth. see Mazur, Cynthia S.

Bullis, Rosemary A., jt. auth. see Bullis, Howard C.

Bullis, W. M., ed. see International Symposium on Very Large Scale Integr.

Bullis, W. Murray. Semiconductor Characterization: Present Status & Future Needs: Gaithersburg, MD, January 30-February 2, 1995. Seiler, D. G. & Diebold, A. C., eds. (Illus.). 730p. 1996. text 84.95 (*1-56396-503-8*) Spr-Verlag.

Bullitt, Alexander C. Rambles in the Mammoth Cave During the Year 1844 by a Visiter. LC 85-6698. (Illus.). 134p. 1985. pap. 5.95 (*0-939748-16-9*) Cave Bks MO.

Bullitt, Dorothy. Filling the Void: Six Steps from Loss to Fulfillment. 1996. 19.50 (*0-614-20429-1*, Scribners Ref) Mac Lib Ref.

Bullitt, Dorothy, jt. auth. see Wickwire, Jim.

Bullitt, Harriet & Woods, Wilfrid R. Chihuly: Icicles. LC 97-43757. (Illus.). 64p. 1997. 20.00 (*1-57684-006-9*) Portland Pr.

Bullitt-Jonas, Margaret. Holy Hunger: A Memoir of Desire. 2000. pap. 13.00 (*0-375-70087-0*) Knopf.

— Holy Hunger: A Memoir of Desire. LC RC552.C65B85 1999. 272p. 1998. 23.00 (*0-375-40094-X*) Random.

Bullitt, Stimson. Ancestral Histories of Scott Bullitt & Dorothy Stimson. LC 94-60563. (Illus.). 408p. 1999. 29.95 (*0-9631630-4-3*) Willows WA.

— River Dark & Bright: A Memoir. (Illus.). 400p. 1999. pap. text 15.95 (*0-9631630-6-X*) Willows WA.

— To Be a Politician. 448p. 1994. pap. 15.95 (*0-9631630-3-5*) Willows WA.

— To Be a Politician. rev. ed. LC 75-43310. 312p. reprint ed. pap. 96.80 (*0-8357-8767-2*, 203368500087) Bks Demand.

Bullitt, W. C., ed. see Freud, Sigmund.

Bullitt, William C., jt. auth. see Freud, Sigmund.

Bullivant, Brian M. Pluralism: Cultural Maintenance & Evolution. 126p. 1984. 69.00 (*0-905028-27-9*, Pub. by Multilingual Matters); pap. 24.95 (*0-905028-26-0*, Pub. by Multilingual Matters) Taylor & Francis.

Bullivant, Keith. The Future of German Literature. 224p. 1993. text 39.50 (*0-85496-978-0*) Berg Pubs.

— Realism Today: Aspects of the Contemporary West German Novel. LC 86-31018. 257p. 1987. 19.50 (*0-85496-521-1*) Berg Pubs.

Bullivant, Keith, ed. After the "Death of Literature" German Writing of the 1970s. LC 87-26796. 421p. 1989. 19.50 (*0-85496-017-6*) Berg Pubs.

— Beyond 1989: Re-Reading German Literature since 1945. LC 96-53154. (Modern German Studies: Vol. 3). 192p. 1997. 45.00 (*1-57181-037-4*); pap. 15.50 (*1-57181-038-2*) Berghahn Bks.

— The Modern German Novel. LC 86-32683. 314p. 1987. 19.50 (*0-85496-522-X*) Berg Pubs.

Bullivant, Lucy. International Interior Design, Vol. 4. (Illus.). 256p. 1993. 65.00 (*1-55859-235-0*) Abbeville Pr.

— International Interior Design 4. (Illus.). 256p. 1993. 65.00 (*1-55859-322-5*) Abbeville Pr.

***Bullivant, Lucy.** Kid Size: The Material World of Childhood. LC 98-129596. 1999. pap. 45.00 (*88-8118-254-8*) Skira IT.

Bullivant, Roger A. & Bradbury, H. W. Underpinning: A Practical Guide. 208p. 1996. text 75.00 (*0-632-04004-1*) Blackwell Sci.

Bullmore, Michael A. St. Paul's Theology of Rhetorical Style: An Examination of I Corinthians 2.1-5 - In the Light of First Century Graeco-Roman Rhetorical Culture. (Christian Universities Press Ser.). (Orig.). 1995. pap. 49.95 (*1-57309-018-2*); text 69.95 (*1-57309-019-0*) Intl Scholars.

Bulloch, Anthony, et al. Images & Ideologies: Self-Definition in the Hellenistic World. LC 92-10371. (Hellenistic Culture & Society Ser.: Vol. 12). 1993. 65.00 (*0-520-07526-9*, Pub. by U CA Pr) Cal Prin Full Svc.

Bulloch, David. Whalewatcher's Handbook: A Field Guide to the Whales, Dolphins, & Porpoises of North America. (Illus.). 128p. 1993. pap. 13.95 (*1-55821-232-9*) Lyons Pr.

Bulloch, Gavin, et al. Operations in Troubled States: Post-Cold War Operations & Peace Talks. 87p. (C). 1998. reprint ed. pap. text 30.00 (*0-7881-3877-4*) DIANE Pub.

***Bulloch, Ivan.** An Acrobat. rev. ed. (I Want to Be Ser.). (Illus.). (J). 2000. 9.95 (*1-58728-080-9*); pap. 5.95 (*1-58728-086-8*) Two Can Pub.

— An Actor. rev. ed. (I Want to Be Ser.). (Illus.). (J). 2000. 9.95 (*1-58728-081-7*); pap. 5.95 (*1-58728-087-6*) Two Can Pub.

— The Big Play Book. rev. ed. (Illus.). (J). 2000. 19.95 (*1-58728-535-5*) Two Can Pub.

Bulloch, Ivan. Cartoons & Animation. (Arts & Crafts Skills Ser.). 1999. pap. text 6.95 (*0-516-26342-0*) Childrens.

***Bulloch, Ivan.** A Clown. rev. ed. (I Want to Be Ser.). (Illus.). (J). 2000. 9.95 (*1-58728-082-5*); pap. 5.95 (*1-58728-088-4*) Two Can Pub.

— Cook. rev. ed. (Let's Ser.). (Illus.). (J). 2000. 9.95 (*1-58728-025-6*); pap. 4.95 (*1-58728-029-9*) Two Can Pub.

— Cooking. (I Can Do It Ser.). (Illus.). (J). 2000. 12.95 (*1-58728-510-X*) Two Can Pub.

— Cooking. rev. ed. (I Can Do It Ser.). (Illus.). (J). 2000. pap. 5.95 (*1-58728-511-8*) Two Can Pub.

— A Cowboy. rev. ed. (I Wish I Were Ser.). (Illus.). (J). 2000. 9.95 (*1-58728-035-3*); pap. 4.95 (*1-58728-039-6*) Two Can Pub.

— A Fairy. rev. ed. (I Wish I Were Ser.). (Illus.). (J) 2000. 9.95 (*1-58728-036-1*); pap. 4.95 (*1-58728-040-X*) Two Can Pub.

— Gardening. rev. ed. (I Can Do It Ser.). (Illus.). (J). 2000. 12.95 (*1-58728-500-2*); pap. 5.95 (*1-58728-501-0*) Two Can Pub.

— A Juggler. rev. ed. (I Want to Be Ser.). (Illus.). (J). 2000. 9.95 (*1-58728-083-3*); pap. 5.95 (*1-58728-089-2*) Two Can Pub.

— A Magician. rev. ed. (I Want to Be Ser.). (Illus.). (J). 2000. 9.95 (*1-58728-084-1*); pap. 5.95 (*1-58728-090-6*) Two Can Pub.

— Make Toys. rev. ed. (Let's Ser.). (Illus.). (J). 2000. 9.95 (*1-58728-028-0*); pap. 4.95 (*1-58728-032-9*) Two Can Pub.

— Measure. rev. ed. (Action Math Ser.). (Illus.). (J). 2000. pap. 4.95 (*1-58728-051-5*) Two Can Pub.

— Paint. rev. ed. (Let's Ser.). (Illus.). (J). 2000. 9.95 (*1-58728-026-4*) Two Can Pub.

— Patterns. rev. ed. (Action Math Ser.). (Illus.). (J). 2000. pap. 4.95 (*1-58728-053-1*) Two Can Pub.

— A Pirate. rev. ed. (I Wish I Were Ser.). (Illus.). (J) 2000. 9.95 (*1-58728-034-5*); pap. 4.95 (*1-58728-038-8*) Two Can Pub.

Bulloch, Ivan. Play with Models. LC 94-14248. (Play with Crafts Ser.). 24p. (J). (ps-2). 1995. lib. bdg. 19.95 (*0-87614-866-6*, Carolrhoda) Lerner Pub.

***Bulloch, Ivan.** Play with Paper. rev. ed. (Let's Ser.) (Illus.). (J). 2000. 9.95 (*1-58728-027-2*); pap. 4.95 (*1-58728-031-0*) Two Can Pub.

— A Princess. rev. ed. (I Wish I Were Ser.). (Illus.). (J). 2000. 9.95 (*1-58728-033-7*); pap. 4.95 (*1-58728-037-X*) Two Can Pub.

— A Puppeteer. rev. ed. (I Want to Be Ser.). (Illus.). (J). 2000. 9.95 (*1-58728-085-X*); pap. 5.95 (*1-58728-091-4*) Two Can Pub.

— Sands Like Smelly! rev. ed. (My Turn Ser.). (Illus.). (J). 2000. 4.95 (*1-58728-011-6*) Two Can Pub.

— Shapes. rev. ed. (Illus.). (J). 2000. pap. 4.95 (*1-58728-054-X*) Two Can Pub.

***Bulloch, Ivan & James, Diana.** Paint. (Let's Ser.). (Illus.). (J). 2000. pap. 4.95 (*1-58728-030-2*) Two Can Pub.

Bulloch, Ivan, et al. Games. LC 96-49562. (Action Math Ser.). (Illus.). 32p. (J). (gr. k-3). 1998. write for info. (*0-7166-4900-4*) World Bk.

— Measure. LC 96-49797. (Action Math Ser.). (Illus.). 32p. (J). (gr. k-3). 1997. 10.00 (*0-7166-4906-3*) World Bk.

— Patterns. LC 96-49559. (Action Math Ser.). (Illus.). 32p. (J). (gr. k-3). 1997. write for info. (*0-7166-4902-0*) World Bk.

— Shapes. LC 96-49558. (Action Math Ser.). (Illus.). 32p. (J). (gr. k-3). 1997. write for info. (*0-7166-4904-7*) World Bk.

Bulloch, J. G. Bailey: The Baillies of Inverness, Scotland, & Some of Their Descendants in the U. S. 86p. 1952. reprint ed. pap. 17.00 (*0-8328-2626-X*); reprint ed. lib. bdg. 27.00 (*0-8328-2625-1*) Higginson Bk Co.

— The Cuthberts, Barons of Castle Hill & Their Descendants in South Carolina & Georgia. (Illus.). 1993. reprint ed. pap. 19.00 (*0-8328-1395-8*); reprint ed. lib. bdg. 29.00 (*0-8328-1394-X*) Higginson Bk Co.

— Glen. History of the Glen Family of South Carolina & Georgia. 134p. 1991. reprint ed. pap. 22.00 (*0-8328-1972-7*); reprint ed. lib. bdg. 32.00 (*0-8328-1971-9*) Higginson Bk Co.

Bulloch, James, tr. The Scots Confession of 1560. (C). 1989. pap. 25.00 (*0-86153-063-2*, Pub. by St Andrew) St Mut.

Bulloch, James, jt. auth. see Drummond, Andrew L.

Bulloch, John. Death of a Country: The Civil War in Lebanon LC 77-366205. 202p. 1977. write for info. (*0-297-77288-0*) Weidenfeld & Nicolson.

— Studies on the Text of Shakespeare. LC 75-39557. reprint ed. 41.50 (*0-404-01227-2*) AMS Pr.

Bulloch, John M. Gordon. The Gordons in Forfarshire, with the Lairds of Ashludie, Dnavourd, Tryiew, Threave & Charleton. 31p. 1997. reprint ed. pap. 6.00 (*0-8328-8795-1*); reprint ed. lib. bdg. 16.00 (*0-8328-8794-3*) Higginson Bk Co.

— Gordon. The Gordons of Nethermuir. 52p. 1997. reprint ed. pap. 10.50 (*0-8328-8797-8*); reprint ed. lib. bdg. 20.50 (*0-8328-8796-X*) Higginson Bk Co.

Bulloch, John M., ed. Gordon: The House of Gordon, 3 vols., Set. (Illus.). 1992. reprint ed. pap. 249.50 (*0-8328-2477-1*); reprint ed. lib. bdg. 275.00 (*0-8328-2476-3*) Higginson Bk Co.

Bulloch, Joseph G. Bailey. History & Genealogy of the Family of Baillie of Dunain, Duchfour & Lamington, with a Short Sketch of McIntosh, Bulloch & Other Families. 111p. 1997. reprint ed. pap. 18.00 (*0-8328-7325-X*); reprint ed. lib. bdg. 28.00 (*0-8328-7324-1*) Higginson Bk Co.

— Bayard. History & Genealogy of the Families of Bayard, Houstoun of Ga. & the Descent of the Bolton Family from Assheton, Byron & Hulton of Hulton Park. (Illus.). 76p. 1997. reprint ed. pap. 14.00 (*0-8328-7427-2*); reprint ed. lib. bdg. 24.00 (*0-8328-7426-4*) Higginson Bk Co.

— Bellinger. History & Genealogy of the Families of Bellinger & DeVeaux, & Other Families. 109p. 1997. reprint ed. pap. 18.00 (*0-8328-7481-7*); reprint ed. lib. bdg. 28.00 (*0-8328-7480-9*) Higginson Bk Co.

Bulloch, Kathleen. Bargains Connecticut: A Shopper's Guide to Connecticut's Discount, Bargain & Factory Outlet Stores. 360p. 1996. pap. 16.95 (*1-887870-02-4*) Ashlor Pubng.

Bulloch, Kathleen & Hall, Heidi. Consign Connecticut: A Shopper's Guide to Connecticut's Consignment Stores. 2nd rev. ed. 380p. (Orig.). 1996. pap. 16.95 (*1-887870-01-6*) Ashlor Pubng.

— Consign Connecticut: A Shopper's Guide to Connecticut's Consignment Stores 1995-1996 Edition. 364p. 1995. pap. 15.95 (*1-887870-00-8*) Ashlor Pubng.

Bulloch, Kathleen L. The Phantom Tollbooth: Literature Unit. (Illus.). 48p. (Orig.). 1994. pap., student ed. 7.95 (*1-55734-431-0*) Tchr Create Mat.

Bullock, ed. Adult Health Nursing. (C). 1990. text. write for info. (*0-321-01538-X*) Addson-Wesley Educ.

Bullock, A. Richard. Sabbatical Planning: For Clergy & Congregations. pap. 8.25 (*1-56699-019-X*) Alban Inst.

Bullock, Alan. Has History a Future? 10p. (Orig.). 1977. pap. text 10.50 (*0-8191-5846-1*) U Pr of Amer.

***Bullock, Alan.** Hitler: A Study in Tyranny. 848p. 1999. 14.98 (*1-56852-036-0*) W S Konecky Assocs.

Bullock, Alan. Hitler: A Study in Tyranny. abr. ed. LC 90-55030. 512p. 1991. reprint ed. pap. 17.00 (*0-06-092020-3*, Perennial) HarperTrade.

— Hitler & Stalin: Parallel Lives. LC 92-56376. 1993. pap. 23.00 (*0-679-72994-1*) Vin Bks.

— Meeting Teachers' Management Needs. 184p. 1990. 85.00 (*1-870167-05-8*, Pub. by P Francis) St Mut.

— Natalia Ginzburg: Human Relationships in a Changing World. LC 90-39079. (Women's Ser.). 269p. 1991. 59.50 (*0-85496-178-X*) Berg Pubs.

— Norton Dictionary of Modern Thought. LC 99-24581. 1999. 59.95 (*0-393-04696-6*) Norton.

— The Past & the Future. 48p. (Orig.). 1982. pap. text 12.50 (*0-8191-5871-2*) U Pr of Amer.

Bullock, Alan, jt. contrib. by see Pimlott, John.

Bullock, Alan, ed. see Oxford University, British Commonwealth Group Staf.

Bullock, Alice. Living Legends: Stories of Early New Mexico. LC 72-90383. (Illus.). 1978. pap. 6.95 (*0-913270-06-7*) Sunstone Pr.

— Loretto & the Miraculous Staircase: How a Famous Staircase Was Built. LC 78-18526. (Illus.). 1978. pap. 2.95 (*0-931270-80-4*) Sunstone Pr.

— Monumental Ghosts: Legends. LC 85-8164. 48p. (Orig.). 1987. pap. 5.95 (*0-86534-029-3*) Sunstone Pr.

— Mountain Villages: Historic Sites in New Mexico. 3rd ed. LC 81-5687. (Illus.). 1991. pap. 8.95 (*0-913270-13-X*) Sunstone Pr.

Bullock, Alison & Thomas, Hywel. Schools at the Centre? A Study of Decentralisation. LC 96-26284. (Illus.). 248p. (C). 1997. pap. 25.99 (*0-415-12911-7*) Routledge.

Bullock, Angela. Making Teddy Bears in Miniature. LC 98-186640. (Illus.). 96p. (Orig.). 1997. pap. 19.95 (*0-87588-497-0*, H5382) Hobby Hse.

Bullock, Barbara L. Pathophysiology: Adaptations & Alterations in Function. 4th ed. LC 95-32143. 1,296p. 1995. text 63.95 (*0-397-55164-9*) Lppncott W & W.

Bullock, Barbara L. & Henze, Reet. Focus on Pathophysiology. LC 99-16400. 1,200p. 1999. pap. text 44.95 (*0-7817-1736-1*) Lppncott W & W.

Bullock, Brenda. A Pocket with a Hole. large type ed. 1997. 24.95 (*0-7531-5034-4*, Pub. by ISIS Lrg Prnt) Transaction Pubs.

Bullock, C. Hassell. An Introduction to the Old Testament Poetic Books. 29.99 (*0-8024-4141-6*, 185) Moody.

Bullock, C. Hassell. An Introduction to the Old Testament Prophetic Books. 391p. 29.99 (*0-8024-4142-4*, 186) Moody.

Bullock, Caroline C., jt. ed. see Whitney, Annie W.

Bullock, Cary. A Guide to Energy Services Companies. LC 99-52102. (Illus.). 185p. 2000. 82.00 (*0-88173-292-3*, 0421) Fairmont Pr.

Bullock, Charles & Mahon, Michael. Introduction to Recreation Services for People with Disabilities: A Person-Centered Approach. (Illus.). 464p. 1997. text 44.95 (*1-57167-069-6*) Sagamore Pub.

Bullock, Charles J. Economic Essays. LC 68-16915. (Essay Index Reprint Ser.). 1977. 26.95 (*0-8369-0263-7*) Ayer.

— Essays on the Monetary History of the United States. LC 69-18301. 292p. 1969. reprint ed. lib. bdg. 35.00 (*0-8371-0332-0*, BUMH, Greenwood Pr) Greenwood.

— The Finances of the United States from Seventeen Seventy-Five to Seventeen Eighty-Nine: With Special Reference to the Budget. LC 79-12742. (Perspectives in American History Ser.: No. 52). (Illus.). viii, 157p. 1979. reprint ed. lib. bdg. 29.50 (*0-87991-821-7*) Porcupine Pr.

B

An Asterisk (*) at the beginning of an entry indicates that the title is appearing for the first time.

B

Bullock, Charles S., 3rd. The Georgia Political Almanac: The General Assembly 1991-1992. Holiman, Michael R., ed. (Illus.). 282p. (Orig.). (C). 1991. pap. 49.95 (0-9631729-0-5) Cornerstn GA.

— The Georgia Political Almanac: The General Assembly 1993-1994. Holiman, Michael R., ed. (Illus.). 321p. (Orig.). (C). 1993. pap. 45.00 (0-9631729-1-3) Cornerstn GA.

Bullock, Charles S., III. The Georgia Political Almanac: The General Assembly 1995-1996. Holiman, Michael R., ed. (Illus.). 346p. (Orig.). (C). 1995. pap. 45.00 (0-9631729-2-1) Cornerstn GA.

Bullock, Charles S., 3rd. The Georgia Political Almanac: The General Assembly 1997-1998. Holiman, Michael R., ed. (Illus.). 350p. (Orig.). 1997. pap. 45.00 (0-9631729-4-8) Cornerstn GA.

Bullock, Charles S., III. The Partisan, Racial, & Gender Makeup of Georgia County Offices. LC 93-19837. (Public Policy Research Ser.). 1993. 5.00 (0-89854-168-9) U of GA Inst Govt.

Bullock, Charles S., III & Johnson, Loch K. Runoff Elections in the United States. LC 92-53626. (Thornton H. Brooks Series in American Law & Society). xxii, 206p. (C). 1992. 39.95 (0-8078-2053-9) U of NC Pr.

Bullock, Charles S., III & Rozell, Mark J., eds. The New Politics of the Old South: An Introduction to Southern Politics. LC 97-36019. 296p. (Orig.). 1998. 63.00 (0-8476-8612-4); pap. 19.95 (0-8476-8613-2) Rowman.

Bullock, Charles S., III, jt. auth. see Gaddie, Ronald Keith.

Bullock, Charles S., III, ed. see Cubbage, Frederick W. & O'Laughlin, Jay.

Bullock, Chris & Peck, David, compiled by. Guide to Marxist Literary Criticism. LC 79-3627. 192p. 1980. 32.50 (0-253-13144-8) Ind U Pr.

***Bullock, Craig.** The Path to Healing: Experiencing God as Love. 1999. pap. 14.95 (1-929342-04-7) Olde Ridge Bk.

Bullock, D. J. & Goldspink, C. R., eds. Management, Welfare & Conservation of Park Deer. 107p. 1992. pap. 30.00 (0-900767-79-0, Pub. by Univs Fed Animal Welfare) St Mut.

Bullock, David W., jt. ed. see Glasser, Stanley R.

Bullock-Davies, Constance. English Pronunciation from the Fifteenth to the Eighteenth Century: A Handbook to the Study of Historical Grammar. LC 75-109726. 180p. 1970. reprint ed. lib. bdg. 55.00 (0-8371-4216-4, DAEP, Greenwood Pr) Greenwood.

Bullock, Diane, et al. DB2 Universal Database & SAP R/3 Version 4. (IBM DB2 Certification Guide Ser.). 514p. 1999. pap. text 54.99 (0-13-082426-7) P-H.

Bullock, Donald H. Programmed Instruction. Langdon, Danny G., ed. LC 77-25108. (Instructional Design Library). (Illus.). 112p. 1978. 27.95 (0-87778-118-4) Educ Tech Pubns.

Bullock, Edna, jt. auth. see Bullock-Wilson, Barbara.

Bullock, Eulala, compiled by. Sermons of Evangelist Rolfe Barnard, Vol. 3. 1984. pap. 4.99 (1-56632-091-7) Revival Lit.

— Sermons of Evangelist Rolfe Bernard, 1904-1969, Vol. 1. (C). 1985. pap. 4.99 (1-56632-086-0) Revival Lit.

— Sermons of Evangelist Rolfe Bernard, 1904-1969, Vol. 2. 1984. pap. 4.99 (1-56632-087-9) Revival Lit.

Bullock, Freddy. LAX: Los Angeles International Airport. LC 98-36676. (Airport Ser.). (Illus.). 112p. 1998. pap. 15.95 (0-7603-0653-2) MBI Pubg.

— Pacific Glory: Airlines of the Great Ocean. LC 99-27102. (Illus.). 112p. 1999. pap. 24.95 (0-7603-0700-8, 128433AP) MBI Pubg.

Bullock, Gillian R. Techniques in Immunocytochemistry, Vol. 1. Petrusz, Peter, ed. 306p. 1986. pap. text 58.00 (0-12-140404-8) Acad Pr.

— Techniques in Immunocytochemistry, Vol. 2. Petrusz, Peter, ed. 290p. 1986. pap. text 58.00 (0-12-140405-6) Acad Pr.

— Techniques in Immunocytochemistry, Vol. 3. Petrusz, Peter, ed. 241p. 1988. reprint ed. pap. text 58.00 (0-12-140406-4) Acad Pr.

— Techniques in Immunocytochemistry, Vol. 4. Petrusz, Peter, ed. 400p. 1989. text 104.00 (0-12-140407-2) Acad Pr.

Bullock, Gillian R., et al, eds. Techniques in Diagnostic Pathology Vol. 2: ELISA Techniques - New Developments & Practical Applications in a Broad Field. (Illus.). 176p. 1991. text 83.00 (0-12-681912-2) Acad Pr.

Bullock, Gillian R. & Petrusz, Peter. Techniques in Immunocytochemistry, Vol. 3. 1985. text 104.00 (0-12-140403-X) Acad Pr.

Bullock, Gloria S. & Crocitto, Jane B. Shopping at the Ani-Mall. Weinberger, Jane, ed. LC 90-70908. (Illus.). 44p. (J). (ps-3). 1991. pap. 3.95 (0-932433-72-3) Windswept Hse.

Bullock, Harold B. The Battle for the Worlds. 2nd rev. ed. Anderson, Jean, ed. (Tarlian Adventures Ser.: Vol. 1). 120p. (J). (gr. 2-5). Date not set. reprint ed. pap. write for info. (1-929248-00-8) Golden Oak Pubs.

— The City in the Clouds. Dumas, Barbara, ed. (Tarlian Adventures Ser.: Vol. 5). 120p. (J). (gr. 2-5). 2001. pap. write for info. (1-929248-08-3) Golden Oak Pubs.

— Consider Jesus Christ. Dumas, Barbara, ed. 50p. 1999. pap. write for info. (1-929248-27-X) Golden Oak Pubs.

— The Crystal Castle. Dumas, Barbara, ed. (Tarlian Adventures Ser.: Vol. 2). 140p. (J). (gr. 2-5). 1999. pap. write for info. (1-929248-02-4) Golden Oak Pubs.

— The Dragon of Raldan. Dumas, Barbara, ed. (Tarlian Adventures Ser.: Vol. 3). 120p. (J). (gr. 2-5). 1999. pap. write for info. (1-929248-04-0) Golden Oak Pubs.

— The Dreamweaver. Dumas, Barbara, ed. (Tarlian Adventures Ser.: Vol. 4). 120p. (J). (gr. 2-5). 2000. pap. write for info. (1-929248-06-7) Golden Oak Pubs.

— God Is Speaking to You. Dumas, Barbara, ed. 100p. 1999. pap. write for info. (1-929248-25-3) Golden Oak Pubs.

Bullock, Hazel J. Grammaire Francaise: Methode Orale. (C). 1949. 24.00 (0-89197-493-8); pap. text 15.50 (0-89197-775-9) Irvington.

Bullock, Helen. Williamsburg Art of Cookery. LC 43-6700. (Illus.). 276p. (Orig.). 1966. 14.95 (0-910412-30-8) Colonial Williamsburg.

Bullock, Henry A. A History of Negro Education in the South: From 1619 to the Present. LC 67-20873. 355p. reprint ed. pap. 110.10 (0-7837-2057-2, 204233200004) Bks Demand.

Bullock, Ian, jt. auth. see Barrow, Logie.

Bullock, J., et al. Physiology. 2nd ed. (National Medical Ser.). (Illus.). 501p. 1991. 25.00 (0-683-06258-1) Lppncott W & W.

Bullock, J. A., jt. ed. see Harper, D. M.

Bullock, J. Benbow. Art for Instant Printing. (Illus.). 100p. (Orig.). 1982. pap. 8.95 (0-937024-03-1) Gourmet Guides.

— Stars for Lincoln, Doctors & Dogs. LC 80-66936. (Illus.). 100p. (Orig.). 1981. pap. 4.95 (0-937024-00-7) Gourmet Guides.

Bullock, J. Floyd. The Clingan Clan: Family History 1600-1981 (Clingan Family & Descendants) 1981. pap. 17.00 (0-916660-21-4) Hse of York.

Bullock, Jack. Combo Sounds of the Big Band Era Vol. 2: Eb Instruments. 28p. 1989. reprint ed. pap. 7.00 (0-7692-1400-2, SB291) Wrner Bros.

Bullock, Jack, ed. Bebop Bass. 44p. (Orig.). (C). 1994. pap. text 6.50 (0-7692-0968-8, SB106) Wrner Bros.

Bullock, Jack & Maiello, Anthony. Belwin 21st Century Band Method: Level 2, B Clarinet. Proctor, Thom, ed. 32p. (Orig.). 1997. pap. text 5.95 (1-57623-998-5, B21204) Wrner Bros.

Bullock, Jack, ed. see Lee, William.

Bullock, Jackson F. The People's Biographer Workbook. 2nd ed. 182p. 1995. pap., student ed. 19.95 (0-9639778-0-6); spiral bd. 19.95 (0-9639778-1-4) Peoples Biographer.

— The People's Biographer Workbook (Afrocentric Version) A Structured Biography Writing Guide for the Nonprofessional Writer. (Illus.). 182p. 1996. pap., wbk. ed. 19.95 (0-9639778-4-9) Peoples Biographer.

— The People's Biographer Workbook (Christian Version) A Structured Biography Writing Guide for the Nonprofessional Writer. (Illus.). 182p. (Orig.). 1996. pap. 19.95 (0-9639778-5-7) Peoples Biographer.

***Bullock, James, et al, eds.** Shaping Projects. 2000. 21.45 (0-932633-48-X) Dorset Hse Pub Co.

Bullock, James R., ed. Introduction to Public Speaking. (C). 1998. text. write for info. (0-321-01203-8) Addson-Wesley Educ.

Bullock, Jeffrey F. Preaching with a Cupped Ear: Hans-Georg Gadamer's Philosophical Hermeneutics As Postmodern Wor(l)d. LC 97-27265. (Berkeley Insights in Linguistics & Semiotics Ser.: Vol. 34). X, 204p. (C). 1999. text 46.95 (0-8204-3898-7) P Lang Pubng.

Bullock, Jocelyn. I Can Do Anyhting! Melpomene Institutes Activity Book for Girls. 45p. (J). (ps-6). 1998. pap. 6.00 (0-9651137-1-X) Melpomene Inst.

Bullock, John. The Rootes Brothers: Story of a Motoring Empire. (Illus.). 256p. 1994. 34.95 (1-85260-454-9, Pub. by J H Haynes & Co) Motorbooks Intl.

Bullock, John, et al. NMS Physiology. 4th ed. 575p. 27.00 (0-683-30603-0) Lppncott W & W.

— Physiology. 3rd ed. LC 93-23683. (National Medical Series for Independent Study). (Illus.). 648p. 1995. 25.00 (0-683-06259-X) Lppncott W & W.

Bullock, Joyce, ed. COGEL Blue Book, 1990-91: Campaign Finance, Ethics & Lobby Law. 8th ed. 200p. 1990. pap. 45.00 (0-87292-956-6, C-173 090) Coun State Govts.

Bullock, Karen O. The Writings of Justin Martyr. LC 98-21265. (Shepherd's Notes Ser.). 1999. 5.95 (0-8054-9220-8) Broadman.

Bullock, Kathleen. A Friend for Mitzi Mouse. LC 90-31559. (Illus.). 40p. (J). (ps-1). 1990. pap. 13.95 (0-671-68867-7) Litle Simon.

— It Chanced to Rain. LC 87-32070. (Illus.). (J). (ps-1). 1992. pap. 3.95 (0-671-77820-X) S&S Bks Yung.

— The Rabbits Are Coming! (J). (ps). 1991. pap. 13.95 (0-671-72963-2) S&S Bks Yung.

— She'll Be Comin' Round the Mountain. LC 92-17340. (J). 1993. mass mkt. 14.00 (0-671-79153-2) S&S Bks Yung.

Bullock, Kathryn R., ed. see Symposium on Advances in Lead-Acid Batteries Staff.

Bullock, Lyndal M., et al, eds. Improving the Social Skills of Children with Emotional/Behavioral Disorders. 120p. 1996. pap. 22.00 (0-86586-283-4) Coun Exc Child.

— Understanding Individual Differences: Highlights from the National Symposium of What Educators Should. 50p. 1996. pap. 13.95 (0-86586-288-5) Coun Exc Child.

***Bullock, Lyndal M. & Gable, Robert A.** Implementing the 1997 IDEA: New Challenges & Opportunities for Serving Students. 1998. pap. 19.95 (0-86586-337-7) Coun Exc Child.

***Bullock, Lyndal M. & Menendez, Anthony L.** Historical Chronology of the Council for Children with Behavioral Disorders, 1964-1999. (What Works for Children & Youth with Emotional/Behavior Disorders Ser.). 59p. 1999. pap. 11.40 (0-86586-351-2) Coun Exc Child.

Bullock, Lyndal M., et al. Educational Aspects of Behavioral Problems in Children & Youth, Vol. 1. LC 74-1011. 437p. 1974. text 38.50 (0-8422-5159-6) Irvington.

— Educational Aspects of Behavioral Problems in Children & Youth, Vol. 2. LC 74-1011. 225p. 1974. text 32.50 (0-8422-5160-X) Irvington.

***Bullock, Lyndal M., et al.** Preparation of Teachers of Students with Emotional/Behavioral Disorders. 122p. 1998. pap. 19.95 (0-86586-321-0) Coun Exc Child.

Bullock, Marcus, ed. Walter Benjamin Vol. 1: Selected Writings, 1913-1926. 1996. 35.00 (0-614-20693-6) HUP.

Bullock, Marcus, ed. see Benjamin, Walter.

Bullock, Mary B. & Litwak, Robert S., eds. The United States & the Pacific Basin: Changing Economic & Security Relationships. (Woodrow Wilson Center Special Studies: No. 2). 80p. 1991. pap. text 7.00 (0-943875-31-5) W Wilson Ctr Pr.

Bullock, Mary B., jt. ed. see Garby, Craig C.

***Bullock, Melissa.** Cadenza: The Literary Annual of Hume Fogg. 2000. write for info. (1-930142-51-X) Write Together.

Bullock, Merry, ed. The Development of Intentional Action: Cognitive, Motivational, & Interactive Processes. (Contributions to Human Development Ser.: Vol. 22). (Illus.). x, 84p. 1991. 64.50 (3-8055-5411-7) S Karger.

Bullock, Michael, tr. see Bachmann, Ingeborg.

Bullock, Michael, tr. see Frisch, Max.

Bullock, Michael, tr. see Goll, Yvan.

Bullock, Michael, tr. see Jaspers, Karl.

Bullock, Michael, tr. see Worringer, Wilhelm.

Bullock, Nigel, et al. Essential Urology. 2nd ed. LC 93-20138. (Illus.). 384p. 1993. pap. text 36.00 (0-443-04807-X) Church.

Bullock, P. & Gregory, P. Soils in the Urban Environment. 1991. 95.00 (0-632-02988-9) Blackwell Sci.

***Bullock, Patrick & North, Patsy.** Charcoal Pocket Studio. (Illus.). 48p. (YA). (gr. 7). 2000. write for info. (0-8230-5628-7) Watsn-Guptill.

Bullock, Paul. Aspiration vs. Opportunity: 'Careers' in the Inner City. LC 73-620101. (Policy Papers in Human Resources & Industrial Relations Ser.: No. 20). 180p. 1973. 10.00 (0-87736-122-3); pap. 5.00 (0-87736-123-1) U of Mich Inst Labor.

— CETA at the Crossroads: Employment Policy & Politics. (Monograph & Research Ser.: No. 29). 280p. 1981. 8.50 (0-89215-113-7) U Cal LA Indus Rel.

— Youth Training & Employment: From New Deal to New Federalism. (Monograph & Research Ser.: No. 43). 359p. 1985. 15.00 (0-89215-133-1) U Cal LA Indus Rel.

Bullock, Penelope L. The Afro-American Periodical Press, 1838-1909. fac. ed. LC 81-1712. (Illus.). 344p. 1981. reprint ed. pap. 106.70 (0-7837-7938-0, 204769400008) Bks Demand.

Bullock, Peter, et al. Deciphering Anasazi Violence: With Regional Comparisons to Meso American & Woodland Cultures. (Illus.). 150p. 1998. pap. 20.00 (0-9665859-0-9) HRM Bks.

Bullock, R. J. Improving Job Satisfaction. (Studies in Productivity: Highlights of the Literature Ser.: Vol. 35). 45p. 1984. pap. 55.00 (0-08-030967-4) Work in Amer.

Bullock, Ralph W. In Spite of Handicaps: Brief Biographical Sketches with Discussion Outlines of Outstanding Negroes Now Living Who Are Achieving Distinction in Various Lines of Endeavor. LC 68-25602. (Essay Index Reprint Ser.). 1977. 23.95 (0-8369-0264-5) Ayer.

Bullock, Richard. The St. Martin's Manual for Writing in the Disciplines: A Guide for Faculty. 76p. 1994. pap. text 6.95 (0-312-09573-2) St Martin.

Bullock, Richard, et al, eds. The Politics of Writing Instruction: Postsecondary. LC 90-5217. 311p. (Orig.). (C). (gr. 13). 1991. pap. text 27.50 (0-86709-272-6, 0272, Pub. by Boynton Cook Pubs) Heinemann.

Bullock, Richard, jt. ed. see Bissex, Glenda L.

Bullock, Richard H., ed. Why Workshop? Changing Course in 7-12 English. LC 98-24010. (Illus.). 160p. 1998. pap. text 17.50 (1-57110-084-9) Stenhse Pubs.

Bullock, Richard L., jt. ed. see Gertsch, Richard E.

Bullock, Robert. The Great Plains: A Young Reader's Journal. LC 86-81461. (Wilderness Habitat Ser.). (Illus.). 64p. (Orig.). (J). (gr. k-8). 1987. pap. 7.95 (0-943972-10-8) Homestead WY.

— The Rocky Mountains: A Young Reader's Journal. LC 93-77117. (Illus.). 64p. (Orig.). (J). (gr. k-5). 1994. pap. 8.95 (0-943972-18-3) Homestead WY.

***Bullock, Robert.** Silent Song. deluxe ed. (Illus.). 32p. 1999. pap. 14.95 (1-929278-00-4) RBullock Ent.

Bullock, Robert M., 3rd & White, Robert. Bullock on Boxes. LC 90-83309. (Illus.). 72p. 1991. pap. text 10.95 (0-9624191-5-X) Audio Amateur.

Bullock, Robin. Midnight Howl: Intermediate Level. 72p. 1997. pap. 11.95 (0-7866-2072-2, 96006) Mel Bay.

***Bullock, Roger.** Secure Treatment Outcomes (P) The Care Careers of Very Difficult Adolescents. LC 98-70908. (Dartington Social Research Ser.). 155p. 1998. 51.95 (1-84014-498-X) Ashgate Pub Co.

Bullock, Roger & Little, Michael. Secure Treatment Outcomes (P) The Care Careers of Very Difficult Adolescents. Millham, Spencer, ed. LC 98-70908. (Dartington Social Research Ser.: Vol. 2). (Illus.). 180p. 1998. pap. 16.95 (1-84014-458-0, Pub. by Ashgate Pub) Ashgate Pub Co.

Bullock, Roger, et al. Children Returning Home: The Re-Unification of Families. LC 98-34053. (Dartington Social Research Ser.). xi, 261p. 1998. pap. 16.95 (1-84014-496-3, Pub. by Ashgate Pub); text 51.95 (1-84014-494-7, Pub. by Ashgate Pub) Ashgate Pub Co.

— Going Home: The Return of Children Separated from Their Families. 272p. 1993. pap. 26.95 (1-85521-329-X, Pub. by Dartmth Pub) Ashgate Pub Co.

— Research in Practice: Experiments in Development & Information Design. LC 98-70903. (Dartington Social Research Ser.: Vol. 3). 120p. 1998. pap. 16.95 (1-84014-459-9, Pub. by Ashgate Pub) Ashgate Pub Co.

Bullock, Roger, jt. ed. see Harrigan, Stuart.

***Bullock, Ross, et al, eds.** Neuromonitoring in Brain Injury. LC 99-46769. (Acta Neurochirurgica Ser.: Suppl. 75'). (Illus.). 80p. 1999. 54.00 (3-211-83379-X) Spr-Verlag.

Bullock, Ross, jt. ed. see Reilly, Peter.

Bullock, Scott R. Transceiver System Design for Digital Communications. Breed, Gary A. & Hammond, Crawford, eds. (Illus.). 432p. 1995. 54.00 (1-884932-46-0) Noble Pubng.

***Bullock, Shan F.** Thomas Andrews, Shipbuilder. LC 99-196652. 1999. 22.95 (0-85640-655-4, Pub. by Blackstaff Pr) Dufour.

Bullock, Shan F. A Titanic Hero. 22.95 (0-8488-0928-9) Amereon Ltd.

Bullock, Steven C. Revolutionary Brotherhood: Freemasonry & the Transformation of the American Social Order, 1730-1840. LC 95-39554. (Published for the Omohundro Institute of Early American History & Culture, Williamsburg, Virginia Ser.). (Illus.). 448p. 1996. 49.95 (0-8078-2282-5) U of NC Pr.

— Revolutionary Brotherhood: Freemasonry & the Transformation of the American Social Order, 1730-1840. LC 95-39554. (Published for the Omohundro Institute of Early American History & Culture, Williamsburg, Virginia Ser.). (Illus.). 448p. 1998. pap. 19.95 (0-8078-4750-X) U of NC Pr.

Bullock, Susan. Women & Work. (Women & World Development Ser.). (C). 1994. text 59.95 (1-85649-117-X, Pub. by Zed Books); text 22.50 (1-85649-118-8, Pub. by Zed Books) St Martin.

Bullock, Terry L. & Hesse, Karl D. Reading in the Social Studies Classroom. 64p. 1981. pap. 8.95 (0-8106-3202-0) NEA.

Bullock, Theodore H. How Do Brains Work? Papers of a Comparative Neurophysiologist. LC 93-17434. (Contemporary Neuroscientists Ser.). (Illus.). 656p. 1993. 176.00 (0-8176-3535-1) Birkhauser.

Bullock, Theodore H., ed. Contributions to Neuroethology: In Memory of Walter F. Heiligenberg International Symposium, La Joll, California, January 1995. (Brain, Behavior & Evolution Ser.: Vol. 50, Suppl. 1, 1997). (Illus.). iv, 88p. 1997. pap. 38.25 (3-8055-6533-X) S Karger.

Bullock, Theodore H., jt. ed. see Basar, E.

Bullock, Thomas & Knight, Greg R. Thomas Bullock Journal. 101p. 1994. 39.95 (0-910523-09-6) Grandin Bk Co.

Bullock, Tom. Astronomy: Second Contact. 4th ed. 544p. 1996. per. 87.95 (0-7872-2428-6, 41242801) Kendall-Hunt.

Bullock, Walter, jt. auth. see Archer, Daniel.

Bullock, Waneta B. & Loveless, Ganelle. ABC Mazes. (Ann Arbor Educational Ser.). (Illus.). 56p. (J). (gr. k-1). 1979. pap. 8.00 (0-87879-713-0, Ann Arbor Div) Acad Therapy.

Bullock, Waneta B., jt. auth. see Vitale, Barbara M.

Bullock, William, jt. auth. see Maidment, Robert.

Bullock, William J. Bach Cantatas Requiring Limited Resources: A Guide to Editions. LC 84-2337. 58p. (C). 1984. lib. bdg. 20.50 (0-8191-3863-0) U Pr of Amer.

Bullock, William P., Jr., jt. ed. see Rogers, Jerry S.

Bullock-Wilson, Barbara & Bullock, Edna. Edna's Nudes. LC 94-45672. (Illus.). 112p. (Orig.). 1995. pap. 28.95 (0-88496-393-4) Capra Pr.

Bullock, Wynn. Wynn Bullock. LC 98-86907. (Masters of Photography Ser.). (Illus.). 96p. 1998. 18.95 (0-89381-827-5) Aperture.

Bullock, Wynn, photos by. Bullock Wynn: The Enchanted Landscape, Photographs 1940-1975. (Illus.). 120p. 1993. 68.00 (0-89381-546-2) Aperture.

Bullokar, John. An English Expositor: Teaching the Interpretation of the Hardest Words Used in Our Language. (Anglistica & Americana Ser.: No. 71). 224p. 1971. reprint ed. 70.00 (3-487-04070-0) G Olms Pubs.

Bullokar, William. Booke at Large (Fifteen Eighty) & Brief Grammar for English (Fifteen Eighty-Six) LC 76-55723. 168p. 1977. reprint ed. 50.00 (0-8201-1287-9) Schol Facsimiles.

— Bullokars Booke at Large for the Amendment of Orthographie for English Speech. LC 68-54622. (English Experience Ser.: No. 24). 110p. 1968. reprint ed. 25.00 (90-221-0024-3) Walter J Johnson.

***Bullon-Fernandez, Maria.** Fathers & Daughters in Gower's Confessio Amantis: Authority, Family, State & Writing. LC 99-57065. (Publications of the John Gower Society). 320p. 2000. 90.00 (0-85991-578-6, DS Brewer) Boydell & Brewer.

Bullough, Bonnie. The Elusive Eden. 2nd ed. LC 95-82034. 678p. (C). 1996. pap. 59.38 (0-07-047908-9) McGraw.

— Gender Blending. LC 96-51743. (Illus.). 524p. 1997. 34.95 (1-57392-124-6) Prometheus Bks.

Bullough, Bonnie, et al, eds. How I Got into Sex. LC 96-46523. 480p. 1997. 29.95 (1-57392-115-7) Prometheus Bks.

Bullough, Bonnie & Bullough, Vern, eds. Nursing Issues for the Nineties & Beyond. LC 92-49817. 248p. (C). 1994. text 29.95 (0-8261-8050-7) Springer Pub.

Bullough, Bonnie & Rosen, George. Preventive Medicine in the United States 1900-1990: Trends & Interpretations. LC 92-20428. 1992. 15.95 (0-88135-180-6, Sci Hist); pap. 11.95 (0-88135-177-6, Sci Hist) Watson Pub Intl.

Bullough, Bonnie, jt. auth. see Bullough, Vern L.

Bullough, Bonnie, jt. ed. see Bullough, Vern L.

Bullough, Edward. Aesthetics: Lectures & Essays. Wilkinson, Elizabeth M., ed. LC 77-21814. 158p. 1977. reprint ed. lib. bdg. 49.75 (0-8371-9789-9, WIAE, Greenwood Pr) Greenwood.

Bullough, Edward, tr. see Gilson, Etienne.

Bullough, Geoffrey. Narrative & Dramatic Sources of Shakespeare, Vol. 8. 1975. text 99.00 (0-231-08898-1) Col U Pr.

Bullough, Geoffrey, ed. see Milton, John.

Bullough, Margaret, ed. see Milton, John.

Bullough, Robert V., Jr. Democracy in Education: Boyd H. Bode. LC 80-84621. 258p. 1981. lib. bdg. 36.95 (0-930390-37-7) Gen Hall.

Bullough, Robert V., Sr. Display Boards. Duane, James E., ed. LC 80-21332. (Instructional Media Library: Vol. 3). (Illus.). 112p. 1981. 27.95 (0-87778-163-X) Educ Tech Pubns.

An Asterisk (*) at the beginning of an entry indicates that the title is appearing for the first time.

Bullough, Robert V. First Year Teacher: A Case Study. 176p. 1989. pap. text 18.95 (*0-8077-2934-5*) Tchrs Coll.
— The Forgotten Dream of American Public Education. LC 88-6786. 158p. 1988. reprint ed. pap. 49.00 (*0-608-06851-9*, 206705700009) Bks Demand.

Bullough, Robert V., Sr. Multi-Image Media. Duane, James E., ed. LC 80-21341. (Instructional Media Library: Vol. 9). (Illus.). 128p. 1981. 27.95 (*0-87778-169-9*) Educ Tech Pubns.
— Photography. Duane, James E., ed. LC 80-21333. (Instructional Media Library: Vol. 11). (Illus.). 104p. 1981. 27.95 (*0-87778-171-0*) Educ Tech Pubns.

Bullough, Robert V. & Baughman, Kerrie. "First-Year Teacher" Eight Years Later: An Inquiry into Teacher Development. LC 97-14053. 386p. (Orig.). 1997. text 46.00 (*0-8077-3651-1*); pap. text 20.95 (*0-8077-3650-3*) Tchrs Coll.

Bullough, Robert V., Jr. & Gitlin, Andrew. Becoming a Student of Teaching: Methodologies for Exploring Self & School Context. LC 94-28785. (Critical Education Practice Ser.: Vol. 2). 288p. 1994. text 51.00 (*0-8153-0916-3*, SS853); pap. text 22.95 (*0-8153-1624-0*) Garland.

Bullough, Robert V., Jr., et al. Human Interests in the Curriculum: Teaching & Learning in a Technological Society. 160p. (C). 1984. pap. text 16.95 (*0-8077-2745-8*) Tchrs Coll.
— Human Interests in the Curriculum: Teaching & Learning in a Technological Society. LC 83-10063. 155p. 1984. reprint ed. pap. 48.10 (*0-608-02763-4*, 206382900007) Bks Demand.

Bullough, Vern. Sex, Society & History. 1976. 15.00 (*0-88202-154-0*) Watson Pub Intl.

Bullough, Vern, ed. The Frontiers of Sex Research. LC 79-2462. 198p. (C). 1979. pap. 18.95 (*0-87975-113-4*) Prometheus Bks.

Bullough, Vern & Brundage, James A., eds. Sexual Practices & the Medieval Church. LC 80-85227. 289p. 1982. reprint ed. pap. 23.95 (*0-87975-268-8*) Prometheus Bks.

Bullough, Vern, et al. Florence Nightingale & Her Era: A Collection of New Scholarship. LC 89-25949. 400p. 1990. text 20.00 (*0-8240-6998-6*, SS629) Garland.
— Issues in Nursing: An Annotated Bibliography. LC 84-48758. 600p. 1985. text 25.00 (*0-8240-8768-2*) Garland.

Bullough, Vern, jt. auth. see Freeman, Sarah.

Bullough, Vern, jt. ed. see Bullough, Bonnie.

***Bullough, Vern L.** Encyclopedia of Birth Control. 2001. lib. bdg. 75.00 (*1-57607-181-2*) ABC-CLIO.

Bullough, Vern L. Sexual Variance in Society & History. LC 79-26504. 733p. reprint ed. pap. 200.00 (*0-608-09272-X*, 205414600004); reprint ed. pap. 200.00 (*0-608-20616-4*, 2054584) Bks Demand.
— The Society for the Scientific Study of Sex: A Brief History. 44p. 1989. pap. write for info. (*0-318-65755-4*) FSS Sexuality.

***Bullough, Vern L., et al, eds.** American Nursing: A Biographical Dictionary. (Illus.). 360p. 2000. text 69.95 (*0-8261-1296-X*) Springer Pub.

***Bullough, Vern L. & Brundage, James A., eds.** Handbook of Medieval Sexuality. 440p. 2000. pap. 27.95 (*0-8153-3662-4*) Garland.

Bullough, Vern L. & Brundage, James A., eds. Handbook of Medieval Sexuality: A Book of Essays. LC 95-52021. (Reference Library of the Humanities: Vol. 1696). 464p. 1996. text 80.00 (*0-8153-1287-3*, H1696) Garland.

Bullough, Vern L. & Bullough, Bonnie. Contraception: A Guide on Birth Control Methods. 2nd ed. LC 97-23707. (Illus.). 216p. 1997. pap. text 18.95 (*1-57392-159-9*) Prometheus Bks.
— Cross Dressing, Sex, & Gender. LC 92-32030. 400p. (Orig.). (C). 1993. text 54.95 (*0-8122-3163-5*); pap. text 18.95 (*0-8122-1431-5*) U of Pa Pr.
— Sexual Attitudes: Myths & Realities. LC 94-47645. 281p. 1995. 31.95 (*0-87975-949-6*) Prometheus Bks.
— The Subordinate Sex: A History of Attitudes Towards Women. LC 72-91079. 383p. reprint ed. pap. 118.80 (*0-608-10727-1*, 201493000093) Bks Demand.
— Women & Prostitution: A Social History. LC 86-43207. 390p. 1987. pap. 22.95 (*0-87975-372-2*) Prometheus Bks.

Bullough, Vern L. & Bullough, Bonnie, eds. Human Sexuality: An Encyclopedia, 2 vols. LC 93-32686. (Illus.). 668p. 1994. text 50.00 (*0-8240-7972-8*, SS685) Garland.

Bullough, Vern L., et al. The Subordinated Sex: A History of Attitudes Toward Women. rev. ed. LC 87-23292. 488p. 1988. pap. 24.95 (*0-8203-1003-4*) U of Ga Pr.

Bullough, Vern L., jt. auth. see Freeman, Sarah.

Bullough, W. A., jt. auth. see Tomlinson, Geoffrey R.

Bullrich, Kurt. Die Farbigen Dammerungserscheinngen. 100p. 1982. 17.95 (*0-8176-1355-2*) Birkhauser.

Bullrich, Silvina. Tomorrow I'll Say, Enough. Miller, Yvette E. et al, eds. Smith, Julia S., tr. from SPA. LC 95-21098. (Discoveries Ser.). 192p. (Orig.). (C). 1996. pap. 15.95 (*0-935480-70-6*) Lat Am Lit Rev Pr.

Bullshows, Harry & Gilliland, Hap. Legends of Chief Bald Eagle. (J). (gr. 2-10). 1997. pap. 1.95 (*0-89992-052-7*) Coun India Ed.

Bullwinkle, Davis A., compiled by. African Women: A General Bibliography, 1976-1985, 9. LC 88-37379. (African Special Bibliographic Ser.: No. 9). 354p. 1989. lib. bdg. 75.00 (*0-313-26607-7*, BAK, Greenwood Pr) Greenwood.
— Women of Eastern & Southern Africa: A Bibliography, 1976-1985, 11. LC 89-2154. 570p. 1989. lib. bdg. 85.00 (*0-313-26606-9*, BWM, Greenwood Pr) Greenwood.
— Women of Northern, Western, & Central Africa: A Bibliography, 1976-1985, 10. LC 89-2160. (African Special Bibliographic Ser.: No. 10). 628p. 1989. lib. bdg. 85.00 (*0-313-26609-3*, BWY, Greenwood Pr) Greenwood.

Bulmahn, Heinz. Adolf Glassbrenner: His Development from "Jungdeutscher" to "Vormarzler" (German Language & Literature Monographs: No. 6). x, 159p. 1978. 39.00 (*90-272-0966-9*, GLLM 6) J Benjamins Pubng Co.

Bulman-Fleming, Barbara. Hemispheric Specialisation in Animals & Humans: A Special Issue of Laterality. 1998. 64.95 (*0-86377-964-6*) L Erlbaum Assocs.

Bulman, George. Play the Game: Volleyball. (Illus.). 80p. 1998. pap. 10.95 (*0-7063-7683-8*, Pub. by WrLock) Sterling.
— Volleyball. LC 96-12405. (Know the Sport Ser.). 48p. 1996. pap. 5.95 (*0-8117-2829-3*) Stackpole.

Bulman, James C. The Heroic Idiom of Shakespearean Tragedy. LC 84-40061. 256p. 1985. 36.50 (*0-87413-271-1*) U Delaware Pr.
— Shakespeare. LC 95-12968. 224p. (C). 1995. pap. 24.99 (*0-415-11626-0*) Routledge.

Bulman, James C., jt. ed. see Braumuller, A. R.

Bulman, Joan. Strindberg & Shakespeare: Shakespeare's Influence on Strindberg's Historical Drama. LC 73-153482. (Studies in Comparative Literature: No. 35). 1971. reprint ed. lib. bdg. 75.00 (*0-8383-1239-X*) M S G Haskell Hse.

Bulman, Nachman, tr. see Kitov, Eliyahu, et al.

Bulman, Nathan, tr. see Kitov, Eliyahu.

Bulman, O. M. Treatise on Invertebrate Paleontology Pt. V: Graptolithina. rev. ed. Moore, Raymond C., ed. LC 53-12913. (Illus.). 195p. 1970. 16.75 (*0-8137-3123-2*) Geol Soc.

Bulman, Philip M. Caught in the Mix: An Oral Portrait of Homelessness. LC 92-43385. 224p. 1993. 57.95 (*0-86569-229-7*, T229, Auburn Hse) Greenwood.

Bulman, R. S. & Cooper, J. R., eds. Speciation of Fission & Activation Products in the Environment. 434p. 1986. mass mkt. 155.50 (*0-85334-422-1*) Elsevier.

Bulman, Raymond F. A Blueprint for Humanity: Paul Tillich's Theology of Culture. 248p. 1972. 36.50 (*0-8387-5000-1*) Bucknell U Pr.
— The Lure of the Millennium: The Year 2000 & Beyond. rev. ed. LC 99-18537. (Illus.). 250p. 1999. pap. 18.00 (*1-57075-253-2*) Orbis Bks.

Bulman, Raymond F. & Parella, Frederick J., eds. Paul Tillich: A New Catholic Assessment. 360p. (Orig.). 1994. pap. text 19.95 (*0-8146-5828-8*, M Glazier) Liturgical Pr.

Bulmash, Gary F. Mastering Adjusting Entries: Accruals & Deferrals. 10th unabridged ed. 150p. 1989. pap. text 39.00 (*1-884826-25-3*) AIPB.

Bulmer. Citizenship Today: The Contemporary Relevance of T. H. Marshall. 256p. 1996. 65.00 (*1-85728-471-2*, Pub. by UCL Pr Ltd); pap. 24.95 (*1-85728-472-0*, Pub. by UCL Pr Ltd) Taylor & Francis.
— Social Research in Developing Countries: Surveys & Censuses in the Third World. 383p. 1993. pap. 32.50 (*1-85728-137-3*, Pub. by UCL Pr Ltd) Taylor & Francis.

Bulmer, Charles, jt. auth. see Carmichael, John, Jr.

Bulmer, David. Functional Anatomy of the Urogenital System. (Illus.). 184p. 1974. pap. 27.95 (*0-8464-0444-3*) Beekman Pubs.

Bulmer, Judith. Kid Kapers: Using Science for Learning Language. LC 94-67964. 1994. pap. text 10.95 (*0-9642403-0-0*) Sci & Lang Pr.
— Smart Kids: 101 Ways to Increase Language, Reading, Writing & Math Skills. LC 97-92576. 128p. 1998. pap. 10.95 (*0-9642403-1-9*) Sci & Lang Pr.

Bulmer, M. G. The Biology of Twinning in Man. LC 71-498413. 215p. reprint ed. pap. 66.70 (*0-8357-7246-2*, 205131300094) Bks Demand.
— Principles of Statistics. LC 78-72991. 252p. (C). 1979. reprint ed. pap. 8.95 (*0-486-63760-3*) Dover.

Bulmer, Martin. The Chicago School of Sociology: Institutionalization, Diversity, & the Rise of Sociological Research. LC 84-8494. (Illus.). xx, 306p. 1997. pap. text 15.95 (*0-226-08005-6*) U Ch Pr.
— The Chicago School of Sociology: Institutionalization, Diversity, & the Rise of Sociological Research. LC 84-8494. (The Heritage of Sociology Ser.). 305p. Date not set. reprint ed. pap. 94.60 (*0-608-20671-7*, 207210800003) Bks Demand.
— Essays on the History of British Sociological Research. (Illus.). 273p. 1985. text 69.95 (*0-521-25477-9*) Cambridge U Pr.
— Racism. LC 99-21004. (Oxford Readers Ser.). 400p. (C). 1999. pap. text 21.95 (*0-19-289300-9*) OUP.
— The Social Basis of Community Care. LC 87-988. 247p. 1987. 55.00 (*0-04-361072-2*); pap. 18.95 (*0-04-361073-0*) Routledge.
— Working-Class Images of Society. (Modern Revivals in Sociology Ser.). 296p. (Orig.). (C). 1994. text 61.95 (*0-7512-0288-6*, Pub. by Gregg Revivals) Ashgate Pub Co.

Bulmer, Martin, ed. Sociological Research Methods. 2nd ed. 450p. (C). 1984. pap. 18.95 (*0-333-37346-4*) Transaction Pubs.
— Sociological Research Methods. 2nd ed. 450p. 1999. pap. 29.95 (*0-87855-814-4*) Transaction Pubs.

Bulmer, Martin, et al, eds. The Goals of Social Policy. 224p. 1989. text 49.95 (*0-04-445131-8*) Routledge.

Bulmer, Martin & Solomos, John. Ethnic & Racial Studies Today. LC 98-30802. 1999. write for info. (*0-415-18172-0*); pap. 24.99 (*0-415-18173-9*) Routledge.

Bulmer, Martin & Warwick, Donald P., eds. Social Research in Developing Countries: Surveys & Censuses in the Third World. LC 83-6970. (Social Development in the Third World Ser.). (Illus.). 401p. reprint ed. pap. 124.40 (*0-8357-7524-0*, 203603100097) Bks Demand.

Bulmer, Martin, et al. Directory of Social Research Organisations in the United Kingdom. 2nd ed. 416p. 1998. pap. 75.00 (*0-7201-2371-2*) Continuum.
— Social Science & Social Policy. (Contemporary Social Research Ser.: No. 12). 272p. (C). 1987. text 49.95 (*0-04-312025-3*); pap. text 19.95 (*0-04-312026-1*) Routledge.

Bulmer, Michael. Theoretical Evolutionary Ecology. LC 93-34424. (Illus.). 332p. (C). 1994. text 65.00 (*0-87893-079-5*); pap. text 39.95 (*0-87893-078-7*) Sinauer Assocs.

Bulmer, Miriam, ed. see Irvine, Ronald A. & Clore, Walter J.

Bulmer, Miriam, ed. see O'Connell, Caroline & Davenport, Megan.

Bulmer, Peter R., jt. auth. see Sheperd, Stewart R.

***Bulmer, Robert.** Essential Cyprus. 2nd ed. (AAA Essential Guides Ser.). 128p. 2000. pap. 8.95 (*0-658-00627-4*, 006274) NTC Contemp Pub Co.

Bulmer, Simon. The Changing Agenda in West German Public Policy. (Association for the Study of German Politics Ser.). 206p. 1989. text 67.95 (*1-85521-041-X*, Pub. by Dartmth Pub) Ashgate Pub Co.
— The Federal Republic of Germany & the European Community. 224p. 1987. text 60.00 (*0-04-382045-X*); pap. text 21.95 (*0-04-382046-8*) Routledge.

Bulmer, Simon. Germanys European Diplomacy. text. write for info. (*0-7190-5854-6*, Pub. by Manchester Univ Pr) St Martin.
— Germany's European Diplomacy. pap. write for info. (*0-7190-5855-4*, Pub. by Manchester Univ Pr) St Martin.

Bulmer-Thomas, Barbara. Journey Through Mexico. LC 90-10950. (Illus.). 32p. (J). (gr. 3-5). 1991. pap. 4.95 (*0-8167-2117-3*) Troll Communs.

Bulmer-Thomas, Victor. The Economic History of Latin America since Independence. LC 93-36441. (Latin American Studies: No. 77). (Illus.). 505p. (C). 1995. text 80.00 (*0-521-36329-2*); pap. text 22.95 (*0-521-36872-3*) Cambridge U Pr.
— Input-Output Analysis in Developing Countries: Sources, Methods, & Applications. LC 81-19826. (Illus.). 313p. reprint ed. pap. 97.10 (*0-8357-7525-9*, 203603200097) Bks Demand.
— The United States & Latin America: The New Agenda. 420p. 1999. pap. text 24.95 (*0-674-92596-3*) HUP.

Bulmer-Thomas, Victor, ed. Britain & Latin America: A Changing Relationship. (Illus.). 256p. (C). 1989. text 59.95 (*0-521-37205-4*) Cambridge U Pr.

Bulmer-Thomas, Victor, et al, eds. Mexico & the North American Free Trade Agreement. LC 94-5688. (Who Will Benefit? Ser.). 1994. text 55.00 (*0-312-12176-8*) St Martin.

***Bulmer-Thomas, Victor & Dunkerley, James, eds.** The United States & Latin America: The New Agenda. 420p. 1999. text 39.95 (*0-674-92595-5*) HUP.

Bulmore, Lawrence, jt. auth. see Lanyen, Milton.

Bulnes Aldunate, Jose M., ed. see Universidad de Puerto Rico, Centro de Investigacio.

Bulock, Lynn. And Mommy Makes Three. (Romance Ser.). 1996. per. 3.25 (*0-373-19154-5*, 1-19154-3) Silhouette.
— Dalton's Dilemma. LC 98-13725. 1998. pap. 9.99 (*1-57673-238-X*, Palisades OR) Multnomah Pubs.
— Dalton's Dilemma. large type ed. LC 98-48573. 1999. 30.00 (*0-7862-1745-6*) Thorndike Pr.
— Gifts of Grace. (Love Inspired Ser.: No. 80). 1999. per. 4.50 (*0-373-87080-9*, 1-87080-7) Harlequin Bks.
— Heart Games. large type ed. LC 92-14125. 231p. 1992. reprint ed. lib. bdg. 13.95 (*1-56054-442-2*) Thorndike Pr.

***Bulock, Lynn.** Island Breeze. LC 98-27819. 1999. pap. 6.99 (*1-57673-398-X*, Palisades OR) Multnomah Pubs.
— Looking for Miracles, Vol. 97. (Love Inspired Ser.). 2000. mass mkt. 4.50 (*0-373-87103-1*, Steeple Hill) Harlequin Bks.

Bulock, Lynn. The Promise of Summer. large type ed. 154p. 1993. reprint ed. pap. 13.95 (*1-56054-677-8*) Thorndike Pr.
— Surprise Package: (Under the Mistletoe) (Romance Ser.). 1994. per. 2.75 (*0-373-19053-0*, 1-19053-7) Silhouette.
— Surrender. LC 1997. 286p. 1997. pap. 9.99 (*1-57673-104-9*, Multnomah Bks) Multnomah Pubs.

Buloff, Joseph. From the Old Marketplace. LC 90-4649. (Illus.). 344p. 1991. text 25.95 (*0-674-32503-6*, BULFRO) HUP.
— From the Old Marketplace. Singer, Joseph, tr. from YID. 344p. 1992. pap. text 12.95 (*0-674-32504-4*) HUP.

Bulos, Dan & Forsman, Sarah. OLAP Database Design: Delivering on the Promise of the Data Warehouse. 400p. 1999. pap. text 49.95 (*1-55860-525-8*, Pub. by Morgan Kaufmann) Harcourt.

Bulos, Marjorie & Teymur, Necdet, eds. Housing: Design, Research, Education. (Ethnoscapes: Current Challenges in the Environmental Social Science Ser.). 288p. 1993. 72.95 (*1-85628-515-4*, Pub. by Avebry) Ashgate Pub Co.

Bulosan, Carlos. America Is in the Heart. (American Autobiography Ser.). 326p. 1995. reprint ed. lib. bdg. 89.00 (*0-7812-8467-8*) Rprt Serv.

Bulosan, Carlos. America Is in the Heart. LC 73-13007. 352p. 1973. reprint ed. pap. 13.95 (*0-295-95289-X*) U of Wash Pr.

Bulosan, Carlos. The Cry & the Dedication. Juan, E. San, Jr., ed. & intro. by. LC 94-29767. (Asian American History & Culture Ser.). (C). 1995. pap. text 22.95 (*1-56639-296-9*); lib. bdg. 69.95 (*1-56639-295-0*) Temple U Pr.

Bulosan, Carlos, Jr. & San Juan, E. The Philippines Is in the Heart: A Collection of Short Stories. (Illus.). 1979. pap. 15.00 (*971-10-0306-6*, Pub. by New Day Pub) Cellar.

Bulot, Regis. Relais et Chateaux: Relais Gourmand, 1994. (FRE.). 612p. 1994. 14.95 (*0-614-00405-5*, 2950788904) Fr & Eur.

***Bulow & Cramer.** Cramer-Bulow: Etudes. 1999. pap. 7.95 (*963-9059-41-2*) Kone Music.

Bulow, Bernhard H. Imperial Germany. Lewenz, Marie A., tr. LC 78-12268. (Illus.). 342p. 1979. reprint ed. lib. bdg. 65.00 (*0-313-21176-0*, BUIG, Greenwood Pr) Greenwood.

Bulow, Ernie. Navajo Taboos. (Illus.). 216p. 1991. 19.95 (*0-914001-02-7*); pap. 12.95 (*0-914001-01-9*) Buffalo Med.

Bulow, Hans Von, see Von Bulow, Hans.

Bulow-Jacobsen, Adam, jt. auth. see Ryholt, K. S. B.

Bulpett, C. W., ed. King of the Wa-Kikuyu. (Illus.). 320p. 1968. reprint ed. 45.00 (*0-7146-1638-9*, Pub. by F Cass Pubs) Intl Spec Bk.

Bulpitt, Christopher J. Randomised Controlled Clinical Trials. LC 96-41439. 1983. text 139.50 (*90-247-2749-9*) Kluwer Academic.
— Randomised Controlled Clinical Trials. 2nd ed. LC 96-41439. 448p. (C). 1996. text 205.50 (*0-7923-4257-7*) Kluwer Academic.

Bulsara, Adi, jt. ed. see Kadtke, James B.

Bulsara, J. Perspectives in Social Welfare in India. 226p. 1984. 22.95 (*0-318-36854-4*) Asia Bk Corp.

Bulsara, Sohrab J., tr. Aerpatastan & Niragastan: Or, the Code of the Holy Doctorship, etc. LC 74-21249. reprint ed. 57.50 (*0-404-12800-9*) AMS Pr.

Bulsari, A. B., ed. Neural Networks for Chemical Engineers. LC 95-9927. (Computer-Aided Chemical Engineering Ser.: Vol. 6). 694p. 1995. 310.50 (*0-444-82097-3*) Elsevier.

Bulson, P. S. Explosions & Structures. LC 98-116254. (Illus.). xxxi, 236p. (C). 1997. 110.00 (*0-419-16930-X*, E & FN Spon) Routledge.

Bulson, P. S., ed. Aluminium Structural Analysis: Recent European Advances. (Illus.). 380p. (C). (gr. 13). 1992. text 185.00 (*1-85166-660-5*) Elsevier Applied Sci.
— Engineering Structures: Developments in the Twentieth Century. 418p. 1983. 32.00 (*0-86292-105-8*) Am Soc Civil Eng.
— Rapidly Assembled Structures. LC 91-70382. (Topics in Engineering Ser.: Vol. 8). 314p. 1991. 115.00 (*1-56252-063-6*) Computational Mech MA.
— Structures under Shock & Impact. LC 89-61081. (SUSI Ser.: Vol. 1). 541p. 1989. 149.00 (*0-945824-21-1*) Computational Mech MA.
— Structures under Shock & Impact: Proceedings of the First International Conference (SUSI '89), Cambridge, MA, 11-13 July, 1989. 534p. 1989. 227.50 (*0-444-88024-0*) Elsevier.

Bulst, Neithard & Genet, Jean, eds. Medieval Lives & the Historian: Studies in Medieval Prosopography. 1986. pap. 19.95 (*0-918720-70-2*); boxed set 39.95 (*0-918720-69-9*) Medieval Inst.

Bulst, Neithard, tr. see Glaber, Rodulfus.

Bultema, Harry. Commentary on Daniel. LC 88-777. 368p. 1992. pap. 12.99 (*0-8254-2262-0*) Kregel.

Bultema, Patrick. Fifth Annual International Help Desk Conference: Monday Proceedings. Etchison, Jim et al, eds. (Illus.). (Orig.). pap. text. write for info. (*1-57125-005-0*) Help Desk Inst.
— Fifth Annual International Help Desk Conference: Tuesday Proceedings. Etchison, Jim et al, eds. (Illus.). (Orig.). pap. text. write for info. (*1-57125-006-9*) Help Desk Inst.
— Fifth Annual International Help Desk Conference Overview. Etchison, Jim et al, eds. (Illus.). (Orig.). pap. text. write for info. (*1-57125-008-5*) Help Desk Inst.
— Fifth International Help Desk Conference: Wednesday-Thursday Proceedings. Etchison, Jim et al, eds. (Illus.). (Orig.). pap. text. write for info. (*1-57125-007-7*) Help Desk Inst.
— The Help Desk Salary Survey, 1994. Etchison, Jim et al, eds. (Illus.). (Orig.). pap. text. write for info. (*1-57125-010-7*) Help Desk Inst.
— How to Design & Write Effective Customer Satisfaction Surveys. Etchison, Jim & Rhoades-Baum, Patrice, eds. (Orig.). (C). pap. write for info. (*1-57125-003-4*) Help Desk Inst.

Bultema, Patrick, et al, eds. Glossary of Help Desk Terms. 36p. (Orig.). pap. write for info. (*1-57125-013-1*) Help Desk Inst.
— 1994 Help Desk & Customer Support Practices Report. (Illus.). 58p. (Orig.). pap. write for info. (*1-57125-012-3*) Help Desk Inst.
— The 1994-1995 Help Desk Buyer's Guide: A Comprehensive Directory of Help Desk Products & Services. (Illus.). 106p. (Orig.). pap. write for info. (*1-57125-011-5*) Help Desk Inst.
— The 6th Annual International Help Desk Conference & Expo. (Illus.). 1144p. (Orig.). pap. write for info. (*1-57125-021-2*) Help Desk Inst.

Bultema, Patrick, ed. see Arambulo, Hector & Jenkins, Connie.

Bultema, Patrick, ed. see Case, Gary & Rhoades-Baum, Patrice.

Bultema, Patrick, ed. see Eliot, Lance B.

Bultema, Patrick, ed. see LaBounty, Char.

Bultema, Patrick, ed. see Levinger, Michael.

Bultema, Patrick, ed. see Melanson, Mia S.

Bultema, Patrick, ed. see Muns, Ron.

Bultema, Patrick, ed. see Murtagh, Steven J.

Bultema, Patrick, ed. see Zawacki, Robert A. & Zawacki, Laura L.

Bulter. Progress in Biophysics & Molecular Biology, Vol. 21. 1970. 100.00 (*0-08-015696-7*, Pergamon Pr) Elsevier.

Bulter, Anthony R. Problems in Physical Organic Chemistry. LC 72-617. 115p. reprint ed. pap. 35.70 (*0-608-10209-1*, 201697200005) Bks Demand.

B

Bulterman, M. K. & Kuijer, M., eds. Compliance with Judgments of International Courts. LC 95-43180. 1995. lib. bdg. 81.50 (*90-411-0157-8*, Pub. by M Nijhoff) Kluwer Academic.

Bultheel, Adhemar. Laurent Series & Their Pade Approximation. (Operator Theory Ser.: No. 27). 270p. 1987. 123.00 (*0-8176-1940-2*) Birkhauser.

Bultheel, Adhemar & Van Barel, Marc. Linear Algebra, Rational Approximation Orthogonal Polynomials. LC 97-40610. (Studies in Computational Mathematics: 6). 464p. 1997. 158.00 (*0-444-82872-9*) Elsevier.

Bultheel, Adhemar, et al. Orthogonal Rational Functions. LC 98-11646. (Monographs on Applied & Computational Mathematics: No. 5). (Illus.). 384p. (C). 1999. text 59.95 (*0-521-65006-2*) Cambridge U Pr.

Bulthoff, Heinrich H., jt. ed. see Tarr, Michael J.

Bulthuis, A., jt. auth. see Henderson-Sellers, Brian.

***Bulthuis, Lenae.** Guess What, Jesus? My Prayer Diary. LC 99-29531. (Illus.). 175p. (YA). 1999. per. 7.95 (*1-56212-475-7*, 1701-0405) CRC Pubns.

— It's Me, Jesus: My Prayer Diary. LC 99-47616. 175p. 1999. pap. 7.95 (*1-56212-504-4*, 160455) CRC Pubns.

***Bultinck, Christina.** The Idiots I Met Using a Stupid Guide to Dating. 2000. 24.95 (*0-9668600-5-5*) InfoKey.

— Internet Expert's Guide to Online Marketing: 2000 Style. 100p. 2000. 24.95 (*0-9668600-8-X*) InfoKey.

— Internet Expert's Guide to Online Research: 2000 Style. Harkiewicz, Monica, ed. 100p. 2000. 24.95 (*0-9668600-9-8*) InfoKey.

— An Internet Expert's Guide to Online Travel: 2000 Style. 100p. 2000. 24.95 (*0-9668600-7-1*) InfoKey.

— An Internet Expert's Guide to Starting an Online Business: 2000 Style. 100p. 2000. 24.95 (*0-9668600-6-3*) InfoKey.

— The Job Seekers Bible. 200p. 2000. 39.95 (*0-9668600-1-2*) InfoKey.

Bultinck, Christina. The Recruiter's Bible: Best Guide to Free Online Recruiting Resources. 2nd ed. 98p. 1999. pap. 80.00 (*0-9668600-3-9*) InfoKey.

***Bultinck, Christina.** A Stupid Guide to Europe Won't Help When You Are at a Bus Stop at 2 a.m. in the Rain... Find Out What You Really Need to Know... 2000. write for info. (*0-9668600-4-7*) InfoKey.

***Bultinck, Christina & Bultinck, Nicole.** ABCs of Online Buying - Annoying Business Commerce & E-Customers from Hell! Have We All Gone Insane? 2000. 12.95 (*0-9668600-0-4*) InfoKey.

Bultinck, Christina & Johnston-Czarnecki, Christy. A Native's Guide to Chicago's South Suburbs. LC 98-85577. (Illus.). 1999. pap. 12.95 (*0-9642426-1-3*) Lake Claremont.

Bultinck, Nicole, jt. auth. see Bultinck, Christina.

Bultman, Bethany E. Reflections of the South. 1997. 14.95 (*1-85833-697-X*, Pub. by CLib Bks) Whitecap Bks.

Bultman, Bethany E., jt. auth. see Church, Beverly R.

Bultmann, Phyllis. Current Research in British Studies, Vol. 7. 7th ed. Bultmann, William, ed. 165p. 1975. pap. text 30.95 (*0-89126-017-X*) MA-AH Pub.

Bultmann, Rudolf. Faith & Understanding. Funk, Robert W., ed. Smith, Louise P., tr. LC 86-45901. (Fortress Texts in Modern Theology Ser.). 352p. 1987. pap. 29.00 (*0-8006-3202-8*, 1-3202, Fortress Pr) Augsburg Fortress.

— The Great Depression & Its Fifty-Year Shadow. (Occasional Papers: No. 18). 1986. pap. 5.95 (*0-318-23336-3*) WWU CPNS.

— Jesus & the Word. (Hudson River Editions Ser.). 226p. 1982. reprint ed. 40.00 (*0-684-17596-7*, Scribners Ref) Mac Lib Ref.

— Jesus Christ & Mythology. 94p. (C). 1981. pap. text 16.20 (*0-02-305570-7*, Macmillan Coll) P-H.

— The New Testament & Mythology & Other Basic Writings. Ogden, Schubert M., ed. & tr. by. LC 84-47921. 192p. 1984. pap. 14.00 (*0-8006-2442-4*, 1-2442, Fortress Pr) Augsburg Fortress.

— What Is Theology? A New Agenda for Theology. Hrrisville, Roy A., tr. LC 96-40256. (Fortress Texts in Modern Theology Ser.). 256p. 1997. pap. 22.00 (*0-8006-3088-2*, 1-3088, Fortress Pr) Augsburg Fortress.

Bultmann, William, ed. see Bultmann, Phyllis.

Bulusu, Surya N., ed. Chemistry & Physics of Energetic Materials. (C). 1990. text 361.00 (*0-7923-0745-3*) Kluwer Academic.

Bulutay, T. Employment, Unemployment & Wages in Turkey. xvi, 358p. 1995. 31.50 (*92-2-109193-7*) Intl Labour Office.

Bulver, Kathryn M. La Femme-Demon: Figurations de la Femme Dans la Litterature Fantastique. (FRE.). VIII, 143p. (C). 1995. text 37.95 (*0-8204-2433-1*) P Lang Pubng.

Bulwer, E. L. & Brongham, Lord. The Fallen Star or, the History of a False Religion: Also, a Dissertation on the Origin of Evil. 136p. 1996. reprint ed. pap. 13.95 (*1-56459-685-0*) Kessinger Pub.

Bulwer, John. Chirologia, 2 vols. in 1. LC 75-147955. (Language, Man & Society Ser.). reprint ed. 62.50 (*0-404-08205-X*) AMS Pr.

Bulwer Lytton, Edward. Alice or the Mysteries. 437p. 1972. reprint ed. spiral bd. 18.50 (*0-7873-1112-X*) Hlth Research.

— Alice or the Mysteries (1877) 440p. 1996. reprint ed. pap. 18.00 (*1-56459-691-5*) Kessinger Pub.

— Bulwer & Macready: A Chronicle of the Early Victorian Theatre. Shattuck, Charles H., ed. LC 57-6957. 285p. reprint ed. pap. 88.40 (*0-8357-7475-9*, 202226700026) Bks Demand.

***Bulwer Lytton, Edward.** Calderon the Courtier. 30p. 1999. reprint ed. pap. 5.00 (*0-7661-0793-0*) Kessinger Pub.

Bulwer Lytton, Edward. Caxtons: A Family Picture (1849) 270p. 1999. reprint ed. pap. 19.95 (*0-7661-0780-9*) Kessinger Pub.

— The Caxtons, a Family Picture, 3 vols., Set. (BCL1-PR English Literature Ser.). 1992. reprint ed. lib. bdg. 225.00 (*0-7812-7590-3*) Rprt Serv.

— The Coming Race. 144p. 1967. reprint ed. spiral bd. 14.00 (*0-7873-0574-X*) Hlth Research.

— The Coming Race. 211p. 1973. reprint ed. 9.95 (*0-932785-07-7*) Philos Pub.

— The Coming Race: A First in Science Fiction. LC 88-33971. (Banquo Bks.). 128p. 1989. reprint ed. pap. 7.95 (*0-88007-174-5*) Woodbridge Pr.

***Bulwer Lytton, Edward.** Darnley (1877) 46p. 1999. reprint ed. pap. 7.00 (*0-7661-0810-4*) Kessinger Pub.

Bulwer Lytton, Edward. Devereux. 232p. 1999. reprint ed. pap. 19.95 (*0-7661-0782-5*) Kessinger Pub.

— Disowned (1852) 226p. 1999. reprint ed. pap. 19.95 (*0-7661-0783-3*) Kessinger Pub.

— Dramatic Works of the Right Hon. Lord Lytton: Comprising; the Duchess De la Valliere, Richelieu, the Lady of Lyons, Money, Not So Bad As We Seem. LC 71-39197. (Select Bibliographies Reprint Ser.). 1977. reprint ed. 29.95 (*0-8369-6799-2*) Ayer.

***Bulwer Lytton, Edward.** Duchess de la Valliere (1837) 66p. 1999. reprint ed. pap. 7.00 (*0-7661-0803-1*) Kessinger Pub.

Bulwer Lytton, Edward. England & the English. Meacham, Standish, ed. LC 71-114959. (Classics of British Historical Literature Ser.). 1992. pap. text 3.45 (*0-226-08015-3*, P384) U Ch Pr.

— England & the English. Meacham, Standish, ed. LC 71-114959. (Classics of British Historical Literature Ser.). (C). 1995. lib. bdg. 27.00 (*0-226-08014-5*) U Ch Pr.

Bulwer Lytton, Edward. England & the English. Meacham, Standish, ed. & intro. by. LC 71-114959. (Classics of British Historical Literature Ser.). 464p. Date not set. reprint ed. pap. 143.90 (*0-608-20672-5*, 207210900003) Bks Demand.

— Ernest Maltravers (1837) 196p. 1999. reprint ed. pap. 17.95 (*0-7661-0794-9*) Kessinger Pub.

Bulwer Lytton, Edward. Eugene Aram: A Tale, 3 vols., 2 bks., Set. LC 79-8158. reprint ed. 84.50 (*0-404-61995-9*) AMS Pr.

***Bulwer Lytton, Edward.** Eugene Aram (1831) 222p. 1999. reprint ed. pap. 17.95 (*0-7661-0791-4*) Kessinger Pub.

Bulwer Lytton, Edward. Falkland (1827) 50p. 1999. reprint ed. pap. 7.50 (*0-7661-0801-5*) Kessinger Pub.

***Bulwer Lytton, Edward.** Godolphin. 160p. 1999. reprint ed. pap. 16.95 (*0-7661-0790-6*) Kessinger Pub.

Bulwer Lytton, Edward. Harold: The Last of the Saxon Kings. 266p. 1999. reprint ed. pap. 24.95 (*0-7661-0756-6*) Kessinger Pub.

— Kenelm Chillingly (1892) 252p. 1999. reprint ed. pap. 19.95 (*0-7661-0781-7*) Kessinger Pub.

***Bulwer Lytton, Edward.** Lady of Lyons or Love & Pride (1838) 40p. 1999. reprint ed. pap. 7.00 (*0-7661-0804-X*) Kessinger Pub.

Bulwer Lytton, Edward. The Last Days of Pompeii. Date not set. lib. bdg. 27.95 (*0-8488-1959-4*) Amereon Ltd.

— The Last Days of Pompeii. 308p. 1983. reprint ed. lib. bdg. 41.95 (*0-89966-309-5*) Buccaneer Bks.

— The Last Days of Pompeii. 435p. 1996. reprint ed. pap. 27.95 (*1-56459-590-0*) Kessinger Pub.

— The Last of the Barons, 3 vols., 2 bks., Set. LC 79-8159. reprint ed. 84.50 (*0-404-62176-7*) AMS Pr.

***Bulwer Lytton, Edward.** Last of the Barons (1843) 350p. 1999. reprint ed. pap. 24.95 (*0-7661-0797-3*) Kessinger Pub.

— Leila or the Siege of Granada. 86p. 1999. reprint ed. pap. 14.95 (*0-7661-0792-2*) Kessinger Pub.

— Lucretia or the Children of Night (1853) 238p. 1999. reprint ed. pap. 18.00 (*0-7661-0796-5*) Kessinger Pub.

— Money (1840) 54p. 1999. reprint ed. pap. 7.00 (*0-7661-0807-4*) Kessinger Pub.

Bulwer Lytton, Edward. My Novel. 602p. 1999. reprint ed. pap. 35.00 (*0-7661-0784-1*) Kessinger Pub.

***Bulwer Lytton, Edward.** Night & Morning (1845) 254p. 1999. reprint ed. pap. 19.95 (*0-7661-0789-2*) Kessinger Pub.

— Not So Bad As We Seem: Or Many Sides to a Character. 44p. 1999. reprint ed. pap. 7.00 (*0-7661-0806-6*) Kessinger Pub.

Bulwer Lytton, Edward. Parisians (1872) 332p. 1999. reprint ed. pap. 24.95 (*0-7661-0787-6*) Kessinger Pub.

— Paul Clifford. 228p. 1999. reprint ed. pap. 17.95 (*0-7661-0800-7*) Kessinger Pub.

***Bulwer Lytton, Edward.** Pausanias the Spartan (1859) 96p. 1999. reprint ed. pap. 14.95 (*0-7661-0795-7*) Kessinger Pub.

Bulwer Lytton, Edward. Pelham: Or the Adventures of a Gentleman. LC 77-88085. 512p. reprint ed. pap. 158.80 (*0-8357-7934-3*, 205700700002) Bks Demand.

***Bulwer Lytton, Edward.** Pelham or Adventures of a Gentleman (1828) 230p. 1999. reprint ed. pap. 19.95 (*0-7661-0799-X*) Kessinger Pub.

Bulwer Lytton, Edward. Pilgrims of the Rhine (1840) 116p. 1999. reprint ed. pap. 12.95 (*0-7661-0786-8*) Kessinger Pub.

***Bulwer Lytton, Edward.** Richelieu: or The Conspiracy (1839) 84p. 1999. reprint ed. pap. 12.00 (*0-7661-0805-8*) Kessinger Pub.

Bulwer Lytton, Edward. Rienzi: The Last of the Roman Tribunes. (BCL1-PR English Literature Ser.). 1992. reprint ed. lib. bdg. 99.00 (*0-7812-7591-1*) Rprt Serv.

— Rienzi: The Last of the Roman Tribunes. LC 70-145150. 1971. reprint ed. 69.00 (*0-403-01079-9*) Scholarly.

***Bulwer Lytton, Edward.** Rienzi: The Last of the Tribunes (1848) 246p. 1999. reprint ed. pap. 19.95 (*0-7661-0798-1*) Kessinger Pub.

— Rightful Heir (1868) 52p. 1999. reprint ed. pap. 7.00 (*0-7661-0808-2*) Kessinger Pub.

Bulwer Lytton, Edward. Strange Story. 499p. 1996. reprint ed. spiral bd. 27.00 (*0-7873-1094-8*) Hlth Research.

— A Strange Story & the Haunted & the Haunters: Or the House & the Brain. 500p. 1992. reprint ed. pap. 25.95 (*1-56459-000-3*) Kessinger Pub.

— Vril: The Power of the Coming Race. 246p. 1997. reprint ed. pap. 19.95 (*0-7661-0105-3*) Kessinger Pub.

***Bulwer Lytton, Edward.** Walpole: or Every Man Has His Price. 36p. 1999. reprint ed. pap. 5.00 (*0-7661-0809-0*) Kessinger Pub.

Bulwer Lytton, Edward. What Will He Do with It? 438p. 1999. reprint ed. pap. 29.95 (*0-7661-0788-4*) Kessinger Pub.

— Zanoni. 398p. 1970. reprint ed. pap. 23.00 (*0-7873-0573-1*) Hlth Research.

— Zanoni: A Rosicrucian Tale. 408p. 1997. reprint ed. pap. 21.50 (*0-7661-0104-5*) Kessinger Pub.

— Zanoni: A Rosicrucian Tale. 2nd ed. LC 78-157505. 462p. 1989. reprint ed. pap. 18.95 (*0-8334-0017-7*, Pub. by Garber Comm) Anthroposophic.

— Zicci. 48p. 1999. reprint ed. pap. 7.00 (*0-7661-0785-X*) Kessinger Pub.

Bulwer Lytton, Edward & Ainsworth, William H. Cult Criminals: The Newgate Novels (1830-1847), 6 vols. John, Juliet, ed. LC 97-26685. 2712p. (C). 1998. 620.00 (*0-415-14383-7*) Routledge.

Bulwer Lytton, Edward & Devey, Louisa. Letters of the Late Edward Bulwer, Lord Lytton, to His Wife. LC 79-148815. reprint ed. 49.50 (*0-404-08884-8*) AMS Pr.

Bulwer Lytton, Edward & Swinburne, Algernon Charles. The New Timon: A Romance of London. Nadel, Ira B. et al, eds. 320p. 1986. lib. bdg. 20.00 (*0-8240-8619-8*) Garland.

Bulychev, Kir. Earth & Elsewhere. 1985. 22.95 (*0-02-518240-4*) Macmillan.

Bulychev, Kirill. Gusliar Wonders. 1985. 16.95 (*0-02-518010-X*) Macmillan.

Bulychev, Nikolai S. & Fotieva, Nina N. Design & Construction of Reinforced Underground Structures in the Russian Federation: Three Case Studies. (Foreign Technology Assessment Ser.). 147p. (Orig.). 1994. pap. 55.00 (*1-881874-11-7*) Global Cnslts.

Bulygin, E., jt. auth. see Alchourron, C. E.

Bulyzhenkov, V., et al, eds. Genetic Approaches in the Prevention of Mental Disorders. (Illus.). 128p. 1990. 66.95 (*0-387-52244-1*) Spr-Verlag.

Buma, Joan. Hands on Nature. (C). 1991. pap. text. write for info. (*0-201-57915-4*) Addison-Wesley.

Buma, Joan W. Look What I Made! 40 Craft Ideas & 120 Related Activities for Children Ages 2 to 5. (Illus.). 96p. 1991. pap. 9.95 (*1-55958-073-9*) Prima Pub.

— Look What I Made Now Vol. II: Interactive Nature Activities for Young Children. (Look What I Made! Ser.). (Illus.). 96p. 1991. pap. 9.95 (*1-55958-176-X*) Prima Pub.

***Bumagin, Michael.** Exploring Ft. Worth with Children. (Illus.). (J). 2000. pap. text. write for info. (*1-55622-734-5*) Wordware Pub.

Bumagin, Victoria E. & Hirn, Kathryn F. Helping the Aging Family: A Guide for Professionals. 320p. 1990. reprint ed. 38.95 (*0-8261-7530-9*) Springer Pub.

Bumann, Richard L. Colony Olivenhain. LC 81-90363. (Illus.). 112p. 1981. 15.95 (*0-9607112-0-1*) Bumann Spec Works.

Bumas, E. Shaskan. The Price of Tea in China. LC 94-18665. (Associated Writing Programs Awards for Short Fiction Ser.). 216p. (C). 1995. 22.95 (*0-87023-930-9*) U of Mass Pr.

Bumas, Lester O. Intermediate Microeconomics: Neoclassical & Factually-Oriented Models. LC 99-41505. 560p. 2000. text 79.95 (*0-7656-0520-1*) M E Sharpe.

Bumb, B. L., et al. Ghana Policy Environment & Fertilizer Sector Development. LC 94-13875. (Technical Bulletin Ser.: Vol. T-41). 1994. pap. text 4.00 (*0-88090-106-3*) Intl Fertilizer.

Bumb, Balu L. Global Fertilizer Perspective, 1960-95: The Dynamics of Growth & Structural Change. LC 89-15595. (Technical Bulletin Ser.: No. T-34). (Illus.). 124p. (Orig.). 1989. pap. text 100.00 (*0-88090-079-2*) Intl Fertilizer.

— Global Fertilizer Perspective, 1980-2000: The Challenges in Structural Transformation. LC 95-6535. (Technical Bulletins Ser.: Vol. NaT-42). 1995. 50.00 (*0-88090-109-8*) Intl Fertilizer.

Bumb, Philip A. My College Ring Between My Toes. (Illus.). 106p. (Orig.). 1996. pap. 12.95 (*0-9652388-5-7*) M C Bumb.

Bumba, Lincoln, jt. auth. see Sissors, Jack Z.

Bumba, Vaclav & Kleczek, Josip, eds. Basic Mechanisms of Solar Activity. (Symposia of the International Astronomical Union Ser.: Vol. 71). 1976. pap. text 112.00 (*90-277-0681-6*); lib. bdg. 187.00 (*90-277-0680-8*) Kluwer Academic.

Bumbalo, V. Adam & the Experts. 1990. pap. 6.95 (*0-88145-087-1*) Broadway Play.

Bumbeck, David, jt. auth. see Brown, Danny.

Bumbera, Marlene C. The Civil War Letters of Cpl. John H. Strathern: Eighth Pennsylvania Reserve Volunteer Corps. LC 95-206643. 146p. 1994. per. 19.95 (*1-55856-175-7*, 074) Closson Pr.

Bumberry, William M., jt. auth. see Whitaker, Carl A.

Bumble, Stan. Computer Generated Physical Properties. LC 99-19200. 2000. 89.95 (*1-56670-329-8*) Lewis Pubs.

— Computer Simulated Plant Design for Waste Minimization/Pollution Prevention. LC 99-57318. (Computer Modelling for Environmental Management Ser.). 208p. 2000. boxed set 129.95 (*1-56670-352-2*, L1352) Lewis Pubs.

Bumcrot, Curt. Essential Learning Objectives. 17p. 1994. pap. text 5.00 (*1-888786-00-0*) BSA&ES.

Bumcrot, Curt & Bumcrot, Jennifer. Achieving Peak Performance Grade 6. 16p. (Orig.). 1996. pap. text, wbk. ed. 5.00 (*1-888786-11-6*) BSA&ES.

— Achieving Peak Performance Practice Test Grade 6. 26p. (Orig.). 1996. pap. text, wbk. ed. 5.00 (*1-888786-12-4*) BSA&ES.

Bumcrot, Curt & Bumcrot, Jenny. Achieving Peak Performance Grade 1. 20p. 1991. pap. text 5.00 (*1-888786-01-9*) BSA&ES.

— Achieving Peak Performance Grade 3. 24p. 1991. pap. text 5.00 (*1-888786-05-1*) BSA&ES.

— Achieving Peak Performance Grade 2. 20p. 1991. pap. text 5.00 (*1-888786-03-5*) BSA&ES.

— Achieving Peak Performance Grade 4. 24p. (Orig.). 1994. pap. text 5.00 (*1-888786-07-8*) BSA&ES.

— Achieving Peak Performance Grade 5. 19p. (Orig.). 1995. pap. text 5.00 (*1-888786-09-4*) BSA&ES.

— Achieving Peak Performance Practice Test. 23p. (J). (gr. 3). 1991. pap. text 5.00 (*1-888786-06-X*) BSA&ES.

— Achieving Peak Performance Practice Test. (Illus.). 14p. (J). (gr. 1). 1991. pap. text 5.00 (*1-888786-02-7*) BSA&ES.

— Achieving Peak Performance Practice Test. (Illus.). 18p. (J). (gr. 2). 1991. pap. text 5.00 (*1-888786-04-3*) BSA&ES.

— Achieving Peak Performance Practice Test. (Illus.). 26p. (J). (gr. 4). 1994. pap. text 5.00 (*1-888786-08-6*) BSA&ES.

— Achieving Peak Performance Practice Test. (Illus.). 26p. (J). (gr. 5). 1995. pap. text 5.00 (*1-888786-10-8*) BSA&ES.

Bumcrot, Curt, et al. Achieving Peak Performance Grade 7. 18p. 1999. pap. text 5.00 (*1-888786-13-2*) BSA&ES.

— Achieving Peak Performance Practice Test. 26p. (J). (gr. 7-8). 1999. pap. text, wbk. ed. 4.00 (*1-888786-14-0*) BSA&ES.

Bumcrot, Jennifer, jt. auth. see Bumcrot, Curt.

Bumcrot, Jenny, jt. auth. see Bumcrot, Curt.

Bumcrot, Robert J., jt. auth. see Althoen, Steven C.

Bumgardner, Joyce C. Helping Students Learn to Write: An Idea Book for K-7 Teachers. LC 95-12816. (Illus.). 288p. (C). 1995. pap. text 33.00 (*0-205-17571-6*) Allyn.

— The New My Writing Book. (Illus.). 72p. (J). (gr. 2-6). 1998. pap. 5.95 (*0-9624260-1-6*) Froggie Pr.

Bumgarner, John R. The Health of the Presidents: The Forty-One United States Presidents Through 1993 from a Physician's Point of View. LC 93-42000. 344p. 1994. lib. bdg. 38.50 (*0-89950-956-8*) McFarland & Co.

— Parade of the Dead: A U. S. Army Physician's Memoir of Imprisonment by the Japanese, 1942-1945. LC 95-6015. (Illus.). 222p. 1995. lib. bdg. 21.95 (*0-7864-0131-1*) McFarland & Co.

— Sarah Childress Polk: A Biography of the Remarkable First Lady. LC 97-9684. 176p. 1997. pap. 26.50 (*0-7864-0366-7*) McFarland & Co.

***Bumgarner, John Reed.** P. K. Life in a Methodist Parsonage. LC 99-93768. 2000. pap. 10.95 (*0-533-13149-9*) Vantage.

Bumgarner, Marlene A. New Book of Whole Grains. LC 97-5727. (Illus.). 1997. pap. 16.95 (*0-312-15601-4*) St Martin.

— Organic Cooking for (Not-So-Organic) Mothers. LC 80-23089. (Illus.). 160p. 1984. spiral bd. 7.95 (*0-938006-00-2*) Chesbro.

***Bumgarner, Marlene A.** Working with School-Age Children: Before & After School Care. LC 98-45605. (Illus.). xx, 322p. (C). 1998. pap. text 30.95 (*1-55934-948-4*, 948-4) Mayfield Printing.

Bumgarner, Matthew C. History of the Carolina & North-Western Railway: The Route of the Carolina & North-Western Railway. (Illus.). 200p. 1996. 49.95 (*1-57072-052-5*) Overmountain Pr.

Bumgarner, Norma J. Mothering Your Nursing Toddler. 2nd rev. ed. (Illus.). 308p. 1999. pap. 12.95 (*0-912500-52-2*) La Leche.

The handbook for mothers who breastfeed their children past infancy has been revised & updated. Norma Jane Bumgarner puts the experience of nursing an older baby or child in perspective, within the context of the entire mother-child relationship. She cites biological, cultural & historical evidence in support of extended breastfeeding & shares stories gleaned from thousands of families in which nursing & natural weaning have been the norm. *Publisher Paid Annotation.*

Bumgarner, Pete. Church Government According to God's Standard. 102p. (Orig.). 1995. pap. 5.95 (*0-9650768-0-6*) STC Pubns.

— Gobierno de la Iglesia Conforme a las Normas de Dios. (SPA.). 101p. (Orig.). 1996. pap. 5.95 (*0-9650768-1-4*) STC Pubns.

Bumgartner, Louis E. Jose del Valle of Central America. LC 63-9007. 314p. reprint ed. pap. 97.40 (*0-8357-9109-2*, 201789000010) Bks Demand.

Bumiller, Elisabeth. May You Be the Mother of a Hundred Sons: A Journey among the Women of India. 320p. 1991. pap. 12.00 (*0-449-90614-0*) Fawcett.

— The Secrets of Mariko. 1996. pap. 14.00 (*0-679-77262-6*) McKay.

— The Secrets of Mariko: A Year in the Life of a Japanese Woman & Her Family. Date not set. pap. 13.00 (*0-614-25848-0*) Vin Bks.

Bumiller, Kristin. The Civil Rights Society: The Social Construction of Victims. LC 87-45485. 172p. 1992. reprint ed. pap. text 14.95 (*0-8018-4510-6*) Johns Hopkins.

An Asterisk (*) at the beginning of an entry indicates that the title is appearing for the first time.

Bumke, Joachim. The Concept of Knighthood in the Middle Ages. Jackson, Erika, tr. from GER. LC 79-8840. (Studies in the Middle Ages: No. 2). 278p. 1982. 34.50 (*0-404-18034-5*) AMS Pr.

***Bumke, Joachim.** Courtly Culture: Literature & Society in the High Middle Ages. LC 00-26079. (Illus.). 770p. 2000. pap. 24.95 (*1-58567-051-0*, Pub. by Overlook Pr) Penguin Putnam.

Bumke, Joachim. Die Vier Fassungen der "Nibelungenklage" Untersuchungen zur Ueberlieferungsgeschichte & Textkritik der Hoefischen Epik im 13. Jahrhundert. (Quellen und Forschungen zur Literatur und Kulturgeschichte: Vol. 8(242)). (GER., Illus.). xiv, 746p. (C). 1996. lib. bdg. 207.40 (*3-11-015076-X*) De Gruyter.

Bumm, F. Deutschlands Gesundheitsverhaltnisse Unter Dem Einfluss Des Weltkrieges, 2 vols. (Wirtschafts-Und Sozialgeschichte des Weltkrieges (Osterreichische Und Ungarische Serie)). 1928. 250.00 (*0-317-27441-4*) Elliots Bks.

Bump, Charles W. Down the Historic Susquehanna from Otsego to the Chesapeake. 184p. 1996. reprint ed. pap. 18.00 (*1-887530-03-7*) RSG Pub.

Bump, Daniel. Algebraic Geometry & the Theory of Curves. LC 98-42147. 1999. 38.00 (*981-02-3561-5*) World Scientific Pub.

— Automorphic Forms & Representations. (Studies in Advanced Mathematics: Vol. 55). (Illus.). 588p. (C). 1999. pap. text 39.95 (*0-521-65818-7*) Cambridge U Pr.

— Automorphic Forms on GL (3r R) (Lecture Notes in Mathematics Ser.: Vol. 1083). xi, 184p. 1984. pap. 31.10 (*0-387-13864-1*) Spr-Verlag.

Bump, Edward A. & Malaker, Kamal. Radioprotectors: Chemical, Biological, & Clincial Perspectives. LC 97-22136. 448p. 1997. boxed set 159.95 (*0-8493-4756-4*) CRC Pr.

Bump, Linda A. Sport Psychology Study Guide. (Illus.). 432p. 1989. pap. text, student ed. 32.00 (*0-87322-023-4*, ACEP0204) Human Kinetics.

Bumpass, Larry, jt. auth. see Sweet, James A.

Bumpass, Larry L. & Westoff, Charles F. The Later Years of Childbearing. LC 74-120751. 184p. reprint ed. pap. 57.10 (*0-7837-1406-8*, 204176000023) Bks Demand.

Bumppo, Natalie, jt. auth. see Bumppo, Natty.

Bumppo, Natty. The Columbus Book of Euchre. LC 81-68103. (Illus.). 72p. 1982. pap. 2.75 (*0-9604894-2-8*) Borf Bks.

— The Columbus Book of Euchre. 2nd rev. ed. LC 99-72146. (Illus.). 90p. 1999. pap. 7.78 (*0-9604894-6-0*) Borf Bks.

— Dear Sir (You Cur) And Other Letters from, to & about Natty Bumppo. unabridged ed. LC 98-71434. 287p. 1998. pap. 13.75 (*0-9604894-5-2*) Borf Bks.

— Lonely Hearts. LC 91-78489. (Illus.). 325p. (Orig.). 1992. pap. 9.75 (*0-9604894-4-4*) Borf Bks.

Bumppo, Natty, ed. The Sackbut Tapes: An Oral Nonfiction Novel Told by the Characters. unabridged ed. LC 98-71161. (Illus.). 304p. 1998. pap. 18.75 (*0-9604894-3-6*) Borf Bks.

Bumppo, Natty & Bumppo, Natalie. Ideas for a Better America. LC 80-66966. (Illus.). 80p. 1980. pap. 3.75 (*0-9604894-0-1*) Borf Bks.

Bumpus, Jerry. The Civilized Tribes: New & Selected Stories. LC 95-10311. 1995. pap. 14.95 (*1-884836-08-9*) U Akron Pr.

— The Civilized Tribes: New & Selected Stories. LC 95-10311. 277p. (C). 1995. 24.95 (*1-884836-07-0*) U Akron Pr.

— Dawn of the Flying Pigs. LC 91-43829. (Illus.). 144p. 1992. pap. 12.50 (*0-914140-16-7*) Carpenter Pr.

— The Happy Convent. LC 89-50876. (Illus.). 176p. 1989. pap. 15.00 (*0-913204-23-4*) December Pr.

— Heroes & Villains. LC 84-25945. 258p. 1986. 15.95 (*0-914590-92-8*); pap. 6.95 (*0-914590-93-6*) Fiction Coll.

Bumpus, Judith. Impressionist Gardens. (Illus.). 80p. 1998. pap. 9.95 (*0-7148-3813-6*) Phaidon Pr.

— Reginald Brill. (Illus.). 128p. 1999. text 43.95 (*1-84014-696-6*, Pub. by Ashgate Pub) Ashgate Pub Co.

— Van Gogh's Flowers. LC 98-231821. (Illus.). 80p. 1998. pap. 9.95 (*0-7148-3814-4*) Phaidon Pr.

Bumpus, Peter, ed. see Paulin, Tony.

Bumpus, Peter, ed. see Sorensen, Ralph.

***Bumpus, Winston, et al.** Common Information Model: Implementing the Object Model for Enterprise Management. LC 99-89371. 316p. 1999. 49.99 (*0-471-35342-6*) Wiley.

Bumpus, Winston, jt. auth. see Sturm, Rick.

Bumslag, Naomi & Michaels, Dia L. A Woman's Guide to Yeast Infections. Zion, Claire, ed. 288p. (Orig.). 1992. mass mkt. 5.99 (*0-671-74699-5*) PB.

***Bumstead, William W.** Buying & Selling Business: Including Forms, Formulas, & Industry Secrets, 1. LC 97-29025. 352p. 1998. 87.95 (*0-471-24336-1*) Wiley.

Bumsted, J. M. Henry Alline, Seventeen Forty-Eight to Seventeen Eighty-Four. LC 73-24664. (Canadian Biographical Studies). 128p. reprint ed. pap. 39.70 (*0-608-12847-3*, 202359800033) Bks Demand.

— A History of the Canadian Peoples. (Illus.). 480p. 1998. pap. text 34.95 (*0-19-541200-1*) OUP.

— Land, Settlement, & Politics on Eighteenth-Century Prince Edward Island. 256p. 1987. 65.00 (*0-7735-0566-0*, Pub. by McG-Queens Univ Pr) CUP Services.

— The Peoples of Canada: A Post-Confederation History, Vol. 2. (Illus.). 456p. (C). 1993. pap. text 32.00 (*0-19-540914-0*) OUP.

— The Peoples of Canada: A Pre-Confederation of Words. (Illus.). 456p. 1992. pap. text 35.00 (*0-19-540690-7*) OUP.

— The Pilgrim's Progress: The Ecclesiastical History of the Old Colony. (Outstanding Studies in Early American History). 407p. 1989. reprint ed. 25.00 (*0-8240-6174-8*) Garland.

Bumsted, J. M., ed. Interpreting Canada's Past: Post-Confederation, Vol. 2. 2nd ed. 724p. (C). 1993. pap. text 32.00 (*0-19-540947-7*) OUP.

— Interpreting Canada's Past: Pre-Confederation, Vol. I. 2nd ed. 730p. (C). 1993. pap. text 32.00 (*0-19-540946-9*) OUP.

Bumsted, Keith & Reeser, Kelly. Please Call the Tower! A Pilot's Guide to FAA Enforcement Program. (Illus.). 235p. 1994. pap. 14.95 (*0-9670342-0-5*) Paragon Commns Inc.

***Bumsted, Lee.** Hot Showers! Maine Coast Lodging for Kayakers & Sailors. 2nd rev. ed. LC 00-130436. (Illus.). 250p. 2000. pap. 18.95 (*1-879418-62-2*) Audenreed Pr.

Bumsted, Robert M., jt. ed. see Smith, James D.

Bun, Friedrich Von, see Bainum, Peter M. & Von Bun, Friedrich.

Bun, Un Ho. Pak Mei Kung Fu. 96p. 1996. pap. 17.95 (*0-901764-19-1*, 93327) P H Crompton.

— Praying Mantis Kung Fu. 96p. 1998. pap. 17.95 (*0-901764-09-4*, 93328) P H Crompton.

Bun Woong Kim, et al. Korean Public Administration: Managing the Uneven Development. LC 97-71676. (Illus.). 400p. 1998. 27.95 (*1-56591-080-X*, Pub. by Hollym Bks) Weatherhill.

Bunak, Viktor V., et al. Contributions to the Physical Anthropology of the Soviet Union. Howells, William W., tr. LC 60-1045. (Harvard University. Peabody Museum of Archaeology & Ethnology. Antiquities of the New World Ser.: Vol. 1, No. 2). reprint ed. lib. bdg. 47.50 (*0-404-52642-X*) AMS Pr.

Bunbongkarn, Suchit. State of the Nation: Thailand. (Illus.). 117p. (Orig.). (C). 1997. pap. text 35.00 (*0-7881-3708-5*) DIANE Pub.

Bunbury, Bill. Timber for Gold: Life on the Goldfields Woodlines. 216p. 1997. pap. 19.95 (*1-86368-197-3*, Pub. by Fremantle Arts) Intl Spec Bk.

Bunbury, Rhonda, ed. Children's Choices: Reading at Home & at School. 1995. pap. 70.00 (*0-949823-53-8*, Pub. by Deakin Univ) St Mut.

Bunce. Chemistry in Nursing. 1998. text 49.00 (*0-697-33084-2*) McGraw.

— The Global Community, Bk. 3. Date not set. pap. text. write for info. (*0-582-06796-0*, Pub. by Addison-Wesley) Longman.

Bunce, Arthur C. Economic Nationalism & the Farmer. 1977. 17.95 (*0-8369-6968-5*, 7849) Ayer.

Bunce, Betty H. Building a Language-Focused Curriculum for the Preschool Classroom Vol. II: A Planning Guide, vol. 2. 480p. 1995. pap. 55.00 (*1-55766-192-8*) P H Brookes.

Bunce, Chip G. Totally Bogus Men: A Social Guide for the American Woman. (Illus.). 76p. 1996. pap. 6.95 (*1-57854-000-3*) Hope Manor.

Bunce, Diane M. Chemistry & Our Changing Times. 7th ed. 1995. pap. text, student ed. 31.67 (*0-13-518820-2*) P-H.

Bunce, Donald F., 2nd. Atlas of Arterial Histology. LC 72-13843. (Illus.). 250p. 1974. 37.50 (*0-87527-096-4*) Green.

Bunce, Eda H. Beyond the Fence: A Book to Read to Your Favorite Dog. (Illus.). 72p. (Orig.). 1990. pap. 5.95 (*0-9628141-0-5*) Blkberry Pr.

Bunce, Fredrick. Dictionary of Buddhist & Hindu Iconography: Objects, Devices, Concepts, Rites & Related Terms. LC 97-901206. (Illus.). (C). 1997. 98.00 (*81-246-0061-9*, Pub. by DK Pubs Ind) S Asia.

Bunce, Fredrick W. An Encyclopaedia of Buddhist Deities, Demigods, Godlings, Saints & Demons: With Special Focus on Iconographic Attributes. LC 94-900634. 1998. pap. 1600.00 (*81-246-0020-1*, Pub. by Print Hse) St Mut.

***Bunce, Fredrick W.** An Encyclopaedia of Hindu Deities, Demi-Gods, Godlings, Demons & Heroes: With Special Focus on Iconographic Attributes, Vols. 1-3, Set. (Illus.). 1627p. 2000. 325.00 (*81-246-0145-3*, Pub. by D K Printwrld) Nataraj Bks.

Bunce, Gerry M., ed. High Energy Spin Physics, 1982. LC 83-70154. (AIP Conference Proceedings Ser.: No. 95). 637p. 1983. lib. bdg. 44.00 (*0-88318-194-0*) Am Inst Physics.

Bunce, Harold L. & Gardner, John. Privatization of Fannie Mae & Freddie Mac: Desirability & Feasibility. (Illus.). 212p. (Orig.). (C). 1997. pap. text 50.00 (*0-7881-3754-9*) DIANE Pub.

Bunce, Joanne. Ultimate Power. 64p. 1990. pap. 2.95 (*0-88144-150-3*) Christian Pub.

Bunce, John W., jt. auth. see Brewer, James W.

Bunce, Lodie, ed. The Magic of Method Selling. (Illus.). 163p. 1994. per. write for info. (*0-9641729-0-9*) eDreampubng.

Bunce, Michael. The Countryside Ideal: Anglo-American Images of Landscape. LC 93-33662. (Illus.). 256p. (C). 1994. pap. 25.99 (*0-415-10435-1*, B7047) Routledge.

— The Countryside Ideal: Anglo-American Images of Landscape. LC 93-33662. (Illus.). 256p. (C). (gr. 13). 1994. 85.00 (*0-415-10434-3*, B7043) Routledge.

Bunce, Philip J., jt. auth. see Farquhar, Erin.

Bunce, R. G., et al, eds. Landscape Ecology & Agroecosystems. 256p. 1993. lib. bdg. 99.95 (*0-87371-918-2*, L918) Lewis Pubs.

Bunce, R. G. & Howard, D. C., eds. Species Dispersal in Agricultural Habitats. (Illus.). 296p. 1992. text 55.00 (*1-85293-076-4*) St Martin.

***Bunce, Steve & Mee, Bob.** Boxing Greats: An Illustrated History of the Legends of the Ring. LC 98-72148. (Illus.). 256p. 1998. 24.98 (*0-7624-0402-7*, Courage) Running Pr.

Bunce, Tim, jt. auth. see Descartes, Alligator.

Bunce, Valerie. Do New Leaders Make a Difference? Executive Succession & Public Policy under Capitalism & Socialism. LC 81-2124. 311p. 1981. reprint ed. pap. 96.50 (*0-7837-9308-1*, 206004800004) Bks Demand.

— Subversive Institutions: The Design & the Destruction of Socialism & the State. LC 98-38293. (Cambridge Studies in Comparative Politics). 324p. (C). 1999. text 54.95 (*0-521-58449-3*); pap. text 19.95 (*0-521-58592-9*) Cambridge U Pr.

Bunce, Vincent. Japan. LC 93-20426. (Places & People Ser.). (Illus.). 32p. (J). (gr. 5-8). 1994. lib. bdg. 20.80 (*0-531-14270-1*) Watts.

— Japan. (Places & People Ser.). (Illus.). 32p. (J). (gr. 5-8). 1996. reprint ed. pap. 6.95 (*0-531-15293-6*) Watts.

Bunce, Vincent & Morgan, Wendy. Living in St. Lucia. LC 96-229119. (Cambridge Primary Geography Ser.). 48p. (C). 1996. pap. 9.95 (*0-521-55658-9*) Cambridge U Pr.

***Bunce, Vincent J.** Volcanoes. LC 99-38579. (Restless Planet Ser.). (Illus.). 48p. (J). 2000. lib. bdg. 25.69 (*0-7398-1327-7*) Raintree Steck-V.

Bunce, William C., ed. Standards for Art Libraries & Fine Arts Slide Collections. (Occasional Papers: No. 2). 48p. (Orig.). 1983. pap. 10.00 (*0-942740-01-7*) Art Libs Soc.

Bunch, Allan. The Basics of Community Information Work. 2nd ed. LC 93-41770. (Illus.). 185p. 1993. reprint ed. pap. 57.40 (*0-608-07771-2*, 206785900010) Bks Demand.

— Community Information Services: Their Origin, Scope & Development. LC 82-201446. 176p. 1982. reprint ed. pap. 54.60 (*0-7837-9262-X*, 206000100004) Bks Demand.

Bunch, Beverly S., jt. auth. see Keel, Thomas M.

Bunch, Brian, jt. auth. see Hellemans, Alexander.

Bunch, Bryan. Handbook of Current Health & Medicine. 632p. 1994. 60.00 (*0-8103-9551-7*) Gale.

— The Henry Holt Almanac of Current Science & Technology: A Sourcebook of Facts & Analysis Covering the Most Important Events in Science & Technology. 704p. 1995. 50.00 (*0-8050-1829-8*) H Holt & Co.

— The Kingdom of Infinite Number: A Field Guide. 368p. 1999. text 23.95 (*0-7167-3388-9*, Sci Am Lib) W H Freeman.

— Reality's Mirror: Exploring the Mathematics of Symmetry. LC 89-33271. 286p. 1989. 19.95 (*0-471-50127-1*) Wiley.

Bunch, Bryan, ed. The Facts on File Scientific Yearbook, 1986. LC 85-642413. 221p. reprint ed. pap. 68.60 (*0-7837-1220-0*, 204175100023) Bks Demand.

— The Family Encyclopedia of Disease: A Complete Guide to Symptoms & Illnesses. LC 99-212480. (Illus.). 480p. 1998. pap. text 29.95 (*0-7167-3432-X*) W H Freeman.

Bunch, Bryan & Hellemans, Alexander. The Timetables of Technology. 512p. 1994. pap. 20.00 (*0-671-88767-X*, Touchstone) S&S Trade Pap.

***Bunch, Bryan & Tesar, Jenny.** The Penguin Desk Encyclopedia of Science & Mathematics. (Illus.). 704p. 2000. 40.00 (*0-670-88528-2*, Viking) Viking Penguin.

Bunch, Bryan, et al. The What, How & Why of Your Child's Health: The Family Encyclopedia of Disease; The Practical Pediatrician; Baby Steps, 3 vols., Set. (Illus.). 1998. pap. text 39.95 (*0-7167-3440-0*) W H Freeman.

Bunch, Bryan, jt. auth. see Hellemans, Alexander.

Bunch, Bryan H. Math. (Step Ahead Plus Workbks.). (Illus.). (J). (gr. 3-4). 1984. pap., wbk. ed. 2.09 (*0-307-23578-5*, 03578, Goldn Books) Gldn Bks Pub Co.

— Math. (Step Ahead Plus Workbks.). (Illus.). 32p. (J). (gr. 4-5). 1984. pap., wbk. ed. 2.09 (*0-307-23579-3*, 03579, Goldn Books) Gldn Bks Pub Co.

Bunch, Bryan H. & Finklestein, Iris. Math. (Step Ahead Plus Workbks.). (Illus.). 32p. (J). (gr. 5-6). 1984. pap., wbk. ed. 2.09 (*0-307-23580-7*, 03580) Gldn Bks Pub Co.

Bunch, Charlotte & Reilly, Niamh. Demanding Accountability: The Global Campaign & Tribunal for Women's Human Rights. 165p. (Orig.). 1994. pap. 14.95 (*0-912917-29-6*) UNIFEM.

Bunch, Chris. The Demon King. LC 97-32282. 528p. 1998. mass mkt. 12.99 (*0-446-67327-7*, Pub. by Warner Bks) Little.

— The Demon King. 560p. 1999. mass mkt. 6.99 (*0-446-60647-2*, Pub. by Warner Bks) Little.

***Bunch, Chris.** The Empire Stone. 560p. 2000. mass mkt. 6.99 (*0-446-60886-6*, Aspect) Warner Bks.

— Firemask. (Last Legion Ser.: No. 2). 2000. mass mkt. 6.99 (*0-451-45687-4*, ROC) NAL.

Bunch, Chris. The Last Legion. Vol. 1. 344p. 1999. mass mkt. 6.99 (*0-451-45686-6*, ROC) NAL.

Bunch, Chris. The Seer King. LC 96-22487. 528p. (Orig.). 1997. mass mkt. 13.99 (*0-446-67282-3*, Pub. by Warner Bks) Little.

Bunch, Chris. The Seer King. 560p. (Orig.). 1998. mass mkt. 6.99 (*0-446-60524-7*, Pub. by Warner Bks) Little.

***Bunch, Chris.** Stormforce. (Last Legion Ser.: Vol. 3). 2000. mass mkt. 6.99 (*0-451-45688-2*, ROC) NAL.

Bunch, Chris. The Warrior King. LC 98-29609. 384p. 1999. mass mkt. 14.99 (*0-446-67456-7*, Pub. by Warner Bks) Little.

— The Warrior King. 448p. 2000. mass mkt. 6.99 (*0-446-60790-8*, Aspect) Warner Bks.

Bunch, Chris, jt. auth. see Cole, A.

Bunch, Chris, jt. auth. see Cole, Allan.

Bunch, Cindy. Created for Relationships. (Created Male & Female Bible Studies). 64p. (Orig.). 1993. pap., wbk. ed. 4.99 (*0-8308-1136-2*, 1136) InterVarsity.

***Bunch, Cindy.** Jesus' Final Week. (LifeGuide Bible Studies). 2000. pap. 4.99 (*0-8308-3091-X*) InterVarsity.

Bunch, Cindy. Women Facing Temptation. (Created Male & Female Bible Studies). 64p. (Orig.). 1993. pap., wbk. ed. 4.99 (*0-8308-1138-9*, 1138) InterVarsity.

Bunch, Cindy, ed. Small Group Idea Book: Resources to Enrich Community, Worship & Prayer, Nurture & Outreach. LC 95-26744. 120p. (Orig.). 1996. pap. 7.99 (*0-8308-1167-2*, 1167) InterVarsity.

Bunch, Cindy & Hotaling, Scott. Christian Virtues. (LifeGuide Bible Studies). 64p. (Orig.). 1997. pap., wbk. ed. 4.99 (*0-8308-1079-X*, 1079) InterVarsity.

— Following God Together. (Created Male & Female Bible Studies). 64p. (Orig.). 1993. pap., wbk. ed. 4.99 (*0-8308-1135-4*, 1135) InterVarsity.

Bunch, Cindy & Wallace, Brian. Created Female. (Created Male & Female Bible Studies). 64p. (Orig.). 1993. pap., wbk. ed. 4.99 (*0-8308-1132-X*, 1132) InterVarsity.

Bunch, Cindy, jt. auth. see Wallace, Brian.

***Bunch, David R.** The Heartacher & the Warehouseman. 96p. 2000. pap. 12.95 (*0-9631203-7-9*, Anamnesis) Anamnesis Pr.

Bunch, Glynn H. The Chosen. LC 78-51038. 1979. 19.95 (*0-87949-112-4*) Ashley Bks.

Bunch, Josephine. Prayers for Everyday Use. 128p. 1994. pap. 7.95 (*1-85311-059-0*, 854, Pub. by Canterbury Press Norwich) Morehouse Pub.

Bunch, Lewis, ed. see Woodard, Lynette & Cook, Kevin.

Bunch, M. A. Dynamics of the Singing Voice. 2nd rev. ed. (Illus.). 208p. 1993. pap. 39.00 (*0-387-82394-8*) Spr-Verlag.

— Dynamics of the Singing Voice. 3rd ed. (Illus.). 196p. 1995. pap. text 42.00 (*3-211-82623-8*) Spr-Verlag.

Bunch, M. E., jt. ed. see Paillat, P. M.

Bunch, Meribeth. Creating Confidence: How to Develop Your Personal Power & Presence. 1999. pap. 17.95 (*0-7494-2782-5*) Kogan Page Ltd.

— Dynamics of the Singing Voice. 3rd ed. LC 94-35638. 196p. 1995. pap. 39.00 (*0-387-82623-8*) Spr-Verlag.

— Dynamics of the Singing Voice. 4th ed. LC 97-5468. 196p. 1997. 44.00 (*3-211-82985-7*) Spr-Verlag.

Bunch, Michael A. Core Curriculum in Architectural Education. LC 93-8671. 1993. 89.95 (*0-7734-2211-0*) E Mellen.

Bunch, Nancy G. Urban Growth in Austin. (Special Project Reports). 189p. 1986. pap. 8.00 (*0-89940-853-2*) LBJ Sch Pub Aff.

***Bunch, Ralph.** Nuts: A Russian Fairy Tale. (Illus.). 84p. (YA). (gr. 3 up). 2000. 19.95 (*1-58151-058-6*, Pub. by BookPartners) Midpt Trade.

Bunch, Randy. Healing: The Gospel Truth. (Book Sermon Ser.). (Orig.). pap. 3.95 (*0-940487-13-6*) Jubilee CA.

— Living above Scandal. (Book Sermon Ser.). 48p. (Orig.). 1993. pap. 3.95 (*0-940487-11-X*) Jubilee CA.

— Offenses: Keeping the Church from Stumbling. 47p. (Orig.). pap. 3.95 (*0-940487-10-1*) Jubilee CA.

Bunch, Richard A. Night Blooms: Reflections. Mycue, Edward, ed. (Took Modern Essays in English Ser.: No. 1). (Illus.). 54p. (Orig.). 1992. pap. 5.00 (*1-879457-30-X*) Norton Coker Pr.

— Sacred Spaces. 20p. 1998. pap. 4.95 (*1-883938-35-X*) Dry Bones Pr.

— Summer Hawk. Mycue, Edward, ed. (Took Modern Poetry in English Ser.: No. 21). (Illus.). 28p. (Orig.). 1991. pap. 3.00 (*1-879457-23-7*) Norton Coker Pr.

— Wading the Russian River. Mycue, Edward, ed. (Took Modern Poetry in English Ser.: No. 41). (Illus.). 28p. (Orig.). 1993. pap. 5.00 (*1-879457-43-1*) Norton Coker Pr.

Bunch, Robert. Invisible Marijuana & Psychedelic Mushroom Gardens. LC 98-85396. 150p. 1998. pap. 17.95 (*1-55950-169-3*, 85276) Loompanics.

Bunch, Robert N. Hydroponic Heroin: How to Grow Opium Poppies Without Soil. LC 98-66073. (Illus.). 94p. 1998. pap. 12.95 (*1-55950-178-2*, 85278) Loompanics.

Bunch, Roland. Two Ears of Corn: A Guide to People-Centered Agricultural Improvement. 2nd ed. (Illus.). 250p. (Orig.). 1985. pap. 7.95 (*0-942716-03-5*) World Neigh.

Bunch, S. Teaching English Naturally Module 1. 1985. text 177.37 (*0-201-19281-0*) Addison-Wesley.

— Teaching English Naturally Module 2. 1985. text 177.37 (*0-201-19282-9*) Addison-Wesley.

— Teaching English Naturally Module 3. 1983. text 156.20 (*0-201-19283-7*) Addison-Wesley.

Bunch, Taylor G. Exodus & Advent Movements: In Type & Antitype. LC 96-61046. 288p. 1997. reprint ed. per. 11.95 (*1-57258-121-2*) Teach Servs.

— The Road to Happiness. LC 97-29357. 1997. pap. 8.99 (*0-8280-1322-5*) Review & Herald.

Bunch, Wilton H., et al. Modern Management of Myelomeningocele. LC 75-161035. (Illus.). 320p. 1972. 22.50 (*0-87527-097-2*) Green.

Bunchanan, Ian, ed. A Deleuzian Century? SAQ Special Issue, Vol. 96. 300p. 1997. pap. text 12.00 (*0-8223-6451-4*) Duke.

Bunchbinder, jt. auth. see Baird.

Bunche, Ralph J. An African-American in South Africa: The Travel Notes of Ralph J. Bunche, September 28, 1937 - January 1, 1938. Edgar, Robert R., ed. (Illus.). 414p. 1992. text 40.00 (*0-8214-1021-0*) Ohio U Pr.

— The Political Status of the Negro in the Age of FDR. Grantham, Dewey W., ed. LC 72-96327. (Illus.). 715p. Date not set. reprint ed. pap. 200.00 (*0-608-20617-2*, 205458500003) Bks Demand.

Buncher, C. Ralph & Tsay, Jia-Yeong, eds. Statistics in the Pharmaceutical Industry. 2nd ed. LC 93-6362. (Statistics: Textbooks & Monographs: Vol. 140). (Illus.). 592p. 1993. text 180.00 (*0-8247-9073-1*) Dekker.

Buncher, Lyn, jt. auth. see Philips, Georges.

Bunchman, Janis & Briggs, Stephanie B. Pictures & Poetry: Activities for Creating. LC 93-72681. (Illus.). 64p. (J). (gr. 3-7). 1994. text 18.65 (*0-87192-273-8*) Davis Mass.

***Bunchua, Kirti.** The Bases of Values in Time of Change: Chinese & Westerrn Chinese Philosophical Studies, No. 16. LC 98-44462. 1998. pap. 17.50 (1-56518-114-X) Coun Res Values.

Bunck, Julie M. Fidel Castro & the Quest for a Revolutionary Culture in Cuba. LC 93-13387. 256p. (C). 1994. 40.00 (0-271-01086-X); pap. 17.95 (0-271-01087-8) Pa St U Pr.

Bunck, Julie M., jt. auth. see Fowler, Michael R.

Buncke, Harry J. Microsurgery: Transplantation-Replantation: An Atlas-Text. LC 90-6142. 832p. 1991. text 275.00 (0-8121-0981-3) Lppncott W & W.

Buncombe, Matthew. The Substance of Consciousness: An Argument for Interactionism. LC 95-79845. (Avebury Series in Philosophy). 240p. 1995. 82.95 (1-85972-271-7, Pub. by Avebry) Ashgate Pub Co.

Bund, Heinrich, tr. see Von Mises, Ludwig.

Bunday, Brian D. An Introduction to Queueing Theory. LC 96-218411. (An Arnold Publication). 224p. 1996. pap. 39.95 (0-340-66239-5, Pub. by E A) OUP.

Bunde, A. & Havlin, Shlomo, eds. Fractals & Disordered Systems. (Illus.). xiv, 350p. 1991. 64.50 (0-387-54070-9) Spr-Verlag.

— Fractals & Disordered Systems. enl. rev. ed. 430p. 1995. 69.95 (0-387-56219-2) Spr-Verlag.

— Fractals in Science: An Interdisciplinary Approach. (Illus.). 314p. 1995. 59.95 (0-387-56221-4) Spr-Verlag.

— Fractals in Science: An Interdisciplinary Approach. LC 94-207946. (Illus.). 298p. 1995. reprint ed. 59.00 (0-387-56220-6) Spr-Verlag.

Bunde, Armin & Havlin, Shlomo, eds. Fractals & Disordered Systems. 2nd ed. LC 95-41926. 408p. 1996. 69.95 (3-540-56219-2) Spr-Verlag.

Bundelmann, Felix. The Language of Sophocles: Communality, Communication & Involvement. LC 99-13645. (Cambridge Classical Studies). 312p. (C). 1999. 64.95 (0-521-66040-8) Cambridge U Pr.

Bunder, Roland. Deux Epis de Mais.Tr. of Two Ears of Corn. (FRE., Illus.). 250p. 1985. pap. 8.00 (0-942716-01-9) World Neigh.

— Dos Mazorcas de Maiz.Tr. of Two Ears of Corn. (SPA., Illus.). 250p. 1985. pap. 8.00 (0-942716-02-7) World Neigh.

Bunders, Joske, et al, eds. Biotechnology: Building on Farmers' Knowledge. (Illus.). 240p. (C). 1998. pap. text 35.00 (0-7881-7309-X) DIANE Pub.

Bunders, Joske F. Participative Strategies for Science-Based Innovations. 1995. pap. 25.00 (90-5383-342-0) Paul & Co Pubs.

Bunders, Joske F., ed. Managing the Gap Between Needs & Options. 96p. (Orig.). 1993. pap. 20.00 (90-5383-173-8, Pub. by VU Univ Pr) Paul & Co Pubs.

Bunders, Joske F. & Broerse, Jacqueline E., eds. Appropriate Biotechnology in Small-Scale Agriculture: How to Reorient Research & Development. 176p. (Orig.). 1991. pap. text 32.50 (0-85198-770-2) OUP.

Bundesanstalt fur Arbeitsschutz Staff. Phanologische Entwickungsstadien Monotyler, Dikotyler Pflanzen: English/French/German/Spanish. (ENG, FRE, GER & SPA.). 590p. 1997. 150.00 (0-320-00449-X) Fr & Eur.

***Bundesbank, Deutsche.** The Monetary Transmission Process: Recent Developments & Lessons for Europe. LC 00-42080. (Illus.). 2000. write for info. (0-312-23766-9) St Martin.

Bundesen, Lynne. One Prayer at a Time: A Day-to-Day Path to Spiritual Growth. LC 95-37511. 240p. 1995. 19.50 (0-684-81114-6) S&S Trade.

— One Prayer at a Time: A Day-to-Day Path to Spiritual Growth. 240p. 1998. pap. 10.00 (0-684-82546-5) S&S Trade.

— One Prayer at a Time: A Day-to-Day Path to Spiritual Growth. large type ed. 223p. 1996. 20.95 (0-7838-1704-5, G K Hall Lrg Type) Mac Lib Ref.

— So the Woman Went Her Way: A Personal Journey. 176p. (Orig.). 1993. pap. 10.00 (0-671-67702-0, Touchstone) S&S Trade Pap.

Bundesen, Lynne & Marks, Kristin. Click. LC 97-809. 256p. 1997. per. 15.00 (0-684-83215-1) S&S Trade Pap.

***Bundey, Nikki.** Drought & People. LC 00-9387. (Science of Weather Ser.). (Illus.). 2001. lib. bdg. write for info. (1-57505-498-1, Carolrhoda) Lerner Pub.

— Drought & the Earth. LC 00-9388. (Science of Weather Ser.). (Illus.). 2001. lib. bdg. write for info. (1-57505-473-6, Carolrhoda) Lerner Pub.

— Ice & People. (Science of Weather Ser.). (Illus.). 32p. (J). (gr. 4-7). 2000. 21.27 (1-57505-497-3) Lerner Pub.

— Ice & the Earth. LC 00-27160. (Science of Weather Ser.). (Illus.). 32p. (J). (gr. 4-7). 2000. 21.27 (1-57505-472-8, Carolrhoda) Lerner Pub.

— In the Gym. LC 98-25064. (First Sports Science Ser.). (Illus.). 32p. (J). (gr. 2-4). 1999. 21.27 (1-57505-358-6, Carolrhoda) Lerner Pub.

Bundey, Nikki. In the Park. LC 97-25961. (First Sports Science Ser.). (Illus.). 32p. (J). (ps-3). 1997. 21.27 (1-57505-277-6, Carolrhoda) Lerner Pub.

— In the Snow. LC 96-40013. (First Sports Science Ser.). (Illus.). (J). 1996. 19.93 (1-57505-086-2, Carolrhoda) Lerner Pub.

— On a Bike. LC 97-25359. (First Sports Science Ser.). 32p. (J). (gr. 1-2). 1997. 21.27 (1-57505-278-4, Carolrhoda) Lerner Pub.

— On the Field. LC 98-24379. (First Sports Science Ser.). (Illus.). 32p. (J). (gr. 2-4). 1999. 21.27 (1-57505-357-8, Carolrhoda) Lerner Pub.

***Bundey, Nikki.** Rain & People. LC 99-39664. (Science of Weather Ser.). (Illus.). 32p. (J). (gr. 4-7). 2000. lib. bdg. 21.27 (1-57505-494-9, Carolrhoda) Lerner Pub.

— Rain & the Earth. LC 99-40958. (Science of Weather Ser.). (Illus.). 32p. (J). (gr. 4-7). 2000. lib. bdg. 21.27 (1-57505-469-8, Carolrhoda) Lerner Pub.

— Snow & People. LC 00-27664. (Science of Weather Ser.). (Illus.). 32p. (J). (gr. 4-7). 2000. 21.27 (1-57505-496-5, Carolrhoda) Lerner Pub.

— Snow & the Earth. LC 00-27919. (Science of Weather Ser.). (Illus.). 32p. (J). (gr. 4-7). 2000. 21.27 (1-57505-471-X, Carolrhoda) Lerner Pub.

— Storms & the Earth. LC 00-9386. (Science of Weather Ser.). (Illus.). (J). 2001. lib. bdg. write for info. (1-57505-474-4, Carolrhoda) Lerner Pub.

— Wind & People. LC 00-23716. (Science of Weather Ser.). (Illus.). 32p. (J). (gr. 4-7). 2000. 21.27 (1-57505-495-7, Carolrhoda) Lerner Pub.

— Wind & the Earth. LC 00-23715. (Science of Weather Ser.). (Illus.). 32p. (J). (gr. 4-7). 2000. 21.27 (1-57505-470-1, Carolrhoda) Lerner Pub.

Bundgaard, Helle. Indian Art Worlds in Conflict: Local, Regional, & National Discourses on Orissan Patta Paintings. (NIAS Monographs: Vol. 80). (Illus.). 368p. 1998. text 55.00 (0-7007-0986-X, Pub. by Curzon Pr Ltd) UH Pr.

Bundgaard, J. A. Parthenon & the Mycenaean City on the Heights. (Publications of the National Museum: No. 1, Pt. 17). (Illus.). 244p. (C). 1976. pap. 33.00 (87-480-6701-6, Pub. by Aarhus Univ Pr) David Brown.

***Bundles, Alelia.** Beekman: Computer Confluence word 97 Blue Ribbon Edition. 3rd ed. 1998. 69.00 (0-201-56125-5) Addisn-Wesley Iberoamer.

— Capron with Select Word. 1998. 72.00 (0-201-61218-6) Addison-Wesley.

Bundles, Alelia. Madam C. J. Walker: Entrepreneur. Huggins, Nathan I., ed. (Black Americans of Achievement Ser.). (Illus.). 124p. (YA). (gr. 5 up). 1991. lib. bdg. 19.95 (1-55546-615-X) Chelsea Hse.

— Madam C. J. Walker: Entrepreneur. Huggins, Nathan I., ed. (Black Americans of Achievement Ser.). (Illus.). 124p. (YA). (gr. 5 up). 1992. pap. 8.95 (0-7910-0251-9) Chelsea Hse.

Bundles, A'Lelia. On Her Own Ground. 2001. write for info. (0-684-82582-1) Simon & Schuster.

Bundock, Michael. Shipping Law Handbook. ring bd. 125.00 (1-85044-889-2) LLP.

Bundrant, C. Arthur. The Missing Myna. (Illus.). 100p. (Orig.). (J). (gr. 6). 1996. pap. 6.95 (1-57502-142-0) Morris Pubng.

Bundred, Nigel J., jt. auth. see Mansel, Robert E.

Bundren, Mary R. Travel Wise with Children: 101 Educational Travel Tips for Families. LC 98-71473. (Illus.). 176p. 1998. pap. 12.95 (0-9645685-3-5, Pub. by Inprint Pub OK) BookWorld.

Bundrum, Ken. The Fighting Stevensons: Honor & War. 48p. (YA). (gr. 8 up). 1998. pap. 8.00 (0-8059-4460-5) Dorrance.

***Bundschuh, Rick.** Heat Burn: Blazing Hot Worship - A Six-Week Study of the Psalms. Reeves, Dale, ed. (Empowered Youth Products Ser.). 80p. 1999. pap. text 14.99 (0-7847-0930-0) Standard Pub.

Bundschuh, Rick. Magnetic Teaching: Making God's Word Stick in the Lives of Your Teens. Durden, Leslie & Reeves, Dale, eds. LC 98-5818. (Empowered Youth Products Ser.). (Illus.). 112p. 1998. pap. 9.99 (0-7847-0824-X, 26-23330) Standard Pub.

Bundschuh, Rick & Finley, Tom. High School Talksheets - Psalms & Proverbs: Fifty Discussion Starters from the Scriptures. 112p. 1995. pap. 12.99 (0-310-49131-2) Zondervan.

— Junior High Talksheets: Psalms & Proverbs: 50 Discussion Starters from Scripture. LC 94-16425. 112p. 1994. pap. 12.99 (0-310-49141-X) Zondervan.

— Kickstarters: 101 Ingenious Intros to Just about Any Bible Lesson. LC 96-46631. 128p. 1997. pap. 12.99 (0-310-21527-7) Youth Spec.

Bundschuh, Rick & Von Trutzschler, E. G. Crash Course in Youth Ministry: Everything You Need to Know from Adolescence to Zits. LC 96-45054. 96p. 1997. pap. 8.99 (0-310-21528-5) Youth Spec.

— Incredible Questionnaires for Youth Ministry: 50 Ways to Find Out All Sorts of Neat Stuff about Your Kids. 112p. 1996. pap. 14.99 (0-310-20770-3) Zondervan.

Bundt, Leslie. Music Therapy: Art Beyond Words. 224p. (C). 1994. pap. 27.99 (0-415-08703-1) Routledge.

Bundy, Alan. Computer Model Math Reasoning. 1984. text 89.00 (0-12-141250-4) Acad Pr.

Bundy, Alan, ed. Catalogue of Artificial Intelligence Techniques. 4th rev. ed. LC 96-41821. 135p. 1996. pap. 29.00 (3-540-59323-3) Spr-Verlag.

— Catalogue of Artificial Intelligence Tools. 2nd rev. ed. (Symbolic Computation Ser.). iv, 168p. 1986. pap. 29.70 (0-387-16893-1) Spr-Verlag.

Bundy, Alan, et al, eds. Catalogue of Artificial Intelligence Techniques. 3rd ed. (Symbolic Computation - Artificial Intelligence Ser.). 190p. 1990. 35.95 (0-387-52959-4) Spr-Verlag.

Bundy, Alan, ed. see International Conference on Automated Deduction St.

Bundy, Albert L. Radiology & the Law. LC 87-14510. 238p. 1994. reprint ed. pap. 73.80 (0-608-03393-6, 206409000008) Bks Demand.

Bundy, Alison. A Bad Business: Short Fictions of Alison Bundy. LC 85-5214. (Lost Roads Ser.: No. 27). 56p. (Orig.). 1985. pap. 6.95 (0-918786-31-2) Lost Roads.

— Duncecap: Stories. LC 98-127151. (Burning Deck Fiction Ser.). 128p. 1998. pap. 10.00 (1-886224-23-4) Burning Deck.

— Duncecap: Stories. limited ed. LC 98-127151. (Fiction Ser.). 128p. 1998. pap. 20.00 (1-886224-24-2) Burning Deck.

— Tale of a Good Cook. 32p. 4.00 (0-945926-27-8) Paradigm RI.

Bundy, Andrew, jt. auth. see Harris, Wilson.

Bundy, Barbara. The Future of the Pacific Rim: Scenarios for Regional Cooperation. LC 94-2982. 288p. 1994. pap. 20.95 (0-275-95088-3) Greenwood.

Bundy, Barbara K., et al, eds. The Future of the Pacific Rim: Scenarios for Regional Cooperation. LC 94-2982. 288p. 1994. 65.00 (0-275-94699-1, Praeger Pubs) Greenwood.

Bundy, Clarence C., et al. Dairy Production. 4th ed. 1977. 31.52 (0-13-197079-8) P-H.

Bundy, Clarence E. Swine Production. 5th ed. LC 84-115065. (Agriculture Ser.). 1984. 30.00 (0-13-879767-6) P-H.

Bundy, Clarence E., et al. Livestock & Poultry Production. 4th ed. 1975. text 31.52 (0-13-538579-2) P-H.

— Swine Production. 4th ed. (gr. 10-12). 1976. text 31.52 (0-13-879783-8) P-H.

Bundy, David. One Hundred Acres-More or Less: History of Bow, New Hampshire. LC 75-38922. (Illus.). 576p. 1975. 20.00 (0-914016-24-5) Phoenix Pub.

Bundy, David D. Keswick: A Bibliographic Introduction to the Higher Life Movements. LC 76-369083. (Occasional Bibliographic Papers of the B. L. Fisher Library: No. 3). 89p. 1975. 3.00 (0-914368-03-6) Asbury Theological.

***Bundy, David Dale.** Sorcerers, Saints, & Sages: An Encyclopedia of Holy People in World Religion, 4 Vols. 2001. lib. bdg. 375.00 (1-57607-119-7) ABC-CLIO.

Bundy, F. P., ed. see Conference on Very High Pressure.

Bundy, Frank J. The Administration of the Illyrian Provinces of the French Empire, 1809-1813. (Modern European History Ser.). 696p. 1987. text 20.00 (0-8240-8032-7) Garland.

Bundy, Mary Lee. Activism in American Librarianship, 1962-1973, 58. Stielow, Frederick J., ed. LC 87-236. (Contributions in Librarianship & Information Science Ser.: No. 58). 217p. 1987. 57.95 (0-313-24602-5, BUA/) Greenwood.

Bundy, Mary Lee. Metropolitan Public Library Users. 1968. pap. 3.50 (0-911808-03-5) U of Md Lib Serv.

— Reader in Research Methods for Librarianship. Wasserman, Paul & Araghi, Gayle, eds. LC 70-86858. 363p. 1983. lib. bdg. 69.50 (0-313-24045-0, ZRM/, Greenwood Pr) Greenwood.

Bundy, Mary Lee & Goodstein, Sylvia, eds. Library's Public Revisited. (Student Contribution Ser.: No. 1). 1967. pap. 3.00 (0-911808-01-9) U of Md Lib Serv.

Bundy, Mary Lee, jt. ed. see Wasserman, Paul.

Bundy, McGeorge. Strength of Government. LC 68-54016. (Godkin Lectures: 1968). 125p. 1968. 22.00 (0-674-84300-2) HUP.

Bundy, McGeorge, et al. Reducing Nuclear Danger: The Road Away from the Brink. 128p. 1993. 14.95 (0-87609-149-4) Coun Foreign.

— Reducing Nuclear Danger: The Road Away from the Brink. 107p. 1993. pap. text 12.95 (0-87609-170-2) Coun Foreign.

Bundy, McGeorge, ed. see Acheson, Dean.

Bundy, Miriam. The Celebration of Womanhood. pap. 9.99 (0-8024-2736-7, 106) Moody.

Bundy, Miriam & Bundy, Stuart. Restoring the Soul: Experiencing God's Grace in Time of Crisis. 119p. 1999. pap. 10.99 (0-8024-6743-1) Moody.

Bundy, Peg, pseud. Pig Out with Peg: Secrets from the Bundy Family Kitchen. 1990. pap. 8.95 (0-380-76431-8, Avon Bks) Morrow Avon.

Bundy, Peter P. Finding the Forest. x, 157p. 1999. 18.50 (0-9671940-0-8, Pub. by Masconomo Forestry); pap. 12.95 (0-9671940-1-6, Pub. by Masconomo Forestry) Adventure Pubs.

Bundy, Stuart, jt. auth. see Bundy, Miriam.

Bundy, Wayne M. The Art of Discovery: Fueling Innovation for Company Growth. Christopher, Bill, ed. LC 97-65793. (Management Library). (Illus.). 90p. (Orig.). 1997. pap. 12.95 (1-56052-438-3) Crisp Pubns.

Bundy, William P. A Tangled Web: The Making of Foreign Policy in the Nixon Presidency. LC 97-35585. (Illus.). 768p. 1998. 35.00 (0-8090-9151-8) Hill & Wang.

— A Tangled Web: The Making of Foreign Policy in the Nixon Presidency. (Illus.). 672p. 1999. pap. 16.00 (0-8090-1624-9) Hill & Wang.

Bunea, S. Paul. DTH: The New Cosmic Constant. 88p. 1998. pap. 8.00 (0-8059-4405-2) Dorrance.

Buneman, Peter, ed. see Conference on Database Theory Staff, et al.

Bunemann, Otto. Roses. 160p. 1994. pap. 14.95 (0-8120-1818-4) Barron.

Bunett, Rob, ed. see Gibson, Melinda.

Bung, K. Toward a Theory of Programmed Learning Foreign Language. (Janua Linguarum, Series Didactica: No. 1). 1973. text 55.40 (90-279-2383-3) Mouton.

Bungartz, H. J., et al, eds. High Performance Scientific & Engineering Computing: Proceedings of the International FORTWIHR Conference on HPSEC, Munich, March 16-18, 1998. LC 99-30073. (Lecture Notes in Computational Science & Engineering Ser.: Vol. 8). x, 470p. 1999. pap. 95.00 (3-540-65730-4) Spr-Verlag.

***Bungartz, H. J., et al, eds.** Lectures on Applied Mathematics: Proceedings of the Symposium Organized by the Sonderforschungsbereich 438 "Mathematical Modeling, Simulation & Intelligent Systems" on the Occasion of Karl-Heinz Hoffmann's 60th Birthday, Munich, June 30-July 1, 1999. ix, 329p. 2000. 84.00 (3-540-66734-2) Spr-Verlag.

Bungay, E. W. G. Electrical Cables Handbook. 2nd ed. 1990. 107.00 (0-8493-7710-2, Q) CRC Pr.

Bungay, Henry R. Basic Biochemical Engineering: Text & Disk with 100 Plus Programs. 2nd ed. (Illus.). 267p. (C). 1993. pap. text 38.00 (0-9639308-1-8) BiLine Assocs.

— Basic Environmental Engineering: Text & Disk with 100 Plus Programs. 2nd ed. (Illus.). 282p. (C). 1992. pap. text 38.00 (0-9639308-0-X) BiLine Assocs.

— Environmental Systems Engineering. LC 97-31778. 224p. 1997. text 107.50 (0-7923-8049-5, D Reidel) Kluwer Academic.

Bungay, P. M., et al, eds. Synthetic Membranes: Science, Engineering & Applications. 1986. text 306.50 (90-277-2293-5) Kluwer Academic.

***Bunge, Charles A.** From Past-Present to Future-Perfect: A Tribute to Charles A. Bunge & the Challenges of Contemporary Reference Service. Ferguson, Chris D., ed. LC 99-27773. (Reference Librarian Ser.: Vol. 31, No. 66). 199p. (C). 1999. text 49.95 (0-7890-0767-3) Haworth Pr.

Bunge, Charles A. & Katz, Bill, eds. Rothstein on Reference . . . With Some Help from Friends. LC 89-19886. (Reference Librarian Ser.: Nos. 25 & 26). (Illus.), 646p. 1990. text 17.95 (0-86656-840-9) Haworth Pr.

Bunge, Frederica M. Oceania: A Regional Study. 588p. 1985. boxed set 22.00 (0-16-023928-1) USGPO.

Bunge, H. J. Textures of Materials: ICOTOM-10. (Materials Science Forum Ser.: Vols. 157-162). (Illus.). 2168p. (C). 1994. text 516.00 (0-87849-681-5, Pub. by Trans T Pub) Enfield Pubs NH.

Bunge, H. J., ed. Directional Properties of Materials: Proceedings of a Symposium. (Illus.). 265p. 1988. 60.00 (3-88355-136-8, Pub. by DGM Metallurgy Info) IR Pubns.

— Experimental Techniques of Texture Analysis: Proceedings of a Workshop. (Illus.). 454p. 1986. 69.00 (3-88355-101-5, Pub. by DGM Metallurgy Info) IR Pubns.

— Theoretical Methods of Texture Analysis: Proceedings of a Workshop. (Illus.). 452p. 1987. 85.00 (3-88355-119-8, Pub. by DGM Metallurgy Info) IR Pubns.

Bunge, H. J., et al. The Determination of Integrated Intensities from Polycrystalline Samples with Preferred Orientation: A Special Issue of the Journal Crystallography Reviews. 44p. 1989. pap. text 39.00 (2-88124-723-7) Gordon & Breach.

***Bunge, John.** Open Chord Advantage: Play Open String Chords in Any Key Without Returning or Using a Capriccio. (Illus.). 80p. 1999. pap. 14.95 (1-56922-197-9) Creat Cncpts.

Bunge, M., ed. see Exact Philosophy Symposium Staff.

***Bunge, Marcia, ed.** The Child in Christian Thought. 2000. pap. 20.00 (0-8028-4693-9) Eerdmans.

Bunge, Marcia, tr. & intro. see Herder, J. G., ed.

Bunge, Mario. Causality & Modern Science. LC 78-74117. (Illus.). 395p. (C). 1979. reprint ed. pap. 12.95 (0-486-23728-1) Dover.

— Dictionary of Philosophy. 320p. 1999. 59.95 (1-57392-257-9) Prometheus Bks.

— Finding Philosophy in Social Science. LC 96-4399. (Illus.). 448p. 1996. 50.00 (0-300-06606-6) Yale U Pr.

— Method, Model & Matter. LC 72-86102. (Synthese Library: No. 44). 204p. 1972. text 140.00 (90-277-0252-7, D Reidel) Kluwer Academic.

— The Mind-Body Problem: A Psychobiological Approach. (Foundations & Philosophy of Science & Technology Ser.: Vol. 1). (Illus.). 245p. 1980. 121.00 (0-08-024720-2, Pub. by Pergamon Repr) Franklin.

***Bunge, Mario.** Philosophy in Crisis: The Need for Reconstruction. 250p. 2001. 33.00 (1-57392-843-7) Prometheus Bks.

Bunge, Mario. Philosophy of Physics. LC 72-86103. (Synthese Library: No. 45). 258p. 1972. text 152.50 (90-277-0253-5, D Reidel) Kluwer Academic.

— Philosophy of Science. LC 97-22359. 1028p. 1998. write for info. (0-7658-0415-8) Transaction Pubs.

— Philosophy of Science Vol. 1: From Problem to Theory. rev. ed. LC 97-22359. 607p. 1999. pap. 39.95 (0-7658-0413-1) Transaction Pubs.

— Philosophy of Science Vol. 2: From Explanation to Justification. rev. ed. LC 97-22359. 374p. 1998. pap. text 34.95 (0-7658-0414-X) Transaction Pubs.

— Scientific Materialism. 233p. 1981. lib. bdg. 112.00 (90-277-1304-9, D Reidel) Kluwer Academic.

— Social Science under Debate: A Philosophical Perspective. LC 98-146375. (Illus.). 672p. 1998. text 85.00 (0-8020-4298-8) U of Toronto Pr.

— The Sociology-Philosophy Connection. LC 99-25391. 197p. 1999. 29.95 (1-56000-416-9) Transaction Pubs.

— Studies in the Foundations, Methodology & Philosophy of Science, 4 vols. Incl. Vol. 3, Pt. 2. Search for Truth. LC 71-163433. (Illus.). viii, 374p. 1967. 77.95 (0-387-03995-3); LC 71-163433. write for info. (0-318-55829-7) Spr-Verlag.

— Treatise on Basic Philosophy, 8 vols. 1900. pap. text 295.00 (0-7923-0552-3, D Reidel); lib. bdg. 595.00 (0-7923-0551-5, D Reidel) Kluwer Academic.

— Treatise on Basic Philosophy: Epistemology & Methodology I. 424p. 1983. lib. bdg. 187.00 (90-277-1511-4, D Reidel) Kluwer Academic.

— Treatise on Basic Philosophy: Epistemology & Methodology II, Vol. 6. 308p. 1983. pap. text 78.50 (90-277-1635-8, D Reidel); lib. bdg. 146.00 (90-277-1634-X, D Reidel) Kluwer Academic.

— Treatise on Basic Philosophy Vol. 7: Epistemology & Methodology III: Philosophy of Science & Technology Pt. II: Life Science, Social Science & Technology. 353p. 1985. pap. text 67.50 (90-277-1914-4, D Reidel); lib. bdg. 138.00 (90-277-1913-6, D Reidel) Kluwer Academic.

— Treatise on Basic Philosophy Vol. 8: Ethics: The Good & the Right. 448p. (C). 1989. lib. bdg. 198.00 (90-277-2839-9, D Reidel) Kluwer Academic.

— Treatise on Basic Philosophy, Vol. 7: Epistemology & Methodology III: Philosophy of Science & Technology Pt I: Formal & Physical Sciences. 272p. 1985. pap. text 57.50 (90-277-1904-7, D Reidel); lib. bdg. 112.00 (90-277-1903-9, D Reidel) Kluwer Academic.

An Asterisk (*) at the beginning of an entry indicates that the title is appearing for the first time.

***Bunge, Mario, ed.** Critical Approaches to Science & Philosophy: Essays in Honor of Karl R. Popper. LC 98-4673. (Science & Technology Studies). 481p. 1998. pap. text 29.95 (*0-7658-0427-1*) Transaction Pubs.

Bunge, Mario, ed. The Methodological Unity of Science. LC 73-83554. (Theory & Decision Library: No. 3). 1973. lib. bdg. 112.00 (*90-277-0354-X*) Kluwer Academic.

— The Methodological Unity of Science. LC 73-83554. (Theory & Decision Library: No. 3). 1973. pap. text 73.50 (*90-277-0404-X*) Kluwer Academic.

Bunge, Mario & Ardila, R. Philosophy of Psychology. (Illus.). 320p. 1987. text 111.95 (*0-387-96442-8*) Spr-Verlag.

Bunge, Mario, jt. auth. see Mahner, M.

Bunge, Mary B. & Mensching, Teresa B., eds. Defining & Applying Effective Teaching Strategies for Library Instruction. (Library Orientation Ser.: No. 18). 133p. 1989. pap. 35.00 (*0-87650-252-4*) Pierian.

Bunge, Nancy. Nathaniel Hawthorne: A Study of the Short Fiction. (Twayne's Studies in Short Fiction). 180p. 1993. 29.00 (*0-8057-0852-9*, Twyne) Mac Lib Ref.

Bunge, Wilfred F. Warmly Weston: A Luther College Life. LC 98-85141. (Luther Legacy Ser.: Vol. 2). (Illus.). 183p. 1998. pap. 15.00 (*0-9620861-1-8*) Luther Coll Pr.

Bunger, James W. & Li, Norman C., eds. Chemistry of Asphaltenes: Based on a Symposium. LC 81-19053. (Advances in Chemistry Ser.: No. 195). (Illus.). 269p. reprint ed. pap. 83.40 (*0-608-04433-4*, 205256900012) Bks Demand.

Bungert, Klauspeter. Cesar Franck - Die Musik und das Denken: Das Gesamtwerk, Neubetrachtet fur Horer, Wissenschaftler und Ausubende Musiker - Mit Einer Allgemeinen Erorterung zum Ineinandergreifen von Form und Klingendem Satz. Von Albrecht, Michael, ed. (Quellen und Studien zur Musikgeschichte von der Antike bis in die Gegenwart: Bd. 34). (GER.). 219p. 1996. 42.95 (*3-631-30354-8*) P Lang Pubng.

Bungey, J. H., jt. auth. see Mosley, W. H.

Bungey, John H. & Millard. Testing of Concrete in Structures. 3rd ed. (Illus.). 296p. 1996. text 138.00 (*0-7514-0241-9*, Pub. by B Acad & Prof) Routldge.

Bungey, Lloyd. Pioneering Aviation in the West. 328p. 1992. pap. 22.95 (*0-88839-271-0*) Hancock House.

Bungs, Dzintra. The Baltic States: Problems & Prospects of Membership in the European Union. LC 98-230443. (Aktuelle Materialien zur Internationalen Politik Ser.). 130 p. 1998. write for info. (*3-7890-5591-3*) Nomos Verlags.

Bungus, Petrus. Numerorum Mysteria. (GER.). 1983. reprint ed. write for info. (*3-487-07297-1*) G Olms Pubs.

Buni, Andrew. Robert L. Vann of the Pittsburgh Courier: Politics & Black Journalism. LC 73-7700. (Illus.). 432p. 1974. text 29.95 (*0-8229-3274-1*) U of Pittsburgh Pr.

Bunick, Nick. In God's Truth. LC 98-73382. (Illus.). 232p. 1999. pap. 12.95 (*1-57174-129-1*) Hampton Roads Pub Co.

Bunick, Nick, jt. auth. see Virtue, Doreen.

Bunie, Andrew, jt. auth. see Boyle, Sheila T.

Bunim, Amos. Ethics from Sinai, 3 vols., Set. 1964. 39.95 (*0-87306-002-4*); pap. 24.95 (*0-87306-003-2*) Feldheim.

— A Fire in His Soul! Irving Bunim, 1901-1980: The Man & His Impact on American Orthodox Jewry. (Illus.). 528p. 1989. pap. 17.95 (*0-87306-474-7*) Feldheim.

***Bunim, Irving M.** Ethics from Sinai: A Wide-Ranging Commentary on Pirkei Avos. LC 00-27914. (ENG & ARC.). 2000. write for info. (*1-58330-392-8*) Feldheim.

Bunim, Miriam S. Space in Medieval Painting & the Forerunners of Perspective. (BCL Ser. I). (Illus.). reprint ed. 32.50 (*0-404-01229-9*) AMS Pr.

Bunimovich, A. I. & Dubinskii, A. V. Mathematical Models & Methods of Localized Interaction Theory. (Series on Advances in Mathematics). 244p. 1995. text 86.00 (*981-02-1743-9*) World Scientific Pub.

Bunimovich, L. A., et al, eds. Sinai's Moscow Seminar on Dynamical Systems. LC 91-640741. (American Mathematical Society Translations Ser.: Series 2, Vol. 171). 247p. 1995. text 95.00 (*0-8218-0456-1*, TRANS2/171) Am Math.

***Bunimovich, L. A., et al.** Dynamical Systems, Ergodic Theory & Applications. 2nd enl. rev. ed. (Encyclopaedia of Mathematical Sciences Ser.). 400p. 2000. 106.00 (*3-540-66316-9*) Spr-Verlag.

Bunin, jt. auth. see Cozzola.

Bunin, Barry A., ed. The Combinatorial Index. LC 97-81368. (Illus.). 322p. 1998. text 79.95 (*0-12-141340-3*) Morgan Kaufmann.

Bunin, Catherine & Bunin, Sherry. Is That Your Sister? A True Story of Adoption. (Illus.). 32p. (J). (gr. 2-6). 1992. reprint ed. 14.95 (*0-9611872-6-3*) Our Child Pr.

Bunin, D. A., et al. Deutsch-Russisches Worterbuch fur Eisenbahnwessen.Tr. of German-Russian Railway Dictionary. (GER & RUS.). 531p. 1957. 14.95 (*0-7859-0796-3*, M9060) Fr & Eur.

Bunin, G. M. & Kemezuk, N. K. German-Russian Dictionary of Mineral Processing & Use: Deutsch-Russisches Woerterbuch der Aufbereitung und Verarbeitung Mineralischer. (GER & RUS.). 519p. 1983. 95.00 (*0-8288-1920-3*, M1987) Fr & Eur.

***Bunin, Ivan.** The Liberation of Tolstoy: A Tale of Two Writers. 2001. 35.00 (*0-8101-1752-5*) Northwestern U Pr.

Bunin, Ivan A. Cursed Days: Diary of a Revolution. Marullo, Thomas G., tr. from RUS. LC 97-52822. 186p. 1998. text 28.50 (*1-56663-186-6*) I R Dee.

— Dark Avenues. unabridged ed. (World Classic Literature Ser.). (RUS.). pap. 6.95 (*2-87714-275-2*, Pub. by Bookking Intl) Distribks Inc.

— The Gentleman from San Francisco & Other Stories. Richards, David & Lund, Sophie, trs. 224p. 1992. pap. 12.95 (*0-14-018552-6*, Penguin Classics) Viking Penguin.

— In a Far Distant Land. Bowie, Robert, tr. from RUS. & pref. by. LC 82-21296. 1983. pap. 8.50 (*0-938920-27-8*) Hermitage Pubs.

— The Life of Arseniev: Youth. Struve, Gleb et al, trs. from RUS. (Studies in Russian Literature & Theory). 300p. 1994. 54.95 (*0-8101-1187-X*); pap. 17.95 (*0-8101-1172-1*) Northwestern U Pr.

— Memories & Portraits. LC 68-8053. (Illus.). 217p. 1968. reprint ed. lib. bdg. 49.75 (*0-8371-0033-X*, BUMP, Greenwood Pr) Greenwood.

— The Well of Days. 314p. Date not set. 24.95 (*0-8488-2220-X*) Amereon Ltd.

— The Well of Days. Struve, Gleb & Miles, H., trs. from RUS. 351p. 1976. reprint ed. 45.00 (*0-86527-326-X*) Fertig.

Bunin, Keith. The Principality of Sorrows. 68p. 1997. pap. 5.60 (*0-87129-767-1*, P82) Dramatic Pub.

Bunin, Patricia A. Do You Think We Could Have Made It & Other Love Poems for the Separated & Divorced. LC 77-91010. 1977. pap. 3.95 (*0-930946-01-4*) Newaves Pub.

Bunin, Pauline. Death of a Marriage. LC 94-71240. 238p. (Orig.). 1995. pap. 14.95 (*1-884866-00-X*) Cosmos Bks.

Bunin, Rachel B. Corel WordPerfect 7 for Windows 95: Illustrated Standard Edition. (Illustrated Ser.). (Illus.). 192p. (C). 1996. pap. 21.95 (*0-7600-3750-7*) Course Tech.

— WordPerfect 6.1 for Windows, Incl. instr. resource kit, test bank, transparency. (Illustrated Ser.). (Illus.). 224p. 1995. text, mass mkt. 20.95 incl. 3.5 ld (*0-7600-3481-8*) Course Tech.

Bunin, Rachel B. & Ericksen, Linda. Corel WordPerfect 7 for Windows 95: Illustrated PLUS Edition. 10th ed. (Illustrated Ser.). (Illus.). 192p. (C). 1997. pap. 38.95 (*0-7600-3755-8*) Course Tech.

— Corel WordPerfect 7 for Windows 95: Standard Edition: A Second Course. 10th ed. (Illustrated Ser.). (Illus.). 800p. (C). 1997. pap. 21.95 (*0-7600-5188-7*) Course Tech.

Bunin, Sherry. Dear Great American Writers School. 176p. (YA). (gr. 5). 1997. mass mkt. 4.50 (*0-440-22038-6*) Dell.

— Dear Great American Writers School. LC 94-27265. 176p. (J). (gr. 5-9). 1995. 15.00 (*0-395-71645-4*) HM.

— Dear Great American Writers School. (J). 1997. 9.60 (*0-606-11245-6*, Pub. by Turtleback) Demco.

Bunin, Sherry, jt. auth. see Bunin, Catherine.

Buning, Hans K. & Letterman, T. Propositional Logic: Deduction & Algorithms. LC 98-38806. (Cambridge Tracts in Theoretical Computer Science Ser.: No. 48). (Illus.). 420p. (C). 1998. 74.95 (*0-521-63017-7*) Cambridge U Pr.

Buning, Herbert & Naeve, Peter, eds. Computational Statistics. 348p. 1981. text 89.25 (*3-11-008419-8*) De Gruyter.

Buning, J. E. & Schooneveld, C. H. van. The Sentence Intonation of Contemporary Standard Russian As a Linguistic Structure. (Description & Analysis of Contemporary Standard Russian: No. 3). 1961. 43.10 (*3-11-000021-0*) Mouton.

Buning, Marius, jt. ed. see Oppenheim, Lois.

Buning, Sietze. Purpaleanie & Other Permutations. LC 78-61207. 1978. pap. 5.95 (*0-931940-00-1*) Middleburg Pr.

— Style & Class. LC 82-14541. 1982. pap. 7.95 (*0-931940-06-0*) Middleburg Pr.

Buning, W. De Cock & Alting, J. H. Netherlands & the World War Vol. 3: Studies in the War History of Neutral: Effect of the War Upon the Colonies. (Economic & Social History of the World War Ser.). 1928. 60.00 (*0-686-83636-7*) Elliots Bks.

Bunis, David M. A Guide to Reading & Writing Judezmo. 49p. 1975. pap. 5.00 (*0-917288-01-7*) Adelantre.

Bunis, David M. & Sunshine, Andrew. Yiddish Linguistics: A Classified Bilingual Index of Yiddish Serials & Collections, 1913-1958. LC 93-34051. 216p. 1994. reprint ed. text 10.00 (*0-8240-9758-0*, H175) Garland.

Bunis, Marty. Collector's Guide to Novelty Radios. (Illus.). 224p. 1994. pap. 18.95 (*0-89145-612-0*, 3881) Collector Bks.

Bunis, Marty & Bunis, Sue. Collector's Guide to Antique Radios: Collectors Guide to Antiques. 4th rev. ed. LC 97-101891. (Illus.). 248p. 1996. pap. 18.95 (*0-89145-712-7*, 4705) Collector Bks.

— Collector's Guide to Transistor Radios: Identification & Values. 2nd ed. 320p. 1996. pap. 16.95 (*0-89145-704-6*, 4652) Collector Bks.

Bunis, Marty, jt. auth. see Breed, Robert.

Bunis, Sue, jt. auth. see Bunis, Marty.

Bunjes, Werner E. English-German Medical & Pharmaceutical Dictionary. 696p. 195.00 (*0-8288-1832-0*, M7106) Fr & Eur.

— German-English Medical & Pharmaceutical Dictionary. 3rd ed. 574p. 1981. 185.00 (*0-8288-1833-9*, M8736) Fr & Eur.

Bunjes, Werner E., jt. auth. see Lejeune, F.

Bunk, B., et al, eds. Lattice Gauge Theory: A Challenge in Large-Scale Computing. LC 86-15155. (NATO ASI Series B, Physics: Vol. 140). 342p. 1986. 95.00 (*0-306-42376-2*, Plenum Trade) Perseus Pubng.

Bunk, W., ed. Advanced Structural & Functional Materials: Proceedings of an International Seminar Organized by Deutsche Forschungsanstalt fur Luft & Raumfahrt, DLR, Koln, June 1991. (Illus.). vi, 219p. 1991. 75.95 (*0-387-53783-X*) Spr-Verlag.

Bunke, H., ed. Advances in Structural & Syntactic Pattern Recognition: Proceedings of the International Workshop on Structural & Syntactic Pattern Recognition, Bern, Switzerland, August 26-28, 1992. LC 92-41024. (Series in Machine Perception & Artificial Intelligence: Vol. 5). 636p. 1993. text 121.00 (*981-02-1183-X*) World Scientific Pub.

Bunke, H. & Sanfeliu, A., eds. Syntactic & Structural Pattern Recognition: Theory & Applications. 564p. (C). 1990. text 99.00 (*9971-5-0552-5*); pap. text 61.00 (*9971-5-0566-5*) World Scientific Pub.

Bunke, H., et al. Document Image Analysis. (Series in Machine Perception & Artificial Intelligence). 208p. 1994. text 61.00 (*981-02-2046-4*) World Scientific Pub.

Bunke, H., jt. auth. see Wang, P. S.

Bunke, Helga & Bunke, Olaf, eds. Statistical Inference in Linear Models Vol. 1: Statistical Methods of Model Building. Bibby, John & Basch, Michal, trs. LC 83-21675. (Wiley Series in Probability & Mathematical Statistics). 614p. reprint ed. pap. 190.40 (*0-8357-3395-5*, 203965200001) Bks Demand.

Bunke, Horst, et al, eds. Modelling & Planning for Sensor Based Intelligent Robot Systems. (Series in Machine Perception & Artificial Intelligence: Vol. 21). 550p. 1995. text 99.00 (*981-02-2238-6*) World Scientific Pub.

Bunke, Olaf, jt. ed. see Bunke, Helga.

Bunke, Ulrich & Olbrich, Martin. Selberg Zeta & Theta Functions: A Differential Operator Approach. LC 95-4564. (Mathematical Research Ser.: Vol. 83). 168p. 1995. pap. text 73.45 (*3-05-501690-4*, Pub. by Akademie Verlag) Wiley.

Bunker, Barbara, et al. Student's Guide to Conducting Social Science Research. LC 74-11814. 120p. (C). 1975. pap. 16.95 (*0-87705-238-7*, Kluwer Acad Hman Sci) Kluwer Academic.

Bunker, Barbara B. & Alban, Billie T. Large Group Interventions: Engaging the Whole System for Rapid Change. LC 96-26883. (The Jossey-Bass Business & Management Ser.). 1996. 30.95 (*0-7879-0324-8*) Jossey-Bass.

Bunker, Barbara B. & Rubin, Jeffrey Z. Conflict, Cooperation, & Justice: Essays Inspired by the Work of Morton Deutsch. LC 94-46743. (Conflict Resolution Ser.). 478p. 1995. text 44.95 (*0-7879-0069-9*) Jossey-Bass.

***Bunker, Barbara Benedict, et al.** A Student's Guide to Conducting Social Science Research. 120p. (YA). (gr. 6-12). 1999. 16.95 (*0-936386-78-9*) Creative Learning.

Bunker, C., jt. auth. see Johnson, N. I.

Bunker, C. W. Bunker Family, Branches Early Identified with Charlestown & Nantucket, Mass., & Delaware & Maryland, As Well As Early Bunkers & Those in Europe. 797p. 1993. reprint ed. pap. 115.00 (*0-8328-3557-9*); reprint ed. lib. bdg. 125.00 (*0-8328-3556-0*) Higginson Bk Co.

Bunker, Chris, jt. auth. see Johnson, Norman.

Bunker, D. & Dickenson, A. Theory of Elementary Gas Reaction Rates. (International Encyclopedia of Physical Chemistry & Chemical Physics Ser.: Vol. 1, TF 19). 1966. 57.00 (*0-08-011804-6*, Pub. by Pergamon Repr) Franklin.

Bunker, Dorothy, jt. auth. see Roberts, Sue N.

Bunker, Dusty. Numerology & Your Future. 256p. 1980. pap. 16.95 (*0-914918-18-4*, Whitford) Schiffer.

— Numerology, Astrology & Dreams. Lockhart, Julie, ed. LC 87-62095. (Illus.). 236p. 1987. pap. 19.95 (*0-914918-74-5*, Whitford) Schiffer.

— Quintiles & Tredeciles: The Geometry of the Goddess. LC 89-51667. (Illus.). 182p. (C). 1989. pap. 12.95 (*0-914918-69-9*, Whitford) Schiffer.

Bunker, Dusty, et al. Birthday Numerology. LC 82-60411. 240p. 1982. pap. 13.95 (*0-914918-39-7*, Whitford) Schiffer.

Bunker, Dusty, jt. auth. see Javane, Faith.

Bunker, Eddie. Little Boy Blue. LC 97-16103. 320p. 1997. text 22.95 (*0-312-16907-8*) St Martin.

***Bunker, Edward.** The Animal Factory. 208p. 2000. reprint ed. pap. 11.95 (*0-312-26711-8*, Minotaur) St Martin.

Bunker, Edward. Dog Eat Dog. 240p. 1996. 22.95 (*0-312-14314-1*) St Martin.

— Dog Eat Dog. 240p. 1997. pap. 12.95 (*0-312-16818-7*) St Martin.

***Bunker, Edward.** Education of a Felon: A Memoir. LC 99-55061. 294p. 2000. text 25.95 (*0-312-25315-X*) St Martin.

Bunker, Edward. Little Boy Blue. 240p. 1998. pap. 13.95 (*0-312-19504-4*, Pub. by Tor Bks) St Martin.

Bunker, Ellen L., jt. auth. see Thompson, Melody M.

Bunker, Emma C. Ancient Bronzes of the Eastern Eurasian Steppes: From the Arthur M. Sackler Collections. LC 97-71766. (Illus.). 400p. 1997. 75.00 (*0-8109-6348-5*, Pub. by Abrams) Time Warner.

Bunker, Emma C., jt. auth. see So, Jenny F.

Bunker, Frank F. The Junior High School Movement - Its Beginnings. LC 83-45417. reprint ed. 41.00 (*0-404-20047-8*) AMS Pr.

Bunker, Gary L. & Bitton, Davis. The Mormon Graphic Image, 1834-1914: Cartoons, Caricatures, & Illustrations. LC 83-1305. (University of Utah Publications in the American West: No. 16). 164p. reprint ed. pap. 50.90 (*0-8357-3274-6*, 203949500013) Bks Demand.

Bunker, Gerald E. The Peace Conspiracy: Wang Ching-Wei & the China War, 1937-1941. LC 78-180149. (Harvard East Asian Ser.: No. 67). 342p. reprint ed. pap. 106.10 (*0-608-30389-5*, 200548600054) Bks Demand.

Bunker, Harris F. Principios Fundamentales de Evaluacion para Educadores. 4th ed. 156p. 1976. 4.00 (*0-8477-2730-0*); pap. 3.00 (*0-8477-2702-5*) U of PR Pr.

Bunker, John. Heroes in Dungarees: The Story of the American Merchant Marine in World War II. LC 95-6785. (Illus.). 392p. 1995. 34.95 (*1-55750-093-2*) Naval Inst Pr.

Bunker, John G. Liberty Ships. LC 79-6103. (Navies & Men Ser.). (Illus.). 1980. reprint ed. lib. bdg. 31.95 (*0-405-13032-5*) Ayer.

Bunker, John Michael & Pressler, Karen L. Edgar Cayce & the Urantia Book. (Illus.). 252p. 1996. 24.90 (*0-9669774-0-8*) J M Bunker.

Bunker, Linda, jt. auth. see Owens, DeDe.

Bunker, Linda, jt. auth. see Rotella, Robert.

Bunker, Linda K. & Rotella, R. J., eds. Sport Psychology: Psychological Consideration in Maximizing Sport Psychology. 1985. 34.95 (*0-932392-20-2*) Mouvement Pubns.

Bunker, Linda K., jt. auth. see Owens, DeDe.

Bunker, M. N. What Handwriting Tells You: About Yourself, Your Friends, & Famous People. 1965. 26.95 (*0-911012-02-8*) Burnham Inc.

Bunker, Mary P. Long Island Genealogies: Being Kindred Descendants of Thomas Powell of Bethpage, L.I., 1688. (Illus.). 350p. 1989. reprint ed. lib. bdg. 58.00 (*0-8328-0574-2*) Higginson Bk Co.

Bunker, Matthew D. Justice & the Media: Reconciling Fair Trials & a Free Press. LC 96-38168. (Communication Ser.). 160p. 1996. 29.95 (*0-8058-2168-6*) L Erlbaum Assocs.

***Bunker, Merton W., Jr. & Moore, Wayne D.** National Fire Alarm Code Handbook, 1, 3. 3rd ed. LC 99-75955. 422p. 2000. 18.00 (*0-87765-445-X*, 72HB99) Natl Fire Prot.

Bunker, Merton W., Jr., jt. ed. see Moore, Wayne D.

Bunker, Paul D. Bunker's War: The World War II Diary of Colonel Paul D. Bunker. Barlow, Keith A., ed. 309p. 1998. text 28.00 (*0-7881-5799-X*) DIANE Pub.

Bunker, Philip R. & Jensen, Per. Molecular Symmetry & Spectroscopy. 2nd ed. 768p. 1998. 81.50 (*0-660-17519-3*) NRC Res Pr.

Bunker, Robert, jt. auth. see Thorp, Raymond W.

Bunker, Stephen G. Peasants Against the State: The Politics of Market Control in Bugisu, Uganda, 1900-1983. LC 85-20894. x, 302p. 1991. pap. text 17.95 (*0-226-08031-5*) U Ch Pr.

— Peasants Against the State: The Politics of Market Control in Bugisu, Uganda, 1900-1983. LC 85-20894. 296p. 1987. text 29.95 (*0-252-01288-7*) U of Ill Pr.

— Underdeveloping the Amazon: Extraction, Unequal Exchange, & the Failure of the Modern State. (Illus.). xvi, 294p. 1988. pap. text 17.95 (*0-226-08032-3*) U Ch Pr.

— Underdeveloping the Amazon: Extraction, Unequal Exchange, & the Failure of the Modern State. LC 83-18197. 296p. 1985. text 29.95 (*0-252-01121-X*) U of Ill Pr.

Bunker, Stephen G., jt. ed. see Ciccantell, Paul S.

Bunker, Stimson, Solien & Jacob, Inc. Staff. Site Planning for Affordable Housing: Four Case Studies in Falmouth, Massachusetts. (Illus.). (Orig.). (C). 1988. pap. text. write for info. (*0-929072-00-6*) Bunker Stimson.

Bunkers, Laurie, ed. see First United Nursery School Parents & Teachers.

Bunkers, Suzanne L. All Will Yet Be Well: The Diary of Sarah Gillespie Huftalen, 1873-1952. LC 93-32516. (Bur Oak Original Ser.). (Illus.). 346p. 1993. text 46.95 (*0-87745-421-3*); pap. text 17.95 (*0-87745-422-1*) U of Iowa Pr.

— A Confederate Girl: The Diary of Carrie Berry, 1864. Steele, Christy & Todd, Ann, eds. LC 99-29044. (Diaries, Letters & Memoirs Ser.). 32p. (J). (gr. 2-7). 2000. lib. bdg. 22.60 (*0-7368-0343-2*, Blue Earth Bks) Capstone Pr.

— In Search of Susanna. LC 96-3396. (Singular Lives Ser.). (Illus.). 270p. (Orig.). 1996. pap. 19.95 (*0-87745-538-4*) U of Iowa Pr.

***Bunkers, Suzanne L.** A Pioneer Farm Girl: The Diary of Sarah Gillespie, 1877-1878. (Diaries, Letters & Memoirs Ser.). 32p. (J). (gr. 2-7). 1999. 21.00 (*0-516-21340-7*) Childrens.

Bunkers, Suzanne L. & Hodgson, Ann, eds. A Pioneer Farm Girl: The Diary of Sarah Gillespie, 1877-1878. LC 99-15273. (Diaries, Letters & Memoirs Ser.). 32p. (J). (gr. 2-7). 2000. lib. bdg. 22.60 (*0-7368-0347-5*, Blue Earth Bks) Capstone Pr.

Bunkers, Suzanne L. & Huff, Cynthia A., eds. Inscribing the Daily: Critical Essays on Women's Diaries. LC 95-31825. 312p. 1996. pap. 18.95 (*1-55849-011-6*); text 55.00 (*1-55849-010-8*) U of Mass Pr.

Bunkin, Alexey, jt. auth. see Voliak, Konstantin.

Bunkin, F. V. Lasers in Acoustics. (Laser Science & Technology Ser.). 177p. 1991. 130.00 (*3-7186-5061-4*, Harwood Acad Pubs) Gordon & Breach.

Bunkin, F. V., ed. Nonlinear Optics & Acoustics of Fluids. (Proceedings of the Institute of General Physics of the Academy of Sciences of the U. S. S. R. Ser.: Vol. 6). 172p. 1989. text 165.00 (*0-941743-28-4*) Nova Sci Pubs.

Bunkin, F. V. & Voliak, K. I., eds. Oceanic Remote Sensing. (Proceedings of the Institute of General Physics of the Academy of Sciences of the U. S. S. R. Ser.: Vol. 1). 222p. (C). 1988. text 165.00 (*0-941743-12-8*) Nova Sci Pubs.

Bunkley, Anita Richmond. African-American Writers Reading Group Guide. 1997. pap. write for info. (*0-452-15549-5*) NAL.

— Balancing Act. 400p. 1998. mass mkt. 6.99 (*0-451-18483-1*, Sig) NAL.

— Black Gold. 448p. 1995. mass mkt. 6.99 (*0-451-17973-0*, Sig) NAL.

— Black Gold. large type ed. LC 94-4869. 592p. 1994. reprint ed. lib. bdg. 23.95 (*0-8161-7434-2*, G K Hall Lrg Type) Mac Lib Ref.

***Bunkley, Anita Richmond.** Emily: The Yellow Rose. 243p. 1999. 19.99 (*0-9624012-1-8*, Pub. by Rinard Pub) Replica Bks.

Bunkley, Anita Richmond. Starlight Passage. 1997. mass mkt. 6.99 (*0-451-19037-8*, Sig) NAL.

— Starlight Passage. 1999. pap. 5.99 (*0-451-18482-3*, Sig) NAL.

— Starlight Passage. large type ed. LC 96-43569. 650p. 1996. lib. bdg. 24.95 (*0-7862-0922-4*) Thorndike Pr.

B

— Steppin' out with Attitude: Sister Sell Your Dream. LC 98-23754. 320p. 1998. pap. 12.50 (*0-06-095288-1*) HarpC.

Bunkley, Anita Richmond, et al. Girlfriends. 368p. 1999. mass mkt. 5.99 (*0-06-101369-2*, Harp PBks) HarpC.

— Sisters. 352p. 1996. mass mkt. 6.99 (*0-451-19100-5*, Sig) NAL.

Bunkley, Crawford B. The African-American Network: Get Connected to More Than 5,000 Prominent People & Organizations in the African-American Community. LC 96-18097. 560p. 1996. pap. 14.95 (*0-452-27493-1*, Plume) Dutton Plume.

Bunkley, Josephine M. The Nun Who Escaped: A True Story. abr. rev. ed. LC 98-67306. Orig. Title: Miss Bunkley's Book: The Testimony of an Escaped Novice. 106p. 1998. reprint ed. pap. 11.95 (*1-889298-84-0*) Rhwymbooks.

***Bunkov, Yuriy M. & Godfrin, Henri.** Topological Defects & the Non-Equilibrium Dynamics. 396p. 2000. pap. 66.00 (*0-7923-6205-5*) Kluwer Academic.

***Bunkowske, Bernice.** Dreams Dawn in Africa. Mueller, Louise & Brauer, Janice K., eds. 172p. 1999. pap. 6.00 (*0-9677375-0-8*) Lutheran Womens.

Bunn, Alfred. Old England & New England, in a Series of Views Taken on the Spot, 2 vols., 1 bk. LC 68-20213. (Illus.). 1972. reprint ed. 26.95 (*0-405-08330-0*, Pub. by Blom Pubns) Ayer.

Bunn, D. S., et al. The Barn Owl. LC 82-72126. (Illus.). 264p. 1982. 32.50 (*0-931130-09-3*) Harrell Bks.

Bunn, David. B. (Illus.). 115p. 1997. 200.00 (*1-888979-06-2*) D Bunn.

— D. (Illus.). 47p. 1997. 200.00 (*1-888979-05-4*) D Bunn.

— David Bunn: Because I Love You. (Illus.). 88p. (Orig.). 1998. pap. 15.00 (*1-888979-07-0*) D Bunn.

— Discipline & Bayonets. (Illus.). 130p. 1996. 275.00 (*1-888979-02-X*) D Bunn.

— Displacements: South African Works on Paper 1984-1994. 1994. pap. 35.00 (*0-8101-5012-3*) Northwestern U Pr.

— The Guide for the Perplexed. (Illus.). 155p. 1996. 275.00 (*1-888979-01-1*) D Bunn.

— Love Among the Artists. (Illus.). 160p. 1996. 275.00 (*1-888979-00-3*) D Bunn.

— The Sea Is a Magic Carpet (Liverpool) (Illus.). 198p. 1997. 200.00 (*1-888979-03-8*) D Bunn.

— The Sea Is a Magic Carpet (Los Angeles) (Illus.). 202p. 1997. 200.00 (*1-888979-04-6*) D Bunn.

Bunn, David, et al, eds. From South Africa: New Writing, Photographs & Art. (Illus.). 504p. 1997. pap. 19.95 (*0-226-08036-6*) U Ch Pr.

— From South Africa: New Writing, Photographs & Art. (Illus.). 504p. 1998. lib. bdg. 57.00 (*0-226-08035-8*) U Ch Pr.

— Writers from South Africa: TriQuarterly 69: Fourteen Writers on Culture, Politics & Literary Theory & Activity in South Africa. 128p. 1991. pap. 6.50 (*0-916384-03-9*, TriQuart) Northwestern U Pr.

Bunn, Derek W. & Larsen, Erik, eds. Systems Modelling for Energy Policy. LC 96-47600. 342p. 1997. 129.95 (*0-471-95794-1*) Wiley.

Bunn, Don. Classic & Collectible Trucks LC 97-75814. 144p. 1998. write for info. (*0-7853-2797-5*) Pubns Intl Ltd.

— Classic Ford F-Series Pickup Trucks, 1948-1956. LC 98-34963. (Pickup Color History Ser.). (Illus.). 128p. 1998. pap. 21.95 (*0-7603-0483-1*) MBI Pubg.

— Dodge Power Wagons 1940-1980 Photo Archive. LC 98-71288. (Illus.). 128p. 1998. pap. 29.95 (*1-882256-89-1*) Iconografix.

— Dodge Trucks. LC 96-8851. (Crestline Ser.). (Illus.). 320p. 1996. 44.95 (*0-7603-0118-2*) MBI Pubg.

— Encyclopedia of Chevrolet Trucks. LC 99-31698. (Illus.). 320p. 1999. 44.95 (*0-7603-0565-X*, 128933AP, Pub. by MBI Pubg) Motorbooks Intl.

Bunn, Don, ed. Dodge Pickups 1939-1978 Photo Album. LC 97-75277. (Photo Album Ser.). (Illus.). 112p. 1998. pap. 19.95 (*1-882256-82-4*) Iconografix.

— White Trucks 1900-1937 Photo Archive: Photographs from the National Automotive History Collection of the Detroit Public Library. LC 97-75276. (Illus.). 128p. 1998. pap. 29.95 (*1-882256-80-8*) Iconografix.

Bunn, Don & Mueller, Mike. Dodge Pickup Color History: Dodge Pickups & Light Duty Trucks, Panels, Vans, Military Trucks, Power Wagon Swetsides, Custom Sports Specials, Dakotas, T300s & More 1916-1996. LC 96-14080. (Color History Ser.). (Illus.). 128p. 1996. pap. 21.95 (*0-7603-0170-0*) MBI Pubg.

Bunn, Don, jt. auth. see Brownell, Tom.

Bunn, George. Arms Control by Committee: Managing Negotiations with the Russians. LC 92-13995. (Studies in International Security & Arms Control). 360p. (C). 1992. 45.00 (*0-8047-2039-8*) Stanford U Pr.

Bunn, George, et al. Nuclear Disarmament: How Much Have the Five Nuclear Powers Promised in the Non-Proliferation Treaty? (Global Security Issues Ser.). 32p. 1994. pap. text 10.00 (*1-884179-01-0*) Lawyers Alliance.

Bunn, Ivan, jt. auth. see Geis, Gilbert.

Bunn, James H. The Dimensionality of Signs, Tools, & Models: An Introduction. LC 80-8151. (Advances in Semiotics Ser.). (Illus.). 214p. reprint ed. pap. 66.40 (*0-608-18247-8*, 205669500081) Bks Demand.

Bunn, James L. Parents - Single Or Otherwise - Their Sex, Stress, Struggles & Survival: Index of New Information & Reference Research Bible. rev. ed. 191p. 1997. 47.50 (*0-7883-1610-9*); pap. 44.50 (*0-7883-1611-7*) ABBE Pubs Assn.

Bunn, Julie A. To Trade or Not to Trade? The Basel Convention & the Transboundary Movement & Disposal of Hazardous Wastes. (Pew Case Studies in International Affairs). 50p. (C). 1997. pap. text 3.50 (*1-56927-219-0*) Geo U Inst Dplmcy.

Bunn, Matthew. Foundation for the Future: The ABM Treaty & National Security. LC 90-55446. 222p. (Orig.). (C). 1990. pap. 20.00 (*0-685-46143-2*) Arms Control.

— Narrative of Matthew Bunn. LC 94-14739. 60p. 1995. pap. 9.95 (*0-87770-531-3*) Ye Galleon.

Bunn, Michele D., jt. auth. see Hutt.

Bunn, Paul A., et al, eds. Clinical Experiences with Platinum & Etoposide Therapy in Lung Cancer. (Journal: Oncology: Vol. 49, Suppl. 1, 1992). (Illus.). iv, 76p. 1992. pap. 24.50 (*3-8055-5639-X*) S Karger.

Bunn, Paul A., Jr. & Veronesi, U., eds. Current Topics in Lung Cancer. (ESO Monographs). vii, 82p. 1991. 56.95 (*0-387-54301-5*) Spr-Verlag.

Bunn, Paul A., jt. ed. see Kane, Madeleine A.

***Bunn, Robert A. C.** The Warriors Legacy. LC 98-88881. 112p. 1999. pap. 8.95 (*1-56167-469-9*, Five Star Spec Ed) Am Literary Pr.

Bunn, Ronald F. German Politics & the Spiegel Affair: A Case Study of the Bonn System. LC 68-21803. 256p. 1968. reprint ed. pap. 79.40 (*0-7837-9874-1*, 206060000006) Bks Demand.

Bunn, Stephen J., jt. ed. see Powis, David A.

Bunn, T. Davis. The Amber Room. 336p. (Orig.). 1992. pap. 9.99 (*1-55661-285-0*) Bethany Hse.

— Berlin Encounter. (Rendezvous with Destiny Ser.: Bk. 4). 192p. 1995. pap. 8.99 (*1-55661-382-2*) Bethany Hse.

— Berlin Encounter. large type ed. LC 97-35681. 227p. 1997. 22.95 (*0-7862-1234-9*) Thorndike Pr.

***Bunn, T. Davis.** The Book of Hours: A Novel. LC 99-89593. 324p. 2000. pap. 12.99 (*0-7852-7088-4*) Nelson.

Bunn, T. Davis. Deadly Games. 1997. 22.99 (*0-614-20654-5*) Bantam.

— Dream Voyagers. LC 99-6409. 352p. 1999. pap. text 11.99 (*0-7642-2180-9*) Bethany Hse.

— Florian's Gate. (Priceless Collection). 352p. 1992. pap. 9.99 (*1-55661-244-3*) Bethany Hse.

— Gibraltar Passage. (Rendezvous with Destiny Ser.: No. 2). 192p. 1994. pap. 8.99 (*1-55661-380-6*) Bethany Hse.

— Gibraltar Passage. large type ed. LC 97-260. (Christian Fiction Ser.). 244p. 1997. 22.95 (*0-7862-1067-2*) Thorndike Pr.

— The Gift. LC 94-25695. 144p. 1994. text 11.99 (*1-55661-527-2*, 231527) Bethany Hse.

***Bunn, T. Davis.** The Great Divide. LC 99-86341. 384p. 2000. 19.95 (*0-385-49615-X*) Doubleday.

— The Great Divide. 2000. 22.95 (*1-57856-374-7*) Waterbrook Pr.

Bunn, T. Davis. In the Shadows of Victory: Rendezvous with Destiny. 1998. 12.99 (*0-88486-195-3*, Inspirational Pr) Arrowood Pr.

— Istanbul Express. LC 95-45262. (Rendezvous with Destiny ser.: Vol. 5). 28p. 1995. pap. 8.99 (*1-55661-383-0*) Bethany Hse.

— Istanbul Express. large type ed. LC 98-10006. 1998. 21.95 (*0-7862-1407-4*) Thorndike Pr.

— Light & Shadow. LC 50-6541. 160p. (Orig.). (YA). (gr. 7-12). 1995. pap. 5.99 (*0-7814-0116-X*) Chariot Victor.

— The Messenger. 142p. 1995. text 11.99 (*1-55661-669-4*) Bethany Hse.

— Music Box: Her Mother's Exquisite Little Gift, Long Hidden Away, Held Such Bittersweet Memories. LC 96-25299. 192p. 1996. text 11.99 (*1-55661-900-6*) Bethany Hse.

— Music Box: Her Mother's Exquisite Little Gift, Long Hidden Away, Held Such Bittersweet Memories. large type ed. LC 96-40163. 218p. 1997. 21.95 (*0-7862-1011-7*) Thorndike Pr.

— One False Move. LC 96-38695. 400p. (Orig.). 1997. pap. 12.99 (*0-7852-7368-9*) Nelson.

— One Shenandoah Winter: A Novel. LC 98-19987. 128p. 1998. 12.99 (*0-7852-7217-8*) Nelson.

— A Passage Through Darkness. 400p. 1999. 10.99 (*0-88486-254-2*) Arrowood Pr.

— The Presence. 352p. (Orig.). 1990. pap. 9.99 (*1-55661-137-4*) Bethany Hse.

***Bunn, T. Davis.** The Presence. 352p. (Orig.). 1999. pap. 10.99 (*0-7642-2301-1*) Bethany Hse.

Bunn, T. Davis. Princess Bella & the Red Velvet Hat. 32p. 1998. text 14.99 (*0-7642-2097-7*) Bethany Hse.

— Promises to Keep. 4p. (Orig.). 1991. pap. 10.99 (*1-55661-213-3*) Bethany Hse.

— The Quilt. LC 93-2413. 128p. 1993. text 11.99 (*1-55661-345-8*) Bethany Hse.

— Rhineland Inheritance. (Rendezvous with Destiny Ser.: No. 1). 224p. 1993. pap. 8.99 (*1-55661-347-4*) Bethany Hse.

— Rhineland Inheritance. large type ed. 285p. 1995. 20.95 (*0-7838-1388-0*, G K Hall Lrg Type) Mac Lib Ref.

— Sahara Crosswind. LC 94-38348. (Rendezvous with Destiny Ser.: Bk. 3). 192p. 1994. pap. 8.99 (*1-55661-381-4*) Bethany Hse.

— Tidings of Comfort & Joy. LC 97-15551. (Illus.). 128p. 1997. 12.99 (*0-7852-7203-8*) Nelson.

— To the Ends of the Earth: A Novel of the Byzantine Empire. LC 95-34248. 352p. 1997. pap. 12.99 (*0-7852-7214-3*) Nelson.

***Bunn, T. Davis.** The Ultimatum. LC 98-53794. 324p. 1999. pap. 12.99 (*0-7852-7086-8*) Nelson.

Bunn, T. Davis. The Warning: A Novel. LC 97-40781. 324p. (Orig.). 1998. pap. 12.99 (*0-7852-7516-9*) Nelson.

— Winter Palace. (Priceless Collection: No. 3). 352p. (Orig.). 1993. pap. 9.99 (*1-55661-324-5*) Bethany Hse.

Bunn, T. Davis, jt. auth. see Oke, Janette.

Bunn, Thomas. Worse Than Death. large type ed. LC 90-34618. 407p. 1990. reprint ed. lib. bdg. 19.95 (*1-56054-005-2*) Thorndike Pr.

***Bunn, Verne A.** Buying & Selling a Small Business. (Illus.). 2000. pap. 6.95 (*0-87891-245-2*) Res & Educ.

Bunn, Verne A. Buying & Selling a Small Business. Bruchey, Stuart & Carosso, Vincent P., eds. LC 78-18955. (Small Business Enterprise in America Ser.). (Illus.). 1979. reprint ed. lib. bdg. 17.95 (*0-405-11459-1*) Ayer.

Bunn, William. Biennial Message of William M. Bunn, Governor of Idaho. (Shorey Historical Ser.). 22p. reprint ed. pap. 10.00 (*0-8466-0047-1*, S47) Shoreys Bkstore.

Bunnag, Krachang, tr. see Suriyabongs, Luang.

Bunnag, Tej. The Provincial Administration of Siam, 1892-1915. (East Asian Historical Monographs). 1978. 29.95 (*0-19-580343-4*) OUP.

Bunnell, A. O. Dansville, NY. (Illus.). 267p. 1993. reprint ed. lib. bdg. 32.00 (*0-8328-2859-9*) Higginson Bk Co.

Bunnell, Adam. Before Infallibility: Liberal Catholicism in Biedermeier Vienna. LC 88-45618. 240p. 1990. 37.50 (*0-8386-3344-7*) Fairleigh Dickinson.

***Bunnell, David & Brate, Adam.** Making the Cisco Connection: The Story Behind the Real Internet Superpower. 240p. 2000. text 24.95 (*0-471-35711-1*) Wiley.

***Bunnell, David & Luecke, Richard A.** The e-Bay Phenomenon: Business Secrets Behind the World's Hottest Internet Company. 224p. 2000. 24.95 (*0-471-38490-9*) Wiley.

Bunnell, David E. Sea Caves of Anacapa Island. LC 93-22206. 207p. 1993. pap. 15.00 (*0-87461-093-1*) McNally & Loftin.

— Sea Caves of Santa Cruz Island. LC 88-37249. (Illus.). 124p. 1991. 12.00 (*0-87461-076-1*) McNally & Loftin.

Bunnell, Deb T. My First Spanish ABC Picture Coloring Book. (Illus.). 24p. (J). 1998. pap. 2.50 (*0-486-40358-0*) Dover.

***Bunnell, Deb T.** Picture Crossword Puzzles. (Illus.). (J). 1999. pap. 2.95 (*0-486-40798-5*) Dover.

Bunnell, Gene. Planning Gain in Theory & Practice. (Progress in Planning Ser.: No. 44-1). 114p. 1995. pap. 112.50 (*0-08-042646-8*, Pergamon Pr) Elsevier.

Bunnell, James C. Power Management That Works! 92p. 1996. mass mkt. 24.95 (*0-929392-22-1*) Annabooks.

Bunnell, Jean. Children at Shaker Village: Rural Life in the 19th Century, Using Primary Sources to Learn about History. (Illus.). 54p. (Orig.). (J). (gr. 5-9). 1991. pap. text 25.00 (*0-915836-16-5*) United Soc Shakers.

— You Decide! Making Responsible Choices. 1998. pap. 10.95 (*1-56822-427-3*) Instruct Fair.

Bunnell, Lafayette H. Discovery of the Yosemite: And the Indian War of 1851 Which Led to That Event. Medley, Steven P., ed. (High Sierra Classics Ser.). 340p. (C). 1990. reprint ed. pap. 9.95 (*0-939666-58-8*) Yosemite Assn.

— Discovery of the Yosemite & the Indian War of 1851. LC 72-146854. (Select Bibliographies Reprint Ser.). 1977. reprint ed. 23.95 (*0-8369-5621-4*) Ayer.

— Discovery of the Yosemite in 1851. Jones, William R., ed. (Illus.). 1977. reprint ed. pap. 3.95 (*0-89646-021-5*) Vistabooks.

— Winona & Its Environs on the Mississippi in Ancient & Modern Days. (Illus.). 694p. 1997. reprint ed. lib. bdg. 72.00 (*0-8328-6818-3*) Higginson Bk Co.

Bunnell, Paul J. Cemetery Inscriptions of Barnstable, Massachusetts & Its Villages, 1600-1900, with Corrections & Additions. 434p. 1995. pap. text 32.00 (*0-7884-0176-9*) Heritage Bk.

— Cemetery Inscriptions of the Town of Barnstable, Massachusetts, & Its Villages, 1600-1900. 430p. 1992. pap. 30.00 (*1-55613-652-8*) Heritage Bk.

— The House of Robinson. (Illus.). 226p. (Orig.). 1995. pap. text 19.00 (*0-7884-0191-2*) Heritage Bk.

— The New Loyalist Index, Vol. 1. 525p. (Orig.). 1989. pap. 38.50 (*1-55613-234-4*) Heritage Bk.

— New Loyalist Index, Vol. 2. xii, 218p. 1996. pap. 22.00 (*0-7884-0400-8*, B844) Heritage Bk.

— New Loyalist Index Vol. 3: Including Cape Cod & Islands, Massachusetts, New Hampshire, New Jersey & New York Loyalists. 195p. 1998. pap. 21.00 (*0-7884-0987-5*, B859) Heritage Bk.

— Research Guide to Loyalist Ancestors: A Directory to Archives, Manuscripts, & Published Sources. 146p. (Orig.). 1990. pap. 17.00 (*1-55613-357-X*) Heritage Bk.

***Bunnell, Paul J.** Research Guide to Loyalist Ancestors: A Directory to Archives, Manuscripts, Published & Electronic Sources. rev. ed. 178p. 2000. pap. 19.00 (*0-7884-1425-9*, 1425) Heritage Bk.

***Bunnell, Peter & Creeley, Robert.** Walter Chappell: Vintage Photographs 1954-1978. (Illus.). 20p. 2000. 50.00 (*0-9670774-1-9*) R Horowitz LLC.

Bunnell, Peter C. Clarence H. White: The Reverence for Beauty. Richelson, Paul W., ed. LC 86-81613. (Illus.). 80p. (Orig.). 1986. pap. text 19.95 (*0-933041-01-2*) Gallery Fine Art Ohio U.

— Degrees of Guidance: Essays on Twentieth-Century American Photography. (Illus.). 264p. (C). 1993. text 80.00 (*0-521-32751-2*) Cambridge U Pr.

— Minor White: The Eye That Shapes. Guthrie, Jill, ed. LC 88-83824. (Illus.). 310p. 1989. pap. text 25.00 (*0-943012-09-0*) Prince U Art.

Bunnell, Peter C., ed. The Aesthetics of French Photography Studies. LC 76-24672. (Sources of Modern Photography Ser.). (FRE., Illus.). 1979. lib. bdg. 38.95 (*0-405-09983-5*) Ayer.

— Nonsilver Printing Processes: Four Selections, 1886-1927. LC 72-9221. (Literature of Photography Ser.). 1975. 24.95 (*0-405-04928-5*) Ayer.

Bunnell, Peter C., intro. Ruth Bernhard: The Collection of Ginny Williams. (Illus.). 50p. 1993. 65.00 (*1-881138-04-6*); pap. 40.00 (*0-685-71951-0*) Tallgrass Pr.

Bunnell, Peter C., tr. Alfred Stieglitz: Photographs from the Collection of Georgia O'Keeffe. (Illus.). 56p. (Orig.). 1993. pap. 45.00 (*0-935037-85-3*) G Peters Gallery.

Bunnell, Peter C. & Sobieszek, Robert A., eds. The Literature of Photography, 62 bks., Set. 1973. 1301.50 (*0-405-04889-0*) Ayer.

— The Sources of Modern Photography Series, 51 bks., Vol. 26. (Illus.). 1979. lib. bdg. 1393.00 (*0-405-18980-X*) Ayer.

— The Sources of Modern Photography Series, 51 bks., Vols. 1[00ad]25. (Illus.). 1979. lib. bdg. 1393.00 (*0-405-09597-X*) Ayer.

— The Universal Exposition of 1900: Two Catalogues. LC 76-23041. (Sources of Modern Photography Ser.). (Illus.). 1979. lib. bdg. 20.95 (*0-405-09603-8*) Ayer.

— Willi Warstat on the Aesthetics of Art Photography, Two Selections: Original Anthology. LC 76-24679. (Sources of Modern Photography Ser.). (GER., Illus.). 1979. lib. bdg. 15.95 (*0-405-09659-3*) Ayer.

Bunnell, Peter C., et al. Photography at Princeton: Celebrating Twenty-Five Years of Collecting & Teaching the History of Photography. Guthrie, Jill, ed. LC 98-86438. (Illus.). (Orig.). Date not set. pap. text 30.00 (*0-943012-26-0*, 98-86438) Prince U Art.

Bunnell, Peter C., ed. see Adams, Robert, et al.

Bunnell, Peter C., ed. see Benthe, Arnold.

Bunnell, Peter C., ed. see Chevalier, Charles.

Bunnell, Peter C., ed. see Davanne, A.

Bunnell, Peter C., ed. see De Saint-Victor, Niepce.

Bunnell, Peter C., ed. see Demacy, Robert & Demachy, C. Puyo.

Bunnell, Peter C., ed. see Dillaye, Frederic.

Bunnell, Peter C., ed. see Eder, Josef-Maria.

Bunnell, Peter C., ed. see Engrand, Bernard.

Bunnell, Peter C., ed. see Evrard-Blanquart, L. D.

Bunnell, Peter C., ed. see Figuier, Louis.

Bunnell, Peter C., ed. see Graff, Werner.

Bunnell, Peter C., ed. see Great Britain, Patent Office Staff.

Bunnell, Peter C., ed. see Guerronnan, Anthony.

Bunnell, Peter C., ed. see Ken, Alexander.

Bunnell, Peter C., ed. see Kodak Staff.

Bunnell, Peter C., ed. see Kuhn, Willy.

Bunnell, Peter C., ed. see Lacan, Ernest.

Bunnell, Peter C., ed. see Lecuyer, Raymond.

Bunnell, Peter C., ed. see Lo Duca, Joseph M.

Bunnell, Peter C., ed. see Martin, Anton.

Bunnell, Peter C., ed. see Masuren-Matthies.

Bunnell, Peter C., ed. see Mentienne, A.

Bunnell, Peter C., ed. see Nadar, Gaspard F.

Bunnell, Peter C., ed. see Pierson & Mayer, J. P.

Bunnell, Peter C., ed. see Poore, Henry R.

Bunnell, Peter C., ed. see Snelling, Henry H. & Anthony, E.

Bunnell, Peter C., jt. ed. see Sobieszek, Robert A.

Bunnell, Peter C., ed. see Stenger, Erich.

Bunnell, Peter C., ed. see Stotz, Gustaf, et al.

Bunnell, Peter C., ed. see Thierry, J.

Bunnell, Peter C., ed. see Van Monckhoven, Desire.

Bunnell, Peter C., ed. see Vogel, Hermann.

Bunnell, Peter C., ed. see Von Rohr, Moritz.

Bunnell, Peter C., ed. see Whiting, John R.

Bunnell, Peter C., ed. see Woodbury, Walter E.

Bunnell, W. S. J. M. Synge's The Playboy of the Western World. rev. ed. (Brodie's Notes Ser.). 59p. 1993. pap. 5.95 (*0-333-58206-3*, Pub. by Macmillan) Trans-Atl Phila.

— Sean O'Casey's Juno & the Paycock. rev. ed. (Brodie's Notes Ser.). 59p. 1993. pap. 5.95 (*0-333-58163-6*, Pub. by Macmillan) Trans-Atl Phila.

Bunnen, Lucinda & Smith, Virginia W. Alaska: Trail Tales & Eccentric Detours. (Illus.). 80p. 1992. 75.00 (*1-882313-00-3*) Ice Hse Pr.

— Scoring in Heaven: Gravestones & Cemetery Art of the American Sunbelt States. (Illus.). 176p. 1991. 60.00 (*0-89381-474-1*) Aperture.

Bunnenberg-Waterman, Christin. German, Just Enough Book. (Hugo's Language Courses Ser.). 128p. (Orig.). 1995. pap. 5.95 (*0-85285-222-3*) Hunter NJ.

Bunner, Henry C. Jersey Street & Jersey Lane. LC 74-94705. (Short Story Index Reprint Ser.). 1977. 19.95 (*0-8369-3083-5*) Ayer.

— Love in Old Cloathes & Other Stories. LC 78-94706. (Short Story Index Reprint Ser.). (Illus.). 1977. 20.95 (*0-8369-3084-3*) Ayer.

— Made in France. LC 71-94707. (Short Story Index Reprint Ser.). (Illus.). 1977. 17.95 (*0-8369-3085-1*) Ayer.

— More "Short Sixes" 1972. reprint ed. lib. bdg. 21.50 (*0-8422-8015-4*) Irvington.

— Short Sixes: Stories to Be Read While the Candle Burns. 1972. reprint ed. lib. bdg. 30.00 (*0-8422-8014-6*) Irvington.

— Stories: Second Stories, Vol. 1. LC 72-5900. (Short Story Index Reprint Ser.). 1977. reprint ed. 25.95 (*0-8369-4194-2*) Ayer.

— Suburban Sage. LC 76-90578. (Short Story Index Reprint Ser.). 1977. 17.95 (*0-8369-3061-4*) Ayer.

— Zadoc Pine & Other Stories. LC 70-94704. (Short Story Index Reprint Ser.). 1977. 20.95 (*0-8369-3086-X*) Ayer.

Bunner, W. In-Plant Industrial Chemical Spill Responsibility. (Industrial Health & Safety Ser.). 1991. text. write for info. (*0-442-00231-9*, VNR) Wiley.

Bunnett. Physical Geography in Diagrams. 4th ed. Date not set. pap. text. write for info. (*0-582-22507-8*, Pub. by Addison-Wesley) Longman.

Bunnett, Fanny E., tr. see Gervinus, Georg G.

Bunnett, Joseph F., et al. Arsenic & Old Mustard: Chemical Problems in the Destruction of Old Arsenical & 'Mustard' Munitions. LC 98-24599. (NATO Science Ser.). 200p. 1998. write for info. (*0-7923-5175-4*) Kluwer Academic.

An Asterisk (*) at the beginning of an entry indicates that the title is appearing for the first time.

Bunnett, Rochelle. Amigos en la Escuela. LC 96-72088. (SPA., Illus.). 32p. (J). (gr. k-3). 1997. 12.95 (*1-887734-15-5*) Star Brght Bks.
— Friends at School. LC 95-31712. (Illus.). 32p. (gr. k-3). 1995. 12.95 (*1-887734-01-5*) Star Brght Bks.
— Friends in the Park. (Illus.). 32p. (J). 1993. 7.95 (*1-56288-347-X*) Checkerboard.
— Friends Together: More Alike Than Different. (Illus.). 12p. (J). (gr. k-4). 1993. teacher ed. 24.95 (*1-56288-429-8*) Checkerboard.

Bunnett, Sara, ed. see Telfer, George F.

Bunney, Gayle. Horse Stories: Riding with the Wind. 1998. pap. 11.95 (*1-55105-124-9*) Lone Pine.

***Bunney, Gayle.** My Life with Dogs. 144p. 1999. pap. 11.95 (*1-55105-152-4*) Lone Pine.

Bunney, Mary H., et al. Viral Warts: Biology & Treatment. 2nd ed. (Illus.). 192p. 1992. text 85.00 (*0-19-262062-2*) OUP.

Bunney, Ron. Eye of the Eagle. 156p. (YA). 1995. pap. 9.95 (*1-86368-126-4*, Pub. by Fremantle Arts) Intl Spec Bk.

Bunney, Ron. Sink or Swim. 200p. (YA). 1999. pap. 12.95 (*1-86368-238-4*, Pub. by Fremantle Arts) Intl Spec Bk.

Bunney, William E., Jr., et al, eds. Neuropsychopharmacology: Proceedings of the XVIth C. I. N. P. Congress, Munich, August, 15-19 1988. 2 vols., Set. (Illus.). 928p. 1990. 368.00 (*0-387-50252-1*) Spr-Verlag.

Bunney, William E., Jr., ed. see Collegium Internationale Neuro-Psychopharmacologic.

Bunney, William E., Jr., jt. ed. see Usdin, Earl.

Bunni, Nael G. Construction Insurance. 334p. 1986. 106.25 (*0-85334-438-8*) Elsevier.
— Construction Insurance. (C). 1986. 560.00 (*0-7855-4246-9*, Pub. by Witherby & Co) St Mut.
— The FIDIC Form of Contract. 4th ed. (Red Bk.). (Illus.). 464p. 1991. 160.00 (*0-632-02514-X*) Blackwell Sci.

Bunni, Nael G. & International Federation of Consulting Engineers S. The FIDIC Form of Contract: The Fourth Edition of the Red Book. 2nd ed. LC 97-23160. 1997. 150.00 (*0-632-04079-3*) Blackwell Sci.

Bunnin, Brad. The Writer's Legal Companion. 3rd ed. 1998. pap. write for info. (*0-201-36096-9*) Addison-Wesley.

***Bunnin, Brad & Beren, Peter.** The Writer's Legal Companion: The Complete Handbook for the Working Writer. 3rd ed. LC 98-86943. 368p. 1998. pap. text 18.50 (*0-7382-0031-X*) Perseus Pubng.

Bunnin, Nicholas & Tsui-James, E. P., eds. The Blackwell Companion to Philosophy. LC 95-6545. 600p. (C). 1996. pap. 31.95 (*0-631-18789-8*) Blackwell Pubs.

***Bunning, Jim, ed.** The Future of Social Security for This Generation & the Next: Congressional Hearing. (Illus.). 137p. (C). 1999. reprint ed. pap. text 25.00 (*0-7881-8446-6*) DIANE Pub.
— The Future of Social Security for This Generation & the Next: Current State of Public Opinion on the Future of Social Security: Congressional Hearing. (Illus.). 72p. (C). 2000. reprint ed. pap. text 20.00 (*0-7881-8992-1*) DIANE Pub.

Bunning, Joan. Learning the Tarot: A Tarot Book for Beginners. LC 98-23461. (Illus.). 320p. 1998. pap. 14.95 (*1-57863-048-7*) Weiser.

Bunning, T. J., et al, eds. Liquid Crystal Materials & Devices Vol. 559: Materials Research Society Symposium Proceedings. LC 99-37083. 284p. 1999. text 68.00 (*1-55899-466-1*) Materials Res.
— Liquid Crystals for Advanced Technologies. (MRS Symposium Proceedings Ser.: Vol. 425). 346p. 1996. 74.00 (*1-55899-328-2*, 425) Materials Res.

Bunno, Michiaki, jt. ed. see Sadanaga, Ryoichi.

Bunny, Edmund. Of Divorce for Adulterie & Marrying Againe: That There Is No Sufficient Warrant So to Do. (English Experience Ser.: No. 781). 1977. reprint ed. lib. bdg. 20.00 (*90-221-0781-7*) Walter J Johnson.

Bunschoten, Raoul. Metaspaces. (Illus.). 32p. pap. 23.00 (*1-901033-80-5*, Pub. by Black Dog Pubg) RAM Publications.

Bunschoten, Raoul, intro. A Passage Through Silence & Light. (Illus.). 48p. 1997. 17.95 (*0-9521773-5-8*, Pub. by Black Dog Pubg) RAM Publications.

Bunse, Lois. Caught by Gesture. unabridged ed. (Modern Poetry in English Ser.: No. 44). (Illus.). 28p. (Orig.). 1994. pap. 6.00 (*1-879457-47-4*) Norton Coker Pr.
— Flowers in Disturbed Places. Mycue, Edward, ed. (Took Modern Poetry in English Ser.: No. 34). (Illus.). 32p. (Orig.). 1993. pap. 6.00 (*1-879457-36-9*) Norton Coker Pr.

Bunsell, A. R., ed. Fibre Reinforcements for Composite Materials. (Composite Materials Ser.: No. 2). x,538p. 1988. 276.00 (*0-444-42801-1*) Elsevier.

Bunsell, A. R. & Berger, Marie-H. Ceramic Fibers. LC 99-19119. (Illus.). 320p. 1999. text 150.00 (*0-8247-1951-4*) Dekker.

Bunsell, A. R., jt. auth. see Harris, Bryan.

Bunselmeyer, Robert E. The Cost of the War, 1914-1919: British Economic War Aims & the Origins of Reparation. LC 75-14078. 240p. (C). 1975. lib. bdg. 35.00 (*0-208-01551-5*, Archon Bks) Shoe String.

***Bunsen, Rick.** Merry Christmas, Space Ranger. (Toy Story 2 Ser.). (Illus.). (J). 2000. pap. 3.29 (*0-307-13270-6*, Goldn Books) Gldn Bks Pub Co.

Bunsen, Rick. Rudolph the Red-Nosed Reindeer. LC 97-74892. (Little Golden Bks.). 24p. (J). 1998. 2.29 (*0-307-98829-5*, 98829, Goldn Books) Gldn Bks Pub Co.

Bunsey, Michael & Sanberg, Paul. Prescription Narcotics: The Addictive Painkillers. (Encyclopedia of Psychoactive Drugs Ser.: No. 1). (Illus.). 124p. (YA). (gr. 7 up). 1986. lib. bdg. 19.95 (*0-87754-770-X*) Chelsea Hse.

Bunshah, R. F. & Weissmantel, Christian. Handbook of Hard Coatings LC 99-27318. 399p. 1999. 145.00 (*0-8155-1438-7*) Noyes.

Bunshah, Rointan F., ed. Handbook of Deposition Technologies for Films & Coatings: Science, Applications & Technology. 2nd ed. LC 93-30751. (Illus.). 835p. 1994. 179.00 (*0-8155-1337-2*) Noyes.

Bunson. The Whole Number Book. 1995. 84.00 (*0-517-88445-3*) Random Hse Value.

Bunson, Margaret. Encyclopedia of Ancient Egypt. LC 99-11512. 1999. 9.99 (*0-517-20380-4*) Random Hse Value.
— Father Damien. rev. ed. LC 97-66785. 1997. pap. text 11.95 (*0-87973-916-9*) Our Sunday Visitor.

***Bunson, Margaret & Bunson, Stephen.** Faith in the Wilderness: The Story of the Catholic Indian Missions. LC 00-130351. (Illus.). 450p. 2000. pap. 17.95 (*0-87973-745-X*) Our Sunday Visitor.

Bunson, Margaret, jt. auth. see Bunson, Matthew.

Bunson, Margaret R. A Dictionary of Ancient Egypt. (Illus.). 312p. 1995. pap. 16.95 (*0-19-509989-3*) OUP.
— The Encyclopedia of Ancient Egypt. 288p. 1991. 45.00 (*0-8160-2093-0*) Facts on File.

Bunson, Margaret R., compiled by. John Paul II's Book of Mary. LC 95-73143. 208p. 1996. 12.95 (*0-87973-578-3*) Our Sunday Visitor.

Bunson, Margaret R. & Bunson, Matthew E. Kateri Tekakwitha. LC 92-61548. (Saints You Should Know Ser.). (Illus.). 56p. (Orig.). (J). 1993. 7.95 (*0-87973-786-7*, 786) Our Sunday Visitor.
— Lives of the Saints You Should Know. LC 94-67356. (Illus.). 150p. (Orig.). 1994. pap. 8.95 (*0-87973-576-7*, 576) Our Sunday Visitor.
— Lives of the Saints You Should Know, Vol. 2. LC 94-67356. (Illus.). 160p. (Orig.). (YA). (gr. 5 up). 1996. pap. 8.95 (*0-87973-753-0*) Our Sunday Visitor.
— St. Francis of Assisi. LC 91-68358. (Saints You Should Know Ser.). 56p. 1996. pap. 5.95 (*0-87973-557-0*) Our Sunday Visitor.
— St. Joan of Arc. LC 91-68359. (Saints You Should Know Ser.). 56p. 1996. 7.95 (*0-87973-784-0*); pap. 5.95 (*0-87973-558-9*) Our Sunday Visitor.
— St. Patrick. LC 92-61547. (Saints You Should Know Ser.). (Illus.). 56p. (J). 1993. 7.95 (*0-87973-785-9*, 785) Our Sunday Visitor.

Bunson, Margaret R., jt. auth. see Bunson, Stephen M.

***Bunson, Matthew.** The Complete Christie: An Agatha Christie Encyclopedia. (Illus.). 496p. 2000. pap. 18.95 (*0-671-02831-6*, PB Trade Paper) PB.
— The Complete Christie: An Agatha Christie Encyclopedia. (Illus.). 496p. 2000. 35.00 (*0-7434-0785-7*) S&S Trade.
— Our Sunday Visitor's 2000 Catholic Almanac. LC 73-641001. 608p. 1999. pap. 28.95 (*0-87973-905-3*) Our Sunday Visitor.

Bunson, Matthew. Prophecies - 2000: Predictions, Revelations, & Visions for the New Millennium. LC 98-51027. 160p. 1999. per. 12.00 (*0-671-01917-1*, WSP) PB.

***Bunson, Matthew.** The Vampire Encyclopedia. LC 00-39366. (Illus.). 320p. 2000. 9.99 (*0-517-16206-7*) Bell T.

Bunson, Matthew. The Wisdom Teachings of the Dalai Lama. LC 97-35805. 1997. pap. 12.95 (*0-452-27927-5*, Plume) Dutton Plume.

***Bunson, Matthew, ed.** Our Sunday Visitor's 2001 Catholic Almanac. 608p. 2000. 28.95 (*0-87973-907-X*); pap. 23.95 (*0-87973-906-1*) Our Sunday Visitor.

***Bunson, Matthew & Bunson, Margaret.** Apostle of the Alleghenies. 1999. pap. 9.95 (*0-87973-399-3*) Our Sunday Visitor.

Bunson, Matthew E. Angels A to Z: A Who's Who of the Heavenly Host. 288p. 1996. pap. 14.00 (*0-517-88537-9*) Crown Pub Group.
— A Dictionary of the Roman Empire. (Illus.). 512p. 1995. pap. 19.95 (*0-19-510233-9*) OUP.
— The Encyclopedia of the Middle Ages. LC 94-33232. 512p. (YA). 1995. 50.00 (*0-8160-2456-1*) Facts on File.
— Encyclopedia of the Roman Empire. (Illus.). 512p. 1994. lib. bdg. 50.00 (*0-8160-2135-X*) Facts on File.
— Encyclopedia Sherlockiana: The Complete A-to-Z Guide to the World of the Great Detective. LC 94-10714. (Illus.). 352p. 1994. 25.00 (*0-671-79826-X*) Macmillan.
— Encyclopedia Sherlockiana: The Complete A-to-Z Guide to the World of the Great Detective. 326p. 1997. 16.00 (*0-02-861679-0*) Macmillan.

Bunson, Matthew E., jt. auth. see Bunson, Margaret R.

Bunson, Stephen, et al. John Paul II's Book of Saints. LC 98-67328. (Illus.). 384p. 1999. 19.95 (*0-87973-934-7*) Our Sunday Visitor.

Bunson, Stephen, jt. auth. see Bunson, Margaret.

Bunson, Stephen M. & Bunson, Margaret R. Encyclopedia of Ancient Mesoamerica. LC 95-13085. (Illus.). 336p. 1996. 45.00 (*0-8160-2402-2*) Facts on File.

Bunson, Stephen M., tr. see Guilaine, Jean, ed.

Bunster, Ximena B. & Chaney, Elsa M. Sellers & Servants: Working Women in Lima, Peru. LC 85-6529. 252p. 1985. 59.95 (*0-275-90067-3*, C0067, Praeger Pubs) Greenwood.
— Sellers & Servants: Working Women in Lima, Peru. LC 88-10356. (Illus.). 267p. (C). 1988. pap. 18.95 (*0-89789-171-6*, Bergin & Garvey) Greenwood.

Bunston, Bill, jt. auth. see Badrocke, Mike.

Bunt, A. C. Media Mixes for Container Grown Plants. (Illus.). 332p. 1988. pap. 129.95 (*0-04-635016-0*) Thomson Learn.

Bunt, G. H. William of Palerne: An Alliterative Romance. xii, 488p. 1985. 89.50 (*90-6088-094-3*, Pub. by Boumas Boekhuis) Gen Publ ON.

***Bunt, Gary.** Virtually Islamic. 224p. 2000. 55.00 (*0-7083-1612-3*, Pub. by U Wales Pr); pap. 29.95 (*0-7083-1611-5*, Pub. by U Wales Pr) Paul & Co Pubs.

Bunt, Gerrit H. Alexander the Great in the Literature of Medieval Britain. 111p. 1994. pap. 27.50 (*90-6980-071-3*, Pub. by Egbert Forsten) Hodlder & Stoughton.

Bunt, Harry C., et al, eds. Multimodal Human-Computer Communication: Systems, Techniques, & Experiments. LC 98-3460. (Lecture Notes in Computer Science: Vol. 1374). viii, 345p. 1998. pap. 59.00 (*3-540-64380-X*) Spr-Verlag.

Bunt, Harry C. & Tomita, Masaru. Recent Advances in Parsing Technology. LC 96-25047. (Text, Speech, & Language Technology). 1996. text 130.50 (*0-7923-4152-X*) Kluwer Academic.

***Bunt, Jonathan, ed.** The Starter Oxford Japanese Dictionary. 400p. 2000. pap. 14.95 (*0-19-860197-2*) OUP.

Bunt, Lucas N., et al. The Historical Roots of Elementary Mathematics. (Illus.). 320p. 1988. reprint ed. pap. text 8.95 (*0-486-25563-8*) Dover.

Bunt, Richard B., jt. auth. see Tremblay, Jean-Paul.

Bunt, Sandra K. The Other Side of the Desk. LC 90-71374. (Illus.). 135p. (Orig.). (J). (gr. 3-6). 1992. pap. 7.95 (*0-932433-80-4*) Windswept Hse.

Bunt, T. J., ed. Vascular Graft Infections. (Illus.). 420p. 1994. 69.00 (*0-87993-576-6*) Futura Pub.

Buntain, Fulton & Donaldson, Hal. One Man's Compassion. 256p. 1989. mass mkt. 5.99 (*0-88368-214-1*) Whitaker Hse.

Buntain, Mark. Waging Spiritual Warfare. 32p. 1993. pap. 1.95 (*0-88243-455-1*, 02-0455) Gospel Pub.

Buntain, Mark, et al. Miracle in the Mirror. LC 81-70999. (Illus.). 16p. 1982. reprint ed. mass mkt. 4.99 (*0-87123-352-5*) Bethany Hse.

Buntain, William L., ed. Management of Pediatric Trauma. LC 93-47168. (Illus.). 788p. 1995. text 185.00 (*0-7216-4547-X*, W B Saunders Co) Harcrt Hlth Sci Grp.

Buntaine, Robert R., ed. see Brucer, Marshall.

Bunte, Hermann-Josef. Lexikon Des Rechts der Wirtschafts, Zur Fortsetzung. (GER.). 1993. 195.00 (*0-7859-8394-5*, 3472001372) Fr & Eur.

***Bunte, Jim, et al.** Vintage Toys: Robots & Space Toys, Vol. 1. Vol. 1. (Illus.). 192p. 2000. pap. 26.95 (*1-58221-025-X*, AT1025, Antique Trader) Krause Pubns.

Bunte, Pamela A. & Franklin, Robert J. From the Sands to the Mountain: Change & Persistence in a Southern Paiute Community. LC 87-25507. (Studies in the Anthropology of North American Indians). 355p. 1987. reprint ed. pap. 110.10 (*0-608-03488-6*, 206420300008) Bks Demand.

Bunte, Wolfgang. Rabbinische Traditionen Bei Nikolaus von Lyra: Ein Beitrag zur Schriftauslegung des Spatmittelalters. (Judentum und Umwelt Ser.: Bd. 58). (GER., Illus.). 324p. 1994. 52.95 (*3-631-48015-6*) P Lang Pubng.
— Religionsgesprache Zwischen Christen un Juden in Den Niederlanden (1100-1500) (Judentum und Umwelt Ser.: Bd. 27). (GER., Illus.). 812p. 1990. 115.80 (*3-631-42963-0*) P Lang Pubng.
— Die Zerstorung Jerusalems in der Mittelniederlandischen Literatur (1100-1600) (Judentum und Umwelt Ser.: Bd. 33). (GER.). 802p. 1992. 99.30 (*3-631-44438-9*) P Lang Pubng.

Bunte, Wolfgang, ed. Anonymus, Tractatus Adversus Judaeum (1122) (Judentum und Umwelt Ser.: Bd. 40). (GER.). 192p. 1993. 36.80 (*3-631-45826-6*) P Lang Pubng.

Buntfuss, Markus. Tradition und Innovation: Die Funktion der Metapher in der Theologischen Theoriesprache. (Theologische Bibliothek Toepelmann Ser.: Vol. 84). (GER.). xxi, 240p. (C). 1997. lib. bdg. 98.70 (*3-11-015575-3*) De Gruyter.

Buntin, Kathleen R. All Alone: Surviving the Loss of Your Spouse. LC 94-40691. iv, 155p. 1995. pap. 7.95 (*0-87579-933-7*) Deseret Bk.

Buntin, Phillip R. Color Kansas Characters Poster/Coloring Book. 64p. (Orig.). (J). (gr. 2 up). 1996. pap. 6.95 (*1-882404-09-2*) KS Herit Ctr.
— Kansas Symbols Coloring Book. 16p. (Orig.). (J) (gr. k up). 1993. pap. 2.95 (*1-882404-06-8*) KS Herit Ctr.
— Oklahoma Symbols Coloring Book. 16p. (J). (ps up). 1997. pap. 2.95 (*1-882404-10-6*) KS Herit Ctr.

Bunting. Human Sexuality. 20th ed. 1995. 12.74 (*1-56134-360-9*) McGraw.
— Human Sexuality 1999-2000 Edition. 24th ed. 1999. pap., student ed. 16.56 (*0-07-041171-9*) McGraw.
— Human Sexuality 1996/97. 21st annot. ed. 1996. teacher ed. (*0-697-31602-5*, WCB McGr Hill) McGrw-H Hghr Educ.
— Peepers. LC 99-6292. 2000. 15.00 (*0-15-260297-6*) Harcourt.

***Bunting & Lyon, Inc. Staff.** Private Independent Schools 2000. 2000. 122.22 (*0-913094-53-6*) Bunting.

Bunting, A. H., jt. ed. see Summerfield, R. J.

Bunting, A. M. Bunting Family: Our People & Ourselves. (Illus.). 245p. 1991. reprint ed. pap. 39.50 (*0-8328-1790-2*); reprint ed. lib. bdg. 49.50 (*0-8328-1789-9*) Higginson Bk Co.

Bunting, Alison, ed. see Thompson, Laurie Lynn Lightner.

Bunting, Alison, ed. see Wood, M. Sandra.

Bunting, Bainbridge. Harvard: An Architectural History. Floyd, Margaret H., ed. (Illus.). 352p. 1985. 37.95 (*0-674-37290-5*) Belknap Pr.
— Harvard: An Architectural History. Floyd, Margaret H., ed. (Belknap Press). (Illus.). 368p. 1998. pap. 29.95 (*0-674-37291-3*) HUP.
— Houses of Boston's Back Bay: An Architectural History 1840-1917. LC 66-21334. (Illus.). 511p. 1967. 40.00 (*0-674-40900-0*) Belknap Pr.
— Houses of Boston's Back Bay: An Architectural History 1840-1917. LC 66-21334. (Illus.). 511p. 1975. pap. text 14.95 (*0-674-40901-9*) Belknap Pr.

***Bunting, Basil & Makin, Peter.** Basil Bunting on Poetry. LC 99-15161. (Illus.). 304p. 1999. 42.00 (*0-8018-6166-7*) Johns Hopkins.

Bunting, Christine, ed. Reference Tools for Fine Arts Visual Resources Collections. (Occasional Papers: 4). 56p. 1984. pap. 12.00 (*0-942740-02-5*) Art Libs Soc.

Bunting, David. Statistical View of the Trusts: A Manual of Large American Industrial & Mining Corporations Active Around 1900, 9. LC 72-9824. (Contributions in Economics & Economic History Ser.: No. 9). 311p. 1974. 75.00 (*0-8371-6624-1*, BOM/) Greenwood.

Bunting, E. S., ed. Production & Utilisation of Protein in Oilseed Crops. 390p. 1981. text 195.50 (*90-247-2532-1*) Kluwer Academic.

Bunting, Elaine & D'Amario, Patricia. Counties of Central Maryland. LC 98-26671. (Our Maryland Counties Ser.). (Illus.). 160p. (J). 1998. 19.95 (*0-87033-503-0*) Cornell Maritime.
— Counties of Northern Maryland. LC 99-58076. (Our Maryland Counties Ser.). (Illus.). 172p. (J). (gr. 3-6). 2000. 19.95 (*0-87033-520-0*, Tidewtr Pubs) Cornell Maritime.

Bunting, Eleanor E. & Kaye, Penelope. Breaking Away: An Open Lab Approach to Writing. 2nd ed. 336p. (C). 1992. per. 28.95 (*0-8403-8113-1*) Kendall-Hunt.

Bunting, Eleanor E., jt. auth. see Ambrose, Martha.

Bunting, Eve. The Big Red Barn. LC 78-12186. (Let Me Read Ser.). (Illus.). 32p. (J). (gr. k-3). 1979. pap. 6.95 (*0-15-611938-2*, Voyager Bks) Harcourt.
— Blackwater. LC 99-24895. (Illus.). 160p. (J). (gr. 5 up). 1999. 15.95 (*0-06-027838-2*) HarpC.
— Blackwater. LC 99-24895. (Illus.). 160p. (J). (gr. 5 up). 1999. lib. bdg. 15.89 (*0-06-027843-9*) HarpC.

***Bunting, Eve.** Blackwater. LC 99-24895. 160p. (J). (gr. 4-7). 2000. mass mkt. 4.95 (*0-06-440890-6*, HarpTrophy) HarpC Child Bks.

Bunting, Eve. The Blue & the Gray. LC 95-30902. (Illus.). 32p. (J). (gr. 1-4). 1996. 14.95 (*0-590-60197-0*) Scholastic Inc.

***Bunting, Eve.** The Butterfly House. LC 98-16349. (Illus.). 32p. (J). (gr. k-3). 1998. 15.95 (*0-590-84884-4*) Scholastic Inc.

Bunting, Eve. Can You Do This Old Badger? LC 98-39809. (Illus.). 32p. (J). 2000. 15.00 (*0-15-201654-6*, Harcourt Child Bks) Harcourt.
— Cheyenne Again. LC 94-43287. (Illus.). 32p. 1995. 14.95 (*0-395-70364-6*, Clarion Bks) HM.
— The Cloverdale Switch. LC 79-2404. (YA). (gr. 7 up). 1979. 9.82 (*0-397-31866-9*); lib. bdg. 12.89 (*0-397-31867-7*) HarpC Child Bks.
— Coffin on a Case. LC 92-855. 96p. (J). (gr. 4-7). 1992. 14.95 (*0-06-020273-4*) HarpC Child Bks.
— Coffin on a Case. LC 92-855. (Trophy Bk.). 112p. (J). (gr. 4-7). 1993. pap. 4.95 (*0-06-440461-7*, HarpTrophy) HarpC Child Bks.

Bunting, Eve. Coffin on a Case. (Trophy Mystery Ser.). 1993. 9.60 (*0-606-05210-0*, Pub. by Turtleback) Demco.
— Compartiendo a Susan. 1995. pap. text 7.95 (*958-04-3151-5*) Norma SA.

Bunting, Eve. Dandelions. LC 94-27104. (Illus.). 48p. (J). (gr. k-5). 1995. 16.00 (*0-15-200050-X*, Harcourt Child Bks) Harcourt.
— Day Before Christmas. (Illus.). 32p. (J). (ps-3). 1992. 16.00 (*0-89919-866-X*, Clarion Bks) HM.

***Bunting, Eve.** Day Before Christmas. (Illus.). 32p. (J). (ps-3). 2000. pap. 5.95 (*0-618-05150-3*, Clarion Bks) HM.

Bunting, Eve. The Day the Whale Came. LC 96-49816. (Illus.). 32p. (J). (gr. 2-4). 1998. 16.00 (*0-15-201456-X*) Harcourt.
— Days of Summer. (J). 2001. write for info. (*0-15-201840-9*) Harcourt.
— A Day's Work. LC 93-38357. (Illus.). 32p. (J). (gr. k-3). 1994. pap. 5.95 (*0-395-84518-1*, Clarion Bks) HM.
— A Day's Work. (Illus.). 32p. (J). 1994. 15.00 (*0-395-67321-6*) HM.
— A Day's Work. (J). 1997. 11.15 (*0-606-11243-X*, Pub. by Turtleback) Demco.

***Bunting, Eve.** Dear Wish Fairy. LC 00-35814. (Hello Reader! Ser.). (Illus.). (J). 2000. write for info. (*0-439-20634-0*) Scholastic Inc.

Bunting, Eve. December. LC 96-21148. (Illus.). 40p. (J). (gr. 1-5). 1997. 16.00 (*0-15-201434-9*, Harcourt Child Bks) Harcourt.

***Bunting, Eve.** December. (Illus.). 40p. (J). (ps-3). 2000. pap. 6.00 (*0-15-202422-0*, Harcourt Child Bks) Harcourt.

Bunting, Eve. Demetrius & the Golden Goblet. LC 79-14865. (Illus.). 48p. (J). (gr. 1-5). 1980. 8.95 (*0-15-223186-2*, Harcourt Child Bks) Harcourt.

***Bunting, Eve.** Doll Baby. LC 99-57808. (Illus.). 48p. (J). (gr. 4-7). 2000. 15.00 (*0-395-93094-4*, Clarion Bks) HM.

Bunting, Eve. Ducky. LC 95-25874. (Illus.). 32p. (J). (ps-1). 1997. 15.00 (*0-395-75185-3*, Clarion Bks) HM.
— Face at the Edge of the World. LC 85-2684. 192p. (J). (gr. 7 up). 1988. pap. 6.95 (*0-89919-800-7*, Clarion Bks) HM.

Bunting, Eve. Face at the Edge of the World. 1988. 12.05 (*0-606-12282-6*, Pub. by Turtleback) Demco.

Bunting, Eve. Fifteen. (FastBack Romance Ser.). 1984. 11.27 (*0-606-00277-4*, Pub. by Turtleback) Demco.
— Flower Garden. LC 92-25766. (Illus.). 32p. (J). (ps-3). 1994. 15.00 (*0-15-228776-0*) Harcourt.
— Flower Garden. (Illus.). 32p. (J). (ps-3). 1999. pap. 24.95 (*0-15-201968-5*) Harcourt.
— Flower Garden. (Illus.). 32p. (J). 2000. pap. 6.00 (*0-15-202372-0*, Voyager Bks) Harcourt.

B

— Fly Away Home. Giblin, James C., ed. (Illus.). 32p. (J). (ps-2). 1991. 16.00 (*0-395-55962-6*, Clarion Bks) HM.
— Fly Away Home. (Illus.). 32p. (J). (ps-3). 1993. pap. 5.95 (*0-395-66415-2*, Clarion Bks) HM.
— Fly Away Home. (J). 1991. 11.15 (*0-606-05294-1*, Pub. by Turtleback) Demco.
— The Followers. (Author's Signature Collection). (Illus.). 40p. (J). (gr. 3-8). 1992. lib. bdg. 12.79 (*0-89565-764-3*) Childs World.
— For Always. (FastBack Romance Ser.). 1984. 11.27 (*0-606-00275-8*, Pub. by Turtleback) Demco.
*Bunting, Eve. Ghost's Hour, Spook's Hour. LC 86-31674. (Carry-Along Book & Cassette Favorites Ser.). 32p. (J). (gr. k-3). 1999. pap. 9.95 incl. audio (*0-395-95756-7*, 111277) Clar Call Bks.
Bunting, Eve. Ghost's Hour, Spook's Hour. LC 86-31674. (Illus.). 32p. (J). (ps-1). 1987. 16.00 (*0-89919-484-2*, Clarion Bks) HM.
— Ghost's Hour, Spook's Hour. LC 86-31674. (Illus.). 32p. (J). (ps). 1989. pap. 6.95 (*0-395-51583-1*, Clarion Bks) HM.
— Ghost's Hour, Spook's Hour. (Illus.). 1p. (J). 1990. pap. 9.95 incl. audio (*0-395-56244-9*, Clarion Bks) HM.
Bunting, Eve. Ghost's Hour, Spook's Hour. 1987. 11.15 (*0-606-01163-3*, Pub. by Turtleback) Demco.
Bunting, Eve. The Ghosts of Departure Point. LC 81-48602. 113p. (J). (gr. 6 up). 1982. 12.95 (*0-397-31997-5*); lib. bdg. 10.89 (*0-397-31998-3*) HarpC Child Bks.
— Ghosts of Departure Point. (J). 1984. mass mkt. 2.50 (*0-590-42361-4*) Scholastic Inc.
— Girl in the Painting. (FastBack Romance Ser.). 1984. 11.27 (*0-606-00291-X*, Pub. by Turtleback) Demco.
— Going Home. LC 95-35323. (Illus.). 32p. (J). (ps-3). 1996. 14.95 (*0-06-026296-6*); lib. bdg. 14.89 (*0-06-026297-4*) HarpC Child Bks.
— Going Home. LC 95-35323. (Illus.). 32p. (J). (ps-3). 1998. pap. 5.95 (*0-06-443509-1*, HarpTrophy) HarpC Child Bks.
— Happy Birthday, Dear Duck. LC 87-15694. (Illus.). 32p. (J). (ps-1). 1988. 16.00 (*0-89919-541-5*, Clarion Bks) HM.
— Happy Birthday, Dear Duck. LC 87-15694. (Illus.). 32p. (J). (ps). 1990. pap. 6.95 (*0-395-52594-2*, Clarion Bks) HM.
Bunting, Eve. Happy Birthday, Dear Duck. (J). 1988. 11.15 (*0-606-03417-X*, Pub. by Turtleback) Demco.
Bunting, Eve. The Happy Funeral. LC 81-47719. (Illus.). 48p. (J). (gr. k-4). 1982. 11.95 (*0-06-020893-7*) HarpC Child Bks.
— The Haunting of SafeKeep. LC 84-48354. (Lippincott Page-Turner Ser.). 160p. (YA). (gr. 7 up). 1985. lib. bdg. 12.89 (*0-397-32113-9*) HarpC Child Bks.
Bunting, Eve. Hey Diddle Diddle, the Cat Plays the Fiddle. 24p. (ps up). pap. 9.95 (*0-694-01434-6*) HarpC.
Bunting, Eve. The Hideout. D'Andrade, Diane, ed. LC 90-45515. 144p. (J). (gr. 4-7). 1991. 14.95 (*0-15-233990-6*) Harcourt.
— The Hideout. LC 90-45515. (Illus.). 144p. (J). (gr. 3-7). 1993. pap. 6.00 (*0-15-233991-4*) Harcourt.
— The Hideout. (J). 1993. 10.10 (*0-606-12333-4*, Pub. by Turtleback) Demco.
— How Many Days to America? A Thanksgiving Story. LC 88-2590. (Illus.). 32p. (J). (gr. k-4). 1988. 16.00 (*0-89919-521-0*, Clarion Bks) HM.
— How Many Days to America? A Thanksgiving Story. (J). 1988. 11.15 (*0-606-03816-7*, Pub. by Turtleback) Demco.
— How Many Days to America: A Thanksgiving Story. (Illus.). 32p. (J). (ps-3). 1990. pap. 5.95 (*0-395-54777-6*, Clarion Bks) HM.
*Bunting, Eve. How Many Days to America? A Thanksgiving Story with Book. (ps-3). 2000. pap. 9.95 incl. audio (*0-618-04082-X*) HM.
Bunting, Eve. I Am the Mummy Heb-Nefer. LC 95-46927. (Illus.). 32p. (J). 1997. 15.00 (*0-15-200479-3*) Harcourt.
*Bunting, Eve. I Am the Mummy Heb-Nefert. (Illus.). 32p. (J). (ps-3). 2000. pap. 6.00 (*0-15-202464-6*, Harcourt Child Bks) Harcourt.
Bunting, Eve. I Don't Want to Go to Camp. LC 95-75747. (Illus.). 32p. (J). (gr. k-2). 1996. 14.95 (*1-56397-393-6*) Boyds Mills Pr.
— I Have an Olive Tree. LC 98-7213. (Joanna Cotler Bks.). (Illus.). 32p. (J). (ps-3). 1999. 14.95 (*0-06-027573-1*) HarpC Child Bks.
— I Have an Olive Tree. LC 98-7213. (Joanna Cotler Bks.). (Illus.). 40p. (J). (ps-3). 1999. lib. bdg. 14.89 (*0-06-027574-X*) HarpC Child Bks.
*Bunting, Eve. I Have an Olive Tree. unabridged ed. (J). (ps). 2000. 10.00 incl. audio (*0-7887-3512-8*, 95865E5) Recorded Bks.
— I Like the Way You Are. LC 99-16607. (Illus.). 48p. (J). (gr. k-4). 2000. 15.00 (*0-395-89066-7*, Clarion Bks) HM.
Bunting, Eve. If I Asked You, Would You Stay? LC 82-49052. (Lippincott Page-Turner Ser.). 160p. (YA). (gr. 7 up). 1984. lib. bdg. 12.89 (*0-397-32066-3*) HarpC Child Bks.
— If I Asked You, Would You Stay? LC 82-49052. (Lippincott Page-Turner Ser.). 160p. (YA). (gr. 7 up). 1987. mass mkt. 3.95 (*0-06-447023-7*, HarpTrophy) HarpC Child Bks.
— The In-Between Days. LC 93-45674. (Illus.). 128p. (YA). (gr. 3-7). 1994. 14.95 (*0-06-023609-4*) HarpC Child Bks.
— The In-Between Days. LC 93-45674. (Trophy Bk.). (Illus.). 128p. (YA). (gr. 2-5). 1996. pap. 4.95 (*0-06-440563-X*, HarpTrophy) HarpC Child Bks.
— The In-Between Days. (YA). (gr. 4 up). 1996. 9.05 (*0-606-08782-6*, Pub. by Turtleback) Demco.
— In the Haunted House. (Illus.). 32p. (J). (ps-3). 1994. pap. 5.95 (*0-395-69942-8*, Clarion Bks) HM.
— In the Haunted House. (Illus.). 1995. pap. 8.95 incl. audio (*0-395-72089-3*) Ticknor & Flds Bks Yng Read.
— In the Haunted House. 1990. 11.15 (*0-606-07701-4*, Pub. by Turtleback) Demco.
— Is Anybody There? LC 87-45881. 176p. (J). (gr. 4-7). 1988. 13.00 (*0-397-32302-6*) HarpC Child Bks.
— Is Anybody There? LC 87-45881. 176p. (J). (gr. 4-7). 1990. pap. 4.95 (*0-06-440347-5*, HarpTrophy) HarpC Child Bks.
— Is Anybody There? (J). 1988. 10.05 (*0-606-02905-2*, Pub. by Turtleback) Demco.
— The Island of One. (Eve Bunting Collection). (Illus.). 40p. (J). (gr. 3-8). 1992. lib. bdg. 12.79 (*0-89565-768-6*) Childs World.
— Jumping the Nail. LC 94-11090. (Illus.). 160p. (YA). (gr. 7-12). 1993. pap. 6.00 (*0-15-241358-8*) Harcourt.
Bunting, Eve. Just Like Everyone Else. (FastBack Romance Ser.). 1984. 11.27 (*0-606-00321-5*, Pub. by Turtleback) Demco.
Bunting, Eve. Lady's Girl. (Eve Bunting Collection). (Illus.). 40p. (J). (gr. 3-8). 1992. lib. bdg. 12.79 (*0-89565-777-5*) Childs World.
*Bunting, Eve. Little Badger, Terror of the Seven Seas. LC 00-8451. (Illus.). (J). 2001. write for info. (*0-15-202395-X*, Harcourt Child Bks) Harcourt.
— Maggie the Freak. (FastBack Romance Ser.). 1984. 11.27 (*0-606-00339-8*, Pub. by Turtleback) Demco.
Bunting, Eve. The Man Who Could Call down Owls. LC 83-17568. (Illus.). 32p. (J). (gr. k-3). 1984. lib. bdg. 16.00 (*0-02-715380-0*, Mac Bks Young Read) S&S Childrens.
— Market Day. LC 95-5604. (Illus.). 32p. (J). (ps-3). 1996. 15.95 (*0-06-025364-9*); lib. bdg. 15.89 (*0-06-025368-1*) HarpC Child Bks.
— Market Day. LC 95-5604. (Illus.). 32p. (J). (ps-3). 1999. pap. 5.95 (*0-06-443517-2*, HarpTrophy) HarpC Child Bks.
— The Mask. (Eve Bunting Collection). (Illus.). 40p. (J). (gr. 3-8). 1992. lib. bdg. 12.79 (*0-89565-769-4*) Childs World.
*Bunting, Eve. The Memory String. LC 99-42771. (Illus.). 40p. (J). (ps-3). 2000. 15.00 (*0-395-86146-2*, Clarion Bks) HM.
Bunting, Eve. The Mirror Planet. (Author's Signature Collection). (Illus.). 40p. (J). (gr. 3-8). 1992. lib. bdg. 12.79 (*0-89565-767-8*) Childs World.
— Moonstick: The Seasons of the Sioux. LC 95-44865. (Joanna Cotler Bks.). (Illus.). 32p. (J). (gr. k-4). 1997. 15.95 (*0-06-024804-1*) HarpC.
*Bunting, Eve. Moonstick: The Seasons of the Sioux. LC 95-44865. (Illus.). 32p. (J). (gr. k-4). 2000. pap. 5.95 (*0-06-443619-5*) HarpC Child Bks.
— Moonstick: The Seasons of the Sioux, Class Set. unabridged ed. (J). 1997. boxed set 167.80 incl. audio (*0-7887-3927-1*, 46348) Recorded Bks.
— Moonstick: The Seasons of the Sioux, Homework. unabridged ed. (J). 1997. boxed set 31.70 incl. audio (*0-7887-1832-0*, 40612) Recorded Bks.
Bunting, Eve. The Mother's Day Mice. LC 85-13991. (Illus.). 32p. (J). (ps-3). 1986. 15.00 (*0-89919-387-0*, Clarion Bks) HM.
— The Mother's Day Mice. LC 85-13991. (Illus.). 32p. (J). (ps-3). 1988. pap. 5.95 (*0-89919-702-7*, Clarion Bks) HM.
— The Mother's Day Mice. LC 85-13991. (Carry-Along Book & Cassette Favorites Ser.). (Illus.). (J). (ps-3). 1989. pap. 9.95 incl. audio (*0-89919-895-3*, 111302, Clarion Bks) Ticknor & Flds Bks Yng Read.
— Mother's Day Mice. (J). 1986. 11.15 (*0-606-04130-3*, Pub. by Turtleback) Demco.
— My Backpack. LC 96-83934. (Illus.). 32p. (J). (ps). 1997. 14.95 (*1-56397-433-9*) Boyds Mills Pr.
Bunting, Eve. Nasty Stinky Sneakers. (J). 1995. 10.30 (*0-606-07937-8*) Turtleback.
Bunting, Eve. Nasty, Stinky Sneakers. LC 93-34641. 112p. (J). (gr. 4-7). 1994. 14.95 (*0-06-024236-1*); lib. bdg. 14.89 (*0-06-024237-X*, J Cotler) HarpC Child Bks.
— Nasty, Stinky Sneakers. LC 93-34641. 128p. (J). (gr. 4-7). 1995. pap. 4.95 (*0-06-440507-9*, HarpTrophy) HarpC Child Bks.
— Night of the Gargoyles. LC 93-8160. (Illus.). 32p. (J). (gr. 3 up). 1994. 14.95 (*0-395-66553-1*, Clarion Bks) HM.
— Night of the Gargoyles. (Illus.). 32p. (J). (gr. k-3). 1999. pap. 7.95 (*0-395-96887-9*, Clarion Bks) HM.
— Night Tree. LC 90-36178. (Illus.). 32p. (J). (ps-3). 1991. 13.95 (*0-15-257425-5*, Harcourt Child Bks) Harcourt.
— Night Tree. LC 90-36178. (Illus.). 32p. (C). (ps-3). 1994. pap. 6.00 (*0-15-200121-2*) Harcourt.
Bunting, Eve. Night Tree. 1994. 11.45 (*0-606-12452-7*) Turtleback.
Bunting, Eve. No Nap. LC 88-35256. (Illus.). 32p. (J). (ps-1). 1989. 15.95 (*0-89919-813-9*, Clarion Bks) HM.
— No Nap. (Illus.). 32p. (J). (ps-1). 1996. pap. 5.95 (*0-395-77283-4*, Clarion Bks) HM.
— No Nap. 1989. 11.15 (*0-606-08834-2*, Pub. by Turtleback) Demco.
Bunting, Eve. Nobody Knows but Me. (FastBack Romance Ser.). 1984. 11.27 (*0-606-00352-5*, Pub. by Turtleback) Demco.
Bunting, Eve. Noche de Humo. De Aragon Andujar, Gloria, tr. LC 98-15863.Tr. of Smoky Night. (SPA., Illus.). 36p. (Orig.). (J). 1999. pap. 6.00 (*0-15-201946-4*) Harcourt.
— Oh, Rick! (Author's Signature Collection). (Illus.). 40p. (J). (gr. 3-8). 1992. lib. bdg. 12.79 (*0-89565-774-0*) Childs World.
Bunting, Eve. Oh, Rick! (FastBack Romance Ser.). 1984. 11.27 (*0-606-00364-9*, Pub. by Turtleback) Demco.
Bunting, Eve. On Call Back Mountain. LC 96-19983. (Illus.). 32p. (J). 1997. 15.95 (*0-590-25929-6*) Scholastic Inc.
— Once Upon a Time. LC 94-47220. (Illus.). 32p. (J). (gr. 2-5). 1995. 14.95 (*1-878450-59-X*, 711) R Owen Pubs.
Bunting, Eve. One Candle. 32p. (ps). 14.89 (*0-06-028116-2*) HarpC.
— One Candle. (Illus.). 32p. (ps-3). 14.95 (*0-06-028115-4*) HarpC.
Bunting, Eve. Our Sixth-Grade Sugar Babies. LC 90-5487. (Trophy Bk.). 160p. (J). (gr. 4-7). 1992. pap. 4.95 (*0-06-440390-4*, HarpTrophy) HarpC Child Bks.
Bunting, Eve. Our Sixth-Grade Sugar Babies. (J). 1992. 10.05 (*0-606-06150-9*, Pub. by Turtleback) Demco.
— OUR 6 GRADE SUGAR BABY. LC 90-5487. 160p. (J). (gr. 4-6). 1990. lib. bdg. 13.89 (*0-397-32452-9*) HarpC Child Bks.
Bunting, Eve. Our Teacher's Having a Baby. (Illus.). 32p. (J). (ps-3). 1992. 15.00 (*0-395-60470-2*, Clarion Bks) HM.
— A Perfect Father's Day. (Illus.). 32p. (J). (ps-3). 1993. pap. 5.95 (*0-395-66416-0*, Clarion Bks) HM.
*Bunting, Eve. A Perfect Father's Day. (Illus.). 32p. (J). 2000. 9.95 (*0-618-04079-X*, Clarion Bks) HM.
Bunting, Eve. A Picnic in October. LC 98-20044. (Illus.). 32p. (J). (gr. k-5). 1999. 16.00 (*0-15-201656-2*, Harcourt Child Bks) Harcourt.
— The Pumpkin Fair. LC 96-20626. (Illus.). 32p. (J). (ps-1). 1999. 15.00 (*0-395-70060-4*, Clarion Bks) HM.
— Red Fox Running. 32p. (J). (ps-3). 1993. 15.95 (*0-395-58919-3*, Clarion Bks) HM.
— Red Fox Running. (Illus.). 32p. (J). (ps-3). 1996. pap. 5.95 (*0-395-79723-3*) HM.
— Red Fox Running. LC 92-27. 1993. 11.15 (*0-606-10293-0*, Pub. by Turtleback) Demco.
— Ride When You're Ready. (Author's Signature Collection). (Illus.). 40p. (J). (gr. 3-8). 1992. lib. bdg. 12.79 (*0-89565-776-7*) Childs World.
— Rudi's Pond. LC 98-51338. (Illus.). 32p. (J). (gr. k-2). 1999. 15.00 (*0-395-89067-5*, Clarion Bks) HM.
— Scary, Scary Halloween. LC 86-2642. (Illus.). 32p. (J). (ps-1). 1986. 15.00 (*0-89919-414-1*, Clarion Bks) HM.
— Scary, Scary Halloween. LC 86-2642. (Illus.). 32p. (J). (ps-3). 1988. pap. 5.95 (*0-89919-799-X*, Clarion Bks) HM.
— Scary, Scary Halloween. (J). 1986. 11.15 (*0-606-02339-9*, Pub. by Turtleback) Demco.
— The Sea World Book of Sharks. LC 79-63920. (Sea World Press Ser.). (Illus.). 80p. (J). (gr. 4-7). 1984. pap. 9.95 (*0-15-271952-0*, Harcourt Child Bks) Harcourt.
— The Sea World Book of Whales. LC 85-16409. (Sea World Press Ser.). (Illus.). 96p. (J). (gr. 4-7). 1987. reprint ed. 14.95 (*0-15-271948-2*, Harcourt Child Bks); reprint ed. pap. 9.95 (*0-15-271953-9*, Harcourt Child Bks) Harcourt.
— Secret Place. LC 95-20466. (Illus.). 32p. (J). (ps-3). 1996. 15.00 (*0-395-64367-8*, Clarion Bks) HM.
— Sharing Susan: A Novel. 1994. 9.05 (*0-606-05998-9*, Pub. by Turtleback) Demco.
— Sixth-Grade Sleepover. LC 86-4679. 96p. (J). (gr. 4-7). 1986. 13.95 (*0-15-275350-8*, Harcourt Child Bks) Harcourt.
— Smoky Night. LC 93-14885. (Illus.). 32p. (J). (ps-3). 1994. 16.00 (*0-15-269954-6*) Harcourt.
— Smoky Night. (Illus.). 1995. 15.00 (*0-15-201035-1*) Harcourt.
— Smoky Night. (J). 1996. 15.00 (*0-15-201541-8*, Harcourt Child Bks) Harcourt.
*Bunting, Eve. Smoky Night. LC 93-14885. (Illus.). 36p. (J). (ps-3). 1999. pap. 6.00 (*0-15-201884-0*) Harcourt.
Bunting, Eve. So Far from the Sea. LC 97-28176. (Illus.). 32p. (J). (gr. 2-5). 1998. 15.00 (*0-395-72095-8*, Clarion Bks) HM.
— Some Frog! LC 96-24844. (Illus.). 48p. (J). (gr. 2-4). 1998. 15.00 (*0-15-277082-8*) Harcourt.
— Someday a Tree. LC 92-24074. (Illus.). 32p. (J). (gr. k-3). 1993. 15.00 (*0-395-61309-4*, Clarion Bks) HM.
— Someday a Tree. LC 92-24074. (Illus.). 32p. (J). (ps-3). 1996. pap. 5.95 (*0-395-76478-5*, Clarion Bks) HM.
Bunting, Eve. Someday a Tree. 1993. 11.15 (*0-606-08874-1*, Pub. by Turtleback) Demco.
Bunting, Eve. Someone Is Hiding on Alcatraz Island. 144p. (YA). 1986. pap. 4.99 (*0-425-10294-7*, Berkley-Pacer) Berkley Pub.
Bunting, Eve. Someone Is Hiding on Alcatraz Island. (J). 1986. 9.60 (*0-606-03297-5*, Pub. by Turtleback) Demco.
Bunting, Eve. SOS Titanic. 256p. (YA). (gr. 7 up). 1996. pap. 6.00 (*0-15-201305-9*) Harcourt.
— SOS Titanic. LC 95-10712. (Illus.). 256p. (YA). (gr. 7 up). 1996. 13.00 (*0-15-200271-5*) Harcourt.
Bunting, Eve. SOS Titanic. (J). 1996. 11.10 (*0-606-09878-X*, Pub. by Turtleback) Demco.
Bunting, Eve. The Space People. (Author's Signature Collection). (Illus.). 40p. (J). (gr. 3-8). 1992. lib. bdg. 12.79 (*0-89565-765-1*) Childs World.
— Spying on Miss Muller. 1996. mass mkt. 4.50 (*0-449-70455-6*) Fawcett.
— Spying on Miss Muller. LC 94-15003. 192p. (J). (gr. 4-6). 1995. 15.00 (*0-395-69172-9*, Clarion Bks) HM.
— St. Patrick's Day in the Morning, 001. LC 79-15934. (Illus.). 32p. (J). (ps-3). 1980. 15.00 (*0-395-29098-8*, Clarion Bks) HM.
— St. Patrick's Day in the Morning. LC 79-15934. (Illus.). 32p. (J). (ps-3). 1983. pap. 5.95 (*0-89919-162-2*, Clarion Bks) HM.
*Bunting, Eve. St. Patrick's Day in the Morning. (ps-3). 2000. pap. 9.95 incl. audio (*0-618-04083-8*) HM.
Bunting, Eve. A Sudden Silence. 112p. (J). 1990. mass mkt. 4.50 (*0-449-70362-2*, Juniper) Fawcett.
— A Sudden Silence. LC 87-26969. 112p. (YA). (gr. 7 up). 1988. 14.95 (*0-15-282058-2*) Harcourt.
— A Sudden Silence. 1990. 9.60 (*0-606-04816-2*, Pub. by Turtleback) Demco.
Bunting, Eve. The Summer of Riley. 140p. lib. bdg. 15.89 (*0-06-029142-7*) HarpC.
— The Summer of Riley. 140p. (gr. 5 up). 15.95 (*0-06-029141-9*) HarpC.
— The Summer Of Riley. 140p. (gr. 5 up). mass mkt. 4.95 (*0-06-440927-9*) HarpC.
Bunting, Eve. Summer Wheels. LC 90-21051. (Illus.). 48p. (J). (gr. 1-5). 1992. 14.95 (*0-15-207000-1*, Harcourt Child Bks) Harcourt.
— Summer Wheels. LC 90-49758. (ACE., Illus.). 56p. (J). (gr. 2-7). 1996. pap. 6.00 (*0-15-200988-4*, Voyager Bks) Harcourt.
Bunting, Eve. Summer Wheels. 1996. 11.20 (*0-606-09912-3*, Pub. by Turtleback) Demco.
Bunting, Eve. Sunflower House. LC 95-5422. (Illus.). 32p. (J). (ps-1). 1996. 15.00 (*0-15-200483-1*) Harcourt.
— Sunflower House. LC 95-5422. (Illus.). 32p. (J). 1999. pap. 6.00 (*0-15-201952-9*) Harcourt.
— Sunshine Home. LC 93-570. (Illus.). 32p. (J). (gr. k-3). 1994. 16.00 (*0-395-63309-5*, Clarion Bks) HM.
— Surrogate Sister. LC 83-49483. 192p. (YA). (gr. 7 up). 1984. lib. bdg. 13.89 (*0-397-32099-X*) HarpC Child Bks.
— Swan in Love. LC 98-7906. (Illus.). 32p. (J). (gr. k-3). 2000. 16.00 (*0-689-82080-1*) Atheneum Yung Read.
— Terrible Things: An Allegory of the Holocaust. rev. ed. (Illus.). 24p. (J). (gr. 1-4). 1989. reprint ed. pap. 6.95 (*0-8276-0507-2*) JPS Phila.
— Train to Somewhere. LC 95-6787. (Illus.). 32p. (J). (gr. k-3). 1996. 16.00 (*0-395-71325-0*, Clarion Bks) HM.
*Bunting, Eve. Train to Somewhere. (Illus.). 32p. (J). (gr. k-3). 2000. pap. 5.95 (*0-618-04031-5*, Clarion Bks) HM.
Bunting, Eve. Trouble on the T-Ball Team. LC 94-43699. (Illus.). 32p. (J). (gr. k-3). 1997. 13.95 (*0-395-66060-2*, Clarion Bks) HM.
— A Turkey for Thanksgiving. (Illus.). 32p. (J). (ps-1). 1991. 15.00 (*0-89919-793-0*, Clarion Bks) HM.
— A Turkey for Thanksgiving. LC 90-21871. (Illus.). 32p. (J). (ps-3). 1995. pap. 5.95 (*0-395-74212-9*, Clarion Bks) HM.
— Turkey for Thanksgiving. 1995. 11.15 (*0-606-08322-7*, Pub. by Turtleback) Demco.
— Turkey for Thanksgiving. unabridged ed. (Illus.). 32p. (J). (ps-1). 1997. 9.95 incl. audio (*0-395-85812-7*, 11212, Clarion Bks) HM.
— Twinnies. LC 96-7645. (Illus.). 32p. (J). (ps-3). 1997. 15.00 (*0-15-291592-3*) Harcourt.
— Two Different Girls. (Author's Signature Collection). (Illus.). 40p. (J). (gr. 3-8). 1992. lib. bdg. 12.79 (*0-89565-772-4*) Childs World.
— The Undersea People. (Author's Signature Collection). (Illus.). 40p. (J). (gr. 3-8). 1992. lib. bdg. 12.79 (*0-89565-766-X*) Childs World.
— The Valentine Bears. (Illus.). 32p. (J). (gr. 3). 1984. 15.00 (*0-89919-138-X*, Clarion Bks) HM.
— The Valentine Bears. LC 82-9577. (Illus.). 32p. (J). (ps-3). 1985. pap. 5.95 (*0-89919-313-7*, Clarion Bks) HM.
— The Waiting Game. LC 80-8793. 64p. (YA). (gr. 7 up). 1981. 12.95 (*0-397-31941-X*) HarpC Child Bks.
— The Wall. (Illus.). 32p. (J). (ps-3). 1990. 15.00 (*0-395-51588-2*, Clarion Bks) HM.
— The Wall. (Illus.). 32p. (J). (ps-3). 1992. pap. 5.95 (*0-395-62977-2*, Clarion Bks) HM.
— Wall. (Reading Rainbow Bks.). (J). 1990. 11.15 (*0-606-02239-2*, Pub. by Turtleback) Demco.
— Wanna Buy an Alien? LC 95-51091. (Illus.). 96p. (J). (gr. 2-5). 2000. 14.00 (*0-395-69719-0*, Clarion Bks) HM.
— The Wednesday Surprise. LC 88-12117. (Illus.). 32p. (J). (ps-3). 1989. 16.00 (*0-89919-721-3*, Clarion Bks) HM.
— The Wednesday Surprise. (Illus.). 32p. (J). (ps-3). 1990. pap. 5.95 (*0-395-54776-8*, Clarion Bks) HM.
Bunting, Eve. The Wednesday Surprise. (Illus.). (J). (ps-3). 1993. pap. 9.95 incl. audio (*0-395-58699-2*, Clarion Bks) HM.
Bunting, Eve. Wednesday Surprise. 1989. 11.15 (*0-606-04576-7*, Pub. by Turtleback) Demco.
*Bunting, Eve. Who Was Born This Special Day. LC 99-27675. (J). 2000. 16.00 (*0-689-82302-9*) Atheneum Yung Read.
Bunting, Eve. The Wild Horses. (Author's Signature Collection). (Illus.). 40p. (J). (gr. 3-8). 1992. lib. bdg. 12.79 (*0-89565-778-3*) Childs World.
— Will You Be My POSSLQ. LC 87-322. 160p. (YA). (gr. 7 up). 1987. 12.95 (*0-15-297399-0*, Harcourt Child Bks) Harcourt.
*Bunting, Eve. Your Move. LC 96-18603. (Illus.). 32p. (C). 1998. 16.00 (*0-15-200181-6*) Harcourt.
*Bunting, Eve & Brett, Jan. Scary, Scary Halloween. (Illus.). 32p. (J). (ps-3). 1999. pap. 9.95 incl. audio (*0-395-95757-5*, Clarion Bks) HM.
Bunting, G. S. A Revision of Spathiphyllum (Araceae) (Memoirs Ser.: Vol. 10 (3)). (Illus.). 54p. 1960. pap. 8.00 (*0-89327-037-7*) NY Botanical.
Bunting, James. Charles Darwin: A Biography. 126p. 1974. pap. 24.95 (*0-8464-1459-7*) Beekman Pubs.
Bunting, Jane. My First ABC. LC 93-15153. (Illus.). 32p. (J). (gr. k-1). 1993. 12.95 (*1-56458-403-8*) DK Pub Inc.
— My First ABC. (Illus.). (J). (ps). 15.95 (*0-590-24127-3*) Scholastic Inc.
— My First Action Word Book: A Picture Dictionary of 1,000 First Words. LC 95-44260. 40p. (J). (ps-3). 1996. 14.95 (*0-7894-0463-X*) DK Pub Inc.
— My First Action Word Book: A Picture Dictionary of 1,000 First Words. (Illus.). 48p. (J). 17.99 (*0-590-24897-9*) Scholastic Inc.
Bunting, Janet. Christmas Carols to Play & Sing: A Piano Keyboard Book. (Illus.). 24p. (J). 1995. 9.95 (*0-689-80353-2*) S&S Childrens.
— My First Recorder Book. (Illus.). 32p. (J). (gr. 2-6). 1989. pap. 14.95 (*0-8120-7618-4*) Barron.

Bunting, John R. The Hidden Face of Free Enterprise: The Strange Economics of the American Businessman. LC 81-13353. 248p. 1981. reprint ed. lib. bdg. 65.00 (*0-313-23218-0*, BUHI, Greenwood Pr) Greenwood.

Bunting, Josiah. An Education for Our Time. LC 98-24842. 304p. 1998. 24.95 (*0-89526-369-6*) Regnery Pub.

***Bunting, Josiah.** An Education for Our Time. 2000. pap. 14.95 (*0-89526-222-3*) Regnery Pub.

Bunting, Josiah. The Lionheads. LC 78-188356. 214p. 1972. 19.95 (*0-8076-0632-4*, Pub. by Braziller) Norton.

Bunting, Madeleine. Model Occupation: The Channel Islands under German Rule, 1940-1945. (Illus.). 384p. 1998. pap. 15.95 (*0-00-637973-7*, Pub. by HarpC) Trafalgar.

Bunting, Marie-France, jt. auth. see Comeau, Raymond F.

Bunting, Mark. Virtual Power. LC 97-1706. 1997. 22.50 (*0-684-81482-X*) S&S Trade.

Bunting, Peter G., ed. Private Independent Schools, 1999: The Bunting & Lyon Blue Book. 52nd ed. LC 72-122324. (Illus.). 616p. 1999. 100.00 (*0-913094-52-8*) Bunting.

Bunting, Rebecca. Teaching about Language in the Primary Years. LC 97-197210. (Roehampton Student Texts Ser.). 144p. 1997. pap. 24.95 (*1-85346-422-8*, Pub. by David Fulton) Taylor & Francis.

Bunting, Richard L., jt. auth. see Benton, Allen H.

Bunting, Robert. The Pacific Raincoast: Environment & Culture of an American Eden, 1778-1900. LC 96-9655. (Development of Western Resources Ser.). 256p. 1996. 29.95 (*0-7006-0805-2*) U Pr of KS.

Bunting, Robert F., Jr., jt. auth. see Hudson, Janice.

Bunting, Roger K. The Chemistry of Photography. (Illus.). 168p. (Orig.). 1987. pap. text 14.95 (*0-9616724-0-4*) Photoglass Pr.

Bunting, Sheila. Rosemarie Parse: Health As Human Becoming. LC 92-49481. (Notes on Nursing Theories Ser.: Vol. 5). (Illus.). 60p. (C). 1992. 22.95 (*0-8039-4795-X*); pap. 9.95 (*0-8039-4549-3*) Sage.

Bunting, Stephen C., jt. auth. see Wright, R. Gerald.

Bunting, Susan. Annual Editions: Human Sexuality, 97-98. 22nd ed. 256p. (C). 1997. text 12.25 (*0-697-37296-0*) Brown & Benchmark.

— Human Sexuality: 1996-1997. annuals 21st ed. 256p. (C). 1996. text. write for info. (*0-697-31601-7*) Brown & Benchmark.

***Bunting, Susan.** Human Sexuality 2000-2001. 25th ed. (Annual Editions Ser.). 240p. (C). 1999. pap. 16.56 (*0-07-236408-4*) McGrw-H Hghr Educ.

Bunting, Susan J. Human Sexuality, 98-99. 23rd ed. (Annual Ser.). (Illus.). 240p. 1998. pap. text 12.25 (*0-697-39183-3*, Dshkn McG-Hill) McGrw-H Hghr Educ.

***Bunting, Trudi.** Canadian Cities in Transition: The Twenty-First Century. 2nd ed. 576p. 1999. pap. text 35.00 (*0-19-541288-5*) OUP.

Bunting, W. H. A Day's Work Pt. I: A Sampler of Historic Maine Photographs, 1860-1920. LC 97-33305. (Illus.). 384p. 1997. 55.00 (*0-88448-188-3*); pap. 35.00 (*0-88448-189-1*) Tilbury Hse.

— A Day's Work Pt. II: A Sampler of Historic Maine Photographs, 1860-1920. (Illus.). 2000. 55.00 (*0-88448-206-5*); pap. 35.00 (*0-88448-207-3*) Tilbury Hse.

Bunting, W. H., jt. auth. see Shettleworth, Earle G., Jr.

Bunting, William H. Portrait of a Port: Boston, 1852-1914. 544p. (C). 1994. pap. text 22.95 (*0-674-69076-1*) HUP.

Buntline, Ned. Buffalo Bill: His Adventures in the West. LC 74-15731. (Popular Culture in America Ser.). (Illus.). 320p. (YA). (gr. 7 up). 1975. reprint ed. 25.95 (*0-405-06366-0*) Ayer.

Buntman, Peter H. Help for Moms with Hyperactive Kids. 75p. 1998. pap. 11.95 (*0-9623986-2-4*) Ctr Fam Life.

— How to Live with Your Teenager, Vol. II. 176p. pap. 14.95 (*0-9623986-0-8*) Ctr Fam Life.

— Living with ADHD Children: A Handbook for Parents, 2 cass. unabridged ed. 80p. 1998. pap. 19.95 incl. audio (*0-9623986-3-2*) Ctr Fam Life.

— Winning the Parent-Teenager Conflict Game. 180p. (Orig.). 1990. pap. 14.95 (*0-685-28061-6*) Ctr Fam Life.

Buntman, Peter H. & Saris, Eleanor M. How to Live Harmoniously with Your Children & Teens Series. 30p. 1990. pap. 37.50 incl. audio (*0-9623986-1-6*) Ctr Fam Life.

— How to Live with Your Teenagers: A Survivor's Handbook for Parents. 168p. 1990. reprint ed. pap. 14.95 (*0-9603124-0-4*) Ctr Fam Life.

Bunton, George W. The Tides. LC 67-2157. (Bernice P. Bishop Museum Special Publications: No. 54). (Illus.). 24p. reprint ed. pap. 30.00 (*0-608-17288-X*, 203032400068) Bks Demand.

Bunton, Richard. AC/DC: Hell Ain't No Bad Place to Be. (Illus.). 96p. 1997. pap. 19.95 (*0-7119-0061-2*, OP 41771) Omnibus NY.

Bunton, Robin, et al, eds. The Sociology of Health Promotion: Critical Analyses of Consumption, Lifestyle & Risk. 224p. (C). 1995. pap. 25.99 (*0-415-11647-3*, C0100) Routledge.

Bunton, Robin, jt. auth. see Petersen, Alan R.

***Bunton, William J.** Death of an Aquanaut. LC 99-66260. (Illus.). 69p. 2000. 19.95 (*0-941332-81-0*, B1001) Best Pub Co.

Buntrock. Conference Terminology. (ENG, FRE, GER & RUS.). 181p. 1989. 29.95 (*0-8288-7635-5*) Fr & Eur.

***Buntrock, Susan.** Finger Skate Board Tricks & Tips. (Illus.). 32p. (J). (gr. 4-7). 2000. pap. 7.95 (*0-439-19453-9*) Scholastic Inc.

Bunuel, Luis. Las Tres de la Madrugada: Level A. text 7.95 (*0-88436-061-X*) EMC-Paradigm.

— An Unspeakable Betrayal: Selected Writings of Luis Bunuel. White, Garrett, tr. from FRE. LC 99-43048. 230p. 2000. pap. 30.00 (*0-520-20840-4*, Pub. by U CA Pr) Cal Prin Full Svc.

Bunuel, Luis & Dali, Salvador. Un Chien Andalou. unabridged ed. (Illus.). 38p. 1994. pap. 13.95 (*0-571-17372-1*) Faber & Faber.

Bunwaree, jt. auth. see Heward.

Bunyan, Chris. Head Without Skin. 100p. 1999. pap., per. 10.00 (*0-9650975-1-X*) Bite Your Tongue.

Bunyan, Ian, et al. No Ordinary Journey: John Rae, Arctic Explorer 1813-1893. (Illus.). 128p. 1993. 65.00 (*0-7735-1106-7*, Pub. by McG-Queens Univ Pr); pap. 24.95 (*0-7735-1107-5*, Pub. by McG-Queens Univ Pr) CUP Services.

Bunyan, John. All Loves Excelling. 120p. 1998. pap. 4.99 (*0-85151-739-0*) Banner of Truth.

Bunyan, John. Baptism & Church Communion. 26p. pap. 2.99 (*0-9652883-3-1*) Audubon Pr.

— El Corredor Celestial.Tr. of Heavenly Footman. write for info. (*0-7899-0312-1*, 497466) Editorial Unilit.

Bunyan, John. The Fear of God. rev. ed. Kistler, Don, ed. LC 99-220857. 220p. 1999. 19.95 (*1-57358-084-8*) Soli Deo Gloria.

— Grace Abounding: To the Chief of Sinners. 201p. 1993. mass mkt. 5.99 (*0-88368-259-1*) Whitaker Hse.

— Grace Abounding: With Other Spiritual Autobiographies. Stachniewski, John & Pacheco, Anita, eds. (Oxford World's Classics Ser.). 336p. 1998. pap. 8.95 (*0-19-282132-6*) OUP.

— Grace Abounding to the Chief of Sinners. Owens, W. R., ed. & intro. by. 144p. 1987. pap. 10.95 (*0-14-043280-9*) Viking Penguin.

— Grace Abounding to the Chief of Sinners: John Bunyan's Autobiography. 243p. 1998. pap. 11.99 (*1-84030-017-5*) Emerald House Group Inc.

— Heavenly Footman. 1988. pap. 4.99 (*1-85792-177-1*, Pub. by Christian Focus) Spring Arbor Dist.

— The Heavenly Footman: A Description of the Man That Gets to Heaven. Fanella, John J., ed. (Collection of Classics Ser.). 62p. 1996. pap. text 2.95 (*1-879089-21-1*) B Graham Ctr.

— The Holy War. (Illus.). 192p. 1998. pap. 10.99 (*1-84030-026-4*) Emerald House Group Inc.

— Holy War. 13.50 (*1-85792-028-7*, Pub. by Christian Focus) Spring Arbor Dist.

***Bunyan, John.** How to Pray in the Spirit: Thirty-One Devotional Readings on Personal Prayer. Parkhurst, Louis Gifford, ed. LC 98-42500. 144p. 1998. pap. text 9.99 (*0-8254-2085-7*) Kregel.

— Journey to Hell. LC 99-43318. 278p. 1999. pap. 7.99 (*0-88368-583-3*) Whitaker Hse.

Bunyan, John. Lessons from Nature: Poems for Boys & Girls. Sanseri, Gary & Sanseri, Wanda, eds. LC 98-70028. (Illus.). 124p. (J). 1998. reprint ed. 19.95 (*1-880045-19-2*) Back Home Indust.

— The Life & Death of Mr. Badman: Presented to the World in a Familiar Dialogue Between Mr. Wiseman & Mr. Attentive. Forrest, James F. & Sharrock, Roger, eds. (Oxford English Texts Ser.). (Illus.). 232p. 1988. text 85.00 (*0-19-812742-1*) OUP.

— Miscellaneous Works: Some Gospel Truths Opened, a Vindication of Some Gospel Truths Opened, & a Few Sighs from Hell, Vol. 1. Underwood, T. L. & Sharrock, Roger, eds. (Oxford English Texts Ser.). (Illus.). 458p. 1980. 115.00 (*0-19-812730-8*) OUP.

— The Miscellaneous Works of John Bunyan Vol. 3: Christian Behavior, the Holy City, the Resurrection of the Dead. McGee, James S., ed. (Oxford English Texts Ser.). (Illus.). 512p. 1987. 95.00 (*0-19-812731-6*) OUP.

— The Miscellaneous Works of John Bunyan Vol. 4: A Defence of the Doctrine of Justification, A Confession of My Faith, Differences in Judgment about Water-Baptism, Peaceable Principles & True, A Case of Conscience Resolved, Questions about the Nature & Perpetuity of the Seventh-Day-Sabbath. Underwood, Ted L., ed. (Oxford English Texts Ser.). (Illus.). 464p. 1990. 115.00 (*0-19-812732-4*) OUP.

— The Miscellaneous Works of John Bunyan Vol. 5: The Barren Fig-Tree, The Strait Gate, The Heavenly Foot-Man. Midgley, Graham, ed. (Oxford English Texts Ser.). (Illus.). 224p. 1986. 85.00 (*0-19-812733-2*) OUP.

— The Miscellaneous Works of John Bunyan Vol. 6: The Poems, Vol. 6. Midgley, E. G., ed. (Oxford English Texts Ser.). (Illus.). 470p. 1980. 115.00 (*0-19-812734-0*) OUP.

— The Miscellaneous Works of John Bunyan Vol. 7: Solomon's Temple Spiritualized, The House of the Forest of Lebanon, The Water of Life, Vol. 7. Midgley, Graham, ed. (Oxford English Texts Ser.). (Illus.). 288p. 1989. 95.00 (*0-19-812735-9*) OUP.

— The Miscellaneous Works of John Bunyan Vol. 8: Instruction for the Ignorant; Light for Them That Sit in Darkness; Saved by Grace; Come, Welcome to Jesus Christ. Greaves, Richard L., ed. (Oxford English Texts Ser.). (Illus.). 470p. 1979. 98.00 (*0-19-812736-7*) OUP.

— The Miscellaneous Works of John Bunyan Vol. 9: A Treatise of the Fear of God, the Greatness of the Soul, a Holy Life, Vol. 9. Greaves, Richard L., ed. (Oxford English Texts Ser.). (Illus.). 412p. 1981. 118.00 (*0-19-812737-5*) OUP.

— The Miscellaneous Works of John Bunyan Vol. 10: Seasonable Counsel & a Discourse upon the Pharisee & the Publicane. Watkins, Owen C., ed. (Oxford English Texts Ser.). (Illus.). 304p. 1988. 79.00 (*0-19-812738-3*) OUP.

— The Miscellaneous Works of John Bunyan Vol. 11: Good News for the Vilest of Men; The Advocateship of Jesus Christ. Greaves, Richard L., ed. (Oxford English Texts Ser.). (Illus.). 276p. 1985. 75.00 (*0-19-812739-1*) OUP.

— The Miscellaneous Works of John Bunyan Vol. 13: Israel's Hope Encouraged; The Desire of the Righteous Granted; The Saints Privilege & Profit; Christ a Compleat Saviour; The Saints Knowledge of Christ's Love; Of Antichrist, & His Ruine, Vol. 13. Owens, W. R. & Sharrock, Roger, eds. (Illus.). 576p. (C). 1994. 110.00 (*0-19-812368-X*) OUP.

— My Sojourn in Heaven & Stopover in Hell. Relfe, Mary S., ed. 128p. Date not set. pap. 6.00 (*0-9607986-3-3*) League Prayer.

— The New Pilgrim's Progress. LC 89-36626. 224p. 1989. pap. 10.99 (*0-929239-13-X*) Discovery Hse Pubs.

— La Oracion. (SPA.). 148p. 1990. pap. 4.99 (*0-85151-408-1*) Banner of Truth.

— Order & Cause of Salvation & Damnation Chart. pap. 3.99 (*0-87377-028-5*) GAM Pubns.

— Pictorial Pilgrim's Progress. (J). (gr. 2-7). 1960. pap. 5.99 (*0-8024-0019-1*, 554) Moody.

— The Pilgrim's Progress. 384p. 1993. mass mkt. 2.49 (*1-55748-345-0*) Barbour Pub.

— The Pilgrim's Progress. (Essential Christian Library Ser.). 432p. 1998. 9.97 (*1-57748-262-X*) Barbour Pub.

***Bunyan, John.** The Pilgrim's Progress. (Deluxe Christian Classics). 304p. 2000. 9.97 (*1-57748-916-0*) Barbour Pub.

Bunyan, John. The Pilgrim's Progress. Keeble, N. H., ed. & intro. by. LC 99-192015. (Oxford World's Classics Ser.). 336p. 1998. pap. 7.95 (*0-19-283400-2*) OUP.

— The Pilgrim's Progress. 400p. 1981. mass mkt. 6.99 (*0-88368-096-3*) Whitaker Hse.

— Pilgrim's Progress. LC 99-19873. (Nelson's Royal Classic Ser.: Vol. 1). 320p. 1999. 18.99 (*0-7852-4222-8*) Nelson.

***Bunyan, John.** Pilgrim's Progress. (Classics of World Literature Ser.). 1998. pap. 5.95 (*1-85326-468-7*, 4687WW, Pub. by Wrdsworth Edits) NTC Contemp Pub Co.

Bunyan, John. Pilgrims Progress. 384p. 1998. pap. 3.97 incl. audio (*0-916441-24-5*) Barbour Pub.

— The Pilgrim's Progress. Helms, Hal M., ed. LC 81-85770. (Living Library). (Illus.). 268p. 1982. pap. 12.95 (*0-941478-02-5*, 930-033, Pub. by Paraclete MA) BookWorld.

Bunyan, John. Pilgrim's Progress. unabridged ed. (Illus.). 379p. 1992. pap. 9.99 (*0-907927-74-2*) Emerald House Group Inc.

Bunyan, John. The Pilgrim's Progress: A Modern-Day Abridgement for Today's Reader. (Little Library Ser.). 48p. 1995. pap. text 0.99 (*1-55748-648-4*) Barbour Pub.

— Pilgrim's Progress: John Bunyan's Immortal Allegory (Condensed & Adapted for Coloring) Cantelon House Publishers Staff, ed. & intro. by. 174p. (YA). (gr. 6-12). 1994. pap. text 19.95 (*0-9642116-0-2*) Cantelon Hse.

— The Pilgrim's Progress: One Man's Search for Eternal Life - a Christian Allegory. 23.95 (*0-8488-0141-5*) Amereon Ltd.

— The Pilgrim's Progress: One Man's Search for Eternal Life - a Christian Allegory. Larsen, Dan, ed. (Young Reader's Christian Library). (Illus.). 224p. (J). (gr. 4-8). 1989. pap. text 1.39 (*1-55748-099-0*) Barbour Pub.

— The Pilgrim's Progress: One Man's Search for Eternal Life - a Christian Allegory. 1976. lib. bdg. 26.95 (*0-89968-156-5*, Lghtyr Pr) Buccaneer Bks.

— The Pilgrim's Progress: One Man's Search for Eternal Life - a Christian Allegory. (Classics Ser.). mass mkt. 4.99 (*0-8024-0012-4*, 392) Moody.

— The Pilgrim's Progress: One Man's Search for Eternal Life - a Christian Allegory. 1964. mass mkt. 5.95 (*0-451-52399-7*, CE1813, Sig Classics) NAL.

— The Pilgrim's Progress: One Man's Search for Eternal Life - a Christian Allegory. Sharrock, Roger, ed. 384p. 1965. pap. 7.99 (*0-14-043004-0*, Penguin Classics) Viking Penguin.

— Pilgrim's Progress: One Man's Search for Eternal Life - a Christian Allegory. 304p. (gr. 11). 1989. mass mkt. 5.99 (*0-8007-8609-2*, Spire) Revell.

— The Pilgrim's Progress: One Man's Search for Eternal Life - a Christian Allegory. large type ed. 416p. 1982. 27.99 (*0-7089-8072-4*, Charnwood) Ulverscroft.

— The Pilgrim's Progress: One Man's Search for Eternal Life - a Christian Allegory. 1979. reprint ed. 35.99 (*0-85151-259-3*) Banner of Truth.

— The Pilgrim's Progress: One Man's Search for Eternal Life - a Christian Allegory. 256p. 1973. reprint ed. pap. 3.95 (*0-310-22142-0*, 6610S) Zondervan.

— The Pilgrim's Progress from This World to That Which Is to Come. (BCL1-PR English Literature Ser.). 352p. 1992. reprint ed. lib. bdg. 89.00 (*0-7812-7326-9*) Rprt Serv.

— The Pilgrim's Progress in Modern English. rev. ed. Hazelbaker, L. Edward, ed. LC 98-72704. Orig. Title: The Pilgrim's Progress. (Illus.). 450p. 1998. pap. 12.99 (*0-88270-757-4*, Bridge) Bridge-Logos.

— Pilgrim's Progress in Today's English. 1964. pap. 8.99 (*0-8024-6520-X*) Moody.

— Pilgrim's Progress (1902) 466p. 1998. reprint ed. pap. 29.95 (*0-7661-0600-4*) Kessinger Pub.

— Prayer. (Puritan Paperbacks Ser.). Orig. Title: Praying in the Spirit. 172p. 1989. reprint ed. pap. 6.99 (*0-85151-090-6*) Banner of Truth.

— El Progreso Del Peregrino Ilustrado. Orig. Title: Pilgrim's Progress Illustrated. (SPA., Illus.). 256p. 1981. mass mkt. 5.99 (*0-8254-1096-7*, Edit Portavoz) Kregel.

— The Riches of Bunyan. abr. ed. Sanna, Ellyn, ed. (Essential Christian Library Ser.). 352p. 1998. reprint ed. 9.97 (*1-57748-345-6*) Barbour Pub.

— Target Earth! A Victorian children's story based on John Bunyan's The Holy War. LC 82-61244. (Victorian Children's Classics Ser.). 178p. 1982. pap. 6.99 (*0-88270-536-9*) Bridge-Logos.

Bunyan, John. Visions of Heaven & Hell. 63p. 1997. pap. 3.00 (*0-944379-36-2*) CPA Bk Pub.

Bunyan, John. Visions of Heaven & Hell. LC 98-26070. 158p. 1998. pap. 6.99 (*0-88368-541-8*) Whitaker Hse.

— The Works of John Bunyan, 3 vols. Offor, George, ed. 2400p. 1992. reprint ed. 116.99 (*0-85151-598-3*) Banner of Truth.

— The Works of John Bunyan: With an introd. to each treatise, notes & a sketch of his life, times & contemporaries., 3 vols. Offor, George, ed. LC 78-154136. reprint ed. lib. bdg. 510.00 (*0-404-09250-0*) AMS Pr.

— Your Victory in Christ. LC 97-51787. 291p. 1997. pap. 6.99 (*0-88368-518-3*) Whitaker Hse.

Bunyan, John & Leavell, L. P. El Progreso Del Peregrino: Pilgrims Progress. Duffer, Hiram F., Jr., tr. from ENG. (SPA.). 1968. reprint ed. pap. 7.50 (*0-311-37006-3*) Casa Bautista.

Bunyan, John & Taylor, Helen. Christiana's Journey: A Victorian children's story based on John Bunyan's Pilgrim's progress, part 2. LC 82-70860. (Victorian Children's Classics Ser.). 176p. 1982. pap. 6.99 (*0-88270-533-4*) Bridge-Logos.

Bunyan, John & Thomas, James H. Pilgrim's Progress in Today's English. 1999. lib. bdg. 23.95 (*1-56723-201-9*) Yestermorrow.

Bunyan, John & Thomas, John H. Peregrino: El en un Castellano Actualizado.Tr. of Pilgrim's Progress in Today's English. (SPA.). 138p. 1996. 14.99 (*0-8254-1095-9*, Edit Portavoz) Kregel.

Bunyan, John, et al. How They Found Christ: In Their Own Words. 2nd rev. ed. Freeman, Bill, ed. LC 97-78492. (Illus.). 201p. 1998. pap. 9.95 (*0-914271-94-6*) Mnstry Pubns.

Bunyan, John A. Why Video Works? New Applications for Management. LC 86-21106. (Professional Librarian Ser.). (Illus.). 203p. 1988. 40.00 (*0-86729-079-X*, Hall Reference) Macmillan.

Bunyan, P. T. A First Biology Course. 240p. (C). 1994. pap. 19.95 (*0-85950-339-9*, Pub. by S Thornes Pubs) Trans-Atl Phila.

Bunyan, Patrick. All Around the Town: Amazing Manhattan Facts & Curiosities. LC 99-19769. (Illus.). 376p. 1999. pap. 19.95 (*0-8232-1941-0*, Pub. by Fordham) BookMasters.

***Bunyan, Patrick.** All Around the Town: Amazing Manhattan Facts & Curiosities. LC 99-19769. (Illus.). 376p. 1999. 35.00 (*0-8232-1940-2*, Pub. by Fordham) BookMasters.

Bunyan, Tony. Secrecy, Democracy & the Third Pillar of the European Union. 1999. 15.95 (*0-7494-2604-7*) Kogan Page Ltd.

***Bunyard, Britt.** Walking to Singapore. (Illus.). 492p. 2000. pap. 25.95 (*0-595-00086-X*, Writers Club Pr) iUniversecom.

Bunyard, Edward A. A Handbook of Hardy Fruits More Commonly Grown in Great Britain: Apples & Pears Stone & Bush Fruits Nuts. 1990. 100.00 (*0-948251-41-7*, Pub. by Picton) St Mut.

Bunyard, Peter. GAIA in Action: Science of the Living Earth. 1997. pap. text 24.95 (*0-86315-202-3*, Pub. by Floris Bks) Anthroposophic.

Bunye, Maria V., jt. auth. see Yap, Elsa P.

Bunz, Joachim. Neuschwanstein. (Opus Ser.: Vol. 33). (GER & ENG.). 60p. 1999. 42.00 (*3-930698-33-1*, Pub. by Edition A Menges) Natl Bk Netwk.

Bunzel, John A. The American Small Businessman. Bruchey, Stuart & Carosso, Vincent P., eds. LC 78-18956. (Small Business Enterprise in America Ser.). (Illus.). 1979. reprint ed. lib. bdg. 28.95 (*0-405-11460-5*) Ayer.

Bunzel, John H. Affirmative Action in Higher Education: A Dilemma of Conflicting Principles. LC 98-26093. (Essays in Public Policy Ser.: No. 89). 1998. pap. 5.00 (*0-8179-5942-4*) Hoover Inst Pr.

— Anti-Politics in America: Reflections on the Anti-Political Temper & Its Distortions of the Democratic Process. LC 78-27675. 291p. 1979. reprint ed. lib. bdg. 49.50 (*0-313-20834-4*, BUAP, Greenwood Pr) Greenwood.

— Race Relations on Campus: Stanford Students Speak. (Portable Stanford Bks.). 192p. (Orig.). 1992. pap. 12.95 (*0-916318-49-4*) Stanford Alumni Assn.

Bunzel, Mark J. & Morris, Sandra K. Multimedia Applications Development: Using Indeo Video & DVI Technology. 2nd ed. LC 93-23188. (Intel Ser.). 309p. 1993. 45.00 (*0-07-043300-3*) McGraw.

Bunzel, Reed. Pay for Play. 240p. (Orig.). 1992. mass mkt. 4.50 (*0-380-76589-6*, Avon Bks) Morrow Avon.

Bunzel, Ruth L. Chichicastenango: A Guatemalan Village. (American Ethnological Society Publications: No. 22). reprint ed. 45.00 (*0-404-58172-2*) AMS Pr.

— The Pubelo Potter: A Study of Creative Imagination in Primitive Art. LC 73-82257. (Columbia Univ. Contributions to Anthropology Ser.: Vol. 8). (Illus.). reprint ed. 55.00 (*0-404-50558-9*) AMS Pr.

— The Pueblo Potter: A Study of Creative Imagination in Primitive Art. (Illus.). 134p. 1972. reprint ed. pap. 7.95 (*0-486-22875-4*) Dover.

— Zuni Katcinas: 47th Annual Report, B. A. E. LC 72-13917. (Beautiful Rio Grande Classics Ser.). (Illus.). 358p. 1984. reprint ed. lib. bdg. 40.00 (*0-87380-099-0*) Popular E Commerce.

— Zuni Texts. LC 73-3551. (American Ethnological Society Publications: No. 15). reprint ed. 42.50 (*0-404-58165-X*) AMS Pr.

Bunzel, Tom. Digital Video on the PC. LC 97-164260. 250p. 1997. pap. 27.95 (*0-941845-21-4*) Micro Pub Pr.

Bunzell, R. Zuni Ceremonialism: Three Studies. LC 96-10861. 369p. (C). 1992. pap. 20.95 (*0-8263-1376-0*) U of NM Pr.

Bunzl, John. Introducing Philosophy. 492p. (C). 1998. per. 32.95 (*0-7872-5621-8*, 41562101) Kendall-Hunt.

Bunzl, Martin. The Context of Explanation. LC 92-47382. 172p. (C). 1993. text 120.50 (*0-7923-2153-7*) Kluwer Academic.

B

— Real History: Reflections on Historical Practice. LC 97-9101. (Philosophical Issues in Science Ser.). 160p. (C). 1997. 70.00 (*0-415-15961-X*); pap. 22.99 (*0-415-15962-8*) Routledge.

*****Buob, Patricia & Eyre, Sally.** Poetic Concoctions: Grades 2-4. (Illus.). 64p. 1999. pap., teacher ed. 6.95 (*1-889369-38-1*, TI0800) Teaching Ink.

Buobnov, B. M. & Golitsyn, G. S. Convection in Rotating Fluids. LC 95-3068. (Fluid Mechanics & Its Applications Ser.: Vol. 29). 232p. (C). 1995. text 162.50 (*0-7923-3371-3*) Kluwer Academic.

Buol, S. W. Soil Genesis & Classification. 4th ed. LC 97-5055. (Illus.). 1997. 59.95 (*0-8138-1464-2*) Iowa St U Pr.

Buomaupina, Maryann, ed. see D'Amato, James J.

*****Buonaiuto, Sheila.** The Yielded Life Bk. 2: A Spiritual Journey. 128p. 2000. pap. 7.00 (*0-939241-70-6*) Faith Print.

Buonaparte, Napoleon. The Diaries. (Great Commanders Ser.). 288p. 1994. reprint ed. 30.00 (*1-56515-008-2*) Collect Reprints.

Buonarroti & Nims, John F. The Complete Poems of Michaelangelo. LC 98-7704. 1998. 25.00 (*0-226-08033-1*) U Ch Pr.

Buonarroti, Michelangelo. The Complete Poetry of Michelangelo. Alexander, Sidney, ed. & tr. by. from ITA. LC 91-16240. (Illus.). 317p. (C). 1993. reprint ed. pap. 19.95 (*0-8214-1049-0*) Ohio U Pr.

— I Sonetti di Michelangelo: The 78 Sonnets of Michelangelo with Verse Translation. Symonds, J. A., tr. (ENG & ITA.). 94p. 1997. pap. text 19.50 (*1-58085-005-7*) Interlingua VA.

— Life Drawings of Michelangelo. (Fine Art Ser.). (Illus.). 48p. 1980. pap. 4.95 (*0-486-23876-8*) Dover.

Buonarroti, Michelangelo, jt. auth. see Nagel, Alexander.

*****Buonassisi, Rosario.** Pizza: From Its Italian Origins to the Modern Table. (Illus.). 168p. 2000. pap. 24.95 (*1-55209-321-2*) Firefly Bks Ltd.

*****Buonaventura, Wendy.** Beauty & the East: A Book of Oriental Body Care. (Illus.). 2000. pap. 17.95 (*1-56656-387-9*) Interlink Pub.

Buonaventura, Wendy. The Book of Oriental Body Care. LC 99-203022. (Illus.). 1997. pap. 29.95 (*0-86356-081-4*, Pub. by Saqi) Intl Spec Bk.

— Serpent of the Nile: Women & Dance in the Arab World. (Illus.). 224p. 1998. reprint ed. pap. 35.00 (*0-86356-073-3*, Pub. by Saqi) Intl Spec Bk.

— Serpent of the Nile: Women & Dance in the Arab World. rev. ed. LC 89-15393. (Illus.). 208p. 1998. pap. text 35.00 (*1-56656-300-3*) Interlink Pub.

Buongiorno, Benedetto & Garland, Robert R. Real Estate Accounting & Reporting Manual, No. 2731, No. 2731. annuals rev. ed. 976p. 1989. boxed set, suppl. ed. 155.00 (*0-7913-0395-0*) Warren Gorham & Lamont.

— Real Estate Accounting & Reporting Manual, No. 2731, No. 2731. rev. ed. 976p. 1991. text, suppl. ed. 57.00 (*0-7913-0792-1*) Warren Gorham & Lamont.

Buonicore, Anthony J., ed. Software Package in Support of ASTM Standard Practice for Environmental Site Assessments: Transaction Screen Process, User's Guide, E1528-93. (ASTM Manual Ser.: MNL24). 54p. 1995. text 99.00 (*0-8031-2063-X*, MNL24) ASTM.

— User's Guide Software Package in Support of ASTM Standard Practice for Environmental Site Assessments: Transaction Screen Process (E1528-96) LC 97-4531. (Manual Ser.: Vol. 24). (Illus.). 53p. 1997. pap. text 110.00 (*0-8031-2074-5*, MNL24) ASTM.

— User's Guide Software Package in Support of ASTM Standard Practice for Environmental Site Assessments: Transaction Screen Process (E1528-96) LC 97-4530. (Manual Ser.: Vol. 24A). (Illus.). 80p. 1997. pap. text 131.00 (*0-8031-2075-3*, MNL24A) ASTM.

Buonicore, Anthony J. & Theodore, Louis. Industrial Control Equipment for Gaseous Pollutants, 2 vols, Vol. 1. LC 74-25260. (Uniscience Ser.). 209p. 1975. 65.00 (*0-87819-067-8*, TD885, CRC Reprint) Franklin.

— Industrial Control Equipment for Gaseous Pollutants, 2 vols, Vol. 2. LC 74-25260. (Uniscience Ser.). 168p. 1975. 44.00 (*0-87819-068-6*, CRC Reprint) Franklin.

Buonicore, Anthony J., jt. auth. see Theodore, Louis.

Buonicore, Anthony J., ed. see Air & Waste Management Association Staff.

Buonicore, Anthony J., jt. ed. see Theodore, Louis.

Buono. Designing Organizations for a Changing World: A Primer on Organization Theory. 300p. pap. text. write for info. (*0-471-13846-0*) Wiley.

Buono, Anthony & Nemerson, Roy. The Race Against Junk Food Vol. 1: Starring the Snak Posse. Orchanian, Robert, ed. (The Adventures in Good Nutrition Ser.). (Illus.). 40p. (J). (ps-3). 1997. per. 9.95 (*0-9658108-0-1*) HCom.

Buono, Anthony F. & Nichols, Lawrence T. Corporate Policy, Values & Social Responsibility. LC 85-6422. 227p. 1985. 67.95 (*0-275-90068-1*, C0068, Praeger Pubs) Greenwood.

Buono, Anthony F., jt. auth. see Bowditch, James L.

Buono, Anthony M. Active Participation at Mass: What It Is & How to Attain It. LC 93-41295. 124p. 1994. pap. 5.95 (*0-8189-0682-0*) Alba.

*****Buono, Anthony M.** The Greatest Marian Prayers: Their History, Meaning & Usage. LC 99-22492. xx, 168p. 1999. pap. 9.95 (*0-8189-0861-0*) Alba.

Buono, Anthony M. Praying with the Church. LC 90-33607. 152p. (Orig.). 1990. pap. 6.95 (*0-8189-0579-4*) Alba.

Buono, Anthony M., ed. Favorite Prayers to Our Lady. large type ed. (Illus.). 150p. 1989. pap. 4.95 (*0-89942-919-X*, 919/04) Catholic Bk Pub.

Buono, Anthony M., ed. see Noe, Virgilio.

Buono, Barbara Del, see Del Buono, Barbara.

Buono, Barbara Del, see Del Buono, John & Del Buono, Barbara.

*****Buono, Christopher L., ed.** The Writers' Journal Guide to the Writing Life. 192p. 2000. pap. 14.95 (*0-9678103-0-2*, 320) Writers Journal.

Buono, Gloria M. The Painting Ballerina. (Illus.). 80p. (J). (gr. 3 up). 1999. pap. 12.95 (*0-9669818-0-4*) AabaGlo.

Buono, John Del, see Del Buono, John.

Buonocore. Diccionario de Bibliotecologia. 2nd ed. (SPA.). 458p. 1976. 39.95 (*0-8288-5586-2*, S12239) Fr & Eur.

Buonocore, Michelina. The Last Portrait: Selected Poems. (Living Poets' Library: No. 37). (Illus.). 54p. 1987. pap. 5.95 (*0-934218-38-2*) Dragons Teeth.

Buonomo, Leonardo. Backward Glances: Exploring Italy, Reinterpreting America (1831-1866) LC 95-10317. 120p. 1995. 28.50 (*0-8386-3649-7*) Fairleigh Dickinson.

Buononato, Sharon. Sentamental Holidays. (Illus.). 50p. 1999. pap. 10.95 (*1-57377-066-3*) Easl Pubns.

— Sentimental Seasons, Vol. 1. (Illus.). 64p. 1998. pap. 9.95 (*1-57377-038-8*) Easl Pubns.

Buonopane, Marguerite D. The North End Italian Cookbook. 4th rev. ed. LC 96-27596. (Illus.). 256p. 1996. pap. 14.95 (*1-56440-990-2*) Globe Pequot.

Buotolo, Robert A. Inspiration at Work: Igniting the Entrepreneurial Spirit of the Individual & the Corporation. 160p. (Orig.). 1997. pap. 14.95 (*0-9651541-0-6*) Dona Nobis Pacem.

*****Buoye, Thomas M.** Manslaughter, Markets & Moral Economy: Violent Disputes over Property Rights in 18th-Century China. (Cambridge Studies in Chinese History, Literature & Institutions). (Illus.). 288p. (C). 2000. 59.95 (*0-521-64045-8*) Cambridge U Pr.

Buoye, Thomas M. A Study Guide for "The Chinese" 109p. 1992. pap. text 10.00 (*0-89264-104-5*) Ctr Chinese Studies.

Buppert, Carolyn. The Nurse Practitioner's Business Practice & Legal Guide. LC 98-39952. 496p. 1999. 79.00 (*0-8342-1185-8*, 11858) Aspen Pub.

*****Buppert, Carolyn.** Primary Care Provider's Guide to Reimbursement & Quality Audits. 2000. 89.00 (*0-8342-1744-9*) Aspen Pub.

Buqeoli, N. G. Russia in Transition: Left, Right or Center? LC 97-212349. 205p. 1997. 85.00 (*1-56072-488-9*) Nova Sci Pubs.

Bur, Jacques. How to Understand the Virgin Mary. (Illus.). 142p. (C). 1996. pap. 19.95 (*0-8264-0946-6*) Continuum.

Burac, Robert, jt. auth. see Peguy, Charles.

Burac, Robert, ed. see Peguy, Charles.

Burack, Alexandra. On the Verge. 32p. 1997. pap. 8.00 (*1-887628-03-7*) Plinth Bks.

Burack, Cynthia. The Problem of the Passions: Feminism, Psychoanalysis & Social Theory. 200p. (C). 1995. pap. text 16.50 (*0-8147-1252-5*) NYU Pr.

Burack, Elmer H. Corporate Resurgence & the New Employment Relationships: After the Reckoning. LC 92-16207. 240p. 1992. 55.00 (*0-89930-789-2*, BKU, Quorum Bks) Greenwood.

— Creative Human Resource Planning & Applications. 2nd ed. LC 87-35696. (Illus.). 261p. 1994. reprint ed. pap. text, spiral bd. 34.95 (*0-942560-16-7*) Brace-Park.

Burack, Elmer H. & Mathys, Nicholas J. Career Management in Organizations: A Practical Human Resource Planning Approach. 427p. (C). 1990. pap., spiral bd. 34.95 (*0-942560-02-7*) Brace-Park.

— Human Resource Planning: A Pragmatic Approach to Manpower Staffing & Development. 3rd rev. ed. 422p. 1996. 49.95 (*0-942560-01-9*) Brace-Park.

Burack, Elmer H. & Torda, Florence. The Manager's Guide to Change. 226p. 1989. spiral bd. 19.95 (*0-942560-14-0*) Brace-Park.

Burack, Jacob A., et al, eds. Handbook of Mental Retardation & Development. (Illus.). 764p. (C). 1998. text 80.00 (*0-521-44123-4*); pap. text 29.95 (*0-521-44668-6*) Cambridge U Pr.

Burack, Jacob A. & Enns, James T., eds. Attention, Development & Psychopathology. LC 97-3395. 414p. 1997. lib. bdg. 50.00 (*1-57230-198-8*) Guilford Pubns.

Burack, Jonathan, ed. Editorial Cartoons by Kids, 1994. (Illus.). 197p. (Orig.). 1994. pap. 7.95 (*1-55933-060-0*) Zino Pr.

— Understanding & Creating Editorial Cartoons: A Resource Guide. (Illus.). 200p. 1994. teacher ed., ring bd. 39.95 (*1-55933-015-5*, 4507BK) Know Unltd.

Burack, Marsha J. Reiki Healing Yourself & Others: A Photo-Instructional Art Book. 160p. 1995. pap. text 24.95 (*1-880441-39-X*) Reiki Heal.

*****Burack, Orah R., et al.** Workbook for Training CNAs in Ethics: Accompanies Text 1307-9. 96p. 2000. pap. text. write for info. (*0-8261-1308-7*) Springer Pub.

Burack, Sylvia, ed. The Big Book of Folktale Plays. LC 90-16928. 336p. (J). (gr. 3-7). 1991. pap. 12.00 (*0-8238-0294-9*) Kalmbach.

— The Big Book of Large-Cast Plays: Twenty-Seven One-Act Plays for Young Actors. LC 94-32725. 350p. (J). 1994. text 13.95 (*0-8238-0302-3*) Kalmbach.

Burack, Sylvia K. How to Write & Sell Your Articles. LC 97-20266. 112p. 1997. pap. 8.95 (*0-87116-182-6*) Writer.

Burack, Sylvia K., ed. Great American Events on Stage. LC 96-32197. 232p. (J). (gr. 4-9). 1996. pap. 16.95 (*0-8238-0305-8*) Kalmbach.

— Thirty Plays from Favorite Stories. LC 97-1039. (Orig.). (J). (gr. 3-7). 1997. pap. 15.95 (*0-8238-0306-6*) Kalmbach.

*****Burack, Sylvia K., ed.** The Writer's Handbook. 65th ed. 900p. 2000. 32.95 (*0-87116-188-5*) Writer.

Burack, Sylvia K., ed. The Writer's Handbook, 1999 Edition. 63rd enl. rev. ed. 900p. 1998. 29.95 (*0-87116-184-2*) Writer.

— The Writer's Handbook, 2000 Edition. 64th rev. ed. LC 36-28596. 919p. 1999. 32.95 (*0-87116-187-7*) Writer.

Burack-Weiss, Ann & Brennan, Frances C. Gerontological Social Work Supervision. LC 91-339. 148p. (Orig.). 1991. pap. text 14.95 (*1-56024-182-9*) Haworth Pr.

— Gerontological Social Work Supervision. LC 91-339. 148p. (Orig.). 1991. lib. bdg. 39.95 (*0-86656-827-1*) Haworth Pr.

Burack-Weiss, Ann, jt. auth. see Silverstone, Barbara.

Buracree, Tom, jt. auth. see Pargh, Andy.

Buragas, Robert, jt. auth. see Flying Models Staff.

Buraglia, Antonio C., photos by. Casa Moderna: Half a Century of Domestic Architecture. (SPA., Illus.). 242p. 1997. 50.00 (*958-9393-24-1*) Villegas Pub.

Burago, Iurii D. & Mazya, V. G. A Potential Theory & Function Theory for Irregular Regions. LC 69-15004. (Seminars in Mathematics Ser.: Vol. 3). 76p. reprint ed. pap. 30.00 (*0-608-10044-7*, 202069500018) Bks Demand.

Burago, Yu D., et al, eds. Geometry III: Theory of Surfaces. Primrose, E., tr. from RUS. LC 92-16958. (Encyclopedia of Mathematical Sciences Ser.: Vol. 48). (Illus.). xii, 244p. 1992. 118.95 (*0-387-53377-X*) Spr-Verlag.

Burago, Yu D. & Zalgaller, V. A. Geometric Inequalities. (Grundlehren der Mathematischen Wissenschaften Ser.: Band 285). (Illus.). 350p. 1988. 158.95 (*0-387-13615-0*) Spr-Verlag.

Burak. Cyberhound's Guide to International Discussion Groups. 1996. 79.00 (*0-7876-1019-4*) Visible Ink Pr.

— Cyberhound's Guide to Internet Databases. 2nd ed. 1996. 104.00 (*0-7876-0935-8*) Gale.

Burak, Hally, ed. see Bourgeois, Paulette.

Burak, Patricia. Crisis Management in a Cross-Cultural Setting. rev. ed. 60p. 1995. pap. text 15.00 (*0-912207-18-3*) NAFSA Washington.

Burakoff, Alexis. On the Ice: Kids' Views & Interviews with Famous (& Not So Famous) Skaters. Econoply, Pamela & Burakoff, Suzanne, eds. LC 95-125140. (Kids' Views & Interviews Ser.: Vol. 1). (Illus.). 100p. (Orig.). (J). (gr. 2-9). 1994. pap. 11.95 (*0-9640792-0-8*) Hare & Hatter.

Burakoff, Gerald. How to Play the Recorder. 40p. 1996. pap. 5.95 (*0-8256-2320-0*, AM 35551) Music Sales.

— Step One: Play Recorder. (Illus.). 32p. 1998. pap. 5.95 (*0-8256-1645-X*, AM945604) Music Sales.

Burakoff, Gerald & Burakoff, Sonya. The Classroom Recorder, 2 bks., Bk. 1. 1970. 3.25 (*0-913334-00-6*, CM1001) Consort Music.

— The Classroom Recorder, 2 bks., Bk. 2. 1972. 3.25 (*0-685-51174-X*, CM1013) Consort Music.

Burakoff, Gerald & Strickland, Willy. The Duet Recorder, 2 bks., Bk. 1. 1970. 4.00 (*0-913334-01-4*, CM1002) Consort Music.

— The Duet Recorder, 2 bks., Bk. 2. 1972. 4.00 (*0-913334-13-8*, 1015) Consort Music.

— The Duet Recorder, 2 bks., Bks. 1-2. 1970. 4.00 (*0-685-74374-8*) Consort Music.

— First Performance. 1974. 4.00 (*0-913334-20-0*, CM1024) Consort Music.

— The Holiday Recorder. 1970. 4.00 (*0-913334-02-2*, CM1008) Consort Music.

— The Quartet Recorder, 2 bks., Bk. 1. 1975. 4.00 (*0-913334-21-9*, CM1025) Consort Music.

— The Quartet Recorder, 2 bks., Bk. 2. 1976. 4.00 (*0-913334-33-2*, CM1031) Consort Music.

— The Quartet Recorder, 2 bks., Bks. 1-2. 1975. 4.00 (*0-685-74377-2*) Consort Music.

— The Trio Recorder, 2 bks., Bk. 1. 1975. 4.00 (*0-913334-24-3*, CM1028) Consort Music.

— The Trio Recorder, Bk. 2. 1977. 4.00 (*0-685-74376-4*, CM1042) Consort Music.

— The Trio Recorder, 2 bks., Bks. 1-2. 1975. 4.00 (*0-685-74375-6*) Consort Music.

Burakoff, Gerald, ed. see Staeps, Hans U.

Burakoff, Sonya, jt. auth. see Burakoff, Gerald.

Burakoff, Suzanne, jt. auth. see McPhee, Jonathan.

Burakoff, Suzanne, ed. see Burakoff, Alexis.

Burakowski, Tadeusz & Wierzchon, Tadeusz. Surface Engineering of Metals. LC 98-42176. (Materials Science & Technology Ser.). 608p. 1998. boxed set 104.95 (*0-8493-8225-4*) CRC Pr.

Burall, Paul. Green Design. (Issues in Design Ser.). (Illus.). 88p. (C). 1991. pap. 19.95 (*0-85072-284-5*, Pub. by Design Council Bks) Ashgate Pub Co.

— Product Development & the Environment. LC 95-40205. 232p. 1996. 69.95 (*0-566-07659-4*, Pub. by Gower) Ashgate Pub Co.

Burana, Carmina. Concordantia in Carmina Burana. (Alpha-Omega Ser.: Reihe B, Bd. XII). (GER.). x, 887p. 1996. 235.00 (*3-487-10253-6*) G Olms Pubs.

Burandt, Gary & Giges, Nancy. Moscow Meets Madison Avenue: The Adventures of the First American Adman in the U. S. S. R. LC 92-52609. (Illus.). 208p. 1992. 22.50 (*0-88730-570-9*, HarpBusn) HarpInfo.

Burandt, Harriet & Dale, Shelley. Tales from the Home Place: Adventures of a Texas Farm Girl. LC 96-38191. 160p. (J). (gr. 4-6). 1997. 14.95 (*0-8050-5075-2*, Bks Young Read) H Holt & Co.

*****Burandt, Harriet, et al.** Tales from the Homeplace: Adventures of Texas Farm Girl. 160p. (J). (gr. 4-6). 1999. pap. 3.99 (*0-440-41494-6*) BDD Bks Young Read.

Burandt, Ulrich. Updating Ergonomics. 144p. 1996. pap. text 29.00 (*3-931126-05-6*, Pub. by Die Gestalten) Consort Bk Sales.

Buranelli, Prosper, et al, eds. The Cross Word Puzzle Book. LC 74-8834. 132p. 1974. reprint ed. 11.95 (*0-405-06191-9*) Ayer.

Buranelli, Prosper, et al. Simon & Schuster 75th Anniversary Vintage Crossword Treasury. 96p. 1999. per. 9.00 (*0-684-85637-9*) S&S Trade.

Buranelli, Vincent. Edgar Allan Poe. 2nd ed. (United States Authors Ser.: No. 4). 168p. 1977. 28.95 (*0-8057-7189-1*) Macmillan.

Buranelli, Vincent, ed. Edgar Allan Poe. LC 77-7265. (Twayne's United States Authors Ser.). 166p. (C). 1977. pap. text 4.95 (*0-672-61502-9*, Bobbs) Macmillan.

— The Trial of Peter Zenger. LC 75-31814. (Illus.). 152p. 1975. reprint ed. lib. bdg. 35.00 (*0-8371-8444-4*, ZEPZ, Greenwood Pr) Greenwood.

Buranelli, Vincent, jt. auth. see Wolfson, Murray.

Buranen, Lise & Roy, Alice M., eds. Perspectives on Plagiarism & Intellectual Property in a Postmodern World. LC 99-11407. (Illus.). 304p. (C). 1999. text 71.50 (*0-7914-4079-6*); pap. text 23.95 (*0-7914-4080-X*) State U NY Pr.

Burani, D. H. The Future of Pakistan. 1985. 34.00 (*0-8364-1266-4*, Pub. by Promilla) S Asia.

Burani, Johanna C. Cholesterol in School Age Children: A Program to Develop Awareness. (Illus.). 88p. 1990. spiral bd. 39.95 (*1-879339-12-9*) Infinity Impress.

— Meal Planning for Diabetes in Pregnancy: Practical Applications. 60p. 1990. spiral bd. 29.95 (*1-879339-13-7*) Infinity Impress.

Buranov, Yuri. Lenin's Will: Falsified & Forbidden. LC 94-15108. (Illus.). 241p. (C). 1994. 33.95 (*0-87975-886-4*) Prometheus Bks.

Buras, A. J. & Lindner, M. Heavy Flavours II. (Advanced Series on "Directions in High Energy Physics": Vol. 15). 800p. 1997. text 147.00 (*981-02-2215-7*) World Scientific Pub.

Buras, A. J. & Lindner, M., eds. Heavy Flavours. (Directions in High Energy Physics Ser.: Vol. 10). 650p. (C). 1992. pap. 81.00 (*981-02-0822-7*); text 143.00 (*981-02-0821-9*) World Scientific Pub.

Buras, Janice P. Way down Yonder in Plaquemines. LC 96-7767. (Illus.). 256p. 1996. pap. 14.95 (*1-56554-229-0*) Pelican.

Buras, Nathan. Reflections on Hydrology: Science & Practice. LC 97-43345. x, 314p. 1997. 35.00 (*0-87590-874-8*) Am Geophysical.

Buras, Nathan, ed. Management of Water Resources in North America: Anticipating the 21st Century: Proceedings of the Engineering Foundation Conference Tucson, Arizona, September 4-8, 1995, Vol. III. LC 95-35421. 160p. 1995. 22.00 (*0-7844-0113-6*) Am Soc Civil Eng.

Buratti, James. Mountain Biking Ohio: A Guide to Singletrack Trails in the Buckeye State. LC 97-91767. (Illus.). 56p. (Orig.). 1997. pap. 10.95 (*0-9657566-0-2*) Single Track Pr.

— Mountain Biking Ohio: A Guide to Singletrack Trails in the Buckeye State. 2nd rev. ed. (Illus.). 96p. (Orig.). 1999. pap. 11.95 (*0-9657566-1-0*) Single Track Pr.

Burattini, E. & Balerna, A., eds. Biomedical Applications of Synchroton Radiation. LC 95-8172. (International School of Physics Enrico Fermi Ser.: Vol. 128). 412p. (YA). (gr. 12). 1996. 127.00 (*90-5199-248-3*, 248-3) IOS Press.

*****Buratto, Lucio.** Cataract Surgery in Complicated Cases. 450p. (C). 2000. text 145.00 (*1-55642-467-1*) SLACK Inc.

Buratto, Lucio. Corneal Topography: The Clinical Atlas.Tr. of Corneale Topografia. (Illus.). 476p. 1996. 135.00 (*1-55642-306-3*, 63063) SLACK Inc.

— Phacoemulsification: Principles & Techniques. LC 97-34823. (Illus.). 544p. 1997. text 195.00 (*1-55642-360-8*, 63608) SLACK Inc.

*****Buratto, Lucio & Brint, Stephen.** LASIK: Surgical Techniques & Complications. 2nd ed. LC 99-46441. 624p. 1999. 215.00 (*1-55642-432-9*) SLACK Inc.

— LASIK: Surgical Techniques & Complications. 2nd ed. (SPA., Illus.). 624p. 2000. 215.00 (*1-55642-446-9*) SLACK Inc.

Buratto, Lucio & Brint, Stephen F. Lasik: Principles & Techniques. LC 97-31540. (Illus.). 464p. 1997. text 149.00 (*1-55642-371-3*, 63713) SLACK Inc.

*****Buratto, Lucio, et al.** Pterygium Surgery. 200p. (C). 2000. pap. text 59.00 (*1-55642-492-2*) SLACK Inc.

— Viscoelastics in Ophthalmic Surgery. (Illus.). 500p. 1999. 145.00 (*1-55642-448-5*) SLACK Inc.

Burawoy, Michael. Manufacturing Consent: Changes in the Labor Process under Monopoly Capitalism. LC 79-10188. xviii, 286p. (C). 1982. pap. text 16.00 (*0-226-08038-2*) U Ch Pr.

— Marxist Inquiries: Studies of Labor, Class & States. 338p. 1983. lib. bdg. 36.00 (*0-226-08039-0*) U Ch Pr.

Burawoy, Michael & Lukacs, Janos. The Radiant Past: Ideology & Reality in Hungary's Road to Capitalism. 232p. 1992. 28.95 (*0-226-08041-2*) U Ch Pr.

— The Radiant Past: Ideology & Reality in Hungary's Road to Capitalism. xvi, 232p. 1994. pap. text 13.95 (*0-226-08042-0*) U Ch Pr.

Burawoy, Michael & Skocpol, Theda, eds. Marxist Inquiries: Studies of Labor, Class & States (Supplement to the American Journal of Sociology) 338p. (C). 1983. pap. text 18.00 (*0-226-08040-4*) U Ch Pr.

Burawoy, Michael & Verdery, Katherine, eds. Uncertain Transition: Ethnographies of Change in the Postsocialist World. 320p. (C). 1999. pap. 23.95 (*0-8476-9043-1*); text 65.00 (*0-8476-9042-3*) Rowman.

Burawoy, Michael, et al. Ethnography Unbound: Power & Resistance in the Modern Metropolis. LC 91-8552. 280p. 1991. 50.00 (*0-520-07320-7*, Pub. by U CA Pr); pap. 18.95 (*0-520-07322-3*, Pub. by U CA Pr) Cal Prin Full Svc.

*****Burawoy, Michael, et al.** Global Ethnography: Forces, Connections & Imaginations in a Postmodern World. LC 99-53114. 410p. 2000. pap. 17.95 (*0-520-22216-4*, Pub. by U CA Pr) Cal Prin Full Svc.

— Global Ethnography: Forces, Connections, & Imaginations in a Postmodern World. LC 99-53114. 410p. 2000. 48.00 (*0-520-22215-6*, Pub. by U CA Pr) Cal Prin Full Svc.

Burayidi, Michael A. Multiculturalism in a Cross-National Perspective. 416p. 1996. 67.50 (*0-7618-0592-3*); pap. 39.50 (*0-7618-0593-1*) U Pr of Amer.

An Asterisk (*) at the beginning of an entry indicates that the title is appearing for the first time.

Burayidi, Michael A., ed. Urban Planning in a Multicultural Society. LC 99-18013. 280p. 2000. 65.00 (*0-275-96125-7*, Praeger Pubs) Greenwood.

Burayidi, Michael A., jt. auth. see Kisubi, Alfred T.

Burba, Keith V., jt. auth. see Burba, Linda J.

Burba, Linda J. & Burba, Keith V. T-R-A-I-N up the Children. 112p. 1985. pap. 7.99 (*0-8341-1062-8*) Beacon Hill.

Burbach, J. H., compiled by. The Catholic Religion: Illustrated & Explained for Child, Adult & Convert. LC 92-60087. (Illus.). 186p. 1993. reprint ed. pap. 9.00 (*0-89555-457-7*) TAN Bks Pubs.

Burbach, J. P. & De Wied, D., eds. Brain Functions in Neuropeptides: A Current View. (Illus.). 142p. (C). 1993. 49.00 (*1-85070-453-8*) Prthnon Pub.

Burbach, K., jt. auth. see Kuhn, K.

Burbach, Roger & Flynn, Patricia. Agribusiness in the Americas. LC 80-17114. 314p. 1980. reprint ed. pap. 97.40 (*0-7837-9609-9*, 206036600005) Bks Demand.

Burbach, Roger & Flynn, Patricia, eds. The Politics of Intervention: The United States in Central America. LC 83-42526. 272p. 1984. pap. 12.00 (*0-85345-635-6*, Pub. by Monthly Rev) NYU Pr.

Burbach, Roger, et al. Globalization & Its Discontents. LC 96-28837. 192p. 1996. 49.95 (*0-7453-1171-7*, Pub. by Pluto GBR); pap. 17.95 (*0-7453-1170-9*, Pub. by Pluto GBR) Stylus Pub VA.

***Burbach, Roger, et al.** Globalization & Post-Modern Politics: From Zapatistas to High Tech Robber Barons. LC 00-9741. 2001. write for info. (*0-7453-1649-2*) Pluto GBR.

Burbach, Roger, jt. ed. see Danaher, Kevin.

Burban, Lisa L. & Anderson, John W. Storms over the Urban Forest: Planning, Responding, & Regreening - A Community Guide to Natural Disaster Relief. 2nd ed. (Illus.). 152p. (Orig.). 1996. reprint ed. pap. text 30.00 (*0-7881-2948-1*) DIANE Pub.

***Burbank, Charles W.** Welfare & the Ideology of Power: Confessions of a Welfare Worker. 149p. 1999. pap. 12.95 (*0-9676145-0-3*) Rosetta Pub.

Burbank, David T. Reign of Rabble: The St. Louis General Strike of 1877. LC 66-21658. 208p. 1966. 35.00 (*0-678-00186-3*) Kelley.

Burbank, Doreen C. Short-Cut Quilts: Sixty Patterns for Creating Quilts from 5" Squares. Linch-Zadel, Lauri, ed. (Illus.). 144p. (Orig.). 1994. pap. 19.95 (*0-943721-13-X*) Leman Pubns.

Burbank, Garin. When Farmers Voted Red: The Gospel of Socialism in the Oklahoma Countryside, 1910-1924, 53. LC 76-5259. (Contributions in American History Ser.: No. 53). (Illus.). 225p. 1977. 55.00 (*0-8371-8903-9*, BSO/, Greenwood Pr) Greenwood.

Burbank, Jane & Ransel, David L. Imperial Russia: New Histories for the Empire. LC 98-17132. (Indiana-Michigan Series in Russian & East European Studies). (Illus.). 352p. 1998. 39.95 (*0-253-33462-4*); pap. 24.95 (*0-253-21241-3*) Ind U Pr.

***Burbank, Jeff.** License to Steal: Nevada's Gaming Control System in the Megaresort Age. LC 99-50648. (The/Gaming Studies). (Illus.). 272p. 2000. 29.95 (*0-87417-339-6*) U of Nev Pr.

Burbank, John, ed. & tr. see Jakobson, Roman.

Burbank, John, ed. & tr. see Mukarovsky, Jan.

Burbank, John, tr. see Mukarovsky, Jan.

Burbank, Jon, ed. Culture Shock! Nepal. (Illus.). 250p. 1991. pap. 12.95 (*1-55868-076-4*) Gr Arts Ctr Pub.

Burbank, Luther. Harvest of the Years. 1998. reprint ed. 40.00 (*0-936128-84-4*) De Young Pr.

— Why I Am an Infidel. (Little Blue Bk.). 1991. pap. 10.00 (*0-936128-77-1*) De Young Pr.

Burbank, Patricia M., jt. auth. see Swonger, Alvin K.

Burbank, Richard D. Charles Wuorinen: A Bio-Bibliography, 49. LC 93-28492. (Bio-Bibliographies in Music Ser.: No. 49). 352p. 1993. lib. bdg. 75.00 (*0-313-25399-4*, Greenwood Pr) Greenwood.

— Twentieth Century Music. LC 80-25040. 509p. 1984. reprint ed. pap. 157.80 (*0-608-02845-2*, 206391200007) Bks Demand.

Burbank, Stephen B. Rule Eleven in Transition: The Report of the Third Circuit Task Force on Federal Rule of Civil Procedure 11. LC 89-80411. 216p. (Orig.). 1989. pap. 20.00 (*0-938870-41-6*) Am Judicature.

Burbank, Toni, ed. see Gardner, Richard A.

Burbank, Victoria K. Fighting Women: Anger & Aggression in Aboriginal Australia. LC 93-20568. 1994. 50.00 (*0-520-08307-5*, Pub. by U CA Pr); pap. 19.95 (*0-520-08308-3*, Pub. by U CA Pr) Cal Prin Full Svc.

Burbank, W. H. Photographic Printing Methods: A Practical Guide to the Professional & Amateur Worker. 3rd ed. LC 72-9185. (Literature of Photography Ser.). 1978. reprint ed. 20.95 (*0-405-04896-3*) Ayer.

Burbatti, Guido L. & Formenti, Laura. The Milan Approach to Family Therapy. LC 87-19595. 221p. 1988. 40.00 (*0-87668-972-1*) Aronson.

— The Milan Approach to Family Therapy. LC 87-19595. 232p. 1993. reprint ed. pap. 30.00 (*0-87668-161-5*) Aronson.

Burbatti, Guido L., et al. Systemic Psychotherapy with Families, Couples, & Individuals. LC 92-9280. 224p. 1993. 45.00 (*0-87668-390-1*) Aronson.

***Burberick, Stanford.** Mainstream PSI: Psychic Abilities in the Real World. 1999. 22.95 (*1-57174-133-X*) Hampton Roads Pub Co.

Burberry. Environment & Services. 7th ed. 1992. pap. text. write for info. (*0-582-21231-6*, Pub. by Addison-Wesley) Longman.

— Mitchells Enviro & Service. (C). 1997. pap. 62.95 (*0-582-24521-4*, Pub. by Addison-Wesley) Longman.

Burberry, R. A. VHF & UHF Antennas. (Electromagnetic Waves Ser.: No. 35). 320p. 1992. text 98.00 (*0-86341-269-6*, EW035) INSPEC Inc.

Burbick, Joan. Healing the Republic: The Language of Health & the Culture of Nationalism in Nineteenth-Century America. LC 93-32395. (Cambridge Studies in American Literature & Culture: No. 82). 367p. (C). 1994. text 69.95 (*0-521-45434-4*) Cambridge U Pr.

Burbidge, Brinsley. The Scottish Garden: Book of the Scottish Garden. (Illus.). 168p. (C). 1989. 31.00 (*0-948473-12-6*, Pub. by Royal Botanic Edinburgh) Balogh.

Burbidge, F. W. The Gardens of the Sun: A Naturalist's Journal of Borneo & the Sulu Archipelago. (Oxford in Asia Hardback Reprints Ser.). (Illus.). 408p. 1989. 35.00 (*0-19-588930-4*) OUP.

Burbidge, Geoffrey, ed. Annual Review of Astronomy & Astrophysics, Vol. 36. LC 63-8846. 692p. 1998. text 70.00 (*0-8243-0936-7*) Annual Reviews.

***Burbidge, Geoffrey, ed.** Annual Review of Astronomy & Astrophysics, Vol. 37. LC 63-8846. 689p. 1999. 140.00 (*0-8243-0937-5*) Annual Reviews.

Burbidge, Geoffrey R., ed. Annual Review of Astronomy & Astrophysics, Vol. 33. LC 63-8846. 1995. text 60.00 (*0-8243-0933-2*) Annual Reviews.

— Annual Review of Astronomy & Astrophysics, Vol. 34. LC 63-8846. 1996. text 65.00 (*0-8243-0934-0*) Annual Reviews.

Burbidge, Geoffrey R., et al, eds. Annual Review of Astronomy & Astrophysics, Vol. 12. LC 63-8846. (Illus.). 1974. text 53.00 (*0-8243-0912-X*) Annual Reviews.

— Annual Review of Astronomy & Astrophysics, Vol. 13. LC 63-8846. (Illus.). 1975. text 53.00 (*0-8243-0913-8*) Annual Reviews.

— Annual Review of Astronomy & Astrophysics, Vol. 14. LC 63-8846. (Illus.). 1976. text 53.00 (*0-8243-0914-6*) Annual Reviews.

— Annual Review of Astronomy & Astrophysics, Vol. 16. LC 63-8846. (Illus.). 1978. text 53.00 (*0-8243-0916-2*) Annual Reviews.

— Annual Review of Astronomy & Astrophysics, Vol. 17. LC 63-8846. (Illus.). 1979. text 53.00 (*0-8243-0917-0*) Annual Reviews.

— Annual Review of Astronomy & Astrophysics, Vol. 18. LC 63-8846. (Illus.). 1980. text 53.00 (*0-8243-0918-9*) Annual Reviews.

— Annual Review of Astronomy & Astrophysics, Vol. 19. LC 63-8846. (Illus.). 1981. text 53.00 (*0-8243-0919-7*) Annual Reviews.

— Annual Review of Astronomy & Astrophysics, Vol. 20. LC 63-8846. (Illus.). 1982. text 53.00 (*0-8243-0920-0*) Annual Reviews.

— Annual Review of Astronomy & Astrophysics, Vol. 21. LC 63-8846. (Illus.). 1983. text 53.00 (*0-8243-0921-9*) Annual Reviews.

— Annual Review of Astronomy & Astrophysics, Vol. 22. LC 63-8846. (Illus.). 1984. text 53.00 (*0-8243-0922-7*) Annual Reviews.

— Annual Review of Astronomy & Astrophysics, Vol. 23. LC 63-8846. (Illus.). 1985. text 53.00 (*0-8243-0923-5*) Annual Reviews.

— Annual Review of Astronomy & Astrophysics, Vol. 24. LC 63-8846. (Illus.). 1986. text 53.00 (*0-8243-0924-3*) Annual Reviews.

— Annual Review of Astronomy & Astrophysics, Vol. 25. LC 63-8846. (Illus.). 1987. text 53.00 (*0-8243-0925-1*) Annual Reviews.

— Annual Review of Astronomy & Astrophysics, Vol. 27. LC 63-8846. 1989. text 53.00 (*0-8243-0927-8*) Annual Reviews.

— Annual Review of Astronomy & Astrophysics, Vol. 28. LC 63-8846. 1990. text 53.00 (*0-8243-0928-6*) Annual Reviews.

— Annual Review of Astronomy & Astrophysics, Vol. 29. LC 63-8846. 1991. text 53.00 (*0-8243-0929-4*) Annual Reviews.

— Annual Review of Astronomy & Astrophysics, Vol. 30. LC 63-8846. 1992. text 57.00 (*0-8243-0930-8*) Annual Reviews.

— Annual Review of Astronomy & Astrophysics, Vol. 31. (Illus.). 1993. text 57.00 (*0-8243-0931-6*) Annual Reviews.

— Annual Review of Astronomy & Astrophysics, Vol. 32. LC 63-8846. (Illus.). 1994. text 60.00 (*0-8243-0932-4*) Annual Reviews.

— Annual Review of Astronomy & Astrophysics, Vol. 35. LC 63-8846. 1997. text 70.00 (*0-8243-0935-9*) Annual Reviews.

Burbidge, John, ed. Beyond Prince & Merchant: Citizen Participation & the Rise of Civil Society. 308p. 1997. pap. 29.95 (*1-888753-09-9*) PACT Pubns.

Burbidge, John L. Period Batch Control. (Oxford Series on Advanced Manufacturing: Vol. 12). (Illus.). 276p. 1996. text 99.95 (*0-19-856400-7*) OUP.

— Production Flow Analysis for Planning Group Technology. (Oxford Series on Advanced Manufacturing: No. 8). (Illus.). 304p. 1989. 69.95 (*0-19-859183-7*) OUP.

— Production Flow Analysis for Planning Group Technology. (Oxford Series on Advanced Manufacturing: No. 8). (Illus.). 188p. 1997. reprint ed. pap. text 44.95 (*0-19-856459-7*) OUP.

Burbidge, John W. Being & Will: An Essay in Philosophical Theology. LC 76-45934. 214p. reprint ed. pap. 66.40 (*0-8357-9484-9*, 201352700086) Bks Demand.

— Hegel on Logic & Religion: The Reasonableness of Christianity. LC 91-19111. (SUNY Series in Hegelian Studies). 184p. (C). 1992. pap. text 21.95 (*0-7914-1018-8*) State U NY Pr.

***Burbidge, John W.** Historical Dictionary of Hegelian Philosophy. LC 00-41285. (Historical Dictionaries of Religions, Philosophies & Movements Ser.). 2000. write for info. (*0-8108-3878-8*) Scarecrow.

Burbidge, John W. On Hegel's Logic: Fragments of a Commentary. 292p. (C). 1995. pap. 17.50 (*0-391-03902-4*) Humanities.

— Real Process: How Logic & Chemistry Combine in Hegel's Philosophy of Nature. (Toronto Studies in Philosophy). 304p. 1996. text 75.00 (*0-8020-0897-6*) U of Toronto Pr.

— Within Reason: A Guide to Non-Deductive Reasoning. 192p. 1990. pap. 14.95 (*0-921149-55-7*) Broadview Pr.

Burbidge, John W., ed. see Fackenheim, Emil L.

Burbidge, John W., ed. see Hegel, Georg Wilhelm Friedrich.

Burbidge, John W., ed. see Smith, Wilfred C.

Burbidge, John W., tr. see D'Hondt, Jacques & Roland, Nelson.

Burbidge, Lee E. For Sale by Owner: How to Sell Your Home Yourself & Save Thousands of Dollars. rev. ed. (Illus.). 81p. 1992. pap. 69.95 (*0-9668470-0-8*) L E Burbidge.

Burbidge, Nicky. Letters. 142p. 1996. pap. text 13.95 (*0-19-442149-X*) OUP.

Burbridge, Edward K. Chicago Boy: The Life & Crimes of a Southside Street Fighter. Burbridge, Maxine, ed. LC 91-76856. 305p. (Orig.). 1998. pap. 25.00 (*0-9631261-0-5*) LA & Chi Riv Undgrd.

— The Landlady's Daughter. 210p. (Orig.). Date not set. pap. 25.00 (*0-9631261-1-3*) LA & Chi Riv Undgrd

Burbridge, Gary, ed. & intro. see Ball, John.

Burbridge, Izabel M., tr. see Novaes, Sylvia C.

Burbridge, Maxine, ed. see Burbridge, Edward K.

***Burbridge, Pauline.** Quilt Studio: Innovative Techniques for Confident & Creative Quiltmaking & Design. LC 99-43585. (Illus.). 160p. 2000. pap. 29.95 (*0-8442-2082-5*, 20825, Quilt Dgst Pr) NTC Contemp Pub Co.

Burbules, Nicholas C. Dialogue in Teaching: Theory & Practice. LC 92-44879. (Advances in Contemporary Educational Thought Ser.: Vol. 10). 208p. (C). 1993. text 43.00 (*0-8077-3242-7*); pap. text 21.95 (*0-8077-3241-9*) Tchrs Coll.

Burbules, Nicholas C. & Callister, Thomas. Watch It: The Risky Promises & Promising Risks of Information Technology for Education. LC 99-49176. 240p. 1999. text 60.00 (*0-8133-9083-4*) Westview.

— Watch IT: The Risky Promises & Promising Risks of Information Technology for Education. LC 99-49176. 240p. 2000. pap. text 24.00 (*0-8133-9082-6*) Westview.

Burbules, Nicholas C. & Torres, Carlos A. Globalization & Education: Critical Perspectives LC 99-23276. (Social Theory, Education & Cultural Change Ser.). 1999. pap. 21.99 (*0-415-92047-7*) Routledge.

***Burbules, Nicholas C. & Torres, Carlos Alberto, eds.** Globalization & Education: Critical Perspectives. LC 99-23276. (Social Theory, Education & Cultural Change Ser.). 384p. (C). 2000. text. write for info. (*0-415-92048-5*) Routledge.

Burbules., Nicholas C., jt. auth. see Phillips, D. C.

Burbules, Nicholas C., ed. see Hansen, David T.

Burby, Liza. Bonnie Blair. LC 96-53333. (Making Their Mark Ser.). (J). 1997. lib. bdg. 15.93 (*0-8239-5066-2*, PowerKids) Rosen Group.

— Mae Jemison. LC 96-37466. (Making Their Mark Ser.). (J). (gr. 2-4). 1997. lib. bdg. 15.93 (*0-8239-5027-1*, PowerKids) Rosen Group.

Burby, Liza N. Blizzards. LC 98-15979. (Extreme Weather Ser.). 24p. (J). (gr. k-4). 1999. 18.60 (*0-8239-5291-6*, PowerKids) Rosen Group.

— Bulimia Nervosa: The Secret Cycle of Bingeing & Purging. LC 98-16888. (Teen Health Library of Eating Disorder Prevention). (Illus.). 64p. (YA). (gr. 7-12). 1998. lib. bdg. 17.95 (*0-8239-2762-8*, EDBULI) Rosen Group.

— A Day in the Life of a Carpenter. LC 98-23984. (Kids' Career Library). 24p. (J). (gr. k-4). 1999. 17.26 (*0-8239-5301-7*, PowerKids) Rosen Group.

— A Day in the Life of a Chef. LC 98-20258. (Kids' Career Library). 24p. (J). (gr. k-4). 1999. 17.26 (*0-8239-5298-3*, PowerKids) Rosen Group.

— A Day in the Life of a Librarian. LC 98-4775. (Kids' Career Library). 24p. (J). (gr. k-4). 1999. 17.26 (*0-8239-5304-1*) Rosen Group.

— A Day in the Life of a Mayor: Featuring New York City Mayor Rudy Giuliani. LC 98-8546. (Kids' Career Library). 24p. (J). (gr. k-4). 1999. 17.26 (*0-8239-5303-3*) Rosen Group.

— A Day in the Life of a Nurse. LC 98-7544. (Kids' Career Library). (Illus.). 24p. (J). (gr. k-4). 1999. 17.25 (*0-8239-5302-5*, PowerKids) Rosen Group.

— A Day in the Life of a Park Ranger. LC 98-7671. (Kids' Career Library). 24p. (J). (gr. k-4). 1999. 17.26 (*0-8239-5300-9*, PowerKids) Rosen Group.

— A Day in the Life of a Professional Golfer. LC 98-5643. (Kids' Career Library). 24p. (J). (gr. k-4). 1999. 17.26 (*0-8239-5299-1*, PowerKids) Rosen Group.

— A Day in the Life of a Sculptor. LC 98-4608. (Kids' Career Library). 24p. (J). (gr. k-4). 1999. 17.26 (*0-8239-5305-X*) Rosen Group.

— Electrical Storms. LC 98-7565. (Extreme Weather Ser.). 24p. (J). (gr. k-4). 1999. 18.60 (*0-8239-5294-0*, PowerKids) Rosen Group.

— Elizabeth Blackwell. LC 96-41732. (Making Their Mark Ser.). (J). 1996. lib. bdg. 15.93 (*0-8239-5022-0*, PowerKids) Rosen Group.

— Gabrielle Reece, Star Volleyball Player. LC 96-54269. (Making Their Mark Ser.). (J). 1997. lib. bdg. 15.93 (*0-8239-5067-0*, PowerKids) Rosen Group.

— Hail. LC 98-7566. (Extreme Weather Ser.). 24p. (J). (gr. k-4). 1999. 18.60 (*0-8239-5293-2*, PowerKids) Rosen Group.

— Heatwaves & Droughts. LC 98-19930. (Extreme Weather Ser.). 24p. (J). (gr. k-4). 1999. 18.60 (*0-8239-5292-4*, PowerKids) Rosen Group.

— Jackie Joyner-Kersee. LC 96-53335. (Making Their Mark Ser.). (J). 1997. lib. bdg. 15.93 (*0-8239-5064-6*, PowerKids) Rosen Group.

— Jane Goodall. LC 96-41730. (Making Their Mark Ser.). (Illus.). 24p. (J). (gr. 2-4). 1997. lib. bdg. 15.93 (*0-8239-5025-5*, PowerKids) Rosen Group.

— Kristi Yamaguchi. LC 96-53334. (Making Their Mark Ser.). (J). 1997. lib. bdg. 15.93 (*0-8239-5065-4*, PowerKids) Rosen Group.

— Leaders of Women's Suffrage. (History Makers Ser.). (Illus.). (YA). (gr. 4-12). 1998. lib. bdg. 22.45 (*1-56006-367-X*) Lucent Bks.

— Margaret Mead. LC 96-41733. (Making Their Mark Ser.). (J). 1997. lib. bdg. 15.93 (*0-8239-5026-3*, PowerKids) Rosen Group.

— Marie Curie. LC 96-41734. (Making Their Mark Ser.). (J). 1997. lib. bdg. 15.93 (*0-8239-5024-7*, PowerKids) Rosen Group.

— Monica Seles. LC 96-30002. (Making Their Mark Ser.). (J). 1997. lib. bdg. 15.93 (*0-8239-5068-9*, PowerKids) Rosen Group.

— Pueblo Indians. (Junior Library of American Indians). (J). 1994. 13.15 (*0-606-08044-9*) Turtleback.

— Rachel Carson. LC 96-41731. (Making Their Mark Ser.). (J). 1997. lib. bdg. 15.93 (*0-8239-5023-9*, PowerKids) Rosen Group.

— Sheryl Swoopes, All-Star Basketball Player. LC 96-54268. (Making Their Mark Ser.). (J). 1997. lib. bdg. 15.93 (*0-8239-5069-7*, PowerKids) Rosen Group.

— Tornadoes. LC 97-52012. (Extreme Weather Ser.). 24p. (J). 1998. 18.60 (*0-8239-5289-4*) Rosen Group.

— Tropical Storms & Hurricanes. LC 98-19931. (Extreme Weather Ser.). 24p. (J). (gr. k-4). 1999. 13.95 (*0-8239-5290-8*, PowerKids) Rosen Group.

Burby, Raymond J. Communicating with People: The Supervisor's Introduction to Verbal Communication & Decision-Making. LC 78-109507. (Supervision Ser.). 1970. pap. text 14.95 (*0-201-00735-5*) Addison-Wesley.

— Managing with People. 1968. pap. text 9.00 (*0-201-00723-1*) Addison-Wesley.

Burby, Raymond J., ed. Cooperating with Nature: Confronting Natural Hazards with Land-Use Planning for Sustainable Communities. LC 98-12415. 368p. 1998. 51.75 (*0-309-06362-0*, Joseph Henry Pr) Natl Acad Pr.

Burby, Raymond J., et al. Cities under Water: Ten Cities' Efforts to Manage Floodplain Land Use. (Program on Environment & Behavior Monograph Ser.: No. 47). 240p. (Orig.). (C). 1988. pap. 20.00 (*0-685-28121-3*) Natural Hazards.

— Making Governments Plan: State Experiments in Managing Land Use. LC 97-2189. (Illus.). 200p. 1997. text 32.50 (*0-8018-5623-X*) Johns Hopkins.

Burcaw, G. Ellis. Introduction to Museum Work. 3rd ed. LC 97-4695. (American Association for State & Local History Book Ser.). 240p. 1997. 65.00 (*0-7619-8925-0*); pap. 25.95 (*0-7619-8926-9*) AltaMira Pr.

Burcaw, Robert T., ed. Moravian Book of Worship Manual for Worship Planners. 146p. 1995. pap., student ed. 6.00 (*1-878422-19-7*) Moravian Ch in Amer.

Burce, Dan W. What Every Woman Needs to Know about Thru-Hiking. LC 93-72959. 100p. 1998. pap. 9.95 (*0-9636342-2-4*) Ctr AT Studies.

***Burcell, Robin.** Every Move She Makes. 400p. 1999. mass mkt. 6.50 (*0-06-101432-X*) HarpC.

Burch. Aid Technology & Export Subsidies. 55.95 (*1-85628-104-3*) Ashgate Pub Co.

Burch. Cost & Management Accounting. Date not set. pap. text, teacher ed. write for info. (*0-314-03327-0*); pap. text, student ed. write for info. (*0-314-03329-7*) West Pub.

— GED Science Book. (YA - Adult Education Ser.). 1995. pap. 10.95 (*0-538-71105-1*) S-W Pub.

Burch. In & Out of Synch. 1991. 51.95 (*0-85967-867-9*) Ashgate Pub Co.

Burch, Alison, tr. see Al-Maghut, Muhammad.

Burch, Allen W., ed. see Anderson, Lynn M.

Burch, Amy, jt. illus. see Thomas, Eric.

Burch, Barron T., see Burch, Ronnie, pseud.

Burch, Betty A. The Assimilation Experience of Five American White Ethnic Novelists of the Twentieth Century. LC 90-39828. (European Immigrants & American Society Ser.). 272p. 1990. reprint ed. text 20.00 (*0-8240-7423-8*) Garland.

Burch, Beverly. On Intimate Terms: The Psychology of Difference in Lesbian Relationships. 192p. (C). 1993. text 21.50 (*0-252-01801-X*) U of Ill Pr.

— Other Women: Lesbian Experience & Psychoanalytic Theory of Women. LC 96-41400. 190p. 1997. 41.50 (*0-231-10602-5*); pap. 16.50 (*0-231-10603-3*) Col U Pr.

Burch-Brown, Carol & Rigsbee, David. Trailers. LC 96-6014. (Illus.). 112p. (Orig.). 1996. pap. 16.95 (*0-8139-1680-1*) U Pr of Va.

Burch, Byron. Brewing Quality Beers. 2nd ed. 1993. pap. 6.95 (*0-9604284-2-9*) Joby Bks.

Burch, C. Beth. Writing for Your Portfolio. LC 98-14844. 473p. 1998. pap. text 38.00 (*0-205-27159-6*) Allyn.

Burch, C. Beth, jt. auth. see Woodman, Leonora.

Burch, Cindy. The Dove's Nest Restaurant (Cookbook) New American Recipes from a Historic Texas Town. LC 96-86128. (Illus.). 144p. 1996. pap. 17.95 (*0-9653257-0-9*) Doves Nest.

Burch, Claire. Goodbye My Coney Island Baby. 329p. 1991. reprint ed. pap. 19.95 (*0-916147-14-2*) Regent Pr.

— Homeless in the Eighties. (Illus.). 120p. 1989. pap. 9.95 (*0-916147-09-6*) Regent Pr.

— Homeless in the Nineties: Selected Poetry. 650p. 1992. pap. 17.95 (*0-916147-19-3*) Regent Pr.

B

An Asterisk (*) at the beginning of an entry indicates that the title is appearing for the first time.

— Homeless in the Nineties: Selected Poetry. rev. ed. (Illus.). 665p. 1999. 34.95 (*1-889059-22-6*) Regent Pr.

— Solid Gold Illusion. (Illus.). 116p. 1991. lib. bdg. 125.00 (*0-916147-15-0*) Regent Pr.

— Stranger in the Family. LC 76-173211. 1972. 6.95 (*0-672-51566-0*, Bobbs) Macmillan.

— Stranger in the Family: A Guide to Living with the Emotionally Disturbed. 214p. 1998. pap. 30.00 (*0-916147-25-8*) Regent Pr.

— Stranger on the Planet: The Small Book of Laurie. 175p. 1997. pap. 10.00 (*0-916147-67-3*) Regent Pr.

— What Really Killed Rosebud? 250p. 1996. pap. 14.00 (*0-916147-69-X*) Regent Pr.

— You Be the Mother Follies. ii, 142p. 1991. reprint ed. pap. 14.95 (*0-916147-13-4*) Regent Pr.

Burch, Claire, ed. see Freedman, Don & Harvey, Elinor.

Burch, David. Academic Freedom: A Selected Bibliography Commemorating the Symposium on Academic Freedom. 23p. (Orig.). 1987. pap. 10.00 (*0-935630-21-X*) U of Tex Tarlton Law Lib.

— Faculty Writings - 1987. (Legal Bibliography Ser.: No. 31A). 45p. 1987. pap., suppl. ed. 30.00 (*0-935630-17-1*) U of Tex Tarlton Law Lib.

— Fundamentals of Kayak Navigation. 3rd ed. LC 99-23964. (Illus.). 336p. 1999. pap. text 14.95 (*0-7627-0473-X*) Globe Pequot.

Burch, David, compiled by. Faculty Writings - 1989-90. (Legal Bibliography Ser.: No. 34). 1992. pap. 125.00 (*0-935630-38-4*) U of Tex Tarlton Law Lib.

— Faculty Writings, 1988-89. (Legal Bibliography Ser.: No. 31B). 42p. 1989. suppl. ed. 30.00 (*0-935630-31-7*) U of Tex Tarlton Law Lib.

Burch, David, et al, eds. Globalization & Agri-Food Restructuring: Perspectives from the Australasia Region. 368p. 1996. text 91.95 (*1-85972-380-2*, Pub. by Avebry) Ashgate Pub Co.

— Restructuring Global & Regional Agricultures: Transformation in Australasian Agri-Food Economies & Spaces. LC 98-74503. 14p. 1999. text 74.95 (*1-84014-975-2*) Ashgate Pub Co.

Burch, David F. Emergency Navigation: Pathfinder Techniques for the Inquistive & Prudent Mariner. rev. ed. 1990. pap. text 16.95 (*0-87742-260-5*) Intl Marine.

— Emergency Navigation: Pathfinding Techniques for the Inquisitive & Prudent Mariner. rev. ed. 260p. 1990. pap. 16.95 (*0-07-156558-2*) McGraw.

— The Starfinder Book. (Illus.). 86p. 1990. pap. 12.95 (*0-939837-08-0*) Paradise Cay Pubns.

Burch, David R. & Young, Stephen E., eds. Conference on the Global Responsibility of Law Librarians Proceedings: October 18-21, 1989, the University of Texas School of Law, Austin, Texas. LC 90-38909. xiii, 256p. 1990. reprint ed. 45.00 (*0-8377-0359-X*, Rothman) W S Hein.

Burch, Deryl. Estimating Excavation. LC 97-26971. (Illus.). 448p. 1997. pap. 39.50 (*0-934041-96-2*) Craftsman.

Burch, Douglas M. Moist: A Pc Program for Predicting Heat & Moisture Transfer in Building Envelopes, Release 3.0. 53p. 1997. pap. 5.00 (*0-16-054692-3*) USGPO.

Burch, Elizabeth & Sachs, Judith. Natural Healing for the Pregnant Woman. LC 96-43824. 336p. 1997. pap. 14.00 (*0-399-52308-1*, Perigee Bks) Berkley Pub.

Burch, Ernest S., Jr. The Inupiaq Eskimo Nations of Northwest Alaska. LC 98-14682. (Illus.). xvii, 473p. 1998. 49.95 (*0-912006-95-1*, 6951) U of Alaska Pr.

— Inupiaq Eskimo Nations of Northwest Alaska. LC 98-14682. (Illus.). xvii, 473p. 1998. pap. 31.95 (*0-912006-96-X*, 696X) U of Alaska Pr.

***Burch, Ernest S., Jr., ed.** International Directory of Arctic Social Scientists. 221p. 1999. reprint ed. pap. text 35.00 (*0-7881-7804-0*) DIANE Pub.

Burch, Ernest S. & Ellanna, Linda J., eds. Key Issuers in Hunter-Gatherer Research. 534p. 1994. 65.00 (*0-85496-375-8*, Pub. by Berg Pubs); pap. 24.50 (*0-85496-376-6*, Pub. by Berg Pubs) NYU Pr.

Burch, Ernest S., Jr. & Forman, Werner. The Eskimos. LC 87-40549. (Illus.). 128p. 1988. 29.95 (*0-8061-2126-2*) U of Okla Pr.

Burch, Francis F., tr. see Henry, Paul.

Burch, Genevieve. Alcohol Prevention in Five Secondary Schools. 68p. (Orig.). 1980. pap. 4.50 (*1-55719-100-X*) U NE CPAR.

— Assessment of the Primary Health Care Needs of North & South Omaha. 159p. (Orig.). 1981. pap. 10.50 (*1-55719-046-1*) U NE CPAR.

— National Juvenile Justice Program Collaboration: Auxiliary Appendixes. 164p. (Orig.). 1978. pap. 10.00 (*1-55719-053-4*) U NE CPAR.

— National Juvenile Justice Program Collaboration: Evaluation Report. 175p. (Orig.). 1978. pap. 11.00 (*1-55719-038-0*) U NE CPAR.

Burch, Genevieve & Davis, Carole M. Utilization of Services by Omaha's Older Mexican-Americans. 72p. (Orig.). 1979. pap. 4.50 (*1-55719-096-8*) U NE CPAR.

Burch, Geoff. The Art & Science of Business Persuasion: Mastering the Power of Getting What You Want. LC 95-50089. (Illus.). 244p. 1996. 18.95 (*1-55972-354-8*, Birch Ln Pr) Carol Pub Group.

Burch, George B. Alternative Goals in Religion: Love, Freedom, Truth. LC 72-82248. 128p. reprint ed. pap. 39.70 (*0-7837-6907-5*, 204673700003) Bks Demand.

— Early Medieval Philosophy. LC 70-148207. (Biography Index Reprint Ser.). 1977. 18.95 (*0-8369-8054-9*) Ayer.

— Nuggets of Gold: Surgeons Quotes. 1999. pap. text 9.99 (*1-889893-29-3*) Emerald House Group Inc.

Burch, George E. A Primer of Cardiology. 4th ed. LC 78-135690. 366p. reprint ed. pap. 104.40 (*0-608-17756-3*, 2056503); reprint ed. pap. 113.50 (*0-608-09979-1*, 201452800090) Bks Demand.

Burch, George E. & DePasquale, Nicholas. The History of Electrocardiography. (Illus.). 309p. 1990. reprint ed. 125.00 (*0-930405-21-8*) Norman SF.

Burch, Gladys. Famous Violinists for Young People. LC 75-38316. (Biography Index Reprint Ser.). (YA). (gr. 7 up). 1977. reprint ed. 21.95 (*0-8369-8118-9*) Ayer.

Burch, Glen. Notes on Titus. 36p. (Orig.). 1995. pap. 3.00 (*1-880573-25-3*) Bible Search Pubns.

— Tithing: And Other Gifts. 20p. (Orig.). 1994. pap. 2.00 (*1-880573-13-X*) Bible Search Pubns.

Burch, Helaine. Asleep in Christ. 144p. 1999. pap. 15.00 (*1-880573-53-9*) Bible Search Pubns.

***Burch, Hobart & Burch, Jan.** Bubba Justice in Key West: Pooping on the Public in Paradise. Dageforde, Linda J., ed. LC 99-27501. (Illus.). 160p. 1999. pap. 12.95 (*1-886225-42-7*, 1500) Dageforde Pub.

Burch, Hobart A. Social Welfare Policy Analysis & Choices. LC 98-8165. 394p. 1998. 49.95 (*0-7890-0602-2*); pap. 24.95 (*0-7890-0603-0*) Haworth Pr.

Burch, Hobbart A. The Why's of Social Policy: Perspective on Policy Preferences. LC 91-10856. 256p. 1991. 59.95 (*0-275-94006-3*, C4006, Praeger Pubs) Greenwood.

Burch, Hobbart A., ed. Basic Social Policy & Planning: Strategies & Practice Methods. LC 95-43400. (Illus.). 341p. (C). 1996. 49.95 (*0-7890-6026-4*) Haworth Pr.

— Basic Social Policy & Planning: Strategies & Practice Methods. LC 95-43400. 341p. (C). 1997. pap. 19.95 (*0-7890-0218-3*) Haworth Pr.

Burch, Holly, ed. The Massachusetts Political Almanac: The Legislature, 1998 Edition, Vol. 1. rev. ed. 359p. 1998. pap. 45.00 (*0-926766-21-X*) Ctr Leader Stu.

Burch, Holly & Barnes, Carolyn, eds. The Massachusetts Political Almanac, 1998, 2 vols., Set. rev. ed. 1998. pap. 75.00 (*0-926766-23-6*) Ctr Leader Stu.

***Burch, J. L., ed.** The Image Mission. LC 99-56951. 506p. 1999. write for info. (*0-7923-6111-3*) Kluwer Academic.

Burch, J. M., jt. auth. see Gerrard, A.

Burch, J. M., jt. auth. see Gerrard, Anthony.

Burch, James L. & Waite, J. H., Jr., eds. Solar System Plasma in Space & Time. LC 94-25481. (Geophysical Monographs: Vol. 84). 295p. 1994. 57.00 (*0-87590-041-0*) Am Geophysical.

Burch, Jan, jt. auth. see Burch, Hobart.

Burch, Jennings M. They Cage the Animals at Night. 292p. 1985. mass mkt. 5.99 (*0-451-15941-1*, Sig) NAL.

— They Cage the Animals at Night. 1984. 10.09 (*0-606-00777-6*, Pub. by Turtleback) Demco.

Burch, Joann J. Chico Mendes: Defender of the Rain Forest. LC 93-1198. (Gateway Greens Ser.). (Illus.). 48p. (J). (gr. 2-4). 1994. lib. bdg. 20.90 (*1-56294-413-4*) Millbrook Pr.

— A Fairy-Tale Life: A Story about Hans Christian Andersen. (Creative Minds Ser.). (Illus.). 64p. (J). (gr. 3-6). 1994. pap. 5.95 (*0-87614-642-6*, First Ave Edns); lib. bdg. 19.93 (*0-87614-829-1*, Carolrhoda) Lerner Pub.

— Fine Print: A Story about Johann Gutenberg. (Creative Minds Biographies Ser.). (Illus.). 64p. (J). (gr. 3-6). 1991. lib. bdg. 19.93 (*0-87614-682-5*, Carolrhoda) Lerner Pub.

— Fine Print: A Story about Johann Gutenberg. (Illus.). 56p. (J). (gr. 3-6). 1992. pap. 5.95 (*0-87614-565-9*, First Ave Edns) Lerner Pub.

— Jefferson Davis: President of the Confederacy. LC 97-18046. (Historical American Biographies Ser.). (Illus.). 128p. (YA). (gr. 6 up). 1998. lib. bdg. 20.95 (*0-7660-1064-3*) Enslow Pubs.

— Kenya: Africa's Tamed Wilderness. 2nd rev. ed. LC 96-18445. (Discovering Our Heritage Ser.). (Illus.). 128p. (J). (gr. 4 up). 1996. lib. bdg. 14.95 (*0-382-39539-5*, Dillon Silver Burdett) Silver Burdett Pr.

— Marian Wright Edelman, Children's Champion. LC 94-2260. (Gateway Biographies Ser.). (Illus.). 48p. (J). (gr. 2-4). 1994. pap. 6.95 (*1-56294-742-7*); lib. bdg. 20.90 (*1-56294-457-6*) Millbrook Pr.

Burch, John B. Mollusks of Michigan. (Illus.). (C). text. write for info. (*0-472-09650-8*); pap. text. write for info. (*0-472-06650-1*) U of Mich Pr.

Burch, John G. & Sardinas, Joseph L. Computer Control & Audit: A Total Systems Approach. LC 78-9093. (Illus.). 508p. reprint ed. pap. 157.50 (*0-608-17412-2*, 205644200067) Bks Demand.

***Burch, Julie A.** Traveling Simplified: A Step-by-Step Guide Perfect for Anyone. (Illus.). 96p. 2000. pap. 9.95 (*0-9672276-0-7*) Samson FL.

Burch, Kathleen. Indicia... A Romance: Book & Game. (Illus.). 1990. boxed set 38.00 (*0-936050-07-1*) Burning Bks.

Burch, Kurt. "Property" & the Making of the International System. LC 97-21297. (Critical Perspectives Ser.). 195p. 1998. 49.95 (*1-55587-622-6*) L Rienner.

Burch, Kurt & Denemark, Robert A. Constituting International Political Economy. LC 97-13955. (International Political Economy Yearbook Ser.). 1997. 52.00 (*1-55587-660-9*) L Rienner.

Burch, Laurel. Fantastic Felines. LC 96-45230. 1997. 29.95 (*0-8118-1644-3*) Chronicle Bks.

Burch, M. Refinishing Pine Furniture. 1983. pap. 2.95 (*0-88266-205-8*, Storey Pub) Storey Bks.

Burch, M., jt. auth. see Archer, N.

Burch, Margaret. Bountiful Blooms: Preserving Flowers with Colour. (Illus.). 106p. 1994. 19.95 (*1-86351-101-6*, Pub. by Sally Milner) Sterling.

Burch, Marilyn. Phonics Seatwork. (J). (gr. 1-3). 1985. pap. 8.99 (*0-8224-5543-9*) Fearon Teacher Aids.

— Shape-a-Sound. (J). (gr. 1-3). 1986. pap. 6.99 (*0-8224-6394-6*) Fearon Teacher Aids.

***Burch, Marilyn.** Word Family Stationary: 40 Adorable, Reproducible Sheets with Word Banks & Companion Activities. (Illus.). 48p. 2000. pap. 9.95 (*0-439-12973-7*) Scholastic Inc.

Burch, Mark. Simplicity Study Circles: A Step-by-Step Guide. 72p. 1998. pap. text 10.00 (*0-86571-368-5*) New Soc Pubs.

Burch, Mark A. Simplicity: Notes, Stories & Exercises for Developing Unimaginable Wealth. 144p. 1995. pap. 12.95 (*0-86571-323-5*) New Soc Pubs.

***Burch, Mark A.** Stepping Lightly: Simplicity for People & the Planet. 224p. 2000. pap. 15.95 (*0-86571-423-1*, Pub. by New Soc Pubs) Consort Bk Sales.

Burch, Martin & Holliday, Ian. The British Cabinet System. LC 95-4954. 272p. (C). 1995. pap. text 28.00 (*0-13-206194-5*) P-H.

Burch, Mary R. The Border Collie: An Owner's Guide to a Happy, Healthy Pet. 1996. 12.95 (*0-87605-492-0*) Howell Bks.

Burch, Maxie B. The Evangelical Historians: The Historiography of George Marsden, Nathan Hatch, & Mark Noll. LC 95-43830. 136p. 1996. lib. bdg. 29.50 (*0-7618-0179-0*) U Pr of Amer.

Burch, Monte. Building Small Barns, Sheds & Shelters. Stetson, Fred, ed. LC 82-15439. (Illus.). 248p. 1982. pap. 14.95 (*0-88266-245-7*, Garden Way Pub) Storey Bks.

— Complete Guide to Building Log Homes. LC 90-39505. (Illus.). 416p. (Orig.). 1990. pap. 19.95 (*0-8069-7486-9*) Sterling.

— How to Build Fifty Classic Furniture Reproductions. LC 92-41776. (Illus.). 320p. 1993. pap. 19.95 (*0-8069-0302-3*) Sterling.

— How to Build Small Barns & Outbuildings. Watson, Ben, ed. LC 91-57948. (Illus.). 288p. 1992. 29.95 (*0-88266-774-2*, Garden Way Pub); pap. 18.95 (*0-88266-773-4*, Garden Way Pub) Storey Bks.

— Monte Burch's Black Bass Basics: Techniques for Largemouth, Smallmouth, Kentuckies. LC 94-69861. (Illus.). 192p. 1994. pap. 12.95 (*1-879206-20-X*) Outdoor World Pr.

— Monte Burch's Pole Building Projects: Over 25 Low-Cost Plans. LC 92-56148. (Illus.). 208p. 1993. 27.95 (*0-88266-860-9*, Garden Way Pub); pap. 18.95 (*0-88266-859-5*, Garden Way Pub) Storey Bks.

— North American Hunting Adventures. Miller, Bill, ed. LC 87-613212. (Hunter's Information Ser.). (Illus.). 208p. 1988. write for info. (*0-914697-09-9*) N Amer Outdoor Grp.

— Sixty-Four Yard & Garden Projects You Can Build Yourself. Matthews, John & Balmuth, Deborah, eds. LC 94-13330. (Illus.). 192p. 1994. 28.95 (*0-88266-834-X*, Storey Pub); pap. 17.95 (*0-88266-846-3*, Storey Pub) Storey Bks.

Burch, Monte, jt. auth. see Brauer, Denny.

Burch, Noel. Life to Those Shadows. Brewster, Ben, ed. & tr. by. LC 90-50406. (Illus.). 317p. 1991. 60.00 (*0-520-07143-3*, Pub. by U CA Pr); pap. 24.95 (*0-520-07144-1*, Pub. by U CA Pr) Cal Prin Full Svc.

— Theory of Film Practice. Lane, Helen R., tr. LC 80-8676. (Illus.). 188p. reprint ed. pap. 58.30 (*0-608-09115-4*, 206974700005) Bks Demand.

Burch, Noel, tr. see Hodeir, Andre.

Burch, Pamala F., jt. auth. see Ettinger, Alice G.

Burch, Philip H. Elites in American History: The Civil War to the New Deal, Vol. 2. LC 80-11287. 496p. 1981. 49.50 (*0-8419-0595-9*); pap. 29.50 (*0-8419-0705-6*) Holmes & Meier.

Burch, Philip H., Jr. Elites in American History Vol. 1: The Federalist Years to the Civil War. LC 80-11287. 355p. 1981. 49.50 (*0-8419-0594-0*) Holmes & Meier.

— Elites in American History Vol. 3: The New Deal to the Carter Administration. LC 80-11528. 534p. (C). 1980. 49.50 (*0-8419-0565-7*); pap. 29.50 (*0-8419-0566-5*) Holmes & Meier.

Burch, Philip H. Research in Political Economy Pt. A: The American Right Wing Takes Command: Key Executive Appointments. 442p. 78.50 (*0-7623-0377-8*) Jai Pr.

Burch, Preston M. & Bower, Alex. Training Thoroughbred Horses. LC 92-25146. 1992. 19.95 (*0-929346-19-X*) R Meerdink Co Ltd.

Burch, R. L., jt. auth. see Russell, W. M.

Burch, Regina A. Love Is All You Need. 242p. 1998. pap. 12.95 (*1-880849-10-0*) Chapel Hill NC.

Burch, Robert. Christmas with Ida Early. LC 85-5680. 158p. (J). (gr. 3-7). 1985. pap. 4.99 (*0-14-031971-9*, PuffinBks) Peng Put Young Read.

— Christmas with Ida Early. 1985. 10.09 (*0-606-00267-7*, Pub. by Turtleback) Demco.

— D. J.'s Worst Enemy: A Novel by Robert Burch. LC 92-44783. (Brown Thrasher Bks.). (Illus.). 144p. (J). (gr. 4-6). 1993. reprint ed. 19.95 (*0-8203-1554-0*) U of Ga Pr.

— Ida Early Comes over the Mountain. 152p. (J). (gr. 3-7). 1982. pap. 2.50 (*0-380-57091-2*, Avon Bks) Morrow Avon.

— Ida Early Comes over the Mountain. (J). (gr. 4 up). 1990. pap. 4.99 (*0-14-034534-5*, PuffinBks) Peng Put Young Read.

— Ida Early Comes over the Mountain. (J). 1990. 9.09 (*0-606-04701-8*, Pub. by Turtleback) Demco.

— Ida Early Gives Lessons. 1999. pap. write for info. (*0-670-81566-7*) Viking Penguin.

— A Peircean Reduction Thesis: The Foundations of Topological Logic. (Philosophical Inquiries Ser.: No. 1). 128p. 1991. 30.00 (*0-89672-247-3*) Tex Tech Univ Pr.

— Queenie Peavy. 160p. (J). (gr. 3-7). 1987. pap. 4.99 (*0-14-032305-8*, PuffinBks) Peng Put Young Read.

— Queenie Peavy. (J). 1966. 9.09 (*0-606-04394-2*, Pub. by Turtleback) Demco.

— Renfroe's Christmas: A Novel by Robert Burch. LC 92-44773. (Brown Thrasher Bks.). (Illus.). 56p. (J). (gr. 3-7). 1993. reprint ed. 19.95 (*0-8203-1553-2*) U of Ga Pr.

— Skinny. LC 89-28225. (Brown Thrasher Bks.). 128p. (J). (gr. 7 up). 1990. reprint ed. 19.95 (*0-8203-1223-1*) U of Ga Pr.

— Traveling Bird. (J). (gr. 1-4). 1959. 9.95 (*0-8392-3038-9*) Astor-Honor.

— Tyler, Wilkin & Skee. LC 89-28245. (Brown Thrasher Bks.). 160p. (J). (gr. 4-6). 1990. reprint ed. 19.95 (*0-8203-1194-4*) U of Ga Pr.

Burch, Robert E. Trial Handbook for Tennessee Lawyers. LC 79-83775. 450p. 1993. suppl. ed. 52.50 (*0-317-03164-3*) West Group.

— Trial Handbook for Tennessee Lawyers. 2nd ed. LC 95-76595. 450p. 125.00 (*0-317-00394-1*) West Group.

Burch, Ronnie, pseud. Power of Prayer. (Illus.). 115p. (C). 1989. student ed. write for info. (*0-318-66288-4*) B T Burch.

***Burch, T. Bice.** Ancient Tortures. 272p. 1999. pap. 17.95 (*1-58444-010-4*, Looking Glass Pr) DiscUs Bks.

Burch, Thomas K., ed. Demographic Behavior: Interdisciplinary Perspectives on Decision Making. (AAAS Selected Symposium Ser.: No. 45). 45p. 1980. text 54.50 (*0-89158-785-3*) Westview.

Burch, Vacher. Anthropology & the Apocalypse: An Interpretation of "The Book of Revelation" in Relation to the Archaeology, Folklore & Religious Literature & Ritual of the Near East. 1977. lib. bdg. 59.95 (*0-8490-1437-9*) Gordon Pr.

— The Orphic Mysteries in Syria & Early Christianity. 1990. pap. 4.95 (*1-55818-125-3*) Holmes Pub.

Burch, Virginia M. Salukis. (Illus.). 192p. 1990. 9.95 (*0-86622-771-7*, KW-189) TFH Pubns.

Burch, Warner M. Endocrinology. 3rd ed. (House Officer Ser.). (Illus.). 240p. 1994. 21.95 (*0-683-01131-6*) Lppncott W & W.

Burch, William R., et al, eds. Ecosystem Management: Adaptive Strategies for Natural Resource Organizations in the Twenty-First Century. LC 98-30049. 200p. 1998. 65.00 (*1-56032-606-9*); pap. 25.95 (*1-56032-607-7*) Hemisp Pub.

Burch, William R. & DeLucca, Donald R. Measuring the Social Impact of Natural Resource Policies. LC 83-12378. 232p. reprint ed. pap. 72.00 (*0-7837-5858-8*, 204557700006) Bks Demand.

Burch, William R., jt. auth. see Field, Donald R., Jr.

Burch, William R., Jr., jt. auth. see Field, Donald R.

Burchall, Larry. The Other Side. 120p. 1991. per. write for info. (*0-8187-0149-8*) Harlo Press.

Burcham, Carl. White Dolphin Blues. LC 98-88646. 1999. 24.50 (*0-88739-213-X*); pap. 13.95 (*0-88739-212-1*) Creat Arts Bk.

Burcham, Nancy A. Combating Sexual Harassment in Schools. 87p. (YA). (gr. 7-12). 1995. pap. 6.95 (*1-57515-050-6*) PPI Pubng.

— Survival Source: When Parents Divorce. 73p. (YA). (gr. 7-12). 1993. pap. 6.95 (*1-57515-036-0*) PPI Pubng.

Burcham, W. E. Nuclear Physics: An Introduction. 2nd ed. LC 73-164480. (Longman Text Ser.). 706p. reprint ed. pap. 200.00 (*0-608-10172-9*, 201190400080) Bks Demand.

Burcham, W. E. & Jobes, M. Nuclear & Partcl Physics. LC 94-13700. (C). 1995. pap. text 61.95 (*0-582-45088-8*, Pub. by Addison-Wesley) Longman.

Burchard, jt. auth. see Hennefeld.

Burchard, Arliss. No Fail Art Projects: Ninety-Nine Successful Lessons for the Primary Grades. 230p. 1990. pap. 24.95 (*0-13-622481-4*) P-H.

***Burchard, Bill.** Inside AutoCAD 2000. LC 99-63018. (Illus.). 1999. pap. 49.99 (*0-7357-0851-7*) New Riders Pub.

— Inside AutoCAD 2000. (Illus.). 1500p. 2000. 55.00 (*0-7357-0947-5*) New Riders Pub.

Burchard, Christoph. Gesammelte Studien Zu Joseph Und Aseneth: Berichtigt Und Erganzt Herausgegeben Mit Unterstutzung Von Carsten Burfeind. (ENG, FRE & GER.). 520p. 1996. 168.00 (*90-04-10628-6*) Brill Academic Pubs.

***Burchard, Elizabeth & Carlone, Judith.** 19 Years in a New Age Cult &Torn from the Arms of Satan. (Illus.). 330p. (C). 1999. pap. 14.95 (*1-881374-05-X*, Pub. by Ace Acad) Amazon Com.

Burchard, Elizabeth, ed. & photos by see Mangano, Christina.

Burchard, Elizabeth R. Ace's Exambusters Biology Study. 2nd ed. (Exambusters Ser.). 384p. (YA). (gr. 7 up). 2000. reprint ed. pap. 10.95 (*1-881374-94-7*, Exambusters) Ace Acad.

— Ace's Exambusters Chemistry Study. 2nd ed. (Exambusters Ser.). 384p. (YA). (gr. 7 up). 2000. reprint ed. pap. 10.95 (*1-881374-93-9*, Exambusters) Ace Acad.

— Ace's Exambusters English Vocabulary Study. (Exambusters Ser.). (YA). (gr. 7 up). 2000. reprint ed. pap. 10.95 (*1-881374-85-8*, Exambusters) Ace Acad.

— French in a Flash. 180p. 1999. 8.95 (*1-928804-01-2*) Avocado Pr.

Burchard, Elizabeth R., ed. Ace's Exambusters Algebra II-Trigonometry Study. 2nd ed. (Exambusters Ser.). 384p. 2000. reprint ed. pap. 10.95 (*1-881374-89-0*) Ace Acad.

— Ace's Exambusters American History Study. 2nd ed. (Exambusters Ser.). 384p. 2000. reprint ed. pap. 10.95 (*1-881374-83-1*) Ace Acad.

— Ace's Exambusters Arithmetic Study. 2nd ed. (Exambusters Ser.). 384p. 2000. reprint ed. pap. 10.95 (*1-881374-91-2*) Ace Acad.

— Ace's Exambusters Earth Science--Geology Study. 2nd ed. (Exambusters Ser.). 384p. 2000. reprint ed. pap. 10.95 (*1-881374-88-2*) Ace Acad.

— Ace's Exambusters French Study. 2nd ed. (Exambusters Ser.). 384p. (YA). (gr. 7 up). 2000. reprint ed. pap. 10.95 (*1-881374-86-6*) Ace Acad.

— Ace's Exambusters Geometry Study. 2nd ed. (Exambusters Ser.). 384p. (YA). (gr. 7 up). 2000. reprint ed. pap. 10.95 (*1-881374-90-4*) Ace Acad.

***Burchard, Elizabeth R., ed.** Ace's Exambusters German Study. (Exambusters Ser.). 384p. (C). 2000. pap. 10.95 (*1-881374-98-X*) Ace Acad.

Burchard, Elizabeth R., ed. Ace's Exambusters GMAT Study. (Exambusters Ser.). 384p. (Orig.). (C). 2000. reprint ed. pap. 10.95 (*1-881374-79-3*) Ace Acad.

— Ace's Exambusters GRE Study. (Exambusters Ser.). 384p. (Orig.). (C). 2000. reprint ed. pap. 10.95 (*1-881374-80-7*) Ace Acad.

***Burchard, Elizabeth R., ed.** Ace's Exambusters Italian Study. (Exambusters Ser.). 384p. (C). 2000. pap. 10.95 (*1-881374-99-8*) Ace Acad.

Burchard, Elizabeth R., ed. Ace's Exambusters MCAT Study. (Exambusters Ser.). 384p. (C). 2000. reprint ed. pap. 10.95 (*1-881374-81-5*) Ace Acad.

— Ace's Exambusters More Sign Language Study, 3 parts, Part 2. Mangano, Christina, tr. (Exambusters Ser.). (Illus.). 250p. (Orig.). 2000. reprint ed. pap. 10.95 (*1-881374-78-5*) Ace Acad.

— Ace's Exambusters New SAT Study. 2nd ed. (Exambusters Ser.). 384p. (YA). (gr. 7 up). 2000. reprint ed. pap. 10.95 (*1-881374-84-X*) Ace Acad.

— Ace's Exambusters Physics Study. 2nd ed. (Exambusters Ser.). 384p. (YA). (gr. 7 up). 2000. reprint ed. pap. 10.95 (*1-881374-87-4*) Ace Acad.

— Ace's Exambusters World History Study. 2nd ed. (Exambusters Ser.). 384p. (YA). (gr. 7 up). 2000. reprint ed. pap. 10.95 (*1-881374-82-3*) Ace Acad.

Burchard, Elizabeth R., ed. see Bernstock, Peter.

Burchard, Elizabeth R., ed. see Brick, Gary.

Burchard, Elizabeth R., ed. see Lopez-Solar, Joyce.

Burchard, Irene H., jt. auth. see Wagner, Muriel G.

Burchard, John D. & Burchard, Sara N., eds. Prevention of Delinquent Behavior. LC 86-26095. (Primary Prevention of Psychopathology Ser.: No. 10). 376p. 1987. reprint ed. pap. 116.60 (*0-608-01457-5*, 205950100001) Bks Demand.

***Burchard, K. W. & Gann, D. S.** The Clinical Handbook of Surgical Critical Care. LC 98-22291. (Clinical Handbook Ser.). (Illus.). 360p. 2000. pap. 29.50 (*1-85070-633-6*) Prthnon Pub.

Burchard, Marshall & Burchard, S. H. Sports Hero, Billie Jean King LC 74-16623. (Sports Hero Biographies Ser.). 93p. (J). 1975. pap. write for info. (*0-399-20416-4*) Putnam Pub Group.

Burchard, Peter. Glory. 1989. pap. 9.95 (*0-312-04643-X*) St Martin.

— Lincoln & Slavery. LC 98-12464. (Illus.). 208p. (J). (gr. 7 up). 1999. 17.00 (*0-689-81570-0*) S&S Childrens.

— "We'll Stand by the Union" Robert Gould Shaw & the Black 54th Massachusetts Regiment. Scott, John A., ed. LC 92-37132. (Makers of America Ser.). (Illus.). 144p. (YA). (gr. 7-12). 1993. 19.95 (*0-8160-2609-2*) Facts on File.

Burchard, Peter D. Carver: A Great Soul. LC 97-91825. (Illus.). 88p. (Orig.). 1998. pap. 8.95 (*0-9658023-0-2*) Serpent Wise.

Burchard, Rachael C. Hallelujah Hopscotch - Musical. 55p. 1986. reprint ed. pap. 4.95 (*0-87129-014-6*, H56) Dramatic Pub.

— Troupers & Tramps: One Person Plays. Zapel, Arthur L., ed. LC 93-38914. 144p. (Orig.). 1994. pap. 10.95 (*1-56608-001-0*, B148) Meriwether Pub.

Burchard, S. H., jt. auth. see Burchard, Marshall.

Burchard, Sara N., jt. ed. see Burchard, John D.

Burchard, Therese J., ed. Let It Be: Advent & Christmas Meditations for Women. LC 98-18349. 112p. 1998. pap. 9.95 (*0-8245-1767-9*, Crsrd) Crossroad NY.

Burchardi. Current Topics in Intensive Care. 4th ed. 1997. pap. text 75.00 (*0-7020-2161-X*) Bailliere Tindall.

Burchardt, F. A., ed. The Economics of Full Employment: Six Studies in Applied Economics. LC 67-16340. (Reprints of Economic Classics Ser.). vii, 213p. 1967. reprint ed. lib. bdg. 35.00 (*0-678-00212-6*) Kelley.

Burchardt, J. L. Travels in Nubia. 656p. 1990. 140.00 (*1-85077-172-3*, Pub. by Darf Pubs Ltd) St Mut.

Burche, Jay. How to Create a Tax Shelter for a Travel Agency. 84p. 1979. 50.00 (*0-933796-00-5*) Newport Bch Rent.

***Burchell.** Carbon Materials for Advanced Technologies. 558p. 1999. 172.50 (*0-08-042683-2*) Elsevier.

***Burchell, David.** A Life Downunder. large type ed. 416p. 1999. 31.99 (*0-7089-9120-3*) Ulverscroft.

Burchell, E. M., et al. South African Criminal Law & Procedure: General Principles of Criminal Law, Vol. I. 2nd ed. 576p. 1982. write for info. (*0-7021-1345-X*, Pub. by Juta & Co); pap. write for info. (*0-7021-1346-8*, Pub. by Juta & Co) Gaunt.

Burchell, Graham, et al, eds. The Foucault Effect: Studies in Governmental Rationality. LC 91-10456. 320p. 1991. pap. 22.50 (*0-226-08045-5*) U Ch Pr.

— The Foucault Effect: Studies in Governmental Rationality. LC 91-10456. 318p. 1999. lib. bdg. 67.00 (*0-226-08044-7*) U Ch Pr.

Burchell, H. B., jt. ed. see Meijler, F. L.

***Burchell, J.** Personality Rights & Freedom of Expression: The Modern Actio Injuriarum. LC 99-223774. 448p. 1999. pap. 74.50 (*0-7021-4810-5*, Pub. by Juta & Co) Gaunt.

Burchell, J. M. The Law of Defamation in South Africa. 392p. 1985. 53.00 (*0-7021-1567-3*, Pub. by Juta & Co); pap. 49.00 (*0-7021-4040-6*, Pub. by Juta & Co) Gaunt.

— Principles of Delict. 292p. 1993. pap. 29.50 (*0-7021-2941-0*, Pub. by Juta & Co) Gaunt.

Burchell, J. M. & Milton, J. R. Principles of Criminal Law. 1991. pap. 45.00 (*0-7021-2639-X*, Pub. by Juta & Co) Gaunt.

Burchell, J. M., jt. auth. see Milton, J. R.

Burchell, Jenny. Polite or Commercial Concerts? Concert Management & Orchestral Repertoire in Edinburgh, Bath, Oxford, Manchester & Newcastle, 1730-1799. LC 96-1839. (Outstanding Dissertations in Music from British Universities Ser.). (Illus.). 432p. 1996. text 105.00 (*0-8153-2462-6*) Garland.

Burchell, Jim & Sunter, F. W. Design & Build in Timber Frame. LC 86-16481. 86p. 1987. reprint ed. pap. 30.00 (*0-608-03593-9*, 206441600009) Bks Demand.

Burchell, Jonathan & Milton, John. Cases & Materials on Criminal Law. 2nd ed. LC 98-110116. 734p. 1997. pap. 61.00 (*0-7021-3854-1*, Pub. by Juta & Co) Gaunt.

Burchell, Jonathan M. South African Criminal Law & Procedure: General Principles of Criminal Law. 3rd ed. LC 98-110447. 430p. 1997. 129.00 (*0-7021-3855-X*, Pub. by Juta & Co) Gaunt.

Burchell, Louise & Lalonde, Catherine. Eliza's Best Wednesday. (Illus.). 64p. (J). 1990. 12.95 (*1-55074-006-7*) Kids Can Pr.

Burchell, Mary. It's Rumoured in the Village. (Harlequin Romance Ser.: 3 Vols. in 1). 192p. 1983. pap. 3.95 (*0-373-20077-3*) Harlequin Bks.

***Burchell, Robert W., et al.** The Costs of Sprawl--Revisited. LC 98-61200. (Report/Transit Cooperative Research Program Ser.). 1998. 62.00 (*0-309-06306-X*) Natl Acad Pr.

Burchell, Robert W., et al. Development Impact Assessment Handbook. LC 93-61040. 326p. 1994. pap. text 89.95 (*0-87420-743-6*, D86) Urban Land.

— Regional Housing Opportunities for Lower Income Households: A Resource Guide to Affordable Housing & Regional Mobility Strategies. 236p. (Orig.). (C). 1995. pap. text 45.00 (*0-7881-2134-0*) DIANE Pub.

Burcher, Honour C. Pioneers & Their Better Halves. 240p. (C). 1990. 50.00 (*0-9589309-0-2*, Pub. by Boolarong Pubns) St Mut.

Burchers, Bryan, et al. Vocabulary Cartoons: SAT Word Power. 2nd rev. ed. (Illus.). 344p. (YA). (gr. 7-12). 1997. pap. 12.95 (*0-9652422-8-5*) New Monic Bks.

Burchers, Sam, III, et al. Vocabulary Cartoons: Elementary Edition. (Illus.). 250p. (J). (gr. 1-4). 1998. pap. 12.95 (*0-9652422-7-7*) New Monic Bks.

***Burchers, Sam, Jr., et al.** Vocabulary Cartoons II: SAT Word Power. (Illus.). 344p. (YA). (gr. 7-12). 2000. pap. 12.95 (*0-9652422-6-9*) New Monic Bks.

Burchert, Frank. De-Konstruktionen Als Funktionale Projektionen. (Europaische Hochschulschriften Ser.: Reihe 21, Bd. 176). (GER., Illus.). 161p. 1996. 35.95 (*3-631-30796-9*) P Lang Pubng.

Burchert, Hans-Jurgen, jt. ed. see Blasius, Karl H.

Burchett, Jay. Lob to Win: When to Lob. 2nd ed. (Illus.). 57p. (Orig.). (C). 1991. pap. 7.95 (*1-882013-02-6*) Newport Pub Hse.

— Smoke Away: Quit Smoking Now. 31p. (Orig.). 1989. pap. 4.95 (*0-929013-04-2*) Newport Pub Hse.

Burchett, Josiah. A Complete History of the Most Remarkable Transactions at Sea. Hattendorf, John B., ed. LC 95-2179. 944p. 1995. 150.00 (*0-8201-1489-8*) Schol Facsimiles.

Burchett, Margaret & Johnson, Krystyna. Native Australian Plants: Horticulture & Uses. 424p. 1996. 59.95 (*0-614-25732-8*, Pub. by New South Wales Univ Pr) Intl Spec Bk.

***Burchett, Marjorie F., et al.** California Title Insurance Practice - 12/99 Update. 2nd ed. Briggs, Donald R., ed. LC 97-65421. 352p. 1999. ring bd. 77.00 (*0-7626-0374-7*, RE-32622) Cont Ed Bar-CA.

Burchett, Michael, jt. auth. see Dando, Marc.

Burchett, P. Jay & Evans, M. Ann. Border to Terrorism. 295p. (Orig.). 1988. pap. 4.95 (*0-929013-03-4*) Newport Pub Hse.

Burchett, Wilfred G. Vietnam: Inside Story of the Guerrilla War. 2nd ed. LC 65-18719. (Illus.). 264p. reprint ed. pap. 81.90 (*0-8357-3584-2*, 203424900089) Bks Demand.

— Vietnam North. LC 66-28970. 207p. reprint ed. pap. 64.20 (*0-8357-3585-0*, 203425000089) Bks Demand.

Burchette, T., jt. ed. see Wright, V. P.

Burchfiel, B. C. Geology of Romania. LC 75-32832. (Geological Society of America, Special Paper: No. 158). 112p. reprint ed. pap. 34.80 (*0-608-13543-7*, 202546900044) Bks Demand.

Burchfiel, B. C., et al, eds. The South Tibetan Detachment System, Himalayan Orogen: Extension Contemporaneous with & Parallel to Shortening in a Collisional Mountain Belt. (Special Papers: No. 269). (Illus.). 1992. pap. 9.38 (*0-8137-2269-1*) Geol Soc.

Burchfiel, Kenneth J. Biotechnology & the Federal Circuit: 1997 Supplement. (Orig.). 1997. pap. 65.00 (*1-57018-062-8*, 1062) BNA Books.

Burchfield, Charles. Charles Burchfield's Journals: The Poetry of Place. Townsend, J. Benjamin, ed. LC 91-17389. (Illus.). 768p. (C). 1992. text 74.50 (*0-7914-0991-0*) State U NY Pr.

Burchfield, Ellen, jt. auth. see Hall, Betty L.

Burchfield, Faye B. Taking Back the Dream LC 97-75553. 137 p. 1997. write for info. (*0-9639878-6-0*) Parnassus Pubng.

Burchfield, Jerry, et al. Photography in Focus. 5th ed. (Illus.). 448p. 1996. pap. 30.95 (*0-8442-5782-6*, 57826) NTC Contemp Pub Co.

— Photography in Focus. 5th rev. ed. LC 94-68802. (Illus.). 448p. (C). 1996. text 27.95 (*0-8442-5781-8*, 57818) NTC Contemp Pub Co.

Burchfield, Joe D. Lord Kelvin & the Age of the Earth. (Illus.). xx, 280p. 1990. pap. text 27.00 (*0-226-08043-9*) U Ch Pr.

Burchfield, Kenneth. Biotechnology & the Federal Circuit with 1997 Supplement. 500p. 1995. pap. 165.00 (*0-87179-860-3*) BNA Books.

Burchfield, Robert W., ed. The Cambridge History of the English Language Vol. 5: English in Britain & Overseas: Origins & Development, Vol. 5. (Illus.). 685p. (C). 1995. text 120.00 (*0-521-26478-2*) Cambridge U Pr.

— Studies in Lexicography. (Illus.). 240p. 1987. 65.00 (*0-19-811945-3*) OUP.

Burchfield, Robert W. & Aarsleff, Hans. The Oxford English Dictionary & the State of the Language. LC 88-600085. 56p. 1988. 3.95 (*0-8444-0602-3*) Lib Congress.

Burchhardt, Jacob, et al. Weltgeschichtliche Betrachtungen. Mayer, J. P., ed. LC 78-67340. (European Political Thought Ser.). (GER.). 1979. reprint ed. lib. bdg. 37.95 (*0-405-11683-7*) Ayer.

***Burchiel, Kim J.** Pain Surgery, 2 vols., Set. (Illus.). 864p. 2000. 179.00 (*0-86577-912-0*) Thieme Med Pubs.

Burchill & Linklater, Scott. Theories of International Relations. 280p. 1996. text 59.95 (*0-312-16244-8*) St Martin.

Burchill, James V., et al. The Cold, Cold Hand: More Stories of Ghosts & Haunts from the Appalachian Foothills. LC 97-25332. (Ghosts & Haunts from the Appalachian Foothills Ser.: Vol. 2). 192p. 1997. pap. 9.95 (*1-55853-543-8*) Rutledge Hill Pr.

— Ghosts & Haunts from the Appalachian Foothills. LC 93-30419. 192p. (Orig.). (J). 1993. pap. 9.95 (*1-55853-253-6*) Rutledge Hill Pr.

Burchill, John, jt. auth. see Metz, Barbara.

Burchill, Julie. Diana. (Illus.). 240p. 1998. 29.95 (*0-297-82418-X*, Pub. by Weidenfeld & Nicolson) Trafalgar.

— From School to University. 1982. pap. text 6.50 (*0-08-028472-8*, Pergamon Pr) Elsevier.

***Burchill, Richard, et al, eds.** Economic, Social & Cultural Rights: Their Implementation in United Kingdom Law. lvii, 174p. 1999. pap. 18.50 (*0-9535234-0-3*, Pub. by U of Nottngham) Gaunt.

Burchill, Scott. Theories of International Relationship. 288p. 1996. pap. 21.95 (*0-312-16245-6*) St Martin.

***Burchinal, Lee & Lukas, Dale.** The Lithuanian Publishers Directory. LC 99-13922. 207p. 1999. pap. 49.50 (*1-57387-076-5*) Info Today Inc.

***Burchsted, Albert.** Laboratory Manual for General Biology I. 320p. (C). 1999. pap. text 36.95 (*0-7872-6095-7*, 41609601) Kendall-Hunt.

Burci, Stefano. Preparing National Regulations for Water Resources Mgnt: Principles & Practice. (Legislative Studies: 52). 400p. 1994. 43.00 (*92-5-103462-1*, F34621, Pub. by FAO) Bernan Associates.

Burciaga, Jose A. Spilling the Beans: Loteria Chicana. LC 95-68912. 142p. 1994. pap. 12.95 (*1-877741-11-6*) J Odell Editions.

— Undocumented Love: Amor Indocumentado. (Illus.). 173p. 1992. pap. 12.00 (*0-9624536-3-3*) Chusma Hse

— Weedee Peepo: A Collection of Essays - Una Coleccion de ensayos. 2nd ed. De La Fuente, Patricia, ed. (Illus.). 207p. (Orig.). 1992. reprint ed. pap. text 10.95 (*0-938738-06-2*) U TX Pan Am Pr.

Burciaga, Jose A., tr. from SPA. In Few Words/En Pocas Palabras: A Compendium of Latino Folk Wit & Wisdom. 288p. (Orig.). 1996. pap. 14.95 (*1-56279-093-5*) Mercury Hse Inc.

Burck, Charlotte & Daniel, Gwyn. Gender & Family Therapy. 176p. 1995. pap. text 27.00 (*1-85575-072-4*, Pub. by H Karnac Bks Ltd) Other Pr LLC.

Burck, Charlotte & Speed, Bebe, eds. Gender, Power & Relationships. LC 94-13591. 225p. (C). 1994. pap. 25.99 (*0-415-10637-0*, B4169) Routledge.

Burck, Erich. Die Erzahlungskunst des T. Livius. (GER.). xxviii, 244p. 1964. 60.00 (*0-318-71082-X*) G Olms Pubs.

— Problemata, Forschungen Zur Klassischen Philologie, Heft 11: Die Erzahlungskunst des T. Livius. xxviii, 244p. 1964. 55.00 (*3-296-10910-2*) G Olms Pubs.

Burck, Frances W. Babysense: A Practical & Supportive Guide to Baby Care. 2nd ed. 1991. pap. 17.95 (*0-312-05056-9*) St Martin.

Burck, Gordon M., jt. auth. see Flowerree, Charles C.

Burck, K. B., et al. Oncogenes: An Introduction to the Concept of Cancer Genes. xv, 300p. 1989. reprint ed. 75.00 (*0-387-96423-1*) Spr-Verlag.

Burck, K. B., jt. auth. see Larrick, J. W.

Burckardt. Greeks & Greek Civilization. 496p. 1999. pap. 16.95 (*0-312-24447-9*) St Martin.

Burckel, Robert B. Characterization of C(X) among Its Subalgebras. (Lecture Notes in Pure & Applied Mathematics Ser.: Vol. 6). (Illus.). 176p. 1972. pap. text 135.00 (*0-8247-6038-7*) Dekker.

Burckel, Robert B., tr. see Bauer, Heinz.

Burckel, Robert B., tr. see Remmert, Reinhold.

Burckert, H. J. A Resolution Principle for a Logic with Restricted Quantifiers. Siekmann, Joerg H., ed. (Lecture Notes in Artificial Intelligence Ser.: Vol. 568). x, 116p. 1991. 30.00 (*0-387-55034-8*) Spr-Verlag.

Burckhalter, David. Among Turtle Hunters & Basket Makers: Adventures with the Seri Indians. (Illus.). 160p. 1999. pap. 16.95 (*1-887896-13-9*, Rio Nuevo) Treas Chest Bks.

Burckhalter, David L., photos by. La Vida Nortena: Photographs of Sonora, Mexico. LC 97-31020. (Illus.). xviii, 105p. 1998. pap. 19.95 (*0-8263-1849-5*) U of NM Pr.

***Burckhardt, Ann.** Calabazas. LC 98-18383. (Primeros Lectores Ciencias: Alimentos Ser.). 1999. 14.00 (*1-56065-786-3*) Capstone Pr.

— Manzanas. LC 98-18749. (Primeros Lectores Ciencias: Alimentos Ser.). 1999. 14.00 (*1-56065-785-5*) Capstone Pr.

Burckhardt, Ann. Primeros Lectores Ciencias: Alimentos, 2 vols. 1999. pap. text 28.00 (*0-7368-0144-8*, Cpstone High Low) Capstone Pr.

— Writing about Food & Families, Fashion & Furnishings. LC 83-10843. 136p. 1984. reprint ed. pap. 42.20 (*0-608-06881-0*, 206708900009) Bks Demand.

Burckhardt, Ann L. Corn. (Early-Reader Science Foods Ser.). (Illus.). 24p. (J). (gr. k-3). 1996. 13.25 (*0-516-20277-4*) Childrens.

— Foods Series, 4 bks. Incl. Apples. LC 96-26564. 24p. (J). (gr. 1-2). 1996. lib. bdg. 13.75 (*1-56065-448-1*, Bridgestone Bks); Corn. LC 96-26570. 24p. (J). (gr. 1-2). 1996. lib. bdg. 13.75 (*1-56065-450-3*, Bridgestone Bks); Potatoes. LC 96-26569. 24p. (J). (gr. 1-2). 1996. lib. bdg. 13.75 (*1-56065-451-1*, Bridgestone Bks); Pumpkins. LC 96-26561. 24p. (J). (gr. 1-2). 1996. lib. bdg. 13.75 (*1-56065-449-X*, Bridgestone Bks); 55.00 (*1-56065-633-6*, Bridgestone Bks) Capstone Pr.

— Multicultural Cookbooks, 4 bks. Incl. People of Africa & Their Food. LC 96-25943. (Illus.). 48p. (J). (gr. 3-4). 1996. lib. bdg. 19.00 (*1-56065-434-1*, Cpstone High Low); People of China & Their Food. LC 96-24789. (Illus.). 48p. (J). (gr. 3-4). 1996. lib. bdg. 19.00 (*1-56065-433-3*, Cpstone High Low); People of Mexico & Their Food. LC 96-24787. (Illus.). 48p. (J). (gr. 3-4). 1996. lib. bdg. 19.00 (*1-56065-432-5*, Cpstone High Low); People of Russia & Their Food. (Illus.). 48p. (J). (gr. 3-4). 1996. lib. bdg. 19.00 (*1-56065-435-X*, Cpstone High Low); 76.00 (*1-56065-639-5*, Cpstone High Low) Capstone Pr.

— The People of Africa & Their Food. (Multicultural Cookbooks Ser.). (Illus.). 48p. (J). (gr. 3-7). 1996. 19.00 (*0-516-20261-8*) Childrens.

— The People of China & Their Food. (Multicultural Cookbooks Ser.). (Illus.). 48p. (J). (gr. 3-7). 1996. 19.00 (*0-516-20260-X*) Childrens.

— The People of Mexico & Their Food. (Multicultural Cookbooks Ser.). (Illus.). 48p. (J). (gr. 3-7). 1996. 19.00 (*0-516-20259-6*) Childrens.

— Potatoes. (Early-Reader Science Foods Ser.). (Illus.). 24p. (J). (gr. k-3). 1996. 13.25 (*0-516-20278-2*) Childrens.

— Pumpkins. (Early-Reader Science Foods Ser.). (Illus.). 24p. (J). (gr. k-3). 1996. 13.25 (*0-516-20276-6*) Childrens.

Burckhardt, Ann L., jt. auth. see Germaine, Elizabeth.

Burckhardt, C. H., et al. Das Gefieder des Huhnes: Abbild des Tieres und seiner Haltung. (Tierhaltung Ser.: No. 9). (GER., Illus.). 67p. 1980. 27.50 (*0-8176-1137-1*) Birkhauser.

Burckhardt, George E. Individuum und Allgemeinheit in Platos Politeia. (Abhandlungen Zur Philosophie und Ihrer Geschichte Ser.: No. 40). 66p. 1981. reprint ed. 20.00 (*3-487-06790-0*) G Olms Pubs.

Burckhardt, Jacob. The Age of Constantine the Great. Hadas, Moses, tr. 400p. 1983. pap. 17.95 (*0-520-04680-3*, Pub. by U CA Pr) Cal Prin Full Svc.

— The Architecture of the Italian Renaissance. Murray, Peter, ed. Palmes, James C., tr. LC 83-18113. (Illus.). 320p. 1985. 50.00 (*0-226-08047-1*) U Ch Pr.

— The Architecture of the Italian Renaissance. Murray, Peter, ed. Palmes, James C., tr. LC 83-18113. (Illus.). 320p. 1987. pap. 29.95 (*0-226-08049-8*) U Ch Pr.

— The Civilization of the Renaissance in Italy. 432p. 1995. 17.95 (*0-679-60169-4*) Modern Lib NY.

— The Civilization of the Renaissance in Italy. Middlemore, S. G., tr. 416p. 1990. pap. 14.95 (*0-14-044534-X*, Penguin Classics) Viking Penguin.

— The Civilization of the Renaissance in Italy. rev. ed. Middlemore, S. G., tr. LC 96-137969. (Arts & Letters Ser.). (Illus.). 424p. (C). 1995. pap. 14.95 (*0-7148-3363-0*, Pub. by Phaidon Press) Phaidon Pr.

— The Greeks & Greek Civilization. Stern, Sheila, tr. LC 98-30107. 448p. 1998. text 27.95 (*0-312-19276-2*) St Martin.

— Judgments on History & Historians. Zohn, Harry, tr. from ENG. LC 98-17504. 1999. 17.00 (*0-86597-206-0*); pap. 9.00 (*0-86597-207-9*) Liberty Fund.

— The Letters of Jacob Burckhardt. Dru, Alexander, tr. from GER. LC 75-8821. (Illus.). 242p. 1975. reprint ed. lib. bdg. 65.00 (*0-8371-8114-3*, BULE, Greenwood Pr) Greenwood.

— Reflections on History. LC 78-24385. Orig. Title: Force & Freedom. 1979. reprint ed. 15.00 (*0-913966-37-1*); reprint ed. pap. 7.00 (*0-913966-38-X*) Liberty Fund.

Burckhardt, Jacqueline & Curiger, Bice. Meret Oppenheim: Beyond the Teacup. LC 95-81295. (Illus.). 176p. 1997. pap. 29.95 (*0-916365-46-8*) Dist Art Pubs.

Burckhardt, Johann L. Bemerkungen Uber die Beduinen und Wahaby, Gesammelt Wehrend Seiner Reise Im Morgenlande. (Illus.). xii, 608p. reprint ed. write for info. (*0-318-71494-9*) G Olms Pubs.

— Reisen in Arabien. (Illus.). xiv, 706p. reprint ed. write for info. (*0-318-71495-7*) G Olms Pubs.

Burckhardt, John L. Arabic Proverbs. 296p. (C). 1988. 200.00 (*1-85077-183-9*, Pub. by Darf Pubs Ltd) St Mut.

— Arabic Proverbs: Manners & Customs of the Modern Egyptians. (ARA & ENG.). 1993. 18.00 (*0-86685-561-0*) Intl Bk Ctr.

— Arabic Proverbs: or The Manners & Customs of the Modern Egyptians, Illustrated from Their Proverbial Sayings Current at Cairo, Translated & Explained. 296p. (C). 1992. pap. 21.50 (*0-7007-0185-0*, Pub. by Curzon Pr Ltd) Paul & Co Pubs.

— Some Accounts of the Travels in Egypt & Nubia. 2nd ed. 1971. 59.00 (*0-403-03692-5*) Scholarly.

— Some Accounts of Travels in Egypt & Nubia. reprint ed. lib. bdg. 79.00 (*0-7812-0741-X*) Rprt Serv.

— Travels in Nubia. LC 74-15014. reprint ed. 71.50 (*0-404-12009-1*) AMS Pr.

— Travels in Syria & the Holy Land. 668p. (C). 1992. 140.00 (*1-85077-189-8*, Pub. by Darf Pubs Ltd) St Mut.

— Travels in Syria & the Holy Land. LC 77-87614. (Illus.). 720p. 1983. reprint ed. 76.50 (*0-404-16437-4*) AMS Pr.

Burckhardt, Lucius. The Werkbund. 118p. 1987. 120.00 (*0-85072-108-3*) St Mut.

B

An Asterisk (*) at the beginning of an entry indicates that the title is appearing for the first time.

Burckhardt, P., et al, eds. Nutritional Aspects of Osteoporosis. LC 98-13311. (Serono Symposia, U. S. A. Ser.). (Illus.). 296p. 1998. 135.00 (*0-387-98494-1*) Spr-Verlag.

Burckhardt, Rudy. Mobile Homes. Elmslie, Kenward, ed. LC 79-90670. (Illus.). 1980. 15.00 (*0-915990-18-0*); pap. 7.50 (*0-915990-19-9*) Z Pr.

***Burckhardt, Rudy.** Wayward Glimpses. (Illus.). 2000. 50.00 (*1-57687-070-7*, pwerHse Bks) pwerHse Cultrl.

Burckhardt, Rudy & Pettet, Simon. Conversations with Rudy Burckhardt about Everything. (Illus.). 72p. (Orig.). 1987. pap. 12.00 (*0-931428-20-3*) Vehicle Edns.

— Talking Pictures: The Photographs of Rudy Burckhardt, 1933-1988. LC 94-19134. (Illus.). 256p. (Orig.). 1994. pap. 26.95 (*0-944072-42-9*) Zoland Bks.

Burckhardt, Rudy, jt. auth. see Katz, Vincent.

Burckhardt, Sigurd. The Drama of Language: Essays on Goethe & Kleist. LC 77-97492. 187p. reprint ed. pap. 58.00 (*0-8357-6604-7*, 203524900094) Bks Demand.

Burckhardt-Stuker, Ruth. Versuche zur Experimentellen Alalgetika-Abhaengigkeit Bei der Ratte. (European University Studies: Ser. 6, Vol. 107). (GER.). 284p. 1983. 41.00 (*3-261-03277-4*) P Lang Pubng.

Burckhardt, Titus. Alchemy: Science of the Cosmos, Science of the Soul. rev. ed. Stoddart, William, tr. from GER. 206p. 1997. reprint ed. pap. 14.95 (*1-887752-11-0*) Fons Vitae.

— Art of Islam: Language & Meaning. 220p. 1996. 69.95 (*0-614-21569-2*, 1526); pap. 39.95 (*0-614-21568-4*, 1526) Kazi Pubns.

— Chartres: And the Birth of the Cathedral. Stoddart, William, tr. from GER. (Illus.). 135p. (Orig.). 1996. 47.50 (*0-941532-23-2*); pap. 37.50 (*0-941532-21-6*) Wrld Wisdom Bks.

— Fez: City of Islam. 176p. 1996. 39.95 (*0-614-21576-5*, 297) Kazi Pubns.

— Fez, City of Islam. Stoddart, William, tr. from GER. (Illus.). 136p. 1992. 34.95 (*0-946621-17-9*, Pub. by Islamic Texts) Intl Spec Bk.

— An Introduction to Sufi Doctrine. 156p. (C). 1988. pap. text 8.50 (*1-56744-217-X*) Kazi Pubns.

— An Introduction to Sufism: The Mystical Dimensions of Islam. 126p. 1990. pap. 11.00 (*1-85274-070-1*, Pub. by Aqrn Pr) Harper SF.

— Mirror of the Intellect: Essays on Traditional Science & Sacred Art. Stoddart, William, ed. & tr. by. from GER. 269p. 1987. 26.95 (*0-946621-08-X*, Pub. by Islamic Texts) Intl Spec Bk.

— Mystical Astrology According to Ibn Arabi. 2nd ed. Rauf, Bulent, tr. from FRE. (Illus.). 52p. (Orig.). 1977. reprint ed. pap. 8.00 (*0-904975-09-6*, Pub. by Beshara) New Leaf Dist.

— Sacred Art in East & West: Its Principles & Methods. 160p. 1996. pap. 19.95 (*0-614-21587-0*, 1095) Kazi Pubns.

— Sacred Art in East & West: Its Principles & Methods. 2nd ed. Northbourne, Lord, tr. from FRE. (Illus.). 160p. 1986. pap. 15.95 (*0-900588-11-X*) S Perennis.

Burckhardt, Titus, ed. Mirror of the Intellect: Essays on Traditional Science & Sacred Art. Stoddart, William, tr. LC 87-10103. (SUNY Series in Islam). 269p. 1987. text 21.50 (*0-88706-683-6*) State U NY Pr.

Burckhardt, Titus, tr. see Ad-Darqawi, Shaikh A.

Burckhardt, Titus, tr. see Al-Jili, Abd A.

Burckhardt, Titus, tr. see Ibn al-Arabi.

Burckle, L. H., jt. ed. see Saito, T.

***Burckle Publishing Staff.** Greater Cincinnati Close Up. 2nd rev. ed. Orig. Title: Cincinnati Without Fears or Tears. (Illus.). 1998. pap. 13.50 (*1-889072-01-X*) Burckle Pubng.

Burckmyer, Becky. Why Does My Boss Hate My Writing? Twenty Questions Smart Business Writers Ask Before They Print. LC 98-26691. 224p. 1999. pap. 8.95 (*1-58062-057-4*) Adams Media.

Burd, Barry A. Computer Science: The Beginning. (Illus.). 500p. (C). 1995. pap. text. write for info. (*0-201-60263-6*) Addison-Wesley.

— Laboratory Manual for Pascal by Example: From Practice to Principle in Computer Science. (Illus.). (C). 1995. pap. text, lab manual ed. 16.95 (*0-15-568164-8*) OUP.

— Pascal by Example: From Practice to Principle in Computer Science. (Illus.). 1008p. (C). 1995. pap. text 65.00 (*0-15-568162-1*) OUP.

Burd, D., jt. ed. see Beltz, Barbara.

Burd, Frank. Civil War Battlefield Parks. (Illus.). 32p. 1997. pap. 4.00 (*1-890541-07-9*) Americana Souvenirs & Gifts.

— Civil War Book of Facts. (Illus.). 32p. 1997. pap. 4.00 (*1-890541-08-7*) Americana Souvenirs & Gifts.

— Philadelphia. (Illus.). 64p. (Orig.). 1989. write for info. (*0-318-64677-3*) Phil Post Card.

Burd, Jack. Jack Burd's Civil War Sourcebook, 1999-2000. 4th rev. ed. 268p. 1998. pap. 14.95 (*1-57427-087-7*, Rockbridge) Howell Pr VA.

***Burd, Stephen D.** Systems Architecture: Hardware & Software in Information Systems. 2nd ed. (Miscellaneous/Catalogs Ser.). (C). 1998. 62.95 (*0-7600-4960-2*) Course Tech.

Burd, Van A. Christmas Story: John Ruskin's Venetian Letters of 1876-1877. LC 89-40236. (Illus.). 296p. 1991. 42.50 (*0-87413-373-4*) U Delaware Pr.

Burd, Van A., ed. see Ruskin, John.

Burd, Van A., ed. see Ruskin, John J.

Burd, W. E. Properties & Evaluation of Carpenter Pyrowear Alloy 53 for Extended Gear Life. (1984 Fall Technical Meeting Ser.: Vol. 84FTM10). 9p. 1984. pap. text 30.00 (*1-55589-092-X*) AGMA.

***Burda, Cindy.** Cooking & Dining Outdoors. LC 99-53764. (Backyard Living Ser.). 128p. 2000. pap. 16.95 (*0-7370-2038-5*) T-L Custom Pub.

Burda, Cindy. Salsa Lover's Kit Booklet & Kit. LC 98-53005. (Illus.). 64p. 1999. 32.95 (*1-57990-123-9*, Pub. by Lark Books) Random.

***Burda, Cindy.** Weekend Woodworking for the Garden. LC 99-44117. (Illus.). 2000. 27.95 (*0-8069-2048-3*) Sterling Pub.

— Wind Toys That Spin, Sing, Twirl & Whirl. (Illus.). 2000. pap. 14.95 (*0-8069-4331-9*) Sterling.

Burda, Cindy. Wind Toys That Spin, Sing, Whirl & Twirl. LC 98-47127. 1999. 24.95 (*0-8069-3934-6*) Sterling.

Burda, Cindy, jt. auth. see Sheldon, Kathy.

Burda, Cindy, ed. see Waszek, Glen.

Burda, Joan M. A Desk Guide to Federal Consumer Law. LC 98-14300. 1998. write for info. (*1-57073-541-7*) Amer Bar Assn.

Burda, Margaret. Amazing States. (Illus.). 160p. (J). (gr. 4-8). 1984. student ed. 14.99 (*0-86653-205-6*, GA 546) Good Apple.

Burda, Michael. Macroeconomics: A European Text. 2nd ed. (Illus.). 638p. 1997. text 85.00 (*0-19-877469-9*) OUP.

Burda, Michael & Wyplosz, Charles. Macroeconomics: A European Text. 2nd ed. LC 96-24643. (Illus.). 638p. 1997. pap. text 49.95 (*0-19-877468-0*) OUP.

Burda Staff, ed. Flower of the Month. (Burda Bks.). 5.95 (*0-686-64663-0*, B804) Toggitt.

— Sampler of the Month. (Burda Bks.). 5.95 (*0-686-64664-9*, B805) Toggitt.

Burdall, Jane. Nurse on Vacation. large type ed. (Dales Large Print Ser.). 262p. 1997. pap. 18.99 (*1-85389-713-2*) Ulverscroft.

— Sister Adames' Dilemma. large type ed. (Dales Large Print Ser.). 275p. 1997. pap. 18.99 (*1-85389-714-0*) Ulverscroft.

Burde, Archana S., jt. auth. see Krishnaswamy, N.

Burde, Gerhard & Zieschang, Heiner. Knots. (Studies in Mathematics: Vol. 5). xii, 399p. 1985. 89.95 (*3-11-008675-1*) De Gruyter.

Burdea, Grigore C. Force & Touch Feedback for Virtual Reality. LC 96-15428. 360p. 1996. 82.50 (*0-471-02141-5*) Wiley.

Burdea, Grigore C. & Copiffet, Philippe. Virtual Realty Technology. 400p. 1994. 93.50 (*0-471-08632-0*) Wiley.

Burdekin, Katharine. The End of This Day's Business. LC 89-34897. 188p. 1989. pap. 8.95 (*1-55861-009-X*) Feminist Pr.

— Proud Man. LC 93-22845. 360p. 1993. 35.00 (*1-55861-070-7*); pap. 14.95 (*1-55861-067-7*) Feminist Pr.

— Swastika Night. LC 85-12980. 208p. (Orig.). 1985. reprint ed. pap. 9.95 (*0-935312-56-0*) Feminist Pr.

Burdekin, Richard C. & Burkett, Paul. Distributional Conflict & Inflation: Theoretical & Historical Perspectives. 240p. 1996. text 65.00 (*0-312-15994-3*) St Martin.

***Burden.** Elements of Architectural Design. 2nd ed. 352p. 2000. pap. text 49.95 (*0-471-37117-3*) Wiley.

— Environmental Monitoring Handbook. 2002. 125.00 (*0-07-135176-0*) McGraw.

— Introduction to the World's Religions: A Handbook. (Religion Ser.). 2002. pap. 27.50 (*0-534-50593-7*) Wadsworth Pub.

— Management Discipline. 400p. 1995. pap. 53.95 (*0-471-36521-1*) Wiley.

Burden. Management Discipline Professional Cop. 1995. pap. text 25.00 (*0-471-36518-1*) Wiley.

— Numerical Analysis. 3rd ed. (Mathematics Ser.). 1985. teacher ed. 14.00 (*0-87150-858-3*) PWS Pubs.

— Numerical Methods. 2nd ed. LC 97-47340. 511p. 1998. mass mkt. 98.95 (*0-534-35187-5*) Brooks-Cole.

— Numerical Methods. 2nd ed. 1998. pap. 25.00 (*0-534-35185-9*) Brooks-Cole.

— Software Numerical Analysis. 5th ed. (Mathematics Ser.). 1993. pap., student ed. 33.95 (*0-534-93221-5*) PWS Pubs.

Burden & Byrd. Methods for Effective Teaching. 2nd ed. LC 98-34489. 418p. 1998. pap. text 59.00 (*0-205-29193-7*) P-H.

Burden, Bob. Flaming Carrot Comics Presents, The Wild Shall Wild Remain! LC 99-190207. (Collected Album Ser.). 232 p. 1997. write for info. (*1-56971-322-7*) Dark Horse Comics.

Burden, Bob, jt. auth. see Williams, Marion.

Burden, C. J. & Robson, B. A., eds. Nuclear & Particle Physics. 468p. (C). 1990. text 113.00 (*981-02-0235-0*) World Scientific Pub.

Burden, C. J., jt. auth. see Bazhanov, V. V.

Burden, David W. & Whitney, Donald B. Biotechnology: Proteins to PCR: A Course in Strategies & Lab Techniques. LC 95-4897. 317p. 1995. pap. 43.50 (*0-8176-3843-1*); text 87.50 (*0-8176-3756-7*) Birkhauser.

Burden, Dianne. Woman Client: Providing Human Services in a Changing World. 1986. pap. 14.95 (*0-422-79780-4*, Pub. by Tavistock) Routldge.

Burden, Ernest. Elements of Architectural Design: A Visual Resource. (Architecture Ser.). (Illus.). 280p. 1994. pap. 44.95 (*0-471-28552-3*, VNR) Wiley.

Burden, Ernest. Illustrated Dictionary of Architecture. LC 98-4757. (Illus.). 400p. 1998. 49.95 (*0-07-008987-6*); pap. 39.95 (*0-07-008988-4*) McGraw.

Burden, Ernest. Perspective Grid Sourcebook: Computer Generated Tracing Guides for Architectural & Interior Design Drawings. 208p. 1991. pap. 54.95 (*0-471-28866-7*, VNR) Wiley.

Burden, Ernest E. Building Facades: Faces, Figures, & Ornamental Details. 2nd ed. (Illus.). 275p. 1996. 59.95 (*0-07-008959-0*) McGraw.

— Elements of Architectural Design. LC 93-29677. 1994. pap. 44.95 (*0-442-01339-6*, VNR) Wiley.

— Entourage: A Tracing File for Architects & Interior Design. 3rd ed. 1996. pap. text 79.95 incl. cd-rom (*0-07-853032-6*) McGraw.

— Entourage: A Tracing File for Architects & Interior Designers. 3rd ed. LC 95-26013. (Illus.). 308p. 1995. pap. 44.95 (*0-07-008944-2*) McGraw.

— Entourage: A Tracing File for Architects & Interior Designers. 3rd ed. (Illus.). 1996. 49.95 (*0-07-852861-5*) McGraw.

— The Perspective Grid Sourcebook: Computer-Generated Tracing Guides for Architecture & Interior Design Drawings. (Illus.). 224p. 1991. pap. 47.95 (*0-442-21132-5*, VNR) Wiley.

— Visionary Architecture: Unbuilt Works of the Imagination. 240p. 1999. 49.95 (*0-07-008994-9*) McGraw.

Burden, Gail & Bryant, Steven A. Laboratory & Radiologic Tests for Primary Eye Care. LC 96-18185. 252p. 1996. pap. text 40.00 (*0-7506-9755-5*) Buttrwrth-Heinemann.

Burden-Hyde, Harryett. In Defense of Martha. unabridged ed. 71p. 1996. pap. 6.25 (*0-89137-467-1*, 74671) Quality Pubns.

Burden, Jean. Journey Toward Poetry. (Orig.). 1967. 8.95 (*0-8079-0145-8*) October.

— Taking Light from Each Other. (University of Central Florida Contemporary Poetry Ser.). 96p. (C). 1992. 19.95 (*0-8130-1113-2*); pap. 10.95 (*0-8130-1114-0*) U Press Fla.

Burden, John A., jt. ed. see Wright, Richard A.

Burden, Maria S. Professor T. S. C. Lowe & His Mountain Railway. 1993. pap. 5.50 (*0-87505-402-1*) Borden.

Burden, Maria Schell. The Life & Times of Robert G. Fowler: The Greatest Aviator in the World. (Illus.). 160p. 1999. pap. 18.00 (*0-87505-369-6*) Borden.

Burden, Michael. Garrick, Arne & the Masque of Alfred: A Case Study in National, Theatrical & Musical Politics. LC 93-49808. (Illus.). 172p. 1994. text 79.95 (*0-7734-9132-5*) E Mellen.

Burden, Michael, ed. Henry Purcell's Operas: The Complete Texts. LC 98-33457. (Illus.). 544p. 2000. text 120.00 (*0-19-816445-9*) OUP.

— Performing the Music of Henry Purcell. (Illus.). 320p. 1996. text 85.00 (*0-19-816442-4*) OUP.

***Burden, Michael, ed.** A Woman Scorn'd: Responses to the Dido Myth. LC 99-237352. (Illus.). 304p. 2000. pap. 16.00 (*0-571-17699-2*) Faber & Faber.

Burden, Nancy. Ambulatory Surgical Nursing. (Illus.). 754p. 1993. text 73.50 (*0-7216-2897-4*, W B Saunders Co) Harcrt Hlth Sci Grp.

— Ambulatory Surgical Nursing: Clinical. 2002. pap. text. write for info. (*0-7216-5696-X*, W B Saunders Co) Harcrt Hlth Sci Grp.

Burden, Nancy, et al. Ambulatory Surgical Nursing. 2nd ed. LC 99-31873. 795p. 1999. text 60.00 (*0-7216-6847-X*, W B Saunders Co) Harcrt Hlth Sci Grp.

Burden, Pat. Bury Him Kindly. large type ed. 296p. 1992. 27.99 (*0-7505-0368-8*, Pub. by Mgna Lrg Print) Ulverscroft.

— Wreath of Honesty. large type ed. 368p. 1992. 27.99 (*0-7089-2583-9*) Ulverscroft.

Burden-Patmon, Denise. Imani's Gift at Kwanzaa. (Illus.). 32p. (J). (ps-3). 1993. pap. 4.95 (*0-671-79841-3*) S&S Bks Yung.

— Imani's Gift at Kwanzaa. (J). 1993. 10.15 (*0-606-05372-7*, Pub. by Turtleback) Demco.

Burden, Paul R. Classroom Management & Discipline, K-12: Methods to Facilitate Cooperation & Instruction. LC 94-5432. 400p. (C). 1995. pap. text 44.06 (*0-8013-1185-3*) Longman.

***Burden, Paul R.** Powerful Classroom Management Strategies: Motivating Students to Learn. LC 99-50711. (One-Off Ser.). 160p. 2000. pap. 21.95 (*0-7619-7563-2*); lib. bdg. 49.95 (*0-7619-7562-4*) Corwin Pr.

Burden, Paul R., jt. auth. see Schell, Leo M.

Burden, Richard L. & Faires, Douglas J. Numerical Analysis. 6th ed. LC 96-27594. (Mathematics Ser.). 776p. (C). 1996. mass mkt. 106.95 (*0-534-95532-0*) Brooks-Cole.

— Numerical Analysis: Instructor's Solution Manual. 6th ed. (C). 1997. text, teacher ed. write for info. (*0-534-95366-2*) Brooks-Cole.

— Numerical Analysis: Study Guide. 6th ed. (Mathematics Ser.). (C). 1997. text, mass mkt., student ed. 30.00 incl. disk (*0-534-95533-9*) Brooks-Cole.

Burden, Richard L. & Faires, J. Douglas. Numerical Analysis. 3rd ed. (C). 1985. mass mkt. 41.50 (*0-87150-857-5*) PWS Pubs.

— Numerical Analysis. 4th ed. (Math). 784p. (C). 1988. mass mkt. 51.00 (*0-534-91585-X*) PWS Pubs.

— Numerical Analysis. 5th ed. LC 92-32192. 784p. 1993. text 78.95 (*0-534-93219-3*) PWS Pubs.

Burden, Richard L., et al. Numerical Analysis. 1978. pap. text 22.00 (*0-87150-243-7*) PWS Pubs.

Burden, Richard L., jt. auth. see Faires, J. Douglas.

Burden, Robert L. & Williams, Marion. Thinking Through the Curriculum. LC 97-14932. 216p. (C). 1998. 75.00 (*0-415-17201-2*); pap. 24.99 (*0-415-17202-0*) Routledge.

Burden, Shirley C. Chairs. (Illus.). 52p. 1985. 22.95 (*0-89381-204-8*) Aperture.

Burden, Shirley C., photos by. Presence. deluxe limited ed. (Illus.). 96p. 1981. 250.00 (*0-89381-076-2*) Aperture.

Burden, Terry L. The Kerygma of the Wilderness Traditions in the Hebrew Bible. LC 93-43277. (American University Studies, VII, Theology & Religion: Vol. 163). 259p. (C). 1994. text 47.95 (*0-685-75337-9*) P Lang Pubng.

Burden, Vera. Discovering the Ridgeway. 1989. pap. 25.00 (*0-85263-990-2*, Pub. by Shire Pubns) St Mut.

Burden, Vera, jt. auth. see Clarke, Howard.

Burden, Virginia, et al. North Carolina Museum of Art: Handbook of the Collections. LC 97-76050. (Illus.). 288p. 1998. 50.00 (*0-88259-978-X*) NCMA.

Burden, William A. The Struggle for Airways in Latin America. Wilkins, Mira, ed. LC 76-29797. (European Business Ser.). (Illus.). 1977. reprint ed. lib. bdg. 35.95 (*0-405-09716-6*) Ayer.

Burdenko, Igor & Biehler, Scott. Overcoming Paralysis: Into the Water & Out of the Wheelchair. LC 99-20886. (Illus.). 241p. 1999. pap. text 14.95 (*0-89529-883-X*, Avery) Penguin Putnam.

Burdeos, Ray. The Steward & the Captain's Daughter. (Illus.). vii, 184p. 1999. 22.95 (*0-9671151-0-8*) LBurdeos Pubs.

Burder, G., ed. see Watts, Isaac.

Burder, John. Sixteen Millimeter Film Cutting. (Media Manuals Ser.). 164p. 1976. pap. 29.95 (*0-240-50857-2*) Buttrwrth-Heinemann.

— The Technique of Editing 16mm Films. 5th ed. LC 88-21280. (Library of Communication Techniques). (Illus.). 144p. reprint ed. pap. 44.70 (*0-608-06250-2*, 206657900008) Bks Demand.

Burdeshaw, Jane & McClain, Cindy. Music for Today's Preschoolers. (Illus.). 39p. (Orig.). (J). (ps-k). 1995. pap. text 10.95 (*1-56309-158-5*, N958103, New Hope) Womans Mission Union.

Burdett, A. L., ed. Arab Dissident Movements 1905-1955, 4 vols. 3000p. 1996. reprint ed. lib. bdg. 795.00 (*1-85207-680-1*, Pub. by Archive Editions) N Ross.

— The Arab League: British Documentary Sources 1943-1963, 10 vols. (ARA & FRE.). 6000p. 1995. reprint ed. lib. bdg. 2495.00 (*1-85207-610-0*, Pub. by Archive Editions) N Ross.

— Caucasian Boundaries: Documents & Maps, 1802-1946. LC 97-178705. (Illus.). 1996. reprint ed. lib. bdg. 395.00 (*1-85207-960-6*, Pub. by Archive Editions) N Ross.

— Civil Aviation, 1920-1962, 8 vols. 5500p. 1994. reprint ed. lib. bdg. 1495.00 (*1-85207-477-9*, Pub. by Archive Editions) N Ross.

— Communications & Transport, 1860-1960, 9 vols. (Illus.). 5200p. 1995. reprint ed. lib. bdg. 1495.00 (*1-85207-620-8*, Pub. by Archive Editions) N Ross.

— The Historical Boundaries Between Bosnia, Croatia, Serbia: Documents & Maps, 1815-1945, 2 vols. 750p. 1995. reprint ed. lib. bdg. 395.00 (*1-85207-965-7*, Pub. by Archive Editions) N Ross.

— Islamic Movements in the Arab World, 1913-1966, 4 vols. 2000p. 1998. lib. bdg. 1295.00 (*1-85207-800-6*) N Ross.

— Persian Gulf & Red Sea Naval Reports, 1820-1960, 15 vols. 11,000p. 1993. reprint ed. lib. bdg. 3995.00 (*1-85207-450-7*, Pub. by Archive Editions) N Ross.

— Records of Defense & Military Policy in the Gulf States & Saudi Arabia, 1920-1960, 12 vols. 8000p. 1994. reprint ed. lib. bdg. 2495.00 (*1-85207-500-7*, Pub. by Archive Editions) N Ross.

— Records of Kuwait, 1961-1965, 6 vols. 1997. reprint ed. lib. bdg. 995.00 (*1-85207-775-1*, Pub. by Archive Editions) N Ross.

— Records of Oman, 1961-1965, 5 vols. 1997. reprint ed. lib. bdg. 995.00 (*0-614-25970-3*, Pub. by Archive Editions) N Ross.

— Records of Qatar: Primary Documents, 1961-1965, 5 vols. (Arabian Regional Records Ser.). 1997. reprint ed. lib. bdg. 995.00 (*1-85207-780-8*, Pub. by Archive Editions) N Ross.

— Records of the Hijaz, 1798-1925, 8 vols. 5000p. 1996. reprint ed. lib. bdg. 1995.00 (*1-85207-655-0*, Pub. by Archive Editions) N Ross.

— Records of the Persian Gulf Pearl Fisheries, 1857-1962, 4 vols. (Illus.). 2000p. 1995. reprint ed. lib. bdg. 795.00 (*1-85207-605-4*, Pub. by Archive Editions) N Ross.

Burdett, A. L., jt. ed. see Asser, M.

Burdett, A. L., jt. ed. see Tuson, P.

Burdett, Anita L., ed. Water Resources in the Arabian Peninsula, 1921-1960, 2 vols. LC 98-195898. 1500p. 1998. lib. bdg. 595.00 (*1-85207-795-6*) N Ross.

***Burdett, Carolyn.** Olive Schreiner & the Progress of Feminism: Evolution, Gender, Empire. LC 00-33304. 2000. write for info. (*0-312-23763-4*) St Martin.

Burdett, Charles. Chances & Changes. LC 79-76921. (American Fiction Reprint Ser.). 1977. reprint ed. 16.95 (*0-8369-7000-4*) Ayer.

Burdett, Charles F. Vincenzo Cardarelli & His Contemporaries: Fascist Politics & Literary Culture. LC 98-47246. 236p. 1999. text 70.00 (*0-19-815978-1*) OUP.

Burdett, Corinne. Moving Beyond Adultry & Divorce. 75p. 1999. pap. 7.95 (*1-880710-37-4*) Monterey Pacific.

Burdett, Gerald L. & Soffen, Gerald A., eds. The Human Quest in Space, 24th Goddard Memorial Symposium, Mar. 20-21, 1986, Greenbelt, MD. (Science & Technology Ser.: Vol. 65). (Illus.). 312p. 1987. 55.00 (*0-87703-262-9*, Am Astronaut Soc); pap. 45.00 (*0-87703-263-7*, Am Astronaut Soc) Univelt Inc.

Burdett, Harold N. Yesteryear in Annapolis. LC 74-26773. (Illus.). 102p. 1974. reprint ed. pap. 31.70 (*0-608-02455-4*, 206309900004) Bks Demand.

Burdett, J. K. Chemical Bonding: A Dialogue. LC 97-173765. 172p. 1997. 140.00 (*0-471-97129-4*); pap. 55.00 (*0-471-97130-8*) Wiley.

Burdett, Jeremy K. Chemical Bonding in Solids. (Topics in Inorganic Chemistry Ser.). (Illus.). 336p. (C). 1995. text 71.95 (*0-19-508991-X*); pap. text 46.95 (*0-19-508992-8*) OUP.

— Molecular Shapes: Theoretical Models of Inorganic Stereochemistry. LC 80-15463. (Wiley-Interscience Publications). 301p. reprint ed. pap. 93.40 (*0-7837-2388-1*, 204007300006) Bks Demand.

Burdett, Jeremy K., jt. auth. see Albright, Thomas A.

Burdett, Jeremy K., ed. & tr. see Jean, Yves & Volatron, Francois.

***Burdett, John.** A Personal History of Thirst. 301p. 1999. reprint ed. text 23.00 (*0-7881-6629-8*) DIANE Pub.

Burdett, Lois. A Child's Portrait of Shakespeare. (Illus.). 64p. (YA). (gr. 2 up). 1995. pap. 8.95 (*0-88753-261-6*); text 19.95 (*0-88753-263-2*) Black Moss.

— Child's Portrait of Shakespeare. (Shakespeare Can Be Fun! Ser.). 1995. 12.15 (*0-606-07364-7*, Pub. by Turtleback) Demco.

***Burdett, Lois.** Hamlet for Kids. (Shakespeare Can Be Fun Ser.). (Illus.). 64p. (YA). (gr. 2 up). 2000. pap. 8.95 (*1-55209-530-4*); lib. bdg. 19.95 (*1-55209-522-3*) Firefly Bks Ltd.

— Hamlet for Kids. (Shakespeare Can Be Fun! Ser.). (Illus.). (J). 2000. 14.30 (*0-606-18136-9*) Turtleback.

Burdett, Lois. Macbeth for Kids. (Illus.). 64p. (YA). (gr. 3 up). 1996. text. write for info. (*0-88753-287-X*, Pub. by Black Moss) Firefly Bks Ltd.

— Macbeth for Kids. (Shakespeare Can Be Fun! Ser.). 1996. 14.15 (*0-606-12762-3*, Pub. by Turtleback) Demco.

— MacBeth for Kids. LC 96-900262. (Illus.). 64p. (YA). (gr. 2-7). 1996. pap. 8.95 (*0-88753-279-9*) Black Moss.

— A Midsummer Night's Dream: For Kids. (Shakespeare Can Be Fun Ser.). (Illus.). 64p. (J). (gr. 2 up). 1997. pap. 8.95 (*1-55209-124-4*); lib. bdg. 19.95 (*1-55209-130-9*) Firefly Bks Ltd.

— A Midsummer Night's Dream for Kids. (Shakespeare Can Be Fun! Ser.). 1997. 14.15 (*0-606-12767-4*, Pub. by Turtleback) Demco.

— Romeo & Juliet: For Kids. (Shakespeare Can Be Fun Ser.). (Illus.). 64p. (J). (gr. 2-7). 1998. pap. 8.95 (*1-55209-229-1*) Firefly Bks Ltd.

— Romeo & Juliet for Kids. (Shakespeare Can Be Fun Ser.). (Illus.). 64p. (J). (gr. 3-9). 1998. lib. bdg. 19.95 (*1-55209-244-5*) Firefly Bks Ltd.

— The Tempest: For Kids. LC 98-932685. (Illus.). 64p. (YA). (gr. 2-7). 1999. lib. bdg. 19.95 (*1-55209-355-7*) Firefly Bks Ltd.

Burdett, Lois & Coburn, Christine. Twelfth Night for Kids. (Shakespeare Can Be Fun Ser.). (Illus.). 40p. (J). (gr. 2 up). 1995. pap. 8.95 (*0-88753-233-0*) Black Moss.

Burdett, Lois & Coburn, Christine, eds. Twelfth Night. (Shakespeare Can Be Fun! Ser.). (J). 1994. 14.15 (*0-606-08325-1*, Pub. by Turtleback) Demco.

Burdett, Lois, jt. auth. see Shakespeare, William.

Burdett, Marilyn, jt. auth. see Boutillette, Linda K.

Burdett, Marilyn J., jt. auth. see Boutillette, Linda K.

Burdett, Nora. Patchwork of Programs 2 for Women's Ministries. LC 99-18664. 88p. 1999. pap. text 15.99 (*0-8341-1774-6*) Beacon Hill.

Burdett, Nora & Keller, Karen. A Patchwork of Programs for Women's Ministries. (Illus.). 160p. 1994. pap. 19.99 (*0-8341-1477-1*, 73546) Beacon Hill.

Burdett, Osbert. Beardsley Period. LC 75-79196. 1969. reprint ed. 46.00 (*0-8154-0297-X*) Cooper Sq.

— Beardsley Period: An Essay in Perspective. 1971. reprint ed. 6.00 (*0-403-00881-6*) Scholarly.

— The Beardsley Period: An Essay in Perspective. (BCL1-PR English Literature Ser.). 302p. 1992. reprint ed. lib. bdg. 89.00 (*0-7812-7047-2*) Rprt Serv.

— The Brownings. 1988. reprint ed. lib. bdg. 59.00 (*0-7812-0416-X*) Rprt Serv.

— The Brownings. LC 78-144919. 345p. 1929. reprint ed. 65.00 (*0-403-00882-4*) Scholarly.

— Critical Essays. LC 79-99685. (Essay Index Reprint Ser.). 1977. 20.95 (*0-8369-1346-9*) Ayer.

— The Idea of Coventry Patmore. (BCL1-PR English Literature Ser.). 213p. 1992. reprint ed. lib. bdg. 79.00 (*0-7812-7614-4*) Rprt Serv.

— The Reverend Smith, Sidney. LC 72-144920. 303p. 1934. reprint ed. 39.00 (*0-403-00883-2*) Scholarly.

— The Two Carlyles. LC 78-164591. (Select Bibliographies Reprint Ser.). 1977. reprint ed. 23.95 (*0-8369-5875-6*) Ayer.

— The Two Carlyles. LC 71-130269. (English Biography Ser.: No. 31). 1970. reprint ed. lib. bdg. 75.00 (*0-8383-1176-8*) M S G Haskell Hse.

— William Blake. LC 74-1127. (Studies in Blake: No. 3). 1974. lib. bdg. 75.00 (*0-8383-2021-X*) M S G Haskell Hse.

Burdett, Richard. Richard Rogers Partnership: Works & Projects. (Illus.). 276p. (Orig.). 1996. pap. 50.00 (*1-885254-32-6*, Pub. by Monacelli Pr) Penguin Putnam.

Burdett, Richard & Cork, Richard. Robert Mason: Broadgate Paintings & Drawings, 1989-1990. (Illus.). 63p. (Orig.). 1990. pap. 18.95 (*1-873175-00-0*) Yale Ctr Brit Art.

Burdett, Rosalind. Essential Scandinavian Style. (Illus.). 96p. 1998. pap. 12.95 (*0-7063-7748-6*, Pub. by WrLock) Sterling.

Burdett, William H. The Roads of Arkansas. (Illus.). 124p. 1990. pap. 13.95 (*0-940672-53-7*) Shearer Pub.

Burdett, William H., ed. Roads of New Mexico. (Illus.). 128p. 1990. pap. 14.95 (*0-940672-52-9*) Shearer Pub.

— The Roads of North Carolina. (Illus.). 80p. 1989. pap. 12.95 (*0-940672-48-0*) Shearer Pub.

Burdette, David & Richard, Kevin. UNIX Communications & Networking. LC 94-32471. 246p. 1994. pap. 19.95 (*1-55828-388-9*, MIS Pr) IDG Bks.

Burdette, Glenn, ed. see Somis, Giovanni B.

***Burdette, Robert J.** The Drums of the 47th. LC 99-36036. (Prairie State Bks.). 2000. 14.95 (*0-252-06853-X*) U of Ill Pr.

Burdette, Robert J. Hawk-Eyes. LC 74-166674. (Illus.). 1971. 21.00 (*0-403-01436-0*) Scholarly.

— The Rise & Fall of the Mustache. LC 71-91074. (American Humorists Ser.). 1878. reprint ed. lib. bdg. 22.50 (*0-8398-0179-3*) Irvington.

— The Rise & Fall of the Mustache & Other Hawk - Eyetems. LC 88-23013. (Iowa Heritage Collection). (Illus.). 328p. 1988. reprint ed. pap. 9.95 (*0-8138-0138-9*) Iowa St U Pr.

— Smiles Yoked with Sighs. LC 76-139757. (Granger Index Reprint Ser.). 1977. 19.95 (*0-8369-6211-7*) Ayer.

Burdette, Robert K. The Saga of Prayer: The Poetry of Dylan Thomas. LC 68-23203. (Studies in English Literature: No. 67). 160p. 1973. text 35.40 (*90-279-2072-9*) Mouton.

Burdette, Roger W. & Thieme-Busch, Carolyn A. Digital Imaging for Mini-Labs. 200p. 1993. pap. 55.00 (*0-9637554-0-4*) Burdette Assocs.

Burdette, Walter. Cancer: Etiology, Diagnosis & Treatment. LC 97-25674. (Illus.). 576p. 1997. text 39.00 (*0-07-008992-2*) McGraw-Hill HPD.

Burdette-Watkins, Mary, jt. auth. see Tinney, James.

Burdge, Geoffrey & Esener, Sadik C., eds. Spatial Light Modulators. LC 97-65313. (Trends in Optics & Photonics Ser.: Vol. 14). (Illus.). 284p. 1997. pap. 55.00 (*1-55752-487-4*) Optical Soc.

Burdge, Rabel J. A Community Guide to Social Impact Assessment. LC 93-87340. 200p. (Orig.). (C). 1995. pap. text 18.95 (*0-941042-17-0*) Soc Ecology Pr.

— A Conceptual Approach to Social Impact Assessment: Collection of Writings by Rabel J. Burdge & Colleagues. 274p. (Orig.). (C). 1994. pap. 18.95 (*0-941042-16-2*) Soc Ecology Pr.

Burdge-Rezvan, Jerena, ed. see Grant, Ann C.

Burdge-Rezvan, Jerena, ed. see Miller, Susan E.

Burdi, A. R., jt. ed. see Vig, K. L.

Burdich, Quentin N., pref. Who's Who in Intellectual Property. (Annual Ser.). 441p. 1989. text 239.00 (*0-929432-00-2*) WWIP NY.

Burdick. Detroit Publishing Company Handbook & Supplement. rev. ed. 96p. 1986. reprint ed. pap. 4.95 (*0-686-40532-3*) Deltiologists Am.

Burdick, Carol. Woman Alone: A Farmhouse Journal. 2nd ed. LC 98-16787. (Illus.). 224p. 1998. reprint ed. pap. 14.95 (*0-8397-8643-3*) Eriksson.

Burdick, Charles B. An American Island in Hitler's Reich: The Bad Nauheim Internment. (Illus.). 120p. (C). 1988. 32.95 (*0-944109-01-2*); pap. 18.95 (*0-944109-00-4*) Margraf Pubns Grp.

— The End of the Prinz Eugen (1x300) (Illus.). 90p. 1996. pap. 20.00 (*0-944109-10-1*) Margraf Pubns Grp.

— Germany's Military Strategy & Spain in World War Two. LC 68-26994. (Illus.). 256p. reprint ed. pap. 79.40 (*0-608-18105-6*, 203223700078) Bks Demand.

Burdick, Charles K. Law of the American Constitution: Its Origins & Development. xviii, 687p. 1987. reprint ed. 65.00 (*0-8377-1948-8*, Rothman) W S Hein.

Burdick, Charles K. & Burdick, Francis M. The Law of the American Constitution: Its Origin & Development. 687p. 1996. reprint ed. 175.00 (*1-56169-217-4*) Gaunt.

Burdick Corporation Staff. Technicians ECG Analyzer. 1p. 1973. pap. 7.51 (*0-13-898610-X*) P-H.

Burdick, David L., tr. see Basov, N. G., ed.

Burdick, David L., tr. see Tsytovich, Vadim N.

Burdick, Donald L., jt. auth. see Leffler, William L.

Burdick, Donald W. Las Epistolas de Juan. (Comentario Biblico Portavoz Ser.). (SPA.). 128p. 1996. pap. 6.99 (*0-8254-1088-6*, Edit Portavoz) Kregel.

Burdick, Eugene. The Blue of Capricorn. LC 61-14728. 322p. 1987. reprint ed. mass mkt. 5.95 (*0-935180-36-2*) Mutual Pub HI.

— Fail-Safe. 23.95 (*0-8488-0437-6*) Amereon Ltd.

Burdick, Eugene & Brodbeck, Arthur J., eds. American Voting Behavior. LC 77-7237. (Illus.). 475p. 1977. lib. bdg. 35.00 (*0-8371-9668-X*, BUAV, Greenwood Pr) Greenwood.

***Burdick, Eugene & Wheeler, Harvey.** Fail Safe. LC 98-35935. 286p. 1999. pap. 14.00 (*0-88001-654-X*) HarpC.

Burdick, Eugene, jt. auth. see Lederer, William J.

Burdick, Faye, ed. see Hoskins Ginn, Karen.

Burdick, Faye, ed. see Nishioka, Rodger Y.

Burdick, Faye, ed. see Nishioka, Roger, et al.

Burdick, Faye, ed. see Turnage, Lynn.

Burdick, Faye, ed. see Tuttle, Bob.

Burdick, Francis M. Law of Partnership, Including Limited Partnerships. lii, 422p. 1983. reprint ed. 45.00 (*0-8377-0333-6*, Rothman) W S Hein.

***Burdick, Francis M.** Law of the American Constitution: Its Origins & Development. xviii, 687p. 1999. reprint ed. 180.00 (*1-56169-487-8*) Gaunt.

— The Law of Torts: A Concise Treatise on the Civil Liability at Common Law & under Modern Statutes for Actionable Wrongs to Person & Property. lxxx, 501p. 1999. reprint ed. 146.50 (*1-56169-552-1*, 18166) Gaunt.

Burdick, Francis M., jt. auth. see Burdick, Charles K.

Burdick, George. California's Smith River. 80p. 1993. pap. 9.95 (*1-878175-63-7*) F Amato Pubns.

Burdick, Gerry & Burdick, Julie. Puzzling about South Dakota. (Illus.). 61p. (Orig.). (J). (gr. 8 up). 1992. pap. 4.95 (*0-9632844-0-1*, 050111557) Dakota Desktop.

Burdick, Harris & Van Allsburg, Chris. The Mysteries of Harris Burdick, 001. 32p. 1984. 17.95 (*0-395-35393-9*) HM.

Burdick, Howard E. Digital Imaging: Theory & Applications. LC 96-50397. (Illus.). 313p. 1997. 50.00 incl. cd-rom (*0-07-913059-3*) McGraw.

Burdick, Jacques. Savory Stews. LC 94-27242. 1995. 23.00 (*0-449-90545-4*) Fawcett.

Burdick, John. Anastacia's Daughters: Popular Christianity & the Politics of Race in Contemporary Brazil. LC 98-16293. 256p. (C). 1998. 75.00 (*0-415-91259-8*); pap. 21.99 (*0-415-91260-1*) Routledge.

— Looking for God in Brazil: The Progressive Catholic Church in Urban Brazil's Religious Arena. LC 92-32556. (C). 1993. 58.00 (*0-520-08000-9*, Pub. by U CA Pr) Cal Prin Full Svc.

— Looking for God in Brazil: The Progressive Catholic Church in Urban Brazil's Religious Arena. LC 92-32556. (Illus.). 280p. (C). 1996. pap. 16.95 (*0-520-20503-0*, Pub. by U CA Pr) Cal Prin Full Svc.

***Burdick, John.** William Morris: Redesigning the World. (Illus.). 128p. 1998. 16.98 (*1-57717-058-X*) Todtri Prods.

***Burdick, John & Hewitt, W. E.** The Church at the Grassroots in Latin America: Perspectives on Thirty Years of Activism. LC 99-37527. 240p. 2000. 62.50 (*0-275-96659-3*, Praeger Pubs) Greenwood.

Burdick, Julie, jt. auth. see Burdick, Gerry.

Burdick, Kathy, et al. Fun & Fantasy Resource Guide, Vol. 3498. Corker, Joanne, ed. (Learn to Read Resource Guide Ser.). (Illus.). 80p. 1996. pap. text, teacher ed. 25.98 (*1-57471-145-8*, 3498) Creat Teach Pr.

— Science Resource Guide, Vol. 3497. Williams, Rozanne L., ed. (Learn to Read Resource Guide Ser.). (Illus.). 80p. 1996. pap. text 25.98 (*1-57471-144-X*, 3497) Creat Teach Pr.

Burdick, Linda, ed. see Giberson, Dudley F.

Burdick, Michael A. For God & Fatherland: Religion & Politics in Argentina. LC 95-3597. (SUNY Series in Religion, Culture, & Society). 283p. (C). 1996. text 64.50 (*0-7914-2743-9*); pap. text 21.95 (*0-7914-2744-7*) State U NY Pr.

Burdick, Nancilu B. Family Ties: Old Quilt Patterns from New Cloth. LC 91-21340. (Illus.). 128p. (Orig.). 1991. pap. 19.95 (*1-55853-134-3*) Rutledge Hill Pr.

— Legacy: The Story of Talula Gilbert Bottoms & Her Quilts. LC 88-11534. (Illus.). 1993. pap. 18.95 (*1-55853-236-6*) Rutledge Hill Pr.

Burdick, Neal S., ed. The Adirondack Mountain Club Forest Preserve Series, 8 vols., Set. 2nd rev. ed. LC 93-28207. (Illus.). 1994. reprint ed. pap. write for info. (*0-935272-64-X*) ADK Mtn Club.

Burdick, Neal S., ed. see Goodwin, Tony.

Burdick, Neal S., ed. see Haberl, Arthur W.

Burdick, Neal S., ed. see Heilman, Carl E., II & Thomas-Train, David.

Burdick, Neal S., ed. see Laing, Linda & Freeman, Jack.

Burdick, Neal S., ed. see O'Shea, Peter V.

Burdick, Neal S., ed. see Steinberg, Michael.

Burdick, Neal S., ed. see Wadsworth, Bruce.

Burdick, Neal S., ed. see Wadsworth, Bruce & Cagle, Laurence T.

Burdick, Neal S., ed. see Wadsworth, Bruce, et al.

Burdick, Neal S., ed. see Winkler, John E.

Burdick, Patricia, et al. Collections Guide: Moving Image Collections of Northeast Historic Film. LC 95-69956. (Illus.). 64p. (Orig.). 1995. pap. 9.95 (*0-964693-0-5*) NE Historic.

Burdick, Richard A. & Graybill, eds. Confidence Intervals on Variance Components. (Statistics: Textbooks & Monographs: Vol. 127). (Illus.). 224p. 1992. text 137.50 (*0-8247-8644-0*) Dekker.

Burdick, Robert. Essential Windows CE Application Programming. LC 98-50464. 460p. 1999. pap. 49.99 incl. cd-rom (*0-471-32747-6*) Wiley.

Burdick, Suzanne & Taylor, Belinda, eds. Theatre Directory San Francisco Bay Area. 9th rev. ed. 161p. 1998. reprint ed. pap. 18.00 (*1-892543-00-1*) Theatre Bay Area.

Burdick, Suzanne, jt. ed. see Taylor, Belinda.

Burdick, Usher L. Marquis de Mores at War in the Bad Lands. 27p. 1986. pap. 4.95 (*0-87770-379-5*) Ye Galleon.

— Marquis Demores at War in the Bad Lands. (Shorey Historical Ser.). 27p. pap. 10.00 (*0-8466-0220-2*, S220) Shoreys Bkstore.

Burdick, Virginia M. Captain Thomas Macdonough: Delaware Born Hero of the Battle of Lake Champlain. LC 91-73590. (Illus.). 100p. (Orig.). 1991. pap. 4.00 (*0-924117-04-4*) Delaware HP.

***Burdick, William, ed.** 2000 Year Book of Emergency Medicine. (Illus.). 400p. 2000. 88.00 (*0-323-01598-5*) Mosby Inc.

Burdick, William L. The Bench & Bar of Other Lands. LC 39-32691. xii, 652p. 1982. reprint ed. lib. bdg. 47.50 (*0-89941-163-0*, 302090) W S Hein.

— The Principles of Roman Law & Their Relation to Modern Law. LC 89-46051. xii, 748p. 1989. reprint ed. 125.00 (*0-912004-77-0*) Gaunt.

Burdin, Joel L. Prioritizing Instruction: The Imperative Is of the Now. LC 96-60905. (NCPEA Yearbook Ser.). 344p. 1996. text 49.95 (*1-56676-473-4*) Scarecrow.

Burdin, Joel L., ed. School Leadership: A Contemporary Reader. LC 88-19104. 448p. 1989. pap. 138.90 (*0-608-05605-7*, 206606300006) Bks Demand.

Burdine, James M., ed. see Sanders, Ed, et al.

Burdisso, R. A. & Fuller, C. R., eds. Second Conference on Recent Advances in Active Control of Sound & Vibration. LC 93-60248. 1100p. 1993. text 99.95 (*1-56676-038-0*) Technomic.

Burditt, Faraday & Holley, Cynthia. Every Day in Every Way. (J). (ps). 1989. pap. 13.99 (*0-8224-2507-6*) Fearon Teacher Aids.

— Resources for Every Day in Every Way. 1989. pap. 17.99 (*0-8224-2508-4*) Fearon Teacher Aids.

Burditt, Faraday, jt. auth. see Holley, Cynthia.

Burditt, Roberta. Buck Naked. 1998. mass mkt. 5.99 (*0-345-40137-9*) Ballantine Pub Grp.

— Buck Naked Sequel. 1998. write for info. (*0-345-40138-7*) Ballantine Pub Grp.

— Shooting Star. 1998. 23.00 (*0-345-40139-5*) Ballantine Pub Grp.

***Burdman, Jessica R.** Collaborative Web Development: Strategies & Best Practices for Web Teams. LC 99-36736. 251p. 2000. pap. 34.95 incl. cd-rom (*0-201-43331-1*) Addison-Wesley.

Burdock, Eugene I., et al, eds. The Behavior of Psychiatric Patients: Quantitative Techniques for Evaluation. LC 82-2364. (Experimental & Clinical Psychiatry Ser.: No. 7). 603p. reprint ed. pap. 187.00 (*0-7837-0889-0*, 204119500019) Bks Demand.

Burdock, George A. Encyclopedia of Food & Color Additives. LC 96-42689. 1104p. 1996. boxed set 399.95 (*0-8493-9412-0*); boxed set 399.95 (*0-8493-9413-9*); boxed set 399.95 (*0-8493-9414-7*) CRC Pr.

— Encyclopedia of Food & Color Additives. LC 96-42689. 1996. write for info. (*0-8493-9416-3*) CRC Pr.

— Fenaroli's Handbook of Flavor Ingredients Vols. I & II, 2 vols., Set. 3rd ed. 1376p. 1994. 400.00 (*0-8493-2712-1*, 2712) CRC Pr.

Burdock, George A., ed. Fenaroli's Handbook of Flavor Ingredients: Adapted from the Italian Language Works of Giovanni Fenaroli, 1. 3rd ed. LC 94-17801. 368p. 1994. lib. bdg. 130.00 (*0-8493-2710-5*) CRC Pr.

— Fenaroli's Handbook of Flavor Ingredients: Adapted from the Italian Language Works of Giovanni Fenaroli, 2. 3rd ed. LC 94-17801. 1024p. 1994. boxed set 325.95 (*0-8493-2711-3*) CRC Pr.

Burdon, Christopher. Stumbling on God: Faith & Vision in Mark's Gospel. LC BS2585.2.B87. 120p. reprint ed. pap. 37.20 (*0-7837-5552-X*, 204532700005) Bks Demand.

Burdon, J. & Leather, Simon R. Pests, Pathogens & Plant Communities. 1990. 155.00 (*0-632-02561-1*) Blackwell Sci.

Burdon, James C., et al. Hemichordata, Tunicata, Cephalochordata. (Zoological Catalogue of Australia Ser.: Vol. 34). (Illus.). 79.95 (*0-643-06036-7*, Pub. by CSIRO) Accents Pubns.

Burdon, R. H., jt. auth. see Adams, R. L.

Burdon, R. H., ed. see Sharpe, P. T.

Burdon, Ronald L. The Elder Care Handbook: Resources & Guidance for Persons Helping Older Family Members. 92p. 1995. pap. 11.95 (*0-9647559-1-2*) Am Wellness.

— The University of Kentucky Elder Care Handbook: Resources & Guidance for University Employees Helping Older Family Members. 88p. 1995. pap. write for info. (*0-9647559-0-4*) Am Wellness.

Burdon, Roy H., jt. ed. see Rice-Evans, Catherine A.

Burds, Jeffrey. Peasant Dreams & Market Politics: Labor Migration & the Russian Village, 1861-1905. LC 97-33876. (Pitt Series in Russian & East European Studies). (Illus.). 407p. 1998. pap. 22.95 (*0-8229-5655-1*); text 50.00 (*0-8229-4049-3*) U of Pittsburgh Pr.

Burdsall, Harold H., Jr. A Contribution to the Taxonomy of the Genus Phanerochaete (Corticiaceae, Aphyllophorales) (Mycologia Memoirs Ser.: No. 10). (Illus.). 170p. 1985. lib. bdg. 39.00 (*3-7682-1392-7*) Lubrecht & Cramer.

Burduck, Michael L. Grim Phantasms: Fear in Poe's Short Fiction. LC 92-19852. (Studies in Nineteenth-Century American Literature: Vol. 2). 176p. 1992. text 25.00 (*0-8153-0070-0*, H1644) Garland.

Burdukiewicz, Jan M. The Late Pleistocene Shouldered Point Assemblages in Western Europe. (Illus.). ix, 253p. 1986. pap. 94.50 (*90-04-08100-3*) Brill Academic Pubs.

***Burdyuzha, V. & Kohzin, G., eds.** The Future of the Universe & the Future of Our Civilization. 400p. 2000. 96.00 (*981-02-4264-6*) World Scientific Pub.

Burdzhalov, E. N. Russia's Second Revolution: The February 1917 Uprising in Petrograd. Raleigh, Donald J., ed. & tr. by. LC 86-45955. (Indiana-Michigan Series in Russian & East European Studies). (Illus.). 412p. 1987. 18.50 (*0-253-35037-9*) Ind U Pr.

Bure, J., et al. Dictionary of Milling Technology. (ENG, GER, ITA & SPA.). 136p. 1980. pap. 24.95 (*0-8288-0032-4*, F10139) Fr & Eur.

Bureau European des Unions de Consommateurs Staff. After Sales Service in the European Economic Community. 281p. 1977. pap. text 53.00 (*0-86010-056-1*) G & T Inc.

Bureau, G. & Multon, J. L., eds. Food Packaging Technology, 2 vols., Set. LC 94-47052. (FRE., Illus.). 800p. 1995. 150.00 (*1-56081-682-1*, Wiley-VCH) Wiley.

— Food Packaging Technology, Vol. 1. (Illus.). 450p. 1995. 160.00 (*1-56081-932-4*, Wiley-VCH) Wiley.

Bureau, G. & Multon, J. L., eds. Food Packaging Technology, Vol. 1. 367p. 1995. 215.00 (*0-471-18641-4*) Wiley.

Bureau, G. & Multon, J. L., eds. Food Packaging Technology, Vol. 2. (Illus.). 400p. 1995. 160.00 (*1-56081-933-2*, Wiley-VCH) Wiley.

Bureau, G. & Multon, J. L., eds. Food Packaging Technology, 2 vols., Vol. 2. 742p. 1995. 375.00 (*0-471-18604-X*); 215.00 (*0-471-18642-2*) Wiley.

Bureau, Jacques. Computers Dictionary: Dictionnaire de l'Informatique. (FRE.). 399p. 1981. pap. 19.95 (*0-8288-4441-0*, M6053) Fr & Eur.

Bureau of American Ethnology Staff. List of Publications with Index. 1988. reprint ed. lib. bdg. 49.00 (*0-7812-0015-6*) Rprt Serv.

Bureau of Biological Survey Staff. Biological Survey Reports, 12 vols., Set. 1993. reprint ed. lib. bdg. 900.00 (*0-7812-5140-0*) Rprt Serv.

Bureau of Business Practice. Fingertip Guide to Payroll. LC 98-184567. 48 p. 1998. write for info. (*0-87622-760-4*) Aspen Pub.

***Bureau of Business Practice Staff.** Beyond Theory, Behavioral Safety in Action: 10 Case Studies of Behavior Change Programs. LC 99-172239. 110 p. 1998. write for info. (*0-87622-763-9*) Aspen Pub.

— Bloodborne Pathogens: Safety Program Planner : Management Manual. LC 99-171883. 336 p. 1998. write for info. (*0-87622-764-7*) Aspen Pub.

Bureau of Business Practice Staff. The Complete Retirement Workshop: Your Guide to Planning a Secure & Rewarding Future. LC 92-37107. 1993. 24.95 (*0-13-501314-3*) Aspen Pub.

— Continuous Improvement: Lessons from the Baldrige Winners. LC 98-171044. iv, 64 p. 1997. write for info. (*0-87622-730-2*) Aspen Pub.

— Credit & Collection Manager's Guides, 1993-94. 3rd ed. (C). 1993. pap. 59.95 (0-13-189953-8) P-H.

— FMLA: Employees in the Hot Seat : 38 Cases That Explain Potential Legal Pitfalls. LC 98-145545. 48 p. 1997. write for info. (0-87622-737-X) Aspen Pub.

Bureau of Business Practice Staff. The Human Resources Casebook: 20 Cases, Comments & Checklists on Critical Employment Law Issues. 47 p. 1997. write for info. (0-87622-738-8) Aspen Pub.

Bureau of Business Practice Staff. The Human Side of Supervision. (C). 1992. 11.95 (0-13-444167-2, Macmillan Coll) P-H.

— The Legal Side of Supervision. (C). 1992. pap. 11.95 (0-13-529934-9, Macmillan Coll) P-H.

***Bureau of Business Practice Staff.** Managing a Flexible Workforce. LC 99-182040. 112 p. 1998. write for info. (0-87622-774-4) Aspen Pub.

Bureau of Business Practice Staff. 1999 Human Resource Management: Issues & Trends. LC 99-183961. 1998. write for info. (0-87622-782-5) Aspen Pub.

Bureau of Business Practice Staff. Office Safety: The Guide to Tackling Today's Office Hazards. LC 98-178878. 110 p. 1997. write for info. (0-87622-744-2) Aspen Pub.

Bureau of Business Practice Staff. The Secretary's Help Desk. LC 98-184566. 94 p. 1997. write for info. (0-87622-741-8) Aspen Pub.

***Bureau of Business Practice Staff.** Secrets of Great Supervision: How to Bring Out the Best in Your People. LC 98-179373. 80p. 1999. ring bd. 225.00 (0-87622-742-6) Aspen Pub.

Bureau of Business Practice Staff. Speed Reading: The Computer Course, Apple IIC. write for info. (0-318-58237-6) P-H.

— Speed Reading: The Computer Course, Apple Version. 1984. text 89.00 incl. Apple II (0-13-833880-9, Macmillan Coll) P-H.

— 25 Strategies for Sensational Service. LC 98-178865. 95 p. 1997. write for info. (0-87622-740-X) Aspen Pub.

— Wage & Hour Compliance Handbook: Practical Guide to Law & Administration. LC 98-133379. 142 p. 1997. write for info. (0-87622-748-5) Aspen Pub.

Bureau of Business Practice Staff. The Winning Edge: Strategies for Office Professionals. LC 98-206651. 48p. 1996. write for info. (0-87622-688-8) Aspen Pub.

Bureau of Business Research Staff. Economic Projections, Nineteen Eighty-Four to Nineteen Ninety-Five. 1984. 15.00 (0-318-03898-6) Bur Busn Res U Nebr.

— Health Care Containment: The Managerial Approach. 1978. 7.50 (0-686-28414-3) Bur Busn Res U Nebr.

Bureau of Deep Mine Safety & Mining & Reclamation. Annual Report on Mining Activities, 1983. Nichols, Patsie, ed. 420p. (C). 1983. 8.35 (0-8182-0060-X) Commonweal PA.

— Annual Report on Mining Activities, 1986. 117th ed. Nichols, Patsie, ed. 536p. 1986. pap. text 8.35 (0-8182-0096-0) Commonweal PA.

— 1982 Annual Report on Mining Activities. Patsie, Nichols & Keffer, Gloria, eds. 485p. (C). 1982. 8.05 (0-8182-0028-6) Commonweal PA.

Bureau of Deep Mine Safety, Mining & Reclamation S. Annual Report on Mining Activities, 1984. Nichols, Patsie, ed. 400p. (C). 1984. 7.15 (0-8182-0068-5) Commonweal PA.

Bureau of Econ & Bus Research Staff. Statistical Abstract of Utah, 1996: Centennial Edition. 13th ed. Gillam, Diane S., ed. 518p. (Orig.). (C). 1996. pap. 40.00 (0-942486-11-0) Univ Utah.

Bureau of Economic & Business Research Staff, Univ, ed. Utah Statistical Abstract, 1983. 9th ed. (Illus.). 396p. (Orig.). 1983. 25.00 (0-942486-04-8) Univ Utah.

Bureau of Engineering Research The University of T, ed. Project Materials Management Handbook. 372p. 1989. text 75.00 (0-685-31295-X, CPMMH) Am Soc Civil Eng.

Bureau of Land Management Staff, jt. auth. see Forest Service Staff.

Bureau of Language Services, International Monetar. IMF Glossary: English, French, Spanish. 4th ed. 1992. pap. 15.00 (1-55775-267-2) Intl Monetary.

Bureau of Legislative Affairs of the State Council, compiled by. Laws & Regulations of the People's Republic of China Governing Foreign-Related Matters, 1949-1992, 4 vols. (CHI & ENG.). 2684p. 1994. 455.00 (0-614-11839-5, Pub. by HUWEI Cnslts) Am Overseas Bk Co.

Bureau of Mines Staff. First Aid. 1997. pap. 6.25 (1-883205-20-4) Intl Med Pub.

Bureau of Municipal Research, Newark, NJ Staff, et al. Urban Police: Selected Surveys on Police Problems in Newark & a Reorganization Plan for the Chicago Police Department. (Police in America Ser.). 1971. reprint ed. 33.95 (0-405-03375-3, 16954) Ayer.

Bureau of National Affairs Communications Staff, jt. auth. see Cornish, Tony.

Bureau of National Affairs Staff. The Consumer Product Safety Act: Texts, Analysis, Legislative History. LC 72-95897. 463p. reprint ed. pap. 143.60 (0-608-14110-0, 202430300037) Bks Demand.

— Federal Labor & Employment Laws. LC 85-9086. 322p. reprint ed. pap. 99.90 (0-7837-4602-4, 204432100002) Bks Demand.

— Hazardous Materials Transport Guide. LC 84-19919. 377p. reprint ed. pap. 116.90 (0-7837-4603-2, 204432200002) Bks Demand.

— Highlights of the New Pension Reform Law: Text of Act, Statement of the Managers, Editoral Analysis. LC 74-188898. 369p. reprint ed. pap. 114.40 (0-608-12749-3, 202433900037) Bks Demand.

— The Job Safety & Health Act of 1970: Text, Analysis, Legislative History. LC 78-156236. 348p. reprint ed. pap. 107.90 (0-608-14106-2, 202430700037) Bks Demand.

— Labor Relations Yearbook, 1979. LC 66-19726. 558p. pap. 173.00 (0-608-14105-4, 202430800037) Bks Demand.

Bureau of National Affairs, Washington, D. C. Staf. Dress Policies & Casual Dress Days. LC 98-210012. (Personnel Policies Forum Surveys Ser.). (Illus.). 72p. 1998. 50.00 (1-55871-364-6) BNA.

Bureau of Standards Staff. Bibliography on the Measurement & Gaging of Gears. (Technical Papers: Vol. P119). (Illus.). 31p. 1943. pap. text 30.00 (1-55589-297-3) AGMA.

Bureau of the Census Administration Staff, jt. auth. see U. S. Department of Commerce, Economics & Statistics Staff.

Bureau Of the Census Staff, ed. Government Dossier: An Inventory of Government Information about Individuals. LC 69-19367. 1969. reprint ed. 19.95 (0-405-00015-4) Ayer.

Bureau of the Census Staff, jt. auth. see U. S. Department of Commerce, Economics & Statisti.

Bureau of the Census Staff, jt. auth. see U. S. Department of Commerce, Economics & Statistics Staff.

Bureau Veritas Staff. Gas & Chemical Ships Safety Handbook. 47p. 1986. pap. 85.00 (1-85044-089-1) LLP.

— Ship Safety Handbook. 3rd ed. 346p. 1995. pap. 90.00 (1-85044-814-0) LLP.

Burek, Deborah M., ed. Cemeteries in the U. S. 2000p. 1994. 160.00 (0-8103-9245-3, 101954) Gale.

Burek, John Van, see Tremblay.

Burek, John Van, see Van Burek, John.

Burek, John Van, see Tremblay.

Burek, Peter J. Plattentektonische Probleme in der Weiteren Umgebung Arabiens Sowie der Danakil Afar-Senke. (Geotektonische Forschungen Ser.: Vol. 47). (GER.). ii, 100p. 1974. 33.00 (3-510-50013-X, Pub. by E Schweizerbartsche) Balogh.

Burelbach, Frederick M., jt. ed. see Alvarez-Altman, Grace.

Burell, Barbara C. A Woman's Place Is in the House: Campaigning for Congress in the Feminist Era. 224p. (Orig.). 1996. pap. text 20.95 (0-472-08384-8, 08384) U of Mich Pr.

Bureloff, Morris & Johnson, Connie. Calculators, Number Patterns, & Magic. (Illus.). 64p. (J). (gr. 4-11). 1977. pap. text 8.50 (0-918932-49-1, AE-1540) Activity Resources.

Buren, Abigail Van, see Van Buren, Abigail.

Buren, Ariane Van, see Van Buren, Ariane, ed.

Buren, Augustus H. Van, see Van Buren, Augustus H.

Buren, Daniel. Achtung! Texte 1969-1994. Fietzek, G. & Inboden, G., eds. (GER., Illus.). 454p. 1995. text 11.00 (3-364-00313-0) Gordon & Breach.

— Daniel Buren. 1997. 49.95 (3-928762-62-1, Pub. by Richter Verlag) Dist Art Pubs.

***Buren, Daniel.** Repertoire. 116p. 1999. 50.00 (4-7713-3405-6, Pub. by Korinsha) Dist Art Pubs.

Buren, E. Douglas Van, see Van Buren, E. Douglas.

Buren, Elizabeth Van, see Van Buren, Elizabeth.

Buren, Gunther Von, see Von Buren, Gunther.

Buren, James G. Van, see Van Buren, James G.

Buren, Jane S. Van, see Van Buren, Jane S.

Buren, John Van, see Van Buren, John.

Buren, John Van, see Kisiel, Theodore J. & Van Buren, John, eds.

Buren, Kathleen Von, see Singer, Barbara & Von Buren, Kathleen.

Buren, Kelly A. Van, see Van Buren, Kelly A.

Buren, Marjorie J. Van, see Van Buren, Marjorie J.

Burenkov, A. F., et al. Tables of Ion Implantation Spatial Distribution. viii, 462p. 1986. text 421.00 (2-88124-071-2) Gordon & Breach.

Burenkov, Sergei, ed. Medicine & Health Care in the U. S. S. R. LC 85-14460. 315p. 1985. 47.50 (0-8236-3310-1, 03310) Intl Univs Pr.

Bures, Donald. Abelian Subalgebras of Von Neumann Algebras. LC 52-42839. (Memoirs Ser.: No. 1/110). 127p. 1971. pap. 16.00 (0-8218-1810-4, MEMO/1/110) Am Math.

Bures, Jan, et al. Conditioned Taste Aversion: Memory of a Special Kind. (Oxford Psychology Ser.: No. 31). (Illus.). 192p. 1998. text 105.00 (0-19-852347-5) OUP.

Bures, Ruth A. Here Comes Christmas. 40p. (J). (gr. k-8). 1982. pap. 14.95 (0-86704-008-4) Clarus Music.

Buresch, Karl. Aus Lydien. (Subsidia Epigraphica Ser.: Vol. VII). (GER.). xv, 226p. 1977. reprint ed. 40.00 (3-487-06264-X) G Olms Pubs.

Buret, Frederic. Syphilis Today & among the Ancients, 3 vols. in 2. LC 72-9627. reprint ed. 81.50 (0-404-57422-X) AMS Pr.

Buretta, Marie. Data Replication: Tools & Techniques for Managing Distributed Information. LC 96-44019. 384p. 1997. pap. 54.99 (0-471-15754-6) Wiley.

***Burfeind, James W.** Juvenile Delinquency. (Criminal Justice Ser.). 2002. 5.25 hd 45.00 (0-534-53301-9) Wadsworth Pub.

Burfeindt-Moral, H. & Burfeindt-Moral, Zacher. Langenscheidt Satzlexikon des Englischen Geschaeftsbriefes. (ENG & GER.). 400p. 1981. 45.00 (0-8288-0088-X, M6087) Fr & Eur.

Burfeindt-Moral, H. & Rohrbacher. Langenscheidt Satzlexikon des Franzoesischen Geschaeftsbriefes. (FRE & GER.). 399p. 1981. 45.00 (0-8288-1271-3, M7165) Fr & Eur.

Burfeindt-Moral, H., et al. Langenscheidt Satzlexikon des Spanischen Geschaeftsbriefes. 5th ed. (GER & SPA.). 395p. 1982. 45.00 (0-8288-0822-8, S29928) Fr & Eur.

Burfeindt-Moral, Zacher, jt. auth. see Burfeindt-Moral, H.

Burfield, Eva. After Midnight. large type ed. 432p. 1987. 27.99 (0-7089-1651-1) Ulverscroft.

— A Chair to Sit On. large type ed. 368p. 1986. 27.99 (0-7089-1414-4) Ulverscroft.

— The Long Winter. large type ed. 320p. 1987. 27.99 (0-7089-1608-2) Ulverscroft.

— The New Mrs. Rainier. large type ed. 336p. 1987. 27.99 (0-7089-1581-7) Ulverscroft.

— Out of Yesterday. large type ed. 320p. 1987. 27.99 (0-7089-1622-8) Ulverscroft.

— The White Prison. large type ed. 352p. 1986. 27.99 (0-7089-1498-5) Ulverscroft.

— Yellow Kowhai. large type ed. 352p. 1987. 27.99 (0-7089-1708-9) Ulverscroft.

Burfield, Lori, ed. see Levitan, Diane & Wildman, Jeanne.

Burfoot. Encyclopedia of Reproductive Technology. LC 98-53131. 1999. text 85.00 (0-8133-6658-5, Pub. by Westview) HarpC.

Burfoot, Amby. The Principles of Running: Practical Lessons from My First 100,000 Miles. LC 99-17991. 1999. 15.95 (1-57954-038-4) Rodale Pr Inc.

***Burfoot, Amby.** The Runner's Guide to the Meaning of Life: What 35 Years of Running Have Taught Me About Winning, Losing, Happiness, Humility, & the Human Heart. LC 99-89556. 144p. 2000. pap. 14.95 (1-57954-263-8) Rodale Pr Inc.

Burfoot, Amby, ed. Runner's World Complete Book of Running: Everything You Need to Know to Run for Fun, Fitness & Competition. LC 96-53296. (Illus.). 320p. 1997. 24.95 (0-87596-354-4) Rodale Pr Inc.

***Burfoot, Amby, ed.** Runner's World Complete Book of Running: Everything You Need to Know to Run for Fun, Fitness, & Competition. 320p. 1999. pap. 15.95 (1-57954-186-0) Rodale Pr Inc.

Burfoot, Annette. Reproductive Technologies. 800p. Date not set. text 100.00 (0-8153-0148-0) Garland.

Burford. Vision of Steven. 1972. 5.95 (0-02-518120-3) Macmillan.

Burford, Alison. Land & Labor in the Greek World. LC 92-19191. (Ancient Society & History Ser.). 320p. 1993. text 40.00 (0-8018-4463-0) Johns Hopkins.

Burford, Barbara. The Threshing Floor. LC 87-7411. 214p. (Orig.). 1987. pap. 7.95 (0-932379-27-3); lib. bdg. 16.95 (0-932379-28-1) Firebrand Bks.

Burford, Betty. Chocolate by Hershey: A Story about Milton S. Hershey. (Creative Minds Ser.). (Illus.). 64p. (J). (gr. 3-6). 1994. pap. 5.95 (0-87614-641-8, Carolrhoda); lib. bdg. 19.93 (0-87614-830-5, Carolrhoda) Lerner Pub.

Burford, Betty M. Al Gore: United States Vice President. LC 93-47475. (People to Know Ser.). (Illus.). 128p. (YA). (gr. 6 up). 1994. lib. bdg. 20.95 (0-89490-496-5) Enslow Pubs.

Burford, Bill, ed. Granta 26: Travel. 1989. pap. 7.95 (0-14-012356-3, Penguin Bks) Viking Penguin.

Burford, Catherine, ed. see Burford, Thomas.

***Burford, Duncan, ed.** Ship of Thought: Essays on Psychoanalysis & Learning. (Encyclopedia of Psychoanalysis: Vol. 4). 250p. 2000. pap. 29.99 (1-900877-25-2, Pub. by Rebus Pr Ltd) Intl Spec Bk.

Burford, E. J. The Orrible Synne. LC 74-172023. (Illus.). 220p. 1979. pap. 7.95 (0-7145-1126-9) M Boyars Pubs.

Burford, E. J. & Shulman, Sandra. Of Bridles & Burnings: The Punishment of Women. 1992. write for info. (0-318-69233-3) St Martin.

Burford, Freda. A Cotswold Suite for SATB Recorders. (Contemporary Consort Ser.: No. 25). i, 25p. 1993. pap. text 12.00 (1-56571-075-4, CC025) PRB Prods.

— Seven Ghostly Fancies, for SAT Recorders. (Contemporary Consort Ser.: No. 23). 8p. 1992. pap. text 3.50 (1-56571-068-1, CC023) PRB Prods.

— Six Thumbnail Sketches for Two Alto Recorders. (Contemporary Consort Ser.: No. 16). 6p. 1991. pap. text 2.00 (1-56571-033-9) PRB Prods.

— The Turn of the Year, for Four Viols. (Charney Manor Ser.: No. 2). i, 16p. 1991. pap. text 9.00 (1-56571-037-1) PRB Prods.

***Burford, Gale & Hudson, Joe.** Conferencing Practices in Community Work with Families. (Modern Applications of Social Work Ser.). 352p. 2000. pap. text 30.95 (0-202-36122-5); lib. bdg. 59.95 (0-202-36121-7) Aldine de Gruyter.

Burford, Grace G. Desire, Death & Goodness: The Conflict of Ultimate Values in Theravada Buddhism. LC 90-5969. (New Perspectives in Philosophical Scholarship Series: Texts & Issues: Vol. 1). 227p. (C). 1991. text 38.95 (0-8204-1242-2) P Lang Pubng.

Burford Hibbert, Eleanor Alice, see Carr, Philippa, pseud.

Burford Hibbert, Eleanor Alice, see Holt, Victoria, pseud.

Burford Hibbert, Eleanor Alice, see Plaidy, Jean, pseud.

***Burford, J.** Beginner's Guide to Numerology & Relationships. 1998. mass mkt. 11.95 (0-340-72450-1, Pub. by Hodder & Stought Ltd) Trafalgar.

Burford, Jack. I Do times 2: The Story of Jacob (And Rachel & Leah) - A Musical. 1999. pap. 5.00 (1-57514-332-1, 0070) Encore Perform Pub.

Burford, John. LRRP Team Leader. 1994. mass mkt. 4.99 (0-8041-1051-4) Ivy Books.

— LRRP's in Action. (Combat Troops in Action Ser.). (Illus.). 50p. 1994. pap. 9.95 (0-89747-313-2) Squad Sig Pubns.

***Burford, John C.** Numerology & Relationships: A Beginner's Guide. (Headway Guides for Beginners Ser.). (Illus.). 96p. 2000. pap. 11.95 (0-340-77487-8, Pub. by Headway) Trafalgar.

Burford, Miles. Days of a Fledgling. LC 97-51547. 256p. 1998. 24.95 (1-56474-262-8) Fithian Pr.

***Burford, Miles.** Fledgling No More: A Novel. 448p. 2000. 26.95 (1-56474-342-X) Fithian Pr.

Burford, Miles. If You Stretch Far Enough You Can See the Bay: And Other Stories. LC 99-11190. 128p. 1999. 19.95 (1-56474-307-1) Fithian Pr.

Burford, Pamela. A Class Act. (Temptation Ser.). 1999. per. 3.75 (0-373-25846-1, 1-25846-6) Harlequin Bks.

— A Hard-Hearted Hero. (Temptation Ser.: No. 644). 1997. per. 3.50 (0-373-25744-9, 1-25744-3) Harlequin Bks.

— His Secret Side. LC 96-2517. (Intrigue Ser.). 248p. 1996. per. 3.75 (0-373-22360-9, 1-22360-1) Harlequin Bks.

— In the Dark (The Wrong Bed) (Temptation Ser.: No. 723). 1999. per. 3.75 (0-373-25823-2, 1-25823-5) Harlequin Bks.

— Jacks Are Wild. 1997. per. 3.50 (0-373-25758-9, 1-25758-3) Harlequin Bks.

***Burford, Pamela.** Love's Funny That Way. (Temptation Ser.). 2000. mass mkt. 3.99 (0-373-25912-3, 1259126) Harlequin Bks.

Burford, Pamela. Orages au Paradis. (Rouge Passion Ser.: No. 485). (FRE.). 1998. mass mkt. 3.50 (0-373-37485-2, 1-37485-9) Harlequin Bks.

— Twice Burned. (Double Dare Ser.). 1997. per. 3.75 (0-373-22420-6, 1-22420-3) Harlequin Bks.

Burford, Pamela & Ryan, Patricia. Summer Heat. (Temptation Ser.: Vol. 696). 1998. per. 3.75 (0-373-25796-1, 1-25796-3) Harlequin Bks.

Burford, Robert & Catherwood, F. Description of a View of the Great Temple of Karnak. (Illus.). 18p. 1988. reprint ed. pap. 12.50 (0-933175-16-7) Van Siclen Bks.

Burford, S. Franklin. The Snowshoe Story: Business, Politics & the Judiciary in West Virginia. 184p. 1993. 19.95 (0-9633805-0-8) Kerens Hill Pubns.

Burford, Thomas. Autograph Collecting - with the Stars. (Illus.). 20p. (Orig.). 1997. pap. 4.95 (0-9619758-7-3) Celeb Access.

— Celebrity Access - The Directory: Or How & Where to Write the Rich & Famous, 1997-1998. rev. ed. Burford, Catherine, ed. 350p. 1997. pap. 21.95 (0-9619758-5-7) Celeb Access.

— Fund Raising with the Stars. (Illus.). 18p. (Orig.). 1997. pap. 4.95 (0-9619758-9-X) Celeb Access.

Burford, Tim. Backpacking Chile & Argentina: A Bradt Hiking Guide. 4th ed. LC 98-30149. (Illus.). 380p. 1998. pap. 17.95 (1-898323-70-4, Pub. by Bradt Pubns) Globe Pequot.

— Backpacking in Central America. LC 95-48122. (Bradt Hiking Guides Ser.). (Illus.). 330p. 1996. pap. 15.95 (1-56440-817-5, Pub. by Bradt Pubns) Globe Pequot.

— Backpacking in Mexico. LC 96-47776. (Bradt Guides Ser.). (Illus.). 248p. 1997. pap. 16.95 (1-898323-56-9, Pub. by Bradt Pubns) Globe Pequot.

— Georgia: The Bradt Travel Guide. LC 99-14879. (Illus.). 288p. 1999. pap. 17.95 (1-898323-98-4, Pub. by Bradt Pubns) Globe Pequot.

— Hiking Guide to Poland & the Ukraine. (Bradt Hiking Guides Ser.). (Illus.). 372p. 1994. pap. 15.95 (1-56440-551-6, Pub. by Bradt Pubns) Globe Pequot.

— Hiking Guide to Romania. 2nd ed. LC 96-15659. (Bradt Hiking Guides Ser.). (Illus.), 326p. 1996. pap. 15.95 (1-56440-950-3, Pub. by Bradt Pubns) Globe Pequot.

— The Rough Guide to Romania. 2nd ed. (Rough Guides Ser.). (Illus.). 400p. 1998. pap. 17.95 (1-85828-305-1, Penguin Bks) Viking Penguin.

Burford, William. A Beginning. 1966. 4.50 (0-393-04286-3) Norton.

— A Beginning. (C). 1966. pap. 1.95 (0-393-04279-0, 3) Norton.

Burford, William, ed. & tr. see Proust, Marcel.

Burg. Introduction to Comparative Politics. 3rd ed. (C). 2000. pap. text. write for info. (0-321-02540-7) Addson-Wesley Educ.

Burg, ed. Intro Compar Pol. 3rd ed. (C). 1999. text 29.66 (0-673-99486-4) Addison-Wesley.

Burg, Annegret. Downtown Berlin: Building the Metropolitan Mix. Shimmann, Hans, ed. (Illus.). 224p. 1995. pap. 65.00 (3-7643-5063-6, Pub. by Birkhauser) Princeton Arch.

— Kollhoff: Architekten Kollhoff und Timmermann, Examples - Esempi - Beispiele. LC 98-38513. (ENG, GER & ITA., Illus.). 205p. 1998. 75.00 (3-7643-5771-1, Pub. by Birkhauser) Princeton Arch.

— Kollhoff: Examples, Esempi, Beispiele: Architekten Kollhoff und Timmermann. LC 98-38513. (ENG, GER & ITA.). 1998. 75.00 (0-8176-5771-1) Birkhauser.

Burg, Annegret & Redecke, Sebashan, eds. Chancellery & Office of the President of the Federal Republic of Germany. (GER., Illus.). 240p. 1996. pap. text 65.00 (3-7643-5203-5, Pub. by Birkhauser) Princeton Arch.

Burg, Annegret & Redecke, Sebastian, eds. Chancellery & Office of the President of the Federal Republic of Germany. (GER., Illus.). 240p. 1995. 80.00 (3-7643-5204-3, Pub. by Birkhauser) Princeton Arch.

Burg, Annegret & Stimmann, Hans, eds. Downtown Berlin: Building the Metropolitan Mix. (Illus.). 224p. 1995. 79.00 (3-7643-5062-8, Pub. by Birkhauser) Princeton Arch.

Burg, Barbara A., et al, eds. Guide to African American & African Primary Sources at Harvard University. 304p. 2000. boxed set 125.00 (1-57356-339-0) Oryx Pr.

Burg, Barbara A., ed. see Worger, William H., et al.

Burg, Barry Richard. An American Seafarer in the Age of Sail: The Intimate Diaries of Philip C. Van Buskirk 1851-1870. LC 93-29923. 248p. 1994. 35.00 (0-300-05637-0) Yale U Pr.

— Richard Mather of Dorchester. LC 75-41987. 223p. reprint ed. pap. 69.20 (0-7837-5781-6, 204544700006) Bks Demand.

— Sodomy & the Pirate Tradition: English Sea Rovers in the Seventeenth Century Caribbean. 2nd rev. ed. LC 94-25521. Orig. Title: Sodomy & the Perception of Evil. (C). 1995. reprint ed. pap. 15.95 (0-8147-1236-3); reprint ed. text 37.50 (0-8147-1235-5) NYU Pr.

Burg, Bob. Endless Referrals: Network Your Everyday Contacts into Sales. LC 98-33518. 257p. 1998. pap. 14.95 (0-07-008997-3) McGraw.

— Memory System Remember: Everything You Need to, When You Need To. 1992. pap. 12.95 (1-55825-063-8) Worldwide Ch God.

An Asterisk (*) at the beginning of an entry indicates that the title is appearing for the first time.

B

An Asterisk (*) at the beginning of an entry indicates that the title is appearing for the first time.

— Constitution: Foundation & Freedom. 1990. teacher ed. 36.50 (*0-15-371606-1*) Harcourt Schl Pubs.

— Delivery of Justice. Date not set. text. write for info. (*0-314-71681-5*) West Pub.

— Helping Professions: A Career Sourcebook. LC 99-30488. (Family Studies). 206p. 1999. 22.95 (*0-534-36475-6*) Brooks-Cole.

***Burger.** Human Services in Contemporary America. 5th ed. LC 99-30486. (Counseling Ser.). 1999. pap. 71.95 (*0-534-35830-6*) Brooks-Cole.

Burger. Munchhausen. unabridged ed. (World Classic Literature Ser.). (GER.). pap. 5.95 (*3-89507-001-7*, Pub. by Bookking Intl) Distribks Inc.

— Personality. 2nd ed. (Psychology Ser.). 1989. text, teacher ed. write for info. (*0-534-11665-5*) Brooks-Cole.

***Burger.** Personality. 5th ed. (Psychology Ser.). (C). 2000. text 18.00 (*0-534-36858-1*) Wadsworth Pub.

Burger. Personality ,Theory & Research. (Psychology). 1986. teacher ed. write for info. (*0-534-06127-3*) Wadsworth Pub.

***Burger.** Waltham Book of Companion Animal Nutrition. 150p. 1999. pap. text 45.00 (*0-7506-3337-9*) Buttrwrth-Heinemann.

Burger & Scheithauer. Tumors of the Central Nervous System. (AFIP Atlas of Tumor Pathology Ser.: Vol. 10). (Illus.). 452p. 1994. pap. text 60.00 (*1-881041-10-7*) Am Registry Path.

Burger, jt. auth. see Redington.

Burger, R., jt. auth. see Harrington, J.

Burger, A. Food Economics. 236p. (C). 1985. 75.00 (*963-05-3880-6*, Pub. by Akade Kiado) St Mut.

Burger, Alan R., et al, eds. Marxism, Science, & the Movement of History. (Philosophical Currents Ser.: Vol. 127). vi, 298p. (Orig.). 1980. pap. 35.00 (*90-6032-186-3*, Pub. by B R Gruner) Humanities.

Burger, Albert E. Building High Loan/Share Ratios: Challenges & Strategies. 47p. 1993. pap. 100.00 (*1-880572-10-9*) Filene Res.

Burger, Albert E., ed. U. S. Trade Deficit - Causes, Consequences & Cures: Proceedings of the Twelfth Annual Economic Policy Conference of the Federal Reserve Bank of St. Louis. (C). 1989. lib. bdg. 95.50 (*0-89838-292-0*) Kluwer Academic.

Burger, Albert E. & Dacin, Tina. Field of Membership: An Evolving Concept. 68p. 1992. pap. 100.00 (*1-880572-02-8*) Filene Res.

Burger, Albert E. & Lypny, Gregory J. Taxation of Credit Unions. 68p. 1991. pap. 100.00 (*1-880572-01-X*) Filene Res.

Burger, Albert E. & Zellmer, Mary. Strategic Opportunities in Serving Low to Moderate Income Members. 42p. 1995. pap. 100.00 (*1-880572-19-2*) Filene Res.

Burger, Albert E., et al. The Digital Revolution: Delivering Financial Services in the Future. 50p. 1997. pap. 100.00 (*1-880572-27-3*) Filene Res.

— Technology Strategies of Best Practice Credit Unions: Today, the Near Future, & the Far Future. 183p. 1997. pap. 100.00 (*1-880572-28-1*) Filene Res.

Burger, Alexander. Deregulierungspotentiale in der Gesetzlichen Rentenversicherung: Reformnotwendigkeiten vs. Reformmoglichkeiten. (GER., Illus.). 282p. 1996. 54.95 (*3-631-30791-8*) P Lang Pubng.

Burger, Alfred. Drugs & People: Medications, Their History & Origins, & the Way They Act. rev. ed. LC 88-12218. 186p. 1988. pap. 57.70 (*0-7837-8438-4*, 204924200010) Bks Demand.

— Searching, Teaching & Writing - What Fun. (Illus.). 167p. (Orig.). 1988. pap. 9.95 (*0-9621746-0-2*) A Burger.

— Understanding Medications: What the Label Doesn't Tell You. LC 95-17498. 220p. 1995. text 45.00 (*0-8412-3210-5*, Pub. by Am Chemical); pap. text 24.95 (*0-8412-3246-6*, Pub. by Am Chemical) OUP.

Burger, Alfred, ed. Drugs Affecting the Central Nervous System. LC 67-21205. (Medicinal Research Ser.: Vol. 2). 453p. reprint ed. pap. 140.50 (*0-608-17102-6*, 202713400054) Bks Demand.

— Drugs Affecting the Peripheral Nervous System. LC 66-22491. (Medicinal Research Ser.: Vol. 1). 644p. reprint ed. pap. 199.70 (*0-608-16904-8*, 202709100054) Bks Demand.

Burger, Anna. The Agriculture of the World. 320p. 1994. 79.95 (*1-85628-609-6*, Pub. by Avebry) Ashgate Pub Co.

Burger-Arndt, Renate. Zur Bedeutung Von Stickstoffeintraegen Fuer Naturnahe Vegetationseinheiten In Mitteleuropa. (Dissertationes Botanicae Ser.: Band 220). (Illus.). 226p. 1994. pap. 65.00 (*3-443-64130-X*, Pub. by Gebruder Borntraeger) Balogh.

Burger, Ary, et al. Defining the Nonprofit Sector: The Netherlands. (Working Papers of the Johns Hopkins Comparative Nonprofit Sector Project: Vol. 23). (Illus.). 29p. 1997. pap. text 6.00 (*1-886333-28-9*) JH Univ Inst Pol Studies.

Burger, Ary, jt. auth. see Veldheer, Vic.

Burger, August. Le Baron de Munchausen. unabridged ed. (FRE.). Date not set. reprint ed. pap. 6.95 (*2-87714-360-0*, Pub. by Bookking Intl) Distribks Inc.

Burger, Barbara L., compiled by. Guide to the Holdings of the Still Picture Branch of the National Archives. LC 90-5834. (Illus.). 176p. 1991. 25.00 (*0-911333-83-5*, 100043) National Archives & Recs.

Burger, Betty, jt. auth. see Burger, Charles.

Burger, Bruce. Esoteric Anatomy: The Body As Consciousness. LC 96-37686. (Illus.). 250p. (Orig.). 1998. pap. 22.50 (*1-55643-224-0*) North Atlantic.

Burger, C. W., et al, eds. Sermon Guides for Preaching in Easter, Ascension, & Pentecost. LC 88-3574. 292p. reprint ed. pap. 90.60 (*0-8357-4358-6*, 203718600007) Bks Demand.

Burger, Charles & Burger, Betty. Christian Eclectic Readers, 5 vols. rev. ed. LC 98-22586. Orig. Title: McGuffey Eclectic Readers. (Illus.). 1029p. 1998. pap., student ed. 50.00 (*0-8028-4480-4*) Eerdmans.

Burger, Christa, jt. auth. see Burger, Peter.

Burger, Dan, ed. Death Row. (Illus.). 254p. (Orig.). 1993. pap. 19.95 (*0-9624857-2-1*) Bobit Pubng.

***Burger, Dan & Genat, Robert.** Impala, 1958-2000. (Illus.). 128p. 2000. pap. 21.95 (*0-7603-0805-5*, 130683AP, Pub. by MBI Pubg) Motorbooks Intl.

Burger, Dan & Little, Amy, eds. Death Row 1992. (Illus.). 228p. 1989. 19.95 (*0-685-52364-0*) Bobit Pubng.

Burger, Dan, jt. auth. see Knapp, Robert R.

Burger Davis, Vema. My Chosen Trails: A Wyoming Woman's Recollections Through the Twentieth Century. LC 98-96028. (Illus.). 200p. 1998. pap. 12.95 (*0-9663347-0-1*) Deep Creek.

Burger, Delores. Women Who Changed the Heart of the City: The Untold Story of the City Rescue Mission Movement. LC 96-32054. 160p. 1997. pap. 10.99 (*0-8254-2146-2*) Kregel.

Burger, Dieter. Quantifizierung Quartaerer Subtropischer Verwitterung auf Kalk. (Relief, Boden, Palaeoklima Ser.: Band 7). (GER., Illus.). xiv, 132p. 1992. pap. 40.00 (*3-443-09007-9*, Pub. by Gebruder Borntraeger) Balogh.

Burger, Dionys, jt. auth. see Abbott, Edwin A.

Burger, E., et al, eds. Environmental Chemical Exposures & Immune System Integrity. LC 87-618327. (Advances in Modern Environmental Toxicology Ser.: Vol. 13). (Illus.). 259p. 1987. 65.00 (*0-911131-14-0*) Specialist Journals.

***Burger, E. & Starbird, M.** The Heart of Mathematics: A Guide to Effective Thinking. (TIMS Ser.). (Illus.). 680p. 1999. 65.00 (*0-387-98811-4*) Spr-Verlag.

***Burger, Edward B.** Exploring the Number Jungle: A Journey into Diophantine Analysis. (STML Ser.). 144p. 2000. 20.00 (*0-8218-2640-9*) Am Math.

***Burger, Edward B. & Starbird, Michael.** The Heart of Mathematics: An Invitation to Effective Thinking. xii, 646p. (C). 1999. text 69.95 (*1-55953-407-9*) Key Coll.

— The Heart of Mathematics: An Invitation to Effective Thinking. (Illus.). xxvi, 646p. (C). 1999. text 79.95 incl. cd-rom (*1-930190-01-8*) Key Coll.

Burger, Edward J. Better Science by Litigators, Better Management by Courts: Drawing on the Pre-Daubert Experience in the Post-Daubert Era LC 99-165581. 37p. 1997. pap. write for info. (*0-937299-52-9*) Natl Legal Ctr Pub Interest.

— A Better Way of Doing Business: A Proactive Approach to Scientific Controversy LC 99-165609. 29p. 1997. pap. write for info. (*0-937299-57-X*) Natl Legal Ctr Pub Interest.

Burger, Edward J., Jr. Science at the White House: A Political Liability. LC 80-81425. 208p. 1981. text 35.00 (*0-8018-2433-8*) Johns Hopkins.

Burger, Edward J., ed. Risk. 288p. 1993. pap. text 20.95 (*0-472-08222-1*, 08222) U of Mich Pr.

Burger, Erich. Data Processing Dictionary: Englisch - Deutsch - Franzosisch - Russisch. 903p. 1989. 195.00 (*0-8288-2479-7*) Fr & Eur.

— Dictionary of Information Science: In English, French, German, Russian, 2 vols., Set. 2nd ed. (ENG, FRE, GER & RUS.). 904p. 1991. lib. bdg. 195.00 (*0-8288-3843-7*) Fr & Eur.

— Elsevier's Dictionary of Information Science: English, German, French & Russian, 2 vols. (ENG, FRE, GER & RUS.). 960p. 1988. 350.00 (*0-8288-0267-X*, M9889) Fr & Eur.

Burger, Erich & Korzak, Gunter. Dictionary of Robot Technology. (ENG, FRE, GER & RUS.). 276p. 1986. 124.50 (*0-444-99519-6*) Elsevier.

— Elsevier's Dictionary of Robot Technology in English, German, French & Russian. 2nd ed. (ENG, FRE, GER & RUS.). 276p. 1986. 195.00 (*0-8288-0681-0*, F126504) Fr & Eur.

Burger, Evelin & Fiebig, Johannes. The Complete Book of Tarot Spreads. LC 96-52303. (Illus.). 192p. 1997. pap. 7.95 (*0-8069-9505-X*) Sterling.

Burger, G., et al. Radiation Protection Quantities for External Exposure, Vol. 9. (Commission of the European Communities Ser.). viii, 260p. 1981. text 277.00 (*3-7186-0063-3*) Gordon & Breach.

Burger, Gerry, jt. auth. see Hendrickson, Steve.

Burger, Glenn, ed. A Lyttel Cronycle: Richard Pynson's Translation (c. 1520) of La Fleur des Histoires de la Terre d'Orient (1307) Hetoum. (Illus.). 286p. (C). 1988. text 50.00 (*0-8020-2626-5*) U of Toronto Pr.

Burger, H. & Boulet, M., eds. A Portrait of the Menopause: Expert Reports on Medical & Therapeutic Strategies for the 1990's. (Illus.). 110p. (C). 1991. 45.00 (*1-85070-357-4*) Prthnon Pub.

Burger, H. D. Seedling of Some Tropical Trees & Shrubs Mainly of South-East Asia. 399p. 1989. pap. 1250.00 (*81-7089-107-8*, Pub. by Intl Bk Distr) St Mut.

Burger, H. Robert. Exploration Geophysics of the Shallow Subsurface. LC 91-30335. 489p. 1992. 105.00 (*0-13-296773-1*) P-H.

Burger, H. Robert, ed. Options for Tunnelling, 1993. LC 93-15219. (Developments in Geotechnical Engineering Ser.: Vol. 74). 936p. 1993. 220.00 (*0-444-89935-9*) Elsevier.

Burger, Habil E. Dictionary of Automatic Data Processing. (ENG, FRE, GER, RUS & SLO.). 480p. 1980. 80.00 (*0-569-08521-7*) St Mut.

Burger, Harald. Das Gesprach in den Massenmedien. (GER.). vii, 438p. (C). 1991. lib. bdg. 138.50 (*3-11-012215-4*) De Gruyter.

— Sprache der Massenmedien: Eine Einfuhrung. 2nd rev. ed. (Sammlung Goschen Ser.: No. 2225). 388p. (C). 1990. pap. 22.95 (*3-11-012306-1*) De Gruyter.

— Zeit und Ewigkeit: Studien zum Wortschatz der Geistlichen Texte des Alt-und Fruehmittelhochdeutschen. LC 74-174177. (Studia Linguistica Germanica: Vol. 6). (C). 1972. 90.00 (*3-11-003995-8*) De Gruyter.

Burger, Harry & Borowsky, Larry. Biancastella: A Jewish Partisan in World War II. LC 96-52672. (Illus.). 172p. 1997. 24.95 (*0-87081-397-8*) Univ Pr Colo.

Burger, Henry & De Kretser, David, eds. The Testis. 2nd ed. LC 86-42904. (Comprehensive Endocrinology Ser.). (Illus.). 605p. 1989. reprint ed. pap. 187.60 (*0-608-07257-5*, 206748400009) Bks Demand.

Burger, Henry G. Wordtree: A Transitive Cladistic for Solving Physical & Social Problems. LC 84-13007. 380p. 1984. 149.00 (*0-936312-00-9*) Wordtree.

Burger, Hillel S. & Brown, Ian W. The Hall of the North American Indian. Isaac, Barbara, ed. LC 90-60688. (Peabody Museum Press Ser.). (Illus.). 136p. 1990. pap. 25.00 (*0-87365-811-6*) Peabody Harvard.

Burger, Hzn D. Seedlings of Some Tropical Trees & Shrubs Mainly of South East Asia 1989. 1989. 230.00 (*81-7089-110-8*, Pub. by Intl Bk Distr) St Mut.

Burger, I. H., ed. The Waltham Book of Companion Animal Nutrition. (Waltham Centre for Pet Nutrition Ser.: Vol. 2). 150p. 1993. pap. text 45.00 (*0-08-040844-3*, Pergamon Pr) Elsevier.

— The Waltham Book of Companion Animal Nutrition. (Waltham Centre for Pet Nutrition Ser.: Vol. 2). (Illus.). 150p. 1993. text 70.00 (*0-08-040843-5*, Pergamon Pr) Elsevier.

Burger, Irene T., jt. auth. see Rand, Mary E.

Burger, J. & Olla, B. L. Behavior of Marine Animals Vol. 5: Shorebirds: Breeding, Behavior & Populations. LC 79-167675. (Illus.). 452p. (C). 1984. text 115.00 (*0-306-41590-9*, Kluwer Plenum) Kluwer Academic.

— Behavior of Marine Animals Vol. 6: Shorebirds: Migration & Foraging Behavior. LC 79-167675. (Illus.). 344p. (C). 1984. text 105.00 (*0-306-41591-7*, Kluwer Plenum) Kluwer Academic.

Burger, J. F. African Adventures. (Illus.). 222p. 1993. 35.00 (*0-940143-77-1*) Safari Pr.

— African Campfire Nights. (Illus.). 192p. 1993. 32.50 (*0-940143-82-8*) Safari Pr.

— African Jungle Memories. (Illus.). 192p. 1993. 32.50 (*0-940143-83-6*) Safari Pr.

— Horned Death. (Illus.). 342p. 1992. 35.00 (*0-940143-66-6*) Safari Pr.

Burger, J. M. Desire for Control: Personality, Social, & Clinical Perspectives. (Social - Clinical Psychology Ser.). (Illus.). 208p. (C). 1992. 39.50 (*0-306-44072-5*, Plenum Trade) Perseus Pubng.

Burger, Jacques, et al. Thermal Methods of Oil Recovery. (Illus.). 448p. (C). 1985. 665.00 (*2-7108-0493-X*, Pub. by Edits Technip) Enfield Pubs NH.

Burger, James A., jt. ed. see Almond, Harry H.

Burger, Jan J., et al, eds. Atmospheric Physics from Spacelab. (Astrophysics & Space Science Library: No. 61). 1976. text 205.50 (*90-277-0768-5*) Kluwer Academic.

Burger, Jeff. La Biblia del Multimedia. (SPA.). 672p. (C). 1993. pap. text 28.66 (*0-201-63101-6*) Addison-Wesley.

— The Murphy's Law Midi Book. Orig. Title: Advanced Midi User's Guide. 94p. (C). 1987. pap. 19.95 (*0-939067-56-0*) Alexander Pub.

— Oberheim Matrix-Six: Getting the Most Out of Your. Alexander, Peter L., ed. (Illus.). 102p. (C). 1987. pap. text 19.95 (*0-939067-17-X*) Alexander Pub.

Burger, Jerry M. Personality. 2nd ed. 525p. (C). 1989. mass mkt. 51.50 (*0-534-11664-7*) Brooks-Cole.

— Personality. 3rd ed. (Psychology Ser.). 1993. pap., student ed. 19.95 (*0-534-17222-9*) Brooks-Cole.

— Personality. 3rd ed. (C). 1993. text 45.50 (*0-534-17220-2*) Brooks-Cole.

— Personality: Theory & Research. 510p. (C). 1986. mass mkt. 35.00 (*0-534-06126-5*) Brooks-Cole.

— Personality: Theory & Research. 4th ed. LC 96-3311. (Psychology Ser.). 590p. 1996. text 52.25 (*0-534-33924-7*) Brooks-Cole.

— Personality: Theory & Research. 4th ed. 1997. text, teacher ed. write for info. (*0-534-34562-X*) Brooks-Cole.

— Study Guide for Personality: Theory & Research. 4th ed. (Miscellaneous/Catalogs Ser.). 1997. mass mkt., student ed. 15.75 (*0-534-34561-1*) Brooks-Cole.

Burger, Joanna. A Naturalist along the Jersey Shore. LC 95-52724. (Illus.). 287p. (C). 1996. pap. 18.95 (*0-8135-2300-1*); text 40.00 (*0-8135-2299-4*) Rutgers U Pr.

— Oil Spills. LC 96-8340. (Illus.). 228p. (C). 1997. text 29.95 (*0-8135-2338-9*) Rutgers U Pr.

— Pattern, Mechanism, & Adaptive Significance of Territoriality in Herring Gulls (Larus argentatus) 92p. 1984. 12.50 (*0-943610-41-9*) Am Ornithologists.

Burger, Joanna, ed. Before & after an Oil Spill: The Arthur Kill. (Illus.). 320p. (C). 1994. text 50.00 (*0-8135-2095-9*) Rutgers U Pr.

— Seabirds & Other Marine Vertebrates: Competition, Predation, & Other Interactions. 312p. 1989. text 72.50 (*0-231-06362-8*) Col U Pr.

***Burger, Joanna, et al, eds.** Protecting the Commons: A Framework for Resource Management in the Americas. (Illus.). 328p. 2000. 60.00 (*1-55963-737-4*, Shearwater Bks); pap. 30.00 (*1-55963-738-2*, Shearwater Bks) Island Pr.

Burger, Joanna & Gochfeld, Michael. The Black Skimmer: The Social Dynamics of a Colonial Species. (Illus.). 416p. 1990. text 61.50 (*0-231-07106-X*) Col U Pr.

***Burger, Joanna & Gochfeld, Michael.** 25 Nature Spectacles in New Jersey. LC 99-43253. (Illus.). 272p. 2000. pap. 20.00 (*0-8135-2766-X*); text 45.00 (*0-8135-2791-0*) Rutgers U Pr.

Burger, Joanna, jt. auth. see Gochfeld, Michael.

Burger, Joanne. SF Published in 1977. (Orig.). 1978. pap. 4.00 (*0-916188-08-6*) J Burger.

Burger, John. Intro to Insurance Company Profitability. (Step One Ser.). 130p. spiral bd. 34.95 (*1-57974-027-8*, Pub. by Life Office) PBD Inc.

Burger, John, jt. auth. see Brown, Barbara F.

Burger, John F., ed. Contributions to the Knowledge of Diptera: A Collection of Articles on Diptera Commemorating the Life & Works of Graham B. Fairchild. LC 99-26227. (Memoirs on Entomology, International Ser.: Vol. 14). (Illus.). 656p. 1999. 80.00 (*1-56665-071-2*) Assoc Pubs FL.

Burger, John F., jt. auth. see Fairchild, Graham B.

Burger, John R. Basic Digital Electronics: With an Emphasis on Practical Design & VLSI. LC 94-27391. 544p. (Orig.). 1995. pap. 48.50 (*0-89464-954-X*) Krieger.

— Basic Digital Electronics: With an Emphasis on Practical Design & VSLI. (Illus.). 544p. (C). 1995. lib. bdg. 64.50 (*0-89464-907-8*) Krieger.

— One-Handed Histories: The Eroto-Politics of Gay Male Video Pornography. LC 93-15575. 143p. 1994. pap. 14.95 (*1-56023-852-6*) Haworth Pr.

— One-Handed Histories: The Eroto-Politics of Gay Male Video Pornography. LC 93-15575. 143p. 1995. lib. bdg. 39.95 (*1-56024-860-2*) Haworth Pr.

Burger, K., et al, eds. Agricultural Economics & Policy: International Challenges for the Nineties: Essays in Honour of Prof. J. De Veer. (Developments in Agricultural Economics Ser.: No. 7). xii,214p. 1991. 124.50 (*0-444-88974-4*) Elsevier.

Burger, Kenneth & Ray, Alvin. Managing Diversity: A Practical Guide. abr. ed. (Illus.). 70p. 1997. pap. text 14.95 (*0-936295-74-0*) FPMI Comns.

***Burger, Kenneth A. & Ray, Alvin E.** The Manager's Survival Guide to Organizational Change. 1999. pap. 14.95 (*0-936295-92-9*) FPMI Comns.

Burger, Kenneth A. & Ray, Alvin E. A Practical Guide to Self Managed Teams. abr. ed. (Illus.). 62p. 1997. pap. text 14.95 (*0-936295-76-7*) FPMI Comns.

Burger, Konrad. Supplement Zu Hain und Panzer: Beitraege Zur Inkunabelbibliographie. vii, 440p. 1966. reprint ed. 160.00 (*0-318-71749-2*) G Olms Pubs.

Burger, Leslie & Rahm, Debra L. Red Cross/Red Crescent. LC 96-384. (J). 1996. 22.60 (*0-8225-2698-0*, Lerner Publctns) Lerner Pub.

— Sister Cities: A World of Difference. LC 95-3424. (International Cooperation Ser.). (J). 1996. lib. bdg. 22.60 (*0-8225-2697-2*, Lerner Publctns) Lerner Pub.

— United Nations High Commissioner for Refugees. LC 95-45058. (J). 1996. lib. bdg. 22.60 (*0-8225-2699-9*) Lerner Pub.

Burger, Louisa M. Shake My Hand. (Illus.). 72p. 1990. 7.50 (*0-912449-36-5*) Floating Island.

— Swing That Pail. (Illus.). 72p. (Orig.). 1991. pap. 7.50 (*0-912449-37-3*) Floating Island.

— They're God's. 48p. 1993. pap. 9.95 (*0-912449-45-4*) Floating Island.

Burger, Lynn T., jt. auth. see Hamm, Russell L.

Burger, Maria, jt. ed. see Field, Richard J.

Burger, Mary. Bleeding Optimist. 91p. 1995. pap. write for info. (*0-9649033-1-8*) Xurban.

Burger, Max M., et al, eds. Cell to Cell Interaction. (Illus.). xx, 252p. 1990. 172.25 (*3-8055-5322-6*) S Karger.

Burger, Max M., jt. ed. see Lash, James W.

***Burger, Maya & Schreiner, Peter, eds.** The Perception of the Elements in the Hindu Tradition. (Studia Religiosa Helvetica Jahrbuch: Vol. 4-5). 215p. 2000. pap. 29.95 (*3-906764-61-3*) P Lang Pubng.

Burger, Nash K. & McHaney, Pearl A. The Road to West 43rd Street. LC 95-11739. (Illus.). 192p. 1995. 25.00 (*0-87805-793-5*) U Pr of Miss.

***Burger, Norman F.** Christian Citizenship in Church & State: Bible Study. 1999. 37.99 (*0-8100-0877-7*) Northwest Pub.

Burger, Peter. The Decline of Modernism. Walker, Nicholas, tr. from GER. (Literature & Philosophy Ser.). 220p. 1992. 40.00 (*0-271-00889-X*); pap. 17.95 (*0-271-00890-3*) Pa St U Pr.

— Digital Design: A Practical Course. LC 91-34660. 464p. (C). 1992. reprint ed. lib. bdg. 64.50 (*0-89464-675-3*) Krieger.

— Theory of the Avant-Garde. Shaw, Michael, tr. from GER. LC 83-10549. (Theory & History of Literature Ser.: Vol. 4). 190p. (C). 1974. pap. 13.95 (*0-8166-1068-1*) U of Minn Pr.

Burger, Peter & Burger, Christa. The Institutions of Art. Kruger, Loren, tr. from GER. LC 91-42754. (Modern German Culture & Literature Ser.). xx, 170p. 1992. text 50.00 (*0-8032-1223-2*) U of Nebr Pr.

Burger, Peter C. & Vogel, F. Stephen. Surgical Pathology of the Nervous System & Its Coverings. 2nd ed. LC 81-16250. (Illus.). 755p. reprint ed. pap. 200.00 (*0-8357-6557-1*, 203592200097) Bks Demand.

Burger, Peter C., et al. Surgical Pathology of the Nervous System & Its Coverings. 3rd ed. (Illus.). 737p. 1990. text 187.00 (*0-443-08687-7*) Church.

Burger, Richard L. Chavin: And the Origins of the Andean Civilization. LC 92-80337. (Illus.). 248p. 1995. pap. 29.95 (*0-500-27816-4*, Pub. by Thames Hudson) Norton.

— The Prehistoric Occupation of Chavin de Huantar, Peru. LC 83-1389. (University of California Publications in Anthropology: No. 14). 421p. reprint ed. pap. 130.60 (*0-7837-7473-7*, 204919500010) Bks Demand.

Burger, Robert. Cooling Tower Technology: Maintenance, Upgrading & Rebuilding. 2nd ed. LC 89-45177. 280p. 1989. pap. text 89.00 (*0-88173-089-0*) Fairmont Pr.

Burger, Robert E. The Chess of Bobby Fischer. rev. ed. (Great Chess Ser.). 350p. 1994. pap. 24.95 (*1-886040-12-5*) Hypermodern Pr.

Burger, Robert E., jt. auth. see Bassler, Thomas J.

An Asterisk (*) at the beginning of an entry indicates that the title is appearing for the first time.

Burger, Robert H. Information Policy: A Framework for Evaluation & Policy Research. LC 92-42683. 216p. 1993. pap. 39.50 (*1-56750-018-8*); text 73.25 (*0-89391-890-3*) Ablx Pub.

Burger, Robert H. & Sullivan, Helen F. Eastern Europe: A Bibliographic Guide to English Language Publications, 1986-1993. xiv, 254p. 1995. lib. bdg. 67.50 (*1-56308-047-8*) Libs Unl.

Burger, Robert H., jt. auth. see Sullivan, Helen F.

***Burger, Roger.** Open Heart: A Brief Collection of Wrods, Written from Inside One Man's Heart. 48p. 1999. pap. 7.95 (*0-9675717-0-7*) Open Heart IA.

Burger, Ronna. The Phaedo: A Platonic Labyrinth. LC 99-19016. 310p. (C). 2000. reprint ed. pap. 25.00 (*1-890318-58-2*) St Augustines Pr.

— Speech & Deed in Aristotle's Ethics. (C). (gr. 13). 1999. 35.00 (*0-415-90246-0*) Routledge.

Burger, Ronna, ed. see Benardete, Seth, et al.

Burger, Rudolph E. Color Management Systems. 64p. 32.50 (*0-614-25536-8*, 00PO44477) Print Indus Am.

Burger, Sandra & Knight, A. P. Horse Owner's Field Guide to Toxic Plants. (Illus.). 200p. 1996. pap. text 26.50 (*0-914327-62-3*) Breakthrgh NY.

Burger, Sarah G., et al. Nursing Homes: Getting Good Care There. LC 95-52755. (Working Caregiver Ser.). 176p. 1996. pap. 14.95 (*0-915166-97-6*, Amrcn Source Bks) Impact Pubs CA.

Burger, Thomas. Max Weber's Theory of Concept Formation: History, Laws, & Ideal Types. 2nd ed. LC 74-31592. xx, 293p. 1986. pap. text 23.95 (*0-8223-0736-7*) Duke.

***Burger, Thomas, ed.** Maria Sibylla Merian: The New Book of Flowers. LC 99-62668. (Illus.). 96p. 1999. 25.00 (*3-7913-2080-7*, Pub. by Prestel) te Neues.

Burger, Udo. The Way to Perfect Horsemanship. Bartle, Nicole, tr. 1998. 75.00 (*0-85131-724-3*) Trafalgar.

— The Way to Perfect Horsemanship. LC 98-85575. (Illus.). 1999. 26.00 (*1-57076-129-9*, Trafalgar Sq Pub) Trafalgar.

Burger, Warren E., et al. The American Heritage History of the Bill of Rights, 10 vols. (Illus.). (YA). (gr. 7 up). 1991. lib. bdg. 199.00 (*0-382-24190-8*) Silver Burdett Pr.

Burger, Wilhelm & Bhanu, Bir. Qualitative Motion Planning. LC 92-13870. (International Series in Engineering & Computer Science, VLSI, Computer Architecture, & Digital Screen Processing: Vol. 184). 224p. (C). 1992. text 139.50 (*0-7923-9251-5*) Kluwer Academic.

Burger, William. American Crime & Punishment: The Religious Origins of American Criminology. 176p. (C). 1994. text 24.95 (*1-883218-08-X*); pap. text 18.95 (*1-883218-09-8*) Vande Vere.

— Radar Observer's Handbook. 7th ed. (C). 1987. 125.00 (*0-85174-443-5*) St Mut.

Burgers, G. J. Constructing Messapian Landscapes: Settlement Dynamics, Social Organization & Culture Contact in the Margins of Graeco - Roman Italy. LC 98-139114. (Dutch Monographs on Ancient History & Archaeology: Vol. 18). (Illus.). 342p. 1998. 97.00 (*90-5063-508-3*, Pub. by Gieben) J Benjamins Pubng Co.

Burgers, H. S. Leonardo da Vinci's Psychology of the Twelve Types. Van Rood, A., tr. LC 84-90396. 1984. 10.95 (*0-87212-184-4*) Libra.

Burgers, Herman & Danelius, Hans. The United Nations Convention Against Torture. (C). 1988. lib. bdg. 119.50 (*90-247-3609-9*) Kluwer Academic.

Burgers, Robert L. Power Lines. 1984. pap. 6.55 (*0-89137-317-9*) Quality Pubns.

Burgerson, J. J., ed. see American Institute of Physics Staff.

Burgert, Annette K. Eighteenth Century Emigrants from German Speaking Lands to North America, Vol. 2: The Western Palatinate. LC 83-60349. (Pennsylvania German Folklore Ser.: Vol. 19). (Illus.). xvi, 405p. 1985. 40.00 (*0-317-56482-X*) Penn German Soc.

— Eighteenth Century Emigrants from Langenselbold In Hesse To America / LC 97-94347. xvi, 192 p. 1997. write for info. (*1-882442-15-6*) AKB Pubns.

— Eighteenth Century Emigrants from the Northern Alsace to America. LC 92-74115. 754p. 1992. 49.50 (*1-882442-00-8*, 1416) Picton Pr.

Burgert, Annette K. & Jones, Henry Z., Jr. Westerwald to America: Some Eighteenth Century Immigrants. LC 89-60829. 284p. 1998. 32.50 (*0-929539-32-X*, 1132) Picton Pr.

Burges, H. D., ed. Microbial Control of Pests & Plant Diseases, 1970 to 1980. LC 80-41480. 960p. 1981. text 272.00 (*0-12-143360-9*) Acad Pr.

Burges, H. Denis. Formulation of Microbial Biopesticides: Beneficial Microorganisms, Nematodes, & Seed Treatments. LC 98-70274. (Illus.). 496p. 1998. write for info. (*0-412-62520-2*) Kluwer Academic.

Burgeson, Nancy. The Baby-Sitter's Guide. LC 91-14959. (Survival Guide Ser.). (Illus.). 32p. (J). (gr. 5-9). 1997. pap. 1.95 (*0-8167-2467-9*) Troll Communs.

— The Money Book for Kids. LC 91-15108. (Survival Guide Ser.). (Illus.). 32p. (J). (gr. 5-9). 1991. pap. 1.95 (*0-8167-2465-2*) Troll Communs.

— My Family History. LC 92-3086. (Family Guide Ser.). (Illus.). 32p. (J). (gr. 4-7). 1997. pap. 1.95 (*0-8167-2794-5*) Troll Communs.

Burgess. The Composition Connection. (C). 1995. pap. text 26.76 (*0-395-73875-X*) HM.

— Encyclopedia Sermon Illustrations. 1988. 19.95 (*0-570-08243-9*) Concordia.

— First Certificate Gold Exam Maximiser. 1996. pap. text. write for info. (*0-582-25301-2*, Pub. by Addison-Wesley) Longman.

— Needles Solutions to a Problem. (C). 1995. pap. text 23.96 (*0-395-72312-4*) HM.

— New British History, Founding a Modern State, 1500-1707. 224p. Date not set. text 59.50 (*1-86064-190-3*, Pub. by I B T) St Martin.

— Principles of Systems & Network. pap. text. write for info. (*0-471-82303-1*) Wiley.

— Researching Connection. (C). 1995. pap. text 26.76 (*0-395-73874-1*) HM.

— Small Business Management Fundamentals. 6th ed. 1993. 45.93 (*0-07-061222-6*) McGraw.

— Techniques of Writing. (C). 1995. pap. text 7.56 (*0-395-73787-7*) HM.

— World Civilizations. (C). 1995. pap. text 36.76 (*0-395-72310-8*) HM.

***Burgess & Stewart.** Meet Peter Cottontail. (Illus.). (J). 2000. pap. 1.00 (*0-486-41030-7*) Dover.

— Peter Cottontail Mazes. (Little Activity Bks.). (Illus.). (J). 2000. pap. 1.00 (*0-486-40968-6*) Dover.

Burgess, jt. auth. see Acklam.

Burgess, A. W., jt. auth. see Hazelwood, Robert R.

Burgess, Adam. Divided Europe: The Culture of Moral Superiority. LC 97-20419. 240p. 1997. 54.95 (*0-7453-1262-4*, Pub. by Pluto GBR) Stylus Pub VA.

Burgess, Adam. Divided Europe: The New Domination of the East. 240p. 1997. pap. 19.95 (*0-7453-1257-8*, Pub. by Pluto GBR) Stylus Pub VA.

Burgess, Adrian. The Burgess Book of Lies. LC 99-186247. 464p. 1999. pap. 24.95 (*0-89886-641-3*) Mountaineers.

Burgess, Adrian & Burgess, Alan. Burgess Book of Lies. (Illus.). 480p. 1994. 30.00 (*0-938567-38-1*) Mountaineers.

Burgess, Alan. The Small Woman. large type ed. 486p. 1973. 27.99 (*0-85456-166-8*) Ulverscroft.

— The Small Woman. 1993. reprint ed. 35.95 (*1-56849-184-0*) Buccaneer Bks.

Burgess, Alan, jt. auth. see Burgess, Adrian.

Burgess, Alan, jt. auth. see Gardner, Ava.

Burgess, Allan. From Twisted Ear to Reverent Tear. (Illus.). 96p. (YA). (gr. 7-12). 1983. 5.98 (*0-941518-25-6*) Perry Enterprises.

Burgess, Allan K. Be of Good Cheer. 1997. 11.95 (*1-57008-301-0*) Bookcraft Inc.

— Teach Me to Walk in the Light. 1995. pap. 8.95 (*1-57008-180-8*) Bookcraft Inc.

Burgess, Allan K. & Molgard, Max H. A Child's Book of Mormon Activity Book, 2 bks., Bk. 1. (J). 1987. pap. 3.95 (*0-88494-625-8*) Bookcraft Inc.

— Fun for Family Night, No. 1. 1990. pap. 11.95 (*0-88494-754-8*) Bookcraft Inc.

— My Baptism Activity & Memory Book. (Illus.). 21p. 1997. pap., student ed. 4.95 (*1-57345-250-5*) Deseret Bk.

— Straight Talk about Gospel Principles. 1994. 10.95 (*0-88494-953-2*) Bookcraft Inc.

Burgess, Ann. Psychiatric Nursing in the 21st Century: Preparing for Primary Mental Health Care. LC 96-8408. 736p. (C). 1996. pap. text 49.95 (*0-8385-8087-4*, A8087-7) Appleton & Lange.

***Burgess, Ann Carroll.** Atlanta. (Alive! Guides Ser.). (Illus.). 300p. 2000. pap. 15.95 (*1-55650-911-1*) Hunter NJ.

Burgess, Ann W. Advance Practice of Psychiatric Nursing. LC 97-11817. 544p. 1997. pap. text 47.95 (*0-8385-0181-8*, A-0181-6) Appleton & Lange.

— Rape & Sexual Assault I: A Research Handbook. LC 83-48217. (Reference Library of Social Science). 452p. 1984. text 25.00 (*0-8240-9049-7*) Garland.

Burgess, Ann W., ed. Rape & Sexual Assault. LC 87-23624. 354p. 1988. text 20.00 (*0-8240-8528-0*, SS361) Garland.

Burgess, Ann W. & Hartman, Carol R., eds. Sexual Exploitation of Patients by Health Professionals, 4. LC 86-9318. (Sexual Medicine Ser.: Vol. 4). 207p. 1986. 65.00 (*0-275-92171-9*, C2171, Praeger Pubs) Greenwood.

Burgess, Ann W. & Ressler, Robert K. Sexual Homicide: Patterns & Motives. 1995. pap. 25.00 (*0-02-874063-7*) Free Pr.

Burgess, Ann W., et al. Sexual Assault of Children & Adolescents. 245p. 1978. 16.00 (*0-318-17072-8*) Kempe Nat Ctr.

— Sexual Assault of Children & Adolescents. LC 77-10217. 250p. 1978. 20.95 (*0-669-01892-9*) Lxngtn Bks.

Burgess, Ann W., jt. auth. see Holmstrom, Lynda L.

Burgess, Ann W., jt. ed. see Hazelwood, Robert R.

Burgess, Ann W., ed. see National Research Council, Panel on Violence Again.

***Burgess, Ann Wolbert.** Violence Through a Forensic Lens. 335p. 2000. pap. 29.95 (*1-930745-00-1*) Nursing Spect.

Burgess, Ann Wolbert, jt. auth. see Prentky, R. A.

Burgess, Anna. The Do-It-Yourself Drawing Book. (Illus.). 64p. (Orig.). (J). (gr. 2 up). 1997. pap. 6.95 (*0-8167-3626-X*, Watermill Pr) Troll Communs.

— The Do-It-Yourself First Craft Book. (Illus.). 64p. (Orig.). (J). (gr. 2 up). 1997. pap. 5.95 (*0-8167-3954-4*, Watermill Pr) Troll Communs.

— The Do-It-Yourself Lettering Book. (Illus.). 64p. (J). (gr. 4-7). 1996. pap. 6.95 (*0-8167-3036-9*) Troll Communs.

— Do-It-Yourself Project Book. (J). (gr. 4-7). 1997. pap. 6.95 (*0-8167-3343-0*) Troll Communs.

Burgess, Anthony. Un Agent Qui Vous Veut du Bien. (FRE.). 1973. pap. 10.95 (*0-7859-1746-2*, 2070363945) Fr & Eur.

— Byrne. LC 97-17247. 160p. 1997. 20.00 (*0-7867-0456-X*) Carroll & Graf.

— Byrne. 160p. 1998. pap. 10.95 (*0-7867-0575-2*) Carroll & Graf.

— A Clockwork Orange. 1996. lib. bdg. 31.95 (*1-56849-511-0*) Buccaneer Bks.

— A Clockwork Orange. 2nd ed. 208p. 1995. pap. 11.00 (*0-393-31283-6*, Norton Paperbks) Norton.

Burgess, Anthony. A Clockwork Orange: Burgess,&Anthony. abr. ed. 1996. audio 12.00 (*0-694-51752-6*, CPN 1417) HarperAudio.

Burgess, Anthony. The Complete Enderby: Comprising Inside Mr. Enderby, Enderby Outside, The Clockwork Testament & Enderby's Dark Lady. 640p. 1996. pap. 15.95 (*0-7867-0248-6*) Carroll & Graf.

— A Dead Man in Deptford. 272p. 1995. 21.00 (*0-7867-0192-7*) Carroll & Graf.

— A Dead Man in Deptford. 288p. 1996. pap. 11.95 (*0-7867-0321-0*) Carroll & Graf.

— The Doctor Is Sick. 272p. 1997. reprint ed. pap. 12.00 (*0-393-31602-5*) Norton.

— Earthly Powers. 608p. 1994. pap. 15.95 (*0-7867-0026-2*) Carroll & Graf.

— Ernest Hemingway. LC 98-75021. (Literary Lives Ser.). 1999. reprint ed. pap. 12.95 (*0-500-26017-6*, Pub. by Thames Hudson) Norton.

Burgess, Anthony. Ernest Hemingway & His World. LC 79-302450. 128 p. 1978. 4.50 (*0-500-13062-0*) Thames Hudson.

Burgess, Anthony. Here Comes Everybody. 1988. 10.95 (*0-09-952570-4*) Arrow Bks.

— Honey for the Bears. rev. ed. 256p. 1996. pap. 12.00 (*0-393-31441-3*, Norton Paperbks) Norton.

— The Kingdom of the Wicked. 470p. 1990. pap. 5.95 (*0-671-72955-1*) PB.

— The Long Day Wanes: A Malayan Trilogy. 512p. 1993. pap. 13.95 (*0-393-30943-6*) Norton.

— Nothing Like the Sun: A Magnificent, Bawdy Telling of Shakespeare's Love. 240p. 1996. pap. 12.00 (*0-393-31507-X*) Norton.

— One Hand Clapping. 1999. pap. 11.95 (*0-7867-0631-7*) Carroll & Graf.

— One Man's Chorus: The Uncollected Writings. Forkner, Benjamin, ed. & intro. by. 400p. 1998. 25.00 (*0-7867-0568-X*) Carroll & Graf.

— One Man's Chorus: The Uncollected Writings. 400p. 2000. pap. text 14.95 (*0-7867-0699-6*) Carroll & Graf.

— Piano Players. 22.95 (*0-8488-1332-4*) Amereon Ltd.

— The Pianoplayers. 1987. reprint ed. pap. 4.95 (*0-685-19178-8*, WSP) PB.

— Shakespeare. LC 94-5667. 251p. 1994. pap. 13.95 (*1-56663-056-8*, Elephant Paperbacks) I R Dee.

— Spiritual Refining: The Anatomy of True & False Conversion. 288p. 1996. 27.95 (*0-9641803-5-9*) Internat Outreach.

— Spiritual Refining: The Anatomy of True & False Conversion. 247p. 1998. 27.95 (*1-892838-00-1*) Internat Outreach.

— The Wanting Seed. 288p. 1996. reprint ed. pap. 13.00 (*0-393-31508-8*) Norton.

— You've Had your Time: Being the Second Part of the Confessions of Anthony Burgess. LC 91-161019. xi, 403p. 1990. write for info. (*0-434-09821-3*) Buttrwrth-Heinemann.

Burgess, Anthony, jt. auth. see Maruta, Hiroshi.

Burgess, Anthony, jt. auth. see Peterson, Wallace C.

Burgess, Anthony, ed. see Defoe, Daniel.

Burgess, Anthony, tr. see Rostand, Edmond.

Burgess, Anthony, tr. & intro. see Sophocles.

Burgess, Arene. A Collector's Guide to Souvenir Plates. (Illus.). 224p. 1996. pap. 19.95 (*0-7643-0099-7*) Schiffer.

— 19th Century Wooden Boxes. LC 97-67261. (Schiffer Book for Collectors Ser.). (Illus.). 160p. 1997. pap. 29.95 (*0-7643-0319-8*) Schiffer.

Burgess, B. H. Burgess Genealogy: Kings Co., Nova Scotia Branch of the Descendants of Thomas & Dorothy Burgess. (Illus.). 99p. 1990. reprint ed. pap. 18.50 (*0-8328-1451-2*); reprint ed. lib. bdg. 28.50 (*0-8328-1450-4*) Higginson Bk Co.

Burgess, Barbara, ed. see Green, John L., Jr.

Burgess, Barbara Hood. Fred Field. (J). 1995. 9.09 (*0-606-07541-0*) Turtleback.

Burgess, Bernard H. What's Holding You Back? LC 98-90352. (Illus.). vi, 240p. 1998. pap. 14.95 (*0-9664764-0-9*) B H Burgess.

Burgess, Beverly. Personal Evangelism Training, Vol. 2. 152p. 1991. pap., student ed. 11.99 (*0-8341-1410-0*) Beacon Hill.

Burgess, Beverly. You Can Be a Witnessing Christian. (Christian Living Ser.). 56p. 1990. pap. 3.50 (*0-8341-1375-9*) Beacon Hill.

Burgess, Beverly C. Chicken Little Conquers Fear. LC 88-113780. 28p. (Orig.). (J). (gr. 1-3). 1987. pap. 4.98 (*0-89274-414-6*, HH-414) Harrison Hse.

Burgess, Beverly C. Daniel & the Lion's Den. (Men of God Ser.). (Illus.). 32p. (Orig.). (J). 1992. pap. 4.98 (*1-879470-03-9*) Burgess Pub.

— God Are You Really Real? (Illus.). 30p. (Orig.). (J). (gr. 1-3). 1985. pap. 2.49 (*0-89274-309-3*, HH-309) Harrison Hse.

— God Has All the Answers. (Illus.). 36p. (Orig.). (J). (ps-5). 2.49 (*1-879470-05-5*) Burgess Pub.

— God Is My Best Friend. (Illus.). 32p. (Orig.). (J). (gr. 1-3). 1986. pap. 2.49 (*0-89274-293-3*, HH-293) Harrison Hse.

— God Is Never Too Busy to Listen. (Illus.). 28p. (Orig.). (J). (gr. 1-3). 1987. pap. 2.49 (*0-89274-457-X*, HH-457) Harrison Hse.

— God Loves My Teddy Bear Too! (Illus.). 32p. (Orig.). (J). (ps-5). 2.49 (*1-879470-04-7*) Burgess Pub.

— How Can I Please You, God? (Illus.). 32p. (J). (ps-5). 1991. reprint ed. 4.98 (*1-879470-00-4*) Burgess Pub.

— Is Easter Just for Bunnies? LC 93-125068. (Illus.). 30p. (Orig.). (J). (ps-k). 1985. pap. 2.49 (*0-89274-310-7*) Harrison Hse.

— Jack & the Beanstalk. 28p. (J). (gr. k-6). 1985. pap. 4.98 (*0-89274-384-0*, HH-384) Harrison Hse.

Burgess, Beverly C. The Little Red Hen. LC 86-140407. (Illus.). 32p. (J). (gr. 1-3). 1984. pap. 4.98 (*0-89274-312-3*, HH-312) Harrison Hse.

— Little Red Riding Hood. LC 86-140386. (Illus.). 32p. (Orig.). (J). (gr. 1-3). 1983. pap. 4.98 (*0-89274-289-5*, HH-289) Harrison Hse.

Burgess, Beverly C. Personal Evangelism Training, Vol. 1. 168p. 1985. pap., student ed. 10.99 (*0-8341-1058-X*) Beacon Hill.

— Prayers for Pre-Schoolers. (Illus.). (Orig.). (J). (ps-2). 1991. pap. 4.98 (*1-879470-02-0*) Burgess Pub.

— Seedtime Stories: Bedtime Stories with Poems & Devotionals. (Illus.). (Orig.). (J). (gr. 2-6). 1991. pap. 4.98 (*1-879470-01-2*) Burgess Pub.

— Shadrach, Meshach, & Abednego. (Men of God Ser.). (Illus.). 32p. (Orig.). (J). 1996. 4.98 (*1-879470-06-3*) Burgess Pub.

— Three Bears in the Ministry. 32p. (Orig.). (J). (ps). 1982. pap. 4.98 (*0-89274-252-6*) Harrison Hse.

— Three Little Pigs. (Illus.). 30p. (Orig.). 1982. pap. 4.98 (*0-89274-283-6*) Harrison Hse.

Burgess, Bob. Diving off the Beaten Track: Best of the Caribbean & Bahamas. LC 93-29753. (Illus.). 128p. 1995. pap. 18.95 (*1-881652-03-3*) Aqua Quest.

Burgess, C. & Jones, D. G., eds. Spectrophotometry, Luminescence & Colour; Science & Compliance: Papers Presented at the 2nd Joint Meeting of the UV Spectrometry Group of the U. K. & the Council for Optical Radiation Measurements of the U. S. A., Ridge, NH, U. S. A., 20-23 June, 1994. LC 95-12166. (Analytical Spectroscopy Library: Vol. 6). 448p. 1995. 272.50 (*0-444-81718-2*) Elsevier.

Burgess, C. & Knowles, A. Standards in Absorption Spectrometry. (Techniques in Visible & Ultraviolet Spectrometry Ser.). (C). 1981. text 29.95 (*0-412-22470-4*, 2230) Chapman & Hall.

Burgess, C. F., ed. see Gay, John.

***Burgess, C. P. & Myers, R. C., eds.** General Relativity & Relativistic Astrophysics: Eighth Canadian Conference. (AIP Conference Proceedings Ser.: Vol. 493). (Illus.). 343p. 1999. 100.00 (*1-56396-905-X*, Pub. by Am Inst Physics) Spr-Verlag.

***Burgess, Chris.** English Skills: Creative Writing Module. (J). (gr. 4-8). 1999. pap. 35.00 (*0-7217-0607-X*, Pub. by Schofield) St Mut.

— English Skills: Spelling Module. (J). (gr. 4-8). 1999. pap. 35.00 (*0-7217-0605-3*, Pub. by Schofield) St Mut.

— English Skills: Vocabulary Module. (J). (gr. 4-8). 1999. pap. 35.00 (*0-7217-0606-1*, Pub. by Schofield) St Mut.

— English Skills: Written Communication Module. (J). (gr. 4-8). 1999. pap. 35.00 (*0-7217-0603-7*, Pub. by Schofield) St Mut.

— Study Reading Modules: (A) Antelope. (J). 1999. pap. 19.95 (*0-7217-0504-9*, Pub. by Schofield) St Mut.

— Study Reading Modules: (B) Bear. (J). 1999. pap. 19.95 (*0-7217-0505-7*, Pub. by Schofield) St Mut.

— Study Reading Modules: (C) Crocodile. (J). 1999. pap. 19.95 (*0-7217-0506-5*, Pub. by Schofield) St Mut.

— Study Reading Modules: (D) Dolphin. (J). 1999. pap. 19.95 (*0-7217-0507-3*, Pub. by Schofield) St Mut.

— Study Reading Modules: (E) Elephant. (J). 1999. pap. 19.95 (*0-7217-0508-1*, Pub. by Schofield) St Mut.

— Study Reading Modules: (F) Frog. (J). 1999. pap. 19.95 (*0-7217-0509-X*, Pub. by Schofield) St Mut.

— Study Reading Modules: (G) Goldfinch. (J). 1999. pap. 19.95 (*0-7217-0510-3*, Pub. by Schofield) St Mut.

— Study Reading Modules: (H) Horse. (J). 1999. pap. 19.95 (*0-7217-0511-1*, Pub. by Schofield) St Mut.

— Study Reading Modules: (I) Ibis. (J). 1999. pap. 19.95 (*0-7217-0512-X*, Pub. by Schofield) St Mut.

— Study Reading Modules: (J) Jaguar. (J). 1999. pap. 19.95 (*0-7217-0513-8*, Pub. by Schofield) St Mut.

— Study Reading Modules: (K) Kangaroo. (J). 1999. pap. 19.95 (*0-7217-0514-6*, Pub. by Schofield) St Mut.

— Study Reading Modules: (L) Lion. (J). 1999. pap. 19.95 (*0-7217-0498-0*, Pub. by Schofield) St Mut.

— Study Reading Modules: (M) Mole. (J). 1999. pap. 19.95 (*0-7217-0499-9*, Pub. by Schofield) St Mut.

— Study Reading Modules: (N) Nightingale. (J). 1999. pap. 19.95 (*0-7217-0500-6*, Pub. by Schofield) St Mut.

— Study Reading Modules: Teacher's Book. 1999. pap., teacher ed. 30.00 (*0-7217-0515-4*, Pub. by Schofield) St Mut.

Burgess, Clifford S., et al, eds. Grammatical Relations: Theoretical Approaches to Empirical Questions. 485p. 1996. 54.95 (*1-57586-003-1*); pap. 20.95 (*1-57586-002-3*) CSLI.

***Burgess, Colin.** Teacher in Space: Christa McAuliffe & the Challenger Legacy. LC 99-56385. (Illus.). 144p. 2000. pap. 24.95 (*0-8032-6182-9*, Bison Books) U of Nebr Pr.

Burgess, Colin, et al. Standards & Best Practice in Absorption Spectrometry. LC 98-53003. 1999. 115.00 (*0-632-05313-5*) Blackwell Sci.

Burgess, Colin, jt. auth. see Champ, Jack.

***Burgess, Connie, ed.** The Children's Way to Metrowest: A Guide to Family Fun in the 'Burbs. (Illus.). 387p. 2000. 15.95 (*0-9679651-0-1*) Wayland Schl.

Burgess, Craig E., jt. auth. see Edgar, Danny K.

Burgess, D. R., et al. Thermochemical & Chemical Kinetic Data for Fluorinated Hydrocarbons. (Illus.). 174p. (C). 1997. reprint ed. pap. text 45.00 (*0-7881-3783-2*) DIANE Pub.

Burgess, Dana. The Complete Idiot's Guide to Classical Mythology. 352p. 1998. pap. text 16.95 (*0-02-862385-1*) Macmillan Gen Ref.

Burgess, David. Total Quality Counseling: A Comprehensive Manual for Elementary & Middle School Counselors. 151p. (Orig.). 1991. pap., teacher ed. 22.95 (*1-884063-44-6*) Mar Co Prods.

***Burgess, David C., et al.** Drafting Business Contracts: Principles, Techniques & Forms - 11/98 Update. Brown, Wendy L., ed. LC 94-79264. 364p. 1998. ring bd. 52.00 (*0-7626-0273-2*, BU-30802) Cont Ed Bar-CA.

Burgess, David F. Encyclopedia of Sermon Illustrations. 248p. 1988. 19.95 (*0-570-04243-7*, 15-2196) Concordia.

Burgess, David R. & Corbett, Gordon. The Teaching Tank Discovery Book. (Illus.). 102p. (J). (gr. k up). 1996. teacher ed., spiral bd. 21.95 (*0-9633907-1-6*) Captivation.

Burgess, David R. & Reinbold, Paul J. The Teaching Tank Discovery Book. (Illus.). 112p. (C). 1992. spiral bd., lab manual ed. 21.95 (*0-9633907-0-8*) Captivation.

Burgess, David R., et al. The Teaching Tank Discovery Book, Vol. 3. (Illus.). 108p. teacher ed. 23.95 (*0-9633907-2-4*) Captivation.

***Burgess, David S.** Fighting for Social Justice: The Life Story of David S. Burgess. (Illus.). 304p. 2001. 34.95 (*0-8143-2899-7*) Wayne St U Pr.

Burgess, Donald. A Horse of White Clouds: Poems from Lusophone Africa. LC 89-32437. (Monographs in International Studies, Africa: No. 55). 213p. 1989. reprint ed. pap. 66.10 (*0-7837-9598-X*, 206035500005) Bks Demand.

Burgess, Donald, jt. auth. see Henchey, Norman.

Burgess, Doris. Imperialism in the 1990S. Bush, Ray, ed. (C). 1996. text 59.95 (*0-7453-0376-5*); pap. text 18.95 (*0-7453-0377-3*) Westview.

Burgess, Douglas K., jt. auth. see McElrath, Joseph R.

Burgess-Durso, Lori, jt. auth. see Durso, Joseph M.

Burgess, Dwight E. My Old Cowboy Boots. LC 92-81560. (Illus.). 83p. 1992. pap. 11.95 (*1-879984-00-8*) Premier KS.

— Strong, Proud, & above All, Free: A Collection of Cowboy Poetry. unabridged ed. LC 96-17594. (Illus.). 80p. (J). 1996. pap. 11.95 (*1-879984-25-3*) Premier KS.

Burgess, Ebenezer. Burgess Genealogy Memorial of the Family of Thomas & Dorothy Burgess, Who Were Settled at Sandwich, in the Plymouth Colony in 1637. (Illus.). 212p. 1989. reprint ed. pap. 26.50 (*0-8328-0345-6*); reprint ed. lib. bdg. 36.50 (*0-8328-0344-8*) Higginson Bk Co.

— Surya-Siddhanta: A Text Book of Hindu Astronomy (1858) 364p. 1998. reprint ed. pap. 24.95 (*0-7661-0712-4*) Kessinger Pub.

Burgess, Edward E. Christ, the Crown of the Torah. 220p. 1986. pap. 8.95 (*0-310-41621-3*, 9942P) Zondervan.

Burgess, Eric. By Jupiter: Odysseys to a Giant. LC 82-4139. (Illus.). 192p. 1982. text 46.50 (*0-231-05176-X*) Col U Pr.

— Outpost on Apollo's Moon. (Illus.). 288p. (C). 1993. 44.00 (*0-231-07666-5*) Col U Pr.

— To the Red Planet. LC 78-6911. (Illus.). 181p. 1978. text 54.00 (*0-231-04392-9*) Col U Pr.

Burgess, Eric, ed. Fourth Western Regional AAS Meeting, Aug. 1-3, 1961, San Francisco CA. LC 57-43769. (Advances in the Astronautical Sciences Ser.: Vol. 9). 910p. 1963. 45.00 (*0-87703-010-3*, Am Astronaut Soc) Univelt Inc.

— Interplanetary Missions, 9th Annual AAS Meeting, Jan. 15-17, 1963, Los Angeles, CA. LC 57-43769. (Advances in the Astronautical Sciences Ser.: Vol. 13). 690p. 1963. 45.00 (*0-87703-014-6*, Am Astronaut Soc) Univelt Inc.

Burgess, Eric, jt. auth. see Murray, Bruce C.

Burgess, Eric, jt. ed. see Jacobs, Horace.

Burgess, Ernest M. & Rappoport, Albert. Physical Fitness: A Guide for Individuals with Lower Limb Loss. (Illus.). 245p. (Orig.). (C). 1993. pap. text 40.00 (*1-56806-432-2*) DIANE Pub.

Burgess, Ernest W. Personality & the Social Group. 230p. 1977. 18.95 (*0-8369-0066-9*) Ayer.

Burgess, Ernest W., ed. The Urban Community. LC 71-175038. (BCL Ser. I). reprint ed. 39.50 (*0-404-01235-3*) AMS Pr.

Burgess, Ernest W. & Bogue, Donald J., eds. Urban Sociology. LC 67-5821. (Phoenix Bks.). (Illus.). 335p. reprint ed. pap. 103.90 (*0-608-09273-8*, 205414700004); reprint ed. pap. 103.90 (*0-608-20618-0*, 205458600003) Bks Demand.

Burgess, Ernest W., jt. auth. see Park, Robert Ezra.

Burgess, Eugene W. & Harbison, Frederick H. Casa Grace in Peru: Second Case Study in an NPA Series on United States Business Performance Abroad. Bruchey, Stuart, ed. LC 80-557. (Multinational Corporations Ser.). (Illus.). 1981. reprint ed. lib. bdg. 19.95 (*0-405-13353-7*) Ayer.

***Burgess, Francis.** Organ Fifty Years Hence. 176p. 2000. reprint ed. lib. bdg. 59.00 (*0-7812-9314-6*) Rprt Serv.

Burgess, Frank. No Small Change: 100 Years of Sutton High Street. 1985. pap. 35.00 (*0-907335-09-8*, Pub. by Sutton Libs & Arts) St Mut.

— Now & Then: More Views of Sutton Old & New: A Photographic Record & Commentary on Sutton Away from the High Street. (C). 1985. pap. 25.00 (*0-907335-13-6*, Pub. by Sutton Libs & Arts) St Mut.

Burgess, Frank G. Are You a Bromide? LC 75-96875. reprint ed. lib. bdg. 17.50 (*0-8398-0180-7*) Irvington.

Burgess, Frederick. Tombstone Lettering on Slate. (Illus.). 1991. reprint ed. pap. 6.50 (*0-930194-20-9*) Ctr Thanatology.

Burgess, G., ed. see Wogan-Browne, Jocelyn.

***Burgess, Gail.** 911 Urgent Dating Solutions. 210p. 1999. pap. 14.98 (*0-9668986-0-5*) Any Key Pr.

Burgess, Gail, ed. see Hanzarotta, Suzette.

Burgess, Gelett. Burgess Unabridged: A New Dictionary of Words You Have Always Needed. LC 83-46013. (Classics of Modern American Humor Ser.). (Illus.). reprint ed. 27.50 (*0-404-19928-3*) AMS Pr.

— Goops & How to Be Them: A Manual of Manners for Polite Infants. LC 68-55630. (Illus.). 88p. (J). (ps-4). 1968. reprint ed. pap. 3.95 (*0-486-22233-0*) Dover.

— The Little Father. (Sunburst Ser.). (Illus.). 32p. (J). (ps-3). 1987. pap. 3.95 (*0-374-44486-2*) FS&G.

— The Master of Mysteries: Problems Solved by Astro, Seer of Secrets & His Love Affair with Valeska Wynne, His Assistant. LC 75-32736. (Literature of Mystery & Detection Ser.). (Illus.). 1976. reprint ed. 40.95 (*0-405-07865-X*) Ayer.

— More Goops & How Not to Be Them: A Manual of Manners for Impolite Infants. LC 68-55531. (Illus.). 88p. (J). (ps-4). 1968. reprint ed. pap. 3.95 (*0-486-22234-9*) Dover.

— Purple Cow--Handset Type. 1987. pap. 7.95 (*0-89979-039-9*) British Am Bks.

— Romance of the Commonplace. LC 68-57308. (Essay Index Reprint Ser.). 1977. 21.95 (*0-8369-0103-7*) Ayer.

Burgess, Gelett & Wells, Carolyn. Purple Cow & Its Parodies. 1987. pap. 4.95 (*0-89979-038-0*) British Am Bks.

Burgess, George. Success Without Success. 203p. 1995. mass mkt. 5.99 (*0-88368-369-5*) Whitaker Hse.

Burgess, George H., et al. Centennial History of the Pennsylvania Railroad Company, 1846-1946. LC 75-41750. (Companies & Men: Business Enterprises in America Ser.). (Illus.). 1976. reprint ed. 67.95 (*0-405-08067-0*) Ayer.

Burgess, Giles H., Jr. The Economics of Regulation & Antitrust. LC 94-19446. (Series in Economics). 484p. (C). 1997. 94.00 (*0-06-501099-X*) Addson-Wesley Educ.

Burgess, Giles H., Jr., ed. Antitrust & Regulation. (International Library of Critical Writings in Business History: Vol. 4). 544p. 1991. 210.00 (*1-85278-451-2*) E Elgar.

Burgess, Glenn. Absolute Monarchy & the Stuart Constitution. LC 95-20647. 229p. 1996. 37.00 (*0-300-06532-9*) Yale U Pr.

— The Politics of the Ancient Constitution: An Introduction to English Political Thought, 1600-1642. LC 92-17255. 256p. (C). 1993. 50.00 (*0-271-00903-9*); pap. 18.95 (*0-271-00926-8*) Pa St U Pr.

***Burgess, Gloria J.** Journey of the Rose. 72p. 1998. 14.00 (*1-892864-01-0*) Jazz Media.

Burgess, Glyn S. The Old French Narrative Lay: An Analytical Bibliography. 148p. (C). 1997. reprint ed. 60.00 (*0-85991-478-X*) Boydell & Brewer.

Burgess, Glyn S., et al, eds. Spirit of the Court: Selected Proceedings of the Congress of the International Courtly Literature Society, Toronto 1983. 416p. 1985. 110.00 (*0-85991-176-4*) Boydell & Brewer.

Burgess, Glyn S., tr. Two Medieval Outlaws: The Romances of Eustace the Monk & Fouke Fitz Waryn. LC 96-45609. 224p. 1997. 60.00 (*0-85991-438-0*, DS Brewer) Boydell & Brewer.

Burgess, Glyn S., tr. from FRE. The Song of Roland. LC 90-183545. (Classics Ser.). 224p. 1990. pap. 8.95 (*0-14-044532-3*, Penguin Classics) Viking Penguin.

Burgess, Glyn S. & Busby, Keith, trs. The Lasi of Marie de France. (Penguin Classics Ser.). 164p. 1986. pap. 10.95 (*0-14-044759-8*, Penguin Bks) Viking Penguin.

Burgess, Gordon J. A Computer-Assisted Analysis of Goethe's "Die Wahlverwandtschaften" The Enigma of Elective Affinities. LC 99-21195. (Studies in German Language & Literature: Vol. 23). 278p. 1999. text 89.95 (*0-7734-8032-3*) E Mellen.

— Die Wahrheit Mit Lachendem Munde: Comedy & Humour in the Novels of Christian Weise. Saphr, Blake L., ed. (Berner Beitraege zur Barockgermanistik Ser.: Vol. 8). (Illus.). 240p. 1990. pap. 23.00 (*3-261-04187-0*) P Lang Pubng.

Burgess, Graham. Chess Highlights of the 20th Century. 208p. 1999. bds. 27.50 (*1-901983-21-8*, Pub. by Gambit) BHB Intl.

— The Complete Alekhine. 256p. 1995. pap. 22.95 (*0-8050-2425-5*, Pub. by Batsford Chess) H Holt & Co.

***Burgess, Graham.** The Gambit Guide to the Torre Attack: An Easy to Learn Opening with Real Practical Sting. (Illus.). 192p. 2000. pap. 22.95 (*1-901983-17-X*, Pub. by Gambit) BHB Intl.

Burgess, Graham. Gambits. 1995. pap. 12.00 (*0-8050-3898-1*) H Holt & Co.

— King's Indian for the Attacking Player. 176p. 1995. pap. 19.95 (*0-8050-2936-2*, Pub. by Batsford Chess) H Holt & Co.

***Burgess, Graham.** King's Indian for the Attacking Player: Popular. (Chess Bks.). (Illus.). 1999. pap. text 17.95 (*0-7134-8566-3*) B T B.

Burgess, Graham. The Mammoth Book of Chess. LC 97-12079. (Mammoth Book Ser.). (Illus.). 5454p. 1997. pap. 11.95 (*0-7867-0431-4*) Carroll & Graf.

***Burgess, Graham.** The Mammoth Book of Chess: Featuring Internet & Computer Games. (Illus.). 512p. 2000. pap. 11.95 (*0-7867-0725-9*, Pub. by Carroll & Graf) Publishers Group.

Burgess, Graham. Queen's Gambit for the Attacking Player. 1995. pap. 19.95 (*0-8050-3581-8*, Pub. by Batsford Chess) H Holt & Co.

— Winning with the Smith Morra-Gambit. (Batsford Chess Library). 1995. pap. 19.95 (*0-8050-3574-5*, Pub. by Batsford Chess) H Holt & Co.

Burgess, Graham, et al. The Mammoth Book of the World's Greatest Chess Games. (Mammoth Book Ser.). (Illus.). 512p. 1998. pap. 10.95 (*0-7867-0587-6*) Carroll & Graf.

Burgess, Graham, jt. auth. see Nunn, John.

Burgess, Guy M., jt. auth. see Burgess, Heidi.

Burgess, Harl Donald & Johnston, Elbert Felton. The Burgess Family. viii, 198p. 1997. 30.00 (*0-944619-50-9*) Gregath Pub Co.

Burgess, Harold, ed. see Wood, Laurence W.

Burgess, Harold W., ed. see Kelsey, Morton T.

Burgess, Heidi & Burgess, Guy M. Encyclopedia of Conflict Resolution. LC 97-8637. 356p. 1997. lib. bdg. 75.00 (*0-87436-839-1*, FN-1646) ABC-CLIO.

Burgess, Hilary. Enquiry & Action: Introducing Problem-Led Learning for Social Work Education. 152p. (Orig.). 1992. pap. text 25.00 (*1-871177-29-4*, Pub. by Whiting & Birch) Paul & Co Pubs.

Burgess, Hovey. Circus Techniques: Juggling, Equilibristics, Vaulting. rev. ed. LC 89-28751. (Illus.). 162p. 1990. pap. 19.95 (*0-917643-06-2*) B Dube.

Burgess, Hugh. Dwell Within These Distances, Vol. 10. 50p. 1982. pap. 3.95 (*0-932616-08-9*) Brick Hse Bks.

Burgess, J. Ions in Solution: Basic Principles of Chemical Interactions. 200p. 1988. pap. text 41.95 (*0-470-21059-1*) P-H.

***Burgess, J. & Tobe, M. L.** Inorganic Reaction Mechanisms. 688p. 2000. pap. text 66.00 (*0-582-23677-0*) Pearson Educ.

Burgess-Jackson, Keith. Rape: A Philosophical Investigation. (Applied Legal Philosophy Ser.). (Illus.). 256p. 1996. text 87.95 (*1-85521-485-7*, Pub. by Dartmth Pub) Ashgate Pub Co.

Burgess-Jackson, Keith, ed. A Most Detestable Crime: New Philosophical Essays on Rape. LC 98-26835. 328p. 1999. text 45.00 (*0-19-512075-2*) OUP.

Burgess-Jackson, Keith, jt. auth. see Copi, Irving.

Burgess-Jackson, Keith, jt. auth. see Copi, Irving M.

Burgess, James, ed. see Grunwedel, Albert.

Burgess, James M. Chronicles of St. Mark's Parish, Santee Circuit, & Williamsburg Township, South Carolina, 1731-1885. 108p. 1991. reprint ed. pap. 12.50 (*0-89308-458-1*, SC 92) Southern Hist Pr.

Burgess, Jan. Food & Digestion. (How Our Bodies Work Ser.). (Illus.). 48p. (J). (gr. 5-8). 1988. lib. bdg. 12.95 (*0-382-09704-1*) Silver Burdett Pr.

— Heart & Blood. (How Our Bodies Work Ser.). (Illus.). 48p. (J). (gr. 5-8). 1988. lib. bdg. 12.95 (*0-382-09700-9*) Silver Burdett Pr.

— Psychic Sleuths: How Psychic Information Is Used to Solve Crimes. LC 93-40593. (J). 1994. pap. 5.95 (*0-382-24741-8*, New Dscvry Bks) Silver Burdett Pr.

Burgess, Jay. The Basics of Java Animation. (Management Briefings Ser.). 39p. 1996. pap. 85.00 (*1-884842-64-X*, QA76) SIGS Bks & Multimedia.

Burgess, Jeff. Quattro Pro Quick Reference Guide. (DDC Quick Reference Guides Ser.). 1990. spiral bd. 12.00 (*1-56243-001-7*, Q-17) DDC Pub.

Burgess, Jim, jt. auth. see Berg, Jeff.

Burgess, Joe. Basic Air Conditioning. Gorham, Kelly, ed. (Illus.). 24p. 1994. student ed. 7.00 (*0-8064-0005-6*, A42) Bergwall.

Burgess, Joe H., ed. see Gadski, Mary Ellen.

Burgess, John. Black Gospel, White Church. 128p. 1985. 7.95 (*0-8164-2380-6*) Harper SF.

— Metal Ions in Solutions. (Chemical Science Ser.). 481p. 1980. pap. text 39.95 (*0-470-26987-1*) P-H.

— The Mob: Organized Crime in America. 70p. (Orig.). (YA). (gr. 7-12). 1996. pap. 6.95 (*1-57515-094-8*) PPI Pubng.

— Psychic & Spirit Phenomena: Believers & Skeptics. 94p. (YA). (gr. 7-12). 1991. pap. 6.95 (*1-57515-008-5*) PPI Pubng.

Burgess, John, et al. Introduction to Macroeconomics. LC 98-209029. 352p. 1998. 72.95 (*0-7329-3716-7*, Pub. by Macmill Educ); pap. 36.95 (*0-7329-3717-5*, Pub. by Macmill Educ) Paul & Co Pubs.

Burgess, John, jt. auth. see Bartecki, Adam.

Burgess, John, jt. ed. see Kniest, Paul.

Burgess, John A. Design Assurance for Engineers & Managers: A Guide for Engineers. (Mechanical Engineering Ser.: Vol. 35). (Illus.). 320p. 1984. text 95.00 (*0-8247-7258-X*) Dekker.

Burgess, John F. Designing for Humans: The Human Factor in Engineering. (Illus.). 450p. 1987. text 39.95 (*0-89433-278-3*) Petrocelli.

Burgess, John F., jt. auth. see Steinhoff, Daniel.

Burgess, John H. Christian Pagan: A Naturalistic Survey of Christian History. (Illus.). 1968. 7.00 (*0-912084-04-9*) Mimir.

— Human Factors in Built Environments. LC 81-184028. 137p. (C). 1982. 30.00 (*0-915250-38-1*) Environ Design.

— System Design Approaches to Public Services. LC 76-737. (Illus.). 300p. 1978. 38.50 (*0-8386-1892-8*) Fairleigh Dickinson.

Burgess, John P. The East German Church & the End of Communism: Essays on Religion, Democratization & Christian Social Ethics. LC 96-21158. 200p. (C). 1997. text 42.00 (*0-19-511098-6*) OUP.

— In Whose Image? Science, Faith, & the New Genetics. LC 98-11934. 168p. 1998. pap. 15.95 (*0-664-50025-0*) Geneva Press.

— Why Scripture Matters: Reading the Bible in a Time of Church Crisis. LC 98-17301. 208p. 1998. pap. 20.00 (*0-664-25708-9*) Westminster John Knox.

Burgess, John P. & Rosen, Gideon. A Subject with No Object: Strategies for Nominalistic Interpretation of Mathematics. (Illus.). 272p. 1997. text 48.00 (*0-19-823615-8*) OUP.

***Burgess, John P. & Rosen, Gideon.** A Subject with No Object: Strategies for Nominalistic Interpretation of Mathematics. (Illus.). 272p. 2000. pap. text 19.95 (*0-19-825012-6*) OUP.

Burgess, John P., jt. auth. see Boolos, George.

Burgess, John P., jt. auth. see Spence, Robert.

Burgess, John S. Guilds of Peking. LC 77-127446. (Columbia Studies in the Social Sciences: No. 308). 270 p. 1970. reprint ed. 27.50 (*0-404-51308-5*) AMS Pr.

***Burgess, John W.** Civil War & the Constitution, 1859-1865. (American History Ser.). 2000. pap. 34.95 (*1-58798-014-2*) Beard Bks.

Burgess, John W. The Foundations of Political Science. rev. ed. LC 93-32627. 172p. (C). 1993. pap. 21.95 (*1-56000-711-7*) Transaction Pubs.

— The Middle Period, 1817-1858. LC 79-37301. (Black Heritage Library Collection). 1977. reprint ed. 41.95 (*0-8369-8938-4*) Ayer.

***Burgess, John W.** Political Science & Comparative Constitutional Law. 2000. reprint ed. write for info. (*1-57588-640-5*) W S Hein.

Burgess, John W. Recent Changes in American Constitutional Theory. LC 76-172206. (Right Wing Individualist Tradition in America Ser.). 1972. reprint ed. 19.95 (*0-405-00417-6*) Ayer.

— Reconstruction & the Constitution. LC 72-457. reprint ed. 29.50 (*0-404-00010-X*) AMS Pr.

— Reminiscences of an American Scholar. LC 34-2217. reprint ed. 20.00 (*0-404-01236-1*) AMS Pr.

— The Sanctity of Law: In What Does It Consist? LC 89-45852. 360p. 1989. reprint ed. 85.00 (*0-912004-72-X*) Gaunt.

Burgess, John W. The Sanctity of Law: In What Does It Consist? 360p. 1996. reprint ed. 90.00 (*1-56169-224-7*) Gaunt.

Burgess, Joseph A. & Gros, Jeffrey. Growing Consensus: Church Dialogues in the United States 1962-1991. LC 93-27753. (Ecumenical Documents Ser.: No. V). 704p. (Orig.). 1995. pap. 34.95 (*0-8091-3382-2*) Paulist Pr.

Burgess, Joseph A. & Gros, Jeffrey, eds. Building Unity: Ecumenical Dialogues with Roman Catholic Participation in the U. S. A. LC 88-28890. (Ecumenical Documents Ser.). 1989. pap. 14.95 (*0-8091-3040-8*) Paulist Pr.

Burgess, Karen E. Home Is Where the Dog Is: Art in the Back Yard. LC 95-45982. (Folk Art & Artists Ser.). (Illus.). 72p. (C). 1996. 32.50 (*0-87805-879-6*); pap. 16.95 (*0-87805-880-X*) U Pr of Miss.

Burgess, Katrina, jt. ed. see Lowenthal, Abraham F.

***Burgess, Kawika.** Jonah Kuhio Kalanianayole. (Illus.). 37p. (YA). (gr. 10-12). 1999. write for info. (*0-9665331-1-9*) UHH Hale Kuamoo.

Burgess, Kawika, ed. see Kai, Mahele Kumuwaiwai.

Burgess, Kenneth F. Burgess: Colonists of New England & Nova Scotia. (Illus.). 134p. 1991. reprint ed. pap. 24.00 (*0-8328-2214-0*); reprint ed. lib. bdg. 34.00 (*0-8328-2213-2*) Higginson Bk Co.

Burgess, Kevin. Solid-Phase Organic Synthesis. LC 99-30796. 277p. 1999. 69.95 (*0-471-31825-6*) Wiley.

Burgess, Kevin L., jt. auth. see Passino, Kevin M.

Burgess, Kim, jt. auth. see Niezen, Ronald.

Burgess, L. B. This Side of the Stars. 1950. 15.95 (*0-87505-356-4*) Borden.

Burgess, Larry E. Daniel Smiley of Mohonk: A Naturalist's Life. LC 96-43727. (Illus.). 130p. 1996. pap. 14.50 (*0-935796-82-7*, 82) Purple Mnt Pr.

— Mohonk: Its People & Spirit: A History of One Hundred Years of Growth & Service. rev. ed. LC 80-15087. (Illus.). 123p. 1993. pap. 15.00 (*0-935796-42-8*) Purple Mnt Pr.

Burgess, Larry E., jt. auth. see Sandos, James A.

Burgess, Lauren C. An Uncommon Soldier: The Civil War Letters of Sarah Rosetta Wakeman, Alias Private Lyons Wakeman, 153rd Regiment, New York State Volunteers. LC 94-76283. (Illus.). 120p. 1994. 25.00 (*0-9634895-1-8*) Minerva Ctr.

Burgess, Lauren C., ed. see Wakeman, Sarah.

Burgess, Laurie. Excellence for Communicators. 150p. (C). 1990. pap. 60.00 (*0-947173-06-4*, Pub. by Boolarong Pubns) St Mut.

Burgess, Lawrence P. & Goode, Richard L. Reanimation of the Paralyzed Face. Steirnberg, Charles M., ed. (American Academy of Facial Plastic & Reconstructive Surgery (AAFPRS) Ser.: Vol. 13). (Illus.). 72p. 1994. 85.00 (*0-86577-519-2*) Thieme Med Pubs.

***Burgess-Lent, Susan.** In the Borderlands. 2000. pap. 18.00 (*0-7388-2159-4*) Xlibris Corp.

Burgess, Leonard R. Top Executive Pay Package. LC 63-8414. 1963. 19.95 (*0-02-904990-3*) Free Pr.

Burgess, Lesley, jt. auth. see Addison, Nicholas.

Burgess, Linda. Between Friends. LC 94-230531. 184p. 1994. pap. 24.95 (*0-908569-88-2*, Pub. by Univ Otago Pr) Intl Spec Bk.

— On the Grapevine. LC 96-223431. 200p. 1996. pap. 24.95 (*1-877133-12-4*) Intl Spec Bk.

— Remember Me: Short Stories. LC 98-107004. 136p. 1997. pap. 21.95 (*1-877133-35-3*, Pub. by Univ Otago Pr) Intl Spec Bk.

Burgess, Lynn. Family Reunion. (Illus.). 16p. (J). (ps-k). 1998. pap. 5.95 (*0-9655442-7-3*) Busn Word.

Burgess, Lynn H., jt. auth. see Tompkins, Leslie C.

Burgess, Lynne H. For Truly to See Your Face. 64p. 1996. pap. 10.95 (*1-887649-01-8*) Black Hat Pr.

Burgess, M. Elaine. Negro Leadership in a Southern City. 1962. pap. 17.95 (*0-8084-0231-5*) NCUP.

Burgess, Mallory. Beloved Heart. 480p. 1997. mass mkt. 4.99 (*0-8217-5669-9*, Zebra Kensgtn) Kensgtn Pub Corp.

— Beloved Honor. 384p. 1995. mass mkt. 4.99 (*0-8217-4968-4*, Pinncle Kensgtn) Kensgtn Pub Corp.

— Beloved Honor. 1995. pap. 4.99 (*0-8217-4936-6*) NAL.

— Beloved Lord. 1996. pap. 4.99 (*0-8217-5318-5*) NAL.

— Passion Fire. 400p. 1988. pap. 3.95 (*0-380-75381-2*, Avon Bks) Morrow Avon.

— Passion Star. 432p. 1988. pap. 3.95 (*0-380-75383-9*, Avon Bks) Morrow Avon.

Burgess, Marjorie L. Walking on the Road of Life. (Orig.). 1997. pap. write for info. (*1-57553-493-2*) Watermrk Pr.

***Burgess, Marjorie Laura.** Life! It's More Than a Notion. LC 99-96748. 2000. pap. 7.95 (*0-533-13334-3*) Vantage.

Burgess, Mark. Advanced Visual Basic. 416p. 1993. pap. 39.95 incl. disk (*0-201-60828-6*) Addison-Wesley.

***Burgess, Mark.** Follow the Kite. (J). 1998. pap. 9.95 (*0-00-136053-1*, Pub. by HarpC) Trafalgar.

Burgess, Mark. Night, Night! (Illus.). 12p. (J). (ps). 1996. bds. 2.99 (*0-689-80673-6*) Litle Simon.

— Teddy Bear's Picnic. 24p. (ps-1). 1999. pap. 5.99 (*0-14-056462-4*, PuffinBks) Peng Put Young Read.

An Asterisk (*) at the beginning of an entry indicates that the title is appearing for the first time.

— Using Clarion Database Developer: Includes Version 3. 2nd ed. 1995. pap. write for info. (*0-201-63297-7*) Addison-Wesley.

Burgess, Marvin F. Rebuilding Downtrodden Job Market & Madhouse Society. LC 95-46537. 257p. 1996. 39.00 (*1-56072-283-5*) Nova Sci Pubs.

Burgess, Mary A., jt. auth. see Clarke, Boden.

Burgess, Mary A., jt. auth. see Reginald, Robert.

Burgess, Mary A., jt. compiled by see Reginald, Robert.

Burgess, Mary A., ed. see Berger, Albert I.

Burgess, Mary A., ed. see Clay, William L., Sr.

Burgess, Mary A., ed. see Estavan, Lawrence.

Burgess, Mary A., ed. see Martin, Abigail A.

Burgess, Mary A., ed. see Shumway, Burgess M.

Burgess, Mary A., ed. see Weinkauf, Mary S.

Burgess, Mary W. The Campbell Chronicles: Samuel Campbell of Lancaster County, Pennsylvania, & His Descendants. LC 87-6311. (Borgo Family Histories Ser.: No. 3). (Illus.). 128p. Date not set. pap. write for info. (*0-89370-478-4*) Millefleurs.

Burgess, Maryanne. Designer Source Listing, Vol. 5. 186p. (Orig.). 1992. pap. 17.95 (*0-9616741-4-8*) Carikean Pub.

— Designer Source Listing, 1997-1998. 144p. 1997. pap. 17.95 (*0-9616741-7-2*) Carikean Pub.

Burgess, Matt, jt. auth. see Holden, Nigel.

Burgess, Melvin. The Baby & Fly Pie: Could a Kidnapped Baby be the Key to a Better Life for Three Homeless Kids? LC 95-44496. 192p. (YA). (gr. 7 up). 1996. mass mkt. 16.00 (*0-689-80489-X*) S&S Bks Yung.

***Burgess, Melvin.** The Copper Treasure. LC 99-33350. 96p. (J). 2000. 15.95 (*0-8050-6381-1*) H Holt & Co.

Burgess, Melvin. Cry of the Wolf. LC 91-47690. 1994. 10.05 (*0-606-06298-X*, Pub. by Turtleback) Demco.

— The Earth Giant. LC 96-52571. 160p. (J). (gr. 3-7). 1997. 15.95 (*0-399-23187-0*, G P Putnam) Peng Put Young Read.

***Burgess, Melvin.** The Earth Giant. 154p. (gr. 3-7). 1999. pap. 4.99 (*0-698-11765-4*) Putnam Pub Group.

— Junk. 2000. pap. 10.95 (*0-413-73840-X*, Methuen Drama) Methn.

— Kite. LC 99-46872. 192p. (YA). (gr. 5-9). 2000. 16.00 (*0-374-34228-8*) FS&G.

Burgess, Melvin. Smack. LC 97-40629. 288p. (YA). (gr. 8 up). 1998. pap. 16.95 (*0-8050-5801-X*) H Holt & Co.

— Smack. LC 97-40629. 304p. (YA). (gr. 7-12). 1999. mass mkt. 6.99 (*0-380-73223-8*, Avon Bks) Morrow Avon.

Burgess, Michael. The British Tradition of Federalism. LC 95-2304. 240p. 1995. 39.50 (*0-8386-3618-7*) Fairleigh Dickinson.

— CSUSB Faculty Authors, Composers, & Playwrights: A Bibliography of Thirty Years of Published Monographs & Recordings, 1965-1995. LC 95-53822. 1996. write for info. (*0-945486-10-3*); pap. 5.30 (*0-945486-11-1*) CSU SBRVFAM.

***Burgess, Michael.** Federalism & European Union: Building of Europe, 1950-2000. LC 99-53300. 363p. (C). 2000. text. write for info. (*0-415-22646-5*) Routledge.

Burgess, Michael. Federalism & European Union: Political Ideas, Influences & Strategies in the European Community, 1972-1986. 256p. 1989. 47.50 (*0-415-00498-5*) Routledge.

***Burgess, Michael.** Federalism & European Union: The Building of Europe, 1950-2000. LC 99-53300. 363p. 2000. pap. 31.99 (*0-415-22647-3*) Routledge.

Burgess, Michael. A Guide to Science Fiction & Fantasy in the Library of Congress Classification Scheme. 2nd ed. LC 87-6308. (Borgo Cataloging Guides Ser.: No. 1). 168p. 1988. pap. 21.00 (*0-89370-927-1*) Millefleurs.

— House of the Burgesses. 2nd ed. LC 87-6316. (Borgo Family Histories Ser.: No. 1). xx, 708p. 1994. pap. 55.00 (*0-89370-479-2*) Millefleurs.

— The Kosnick Connection: A History of the Krsnic-Kosnick & Kapel Families in Slovenija & America. LC 87-6386. (Borgo Family Histories Ser.: No. 4). (Illus.). 96p. Date not set. pap. write for info. (*0-89370-477-6*) Millefleurs.

— Letters to Uncle Mike. 172p. 1998. pap. 10.95 (*0-9657638-0-3*) Saddle Mtn.

***Burgess, Michael.** Letters to Uncle Mike. 2nd ed. 172p. 2000. pap. 14.00 (*0-9657638-5-4*) Saddle Mtn.

Burgess, Michael. Lords Temporal & Lords Spiritual: A Chronological Checklist of the Popes, Patriarchs, Katholikoi & Independent Archbishop & Metropolitans of the Monarch, Autocephalous Churches of the Christian East & West. 2nd ed. LC 87-6319. (Stokvis Studies in Historical Chronology & Thought: No. 1). 336p. 1995. pap. 31.00 (*0-89370-426-1*) Millefleurs.

***Burgess, Michael.** More Letters to Uncle Mike. 200p. 2000. pap. 14.00 (*0-9657638-6-2*) Saddle Mtn.

Burgess, Michael. Mystery & Detective Fiction in the Library of Congress Classification Scheme. LC 84-12344. (Borgo Cataloging Guides Ser.: No.2). 184p. 1987. pap. 23.00 (*0-89370-918-2*) Millefleurs.

— Uncle Mike's Guide to the Real Oregon Coast. 2nd ed. 1997. pap. text 14.95 (*0-9657638-1-1*) Saddle Mtn.

— The Work of Robert Reginald: An Annotated Bibliography & Guide. enl. rev. ed. Clarke, Boden, ed. LC 87-6306. (Bibliographies of Modern Authors Ser.: No. 5). 176p. 1992. pap. 21.00 (*0-8095-1505-9*, 15318070) Millefleurs.

Burgess, Michael, ed. Canadian Federalism. 1991. text 65.00 (*0-7185-1334-7*) St Martin.

— Federalism & Federation in Western Europe. xx, 192p. (C). 1986. text 90.00 (*0-7099-3955-8*, Pub. by C Helm) Routldge.

Burgess, Michael & Gagnon, Alain G., eds. Comparative Federalism & Federation: Competing Traditions & Future Directions. LC 93-93310. 250p. 1993. text 60.00 (*0-8020-0527-6*); pap. text 19.95 (*0-8020-6965-7*) U of Toronto Pr.

Burgess, Michael & Ryan, Beverly A. Western Fiction in the Library of Congress Classification Scheme. LC 87-6309. (Borgo Cataloging Guides Ser.: No. 3). 48p. 1988. pap. 13.00 (*0-89370-922-0*) Millefleurs.

Burgess, Michael, et al. The State & Province Vital Records Guide. LC 87-6312. (Borgo Reference Guides Ser.: No. 5). 96p. 1993. pap. 15.00 (*0-89370-915-8*) Millefleurs.

Burgess, Michael, ed. see Bloomberg, Marty & Barrett, Buckley B.

Burgess, Michael, ed. see Bourquin, David R.

Burgess, Michael, ed. see Clay, William L., Sr.

Burgess, Michael, ed. see Shumway, Burgess M.

Burgess, Michael, ed. see Weinkauf, Mary S.

***Burgess, Michael A.** Money You Need It. 118p. 1999. pap. write for info. (*0-7392-0459-9*, PO3766) Morris Pubng.

Burgess, Michael M. & Woodrow, Brian E., eds. Contemporary Issues in Pediatric Ethics. LC 91-31141. 124p. 1991. lib. bdg. 59.95 (*0-7734-9673-4*) E Mellen.

Burgess, Mike. The Unexplained, 4 bks. Incl. Magic & Magicians. (Illus.). 48p. (J). (gr. 3-4). 1991. lib. bdg. 19.00 (*1-56065-044-3*, Cpstone High Low); 76.00 (*1-56065-666-2*, Cpstone High Low) Capstone Pr.

***Burgess, Miranda.** British Fiction & the Production of Socal Order: 1740-1830. (Cambridge Studies in Romanticism: Vol. 43). (Illus.). 291p. (C). 2000. Price not set. (*0-521-77329-6*) Cambridge U Pr.

Burgess, Moira. Imagine a City: Glasgow in Fiction LC 98-188464. 351 p. 1998. write for info. (*1-874640-78-5*) Argyll Pubng.

— The Other Voice: Scottish Women's Writing since 1808. LC 87-63143. 290p. 1988. 27.50 (*0-685-31955-5*); pap. 12.95 (*0-685-31956-3*) Dufour.

Burgess, Moira, ed. Other Voice. LC 87-63413. 1988. 27.50 (*0-948275-39-1*); pap. 12.95 (*0-948275-31-6*) Dufour.

— The Other Voice: Scottish Women's Writing since 1808. LC 87-63413. 290p. 1988. 27.50 (*0-318-39994-6*) Dufour.

Burgess, Molgard. Fun for Family Night, Vol. 2. 1992. pap. 11.95 (*0-88494-817-X*) Bookcraft Inc.

— Gospel in Action: Stories That Teach & Inspire. 1992. 9.95 (*0-88494-836-6*) Bookcraft Inc.

***Burgess, Muriel.** Shirley: An Appreciation of the Life of Shirley Bassey. 1998. 29.95 (*0-7126-7918-9*, Pub. by Random) Trafalgar.

Burgess, N. G. The Photograph Manual. 8th ed. LC 72-9186. (Literature of Photography Ser.). 1973. reprint ed. 24.95 (*0-405-04897-1*) Ayer.

Burgess, N. T. Quality Assurance of Welded Construction. 2nd ed. 214p. 1989. mass mkt. 87.50 (*1-85166-274-X*) Elsevier.

Burgess, Nancy & Sisters of the Living Word. Hearts Full of Compassion: Inspirations in the Lives of Ordinary Women. 148p. 1999. pap. 7.95 (*0-9668749-1-9*) Save-A-Barn.

Burgess, Nancy, jt. auth. see Churchill, Karen L.

Burgess, Neil. The Hippocampal & Pariental Foundations of Spatial Cognition. (Illus.). 502p. text. write for info. (*0-19-852453-6*) OUP.

Burgess, Neil, et al, eds. The Hippocampal & Parietal Foundations of Spatial Cognition. (Illus.). 504p. 1999. pap. text 54.50 (*0-19-852452-8*) OUP.

Burgess, Norma J., jt. ed. see Brown, Eurnestine.

Burgess, Patricia. Classic Main Courses. 192p. 1996. 17.98 (*0-7858-0576-1*) Bk Sales Inc.

— Cosmetic Surgery Without Fear: How to Make Safe Choices & Informed Decisions. 304p. 1999. pap. 24.95 (*0-9667630-0-9*, Pub. by Cosmetic Surgery) ACCESS Pubs Network.

Burgess, Patricia S., et al. GRE Success. 2nd ed. (Peterson's Test Success Ser.). (Illus.). 361p. 1998. pap. 16.95 incl. cd-rom (*0-7689-0022-0*) Petersons.

Burgess, Paul L. & Kingston, Jerry L. An Incentives Approach to Improving the Unemployment Compensation System. LC 87-23128. 273p. 1987. text 24.00 (*0-88099-049-X*); pap. text 14.00 (*0-88099-048-1*) W E Upjohn.

Burgess, Pete, tr. see Lecher, Wolfgang & Platzer, Hans-Wofgang.

Burgess, Peter. How to Build, Modify & Power Tune Cylinder Heads. (Illus.). 128p. 1999. pap. 24.95 (*1-901295-45-1*) Vloce Pub.

— How to Power Tune the MGB 4-Cylinder Engine. (Illus.). 112p. 1996. pap. 19.95 (*1-874105-61-8*, Pub. by Vloce Pub) Motorbooks Intl.

— Selected Quotations from East & West. 244p. 1983. pap. 7.95 (*9971-947-28-5*) Heian Intl.

— Survey of Company Car Schemes, 1993-94. 160p. 1993. 135.00 (*0-85459-768-9*, Pub. by Tolley Pubng) St Mut.

Burgess, Peter, et al. A-Z of Tropical Fish Diseases & Health Problems. (Illus.). 392p. 1998. 24.95 (*1-58245-049-8*) Howell Bks.

Burgess, Peter, jt. auth. see Bailey, Mary.

Burgess, Philip M. & Kelly, Michael. Profile of Western North America: Indicators of an Emerging Economic Region. LC 94-31787. (Economic Regions: Statistical Handbook Ser.). 1994. 39.95 (*1-55591-907-3*) Fulcrum Pub.

Burgess, Phillip, jt. auth. see Ross, Stan.

Burgess, R. Beyond the First Degree: Graduate Education, Lifelong Learning, & Careers. Burgess, Robert G., ed. LC 97-20166. (Illus.). 176p. 1998. pap. 35.95 (*0-335-19976-3*) OpUniv Pr.

Burgess, R. & Kinghorn, Robert. Speyside Railways: Exploring the Remains of the Great North of Scotland Railway & Its Environs. (Illus.). 128p. 1988. pap. 17.80 (*0-08-036411-X*, Pub. by Aberdeen U Pr) Macmillan.

Burgess, R. H., ed. Manufacture & Processing of PVC. (Illus.). 276p. (C). (gr. 13). 1981. 140.00 (*0-85334-972-X*, E & FN Spon) Routledge.

Burgess, R. W., ed. The Chronicle of Hydatius: And the Consularia Constantinopolitana. LC 92-18516. (Classical Monographs). (Illus.). 288p. 1993. 75.00 (*0-19-814787-2*, Clarendon Pr) OUP.

Burgess, Reginald. Linux, DOS, & Windows: A How to Build Yourself a 95/NT, 2000 Microsoft Active Directory Clone Now with NDS Networking! (Illus.). 267p. 1999. pap. 37.95 (*1-891950-03-7*) Amer Group Pub.

— Linux, DOS, & Windows . . . How to Build Yourself a 95/NT Clone: Available CD with Linux Operating System, Netscape Browser, Real Audio Player, Caldera 1.3 O/S & 2nd CD with Apps. 160p. 1997. pap. 27.95 incl. cd-rom (*1-891950-02-9*, 98190201) Amer Group Pub.

— 1 Linux Way to Do DOS, & Windows: Building Microsoft Gates' Business @ the Speed of Thought "Digital Nervous System" Using Oracle 8, NDS, JAVA, & WINE: Get an up to Date 2 CD-ROM Red Hat 5.2 Based Linux O/S with Netscape, DB's & Apps, Real Audio Player, & 2.2 Kernel; Which Runs MS Windows Apps & Has Extra Windofiles & Flaw Proofs. 249p. 1999. mass mkt. 37.95 incl. cd-rom (*1-891950-10-X*) Amer Group Pub.

— 1 Linux Way to Do DOS, & Windows: Building Microsoft Gates' Business @ the Speed of Thought "Digital Nervous System" Using the Value of Sybase as a Clone to SQL Server: Get an up to Date 2 CD-ROM Red Hat 5.2 Based Linux O/S with Netscape, DB's & Apps, Real Audio Player, & 2.2 Kernel; Which Runs MS Windows Apps & Has Extra Windows Files & Flaw Proofs. 249p. 1999. mass mkt. 37.95 incl. cd-rom (*1-891950-12-6*) Amer Group Pub.

— 1 Linux Way to Do DOS, & Windows: BuildingMicrosoft Gates' Business @ the Speed of Thought "Digital Nervous System" Using Open Source Postgres SQL, NDS, JAVA & WINE: Get an up to Date 2 CD-ROM Red Hat 5.2 Based Linux O/S with Netscape, SQL DB's & Apps, Real Audio Player, & 2.2 Kernel; Which Runs MS Windows Apps & Has Extra Windows Files & Flaw Proofs. 249p. 1999. mass mkt. 37.95 incl. cd-rom (*1-891950-11-8*) Amer Group Pub.

Burgess, Reginald P. 1 Microsoft Way . . . A Cookbook to Breaking Bill Gates Windows Monopoly Without Breaking Windows: Available CD-ROM with Linux Files to Build a 95-NT Clone with Mandrake Red Hat 5.3.2 Linux O/S & Wine Included. 208p. 1998. pap. 17.95 (*1-891950-08-8*) Amer Group Pub.

Burgess, Richard. Developing Your Own 32-Bit Operating System. (Illus.). 768p. (Orig.). 1995. 49.99 (*0-672-30655-7*) Sams.

— Fundamentals of EEG Technology. 2nd ed. 1998. text. write for info. (*0-397-51858-7*) Lppncott W & W.

Burgess, Richard J. The Art of Record Production. LC 98-185923. 228p. (C). 1997. pap. text 19.95 (*0-7119-5552-2*, OP47821) Omnibus NY.

Burgess, Richard R., ed. The Naval Aviation Guide. 5th ed. (Illus.). 488p. 1996. 27.95 (*1-55750-611-6*) Naval Inst Pr.

***Burgess, Robert.** Theatre Models in Paper & Carc. 160p. 1999. pap. text 24.95 (*1-86108-110-3*) Guild Master.

Burgess, Robert, jt. ed. see Katz, William A.

Burgess, Robert F. The Cave Divers. LC 96-39661. (Illus.). 352p. 2000. pap. 19.95 (*1-881652-11-4*) Aqua Quest.

— Handbook of Trailer Sailing. 2nd ed. 240p. 1992. pap. 19.95 (*0-87742-343-1*, 60329) Intl Marine.

— Handbook of Trailer Sailing. 2nd ed. 1992. 19.95 (*0-07-008981-7*) McGraw.

Burgess, Robert F. & Clausen, Carl J. Florida's Golden Galleons. (Florida Classics Ser.). Orig. Title: Gold, Galleons & Archaeology. (Illus.). 195p. (Orig.). 1982. pap. 17.95 (*0-912451-07-6*) Florida Classics.

Burgess, Robert G. Howard Becker on Education. LC 95-5372. (Modern Educational Thought Ser.). 128p. 1995. 108.95 (*0-335-19091-X*) OpUniv Pr.

— Howard Becker on Education. LC 95-5372. (Modern Educational Thought Ser.). 14.99p. 1995. pap. 23.95 (*0-335-19090-1*) OpUniv Pr.

— In the Field: An Introduction to Field Research. (Contemporary Social Research Ser.: No. 8). 180p. 1984. text 34.95 (*0-04-312017-2*); pap. text 14.95 (*0-04-312018-0*) Routledge.

Burgess, Robert G., ed. Educational Research & Evaluation: For Policy & Practice? (Social Research & Educational Studies: Vol. 13). 224p. 1993. 85.00 (*0-7507-0188-9*, Falmer Pr); pap. 34.95 (*0-7507-0189-7*, Falmer Pr) Taylor & Francis.

— Essays in Educational Ethnography. 192p. 1996. 72.00 (*0-7507-0274-5*, Falmer Pr); pap. 27.50 (*0-7507-0275-3*, Falmer Pr) Taylor & Francis.

— Field Research: A Source Book & Field Manual. (Contemporary Social Research Ser.: No. 4). 228p. (C). 1982. pap. text 39.95 (*0-04-312014-8*) Routledge.

— Postgraduate Education & Training in the Social Sciences: Processes & Products. (Higher Education Policy Ser.: No. 19). 240p. 1994. 59.95 (*1-85302-533-X*) Taylor & Francis.

— The Research Process in Educational Settings: Ten Case Studies. 275p. 1984. pap. 34.95 (*0-905273-91-5*, Falmer Pr) Taylor & Francis.

— Studies in Qualitative Methodology, Vol. 5. 216p. 1995. 73.25 (*1-55938-902-8*) Jai Pr.

— Studies in Qualitative Methodology, Vol. 6. Date not set. 73.25 (*0-7623-0053-1*) Jai Pr.

— Studies in Qualitative Methodology: Learning about Fieldwork, Vol. 3. 237p. 1992. 73.25 (*1-55938-246-5*) Jai Pr.

— Studies in Qualitative Methodology Vol. 1: Conducting Qualitative Research. 257p. 1988. 73.25 (*0-89232-762-6*) Jai Pr.

— Studies in Qualitative Methodology Vol. 2: Reflections on Field Experience. 238p. 1990. 73.25 (*1-55938-023-3*) Jai Pr.

— Studies in Qualitative Methodology Vol. 4: Issues in Qualitative Research. 296p. 1994. 73.25 (*1-55938-569-3*) Jai Pr.

Burgess, Robert G. & Society for Research into Higher Education Staff. Beyond the First Degree: Graduate Education, Lifelong Learning, & Careers. LC 97-20166. (Illus.). 176p. 1998. 115.00 (*0-335-19977-1*) OpUniv Pr.

Burgess, Robert G., et al. Implementing In-Service Education & Training. LC 92-39890. 196p. 1993. 99.95 (*0-7507-0184-6*, Falmer Pr); pap. 34.95 (*0-7507-0185-4*, Falmer Pr) Taylor & Francis.

Burgess, Robert G., jt. ed. see Bryman, Alan.

Burgess, Robert G., ed. see Burgess, R.

Burgess, Robert H. Coasting Schooner: The Four-Master Albert F. Paul. LC 77-10554. (Mariners Museum Publication Ser.: No. 35). (Illus.). 269p. 1978. 17.50 (*0-917376-31-5*) Mariners Mus.

— This Was Chesapeake Bay. LC 63-20545. (Illus.). 218p. 1963. 24.95 (*0-87033-125-6*, Tidewtr Pubs) Cornell Maritime.

Burgess, Robert H., ed. see Gregory, Hugh M.

Burgess, Robert O. Amy's Gold. LC 85-62546. (Illus.). 234p. 1985. 17.95 (*0-9615504-0-6*) Sweetwater Pr.

— Comes a Pale Horse. deluxe ed. LC 98-90836. (Illus.). 540p. (YA). 1998. 26.95 (*0-9615504-7-3*) Sweetwater Pr.

***Burgess, Robert S.** To Try the Bloody Law: The Story of Mary Dyer. LC 00-102840. (Illus.). 144p. 2000. 19.95 (*0-923687-56-4*) Celo Valley Bks.

Burgess, Rod. Labour Shelter & Global Capitalism. (Development & Underdevelopment Ser.). 272p. (C). 1998. 65.00 (*0-415-08841-0*); pap. 24.99 (*0-415-08842-9*) Routledge.

Burgess, Rod, et al, eds. The Challenge of Sustainable Cities: Neoliberalism & Urban Strategies in Developing Countries. LC 96-34469. 288p. 1997. pap. 25.00 (*1-85649-480-2*); text 65.00 (*1-85649-479-9*, Pub. by Zed Books) St Martin.

Burgess, Roger A., ed. Progress in Construction Science & Technology, Vol. 1. LC TA0145.P76. 330p. reprint ed. pap. 102.30 (*0-608-09988-0*, 201550200001) Bks Demand.

— Progress in Construction Science & Technology, Vol. 2. LC TA0145.P7. 251p. reprint ed. pap. 77.90 (*0-608-09989-9*, 201550200002) Bks Demand.

***Burgess, Ron.** Laughing Lessons: 149 2/3 Ways to Make Teaching & Learning Fun. LC 99-56599. (Illus.). 176p. 2000. pap., teacher ed. 21.95 (*1-57542-075-9*) Free Spirit Pub.

***Burgess, Ronald.** Clown Jokes & Walkaround Gags. LC 98-42629. 1998. pap. 10.00 (*0-941599-35-3*) Piccadilly Bks.

— Son of Clown Jokes & Walkaround Gags. (Illus.). 64p. 2000. pap. 8.00 (*0-941599-46-9*, Pub. by Piccadilly Bks) Empire Pub Srvs.

Burgess, Ronald D. The New Dramatists of Mexico, 1967-1985. LC 90-40023. 176p. 1991. text 23.00 (*0-8131-1727-5*) U Pr of Ky.

Burgess, Ronald R., ed. see International Symposium on Silicon Materials, Science & Technology Staff.

Burgess, Rosemary & Kinghorn, Robert. Moray Coast Railways: Exploring the Remains & Environs of the Great North of Scotland & Highland Railways in Morayshire & Banffshire. (Illus.). 140p. 1990. pap. text 17.75 (*0-08-037970-2*, Pergamon Pr) Elsevier.

Burgess, Roy. Early New Englanders & Kin. xii, 503p. (Orig.). 1992. pap. 35.00 (*1-55613-644-7*) Heritage Bk.

Burgess, Russel W. Real Estate Home Inspection: A Comprehensive Study. 2nd rev. ed. LC 93-50826. 454p. (C). 1994. pap. 74.95 (*0-7931-0867-5*, 1531-0102, Real Estate Ed) Dearborn.

Burgess, Russell. Real Estate Home Inspection: Mastering the Profession. 3rd ed. LC 98-39641. 1998. pap. 86.95 (*0-7931-2913-3*) Dearborn.

Burgess, Ruth. At Ground Level. (Illus.). 1987. 25.00 (*0-947988-21-1*, Pub. by Wild Goose Pubns) St Mut.

Burgess, Samuel B. Understanding the Autopsy. LC 92-74142. (Illus.). 224p. (Orig.). 1993. pap. 22.50 (*0-923687-26-2*) Celo Valley Bks.

Burgess, Scott A. The Work of Dean Ing: An Annotated Bibliography & Guide. Clarke, Boden, ed. LC 87-827. (Bibliographies of Modern Authors Ser.: No. 11). 82p. 1990. pap. 15.00 (*0-89370-495-4*) Millefleurs.

— The Work of Reginald Bretnor: An Annotated Bibliography & Guide. Clarke, Boden, ed. LC 85-31405. (Bibliographies of Modern Authors Ser.: No. 8). 122p. 1989. pap. 17.00 (*0-89370-487-3*) Millefleurs.

Burgess, Scott A., ed. see Coblentz, Stanton A. & Elliot, Jeffrey M.

***Burgess, Simon.** Stafford Cripps: A Political Life. 352p. 1999. 50.00 (*0-575-06565-6*, Pub. by Indigo) Trafalgar.

Burgess, Stanley M. Holy Spirit: Ancient Christian Traditions. 216p. 1984. pap. 19.95 (*0-913573-10-8*) Hendrickson MA.

— The Holy Spirit: Eastern Christian Traditions. 260p. (Orig.). 1989. pap. 19.95 (*0-913573-81-7*) Hendrickson MA.

— Holy Spirit: Medieval Roman Catholic & Reformation Traditions, 6th-16th Centuries. LC 96-10723. 252p. 1997. pap. 19.95 (*1-56563-139-0*) Hendrickson MA.

Burgess, Stanley M. & McGee, Gary B. Dictionary of Pentecostal & Charismatic Movements. Alexander, Patrick H., ed. 960p. 1988. 39.99 (*0-310-44100-5*) Zondervan.

Burgess, Stephen F. Smallholders & Political Voice in Zimbabwe. LC 97-7904. 238p. 1997. 39.50 (*0-7618-0741-1*) U Pr of Amer.

Burgess, Stewart. Preschool Readiness Guidebook. deluxe ed. (Illus.). 176p. Date not set. write for info. (*1-929651-14-7*) Brllnt Begnngs.

Burgess, Sullivan, jt. auth. see Kelly, Fred C.

***Burgess, Susan & Shenstone, William.** So Obstinately Loyal: James Moody, 1744-1809. (Illus.). 392p. 1999. 39.95 (*0-88629-355-3*) McG-Queens Univ Pr.

Burgess, Susan R. Contest for Constitutional Authority: The Abortion & War Powers Debates. LC 91-34979. xiv, 178p. 1992. 29.95 (*0-7006-0522-3*) U Pr of KS.

— Contest for Constitutional Authority: The Abortion & War Powers Debates. LC 91-34979. xiv, 178p. 1994. pap. 14.95 (*0-7006-0629-7*) U Pr of KS.

Burgess, Terry, jt. auth. see Barnard, Andy.

Burgess, Thomas. Greeks in America: An Account of Their Coming, Progress, Customs, Living & Aspirations. LC 72-129392. (American Immigration Collection. Series 2). (Illus.). 1977. reprint ed. 21.95 (*0-405-00547-4*) Ayer.

— Selecting an On-Site Manager, GAP19. 2nd ed. 32p. (C). 1996. pap. 17.50 (*0-944715-46-X*) CAI.

Burgess, Thomas N. Take Me under the Sea: The Dream Merchants of the Deep. LC 93-87618. (Illus.). 272p. (Orig.). 1994. pap. 13.95 (*0-9639840-0-4*) Ocean Archives.

Burgess, Thornton W. The Adventures of Bob White. 18.95 (*0-88411-776-6*) Amereon Ltd.

— The Adventures of Bob White. (J). 1992. reprint ed. lib. bdg. 17.95 (*0-89966-994-8*) Buccaneer Bks.

— Adventures of Bobby Coon. (J). 18.95 (*0-8488-0383-3*) Amereon Ltd.

— The Adventures of Bobby Coon. (J). 1992. reprint ed. lib. bdg. 17.95 (*0-89966-992-1*) Buccaneer Bks.

— The Adventures of Bobby Raccoon. LC 94-44605. (Illus.). 96p. (J). 1995. pap. text 1.00 (*0-486-28617-7*) Dover.

— The Adventures of Buster Bear. (J). 19.95 (*0-8488-0354-X*) Amereon Ltd.

— The Adventures of Buster Bear. (Bedtime Story Bks.). (J). 1986. reprint ed. lib. bdg. 17.95 (*0-89966-525-X*) Buccaneer Bks.

— The Adventures of Buster Bear. LC 92-36949. (Children's Thrift Classics Ser.). (Illus.). 96p. (J). 1993. reprint ed. pap. 1.00 (*0-486-27564-7*) Dover.

— Adventures of Chatterer the Red Squirrel. (J). 18.95 (*0-8488-0376-0*) Amereon Ltd.

— The Adventures of Chatterer the Red Squirrel. unabridged ed. LC 92-14627. (Children's Thrift Classics Ser.). (Illus.). 96p. (J). 1992. reprint ed. pap. 1.00 (*0-486-27399-7*) Dover.

— The Adventures of Danny Meadow Mouse. (J). 18.95 (*0-8488-0377-9*) Amereon Ltd.

— The Adventures of Danny Meadow Mouse. LC 92-36950. (Illus.). 96p. (J). 1993. reprint ed. pap. 1.00 (*0-486-27565-5*) Dover.

— The Adventures of Grandfather Frog. (J). (gr. 5-6). 18.95 (*0-88411-777-4*) Amereon Ltd.

— The Adventures of Grandfather Frog. unabridged ed. LC 92-13146. (Children's Thrift Classics Ser.). (Illus.). 96p. (J). 1992. reprint ed. pap. text 1.00 (*0-486-27400-4*) Dover.

— The Adventures of Jerry Muskrat. (J). (gr. 5-6). 18.95 (*0-88411-782-0*) Amereon Ltd.

— The Adventures of Jerry Muskrat. (Illus.). 96p. (J). 1993. reprint ed. pap. text 1.00 (*0-486-27817-4*) Dover.

— The Adventures of Jimmy Skunk. (J). 18.95 (*0-8488-0384-1*) Amereon Ltd.

— The Adventures of Jimmy Skunk. (Illus.). 128p. (J). (ps-3). 1987. pap. 2.95 (*0-316-11662-9*) Little.

— The Adventures of Jimmy Skunk. (J). 1992. reprint ed. lib. bdg. 17.95 (*0-89966-993-X*) Buccaneer Bks.

— The Adventures of Jimmy Skunk. (Children's Thrift Stories Ser.). (Illus.). 96p. (J). 1994. reprint ed. pap. 1.00 (*0-486-28023-3*) Dover.

— The Adventures of Johnny Chuck. (J). (gr. 5-6). 18.95 (*0-88411-787-1*) Amereon Ltd.

— The Adventures of Johnny Chuck. (J). 1992. reprint ed. lib. bdg. 17.95 (*0-89966-991-3*) Buccaneer Bks.

— The Adventures of Johnny Chuck. unabridged ed. LC 94-29788. (Children's Thrift Classics Ser.). (Illus.). 96p. (J). 1995. pap. text 1.00 (*0-486-28353-4*) Dover.

— The Adventures of Lightfoot the Deer. (J). 19.95 (*0-8488-0393-0*) Amereon Ltd.

— The Adventures of Mister Mocker. (J). 18.95 (*0-8488-0378-7*) Amereon Ltd.

— Adventures of Mr. Mocker. 120p. 1977. reprint ed. lib. bdg. 17.95 (*0-89966-271-4*) Buccaneer Bks.

— The Adventures of Ol' Mistah Buzzard. (J). (gr. 5-6). 18.95 (*0-88411-784-7*) Amereon Ltd.

— The Adventures of Old Man Coyote. (J). (gr. 5-6). 18.95 (*0-88411-781-2*) Amereon Ltd.

— The Adventures of Old Man Coyote. LC 96-45610. (Children's Thrift Classics Ser.). (Illus.). 96p. (J). 1998. reprint ed. pap. text 1.00 (*0-486-29646-6*) Dover.

— The Adventures of Old Mr. Toad. (J). (gr. 5-6). 18.95 (*0-88411-785-5*) Amereon Ltd.

— The Adventures of Old Mr. Toad. LC 98-21597. (Illus.). 80p. (J). 1998. pap. 1.00 (*0-486-40385-8*) Dover.

— The Adventures of Ol'Mistah Buzzard. (J). 1992. reprint ed. lib. bdg. 17.95 (*0-89966-995-6*) Buccaneer Bks.

— Adventures of Paddy the Beaver. (J). 18.95 (*0-8488-0379-5*) Amereon Ltd.

— Adventures of Paddy the Beaver. (Bedtime Story Bks.). (J). 1986. reprint ed. lib. bdg. 17.95 (*0-89966-528-4*) Buccaneer Bks.

— Adventures of Peter Cottontail. (J). 18.95 (*0-8488-0353-1*) Amereon Ltd.

— The Adventures of Peter Cottontail. (Illus.). (J). (ps-8). 1990. reprint ed. lib. bdg. 18.95 (*0-89966-664-7*) Buccaneer Bks.

— The Adventures of Peter Cottontail, Vol. 100. large type ed. (Illus.). 64p. (J). 1991. reprint ed. pap. 1.00 (*0-486-26929-9*) Dover.

— The Adventures of Poor Mrs. Quack. (J). (gr. 5-6). 18.95 (*0-88411-775-8*) Amereon Ltd.

— The Adventures of Poor Mrs. Quack, Vol. 100. (Illus.). 96p. (J). 1993. reprint ed. pap. text 1.00 (*0-486-27818-2*) Dover.

— The Adventures of Prickly Porky. (J). (gr. 5-6). 18.95 (*0-88411-783-9*) Amereon Ltd.

— The Adventures of Prickly Porky. unabridged ed. (Children's Thrift Classics Ser.). (Illus.). 80p. (J). (gr. 1). 1998. reprint ed. pap. 1.00 (*0-486-29170-7*) Dover.

— The Adventures of Reddy Fox. (J). 18.95 (*0-8488-0380-9*) Amereon Ltd.

— The Adventures of Reddy Fox. large type ed. (Children's Thrift Classics Ser.). (Illus.). 64p. (J). 1991. reprint ed. pap. 1.00 (*0-486-26930-2*) Dover.

— The Adventures of Reddy Fox. (J). 1992. reprint ed. lib. bdg. 17.95 (*0-89966-990-5*) Buccaneer Bks.

— Adventures of Sammy Jay. (J). 15.95 (*0-8488-0381-7*) Amereon Ltd.

— Adventures of Unc' Billy Possum. (J). 18.95 (*0-8488-0382-5*) Amereon Ltd.

— Billy Mink. (J). 18.95 (*0-8488-0397-3*) Amereon Ltd.

— Billy Mink. 91p. (J). 1981. reprint ed. lib. bdg. 17.95 (*0-89966-352-4*); reprint ed. lib. bdg. 17.95 (*0-89967-026-1*, Harmony Rain) Buccaneer Bks.

— Blacky the Crow. (J). 18.95 (*0-8488-0394-9*) Amereon Ltd.

— Blacky the Crow. LC 99-10879. (Illus.). 80p. 1999. pap. text 1.00 (*0-486-40550-8*) Dover.

— Blacky the Crow. 93p. (J). 1981. reprint ed. lib. bdg. 17.95 (*0-89966-351-6*); reprint ed. lib. bdg. 17.95 (*0-89967-025-3*, Harmony Rain) Buccaneer Bks.

— Bowser the Hound. (J). 19.95 (*0-8488-0391-4*) Amereon Ltd.

Burgess, Thornton W. Burgess Animal Book for Children. (J). 28.95 (*0-8488-0716-2*) Amereon Ltd.

— Burgess Bird Book for Children. (J). 24.95 (*0-8488-0404-X*) Amereon Ltd.

— Burgess Flower Book for Children. 21.95 (*0-8488-0717-0*) Amereon Ltd.

— Burgess Sea Shore Book for Children. (J). 26.95 (*0-8488-0403-1*) Amereon Ltd.

Burgess, Thornton W. Buster Bear's Twins. (J). 19.95 (*0-8488-0396-5*) Amereon Ltd.

— Buster Bear's Twins. LC 99-25510. (Children's Thrift Classics Ser.). 80p. 1999. pap. text 1.00 (*0-486-40790-X*) Dover.

— Buster Bear's Twins. (J). 1992. reprint ed. lib. bdg. 17.95 (*0-89966-981-6*) Buccaneer Bks.

— Dear Old Briar Patch. (J). 18.95 (*0-8488-0402-3*) Amereon Ltd.

— Favorite Thornton Burgess Animal Stories, 5 vols. (J). (gr. 4-7). 1992. pap. 5.00 (*0-486-27402-0*) Dover.

— Favorite Thornton Burgess Animal Stories, 5 vols. (Illus.). (J). (gr. 4-7). 1993. pap. 6.00 (*0-486-27634-1*) Dover.

— Happy Jack. (J). 19.95 (*0-8488-0389-2*) Amereon Ltd.

— Jerry Muskrat at Home. (J). 18.95 (*0-8488-0399-X*) Amereon Ltd.

— Jerry Muskrat at Home. (Smiling Pool Ser.). (J). 1986. reprint ed. lib. bdg. 17.95 (*0-89966-527-6*) Buccaneer Bks.

— Lightfoot the Deer. LC 97-42201. (Children's Thrift Classics Ser.). (Illus.). (J). 1998. pap. 1.00 (*0-486-40100-6*) Dover.

— Lightfoot the Deer. (Green Forest Ser.). (J). 1986. reprint ed. lib. bdg. 17.95 (*0-89966-526-8*) Buccaneer Bks.

— Listen & Read the Adventures of Peter Cottontail. (Illus.). 96p. (Orig.). (J). 1996. pap. text 5.95 incl. audio (*0-486-29101-4*) Dover.

— Little Joe Otter. (J). 18.95 (*0-8488-0398-1*) Amereon Ltd.

— Little Joe Otter. 103p. (J). 1981. reprint ed. lib. bdg. 17.95 (*0-89966-353-2*); reprint ed. lib. bdg. 17.95 (*0-89967-027-X*, Harmony Rain) Buccaneer Bks.

— Longlegs the Heron. (J). 19.95 (*0-8488-0400-7*) Amereon Ltd.

— Longlegs the Heron. (J). 1992. reprint ed. lib. bdg. 17.95 (*0-89966-979-4*) Buccaneer Bks.

— Mother West Wind's Children. (Nature-Story Bks.). (Illus.). 156p. (J). (gr. k-3). 1985. pap. 12.95 (*0-316-11657-2*) Little.

— Mother West Wind's Neighbors. LC 68-21862. (Nature-Story Bks.). (Illus.). 148p. (J). (gr. k-3). 1985. pap. 12.95 (*0-316-11656-4*) Little.

— Mother West Wind's Neighbors. (Illus.). 160p. (J). 1992. reprint ed. lib. bdg. 14.95 (*0-89966-901-8*) Buccaneer Bks.

— Mrs. Peter Rabbit. (J). 18.95 (*0-8488-0390-6*) Amereon Ltd.

— Mrs. Peter Rabbit. unabridged ed. LC 96-21745. (Children's Thrift Classics Ser.). (Illus.). 96p. (J). 1998. reprint ed. pap. text 1.00 (*0-486-29376-9*) Dover.

— Old Granny Fox. (J). 18.95 (*0-8488-0392-2*) Amereon Ltd.

— Old Mother West Wind. (J). 16.95 (*0-8488-0385-X*) Amereon Ltd.

— Old Mother West Wind. LC 89-20088. (Illus.). 90p. (J). (gr. 2-4). 1995. 18.95 (*0-8050-1005-X*, Bks Young Read) H Holt & Co.

— Old Mother West Wind. (Old Mother West Wind Bks.: Vol. 1). (Illus.). 152p. (J). 1996. 9.95 (*1-883684-11-0*) Peninsula MA.

— Old Mother West Wind. (J). 1985. 16.05 (*0-606-03992-9*, Pub. by Turtleback) Demco.

— Old Mother West Wind. anniversary ed. (Nature-Story Bks.). (Illus.). 140p. (J). (gr. k-3). 1985. pap. 12.95 (*0-316-11655-6*) Little.

Burgess, Thornton W. Old Mother West Wind. (Illus.). 160p. (J). 1992. reprint ed. lib. bdg. 14.95 (*0-89966-900-X*) Buccaneer Bks.

Burgess, Thornton W. Old Mother West Wind. unabridged ed. LC 95-36751. (Children's Thrift Classics Ser.). (Illus.). 112p. (J). 1995. reprint ed. pap. text 1.00 (*0-486-28849-8*) Dover.

— Old Mother West Wind & 6 Other Stories. (J). 1996. pap., boxed set 7.00 (*0-486-29455-2*) Dover.

— Old Mother West Wind's Animal Friends. Date not set. lib. bdg. 19.95 (*0-88411-779-0*, Aeonian Pr) Amereon Ltd.

— Old Mother West Wind's Children. (J). 18.95 (*0-8488-0386-8*) Amereon Ltd.

— Old Mother West Wind's Children. (Old Mother West Wind Bks.: Vol. 2). (Illus.). 152p. (J). 1996. 9.95 (*1-883684-12-9*) Peninsula MA.

— Old Mother West Wind's "How" Stories. 19.95 (*0-88411-780-4*) Amereon Ltd.

— Old Mother West Wind's Neighbors. (J). (gr. 5-6). 19.95 (*0-88411-786-3*) Amereon Ltd.

— Old Mother West Wind's "When" Stories. (J). 21.95 (*0-8488-0387-6*) Amereon Ltd.

— Old Mother West Wind's "Where" Stories. (J). 18.95 (*0-8488-0388-4*) Amereon Ltd.

— Old Mother West Wind's "Why" Stories. 19.95 (*0-88411-778-2*) Amereon Ltd.

— Peter Cottontail. LC 96-2982. (Little Activity Bks.). (Illus.). 12p. (J). 1996. pap. 1.00 (*0-486-29369-6*) Dover.

— Tales from the Storyteller's House. (J). 19.95 (*0-8488-0930-0*) Amereon Ltd.

— Tommy & the Wishing Stone. (J). 19.95 (*0-8488-0932-7*) Amereon Ltd.

— Tommy's Change of Heart. (J). 19.95 (*0-8488-1418-5*) Amereon Ltd.

— Tommy's Wishes Come True. (J). 19.95 (*0-8488-1419-3*) Amereon Ltd.

— While Story-Log Burns. (J). 18.95 (*0-8488-0401-5*) Amereon Ltd.

— Whitefoot the Wood Mouse. (J). 18.95 (*0-8488-0395-7*) Amereon Ltd.

— Whitefoot the Wood Mouse. (J). 1992. reprint ed. lib. bdg. 17.95 (*0-89966-980-8*) Buccaneer Bks.

***Burgess, Thornton W. & Cady, Harrison.** The Adventures of Paddy the Beaver. LC 00-38418. (Children's Thrift Classics). (J). 2000. pap. write for info. (*0-486-41305-5*) Dover.

Burgess, Thornton W. & Stewart, Pat. Peter Cottontail Dot-to-Dot. (Illus.). 32p. (J). 1998. pap. 1.00 (*0-486-40355-6*) Dover.

Burgess, Thornton W., jt. auth. see Harris, Joel Chandler.

Burgess, Thornton W., jt. auth. see Milne, A. A., pseud.

Burgess, Thorton W. The Boy Scouts in a Trapper's Camp. (Illus.). 336p. Date not set. reprint ed. lib. bdg. 25.95 (*0-8488-2185-8*) Amereon Ltd.

— The Boy Scouts of Woodcraft Camp. (Illus.). 338p. Date not set. reprint ed. lib. bdg. 25.95 (*0-8488-2186-6*) Amereon Ltd.

— The Boy Scouts on Lost Trail. (Illus.). 364p. Date not set. reprint ed. lib. bdg. 26.95 (*0-8488-2183-1*) Amereon Ltd.

— The Boy Scouts on Swift River. (Illus.). 338p. Date not set. reprint ed. lib. bdg. 25.95 (*0-8488-2184-X*) Amereon Ltd.

Burgess, Tom. Documents on Instrumental Music. 145p. 1989. reprint ed. pap. 4.99 (*0-89900-355-9*) College Pr Pub.

Burgess, Tony. The Hellmouths of Bewdley. LC 96-932469. 180p. 1997. pap. 12.00 (*1-55022-315-1*, Pub. by ECW) Genl Dist Srvs.

Burgess, Trish, ed. Annual Obituary, 1985. 85th ed. 749p. 1988. 100.00 (*0-912289-82-1*) St James Pr.

— Annual Obituary, 1986. 86th ed. 1989. 100.00 (*1-55862-013-3*) St James Pr.

— Annual Obituary, 1987. 87th ed. 1990. 100.00 (*1-55862-021-4*) St James Pr.

— Annual Obituary, 1988. 88th ed. 760p. 1990. 100.00 (*1-55862-050-8*) St James Pr.

Burgess, Tyrell, et al. Learning for Living: Higher Education in East London, 1890-1992. LC 94-46791. (Illus.). 185p. (C). 1995. pap. 19.95 (*0-485-12092-5*, Pub. by Athlone Pr); text 49.95 (*0-485-11434-8*, Pub. by Athlone Pr) Humanities.

Burgess, Tyrrell, jt. auth. see Swann, Joanna.

Burgess, W. A. Cowards. LC 96-52574. 1997. text 20.95 (*0-312-15503-4*) St Martin.

Burgess, W. H. Chronic Disease (1907) 320p. 1998. reprint ed. pap. 24.95 (*0-7661-0516-4*) Kessinger Pub.

Burgess, Warren, et al. Dr. Burgess's Atlas of Marine Aquarium Fishes. 736p. 1988. 79.95 (*0-86622-896-9*, H-1100) TFH Pubns.

Burgess, Warren E. The ABCs of Marine Aquariums. (Illus.). 94p. 1989. 9.95 (*0-86622-764-4*, KW-154) TFH Pubns.

— An Atlas of Freshwater & Marine Catfishes: A Preliminary Survey of the Siluriformes. (Illus.). 784p. 1989. pap. 69.95 (*0-86622-131-X*, H-1097) TFH Pubns.

Burgess, Warren E. Colored Atlas of Miniature Catfish. (Illus.). 352p. 1992. text 23.95 (*0-86622-441-6*, TS183) TFH Pubns.

Burgess, Warren E. A Complete Introduction to Marine Aquariums. (Complete Introduction to...Ser.). (Illus.). 128p. (Orig.). 1987. pap. 8.95 (*0-86622-351-7*, CO-021S) TFH Pubns.

— Corydoras Catfishes. (Illus.). 64p. 1997. 12.95 (*0-7938-0212-1*, WW-046) TFH Pubns.

***Burgess, Warren E.** Dr. Burgess's Atlas of Marine Aquarium Fishes. 3rd ed. (Illus.). 2000. 79.95 (*0-7938-0575-9*) TFH Pubns.

Burgess, Warren E. Marine Aquaria. (Illus.). 96p. text 9.95 (*0-87666-533-4*, KW-088) TFH Pubns.

Burgess, Warren E., et al. Dr. Burgess's Mini Marine Atlas. (Illus.). 1024p. 1997. 35.95 (*0-7938-0032-3*, H-1107) TFH Pubns.

Burgess, Warren E., jt. auth. see Axelrod, Herbert R.

Burgess, Warren E., ed. see Kobayagawa, Midori.

Burgess, William. Bible in Shakespeare. LC 68-24900. (Studies in Shakespeare: No. 24). 1969. reprint ed. lib. bdg. 75.00 (*0-8383-0921-6*) M S G Haskell Hse.

Burgess, William, et al. Ventilation for Control of the Work Enviorment. LC 88-31463. 496p. 1989. 110.00 (*0-471-89219-X*) Wiley.

Burgess, William A. Recognition of Health Hazards in Industry: A Review of Materials & Processes. 560p. 1995. 94.95 (*0-471-57716-2*) Wiley.

Burgess, William J. Piercing the Shields of Justice: Inside the ATF. LC 95-45086. (Illus.). 224p. 1995. 25.00 (*1-55618-156-6*) Brunswick Pub.

Burgess-Wise, David. The Ultimate Race Car. LC 98-32294. 1999. 29.95 (*0-7894-4182-9*) DK Pub Inc.

Burgess-Wise, David, jt. auth. see Montagu, Lord.

Burgess, Yvonne. Say a Little Mantra for Me. (Writers Ser.). 166p. 1995. reprint ed. pap. text 12.95 (*0-86975-467-X*, Pub. by Ravan Pr) Ohio U Pr.

Burgest, David R. Proverbs for the Young . . . And the Not So Young. (Illus.). 75p. (Orig.). (YA). (gr. 7-12). 1989. pap. write for info. (*0-318-65788-0*) Self-Taught Pubs.

— Reflections on the Thoughts of a Young Black Male: Collection of My Childhood Poetry. (Illus.). 127p. (Orig.). 1992. pap. write for info. (*0-9624077-0-4*) Self-Taught Pubs.

— Social Work Practice with Minorities. 2nd ed. LC 89-32068. 362p. 1989. 42.00 (*0-8108-2207-5*) Scarecrow.

Burget & Menick. Aesthetic Restoration of Nasal Defects. (Illus.). 304p. 1992. text 160.00 (*0-8016-0909-7*) Mosby Inc.

— Aesthetic Restoration of Nasal Defects. (Illus.). 615p. (C). (gr. 13). 1993. text 195.00 (*0-8016-7443-3*, 00909) Mosby Inc.

Burgett, B. Progressive Double Bass Drumming, Vol. 1. 88p. 1994. otabind 10.95 (*0-7935-3155-1*, 06621767) H Leonard.

***Burgett, Bruce.** American Sex. 1999. 30.00 (*0-226-08059-5*); pap. text 15.00 (*0-226-08060-9*) U Ch Pr.

Burgett, Bruce. Sentimental Bodies: Sex, Gender, & Citizenship in the Early Republic. LC 98-6479. 217p. 1998. text 39.50 (*0-691-01559-7*, Pub. by Princeton U Pr) Cal Prin Full Svc.

Burgett, D. M., et al. Nectar & Pollen Plants of Oregon & the Pacific Northwest: An Illustrated Guide to Plants Used by Honey Bees. enl. rev. ed. (Illus.). 151p. (Orig.). (C). 1989. pap. 11.95 (*0-9624785-0-4*) Honeystone Pr.

***Burgett, Donald R.** Currahee! A Paratrooper's Account of the Normandy Invasion. LC 99-32520. (Illus.). 256p. 1999. 24.95 (*0-89141-681-1*) Presidio Pr.

— Currahee! A Screaming Eagle at Normandy. 256p. 2000. mass mkt. 6.50 (*0-440-23630-4*) Dell.

— Currahee! A Screaming Eagle at Normandy. large type ed. LC 00-35069. 216p. 2000. 26.95 (*0-7838-9080-X*) Mac Lib Ref.

Burgett, Donald R. Currahee! 'We Stand Alone!' A Paratrooper's Account of the Normandy Invasion. LC 68-143790. 190p. 1968. write for info. (*0-09-000680-1*) Arrow Bks.

— The Road to Arnhem: A Screaming Eagle in Holland. LC 99-35435. 360p. 1999. 24.95 (*0-89141-682-X*) Presidio Pr.

***Burgett, Donald R.** Seven Roads to Hell: A Screaming Eagle at Bastogne. 288p. 2000. mass mkt. 6.50 (*0-440-23627-4*) Dell.

Burgett, Donald R. Seven Roads to Hell: A Screaming Eagle at Bastogne. LC 98-51693. (Illus.). 256p. 1999. 24.95 (*0-89141-680-3*) Presidio Pr.

***Burgett, Donald R.** Seven Roads to Hell: A Screaming Eagle at Bastogne. large type ed. (G. K. Hall American History Ser.). 2000. 27.95 (*0-7838-8994-1*, G K Hall Lrg Type) Mac Lib Ref.

Burgett, Gordon. Empire-Building by Writing & Speaking: A How-to Guide for Communicators, Entrepreneurs, & Other Information-Merchants. (Illus.). 208p. (Orig.). 1987. 15.95 (*0-910167-03-6*); pap. 12.95 (*0-910167-02-8*) Comm Unltd CA.

***Burgett, Gordon.** How to Create Your Own Super Second Life: What Are You Going to Do with Your Extra 30 Years? (Illus.). 240p. 1999. pap. 19.95 (*0-910167-60-5*, AgeMasters) Comm Unltd CA.

Burgett, Gordon. How to Sell More Than Seventy-Five Percent of Your Freelance Writing. LC 94-40325. 256p. (Orig.). 1990. pap. 12.95 (*1-55958-035-6*) Prima Pub.

— How to Sell More Than Seventy-Five Percent of Your Freelance Writing. 2nd expanded rev. ed. LC 94-40325. 240p. (Orig.). 1995. pap. 14.00 (*1-55958-689-3*) Prima Pub.

— Niche Marketing for Writers, Speakers, & Entrepreneurs: How to Make Yourself Indispensable, Slightly Immortal, & Lifelong Rich in 18 Months! 192p. (Orig.). 1993. pap. 14.95 (*0-910167-22-2*) Comm Unltd CA.

— Publishing to Niche Markets. rev. ed. (Illus.). 200p. (Orig.). 1995. pap. 14.95 (*0-910167-27-3*) Comm Unltd CA.

— Sell & Resell Your Magazine Articles. LC 97-15359. 224p. 1997. 17.99 (*0-89879-799-3*, Wrtrs Digest Bks) F & W Pubns Inc.

— Standard Marketing Procedures for Dentists. (Illus.). 224p. (Orig.). 1997. pap. 149.00 incl. disk (*0-910167-36-2*, Dental Commun) Comm Unltd CA.

— The Travel Writer's Guide: How to Earn at Least Twice What You Spend on Travel by Writing Newspaper & Magazine Articles. (Illus.). 304p. (Orig.). 1991. pap. 14.95 (*1-55958-115-8*) Prima Pub.

— The Travel Writer's Guide: How to Earn at Least Twice What You Spend on Travel by Writing Newspaper & Magazine Articles. 2nd rev. ed. LC 94-20626. (Illus.). 320p. (Orig.). 1994. pap. 14.95 (*1-55958-561-7*) Prima Pub.

— Treasure & Scavenger Hunts: How to Plan, Create, & Give Them. (Illus.). 128p. 1994. pap. 9.95 (*0-910167-25-7*) Comm Unltd CA.

Burgett, Gordon & Franklin, Reece. Standard Marketing Procedures for Dentists. 2nd rev. ed. 188p. (Orig.). 1998. ring bd. 149.00 incl. disk (*0-910167-45-1*, Dental Commun) Comm Unltd CA.

Burgett, Shirley, jt. auth. see Svanevik, Michael.

Burggraaf, A. J., ed. Fundamentals of Inorganic Membrane. LC 97-100976. (Membrane Science & Technology Ser.: Vol. 4). 708p. 1996. text 359.00 (*0-444-81877-4*) Elsevier.

Burggraaf, A. J., et al. Inorganic Membranes. 632p. 1992. text 175.00 (*0-87849-625-4*, Pub. by Trans T Pub) Enfield Pubs NH.

Burggraaf, Y., tr. see Nannenga-Bremekamp, N. E.

Burggraf, Frederick. Thinking Connections Book B: Concept Maps for Life Science. (Illus.). 140p. (J). (gr. 7-12). 1998. pap. 22.95 (*0-89455-701-7*, MP5101) Crit Think Bks.

Burggraf, Linda P. Consuming Passions. limited ed. 21p. 1984. pap. 7.95 (*0-944754-06-6*) Pudding Hse Pubns.

Burggraf, Shirley P. Feminine Economy & Economic Man: Reviving the Role of Family in the Post-Industrial Age. 304p. 1998. pap. text 15.00 (*0-7382-0036-0*) Perseus Pubng.

Burggraf, Virginia & Barry, Richard. Gerontological Nursing: Current Practice & Research. 336p. 1996. pap. 35.00 (*1-55642-284-9*, 32849) SLACK Inc.

Burggraf, Virginia & Barry, Richard, Sr. Gerontological Nursing: Current Practice & Research Faculty Guide. (Illus.). 64p. 1997. pap. text, teacher ed. Price not set. (*1-55642-359-4*, 33594) SLACK Inc.

Burggraf, Virginia & Stanley, Mickey, eds. Nursing the Elderly: A Care Plan Approach. LC 87-37937. (Illus.). 461p. 1989. reprint ed. pap. 143.00 (*0-608-07305-9*, 206753300009) Bks Demand.

Burggren. Human Anatomy & Physiology: The Integrated Approach. (C). 1996. text. write for info. (*0-03-000564-7*) Harcourt Coll Pubs.

Burggren, Warren W. & Keller, Bradley B., eds. Development of Cardiovascular Systems: Molecules to Organisms. LC 96-44920. (Illus.). 376p. (C). 1998. text 80.00 (*0-521-56072-1*) Cambridge U Pr.

Burggren, Warren W., jt. ed. see Feder, Martin E.

Burgh, A. Wallen. Sumida, Edition I. 222p. 1959. write for info. (*0-318-57674-0*) Rural Life.

Burgh, Adriaan Van der, see Van der Burgh, Adriaan, ed.

Burgh, Anita. The Azure Bowl: Daughters of a Granite Land Trilogy, Vol. I. 448p. 1992. 24.95 (*0-7011-3461-5*, Pub. by Chatto & Windus) Trafalgar.

— Breeders. 512p. 1997. pap. 17.95 (*0-7528-0383-2*, Pub. by Orion Pubng Grp) Trafalgar.

— Lottery. large type ed. (Magna Large Print Ser.). 598p. 1997. 27.99 (*0-7505-0992-9*) Ulverscroft.

***Burgh, Hugo de.** Investigative Journalism: Context & Practice. LC 99-43659. 336p. 2000. pap. 26.99 (*0-415-19054-1*) Routledge.

Burgh, Hugo De, see De Burgh, Hugo, ed.

Burgh Norman, John E. De, see De Burgh Norman, John E., ed.

***Burgh, Rene.** Sewing Classic Clothes That Fit. (Illus.). 144p. 2000. 22.99 (*1-55870-570-8*, Betrwy Bks) F & W Pubns Inc.

Burghagen, M. M., tr. see Belitz, H. D. & Grosch, W.

Burghardt, Andrew F. Borderland, a Historical & Geographical Study of Burgenland, Austria. LC 62-15992. 389p. reprint ed. pap. 120.60 (*0-8357-7350-7*, 201535600001) Bks Demand.

Burghardt, Carl R., ed. Readings in Rhetorical Criticism. 2nd rev. ed. LC 99-56715. 682p. (C). 2000. pap. text 47.50 (*1-891136-03-8*) Strata Pub Co.

Burghardt, David M. Introduction to Engineering Design & Problem Solving. LC 98-18378. 240p. 1998. pap. 27.50 (*0-07-012188-5*) McGraw.

Burghardt, E., et al, eds. Surgical Gynecologic Oncology. LC 92-49606. 1993. 249.00 (*0-86577-473-0*) Thieme Med Pubs.

Burghardt, E., et al. Colposcopy, Cervical Pathology: Textbook & Atlas. 3rd ed. Ostor, Andrew G. & Tamussino, Karl, trs. from GER. LC 98-6919. 1998. 139.00 (*0-86577-634-2*); 139.00 (*3-13-659903-9*) Thieme Med Pubs.

Burghardt, Erich. Colposcopy: Cervical Pathology. 2nd ed. Oster, Andrew G., tr. (Illus.). 249p. 1991. 135.00 (*0-86577-348-3*) Thieme Med Pubs.

Burghardt, Galen. Treasury Options for Institutional Investors. Kirshner, Susan & CBOT Market & Product Development Department Staff, eds. LC 98-179873. 120p. 1997. pap. 25.00 (*0-917456-05-X*) Chicago Bd Trade.

Burghardt, Galen D. Eurodollar Futures & Options. (Institutional Investor Publications). 1991. text 65.00 (*1-55738-159-3*, Irwn Prfssnl) McGraw-Hill Prof.

Burghardt, Galen D. & Belton, Terrence M. The Treasury Bond Basis: An In-Depth Analysis for Hedgers, Speculators & Arbitrageurs. rev. ed. 225p. 1993. text 65.00 (*1-55738-479-7*, Irwn Prfssnl) McGraw-Hill Prof.

Burghardt, Gordon M., ed. see Rand, A. Stanley.

Burghardt, M. David. Introduction Engineering Profession. 2nd ed. LC 94-26512. 304p. (C). 1997. pap. text 59.00 (*0-673-99371-X*) Addison-Wesley.

***Burghardt, M. David & Harbach, James A.** Engineering Thermodynamics. 4th ed. LC 99-13153. 894p. (C). 1999. 90.00 (*0-87033-521-9*) Cornell Maritime.

Burghardt, Raymond F., et al. Who Needs Embassies? How U. S. Missions Abroad Help Shape Our World. Locke, Mary E. & Yost, Casimir A., eds. LC 98-125133. (Institute for the Study of Diplomacy Monograph Ser.). 133p. 1997. pap. 7.00 (*0-934742-91-X*) Geo U Inst Dplmcy.

Burghardt, Rita, jt. auth. see Long, Steve.

Burghardt, Stephen. Organizing for Community Action. LC 82-6034. (Sage Human Services Guides Ser.: No. 27). 120p. 1982. reprint ed. pap. 37.20 (*0-608-01190-8*, 205948800001) Bks Demand.

Burghardt, Stephen & Fabricant, Michael. Working under the Safety Net: Policy & Practice with the New American Poor. LC 86-27970. (Sage Human Services Guide Ser.: No. 13). 180p. 1987. reprint ed. pap. 55.80 (*0-608-04302-8*, 206508100012) Bks Demand.

Burghardt, Steve. The Other Side of Organizing: Personal Dilemmas & Political Demands. 248p. 1982. 22.95 (*0-87073-630-2*); pap. 15.95 (*0-87073-631-0*) Schenkman Bks Inc.

Burghardt, Steve, jt. auth. see Fabricant, Michael B.

Burghardt, W. J., et al, eds. St. Maximus the Confessor: The Ascetic Life, the Four Centuries on Charity. LC 55-8642. (Ancient Christian Writers Ser.: No. 21). 293p. 1955. 19.95 (*0-8091-0258-7*) Paulist Pr.

Burghardt, Walter, jt. auth. see Murray, John C.

Burghardt, Walter J. Christ in Ten Thousand Places: Homilies Toward a New Millennium. LC 99-33816. 288p. 1999. pap. 19.95 (*0-8091-3905-7*) Paulist Pr.

***Burghardt, Walter J.** Hear the Just Word & Live It. 96p. 2000. pap. 5.95 (*0-8091-3930-8*) Paulist Pr.

Burghardt, Walter J. Let Justice Roll down Like Waters: Biblical Justice Homilies Throughout the Year. LC 97-37897. 320p. 1998. pap. 19.95 (*0-8091-3765-8*) Paulist Pr.

***Burghardt, Walter J.** Long Have I Loved You: A Theologian Reflects on His Church. LC 99-40097. 500p. 2000. pap. 20.00 (*1-57075-296-6*) Orbis Bks.

Burghardt, Walter J. Love is a Flame of the Lord: More Homilies on the Just Word. LC 95-22767. 192p. (Orig.). 1996. pap. 14.95 (*0-8091-3603-1*) Paulist Pr.

— Preaching: The Art & the Craft. 256p. 1987. pap. 14.95 (*0-8091-2906-X*) Paulist Pr.

— Preaching the Just Word. LC 96-15779. 224p. 1998. 27.50 (*0-300-06768-2*); pap. 14.95 (*0-300-07721-1*) Yale U Pr.

— Speak the Word with Boldness: Homilies for Risen Christians. LC 94-4905. 400p. (Orig.). 1994. pap. 14.95 (*0-8091-3470-5*) Paulist Pr.

— Still Proclaiming Your Wonders: Homilies for the '80s. 256p. (Orig.). 1984. pap. 9.95 (*0-8091-2632-X*) Paulist Pr.

Burghardt, Walter J., et al, eds. Arnobius of Sicca, the Case Against the Pagans, Vol. 1. (Ancient Christian Writers Ser.: No. 7). 372p. 1949. 22.95 (*0-8091-0248-X*) Paulist Pr.

— Arnobius of Sicca, the Case Against the Pagans, Vol. 2. LC 78-62458. (Ancient Christian Writers Ser.: No. 8). 659p. 1949. 19.95 (*0-8091-0249-8*) Paulist Pr.

— Athenagoras, Embassy for the Christians, the Resurrection of the Dead. LC 56-11421. (Ancient Christian Writers Ser.: No. 23). 193p. 1956. 14.95 (*0-8091-0036-3*) Paulist Pr.

— The Didache, the Epistle of Barnabas, the Epistle & Martyrdom of St. Polycarp, the Fragments of Papias, the Epistle of Diognetus. LC 78-62453. (Ancient Christian Writers Ser.: No. 6). 241p. 1948. 19.95 (*0-8091-0247-1*) Paulist Pr.

— Egeria, Diary of a Pilgrimage. LC 70-119159. (Ancient Christian Writers Ser.: No. 38). 292p. 1970. 24.95 (*0-8091-0029-0*) Paulist Pr.

— Firmicus Maternus, the Error of the Pagan Religions. (Ancient Christian Writers Ser.: No. 37). 1970. 18.95 (*0-8091-0039-8*) Paulist Pr.

— Julianus Pomerius, the Contemplative Life. LC 78-62457. (Ancient Christian Writers Ser.: No. 4). 220p. 1947. 16.95 (*0-8091-0245-5*) Paulist Pr.

— Origen, Prayer, Exhortation to Martyrdom. LC 78-62467. (Ancient Christian Writers Ser.: No. 19). 261p. 1954. 29.95 (*0-8091-0256-0*) Paulist Pr.

— Origen, the Song of Songs: Commentary & Homilies. LC 57-11826. (Ancient Christian Writers Ser.: No. 26). 491p. 1957. 24.95 (*0-8091-0261-7*) Paulist Pr.

— Rufinus: A Commentary of the Apostles' Creed. LC 78-62468. (Ancient Christian Writers Ser.: No. 20). 167p. 1955. 14.95 (*0-8091-0257-9*) Paulist Pr.

— St. Athanasius: The Life of St. Antony. LC 78-62454. (Ancient Christian Writers Ser.: No. 10). 155p. 1950. 24.95 (*0-8091-0250-1*) Paulist Pr.

— Tertullian, the Treatise Against Hermogenes. LC 56-13257. (Ancient Christian Writers Ser.: No. 24). 179p. 1956. 14.95 (*0-8091-0148-3*) Paulist Pr.

— Tertullian, Treatise on Marriage & Remarriage: To His Wife, an Exhortation to Chastity Monogamy. LC 78-62462. (Ancient Christian Writers Ser.: No. 13). 103p. 1951. 14.95 (*0-8091-0149-1*) Paulist Pr.

— Tertullian, Treatise on Penance: On Penitence & on Purity. LC 58-10746. (Ancient Christian Writers Ser.: No. 28). 138p. 1959. 21.95 (*0-8091-0150-5*) Paulist Pr.

Burghardt, Walter J., et al. A New Look at Preaching, Vol. 7. 164p. 1989. pap. 24.00 (*0-86217-074-5*, Pub. by Veritas Pubns) St Mut.

Burghardt, Walter J., ed. see Augustine, Saint.

Burghardt, Walter J., ed. see Cyprian, Saint.

Burghardt, Walter J., ed. see Gregory, Saint.

Burghardt, Walter J., ed. see Irenaeus, Saint.

Burghardt, Walter J., ed. see John Chrysostom, Saint.

Burghardt, Walter J., ed. see Methodius, Saint.

Burghardt, Walter J., ed. see Prosper, Saint.

Burghardt, Wolfgang & Hoelker, Klaus, eds. Text Processing. (Research in Text Theory Ser.). 466p. (C). 1979. text 142.35 (*3-11-007565-2*) De Gruyter.

Burghart, Johannes, jt. ed. see Lawler, Thomas C.

Burghart, Judy. Living in the U. S. A. 160p. 1990. pap. 10.55 (*0-8442-7694-4*) NTC Contemp Pub Co.

— Living in the U. S. A. 2nd ed. 160p. 1990. pap. 10.55 (*0-8442-7695-2*) NTC Contemp Pub Co.

Burgher, Goldene F. Washington County, Tennessee Wills, 1777-1872. (Illus.). 144p. 1983. pap. 25.00 (*0-89308-285-6*) Southern Hist Pr.

Burgher, Martha M., jt. auth. see Holmes, Scott.

Burgher, Peter H. Changement: Understanding & Managing Business. LC 78-19576. 1979. text 39.95 (*0-669-02569-0*) Agnes Press.

— Professional Excellence: System for Managing Professionals. LC 85-7296. 160p. 1986. 29.95 (*0-936033-00-2*) Agnes Press.

Burghes, D. N. & Borrie, M. S. Modelling with Differential Equations. LC 80-41936. (Mathematics & Its Applications Ser.). 172p. 1982. pap. text 41.95 (*0-470-27360-7*) P-H.

Burghes, D. N. & Wood, A. D. Mathematical Models in the Social Management & Life Sciences. LC 79-40989. (Mathematics & Its Applications Ser.). 287p. 1980. pap. text 41.95 (*0-470-27073-X*) P-H.

Burghley, Michael & Burghley, Nancy. The Rising Tide of Change. (Illus.). 69p. (Orig.). 1986. pap. 5.95 (*0-935427-12-0*) Foundation Hse.

Burghley, Nancy, jt. auth. see Burghley, Michael

***Burghoff, Gary & Pets: Part of the Family Editors.** The Wonderful Thing about Pets: Remarkable Stories About the Animals Who Share Our Lives. LC 99-89629. 208p. 2000. 18.95 (*1-57954-187-9*) Rodale Pr Inc.

Burghorn, Jim. Problem Solving Simplified: A Common Sense Approach to Solving Complex Problems. 115p. (Orig.). 1997. pap. 39.95 (*0-9640615-1-1*) Comm Sense Pubns.

Burghorn, Jim & Gudenas, Ingrid. Hats & Stats: The Keys to Success at Work. LC 94-94224. (Illus.). 97p. 1994. pap. 39.95 (*0-9640615-0-3*) Comm Sense Pubns.

Burght, Gregor Van Der, see Van Der Burght, Gregor.

Burght, Grvander. Corporate Law in Practice. LC 98-28446. 1998. 103.00 (*90-411-0749-5*) Kluwer Law Intl.

Burght, Van D. Corporate Law. 1988. lib. bdg. 81.00 (*90-6544-337-1*) Kluwer Academic.

Burgi, Philip H., ed. Model-Prototype Correlation of Hydraulic Structures. (Symposium Proceedings Ser.). 488p. 1988. 49.00 (*0-87262-669-5*) Am Soc Civil Eng.

Burgie, I. Lord Burgie: Wish You Were Here & Others. (Piano-Vocal-Guitar Ser.). 1989. 9.95 (*0-89524-420-9*, 02500560) Cherry Lane.

Burgie, Irving. Caribbean Souvenir Songbook. Okun, Milton, ed. pap. 5.95 (*0-685-75219-4*); audio 10.00 (*0-685-75220-8*) Cherry Lane.

— Your Caribbean Souvenir Song Book. Phillips, Mark, ed. (Illus.). (Orig.). 1990. pap. text 12.95 (*0-89524-404-7*) Cherry Lane.

Burgiel, Stanley W., jt. ed. see Cohen, Sheldon.

Burgiere, Andre. Diccionario de Ciencias Historicas. (SPA.). 686p. 1991. 175.00 (*0-7859-3357-3*, 8446000377) Fr & Eur.

Burgiere, Andre, ed. A History of Family Life, 2 vols. Wilson, Andrew et al, trs. LC 95-23811.Tr. of Histoire de la Famille. write for info. (*0-674-39674-X*) HUP.

Burgin, C. David, ed. see Lucius, Jim.

Burgin, C. David, ed. see Torrez, Andrew.

Burgin, David. Great Moments: The Official Book of the 1998 World Series. 1998. pap. 19.95 (*0-942627-34-2*) Woodford Pubng.

Burgin, Diana, tr. see Bulgakov, Mikhail Afanasevich.

Burgin, Diana L. Richard Burgin: A Life in Verse. (Illus.). 230p. (Orig.). 1989. pap. 19.95 (*0-89357-196-2*) Slavica.

— Sophia Parnok: The Life & Work of Russia's Sappho. LC 94-1266. (Cutting Edge: Lesbian Life & Literature Ser.). (C). 1994. text 55.00 (*0-8147-1190-1*); pap. text 19.50 (*0-8147-1221-5*) NYU Pr.

Burgin, John C. Teaching Singing. LC 72-10594. 290p. 1973. 32.00 (*0-8108-0565-0*) Scarecrow.

Burgin, Miron, ed. Handbook of Latin American Studies, Vol. 6: 1940. LC 36-32633. xvi, 570p. 1963. 35.00 (*0-8130-0032-7*) U Press Fla.

— Handbook of Latin American Studies, Vol. 7: 1941. LC 36-32633. xv, 549p. 1963. 35.00 (*0-8130-0033-5*) U Press Fla.

— Handbook of Latin American Studies, Vol. 8: 1942. LC 36-32633. xv, 521p. 1963. 35.00 (*0-8130-0034-3*) U Press Fla.

Burgin, Miron, jt. ed. see Hanke, Lewis.

Burgin, Patricia. The Powerful Percent: Student at the Heart of the Great Commission. 141p. (C). Date not set. pap. 7.95 (*0-9629245-0-4*) WSN Pr.

Burgin, Richard. Fear of Blue Skies. LC 97-21604. (Poetry & Fiction Ser.). 184p. 1997. 19.95 (*0-8018-5745-7*) Johns Hopkins.

***Burgin, Richard.** Ghost Quartet. LC 99-26624. 288p. 1999. 25.95 (*0-8101-5095-6*, TriQuart) Northwestern U Pr.

Burgin, Richard. Man Without Memory: Stories. LC 88-20854. (Illinois Short Fiction Ser.). 136p. 1989. 14.95 (*0-252-01602-5*) U of Ill Pr.

— Private Fame. (Illinois Short Fiction Ser.). 168p. 1991. 16.95 (*0-252-01843-5*) U of Ill Pr.

Burgin, Richard, ed. Jorge Luis Borges: Conversations. LC 98-36711. (Literary Conversations Ser.). 256p. 1998. pap. 17.00 (*1-57806-076-1*) U Pr of Miss.

Burgin, Richard, ed. see Borges, Jorge Luis.

Burgin, Robert, et al, eds. Library Overdues: Analysis, Strategies & Solutions to the Problem. LC 84-19736. (Library & Archival Security: Vol. 6, Nos. 2-3). 135p. 1985. text 39.95 (*0-86656-376-8*) Haworth Pr.

Burgin, Victor. In Different Spaces: Place & Memory in Visual Culture. LC 95-48900. (Illus.). 329p. (C). 1996. 48.00 (*0-520-20298-8*, Pub. by U CA Pr); pap. 18.95 (*0-520-20299-6*, Pub. by U CA Pr) Cal Prin Full Svc.

— Some Cities. LC 95-50336. (Illus.). 224p. (C). 1996. pap. 19.95 (*0-520-20636-3*, Pub. by U CA Pr) Cal Prin Full Svc.

Burgin, Victor. Venise. (Illus.). 72p. 1997. pap. 24.95 (*0-901033-10-3*, Pub. by Art Bks Intl) Partners Pubs Grp.

Burgin, Victor. Venise. 72p. 1997. pap. 24.95 (*1-901033-10-4*, Pub. by Black Dog Pubg) RAM Publications.

Burgin, Victor, et al. Formations of Fantasy. 240p. 1987. pap. 14.95 (*0-416-31220-9*, 1202) Routledge.

— Victor Burgin: History Painting. (Illus.). 52p. (Orig.). 1995. 15.00 (*0-9645577-0-3*) U Buff Art Gall.

Burgin, William G., jt. auth. see Griffin, Kenneth D.

Burgio, G. Roberto, et al, eds. Primum Non Nocere Today - a Symposium on Pediatric Bioethics: Proceedings of the International Symposium on Pediatric Bioethics, Pavia, 26-28 May 1994. LC 94-40670. (International Congress Ser.: Vol. 1071). 186p. 1994. 158.50 (*0-444-81920-7*) Elsevier.

Burgio, G. Roberto & Lantos, John D., eds. Primum Non Nocere Today. 2nd ed. LC 98-47922. (International Congress Ser.). 190p. 1998. 161.00 (*0-444-82923-7*, Excerpta Medica) Elsevier.

Burgio, Kathryn L., et al. Staying Dry: A Practical Guide to Bladder Control. LC 89-45480. 176p. 1989. pap. 12.95 (*0-8018-3909-2*); text 30.00 (*0-8018-3912-2*) Johns Hopkins.

Burgis, Alan. Full Circle. (C). 1988. 35.00 (*0-7855-3516-0*, Pub. by Rivelin Grapheme Pr) St Mut.

***Burgis, Donald.** Let's Get Down to Business. Noresta, Anthony, ed. (Illus.). 148p. 2000. spiral bd. 20.00 (*0-9701633-0-4*) Hisp Inst for Res.

Burgis, Mary J. & Morris, Pat. The Natural History of Lakes. (Illus.). 224p. 1987. text 39.95 (*0-521-30793-7*) Cambridge U Pr.

Burgis, Nina, ed. see Dickens, Charles.

Burgis, Nina, ed. see Trollope, Anthony.

***Burgisser, Peter.** Completeness & Reduction Algebraic Complexity Theology. Becker, E. et al, eds. (Algorithms & Computations in Mathematics: 7). (Illus.). 170p. 2000. 79.95 (*3-540-66752-0*) Spr-Verlag.

Burgisser, Peter, et al. Algebraic Complexity Theory. LC 96-29754. (Grundlehren der Mathematischen Wissenschaften Ser.: Vol. 315). 655p. 1997. 139.50 (*3-540-60582-7*) Spr-Verlag.

***Burgland, Lane A.** Reading the Bible with Understanding. 144p. 1998. pap., teacher ed. 9.99 (*0-570-01555-3*, 22-2547GJ) Concordia.

Burglass, Milton E., ed. see Schaefer, Faith S.

***Burglund, John F.** Expositions in Modern Mathematics. 312p. 2000. write for info. (*1-58692-025-1*) Copyright Mgmt.

Burgmaier, Lynn. The Man from Right Field. LC 98-90372. 1998. 19.95 (*0-533-12770-X*) Vantage.

Burgman, Mark A., jt. auth. see Ferson, S.

Burgmann, Meredith. Green Bans, Red Union: Environmental Activism & the New South Wales Builders Labourer's Federation. LC 99-180953. 320p. 1998. pap. 29.95 (*0-86840-760-7*, Pub. by New South Wales Univ Pr) Intl Spec Bk.

Burgmann, Petra. Feeding Your Pet Bird. 144p. 1993. pap. 11.95 (*0-8120-1521-5*) Barron.

Burgmann, Verity. Power & Protest: Movements for Change in Australian Society. 240p. (Orig.). 1992. pap. text 18.95 (*1-86373-211-X*, Pub. by Allen & Unwin Pty) Paul & Co Pubs.

— Revolutionary Industrial Unionism: The Industrial Workers of the World in Australia. LC 95-3722. (Illus.). 358p. (C). 1995. text 59.95 (*0-521-47123-0*) Cambridge U Pr.

Burgmeier, Arline, et al. Lexis: Academic Vocabulary Study for ESL Students. 240p. (C). 1990. pap. text 31.53 (*0-13-535022-0*) P-H.

Burgmeier, James L., et al. Calculus with Applications. 640p. (C). 1990. teacher ed. write for info. (*0-318-65085-1*) McGraw.

Burgmueller, F. Twenty-Five Easy & Progressive Studies for the Piano, Opus 100. Hoffman, Carl, ed. (Carl Fischer Music Library: No. 324). 1909. pap. 6.50 (*0-8258-0107-9*, L324) Fischer Inc NY.

— Twenty-Five Easy & Progressive Studies for the Piano Opus 100 Complete. 36p. 1986. pap. 4.95 (*0-7935-2556-X*) H Leonard.

Burgner, Goldene F. Carter County, Tennessee, Marriages, 1796-1870. 150p. 1987. pap. 25.00 (*0-89308-601-0*, TN 100) Southern Hist Pr.

— Greene County Minutes of the Court of Common Pleas, 1783-1795. 280p. 1982. 27.50 (*0-89308-278-3*, TN 29) Southern Hist Pr.

— Greene County Tax Digests, 1809-1817. 250p. 1986. 27.50 (*0-89308-277-5*, TN 36) Southern Hist Pr.

— Greene County, Tennessee, Chancery Court Minutes, 1825-1876. 371p. 1987. 38.50 (*0-89308-602-9*, TN 102) Southern Hist Pr.

— Greene County Tennessee, Marriages, 1783 to 1868. 396p. 1981. 35.00 (*0-89308-202-3*) Southern Hist Pr.

— Greene County Wills, 1783-1890. 150p. 1981. 27.50 (*0-89308-203-1*) Southern Hist Pr.

— Washington County, Tennessee, Marriages, 1780-1870. (Illus.). 224p. 1985. 27.50 (*0-89308-564-2*, TN 89) Southern Hist Pr.

Burgoa, Francisco De, see De Burgoa, Francisco.

Burgon, Dean J. The Last Twelve Verses of Mark. 1996. pap. 15.00 (*1-888328-00-2*) D Burgon Soc.

Burgon, Dean J. Unholy Hands on the Bible: An Introduction to Textual Criticism. 1990. 34.99 (*1-878442-63-5*) Sovreign Grace Pubs.

B

Burgon, John W. Unholy Hands on the Bible: The Works of John W. Burgon, Vol. 1. abr. ed. (New Testament Text Ser.). 608p. (C). 1989. text 24.95 (0-685-30023-4) Sovereign Grace Pubs.

Burgoon, Judee K., et al. Interpersonal Adaptation: Dyadic Interaction Patterns. (Illus.). 352p. (C). 1995. text 54.95 (0-521-45120-5) Cambridge U Pr.

— Nonverbal Communication: The Unspoken Dialogue. 2nd ed. 535p. (C). 1995. pap. 41.25 (0-07-008995-7) McGraw.

Burgoon, Michael, ed. Communication Yearbook, No. 5. 885p. (C). 1982. text 59.95 (0-87855-447-5) Transaction Pubs.

— Communication Yearbook, No. 6. LC 76-45943. (Illus.). 968p. reprint ed. pap. 200.00 (0-7837-1121-2, 204165100006) Bks Demand.

Burgoon, Michael, et al. Human Communications. 3rd ed. (C). 1993. 65.00 (0-8039-5076-4); pap. 28.00 (0-8039-5077-2) Sage.

Burgos, ed. see Apollinaire, Guillaume.

***Burgos-Debray, Elizabeth.** Me Llamo Rigoberta Menchu y As. (SPA.). 1998. pap. 19.98 (968-23-1315-5) Siglo XXI.

Burgos-Debray, Elizabeth, ed. see Menchu, Rigoberta.

Burgos, Julia de. El Mar y Tu. LC 81-68710. (Illus.). 1981. pap. 6.75 (0-940238-46-2) Ediciones Huracan.

Burgos, Julia De, see De Burgos, Julia.

Burgos, Pedro J. Epistolas de Viajes. LC 85-20311. (SPA.). 266p. 1986. pap. 11.00 (0-8477-3519-2) U of PR Pr.

Burgos, Villaneuve. Guia Propuestas y Tesis. (SPA.). 78p. 1992. pap. write for info. (0-929441-28-1) Pubns Puertorriquenas.

Burgos, William, et al. The Commuter Nation: Perspectives on Puerto Rican Migration. 1994. pap. 13.75 (0-8477-2498-0) U of PR Pr.

Burgoyne, Arthur G. Homestead: A Complete History of the Struggle Between the Carnegie Steel Co. & the Amalgamated Assoc. of Iron & Steel Workers. LC 68-55495. viii, 298p. 1971. reprint ed. 45.00 (0-678-00872-8) Kelley.

— The Homestead Strike of Eighteen Ninety-Two. LC 79-4702. (Illus.). 352p. (C). 1979. reprint ed. pap. 15.95 (0-8229-5310-2); reprint ed. text 49.95 (0-8229-3405-1) U of Pittsburgh Pr.

***Burgoyne, Bernard, ed.** Drawing the Soul: Models & Schemas in Psychoanalysis. 260p. 2000. pap. 29.99 (1-900877-02-3, Pub. by Rebus Pr Ltd) Intl Spec Bk.

***Burgoyne, Bernard & Sullivan, Mary, eds.** The Klein-Lacan Dialogues. LC 99-13501. 180p. 1999. pap. 18.95 (1-892746-16-6, 46166) Other Pr LLC.

Burgoyne, Bruce E. Canada During the American Revolutionary War. 222p. 1998. pap. 20.50 (0-7884-0857-7, B874) Heritage Bk.

— Defeat, Disaster, & Dedication. xiv, 142p. 1997. pap. 12.00 (0-7884-0715-5, B873) Heritage Bk.

— The Diary of Lieutenant Von Bardeleben: And Other Von Donop Regiment Documents. 211p. 1998. pap. 21.00 (0-7884-1054-7, No. B872) Heritage Bk.

— Enemy Views: The American Revolutionary War As Recorded by the Hessian Participants. LC 97-136578. (Illus.). xxxi, 616p. (Orig.). 1996. pap. 40.50 (0-7884-0563-2, B867) Heritage Bk.

— George Pausch's Journal & Reports of the Campaign in America. 148p. (Orig.). 1996. pap. 19.50 (0-7884-0531-4, B862) Heritage Bk.

— The Hesse-Cassel Mirbach Regiment in the American Revolution. LC 98-210009. 140p. 1998. pap. 17.00 (0-7884-0940-9, B875) Heritage Bk.

— A Hessian Report on the People, the Land, the War: Eighteenth Century America As Noted in the Diary of Chaplain Philipp Waldeck. LC 95-237821. 206p. (Orig.). 1995. pap. 17.50 (0-7884-0252-8) Heritage Bk.

***Burgoyne, Bruce E.** The 3rd English-Waldeck Regiment in the American Revolution. (Illus.). 323p. 1999. pap. 31.50 (0-7884-1301-5, B877) Heritage Bk.

Burgoyne, Bruce E., ed. Diaries of Two Ansbach Jaegers. LC 97-194982. (Illus.). xii, 166p. 1997. pap. 17.00 (0-7884-0655-8, B869) Heritage Bk.

— A Hessian Officer's Diary of the American Revolution Translated from An Anonymous Ansbach-Bayreuth Diary As Originally Written by Johann Ernst Prechtel. (Illus.). 317p. (Orig.). 1994. pap. text 24.50 (0-7884-0107-6) Heritage Bk.

Burgoyne, Bruce E., tr. from GER. Diaries of a Hessian Chaplain & the Chaplain's Assistant. 50p. (Orig.). (C). 1990. pap. 4.00 (0-939016-17-6) Johannes Schwalm Hist.

Burgoyne, Bruce E., tr. see Barth, R. Carl, ed.

Burgoyne, John. The Dramatic & Poetical Works of the Late Lieut. Gen. J. Burgoyne. LC 77-2932. 520p. 1977. reprint ed. 75.00 (0-8201-1285-2) Schol Facsimiles.

— State of the Expedition from Canada, As Laid Before the House of Commons. LC 70-77104. (Eyewitness Accounts of the American Revolution Ser.). 1969. reprint ed. 23.95 (0-405-01146-6) Ayer.

Burgoyne, John & Reynolds, Michael, eds. Management Learning: Integrating Perspectives in Theory & Practice. 368p. 1997. 85.00 (0-8039-7643-7); pap. 35.00 (0-8039-7644-5) Sage.

Burgoyne, John G., jt. ed. see Livian, Yves F.

Burgoyne, Patrick & Faber, Liz. Internet Design Project. Blackwell, Lewis, ed. (Illus.). 250p. 1998. 27.50 (0-7893-0124-5, Pub. by Universe) St Martin.

— The New Internet Design Project: The Best of Graphic Art on the Web Reloaded. (Illus.). 144p. 1999. pap. 29.95 (0-7893-0362-0, Pub. by Universe) St Martin.

Burgoyne, Patrick & Leslie, Jeremy. Board: Surf, Skate, Snow Graphics. LC 97-38235. 1998. pap. write for info. (0-8230-0528-3) Watsn-Guptill.

Burgoyne, R. D. & Peterson, O. M., eds. Landmarks in Intracellular Signalling. (Landmarks in Science & Medicine Ser.: Vol. 2). (Illus.). 280p. (C). 1997. pap. text 34.00 (1-85578-101-8, Pub. by Portland Pr Ltd) Ashgate Pub Co.

Burgoyne, Robert. Bertolucci's 1900: A Narrative & Historical Analysis. LC 90-12355. (Contemporary Film & Television Ser.). (Illus.). 184p. reprint ed. pap. 57.10 (0-608-10539-2, 207115900009) Bks Demand.

— Film Nation: Hollywood Looks at U. S. History. LC 97-5919. (Illus.). 160p. (C). 1997. pap. 14.95 (0-8166-2071-7); text 39.95 (0-8166-2070-9) U of Minn Pr.

Burgoyne, Suzanne, et al. Teaching & Performing: Ideas for Energizing Your Classes. LC 96-46235. (Orig.). 1996. pap. 24.95 (0-912150-44-0) Atwood Pub LLC.

Burgoyne, Suzanne, jt. tr. see Friedman, Donald F.

Burgoyne, Thomas H. The Light of Egypt: The Science of the Soul & the Stars, 2 vols. 114p. 1980. pap. 34.00 (0-89540-125-8, SB-125) Sun Pub.

— The Light of Egypt: or The Science of the Soul & the Stars, 2 vols. (Illus.). 600p. 1980. pap. 34.00 (0-89540-064-2, SB-064, Sun Bks) Sun Pub.

Burgraff, Roger. Persuasion Power Skills. 13p. 1991. pap. text 79.50 incl. audio (0-88432-436-2, S03040) Audio-Forum.

— Skills for Management Effectiveness, Set 6. 28p. 1991. pap. 79.50 incl. audio (0-88432-437-0, S03050) Audio-Forum.

Burgreen, David. Design Methods for Power Plant Structures. 446p. 1970. reprint ed. 48.00 (0-916877-03-5) Arcturus Pubs.

— Elements of Thermal Stress Analysis. 462p. 1971. reprint ed. 48.00 (0-916877-02-7) Arcturus Pubs.

— Pressure Vessel Analysis. 363p. 1979. 48.00 (0-916877-05-1) Arcturus Pubs.

— Principles of Piping Analysis. 483p. 1977. 48.00 (0-916877-04-3) Arcturus Pubs.

Burgstahler. New Kids on the Net. LC 98-172243. 190p. (C). 1997. pap. text 24.95 (0-205-27698-9) P-H.

Burgstahler, Sheryl. New Kids on Net: A Tutorial for Teachers, Parents & Students. 214p. 1998. pap. text 24.95 (0-205-28594-5) Allyn.

Burgstahler, Sheryl. New Kids on the Net: A Tutorial. LC 97-150029. 252p. (C). 1996. pap. text 24.95 (0-205-19872-4) Allyn.

— New Kids on the Net: Activities for K-12. 199p. (J). (gr. k-12). 1996. pap. text 24.95 (0-205-19873-2) Allyn.

— New Kids on the Net: Internet Activities in Elementary Language Arts. 232p. 1999. pap. text 24.95 (0-205-30587-3) Allyn.

Burgstahler, Sheryl, et al. Universal Access: Electronic Resources in Libraries. 1998. 75.00 (0-8389-3490-0) ALA.

Burgstaller, Andre. Property & Prices: Towards a Unified Theory of Value. (Illus.). 254p. (C). 1995. text 59.95 (0-521-41903-4) Cambridge U Pr.

Burgstaller, Signe. United Nations Conflict Management: An Institutionalist Perspective. (Illus.). 91p. (Orig.). (C). 1995. pap. text 25.00 (0-7881-2177-4) DIANE Pub.

Burguera, Jose Luis. Flow Injection Atomic Spectroscopy. (Practical Spectroscopy Ser.: Vol. 7). (Illus.). 368p. 1989. text 199.00 (0-8247-8059-0) Dekker.

Burguiere, Andre. Dictionnaire Des Sciences Historiques. (FRE.). 704p. 1986. pap. 125.00 (0-7859-7742-2, 2130393616) Fr & Eur.

Burguiere, Andre, et al, eds. A History of the Family Vol. 1: Distant Worlds, Ancient Worlds, Vol. I. (Illus.). 704p. 1996. 39.95 (0-674-39675-8) HUP.

— A History of the Family Vol. 2: The Impact of Modernity. (Illus.). 600p. 1996. 39.95 (0-674-39676-6) HUP.

***Burguiere, Andre & Grew, Raymond, eds.** The Construction of Minorities: Cases for Comparison Across Time & Around the World. (Comparative Studies in Society & History Book). (Illus.). 320p. (C). 2000. text 59.50 (0-472-09737-7, 09737); pap. text 22.95 (0-472-06737-0, 06737) U of Mich Pr.

***Burguieres, Cheryl C.** One Centimeter. 2nd ed. (Illus.). 1999. 21.95 (0-87719-368-1) Gulf Pub.

Burgum, Ian, jt. auth. see Atterbury, Paul.

Burgum, Ian, jt. auth. see Keen, Richard.

Burgunder, Lee B. Legal Aspects of Managing Technology. LC 94-37946. (Illus.). 448p. (C). 1994. mass mkt. 60.95 (0-538-82664-9) S-W Pub.

— Managing the Legal Aspects of Technology. 2nd ed. 2000. pap. 67.95 (0-324-02720-6) Thomson Learn.

***Burgunder, Lee B.** Pre-Release: Managing the Legal Aspects of Technology. 2nd ed. (SWC-General Business Ser.). 1999. pap. 35.00 (0-324-04077-6) Thomson Learn.

Burgundy Group, Inc. Staff. Top of the House. 112p. 1995. pap. text, spiral bd. 39.95 (0-7872-0815-9) Kendall-Hunt.

Burgwin, Marion A., jt. ed. see Genoways, Hugh H.

Burgwinkle, William, et al, eds. Significant Others: Gender & Culture in Film & Literature East & West. LC 93-7608. (Literary Studies: Vol. 6). 136p. 1993. pap. text 15.00 (0-8248-1564-5) Coll Lang Ling & Lit.

Burgwinkle, William E. Love for Sale: Materialist Readings of the Troubadour Razo Corpus. LC 97-30606. (New Middle Ages Ser.: Vol. 5). (Illus.). 360p. 1997. text 70.00 (0-8153-2842-7, H2067) Garland.

Burgwyn, H. James. Italian Foreign Policy in the Interwar Period, 1918-1940. LC 96-43874. (Foreign Policies of the Great Powers Ser.). 240p. 1997. 65.00 (0-275-94877-3, Praeger Pubs) Greenwood.

— The Legend of the Mutilated Victory: Italy, the Great War, & the Paris Peace Conference, 1915-1919, 38. LC 92-45082. (Contributions to the Study of World History Ser.: No. 38). 368p. 1993. 57.95 (0-313-28885-2, GM8885, Greenwood Pr) Greenwood.

Burham, David. The Role of the Media in Controlling Corruption. (Criminal Justice Center Monogrpahs). 1978. pap. text 3.00 (0-318-37486-2) John Jay Pr.

Burhan, Faysad. The Solution to the Muslim Crisis. 2nd ed. 185p. 1996. pap. 9.95 (0-9653790-0-0) Inst Arabic & Islamic.

Burhan-Stipanov, Linda & Barry, Kathleen C. Cancer Education Resources for American Indians & Alaska Natives. (Illus.). 73p. (Orig.). (C). 1996. pap. text 20.00 (0-7881-3001-3) DIANE Pub.

Burhans, Clinton S. The Would-Be Writer. 3rd ed. LC 74-133494. 400p. reprint ed. pap. 124.00 (0-608-30122-1, 201261700082) Bks Demand.

— The Would-Be Writer. 3rd ed. LC 74-13349. 444p. 1971. reprint ed. pap. 137.70 (0-608-10409-4, 202169700023) Bks Demand.

Burhans, Robert D. The First Special Service Force: A War History of the North Americans, 1942-1944. (Illus.). 376p. 1996. reprint ed. 39.95 (0-89839-261-6) Battery Pr.

Burhans, S., Jr. Burhans: Descendants from the First Ancestor in America, Jacob Burhans, 1660, & His Son, Jan Burhans, 1663. (Illus.). 799p. 1991. reprint ed. pap. 114.00 (0-8328-1896-8); reprint ed. lib. bdg. 124.00 (0-8328-1895-X) Higginson Bk Co.

Burhans, William A., tr. see Triandafillov, V. K. & Kipp, Jacob W.

Burhanuddin, Muhammed & Taher, Mohamed. Indian Contribution to American Studies: An Assessment. LC 98-902730. (C). 1997. 52.50 (81-7488-471-8, Pub. by Anmol) S Asia.

Burhenne, W. E., ed. International Environmental Law: Droit International de l'environnement/Internationales Umweltrecht. 1997. ring bd. 477.00 (90-411-0757-6) Kluwer Law Intl.

Burhenne, Wolfgang E., ed. International Environmental Soft Law: Collection of Relevant Instruments. LC 92-39157. 304p. (C). 1993. lib. bdg. 402.00 (0-7923-2070-0) Kluwer Academic.

Burhenne, Wolfgang E. & Robinson, Nicholas A., eds. International Protection of the Environment: Conservation in Sustainable Development, 6 vols., Set. LC 95-195899. 1995. ring bd. 595.00 (0-379-10295-1) Oceana.

Burher, Brett, jt. auth. see Christensen, Ken.

Buri, Fritz. The Buddha-Christ As the Lord of the True Self: The Religious Philosophy of the Kyoto School & Christianity. Oliver, Harold H., tr. LC 97-15884. 320p. 1997. text 35.00 (0-86554-536-7, MUP/H410) Mercer Univ Pr.

— Theology of Existence. Oliver, Harold H., tr. 128p. 1965. 6.00 (0-87921-001-X) Attic Pr.

Buria, Maria E. Billy the Bean. (Illus.). 36p. (Orig.). (J). (ps). 1989. pap. 5.95 (1-878926-04-7) Colorful Lrngs.

***Buria, Maria E.** Larousse Active dictionary for Beginners Spanish: Pictures, Songs, Activities & Pronunciation. (Illus.). 64p. (YA). 2000. 15.95 (2-03-540170-4, Larousse LKC) LKC.

Buriak, Philip & Osborne, Edward W. Physical Science Applications in Agriculture. 500p. 1996. text 58.75 (0-8134-3013-5); text, teacher ed. 9.95 (0-8134-3014-3) Interstate.

— Physical Science Applications in Agriculture I Teacher's Guide. 1998. teacher ed. 40.00 (0-8134-3037-2, 3037) Interstate.

— Physical Science Applications in Agriculture II Teacher's Guide. 1998. teacher ed. 40.00 (0-8134-3038-0, 3038) Interstate.

Burian, Edward R., ed. Modernity & the Architecture of Mexico. LC 96-2758. (Illus.). 240p. 1997. 40.00 (0-292-70852-1); pap. 19.95 (0-292-70853-X) U of Tex Pr.

Burian, J. M., ed. from CZE. The Secret of Theatrical Space: The Memoirs of Josef Svoboda. (Illus.). 144p. 1995. pap. 29.95 (1-55783-216-1) Applause Theatre Bk Pubs.

***Burian, Jarka M.** Modern Czech Theatre: Reflector & Conscience of a Nation. LC 99-58328. (Studies in Theatre History & Culture). (Illus.). 280p. 2000. text 37.95 (0-87745-711-5); pap. text 18.95 (0-87745-722-0) U of Iowa Pr.

Burian, Peter, ed. Directions in Euripidean Criticism: A Collection of Essays. LC 84-25950. viii, 237p. (C). 1985. 31.95 (0-8223-0610-7) Duke.

Burian, Peter, tr. Aeschylus: The Suppliants. 116p. 1991. text 27.95 (0-691-06867-4, Pub. by Princeton U Pr) Cal Prin Full Svc.

***Burian, Peter & Caputo, Robert.** National Geographic Photography Field Guide: Secrets to Making Great Pictures. LC 99-23595. 352p. 1999. per. 24.95 (0-7922-7498-9, Pub. by Natl Geog) S&S Trade.

Burian, Peter & Swann, Brian, trs. The Phoenician Women. (Greek Tragedy in New Translations Ser.). 112p. 1992. pap. 7.95 (0-19-507708-3) OUP.

Burian, Peter, ed. see Else, Gerald F.

Burian, Peter, tr. see Aeschylus.

Burian, Peter H. Aristophanes: Birds. 1991. pap. text 7.00 (0-929524-64-0) Bryn Mawr Commentaries.

Burian, Peter K. & Maschke, Thomas. Minolta Maxxum 700si/500si/400si/300si. 3rd rev. ed. Ohlig, Hayley, tr. from GER. (Magic Lantern Guides Ser.). (Illus.). 176p. (Orig.). (C). 1997. pap. 19.95 (1-883403-08-1, H 122, Silver Pixel Pr) Saunders Photo.

Burian, Peter K. & Richter, Gunter. Nikon N50-F50. Ohlig, Hayley, tr. from GER. LC 95-128048. (Magic Lantern Guides Ser.). (Illus.). 176p. (Orig.). (C). 1998. pap. 19.95 (1-883403-13-8, H 134, Silver Pixel Pr) Saunders Photo.

***Burian, Peter K., et al.** National Geographic Photography Field Guide: Secrets to Making Great Pictures. LC 99-23595. (Illus.). 1999. write for info. (0-7922-7496-2) Natl Geog.

Burian, Peter K., jt. auth. see Lothert, Gunter.

Burian, Peter K., jt. auth. see Maschke, Thomas.

Burian, Peter K., jt. auth. see Richter, Gunter.

Burian, Richard M., jt. ed. see Brandon, Robert N.

***Burian, Steven K.** Revision of the Genus Leptophlebia in North America: Ephemeroptera: Leptophlebiidae. LC 00-102481. (Bulletin Ser.: Vol. 13, No. 3). (Illus.). 60p. 2000. pap. text 15.00 (0-86727-138-8) Ohio Bio Survey.

Burich, Nancy J., ed. Alexander the Great: A Bibliography. LC 72-114734. 177p. reprint ed. pap. 54.90 (0-8357-9358-3, 201131100076) Bks Demand.

Burich, Tracy A., jt. auth. see Kevesdy, K. Mark.

Buridan, Jean. Iohannis Buridani, Quaestiones Super Libris Quattuor de Caelo et Mundo. Moody, Ernest A., ed. (Mediaeval Academy of America Publications). 1942. 40.00 (0-527-01704-3) Periodicals Srv.

— Jean Buridan's Logic. 392p. 1985. lib. bdg. 195.50 (90-277-1918-7, D Reidel) Kluwer Academic.

***Burillier, Herve.** Celestial Sites, Celestial Splendors. LC QB64.B82 2000. (Illus.). 192p. 2000. pap. 14.95 (0-521-66773-9) Cambridge U Pr.

Burilova, Milena. Sensem. (CZE., Illus.). 122p. (Orig.). (J). (gr. 3-9). 1992. text 24.50 (0-930329-62-7) Kabel Pubs.

— Sensem. (CZE., Illus.). 121p. (Orig.). (J). (gr. 3-9). 1994. pap. 24.50 (0-685-71259-1) Kabel Pubs.

Burin, Frederic S., ed. see Kircheimer, Otto.

Buring, Daneel. Lesbian & Gay Memphis: Building Communities Behind the Magnolia Curtain. LC 97-41476. (Studies in American Popular History & Culture). 284p. 1997. text 61.00 (0-8153-2990-3) Garland.

Buring, Julie, jt. auth. see Hennekens, Charles.

Buringa, Joke. Bibliography on Women in Yemen. Colburn, Marta, ed. (Yemen Development Ser.). 158p. (C). 1992. 10.00 (1-882557-00-X) Am Inst Yemeni.

Buringh, P. Introduction to Study of Soils in Tropical & Subtropical Regions. 124p. 1992. pap. 175.00 (81-7089-186-8, Pub. by Intl Bk Distr) St Mut.

Burington, Richard S. Handbook of Mathematical Tables & Formulas. 5th ed. LC 78-39634. (Illus.). 480p. (C). 1973. 80.00 (0-07-009015-7) McGraw.

Buriot, Henri, tr. see Croce, Benedetto.

Burish, Thomas G., et al, eds. Cancer, Nutrition, & Eating Behavior: A Biobehavioral Perspective. LC 84-28731. 252p. reprint ed. pap. 78.20 (0-7837-1985-X, 204225900002) Bks Demand.

Buritica, P. & Hennen, J. F. Pucciniosireae: Uredinales, Pucciniaceae. LC 79-27151. (Flora Neotropica Monographs: No. 24). (Illus.). 50p. 1980. pap. 7.75 (0-89327-219-1) NY Botanical.

Burjan, V., et al. Prehl'ad Matematika 1, 2 (A Survey of Mathematics 1, 2), Vol. 2. (SLO.). 240p. 1997. pap. write for info. (80-08-02490-9, Pub. by Slov Pegagog Naklad) IBD Ltd.

Burk, Bill E. Dot . . . Dot . . . Dot. LC 87-28895. 232p. 1987. 14.95 (0-942179-03-X) Shelby Hse.

— Early Elvis: The Sun Years. Burk, Connie L., ed. LC 97-91716. (Illus.). 224p. 1997. 24.95 (1-879207-51-6) Propwash Pub.

— Early Elvis: The Tupelo Years. limited ed. Burk, Connie L., ed. (Illus.). 192p. 1994. 24.95 (1-879207-50-8) Propwash Pub.

— Elvis: Through My Eyes. limited ed. Burk, Connie L., ed. (Illus.). 200p. 1996. 24.95 (1-879207-16-8) Propwash Pub.

— Elvis in Canada. Burk, Connie L., ed. LC 96-92442. (Illus.). 1996. pap. 16.95 (1-879207-24-9) Propwash Pub.

— Elvis Through My Eyes. Burk, Connie L., ed. LC 81-91523. (Illus.). 196p. 1987. 16.95 (0-942179-00-5) Shelby Hse.

Burk, Bill E., jt. auth. see Jones, Ira.

Burk, Bruce. Game Bird Carving. (Illus.). 400p. 1988. 39.95 (0-8329-0439-2, Winchester Pr) New Win Pub.

— Waterfowl Studies: Dabbling & Whistling Ducks. LC 84-51284. (Waterfowl Studies: Vol. I). (Illus.). 240p. 1984. 35.00 (0-88740-025-6) Schiffer.

— Waterfowl Studies: Diving Ducks. LC 84-51283. (Waterfowl Studies: Vol. II). (Illus.). 280p. 1984. 39.95 (0-88740-026-4) Schiffer.

— Waterfowl Studies: Geese & Swans. LC 84-51260. (Waterfowl Studies: Vol. III). (Illus.). 200p. 1984. 29.95 (0-88740-027-2) Schiffer.

Burk, Celine, ed. see Clark, Beverly.

Burk, Connie L., ed. see Burk, Bill E.

Burk, Cornelius F., Jr. & Horton, Forest W., Jr. InfoMap: A Complete Guide to Discovering Corporate Information Resources. 2nd ed. (Illus.). 254p. (C). 1991. reprint ed. text 42.95 (0-9606408-6-X) Info Mgmt Pr.

Burk, Dale A. Camp Cookbook: Featuring Camp Recipes for Fixing Both at Home & in the Field. (Illus.). 216p. 1994. pap. text 12.95 (0-912299-52-5) Stoneydale Pr Pub.

— Elmer Sprunger: Wildlife Artist. LC 82-99860. (Illus.). 104p. (Orig.). 1982. 12.95 (0-686-46594-6); pap. 8.95 (0-912299-06-1) Stoneydale Pr Pub.

— Great Bear, Wild River. LC 77-81463. (Illus.). 160p. 1977. pap. 7.95 (0-912299-10-X) Stoneydale Pr Pub.

— Montana Fishing. 2nd rev. ed. LC 82-99817. (Illus.). 152p. 1983. pap. 5.95 (0-912299-08-8) Stoneydale Pr Pub.

— Montana Hunting Guide. exp. rev. ed. LC 83-60660. (Illus.). 188p. 1985. pap. 13.95 (0-912299-16-9) Stoneydale Pr Pub.

— Montana Hunting Guide. 3rd exp. rev. ed. LC 83-60660. (Illus.). 188p. 1985. 18.95 (0-912299-19-3) Stoneydale Pr Pub.

— New Interpretations. 3rd ed. LC 82-99859. (Illus.). 204p. 1982. reprint ed. pap. 14.95 (0-912299-07-X) Stoneydale Pr Pub.

An Asterisk (*) at the beginning of an entry indicates that the title is appearing for the first time.

Burk, Donna & Snider, Allyn. Invitations to Problem Solving with Story Boxes: Kindergarten, Incl. blackline masters. LC 94-75511. (Illus.). 182p. (C). 1994. teacher ed., spiral bd. 35.00 (*1-886131-26-0*, SBK) Math Lrning.

— Posing & Solving Problems with Story Boxes: First & Second Grade, Incl. blackline masters. LC 94-75180. (Illus.). 218p. (C). 1994. teacher ed., spiral bd. 38.00 (*1-886131-25-2*, SB12) Math Lrning.

Burk, Donna, et al. Arithmetic. (Box It or Bag It Mathematics Ser.). (Illus.). 97p. (C). 1988. teacher ed., ring bd. 17.00 (*1-886131-07-4*, BB6) Math Lrning.

— Box It or Bag It Mathematics, 9 vols., Set. (Illus.). (C). 1988. teacher ed., ring bd. 80.00 (*1-886131-11-2*, BBT) Math Lrning.

— Box It or Bag It Mathematics: Teachers Resource Guide - First-Second, Incl. blackline masters. LC 88-61046. (Illus.). 296p. (C). 1988. teacher ed., spiral bd. 39.50 (*1-886131-01-5*, BB12) Math Lrning.

— Box It or Bag It Mathematics: Teachers Resource Guide - Kindergarten, Incl. blackline masters. LC 87-63571. (Illus.). 232p. (C). 1988. teacher ed., spiral bd. 36.00 (*1-886131-00-7*, BBK) Math Lrning.

— Introduction to Measuring. (Box It or Bag It Mathematics Ser.). (Illus.). 45p. (C). 1988. teacher ed., ring bd. 8.00 (*1-886131-03-1*, BB2) Math Lrning.

— Math Excursions No. 1: Project-Based Mathematics for First Graders. LC 91-46272. (Illus.). 259p. (C). 1992. pap. text 29.50 (*0-435-08331-7*, 08331) Heinemann.

— Math Excursions No. 2: Project-Based Mathematics for Second Graders. LC 91-15387. 218p. (C). 1991. pap. text 29.50 (*0-435-08321-X*, 08321) Heinemann.

— Math Excursions No. K: Project-Based Mathematics for Kindergarteners. 2nd rev. ed. LC 92-16735. (Math Excursions Ser.). 299p. (YA). 1993. pap. text 25.00 (*0-435-08345-7*, 08345) Heinemann.

— Money. (Box It or Bag It Mathematics Ser.). (Illus.). 66p. (C). 1988. teacher ed., ring bd. 9.00 (*1-886131-08-2*, BB7) Math Lrning.

— Pattern. (Box It or Bag It Mathematics Ser.). (Illus.). 67p. (C). 1988. teacher ed., ring bd. 12.00 (*1-886131-06-6*, BB5) Math Lrning.

— Place Value Addition & Subtraction. (Box It or Bag It Mathematics Ser.). (Illus.). 66p. (C). 1988. teacher ed., ring bd. 9.50 (*1-886131-10-4*, BB9) Math Lrning.

— Place Value Counting. (Box It or Bag It Mathematics Ser.). (Illus.). 57p. (C). 1988. teacher ed., ring bd. 8.00 (*1-886131-09-0*, BB8) Math Lrning.

— Reading, Writing & Understanding Numerals 0-10. (Box It or Bag It Mathematics Ser.). (Illus.). 60p. (C). 1988. teacher ed., ring bd. 9.50 (*1-886131-05-8*, BB4) Math Lrning.

— Shapes. (Box It or Bag It Mathematics Ser.). (Illus.). 73p. (C). 1988. teacher ed., ring bd. 12.00 (*1-886131-02-3*, BB1) Math Lrning.

— Understanding Measuring. (Box It or Bag It Mathematics Ser.). (Illus.). 33p. (Orig.). (C). 1988. teacher ed., ring bd. 5.50 (*1-886131-04-X*, BB3) Math Lrning.

***Burk, Dorsey.** How Do You Tell a Hungry Soul She Cannot Have a Bible? (Illus.). 128p. 1998. pap. 10.00 (*1-56722-255-2*) Word Aflame.

— Where Angels Dwell. 128p. 2000. pap. 9.95 (*1-56722-254-4*) Word Aflame.

Burk, Elowese, ed. see Garton, Shirley W. & Garton, Brad.

***Burk Evans, Anita.** Do You Ever Think of Me. limited ed. LC 98-93896. 140p. 1998. 19.95 (*0-9700546-0-2*) B Evans Pubng.

Burk, Frank. Lebesgue Measure & Integration: An Introduction. LC 97-6510. 312p. 1997. 89.95 (*0-471-17978-7*) Wiley.

Burk, Frank D. Evolution by Chance or by Design. (Illus.). 176p. (C). 1994. pap. 8.95 (*0-87961-237-1*) Naturegraph.

Burk, G., jt. auth. see Hamm, G.

***Burk, Gay.** Dangerous Vision. Starke, David & Wasner, Colleen, eds. LC 99-70688. 222p. 1999. pap. 12.95 (*0-9654023-1-2*) Malamalama Pr.

Burk, George A. The Bridge Never Crossed: A Survivor's Search for Meaning. LC 98-89869. (Illus.). 170p. 1999. pap. 16.95 (*1-888725-16-8*) Sci & Human Pr.

Burk, Isabel. Guide for School-Based Drug Policy & Advisory Councils. LC 98-74888. 104p. (C). 1998. pap. text 19.95 (*0-9655436-5-X*) Balance Grp.

Burk, James. Values in the Marketplace: The American Stock Market under Federal Securities Law. (Studies in North America: No. 2). x, 207p. (C). 1988. lib. bdg. 79.25 (*3-11-011714-2*) De Gruyter.

Burk, James, ed. The Adaptive Military: Armed Forces in a Turbulent World. 2nd ed. LC 98-28518. 226p. 1998. pap. 24.95 (*0-7658-0472-7*) Transaction Pubs.

Burk, James, ed. see Janowitz, Morris.

Burk, Janelle M. The Planting: A Book of Seasons. (Illus.). 96p. 1988. 9.95 (*0-9615736-1-9*) Milestone Pr.

Burk, Janelle M., jt. auth. see McFadden, Alneer A.

Burk, John N. The Life & Works of Beethoven: Music Book Index. 483p. 1993. reprint ed. lib. bdg. 99.00 (*0-7812-9572-6*) Rprt Serv.

Burk, John N., ed. see Howe, Mark A.

Burk, Juli. Guidebook to the Theatre. 160p. (C). 1997. per. 29.95 (*0-7872-4157-1*, 41415701) Kendall-Hunt.

***Burk, Juli.** Guidebook to the Theatre. 2nd ed. 150p. (C). 1999. per. 30.95 (*0-7872-6087-8*) Kendall-Hunt.

Burk, Karen B., jt. auth. see Webster, Douglas W.

Burk, Kathleen. Morgan Grenfell, 1838 to 1988: The Biography of a Merchant Bank. (Illus.). 364p. 1990. text 42.00 (*0-19-828306-7*) OUP.

— United States & the European Alliance Since 1945. 1999. 68.00 (*1-85973-277-1*) Berg Pubs.

Burk, Kathleen & Cairncross, Alec. Good-Bye, Great Britain: The Nineteen Seventy-Six IMF Crisis. LC 91-42929. 256p. (C). 1992. 42.50 (*0-300-05728-8*) Yale U Pr.

Burk, Margaret & Hudson, Gary. Final Curtain: Eternal Resting Places of Stars, Celebrities, Moguls, Misers, Misfits & Their Stories. LC 96-45257. 256p. 1996. pap. 18.95 (*0-929765-53-2*) Seven Locks Pr.

Burk, Margaret, ed. see Cotten, Patricia M.

Burk, Margaret T. Are the Stars Out Tonight? The Story of the Famous Ambassador & Cocoanut Grove ... Hollywood's Hotel. (Illus.). 190p. 1980. text 15.00 (*0-937806-00-5*) M Burk.

Burk, Patsy Ward. The Knife Struck Four. 288p. mass mkt. 4.99 (*1-55197-051-1*) Picasso Publ.

Burk, Raymond F., ed. Selenium in Biology & Human Health. LC 93-4691. 1993. 87.95 (*0-387-94080-4*) Spr-Verlag.

Burk, Robert F. The Corporate State & the Broker State: The DuPonts & American National Politics, 1925-1940. (Illus.). 384p. 1990. 49.95 (*0-674-17272-8*) HUP.

— Dwight D. Eisenhower: Hero & Politician. (Twayne's Twentieth Century American Biography Ser.: No. 2). 232p. (C). 1986. 33.00 (*0-8057-7752-0*) Macmillan.

— The Eisenhower Administration & Black Civil Rights. fac. ed. LC 84-2312. (Twentieth-Century America Ser.). (Illus.). 302p. 1984. pap. 93.70 (*0-7837-7685-3*, 204743800007) Bks Demand.

— Never Just a Game: Players, Owners & American Baseball to 1920. LC 93-22719. (Illus.). xviii, 284p. (C). 1994. 45.00 (*0-8078-2122-5*) U of NC Pr.

***Burk, Robert Fredrick.** Much More Than a Game: Players, Owners & American Baseball since 1921. LC 00-41774. (Illus.). 2001. pap. write for info. (*0-8078-4908-1*) U of NC Pr.

Burk, Robin. UNIX Unleashed, 3rd Edition. 3rd ed. LC 98-89270. 1998. 49.99 (*0-672-31411-8*) Sams.

Burk, Robin & Causey, James. Teach Yourself MCSE TCP/IP in 14 Days: MCSE Exam Preparation Guide. LC 98-139091. 576p. 1998. pap. 35.00 (*0-672-31167-4*) Sams.

Burk, Robin & Spoortack, Mark A. Sams' Teach Yourself MCSE Networking Essentials in 14 Days: MCSE Exam G. LC 97-81442. 448p. 1998. 35.00 (*0-672-31175-5*) Sams.

Burk, Robin, et al. UNIX Unleashed: System Administrator's Edition. 2nd ed. 1392p. 1997. pap. 59.99 (*0-672-30952-1*) Sams.

Burk, Ronald L. & Ackerman, Norman. Small Animal Radiology: A Diagnostic Atlas & Text. LC 86-12994. (Illus.). 390p. reprint ed. pap. 120.90 (*0-7837-1616-8*, 204190800024) Bks Demand.

— Small Animal Radiology & Ultrasonography: A Diagnostic Atlas & Text. 2nd ed. Kersey, Ray, ed. (Illus.). 560p. 1996. text 120.00 (*0-7216-5270-0*, W B Saunders Co) Harcrt Hlth Sci Grp.

Burk, Ted, jt. auth. see Grier, James W.

Burk, W. R. A Bibliography of North American Gasteromycetes I: Phalales. 200p. 1981. pap. text 65.00 (*3-7682-1262-9*) Lubrecht & Cramer.

Burka, Christa F. Pearls of Consciousness. 73p. (Orig.). 1987. pap. 5.95 (*0-914732-20-X*) Bro Life Inc.

Burka, Jane B. Procrastination: Why You Do It, What to Do about It. 1990. pap. 12.00 (*0-201-55089-X*) Addison-Wesley.

— Procrastination: Why You Do It, What to Do about It. 1990. pap. 6.95 (*0-201-57037-8*) Addison-Wesley.

Burka, Jane B. & Yuen, Lenora. Procrastination: Why You Do It, What to Do about It. (Illus.). 256p. 1983. pap. 9.95 (*0-201-10191-2*) Addison-Wesley.

Burkam, Anita, ed. see Kelley, Owen.

Burkan, Peggy D. Guiding Yourself. LC 83-91310. 101p. (Orig.). pap. 7.95 (*0-935616-12-8*) Reunion Pr.

Burkan, Peggy D. & Burkan, Tolly. Guiding Yourself into a Spiritual Reality. LC 83-91310. 125p. (Orig.). 1984. pap. 10.00 (*0-935616-09-8*) Reunion Pr.

Burkan, Peggy D., jt. auth. see Burkan, Tolly.

Burkan, Tolly. Winning the Jackpot: Creating Wealth & Abundance. 175p. 1996. pap. text 12.95 (*1-885223-44-7*) Beyond Words Pub.

Burkan, Tolly & Burkan, Peggy D. Firewalking. write for info. (*0-318-58405-0*) Reunion Pr.

Burkan, Tolly & Rosin, Mark B. Dying to Live. LC 84-62759. (Illus.). 228p. (Orig.). 1985. pap. 15.00 (*0-935616-03-9*) Reunion Pr.

Burkan, Tolly, jt. auth. see Burkan, Peggy D.

Burkan, Wayne. Wide-Angle Vision: Beat Your Competition by Focusing on Fringe Competitors, Lost Customers & Rogue Employees. LC 96-10239. 275p. 1996. 27.95 (*0-471-13416-3*) Wiley.

Burkar, W. & Schmortz, K. Grinding & Polishing. 345p. 1989. 295.00 (*0-86108-079-3*, Pub. by Fuel Metallurgical Jrnl) St Mut.

Burkard, Hans-Jurgen, photos by. Stern Portfolio: Hans-Jurgen Burkard. (Illus.). 96p. 1998. pap. 19.95 (*3-570-12295-6*) te Neues.

Burkard, Martha R., jt. auth. see Anderson, Pauline C.

Burkard, Michael. Entire Dilemma: Poems. LC 97-47221. 60p. 1998. 20.95 (*1-889330-17-5*); pap. 12.95 (*1-889330-18-3*) Sarabande Bks.

— The Fires They Kept. LC 86-61224. 104p. 1986. 16.95 (*0-915371-02-2*); pap. 8.95 (*0-915371-03-0*) Metro Bk Co.

— In a White Light. LC 77-94478. 49p. 1977. per. 3.75 (*0-934332-00-2*) LEpervier Pr.

— My Secret Boat: A Notebook of Prose & Poems. 1991. pap. 8.95 (*0-393-30748-4*) Norton.

***Burkard, Michael.** Pennsylvania Collection Agency. 90p. 2001. pap. 14.00 (*1-930974-00-0*) New Issues MI.

— Unsleeping. LC 00-30130. 88p. 2000. 20.95 (*1-889330-52-3*); pap. 12.95 (*1-889330-53-1*) Sarabande Bks.

***Burkard, Patricia.** Leaves in Bloom. 1999. pap. write for info. (*1-58235-218-6*) Watermrk Pr.

Burkard, Rainer E., ed. see Goos, G.

***Burkard, Richard.** The Archpriest of Hita & the Imitators of Ovid: A Study in the Ovidian Background of the Libro de Buen Amor. (Estudios de Literatura Medieval Ser.: Vol. 1). 200p. 1999. pap. 16.50 (*0-936388-84-6*) Juan de la Cuesta.

Burkard, Tom. The Ultimate Mickey Mantle Trivia Book. LC 97-12712. (Illus.). 128p. 1997. pap. 9.95 (*0-8065-1893-6*, Citadel Pr) Carol Pub Group.

Burkardt, Matthias, et al, eds. Structure of the Nt Meson: New Mexico State University, 8-9 March 1996. 150p. 1997. 34.00 (*981-02-3159-8*) World Scientific Pub.

Burkart, Edward I., jt. ed. see Van Essen, Arthur.

Burkart, Gary P. The Parish Life Coordinator: An Institute for Pastoral Life Study. LC 92-26970. 140p. (Orig.). 1992. pap. 8.95 (*1-55612-569-0*, LL1569) Sheed & Ward WI.

Burkart, Jeffrey E. Sure Can Use a Little Good News: 12 Gospel Plays in Rhyme. LC 96-5315. (Illus.). 112p. 1996. 13.99 (*0-570-04866-4*, 12-3357) Concordia.

Burkart, M., ed. see Council of Educators in Landscape Architecture Sta.

Burkart, O. Automatic Verification of Sequential Infinite-State Processes. (Lecture Notes in Computer Science Ser.: Vol. 1354). x, 163p. 1998. pap. 37.00 (*3-540-63982-9*) Spr-Verlag.

Burke. American Feminist Playwrights. 1997. pap. 18.00 (*0-8057-1620-3*, Twyne) Mac Lib Ref.

Burke. Autumn Activities. 16p. 1996. pap., wbk. ed. 2.95 (*1-55734-809-X*) Tchr Create Mat.

— Circles. 288p. Date not set. 24.00 (*0-7432-0008-X*) S&S Trade.

Burke. Emergency Management of Athletic Injuries. 416p. (C). 1987. pap. 165.00 (*0-02-317090-5*, Macmillan Coll) P-H.

— Enfermeria Gerontologica. 2nd ed. (C). 1998. text 49.04 (*84-8174-308-9*, Pub. by Mosby-Doyma Libros) Mosby Inc.

— Just Because I'm Smiling Doesn't Mean I'm Happy. 1990. 18.95 (*0-671-72693-5*, Pocket Books) PB.

— Marketing & Selling the Travel Product. 2nd ed. (Hospitality, Travel & Tourism Ser.). 1998. teacher ed. 12.00 (*0-8273-7649-9*) Delmar.

— Marketing & Selling the Travel Product. 2nd ed. LC 99-43258. (Hospitality, Travel & Tourism Ser.). (C). 1999. pap. 56.95 (*0-8273-7648-0*) Delmar.

— 1996 Title Insurance. 1996. 75.00 (*0-316-11826-5*, Aspen Law & Bus) Aspen Pub.

— Project Management. 3rd ed. LC 99-13356. 2000. pap. text 42.00 (*0-471-98762-X*) Wiley.

— Red Acre Farm. (J). 1995. 14.95 (*0-8050-2047-0*) H Holt & Co.

Burke. Windbreaks. pap. text. write for info. (*0-7506-8951-X*) Buttrwrth-Heinemann.

Burke & Kranhold. Big Fearon Bulletin Board Book. 1978. pap. 21.99 (*0-8224-0702-7*) Fearon Teacher Aids.

Burke, jt. auth. see Lea.

***Burke, A. M.** Key to Ancient Parish Registers of England & Wales. fac. ed. 163p. 2000. reprint ed. 29.95 (*0-7404-0378-8*) Higginson Bk Co.

Burke, Abbot G. An Eagle's Flight: Autobiography of a Gnostic Orthodox Christian. LC 95-170302. 500p. (Orig.). 1994. pap. 17.95 (*0-932104-06-1*) St George Pr.

Burke, Abbot G. Magnetic Therapy. LC 80-22941. 92p. 1987. reprint ed. pap. 8.95 (*0-87516-588-5*) DeVorss.

Burke, Abbot G. Simply Heavenly! The Monastery Vegetarian Cookbook. (Illus.). 349p. (Orig.). pap. 19.95 (*0-932104-00-2*) St George Pr.

— Simply Heavenly! The Monastery Vegetarian Cookbook. rev. ed. (Illus.). 326p. (Orig.). 1995. pap. 19.95 (*0-932104-07-X*) St George Pr.

Burke, Adam. Pocket Guide to Self-Hypnosis. LC 97-12914. (Crossing Press Pocket Ser.). (Illus.). 112p. 1997. pap. 6.95 (*0-89594-824-9*) Crossing Pr.

Burke, Adolf M. Germany in Europe, 1945-1992. (Orig.). 2001. pap. 9.95 (*0-7509-2058-0*, Pub. by Sutton Publng) Intl Pubs Mktg.

Burke, Al. Misery in the Name of Freedom: The United States in Nicaragua, 1909-1988. LC 88-6740. (Illus.). 200p. (Orig.). (C). 1988. pap. 8.95 (*0-929004-01-9*, E183.8.N5B87) Sea Otter Pr.

Burke, Alan. My Naked Soul. (Illus.). 1968. 3.95 (*0-87212-021-X*) Libra.

Burke, Albert L. He That Hath an Ear. 101p. (Orig.). 1982. pap. 3.50 (*0-9608662-0-5*) Eleventh Hour.

Burke, Allen & Virmani, Renu. Tumors of the Heart & Great Vessels. (AFIP Atlas of Tumor Pathology Ser.: Vol. 16). (Illus.). 231p. 1996. pap. text 58.00 (*1-881041-20-4*) Am Registry Path.

Burke, Amy M. Math Libs. (Illus.). 93p. (J). (gr. 4-6). 1996. pap., wbk. ed. 14.99 (*0-89824-223-1*) Royal Fireworks.

— Not Just Grammar. 38p. (J). (gr. 4-6). 1996. pap., wbk. ed. 9.99 (*0-89824-222-3*) Royal Fireworks.

— Not Just Schoolwork, Vol. 2. (Orig.). (J). (gr. 4-12). 1993. pap. 21.95 (*1-878347-24-1*) NL Assocs.

— Not Just Schoolwork, Vol. 3. (Orig.). (J). (gr. 4-12). 1993. pap. 21.95 (*1-878347-25-X*) NL Assocs.

— Not Just Schoolwork, Vol. 4. rev. ed. (Illus.). 112p. (Orig.). 1994. pap. text 21.95 (*1-878347-34-9*) NL Assocs.

— Parent Points. 44p. (J). 1996. pap. 9.99 (*0-89824-224-X*) Royal Fireworks.

— Tools of the Trade, Vol. 2. 40p. 1993. pap. 7.95 (*1-878347-33-0*) NL Assocs.

Burke, Amy M. & Wallace, Roger. Not Just Schoolwork. LC 76-9524. 201p. (Orig.). (J). (gr. 3-12). 1990. pap. 32.95 (*0-8290-0354-1*) NL Assocs.

Burke, Amy M., jt. auth. see Levy, Nathan.

Burke, Anne. A. J. M. Smith: An Annotated Bibliography. 103p. (C). 1983. pap. 9.00 (*0-920763-66-9*, Pub. by ECW) Genl Dist Srvs.

***Burke, Anne.** Crystal Forest of the Green Goddess. 2000. pap. text 8.95 (*0-7880-1440-4*) CSS.

Burke, Anne. Raymond Knister: An Annotated Bibliography. 322p. (C). 1981. pap. 9.00 (*0-920763-54-5*, Pub. by ECW) Genl Dist Srvs.

— Twelve Lessons for Confirmation in Secondary Schools. (C). 1988. 30.00 (*0-85439-091-X*, Pub. by St Paul Pubns) St Mut.

***Burke, Anne, ed.** Imprints & Casualities: Women & Language, Reinventing Memory. (Selected Readings from the Living Archives of the Feminist Caucus of the League of Canadian Poets: Vol. 2). 160p. 2000. pap. text 12.75 (*1-896647-24-3*) Genl Dist Srvs.

Burke, Anne, et al. Open 24 Hours: Featuring 5 Canadian Poets. LC 98-111657. 108p. 1997. pap. text 10.50 (*0-921411-64-2*) Genl Dist Srvs.

Burke, Arleigh. Best of Admiral Burke. Hubbard, Douglass H., ed. (Orig.). 1987. pap. 2.00 (*0-934841-13-6*) Adm Nimitz Foun.

Burke, Arthur M. Key to the Ancient Parish Registers of England & Wales. (Illus.). 163p. 1996. reprint ed. pap. 18.00 (*0-8063-0445-6*, 800) Genealog Pub.

***Burke, Arthur M.** The Prominent Families of the United States of America. 510p. 1999. pap. 37.50 (*0-8063-1308-0*) Clearfield Co.

***Burke, Ashworth P.** Burke's Family Records. 709p. 1999. 50.00 (*0-8063-4505-5*) Clearfield Co.

— Burke's Family Records. (Illus.). 709p. 1999. reprint ed. lib. bdg. 69.50 (*0-8328-9848-1*) Higginson Bk Co.

Burke, Ashworth P., jt. auth. see Burke, John B.

Burke, B., jt. auth. see Kolker, Aliza Meredith.

Burke, B. Meredith, jt. auth. see Kolker, Aliza.

Burke, Barbara, ed. see LoBue, Tony.

Burke, Barlow. Natural Resources: Cases & Materials. 398p. (C). 1998. 44.95 (*0-87084-108-4*) Anderson Pub Co.

Burke, Barlow, Jr. Personal Property in a Nutshell. 2nd ed. LC 83-6519. (Nutshell Ser.). 399p. (C). 1993. pap. 21.00 (*0-314-01700-3*) West Pub.

Burke, Barlow, et al. Fundamentals of Property Law. LC 99-62382. 800p. 1999. write for info. (*0-327-01258-7*, 1113010) LEXIS Pub.

Burke, Barlow, Jr., et al. Mineral Law, Teacher's Manual to Accompany Cases & Materials On. (American Casebook Ser.). 175p. (C). 1995. pap. text, teacher ed. write for info. (*0-314-04809-X*) West Pub.

Burke, Bernard. Burke's American Families with British Ancestry. LC 74-32428. (Illus.). 542p. 1996. reprint ed. 47.50 (*0-8063-0662-9*) Genealog Pub.

— A Genealogical History of the Dormant, Abeyant, Forfeited, Extinct Peerages of the British Empire. (Illus.). 642p. 1996. reprint ed. 40.00 (*0-8063-0789-7*) Genealog Pub.

— The General Armory of England, Scotland, Ireland & Wales: Comprising a Registry of Armorial Bearings from the Earliest to the Present Time. 3 vols. lxxii, 1185p. 1996. reprint ed. pap. 40.00 (*0-7884-0558-6*, B866) Heritage Bk.

Burke, Bernard F., et al, eds. Planetary Systems - Formation, Evolution & Detection: Proceedings of the 1st International Conference, Held in Pasadena, California on December 8-10, 1992. LC 94-20181. 1994. text 323.00 (*0-7923-2895-7*) Kluwer Academic.

Burke, Bernard F. & Graham-Smith, Francis. An Introduction to Radio Astronomy. (Illus.). 309p. (C). 1996. text 80.00 (*0-521-55454-3*); pap. text 34.95 (*0-521-55604-X*) Cambridge U Pr.

Burke, Bernard V. Ambassador Frederic Sackett & the Collapse of the Weimar Republic, 1930-1933: The United States & Hitler's Rise to Power. (Illus.). 344p. (C). 1995. text 57.95 (*0-521-47005-6*) Cambridge U Pr.

Burke, Betty. Anne of Green Gables: A Literature Unit. Cain, Janet, ed. (Illus.). 48p. 1994. student ed. 7.95 (*1-55734-438-8*) Tchr Create Mat.

— Peter Pan: A Literature Unit. Cain, Janet, ed. (Illus.). 48p. (Orig.). 1994. student ed. 7.95 (*1-55734-433-7*) Tchr Create Mat.

***Burke, Betty.** Spring Activities. (Illus.). 32p. 1999. pap., teacher ed. 2.95 (*1-55734-799-9*, TCM799) Tchr Create Mat.

Burke, Betty. Summer Activities. (Illus.). 1996. pap., teacher ed. 2.95 (*1-55734-808-1*, TCM808) Tchr Create Mat.

— Winter Activities. (Illus.). 1996. pap., teacher ed. 2.95 (*1-55734-798-0*, TCM798) Tchr Create Mat.

Burke, Betty & Cain, Janet. Heroes. (Interdisciplinary Units Ser.). (Illus.). 1994. 14.95 (*1-55734-605-4*) Tchr Create Mat.

Burke, Betty & Teacher Created Materials Staff. Celebrate Our Similarities: Primary. 176p. (J). (gr. 1-3). 1997. pap. 15.95 (*1-55734-508-2*) Tchr Create Mat.

Burke, Beverley, jt. auth. see Dalrymple, Jane.

Burke, Bill. Mine Fields. 120p. 1995. 50.00 (*0-932526-50-0*) Nexus Pr.

— Mine Fields. deluxe ed. 1995. 300.00 (*0-932526-79-9*) Nexus Pr.

Burke, Bill E. Elvis-A Thirty Year Chronicle. (Illus.). 351p. 1985. 14.95 (*0-932117-02-3*) Osborne Enterps.

Burke, Billie. With a Feather on My Nose. (American Autobiography Ser.). 272p. 1995. reprint ed. lib. bdg. 79.00 (*0-7812-8468-6*) Rprt Serv.

Burke, Bink, jt. auth. see Reinert, Andy.

Burke, Bob. The Dewey Bartlett Legacy. Franks, Kenny A. & Campbell, Gini M., eds. (Oklahoma Statesmen Ser.). (Illus.). 215p. 1995. 20.00 (*1-885596-01-4*) OK Heritage.

— The Eloquent Congressman. Franks, Kenny et al, eds. (Oklahoma Statesmen Ser.). 100p. 1994. 20.00 (*1-885596-00-6*) OK Heritage.

— From Oklahoma to Eternity: The Life of Wiley Post & the Winnie Mae. Franks, Kenny A. & Moore Campbell, Gini, eds. LC 97-69054. (Oklahoma Trackmaker Ser.). (Illus.). 224p. 1998. 24.95 (*1-885596-07-3*) OK Heritage.

— Like a Prairie Fire: A History of the Assemblies of God in Oklahoma. Cunningham, Robert C. & Womack, David A., eds. (Illus.). 518p. 12.00 (*0-9641325-0-8*) OK Dist Coun.

***Burke, Bob.** Out from the Shadows: The Life of John J. Harden. Franks, Kenny & Campbell, Gini Moore, eds. LC 98-67123. (Oklahoma Trackmaker Ser.). 224p. 1998. 16.95 (*1-885596-09-X*) OK Heritage.

Burke, Bob & Creel, Von R. Mike Monroney: Oklahoma Liberal. Franks, Kenny A. & Moore Campbell, Gini, eds. LC 96-71238. (Oklahoma Statesmen Ser.: Vol. IV). (Illus.). 210p. 1997. 20.00 (*1-885596-04-9*) OK Heritage.

***Burke, Bob & Franks, Kenny.** Abe Lemons: Court Magician. Campbell, Gini Moore & Dabney, Eric, eds. LC 99-65514. (Oklahoma Trackmaker Ser.). (Illus.). 371p. 1999. 24.95 (*1-885596-14-6*) OK Heritage.

— Glen D. Johnson, Sr. Vol. III: The Road to Washington. Campbell, Gini Moore, ed. (Oklahoma Statesmen Ser.). (Illus.). 152p. 1996. 15.00 (*1-885596-05-7*) OK Heritage.

***Burke, Bob & Miles-LaGrange, Vicki.** A Passion for Equality: The Life of Jimmy Stewart. Franks, Kenny & Campbell, Gini Moore, eds. LC 99-70170. (Oklahoma Trackmaker Ser.). (Illus.). 224p. 1999. 18.95 (*1-885596-12-X*) OK Heritage.

***Burke, Bob & Monson, Angela.** Roscoe Dunjee Vol. V: Chamption of Civil Rights. Campbell, Gini Moore, ed. (Oklahoma Statesmen Ser.). (Illus.). 186p. 1998. 15.00 (*1-885596-08-1*) OK Heritage.

***Burke, Bob & Parr, Royse.** Glory Days of Summer: The History of Baseball in Oklahoma. Campbell, Gini Moore, ed. LC 99-62506. (Oklahoma Horizons Ser.). (Illus.). 480p. 1999. 39.95 (*1-885596-13-8*) OK Heritage.

***Burke, Bob & Womack, David A.** Push Back the Darkness: The Story of Don Stamps & the Full Life Study Bible. 2nd ed. (Illus.). 261p. 2000. reprint ed. pap. write for info. (*0-7361-0168-3*) Life Pubs Intl.

Burke, Bob, et al. American Jurist: The Life of Judge Alfred P. Murrah. Campbell, Gini Moore, ed. LC 96-67015. (Oklahoma Trackmaker Ser.). (Illus.). 398p. 1996. 22.95 (*0-86546-090-6*) OK Heritage.

Burke, Bob, jt. auth. see Thompson, Ralph G.

Burke, Bobbye. Daddy's Little Girl. (Illus.). 32p. (ps-3). 5.25 hd 5.95 (*0-06-443657-8*) HarpC.

— Daddy's Little Girl. 32p. (J). Date not set. 6.95 (*0-694-01449-4*, HarpFestival) HarpC Child Bks.

— Daddy's Little Girl. 32p. (J). (ps-3). Date not set. 14.95 (*0-06-028722-5*) HarpC Child Bks.

Burke, Carol. Vision Narratives of Women in Prison. LC 91-3516. 208p. (C). 1992. text 28.00 (*0-87049-727-8*) U of Tenn Pr.

Burke, Carol & Tinsley, Molly B. The Creative Process. 4th ed. LC 92-50043. 186p. (C). 1992. pap. text 22.95 (*0-312-06117-X*) St Martin.

Burke, Carol S., jt. auth. see Russell, Louise B.

Burke, Carolyn. Becoming Modern: The Life of Mina Loy. LC 95-13118. 494p. 1996. text 35.00 (*0-374-10964-8*) FS&G.

— Becoming Modern: The Life of Mina Loy. LC 97-12745. 503p. 1997. pap. 19.95 (*0-520-21089-1*, Pub. by U CA Pr) Cal Prin Full Svc.

Burke, Carolyn & Schor, Naomi, eds. Engaging with Irigaray: Feminist Philosophy & Modern European Thought. LC 94-6815. (Gender & Culture Ser.). 428p. 1994. 76.00 (*0-231-07896-X*); pap. 20.00 (*0-231-07897-8*) Col U Pr.

Burke, Carolyn, jt. auth. see Short, Kathy G.

Burke, Carolyn, tr. see Irigaray, Luce.

Burke, Catherine, ed. Psychosocial Dimensions of Oncology Nursing Care. LC 98-68085. 218p. 1998. pap. text 18.00 (*1-890504-06-8*) Oncology Nursing.

Burke, Cathryn B. & Raia, Susan P. Soul Traditional Southern Food Practices, Customs, & Holidays. LC 95-17614. (Ethnic & Regional Food Practices - A Ser.). 1995. 10.00 (*0-88091-144-1*) Am Dietetic Assn.

Burke, Charles H. How to Build an Internet Service Company: From A to Z. 2nd ed. LC 96-69435. (Illus.). 280p. 1997. mass mkt. 49.95 (*0-935563-03-2*) Social Sys Pr.

***Burke, Charlotte.** Journey's End. 1999. pap. write for info. (*1-58235-100-7*) Watermrk Pr.

Burke, Charlotte. Life's Journey. 1997. pap. write for info. (*1-57553-583-1*) Watermrk Pr.

Burke, Chris & Garitta, Robert. Gurds Autoduel: Roleplaying in the World of Car Wars. 2nd ed. Haring, Scott, ed. (Illus.). 128p. 1997. pap. 19.95 (*1-55634-240-3*, 6003, Pub. by S Jackson Games) BookWorld.

Burke, Christopher. Paul Renner: The Art of Typography. LC 98-41025. (Illus.). 220p. 1999. pap. 35.00 (*1-56898-158-9*) Princeton Arch.

***Burke, Christopher Matthew.** When Appearances Do Matter: The Development of Representation Jurisprudence, 89. LC 98-41416. (Contributions in Legal Studies: Vol. 89). 224p. 1999. 59.95 (*0-313-30751-2*, Greenwood Pr) Greenwood.

***Burke, Claire.** Kenntnisse: Advanced German Course. LC 98-48145. 1999. pap. text. write for info. (*0-415-16394-3*) Routledge.

— Kenntnisse Cassettes: Advanced German Course. LC 98-48145. 1999. audio. write for info. (*0-415-16396-X*) Routledge.

***Burke, Claire, et al.** Kenntnisse: Teacher's Book. LC 98-48145. 104p. 1999. pap. write for info. (*0-415-16395-1*) Routledge.

Burke, Clifford. Exploring Washington's Smaller Cities. (Illus.). 262p. 1987. pap. 10.95 (*0-931849-03-9*) Quartzite Bks.

— Sacred Places. 64p. 1993. pap. 10.00 (*1-883384-00-1*) Dsrt Rose NM.

— Skull Drawings & Bone Songs. (Illus.). 48p. 1998. pap. 35.00 (*1-883384-01-X*) Dsrt Rose NM.

***Burke, Clifford.** Talking with Raven: Poems. 35p. 1999. pap. write for info. (*1-58249-004-X*) Grey Spider.

Burke, Colin. Information & Secrecy: Vannevar Bush, Ultra, & the Other Memex. LC 93-39656. (Illus.). 487p. 1993. 52.00 (*0-8108-2783-2*) Scarecrow.

Burke, Cormac. Covenanted Happiness: Love & Commitment in Marriage. 2nd ed. 272p. (Orig.). 1999. pap. 9.95 (*1-889334-15-4*) Scepter Pubs.

Burke, Cornelius G. The Collector's Haydn. LC 77-28259. (Keystone Books in English: No. KB 7). 316p. 1978. reprint ed. lib. bdg. 65.00 (*0-313-20239-7*, BUCH, Greenwood Pr) Greenwood.

Burke, Cristine S. Marcy Wigglewasher & the Bad News Bully. Faccenda, Ann B., ed. (Marcy Wigglewasher Ser.). (Illus.). 24p. (Orig.). (J). (gr. k-5). 1995. pap. 3.95 (*0-9638237-2-8*) Playgrnd Bks.

— Marcy Wigglewasher's Not So Boring Summer. Faccenda, Ann B., ed. (Marcy Wigglewasher Ser.). (Illus.). 24p. (Orig.). (J). (gr. k-5). 1995. pap. 3.95 (*0-9638237-1-X*) Playgrnd Bks.

— Marcy Wigglewasher's Small Adventure. Faccenda, Ann B., ed. (Marcy Wigglewasher Ser.). (Illus.). 24p. (Orig.). (J). (gr. k-5). 1995. pap. 3.95 (*0-9638237-3-6*) Playgrnd Bks.

Burke, D. Diligence. 1998. pap. 5.99 (*0-89274-747-1*, HH-747) Harrison Hse.

Burke, D. The Street French Slang Dictionary & Thesaurus. LC 98-106201. (FRE.). 223p. 1997. pap. 16.95 (*0-471-16806-8*) Wiley.

Burke, D. Barlow, Jr. Federal Mortgage Set. 526p. 1990. 145.00 (*0-316-11729-3*, Aspen Law & Bus) Aspen Pub.

— Law of Federal Mortgage Documents. 500p. 1989. 145.00 (*0-316-11701-3*, Aspen Law & Bus) Aspen Pub.

— Law of Real Estate Brokers. LC 81-81531. 448p. 1983. 95.00 (*0-316-11676-9*, Aspen Law & Bus) Aspen Pub.

— Law of Real Estate Brokers: Essential Documents for Representing the Older Client. 896p. 1992. 145.00 (*0-316-11700-5*, Aspen Law & Bus) Aspen Pub.

— The Law of Title Insurance. 592p. 1987. 95.00 (*0-316-11707-2*, Aspen Law & Bus) Aspen Pub.

— Law of Title Insurance. 2nd ed. 1052p. 1999. ring bd. 145.00 (*0-316-11788-9*, 17889) Aspen Law.

***Burke, D. Barlow.** Law of Title Insurance. 3rd ed. LC 00-44796. 2000. write for info. (*0-7355-1503-4*) Panel Pubs.

Burke, D. Barlow. Real Estate Law, Set. 2nd ed. 999p. 1998. ring bd. 145.00 (*0-316-11781-1*, Aspen Law & Bus) Aspen Pub.

Burke, D. Barlow, Jr. Real Estate Transactions. (Examples & Explanations Ser.). 512p. 1993. 60.00 (*0-316-11773-0*, 17730) Aspen Law.

Burke, D. Barlow. Real Estate Transactions: Examples & Explanations. 2nd ed. LC 99-17231. 552p. 1999. pap. text 33.95 (*0-7355-0054-1*) Panel Pubs.

— Title: 1995 Supplement. 1995. 70.00 (*0-316-11635-1*, Aspen Law & Bus) Aspen Pub.

— Title Insurance. 2nd ed. 1993. 145.00 (*0-316-11737-4*, Aspen Law & Bus) Aspen Pub.

***Burke, Dan, et al.** Methods in Yeast Genetics: A Cold Spring Harbor Laboratory Course Manual. LC 00-31721. (Illus.). 2000. pap. write for info. (*0-87969-588-9*) Cold Spring Harbor.

Burke, Dan, et al. Software Marketing Practices: Your One Reference Source for Creating Effective Marketing Budgets. (Illus.). 346p. 1997. 795.00 (*1-58128-007-6*, QR) Culpepper.

Burke, Daniel. Beyond Interpretation: Studies in the Modern Short Story. xii, 179p. 1991. 37.50 (*0-87875-394-X*) Whitston Pub.

Burke, Daniel, ed. see De La Salle, John B.

Burke, David. Biz Talk-1: American Business Slang & Jargon. Graul, Robert, ed. (Illus.). 256p. (Orig.). 1993. pap. 16.95 (*1-879440-17-2*) Optima CA.

— Biz Talk-2: More Slang, Idioms & Jargon Used in American Business. LC 98-145145. (Illus.). 300p. 1997. pap. text 18.95 (*1-879440-19-9*) Optima CA.

— Road Through the Wilderness: The Story of the Transcontinental Railway. (Illus.). 296p. 39.95 (*0-86840-140-4*, Pub. by New South Wales Univ Pr) Intl Spec Bk.

***Burke, David.** Spy TV: Just Who is the Digital TV Revolution Overthrowing? Make Sure It's Not You! 1999. pap. 9.95 (*1-899866-25-6*) Slab-O-Concrete Pubns.

Burke, David. Street French I: The Best of French Slang. 2nd ed. LC 96-4202. 272p. 1996. pap. 15.95 (*0-471-13898-3*) Wiley.

— Street French 3: The Best of Naughty French, Vol. III. LC 97-5827. (FRE.). 256p. 1997. pap. 15.95 (*0-471-13900-9*) Wiley.

— Street French 2: The Best of French Idioms. 2nd ed. LC 96-15950. 1996. pap. 15.95 (*0-471-13899-1*) Wiley.

— Street German: The Best of German Idioms, No. 1. Graul, Robert, ed. (Illus.). 320p. (Orig.). 1996. pap. 16.95 (*1-879440-21-0*) Optima CA.

***Burke, David.** Street Italian 1: The Best of Italian Slang. (Street Language Ser.). (ITA & ENG.). 256p. 2000. pap. 15.95 (*0-471-38438-0*) Wiley.

Burke, David. Street Spanish 1: The Best of Spanish Slang. LC 97-21377. (SPA., Illus.). 256p. 1997. pap. 15.95 (*0-471-17970-1*) Wiley.

***Burke, David.** Street Spanish Slang Dictionary & Thesaurus. LC 99-25550. 267p. 1999. pap. 16.95 (*0-471-16834-3*) Wiley.

Burke, David. Street Spanish 2: The Best of Spanish Idioms. (SPA.). 224p. 1998. pap. 15.95 (*0-471-17971-X*) Wiley.

— Street Spanish 3: The Best of Naughty Spanish. LC 98-12974. (SPA.). 256p. 1998. pap. 15.95 (*0-471-17972-8*) Wiley.

***Burke, David.** Street Speak 2: American Slang & Idioms Used by Everyone. 232p. 2000. pap. 21.95 (*1-891888-06-4*, Pub. by Slangman Pubng) IPG Chicago.

Burke, David. Street Speak 1 The Best of American Slang & Idioms. 1999. pap. text 16.95 (*1-891888-08-0*) Slangman Pubng.

— Street Talk 1: How to Speak & Understand American Slang. LC 92-149368. (Illus.). 256p. 1991. pap. 16.95 (*1-879440-00-8*) Optima CA.

— Street Talk 3: The Best of American Idioms. LC 93-84787. (Illus.). 336p. (C). 1995. pap. 18.95 (*1-879440-12-1*) Optima CA.

— Street Talk 2: Slang Used in Popular American Television Shows (plus slang used by teens, rappers & surfers) LC 92-81410. (Illus.). 286p. (Orig.). (C). 1992. pap. 16.95 (*1-879440-06-7*) Optima CA.

***Burke, David.** Traveler's Companion Guide to Mediterranean France. 2nd ed. (Illus.). 368p. 2000. pap. text 23.95 (*0-7627-0607-4*) Globe Pequot.

Burke, David & Harrington, David. Street Talk Student Book: Essential American Slang & Idioms. Wright, Debbie, ed. (Illus.). 144p. (C). 1998. pap. text 14.95 (*1-891888-09-9*) Slangman Pubng.

Burke, David & Price, Tom. British Motor Museums: The Comprehensive Guide to the Vehicle Collections of Britain. (Illus.). 144p. 1999. pap. 17.95 (*1-901295-39-7*, 128175AE, Pub. by Vloce Pub) Motorbooks Intl.

Burke, David & Reingold, Carmel B. Cooking with David Burke. LC 93-48909. 1995. 32.50 (*0-394-58343-4*) Knopf.

***Burke, David & Tse, Peter.** Dictionary of Essential American Slang No. 3. 2000. pap. 12.95 (*1-879440-29-6*) Optima CA.

Burke, David C. & Murray, D. Duncan. Handbook of Spinal Cord Medicine. LC 76-359743. (Illus.). 100p. reprint ed. pap. 31.00 (*0-608-09639-3*, 205441500001) Bks Demand.

Burke, Deborah M., jt. ed. see Light, Leah L.

***Burke, Debra D. & Brown-Walker, Sheila M.** Legal Liabilities at Bayshore Science. LC 00-44608. 2000. write for info. (*0-13-012500-8*) P-H.

Burke, Deidre. Food & Fasting. LC 93-537. (Comparing Religions Ser.). (Illus.). 32p. (J). (gr. 4-8). 1993. lib. bdg. 22.83 (*1-56847-034-7*) Raintree Steck-V.

Burke, Delta & Lipsitz, Alexis. Delta Style: Eve Wasn't a Size 6 & Neither Am I. LC 97-31523. 176p. 1998. text 24.95 (*0-312-15454-2*) St Martin.

— Delta Style: Eve Wasn't a Size 6 & Neither Am I. (Illus.). 256p. 1998. pap. 13.99 (*0-312-19855-8*) St Martin.

Burke, Dennis. Breaking Financial Barriers. 100p. 1997. pap. 5.00 (*1-890026-04-2*) D Burke Min.

— Grace-Power Beyond Your Ability. 96p. 1992. mass mkt. 5.99 (*0-89274-904-0*, HH-904) Harrison Hse.

— How to Meditate God's Word. 64p. 1982. mass mkt. 5.99 (*0-89274-241-0*, HH-241) Harrison Hse.

— The Law of the Wise. 64p. (Orig.). 1995. mass mkt. 5.99 (*0-89274-777-3*, HH-777) Harrison Hse.

— Yielding to the Holy Spirit. 80p. 1993. mass mkt. 5.99 (*0-89274-468-5*, HH-468) Harrison Hse.

— You Can Conquer Life's Conflicts. 128p. 1988. pap. 5.99 (*0-89274-524-X*, HH-524) Harrison Hse.

Burke-DeValeria, Jeanne, jt. auth. see DeValeria, Dennis.

***Burke, Diana.** Matchmakers.com. (Full House Sisters Ser.). (Illus.). 160p. (J). (gr. 4-6). 2000. per. 3.99 (*0-671-04091-X*, Minstrel Bks) PB.

— Will You Be My Valentine? (Full House Sisters Ser.). 160p. (J). (gr. 4-7). 2000. mass mkt. 3.99 (*0-671-04086-3*, Minstrel Bks) PB.

Burke, Dianne O. Rhyme along Treasury. 80p. (J). (ps). 1997. 10.95 (*1-56565-740-3*) Lowell Hse Juvenile.

Burke, Dianne O'Quinn. Itsy-Bitsy Spider. (Rhyme-Along Board Bks.). 12p. (J). (gr. k-1). 1999. reprint ed. pap. 4.95 (*1-56565-092-1*, 00921W, Pub. by Lowell Hse) NTC Contemp Pub Co.

Burke, Dolores L. A New Academic Marketplace, 30. LC 88-15445. (Contributions to the Study of Education Ser.: No. 30). 208p. 1988. 55.00 (*0-313-26383-3*, BNE/, Greenwood Pr) Greenwood.

— Physicians in the Academic Marketplace, 53. LC 91-28327. (Contributions to the Study of Education Ser.: No. 53). 184p. 1991. 52.95 (*0-313-27850-4*, BYE/, Greenwood Pr) Greenwood.

Burke, Doreen B. American Paint Metropolitan Museum. (Illus.). 0.00 (*0-691-04003-6*) Princeton U Pr.

Burke, Doreen B. A Catalogue of Works by Artists Born Between 1846-1864. (American Paintings in the Metropolitan Museum of Art Ser.: Vol. 3). 524p. 1980. 75.00 (*0-87099-244-9*) Metro Mus Art.

— J. Alden Weir. (Illus.). 313p. 1983. 50.00 (*0-8453-4779-9*, Cornwall Bks) Assoc Univ Prs.

— J. Alden Weir: An American Impressionist Painter. LC 83-47901. (Illus.). 320p. 1991. reprint ed. pap. 19.95 (*0-87413-263-0*) U Delaware Pr.

Burke, Doris. The Family. 192p. 1999. pap. 11.95 (*1-56315-130-8*) SterlingHse.

Burke, Dorothy. Easy Lotus Notes 5. (Easy Ser.). 1998. pap. 19.99 (*0-7897-1813-8*) Que.

— How to User Lotus Notes 5. (How to Use ... (Que) Series). 325p. 1999. pap. text 24.99 (*0-672-31505-X*) Sams.

Burke, Dorothy & Calabria, Jane. Ten Minute Guide to Lotus Notes 4.6. LC 97-80536. (10 Minute Guide Ser.). 213p. 1997. pap. text 14.99 (*0-7897-1536-8*) Que.

Burke, Dorothy, jt. auth. see Calabria, Jane.

Burke, E. A., jt. auth. see Uytenbogaardt, E. W.

Burke, E. P. An Historical Essay on the Laws & the Government of Rome: Designed As an Introduction to the Study of the Civil Law. LC 93-79713. 318p. 1994. reprint ed. 90.00 (*1-56169-071-6*) Gaunt.

Burke, Ed, et al. Training Nutrition: The Diet & Nutrition Guide for Peak Performance. LC 92-53280. (Illus.). 180p. (Orig.). (C). 1996. pap. text 20.00 (*1-884125-22-0*) Cooper Pubng.

Burke, Edmund. An Account of the European Settlements in America, 2 vols. LC 77-141082. (Research Library of Colonial Americana). 1972. reprint ed. 58.95 (*0-405-03277-3*) Ayer.

— Account of the European Settlements in America, 6 pts. in 2 vols., Set. reprint ed. 30.00 (*0-404-01237-X*) AMS Pr.

— Edmund Burke: A Philosophical Inquiry into the Origin of Our Ideas of the Sublime & Beautiful. Boulton, James T., ed. LC 68-27583. 1968. pap. 15.00 (*0-268-00085-9*) U of Notre Dame Pr.

— Edmund Burke: Selected Writings & Speeches. Stanlis, Peter J., ed. LC 97-15176. (Gateway Ser.). 584p. 1997. pap. 14.95 (*0-89526-407-2*, Gateway Editions) Regnery Pub.

— Further Reflections on the Revolution in France. Ritchie, Daniel E., ed. LC 91-33265. 361p. (C). 1992. 18.00 (*0-86597-098-X*); pap. 7.50 (*0-86597-099-8*) Liberty Fund.

— Letter to a Member of the National Assembly. LC 90-36404. 84p. 1990. reprint ed. 40.00 (*1-85477-037-3*) Continuum.

— A Letter to the Sheriffs of Bristol: A Speech at Bristol on Parliamentary Conduct; a Letter to a Noble Lord. Murison, W., ed. LC 76-29423. reprint ed. 34.00 (*0-404-15344-5*) AMS Pr.

— Letters, Speeches & Tracts on Irish Affairs. Arnold, Matthew, ed. LC 75-28809. reprint ed. 72.50 (*0-404-13802-0*) AMS Pr.

— The Natural Pharmacist Guide to Creatine & Sports Performance. LC 98-48204. 208p. 1999. pap. 6.99 (*0-7615-1614-X*) Prima Pub.

— Of the Sublime & Beautiful. 1986. reprint ed. pap. 28.95 (*0-935005-28-5*); reprint ed. lib. bdg. 45.95 (*0-935005-27-7*) Lincoln-Rembrandt.

— Off-Season Training for Cyclists. LC 98-135336. (Illus.). 200p. 1997. pap. text 14.95 (*1-884737-40-4*) VeloPress.

***Burke, Edmund.** On Empire, Liberty & Reform: Speeches & Letters. 416p. 2000. pap. 15.00 (*0-300-08147-2*) Yale U Pr.

Burke, Edmund. A Philosophy Enquiry into the Origin of Our Ideas of the Sublime & Beautiful. Phillips, Adam, ed. & intro. by. (Oxford World's Classics Ser.). 202p. 1998. pap. 9.95 (*0-19-283580-7*) OUP.

— Philosophy of Edmund Burke: A Selection from His Speeches & Writings. Bredvold, Louis I. & Ross, Ralph G., eds. 288p. 1960. pap. text 16.95 (*0-472-06121-6*, 06121, Ann Arbor Bks) U of Mich Pr.

— Pre-Revolutionary Writings. Harris, Ian, ed. (Cambridge Texts in the History of Political Thought Ser.). 406p. (C). 1993. text 59.95 (*0-521-36227-X*); pap. text 19.95 (*0-521-36800-6*) Cambridge U Pr.

— Prelude to Protectorate in Morocco: Precolonial Protest & Resistance, 1860-1912. LC 75-43228. (Illus.). 328p. 1996. lib. bdg. 30.00 (*0-226-08075-7*) U Ch Pr.

— Prelude to Protectorate in Morocco: Precolonial Protest & Resistance, 1860-1912. LC 75-43228. (Studies in Imperialism Ser.). 328p. Date not set. reprint ed. pap. 101.70 (*0-608-20619-9*, 205458700003) Bks Demand.

— Reflections on the Revolution in France. Pocock, J. G. A., ed. LC 86-31894. (HPC Classics Ser.). 294p. (C). 1987. lib. bdg. 29.95 (*0-87220-021-3*) Hackett Pub.

— Reflections on the Revolution in France. Pocock, J. G., ed. & intro. by. LC 86-31894. (HPC Classics Ser.). 294p. (C). 1987. pap. text 9.95 (*0-87220-020-5*) Hackett Pub.

***Burke, Edmund.** Reflections on the Revolution in France. Mitchell, L. G., ed. (Oxford World's Classics Ser.). 352p. 1999. pap. 8.95 (*0-19-283978-0*) OUP.

Burke, Edmund. Reflections on the Revolution in France. LC 87-61365. (Great Books in Philosophy). 253p. 1987. pap. 7.95 (*0-87975-411-7*) Prometheus Bks.

— Reflections on the Revolution in France: Burke. Mahoney, Thomas H., ed. 352p. (C). 1955. pap. text 7.33 (*0-02-420190-1*, Macmillan Coll) P-H.

***Burke, Edmund.** Select Works of Edmund Burke: Miscellaneous Writings. xix, 289p. 1999. 18.00 (*0-86597-168-4*); pap. 9.00 (*0-86597-169-2*) Liberty Fund.

Burke, Edmund. Selected Letters of Edmund Burke. Mansfield, Harvey C., Jr., ed. LC 83-18138. 508p. 1984. 42.00 (*0-226-08068-4*) U Ch Pr.

— Selected Writings & Speeches. Stanlis, J. Peter, ed. 1990. 21.75 (*0-8446-1094-1*) Peter Smith.

— Selected Writings of Edmund Burke. Bate, Walter Jackson, ed. LC 75-9946. 536p. 1975. reprint ed. lib. bdg. 35.00 (*0-8371-8122-4*, BUSEW, Greenwood Pr) Greenwood.

— Speeches. Selby, F. G., ed. LC 73-9127. 328p. 1974. reprint ed. lib. bdg. 69.50 (*0-8371-6984-4*, BUSP, Greenwood Pr) Greenwood.

— Speeches on the American War & Letters to the Sheriffs of Bristol. LC 72-8666. (American Revolutionary Ser.). 272p. reprint ed. lib. bdg. 37.50 (*0-8398-0191-2*) Irvington.

— A Vindication of Natural Society. LC 81-84826. (Illus.). 130p. 1982. reprint ed. pap. text 5.00 (*0-86597-010-6*) Liberty Fund.

An Asterisk (*) at the beginning of an entry indicates that the title is appearing for the first time.

— A Vindication of Natural Society. Pagano, Frank N., ed. & intro. by. LC 81-84826. (Illus.). 130p. 1982. reprint ed. 12.00 (*0-86597-009-2*) Liberty Fund.

— Works, 12 vols. reprint ed. 895.00 (*0-403-04342-5*) Somerset Pub.

— The Works, 12 vols. in 6, Set. (Anglistica & Americana Ser.: No. 155). 1975. reprint ed. 1105.00 (*3-487-05619-4*) G Olms Pubs.

— The Works of Edmund Burke, 12 vols., Set. 1987. reprint ed. lib. bdg. 895.00 (*0-7812-0439-9*) Rprt Serv.

— The Writings & Speeches of Edmund Burke: Party, Parliament & the American Crisis, 1766-1774, Vol. 2. Langford, Paul, ed. 526p. (C). 1981. text 135.00 (*0-19-822416-8*) OUP.

— The Writings & Speeches of Edmund Burke Vol. III: Party, Parliament & the American Crisis, 1774-1780. Elofson, Warren M., ed. 734p. (C). 1996. text 150.00 (*0-19-822414-1*, 7708) OUP.

— The Writings & Speeches of Edmund Burke Vol. III: The French Revolution, 1790-1794. Mitchell, L. G., ed. 568p. 1990. text 140.00 (*0-19-822422-2*) OUP.

— The Writings & Speeches of Edmund Burke Vol. VI: Vol. VI: India: The Launching of the Hastings Impeachment 1786-1788. Marshall, P. J., ed. 524p. 1991. text 140.00 (*0-19-821788-9*) OUP.

— The Writings & Speeches of Edmund Burke Vol. IX: Vol. IX: The Revolutionary War, 1794-1797, & Ireland. McDowell, Robert B., ed. 740p. 1992. text 170.00 (*0-19-821787-0*) OUP.

***Burke, Edmund.** The Writings & Speeches of Edmund Burke Volume Vii: India: The Hastings Trial 1789-1794. Marshall, Peter, ed. 744p. 2000. text 125.00 (*0-19-820809-X*) OUP.

Burke, Edmund, III, ed. Islam, Politics, & Social Movements. 330p. 1996. pap. 45.00 (*0-614-21513-7*, 593) Kazi Pubns.

— Struggle & Survival in the Modern Middle East. 395p. 1996. pap. 16.00 (*0-614-21631-1*, 1173) Kazi Pubns.

— Struggle & Survival in the Modern Middle East. 395p. 1994. 60.00 (*0-520-07566-8*, Pub. by U CA Pr); pap. 19.95 (*0-520-07988-4*, Pub. by U CA Pr) Cal Prin Full Svc.

***Burke, Edmund & Bromwich, David.** On Empire, Liberty & Reform. LC 99-45105. (Lewis Walpole Series in 18th Century Culture & History). 416p. 2000. 40.00 (*0-300-08146-4*) Yale U Pr.

Burke, Edmund & Carter, Michael. Practice & Theory of Automated Timetabling II: Second International Conference, PATAT/97, Toronto, Canada, August 20-22, 1997, Selected Papers. Goos, G. et al, eds. LC 98-39445. (Lecture Notes in Computer Science Ser.: Vol. 1408). xii, 273p. 1998. pap. 49.00 (*3-540-64979-4*) Spr-Verlag.

Burke, Edmund & Fahey, Thomas D. Phosphatidylserine (Ps) (Good Health Guides Ser.). pap. 3.95 (*0-87983-979-1*, 39791K, Keats Publng) NTC Contemp Pub Co.

Burke, Edmund & Foxley, Eric. Logic & Its Applications. 380p. 1996. pap. 59.00 (*0-13-030263-5*) P-H.

Burke, Edmund & Kramnick, Isaac. Portable Edmund Burke. LC 98-41476. 544p. 1999. pap. 16.95 (*0-14-026760-3*, PuffinBks) Peng Put Young Read.

Burke, Edmund, III & Lapidus, Ira M., eds. Islam, Politics, & Social Movements. (Comparative Studies on Muslim Societies: No. 5). 1988. pap. 15.95 (*0-520-06868-8*, Pub. by U CA Pr) Cal Prin Full Svc.

Burke, Edmund & Paine, Thomas. Reflections on the Revolution in France: Burke. 520p. 1969. pap. 5.95 (*0-385-08190-1*, Anchor NY) Doubleday.

Burke, Edmund & Ross. Practice & Theory of Automated Timetabling: First International Conference, Edinburgh, U.K., August 29-Septmber 1, 1995:Selected Papers, Vol. 115. LC 96-35279. (Lecture Notes in Computer Science Ser.). xiii, 381p. 1996. 62.00 (*3-540-61794-9*) Spr-Verlag.

Burke, Edmund H. History of Archery. LC 70-138579. 224p. 1971. reprint ed. lib. bdg. 35.00 (*0-8371-5778-1*, BUHA, Greenwood Pr) Greenwood.

Burke, Edmund J. & Gravelle, Brent. Wellness & Chiropractic. (Illus.). 304p. 1997. pap. 29.95 (*0-614-24660-1*) Mouvement Pubns.

— Wellness & Chiropractic. (Illus.). 304p. 1997. pap. text 29.95 (*0-614-26225-9*) Mouvement Pubns.

Burke, Edmund J. & Michael, Ernest D. Laboratory Experiences in Exercise Physiology. 2nd ed. 1990. student ed. 24.95 (*0-614-24658-X*) Mouvement Pubns.

Burke, Edmund M. Corporate Community Relations: The Principle of the Neighbor of Choice. LC 98-27837. 208p. 1999. 55.00 (*1-56720-192-X*, Quorum Bks); pap. 19.95 (*0-275-96471-X*, Praeger Pubs) Greenwood.

— A Participatory Approach to Urban Planning. LC 78-31107. 304p. 1979. 42.95 (*0-87705-393-6*, Kluwer Acad Hman Sci) Kluwer Academic.

***Burke, Edmund R.** Creatine: What You Need to Know. 48p. 1999. pap. 3.95 (*0-89529-978-X*, Avery) Penguin Putnam.

Burke, Edmund R. Cycling Health & Physiology: Using Sport Science to Improve Your Riding & Racing. 2nd ed. LC 97-42785. (Illus.). 240p. 1998. pap. 17.95 (*0-941950-34-4*) Vitesse Pr.

***Burke, Edmund R.** D-Pinitol: What You Need to Know. 48p. 1999. pap. 3.95 (*1-58333-012-7*, Avery) Penguin Putnam.

— D-Ribose: What You Need to Know. 48p. 1999. pap. 3.95 (*0-89529-981-X*, Avery) Penguin Putnam.

Burke, Edmund R. Healing Sports Injuries with Good Nutrition. LC 98-168668. (Sports Nutrition Guides Ser.). 48p. 1998. pap. 3.95 (*0-87983-857-4*, 38574K, Keats Publng) NTC Contemp Pub Co.

— Herbs for Sports Performance, Energy & Recovery. (Sports Nutrition Guides Ser.). 48p. 1998. pap. 3.95 (*0-87983-854-X*, 3854XK, Keats Publng) NTC Contemp Pub Co.

— Optimal Muscle Recovery: Your guide to Achieving Peak Physical Perfromance. 224p. 1999. pap. text 14.95 (*0-89529-884-8*, Avery) Penguin Putnam.

— Pre-Exercise, Competition & Post-Exercise Nutrition for Maximum Performance. LC 98-168656. (Sports Nutrition Guides Ser.). 48p. 1998. pap. 3.95 (*0-87983-850-7*, 38507K, Keats Publng) NTC Contemp Pub Co.

— Serious Cycling. LC 94-17276. (Illus.). 272p. 1994. pap. 18.95 (*0-87322-759-X*, PBUR0759) Human Kinetics.

— Women's Sports Nutrition. LC 98-168663. (Sports Nutrition Guides Ser.). 48p. 1998. pap. 3.95 (*0-87983-852-3*, 38523K, Keats Publng) NTC Contemp Pub Co.

Burke, Edmund R., ed. Complete Home Fitness Handbook. LC 95-38818. (Illus.). 256p. (Orig.). 1995. pap. 15.95 (*0-87322-994-0*, PBUR0994) Human Kinetics.

— High-Tech Cycling. LC 95-81020. (Illus.). 312p. (Orig.). 1995. pap. 19.95 (*0-87322-535-X*, PBUR0535) Human Kinetics.

— Precision Heart Rate Training. LC 97-44079. (Illus.). 224p. 1998. pap. 15.95 (*0-88011-770-2*, PBUR0770) Human Kinetics.

Burke, Edmund R. & Gastelu, Daniel. Avery's Sports Nutrition Almanac. 336p. 1999. pap. text 9.95 (*0-89529-885-6*, Avery) Penguin Putnam.

Burke, Edmund R. & Newsom, Mary M., eds. Medical & Scientific Aspects of Cycling. LC 87-3321. (Illus.). 272p. 1988. reprint ed. pap. 84.40 (*0-608-07072-6*, 206728600008) Bks Demand.

***Burke, Edmund R. & Pavelka, Ed.** The Complete Book of Long-Distance Cycling: Build the Strength, Skills & Confidence to Ride as Far as Possible. 288p. 2000. pap. 19.95 (*1-57954-199-2*) Rodale Pr Inc.

Burke, Edmund R., jt. auth. see Carmichael, Chris.

Burke, Edmund R., tr. see Klausen, Klaus, et al.

Burke, Edward M., jt. auth. see Sautter, R. Craig.

Burke, Elizabeth, ed. see Rosen, Kenneth.

Burke, Emily. Pleasure & Pain: Reminiscences of Georgia in the 1840's. 100p. 1991. 15.00 (*0-88322-006-7*) Beehive GA.

Burke, Ethel. Ethel Burke's What I Hate about Christmas. LC 95-14807. 144p. (Orig.). 1995. pap. 8.00 (*0-399-52165-8*, Perigee Bks) Berkley Pub.

Burke, Eugene F., jt. auth. see Hunter, David R.

Burke, F. D., et al, eds. Principles of Hand Surgery. (Illus.). 392p. 1989. text 75.00 (*0-443-03466-4*) Church.

Burke, F. D., et al. Principles of Hand Surgery. LC 88-35268. (Illus.). 382p. 1990. reprint ed. pap. 118.50 (*0-7837-9747-8*, 206047500005) Bks Demand.

Burke, Fielding. Call Home the Heart. 1999. lib. bdg. 31.95 (*1-56723-173-X*) Yestermorrow.

— Call Home the Heart. LC 83-5606. (Novels of the Thirties Ser.). 496p. 1983. reprint ed. pap. 9.95 (*0-935312-15-3*) Feminist Pr.

Burke, Frank. Fellini. LC 96-38444. 1996. 33.00 (*0-8057-3893-2*, Twyne) Mac Lib Ref.

— Fellini. LC 96-38444. (Illus.). 275p. 1996. pap. 20.00 (*0-8057-3894-0*, Twyne) Mac Lib Ref.

— UNIX System Administration. 175p. (C). 1987. text. write for info. (*0-318-61789-7*) SCP.

Burke, Frank G. Research & the Manuscript Tradition. LC 97-15729. 310p. 1997. 47.50 (*0-8108-3348-4*) Scarecrow.

Burke, Frank M. & Berry, Buford. Tax Practice Handbook. LC 85-16899. 436p. 1985. text 39.95 (*0-13-884735-5*) P-H.

Burke, Frank M., Jr. & Starcher, Mark L. Oil & Gas Taxation in Nontechnical Language. LC 93-13053. 280p. 1993. 25.00 (*0-87814-397-1*) PennWell Bks.

Burke, Fred. Africa's Quest for Order. 1990. 16.50 (*0-8446-0526-3*) Peter Smith.

Burke, Fred, tr. see Hoshino, Yukinobu.

Burke, Fred G. Local Government & Politics in Uganda. LC 64-16919. 286p. reprint ed. pap. 88.70 (*0-608-15215-3*, 202740900055) Bks Demand.

— Public Education: Who's in Charge? LC 89-38008. 205p. 1990. 55.00 (*0-275-93402-0*, C3402, Greenwood Pr) Greenwood.

— Tanganyika: Preplanning. LC 65-25989. (National Planning Ser.: No. 3). 138p. reprint ed. pap. 42.80 (*0-608-13740-5*, 202039600017) Bks Demand.

Burke, George. Gnostic Christianity: An Introduction. LC 94-173286. 100p. (Orig.). pap. 7.95 (*0-932104-05-3*) St George Pr.

— Simply Heaven! The Monastery Vegetarian Cookbook. 1996. pap. 19.95 (*0-614-19373-7*) Macmillan.

Burke, Gerald. Teachers & the Economy. 132p. (C). 1985. 59.00 (*0-7300-0373-6*, Pub. by Deakin Univ) St Mut.

Burke, Gerald & Rumberger, Russell W., eds. The Future Impact of Technology on Work & Education, Vol. 3. 225p. 1987. pap. write for info. (*0-318-66777-0*) Taylor & Francis.

Burke, Gill. Housing & Social Justice: The Role of Policy in British Housing. LC 79-42624. (Social Policy in Modern Britain Ser.). 239p. reprint ed. pap. 74.10 (*0-608-18741-0*, 203034400068) Bks Demand.

Burke, Glenn & Sherman, Erik. Out at Home: The Glenn Burke Story. Sherman, Michael, ed. 128p. (Orig.). 1995. pap. 14.95 (*0-9648158-0-X*) Excel Pubng.

Burke, Greg, jt. auth. see John Paul, II, pseud.

***Burke, Gwendolyn, et al.** Handbook of Environmental Management & Technology. 2nd ed. LC 99-43061. 832p. 2000. 149.00 (*0-471-34910-0*) Wiley.

***Burke, H. Dale.** Different by Design: God's Master Plan for Harmony Between Men & Women in Marriage. LC 99-86116. 2000. pap. 12.99 (*0-8024-8197-3*) Moody.

Burke, H. Dale. A Love That Never Fails: 1 Corinthians 13. (Guidelines for Living Ser.). 208p. 1999. pap. 9.99 (*0-8024-8198-1*) Moody.

Burke, Harriet, et al. People, Promise & Community: A Practical Guide to Creating & Sustaining Small Communities of Faith. 160p. (Orig.). 1996. pap 16.95 (*0-8091-3665-1*) Paulist Pr.

***Burke, Heather.** Meaning & Ideology in Historical Archaeology: Style, Social Identity & Capitalism in an Australian Town. LC 99-37715. (Contributions to Global Historical Archaeology Ser.). 276p. 1999. 79.95 (*0-306-46066-1*) Kluwer Academic.

Burke-Hengen, Mary & Gillespie, Timothy D., eds. Building Community: Social Studies in the Middle School Years. LC 95-8643. 227p. 1995. pap. text 25.00 (*0-435-08904-8*, 08904) Heinemann.

***Burke, Herbert.** Of the Secret Earth. LC 99-45862. 88p. 1998. pap. 9.75 (*0-920635-12-1*) Genl Dist Srvs.

Burke, Howard. Lead Sheet Interpretations: Swing & Latin Styles. (Illus.). 55p. (Orig.). (C). 1993. pap. 8.95 (*1-56516-059-2*) H Leonard.

Burke, J., et al. The Emergence of the Modern World: 1300-1815. (C). 1971. pap. text 17.95 (*0-686-80324-8*) Irvington.

Burke, J. E. Kinectics of Phase Transformations in Metals. LC 65-26345. 1965. 106.00 (*0-08-011214-5*, Pub. by Pergamon Repr) Franklin.

— Progress in Ceramic Science, Vol. 4. 1966. 133.00 (*0-08-011842-9*, Pub. by Pergamon Repr) Franklin.

Burke, J. E., jt. auth. see Beebee, T.

Burke, J. Martin & Friel, Michael K. Taxation of Individual Income. 5th ed. LC 98-10265. (Casebook Ser.). 1998. 60.00 (*0-8205-3170-7*) Bender.

Burke, J. Martin & Friel, Micheal K. Taxation of Individual Income. 1992. teacher ed. write for info. (*0-8205-0422-X*) Bender.

Burke, Jack. Creating Customer Connections: How to Make Customer Service a Profit Center for Your Company. LC 96-76108. 375p. (Orig.). 1997. pap. 29.95 (*1-56343-149-1*) Silver Lake.

— Natural Way to Better Golf. 1997. pap. 11.00 (*0-684-84255-6*) S&S Trade.

Burke, Jackie C. Capital Horse Country: A Rider's & Spectator's Guide. LC 94-6658. (Illus.). 294p. 1994. pap. 14.95 (*0-939009-80-3*, EPM) Howell Pr VA.

— Equal to the Challenge: Pioneering Women of Horse Sports. LC 97-1898. 198p. 1997. 19.95 (*0-87605-727-X*) Howell Bks.

Burke, Jackson & Ettenberg, Eugene M. John S. Fass & the Hammer Creek Press. (Illus.). 56p. 1998. 35.00 (*1-56792-086-1*) Godine.

***Burke, James.** The Knowledge Web: From Electronic Agents to Stonehenge & Back--And Other Journeys Through Knowledge, 1. LC 99-24539. 320p. 1999. 24.50 (*0-684-85934-3*) S&S Trade.

— The Knowledge Web: From Electronic Agents to Stonehenge & Back--And Other Journeys Through Knowledge. (Illus.). 288p. 2000. pap. 14.00 (*0-684-85935-1*, Touchstone) S&S Trade Pap.

Burke, James. What Are the Chances? Risks & Odds in Everyday Life. (Illus.). 128p. 1992. pap. 8.95 (*0-8065-1334-9*, Citadel Pr) Carol Pub Group.

Burke, James & Ornstein, Robert E. The Axemaker's Gift: A Double-Edged History of Human Culture. 2nd ed. LC 97-182361. (Illus.). 368p. 1997. reprint ed. pap. 15.95 (*0-87477-856-5*, Tarcher Putnam) Putnam Pub Group.

Burke, James & Resnick, Barry. Marketing & Selling the Travel Product. 332p. 1991. pap., teacher ed. write for info. (*0-538-70278-8*) S-W Pub.

Burke, James A., II, ed. Win Win: Student Book. 2nd ed. (Illus.). 65p. (Orig.). (YA). (gr. 9-12). 1996. pap. text 4.59 (*1-878227-39-4*) Peace Educ.

Burke, James A., II, ed. see Bachay, Judith.

Burke, James A., II, ed. see Brunt, Elyse.

Burke, James A., II, ed. see Carlebach, Diane.

Burke, James A., II, ed. see Carlebach, Diane & Dickmann, Catherine H.

Burke, James A., II, ed. see Diekman, Catherine H.

Burke, James A., II, ed. see Lewis, Rick & Smith, Judy.

Burke, James A., II, ed. see Rizzo, Sandy T., et al.

Burke, James A., II, ed. see Schmidt, Fran, II.

Burke, James A., II, ed. see Schmidt, Fran, et al.

Burke, James D. Bob Kolbrener Photographs: Twenty-Five Years in the American West. Steiner, Mary A., ed. (Illus.). 48p. (Orig.). 1993. pap. 16.95 (*0-89178-038-6*) St Louis Art Mus.

Burke, James D., ed. Space Manufacturing 1983. LC 57-43769. (Advances in the Astronautical Sciences Ser.: Vol. 53). (Illus.). 496p. 1983. pap. 60.00 (*0-87703-189-4*, Am Astronaut Soc) Univelt Inc.

Burke, James E. Pension Plan Management Manual: Cumulative Supplementation. 592p. 1991. supp. ed. 52.25 (*0-7913-0973-8*) Warren Gorham & Lamont.

Burke, James F. Desire Against the Law: The Juxtaposition of Contraries in Early Medieval Spanish Literature. LC 97-38396. (Figurae Ser.). 1998. write for info. (*0-8047-2936-0*) Stanford U Pr.

— History & Vision: The Figural Structure of the Libro del Cavallero Zifar. (Monografias A Ser.: Vol. XXVIII). 155p. (Orig.). (C). 1972. pap. 41.00 (*0-900411-58-9*, Pub. by Tamesis Bks Ltd) Boydell & Brewer.

— Structures from the Trivium in the "Cantar de Mio Cid" (Romance Ser.: No. 66). 256p. 1992. text 55.00 (*0-8020-5947-3*) U of Toronto Pr.

***Burke, James F.** Vision, the Gaze & the Function of the Senses in Celestina. LC 99-53135. (Studies in Romance Literatures). 2000. write for info. (*0-271-02038-5*) Pa St U Pr.

Burke, James J. Power Distribution Engineering: Fundamentals & Applications. LC 94-11103. (Electrical Engineering & Electronics Ser.: Vol. 88). (Illus.). 376p. 1994. text 125.00 (*0-8247-9237-8*) Dekker.

Burke, James Lee. Black Cherry Blues. large type ed. LC 96-41033. 1996. lib. bdg. 24.95 (*1-57490-070-6*, Beeler LP Bks) T T Beeler.

— Black Cherry Blues. 336p. 1990. reprint ed. mass mkt. 6.99 (*0-380-71204-0*, Avon Bks) Morrow Avon.

— Burning Angel. LC 94-41921. 464p. 1996. mass mkt. 6.99 (*0-7868-8904-7*, Pub. by Hyperion) Time Warner.

— Burning Angel. limited ed. 340p. 1995. boxed set 125.00 (*0-9631925-3-1*) B E Trice.

— Cadillac Jukebox. 352p. 1996. 22.95 (*0-7868-6175-4*, Pub. by Hyperion) Time Warner.

— Cadillac Jukebox. 464p. 1997. mass mkt. 6.99 (*0-7868-8918-7*, Pub. by Hyperion) Time Warner.

— Cadillac Jukebox. large type ed. LC 96-35550. (Large Print Bks.). 1996. 27.95 (*1-56895-375-5*, Compass) Wheeler Pub.

— Cadillac Jukebox. limited ed. 303p. 1996. boxed set 150.00 (*0-9631925-5-8*) B E Trice.

— Cimarron Rose. LC 96-30745. 304p. 1997. 24.45 (*0-7868-6258-0*, Pub. by Hyperion) Time Warner.

— Cimarron Rose. (J). 1998. mass mkt. 7.99 (*0-7868-8930-6*, Pub. by Hyperion) Time Warner.

— Cimarron Rose. large type ed. LC 97-43874. (Large Print Bks.). 1998. 26.95 (*1-56895-527-8*) Wheeler Pub.

— Cimarron Rose. limited ed. 288p. 1997. boxed set 150.00 (*0-9631925-9-0*) B E Trice.

— Connections. rev. ed. LC 95-12751. 304p. 1995. pap. 24.95 (*0-316-11672-6*) Little.

— Convict. Date not set. lib. bdg. 24.95 (*0-8488-1775-3*) Amereon Ltd.

— The Convict & Other Stories. 2001. mass mkt. 6.99 (*0-7868-8965-9*) Hyperion.

— Conviction: A Novel. LC 95-15701. 160p. (J). 1995. pap. 10.45 (*0-7868-8143-7*, Pub. by Hyperion) Time Warner.

— The Day the Universe Changed. rev. ed. LC 95-12752. 352p. 1995. pap. 24.95 (*0-316-11704-8*) Little.

— Dixie City Jam. LC 93-36228. 352p. 1994. 22.95 (*0-7868-6019-7*, Pub. by Hyperion) Time Warner.

— Dixie City Jam. 512p. 1995. mass mkt. 5.99 (*0-7868-8900-4*, Pub. by Hyperion) Time Warner.

— Half of Paradise: A Novel. Date not set. lib. bdg. 24.95 (*0-8488-1778-8*) Amereon Ltd.

— Half of Paradise: A Novel. LC 95-2246. 288p. (J). 1995. pap. 10.95 (*0-7868-8117-8*, Pub. by Hyperion) Time Warner.

— Half of Paradise: A Novel. 469p. (J). 1998. mass mkt. 6.50 (*0-7868-8946-2*, Pub. by Hyperion) Time Warner.

***Burke, James Lee.** Heartwood. 400p. 2000. mass mkt. 7.50 (*0-440-22401-2*) Dell.

Burke, James Lee. Heartwood. LC 98-40419. 341p. 1999. 24.95 (*0-385-48843-2*) Doubleday.

***Burke, James Lee.** Heartwood. LC 99-34270. 1999. 24.95 (*0-375-40849-5*) Random Hse Lrg Prnt.

— Heartwood. limited ed. 341p. 1999. boxed set 150.00 (*1-890885-08-8*) B E Trice.

Burke, James Lee. Heaven's Prisoners. abr. ed. LC 00-5260. 288p. 1996. per. 5.99 (*0-671-51741-4*) PB.

— Heaven's Prisoners. large type ed. LC 97-16004. 1997. lib. bdg. 24.95 (*1-57490-086-2*, Beeler LP Bks) T T Beeler.

— In Electric Mist with Co. 352p. 1994. reprint ed. mass mkt. 6.99 (*0-380-72121-X*, Avon Bks) Morrow Avon.

— In the Electric Mist with Confederate Dead: A Novel. LC 92-26615. 352p. 1993. 19.95 (*1-56282-882-7*, Pub. by Hyperion) Time Warner.

— Lay Down My Sword & Shield. Date not set. lib. bdg. 24.95 (*0-8488-1779-6*) Amereon Ltd.

— Lay Down My Sword & Shield. LC 94-33421. 240p. (J). 1995. pap. 10.45 (*0-7868-8039-2*, Pub. by Hyperion) Time Warner.

***Burke, James Lee.** Lay Down My Sword & Shield. 389p. 1999. mass mkt. 6.50 (*0-7868-8950-0*, Pub. by Hyperion) Time Warner.

Burke, James Lee. The Lost Get-Back Boogie. Date not set. lib. bdg. 24.95 (*0-8488-1780-X*) Amereon Ltd.

— The Lost Get-Back Boogie. LC 94-33419. 256p. (J). 1995. pap. 10.45 (*0-7868-8101-1*, Pub. by Hyperion) Time Warner.

— The Lost Get-Back Boogie. LC 86-10662. 241p. 1986. 16.95 (*0-8071-1334-4*) La State U Pr.

***Burke, James Lee.** The Lost Get-Back Boogie. large type ed. 343p. 2000. lib. bdg. 28.95 (*1-58547-053-8*) Ctr Point Pubg.

Burke, James Lee. The Lost Get-Back Boogie. 256p. (J). 1997. reprint ed. mass mkt. 5.99 (*0-7868-8934-9*, Pub. by Hyperion) Time Warner.

***Burke, James Lee.** A Morning for Flamingos. 1999. pap. 9.98 (*0-671-04408-7*) PB.

Burke, James Lee. A Morning for Flamingos. large type ed. LC 98-26235. 1998. 24.95 (*1-57490-155-9*, Beeler LP Bks) T T Beeler.

— Morning for Flamingos. 336p. 1991. reprint ed. mass mkt. 6.99 (*0-380-71360-8*, Avon Bks) Morrow Avon.

— The Neon Rain. 288p. 1992. per. 6.99 (*0-671-75644-3*) PB.

— The Neon Rain. large type ed. 377p. 1991. 21.95 (*1-85089-413-2*, Pub. by ISIS Lrg Prnt) Transaction Pubs.

— The Pinball Effect: How Renaissance Water Gardens Made the Carburetor Possible & Other Journeys Through Knowledge. 336p. 1997. pap. 15.95 (*0-316-11610-6*) Little.

— A Present for Santa. 256p. 1989. pap. 3.95 (*0-380-70483-8*, Avon Bks) Morrow Avon.

— A Present for Santa. 304p. 1986. 16.95 (*0-685-14542-5*) St Martin.

B

***Burke, James Lee.** Purple Cane Road: A Novel. LC 99-54080. 330p. 2000. 24.95 (0-385-48844-0) Doubleday.
— Purple Cane Road: A Novel. large type ed. LC 00-21643. 528p. 2000. 24.95 (0-375-43055-5) Random Hse Lrg Prnt.
Burke, James Lee. Stained White Radiance. 336p. 1993. reprint ed. mass mkt. 6.99 (0-380-72047-7, Avon Bks) Morrow Avon.
— Sunset Limited. 416p. 1999. mass mkt. 7.50 (0-440-22398-9, Island Bks) Dell.
— Sunset Limited. LC 97-23893. 320p. 1998. 24.95 (0-385-48842-4) Doubleday.
— Sunset Limited. large type ed. LC 98-8710. 1998. 28.95 (0-7838-0331-1, G K Hall Lrg Type) Mac Lib Ref.
***Burke, James Lee.** Sunset Limited. large type ed. LC 98-8710. 429p. 2000. pap. 26.95 (0-7838-0332-X, G K Hall Lrg Type) Mac Lib Ref.
Burke, James Lee. Texas City, 1947. deluxe ed. 30p. 1992. 75.00 (0-935716-61-0) Lord John.
— To the Bright & Shining Sun. Date not set. lib. bdg. 24.95 (0-8488-1776-1) Amereon Ltd.
— To the Bright & Shining Sun. LC 94-35202. 224p. (J). 1995. pap. 10.45 (0-7868-8012-0, Pub. by Hyperion) Time Warner.
— To the Bright & Shining Sun 2001. mass mkt. 6.50 (0-7868-8968-3) Disney Pr.

Burke, James Lee. Two for Texas. Date not set. lib. bdg. 18.95 (0-8488-1777-X) Amereon Ltd.
Burke, James Lee. Two for Texas. LC 94-32465. 148p. (J). 1995. pap. 10.45 (0-7868-8011-2, Pub. by Hyperion) Time Warner.
Burke, James Lee. Two for Texas. 192p. 2000. mass mkt. 6.50 (0-7868-8970-5, Pub. by Hyperion) Time Warner.
***Burke, Jan.** Bones. LC 99-22207. (Irene Kelly Mystery Ser.: No. 7). 384p. 1999. 22.50 (0-684-85551-8) S&S Trade.
Burke, Jan. Dear Irene: An Irene Kelly Mystery. 1996. mass mkt. 5.50 (0-380-72556-8, Avon Bks) Morrow Avon.
***Burke, Jan.** Flight. (Irene Kelly Mysteries Ser.). 2000. 23.00 (0-684-85552-6) Simon & Schuster.
Burke, Jan. Goodnight Irene. 256p. 1994. mass mkt. 5.99 (0-380-72279-8, Avon Bks) Morrow Avon.
— Goodnight, Irene. large type ed. 1996. 25.99 (0-7089-3287-8) Ulverscroft.
— Hocus: An Irene Kelly Mystery. (Irene Kelly Mystery Ser.). 480p. 1998. mass mkt. 6.99 (0-06-104439-3) HarpC.
— Hocus: An Irene Kelly Mystery. LC 96-34414. 336p. 1997. 22.00 (0-684-80344-5); write for info. (0-684-00492-5) S&S Trade.
— Hocus: An Irene Kelly Mystery. large type ed. LC 97-36272. 1997. lib. bdg. 24.95 (1-57490-106-0, Beeler LP Bks) T T Beeler.
— Liar: An Irene Kelly Mystery. (Irene Kelly Mystery Ser.). 400p. 1999. mass mkt. 6.99 (0-06-104440-7) HarpC.
— Liar: An Irene Kelly Mystery. LC 98-10197. 320p. 1998. 23.00 (0-684-80345-3) S&S Trade.
— Sweet Dreams, Irene. 256p. 1995. mass mkt. 4.99 (0-380-72350-6, Avon Bks) Morrow Avon.
— Sweet Dreams, Irene. LC 93-31179. 1994. 18.00 (0-671-78210-X) S&S Trade.
Burke, Jane K. Self Discovery & Manifestation. (Orig.). 1995. pap. 9.95 (0-929377-00-1) Burke-Srour Pubns Inc.
Burke, Janice P., et al, eds. The Development of Standardized Clinical Evaluations in Mental Health. LC 88-656. (Occupational Therapy in Mental Health Ser.: Vol. 8, No. 1). (Illus.). 94p. 1988. text 39.95 (0-86656-729-1) Haworth Pr.
Burke, Jeffrey. Island Lighthouse Inn: A Chronicle. LC 96-37601. (Illus.). 208p. 1997. 21.95 (0-8298-1162-1) Pilgrim OH.
***Burke, Jennifer S.** Cloudy Days. (Welcome Bks.). (Illus.). (J). 2000. 13.50 (0-516-23117-0) Childrens.
— Cloudy Days. (Weather Report Ser.). (Illus.). 24p. (J). (ps-2). 2000. pap. write for info. (0-516-23042-5) Childrens.
— Cold Days. (Welcome Bks.). (Illus.). (J). 2000. 13.50 (0-516-23118-9) Childrens.
— Cold Days. LC 00-27736. (Weather Report Ser.). (Illus.). 24p. (J). (ps-2). 2000. pap. write for info. (0-516-23043-3) Childrens.
— Hot Days. (Weather Report Ser.). (Illus.). 24p. (J). (ps-2). 2000. pap. 4.95 (0-516-23044-1) Childrens.
— Hot Days. (Welcome Bks.). (Illus.). (J). 2000. 13.50 (0-516-23119-7) Childrens.
— Ovals. (Welcome Bks.). (Illus.). (J). 2000. 13.50 (0-516-23076-X) Childrens.
— Ovals. (City Shapes Ser.). (Illus.). 24p. (J). (ps-2). 2000. pap. 4.95 (0-516-23001-8) Childrens.
— Rainy Days. LC 00-24623. (Weather Report Ser.). (Illus.). 24p. (J). (ps-2). 2000. pap. 4.95 (0-516-23045-X) Childrens.
— Rainy Days. (Welcome Bks.). (Illus.). (J). 2000. 13.50 (0-516-23120-0) Childrens.
— Rectangles. (Welcome Bks.). (Illus.). (J). 2000. 13.50 (0-516-23077-8) Childrens.
— Rectangles. (City Shapes Ser.). (Illus.). 24p. (J). (ps-2). 2000. pap. 4.95 (0-516-23002-6) Childrens.
— Squares. (Welcome Bks.). (Illus.). (J). 2000. 13.50 (0-516-23078-6) Childrens.
— Squares. (City Shapes Ser.). (Illus.). 24p. (J). (ps-2). 2000. pap. write for info. (0-516-23003-4) Childrens.
— Stars. (Welcome Bks.). (Illus.). (J). 2000. 13.50 (0-516-23079-4) Childrens.
— Stars. (City Shapes Ser.). (Illus.). 24p. (J). (ps-2). 2000. pap. 4.95 (0-516-23004-2) Childrens.
— Sunny Days. (Welcome Bks.). (Illus.). (J). 2000. 13.50 (0-516-23121-9) Childrens.
— Sunny Days. LC 00-23355. (Weather Report Ser.). (Illus.). 24p. (J). (ps-2). 2000. pap. write for info. (0-516-23046-8) Childrens.
— Triangles. (Welcome Bks.). (Illus.). (J). 2000. 13.50 (0-516-23080-8) Childrens.
— Triangles. (City Shapes Ser.). (Illus.). 24p. (J). (ps-2). 2000. pap. write for info. (0-516-23005-0) Childrens.
— Windy Days. (Welcome Bks.). (Illus.). (J). 2000. 13.50 (0-516-23122-7) Childrens.
— Windy Days. LC 00-24584. (Weather Report Ser.). (Illus.). 24p. (J). (ps-2). 2000. pap. write for info. (0-516-23047-6) Childrens.
Burke, Jerome T. Black Point. LC 93-80487. 325p. (Orig.). 1994. pap. text 12.00 (0-9639096-0-6) HollyCourt Pr.
Burke, Jim. The English Teacher's Companion: A Complete Guide to Classroom Curriculum & the Profession. LC PE65.B87 1999. 1999. pap. text 24.00 (0-86709-475-3, Pub. by Boynton Cook Pubs) Heinemann.
— I Hear America Reading: Why We Read What We Read. LC 99-33312. 1999. pap. text 12.50 (0-325-00134-0) Heinemann.
***Burke, Jim.** Reading Reminders: Tools, Tips, & Techniques. 224p. 2000. pap. text 21.00 (0-86709-500-8) Boynton Cook Pubs.
— Reading the Future. pap. write for info. (0-86709-497-4, Pub. by Boynton Cook Pubs) Heinemann.
***Burke, Jim & Prater, Carol.** I'will Grant You That: A Step-By-Step Guide To Finding Funds, Designing Winning Projects, & Writing Powerful Grant Proposals. LC 00-22502. 2000. pap. text 25.00 (0-325-00197-9) Heinemann.
Burke, Jim, jt. auth. see Bulla, Clyde R.
Burke, Joan, ed. & intro. see H. D., pseud.
Burke, John. Bridge of Triangles. LC 94-220359. 2000. pap. 19.95 (0-7022-2639-4, Pub. by Univ Queensland Pr) Intl Spec Bk.
— The English Inn. LC 81-4292. (Illus.). 240p. 1981. 39.50 (0-8419-0706-4) Holmes & Meier.
***Burke, John.** A Good News Spirituality: Finding Holiness in Parish Life. 240p. 2000. pap. 14.95 (0-8091-3963-4) Paulist Pr.
Burke, John. Intronet: A Beginner's Guide to Searching the Internet. LC 98-45722. 100p. 1999. pap. 29.95 (1-55570-351-8) Neal-Schuman.
— Learning the Internet: A Workbook for Beginners. 138p. (Orig.). 1996. pap., wbk. ed. 49.95 incl. disk (1-55570-303-8) Neal-Schuman.
— Learning the Internet: A Workbook for Beginners. (Illus.). 138p. (Orig.). 1996. pap., wbk. ed. 32.95 (1-55570-248-1) Neal-Schuman.
— The Legend of Baby Doe: The Life & Times of the Silver Queen of the West. LC 89-32800. (Illus.). xiii, 256p. 1989. pap. 13.95 (0-8032-6103-9, Bison Books) U of Nebr Pr.
— Those Magnificent Men in Flying Machines. 20.95 (0-8488-0374-4) Amereon Ltd.
— Web Databases with Cold Fusion 3. LC 97-44548. (Illus.). 480p. 1997. pap. 49.95 incl. cd-rom (0-07-913092-5) McGraw.
Burke, John, ed. Outcomes, Learning & the Curriculum: Implications for NVQs & Other Qualifications. LC 94-24819. 274p. 1994. 95.00 (0-7507-0288-5, Falmer Pr); pap. 27.95 (0-7507-0289-3, Falmer Pr) Taylor & Francis.
Burke, John & Ethylene Producers Staff, eds. Proceedings of the 9th Ethylene Producers' Conference. (Ethylene Producers Ser.). 850p. 1997. 170.00 (0-8169-0743-9, T-104) Am Inst Chem Eng.
Burke, John B. Burke's Extinct & Dormant Baronetcies of England, Ireland & Scotland. 2nd ed. (Illus.). 644p. 1999. reprint ed. pap. 47.50 (0-8063-0739-0, Pub. by Clearfield Co) ACCESS Pubs Network.
— A Genealogical & Heraldic History of the Commoners of Great Britain & Ireland: Reprinted with the index to Pedigrees in Burke's Commoners, 4 vols. LC 76-44267. (Illus.). 3113p. 1998. reprint ed. pap. 200.00 (0-8063-0742-0) Clearfield Co.
***Burke, John B.** The General Armory of England, Scotland, Ireland & Wales. 1185p. 2000. pap. write for info. (0-8063-4947-6) Clearfield Co.
Burke, John B. The Roll of Battle Abbey. 113p. 2000. pap. 17.50 (0-8063-0807-9, 840) Clearfield Co.
— Studies in Genesis. 1979. pap. 5.99 (0-88469-048-2) BMH Bks.
Burke, John B. & Burke, Ashworth P. A Genealogical & Heraldic History of the Commoners of Great Britain & Ireland, 2 vols. 888p. 1997. pap. 65.00 (0-8063-0415-4) Clearfield Co.
Burke, John C. Decreasing Classroom Behavior Problems: Practical Guidelines for Teachers. (Illus.). 206p. (Orig.). (C). 1992. pap. 39.95 (1-879105-37-3, 0221) Thomson Learn.
Burke, John D. Advertising in the Marketplace. 2nd ed. 1980. text 73.44 (0-07-009035-1) McGraw.
Burke, John E. The Burden of the South, in Verse. LC 70-170690. (Black Heritage Library Collection). 1977. reprint ed. 20.95 (0-8369-8880-9) Ayer.
— Chivalry, Slavery & Young America. LC 74-170691. (Black Heritage Library Collection). 1977. reprint ed. 21.95 (0-8369-8881-7) Ayer.
— An Historical-Analytic Study of the Legislative & Political Origins of the Public Broadcasting Act of 1967. Sterling, Christopher H., ed. LC 78-21717. (Dissertations in Broadcasting Ser.). (Illus.). 1980. lib. bdg. 30.95 (0-405-11756-6) Ayer.
Burke, John G. Origins of the Science of Crystals. LC 66-13584. 208p. reprint ed. pap. 64.50 (0-608-15837-2, 203142700074) Bks Demand.
Burke, John G., et al, eds. Cook's Index, Vol. 1. 536p. 1989. 55.00 (0-934272-09-3) J G Burke Pub.
— Cook's Index, Vol. 2. 280p. 1997. 55.00 (0-934272-31-X) J G Burke Pub.
— Dictionary of Contemporary Quotations, Vol. 6. 302p. 1987. 45.00 (0-934272-13-1) J G Burke Pub.
Burke, John G. & Eakin, Marshall C. Technology & Change. (Illus.). 1979. pap., student ed. write for info. (0-87835-087-X) Thomson Learn.
Burke, John G. & Kehde, Ned, eds. Dictionary of Contemporary Quotations, Vol. 7. 312p. 1990. 55.00 (0-934272-25-5) J G Burke Pub.
— Dictionary of Contemporary Quotations, Vol. 8. 332p. 1994. 55.00 (0-934272-32-8) J G Burke Pub.
— Dictionary of Contemporary Quotations, Vol. 9. 1998. 55.00 (0-934272-45-X) J G Burke Pub.
Burke, John J. From Home & Abroad: American & British Writers in Philadelphia, 1800-1910. LC 94-20121. 108p. (Orig.). (C). reprint ed. pap. text 22.50 (0-8191-9592-8); reprint ed. lib. bdg. 41.50 (0-8191-9591-X) U Pr of Amer.
***Burke, John J.** Neal-Schuman Library Technology Companion: A Basic Guide for Library Staff. 250p. 2000. pap. 45.00 (1-55570-398-4) Neal-Schuman.
Burke, John J. The Political Foundation of Law & the Need for Theory with Practical Value: The Theories of Ronald Dworkin & Roberto Unger. 319p. (Orig.). 1992. 64.95 (1-880921-46-4); pap. text 44.95 (1-880921-05-7) Austin & Winfield.
— The Writer in Pennsylvania, 1681-1981. LC 81-85496. 93p. 1982. pap. 5.95 (0-686-36440-6) St Joseph.
— The Writer in Philadelphia, 1682-1982. LC 81-51298. 84p. 1981. pap. 5.95 (0-686-36439-2) St Joseph.
***Burke, John J., ed.** Catholic Prayer Book for the Marine Corps. 66p. 1999. reprint ed. pap. 5.95 (0-912141-81-6) Roman Cath Bks.
Burke, John J. & Kay, Donald, eds. The Unknown Samuel Johnson. LC 81-70159. 195p. reprint ed. pap. 60.50 (0-608-17150-6, 202736300055) Bks Demand.
Burke, John J. & Puskar, Arno. The Estonian Securities Market. LC 98-12224. 1998. 75.00 (1-57823-050-0) Juris Pubng.
Burke, John J., Jr., ed. see Alabama Symposium on English & American Literature.
Burke, John P. The Institutional Presidency. (Interpreting American Politics Ser.). 288p. 1992. text 45.00 (0-8018-4315-4); pap. text 15.95 (0-8018-4316-2) Johns Hopkins.
***Burke, John P.** The Institutional Presidency: Organizing & Managing the White House from FDR to Clinton. 2nd ed. LC 00-36539. (Interpreting American Politics Ser.). 296p. 2000. pap. write for info. (0-8018-6501-8) Johns Hopkins.
— Presidential Transitions: From Politics to Practice. 430p. 2000. 65.00 (1-55587-916-0) L Rienner.
Burke, John P. & Greenstein, Fred I. How Presidents Test Reality: Decisions on Vietnam, 1954 & 1965. 344p. 1991. pap. 16.95 (0-87154-176-9) Russell Sage.
Burke, John P., et al. How Presidents Test Reality: Decisions on Vietnam, 1954 & 1965. LC 89-6431. 320p. 1989. 42.50 (0-87154-175-0) Russell Sage.
Burke, John P., jt. auth. see Brownell, Herbert.
Burke, John R., jt. auth. see Lea, Susan M.
Burke, John W., ed. Competency Based Education & Training. 220p. 1989. 79.95 (1-85000-626-1, Falmer Pr); pap. 37.95 (1-85000-627-X, Falmer Pr) Taylor & Francis.
Burke, Johnny, jt. auth. see Leeds, Michael.
Burke, Jonathan. Four Stars for Danger. large type ed. 320p. 1992. 27.99 (0-7089-2584-7) Ulverscroft.
— Gossip to the Grave. large type ed. (Linford Mystery Library). 320p. 1988. pap. 16.99 (0-7089-6512-1) Ulverscroft.
— Someone Lying, Someone Dying. large type ed. 1991. 27.99 (0-7089-2549-9) Ulverscroft.
— The Weekend Girls. large type ed. (Linford Mystery Library). 320p. 1987. pap. 16.99 (0-7089-6456-7, Linford) Ulverscroft.
Burke, Joseph F. Contemporary Approaches to Psychotherapy & Counseling: The Self-Regulation & Maturity Model. LC 88-39587. 427p. (C). 1989. text 57.95 (0-534-10146-1) Brooks-Cole.
Burke, Joseph M. Representing a Claimant in a Workers' Compensation Case. LC 93-86314. 154p. 1993. pap. text 45.00 (0-944490-56-5) Mass CLE.
Burke, Judy, ed. Look What You Can Make with Paper Bags. LC 97-77904. (Illus.). 48p. (J). (ps-7). 1999. pap. 5.95 (1-56397-717-6) Boyds Mills Pr.
Burke, Julian F. The Human Genome. (C). 1997. pap. text. write for info. (0-582-27655-1, Pub. by Addison-Wesley) Longman.
— PCR: Essential Techniques. LC 96-28414. 168p. 1996. pap. 47.95 (0-471-95697-X) Wiley.
Burke, June K. Creation, Its Laws & You. (Illus.). (Orig.). 1993. pap. 9.95 (0-929377-01-X) Burke-Srour Pubns Inc.
— You Are Unique. (Orig.). 1995. pap. 9.95 (0-929377-03-6) Burke-Srour Pubns Inc.
Burke, Karen C. Federal Income Taxation of Corporations & Stockholders in a Nutshell. 4th ed. (Nutshell Ser.). 300p. (C). 1996. pap. 21.00 (0-314-06641-1) West Pub.
— Federal Income Taxation of Partnerships in a Nutshell. (Nutshell Ser.). 356p. (C). 1992. pap. text 17.00 (0-314-00250-2) West Pub.
Burke, Karen C., jt. auth. see Weidenbruch, Peter P., Jr.
Burke, Karen M., jt. ed. see LeMone, Priscilla.
Burke, Kate. Searching in New York: A Reference Guide to Public & Private Records. (ISC State Search Bks.: No. 5). 270p. (Orig.). 1987. pap. text 15.95 (0-942916-10-7) ISC Pubns.
Burke, Kate, ed. see Charuhas, Chris.
Burke, Kathleen, et al. Intermediate Microeconomics: A Workbook. Dawes, Dana C., ed. (Illus.). 186p. (C). 1998. pap. text, wbk. ed. 28.00 (1-878437-94-1) Pac Crest Soft.
Burke, Katie. Lightning Bug Thunder. LC 98-930990. (Illus.). 32p. (J). (ps-4). 1998. 14.95 (1-55209-271-2) Firefly Bks Ltd.
Burke, Katy. The Handbook for Non-Macho Sailors. write for info. (0-318-59568-0) S&S Trade.
Burke, Kay. Designing Professional Portfolios for Change. LC 96-80215. (Illus.). 184p. (Orig.). 1997. pap. 25.95 (1-57517-056-6, 1488) SkyLght.
— How to Assess Authentic Learning. (Mindful School Ser.). 184p. (Orig.). (C). 1998. pap. text 31.00 (0-205-29265-8, Longwood Div) Allyn.
— How to Assess Authentic Learning. LC 93-78419. (Mindful School Ser.). (Illus.). 192p. (Orig.). 1993. pap. text 26.95 (0-932935-75-3) SkyLght.
— Portfolio Connection. 196p. 1998. pap. 31.00 (0-205-29267-4) P-H.
— What to Do with the Kid Who . . . Developing Cooperation, Self-Discipline, & Responsibility in the Classroom. LC 92-64102. 352p. 1992. pap. 41.95 (0-932935-42-7) SkyLght.
Burke, Kay, ed. Authentic Assessment: A Collection. LC 92-62484. (Orig.). 1992. pap. text 23.95 (0-932935-51-6) SkyLght.
— Managing the Interactive Classroom: A Collection of Articles. LC 95-78185. (Illus.). 144p. (Orig.). 1995. pap. 14.95 (1-57517-002-7, 1343) SkyLght.
— Professional Portfolios: A Collection of Articles. LC 96-77237. 192p. (Orig.). 1996. pap. 23.95 (1-57517-013-2, 1462) SkyLght.
Burke, Kay, et al. The Portfolio Connection. LC 94-78532. (Mindful School Ser.). 196p. 1994. pap. 26.95 (0-932935-78-8) SkyLght.
Burke, Keast, jt. auth. see Holtermann, Bernard O.
Burke, Ken R., ed. see Edwards, David.
Burke, Ken R., ed. see McKinley, Michael.
Burke, Ken R., ed. see Ortho Books Staff.
Burke, Ken R., ed. see Sinnes, A. Cort.
Burke, Ken R., ed. see Wolfe, Rex & McNair, James.
Burke-Kennedy, Declan. Leonie. LC 96-101809. 270p. 1995. 28.00 (1-85371-501-8, Pub. by Poolbeg Pr) Dufour.
— Leonie. 304p. 1996. pap. 14.95 (1-85371-542-5, Pub. by Poolbeg Pr) Dufour.
Burke, Kenneth. Attitudes Toward History. 3rd ed. 1984. pap. 17.95 (0-520-04148-8, Pub. by U CA Pr) Cal Prin Full Svc.
— Collected Poems, 1915-1967. LC 67-29786. 318p. reprint ed. pap. 98.60 (0-7837-4756-X, 204450300003) Bks Demand.
— Counter-Statement. LC 68-20356. 1968. pap. 15.95 (0-520-00196-6, Pub. by U CA Pr) Cal Prin Full Svc.
— A Grammar of Motives. LC 69-16741. 1969. reprint ed. pap. 18.95 (0-520-01544-4, Pub. by U CA Pr) Cal Prin Full Svc.
— Language As Symbolic Action: Essays on Life, Literature, & Method. LC 66-27655. 1966. reprint ed. pap. 19.95 (0-520-00192-3, Pub. by U CA Pr) Cal Prin Full Svc.
— On Symbols & Society. (Heritage of Sociology Ser.). 342p. 1989. pap. text 17.00 (0-226-08078-1) U Ch Pr.
— On Symbols & Society. (Heritage of Sociology Ser.). 352p. 1989. lib. bdg. 39.95 (0-226-08077-3) U Ch Pr.
— Permanence & Change: An Anatomy of Purpose. 3rd ed. 1984. pap. 17.95 (0-520-04146-1, Pub. by U CA Pr) Cal Prin Full Svc.
— The Philosophy of Literary Form. 1974. reprint ed. pap. 19.95 (0-520-02483-4, Pub. by U CA Pr) Cal Prin Full Svc.
— A Rhetoric of Motives. LC 69-16742. 1969. reprint ed. pap. 18.95 (0-520-01546-0, Pub. by U CA Pr) Cal Prin Full Svc.
— The Rhetoric of Religion: Studies in Logology. 1970. pap. 16.95 (0-520-01610-6, Pub. by U CA Pr) Cal Prin Full Svc.
— Terms for Order. Hyman, Stanley E., ed. LC PN0511.B7962. 206p. reprint ed. pap. 63.90 (0-608-18382-2, 205621800056) Bks Demand.
Burke, Kenneth, et al. Surrealism Pro & Con. 1973. pap. 6.50 (0-910664-27-7) Gotham.
Burke, Kevin, jt. auth. see Burke, Timothy.
Burke, Kevin C., jt. ed. see Crowley, Thomas J.
***Burke, Kevin F.** The Ground Beneath the Cross: The Theology of Ignacio Ellacuria. LC 99-38855. 256p. 2000. text 55.00 (0-87840-761-8) Georgetown U Pr.
Burke, Larry. The Baseball Chronicles: A Decade-by-Decade History of the All-American Pastime. 1996. 19.98 (0-7651-9603-4) Smithmark.
Burke, Larry, jt. auth. see Bench, Johnny.
Burke, Larry, jt. auth. see Ripken, Cal, Sr.
Burke, Laura & Murphy, Judy, eds. Charting by Exception: Cost Effective in Nursing Documentation. (Orig.). 1989. pap. text 41.95 (0-8273-4216-0) Delmar.
Burke, Laura J. & Murphy, Judith A. Charting by Exception Applications. 2nd ed. LC 94-10957. 512p. (C). 1995. pap. 169.95 (0-8273-6048-7) Delmar.
Burke, Leo T. A Universal Theory: The Science of Metaphysics. 282p. 1999. pap. 12.95 (1-891929-21-6) Four Seasons.
Burke, Lew. Lew Burke's Dog Training. (Illus.). 255p. 1976. 17.95 (0-87666-656-X, H-962) TFH Pubns.
***Burke, Lillian.** Computers in Allied Health. LC 99-42918. (Illus.). 242p. (C). 1999. pap. text 30.67 (0-13-083199-9) P-H.
Burke, Lisa. 7 Steps to Stress Free Teaching: A Stress Prevention Planning Guide for Teachers. 158p. 1999. pap., teacher ed. 19.95 (0-9668233-5-4) Educators Lighthse.

An Asterisk (*) at the beginning of an entry indicates that the title is appearing for the first time.

— 7 Steps to Stress Free Teaching Plan Book. 96p. 1999. spiral bd., wbk. ed. 9.95 (*0-9668233-1-1*) Educators Lighthse.

Burke, Lisa-Lin. Straw Hat. LC 98-93645. 128p. (Orig.). (C). 1998. pap. 10.00 (*1-57579-135-8*) Pine Hill Pr.

Burke, Louis. Basic & Advanced Colposcopy. 2nd ed. 1999. 195.00 (*0-8385-0651-8*, Medical Exam) Appleton & Lange.

Burke, Louise. The Complete Guide to Food for Sports Performance: Peak Nutrition for Your Sport. 2nd rev. ed. (Illus.). 392p. (Orig.). 1996. pap. 16.95 (*1-86373-916-5*, Pub. by Allen & Unwin Pty) IPG Chicago.

Burke, Louise & Deakin, Vicki. Clinical Sports Nutrition. 256p. 1995. text 59.00 (*0-07-470085-5*) McGraw-Hill HPD.

Burke, Louise, jt. auth. see Hawley, John.

Burke, Louise L. & Ready, Keith F. Parks, Preserves & Rivers: A Guide to Outdoor Adventures in Virginia's Capital Region. LC 85-7255. (Illus.). 285p. (Orig.). 1985. pap. 3.00 (*0-9615016-0-X*) Metro Found.

***Burke, Lucy, et al, eds.** Routledge Language & Cultural Theory Reader. LC 99-47377. (Research in Cultural & Media Studies). 560p. (C). 2000. text. write for info. (*0-415-18680-3*) Routledge.

***Burke, Lucy, et al.** Routledge Language & Cultural Theory Reader. LC 99-47377. 464p. 2000. pap. write for info. (*0-415-18681-1*) Routledge.

Burke, Lydia. The Devil & Jessie Webster. (Intimate Moments Ser.). 1994. per. 3.50 (*0-373-07594-4*, 1-07594-4) Harlequin Bks.

Burke, Lynne & McColman, John. Scanner Master D. C., Delaware, Maryland & Virginia Guide: The Public Safety/Radio Communications Reference. 4th ed. (Illus.). 432p. 1996. pap. 29.95 (*0-939430-34-7*) Scanner Master.

Burke, M. G., et al, eds. Understanding Microstructure: Proceedings of the 29th Annual Technical Meeting of the International Metallographic Society Held in Pittsburgh, Penn., 1996. LC 97-61021. (Microstructural Science Ser.: Vol. 24). 225p. 1997. 93.00 (*0-87170-611-3*, 6509) ASM.

Burke, Marc E. Coming Out of the Blue: British Police Officers Talk about Their Lives on the Job As Lesbians, Gays & Bisexuals. 272p. 1993. pap. text 21.95 (*0-304-32714-X*) Continuum.

Burke, Marcus. Distant Echoes: Painted Reliefs & Drawings by Miguel Zapata. McDougall, Betsey, ed. LC 86-62683. (Illus.). 43p. (Orig.). 1986. pap. 8.00 (*0-935937-02-1*) Meadows Mus.

Burke, Marcus, et al. A Selection of Spanish Masterworks from the Meadows Museum. LC 86-62402. (Illus.). 16p. (Orig.). 1986. pap. 4.00 (*0-935937-01-3*) Meadows Mus.

Burke, Marcus B. Mexican Art Masterpieces. (Illus.). 120p. 1998. 34.50 (*0-88363-598-4*) H L Levin.

Burke, Marcus B. & Davenport Museum of Art (Davenport, Iowa) Staff. Treasures of Mexican Colonial Painting: The Davenport Museum of Art Collection. LC 97-39015. (Illus.). 160p. 1998. 45.00 (*0-89013-357-3*) Museum NM Pr.

Burke, Marcus B., et al. Collections of Paintings in Madrid, 1601-1755, Pts. 1 & 2. LC 97-21522. (Documents for the History of Collecting Ser.: Spanish Inventories). 1082p. 1997. 150.00 (*0-89236-496-3*, Pub. by J P Getty Trust) OUP.

Burke, Margaret B., et al. Cancer Chemotherapy: Nursing Process. 2nd ed. (Nursing Ser.). 752p. (C). 1996. 62.50 (*0-86720-718-3*) Jones & Bartlett.

— Chemotherapy Care Plans. 2nd ed. LC 97-41987. (Nursing Ser.). 587p. 1997. spiral bd. 34.95 (*0-7637-0424-5*) Jones & Bartlett.

Burke, Margaret B., jt. ed. see Winningham, Maryl.

Burke, Margaret G., jt. auth. see Raven, Peter H.

Burke, Margaret R., ed. Bowdoin College Museum of Art: Handbook of the Collections. LC 81-66892. (Illus.). (Orig.). 1981. pap. 10.00 (*0-916606-01-5*) Bowdoin Coll.

Burke, Maria E. & Hall, Hazel. Navigating Business Information Sources: A Practical Guide for Information. 260p. 1998. pap. 65.00 (*1-85604-258-8*, LAP2588, Pub. by Library Association) Bernan Associates.

Burke, Marie L. Swami Vivekananda in the West: New Discoveries: His Prophetic Mission, Vol. 1. (Illus.). 515p. text 9.95 (*0-87481-218-6*, Pub. by Advaita Ashrama) Vedanta Pr.

— Swami Vivekananda in the West Pt. III: New Discoveries the World Teacher. (ENG & SAN., Illus.). 639p. 1987. 8.95 (*0-87481-418-9*, Pub. by Advaita Ashrama) Vedanta Pr.

— Swami Vivekananda in the West Vol. II: New Discoveries. (Illus.). 457p. 1985. 8.95 (*81-85301-15-8*, Pub. by Advaita Ashrama) Vedanta Pr.

— Swami Vivekananda in the West Vol. 6, Pt. 2: New Discoveries - A New Gospel. (Illus.). 461p. 1988. 8.95 (*0-87481-221-6*, Pub. by Advaita Ashrama) Vedanta Pr.

Burke, Marie L. & Sister Gargi. Swami Trigunatita: His Life & Work. LC 98-138868. (Illus.). 434p. (Orig.). 1997. pap. 16.95 (*0-9612388-3-6*) Vedanta Soc N Cal.

***Burke, Marjorie A., et al, eds.** Women's Uncommon Prayers: Our Lives Revealed, Nurtured, Celebrated. 370p. 2000. 23.00 (*0-8192-1864-2*) Morehouse Pub.

Burke, Marthy C. Life & Adventures of Calamity Jane: By Herself. (Illus.). 14p. 1979. pap. 2.95 (*0-87770-220-9*) Ye Galleon.

Burke, Martin J. The Conundrum of Class: Public Discourse on the Social Order in America. LC 95-7081. 322p. 1995. pap. text 16.95 (*0-226-08081-1*) U Ch Pr.

— The Conundrum of Class: Public Discourse on the Social Order in America. LC 95-7081. 322p. 1995. lib. bdg. 47.50 (*0-226-08080-3*) U Ch Pr.

Burke, Mary. Primary Care for the Older Adult. (Illus.). 550p. 1999. text 54.95 (*0-8151-8916-8*, 31744) Mosby Inc.

***Burke, Mary, et al, eds.** Women, Writing & the Reproduction of Culture in Tudor & Stuart Britain. LC 99-16570. 320p. 1999. pap. text 29.95 (*0-8156-2815-3*) Syracuse U Pr.

Burke, Mary & Sherman, S., eds. Gerontological Nursing: Issues & Opportunities. 98p. (C). 1993. pap. text 23.95 (*0-88737-572-3*, 14-2510) Natl League Nurse.

Burke, Mary & Sherman, Susan, eds. Ways of Knowing & Caring for Older Adults. LC 93-38938. 1993. 25.95 (*0-88737-593-6*) Natl League Nurse.

Burke, Mary & Walsh, Mary. Gerontologic Nursing: Wholistic Care of the Older Adult. 2nd ed. (Illus.). 640p. (C). (gr. 13). 1996. pap. text 36.00 (*0-8151-1331-5*, 28200) Mosby Inc.

Burke, Mary A. Organizing Multimedia Information: Principles & Practice of Information Retrieval. LC 98-36866. 250p. 1999. 78.95 (*0-566-08171-7*) Ashgate Pub Co.

Burke, Mary A. & Liljenstolpe, Carl. Creative Fund Raising: A Guide for Success. Machosky, Brenda, ed. LC 92-54369. (Fifty-Minute Ser.). 111p. (Orig.). 1993. pap. 10.95 (*1-56052-181-3*) Crisp Pubns.

Burke, Mary A., jt. auth. see Liljenstolpe, Carl.

Burke, Mary Alice H. Elizabeth Nourse, 1859-1938: A Salon Career. LC 82-600496. (Illus.). 280p. 1983. text 60.00 (*0-87474-298-6*, BUEN) Smithsonian.

Burke, Mary G. Japanese Art: Personal Selections from the Mary & Jackson Burke Collection. 1993. pap. write for info. (*1-882865-00-6*) Morikami Mus.

Burke, Mary H. Few Precious Memories. LC 98-90073. 1998. pap. 14.95 (*0-533-12704-1*) Vantage.

Burke, Mary T. & Miranti, Judith G. Counseling: The Spiritual Dimension. 191p. 1995. pap. text 17.95 (*1-55620-145-1*, 72575) Am Coun Assn.

Burke, Maryellen, jt. ed. see Randall, Peter E.

***Burke, Maurice R.** Learning Mathematics for a New Century: 2000 Yearbook, National Council of Teachers of Mathematics. (Illus.). 2000. 29.95 (*0-87353-479-4*) NCTM.

Burke, Michael. Handbook of Machine Vision Engineering, 2. LC 92-32983. 1996. text 79.95 (*0-442-30900-7*, VNR) Wiley.

— Handbook of Machine Vision Engineering, 3. LC 92-32983. 1998. text 79.95 (*0-442-30901-5*, VNR) Wiley.

Burke, Michael, jt. auth. see Wildbur, Peter.

Burke, Michael E., ed. Mexico: An Illustrated History. LC 99-25595. (Hippocrene Illustrated Histories Ser.). (Illus.). 150p. 1999. 11.95 (*0-7818-0690-9*) Hippocrene Bks.

Burke, Michael E. & Pigeon, Robert L., eds. Law, Authority, & Society: Readings in Ancient & Medieval Social Thought. LC 95-34404. 1995. text 25.00 (*0-938289-53-5*, 289535) Combined Pub.

Burke, Michelle M. The Valuable Office Professional: For Administrative Assistants, Office Managers, Secretaries & Other Support Staff. Glenn, Mary, ed. 192p. (Orig.). 1996. pap. 17.95 (*0-8144-7888-3*) AMACOM.

Burke, Michelle Prater. Ideals' Guide to Literary Places in the U. S. LC 98-26945. 1998. pap. 19.00 (*0-8249-4093-8*) Ideals.

Burke, Mickie. Gerontologic Nursing: Wholistic Care of the Older Adult. 2nd ed. (Illus.). teacher ed. write for info. (*0-8151-1332-3*) Mosby Inc.

Burke, Mike. Applied Ergonomics Handbook. 272p. 1991. lib. bdg. 85.00 (*0-87371-367-2*, L367) Lewis Pubs.

— Ergonomic Assessment & Intervention Planning. LC 97-36248. 320p. 1997. vinyl bd. 47.00 (*0-8342-1006-1*, 21006) Aspen Pub.

— Ergonomics Analysis & Problem Solving Database. 48p. 1993. lib. bdg. 335.00 (*0-87371-651-5*, L651) Lewis Pubs.

Burke, Nancy. Gender & Envy. LC 98-2534. 448p. (C). 1998. pap. 24.99 (*0-415-91628-3*) Routledge.

— Gender & Envy. LC 98-2534. 448p. (C). 1998. 85.00 (*0-415-91627-5*) Routledge.

— Hey Baby, What's Your Sign? The Astrological Baby Name Book. 1998. mass mkt. 7.99 (*0-425-16423-3*) Berkley Pub.

— Hey Baby, What's Your Sign? The Astrological Baby Name Book. 1999. pap. 14.95 (*0-425-17046-2*) Berkley Pub.

— Teachers Are Special: A Tribute to Those Who Educate, Encourage & Inspire. LC 97-32797. 64p. 1998. 5.99 (*0-517-20264-6*) Random Hse Value.

Burke, Nancy, jt. auth. see Pressman, Alan H.

Burke, Omar M. Among the Dervishes. 203p. 1973. 22.00 (*0-900860-17-0*, Pub. by Octagon Pr) ISHK.

— Among the Dervishes. 2nd ed. 203p. 1993. pap. 15.00 (*0-86304-018-7*, Pub. by Octagon Pr) ISHK.

Burke, P. A. & Forse, R. A. Injury & Sepsis Survival: Basic Mechanisms & Medical Treatment. (Illus.). Date not set. text. write for info. (*0-8247-9483-4*) Dekker.

Burke, P. G., et al, eds. Atoms in Astrophysics. LC 82-22517. (Physics of Atoms & Molecules Ser.). 374p. 1983. 95.00 (*0-306-41097-4*, Plenum Trade) Perseus Pubng.

Burke, P. G. & Berrington, K. A., eds. Atomic & Molecular Processes: An R-Matrix Approach. LC 93-16062. (Illus.). 416p. 1993. 143.00 (*0-7503-0199-6*) IOP Pub.

Burke, P. G. & Joachain, C. J. Photon & Electron Collisions with Atoms & Molecules: Proceedings of the Second European Study Conference Held in Belfast, Northern Ireland, July 23-26, 1996. LC 97-29100. (Physics of Atoms & Molecules Ser.). 378p. (C). 1997. text 125.00 (*0-306-45692-3*, Kluwer Plenum) Kluwer Academic.

— Theory of Electron-Atom Collisions Pt. 1: Potential Scattering. (Physics of Atoms & Molecules Ser.). (Illus.). 270p. (C). 1995. text 83.00 (*0-306-44546-8*, Kluwer Plenum) Kluwer Academic.

Burke, P. G. & West, J. B., eds. Electron - Molecule Scattering & Photoionization. LC 88-19610. (Physics of Atoms & Molecules Ser.). (Illus.). 282p. 1988. 79.50 (*0-306-42998-5*, Plenum Trade) Perseus Pubng.

Burke, P. G., tr. see Drukarev, Gregorii F., ed.

Burke, Pam. Above Your Dreams God Has a Plan. 50p. (Orig.). 1997. pap. 6.00 (*1-57502-413-6*, P01280) Morris Pubng.

Burke, Pat. Post-Synodal Apostolic Exhortations. Miller, J. Michael, ed. 1998. 49.95 incl. cd-rom (*0-87973-290-3*) Our Sunday Visitor.

Burke, Patricia A. Breathe Deeply: Healing Stories for the Soul. LC 95-788148. (Illus.). 176p. (Orig.). 1995. pap. 12.00 (*1-879418-95-9*) Audenreed Pr.

Burke, Patricia D., jt. ed. see Overmier, J. Bruce.

Burke, Patrick. Eastern Europe. LC 96-35487. (Country Fact Files Ser.). (Illus.). 48p. (J). (gr. 4-8). 1997. lib. bdg. 24.26 (*0-8172-4628-2*) Raintree Steck-V.

Burke, Patrick. Germany. (Modern Industrial World Ser.). (Illus.). 48p. (J). (gr. 6-8). 1995. lib. bdg. 24.26 (*1-56847-357-5*) Raintree Steck-V.

— Revolution in Europe, 1989. (Revolution Ser.). (Illus.). 48p. (J). (gr. 4-6). 1996. lib. bdg. 24.26 (*1-56847-422-9*) Raintree Steck-V.

— Who's Who in Nuclear Weapons. LC 88-30078. 398p. 1989. lib. bdg. 115.00 (*0-313-26590-9*, BWW/, Greenwood Pr) Greenwood.

Burke, Patrick & Van Der Veken, Jan, eds. Merleau-Ponty in Contemporary Perspective. LC 92-38343. (Phaenomenologica Ser.: Vol. 129). 236p. 1993. text 134.50 (*0-7923-2142-1*) Kluwer Academic.

Burke, Paul. If Your Name's Not Jack, Get Out of That Box: Overcoming the Barriers to Success. 200p. 1994. pap. 14.95 (*0-9638826-0-0*) Illumin Pr.

— A Picture of Subsidized Households in 1997: United States: Totals & Agencies with over 500 Units. (Illus.). 109p. 1998. pap. text 25.00 (*0-7881-7389-8*) DIANE Pub.

Burke, Paul W. Annotations to the Homeowners' Policy. 3rd ed. LC 97-1118. 1997. pap. 109.95 (*1-57073-387-2*) Amer Bar Assn.

Burke, Peter. The Art of Conversation. LC 93-10831. 178p. 1993. text 42.50 (*0-8014-2956-0*); pap. text 15.95 (*0-8014-8167-8*) Cornell U Pr.

— The Drowning Dream. LC 98-218961. 264p. 1998. pap. 16.95 (*1-86368-214-7*, Pub. by Fremantle Arts) Intl Spec Bk.

— The European Renaissance: Centres & Peripheries. LC 98-5901. (Making of Europe Ser.). (Illus.). 240p. 1998. 24.95 (*0-631-19845-8*) Blackwell Pubs.

— The European Renaissance: The Philosophical Debates. LC 98-13166. (Illus.). 320p. 1998. 27.95 (*0-631-20955-7*) Blackwell Pubs.

— The Fabrication of Louis XIV. (Illus.). 288p. 1992. pap. 18.00 (*0-300-05943-4*) Yale U Pr.

— The Fortunes of the Courtier: The European Reception of Castiglione's Cortegiano. LC 95-17617. (Series in the History of the Book). (Illus.). 222p. 1996. pap. 18.95 (*0-271-01517-9*) Pa St U Pr.

— The Fortunes of the Courtier: The European Reception of Castiglione's Cortegiano. LC 95-17617. (Series in the History of the Book). (Illus.). 222p. 1996. 45.00 (*0-271-01516-0*) Pa St U Pr.

— The French Historical Revolution: The Annales School, 1929-89. LC 90-70699. (Key Contemporary Thinkers Ser.). 180p. 1991. pap. 12.95 (*0-8047-1837-7*) Stanford U Pr.

— History & Social Theory. LC 92-54434. 208p. 1993. text 42.50 (*0-8014-2861-0*); pap. text 15.95 (*0-8014-8100-7*) Cornell U Pr.

— The Italian Renaissance: Culture & Society in Italy. 2nd ed. LC 98-48379. 2p. 1999. 19.95 (*0-691-00678-4*, Pub. by Princeton U Pr) Cal Prin Full Svc.

— The Italian Renaissance Culture & Society in Italy. (Illus.). 340p. 1987. pap. text 17.95 (*0-691-02838-9*, Pub. by Princeton U Pr) Cal Prin Full Svc.

— Montaigne. (Past Masters Ser.). 90p. 1983. pap. text 6.95 (*0-19-287522-1*) OUP.

— Photographs at the Frontier: Aby Warburg in America, 1895-1896. (Illus.). 160p. 1998. 45.00 (*1-85894-067-2*) U of Wash Pr.

— Popular Culture in Early Modern Europe. rev. ed. (Illus.). 416p. 1994. pap. 31.95 (*1-85928-102-8*, Pub. by Scolar Pr) Ashgate Pub Co.

— The Renaissance. 2nd ed. 1996. text 11.95 (*0-333-37201-8*, Pub. by Macmillan) St Martin.

***Burke, Peter.** A Social History of Knowledge. 2000. 64.95 (*0-7456-2484-7*, Pub. by Polity Pr); pap. 27.95 (*0-7456-2485-5*, Pub. by Polity Pr) Blackwell Pubs.

Burke, Peter. Varieties of Cultural History. LC 97-15063. 256p. 1997. text 42.50 (*0-8014-3491-2*); pap. text 16.95 (*0-8014-8492-8*) Cornell U Pr.

— Venice & Amsterdam: A Study of Seventeenth-Century Elites. Leigh, Sue, ed. LC 94-27628. 180p. 1994. pap. 22.95 (*0-7456-1324-1*) Blackwell Pubs.

— Venice & Amsterdam: A Study of Seventeenth-Century Elites. Leigh, Sue, ed. LC 94-27628. (Illus.). 180p. 1994. 55.95 (*0-7456-1343-8*) Blackwell Pubs.

Burke, Peter, ed. Critical Essays on Michel Foucault. (Critical Thoughts Ser.: Vol. 2). 233p. 1992. 65.95 (*0-85967-854-7*, Pub. by Scolar Pr) Ashgate Pub Co.

— History of Italian Art, 2 vols., Set. Dorey, Claire & Bianchini, Ellen, trs. from ITA.Tr. of Storia dell'Arte Italiana. (Illus.). 864p. 1995. 128.00 (*0-7456-1364-0*) Blackwell Pubs.

— History of Italian Art, Vol. I. Dorey, Claire & Bianchini, Ellen, trs.Tr. of Storia dell'Arte Italiana. (Illus.). 350p. 1995. 64.95 (*0-7456-0694-6*) Blackwell Pubs.

— History of Italian Art, Vol. II. Dorey, Claire & Bianchini, Ellen, trs.Tr. of Storia dell'Arte Italiana. (Illus.). 350p. 1995. 64.95 (*0-7456-0695-4*) Blackwell Pubs.

— New Perspectives on Historical Writing. 280p. 1992. text 35.00 (*0-271-00827-X*); pap. text 15.95 (*0-271-00834-2*) Pa St U Pr.

Burke, Peter, et al, eds. Programming for Staff Development: Fanning the Flame. 224p. 1990. pap. 34.95 (*1-85000-752-7*, Falmer Pr) Taylor & Francis.

***Burke, Peter & Briggs, Asa.** A Short History of the Media. 2001. 59.95 (*0-7456-2374-3*, Pub. by Polity Pr); pap. 24.95 (*0-7456-2375-1*, Pub. by Polity Pr) Blackwell Pubs.

***Burke, Peter & Cigno, Katy.** Learning Disabilities in Children. LC 99-87589. (Working Together for Children, Young People & Their Families Ser.). 2000. pap. write for info. (*0-632-05104-3*) Blackwell Sci.

Burke, Peter & Cigno, Katy. Support for Families. 176p. (C). 1996. 63.95 (*1-85628-983-4*, Pub. by Avebry) Ashgate Pub Co.

Burke, Peter & Porter, Roy, eds. Languages & Jargons: Contributions to a Social History of Language. 2nd rev. ed. 214p. 1996. 30.95 (*0-7456-1279-2*, Pub. by Polity Pr) Blackwell Pubs.

Burke, Peter, jt. auth. see Jaramillo, Alvaro.

Burke, Peter, ed. see Thomas, Keith.

Burke, Peter J., jt. auth. see Knoke, David.

Burke, Phoebe, ed. see Saint Louis Art Museum Staff.

Burke, Phyllis. Atomic Candy. LC 88-7660. 367p. 1990. pap. 9.95 (*0-87113-364-4*, Atlntc Mnthly) Grove-Atltic.

— Gender Shock: Exploding the Myths of Male & Female. 336p. 1997. pap. 14.95 (*0-385-47718-X*, Anchor NY) Doubleday.

Burke, Polly, jt. auth. see Cunningham, Bill.

Burke, Quentin, ed. see Wright, Harold Bell.

Burke, R. D., et al, eds. Echinoderm Biology: Proceedings of the Sixth International Echinoderm Conference, Victoria, 23-28 August 1987. 832p. (C). 1988. text 180.00 (*90-6191-755-7*, Pub. by A A Balkema) Ashgate Pub Co.

Burke, Rachel, ed. see Shakespeare, William.

Burke, Ray & Herron, Ron. La Crianza Practica de los Hijos: Una Guia Paso a Paso Para Formar Hijos Responsables y Hogares Felices. Cardenas, Margarita, tr. 127p. 1998. pap. 14.95 (*0-938510-94-0*, 39-006) Boys Town Pr.

Burke, Raymond V. & Herron, Ronald W. Common Sense Parenting: A Proven Step-by-Step Guide for Raising Responsible Kids & Building Happy Families. 2nd rev. ed. (Illus.). 216p. 1996. pap. text 14.95 (*0-938510-77-0*, 39-002) Boys Town Pr.

Burke, Richard. A Guide to TCP-IP. 612p. (C). 1998. pap. 57.95 (*0-7600-5080-5*) Course Tech.

***Burke, Richard.** MCSE Guide to TCP/IP on Microsoft Windows NT 4.0. (Illus.). 4000p. 1999. pap. 60.95 incl. cd-rom (*0-619-01577-2*) Course Tech.

Burke, Richard. MCSE TCP/IP Exam Prep. 10th ed. LC 98-16108. (Exam Prep Ser.). 376p. (C). 1998. mass mkt. 49.99 (*1-57610-239-4*) Coriolis Grp.

Burke, Richard C., ed. Instructional Television: Bold New Venture. LC 70-143243. 158p. reprint ed. pap. 49.00 (*0-608-18631-7*, 205602400044) Bks Demand.

Burke, Richard E., ed. see Anderson, Robert H., et al.

Burke, Richard R. Communicating with Students in Schools: A Workbook for Practitioners & Teachers in Training. 180p. 1984. student ed. 14.75 (*0-8191-3878-9*) U Pr of Amer.

— Communicating with Students in Schools: Exercises in Motivation & School Discipline Through Rapport. 3rd ed. 168p. (Orig.). (C). 1994. pap. text 19.95 (*0-8191-9726-2*) U Pr of Amer.

***Burke, Robert.** Counter-Terrorism for Emergency Responders. LC 99-29184. 368p. 1999. boxed set 69.95 (*1-56670-363-8*) Lewis Pubs.

Burke, Robert. Hazardous Materials Chemistry for Emergency Responders: Street Chemistry. LC 96-31459. 368p. 1997. boxed set 69.95 (*1-56670-174-0*) CRC Pr.

Burke, Robert B. Opus Majus of Roger Bacon. (Illus.). 876p. 1998. reprint ed. pap. 75.00 (*0-7661-0421-4*) Kessinger Pub.

***Burke, Robert B., tr.** The Opus Majus of Roger Bacon, 2 vols. (Medieval & Renaissance Philosophy Ser.). 854p. 2000. 280.00 (*1-85506-856-7*) Thoemmes Pr.

Burke, Robert E. The New Era & the New Deal, 1920-1940. LC 87-7987. (Goldentree Bibliographies Series in American History). (C). 1981. text 27.95 (*0-88295-537-3*); pap. text 19.95 (*0-88295-581-0*) Harlan Davidson.

— Olson's New Deal for California. LC 82-984. (Illus.). 279p. 1982. reprint ed. lib. bdg. 65.00 (*0-313-23414-0*, BUON, Greenwood Pr) Greenwood.

Burke, Robert W., ed. see International Committee on Museum Security Staff.

Burke, Robin. System Administrator's Guide to Windows NT Server 5. 1000p. 1999. 49.99 (*0-7897-1307-1*, Pub. by Macmillan) S&S Trade.

Burke, Robin, ed. AI Applications in Knowledge Navigation & Retrieval: Papers from the 1995 Fall Symposium. (Technical Reports). (Illus.). 155p. 1995. spiral bd. 25.00 (*0-929280-95-4*) AAAI Pr.

Burke, Roger. The Last Cowboy. (Orig.). 1989. pap. 10.00 (*0-685-26592-7*) Columbia Rvr Bk Co.

Burke, Roland, jt. auth. see Duarte, Joe.

Burke, Roma N. Journey from Yesterday. LC 85-62500. 112p. (Orig.). 1985. pap. 7.95 (*0-88100-050-7*) Natl Writ Pr.

— Whiskers, a Kitten's Story. LC 87-62417. 120p. (J). (gr. 3-8). 1988. pap. 8.95 (*0-88100-058-2*) Natl Writ Pr.

Burke, Ronald. Hopes & Words & Ordinary Things. 39p. (YA). (gr. 10 up). 1974. pap. 3.50 (*0-87129-816-3*, H28) Dramatic Pub.

— The Saga of Katy & the Gamblin' Lady. 32p. 1974. pap. 3.50 (*0-87129-687-X*, S10) Dramatic Pub.

B

An Asterisk (*) at the beginning of an entry indicates that the title is appearing for the first time.

— The Small World of Millie McIvor. 1974. 3.50 (*0-87129-506-7*, S41) Dramatic Pub.

Burke, Ronald J. Women in Corporate Management. LC 97-23235. 1997. lib. bdg. 80.00 (*0-7923-4664-5*) Kluwer Academic.

***Burke, Ronald J. & Mattis, Mary C.** Women on Corporate Boards of Directors: International Challenges & Opportunities. LC 99-89697. (Issues in Business Ethics Ser.). 2000. write for info. (*0-7923-6162-8*) Kluwer Academic.

Burke, Ronald J., jt. ed. see Cooper, Cary L.

Burke, Ronald J., jt. ed. see Davidson, Marilyn J.

Burke, Ronald K. American Public Discourse: A Multicultural Perspective. LC 92-14800. 338p. (Orig.). (C). 1992. pap. text 35.00 (*0-8191-8753-4*); lib. bdg. 59.50 (*0-8191-8752-6*) U Pr of Amer.

— Samuel Ringgold Ward: Christian Abolitionist. LC 94-42751. (Studies in African American History & Culture). (Illus.). 176p. 1995. text 15.00 (*0-8153-1930-4*) Garland.

Burke, Ronald R., jt. ed. see Allsopp, Michael E.

Burke, Ronald S. & Bittel, Lester R. Introduction to Management Practice. LC 80-19088. (Illus.). 608p. 1980. text 65.46 (*0-07-009042-4*) McGraw.

***Burke, Rory.** Managing Your Bluewater Cruise. 2000. pap. 29.95 (*0-473-03822-6*) PROMATEC Intl.

Burke, Rory. Project Management. 3rd ed. pap. text, teacher ed. write for info. (*0-471-72036-4*) Wiley.

***Burke, Rory.** Project Management: Planning & Control Techniques. 3rd ed. 346p. 2000. pap. 29.95 (*0-620-23414-8*) Red Roof Design.

Burke, Ruby J., jt. ed. see Brackney, William H.

Burke, Russell E., jt. auth. see Chew, Paul A.

Burke, Russell E., III, ed. see Boyle, Richard J.

Burke, Ruth E. The Games of Poetics: Ludic Criticism & Postmodern Fiction. LC 92-20765. (American University Studies: Comparative Literature: Ser. III, Vol. 47). XIV, 149p. (C). 1993. text 38.95 (*0-8204-1943-5*) P Lang Pubng.

— The Games of Poetics: Ludic Criticism & Postmodern Fiction. LC 92-20765. (American University Studies, Comparative Literature Ser.: No. III, Vol. 47). (Illus.). 208p. (C). 1994. text 39.95 (*0-8204-1942-7*) P Lang Pubng.

Burke, S. M. Akbar: The Greatest Mogul. 262p. 1989. reprint ed. 24.00 (*0-317-99945-1*, Pub. by M Manoharial) Coronet Bks.

— Mainsprings of Indian & Pakistani Foreign Policies. LC 74-78992. 318p. reprint ed. pap. 98.60 (*0-608-16068-7*, 203320800084) Bks Demand.

Burke, S. M. & Quraishi, Salim A. The British Raj in India: An Historical Review. (Illus.). 714p. 1997. reprint ed. pap. text 38.00 (*0-19-577734-4*) OUP.

— Quaid-i-Azam Mohammad Ali Jinnah: His Personality & His Politics. LC 98-107916. (The Jubilee Ser.). 428p. 1997. 39.95 (*0-19-577783-2*) OUP.

Burke, Sally. American Feminist Playwrights. 1996. 33.00 (*0-8057-7830-6*, Hall Reference) Macmillan.

Burke, Sally, jt. ed. see Albright, Martina.

Burke, Samuel M. & Din Quraishi, Salim A. The British Raj in India: An Historical Review. (Illus.). 714p. 1995. text 75.00 (*0-19-577569-4*) OUP.

Burke, Sara Z. Seeking the Highest Good: Social Service & Gender at the University of Toronto, 1888-1937. (Studies in Gender & History). (Illus.). 200p. 1996. text 55.00 (*0-8020-0782-1*); pap. text 17.95 (*0-8020-7146-5*) U of Toronto Pr.

Burke, Sarah A., ed. Developing Your Documentation Manual: A Guide for Commercial Bankers. LC 88-32921. 44p. 1988. pap. text 50.00 (*0-936742-60-7*, 32231) Robt Morris Assocs.

— Management Information Reports: Content & Design. LC 90-27329. (Illus.). 56p. (Orig.). 1991. pap. text 34.00 (*0-936742-80-1*, 32491) Robt Morris Assocs.

Burke, Sarah A., jt. ed. see Behr, Joan H.

Burke, Sarah A., ed. see Lewis, Robert E.

Burke, Sarah A., ed. see McKinley, John E.

Burke, Sarah A., ed. see Oleksiw, Andrew.

Burke, Sarah A., ed. see Strischek, Dev.

Burke, Sarah A., ed. see Temple, Douglas M.

Burke, Sean. Authorship: From Plato to the Postmodern. 384p. 1996. pap. 27.50 (*0-7486-0618-1*, Pub. by Edinburgh U Pr) Col U Pr.

— The Death & Return of the Author: Criticism & Subjectivity in Barthes, Foucault, & Derrida. 240p. 1993. pap. 25.00 (*0-7486-0361-1*, Pub. by Edinburgh U Pr) Col U Pr.

***Burke, Sean.** The Death & Return of the Author: Criticism & Subjectivity in Barthes, Foucault & Derrida. 264p. 1998. pap. 28.00 (*0-7486-1006-5*, Pub. by Edinburgh U Pr) Col U Pr.

Burke, Sharman. Understanding the Tarot. LC 97-28817. 128p. 1998. pap. 15.95 (*0-312-17913-8*) St Martin.

Burke, Sharon O., jt. auth. see Roberts, Carol A.

***Burke, Sheila, et al.** Social Security & Medicare. LC 99-50627. 2000. 20.95 (*0-8157-1283-9*) Brookings.

Burke, Shelly & Whited, Martha. How to Find Your Perfect Job in Nursing. 220p. 1997. pap. write for info. (*1-57579-052-1*) Pine Hill Pr.

Burke, Shirley R. Human Anatomy & Physiology. 3rd ed. (C). 1991. mass mkt. 48.95 (*0-8273-4853-3*) Delmar.

— Human Anatomy & Physiology Instructor's Guide. 3rd ed. 1992. pap., teacher ed. 16.00 (*0-8273-4854-1*) Delmar.

— Human Anatomy & Physiology Workbook. 3rd ed. 1993. pap., lab manual ed. 18.95 (*0-8273-5047-3*) Delmar.

Burke, Stanley & Peterson, Roy. The Day of the Glorious Revolution. 43p. 1974. 1.99 (*0-88862-067-5*, Pub. by J Lorimer) Formac Dist Ltd.

— Frog Fables & Beaver Tales. 45p. 1973. 9.95 (*0-88862-048-9*, Pub. by J Lorimer) Formac Dist Ltd.

Burke, Stephen. Surrender. LC 98-93802. 272p. (Orig.). 1999. pap. 12.95 (*0-9668940-0-6*) DayBue Pubg.

Burke, Susan, jt. auth. see Croce, Nicholas J.

Burke, Susan E. Creating a Quality ESL Program. LC 98-16037. 102p. 1998. pap. 15.50 (*1-56212-343-2*, 1700-5010) CRC Pubns.

Burke, Susan M. & Hill, Matthew H., eds. From Pennsylvania to Waterloo: Pennsylvania-German Folk Culture in Transition. (Illus.). 148p. (C). 1991. pap. 29.95 (*0-9695578-0-9*) W Laurier U Pr.

Burke, Suzanne. Ollie Owl. Jordan, Alton, ed. (I Can Eat an Elephant Ser.). (Illus.). (J). (gr. k-3). 1984. 7.95 (*0-89868-015-8*, Read Res); pap. 3.95 (*0-89868-048-4*, Read Res) ARO Pub.

— Our Parade. Jordan, Alton, ed. (I Can Eat an Elephant Ser.). (Illus.). (J). (gr. k-3). 1984. 7.95 (*0-89868-017-4*, Read Res); pap. 3.95 (*0-89868-050-6*, Read Res) ARO Pub.

Burke, T., et al, eds. DNA Fingerprinting: Approaches & Applications. (Experientia Supplementum Ser.: Vol. 58). 410p. 1991. 176.00 (*0-8176-2562-3*) Birkhauser.

Burke, T. A., ed. Polly Peablossom's Wedding & Other Tales. 1972. reprint ed. lib. bdg. 32.00 (*0-8422-8157-6*) Irvington.

Burke, T. E. Questions of Belief. 121p. (C). 1995. 61.95 (*1-85628-988-5*, Pub. by Avebry) Ashgate Pub Co.

Burke, T. Patrick. Intro to the Major Religions: An Introduction with Texts. (Illus.). 320p. (C). 1995. 72.95 (*1-55786-714-3*) Blackwell Pubs.

— Intro to the Major Religions: An Introduction with Texts. (Illus.). 320p. (C). 1996. pap. 31.95 (*1-55786-715-1*) Blackwell Pubs.

— Learning Arithmetic Using the Graphing Calculator. (Illus.). vi, 400p. 1997. spiral bd. 45.00 (*0-9657238-0-1*) Calculator Trning.

— No Harm: Ethical Principles for a Free Market. LC 93-12444. 1993. 24.95 (*1-55778-618-6*) Paragon Hse.

— Quick Reference: Arithmetic with the TI-82 or TI-83. (Illus.). 1998. spiral bd. 15.00 (*0-9657238-4-4*) Calculator Trning.

Burke, T. Patrick, jt. text see Friedman, Maurice S.

Burke, Terrill M. Dolphin Magic: Adepts vs. Inepts. LC 93-90146. (Dolphin Ser.: Bk. 2). 302p. (Orig.). (J). (gr. 4 up). 1993. pap. 12.25 (*1-880485-69-9*) Alpha-Dolphin.

— Dolphin Magic: The Ancient Knowledge. LC 93-90146. (Dolphin Ser.: Bk. 3). 372p. (Orig.). (J). (gr. 4 up). 1994. pap. 12.25 (*1-880485-51-6*) Alpha-Dolphin.

— Dolphin Magic: The First Encounter. LC 93-90146. (Dolphin Ser.: Bk. 1). 320p. (Orig.). (J). (gr. 4 up). 1992. pap. 12.25 (*1-880485-65-6*) Alpha-Dolphin.

— Dolphin Magic: The Unexpected Stranger. LC 95-75716. (Dolphin Ser.). 368p. (Orig.). (J). (gr. 4 up). 1995. pap. 12.25 (*1-880485-54-0*) Alpha-Dolphin.

— Dolphin Magic: Unobstructed Universes. LC 95-94972. (Dolphin Ser.). 358p. (Orig.). (J). (gr. 4 up). 1996. pap. 12.25 (*1-880485-56-7*) Alpha-Dolphin.

— I Love Gee-Gees Bk. 1. LC 94-71391. (Illus.). 76p. (Orig.). (J). (gr. 1-4). 1995. pap. 7.95 (*1-880485-62-1*) Alpha-Dolphin.

— I Love Gee-Gees Bk. 2. LC 95-95121. (Illus.). 96p. (J). (gr. 1-4). 1996. pap. 7.95 (*1-880485-53-2*) Alpha-Dolphin.

— Mind One, Pt. 1. LC 95-90145. 208p. (Orig.). (YA). (gr. 6 up). 1993. pap. 9.99 (*1-880485-61-3*) Alpha-Dolphin.

— Mind One, Pt. 2. LC 95-90145. 165p. (Orig.). (YA). (gr. 6 up). 1996. pap. 9.99 (*1-880485-58-3*) Alpha-Dolphin.

Burke, Terry & Shackleton, J. R. Trouble in Store? U. K. Retailing in the 1990s. (IEA Hobart Paper Ser.: No. 130). 92p. 1996. pap. 24.50 (*0-255-36374-5*, Pub. by Inst Economic Affairs) Coronet Bks.

Burke, Terry, et al. Competition in Theory & Practice. 270p. 1988. lib. bdg. 69.95 (*0-7099-5005-5*, Pub. by C Helm) Routldge.

Burke, Theresa K. & Cullen, Barbara. Rachel's Vineyard: A Psych. & Spirit. Journey of Post-Abortion Healing. LC 95-20262. 167p. (Orig.). 1995. pap. 12.95 (*0-8189-0719-3*) Alba.

Burke, Theta. And We Have Touched. LC 78-67725. (Orig.). 1978. pap. 5.95 (*0-916872-05-X*) Delafield Pr.

— Connections. 1993. spiral bd. 12.95 (*0-916872-09-2*) Delafield Pr.

— I've Heard Your Feelings. LC 76-7103. 1976. 8.95 (*0-916872-01-7*); pap. 5.95 (*0-916872-00-9*) Delafield Pr.

— Loving Who You Are Where You Are. LC 82-71079. 80p. 1982. pap. 5.95 (*0-916872-07-6*) Delafield Pr.

— So Speaks My Sea. 80p. (Orig.). 1995. pap. 7.95 (*0-916872-10-6*) Delafield Pr.

— Sounds of Yourself. LC 76-48010. 1977. pap. 5.95 (*0-916872-02-5*) Delafield Pr.

— When You Can't See a Way. LC 85-72772. 80p. (Orig.). 1987. pap. 5.95 (*0-916872-08-4*) Delafield Pr.

Burke, Thomas. English Night-Life: From Norman Curfew to Present. 1972. 24.95 (*0-405-18114-0*, 1329) Ayer.

— Limehouse Nights. LC 73-103498. (Short Story Index Reprint Ser.). 1977. 21.95 (*0-8369-3240-4*) Ayer.

— Night-Pieces: Eighteen Tales. LC 78-150539. (Short Story Index Reprint Ser.). 1977. reprint ed. 20.95 (*0-8369-3836-4*) Ayer.

— Pleasantries of Old Quong, Vol. 1. LC 72-5861. (Short Story Index Reprint Ser.). 1977. reprint ed. 23.95 (*0-8369-4195-0*) Ayer.

— Tea-Shop in Limehouse. LC 77-103499. (Short Story Index Reprint Ser.). 1977. 20.95 (*0-8369-3241-2*) Ayer.

Burke, Thomas, ed. see Croce, Nicholas J. & Burke, Susan.

Burke, Thomas A., et al, eds. Regulating Risk: The Science & Politics of Risk. LC 93-61119. (Illus.). 102p. 1993. pap. 25.00 (*0-944398-13-8*) ILSI.

Burke, Thomas E., Jr. Mohawk Frontier: The Dutch Community of Schenectady, New York, 1661-1710. LC 91-55237. 264p. 1991. text 39.95 (*0-8014-2541-7*) Cornell U Pr.

Burke, Thomas J., ed. The Christian Vision: Man & Morality, Vol. 2. LC 85-81263. 174p. 1989. pap. 5.00 (*0-916308-96-0*) Hillsdale Coll Pr.

— The Christian Vision: Man & State: Religion, Society & the Constitution. LC 88-80609. 143p. 1989. 5.00 (*0-916308-87-1*) Hillsdale Coll Pr.

— The Christian Vision Vol. 3: Man & Mind: A Christian Theory of Personality. LC 85-81263. 230p. 1989. pap. 5.00 (*0-916308-90-1*) Hillsdale Coll Pr.

Burke, Thomas P. The Reluctant Vision: An Essay in the Philosophy of Religion. LC 73-88354. 142p. (Orig.). reprint ed. pap. 44.10 (*0-608-16331-7*, 202688300053) Bks Demand.

Burke, Tim, et al. Major League Dad. LC 94-3069. 200p. 1994. 16.99 (*1-56179-212-8*) Focus Family.

— Writing Device Drivers: Tutorial & Reference. 1140p. 1995. pap. 74.95 (*1-55558-141-2*, Digital DEC) Buttrwrth-Heinemann.

Burke, Timothy. Cocoa Puppy. LC 89-50890. (Illus.). 32p. (Orig.). (J). (ps-3). 1989. 5.00 (*0-9623227-0-9*) Thunder & Ink.

— Lifebuoy Men, Lux Women: Commodification, Consumption, & Cleanliness in Modern Zimbabwe. LC 95-44291. (Body, Commodity, Text Ser.). (Illus.). 312p. 1996. text 49.95 (*0-8223-1753-2*); pap. text 17.95 (*0-8223-1762-1*) Duke.

Burke, Timothy & Burke, Kevin. Saturday Morning Fever: Tuning in to Cartoon Culture. LC 98-15719. (Illus.). 256p. 1998. pap. 17.95 (*0-312-16996-5*, St Martin Griffin) St Martin.

Burke, Timothy R. Tugboats in Action. LC 93-9131. (J). (gr. k-3). 1993. lib. bdg. 15.95 (*0-8075-8112-7*) A Whitman.

— Tugboats in Action. (J). 1997. 12.15 (*0-606-12014-9*, Pub. by Turtleback) Demco.

— Tugboats in Action. (Illus.). 32p. (J). (gr. k-3). 1997. reprint ed. pap. 6.95 (*0-8075-8113-5*) A Whitman.

Burke, Tina, et al. Cowpuncher Poetry: A Collection of Campfire Stories. Curtis, Nancy, ed. (Illus.). 1986. 3.95 (*0-931271-01-0*) Hi Plains Pr.

Burke, Tom. Dewey's New Logic: A Reply to Russell. LC 94-1618. 300p. 1994. 32.00 (*0-226-08069-2*) U Ch Pr.

— Dewey's New Logic: A Reply to Russell. (Illus.). 288p. 1998. pap. text 17.00 (*0-226-08070-6*) U Ch Pr.

Burke, Tom, ed. see Judd, Cameron.

Burke, Tom, ed. see Kosser, Michael.

Burke, Tom J., jt. auth. see Holms, John P.

Burke, V., jt. auth. see Gracey, Michael.

Burke, Victor Lee. Clash of Civilizations. LC 96-46006. 1997. 60.95 (*0-7456-1198-2*) Blackwell Pubs.

Burke, Vikk. Aim Your Child Like An Arrow. Date not set. pap. 5.00 (*1-890026-01-8*) D Burke Min.

Burke, Vincent, jt. auth. see Selfe, David.

Burke, Virginia M., ed. Paragraph in Context. LC 79-92274. (Composition & Rhetoric Ser.). (C). 1969. pap. write for info. (*0-672-60906-1*, CR20, Bobbs) Macmillan.

Burke, Virginia M., jt. ed. see Banks, Phyllis M.

Burke, Virginia M., jt. ed. see Corbett, Edward P.

Burke, W., et al, eds. Soil Structure Assessment. 99p. (C). 1986. text 58.00 (*90-6191-656-9*, Pub. by A A Balkema) Ashgate Pub Co.

Burke, W., ed. see Dicker, A.

Burke, W. P. Irish Priests in Penal Times. 1914. 27.50 (*0-7165-0034-5*, Pub. by Irish Acad Pr) Intl Spec Bk.

Burke, W. S. Official Military History of Kansas Regiments During the War for the Suppression of the Great Rebellion. 464p. (C). 1995. text 40.00 (*1-878882-07-4*) KS Heritage Pr.

Burke, W. Steven & Young, Alvin L., prefs. Symbol, Substance, Science - The Societal Issues of Food Biotechnology: Conference Proceedings, June 28 & 29, 1993. xi, 146p. (Orig.). 1993. pap. text 20.00 (*0-945597-24-X*) NC Biotech Ctr.

Burke, W. Warner. Organizational Development. (C). 1998. text 44.00 (*0-673-39018-7*) Addson-Wesley Educ.

— Organizational Development: A Normative View. LC 86-26474. 189p. (C). 1987. pap. text 26.95 (*0-201-10697-3*) Addison-Wesley.

— Organizational Development: A Normative View. 2nd ed. LC 93-14813. 240p. (C). 1993. pap. text 37.00 (*0-201-50835-4*) Addison-Wesley.

Burke, W. Warner, ed. Current Issues & Strategies in Organization Development. LC 76-28755. 448p. 1977. 52.00 (*0-87705-270-0*, Kluwer Acad Hman Sci) Kluwer Academic.

— Managing Organizational Change. LC 95-14148. 1995. 29.95 (*0-8144-6713-X*) AMACOM.

Burke, Wallace E. He Who Conquers. rev. ed. LC 93-94266. (Anasazi Ser.: Bk. I). (Illus.). 390p. (Orig.). 1994. reprint ed. pap. 12.95 (*0-9639014-0-0*) WEB Pubng.

— Night Hawk. (Anasazi Ser.: Bk. II). (Illus.). 225p. (Orig.). (YA). 1994. pap. 10.95 (*0-9639014-1-9*) WEB Pubng.

Burke, Wallace E., ed. see Wartell, Matthew L.

Burke, Walter F., jt. auth. see Tansey, Michael J.

***Burke, Warner, et al.** Business Climate Shifts: Profiles of Change Makers. LC 99-37788. 256p. 1999. text 24.95 (*0-7506-7186-6*) Buttrwrth-Heinemann.

Burke-Weiner, Kimberly. The Maybe Garden. Roehm, Michelle, ed. (Illus.). 36p. (J). (gr. 1-4). 1992. 14.95 (*0-941831-56-6*); pap. 7.95 (*0-941831-57-4*) Beyond Words Pub.

— Penny Wishes. LC 96-77306. (Illus.). 32p. (J). (gr. 3-6). 1996. 15.95 (*0-9634637-3-X*); pap. 8.95 (*0-9634637-4-8*) Inquir Voices.

Burke, William. Additional Reasons for Our Immediately Emancipating Spanish America. LC 73-128426. reprint ed. 27.50 (*0-404-01240-X*) AMS Pr.

— The International Law of the Sea: Library Edition, 2 vols. 918p. 1993. ring bd. 100.00 (*1-879581-10-8*) Lupus Pubns.

— International Law of the Sea: Student Edition. 902p. 1999. student ed., ring bd. 75.00 (*1-879581-65-5*) Lupus Pubns.

— Protect Us from All Anxiety: Meditations for the Depressed. (Illus.). 274p. 1998. pap. 9.95 (*0-87946-184-5*, 274) ACTA Pubns.

— Shua. LC 90-8566. (Illus.). 110p. (Orig.). 1990. pap. 8.95 (*0-87946-050-4*, 119) ACTA Pubns.

Burke, William F., Jr., jt. auth. see Jackson, Joe.

Burke, William H. The Handbook of Forensic Rehabilitation. LC 94-41909. 304p. (Orig.). 1995. pap. 34.50 (*1-882855-31-0*) HDI Pubs.

— Sexuality after TBI. 2nd ed. (Professional Series on Traumatic Brain Injury: Vol. 10). 68p. 1995. pap. 9.50 (*1-882855-41-8*) HDI Pubs.

Burke, William H., ed. Accessing Community Resources: Discharge Planning. 2nd ed. (Professional Series on Traumatic Brain Injury: Vol. 13). 80p. 1996. pap. 9.50 (*1-882855-48-5*) HDI Pubs.

— Applied Behavior Analysis in Brain Injury Rehabilitation. 2nd ed. (Professional Series on Traumatic Brain Injury: Vol. 2). 68p. (Orig.). 1996. pap. 9.50 (*1-882855-43-4*) HDI Pubs.

— Brain Injury Rehabilitation: Adaptive Driving after TBI. 2nd rev. ed. (Professional Series on Traumatic Brain Injury: Vol. 5). 40p. 1996. pap. 9.50 (*1-882855-52-3*) HDI Pubs.

— Brain Injury Rehabilitation: Managing Anger & Aggression. 2nd rev. ed. (Professional Series on Traumatic Brain Injury: Vol. 6). 60p. 1996. pap. 9.50 (*1-882855-53-1*) HDI Pubs.

— Brain Injury Rehabilitation with Children & Adolescents. 2nd rev. ed. (Professional Series on Traumatic Brain Injury: Vol. 12). 76p. 1996. pap. 9.50 (*1-882855-50-7*) HDI Pubs.

— Community Living Skills Development: Teaching Methods. 2nd rev. ed. (Professional Series on Traumatic Brain Injury: Vol. 3). 76p. (Orig.). 1996. pap. 9.50 (*1-882855-44-2*) HDI Pubs.

— Developing Adaptive Work Behaviors. (Professional Series on Traumatic Brain Injury: Vol. 17). 52p. (Orig.). 1988. pap. 9.50 (*1-882855-24-8*) HDI Pubs.

— Developing Motivation. 2nd ed. (Professional Series on Traumatic Brain Injury: Vol. 11). 56p. (Orig.). 1996. pap. 9.50 (*1-882855-42-6*) HDI Pubs.

— Developing Self Control. 2nd rev. ed. (HDI Professional Series on Traumatic Brain Injury: Vol. 14). (Illus.). 64p. 1997. pap. 9.50 (*1-882855-59-0*) HDI Pubs.

— Developing Social Skills, 20 vols. 2nd rev. ed. (HDI Professional Series on Traumatic Brain Injury). 64p. (Orig.). 1997. pap. 9.50 (*1-882855-57-4*) HDI Pubs.

— Developing the TBI Rehab Plan. (Professional Series on Traumatic Brain Injury: Vol. 4). 48p. (Orig.). 1988. pap. 9.50 (*1-882855-11-6*) HDI Pubs.

— The HDI Professional Series on Traumatic Brain Injury Rehabilitation, Vols. 1-20. (Orig.). 1995. pap. 175.00 (*1-882855-29-9*) HDI Pubs.

— Head Injury Rehabilitation: An Overview. (Professional Series on Traumatic Brain Injury: Vol. 1). 48p. 1996. pap. 9.50 (*1-882855-08-6*) HDI Pubs.

— Increasing Self Awareness. (Professional Series on Traumatic Brain Injury: Vol. 15). 48p. (Orig.). 1988. pap. 9.50 (*1-882855-22-1*) HDI Pubs.

— Management of Communication & Language Deficits. (Professional Series on Traumatic Brain Injury: Vol. 20). 56p. (Orig.). 1996. pap. 9.50 (*1-882855-27-2*) HDI Pubs.

— Management of Memory Disorders. 2nd ed. (Professional Series on Traumatic Brain Injury: Vol. 8). 44p. (Orig.). 1995. pap. 9.50 (*1-882855-39-6*) HDI Pubs.

— Managing Attention Deficits. 2nd rev. ed. (Professional Series on Traumatic Brain Injury: Vol. 7). 52p. 1996. pap. 9.50 (*1-882855-49-3*) HDI Pubs.

— The Role of the Family in TBI Rehab. 2nd rev. ed. (Professional Series on Traumatic Brain Injury: Vol. 19). 56p. 1996. pap. 9.50 (*1-882855-46-9*) HDI Pubs.

— Supported Employment & TBI. 2nd ed. (Professional Series on Traumatic Brain Injury: Vol. 18). 64p. (Orig.). 1995. pap. 9.50 (*1-882855-38-8*) HDI Pubs.

— Teaching Job Seeking Skills. (Professional Series on Traumatic Brain Injury: Vol. 16). 100p. (Orig.). 1988. pap. 9.50 (*1-882855-23-X*) HDI Pubs.

Burke, William J. & Bradbury, Carl W. Accounting Systems for Law Offices. 1978. ring bd. 220.00 incl. cd-rom (*0-8205-1014-9*) Bender.

Burke, William K. A New Approach to Shakespeare's Early Comedies: Theoretical Foundations. LC 93-95042. (Theoretical Foundations Ser.). 1998. 24.95 (*0-533-10933-7*) Vantage.

Burke, William L. Applied Differential Geometry. LC 84-14952. (Illus.). 416p. 1985. pap. text 52.95 (*0-521-26929-6*) Cambridge U Pr.

Burke, William M. History & Functions of Central Labor Unions. LC 71-7666. (Columbia University. Studies in the Social Sciences: No. 30). reprint ed. 32.50 (*0-404-51030-2*) AMS Pr.

Burke, William T., et al. Marvin: Poetry & Dialysis. (Illus.). 48p. 1988. pap. 3.95 (*0-944231-03-9*) Slvr Wings CA.

Burke, William T., jt. auth. see McDougal, Myres S.

Burke, Wyatt W. Organization Development: Principles & Practices. fac. ed. LC 81-83134. (Illus.). 416p. 1982. reprint ed. pap. 129.00 (*0-7837-8214-4*, 204791400008) Bks Demand.

Burkel, Christoph J. Hans Scharoun. (Studio Paperback Ser.). (Illus.). 182p. 1993. pap. 29.95 (*3-7643-5581-6*, Pub. by Birkhauser) Princeton Arch.

Burkel, E. Springer Tracts in Modern Physics Vol. 125: Inelastic Scattering of X-Rays with Very High Resolution. Hohler, G. & Niekisch, E. A., eds. (Illus.). 130p. 1991. 97.95 (*0-387-54418-6*) Spr-Verlag.

Burkel, William E., jt. auth. see Woodburne, Russell T.

Burkert, Andreas, et al, eds. Galactic Chemodynamics 4 Vol. 112: The History of the Milky Way & Its Satellite Systems. (ASP Conference Series Catalog). 216p. 1996. 34.00 (*1-886733-32-5*) Astron Soc Pacific.

Burkert, H. & Nagel, G. A., eds. Neue Erfahrungen Mit Oxazaphosphorinen unter Besonderer Beruecksichtigung des Uroprotektors Uromitexan. (Beitraege Zur Onkologie, Contributions to Oncology Ser.: Band 5). (Illus.). 126p. 1980. pap. 25.25 (*3-8055-1381-X*) S Karger.

Burkert, Nancy E. Valentine & Orson. (Floyd Yearout Bks.). (Illus.). 56p. (J). (gr. 5 up). 1989. 16.95 (*0-374-38078-3*) FS&G.

Burkert, Ulrich. Molecular Mechanics. 340p. 1982. pap. text 59.00 (*0-8412-0885-9*, Pub. by Am Chemical) OUP.

Burkert, Ulrich & Allinger, Norman L., eds. Molecular Mechanics. LC 82-11442. (ACS Monograph: No. 177). 340p. 1982. text 85.00 (*0-8412-0584-1*, Pub. by Am Chemical) OUP.

Burkert, V. B., et al, eds. N* Physics & Nonpertubative Quantum Chromodynamics: Proceedings of the Joint ECT*/Jefferson Lab Workshop, May 18-29, 1998, Trento, Italy. LC 99-15826. (Few-Body Systems Ser.: Vol. 11). 380p. 1999. 99.00 (*3-211-83299-8*) Spr-Verlag.

Burkert, Walter. Ancient Mystery Cults. (Carl Newell Jackson Lectures). 176p. 1989. pap. 15.00 (*0-674-03387-6*) HUP.

— Creation of the Sacred: Tracks of Biology in Early Religions. LC 95-44787. 272p. (C). 1996. 33.95 (*0-674-17569-7*) HUP.

— Creation of the Sacred: Tracks of Biology in Early Religions. 272p. 1998. pap. text 15.95 (*0-674-17570-0*) HUP.

— Greek Religion. Raffan, John, tr. LC 84-25209. (GER.). 512p. 1987. pap. 19.50 (*0-674-36281-0*) HUP.

— Homo Necans: Interpretationen altgriechischer Opferriten und Mythen. LC 72-83051. (Religionsgeschichtliche Versuche und Vorarbeiten Ser.: Vol. 32). 356p. (C). 1972. 106.15 (*3-11-003875-7*) De Gruyter.

— Homo Necans: Interpretationen Altgriechischer Opferriten und Mythen. 2nd ed. (Religionsgeschichtliche Versuche und Vorarbeiten Ser.: Vol. 32). (GER.). xii, 378p. (C). 1997. pap. text 55.70 (*3-11-015098-0*); lib. bdg. 120.00 (*3-11-015099-9*) De Gruyter.

— Homo Necans: The Anthropology of Ancient Greek Sacrificial Ritual & Myth. Bing, Peter, tr. from GER. LC 77-93473. (Illus.). 360p. (C). 1983. pap. 17.95 (*0-520-05875-5*, Pub. by U CA Pr) Cal Prin Full Svc.

— Klassisches Altertum & Antikes Christentum: Probleme Einer Uebergreifenden Religionswissenschaft. (Hans - Lietzmann - Vorlesungen Ser.: Vol. 1). (GER.). xii, 52p. (Orig.). 1996. pap. text 20.75 (*3-11-015543-5*) De Gruyter.

— Lore & Science in Ancient Pythagoreanism. Minar, Edwin L., Jr., tr. LC 70-162856. 543p. reprint ed. pap. 168.40 (*0-7837-2230-3*, 205732000004) Bks Demand.

— The Orientalizing Revolution: Near Eastern Influence on Greek Culture in the Early Archaic Age. (Revealing Antiquity Ser.: No. 5). (Illus.). 256p. 1992. 35.00 (*0-674-64363-1*) HUP.

— The Orientalizing Revolution: Near Eastern Influence on Greek Culture in the Early Archaic Age. Pinder, Margaret E., tr. (Revealing Antiquity Ser.: No. 5). (Illus.). 240p. (C). 1995. pap. text 16.50 (*0-674-64364-X*) HUP.

— Structure & History in Greek Mythology & Ritual. LC 78-62856. (Sather Classical Lectures: No. 47). 1980. pap. 17.95 (*0-520-04770-2*, Pub. by U CA Pr) Cal Prin Full Svc.

— Structure & History in Greek Mythology & Ritual. LC 78-62856. (Sather Classical Lectures: No. 47). (Illus.). 246p. reprint ed. pap. 76.30 (*0-7837-4755-1*, 204450200003) Bks Demand.

***Burkert, Walter.** Wild Origins. 1999. 22.00 (*0-226-08085-4*) U Ch Pr.

Burkert, Walter & Stolz, Fritz, eds. Hymnen der Alten Welt Im Kulturvergleich. (Orbis Biblicus et Orientalis Ser.: Vol. 131). (GER.). 123p. 1994. text 26.75 (*3-7278-0929-9*, Pub. by Presses Univ Fribourg) Eisenbrauns.

Burkert, Walter, ed. see Diels, Hermann.

Burkes, E. Jeff, Jr. & Wood, Matthew T. Dental Assisting Manual II: Basic Sciences. 3rd ed. LC 79-10801. (Illus.). 124p. 1980. pap. 38.50 (*0-608-05226-4*, 206576300001) Bks Demand.

Burkes, E. Jeff, Jr., jt. auth. see Wood, Matthew T.

***Burkes, Shannon.** Death in Qoheleth & Egyptian Biographies of the Late Period. LC 99-38480. 312p. 1999. 45.00 (*0-88414-005-9*, 062170, Pub. by Soc Biblical Lit) Scholars Pr GA.

Burket, Jerri, ed. see McLaurin, Joe M.

Burket, Larry & Temple, Todd. Money Matters Workbook for Teens (11-14) (YA). 1998. pap., wbk. ed. 12.99 (*0-8024-6345-2*) Moody.

Burket, William H. Union Beach. LC 98-87444. (Images of America Ser.). (Illus.). 128p. 1998. pap. 18.99 (*0-7524-0939-5*) Arcadia Publng.

Burkett. Get a Grip on Your Money. 1995. pap., student ed. 7.50 (*1-56427-071-8*) Christian Fin Concepts.

— Introductory Chemistry. 304p. 1997. spiral bd. 33.75 (*0-8151-1328-5*) McGraw.

— Surviving the Money Jungle. 1995. pap. 9.50 (*1-56427-070-X*) Christian Fin Concepts.

— Surviving the Money Jungle. 1995. pap. 7.50 (*1-56427-069-6*) Focus Family.

Burkett, Allan R. & Sevenair, John P. Introductory Chemistry. 848p. (C). 1997. text. write for info. (*0-07-114035-2*, WCB McGr Hill) McGrw-H Hghr Educ.

Burkett, Allen & Burkett, Larry. Your Child & Money. 1999. pap. 9.99 (*0-8024-2854-1*) Moody.

Burkett, Anne P. & Sherman, Steve. The Official Lite Unauthorized Biography of J. Danforth Quayle. (Illus.). 160p. (Orig.). 1992. pap. 6.95 (*0-9623992-4-8*) Electric Strawberry.

Burkett, B. G. & Whitley, Glenna. Stolen Valor: How the Vietnam Generation Was Robbed of Its Heroes & Its History. (Illus.). 692p. 1998. 31.95 (*0-9667036-0-X*) Verity Pr Inc.

Burkett, Brigitte. 18th Century Emigrants from Baden Wurttemberg, Vol. I. LC 96-69155. (Illus.). 428p. 1996. 49.50 (*0-89725-244-6*, 1639) Picton Pr.

— Genealogical Data Extracted from the Boston Selectmen's Minute, 1736-1775. 486p. (Orig.). 1993. pap. text 33.00 (*1-55613-880-6*) Heritage Bk.

— 19th Century Emigrants from Baden-Wurttemberg Vol. 1: The Enzkreis. LC 97-68243. 450p. 1997. 45.00 (*0-89725-292-6*, 1797) Picton Pr.

Burkett, Christopher, photos by. Intimations of Paradise: Photographs by Christopher Burkett. (Illus.). 184p. 1999. 65.00 (*0-9670216-0-X*) W Wind.

— Robert Frost Seasons. (Illus.). 120p. 1995. 50.00 (*0-8050-2433-6*) H Holt & Co.

Burkett, David & Narcisco, John. Declare Yourself: Discovering the Me in Relationships. LC 75-11802. (Illus.). 1975. 11.95 (*0-13-197582-X*, Spectrum IN) Macmillan Gen Ref.

Burkett, David, jt. auth. see Narciso, John.

Burkett, David W. Writing Science News for the Mass Media. 2nd rev. ed. LC 72-84334. 224p. reprint ed. pap. 69.50 (*0-608-18162-5*, 203286300081) Bks Demand.

Burkett, Delbert. The Son of Man Debate: A History & Evaluation. LC 99-19515. (Society for New Testament Studies Monograph Ser.: No. 107). 190p. 2000. 54.95 (*0-521-66306-7*) Cambridge U Pr.

— The Son of the Man in the Gospel of John. (JSNT Supplement Ser.: No. 56). 188p. (C). 1991. 57.50 (*1-85075-292-3*, Pub. by Sheffield Acad) CUP Services.

***Burkett, Elinor.** The Baby Boon: How Family-Friendly America Cheats the Childless. LC HQ755.8.B857 2000. 272p. 2000. 24.50 (*0-684-86303-0*) Free Pr.

Burkett, Elinor. The Gravest Show on Earth. 1999. pap. 23.95 (*0-670-85230-9*) Viking Penguin.

— The Gravest Show on Earth: America in the Age of AIDS. 416p. 1996. pap. 15.00 (*0-312-14607-8*) St Martin.

— The Right Women: A Journey Through the Heart of Conservative America. LC 97-29501. 288p. 1998. 22.50 (*0-684-83308-5*) S&S Trade.

— The Right Women: A Journey Through the Heart of Conservative America. 288p. 1999. pap. 14.00 (*0-684-85202-0*) S&S Trade.

Burkett, Eva M. American English Dialects in Literature. LC 78-17742. 222p. 1978. 24.00 (*0-8108-1151-0*) Scarecrow.

— Writing in Subject-Matter Fields: A Bibliographic Guide, with Annotations & Writing Assignments. LC 76-30397. 204p. 1977. 21.00 (*0-8108-1012-3*) Scarecrow.

Burkett, Jerri L. The Huber-Hoover Family History Index. 96p. 1993. 9.95 (*1-883294-03-7*) Masthof Pr.

***Burkett, Joe.** Tayshas. LC 99-91313. 192p. 2000. 18.95 (*0-8034-9400-9*, Avalon Bks) Bouregy.

Burkett, K. D., jt. auth. see Watson, Jude.

***Burkett, Kathryn Lewis & Parker, Donald.** Hancock County, Illinois: A Pictorial History. LC 00-23264. 2000. write for info. (*1-57864-101-2*) Donning Co.

Burkett, Larry. Biblical Principles for Business Workbook. (Christian Financial Concepts Ser.). 66p. 1989. 7.00 (*1-56427-102-1*) Christian Fin Concepts.

— Business by the Book: An Updated Edition of the Bestselling Classic. LC 97-43793. 240p. 1998. 14.99 (*0-7852-7141-4*) Nelson.

— Cash Organizer. 1994. pap. 14.99 (*0-8024-7059-9*) Moody.

— Christian Financial Counselor's Manual. (Christian Financial Concepts Ser.). 73p. 1991. pap. 5.00 (*1-56427-075-0*) Christian Fin Concepts.

— Christian Financial Counselor's Self-Study Course. (Christian Financial Concepts Ser.). 200p. 1991. ring bd. 50.00 (*1-56427-076-9*) Christian Fin Concepts.

— The Coming Economic Earthquake. 1991. 15.99 (*0-8024-1526-1*) Moody.

— The Coming Economic Earthquake: Updated & Expanded for the Clinton Agenda. rev. ed. pap. 11.99 (*0-8024-1539-3*, 335) Moody.

— Como Manejar Su Dinero. Orig. Title: How to Manage Your Money. (SPA., Illus.). 128p. 1993. pap. 6.99 (*0-8254-1097-5*, Edit Portavoz) Kregel.

— Complete Financial Guide for Couples. 228p. 1993. pap. 10.99 (*1-56476-130-4*, 6-3130, Victor Bks) Chariot Victor.

— The Complete Financial Guide for Young Couples. 200p. 1989. 18.99 (*0-89693-634-1*, 6-1634, Victor Bks) Chariot Victor.

— Complete Guide to Managing Your Money, 3 vols. in 1. 576p. 1996. 12.99 (*0-88486-132-5*) Arrowood Pr.

— Compras Mayores. (Serie Conceptos Cristianos Financieros (Christian Financial Concepts) Ser.).Tr. of Major Purchases. (SPA.). 120p. 1995. 3.29 (*0-7899-0018-1*, 497249) Editorial Unilit.

***Burkett, Larry.** Crisis Control in the New Millennium. LC 99-43088. 256p. 1999. 21.99 (*0-7852-6939-8*) Nelson.

— El Cuaderno de Planificacion Financiera.Tr. of Financial Planning Workbook. 10.99 (*1-56063-573-8*, 497253) Editorial Unilit.

Burkett, Larry. El Cuaderno de Planificacion Financiera.Tr. of Financial Planning Workbook. (SPA.). 110p. 1995. write for info. (*0-614-24357-2*); pap. write for info. (*0-614-27022-7*) Editorial Unilit.

— Dando y Diezmando. (Serie Conceptos Cristianos Financieros (Christian Financial Concepts) Ser.).Tr. of Giving & Tithing. (SPA.). 100p. 1995. 3.29 (*0-7899-0019-X*, 497250) Editorial Unilit.

***Burkett, Larry.** Debt-Free Living. 1999. pap. 16.99 (*0-8024-4229-3*) Moody.

Burkett, Larry. Debt-Free Living: How to Get Out of Debt (and Stay Out) 1989. 17.99 (*0-8024-2549-6*) Moody.

***Burkett, Larry.** Different Kind of Party. (Illus.). (J). 2000. 7.99 (*0-8024-0983-0*) Moody.

Burkett, Larry. Dollars & Sense: Bible Wisdom for the Faithful Steward. 1993. mass mkt. 4.97 (*1-55748-415-5*) Barbour Pub.

— Dollars & Sense: Bible Wisdom for the Faithful Steward. LC 98-101316. 91p. 1997. lthr. 5.97 (*1-57748-093-7*) Barbour Pub.

— La Familia y Sus Finanzas. Orig. Title: Your Finances in Changing Times. (SPA., Illus.). 160p. 1990. pap. 6.99 (*0-8254-1098-3*, Edit Portavoz) Kregel.

— Family Budget Workbook. 1993. wbk. ed. 12.99 (*0-8024-7320-2*) Northfield Pub.

— The Family Budget Workbook: Gaining Control of Your Personal Finances. (Orig.). 1993. pap., wbk. ed. 12.99 (*1-881273-20-2*) Northfield Pub.

— The Financial Guide for the Single Parent. LC 97-199530. 240p. 1997. pap. 11.99 (*0-8024-2738-3*, 338) Moody.

***Burkett, Larry.** Financial Parenting: Showing Your Kids That Money Matters. 1999. pap. 12.99 (*0-8024-3085-6*) Moody.

Burkett, Larry. The Financial Planning Organizer. ring bd. 29.99 (*0-8024-2553-4*, 340) Moody.

— Financial Planning Workbook. 1990. pap. 12.99 (*0-8024-2545-3*, 341) Moody.

— Financial Planning, 1991 Edition. (Christian Financial Concepts Ser.). 62p. 1991. teacher ed. 6.00 (*1-56427-052-1*) Christian Fin Concepts.

— Financing Your College Education. 2000. pap. 7.99 (*0-8024-0980-6*) Moody.

— Finanzas Personales. (Serie Conceptos Cristianos Financieros (Christian Financial Concepts) Ser.).Tr. of Personal Finances. (SPA.). 110p. 1995. 3.29 (*0-7899-0021-1*, 497252) Editorial Unilit.

— Finding the Career That Fits You. 1998. pap. text 29.99 (*0-8024-2522-4*) Moody.

— Getting Your First Credit Card. 2000. pap. 7.99 (*0-8024-0979-2*) Moody.

— Giving & Tithing. 1998. pap. 6.99 (*0-8024-3737-0*) Moody.

— Great Is Thy Faithfulness: 365 Daily Devotions. LC 99-193161. 384p. 1998. 17.99 (*1-57748-374-X*) Barbour Pub.

— Guia para el Presupuesto Familia. (Serie Enfoque a la Familia - Focus on the Family Ser.).Tr. of Guide to Family Budgeting. (SPA.). 1995. 1.99 (*1-56063-068-X*, 497444) Editorial Unilit.

***Burkett, Larry.** Home for the Hampster. (Illus.). (J). 2000. 7.99 (*0-8024-0982-2*) Moody.

— How Much Is Enough? 30 Days to Personal Revival. 142p. 1999. pap. text 7.95 (*0-7673-9559-X*, LifeWy Press) LifeWay Christian.

Burkett, Larry. How to Manage Your Money. (Christian Financial Concepts Ser.). 66p. 1990. teacher ed. 6.00 (*1-56427-012-2*) Christian Fin Concepts.

— How to Manage Your Money. rev. ed. pap., wbk. ed. 12.99 (*0-8024-2543-7*, 342) Moody.

— The Illuminati. 320p. 1991. pap. 12.99 (*0-8407-7685-3*) Nelson.

— The Illuminati. 384p. 1996. mass mkt. 5.99 (*0-7852-7529-0*) Nelson.

— Inversiones Seguras.Tr. of Sound Investment. (SPA.). 110p. 1995. write for info. (*0-7899-0020-3*) Editorial Unilit.

— Investing for the Future. rev. ed. 264p. 1997. pap. 10.99 (*1-56476-631-4*, Victor Bks) Chariot Victor.

— Investing Through Your Building Years. (Seasons of Investing Ser.). 144p. (Orig.). 1993. pap. 7.99 (*1-56476-097-9*, 6-3097, Victor Bks) Chariot Victor.

— Larry Burkett's Bill Organizer. 1997. pap. text 14.99 (*0-8024-7061-0*) Moody.

— Larry Burkett's Little Instruction Book on Managing Your Money. 160p. 1997. pap. 6.99 (*1-56292-152-5*) Honor Bks OK.

***Burkett, Larry.** Last Chance for Camp. (Illus.). (J). 2000. 7.99 (*0-8024-0985-7*) Moody.

Burkett, Larry. Libertad Financiera. (Serie Conceptos Cristianos Financieros (Christian Financial Concepts) Ser.).Tr. of Financial Freedom. (SPA.). 82p. 1995. 3.29 (*0-7899-0022-X*, 497247) Editorial Unilit.

***Burkett, Larry.** Money in Marriage: A Biblical Approach, 2 vols. 1999. pap. 19.99 (*0-8024-4230-7*) Moody.

— Money in Marriage System: A Biblical Approach. 1999. pap. 34.99 (*0-8024-4231-5*) Moody.

Burkett, Larry. Money Management for College Students. (C). 1998. pap., wbk. ed. 11.99 (*0-8024-6347-9*) Moody.

— Paying for Your First Car. 2000. pap. 7.99 (*0-8024-0978-4*) Moody.

— Personal Finances. LC 99-158330. 1998. pap. 6.99 (*0-8024-3738-9*) Moody.

— Planes de Seguros. (Serie Conceptos Cristianos Financieros (Christian Financial Concepts) Ser.).Tr. of Insurance Plans. (SPA.). 100p. 1995. pap. 3.29 (*0-7899-0017-3*, 497251) Editorial Unilit.

— Renting Your First Apartment. 2000. pap. 7.99 (*0-8024-0981-4*) Moody.

***Burkett, Larry.** Sarah & the Art Contest. (Illus.). (J). 2000. 7.99 (*0-8024-0984-9*) Moody.

Burkett, Larry. Solar Flare. large type ed. 1998. 22.95 (*0-7862-1323-X*) Thorndike Pr.

— The Thor Conspiracy: The Seventy-Hour Countdown to Disaster. 1996. pap. 12.99 (*0-7852-7200-3*) Nelson.

— Usando Su Dinero Sabiamente.Tr. of Using Your Money Wisely. (SPA.). 1995. 9.99 (*1-56063-503-7*, 497245) Editorial Unilit.

Burkett, Larry. Using Your Money Wisely: Biblical Principles under Scrutiny. pap. 10.99 (*0-8024-3429-0*, 346) Moody.

Burkett, Larry. Victory over Debt: Rediscovering Financial Freedom. 1992. pap. 8.99 (*0-8024-7300-8*) Moody.

— Victory over Debt: Rediscovering Financial Freedom. 1992. pap. 10.99 (*1-881273-00-8*) Northfield Pub.

— La Vida Libre de Deudas.Tr. of Debt-Free Living. (SPA.). 297p. 1995. 8.99 (*1-56063-504-5*, 497246) Editorial Unilit.

— What Ever Happened to the American Dream? 224p. 17.99 (*0-8024-7175-7*, 347) Moody.

— Where Your Treasure Is: Your Attitude on Finances. LC 96-207826. (Stewardship Ser.: Bk. 2). 1996. pap. 5.99 (*0-8024-2804-5*) Moody.

— Women Leaving the Workplace: How to Make the Transition from Work to Home. LC 96-200719. 18.99 (*0-8024-9161-8*, 348) Moody.

— The Word on Finances: Topical Scriptures & Commentary. LC 95-111037. 300p. pap. 14.99 (*0-8024-9238-X*, 349) Moody.

— Your Complete Guide to Financial Security: How to Invest & Prepare for Your Future Peace of Mind, 2 vols. in 1. 512p. 1998. 12.99 (*0-88486-170-8*, Inspirational Pr) Arrowood Pr.

— Your Finances in Changing Times. pap. 9.99 (*0-8024-2548-8*, 350) Moody.

Burkett, Larry & Fuller, Cheri. The Financial Guide for the Single Parent. 112p. 1997. pap., wbk. ed. 12.99 (*0-8024-2739-1*, 339) Moody.

Burkett, Larry & Osborne, Rick. Financial Parenting: Showing Your Kids That Money Matters. LC 96-9882. 224p. 1996. 16.99 (*0-7814-0305-7*, Chariot Bks) Chariot Victor.

— Your Child: Wonderfully Made: Discovering God's Unique Plan. 200p. 1998. 18.99 (*0-8024-2851-7*) Moody.

Burkett, Larry & Taylor, Michael E. Hope When It Hurts: A Personal Testimony of How to Deal with the Impact of Cancer. LC 98-209852. Orig. Title: Damaged but Not Broken. 1998. pap. 12.99 (*0-8024-8243-0*) Moody.

— Money Before Marriage: A Financial Workbook for Engaged Couples. LC 96-207828. wbk. ed. 14.99 (*0-8024-6389-4*, 343) Moody.

Burkett, Larry & Temple, Todd. Money Matters Workbook for Teens (15-18) (YA). 1998. pap., wbk. ed. 12.99 (*0-8024-6346-0*) Moody.

Burkett, Larry, et al. 50 Money-Making Ideas for Kids. LC 97-25841. (Illus.). 148p. (Orig.). (J). (gr. 3-9). 1997. pap. 9.99 (*0-8499-4045-1*) Tommy Nelson.

Burkett, Larry, jt. auth. see Burkett, Allen.

Burkett, Larry, jt. auth. see Ellis, Lee.

Burkett, Lee N. Beginning Weight Training. (C). 1994. 17.33 (*0-205-15946-X*, Macmillan Coll) P-H.

Burkett, Lucille F. Barbadian Fairy Tales. Roberts, Anne F., ed. (Illus.). 38p. (Orig.). (J). (gr. 1 up). 1987. pap. 5.00 (*0-317-62575-6*) Libr Commns Servs.

***Burkett, Lynnell.** The Future of Newspapers: 20 Leaders Talk about the Future of Newspapers. 58p. 1999. pap. 7.50 (*0-9656018-8-9*) NMC.

— Future Voice: Editorial Pages: Newspapers' Overlooked Strategic Tool. (Illus.). 92p. 1999. pap. 13.50 (*0-9656018-7-0*) NMC.

***Burkett, Paul.** Development Crisis & Class Struggle. LC 99-45205. 2000. text. write for info. (*0-312-23250-0*) St Martin.

Burkett, Paul. Marx & Nature: A Red & Green Perspective. LC 98-42328. 336p. 1999. text 45.00 (*0-312-21940-7*) St Martin.

Burkett, Paul, jt. auth. see Burdekin, Richard C.

Burkett, Randall K. Garveyism As a Religious Movement: The Institutionalization of a Black Civil Religion. LC 78-15728. (American Theological Library Association Monograph: No. 13). 242p. 1978. 35.00 (*0-8108-1163-4*) Scarecrow.

Burkett-Sevenai. Introductory Chemistry. 1997. pap. 23.44 (*0-8151-1327-7*) McGraw.

— Introductory Chemistry. 1997. teacher ed. 13.75 (*0-697-41041-2*, WCB McGr Hill) McGrw-H Hghr Educ.

Burkett, Warren. News Reporting: Science, Medicine, & High Technology. LC 85-23102. 170p. 1986. reprint ed. pap. 52.70 (*0-608-00080-9*, 206084300006) Bks Demand.

Burkett, William R. Bloodsport. 304p. 1998. mass mkt. 5.99 (*0-06-105822-X*, HarperPrism) HarpC.

***Burkett, William R. & Alexander, James Edwin.** The Fall of David Hall. 224p. 2000. pap. 16.50 (*0-939965-17-8*) Macedon Prod.

***Burkett, Wynn McClenahan.** Life after Baby: From Professional Woman to Beginner Parent. (Illus.). 2000. pap. write for info. (*1-885171-44-7*, Pub. by Wldcat Canyon) Publishers Group.

Burkey, Stan. People First: A Guide to Self-Reliant Participatory Rural Development. 256p. (C). 1993. text 55.00 (*1-85649-081-5*, Pub. by Zed Books) St Martin.

— People First: A Guide to Self-Reliant Participatory Rural Development. 256p. (C). 1996. text 25.00 (*1-85649-082-3*, Pub. by Zed Books) St Martin.

Burkhalter, Holly, jt. auth. see Fitzpatrick, John.

Burkhalter, Howard J. & Pollock, Allen. Supplement to Railway Stamps. 52p. 1988. pap. 5.00 (*0-935991-03-4*) Am Topical Assn.

B

Burkhalter, Mary L. Active Children's Literature: Alphabet Story, Colors, Mister Prince. (Illus.). 50p. (J). (gr. k-4). 1998. pap. 20.00 (*0-934284-09-1*) Jolean Pub Co.
— Educational Games Rules & Regulations for Educational Games: Tens (Card Game), Warfare & Great Sage (Board Games) 18p. (J). (gr. 3-12). 1998. pap. 110.00 (*0-934284-10-5*) Jolean Pub Co.
— Emperor of Kings. 1980. pap. 35.00 (*0-934284-01-6*) Jolean Pub Co.
— Fare to Hoboken. 1998. pap. 35.00 (*0-934284-07-5*) Jolean Pub Co.
— The 5000th Year of Reason. 210p. 1998. pap. 35.00 (*0-934284-03-2*) Jolean Pub Co.
— How to Live. (Orig.). 1983. pap. 5.00 (*0-934284-02-4*) Jolean Pub Co.
— Joyful Songs: Pepsi Anthem, Making Love Again, Winner on Top, Etc. 20p. 1998. pap. 20.00 (*0-934284-05-9*) Jolean Pub Co.
— Kissed Grass. LC 23-138. (Orig.). 1979. pap. 7.50 (*0-934284-00-8*) Jolean Pub Co.
— The Lion & the Rose: Songs Included. 160p. 1998. pap. 50.00 (*0-934284-06-7*) Jolean Pub Co.
— Literary Mate. 90p. 1998. pap. 150.00 (*0-934284-08-3*) Jolean Pub Co.
— Poems for the City & the Country Too. 30p. 1998. pap. 20.00 (*0-934284-11-3*) Jolean Pub Co.
— Skeeterball (Rules & Regulations) 20p. 1999. pap. 20.00 (*0-934284-12-1*) Jolean Pub Co.
— Sweet Songs of Manhattan: Songs Included. 1998. pap. 50.00 (*0-934284-04-0*) Jolean Pub Co.

Burkhalter, William E. Medical Department, United States Army, Surgery in Vietnam, Orthopedic Surgery. 238p. 1995. boxed set 24.00 (*0-16-061320-5*) USGPO.

Burkhanov, G. S., jt. auth. see Devyatykh, G. G.

Burkhard, Arthur. Grillparzer Im Ausland. (GER., Illus.). 1969. pap. 8.00 (*0-917324-07-2*) German Bk Ctr.

Burkhard, Arthur, tr. see Grillparzer, Franz.

***Burkhard, Balthasar.** Shadow. (Illus.). 240p. 2000. 60.00 (*3-907044-96-7*) Lars Muller.

Burkhard, Barbara, jt. auth. see Domjan, Michael P.

***Burkhard, Bud.** French Marxism Between the Wars: Henri Lefebure & the "Philosophies" LC 99-54681. 270p. 2000. 54.95 (*1-57392-722-8*, Humanity Bks) Prometheus Bks.

Burkhard-Ebin, Barbara, jt. auth. see Domjan, Michael.

Burkhard, Gudrun. Taking Charge: Your Life Patterns & Their Meaning. 1998. pap. 16.95 (*0-86315-253-8*, Pub. by Floris Bks) Gryphon Hse.

Burkhard, Henke, et al, eds. Unwrapping Goethe's Weimar: Essays in Cultural Studies & Local Knowledge. LC 99-42723. (Studies in German Literature, Linguistics & Culture). 300p. 1999. 55.00 (*1-57113-194-9*, Pub. by Camden Hse) Boydell & Brewer.

Burkhard, James R. Partnership & L. L. C. Litigation Manual: Actions for Accounting & Other Remedies. LC 95-76587. 333p. 1995. 215.00 (*0-8318-0689-3*, B689/B746) Am Law Inst.

Burkhard, James R., et al. South Carolina Limited Liability Companies & Limited Liability Partnerships. 2nd ed. 812p. 1997. ring bd. 100.00 (*0-943856-75-2*, 685) SC Bar CLE.

Burkhard, Johanna. Comfort Food Cookbook. (Illus.). 192p. 1998. pap. 17.95 (*1-896503-73-X*, Pub. by R Rose Inc) Firefly Bks Ltd.
— Fast & Easy Cooking. (Illus.). 192p. 1999. pap. 17.95 (*1-896503-81-0*, Pub. by R Rose Inc) Firefly Bks Ltd.

Burkhard, John, tr. see Lafont, Ghislain.

Burkhard, Leo & Salm, Luke. Encounters: De la Salle at Parmenie. (Illus.). 87p. 1983. pap. 5.00 (*1-884904-14-9*) Christian Brothers.

Burkhard, Leo C. Beyond the Boundaries: A Story of John Baptist de la Salle, Patron of All Teachers. rev. ed. LC 94-71314. (Illus.). 192p. 1994. pap. 12.40 (*1-884904-04-1*) Christian Brothers.

Burkhard, Marianne & Clausen, Jeanette, eds. Women in German Yearbook Four: Feminist Studies & German Culture. (Illus.). 234p. (Orig.). (C). 1988. pap. text 22.50 (*0-8191-6704-5*); lib. bdg. 45.00 (*0-8191-6703-7*) U Pr of Amer.

Burkhard, Marianne, ed. see Staiger, Emil.

Burkhard, Walter A. C for Programmers. 562p. (C). 1988. pap. 49.95 (*0-534-08856-2*) PWS Pubs.

Burkhardt, A. & Meyer-Breiting, E. Tumours of the Larynx. (Illus.). 240p. 1988. 224.00 (*0-387-16342-5*) Spr-Verlag.

Burkhardt, A., jt. auth. see Gebbers, J. O.

Burkhardt, Al. The Archimedeams. (Illus.). 32p. (gr. 8-12). 1999. pap. text 18.95 (*0-914534-17-3*, 130) Stokes.

Burkhardt, Ann, jt. auth. see Gillen, Glen.

Burkhardt, Ann M. House Detective: A Guide to Researching Birmingham Buildings. Bowhser, Alice M., ed. LC 77-608282. (Illus.). 64p. (Orig.). 1988. pap. 9.95 (*0-87651-994-X*) Birmingham Hist Soc.
— Town Within a City: A History of Five Points South Neighborhood. Bowsher, Alice M., ed. (Illus.). 92p. 1982. pap. 16.95 (*0-943994-13-6*) Birmingham Hist Soc.

Burkhardt, Armin, ed. Speech Acts, Meaning & Intentions: Critical Approaches to the Philosophy of J. R. Searle. (Foundations of Communication & Cognition Ser.). v, 428p. (C). 1990. lib. bdg. 136.95 (*3-11-011300-7*) De Gruyter.

Burkhardt, Armin & Fritzsche, K. Peter, eds. Sprache Im Umbruch: Politischer Sprachwandel Im Zeichen Von "Wende" und "Vereinigung" (Sprache, Politik, Oeffentlichkeit Ser.: Bd. 1). (GER.). xxi, 314p. (C). 1992. lib. bdg. 113.85 (*3-11-013613-9*) De Gruyter.

Burkhardt, Arne, jt. auth. see Seifert, Gerhard.

Burkhardt, Barbara. Dressage from A to X: The Definitive Guide to Riding & Competing. LC 99-17915. 1999. 27.50 (*1-57076-100-0*) Trafalgar.

Burkhardt, Bernd. Hegels Wissenschaft der Logik Im Spannungsfeld der Kritik. (Studien und Materialien Zur Geschichte der Philosophie: Bd. 18). (GER.). xiv, 562p. 1993. write for info. (*3-487-09769-9*) G Olms Pubs.

Burkhardt, D. C. Rolling Dreams: Portraits of the Northwest's Railroad Heritage. LC 98-140229. (Illus.). 88p. 1997. pap. 38.00 (*0-9661042-7-7*) Rolling Dreams.

Burkhardt, D. C. Jesse. Backwoods Railroads: Branchlines & Shortlines of Western Oregon. LC 93-42338. (Illus.). 168p. 1994. 45.00 (*0-87422-104-8*) Wash St U Pr.

Burkhardt, F. A. Boucher Family, Bowsher, Bauscher, Bausher, Bousher, Comprising a Genealogy of Branches of Strawn, Harpster, Tedrow, Cryfer, et al: Descendants of Daniel Boucher of Albany Township, Berks Co., PA, with Notes of Other Boucher Families. (Illus.). 402p. 1992. reprint ed. pap. 62.00 (*0-8328-2644-8*); reprint ed. lib. bdg. 72.00 (*0-8328-2643-X*) Higginson Bk Co.

Burkhardt, Frederick & Smith, Sydney. A Calendar of the Correspondence of Charles Darwin, 1821-1882. 2nd ed. (Illus.). 748p. (C). 1994. text 160.00 (*0-521-43423-8*) Cambridge U Pr.

Burkhardt, Frederick, ed. see Darwin, Charles.

Burkhardt, Frederick, ed. see James, William.

Burkhardt, Frederick H., ed. Cleavage in Our Culture. LC 74-90619. (Essay Index Reprint Ser.). 1977. 23.95 (*0-8369-1396-5*) Ayer.

Burkhardt, Frederick H., ed. see James, William.

Burkhardt, G., et al, eds. Astronomy & Astrophysics Abstracts Vol. 64, Pt. 2: Literature 1995. x, 1666p. 1996. 371.00 (*3-540-61552-0*) Spr-Verlag.
— Astronomy & Astrophysics Abstracts, Vol. 50 A & B: Literature 1989, Pt. 2, Set. xxvii, 1429p. 1990. 334.95 (*0-387-52889-X*) Spr-Verlag.
— Astronomy & Astrophysics Abstracts, Vol. 52: Literature 1990, Pt. 2, Vols. A & B, 2 vols., Set. 1556p. 1991. 366.95 (*0-387-54336-8*) Spr-Verlag.
— Astronomy & Astrophysics Abstracts, Vol. 53: Literature 1991, Pt. 1. xviii, 1625p. 1992. 398.95 (*0-387-55314-2*) Spr-Verlag.
— Astronomy & Astrophysics Abstracts, Vol. 54: Literature 1991, 2 vols., Set. 1648p. 1992. 398.95 (*0-387-55795-4*) Spr-Verlag.
— Astronomy & Astrophysics Abstracts, Vol. 55A & 55B: Literature, 1992, Pt. 1, 2 vols., Set. x, 1447p. 1993. 405.95 (*0-387-56436-5*) Spr-Verlag.
— Literature, 1990, Pt. 1. (Astronomy & Astrophysics Abstracts Ser.: Vol. 51). viii, 1526p. 1991. 358.95 (*0-387-53533-0*) Spr-Verlag.
— Literature, 1998 Pt. 1: A Publication of the Astronomisches Rechen-Institut Heidelberg Produced in Cooperation with the Fachinformationszentrum Karlsruhe & the Institution of Electrical Engineering, U. K. (Astronomy & Astrophysics Abstracts Ser.: Vol. 69). xviii, 1931p. 1999. 399.00 (*3-540-65481-X*) Spr-Verlag.
— Literature, 1997. (Astronomy & Astrophysics Abstracts Ser.: Vol. 68). xviii, 1794p. 1998. 375.00 (*3-540-64596-9*) Spr-Verlag.
— Literature, 1993, 2 vols., Vols. A & B, Pt. 1. (Astronomy & Astrophysics Abstracts Ser.: Vol. 57). x, 1663p. 1994. 325.95 (*0-387-57721-1*) Spr-Verlag.

Burkhardt, G & Esser, U., eds. Astronomy & Astrophysics Abstracts. 2208p. 1994. 359.95 (*3-540-58554-0*) Spr-Verlag.

Burkhardt, Gerhard. Klopstock, Friedrich Gottlieb: Werke und Briefe. Historisch-Kritische Ausgabe Section Addenda; Klopstock-Bibliographie, Vol. 1. xii, 340p. (C). 1975. 150.75 (*3-11-004896-5*) De Gruyter.

Burkhardt, Gina, jt. auth. see Petri, Mart.

Burkhardt, H., et al, eds. Computer Vision - ECCV '98: 5th European Conference on Computer Vision, Freiburg, Germany, June 2-6, 1998. Proceedings. LC 98-25892. (Lecture Notes in Computer Science Ser.: Vol. I, Vol. 1406). xvi, 927p. 1998. pap. 96.00 (*3-540-64569-1*) Spr-Verlag.
— Computer Vision - ECCV '98: 5th European Conference on Computer Vision, Freiburg, Germany, June 2-6, 1998. Proceedings. LC 98-25892. (Lecture Notes in Computer Science Ser.: Vol. II, Vol. 1407). xvi, 881p. 1998. pap. 99.00 (*3-540-64613-2*) Spr-Verlag.

Burkhardt, Hans. Logik und Semiotik in der Philosophie von Leibniz. (Analytica Ser.). 488p. 1980. lib. bdg. 132.00 (*3-88405-001-X*) Philosophia Pr.

Burkhardt, Hans & Smith, Barry, eds. Handbook of Metaphysics & Ontology, 2 vols., Set. (Analytica Ser.). xxiv, 1005p. 1991. 380.00 (*3-88405-080-X*) Philosophia Pr.

Burkhardt, Hugh. The Real World & Mathematics. 188p. (C). 1981. pap. text 14.95 (*0-216-91084-6*) Birkhauser.

Burkhardt, Mitch. Willie Mays: Baseball Legend. (Black American Ser.). (Illus.). 192p. (YA). 1992. mass mkt. 3.95 (*0-87067-587-7*, Melrose Sq) Holloway.

Burkhardt-Nathaniel. Ethics & Issues in Contemporary Nursing. LC 97-38418. 384p. (C). 1998. mass mkt. 45.95 (*0-8273-7702-9*) Delmar.
— IML Ethics & Issues in Contemporary Nursing. (Home Care Aide Ser.). 64p. 1998. teacher ed. 12.00 (*0-8273-7703-7*) Delmar.

Burkhardt, Richard W., Jr. The Spirit of System: Lamarck & Evolutionary Biology. (Illus.). 288p. 1990. text 29.00 (*0-674-83317-1*) HUP.
— The Spirit of System: Lamarck & Evolutionary Biology. (Illus.). 320p. (C). 1995. pap. text 20.50 (*0-674-83318-X*) HUP.

Burkhardt, Richard W., jt. auth. see Walker, Janet R.

Burkhardt, Sandra A. & Rotatori, Anthony F., eds. Treatment & Prevention of Childhood Sexual Abuse. 220p. 1995. 34.95 (*1-56032-320-5*) Taylor & Francis.

Burkhardt, W. First Steps in Mathematica. 100p. 1995. 24.95 (*3-540-19875-X*) Spr-Verlag.

Burkhardt, Werner. First Steps in Maple. Stewart, M. J., tr. 118p. 1995. pap. 19.95 (*3-540-19874-1*) Spr-Verlag.
— First Steps in Maple. Stewart, M. J., tr. from GER. LC 94-38691. (Illus.). 118p. 1995. 19.95 (*0-387-19874-1*) Spr-Verlag.
— First Steps in Mathematica. LC 94-25687. Orig. Title: Erste Schritte mit Mathematica. 128p. 1994. write for info. (*0-387-19875-X*) Spr-Verlag.

Burkhardt, Willi P., jt. auth. see Dumler, Helmut.

Burkhart, A. G., Jr. Aymond: A Novel. LC 96-45294. 160p. (Orig.). 1997. pap. 14.95 (*0-86534-258-X*) Sunstone Pr.

Burkhart, Ann M. How to Study Law & Take Law Exams in a Nutshell. Stein, Robert A., ed. LC 96-32165. (Nutshell Ser.). 366p. (C). 1996. pap. 21.50 (*0-314-06596-2*) West Pub.

***Burkhart, Ann M., et al.** Fundamentals of Property Law. 125p. 1999. pap., teacher ed. write for info. (*0-327-01287-0*, 1112910) LEXIS Pub.

Burkhart, Ann M., jt. auth. see Bernhardt, Roger H.

***Burkhart, Bryan & Hunt, David.** Airstream: The History of the Land Yacht. LC 99-39938. (Illus.). 144p. 2000. pap. 19.95 (*0-8118-2471-3*) Chronicle Bks.

Burkhart, Charles. Anthology for Musical Analysis. 5th ed. 640p. (C). 1994. pap. text 62.00 (*0-03-055318-0*, Pub. by Harcourt Coll Pubs) Harcourt.
— The Pleasure of Miss Pym. LC 87-5829. reprint ed. pap. 43.40 (*0-608-20099-9*, 2071371) Bks Demand.

Burkhart, Christina. Surf Sammy's New Computer: A Surf Sammy & Friends Computer Adventure. LC 97-92821. (A Surf Sammy & Friends Computer Adventure Ser.). (Illus.). 32p. (J). (ps-k). 1999. 14.95 (*0-9662025-0-3*) Roof Publ.

Burkhart, Dagmar, jt. auth. see Leitner, Andreas.

Burkhart, Elizabeth, jt. auth. see Androwich, Ida.

Burkhart, F., ed. Neue Aspekte in der Behandlung der Herzinsuffizienz: Oberrheinisches Kardiologen - Symposium. (Journal: Cardiology: Vol. 65, Suppl. 1, 1980). (Illus.). 1980. pap. 16.75 (*3-8055-0652-X*) S Karger.

Burkhart, Harold E., jt. auth. see Avery, Thomas E.

***Burkhart, James.** Quantitative & Qualitative Reasoning Skills. 188p. (C). 1999. per. 20.95 (*0-7872-6378-8*, 41637801) Kendall-Hunt.

Burkhart, Janice, jt. auth. see American-French Genealogical Society Staff.

Burkhart, Joyce L. & Mercer, Deborah B. Scripture Concepts for Children Activity-Story Book: Building Godly Character, Vol. 2. (Illus.). 43p. (J). (ps-2). 1994. pap. 8.00 (*0-9633166-1-3*) Joyce Burkhart.
— Scripture Concepts for Children Activity-Story Book Vol. 1: Building Godly Self-Esteem. (Illus.). 43p. (Orig.). (J). (ps-2). 1991. pap. 8.00 (*0-9633166-0-5*) Joyce Burkhart.

Burkhart, Judith A., jt. auth. see Gunnar, Peter M.

Burkhart, Larry L. The Good Fight: Medicine in Colonial Pennsylvania. (Studies in Historical Demography). 360p. 1989. reprint ed. text 25.00 (*0-8240-3395-7*) Garland.

Burkhart, Linda J. Using Computers & Speech Synthesis to Facilitate Communicative Interaction with Young & or Severely Handicapped Children. LC 87-71763. (Illus.). (C). 1987. student ed. 24.95 (*0-9619338-0-1*) L J Burkhart.

Burkhart, Lona, jt. auth. see Turmon, Ramona.

Burkhart, Louise M. Holy Wednesday: A Nahua Drama from Early Colonial Mexico. (New Cultural Studies). (Illus.). 320p. 1996. text 42.95 (*0-8122-3342-5*); pap. text 18.95 (*0-8122-1576-1*) U of Pa Pr.

Burkhart, Lynne C. Old Values in a New Town: The Politics of Race & Class in Columbia, Maryland. LC 80-26556. 165p. 1981. 45.00 (*0-275-90588-8*, C0588, Praeger Pubs) Greenwood.

Burkhart, Marianne C., jt. ed. see Waife, Ronald S.

Burkhart, Nellie K. Dike: Genealogy of the Dike & Torrance Families, from 1623 & 1701. 54p. 1997. reprint ed. pap. 11.00 (*0-8328-8300-X*); reprint ed. lib. bdg. 21.00 (*0-8328-8299-2*) Higginson Bk Co.

Burkhart, Patrick J. & Reuss, Suzanne. Successful Strategic Planning: A Guide for Nonprofit Agencies & Organizations. (Illus.). 80p. (C). 1993. pap. text 16.95 (*0-8039-4799-2*) Sage.

Burkhart, Rob. To Be Like Jesus. LC 89-82758. (Sunday School Staff Training Book of the Year Ser.). 110p. 1990. pap. 2.95 (*0-88243-658-9*, 02-0658) Gospel Pub.

Burkhart, Robert E. Shakespeare's Bad Quartos: Deliberate Abridgements Designed for Performance by Reduced Cast. (Studies in English Literature: No. 101). (Illus.). 124p. 1975. pap. text 32.35 (*90-279-3276-X*) Mouton.

Burkhart, Stephen S. Laser Burn. LC 94-36631. 1994. 19.95 (*1-880510-26-X*) State House Pr.

Burkhart, W. Eugene, Jr. Decorating Christmas Trees. (Illus.). 64p. (Orig.). 1985. pap. 8.95 (*0-9615199-0-8*) Burkharts.

Burkhart, Walter. Neues Lexikon der Vornamen. (GER.). 29.95 (*0-7859-8328-7*, 3404603435) Fr & Eur.

Burkhart, Wanda. Submitting to a Sinning Husband. 64p. 1984. pap. 2.95 (*0-88144-042-6*) Christian Pub.

Burkhauser, Jude, ed. Glasgow Girls: Women in Art & Design, 1880-1920. LC 93-84475. (Illus.). 264p. 1993. 120.00 (*0-9636985-0-8*) Red Ochre Pr.

Burkhauser, Richard, et al. Income Mobility & the Middle Class. LC 97-114871. (Studies on Understanding Economic Inequality). 50p. (Orig.). 1996. pap. 9.95 (*0-8447-7075-2*, AEI Pr) Am Enterprise.

Burkhauser, Richard V., ed. Pensions in a Changing Economy. LC 93-2155. 1993. pap. 15.00 (*0-86643-078-4*) Empl Benefit Res Inst.

Burkhauser, Richard V. & Haveman, Robert H. Disability & Work: The Economics of American Policy. LC 82-113. (Policy Studies in Employment & Welfare: No. 38). 141p. 1982. reprint ed. pap. 43.80 (*0-608-04076-2*, 206480800011) Bks Demand.

Burkhead, Jesse & Welborn, David M. Intergovernmental Relations in the American Administrative State: The Johnson Presidency. LC 89-31697. (Administrative History of the Johnson Presidency Ser.). 336p. 1989. text 40.00 (*0-292-73849-8*) U of Tex Pr.

Burkhead, Jesse, et al. Input & Output in Large-City High Schools. LC 67-16845. (Education in Large Cities Ser.: No. 2). 122p. reprint ed. pap. 37.90 (*0-608-15212-9*, 202740600055) Bks Demand.

Burkhead, Jesse, jt. auth. see Premchand, A.

Burkhead, N. M., jt. auth. see Jenkins, R. E.

Burkhead, Wayne Z., Jr., ed. Rotator Cuff Disorders. LC 95-14112. (Illus.). 512p. 1996. 129.00 (*0-683-01215-0*) Lppncott W & W.

Burkhill, John C. The Theory of Ordinary Differential Equations. LC 76-369325. (Longman Mathematical Texts Ser.). 130p. reprint ed. pap. 40.30 (*0-608-30310-0*, 201356300087) Bks Demand.

Burkhill, T. Alec. The Evolution of Christian Thought. fac. ed. LC 76-127601. 516p. 1971. reprint ed. pap. 160.00 (*0-608-01010-3*, 206186800012) Bks Demand.

Burkhold. Living in the U. S. A., Bk. 3. 160p. 1990. pap. 10.55 (*0-8442-7696-0*) NTC Contemp Pub Co.
— Living in the U. S. A., Bks. 1, 2 & 3. 1990. pap., teacher ed. 14.05 (*0-8442-7697-9*) NTC Contemp Pub Co.

Burkholder, Charles E., jt. auth. see Crilley, Raymond E.

Burkholder, Charles E., jt. auth. see Crilley, Raymond E., Sr.

Burkholder, Charles E., jt. auth. see Crilley, Raymond E.

Burkholder, Clyde. Ox-Bow Incident Notes. (Cliffs Notes Ser.). 56p. 1974. pap. 4.95 (*0-8220-0971-4*, Cliff) IDG Bks.

Burkholder, Craton R. Emergency Care for Cats & Dogs: First Aid for Your Pets. LC 87-3726. (Illus.). 176p. 1987. 23.95 (*0-935576-19-3*) Kesend Pub Ltd.
— Emergency Care for Cats & Dogs: First Aid for Your Pets. LC 87-3726. (Illus.). 172p. 1995. pap. 15.95 (*0-935576-18-5*) Kesend Pub Ltd.

Burkholder, D. L., et al. Ecole d'Ete de Probabilites de Saint-Flour XIX - 1989. (Lecture Notes in Mathematics Ser.: Vol. 1464). 256p. 1991. 50.95 (*0-387-53841-0*) Spr-Verlag.

Burkholder, Dan. Making Digital Negatives for Contact Printing: A Step-by-Step Guide to Affordable Enlarged Negatives for Platinum, Silver, & Other Printing Processes. 2nd rev. ed. (Illus.). 350p. 1999. pap. 34.95 (*0-9649638-6-8*) Bladed Iris.
Completely revised & updated in this 1999 second edition, Dan Burkholder's award-winning book is a step-by-step guide to making affordable enlarged negatives for contact printing on silver, platinum, palladium & other contact printing processes. Exciting new techniques for making negatives with desktop printers are now included, as well as tips for using the latest imaging software. Photo Eye, the world's largest distributor of photography books, called it a "revolutionary book on this innovative & affordable technique." Jerry Uelsmann said of the book, "Making Digital Negatives is indispensable. It is clear, concise & insightful." In addition to the easy to follow text, illustrations & photographs, Burkholder's book includes a CD-ROM with calibration utilities, test images & demo software (both Mac & PC) & a separate color calibration print. Photographers wishing to combine the power & precision of digital imaging with the beauty & permanence of traditional photographic printing will find this book invaluable. Contact Bladed Iris Press, PO Box 111877, Carrollton, TX 75011-1877; phone 972-242-9819, fax: 972-242-9651; e/mail: bladediris@aol.com: www.danburkholder.com.
Publisher Paid Annotation.

Burkholder, David. Ye Fathers. 358p. 1995. 11.15 (*0-7399-0199-0*, 2112) Rod & Staff.
— Young Man, Be Strong. 248p. 1988. 9.25 (*0-7399-0138-9*, 2485) Rod & Staff.
— Young Man, Be Strong. Zelinski, Andrew, tr. (SPA.). 270p. 1998. pap. 5.80 (*0-7399-0139-7*, 2485.1) Rod & Staff.

***Burkholder, Ferner L., et al.** Friends Made, Moments Shared, Memories for Life: An Oral History of VMSB 343 United States Marine Corps in World War II. LC 00-30973. (Illus.). 2000. pap. write for info. (*0-9667269-4-4*) Lemieux Intl Ltd.

Burkholder, Galen C. Daddy, Are You Santa Claus? (Mommy, Why...Ser.). (Illus.). 24p. (Orig.). (J). 1995. pap. 3.99 (*1-56043-159-8*) Destiny Image.
— Daddy, Does God Take a Vacation? (Mommy, Why...Ser.). (Illus.). 24p. (Orig.). (J). 1995. pap. 3.99 (*1-56043-153-9*) Destiny Image.

Burkholder, Grace. An Arabian Collection: Artifacts from the Eastern Province. (Illus.). 224p. (Orig.). (C). 1984. pap. text. write for info. (*0-9613535-0-3*) GB Pubns.

Burkholder, H. C., ed. High Level Nuclear Waste Disposal. LC 86-14015. xvii, 914p. 1986. text 230.00 (*0-935470-29-8*) Gordon & Breach.

Burkholder, J. Lawrence. The Problem of Social Responsibility from the Perspective of the Mennonite Church. 238p. (Orig.). 1989. reprint ed. pap. text 25.00 (*0-936273-14-3*) Inst Mennonite.

An Asterisk (*) at the beginning of an entry indicates that the title is appearing for the first time.

Burkholder, J. Peter. All Made of Tunes: Charles Ives & the Uses of Musical Borrowing. LC 95-13537. 1995. 37.50 (*0-300-05642-7*) Yale U Pr.
— Study & Listening Guide. 5th ed. (C). 1996. pap. text, student ed. 18.25 (*0-393-96905-3*) Norton.
Burkholder, J. Peter, ed. Charles Ives & His World. LC 96-21393. 464p. 1996. text 55.00 (*0-691-01164-8*, Pub. by Princeton U Pr); pap. text 19.95 (*0-691-01163-X*, Pub. by Princeton U Pr) Cal Prin Full Svc.
Burkholder, J. Peter, jt. ed. see Block, Geoffrey H.
Burkholder, John & O'Connor, D. Thomas. Kemple Glass, 1945-1970. LC 97-168260. (Illus.). 160p. 1997. 44.95 (*1-57080-012-X*, 4085); pap. 34.95 (*1-57080-009-X*, 4084) Antique Pubns.
Burkholder, Kathy J. Plant Identification Characteristics for Deciduous Trees & Shrubs - Lesson Plans. King, Muriel N., ed. (Illus.). 112p. (C). 1995. pap. text, teacher ed. 24.95 (*1-56502-006-5*, 2214G) Ohio Agri Educ.
***Burkholder, Kelly.** Diaries & Journals. LC 00-28432. (Artistic Adventures Ser.). 2000. write for info. (*1-57103-352-1*) Rourke Pr.
— Pen Pals. LC 00-28434. (Artistic Adventures Ser.). 2000. write for info. (*1-57103-353-X*) Rourke Pr.
— Plays. LC 00-36927. (Artistic Adventures Ser.). 2000. pap. write for info. (*1-57103-357-2*) Rourke Bk Co.
— Poetry. LC 00-25371. (Artistic Adventures Ser.). (Illus.). (J). 2000. write for info. (*1-57103-354-8*) Rourke Bk Co.
— Puppets. LC 00-25372. (Artistic Adventures Ser.). (Illus.). (J). 2000. write for info. (*1-57103-355-6*) Rourke Bk Co.
— Stories. LC 00-25373. (Artistic Adventures Ser.). (Illus.). (J). 2000. write for info. (*1-57103-356-4*) Rourke Bk Co.
Burkholder, Kendra. Whom Shall I Fear? 228p. 1996. 8.90 (*0-7399-0158-3*, 2469) Rod & Staff.
Burkholder, Lester. Pennsylvania Mennonites in Mexico. (Illus.). 145p. 1998. pap. 9.95 (*1-883294-73-8*) Masthof Pr.
Burkholder, Mark A. Biographical Dictionary of Councilors of the Indies, 1717-1808. LC 86-401. 231p. 1986. lib. bdg. 79.50 (*0-313-24024-8*, BBC/, Greenwood Pr) Greenwood.
— Politics of a Colonial Career: Jose Baquijano & the Audiencia of Lima. LC 80-52279. 205p. reprint ed. pap. 63.60 (*0-608-15372-9*, 202932200060) Bks Demand.
— Politics of a Colonial Career: Jose Baquijano & the Audiencia of Lima. 2nd ed. LC 89-35964. (Latin American Silhouettes Ser.). 184p. (C). 1989. reprint ed. pap. 17.95 (*0-8420-2352-6*) Scholarly Res Inc.
— Politics of a Colonial Career: Jose Baquijano & the Audiencia of Lima. 2nd ed. LC 89-35964. (Latin American Silhouettes Ser.). 184p. (C). 1990. reprint ed. 45.00 (*0-8420-2353-4*) Scholarly Res Inc.
***Burkholder, Mark A., ed.** Administrators of Empire. LC 98-24125. (Expanding World Ser.: No. 22). 378p. 1998. text 130.95 (*0-86078-527-0*) Ashgate Pub Co.
Burkholder, Mark A. & Chandler, D. S. Biographical Dictionary of Audiencia Ministers in the Americas, 1687-1821. LC 82-925. 491p. 1982. lib. bdg. 135.00 (*0-313-22038-7*, BBD/, Greenwood Pr) Greenwood.
Burkholder, Mark A. & Johnson, Lyman L. Colonial Latin America. 3rd ed. LC 97-24114. (Illus.). 384p. (C). 1997. text 59.95 (*0-19-510535-4*); pap. text 25.95 (*0-19-510536-2*) OUP.
***Burkholder, Mark A. & Johnson, Lyman L.** Colonial Latin America. 4th ed. (Illus.). 400p. (C). 2000. pap. text 27.95 (*0-19-513702-7*) OUP.
Burkholder, Nelson D. I Remember... Reminiscing on 78 Years of Mennonite Life in Denbigh. Williams, Angie B., ed. LC 97-222107. 150p. (Orig.). 1997. pap. 9.95 (*1-57502-596-5*, PO1711) Morris Pubng.
Burkholder, Nicholas C., jt. auth. see Beatty, Richard H.
burkholder, peter. Concise History of Western Music: Study Guide. pap. 12.00 (*0-393-97171-6*) Norton.
Burkholder, Peter M. Atlas of Human Glomerular Pathology: Correlative Light, Immunofluorescence, & Ultrastructural Histology. LC 74-13371. 448p. reprint ed. pap. 138.90 (*0-8357-5842-7*, 205540600019) Bks Demand.
Burkholder, Robert E. & Myerson, Joel. Critical Essays on Ralph Waldo Emerson. LC 82-15831. (Critical Essays on American Literature Ser.). ix, 530p. 1983. write for info. (*0-8161-8305-8*) Mac Lib Ref.
— Emerson: An Annotated Secondary Bibliography. LC 84-15352. (Series in Bibliography). 864p. 1985. 130.00 (*0-8229-3502-3*) U of Pittsburgh Pr.
Burkholder, Robert E. & Myerson, Joel, contrib. by. Ralph Waldo Emerson: An Annotated Bibliography of Criticism, 1980-1991, 18. LC 93-45954. (Bibliographies & Indexes in American Literature Ser.). 248p. 1994. lib. bdg. 79.50 (*0-313-29150-0*) Greenwood.
Burkholder, Robert E., jt. ed. see Mott, Wesley T.
Burkholder, Rosene. Learning Our Letters. (Jewel Book Ser.: Set 5). (Illus.). 32p. (J). (ps-2). 1994. pap. 2.55 (*0-7399-0050-1*, 2580) Rod & Staff.
Burkholder, Thomas R., jt. auth. see Campbell, Karlyn K.
Burkholz, Herbert. Brain Damage. 288p. 1992. text 20.00 (*0-689-12009-5*) Atheneum Yung Read.
— Writer in Residence. 1992. 24.95 (*0-685-53582-7*) Permanent CA.
— Writer in Residence. LC 91-29696. 310p. 1992. 24.95 (*1-877946-11-7*) Permanent Pr.
Burkholz, Mathew L. & Kaplan, Linda L. Copper Art Jewelry: A Different Luster. LC 92-60623. (Illus.). 176p. 1992. text 49.95 (*0-88740-419-7*) Schiffer.
Burkholz, Matthew L. The Bakelite Collection. LC 97-67289. 256p. 1997. 59.95 (*0-7643-0016-4*) Schiffer.
Burki. Pakistan. 3rd ed. LC 98-55927. 272p. 2000. pap. 26.00 (*0-8133-3621-X*, Pub. by Westview) HarpC.
Burki, David & Ward, Robert. MS-DOS System Programming. 3rd ed. 830p. 1994. pap. 39.95 incl. disk (*0-87930-445-6*) C M P Books.
Burki, Shahid J. Historical Dictionary of Pakistan. LC 91-13610. (Asian Historical Dictionaries Ser.: No. 3). (Illus.). 292p. 1991. 37.00 (*0-8108-2411-6*) Scarecrow.
— Pakistan: The Continuing Search for Nationhood. 2nd rev. ed. (Nations of Contemporary Asia Ser.). 243p. (C). 1991. pap. 21.50 (*0-8133-8101-0*) Westview.
***Burki, Shahid J., et al, eds.** Beyond the Center: Decentralizing the State. (Latin American & Caribbean Studies). (SPA.). 128p. 1999. pap. 30.00 (*0-8213-4582-6*, 14582) World Bank.
Burki, Shahid J. & Perry, Guillermo. M As All a del Consenso de Washington: La Hora de la Reforma Institucional. LC 98-37364. (World Bank Latin American & Caribbean Studies Ser.). 184p. 1998. pap. 22.00 (*0-8213-4347-5*) World Bank.
Burki, Shahid J. & Perry, Guillermo E. Beyond the Washington Consensus: Institutions Matter. (Latin American & Caribbean Studies). 168p. 1998. 30.00 (*0-8213-4282-7*, 14282) World Bank.
— The Long March: A Reform Agenda for Latin America & the Caribbean in the Next Decade. LC 97-13357. (Latin American & Caribbean Studies). 132p. 1997. pap. 22.00 (*0-8213-3985-0*, 13985) World Bank.
— The Long March: A Reform Agenda for Latin America & the Caribbean in the Next Decade (Spanish) (Latin American & Caribbean Studies). 148p. 1998. pap. 22.00 (*0-8213-4281-9*, 14281) World Bank.
***Burki, Shahid J. & Perry, Guillermo E., eds.** Annual World Bank Conference on Development in Latin America & the Caribbean 1998 Proceedings: Banks & Capial Markets - Sound Financial Systems for the 21st Century. 264p. 1999. pap. 30.00 (*0-8213-4520-6*, 14520) World Bank.
Burki, Shahid J., et al. Annual World Bank Conference on Development in Latin America, 1997: Trade: Toward Open Regionalism. (Latin American & Caribbean Studies). 288p. 1998. pap. 40.00 (*0-8213-4272-X*, 14272) World Bank.
— Annual World Bank Conference on Development in Latin American & in the Caribbean, 1996: Poverty & Inequality (Proceedings of a Conference Held in Bogota, Colombia) (Latin American & Caribbean Studies). 352p. 1998. pap. 22.00 (*0-8213-3984-2*, 13984) World Bank.
***Burki, Shahid J., et al.** Beyond the Center: Decentralizing the State. LC 99-15991. (Latin American & Caribbean Studies). 116p. 1999. pap. 30.00 (*0-8213-4521-4*, 14521) World Bank.
Burki, Shahid J., jt. ed. see LaPorte, Robert, Jr.
Burki, Shahid Javed. Historical Dictionary of Pakistan. 2nd ed. Woronoff, Jon, ed. & frwd. by. LC 99-10725. (Oceanic Historical Dictionaries: No. 33). (Illus.). 560p. 1999. 89.50 (*0-8108-3634-3*) Scarecrow.
Burki, Shahid Javed & Edwards, Sebastian. Dismantling the Populist State: The Unfinished Revolution in Latin America & the Caribbean. LC 96-174880. (World Bank Latin American & Caribbean Studies). 44p. 1996. pap. 22.00 (*0-8213-3689-4*, 13689) World Bank.
— Latin America after Mexico: Quickening the Pace. LC 96-22783. (World Bank Latin American & Caribbean Studies). 40p. 1996. pap. 22.00 (*0-8213-3629-0*, 13629) World Bank.
Burkil, A. A Dictionary of Economic Products of Malaya, Vols. 1-2 Rep. (C). 1986. 600.00 (*0-7855-2285-9*, Pub. by Scientific) St Mut.
Burkill, H. M. The Useful Plants of West Tropical Africa, Vol. 4. 968p. 1997. 140.00 (*1-900347-13-X*, Pub. by Royal Botnic Grdns) Balogh.
— The Useful Plants of West Tropical Africa Vol. 1: Families A-D. LC 99-161006. (Illus.). 960p. 1985. 140.00 (*0-947643-01-X*, Pub. by Royal Botnic Grdns) Balogh.
— The Useful Plants of West Tropical Africa Vol. 2: Families E - I. xii, 636p. 1994. 100.00 (*0-947643-56-7*, Pub. by Royal Botnic Grdns) Balogh.
— The Useful Plants of West Tropical Africa Vol. 3: Families J-L. (Illus.). xi, 855p. 1995. 120.00 (*0-947643-64-8*, Pub. by Royal Botnic Grdns) Balogh.
Burkill, I. H. Notes from a Journey to Nepal. (C). 1977. text 100.00 (*0-89771-572-1*, Pub. by Intl Bk Distr) St Mut.
Burkill, I. H., ed. Notes from a Journey to Nepal. x, 81p. 1977. reprint ed. 41.00 (*0-7855-3067-3*, Pub. by Intl Bk Distr) St Mut.
Burkill, John C. The Lebesgue Integral. (Cambridge Tracts in Mathematics & Mathematical Physics: No. 40). 95p. reprint ed. pap. 27.10 (*0-608-15697-3*, 2031624) Bks Demand.
Burkill, T. A., ed. see Winter, Paul.
Burkin, A. R. Extractive Metallurgy of Nickel. LC 86-28942. (Critical Reports on Applied Chemistry). 160p. 1987. 475.00 (*0-471-91425-8*) Wiley.
***BURKIN, A R.** Theory & Principle. 1999. 45.00 (*1-86094-184-2*) World Scientific Pub.
Burkinshaw, Bill. Introducing Radio Control Model Aircraft. (Illus.). 108p. 1995. pap. 16.95 (*1-85486-116-6*, Pub. by Nexus Special Interests) Trans-Atl Phila.
Burkinshaw, Owen, jt. auth. see Aliprantis, Charalambos.
Burkinshaw, Owen, jt. auth. see Aliprantis, Charalambos D.
Burkinshaw, Robert K. Pilgrims in Lotus Land: Conservative Protestantism in British Columbia, 1917-1981. LC 95-235185. (McGill-Queen's Studies in the History of Religion Ser.). 376p. 1995. 55.00 (*0-7735-1286-1*, Pub. by McG-Queens Univ Pr) CUP Services.
Burkitt. Essential Surgery. 2nd ed. 1995. text 56.00 (*0-443-04805-3*, W B Saunders Co) Harcrt Hlth Sci Grp.
Burkitt, A. N., jt. auth. see Heermann, D. W.
Burkitt, Brian, jt. auth. see Hutchinson, Frances.
Burkitt, Denis P., jt. ed. see Trowell, H. C.
Burkitt, F. C. Jewish & Christian Apocalypses. (British Academy, London, Schweich Lectures on Biblical Archaeology Series, 1930). 1969. reprint ed. pap. 25.00 (*0-8115-1255-X*) Periodicals Srv.
Burkitt, F. Crawford. The Earliest Sources for the Life of Jesus. 1977. lib. bdg. 59.95 (*0-8490-1736-X*) Gordon Pr.
Burkitt, Francis C. Church & Gnosis: A Study of Christian Thought & Speculation in the Second Century. LC 77-84696. (Morse Lectures: 1931). reprint ed. 37.50 (*0-404-16104-9*) AMS Pr.
— Early Christianity Outside the Roman Empire: Two Lectures Delivered at Trinity College, Dublin. LC 82-45806. (Orthodoxies & Heresies in the Early Church Ser.). 1983. reprint ed. 27.50 (*0-404-62375-1*) AMS Pr.
— The Religion of the Manichees: Donnellan Lectures for 1924. LC 77-84698. reprint ed. 34.50 (*0-404-16105-7*) AMS Pr.
Burkitt, Francis H. Early Eastern Christianity: St. Margaret's Lectures, 1904, on the Syriac-Speaking Church. LC 82-45809. (Orthodoxies & Heresies in the Early Church Ser.). reprint ed. 37.50 (*0-404-62378-6*) AMS Pr.
Burkitt, H. George, et al. Essential Surgery. (Illus.). 771p. 1990. pap. text 55.00 (*0-443-03593-8*) Church.
— Wheater's Functional Histology: A Text & Colour Atlas. 3rd ed. LC 93-7323. (Illus.). 416p. 1993. pap. text 58.00 (*0-443-04691-3*) Church.
Burkitt, H. George, jt. auth. see Wheater, Paul R.
Burkitt, Ian. Social Selves: Theories of the Social Formation of Personality. 240p. (C). 1992. 45.00 (*0-8039-8384-0*); pap. 14.99 (*0-8039-8385-9*) Sage.
Burkitt, Lemuel & Read, Jesse. A Concise History of the Kehukee Bapist Association from Its Original Rise to the Present Time. rev. ed. Gaustad, Edwin S., ed. LC 79-52591. (Baptist Tradition Ser.). 1980. reprint ed. lib. bdg. 31.95 (*0-405-12458-9*) Ayer.
Burkitt, Miles C. Our Early Ancestors: An Introductory Study of Mesolithic, Neolithic, & Copper Age Cultures in Europe & Adjacent Regions. LC 72-80142. (Illus.). 1972. reprint ed. 18.95 (*0-405-08331-9*, Pub. by Blom Pubns) Ayer.
— Prehistory: Study of Early Cultures in Europe & the Mediterranean Basin. 2nd ed. LC 73-169752. (Select Bibliographies Reprint Ser.). 1977. reprint ed. 42.95 (*0-8369-5972-8*) Ayer.
Burkle, Candace R. & Marshak, David. HM Study Skills Program: Level I Student Text. Morimoto, Kiyo et al, eds. 96p. 1980. teacher ed. 5.95 (*0-88210-111-0*); pap. text 5.95 (*0-88210-110-2*) Natl Assn Principals.
Burkle, Diane, et al. Big Fearon Book of Dinosaurs. (J). (gr. 1-3). 1989. pap. 12.99 (*0-8224-0698-5*) Fearon Teacher Aids.
Burkle, Frank. HM Study Skills Program: Level B Student Text. Phipps, Paula & Marshak, David, eds. (Illus.). 83p. 1986. teacher ed. 8.50 (*0-939327-01-5*); pap. text 4.75 (*0-939327-00-7*) NAES Alexandria.
Burkle, Horst, ed. Grundwerte Menschlichen Verhaltens in Den Religionen. (Religionswissenschaft Ser.: Ed. 6). (GER.). 221p. 1993. 46.80 (*3-631-44740-X*) P Lang Pubng.
Burkle, Horst, ed. see Puttanil, Thomas.
***Burkle, Margot.** Love & Remembrance: A Memory Book for Parents Whose Child Has Died. 1998. 6.95 (*1-56123-104-5*) Centering Corp.
Burkle, William C., ed. see Walton, George.
***Burkle-Young, Francis A.** Papal Election in the Age of Transition, 1878-1922. 224p. 2000. 50.00 (*0-7391-0114-5*) Lxngtn Bks.
Burkle-Young, Francis A. Passing the Keys: Cardinals, Conclaves & the Election of the Next Pope. LC 99-29538. 480p. 1999. 35.00 (*1-56833-130-4*, Pub. by Madison Bks UPA) Natl Bk Netwk.
Burkle-Young, Francis A. & Maley, Saundra R. The Art of the Footnote: The Intelligent Student's Guide to the Art & Science of Annotating Texts. LC 96-16362. 242p. 1996. pap. text 16.50 (*0-7618-0348-3*); lib. bdg. 38.50 (*0-7618-0347-5*) U Pr of Amer.
— The Research Guide for the Digital Age: A New Handbook to Research & Writing for the Serious Student. LC 97-16464. 352p. (C). 1997. pap. 23.50 (*0-7618-0779-9*) U Pr of Amer.
Burkle-Young, Francis A., jt. auth. see Doerrer, Michael L.
Burklin, C. R. The Process Plant Designer's Pocket Handbook of Codes & Standards. LC 79-17599. 184p. 1979. reprint ed. pap. 57.10 (*0-608-00832-X*, 206162200010) Bks Demand.
Burklin, Thorsten. Balance und Krise. (Studien und Materialien Zur Geschichte der Philosophie: Bd. 47). (GER.). viii, 212p. 1997. write for info. (*3-487-10561-6*) G Olms Pubs.
***Burklo, Jim.** Open Christianity: Home by Another Road. 2000. pap. write for info. (*0-933670-05-2*) Rising Star.
Burklow, Brad. Parent's Solution to a Problem Child. (Illus.). 104p. 1995. pap. 11.95 (*0-933025-38-6*) Blue Bird Pub.
Burkman, Allan M., jt. auth. see Patil, Popat N.
Burkman, Katherine. Simon Gray: A Casebook. LC 92-319493. (Casebooks on Modern Dramatists Ser.: Vol. 13). 228p. 1992. text 20.00 (*0-8240-5758-9*, H1362) Garland.
Burkman, Katherine H. The Arrival of Godot: Ritual Patterns in Modern Drama. LC 85-45786. 176p. 1986. 32.50 (*0-8386-3264-5*) Fairleigh Dickinson.
Burkman, Katherine H., ed. Myth & Ritual in the Plays of Samuel Beckett. LC 86-46026. 176p. 1987. 32.50 (*0-8386-3299-8*) Fairleigh Dickinson.
Burkman, Katherine H. & Kundert-Gibbs, John L., eds. Pinter at Sixty. LC 92-35160. (Drama & Performance Studies). 240p. 1993. 36.95 (*0-253-34499-9*); pap. 15.95 (*0-253-20811-4*) Ind U Pr.
Burkman, Katherine H. & Roof, Judith, eds. Staging the Rage: The Web of Misogyny in Modern Drama. LC 97-48456. 272p. 1998. 42.50 (*0-8386-3763-9*) Fairleigh Dickinson.
Burkman, Kay. Champ. 47p. 1985. pap. 5.95 (*0-86492-058-X*, Pub. by Goose Ln Edits) Genl Dist Srvs.
Burkman, Kip. The Stroke Recovery Book: A Guide for Patients & Families. LC 98-6547. (Illus.). 172p. 1998. pap. 14.95 (*1-886039-30-5*) Addicus Bks.
Burkman, Ronald. Handbook of Contraception & Abortion. 1989. 32.95 (*0-316-09167-7*, Little Brwn Med Div) Lppncott W & W.
Burkman, Thomas W., ed. The Occupation of Japan: Arts & Culture. 262p. (C). 1984. lib. bdg. 19.25 (*0-9606418-5-8*) Genl D MacArthur Fnd.
— The Occupation of Japan: The International Context. 308p. (C). 1984. lib. bdg. 19.25 (*0-9606418-4-X*) Genl D MacArthur Fnd.
Burko, Lior M., ed. see International Research Workshop on Internal Struct.
Burkoff, John M. Criminal Defense Ethics: Law & Liability. LC 86-6092. 1986. ring bd. 140.00 (*0-87632-498-7*) West Group.
— Search Warrant Law Deskbook, Vol. 1. LC 86-26336. (Criminal Law Ser.). 1987. ring bd. 125.00 (*0-87632-530-4*) West Group.
Burkoff, John M. & Hudson, Hope L. Ineffective Assistance of Counsel, 1 vol. LC 93-26454. (Criminal Law Ser.). 1993. ring bd. 120.00 (*0-87632-919-9*) West Group.
Burkoff, Stanley T., et al. Short Tall Bridge Tales: Funny Stories about Tricky Hands. 192p. (Orig.). 1996. pap. 13.95 (*1-888745-00-2*, 4-1996-1) Zookeeper Pubng.
Burkowsky, Mitchell R. Orientation to Language & Learning Disorders in Children. LC 75-176182. 304p. 1973. 16.50 (*0-87527-098-0*) Green.
Burks, Alice R. & Burks, Arthur W. The First Electronic Computer: The Atanasoff Story. LC 87-25547. 400p. (C). 1989. pap. text 29.95 (*0-472-08104-7*, 08104) U of Mich Pr.
Burks, Ardath W. & Rogow, Arnold A. The Government of Japan. LC 82-6136. (Crowell Comparative Government Ser.). 283p. 1982. reprint ed. lib. bdg. 65.00 (*0-313-23575-9*, BUGJ, Greenwood Pr) Greenwood.
Burks, Ardath W., jt. auth. see Beck, Clark L.
Burks, Arthur W. Chance, Cause, Reason: An Inquiry into the Nature of Scientific Evidence. LC 74-11617. 1994. pap. text 12.50 (*0-226-08088-9*, P836) U Ch Pr.
Burks, Arthur W., jt. auth. see Burks, Alice R.
Burks, B. D. The Mayflies, or Ephemeroptera, of Illinois. LC 75-2296. (Illus.). viii, 216p. 1975. reprint ed. 15.00 (*0-911836-06-3*) Entomological Repr.
Burks, Barbara S., et al. The Promise of Youth: Follow-up Studies of a Thousand Gifted Children. (Genetic Studies of Genius: Vol. III). xiv, 508p. 1930. 65.00 (*0-8047-0011-7*) Stanford U Pr.
Burks, Bennette D. & Minnis, Mary M. Onsite Wastewater Treatment Systems. LC 94-76249. 320p. (C). 1994. pap. text 49.95 (*0-9641049-0-3*) Hogarth Hse.
Burks, Brian. Runs with Horses. LC 95-8460. 128p. (J). (gr. 7 up). 1995. 12.00 (*0-15-200264-2*, Harcourt Child Bks) Harcourt.
— Runs with Horses. LC 95-8460. 128p. (YA). (gr. 7 up). 1995. pap. 5.00 (*0-15-200994-9*, Harcourt Child Bks) Harcourt.
— Runs with Horses. 1995. 10.10 (*0-606-09802-X*, Pub. by Turtleback) Demco.
— Soldier Boy. LC 96-30289. 160p. (J). 1997. 12.00 (*0-15-201218-4*); pap. 5.00 (*0-15-201219-2*) Harcourt.
— Walks Alone. LC 97-14738. 115p. (J). (gr. 5-8). 1998. 16.00 (*0-15-201612-0*, Harcourt Child Bks) Harcourt.
***Burks, Brian.** Walks Alone. (YA). (gr. 5-8). 2000. pap. 6.00 (*0-15-202472-7*, Harcourt Child Bks) Harcourt.
Burks, Brian. Wrango. LC 99-12381. 118p. (J). (gr. 4-8). 1999. 16.00 (*0-15-201815-8*, Harcourt Child Bks) Harcourt.
Burks, Brian, jt. auth. see Paulsen, Gary.
Burks, Catherine. Different Friends, 5 bks. Incl. Vol. 1. Hi! Let's Meet Billy. (Illus.). (J). (gr. 1-5). 1998. pap. 6.95 (*1-892750-00-7*); Vol. 2. Hi! Let's Meet Pete. (Illus.). (J). (gr. 1-5). 1998. pap. 6.95 (*1-892750-01-5*); Vol. 3. Hi! Let's Meet Sam. (Illus.). (J). (gr. 1-5). 1998. pap. 6.95 (*1-892750-02-3*); Vol. 4. Hi! Let's Meet Bertha. (Illus.). (J). (gr. 1-5). 1998. pap. 6.95 (*1-892750-03-1*); Vol. 5. Hi! Let's Meet Doris. (Illus.). (J). (gr. 1-5). 1998. pap. 6.95 (*1-892750-05-8*); 34.75 (*1-892750-04-X*) Diff Friends.
Burks, Charlie. Gauze, Violins, Etc. (Illus.). 28p. (Orig.). 1996. pap. 6.00 (*1-890654-01-9*) Wood Work.
***Burks, Cramer.** Spy Toys: A History & Price Guide. LC 96-61344. (Illus.). 160p. 1999. pap. 19.95 (*1-887790-04-7*) Windmill Group.
Burks, David B., et al. Against the Grain: The Mission of Harding University. (Illus.). 325p. 1998. text 19.95 (*0-9670747-0-3*) Harding Univ.
Burks, David C., ed. Place of the Wild: A Wildlands Anthology. LC 94-29221. (Illus.). 288p. 1994. pap. 17.95 (*1-55963-342-5*); text 38.00 (*1-55963-341-7*) Island Pr.
Burks, Eddie & Cribbs, Gillian. Ghosthunter: Investigating the World of Ghosts & Spirits. (Illus.). 416p. 1996. mass mkt. 15.95 (*0-7472-4717-X*, Pub. by Headline Bk Pub) Trafalgar.
***Burks, Jack S. & Johnson, Kenneth P.** Multiple Sclerosis: Diagnosis, Medical Management & Rehabilitation. LC 00-35858. (Illus.). 2000. write for info. (*1-888799-35-8*) Demos Medical.
***Burks, James Edward.** Bid Me Come: A Christian's Walk in Faith. 80p. 2000. pap. 8.95 (*1-930621-03-5*, Pub. by Universal SC) BookWorld.
Burks, James F., jt. ed. see Therio, Adrien.

B

Burks, Jayne, jt. auth. see Rubenstein, Melvin.

Burks, Jean M., jt. auth. see Rieman, Timothy D.

Burks, Lorna. I Die Daily. (American Autobiography Ser.). 208p. 1995. reprint ed. lib. bdg. 79.00 (*0-7812-8469-4*) Rprt Serv.

Burks, Richard V. The Future of Communism in Europe. LC 68-64186. (Franklin Memorial Lectures Ser.: Vol. 17). 286p. reprint ed. pap. 88.70 (*0-608-16484-4*, 202763300055) Bks Demand.

Burks, Ron & Burks, Vicki. Damaged Disciples: Casualties of Authoritarian Churches & the Shepherding Movement. 176p. 1992. pap. 8.99 (*0-310-57611-3*) Zondervan.

Burks-Shiver, Jacqueline. Something's Out There. 30p. 1996. pap. 5.95 (*0-9654212-0-1*) Burks-Shiver.

— Tapping Through. Allman, Eileen, ed. 30p. 1996. pap. 5.95 (*0-9654212-1-X*) Burks-Shiver.

Burks, Susan L. Managing Your Migraine: A Migraine-Sufferer's Practical Guide. LC 94-4712. 264p. 1994. pap. 14.50 (*0-89603-324-4*) Humana.

Burks, T. F., jt. ed. see Nahas, Gabriel G.

Burks, Vicki, jt. auth. see Burks, Ron.

Burks, William B. & Weston, Thomas G. Partnership for Peace vs. Relations with Russia. (Pew Case Studies in International Affairs). 50p. (C). 1996. pap. text 3.50 (*1-56927-468-1*, GU Schl Foreign) Geo U Inst Dplmcy.

Burl. State Models. 80p. 2001. pap. 12.00 (*0-13-081226-9*) P-H.

***Burl, Aubrey.** Circles of Stone: 3500-900 B.C. (Illus.). 224p. 1999. 45.00 (*1-86046-661-3*, Pub. by Harvill Press) FS&G.

— Danse Macabre: Francois Villon: Poetry & Murder in Medieval Paris. (Illus.). 224p. 2000. 18.95 (*0-7509-2177-3*) Sutton Publng.

Burl, Aubrey. From Carnac to Callanish: The Prehistoric Stone Rows of Britain, Ireland, & Brittany. LC 93-19539. (Illus.). 380p. 1993. 55.00 (*0-300-05575-7*) Yale U Pr.

— Great Stone Circles: Fables, Fictions, Facts. LC 98-34056. (Illus.). 216p. 1999. 30.00 (*0-300-07689-4*) Yale U Pr.

— Prehistoric Astronomy & Ritual. (Archaeology Ser.: No. 32). (Illus.). 32p. 1983. pap. 10.50 (*0-85263-621-0*, Pub. by Shire Pubns) Parkwest Pubns.

— Prehistoric Henges. (Archaeology Ser.: No. 66). (Illus.). 64p. 1989. pap. 10.50 (*0-7478-0123-1*, Pub. by Shire Pubns) Parkwest Pubns.

— Prehistoric Stone Circles, 9. (Archaeology Ser.: No. 98). (Illus.). 52p. 1999. pap. 10.50 (*0-85263-962-7*, Pub. by Shire Pubns) Parkwest Pubns.

— Stone Circles: A Guide to the Megalithic Rings of Britain, Ireland & Brittany. LC 94-23685. 1995. 14.00 (*0-300-06331-8*) Yale U Pr.

***Burl, Aubrey.** Stone Circles of Britain, Ireland & Brittany. LC 99-87909. (Illus.). 416p. 2000. 60.00 (*0-300-08347-5*) Yale U Pr.

Burl, Jeffrey B. Linear Optimal Control. LC 98-36516. 432p. (C). 1998. 95.00 (*0-201-80868-4*, Prentice Hall) P-H.

Burlaga, Leonard F. Interplanetary Magnetohydrodynamics. (International Series in Astronomy & Astrophysics: No. 8). (Illus.). 272p. 1995. text 90.00 (*0-19-508472-1*) OUP.

Burlage, L. Charles. Let the River Flow. (Illus.). 500p. (Orig.). 1986. pap. 14.95 (*0-9616208-0-3*) Burlage Corp.

Burlage, Robert S., et al, eds. Techniques in Microbial Ecology. LC 96-49666. (Illus.). 480p. (Orig.). 1998. spiral bd. 65.00 (*0-19-509223-6*) OUP.

Burlak, Raelle. Fabric Painting. LC 98-110377. (Illus.). 96p. 1997. pap. text 14.95 (*1-86351-207-1*, Pub. by Sally Milner) Sterling.

Burlakoff, Nikolai & Lindahl, Carl, eds. Folklore on Two Continents: Essays in Honor of Linda Degh. LC 81-141572. (Illus.). 388p. (Orig.). (C). 1980. pap. 12.95 (*0-915305-01-1*) Trickster Pr.

***Burlakova, E. B., ed.** Consequences of the Chernobyl Catastrophe on Human Health. 278p. 1999. lib. bdg. 129.00 (*1-56072-699-7*) Nova Sci Pubs.

Burlakova, E. B., ed. Radiobiological Disasters: Consequences of Accidents at Nuclear Power Stations. 257p. (C). 1994. lib. bdg. 145.00 (*1-56072-195-2*) Nova Sci Pubs.

Burlamaqui, Jean-Jaques. Principes du Droit Naturel. xxiv, 473p. 1984. reprint ed. 95.00 (*3-487-07400-1*) G Olms Pubs.

— The Principles of Natural & Politic Law. 5th ed. Nugent, Thomas, tr. LC 70-38249. (Evolution of Capitalism Ser.). 500p. 1972. reprint ed. 38.95 (*0-405-04114-4*) Ayer.

***Burlamaqui, Leonardo, et al.** Institutions & the Role of the State. LC 00-34731. (New Horizons in Institutional & Evolutionary Economics Ser.). 2000. write for info. (*1-84064-311-0*) E Elgar.

Burland, C. A., comment. Codex Fejervary-Mayer. fac. ed. (Codices Selecti C Ser.: Vol. XXVI). 46p. 1971. lthr. 320.00 (*3-201-00764-1*, Pub. by Akademische Druck-und) Balogh.

Burland, C. A., intro. Codex Egerton 1895. fac. ed. (Codices Selecti C Ser.: Vol. VII). 1965. lthr. 427.00 (*3-201-00758-7*, Pub. by Akademische Druck-und) Balogh.

— Codex Laud. fac. ed. (Codices Selecti C Ser.: Vol. XI). (Illus.). 48p. 1966. lthr. 320.00 (*3-201-00761-7*, Pub. by Akademische Druck-und) Balogh.

Burland, Cottie A. Ancient China. (Great Civilization Ser.). (Illus.). (J). (gr. 4-8). 1974. reprint ed. 13.95 (*0-7175-0018-7*) Dufour.

— Ancient Egypt. (Great Civilization Ser.). (Illus.). (J). (gr. 4-8). 1974. reprint ed. 13.95 (*0-7175-0014-4*) Dufour.

— Ancient Rome. (Great Civilization Ser.). (Illus.). (J). (gr. 4-8). 1974. reprint ed. 13.95 (*0-7175-0015-2*) Dufour.

— The Arts of the Alchemists. LC 79-8598. reprint ed. 49.50 (*0-404-18451-0*) AMS Pr.

— Way of the Buddha. (Way Ser.). 64p. (J). (gr. 3-7). 1988. pap. 10.95 (*0-7175-0590-1*) Dufour.

Burland, Harris. Dacobra: or The White Priests of Ahriman. 1979. reprint ed. 8.50 (*0-686-53053-5*) Bookfinger.

Burland, J. B. & Mitchell, J. M., eds. Piling & Deep Foundations: Proceedings of the 3rd International Conference, London, 15-18 May 1989. 700p. (C). 1989. text 304.00 (*90-6191-889-8*, Pub. by A A Balkema) Ashgate Pub Co.

Burlant, Arlene. Secrets of Lactose-Free Cooking: Over 150 Easy-to-Make & Delicious Dairy-Free Recipes - From Breakfast to Dinner. LC 95-50595. 192p. 1996. pap. 13.95 (*0-89529-724-8*, Avery) Penguin Putnam.

Burlatskiy. The Renovation of Socialism. Date not set. text. write for info. (*0-08-037102-7*, Pergamon Pr) Elsevier.

***Burleigh.** Hercules. (Illus.). (J). 1999. 25.26 (*0-7398-1482-6*) Raintree Steck-V.

Burleigh. Home Run: Story of Babe Ruth. (J). 1998. 16.00 (*0-15-202115-9*) Harcourt.

Burleigh, Anne H. Journey up the River. LC 94-77461. 220p. (Orig.). 1994. pap. 11.95 (*0-89870-468-5*) Ignatius Pr.

Burleigh, Anne H., ed. Education in a Free Society. LC 73-78807. 188p. 1973. 8.00 (*0-913966-00-2*) Liberty Fund.

Burleigh, Charles. The Genealogy & History of the Guild Guile & Gile Family. (Illus.). 381p. 1989. reprint ed. pap. 57.00 (*0-8328-0620-X*); reprint ed. lib. bdg. 65.00 (*0-8328-0619-6*) Higginson Bk Co.

— The Genealogy & History of the Ingalls Family Giving the Descendants of Edmund Ingalls Who Settled in Lynn, Mass. in 1629. (Illus.). 324p. reprint ed. pap. 48.50 (*0-8328-0706-0*); reprint ed. lib. bdg. 56.50 (*0-8328-0705-2*) Higginson Bk Co.

— The Genealogy of the Burley or Burleigh Family of America. (Illus.). 200p. 1989. reprint ed. pap. 40.00 (*0-8328-0349-9*); reprint ed. lib. bdg. 48.00 (*0-8328-0348-0*) Higginson Bk Co.

Burleigh, Charles C. Thoughts on the Death Penalty. LC 82-45657. (Capital Punishment Ser.). 1983. reprint ed. 37.50 (*0-404-62404-9*) AMS Pr.

Burleigh, David & Sato, Hiroaki, eds. Autumn Stone in the Woods: A Tribute to Lindley Williams Hubbell. LC 97-68801. 144p. 1997. pap. 11.95 (*1-889087-03-3*) P S A Pr.

Burleigh, Douglas D., jt. ed. see Winzbach, Richard N.

Burleigh, Harry T. Negro Spirituals, 2 vols. in 1. LC 74-24262. reprint ed. 45.00 (*0-404-12874-2*) AMS Pr.

Burleigh, John S., ed. Augustine: Earlier Writings. LC 53-13043. (Library of Christian Classics). 410p. 1979. pap. 28.95 (*0-664-24162-X*) Westminster John Knox.

Burleigh, Marta. There Is a Choice. LC 93-61661. 336p. 1994. pap. 12.95 (*0-9639519-3-9*) Whitewing Pr.

Burleigh, Michael. Confronting the Nazi Past. (History Today Bk.). (Illus.). 198p. 1998. pap. 19.95 (*1-85585-411-2*, Pub. by Collins & Br) Trafalgar.

— Confronting the Nazi Past. LC 96-25793. 200p. 1996. text 39.95 (*0-312-16353-3*) St Martin.

— Ethics & Extermination: Reflections on Nazi Genocide. LC 96-47660. 274p. (C). 1997. text 54.95 (*0-521-58211-3*); pap. text 17.95 (*0-521-58816-2*) Cambridge U Pr.

***Burleigh, Michael.** The Third Reich: A New History. (Illus.). 864p. 2000. 40.00 (*0-8090-9325-1*) Hill & Wang.

Burleigh, Michael & Wipperman, Wolfgang. The Racial State: Germany, 1933-1945. (Illus.). 416p. (C). 1991. 54.95 (*0-521-39114-8*) Cambridge U Pr.

— The Racial State: Germany, 1933-1945. (Illus.). 402p. (C). 1993. pap. text 24.95 (*0-521-39802-9*) Cambridge U Pr.

Burleigh, Nina. A Very Private Woman: The Life & Unsolved Murder of Presidential Mistress Mary Meyer. 368p. 1999. pap. 13.95 (*0-553-38051-6*) Bantam.

Burleigh, Robert. Black Whiteness: Admiral Byrd Alone in the Antarctic. LC 96-21999. (Illus.). 40p. (J). (gr. 2-7). 1998. 16.00 (*0-689-81299-X*) S&S Childrens.

***Burleigh, Robert.** Edna. LC 99-42667. (Illus.). 32p. (J). (gr. k-4). 2000. lib. bdg. 16.99 (*0-531-33246-2*) Orchard Bks Watts.

Burleigh, Robert. Flight. LC 90-35401. (Illus.). 32p. (J). (ps up). 1997. pap. 5.99 (*0-698-11425-6*, PapStar) Peng Put Young Read.

— Flight. 1997. 11.15 (*0-606-11336-3*, Pub. by Turtleback) Demco.

— Flight: The Journey of Charles Lindbergh. LC 90-35401. (Illus.). 32p. (J). (ps-3). 1991. 15.95 (*0-399-22272-3*, Philomel) Peng Put Young Read.

***Burleigh, Robert.** Goal. LC 98-33181. 2001. write for info. (*0-15-201789-5*) Harcourt.

Burleigh, Robert. Hercules. LC 98-4989. 32p. (J). 1999. 16.00 (*0-15-201667-8*, Harcourt Child Bks) Harcourt.

— Home Run. (J). (gr. 1-5). 1998. 24.26 (*0-8172-5764-0*) Raintree Steck-V.

— Home Run: The Story of Babe Ruth. LC 95-10038. (Illus.). 32p. (J). (gr. k-4). 1998. 16.00 (*0-15-200970-1*) Harcourt.

— Hoops. LC 96-18440. (Illus.). 32p. (J). (gr. k up). 1997. 16.00 (*0-15-201450-0*) Harcourt.

Burleigh, Robert. I Love Going Through This Book. (Illus.). 40p. (J). (ps-3). 5.95 (*0-06-443647-0*) HarpC.

— I Love Going Through This Book. LC 99-88386. 40p. (J). (ps-3). 2001. 15.95 (*0-06-028805-1*); lib. bdg. 15.89 (*0-06-028806-X*) HarpC Child Bks.

Burleigh, Robert. It's Funny Where Ben's Train Takes Him. LC 98-10483. (Illus.). 32p. (J). (ps-2). 1999. 15.95 (*0-531-30106-0*) Orchard Bks Watts.

— A Man Named Thoreau. LC 85-7947. (Illus.). 48p. (J). (gr. 3 up). 1985. 15.00 (*0-689-31122-2*) Atheneum Yung Read.

— Messenger, Messenger. LC 98-20566. (J). 2000. 17.00 (*0-689-82103-4*) Atheneum Yung Read.

— Who Said That? LC 96-19985. (J). 1995. 15.95 (*0-8050-4394-2*) H Holt & Co.

***Burleigh, Robert & Gore, Leonid.** The Secrets of the Great Houdini. LC 00-38057. (Illus.). 2002. write for info. (*0-689-83267-2*) Atheneum Yung Read.

***Burleigh, Robert, et al.** Edna. LC 99-42667. (Illus.). 32p. (J). (gr. k-4). 2000. 15.95 (*0-531-30246-6*) Orchard Bks Watts.

Burleigh, Ruth M. Grandma & the Hills Vol. 1: Spirit of the Hills. (Orig.). 1995. pap. 7.00 (*1-887804-02-1*) Cent Mont Pubng.

Burleigh, William G. Revenue Agent: Life & Death Exploits of a Prohibition Agent in West Virginia. 2nd ed. Wallace, David B., ed. & photos by by. (Illus.). 52p. 1995. pap. 4.75 (*1-889074-00-4*) Elkhorn Pr.

Burlend, Edward, jt. auth. see Burlend, Rebecca.

Burlend, Rebecca & Burlend, Edward. A True Picture of Emigration. Quaife, Milo M., ed. LC 86-25114. (Illus.). xxxi, 167p. 1987. reprint ed. pap. text 10.95 (*0-8032-6083-0*, Bison Books) U of Nebr Pr.

***Burles, Heather.** Smouldering Incense, Hammered Brass: A Syrian Interlude. 190p. 1999. pap. 14.95 (*0-88801-237-3*, Pub. by Turnstone Pr) Genl Dist Srvs.

Burles, Kenneth T. Broken Bones. LC 98-22379. (Learning about Your Health Ser.). (J). 1998. (*1-57103-253-3*) Rourke Pr.

— Broken Bones. LC 98-3422. (Learning about Your Health Ser.). (J). 1998. 19.93 (*0-86625-652-0*) Rourke Pubns.

— Fever. LC 98-7654. (Learning about Your Health Ser.). 32p. (J). (ps-4). 1998. 14.95 (*1-57103-256-8*) Rourke Pr.

— Fever. LC 98-3423. (Learning about Your Health Ser.). (J). 1998. 14.95 (*0-86625-651-2*) Rourke Pubns.

— Tonsillitis. LC 98-22381. (Learning about Your Health Ser.). 32p. (J). (ps-4). 1998. 14.95 (*1-57103-257-6*) Rourke Pr.

Burles, Mark. Chinese Policy Toward Russia & the Central Asian Republics. LC 99-21022. (Illus.). xi, 76p. 1999. pap. 15.00 (*0-8330-2731-X*, MR-1045-AF) Rand Corp.

***Burles, Mark & Shulsky, Abram N.** Patterns in China's Use of Force: Evidence from History & Doctrinal Writings. LC 99-88091. xv, 106p. (C). 2000. pap. 12.00 (*0-8330-2804-9*, MR-1060-AF) Rand Corp.

Burleson. Communication Yearbook, Vol. 19. 89.95 (*0-7619-0165-5*) Sage.

Burleson. High Performance Oracle8 Tuning. 650p. 1997. 49.99 incl. cd-rom (*1-57610-217-3*) Coriolis Grp.

— Virology: A Laboratory Manual. 17p. 1992. teacher ed. 6.00 (*0-12-144731-6*) Acad Pr.

Burleson, Bob. Runic Meaning in Texas Cattle Brands: Plays of the Organic Theatre. 2nd rev. ed. LC 94-61670. (Illus.). 541p. 1995. 24.95 (*0-913699-89-6*); pap. 16.95 (*0-913699-88-8*) Worksworth.

Burleson, Bob & Riskind, David H. Backcountry Mexico: A Traveler's Guide & Phrase Book. (Illus.). 335p. 1986. pap. 14.95 (*0-292-70755-X*) U of Tex Pr.

Burleson, Brant, et al, eds. The Communication of Social Support: Messages, Interactions, Relationships, & Community. LC 93-40639. 304p. (C). 1994. text 48.00 (*0-8039-4350-4*); pap. text 21.50 (*0-8039-4351-2*) Sage.

Burleson, Brant R., ed. Communication Yearbook. 500p. 1996. 85.00 (*0-7619-0686-X*) Sage.

— Communication Yearbook, Vol. 18. (Illus.). 610p. 1994. 79.95 (*0-8039-5925-7*) Sage.

— Communication Yearbook, Vol. 19. 544p. 1995. 59.95 (*0-8309-0165-5*) Sage.

***Burleson, Clyde W.** Deep Challenges Our Quest for Energy Beneath the Sea. 1998. 24.95 (*0-88415-219-7*) Gulf Pub.

Burleson, Clyde W. The Jennifer Project. LC 97-2882. (Illus.). 180p. (C). 1997. pap. 13.95 (*0-89096-764-4*) Tex A&M Univ Pr.

Burleson, Clyde W. & Burleson, Suzy W. A Guide to the Texas Medical Center. (Illus.). 160p. 1987. pap. 7.95 (*0-292-72727-5*) U of Tex Pr.

***Burleson, Derick.** Ejo. 2000. 18.95 (*0-299-17020-9*); pap. 11.95 (*0-299-17024-1*) U of Wis Pr.

Burleson, Derick, ed. see Ali, Agha Shahid, et al.

Burleson, Donald. High Performance Oracle Data Warehousing. 10th ed. LC 98-123570. 450p. (C). 1997. mass mkt. 39.99 (*1-57610-154-1*) Coriolis Grp.

Burleson, Donald K. Inside the DB Object Model. LC 98-6349. 1998. lib. bdg. 69.95 (*0-8493-1807-6*) CRC Pr.

— Managing Distributed Databases: Building Bridges Between Database Islands. LC 95-48350. 384p. 1995. pap. 59.99 (*0-471-08623-1*) Wiley.

— Oracle Databases on the Web. 10th ed. LC 97-154645. 592p. (C). 1997. mass mkt. 39.99 (*1-57610-099-5*) Coriolis Grp.

— Oracle SAP Administration. Estabrook, Virginia & Russell, Deborah, eds. (Illus.). 352p. 1999. pap. 32.95 (*1-56592-696-X*) OReilly & Assocs.

— Practical Application of Object-Oriented Techniques to Relational Databases. 250p. 1994. 64.99 (*0-471-61225-1*) Wiley.

Burleson, Donald R. Arroyo. LC 98-93529. 258p. 1999. pap. 14.95 (*0-9649580-2-3*) Black Mesa.

— Beyond the Lamplight: Stories from the Dark. Aniolowski, Scott D., ed. LC 96-69853. (Illus.). 340p. (Orig.). 1996. pap. 14.95 (*1-57502-274-5*, PO971) Morris Pubng.

— Flute Song. LC 95-96038. 214p. 1995. pap. 9.95 (*0-9649580-0-7*) Black Mesa.

— H. P. Lovecraft: A Critical Study, 5. LC 82-24186. (Contributions to the Study of Science Fiction & Fantasy Ser.: No. 5). 243p. 1983. 59.95 (*0-313-23255-5*, BUL/, Greenwood Pr) Greenwood.

— Lovecraft: Disturbing the Universe. LC 90-37366. 184p. 1990. text 24.95 (*0-8131-1728-3*) U Pr of Ky.

— The Roswell Crewman. 2nd rev. ed. LC 95-96038. 220p. 1997. reprint ed. pap. 12.95 (*0-9649580-1-5*) Black Mesa.

Burleson, Florence G., et al. Virology: A Laboratory Manual. (Illus.). 250p. 1992. spiral bd. 21.00 (*0-12-144730-8*) Acad Pr.

Burleson, Gary B., et al, eds. Methods in Immunotoxicology, Vol. 1. LC 95-979. 552p. 1995. 339.50 (*0-471-56196-7*, Wiley-Liss) Wiley.

Burleson, Gary R., et al, eds. Methods in Immunotoxicology, 2 vols. LC 95-979. 1048p. 1995. 350.00 (*0-471-30597-9*, Wiley-Liss) Wiley.

— Methods in Immunotoxicology, Vol. 2. LC 95-979. 496p. 1995. 339.50 (*0-471-56197-5*, Wiley-Liss) Wiley.

Burleson, Joe, ed. see Kelley, Sandy.

Burleson, Noyce, jt. auth. see Moliere.

Burleson, Scott, jt. auth. see Carter, W. Horace.

Burleson, Suzy W., jt. auth. see Burleson, Clyde W.

Burlew, A. Kathleen, et al, eds. African American Psychology: Theory, Research, & Practice. (Illus.). 400p. (C). 1992. 55.00 (*0-8039-4765-8*); pap. 28.00 (*0-8039-4766-6*) Sage.

Burlew, John S., ed. Algal Culture: From Laboratory to Pilot Plant. (Illus.). 366p. 1953. 20.00 (*0-87279-611-6*, 600) Carnegie Inst.

Burlew, John S., intro. The Connecticut Walk Book. 16th ed. (Illus.). 1990. 15.96 (*0-9619052-1-2*) CT Forest & Pk Assn.

***Burley.** Hatha-Yoga: Its Context, Theory & Practice. 2000. 29.50 (*81-208-1705-2*, Pub. by Motilal Bnarsidass); pap. 18.50 (*81-208-1706-0*, Pub. by Motilal Bnarsidass) S Asia.

Burley, Adam, et al. Questions on the De Anima of Aristotle. (Studien und Texte zur Geistesgeschichte des Mittelalters). (ENG & LAT.). lxiv, 179p. 1996. 97.00 (*90-04-10655-3*) Brill Academic Pubs.

Burley-Allen. Listening: The Forgotten Skill & Managing Assertively:How to Improve Your People Skills. 2nd ed. 418p. pap. 29.90 (*0-471-12376-5*) Wiley.

Burley-Allen, Madelyn. Listening - The Forgotten Skill: A Self-Teaching Guide. 2nd ed. (Self-Teaching Guides Ser.). 208p. 1995. pap. 16.95 (*0-471-01587-3*) Wiley.

— Managing Assertively: How to Improve Your People Skills. 2nd ed. LC 94-32607. (Self-Teaching Guides Ser.). 240p. 1995. pap. 17.95 (*0-471-03971-3*) Wiley.

— Memory Skills in Business. (Better Management Skills Ser.). 1990. pap. 12.95 (*0-7494-0153-2*) Kogan Page Ltd.

Burley-Allen, Madelyn, jt. auth. see Crisp, Michael G.

Burley, D. M., et al, eds. Pharmaceutical Medicine. 2nd ed. 384p. 1993. text 80.00 (*0-340-52517-7*, Pub. by E A) OUP.

Burley, David, jt. auth. see James, Glyn.

Burley, David G. A Particular Condition in Life: Self-Employment & Social Mobility in Mid-Victorian Brantford, Ontario. 328p. 1994. 60.00 (*0-7735-1199-7*, Pub. by McG-Queens Univ Pr) CUP Services.

Burley, David V., et al. Prophecy of the Swan: The Upper Peace River Fur Trade of 1794-1823. 1996. pap. 25.95 (*0-7748-0545-5*) U of Wash Pr.

Burley, Edith I. Servants of the Honourable Company: Work, Discipline & Conflict in the Hudson's Bay Company, 1770-1870. (Canadian Social History Ser.). (Illus.). 230p. 1998. pap. text 22.95 (*0-19-541296-6*) OUP.

Burley, Gertrude S., jt. auth. see Gard, Robert E.

Burley, Gibson J. & Speight, Martin R. The Adoption of Agricultural Practices for the Development of Heritable Resistance to Pests & Pathogens in Forest Crops. 1980. 60.00 (*0-85074-057-6*) St Mut.

Burley, J. & Nikles, D. C. Selection & Breeding to Improve Some Tropical Conifers, 2 Vols., 1. 1972. 110.00 (*0-85074-026-6*) St Mut.

— Selection & Breeding to Improve Some Tropical Conifers, 2 Vols., 2. 1972. 110.00 (*0-85074-027-4*) St Mut.

Burley, J. & Nikles, G. Tropical Provenance & Progeny Research & International Cooperation. 1973. 100.00 (*0-85074-022-3*) St Mut.

Burley, J. & Palmer, E. R. Pulp & Wood Densitometric Properties of Pinus Caribaea from Fiji. 1979. 50.00 (*0-85074-046-0*) St Mut.

Burley, J. & Wood, P. J. A Manual on Species & Provenance Research with Particular Reference to the Tropics. 1976. 62.50 (*0-85074-016-9*) St Mut.

— A Manual on Species & Provenance Research with Particular Reference to the Tropics. 1977. 30.00 (*0-85074-024-X*) St Mut.

— Manual Sobre Investigaciones de Especies y Procedencias con Referencia Especial a Los Tropicos. 1979. 50.00 (*0-85074-058-4*) St Mut.

Burley, J., jt. auth. see Armitage, F. B.

Burley, Joanne, jt. auth. see Scales, Alice M.

Burley, Justine, ed. The Genetic Revolution & Human Rights: The Oxford Amnesty Lectures 1998. (Popular Science Ser.). 220p. 1999. pap. 14.95 (*0-19-286201-4*) OUP.

Burley, Kay, jt. auth. see Hopkins, Cathy.

Burley, M. A. & Coleman, M. J., eds. Fifteenth National Passive Solar Conference Proceedings. (Illus.). 550p. (Orig.). (C). 1990. per. 100.00 (*0-89553-206-9*) Am Solar Energy.

— Solar 90: Annual Conference Proceedings of the American Solar Energy Society. (Illus.). 515p. (Orig.). (C). 1990. per. 100.00 (*0-89553-163-1*) Am Solar Energy.

Burley, N. T., jt. ed. see Parker, P. G.

Burley, Nancy, jt. auth. see Willson, Mary F.

Burley, Peter & Foster, John, eds. Economics & Thermodynamics: New Perspectives on Economic Analysis. LC 94-18357. (Recent Economic Thought Ser.). 272p. (C). 1994. lib. bdg. 106.00 (*0-7923-9446-1*) Kluwer Academic.

Burley, Philip K., ed. & intro. see Stead, W. T. & Woodman, Pardoe.

An Asterisk (*) at the beginning of an entry indicates that the title is appearing for the first time.

Burley, R. W. & Vadehra, D. The Avian Egg: Chemistry & Biology. LC 88-28191. 472p. 1989. 265.00 (*0-471-84995-2*) Wiley.

Burley, S. Contemporary Community Nursing. Chilton, S. et al, eds. 256p. (Orig.). 1997. pap. 32.50 (*1-56593-822-4*, 1616) Singular Publishing.

Burley, S., jt. auth. see Arden, M.

***Burley, W. J.** Death in Willow Pattern. large type unabridged ed. 251p. 1999. 25.95 (*0-7531-5994-5*, 159945, Pub. by ISIS Lrg Prnt) ISIS Pub.

Burley, W. J. A Taste of Power. large type ed. (Magna Large Print Ser.). 434p. 1998. 29.99 (*0-7505-1169-9*, Pub. by Mgna Lrg Print) Ulverscroft.

— Wycliffe & Death in Stanley Street. large type ed. (Magna Large Print Ser.). 295p. 1997. 27.50 (*0-7505-1143-5*, Pub. by Mgna Lrg Print) Ulverscroft.

— Wycliffe & How to Kill a Cat. large type ed. (Magna Large Print Ser.). 303p. 1997. 27.50 (*0-7505-1120-6*) Thorndike Pr.

***Burley, W. J.** Wycliffe & the Cycle of Death. 2000. pap. 8.95 (*0-552-14109-7*, Pub. by Transworld Publishers Ltd) Trafalgar.

— Wycliffe & the Dead Flautist. 2000. pap. 8.95 (*0-552-14264-6*, Pub. by Transworld Publishers Ltd) Trafalgar.

Burley, W. J. Wycliffe & the Four Jacks. 1994. mass mkt. 5.99 (*0-552-14267-0*) Bantam.

***Burley, W. J.** Wycliffe & the Last Rites. 2000. pap. 8.95 (*0-552-14265-4*, Pub. by Transworld Publishers Ltd) Trafalgar.

Burley, W. J. Wycliffe & the Pea Green Boat. 208p. 1993. mass mkt. 4.99 (*0-552-12804-X*) Bantam.

— Wycliffe & the Quiet Virgin. 176p. 1988. mass mkt. 2.95 (*0-380-70510-9*, Avon Bks) Morrow Avon.

— Wycliffe & the Redhead. LC 98-33885. 192p. 1998. text 20.95 (*0-312-19374-2*) St Martin.

— Wycliffe & the Schoolgirls. 1987. mass mkt. 3.95 (*0-552-12805-8*) Bantam.

***Burley, W. J.** Wycliffe & the Tangled Web. 2000. pap. 8.95 (*0-552-14268-9*, Pub. by Transworld Publishers Ltd) Trafalgar.

Burley, W. J. Wycliffe & the Three-Toed Pussy. large type ed. (Magna Large Print Ser.). 320p. 1996. 25.99 (*0-7505-0963-5*, Pub. by Mgna Lrg Print) Ulverscroft.

— Wycliffe & Winsor Blue. 1997. mass mkt. 6.99 (*0-552-13436-8*) Bantam.

***Burley, W. J.** Wycliffe's Wild Goose Chase. (J). 2000. pap. 8.95 (*0-552-14269-7*, Pub. by Transworld Publishers Ltd) Trafalgar.

Burley, Walter. In Physicam Aristotelis Expositio Et Quaestiones. 200p. 1972. reprint ed. write for info. (*3-487-04143-X*) G Olms Pubs.

***Burley, Walter.** On the Purity of the Art of Logic: The Shorter & the Longer Treatises. Spade, Paul V., tr. 384p. 2000. 60.00 (*0-300-08200-2*) Yale U Pr.

Burliegh, David, ed. Black Belt Client/Server Software Development. (Black Belt Ser.). (Illus.). 352p. 1997. pap. 34.95 (*0-87930-498-7*) C M P Books.

Burlin, Bernadine E. Hero: Personal Experiences with Darwin Gross. LC 99-163303. 202p. 1998. pap. 16.95 (*0-931689-49-X*) Be Good To Your Self.

***Burlin, Carl.** Personal Investment Planning. 560p. 1999. pap. 120.00 (*0-85297-561-9*, Pub. by Chartered Bank) St Mut.

Burlina, A. & Galzigna, L. Clinical Enzymology Symposia Vl. 4: Proceedings of the 10th International Symposium 1984. 212p. 1984. text 64.00 (*1-57235-051-2*) Piccin Nuova.

— Clinical Enzymology Symposia Vol. 1: Proceedings of the 7th International Symposium, April 1976. 382p. 1977. text 28.00 (*1-57235-048-2*) Piccin Nuova.

— Clinical Enzymology Symposia Vol. 2: Proceedings of the 8th International Symposium, April 1978. 646p. 1980. text 36.00 (*1-57235-049-0*) Piccin Nuova.

— Clinical Enzymology Symposia Vol. 3: Proceedings of the 9th International Symposium, April 1980. 222p. 1980. text 24.00 (*1-57235-050-4*) Piccin Nuova.

— Clinical Enzymology Symposia Vol. 5: Proceedings of the 11th International Symposium 1984. 212p. 1986. pap. text 24.00 (*1-57235-052-0*) Piccin Nuova.

Burling, Ed. Human Biology Lab Book. 1998. text, lab manual ed. 10.11 (*1-56870-327-9*) RonJon Pub.

Burling, Irving R., jt. auth. see Whitsett, David A.

Burling, Marlene L. Grandma Tell Me the Easter Story. (Illus.). 45p. (J). (gr. k-4). 1998. pap. 7.25 (*1-55630-889-2*) Brentwood Comm.

Burling, Robbins. Hill Farms & Padi Fields: Life in Mainland SE Asia. LC 98-127592. x, 170p. (C). 1992. reprint ed. pap. text 12.95 (*1-881044-00-9*) ASU Prog SE Asian.

***Burling, Robbins.** Learning a Field Language. 112p. (C). 2000. pap. 9.95 (*1-57766-123-0*) Waveland Pr.

Burling, Robbins. Patterns of Language: Structure, Variation, Change. (Illus.). 461p. 1992. pap. text 39.95 (*0-12-144920-3*) Acad Pr.

— Proto Lolo-Burmese. LC 66-64406. (General Publications: Vol. 43). (Orig.). 1967. pap. text 16.00 (*0-87750-131-9*) Res Inst Inner Asian Studies.

Burling, William J. A Checklist of New Plays & Entertainments on the London Stage, 1700-1737. LC 90-56230. 240p. 1993. 35.00 (*0-8386-3451-6*) Fairleigh Dickinson.

***Burling, William J.** Summer Theatre in London, 1661-1820 & the Rise of the Haymarket Theatre. LC 99-42203. 328p. 2000. 45.00 (*0-8386-3811-2*) Fairleigh Dickinson.

Burlingame. The Newmans of Hollywood. 2000. 32.50 (*0-02-864770-X*) S&S Trade.

***Burlingame, A. L., et al, eds.** Mass Spectrometry in Biology & Medicine. LC 99-23633. 592p. 1999. 150.00 (*0-89603-799-1*) Humana.

Burlingame, A. L. & Carr, Steven A., eds. Mass Spectrometry in the Biological Sciences. LC 95-38333. 584p. 1996. 175.00 (*0-89603-340-6*) Humana.

***Burlingame, Anne & Horn, Barbara, eds.** Philbrook: The Perfect Setting, 2000. 128p. 1999. 16.95 (*0-86659-019-6*) Philbrook Mus Art.

Burlingame, Anne E. Battle of the Books in Its Historical Setting. LC 68-54230. 1969. reprint ed. 30.00 (*0-8196-0224-8*) Biblo.

Burlingame, Beverley, jt. ed. see Gottesman, Alice J.

Burlingame, Burl. Advance Force-Pearl Harbor. (Illus.). 480p. (Orig.). 1993. pap. 22.00 (*0-9629227-1-4*) Pacific Mono.

Burlingame, Burl, jt. auth. see Brown, DeSoto.

Burlingame, Burt B., jt. auth. see Shultis, Arthur.

Burlingame, Dwight, ed. Library Development: A Future Imperative. LC 89-33331. (Journal of Library Administration: Vol. 12, No. 4). 152p. 1990. text 39.95 (*1-56024-030-X*) Haworth Pr.

— Library Fundraising: Models for Success. 95p. (Orig.). 1995. pap. 30.00 (*0-8389-0657-5*, 0657-5-2045) ALA.

Burlingame, Dwight F. Critical Issues in Fund Raising. LC 96-39628. (NSFRE-Wiley Fund Development Ser.). 266p. 1997. 45.00 (*0-471-17465-3*) Wiley.

Burlingame, Dwight F., ed. The Responsibilities of Wealth. LC 91-17000. (Philanthropic Studies). (Illus.). 164p. 1992. text 25.00 (*0-253-31279-5*) Ind U Pr.

Burlingame, Dwight F. & Young, Dennis R., eds. Corporate Philanthropy at the Crossroads. LC 96-3321. (Philanthropic Studies). (Illus.). 200p. 1996. text 29.95 (*0-253-33077-7*) Ind U Pr.

Burlingame, E. W. A Treasury of Buddhist Stories from the Dhammapada Commentary. 250p. 1996. 12.00 (*955-24-0147-X*, Pub. by Buddhist Pub Soc) Vipassana Res Pubns.

Burlingame, Eileen C., jt. ed. see Struble, Leslie J.

Burlingame, Eugene W. Buddhist Legends: Translated from the Original Pali Text of the Dhammapada Commentary, 3 vols., Set. 1999. reprint ed. 110.00 (*81-215-0879-7*, Pub. by M Manoharial) Coronet Bks.

— Buddhist Parables. (C). 1991. reprint ed. 22.00 (*81-208-0738-3*, Pub. by Motilal Bnarsidass) S Asia.

Burlingame, Eugene W., tr. from PLI. Buddhist Legends, 3 vols. (C). 1979. reprint ed. 97.00 (*0-86013-057-6*, Pub. by Pali Text) Elsevier.

Burlingame, Eugene W., tr. see Dhammapadatthakatha.

Burlingame, Gary M., jt. ed. see Fuhriman, Addie.

Burlingame, Joan & Blaschko, Thomas M. Assessment Tools for Recreational Therapy: Red Book, No. 1. 2nd ed. 310p. (C). 1997. reprint ed. 40.00 (*1-882883-31-4*, 160) Idyll Arbor.

Burlingame, Joan & Skalko, Thomas K. Idyll Arbor's Glossary for Therapists. LC 97-19810. (Illus.). 294p. 1997. pap. 35.00 (*1-882883-14-4*, 320) Idyll Arbor.

Burlingame, Joan, ed. see Cunninghis, Richelle N. & Best-Martini, Elizabeth.

Burlingame, Joan, ed. see Hoss, M. A.

***Burlingame, Jon.** Sound & Vision: 60 Years of Motion Picture Soundtracks. (Illus.). 288p. 2000. pap. write for info. (*0-8230-8427-2*) Watsn-Guptill.

— TV's Biggest Hits: The Story of Television Themes from "Dragnet" to "Friends" (Illus.). 338p. 2000. reprint ed. 25.00 (*0-7881-9319-8*) DIANE Pub.

Burlingame, Jon & Asner, Edward. For the Record: The Struggle & Ultimate Political Rise of American Recording Musicians Within Their Labor Movement LC 97-68160. xv, 106 p. 1997. write for info. (*0-9658464-0-7*) Rec Musicians.

Burlingame, Merrill G., ed. & frwd. see Callaway, Lew L., Jr.

Burlingame, Michael. The Inner World of Abraham Lincoln. LC 93-34650. (Illus.). 416p. 1994. 29.95 (*0-252-02086-3*) U of Ill Pr.

— The Inner World of Abraham Lincoln. 416p. 1997. 18.95 (*0-252-06667-7*) U of Ill Pr.

Burlingame, Michael & Ettlinger, John R., eds. Inside Lincoln's White House: The Complete Civil War Diary of John Hay. 1999. pap. 22.95 (*0-8093-2262-5*) S Ill U Pr.

Burlingame, Michael, jt. auth. see Hay, John.

Burlingame, Michael, jt. auth. see Nicolay, John G.

Burlingame, Michael, ed. see Brooks, Noah.

Burlingame, Michael, ed. see Hay, John.

Burlingame, Michael, ed. see Stevens, Walter B.

Burlingame, Michael, ed. & intro. see Stoddard, William O.

Burlingame, Roger. Don't Let Them Scare You. LC 73-212184. (Illus.). 352p. 1974. reprint ed. lib. bdg. 65.00 (*0-8371-6146-0*, BUSY, Greenwood Pr) Greenwood.

— Engines of Democracy: Inventions & Society in Mature America. LC 75-22804. (America in Two Centuries Ser.). (Illus.). 1976. reprint ed. 53.95 (*0-405-07676-2*) Ayer.

— General Billy Mitchell: Champion of Air Defense. LC 77-26823. (They Made America Ser.). (Illus.). 212p. 1978. reprint ed. lib. bdg. 35.00 (*0-313-20170-6*, BUGM, Greenwood Pr) Greenwood.

— March of the Iron Men: A Social History of Union Through Invention. LC 75-22805. (America in Two Centuries Ser.). (Illus.). 1976. reprint ed. 46.95 (*0-405-07677-0*) Ayer.

— Of Making Many Books: A Hundred Years of Reading, Writing, & Publishing. LC 96-14230. (History of the Bk.). (Illus.). 386p. 1996. reprint ed. 55.00 (*0-271-01619-1*); reprint ed. pap. 19.95 (*0-271-01611-6*) Pa St U Pr.

***Burlingame, Virginia S.** Ethnogerocounseling: Counseling Ethnic Elders & Their Families. LC 98-28250. (Series on Life Styles & Issues in Aging). 1998. 39.95 (*0-8261-1217-X*) Springer Pub.

Burlingame, Virginia S. Gerocounseling: Counseling Elders & Their Families. LC 94-43090. (Life Styles & Issues in Aging Ser.). 232p. 1995. 36.95 (*0-8261-8820-6*) Springer Pub.

Burlingham, Bo, jt. auth. see Stack, Jack.

Burlingham-Brown, Barbara. Why Didn't She Keep Me? Answers to the Question Every Adopted Child Asks. 2nd rev. ed. LC 93-29241. 183p. 1994. pap. 12.95 (*1-888698-14-4*, Langford Bks) Diamond Communications.

Burlingham, Cynthia, ed. William Brice: Works on Paper, 1982-1992. LC 93-16424. 1993. 25.00 (*0-9628762-1-3*) Grunwald Arts.

Burlingham, Cynthia & Shepherd, Elizabeth, eds. In the Sculptor's Landscape: Celebrating Twenty-Five Years of the Franklin D. Murphy Sculpture Garden. LC 93-667. 1993. 25.00 (*0-943739-17-9*) F S Wight Art.

Burlingham, Dorothy. Twins: A Study of Three Pairs of Twins (with 30 Charts) LC 53-6599. 230p. reprint ed. pap. 71.30 (*0-608-11208-9*, 201070200070) Bks Demand.

Burlingham, Dorothy T., jt. auth. see Freud, Anna.

Burlingham, William J. A Critical Analysis of Monoclonal Therapy in Transplantation. 304p. 1991. lib. bdg. 139.00 (*0-8493-6821-9*, RC1235) CRC Pr.

Burlington County GSC Staff. Kettle's On. LC 90-34910. 1994. 11.95 (*0-87197-275-1*) Favorite Recipes.

Burlington, Felipe. Alabanza y Adoracion: Canciones Contemporaneas.Tr. of Contemporary Hymns. (SPA.). 48p. 1997. pap. text 4.99 (*0-311-32249-2*) Casa Bautista.

***Burlington Fine Arts Club, London Staff.** Catalogue of an Exhibition of Objects of Indigenous American Art. (LC History-America-E). 85p. 1999. reprint ed. lib. bdg. 69.00 (*0-7812-4280-0*) Rprt Serv.

***Burlinson, Kathryn.** Christina Rossetti. (Writers & Their Works Ser.). 112p. 1998. pap. text 19.00 (*0-7463-0846-9*, Pub. by Northcote House) U Pr of Miss.

Burlison, James. Compendium for Five. 184p. 1999. 17.00 (*0-8059-4724-8*) Dorrance.

Burlison, Steve, jt. ed. see Anderson, Joy.

Burlitch, J. M. Chemical Synthesis in the Laboratory: An Advanced Course. 280p. (C). 1993. text 42.00 (*981-02-0449-3*); pap. text 28.00 (*981-02-0450-7*) World Scientific Pub.

Burls, Amanda, jt. ed. see Bradley, Peter.

Burls, Christine, tr. see Christophe, Francine.

Burman, B. K. Beyond Mandal & After: Backward Classes in Perspective. (C). 1992. 16.00 (*81-7099-384-9*, Pub. by Mittal Pubs Dist) S Asia.

Burman, B. R. Religion & Politics in Tibet. 180p. 1979. 14.95 (*0-7069-0801-5*) Asia Bk Corp.

***Burman, Barbara.** The Culture of Sewing: Gender, Consumption & Homedressmaking. (Dress, Body & Culture Ser.). 1999. pap. text 19.50 (*1-85973-208-9*, Pub. by Berg Pubs) NYU Pr.

Burman, Barbara, ed. The Culture of Sewing: Gender, Consumption & Homedressmaking. (Dress, Body, Culture Ser.). (Illus.). 288p. 1999. 65.00 (*1-85973-203-8*, Pub. by Berg Pubs) NYU Pr.

***Burman, C. P.** Genesis: The Beginning - An Analysis for the Layman. 80p. 1998. pap. 14.95 (*1-890035-10-6*) New Centry Pr.

Burman, Donna L., jt. ed. see White, Suzanne S.

Burman, Edward. The Assassins: Holy Killers of Islam. (Illus.). 208p. (Orig.). 1988. pap. 12.95 (*1-85274-027-2*, Pub. by Crucible Pr) Cavendish Bks.

— Supremely Abominable Crimes: The Trial of the Knights of Templar. 304p. 1995. 21.95 (*0-85031-928-5*) Allison & Busby.

— The Templars: Knights of God. 208p. 1987. pap. 12.95 (*0-89281-221-4*) Inner Tradit.

Burman, Elizabeth. Whose Eyes Are These? LC 97-6790. (J). (ps-1). 1997. 14.99 (*0-8499-1464-7*) Tommy Nelson.

Burman, Erica. Deconstructing Developmental Psychology. LC 93-5880. (Critical Psychology Ser.). 208p. (C). 1994. pap. 24.99 (*0-415-06438-4*) Routledge.

— Deconstructing Feminist Psychology. (Gender & Psychology Ser.: Vol. 10). 224p. (C). 1997. 45.00 (*0-8039-7639-9*); pap. 14.99 (*0-8039-7640-2*) Sage.

Burman, Erica, et al. Challenging Women: Psychology's Exclusions, Feminist Possibilities. LC 95-30473. 210p. 1995. 103.95 (*0-335-19511-3*); pap. 31.95 (*0-335-19510-5*) OpUniv Pr.

Burman, Eva & Ling, Lorraine. Values in Education. LC 98-120480. 240p. (C). 1997. pap. 20.99 (*0-415-15738-2*) Routledge.

— Values in Education. LC 98-120480. 240p. (C). 1997. 75.00 (*0-415-15737-4*) Routledge.

Burman, Howard. An O. Henry Christmas. 64p. 1998. pap. 5.00 (*0-87440-066-X*) Bakers Plays.

***Burman, John F.** The Hollywood Reporter Director Power '98. (Illus.). 20p. 1998. reprint ed. 25.00 (*0-941140-76-8*) Hollywood Rep.

— The Hollywood Reporter Star Power '98: Actors & Actresses. (Illus.). 16p. 1998. reprint ed. 25.00 (*0-941140-75-X*) Hollywood Rep.

— The Hollywood Reporter Star Power '99: Actors & Actresses. (Illus.). 32p. 1999. reprint ed. 35.00 (*0-941140-77-6*) Hollywood Rep.

Burman, L. G., jt. ed. see Nordbring, F.

Burman, Leonard. The Tax Treatment of Employment-Based Health Insurance. (Illus.). 59p. (Orig.). (C). 1994. pap. text 30.00 (*0-7881-1090-X*) DIANE Pub.

Burman, Leonard E. The Labyrinth of Capital Gains Tax Policy: A Guide for the Perplexed. LC 99-6203. 1999. 26.95 (*0-8157-1270-7*) Brookings.

Burman, Lin, tr. see Pare, Francois.

Burman, Madeleine L. Code of the Prophets. LC 84-90888. (Illus.). 112p. (Orig.). 1984. 4.95 (*0-9613283-0-4*); pap. 6.95 (*0-317-00778-5*) M L Burman.

Burman, P. Conserving the Railway Heritage. 244p. (C). (gr. 13). 1996. pap. 55.00 (*0-419-21280-9*) Routledge.

Burman, P. J. Precedence Networks for Project Planning & Control. 1980. pap. text 20.00 (*0-9606344-0-1*) Blitz Pub Co.

Burman, Peter, jt. auth. see Binney, Marcus.

Burman, R. D. & Pochop, L. O. Evaporation, Evapotranspiration & Climatic Data. LC 94-229734. (Developments in Atmospheric Science Ser.: 22). 302p. 1994. 200.50 (*0-444-81940-1*) Elsevier.

Burman, Richard. Manufacturing Management: Principles & Systems. LC 94-44158. 1995. 19.95 (*0-07-709044-6*) McGraw.

Burman, Shirley, jt. auth. see Levinson, Nancy S.

Burman, Stephen. America & the Modern World: Transcendence of United States Hegemony. 224p. 1991. text 45.00 (*0-312-01971-8*) St Martin.

— The Black Progress Question: Explaining the African-American Predicament. (Sage Series on Race & Ethnic Relations: Vol. 9). 240p. 1994. 52.00 (*0-8039-5060-8*); pap. 24.00 (*0-8039-5061-6*) Sage.

Burman, Thomas E. Religious Polemic & the Intellectual History of the Mozarabs, c.1050-1200. LC 94-33776. (Studies in Intellectual History: 52). 1994. 118.00 (*90-04-09910-7*) Brill Academic Pubs.

Burmanni, N. L. Flora Indica. 331p. (C). 1984. 180.00 (*0-7855-3244-7*, Pub. by Scientific) St Mut.

Burmanno, Petro, ed. see Petronius.

Burmaster, Orvis C., ed. see Axelrod, David.

Burmaster, Orvis C., ed. see Baker, David.

Burmaster, Orvis C., ed. see Barnes, Dick.

Burmaster, Orvis C., ed. see Beasley, W. Conger, Jr.

Burmaster, Orvis C., ed. see Davis, H. L.

Burmaster, Orvis C., ed. see Deal, Susan S.

Burmaster, Orvis C., ed. see Fay, Julie.

Burmaster, Orvis C., ed. see Ferril, Thomas H.

Burmaster, Orvis C., ed. see Hall, Hazel.

Burmaster, Orvis C., ed. see Haste, Gwendolen.

Burmaster, Orvis C., ed. see Hess, Sonya.

Burmaster, Orvis C., ed. see Hogue, Cynthia.

Burmaster, Orvis C., ed. see Krieger, Robert.

Burmaster, Orvis C., ed. see Schenker, Donald.

Burmeister. Mathematical Theories of Economic Growth. 464p. 1993. 79.95 (*0-7512-0177-4*) Ashgate Pub Co.

Burmeister. Sea Connective Heat Transfer. 2nd ed. 640p. 1994. pap. text 140.00 (*0-471-05017-2*) Wiley.

Burmeister, Alice & Monte, Tom. The Touch of Healing: Energizing the Body, Mind & Spirit with the Art of Jin Shin Jyutsu. LC 96-36960. (Illus.). 208p. 1997. pap. 15.95 (*0-553-37784-1*) Bantam.

Burmeister-Brown, Susan & Davies, Linda, eds. Glimmer Train Stories. (Illus.). 168p. (Orig.). 1996. pap. 9.95 (*1-880966-17-4*) Glimmer Train Pr.

— Glimmer Train Stories. (Illus.). 168p. (Orig.). 1997. pap. 9.95 (*1-880966-21-2*) Glimmer Train Pr.

— Glimmer Train Stories. (Illus.). 168p. (Orig.). 1997. pap. 9.95 (*1-880966-22-0*) Glimmer Train Pr.

— Glimmer Train Stories. (Illus.). 168p. (Orig.). 1997. pap. 9.95 (*1-880966-23-9*) Glimmer Train Pr.

— Glimmer Train Stories. (Illus.). 168p. (Orig.). 1997. pap. 9.95 (*1-880966-24-7*) Glimmer Train Pr.

— Glimmer Train Stories. (Illus.). 168p. (Orig.). 1998. pap. 9.95 (*1-880966-25-5*) Glimmer Train Pr.

Burmeister, E., jt. ed. see Becker, R.

Burmeister, Eva E. Forty-Five in the Family: The Story of a Home for Children. LC 76-100147. 247p. 1970. reprint ed. lib. bdg. 65.00 (*0-8371-3259-2*, BUFA, Greenwood Pr) Greenwood.

Burmeister, George & Kreith, Frank. Energy Management & Conservation. 400p. 1992. pap. text 45.00 (*1-55516-375-0*, 4115) Natl Conf State Legis.

Burmeister, George & Mahoney, Kate. Alternative Transportation Fuels: Options for State Legislatures. (State Legislative Reports: Vol. 17, No. 9). 26p. 1992. pap. 15.00 (*1-55516-281-9*, 7302-1709) Natl Conf State Legis.

Burmeister, George & Sikkema, Eric. Home Energy Rating Systems. (State Legislative Reports: Vol. 18, No. 10). 9p. 1993. 15.00 (*1-55516-097-2*, 7302-1810) Natl Conf State Legis.

— Wind-Generated Electricity. (State Legislative Reports: Vol. 18, No. 7). 7p. 1993. 15.00 (*1-55516-099-9*, 7302-1807) Natl Conf State Legis.

Burmeister, Joachim. Musical Poetics. Palisca, Claude V., ed. Rivera, Benito V., tr. & intro. by. LC 92-33207. (Music Theory Translation Ser.). (ENG & LAT.). 336p. (C). 1993. 62.00 (*0-300-05110-7*) Yale U Pr.

Burmeister, Jody. Hanna Meets a Mud Wump. LC 96-71183. (Illus.). 75p. (J). (gr. 1-5). 1997. 16.95 (*1-882792-37-8*) Proctor Pubns.

Burmeister, Kerstin. Auberbudgetare Aktivitaten des Bundes Vol. XXV: Eine Analyse der Nebenhaushalte des Bundes under Besonderer Berucksichtigung der Finanzhistorischen Entwicklung. (Europaische Hochschulschriften: Reihe 5: Bd. 2036). (GER., Illus.). XXV, 400p. 1996. pap. 63.95 (*3-631-31228-8*) P Lang Pubng.

Burmeister, L. C., jt. ed. see Faghri, M.

Burmeister, Lou E. Words--From Print to Meaning. (Education Ser.). 1975. 8.90 (*0-201-00770-3*) Addison-Wesley.

Burmeister, Louis C. Convective Heat Transfer. 2nd ed. LC 93-1032. 640p. 1993. 140.00 (*0-471-57709-X*) Wiley.

Burmeister, Louis C. Elements of Thermal-Fluid System Design. LC 97-17164. 593p. (C). 1997. 105.00 (*0-13-660218-5*) P-H.

Burmeister, Margit & Ulanovsky, Levy, eds. Pulsed-Field Gel Electrophoresis: Protocols, Methods & Theories. LC 92-1475. (Methods in Molecular Biology Ser.: Vol. 12). (Illus.). 488p. 1992. 99.50 (*0-89603-229-9*) Humana.

B

An Asterisk (*) at the beginning of an entry indicates that the title is appearing for the first time.

Burmeister, Michelle. Medical Domain. 365p. mass mkt. 4.99 (*1-896329-14-4*) Picasso Publ.

Burmeister, Steve, jt. ed. see Pilon, Pierre.

***Burmester, G. R. & Pezzuto, A.** Color Atlas of Immunology. (Illus.). 293p. 2001. pap. 29.00 (*0-86577-964-3*) Thieme Med Pubs.

Burmester, Helen S. The Seven Rays Made Visual: An Illustrated Introduction to the Teaching on the Seven Rays. LC 85-63216. (Illus.). 142p. (Orig.). 1986. pap. 14.95 (*0-87516-563-X*) DeVorss.

Burn. Age of Equipoise. 344p. 1994. 69.95 (*0-7512-0296-7*) Ashgate Pub Co.

Burn. Developing Group Skills. 2002. 40.00 (*0-534-52671-3*) Wadsworth Pub.

Burn, A. J., et al, eds. Integrated Pest Management. 474p. 1988. text 157.00 (*0-12-145740-0*) Acad Pr.

Burn, Alan. The Fighting Captain: The Story of Frederic Walker & the Battle of the Atlantic. (Illus.). 204p. (C). 1998. pap. 29.50 (*0-85052-555-1*, Pub. by Leo Cooper) Trans-Atl Phila.

***Burn, Alan.** Fighting Commodores: Convoy Commanders in the Second World War. LC 98-68697. (Illus.). 256p. 1999. 34.95 (*1-55750-283-8*) Naval Inst Pr.

Burn, Andrew R. Alexander the Great & the Hellenistic Empire. LC 83-45724. reprint ed. 33.50 (*0-404-20048-6*) AMS Pr.

— History of Greece. 1966. pap. 13.95 (*0-14-013751-3*) Viking Penguin.

— Persia & the Greeks: The Defense of the West, 546-478 B. C. rev. ed. LC 83-40516. 640p. 1984. 65.00 (*0-8047-1235-2*) Stanford U Pr.

— The World of Hesiod. LC 66-29859. 262p. 1972. reprint ed. 18.95 (*0-405-08332-7*, Pub. by Blom Pubns) Ayer.

Burn, Ashley, jt. auth. see Ahuja, B. N.

Burn, Barbara. Horseless Rider. LC 97-4490. 1997. 27.95 (*0-87605-745-8*) Howell Bks.

— Masterpieces from the Metropolitan Museum of Art. 1997. 39.50 (*0-87099-677-0*) Metro Mus Art.

— Metropolitan Children. (Illus.). 112p. 1984. 16.95 (*0-87099-373-9*) Metro Mus Art.

— Metropolitan Museum Journal. (Canadian Museum of Civilization Mercury Ser.: Vol. 29). 350p. 1994. lib. bdg. 66.00 (*0-226-52126-5*) U Ch Pr.

— Practical Guide to Impractical Pets. LC 97-1822. 352p. 1997. 27.95 (*0-87605-724-5*) Howell Bks.

***Burn, Barbara.** A Practical Guide to Impractical Pets: 84 Exotic Pets & How to Live with Them Successfully. rev. ed. (Illus.). 372p. 1999. reprint ed. text 28.00 (*0-7881-6663-8*) DIANE Pub.

Burn, Barbara, ed. Masterpieces of the Metropolitan Museum of Art. LC 93-7966. (Illus.). 320p. 1993. 50.00 (*0-8212-2047-0*, Pub. by Bulfinch Pr) Little.

Burn, Barbara, ed. Metropolitan Museum Journal, Vol. 8 1985. 35.00 (*0-226-52105-2*) U Ch Pr.

— Metropolitan Museum Journal, Vol. 9 1985. 35.00 (*0-226-52106-0*) U Ch Pr.

— Metropolitan Museum Journal, Vol. 10 1985. 35.00 (*0-226-52107-9*) U Ch Pr.

— Metropolitan Museum Journal, Vol. 11 1985. 35.00 (*0-226-52108-7*) U Ch Pr.

— Metropolitan Museum Journal, Vol. 12 1985. 35.00 (*0-226-52109-5*) U Ch Pr.

— Metropolitan Museum Journal, Vol. 17 1985. 35.00 (*0-226-52114-1*) U Ch Pr.

— Metropolitan Museum Journal, Vol. 18. 1985. 35.00 (*0-226-52116-8*) U Ch Pr.

— Metropolitan Museum Journal, Vol. 22. 1988. lib. bdg. 50.00 (*0-226-52119-2*) U Ch Pr.

— Metropolitan Museum Journal, Vol. 25 1990. lib. bdg. 60.00 (*0-226-52122-2*) U Ch Pr.

Burn, Barbara, ed. Metropolitan Museum Journal, Vol. 31. (Illus.). 1996. lib. bdg. 70.00 (*0-226-52127-3*) U Ch Pr.

— Metropolitan Museum Journal, Vol. 33. 1999. lib. bdg. 77.00 (*0-226-52131-1*) U Ch Pr.

— Metropolitan Museum Journal Vol. 30. 200p. 1995. lib. bdg. 60.00 (*0-226-08116-8*) U Ch Pr.

— Metropolitan Museum Journal Vol. 32: Metropolitan Museum of Art. 200p. 1998. lib. bdg. 70.00 (*0-226-52128-1*) U Ch Pr.

— Metropolitan Museum Journal, (1991) Vol. 27: Essays in Memory of Guy C. Bauman. (Illus.). 192p. 1992. lib. bdg. 60.00 (*0-226-52124-9*) U Ch Pr.

Burn, Barbara, ed. see Metropolitan Museum of Art Staff.

Burn, Barbara B. The Contribution of International Educational Exchange to the International Education of Americans: Projections for the Year 2000. (Occasional Papers on International Educational Exchange: No. 26). (Orig.). 1990. pap. 5.00 (*1-882036-06-9*) Coun Intl Ed.

Burn, Barbara B., ed. Integrating Study Abroad into the Undergraduate Liberal Arts Curriculum: Eight Institutional Case Studies, 44. LC 90-22620. (Contributions to the Study of Education Ser.: No. 44). 160p. 1991. 49.95 (*0-313-27780-X*, BIQ, Greenwood Pr) Greenwood.

Burn, Barbara B., et al, eds. Study Abroad Programmes, Vol. 1. (Higher Education Policy Ser.: No. 11). 280p. 1990. 49.95 (*1-85302-522-4*) Taylor & Francis.

Burn, Billie. An Island Named Daufuskie. LC 91-31046. (Illus.). 616p. 1991. 24.95 (*0-87152-454-6*) Reprint.

— Stirrin' the Pots on Daufuskie. 212p. (Orig.). 1985. pap. 9.50 (*0-9614670-0-2*) Burn Books.

Burn, Bob & Chetwynd, Amanda. A Cascade of Numbers: An Introduction to Number Theory. (An Arnold Publication). 160p. 1998. pap. 19.95 (*0-340-65251-9*, Pub. by E A) OUP.

Burn, Bob, et al. Teaching Undergraduate Mathematics. LC 98-24247. 1998. 48.00 (*1-86094-115-X*, Pub. by Imperial College) World Scientific Pub.

Burn, Bonnie E. Flip Chart Power: Secrets of the Masters. LC 95-53700. (Illus.). 144p. 1996. pap. 29.95 (*0-88390-485-3*) Jossey-Bass.

***Burn, Bonnie E. & Payment, Maggie.** Assessments A to Z: A Collection of 50 Questionnaires, Instruments & Inventories. LC 00-26940. 224p. 2000. 49.95 (*0-7879-4509-9*) Jossey-Bass.

Burn, D. Benchmarking the Human Resources Function. 1996. pap. 145.00 (*1-85953-072-9*, Pub. by Tech Comm) St Mut.

***Burn, David & Bell, Chris.** The Instant Guide to Cats. LC 99-50246. 2000. 4.99 (*0-517-12357-6*) Random Hse Value.

***Burn, David & Fitzsimons, C.** Instant Guide to Horses. LC 99-50245. (Illus.). 2000. 4.99 (*0-517-20832-6*) Random Hse Value.

Burn, Derek. Achieving Corporate Success Through People: Making Competencies Impact on the Bottom Line. (Financial Times Management Briefings Ser.). 1997. pap. 89.50 (*0-273-63306-6*, Pub. by F T P-H) Trans-Atl Phila.

— Benchmarking the Human Resources Function. (Financial Times Management Briefings Ser.). 1997. pap. 94.50 (*0-273-63171-3*, Pub. by F T P-H) Trans-Atl Phila.

Burn, E. H. Maudsley & Burn's Land Law - Cases & Materials. 6th ed. 960p. 1992. pap. 58.00 (*0-406-60988-8*, UK, MICHIE) LEXIS Pub.

— Maudsley & Burn's Trusts & Trustees: Cases & Materials. 1996. pap. write for info. (*0-406-01445-0*, MBTTSSC, MICHIE) LEXIS Pub.

Burn, Geoffrey, et al, eds. Theory & Formal Methods: Proceedings of the 1st Imperial College Department of Computing Workshop on Theory & Formal Methods, Isle of Thorns Conference Centre, Chelwood Gate, Sussex, UK, March 1993. LC 93-25444. (Workshops in Computing Ser.). 1993. 77.95 (*0-387-19842-3*) Spr-Verlag.

Burn, Ian. Dialogue: Australian Studies in Art History. (Illus.). 208p. (Orig.). 1992. pap. text 19.95 (*1-86373-086-9*, Pub. by Allen & Unwin Pty) Paul & Co Pubs.

Burn, James D. Three Years among the Working-Classes in the United States During the War. LC 74-22735. reprint ed. 39.50 (*0-404-58487-X*) AMS Pr.

Burn, Janice M. & Martinsons, Maris G., eds. Information Technology & the Challenge for Hong Kong. LC 98-170595. (Illus.). 416p. 1997. pap. 52.50 (*962-209-420-1*, Pub. by HK Univ Pr) Coronet Bks.

Burn, John, II, jt. auth. see Fox, Peter.

Burn, Julie K. Opportunities in Computer Systems Careers. rev. ed. (Opportunities In . . . Ser.). (Illus.). 160p. pap. 11.95 (*0-8442-4599-2*, 45992, Natl Textbk Co) NTC Contemp Pub Co.

Burn, June. Living High: An Unconventional Autobiography. LC 92-70139. (Illus.). 292p. 1992. pap. 15.95 (*0-9634562-0-2*) Griffin Bay Bk.

Burn, L. Introduction to Medical Manipulation. 1985. text 57.00 (*0-85200-878-3*) Kluwer Academic.

***Burn, Loic.** Back & Neck Pain: The Facts. (The Facts Ser.). (Illus.). 224p. 2000. pap. text 19.95 (*0-19-263077-6*) OUP.

Burn, Loic. Musculoskeletal Medicine: The Spine. (C). 1990. text 173.50 (*0-7923-8913-1*) Kluwer Academic.

Burn, Loic, jt. auth. see Paterson, John K.

Burn, Loic, jt. ed. see Paterson, John K.

Burn, Lucilla. The British Museum Book of Greek & Roman Art. LC 91-75165. (Illus.). 224p. 1992. pap. 24.95 (*0-500-27657-9*, Pub. by Thames Hudson) Norton.

— Greek Myths. (Legendary Past Ser.). (Illus.). 80p. 1991. pap. 12.95 (*0-292-72748-8*) U of Tex Pr.

— The Meidias Painter. (Oxford Monographs on Classical Archaeology). (Illus.). 160p. 1988. 84.00 (*0-19-813221-2*) OUP.

Burn, R. P. Groups: A Path to Geometry. (Illus.). 254p. 1987. pap. text 31.95 (*0-521-34793-9*) Cambridge U Pr.

— Numbers & Functions: Steps to Analysis. (Illus.). 352p. (C). 1992. text 80.00 (*0-521-41086-X*) Cambridge U Pr.

— Numbers & Functions: Steps to Analysis. (Illus.). 350p. (C). 1994. pap. text 30.95 (*0-521-45773-4*) Cambridge U Pr.

***Burn, R. P.** Numbers & Functions: Steps to Analysis. 350p. 2000. pap. write for info. (*0-521-78836-6*) Cambridge U Pr.

Burn, R. P. A Pathway into Number Theory. 2nd ed. (Illus.). 267p. (C). 1996. pap. text 27.95 (*0-521-57540-0*) Cambridge U Pr.

Burn, Robert, des. Campbell, Ken a Few Ways Through the Window. (Illus.). 1990. pap. 52.00 (*0-905836-69-3*, Pub. by Museum Modern Art) St Mut.

— Campbell, Ken a Few Ways Through the Window. deluxe limited ed. (Illus.). 1990. pap. 80.00 (*0-7855-2661-7*, Pub. by Museum Modern Art) St Mut.

Burn, Shawn M. The Social Psychology of Gender. LC 95-15698. (Social Psychology Ser.). 233p. (C). 1995. pap. 28.44 (*0-07-009182-X*) McGraw.

***Burn, Shawn M.** Women Across Cultures: A Global Perspective. LC 99-32736. 1999. pap. text 33.95 (*1-55934-990-5*) Mayfield Pub.

Burn, Skye. The Crystal Gazer. (Illus.). 96p. (Orig.). 1988. pap. 7.00 (*0-944920-00-4*) Bellowing Ark Pr.

Burn, William L. The British West Indies. LC 73-21259. (Illus.). 196p. 1975. reprint ed. lib. bdg. 55.00 (*0-8371-6138-X*, BUBW, Greenwood Pr) Greenwood.

Burnaby, Barbara, jt. ed. see Campbell, Pat.

Burnaby, Barbara, jt. ed. see Herriman, Michael.

Burnaby, Barbara, jt. ed. see Ricento, Thomas K.

Burnaby, Barbara J., jt. ed. see Campbell, Pat.

Burnaby, Frederick. A Ride to Khiva: Travels & Adventure in Central Asia. LC 97-14306. 414p. 1997. pap. 13.95 (*0-19-288050-0*) OUP.

— A Ride to Khiva: Travels & Adventures in Central Asia. LC 79-115513. (Russia Observed Ser., No. 1). 1970. reprint ed. 23.95 (*0-405-03010-X*) Ayer.

Burnaby, John, ed. Augustine: Later Works. LC 55-5022. (Library of Christian Classics). 356p. 1980. reprint ed. pap. 28.95 (*0-664-24165-4*) Westminster John Knox.

Burnaby, Sherrard B. Elements of the Jewish Muhammadan Calendars. 1976. lib. bdg. 59.95 (*0-8490-1757-2*) Gordon Pr.

Burnacini, Lodovico O. Vestalische Ewige Feuer (Il Fuoco Eterno) LC 68-21208. (GER., Illus.). 1972. reprint ed. 38.95 (*0-405-08333-5*) Ayer.

Burnaford, Gail E., et al, eds. Teachers Doing Research: Practical Possibilities. 216p. 1996. pap. 18.50 (*0-8058-2254-2*) L Erlbaum Assocs.

***Burnaford, Gail E., et al, eds.** Teachers Doing Research: The Power of Action Through Inquiry. 2nd ed. 264p. 2000. pap. write for info. (*0-8058-3589-X*) L Erlbaum Assocs.

Burnaford, Gail E., jt. auth. see Joseph, Pamela B.

Burnall, Arthur C. & Tiale, P. A., eds. The Voyage of John Huyghen Van Linschoten to the East Indies: From the Old English Translation of 1598, 2 vols. (C). 1988. 50.00 (*81-206-0420-2*, Pub. by Asian Educ Servs) S Asia.

Burnam, Alma A. Genealogy of the Burnam-Berry Family & Genealogy of the Berry-Gilbert Family. (Illus.). 133p. 1998. ring bd. 45.00 (*0-9653419-3-3*) Lazuli Pr.

Burnam, Edna Mae. Edna-Mae Burnam's Dozen a Day, Bk. 1. (Illus.). 32p. 1950. 3.95 (*0-87718-031-8*, E50213) Willis Music Co.

Burnam, Jesse. Capt. Jesse Burnam: A Texas Pioneer. LC 96-90661. 85p. 1997. write for info. (*0-87244-089-3*) Texian.

***Burnam, John C.** Dog Tags of Courage: The Turmoil of War & the Rewards of Companionship. 320p. 2000. 24.95 (*1-882897-42-0*) Lost Coast.

Burnam, Tom. Dictionary of Misinformation. (J). 1975. 19.95 (*0-690-00147-9*) HarpC Child Bks.

Burnand, Gordon. Building Confidence with Human Problems: A Workbook. 151p. 1991. pap. 75.00 (*0-907774-06-7*, Pub. by Ldrship Ltd) St Mut.

— Focal Problems, Theory & Support in Stories & Myths. rev. ed. 252p. 1986. 90.00 (*0-907774-04-0*, Pub. by Ldrship Ltd) St Mut.

— Strategies of Living in Different Societies. 177p. 1985. 75.00 (*0-907774-02-4*, Pub. by Ldrship Ltd) St Mut.

— Via Focal Problems. 275p. 1982. text 75.00 (*0-907774-00-8*, Pub. by Ldrship Ltd) St Mut.

Burnand, K. C. & Young, A. E. The New Aird's Companion in Surgical Studies. (Illus.). 1440p. 1993. text 147.00 (*0-443-03831-7*) Church.

***Burnand, K. G. & Young, A. E., eds.** The New Aird's Companion in Surgical Studies. 2nd ed. (Illus.). 1248p. 1998. text. write for info. (*0-443-05326-X*) Church.

***Burnard.** Amazing Adventures of Soupy Boy. (J). 2000. pap. 6.95 (*0-440-86365-1*, Pub. by Transworld Publishers Ltd) Trafalgar.

Burnard. Health Care Computing. 1996. 48.95 (*0-412-60530-9*) Chapman & Hall.

***Burnard, Bonnie.** A Good House: A Novel. LC 99-87022. 320p. 2000. 25.00 (*0-8050-6495-8*) H Holt & Co.

— A Good House: A Novel. 2001. pap. write for info. (*0-8050-6496-6*) St Martin.

Burnard, Bonnie. Women of Influence. 120p. 1995. reprint ed. pap. 9.95 (*0-919926-82-7*, Pub. by Coteau) Genl Dist Srvs.

Burnard, Bonnie, ed. The Old Dance: Love Stories of One Kind or Another. 368p. 1986. mass mkt. 5.95 (*0-919926-56-8*, Pub. by Coteau) Genl Dist Srvs.

Burnard, Bonnie, selected by. Stag Line: Stories by Men. 220p. 1995. pap. 12.95 (*1-55050-061-9*, Pub. by Coteau) Genl Dist Srvs.

Burnard, D. Bullysaurus Gladiator. (Illus.). (J). mass mkt. 7.95 (*0-340-68979-X*, Pub. by Hodder & Stought Ltd) Trafalgar.

— Read Alone Bullysaurus. (Illus.). (J). 1996. mass mkt. 7.95 (*0-340-64855-4*, Pub. by Hodder & Stought Ltd) Trafalgar.

Burnard, Damon. The Amazing Adventures of Soupy Boy. LC 97-47163. (Illus.). 96p. (J). (gr. 3-5). 1998. pap. 4.50 (*0-395-91225-3*) HM.

— Burger. LC 97-47164. (J). (gr. 2-5). 1998. pap. 4.50 (*0-395-91315-2*) HM.

Burnard, Damon. Pork & Beef's Great Adventure. LC 97-8817. 48p. (J). (gr. 2-3). 1998. 15.00 (*0-395-86765-7*) HM.

***Burnard, Damon.** Pork & Beef's Great Adventure. (Illus.). (J). 2000. pap. 5.95 (*0-618-07037-0*) HM.

Burnard, Lou & Aston, Guy. The BNC Handbook: Exploring the British National Corpus with SARA. 256p. 1998. 70.00 (*0-7486-1054-5*, Pub. by Edinburgh U Pr); pap. 25.00 (*0-7486-1055-3*, Pub. by Edinburgh U Pr) Col U Pr.

Burnard, Philip. Acquiring Interpersonal Skills: A Handbook of Experiential Learning for Health Professionals. 2nd ed. 1996. pap. 38.25 (*1-56593-767-8*, 1492) Singular Publishing.

— Coping with Stress in the Health Professions: A Practical Guide. (Therapy in Practice Ser.: No. 21). 22.50 (*0-412-38910-X*) Chapman & Hall.

— Counseling Skills for Health Professionals. (Therapy in Practice Ser.). 250p. 1989. pap. 15.95 (*0-412-32000-2*) Chapman & Hall.

— Counseling Skills for Health Professionals. 2nd ed. 272p. 1994. 42.50 (*1-56593-312-5*, 0635) Singular Publishing.

— Counseling Skills for Health Professionals. 3rd ed. (Illus.). 336p. 1999. pap. 28.95 (*0-7487-3976-9*) Standard Pub.

— Effective Communication Skills for Health Professionals: A Manual for Writers. LC 92-20116. (Therapy in Practice Ser.: Vol. 32). 232p. 1992. pap. 46.50 (*1-56593-014-2*, 0257) Singular Publishing.

— Experimental Learning in Action. 190p. 1991. 66.95 (*1-85628-261-9*, Pub. by Avebry) Ashgate Pub Co.

— Health Care Computing: A Survival Guide for PC Users. 212p. 1994. pap. 29.95 (*1-56593-414-8*, 1080) Singular Publishing.

— Health Care Computing: A Survival Guide for PC Users. 2nd ed. 224p. 1996. pap. text 45.00 (*1-56593-755-4*, 1468) Singular Publishing.

— Learning Human Skills: An Experiential & Reflective Guide for Nurses. 3rd ed. LC 95-30494. (Illus.). 288p. 1995. pap. text 37.50 (*0-7506-2441-8*) Buttrwrth-Heinemann.

— Personal Computing for Health Professionals. 144p. 1993. pap. 49.50 (*1-56593-149-1*, 0461) Singular Publishing.

— Practical Counselling & Helping. LC 98-49632. 1999. pap. write for info. (*0-415-18883-0*) Routledge.

— Teaching Interpersonal Skills: A Handbook of Experiential Learning for Health Professionals. Campling, Jo, ed. (Therapy in Practice Ser.: No. 10). 204p. 1990. pap. 23.00 (*0-412-34590-0*, A4190) Chapman & Hall.

— Training Games for Interpersonal Skills: 107 Experiential Learning Activities for Trainers. 288p. 1996. ring bd. 99.95 (*0-07-009186-2*) McGraw.

— Writing for Health Professionals: A Manual for Writers. LC 92-20116. (Therapy in Practice Ser.: Vol. 32). 1992. 41.50 (*1-56593-074-6*, 0371) Singular Publishing.

— Writing for Health Professionals: A Manual for Writers. 2nd ed. (Illus.). 256p. 1996. pap. 38.25 (*1-56593-765-1*, 1488) Singular Publishing.

Burnard, Philip & Hulatt, Ian, eds. Nurses Counselling: The View from the Practitioners. LC 96-14626. 192p. 1996. pap. text 40.00 (*0-7506-2004-8*) Buttrwrth-Heinemann.

Burnard, Philip, jt. auth. see Gijbels, Harry.

Burnard, Philip, jt. auth. see Harrison, Judy.

Burnard, Philip, jt. auth. see Mwale, Genevieve.

Burnard, Philip, jt. ed. see Morrison, Paul.

Burnard, Sonia. Developing Child's Behaviour in the Classrooms: A Practical Guide for Teachers & Students. LC 98-111018. 165p. 1998. text 89.95 (*0-7507-0820-4*) Taylor & Francis.

Burnard, Sonia & Yaxley, Heather. Managing Children's Behaviour in the Classroom: A Practical Guide for Teachers & Students. LC 98-111018. 160p. 1997. pap. 27.95 (*0-7507-0722-4*, Falmer Pr) Taylor & Francis.

Burnay, S. G., et al, eds. Applications of Thermal Imaging. (Illus.). 272p. 1988. 154.00 (*0-85274-421-8*) IOP Pub.

Burnbaum, Steve. Walt Disney World, 1990: The Official Guide. 1989. pap. 10.95 (*0-380-71004-8*, Avon Bks) Morrow Avon.

Burndred, S. Mathematics: Attainment Tests. (National Curriculum 11-14 Year Olds Ser.). 192p. (C). 1991. 60.00 (*1-870941-63-2*) St Mut.

Burne, Alfred H. The Agincourt War. LC 75-17190. 359p. 1976. reprint ed. lib. bdg. 41.50 (*0-8371-8300-6*, BUAW, Greenwood Pr) Greenwood.

— The Agincourt War: A Military History of the Latter Part of the Hundred Years War, 1369-1453. LC 90-23265. 368p. 1991. 37.50 (*1-85367-087-1*, 5457) Stackpole.

— The Battlefields of England. (Illus.). 560p. 1996. 44.95 (*1-85367-228-9*, Pub. by Greenhill Bks) Stackpole.

***Burne, Alfred H.** The Crecy War. (Wordsworth Military Library). (Illus.). 366p. 1999. pap. 12.99 (*1-84022-210-7*, Pub. by Wrdsworth Edits) Combined Pub.

Burne, Alfred H. The Crecy War: A Military History of the Hundred Years' War from 1337 to the Peace of Bretigny, 1360. LC 75-17195. (Illus.). 366p. 1976. reprint ed. lib. bdg. 69.50 (*0-8371-8301-4*, BUCW, Greenwood Pr) Greenwood.

— The Crecy War: A Military History of the 100 Years War from 1337-1360. 368p. 1991. 37.50 (*1-85367-081-2*, 5484) Stackpole.

***Burne, Alfred H.** Lee, Grant & Sherman: A Study in Leadership in the 1864-1865 Campaign. 2000. reprint ed. pap. 16.95 (*0-7006-1073-1*) U Pr of KS.

— Lee, Grant & Sherman: A Study in Leadership in the 1864-65 Campaign. (Modern War Studies). 2000. 29.95 (*0-7006-1072-3*) U Pr of KS.

***Burne, Arthur H.** Agincourt War. 359p. 1999. pap. 12.99 (*1-84022-211-5*) Wrdsworth Edits.

Burne, Charlotte S., ed. Handbook of Folklore. enl. rev. ed. (Folk-Lore Society, London Monographs: Vol. 73). 1969. reprint ed. pap. 35.00 (*0-8115-0533-2*) Periodicals Srv.

Burne, Jerome, ed. Chronicle of the World. 1990. 49.95 (*0-685-34644-7*) P-H.

Burne-Jones, Edward. The Pre-Raphaelite Drawings of Edward Burne-Jones. (Art Library). (Illus.). 44p. (Orig.). 1981. pap. 4.95 (*0-486-24113-0*) Dover.

Burne-Jones, Edward C. Burne-Jones Talking, His Conversations, 1895-1898: Preserved by His Studio Assistant, Thomas Rooke. Lago, Mary, ed. LC 81-51062. 231p. reprint ed. pap. 71.70 (*0-7837-2358-X*, AU0042300006) Bks Demand.

Burne-Jones, Georgiana M. Memorials of Edward Burne-Jones, 2 Vols. LC 74-179508. (Select Bibliographies Reprint Ser.). 1977. reprint ed. 47.95 (*0-8369-6637-6*) Ayer.

— Memorials of Edward Burne-Jones, 2 vols., 1 bk. LC 71-174396. (Illus.). 704p. 1972. reprint ed. 38.95 (*0-405-08334-3*, Pub. by Blom Pubns) Ayer.

— Memorials of Edward Burne-Jones, 2 vols., Vol. I: 1833-1867. 352p. (C). 1993. 50.00 (*0-85331-631-7*) Lund Humphries.

— Memorials of Edward Burne-Jones, 2 vols., Vol. II: 1868-1898. 424p. (C). 1993. 50.00 (*0-85331-632-5*, Pub. by Lund Humphries) Antique Collect.

Burne, Martin. A Woman Furiously Sweeping: God's Loving Pursuit of Each Person. 1990. pap. 11.95 (*0-87193-278-4*) Dimension Bks.

Burne, R. & Binchy, William. Annual Review of Irish Law, 1992. 1994. 95.00 (*1-85800-001-7*) Intl Spec Bk.

An Asterisk (*) at the beginning of an entry indicates that the title is appearing for the first time.

Burnell, A. C., jt. auth. see Yule, Henry.

Burnell, A. C., jt. auth. see Yule, Henry A.

Burnell, Adrienne L., jt. auth. see Burnell, George M.

Burnell, Barbara S. Technological Change & Women's Work Experience: Alternative Methodological Perspectives. LC 92-38705. 224p. 1993. 57.95 (*0-89789-292-5*, H292, Bergin & Garvey) Greenwood.

Burnell, Diana P. Study Guide to Activities Therapy. fac. ed. LC 75-28928. 189p. pap. 58.60 (*0-7837-7439-7*, 204723300006) Bks Demand.

Burnell, Dick. Vesuvius & Other Latin Plays. (Illus.). 88p. (C). 1991. pap. text 12.95 (*0-521-40959-4*) Cambridge U Pr.

Burnell, George M. & Burnell, Adrienne L. Clinical Management of Bereavement: A Handbook for Health Care Professionals. 192p. 1989. 38.95 (*0-89885-424-5*, Kluwer Acad Hman Sci) Kluwer Academic.

Burnell-Gray, J. S., jt. ed. see Datta, P. K.

Burnell, Ivan G. Power of Positive Doing: Twelve Strategies for Taking Control of Your Life. (Orig.). 1990. pap. 14.95 (*0-9625806-0-0*) IPD Pubg.

— Power of Positive Doing: 12 Strategies for Taking Control of Your Life. rev. ed. LC 99-94026. 240p. (Orig.). 1999. pap. 14.95 (*0-9625806-3-5*) IPD Pubg.

— Say Yes to Life: Get Out of Your Own Way. (Illus.). 168p. (Orig.). 1997. pap. 7.95 (*0-9625806-2-7*) IPD Pubg.

Burnell, John. Bombay in the Days of Queen Anne: Being an Account of the Settlement. (C). 1997. 34.00 (*81-215-0775-8*, Pub. by M Manoharial) Coronet Bks.

***Burnell, Mark.** The Rhythm Section. LC 99-44292. 384p. 2000. 25.00 (*0-06-019465-0*) HarpC.

— The Rhythm Section. 496p. 2000. mass mkt. 6.99 (*0-06-103001-5*, Avon Bks) Morrow Avon.

***Burnell, Peter J.** Democracy Assistance: International Co-Operation for Democratization. LC 00-34067. 2000. write for info. (*0-7146-8144-X*, Pub. by F Cass Pubs) Intl Spec Bk.

Burnell, Peter J. Foreign Aid in a Changing World. LC 97-9043. (Issues in Third World Politics Ser.). 268p. 1997. 119.95 (*0-335-19525-3*); pap. 37.95 (*0-335-19524-5*) OpUniv Pr.

Burnell, Peter J. & Calvert, Peter. The Resilience of Democracy: Persistent Practice, Durable Ideas. LC 98-52186. (Democratization Studies). 288p. 1999. pap. 24.50 (*0-7146-8026-5*, Pub. by F Cass Pubs) Intl Spec Bk.

Burnell, Peter J. & Calvert, Peter, eds. The Resilience of Democracy: Persistent Practice, Durable Ideas. LC 98-52186. (Democratization Studies). 13p. 1999. 57.50 (*0-7146-4965-1*, Pub. by F Cass Pubs) Intl Spec Bk.

***Burnell, Peter J. & Ware, Alan, eds.** Funding Democratization. LC 98-2898. 224p. 1998. text 79.95 (*0-7190-5033-2*, Pub. by Manchester Univ Pr) St Martin.

Burnell, S. J., et al, eds. Next Generation Infrared Space Observatory. LC 92-32222. 1992. text 171.00 (*0-7923-1983-4*) Kluwer Academic.

Burner, David. John F. Kennedy & a New Generation. LC 88-1958. (Library of American Biography). 189p. (C). 1997. pap. 21.20 (*0-673-39810-2*) Addson-Wesley Educ.

— Making Peace with the '60s. LC 96-3336. 286p. 1996. text 34.50 (*0-691-02660-2*, Pub. by Princeton U Pr) Cal Prin Full Svc.

— Making Peace with the '60s. 304p. 1987. reprint ed. pap. text 16.50 (*1-881089-21-5*) Brandywine Press.

— Making Peace with the 60s. (Illus.). 302p. (C). 1996. pap. text 14.95 (*0-691-05953-5*, Pub. by Princeton U Pr) Cal Prin Full Svc.

— The Politics of Provincialism: The Democratic Party in Transition, 1918-1932. 320p. 1986. pap. 17.00 (*0-674-68940-2*) HUP.

Burner, David & Marcus, Anthony, eds. Turning Points Vol. I: Making Decisions in American History. 262p. (C). 1999. pap. text 18.50 (*1-881089-51-7*) Brandywine Press.

— Turning Points Vol. II: Making Decisions in American History. 240p. 1999. pap. 18.50 (*1-881089-54-1*) Brandywine Press.

Burner, David & West, Thomas R. The Torch Is Passed: The Kennedy Brothers & American Liberalism. 2nd ed. (Series in American History: No. 4). 321p. (C). 1992. reprint ed. pap. 12.50 (*1-881089-03-7*) Brandywine Press.

Burner, David, et al. America: A Portrait in History. 2nd ed. Incl. Vol. 1. 2nd ed. 1978. pap. text 16.95 (*0-13-024232-2*); (Illus.). 1978. write for info. (*0-318-54910-7*) P-H.

— Firsthand America: A History of the United States, 2 vols. 5th ed. (Illus.). 1144p. (C). 1998. 47.95 (*1-881089-76-2*) Brandywine Press.

***Burner, David, et al.** Firsthand America: A History of the United States. 6th rev. ed. (Illus.). 1144p. (C). 2000. text 47.95 (*1-881089-92-4*) Brandywine Press.

Burner, David, et al. Firsthand America Vol. 1: A History of the United States. 5th ed. (Illus.). 592p. (C). 1998. pap. text 38.75 (*1-881089-77-0*) Brandywine Press.

***Burner, David, et al.** Firsthand America Vol. 1: A History of the United States. 6th rev. ed. (Illus.). 592p. 2000. pap. text 38.75 (*1-881089-93-2*) Brandywine Press.

Burner, David, et al. Firsthand America Vol. I: A History of the United States (to 1877) 4th ed. (Illus.). 576p. (C). 1996. pap. text 35.75 (*1-881089-62-2*) Brandywine Press.

— Firsthand America Vol. 2: A History of the United States. 5th ed. (Illus.). 640p. (C). 1998. pap. text 38.75 (*1-881089-78-9*) Brandywine Press.

***Burner, David, et al.** Firsthand America Vol. II: A History of the United States. 6th rev. ed. (Illus.). 640p. 1999. pap. text 38.75 (*1-881089-94-0*) Brandywine Press.

Burner, David, et al. Firsthand America Vol. II: A History of the United States (Since 1865) 4th ed. (Illus.). 624p. (C). 1996. pap. text 35.75 (*1-881089-63-0*) Brandywine Press.

Burner, David, jt. auth. see Marcus.

Burner, David, jt. auth. see Marcus, Robert D.

Burner, David, jt. ed. see Marcus, Robert D.

Burner, Eric R. And Gently He Shall Lead Them: Robert Parris Moses & Civil Rights in Mississippi. (Illus.). 272p. (C). 1994. text 45.00 (*0-8147-1209-6*) NYU Pr.

— And Gently He Shall Lead Them: Robert Parris Moses & Civil Rights in Mississippi. (Illus.). 272p. (C). 1995. pap. text 18.50 (*0-8147-1250-9*) NYU Pr.

Burnes, A. Patricia & Nees-Hatlen, Virginia, eds. Connections: Interdisciplinary Approaches to Teaching. LC 83-62569. 171p. (Orig.). 1983. pap. 5.95 (*0-915032-97-X*) Natl Poet Foun.

Burnes, Alexander. Travels in to Bokhara Being the Account of a Journey from India to Cabool, Tartary & Persia: Also, Narrative of a Voyage on the Indus from the Sea to Lahore, 3 vols., Set. (C). 1992. reprint ed. 72.50 (*81-206-0792-9*, Pub. by Asian Educ Servs) S Asia.

Burnes, Bernard. Managing Change: A European Perspective. 2nd ed. (Illus.). 384p. (Orig.). 1996. pap. 62.50 (*0-273-61118-6*, Pub. by Pitman Pub) Trans-Atl Phila.

Burnes, Bernard, jt. ed. see Dale, Barrie.

Burnes, Caroline. Bewitching Familiar. LC 95-23268. 249p. 1995. mass mkt. 3.50 (*0-373-22343-9*, 1-22343-7) Harlequin Bks.

— A Christmas Kiss. 1996. per. 3.75 (*0-373-22399-4*, 1-22399-9) Harlequin Bks.

— Cutting Edge. (Intrigue Ser.). 1994. per. 2.99 (*0-373-22267-X*, 1-22267-8) Harlequin Bks.

— Familiar Fire: Fear Familiar Mystery. (Intrigue Ser.: No. 452). 1998. per. 3.75 (*0-373-22452-4*, 1-22452-6) Harlequin Bks.

— Familiar Heart. (Intrigue Ser.: No. 426). 1997. per. 3.75 (*0-373-22426-5*, 1-22426-0) Harlequin Bks.

***Burnes, Caroline.** Familiar Obsession: Fear Familiar. (Intrigue Ser.: Bk. 570). 2000. per. 4.25 (*0-373-22570-9*, 1-22570-5) Harlequin Bks.

Burnes, Caroline. Familiar Remedy. LC 97-10567. 248p. 1994. mass mkt. 2.99 (*0-373-22293-9*, 1-22293-4) Harlequin Bks.

— Familiar Tale: (Fear Familiar Mystery) LC 95-13557. (Intrigue Ser.). 249p. 1995. per. 3.50 (*0-373-22322-6*, 1-22322-1) Harlequin Bks.

— Familiar Valentine (Fear Familiar) Fear Familiar. (Intrigue Ser.: No. 502). 1999. per. 3.99 (*0-373-22502-4*, 1-22502-8) Harlequin Bks.

— Fatal Ingredients. (Intrigue Ser.). 1992. pap. 2.89 (*0-373-22204-1*, 1-22204-1) Harlequin Bks.

— Fear Familiar. (Men at Work Ser.: Vol. 38). 1998. mass mkt. 4.50 (*0-373-81050-4*, 1-81050-6) Harlequin Bks.

— Flesh & Blood. (Intrigue Ser.). 1993. per. 2.99 (*0-373-22241-6*, 1-22241-3) Harlequin Bks.

— Hoodwinked. (Intrigue Ser.). 1993. mass mkt. 2.99 (*0-373-22229-7*, 1-22229-8) Harlequin Bks.

— Midnight Prey: Lawman. (Intrigue Ser.). 1997. per. 3.75 (*0-373-22409-5*, 1-2409-6) Harlequin Bks.

— Remember Me, Cowboy. (Intrigue Ser.: Vol. 485). 1998. per. 3.99 (*0-373-22485-0*, 1-22485-6) Harlequin Bks.

— Shades of Familiar. 1994. per. 2.99 (*0-373-22277-7*, 1-22277-7) Harlequin Bks.

***Burnes, Caroline.** Texas Midnight. (Intrigue Ser.: Vol. 554). 2000. per. 4.25 (*0-373-22554-7*) Harlequin Bks.

Burnes, Caroline. Thrice Familiar. (Intrigue Ser.). 1993. mass mkt. 2.99 (*0-373-22256-4*, 1-22256-1) Harlequin Bks.

— Too Familiar. (Intrigue Ser.). 1993. pap. 2.89 (*0-373-22215-7*, 1-22215-7) Harlequin Bks.

Burnes, Caroline, jt. auth. see York, Rebecca.

Burnes, Jennifer J., jt. auth. see Benson, Bobbi L.

Burnes, Tony. Natural Law & Political Ideology in the Philosophy of Hegel. LC 95-83286. (Avebury Series in Philosophy). 208p. 1996. 72.95 (*1-85972-040-4*, Pub. by Avebry) Ashgate Pub Co.

Burness, Don, compiled by. Echoes of the Sunbird: An Anthology of Contemporary African Poetry. (Monographs in International Studies, Africa: No. 62). 224p. (Orig.). (C). 1993. pap. text 17.00 (*0-89680-173-X*) Ohio U Pr.

Burness, Don, ed. Wanasema: Conversations with African Writers. LC 85-5064. (Monographs in International Studies, Africa: No. 46). 103p. 1985. pap. text 11.00 (*0-89680-129-2*) Ohio U Pr.

Burness, Donald. Fire: Six Writers from Angola, Mozambique, & Cape Verde. LC 77-3840. (ENG & POR.). 148p. 1977. 16.00 (*0-914478-51-6*, Three Contnts); pap. 10.00 (*0-914478-52-4*, Three Contnts) L Rienner.

— On the Shoulder of Marti: Cuban Literature of the Angolan War. (Illus.). 203p. (Orig.). 1996. pap. 16.00 (*0-89410-768-2*, Three Contnts) L Rienner.

Burness, Donald, compiled by. Critical Perspectives on Lusophone Literature from Africa. LC 80-53348. (Illus.). 307p. 1981. 29.95 (*0-89410-015-7*, Three Contnts); pap. 16.95 (*0-89410-016-5*, Three Contnts) L Rienner.

Burness, Edwina, jt. auth. see Salmon, Vivian.

Burness, Paul. The Tragic Charge of the Light Horse at Gallipoli. LC 96-150363. 1996. pap. text 16.95 (*0-86417-782-8*, Pub. by Kangaroo Pr) Seven Hills Bk.

Burness, Tad. Cars of Early Thirties. pap. text 83.00 (*0-685-15938-8*) Bodmin Bks.

— Cars of the Early Thirties. LC 73-93376. 287p. reprint ed. pap. 89.00 (*0-608-16742-8*, 205218700053) Bks Demand.

— Cars of the Early Twenties. LC 68-56614. 291p. reprint ed. pap. 90.30 (*0-608-16733-9*, 205218600053) Bks Demand.

— Ultimate Car Spotters Guide, 1946-1969. LC 98-84622. (Illus.). 384p. 1998. pap. 21.95 (*0-87341-629-5*, UCSG) Krause Pubns.

Burnet. Immunological Surveillance. 1970. 15.00 (*0-08-017481-7*, Pergamon Pr) Elsevier.

Burnet & Eason. Essentials of Accounting Key for Practice. 7th ed. (Swc-Accounting). 1990. 13.25 (*0-538-80689-3*) S-W Pub.

Burnet, et al. Essentials of Accounting. 6th ed. (Swc-Accounting Ser.). 1987. student ed. 12.75 (*0-538-01491-1*) S-W Pub.

Burnet, Bishop G. History of His Own Time. 516p. 1994. pap. 10.95 (*0-460-87172-2*, Everyman's Classic Lib) Tuttle Pubng.

Burnet, David. Introduction to Housing Law. 221p. 1996. pap. 40.00 (*1-85941-190-8*, Pub. by Cavendish Pubng) Gaunt.

Burnet, David & Harpwood, Vivienne. A-Level Law Workbook. 90p. 1995. pap. 22.00 (*1-85941-003-0*, Pub. by Cavendish Pubng) Gaunt.

Burnet, David, jt. auth. see Skone, John.

Burnet, Frank M. Integrity of the Body: A Discussion of Modern Immunological Ideas. LC 62-8180. (Books in Biology: No. 3). (Illus.). 199p. 1962. 26.95 (*0-674-45650-5*) HUP.

— Intrinsic Mutagenesis: A Genetic Approach to Aging. LC 74-6978. (Wiley Biomedical-Health Publication Ser.). 253p. reprint ed. pap. 78.50 (*0-7837-3434-4*, 205775500008) Bks Demand.

Burnet, Gilbert. Bishop Burnet's History of His Own Time, 6 vols., Set. Routh, Martin J., ed. 1969. reprint ed. 865.00 (*0-685-66438-4*, 05102325) G Olms Pubs.

— Gilbert Burnet's Discourse of the Pastoral Care. Cornwall, Robert D., ed. LC 97-29272. (Texts & Studies in Religion: Vol. 76). 260p. 1997. text 89.95 (*0-7734-8537-6*) E Mellen.

— The History of the Reformation of the Church of England, 7 vols. rev. ed. LC 83-45575. reprint ed. write for info. (*0-404-19893-7*) AMS Pr.

— Some Passages of the Life & Death of the Right Honourable John Earl of Rochester. (Anglistica & Americana Ser.: No. 28). 182p. 1969. reprint ed. 70.00 (*0-685-66439-2*, 05102151) G Olms Pubs.

***Burnet, Gilbert, ed.** The Boyle Lectures (1692-1732) A Defence of Natural & Revealed Religion, Being an Abridgement of the Sermons Preached at the Lectures Founded by Robert Boyle, 4 vols. 1950p. 2000. 475.00 (*1-85506-813-3*) Thoemmes Pr.

Burnet, Jacob. Notes on the Early Settlement of the North-Western Territory. LC 75-90. (Mid-American Frontier Ser.). 1975. reprint ed. 41.95 (*0-405-06857-3*) Ayer.

Burnet, James. Of the Origin & Progress of Language, 6 vols., Set. (Anglistica & Americana Ser.: No. 138). 1974. reprint ed. 865.00 (*3-487-05432-9*) G Olms Pubs.

Burnet, Jean. Next-Year Country: A Study of Rural Social Organization in Alberta. LC HN0110.H3B8. (Social Credit in Alberta: Its Background & Development Ser.: No. 3). 204p. reprint ed. pap. 63.30 (*0-8357-8248-4*, 203407200088) Bks Demand.

Burnet, John. Essays & Addresses. LC 68-54335. (Essay Index Reprint Ser.). 1977. reprint ed. 20.95 (*0-8369-0265-3*) Ayer.

— Platonism. 5. LC 83-1503. (Sather Classical Lecture: Vol. 5). 130p. (C). 1983. reprint ed. lib. bdg. 42.50 (*0-313-23699-2*, BUPL, Greenwood Pr) Greenwood.

Burnet, John, ed. Opera, 5 vols. Incl. Vol. 2. Parmenides, Philebus, Symposium, Phaedrus, Alcibiades 1 & 2, Hipparchus, Amatores. 2nd ed. 410p. 1922. text 35.00 (*0-19-814541-1*); Vol. 3. Theages, Charmides, Laches, Lysis, Euthydemus, Protagoras, Gorgias, Meno. Hippias Maior, Hippas Minor, Io, Menexenus. Plato. 524p. 1922. text 35.00 (*0-19-814542-X*); Vol. 4. Clitopho, Respublica, Timaeus, Critias. Plato. 554p. 1922. text 35.00 (*0-19-814544-6*); Vol. 5. Minos, Leges, Epinomis, Epistulae, Definitiones. Plato. 610p. 1922. text 55.00 (*0-19-814546-2*); write for info. (*0-318-54865-8*) OUP.

Burnet, John, ed. see Aristotle.

Burnet, John, ed. see Plato.

Burnet, M., jt. auth. see Andrewes, C.

Burnet, Margaret. Letters from Lady Margaret Burnet. LC 74-39562. (Bannatyne Club, Edinburgh. Publications: No. 24). reprint ed. 32.50 (*0-404-52730-2*) AMS Pr.

Burnet, Mary E., et al. Essentials Of Accounting Text. 6th ed. (SWC-Accounting). (C). 1987. mass mkt. 25.00 (*0-538-01490-3*, A49) S-W Pub.

Burnet, Regula. Green Ink. LC 98-35741. 1998. pap. 5.00 (*0-88734-757-6*) Players Pr.

Burnet, Thomas, ed. Remarks on John Locke: With Locke's Replies. (C). 1989. 60.00 (*0-907839-43-6*, Pub. by Brynmill Pr Ltd) St Mut.

Burnett. Book of Sequences. 18.00 (*0-06-061199-5*) HarpC.

— Promotion Management. (C). 1992. pap., teacher ed. 4.76 (*0-395-56554-5*) HM.

— Puck of Pool's Hill. (Children's Library). 1998. pap. 3.95 (*1-85326-138-6*, 1386WW, Pub. by Wrdsworth Edits) NTC Contemp Pub Co.

— Shakespeare & Ireland. LC 97-14277. 220p. 1997. text 59.95 (*0-312-17628-7*) St Martin.

— Sporting Scotland. (Illus.). 88p. 1995. pap. 6.95 (*0-948636-66-1*, 36661, Pub. by Natl Mus Scotland) A Schwartz & Co.

***Burnett.** Technical Communication. 5th ed. 2000. 52.25 (*0-534-56098-9*) Wadsworth Pub.

Burnett, et al. Business Communication: Strategies for Success. rev. ed. LC 95-69677. 1997. student ed. 67.95 (*0-87393-499-7*) Dame Pubns.

— Business Communication: Strategies for Success Study Guide. rev. ed. 1997. pap., student ed. 23.95 (*0-87393-600-0*) Dame Pubns.

Burnett, ed. see Thornton, Mark & Manning, John.

Burnett, Catherine M. & Manary, Adria H. Touched by a Rainbow: A Collection of Poems That Will Inspire the Soul & Bring Generations Together in Harmony of Thought. LC 98-73002. (Illus.). 144p. 1998. pap. 11.95 (*0-9665830-1-9*) Angel Power Pr.

Thirty-six years ago, Adria Manary was in the first grade. Catherine Burnett was her caring & memorable teacher. How they have come together to compile an exquisite array of poems that will touch the hearts of all generations & generations to come. ***Publisher Paid Annotation.***

Burnett, Alan, et al, eds. Cambridge Medical Reviews: Haematological Oncology, Vol. 3. (Illus.). 258p. (C). 1994. text 95.00 (*0-521-44208-7*) Cambridge U Pr.

***Burnett, Alexander F.** Clinical Obstetrics & Gynecology: A Problem-Based Approach. LC 00-39760. (Illus.). 450p. (C). 2000. pap. 32.95 (*0-632-04353-9*) Blackwell Sci.

Burnett, Allster D., jt. auth. see Watson, Ian.

Burnett, Amy. The Yoke of Christ: Martin Bucer & Christian Discipline. LC 93-47542. (Sixteenth Century Essays & Studies: Vol. 26). 256p. 1994. 40.00 (*0-940474-28-X*, SCJP) Truman St Univ.

Burnett, Andrew. Coins. LC 91-9181. (Interpreting the Past Ser.: No. 3). (Illus.). 64p. 1991. pap. 13.95 (*0-520-07628-1*, Pub. by U CA Pr) Cal Prin Full Svc.

Burnett, Andrew, jt. auth. see Johns, Catherine.

Burnett, Anne P. The Art of Bacchylides. (Martin Classical Lectures: No. 29). 224p. 1985. 25.00 (*0-674-04666-8*) HUP.

Burnett, Anne P. Revenge in Attic & Later Tragedy. LC 97-22677. (Sather Classical Lectures). 384p. 1997. 42.00 (*0-520-21096-4*, Pub. by U CA Pr) Cal Prin Full Svc.

Burnett, Archie, ed. see Housman, Alfred E.

Burnett, Arthur C. Yankees in the Republic of Texas: Their Origin & Impact. 1952. 7.50 (*0-685-05007-6*) A Jones.

Burnett-Balga, Beth & Duke, Kenneth L. Test Preparation Guide for FLMI 315: Legal Aspects of Life & Health Insurance (Canada) rev. ed. (FLMI Insurance Education Program Ser.). 139p. pap. 18.00 (*1-57974-026-X*, Pub. by Life Office) PBD Inc.

Burnett-Balga, Beth, et al. Prep Pak for FLMI 280. (FLMI Insurance Education Program Ser.). 259p. 1999. spiral bd. 24.00 (*1-57974-030-8*) PBD Inc.

Burnett, Ben G. Political Groups in Chile: The Dialogue Between Order & Change. LC 70-135759. (Latin American Monographs: No. 21). 333p. reprint ed. pap. 103.30 (*0-8357-7730-8*, 203608700002) Bks Demand.

Burnett, Ben G. & Troncoso, Moises P. The Rise of the Latin American Labor Movement. 1960. 12.95 (*0-8084-0406-7*) NCUP.

Burnett, Betty. St. Louis at War: The Story of a City, 1941-1945. LC 87-15591. (Illus.). 175p. 1987. 14.95 (*0-935284-52-4*) Patrice Pr.

Burnett, Betty, ed. The Flood of Nineteen Ninety-Three: Stories from a Midwestern Disaster. (Illus.). 188p. (Orig.). 1994. pap. 10.95 (*1-880397-06-4*) Patrice Pr.

Burnett, Betty, ed. see Alleman, Roy V.

Burnett, Betty, ed. see Franzwa, Gregory M.

Burnett, Betty, jt. ed. see Franzwa, Gregory M.

Burnett, Betty, ed. see Shutz, Byron.

Burnett, C. S., ed. see D'Alverny, Marie-Therese.

Burnett, Carol. One More Time. 352p. 1987. mass mkt. 4.95 (*0-380-70449-8*, Avon Bks) Morrow Avon.

— Selected from One More Time: A Memoir. abr. ed. (Writers' Voices Ser.). (Illus.). 64p. 1989. pap. text 3.95 (*0-929631-03-X*, Signal Hill) New Readers.

Burnett, Carolyn M. The First Texans: 12 Native American Tribes. LC 94-16986. 160p. (J). (gr. 6-7). 1995. 14.95 (*0-89015-980-7*) Sunbelt Media.

Burnett, Catherine, jt. auth. see McCabe, Neil.

Burnett, Cathy, jt. ed. see Fenner, Arnie.

Burnett, Charles. The Introduction of Arabic Learning into England. LC 98-157808. (Panizzi Lectures, 1996 Ser.). (Illus.). 112p. 1998. pap. text 32.00 (*0-7123-4545-0*) U of Toronto Pr.

— Magic & Divination in the Middle Ages: Texts & Techniques in the Islamic & Christian Worlds. LC 96-30650. (Collected Studies: Vol. CS557). 384p. 1996. 109.95 (*0-86078-615-3*, Pub. by Variorum) Ashgate Pub Co.

Burnett, Charles, et al, eds. The Abbreviation of the Introduction to Astrology: Together with the Medieval Latin Translation of Adelard of Bath. Yamamoto, Keiji et al, trs. LC 94-2489. (Islamic Philosophy, Theology & Science, Studies & Texts Ser.: Vol. 15). 1994. 75.00 (*90-04-09997-2*) Brill Academic Pubs.

Burnett, Charles & Jacquart, Danielle, eds. Constantine the African & Ali ibn al-Abbas al-Magusi: The Pantegni & Related Texts. LC 94-33854. (Studies in Ancient Medicine: Vol. 10). 1994. 107.50 (*90-04-10014-8*) Brill Academic Pubs.

Burnett, Charles, jt. auth. see D'Alverny, Marie-Therese.

Burnett, Charles, ed. see Adelard.

Burnett, Charles, ed. see D'Alverny, Marie T.

Burnett, Charles, ed. see D'Alverny, Marie-Therese.

Burnett, Charles, ed. see Mashar, Abu.

Burnett, Charles J. & Bennett, Helen. The Green Mantle: A Celebration of the Revival in 1687 of the Most Ancient & Most Noble Order of the Thistle. (Illus.). 20p. 1995. pap. 3.50 (*0-948636-07-6*, 6076, Pub. by Natl Mus Scotland) A Schwartz & Co.

Burnett, Charles J. & Dennis, Mark. Scotland's Heraldic Heritage: The Lion Rejoicing. (Discovering Historic Scotland Ser.). (Illus.). 104p. 1997. pap. 26.00 (*0-11-495784-3*, Pub. by Statnry Office) Balogh.

Burnett, Claudine. From Fields to Oil Town: A Tour of Huntington Beach, 1901-1922. (Illus.). (Orig.). 1995. pap. text 12.95 (*1-881903-08-7*) DW Artworks.
— Haunted Long Beach. (Illus.). 83p. 1996. pap. 11.00 (*0-9610250-1-8*) Hist Soc of Long Bch.

Burnett, Constance B. Five for Freedom: Lucretia Mott, Elizabeth Cady Stanton, Lucy Stone, Susan B. Anthony, Carrie Chapman Catt. LC 68-8734. (Illus.). 317p. 1968. reprint ed. lib. bdg. 69.50 (*0-8371-0034-8*, BUFF, Greenwood Pr) Greenwood.

***Burnett, D. Graham.** Masters of All They Surveyed: Exploration, Geography & a British El Dorado. LC 99-98199. 1999. 45.00 (*0-226-08120-6*) U Ch Pr.

Burnett, Dan. A Cowboy Never Lies. LC 96-92293. 208p. (Orig.). 1996. pap. 12.95 (*0-9652375-0-8*, 360-826-4130) New West Pr.
— A Cowboy Never Lies 2. LC 98-67159. 1999. pap. 12.95 (*0-9652375-1-6*, 360-826-4130) New West Pr.

Burnett, Dana D., et al. Academic Integrity Matters. LC 97-51743. 1997. write for info. (*0-931654-23-8*) National Assn Blk Acct.

Burnett, Darlene, jt. ed. see Beede, Martha.

Burnett, David. God's Mission: Healing the Nations. 1996. 5.99 (*0-947697-46-2*) O M Lit.
— The Spirit of Hinduism. 1993. 10.99 (*1-85424-194-X*) O M Lit.

Burnett, David, et al, eds. Microelectronic Device Technology II. LC 99-184109. (Proceedings of SPIE Ser.: Vol. 3506). 364p. 1998. 89.00 (*0-8194-2965-1*) SPIE.

***Burnett, David & Tsuchiya, Toshiaki, eds.** Microelectric Device Technology III. 314p. 1999. pap. text 72.00 (*0-8194-3478-7*) SPIE.

Burnett, David, jt. auth. see Bardon, Jonathan.

Burnett, David G. The Healing of the Nations: The Biblical Basis of the Mission of God. (Biblical Classics Library: Vol. 18). 230p. 1996. reprint ed. mass mkt. 5.99 (*0-85364-742-9*, Pub. by Paternoster Pub) OM Literature.

Burnett, David S. Finite Element Analysis: From Concepts to Applications Solutions Manual. student ed. write for info. (*0-201-10258-7*) Addison-Wesley.

***Burnett, Deborah.** Comfortable Living by Design: Down-to-Earth Decorating Advice for a Warm & Friendly Home. 240p. 1999. pap. 14.95 (*0-9672167-0-2*) Humble Abund.

Burnett, E. C. Letters of Members of the Continental Congress, 1774-1789, Vols. 3, 4, 5, & 6. 1990. 74.00 (*0-8446-1095-X*) Peter Smith.

Burnett, E. K. Inlaid Stone & Bone Artifacts from Southern California. fac. ed. (New York Museum of the American Indian Heye Foundation Ser.: Vol. XIII). (Illus.). 131p. (C). 1944. reprint ed. pap. text 14.38 (*1-55567-806-8*) Coyote Press.

Burnett, E. K., ed. see Ewers, John C.

Burnett, Ed. Database Marketing: The New Profit Frontier. 200p. 1996. pap. 39.95 (*0-9645356-2-9*) Morris-Lee Pub.
— Growing Your Small Business: A Marketing Handbook of Proven Promotional Ideas for Entrepreneurs. LC 96-76846. 139p. (Orig.). 1996. pap. 14.95 (*0-9645356-1-0*) Morris-Lee Pub.

Burnett, Elizabeth, ed. see Cote, Richard N.

Burnett, F. Gerald & Kafka, Gerald A. Litigation of Federal Tax Controversies. 2094p. 1986. pap. text 125.00 (*0-07-009069-6*) Shepards.

Burnett, Frances Hodgson. Editha's Burglar. LC 94-19127. (Illus.). 54p. (J). (gr. k-8). 1994. 14.95 (*1-55709-244-3*) Applewood.
— A Fair Barbarian. 285p. 1995. reprint ed. pap. 15.95 (*0-89301-187-8*) U of Idaho Pr.
— Haworth's. LC 79-3328. reprint ed. 44.50 (*0-404-61799-9*) AMS Pr.
— El Jardin Secreto. Ulsamer, Aurora & Santander, Rafael D., trs.Tr. of Secret Garden. (SPA., Illus.). 128p. 1996. reprint ed. pap. text 3.95 (*0-486-29199-5*) Dover.
— Jarl's Daughter & Other Novelettes. LC 75-94708. (Short Story Index Reprint Ser.). 1977. 17.95 (*0-8369-3087-8*) Ayer.
— Lady of Quality. 22.95 (*0-8488-0252-7*) Amereon Ltd.
— The Land of the Blue Flower. LC 93-19968. (Illus.). 48p. (J). (ps-5). 1993. reprint ed. 15.95 (*0-915811-46-4*, Starseed) H J Kramer Inc.
— Little Lord Fauntleroy. (J). 21.95 (*0-8488-0792-8*) Amereon Ltd.
— Little Lord Fauntleroy. (Illus.). 160p. (YA). (gr. 5 up). 1993. 18.95 (*0-87923-958-1*) Godine.
— Little Lord Fauntleroy. LC 95-15325. (Everyman's Library of Children's Classics). (Illus.). (J). 1995. 13.95 (*0-679-44474-2*, Evrymans Lib Childs) Knopf.
— Little Lord Fauntleroy. (Illus.). 256p. (YA). (gr. 5 up). 1996. pap. 4.99 (*0-14-036753-5*, PuffinBks) Peng Put Young Read.
— Little Lord Fauntleroy. (Illus.). (J). 21.95 (*0-590-74607-3*) Scholastic Inc.
— Little Lord Fauntleroy. (J). 1997. pap. 2.95 (*0-8167-1465-7*) Troll Communs.
— Little Lord Fauntleroy. (Puffin Classics). (J). 1994. 9.09 (*0-606-09560-8*, Pub. by Turtleback) Demco.
— Little Lord Fauntleroy. (Children's Library). 1998. pap. 3.95 (*1-85326-130-0*, 1300WW, Pub. by Wrdsworth Edits) NTC Contemp Pub Co.
— Little Lord Fauntleroy. large type ed. (Large Print Heritage Ser.). 272p. (YA). (gr. 7-12). 1997. lib. bdg. 28.95 (*1-58118-002-0*, 21965) LRS.
— Little Lord Fauntleroy. (Illus.). 252p. (J). 1981. reprint ed. lib. bdg. 21.95 (*0-89966-288-9*) Buccaneer Bks.

Burnett, Frances Hodgson. Little Lord Fauntleroy, Homework Set. unabridged ed. (J). (gr. 5). 1997. boxed set 56.24 incl. audio (*0-7887-1840-1*, 40620) Recorded Bks.

Burnett, Frances Hodgson. A Little Princess. (J). 16.95 (*0-8488-1253-0*) Amereon Ltd.
— A Little Princess. 300p. (J). 1977. lib. bdg. 15.95 (*0-89967-005-9*, Harmony Rain) Buccaneer Bks.

***Burnett, Frances Hodgson.** A Little Princess. LC 00-31778. (Juvenile Classics). (Illus.). 2000. pap. write for info. (*0-486-41446-9*) Dover.

Burnett, Frances Hodgson. A Little Princess. LC 63-15435. (Illus.). 336p. (J). (gr. 4-7). 1999. 16.95 (*0-397-30693-8*) HarpC Child Bks.
— A Little Princess. LC 99-27022. (Illus.). 40p. (J). (ps-3). 2000. 16.95 (*0-06-027891-9*) HarpC Child Bks.

***Burnett, Frances Hodgson.** A Little Princess. LC 97-43631. (Illus.). 40p. (J). (ps-3). 2000. lib. bdg. 16.89 (*0-06-029010-2*) HarpC Child Bks.
— A Little Princess. (Illus.). 44p. 1998. pap. 5.25 (*0-19-422875-4*) OUP.

Burnett, Frances Hodgson. A Little Princess. LC 94-43353. (Illustrated Junior Library). (Illus.). 288p. (J). (gr. 4-7). 1995. 14.95 (*0-448-40949-6*, G & D) Peng Put Young Read.
— A Little Princess. (Illus.). 304p. (YA). (gr. 4-7). 1995. pap. 4.99 (*0-14-036688-1*, PuffinBks) Peng Put Young Read.
— A Little Princess. LC 93-14000. (Step into Classics Ser.). 107p. (J). (gr. 2-6). 1994. pap. 3.99 (*0-679-85090-2*) Random.
— A Little Princess. (Bullseye Step into Classics Ser.). 108p. (J). (gr. 2-6). 1994. pap. 2.99 (*0-685-71036-X*) Random Bks Yng Read.

***Burnett, Frances Hodgson.** A Little Princess. (Unabridged Classics Ser.). 224p. (YA). 2000. pap. 5.98 (*0-7624-0548-1*, Courage) Running Pr.

Burnett, Frances Hodgson. A Little Princess. (Illus.). (J). 22.95 (*0-590-24079-X*) Scholastic Inc.
— A Little Princess. 256p. (J). (gr. 4-7). 1995. pap. 3.99 (*0-590-54307-5*, Apple Classics) Scholastic Inc.

***Burnett, Frances Hodgson.** A Little Princess. (Illus.). 272p. (gr. 4-7). 2000. pap. 4.99 (*0-439-10137-9*) Scholastic Inc.

Burnett, Frances Hodgson. A Little Princess. LC 87-15485. (Illus.). 48p. (J). (gr. 3-6). 1988. lib. bdg. 19.95 (*0-8167-1201-8*) Troll Communs.
— A Little Princess. (J). 1997. pap. 2.95 (*0-89375-500-1*) Troll Communs.
— A Little Princess. LC 87-15485. (Illus.). 48p. (J). (ps-3). 1998. pap. 5.95 (*0-8167-1202-6*) Troll Communs.
— A Little Princess. (Children's Library). (J). Date not set. pap. 3.95 (*1-85326-136-X*, 136XWW, Pub. by Wrdsworth Edits) NTC Contemp Pub Co.

Burnett, Frances Hodgson. Little Princess. 1997. pap. text 12.95 (*0-14-086079-7*, PuffinBks) Peng Put Young Read.

Burnett, Frances Hodgson. A Little Princess. abr. ed. (Children's Thrift Classics Ser.). (Illus.). 96p. (J). (gr. 1). 1996. pap. 1.00 (*0-486-29171-5*) Dover.
— A Little Princess. large type ed. (Large Print Heritage Ser.). 324p. (YA). 1998. lib. bdg. 31.95 (*1-58118-021-7*, 21998) LRS.
— A Little Princess. 232p. (J). 1981. reprint ed. lib. bdg. 15.95 (*0-89966-327-3*) Buccaneer Bks.
— A Little Princess. LC 88-46102. (Illus.). 192p. (YA). (gr. 5 up). 2000. reprint ed. 18.95 (*0-87923-784-8*) Godine.
— A Little Princess. LC 63-15435. (Trophy Bk.). (Illus.). 336p. (J). (gr. 4-7). 1987. reprint ed. pap. 4.95 (*0-06-440187-1*, HarpTrophy) HarpC Child Bks.
— A Little Princess, Set. unabridged ed. (YA). (gr. 3 up). 1995. 24.95 incl. audio (*0-945353-94-4*, H90394, Pub. by Audio Partners) Publishers Group.
— A Little Princess: Picture Book. (Illus.). 32p. (J). (gr. k-2). 1995. pap. 2.95 (*0-590-55204-X*) Scholastic Inc.
— A Little Princess Book & Charm. (Charming Classic Bks.). (Illus.). 336p. (YA). (gr. 4-7). 1999. 5.95 (*0-694-01236-X*, HarpFestival) HarpC Child Bks.

***Burnett, Frances Hodgson.** Little Princess Coloring Book. (Illus.). 48p. (J). 1999. pap. 2.95 (*0-486-40561-3*) Dover.

Burnett, Frances Hodgson. Little Princess Paper Dolls. (J). (ps-3). 1999. pap. 7.95 (*0-694-00970-9*, HarpFestival) HarpC Child Bks.

***Burnett, Frances Hodgson.** Little Princess/The Secret Garden. 480p. 1999. reprint ed. 8.98 (*0-7624-0564-3*) Running Pr.

Burnett, Frances Hodgson. The Lost Prince. (J). 25.95 (*0-8488-0691-3*) Amereon Ltd.
— The One I Knew the Best of All. LC 79-8779. (Signal Lives Ser.). 1980. reprint ed. lib. bdg. 39.95 (*0-405-12828-2*) Ayer.
— Racketty-Packetty House. LC 75-8531. (Illus.). 64p. (J). (gr. 2-5). 1975. 12.95 (*0-397-31642-9*) HarpC Child Bks.
— Sara Crewe. 96p. (J). (gr. 3-7). 1986. pap. 3.50 (*0-590-42323-1*) Scholastic Inc.
— Sara Crewe, or, What Happened at Miss Minchin's. 59p. (J). (gr. 1 up). 1996. pap. 5.50 (*0-87129-734-5*, SB5) Dramatic Pub.
— Sara Crewe, or, What Happened at Miss Minchin's. 1981. 8.60 (*0-606-01169-2*, Pub. by Turtleback) Demco.
— The Secret Garden. (J). 22.95 (*0-8488-0692-1*) Amereon Ltd.
— The Secret Garden. (Andre Deutsch Classics). 251p. (J). (gr. 5-8). 1996. 9.95 (*0-233-99075-5*, Pub. by Andre Deutsch) Trafalgar.
— The Secret Garden. (Classics Ser.). (Illus.). 256p. (J). 1987. mass mkt. 3.95 (*0-553-21201-X*, Bantam Classics) Bantam.
— The Secret Garden. (Classics for Young Readers Ser.). 64p. (J). 1994. 5.98 (*0-86112-982-2*) Brimax Bks.
— The Secret Garden. 1977. 21.95 (*0-89967-001-6*, Harmony Rain) Buccaneer Bks.
— The Secret Garden. 288p. (J). 1987. pap. 4.50 (*0-440-40055-4*) Dell.
— The Secret Garden. 288p. (YA). (gr. k-6). 1989. mass mkt. 4.50 (*0-440-97709-6*, Dell Trade Pbks) Dell.
— The Secret Garden. (Illus.). 96p. (J). (gr. 4-7). 1994. pap. 1.00 (*0-486-28024-1*) Dover.

***Burnett, Frances Hodgson.** The Secret Garden. LC 99-32232. (Illus.). 288p. (J). 1999. pap. text 3.00 (*0-486-40784-5*) Dover.

Burnett, Frances Hodgson. The Secret Garden. LC 86-22780. (Illus.). 240p. (J). (gr. 4-6). 1995. 19.95 (*0-8050-0277-4*, Bks Young Read) H Holt & Co.
— The Secret Garden. 368p. (J). (gr. 4 up). 1998. 16.95 (*0-397-32165-1*) Lppncott W & W.
— The Secret Garden. (J). 1987. mass mkt. 3.95 (*0-451-52417-9*, Sig Classics) NAL.
— The Secret Garden. Butts, Dennis, ed. & intro. by. (World's Classics Ser.). 360p. (J). 1987. pap. 7.95 (*0-19-281772-8*) OUP.
— The Secret Garden. (Classics for Young Readers Ser.). (Illus.). 298p. (J). (gr. 1-4). 1994. pap. 4.99 (*0-14-036666-0*, PuffinBks) Peng Put Young Read.
— The Secret Garden. (Illustrated Junior Library). (Illus.). 320p. (YA). 1996. 15.99 (*0-448-41250-0*, G & D) Peng Put Young Read.
— The Secret Garden. (Classics Ser.). (Illus.). 52p. (J). 1994. text 3.50 (*0-7214-1657-8*, Ladybrd) Penguin Putnam.
— The Secret Garden. Hanft, Joshua, ed. (Great Illustrated Classics Ser.: Vol. 38). (Illus.). 240p. (J). (gr. 3-6). 1994. 9.95 (*0-86611-989-2*) Playmore Inc.
— The Secret Garden. LC 93-18509. (Step into Classics Ser.). (Illus.). 128p. (J). (gr. 2-7). 1993. pap. 3.99 (*0-679-84751-0*, Pub. by Random Bks Yng Read) Random.
— The Secret Garden. 304p. (J). (gr. 4-7). 1987. pap. 3.50 (*0-590-43346-6*, Apple Classics) Scholastic Inc.
— The Secret Garden. (Illus.). (J). 1999. 22.95 (*0-590-24077-3*) Scholastic Inc.
— The Secret Garden. 288p. (J). 1990. pap. 2.50 (*0-8125-0501-8*, Pub. by Tor Bks) St Martin.
— The Secret Garden. (YA). 1991. mass mkt. 3.99 (*0-8125-1910-8*, Pub. by Tor Bks) St Martin.
— The Secret Garden. LC 87-15490. (Illustrated Classics Ser.). (Illus.). 48p. (J). (gr. 3-6). pap. text 5.95 (*0-8167-1204-2*) Troll Communs.
— The Secret Garden. LC 87-15490. (Illustrated Classics Ser.). (Illus.). (J). (gr. 3-6). 1988. lib. bdg. 12.89 (*0-8167-1203-4*) Troll Communs.
— The Secret Garden. (Deluxe Watermill Classic Ser.). 288p. (YA). 1991. pap. 3.95 (*0-8167-2559-4*) Troll Communs.
— The Secret Garden. (Deluxe Watermill Classic Ser.). 288p. (YA). 1992. 9.49 (*0-8167-2558-6*) Troll Communs.
— The Secret Garden. (J). 1987. 9.09 (*0-606-01340-7*, Pub. by Turtleback) Demco.
— The Secret Garden. (Children's Library). (J). 1998. pap. 3.95 (*1-85326-104-1*, 1041WW, Pub. by Wrdsworth Edits) NTC Contemp Pub Co.

Burnett, Frances Hodgson. Secret Garden. 304p. (J). (gr. 3-5). pap. 4.95 (*0-8072-1412-4*) Listening Lib.
— Secret Garden. (Oxford World Classics Ser.). 368p. (J). 2000. pap. 7.95 (*0-19-283596-3*) OUP.

Burnett, Frances Hodgson. Secret Garden. Lurie, Alison, ed. & intro. by. LC 98-54731. 304p. 1999. pap. 5.95 (*0-14-118218-0*, PuffinBks) Peng Put Young Read.
— Secret Garden, 1 vol. 320p. (gr. 4-7). 1999. pap. text 3.99 (*0-439-09939-0*) Scholastic Inc.
— The Secret Garden. LC 99-223460. (Illus.). 352p. (J). (ps up). 2000. 21.95 (*0-688-14582-5*, Wm Morrow) Morrow Avon.

Burnett, Frances Hodgson. The Secret Garden. abr. ed. (Children's Classics Ser.). (J). mass mkt. 14.95 (*1-85998-078-3*) Trafalgar.
— The Secret Garden. abr. ed. (Children's Classics Ser.). (J). 1997. mass mkt. 16.95 incl. audio (*1-85998-748-6*) Trafalgar.

Burnett, Frances Hodgson. The Secret Garden. adapted ed. LC 97-20757. (Illus.). 32p. (J). (ps-2). 1998. 14.95 (*0-06-027853-6*) HarpC.
— The Secret Garden. large type ed. (Large Print Heritage Ser.). 388p. (YA). (gr. 7-12). 1997. lib. bdg. 32.95 (*1-58118-000-4*, 21490) LRS.
— The Secret Garden. large type ed. 380p. (J). 1996. reprint ed. lib. bdg. 24.00 (*0-939495-02-3*) North Bks.
— The Secret Garden. 302p. (J). 1981. reprint ed. lib. bdg. 21.95 (*0-89966-326-5*) Buccaneer Bks.
— The Secret Garden. LC 86-45534. (Illus.). 192p. (YA). (gr. 5 up). 2000. reprint ed. 18.95 (*0-87923-649-3*) Godine.
— The Secret Garden. LC 62-17457. (Trophy Bk.). (Illus.). 368p. (J). (gr. 4 up). 1998. reprint ed. pap. 4.95 (*0-06-440188-X*, HarpTrophy) HarpC Child Bks.
— The Secret Garden. 248p. (J). 1998. reprint ed. lib. bdg. 24.00 (*1-58287-069-1*) North Bks.
— The Secret Garden. unabridged ed. (Illus.). 200p. (J). 1993. 25.00 (*0-88363-202-0*) H L Levin.
— The Secret Garden. unabridged ed. (Wordsworth Classics). (YA). (gr. 6-12). 1998. 5.27 (*0-89061-104-1*, R1041WW, Jamestwn Pub) NTC Contemp Pub Co.

Burnett, Frances Hodgson. The Secret Garden, Set. abr. ed. Baxter, Beth, ed. (J). (gr. 3-7). 1986. pap. 12.95 incl. audio (*1-882071-05-0*, 006) B&B Audio.

Burnett, Frances Hodgson. The Secret Garden, Set. unabridged ed. (YA). (gr. 5 up). 1997. 24.95 incl. audio (*1-57270-040-8*, H61040, Pub. by Audio Partners) Publishers Group.
— The Secret Garden; A Little Princess; Little Lord Fauntleroy. LC 95-14138. 576p. (J). 1995. 11.99 (*0-517-14748-3*) Random Hse Value.
— Secret Garden Book & Charm. adapted ed. (Illus.). 368p. (J). (gr. 4-7). 1998. 5.95 (*0-694-01110-X*) HarpC.
— The Secret Garden Coloring Book. (Illus.). (J). (gr. 4-7). 1993. pap. 2.95 (*0-486-27680-5*) Dover.
— The Secret Garden, Musical. 107p. (J). (gr. 1 up). 1997. pap. 5.95 (*0-87129-652-7*, S34) Dramatic Pub.
— The Secret Garden Paper Dolls. adapted ed. (Illus.). 24p. (J). (ps-3). 1998. 7.95 (*0-694-00969-5*) HarpC Child Bks.
— Secret Garden, with Charm, Key-Shaped. LC 93-244268. (Illus.). 48p. (J). (ps-3). 1993. pap. 12.95 (*0-590-47173-2*) Scholastic Inc.
— The Shuttle. 22.95 (*0-8488-0253-5*) Amereon Ltd.
— Surly Tim & Other Stories. LC 77-103500. (Short Story Index Reprint Ser.). 1977. 21.95 (*0-8369-3242-0*) Ayer.
— T. Tembaron. 22.95 (*0-8488-0254-3*) Amereon Ltd.
— That Lass O'Lowries. LC 97-156750. (Pocket Classics Ser.). 160p. 1997. pap. 10.95 (*0-7509-1410-6*, Pub. by Sutton Pub Ltd) Intl Pubs Mktg.
— That Lass O'Lowries, 2 vols., 1 bk. LC 79-3329. reprint ed. 44.50 (*0-404-61798-0*) AMS Pr.
— Through One Administration. LC 67-29260. reprint ed. pap. text 6.95 (*0-89197-965-4*); reprint ed. lib. bdg. 19.50 (*0-8398-0181-5*) Irvington.

***Burnett, Frances Hodgson.** The White People. LC 99-80178. 164p. 2000. write for info. (*1-893766-17-9*) Aeon Pub Co.

***Burnett, Frances Hodgson & Konigsburg, E. L.** The Secret Garden. (Classics Ser.). 304p. (J). 1999. pap. 3.99 (*0-689-83141-2*) Aladdin.

***Burnett, Frances Hodgson, et al.** The Secret Garden. LC 99-33392. (Young Classics Ser.). (J). 1999. write for info. (*0-7894-4943-9*) DK Pub Inc.

Burnett, Frances Hodgson, jt. auth. see Cotler, Amy.

Burnett, G. Jersey Central Diesels. Bernet, Gerard E., ed. LC 89-50012. 192p. 1991. 48.00 (*0-9618503-7-X*) Withers Pub.

Burnett, Gail, ed. Inner Strings, Poetry. 1980. pap. 3.00 (*0-318-03121-3*) Aegis Pub Co.
— Thyrsus-Poems. 1985. pap. 6.00 (*0-318-03122-1*) Aegis Pub Co.
— Thyrsus II. 1990. pap. 12.00 (*0-685-60195-1*) Aegis Pub Co.

Burnett, Gail, jt. auth. see Boa, Kenneth.

***Burnett, Gail Lemley.** Muscular Dystrophy. rev. ed. LC 00-8401. (Health Watch Ser.). (Illus.). 48p. (YA). (gr. 5 up). 2000. lib. bdg. 18.95 (*0-7660-1651-X*) Enslow Pubs.

Burnett, Gary. H. D. Between Image & Epic: The Mysteries of Her Poetics. LC 89-27653. (Studies in Modern Literature: No. 111). 206p. (C). reprint ed. 63.90 (*0-8357-2042-X*, 207070100004) Bks Demand.

Burnett, Gene M. Florida's Past, Vol. II. 1997. pap. text 12.95 (*1-56164-139-1*) Pineapple Pr.
— Florida's Past Vol. 1: People & Events That Shaped the State. LC 86-15048. (Illus.). 278p. 1996. pap. 12.95 (*1-56164-115-4*) Pineapple Pr.
— Florida's Past Vol. 3: People & Events That Shaped the State. LC 91-15048. (Illus.). 277p. 1996. pap. 12.95 (*1-56164-117-0*) Pineapple Pr.

Burnett, George. Breadman's Healthy Bread. 288p. 1992. 15.00 (*0-688-12025-3*, Wm Morrow) Morrow Avon.

Burnett, Georgellen. We Just Toughed It Out: Women Heads of Households on the Llano Estacado. (Southwestern Studies Ser.: No. 90). 65p. 1990. pap. 10.00 (*0-87404-176-7*) Tex Western.

Burnett, Granville. Up from Harlem. 80p. 1991. pap. 5.95 (*0-936369-21-3*) Son Rise Pubns.

Burnett-Hall, Richard. Environmental Law, Vol. 1. 1994. 200.00 (*0-421-47090-9*, Pub. by Sweet & Maxwll) Gaunt.

Burnett, Hallie & Burnett, Whit. Fiction Writers Hdbk. 224p. 1993. reprint ed. pap. 13.00 (*0-06-273169-6*, Harper Ref) HarpC.

Burnett, I. Emett, jt. auth. see Pankake, Anita M., Jr.

Burnett, J. J. Sketches of Tennessee's Pioneer Baptist Preachers: History of Baptist Beginnings in the Several Associations in the State. (Illus.). 576p. 1985. reprint ed. 21.95 (*0-932807-11-9*) Overmountain Pr.

Burnett, Jacquetta H., et al. Anthropology & Education: An Annotated Bibliographic Guide. LC 73-94324. (Bibliographies Ser.). 168p. 1974. 15.00 (*0-87536-231-1*); pap. 10.00 (*0-87536-232-X*) HRAFP.

Burnett, Jacquetta H., jt. ed. see Kimball, Solon T.

Burnett, James. The Music of Gustav Mahler. LC 84-29790. 232p. 1985. 36.50 (*0-8386-3167-3*) Fairleigh Dickinson.

Burnett, James, jt. auth. see Gammond, Peter.

Burnett-James, David. Ravel. (Illustrated Lives of the Great Composers Ser.). (Illus.). 144p. 1987. pap. 17.95 (*0-7119-0987-3*, OP44015) Omnibus NY.
— Sibelius. (Illustrated Lives of the Great Composers Ser.). (Illus.). 128p. 1989. pap. 17.95 (*0-7119-1683-7*, OP45004) Omnibus NY.

Burnett, Jane. Crucigramas Para Estudiantes. (SPA., Illus.). 30p. 1990. pap. 14.60 (*0-8442-7229-9*, Natl Textbk Co) NTC Contemp Pub Co.
— Easy Spanish Crossword Puzzles. (SPA., Illus.). 64p. 1994. pap. 4.95 (*0-8442-7244-2*, 72442, Natl Textbk Co) NTC Contemp Pub Co.

Burnett, Jefferson G. & Orem, Donna, compiled by. Questions & Answers on Gift Substantiation & Quid Pro Quo Disclosure Statement Requirements for Private Schools. 40p. 1994. 29.95 (*0-89964-308-6*, 28001) Coun Adv & Supp Ed.

Burnett, Jim. Tee Times. LC 97-28121. 1997. 24.50 (*0-684-83128-7*) S&S Trade.

Burnett, Joanne. Piaget's Babies: The First Two Years of Life: Child Development for the Intellectual. 200p. (Orig.). 1995. pap. 21.95 (*0-9647389-0-2*) J Burnett.
— Take Charge of Your Baby's Development: From Day One Through Toilet-Training, Boy Version. (Illus.). 340p. (Orig.). 1995. pap., ring bd. 54.95 (*0-9647389-1-0*) J Burnett.
— Take Charge of Your Baby's Development: From Day One Through Toilet-Training, Girl Version. (Illus.). 340p. (Orig.). 1995. pap., ring bd. 54.95 (*0-9647389-2-9*) J Burnett.

An Asterisk (*) at the beginning of an entry indicates that the title is appearing for the first time.

Burnett, John. Destiny Obscure: Autobiographies of Childhood, Education, & Family from the 1820s to the 1920s. LC 93-39254. (Modern British History Ser.). 352p. (C). 1994. pap. 25.99 (*0-415-10401-7*, B4098) Routledge.

— A History of the Cost of Living. (Modern Revivals in Economic & Social History Ser.). 366p. 1993. 69.95 (*0-7512-0161-8*, Pub. by Gregg Pub) Ashgate Pub Co.

— Liquid Pleasures: Social History of Drinks in Modern Britain. LC 98-54588. 1999. pap. 24.99 (*0-415-13182-0*); text. write for info. (*0-415-13181-2*) Routledge.

— Useful Toil: Autobiographies of Working People from the 1820s to the 1920s. LC 93-39961. 352p. (C). 1994. pap. 25.99 (*0-415-10399-1*, B4447) Routledge.

Burnett, John & Oddy, Derek J., eds. The Origins & Development of Food Policies in Europe. LC 93-5647. 1994. 64.00 (*0-7185-1474-2*) St Martin.

Burnett, John, jt. auth. see Moriarty, Sandra.

Burnett, John, jt. auth. see Putnam, Robert E.

Burnett, John, jt. auth. see Wells, William.

Burnett, John, ed. see Oddy, Dereka J.

Burnett, John A., jt. auth. see Mayer, Lawrence C.

Burnett, John H. Mycogenetics: An Introduction to the General Genetics of Fungi. LC 74-13143. 389p. reprint ed. pap. 120.60 (*0-608-18413-6*, 203043500069) Bks Demand.

Burnett, John H., jt. ed. see Polunin, Nicholas.

Burnett, John J. Promotion Management. (C). 1992. text 75.96 (*0-395-56553-7*) HM.

***Burnett, Karen Gedig.** Simon's Hook: A Story about Teases & Put-Downs. LC 99-71709. (Illus.). 40p. (J). (gr. 1-4). 1999. 14.95 (*0-9668530-0-8*); pap. 8.95 (*0-9668530-1-6*) GR Pubg.

Burnett, Keith, ed. Spectral Line Shapes: Proceedings, 6th International Conference, Boulder, CO, July, 1982, Vol. 2. 1057p. 1983. 300.00 (*3-11-008846-0*) De Gruyter.

— Ultracold Atoms & Bose-Einstein-Condensation: Trends in Optics & Photonics. LC 96-69617. (TOPS Ser.: Vol. 7). 300p. (Orig.). 1996. pap. 55.00 (*1-55752-465-3*) Optical Soc.

Burnett, Keith, et al, eds. Bose-Einstein Condensation: An Introduction. (Illus.). 180p. (Orig.). (C). 1996. pap. text 50.00 (*0-7881-3740-9*) DIANE Pub.

Burnett, Ken. The Project Management Paradigm. LC 98-2641. (Practitioner Ser.). xiv, 266p. 1998. pap. 79.95 (*3-540-76238-8*) Spr-Verlag.

— Relationship Fundraising. (Illus.). 332p. 1995. 40.00 (*0-9518971-0-1*) Precept Pr.

— Strategic Customer Alliances: How to Win, Manage & Develop Key Account Business in the 1990s. 1994. 35.00 (*0-7863-0144-9*, Irwn Prfssnl) McGraw-Hill Prof.

Burnett, Leo. 100 Leos: Wit & Wisdom from Leo Burnett. (Illus.). 128p. 1995. pap. 6.95 (*0-8442-3420-6*, NTC Business Bks) NTC Contemp Pub Co.

Burnett, Lou. Reveries of an Artist. 165p. (Orig.). (YA). 1996. pap. write for info. (*1-57502-253-2*, P0935) Morris Pubng.

Burnett, Margaret. Indians Don't Kiss. 202p. (Orig.). 1996. pap. 16.00 (*0-7486-6212-X*, Pub. by Polygon) Subterranean Co.

***Burnett, Mark.** Survivor! (Illus.). 240p. 2000. pap. 19.95 (*1-57500-143-8*, Pub. by TV Bks) HarpC.

Burnett, Mark T. & Manning, John. New Essays on Hamlet. LC 93-4052. (Hamlet Collection: No. 1). 1994. 52.50 (*0-404-62311-5*) AMS Pr.

***Burnett, Mark Thornton & Wray, Ramona.** Shakespeare, Film, Fin de Siecle. LC 99-59390. 2000. 42.00 (*0-312-23148-2*) St Martin.

Burnett, Mary S. Heartwaves: Daily Meditations for Children. LC 97-23003. 192p. (Orig.). (J). (gr. 2-7). 1997. pap. text 17.95 (*0-89390-396-5*) Resource Pubns.

Burnett, Mary W. The Principles of Occult Healing. 2nd ed. 135p. 1996. reprint ed. spiral bd. 12.00 (*0-7873-0133-7*) Hlth Research.

— The Principles of Occult Healing (1918) 136p. 1996. reprint ed. pap. 10.95 (*1-56459-888-8*) Kessinger Pub.

Burnett, Mary W., ed. The Principles of Occult Healing. 135p. 1981. pap. 14.00 (*0-89540-072-3*, SB-072) Sun Pub.

Burnett, Michael. Jamaican Music. (Topics in Music Ser.). (Illus.). 48p. 1985. pap. text 10.95 (*0-19-321333-8*) OUP.

— Jazz. (Topics in Music Ser.). (Illus.). 48p. 1986. pap. text 10.95 (*0-19-321336-2*) OUP.

Burnett, Neil. Turning Assets into Prosperity: How to Trade Your Way to Financial Success. 206p. 1982. pap. 7.95 (*0-940986-03-5*) ValuWrite.

Burnett, Nicholas & Harrington, Steve. The Best Adventure Yet. (Illus.). 100p. (Orig.). (J). (gr. 1-7). 1996. pap. 5.95 (*0-9624629-6-9*) Maritime Pr.

Burnett, Oscar, ed. Ecumenical Perspectives 1989. (Ecumenicom Ser.). 32p. (Orig.). 1990. pap. 2.00 (*0-9614976-2-9*) Archives Belmont.

Burnett, P. A., jt. ed. see D'Arcy, C. J.

Burnett, Patricia H. True Colors: An Artist's Journey from Beauty Queen to Feminist. 183p. 1995. 29.95 (*1-879094-48-7*) Momentum Bks.

Burnett, Peter H. Recollections & Opinions of an Old Pioneer. LC 76-87661. (American Scene Ser.). 1969. reprint ed. lib. bdg. 55.00 (*0-306-71765-4*) Da Capo.

***Burnett, R. George, et al.** Wisconsin Trial Practice. LC 99-34642. 1999. ring bd. 145.00 (*1-57862-033-3*) State Bar WI.

Burnett, Rachel. IT, Business Management & Law. (C). Date not set. text 39.95 (*1-85554-804-6*) Blackwell Pubs.

— Outsource IT: The Legal Contract. LC 97-47695. 175p. 1998. 96.95 (*0-566-07698-5*, Pub. by Gower) Ashgate Pub Co.

Burnett, Raymond G. Menopause. (Illus.). 144p. 1987. pap. 12.75 (*0-8092-4677-5*, 467750, Contemporary Bks) NTC Contemp Pub Co.

Burnett, Rebecca & Ewald, Helen R. Business Communication. LC 96-46561. 665p. (C). 1996. 89.00 (*0-205-16243-6*) Allyn.

Burnett, Rebecca E. Careers for Numbers Crunchers: And Other Quantitative Types. LC 92-24334. (Careers for You Ser.). (Illus.). 192p. 1994. pap. 9.95 (*0-8442-8137-9*, 81379, VGM Career) NTC Contemp Pub Co.

— Careers for Numbers Crunchers: And Other Quantitative Types. LC 92-24334. (Careers for You Ser.). (Illus.). 192p. 1994. 14.95 (*0-8442-8136-0*, 81360, VGM Career) NTC Contemp Pub Co.

— Technical Communication. 2nd ed. 668p. (C). 1990. pap. 39.95 (*0-534-12426-7*) Wadsworth Pub.

— Technical Communication. 3rd ed. 680p. 1993. mass mkt. 41.00 (*0-534-19932-1*) Wadsworth Pub.

— Technical Communication. 4th ed. LC 96-44283. (Freshman English/Advanced Writing Ser.). (C). 1996. 46.50 (*0-534-51605-X*) Wadsworth Pub.

Burnett, Reggi. Adam's Table. 2nd rev. ed. LC 93-61037. 96p. 1994. otabind 8.95 (*0-945383-59-2*) Teach Servs.

Burnett, Robert. The Global Jukebox: The International Music Industry. LC 95-9247. 192p. (C). 1996. pap. 22.99 (*0-415-09276-0*) Routledge.

— The Global Jukebox: The International Music Industry. LC 95-9247. 192p. (C). 1996. 70.00 (*0-415-09275-2*) Routledge.

Burnett, Robert, ed. see Cushman, Helen B.

Burnett, Robin. Law of International Business Transactions. 296p. 1994. 64.00 (*1-86287-131-0*, Pub. by Federation Pr) Gaunt.

***Burnett, Robin.** Law of International Business Transactions. 2nd ed. LC 99-205177. 338p. 1999. pap. 59.00 (*1-86287-299-6*, Pub. by Federation Pr) Gaunt.

Burnett, Robin. The Pillbug Project: A Guide to Investigation. (Illus.). 110p. 1992. pap. text 16.50 (*0-87355-109-5*) Natl Sci Tchrs.

Burnett, Robyn K. & Luebbering, Ken. German Settlement in Missouri: New Land, Old Ways. Schroeder, Rebecca B., ed. (Missouri Heritage Readers Ser.). (Illus.). 128p. (C). 1996. pap. 8.95 (*0-8262-1094-5*) U of Mo Pr.

Burnett, Ron. These Images Which Rain down into the Imaginary. LC 94-48674. 368p. 1995. pap. 16.95 (*0-253-20977-3*) Ind U Pr.

Burnett, Ron, ed. Explorations in Film Theory: Selected Essays from "Cine-Tracts" LC 89-46337. (Illus.). 318p. 1991. 42.00 (*0-253-31282-5*) Ind U Pr.

Burnett, Rosalie, et al, eds. Accounting for Relationships: Explanation, Representation & Knowledge. (Illus.). 480p. 1988. text 75.00 (*0-416-41410-9*) Routledge.

Burnett, Sarah. A Passion for Color: Creating Brilliant Custom Yarns from Simple Natural Dyes, with 20 Exclusive Knit Designs for Adults & Children. (Illus.). 160p. 1990. text 39.95 (*0-02-518625-6*) Macmillan.

Burnett, Sarah & Octopus, Conran. A Passion for Color. Petrini, Elisa, ed. 160p. 1990. 39.95 (*0-685-32663-2*) Macmillan Info.

Burnett, Sarah & Saifuddin, Asif. Exercises in Diagnostic Imaging. 150p. 1997. text 52.00 (*90-5702-017-3*, Harwood Acad Pubs); pap. text 22.00 (*90-5702-018-1*, Harwood Acad Pubs) Gordon & Breach.

Burnett Smith, Barbara, et al. 'Tis the Season for Murder: Christmas Crimes. 1998. per. 6.99 (*0-373-26290-6*, 1-26290-6, Wrldwide Lib) Harlequin Bks.

***Burnett Smith, Mary.** Miss Ophelia. 288p. 1998. reprint ed. pap. 13.00 (*0-688-16357-2*, Quil) HarperTrade.

Burnett, Stanton H., et al. The Italian Guillotine: Operation Clean Hands & the Overthrow of Italy's First Republic. LC 98-12811. 352p. 1998. 62.00 (*0-8476-8877-1*); pap. 22.95 (*0-8476-8878-X*) Rowman.

Burnett, Stephen G. From Christian Hebraism to Jewish Studies: Johannes Buxtorf (1564-1629) & Hebrew Learning in the Seventeenth Century. LC 96-16632. (Studies in the History of Christian Thought, 0081-8607: Vol. 68). 1996. 109.50 (*90-04-10346-5*) Brill Academic Pubs.

***Burnett, Steven.** Windows 2000 & UNIX Integration Guide. (Network Professional's Library). 544p. 2000. pap. 49.99 (*0-07-212167-X*) McGrw-H Intl.

Burnett, Stuart, jt. auth. see Holland, James.

Burnett, T. A. J., ed. see Browning, Robert.

***Burnett, Tommy I.** Roxie's Country Cookbook. (Illus.). 300p. 1999. 18.95 (*0-9673603-0-7*) Country Road.

Burnett, V. Compton, tr. see Steiner, Rudolf.

Burnett, Vena & Weiss, Jennifer. Colon Cleanse the Easy Way. 15p. Date not set. pap. 2.95 (*0-913923-42-7*) Woodland UT.

— Limpiar el Colon (Colon Cleanse) (SPA.). 1985. pap. 3.95 (*0-913923-51-6*) Woodland UT.

Burnett, Virgil. A Comedy of Eros. 112p. 1984. pap. write for info. (*0-88984-055-5*) Porcup Quill.

— Towers at the Edge of a World. 216p. 1983. pap. write for info. (*0-88984-082-2*) Porcup Quill.

Burnett, W. C. & Riggs, S. R., eds. Phosphate Deposits of the World Vol. 3: Genesis of Neogene to Recent Phosphorites. (World & Regional Geology Ser.). (Illus.). 480p. (C). 1990. text 175.00 (*0-521-33370-9*) Cambridge U Pr.

Burnett, W. R. Captain Lightfoot. 224p. reprint ed. lib. bdg. 21.95 (*0-89190-495-6*, Rivercity Pr) Amereon Ltd.

— High Sierra. 1982. reprint ed. lib. bdg. 16.95 (*0-89966-422-9*) Buccaneer Bks.

— Little Caesar. 156p. 1986. pap. 3.50 (*0-88184-235-4*) Carroll & Graf.

— Little Caesar. 316p. 1994. 35.00 (*1-883402-78-6*) S&S Trade.

— Little Caesar. 308p. reprint ed. lib. bdg. 20.95 (*0-89190-485-9*, Rivercity Pr) Amereon Ltd.

Burnett, Whit. Maker of Signs. LC 79-106252. (Short Story Index Reprint Ser.). 1977. 20.95 (*0-8369-3289-7*) Ayer.

Burnett, Whit, ed. Spirit of Man. LC 68-58775. (Essay Index Reprint Ser.). 1977. 24.95 (*0-8369-0036-7*) Ayer.

Burnett, Whit, jt. auth. see Burnett, Hallie.

Burnett, William. Laboratory Manual for Principles of Biology I. 132p. (C). 1996. spiral bd. 17.95 (*0-7872-2105-8*) Kendall-Hunt.

— Laboratory Manual for Principles of Biology I. 2nd ed. 164p. (C). 1998. spiral bd. 29.95 (*0-7872-5120-8*, 41512001) Kendall-Hunt.

Burnett, William & Henderson, Stanley D. Cases & Comment on Contracts. 7th ed. LC 98-150315. (University Casebook Ser.). 950p. 1998. text 42.00 (*1-56662-590-4*) Foundation Pr.

Burnett, William G. The Prison Camp at Andersonville. (Civil War Ser.). (Illus.). 44p. 1995. pap. 4.95 (*0-915992-84-1*) Eastern National.

Burnett, William R. Le Capitaine Lightfoot. (FRE.). 1984. pap. 15.95 (*0-7859-2002-1*, 2070376141) Fr & Eur.

— Le Petit Cesar. (FRE.). 256p. 1987. pap. 11.95 (*0-7859-2068-4*, 2070378527) Fr & Eur.

— Quand la Ville Dort. (FRE.). 310p. 1989. pap. 11.95 (*0-7859-2133-8*, 2070382087) Fr & Eur.

Burnett, Yumiko M., tr. see Rodieck, Jorma.

Burnette, jt. auth. see McAnulty.

***Burnette, Ada, et al.** FTCE Administrative. (C). 2000. per. 22.50 (*1-58197-072-2*) XAM.

— PRAXIS Administrative. (Praxis Ser.). (C). 2000. per. 40.00 (*1-58197-050-1*) XAM.

Burnette, Allyson C. Pocket Power No. 6: Travel. Leonard, Joseph M., ed. 48p. (Orig.). 1988. pap. 2.95 (*0-945893-05-1*) Pocket Power.

Burnette, Alma. A Journal. Miller, Lafe, ed. (Illus.). 32p. (Orig.). (J). (gr. 1-8). 1994. 2.95 (*1-886452-04-9*) Amer Recycling.

— Omi-Tutu-Kekere. Miller, Lafe, ed. (Illus.). 28p. (Orig.). (J). (gr. 1-8). 1994. 2.95 (*1-886452-02-4*) Amer Recycling.

— Sukoshi No-Kireina-Kuuki. Miller, Lafe, ed. (Illus.). 28p. (Orig.). (J). (gr. 1-8). 1994. 2.95 (*1-886452-03-2*) Amer Recycling.

— Ukandoit. Miller, Lafe, ed. (Illus.). 28p. (Orig.). (J). (gr. 1-8). 1994. 2.95 (*1-886452-00-8*) Amer Recycling.

— Vanishing-No-More. Miller, Lafe, ed. (Illus.). 28p. (Orig.). (J). (gr. 1-8). 1994. 2.95 (*1-886452-01-6*) Amer Recycling.

Burnette, Brenda E., jt. auth. see Chicone, Jerry, Jr.

Burnette, Jeff. Good Credit a Valuable Asset: A Consumer Credit Reference Guide. LC 88-70546. 84p. (Orig.). 1988. pap. 12.95 (*0-945838-00-X*) Burnette Assocs.

***Burnette, Melanie M.** 365 Bible Prayers for Children. 244p. (J). 2000. 7.99 (*0-517-16207-5*) Random Hse Value.

Burnette, Melanie M. 365 Read-To-Me Prayers for Children. 1999. 10.99 (*0-8054-9387-5*) Broadman.

— 365 Read to Me Bedtime Stories: A Story a Day from the Creation to the Resurrection. (J). 1998. 10.99 (*0-8054-9338-7*) Broadman.

Burnette, Patricia. Prayer Journal, 1. 63p. 1998. ring bd. 14.99 (*0-9668295-0-6*) Word of Wis.

Burnette, Robert B. The Baptism into the Holy Spirit. (Holy Spirit Ser.: Vol. 1). 64p. 1991. pap. 3.95 (*1-881202-09-7*) Anointed Pubns.

— The Equippers: Apostles, Prophets, Evangelists, Pastors, & Teachers. 64p. 1991. pap. 3.95 (*1-881202-08-9*) Anointed Pubns.

— The Gifts of the Holy Spirit. (Holy Spirit Ser.: Vol. 2). 64p. 1990. pap. 3.95 (*1-881202-03-8*) Anointed Pubns.

— Holy Spirit Baptism. 86p. 1990. student ed. 9.95 (*1-881202-02-X*) Anointed Pubns.

— Jesus: The Miracle Worker & the Gifts of the Holy Spirit. 64p. 1992. pap. 3.95 (*1-881202-12-7*) Anointed Pubns.

— Let's Talk about Salvation. 56p. 1990. pap. 3.95 (*1-881202-06-2*) Anointed Pubns.

— Let's Talk about the Bible. 68p. 1990. pap. 3.95 (*1-881202-07-0*) Anointed Pubns.

— Let's Talk about the Church. 56p. 1990. pap. 3.95 (*1-881202-05-4*) Anointed Pubns.

— Let's Talk about Witnessing. 68p. 1992. pap. 3.95 (*1-881202-10-0*) Anointed Pubns.

— Life with Jesus. 48p. 1988. pap. 2.95 (*1-881202-00-3*) Anointed Pubns.

— Manna for the Hungry-Hearted. 56p. 1989. pap. 3.95 (*1-881202-01-1*) Anointed Pubns.

— Praying with the Holy Spirit. (Holy Spirit Ser.: Vol. 3). 64p. 1990. pap. 3.95 (*1-881202-04-6*) Anointed Pubns.

— What's Your Objection to Holy Spirit Baptism? 90p. 1992. student ed. 9.95 (*1-881202-11-9*) Anointed Pubns.

Burnette, Ronald, et al. Solutions to Practice Sets to Accompany Hanson-Hamre-Walgenbach Principles of Accounting, 6-E & Financial Accounting, 7-E. 134p. (C). 1993. 7.50 (*0-03-097393-7*) Dryden Pr.

Burney, Anna C. Tempi Moderni. (ITA.). 204p. (C). 1982. pap. text 40.00 (*0-03-059557-6*) Harcourt Coll Pubs.

Burney, C. F. Israel's Settlement in Canaan: The Biblical Tradition & Its Historical Background. 3rd ed. (British Academy, London, Schweich Lectures on Biblical Archaeology Series, 1930). 1969. reprint ed. pap. 25.00 (*0-8115-1259-2*) Periodicals Srv.

Burney, Charles. An Account of the Musical Performances in Westminster Abbey. LC 78-31784. (Music Reprint Ser.). 1979. reprint ed. 39.50 (*0-306-79524-8*) Da Capo.

— Dr. Charles Burney's Continental Travels. LC 76-26048. reprint ed. 37.50 (*0-404-12920-X*) AMS Pr.

— Memoirs of Dr. Charles Burney, 1726-1769. Klima, Slava et al, eds. LC 87-6060. xl, 233p. 1988. text 55.00 (*0-8032-1197-X*) U of Nebr Pr.

— The Present State of Music in France & Italy. fac. ed. (Monuments of Music & Music Literature in Facsimile Ser., Series II: Vol. 70). 1969. lib. bdg. 50.00 (*0-8450-2270-9*) Broude.

— The Present State of Music in France & Italy. 2nd ed. LC 74-24263. 1976. reprint ed. 55.00 (*0-404-12875-0*) AMS Pr.

— The Present State of Music in Germany, The Netherlands & United Provinces. fac. ed. (Monuments of Music & Music Literature in Facsimile Ser., Series II: Vol. 117). 1969. lib. bdg. 125.00 (*0-8450-2317-9*) Broude.

Burney, Cindy, jt. auth. see Parris, Sonia L.

***Burney, Deborah.** Speaking in Prophetic Voice. 100p. 2000. pap. 14.95 (*1-883866-19-7*) Clarion Pub.

***Burney, Elizabeth.** Crime & Banishment: Nuisance & Exclusion in Social Housing. (Criminal Policy Ser.). 159p. 1999. pap. 36.00 (*1-872870-79-1*, 18472, Pub. by Waterside Pr) Gaunt.

Burney, Elizabeth. Sentencing Young People: The Effects of the Criminal Justice Act 1982. 120p. 1985. 46.95 (*0-566-05127-3*) Ashgate Pub Co.

Burney, Fanny. Camilla. Bloom, Edward A. & Bloom, Lillian D., eds. (Oxford World's Classics Ser.). (Illus.). 990p. 1999. pap. 13.95 (*0-19-283908-X*) OUP.

— The Early Journals & Letters of Fanny Burney: The Streatham Years, 1778-1779, Vol. III. Troide, Lars E., ed. (Illus.). 512p. 1994. 70.00 (*0-7735-0527-X*, Pub. by McG-Queens Univ Pr) CUP Services.

— The Early Journals & Letters of Fanny Burney: 1768-1773, Vol. I. Troide, Lars E., ed. 406p. 1988. 70.00 (*0-7735-0538-5*, Pub. by McG-Queens Univ Pr) CUP Services.

— The Early Journals & Letters of Fanny Burney: 1774-1777, Vol. II. Troide, Lars E., ed. 550p. (C). 1991. text 70.00 (*0-7735-0539-3*, Pub. by McG-Queens Univ Pr) CUP Services.

— Evelina: Or the History of a Young Lady's Entrance into the World. Bloom, Edward A., ed. & intro. by. (Oxford World's Classics Ser.). (Illus.). 462p. 1998. pap. 9.95 (*0-19-283396-0*) OUP.

— Fanny Burney: Selected Letters & Journals. Hemlow, Joyce, ed. (Illus.). 410p. 1986. 55.00 (*0-19-818528-6*) OUP.

— The Journals & Letters of Fanny Burney (Madame d'Arblay), 2 vols., Vols. IX & X. Derry, Warren, ed. (Illus.). 1,090p. (C). 1982. text 275.00 (*0-19-812508-9*) OUP.

— The Journals & Letters of Fanny Burney (Madame d'Arblay), 1812-1814 Vol. 7: Letters 632-834, Vol. 7. Bloom, Edward A. et al, eds. (Illus.). (C). 1979. 105.00 (*0-19-812468-6*) OUP.

— The Journals & Letters of Fanny Burney (Madame d'Arblay), 1815 Vol. 8: Letters 835-934. Hughes, Peter et al, eds. (Illus.). (C). 1980. 109.00 (*0-19-812507-0*) OUP.

— Journals of Fanny Burney (Madam D'Arblay), 12 vols. Incl. Set. Mayfair, 1818-1824, Letters, 1180-1354. (Illus.). 1,134p. 1984. text 225.00 (*0-19-812563-1*); Vol. 1. 1791 to 1792, Letters 1-39. Hemlow, Joyce, ed. 1972. 58.00 (*0-19-811498-2*); Vol. 3. Great Bookham, 1793-1797. Hemlow, Joyce. (Illus.). (C). 1973. 58.00 (*0-19-812419-8*); Vol. 4. West Humble, 1797-1801. Hemlow, Joyce, ed. (Illus.). 560p. 1973. 110.00 (*0-19-812432-5*); Vol. 5. West Humble & Paris, 1801-1803, Letters 423-549. Hemlow, Joyce, ed. 1976. 79.00 (*0-19-812467-8*); Vol. 6. France, 1803-1812, Letters 550-631. Hemlow, Joyce, ed. (C). 1976. 72.00 (*0-19-812516-X*); Vol. 12. Mayfair, 1825-1840, Letters, 1355-1521. Hemlow, Joyce. 74.50 (Illus.). write for info. (*0-318-54852-6*) OUP.

— The Witlings. Delery, Clayton J., ed. (Early Women Writers 1650-1800 Ser.: No. 3). 161p. 1995. 29.95 (*0-937191-55-8*) Mich St U Pr.

— The Witlings & the Woman Hater by Frances Burney. Sabor, Peter & Sill, Geoffrey M., eds. LC 97-28194. (Pickering Woman's Classics Ser.). 204p. Date not set. 55.00 (*1-85196-360-X*, Pub. by Pickering & Chatto) Ashgate Pub Co.

Burney, Fanny & Cooke, Stewart J. Evelina: Or the History of a Young Lady's Entrance into the World: Authoritative Text, Contexts & Contemporary Reactions & Criticisms. LC 96-54869. (Norton Critical Editions Ser.). (C). 1998. pap. text 13.25 (*0-393-97158-9*) Norton.

***Burney, Frances.** Cecilia: Memoirs of an Heiress. (Oxford World's Classics Ser.). 1,056p. 1999. pap. 12.95 (*0-19-283909-8*) OUP.

Burney, Frances. The Complete Plays of Frances Burney: Comedies & Tragedies, Set, Vols. 1 & 2. Sill, Geoffrey M. et al, eds. 800p. 1995. text 180.00 (*0-7735-1333-7*) McG-Queens Univ Pr.

— The Early Diary of Frances Burney, 1768-78, 2 Vols. Ellis, Annie R., ed. LC 70-37331. (Select Bibliographies Reprint Ser.). 1977. reprint ed. 52.95 (*0-8369-6678-3*) Ayer.

— Evelina. Doody, Margaret Anne, ed. & intro. by. 544p. 1994. pap. 11.95 (*0-14-043347-3*, Penguin Classics) Viking Penguin.

— The Wanderer. Doody, Margaret Anne et al, eds. (Oxford World's Classics Ser.). 1008p. 1999. pap. 15.95 (*0-19-283758-3*) OUP.

Burney, Frances, jt. auth. see More, Hannah.

***Burney, H. S., et al, eds.** Chlor-Alkali & Chlorate Technology: R. B. MacMullin Memorial Symposium. 278p. 1999. 62.00 (*1-56677-244-3*, PV 99-21) Electrochem Soc.

Burney, I. H. No Illusions, Some Hope & Fears: The Outlook Editorials of I. H. Burney. 564p. 1996. 35.00 (*0-19-577687-9*) OUP.

Burney, Ian A. Bodies of Evidence: Medicine & the Politics of the English Inquest, 1830-1926. LC 99-29328. 1999. 39.95 (*0-8018-6240-X*) Johns Hopkins.

B

An Asterisk (*) at the beginning of an entry indicates that the title is appearing for the first time.

Burney, Jan. Ettore Sottsass. Pawley, Martin, ed. (Design Heroes Ser.). (Illus.). 192p. 1992. 24.95 (*0-8008-2468-7*) Taplinger.

Burney, Joan R. The Keepers Vol. 1: A Merry Heart Doeth Good. (Illus.). 218p. (Orig.). 1987. pap. 10.00 (*0-9626645-0-2*) J Burney.

— The Keepers Vol. I: A Merry Heart Doeth Good. (Illus.). 218p. (Orig.). 1996. pap. write for info. (*1-57579-021-1*) Pine Hill Pr.

— The Keepers Vol. 2: Comes the Dawn. (Illus.). 220p. 1989. pap. 10.00 (*0-9626645-1-0*) J Burney.

— The Keepers Vol. II: Comes the Dawn. (Illus.). 211p. (Orig.). 1996. pap. write for info. (*1-57579-022-X*) Pine Hill Pr.

— The Keepers Vol. III: Hyacinth's for the Soul. (Illus.). (Orig.). 1997. pap. write for info. (*1-57579-023-8*) Pine Hill Pr.

Burney, Joan R., jt. auth. see Chandler, Phyllis.

Burney, Joan R., jt. auth. see Pedersen, Mary J.

Burney, John M. Training the Bourgeoisie: The University of Toulouse in the Nineteenth Century-Faculties & Students in Provincial France. (Modern European History Ser.). 392p. 1987. text 15.00 (*0-8240-8033-5*) Garland.

***Burney-Nissen, Laura.** Strategies for Integrating Substance Abuse Treatment & the Juvenile Justice System: A Practical Guide. 239p. (C). 2000. pap. text 35.00 (*0-7567-0166-X*) DIANE Pub.

Burney, Pierre. Orthographie. 128p. 1967. 9.95 (*0-8288-7462-X*) Fr & Eur.

Burney, Robert. Codependence - The Dance of Wounded Souls: A Cosmic Perspective of Codependence & the Human Condition. LC 95-95029. 128p. (Orig.). 1996. pap. 14.95 (*0-9648383-1-1*) Joy To You.

Burney, Sarah H. The Letters of Sarah Harriet Burney. Clark, Lorna J., ed. LC 94-49167. 1997. 85.00 (*0-8203-1746-2*) U of Ga Pr.

Burney, Simon. Cyclo-Cross. 2nd ed. LC 96-37531. (Illus.). 160p. 1996. pap. 14.95 (*1-884737-20-X*) VeloPress.

Burney, Tracy L. If You Could Be. (Illus.). ix, 16p. (J). (ps-6). 1997. pap. text 4.95 (*0-9666663-0-5*) T B Bks.

Burnfield, Alexander. Multiple Sclerosis: A Personal Exploration. (Illus.). 192p. (Orig.). 1997. pap. 14.95 (*0-285-65018-1*, Pub. by Souvenir Pr Ltd) IPG Chicago.

Burnford, Sheila. The Incredible Journey. LC 96-216595. (J). 1996. 15.95 (*0-385-32279-8*, Delacorte Pr Bks) BDD Bks Young Read.

— The Incredible Journey. (J). (gr. 6-8). 18.95 (*0-88411-099-0*) Amereon Ltd.

— The Incredible Journey. (Illus.). 160p. (J). (gr. 5-7). 1995. mass mkt. 4.99 (*0-440-22670-8*) BDD Bks Young Read.

— The Incredible Journey. 160p. (J). 1997. pap. 4.99 (*0-440-41324-9*) Dell.

Burnford, Sheila. The Incredible Journey. 148p. pap. 4.99 (*0-8072-8323-1*) Listening Lib.

Burnford, Sheila. The Incredible Journey. (J). 10.00 (*0-614-30526-8*) NAVH.

— The Incredible Journey. large type ed. (Illus.). (J). 1995. 42.50 (*0-614-09589-1*, L-34835-00) Am Printing Hse.

Burnford, Sheila Every. The Incredible Journey. (J). 1996. 9.60 (*0-606-00867-5*, Pub. by Turtleback) Demco.

Burnham & Bennett Staff. Plan of Chicago. LC 93-14988. (Illus.). 268p. 1993. reprint ed. 75.00 (*1-878271-41-5*) Princeton Arch.

***Burnham, Alexander, ed.** We Write for Our Own Time: Selected Essays from Seventy-Five Years of the Virginia Quarterly Review. LC 99-36026. 512p. 2000. 60.00 (*0-8139-1914-2*); pap. 19.95 (*0-8139-1983-5*) U Pr of Va.

Burnham, Archie C., Jr. & Abrams, Bernard S. Roadway Through the MUTCD: Vision & Other Human Factors in the Manual on Uniform Traffic Control Devices. LC 98-44993. (Illus.). 101p. 1998. spiral bd. 35.00 (*0-913875-51-1*, 5511-N) Lawyers & Judges.

Burnham, Audrey & Rand Drug Policy Research Center Staff. Review & Evaluation of the Substance Abuse & Mental Health Services Block Grant Allotment Formula. LC 97-29269. 1998. pap. 20.00 (*0-8330-2548-1*) Rand Corp.

Burnham, Barry & Wacher, John. The Small Towns of Roman Britain. LC 90-41007. (Illus.). 388p. 1991. 60.00 (*0-520-07303-7*, Pub. by U CA Pr) Cal Prin Full Svc.

Burnham, Bill. The Electronic Commerce Report. LC 98-10373. 400p. 1998. 29.95 (*0-07-009238-9*) McGraw.

— A Fascination with Falcons: A Biologist's Adventures from Greenland to the Tropics. 216p. 1997. pap. 29.95 (*0-88839-415-2*) Hancock House.

Burnham, Bill, jt. auth. see Burnham, Mary.

***Burnham, Brad.** Hammerhead Shark. LC 00-24762. (Underwater World of Sharks Ser.). (Illus.). (J). 2000. write for info. (*0-8239-5584-2*, PowerKids) Rosen Group.

— The Mako Shark. LC 00-25483. (Underwater World of Sharks Ser.). (Illus.). (J). 2000. write for info. (*0-8239-5585-0*, PowerKids) Rosen Group.

— The Sand Tiger Shark. LC 99-59153. (Underwater World of Sharks Ser.). (Illus.). (J). 2000. lib. bdg. write for info. (*0-8239-5707-1*) Rosen Group.

— The Whale Shark. LC 00-22375. (Illus.). 2000. write for info. (*0-8239-5587-7*) Rosen Group.

Burnham, Byron R. Evaluating Human Resources & the Organization. (Professional Practices in Adult Education & Human Resource Development Ser.). 142p. (C). 1995. lib. bdg. 21.00 (*0-89464-680-X*) Krieger.

Burnham, C. G., ed. Second World Congress on Superconductivity. 400p. (C). 1992. text 114.00 (*981-02-0618-6*) World Scientific Pub.

Burnham, C. Wayne, et al. Thermodynamic Properties of Water to 1,000 C & 10,000 Bars. LC 73-96715. (Geological Society of America, Special Paper: No. 132). 104p. reprint ed. pap. 32.30 (*0-608-15643-4*, 203186600077) Bks Demand.

Burnham, Carol. Attic Light. LC 96-3049. 1997. 22.00 (*1-877946-88-5*) Permanent Pr.

Burnham, Charles. The Linkman. large type ed. (Linford Western Library). 272p. 1995. pap. 16.99 (*0-7089-7748-0*, Linford) Ulverscroft.

— The Nighthawk. large type ed. (Linford Western Library). 256p. 1997. pap. 16.99 (*0-7089-5002-7*, Linford) Ulverscroft.

Burnham, Christopher C. Writing from the Inside Out. 296p. (C). 1988. pap. text 3.00 (*0-15-597866-7*) Harcourt Coll Pubs.

Burnham, Clara L. Sweet Clover: A Romance of the White City. LC 92-70330. (Great Lakes Romances Ser.). 256p. (Orig.). 1992. reprint ed. pap. 8.95 (*0-923048-80-4*) Bigwater Pub.

— West Point Wooing & Other Stories. LC 79-94709. (Short Story Index Reprint Ser.). 1977. 20.95 (*0-8369-3088-6*) Ayer.

Burnham, Clint. Be Labour Reading. 100p. 1997. pap. 12.00 (*1-55022-344-5*, Pub. by ECW) LPC InBook.

— The Jamesonian Unconscious: The Aesthetics of Marxist Theory. Fish, Stanley Eugene & Jameson, Fredric, eds. LC 94-41965. (Post-Contemporary Interventions Ser.). 272p. 1995. text 49.95 (*0-8223-1585-8*); pap. text 17.95 (*0-8223-1613-7*) Duke.

— Steven McCaffery. (Canadian Author Studies). 55p. 1997. pap. 9.95 (*1-55022-326-7*, Pub. by ECW) LPC InBook.

Burnham, Colin. Classic Volkswagen: Colour Classics. (Illus.). 128p. 1996. pap. 10.95 (*1-85532-651-5*, Pub. by Ospry) Stackpole.

Burnham, Daniel. The World's Columbian Exposition, 2 vols. Draper, Joan E. & Hines, Thomas, eds. (Illus.). 8500p. 1989. text 125.00 (*0-8240-3723-5*) Garland.

Burnham, Daniel H. & Bennett, Edward H. Plan of Chicago Prepared under the Direction of the Commercial Club During the Years 1906, 1907, 1908. Moore, Charles, ed. LC 71-75303. (Architecture & Decorative Art Ser.: Vol. 29). (Illus.). 1970. reprint ed. lib. bdg. 125.00 (*0-306-71261-X*) Da Capo.

Burnham, David. Above the Law: Secret Deals, Political Fixes, Misadventure U. S. Department of Justice. 448p. 1996. 27.50 (*0-684-80699-1*) S&S Trade.

Burnham, Deborah. Anna & the Steel Mill. LC 94-31356. 75p. 1995. 16.50 (*0-89672-345-3*) Tex Tech Univ Pr.

Burnham, Dorothy K. Cut My Cote. (Illus.). 36p. 1994. pap. write for info. (*0-88854-046-9*) Royal Ontario.

— To Please the Caribou. (Illus.). 328p. 1996. 60.00 (*0-88854-399-9*); pap. write for info. (*0-88543-964-3*) Royal Ontario.

— Unlike the Lilies: Doukhobor Textile Traditions in Canada. (Illus.). 112p. 1994. pap. write for info. (*0-88854-322-0*) Royal Ontario.

— Warp & Weft: A Textile Terminology. (Illus.). 232p. 1994. write for info. (*0-88854-256-9*) Royal Ontario.

Burnham, Dorothy K., jt. auth. see Burnham, Harold B.

Burnham, Guy. The Lake Superior Country in History & in Story. (Illus.). 464p. 1996. reprint ed. pap. 19.50 (*1-889924-00-8*) Paradigm Pr WI.

Burnham, Harold B. & Burnham, Dorothy K. Keep Me Warm One Night: Early Handweaving in Eastern Canada. LC 72-83388. (Illus.). 1972. 80.00 (*0-8020-1896-3*) U of Toronto Pr.

Burnham, J. H. History of Bloomington & Normal, in McLean Co., Ill. (Illus.). 145p. 1997. reprint ed. pap. 19.50 (*0-8328-5713-0*); reprint ed. lib. bdg. 27.50 (*0-8328-5712-2*) Higginson Bk Co.

Burnham, James. Coming Defeat of Communism. LC 68-8735. (Illus.). 278p. 1968. reprint ed. lib. bdg. 65.00 (*0-8371-0035-6*, BUDC, Greenwood Pr) Greenwood.

— Congress & the American Tradition. LC 96-20943. 363p. 1996. pap. 12.95 (*0-89526-717-9*, Gateway Editions) Regnery Pub.

— The Machiavellians. LC 70-117762. (Essay Index Reprint Ser.). 1977. 19.95 (*0-8369-1785-5*) Ayer.

— The Machiavellians: Defenders of Freedom. LC 87-23253. 246p. 1987. pap. 7.95 (*0-89526-785-3*) Regnery Pub.

— The Managerial Revolution: What Is Happening in the World. LC 71-138102. 285p. 1972. reprint ed. lib. bdg. 38.50 (*0-8371-5678-5*, BUMR, Greenwood Pr) Greenwood.

— Suicide of the West: An Essay on the Meaning & Destiny of Liberalism. LC 64-14211. 320p. 1985. reprint ed. pap. 9.95 (*0-89526-822-1*) Regnery Pub.

Burnham, James, jt. auth. see Wood, Stephen.

Burnham, Janelle, et al. Inspirational Romance Reader No. 3: Historical Collection. 400p. 1999. pap. 4.97 (*1-57748-605-6*) Barbour Pub.

Burnham, Janet Hayward. Love Takes a Country Road, Vol. 1. LC 99-21839. 1999. pap. 21.95 (*0-7838-8614-4*) Thorndike Pr.

Burnham, Joan M., tr. see Dalichow, Irene & Booth, Mike.

Burnham, Joan M., tr. see Rilke, Rainer Maria.

Burnham, John C. Bad Habits: Drinking, Smoking, Taking Drugs, Gambling, Sexual Misbehavior & Swearing in American History. (Illus.). 385p. (C). 1994. pap. text 20.00 (*0-8147-1224-X*) NYU Pr.

— How Superstition Won & Science Lost: Popularizing Science & Health in the United States. LC 86-31360. 381p. 1987. reprint ed. pap. 118.20 (*0-7837-5659-3*, 205908500005) Bks Demand.

— Jelliffe: American Psychoanalyst & Physician. McGuire, William, ed. LC 83-1076. (Illus.). 344p. 1983. 30.00 (*0-226-08114-1*) U Ch Pr.

— Psychoanalysis & American Medicine, 1894-1918: Medicine, Science, & Culture. LC 67-31293. (Psychological Issues Monographs: No. 20, Vol. 5, No. 4). 249p. (Orig.). 1967. 37.50 (*0-8236-5100-2*) Intl Univs Pr.

Burnham, John C., ed. see Kempf, Edward J.

Burnham, John H., jt. ed. see Prince, Ezra M.

Burnham, John M. Integrative Facilities Management. LC 93-14481. (APICS Ser.). 300p. 1993. 47.50 (*1-55623-679-4*, Irwn Prfssnl) McGraw-Hill Prof.

— Just-in-Time in a Major Process Industry: Case Studies of JIT Implementation at ALCOA. American Production & Inventory Control Society St, ed. LC 86-72791. 115p. 1986. pap. 20.00 (*0-935406-87-5*) Am Prod & Inventory.

Burnham, John M., jt. auth. see Fogarty, Donald W.

Burnham, Jon. The Winning Pitch. 154p. (Orig.). 1995. pap. 7.95 (*1-883928-10-9*) Longwood.

Burnham, June, tr. see Laidi, Zaki.

Burnham, K. P., et al. Design & Analysis Methods for Fish Survival Experiments Based on Release - Recapture. LC 87-70785. (Monograph Ser.: No. 5). 437p. 1987. text 37.00 (*0-913235-41-5*, 520.05C) Am Fisheries Soc.

Burnham, K. P., jt. auth. see Anderson, D. A.

Burnham, Kenneth E. God Comes to America: Father Divine & the Peace Mission Movement. LC 78-27677. 170p. 1995. 40.00 (*0-931186-01-3*) Lambeth Pr.

***Burnham, Linda.** Arizona: A Guide to Unique Places. 3rd ed. (Off the Beaten Path Ser.). (Illus.). 2001. pap. 12.95 (*0-7627-0803-4*) Globe Pequot.

Burnham, Linda F. Bob & Bob: The First Five Years. LC 80-67655. (Illus.). 100p. (Orig.). 1980. pap. 12.00 (*0-937122-00-9*) Astro Artz Eighteenth St.

Burnham, Linda F. & Durland, Steven, eds. The Citizen Artist: 20 Years of Art in the Public Arena. LC 98-70739. (Thinking Publicly: No. 2). (Illus.). 384p. 1998. pap. 18.00 (*1-883831-10-5*, 810561) Critical Pr.

***Burnham, Mary & Burnham, Bill.** Hike America: Virginia. (Illus.). 2000. pap. 17.95 (*0-7627-0763-1*) Globe Pequot.

Burnham, Mayumi, ed. & tr. see Shioda, Yoshihiko & Ina, Fumio.

Burnham, Michael, jt. auth. see Riley, Jan.

Burnham, Michelle. Captivity & Sentiment: Cultural Exchange in American Literature, 1682-1861. LC 96-49268. (Re-Encounters with Colonialism Ser.). (Illus.). 223p. 1997. 35.00 (*0-87451-818-0*) U Pr of New Eng.

Burnham, Michelle. Captivity & Sentiment: Cultural Exchange in American Literature, 1682-1861. LC 96-49268. (Reencounters with Colonialism Ser.). (Illus.). 223p. 1997. pap. 17.95 (*1-58465-016-8*) U Pr of New Eng.

Burnham, Murry & Tinsley, Russell. Murry Burnham's Hunting Secrets. LC 83-13315. (Illus.). 244p. 1983. 17.95 (*0-8329-0343-4*, Winchester Pr) New Win Pub.

Burnham, Nellie. Knitted Toys & Dolls: Complete Instructions for 17 Easy-to-Do Projects. (Illus.). 32p. (Orig.). 1982. pap. 2.95 (*0-486-24148-3*) Dover.

Burnham, Patricia G. Playtraining Your Dog. (Illus.). 256p. 1985. pap. 11.95 (*0-312-61691-0*) St Martin.

Burnham, Patricia M. & Giese, Lucretia H., eds. Redefining American History Painting. (Illus.). 427p. (C). 1995. text 105.00 (*0-521-46059-X*) Cambridge U Pr.

Burnham, Patricia M., et al. John Trumbull: The Hand & Spirit of a Painter. Cooper, Helen, ed. (Illus.). 308p. 1982. pap. 25.00 (*0-89467-024-7*) Yale Art Gallery.

Burnham, Peter. The Political Economy of Postwar Reconstruction. LC 91-164362. xiv, 228 p. 1990. write for info. (*0-333-48289-1*) Macmillan.

— Surviving the Research Process in Politics. LC 97-40768. 1997. pap. 24.95 (*1-85567-447-5*) Bks Intl VA.

Burnham, Peter, ed. Research Process in Politics & International Relations. LC 97-40768. 210p. 1997. 75.00 (*1-85567-446-7*) Bks Intl VA.

Burnham, Philip. Gbaya. LC 96-15575. (Heritage Library of African Peoples: Set 3). (Illus.). 64p. (YA). (gr. 7-12). 1996. lib. bdg. 16.95 (*0-8239-1995-1*, D1995-1) Rosen Group.

***Burnham, Philip.** Indian Country, God's Country: Native Americans & the National Parks. LC 99-50934. (Illus.). 384p. 2000. 27.50 (*1-55963-667-X*) Island Pr.

Burnham, Philip. The Politics of Cultural Difference in Northern Cameroon. 272p. 1996. text 45.00 (*1-56098-694-8*) Smithsonian.

Burnham, Philip, jt. auth. see Lederer, Richard.

Burnham, Phillip & Lederer, Richard. Basic Verbal Skills. 2nd ed. 243p. (gr. 9-12). 1980. student ed. 10.06 (*0-88334-130-1*, 76104); pap. text 16.32 (*0-88334-134-4*, 76106) Longman.

— Basic Verbal Skills for the Middle School. 1976. 9.15 (*0-8013-0071-1*, 75735); student ed. 18.66 (*0-88334-073-9*, 76066) Longman.

— Basic Verbal Skills for the Middle School Grammar & Punctuation Workbook. 1976. 5.88 (*0-88334-074-7*, 76067); student ed. 9.15 (*0-8013-0072-X*, 75736) Longman.

Burnham, R. & Hogan, R. The Cork Dramatic Society: Lost Plays of the Irish Renaissance, Vol. III. 1985. pap. 3.95 (*0-912262-82-6*) Proscenium.

Burnham, R. Peter. The Least Shadow. (Juniper Bks.: Vol. 63). 84p. (Orig.). 1996. pap. 12.00 (*1-55780-149-5*) Juniper Pr ME.

Burnham, Richard. Housing Ourselves: Creating Affordable, Sustainable Shelter. 1998. 59.95 (*0-07-009236-2*); pap. 36.95 (*0-07-009237-0*) McGraw.

Burnham, Richard, jt. auth. see Hogan, Robert T.

Burnham, Robert, Jr. Burnham's Celestial Handbook: An Observer's Guide to the Universe Beyond the Solar System, Vol. 3. (Illus.). 1979. pap. 14.95 (*0-486-23673-0*) Dover.

Burnham, Robert. Comet Hale-Bopp: Find & Enjoy the Great Comet. (Illus.). 64p. (C). 1997. pap. 13.95 (*0-521-58636-4*) Cambridge U Pr.

— Great Comets. LC 98-50546. (Illus.). 230p. 1999. pap. 21.95 (*0-521-64600-6*) Cambridge U Pr.

***Burnham, Robert, contrib. by.** Night Sky: An Explore Your World Handbook. LC 99-35934. (Illus.). 192p. 1999. pap. 13.95 (*1-56331-801-6*) Discovery.

Burnham, Robert, Jr. & Luft, Herbert A. Burnham's Celestial Handbook: An Observer's Guide to the Universe Beyond the Solar System, 1. LC 77-82888. (Illus.). 1978. reprint ed. pap. 14.95 (*0-486-23567-X*) Dover.

— Burnham's Celestial Handbook: An Observer's Guide to the Universe Beyond the Solar System, 2. LC 77-82888. (Illus.). 1978. reprint ed. pap. 14.95 (*0-486-23568-8*) Dover.

Burnham, Robert, et al. Advanced Skywatching. O'Byrne, John, ed. LC 97-22875. (Nature Company Guides Ser.). (Illus.). 288p. (gr. 9). 1997. 24.95 (*0-7835-4941-5*) Time-Life.

Burnham, Robert E. Who Are the Finns? A Study in Prehistory. LC 76-44701. reprint ed. 32.50 (*0-404-15913-3*) AMS Pr.

Burnham, Roderick H. Burnham: Genealogical Records of Thomas Burnham. 2nd ed. 292p. 1991. reprint ed. pap. 45.50 (*0-8328-2107-1*); reprint ed. lib. bdg. 55.50 (*0-8328-2106-3*) Higginson Bk Co.

— The Burnham Family; or Genealogical Records of the Descendants of the Four Emigrants of the Name, Who Were among the Early Settlers in America. (Illus.). 546p. 1989. reprint ed. pap. 84.00 (*0-8328-0351-0*); reprint ed. lib. bdg. 94.00 (*0-8328-0350-2*) Higginson Bk Co.

— Burt. Genealogical Records of Henry & Eulalia Burt, the Emigrants, Who Early Settled at Springfield, Ma., & Their Descendants Through Nine Generations, 1640-1891. 347p. 1996. reprint ed. pap. 47.00 (*0-8328-5434-4*); reprint ed. lib. bdg. 57.00 (*0-8328-5433-6*) Higginson Bk Co.

Burnham, Saranne D. Three River Junction: A Story of an Alaskan Bald Eagle Preserve. (Illus.). 32p. (J). (gr. 1-4). 1997. 15.95 (*1-56899-441-9*); 19.95 incl. audio (*1-56899-443-5*, BC7003); pap. 5.95 (*1-56899-442-7*) Soundprints.

— Three River Junction: A Story of an Alaskan Bald Eagle Preserve, Incl. plush toy. (Illus.). 36p. (J). (gr. 1-4). 1997. 26.95 (*1-56899-444-3*); 31.95 incl. audio (*1-56899-445-1*) Soundprints.

— Three River Junction: A Story of an Alaskan Bald Eagle Preserve, Incl. toy. (Illus.). 36p. (J). (gr. 1-4). 1997. pap. 16.95 (*1-56899-446-X*); pap. 19.95 incl. audio (*1-56899-447-8*) Soundprints.

Burnham Schwartz, John. Reservation Road. LC 98-14580. 292p. 1998. 24.00 (*0-375-40263-2*) Knopf.

— Reservation Road. 1999. pap. 13.00 (*0-375-70273-3*) Knopf.

— Reservation Road. large type ed. LC 98-48521. 1999. 30.00 (*0-7862-1740-5*, G K Hall Lrg Type) Mac Lib Ref.

***Burnham, Scott.** Beethoven & His World. (Illus.). 300p. 2000. 55.00 (*0-691-07072-5*); pap. 19.95 (*0-691-07073-3*) Princeton U Pr.

Burnham, Scott. Beethoven Hero. LC 95-8981. 232p. 1995. text 32.50 (*0-691-04407-4*, Pub. by Princeton U Pr) Cal Prin Full Svc.

***Burnham, Scott.** Beethoven Hero. 2000. pap. text 18.95 (*0-691-05058-9*, Pub. by Princeton U Pr) Cal Prin Full Svc.

Burnham, Scott, ed. see Marx, A. B.

Burnham, Scott J. The Contract Drafting Guidebook: 1992 Edition. 511p. 1992. text 60.00 (*0-87473-958-6*, 60712-10, MICHIE) LEXIS Pub.

— Drafting Contract: 1987 Edition. 1987. pap. text. write for info. (*0-87473-332-4*, 10635-10, MICHIE) LEXIS Pub.

— Drafting Contracts, 1993. 2nd ed. 1993. pap. 20.00 (*0-87473-313-8*, 10634-10, MICHIE) LEXIS Pub.

Burnham, Scott J., jt. auth. see Rosett, Arthur.

Burnham, Sophy. Angel Letters. 160p. 1996. pap. 12.00 (*0-345-37866-0*) Ballantine Pub Grp.

— A Book of Angels. 1995. mass mkt. 6.99 (*0-345-40057-7*) Ballantine Pub Grp.

— A Book of Angels: Reflection on Angels Past & Present & True Stories of How They Touch Our Lives. large type ed. (Illus.). 256p. 1991. pap. 12.95 (*0-8027-2661-5*) Walker & Co.

— A Book of Angels: Reflections on Angels Past & Present & True Stories of How They Touch Our Lives. (Illus.). 256p. 1990. pap. 12.00 (*0-345-36157-1*) Ballantine Pub Grp.

— A Book of Angels: Reflections on Angels Past & Present & True Stories of How They Touch Our Lives. 320p. 1994. pap. 10.00 (*0-345-37355-3*) Ballantine Pub Grp.

— The Ecstatic Journey: The Transforming Power of Mystical Experience. LC 97-23311. 320p. 1997. 25.00 (*0-345-39507-7*) Ballantine Pub Grp.

— The Ecstatic Journey: The Transforming Power of Mystical Experience. 323p. 1999. reprint ed. text 23.00 (*0-7881-6252-7*) DIANE Pub.

— The Ecstatic Journey: Walking the Mystical Path in Everyday Life. 1999. pap. 14.00 (*0-345-42479-4*) Ball Well.

— For Writers Only. 224p. 1996. pap. 11.00 (*0-345-40405-X*) Ballantine Pub Grp.

Burnham, Stanley. America's Bimodal Crisis: Black Intelligence in White Society. 3rd ed. 160p. 1993. 10.00 (*0-936396-06-7*) Foun Human GA.

Burnham, Sue. Shinkansen Readers: A Sumo Story, C Level. 3.95 (*0-8219-1680-7*) EMC-Paradigm.

— Shinkansen Readers: Cheesecake Crepes in Kyoto, B level. 3.95 (*0-8219-1679-3*) EMC-Paradigm.

An Asterisk (*) at the beginning of an entry indicates that the title is appearing for the first time.

— Shinkansen Readers: I Want to be a Samurai, A Level. 3.95 (*0-8219-1676-9*) EMC-Paradigm.
— Shinkansen Readers: Nightmare on Dan's Street, A Level. 3.95 (*0-8219-1674-2*) EMC-Paradigm.
— Shinkansen Readers: Satodo Surfs the Net, A Level. 3.95 (*0-8219-1675-0*) EMC-Paradigm.
— Shinkansen Readers: Teacher's Activity Book. 14.95 (*0-8219-1683-1*) EMC-Paradigm.
— Shinkansen Readers: Temples in Kyoto, Soccer in Osaka, C level. 3.95 (*0-8219-1681-5*) EMC-Paradigm.
— Shinkansen Readers: To Yuki from Michael, B Level. 3.95 (*0-8219-1677-7*) EMC-Paradigm.
— Shinkansen Readers: Toyotomi Faces the Monsters, B level. 3.95 (*0-8219-1678-5*) EMC-Paradigm.
***Burnham, T. Lee.** A Parent Toolkit for Success with Children. 150p. 1999. 20.00 (*0-9676686-0-3*) Rocky Mtn Ctr.
***Burnham, Terry & Phelan, Jay.** Mean Genes: From Sex to Money to Food--Taming Our Primal Instincts. 224p. 2000. text 24.00 (*0-7382-0230-4*, Pub. by Perseus Pubng) HarpC.
Burnham, Trudie. Innovative Soy Cooking. LC 98-26030. (Specialty Cookbook Ser.). (Illus.). 96p. 1998. pap. 6.95 (*0-89594-962-8*) Crossing Pr.
Burnham, Virginia S., jt. auth. see Hampton, William H.
Burnham, W. Dean. Presidential Ballots, 1836-1892. LC 75-22806. (America in Two Centuries Ser.). 1976. reprint ed. 78.95 (*0-405-07678-9*) Ayer.
Burnham, Walter D., ed. The American Prospect Reader in American Politics. LC 94-23157. 400p. (Orig.). (C). 1994. pap. text 19.95 (*1-56643-012-7*, Chatham House Pub) Seven Bridges.
Burnham, Weldon. General Chemistry Lab Studies. 3rd ed. 442p. (C). 1998. per. 42.95 (*0-7872-5184-4*, 41518401) Kendall-Hunt.
***Burnham, Weldon.** General Chemistry Lab Studies. 4th ed. 442p. (C). 2000. per. 43.95 (*0-7872-7242-6*) Kendall-Hunt.
Burnham, Weldon S. General Chemistry Laboratory Studies. 2nd ed. 448p. (C). 1996. pap. text, per. 35.95 (*0-7872-2437-5*) Kendall-Hunt.
Burnham, William. Introduction to the Law & Legal System of the U. S. (American Casebook Ser.). 625p. (C). 1995. pap. text 45.00 (*0-314-06661-6*) West Pub.
Burnham, William, jt. auth. see Danilenko, G. M.
Burnham, William H. Great Teachers & Mental Health: A Study of Seven Educational Hygienists. LC 72-156623. (Essay Index Reprint Ser.). 1977. reprint ed. 26.95 (*0-8369-2273-5*) Ayer.
Burnhans, William, tr. see Rossi, Jacques.
Burnharn, Fredrick. Scouting on Two Continents. 1993. reprint ed. 35.00 (*1-879356-31-7*) Wolfe Pub Co.
— Taking Chances. 140p. 1994. reprint ed. 35.00 (*1-879356-32-5*) Wolfe Pub Co.
Burnheim, John. Is Democracy Possible? 1986. pap. 16.95 (*0-520-06596-4*, Pub. by U CA Pr) Cal Prin Full Svc.
***Burnie, Brian.** Foundations: Society, Challenge & Change. 2nd ed. 320p. 1999. 29.95 (*1-55077-109-4*) Thompson Educ.
Burnie, David. Animals: How They Work. LC 93-43404. (Illus.). 48p. (J). 1994. 14.95 (*0-8069-0742-8*) Sterling.
— El Arbol. (SPA.). 1995. 18.95 (*84-372-3708-4*) Santillana.
***Burnie, David.** Bird. (Eyewitness Books). (J). (gr. 4-7). 2000. 19.99 (*0-7894-6550-7*) DK Pub Inc.
— Bird. (Eyewitness Books). (J). (gr. 4-7). 2000. 15.95 (*0-7894-5800-4*) DK Pub Inc.
Burnie, David. The Concise Encyclopedia of the Human Body. LC 95-15134. (Illus.). 160p. (YA). (gr. 5 up). 1995. 19.95 (*0-7894-0204-1*, 5-70617) DK Pub Inc.
— Dictionary of Nature. LC 93-30696. (J). (gr. 3 up). 1994. 19.95 (*1-56458-473-9*) DK Pub Inc.
***Burnie, David.** Earth. (Concise Encyclopedias Ser.). 192p. (YA). (gr. 5-9). 2000. pap. text 5.95 (*0-7894-6105-6*, D K Ink) DK Pub Inc.
Burnie, David. Evolution. LC 98-52940. (Get a Grip On... Ser.). (Illus.). 192p. (gr. 7). 1998. pap. 14.95 (*0-7370-0036-8*) T-L Custom Pub.
— Flowers: Investigate the Colorful World of Flowers, Fruits, & Seeds. LC 91-58209. (Eyewitness Explorers Ser.). (Illus.). (J). (gr. k-3). 1992. 9.95 (*1-56458-023-7*) DK Pub Inc.
— Forest. LC 98-17808. (Inside Guides Ser.). (J). 1998. write for info. (*0-7894-3492-X*) DK Pub Inc.
***Burnie, David.** Human Body. (Concise Encyclopedias Ser.). 160p. (YA). (gr. 5-9). 2000. pap. text 5.95 (*0-7894-6104-8*, D K Ink) DK Pub Inc.
Burnie, David. Insects & Spiders. Time-Life Books Editors, ed. LC 96-28417. (Nature Company Discoveries Library). (Illus.). 64p. (J). (gr. 4-7). 1999. 16.00 (*0-7835-4881-8*) Time-Life.
***Burnie, David.** The Kingfisher Illustrated Animal Encyclopedia. (Illus.). 320p. (YA). 2000. 27.95 (*0-7534-5283-9*) LKC.
Burnie, David. Light. LC 92-7661. (Eyewitness Books). (Illus.). 64p. (J). (gr. 4-7). 1992. 15.95 (*1-879431-79-3*) DK Pub Inc.
— Machines & How They Work. LC 91-60147. (See & Explore Library). (Illus.). 64p. (J). (gr. 3 up). 1991. 12.95 (*1-879431-15-7*) DK Pub Inc.
— Mammals. LC 92-54312. (Eyewitness Explorers Ser.). (Illus.). 64p. (J). (gr. 4-7). 1993. 9.95 (*1-56458-228-0*) DK Pub Inc.
— Microlife. LC 97-18888. (Inside Guides Ser.). (J). (gr. 3-6). 1997. write for info. (*0-7894-2036-8*) DK Pub Inc.
***Burnie, David.** Plant. (Eyewitness Books). (Illus.). (J). (gr. 4-7). 2000. 19.99 (*0-7894-6563-9*) DK Pub Inc.
— Plant. (Eyewitness Books). (J). (gr. 4-7). 2000. 15.95 (*0-7894-5812-8*) DK Pub Inc.
Burnie, David. Seashore. LC 93-31075. (Eyewitness Explorers Ser.). (Illus.). 64p. (J). (gr. k-3). 1994. 9.95 (*1-56458-323-6*) DK Pub Inc.
— Tree. (Eyewitness Books). (J). (gr. 4-7). 2000. 19.99 (*0-7894-6554-X*) DK Pub Inc.
— Tree. (Eyewitness Books). (J). (gr. 4-7). 2000. 15.95 (*0-7894-5820-9*) DK Pub Inc.
Burnie, David. Tree. LC 88-1572. (Eyewitness Books). (Illus.). 64p. (J). (gr. 5 up). 1988. 19.00 (*0-394-89617-3*, Pub. by Knopf Bks Yng Read) Random.
— Tree. LC 88-1572. (Eyewitness Books). (Illus.). 64p. (J). (gr. 5 up). 1988. lib. bdg. 20.99 (*0-394-99617-8*, Pub. by Knopf Bks Yng Read) Random.
Burnie, David, et al. Man Changes the World. LC 98-25947. (Earth, Its Wonders, Its Secrets Ser.). 1999. write for info. (*0-7621-0115-6*) RD Assn.
Burnie, David A. Animals. LC 92-15434. (Picture Pockets Ser.). (J). 1993. pap. 13.00 (*0-671-79130-3*) S&S Bks Yung.
— How Nature Works: 100 Ways Parents & Kids Can Share the Secrets of Nature. LC 91-12432. (Illus.). 192p. (J). (gr. 3 up). 1991. 24.00 (*0-89577-391-0*, Pub. by RD Assn) Penguin Putnam.
***Burnie, Geoffrey.** Flowers. LC 99-88296. (Little Guides Ser.). (Illus.). 320p. 2000. reprint ed. 14.95 (*1-875137-75-0*) Weldon Owen.
Burnie, James P., ed. see Matthews, Ruth.
Burnie, Joan. Postbus Country: Glimpses of Rural Scotland. (Illus.). 128p. 1995. 24.95 (*0-86241-484-9*, Pub. by Canongate Books) Interlink Pub.
— Scotland the Worst! A Collection of the Truly Awful, Incredibly Trivial & Totally Unspeakable. 156p. 1996. pap. 11.95 (*0-86241-553-5*, Pub. by Canongate Books) Interlink Pub.
Burnie, Richard. Monumental Mazes. LC 98-49317. (Illus.). 32p. 1999. 14.95 (*0-375-80155-3*) Knopf.
Burnier, Francis. 404 & the Marsh Creek Farmer: Confession of the Marsh Creek Farmer. 80p. 1999. pap. 8.00 (*0-8059-4663-2*) Dorrance.
Burnier, Radha. Human Regeneration: Lectures & Discussions. 1991. pap. 12.95 (*81-7059-169-4*, 8550, Quest) Theos Pub Hse.
Burnier, Radha. No Other Path to Go. 1985. pap. 5.50 (*81-7059-276-3*, Quest) Theos Pub Hse.
***Burnies, Caroline.** Familiar Christmas: Fear Familiar, No. 542. (Intrigue Ser.). 1999. mass mkt. 3.99 (*0-373-22542-3*) Harlequin Bks.
Burnill, Richard. Ishi, in Both Worlds: Biography of the Last Reported Yahi Indian of California, 3 vols. LC 97-94013. (Illus.). (J). (gr. 4-12). Date not set. 22.95 (*1-878464-50-7*); pap. 12.95 (*1-878464-51-5*) Anthro Co.
Burnim, Kalman A. & Highfill, Philip H., Jr. John Bell, Patron of British Theatrical Portraiture: A Catalog of His Theatrical Portraits in His Editions of "Bell's Shakespeare" & "Bell's British Theatre" LC 97-4085. (Illus.). 416p. 1997. 60.00 (*0-8093-2123-8*) S Ill U Pr.
Burnim, Kalman A., ed. see Hill, Aaron & Popple, William.
Burningham, Bradd. The Sad Eye. 208p. 1991. pap. 12.95 (*0-86492-093-8*, Pub. by Goose Ln Edits) Genl Dist Srvs.
Burningham, David, et al. Teach Yourself Economics. (Illus.). 416p. 1995. pap. 12.95 (*0-8442-3918-6*, Teach Yrslf) NTC Contemp Pub Co.
Burningham, Hilary, ed. see Shakespeare, William.
***Burningham, J.** Simp. 1999. pap. write for info. (*0-09-940077-4*, Pub. by Random) Random House.
Burningham, John. The Baby. (J). 1975. 3.95 (*0-690-00900-3*) HarpC Child Bks.
— The Baby. 2nd ed. LC 93-24277. (Illus.). 24p. (J). (ps). 1994. 6.95 (*1-56402-334-6*) Candlewick Pr.
— The Blanket. (J). 1966. 3.95 (*0-690-01269-1*) HarpC Child Bks.
— Cannonball Simp. LC 93-32369. (Illus.). 32p. (J). (ps up). 1994. 15.95 (*1-56402-338-9*) Candlewick Pr.
— Cannonball Simp. 1995. 11.19 (*0-606-07336-1*, Pub. by Turtleback) Demco.
— Cloudland. (Illus.). 48p. (J). (gr. k-3). 1999. pap. 7.99 (*0-517-88589-1*, Pub. by Crown Bks Yng Read) Random.
— Cloudland. LC 95-49467. (J). 1996. lib. bdg. 19.00 (*0-05-170929-5*) Crown Pub Group.
— Cloudland. LC 95-49467. 48p. (J). 1996. 19.00 (*0-517-70928-7*); lib. bdg. 20.99 (*0-517-70929-5*) Random Hse Value.
— The Dog. LC 76-17626. (Illus.). (J). (ps-1). 1977. lib. bdg. 11.89 (*0-690-01272-1*) HarpC Child Bks.
— The Dog. LC 76-17626. (Illus.). (J). (ps-1). 1985. 3.95 (*0-694-00006-X*) HarpC Child Bks.
— Dog. (J). 1966. 3.95 (*0-690-01271-3*) HarpC Child Bks.
— The Dog. 2nd ed. LC 93-10344. (Illus.). 24p. (J). (ps). 1994. 6.95 (*1-56402-326-5*) Candlewick Pr.
— Friend. (J). 1966. 3.95 (*0-690-01273-X*) HarpC Child Bks.
— The Friend. LC 93-10331. (Illus.). 24p. (J). (ps). 1996. reprint ed. pap. 2.99 (*1-56402-931-X*) Candlewick Pr.
— The Friend. 2nd ed. LC 93-10331. (Illus.). 24p. (J). (ps-2). 1994. 6.95 (*1-56402-327-3*) Candlewick Pr.
— Harvey Slumfenburger's Christmas Present. LC 92-54957. (Illus.). 48p. (J). (ps-3). 1996. reprint ed. pap. 7.99 (*1-56402-978-6*) Candlewick Pr.
***Burningham, John.** Harvey Slumfenburger's Present. 48p. (J). (ps-3). 2000. 6.99 (*0-7636-1378-9*) Candlewick Pr.
Burningham, John. Hey! Get off Our Train. (Illus.). 48p. (J). (gr. 1-5). 1999. pap. 7.99 (*0-517-88204-3*, Pub. by Crown Bks Yng Read) Random.
Burningham, John. Hey! Get off Our Train. LC 89-15802. 1994. 13.19 (*0-606-06458-3*, Pub. by Turtleback) Demco.
— John Burningham's ABC. (Illus.). 14p. (J). (ps). 1999. 6.99 (*0-517-80065-9*, Pub. by Crown Bks Yng Read) Random.
Burningham, John. John Burningham's France. LC 98-3523. (J). 1998. 24.95 (*0-7894-2557-2*, D K Ink) DK Pub Inc.
— John Patrick Norman McHennessy - The Boy Who Was Always Late. (Illus.). 40p. (J). (gr. k-3). 1999. pap. 7.99 (*0-517-88595-6*, Pub. by Crown Bks Yng Read) Random.
— Mr. Grumpy's Outing: Big Book. LC 77-159507. (Illus.). 32p. (J). (ps-3). 1995. pap. 19.95 (*0-8050-3854-X*) H Holt & Co.
— Mr. Gumpy's Motor Car. LC 75-4582. (Illus.). 43p. (J). (ps-3). 1976. lib. bdg. 17.89 (*0-690-00799-X*) HarpC Child Bks.
— Mr. Gumpy's Motor Car. (Illus.). (J). (ps-3). 1993. 18.82 (*0-690-00798-1*, 175231) HarpC Child Bks.
— Mr. Gumpy's Outing. LC 77-159507. (Illus.). 32p. (J). (ps-2). 1995. 14.95 (*0-8050-0708-3*, Bks Young Read); pap. 5.95 (*0-8050-1315-6*, Bks Young Read) H Holt & Co.
Burningham, John. Mr. Gumpy's Outing. (J). 1970. 11.15 (*0-606-04482-5*, Pub. by Turtleback) Demco.
Burningham, John. The School. (J). 1975. 3.95 (*0-690-00902-X*) HarpC Child Bks.
— The Shopping Basket. LC 80-7987. (Illus.). 32p. (J). (ps-2). 1980. lib. bdg. 13.89 (*0-690-04083-0*) HarpC Child Bks.
— The Shopping Basket. LC 95-25945. (Illus.). 32p. (J). (ps up). 1997. reprint ed. pap. 5.99 (*0-7636-0098-9*) Candlewick Pr.
— The Shopping Basket. 2nd ed. (Illus.). 32p. (J). 1996. 15.99 (*1-56402-688-4*) Candlewick Pr.
— Time to Get Out of the Bath, Shirley. LC 76-58503. (Illus.). 32p. (J). (gr. k-2). 1978. 13.95 (*0-690-01378-7*); 13.89 (*0-690-01379-5*) HarpC Child Bks.
— Whadayamean. LC 98-44159. 1999. 19.00 (*0-375-80177-4*) Knopf.
***Burningham, John.** Whaddayamean. (Illus.). 48p. (J). (gr. k-3). 1999. 18.95 (*0-517-80066-7*, Pub. by Crown Bks Yng Read); lib. bdg. 20.99 (*0-517-80067-5*, Pub. by Crown Bks Yng Read) Random.
Burningham, Robin. Hawaiian Word Book. (HAW., Illus.). 104p. (Orig.). 1983. pap. 19.95 incl. audio (*1-880188-60-0*) Bess Pr.
Burningham, Robin Y. Hawaiian Word Book. (HAW., Illus.). 104p. (Orig.). 1983. pap. 11.95 (*0-935848-12-6*) Bess Pr.
Burningham, Veronica. Weaving Without a Loom. 1998. pap. 16.95 (*0-85532-818-5*, Pub. by Srch Pr) A Schwartz & Co.
Burnip, John, tr. & illus. see Yovkov, Yordan.
Burnip, M. S. & Newton, A. Non-Woven Fabrics. 105p. 1970. 95.00 (*0-7855-7208-2*) St Mut.
Burnip, M. S. & Thomas, J. H. The Production & Properties of Knitted & Woven Fabrics. 139p. 1969. 90.00 (*0-7855-7214-7*) St Mut.
***Burniske, R. W. & Monke, Lowell.** Breaking Down the Digital Walls: Learning to Teach in a Post-Modem World. (C). 2000. pap. text 19.95 (*0-7914-4754-5*) State U NY Pr.
— Breaking Down the Digital Walls: Learning to Teach in a Post-Modem World. (C). 2001. text 59.50 (*0-7914-4753-7*) State U NY Pr.
Burnisky, David L. The Personalites of Melvin Hill Cemetary Phelps, Ontario Co., NY. (Illus.). 269p. 1996. pap. 28.50 (*0-7884-0383-4*, B868) Heritage Bk.
Burnley, David. A Guide to Chaucer's Language. LC 83-10523. 264p. (Orig.). (C). 1994. pap. text 15.95 (*0-8061-2665-5*) U of Okla Pr.
— The History of the English Language: A Source Book. 400p. (C). 1992. text 66.50 (*0-582-02522-2*, 79004) Longman.
— History of the English Language: Sourcebook. 392p. (C). 1995. pap. 50.00 (*0-582-02521-4*, 79005) Longman.
Burnley, Eric. Surf Fishing the Atlantic Coast. LC 88-39541. (Illus.). 192p. (Orig.). 1989. pap. 14.95 (*0-8117-2301-1*) Stackpole.
Burnley, Ian, et al. Immigration & Australian Cities. 167p. 1997. pap. 34.00 (*1-86287-258-9*, Pub. by Federation Pr) Gaunt.
Burnley, J. D. Courtliness & Literature in Medieval England. LC 97-8831. (Longman Medieval & Renaissance Library). (C). 1998. text 62.81 (*0-582-29215-8*) Longman.
Burnner, Jose J., jt. ed. see Puryear, Jeffrey M.
Burnnett, Carroll. Kikko's Tracks. (Illus.). 28p. (Orig.). (J). (ps up). 1988. pap. 6.95 (*0-9619414-1-3*) Foto Fantasi Pr.
Burns. Criminal Injuries Compensation. 2nd ed. 416p. 1992. boxed set 100.00 (*0-409-80907-1*, MICHIE) LEXIS Pub.
— Dreyfus Affair. LC 98-86157. 1998. pap. text 12.95 (*0-312-11167-3*) St Martin.
— France & the Dreyfus Affair. LC 98-86157. 210p. 1998. text 39.95 (*0-312-21813-3*) St Martin.
***Burns.** Fundamentals of Chemistry. 3rd ed. 1999. suppl. ed. write for info. (*0-13-018817-4*) P-H.
— Fundamentals of Chemistry in the Laboratory. 3rd ed. 1999. pap. 47.00 (*0-13-080160-7*) P-H.
Burns. Fundamentals Of Chemistry. 3rd ed. LC 98-27231. 744p. 1999. 82.00 (*0-13-918665-4*) P-H.
***Burns.** Government by the People. 3rd ed. 199p. 2000. pap., student ed. 16.00 (*0-13-013950-5*) P-H.
— Government by the People. 17th ed. 1998. 62.33 (*0-13-011116-3*) P-H.
— Government by the People. 18th ed. 1999. 22.33 (*0-13-083885-3*) P-H.
Burns. Gracie. 1999. pap. 9.98 (*0-671-04409-5*) PB.
— Hematology. 1999. pap. text. write for info. (*0-7216-4693-X*, W B Saunders Co) Harcrt Hlth Sci Grp.
***Burns.** Hist & Cell Bio Review. 2001. text. write for info. (*0-323-00834-8*) Harcourt.
Burns. Pathfinder. 1998. mass mkt. 6.99 (*0-8041-1602-4*) Ivy Books.
— Polyester Molding Compounds. (Plastics Engineering Ser.: Vol. 2). (Illus.). 352p. 1982. text 160.00 (*0-8247-1280-3*) Dekker.
— Principles of Electrical Circuits. (West Engineering Ser.). 1987. pap., student ed. 16.95 (*0-534-93868-X*); text 60.50 (*0-534-93812-4*); trans. 92.95 (*0-534-93869-8*) PWS Pubs.
— Rocks & Minerals Coloring Book. (Illus.). (J). pap. 2.95 (*0-486-28645-2*) Dover.
— Shinny's Girls & Other Stories. (NFS Canada Ser.). 208p. pap. 15.95 (*0-88922-272-X*, Pub. by Talonbks) Genl Dist Srvs.
— Sociology: Perspectives & Approaches. (C). 1999. pap. text 36.00 (*0-205-27856-6*, Macmillan Coll) P-H.
— Understanding Nursing Research. (C). 1995. pap. text, student ed. 18.95 (*0-7216-4437-6*) Harcourt.
Burns & Oates. The Key to Baroque Art. (Key to Art Guide Bks.). (Illus.). 80p. 1994. pap. 20.00 (*0-85532-665-4*, Pub. by Srch Pr) St Mut.
— The Key to Gothic Arts. (Illus.). 80p. 1994. pap. 25.00 (*0-85532-663-8*, Pub. by Srch Pr) St Mut.
— The Key to Modern Art of the Early 20th Century. (Key to Art Guide Bks.). (Illus.). 80p. (Orig.). 1994. pap. 25.00 (*0-85532-664-6*, Pub. by Srch Pr) St Mut.
— The Key to Painting. (Key to Art Guide Bks.). (Illus.). 80p. (Orig.). 1994. pap. 20.00 (*0-85532-662-X*, Pub. by Srch Pr) St Mut.
— The Key to Renaissance Art. (Key to Art Guide Bks.). (Illus.). 80p. (Orig.). 1994. pap. 20.00 (*0-85532-666-2*, Pub. by Srch Pr) St Mut.
— The Key to Romantic & Impressionist Art. (Key to Art Guide Bks.). (Illus.). 80p. (Orig.). 1994. pap. 20.00 (*0-85532-667-0*, Pub. by Srch Pr) St Mut.
Burns, jt. auth. see Jenkinson.
Burns, jt. auth. see Mason.
Burns, jt. auth. see Peltason.
***Burns & McDonnell Engineering Company Staff & National Rural Electric Cooperative Association Staff.** Design Guide for Rural Substations. LC 99-88739. (Illus.). 1999. pap. write for info. incl. cd-rom (*0-917599-29-2*) Natl Rural.
***Burns, A. August, et al.** Donde No Hay Doctor para Mujeres: Un Manual para la Salud de la Mujer. De Avila, Lisa, tr.Tr. of Where Women Have No Doctor. (SPA.). 5p. 1999. pap. 20.00 (*0-942364-31-7*) Hesperian Found.
Burns, A. August, et al. Where Women Have No Doctor: A Health Guide for Women. Niemann, Sandy, ed. LC 97-19421. 1997. pap. 20.00 (*0-942364-25-2*) Hesperian Found.
Burns, A. B., et al, eds. Desorption Induced by Electronic Transitions, DIET V: Proceedings of the Fifth International Workshop, Taos, NM, March 31-April 4, 1992. (Surface Sciences Ser.: Vol. 31). (Illus.). 360p. 1993. 130.95 (*0-387-56473-X*) Spr-Verlag.
***Burns, A. P., ed.** Multiphase '99: Frontier Technology Comes of Age: Proceedings of the 9th International Conference on Multiphase; Frontier Technology Comes of Age Held in Cannes, France, 1999. (BHR Group Conference Ser.: No. 35). 606p. 1999. 530.00 (*1-86058-212-5*) Prof Eng Pubng.
Burns, A. R., et al, eds. Desorption Induced by Electron Transitions Diet V: Proceedings of the Fifth International Workshop, Taos, NM, March 31-April 4, 1992. LC 93-7305. (Surface Sciences Ser.: Vol. 31). 1993. write for info. (*3-540-56473-X*) Spr-Verlag.
Burns, Aaron, ed. The ITC Typeface Collection. (Illus.). 572p. 1982. 49.95 (*0-9608034-0-8*) Intl Typeface.
Burns, Adele B., ed. see APLIC International Staff.
Burns, Adrienne. Heart Untamed. 1999. mass mkt. 5.99 (*0-515-12507-5*, Jove) Berkley Pub.
***Burns, Adrienne.** It Takes Two. 2000. mass mkt. 5.99 (*0-515-12751-5*, Jove) Berkley Pub.
— Three's a Charm. (Magical Love Ser.). 2000. mass mkt. 5.99 (*0-515-12907-0*, Jove) Berkley Pub.
Burns, Ailsa & Scott, Cath. Mother-Headed Families & Why They Have Increased. 232p. 1994. text 49.95 (*0-8058-1440-X*) L Erlbaum Assocs.
Burns, Ailsa, jt. ed. see Grieve, Norma.
Burns, Alan. Real-Time Systems & Their Programming. 2nd ed. 688p. (C). 1996. 58.00 (*0-201-40365-X*) Addison-Wesley.
Burns, Alan, ed. Towards Ada 9X. LC 91-59041. (Studies in Computer & Communications Systems: Vol. 2). 201p. (gr. 12). 1992. 70.00 (*90-5199-075-8*, Pub. by IOS Pr) IOS Press.
Burns, Alan & Wellings, Andy. Concurrency in ADA. LC 98-150778. (Illus.). 412p. 1998. pap. text 32.95 (*0-521-62911-X*) Cambridge U Pr.
— HRT-HOOD: A Structured Design Method for Hard Real-Time ADA Systems. LC 95-7584. (Real-Time Safety Critical Systems Ser.: Vol. 3). 330p. 1995. 177.50 (*0-444-82164-3*) Elsevier.
Burns, Alan, et al. Red Dust Two: New Writing. LC 72-127954. 1972. 4.25 (*0-87376-019-0*) Red Dust.
— A Review of Ada Tasking. (Lecture Notes in Computer Science Ser.: Vol. 262). viii, 141p. 1989. 22.00 (*0-387-18008-7*) Spr-Verlag.
Burns, Alan C. History of the British West Indies. 1976. lib. bdg. 59.95 (*0-8490-1989-3*) Gordon Pr.
Burns, Alastair, jt. auth. see Bhugra, Dinesh K. L.
Burns, Alfred. From Austria to Hawaii: Odyssey of a Classicist. LC 93-37803. (Hawaii Classical Studies: Vol. 1). 292p. (C). 1994. text 49.95 (*0-8204-2400-5*) P Lang Pubng.

B

An Asterisk (*) at the beginning of an entry indicates that the title is appearing for the first time.

Burns, Alistair, et al. Alzheimer's Disease: A Medical Companion. LC 94-37632. 232p. 1995. pap. 39.95 (*0-632-03731-8*) Blackwell Sci.

Burns, Allan F. Maya in Exile: Guatemalans in Florida. LC 92-22774. (Illus.). 224p. 1993. 59.95 (*1-56639-035-4*); pap. 18.95 (*1-56639-036-2*) Temple U Pr.

Burns, Allan F., tr. An Epoch of Miracles: Oral Literature of the Yucatec Maya. (Texas Pan American Ser.). (Illus.). 282p. (C). 1983. text 27.50 (*0-292-72037-8*) U of Tex Pr.

***Burns, Alvin C. & Bush, Ronald F.** Marketing Research. 3rd ed. LC 99-47150. 640p. 1999. 105.00 (*0-13-014411-8*) P-H.

Burns, Andy, jt. auth. see Burns, Diane.

Burns, Angela. Ants, Nanny Goats & Zebras: Poems for Elizabeth. (Illus.). 58p. (J). (ps). 1997. pap. 8.95 (*0-9643659-2-8*) Watermarks.

Burns, Anne. Collaborative Action Research for English Language Teachers. LC 99-208715. (Language Teaching Library). (Illus.). 271p. (C). 1999. 54.95 (*0-521-63084-3*); pap. 20.95 (*0-521-63895-X*) Cambridge U Pr.

Burns, Annie W. Marriages in Woodford County: For the Period of Years 1788 to 1851. 32p. 1997. reprint ed. pap. 7.00 (*0-8328-6741-1*) Higginson Bk Co.

— Record of Marriages in Shelby County: For the Period of Years 1788 to 1851. 98p. 1997. reprint ed. pap. 18.00 (*0-8328-6739-X*) Higginson Bk Co.

— Record of Wills in Woodford County: For the Period of Years 1788 to 1851. 88p. 1997. reprint ed. pap. 16.50 (*0-8328-6742-X*) Higginson Bk Co.

Burns, Annie W., compiled by. Revolutionary War Pensions of Soldiers Who Settled in Fayette Co., Kentucky. 121p. 1996. reprint ed. pap. 17.00 (*0-8328-5198-1*) Higginson Bk Co.

Burns, Anthony, jt. auth. see Graham-Brown, Bobin A.

***Burns, Arnold I.** Laugh Factory. LC 99-90821. 1999. 25.00 (*0-7388-0534-3*); pap. 18.00 (*0-7388-0535-1*) Xlibris Corp.

— Laughing Stock. LC 00-190491. 155p. 2000. 25.00 (*0-7388-1788-0*); pap. 18.00 (*0-7388-1789-9*) Xlibris Corp.

Burns, Arthur. The Diocesan Revival in the Church of England C.1800-1870. LC 98-54618. (Illus.). 358p. 1999. text 82.00 (*0-19-820784-0*) OUP.

Burns, Arthur & Williams, Edward. Federal Work, Security & Relief Programs. LC 71-166956. (Research Monographs: Vol. 24). 1971. reprint ed. lib. bdg. 19.50 (*0-306-70356-4*) Da Capo.

Burns, Arthur E. & Watson, Donald S. Government Spending & Economic Expansion. LC 75-173452. (FDR & the Era of the New Deal Ser.). 174p. 1972. reprint ed. lib. bdg. 27.50 (*0-306-70368-8*) Da Capo.

Burns, Arthur F. Business Cycle in a Changing World. LC 69-12462. (Business Cycles Ser.: No. 18). 366p. 1969. 95.70 (*0-87014-200-3*, 67) Natl Bur Econ Res.

— The Business Cycle in a Changing World. LC 69-12462. (National Bureau of Economic Research, Studies in Business Cycles: Vol. 18). 368p. reprint ed. pap. 114.10 (*0-8357-2601-0*, 201596700006) Bks Demand.

— The Frontiers of Economic Knowledge. (General Ser.: No. 57). 397p. 1954. reprint ed. 102.30 (*0-87014-056-6*) Natl Bur Econ Res.

— The Frontiers of Economic Knowledge: Essays. LC 75-19695. (National Bureau of Economic Research Ser.). (Illus.). 1975. reprint ed. 31.95 (*0-405-07576-6*) Ayer.

— Production Trends in the United States since 1870. xxxii, 363p. 1964. reprint ed. 49.50 (*0-678-00024-7*) Kelley.

— Production Trends in the United States since 1870. (General Ser.: No. 23). 396p. 1934. reprint ed. 103.00 (*0-87014-022-1*) Natl Bur Econ Res.

— Prosperity Without Inflation. LC 58-7634. (Millar Lectures). 102p. reprint ed. pap. 31.70 (*0-7837-5570-8*, 204534800005) Bks Demand.

Burns, Arthur F., ed. Wesley Clair Mitchell: The Economic Scientist. (General Ser.: No. 53). 401p. 1952. reprint ed. 104.30 (*0-87014-052-3*) Natl Bur Econ Res.

Burns, Arthur F. & Mitchell, Wesley C. Measuring Business Cycles. LC 46-6004. (National Bureau of Economic Research, Studies in Business Cycles: No. 2). 590p. reprint ed. pap. 182.90 (*0-8357-3244-4*, 205713800011) Bks Demand.

— Measuring Business Cycles. (Business Cycles Ser.: No. 2). 590p. 1946. reprint ed. 153.40 (*0-87014-085-X*) Natl Bur Econ Res.

Burns, Arthur F., et al. The Anguish of Central Banking. LC 81-482170. (Per Jacobsson Lectures: 1979). 55p. reprint ed. pap. 30.00 (*0-8357-5484-7*, 201926200011) Bks Demand.

Burns, Arthur R. Money & Monetary Policy in Early Times. 1976. lib. bdg. 59.95 (*0-8490-2275-4*) Gordon Pr.

Burns, Augustus M., III, jt. auth. see Pleasants, Julian M.

Burns, B. G. Rosie's Roses: An Accounting Practice Set. 75p. 1993. pap. 15.00 (*0-409-30843-9*, Austral, MICHIE) LEXIS Pub.

Burns-Balogh, Pamela. A Reference Guide to Orchidology. (Illus.). 155p. 1989. pap. 34.00 (*3-87429-291-6*, 035268, Pub. by Koeltz Sci Bks) Lubrecht & Cramer.

Burns-Balogh, Pamela & Funk, V. A. A Phylogenetic Analysis of the Orchidaceae. LC 85-600315. (Smithsonian Contributions to Botany Ser.: No. 13). 83p. reprint ed. pap. 30.00 (*0-608-16203-5*, 202713800054) Bks Demand.

Burns, Barbara. All about Siamese Cats. (Illus.). 160p. 1993. 23.95 (*0-86622-665-6*, TS-129) TFH Pubns.

— Channelling: Evolutionary Exercises for Channels. 118p. (Orig.). 1993. pap. 9.95 (*0-929385-35-7*) Light Tech Pubng.

— The Short Stories of Detlev Von Liliencron: Passion, Penury, Patriotism. LC 98-40432. (Studies in German Language & Literature: Vol. 20). 282p. 1998. text 89.95 (*0-7734-8258-X*) E Mellen.

Burns, Barbara, ed. Metropolitan Museum Journal, Vol. 7 1985. 35.00 (*0-226-52104-4*) U Ch Pr.

Burns, Barbara, ed. Percepts, Concepts, & Categories: The Representation & Processing of Information. LC 92-26533. xviii,696p. 1992. 192.00 (*0-444-88734-2*, North Holland) Elsevier.

Burns, Barbara J., jt. auth. see Climent, Carlos E.

Burns, Ben. Nitty Gritty: A White Editor in Black Journalism. LC 95-32890. 288p. 1996. 27.50 (*0-87805-812-5*) U Pr of Miss.

***Burns, Bernard.** Managing Change: A Strategic Approach to Organisational Dynamics. 3rd ed. LC 00-36725. 2000. write for info. (*0-273-64166-2*, Pub. by Pitman Pbg) Trans-Atl Phila.

Burns, Beth & Godin, Seth. If You're Clueless about Getting a Great Job & Want to Know More. LC 98-5445. 208p. 1998. pap. text 15.95 (*0-7931-2882-X*) Dearborn.

Burns, Beth, jt. auth. see Godin, Seth.

Burns, Beth, tr. see Foster, Fred.

***Burns, Bill.** The Carpet Installation Training Handbook. Burns, Richard Dean, ed. LC 99-96189. (Illus.). ix, 200p. 1999. pap. write for info. (*0-9673696-0-6*) Caliber Pubns.

Burns, Bill. Raising Susan: A Man, a Woman, & a Golden Eagle. 284p. 1999. 20.95 (*0-7737-3161-X*) S&S Trade.

— When Pain Strikes. LC 98-26535. (Theory Out of Bounds Ser.). 1998. 62.95 (*0-8166-2948-X*) U of Minn Pr.

***Burns, Bill, ed.** How Did Carpet Get in This House Anyway? large type ed. LC 99-96190. (Illus.). 32p. (J). (gr. 4-6). 2000. pap. write for info. (*0-9673696-2-2*) Caliber Pubns.

Burns, Bill, et al, eds. When Pain Strikes. LC 98-26535. 287p. 1998. pap. 24.95 (*0-8166-2949-8*) U of Minn Pr.

Burns-Bisogno, Louise. Censoring Irish Nationalism: The British, Irish & American Suppression of Republican Images in Film & Television, 1909-1995. LC 97-16582. 223p. 1997. lib. bdg. 45.00 (*0-7864-0405-1*) McFarland & Co.

Burns, Bob, et al, eds. Guernsey: An Island Community of the Atlantic Iron Age. LC 97-122629. (Monographs: Vol. 43). (Illus.). 129p. 1996. pap. 32.00 (*0-947816-44-5*, Pub. by Oxford Univ Comm Arch) David Brown.

Burns, Bob & Burns, Mike. Wilderness Navigation: Finding Your Way Using Maps, Compass, Altimeter, & GPS. LC 98-49711. (Illus.). 112p. 1999. pap. 9.95 (*0-89886-629-4*) Mountaineers.

***Burns, Bob & Michlig, John.** It Came from Bob's Basement: Exploring the Science Fiction & Monster Movie Archive of Bob Burns. LC 00-22400. (Illus.). 2000. pap. 24.95 (*0-8118-2572-8*) Chronicle Bks.

Burns, Bob & Whiteman, Tom. Fresh Start Divorce Recovery Workbook: A Step-by-Step Program for Those Who Are Divorced Or Separated. rev. ed. LC 98-160497. xii, 291p. 1998. pap. 16.99 (*0-7852-7192-9*) Nelson.

Burns, Bobby. Shelter: One Man's Journey from Homelessness to Hope. LC 98-8977. 140p. 1998. 35.00 (*0-8165-1861-0*) U of Ariz Pr.

— Shelter: One Man's Journey from Homelessness to Hope. LC 98-8977. 125p. 1998. pap. 12.95 (*0-8165-1862-9*) U of Ariz Pr.

Burns, Brad. L. L. Bean Fly Fishing for Striped Bass Handbook. LC 98-16674. (Illus.). 192p. 1998. pap. 19.95 (*1-55821-736-3*) Lyons Pr.

Burns, Bradford E., jt. auth. see Cole, John N.

Burns, Bree. Harriet Tubman: And the Fight Against Slavery. (Junior Black Americans of Achievement Ser.). (Illus.). 76p. (J). (gr. 4-7). 1993. lib. bdg. 14.95 (*0-7910-1751-6*) Chelsea Hse.

— Harriet Tubman: And the Fight Against Slavery. (Junior Black Americans of Achievement Ser.). (Illus.). 76p. (J). (gr. 3-6). 1994. pap. 4.95 (*0-7910-1995-0*) Chelsea Hse.

***Burns, Brian.** Encyclopedia of Games. (Illus.). 304p. 2000. 14.98 (*1-58663-096-2*) M Friedman Pub Grp Inc.

Burns, Brian, ed. Footsteps Through History: A Walking Tour of Sturbridge Common & Southbridge. LC 84-60806. (Illus.). 88p. 1984. pap. text 4.95 (*0-917523-01-6*) Worcester County.

Burns, Bruce P. Survival of American Democracy: Virtual Reality vs. Actual Reality, a Metaphor, & Irony of Christianity. LC 96-68693. 233p. (Orig.). 1996. 21.95 (*1-882792-30-0*); pap. 12.95 (*1-882792-25-4*) Proctor Pubns.

Burns, Bryan. The Novels of Thomas Love Peacock. LC 84-19905. 256p. 1985. 53.00 (*0-389-20532-X*, 08094) B&N Imports.

— World Cinema: Hungary. LC 96-16839. (Illus.). 240p. (C). 1996. 38.50 (*0-8386-3722-1*) Fairleigh Dickinson.

***Burns, Bryan Randolph & Meinzen-Dick, Ruth S., eds.** Negotiating Water Rights. 326p. 2000. pap. 25.00 (*1-85339-484-X*, Pub. by Intermed Tech) Stylus Pub VA.

Burns, C. D. Greek Ideals. LC 73-20390. (Studies in Classical Literature: No. 60). 1974. lib. bdg. 75.00 (*0-8383-1767-7*) M S G Haskell Hse.

Burns, C. Delisle, tr. see Drews, Arthur.

***Burns, Cameron.** Selected Climbs in the Desert Southwest: Colorado & Utah. LC 99-6579. (Illus.). 240p. 1999. pap. 22.95 (*0-89886-657-X*) Mountaineers.

Burns, Cameron M. Colorado Ice Climber's Guide. (Illus.). 240p. (Orig.). 1997. pap. 25.00 (*1-57540-086-3*) Falcon Pub Inc.

— How to Get a Job in the Film Industry: A Unique to Getting Started in Hollywood, Vol. I. (How to Get a Job Ser.). (Illus.). 96p. 1998. pap. text 15.95 (*0-9629627-0-8*) Hard Pressed Bks.

— Kilimanjaro & Mount Kenya: A Climbing & Trekking Guide. LC 97-45542. 176p. 1998. pap. 18.95 (*0-89886-557-3*) Mountaineers.

Burns, Cameron M., jt. auth. see Porcella, Stephen F.

Burns, Cameron M., jt. auth. see Porcella, Steven F.

Burns, Candace & Deurbrouck, Jo. The Insiders' Guide to Yellowstone. 2nd ed. (Insiders' Guide Travel Ser.). 1999. pap. 15.95 (*1-57380-130-5*, The Insiders Guide) Falcon Pub Inc.

Burns, Cara M., jt. auth. see Burns, Maureen A.

Burns, Carl O. Dugan & Diamond Carnival Glass 1909-1931: Identification & Values. LC 99-164776. 208p. 1998. pap. 19.95 (*1-57432-082-3*) Collector Bks.

— Imperial Carnival Glass: Identification & Value Guide, Vol. VI. LC 96-139872. 184p. 1996. pap. 18.95 (*0-89145-697-X*, 4644) Collector Bks.

Burns, Caroline, ed. Seeds of Kindness: Garden Thoughts for the Heart. (Cherished Moments Ser.). (Illus.). 64p. 1996. 9.99 (*1-57051-108-X*) Brownlow Pub Co.

Burns, Caroline E., jt. auth. see Burns, Kevan J.

***Burns, Catherine E.** Pocket Reference for Pediatric Primary Care. LC 00-37159. 2001. write for info. (*0-7216-8466-1*, W B Saunders Co) Harcrt Hlth Sci Grp.

Burns, Catherine E., et al. Pediatric Primary Care: A Handbook for Nurse Practitioners. Rader, Ilze, ed. (Illus.). 980p. 1996. text 68.00 (*0-7216-5013-9*, W B Saunders Co) Harcrt Hlth Sci Grp.

***Burns, Catherine E., et al.** Pediatric Primary Care: A Handbook of Nurse Practitioners. 2nd ed. LC 99-47085. (Illus.). 990p. 2000. text 65.00 (*0-7216-8062-3*, W B Saunders Co) Harcrt Hlth Sci Grp.

Burns, Cathy. Alcoholics Anonymous Unmasked: Deception & Deliverance. 128p. 1991. pap. 5.95 (*1-56043-449-X*, Companion Pr) Destiny Image.

— Astrology & Your Future. 20p. 1994. pap. 0.50 (*1-891117-05-X*) Sharing.

— Different Kinds of Friendship. 20p. 1997. pap. 0.50 (*1-891117-09-2*) Sharing.

— Dowsing Is in the Bible. 20p. 1998. pap. 0.50 (*1-891117-13-0*) Sharing.

***Burns, Cathy.** Eastern Star Goddesses. 32p. 2000. 0.50 (*1-891117-16-5*) Sharing.

Burns, Cathy. Eternal Life. 20p. (Orig.). 1990. pap. 0.50 (*1-891117-02-5*) Sharing.

***Burns, Cathy.** Explanation of Some Occult Terms. (Illus.). 28p. 1999. pap. 0.50 (*1-891117-15-7*) Sharing.

Burns, Cathy. Hidden Dangers of Reflexology. 16p. 1997. pap. 0.50 (*1-891117-08-4*) Sharing.

Burns, Cathy. Hidden Secrets of Masonry. 64p. 1990. pap. 4.95 (*0-00-540512-2*) Sharing.

— Hidden Secrets of the Eastern Star: The Masonic Connection. 512p. 1994. pap. 15.95 (*0-00-502181-2*) Sharing.

Burns, Cathy. Hypnosis: Cure or Curse? 16p. 1993. pap. 0.50 (*1-891117-06-8*) Sharing.

***Burns, Cathy.** Masonic & Occult Symbols Illustrated. (Illus.). 552p. 1998. pap. 21.95 (*1-891117-12-2*) Sharing.

Burns, Cathy. Mormonism, Masonry, & Godhood: Can Angels Be Trusted? LC 98-170233. (Illus.). 132p. (Orig.). 1997. pap. 6.95 (*1-891117-01-7*) Sharing.

— A One World Order Is Coming: Who Will Rule? LC 98-126763. 116p. (Orig.). 1997. pap. 5.95 (*1-891117-00-9*) Sharing.

— Questions & Answers about the New Age Movement. 20p. 1989. pap. 0.50 (*1-891117-04-1*) Sharing.

— A Scriptural View of Hell. 40p. 1998. pap. 4.95 (*1-891117-11-4*) Sharing.

— Secure in Christ. LC 98-230781. 136p. 1998. pap. 6.95 (*1-891117-10-6*) Sharing.

— To Catholics, with Love. 12p. 1982. pap. 0.50 (*1-891117-03-3*) Sharing.

— What Is Your I. Q.? 9p. 1981. pap. 0.50 (*1-891117-07-6*) Sharing.

***Burns, Cathy, compiled by.** Pathway to Peace. 72p. 1999. pap. 2.50 (*1-891117-14-9*) Sharing.

Burns, Cecil D. Leisure in the Modern World. 1982. 19.95 (*0-8434-0434-5*) McGrath NH.

Burns, Charles. Big Baby. 96p. 1999. 24.95 (*1-56097-361-7*) Fantagraph Bks.

— Black Hole, No. 1. 40p. 1995. pap. 3.50 (*0-87816-337-9*) Kitchen Sink.

— El Borbah. 72p. 1998. 24.95 (*1-56097-326-9*) Fantagraph Bks.

***Burns, Charles.** Skin Deep: Tales of Doomed Romance. 2000. 24.95 (*1-56097-390-0*) Fantagraph Bks.

Burns, Charles & Panter, Gary. Facetasm. 2nd rev. ed. LC 99-159283. (Illus.). 18p. 1997. 12.95 (*1-889539-05-8*) Gates of Heck.

Burns, Cherle. Stepmotherhood: How to Survive Without Feeling Frustrated, Left Out, or Wicked. LC 86-45083. 240p. 1986. reprint ed. pap. 12.50 (*0-06-097064-2*, PL/7064, Perennial) HarperTrade.

***Burns, Christy L.** Gestural Politics: Stereotype & Parody in Joyce. LC 99-45915. (C). 2000. text 59.50 (*0-7914-4613-1*) State U NY Pr.

— Gestural Politics: Stereotype & Parody in Joyce. LC 99-45915. 2000. pap. 19.95 (*0-7914-4614-X*) State U NY Pr.

Burns, Clarence. Building Your Organization's TQM System: The Unified Total Quality Model. LC 97-7863. (Illus.). 172p. 1997. 28.00 (*0-87389-422-7*, H0963) ASQ Qual Pr.

Burns, Clarias. Mission of Danger. 185p. (Orig.). 1996. pap. 4.95 (*0-9645041-1-1*) Cntryside Pub.

Burns, Clarica. The Evil Tribute. 207p. 1997. pap. 4.95 (*0-9645041-2-X*) Cntryside Pub.

***Burns, Clarica.** Mayan Treasure. 225p. 1999. pap. 4.95 (*0-9645041-5-4*) Cntryside Pub.

Burns, Clarica. Red Herring. 255p. (Orig.). 1995. pap. 4.95 (*0-9645041-0-3*) Cntryside Pub.

***Burns, Clarica.** Wicked Vows. 195p. (Orig.). 1998. pap. 4.95 (*0-9645041-4-6*) Cntryside Pub.

***Burns, Conrad, ed.** Computational Biology: Congressional Hearing. 92p. (C). 1999. reprint ed. pap. text 20.00 (*0-7881-7271-9*) DIANE Pub.

— 8-442, The Internet Tax Freedom Act: Congressional Hearing. 83p. 2000. reprint ed. pap. text 20.00 (*0-7567-0151-1*) DIANE Pub.

— New Charges on 800 Number Providers: Congressional Hearing. 58p. (C). 2000. reprint ed. pap. text 20.00 (*0-7567-0040-X*) DIANE Pub.

Burns, Constance K., jt. ed. see Formisano, Ronald P.

Burns, D. J., jt. auth. see Yelle, Henri.

Burns, D. T., et al. Inorganic Reaction Chemistry: Reactions of the Elements & Their Compounds, Vol. 2B. LC 80-42029. (Analytical Chemistry Ser.). 410p. 1981. text 123.00 (*0-470-27210-4*) P-H.

Burns, Daniel. Technotrends: How to Use Technology to Go Beyond Your Competition. LC 92-56234. 400p. 1994. 16.00 (*0-88730-700-0*, HarpBusn) HarpInfo.

Burns, Danny. Poll Tax Rebellion. (Illus.). 208p. 1992. pap. 10.00 (*1-873176-50-3*, AK Pr San Fran) AK Pr Dist.

Burns, David. College, Alcohol & Choices: An Essential Conversation Guide for Parents & Students. Glunz, Kristen L., ed. 154p. (Orig.). 1996. pap. 24.95 (*1-882145-02-X*, 575) U WI Clearinghse.

— Heating Up. 1999. pap. write for info. (*0-14-012140-4*, Viking); pap. write for info. (*0-670-82797-5*) Viking Penguin.

Burns, David & Wagener, B. Bruce. A Process Approach to Public Speaking. 448p. (C). 1995. pap. text, per. 37.95 (*0-8403-9750-X*) Kendall-Hunt.

— A Process Approach to Public Speaking. 416p. (C). 1996. pap. text, per. 37.95 (*0-7872-3230-0*) Kendall-Hunt.

Burns, David D. Feeling Good: The New Mood Therapy. 480p. 1992. mass mkt. 6.99 (*0-380-71803-0*, Avon Bks) Morrow Avon.

— Feeling Good: The New Mood Therapy. 736p. 1999. pap. 14.00 (*0-380-73176-2*, Avon Bks) Morrow Avon.

***Burns, David D.** Feeling Good: The New Mood Therapy, Vol. 1. rev. ed. (Illus.). 736p. 1999. mass mkt. 7.50 (*0-380-81033-6*, Avon Bks) Morrow Avon.

Burns, David D. Feeling Good Handbook. LC 99-18102. 1999. pap. 17.95 (*0-452-28132-6*) NAL.

— Intimate Connections: The New Clinically Tested Program for Overcoming Loneliness. 1985. mass mkt. 6.99 (*0-451-14845-2*, Sig) NAL.

— Ten Days to Self-Esteem! LC 92-38209. 240p. 1993. pap. 25.00 (*0-688-12708-8*, Wm Morrow) Morrow Avon.

***Burns, David M.** Gateway: Dr. Thomas Walker & the Opening of Kentucky. LC 99-85874. (Illus.). 100p. 2000. pap. 20.00 (*0-9677765-1-1*) Bell County.

— Ten Days to Self-Esteem. LC 92-42449. (Illus.). 336p. 1999. pap. 14.95 (*0-688-09455-4*, Wm Morrow) Morrow Avon.

***Burns, Deb.** Storey's Horse-Lover's Encyclopedia: An English & Western A-to-Z Guide. 480p. 2000. 37.50 (*1-58017-336-5*); pap. 24.95 (*1-58017-317-9*) Storey Bks.

Burns, Deborah. Tips for the Savvy Traveler. large type ed. 338p. (Orig.). 1997. 24.95 (*0-7838-8265-3*, G K Hall Lrg Type) Mac Lib Ref.

— Tips for the Savvy Traveler: The Book to Read Before Taking Any Trip. LC 96-53199. 224p. 1997. pap. 12.95 (*0-88266-971-0*) Storey Bks.

Burns, Deborah & Clarkson, Sarah M. Tips for the Savvy Traveler. LC 86-43042. 224p. (Orig.). 1987. pap. 8.95 (*0-88266-464-6*, Storey Pub) Storey Bks.

Burns, Deborah, ed. see Art, Henry W.

Burns, Deborah, ed. see Daniel, Alfred H.

Burns, Deborah, ed. see Franklin, Stuart.

Burns, Deborah, ed. see Hill, Cherry.

Burns, Deborah, ed. see McBride, Kathleen.

Burns, Deborah, ed. see Mettler, John J., Jr.

Burns, Deborah, ed. see Riotte, Louise.

Burns, Deborah, ed. see Rogers Gessert, Kate.

Burns, Deborah, ed. see Rupp, Rebecca.

Burns, Deborah, ed. see Simmons, Paula.

Burns, Deborah, ed. see Tilgner, Linda.

Burns, Deborah, ed. see Van Leuven, Nancy.

Burns, Deborah E. Pathways to Investigative Skills: Instructional Lessons for Guiding Students from Problem Finding to Final Product, Grades 3-9. 104p. 1990. ring bd. 49.95 incl. sl. (*0-936386-54-1*) Creative Learning.

— Shaker Cities of Peace, Love, & Union: A History of the Hancock Bishopric. LC 92-59965. (Illus.). 262p. 1993. pap. 19.95 (*0-87451-613-7*) U Pr of New Eng.

Burns, Deborah E. & Stevens, Lauren R. Most Excellent Majesty, a History of Mt. Greylock. Wislocki, George, ed. (Illus.). 112p. (Orig.). 1988. pap. 12.95 (*0-9620959-0-7*) Berkshire Natural.

Burns, Dee. Golf 'N' Verse. (Illus.). 112p. 1995. pap. 7.95 (*0-9649460-0-9*) Boomarang Pubng.

Burns, Diane. Cranberries: Fruit of the Bogs. LC 93-29620. (Illus.). 48p. (J). 1994. pap. 7.95 (*0-87614-964-6*, Carolrhoda) Lerner Pub.

— Cranberries: Fruit of the Bogs. LC 93-29620. (Illus.). (J). (ps-5). 1994. lib. bdg. 22.60 (*0-87614-822-4*, Carolrhoda) Lerner Pub.

Burns, Diane. Cranberries: Fruit of the Bogs. (Illus.). (J). 1995. 13.40 (*0-606-18817-7*) Turtleback.

Burns, Diane. Riding the One-Eyed Ford. 2nd ed. (Poetry Ser.). (Illus.). 50p. (Orig.). (C). 1984. reprint ed. pap. 3.50 (*0-936556-05-6*) Contact Two.

— Sugaring Season: Making Maple Syrup. (Illus.). 48p. (J). (gr. 1-5). 1990. pap. 5.95 (*0-87614-554-3*, Carolrhoda) Lerner Pub.

— Sugaring Season: Making Maple Syrup. (Photo Bks.). (Illus.). 32p. (J). (gr. 1-5). 1990. 22.60 (*0-87614-420-2*, Carolrhoda) Lerner Pub.

Burns, Diane & Burns, Andy. Home on the Range: Ranch-Style Riddles. LC 93-19158. (You Must Be Joking! Ser.). (Illus.). 32p. (J). (gr. 1-4). 1994. lib. bdg. 14.60 (0-8225-2341-8, Lerner Publctns) Lerner Pub.

Burns, Diane, ed. see Clifford, H. J., et al.

Burns, Diane L. Berries, Nuts & Seeds. LC 96-11585. (Take-Along Guide Ser.). (Illus.). 48p. (J). (gr. 5-7). 1996. pap. 6.95 (1-55971-573-1, NorthWord Pr) Creat Pub Intl.

— Frogs, Toads, & Turtles. LC 96-37143. (Take-Along Guide Ser.). (Illus.). 48p. (Orig.). (J). (gr. 3-7). 1997. pap. 6.95 (1-55971-593-6, NorthWord Pr) Creat Pub Intl.

Burns, Diane L. Frogs, Toads & Turtles. (Take-Along Guide Ser.). (Illus.). (J). 1997. 12.40 (0-606-18078-8) Turtleback.

Burns, Diane L. Snakes, Salamanders & Lizards. 48p. 1998. pap. 6.95 (1-55971-627-4, NorthWord Pr) Creat Pub Intl.

— Trees, Leaves & Bark. (Take-Along Guide Ser.). 48p. 1998. pap. text 6.95 (1-55971-628-2, NorthWord Pr) Creat Pub Intl.

— Wildflowers, Blooms & Blossoms. LC 97-7754. (Take-Along Guide Ser.). (Illus.). 48p. (J). (gr. 3-7). 1998. pap. 6.95 (1-55971-642-8, NorthWord Pr) Creat Pub Intl.

Burns, Diane L. & Burns, Jill A. Plant a Garden in Your Sneaker! Fun & Outrageous Planting Projects for All Seasons. LC 98-182178. (Illus.). 64p. (J). (gr. 2 up). 1998. pap. 10.95 (0-07-009228-1) McGraw.

Burns, Donald A. & Ciurczak, Emil W., eds. Handbook of Near-Infrared Analysis. (Practical Spectroscopy Ser.: Vol. 13). (Illus.). 712p. 1992. text 250.00 (0-8247-8657-2) Dekker.

Burns, Douglas M. Buddhist Meditation & Depth Psychology. 72p. 1994. 4.50 (955-24-0114-3, Pub. by Buddhist Pub Soc) Vipassana Res Pubns.

Burns, E. Bradford. Kinship with the Land: Regionalist Thought in Iowa, 1894-1942. LC 95-43623. (Illus.). 214p. 1996. text 27.95 (0-87745-534-1) U of Iowa Pr.

— Latin America: A Concise Interpretive History. 6th ed. LC 92-38300. 372p. (C). 1993. pap. text 47.00 (0-13-501321-6) P-H.

— Patriarch & Folk: The Emergence of Nicaragua, 1798-1858. 320p. (C). 1991. 51.95 (0-674-65796-9) HUP.

— The Poverty of Progress: Latin America in the Nineteenth Century. LC 80-51236. 224p. 1980. pap. 17.95 (0-520-05078-9, Pub. by U CA Pr) Cal Prin Full Svc.

Burns, E. Bradford, ed. Latin America: Conflict & Creation: A Historical Reader. LC 92-13345. 336p. (C). 1992. pap. text 39.20 (0-13-526260-7) P-H.

Burns, E. Jane. Arthurian Fictions: Rereading the Vulgate Cycle. LC 85-7325. 220p. reprint ed. pap. 68.20 (0-608-09658-X, 206977300006) Bks Demand.

— Bodytalk: When Women Speak in Old French Literature. (New Cultural Studies). 304p. (Orig.). (C). 1993. text 39.95 (0-8122-3183-X); pap. text 18.50 (0-8122-1405-6) U of Pa Pr.

Burns, E. Robert. Review Questions for Human Histology. LC 95-17810. (Review Questions Ser.). 216p. 1995. 19.95 (1-85070-594-1) Prthnon Pub.

Burns, E. Robert & Cave, M. Donald. Mosby's USMLE Step 1 Reviews: Histology & Cell Biology. LC 95-52478. (Ace the Boards Ser.). (Illus.). 272p. (C). (gr. 13). 1996. pap. text 30.00 incl. audio compact disk (0-8151-1338-2, 27045) Mosby Inc.

Burns, E. Robert & Cve, M. Donald. Ace: Histology. (Illus.). 272p. 1996. text 30.00 incl. disk (0-8151-1335-8, 28954) Mosby Inc.

Burns, E. Timothy. From Risk to Resilience: A Journey with Heart for Our Children. LC 94-76962. (Illus.). 165p. (Orig.). 1995. pap. 15.00 (1-56374-017-6, BB-11) Marco Polo Pubs.

— Our Children, Our Future: Defining the Stakes in a Battle We Must Not Lose. (Illus.). 1991. pap. 14.95 (1-56374-000-1) Marco Polo Pubs.

Burns, Edward. She's the One & the Brothers Mcmullen. 1997. pap. text 14.95 (0-571-19072-3) Faber & Faber.

— Test Accommodations for Students with Disabilities. LC 97-46391. 340p. 1998. text 66.95 (0-398-06844-5); pap. text 49.95 (0-398-06845-3) C C Thomas.

— Three Screenplays. LC 97-15616. (Illus.). 256p. (J). 1998. pap. 15.95 (0-7868-8272-7, Pub. by Hyperion) Time Warner.

— World Civilizations, Vol. 1. 9th ed. LC 96-23844. (C). 1997. pap. 61.25 (0-393-96880-4, Norton Paperbks) Norton.

— World Civilizations, Vol. 2. 9th ed. LC 96-23844. (C). 1997. pap. 44.00 (0-393-96881-2) Norton.

Burns, Edward, ed. The Letters of Carl van Vechten & Gertrude Stein, 1913-1946. 2 vols., Set. LC 85-24343. (Illus.). 901p. 1986. text 145.00 (0-231-06308-3) Col U Pr.

— Technical Strategy for the Treatment, Packaging, & Disposal of Aluminum-Based Spent Nuclear Fuel, Vol. 1. (Illus.). 92p. (C). 1997. pap. text 30.00 (0-7881-4583-5) DIANE Pub.

Burns, Edward, jt. auth. see Simon, David.

Burns, Edward, jt. ed. see Baines, Paul.

Burns, Edward, jt. ed. see Hillis, W. S.

Burns, Edward J. & Greener, Joseph H., eds. One Hundred All-Time Standards for All Organs, EFS165. (Illus.). 128p. 1962. pap. 14.95 (0-8256-2165-8, AM40783) Music Sales.

Burns, Edward M., et al, eds. The Letters of Gertrude Stein & Thornton Wilder. LC 96-17169. (Illus.). 384p. 1997. 35.00 (0-300-06774-7) Yale U Pr.

Burns, Edward N., jt. auth. see Arthur, Lowell J.

Burns, Eleanor. An Amish Quilt in a Day, Variations of Roman Stripe. (Illus.). 46p. 1986. 8.95 (0-922705-05-4) Quilt Day.

— Applique in a Day. LC 95-144765. (Illus.). 88p. 1994. per. 22.95 (0-922705-84-4) Quilt Day.

— Baskets & Flowers Block Party. (Quilter's Block Party Ser.: No. 2). (Illus.). 44p. 1989. 9.95 (0-922705-31-3) Quilt Day.

— Bears in the Woods. LC 98-159926. (Illus.). 127p. 1997. pap. 24.95 (0-922705-95-X) Quilt Day.

— Blazing Star Tablecloth. (Illus.). 24p. 1991. 6.95 (0-922705-24-0) Quilt Day.

— Bunnies & Blossoms. (Illus.). 32p. 1980. pap. 8.95 (0-922705-11-9) Quilt Day.

— Burgoyne Surrounded Quilt in a Day. (Illus.). 64p. 1992. 9.95 (0-922705-36-4) Quilt Day.

— Christmas Quilts & Crafts. (Illus.). 120p. (Orig.). 1995. pap. 24.95 (0-922705-88-7) Quilt Day.

— Country Christmas. 2nd ed. (Illus.). 30p. (Orig.). 1980. pap. 8.95 (0-922705-10-0) Quilt Day.

— Country Flag Wallhanging & Placemats. (Illus.). 18p. 1991. 6.95 (0-922705-25-9) Quilt Day.

— The Diamond Log Cabin. (Illus.). 24p. 1988. pap. 6.95 (0-922705-03-8) Quilt Day.

— A Flying Geese Quilt in a Day. (Illus.). 24p. 1992. 6.95 (0-922705-35-6) Quilt Day.

— Friendship Quilt. 36p. 1988. pap. 6.95 (0-922705-14-3) Quilt Day.

— From Blocks to Quilt. (Illus.). 16p. 1994. 6.95 (0-922705-83-6) Quilt Day.

— Grandmother's Garden Quilt. (Illus.). 180p. 1999. pap. 27.95 (0-922705-97-6) Quilt Day.

— Irish Chain in a Day - Single & Double. (Illus.). 64p. (Orig.). 1986. pap. 8.95 (0-922705-06-2) Quilt Day.

— Jewel Box Quilt. large type ed. (Illus.). 64p. (Orig.). 1997. 18.95 (0-922705-91-7) Quilt Day.

— Kaleidoscope Quilt. (Illus.). 96p. (Orig.). 1996. 14.95 (0-922705-49-6) Quilt Day.

— Last Minute Gifts. 9p. 1991. pap. 6.95 (0-922705-32-1) Quilt Day.

— Log Cabin Christmas Tree Wallhanging. (Illus.). 16p. 1986. 6.95 (0-922705-29-1) Quilt Day.

— Log Cabin Christmas Wreath Wallhanging. (Illus.). 16p. 1986. 6.95 (0-922705-28-3) Quilt Day.

— Lover's Knot Quilt. (Illus.). 59p. (Orig.). 1985. pap. 8.95 (0-922705-04-6) Quilt Day.

— Make a Quilt in a Day Log Cabin. 20th rev. ed. (Illus.). 96p. 1998. pap. 18.95 (0-922705-98-4) Quilt Day.

— May Basket Quilt. (Illus.). 62p. (Orig.). 1987. pap. 8.95 (0-922705-07-0) Quilt Day.

— Morning Star. LC 88-92069. (Illus.). 64p. (Orig.). 1988. pap. text 8.95 (0-922705-12-7) Quilt Day.

— Pioneer Sampler. (Quilt Block Party Ser.: No. 5). (Illus.). 88p. 1993. 14.95 (0-922705-43-7) Quilt Day.

— Quilter's Almanac Block Party, Series No. 3. (Illus.). 56p. 1991. 14.95 (0-922705-34-8) Quilt Day.

— Quilter's Year Block Party, Series No. 1. (Illus.). 40p. 1988. 9.95 (0-922705-30-5) Quilt Day.

— Radiant Star Quilt. (Illus.). 64p. 1990. 9.95 (0-922705-20-8) Quilt Day.

— Recycled Treasures from Grandma's Attic. (Illus.). 32p. 1993. 10.95 (0-922705-42-9) Quilt Day.

— The Sampler: A Machine Sewn Quilt. (Illus.). 125p. (Orig.). 1982. pap. 14.95 (0-922705-08-9) Quilt Day.

— Schoolhouse Wallhanging. (Illus.). 24p. 1987. pap. 6.95 (0-922705-02-X) Quilt Day.

— Star Log Cabin Quilt. (Illus.). 92p. 1995. per. 14.95 (0-922705-86-0) Quilt Day.

— Stars Across America. (Quilter's Block Party Ser.: No. 7). (Illus.). 120p. 1996. 24.95 (0-922705-89-5) Quilt Day.

— Sunbonnet Sue Visits Quilt in a Day. (Illus.). 48p. 1992. 10.95 (0-922705-38-0) Quilt Day.

— Trio of Treasured Quilts. 2nd rev. ed. (Illus.). 150p. (Orig.). 1989. spiral bd. 14.95 (0-922705-18-6) Quilt Day.

— Trip Around the World Quilt. (Illus.). 55p. (Orig.). 1988. pap. 8.95 (0-922705-13-5) Quilt Day.

— Tulip Quilt. (Illus.). 72p. 1991. 9.95 (0-922705-22-4) Quilt Day.

Burns, Eleanor, ed. see Gilbert, Wendy.

Burns, Eleanor, ed. see Martin, Cynthia.

Burns, Eleanor, ed. see Smith, Loretta.

Burns, Eleanor B. A Widow's Dilemma: (It Can Happen to Anyone) Robertson, Ann, ed. & illus. by. 92p. (Orig.). 1996. pap. 6.00 (0-9652990-0-7) E B Burns.

Burns, Elizabeth. Hanky Panky: Traditional Handkerchief Toys. 1991. pap. 4.50 (0-9624152-2-7) E Burns.

— Hanky Panky: Traditional Handkerchief Toys. (Illus.). 24p. (J). (ps-6). 1993. reprint ed. pap. 4.50 (0-9624152-0-0) E Burns.

— Ophelia & Other Poems. 1991. 12.00 (0-7486-6096-8, Pub. by Polygon) Subterranean Co.

Burns, Elizabeth, et al, eds. Original Prints 4: New Writing from Scottish Women. 1992. pap. 10.95 (0-7486-6129-8, Pub. by Edinburgh U Pr) Col U Pr.

Burns, Elizabeth, jt. auth. see Grimes, Jorge.

Burns, Elizabeth M., et al, eds. An Addictions Curriculum for Nurses & Other Helping Professionals, Vol. 1: The Undergraduate Level. LC 93-18559. (Teaching of Nursing Ser.: Vol. 14). 288p. 1993. 46.95 (0-8261-8190-2) Springer Pub.

— An Addictions Curriculum for Nurses & Other Helping Professionals, Vol. 2: The Graduate Level - Advanced Knowledge & Practice. LC 93-18559. (Teaching of Nursing Ser.: Vol. 15). 392p. 1993. pap. 49.95 (0-8261-8191-0) Springer Pub.

Burns, Emile, ed. Handbook of Marxism. 2 Vols. LC 79-119441. (Reference Ser.: No. 44). 1970. reprint ed. lib. bdg. 150.00 (0-8383-1090-7) M S G Haskell Hse.

Burns, Emile, tr. see Engels, Friedrich & Marx, Karl.

Burns, Emile, tr. see Tolstoy, Leo.

Burns, Emily, ed. see Losh, John B.

Burns, Emily E., ed. see Losh, John B.

Burns, Eric. The Autograph: A Modern Fable of a Father & Daughter. LC 97-25505. (Illus.). 69p. 1997. 14.95 (1-57392-167-X) Prometheus Bks.

— The Joy of Books: Confessions of a Lifelong Reader. LC 95-21306. (Illus.). 207p. 1995. 24.95 (1-57392-004-5) Prometheus Bks.

Burns, Eugene. Last King of Paradise. LC 72-10607. (Select Bibliographies Reprint Ser.). 1977. reprint ed. 21.95 (0-8369-7102-7) Ayer.

Burns, Eveline M. Social Security & Public Policy. LC 75-17211. (Social Problems & Social Policy Ser.). 1976. reprint ed. 23.95 (0-405-07483-2) Ayer.

Burns, Eveline M., ed. see Children's Allowance Conference Staff.

Burns, Evelyn F. Anatomy & Physiology. Bushong, Stewart C., ed. LC 98-24889. (Essentials of Medical Imaging Ser.). (Illus.). 130p. 1999. pap. 26.95 (0-07-009231-1) McGraw-Hill HPD.

— Radiographic Imaging. 1992. pap. text, lab manual ed. 16.95 (0-7216-3245-9, W B Saunders Co) Harcrt Hlth Sci Grp.

— Radiographic Imaging: A Guide for Producing Quality Radiographs. (Illus.). 223p. 1992. teacher ed. write for info. (0-7216-3247-5, W B Saunders Co) Harcrt Hlth Sci Grp.

— Radiographic Imaging: A Guide for Producing Quality Radiographs. LC 92-19465. (Illus.). 223p. 1992. text 39.50 (0-7216-3246-7, W B Saunders Co) Harcrt Hlth Sci Grp.

Burns, Frederic J., et al, eds. Radiation Carcinogenesis & DNA Alterations. LC 87-2224. (NATO ASI Series A, Life Sciences: Vol. 124). 630p. 1987. 125.00 (0-306-42495-9, Plenum Trade) Perseus Pubng.

Burns, G. W. Temperature-Electromotive Force Reference Functions & Tables for the Letter-Designated Thermocouple Types Based on the Its-90. 633p. 1993. per. 47.00 (0-16-042295-7) USGPO.

Burns, Gary & Thompson, Robert J., eds. Television Studies: Textual Analysis. LC 88-23170. (Media & Society Ser.). 268p. 1989. 65.00 (0-275-92745-8, C2745, Praeger Pubs) Greenwood.

Burns, Gary, jt. auth. see Allred, Terri.

Burns, Gary, jt. auth. see Sobey, Edwin J.

Burns, Gary, jt. ed. see Thompson, Robert J.

Burns, Gene. Frontiers of Catholicism: The Politics of Ideology in a Liberal World. LC 91-46039. 1994. pap. 17.95 (0-520-08922-7, Pub. by U CA Pr) Cal Prin Full Svc.

Burns, George. Come to Think of It. LC 99-93019. 84p. 1999. pap. write for info. (1-57579-147-1) Pine Hill Pr.

***Burns, George.** Come to Think of It..., 1. 74p. 1999. pap. 9.95 (0-9674274-0-1) II Execs.

Burns, George. Exploring the World of Astronomy. (Try This! Ser.). (Illus.). 48p. (J). (gr. 1-5). 1995. pap. 6.95 (0-531-15745-8) Watts.

— Exploring the World of Astronomy. (Try This! Ser.). 48p. 1995. lib. bdg. 20.00 (0-531-20124-4) Watts.

— Exploring the World of Geology. (Try This! Ser.). (Illus.). 48p. (J). (gr. 3-5). 1995. lib. bdg. 20.80 (0-531-20121-X) Watts.

— George Burns & the One Hundred-Year Dash. large type ed. 1996. 23.95 (0-7838-1689-8, G K Hall Lrg Type) Mac Lib Ref.

— Nature-Guided Therapy: Brief Integrative Strategies for Health & Wellbeing. LC 97-44772. 250p. 1998. 35.95 (0-87630-850-7) Taylor & Francis.

Burns, George W. & Bottino, Paul J. The Science of Genetics. 6th ed. 491p. (C). 1988. 72.80 (0-02-317400-5, Macmillan Coll) P-H.

Burns, Gerald. Boccherini's Minuet. 2nd ed. LC PS3552.U7324. (Lucky Heart Bk.). 62p. reprint ed. pap. 30.00 (0-7837-9099-6, 204984900003) Bks Demand.

— A Book of Spells: First Third. LC 79-2568. (Lucky Heart Bk.). 22p. 1978. reprint ed. pap. 30.00 (0-7837-9098-8, 204984800003) Bks Demand.

— High-Temperature Superconductivity: An Introduction. (Illus.). 199p. 1991. pap. text 31.00 (0-12-146090-8) Acad Pr.

— Letters to Obscure Men. LC 75-40540. (Lucky Heart Bk.). 68p. 1975. reprint ed. pap. 30.00 (0-7837-9097-X, 204984700003) Bks Demand.

— Nations in Public. LC PS3552.B8. (Salt Lick Samplers Ser.). 12p. 1975. reprint ed. pap. 30.00 (0-7837-9158-5, 204985800003) Bks Demand.

— Shorter Poems. LC 92-29476. 128p. 1993. pap. 9.95 (1-56478-026-0) Dalkey Arch.

— Solid State Physics. (C). 1985. text 59.00 (0-12-146070-3) Acad Pr.

— A Thing about Language. 160p. (C). 1989. pap. 18.95 (0-8093-1528-9) S Ill U Pr.

— Toward a Phenomenology of Written Art. LC 79-15699. 64p. 1979. 25.00 (0-914232-36-3); pap. 10.00 (0-914232-35-5) McPherson & Co.

Burns, Gerald & Glazer, A. M., eds. Space Groups for Solid State Scientists. 2nd ed. 343p. 1990. text 65.00 (0-12-145761-3) Acad Pr.

Burns, Gerald, intro. see Dahlberg, Edward.

Burns, Gerard J., jt. ed. see Schramm, Karl.

Burns, Gerard P. & Bank, Simmy, eds. Disorders of the Pancreas: Controversies in Diagnosis & Management. (Illus.). 450p. 1991. 68.01 (0-08-040317-4, Pub. by PPI) McGraw.

— Disorders of the Pancreas: Current Issues in Diagnosis & Management. (Illus.). 506p. 1992. text 82.00 (0-07-105402-2) McGraw-Hill HPD.

Burns, Glen, tr. see Gumbrecht, Hans U.

Burns, Graham, ed. see Euromoney Staff.

Burns, Grant. Librarians in Fiction: A Critical Bibliography. LC 98-10695. 191p. 1998. pap. 29.95 (0-7864-0499-X) McFarland & Co.

— The Nuclear Present: A Guide to Recent Books on Nuclear War, Weapons, the Peace Movement, & Related Issues, with a Chronology of Nuclear Events, 1789-1991. LC 92-32440. 654p. 1992. 73.00 (0-8108-2619-4) Scarecrow.

— Sports Pages: A Critical Bibliography of Twentieth-Century American Novels & Stories Featuring Baseball, Basketball, Football & Other Pursuits. LC 86-31388. 274p. 1987. 29.00 (0-8108-1966-X) Scarecrow.

Burns, H. Donald, et al, eds. Nuclear Imaging in Drug Discovery, Development, & Approval. LC 92-48930. x, 339p. 1992. 63.50 (0-8176-3601-3) Birkhauser.

Burns, H. L., et al, eds. Intelligent Tutoring Systems: Evolutions in Design. 312p. (C). 1991. pap. 36.00 (0-8058-0683-0); text 59.95 (0-8058-0682-2) L Erlbaum Assocs.

Burns, Haggard, ed. see Dew, Greg.

Burns, Helen. The American Banking Community & New Deal Banking Reforms: 1933-1935, 11. LC 72-789. (Contributions in Economics & Economic History Ser.: No. 11). 203p. 1974. 52.95 (0-8371-6362-5, BAB, Greenwood Pr) Greenwood.

Burns, Helen Marie & Carney, Sheila. Praying with Catherine McAuley. Koch, Carl, ed. (Companions for the Journey Ser.). (Illus.). 128p. 1996. pap. 7.95 (0-88489-334-0) St Marys.

Burns, Hilary. Cane, Rush & Willow: Weaving with Natural Materials. (Illus.). 144p. 1998. pap. 24.95 (1-55209-260-7) Firefly Bks Ltd.

Burns, Irma G. Maui's Mittee & the General. 15.95 (0-914916-90-4) Ku Paa.

Burns, J. El Ministerio Juvenil Dinamico.Tr. of Youth Builder. (SPA.). 100. pap. 13.99 (0-7899-0314-8, 497392) Editorial Unilit.

Burns, J. Sobreviviendo a la Adolescencia.Tr. of Surviving Adolescence. (SPA.). 7.99 (0-7899-0432-2, 497397) Editorial Unilit.

Burns, J., et al. Publication Opportunities for Tax Researchers. 241p. 1988. 3.00 (0-685-17962-1) Am Accounting.

Burns, J. A. Growth & Development of the Catholic School System in the United States. LC 78-89156. (American Education: Its Men, Institutions, & Ideas. Series 1). 1974. reprint ed. 23.95 (0-405-01394-9) Ayer.

— The Principles, Origin & Establishment of the Catholic School System in the United States. LC 74-89155. (American Education: Its Men, Institutions, & Ideas. Series 1). 1975. reprint ed. 23.95 (0-405-01393-0) Ayer.

Burns, J. DeWitt. The Cappy's Hill Cadre. 1998. 26.95 (0-9660206-1-8) New Eng Coastal.

Burns, J. H. Lordship, Kingship, & Empire: The Idea of Monarchy, 1400-1525. (Carlyle Lectures). 192p. 1992. text 55.00 (0-19-820206-7) OUP.

— The True Law of Kingship: Concepts of Monarchy in Early Modern Scotland. LC 95-17980. (Illus.). 328p. (C). 1996. text 69.00 (0-19-820384-5, Clarendon Pr) OUP.

Burns, J. H., ed. The Cambridge History of Medieval Political Thought c. 350-c. 1450. 816p. 1988. text 110.00 (0-521-24324-6) Cambridge U Pr.

— The Cambridge History of Medieval Political Thought c. 350-c. 1450. 816p. (C). 1991. pap. text 39.95 (0-521-42388-0) Cambridge U Pr.

— The Cambridge History of Political Thought 1450-1700. 810p. (C). 1995. pap. text 39.95 (0-521-47772-7) Cambridge U Pr.

Burns, J. H., et al, eds. An Introduction to the Principles of Morals & Legislation. 343p. (C). 1970. text 75.00 (0-485-13211-7, Pub. by Athlone Pr) Humanities.

Burns, J. H. & Goldie, Mark, eds. The Cambridge History of Political Thought, 1450-1700. 810p. (C). 1991. text 110.00 (0-521-24716-0) Cambridge U Pr.

Burns, J. H. & Izbicki, Thomas M., eds. Conciliarism & Papalism. LC 96-46495. (Cambridge Texts in the History of Political Thought Ser.). 352p. (C). 1998. text 64.95 (0-521-47089-7); pap. text 23.95 (0-521-47674-7) Cambridge U Pr.

Burns, J. H., ed. see Bentham, Jeremy & Hart, H. L. A.

Burns, J. H., ed. see Gentham, Jeremy.

Burns, J. Patout, ed. War & Its Discontents: Pacifism & Quietism in the Abrahamic Traditions. LC 95-42086. 240p. 1996. 55.00 (0-87840-603-4) Georgetown U Pr.

Burns, J. Patout, ed. Theological Anthropology. LC 81-43080. (Sources of Early Christian Thought Ser.). 136p. (Orig.). 1981. pap. 14.00 (0-8006-1412-7, 1-1412, Fortress Pr) Augsburg Fortress.

Burns, Jabez. 151 Sermon Outlines. LC 86-27520. (Sermon Outline Ser.). 224p. 1987. pap. 11.99 (0-8254-2266-3) Kregel.

— 200 Sermon Outlines. LC 75-92502. (Sermon Outline Ser.). 424p. 1969. reprint ed. pap. 14.99 (0-8254-2264-7) Kregel.

Burns, Jacqueline. How to Have Everything You Want. 19p. 1998. 1.25 (0-9665013-0-6) Life Without.

Burns, James, et al. Government by the People: Brief Edition. 3rd ed. LC 99-45754. 478p. (C). 1999. pap. text 45.00 incl. cd-rom (0-13-011635-1) P-H.

— Government by the People: Texas Version. 2nd ed. LC 97-24091. 896p. 1997. 80.00 (0-13-287186-6) P-H.

Burns, James B. Railroad Mergers & the Language of Unification. LC 97-21854. 232p. 1998. 59.95 (1-56720-166-0, Quorum Bks) Greenwood.

Burns, James F., ed. see Andreas, Barbara K., et al.

Burns, James J. The Colonial Agents of New England. LC 75-29253. (Perspectives in American History Ser.: No. 26). v, 156p. 1975. reprint ed. lib. bdg. 27.50 (0-87991-350-9) Porcupine Pr.

B

An Asterisk (*) at the beginning of an entry indicates that the title is appearing for the first time.

Burns, James M. Congress on Trial: The Legislative Process & the Administrative State. LC 66-29462. 224p. 1966. reprint ed. 50.00 (*0-87752-013-5*) Gordian.
— Leadership. LC 76-5117. 544p. 1982. pap. 18.00 (*0-06-131975-9*, TB 1975, Torch) HarpC.
— Roosevelt: Soldier of Freedom. (Leaders of Our Time Ser.). (Illus.). 640p. 1999. reprint ed. 14.95 (*1-56852-091-3*, Konecky & Konecky) W S Konecky Assocs.
— Roosevelt Lion & the Fox. (Illus.). 588p. 1963. pap. 20.00 (*0-15-678870-5*) Harcourt.
Burns, James M. & Overby, L. Marvin. Cobblestone Leadership: Majority Rule, Minority Power. LC 90-50229. (Julian J. Rothbaum Distinguished Lectures: Vol. 3). 160p. (C). 1990. 22.95 (*0-8061-2314-1*) U of Okla Pr.
Burns, James M., et al. Government by the People: State & Local Politics. 5th ed. (Illus.). 288p. (C). 1987. pap. text. write for info. (*0-318-61093-0*) P-H.
— State & Local Politics: Government by the People. 8th ed. LC 95-23798. 304p. 1995. pap. text 33.40 (*0-13-455866-9*) P-H.
— State & Local Politics: Government by the People. 9th ed. LC 97-38323. 293p. 1997. pap. text 37.00 (*0-13-639568-6*) P-H.
***Burns, James MacGregor.** State & Local Politics: Government by the People. 10th ed. LC 00-35631. 272p. 2000. pap. 33.33 (*0-13-025688-9*) P-H.
Burns, James MacGregor, ed. Government by the People: National, State, & Local. 18th ed. LC 99-15982. 800p. 2000. 74.00 (*0-13-011658-0*) S&S Trade.
Burns, James MacGregor & Cronin. Government by People National. 18th ed. LC 99-15983. 583p. 1999. text 66.00 incl. audio compact disk (*0-13-011656-4*) P-H.
Burns, James MacGregor & Sorenson, Georgia Jones. Dead Center: Clinton-Gore Leadership & the Perils of Moderation. LC 99-34871. 416p. 1999. 27.00 (*0-684-83778-1*) Scribner.
***Burns, James MacGregor, et al.** Government by the People: National. 18th ed. 1999. pap., student ed. 21.00 (*0-13-011754-4*) P-H.
— Government By The People: National, State & Local. 18th ed. 1999. pap., student ed. 21.00 (*0-13-011765-X*) P-H.
Burns, James MacGregor, ed. see Cronin.
Burns, James R. & Eubanks, Darrell. Microcomputers: Business & Personal Applications. 614p. (C). 1988. text 57.00 (*0-314-93159-7*) West Pub.
***Burns, Jane.** Wise Gal Tarot: Amazing Ways to Read Your Fortune! (Illus.). 2000. pap. 9.95 (*0-375-80644-X*) Knopf.
— Wise Gal Tarot: Amazing Ways to Read Your Fortune! 2000. 15.99 (*0-375-90644-4*) Knopf Bks Yng Read.
Burns, Jane, jt. auth. see Gottlieb, Dale.
Burns, Jane, jt. auth. see Rice, Martha.
Burns, Jane O., ed. see Needles, Belverd E.
Burns, Janice A. Sarah's Song: A True Story of Love & Courage. 272p. 1996. mass mkt. 6.50 (*0-446-60343-0*, Pub. by Warner Bks) Little.
Burns, Jasper. Fossil Collecting in the Mid-Atlantic States. LC 90-45388. (Illus.). 208p. 1991. pap. 22.95 (*0-8018-4145-3*); text 42.50 (*0-8018-4121-6*) Johns Hopkins.
— Virginia Fossils: An Educational Activity Book. (Illus.). 40p. (Orig.). (J). (gr. 4-7). 1998. pap. 4.95 (*1-884549-03-9*) VA Mus Natl Hist.
Burns, Jeff. Pentatonic Scales for the Jazz/Rock Keyboardist. 40p. 1997. pap. 9.95 (*0-7935-7679-2*) H Leonard.
Burns, Jeff D., jt. auth. see Steffenhagen, R. A.
***Burns, Jeffrey M.** Disturbing the Peace: A History of the Christian Family Movement, 1949-1974. LC 98-35634. 1999. pap. 25.00 (*0-268-00889-2*, Pub. by U of Notre Dame Pr) Chicago Distribution Ctr.
— Disturbing the Peace A History of the Christian Family Movement, 1949-1974. LC 98-35634. 1999. pap. text 50.00 (*0-268-00888-4*) U of Notre Dame Pr.
***Burns, Jeffrey M., et al, eds.** Keeping Faith: European & Asian Catholic Immigrants. (American Catholic Identities Ser.). 250p. 2000. 50.00 (*1-57075-317-2*); pap. 25.00 (*1-57075-297-4*) Orbis Bks.
Burns, Jerry, photos by. Sunday Best Baking: Over a Century of Secrets from the White Lily Kitchen. LC 98-66370. 276p. 1998. 18.95 (*1-56352-529-1*) Longstreet.
Burns, Jerry, tr. see Foster, Fred.
Burns, Jethro & Eidson, Ken. Complete Jethro Burns Mandolin Book. (Complete Book). 1993. spiral bd. 22.95 (*1-56222-663-0*, 94875) Mel Bay.
***Burns, Jethro & Eidson, Ken.** Complete Jethro Burns Mandolin 2-CD Package. 240p. 1999. pap. 46.95 incl. audio compact disk (*0-7866-4708-6*, 94875CDP) Mel Bay.
Burns, Jethro & Eidson, Ken. Jethro Burns - Bluegrass Mandolin Techniques. 80p. 1982. spiral bd. 9.95 (*0-87166-385-6*, 93807) Mel Bay.
Burns, Jill A., jt. auth. see Burns, Diane L.
***Burns, Jim.** Addicted to God. Simon, Wil, ed. LC 99-47583. 2000. pap. 9.99 (*0-8307-2531-8*) Gospel Lght.
Burns, Jim. Internal Memorandum. 1985. 19.00 (*0-904524-33-7*, Pub. by Rivelin Grapheme Pr) St Mut.
— Out of the Past: Selected Poems, 1961-1986 - Jim Burns. (Illus.). 92p. (C). 1988. pap. 40.00 (*0-947612-27-0*, Pub. by Rivelin Grapheme Pr) St Mut.
— Spirit Wings: Taking Off in Your Relationship with God & Learning to Soar a Spirit-Filled Devotional for Youth. LC 92-15247. 290p. (Orig.). (YA). 1992. pap. 10.99 (*0-89283-783-7*, Vine Bks) Servant.
***Burns, Jim.** Transluminal: The Paintings of Jim Burns. (Illus.). 2000. pap. 21.95 (*1-85585-678-6*) Paper Tiger.
Burns, Jim, ed. Incredible Retreats, 8 vols., Vol. 7. (Fresh Ideas Ser.). 173p. (YA). 1999. pap. 16.99 (*0-8307-2403-6*, Gospel Light) Gospel Lght.
— Missions & Service Projects, 8 vols., Vol. 6. (Fresh Ideas Ser.). 153p. (YA). 1999. pap. 16.99 (*0-8307-1879-6*, Gospel Light) Gospel Lght.
— Worship: For Youth Workers & Teachers. (Fresh Ideas Resources Ser.: Bk. VIII). 1999. pap. 16.99 (*0-8307-2404-4*, Gospel Light) Gospel Lght.
Burns, Jim & Brown, Betty A. Women Chefs: A Collection of Portraits & Recipes from California's Culinary Pioneers. 220p. 1987. pap. 16.95 (*0-943186-37-4*) Aris Bks.
Burns, Jim, jt. auth. see Arterburn, Stephen.
Burns, Jim, jt. auth. see St. Clair, Barry.
Burns, Jim, ed. see Mateljan, George.
Burns, Jimmy. Hand of God. LC 97-13461. (Orig.). 1997. 22.95 (*1-55821-597-2*, 15972) Lyons Pr.
— Spain: A Literary Companion. (Illus.). 256p. 1995. 34.95 (*0-7195-5098-X*); pap. 24.95 (*0-7195-5216-8*) Trafalgar.
Burns, Joanne. Penelope's Knees. 1996. pap. 18.95 (*0-7022-2780-3*, Pub. by Univ Queensland Pr) Intl Spec Bk.
Burns, Joe. HTML Goodies. 1998. pap. 19.99 (*0-7897-1823-5*) Que.
Burns, John. Celebration of the Light: Zen in the Novels of Neil M. Gunn. 1988. 45.00 (*0-389-20780-2*, N8339) B&N Imports.
— The Same River Twice. McHenry, Lauren, ed. LC 97-19371. 80p. (Orig.). 1997. pap. 15.00 (*1-882611-11-X*) Yardbird Bks.
Burns, John & Keys, Kerry S. The Nearing Notebooks. 36p. 1996. pap. 10.00 (*0-930502-23-X*) Pine Pr.
Burns, John, et al. The Answer to Addiction: The Path to Recovery from Alcohol, Drug, Food & Sexual Dependencies. rev. ed. (Illus.). 344p. 1996. pap. 12.95 (*0-914896-41-5*) East Ridge Pr.
Burns, John, jt. auth. see Bradfield, Susi.
Burns, John, jt. auth. see Twenty-Four Magazine Editors.
Burns, John A., jt. auth. see National Park Service, U.S. Department of the Inte.
Burns, John F. Sacramento: Gold Rush Legacy, Metropolitan Destiny. Parks, Lori, ed. LC 98-73490. (Illus.). 350p. 1999. 49.95 (*1-886483-27-2*) Heritge Media.
Burns, John J., Jr., ed. see American Society of Mechanical Engineers Staff.
Burns, John M. Evolutionary Differentiation: Differentiating Gold-Banded Skippers-Autochton Cellus & More (Lepidoptera: Hesperiidae: Pyrginae. LC 84-600229. (Smithsonian Contributions to Zoology Ser.: No. 405). 42p. reprint ed. pap. 30.00 (*0-608-14591-2*, 202481800038) Bks Demand.
Burns, John P., ed. Asian Civil Service Systems: Improving Efficiency & Productivity. 304p. 1994. pap. 25.00 (*981-210-032-6*, Pub. by Times Academic) Intl Spec Bk.
— The Chinese Communist Party's Nomenklatura System. LC 88-35577. (Chinese Studies on China). 214p. (C). (gr. 13). 1989. text 80.95 (*0-87332-543-5*) M E Sharpe.
Burns, John P. & Rosen, Stanley, eds. Policy Conflicts in Post-Mao China: A Documentary Survey with Analysis. LC 86-907. 384p. (gr. 13). 1986. pap. text 36.95 (*0-87332-338-6*, East Gate Bk) M E Sharpe.
— Policy Conflicts in Post-Mao China: A Documentary Survey with Analysis. LC 86-907. (Illus.). 384p. 1986. reprint ed. pap. 119.10 (*0-7837-9991-8*, 206071800006) Bks Demand.
Burns, John P., jt. ed. see Scott, Ian.
Burns, John T. Cosmic Influences on Humans, Animals & Plants: A Select Bibliography. LC 97-3441. (Magill Bibliographies Ser.). 1997. 34.50 (*0-8108-3313-1*) Scarecrow.
— Cycles in Humans & Nature. 300p. 1994. 42.50 (*0-8108-2831-6*) Scarecrow.
***Burns, John T.** Encyclopedia of Cycles in Nature. 2001. lib. bdg. 75.00 (*1-57607-087-5*) ABC-CLIO.
Burns, Joseph, et al, eds. Guide to Managed Care Strategies, 1998: An Annual Report on the Latest Practices & Policies in the New Managed Care Environment. (Illus.). 342p. 1997. pap. 225.00 (*1-57987-029-5*) Faulkner & Gray.
— Hospital Strategies in Managed Care, 2000 Edition: Survival Tactics & Success Strategies for the Age of Managed Care. (Illus.). 368p. 1999. pap. 225.00 (*1-57987-109-7*) Faulkner & Gray.
***Burns, Joseph & Baiggeman, Paula, eds.** Guide to Managed Care Strategies 2000 Edition. (Illus.). 416p. 1999. pap. 245.00 (*1-57987-120-8*) Faulkner & Gray.
Burns, Joseph & Sipkoff, Martin, eds. Hospital Strategies in Managed Care: Survival Tactics & Success Strategies for the Age of Managed Care. (Illus.). 320p. (Orig.). 1997. pap. 195.00 (*1-57987-003-1*) Faulkner & Gray.
Burns, Joseph, jt. ed. see Koizumi, Luci.
Burns, Joseph A., ed. Planetary Satellites. LC 76-7475. 598p. 1977. text 47.00 (*0-8165-0552-7*) U of Ariz Pr.
Burns, Joseph A. & Matthews, Mildred S., eds. Satellites. LC 86-19145. (Space Science Ser.). (Illus.). 1021p. 1986. 72.00 (*0-8165-0983-2*) U of Ariz Pr.
Burns, Joseph G., ed. The Engineering Aesthetics of Tall Buildings. 57p. 1985. 15.00 (*0-87262-450-1*) Am Soc Civil Eng.
Burns, Josephine, jt. auth. see Alderman, Margaret.
Burns, Julie & Bialosiewicz, Frank. The Road to Birth Game. (Technical Notes Ser.: No. 24). (Illus.). 33p. (Orig.). 1983. pap. text 2.00 (*0-932288-71-5*) Ctr Intl Ed U of MA.
Burns, Julie & Swan, Dorothy. Reading Without Books. LC 78-72078. (J). (gr. 4-6). 1979. pap. 9.99 (*0-8224-5830-6*) Fearon Teacher Aids.
Burns, Julie, jt. auth. see Bialosiewicz, Frank.
Burns, Julie, jt. auth. see Kris-Etherton, Penny.
Burns, Julie K. Opportunities in Computer Systems Careers. rev. ed. (Opportunities in...Ser.). (Illus.). 160p. 1996. 14.95 (*0-8442-4598-4*, 45984, Natl Textbk Co) NTC Contemp Pub Co.
Burns, June, jt. auth. see Burns, Tony.
Burns, K., jt. auth. see Ward, G.
Burns, K. M., jt. auth. see Hallenbeck, William H.
***Burns Kallaher, Karen.** Cult Leaders. LC 99-37857. (History Makers Ser.). (Illus.). 144p. (YA). (gr. 6-9). 2000. lib. bdg. 23.70 (*1-56006-593-1*) Lucent Bks.
Burns, Karen L., ed. Guiding Catalog Growth: Sucessful Strategies, Management & Techniques. (Illus.). 325p. 1985. pap. text 79.95 (*0-933641-04-4*) Direct Mkt.
***Burns, Karen Ramey.** The Forensic Anthropology Training Manual. LC 98-50154. 282p. (C). 1999. pap. text 32.20 (*0-13-010576-7*) P-H.
Burns, Kate. Blink Like an Owl! LC 99-227197. (Lift-the-Flap Book Ser.). (Illus.). 12p. (J). 1998. 6.95 (*1-899607-41-2*) Sterling.
— Hide & Seek: In the Jungle. (Hide & Seek Ser.). 14p. (J). (gr. k-3). 1996. 9.95 (*0-316-11821-4*) Little.
— Hide & Seek: In the Ocean. (Hide & Seek Ser.). (Illus.). 14p. (J). (gr. k-3). 1996. 9.95 (*0-316-11823-0*) Little.
— Hide & Seek: In the Sand. (Hide & Seek Ser.). (Illus.). 14p. (J). (gr. k-3). 1996. 9.95 (*0-316-11822-2*) Little.
— Hide & Seek: In the Snow. (Hide & Seek Ser.). 14p. (J). (gr. k-3). 1996. 9.95 (*0-316-11820-6*) Little.
***Burns, Kate.** Jump Like a Frog! 1999. 6.95 (*1-899607-35-8*) Levinson Bks.
— Round & Round the Garden. (Illus.). 16p. (J). 2000. 6.95 (*1-86233-106-5*) Levinson Bks.
— Snap Like a Crocodile! 1999. 6.95 (*1-899607-40-4*) Levinson Bks.
Burns, Kate. Waddle Like a Duck! LC 99-227222. (Lift-the-Flap Book Ser.). (Illus.). 12p. (J). 1998. 6.95 (*1-899607-42-0*) Sterling.
Burns, Kate & Apperley, Dawn. How Does Your Garden Grow? A Pop-Up & Pull-Tab Garden. LC 99-484133. (Illus.). 12p. (J). (ps-1). 1998. 10.95 (*1-899607-51-X*) Sterling.
Burns, Kate & Chambers, Sally. Today I Went to Sea: The Ultimate Nursery Rhyme Activity Book. (Illus.). 8p. (J). (ps-2). 1997. 14.95 (*0-7641-5006-5*) Barron.
Burns, Kate & Petrone, Valeria. Round & Round the Garden. (Finger Puppet Bks.). (Illus.). 16p. (J). 1998. 10.95 (*1-86233-040-9*) Sterling.
***Burns, Kathleen.** Top Students/Top Parents: Reading, Writing, Language. LC 99-95328. (Illus.). 320p. 2000. pap. 20.00 (*0-9672575-0-6*) K Burns.
Burns, Kathryn. Colonial Habits: Convents & the Spiritual Economy of Cuzco, Peru. LC 98-8099. 1999. write for info. (*0-8223-2259-5*); pap. 17.95 (*0-8223-2291-9*) Duke.
Burns, Kathy. Mission Friends Guide. McClain, Cindy, ed. 42p. (Orig.). 1995. pap. text 3.95 (*1-56309-131-3*, W958105) Womans Mission Union.
Burns, Keith, jt. auth. see Adams, Leith.
Burns, Keith, jt. ed. see Adams, Leith.
Burns, Ken. Baseball, the American Epic. (1994 American Antiquarian Society-Lila Wallace-Reader's Digest Fund Lecture). 17p. 1995. pap. 7.00 (*0-944026-61-3*) Am Antiquarian.
***Burns, Ken.** Civil War Telecourse Student Guide. 1999. student ed. write for info. (*0-939009-42-0*, EPM) Howell Pr VA.
Burns, Ken, jt. auth. see Hartwell, Carroll T.
Burns, Ken, jt. auth. see Ward, Geoffrey C.
Burns, Kenneth G., tr. & intro. see Ohsawa, George.
Burns, Kevan J. & Burns, Caroline E. Nurse Saver: An Organizational Too! (Illus.). 24p. 1998. wbk. ed. 25.00 (*0-9663913-0-6*) Nurse Saver.
Burns, Khephra. Black Stars in Orbit: NASA's African-American Astronauts. LC 93-44624. 1995. 14.15 (*0-606-09084-3*, Pub. by Turtleback) Demco.
Burns, Khephra. Mansa Musa: The Lion of Mali. LC 97-50559. (Illus.). (J). 2000. 20.01 (*0-15-200375-4*) Harcourt.
Burns, Khephra & Miles, William. Black Stars in Orbit: NASA's African-American Astronauts. LC 93-44624. (Illus.). 80p. (J). (gr. 3-7). 1995. 20.00 (*0-15-200432-7*, Gulliver Bks); pap. 10.00 (*0-15-200276-6*, Gulliver Bks) Harcourt.
Burns, Khephra, jt. auth. see Taylor, Susan.
Burns, Khephra, jt. ed. see Taylor, Susan L.
Burns Knight, Margy. Las Paredes Hablan - Talking Walls. Kohen, Clarita, tr. (SPA., Illus.). 32p. 1992. pap. 8.95 (*0-88448-157-3*) Tilbury Hse.
— Las Paredes Hablan/Talking Walls: Cuentan Mas Historias/The Stories Continue. Kohen, Clarita, tr. (SPA.). (J). (gr. 3-8). 1996. 17.95 (*0-88448-166-2*); pap. 8.95 (*0-88448-167-0*) Tilbury Hse.
— Quien es de Aqui - Who Belongs Here? Kohen, Clarita, tr. from ENG. (SPA., Illus.). 40p. (J). (gr. 3-8). 1995. 16.95 (*0-88448-158-1*); pap. 8.95 (*0-88448-159-X*) Tilbury Hse.
— Talking Walls. (CHI & ENG., Illus.). 38p. (J). (gr. 2 up). 1995. 18.95 (*1-879600-33-1*); 18.95 (*1-879600-35-8*) Pac Asia Pr.
— Talking Walls. Kohen, Clarita, tr. (ENG & SPA., Illus.). 38p. (J). (gr. 2 up). 1995. 18.95 (*1-879600-32-3*) Pac Asia Pr.
— Talking Walls. Yang, Xeng, tr. (Illus.). 38p. (J). (gr. 2 up). 1995. 18.95 (*1-879600-34-X*) Pac Asia Pr.
— Talking Walls. Ouk, Mory, tr. (CAM., Illus.). 38p. (J). (gr. 2 up). 1995. 18.95 (*1-879600-36-6*) Pac Asia Pr.
— Talking Walls. Dupiechain, Loida S., tr. (ENG & TAG., Illus.). 38p. (J). (gr. 2 up). 1995. 18.95 (*1-879600-38-2*) Pac Asia Pr.
— Talking Walls. Bounking, Vikham & Kaignavongsa, Xay, trs. (ENG & LAO., Illus.). 38p. (J). (gr. 2 up). 1995. 18.95 (*1-879600-37-4*) Pac Asia Pr.
— Talking Walls. (Illus.). 36p. (J). 1993. 19.95 (*1-55082-056-7*, Pub. by Quarry Pr) LPC InBook.
— Talking Walls. LC 91-67867. (Illus.). 40p. (J). (gr. 3-8). 1992. 17.95 (*0-88448-102-6*) Tilbury Hse.
— Talking Walls. (Illus.). 40p. (J). (gr. 3-8). 1995. pap. 8.95 (*0-88448-154-9*) Tilbury Hse.
— Talking Walls: The Stories Continue. LC 96-15123. (Illus.). 40p. (J). (gr. 3-8). 1996. 17.95 (*0-88448-164-6*) Tilbury Hse.
— Talking Walls: The Stories Continue. (Illus.). (J). (gr. 3-8). 1997. pap. 8.95 (*0-88448-165-4*) Tilbury Hse.
— Welcoming Babies. (Illus.). 40p. (J). (ps-4). 1998. pap. 7.95 (*0-88448-124-7*) Tilbury Hse.
— Who Belongs Here? An American Story. (Illus.). 40p. (J). (gr. 3-8). 1993. pap. 8.95 (*0-88448-169-7*) Tilbury Hse.
— Who Belongs Here? Teacher's Guide. (Illus.). 40p. 1995. teacher ed. 9.95 (*0-88448-111-5*) Tilbury Hse.
Burns Knight, Margy & Chan, Thomas V. Talking Walls: The Stories Continue Teacher's Guide. (Illus.). 144p. (J). (gr. 3-8). 1996. pap., teacher ed. 9.95 (*0-88448-168-9*) Tilbury Hse.
— Talking Walls Teacher's Guide. 48p. (Orig.). (J). (gr. 3-8). 1992. pap., teacher ed. 9.95 (*0-88448-106-9*) Tilbury Hse.
Burns Knight, Margy & Sibley O'Brien, Anne. Who Belongs Here? An American Story. (Illus.). 40p. (J). (gr. 3-8). 1993. 16.95 (*0-88448-110-7*) Tilbury Hse.
***Burns, Kristine H., ed.** Women & Music in America since 1900: An Encyclopedia. (Illus.). 736p. 2001. text 150.00 (*1-57356-267-X*) Oryx Pr.
Burns, L. S. & Grebler, L. The Future of Housing Markets: A New Appraisal. (Environment, Development, & Public Policy Ser.). (Illus.). 222p. (C). 1986. 55.00 (*0-306-42313-8*, Plenum Trade) Perseus Pubng.
Burns, Lamont. Down Home Southern Cooking. 1987. pap. 9.50 (*0-9627145-2-6*, Cyrus Pr) Waterside Prodns.
Burns, Landon C. Pat Conroy: A Critical Companion. LC 95-39495. (Critical Companions to Popular Contemporary Writers Ser.). 216p. 1996. 29.95 (*0-313-29419-4*, Greenwood Pr) Greenwood.
Burns, Larry & Osborne, Jan, eds. Student Peer Counseling Training Curriculum. 1985. teacher ed. 95.00 (*1-56117-029-1*); student ed. 3.50 (*1-56117-004-6*); student ed. 3.95 (*1-56117-003-8*) Telesis CA.
Burns, Laura G., jt. auth. see Smith, Bruce T.
Burns, Laurence E., jt. auth. see Thorpe, Geoffrey L.
Burns, Lawrence D., ed. Corn Meal Cookery: A Collection of Heirloom Corn Meal Recipes Dating from 1846. xix, 52p. 1998. pap. write for info. (*0-9665507-0-6*) Simon Pure.
Burns, Leland S. & Friedmann, John, eds. The Art of Planning: Selected Essays of Harvey S. Perloff. LC 85-12470. (Environment, Development, & Public Policy: Public Policy & Social Services Ser.). (Illus.). 378p. (C). 1985. 96.00 (*0-306-42030-9*, Plenum Trade) Perseus Pubng.
Burns, Leslie & Bryant, Nancy. The Business of Fashion: Designing, Manufacturing, Marketing. 1997. teacher ed. 3.50 (*1-56367-074-7*) Fairchild.
Burns, Leslie D. & Bryant, Nancy O. The Busines of Fashion: Designing, Manufacturing, & Marketing. LC 96-85747. (Illus.). 439p. 1997. 63.00 (*1-56367-073-9*) Fairchild.
Burns, Leslie D. & Sproles, George B. Changing Appearances: Understanding Dress in Contemporary Society. LC 93-73072. 323p. 1994. 49.00 (*1-56367-014-3*) Fairchild.
Burns, Leslie D., jt. auth. see Sproles, George B.
Burns, Lillie R. Blacks vs. Black: I Have a Problem Relating to Some Blacks & I Am Black Myself. 28p. 1998. pap. 16.95 (*0-9665476-0-8*) LB Enterp.
Burns, Linda. Vagueness: An Investigation into Natural Languages & the Sorites Paradox. (Reason & Argument Ser.: No. 4). 216p. 1991. lib. bdg. 126.50 (*0-7923-1489-1*, Pub. by Kluwer Academic) Kluwer Academic.
Burns, Linda H. & Covington, Sharon N. Infertility Counseling: A Comprehensive Handbook for Clinicians. LC 98-3822. (Illus.). 648p. 1998. 58.00 (*1-85070-924-6*) Prthnon Pub.
Burns, Linda H., jt. auth. see Ilse, Sherokee.
Burns, Lois, jt. auth. see Maloney, Florence.
Burns, Lois M., jt. auth. see Maloney, Florence C.
Burns, Lori. Bach's Modal Chorales. LC 95-24547. (Harmonologia Ser.: No. 9). 257p. 1995. 54.00 (*0-945193-74-2*) Pendragon NY.
Burns, Louis F. Symbolic & Decorative Art of the Osage People. Sioux, Dhegiha, tr. (Illus.). 124p. (Orig.). 1995. pap. 34.50 (*0-942574-10-9*) Ciga Pr.
Burns, Luisa E., ed. see Naugle, June.
Burns, M., jt. auth. see Devendra, C.
Burns, M. Doug. 12 Days in Walleye Heaven. Barringer, Bernie R., ed. & pref. by. (Illus.). 180p. (Orig.). Date not set. pap. 14.95 (*1-885149-02-6*) Moving Mtn.
Burns, M. Edward, Jr. Pet Peeves: And What to Do about Them. rev. ed. LC 92-6014. (C). 1992. pap. 15.95 (*0-941301-19-2*) CAI.
Burns, M. L., et al, eds. Positron-Electron Pairs in Astrophysics: AIP Conference Proceedings No. 101, Goddard Space Flight Center, 1983. LC 83-71926. 447p. 1983. lib. bdg. 38.50 (*0-88318-200-9*) Am Inst Physics.
Burns, M. Susan, ed. see National Research Council Staff & Alberts, Betty.
Burns, Marcelline, et al. Drug Information Handbook for the Criminal Justice Professional. 925p. 1998. pap. 29.75 (*0-916589-60-9*) Lexi-Comp.
Burns, Margaret. Single Room Maternity Care. 160p. 1996. spiral bd. 85.00 (*1-879575-75-2*) Acad Med Sys.
— Surgical Standards in Obstetrics. 190p. 1995. spiral bd. 95.00 (*1-879575-66-3*) Acad Med Sys.

An Asterisk (*) at the beginning of an entry indicates that the title is appearing for the first time.

Burns, Margarete. Labor & Delivery Policy & Procedure Guideline Manual. 400p. 1996. spiral bd. 115.00 (*1-879575-70-1*) Acad Med Sys.

Burns, Marilyn. About Teaching Mathematics. (Illus.). (J). (gr. k-8). 1992. pap. 27.95 (*0-201-48039-5*) Addison-Wesley.

***Burns, Marilyn.** About Teaching Mathematics: A K-8 Resource. 2nd rev. ed. LC 00-36177. (Illus.). 320p. 2000. pap. 32.95 (*0-941355-25-X*) Math Solns Pubns.

Burns, Marilyn. The Book of Think: Or How to Solve Problems Twice Your Size. (Brown Paper School Bks.). (Illus.). 125p. (YA). (gr. 5 up). 1976. pap. 12.95 (*0-316-11743-9*) Little.

— Book of Think, or, How to Solve a Problem Twice Your Size. (Brown Paper School Bks.). (J). 1976. 18.05 (*0-606-04017-X*, Pub. by Turtleback) Demco.

— A Collection of Math Lessons: From Grades 3 Through 6. (Illus.). 193p. 1987. pap. text 16.95 (*0-941355-00-4*) Math Solns Pubns.

— Collection of Math Lessons: Grades One to Three, Lessons 1-3. (J). 1995. pap. 15.95 (*0-201-48041-7*) Addison-Wesley.

— Collection of Math Lessons: Grades Six to Eight. (J). (gr. 6-8). 1995. pap. 15.95 (*0-201-48042-5*) Addison-Wesley.

— Collection of Math Lessons: Grades Three to Six, Lessons 3-6. 176p. (J). (gr. 3-6). 1995. pap. 15.95 (*0-201-48040-9*) Addison-Wesley.

— 50 Problem-Solving Lessons: The Best of 10 Years from Math Solutions Newletters. 183p. 1996. pap. 15.95 (*0-941355-16-0*) Math Solns Pubns.

— Good for Me! All about Food in 32 Bites. LC 78-6727. (Brown Paper School Bks.). (Illus.). 127p. (YA). (gr. 5 up). 1978. pap. 11.95 (*0-316-11747-1*) Little.

— The Greedy Triangle. LC 94-11308. (Brainy Day Bks.). (Illus.). 40p. (J). (ps-3). 1995. 15.95 (*0-590-48991-7*, Scholastic Ref) Scholastic Inc.

— Hanukkah Book. 1991. 9.09 (*0-606-07607-7*, Pub. by Turtleback) Demco.

— The Hanukkah Book. LC 80-27935. 128p. (YA). (gr. 4-7). 1991. reprint ed. mass mkt. 3.99 (*0-380-71520-1*, Avon Bks) Morrow Avon.

— How Many Feet? How Many Tails? A Book of Math Riddles. LC 96-7970. (Hello Math Reader Ser.). (Illus.). 32p. (J). (ps-3). 1996. pap. 3.50 (*0-590-67360-2*, Cartwheel) Scholastic Inc.

Burns, Marilyn. How Many Feet? How Many Tails? A Book of Math Riddles. LC 96-7970. (Hello Math Reader Ser.). 1996. 8.70 (*0-606-09437-7*, Pub. by Turtleback) Demco.

Burns, Marilyn. I Am Not a Short Adult: Getting Good at Being a Kid. (Brown Paper School Bks.). (Illus.). 125p. (YA). (gr. 5 up). 1977. pap. 12.95 (*0-316-11746-3*) Little.

— The I Hate Mathematics! Book. (Brown Paper School Bks.). (Illus.). 127p. (YA). (gr. 5 up). 1975. pap. 13.95 (*0-316-11741-2*) Little.

— I Hate Mathematics! Book. (Brown Paper School Bks.). (J). 1975. 17.05 (*0-606-04010-2*, Pub. by Turtleback) Demco.

— Math: Facing an American Phobia. LC 97-45225. (Illus.). 164p. 1998. pap. 14.95 (*0-941355-19-5*) Math Solns Pubns.

— Math & Literature (K-3), Bk. 1. 73p. 1995. pap. text 14.95 (*0-941355-07-1*) Math Solns Pubns.

— Math for Smarty Pants. (Brown Paper School Bks.). (J). 1982. 17.05 (*0-606-04019-6*, Pub. by Turtleback) Demco.

— Math for Smarty Pants: or Who Says Mathematicians Have Little Pig Eyes. (Brown Paper School Bks.). (Illus.). 128p. (YA). (gr. 7 up). 1982. pap. 12.95 (*0-316-11739-0*) Little.

— Multiplication, Grade 3. (Math by All Means Ser.). 144p. 1995. pap. text. write for info. (*0-941355-04-7*) Math Solns Pubns.

— The $1.00 Word Riddle Book. (Illus.). 48p. (J). (gr. 3-8). 1990. pap. 7.50 (*0-938587-29-3*) Cuisenaire.

— The $1.00 Word Riddle Book. 48p. (J). (gr. k-5). 1990. pap. text 8.95 (*0-941355-02-0*) Math Solns Pubns.

— One Dollar Word Riddle Book. (J). (gr. 4-7). 1995. pap. 7.50 (*0-201-48025-5*) Addison-Wesley.

— Place Value, Grades 1-2. (Math by All Means Ser.). (Illus.). 208p. 1994. pap. text 23.95 (*0-941355-09-8*) Math Solns Pubns.

— Probability, Grades 3-4. (Math by All Means Ser.). 254p. 1995. pap. text. write for info. (*0-941355-12-8*) Math Solns Pubns.

— Spaghetti & Meatballs for All! A Mathematical Story. LC 96-36082. (Illus.). 40p. (J). (gr. 1-4). 1997. 15.95 (*0-590-94459-2*) Scholastic Inc.

— This Book Is about Time. LC 78-6614. (Brown Paper School Bks.). (Illus.). 128p. (YA). (gr. 5 up). 1978. pap. 13.95 (*0-316-11750-1*) Little.

— Writing in Math Class: A Resource for Grades 2-8. (Illus.). 197p. 1995. pap. text 19.95 (*0-941355-13-6*) Math Solns Pubns.

Burns, Marilyn, ed. Leading the Way: Principals & Superintendents Look at Math Instruction. LC 99-31755. 96p. (Orig.). 1999. pap. 14.95 (*0-941355-21-7*) Math Solns Pubns.

Burns, Marilyn & Humphreys, Cathy. A Collection of Math Lessons: From Grades 6 Through 8. (Illus.). 186p. 1990. pap. text 16.95 (*0-941355-03-9*) Math Solns Pubns.

Burns, Marilyn & Tank, Bonnie. A Collection of Math Lessons: From Grades 1 Through 3. 1988. pap. text 16.95 (*0-941355-01-2*) Math Solns Pubns.

Burns, Marilyn, jt. auth. see Keenan, Sheila.

Burns, Marilyn, jt. auth. see Maccarone, Grace.

Burns, Marilyn, jt. auth. see MacCarone, Grace.

Burns, Marilyn, jt. auth. see Ochiltree, Dianne.

Burns, Marilyn, jt. auth. see Ohanian, Susan.

Burns, Marilyn, jt. auth. see Rocklin, Joanne.

Burns, Marjorie, jt. auth. see Cassie, Brian.

Burns, Marshall L. Modern Physics for Science & Engineering. 578p. (C). 1988. teacher ed. 20.00 (*0-15-562352-4*) Harcourt Coll Pubs.

Burns, Martha. Reading Group Journal Notes in the Margin. 1999. 16.95 (*0-7892-0586-6*) Abbeville Pr.

Burns, Martha S., jt. auth. see Halper, Anita S.

Burns, Mary. Center - Center. 256p. (Orig.). 1993. pap. 14.95 (*0-88922-309-2*) Genl Dist Srvs.

— Pathophysiology: A Programmed Approach. LC 97-41936. (C). 1998. pap. 39.95 (*0-8385-8084-X*) Appleton & Lange.

— The Private Eye: Observing Snow Geese. LC 97-118505. (Illus.). 2244p. 1996. 29.95 (*0-7748-0575-7*) U of Wash Pr.

— Suburbs of the Arctic Circle. 158p. 1988. 12.95 (*0-920806-79-1*, Pub. by Penumbra Pr) U of Toronto Pr.

Burns, Mary F. The Burns Braille Transcription Dictionary. LC 91-40378. 96p. 1992. pap. 19.95 (*0-89128-232-7*) Am Foun Blind.

Burns, Mary R., et al. Review Questions for Health Information Management: RRA & Art Examination Preparation. LC 96-29845. (Review Questions Ser.). 138p. 1997. pap. 19.95 (*1-85070-737-5*) Prthnon Pub.

Burns, Mathew E., jt. auth. see Schultz, Wayne R.

Burns, Maureen. Forgiveness - a Gift You Give Yourself. 145p. (Orig.). 1992. pap. 15.00 (*0-9613084-6-X*) Empey Ent.

Burns, Maureen A. Corre Contu Suenos. (Illus.). 60p. 1987. pap. 10.00 (*0-9613084-1-9*) Empey Ent.

— Getting in Touch - Intimacy. (Illus.). 76p. 1989. pap. 10.00 (*0-9613084-3-5*) Empey Ent.

— Run with Your Dreams. (Illus.). 60p. 1982. pap. 10.00 (*0-9613084-0-0*) Empey Ent.

Burns, Maureen A. & Burns, Cara M. Cara's Story. (Illus.). 54p. 1987. pap. 10.00 (*0-9613084-2-7*) Empey Ent.

Burns, Max. Cottage Water Systems: An Out-of-the-City Guide to Pumps, Plumbing, Water Purification, & Privies. rev. ed. LC 93-94407. (Illus.). 160p. (Orig.). 1993. pap. 24.95 (*0-9696922-0-X*) Firefly Bks Ltd.

— Dock Manual. LC 98-47045. 201p. 1999. pap. 24.95 (*1-58017-098-6*) Storey Bks.

Burns, Meg, jt. auth. see Burns, Philip.

Burns, Melissa C., ed. see Friedman, Jordan.

Burns, Michael. Discovery & Reminiscence: Essays on the Poetry of Mona Van Duyn. LC 97-37474. ix, 158 p. 1998. 32.00 (*1-55728-473-3*) U of Ark Pr.

— Hot Planet. 316p. (Orig.). 1994. pap. 9.50 (*0-9639345-0-3*) Planet Pr.

— It Will Be All Right in the Morning: Poems. LC 98-9298. 80p. 1998. pap. 16.00 (*1-55728-516-0*) U of Ark Pr.

— Rural Society & French Politics: Boulangism & the Dreyfus Affair, 1886-1900. LC 84-3253. (Illus.). 262p. reprint ed. pap. 81.30 (*0-608-06321-5*, 206668300008) Bks Demand.

— The Secret Names: Poems. 64p. 1994. pap. 12.95 (*0-8262-0947-5*) U of Mo Pr.

— Supermarine Spitfire. (Illus.). 192p. 1998. 44.95 (*1-86126-119-5*, Pub. by Crolwood) Motorbooks Intl.

Burns, Michael, ed. Low-Level Radioactive Waste Regulation: Science, Politics, & Fear. (Illus.). 311p. 1987. lib. bdg. 89.95 (*0-87371-026-6*, L026) Lewis Pubs.

— Miller Williams & the Poetry of the Particular. 152p. (C). 1991. text 27.50 (*0-8262-0807-X*) U of Mo Pr.

Burns, Michael & Sanders, Mark, eds. Jumping Pond: Poems & Stories from the Ozarks. 100p. (C). 1983. pap. 5.00 (*0-913785-00-8*) S M S U.

Burns, Michael, et al. And As for Darkness: Poems. Goad, Craig M., ed. 28p. 1987. pap. 3.50 (*0-9616467-1-3*) GreenTower Pr.

Burns, Michael R. Telemarketing: Setting up for Success. 200p. 1987. 22.00 (*0-936840-10-2*) Tech Marketing.

Burns, Mike, jt. auth. see Burns, Bob.

Burns, Mildred L. Values Based Planning for Quality Education. LC 95-60606. 520p. 1995. text 39.95 (*1-56676-284-7*) Scarecrow.

Burns, Morris U. The Dramatic Criticism of Alexander Woollcott. LC 80-12935. 292p. 1980. 26.50 (*0-8108-1299-1*) Scarecrow.

Burns, Morris U., jt. auth. see Woods, Porter S.

Burns, N. D., jt. auth. see Kochhar, A. K.

Burns, N. R. Injunctions: A Practical Handbook. xviii, 108p. 1988. 39.50 (*0-455-20776-3*, Pub. by LawBk Co) Gaunt.

Burns, Nancy. The Formation of American Local Governments: Private Values in Public Institutions. LC 93-46100. (Illus.). 208p. (C). 1994. text 49.95 (*0-19-508275-3*); pap. text 22.95 (*0-19-509093-4*) OUP.

— The Practice of Nursing Research. 3rd ed. 1997. text 59.00 (*0-7216-7572-7*, W B Saunders Co) Harcrt Hlth Sci Grp.

Burns, Nancy & Grove, Susan K. The Practice of Nursing Research: Conduct, Critique & Utilization. 3rd ed. Eoyang, Thomas, ed. (Illus.). 715p. 1997. text 43.95 (*0-7216-3054-5*, W B Saunders Co) Harcrt Hlth Sci Grp.

— The Practice of Nursing Research: Conduct, Critique & Utilization. 3rd ed. (Illus.). 1997. teacher ed. write for info. (*0-7216-3057-X*, W B Saunders Co) Harcrt Hlth Sci Grp.

— Study Guide for Practice of Nursing Research: Conduct, Critique & Utilization. 3rd ed. (Illus.). 715p. 1997. pap. text, student ed. 22.95 (*0-7216-2587-8*, W B Saunders Co) Harcrt Hlth Sci Grp.

— Study Guide for Understanding Nursing Research. 2nd ed. 255p. pap. text. write for info. (*0-7216-8108-5*, W B Saunders Co) Harcrt Hlth Sci Grp.

— Understanding Nursing Research. 208p. 1994. teacher ed. write for info. (*0-7216-4439-2*, W B Saunders Co) Harcrt Hlth Sci Grp.

— Understanding Nursing Research. (Illus.). 560p. 1995. pap. text 32.00 (*0-7216-4436-8*, W B Saunders Co) Harcrt Hlth Sci Grp.

— Understanding Nursing Research. 2nd ed. LC 98-43924. (Illus.). 555p. (C). 1999. pap. write for info. (*0-7216-8106-9*, W B Saunders Co) Harcrt Hlth Sci Grp.

Burns, Natasha. Safari Style. 216p. 1998. 45.00 (*1-55670-859-9*) Stewart Tabori & Chang.

Burns, Ned H., jt. auth. see Lin, T. Y.

Burns, Ned H., jt. ed. see Halvorsen, Grant T.

Burns, Norman. The Tariff of Syria, 1919 to 1932. LC 76-180328. (Mid-East Studies). reprint ed. 42.50 (*0-404-56234-5*) AMS Pr.

Burns, Norman T. Christian Mortalism from Tyndale to Milton. LC 72-75406. 232p. reprint ed. pap. 72.00 (*0-8357-2537-5*, 205715800015) Bks Demand.

Burns, Olive Ann. Cold Sassy Tree. 400p. 1986. pap. 13.95 (*0-385-31258-X*, Delta Trade) Dell.

— Cold Sassy Tree. LC 84-8570. 392p. 1984. 25.00 (*0-89919-309-9*, Pub. by Ticknor & Fields) HM.

— Cold Sassy Tree. (J). 1984. 17.10 (*0-606-02606-1*, Pub. by Turtleback) Demco.

— Leaving Cold Sassy: The Unfinished Sequel to Cold Sassy Tree. 320p. 1994. pap. 12.95 (*0-385-31220-2*, Delta Trade) Dell.

Burns, Olive Ann. Leaving Cold Sassy: The Unfinished Sequel to Cold Sassy Tree. LC 92-5561. 1992. 17.05 (*0-606-06523-7*, Pub. by Turtleback) Demco.

Burns, Olive Ann. Leaving Cold Sassy: The Unfinished Sequel to Cold Sassy Tree. large type ed. LC 92-40634. (General Ser.). 336p. 1994. lib. bdg. 22.95 (*0-8161-5702-2*, G K Hall Lrg Type) Mac Lib Ref.

Burns, Olive Ann, jt. auth. see Center for Learning Network Staff.

Burns, P., jt. auth. see Becher, H.

Burns, Pamela G., ed. see Courtney, Linda J.

Burns, Pat. Excel for Windows 95 Secrets. 888p. 1996. pap. 39.99 (*1-56884-712-2*) IDG Bks.

Burns, Patricia. Keep Safe for Me. large type ed. (Magna Large Print Ser.). 525p. 1997. 27.99 (*0-7505-1000-5*) Ulverscroft.

— The Marriage Mart. large type ed. 1995. 27.99 (*0-7089-3306-8*) Ulverscroft.

— Moonshadow. large type ed. 480p. 1996. 27.99 (*0-7089-3625-3*) Ulverscroft.

Burns, Patricia D., et al. Short Stuff: Poems & Stories for Children. (Illus.). 45p. (J). (gr. 2-5). 1997. pap. 5.00 (*0-9660071-2-3*) BEAR-IN-MIND.

Burns, Patricia H. The Book of Revelation Explained, Vol. 1. LC 82-90898. iv, 57p. 1986. pap. 19.95 (*0-9611368-0-4*) B R E Pub.

Burns, Patrick. Teach Yourself Office 97 for Windows. LC 96-29918. 1120p. 1997. pap. text 24.95 (*1-55828-530-X*, MIS Pr) IDG Bks.

Burns, Patrick, jt. auth. see Conner, Roger.

Burns, Patrick J. CD-Morph! Explore Gryphon Software's Amazing Special Effects & Animation Software. LC 94-20831. 192p. 1994. 39.95 incl. cd-rom (*0-201-40911-9*) Addison-Wesley.

— Using Quattro Pro 5. 2nd ed. (Illus.). 914p. (Orig.). 1993. 29.95 (*1-56529-257-X*) Que.

Burns, Patrick J. & Barrows. Excel 97 Secrets. LC 97-70134. 792p. 1997. pap. 49.99 (*0-7645-3044-5*) IDG Bks.

***Burns, Paul, ed.** April, 12 vols. (Butler's Lives of the Saints Ser.). 237p. (C). 1999. 24.95 (*0-8146-2380-8*) Liturgical Pr.

Burns, Paul, ed. Butler's Lives of the Saints: February. 256p. 2000. 24.95 (*0-8146-2378-6*) Liturgical Pr.

— Butler's Lives of the Saints: January, Set. LC 95-31671. 256p. (Orig.). 1995. 24.95 (*0-8146-2377-8*) Liturgical Pr.

— Butler's Lives of the Saints: September. 304p. 2000. 24.95 (*0-8146-2385-9*) Liturgical Pr.

Burns, Paul, ed. Butler's Lives of the Saints Standing Order, 12 vols. Date not set. 269.50 (*0-8146-2389-1*) Liturgical Pr.

Burns, Paul, ed. March. (Butler's Lives of the Saints Ser.). 293p. 1999. 24.95 (*0-8146-2379-4*) Liturgical Pr.

Burns, Paul, jt. ed. see Cumming, John.

Burns, Paul, jt. ed. see Doyle, Peter.

Burns, Paul, jt. ed. see Farmer, David H.

Burns, Paul, jt. ed. see Jones, Kathleen.

Burns, Paul, tr. see Boff, Leonardo & Boff, Clodovis.

Burns, Paul, tr. see Casaldaliga, Pedro & Vigil, Jose M.

Burns, Paul, tr. see Comblin, Joseph.

Burns, Paul, tr. see Moser, Antonio & Leers, Bernardino.

Burns, Paul, tr. see Munoz, Ronaldo.

Burns, Paul, tr. see Sobrino, Jon.

Burns, Paul C. & Roe, Betty D. Informal Reading Inventory: Preprimer to Twelfth Grade, 4 vols. 4th ed. 218p. (C). 1992. pap. text 39.16 (*0-395-64781-9*) HM.

***Burns, Paul C. & Roe, Betty D.** Informal Reading Inventory: Preprimer to Twelfth Grade. 5th rev. ed. 222p. 1998. spiral bd. write for info. (*0-395-90346-7*) HM Soft Schl Col Div.

Burns, Paul C. & Roe, Betty D. Reading Activities for Today's Elementary Schools. 218p. (C). 1991. reprint ed. pap. text 27.00 (*0-8191-8055-6*) U Pr of Amer.

Burns, Paul C., et al. Teaching Reading in Today's Elementary Schools. 6 vols. 6th ed. 672p. (C). 1995. text 63.96 (*0-395-75293-0*) HM.

— Teaching Reading in Today's Elementary Schools. 6 vols. 6th ed. (C). 1995. text, teacher ed. 11.96 (*0-395-75294-9*) HM.

Burns, Paula. Abby's Search for Cooper. (Illus.). 32p. (J). (gr. k-3). 1996. pap. 7.95 (*0-925168-48-3*) North Country.

Burns, Peggy. The Mail. (Stepping Through History Ser.). (Illus.). 32p. (J). 1994. lib. bdg. 5.00 (*1-56847-249-8*) Raintree Steck-V.

— Money. (Stepping Through History Ser.). (Illus.). 32p. (J). 1994. lib. bdg. 5.00 (*1-56847-248-X*) Raintree Steck-V.

— The News. (Stepping Through History Ser.). (Illus.). 32p. (J). 1995. lib. bdg. 5.00 (*1-56847-342-7*) Raintree Steck-V.

***Burns, Peggy.** Pope John Paul II: Pope for the People. LC 00-36935. (Famous Lives Ser.). (Illus.). 2000. write for info. (*0-8172-5714-4*) Raintree Steck-V.

Burns, Peggy. Stores & Markets. (Stepping Through History Ser.). (Illus.). 32p. (J). (gr. 3-7). lib. bdg. 5.00 (*1-56847-344-3*) Raintree Steck-V.

— Writing. (Stepping Through History Ser.). (Illus.). 32p. (J). 1995. lib. bdg. 5.00 (*1-56847-341-9*) Raintree Steck-V.

Burns, Peggy & Chrisp, Peter. Travel. (Stepping Through History Ser.). (Illus.). 32p. (J). 1995. lib. bdg. 5.00 (*1-56847-343-5*) Raintree Steck-V.

Burns, Peggy & Rowe, Julian. Language & Writing. LC 94-45474. (Legacies Ser.). (Illus.). 48p. (J). (gr. 4-6). 1995. lib. bdg. 24.26 (*1-56847-244-7*) Raintree Steck-V.

Burns, Peter. An Introduction to Tourism & Anthropology. LC 98-37417. 1999. write for info. (*0-415-18626-9*); pap. 24.99 (*0-415-18627-7*) Routledge.

***Burns, Peter C. & Finch, Robert, eds.** Uranium: Mineralogy, Geochemistry & the Environment. (Reviews in Mineralogy Ser.). (Illus.). 679p. 1999. pap. 32.00 (*0-939950-50-2*) Mineralogical Soc.

Burns, Peter D. Standing Ovation: Appreciating the Success You Are! 256p. (Orig.). 1995. pap. 12.95 (*0-9646035-0-0*) Paradigm WI.

Burns, Philip, ed. Dear Uncle George: The Correspondence Between Ezra Pound & Congressman Tinkham of Massachusetts. (Ezra Pound Scholarship Ser.). 234p. 1996. 35.00 (*0-943373-36-0*); pap. 19.95 (*0-943373-37-9*) Natl Poet Foun.

Burns, Philip & Burns, Meg. A Guide to Used Book Dealers of the Mid-Atlantic: Covering Portions of Pennsylvania, New Jersey, Delaware, Maryland, Virginia & Washington, D.C. LC 93-93812. (Illus.). 192p. (Orig.). 1993. pap. 9.95 (*0-9634481-1-0*) Turtle Hill.

Burns, Philip D. Multiple Victims, Multiple Causes: How to Recognize & Stop the Disease of Violence. LC 95-69176. 217p. (Orig.). 1995. 12.95 (*1-887431-50-0*) Sytech Res.

Burns, Phillys B. Iron Lady at Sea: From Shipyard to Voyage: A Story of the Great Iron-Hulled Sailing Ship, Star of India. (Illus.). 108p. (Orig.). (YA). 1988. pap. 6.95 (*0-685-20061-2*) Cove Pr CA.

Burns, R. Grabbits Gadgets: An Accounting Practice Set. 80p. 1990. pap. 16.00 (*0-409-30363-1*, Austral, MICHIE) LEXIS Pub.

Burns, R., ed. Sociological Backgrounds of Adult Education. (Notes & Essays Ser.: No. 41). 1970. pap. text 2.50 (*0-685-76690-X*, NES 41) Syracuse U Cont Ed.

Burns, R., tr. see Novikov, S. P., ed.

Burns, R., tr. see Petrov, Alexander.

Burns, R., tr. see Vrhovac, Duska.

Burns, R. B. Essential Psychology. 2nd ed. 416p. 1991. pap. text 59.00 (*0-7923-8957-3*) Kluwer Academic.

Burns, R. B. & Dobson, C. B. Introductory Psychology. 1984. pap. text 58.00 (*0-85200-491-5*) Kluwer Academic.

Burns, R. B., tr. see Kargapolov, M. I. & Merzljakov, Ju. I.

Burns, R. C. & Kaufman, S. H. Actions, Styles, & Symbols in Kinetic Family Drawings (KFD) An Interpretative Manual. LC 70-186854. 320p. 1987. pap. text 23.95 (*0-87630-228-2*) Brunner-Mazel.

Burns, R. G., tr. see Dubrovin, B. A., et al.

Burns, R. M. The Great Debate on Miracles: From Joseph Glanvill to David Hume. LC 78-75197. 300p. 1981. 39.50 (*0-8387-2378-0*) Bucknell U Pr.

Burns, R. W. British Television: The Formative Years. (History of Technology Ser.: No. 7). 488p. 1986. 125.00 (*0-86341-079-0*, HT007) INSPEC Inc.

***Burns, R. W.** The Life & Times of Alan Dower Blumlein. (IEE History of Technology Ser.: No. 24). 534p. 1999. boxed set 95.00 (*0-85296-773-X*) INSPEC Inc.

Burns, R. W. Television: An International History of the Formative Years. (IEE History of Technology Ser.: No. 22). 656p. 1998. boxed set 120.00 (*0-85296-914-7*, TK, Pub. by INSPEC Inc) Whitehurst & Clark.

Burns, R. W., ed. Radar Development to 1945. (Radar, Sonar, Navigation & Avionics Ser.: No. 2). 528p. 1988. 125.00 (*0-86341-139-8*, RA002) INSPEC Inc.

Burns, Ralph. Mozart's Starling. (Ohio Review Bks.). 72p. 1990. 15.95 (*0-942148-13-4*); pap. 8.95 (*0-942148-12-6*) Ohio Review.

— Swamp Candles. LC 95-50367. (Iowa Poetry Prize, 1995 Ser.). 78p. (Orig.). 1996. pap. 11.95 (*0-87745-539-2*) U of Iowa Pr.

— Us. (CSU Poetry Ser.: No. XII). 43p. (Orig.). 1983. pap. 4.50 (*0-914946-38-2*) Cleveland St Univ Poetry Ctr.

— Windy Tuesday Nights. LC 84-60839. (Illus.). 48p. 1984. pap. 6.00 (*0-915943-03-4*) Milkweed Ed.

Burns, Ralph A. Essentials of Chemistry. 2nd ed. 544p. (Orig.). 1995. pap. text 68.00 (*0-02-317361-0*, Macmillan Coll) P-H.

— Fundamentals of Chemistry. 192p. 1995. pap. text, lab manual ed. 47.00 (*0-13-378480-0*) P-H.

— Fundamentals of Chemistry. 2nd ed. (C). 1995. text 76.00 (*0-02-317351-3*, Macmillan Coll) P-H.

Burns, Ralph O. Basic Bible Truths for New Converts. 30p. 1978. reprint ed. pap. 0.99 (*0-87227-007-6*, RBP5003) Reg Baptist.

Burns, Rebecca, ed. see Battlo, Jean.

Burns, Rebecca C., ed. Parents & Schools: From Visitors to Partners. LC 93-31951. 1993. pap. write for info. (*0-8106-1856-7*) NEA.

B

An Asterisk (*) at the beginning of an entry indicates that the title is appearing for the first time.

Burns, Rex. Blood Line. 204p. 1995. 19.95 (*0-8027-3256-9*) Walker & Co.

— The Leaning Land: A Gabe Wager Mystery. LC 97-3581. 246p. 1997. 22.95 (*0-8027-3306-9*) Walker & Co.

— Success in America: The Yeoman Dream & the Industrial Revolution. LC 75-32482. (Illus.). 224p. 1976. 30.00 (*0-87023-207-X*) U of Mass Pr.

Burns, Rex & Sullivan, Mary R., eds. Crime Classics: The Mystery Story from Poe to the Present. 416p. 1991. reprint ed. pap. 14.95 (*0-14-013128-0*, Penguin Bks) Viking Penguin.

***Burns, R.I. & Chevedden, P.E.** Delayed. 1999. 110.50 (*90-04-11244-8*) Brill Academic Pubs.

Burns, Ric. Donner Party. 592p. 1999. pap. 40.00 (*0-670-84790-9*) Viking Penguin.

Burns, Ric & Sanders, James. New York: An Illustrated History. Ades, Lisa, ed. LC 99-23569. (Illus.). 480p. 1999. 60.00 (*0-679-45482-9*) Knopf.

Burns, Richard. Basic Guide to Gymnastics. 1998. pap. text 7.95 (*1-882180-44-5*) Griffin CA.

Burns, Richard. Cancer. 204p. 1997. pap. 8.97 (*0-9659860-0-4*) R Burns.
Cancer--is there a cure? A fictional tale of the life & death of cancer. ***Publisher Paid Annotation.***

Burns, Richard. High Blood Pressure: What Your Doctor Doesn't Tell You. 1995. pap. 17.95 (*0-949142-40-9*, Pub. by Stirling Pr) Intl Spec Bk.

— Keys to Transformation: Ceri Richards & Dylan Thomas. 137p. 1981. reprint ed. 25.00 (*0-905289-13-7*, Pub. by Enitha Pr); reprint ed. pap. 13.95 (*0-905289-08-0*, Pub. by Enitha Pr) Dufour.

— Learning to Talk. 79p. 1980. reprint ed. pap. 7.95 (*0-905289-71-4*, Pub. by Enitha Pr) Dufour.

— Learning to Talk. 79p. 1982. reprint ed. 11.95 (*0-905289-76-5*, Pub. by Enitha Pr) Dufour.

— Olympism: A Guide to the Histories, Ideals & Sports of the Olympic Games. 1996. pap. text 8.95 (*1-882180-55-0*) Griffin CA.

— Pass Exams & Write Top Essays. 127p. 1995. pap. 14.95 (*0-949142-64-6*, Pub. by Stirling Pr) Intl Spec Bk.

— Roots-Routes. (Illus.). 44p. (Orig.). 1982. pap. 8.00 (*0-914946-32-3*) Cleveland St Univ Poetry Ctr.

Burns, Richard C., jt. auth. see Cohen, Stephen.

Burns, Richard D. A Basic Guide to Soccer. (Official United States Olympic Committee Sports Ser.). 1995. pap. 7.95 (*1-882180-35-6*) Griffin CA.

Burns, Richard D., ed. A Basic Guide to Cycling. (Official United States Olympic Committee Sports Ser.). (Illus.). 128p. (Orig.). (YA). 1997. pap. 7.95 (*1-882180-51-8*) Griffin CA.

— Harry S. Truman: A Bibliography of His Times & Presidency. LC 84-20223. (Twentieth-Century Presidential Bibliography Ser.). 297p. 1984. 85.00 (*0-8420-2219-8*) Scholarly Res Inc.

— Herbert Hoover: A Bibliography of His Times & Presidency. LC 90-28848. (Twentieth-Century Presidential Bibliography Ser.). 224p. 1991. 85.00 (*0-8420-2305-4*) Scholarly Res Inc.

Burns, Richard D., et al, eds. Continuing Dialogue: Men & Issues in Early American History. rev. ed. LC 63-23420. x, 252p. (Orig.). (C). 1964. pap. text 8.50 (*0-87015-141-X*) Pacific Bks.

Burns, Richard D., intro. Encyclopedia of Arms Control & Disarmament, 3 vols., 1. 1488p. 1993. 120.00 (*0-684-19603-4*, Scribners Ref) Mac Lib Ref.

— Encyclopedia of Arms Control & Disarmament, 3 vols., 2. 1488p. 1993. 120.00 (*0-684-19604-2*, Scribners Ref) Mac Lib Ref.

— Encyclopedia of Arms Control & Disarmament, 3 vols., 3. 1488p. 1993. 120.00 (*0-684-19605-0*, Scribners Ref) Mac Lib Ref.

— Encyclopedia of Arms Control & Disarmament, 3 vols., Set. 1488p. 1993. 350.00 (*0-684-19281-0*, Scribners Ref) Mac Lib Ref.

Burns, Richard D., jt. ed. see Brune, Lester H.

Burns, Richard Dean, ed. see Burns, Bill.

Burns, Richard W. & Brooks, Gary D., eds. Curriculum Design in a Changing Society. LC 75-122811. 366p. 1970. 39.95 (*0-87778-003-X*) Educ Tech Pubns.

Burns, Richard W. & Klingstedt, Joe L., eds. Competency-Based Education: An Introduction. LC 73-3133. 180p. 1973. pap. 24.95 (*0-87778-061-7*) Educ Tech Pubns.

Burns, Ridge & Campbell, Pam. Create in Me a Youth Ministry. rev. ed. 204p. 1994. pap. 9.99 (*1-56476-322-6*, 6-3322, Victor Bks) Chariot Victor.

— No Youth Worker Is an Island. 216p. (Orig.). 1992. pap. 10.99 (*0-89693-735-6*, 6-1735, Victor Bks) Chariot Victor.

Burns, Rita. Ezra Nehemiah. (Collegeville Bible Commentary - Old Testament Ser.). 96p. 1985. pap. 4.95 (*0-8146-1418-3*) Liturgical Pr.

Burns, Rob, ed. German Cultural Studies: An Introduction. (Illus.). 376p. 1995. text 59.00 (*0-19-871502-1*); pap. text 18.95 (*0-19-871503-X*) OUP.

Burns, Robert. The Caledonian Musical Museum, 3 vols., Set. LC 72-144553. 1976. reprint ed. 145.00 (*0-404-08520-2*) AMS Pr.

***Burns, Robert.** Doing Business in Asia. 1p. (C). 1999. pap. text 15.95 (*0-7339-0193-X*) Addison-Wesley.

Burns, Robert. Isabella Valancy Crawford & Her Works. (Canadian Author Studies). 51p. (C). 1988. pap. text 9.95 (*0-920763-72-3*, Pub. by ECW) Genl Dist Srvs.

— The Jolly Beggars: or Love & Liberty. 1989. write for info. (*0-946487-02-2*) Luath Pr Ltd.

— The Letters of Robert Burns, 2 vols., Vol. 1. 2nd ed. Ferguson, De Lancey & Roy, G. Ross, eds. (Illus.). 558p. (C). 1986. text 130.00 (*0-19-812478-3*) OUP.

— The Letters of Robert Burns, 2 vols., Vol. 2. 2nd ed. Ferguson, De Lancey & Roy, G. Ross, eds. (Illus.). 550p. (C). 1986. text 110.00 (*0-19-812321-3*) OUP.

— Managing People in Changing Times: Coping with the Human Impact of Organizational Change. 192p. 1993. pap. text 24.95 (*1-86373-356-6*, Pub. by Allen & Unwin Pty) Paul & Co Pubs.

— Poems & Songs. (Thrift Editions Ser.). 96p. 1991. pap. 1.00 (*0-486-26863-2*) Dover.

— Poems & Songs. 2nd ed. Kinsley, James, ed. (Oxford Standard Authors Ser.). 802p. 1971. pap. text 21.00 (*0-19-281114-2*) OUP.

— Poems, Chiefly in the Scottish Dialect. LC 72-153518. reprint ed. 41.50 (*0-404-08977-1*) AMS Pr.

— Poems Chiefly in the Scottish Dialect. LC 91-7154. 252p. 1991. reprint ed. 55.00 (*1-85477-060-8*) Continuum.

— Poems in Scots & English. rev. ed. Law, Donald, ed. (Everyman Paperback Classics Ser.). 256p. (C). 1996. pap. 8.95 (*0-460-87786-0*, Everyman's Classic Lib) Tuttle Pubng.

— Poetry of Robert Burns, 4 vols., Set. Henley, William E. & Henderson, Thomas F., eds. LC 78-113567. reprint ed. 120.00 (*0-404-01250-7*) AMS Pr.

— The Prose Works of Robert Burns. LC 79-144501. reprint ed. 51.00 (*0-404-08509-1*) AMS Pr.

— Robert Burns. (Poets Ser.). 146p. 1993. 5.95 (*0-7117-0401-5*, Pub. by JARR UK) Seven Hills Bk.

— The Robert Burns Select. (Illus.). 124p. (Orig.). 1996. pap. 7.00 (*0-9634992-8-9*) Pretani.

— Selected Poems. Brown, Kenneth, ed. LC 99-204788. (Literature Ser.). 160p. (C). 1998. pap., student ed. 10.95 (*0-521-62683-8*) Cambridge U Pr.

— Selected Poems. McGuirk, Carol, ed. 368p. 1994. pap. 12.95 (*0-14-042382-6*, Penguin Classics) Viking Penguin.

— Songs of Robert Burns. Dick, James C., ed. LC 79-144552. reprint ed. 67.50 (*0-404-08511-3*) AMS Pr.

— Tam O'Shanter: A Tale. limited ed. (Illus.). (C). 1989. 100.00 (*0-948473-17-7*) St Mut.

Burns, Robert, compiled by. The Merry Muses of Caledonia: A Collection of Favourite Scots Songs, Ancient & Modern, Selected for Use of the Crochallan Fencibles (1799) limited ed. 128p. 1999. 90.00 (*1-57003-324-2*) U of SC Pr.

Burns, Robert & Olson, William H. Tam O'Shanter, an American Parallel. 27p. (Orig.). 1995. pap. 3.50 (*0-9640210-1-3*) Jackson Harbor.

— Tam O'Shanter, an American Parallel. (Illus.). 27p. (Orig.). 1995. 12.99 (*0-9640210-3-X*) Jackson Harbor.

***Burns, Robert & Rayment-Pickard, Hugh.** Philosophies of History: From Enlightenment to Post-Modernity. LC 99-56272. 352p. 2000. text 64.95 (*0-631-21236-1*); pap. text 32.95 (*0-631-21237-X*) Blackwell Pubs.

Burns, Robert A. Roman Catholicism: Yesterday & Today. 258p. 1992. pap. 11.95 (*0-8294-0711-1*) Loyola Pr.

Burns, Robert A., jt. auth. see Anderson, Lorin W.

Burns, Robert B. Psychology for Effective Managers: Understanding & Managing Human Behavior in the Workplace. (Illus.). 323p. 1999. pap. 24.95 (*1-875680-34-9*) Woodslane.

Burns, Robert B., jt. auth. see Anderson, Lorin W.

Burns, Robert C. A Guide to Family-Centered Circle Drawings (F-C-C-D) with Symbol Probes & Visual Free Association. LC 90-1935. (Illus.). 160p. 1990. text 30.95 (*0-87630-587-7*) Brunner-Mazel.

— Kinetic-House-Tree-Person Drawings (K-H-T-P) An Interpretative Manual. LC 86-26876. 232p. 1987. text 33.95 (*0-87630-448-X*) Brunner-Mazel.

***Burns, Robert E.** Being Catholic, Being American: The Notre Dame Story, 1842-1934. LC 98-31553. 608p. 1999. 35.00 (*0-268-02156-2*) U of Notre Dame Pr.

— Being Catholic, Being American Vol. 2: The Notre Dame Story, 1934-1952. (Mary & Tim Gray Series for the Study of Catholic Higher Education). 632p. 2000. 35.00 (*0-268-02163-5*, Pub. by U of Notre Dame Pr) Chicago Distribution Ctr.

Burns, Robert E. I Am a Fugitive from a Georgia Chain Gang. 280p. 1990. reprint ed. lib. bdg. 25.95 (*0-89966-688-4*) Buccaneer Bks.

— I Am a Fugitive from a Georgia Chain Gang! LC 97-14202. 288p. 1997. reprint ed. pap. 15.95 (*0-8203-1943-0*, Brown Thrasher) U of Ga Pr.

— I Am a Fugitive from the Georgia Chain Gang! 145p. 1994. 20.00 (*0-88322-013-X*) Beehive GA.

— Irish Parliamentary Politics in the Eighteenth Century, 1714-1730, Vol. 1. LC 88-20941. 1989. 39.95 (*0-8132-0673-1*) Cath U Pr.

— Irish Parliamentary Politics in the Eighteenth Century, 1730-1760, Vol. 2. LC 88-20941. 1990. 49.95 (*0-8132-0710-X*) Cath U Pr.

— The Shape & Form of Puget Sound. LC 84-15354. (Puget Sound Bks.). (Illus.). 114p. (Orig.). (C). 1985. pap. 8.95 (*0-295-96184-8*) U of Wash Pr.

— The Wrath of Allah. (Illus.). 200p. (Orig.). 1994. pap. 12.95 (*1-880628-01-5*) A Ghosh.

Burns, Robert E., jt. auth. see Farrell, Thomas J.

Burns, Robert I. Foundations of Crusader Valencia: Revolt & Recovery, 1257-1263. LC 90-8837. (Diplomatarium Regni Valentiae - Diplomatarium of the Crusader Kingdom of Valencia Ser.: Vol. 2). (Illus.). 456p. 1991. reprint ed. pap. 141.40 (*0-608-07178-1*, 206740300009) Bks Demand.

— Jews in the Notarial Culture: Latinate Wills in Mediterranean Spain, 1250-1350. LC 95-49937. (Illus.). 244p. 1996. 48.00 (*0-520-20393-3*, Pub. by U CA Pr) Cal Prin Full Svc.

— Society & Documentation in Crusader Valencia. LC 84-17828. (Diplomatarium of the Crusader Kingdom of Valencia Ser.). 287p. 1985. reprint ed. pap. 89.00 (*0-608-04624-8*, 206531100003) Bks Demand.

Burns, Robert I. Transition in Crusader Valencia: Years of Triumph. 0.00 (*0-691-05475-4*) Princeton U Pr.

Burns, Robert I. The Worlds of Alfonso the Learned & James the Conqueror: Intellect & Force in the Middle Ages. LC 85-42678. (Illus.). 259p. 1985. reprint ed. pap. 80.30 (*0-608-06387-8*, 206674800008) Bks Demand.

Burns, Robert L. Measurement of the Need for Transporting Pupils: Basis for State Equalization of Transportation Costs. LC 72-176614. (Columbia University. Teachers College. Contributions to Education Ser.: No. 289). reprint ed. 37.50 (*0-404-55289-7*) AMS Pr.

Burns, Robert M. & Bradley, William W. Protective Coatings for Metals. 3rd ed. LC 67-20826. (ACS Monograph: No. 163). 1975. 59.95 (*0-8412-0285-0*); fiche. write for info. (*0-318-50482-0*) Am Chemical.

Burns, Robert P. Evidence in Context: A Trial Evidence Workbook. LC 99-168988. 1998. 34.95 (*1-55681-603-0*) Natl Inst Trial Ad.

— A Theory of the Trial. LC 98-54175. 247p. 1999. 29.95 (*0-691-00727-6*, Pub. by Princeton U Pr) Cal Prin Full Svc.

Burns, Robert P. & Lubet, Steven. Cranbrooke v. Intellex. LC 96-132670. 264p. 1994. pap. 22.95 (*1-55681-409-7*) Natl Inst Trial Ad.

***Burns, Robert P. & Lubet, Steven.** Problems & Materials in Evidence & Trial Advocacy. 2nd ed. LC 99-169128. 1998. 35.95 (*1-55681-631-6*) Natl Inst Trial Ad.

Burns, Robert P., jt. auth. see Lubet, Steven.

***Burns, Robert W.** Ex-Baltimore & Ohio Lines in Northwestern Pennsylvania. (Illus.). 68p. 1999. pap. 20.00 (*0-9677739-0-3*) R W Burns.

Burns, Roberts. Sound Smart: 101 Ways to Turn a Phrase. Bastedo, Suzanne, ed. 90p. 1998. pap. (*0-89716-809-7*, Peanut Btr Pubng) Elton-Wolf Pub.

Burns, Robin J. & Aspeslagh, Robert. Three Decades of Peace Education Around the World: An Anthology. LC 95-25440. (Reference Books in International Education, Vol. 27, Reference Library of Social Science: Vol. 24). 432p. 1996. text 95.00 (*0-8240-5549-7*, SS600) Garland.

Burns, Roger G. Mineralogical Applications of Crystal Field Theory. 2nd ed. (Cambridge Topics in Mineral Physics & Chemistry Ser.: No. 5). (Illus.). 575p. (C). 1993. text 89.95 (*0-521-43077-1*) Cambridge U Pr.

Burns, Ron & Farris, Joey. One Surface Learning. 76p. (Orig.). 1995. pap. text 21.95 (*0-89724-820-1*, EL9590CD) Wrner Bros.

Burns, Ronald M. One Country or Two? LC 76-174566. 297p. reprint ed. pap. 92.10 (*0-608-16143-8*, 202383600034) Bks Demand.

Burns, Ross. The Monuments of Syria: A Historical Guide. (Illus.). 320p. 1999. pap. 24.50 (*1-86064-244-6*, Pub. by I B T) St Martin.

— The Monuments of Syria: A Historical Guide. LC 92-25220. (Illus.). 297p. (C). 1992. text 110.00 (*0-8147-1200-2*) NYU Pr.

— The Monuments of Syria: A Historical Guide. (Illus.). 297p. (C). 1997. pap. text 25.00 (*0-8147-1287-8*) NYU Pr.

— The World War I Album. (Illus.). 304p. 1997. 17.98 (*0-7858-0864-7*) Bk Sales Inc.

— World War II Album. (Illus.). 304p. 1997. 17.98 (*0-7858-0863-9*) Bk Sales Inc.

Burns, Russell M. Silvics of North America Vol. 1: Conifers. 681p. 1991. per. 44.00 (*0-16-027145-2*, Agriculture Dept) USGPO.

Burns, Ruth Blake, jt. auth. see Fischer, Marjorie Hood.

Burns, Sandra, jt. auth. see Farrell, Wallace B.

Burns, Sarah. Inventing the Modern Artist: Art & Culture in Gilded Age America. LC 96-5929. (Illus.). 384p. (C). 1996. 50.00 (*0-300-06445-4*) Yale U Pr.

Burns, Sarah. Inventing the Modern Artist: Art & Culture in Gilded Age America. (Illus.). 392p. 1999. pap. text 20.00 (*0-300-07859-5*) Yale U Pr.

Burns, Sarah, et al, eds. The Art of Desire: Erotic Treasures from the Kinsey Institute. LC 98-144002. (Illus.). 112p. (C). Date not set. pap. 24.95 (*0-9660320-0-4*) Kinsey Inst.

Burns, Scott, ed. Environmental, Groundwater, & Engineering Geology: Applications from Oregon. LC 97-46896. (AEG Special Publications: No. 9). (Illus.). 640p. 1997. lib. bdg. 79.95 (*0-89863-205-6*, 205-6) Star Pub CA.

Burns, Sheila, jt. auth. see Bloom, Ursula.

Burns, Sheila, jt. auth. see Walczak, Yvette.

Burns, Shelley, ed. Violence & Discipline Problems in U. S. Public Schools, 1996-97. (Illus.). 129p. (C). 1999. pap. text 30.00 (*0-7881-7766-4*) DIANE Pub.

Burns, Stan. Exceeding Expectations: The Enterprise Rent-a-Car Story. LC 97-73084. (Illus.). 192p. 1997. write for info. (*0-944641-23-7*) Greenwich Pub Group.

***Burns, Stan.** Saic: The First Thirty Years. LC 99-39998. 1999. write for info. (*1-887656-20-0*) Tehabi Bks.

Burns, Stanley. A Morning's Work: Photographs from the Burns Archive. (Illus.). 248p. 1998. 60.00 (*0-944092-45-4*) Twin Palms Pub.

Burns, Stanley B. Forgotten Marriage: The Painted Tintype & The Decorative Frame, 1860-1910, A Lost Chapter in American Portraiture. LC 94-78617. (Illus.). 240p. 1995. pap. 34.95 (*0-9612958-2-1*) Burns Collection.

— Forgotten Marriage: The Painted Tintype & The Decorative Frame, 1860-1910, A Lost Chapter in American Portraiture. LC 94-78617. (Illus.). 220p. 1995. 65.00 (*0-9612958-1-3*) Burns Collection.

Burns, Stanley G. & Bond, Paul R. Principles of Electronic Circuits. 2nd ed. LC 96-173342. (West Engineering Ser.). 1000p. (C). 1996. mass mkt. 109.95 (*0-534-95494-4*) PWS Pubs.

Burns, Stella E., jt. auth. see Stedman, Oliver H.

***Burns, Stephanie.** Artisitry In Training: Thinking Differently About the Way You Help People to Learn. 273p. 1999. pap. 29.95 (*1-875889-07-8*) Woodslane.

***Burns, Stephen L.** Call from a Distant Shore. 2000. mass mkt. 6.99 (*0-451-45792-7*, ROC) NAL.

Burns, Stephen L. Flesh & Silver. 352p. 1999. mass mkt. 5.99 (*0-451-45752-8*, ROC) NAL.

Burns, Stephen S. & Marston, David A. Who's Who in Security. 398p. 1989. 145.00 (*0-9623775-0-3*) Natl Sec Inst.

Burns, Stephen S. & Marston, David A., eds. Who's Who in the Safety Profession. 413p. 1990. pap. text 145.00 (*0-9623775-1-1*) Natl Sec Inst.

Burns, Stewart. Social Movements of the Nineteen Sixties: Searching for Democracy. (Social Movements Past & Present Ser.). 256p. 1990. 29.95 (*0-8057-9737-8*) Macmillan.

— Social Movements of the 1960's: Searching for Democracy. (Social Movements Past & Present Ser.). 256p. 1990. pap. 20.00 (*0-8057-9738-6*) Macmillan.

Burns, Stewart, ed. Daybreak of Freedom: The Montgomery Bus Boycott. (Illus.). 392p. 1997. 49.95 (*0-8078-2360-0*); pap. text 18.95 (*0-8078-4661-9*) U of NC Pr.

Burns, Stuart L. Stressing & Unstressing in a Tent: A Narrative Reminiscence. LC 87-4211. (Illus.). 207p. 1987. reprint ed. pap. 64.20 (*0-608-00110-4*, 206087500006) Bks Demand.

— Whores Before Descartes: Assorted Poetry & Sordid Prose. LC 80-54381. 96p. (Orig.). (C). 1980. pap. 4.50 (*0-9605326-0-9*) Wash Launderan.

Burns, Suzanne L. Gardens of Light: An Artist's Inspirations on "Growing" (Illus.). 32p. (Orig.). 1994. pap., per. 6.00 (*0-9643461-0-9*) S L Burns.

Burns, Teresa H. Salad Dressings. LC 97-24478. (Specialty Cookbook Ser.). (Illus.). 128p. (Orig.). 1997. pap. 6.95 (*0-89594-895-8*) Crossing Pr.

Burns, Theresa. You're Not My Cat. LC 88-8388. (Illus.). 32p. (J). (ps-3). 1989. 12.95 (*0-397-32340-9*); lib. bdg. 12.89 (*0-397-32341-7*) HarpC Child Bks.

Burns, Thomas. Applied Statics & Strength of Materials. 448p. 1997. teacher ed. write for info. (*0-8273-6960-3*) Delmar.

— Applied Statics & Strength of Materials. abr. rev. ed. LC 96-3965. 640p. 1996. mass mkt. 84.95 (*0-8273-6959-X*) Delmar.

— Fundamental Structrual Steel Design Using LRFD. LC 94-13096. 1995. 14.95 (*0-8273-6222-6*) Delmar.

— Fundamental Structrual Steel Design - ASD: Solutions Manual. 13p. 1994. teacher ed. 14.95 (*0-8273-5706-0*) Delmar.

— Serious Incident Prevention: How to Sustain Accident-Free Operations. LC 99-18581. 208p. 1999. 55.00 (*0-88415-808-X*) Gulf Pub.

Burns, Thomas J. & Coffman, Edward N. Ohio State Institute of Accounting Conference Collected Papers, 1938 to 1963. Brief, Richard P., ed. LC 80-1455. (Dimensions of Accounting Theory & Practice Ser.). 1980. lib. bdg. 25.95 (*0-405-13477-0*) Ayer.

Burns, Thomas R. Aversion to Honor: A Tale of Sexual Harassment Within the Federal Government. 256p. (Orig.). 1997. pap. 14.95 (*1-56184-128-5*) New Falcon Pubns.

Burns, Thomas S. Barbarians Within the Gates of Rome: A Study of Roman Military Policy & the Barbarians, ca. 375-425 A. D. LC 94-12788. (Illus.). 452p. 1995. 35.00 (*0-253-31288-4*) Ind U Pr.

— A History of the Ostrogoths. LC 83-49286. (Illus.). 320p. 1984. pap. 18.95 (*0-253-20600-6*, MB 600) Ind U Pr.

Burns, Thomas S. & Overbeck, Bernhard H. Rome & the Germans As Seen in Coinage. (Illus.). 88p. (Orig.). 1987. pap. text 10.00 (*0-9619281-0-7*) Burns & Overbeck.

Burns, Tim. Break the Curve: The Entrepreneur's Small Business Blueprint. LC 99-187928. (ITBP PROFESSIONAL). 256p. 1998. pap. 19.99 (*1-86152-319-X*) Thomson Learn.

***Burns, Tim.** Entrepreneurship.com. 2000. pap. 19.95 (*1-57410-136-6*) Dearborn.

Burns, Tim. Our Children, Our Future. 15.00 (*0-614-19153-X*) Marco Polo Pubs.

Burns, Timothy, ed. After History? Francis Kukuyama & His Critics. 280p. 1994. lib. bdg. 54.50 (*0-8476-7926-8*) Rowman.

Burns, Tom. Cordoba. (Everything under the Sun Ser.). (Illus.). 176p. 1995. pap. 6.95 (*0-8442-9209-5*, Passprt Bks) NTC Contemp Pub Co.

— Description, Explanation, & Understanding: Selected Writings on the Nature of Society. 312p. 1995. 80.00 (*0-7486-0533-9*, Pub. by Edinburgh U Pr) Col U Pr.

— Granada. (Everything under the Sun Ser.). (Illus.). 176p. 1995. pap. 6.95 (*0-8442-9211-7*, Passprt Bks) NTC Contemp Pub Co.

— Madrid. (Everything under the Sun Ser.). (Illus.). 192p. 1994. pap. 6.95 (*0-8442-9208-7*, Passprt Bks) NTC Contemp Pub Co.

Burns, Tom, ed. Spain. (Everything under the Sun Ser.). 496p. 1995. pap. 12.95 (*0-8442-9210-9*, Passprt Bks) NTC Contemp Pub Co.

Burns, Tom & Andersen, Svein S. Societal Decision-Making: Democratic Challenges to State Technocracy. 243p. 1992. 66.95 (*1-85521-269-2*, Pub. by Dartmth Pub) Ashgate Pub Co.

Burns, Tom & Stalker, George M. The Management of Innovation. 304p. (Orig.). 1994. reprint ed. pap. text 22.00 (*0-19-828878-6*) OUP.

Burns, Tom, ed. see Luhmann, Niklas.

Burns, Tom R. & Baumgartner. Man, Decisions, Society, Vol. 10. (Studies in Cybernetics). xiv, 342p. 1986. text 106.00 (*2-88124-004-6*); pap. text 46.00 (*2-88124-026-7*) Gordon & Breach.

Burns, Tom R. & Ueberhorst, Reinhard. Creative Democracy: Systematic Conflict Resolution & Policymaking in a World of High Science & Technology. LC 88-25292. (Illus.). 194p. 1988. 49.95 (*0-275-92957-4*, C2957, Praeger Pubs) Greenwood.

***Burns, Tony.** Hegel Marx Connection. 2000. text 69.95 (*0-312-23403-1*) St Martin.

***Burns, Tony & Burns, June.** Scroll Saw Art Puzzles. (Illus.). 80p. (Orig.). 1999. pap. 14.95 (*1-56523-116-3*, Pub. by Fox Chapel Pub) IPG Chicago.

Burns, Tracie M., ed. see O'Connor, Michol.

Burns, Virgil, ed. Charlie Brown: A Book of Good Griefs. 1985. 10.95 (*0-685-60163-3*) Entheo Bks.

Burns, Virginia L. Gentle Hunter: Biography of Alice Evans, Bacteriologist. LC 92-73761. (Illus.). 224p. (J). (gr. 5-12). 1993. lib. bdg. 22.00 (*0-9604726-5-7*) Enterprise Pr.

— Lewis Cass-Frontier Soldier. LC 80-81133. (Illus.). 1980. lib. bdg. 17.50 (*0-9604726-1-4*) Enterprise Pr.

— Tall Annie. LC 87-80726. (Illus.). 1987. lib. bdg. 17.50 (*0-9604726-3-0*) Enterprise Pr.

Burns, Virginia L., jt. auth. see Stringer, Christopher.

Burns, Virginia Law. William Beaumont-Frontier Doctor. 2nd rev. ed. LC 78-72566. (Illus.). 166p. 1989. reprint ed. lib. bdg. 17.50 (*0-9604726-4-9*) Enterprise Pr.

Burns, Vivian, jt. auth. see Poinsett, Norma.

***Burns, Walter N.** The Saga of Billy the Kid. LC 99-36553. 336p. 1999. pap. 17.95 (*0-8263-2153-4*) U of NM Pr.

***Burns, Walter Noble.** The Robin Hood of El Dorado: The Saga of Joaquin Murieta, Famous Outlaw of California's Age of Gold. LC 99-26428. 320p. 1999. pap. 17.95 (*0-8263-2155-0*) U of NM Pr.

— Tombstone: An Iliad of the Southwest. LC 99-36552. 440p. 1999. pap. 17.95 (*0-8263-2154-2*) U of NM Pr.

Burns, Wayne. Charles Reade: A Study in Victorian Authorship. LC 61-7182. 360p. 1961. text 37.50 (*0-8290-0161-1*) Irvington.

— Enfin Celine Vint: A Contextualist Reading of Journey to the End of the Night & Death on the Installment Plan. (American University Studies: Romance Languages & Literature: Ser. II, Vol. 85). XII, 238p. (C). 1988. text 37.00 (*0-8204-0678-3*) P Lang Pubng.

— Journey Through the Dark Woods. LC 82-15822. 230p. (Orig.). 1982. pap. 6.95 (*0-9609666-0-9*) Howe St Pr.

Burns, William. Pulse & Other Poems. 30p. (Orig.). 1991. 8.00 (*0-685-48466-1*) Talisman Research.

— Under Pressure: Some Crack Contenders. Wilson, Don D., ed. 48p. 1989. pap. 7.00 (*0-9607756-9-2*) Singular Speech Pr.

Burns, William C. Revival Sermons. 205p. 1981. pap. 7.99 (*0-85151-316-6*) Banner of Truth.

Burns, William C., jt. auth. see Gillespie, Alexander.

Burns, William H. The Voices of Negro Protest in Amercia. LC 80-21197. 88p. 1980. reprint ed. lib. bdg. 49.75 (*0-313-22219-3*, BUVN, Greenwood Pr) Greenwood.

Burns, William J. Economic Aid & American Policy Toward Egypt, 1955-1981. LC 83-20181. 285p. (C). 1985. text 24.50 (*0-87395-868-3*) State U NY Pr.

— The Irometer, Vol. I. 105p. 1997. reprint ed. spiral bd. 12.50 (*0-7873-0134-5*) Hlth Research.

— Masked War: The Story of a Peril That Threatened the United States. LC 76-90168. (Mass Violence in America Ser.). 1969. reprint ed. 31.95 (*0-405-01303-5*) Ayer.

Burns, William K., ed. Optical Fiber Rotation Sensing. (Quantum Electronics Ser.). (Illus.). 390p. 1993. text 94.00 (*0-12-146075-4*) Acad Pr.

Burns, William S. Memoirs of Fourth Missouri Cavalry. (Illus.). 161p. 1988. 20.00 (*0-89029-315-5*) Morningside Bkshop.

Burns-Wolfe, Marty & Mahaffey, Foyne. In Mother Words: Unconventional Wisdom for Moms Raising Daughters. (Illus.). 96p. 1996. pap. 11.95 (*0-7867-0328-8*) Carroll & Graf.

Burns, Y. M. Media Law. 420p. 1990. pap. 98.00 (*0-409-01342-0*, SA, MICHIE) LEXIS Pub.

***Burns, Yvonne.** Administrative Law under the 1996 Constitution. LC 98-189327. xix, 352 p. 1998. write for info. (*0-409-01343-9*) LEXIS Pub.

Burns, Yvonne, ed. Down Syndrome: Moving Through Life. 235p. 1993. pap. 44.75 (*1-56593-140-8*, 0452) Singular Publishing.

Burns, Yvonne R. & MacDonald, Julie, eds. Physiotherapy & the Growing Child. (Illus.). 529p. 1996. text 68.00 (*0-7020-1942-9*, Pub. by W B Saunders) Saunders.

Burnsed, C. Vernon. The Classroom Teacher's Guide to Music Education. LC 98-14203. (Illus.). 200p. 1998. spiral bd. 33.95 (*0-398-06909-3*) C C Thomas.

Burnsed, Cindy. The Adventures of Arlo T. Crispy: Crispy Family Treasure. Foster, Gloria, ed. LC 96-131047. (Arlo T. Crispy Ser.). (Illus.). 32p. (Orig.). (J). (gr. 5). 1995. pap. 4.99 (*0-9639921-9-8*) Mouldings.

Burnshaw, Stanley. Robert Frost Himself. LC 86-20793. (Illus.). xii, 342p. 1986. 19.95 (*0-8076-1164-6*) Braziller.

— Robert Frost Himself. LC 86-20793. (Illus.). 342p. 1989. pap. 12.95 (*0-8076-1234-0*) Braziller.

— The Seamless Web. 1991. pap. 12.50 (*0-8076-0534-4*) Braziller.

Burnshaw, Stanley, et al, eds. The Poem Itself. LC 94-22928. (ENG, FRE, GER, ITA & POR.). 1995. pap. 24.00 (*1-55728-328-1*) U of Ark Pr.

Burnside, C. D. Electro-Magnetic Distance Measurement. (Illus.). 128p. 1971. pap. 25.00 (*0-8464-0363-3*) Beekman Pubs.

— Electromagnetic Distance Measurement. 3rd ed. (Illus.). 228p. 1991. pap. 49.95 (*0-632-03122-0*) Blackwell Sci.

Burnside, Carolyn R. Hail Washington Irving: Eighty-One Years on the Hill. LC 96-96842. (Illus.). 248p. 1996. pap. 12.00 (*0-87012-566-4*) McClain.

HAIL, WASHINGTON IRVING takes you on a nostalgic trip down memory lane & back up the hill to WI. Whether you graduated fifty years ago or in the final class, you will find anecdotes & recollections to bring back Hilltopper memories! *Publisher Paid Annotation.*

Burnside, Irene & Schmidt, Mary G. Working with Older Adults: Group Process. 3rd ed. (Nursing-Health Science Ser.). 544p. (C). 1994. pap. text 45.00 (*0-86720-679-9*) Jones & Bartlett.

Burnside, James R. Exploring the 46 Adirondack High Peaks: With 282 Photos, Maps & Mountain Profiles, Excerpts from the Author's Journal, & Historical Insights. LC 96-94033. (Illus.). 528p. (Orig.). (C). 1996. pap. 24.95 (*0-9624923-2-9*) High Peaks Pr.

— Letting Go: Cost-Based Productivity Soared 106 Percent When Management Loosened the Reins at the GE Business Information Center. LC 92-73013. (Illus.). 132p. (Orig.). 1992. pap. 12.95 (*0-9624923-1-0*) High Peaks Pr.

— The Selling of General Electric. LC 89-51860. 224p. (Orig.). 1990. pap. 14.95 (*0-9624923-0-2*) High Peaks Pr.

Burnside, Janet R., et al. Ohio Rules of Evidence Trial Book. LC 99-61863. 500p. 1999. 75.00 (*0-327-01190-4*, 6353610) LEXIS Pub.

Burnside, John. The Dumb House. 256p. 1998. pap. 17.95 (*0-224-04207-6*, Pub. by Jonathan Cape) Trafalgar.

— A Normal Skin. 64p. 1998. pap. 12.95 (*0-224-04286-6*, Pub. by Jonathan Cape) Trafalgar.

— Swimming in the Flood. LC 96-146257. 64p. 1998. pap. 12.95 (*0-224-04198-3*, Pub. by Jonathan Cape) Trafalgar.

Burnside, Judy D., jt. auth. see Arford, Joanne M.

Burnside, Kathleen M. Childe Hassam in Connecticut. (Illus.). 32p. (Orig.). 1987. pap. 8.00 (*1-880897-11-3*) Lyme Hist.

Burnside, Kevin. Buying a Manufactured Home: How to Get the Most Bang for Your Buck in Today's Housing Market. LC 99-70799. (Home Resources Ser.). (Illus.). 160p. 1999. pap. 14.95 (*1-892495-00-7*, 5007) Van der Plas.

Burnside, Scott & Cairns, Alan. Deadly Innocence. LC 96-132849. 1995. mass mkt. 7.50 (*0-446-60154-3*, Pub. by Warner Bks) Little.

Burnside, William H., jt. auth. see Research & Education Association Staff.

Burnsnali, William J., ed. see Morgenthaler, George W.

Burnstein. Grandmother Book. 1999. text. write for info. (*0-312-24543-2*) St Martin.

Burnstein, Chaya. Hebrew Alphabet Coloring Book, Vol. 181. (Illus.). (J). (gr. k-3). 1986. pap. 2.50 (*0-486-25089-X*) Dover.

Burnstein, Daniel, et al. The Digital MBA. 450p. 1995. pap. text 39.95 (*0-07-882099-5*) Osborne-McGraw.

Burnstein, Ray A., et al, eds. Twenty Beautiful Years of Bottom Physics: Proceedings of the b20 Symposium. LC 98-70174. (AIP Conference Proceedings Ser.: Vol. 424). (Illus.). xv, 385p. 1998. 98.00 (*1-56396-745-6*) Am Inst Physics.

***Burnstine, Lyn.** Anita Trueman Pickett. LC 99-38657. 1999. pap. write for info. (*1-55896-384-7*, Skinner Hse Bks) Unitarian Univ.

Burnstock, G. & Griffith, S. G. Nonadrenergic Innervation of Blood Vessels, 2 vols., Vol. I: Putative Neurotransmitters. LC 87-24283. 176p. 1988. 95.00 (*0-8493-6681-X*, QP109, CRC Reprint) Franklin.

— Nonadrenergic Innervation of Blood Vessels, 2 vols., Vol. II: Regional Innervation. LC 87-24283. 256p. 1988. 140.00 (*0-8493-6682-8*, QP109, CRC Reprint) Franklin.

Burnstock, Geoffrey. Cardiovascular Biology of Purines LC 98-37372. (Developments in Cardiovascular Medicine Ser.). 374p. 1998. 210.00 (*0-7923-8334-6*) Kluwer Academic.

Burnstock, Geoffrey, ed. Autonomic Neuroeffector Mechanisms. (The Autonomic Nervous System Ser.). xii, 580p. 1992. text 198.00 (*3-7186-5135-1*, Harwood Acad Pubs) Gordon & Breach.

— Autonomic Neuroeffector Mechanisms. (Autonomic Nervous System Ser.). xii, 580p. 1995. pap. text 66.00 (*3-7186-5683-3*, Harwood Acad Pubs) Gordon & Breach.

***Burnstock, Geoffrey & Sillito, Adam M., eds.** Nervous Control of the Eye. (Autonomic Nervous System Ser: Vol. 13). 320p. 2000. text 120.00 (*90-5823-018-X*, Harwood Acad Pubs) Gordon & Breach.

***Burnston, Sharon Ann.** Fitting & Proper: 18th Century Clothing from the Collection of the Chester County Historical Society. (Illus.). 122p. 2000. pap. 29.95 (*1-880655-10-1*) Scurlock Pub.

Burnstone, Deborah, tr. see Klee, Ernst, et al, eds.

Burnsworth, Alice, jt. auth. see Walker, Morton.

Burnweit, Richard C., compiled by. Bibliography on California's Congressional Delegation: 1955 to the Present. 256p. 1992. pap. text 30.00 (*1-883638-15-1*) Rose Inst.

Burny, A. & Mammerickx, M., eds. Enzootic Bovine Leukosis & Bovine Leukemia Virus. (Development in Veterinary Virology Ser.). 1986. text 161.50 (*0-89838-846-5*) Kluwer Academic.

Burnyeat, Myles F. The Theaetetus of Plato. LC 89-26936. 372p. (C). 1990. reprint ed. lib. bdg. 37.95 (*0-915144-82-4*) Hackett Pub.

— The Theaetetus of Plato. Levett, M. J., tr. LC 89-26936. 372p. (C). 1990. reprint ed. pap. text 16.95 (*0-915144-81-6*) Hackett Pub.

Burnyeat, Myles F. & Frede, Michael, eds. The Original Sceptics: A Controversy. LC 95-514551. 192p. (Orig.). (C). 1997. pap. text 14.95 (*0-87220-347-6*); lib. bdg. 34.95 (*0-87220-348-4*) Hackett Pub.

Burnyeat, Myles F., ed. see Schofield, Malcolm, et al.

Burnyeat, Myles F., ed. see Vlastos, Gregory.

Buro Destuct Staff. Buro Destruct. 160p. 1999. pap text 39.99 (*3-931126-24-2*, Pub. by Die Gestalten) Consort Bk Sales.

Burogs, Elizabeth. Me Llamo Rigoberta Menchu/Rigoberta Menchu. 1997. pap. text 21.95 (*84-322-4688-3*) Continental Bk.

Buroker, Jill V. Guide to the Critique of Reason. 2001. pap. 25.00 (*0-534-51253-4*) Thomson Learn.

Buroker, Jill V., ed. see Arnauld, Antoine & Nicole, Pierre.

Buroker, Jill Vance. Space & Incongruence. (Synthese Historical Library). 1981. lib. bdg. 129.50 (*90-277-1203-4*) Kluwer Academic.

Buron, Raoul J., jt. auth. see McDonald-Mann, Dana.

Buronson. First of the North Star. (Illus.). 368p. 1995. pap. 19.95 (*1-56931-031-9*) Viz Commns Inc.

— Strain. Vol. 1. (Illus.). 224p. 1999. pap. text 16.95 (*1-56931-319-9*, Viz Comics) Viz Commns Inc.

***Buronson.** Strain, No. 3. (Illus.). (J). 2000. pap. 16.95 (*1-56931-469-1*, Viz Comics) Viz Commns Inc.

— Strain, Vol. 2. 1999. pap. 15.95 (*1-56931-381-4*) Viz Commns Inc.

Buros Institute Staff, et al, eds. Tests in Print V. 1800p. 1999. text 325.00 (*0-910674-51-5*) Buros Inst Mental.

Buros, Oscar K., ed. English Tests & Reviews. LC 75-8109. (Tests in Print Ser.). xxiii, 395p. 1975. text 40.00 (*0-910674-15-9*) U of Nebr Pr.

— Foreign Language Tests & Reviews. LC 75-8110. xxiii, 312p. 1975. text 35.00 (*0-910674-16-7*) U of Nebr Pr.

— Intelligence Tests & Reviews. LC 75-8112. (Tests in Print Ser.). xxvii, 1129p. 1975. 80.00 (*0-8032-1163-5*) U of Nebr Pr.

— Mathematics Tests & Reviews. LC 75-8113. (Tests in Print Ser.). xxv, 435p. 1975. text 35.00 (*0-910674-18-3*) U of Nebr Pr.

— Personality Tests & Reviews II. LC 74-13192. (Tests in Print Ser.). xxxi, 841p. 1975. text 65.00 (*0-910674-19-1*) U of Nebr Pr.

— Reading Tests & Reviews II: A Monograph Consisting of the Reading Sections of the Seventh Mental Measurements Yearbook (1972) & Tests in Print II (1974) LC 70-13495. 285p. reprint ed. pap. 88.40 (*0-608-16454-2*, 202656300050) Bks Demand.

— Science Tests & Reviews. LC 75-8114. (Tests in Print Ser.). xxiii, 296p. 1975. text 35.00 (*0-910674-21-3*) U of Nebr Pr.

— Social Science Tests & Reviews. LC 75-8115. (Tests in Print Ser.). xxiii, 227p. 1975. text 35.00 (*0-910674-22-1*) U of Nebr Pr.

— Vocational Tests & Reviews. LC 75-8116. (Tests in Print Ser.). xxvi, 1087p. 1975. 75.00 (*0-8032-4650-1*) U of Nebr Pr.

Buros, Oscar K., et al, eds. Tests in Print: A Comprehensive Bibliography of Tests for Use in Education, Psychology & Industry. LC 61-16302. 511p. reprint ed. pap. 158.50 (*0-608-14845-8*, 202611000043) Bks Demand.

Burov, Michael, tr. see Tropp, Eduard A., et al.

Burov, Micheal, tr. see Volkov, M. V. & Oganesyan, O. V.

Burow, James H. 2000 Census: Preparations for Dress Rehearsal Leave Many Unanswered Questions. 51p. 1999. pap. text 20.00 (*0-7881-8026-6*) DIANE Pub.

— 2000 Census: Progress Made on Design, but Risks Remain. (Illus.). 92p. 1998. pap. text 20.00 (*0-7881-7208-5*) DIANE Pub.

Burow, James H., et al. Internet & Electronic Dial-Up Bulletin Boards: Information Reported by Federal Organizations. (Illus.). 44p. 1998. pap. text 20.00 (*0-7881-4843-5*) DIANE Pub.

Burow, Johannes, jt. auth. see Borker, Christoph.

Buroway. Writing Fiction: A Guide to Narrative Craft. 5th ed. LC 99-25518. 384p. (C). 1999. pap. 42.00 (*0-321-02689-6*) Addison-Wesley.

Burpee, C. Gaye & Morgan, James N. Household Survey of Grenada, 1985: Findings & Documentation of Procedures. LC 86-217405. (Institute for Social Research, Research Report). (Illus.). 176p. reprint ed. pap. 54.60 (*0-7837-5282-2*, 204502000005) Bks Demand.

Burpee, Charles W. History of Hartford County, 1633-1928, Being a Study of the Makers of the First Constitution & the Story of Their Lives, of Their Descendants & of All Who Have Come, 3 vols. 1383p. 1997. reprint ed. lib. bdg. 216.00 (*0-8328-5655-X*) Higginson Bk Co.

Burpee, L. L. A Guide to Integrated Control of Turfgrass Diseases: Cool Season Turgrasses, Vol. I. Nus, Jeff, ed. 241p. (C). pap. write for info. (*0-9635707-1-4*) GC Super Assn.

Burpee, Lawrence J. Discovery of Canada. LC 74-2412. (Essay Index Reprint Ser.). 1977. reprint ed. 22.95 (*0-518-10161-4*) Ayer.

Burpee, Lawrence J., ed. see La Verendrye, Pierre G.

Burpee Staff, jt. auth. see Hubbard, Juliet A.

Burpee Staff, jt. auth. see Krasda, Martha E.

Burqhardt, ed. see Jerome.

Burquest, Donald A. Phonological Analysis: A Functional Approach. 2nd ed. LC 98-196099. x, 314p. 1998. pap. 29.00 (*1-55671-067-4*) S I L Intl.

Burquest, Donald A. & Laidig, Wyn D., eds. Phonological Studies in Four Languages of Maluku. LC 92-80562. (Publications in Linguistics: No. 108). viii, 232p. (Orig.). 1992. pap. 17.00 (*0-88312-803-9*) S I L Intl.

Burquest, Donald A., jt. auth. see Edmondson, Jerold A.

Burr. An Invitation to Personal Construct Psychology. 148p. 1992. pap. 27.50 (*1-56593-560-8*, 0312) Singular Publishing.

— Lovers I Ching. (Illus.). 144p. 2000. text 19.95 (*0-312-24082-1*) St Martin.

— Statistical Tools for Software Engineering. (C). 1995. mass mkt. 43.00 (*0-412-60600-3*) Chapman & Hall.

Burr & Day. Family Science/Parenting. (Adaptable Courseware Ser.). 1996. 19.75 (*0-534-49715-2*) Brooks-Cole.

Burr & Dipiero. Till You Love Me. (Piano-Vocal-Guitar Ser.). 6p. 1994. pap. 3.95 (*0-7935-4286-3*, 00120024) H Leonard.

Burr, A. & Owen, M. Statistical Methods for Software Quality. (Illus.). 224p. 1996. mass mkt. 43.95 (*1-85032-171-X*) ITCP.

Burr, A. H. Mechanical Analysis & Design. 640p. 1981. teacher ed. write for info. (*0-318-51819-8*) Elsevier.

Burr, Aaron. Memoirs of Aaron Burr, 2 vols., Set. (American Biography Ser.). 1991. reprint ed. lib. bdg. 148.00 (*0-7812-8053-2*) Rprt Serv.

— The Private Journal of Aaron Burr, 2 vols., Set. LC 75-31113. reprint ed. 86.50 (*0-404-13710-5*) AMS Pr.

— The Private Journal of Aaron Burr, 2 vols., Set. (American Biography Ser.). 1991. reprint ed. write for info. (*0-7812-8054-0*) Rprt Serv.

Burr, Alister. Modulation & Coding. (C). 2000. pap. text. write for info. (*0-201-39857-5*) Addison-Wesley.

Burr, Allston, ed. Sir Walter Scott, an Index, Placing the Short Poems in His Novels & His Long Poems & Dramas. LC 76-148632. vi, 130p. 1974. reprint ed. lib. bdg. 55.00 (*0-8371-5994-6*, BUSW, Greenwood Pr) Greenwood.

Burr, Amanda J. New Life for the Old, Old Story: A Guide for Developing Story Sermons. 150p. 1989. 25.00 (*0-945253-06-0*) Thornsbury Bailey Brown.

Burr, Anna R. The Portrait of a Banker, James Stillman. 1975. 36.95 (*0-405-06950-2*, 19126) Ayer.

— Weir Mitchell, His Life & Letters. 1993. reprint ed. lib. bdg. 89.00 (*0-7812-5440-X*) Rprt Serv.

Burr, Anna R., jt. auth. see James, Alice.

Burr, Arthur H. & Cheatham, John B., Jr. Mechanical Analysis & Design. 2nd ed. LC 94-25342. 832p. (C). 1995. 100.00 (*0-02-317265-7*, Macmillan Coll) P-H.

Burr, B. & Harris, H. Financial Choice for Women. (C). 1989. text 35.00 (*1-85631-003-5*, Pub. by Rosters Ltd) St Mut.

Burr, B., jt. auth. see Weisenfeld, M.

Burr, Benjamin, jt. ed. see Helentjaris, Timothy.

Burr, Betty F. Nacodoches Archives, 1835 Entrance Certificates. 1982. 8.95 (*0-911619-02-X*) B F Burr.

Burr, Betty Fagan, prod. Tyrrell County North Carolina Minutes Court of Pleas & Quarter Sessions, 1735-1754, Bk. 1. 137p. (Orig.). 1981. pap. 14.50 (*0-911619-01-1*) B F Burr.

Burr, Bill. Golf for Lefties. LC 97-24829. (Illus.). 128p. (Orig.). 1997. pap. 14.95 (*1-57028-129-7*, 81297H, Mstrs Pr) NTC Contemp Pub Co.

Burr, Brooks M. & Mayden, Richard L. Life History of the Freckled Madtom, Noturus Nocturnus, in Mill Creek, Illinois: Pisces: Ictaluridae. (Occasional Papers: No. 98). 15p. 1982. 1.00 (*0-317-04823-6*) U KS Nat Hist Mus.

Burr, Brooks M. & Warren, Melvin L. A Distributional Atlas of Kentucky Fishes. unabridged ed. (Kentucky Nature Preserves Commission Scientific & Technical Ser.: Vol. 4). (Illus.). xvi, 398p. 1986. pap. 12.84 (*0-9673646-3-9*) KY State Nature.

Burr, Brooks M., jt. auth. see Mayden, Richard L.

Burr, Brooks M., jt. auth. see Page, Lawrence M.

Burr, Carole Reid & Petersen, Roger. Rose Marie Reid: An Extraordinary Life. LC 95-15844. 1995. 15.95 (*1-55503-810-7*, 01111906) Covenant Comms.

Burr, Catherine, et al. Motherhood Is Not for Wimps. 160p. (Orig.). 1996. pap. 7.95 (*0-9635176-7-8*) Walrus Prods.

Burr, Chandler. A Separate Creation: The Search for the Biological Origins of Sexual Orientation. 288p. (J). 1996. 24.45 (*0-7868-6081-2*, Pub. by Hyperion) Time Warner.

— A Separate Creation: The Search for the Biological Origins of Sexual Orientation. (Illus.). 354p. 1999. reprint ed. text 25.00 (*0-7881-6697-2*) DIANE Pub.

Burr, Christina A. Spreading the Light: Women & Labour Reform in Late Nineteenth-Century Toronto. 272p. 1999. text 50.00 (*0-8020-0940-9*); pap. text 18.95 (*0-8020-7908-3*) U of Toronto Pr.

Burr, Claudia, et al. When the Viceroy Came. (Illus.). 32p. (J). (gr. 5-9). 1999. 15.95 (*0-88899-354-4*) Grndwd Bks.

Burr, Claudia, jt. auth. see Libura, Krystyna.

Burr, Clinton. Condo & Villa Vacations Rated: Caribbean, Mexico, & Hawaii. 1993. pap. 17.00 (*0-671-87005-X*, P-H Travel) Prntice Hall Bks.

Burr, Clinton & Burr, Ellen. Resort Properties - Exotic Destinations: Villa & Condo Vacations: Hawaii, Mexico & Caribbean. 1992. pap. 20.00 (*1-881076-00-8*) Resort Prop Owners.

Burr, Clinton S. America's Race Heritage: An Account of the Diffusion of Ancestral Stocks in the United States. LC 76-46069. (Anti-Movements in America Ser.). 1977. reprint ed. lib. bdg. 37.95 (*0-405-09943-6*) Ayer.

Burr, Dan, jt. auth. see Vance, James.

Burr, Daniella, jt. auth. see Dadey, Debbie.

Burr, David. Olivi & Franciscan Poverty: The Origins of the Usus Pauper Controversy. LC 88-39056. (Middle Ages Ser.). 224p. (C). 1989. text 39.95 (*0-8122-8151-9*) U of Pa Pr.

— Olivi's Peaceable Kingdom: A Reading of the Apocalypse Commentary. LC 93-25557. (Middle Ages Ser.). 320p. (C). 1993. text 42.50 (*0-8122-3227-5*) U of Pa Pr.

Burr, Debora. Animals of the Grasslands. (Windows on Nature Ser.). 16p. (J). (gr. 1-4). 1997. pap. 3.99 (*1-884628-41-9*, Flyng Frog) Allied Pub MD.

— Animals of the Ocean. (Windows on Nature Ser.). 16p. (J). (gr. 1-4). 1997. pap. 3.99 (*1-884628-40-0*, Flyng Frog) Allied Pub MD.

— Animals of the Polar Regions. (Windows on Nature Ser.). 16p. (J). (gr. 1-4). 1997. pap. 3.99 (*1-884628-42-7*, Flyng Frog) Allied Pub MD.

B

An Asterisk (*) at the beginning of an entry indicates that the title is appearing for the first time.

— Animals of the Rain Forest. (Windows on Nature Ser.). 16p. (J). (gr. 1-4). 1997. pap. 3.99 (*1-884628-39-7*, Flyng Frog) Allied Pub MD.

Burr, E., jt. ed. see Huff, A.

Burr, Elisabeth. Verb und Varietat. (Romanistische Texte und Studien: Bd. 5). (GER.). 1993. write for info. (*3-487-09762-1*) G Olms Pubs.

Burr, Elisha W., ed. Companion Bird Medicine. LC 86-27606. (Illus.). 261p. reprint ed. pap. 81.00 (*0-608-08709-2*, 206927700003) Bks Demand.

Burr, Elizabeth, tr. from GER. Chiron Dictionary of Greek & Roman Mythology: Gods & Goddesses, Heroes, Places, & Events of Antiquity. LC 93-43989. (Illus.). 320p. (Orig.). 1994. pap. 14.95 (*0-933029-82-9*) Chiron Pubns.

Burr, Ellen, jt. auth. see Burr, Clinton.

Burr, Esther E., jt. auth. see Karlsen, Carol F.

Burr, Feanny. Field & Garden Vegetables of America. (American Horticultural Ser.: Vol. 1). (Illus.). 667p. 1999. reprint ed. pap. 29.00 (*0-929332-10-5*) Amer Botanist.

Burr, Fearing. Field & Garden Vegetables of America. 702p. Date not set. 37.95 (*0-8488-2636-1*) Amereon Ltd.

Burr, George L. New England's Place in the History of Witchcraft. LC 71-164592. (Select Bibliographies Reprint Ser.). 1977. reprint ed. 18.95 (*0-8369-5876-4*) Ayer.

— Persecution & Liberty: Essays in Honor of George Lincoln Burr. LC 68-26467. (Essay Index Reprint Ser.). 1977. reprint ed. 23.95 (*0-8369-0783-3*) Ayer.

Burr, George L., jt. ed. see Lea, Henry C.

Burr, Gillian & Cohen, Marion, eds. Yesterday's Kitchen: Jewish Communities & Their Food Before 1939. LC 93-30054. (Illus.). 225p. 1993. text 19.50 (*0-85303-264-5*, Pub. by M Vallentine & Co) Intl Spec Bk.

***Burr, Ginger.** Fashion Secrets Mother Never Taught You! 92p. 1999. pap. 16.95 (*0-9673572-0-9*) Total Image.

Burr, Gray. Afterlives. 80p. 1996. pap. 9.00 (*1-880286-25-4*) Singular Speech Pr.

— Leaving the House. (Juniper Bks: No. 57). 26p. (Orig.). 1993. pap. 8.00 (*1-55780-120-7*) Juniper Pr ME.

***Burr, H., tr.** Records of the Holy Trinity ("Old Swedes") Church from 1697 to 1773. 772p. 2000. 79.50 (*0-7404-0031-2*) Higginson Bk Co.

Burr, Harold S. Blueprint for Immortality. 104p. 1972. pap. 26.95 (*0-85435-281-3*, Pub. by C W Daniel) Natl Bk Netwk.

Burr, Harold S. Blueprint for Immortality. 5th ed. 192p. pap. 18.95 (*0-8464-4205-1*) Beekman Pubs.

***Burr, Horace.** The Records of Holy Trinity Church, Wilmington, Delaware, 2 vols. in 1. 938p. 1999. pap. 65.00 (*0-8063-4926-3*) Clearfield Co.

Burr, Irving. Statistical Quality Control Methods. (Statistics: Textbooks & Monographs: Vol. 16). (Illus.). 536p. 1976. text 69.75 (*0-8247-6344-0*) Dekker.

Burr, Irving Wingate. Elementary Statistical Quality Control. (Statistics: Textbooks & Monographs: Vol. 25). (Illus.). 432p. 1979. text 69.75 (*0-8247-6686-5*) Dekker.

***Burr, J. Millard & Collins, Robert O.** Africa's Thirty Years' War: Chad, Libya, & the Sudan, 1963-1993. LC 99-10889. 352p. 1999. 65.00 (*0-8133-3566-3*, Pub. by Westview) HarpC.

Burr, Jeanne, ed. Sex Roles: Rights & Values in Conflict. LC 79-3760. 224p. reprint ed. pap. 69.50 (*0-608-18304-0*, 203156400075) Bks Demand.

Burr, Jeanne & Maidens, Melinda, eds. America's Troubled Children. LC 80-20541. 192p. reprint ed. pap. 59.60 (*0-8357-5412-X*, 202289400030) Bks Demand.

Burr, John G. Chemi-& Bioluminescence. LC 85-10423. (Clinical & Biochemical Analysis Ser.: Vol. 16). (Illus.). 632p. (C). 1985. text 230.00 (*0-8247-7277-6*) Dekker.

Burr, John R. World Philosophy: A Contemporary Bibliography, 3. LC 93-18031. (Bibliographies & Indexes in Philosophy Ser.: No. 3). 400p. 1993. lib. bdg. 89.50 (*0-313-24032-9*, BWP/) Greenwood.

Burr, John R., ed. Handbook of World Philosophy: Contemporary Developments Since 1945. LC 80-539. (Illus.). 639p. 1980. lib. bdg. 105.00 (*0-313-22381-5*, BCD/, Greenwood Pr) Greenwood.

***Burr, John R. & Goldinger, Milton.** Philosophy & Contemporary Issues. 8th ed. LC 99-26270. 548p. 1999. pap. text 45.00 (*0-13-020993-7*) P-H.

Burr, John R. & Goldinger, Milton, eds. Philosophy & Contemporary Issues. 7th ed. LC 95-16787. 576p. (C). 1995. pap. text 47.00 (*0-02-317430-7*, Macmillan Coll) P-H.

Burr, John T. SPC Tools for Everyone. LC 93-9436. (Illus.). 77p. 1993. pap. 21.00 (*0-87389-244-5*, H0797) ASQ Qual Pr.

Burr, Judith, et al. Cognetics: Thinking Skills in Language Arts & Social Sciences. 117p. 1991. teacher ed. 89.95 (*1-56602-041-7*); student ed. write for info. (*1-56602-054-9*) Research Better.

— Cognetics: Thinking Skills in Mathematics & Science, No. 2. 121p. 1992. teacher ed. 89.95 (*1-56602-052-2*); student ed. write for info. (*1-56602-053-0*) Research Better.

***Burr, Karen Kaslov.** A Prayer to Thank You. Wise, Noreen, ed. (Book-a-Day Collection). (Illus.). 32p. (J). (ps up). 2000. pap. 5.95 (*1-58584-385-7*) Huckleberry CT.

Burr, M. Coleoptra. Dermaptera-Earwigs. xviii, 217p. 1990. reprint ed. 20.00 (*81-7019-047-9*) Scholarly Pubns.

— Dermaptera. (Illus.). xviii, 238p. 1973. reprint ed. 20.00 (*0-88065-074-5*) Scholarly Pubns.

Burr, M. J., ed. Conveyancing. 304p. 1996. pap. 95.00 (*0-7510-0786-2*, Pub. by HLT Pubns) St Mut.

— Conveyancing Cases. 168p. 1996. pap. 95.00 (*0-7510-0668-8*, Pub. by HLT Pubns) St Mut.

Burr, M. L., ed. Epidemiology of Allergic Diseases. (Monographs in Allergy: Vol. 31). (Illus.). viii, 216p. 1993. 239.25 (*3-8055-5601-2*) S Karger.

Burr, Malcolm, tr. see Arseniev, V. K.

Burr, Merrilee, ed. see Chaney, Alfred.

Burr, Myrth E. The Biblical Story of Ruth & Naomi: Ancestral Line of Christ; She Kept Their Name Alive in Israel. 52p. 1997. pap. text 8.95 (*1-57636-046-6*) SunRise Pbl.

— Mary Fielding Smith: Mother of a Prophet: Her Trek West. 36p. 1997. pap. text 8.95 (*1-57636-038-5*) SunRise Pbl.

— Queen Esther. 48p. 1998. pap. text 8.95 (*1-57636-055-5*) SunRise Pbl.

Burr, Nelson R. Religion in American Life. LC 70-136219. (Goldentree Bibliographies Series in American History). (C). 1971. text 15.95 (*0-88295-507-1*) Harlan Davidson.

Burr, Ralph C., tr. see Poznansky, Alexander.

Burr, Ramiro. The Billboard Guide to Tejano & Regional Mexican Music. LC 98-51910. (Illus.). 288p. 1999. pap. text 18.95 (*0-8230-7691-1*) Watsn-Guptill.

Burr, Richard & Fleagle, Arnold. Developing Your Secret Closet of Prayer: A Strategy for Intimacy with God. LC 99-164972. 200p. 1998. pap. 10.99 (*0-87509-778-2*) Chr Pubns.

***Burr, Robert B.** Trading Bits of Dream. (Chapbook Ser.). 24p. 1999. pap. 8.00 (*1-56439-104-3*, Pub. by Ridgeway) Partners Pubs Grp.

Burr, Robert N. By Reason or Force: Chile & the Balancing of Power in South America, 1830-1905. LC F 3095.B95. (University of California Publications in Social Welfare: No. 77). 332p. reprint ed. pap. 103.00 (*0-7837-4802-7*, 204444900003) Bks Demand.

Burr, Sandra, jt. ed. see Potkay, Adam.

Burr, Stefan A., ed. The Mathematics of Networks. LC 82-18469. (Proceedings of Symposia in Applied Mathematics Ser.: No. 26). 142p. 1983. reprint ed. pap. 25.00 (*0-8218-0031-0*, PSAPM/26) Am Math.

Burr, Stefan A., et al, eds. The Unreasonable Effectiveness of Number Theory. LC 92-24328. (Proceedings of Symposia in Applied Mathematics Ser.: Vol. 46). 125p. 1992. text 28.00 (*0-8218-5501-8*, PSAPM/46) Am Math.

Burr, Susanne, ed. see Schopick, David J.

Burr, Susanne, ed. see Schopick, David J., et al.

Burr, T. J. Rocky Mountain Adventure Collection: The Adventures of a Colorado Mountaineer. LC 91-23499. (Illus.). 320p. (Orig.). 1992. pap. 12.95 (*1-56474-003-X*) Fithian Pr.

Burr, Virginia I., ed. The Secret Eye: The Journal of Ella Gertrude Clanton Thomas, 1848-1889. LC 89-37188. (Gender & American Culture Ser.). (Illus.). xxiv, 470p. (C). 1990. 49.95 (*0-8078-1897-6*); pap. 19.95 (*0-8078-4273-7*) U of NC Pr.

Burr, Vivien. Gender & Social Psychology. LC 97-37617. (Psychology Focus Ser.). (Illus.). 184p. (C). 1998. 50.00 (*0-415-15814-1*); pap. 14.99 (*0-415-15815-X*) Routledge.

— An Introduction to Social Construction. 208p. (C). 1995. pap. 20.99 (*0-415-10405-X*, C0125) Routledge.

Burr, Wesley R. & Klein, Shirley. Reexamining Family Stress: New Theory & Research. (Library of Social Research: Vol. 193). (Illus.). 224p. (C). 1993. text 59.95 (*0-8039-4929-4*); pap. text 26.00 (*0-8039-4930-8*) Sage.

***Burr, William.** Boat Maintenance: The Essential Guide to Cleaning, Painting & Cosmetics. 2000. write for info. (*0-07-135703-3*) Intl Marine.

Burr, William, ed. The Kissinger Transcripts: The Top Secret Talks with Beijing & Moscow: A National Security Archive Documents Reader. 400p. 1999. 30.00 (*1-56584-480-7*, Pub. by New Press NY) Norton.

***Burr, William, ed.** The Kissinger Transcripts: The Top Secret Talks with Beijing & Moscow: A National Security Archive Documents Reader. 544p. 1999. pap. 18.95 (*1-56584-568-4*, Pub. by New Press NY) Norton.

***Burr, William A & Nagi, Dinesh K.** Exercise & Sport in Diabetes LC 99-32280. (Diabetes in Practice Ser.). 208p. 1999. 74.95 (*0-471-98496-5*) Wiley.

Burr, William E. Planning for the Fiber Distributed Data Interface. (Illus.). 102p. (Orig.). (C). 1995. pap. text 40.00 (*0-7881-1233-3*) DIANE Pub.

Burr, William H. Revelations of Antichrist: Concerning Christ & Christianity. LC 79-161340. (Atheist Viewpoint Ser.). 448p. 1972. reprint ed. 31.95 (*0-405-03801-1*) Ayer.

— Self-Contradictions of the Bible. LC 87-61529. 96p. 1998. reprint ed. pap. 19.95 (*1-57392-233-1*) Prometheus Bks.

Burr, William M., Jr. Sailing Tips. (Illus.). 176p. 1989. pap. 10.95 (*0-312-02977-2*) St Martin.

— Sailing Tips: One Thousand New Ways to Solve Old Problems. 1989. pap. 9.95 (*0-318-42736-2*) St Martin.

Burr, Zofia, ed. see Ammons, A. R.

Burra, Neera. Born to Work: Child Labour in India. (Illus.). 320p. 1995. text 24.95 (*0-19-563628-7*) OUP.

— Born to Work: Child Labour in India. (Oxford India Paperbacks Ser.). (Illus.). 320p. 1998. reprint ed. pap. 10.95 (*0-19-564097-7*) OUP.

— Child Labour in the Brass-Ware Industry of Moradabad, Uttar Pradesh, India LC 91-149012. (ARTEP Working Papers). 57 p. 1989. write for info. (*92-2-106708-4*) Intl Labour Office.

Burra, Neera, jt. ed. see Singh, Andrea M.

Burra, Peter. Wordsworth. LC 72-2096. (Studies in Wordsworth: No. 29). 1972. reprint ed. lib. bdg. 75.00 (*0-8383-1486-4*) M S G Haskell Hse.

Burrage, A. A. The Burrage Memorial: A Genealogical History of the Descendants of John Burrage. (Illus.). 265p. 1989. reprint ed. pap. 39.50 (*0-8328-1293-5*); reprint ed. lib. bdg. 49.50 (*0-8328-1292-7*) Higginson Bk Co.

***Burrage, A. M.** Warning Whispers. Adrian, Jack, ed. xiv, 230p. 1999. 38.50 (*1-899562-84-2*) Ash-Tree.

Burrage, Alfred McLelland. Intruders: New Weird Tales. Adrian, Jack, ed. LC 96-113555. 233 p. 1995. write for info. (*1-899562-04-4*) Ash-Tree.

— Some Ghost Stories. 1981. 8.50 (*0-686-69311-6*) Bookfinger.

— Someone in the Room. Reginald, R. & Menville, Douglas A., eds. LC 75-46259. (Supernatural & Occult Fiction Ser.). 1976. reprint ed. lib. bdg. 23.95 (*0-405-08118-9*) Ayer.

***Burrage, Henry S.** Gorges & the Grant of the Province of Maine 1622: A Tercentenary Memoiral. 204p. 2000. reprint ed. 18.50 (*0-7884-1383-X*, 1383) Heritage Bk.

Burrage, Joyce. Clarke County. LC 98-88055. (Images of America Ser.). (Illus.). 128p. 1998. pap. 18.99 (*0-7524-0400-8*) Arcadia Publng.

Burrage, Kevin. Parallel & Sequential Methods for Ordinary Differential Equations. (Monographs on Numerical Analysis). (Illus.). 462p. 1995. text 110.00 (*0-19-853432-9*) OUP.

Burrage, Michael & Torstendahl, Rolf, eds. Professions in Theory & History: Rethinking the Study of the Professions. (SCASSS Ser.). 248p. (C). 1990. text 45.00 (*0-8039-8252-6*) Sage.

Burrall, Elmer E. The Puzzle of the Cross. 1991. pap. 5.25 (*1-55673-278-3*, 9111) CSS OH.

Burras, J. K. & Griffiths, Mark. Manual of Climbers & Wall Plants. (Illus.). 304p. 1995. 39.95 (*0-88192-299-4*) Timber.

Burras, J. K. & Griffiths, Mark, eds. Manual of Climbers & Wall Plants. (New Royal Horticultural Society Dictionary Ser.). (Illus.). 282p. 1994. 72.50 (*0-333-61537-9*, Pub. by Pan) Trans-Atl Phila.

Burrell. Adult Nursing. 3rd ed. 1999. pap. text 75.95 (*0-8385-0364-0*) Appleton & Lange.

Burrell & Nebert, D. Marine Environmental Studies in Boca de Quadra & Smeaton Bay: Physical Oceanography, 1980. (IMS Report: No. R81-5). 59p. 5.25 (*0-914500-12-0*) U of AK Inst Marine.

Burrell, jt. auth. see Feder.

Burrell, jt. auth. see Gibson.

Burrell, A., ed. Milk Quotas in the European Community. 214p. (C). 1989. 55.00 (*0-85198-640-4*) OUP.

Burrell, Angus, jt. auth. see Brewster, Dorothy.

Burrell, Arthur. Cathedral on the Nile: The History of All Saints Cathedral, Cairo. 120p. 1985. 35.00 (*0-7855-1031-1*, Pub. by Amate Pr Ltd) St Mut.

Burrell, Arthur, ed. A Book of Heroic Verse. LC 78-168775. (Granger Index Reprint Ser.). 1977. reprint ed. 23.95 (*0-8369-6295-8*) Ayer.

Burrell, Augustine. The Collected Essays & Addresses of the Rt. Hon. Augustine Birrell, 1880-1920, Set, 3 vols., Vol. I. (BCL1-PR English Literature Ser.). 1992. reprint ed. lib. bdg. 225.00 (*0-7812-7007-3*) Rprt Serv.

Burrell, Barbara, ed. Women & Public Policy. (Policy Studies Journal: Vol. 25:4). 172p. 1997. pap. write for info. (*0-944285-54-6*) Pol Studies.

Burrell, Barbara C. Public Opinion, the First Ladyship, & Hillary Rodham Clinton. Bardes, Barbara, ed. LC 96-29385. (Women in American Politics Ser.: Vol. 1). (Illus.). 172p. 1997. text 39.00 (*0-8153-2142-2*) Garland.

Burrell, Brian. Damn the Torpedoes: Fighting Words, Rallying Cries, & the Hidden History. LC 99-21405. (Illus.). 281p. 1999. 20.00 (*0-07-134262-1*) McGraw.

— Merriam-Webster's Guide to Everyday Math, a Home & Business Reference. LC 98-18147. 384p. 1998. pap. 14.95 (*0-87779-621-1*) Merriam-Webster Inc.

— Merriam-Webster's Pocket Guide to Business & Everyday Math. 368p. 1996. pap. 3.95 (*0-87779-505-3*) Merriam-Webster Inc.

***Burrell, Brian.** The Words We Live By: The Creeds, Mottoes & Pledges That Have Shared America. 369p. 2000. reprint ed. pap. text 26.00 (*0-7881-6979-3*) DIANE Pub.

Burrell, Brian. The Words We Live By: The Creeds, Mottoes, Oaths, & Pledges That Have Shaped America. LC 96-53537. (Illus.). 320p. 1997. 25.50 (*0-684-83001-9*) Free Pr.

Burrell, C. Colston. A Gardener's Encyclopedia of Wildflowers: An Organic Guide to Choosing & Growing over 150 Beautiful Wildflowers. LC 96-25130. (Illus.). 216p. 1997. text 29.95 (*0-87596-723-X*) Rodale Pr Inc.

— Perennial Combinations: Stunning Combinations That Make Your Yard Look Fantastic Right from the Start. LC 98-40152. (Illus.). 352p. 1999. text 29.95 (*0-87596-806-6*) Rodale Pr Inc.

Burrell, C. Colston, ed. Ferns: Wild Things Make a Comeback in the Garden. (21st-Century Gardening Ser.). (Illus.). 112p. 1994. pap. 9.95 (*0-945352-82-4*) Bklyn Botanic.

— The Natural Water Garden: Pools, Ponds, Marshes & Bogs for Backyards Everywhere. (Twenty-First Century Gardening Ser.). 1997. pap. 9.95 (*1-889538-01-9*) Bklyn Botanic.

***Burrell, C. Colston, ed.** Wildflower Gardens: 60 Spectacular Plants & How to Use Them in Your Garden. (Twenty-First Century Gardening Ser.). (Illus.). 112p. 1999. pap. 9.95 (*1-889538-11-6*) Bklyn Botanic.

Burrell, C. Colston & Brooklyn Botanic Garden Botanists, eds. Woodland Gardens: Shade Gets Chic. LC 96-167514. (21st-Century Gardening Ser.). (Illus.). 120p. 1995. pap. 9.95 (*0-945352-90-5*) Bklyn Botanic.

Burrell, C. Colston, jt. auth. see McClure, Susan.

Burrell, C. Colston, jt. auth. see Phillips, Ellen.

Burrell, C. Colston, jt. auth. see Stell, Elizabeth.

Burrell, Clarice. Pocketful of Rainbows. 1967. 5.00 (*0-87511-014-2*); pap. 3.95 (*0-87511-013-4*) Claitors.

Burrell, Cole, ed. The Shady Border: Knockout Plant Combinations That Light up the Shadows. (Twenty-First Century Gardening Ser.). (Illus.). 112p. 1998. pap. 9.95 (*1-889538-06-X*) Bklyn Botanic.

Burrell, D. C. Marine Environmental Studies in Boca de Quadra & Smeaton Bay: Chemical & Geochemical. (IMS Reports: No. R82-2). 307p. 1980. pap. 19.25 (*0-914500-16-3*) U of AK Inst Marine.

Burrell, D. C., et al. Marine Environmental Studies in Boca de Quadra & Smeaton Bay: Physical & Chemical, 1979. (Science Technical Reports: No. R80-1). (Illus.). 144p. pap. 10.50 (*0-914500-10-4*) U of AK Inst Marine.

Burrell, D. C., ed. see International Conference on Port & Ocean Engineeri.

Burrell, Dan L., et al. Perspectives in Christian Education: Focus on Parent & Student Relationships. LC 97-61498. 160p. 1997. pap. write for info. (*1-57921-049-X*) WinePress Pub.

Burrell, Dan L., jt. auth. see Johnson, Philip C.

Burrell, David. Getting In: An Applicant's Guide to Graduate School Admissions. 1997. pap. 30.00 (*0-938609-16-5*) Graduate Group.

Burrell, David & Landau, Yehezkel, eds. Voices from Jerusalem: Jews & Christians Reflect on the Holy Land. 1991. pap. 9.95 (*0-8091-3270-2*) Paulist Pr.

Burrell, David & Malits, Elena. Original Peace: Restoring God's Creation. LC 97-17543. 128p. (Orig.). 1997. pap. 8.95 (*0-8091-3733-X*, 3733-X) Paulist Pr.

Burrell, David, jt. auth. see Cunningham, Paul R.

Burrell, David B. Analogy & Philosophical Language. LC 73-77144. 290p. reprint ed. pap. 89.90 (*0-8357-8696-X*, 203368700087) Bks Demand.

— Exercises in Religious Understanding. LC 74-12566. 253p. reprint ed. pap. 78.50 (*0-608-12698-5*, 202436600036) Bks Demand.

— Freedom & Creation in the Abrahamic Traditions. (Occasional Papers Ser.). iii, 39p. 1995. pap. 4.95 (*1-929218-05-2*) Georgetwn U Ctr Muslim.

— Freedom & Creation in Three Traditions. (C). 1994. pap. text 16.50 (*0-268-00988-0*) U of Notre Dame Pr.

***Burrell, David B.** Friendship & Ways to Truth. LC 00-8603. 128p. 2000. pap. 8.00 (*0-268-02860-5*, Pub. by U of Notre Dame Pr); lib. bdg. 15.00 (*0-268-02859-1*) U of Notre Dame Pr.

Burrell, David B. Knowing the Unknowable God: Ibn-Sina, Maimonides, Aquinas. LC 85-40600. 130p. 1986. pap. text 11.50 (*0-268-01226-1*) U of Notre Dame Pr.

Burrell, David B., tr. see Al-Ghazali.

Burrell, David B., tr. see Al-Ghazali, Muhammad.

Burrell, Elaine G., ed. I Remember When, Vol. 1. (I Remember When Ser.). (Illus.). 64p. 1997. pap. 4.95 (*0-9658429-1-6*) Little Bear.

Burrell, Gibson. Pandemonium: Toward a Retro-Organization Theory. 208p. 1996. 75.00 (*0-8039-7776-X*); pap. 26.95 (*0-8039-7777-8*) Sage.

Burrell, Graham, ed. Aftermath: Along the Way...One Man's War & Peace (1940-1990) (C). 1990. text 35.00 (*0-7223-2544-4*, Pub. by A H S Ltd) St Mut.

Burrell, Joan, jt. auth. see Bourne, Rodger.

Burrell, Katherine S. Through the Eyes of a Child. 40p. 1998. pap. 8.00 (*0-8059-4519-9*) Dorrance.

Burrell, Lenette O., et al. Adult Nursing: Acute & Community Care. 2nd ed. LC 96-12365. (Illus.). 2200p. (C). 1996. pap. text 75.00 (*0-8385-0174-5*, A0174-1) Appleton & Lange.

Burrell, Lional, jt. auth. see Wood, Jonathon.

Burrell, Louis V. The Petals of the Rose: Poems & Epigrams. LC 70-168513. (Black Heritage Library Collection). 1977. reprint ed. 14.95 (*0-8369-8876-0*) Ayer.

Burrell, Martin. Betwixt Heaven & Charing Cross. LC 68-16916. (Essay Index Reprint Ser.). 1977. 20.95 (*0-8369-0266-1*) Ayer.

— Crumbs Are Also Bread. LC 70-86739. (Essay Index Reprint Ser.). 1977. 21.95 (*0-8369-1173-3*) Ayer.

Burrell, Maurice. The Christian Fringe: A Critical Assessment of Seven Religious Alternatives to Mainstream Christianity. 173p. 1997. 23.95 (*1-85311-116-3*, 6320, Pub. by Canterbury Press Norwich) Morehouse Pub.

Burrell, Michael M. Enzymes of Molecular Biology. 2nd ed. (Methods in Molecular Biology Ser.). 1999. 69.50 (*0-89603-708-8*) Humana.

Burrell, Michael M., ed. Enzymes of Molecular Biology. LC 92-45040. (Methods in Molecular Biology Ser.). (Illus.). 384p. 1993. pap., student ed. 69.50 (*0-89603-322-8*) Humana.

— Enzymes of Molecular Biology. LC 92-45040. (Methods in Molecular Biology Ser.: Vol. 16). (Illus.). 384p. 1993. student ed., spiral bd. 59.50 (*0-89603-234-5*) Humana.

Burrell, Paul. In the Royal Manner: Expert Advice on Etiquette & Entertaining from the Former Butler to Diana, Princess of Wales. 144p. 1999. 27.95 (*0-446-52641-X*, Pub. by Warner Bks) Little.

Burrell, Paul B., tr. see Dubois, Jacques, et al.

Burrell, Percival. Suttons Synagogue: or The English Centurion (A Sermon) LC 74-28822. (English Experience Ser.: No. 647). 1974. reprint ed. 15.00 (*90-221-0647-0*) Walter J Johnson.

Burrell, R. Michael & Jarman, R. L., eds. Iran: Political Diaries, 1881-1965, 14 vols. 1997. reprint ed. lib. bdg. 5995.00 (*1-85207-710-7*, Pub. by Archive Editions) N Ross.

Burrell, Robert & Lewis, Daniel M. Experimental Immunological. 6th ed. 134p. (C). 1987. pap. text 33.80 (*0-02-317290-8*, Macmillan Coll) P-H.

Burrell, Robert, et al. Toxicology of the Immune System: A Human Approach. 322p. 1992. 150.00 (*0-471-29069-6*, VNR) Wiley.

Burrell, Roy. The Greeks. (Rebuilding the Past Ser.). (Illus.). 114p. (YA). (gr. 7 up). 1990. 22.95 (*0-19-917161-0*) OUP.

— The Greeks. (Rebuilding the Past Ser.). (Illus.). 112p. (J). (gr. 7 up). 1998. pap. text 14.95 (*0-19-917101-7*) OUP.

An Asterisk (*) at the beginning of an entry indicates that the title is appearing for the first time.

— Oxford First Ancient History. (Rebuilding the Past Ser.). (Illus.). 320p. (J). (gr. 4-8). 1994. bds. 37.95 (*0-19-521058-1*) OUP.

— Oxford First Ancient History. (Rebuilding the Past Ser.). (Illus.). 320p. (J). (gr. 4-8). 1997. reprint ed. pap. 22.95 (*0-19-521373-4*) OUP.

Burrell, Sherry. Families: Explore Family Concepts in a Caring Classroom. Stranich, Helen, ed. (Illus.). 48p. 1991. pap. 6.95 (*1-878727-05-2*) First Teacher.

Burrell, T. D. South African Patent Law & Practice. 2nd ed. 699p. 1985. boxed set 223.00 (*0-409-01355-2*, SA, MICHIE) LEXIS Pub.

Burrelli, Joan, et al. Women, Minorities, & Persons with Disabilities in Science & Engineering, 1996. (Illus.). 283p. (C). 1998. pap. text 35.00 (*0-7881-4902-4*) DIANE Pub.

Burrello, Leonard C. & Greenburg, David E., eds. Leadership & Supervision in Special Services: Promising Ideas & Practices. LC 87-35266. (Special Services in the Schools Ser.: Vol. 4, Nos. 1 & 2). (Illus.). 136p. 1988. text 39.95 (*0-86656-725-9*) Haworth Pr.

***Burrello, Leonard C., et al.** Serving Exceptional Students, Too: How School Leaders Create Unified Systems. 256p. 2000. pap. 32.95 (*0-7619-7698-1*); lib. bdg. 69.95 (*0-7619-7697-3*) Corwin Pr.

Burren, Michael, jt. auth. see Martin, George.

Burren, N. K. Improved Gear Life Through Controlled Shot Peening. (1985 Fall Technical Meeting Ser.: Vol. 85FTM15). 7p. 1985. pap. text 30.00 (*1-55589-108-X*) AGMA.

Burresci, Lawrence G. & Heaney, James B., eds. Cryogenic Optical Systems & Instruments VIII. 242p. 1996. 56.00 (*0-8194-2202-9*) SPIE.

Burrese, Alain. Hard-Won Wisdom from the School of Hard Knocks: How to Avoid a Fight & Things to Do When You Can't or Don't Want To. 272p. 1996. pap. 21.00 (*0-87364-905-2*) Paladin Pr.

Burress, Lee. Battle of the Books: Literary Censorship in the Public Schools, 1950-1985. LC 88-30775. (Illus.). 395p. 1992. 47.50 (*0-8108-2151-6*) Scarecrow.

Burress, Rex. Life on No Creek: Missouri Rural Days. (Illus.). 128p. (Orig.). 1996. pap. 12.00 (*0-9652079-0-0*) Signs of the Seasons.

— Of a Feather: Insights into Nature from Lake Merritt to the Feather River. (Illus.). 145p. (Orig.). 1993. pap. 12.00 (*0-9652079-1-9*) Signs of the Seasons.

Burrett, Jill. Dad's Place: A New Guide for Fathers after Divorce. (Illus.). 160p. 1997. pap. text 16.95 (*0-7063-7641-2*, Pub. by WrLock) Sterling.

Burrett, Tony, tr. see Masson, Christine.

Burrgraeve, Roger & Vervenne, Marc. Swords into Plowshares: Theological Reflections on Peace. (Louvain Theological & Pastoral Monographs). 208p. (Orig.). 1992. pap. 25.00 (*0-8028-0568-X*) Eerdmans.

Burri, Alex, ed. Sprache und Denken (Language & Thought) (ENG & GER.). vi, 384p. 1997. 163.00 (*3-11-015648-2*) De Gruyter.

***Burri, Rene.** Luis Barragan. (Illus.). 2000. 15.95 (*0-7148-3960-4*) Phaidon Pr.

Burri, Rene, photos by. Cuba y Cuba. LC 97-43813. (Motta Photography Ser.). (Illus.). 60p. 1998. 24.95 (*1-56098-781-2*) Smithsonian.

Burri, Rene, jt. auth. see Ruegg, Arthur.

Burridge, Betty, ed. Sonoma County Breeding Bird Atlas: Detailed Maps & Accounts for Our Nesting Birds. LC 95-77779. 216p. 1995. pap. 15.00 (*0-9647516-3-1*) Madrone Audubon.

Burridge, D. M. & Kallen, E., eds. Problems & Prospects in Long & Medium Range Weather Forecasting. (Topics in Atmospheric & Oceanographic Sciences Ser.). (Illus.). 290p. 1983. pap. 34.00 (*0-387-12827-1*) Spr-Verlag.

Burridge, David. Twentieth Century Defences of Britian: Kent. Earle, James, ed. LC 97-30154. (Twentieth Century Defence of Britain Ser.). (Illus.). 85p. 1998. pap. 14.95 (*1-85753-233-3*, Pub. by Brasseys) Brasseys.

Burridge, George N. Green Bay Workhouse: Nau Tug Line. 1996. pap. 25.95 (*0-9629219-1-2*) Wisconsin Mus.

Burridge, J. H. Pastor Russell's Date System: And Teachings on the Person of Christ, the Atonement, Etc. 32p. 1988. reprint ed. pap. 1.95 (*1-883858-45-3*) Witness CA.

— Pastor Russell's Position & Credentials: And His Methods of Interpretation. 32p. 1988. reprint ed. pap. 1.95 (*1-883858-44-5*) Witness CA.

— Pastor Russell's Teachings on the Coming of Christ. 32p. 1988. reprint ed. pap. 1.95 (*1-883858-46-1*) Witness CA.

Burridge, Jeff, ed. see Williams, Anne S.

Burridge, Kate. Syntactic Change in Germanic: Aspects of Language Change in Germanic with Particular Reference to Middle Dutch. LC 92-23195. (Current Issues in Linguistic Theory Ser.: No. 89). xii, 287p. 1992. 76.00 (*1-55619-146-4*) J Benjamins Pubng Co.

Burridge, Kate, jt. auth. see Boerjars, Kersti.

Burridge, Keith, jt. auth. see Landy, Joanne M.

Burridge, Keith R. & Landy, Joanne M. Ready-to-Use Fundamental Motor Skills for Teaching, Remediating & Assessing Young Children. LC 99-22410. (Complete Motor Skills Activities Program Ser.). xxxi, 271p. 1999. pap. 29.95 (*0-13-013941-6*) Prntice Hall Bks.

Burridge, Keith R., jt. auth. see Landy, Joanne M.

Burridge, Kenelm O. Mambu: A Melanesian Millennium. LC 94-42499. (Mythos Ser.). 296p. 1995. text 55.00 (*0-691-04388-4*, Pub. by Princeton U Pr); pap. text 16.95 (*0-691-00166-9*, Pub. by Princeton U Pr) Cal Prin Full Svc.

— Someone, No One: An Essay on Individuality. LC 79-83979. 283p. reprint ed. pap. 87.80 (*0-8357-4200-8*, 203697900006) Bks Demand.

Burridge, Kenneth D., et al. Element Masters: Fantasy Role-Playing Game. 2nd rev. ed. (Illus.). 150p. 1984. pap. 14.95 (*0-930039-01-7*) Escape Ventures.

Burridge, Martin. International Competitive Strategy with Industry Cases. (C). 1993. pap. text. write for info. (*0-201-63185-7*) Addison-Wesley.

Burridge, Michael, ed. see Angino, Richard C.

Burridge, R., et al. Macroscopic Properties of Disordered Media: Proceedings 1981, New York. (Lecture Notes in Physics Ser.: Vol. 154). 307p. 1982. 33.95 (*0-387-11202-2*) Spr-Verlag.

Burridge, Richard A. Four Gospels, One Jesus? A Symbolic Reading. 205p. 1994. pap. text 14.00 (*0-8028-0876-X*) Eerdmans.

Burridge, Robert, ed. Fracture Mechanics. LC 78-24473. (SIAM-AMS Proceedings Ser.: Vol. 12). 169p. 1979. text 30.00 (*0-8218-1332-3*, SIAMS/12) Am Math.

Burridge, Roger & Ormandy, David, eds. Unhealthy Housing: Research, Remedies, & Reform. LC 92-21146. (Illus.). 480p. (C). 1993. 90.00 (*0-419-15410-8*, E & FN Spon) Routledge.

Burrier, Helen. How to Study Mathematics. 2nd ed. 16p. (C). 1988. pap. text 20.00 (*0-13-020884-1*, Pub. by P-H) S&S Trade.

Burriesci, Lawerence G., jt. ed. see Heaney, James B.

Burrill. Geometry Application & Connection. 1995. 55.95 (*0-02-824438-9*) Macmillan.

***Burrill, et al.** Geometry: Integration - Applications - Connections. 1998. student ed. 45.49 (*0-02-825275-6*); wbk. ed. 5.99 (*0-02-825322-1*) Glencoe.

— Geometry: Integration - Applications - Connections, Teacher's Wraparound Edition. 1998. teacher ed. 65.83 (*0-02-825276-4*) Glencoe.

Burrill, Alexander M. A Law Dictionary & Glossary: Containing Full Definitions of the Principal Terms of the Common & Civil Law, 2 vols., Vol. 2. 2nd ed. 658p. 1987. reprint ed. lib. bdg. write for info. (*0-318-62142-8*) W S Hein.

— Law Dictionary & Glossary: Containing Full Definitions of the Principal Terms of the Common & Civil Law, Together with Translations & Explanations of the Various Technical Phrases in Different Languages, Occuring in the Ancient & Modern Reports, & Standard Treaties; Embracing, Also, All the Principal Common & Civil Law Maxims. Compiled on the Basis of Spelman's Glossary, & Adapted to the Jurisprudence of the United States;, 2 vols., Vol. 1. 2nd ed. xxv, 700p. 1987. reprint ed. 145.00 (*0-8377-1946-1*, Rothman) W S Hein.

— A New Law Dictionary & Glossary: Containing Full Definitions of the Principal Terms of the Common & Civil Law, Together with Translations & Explanations of the Various Technical Phrases in Different Languages, Occurring in the Ancient & Modern Reports, & Standard Treatises; Embracing Also All the Principal Common & Civil Law Maxims - Compiled on the Basis of Spelman's Glossary, & Adapted to the Jurisprudence of the United States; LC 97-38481. xviii, 1099p. 1997. reprint ed. lib. bdg. 175.00 (*1-886363-32-3*) Lawbk Exchange.

Burrill, Claude S., jt. auth. see Ledolter, Johannes.

Burrill, Claude W. & Ledolter, Johannes. Achieving Quality Through Continual Improvement. LC 98-15989. 640p. 1998. text 99.95 (*0-471-09220-7*) Wiley.

Burrill, G. Steven & Almassy, Stephen E. Electronics, '91. 60p. (Orig.). 1991. pap. text. write for info. (*1-879161-01-X*) Ernst & Young.

Burrill, Gail & Hopfensperger, Patrick. Exploring Linear Relations: Algebra. Anderson, Cathy et al, eds. (Data-Driven Mathematics Ser.). 208p. (YA). (gr. 7-12). 1997. pap. text, teacher ed. 22.95 (*1-57232-211-X*, 21162) Seymour Pubns.

Burrill, Gail, et al. Data Analysis & Statistics Across the Curriculum. LC 92-16923. (Curriculum & Evaluation Standards for School Mathematics Addenda Ser.: Grades 9-12). (Illus.). 88p. 1992. pap. 16.95 (*0-87353-329-1*) NCTM.

Burrill, Gail F. & Hopfensperger, Patrick. Exploring Linear Relations: Algebra. Anderson, Cathy et al, eds. (Data-Driven Mathematics Ser.). 136p. (Orig.). (YA). (gr. 7-12). 1997. pap. text, student ed. 14.95 (*1-57232-210-1*, 21161) Seymour Pubns.

Burrill, Gary. Away: Maritimers in Massachusetts, Ontario & Alberta. 272p. 1992. 49.95 (*0-7735-0899-6*, Pub. by McG-Queens Univ Pr) CUP Services.

Burrill, John, jt. auth. see Fox, Peter.

Burrill, Kathleen R. The Quatrains of Nesimi Fourteenth-Century Turkic Hurufi. (Publications in Near & Middle East Studies: Ser. A, No. 14). 1972. 138.50 (*90-279-2328-0*) Mouton.

Burrill, Richard. How Magpie Got His Yellow Bill: A Children's Story about Keeping Respect. LC 96-95297. (Illus.). 35p. (J). (gr. 3-7). 1998. per. 9.50 (*1-878464-23-X*) Anthro Co.

— River of Sorrows: Life History of the Maidu-Nisenan Indians. LC 88-25528. (Illus.). 219p. (Orig.). 1988. pap. 9.50 (*0-87961-187-1*) Naturegraph.

Burrill, Richard L. The Human Almanac: People Through Time. 432p. (YA). (gr. 9-12). 1983. pap. 12.95 (*0-943238-00-5*) Anthro Co.

— Protectors of the Land: An Environmental Journey to Understanding the Conservation Ethic. Macias, Regina, ed. (Illus.). 354p. (J). (gr. 3-12). 1994. pap. text 22.95 (*1-878464-02-7*) Anthro Co.

— Somewhere Behind the Eyes Vol. 1: Hocus Focus Aha! (Illus.). 72p. (J). (gr. 4-12). 1999. pap. 12.95 (*1-878464-15-9*) Anthro Co.

— Somewhere Behind the Eyes Vol. 2: Images in the Moon & in the Stars Aha! (Illus.). 100p. (YA). (gr. 9-12). 1998. pap. 12.95 (*1-878464-05-1*) Anthro Co.

— Somewhere Behind the Eyes Vol. 3: Surprise Images in Nature Aha! (Somewhere Behind the Eyes Ser.). (Illus.). 96p. (J). (gr. 4-12). Date not set. pap. text 12.95 (*1-878464-19-1*) Anthro Co.

— Somewhere Behind the Eyes Vol. 4: Other Language Treasures Aha! (Illus.). 85p. (J). (gr. 4-12). Date not set. pap. 12.95 (*1-878464-17-5*) Anthro Co.

— Towards Togetherness: The Cooperative Games, Songs, & Activities Handbook. (Illus.). 112p. (Orig.). (J). (gr. 3-12). 1994. pap. 10.95 (*1-878464-12-4*) Anthro Co.

Burrill, Richard L., ed. Closest to God: Humankind's Search for the Supreme Being. Date not set. pap. 10.95 (*1-878464-07-8*) Anthro Co.

— Muhammad, His Life Story Introduced. (gr. 9-12). Date not set. 17.95 (*1-878464-59-0*) Anthro Co.

Burrill, Russell. New World Order: What's Behind the Headlines. (Illus.). 192p. (Orig.). 1992. pap. 1.95 (*1-882704-00-2*) Seminars Unltd.

Burrill, Steven. Kennebunk: Main Street. (Images of America Ser.). 1995. pap. 16.99 (*0-7524-0236-6*) Arcadia Publng.

Burrill, Steven G. & Norback, Craig T. The Arthur Young Guide to Rating Venture Capital. 192p. 1988. 24.95 (*0-8306-3014-7*) McGraw-Hill Prof.

Burrill, William. Hemingway: The Toronto Years. 332p. 1996. mass mkt. 12.95 (*0-385-25558-6*) Doubleday.

— Naked Eye. 208p. 1998. pap. 13.99 (*1-895837-31-6*) Insomniac.

Burrillo, Ralph. Fragments. 130p. 1997. pap. write for info. (*1-888024-14-3*) Ahead Desktop.

Burrin, Philippe. France under the Germans: Collaboration & Compromise. LC 96-69742. 512p. 1997. 27.50 (*1-56584-323-1*, Pub. by New Press NY) Norton.

— France under the Germans: Collaboration & Compromise. Lloyd, Janet, tr. from FRE. 512p. 1998. pap. 16.95 (*1-56584-439-4*, Pub. by New Press NY) Norton.

— Hitler & the Jews: The Genesis of the Holocaust. Southgate, Patsy, tr. (An Arnold Publication). 192p. 1994. pap. text 19.95 (*0-340-59362-8*, B2933) CUP.

Burrin, Phillippe. New Historicism & Cultural Materialism. 480p. text. write for info. (*0-340-65222-5*, Pub. by E A) Routldge.

Burrington, Gillian A. Equal Opportunities in Librarianship? Gender & Career Aspirations. LC 87-7221. (Library Association Research Publication: Vol. 24). 199p. reprint ed. pap. 61.70 (*0-608-08879-X*, 206951600004) Bks Demand.

Burrington, James D. & Clark, Douglas S., eds. Biocatalysis & Biomimetics. LC 89-307. (ACS Symposium Ser.: No. 392). (Illus.). xi, 172p. 1989. text 45.00 (*0-8412-1611-8*, Pub. by Am Chemical) OUP.

Burrington, Stephen H. Road Kill: How Solo Driving Runs Down the Economy. 3rd unabridged ed. (Illus.). 56p. 1994. pap. 10.00 (*1-892787-03-2*) Conservation Law.

***Burrington, Stephen H. & Heart, Bennet.** Calmar el Trafico. unabridged ed.Tr. of Calm the Traffic. (SPA., Illus.). 2000. 5.00 (*1-892787-04-0*) Conservation Law.

Burrington, Stephen H. & Heart, Bennet. City Routes, City Rights: Building Neighborhoods & Environmental Justice by Fixing Transportation. unabridged ed. (Illus.). 82p. 1998. pap. 15.00 (*1-892787-01-6*) Conservation Law.

Burrington, Stephen H. & Thiebach, Veronika. Take Back Your Streets: How to Protect Communities from Asphalt. 3rd ed. (Illus.). 54p. 1998. pap. 10.00 (*1-892787-02-4*) Conservation Law.

***Burris.** Florida Administrative Practice Manual 99-1, 3 vols. 544p. 1999. ring bd. write for info. (*0-327-01375-3*, 8049618) LEXIS Pub.

Burris. Florida Administrative Practice Manual 99-2, 3 vols., Set. 296p. 1999. ring bd. write for info. (*0-327-01508-X*, 8049619) LEXIS Pub.

Burris, ed. see England, Arthur & Levinson, Harold.

Burris, Barbara. Callie & Zora. LC 96-92676. (Illus.). 96p. (Orig.). (J). (gr. 4-5). 1998. 15.95 (*0-9654197-3-8*) PennyRoyal Bks.

Burris, Beverly. No Room at the Top: Underemployment & Alienation in the Corporation. LC 82-18073. 331p. 1983. 65.00 (*0-275-90954-9*, C0954, Praeger Pubs) Greenwood.

Burris, Beverly H. Technocracy at Work. LC 92-24052. (SUNY Series, the New Inequalities). 243p. (C). 1993. text 64.50 (*0-7914-1495-7*); pap. text 21.95 (*0-7914-1496-5*) State U NY Pr.

Burris, Christopher. The Proper Care of Cats. (TW Ser.). (Illus.). 256p. 1991. text 16.95 (*0-86622-403-3*, TW-103) TFH Pubns.

— The Proper Care of Dogs. (TW Ser.). (Illus.). 256p. 1991. text 16.95 (*0-86622-402-5*, TW-102) TFH Pubns.

***Burris, Christopher.** Proper Care of Dogs. (Illus.). 2000. 12.95 (*0-7938-3155-5*) TFH Pubns.

Burris, Cynthia, ed. see Guerra, Michael.

Burris, Damon A. Doin' It: A Guide to Great Sex. large type ed. 160p. (Orig.). 1997. pap. 7.95 (*0-9657257-0-7*) Goatee Graphics.

***Burris, John.** Blue vs. Black. 256p. 2000. pap. 13.95 (*0-312-26296-5*) St Martin.

Burris, John & Whitney, Catherine. Blue vs. Black: Let's End the Conflict Between Cops & Minorities. LC 99-22180. (Illus.). 256p. 1999. text 23.95 (*0-312-20392-6*) St Martin.

Burris, Johnny, et al. Florida Administrative Practice. 1979-1994, 3 vols., Set. 274p. 1997. ring bd. 270.00 (*0-409-26108-4*, 80490-10, MICHIE) LEXIS Pub.

Burris, Johnny C. Florida Administrative Practice Manual, 98-1. 150p. 1998. ring bd. write for info. (*0-327-00611-0*, 8049617) LEXIS Pub.

Burris, Jon, ed. Through an Open Door: Selections from the Robert A. Hefner III Collection of Contemporary Chines. (Illus.). 140p. 1998. 55.00 (*1-55670-820-3*); pap. text 45.00 (*1-55670-821-1*) Stewart Tabori & Chang.

Burris, Jon, photos by. New Russian Art: Paintings from the Christian Keesee Collection. (Illus.). 138p. 1995. 35.00 (*1-55670-435-6*) Stewart Tabori & Chang.

Burris-Kitchen, Deborah. Female Gang Participation: The Role of African-American Women in the Informal Drug Economy & Gang Activities. LC 97-21694. (Women's Studies: Vol. 17). 224p. 1997. text 89.95 (*0-7734-8617-8*) E Mellen.

Burris-Meyer, Harold, et al. Sound in the Theatre. rev. ed. LC 78-66064. 1979. 16.95 (*0-87830-157-7*, Thtre Arts Bks) Routledge.

Burris, Priscilla & Publications International, Ltd. Editorial Staff. Garden Bunnies. LC 98-130704. (Wonder Window Ser.). (Illus.). 1998. write for info. (*0-7853-2683-9*) Pubns Intl Ltd.

Burris, Quincy G. Richard Doddridge Blackmore: His Life & Novels. (BCL1-PR English Literature Ser.). 219p. 1992. reprint ed. lib. bdg. 79.00 (*0-7812-7440-0*) Rprt Serv.

***Burris, Rob.** Velocette Motorcycles. (Illus.). 176p. 2000. 39.95 (*1-901295-78-8*, 129988AE, Pub. by Vloce Pub) Motorbooks Intl.

Burris, Russell. Computer Network Experiments in Teaching Law. 65p. 1980. 10.00 (*0-318-14010-1*) EDUCOM.

Burris, Sidney. A Day at the Races. LC 89-5295. (University of Utah Press Poetry Ser.). 78p. reprint ed. pap. 30.00 (*0-7837-5539-2*, 204531300005) Bks Demand.

***Burris, Sidney.** Doing Lucretius. (Southern Messenger Poets Ser.). 80p. 2000. 22.50 (*0-8071-2550-4*); pap. 14.95 (*0-8071-2551-2*) La State U Pr.

Burris, Sidney. The Poetry of Resistance: Seamus Heaney & the Pastoral Tradition. LC 89-25502. 182p. (C). 1990. text 32.95 (*0-8214-0951-4*) Ohio U Pr.

Burris, Stanley. Logic for Math & Computer Science. LC 97-15438. 420p. 1997. 78.67 (*0-13-285974-2*) P-H.

Burris, Stanley & McKenzie, Ralph. Decidability & Boolean Representations. LC 81-7902. (Memoirs of the American Mathematical Society Ser.: No. 32/246). 106p. 1981. pap. 16.00 (*0-8218-2246-2*, MEMO/32/246) Am Math.

Burris, Stephen E., jt. auth. see Elliston, Edgar J.

***Burris, Thomas P.** Nuclear Receptors & Genetic Disease. 400p. 2000. 129.95 (*0-12-146160-2*) Acad Pr.

Burris, Val. The Crisis of the New Middle Class. 270p. Date not set. pap. write for info. (*0-275-92366-5*, B2366, Praeger Pubs) Greenwood.

Burris, W. Alan. A Liberty Primer. 2nd ed. LC 83-61673. (Illus.). 562p. (Orig.). (C). 1983. pap. 7.95 (*0-9608490-1-7*) Society Indiv Lib.

Burris, W. H. Revelations of Antichrist. 1972. 59.95 (*0-8490-0950-2*) Gordon Pr.

Burris, William C. & Haynsworth, Clement F., Jr. Duty & the Law: Judge John J. Parker & the Constitution. LC 86-72659. (Illus.). 256p. 1987. 14.95 (*0-938991-08-6*) Colonial Pr AL.

Burrise, Andrea, ed. see O'Neal, Terry.

***Burrison, John A.** Shaping Traditions: Folk Arts in a Changing South. 2000. pap. text 24.95 (*0-8203-2150-8*) U of Ga Pr.

Burrison, John A., ed. Storytellers: Folktales & Legends from the South. LC 88-37143. (Brown Thrasher Bks.). (Illus.). 384p. 1991. pap. 16.95 (*0-8203-1267-3*) U of Ga Pr.

Burrison, John A., jt. auth. see Goizueta Folklife Gallery (Atlanta History Museum) Staff.

Burriss, Craig. Determining Sound Power Levels of Enclosed Gear Drives Using the Sound Intensity Method. (Technical Papers: Vol. 97FTM2). (Illus.). 7p. 1997. pap. text 30.00 (*1-55589-696-0*) AGMA.

Burriss, Eli E. Taboo, Magic, Spirits: A Study of Primitive Elements in Roman Religion. LC 72-114489. 250p. 1972. reprint ed. lib. bdg. 35.00 (*0-8371-4724-7*, BUTA, Greenwood Pr) Greenwood.

***Burriss, T. Moffatt.** World War II Paratrooper Memoir. 2000. 24.95 (*1-57488-258-9*) Brasseys.

Burritt, Elihu. The Learned Blacksmith: The Letters & Journals of Elihu Burritt. (BCL1-PS American Literature Ser.). 241p. 1993. reprint ed. lib. bdg. 79.00 (*0-7812-6948-2*) Rprt Serv.

Burritt, Elihu & Curti, Merle E. The Learned Blacksmith: The Letters & Journals of Elihu Burritt. 1977. 16.95 (*0-8369-7133-7*) Ayer.

Burritt, Mary. Arias. (Mary Burritt Poetry Ser.). 83p. 1996. 24.95 (*0-8263-1696-4*); pap. 9.95 (*0-8263-1697-2*) U of NM Pr.

— The Solera Poems. LC 79-11408. 55p. 1979. pap. 3.75 (*0-934332-11-8*) LEpervier Pr.

Burrluck, Dave. The Player's Guide to Guitar Maintenance. (Illus.). 84p. 1998. pap. 24.95 (*0-87930-549-5*) Miller Freeman.

***Burrluck, Dave.** The PRS Guitar Book: A Complete History of Paul Reed Smith Guitars. limited ed. (Illus.). 126p. 1999. boxed set 75.00 (*0-87930-593-2*) Miller Freeman.

Burron, Arnold. A Layman's Guide to the Great "Reading" Controversy. (Issues Paper #11-94 Ser.). 33p. 1994. pap. text 8.00 (*1-57655-139-3*) Independ Inst.

— What If Teachers Could Choose Their Schools? Opening up the Educational Job Market. (Issue Papers: No. 13-88). 7p. 1988. pap. text 8.00 (*1-57655-081-8*) Independ Inst.

Burros, Marian. Eating Well Is the Best Revenge: Everyday Strategies for Delicious, Healthful Food in 30 Minutes. LC 95-19. 1995. 25.00 (*0-684-80399-2*) S&S Trade.

— Elegant but Easy Cookbook. 1995. 8.98 (*0-88365-914-X*) Galahad Bks.

— 20-Minute Menus: Time-Wise Recipes & Strategic Plans for Freshly Cooked Meals Every Day. 256p. 1995. per. 12.00 (*0-684-80135-3*) S&S Trade Pap.

Burros, Marian & Levine, Lois. Elegant But Easy Cookbook. 214p. 1984. pap. 10.00 (*0-02-009340-3*) Macmillan.

— The New Elegant but Easy Cookbook. LC 97-46884. 352p. 1998. 24.50 (*0-684-83244-5*) S&S Trade.

B

*__Burrough, Bryan.__ Dragonfly: An Epic Adventure of Survival in Outer Space. 544p. 2000. pap. 15.00 (*0-06-093269-4*) HarpC.

__Burrough, Bryan.__ Dragonfly: NASA & the Crisis Aboard Mir. LC 98-43309. (Illus.). 544p. 1998. 26.95 (*0-88730-783-3*) HarpC.

*__Burrough, Bryan.__ Dragonfly: Nasa & the Crisis Aboard Mir. unabridged ed. 1998. audio 25.00 (*0-694-52115-9*, 694523, Pub. by HarperAudio) Lndmrk Audiobks.

__Burrough, Bryan & Helyar, John.__ Barbarians at the Gate: The Rise & Fall of RJR Nabisco. LC 89-45635. (Illus.). 576p. 1992. reprint ed. pap. 16.00 (*0-06-092038-6*, Perennial) HarperTrade.

__Burrough, Peter.__ European Geographic Information Infrastructures: Opportunities & Pitfalls. 208p. 1997. 95.00 (*0-7484-0755-3*, Pub. by Tay Francis Ltd); pap. text 47.95 (*0-7484-0756-1*, Pub. by Tay Francis Ltd) Taylor & Francis.

__Burrough, Peter & Frank, Andrew, eds.__ Geographic Objects with Indeterminate Boundaries. (GISDATA Ser.). 250p. 1996. 89.95 (*0-7484-0386-8*); pap. 49.95 (*0-7484-0387-6*) Taylor & Francis.

__Burrough, Peter A. & McDonnell, Rachel A.__ Principles of Geographical Information Systems. 2nd ed. (Spatial Information Systems Ser.). (Illus.). 346p. (C). 1998. text 104.00 (*0-19-823366-3*); pap. text 49.95 (*0-19-823365-5*) OUP.

__Burroughs.__ Billy Watsons Croker Sack. 18.95 (*0-03-902893-3*) Dryden Pr.

__Burroughs.__ Burrough's Kankakee's Earliest Settlers. 1986. pap. 11.95 (*0-685-18891-4*) Lindsay Pubns.

— Maternity Nursing: An Introductory Text. 7th ed. (C). text. write for info. (*0-8089-2119-3*, Grune & Strat) Harcrt Hlth Sci Grp.

__Burroughs, jt. auth. see Hansen.__

*__Burroughs, A. & Price, D.__ An Atlas of Liver Disease. (Encyclopedia of Visual Medicine Ser.). (Illus.). 140p. 2001. write for info. (*1-84214-012-4*) Prthnon Pub.

__Burroughs, Alan.__ Art Criticism from a Laboratory. LC 70-110267. 277p. 1971. reprint ed. lib. bdg. 65.00 (*0-8371-4493-0*, BUAC, Greenwood Pr) Greenwood.

— John Greenwood in America, 1745-1752: A Monograph. (Illus.). 88p. (Orig.). 1943. pap. write for info. (*1-879886-08-1*) Addison Gallery.

__Burroughs, Arlene.__ Maternity Nursing: An Introductory Text. 6th ed. (Illus.). 1992. pap., teacher ed. write for info. (*0-7216-4507-0*, W B Saunders Co) Harcrt Hlth Sci Grp.

— Maternity Nursing: An Introductory Text. 7th ed. (Illus.). 1997. pap., teacher ed. write for info. (*0-7216-2496-0*, W B Saunders Co) Harcrt Hlth Sci Grp.

— Maternity Nursing: An Introductory Text. 7th ed. Rader, Ilze, ed. LC 97-7111. (Illus.). 608p. 1997. pap. text 31.50 (*0-7216-2473-1*, W B Saunders Co) Harcrt Hlth Sci Grp.

— Study Guide to Accompany Maternity Nursing: An Introductory Text. 6th ed. (Illus.). 224p. 1992. pap. text, student ed. 19.95 (*0-7216-3314-5*, W B Saunders Co) Harcrt Hlth Sci Grp.

*__Burroughs, Augusten.__ Sellevision. 224p. 2000. pap. 11.95 (*0-312-26772-X*, St Martin Griffin) St Martin.

__Burroughs, B. E.__ Legends & Tales of Homeland on the Kankakee. 1923. 16.95 (*0-917914-65-1*) Lindsay Pubns.

__Burroughs, Barkham.__ Barkham Burroughs' Encyclopaedia of Astounding Facts & Useful Information 1889. Burroughs, Miggs, ed. (Illus.). 148p. (Orig.). 1983. reprint ed. pap. 8.95 (*0-9610994-0-2*) Brayden.

__Burroughs, Bob.__ Church Music in the Real World: A Church Musician's Handbook for the Rest of Us. 144p. (Orig.). 1996. pap. 12.95 (*1-889411-00-0*, ESI86B) Tempo Music.

__Burroughs, Bob.__ Walk in Light. 1.25 (*0-687-07165-8*) Abingdon.

__Burroughs, Burt E.__ Burrough's Kankakee's Earliest Settlers. 1986. 24.95 (*0-917914-54-6*) Lindsay Pubns.

__Burroughs, Catherine B.__ Closet Stages: Joanna Baillie & the Theater Theory of British Romantic Women Writers. LC 97-3949. (Illus.). 264p. 1997. text 39.95 (*0-8122-3393-X*) U of Pa Pr.

*__Burroughs, Catherine B., ed.__ Women in British Romantic Theatre: Drama, Performance & Society, 1790-1840. LC 00-21924. (Illus.). 344p. (C). 2000. write for info. (*0-521-66224-9*) Cambridge U Pr.

__Burroughs, Catherine B. & Ehrenreich, Jeffrey D., eds.__ Reading the Social Body. LC 92-40753. (Illus.). 285p. 1993. text 35.00 (*0-87745-401-9*); pap. text 15.95 (*0-87745-402-7*) U of Iowa Pr.

__Burroughs, Charles.__ From Signs to Design: Environmental Process & Reform in Early Renaissance Rome. (Illus.). 358p. 1990. 52.50 (*0-262-02298-2*) MIT Pr.

__Burroughs, David.__ The New Wine Companion. 2nd ed. 244p. 1993. pap. 34.95 (*0-7506-1274-6*) Buttrwrth-Heinemann.

__Burroughs, David & Bezzant, Norman.__ The New Wine Companion. 2nd ed. LC 94-27192. 256p. reprint ed. pap. 79.40 (*0-608-09704-7*, 206987000007) Bks Demand.

— Wine Regions of the World. 2nd ed. LC 79-322312. (Illus.). 431p. reprint ed. pap. 133.70 (*0-608-07411-X*, 206763800009) Bks Demand.

__Burroughs, David, et al.__ Wine Regions of the World. 2nd ed. 1988. pap. 39.95 (*0-7506-0631-2*) Buttrwrth-Heinemann.

__Burroughs, Edgar Rice.__ Apache Devil. 192p. 17.95 (*0-8488-1254-9*) Amereon Ltd.

*__Burroughs, Edgar Rice.__ At the Earth's Core. LC 99-54812. (Bison Frontiers of Imagination Ser.). (Illus.). 296p. 2000. pap. 12.95 (*0-8032-6174-8*, Bison Books) U of Nebr Pr.

__Burroughs, Edgar Rice.__ Chessman of Mars. 220p. 1987. mass mkt. 4.99 (*0-345-35038-3*, Del Rey) Ballantine Pub Grp.

— Deputy Sheriff of Commanche County. 320p. Date not set. 24.95 (*0-8488-2518-7*) Amereon Ltd.

— Efficiency Expert. 224p. Date not set. 21.95 (*0-8488-2520-9*) Amereon Ltd.

— The Gods of Mars. 190p. Date not set. 20.95 (*0-8488-2222-6*) Amereon Ltd.

__Burroughs, Edgar Rice.__ The Gods of Mars, Set. abr. ed. (Mars Ser.). 1996. 16.95 incl. audio (*1-882071-77-8*, 394313, Pub. by B&B Audio) Lndmrk Audiobks.

— The Land That Time Forgot. LC 98-50000. (Illus.). 448p. 1999. pap. 14.95 (*0-8032-6154-3*, Bison Books) U of Nebr Pr.

__Burroughs, Edgar Rice.__ Mars No. 2: Gods of Mars. 190p. 1985. mass mkt. 4.99 (*0-345-32439-0*, Del Rey) Ballantine Pub Grp.

— Mars No. 9: Synthetic Men of Mars. 160p. 1986. mass mkt. 5.99 (*0-345-33930-4*, Del Rey) Ballantine Pub Grp.

— The Monster Men. LC 62-8707. (Illus.). (J). 1962. 25.00 (*0-940724-06-5*) P Hunt.

— The Oakdale Affair. 18.95 (*0-8488-1255-7*) Amereon Ltd.

— The Oakdale Affair. 1976. reprint ed. lib. bdg. 25.95 (*0-89966-041-X*) Buccaneer Bks.

— The Outlaw of Torn. 256p. 22.95 (*0-8488-1256-5*) Amereon Ltd.

— The Outlaw of Torn. 1976. reprint ed. lib. bdg. 10.55 (*0-89966-042-8*) Buccaneer Bks.

— Pellucidar. 22.95 (*0-8488-0933-5*) Amereon Ltd.

— A Princess of Mars. 159p. Date not set. 18.95 (*0-8488-2221-8*) Amereon Ltd.

— A Princess of Mars. 160p. 1985. mass mkt. 4.99 (*0-345-33138-9*, Del Rey) Ballantine Pub Grp.

__Burroughs, Edgar Rice.__ A Princess of Mars. abr. ed. (Mars Ser.). (YA). (gr. 8-12). 1995. 16.95 incl. audio (*1-882071-51-4*, 393368, Pub. by B&B Audio) Lndmrk Audiobks.

__Burroughs, Edgar Rice.__ The Return of Tarzan. 221p. Date not set. 21.95 (*0-8488-2223-4*) Amereon Ltd.

— The Return of Tarzan. 224p. 1984. mass mkt. 5.99 (*0-345-31575-8*, Ballantine) Ballantine Pub Grp.

— Science Fiction Classics. 464p. 1992. 7.98 (*0-89009-582-5*) Bk Sales Inc.

— The Son of Tarzan. 1998. lib. bdg. 27.95 (*1-56723-026-1*) Yestermorrow.

— Tarzan. (Two-in-One Ser.: Nos. 13 & 14). (J). 1997. mass mkt. 6.99 (*0-345-41349-0*, Del Rey) Ballantine Pub Grp.

— Tarzan. LC 98-39041. (Illus.). 32p. (J). (gr. k-4). 1999. 15.99 (*0-7868-0384-3*, Pub. by Disney Pr) Time Warner.

— Tarzan. LC 96-49011. (Children's Thrift Classics Ser.). (Illus.). 96p. (J). 1998. reprint ed. pap. text 1.00 (*0-486-29530-3*) Dover.

— Tarzan & the Jewels of Opar. 1998. mass mkt. 5.99 (*0-345-91423-6*, Del Rey) Ballantine Pub Grp.

*__Burroughs, Edgar Rice.__ Tarzan, Lion Man & Leopard Man. 1999. mass mkt. write for info. (*0-345-41754-2*, Del Rey) Ballantine Pub Grp.

__Burroughs, Edgar Rice.__ Tarzan of the Apes. 22.95 (*0-8488-1257-3*) Amereon Ltd.

— Tarzan of the Apes. 1993. pap. 12.95 incl. audio (*1-882071-43-3*) B&B Audio.

— Tarzan of the Apes. (Tarzan Ser.). 246p. 1984. mass mkt. 5.99 (*0-345-31977-X*, Del Rey) Ballantine Pub Grp.

— Tarzan of the Apes. 228p. 1990. mass mkt. 4.95 (*0-451-52423-3*, Sig Classics) NAL.

— Tarzan of the Apes, 1. (Tarzan of the Apes Ser.). 1999. mass mkt. 4.99 (*0-8125-7238-6*, Pub. by Tor Bks) St Martin.

__Burroughs, Edgar Rice.__ Tarzan of the Apes. (J). 1991. 9.09 (*0-606-12823-9*, Pub. by Turtleback) Demco.

__Burroughs, Edgar Rice.__ Tarzan of the Apes. 320p. 1990. pap. 8.95 (*0-14-018464-3*, Penguin Classics) Viking Penguin.

— Tarzan of the Apes. LC 81-19873. (Step into Classics Ser.). (Illus.). 96p. (J). (gr. 2-7). 1982. pap. 3.99 (*0-394-85089-0*, Pub. by Random Bks Yng Read) Random.

— Tarzan of the Apes. large type ed. 381p. 1994. lib. bdg. 21.95 (*0-7838-1160-8*, G K Hall Lrg Type) Mac Lib Ref.

— Tarzan of the Apes. 1976. reprint ed. lib. bdg. 25.95 (*0-89966-046-0*) Buccaneer Bks.

— Tarzan of the Apes. LC 96-53315. (Thrift Editions Ser.). 224p. 1997. reprint ed. pap. text 2.00 (*0-486-29570-2*) Dover.

*__Burroughs, Edgar Rice.__ Tarzan of the Apes: Adapted by Robin Moore from Edgar Rice Burrough's Tarzan of the Apes. LC 98-52894. (Illus.). 96p. (gr. 2-5). 1999. per. 3.99 (*0-689-82413-0*, 076714003886) S&S Childrens.

__Burroughs, Edgar Rice.__ Tarzan Triumphant: Tarzan & the City of Gold. (Tarzan Ser.). 1997. mass mkt. 6.99 (*0-345-41641-4*, Del Rey) Ballantine Pub Grp.

— Tarzan 2 in 1, Vols. 3 & 4. 1996. mass mkt. 5.99 (*0-345-40830-6*, Del Rey) Ballantine Pub Grp.

*__Burroughs, Edgar Rice.__ Tarzan's Quest. 1999. mass mkt. write for info. (*0-345-41755-0*, Del Rey) Ballantine Pub Grp.

__Burroughs, Edgar Rice.__ The War Chief. 17.95 (*0-8488-1258-1*) Amereon Ltd.

— The Warlord of Mars. 158p. Date not set. 18.95 (*0-8488-2224-2*) Amereon Ltd.

__Burroughs, Edgar Rice.__ The Warlord of Mars. (Martian Tales of Edgar Rice Burroughs). 1997. 16.95 incl. audio (*1-882071-91-3*) B&B Audio.

__Burroughs, Edgar Rice.__ The Warlord of Mars. 158p. 1985. mass mkt. 4.99 (*0-345-32453-6*, Del Rey) Ballantine Pub Grp.

— The Warlord of Mars. 1976. reprint ed. lib. bdg. 21.95 (*0-89966-045-2*) Buccaneer Bks.

__Burroughs, Edgar Rice & Dameron, Ned.__ Marcia of the Doorstep: A Romance. 1999. 60.00 (*1-880418-41-X*); 30.00 (*1-880418-42-8*) D M Grant.

— You Lucky Girl! A Romanic Play. 1999. 60.00 (*1-880418-43-6*) D M Grant.

— You Lucky Girl! A Romantic Play. 172p. 30.00 (*1-880418-44-4*) D M Grant.

__Burroughs, Edgar Rice & Green, John.__ Tarzan Coloring Book. (Illus.). 48p. (J). 1998. pap. 2.50 (*0-486-40359-9*) Dover.

__Burroughs, Edgar Rice & Kaluta, Michael W.__ Edgar Rice Burroughs' Minidoka: 937th Earl of One Mile Series M. (Illus.). 64p. (YA). (gr. 7 up). 1998. 14.95 (*1-56971-280-8*) Dark Horse Comics.

__Burroughs, Edgar Rice & Lansdale, Joe R.__ Tarzan: The Lost Adventure. limited ed. (Illus.). 208p. (YA). (gr. 7 up). 1996. 99.95 (*1-56971-128-3*) Dark Horse Comics.

— Tarzan: The Lost Adventures. 1997. mass mkt. 5.99 (*0-345-41273-7*, Del Rey); mass mkt. 5.99 (*0-614-27738-8*, Del Rey) Ballantine Pub Grp.

— Tarzan Bk. 1: The Lost Adventure. limited ed. (Illus.). 208p. 1996. 19.95 (*1-56971-083-X*) Dark Horse Comics.

__Burroughs, Edgar Rice, jt. auth. see Brady, Clark A.__

__Burroughs, Edgar Rice, jt. auth. see Manning, Russ.__

__Burroughs, Edgar Rice, jt. auth. see Simonson, Walter.__

*__Burroughs, Esther.__ Empowered! rev. ed. Law, Jennifer, ed. 122p. 1999. pap. 8.99 (*1-56309-716-8*, N994101, New Hope) Womans Mission Union.

__Burroughs, Esther.__ A Garden Path to Mentoring: Planting Your Life in Another & Releasing the Fragrance of Christ. LC 97-178225. 136p. 1997. pap. text 12.95 (*1-56309-197-6*, N974101, New Hope) Womans Mission Union.

— Splash the Living Water. LC 98-53422. 192p. 1999. pap. 12.99 (*0-7852-6958-4*) Nelson.

__Burroughs, Eugene B.__ Investment Policy Guidebook for Trustees. 3rd ed. Brzezinski, Mary Jo, ed. LC 94-79003. 225p. 1995. pap. 29.00 (*0-89154-485-2*) Intl Found Employ.

*__Burroughs, Eugene B.__ The Multiemployer 401(K)/DC Plan Guide. LC 99-65787. 211p. 1999. pap. 33.00 (*0-89154-536-0*) Intl Found Employ.

__Burroughs, Eugene B., ed.__ Trustees & Their Professional Advisors. LC 96-76848. 205p. 1996. pap. 33.00 (*0-89154-502-6*) Intl Found Employ.

__Burroughs, Franklin.__ Billy Watson's Croker Sack. LC 97-34307. 1998. pap. 15.95 (*0-8203-1999-6*) U of Ga Pr.

— The River Home: A Return to the Carolina Low Country. LC 97-30908. 1998. pap. 15.95 (*0-8203-1998-8*) U of Ga Pr.

__Burroughs, H. E., jt. auth. see Hansen, Shirley J.__

__Burroughs, J.__ John Burroughs' America. (American Naturalists Ser.). (Illus.). 304p. (J). 1960. 18.95 (*0-8159-5109-4*) Devin.

— John Burroughs' America. (American Naturalists Ser.). (Illus.). 304p. (J). 1965. pap. 9.95 (*0-8159-5114-0*) Devin.

__Burroughs, Jean M.__ Bride of the Santa Fe Trail: A Novel. LC 83-18051. 160p. (Orig.). 1984. pap. 9.95 (*0-86534-042-0*) Sunstone Pr.

__Burroughs, Jeff.__ Jeff Burroughs' Little League Instructional Guide. LC 94-70386. (Illus.). 157p. 1994. pap. 12.95 (*1-56625-009-9*) Bonus Books.

__Burroughs, Jeff, jt. auth. see Hennessy, Tom.__

*__Burroughs, Jeremiah.__ El Contentamiento Cristiano... Una Joya Rara: Aprendiendo a Estar Contentos. abr. ed. Appleby, H. J., ed. Montgomery, Thomas & Negrete, Omar Ibanez, trs. Orig. Title: The Rare Jewel of Christian Contentment. (SPA.). 50p. 1999. pap. 1.19 (*1-928980-07-4*) Pub Faro.

__Burroughs, Jeremiah.__ The Evil of Evils. Kistler, Don, ed. 345p. 1992. reprint ed. 22.95 (*1-877611-48-4*) Soli Deo Gloria.

— The Excellency of a Gracious Spirit. Kistler, Don, ed. 259p. 1996. 24.95 (*1-57358-024-4*) Soli Deo Gloria.

— Gospel Conversation. Kistler, Don, ed. 305p. 1995. 24.95 (*1-877611-91-3*) Soli Deo Gloria.

— Gospel Fear. Kistler, Don, ed. 166p. 1991. 18.95 (*1-877611-31-X*) Soli Deo Gloria.

— Gospel Reconciliation. Kistler, Don, ed. 379p. 1997. 29.95 (*1-57358-042-2*) Soli Deo Gloria.

— Gospel Remission. Kistler, Don, ed. LC 97-104427. 310p. 1995. 26.95 (*1-57358-014-7*) Soli Deo Gloria.

— Gospel Worship. 398p. 1990. 24.95 (*1-877611-12-3*) Soli Deo Gloria.

— Irenicum: Healing the Divisions among God's People. Kistler, Don, ed. 440p. 1997. 29.95 (*1-57358-058-9*) Soli Deo Gloria.

— Learning to Be Happy. 1988. pap. 4.99 (*0-946462-16-X*, Pub. by Evangelical Pr) P & R Pubng.

— The Rare Jewel of Christian Contentment. 1979. pap. 8.50 (*0-85151-091-4*) Banner of Truth.

— The Saints' Happiness: Sermons on the Beatitudes. 264p. 1988. reprint ed. 26.95 (*1-877611-00-X*) Soli Deo Gloria.

— A Treatise of Earthly-Mindedness. rev. ed. Kistler, Don, ed. 219p. 1991. reprint ed. 18.95 (*1-877611-38-7*) Soli Deo Gloria.

__Burroughs, John.__ Accepting the Universe. Lugg, George W., ed. LC 86-31430. 224p. 1987. 15.50 (*0-935834-58-3*) Rainbow Books.

— Bird & Bough. (Works of John Burroughs). 1989. reprint ed. lib. bdg. 79.00 (*0-7812-2193-5*) Rprt Serv.

— Birds & Poets. (Works of John Burroughs). 1989. reprint ed. lib. bdg. 79.00 (*0-7812-2180-3*) Rprt Serv.

— Birds of John Burroughs: A Great Naturalist's Meditations & Essays on Bird Watching. (Illus.). 240p. 1989. pap. 13.95 (*0-87951-312-8*, Pub. by Overlook Pr) Penguin Putnam.

— The Birds of John Burroughs: A Great Naturalist's Meditations & Essays on Bird Watching. LC 87-42888. (Illus.). 240p. 1987. reprint ed. 23.95 (*0-87951-301-2*, Pub. by Overlook Pr) Penguin Putnam.

— The Breath of Life. (Works of John Burroughs). 1989. reprint ed. lib. bdg. 79.00 (*0-7812-2198-6*) Rprt Serv.

— Camping & Tramping with Roosevelt. LC 71-125733. (American Environmental Studies). 1974. reprint ed. 16.95 (*0-405-02658-7*) Ayer.

— Camping & Tramping with Roosevelt. (Works of John Burroughs). 1989. reprint ed. lib. bdg. 79.00 (*0-7812-2194-3*) Rprt Serv.

— Far & Near. (Works of John Burroughs). 1989. reprint ed. lib. bdg. 79.00 (*0-7812-2191-9*) Rprt Serv.

— Field & Study. (Works of John Burroughs). 1989. reprint ed. lib. bdg. 79.00 (*0-7812-2200-1*) Rprt Serv.

— Fresh Fields. (Works of John Burroughs). 1989. reprint ed. lib. bdg. 79.00 (*0-7812-2183-8*) Rprt Serv.

— The Gospel of Nature. 43p. 1990. pap. 5.95 (*1-55709-131-5*) Applewood.

— The Heart of Burrough's Journal. (Works of John Burroughs). 1989. reprint ed. lib. bdg. 79.00 (*0-7812-2202-8*) Rprt Serv.

— In the Catskills. 250p. (Orig.). 1993. reprint ed. lib. bdg. 79.00 (*0-7812-5117-6*) Rprt Serv.

— In the Catskills. rev. ed. (Illus.). 251p. (Orig.). (C). 1988. reprint ed. pap. 12.50 (*0-945677-04-9*) Riverby Bks.

— In the Catskills: Selections from the Writings of John Burroughs. LC 90-45588. (Illus.). 263p. 1990. reprint ed. 34.95 (*0-87797-184-6*) Cherokee.

— Indoor Studies. (Works of John Burroughs). 1989. reprint ed. lib. bdg. 79.00 (*0-7812-2185-4*) Rprt Serv.

— John James Audubon. LC 86-12810. 176p. 1987. 22.95 (*0-87951-259-8*, Pub. by Overlook Pr) Penguin Putnam.

— Leaf & Tendril. (Works of John Burroughs). 1989. reprint ed. lib. bdg. 79.00 (*0-7812-2195-1*) Rprt Serv.

— The Legality of Threat or Use of Nuclear Weapons: A Guide to the Historic Opinion of the International Court of Justice. 169p. 1998. pap. 24.95 (*3-8258-3516-2*) Transaction Pubs.

— Literary Values. (Works of John Burroughs). 1989. reprint ed. lib. bdg. 79.00 (*0-7812-2190-0*) Rprt Serv.

— Literary Values, & Other Papers. LC 76-156624. (Essay Index Reprint Ser.). 1977. reprint ed. 21.95 (*0-8369-2347-2*) Ayer.

— Locusts & Wild Honey. (Works of John Burroughs). 1989. reprint ed. lib. bdg. 79.00 (*0-7812-2181-1*) Rprt Serv.

— My Boyhood. (Works of John Burroughs). 1989. reprint ed. lib. bdg. 79.00 (*0-7812-2201-X*) Rprt Serv.

— Notes on Walt Whitman As Poet & Person. LC 68-24932. (Studies in Whitman: No. 28). 1969. reprint ed. lib. bdg. 75.00 (*0-8383-0922-4*) M S G Haskell Hse.

— Notes on Walt Whitman As Poet & Person. (Works of John Burroughs). 1989. reprint ed. lib. bdg. 79.00 (*0-7812-2177-3*) Rprt Serv.

— Pepacton. (Works of John Burroughs). 1989. reprint ed. lib. bdg. 79.00 (*0-7812-2182-X*) Rprt Serv.

— Riverby. (Works of John Burroughs). 1989. reprint ed. lib. bdg. 79.00 (*0-7812-2186-2*) Rprt Serv.

— Signs & Seasons. (Works of John Burroughs). 1989. reprint ed. lib. bdg. 79.00 (*0-7812-2184-6*) Rprt Serv.

— Squirrels & Other Fur Bearers. (Works of John Burroughs). 1989. reprint ed. lib. bdg. 79.00 (*0-7812-2188-9*) Rprt Serv.

— The Summit of the Years. (Works of John Burroughs). 1989. reprint ed. lib. bdg. 79.00 (*0-7812-2197-8*) Rprt Serv.

— Time & Change. (Works of John Burroughs). 1989. reprint ed. lib. bdg. 79.00 (*0-7812-2196-X*) Rprt Serv.

— Under the Apple Trees. (Works of John Burroughs). 1989. reprint ed. lib. bdg. 79.00 (*0-7812-2199-4*) Rprt Serv.

— Wake Robin. (Works of John Burroughs). 1989. reprint ed. lib. bdg. 79.00 (*0-7812-2178-1*) Rprt Serv.

— Ways of Nature. LC 77-157963. (Essay Index Reprint Ser.). 1977. reprint ed. 21.95 (*0-8369-2217-4*) Ayer.

— Ways of Nature. (Works of John Burroughs). 1989. reprint ed. lib. bdg. 79.00 (*0-7812-2192-7*) Rprt Serv.

— Whitman: A Study. LC 72-131652. 1979. reprint ed. 29.00 (*0-403-00539-6*) Scholarly.

— Whitman a Study. (Works of John Burroughs). 1989. reprint ed. lib. bdg. 79.00 (*0-7812-0010-5*) Rprt Serv.

— Winter Sunshine. (Works of John Burroughs). 1989. reprint ed. lib. bdg. 79.00 (*0-7812-2179-X*) Rprt Serv.

— The Works of John Burroughs. 1989. reprint ed. lib. bdg. 63.00 (*0-685-74129-X*) Rprt Serv.

— Writings of John Burroughs, 26 vols., Set. 1993. reprint ed. lib. bdg. 2054.00 (*0-7812-5141-9*) Rprt Serv.

__Burroughs, John, ed.__ Songs of Nature. LC 79-98077. (Granger Index Reprint Ser.). 1977. 21.95 (*0-8369-6070-X*) Ayer.

__Burroughs, John & Fleck, Richard F.__ Deep Woods. LC 97-32702. (Illus.). 240p. 1998. pap. 17.95 (*0-8156-0416-5*) Syracuse U Pr.

__Burroughs, John & Wiley, Farida A.__ John Burroughs' America: Selections from the Writings of the Naturalist. LC 96-44551. (Illus.). 320p. 1997. reprint ed. pap. text 8.95 (*0-486-29746-2*) Dover.

__Burroughs, Jon & Daniell, Gene S., eds.__ Hiking Guide to Mount Washington & the Presidential Range. 5th ed. LC 92-7552. (Trail Guide Ser.). (Illus.). 192p. 1998. pap. 14.95 (*1-878239-13-9*) AMC Books.

__Burroughs, Jon, jt. auth. see Daniell, Gene.__

__Burroughs, Jon, jt. ed. see Daniel, Eugene S., III.__

__Burroughs, Jon, jt. ed. see Daniell, Gene.__

__Burroughs, Juli, ed. see Wathen, Douglas L.__

__Burroughs, Julian.__ Hudson River Memories. (Illus.). 106p. (Orig.). (C). 1988. pap. 12.50 (*0-945677-02-2*) Riverby Bks.

__Burroughs, Lea.__ Introducing Children to the Arts: A Practical Guide for Children's Librarians & Educators. 356p. (C). 1988. 45.00 (*0-8161-8818-1*, Hall Reference) Macmillan.

__Burroughs, Margaret T., ed. see Allen, Ana M.__

__Burroughs, Miggs, ed. see Burroughs, Barkham.__

An Asterisk (*) at the beginning of an entry indicates that the title is appearing for the first time.

Burroughs, Nigel. Nature's Chicken: The Story of Today's Chicken Farms. LC 92-13799. (Illus.). 32p. (J). (gr. 2 up). 1992. pap. 5.95 (*0-913990-92-2*) Book Pub Co.

Burroughs, Peter, et al, eds. Managing the Business of Empire: Essays in Honour of David Fieldhouse. LC 98-7267. 272p. 1998. 45.00 (*0-7146-4826-4*, Pub. by F Cass Pubs) Intl Spec Bk.

Burroughs, Polly. Guide to Martha's Vineyard. 6th ed. (Illus.). 210p. 1998. pap. text 10.00 (*0-7881-5260-2*) DIANE Pub.

— Guide to Martha's Vineyard. 8th ed. LC 98-48364. (Illus.). 224p. 1999. pap. text 12.95 (*0-7627-0432-2*) Globe Pequot.

— Guide to Nantucket. 8th ed. LC 98-32211. (Illus.). 224p. (Orig.). 1999. pap. text 12.95 (*0-7627-0412-8*) Globe Pequot.

Burroughs, Raymond D., ed. The Natural History of the Lewis & Clark Expedition. 1995. pap. 19.95 (*0-87013-389-6*) Mich St U Pr.

***Burroughs-Saha, Laura.** Out of the Ashes, Into the Wind. 2001. pap. 8.00 (*0-8059-5029-X*) Dorrance.

Burroughs, Sue & Evans, Roy, eds. Play, Language & Socialization. (Special Aspects of Education Ser.: Vol. 8). vi, 264p. 1986. text 137.00 (*0-677-21510-X*); pap. text 36.00 (*0-677-21500-2*) Gordon & Breach.

Burroughs, Tony. The Intenders, Vol. 1. LC 96-86317. (Illus.). 224p. (Orig.). 1996. pap. 13.95 (*0-9654288-0-X*) Dolphin Pr.

— The Intenders Handbook: A Guide to the Intention Process & the Conscious Community. 2nd rev. ed. 55p. 1998. mass mkt. 4.00 (*0-9654288-1-8*) Dolphin Pr.

***Burroughs, Tony.** The Intenders of the Highest Good. 2nd unabridged ed. LC 96-86317. 239p. 1999. mass mkt. 15.00 (*0-9654288-2-6*) Dolphin Pr.

Burroughs, W. Coll. Interviews of Wm. SB. 1997. pap. 14.00 (*0-936756-48-9*) Autonomedia.

Burroughs, W. Jeffrey, jt. auth. see Spickard, Paul R.

Burroughs, W. Jeffrey, jt. ed. see Spickard, Paul R.

***Burroughs, William.** Burroughs Live: Collected Interviews. Lotringer, Sylvere, ed. (Double Agents Ser.). 650p. 2000. pap. 29.95 (*1-58435-010-5*, Pub. by Semiotexte) MIT Pr.

***Burroughs, William J.** The Climate Revealed. (Illus.). 192p. 1999. 39.95 (*0-521-77081-5*) Cambridge U Pr.

Burroughs, William J. The Last Words of Dutch Schultz: Fiction in the Form of a Film Script. (Illus.). 128p. 1993. reprint ed. pap. 10.45 (*1-55970-211-7*, Pub. by Arcade Pub Inc) Time Warner.

— Watching the World's Weather. (Illus.). 208p. (C). 1991. 29.95 (*0-521-34342-9*) Cambridge U Pr.

— Weather Cycles: Real or Imaginary? (Illus.). 221p. (C). 1995. pap. text 22.95 (*0-521-47869-3*) Cambridge U Pr.

***Burroughs, William J., et al.** Weather. (Nature Company Guides Ser.). (Illus.). 288p. 2000. pap. write for info. (*0-7370-0080-5*) Time-Life Educ.

***Burroughs, William James.** Climate Change: A Multidisciplinary Approach. (Illus.). 320p. (C). 2001. Price not set. (*0-521-56125-6*); pap. Price not set. (*0-521-56771-8*) Cambridge U Pr.

Burroughs, William S. The Adding Machine: Collected Essays. 201p. 1986. 16.95 (*0-8050-0000-3*) Seaver Bks.

— The Adding Machine: Selected Essays. LC 92-46690. 216p. (C). 1993. reprint ed. pap. 12.45 (*1-55970-210-9*, Pub. by Arcade Pub Inc) Time Warner.

— Blade Runner: A Movie. LC 78-21584. 1979. pap. 8.95 (*0-912652-46-2*) Blue Wind.

— Burroughs: Letters. 1999. 24.95 (*0-670-81349-4*) Viking Penguin.

— The Burroughs File. 1984. pap. 12.95 (*0-87286-152-X*) City Lights.

— Cities of the Red Night. 352p. 1995. pap. 11.00 (*0-8050-3955-4*) H Holt & Co.

— Collected Interviews of William S. Burroughs. 320p. Date not set. 14.00 (*0-614-14965-7*) Autonomedia.

— Does the Weather Really Matter? The Social Implications of Climate Change. LC 97-492. (Illus.). 242p. (C). 1997. 24.95 (*0-521-56126-4*) Cambridge U Pr.

— Evil River. 2001. 19.95 (*0-670-81351-6*) Viking Penguin.

— The Exterminator. (Fiction Ser.). 176p. 1979. pap. 11.95 (*0-14-005003-5*, Penguin Bks) Viking Penguin.

— Ghost of Chance. LC 95-68012. (High Risk Ser.). (Illus.). 96p. 1995. 14.99 (*1-85242-406-0*, High Risk Bks) Serpents Tail.

— Helnwein: Faces. 1994. 50.00 (*3-7231-0427-4*, Pub. by Edit Stemmle) Dist Art Pubs.

— Interzone. 224p. 1990. pap. 12.95 (*0-14-009451-2*, Penguin Bks) Viking Penguin.

— The Job: Interviews with William S. Burroughs. 224p. 1989. pap. 13.95 (*0-14-011882-9*, Penguin Bks) Viking Penguin.

— Junky. (Fiction Ser.). 176p. 1977. pap. 11.95 (*0-14-004351-9*, Penguin Bks) Viking Penguin.

— Junky. 1994. reprint ed. lib. bdg. 29.95 (*1-56849-537-4*) Buccaneer Bks.

***Burroughs, William S.** Last Words: The Final Journals of William S. Burroughs. Grauerholz, James, ed. LC 99-44259. 320p. 2000. 25.00 (*0-8021-1657-4*, Pub. by Grove-Atltic) Publishers Group.

Burroughs, William S. Letters. 1993. pap. 25.00 (*0-670-77285-2*) Viking Penguin.

— Live Performance, Vol. 1. Hoffman, Kathelin, ed. (Illus.). (C). 12.95 incl. audio (*0-929856-00-7*) Caravan Dreams Prodns.

— Mountain Weather: A Guide for Skiers & Hillwalkers. (Illus.). 111p. 1996. pap. 24.95 (*1-85223-877-1*, Pub. by Crolwood) Trafalgar.

— My Education: A Book of Dreams. 208p. 1996. pap. 11.95 (*0-14-009454-7*, Penguin Bks) Viking Penguin.

— Naked Lunch. LC 91-22972. 288p. 1992. pap. 11.95 (*0-8021-3295-2*, Grove) Grove-Atltic.

— Naked Lunch. 1994. reprint ed. lib. bdg. 29.95 (*1-56849-538-2*) Buccaneer Bks.

— Nova Express. LC 92-18339. 192p. 1992. pap. 12.00 (*0-8021-3330-4*, Grove) Grove-Atltic.

— The Place of Dead Roads. 320p. 1995. pap. 12.00 (*0-8050-3954-6*) H Holt & Co.

— The Place of Dead Roads. 1994. reprint ed. lib. bdg. 29.95 (*1-56849-539-0*) Buccaneer Bks.

— Port of Saints. LC 80-10309. 1980. 49.95 (*0-912652-64-0*); pap. 14.95 (*0-912652-65-9*) Blue Wind.

— Queer. 144p. 1987. pap. 11.95 (*0-14-008389-8*, Penguin Bks) Viking Penguin.

— The Soft Machine. LC 92-18811. 184p. 1992. pap. 12.00 (*0-8021-3329-0*, Grove) Grove-Atltic.

Burroughs, William S., Jr. Speed & Kentucky Ham: Two Novels. 384p. 1993. pap. 14.95 (*0-87951-505-8*, Pub. by Overlook Pr) Penguin Putnam.

Burroughs, William S. The Ticket That Exploded. LC 86-33486. 224p. 1971. pap. 12.00 (*0-8021-5150-7*, Grove) Grove-Atltic.

— Uncommon Quotes, Vol. 1. Hoffman, Kathelin, ed. (Illus.). (C). 1989. audio. write for info. (*0-318-63927-0*) Caravan Dreams Prodns.

— The Western Lands. 272p. 1988. pap. 12.95 (*0-14-009456-3*, Penguin Bks) Viking Penguin.

— The Wild Boys: A Book of the Dead. LC 92-19273. 192p. 1992. pap. 11.00 (*0-8021-3331-2*, Grove) Grove-Atltic.

— Word Virus: The William S. Burroughs Reader. Grauerholz, James & Silverberg, Ira, eds. LC 97-48269. 576p. 1999. 27.50 (*0-8021-1629-9*) Grove-Atltic.

***Burroughs, William S.** Word Virus: The William S. Burroughs Reader. Grauerholz, James & Silverberg, Ira, eds. 576p. 2000. pap. 15.00 (*0-8021-3694-X*, Pub. by Grove-Atltic) Publishers Group.

Burroughs, William S., ed. Granta 52. 224p. 1996. pap. 11.95 (*0-14-014113-8*, Penguin Bks) Viking Penguin.

Burroughs, William S., text. George Condo: Recent Paintings. LC 94-60551. (Illus.). 42p. (Orig.). 1994. pap. write for info. (*1-878283-45-6*) PaceWildenstein.

Burroughs, William S. & Ginsberg, Allen. The Yage Letters. LC 63-12222. (Orig.). 1963. pap. 8.95 (*0-87286-004-3*) City Lights.

Burroughs, William S. & Odier, Daniel. The Job. LC 85-172199. 224 p. 1984. write for info. (*0-7145-4028-5*) M Boyars Pubs.

Burroughs, William S., et al. The Starry Wisdom: A Tribute to H. P. Lovecraft. Mitchell, D. M., ed. (Illus.). 192p. (Orig.). 1996. pap. 15.95 (*1-871592-32-1*) Creation Books.

Burroughs, William S., jt. auth. see Odier, Daniel.

Burrow. Marketing Foundations & Functions. (Marketing Education Ser.). 1994. pap. 5.95 (*0-538-62549-X*) S-W Pub.

Burrow, et al. Thyroid Function & Disease. (Illus.). 352p. 1989. text 105.00 (*0-7216-2190-2*, W B Saunders Co) Harcrt Hlth Sci Grp.

Burrow, Barbara. Christmas Time at Santa's Workshop. (Pop-Up Bks.). (J). 1989. 8.95 (*0-8167-1442-8*) Troll Communs.

Burrow, Colin. Edmund Spenser. (Writers & Their Work Ser.). 95p. (Orig.). 1996. pap. text 17.00 (*0-7463-0750-0*, Pub. by Northcote House) U Pr of Miss.

— Epic Romance: Homer to Milton. LC 92-45882. 336p. (C). 1993. text 59.00 (*0-19-811794-9*, Clarendon Pr) OUP.

Burrow, David. The Camp Counselor's Handbook of over Ninety Games & Activities Just for Rainy Days. 2nd ed. 52p. (Orig.). (C). 1992. pap. 5.95 (*0-9622191-2-6*) McElroy Pub.

— Mastering Leadership in the Christian Camp. (Illus.). 166p. (Orig.). 1996. pap. 14.95 (*0-9622191-6-9*) McElroy Pub.

Burrow, Dee. Sequential Strategies for Math. (Primary Level Ser.). 336p. 1995. pap. text, teacher ed. 55.00 (*0-9641654-1-4*) G W Teal.

Burrow, Gerard N. & Duffy, Thomas P. Medical Complications During Pregnancy. 5th ed. Kersey, Ray, ed. LC 98-38029. (Illus.). viii, 532p. (C). 1999. text. write for info. (*0-7216-7508-5*, W B Saunders Co) Harcrt Hlth Sci Grp.

Burrow, Gerard N. & Dussault, Jean H., eds. Neonatal Thyroid Screening. LC 79-5320. 332p. 1980. reprint ed. pap. 103.00 (*0-608-00382-4*, 206109600007) Bks Demand.

Burrow, Gerard N. & Ferris, Thomas F., eds. Medical Complications During Pregnancy. 4th ed. LC 94-25450. (Illus.). 633p. 1994. text 87.00 (*0-7216-5150-X*, W B Saunders Co) Harcrt Hlth Sci Grp.

Burrow, Gerard N., jt. ed. see Eggo, Margaret C.

Burrow, Giles, jt. auth. see IPM Information Services Staff.

Burrow, J. A. Essays on Medieval Literature. (Illus.). 224p. (C). 1984. text 59.00 (*0-19-811187-8*) OUP.

— Langland's Fictions. LC 92-26820. (Illus.). 144p. 1993. 39.95 (*0-19-811293-9*, Clarendon Pr) OUP.

— Medieval Writers & Their Work: Middle English Literature, 1100-1500. 158p. (C). 1982. pap. text 20.95 (*0-19-289122-7*) OUP.

— Thomas Hoccleve. (Authors of the Middle Ages Ser.: No. 4). 64p. 1994. pap. 18.95 (*0-86078-419-3*, Pub. by Variorum) Ashgate Pub Co.

Burrow, J. A., ed. Sir Gawain & the Green Knight. Stone, Brian, tr. (Classics Ser.). 176p. 1987. pap. 9.95 (*0-14-042295-1*, Penguin Bks) Viking Penguin.

Burrow, J. A., intro. Middle English Literature: British Academy Gollancz Lectures. 262p. 1990. pap. text 29.95 (*0-19-726085-3*) OUP.

Burrow, J. A. & Turville-Petre, Thorlac. A Book of Middle English. (Illus.). 384p. (C). 1996. pap. 30.95 (*0-631-19353-7*) Blackwell Pubs.

Burrow, J. A., ed. see Hoccleve, Thomas.

***Burrow, J. W.** Crisis of Reason: European Thought, 1848-1914. LC 99-59165. (Intellectual History of the West Ser.). (Illus.). 288p. 2000. 29.95 (*0-300-08390-4*) Yale U Pr.

Burrow, J. W., ed. see Darwin, Charles.

Burrow, J. W., ed. see von Humboldt, Wilhelm.

Burrow, James G. Organized Medicine in the Progressive Era: The Move Towards Monopoly. LC 77-894. 232p. reprint ed. pap. 72.00 (*0-608-14681-1*, 202584000046) Bks Demand.

Burrow, James L. Business Principles & Management. 10th ed. (GB - Basic Business Ser.). 1995. 4.95 (*0-538-62469-8*); student ed. 16.95 (*0-538-62468-X*) S-W Pub.

— Business Principles & Management. 10th ed. (GB - Basic Business Ser.). 1995. mass mkt. 185.95 (*0-538-62779-4*) S-W Pub.

— Business Principles & Management. 10th ed. (GB - Basic Business Ser.). 1996. text, suppl. ed. 185.95 (*0-538-62780-8*) S-W Pub.

— Marketing Foundations & Functions. (SB - Marketing Education Ser.). 1994. mass mkt. 59.95 (*0-538-62541-4*); mass mkt. 10.95 (*0-538-62545-7*); mass mkt., wbk. ed. 13.95 (*0-538-62542-2*); mass mkt., wbk. ed. 10.95 (*0-538-62548-1*) S-W Pub.

Burrow, Jim, jt. auth. see Everard, Kenneth E.

Burrow, John. Vegetable Gardening: Spring & Fall. Billac, Pete, ed. LC 95-70123. (Illus.). 128p. (Orig.). 1995. pap. 9.95 (*0-943629-17-9*) Swan Pub.

— Your Front Yard. 136p. 1994. per. 9.95 (*0-943629-12-8*) Swan Pub.

***Burrow, John & Wei, Ian P., eds.** Medieval Futures. LC 00-20945. 224p. 2000. 90.00 (*0-85115-779-3*) Boydell & Brewer.

Burrow, John W. Whigs & Liberals: Continuity & Change in English Political Thought. (Illus.). 176p. 1988. text 49.95 (*0-19-820139-7*) OUP.

Burrow, Kelli J., ed. see Burrow, Tim J.

Burrow, Martha G. Women: A Worldwide View of Their Management Development Needs. LC 76-10796. 31p. reprint ed. pap. 30.00 (*0-608-10862-6*, 205152500091) Bks Demand.

Burrow, Martin. Representation Theory of Finite Groups. LC 92-39061. viii, 184p. 1993. reprint ed. pap. 6.95 (*0-486-67487-8*) Dover.

Burrow, N. Trigant. The Determination of the Position of a Momentary Impression. Colvin, Stephen S., ed. (Of Psychol. Monos.: Vol. 11). 1909. 55.00 (*0-8115-1410-2*) Periodicals Srv.

Burrow, Rufus, Jr. James H. Cone & Black Liberation Theology. LC 93-41759. 278p. 1994. lib. bdg. 38.50 (*0-89950-900-2*) McFarland & Co.

***Burrow, Rufus, Jr.** Personalism: A Critical Introduction. LC 99-43444. 1999. 29.99 (*0-8272-2955-0*) Chalice Pr.

Burrow, Ruth. Fire upon the Earth. 1998. pap. 14.95 (*0-87193-270-9*) Dimension Bks.

Burrow, Thomas & Emeneau, M. B. A Dravidian Etymological Dictionary. 1998. 98.00 (*81-215-0856-8*, Pub. by M Manoharial) Coronet Bks.

Burrow, Thomas & Emeneau, Murray B., eds. A Dravidian Etymological Dictionary. 2nd ed. 1984. 85.00 (*0-19-864326-8*) OUP.

Burrow, Thomas, jt. auth. see Emeneau, Murray B.

Burrow, Tim J. Wild Fish Gourmet Style, Vol. 1. 60p. 1996. pap. text 9.95 (*0-9641654-3-0*) G W Teal.

— Wild Game Gourmet Style. Burrow, Kelli J., ed. (Illus.). (Orig.). 1992. pap. 9.95 (*0-9641654-0-6*) G W Teal.

Burrow, Trigant. The Biology of Human Conflict: An Anatomy of Behavior, Individual & Social. LC 73-14149. (Perspectives in Social Inquiry Ser.). 510p. 1974. reprint ed. 33.95 (*0-405-05495-5*) Ayer.

— A Search for Man's Sanity. Grob, Gerald N., ed. LC 78-22553. (Historical Issues in Mental Health Ser.). 1980. reprint ed. lib. bdg. 50.95 (*0-405-11907-0*) Ayer.

Burroway, Janet. Cutting Stone. 480p. 1993. mass mkt. 4.50 (*1-55817-757-4*, Pinncle Kensgtn) Kensgtn Pub Corp.

— Material Goods. LC 80-12381. 77p. 1980. pap. 16.95 (*0-8130-0670-8*) U Press Fla.

— Writing Fiction: A Guide to Narrative Craft. 2nd ed. LC 86-15217. 396 p. 1987. write for info. (*0-316-11770-6*) Little.

Burroway, Janet, jt. auth. see Lord, John V.

Burrowes. Play Electric Guitar. 1999. text 22.95 (*0-312-24417-7*) St Martin.

***Burrowes, Adjoa J.** Grandma's Purple Flowers. 2000. 15.95 (*1-880000-73-3*) Lee & Low Bks.

Burrowes, Reynold A. Revolution & Rescue in Grenada: An Account of the U. S.-Caribbean Invasion, 203. LC 87-23704. (Contributions in Political Science Ser.: No. 203). 194p. 1988. 37.95 (*0-313-26066-4*, BWV/, Greenwood Pr) Greenwood.

— The Wild Coast: An Account of Politics in West Indies. 350p. 1984. pap. 16.95 (*0-87073-127-0*); text 22.95 (*0-87073-037-1*) Schenkman Bks Inc.

Burrowes, Robert. Essay on the Stile of Doctor Samuel Johnson 1 & 2: From "The Transactions of the Royal Irish Academy" LC 92-22684. (Augustan Reprints Ser.: No. 229). 1992. reprint ed. 14.50 (*0-404-70229-5*, PR3538) AMS Pr.

Burrowes, Robert D. Historical Dictionary of Yemen. LC 94-46534. (Asian Historical Dictionaries Ser.: No. 17). (Illus.). 528p. 1995. 87.50 (*0-8108-2987-8*) Scarecrow.

Burrowes, Robert J. The Strategy of Nonviolent Defense: A Gandhian Approach. LC 95-2223. 367p. (C). 1995. text 49.50 (*0-7914-2587-8*); pap. text 16.95 (*0-7914-2588-6*) State U NY Pr.

Burrowes, Wesley. The Becauseway. (New Abbey Theatre Ser.). 1983. pap. 2.95 (*0-912262-74-5*) Proscenium.

Burrows. Encyclopedia of the Guitar. 1998. 75.00 (*0-02-865028-X*) Macmillan Gen Ref.

— European Social Law. xxxii, 451p. 1996. pap. text 51.95 (*0-471-96537-5*) Wiley.

— Intro Engineering Workbook. 8th ed. 1999. pap., wbk. ed. 21.50 (*0-07-236904-3*) McGraw.

Burrows. Pregnancy at Work. 54.95 (*1-85521-030-4*) Ashgate Pub Co.

Burrows, et al. Electronics. 1986. write for info. (*0-409-10252-0*) Buttrwrth-Heinemann.

Burrows, A. Essays on the Law of Restitution. 344p. 1991. 79.00 (*0-19-825434-2*) OUP.

Burrows, Andersen, tr. see Muller, S.

***Burrows, Andrew.** Cases & Materials on the Law of Restitution. 976p. 1998. pap. text 54.00 (*0-19-876291-7*) OUP.

Burrows, Andrew. Understanding the Law of Obligations. 224p. 1998. 60.00 (*1-901362-38-8*, Pub. by Hart Pub) Northwestern U Pr.

Burrows, Andrew & McKendrick, Ewan, eds. Cases & Materials on the Law of Restitution. LC 96-53050. 976p. 1998. text 105.00 (*0-19-876290-9*) OUP.

Burrows, Anne, et al. Kith & Kin: Sources for Family History. 2nd rev. ed. (Illus.). 1994. pap. 12.00 (*0-7243-0200-X*) Libs So Aus.

Burrows, Arthur A. Grammar Exercises Part One: Elementary-Intermediate ESL. 2nd rev. ed. Clark, Raymond C., ed. (Interplay ESL Ser.). (Illus.). 256p. (Orig.). 1992. pap. text 12.50 (*0-86647-050-6*) Pro Lingua.

Burrows, Arthur A., ed. see Fantini, Alvino E. & Enriquez, Cristina.

Burrows, Arthur A., ed. see Fuchs, Marjorie S., et al.

Burrows, Arthur A., ed. see Hawkinson, Annie & Clark, Raymond C.

Burrows, Arthur A., ed. see Hawkinson, Annie & Moran, Patrick R.

Burrows, Clifford Robert & Edge, K. A., eds. Innovations in Fluid Power: Seventh Bath International Fluid Power Workshop Held at the University of Bath, England, 21st-23rd September 1994. LC 95-24046. (Fluid Power Ser.: Vol. 7). 368p. 1995. 175.00 (*0-86380-170-6*) Wiley.

Burrows, Clifford Robert, ed. see Bath International Fluid Power Workshop.

Burrows, Colin. Processes of Vegetation Change. 340p. 1990. pap. 49.95 (*0-04-580013-8*) Thomson Learn.

***Burrows, C.R. & Edge, K.A., eds.** Power Transmission & Motion Control: Proceedings Bath Workshop Bath, UK 1999. 376p. 1999. 378.00 (*1-86058-205-2*) Prof Eng Pubng.

Burrows, David. The Child Support Act 1991: A Practitioner's Guide. 1993. pap. text 42.00 (*0-406-02353-0*, UK, MICHIE) LEXIS Pub.

— Making the Most of Your Teenage Years. (YA). 1995. pap. 6.99 (*1-56229-456-3*) Pneuma Life Pub.

— A Practitioner's Guide to the Family Law Act, 1996. 170p. 1996. pap. 43.00 (*1-85811-116-1*, Pub. by CLT Prof) Gaunt.

— Sound, Speech, & Music. LC 89-4947. 152p. 1990. 22.50 (*0-87023-685-7*) U of Mass Pr.

— Strategies for Saving the Next Generation. 1995. pap. 6.99 (*1-56229-403-2*) Pneuma Life Pub.

Burrows, David, ed. Butterworths Family Law Guide. 1996. pap. write for info. (*0-406-08141-7*, BFLG, MICHIE) LEXIS Pub.

Burrows, David & Schnoebelen, Anne, eds. Pietro Cesti - (1623-1669) - Giovanni Legrenzi (1626-1690), Vol. 6. (Italian Contata in the Seventeenth Century Ser.). 1986. lib. bdg. 25.00 (*0-8240-8880-8*) Garland.

Burrows, David, jt. auth. see White, Donal L.

Burrows, David J., et al. Myths & Motifs in Literature. LC 72-90546. 448p. (Orig.). (C). 1973. pap. 16.95 (*0-02-905030-8*) Free Pr.

Burrows, David L., ed. see Gasparini, Francesco.

Burrows, Desmond, ed. Chromium: Metabolism & Toxicity. 184p. 1983. 108.00 (*0-8493-5447-1*, QP535, CRC Reprint) Franklin.

Burrows, Dick. Basic Woodworking Techniques. 128p. 10.99 (*1-57215-241-9*, JG2419) World Pubns.

Burrows, Dick, jt. auth. see Kessler, Jane.

***Burrows, Donald.** Handel. (Master Musicians Ser.). (Illus.). 504p. 2000. pap. text 19.95 (*0-19-816649-4*) OUP.

Burrows, Donald, ed. The Cambridge Companion to Handel. LC 96-50935. (Cambridge Companions to Music Ser.). (Illus.). 366p. (C). 1998. text 59.95 (*0-521-45425-5*); pap. text 19.95 (*0-521-45613-4*) Cambridge U Pr.

Burrows, Donald & Ronish, Martha J. A Catalogue of Handel's Musical Autographs. (Illus.). 372p. (C). 1994. text 165.00 (*0-19-315250-9*) OUP.

Burrows, E. G. The Birds under the Earth. 32p. 1997. pap. 7.00 (*0-937669-60-1*) Owl Creek Pr.

— Ethnology of Futuna. (BMB Ser.: No. 138). 1972. reprint ed. 40.00 (*0-527-02244-6*) Periodicals Srv.

— Ethnology of Uvea, Wallis Islands. (BMB Ser.). 1972. reprint ed. 30.00 (*0-527-02253-5*) Periodicals Srv.

— Handsigns for Rain. (Chapbook Ser.: Series 4). 32p. 1989. 5.00 (*0-933573-11-1*) Wayland Pr.

— The House of August. LC 85-7586. 67p. (Orig.). 1985. pap. 6.00 (*0-87886-126-2*, Greenfld Rev Pr) Greenfld Rev Lit.

— Kiva. LC 76-150822. 56p. 1976. 3.50 (*0-87886-077-0*, Greenfld Rev Pr) Greenfld Rev Lit.

— Native Music of the Tuamotus. (BMB Ser.: No. 109). 1974. reprint ed. 25.00 (*0-527-02215-2*) Periodicals Srv.

— Properties: A Play for Voices. (QRL Poetry Bks.: Vol. XX). 1978. 20.00 (*0-614-06366-3*) Quarterly Rev.

— Songs of Urea & Futuna. (BMB Ser.). 1974. reprint ed. 25.00 (*0-527-02291-8*) Periodicals Srv.

B

Burrows, Edmund H. & Leeds, Norman E. Neuroradiology, Vol. 1. LC 80-24709. (Illus.). 556p. 1981. reprint ed. pap. 172.40 (*0-7837-3062-4*, 204274400001) Bks Demand.

— Neuroradiology, Vol. 2. LC 80-24709. (Illus.). 378p. 1981. reprint ed. pap. 117.20 (*0-7837-3063-2*, 204274400002) Bks Demand.

Burrows, Edward E. Specimen. 144p. (Orig.). 1991. pap. 12.95 (*0-9629618-0-9*) Willowby Bks.

Burrows, Edwin G. Atoll Culture: Ethnology of Ifaluk in the Central Carolines. LC 79-110044. 355p. 1970. reprint ed. lib. bdg. 65.00 (*0-8371-4426-4*, BUAT, Greenwood Pr) Greenwood.

Burrows, Edwin G. & Wallace, Mike. Gotham: A History of New York City to 1898. LC 97-39308. (Illus.). 1416p. 1998. 60.00 (*0-19-511634-8*) OUP.

***Burrows, Edwin G. & Wallace, Mike.** Gotham: A History of New York City to 1898, 2 vols. (The History of NYC Ser.). (Illus.). 1350p. 2000. pap. 24.95 (*0-19-514049-4*) OUP.

Burrows, Elaine, ed. British Cinema Source Book. LC 95-236365. 1995. 59.95 (*0-85170-474-3*, Pub. by British Film Inst) Ind U Pr.

Burrows, Elizabeth M. Harp of Destiny. (Illus.). 180p. 1991. pap. 12.95 (*0-945946-13-9*) Cassandra Pr.

— Odyssey of the Apocalypse. 176p. 1994. 29.95 (*1-57087-091-8*) Prof Pr NC.

Burrows, Elsie M. Chlorophyta. (Seaweeds of the British Isles Ser.: Vol. 2). (Illus.). 256p. 1991. pap. 49.95 (*0-11-310002-7*, Pub. by Statnry Office) Balogh.

Burrows, Evelyn. A Feeding Place along the Narrow Way: Poems for the Young & Younger. 24p. 1999. pap. 7.00 (*0-8059-4646-2*) Dorrance.

Burrows, F. J., jt. ed. see Selkirk, D. R.

Burrows, Fredrika A., ed. see Rex, Percy F.

Burrows, G., jt. ed. see Krupinski, Jerzy.

Burrows, G. D., et al, eds. The Neurobiology of Anxiety: Handbook of Anxiety, Vol. 3. 496p. 1990. 253.25 (*0-685-54173-8*) Elsevier.

— Recent Advances in Neuropsychopharmacology: Selected Papers from the 12th Congress of the Collegium Internationale Neuro-Psychopharmacologicum Goteborg, Sweden, 22-26 June, 1980. (Advances in the Biosciences Ser.: 31). (Illus.). 401p. 1981. 87.50 (*0-08-026382-8*, Pergamon Pr) Elsevier.

Burrows, G. W. Puffer Ahoy! (C). 1987. 104.00 (*0-85174-419-2*) St Mut.

Burrows, George M. Commentaries on the Causes, Forms, Symptoms & Treatment, Moral & Medical, of Insanity. LC 75-16693. (Classics of Psychiatry Ser.). 1976. reprint ed. 59.95 (*0-405-07422-0*) Ayer.

***Burrows, George M. & Tyrl, Ronald.** Toxic Plants of North America. 1528p. 2000. 119.95 (*0-8138-2266-1*) Iowa St U Pr.

Burrows, Geraldine. Miss Thornrose & the Rake. LC 99-33907. (Romances Ser.). 1999. 24.95 (*0-7862-2043-0*, Five Star MI) Mac Lib Ref.

Burrows, Giles. No-Strike Agreements & Pendulum Arbitration. IPM Information & Advisory Services Staff, ed. 112p. (C). 1986. 38.00 (*0-85292-388-0*) St Mut.

Burrows, Giles, ed. Determining Pay: A Guide to the Issues. (C). 1990. 100.00 (*0-85292-442-9*, Pub. by IPM Hse) St Mut.

Burrows, Graham, jt. auth. see Davies, Brian.

Burrows, Graham D. & Norman, Trevor R., eds. Psychotropic Drugs: Plasma Concentration & Clinical Response. LC 80-25685. (Experimental & Clinical Psychiatry Ser.: No. 4). (Illus.). 544p. reprint ed. pap. 168.70 (*0-7837-0659-6*, 204099500019) Bks Demand.

Burrows, Graham D. & Stanley, Robb, eds. Contemporary International Hypnosis: Proceedings of the XIIIth International Congress on Hypnosis, Melbourne, Australia, August 6-12, 1994. LC 95-6640. 410p. 1995. 260.00 (*0-471-95829-8*) Wiley.

Burrows, Graham D., jt. ed. see Raphael, Beverly.

Burrows, H. Jackson & Coltart, W. D. Treatment by Manipulation. 36p. 1996. reprint ed. spiral bd. 10.50 (*0-7873-0135-3*) Hlth Research.

Burrows-Hudson, Sally, ed. Standards of Clinical Practice for Nephrology Nursing. rev. expanded ed. 107p. 1999. pap. 50.00 (*0-9653379-1-X*, Pub. by Am Nephrology) Jannetti Pubns.

Burrows, J. F. Cheshire & Fifoot's Law of Contract. 8th ed. 671p. 1992. pap. 126.00 (*0-409-78981-X*, NZ, MICHIE); boxed set 117.00 (*0-409-78968-2*, NZ, MICHIE) LEXIS Pub.

— News Media Law in New Zealand. 3rd ed. 476p. 1991. pap. 49.95 (*0-19-558208-X*, 12309) OUP.

***Burrows, Jack.** Black Sun of the Miwok. LC 99-50772. 2000. 19.95 (*0-8263-2237-9*) U of NM Pr.

Burrows, Jack. John Ringo: The Gunfighter Who Never Was. LC 87-5823. (Illus.). 242p. 1996. pap. 15.95 (*0-8165-1648-0*) U of Ariz Pr.

Burrows, John. Computation into Criticism: A Study of Jane Austen's Novels. 224p. 1987. 75.00 (*0-19-812856-8*) OUP.

Burrows, John H. The Necessity of Myth: A History of the National Negro Business League, 1900-45. LC 82-82259. 236p. (C). 1988. 25.00 (*0-9619848-0-5*) J H Burrows.

Burrows, Judith, tr. see Wenfu, Lu.

Burrows, Julie. Like an Evening Gone. large type ed. 380p. 1989. 27.99 (*0-7089-1954-5*) Ulverscroft.

— No Need for Violence. large type ed. 288p. 1989. 27.99 (*0-7089-1990-1*) Ulverscroft.

Burrows, Ken. Intercourse. 192p. 1993. pap. 9.95 (*0-9637475-4-1*) Ferrows Ent.

Burrows, Lawrence B. Growth Management: Issues, Techniques, & Policy Implications. 160p. 1978. pap. text 21.95 (*0-88285-043-1*) Transaction Pubs.

Burrows, Lila W., et al. My Child, Let Me Take the Wheel! Dealing with Depression. (Illus.). 172p. 1991. 6.95 (*0-936369-29-9*) Son-Rise Pubns.

Burrows, M. Neurobiology of an Insect Brain. (Illus.). 698p. 1996. text 125.00 (*0-19-852344-0*) OUP.

Burrows, Mark S. Jean Gerson & "De Consolatione Theologoae" (1418) The Consolation of a Biblical & Reforming Theology for a Disordered Age. (Beitrage Zur Historischen Theologie Ser.: No. 78). 300p. 1990. 97.50 (*3-16-145600-9*, Pub. by JCB Mohr) Coronet Bks.

Burrows, Maurice, et al. Management for Hospital Doctors. LC 93-37792. 336p. 1994. text 85.00 (*0-7506-0880-3*) Buttrwrth-Heinemann.

Burrows, Michael, jt. auth. see Newman, Lawrence W.

Burrows, Millart. Founders of Great Religions: Being Personal Sketches of Famous Leaders. LC 72-13272. (Essay Index Reprint Ser.). 1977. reprint ed. 25.95 (*0-8369-8148-0*) Ayer.

Burrows, Nanette B., et al. Academy Days: A History of Greenwich Academy from 1826 to 1986. LC 87-23585. (Illus.). 144p. 1987. 30.00 (*0-914659-27-8*) Phoenix Pub.

Burrows, Noreen, jt. auth. see Prechal, Sacha.

Burrows, Paul & Hitiris, Theodore. Macroeconomic Theory: A Mathematical Introduction. LC 73-2779. 224p. reprint ed. pap. 69.50 (*0-608-15785-6*, 203102300073) Bks Demand.

Burrows, R. Living in Mystery. 1990. pap. 28.00 (*0-7220-5095-X*) St Mut.

***Burrows, R.** The Tree Outside the Window. 188p. 2000. pap. 10.95 (*0-87714-560-1*) Denlingers.

Burrows, Raymond M. Symphony Themes. 295p. reprint ed. lib. bdg. 59.00 (*0-685-14863-7*) Rprt Serv.

Burrows, Richard T. Guide to Owning a Labrador Retriever: AKC Rank #1. LC 99-26498. (Illus.). 64p. 1999. 19.95 (*0-7910-5470-5*) Chelsea Hse.

— Guide to Owning a Labrador Retriever: AKC Rank #1. (Guide to Owning Ser.). (Illus.). 64p. 1995. pap. 6.95 (*0-7938-1852-4*, RE-302) TFH Pubns.

Burrows, Rita, jt. auth. see Homer, Arnold.

Burrows, Robyn. Dairies & Daydreams: The Mudgeeraba Story. 149p. (C). 1990. 45.00 (*0-7316-8226-2*, Pub. by Boolarong Pubns) St Mut.

Burrows, Roger. Images, Vol. 1. (Illus.). 100p. (Orig.). 1992. pap. 6.95 (*1-56138-109-8*) Running Pr.

— Images II, Vol. 2. (Illus.). 100p. (Orig.). 1992. pap. 6.95 (*1-56138-110-1*) Running Pr.

— Images III. (Illus.). 100p. (Orig.). 1994. pap. 6.95 (*1-56138-192-6*) Running Pr.

***Burrows, Roger.** Utlimate Coloring Experience: Designs to Stimulate Your Imagination. (Images Ser.). 2000. pap. 6.95 (*0-7624-0695-X*) Running Pr.

Burrows, Roger & Loader, Brian D., eds. Towards a Post-Fordist Welfare State? LC 93-42527. (State of Welfare Ser.). 240p. (C). 1994. pap. 25.99 (*0-415-09967-6*, B4432) Routledge.

Burrows, Roger, et al. Homelessness & Social Policy. LC 97-2330. (Illus.). 288p. (C). 1997. 80.00 (*0-415-15456-1*); pap. 25.99 (*0-415-15457-X*) Routledge.

Burrows, Roger, jt. auth. see Featherstone, Mike.

Burrows, Russell. Bernard DeVoto. LC 97-70323. (Western Writers Ser: Vol. 127). (C). 1997. pap. 4.95 (*0-88430-126-5*) Boise St U W Writ Ser.

Burrows, Russell E. & Rydholm, Fred. The Mystery Cave of Many Faces: A History of Burrows Cave, Bk. I. LC 92-80160. 240p. 1992. 22.00 (*0-9639948-3-2*) Superior Hrtland.

Burrows, Ruth. Ascent to Love: The Spiritual Teaching of St. John of the Cross. 128p. 1987. pap. 14.95 (*0-87193-258-X*) Dimension Bks.

— Before the Living God. 1979. pap. 14.95 (*0-87193-155-9*) Dimension Bks.

— Guidelines for Mystical Prayer. 1978. pap. 14.95 (*0-87193-134-6*) Dimension Bks.

— Through Him, with Him, in Him. (Illus.). 1982. pap. 14.95 (*0-87193-261-X*) Dimension Bks.

— To Believe in Jesus. 1983. pap. 14.95 (*0-87193-154-0*) Dimension Bks.

Burrows, Ruth. The Watchful Heart: Daily Reading with Ruth Burrows. Obbard, Elizabeth R., ed. 1992. pap. 8.95 (*0-87193-283-0*) Dimension Bks.

***Burrows, Simon.** French Exile Journalism & European Politics, 1792-1814. LC 00-34196. (Studies in History). 2001. write for info. (*0-86193-249-8*, Royal Historical Soc) Boydell & Brewer.

Burrows, Susan G. & Gassert, Carole A. En Camino a la Recuperaci,on: Despu,es de Cirugi,a de Corazo,n Abierto: Un Libro Educativo Para el Paciente y Su Familia. LC 92-26284. 56p. 1992. pap. 8.25 (*0-939838-33-8*) Pritchett & Hull.

— Moving Right along after Heart Surgery. large type rev. ed. Hubbard, Karen, ed. (Illus.). 56p. 1999. pap. 6.50 (*0-939838-49-4*) Pritchett & Hull.

Burrows, Susan G., jt. auth. see Gassert, Carole A.

***Burrows, Terry.** Advanced Presentations. 72p. 2000. pap. 6.95 (*0-7894-6851-4*) DK Pub Inc.

Burrows, Terry. The Complete Encyclopedia of the Guitar: The Definitive Guide to the World's Most Popular Instrument. 1999. pap. 20.00 (*0-02-865027-1*) Macmillan.

— The Complete Encyclopedia of the Guitar: The Definitive Guide to the World's Most Popular Instrument. (Illus.). 220p. 1999. pap. 20.00 (*0-02-865026-3*) Macmillan.

***Burrows, Terry.** How to Read Music. (Illus.). 128p. 1999. text 22.95 (*0-312-24159-3*) St Martin.

— Playing Guitar. LC 00-8783. (Keep It Simple Ser.). (Illus.). 352p. 2000. pap. write for info. (*0-7894-5979-5*, Pub. by DK Pub Inc) Pub Resources Inc.

— Visual History of the Twentieth Century. 1999. text 35.00 (*1-85868-688-1*, Pub. by Carlton Bks Ltd) Natl Bk Netwk.

Burrows, Thomas D. & Wood, Donald N. Video Production: Disciplines & Techniques. 7th ed. LC 97-70089. 480p. (C). 1997. text. write for info. (*0-697-32719-1*, WCB McGr Hill) McGrw-H Hghr Educ.

Burrows, Thomas D., et al. Television Production: Disciplines & Techniques. 6th ed. 464p. (C). 1994. per. write for info. (*0-697-20131-7*) Brown & Benchmark.

Burrows, Toby. The Text in the Machine: Electronic Texts in the Humanities. LC 98-49068. (Illus.). 182p. 1999. lib. bdg. 49.95 (*0-7890-0424-0*) Haworth Pr.

Burrows, Toby & Kent, Philip G., eds. Serials Management in Australia & New Zealand: Profile of Excellence. LC 93-13212. (Australian & New Zealand Journal of Serials Librarianship: Vol. 3, Nos. 3-4). (Illus.). 175p. 1993. lib. bdg. 39.95 (*1-56024-453-4*) Haworth Pr.

Burrows, Toby & Stone, Grant, eds. Comics in Australia & New Zealand: The Collections, the Collectors, the Creators. LC 94-1850. (Australian & New Zealand Serials Librarianship Ser.: Vol. 4, No. 3). (Illus.). 115p. 1994. 34.95 (*1-56024-664-2*) Haworth Pr.

***Burrows, William.** By Any Means Necessary. 2001. text (*0-374-11747-0*) FS&G.

***Burrows, William E.** The Infinite Journey: Eyewitness Accounts of NASA & the Age of Space. (Illus.). 240p. 2000. 40.00 (*1-56331-924-1*) Discovery.

Burrows, William E. This New Ocean: A History of the First Space Age. LC 98-3252. 912p. 1998. 34.95 (*0-679-44521-8*) Random.

***Burrows, William E.** This New Ocean: The Story of the First Space Age. 784p. 1999. pap. 15.95 (*0-375-75485-7*) Modern Lib NY.

***Burrows, William E. & Langford, Joseph D.** Programming Business Applications with Microsoft Visual Basic: Version 6.0. 3rd ed. LC 99-89329. 2000. write for info. (*0-07-238408-5*) McGraw.

Burrows, William E. & Langford, Joseph D. Programming Business Applications with Visual Basic. 2nd ed. LC 97-50038. 688p. 1998. pap. 56.88 (*0-07-012143-5*) McGraw.

Burrows, William E., jt. auth. see Langford, Joseph D.

Burrows, William R. New Ministries: The Global Context. LC 80-17261. 192p. (Orig.). 1980. reprint ed. pap. 59.60 (*0-7837-9818-0*, 206054700005) Bks Demand.

Burrows, William R., ed. Redemption & Dialogue: Reading "Redemptoris Missio" & "Dialogue & Proclamation" LC 94-11990. 300p. (Orig.). 1994. pap. 20.00 (*0-88344-935-8*) Orbis Bks.

Burrows, Williams. Critical Mass: The Dangerous Race for Superweapons in a Fragmenting World. 576p. 1994. 25.00 (*0-671-74895-5*) S&S Trade.

Burrup, Percy E. & Brimley, Vern, Jr. Financing Education in a Climate of Change. 4th ed. 308p. (C). 1988. pap. text 38.95 (*0-205-11159-9*, H11596) Allyn.

Burrup, Percy E., et al. Financing Education in a Climate of Change. 7th ed. LC 98-16955. 400p. 1998. 79.67 (*0-205-28783-2*) Allyn.

Burrus, Barbara H. Sharing Four Cultures: A Journey of Love. LC 97-66952. (Illus.). 224p. 1997. 24.95 (*1-57736-045-1*) Providence Hse.

Burrus, Bernie R. Administrative Law & Local Government. LC 63-63661. (Michigan Legal Publications). 139p. 1982. reprint ed. lib. bdg. 39.50 (*0-89941-170-3*, 302120) W S Hein.

— Investigation & Discovery in State Antitrust. (Michigan Legal Publications). vi, 95p. 1986. reprint ed. lib. bdg. 38.50 (*0-89941-486-9*, 304130) W S Hein.

Burrus, C. S. & Parks, Thomas W. DFT/FFT & Convolution Algorithms & Implementation. LC 84-18808. (Topics in Digital Signal Processing Ser.). 256p. 1985. 98.00 (*0-471-81932-8*) Wiley.

— Digital Filter Design. LC 86-32500. (Topics in Digital Signal Processing Ser.). 368p. 1987. 120.00 (*0-471-82896-3*) Wiley.

Burrus, C. S., et al. An Introduction to Wavelets & Wavelet: A Primer. LC 96-53263. 268p. 1997. pap. 54.00 (*0-13-489600-9*) P-H.

Burrus, C. S., ed. see Tolimieri, Richard, et al.

Burrus, Christina. The Art Collectors of Russia: Private Treasures Revealed. (Illus.). 256p. 1994. 69.00 (*1-85043-740-8*, Pub. by I B T) St Martin.

Burrus, Dan & Thomsen, Patti. Advances in Agriculture: A User Friendly Guide to the Latest Technology. 73p. (Orig.). 1991. pap. 9.95 (*1-880136-53-8*) Intl Mgmt Pubns.

— Environmental Solutions: A User Friendly Guide to the Latest Technology. 71p. (Orig.). 1991. pap. 10.95 (*1-880136-51-1*) Intl Mgmt Pubns.

— Medical Advances: A User Friendly Guide to the Latest Technology. 131p. (Orig.). 1991. pap. 12.95 (*1-880136-52-X*) Intl Mgmt Pubns.

— The New Tools of Technology: A User Friendly Guide to the Latest Technology. 187p. (Orig.). 1991. pap. 19.95 (*1-880136-50-3*) Intl Mgmt Pubns.

Burrus, Daniel. Reengineering Yourself: Using Tomorrow's Success Tools to Excel Today. 1996. 16.00 incl. audio (*0-671-57293-8*, 638756) S&S Trade.

Burrus, Daniel & Gittines, Roger. Technotrends: How to Use Technology, Set. abr. ed. 1993. audio 17.00 (*1-55994-791-8*, CPN 2411, Pub. by HarperAudio) Lndmrk Audiobks.

Burrus, Daniel & Gittines, Roger. Technotrends: How You Can Go Beyond Your Competition by Applying Tomorrow's Technology Today. LC 92-56234. (Illus.). 304p. 1993. 25.00 (*0-88730-627-6*, HarpBusn) HarpInfo.

Burrus, Ernest J. Ducrue's Account of the Expulsion of the Jesuits from Lower California (1767-1769) Vol. 2. 1967. 20.00 (*88-7041-502-3*) Jesuit Hist.

Burrus, Ernest J., jt. ed. see Grajales, Gloria.

Burrus, Harry. Bouquet. deluxe ed. LC 88-63413. (Illus.). 75p. 1989. 100.00 (*0-941749-07-X*) Black Tie Pr.

— Cartouche. LC 94-22756. (Illus.). 220p. 1995. pap. 17.95 (*0-941749-33-9*) Black Tie Pr.

— For Deposit Only: Selected Poems, 1960-1975. LC 90-361. (Illus.). 186p. 1990. pap. 12.50 (*0-941749-11-8*); pap. 12.50 (*0-940719-11-8*) Black Tie Pr.

— For Deposit Only: Selected Poems, 1960-1975. limited ed. LC 90-361. (Illus.). 186p. Date not set. pap. 15.00 (*0-941749-12-6*) Black Tie Pr.

— A Game of Rules. deluxe limited ed. LC 88-63408. (Illus.). 96p. Date not set. 45.00 (*0-941749-08-8*); pap. 20.00 (*0-941749-06-1*) Black Tie Pr.

— A Game of Rules. deluxe limited ed. LC 88-63408. (Illus.). 96p. 1989. 30.00 (*0-941749-04-5*) Black Tie Pr.

— I Do Not Sleep with Strangers: Confessions of a Tennis Pro. LC 87-70301. (Illus.). 112p. 1987. 19.95 (*0-941749-01-0*); pap. 13.95 (*0-941749-02-9*) Black Tie Pr.

— The Jaguar Portfolio. LC 91-8198. (Illus.). 128p. (Orig.). 1991. pap. 12.50 (*0-941749-25-8*) Black Tie Pr.

— O!!Zone 98 - International Visual Poetry. (Illus.). 1998. pap. 25.00 (*1-884185-15-0*) O Zone.

— Without Feathers. limited ed. LC 90-36267. (Illus.). 64p. (Orig.). 1990. pap. 12.50 (*0-941749-16-9*) Black Tie Pr.

Burrus, Harry, jt. ed. see Gravis, Peter.

Burrus, J., ed. Thermal Modeling in Sedimentary Basins: 2nd, IFP Exploration & Production Research Conference, Carcans, 1985. (Illus.). 624p. (C). 1986. 725.00 (*2-7108-0504-9*, Pub. by Edits Technip) Enfield Pubs NH.

Burrus, L. D., et al. The Ninth Marines: A History of the Ninth Marine Regiment in World War II; with Lists of the Officers & Men Who Served from Organization to Disbandment, 1942-1945. 1985. reprint ed. 35.95 (*0-89201-116-5*) Zenger Pub.

Burrus, S. S., et al. Four Ancestors: Stories, Songs & Poems from Native North America. LC 95-15250. 96p. (J). (gr. 2-5). 1997. 18.95 (*0-8167-3843-2*) BrdgeWater.

Burrus, Thomas L. & Yaffa, Harold. Energy Natural Environment. 4th ed. 396p. (C). 1990. pap. text 49.00 (*0-536-57733-1*) Pearson Custom.

Burrus, Victoria A. & Goldberg, Harriet, eds. Esopete Ystoriado. (Spanish Ser.: No. 61). xxxiv, 280p. 1990. 30.00 (*0-940639-56-4*) Hispanic Seminary.

***Burrus, Virginia.** Begotten, Not Made: Conceiving Manhood in Late Antiquity. (Figurae Ser.). 2000. 49.50 (*0-8047-3706-1*); pap. text 19.95 (*0-8047-3973-0*) Stanford U Pr.

Burrus, Virginia. Chastity As Autonomy: Women in the Stories of Apocryphal Acts. LC 87-7949. (Studies in Women & Religion: Vol. 23). 184p. 1987. lib. bdg. 79.95 (*0-88946-526-6*) E Mellen.

— The Making of a Heretic: Gender, Authority, & the Priscillianist Controversy. LC 94-33270. (Transformation of the Classical Heritage Ser.: Vol. XXIV). 319p. 1995. 52.50 (*0-520-08997-9*, Pub. by U CA Pr) Cal Prin Full Svc.

***Burruss, Pricellious J.** Transformed Singles. Coleman, Vanessa D. & Johnson, Lisa, eds. (Illus.). 67p. 1999. pap. 7.00 (*0-9667410-1-3*) R Burruss Minist.

Burry, Anthony, jt. auth. see Kellerman, Henry.

Burry, Hugh C., jt. auth. see Penington, Graeme.

Burry, J. H., jt. ed. see Singh, S. P.

Burry, Mark. Expiatory Church of the Sagrada Familia: Barcelona 1884-Antoni Gaudi. (Architecture in Detail Ser.). (C). 1993. pap. 29.95 (*0-7148-2849-1*, Pub. by Phaidon Press) Phaidon Pr.

Bursa, Milan & Pec, Karel. Gravity Field & Dynamics of the Earth. Tauer, J., tr. from CZE. LC 93-4997.Tr. of Tihove Pole a Dynamika Zeme. 1993. 174.95 (*0-387-56817-4*) Spr-Verlag.

Bursch, J. H., jt. ed. see Heintzen, Paul H.

Bursch, Meike. Judentaufe und Fruhneuzeitliches Strafrecht: Die Verfahren Gegen Christian Treu Aus Weener - Ostfriesland, 1720-1728. (Rechtshistorische Reihe Ser.: Bd. 140). (GER.). 168p. 1996. 35.95 (*3-631-49408-4*) P Lang Pubng.

***Bursell, Kaare.** The End of Medicine: How I Learned to Quit Worrying & Love My Disease. 212p. 2000. pap. 15.00 (*0-9700262-7-7*, 1) K Bursell.

Bursell, Rupert D. Liturgy Order & the Law. 362p. 1996. text 80.00 (*0-19-826250-7*); pap. text 28.00 (*0-19-826249-3*) OUP.

Bursen, H. A. Dismantling the Memory Machine: A Philosophical Investigation of Machine Theories of Memory. (Synthese Library: No. 128). 170p. 1978. text 71.50 (*90-277-0933-5*) Kluwer Academic.

Bursevi, Ismail H., tr. see Ibn al-Arabi.

Bursey, Gert. Weight Loss: The Psychological Approach. LC 97-66630. (Illus.). 110p. (Orig.). 1997. pap. 9.50 (*0-9657078-0-6*) Reliable Wght Consult.

***Bursey, Kevin.** Ice Stars: A Celebration of the Artistry, Beauty, & Grace of the Ice Skating World. 1999. pap. 22.95 (*1-57243-343-4*) Triumph Bks.

Bursey, Maurice. Francis Preston Venable of the University of North Carolina. unabridged ed. (Illus.). xi, 111p. 1989. 11.95 (*0-940715-02-3*) Chapel Hill Hist.

Bursey, Maurice M., jt. ed. see Winefordner, James D.

Bursey, Peter, jt. compiled by see Morriss, Roger.

Burshtein, A. I. Introduction to Thermodynamics & Kinetic Theory of Matter. LC 95-11655. 336p. 1995. 79.95 (*0-471-04755-4*, Wiley-Interscience) Wiley.

Bursik, Robert J., Jr. & Grasmick, Harold G. Neighborhoods & Crime: The Dimensions of Effective Community Control. LC 92-29041. 226p. 1992. 37.00 (*0-669-24632-8*) Lxngtn Bks.

Bursik, Rose. Amelia's Fantastic Flight. LC 91-28809. (J). (ps-3). 1995. pap. 5.95 (*0-8050-3386-6*) H Holt & Co.

An Asterisk (*) at the beginning of an entry indicates that the title is appearing for the first time.

— Amelia's Fantastic Flight. LC 91-28809. (Illus.). 32p. (J). (ps-2). 1995. 14.95 (*0-8050-1872-7*, Bks Young Read) H Holt & Co.
— Zoe's Sheep. (J). 1995. 14.95 (*0-8050-2530-8*) H Holt & Co.
— Zoe's Sheep. (Illus.). 89p. (J). 1995. pap. 5.95 (*0-8050-4642-9*) H Holt & Co.
— Zoe's Sheep. LC 93-4519. (J). 1996. 11.15 (*0-606-10105-5*, Pub. by Turtleback) Demco.
Bursill-Hall, G. L., et al, eds. De Ortu Grammaticae. Studies in Medieval Grammar & Linguistic Theory in Memory of Jan Pinborg. LC 90-444. (Studies in the History of the Language Sciences: Vol. 43). x, 372p. 1990. 112.00 (*90-272-4526-6*) J Benjamins Pubng Co.
Bursill, Henry. Hand Shadows & More Hand Shadows: A Series of Novel & Amusing Figures Formed by the Hand. LC 96-48842. (Illus.). 64p. 1997. reprint ed. pap. text 2.50 (*0-486-29513-3*) Dover.
Bursk, Christopher. Cell Count. LC 97-25355. 96p. 1997. 18.95 (*0-89672-385-2*) Tex Tech Univ Pr.
— Little Harbor. (QRL Poetry Bks.: Vol. XXIII). 1982. 20.00 (*0-614-06400-7*) Quarterly Rev.
Bursk, Edward C., ed. Human Relations for Management: The Newer Perspective. LC 70-167320. (Essay Index Reprint Ser.). 1977. reprint ed. 23.95 (*0-8369-2582-3*) Ayer.
Bursk, Edward C. & Blodgett, Timothy B., eds. Developing Executive Leaders. LC 70-160023. (Illus.). 199p. reprint ed. pap. 61.70 (*0-7837-1679-6*, 205721100024) Bks Demand.
Bursk, Edward C. & Chapman, John F., eds. New Decision-Making Tools for Managers: Mathematical Programing As an Aid in the Solving of Business Problems. LC 63-11416. (Illus.). 413p. reprint ed. 133.70 (*0-8357-9168-8*, 201775200007) Bks Demand.
Bursk, Edward C. & Greyser, Stephen A., eds. Cases in Marketing Management. 2nd ed. (Foundations of Marketing Ser.). (Illus.). 240p. 1975. pap. text 30.00 (*0-13-118893-3*) P-H.
Bursley, Gilbert E. Attache Adventures Abroad: The Postwar Decade in Turkey, Greece, Palestine & Equatorial Africa. LC 93-73566. (Illus.). 252p. (Orig.). 1994. pap. 15.50 (*0-9638532-0-1*) Cleary Coll.
Bursnall, William J., et al, eds. Space Shuttle Missions of the 80's, 21st Annual AAS Meeting, Aug. 26-28, 1975, Denver, CO, Pt. 1. LC 57-43769. (Advances in the Astronautical Sciences Ser.: Vol. 32). (Illus.). 598p. 1977. 40.00 (*0-87703-078-2*, Am Astronaut Soc) Univelt Inc.
— Space Shuttle Missions of the 80's, 21st Annual AAS Meeting, Aug. 26-28, 1975, Denver, CO, Pt. 2. LC 57-43769. (Advances in the Astronautical Sciences Ser.: Vol. 32). (Illus.). 766p. 1977. 55.00 (*0-87703-087-1*, Am Astronaut Soc) Univelt Inc.
Burson, James L., jt. auth. see Williams, Philip L.
Burson, James L., jt. ed. see Williams, Phillip L.
Burson, Linda. Play with Shakespeare: A Guide to Producing Shakespeare with Young People. (Illus.). 218p. (Orig.). 1992. pap. 19.95 (*0-932720-51-X*) New Plays Inc.
Burson, Lorraine E. Recruiting & Training Volunteers for Church & Synagogue Libraries. LC 86-9682. (Guide Ser.: No. 14). 32p. 1999. pap. 9.00 (*0-915324-24-5*) CSLA.
***Burson, Matthew.** Our Sunday Visitor's 2000 Catholic Almanac. LC 73-641001. 608p. 1999. 23.95 (*0-87973-904-5*) Our Sunday Visitor.
Burson, Nancy. Faces. (Illus.). 72p. 1993. 45.00 (*0-944092-24-1*) Twin Palms Pub.
Burson, Nancy, et al, photos by. Aperture Vol. 148: Delirium. (Illus.). 80p. (Orig.). 1997. pap. 27.95 (*0-89381-736-8*) Aperture.
Burson, Scott R. & Walls, Jerry. C. S. Lewis & Francis Schaeffer: Lessons for a New Century from the Most Influential Apologists of Our Time. LC 97-43691. 308p. 1998. pap. 14.99 (*0-8308-1935-5*, 1935) InterVarsity.
***Burson, Sherman L.** Locked Out: And Other Tales. Burson, Valerie, ed. 2000. write for info. (*0-9667916-3-0*) Queensbury Pr.
Burson, Therese, ed. see Barey, Pat.
Burson, Valerie, ed. see Burson, Sherman L.
Burssens, Gaston. From the Flemish of Gaston Burssens. Wade, John S., tr. from FLE. LC 82-8756. 21p. (Orig.). 1982. pap. 3.00 (*0-933292-10-4*) Arts End.
Burstall, Dawn, jt. auth. see Turnbull, Geoffrey K.
Burstall, F. E. & Rawnsley, J. H. Twistor Theory for Riemannian Symmetric Spaces. Dold, A. et al, eds. (Lecture Notes in Mathematics Ser.: Vol. 1424). iii, 112p. 1990. 30.95 (*0-387-52602-1*) Spr-Verlag.
Burstall, M. L., jt. auth. see Rueben, B. G.
Burstall, Mike. Pharmaceutical Products, Vol. I-2. (Single Market Review Ser.). 1998. 70.00 (*0-7494-2306-4*) Kogan Page Ltd.
Burstall, Rod M., et al. Programming in POP-2. LC 71-850175. viii, 290 p. 1971. write for info. (*0-85224-197-6*) Edinburgh U Pr.
Burstall, Sara A. Education of Girls in the United States. LC 79-165709. (American Education Ser, No. 2). 1972. reprint ed. 18.95 (*0-405-03698-1*) Ayer.
Burstall, Terry. A Soldier Returns: A Long Tan Veteran Discovers the Other Side of Vietnam. 1990. pap. 16.95 (*0-7022-2252-6*, Pub. by Univ Queensland Pr) Intl Spec Bk.
— The Soldiers' Story: The Battle at Xa Long Tan Vietnam, August 18, 1966. (Illus.). 188p. 1987. pap. 16.95 (*0-7022-2047-7*, Pub. by Univ Queensland Pr) Intl Spec Bk.
— The Soldiers' Story: The Battle at Xa Long Tan Vietnam, August 18, 1966. 1998. reprint ed. pap. 18.95 (*0-7022-3009-X*, Pub. by Univ Queensland Pr) Intl Spec Bk.
— Vietnam: The Australian Dilemma, 1962-1972. 1993. pap. 19.95 (*0-7022-2470-7*, Pub. by Univ Queensland Pr) Intl Spec Bk.
Burstall, Tim. Bulk Water Pipelines. LC 98-227905. 183p. 1997. 74.00 (*0-7277-2609-9*, 2609, Pub. by T Telford) RCH.
Burstein. Democratic Politics. (C). 1998. pap. text 23.00 (*0-15-500325-9*) Harcourt Coll Pubs.
— Management of Hotel & Motel Security. (Occupational Safety & Health Ser.: Vol. 5). (Illus.). 216p. 1980. text 110.00 (*0-8247-1002-9*) Dekker.
— Sleighbed. 2000. 20.00 (*0-06-251616-7*) HarpC.
— Sleighbed. 2000. pap. 14.00 (*0-06-251617-5*) HarpC.
Burstein, Abraham. Ghetto Messenger: Sixty Tales of a Unique Seventy Year Old Messenger 'Boy' LC 72-150540. (Short Story Index Reprint Ser.). 1977. reprint ed. 20.95 (*0-8369-3837-2*) Ayer.
Burstein, Albert H. & Wright, Timothy M. Fundamentals of Orthopedic Biomechanics. (Illus.). 240p. 1994. 57.00 (*0-683-01135-9*) Lppncott W & W.
Burstein, Albert H., jt. auth. see Frankel, Victor H.
Burstein, Alvin G. & Loucks, Sandra. Rorschach Test Scoring. LC 66-66615. 300p. 1989. pap. 39.95 (*0-89116-780-3*) Hemisp Pub.
***Burstein, Andrew.** America's Jubilee. LC 00-20302. 2001. write for info. (*0-375-41033-3*) Knopf.
Burstein, Andrew. The Inner Jefferson. LC 97-150594. 334p. 1997. pap. 14.95 (*0-8139-1720-4*) U Pr of Va.
Burstein, Andrew. Sentimental Democracy: The Evolution of America's Romantic Self-Image. LC 98-52046. 432p. 1999. 28.00 (*0-8090-8535-6*) Hill & Wang.
***Burstein, Andrew.** Sentimental Democracy: The Evolution of America's Romantic Self-Image. 432p. 2000. pap. 15.00 (*0-8090-8536-4*) Hill & Wang.
Burstein, Chaya. A Kid's Catalog of Israel: Revised & Updated for 1998. rev. ed. (Illus.). 288p. 1998. pap. 15.95 (*0-8276-0651-6*) JPS Phila.
Burstein, Chaya. Make Your Own Jewish Calendar Coloring Book. (J). 1995. pap. 2.50 (*0-486-28630-4*) Dover.
Burstein, Chaya M. Benjy's Bible Trails. LC 90-25421. (Illus.). 32p. (J). (gr. 1-5). 1992. pap. 3.95 (*0-929371-27-5*) Kar-Ben.
— A First Jewish Holiday Cookbook. (Activity Bk.). (Illus.). (J). (gr. 3-8). 1979. pap. 9.95 (*0-88482-775-5*) Hebrew Pub.
— The Hebrew Prophets: A Story-Workbook. (Illus.). (Orig.). (J). (gr. 4-6). 1990. pap., student ed. 6.95 (*0-8074-0430-6*, 123932) UAHC.
— The Jewish Kids Catalog. (Illus.). 224p. (J). (gr. 3-7). 1983. pap. 15.95 (*0-8276-0215-4*) JPS Phila.
— The Kids' Catalog of Bible Treasures. LC 99-11591. (Illus.). 142p. (J). (gr. 3-7). 1999. pap. 15.95 (*0-8276-0667-2*) JPS Phila.
— Our Land of Israel. (Illus.). (J). 1995. pap. 12.00 (*0-8074-0527-2*, 127272) UAHC.
— 10 Great Jewish Children's Stories. (Ten Jewish Children's Stories Ser.: Vol. 1). (Illus.). 48p. (J). (ps-3). 1994. 14.95 (*965-483-005-1*) Pitspopany.
— The UAHC Kids Catalog of Jewish Living. LC 91-42815. (Illus.). (J). (gr. 4-6). 1992. pap. 9.95 (*0-8074-0464-0*, 123934) UAHC.
Burstein, Chaya M. & Leiman, Sondra. Our Land of Israel. (Illus.). (J). (gr. 4). 1996. pap., teacher ed. 15.00 (*0-8074-0533-7*, 208037) UAHC.
Burstein, Daniel. Turning the Tables: A Machiavellian Strategy for Dealing with Japan. 256p. 1993. 22.00 (*0-671-78953-8*) S&S Trade.
Burstein, Daniel & De Keijzer, Arne. Big Dragon: China's Future: What It Means for Business, the Economy, & the Global Order. LC 97-50092. 384p. 1998. 24.50 (*0-684-80316-X*) S&S Trade.
Burstein, Daniel & DeKeijzer, Arne J. Big Dragon: The Future of China: What It Means for Business, the Economy, & the Global Order. 416p. 1999. per. 14.00 (*0-684-85366-3*, Touchstone) S&S Trade Pap.
***Burstein, Daniel & Kline, David.** Road Warriors: Dreams & Nightmares along the Information Highway. 466p. 1999. reprint ed. text 25.00 (*0-7881-6621-2*) DIANE Pub.
Burstein, David, jt. ed. see Davies, Jonathan I.
Burstein, E. & Weisbuch, C. Confined Electrons & Photons: New Physics & Applications. LC 95-17270. (NATO ASI Ser.: Ser. B, Vol. 340). (Illus.). 918p. (C). 1995. 215.00 (*0-306-44990-0*, Kluwer Plenum) Kluwer Academic.
Burstein, Ellen. Legwork. (Illus.). 288p. 1994. 22.00 (*0-02-578110-3*) S&S Trade.
Burstein, Emanuel. Federal Income Taxation of Insurance Companies. LC 96-78806. (Illus.). 365p. 1996. 69.00 (*0-9654356-0-1*) Ins Tax Regulation.
***Burstein, Emanuel.** Federal Income Taxation of Insurance Companies: 1998-1999 Supplement. 67p. 1999. pap. text 19.00 (*0-9654356-2-8*) Ins Tax Regulation.
Burstein, G. T., et al. Engineering Materials Selector, 3 vols. (Illus.). 1998. text 875.00 incl. cd-rom (*0-7506-3804-4*) Buttrwrth-Heinemann.
***Burstein, Gabriel.** Macro Trading & Investment Strategies: Macroeconomic Arbitrage in Global Markets. LC 98-39938. (Trading Advantage Ser.). 228p. 1999. 59.95 (*0-471-31586-9*) Wiley.
Burstein, Gerald. Bummy's Basic Parliamentary Guide: An Illustrated Step-by-Step Procedure for Making Meetings Work. LC 96-48243. 120p. 1997. spiral bd. 19.95 (*0-915035-50-2*, 9720B) Dawn Sign.
Burstein, Harvey. Criminal Investigation: An Introduction. LC 97-48655. 336p. (C). 1998. 74.00 (*0-13-575358-9*) P-H.
— Hotel Security Management. LC 74-14039. 138p. 1975. text 33.95 (*0-275-09820-6*, C0069, Praeger Pubs) Greenwood.
— Industrial Security Management. 2nd ed. LC 86-3179. 280p. 1986. 62.95 (*0-275-92002-X*, C2002, Praeger Pubs) Greenwood.
Burstein, Harvey. Introduction to Security. 304p. 1994. 77.00 (*0-13-057051-6*) P-H.
— Introduction to Security. 1999. 61.00 (*0-13-018553-1*, Prentice Hall) P-H.
Burstein, Harvey. Security: A Management Perspective. LC 95-9241. 207p. 1995. 74.00 (*0-13-150657-9*) P-H.
Burstein, Harvey, jt. auth. see Date General Corporation Staff.
Burstein Hewitt, Lonnie. The Little Red Writing Book: A Practical Guide to Writing Your Own Life Story. LC 98-90740. vi, 94p. 1998. pap. 12.95 (*0-966673-0-7*) TellTale Prods.
Burstein, Janet H. Writing Mothers, Writing Daughters: Tracing the Maternal in American Jewish Women's Stories. LC 95-50191. 224p. (C). 1996. 14.95 (*0-252-06555-7*); text 34.95 (*0-252-02252-1*) U of Ill Pr.
Burstein, Jessica. The Grandmother Book. (Illus.). 92p. 1999. text 24.95 (*1-58238-050-3*, Whitman Coin) St Martin.
Burstein, Joel V. State of New York Report of the Law Revision Commission, 6 vols. 1998. reprint ed. 465.00 (*1-57588-428-3*, 300110) W S Hein.
Burstein, John. Slim Goodbody's Healthy Days Diary: Activity Book. (Illus.). 64p. (J). (ps-5). 1983. spiral bd. 5.95 (*0-89845-056-X*, B056X, Caedmon) HarperAudio.
Burstein, Jonathan L., jt. auth. see Hogan, David E.
Burstein, Joseph. Approximation by Exponentials, Their Extensions, & Differential Equations: Extended to Dynamics Identification. unabridged ed. LC 96-76406. (Illus.). 70p. (Orig.). 1997. pap. 22.45 (*0-9607126-3-1*) Metrics Pr.
***Burstein, Joseph.** Battle of Finland: June-August, 1944, Miracle & Milestone of Warfare. LC 99-74218. (Illus.). 60p. 1999. pap. 24.00 (*0-9607126-5-8*) Metrics Pr.
Burstein, Joseph. Exact Solutions of Nonlinear, etc. Differential Equations. unabridged ed. LC 98-91704. (Illus.). 91p. 1998. pap. 85.00 (*0-9607126-4-X*) Metrics Pr.
Burstein, Leigh, et al, eds. Collecting Evaluation Data: Problems & Solutions. LC 85-1848. (Illus.). 318p. 1985. reprint ed. pap. 98.60 (*0-608-01102-9*, 205941100001) Bks Demand.
— The IEA Study of Mathematics III: Student Growth & Classroom Processes. LC 92-15030. (International Studies in Educational Achievement). (Illus.). 351p. 1993. text 122.00 (*0-08-041371-4*, Pergamon Pr) Elsevier.
Burstein, Leigh, et al. Validating National Curriculum Indicators. 109p. 1995. pap. text 15.00 (*0-8330-2333-0*, MR-658-NSF) Rand Corp.
Burstein, M. & Legmann, P. Lipoprotein Precipitation. (Monographs on Atherosclerosis: Vol. 11). (Illus.). viii, 132p. 1982. 84.50 (*3-8055-3512-0*) S Karger.
Burstein, Mark. Much Ado: The Pogofenokee Trivia Book. LC 88-16095. (Illus.). 50p. (Orig.). 1988. pap. 15.00 (*0-945185-02-2*) Spring Hollow Bks.
Burstein, Patricia, jt. auth. see Crimp, Susan.
Burstein, Patricia, jt. auth. see MacFarlane, Ellen B.
Burstein, Paul. Discrimination, Jobs & Politics: The Struggle for Equal Employment Opportunity in the United States. LC 97-30949. 247p. 1998. pap. text 15.95 (*0-226-08136-2*) U Ch Pr.
— Discrimination, Jobs, & Politics: The Struggle for Equal Employment Opportunity in the United States Since the New Deal. LC 85-4802. x, 248p. 1994. pap. text 12.95 (*0-226-08135-4*) U Ch Pr.
Burstein, Paul, ed. Equal Employment Opportunity: Labor Market Discrimination & Public Policy. (Sociology & Economics Ser.). 456p. 1994. pap. text 28.95 (*0-202-30476-0*); lib. bdg. 54.95 (*0-202-30475-2*) Aldine de Gruyter.
Burstein, Paul, jt. auth. see Simon, Julian L.
Burstein, Philip L. Benchmarks for Designing Workers' Compensation Medical Fee Schedules, 1994-1995. 1994. 50.00 (*0-935149-50-3*, WC-94-7) Workers Comp Res Inst.
— Benchmarks for Designing Workers' Compensation Medical Fee Schedules, 1995-1996. LC 96-15348. 127p. (Orig.). 1996. pap. 50.00 (*0-935149-56-2*, WC-96-2) Workers Comp Res Inst.
Burstein, Philip L., ed. The RBRVS As a Model for Workers Compensation Medical Fee Schedules: Pros & Cons. LC 96-28615. 1996. pap. 50.00 (*0-935149-59-7*, WC-96-5) Workers Comp Res Inst.
Burstein, Raya. Visual Perceptual Skill Building Book 1. LC 98-177548. 200p. (J). (gr. k-2). 1998. pap. 21.95 (*0-89455-700-9*, MP4701) Crit Think Bks.
Burstein, Sharon A., et al, eds. Capital Connoisseur. (Illus.). 252p. 1988. 19.95 (*0-9620894-0-0*) LCIH.
Burstein, Stanley M. Graeco-Africana: Studies in the History of Greek Relations with Egypt & Nubia. (Hellenism: Ancient, Mediaeval, Modern Ser.: No. 16). 262p. (C). 1995. text 40.00 (*0-89241-520-7*) Caratzas.
— The Hellenistic Age from the Battle of Ipsos to the Death of Kleopatra VII. (Translated Documents of Greece & Rome Ser.: No. 3). 196p. 1985. pap. text 23.95 (*0-521-28158-X*) Cambridge U Pr.
— The Hellenistic Period in World History. Adas, Michael, ed. (Essays on Global & Comparative History Ser.). 33p. 1995. reprint ed. pap. 6.00 (*0-87229-075-1*) Am Hist Assn.
— Outpost of Hellenism: The Emergence of Heraclea on the Black Sea. LC 74-620189. (University of California Publications: Classical Studies: Vol. 14). 164p. reprint ed. pap. 50.90 (*0-608-18654-6*, 202126800021) Bks Demand.
Burstein, Stanley M., ed. Ancient African Civilizations: Kush & Axum. LC 97-41207. (Illus.). 196p. (C). 1997. text 39.95 (*1-55876-147-0*); pap. text 16.95 (*1-55876-148-9*) Wiener Pubs Inc.
Burstein, Stanley M. & Nagle, D. Brendan, eds. The Ancient World: Readings in Social & Cultural History. LC 94-18200. 323p. 1994. pap. text 32.20 (*0-13-756222-5*) P-H.
Burstein, Stanley M. & Okin, Louis, eds. Panhellenica: Essays in Ancient History. 1980. 15.00 (*0-87291-134-9*) Coronado Pr.
Burstein, Stanley M., et al. Ancient History: Recent Work & New Directions. LC 97-35440. (Publications of the Association of Ancient Historians: No. 5). 120p. 1997. text 21.95 (*0-941690-79-2*) Regina Bks.
— Ancient History: Recent Work & New Directions. LC 97-35440. (Publications of the Association of Ancient Historians: No. 5). 120p. 1997. pap. text 12.95 (*0-941690-78-4*) Regina Bks.
Burstein, Stanley M., ed. see Lewis, Bernard.
Burstein, Sumner, jt. auth. see Schulster, Dennis.
Bursten, Ben. The Manipulator: A Psychoanalytic View. LC 72-92553. 287p. reprint ed. pap. 89.00 (*0-608-30593-6*, 201741700007) Bks Demand.
Bursten, Bruce, jt. auth. see Wilson, Roxy.
Bursten, Bruce E., jt. auth. see Brown, Theodore L.
Bursten, Emanuel. Federal Income Taxation of Insurance Companies, 1997 Annual Supplement. unabridged ed. 56p. 1998. pap. 19.00 (*0-9654356-1-X*) Ins Tax Regulation.
Bursten, Martin A. Escape from Fear. LC 73-8563. (Illus.). 224p. 1973. reprint ed. lib. bdg. 65.00 (*0-8371-6961-5*, BUEF, Greenwood Pr) Greenwood.
Burstiner, Irving. Be Your Own Consultant: 188 Ways to Improve Your Business Operation. LC 95-47107. 256p. 1996. 21.95 (*1-55972-357-2*, Birch Ln Pr) Carol Pub Group.
— Be Your Own Consultant: 188 Ways to Improve Your Business Operation. (Illus.). 211p. 1998. text 22.00 (*0-7881-5802-3*) DIANE Pub.
— How to Start & Run Your Own Retail Business: Expert Advice from a Leading Business Consultant. rev. ed. LC 98-14870. (Illus.). 304p. 1998. pap. text 19.95 (*0-8065-1988-6*, Citadel Pr) Carol Pub Group.
— How to Start & Run Your Own Retail Business: Expert Advice from a Leading Business Consultant & Entrepreneur. LC 93-45560. 1994. pap. 19.95 (*0-8065-1518-X*, Citadel Pr) Carol Pub Group.
— Mail Order Selling: How to Market Almost Anything by Mail. 3rd ed. LC 94-48372. (Small Business Editions Ser.). 292p. 1995. 79.95 (*0-471-09791-8*); pap. 19.95 (*0-471-09759-4*) Wiley.
— The Small Business Handbook. 3rd ed. LC 97-20330. 432p. 1997. per. 20.00 (*0-684-83022-1*, Fireside) S&S Trade Pap.
— The Small Business Handbook: A Comprehensive Guide to Starting & Running Your Own Business. rev. ed. 368p. 1994. pap. 18.00 (*0-671-88108-6*, Fireside) S&S Trade Pap.
— Start & Run Your Own Profitable Service Business. LC 92-31197. (Illus.). 284p. (C). 1992. pap. 19.95 (*0-13-842733-X*) P-H.
Burstinger, Irving, jt. auth. see Coventry, W.
Burstock, G., jt. auth. see Bloom, S. R.
Burston, Betty. Twenty-Four Seven: Street Warfare in Washington D. C. 256p. 1994. mass mkt. 4.95 (*0-87067-951-1*) Holloway.
***Burston, Daniel.** The Crucible of Experience: R. D. Laing & the Crisis of Psychotherapy. LC 99-57332. 2000. 27.95 (*0-674-00217-2*) HUP.
Burston, Daniel. The Legacy of Erich Fromm. LC 90-5348. (Illus.). 288p. 1991. 43.50 (*0-674-52168-4*, BURLEG) HUP.
— The Wing of Madness: The Life & Work of R. D. Laing. 304p. 1996. 37.95 (*0-674-95358-4*) HUP.
— Wing of Madness: The Life & Work of R. D. Laing. 288p. 1998. pap. text 17.95 (*0-674-95359-2*) HUP.
Burston, Patrick. The Castle of Fear. LC 95-50788. (Candlewick Gamebook Ser.). (Illus.). 48p. (J). (gr. k-3). 1996. pap. 5.99 (*1-56402-860-7*) Candlewick Pr.
— The Fairground of Dread. LC 96-38644. (Candlewick Gamebook Ser.). (Illus.). 48p. (Orig.). (J). (gr. 1-3). 1997. pap. 5.99 (*0-7636-0137-3*) Candlewick Pr.
— The Island of Horror. LC 96-127. (Candlewick Gamebook Ser.). (Illus.). 48p. (J). (gr. 1-4). 1996. pap. 5.99 (*1-56402-861-5*) Candlewick Pr.
— The Jungle of Peril. LC 95-26689. (Candlewick Gamebook Ser.). (Illus.). 48p. (J). (gr. k-3). 1996. 5.99 (*1-56402-862-3*) Candlewick Pr.
— The Pirates of Doom: A Choose-Your-Challenge Gamebook. LC 95-46002. (Candlewick Gamebks.). (Illus.). 48p. (Orig.). (J). (gr. k-3). 1996. pap. 5.99 (*1-56402-855-0*) Candlewick Pr.
— Planet of Terror: A Choose-Your-Challenge Gamebook. LC 95-47634. (Candlewick Gamebks.). (Illus.). 48p. (Orig.). (J). (gr. k-3). 1996. pap. 5.99 (*1-56402-851-8*) Candlewick Pr.
— The Sea of Menace: A Pick Your Peril Adventure. LC 97-46489. (Illus.). 32p. (J). (gr. 2-5). 1998. 5.99 (*0-7636-0579-4*) Candlewick Press.
Burston, Paul. What Are You Looking At? Queer Sex, Style & Cinema. LC 95-195143. 179p. 1995. pap. 17.95 (*0-304-34300-5*, Pub. by Cassell) LPC InBook.
Burston, Paul & Richardson, Colin, eds. A Queer Romance: Lesbians, Gay Men, & the Popular Culture. LC 94-10783. (Illus.). 256p. (C). (gr. 13). 1995. 80.00 (*0-415-09617-0*, C0357); pap. 22.99 (*0-415-09618-9*, C0358) Routledge.
Burston, W. H., ed. see Bentham, Jeremy.

An Asterisk (*) at the beginning of an entry indicates that the title is appearing for the first time.

Burstone, Charles J. & Marcotte, Michael R. Problem Solving in Orthodontics: Goal Oriented Treatment Strategies. (Illus.). 250p. write for info. (0-86715-353-9) Quint Pub Co.

Burstone, Charles J., jt. ed. see Nanda, Ravindra.

Burstone, Charles J., jt. ed. see Norton, Louis A.

Burstow, Bonnie. Radical Feminist Therapy: Working in the Context of Violence. (Illus.). 344p. (C). 1992. 58.00 (0-8039-4787-9); pap. 26.95 (0-8039-4788-7) Sage.

Burstyn, Harold L. At the Sign of the Quadrant: An Account of the Contributions to American Hydrography Made by Edmund March Blunt & His Sons. LC 57-59435. (Marine Historical Association, Publication: No. 32). 119p. reprint ed. pap. 36.90 (0-8357-2790-4, 203991600014) Bks Demand.

Burstyn, Joan. Waiting for the Lame Horse. LC 87-73262. 65p. 1987. pap. 9.00 (0-9610346-8-8) Belle Mead Pr.

Burstyn, Joan, ed. Desktop Publishing in the University. 126p. (Orig.). (C). 1991. pap. text 14.95 (0-8156-8116-X) Syracuse U Pr.

Burstyn, Joan N., ed. Educating Tomorrow's Valuable Citizen. LC 95-36801. 229p. (C). 1996. pap. text 19.95 (0-7914-2948-2) State U NY Pr.

Burstyn, Varda. The Rites of Men: Manhood, Politics, & the Culture of Sport. 528p. 1999. pap. 24.95 (0-8020-7725-0); text 60.00 (0-8020-2844-6) U of Toronto Pr.

B

Bursuck, William D., ed. Homework: Issues & Practices for Students with LD. LC 95-14310. 226p. 1995. pap. 29.00 (0-89079-671-8, 7317) PRO-ED.

Bursuck, William D., jt. auth. see Friend, Marilyn P.

Bursztyn, Peter G. Physiology for Sportspeople: A Serious User's Guide to the Body. LC 90-3608. (Illus.). 292p. 1991. text 19.95 (0-7190-3087-0, Pub. by Manchester Univ Pr) St Martin.

Bursztyn, Sylvia. Los Angeles Times Sunday Crossword, Vol. 5. Vol. 5. 1992. pap. 9.00 (0-8129-1917-3, Times Bks) Crown Pub Group.

— Los Angeles Times Sunday Crossword, Vol. 6. 1992. pap. 8.50 (0-8129-1918-1, Times Bks) Crown Pub Group.

— Los Angeles Times Sunday Crossword Omnibus, Vol. 2. 2nd ed. 1998. pap. 11.00 (0-8129-2973-X, Times Bks) Crown Pub Group.

— Los Angeles Times Sunday Crossword Puzzles, Vol. 1. Vol. 1. 1991. pap. 8.50 (0-8129-1910-6, Times Bks) Crown Pub Group.

— Los Angeles Times Sunday Crossword Puzzles, Vol. 2. 1991. pap. write for info. (0-685-47860-2, Times Bks) Crown Pub Group.

— Los Angeles Times Sunday Crossword Puzzles, Vol. 5. 1992. pap. 7.00 (0-8129-2040-6, Times Bks) Crown Pub Group.

— Los Angeles Times Sunday Crossword Puzzles, Vol. 6. 1992. pap. 7.00 (0-8129-2041-4, Times Bks) Crown Pub Group.

— Los Angeles Times Sunday Crossword Puzzles, Vol. 7. Vol. 7. 1992. pap. 8.50 (0-8129-1919-X, Times Bks) Crown Pub Group.

— Los Angeles Times Sunday Crossword Puzzles, Vol. 8. Vol. 8. 1992. pap. 8.50 (0-8129-1920-3, Times Bks) Crown Pub Group.

— Los Angeles Times Sunday Crossword Puzzles, Vol. 15. Vol. 15. 1996. pap. 9.00 (0-8129-2788-5, Times Bks) Crown Pub Group.

— Los Angeles Times Sunday Crossword Puzzles, Vol. 16. 16th ed. 1997. pap. 9.00 (0-8129-2938-1, Times Bks) Crown Pub Group.

***Bursztyn, Sylvia.** Los Angeles Times Sunday Crossword Puzzles, Vol. 19. 64p. 2000. pap. 9.95 (0-8129-3352-4, Times Bks) Crown Pub Group.

Bursztyn, Sylvia & Tunick, Barry. Los Angeles Times Sunday Crossword Puzzles, Vol. 14. 14th ed. Vol. 14. 1995. pap. 9.00 (0-8129-2232-8, Times Bks) Crown Pub Group.

— Los Angeles Times Sunday Crosswork Omnibus, Vol. 1. 128p. 1996. pap. 11.00 (0-8129-2758-3, Times Bks) Crown Pub Group.

Bursztyn, Sylvia, jt. auth. see Tunick, Barry.

Bursztynski, Sue. Potions to Pulsars: Women Doing Science. (True Stories Ser.). 96p. (J). (gr. 3-8). 1996. pap. text 6.95 (1-86448-246-X) IPG Chicago.

***Burt.** After the Hole. 2000. pap. 9.95 (0-552-99531-2, Pub. by Transworld Publishers Ltd) Trafalgar.

Burt. Purchasing & Supply Management. 7th ed. 2002. 68.00 (0-07-229070-6) McGraw.

***Burt.** Sophie. 2000. pap. 10.95 (0-552-99532-0, Pub. by Transworld Publishers Ltd) Trafalgar.

Burt. Textbook of Neuroanatomy. 1993. pap. text 43.00 (0-7216-2199-6, W B Saunders Co) Harcrt Hlth Sci Grp.

Burt, et al, eds. Expert Systems in Electrical Power Engineering. LC 98-114054. 256p. 1998. 119.95 (0-412-75320-0, Chap & Hall NY) Chapman & Hall.

Burt & Hog. Baseball: Easy Sports Reader. (Illus.). 16p. (J). (ps-1). 1996. pap. 2.49 (1-55734-892-8) Tchr Create Mat.

— Basketball: Easy Sports Reader. (Illus.). 16p. (J). (ps-1). 1996. pap. 2.49 (1-55734-893-6) Tchr Create Mat.

— Swimming: Easy Sports Reader. (Illus.). 16p. (J). (ps-1). 1996. pap. 2.49 (1-55734-897-9) Tchr Create Mat.

— Tennis: Easy Sports Reader. (Illus.). 16p. (J). (ps-1). 1996. pap. 2.49 (1-55734-895-2) Tchr Create Mat.

Burt & Stetina, T. Speed & Thrash Metal Guitar Method. 1991. per. 14.95 incl. audio (0-7935-0254-3, 00660171) H Leonard.

Burt, et al. Fine's Wisconsin Evidence, 1988-1993: A Quick Guide to Courtroom Evidence, 3 vols. Dobkin, James A., ed. 1000p. 1995. ring bd., suppl. ed. 270.00 (0-250-40720-5, 81289-10, MICHIE) LEXIS Pub.

Burt, jt. auth. see Aguado.

Burt, jt. auth. see Bader.

Burt, jt. auth. see Stetina, T.

Burt, jt. auth. see Stettina.

Burt, A. Spelling. (Illus.). (J). (gr. 4-6). mass mkt. 6.95 (0-340-72651-2, Pub. by Hodder & Stought Ltd) Trafalgar.

Burt, A. W. Cushman Genealogy & General History. (Illus.). 432p. 1991. reprint ed. pap. 67.00 (0-8328-2046-6); reprint ed. lib. bdg. 77.00 (0-8328-2045-8) Higginson Bk Co.

Burt, Al, Jr. Al Burt's Florida: Snowbirds, Sandcastles, & Self-Rising Crackers. LC 97-9454. (Florida History & Culture Ser.). (Illus.). 192p. 1997. 24.95 (0-8130-1542-1) U Press Fla.

Burt, Al. Becalmed in the Mullet Latitudes: Al Burt's Florida. Martin, Val, ed. LC 83-81677. 350p. (Orig.). 1983. pap. 9.95 (0-912451-10-6) Florida Classics.

***Burt, Al.** The Tropic of Cracker. LC 99-18371. (History & Culture Ser.). (Illus.). 224p. 1999. 24.95 (0-8130-1695-9) U Press Fla.

Burt, Alvin. Florida a Place in the Sun. (Illus.). 244p. 1974. 8.95 (0-685-50329-1) Burda Media.

Burt, Anand, ed. see Osho.

Burt, Andrew L. Noontide Night: A Y2K Novel. 314p. 1999. pap. 12.95 (0-9672984-0-7, NeverWrlds Pr) TechSoft.

Burt, Angela M. A Guide to Better Grammar. 2nd ed. 128p. (C). 1991. pap. 22.00 (0-7487-0537-6, Pub. by S Thornes Pubs) Trans-Atl Phila.

— A Guide to Better Punctuation. 2nd ed. 144p. (C). 1991. pap. 22.00 (0-7487-1122-8, Pub. by S Thornes Pubs) Trans-Atl Phila.

— A Guide to Better Spelling. 2nd ed. 104p. (C). 1991. pap. 22.00 (0-7487-1234-8, Pub. by S Thornes Pubs) Trans-Atl Phila.

Burt, Arthur. Pebbles to Slay Goliath. Walters, Kathie, ed. & intro. by. (Illus.). 64p. 1996. pap. 4.99 (0-9629559-7-3) Good News Min.

— Surrender. LC 97-66741. 1997. pap. 9.99 (0-88419-508-2) Creation House.

Burt, B., ed. see Lee, L., et al.

Burt, Ben. Tradition & Christianity: The Colonial Transformation of a Solomon Islands Society. LC 93-23801. (Studies in Anthropology & History: Vol. 10). 314p. 1994. text 71.00 (3-7186-5449-0) Gordon & Breach.

Burt, Ben & Clerk, Christian. Environment & Development in the Pacific Islands LC 98-200222. (Pacific Policy Paper Ser.). xiii, 299p. 1997. write for info. (0-7315-2351-2) ANU Res Sch.

Burt, Ben, ed. see Kwa'ioloa, Michael.

***Burt, Bernard I.** 100 Best Spas of the World. (Illus.). 2001. pap. 19.95 (0-7627-0807-7) Globe Pequot.

Burt, Bill. Behind the Scenes of NASCAR Racing. LC 96-50987. (Enthusiast Color Ser.). (Illus.). 96p. 1997. pap. 13.95 (0-7603-0348-7) MBI Pubg.

— The King of the Trees. LC 97-62570. 192p. 1998. pap. 10.99 (1-57921-090-2, Pub. by WinePress Pub) BookWorld.

***Burt, Bill.** NASCAR Transporters. (Illus.). 96p. 2000. pap. 13.95 (0-7603-0816-0, 130531AP, Pub. by MBI Pubg) Motorbooks Intl.

Burt, Bill. Stock Car Race Fan's Reference Guide: Understanding Nascar. LC 98-46887. (Illus.). 192p. 1999. 19.95 (0-7603-0509-9) Motorbooks Intl.

Burt, Bill, jt. auth. see Monaco, Richard.

Burt, Brian A. & Ekland, Steven A. Dentistry, Dental Practice & the Community. 5th ed. Fletcher, Judy, ed. LC 98-28551. (Illus.). 395p. (C). 1999. pap. text. write for info. (0-7216-7309-0, W B Saunders Co) Harcrt Hlth Sci Grp.

Burt, Brian A. & Eklund, Stephen A., eds. Dentistry, Dental Practice, & the Community. 4th ed. (Illus.). 347p. 1992. pap. text 45.00 (0-7216-3195-9, W B Saunders Co) Harcrt Hlth Sci Grp.

***Burt, C. M. & American Society of Civil Engineers Staff.** Selection of Irrigation Methods for Agriculture: Committee Report. LC 99-54568. 1999. write for info. (0-7844-0462-3) Am Soc Civil Eng.

Burt, C. Tyler. Phosphorus NMR in Biology. 248p. 1987. 141.00 (0-8493-5842-6, CRC Reprint) Franklin.

Burt, Calvin C. Egyptian Masonic History of the Original & Unabridged Ancient & Ninety-Six Degree Rite of Memphis. 350p. 1993. reprint ed. pap. 27.00 (1-56459-341-X) Kessinger Pub.

***Burt, Catharine W.** Injury Visits to Hospital Emergency Departments: United States, 1992-95. 82p. 1998. pap. 7.00 (0-16-049381-1) USGPO.

Burt, Catharine W., et al. Injury Visits to Hospital Emergency Departments: United States, 1992-95. LC 97-42729. (Vital & Health Statistics Ser.: Series 13, No. 131). 1998. write for info. (0-8406-0536-6) Natl Ctr Health Stats.

Burt, Charles M. & Styles, Stuart W. Drip & Microirrigation: For Trees, Vines & Row Crops. LC 94-79774. (Illus.). 261p. (Orig.). 1994. pap. text 34.95 (0-9643634-0-2) Irrigat Trning.

Burt, Charles M., et al. Fertigation. 300p. 1995. pap. text 34.95 (0-9643634-1-0) Irrigat Trning.

Burt, Cyril L., ed. How the Mind Works. LC 78-105000. (Essay Index Reprint Ser.). 1977. 21.95 (0-8369-1454-6) Ayer.

***Burt, Dan.** You Can Paint Vibrant Watercolors. LC 98-49886. (Illus.). 128p. 1999. 27.99 (0-89134-903-0, 31426, North Lght Bks) F & W Pubns Inc.

Burt, Daniel S. The Biography Book: A Reader's Guide to Nonfiction, Fictional, & Film Biographies of the 500 Most Fascinating Individuals of All Time. 544p. 2001. boxed set 74.50 (1-57356-256-4) Oryx Pr.

— Literary 100: A Ranking of the Most Influential Novelists, Playwrights & Poets of All Time. LC 98-13729. (Illus.). 256p. 1998. 29.95 (0-8065-1956-8, Citadel Pr) Carol Pub Group.

***Burt, Daniel S.** The Literary 100: A Ranking of the Most Influential Novelists, Playwrights & Poets of All Time. (Illus.). 416p. 2001. 35.00 (0-8160-4382-5, Checkmark); pap. 19.95 (0-8160-4383-3, Checkmark) Facts on File.

Burt, David K. Zero-Base Pricing: Achieving World-Class Competitiveness Through Reduced All-in-Costs. 1990. text 50.00 (1-55738-132-1, Irwn Prfssnl) McGraw-Hill Prof.

Burt, David N. Proactive Procurement: The Key to Increased Profits, Productivity, & Quality. (Illus.). 288p. 1984. text 54.20 (0-13-711465-6) P-H.

Burt, David N. & Doyle, Michael F. The American Keiretsu: A Strategic Weapon for Global Competitiveness. LC 92-46913. 251p. 1993. 25.00 (1-55623-852-5, Irwn Prfssnl) McGraw-Hill Prof.

Burt, David N. & Pinkerton, Richard L. A Purchasing Manager's Guide to Strategic Proactive Procurement. LC 95-44558. 240p. 1996. 55.00 (0-8144-0288-7) AMACOM.

***Burt, Denise.** Kangaroos. LC 99-26680. (Nature Watch Ser.). (Illus.). 48p. (J). (gr. 2-5). 2000. 22.60 (1-57505-388-8, Carolrhoda) Lerner Pub.

Burt, Denise. Koalas. LC 98-46097. 48p. (J). (gr. 3-6). 1999. 22.60 (1-57505-380-2, Carolrhoda) Lerner Pub.

Burt, Don. Winning with the American Quarter Horse. LC 95-45235. (Equestrian Library). (Illus.). 256p. 1996. 30.00 (0-385-46813-X) Doubleday.

Burt, Donald. The Pilgrim God: A Preacher Reflects on the Story of Jesus. 312p. (Orig.). 1995. pap. 15.95 (0-8146-2246-1) Liturgical Pr.

Burt, Donald X. Augustine's World: An Introduction to His Speculative Philosophy. LC 96-10254. 306p. Date not set. pap. text 27.50 (0-7618-0295-9); lib. bdg. 57.00 (0-7618-0294-0) U Pr of Amer.

— Friendship & Society: An Introduction to Augustine's Practical Philosophy. LC 99-40410. 248p. 1999. pap. 18.00 (0-8028-4682-3) Eerdmans.

***Burt, E S.** Poetry's Appeal: 19th-Century French Lyric & the Political Space. LC 99-39452. (Meridian Ser.). 1999. pap. text 19.95 (0-8047-3873-4) Stanford U Pr.

Burt, E. S. Reading the Archive: On Texts & Institutions, Yale French Studies, Vol. 77. Vol. 77. 1990. pap. 18.00 (0-300-04540-9) Yale U Pr.

Burt, E. S., ed. see De Man, Paul.

Burt, E. S., ed. see De Man Paul Staff.

Burt, Edmund. Burt's Letters from the North of Scotland. LC 99-215315. (Illus.). 400p. 1998. pap. 25.95 (1-874744-90-4, Pub. by Birlinn Ltd) Dufour.

Burt, Edna W. Looking Good, Living Long, Feeling Great: A Breakthrough 9-Step Program to Help You Look Your Best, Live a Long, Healthy Life & Feel Great in the Process. LC 92-90004. 100p. (Orig.). 1992. pap. 14.95 (0-9631972-0-7) Edna FourCZNS.

Burt, Edward A. Thelephoraceae of North America, 15 Pts. (Illus.). 900p. 1966. reprint ed. lib. bdg. 50.00 (0-945345-04-6) Lubrecht & Cramer.

Burt, Elinor. Spanish Dishes from the Old Clay Pot. rev. ed. (Cookery Ser.). (Illus.). 280p. 1979. reprint ed. pap. 9.95 (0-89496-001-6) Ross Bks.

Burt, Elisabeth V., tr. see Palazzoli, Mara S., et al.

Burt, Elizabeth R., et al. High Fit-Low Fat Vegetarian Cookbook. LC 96-70640. (Illus.). 192p. 1996. spiral bd. 14.95 (0-9649656-1-5) U MI MedSport.

***Burt, Elizabeth V.** Historical Dictionary of Women's Press Organizations: Institutional Profiles, 1881-1999. LC 99-49045. 384p. 2000. lib. bdg. 85.00 (0-313-30661-3) Greenwood.

Burt, Erica. Natural Materials. (Craft Projects Ser.). (Illus.). 32p. (J). (gr. 2-6). 1990. lib. bdg. 11.95 (0-685-46442-3) Rourke Corp.

— Paper. (Craft Projects Ser.). (Illus.). 32p. (J). (gr. 2-6). 1990. lib. bdg. 11.95 (0-685-46443-1) Rourke Corp.

Burt, Eugene C. An Annotated Bibliography of the Visual Arts of East Africa. LC 80-7805. (Traditional Arts of Africa Ser.). 392p. 1980. 25.00 (0-253-17225-X) Ind U Pr.

— East African Art in the Collection of the Seattle Art Museum. LC 85-63342. (Illus.). 32p. (Orig.). 1986. pap. 4.95 (0-932216-20-X) Seattle Art.

— Erotic Art: An Annotated Bibliography with Essays. 500p. 1989. 60.00 (0-8161-8957-9, Hall Reference) Macmillan.

— Ethnoart: Africa, Oceania & the Americas: A Bibliography of Theses & Dissertations. LC 88-7207. 212p. 1988. text 10.00 (0-8240-7545-5) Garland.

Burt, Eugene C., ed. Serials Guide to Ethnoart: A Guide to Serial Publications on Visual Arts of Africa, Oceania, & the Americas, 11. LC 90-40202. (Art Reference Collection Ser.: No. 11). 384p. 1990. lib. bdg. 75.00 (0-313-27332-4, BEM, Greenwood Pr) Greenwood.

Burt, Forrest D. The Effective Writer. 130p. 1978. pap. text 9.95 (0-89641-005-6) American Pr.

Burt, Forrest D. & Machann, Clinton, eds. Selected Letters of Matthew Arnold. LC 92-16553. 270p. (C). 1993. text 49.50 (0-472-10224-9, 10224) U of Mich Pr.

Burt, Forrest D. & Want, Cleve E., eds. Invention & Design. 4th ed. 416p. (C). 1984. pap. 39.06 (0-07-554426-1) McGraw.

Burt, Forrest D., jt. ed. see Machann, Clinton.

Burt-Garrans, Terry. Southern Ontario: Cross-Country Ski Guide. LC 98-126136. (Illus.). 176p. 1994. pap. 11.95 (1-55046-126-5, Pub. by Boston Mills) Genl Dist Srvs.

Burt, George, jt. auth. see Hatfield, James.

Burt, George D. The Art of Film Music. 280p. 1994. pap. text 20.00 (1-55553-270-5) NE U Pr.

Burt, George D., jt. auth. see Hatfield, James.

Burt, H. M. & Burt, S. W. Early Days in New England: Life & Times of Henry Burt of Springfield & Some of His Descendants. (Illus.). 620p. 1989. reprint ed. pap. 78.50 (0-8328-0355-3); reprint ed. lib. bdg. 88.50 (0-8328-0354-5) Higginson Bk Co.

Burt, James, jt. auth. see Aguado, Edward.

Burt, James E. & Barber, Gerald M. Elementary Statistics for Geographers. 2nd ed. LC 95-44912. (Illus.). 638p. 1995. lib. bdg. 65.00 (0-89862-282-4, 2282) Guilford Pubns.

Burt, Jeannie, jt. auth. see White, Gwen.

Burt, Jeffrey A., jt. auth. see Dobkin, James A.

Burt, Jeffrey A., jt. ed. see Dobkin, James A.

Burt, Jim. Hardball. 1987. write for info. (0-318-62540-7) Harcourt.

Burt, Jim & Gola, Hank. Hard Nose: The Story of the 1986 Giants. (Illus.). 1987. 15.95 (0-15-138575-0) Harcourt.

Burt, Jocelyn. Discover the Northern Territory. LC 96-157150. (Illus.). 80p. (C). 1995. pap. 19.95 (1-875560-58-0) Intl Spec Bk.

— Discover Western Australia. (Illus.). 92p. 1996. pap. 19.95 (1-875560-84-X) Intl Spec Bk.

— Discover Western Australia. 1993. 29.95 (1-875560-21-1, Pub. by Univ of West Aust Pr) Intl Spec Bk.

— The Kimberley: Australia's Unique North-West. LC 97-158546. (Illus.). 304p. 1996. pap. 19.95 (1-875560-78-5) Intl Spec Bk.

Burt, John. Robert Penn Warren & American Idealism. LC 87-14742. 256p. (C). 1988. 35.00 (0-300-04067-9) Yale U Pr.

— Work Without Hope: Poems. (Poetry & Fiction Ser.). 80p. (C). 1996. 16.95 (0-8018-5371-0) Johns Hopkins.

Burt, John, ed. see Warren, Robert Penn.

Burt, John S. They Left Their Mark: William Austin Burt & His Sons, Surveyors of the Public Domain. (Illus.). 188p. 1987. 50.00 (0-910845-31-X, 977) Landmark Ent.

Burt, John S. & Hawthorne, W. E. Past & Present of Marshall & Putnam Counties Illinois, with Biographical Sketches of Many Prominent & Leading Citizens & Illustrious Dead. (Illus.). 511p. 1998. reprint ed. lib. bdg. 54.50 (0-8328-7083-8) Higginson Bk Co.

Burt, Joy, jt. auth. see Burt, Ron.

Burt, Katharine N. Red Lady. 1979. mass mkt. 2.50 (0-451-11596-1, AE1596, Sig) NAL.

Burt, Kathleen. Archetypes of the Zodiac. LC 87-45743. (Modern Astrology Library). (Illus.). 576p. (Orig.). 1999. pap. 17.95 (0-87542-088-5) Llewellyn Pubns.

Burt, Leah B. Stenzel, see Welch, Walter L. & Stenzel Burt, Leah B.

Burt, Lizzie & Mercer, Nelda. High Fit-Low Fat. rev. ed. LC 89-23360. (Illus.). 1993. spiral bd. 14.95 (0-87197-260-3) U MI Med Ctr.

Burt, Mala S., ed. Stepfamilies Stepping Ahead: An Eight-Step Program for Successful Family Living. 2nd ed. LC 89-51436. Orig. Title: Stepping Ahead. 96p. (C). 1989. pap. 9.95 (0-9624432-0-4) Stepfamily Assn Amer.

Burt, Mala S. & Burt, Roger B. Stepfamilies: The Step by Step Model of Brief Therapy. 208p. 1996. 26.95 (0-87630-832-9) Brunner-Mazel.

Burt, Marina K., ed. see Teachers of English to Speakers of Other Languages.

***Burt, Martha R.** Homelessness: Programs & the People They Serve: Findings of the National Survey of Homeless Assistance Providers & Clients. (Illus.). 88p. (C). 2000. pap. text 20.00 (0-7881-8754-6) DIANE Pub.

Burt, Martha R. Over the Edge: The Growth of Homelessness in the 1980s. LC 91-18000. (Illus.). 278p. 1992. reprint ed. 45.00 (0-87154-177-7) Russell Sage.

— Over the Edge: The Growth of Homelessness in the 1980s. 278p. 1993. reprint ed. pap. 16.95 (0-87154-178-5) Russell Sage.

Burt, Martha R. & Cohen, Barbara E. America's Homeless: Numbers, Characteristics, & Programs That Serve Them. LC 89-9141. (Reports: No. 89-3). 176p. (Orig.). (C). 1989. pap. text 16.00 (0-87766-472-2); lib. bdg. 43.00 (0-87766-471-4) Urban Inst.

Burt, Martha R., et al. Building Supportive Communities for At-Risk Adolescents: It Takes More Than Services. LC 97-32411. 314p. 1997. pap. 24.95 (1-55798-466-2, 431-703A) Am Psychol.

Burt, Marvin R. Drug Abuse: Its Natural History & the Effectiveness of Current Treatments. 362p. 1979. text 44.95 (0-87073-995-6) Transaction Pubs.

Burt, Marvin R., jt. auth. see Sowder, Barbara J.

Burt, Mary A. Beginning the Walk: A Tool for Developing Your Preschooler's Faith. (Illus.). 184p. (Orig.). 1994. pap. 19.95 (0-9641134-0-6) Prods With A Purpose.

Burt, Mary E. Carr: Genealogy of Joseph Carr of Jamestown, Rhode Island, from "Carr Family Records" & Carried to the 10th Generation. (Illus.). 36p. 1997. reprint ed. pap. 7.00 (0-8328-7857-X); reprint ed. lib. bdg. 17.00 (0-8328-7856-1) Higginson Bk Co.

— Literary Landmarks: A Guide to Good Reading for Young People. 1977. lib. bdg. 59.95 (0-8490-2170-7) Gordon Pr.

Burt, Mary E., ed. Poems That Every Child Should Know: A Selection of the Best Poems of All Times for Young People. LC 71-168776. (Granger Index Reprint Ser.). 1977. reprint ed. 49.92 (0-8369-6296-6) Ayer.

Burt, Mary E. & Cable, Mary B. Eugene Field Book. LC 76-86794. (Granger Index Reprint Ser.). 1977. 17.95 (0-8369-6071-8) Ayer.

Burt, Maxwell S. Delectable Mountains. LC 70-144922. 1971. reprint ed. 29.00 (0-403-00885-9) Scholarly.

— The Diary of a Dude-Wrangler. (BCL1 - United States Local History Ser.). 331p. 1991. reprint ed. lib. bdg. 89.00 (0-7812-6327-1) Rprt Serv.

— Other Side. LC 70-134064. (Essay Index Reprint Ser.). 1977. reprint ed. 23.95 (0-8369-2218-2) Ayer.

***Burt, McKinley, Jr.** African-American Inventors. LC 99-50989. 2000. pap. write for info. (0-89420-344-4) Natl Book.

Burt, McKinley, Jr. Black Inventors of America. 2nd ed. 1989. pap. 12.95 (0-89420-284-7, 296959) Natl Book.

Burt, Nancy V., jt. auth. see Standley, Fred L.

An Asterisk (*) at the beginning of an entry indicates that the title is appearing for the first time.

B

An Asterisk (*) at the beginning of an entry indicates that the title is appearing for the first time.

— Cass County, Michigan: 1880 Federal Census Index. (Illus.). 120p. (Orig.). 1995. pap. 12.00 (0-937505-11-0) Glyndwr Resc.

Burton, Ann M. & Burton, Conrad. Born in Ohio & Living in Southwest Michigan in 1860: Born in Ohio. (Illus.). 1994. fiche 5.00 (0-937505-13-7) Glyndwr Resc.

— Cass County, Michigan: 1870 Census Index. (Illus.). 80p. 1990. pap. 10.00 (0-937505-06-4) Glyndwr Resc.

— Michigan Quakers: Abstracts of 15 Meetings of the Society of Friends 1831-1960. LC 89-82300. (Illus.). 601p. 1989. 50.00 (0-937505-05-6) Glyndwr Resc.

Burton, Ann Mullin. Carroll County, Indiana: 1850 Census Index. pap. write for info. (0-937505-18-8) Glyndwr Resc.

Burton, Anthony. Children's Pleasures. (Illus.). 1996. 49.50 (1-85177-174-3, Pub. by V&A Ent) Antique Collect.

***Burton, Anthony.** Thomas Telford. 224p. 2000. 29.95 (1-85410-652-X, Pub. by Aurum Pr) London Brdge.

— Traction Engines: Two Centuries of Steam Power. (Illus.). 2000. 12.99 (0-7858-1172-9) Bk Sales Inc.

Burton, Anthony. Vision & Accident: The Story of the Victoria & Albert Museum. (Illus.). 256p. 1999. 95.00 (1-85177-292-8, Pub. by V&A Ent) Antique Collect.

Burton, Antoinette. At the Heart of the Empire: Indians & the Colonial Encounter in Late-Victorian Britain. LC 96-29617. 304p. 1998. 55.00 (0-520-20958-3, Pub. by U CA Pr) Cal Prin Full Svc.

— Burdens of History: British Feminists, Indian Women, & Imperial Culture, 1865-1915. LC 94-5722. 390p. 1994. pap. 19.95 (0-8078-4471-3); text 55.00 (0-8078-2161-6) U of NC Pr.

Burton, Antoinette. Politics & Empire in Victorian Britain. text. write for info. (0-312-22997-6) St Martin.

***Burton, Antoinette, ed.** Gender Sexuality & Colonial Modernities. (Routledge Research in Gender & History Ser.). (Illus.). 232p. (C). 1999. text 90.00 (0-415-20068-7) Routledge.

Burton, Art T. Black, Red & Deadly: Black & Indian Gunfighters of the Indian Territories. Eakin, Ed, ed. (Illus.). 288p. 1991. 24.95 (0-89015-798-7); pap. 17.95 (0-89015-994-7) Sunbelt Media.

Burton, Arthur. Modern Humanistic Psychotherapy. LC 67-27947. (Jossey-Bass Behavioral Science Ser.). 188p. reprint ed. 58.30 (0-8357-9335-4, 201391500087) Bks Demand.

— Twelve Therapists: How They Live & Actualize Themselves. LC 72-83966. (Jossey-Bass Behavioral Science Ser.). 342p. reprint ed. pap. 106.10 (0-608-17081-X, 202774700056) Bks Demand.

Burton, Arthur, ed. Encounter: Theory & Practice of Encounter Groups. LC 73-92889. (Jossey-Bass Behavioral Science Ser.). 224p. reprint ed. 63.90 (0-8357-9318-4, 2013911) Bks Demand.

***Burton, Arthur T.** Black, Buckskin & Blue: African American Scouts & Soldiers on the Western Frontier. LC 99-35249. 1999. 24.95 (1-57168-295-3, Eakin Pr) Sunbelt Media.

Burton, Asa. Essays on Some of the First Principles of Metaphysicks, Ethicks, & Theology. LC 73-4839. (History of Psychology Ser.). 432p. 1973. reprint ed. lib. bdg. 60.00 (0-8201-1114-7) Schol Facsimiles.

Burton, Audrey. The Bukharans: A Dynastic, Diplomatic & Commercial History. (Illus.). 360p. 1990. 75.00 (0-7103-0382-3, A4532) Routledge.

— The Bukharans: A Dynastic, Diplomatic & Commercial History 1550-1702. (Illus.). 530p. 1996. 45.00 (0-7007-0417-5, Pub. by Curzon Pr Ltd) Paul & Co Pubs.

Burton, B. Diffusional Creep of Materials. 1977. 36.00 (0-87849-506-1, Pub. by Trans T Pub) Enfield Pubs NH.

Burton, B. P., et al. Phase Equilibria & Crystal Chemistry in Portions of the System SRO-CAO-Bi203-CuO. (Illus.). 49p. (Orig.). (C). 1994. pap. text 30.00 (0-7881-0375-X) DIANE Pub.

Burton, Barry. Let's Weigh the Evidence. LC 83-71271. 95p. 1983. pap. 4.50 (0-937958-17-4) Chick Pubns.

Burton, Ben. The Chicken That Won a Dogfight: The Humor & Hope of an Arkansas Boyhood. LC 92-35636. 159p. 1993. pap. 8.95 (0-87483-258-6) August Hse.

Burton, Benjamin T. Human Nutrition. 3rd ed. (Illus.). 1975. text 39.95 (0-07-009282-6) McGraw.

Burton, Betty. The Girl Now Leaving. large type ed. (Charnwood Large Print Ser.). 544p. 1997. 27.99 (0-7089-8891-1, Charnwood) Ulverscroft.

— Goodbye Piccadilly. large type ed. 544p. 1993. 27.99 (0-7089-8688-9) Ulverscroft.

— Long, Hot Summer. large type ed. 608p. 1996. 27.99 (0-7089-8817-2, Charnwood) Ulverscroft.

— Not Just a Soldier's War. large type ed. (Charnwood Large Print Ser.). 464p. 1997. 27.99 (0-7089-8953-5, Charnwood) Ulverscroft.

— Women Are Bloody Marvellous. large type ed. 1993. 60.00 (0-7066-1017-2, Pub. by Remploy Pr) St Mut.

***Burton, Bill, et al.** Cisco Technical Expert IP Protocol Boxed Set. 1200p. 1999. pap. text, boxed set 99.99 (0-07-135577-4) McGraw.

Burton, Bob. Bail Enforcer: The Advanced Bounty Hunter. (Illus.). 216p. 1990. pap. 16.95 (0-87364-578-2) Paladin Pr.

— Endangered!, 4 bks. Incl. Endangered Birds. LC 95-41128. (Illus.). 64p. (J). (gr. 4 up). 1996. lib. bdg. 26.60 (0-8368-1422-3); Endangered Environments. LC 95-41129. (Illus.). 64p. (J). (gr. 4 up). 1996. lib. bdg. 25.27 (0-8368-1423-1); Endangered Mammals. LC 95-40933. (Illus.). 64p. (J). (gr. 4 up). 1996. lib. bdg. 25.27 (0-8368-1424-X); Endangered Sea Life. LC 95-41127. (Illus.). 64p. (J). (gr. 4 up). 1996. lib. bdg. 26.60 (0-8368-1425-8); (Illus.). (J). 1996. Set lib. bdg. 106.40 (0-8368-1421-5) Gareth Stevens Inc.

Burton, Bob & Thorson, Ralph. The Bounty Hunter. (Illus.). 136p. 1984. pap. 15.00 (0-87364-296-1) Paladin Pr.

Burton, Bob, jt. auth. see Hager, Nicky.

Burton, Bonnie B., jt. auth. see McCarson, Bonnie.

Burton, Bruce, jt. ed. see Wurfel, David.

Burton, Bruce A. Hail! Nene Karenna, The Hymn. Butterfield, Stephen, ed. (Illus.). 292p. 1981. 17.75 (0-9611422-2-7) Security Dupont.

Burton, Bruce A., ed. see Pohl, Frederick J.

Burton, Bryan. Voices of the Wind: Native American Flute Songs. (Illus.). 36p. 1998. 20.95 incl. cd-rom (0-937203-88-2); 20.95 incl. audio (0-937203-89-0) World Music Pr.

Burton, C. Emory. The Poverty Debate: Politics & the Poor in America. LC 92-15992. 200p. 1992. pap. 16.95 (0-275-94436-0, B4436, Praeger Pubs) Greenwood.

— The Poverty Debate: Politics & the Poor in America, 102. LC 92-14353. (Contributions in Sociology Ser.: No. 102). 224p. 1992. 57.95 (0-313-28594-2, BYL, Greenwood Pr) Greenwood.

Burton, Carol, jt. auth. see Donnan, Geoffrey A.

Burton, Caryl & Franckeiss, Anton. Training for Total Quality Management. 1994. ring bd. 271.95 (0-566-07311-0, Pub. by Gower) Ashgate Pub Co.

***Burton, Cassandra.** African-American Education in Westmoreland County, VA. (Images of America Ser.). (Illus.). 128p. 1999. pap. 18.99 (0-7385-0145-X) Arcadia Publng.

Burton, Cassandra K., jt. auth. see Prior, Jennifer Overend.

Burton, Celia & Michael, Norma. A Practical Guide to Project Planning. 160p. 1994. pap. 27.95 (0-89397-396-3) Nichols Pub.

Burton, Charles. Political & Social Change in China since 1978: Contributions in Political Science, 250. LC 89-17208. 225p. 1990. 59.95 (0-313-26834-7, BSQ/, Greenwood Pr) Greenwood.

Burton, Charles V., jt. ed. see Kirkaldy-Willis, William H.

Burton, Cheryl, jt. auth. see Burton, Ann.

Burton-Christie, Douglas. Word in Desert. 352p. 1993. pap. text 27.50 (0-19-508333-4) OUP.

Burton, Clare. The Promise & the Price: Essays on Women & Organisations. 208p. 1991. pap. text 18.95 (0-04-442286-5, Pub. by Allen & Unwin Pty) Paul & Co Pubs.

— Subordination: Feminism & Social Theory. 146p. 1985. text 39.95 (0-86861-718-0, Pub. by Allen & Unwin Pty); pap. text 18.95 (0-86861-710-5, Pub. by Allen & Unwin Pty) Paul & Co Pubs.

Burton, Conrad, jt. auth. see Burton, Ann M.

***Burton, Corinne.** PowerPoint Simple Projects: Intermediate. (Illus.). 96p. 2000. pap., teacher ed. 8.95 (1-57690-441-5, TCM 2441) Tchr Create Mat.

Burton, Craig. A Hatful of Pain. LC 98-86797. (Illus.). 212p. 1999. 19.95 (1-56167-470-2, Five Star Spec Ed) Am Literary Pr.

Burton, Cyndy, jt. auth. see Olsen, Tim.

Burton, Cynthia E., jt. auth. see Cohen-Rosenthal, Edward.

Burton, D. Jeff. Along the Great Western Trail: Trails Between Parleys & Ogden Canyon, Utah. 80p. 1995. pap. 8.95 (1-883992-17-6) IVE Inc.

— Elemental Industrial Hygiene Home Study Course. 360p. 1992. write for info. (0-9623160-0-8) IVE Inc.

— Engineering Control Monograph: 20 Years of D. Jeff Burton Columns from OH&S. 200p. 1998. pap. 59.95 (1-883992-20-6) IVE Inc.

— For Those Who Wonder. 2nd rev. ed. 125p. 1993. 6.95 (0-9623160-3-2) IVE Inc.

— For Those Who Wonder: Managing Religious Questions & Doubts. 3rd ed. 128p. 1994. pap. 8.95 (1-883992-06-0) IVE Inc.

— IAQ & HVAC Workbook. (Illus.). 335p. 1993. 75.00 (0-9623160-7-5) IVE Inc.

— IAQ & HVAC Workbook. 3rd ed. 300p. 1997. spiral bd., wbk. ed. 59.95 (1-883992-16-8) IVE Inc.

— Industrial Hygiene Workbook. 340p. 1993. 45.00 (0-9623160-9-1) IVE Inc.

— Industrial Ventilation Workbook. (Illus.). 314p. (C). 1989. 30.00 (1-883992-04-4) IVE Inc.

— Industrial Ventilation Workbook. 2nd ed. 345p. 1992. student ed. 45.00 (0-9623160-2-4) IVE Inc.

— Industrial Ventilation Workbook. 4th ed. 300p. 1998. spiral bd., wbk. ed. 59.95 (1-883992-05-2) IVE Inc.

— Laboratory Ventilation Workbook. 2nd rev. ed. 350p. (C). 1994. pap. text, wbk. ed. 59.95 (1-883992-02-8) IVE Inc.

— Occupational Health Workbook. 300p. 1997. spiral bd., wbk. ed. 59.95 (1-883992-10-9) IVE Inc.

— Progression: The Afterlife. 80p. 1992. pap. 8.95 (0-9623160-5-9) IVE Inc.

— Semiconductor Exhaust Ventilation Guidebook. 200p. 1995. pap. text 59.95 (1-883992-08-7) IVE Inc.

— Summer Hiking from the Snowbird Tram. 40p. 1977. pap. 8.95 (1-883992-18-4) IVE Inc.

Burton, D. Jeff, jt. auth. see Hemeon, W. C.

Burton, Dan. Making the Federal Government Accountable: Enforcing the Mandate for Effective Financial Management. 51p. (C). 1999. text 20.00 (0-7881-7658-7) DIANE Pub.

Burton, Dan, ed. Enforcement of Penalties Against Violations of the U. S. Embargo on Cuba: Hearing Before the Committee on Relations, U. S. House of Representatives. 52p. (C). 1998. pap. text 20.00 (0-7881-7107-0) DIANE Pub.

— Gulf War Veterans' Illnesses - VA, DOD Continue to Resist Strong Evidence Linking Toxic Causes to Chronic Health Effects: Second Report by the Committee on Government Reform & Oversight, U. S. House of Representatives. 136p. (C). 1998. pap. text 30.00 (0-7881-7030-9) DIANE Pub.

Burton, Daniel. Rainbow of God's Love. 1.25 (0-687-02786-1) Abingdon.

Burton, Daniel F., Jr., et al, eds. Vision for the 1990s: U. S. Strategy & the Global Economy. LC 88-29216. 184p. 1989. text 34.95 (0-88730-248-3, HarpBusn) HarpInfo.

Burton, Danny. Money Laundering: FinCEN Needs to Better Communicate Regulatory Priorities & Time Lines. 54p. (C). 1999. pap. text 20.00 (0-7881-7778-8) DIANE Pub.

***Burton, Danny R.** Crime Technology: Federal Assistance to State & Local Law Enforcement. (Illus.). 52p. (C). 1999. pap. text 20.00 (0-7881-8465-2) DIANE Pub.

Burton, David. Edwin Arlington Robinson: Stages in a New England Poet's Search. LC 86-33144. (Studies in New England Thought & Literature: Vol. 1). 206p. 1987. lib. bdg. 89.95 (0-88946-557-6) E Mellen.

***Burton, David.** Manmade for Murder. 2000. per. 4.99 (0-373-26342-2) Harlequin Bks.

Burton, David. Manmade for Murder. 296p. 1997. 20.95 (1-885173-33-4) Write Way.

***Burton, David.** Savouring the East: Feasts & Stories from Istanbul to Bali. (Illus.). 278p. 2000. reprint ed. pap. text 17.00 (0-7881-9105-5) DIANE Pub.

Burton, David F. Emptiness Appraised: A Critical Study of Nagarjuna's Philosophy. (Critical Studies in Buddhism: Vol. 11). 288p. 1999. text 55.00 (0-7007-1066-3, Pub. by Curzon Pr Ltd) UH Pr.

Burton, David G. The Legend of Bernardo Del Carpio: From Chronicle to Drama. 150p. 1990. 30.00 (0-916379-54-X) Scripta.

Burton, David H. An Anglo-American Plutarch. 304p. (Orig.). (C). 1990. pap. text 26.00 (0-8191-7788-1); lib. bdg. 50.00 (0-8191-7787-3) U Pr of Amer.

— British-American Diplomacy, 1895-1917: Early Years of the Special Relationship. LC 98-24924. (Anvil Ser.). (C). 1998. pap. write for info. (1-57524-048-3) Krieger.

— Cecil Spring Rice: A Diplomat's Life. LC 89-46135. (Illus.). 232p. 1990. 35.00 (0-8386-3395-1) Fairleigh Dickinson.

— Clara Barton: In the Service of Humanity, 148. LC 94-37878. (Contributions in Women's Studies: Vol. 148). 192p. 1995. 55.00 (0-313-28945-X, Greenwood Pr) Greenwood.

— The Learned Presidency: Theodore Roosevelt, William Howard Taft, Woodrow Wilson. LC 86-46327. 224p. 1988. 32.50 (0-8386-3313-7) Fairleigh Dickinson.

— Political Ideas of Justice Holmes. LC 91-55095. 128p. 1992. 29.50 (0-8386-3457-5) Fairleigh Dickinson.

— Taft, Holmes & the 1920s Court: An Appraisal. LC 98-10012. 176p. 1998. 33.50 (0-8386-3768-X) Fairleigh Dickinson.

— Theodore Roosevelt, American Politician: An Assessment. LC 96-29718. 176p. 1997. 29.50 (0-8386-3727-2) Fairleigh Dickinson.

— William Howard Taft: In the Public Service. LC 84-27778. 160p. (C). 1985. pap. text 11.50 (0-89874-829-1) Krieger.

Burton, David H., ed. Holmes-Sheehan Correspondence: The Letters of Justice Oliver Wendell Holmes & Canon Patrick Augustine Sheehan. 2nd rev. ed. LC 93-1717. 96p. 1993. 20.00 (0-8232-1525-3) Fordham.

— Oliver Wendell Holmes, Jr. What Manner of Liberal? LC 78-23645. (American Problem Studies). 168p. 1979. pap. 11.50 (0-88275-793-8) Krieger.

— Progressive Masks: Letters of Oliver Wendell Holmes, Jr., & Franklin Ford. LC 80-54787. 144p. 1982. 27.50 (0-87413-188-X) U Delaware Pr.

Burton, David H., ed. see Taft, William Howard.

Burton, David M. Abstract Algebra. 496p. (C). 1988. text 58.75 (0-697-06761-0, WCB McGr Hill) McGrw-H Hghr Educ.

— Elementary Number Theory. 2nd ed. 480p. (C). 1989. text 56.88 (0-697-05919-7, WCB McGr Hill) McGrw-H Hghr Educ.

— Elementary Number Theory. 3rd ed. LC 92-71359. 400p. (C). 1993. text. write for info. (0-697-13330-3, WCB McGr Hill) McGrw-H Hghr Educ.

— Elementary Number Theory. 3rd ed. 388p. 1994. text 50.63 (0-697-27682-1, WCB McGr Hill) McGrw-H Hghr Educ.

— Elementary Number Theory. 4th ed. LC 97-12797. (International Series in Pure & Applied Mathematics). 432p. (C). 1997. 77.50 (0-07-009466-7) McGraw.

— The History of Mathematics: An Introduction. 3rd ed. LC 96-77659. (International Series in Pure & Applied Mathematics). (C). 1996. text 103.75 (0-07-009465-9) McGraw.

— The History of Mathematics: An Introduction. 3rd ed. LC 94-70130. 698p. (C). 1994. text 51.45 (0-697-16089-0, WCB McGr Hill) McGrw-H Hghr Educ.

Burton, Dawn. Financial Services & the Consumer. LC 93-44350. 144p. (C). 1994. pap. 24.95 (0-415-09962-5, B4155) Thomson Learn.

— Financial Services & the Consumer. LC 93-44350. 144p. (C). (gr. 13). 1994. pap. 53.95 (0-415-09961-7, B4151) Thomson Learn.

Burton, Dee. The American Cancer Society's "Freshstart" 21 Days to Stop Smoking. 1986. mass mkt. 5.50 (0-671-62086-X) PB.

Burton, Dee, et al. Developing School-Based Tobacco Use Prevention & Cessation Programs. 256p. 1994. 49.95 (0-8039-4927-8); pap. 24.00 (0-8039-4928-6) Sage.

Burton, Deirdre. Amores: 12 Stories. LC 98-89530. 290p. 1999. pap. 10.95 (0-9669290-0-4) Saddle Rock Pr.

Burton, Dennis. Central Park Nature Guide. LC 96-45269. 1995. 23.00 (0-8050-4616-X) H Holt & Co.

— Central Park Nature Guide. LC 96-45269. 1997. pap. 12.95 (0-8050-4617-8) H Holt & Co.

Burton, Doris K. Settlements of Uintah County: Digging Deeper. LC 98-61107. (History Ser.). (Illus.). 627p. 1998. 29.95 (0-9665287-0-0) Uintah Cnty Lib.

Burton, Duane. Jury Instructions in Intellectual Property Cases, 3 vols. 2300p. 1978. pap. 609.75 (1-928780-00-8) Big Foot Pr.

— Jury Instructions in Intellectual Property Cases, 2 vols., Set. rev. ed. 2200p. (C). 1996. reprint ed. 599.75 (0-318-68313-X) Big Foot Pr.

— Lost Profits in Patent Infringement Cases. LC TX4-761-60. 800p. 1998. pap. 297.75 (1-928780-01-6) Big Foot Pr.

— Rules of Construction for Patent Claims. 2nd ed. LC TX4-751-39. 230p. 1996. pap. 106.50 (1-928780-02-4) Big Foot Pr.

Burton, Dudley J. The Governance of Energy: Problems, Prospects & Underlying Issues. LC 79-89507. 426p. 1980. 79.50 (0-275-90459-8, C0459, Praeger Pubs) Greenwood.

Burton, Dudley J. & Ravishankar, K. Treatment of Hazardous Petrochemical & Petroleum Wastes: Current, New & Emerging Technologies. LC 89-39093. (Illus.). 268p. 1990. 56.00 (0-8155-1215-5) Noyes.

Burton, Dwight L. Literature Study in the High Schools. 3rd ed. LC 74-94346. viii, 357p. 1970. write for info. (0-03-081119-8) H Holt & Co.

Burton, E. C. Enforcement of Natural Resources Legislation: A Handbook. LC 85-118246. xxvi, 154p. (Orig.). 1984. pap. write for info. (0-459-36910-5) Carswell.

— Journal of a Country Lawyer: Crime, Sin, & Damn Good Fun. (Illus.). 239p. 1995. pap. 17.95 (0-88839-364-4) Hancock House.

***Burton, E. James & Bragg, Steven M.** Sales & Operations for Your Small Business. 240p. 2000. pap. 24.95 (0-471-39704-0) Wiley.

Burton, E. Milby. Charleston Furniture, 1700-1825. LC 73-120917. (Illus.). 160p. 1997. reprint ed. pap. 19.95 (1-57003-147-9) U of SC Pr.

— The Siege of Charleston, 1861-1865. LC 70-120584. xxii, 390p. 1976. pap. 14.95 (0-87249-345-8) U of SC Pr.

Burton, E. Milby & Cutten, George B. South Carolina Silversmiths, 1690-1860 & the Silversmiths of North Carolina. LC 98-65953. (Illus.). 429p. 1998. reprint ed. 30.00 (1-891495-06-2) Oglethorpe Pr.

Burton, Edmund C. & Grant, Robert S. Wheels, Skis & Floats: The Northern Adventures of a Pioneer Pilot. (Illus.). 174p. 1998. pap. 19.95 (0-88839-428-4) Hancock House.

Burton, Edward. An Inquiry into the Heresies of the Apostolic Age. LC 78-63166. (Heresies of the Early Christian & Medieval Era Ser.: Second Ser.). reprint ed. 87.50 (0-404-16179-0) AMS Pr.

Burton, Edward & Brody, Alan. Essentials of Pediatric Radiology. LC 98-34484. 1998. write for info. (3-13-115681-3) Thieme Med Pubs.

***Burton-Edwards, Grace, ed.** BookMarks Vol. 3: Bible Explorations for Older Youth. 144p. (YA). (gr. 9-12). 2000. pap. 16.00 (0-8170-1333-4) Judson.

Burton, Elizabeth. Mean Mean Madeleen - Sweet Sweet Angeleen. unabridged ed. Caso, Adolph, ed. LC 97-24767. (Illus.). 32p. (J). (gr. 2-6). 1997. pap. 12.95 (0-8283-2043-8) Branden Bks.

— Oh No, Steven! An Anthology of Steven Stories. Caso, Adolph, ed. (Illus.). 60p. (J). (gr. 4-9). 1996. pap. 11.95 (0-8283-2019-5) Branden Bks.

Burton, Eric. Collector's Dictionary of Clocks & Watches. 320p. 1999. 45.00 (0-7198-0300-4, Pub. by R Hale Ltd) Seven Hills Bk.

Burton, Eric & Mahang, Lois. Going Places: Picture-Based English, Bk. 2. LC 94-49596. (Illus.). 224p. 1995. pap. text, student ed. 13.60 (0-201-82526-0) Addison-Wesley.

Burton, Eric & Maharg, Lois. Going Places: Picture-Based English, Bk. 1. LC 94-49596. (Illus.). 208p. 1995. pap. text, student ed. 13.60 (0-201-82525-2) Addison-Wesley.

***Burton, Eric James & Bragg, Steven M.** Accounting & Finance for Your Small Business. 2nd ed. LC 00-20096. 350p. 2000. pap. 34.95 (0-471-32360-8) Wiley.

Burton, Ernest D. Syntax of Moods & Tenses of New Testament Greek. 240p. 1993. 35.95 (0-567-01002-3, Pub. by T & T Clark) Bks Intl VA.

— Syntax of the Moods & Tenses in New Testament Greek. LC 76-25360. 240p. 1976. 18.99 (0-8254-2256-6, Kregel Class) Kregel.

Burton, Ernest D., jt. auth. see Stevens, William A.

Burton, Ernest De Witt. Galatians: Critical & Exegetical Commentary. Driver, Samuel R. & Briggs, Charles A., eds. (International Critical Commentary Ser.). 632p. 1921. 39.95 (0-567-05029-7, Pub. by T & T Clark) Bks Intl VA.

Burton, Ernest J. The British Theatre: Its Repertory & Practice, 1100-1900 A. D. LC 77-22954. (Illus.). 271p. 1977. reprint ed. lib. bdg. 65.00 (0-8371-9739-2, BUBT, Greenwood Pr) Greenwood.

Burton, F. Multimedia Guide to Non-Human Primates. 1995. cd-rom 87.00 (0-13-207168-1) P-H.

Burton, Frances. Family Law. 200p. (C). 1990. pap. 60.00 (1-85352-512-X, Pub. by HLT Pubns) St Mut.

— Family Law & Practice. (Legal Practice Course Ser.). 507p. 1997. pap. 38.00 (1-874241-91-0, Pub. by Cavendish Pubng) Gaunt.

Burton, Frances, ed. Family Law: Documents, Forms & Precedents. 200p. (C). 1991. pap. 95.00 (0-7510-0020-5, Pub. by HLT Pubns) St Mut.

Burton, Frances D. Multimedia Guide to Non-Human Primates: The Print Version. LC 96-134652. 2953p. 1995. pap. text 53.00 (0-13-209727-3) P-H.

Burton, Frances D., ed. Social Processes & Mental Abilities in Non-Human Primates: Evidences from Longitudinal Field Studies. LC 92-11041. 308p. 1992. 99.95 (0-7734-9537-1) E Mellen.

Burton, Frances M., jt. auth. see Burton, Paul R.

Burton, Frank, jt. auth. see Nelson-Jones, Rodney.

Burton, Franklin L., ed. see Metcalf & Eddy, Inc. Staff & Tchobanoglous, George.

Burton, Fred, et al, eds. International Business & Europe in Transition. (AIB Series in International Business). 272p. 1996. text 59.95 (0-312-16041-0) St Martin.

An Asterisk (*) at the beginning of an entry indicates that the title is appearing for the first time.

Burton, Frederick R. American Primitive Music, with Special Attention to Songs of the Highways. 1977. lib. bdg. 59.95 (*0-8490-1416-6*) Gordon Pr.

Burton, G. Australian Financial Transactions Law. 572p. 1991. boxed set 91.00 (*0-409-39361-4*, Austral, MICHIE) LEXIS Pub.

— Australian Financial Transactions Law. 572p. 1991. write for info. (*0-409-30361-5*, MICHIE); pap. 57.00 (*0-409-49389-9*, Austral, MICHIE) LEXIS Pub.

***Burton, G.** Talking Television. (An Arnold Publication). 256p. 2000. pap. 24.95 (*0-340-58964-7*, Pub. by E A) OUP.

Burton, G. Allan. Sediment Toxicity Assessment. 480p. 1992. lib. bdg. 110.00 (*0-87371-450-4*, L450) Lewis Pubs.

Burton, G. Allen, Jr. Manual Evaluating Stormwater Effects in Receiving Waters. 250p. 1999. 59.95 (*0-87371-924-7*, L924) Lewis Pubs.

Burton, G. K. Directions in Finance Law. 1990. pap. 54.00 (*0-409-30142-6*, Austral, MICHIE); boxed set 78.00 (*0-409-30348-8*, Austral, MICHIE) LEXIS Pub.

Burton, G. M., et al. Towards a Good Beginning: Teaching Early Childhood Mathematics. 257p. 1984. write for info. (*0-318-61051-5*) Addison-Wesley.

Burton, Gabrielle. Heartbreak Hotel. LC 98-52439. 320p. 1999. reprint ed. pap. 13.50 (*1-56478-167-4*) Dalkey Arch.

— I'm Running Away from Home, but I'm Not Allowed to Cross the Street: A Primer on Women's Liberation. 208p. 1972. 5.00 (*0-912786-00-0*) Know Inc.

Burton, Gail. The Candida Control Cookbook: What You Should Know & What You Should Eat to Manage Yeast Infections. 3rd rev. ed. 240p. 1996. pap. 13.95 (*0-944031-67-6*) Aslan Pub.

Burton, Gail T. Cow Pies & Candle Lights. (Illus.). 128p. 1999. pap. write for info. (*0-7392-0161-1*, PO3111) Morris Pubng.

Burton, Garlinda M. Body Image. (YouthSearch Ser.: Vol. 8). 64p. 1996. pap. 5.95 (*0-687-05599-7*) Abingdon.

— 365 Meditations for Mothers of Teens. LC 96-19805. 336p. 1996. pap. 12.00 (*0-687-10921-3*) Dimen for Liv.

Burton, Geoff, jt. auth. see Caputo, Raffaele.

Burton, George G. Respiratory Care: A Guide to Clinical Practice. 4th ed. LC 96-40216. 1264p. 1997. text 69.95 (*0-397-55165-7*) Lppncott W & W.

— Therapist Driven Protocols. 547p. 1994. spiral bd. 175.00 (*1-879575-48-5*) Acad Med Sys.

Burton, Glyn, et al. Quantitative Methods for Business & Economics. LC 98-27625. (Longman Modular Texts in Business & Economics Ser.). 1998. pap. text. write for info. (*0-582-31165-9*) Longman.

Burton, Grace, et al. Fifth-Grade Book. Leiva, Miriam A., ed. LC 91-45680. (Curriculum & Evaluation Standards for School Mathematics Addenda Ser.). (Illus.). 32p. 1992. pap. 11.95 (*0-87353-315-1*) NCTM.

— First-Grade Book. Leiva, Miriam A., ed. LC 91-25729. (Curriculum & Evaluation Standards for School Mathematics Addenda Ser.: Grades K-6). (Illus.). 24p. 1991. pap. 10.95 (*0-87353-311-9*) NCTM.

— Fourth-Grade Book. Leiva, Miriam A., ed. LC 91-47648. (Curriculum & Evaluation Standards for School Mathematics Addenda Ser.). (Illus.). 32p. 1992. pap. text 11.95 (*0-87353-314-3*) NCTM.

— Kindergarten Book. Leiva, Miriam, ed. LC 91-11590. (Curriculum & Evaluation Standards for School Mathematics Addenda Ser.: Grades K-6). (Illus.). 24p. 1991. pap. 10.95 (*0-87353-310-0*) NCTM.

— Number Sense & Operations. LC 92-41880. (Curriculum & Evaluation Standards for School Mathematics Addenda Ser.: Grades K-6). (Illus.). 56p. 1993. pap. 13.95 (*0-87353-319-4*) NCTM.

— Second-Grade Book. Leiva, Miriam A., ed. LC 92-16408. (Curriculum & Evaluation Standards for School Mathematics Addenda Ser.: Grades K-6). (Illus.). 32p. 1992. pap. 11.95 (*0-87353-312-7*) NCTM.

— Sixth-Grade Book. Leiva, Miriam A., ed. LC 92-16924. (Curriculum & Evaluation Standards for School Mathematics Addenda Ser.: Grades K-6). (Illus.). 32p. (J). (gr. k-6). 1992. pap. 11.95 (*0-87353-316-X*) NCTM.

— Third-Grade Book. Leiva, Miriam A., ed. LC 91-34131. (Curriculum & Evaluation Standards for School Mathematics Addenda Ser.). (Illus.). 32p. (J). (gr. k-6). 1991. pap. 11.95 (*0-87353-313-5*) NCTM.

Burton, Graeme. More Than Meets the Eye: An Introduction to Media Studies. 192p. 1995. text 16.95 (*0-340-50409-9*, A4810, Pub. by E A) St Martin.

— More Than Meets the Eye: An Introduction to Media Studies. 2nd ed. LC 97-961. 256p. 1997. pap. text 19.95 (*0-340-67663-9*, Pub. by E A) OUP.

Burton, Graeme & Dimbleby, Richard. Between Ourselves: An Introduction to Interpersonal Communication. 224p. (Orig.). 1988. text 16.95 (*0-7131-6565-0*, Pub. by E A) St Martin.

— Between Ourselves: An Introduction to Interpersonal Communication. 2nd ed. LC 95-17542. 288p. (Orig.). 1995. pap. text 16.95 (*0-340-60585-5*, Pub. by E A) OUP.

Burton, Graeme, jt. auth. see Dimbleby, Richard.

Burton, Gwendolyn R. W. & Engelkirk, Paul G. Microbiology for the Health Sciences. 5th ed. 464p. 1995. pap. text 25.95 (*0-397-55187-8*) Lppncott W & W.

— Microbiology for the Health Sciences. 6th ed. LC 99-19388. 1999. write for info. (*0-7817-1844-9*) Lppncott W & W.

Burton, Harry E. Discovery of the Ancient World. LC 75-102228. (Select Bibliographies Reprint Ser.). 1977. 27.95 (*0-8369-5113-1*) Ayer.

Burton, Harry P., ed. Famous Stories by Famous Writers. 21.95 (*0-89190-126-4*) Amereon Ltd.

Burton, Heather, jt. auth. see Marti, James.

Burton, Helen. Homeplace & Other Poems. 42p. 1995. 15.95 (*0-9645769-0-2*) H Burton.

— Petals in the Wind. LC 95-95062. (Illus.). 82p. 1997. 17.95 (*0-9645769-1-0*) H Burton.

— A Walk in the Sun. LC 98-92690. (Illus.). 67p. (J). (gr. 4-12). 1998. 16.95 (*0-9645769-2-9*) H Burton.

Burton, Henry. An Apology of Appeale: Also, an Epistle to the True Hearted Nobility. LC 76-57364. (English Experience Ser.: No. 782). 1977. reprint ed. lib. bdg. 20.00 (*90-221-0782-5*) Walter J Johnson.

— For God & the King. LC 76-57365. (English Experience Ser.: No. 783). 1977. lib. bdg. 35.00 (*90-221-0783-3*) Walter J Johnson.

— A Tryall of Private Devotions. LC 77-6863. (English Experience Ser.: No. 856). 1977. reprint ed. lib. bdg. 20.00 (*90-221-0856-2*) Walter J Johnson.

Burton, Hester. Kate Ryder. LC 75-8576. (Illus.). 160p. (J). (gr. 7 up). 1975. 10.95 (*0-690-00978-X*) HarpC Child Bks.

— To Ravensrigg. LC 76-54292. (J). 1977. 10.78 (*0-690-01354-X*) HarpC Child Bks.

Burton, Ian, et al. The Environment as Hazard. 2nd ed. LC 92-33125. 290p. 1993. pap. text 21.95 (*0-89862-159-3*, 2159) Guilford Pubns.

— The Human Ecology of Coastal Flood Hazard in Megalopolis. LC 68-57967. (University of Chicago, Department of Geography, Research Paper Ser.: No. 115). 212p. reprint ed. pap. 65.80 (*0-7837-0394-5*, 204071500018) Bks Demand.

Burton, Ian, jt. ed. see Kates, Robert W.

Burton, Isabel, tr. see Alencar, Jose de.

Burton, Isadel, ed. see Vetalapancavimsati.

Burton, J., et al. Teaching of Human Sexuality in Schools for Health Professionals. (Public Health Papers: No. 57). 1974. pap. text 5.00 (*92-4-130057-4*, 1110057) World Health.

Burton, J. A. Effective Warehousing. 355p. (C). 1988. 65.00 (*0-7855-3771-6*, Pub. by Inst Pur & Supply) St Mut.

— Effective Warehousing. 355p. (C). 1989. 110.00 (*0-7855-4643-X*, Pub. by Inst Pur & Supply) St Mut.

Burton, J. Bryan. Moving Within the Circle: Contemporary Songs & Dances of Native America. (Illus.). 144p. (Orig.). 1994. pap. 29.95 incl. audio compact disk (*0-937203-65-3*); pap. 63.00 incl. sl., audio compact disk (*0-937203-66-1*) World Music Pr.

— Moving Within the Circle: Contemporary Songs & Dances of Native America. annot. ed. (Illus.). 144p. (Orig.). 1992. pap. 29.95 incl. audio (*0-937203-43-2*); pap. 60.00 incl. audio, sl. (*0-937203-50-5*) World Music Pr.

Burton, J. D., et al, eds. Dynamic Processes in the Chemistry of the Upper Ocean. LC 86-72520. (NATO Conference Series IV, Marine Sciences: Vol. 17). 254p. 1986. 69.50 (*0-306-42408-8*, Plenum Trade) Perseus Pubng.

Burton, J. L. Aids to Postgraduate Medicine. 5th ed. (Illus.). 272p. 1988. pap. text 16.95 (*0-443-03548-2*) Church.

— Aids to Postgraduate Medicine. 6th ed. 1994. pap. text 23.00 (*0-443-04913-0*) Church.

— Essentials of Dermatology. 3rd ed. (Illus.). 308p. 1990. pap. 29.95 (*0-443-04082-6*) Church.

Burton, J. M. Honore De Balzac & His Figures of Speech. (Elliott Monographs: Vol. 8). 1921. 25.00 (*0-527-02612-3*) Periodicals Srv.

***Burton, Jack.** Sonoma Picnics: A California Wine Country Travel Companion. LC 99-51721. (Illus.). 168p. 1999. pap. 13.00 (*0-939431-22-X*) Bored Feet Pubns.

Burton, Jack L. Fundamentals Of Electrical Systems Design. LC 99-29976. (Building Systems Design Ser.: Vol. 1). (Illus.). 177p. 1999. pap. text 35.00 incl. disk (*0-13-914029-8*) P-H.

— Fundamentals of HVAC Systems Design, Vol. 2. LC 98-29578. (Building Systems Design Ser.). 159p. 1998. pap. text 52.00 (*0-13-907593-3*) P-H.

— Fundamentals of Interior Lighting Design, Vol. 1. LC 98-3917. (Building Systems Design Ser.: Vol. 1). 118p. 1998. pap. text 49.00 (*0-13-907627-1*) P-H.

— Statics for Building Construction. LC 98-9661. 318p. 1998. 68.00 (*0-13-674300-5*) P-H.

Burton, James & McBride, W. Blan. The Business Owner's Operating Manual: A Step-by-Step Guide to Planning, Operating, & Evaluating Your Business. 10th ed. LC 91-4760. (Modern Accounting Perspectives & Practices Ser.). 352p. 1991. 89.95 (*0-471-87927-4*) Wiley.

Burton, James G. The Pentagon Wars: Reformers Challenge the Old Guard. LC 93-3424. (Illus.). 306p. 1993. 31.95 (*1-55750-081-9*) Naval Inst Pr.

Burton, James H. Evolution of the Income Approach. 260p. 1982. 17.00 (*0-911780-62-9*) Appraisal Inst.

Burton, Jan E. & Rasmussen, Lucinda A. Treating Children with Sexually Abusive Behavior Problems: Guidelines for Child & Parent Intervention. LC 98-6095. (Illus.). 279p. 1998. pap. 29.95 (*0-7890-0473-9*, Maltreatment & Trauma Pr); lib. bdg. 49.95 (*0-7890-0472-0*, Maltreatment & Trauma Pr) Haworth Pr.

Burton, Jane & Taylor, Kim. Exploring the Science of Nature, 4 bks. Incl. Nature & Science of Fossils. LC 98-31770. (Illus.). 32p. (J). (gr. 3 up). 1999. lib. bdg. 15.95 (*0-8368-2183-1*); Nature & Science of Seeds. LC 98-34023. (Illus.). 32p. (J). (gr. 3 up). 1999. lib. bdg. 21.27 (*0-8368-2184-X*); Nature & Science of Shells. LC 98-45673. (Illus.). 32p. (J). (gr. 3 up). 1999. lib. bdg. 15.95 (*0-8368-2185-8*); Nature & Science of Waste. LC 98-35275. (Illus.). 32p. (J). (gr. 3 up). 1999. lib. bdg. 15.95 (*0-8368-2186-6*); (Illus.). (J). (gr. 3 up). 1999. Set lib. bdg. 85.07 (*0-8368-2182-3*) Gareth Stevens Inc.

Burton, Jane & Taylor, Kim. Exploring the Science of Nature: New Releases, 4 bks. Incl. Nature & Science of Autumn. Burton, Jane, photos by. LC 99-21153. (Illus.). 32p. (YA). (gr. 3 up). 1999. lib. bdg. 21.27 (*0-8368-2190-4*); Nature & Science of Spring. Burton, Jane & Taylor, Kim, photos by. LC 99-29593. (Illus.). 32p. (J). (gr. 3 up). 1999. lib. bdg. 21.27 (*0-8368-2188-2*); Nature & Science of Summer. Burton, Jane & Taylor, Kim, photos by. LC 99-30126. (Illus.). 32p. (J). (gr. 3 up). 1999. lib. bdg. 21.27 (*0-8368-2189-0*); Nature & Science of Winter. LC 99-14718. (Illus.). 32p. (J). (gr. 3 up). 1999. lib. bdg. 21.27 (*0-8368-2191-2*); (Illus.). (J). Set lib. bdg. 85.07 (*0-8368-2187-4*) Gareth Stevens Inc.

Burton, Jane & Taylor, Kim. Exploring the Science of Nature Series, 8 bks. Incl. Nature & Science of Leaves. LC 97-8478. 32p. (J). (gr. 2 up). 1997. lib. bdg. 21.27 (*0-8368-1942-X*); Nature & Science of Mud. LC 97-8479. 32p. (J). (gr. 2 up). 1997. lib. bdg. 21.27 (*0-8368-1943-8*); Nature & Science of Rain. LC 97-8480. 32p. (J). (gr. 2 up). 1997. lib. bdg. 21.27 (*0-8368-1944-6*); Nature & Science of Sunlight. LC 97-8481. 32p. (J). (gr. 2 up). 1997. lib. bdg. 21.27 (*0-8368-1946-2*); (J). Set lib. bdg. 148.00 (*0-8368-2101-7*) Gareth Stevens Inc.

— Exploring the Science of Nature Series: New Releases, 4 bks. Incl. Nature & Science of Eggs. LC 98-6330. (Illus.). 32p. (J). (gr. 3 up). 1998. lib. bdg. 21.27 (*0-8368-2105-X*); Nature & Science of Flowers. LC 97-53119. (Illus.). 32p. (J). (gr. 3 up). 1998. lib. bdg. 21.27 (*0-8368-2106-8*); Nature & Science of Patterns. LC 97-53093. (Illus.). 32p. (J). (gr. 3 up). 1998. lib. bdg. 21.27 (*0-8368-2107-6*); Nature & Science of Wings. LC 98-6136. (Illus.). 32p. (J). (gr. 3 up). 1998. lib. bdg. 21.27 (*0-8368-2108-4*); Set pap. 79.74 (*0-8368-2104-1*) Gareth Stevens Inc.

***Burton, Jane & Taylor, Kim.** The Nature & Science of Numbers. LC 00-32248. (Exploring the Science of Nature Ser.). (Illus.). 2000. lib. bdg. write for info. (*0-8368-2193-9*) Gareth Stevens Inc.

Burton, Jane, jt. auth. see Head, Honor.

Burton, Jane, tr. see Sesboue, Bernard.

Burton, Janet. Monastic & Religious Orders in Britain, 1000-1300. (Cambridge Medieval Textbooks Ser.). (Illus.). 367p. (C). 1994. text 69.95 (*0-521-37441-3*); pap. text 22.95 (*0-521-37797-8*) Cambridge U Pr.

— The Monastic Order in Yorkshire, 1069-1215. LC 98-25233. (Cambridge Studies in Medieval Life & Thought: No. 40). 352p. (C). 1999. text 69.95 (*0-521-55229-X*) Cambridge U Pr.

Burton, Janet E. English Episcopal Acta Vol. V: York, 1070-1154, Vol. 5. (English Episcopal Acta Ser.: No. V). (Illus.). 208p. 1988. 80.00 (*0-19-726070-5*) OUP.

***Burton, Jeff.** Untitled. 85p. 1999. 40.00 (*4-915877-74-4*) Synergy Inc.

***Burton, Jeff, photos by.** Dreamland. (Illus.). 2000. 50.00 (*1-57687-076-6*, pwerHse Bks) pwerHse Cultrl.

Burton, Jeffrey. Indian Territory & the United States, 1866-1906: Courts, Government, & the Move for Oklahoma Statehood. LC 94-41039. (Legal History of North America Ser.: Vol. 1). xix, 314p. 1997. pap. 13.95 (*0-8061-2918-2*) U of Okla Pr.

— Indian Territory & the United States, 1866-1906: Courts, Government & the Movement for Oklahoma Statehood. LC 94-41039. (Legal History of North America Ser.: Vol. 1). 336p. 1995. 28.95 (*0-8061-2754-6*) U of Okla Pr.

***Burton, Jehu T.** Trusting God Through Tears: A Story to Encourage. LC 99-86399. 160p. 2000. pap. 10.99 (*0-8010-6161-X*) Baker Bks.

Burton, Jim. Legacy Builders: Dad, What Does Your Life Say to Your Wife & Children? LC 96-60586. 208p. 1996. pap. 11.99 (*1-56384-117-7*, Vital Issue Pr) Huntington Hse.

Burton, Joan. Best Hikes with Children in Western Washington & the Cascades, Vol. 1. 2nd ed. LC 98-3025. (Best Hikes with Children Ser.). (Illus.). 224p. 1998. pap. 14.95 (*0-89886-564-6*) Mountaineers.

— Western Washington & the Cascades, Vol. 2. 2nd ed. LC 98-3025. (Best Hikes with Children Ser.). 230p. 1999. pap. text 14.95 (*0-89886-626-X*) Mountaineers.

Burton, Joan B. Theocritus's Urban Mimes: Mobility, Gender, & Patronage. LC 94-28938. (Hellenistic Culture & Society Ser.: Vol. XIX). 307p. 1995. 48.00 (*0-520-08858-1*, Pub. by U CA Pr) Cal Prin Full Svc.

Burton, John. Atlas of Endangered Species. 2nd ed. 1998. 125.00 (*0-02-865034-4*) S&S Trade.

— The Handbook of Residential Care. LC 93-14836. (Illus.). 240p. 1993. pap. write for info. (*0-415-08636-1*) Routledge.

— The Handbook of Residential Care. LC 93-14836. (Illus.). 240p. (C). 1993. 85.00 (*0-415-08635-3*, B2231) Routledge.

***Burton, John.** Hypnotic Language: Its Structure & Its Uses. 2000. 37.50 (*1-899836-35-7*, Pub. by Crown Hse LPC Group.

Burton, John. An Introduction to the Hadith. (Islamic Surveys Ser.). 256p. 1994. 60.00 (*0-7486-0350-6*, Pub. by Edinburgh U Pr); pap. 28.50 (*0-7486-0435-9*, Pub. by Edinburgh U Pr) Col U Pr.

— Managing Residential Care. LC 97-18305. (Illus.). 280p. (C). 1998. 75.00 (*0-415-16487-7*); pap. 24.99 (*0-415-16488-5*) Routledge.

— Mirador: My Term As Hitler's Guest. 163p. 1986. 29.00 (*0-7212-0766-9*, Pub. by Regency Pr GBR) St Mut.

— The Sources of Islamic Law. 272p. 1990. 80.00 (*0-7486-0108-2*, Pub. by Edinburgh U Pr) Col U Pr.

Burton, John A. Owls of the World. 1990. 19.98 (*0-88486-022-1*) Arrowood Pr.

— 3-D Reptile. LC 99-180636. (Eyewitness Books). (Illus.). 56p. (J). (gr. 4-7). 1998. spiral bd. 16.95 (*0-7894-3452-0*) DK Pub Inc.

Burton, John C. Pour Man's Friend: A Guide & Reference for Bar Personnel. rev. ed. Burton, Nanci L., ed. LC 90-81198. (Illus.). 246p. 1990. per. 14.95 (*0-9624625-0-0*) Aperitifs Pub.

— Pour Man's Friend: Supplementary Workbook. Burton, Nanci L., ed. (Illus.). 96p. (C). 1992. ring bd. 14.95 (*0-9624625-1-9*) Aperitifs Pub.

Burton, John C., et al. Handbook of Accounting & Auditing. 1988. 160.00 (*0-7913-0044-7*) Warren Gorham & Lamont.

— Handbook of Accounting & Auditing. 1991. suppl. ed. 74.75 (*0-685-58524-7*) Warren Gorham & Lamont.

Burton, John F., Jr., ed. New Perspectives in Workers' Compensation. (Frank W. Pierce Memorial Lectureship & Conference Ser.: No. 7). 176p. 1988. pap. text 14.95 (*0-87546-144-1*, ILR Press) Cornell U Pr.

Burton, John F., Jr., jt. auth. see Berkowitz, Monroe.

Burton, John F., Jr., jt. auth. see Yates, Elizabeth H.

Burton, John H. Narratives from Criminal Trials in Scotland, 2 vols. in 1. LC 71-39564. reprint ed. 57.50 (*0-404-09925-4*) AMS Pr.

— Political & Social Economy; Its Practical Applications. LC 68-55499. (Reprints of Economic Classics Ser.). xii, 345p. 1970. reprint ed. 49.50 (*0-678-00621-0*) Kelley.

Burton, John H., ed. Darien Papers. LC 78-39563. (Bannatyne Club, Edinburgh. Publications: No. 90). reprint ed. 72.50 (*0-404-52831-7*) AMS Pr.

Burton, John H., intro. The Works of Jeremy Bentham: Published under the Superintendence of His Executor, John Bowring (1843 Edition), 11 vols., Set. 6640p. 1996. reprint ed. 625.00 (*1-85506-414-6*) Bks Intl VA.

B

Burton, John Hill, ed. Benthamiana: or Select Extracts from the Works of Jeremy Bentham: With an Outline of His Opinions on the Principal Subjects Discussed in His Works. xxiii, 419p. 1998. reprint ed. 135.00 (*1-56169-364-2*) Gaunt.

Burton, John J. Tabanini of Thailand above the Isthmus of Kra. LC 76-56190. (Illus.). 165p. (Orig.). 1978. 15.00 (*0-911836-10-1*) Entomological Repr.

Burton, John K., jt. ed. see Reed, W. Michael.

Burton, John W. Conflict Resolution: Its Language & Processes. LC 96-9224. 1996. pap. 14.95 (*0-8108-3214-3*) Scarecrow.

— A Nilotic World: The Atuot-speaking Peoples of the Southern Sudan, 1. LC 86-31790. (Contributions to the Study of Anthropology Ser.: No. 1). 188p. 1987. 49.95 (*0-313-25501-6*, BND/, Greenwood Pr) Greenwood.

— World Society. LC 71-176252. 192p. reprint ed. pap. 54.80 (*0-608-16434-8*, 2026335) Bks Demand.

Burton, Jonathan. Investment Titans: Investment Insights from the Minds That Move Wall Street. 2000. 24.95 (*0-07-135496-4*) McGraw.

Burton, Julianne. Cinema & Social Change in Latin America: Conversations with Filmmakers. 4th ed. LC 86-11297. (University of Texas at Austin, Institute of Latin American Studies). 320p. reprint ed. pap. 99.20 (*0-608-20863-9*, 207196200003) Bks Demand.

Burton, Julianne, ed. The New Latin American Cinema: An Annotated Bibliography of English-Languages Sources, 1960-1980. LC 83-80377. (Orig.). 1983. pap. 4.00 (*0-918266-17-3*) Smyrna.

Burton, June K., ed. Essays in European History: Selected from the Annual Meetings of the Southern Historical Association, 1986-1987. LC 88-37939. (Illus.). 188p. (Orig.). (C). 1989. pap. text 22.50 (*0-8191-7280-4*) U Pr of Amer.

Burton, June K. & White, Carolyn W. Essays in European History: Selected from the Annual Meetings of the Southern Historical Association, 1988-1989, Vol. II. 256p. 1996. pap. text 32.00 (*0-7618-0317-3*); lib. bdg. 51.00 (*0-7618-0316-5*) U Pr of Amer.

Burton, Katherine. Blessed Andre. 197p. 1996. reprint ed. 19.95 (*0-912141-38-7*) Roman Cath Bks.

Burton, Katherine. One Grey Mouse.Tr. of Une Souris Grise. (Illus.). 24p. (J). 1995. pap. 5.95 (*1-55074-324-4*) Kids Can Pr.

Burton, Katherine. Tess. (Calloway Corners Ser.). 1993. per. 3.50 (*0-373-83280-X*, 1-83280-7) Harlequin Bks.

Burton, Katherine & Fernandes, Eugenie. One Gray Mouse. unabridged ed. (Illus.). 24p. (J). (ps-k). 1997. 12.95 (*1-55074-225-6*, Pub. by Kids Can Pr) Genl Dist Srvs.

Burton, Katherine & Fernandes, Kim. Une Souris Grise.Tr. of Une Souris Grise. (FRE., Illus.). 24p. (J). mass mkt. 6.99 (*0-590-16023-0*) Scholastic Inc.

Burton, Katherine K. In No Strange Land. LC 72-99619. (Essay Index Reprint Ser.). 1977. 22.95 (*0-8369-1551-8*) Ayer.

— Paradise Planters, the Story of Brook Farm. LC 72-2949. reprint ed. 52.50 (*0-404-10714-1*) AMS Pr.

Burton, Ken. Knots: A Step-by-Step Guide to Tying Loops, Hitches, Bends & Dozens of Other Useful Knots. LC 96-69267. (Illus.). 80p. 1998. 12.98 (*0-7624-0067-6*, Courage) Running Pr.

***Burton, Kenneth S., Jr.** Knots: A Step-by-Step Guide to Tying Loops, Hitches, Bends, & Dozens of Other Useful Knots. (Illus.). 80p. 2000. reprint ed. text 25.00 (*0-7881-6921-1*) DIANE Pub.

Burton, Kenneth S., jt. auth. see Rodale's Home Improvement Books Staff.

Burton, Kermit. The Alpha A-B Living Trust Kit. 10th ed. (Non-Lawyer Legal Kit Ser.). 150p. 2000. per. 24.95 (*0-937434-46-9*); ring bd. 24.95 (*0-937434-64-7*) Alpha Publns Amer.

— The Alpha A-B Living Trust Kit: Reference Edition. 2nd ed. (Self-Help Legal Kit Ser.). (Illus.). 172p. 1998. per. 21.95 (*1-57164-127-0*) Alpha Publns Amer.

— The Alpha Annulment Kit: Arizona Edition. 8th ed. (Non-Lawyer Legal Kits Ser.). 110p. 1999. per. 17.95 (*0-937434-15-9*); ring bd. 17.95 (*0-937434-65-5*) Alpha Publns Amer.

— The Alpha Bankruptcy Kit: Chapter 7 Edition. 12th ed. (Non-Lawyer Legal Kits Ser.). 120p. 2000. ring bd. 24.95 (*0-937434-66-3*) Alpha Publns Amer.

— The Alpha Bankruptcy Kit: Chapter 7 Edition. 12th rev. ed. (Non-Lawyer Legal Kit Ser.). 164p. 2000. per. 24.95 (*0-937434-29-9*) Alpha Publns Amer.

— The Alpha Chapter 7 Bankruptcy Kit: Reference Edition. 2nd ed. (Self-Help Legal Ser.). (Illus.). 156p. 1998. per. 21.95 (*1-57164-128-9*) Alpha Publns Amer.

— The Alpha Chapter 13 Bankruptcy Kit: Reference Edition. 2nd ed. (Self-Help Legal Kit Ser.). (Illus.). 156p. 1998. per. 21.95 (*1-57164-129-7*) Alpha Publns Amer.

— The Alpha Chapter 13 Kit. 7th ed. (Non-Lawyer Legal Kits Ser.). 100p. 1999. ring bd. 24.95 (*0-937434-67-1*) Alpha Publns Amer.

— The Alpha Chapter 13 Kit. 7th rev. ed. (Non-Lawyer Legal Kit Ser.). 169p. 1999. per. 24.95 (*0-937434-30-2*) Alpha Publns Amer.

— The Alpha Corporation Kit: Arizona Edition. (Non-Lawyer Legal Kits Ser.). 150p. 1998. per. 24.95 (*0-937434-53-1*); ring bd. 24.95 (*0-937434-90-6*) Alpha Publns Amer.

— The Alpha Corporation Kit: National Edition. 9th ed. (Non-Lawyer Legal Kits Ser.). 180p. 1999. ring bd. 24.95 (*0-937434-68-X*) Alpha Publns Amer.

— The Alpha Corporation Kit: National Edition. 9th rev. ed. (Non-Lawyer Legal Kit Ser.). 180p. 1999. per. 24.95 (*0-937434-31-0*) Alpha Publns Amer.

— The Alpha Corporation Kit: Reference Edition. 2nd ed. (Self-Help Legal Kit Ser.). (Illus.). 163p. 1998. per. 21.95 (*1-57164-130-0*) Alpha Publns Amer.

— The Alpha Divorce Kit: Arizona Edition. 10th ed. (Non-Lawyer Legal Kit Ser.). 116p. 2000. per. 24.95 (*1-57164-126-2*) Alpha Publns Amer.

— The Alpha Divorce Kit: Arizona Edition. 11th ed. (Non-Lawyer Legal Kits Ser.). 116p. 2000. ring bd. 24.95 (*0-937434-69-8*) Alpha Publns Amer.

— The Alpha Divorce Kit: California. 14th rev. ed. (Non-Lawyer Legal Kit Ser.). 166p. 2000. per. 24.95 (*0-937434-10-8*) Alpha Publns Amer.

— The Alpha Divorce Kit: California Edition. 14th ed. (Non-Lawyer Legal Kits Ser.). 155p. 2000. ring bd. 24.95 (*0-937434-70-1*) Alpha Publns Amer.

— The Alpha Divorce Kit: Florida Edition. (Non-Lawyer Legal Kits Ser.). 105p. Date not set. ring bd. 24.95 (*0-937434-86-8*) Alpha Publns Amer.

— The Alpha Divorce Kit: Georgia Edition. (Non-Lawyer Legal Kits Ser.). 105p. Date not set. ring bd. 24.95 (*0-937434-87-6*) Alpha Publns Amer.

— The Alpha Divorce Kit: Idaho Edition. (Non-Lawyer Legal Kits Ser.). 105p. Date not set. per. 24.95 (*0-937434-94-9*) Alpha Publns Amer.

— The Alpha Divorce Kit: New Mexico Edition. 2nd ed. (Non-Lawyer Legal Kits Ser.). 115p. 1999. per. 24.95 (*0-937434-49-3*); ring bd. 24.95 (*0-937434-71-X*) Alpha Publns Amer.

— The Alpha Estate Planning Kit. (Non-Lawyer Legal Kits Ser.). 135p. Date not set. per. 29.95 (*0-937434-88-4*); ring bd. 29.95 (*0-937434-72-8*) Alpha Publns Amer.

— The Alpha Guardianship Kit: Arizona Edition. 5th ed. (Non-Lawyer Legal Kits Ser.). 110p. 1999. per. 17.95 (*0-937434-23-X*); ring bd. 17.95 (*0-937434-73-6*) Alpha Publns Amer.

— The Alpha Home Sales Kit: National Edition. 2nd ed. (Non-Lawyer Legal Kits Ser.). 65p. 1997. ring bd. 15.95 (*0-937434-74-4*) Alpha Publns Amer.

— The Alpha Home Sales Kit: National Edition. 2nd rev. ed. (Non-Lawyer Legal Kit Ser.). 65p. 1997. per. 15.95 (*0-937434-32-9*) Alpha Publns Amer.

— The Alpha Home Sales Kit: Reference Edition. 2nd ed. (Self-Help Legal Kit Ser.). (Illus.). 145p. 1998. per. 16.95 (*1-57164-131-9*) Alpha Publns Amer.

— The Alpha Homestead Kit: Arizona Edition. (Non-Lawyer Legal Kits Ser.). 35p. 1997. ring bd. 8.95 (*0-937434-75-2*) Alpha Publns Amer.

— The Alpha Last Will & Testament Kit. 11th rev. ed. (Non-Lawyer Legal Kit Ser.). 92p. 2000. per. 16.95 (*0-937434-38-8*) Alpha Publns Amer.

— The Alpha Last Will & Testament Kit: National Edition. 11th ed. (Non-Lawyer Legal Kits Ser.). 70p. 2000. ring bd. 16.95 (*0-937434-76-0*) Alpha Publns Amer.

— The Alpha Last Will & Testament Kit: Reference Edition. 2nd ed. (Self-Help Legal Kit Ser.). (Illus.). 101p. 1998. per. 16.95 (*1-57164-132-7*) Alpha Publns Amer.

— The Alpha Limited Liability Company Kit: Arizona Edition. 2nd ed. (Non-Lawyer Legal Kits Ser.). 185p. 1998. ring bd. 24.95 (*0-937434-77-9*) Alpha Publns Amer.

— The Alpha Limited Liability Company Kit: Arizona Edition. 2nd rev. ed. (Non-Lawyer Legal Kit Ser.). 191p. 1998. per. 24.95 (*0-937434-63-9*) Alpha Publns Amer.

— The Alpha Limited Liability Company Kit: National Edition. (Non-Lawyer Legal Kits Ser.). 200p. 1998. per. 24.95 (*0-937434-61-2*); ring bd. 24.95 (*0-937434-62-0*) Alpha Publns Amer.

— The Alpha Limited Liability Company Kit: Reference Edition. 2nd ed. (Self-Help Legal Kit Ser.). (Illus.). 151p. 1998. per. 21.95 (*1-57164-133-5*) Alpha Publns Amer.

— The Alpha Living Trust Kit. 10th rev. ed. (Non-Lawyer Legal Kit Ser.). 107p. 2000. per. 17.95 (*0-937434-33-7*) Alpha Publns Amer.

— The Alpha Living Trust Kit: National Edition. 10th ed. (Non-Lawyer Legal Kits Ser.). 90p. 1999. ring bd. 17.95 (*0-937434-78-7*) Alpha Publns Amer.

— The Alpha Living Trust Kit: Reference Edition. 2nd ed. (Self-Help Legal Kit Ser.). (Illus.). 138p. 1998. per. 18.95 (*1-57164-134-3*) Alpha Publns Amer.

— The Alpha Living Will Kit: Alabama Edition. (Non-Lawyer Legal Kits Ser.). 56p. 1997. ring bd. 12.95 (*1-57164-220-X*) Alpha Publns Amer.

— The Alpha Living Will Kit: Alaska Edition. (Non-Lawyer Legal Kits Ser.). 56p. 1997. ring bd. 12.95 (*1-57164-221-8*) Alpha Publns Amer.

— The Alpha Living Will Kit: Arizona Edition. 2nd ed. (Non-Lawyer Legal Kits Ser.). 56p. 1997. ring bd. 12.95 (*1-57164-222-6*) Alpha Publns Amer.

— The Alpha Living Will Kit: Arkansas Edition. (Non-Lawyer Legal Kits Ser.). 56p. 1997. ring bd. 12.95 (*1-57164-223-4*) Alpha Publns Amer.

— The Alpha Living Will Kit: California Edition. 2nd ed. (Non-Lawyer Legal Kits Ser.). 56p. 1997. ring bd. 12.95 (*1-57164-224-2*) Alpha Publns Amer.

— The Alpha Living Will Kit: Colorado Edition. (Non-Lawyer Legal Kits Ser.). 56p. 1997. ring bd. 12.95 (*1-57164-225-0*) Alpha Publns Amer.

— The Alpha Living Will Kit: Connecticut Edition. (Non-Lawyer Legal Kits Ser.). 56p. 1997. ring bd. 12.95 (*1-57164-226-9*) Alpha Publns Amer.

— The Alpha Living Will Kit: Delaware Edition. (Non-Lawyer Legal Kits Ser.). 56p. 1997. ring bd. 12.95 (*1-57164-227-7*) Alpha Publns Amer.

— The Alpha Living Will Kit: District of Columbia Edition. (Non-Lawyer Legal Kits Ser.). 56p. 1997. ring bd. 12.95 (*1-57164-228-5*) Alpha Publns Amer.

— The Alpha Living Will Kit: Florida Edition. (Non-Lawyer Legal Kits Ser.). 56p. 1997. ring bd. 12.95 (*1-57164-229-3*) Alpha Publns Amer.

— The Alpha Living Will Kit: Georgia Edition. (Non-Lawyer Legal Kits Ser.). 56p. 1997. ring bd. 12.95 (*1-57164-230-7*) Alpha Publns Amer.

— The Alpha Living Will Kit: Hawaii Edition. (Non-Lawyer Legal Kits Ser.). 56p. 1997. ring bd. 12.95 (*1-57164-231-5*) Alpha Publns Amer.

— The Alpha Living Will Kit: Idaho Edition. (Non-Lawyer Legal Kits Ser.). 56p. 1997. ring bd. 12.95 (*1-57164-232-3*) Alpha Publns Amer.

— The Alpha Living Will Kit: Illinois Edition. (Non-Lawyer Legal Kits Ser.). 56p. 1997. ring bd. 12.95 (*1-57164-233-1*) Alpha Publns Amer.

— The Alpha Living Will Kit: Indiana Edition. (Non-Lawyer Legal Kits Ser.). 56p. 1997. ring bd. 12.95 (*1-57164-234-X*) Alpha Publns Amer.

— The Alpha Living Will Kit: Iowa Edition. (Non-Lawyer Legal Kits Ser.). 56p. 1997. ring bd. 12.95 (*1-57164-235-8*) Alpha Publns Amer.

— The Alpha Living Will Kit: Kansas Edition. (Non-Lawyer Legal Kits Ser.). 56p. 1997. ring bd. 12.95 (*1-57164-236-6*) Alpha Publns Amer.

— The Alpha Living Will Kit: Kentucky Edition. (Non-Lawyer Legal Kits Ser.). 56p. 1997. ring bd. 12.95 (*1-57164-237-4*) Alpha Publns Amer.

— The Alpha Living Will Kit: Louisiana Edition. (Non-Lawyer Legal Kits Ser.). 56p. 1997. ring bd. 12.95 (*1-57164-238-2*) Alpha Publns Amer.

— The Alpha Living Will Kit: Maine Edition. (Non-Lawyer Legal Kits Ser.). 56p. 1997. ring bd. 12.95 (*1-57164-239-0*) Alpha Publns Amer.

— The Alpha Living Will Kit: Maryland Edition. (Non-Lawyer Legal Kits Ser.). 56p. 1997. ring bd. 12.95 (*1-57164-240-4*) Alpha Publns Amer.

— The Alpha Living Will Kit: Massachusetts Edition. (Non-Lawyer Legal Kits Ser.). 56p. 1997. ring bd. 12.95 (*1-57164-241-2*) Alpha Publns Amer.

— The Alpha Living Will Kit: Michigan Edition. (Non-Lawyer Legal Kits Ser.). 56p. 1997. ring bd. 12.95 (*1-57164-242-0*) Alpha Publns Amer.

— The Alpha Living Will Kit: Minnesota Edition. (Non-Lawyer Legal Kits Ser.). 56p. 1997. ring bd. 12.95 (*1-57164-243-9*) Alpha Publns Amer.

— The Alpha Living Will Kit: Mississippi Edition. (Non-Lawyer Legal Kits Ser.). 56p. 1997. ring bd. 12.95 (*1-57164-244-7*) Alpha Publns Amer.

— The Alpha Living Will Kit: Missouri Edition. (Non-Lawyer Legal Kits Ser.). 56p. 1997. ring bd. 12.95 (*1-57164-245-5*) Alpha Publns Amer.

— The Alpha Living Will Kit: Montana Edition. (Non-Lawyer Legal Kits Ser.). 56p. 1997. ring bd. 12.95 (*1-57164-246-3*) Alpha Publns Amer.

— The Alpha Living Will Kit: National Edition. 5th ed. (Non-Lawyer Legal Kits Ser.). 236p. 1998. ring bd. 24.95 (*0-937434-80-9*) Alpha Publns Amer.

— The Alpha Living Will Kit: National Edition. 5th rev. ed. (Non-Lawyer Legal Kit Ser.). 236p. 1998. per. 24.95 (*0-937434-34-5*) Alpha Publns Amer.

— The Alpha Living Will Kit: Nebraska Edition. (Non-Lawyer Legal Kits Ser.). 56p. 1997. ring bd. 12.95 (*1-57164-247-1*) Alpha Publns Amer.

— The Alpha Living Will Kit: Nevada Edition. (Non-Lawyer Legal Kits Ser.). 56p. 1997. ring bd. 12.95 (*1-57164-248-X*) Alpha Publns Amer.

— The Alpha Living Will Kit: New Hampshire Edition. (Non-Lawyer Legal Kits Ser.). 56p. 1997. ring bd. 12.95 (*1-57164-249-8*) Alpha Publns Amer.

— The Alpha Living Will Kit: New Jersey Edition. (Non-Lawyer Legal Kits Ser.). 56p. 1997. ring bd. 12.95 (*1-57164-250-1*) Alpha Publns Amer.

— The Alpha Living Will Kit: New Mexico Edition. (Non-Lawyer Legal Kits Ser.). 56p. 1997. ring bd. 12.95 (*1-57164-251-X*) Alpha Publns Amer.

— The Alpha Living Will Kit: New York Edition. (Non-Lawyer Legal Kits Ser.). 56p. 1997. ring bd. 12.95 (*1-57164-252-8*) Alpha Publns Amer.

— The Alpha Living Will Kit: North Carolina Edition. (Non-Lawyer Legal Kits Ser.). 56p. 1997. ring bd. 12.95 (*1-57164-253-6*) Alpha Publns Amer.

— The Alpha Living Will Kit: North Dakota Edition. (Non-Lawyer Legal Kits Ser.). 56p. 1997. ring bd. 12.95 (*1-57164-254-4*) Alpha Publns Amer.

— The Alpha Living Will Kit: Ohio Edition. (Non-Lawyer Legal Kits Ser.). 56p. 1997. ring bd. 12.95 (*1-57164-255-2*) Alpha Publns Amer.

— The Alpha Living Will Kit: Oklahoma Edition. (Non-Lawyer Legal Kits Ser.). 56p. 1997. ring bd. 12.95 (*1-57164-256-0*) Alpha Publns Amer.

— The Alpha Living Will Kit: Oregon Edition. (Non-Lawyer Legal Kits Ser.). 56p. 1997. ring bd. 12.95 (*1-57164-257-9*) Alpha Publns Amer.

— The Alpha Living Will Kit: Pennsylvania Edition. (Non-Lawyer Legal Kits Ser.). 56p. 1997. ring bd. 12.95 (*1-57164-258-7*) Alpha Publns Amer.

— The Alpha Living Will Kit: Rhode Island Edition. (Non-Lawyer Legal Kits Ser.). 56p. 1997. ring bd. 12.95 (*1-57164-260-9*) Alpha Publns Amer.

— The Alpha Living Will Kit: South Carolina Edition. (Non-Lawyer Legal Kits Ser.). 56p. 1997. ring bd. 12.95 (*1-57164-261-7*) Alpha Publns Amer.

— The Alpha Living Will Kit: South Dakota Edition. (Non-Lawyer Legal Kits Ser.). 56p. 1997. ring bd. 12.95 (*1-57164-262-5*) Alpha Publns Amer.

— The Alpha Living Will Kit: Tennessee Edition. (Non-Lawyer Legal Kits Ser.). 56p. 1997. ring bd. 12.95 (*1-57164-263-3*) Alpha Publns Amer.

— The Alpha Living Will Kit: Texas Edition. (Non-Lawyer Legal Kits Ser.). 56p. 1997. ring bd. 12.95 (*1-57164-264-1*) Alpha Publns Amer.

— The Alpha Living Will Kit: Utah Edition. (Non-Lawyer Legal Kits Ser.). 56p. 1997. ring bd. 12.95 (*1-57164-265-X*) Alpha Publns Amer.

— The Alpha Living Will Kit: Vermont Edition. (Non-Lawyer Legal Kits Ser.). 56p. 1997. ring bd. 12.95 (*1-57164-266-8*) Alpha Publns Amer.

— The Alpha Living Will Kit: Virginia Edition. (Non-Lawyer Legal Kits Ser.). 56p. 1997. ring bd. 12.95 (*1-57164-267-6*) Alpha Publns Amer.

— The Alpha Living Will Kit: Washington Edition. (Non-Lawyer Legal Kits Ser.). 56p. 1997. ring bd. 12.95 (*1-57164-268-4*) Alpha Publns Amer.

— The Alpha Living Will Kit: West Virginia Edition. (Non-Lawyer Legal Kits Ser.). 56p. 1997. ring bd. 12.95 (*1-57164-269-2*) Alpha Publns Amer.

— The Alpha Living Will Kit: Wisconsin Edition. (Non-Lawyer Legal Kits Ser.). 56p. 1997. ring bd. 12.95 (*1-57164-270-6*) Alpha Publns Amer.

— The Alpha Living Will Kit: Wyoming Edition. (Non-Lawyer Legal Kits Ser.). 56p. 1997. ring bd. 12.95 (*1-57164-271-4*) Alpha Publns Amer.

— The Alpha Name Change Kit: Arizona Edition. 7th ed. (Non-Lawyer Legal Kits Ser.). 70p. 1999. ring bd. 17.95 (*0-937434-81-7*) Alpha Publns Amer.

— The Alpha Non-Profit Corporation Kit. 5th rev. ed. (Non-Lawyer Legal Kit Ser.). 180p. 1997. per. 24.95 (*0-937434-35-3*) Alpha Publns Amer.

— The Alpha Non-Profit Corporation Kit: National Edition. 5th ed. (Non-Lawyer Legal Kits Ser.). 105p. 1997. ring bd. 24.95 (*0-937434-82-5*) Alpha Publns Amer.

— The Alpha Non-Profit Corporation Kit: Reference Edition. 2nd ed. (Illus.). 163p. 1998. per. 21.95 (*1-57164-135-1*) Alpha Publns Amer.

— The Alpha Partnership Kit. 5th rev. ed. (Non-Lawyer Legal Kit Ser.). 100p. 1999. per. 24.95 (*0-937434-36-1*) Alpha Publns Amer.

— The Alpha Partnership Kit: National Edition. 5th ed. (Non-Lawyer Legal Kits Ser.). 110p. 1999. ring bd. 24.95 (*0-937434-83-3*) Alpha Publns Amer.

— The Alpha Partnership Kit: Reference Edition. 2nd ed. (Self-Help Legal Kit Ser.). (Illus.). 172p. 1998. per. 21.95 (*1-57164-136-X*) Alpha Publns Amer.

— The Alpha Pre-Marriage Kit. 2nd rev. ed. (Non-Lawyer Legal Kit Ser.). 93p. 1997. per. 15.95 (*0-937434-37-X*) Alpha Publns Amer.

— The Alpha Pre-Marriage Kit: National Edition. 2nd ed. (Non-Lawyer Legal Kits Ser.). 71p. 1997. ring bd. 15.95 (*0-937434-84-1*) Alpha Publns Amer.

— The Alpha Pre-Marriage Kit: Reference Edition. 2nd ed. (Self-Help Legal Kit Ser.). (Illus.). 139p. 1998. per. 16.95 (*1-57164-137-8*) Alpha Publns Amer.

— The Alpha Separation Kit: Arizona Edition. 9th ed. (Non-Lawyer Legal Kits Ser.). 116p. 1999. per. 24.95 (*0-937434-59-0*); ring bd. 24.95 (*0-937434-85-X*) Alpha Publns Amer.

Burton, L. C. Who Conquers Me? (Staples South West Region Publications). 1996. pap. write for info. (*1-875560-83-1*, Pub. by Staples) Intl Spec Bk.

Burton, L. DeVere. Agriscience & Technology. 1991. text 32.50 (*0-8273-4016-8*) Delmar.

— Agriscience & Technology. 199p. 1991. pap., teacher ed. 12.75 (*0-8273-4017-6*) Delmar.

— Agriscience & Technology. 199p. 1994. 17.00 (*0-8273-4018-4*) Delmar.

Burton, Larry W., jt. auth. see McDonald, Daniel L.

Burton, Laurel A. Religion & the Family: When God Helps. LC 91-23285. (Illus.). 224p. 1992. pap. 19.95 (*1-56024-197-7*); lib. bdg. 39.95 (*1-56024-192-6*) Haworth Pr.

Burton, Laurel A., ed. The Chaplain-Physician Relationship. (Journal of Health Care Chaplaincy). 78p. 1991. text 39.95 (*1-56024-108-X*) Haworth Pr.

— Making Chaplaincy Work: Practical Approaches. LC 88-541. (Journal of Health Care Chaplaincy: Vol. 1, No. 2). (Illus.). 98p. 1988. text 29.95 (*0-86656-743-7*) Haworth Pr.

Burton, Laurel A. & Handzo, George, eds. Health Care Chaplaincy in Oncology. LC 92-25898. (Journal of Health Care Chaplaincy: Vol. 4, Nos. 1/2). (Illus.). 151p. 1993. 39.95 (*1-56024-200-0*) Haworth Pr.

Burton, Lawrence D. Agriscience & Technology. 2nd ed. (Agriculture Ser.). 1997. mass mkt., lab manual ed. 17.75 (*0-8273-6930-1*) Delmar.

Burton, Lawrence D. Ecology of Fish & Wildlife. LC 94-44242. (Illus.). 416p. (J). 1995. pap. 50.95 (*0-8273-6065-7*) Delmar.

Burton, Lawrence D. Forestry. (C). 1998. pap. text, teacher ed. 12.00 (*0-8273-8011-9*) Delmar.

— Principles of Fish & Wildlife Ecology. (Agriculture Ser.). 1995. pap., teacher ed. 12.00 (*0-8273-6066-5*) Delmar.

Burton, Lee, jt. auth. see Adams, Phillip.

***Burton, Len S.** When No One Pursues: Inside an FBI Investigation. 320p. 1999. 19.95 (*0-9675510-0-5*) Golden Shield.

Burton, Leon. Arts Play: Creative Activities in Art, Music, Dance, & Drama for Young Children. 1981. pap. text 23.95 (*0-201-00201-9*) Addison-Wesley.

— Musicplay: Learning Activities for Young Children. 1979. pap. text 23.95 (*0-201-00883-1*) Addison-Wesley.

— Musicplay: Recordings & Learning Activities for Young Children. 1979. text 44.00 (*0-201-20940-3*) Addison-Wesley.

Burton, Leon, et al. Adventures in Music Listening, Level 2. Cavalier, Debbie, ed. 96p. (C). 1997. pap. text, teacher ed. 49.95 (*0-7692-0264-0*, BMR08202) Wrner Bros.

— Adventures in Music Listening, Level 2. Cavalier, Debbie, ed. 44p. (C). 1997. pap. text, student ed. 2.50 (*0-7692-1657-9*, BMR08202S) Wrner Bros.

— Adventures in Music Listening: Level 1. Cavalier, Debbie, ed. (Illus.). (Orig.). (YA). 1996. pap., teacher ed. 49.95 (*1-57623-392-8*, BMR08201); pap., student ed. 2.50 (*1-57623-393-6*, BMR08201S) Wrner Bros.

— Adventures in Music Listening: Level 1 Big Book. Cavalier, Debbie, ed. (Illus.). (Orig.). (J). 1996. pap. text 49.95 (*1-57623-369-3*, BMR08201B) Wrner Bros.

Burton, Leon H. Bugplay: Activities with Insects for Young Children. 1989. pap., text, teacher ed. 26.95 incl. audio (*0-201-21540-3*) Addison-Wesley.

— Joy in Learning: Making It Happen in Early Childhood Classes. 80p. 1991. pap. 9.95 (*0-8106-0359-4*) NEA.

***Burton, Leon H. & Kudo, Takeo.** SoundPlay: Understanding Music Through Creative Movement. (Illus.). 120p. (C). 2000. pap. Price not set. incl. audio compact disk (*1-56545-130-9*, 3003) MENC.

Burton, Leone, jt. photos by see Stacey, Kaye.

Burton, Lesley & Musselwhite, Brian, eds. An Illustrated History of Fareham. (C). 1989. 39.00 (*1-85455-040-3*, Pub. by Ensign Pubns & Print) St Mut.

Burton, Lesley, jt. auth. see Blain, Jennifer.

Burton, Leslie M., jt. auth. see Burton, Steven J.

Burton, LeVar. Aftermath. 304p. 1997. reprint ed. mass mkt. 6.50 (*0-446-60501-8*, Pub. by Warner Bks) Little.

Burton, Linda, ed. Families & Aging. LC 92-42277. (Generations & Aging Ser.). 161p. 1993. pap. text 23.95 (*0-89503-114-0*) Baywood Pub.

— Stories from Tennessee. LC 82-16016. 431p. reprint ed. pap. 133.70 (*0-608-08626-6*, 206914900003) Bks Demand.

Burton, Linda, et al. What's a Smart Woman Like You Doing at Home? 2nd rev. ed. LC 92-22259. 170p. (Orig.). 1993. pap. 8.95 (*0-9631188-1-1*) Mothers at Home.

Burton, Linda L. Chattanooga Great Places: Plus a Hundred Miles. LC 96-69855. (Illus.). 256p. (Orig.). 1995. pap. 11.95 (*0-9644760-0-2*) Phase II Publ.

— Southeast Great Trips. LC 96-70440. 256p. (Orig.). 1996. pap. 11.95 (*0-9644760-1-0*) Phase II Publ.

Burton, Lisa. Interpersonal Skills for Travel & Tourism. 288p. (Orig.). 1994. pap. 47.50 (*0-582-27946-1*, Pub. by Addison-Wesley) Trans-Atl Phila.

Burton, Lloyd. American Indian Water Rights & the Limits of Law. LC 90-23088. (Development of Western Resources Ser.). xiv, 178p. 1991. pap. 14.95 (*0-7006-0601-7*) U Pr of KS.

Burton, Lombra. Financial System & The Economy: Principles of Money & Banking. 2nd ed. LC 99-20821. 627p. 1999. 87.95 (*0-324-00439-7*) Thomson Learn.

***Burton, Ludima Gus.** Only for a Year. LC 00-190018. 192p. 2000. 18.95 (*0-8034-9415-7*, Avalon Bks) Bouregy.

Burton, M., ed. Magnesium in Clinical Medicine & Therapeutics Journal: Magnesium & Trace Elements, Vol. 10, Nos. 2-4, 1991-92. (Illus.). 252p. 1993. pap. 35.75 (*3-8055-5696-9*) S Karger.

Burton, M., et al. Social Skills for People with Learning Disabilities: A Social Capability Approach. 282p. 1995. pap. 44.75 (*1-56593-194-7*, 0509) Singular Publishing.

Burton, M., jt. auth. see Mackie, K.

Burton, M. E., ed. The Wandering Jew. LC 83-51130. 80p. 1984. 12.95 (*0-938310-02-X*) Volunteer Pubns.

Burton, M. P., jt. auth. see Young, T.

***Burton, Mallory.** Green River Virgins: And Other Passionate Anglers. 2000. 24.95 (*1-58574-142-6*) Lyon Press.

Burton, Mallory. Reading the Water: Stories & Essays of Flyfishing & Life. LC 88-21851. 256p. (Orig.). 1995. pap. 13.95 (*1-879628-10-4*) Keokee ID.

Burton, Margaret & Vosburgh, Marion. A Bibliography of Librarianship. 1976. lib. bdg. 59.95 (*0-8490-1499-9*) Gordon Pr.

Burton, Margaret E., ed. see Caron, D. Phillip.

Burton, Margaret E., ed. see Sax, Sam.

Burton, Margaret E., ed. see Wiliamson, Margaret G.

Burton, Margie, et al. Across the Seasons. Evento, Susan, ed. (Early Connections Ser.). 16p. (gr. k-2). 1998. pap. text 4.25 (*1-892393-61-1*) Benchmark Educ.

— Animal Coverings. Evento, Susan, ed. (Early Connections Ser.). 16p. (J). (gr. k-2). 1998. pap. 4.25 (*1-892393-65-4*) Benchmark Educ.

— Animal Homes. Evento, Susan, ed. (Early Connections Ser.). 16p. (J). (gr. k-2). 1998. pap. 4.25 (*1-892393-58-1*) Benchmark Educ.

— Animals & Their Babies. Evento, Susan, ed. (Early Connections Ser.). 16p. (J). (gr. k-2). 1998. pap. 4.25 (*1-892393-43-3*) Benchmark Educ.

— Animals' Eyes & Ears. Adams, Alison, ed. (Early Connections Ser.). 16p. (J). (gr. k-2). 1998. pap. 4.50 (*1-58344-052-6*) Benchmark Educ.

— Are We Hurting the Earth. Adams, Alison, ed. (Early Connections Ser.). 16p. (J). (gr. k-2). 1999. pap. 4.50 (*1-58344-053-4*) Benchmark Educ.

— Art Around the World. Adams, Alison, ed. (Early Connections Ser.). 16p. (J). (gr. k-2). 1999. pap. 4.50 (*1-58344-054-2*) Benchmark Educ.
— Big Rocks, Little Rocks. Evento, Susan, ed. (Early Connections Ser.). 16p. (J). (gr. k-2). 1998. pap. 4.25 (*1-892393-66-2*) Benchmark Educ.
— Bigger Than, Smaller Than. Evento, Susan, ed. (Early Connections Ser.). 16p. (J). (gr. k-2). 1998. pap. 4.25 (*1-892393-38-7*) Benchmark Educ.
— Birthday Celebrations. Evento, Susan, ed. (Early Connections Ser.). 16p. (J). (gr. k-2). 1998. pap. 4.25 (*1-892393-73-5*) Benchmark Educ.
— Caring for Our Pets. Evento, Susan, ed. (Early Connections Ser.). 16p. (J). (gr. k-2). 1998. pap. 4.25 (*1-892393-60-3*) Benchmark Educ.
— Children As Young Scientists. Adams, Alison, ed. (Early Connections Ser.). 16p. (gr. k-2). 1999. pap. 4.50 (*1-58344-055-0*) Benchmark Educ.
— Cleaning My Room. Adams, Alison, ed. (Early Connections Ser.). 16p. (J). (gr. k-2). 1999. pap. 4.50 (*1-58344-056-9*) Benchmark Educ.
— Clouds. Adams, Alison, ed. (Early Connections Ser.). 16p. (J). (gr. k-2). 1999. pap. text 4.50 (*1-58344-057-7*) Benchmark Educ.
— Community Jobs. Adams, Alison, ed. (Early Connections Ser.). 16p. (J). (gr. k-2). 1999. pap. 4.50 (*1-58344-058-5*) Benchmark Educ.
***Burton, Margie, et al.** Counting Insects. Adams, Alison, ed. (Early Connections Ser.). 16p. (J). (gr. k-2). 1999. pap. 4.50 (*1-58344-059-3*) Benchmark Educ.
Burton, Margie, et al. Counting 1-5. Evento, Susan, ed. (Early Connections Ser.). 16p. (J). (gr. k-2). 1998. pap. 4.25 (*1-892393-28-X*) Benchmark Educ.
— Counting Seeds. Evento, Susan, ed. (Early Connections Ser.). 16p. (J). (gr. k-2). 1998. pap. 4.25 (*1-892393-34-4*) Benchmark Educ.
— Everyday Math. Evento, Susan, ed. (Early Connections Ser.). 16p. (J). (gr. k-2). 1998. pap. 4.25 (*1-892393-35-2*) Benchmark Educ.
— Families. Adams, Alison, ed. (Early Connections Ser.). 16p. (gr. k-2). 1999. pap. 4.50 (*1-58344-060-7*) Benchmark Educ.
***Burton, Margie, et al.** Food Around the World. Adams, Alison, ed. (Early Connections Ser.). 16p. (J). (gr. k-2). 1999. pap. 4.50 (*1-58344-061-5*) Benchmark Educ.
— Friends. Adams, Alison, ed. (Early Connections Ser.). 16p. (J). (gr. k-2). 1999. pap. 4.50 (*1-58344-062-3*) Benchmark Educ.
Burton, Margie, et al. Going Places. Adams, Alison, ed. (Early Connections Ser.). 16p. (J). (gr. k-2). 1999. pap. 4.50 (*1-58344-063-1*) Benchmark Educ.
***Burton, Margie, et al.** Growing Older. Adams, Alison, ed. (Early Connections Ser.). 16p. (J). (gr. k-2). 1999. pap. 4.50 (*1-58344-064-X*) Benchmark Educ.
Burton, Margie, et al. Heat. Adams, Alison, ed. (Early Connections Ser.). 16p. (J). (gr. k-2). 1999. pap. 4.50 (*1-58344-065-8*) Benchmark Educ.
— Homes for People. Evento, Susan, ed. (Early Connections Ser.). 16p. (J). (gr. k-2). 1998. pap. 4.25 (*1-892393-44-1*) Benchmark Educ.
— How Many? Evento, Susan, ed. (Early Connections Ser.). 16p. (J). (gr. k-2). 1998. pap. 4.25 (*1-892393-40-9*) Benchmark Educ.
***Burton, Margie, et al.** How Many Are Left? Adams, Alison, ed. (Early Connections Ser.). 16p. (J). (gr. k-2). 1999. pap. 4.50 (*1-58344-066-6*) Benchmark Educ.
— Insects All Around. Adams, Alison, ed. (Early Connections Ser.). 16p. (J). (gr. k-2). 1999. pap. 4.50 (*1-58344-067-4*) Benchmark Educ.
Burton, Margie, et al. Let's Go. Evento, Susan, ed. (Early Connections Ser.). 16p. (J). (gr. k-2). 1998. pap. 4.25 (*1-892393-45-X*) Benchmark Educ.
— Life in the City. Adams, Alison, ed. (Early Connections Ser.). 16p. (J). (gr. k-2). 1999. pap. 4.50 (*1-58344-069-0*) Benchmark Educ.
— Life on a Farm. Evento, Susan, ed. (Early Connections Ser.). 16p. (J). (gr. k-2). 1998. pap. 4.25 (*1-892393-55-7*) Benchmark Educ.
— Long Ago. Evento, Susan, ed. (Early Connections Ser.). 16p. (J). (gr. k-2). 1998. pap. 4.25 (*1-892393-50-6*) Benchmark Educ.
— Looking Down. Evento, Susan, ed. (Early Connections Ser.). 16p. (J). (gr. k-2). 1998. pap. 4.25 (*1-892393-54-9*) Benchmark Educ.
— Looking for Patterns. Adams, Alison, ed. (Early Connections Ser.). 16p. (J). (gr. k-2). 1999. pap. 4.50 (*1-58344-070-4*) Benchmark Educ.
— Looking for Shapes. Adams, Alison, ed. (Early Connections Ser.). 16p. (J). (gr. k-2). 1999. pap. 4.50 (*1-58344-071-2*) Benchmark Educ.
— Looking into Space. Adams, Alison, ed. (Early Connections Ser.). 16p. (J). (gr. k-2). 1999. pap. 4.50 (*1-58344-072-0*) Benchmark Educ.
— Magnets. Evento, Susan, ed. (Early Connections Ser.). 16p. (J). (gr. k-2). 1998. pap. 4.25 (*1-892393-57-3*) Benchmark Educ.
— Measure Up! Adams, Alison, ed. (Early Connections Ser.). 16p. (J). (gr. k-2). 1999. pap. text 4.50 (*1-58344-073-9*) Benchmark Educ.
— Measuring Time. Evento, Susan, ed. (Early Connections Ser.). 16p. (J). (gr. k-2). 1998. pap. 4.25 (*1-892393-42-5*) Benchmark Educ.
— My Five Senses. Evento, Susan, ed. (Early Connections Ser.). 16p. (J). (gr. k-2). 1998. pap. 4.25 (*1-892393-64-6*) Benchmark Educ.
— Needs & Wants. Evento, Susan, ed. (Early Connections Ser.). 16p. (J). (gr. k-2). 1998. pap. 4.25 (*1-892393-48-4*) Benchmark Educ.
— No One Else Like Me. Evento, Susan, ed. (Early Connections Ser.). 16p. (gr. k-2). 1998. pap. 4.25 (*1-892393-69-7*) Benchmark Educ.
— Numbers Are Everywhere. Evento, Susan, ed. (Early Connections Ser.). 16p. (J). (gr. k-2). 1998. pap. 4.25 (*1-892393-39-5*) Benchmark Educ.
— Ocean Animals. Adams, Alison, ed. (Early Connections Ser.). 16p. (J). (gr. k-2). 1999. pap. text 4.50 (*1-58344-074-7*) Benchmark Educ.
— One for You & One for Me. Adams, Alison, ed. (Early Connections Ser.). 16p. (gr. k-2). 1999. pap. text 4.50 (*1-58344-075-5*) Benchmark Educ.
— Our Money. Adams, Alison, ed. (Early Connections Ser.). 16p. (J). (gr. k-2). 1999. pap. 4.50 (*1-58344-076-3*) Benchmark Educ.
— Parts of a Whole. Evento, Susan, ed. (Early Connections Ser.). 16p. (J). (gr. k-2). 1998. pap. text 4.25 (*1-892393-41-7*) Benchmark Educ.
— Patterns All Around. Evento, Susan, ed. (Early Connections Ser.). 16p. (J). (gr. k-2). 1998. pap. text 4.25 (*1-892393-33-6*) Benchmark Educ.
— People Use Tools. Evento, Susan, ed. (Early Connections Ser.). 16p. (J). (gr. k-2). 1998. pap. text 4.25 (*1-892393-56-5*) Benchmark Educ.
— Playground Fun. Evento, Susan, ed. (Early Connections Ser.). 16p. (J). (gr. k-2). 1998. pap. text 4.25 (*1-892393-62-X*) Benchmark Educ.
— Playing It Safe. Evento, Susan, ed. (Early Connections Ser.). 16p. (J). (gr. k-2). 1998. pap. 4.25 (*1-892393-72-7*) Benchmark Educ.
— The Power of Nature. Adams, Alison, ed. (Early Connections Ser.). 16p. (J). (gr. k-2). 1999. pap. 4.50 (*1-58344-078-X*) Benchmark Educ.
— Reduce, Reuse, & Recycle. Adams, Alison, ed. (Early Connections Ser.). 16p. (J). (gr. k-2). 1999. pap. 4.50 (*1-58344-079-8*) Benchmark Educ.
— Riches from Nature. Adams, Alison, ed. (Early Connections Ser.). 16p. (J). (gr. k-2). 1999. pap. 4.50 (*1-58344-080-1*) Benchmark Educ.
***Burton, Margie, et al.** Rules. Adams, Alison, ed. (Early Connections Ser.). 16p. (J). (gr. k-2). 1999. pap. 4.50 (*1-58344-081-X*) Benchmark Educ.
Burton, Margie, et al. Shapes. Evento, Susan, ed. (Early Connections Ser.). 16p. (J). (gr. k-2). 1998. pap. 4.25 (*1-892393-37-9*) Benchmark Educ.
***Burton, Margie, et al.** Sounds. Adams, Alison, ed. (Early Connections Ser.). 16p. (J). (gr. k-2). 1999. pap. 4.50 (*1-58344-082-8*) Benchmark Educ.
Burton, Margie, et al. Toy Models. Evento, Susan, ed. (Early Connections Ser.). 16p. (J). (gr. k-2). 1998. pap. 4.25 (*1-892393-68-9*) Benchmark Educ.
***Burton, Margie, et al.** Travel Money, U. S. A. Adams, Alison, ed. (Early Connections Ser.). 16p. (J). (gr. k-2). 1999. pap. 4.50 (*1-58344-083-6*) Benchmark Educ.
— Trees. Adams, Alison, ed. (Early Connections Ser.). 16p. (J). (gr. k-2). 1999. pap. 4.50 (*1-58344-084-4*) Benchmark Educ.
— Water Goes Up! Water Comes Down! Adams, Alison, ed. (Early Connections Ser.). 16p. (J). (gr. k-2). 1999. pap. 4.50 (*1-58344-085-2*) Benchmark Educ.
— We Use Numbers. Adams, Alison, ed. (Early Connections Ser.). 16p. (J). (gr. k-2). 1999. pap. 4.50 (*1-58344-086-0*) Benchmark Educ.
Burton, Margie, et al. We Use Water. Evento, Susan, ed. (Early Connections Ser.). 16p. (gr. k-2). 1998. pap. 4.25 (*1-892393-59-X*) Benchmark Educ.
— Weather. Evento, Susan, ed. (Early Connections Ser.). 16p. (J). (gr. k-2). 1998. pap. 4.25 (*1-892393-67-0*) Benchmark Educ.
— What Are My Chances? Adams, Alison, ed. (Early Connections Ser.). 16p. (J). (gr. k-2). 1999. pap. 4.50 (*1-58344-077-1*) Benchmark Educ.
— What Comes in Twos? Evento, Susan, ed. (Early Connections Ser.). 16p. (J). (gr. k-2). 1998. pap. 4.25 (*1-892393-36-0*) Benchmark Educ.
— What People Do. Evento, Susan, ed. (Early Connections Ser.). 16p. (J). (gr. k-2). 1998. pap. text 4.25 (*1-892393-71-9*) Benchmark Educ.
***Burton, Margie, et al.** Where People Live. Adams, Alison, ed. (Early Connections Ser.). 16p. (J). (gr. k-2). 1999. pap. 4.50 (*1-58344-087-9*) Benchmark Educ.
Burton, Margie, et al. With My Mom & Dad. Evento, Susan, ed. (Early Connections Ser.). 16p. (J). (gr. k-2). 1998. pap. text 4.25 (*1-892393-46-8*) Benchmark Educ.
— Working Together. Evento, Susan, ed. (Early Connections Ser.). 16p. (J). (gr. k-2). 1998. pap. 4.25 (*1-892393-47-6*) Benchmark Educ.
Burton, Maria A. Ruiz de, see Ruiz de Burton, Maria A.
Burton, Marilee R. Aaron Awoke. LC 81-48638. (Illus.). 40p. (J). (ps). 1982. 11.95 (*0-06-020891-0*) HarpC Child Bks.
Burton, Marilee R. My Best Shoes. LC 92-33863. (Illus.). 32p. (J). 1994. 14.89 (*0-688-11757-0*, Wm Morrow) Morrow Avon.
Burton, Marilee R. Oliver's Birthday. LC 85-45682. (Illus.). 32p. (J). (ps). 1986. 11.95 (*0-06-020879-1*) HarpC Child Bks.
Burton, Mark & Kellaway, Mike, eds. Developing & Managing High Quality Services for People with Learning Disabilities. LC 97-49091. 299p. 1998. text 67.95 (*1-85742-378-X*, HV3008.G7D46, Pub. by Ashgate Pub) Ashgate Pub Co.
***Burton, Martin N., et al.** Hall & Colman's Diseases of the Ear, Nose & Throat. 15th ed. LC 99-23406. 1999. write for info. (*0-443-06190-4*) Church.
***Burton, Martin Nelson.** The Whale Comedian. LC 98-96954. (Illus.). 32p. (J). (ps-3). 2000. 15.95 (*0-9666490-8-7*, Pub. by London Town Pr) IPG Chicago.
***Burton, Mary.** Bride for McCain. (Historical Ser.: Vol. 502). 2000. per. 4.99 (*0-373-29102-7*) Harlequin Bks.
Burton, Mary. Psychotherapy, Counselling & Primary Mental Health Care: Assessment for Brief or Longer-Term Treatment. LC 98-13952. 270p. 1998. 91.50 (*0-471-97657-1*) Wiley.
***Burton, Mary.** Psychotherapy, Counselling & Primary Mental Health Care: Assessment for Brief or Longer-Term Treatment. LC 98-13952. 270p. 1998. pap. 48.50 (*0-471-98228-8*) Wiley.
Burton, Mary. An Unfaded Garland: Meditations on Light & Silence. 1997. pap. 35.00 (*0-86012-277-8*, Pub. by Srch Pr) St Mut.
Burton, Mary & Watson, M. Counselling People with Cancer. LC 97-34810. 214p. 1998. pap. 45.00 (*0-471-97813-2*) Wiley.
Burton, Mary L. & Clifton, Marion. Portland-Vancouver Bridal Guide, 1990. (Illus.). 380p. (Orig.). 1989. pap. 12.95 (*0-685-29058-1*) Bravo Pubns.
Burton, Mary L. & Wedemeyer, Richard A. In Transition: From the Harvard Business School Club of New York's Personal Seminar in Career Management. 224p. 1991. 20.00 (*0-88730-517-2*, HarpBusn) HarpInfo.
— In Transition: From the Harvard Business School Club of New York's Personal Seminar in Career Management. LC 91-5065. (Illus.). 256p. 1992. pap. 13.00 (*0-88730-571-7*, HarpBusn) HarpInfo.
***Burton, Mary Lou.** Bravo! Event Resource Guide: The Areas's Most Comprehensive Guide to Services for Event Planning. 640p. 2000. pap. 9.95 (*1-884471-23-4*) Bravo Pubns.
— Bridal Resource Guide: Portland Area's Most Comprehensive Guide to Wedding Planning. (Illus.). 624p. 1999. pap. 9.95 (*1-884471-24-2*) Bravo Pubns.
Burton, Mary Lou. Event Resource Guide: Portland, Vancouver, Salem & Outlying Areas, 1999 ed. 1998. pap. text 8.95 (*1-884471-20-X*) Bravo Pubns.
Burton, Mary T. & Whitfield, Donna. Insider's Guide to Direct Marketing for A/E/P & Environmental Consulting Firms. (Insider's Guide Ser.: No. 5). 198p. 1995. pap. text 79.00 (*1-885002-13-0*) Zweig White.
Burton, MaryLou. Event Resource Guide '98: Portland, Vancouver, Salem & Outlying Areas. 1998. pap. 8.95 (*1-884471-18-8*) Bravo Pubns.
Burton, Maureen & Lombra, Raymond E. The Financial System & the Economy. LC 96-26925. 1996. mass mkt. 64.50 (*0-314-09503-9*) West Pub.
Burton, Maurice. Le Dictionnaire en Couleurs des Animaux. (FRE.). 400p. 1974. 75.00 (*0-8288-6024-6*, M6653) Fr & Eur.
Burton, Maurice & Burton, Robert. Enciclopedia de la Vida Animal, 6 vols., Set. 2nd ed. (SPA.). 2770p. 1978. 325.00 (*0-8288-5215-4*, S50508) Fr & Eur.
Burton, Maurice & Burton, Robert, eds. The Marshall Cavendish International Wildlife Encyclopedia, 25 vols. (Illus.). 3000p. 1991. reprint ed. lib. bdg. 499.95 (*0-86307-734-X*) Marshall Cavendish.
Burton, Michael. An Agricultural Policy Model for the U. K. 329p. 1992. 91.95 (*1-85628-295-3*, Pub. by Avebry) Ashgate Pub Co.
— John Henry Faulk: The Making of a Liberated Mind. (Illus.). 204p. 1993. 19.95 (*0-89015-923-8*) Sunbelt Media.
***Burton, Michael.** Veneering: A Foundation Course. LC 99-49675. (Illus.). 160p. 2000. 19.95 (*0-8069-2855-7*) Sterling.
Burton, Michael & Goethe, Johann Wolfgang Von. The Green Snake & the Beautiful Lily. Carlyle, Thomas, tr. 96p. 1999. pap. text 6.95 (*1-869890-07-8*, Pub. by Hawthorn Press) Anthroposophic.
Burton, Michael H. In Celebration of Being Human. 66p. 1991. pap. 7.50 (*0-932776-18-3*) Adonis Pr.
— In the Light of a Child: A Journey Through the 52 Weeks of the Year in Both Hemispheres for Children & for the Child in Each Human Being. LC 97-32633. 60p. (J). 1998. pap. 12.95 (*0-88010-450-3*) Anthroposophic.
— Plays for Grades 2 Through 4. (Illus.). vi, 51p. 1995. spiral bd. 12.95 (*0-945803-22-2*, 00185) R Steiner Col.
Burton, Michael H., tr. see Steiner, Rudolf.
Burton, Mike & Shadbolt, Nigel. POP 11 PROGRAM ART INTEL. 225p. (C). 1987. pap. text 23.75 (*0-201-18049-9*) Addison-Wesley.
Burton, Mike, jt. auth. see Bruce, Vicki.
Burton, Nanci L., ed. see Burton, John C.
Burton, Neill G. & Bettelheim, Charles. China since Mao. LC 78-15623. 130p. reprint ed. pap. 40.30 (*0-7837-6985-7*, 204679700004) Bks Demand.
***Burton, Noel.** How to Manage the IT Help Desk & Call Centre. 320p. 2000. pap. 47.95 (*0-7506-4901-1*) Buttrwrth-Heinemann.
Burton, O. E. A Study in Creative History: The Interaction of the Eastern & Western Peoples to 500 B. C. 1977. lib. bdg. 59.95 (*0-8490-2708-X*) Gordon Pr.
Burton, Orville V. & McMath, Robert C., Jr., eds. Class, Conflict, & Consensus: Antebellum Southern Community Studies, 96. LC 81-1071. (Contributions in American History Ser.: No. 96). (Illus.). 308p. 1982. 75.00 (*0-313-21310-6*, BSC/) Greenwood.
— Toward a New South? Studies in Post-Civil War Southern Communities, 97. LC 81-1666. (Contributions in American History Ser.: No. 97). (Illus.). 319p. 1982. 59.95 (*0-313-22996-1*, BNC/) Greenwood.
Burton, Orville V., jt. auth. see McArthur, Judith N.
Burton, Orville W. In My Father's House Are Many Mansions: Family & Community in Edgefield, South Carolina. LC 84-25830. (Fred W. Morrison Series in Southern Studies). (Illus.). xxi, 480p. 1987. pap. 22.50 (*0-8078-4183-8*) U of NC Pr.
Burton, P. Fieldbus for Industrial Control Systems. 300p. 1997. 87.00 (*0-412-57890-5*, Chap & Hall NY) Chapman & Hall.
Burton, Paul. Escape from Terror: Five Explosive Worlds of Air Combat, Capture, Confinement & Escape from Nazi Germany. Cate, Michael, ed. & tr. by. LC 95-81643. (Illus.). 248p. 1996. 22.50 (*1-886130-03-5*) Cate Media.
Burton, Paul. Microcomputers in Library & Information Services: An Annotated Bibliography. 126p. 1986. text 49.95 (*0-566-03540-5*, Pub. by Gower) Ashgate Pub Co.
Burton, Paul F. Info Management. 1991. 57.50 (*0-412-34130-1*, Chap & Hall NY) Chapman & Hall.
Burton, Paul F. & Petrie, J. Howard. Information Management Technology. rev. ed. (Illus.). 240p. 1991. 51.95 (*0-442-31295-4*) Chapman & Hall.
Burton, Paul R. & Burton, Frances M. Ephraim Stories. (Illus.). 316p. 1999. 16.95 (*0-9650769-0-3*); pap. 16.95 (*0-9650769-1-1*) Stonehll Pub WI.
Burton, Pauline, et al, eds. Bilingual Women: Anthropological Approaches to Second Language Use. 210p. 1994. 49.50 (*0-85496-737-0*, Pub. by Berg Pubs); pap. 19.50 (*0-85496-864-4*, Pub. by Berg Pubs) NYU Pr.
Burton, Paulu. Radio & Television Broadcasting on the European Continent. LC 67-27097. 302p. reprint ed. pap. 93.70 (*0-608-18669-4*, 205589700039) Bks Demand.
Burton, Peter. Amongst the Aliens. 1995. pap. 12.95 (*1-873741-21-9*, Pub. by Millvres Bks) LPC InBook.
— Somerset Maugham: Outlines. 96p. 2000. pap. 9.95 (*1-899791-76-0*) Stewart Tabori & Chang.
Burton, Peter, ed. The Mammoth Book of Gay Short Stories. LC 97-28172. (Mammoth Book Ser.). 512p. 1997. pap. 10.95 (*0-7867-0430-6*) Carroll & Graf.
Burton, Peter & Smith, Richard, eds. Vale of Tears: A Problem Shared. 212p. (Orig.). 1992. pap. 13.95 (*1-873741-05-7*, Pub. by Millvres Bks) LPC InBook.
Burton, Philip. Birds of North America. (Spotter's Guides Ser.). (Illus.). 64p. (YA). (gr. 8-12). 1991. lib. bdg. 12.95 (*0-88110-984-3*, Usborne) EDC.
— Birds of North America. (Spotter's Guides Ser.). (Illus.). 64p. (J). (gr. 7 up). 1992. pap. 4.95 (*0-7460-1145-8*, Usborne) EDC.
— Birds of North America. (Usborne Kid Kits Ser.). (Illus.). (J). (gr. 3-7). 1998. 15.95 (*1-58086-017-6*, Usborne) EDC.
***Burton, Philip.** The Old Latin Gospels: A Study of Their Texts & Language. (Oxford Early Christian Studies). 250p. 2000. text 70.00 (*0-19-826988-9*) OUP.
Burton, Philip, et al. Richard & Philip: The Burtons A Book of Memories. 184p. 1993. 28.00 (*0-7206-0855-4*, Pub. by P Owen Ltd) Dufour.
Burton, Philip W. Advertising Copywriting. 7th ed. 400p. 1994. 39.95 (*0-8442-3200-9*, NTC Business Bks) NTC Contemp Pub Co.
— Advertising Copywriting. 7th ed. LC 96-21090. (Illus.). 400p. 1996. 44.95 (*0-8442-3206-8*, NTC Business Bks) NTC Contemp Pub Co.
Burton, Philip W. & Purvis, Scott C. Which Ad Pulled Best? 8th ed. LC 95-39651. (Illus.). 160p. 1995. pap. 19.95 (*0-8442-3315-3*, NTC Business Bks) NTC Contemp Pub Co.
— Which Ad Pulled Best? Answer Key. 8th ed. pap. 3.95 (*0-8442-3316-1*) NTC Contemp Pub Co.
Burton, R. Kamasutra of Vatsyayana. (Illus.). 187p. 1994. 9.95 (*81-7224-128-3*) Asia Bk Corp.
Burton, R. A. Heat, Bearings & Lubrication: Engineering Analysis of Thermally Coupled Shear Flows & Elastic Solid Boundaries. LC 99-18597. (Illus.). 250p. 1999. 69.00 (*0-387-98798-3*) Spr-Verlag.
Burton, R. F. First Footsteps in East Africa, Vol. 1. 256p. 1986. 200.00 (*1-85077-127-8*, Pub. by Darf Pubs Ltd) St Mut.
— First Footsteps in East Africa, Vol. 2. 288p. 1986. 200.00 (*1-85077-128-6*, Pub. by Darf Pubs Ltd) St Mut.
— First Footsteps in East Africa, Vols. 1 & 2. 1986. 200.00 (*0-7855-1997-1*, Pub. by Darf Pubs Ltd) St Mut.
— Pilgrimage to Al-Madinah & Meccah, Vol. 1. 488p. 1986. 350.00 (*1-85077-125-1*, Pub. by Darf Pubs Ltd) St Mut.
— Pilgrimage to Al-Madinah & Meccah, Vol. 2. 512p. 1986. 350.00 (*1-85077-126-X*, Pub. by Darf Pubs Ltd) St Mut.
— Pilgrimage to Al-Madinah & Meccah, Vols. 1 & 2. 1986. write for info. (*0-7855-2569-6*, Pub. by Darf Pubs Ltd) St Mut.
Burton, R. Lee. Canneries of the Eastern Shore: With Photographs Made Especially for This Book by A. Vernon Taylor. LC 85-41006. (Illus.). 206p. 1986. reprint ed. pap. 63.90 (*0-7837-9074-0*, 204982300003) Bks Demand.
Burton, Ralph A., ed. Bearing & Seal Design in Nuclear Power Machinery: Proceedings of the Symposium on Lubrication in Nuclear Applications, Miami Beach, Florida, June 5-7, 1967. LC 67-27785. 539p. reprint ed. pap. 167.10 (*0-8357-7084-2*, 201680900005) Bks Demand.
Burton, Richard. Arabian Nights. 1997. 20.50 (*0-679-60235-6*) Modern Lib NY.
— Forces in Fiction & Other Essays. LC 70-76896. (Essay Index Reprint Ser.). 1977. 18.95 (*0-8369-0008-1*) Ayer.
— The Kasidah. 128p. 1991. reprint ed. 23.00 (*0-86304-061-6*, Pub. by Octagon Pr) ISHK.
— The Kasidah of Haji Abdu El-Yezdi (1924) 136p. 1998. reprint ed. pap. 16.95 (*0-7661-0172-X*) Kessinger Pub.
— Literary Leaders of America. LC 71-105001. (Essay Index Reprint Ser.). 1977. 21.95 (*0-8369-1455-4*) Ayer.
— Literary Likings. LC 79-37510. (Essay Index Reprint Ser.). 1977. reprint ed. 25.95 (*0-8369-2538-6*) Ayer.
— Little Essays in Literature & Life. LC 74-93322. (Essay Index Reprint Ser.). 1977. 23.95 (*0-8369-1277-2*) Ayer.
— The Look of the West, 1860. LC 63-17030. (Illus.). 363p. reprint ed. 112.60 (*0-8357-9710-4*, 201463000093) Bks Demand.
— Masters of the English Novel. LC 79-90620. (Essay Index Reprint Ser.). 1977. 23.95 (*0-8369-1252-7*) Ayer.

B

— Proteins, Ancient Greeks & T'ang Poetry. 1994. pap. 18.95 (*0-7486-6173-5*, Pub. by Edinburgh U Pr) Col U Pr.

— Selected Papers on Anthropology, Travel & Exploration. LC 72-80499. 240p. 1972. reprint ed. 24.95 (*0-405-08335-1*, Pub. by Blom Pubns) Ayer.

— Selections from Arabian Nights. 390p. 1992. reprint ed. pap. 14.95 (*1-57002-070-1*) Univ Publng Hse.

— Sindh & the Races That Inhabit the Valley of the Indus. (C). 1992. reprint ed. 28.00 (*81-206-0758-9*, Pub. by Asian Educ Servs) S Asia.

— Sir Richard Burton's Travels in Arabia & Africa: Four Lectures from a Huntington Library Manuscript. LC 90-44363. (Illus.). 110p. 1990. 24.95 (*0-87328-131-4*) Huntington Lib.

Burton, Richard, tr. The Perfumed Garden of the Shaykh Nefzawi. 1992. reprint ed. lib. bdg. 21.95 (*0-89968-296-0*, Lghtyr Pr) Buccaneer Bks.

Burton, Richard & Arbuthnot, F. F. The Kama Sutra of Vatsyayana. 224p. 1986. mass mkt. 6.99 (*0-425-09593-2*) Berkley Pub.

Burton, Richard & Arbuthnot, F. F., trs. The Illustrated Kama Sutra: Ananga-Ranga Perfumed Garden, The Classic Eastern Love Texts. (Illus.). 156p. 1991. pap. 19.95 (*0-89281-441-1*) Inner Tradit.

Burton, Richard, et al. Keep Your Hand on the Plow: The African American Presence in the Catholic Church. xii, 124p. (C). 1996. pap. 19.95 (*1-55586-098-2*) US Catholic.

Burton, Richard, ed. see Gibbons, Dave.

Burton, Richard, tr. see Archer, W. G., ed.

Burton, Richard D. Afro-Creole: Power, Opposition, & Play in the Caribbean. LC 96-50046. (Illus.). 320p. 1996. text 45.00 (*0-8014-3249-9*); pap. text 17.95 (*0-8014-8325-5*) Cornell U Pr.

— Baudelaire & the Second Republic: Writing & Revolution. 396p. 1992. text 99.00 (*0-19-815469-0*) OUP.

Burton, Richard D. & Reno, Fred, eds. French & West Indian: Martinique, Guadeloupe, & French Guiana Today. 208p. (C). 1995. text 42.50 (*0-8139-1565-1*); pap. text 18.00 (*0-8139-1566-X*) U Pr of Va.

Burton, Richard F. Biology by Numbers: An Encouragement to Quantitative Thinking. (Illus.). 252p. (C). 1998. text 59.95 (*0-521-57156-1*); pap. text 19.95 (*0-521-57698-9*) Cambridge U Pr.

— The Book of the Sword. (Illus.). 336p. 1987. reprint ed. pap. 9.95 (*0-486-25434-8*) Dover.

— City of the Saints. LC 72-134390. (BCL Ser. II). (Illus.). reprint ed. 82.50 (*0-404-08433-8*) AMS Pr.

— Falconry in the Valley of the Indus. 3rd ed. (Oxford in Asia Historical Reprints Ser.). (Illus.). 88p. 1997. reprint ed. text 21.95 (*0-19-577737-9*) OUP.

— First Footsteps in East Africa: Or, An Exploration of Harar. (Illus.). 544p. 1987. reprint ed. pap. 12.95 (*0-486-25475-5*) Dover.

— First Footsteps in East Africa: or An Exploration of Harar. LC 74-15015. (Illus.). reprint ed. 38.50 (*0-404-12010-5*) AMS Pr.

— Goa & the Blue Mountains: Or, Six Months of Sick Leave. (Illus.). 400p. 1991. 55.00 (*0-520-07610-9*, Pub. by U CA Pr); pap. 19.95 (*0-520-07611-7*, Pub. by U CA Pr) Cal Prin Full Svc.

— The Gold Mines of Midian. Ward, Philip, ed. (Arabia Past & Present Ser.: Vol. 8). (Illus.). 1979. 45.00 (*0-900891-50-5*) Oleander Pr.

— The Gold-Mines of Midian. unabridged ed. LC 95-15866. Orig. Title: The Gold-Mines of Midian & the Ruined Midianite Cities. (Illus.). 416p. 1995. reprint ed. pap. text 10.95 (*0-486-28739-4*) Dover.

— Kama Sutra: The Classic Hindu Treatise on Love & Social Conduct. 256p. 1991. pap. 12.95 (*0-14-019360-X*, Arkana) Viking Penguin.

— The Lake Region of Central Africa: A Picture of Exploration. LC 77-116278. (Illus.). 572p. 1972. reprint ed. 95.00 (*0-403-00442-X*) Scholarly.

— The Lake Regions of Central Africa. LC 94-46004. (Illus.). 576p. 1995. pap. text 14.95 (*0-486-28618-5*) Dover.

— The Land of Midian, 2 vols., Set. (Arabia Past & Present Ser.: Vols. 14-15). (Illus.). 1979. 90.00 (*0-900891-55-6*) Oleander Pr.

— Narrative of Pilgrimage to El Medina & Mecca, 2 vols., Set. (C). 1994. 72.00 (*81-206-0903-4*, Pub. by Asian Educ Servs) S Asia.

— Nile Basin. 2nd ed. LC 65-23403. (Middle East in the 20th Century Ser.). 1967. reprint ed. 25.00 (*0-306-70926-0*) Da Capo.

— Personal Narrative of a Pilgrimage to Al-Madinah & Meccah, Vol. 1. (Illus.). 1964. pap. 11.95 (*0-486-21217-3*) Dover.

— Personal Narrative of a Pilgrimage to Al-Madinah & Meccah, Vol. 2. (Illus.). 1964. pap. 10.95 (*0-486-21218-1*) Dover.

— Physiology by Numbers: An Encouragement to Quantitative Thinking. LC 93-37134. (Illus.). 201p. (C). 1994. text 64.95 (*0-521-42067-9*); pap. text 22.95 (*0-521-42138-1*) Cambridge U Pr.

***Burton, Richard F.** Physiology by Numbers: An Encouragement to Quantitative Thinking. 2nd ed. (Illus.). 200p. (C). 2000. text 64.95 (*0-521-77200-1*); pap. text 24.95 (*0-521-77703-8*) Cambridge U Pr.

— Scinde or the Unhappy Valley, 2 vols. in 1. 623p. 1998. 34.50 (*81-215-0903-3*, Pub. by M Manoharial) Coronet Bks.

Burton, Richard F. Scinde or the Unhappy Valley. 2nd ed. LC 98-906405. 1998. write for info. (*81-206-1292-2*) Asian Educ Servs.

— Sind Revisited. (C). 1997. 42.50 (*81-215-0771-5*, Pub. by M Manoharial) Coronet Bks.

— Sindh & the Races That Inhabit the Valley of the Indus. 1998. 34.00 (*81-215-0823-1*, Pub. by M Manoharial) Coronet Bks.

— Wanderings in West Africa. Orig. Title: Wanderings in West Africa from Liverpool to Fernando Po. (Illus.). 624p. 1991. reprint ed. pap. 13.95 (*0-486-26890-X*) Dover.

— Wit & Wisdom from West Africa: A Book of Proverbial Philosophy, Idioms, Enigmas, & Laconisms. LC 77-79952. 1969. reprint ed. pap. 25.00 (*0-8196-0243-4*) Biblo.

Burton, Richard F., ed. Wit & Wisdom from West Africa. LC 69-18975. 455p. 1969. reprint ed. lib. bdg. 35.00 (*0-8371-1378-4*, BUW&, Greenwood Pr) Greenwood.

Burton, Richard F., tr. King Vikram & the Vampire: Classic Hindu Tales of Adventure, Magic, & Romance. (Illus.). 272p. (Orig.). 1992. pap. 12.95 (*0-89281-475-6*, Park St Pr) Inner Tradit.

— Marc Chagall: Arabian Nights. LC 98-54867. (Pegasus Library). (Illus.). 164p. 1999. 25.00 (*3-7913-2081-5*) te Neues.

Burton, Richard F., tr. see Nafzawi, Umar ibn Muhammad.

Burton, Richard F., tr. see Royal Geography Society.

Burton, Richard F., tr. see Vetalapancavimsati.

Burton, Richard M. & Obel, Borge. Strategic Organizational Diagnosis & Design: Developing Theory for Application. LC 95-22948. 480p. (C). 1995. lib. bdg. 89.95 (*0-7923-9628-6*) Kluwer Academic.

Burton, Richard M. & Obel, Borge, eds. Design Models for Hierarchical Organizations: Computation, Information, & Decentralization. LC 95-30792. 296p. (C). 1995. lib. bdg. 109.00 (*0-7923-9609-X*) Kluwer Academic.

Burton, Richard M., et al. Strategic Organizational Diagnosis & Design: Developing Theory for Application. 2nd ed. LC 98-28277. 1998. 140.00 (*0-7923-8229-3*); pap. 69.95 (*0-7923-8247-1*) Kluwer Academic.

Burton, Robert. Anatomy of Melancholy, 3 vols. Shilleto, A. R., ed. LC 75-39565. reprint ed. 287.50 (*0-404-07822-2*) AMS Pr.

— The Anatomy of Melancholy. 1036p. 1992. reprint ed. pap. 50.00 (*1-56459-003-8*) Kessinger Pub.

— The Anatomy of Melancholy, Vol. II. Kiessling, Nicolas K. et al, eds. (Oxford English Texts Ser.). (Illus.). 452p. 1990. text 135.00 (*0-19-812330-2*) OUP.

— The Anatomy of Melancholy, Vol. III. Faulkner, Thomas C. et al, eds. (Oxford English Texts Ser.). (Illus.). 820p. 1994. text 160.00 (*0-19-812331-0*) OUP.

— The Anatomy of Melancholy, Vol. IV. Bamborough, J. B. & Dodsworth, Martin, eds. (Oxford English Texts Ser.). 384p. 1998. text 110.00 (*0-19-812332-9*) OUP.

***Burton, Robert.** The Anatomy of Melancholy, Vol. VI. Bamborough, J. B. & Dodsworth, Martin, eds. (Oxford English Texts Ser.). 416p. 2001. text 120.00 (*0-19-818486-7*) OUP.

Burton, Robert. The Anatomy of Melancholy: Text "Democritus Junior to the Reader" & "The First Partition", Vol. I. Faulkner, Thomas C. et al, eds. (Illus.). 746p. 1989. text 165.00 (*0-19-812448-1*) OUP.

— The Anatomy of Melancholy: What It Is. LC 72-178. (English Experience Ser.: No. 301). 746p. 1971. reprint ed. 100.00 (*90-221-0301-3*) Walter J Johnson.

— Bird Migration: An Illustrated Account. (Illus.). 160p. 1992. 29.95 (*0-8160-2781-1*) Facts on File.

Burton, Robert. The Daily Telegraph Nature Notes. (Illus.). 112p. 17.95 (*0-340-72884-1*, Pub. by Hodder & Stought Ltd) Trafalgar.

Burton, Robert. The Egg: A Photographic Story of Hatching. LC 93-28365. (Illus.). 40p. (J). (ps-3). 1994. 14.95 (*1-56458-460-7*) DK Pub Inc.

***Burton, Robert.** Egg: A Photographic Story of Hatching. LC 93-28365. (Illus.). 40p. (J). (gr. 1-5). 2000. pap. text 7.95 (*0-7894-6069-6*, D K Ink) DK Pub Inc.

Burton, Robert. The Life & Death of Whales. 2nd enl. rev. ed. (Helix Bks.: No. 378). (Illus.). 186p. (C). 1983. pap. text 15.00 (*0-8226-0378-0*) Littlefield.

— National Audubon Society Concise Birdfeeder Handbook. LC 91-58218. 128p. 1997. pap. 9.95 (*0-7894-1465-1*) DK Pub Inc.

— The National Audubon Society North American Birdfeeder Handbook. rev. ed. (Illus.). 224p. 1995. 24.95 (*0-7894-0337-4*, 6-70523) DK Pub Inc.

— Philosophaster. 310p. 1992. reprint ed. pap. 30.00 (*1-56459-227-8*) Kessinger Pub.

— Wild Animals I Have Known. Kottmeyer, William A. et al, eds. 1962. pap. 7.96 (*0-07-009288-5*) McGraw.

***Burton, Robert & Kress, Stephen W.** The Audubon Backyard Birdwatcher: Birdfeeders & Bird Gardens. LC 99-10809. (Illus.). 400p. 1999. 19.98 (*1-57145-186-2*, Thunder Bay) Advantage Pubs.

Burton, Robert, jt. auth. see Burton, Maurice.

Burton, Robert, jt. ed. see Burton, Maurice.

Burton, Robert A. Cellmates. 1999. mass mkt. 6.50 (*0-440-22656-2*) Dell.

— Cellmates. LC 97-66723. 280p. 1997. 19.95 (*0-9653524-4-7*) Russn Hill Pr.

— Doc-in-a-Box. LC 90-10315. 214p. 1991. 18.95 (*0-939149-47-8*) Soho Press.

— Final Therapy. 304p. (Orig.). 1994. mass mkt. 5.50 (*0-515-11503-7*, Jove) Berkley Pub.

Burton, Robert E. Self-Remembering. rev. ed. LC 95-16125. 240p. 1995. reprint ed. pap. text 14.95 (*0-87728-844-5*) Weiser.

Burton, Robert E. & Rich, Sandra L. Ohio Corporation Law & Practice. (National Corporation Law Ser.). 1992. ring bd. 126.00 (*0-13-633371-0*) Aspen Law.

Burton, Robert G., ed. Natural & Artificial Minds. LC 92-35020. (SUNY Series, Scientific Studies in Natural & Artificial Intelligence). 245p. (C). 1993. text 64.50 (*0-7914-1507-4*); pap. text 21.95 (*0-7914-1508-2*) State U NY Pr.

Burton-Roberts, Noel. Analyzing Sentences: An Introduction to English Syntax. 2nd ed. LC 96-48575. (Learning about Language Ser.). 1997. pap. 27.25 (*0-582-24876-0*) Longman.

***Burton-Roberts, Noel, et al, eds.** Phonological Knowledge: Conceptual & Empirical Issues. (Illus.). 320p. 2000. text 80.00 (*0-19-824127-5*); pap. text 35.00 (*0-19-824129-1*) OUP.

Burton, Rodney, compiled by. Scientific Abstracting & Indexing Periodicals in the British Library: A Guide to SRIS Holdings & Their Use. 4th ed. (Key to British Library Holdings Ser.). 64p. 1991. pap. 36.00 (*0-7123-0780-X*, Pub. by SRIS) L Erlbaum Assocs.

***Burton, Ron.** Illustrated Buyer's Guide: Classic Japanese Motorcycles. (Illus.). 160p. 2000. pap. 17.95 (*0-7603-0765-2*, 130123AP, Pub. by MBI Pubg) Motorbooks Intl.

Burton-Rose, Daniel, et al, eds. The Celling of America: An Inside Look at the U. S. Prison Industry. LC 97-45071. 1997. lib. bdg. 29.95 (*1-56751-141-4*) Common Courage.

— The Celling of America: An Inside Look at the U. S. Prison Industry. LC 97-45071. 264p. 1998. pap. 19.95 (*1-56751-140-6*) Common Courage.

Burton, Rosemary. Prudentius Psychomachia. (Bryn Mawr Latin Commentaries Ser.). 106p. (Orig.). (C). 1989. pap. 7.00 (*0-929524-61-6*) Bryn Mawr Commentaries.

— Travel Geography. 2nd ed. (Illus.). 514p. (Orig.). 1998. reprint ed. pap. 52.50 (*0-582-31558-1*) Trans-Atl Phila.

Burton, Rulon T. The Island That Was Not There. (Illus.). 25p. (J). (gr. 3 up). 1998. 16.95 (*0-9640696-3-6*) Tabernacle Bks.

— We Believe: Doctrines & Principles of the Church of Jesus Christ of Latter Day Saints. 1400p. (Orig.). 1994. lib. bdg. 39.95 (*0-9640696-0-1*) Tabernacle Bks.

— We Believe: Doctrines & Principles of the Church of Jesus Christ of Latter Day Saints. 1200p. (Orig.). 1995. pap. 24.95 (*0-9640696-2-8*) Tabernacle Bks.

Burton, S. The Derbyshire Gritstone Way. (C). 1988. pap. 50.00 (*0-904110-88-5*, Pub. by Thornhill Pr) St Mut.

Burton, S. M. The Art of Astronomical Navigation. (C). 1987. 45.00 (*0-85174-257-2*) St Mut.

Burton, S. W. & Akiskal, H. S., eds. Dysthymic Disorder. 144p. 1990. pap. text 21.00 (*0-88048-600-7*, 8600, Pub. by Royal Coll Psych) Parkwest Pubns.

Burton, Sam W. Disciple Mentoring: Theological Education by Extension. LC 97-49878. 1998. write for info. (*0-87808-279-4*) William Carey Lib.

***Burton, Sarah K.** Study in Britain Handbook: On Course World Study Guide. 2nd ed. Chapman, Kirsten et al, eds. (Illus.). 576p. 1999. pap. 11.95 (*1-898730-31-8*, Pub. by On Course Pubns) Midpt Trade.

Burton, Scott. A Life in the Balance: A Professional Juggler & Comic's Story of Surviving Cancer with Laughter & a Passion for Living. 1997. 15.00 (*0-9658815-0-4*) Inconvenience Prods.

Burton, Sharon. Applying Lotus 2.2. (C). 1991. pap. text, teacher ed. 2.76 (*0-395-56971-0*) HM.

— Applying WordPerfect 5.1 / 5.0. (C). 1991. pap. text, teacher ed. 2.76 (*0-395-56975-3*) HM.

— Business Math Using Calculators. 2nd ed. (C). 1989. mass mkt. 45.95 (*0-538-70062-9*) S-W Pub.

Burton, Sharon & Holloway, Ralph. Keyboarding for the Information Processor. 168p. (gr. 11-12). 1985. teacher ed. write for info. (*0-672-98469-5*); pap, text. write for info. (*0-672-98468-7*) Macmillan.

Burton, Sharon & Shelton, Nelda. Basic Letter & Memo Writing. LC 96-20984. 304p. (C). 1996. text 17.50 (*0-256-22014-X*, Irwn McGrw-H) McGrw-H Hghr Educ.

— Software Solutions: Concepts & Applications. (C). 1991. write for info. (*0-395-53249-3*) HM Soft Schl Col Div.

— Using WordPerfect 5.1. (C). 1991. pap. text. write for info. (*0-395-56952-4*) HM Soft Schl Col Div.

Burton, Sharon & Shelton, Nelda. Writing Letters & Memos: Essential Guidelines. 1997. teacher ed. 16.48 (*0-256-23157-5*, Irwn McGrw-H) McGrw-H Hghr Educ.

Burton, Sharon, et al. Procedures for the Automated Office. 4th ed. LC 97-8716. 401p. 1997. pap. text 56.00 (*0-13-261025-6*) P-H.

***Burton, Sharon, et al.** Procedures for the Automated Office. 5th ed. 416p. 2000. pap. 46.67 (*0-13-025431-2*, Prentice Hall) P-H.

Burton, Sharon, jt. auth. see Perl, Michael.

Burton, Sharon, jt. auth. see Shelton, Nelda.

Burton, Sheryl. When There's a Will There's a Way. LC 98-194328. 114p. 1997. pap. 16.00 (*1-900990-07-5*, Pub. by Natl Childrens Bur) Paul & Co Pubs.

Burton, Shirley & Kiley, Leo, eds. Beyond Addictions, Beyond Boundaries: The Defiant Power of the Human Spirit. (Illus.). 220p. (Orig.). 1986. pap. text 10.95 (*1-55796-000-3*) Brookridge Pub.

Burton, Stacy & Dworkin, Dennis. Trials of Modernity: Europe since 1500. 250p. (C). 1996. text 33.20 (*0-536-59010-9*) Pearson Custom.

Burton, Stephanie K. Music Explosion Book & Tape: Teacher's Manual. rev. ed. Date not set. teacher ed. 34.95 incl. audio (*1-889163-05-8*) Panda Bear Pub.

Burton, Stephanie K. Music Mania. 153p. (Orig.). 1994. pap., teacher ed. 29.95 incl. audio (*1-889163-00-7*); pap., teacher ed. 19.95 (*1-889163-02-3*) Panda Bear Pub.

Burton, Stephanie K. Music Mania Book & CD: Teacher's Manual. 153p. 1994. teacher ed. 33.95 incl. audio compact disk (*1-889163-03-1*) Panda Bear Pub.

***Burton, Stephanie K. & Campbell, Phyllis.** The Curiosity Shop Book & Cassette. 38p. 2000. pap. 17.95 incl. audio (*1-889163-04-X*); pap. 17.95 incl. audio (*1-889163-07-4*) Panda Bear Pub.

— The Curiosity Shop Book & CD. 38p. 2000. pap. 21.95 incl. audio compact disk (*1-889163-06-6*) Panda Bear Pub.

Burton, Stephanie K. & Campbell, Phyllis. Science Times with Nursery Rhymes. (Illus.). (Orig.). (J). (ps-2). 1996. pap., teacher ed. 16.95 (*1-889163-01-5*) Panda Bear Pub.

Burton, Steven J. Contract Law, Selected Source Materials. 312p. (C). 1995. pap. text 12.00 (*0-314-06535-0*) West Pub.

— Judging in Good Faith. (Cambridge Studies in Philosophy & Law). 291p. (C). 1992. text 69.95 (*0-521-41994-8*) Cambridge U Pr.

— Judging in Good Faith. (Cambridge Studies in Philosophy & Law). 291p. 1994. pap. text 21.95 (*0-521-47740-9*) Cambridge U Pr.

— Legal Reason. 2nd ed. 192p. 1995. pap. text 24.95 (*0-316-11489-8*, Aspen Law & Bus) Aspen Pub.

— Principles of Contract Law. LC 95-3030. (American Casebook Ser.). 699p. (C). 1995. 57.50 (*0-314-04972-X*) West Pub.

***Burton, Steven J., ed.** The Path of the Law & Its Influence: The Legacy of Oliver Wendell Holmes. (Cambridge Studies in Philosophy & Law). 384p. 2000. 64.95 (*0-521-63006-1*) Cambridge U Pr.

Burton, Steven J. & Burton, Leslie M. The Encyclopedia of Contemporary Doll Art & International Directory of Doll Artists. (Illus.). 800p. 1996. 89.95 (*0-9653070-1-8*) Collectors Res.

Burton, Steven J. & Eisenberg, Melvin A. Contract Law: Selected Source Materials. 2nd ed. 336p. 1996. pap. text. write for info. (*0-314-20031-2*) West Pub.

— Contract Law, Selected Source Materials. 4th ed. LC 98-27910. (Pamphlet Ser.). 450p. 1998. pap. text 15.50 (*0-314-23301-6*) West Pub.

***Burton, Sue.** The Encyclopedia of Flower-Painting Techniques: A Unique Shape-by-Shape Directory to Painting Beautiful, Realistic Flowers. (Illus.). 160p. 2000. reprint ed. 25.00 (*0-7881-9207-8*) DIANE Pub.

Burton, Susan B, & Miller, May T. A Batch of Patchwork: Beyond the Quilting Bee, 12 Easy Quilts to Make with Friends. LC 97-36647. 128p. 1997. 18.95 (*0-89145-883-2*, 4832, Am Quilters Soc) Collector Bks.

Burton, Susan S. & Laughlin, Minnabell, eds. Proceedings of the Hohokam Conference, 1973. (Contributions to Anthropological Studies: No. 2). 1978. 10.00 (*0-916552-13-6*) Ctr Anthrop Studies.

***Burton, T. L., ed.** Sidrak & Bokkus: A Parallel-Text Edition. (Early English Text Society Original Ser.: 311). (Illus.). 540p. 1999. text 90.00 (*0-19-722315-X*) OUP.

— Sidrak & Bokkus Vol. II, Vol. 2. (Early English Text Society Original Ser.). (Illus.). 508p. 1999. text 85.00 (*0-19-722316-8*) OUP.

Burton, T. L. & Greentree, Rosemary, eds. Chaucer's, Miller's, Reeve's, & Cook's Tales: An Annotated Bibliography, 1900-1992. (Chaucer Bibliographies Ser.: Vol. 5). 287p. 1997. text 75.00 (*0-8020-0874-7*) U of Toronto Pr.

Burton, Terrence T. & Moran, John W. The Future Focused Organization: Complete Organizational Alignment for Breakthrough Results. 256p. (C). 1995. pap. text 19.95 (*0-13-323791-5*) P-H.

Burton, Terry. Christmas Snow. 20p. (J). (ps). 1996. bds. 3.49 (*1-85854-544-7*) Brimax Bks.

— My First Dictionary. 48p. (J). (ps-1). 1997. 7.98 (*1-85854-600-1*) Brimax Bks.

— Santa's Busy Night. 20p. (J). (ps). 1996. bds. 3.49 (*1-85854-545-5*) Brimax Bks.

— Tiger's New Car. (My Big Little Fat Bks.). 20p. (J). (ps). 1997. bds. 3.49 (*1-85854-599-4*) Brimax Bks.

— When Crocodile Is Happy. (My Big Little Fat Bks.). 20p. (J). (ps up). 1997. bds. 3.49 (*1-85854-598-6*) Brimax Bks.

Burton, Theodore E. Financial Crises & Periods of Industrial & Commercial Depressions. LC 74-165618. (Select Bibliographies Reprint Ser.). 1977. reprint ed. 29.95 (*0-8369-5925-6*) Ayer.

— Financial Crises & Periods of Industrial & Commercial Depressions. LC 66-23328. 1983. reprint ed. 21.00 (*0-87034-021-2*) Fraser Pub Co.

— John Sherman. Morse, John T., Jr., ed. LC 76-128948. (American Statesmen Ser.: No. 33). reprint ed. 49.50 (*0-404-50883-9*) AMS Pr.

Burton, Theodore E. & Selden, G. C. A Century of Prices: An Examination of Economic & Financial Conditions As Reflected in Prices, Money Rates, Etc., During the Past 100 Years, with a View to Establish General Principles Which May Aid in Interpreting the Present & Future. LC 96-84378. 118p. 1996. reprint ed. pap. 18.00 (*0-87034-123-5*) Fraser Pub Co.

Burton, Thomas. Serpent-Handling Believers. LC 92-30409. (Illus.). 344p. (Orig.). (C). 1993. pap. 21.95 (*0-87049-788-X*) U of Tenn Pr.

Burton, Thomas D. Introduction to Dynamic Systems Analysis. LC 93-32113. (Series in Mechanical Engineering). 690p. (C). 1994. 87.81 (*0-07-009290-7*) McGraw.

Burton, Thomas G., ed. Tom Ashley, Sam McGee, Bukka White: Tennessee Traditional Singers. LC 79-19655. (Illus.). 251p. reprint ed. pap. 77.90 (*0-8357-6539-3*, 203590100097) Bks Demand.

Burton, Thomas L., jt. ed. see Jackson, Edgar L.

Burton, Thomas M. Stream Ecology. Date not set. 69.95 (*0-87371-818-6*) Lewis Pubs.

Burton, Tim. The Melancholy Death of Oyster Boy: And Other Stories. LC 97-18468. (Illus.). 128p. 1997. 20.00 (*0-688-15681-9*, Wm Morrow); 20.00 (*0-688-15682-7*, Wm Morrow) Morrow Avon.

— The Nightmare Before Christmas. LC 92-54867. (Illus.). 40p. (J). 1993. 15.95 (*1-56282-411-2*, Pub. by Hyprn Child) Little.

An Asterisk (*) at the beginning of an entry indicates that the title is appearing for the first time.

— The Nightmare Before Christmas. LC 92-54867. (Illus.). 40p. (J). 1994. pap. 6.70 (*0-7868-1014-9*, Pub. by Hyprn Ppbks) Little.

Burton, Tim, intro. The Art of Sleepy Hollow. 1999. 29.95 (*0-671-03657-2*) S&S Trade.

***Burton, Tim, intro.** Tim Burton's Sleepy Hollow. 192p. 1999. per. 5.99 (*0-671-03665-3*, PB Hardcover) PB.

Burton, Tim & Salisbury, Mark. Burton on Burton. (Directors on Directors Ser.). (Illus.). 200p. 1995. 22.95 (*0-571-17392-6*) Faber & Faber.

Burton, Tom. Words in Your Ear. (Illus.). 192p. 1999. pap. 14.95 (*1-86254-475-1*, Pub. by Wakefield Pr) BHB Intl.

***Burton, Tony.** These Are a Few of My Favorite Things. (Illus.). 128p. 1999. per. 10.00 (*0-684-85794-4*) S&S Trade Pap.

Burton, Tony, jt. ed. see Baldwin, Mark.

***Burton, Valorie Raquel.** Rich Minds ... Rich Rewards: 50 Ways to Enhance Your Everyday Life. 204p. 1999. pap. 13.95 (*1-930257-00-7*, 0115-73) Pearl Bks TX.

Burton, Velmer S., Jr., jt. ed. see Cullen, Francis T.

Burton, Vernon, et al. Insects, Mites & Other Invertebrates & Their Control in California. rev. ed. LC 81-68756. 126p. 1981. pap. 4.00 (*0-931876-49-4*, 4044) ANR Pubns CA.

Burton, Virginia L. Calico the Wonder Horse. (Illus.). 64p. 1996. pap. 5.95 (*0-395-84541-6*) HM.

— Calico the Wonder Horse. (Illus.). 64p. 1997. 16.00 (*0-395-85735-X*) HM.

— Choo Choo. (Illus.). 48p. (J). (gr. k-3). 1973. 16.00 (*0-395-17684-0*) HM.

— Choo Choo. (Carry-Along Book & Cassette Favorites Ser.). 1p. (J). (gr. k up). 1989. pap. 9.95 incl. audio (*0-395-51168-2*, 482615) HM.

— Choo Choo: The Story of a Little Engine Who Ran Away. LC 37-19461. (Illus.). 56p. (Orig.). (J). (gr. k-8). 1988. pap. 6.95 (*0-395-47942-8*) HM.

— Katy & the Big Snow, 001. (Illus.). 40p. (J). (gr. k-3). 1973. 15.00 (*0-395-18155-0*) HM.

— Katy & the Big Snow, 001. (Illus.). 40p. (J). (gr. k-3). 1974. pap. 6.95 (*0-395-18562-9*, Sandpiper) HM.

— Life Story, 001. (Illus.). 80p. (J). (gr. k-3). 1962. 20.00 (*0-395-16030-8*) HM.

— Life Story. (Illus.). 80p. (J). (gr. k-3). 1989. pap. 9.95 (*0-395-52017-7*) HM.

— The Little House, 001. (Illus.). 44p. (J). (gr. k-3). 1978. 14.95 (*0-395-18156-9*) HM.

— The Little House, 001. LC 88-176374. (Illus.). 44p. (J). (ps-3). 1978. pap. 5.95 (*0-395-25938-X*) HM.

— The Little House. (J). 1969. 11.15 (*0-606-01531-0*, Pub. by Turtleback) Demco.

— Maybelle, the Cable Car. LC 96-9845. (Illus.). 48p. (J). (ps-4). 1997. 16.00 (*0-395-82847-3*) HM.

— Mike Mulligan & His Steam Shovel. (Illus.). (J). (gr. k-3). 1939. lib. bdg. 11.95 (*0-395-06681-6*) HM.

— Mike Mulligan & His Steam Shovel. (J). 1939. 11.15 (*0-606-01106-4*, Pub. by Turtleback) Demco.

— Mike Mulligan & His Steam Shovel. unabridged ed. (Carry-Along Book & Cassette Favorites Ser.). 1p. (J). (ps-4). 1993. pap. 9.95 incl. audio (*0-395-66499-3*, 482618) HM.

— Mike Mulligan & His Steam Shovel: Story & Pictures, 001. (Sandpiper Books Ser.). (Illus.). 44p. (J). (ps-3). 1977. pap. 5.95 (*0-395-25939-8*) HM.

— Mike Mulligan y Su Maquina Maravillosa. 48p. (J). (ps-3). 1997. 16.00 (*0-395-86264-7*); pap. 5.95 (*0-395-86134-9*) HM.

Burton, Virginia Lee. La Casita. 1988. 15.15 (*0-606-10434-8*, Pub. by Turtleback) Demco.

***Burton, Virginia Lee.** Katy & the Big Snow. (Illus.). 40p. (J). (gr. k-3). 1999. 9.95 (*0-395-95991-8*) HM.

Burton, Virginia Lee. Katy & the Big Snow. (J). 1943. 12.15 (*0-606-03726-8*, Pub. by Turtleback) Demco.

— Maybelle the Cable Car. LC 96-9845. (Illus.). 48p. (ps-4). 1997. pap. 5.95 (*0-395-84003-1*) HM.

— Maybelle the Cable Car. LC 96-9845. 1996. 11.15 (*0-606-11607-9*, Pub. by Turtleback) Demco.

— Mike Mulligan & His Steam Shovel: 60th Anniversary Edition. 60th ed. (Sandpiper Books Ser.). (Illus.). 44p. (J). (ps-3). 1977. 14.95 (*0-395-16961-5*) HM.

— Mike Mulligan y Su Maquina Maravillosa. 1997. 11.15 (*0-606-12768-2*, Pub. by Turtleback) Demco.

***Burton, Virginia Lee.** Mike Mulligan Y Su Maquina Maravillosa: Mike Mulligan & His Steam Shovel. (Illus.). 56p. (J). (gr. k-3). 1999. 9.95 (*0-618-01136-6*) HM.

— Song of Robin Hood. (Illus.). (J). 2000. 20.00 (*0-618-07186-5*) HM.

Burton, W., tr. see Achilles, Tatius.

Burton, W. Butler. The Large Scale Characteristics of the Galaxy. (International Astronomical Union Highlights Ser.: No. 84). 1979. lib. bdg. 182.50 (*90-277-1029-5*) Kluwer Academic.

Burton, W. Butler & Hartmann, Dap. Atlas of Galactic Neutral Hydrogen. LC 96-41201. (Illus.). 245p. (C). 1997. text 159.95 (*0-521-47111-7*) Cambridge U Pr.

Burton, W. Butler, et al. The Galactic Interstellar Medium. Bartholdi, P. & Pfenniger, D., eds. LC 92-30271. (Saas-Fee Advanced Course Twenty One Lecture Notes Ser.: Vol. 1991). 1992. 79.95 (*0-387-55805-5*) Spr-Verlag.

Burton, W. Butler, jt. ed. see Wolstencroft, R. D.

***Burton, W. C.** Christmas in My Bones. Bledsoe, Erik, ed. (Illus.). 139p. 1999. pap. 12.95 (*1-878086-79-0*, Pub. by Down Home NC) Blair.

Burton, W. C. "Mutt". Christmas in My Bones. Bledsoe, Erik, ed. (Illus.). 139p. 1991. 14.95 (*1-878086-11-1*, Pub. by Down Home NC) Blair.

Burton, Walter H. An Elementary Compendium of the Law of Real Property. 4th ed. xxxii, 574p. 1998. reprint ed. 180.00 (*1-56169-404-5*) Gaunt.

Burton, Warren. District School As It Was. LC 71-89157. (American Education: Its Men, Institutions, & Ideas. Series 1). 1977. reprint ed. 19.95 (*0-405-01395-7*) Ayer.

— The District School As It Was. LC 76-56993. 1977. reprint ed. 7.95 (*0-918214-01-7*) F E Peters.

***Burton, Wayne.** Closer to Heaven. 1999. pap. 8.99 (*1-55517-431-0*) CFI Dist.

Burton, William C. Burton's Legal Thesauras. 3rd ed. LC 98-16952. 1998. 115.00 (*0-02-864986-9*) Macmillan.

Burton, William C., ed. The Legal Thesaurus. 2nd ed. 1024p. 1992. 27.00 (*0-02-897079-9*) Macmillan.

Burton, William L. Descriptive Bibliography of Civil War Manuscripts in Illinois. LC 65-24627. 410p. reprint ed. pap. 127.10 (*0-608-13175-X*, 201529000001) Bks Demand.

— Melting Pot Soldiers: The Union's Ethnic Regiments. LC 97-50163. (North's Civil War Ser.: No. 4). xvi, 283p. 1998. 32.50 (*0-8232-1827-9*); pap. 19.95 (*0-8232-1828-7*) Fordham.

— Melting Pot Soldiers: The Union's Ethnic Regiments. LC 87-3299. 292p. reprint ed. pap. 90.60 (*0-7837-2175-7*, 204251300004) Bks Demand.

Burton, William W., ed. Conversations about Bernstein. (Illus.). 198p. 1999. reprint ed. text 25.00 (*0-7881-6100-8*) DIANE Pub.

Burton, Yvette, ed. Community Activism & Health Care. 1997. 19.95 (*0-88737-736-X*, 14-736X, NLN Pr) Natl League Nurse.

Burton, Zachary F., et al. Experiments in Molecular Biochemistry: Biochemical Applications. LC 96-1998. (Illus.). 227p. 1997. 34.95 (*0-12-147370-8*) Acad Pr.

Burtschi, Mary. European Journey. LC 83-80653. (Illus.). 72p. 1983. pap. 6.00 (*0-9610554-0-5*) Little Brick Hse.

— James Hall of Lincoln's Frontier World. LC 77-87957. (Illus.). 202p. (C). 1978. 9.95 (*0-9601648-2-0*) Little Brick Hse.

— Vandalia: Wilderness Capital of Lincoln's Land. LC 63-5255. (Illus.). 167p. (C). 1977. 12.00 (*0-9601648-1-2*) Little Brick Hse.

Burtschi, Mary, ed. see Hall, James A.

Burtsell, Richard L. & Callahan, Nelson J. The Diary of Richard L. Burtsell, Priest of New York the Early Years, 1865-1868. 1978. 41.95 (*0-405-10813-3*) Ayer.

Burtt, Alice A. The Diaries of Alice Amelia Burtt, 1907, 1908, 1909. Burtt, M. Edward, ed. 51p. (Orig.). 1993. pap. write for info. (*1-888913-06-1*) M E Burtt.

— Excerpts of the Diaries of Alice Amelia Burtt, 1920-1925. Burtt, M. Edward, ed. i, 62p. (Orig.). 1993. pap. write for info. (*1-888913-05-3*) M E Burtt.

Burtt, Alice A., jt. auth. see Burtt, Walter E.

Burtt, Ann P., jt. auth. see Burtt, M. Edwart.

Burtt, Ann P., tr. see Harvey, Daniel W.

Burtt, Ann P., tr. see Harvey, Nathaniel D.

Burtt, B. L., jt. auth. see Hilliard, O. M.

Burtt, E. H., Jr. An Analysis of Physical, Physiological & Optical Aspects of Avian Coloration with Emphasis on Wood-Warblers. (Ornithological Monographs: Vol. 38). (Illus.). 126p. 1986. 15.00 (*0-943610-47-8*) Am Ornithologists.

Burtt, E. T. The Sense of Animals. (Wykeham Science Ser.: No. 26). 128p. 1974. pap. 18.00 (*0-85109-370-1*) Taylor & Francis.

Burtt, E. T. & Pringle, A. The Senses of Animals. LC 73-77794. (Wykeham Science Ser.: No. 26). 168p. (C). 1974. 18.00 (*0-8448-1153-X*, Crane Russak) Taylor & Francis.

Burtt, Edwin A. Light, Love & Life. 115p. (Orig.). 1986. pap. write for info. (*0-9616132-1-1*) E A Burtt.

— Metaphysical Foundations of Modern Physical Science. 2nd ed. LC 80-15426. (C). 1982. reprint ed. pap. 17.50 (*0-391-01742-X*) Humanities.

***Burtt, Edwin A.** Teachings of the Compassionate Buddha: Early Discourses, the Dhammapada & Later Basic Writing. 2000. pap. 9.95 (*0-451-20077-2*, Sig) NAL.

Burtt, Edwin A., ed. Teachings of the Compassionate Buddha. (Orig.). 1955. mass mkt. 6.99 (*0-451-62711-3*, Ment) NAL.

Burtt, George. Psychographics in Personal Growth. LC 72-95846. 1972. pap. 3.50 (*0-913596-00-0*) Vector Counsel.

— Vector Handbook. LC 71-91981. 1969. pap. 3.50 (*0-913596-03-5*) Vector Counsel.

Burtt, Harold E., jt. auth. see Birnes, William J.

Burtt, J. O., tr. Minor Attic Orators, Vol. 2. Incl. Demades. Dinarchus. Hyperides. Lycurgus. (Loeb Classical Library: No. 395). 15.50 (*0-674-99434-5*) HUP.

Burtt, M. Edward. The Allendale Cemetery. (Illus.). ii, 9p. 1997. pap. write for info. (*1-888913-31-2*) M E Burtt.

— A Brief History of Louis Head, Its Churches & Cemeteries. (Illus.). i, 61p. (Orig.). 1995. pap. write for info. (*1-888913-16-9*) M E Burtt.

— The Cemeteries of East Sable. (Illus.). ii, 45p. 1997. pap. write for info. (*1-888913-26-6*) M E Burtt.

— The Cemeteries of Little Harbour. (Illus.). iii, 52p. 1997. pap. write for info. (*1-888913-29-0*) M E Burtt.

— The Cemeteries of Louis Head. (Illus.). iii, 51p. (Orig.). 1994. pap. write for info. (*1-888913-13-4*) M E Burtt.

— The Cemeteries of Louis Head. rev. ed. (Illus.). 76p. (Orig.). 1996. pap. write for info. (*1-888913-24-X*) M E Burtt.

— The Cemeteries of Osborne Harbour. (Illus.). ii, 114p. 1997. pap. write for info. (*1-888913-33-9*) M E Burtt.

— The Cemeteries of Sable River. (Illus.). ii, 57p. 1997. pap. write for info. (*1-888913-27-4*) M E Burtt.

— The Cemeteries of West Middle Sable. (Illus.). ii, 22p. 1997. pap. write for info. (*1-888913-28-2*) M E Burtt.

— Cyril Giffin's Louis Head of 1973. Giffin, Cyril, tr. i, 28p. (Orig.). 1995. pap. write for info. (*1-888913-17-7*) M E Burtt.

— The Genealogists Index of Cemeteries. (Illus.). iv, 600p. 1997. pap. write for info. (*1-888913-32-0*) M E Burtt.

— History & Remembrances of the Northwood Meadows State Park. (Illus.). 70p. (Orig.). 1994. pap. write for info. (*1-888913-09-6*) M E Burtt.

— The Louis Head Cemetery. (Illus.). i, 27p. (Orig.) 1994. pap. write for info. (*1-888913-12-6*) M E Burtt.

— The Louis Head Cemetery. rev. ed. (Illus.). i, 50p. (Orig.). 1996. pap. write for info. (*1-888913-21-5*) M E Burtt.

— Manual of the Northwood Meadows State Park. (Illus.). 25p. (Orig.). 1991. pap. write for info. (*1-888913-00-2*) M E Burtt.

— North to the Artic, 3 vols., Set. (Illus.). xii, 735p. (Orig.). 1992. pap. write for info. (*1-888913-04-5*) M E Burtt.

— North to the Artic, Vol. 1. (Illus.). v, 255p. (Orig.). 1992. pap. write for info. (*1-888913-01-0*) M E Burtt.

— North to the Artic, Vol. 2. (Illus.). iv, 249p. (Orig.). 1992. pap. write for info. (*1-888913-02-9*) M E Burtt.

— North to the Artic, Vol. 3. (Illus.). iii, 231p. (Orig.). 1992. pap. write for info. (*1-888913-03-7*) M E Burtt.

— The Northfield Cemetery. (Illus.). ii, 17p. 1997. pap. write for info. (*1-888913-35-5*) M E Burtt.

— Old Pictures. (Illus.). 50p. (Orig.). 1995. pap. write for info. (*1-888913-15-0*) M E Burtt.

— The Pride Cemetery. (Illus.). i, 16p. (Orig.). 1994. pap. write for info. (*1-888913-11-8*) M E Burtt.

— The Rockland Cemetery. (Illus.). ii, 38p. 1997. pap. write for info. (*1-888913-30-4*) M E Burtt.

— The Wreck of the Parker M. Whitmore. rev. ed. (Illus.). i, 46p. (Orig.). 1996. pap. write for info. (*1-888913-25-8*) M E Burtt.

— Ye Olde Osborne Cemetery. (Illus.). 13p. (Orig.). 1995. pap. write for info. (*1-888913-18-5*) M E Burtt.

Burtt, M. Edward, et al. The Giffin, Ringer, & Related Families of Nova Scotia. vii, 1526p. 1997. pap. write for info. (*1-888913-34-7*) M E Burtt.

— Olivia Pride Burtt's Nova Scotian Ancestry: The Story of the Prides, Abbotts & Coles. (Illus.). iii, 55p. 1993. pap. write for info. (*1-888913-07-X*) M E Burtt.

Burtt, M. Edward, jt. auth. see Burtt, Walter E.

Burtt, M. Edward, ed. see Burtt, Alice A.

Burtt, M. Edward, ed. see Burtt, Walter E. & Burtt, Alice A.

Burtt, M. Edward, ed. see Harvey, Daniel W.

Burtt, M. Edward, ed. see Harvey, Nathaniel D.

Burtt, M. Edward, ed. see Locke, G. Malcom.

Burtt, M. Edward, ed. see MacMillan, Arnold J., et al.

Burtt, M. Edward, ed. see MacMillan, Floyd B.

Burtt, M. Edwart & Burtt, Ann P. Dana Burtt's Royal Ancestry & Nova Scotian Heritage: The Lineage of Richard Warren of the Mayflower. (Illus.). iv, 135p. (Orig.). 1994. pap. write for info. (*1-888913-08-8*) M E Burtt.

Burtt, Shelley. Virtue Transformed: Political Argument in England, 1688-1740. 192p. (C). 1992. text 52.95 (*0-521-37528-2*) Cambridge U Pr.

Burtt-Smith, Jim. Drop in the Ocean: Ditchings in World War II. 1996. 31.95 (*0-85052-507-1*, Pub. by Leo Cooper) Trans-Atl Phila.

Burtt-Smith, Jim & French, John. A Drop in the Ocean. large type ed. (Ulverscroft Large Print Ser.). (Illus.). 320p. 1997. 27.99 (*0-7089-3786-1*) Ulverscroft.

Burtt, Walter E. & Burtt, Alice A. The Diaries of Walter E. Burtt & Alice A. Burtt, 1906 to 1914. Burtt, M. Edward, ed. ii, 524p. 1998. pap. 50.00 (*1-888913-36-3*) M E Burtt.

Burtt, Walter E. & Burtt, M. Edward. The Ancentral Lines of the Burtt Family: Walter Everett Burtt II. xi, 173p. (Orig.). 1996. pap. write for info. (*1-888913-23-1*) M E Burtt.

Burukovskii, R. N. Key to Shrimps & Lobsters. (Russian Translation Ser.: No. 5). 188p. 1983. 88.00 (*90-6191-296-2*, Pub. by A A Balkema) Ashgate Pub Co.

— Key to Shrimps & Lobsters. 1982. 21.00 (*0-8364-2557-X*, Pub. by Oxford IBH) S Asia.

Burull, Erica J. The Acts: A Musical Based on the Gospel of St. John & the Biblical Acts. LC 96-77687. (Illus.). vii, 94p. (Orig.). 1996. pap. 14.95 (*1-889721-01-8*) E Greenwood Pubs.

— The Crazymakers: A Veterinary Fable (A Musical) LC 99-94014. 125p. 1999. pap. 15.00 (*1-889721-02-5*) E Greenwood Pubs.

Burum, Linda. Asian Pasta. LC 85-15663. 175p. (Orig.). 1985. 22.95 (*0-943186-21-8*); pap. 12.95 (*0-943186-23-4*) Aris Bks.

— Asian Pasta: A Cook's Guide to the Noodles, Wrappers & Pasta Creations of the East. (Illus.). 224p. 1985. pap. 12.45 (*0-201-10833-X*) Addison-Wesley.

***Buruma, Anna.** Fashions of the Past. (Historical Guide to World Costumes Ser.). (Illus.). 2000. 27.95 (*1-85585-727-8*) Collins & Br.

— Fashions of the Past: A Historical Guide to World Costumes. (Illus.). 2000. 27.95 (*1-85585-723-5*) Collins & Br.

***Buruma, Ian.** Anglomania: A European Love Affair. LC 98-27587. 504p. 2000. pap. 14.00 (*0-375-70536-5*) Vin Bks.

Buruma, Ian. India: A Mosaic. Silvers, Robert B. & Epstein, Barbara, eds. LC 99-32297. 285p. 2000. 24.95 (*0-940322-08-0*) NY Rev Bks.

***Buruma, Ian.** The Missionary & the Libertine. LC 99-53744. 320p. 2000. 22.95 (*0-375-50222-X*) Random.

— The Wages of Guilt: Memories of War in Germany & Japan. 330p. 1999. reprint ed. text 25.00 (*0-7881-6655-7*) DIANE Pub.

Buruma, Ian & Richie, Donald. The Japanese Tattoo. LC 79-26738. (Illus.). 120p. 1990. 22.50 (*0-8348-0228-7*) Weatherhill.

Buruma, Ian, jt. auth. see Cobb, Jodi.

Burunat, Julio, jt. auth. see Burunat, Silvia.

Burunat, Silvia & Burunat, Julio. Nuevas Voces Hispanas. (C). text. write for info. (*0-318-69172-8*) Harcourt Coll Pubs.

Burunat, Silvia & Garcia, Ofelia, eds. Veinte Anos de Literatura Cubanoamericana. LC 87-70662. 224p. 1988. 26.00 (*0-916950-77-8*); pap. 16.00 (*0-916950-78-6*) Biling Rev-Pr.

Burusphat, Somsonge. The Structure of Thai Narrative. LC 90-72069. (Publications in Linguistics: No. 98). xiv, 231p. (Orig.). 1991. pap. 18.00 (*0-88312-805-5*) S I L Intl.

Burvikovs, ed. see Konrath, Larry F.

Burvikovs, ed. see Maness, Terry S. & Zietlow, John T.

Burvikovs, ed. see Nelson, Theron R. & Potter, Thomas A.

Burvikovs, ed. see Reid, David A.

Burvikovs, ed. see Ruthstrom, Carl R. & Dykman, Charlene A.

Burvikovs, ed. see Scott, William L.

Burvikovs, ed. see Strong, Robert A.

***Burwash.** Enabling Productivity: Addressing Work-related Issues. 16th ed. 2002. pap. 44.00 (*0-7693-0126-6*, Pub. by Singular Publishing) Thomson Learn.

Burwash, Lynn & McMullin, Cie. All about Me. unabridged ed. (Illus.). 12p. (J). (ps-2). 1998. spiral bd. 10.95 (*0-9668858-0-5*) All About Me.

Burwash, Martin. Great Adventure: The Railroad Legacy of Stevens Pass. LC 98-73479. (Illus.). 128p. 1998. 39.95 (*1-884831-07-9*) Fox Pubns.

***Burwash, Peter.** Dear Teenager: If You Only Knew... LC 99-54679. 128p. 2000. 12.95 (*1-887089-20-9*, Pub. by Torchlght Pub) Natl Bk Netwk.

Burwash, Peter. Improving the Landscape of Your Life. LC 97-35309. 128p. 1999. 12.95 (*1-887089-15-2*) Torchlght Pub.

— The Key to Great Leadership: Rediscovering the Principles of Outstanding Service: Lessons from the Front Lines of the World's Best Service Companies. LC 95-18225. 160p. 1995. pap. 11.95 (*1-887089-01-2*) Torchlght Pub.

— Total Health: The Next Level: Exploding the Myths of America's Diet. Klapper, Michael, ed. LC 97-16674. 160p. 1997. pap. 11.95 (*1-887089-10-1*) Torchlght Pub.

— Who Cares? "A Wake up Call for Service & Leadership" 160p. 1993. pap. 14.95 (*1-883743-00-1*) P Burwash Int.

Burwash, Peter & Tullius, John. Total Tennis: A Complete Guide for Today's Player. (Illus.). 256p. 1991. pap. 14.95 (*0-02-079261-1*) Macmillan.

Burwell, Francis G. & Daalder, Ivo H., eds. The United States & Europe in the Global Arena. LC 99-11219. 1999. text 69.95 (*0-312-22188-6*) St Martin.

Burwell, Helen P. The Burwell Directory of Information Brokers - 1994. 600p. 1994. 79.50 (*0-938519-10-7*) Burwell Ent.

— The Burwell World Directory of Information Brokers 1995. 2nd rev. ed. 1998. pap. 74.38 (*0-938519-14-X*) Burwell Ent.

— Online Competitive Intelligence: Move Your Business to the Top Using Cyber-Intelligence. Sankey, Michael & Ernst, Carl R., eds. 396p. 1999. pap. 25.95 (*1-889150-08-8*, Pub. by Facts on Demand) Natl Bk Netwk.

Burwell, Helen P., ed. Burwell World Directory of Information Brokers 1995. 800p. 1995. pap. text 99.50 (*0-938519-11-5*) Burwell Ent.

Burwell, Jennifer. Notes on Nowhere: Feminist Utopian Logic & Social Transformation. LC 96-31507. (American Culture Ser.). 1997. pap. 19.95 (*0-8166-2639-1*); text 49.95 (*0-8166-2638-3*) U of Minn Pr.

Burwell, John T., ed. Mechanical Wear: Being the Proceedings of a Summer Conference on This Subject Held in June 1948. LC 50-1084. 395p. reprint ed. pap. 122.50 (*0-608-14337-5*, 205196000017) Bks Demand.

Burwell, Michael. North & West. (Illus.). (Orig.). (C). 1989. pap. 3.95 (*0-9623693-0-6*) Heaven Bone Pr.

Burwell, N. Yolanda, jt. ed. see Carlton-LaNey, Iris.

Burwell, Robert L., Jr., ed. see NATO Science Committee Conference on Catalysis Sta.

Burwell, Rose M. Hemingway: The Postwar Years & the Posthumous Novels. (Studies in American Literature & Culture: No. 96). (Illus.). 280p. (C). 1996. pap. text 19.95 (*0-521-56563-4*) Cambridge U Pr.

Burwell, William M. White Acre vs. Black Acre. LC 72-83941. (Black Heritage Library Collection). 1977. 15.95 (*0-8369-8514-1*) Ayer.

***Burwick, Diane M.** How to Implement the CMM. (Illus.). 527p. 1999. 32.00 (*0-9676734-5-3*) Bus Process.

Burwick, Frederick. The Damnation of Newton: Goethe's Color Theory & Romantic Perception. (Quellen und Forschungen zur Sprach und Kulturgeschichte der Germanischen Voelker: NF Band 86 210). vi, 308p. 1986. lib. bdg. 119.25 (*3-11-010765-1*) De Gruyter.

— Illusion & the Drama: Critical Theory of the Enlightenment & Romantic Era. (Illus.). 336p. 1991. 45.00 (*0-271-00732-X*) Pa St U Pr.

***Burwick, Frederick.** Mimesis & Its Romantic Reflections. LC 99-53720. 2000. write for info. (*0-271-02037-7*) Pa St U Pr.

Burwick, Frederick. Poetic Madness & the Romantic Imagination. (Illus.). 376p. 1996. 55.00 (*0-271-01488-1*) Pa St U Pr.

Burwick, Frederick, ed. Approaches to Organic Form. 304p. (C). 1987. text 176.50 (*90-277-2541-1*, D Reidel) Kluwer Academic.

Burwick, Frederick & Pape, Walter, eds. Aesthetic Illusion: Theoretical & Historical Approaches. x, 478p. (C). 1990. lib. bdg. 163.10 (*3-11-011750-9*) De Gruyter.

Burwick, Frederick, jt. ed. see Pape, Walter.

Burwood, Stephen. American Labour, France & the Politics of Intervention, 1945-1952: Workers & the Cold War. LC 98-49633. 277p. 1999. text 89.95 (*0-7734-8232-6*) E Mellen.

Burwood, Stephen, jt. auth. see Eastaway, Nigel A.

Burwood, Stephen, jt. ed. see Dubofsky, Melvyn.

B

Bury, Bob & Fowler, Richard. Imaging Strategy: A Guide for Clinicians. LC 92-22706. 176p. 1992. 55.00 (*0-19-262323-0*) OUP.
— Imaging Strategy: A Guide for Clinicians. LC 92-22706. (Illus.). 176p. 1992. pap. text 27.50 (*0-19-262063-0*) OUP.
Bury, Charles. The One-Minute Business Letter. LC 84-61830. 103p. (Orig.). 1984. pap. 14.95 (*0-9613854-0-5*) Modern Comm Assocs.
Bury, Don & Heischman, Larry. The Buyer's Guide to Business Insurance. Akin, Camille, ed. LC 94-17498. (Illus.). 279p. 1994. pap. 19.95 (*1-55571-162-6*, Oasis Pr) PSI Resch.
Bury, G. Wyman. Land of Uz. 1999. pap. 30.00 (*1-85964-121-0*) Garnet Publishing Ltd.
Bury, George W. Arabia Infelix: Or The Turks in Yamen. 1999. pap. 30.00 (*1-85964-122-9*) Garnet Publishing Ltd.
— Pan-Islam. LC 80-1938. reprint ed. 30.00 (*0-404-18956-3*) AMS Pr.
Bury, J. B., ed. The Decline & Fall of the Roman Empire Vol. I: The History of the Empire from A.D. 180 to 395, Vol. 2. LC 94-27080. 944p. 1996. 23.00 (*0-679-60148-1*) Modern Lib NY.
— The Decline & Fall of the Roman Empire Vol. II: The History of the Empire from A.D. 395 to 1185, 2 vols., Vol. 2. LC 94-27080. 912p. 1996. 22.00 (*0-679-60149-X*) Modern Lib NY.
Bury, J. B., ed. see Freeman, Edward A.
Bury, J. P. France, 1814-1940. 1985. pap. 15.95 (*0-416-37930-3*) Routledge.
— Gambetta & the National Defense. LC 70-80531. 1970. reprint ed. 17.00 (*0-86527-077-5*) Fertig.
Bury, J. P. & Tombs, R. P. Thiers, 1797-1877: A Political Life. 272p. 1986. text 45.00 (*0-04-944013-6*) Routledge.
Bury, John, ed. Gardening in Spanish & English: Para Jardineros, en Ingles y Espanol. LC 88-90532. (Illus.). 120p. (Orig.). 1988. pap. 7.95 (*0-945462-03-4*); lib. bdg. 9.95 (*0-945462-04-2*) Ridgetop Bks.
Bury, John B. A History of Freedom of Thought. LC 74-30844. 246p. 1975. reprint ed. lib. bdg. 35.00 (*0-8371-7935-1*, BUHF, Greenwood Pr) Greenwood.
— History of the Later Roman Empire: From the Death of Theodosius I to the Death of Justinian, 2 vols., Vol. 1. 1958. pap. 12.95 (*0-486-20398-0*) Dover.
— History of the Later Roman Empire: From the Death of Theodosius I to the Death of Justinian, 2 vols., Vol. 2. 1958. pap. 12.99 (*0-486-20399-9*) Dover.
— The Idea of Progress: An Inquiry into Its Origin & Growth. LC 82-6261. 357p. 1982. reprint ed. lib. bdg. 41.50 (*0-313-23374-8*, BUIP, Greenwood Pr) Greenwood.
— Invasion of Europe by the Barbarians. 2000. pap. 13.95 (*0-393-00388-4*) Norton.
— The Life of Saint Patrick. 432p. 1998. pap. 12.95 (*0-486-40037-9*) Dover.
— The Life of St. Patrick: His Place in History. LC 79-175691. (Select Bibliographies Reprint Ser.). 1977. reprint ed. 26.95 (*0-8369-6606-6*) Ayer.
— Selected Essays. Temperley, Harold W., ed. LC 68-30177. (Essay Index Reprint Ser.). 1977. 20.95 (*0-8369-0267-X*) Ayer.
Bury, John B., ed. Byzantine Texts, 5 vols., Set. reprint ed. 313.50 (*0-404-60000-X*) AMS Pr.
Bury, John B., ed. see Gibbon, Edward.
Bury, John B., ed. see Pindar, Peter.
Bury, John P. Gambetta-the National Defense: A Republican Dictatorship in France. LC 77-114490. (Illus.). 341p. 1971. reprint ed. lib. bdg. 65.00 (*0-8371-4818-9*, BUGN, Greenwood Pr) Greenwood.
Bury, Judy, et al, eds. Working with Women & AIDS: Medical, Counselling & Social Issues. LC 92-9967. (Illus.). 176p. (C). 1992. 85.00 (*0-415-07658-7*, A9601); pap. 27.99 (*0-415-07659-5*, A9605) Routledge.
Bury, Karl. Statistical Distributions in Engineering. LC 98-22941. (Illus.). 372p. (C). 1999. 80.00 (*0-521-63232-3*); pap. 34.95 (*0-521-63506-3*) Cambridge U Pr.
Bury, M. R. The Offshore Disposal of Radioactive Waste by Drilled Emplacement: A Feasibility Study. 192p. 1985. lib. bdg. 112.00 (*0-86010-708-6*) G & T Inc.
Bury, Michael & Elston, Mary Ann. Health & Illness in a Changing Society. LC 97-199904. (Illus.). 240p. (C). 1997. 80.00 (*0-415-11514-0*); pap. 25.99 (*0-415-11515-9*) Routledge.
Bury, Patrick. The College of Corpus Christi & of the Blessed Virgin Mary: A History from 1822-1952. (Illus.). 408p. 1995. 60.00 (*0-85115-612-6*) Boydell & Brewer.
Bury, R. G., tr. Laws, 2 vols., 1. (Loeb Classical Library: No. 187, 192). 522p. 1926. text 18.95 (*0-674-99206-7*) HUP.
— Laws, 2 vols., 2. (Loeb Classical Library: No. 187, 192). 590p. 1926. text 18.95 (*0-674-99211-3*) HUP.
Bury, R. G., tr. see Sextus Empiricus.
Bury, Robert G., ed. see Plato.
Bury, Ruth, jt. auth. see Hughes, Griffith R.
Bury, Shirley. Jewellery, 1789-1910: The International Era, 2 Vols., 1. (Illus.). 472p. 1991. 79.50 (*1-85149-148-1*) Antique Collect.
— Jewelry, 1789-1910: The International Era, 2 Vols., 2. (Illus.). 374p. 1991. 79.50 (*1-85149-149-X*) Antique Collect.
Bury St. Edmund's Commissary Court Staff. Wills & Inventories, from the Register of the Commissary of Bury St. Edmund's & the Archdeacon of Sudbury. Tymms, Samuel, ed. (Camden Society, London. Publications, First Ser.: No. 49). reprint ed. 72.50 (*0-404-50149-4*) AMS Pr.
Bury, Stephanie C., ed. see Sutton, Stephen A.
Bury, Stephen. Artists' Books. LC 95-9230. (Illus.). 223p. 1995. 113.95 (*1-85928-163-X*, Pub. by Scolar Pr) Ashgate Pub Co.
— The Cobweb. 448p. 1997. mass mkt. 6.50 (*0-553-57545-7*) Bantam.
— Interface. 640p. 1995. mass mkt. 6.50 (*0-553-57240-7*) Bantam.
— Interspace. 1999. pap. write for info. (*0-451-45482-0*, ROC); pap. write for info. (*0-451-45483-9*, ROC) NAL.
Bury, Tracy. Evidence Based Healthcare: A Practical Guide for Therapists. LC 98-51472. 264p. 1998. pap. text 45.00 (*0-7506-3783-8*) Buttrwrth-Heinemann.

Bury, Viscount. Manual of Rifling & Rifle Sights. fac. ed. (Illus.). 48p. 1995. reprint ed. pap. 11.95 (*1-880677-07-5*) Excalibur AZ.
This is a facsimile editon of an 1864 manual produced for the British National Rifle Association. The book gives details on contemporary rifling, fore sights, middle sights & back sights. In addition, the manual features woodcuts of sights & other inventions by Metford, Bury, the British government, Kerr, Blanch, Turner, Elcho, Vernon & London Armoury Co. Includes four pages of fold-out diagrams at the back of the book. 165 illustrations & woodcuts are featured in the manual. Contact Excalibur Publications, PO Box 35369, Tucson, AZ 85740-5369. Voice: (520) 575-9057. Fax: (520) 575-9068. *Publisher Paid Annotation.*

Buryak, Eugenia. Intellectual Property in the Ex-Soviet Union Republics. Garrison, David L. & Gans, Ludmilla, eds. (ENG & RUS.). 800p. Date not set. 225.00 (*0-9634156-1-1*); ring bd. 225.00 (*0-9634156-0-3*) Skaya Pub.
Buryn, Ed. William Blake Tarot Triumphs. (Illus.). 16p. (Orig.). 1991. pap. 19.95 (*0-916804-04-6*) Ed Buryn Pub.
Buryn, Ed, ed. see Greer, Mary K.
Buryn, Ed, ed. see Lammey, William C.
Burz, Helen L. & Marshall, Kit. Performance-Based Curriculum for Language Arts: From Knowing to Showing. LC 96-35195. (Illus.). 104p. 1997. 55.95 (*0-8039-6508-7*); pap. 24.95 (*0-8039-6509-5*) Corwin Pr.
— Performance-Based Curriculum for Mathematics: From Knowing to Showing. LC 96-12354. (FKS Ser.). (Illus.). 112p. 1996. 55.95 (*0-8039-6495-1*); pap. 24.95 (*0-8039-6496-X*) Corwin Pr.
***Burz, Helen L. & Marshall, Kit.** Performance-Based Curriculum for Music & the Visual Arts: From Knowing to Showing. LC 99-6280. (FKS Ser.). (Illus.). 136p. 1999. pap. 22.95 (*0-7619-7536-5*); lib. bdg. 55.95 (*0-7619-7535-7*) Sage.
Burz, Helen L. & Marshall, Kit. Performance-Based Curriculum for Science: From Knowing to Showing. LC 97-4946. (Illus.). 104p. 1997. 55.95 (*0-8039-6506-0*); pap. 24.95 (*0-8039-6507-9*) Corwin Pr.
— Performance-Based Curriculum for Social Studies: From Knowing to Showing. LC 97-45266. (Illus.). 128p. 1997. 55.95 (*0-8039-6500-1*); pap. 24.95 (*0-8039-6501-X*) Corwin Pr.
***Burzichelli, John & Gergel, Richard J.** Ward LaFrance Fire Trucks, 1916-1978. (Photo Archives Ser.). (Illus.). 128p. 2000. pap. 32.95 (*1-58388-013-5*, 130751AE, Pub. by Iconografix) Motorbooks Intl.
Burzio, Luigi. Italian Syntax. 1986. text 188.00 (*90-277-2014-2*); pap. text 62.50 (*90-277-2015-0*) Kluwer Academic.
— Principles of English Stress. LC 93-43093. (Studies in Linguistics: No. 72). 387p. (C). 1995. text 64.95 (*0-521-44513-2*) Cambridge U Pr.
Burzon, Nancy & Moore, Jean. Reconnecting with People: A Strategy for Organization Success. LC 98-74744. (Crisp Management Library: Vol. 22). 96p. 1998. pap. 12.95 (*1-56052-490-1*) Crisp Pubns.
Burztynski, Sue. Monsters: And Creatures of the Night. 96p. (J). (gr. 3-8). 1996. pap. text 6.95 (*1-86448-245-1*) IPG Chicago.
Burzynski, Denny. Applied Calculus. (Mathematics Ser.). 1996. pap., teacher ed., suppl. ed. 22.00 (*0-534-93403-X*) PWS Pubs.
— Elementary Algebra. (C). 1989. pap. text, teacher ed. 34.00 (*0-03-014369-1*) Harcourt Coll Pubs.
— Elementary Algebra. (C). 1989. pap. text, teacher ed., suppl. ed. 40.50 (*0-03-063907-7*, Pub. by Harcourt Coll Pubs) Harcourt.
— Fundamentals of Math. (C). 1989. pap. text, teacher ed. 34.00 (*0-03-014408-6*) Harcourt Coll Pubs.
— Fundamentals of Math. (C). 1989. pap. text, teacher ed. 25.00 (*0-03-014419-1*) Harcourt Coll Pubs.
— Intermediate Algebra. (C). 1989. pap. text, teacher ed., suppl. ed. 40.50 (*0-03-063904-2*, Pub. by Harcourt Coll Pubs) Harcourt.
— Intermediate Algebra. (C). 1989. pap. text, teacher ed. 34.00 (*0-03-014357-8*); pap. text, student ed. 25.00 (*0-03-014358-6*) Harcourt Coll Pubs.
Burzynski, Denny & Ellis, Wade. Intermediate Algebra. 640p. (C). 1989. pap. text 63.00 (*0-03-063903-4*) SCP.
Burzynski, Denny, et al. Precalculus Using the TI Calculator. (C). 1995. text 65.95 (*0-534-18864-8*) PWS Pubs.
Busa, Antonio, ed. see Seneca, Lucius Annaeus.
Busa, Christopher, ed. Mary Hackett: A Survey. LC 96-70324. (Introductions Ser.: Vol. 1). (Illus.). 48p. 1996. pap. 20.00 (*0-944854-31-1*) Provincetown Arts.
— Provincetown Arts: 1990 Annual. (Joel Meyerowitz Cover Ser.). (Illus.). 184p. (Orig.). 1990. pap. 5.00 (*0-944854-02-8*) Provincetown Arts.
— Provincetown Arts: 1991 Annual. (Long Point Artists Cover Ser.: Vol. 7). (Illus.). 184p. (Orig.). 1991. pap. 6.50 (*0-944854-03-6*) Provincetown Arts.
— Provincetown Arts: 1992 Annual. (Stanley Kunitz Cover Subject Ser.: Vol. 8). (Illus.). 184p. (Orig.). 1992. pap. 6.50 (*0-944854-04-4*) Provincetown Arts.
— Provincetown Arts: 1993 Annual. (Fine Arts Work Center in Provincetown Cover Subject Ser.: Vol. 9). (Illus.). 184p. (Orig.). 1993. pap. 6.50 (*0-944854-10-9*) Provincetown Arts.
— Provincetown Arts: 1994 Annual. (Illus.). 164p. (Orig.). 1994. pap. 6.50 (*0-944854-13-3*) Provincetown Arts.
— Provincetown Arts: 1995 Annual. (Mary Oliver Cover Subject Ser.). (Illus.). 164p. 1995. pap. 6.50 (*0-944854-21-4*) Provincetown Arts.
— Provincetown Arts, 1997 Annual. (John Waters Cover Subject Ser.: Vol. 13). (Illus.). 164p. 1997. pap. 6.50 (*0-944854-32-X*) Provincetown Arts.
— Provincetown Arts, 1996 Annual. (Karen Finley Cover Ser.: Vol. 12). (Illus.). 164p. 1996. pap. 6.50 (*0-944854-30-3*) Provincetown Arts.
Busa, Christopher & Elman, Raymond S., eds. Provincetown Arts: 1988 Annual. (Robert Motherwell Cover Ser.). (Illus.). 184p. (Orig.). 1988. pap. 4.00 (*0-944854-00-1*) Provincetown Arts.
— Provincetown Arts Annual: 1989 Annual. (Annie Dillard Cover Ser.). (Illus.). 184p. (Orig.). 1990. pap. 5.00 (*0-944854-01-X*) Provincetown Arts.
Busa, Christopher, et al. The Narrative Art of Peter Hutchinson: A Retrospective, Vol. 2. LC 94-67733. (Artists Ser.: II). (Illus.). 72p. (Orig.). 1994. pap. text 15.00 (*0-944854-14-1*) Provincetown Arts.
Busa, Christopher, ed. see Levine, Anne-Marie.
Busa, Christopher, ed. see Rhodes, Martha.
Busa, Christopher, ed. & intro. see Hutchinson, Peter.
Busa, Marie. The Winter's Dream. Pacitti, Aleen M., ed. (Illus.). 59p. 1996. pap. text 5.95 (*0-9643424-3-X*) A J Morrison.
Busa, Peter. Life Colors Art: Fifty Years of Painting. (Artists Ser.: Vol. 1). (Illus.). 72p. 1992. pap. 20.00 (*0-944854-05-2*) Provincetown Arts.
Busard, H. L. & Folkerts, M., eds. Robert Chester's Redation of Euclid's Elements, the So-Called Adelard II Version, 2 vols. (Science Networks Historical Studies: Vols. 8 & 9). (Illus.). 960p. 1992. 322.00 (*0-8176-2728-6*) Birkhauser.
Busard, H. L., ed. see Euclid.
Busarello, Giovanni, et al, eds. Morphological & Physical Classification of Galaxies: Proceedings of the Fifth International Workshop of the Osservatorio Astronomico di Capodimonte, Held in Sant'Agata Sui Due Golfi, Italy, September 3-7, 1990. LC 92-1502. (Astrophysics & Space Science Library: Vol. 178). 490p. (C). 1992. text 226.50 (*0-7923-1712-2*) Kluwer Academic.
Busath, jt. auth. see Seegmiller.
Busath, Don, photos by. Salt Lake City in a Different Light. LC 96-70254. (Illus.). 150p. 1996. text 49.95 (*1-57636-025-3*) SunRise Pbl.
Busbee, Jim. Riding Tough. large type ed. (Linford Western Library). 368p. 1985. pap. 16.99 (*0-7089-6186-X*) Ulverscroft.
Busbee, Pauline S. Heart Pine. LC 93-91006. 100p. 1993. 14.95 (*0-9639537-0-2*) Encore Ent.
***Busbee, Shirlee.** At Long Last. 2000. mass mkt. 6.99 (*0-446-60807-6*) Warner Bks.
Busbee, Shirlee. For Love Alone. 421p. 1997. mass mkt. 5.99 (*0-446-60218-3*, Pub. by Warner Bks) Little.
***Busbee, Shirlee.** For Love Alone. 448p. 2000. mass mkt. 6.50 (*0-446-60532-8*) Warner Bks.
Busbee, Shirlee. Gypsy Lady. 1977. mass mkt. 5.50 (*0-380-01824-1*, Avon Bks) Morrow Avon.
— Gypsy Lady. 1999. mass mkt. 3.99 (*0-446-60797-5*, Pub. by Warner Bks) Little.
— Heart for the Taking. 1997. mass mkt. 161.73 (*0-446-16414-3*) Warner Bks.
— Lady Vixen. 544p. 1980. mass mkt. 5.50 (*0-380-75382-0*, Avon Bks) Morrow Avon.
— Love Be Mine. 416p. 1998. mass mkt. 6.99 (*0-446-60530-1*, Pub. by Warner Bks) Little.
— Lovers Forever. 1996. mass mkt. 5.99 (*0-446-60219-1*, Pub. by Warner Bks) Little.
— Midnight Masquerade. 464p. 1988. mass mkt. 5.50 (*0-380-75210-7*, Avon Bks) Morrow Avon.
— Midnight Masquerade. large type ed. (General Ser.). 606p. 1989. lib. bdg. 21.95 (*0-8161-4753-1*, G K Hall Lrg Type) Mac Lib Ref.
— The Spanish Rose. 496p. 1992. reprint ed. 22.00 (*0-7278-4313-3*) Severn Hse.
— The Tiger Lily. 464p. 1985. mass mkt. 5.50 (*0-380-89499-8*, Avon Bks) Morrow Avon.
Busbey, L. White. Uncle Joe Cannon: The Story of a Pioneer American. (History - United States Ser.). 362p. 1992. reprint ed. lib. bdg. 89.00 (*0-7812-6194-5*) Rprt Serv.
Busbin, James W., jt. auth. see Self, Donald R.
Busby. Reagan & the Iran-Contra Affair. LC 98-38451. 1999. text 65.00 (*0-312-21982-2*) St Martin.
***Busby, Ailie.** Hey, Diddle Diddle. (Illus.). 2000. 8.95 (*0-7641-5308-0*) Barron.
Busby, C. Tectonics of Sedimentary Basis. (Illus.). 400p. 1995. 79.95 (*0-86542-245-1*) Blackwell Sci.
Busby, Cathy, jt. ed. see Miller, David M.
Busby, Cathy J. & Ingersoll, Raymond V. Tectonics of Sedimentary Basins. (Illus.). 1997. pap. 61.95 (*0-632-04363-6*) Blackwell Sci.
***Busby, Cecilia.** The Performance of Gender: An Anthropology of Everyday Life in a South Indian Fishing Village. LC 99-86428. (Illus.). 2000. write for info. (*0-485-19571-2*, Pub. by Athlone Pr) Humanities.
Busby, Colin I., et al. A Cultural Resource Overview of the Bureau of Land Management: Coleville, Bodie, Benton & Owens Valley Planning Units, California. (Illus.). 360p. (C). 1979. reprint ed. pap. text 37.50 (*1-55567-391-0*) Coyote Press.
Busby, Cylin. Chicken-Fried Rat: Tales Too Gross to Be True. LC 98-8051. (Illus.). 112p. (J). (gr. 3-7). 1998. pap. 4.95 (*0-06-440701-2*) HarpC.
Busby, D. E. Space Clinical Medicine: A Prospective Look at Medical Problems from Hazards of Space Operations. 276p. 1968. text 106.00 (*90-277-0110-5*) Kluwer Academic.
Busby, D. E., ed. see International Congress of Aviation & Space Medicin.
***Busby, Dan.** Giving from the Heart: A Legacy That Lasts Forever. 32p. 1998. pap. 10.00 (*0-9664049-0-4*) Premiere Publng.
— The Zondervan 2000 Church & Nonprofit Organization Tax & Financial Guide. 208p. 1999. pap. 12.99 (*0-310-22886-7*) Zondervan.
Busby, Daniel D. The Christian's Guide to Worry-Free Money Management: Ten Easy Steps. LC 95-223120. 192p. 1994. pap. 14.99 (*0-310-46231-2*) Zondervan.
— The Zondervan Church & Nonprofit Organization Tax & Financial Guide, 1992. 96p. 1991. pap. 9.99 (*0-310-54271-5*) Zondervan.
— The Zondervan Church & Nonprofit Organization Tax & Financial Guide, 1993. 144p. 1992. pap. 9.99 (*0-310-58691-7*) Zondervan.
— The Zondervan Church & Nonprofit Organization Tax & Financial Guide, 1995. 176p. 1995. pap. 11.99 (*0-310-48641-6*) Zondervan.
— The Zondervan Minister's Tax & Financial Guide, 1993. 144p. 1992. pap. 9.99 (*0-310-58701-8*) Zondervan.
— The Zondervan Minister's Tax & Financial Guide, 1994. 144p. 1993. pap. 14.99 (*0-310-61651-4*) Zondervan.
— The Zondervan Minister's Tax & Financial Guide, 1995. 144p. 1995. pap. 14.99 (*0-310-48651-3*) Zondervan.
— The Zondervan 1999 Church & Nonprofit Organization Tax & Financial Guide: For 1998 Tax Returns. 208p. 1998. pap. 12.99 (*0-310-22538-8*) Zondervan.
Busby, Dave & Hill, Terry. The Heart of the Matter. 78p. 1993. pap. 5.99 (*0-9634057-5-6*) Full Court MI.
Busby, Dean M. The Impact of Violence on the Family: Treatment Approaches for Therapists & Other Professionals. LC 95-40081. 320p. (C). 1996. 58.00 (*0-205-17570-8*) Allyn.
Busby, Douglas L., et al. Reader's Hebrew-English Lexicon of the Old Testament. 720p. 1989. 49.99 (*0-310-36980-0*) Zondervan.
Busby, Eileen R. Royal Winton Porcelain: Ceramice Fit for a King. (Illus.). 1998. pap. 34.95 (*1-57080-047-2*) Antique Pubns.
— Royal Winton Porcelain: Ceramics Fit for a King. (Illus.). 1998. 44.95 (*1-57080-048-0*) Antique Pubns.
Busby, Everett, et al. Readings for Social Work Practice, Vol. 1. LC 72-8103. 174p. 1972. pap. text 14.95 (*0-686-76955-4*) Irvington.
Busby, F. M. Arrow from Earth. 432p. (Orig.). 1995. mass mkt. 5.50 (*0-380-77232-9*, Avon Bks) Morrow Avon.
— The Triad Worlds. 384p. (Orig.). 1996. mass mkt. 5.99 (*0-380-78468-8*, Avon Bks) Morrow Avon.
Busby, H. R. & Houser, Donald R. Plate Bending & Finite Element Analysis of Spur & Helical Gear Tooth Deflection. (1985 Fall Technical Meeting Ser.: Vol. 85FTM4). 10p. 1985. pap. text 30.00 (*1-55589-097-0*) AGMA.
Busby, Harry, ed. see Clark, George.
Busby, Henry R., jt. auth. see Trujillo, David M.
Busby, Keith. Text & Intertext in Medieval Arthurian Literature. Lacy, Norris J., ed. LC 96-2392. 256p. 1996. text 15.00 (*0-8153-2385-9*, H1997) Garland.
Busby, Keith, ed. The Arthurian Yearbook, Vol. II. LC 10-533877. (Illus.). 256p. 1992. text 10.00 (*0-8153-0337-8*, 1458) Garland.
— The Arthurian Yearbook, Vol. 3. LC 10-533877. 286p. 1993. text 10.00 (*0-8153-1539-2*, H18113) Garland.
— The Arthurian Yearbook One. LC 10-533877. (Illus.). 260p. 1991. text 10.00 (*0-8240-7209-X*, 1247) Garland.
— Word & Image in Arthurian Literature: The Arthurian Yearbook. LC 96-2769. 400p. 1996. text 80.00 (*0-8153-2050-7*) Garland.
Busby, Keith & Kooper, Erik, eds. Courtly Literature: Culture & Context. Proceedings of the 5th Triennial Congress of the International Courtly Literature Society, Dalfsen, The Netherlands, 9-16 August, 1986. LC 90-1072. (Utrecht Publications in General & Comparative Literature: Vol. 25). xvi, 621p. 1990. 148.00 (*90-272-2211-8*) J Benjamins Pubng Co.
Busby, Keith, jt. tr. see Burgess, Glyn S.
Busby, Keith, tr. & intro. see De Hodenc, Raoul.
Busby, Ken, ed. see Erwin, Sarah, et al.
Busby, Margaret. Daughters of Africa: An International Anthology of Words & Writings by Women of African Descent & from the Ancient Egyptian to the Present. 1999. pap. text 21.00 (*0-345-91501-1*) Ballantine Pub Grp.
— Family Odyssey. 1997. write for info. (*0-679-44227-8*) Pantheon.
— Family Odyssey. 1998. pap. write for info. (*0-679-75870-4*) Vin Bks.
Busby, Margaret, ed. Daughters of Africa: An International Anthology of Words & Writings by Women of African Descent & from the Ancient Egyptian to the Present. 1152p. 1994. pap. 21.00 (*0-345-38268-4*) One Wrld.
Busby, Mark. Lanford Wilson. LC 87-70029. (Western Writers Ser.: No. 81). (Illus.). 52p. (Orig.). 1987. pap. 4.95 (*0-88430-080-3*) Boise St U W Writ Ser.
— Preston Jones. LC 82-74092. (Western Writers Ser.: No. 58). (Illus.). 52p. (Orig.). 1983. pap. 4.95 (*0-88430-032-3*) Boise St U W Writ Ser.

An Asterisk (*) at the beginning of an entry indicates that the title is appearing for the first time.

— Ralph Ellison. (Twayne's United States Authors Ser.: No. 582). 200p. (C). 1991. 32.00 (*0-8057-7626-5*, Twayne) Mac Lib Ref.

Busby, Mark, ed. New Growth No. 2: Contemporary Short Stories by Texas Writers. LC 93-71686. 280p. (Orig.). 1993. pap. 12.95 (*0-931722-96-9*) Corona Pub.

***Busby, Michael.** Demystifying EDI. 2000. pap. 39.95 (*1-55622-708-6*) Wordware Pub.

— Demystifying TCP/IP. 3rd ed. LC 99-12085. (Illus.). 337p. 1999. pap. 29.95 incl. cd-rom (*1-55622-665-9*) Wordware Pub.

Busby, Michael. Learn Microsoft Office 2000. LC 00-28961. 700p. 1999. pap. write for info. (*1-55622-716-7*) Wordware Pub.

Busby, Michael, jt. auth. see Schatt, Stanley.

Busby, Mike. Demystifying ATM/ADSL. LC 98-3965. 1998. pap. 29.95 (*1-55622-592-X*) Wordware Pub.

Busby, Rebecca L. & Institute of Gas Technology Staff. Natural Gas in Nontechnical Language. LC 99-14115. 200p. 1999. 64.95 (*0-87814-738-1*) PennWell Bks.

***Busby, Russ.** Billy Graham: God's Ambassador. LC 99-45110. (Illus.). 272p. 1999. 39.95 (*0-7370-0065-1*) T-L Custom Pub.

— Billy Graham: God's Ambassador. deluxe ed. 272p. 1999. 50.00 (*1-887656-23-5*) Tehabi Bks.

Busby-Spera, Cathy & Saleeby, Jason, eds. Geologic Guide to the Mineral King Area, Sequoia National Park, California. (Illus.). 44p. (Orig.). 1987. pap. 5.00 (*1-878861-13-1*) Pac Section SEPM.

Busby, Stephen J., et al, eds. Molecular Microbiology. LC 97-32739. (NATO ASI Series H: Vol. 103). viii, 334p. 1998. 129.00 (*3-540-63873-3*) Spr-Verlag.

Busby, Thomas. A General History of Music from the Earliest Times, 2 vols., Set. LC 68-21091. (Music Ser.). 1968. reprint ed. 95.00 (*0-306-71063-3*) Da Capo.

— A Grammar of Music. LC 76-20711. (Music Reprint Ser.). 1976. reprint ed. lib. bdg. 55.00 (*0-306-70789-6*) Da Capo.

Busca Isusi, Jose M. Traditional Basque Cooking: History & Preparation. LC 87-10741. (Basque Ser.). (Illus.). 212p. 1993. pap. 19.95 (*0-87417-202-0*) U of Nev Pr.

***Buscaglia, Edgardo.** Judicial Corruption in Developing Countries: Its Causes & Economic Consequences. (Essays in Public Policy Ser.: No. 95). 16p. 1999. pap. 5.00 (*0-8179-4302-1*) Hoover Inst Pr.

Buscaglia, Edgardo & Long, Clarisa. U. S. Foreign Policy & Intellectual Property Rights in Latin America. LC 97-2576. (Essays in Public Policy Ser.: No. 77). 1997. pap. 5.00 (*0-8179-5822-3*) Hoover Inst Pr.

***Buscaglia, Edgardo & Ratliff, William E.** Law & Economics in Developing Countries. LC 00-27213. 2001. write for info. (*0-8179-9772-5*) Hoover Inst Pr.

Buscaglia, Leo. The Art of Being Fully Human. 1995. 12.00 incl. audio (*0-671-52061-X*, Picture Book Studio) S&S Trade.

— Celebrate Life! 1995. audio 16.00 (*0-671-50602-1*) S&S Trade.

Buscaglia, Leo. Living, Loving & Learning. 1995. 16.00 incl. audio (*0-671-52062-8*) S&S Trade.

Buscaglia, Leo. Loving Each Other: The Challenge of Human Relationships. 1995. audio 16.00 (*0-671-52070-9*) S&S Trade.

Buscaglia, Leo F. Because I Am Human. LC 72-92809. 72p. 1972. 5.95 (*0-913590-06-1*) SLACK Inc.

— Born for Love. LC 91-51071. 298p. 1992. 19.00 (*1-55642-213-X*) SLACK Inc.

— Born for Love: Reflections on Loving. 320p. 1994. reprint ed. pap. 11.00 (*0-449-90929-8*, Columbine) Fawcett.

— Born for Love: Thoughts for Lovers. 1992. 19.00 (*0-679-41393-6*) Random.

— Born for Love: Thoughts for Lovers. large type ed. 1992. 21.00 (*0-679-41381-2*) Random Hse Lrg Prnt.

— Bus Nine to Paradise. LC 85-63187. 276p. 1986. 16.95 (*0-943432-67-7*) SLACK Inc.

— The Disabled & Their Parents: A Counseling Challenge. rev. ed. LC 83-50284. 88p. 1995. pap. 22.95 (*0-8050-1079-3*, Owl) H Holt & Co.

— The Disabled & Their Parents: A Counseling Challenge. 3rd rev. ed. 420p. 1994. pap. 22.95 (*1-55642-257-1*) SLACK Inc.

— The Fall of Freddie the Leaf. LC 81-86645. 32p. 1982. 7.95 (*0-913590-89-4*) SLACK Inc.

— The Fall of Freddie the Leaf: A Story of Life for All Ages. LC 81-86645. (Illus.). 32p. (J). (ps-3). 1983. 9.95 (*0-8050-1064-5*) H Holt & Co.

— Leo Buscaglia's Love Cookbook. 88p. 1995. 29.50 (*0-8050-3725-X*) H Holt & Co.

— Living, Loving & Learning. 288p. 1985. pap. 10.00 (*0-449-90181-5*, Columbine) Fawcett.

— Living, Loving & Learning. LC 81-824284. 264p. 1982. 13.50 (*0-913590-88-6*) SLACK Inc.

— Love. 1996. pap. 10.00 (*0-449-91162-4*) Fawcett.

— Love. LC 72-92810. 147p. 1972. 9.95 (*0-913590-07-X*); 15.00 (*0-685-72905-2*) SLACK Inc.

— Love: A Fairy Tale for Grown-Up Children. 1995. 9.95 (*0-03-063201-3*) Harcourt Coll Pubs.

— Loving Each Other. 208p. 1986. pap. 10.00 (*0-449-90157-2*, Columbine) Fawcett.

— Loving Each Other. LC 84-50590. 208p. 1984. 13.95 (*0-943432-27-8*) SLACK Inc.

— A Memory for Tino. (Illus.). 50p. (J). (ps up). 1988. 12.95 (*1-55642-020-X*) SLACK Inc.

— Papa, My Father. 1989. 12.95 (*1-55642-087-0*) SLACK Inc.

— Personhood. 147p. 1986. pap. 11.00 (*0-449-90199-8*, Columbine) Fawcett.

— Personhood. LC 78-66423. 160p. 1978. 9.95 (*0-913590-63-0*) SLACK Inc.

— Seven Stories of Christmas Love. (Illus.). 112p. 1995. 12.95 (*0-8050-2434-4*) H Holt & Co.

— Seven Stories of Christmas Love. (Illus.). 110p. (J). 1987. 12.95 (*1-55642-019-6*) SLACK Inc.

— The Way of the Bull. LC 73-83777. 176p. 1973. 9.95 (*0-913590-08-8*) SLACK Inc.

Buscaino, Dale & Daniel, Scott. IBM BASIC Decoded & Other Mysteries. 29.95 (*0-317-06580-7*) Blue Cat.

— Superzap: IBM-PC Version 1.0. Moore, David & Trapp, Charles, eds. (Illus.). 104p. 1985. 49.95 incl. disk (*0-932679-00-5*) Blue Cat.

Buscall, R., jt. ed. see Goodwin, J. W.

Buscani, Lisa. Jangle. 88p. 1992. pap. 7.95 (*0-9624287-8-7*) Tia Chucha Pr.

Buscema, John, jt. auth. see Lee, Stan.

Buscemi. 75 Readings Plus. 6th ed. 2000. pap. 17.50 (*0-07-237062-9*) McGraw.

Buscemi, John. Places for Devotion. Philippart, David, ed. (Meeting House Essays Ser.: No. 4). (Illus.). 32p. (Orig.). 1993. pap. 6.00 (*0-929650-68-9*, DEVOT) Liturgy Tr Pubns.

Buscemi, Santi V. A Reader for Developing Writers. 3rd ed. LC 95-43248. 578p. (C). 1996. pap. 32.88 (*0-07-009484-5*) McGraw.

— A Reader for Developing Writers. 4th ed. LC 97-53223. 552p. 1998. pap. 31.88 (*0-07-009490-X*) McGraw.

***Buscemi, Santi V.** 75 Readings: An Anthology. 8th ed. 2001. pap. 10.00 (*0-07-237066-1*) McGraw.

Buscemi, Santi V. 75 Readings Plus. 2nd ed. 1993. 26.87 (*0-07-009353-9*) McGraw.

Buscemi, Santi V., et al, eds. Seventy-Five Readings Plus. 3rd ed. LC 95-19930. (C). 1995. pap. text 18.25 (*0-07-009482-9*) McGraw.

Buscemi, Santi V. & Smith, Charlotte. 75 Readings: An Anthology. 6th ed. LC 96-26255. 496p. (C). 1996. pap. 14.06 (*0-07-052157-3*) McGraw.

— 75 Readings: An Anthology. 7th ed. LC 98-26943. 480p. 1998. pap. 14.06 (*0-07-092067-2*) McGraw.

— 75 Readings Plus. 4th ed. LC 97-21489. 504p. 1997. pap. 25.68 (*0-07-009488-8*) McGraw.

— 75 Readings Plus. 5th ed. LC 99-23204. 480p. 1999. pap. 25.00 (*0-07-229265-2*) McGraw.

Buscemi, Santi V., et al. The Basics: A Rhetoric & Handbook. LC 94-29220. (C). 1994. pap. text 21.25 (*0-07-009405-5*) McGraw.

— The Basics: A Rhetoric & Handbook. 2nd ed. LC 97-7539. 448p. 1997. pap. 28.81 (*0-07-009454-3*) McGraw.

***Buscemi, Santi V., et al.** The Basics: A Rhetoric & Handbook. 3rd ed. LC 99-45939. 2000. write for info. (*0-07-234793-7*) McGrw-H Hghr Educ.

Buscemi, Santi V., jt. auth. see Litzinger, Boyd.

Busch. The Brown Book, 1993-94. 200p. (Orig.). 1994. pap. 14.95 (*0-932053-15-7*) Prime Pubns.

***Busch.** Digital Photography for Dummies. (Quick Reference Ser.). 224p. 2000. spiral bd. 12.99 (*0-7645-0750-8*) IDG Bks.

Busch. Expanding Your Commander. 1985. 18.95 (*0-13-295213-0*) P-H.

Busch. Fast Atom Bombardment Mass Spectrometry. 200p. write for info. (*0-471-24664-6*) Wiley.

Busch. Fundamentals of Dimensional Metrology. 3rd ed. (Mechanical Technology Ser.). 1997. teacher ed. 16.00 (*0-8273-7127-6*) Delmar.

— Fundamentals of Dimensional Metrology. 3rd ed. (Mechanical Technology Ser.). 1998. 44.95 (*0-8273-7709-6*) Delmar.

— The Gold Book, 1990. 816p. (Orig.). 1990. pap. 16.95 (*0-932053-10-6*) Prime Pubns.

— Valley of the Grizzlies. LC 98-51597. 1998. text 24.95 (*0-312-19679-2*) St Martin.

Busch, ed. The Brown Book, 1989-90. 200p. (Orig.). 1990. pap. 13.50 (*0-932053-09-2*) Prime Pubns.

Busch, jt. ed. see Brecher.

Busch, Rainer. German U-Boat Commanders of World War II: A Biographical Dictionary. LC D781.B85713 1999. 1999. 49.95 (*1-55750-186-6*) Naval Inst Pr.

Busch & Wilkie Brothers Foundation Staff. Fundamentals of Dimensional Metrology. 2nd ed. LC 64-12593. 1986. pap., teacher ed. 16.00 (*0-8273-2128-7*) Delmar.

— Fundamentals of Dimensional Metrology. 2nd ed. LC 64-12593. 1989. text 46.95 (*0-8273-2127-9*) Delmar.

***Busch, A. E., ed.** Cardiac Ion Channels. (Cellular Physiology & Biochemistry Ser.: Vol. 9, No. 4-5, 1999). (Illus.). 112p. 1999. pap. 34.00 (*3-8055-7012-0*) S Karger.

***Busch, Akiko.** Geography of Home: Writings on Where We Live. LC 98-46588. (Illus.). 208p. 1999. 19.95 (*1-56898-172-4*) Princeton Arch.

— The Photography of Architecture: Twelve Views. (Illus.). 233p. 1993. pap. 29.95 (*0-471-29369-5*, VNR) Wiley.

Busch, Akiko, ed. Design for Sports: The Cult of Performance. LC 97-36554. (Illus.). 112p. 1998. pap. 19.95 (*1-56898-145-7*) Princeton Arch.

Busch, Alexander. Die Geschichte des Privatdozenten: Eine Soziologische Studie zur Grossbetrieblichen Entwicklung der Deutschen Universitaten. Metzger, Walter P., ed. LC 76-55208. (Academic Profession Ser.).Tr. of History of Privatdocentens: a Sociological Study of the Development of the German University As Big Business. (GER.). 1977. reprint ed. lib. bdg. 17.95 (*0-405-10036-1*) Ayer.

Busch, Alva. Roadside Prey. 320p. 1996. mass mkt. 5.99 (*0-7860-0221-2*, Pinncle Kensgtn) Kensgtn Pub Corp.

Busch, Amy L. Finding Their Voices: Listening to Battered Women Who've Killed. 200p. 1998. 27.95 (*1-56072-618-0*, Nova Kroshka Bks) Nova Sci Pubs.

Busch, Andreas, jt. ed. see Braun, Dietmar.

Busch, Andrew, jt. auth. see Ceaser, James W.

Busch, Andrew E. Horses in Midstream: U. S. Midterm Elections & Their Consequences. LC 99-6654. (Illus.). 254p. (C). 1999. pap. 19.95 (*0-8229-5705-1*); text 45.00 (*0-8229-4105-8*) U of Pittsburgh Pr.

— Outsiders & Openness in the Presidential Nominating System. LC 96-45916. (Policy & Institutional Studies). 248p. 1997. pap. 19.95 (*0-8229-5627-6*); text 45.00 (*0-8229-3976-2*) U of Pittsburgh Pr.

Busch, Arthur W. Aerobic Biological Treatment of Waste Waters: Principles & Practice; a Monograph. LC 70-155639. (Illus.). 432p. reprint ed. pap. 134.00 (*0-8357-8009-0*, 203417100088) Bks Demand.

Busch, Bernd. Hans Meyer-Veden Altona Stadt-Teile. 143p. 1993. 82.00 (*0-685-67848-2*, Pub. by Ernst & Sohn) Wiley.

Busch, Bernd W., jt. auth. see Busch, Eleanore B.

Busch, Brian, ed. see Armstrong, John.

Busch, Brian, ed. see Moore, Donald.

Busch, Brian, ed. see Valley, Jim.

Busch, Briton C. Mudros to Lausanne: Britain's Frontier in West Asia, 1918-1923, Vol. 3. LC 76-21641. 430p. (C). 1976. text 24.50 (*0-87395-265-0*) State U NY Pr.

— The War Against the Seals: A History of the North American Seal Fishery. (Illus.). 432p. 1987. pap. 24.95 (*0-7735-0610-1*, Pub. by McG-Queens Univ Pr) CUP Services.

— Whaling Will Never Do for Me: The American Whaleman in the Nineteenth Century. LC 93-10810. 280p. (C). 1993. 32.50 (*0-8131-1838-7*) U Pr of Ky.

Busch, Briton C., ed. Master of Desolation: The Reminiscences of Capt. Joseph J. Fuller. (American Maritime Library: Vol. 9). (Illus.). xxx, 349p. 1980. 19.95 (*0-913372-21-8*) Mystic Seaport.

Busch, Briton C. & Gough, Barry M., eds. Fur Traders from New England, the Boston Men, 1787-1800: The Narratives of William Dane Phelps, William Sturgis & James Gilchrist Swan. (Northwest Historical Ser.: Vol. 18). 103p. 1996. 29.50 (*0-87062-261-7*) A H Clark.

Busch, Carolyn, jt. auth. see Odden, Allan.

Busch, Charles. Call Me a Vampire Lesbian. 2000. 8.95 (*0-06-016498-0*) HarperTrade.

Busch, Charles. Whores of Lost Atlantis: A Novel. LC 93-1399. 304p. (YA). 1993. 21.45 (*1-56282-786-4*, Pub. by Hyperion) Time Warner.

Busch, Cindy J., jt. auth. see Murray-Plumer, Sara.

Busch, Daniel A. Stratigraphic Traps in Sandstones: Exploration Techniques. LC 74-83506. (American Association of Petroleum Geologists. Memoir Ser.: No. 21). (Illus.). 186p. reprint ed. pap. 57.70 (*0-7837-1652-4*, 204195000024) Bks Demand.

Busch, Daryl H. Reactions of Coordinated Ligands & Homogeneous Catalysis: A Symposium Sponsored by the American Chemical Society, Washington, D.C., March 22-24, 1962. LC 63-13314. (American Chemical Society Advances in Chemistry Ser.: No. 37). 263p. 1963. reprint ed. pap. 81.60 (*0-608-08338-0*, 205125600094) Bks Demand.

Busch, David. Cascading Style Sheets Complete. LC 98-2574. 400p. 1998. pap. 44.95 incl. cd-rom (*0-07-913703-2*) McGraw.

Busch, David. Commodore 128 Subroutine Libra. 1994. mass mkt. write for info. (*0-394-59832-6*) Random.

Busch, David. The Complete Scanner Handbook for Desktop Publishing PC Edition & The Complete Toolkit for the IBM PC: PC Edition & The Complete Toolkit for the IBM PC. 2nd ed. 1992. text 55.00 incl. 5.25 hd (*1-55623-720-0*, Irwn Prfssnl) McGraw-Hill Prof.

***Busch, David.** Guerrilla Guide to Great Graphics with the Gimp. 2000. pap. 39.99 (*0-7615-2407-X*, Prima Tech) Prima Pub.

Busch, David. Macintosh F-X: Tools & Techniques for Outrageous Effects. LC 94-22446. 445p. 1994. pap. 34.95 incl. cd-rom (*1-55828-363-3*, MIS Pr) IDG Bks.

— Microsoft Works Suite 99 at a Glance. LC 98-31459. (At A Glance Ser.). (Illus.). 224p. 1999. pap. 19.99 (*0-7356-0571-8*) Microsoft.

— Photoshop 4 Answers! Certified Tech Support. LC 98-141854. 1998. pap. text 24.99 (*0-07-882456-7*) Osborne-McGraw.

Busch, David D. Astonishing Web Graphics with Kai's Powertools & Plug-Ins. LC 98-29445. (C). 1998. write for info. (*0-12-147616-2*) Acad Pr.

— Astonishing Web Graphics with Kai's Powertools & Plug-Ins. LC 98-29445. (Illus.). 274p. (C). 1998. pap. text 45.95 (*0-12-147615-4*) Acad Pr.

— BASIC Games for Your VIC-20 Computer. 1984. 9.95 (*0-89303-910-1*) P-H.

— Digital Photography. 89p. 1995. pap. 39.95 (*1-55828-448-6*, Cliff) IDG Bks.

— IBM-PC & PCjr Subroutine Cookbook. (Illus.). 315p. 14.95 (*0-317-13056-0*) P-H.

— Keyboard Classroom with Commodore 64: Educational Programs for the Whole Family. (Illus.). 310p. 14.95 (*0-317-13075-7*) P-H.

***Busch, David D.** Mastering StarOffice 5.1 for Linux. 2000. pap. write for info. (*0-7821-2709-6*) Sybex.

Busch, David D. Outrageous Macintosh Filters. LC 95-10900. 1995. pap. 39.95 (*1-55828-429-X*, MIS Pr) IDG Bks.

— Outrageous PC F/X: Tools & Techniques for Outrageous Graphic Effects. 428p. 1994. pap. 34.95 incl. cd-rom (*1-55828-394-3*, MIS Pr) IDG Bks.

— PageMaker 6.5 for Macintosh & Windows. LC 97-104. (Teach Yourself Ser.). 448p. 1997. pap. text 29.95 (*1-55828-539-3*, MIS Pr) IDG Bks.

***Busch, David D.** Painting Amazing Web Images with MetaCreations Painter. 350p. 1999. pap. 45.95 incl. cd-rom (*0-12-147617-0*) Morgan Kaufmann.

Busch, David D. PC-DOS Customized: Create Your Own DOS Commands. rev. ed. 400p. (C). 1988. pap. 18.95 (*0-685-19362-4*) P-H.

— Program Your IBM PC to Program Itself. 1991. 24.95 (*0-8306-6630-3*) McGraw-Hill Prof.

— Shareware Plus: Featuring 4 DOS. 1990. pap. 40.00 (*1-55623-411-2*, Irwn Prfssnl) McGraw-Hill Prof.

— Sorry about the Explosion: A Humorous Guide to Computers. (Personal Computing Ser.). (Illus.). 128p. (C). 1985. pap. 8.50 (*0-13-822834-5*) P-H.

— Supercharging OS-2 Batch Files & Utilities. 320p. 1988. pap. 22.95 (*0-201-13785-2*) Addison-Wesley.

Busch, David D., et al. Hewlett-Packard Official Scanner Handbook. LC 99-22692. (Hewlett-Packard Press Ser.). (Illus.). 520p. 1999. pap. 19.99 (*0-7645-3304-5*) IDG Bks.

Busch, David D., jt. auth. see Stemberg, Thomas G.

Busch, Douglas. Prefaces to Renaissance Literature. LC 65-13837. 126p. 1965. reprint ed. pap. 39.10 (*0-7837-4455-2*, 205798500012) Bks Demand.

Busch, Douglas I. Tides in Time. LC 96-92051. (Illus.). 56p. 1996. 40.00 (*0-88496-413-2*) Capra Pr.

— Tides in Time. deluxe limited ed. LC 96-3015. (Illus.). 56p. 1996. 250.00 (*0-88496-414-0*) Capra Pr.

Busch, Duffy, ed. The Brown Book, 1991-92. (Orig.). 1991. pap. 14.95 (*0-932053-11-4*) Prime Pubns.

— The Gold Book, 1986-87. 640p. (Orig.). 1986. pap. 13.50 (*0-932053-03-3*) Prime Pubns.

— The Gold Book, 1987-88. (Annual Ser.). 680p. (Orig.). 1987. pap. 15.00 (*0-932053-06-8*) Prime Pubns.

— The Gold Book, 1988-89. (Annual Ser.). (Orig.). 1988. pap. 16.00 (*0-932053-07-6*) Prime Pubns.

— The Gold Book, 1991-92. 800p. (Orig.). 1991. pap. 16.95 (*0-932053-12-2*) Prime Pubns.

— The Gold Book, 1992-93. 800p. (Orig.). 1992. pap. 16.95 (*0-932053-14-9*) Prime Pubns.

— Leading Minnesota Companies. 200p. (Orig.). 1991. pap. 16.00 (*0-932053-13-0*) Prime Pubns.

— Leading Twin Cities Companies, 1986-87. (Annual Ser.). 80p. 1987. pap. 10.00 (*0-932053-04-1*) Prime Pubns.

— Metro Phoenix: The Gold Book, 1987. (Annual Ser.). 243p. (Orig.). 1988. pap. 15.00 (*0-932053-05-X*) Prime Pubns.

— Metro Phoenix: The Gold Book, 1988-89. (Annual Ser.). (Orig.). 1988. pap. 15.00 (*0-932053-08-4*) Prime Pubns.

— Twin Cities Gold Book, 1985-86. 600p. (Orig.). 1985. pap. 13.50 (*0-932053-00-9*) Prime Pubns.

Busch, Eleanore B. & Busch, Bernd W. The No-Drugs Guide to Better Health. 223p. 1983. 19.95 (*0-13-623090-3*, Parker Publishing Co); pap. 5.95 (*0-13-623082-2*, Parker Publishing Co) P-H.

Busch, Emily, tr. see Homma, Gaku.

***Busch, Felecia.** The New Nutrition: From Antioxidants to Zinc. LC 99-51841. 336p. 2000. pap. 16.95 (*0-471-34793-0*) Wiley.

Busch, Francis X. Enemies of the State. LC 97-81067. (Notable American Trials Ser.: Vol. 4). viii, 299p. 1998. reprint ed. 75.00 (*1-57588-425-9*, 311680) W S Hein.

— Guilty or Not Guilty? 287p. 1977. 18.95 (*0-8369-8039-5*) Ayer.

— Guilty or Not Guilty? LC 97-81040. (Notable American Trials Ser.: Vol. 2). ix, 287p. 1998. reprint ed. 75.00 (*1-57588-421-6*, 311640) W S Hein.

— Notable American Trial Series, 4 vols. 1998. reprint ed. 240.00 (*1-57588-423-2*, 311330) W S Hein.

— Prisoners at the Bar. LC 97-81066. (Notable American Trials Ser.: Vol. 1). ix, 288p. 1998. reprint ed. 75.00 (*1-57588-424-0*, 311670) W S Hein.

— Prisoners at the Bar: An Account of the Trials of the William Haywood Case, the Sacco-Vanzetti Case, the Loeb-Leopold Case, the Bruno Hauptmann Case. LC 77-126319. (Biography Index Reprint Ser., Vol. 2). 1977. 20.95 (*0-8369-8025-5*) Ayer.

— They Escaped the Hangman. LC 97-81039. (Notable American Trials Ser.: Vol. 3). viii, 301p. 1998. reprint ed. 75.00 (*1-57588-422-4*, 311650) W S Hein.

Busch, Fred. The Ego at the Center of Clinical Technique. LC 94-46740. 280p. 1995. 50.00 (*1-56821-471-5*) Aronson.

— Rethinking Clinical Technique. LC 98-30372. 1998. 40.00 (*0-7657-0183-9*) Aronson.

Busch, Frederick. Absent Friends. LC 91-13846. 288p. 1991. reprint ed. pap. 11.95 (*0-8112-1175-4*, NDP721, Pub. by New Directions) Norton.

— The Children in the Woods: New & Selected Stories. 352p. 1995. pap. 12.00 (*0-449-90979-4*) Fawcett.

— Closing Arguments. 304p. 1993. pap. 10.00 (*0-449-90750-3*, Columbine) Fawcett.

— A Dangerous Profession: A Book about the Writing Life. LC 99-38392. 256p. 1999. pap. 13.00 (*0-7679-0398-6*) Bantam.

— A Dangerous Profession: A Book about the Writing Life. LC 98-7329. 256p. 1998. text 23.95 (*0-312-19255-X*) St Martin.

***Busch, Frederick.** Don't Tell Anyone. 320p. 2000. 25.95 (*0-393-04973-6*) Norton.

Busch, Frederick. Girls: A Novel. 288p. 1998. pap. 12.00 (*0-449-91263-9*) Fawcett.

— Harry & Catherine. LC 90-55711. 304p. 1991. pap. 10.00 (*0-679-73076-1*) Vin Bks.

***Busch, Frederick.** Harry & Catherine: A Love Story. 304p. 2000. pap. 14.00 (*0-393-32076-6*) Norton.

Busch, Frederick. Hawkes: A Guide to His Fictions. LC 72-7765. 214p. 1973. reprint ed. pap. 66.40 (*0-608-07600-7*, 205991500010) Bks Demand.

— Invisible Mending: A Novel. LC 96-29790. 296p. 1997. reprint ed. pap. 12.95 (*0-87074-417-8*) SMU Press.

— Letters to a Fiction Writer. LC 98-54320. 291p. 1999. 25.00 (*0-393-04735-0*) Norton.

***Busch, Frederick.** Letters to a Fiction Writer. 304p. 2000. pap. 13.95 (*0-393-32061-8*) Norton.

Busch, Frederick. Long Way from Home: A Novel. 304p. 1994. reprint ed. pap. 12.00 (*0-449-90922-0*, Columbine) Fawcett.

— The Mutual Friend. LC 93-31458. 240p. 1994. reprint ed. pap. 9.95 (*0-8112-1258-0*, NDP774, Pub. by New Directions) Norton.

B

*__Busch, Frederick.__ The Night Inspector. 304p. 2000. pap. 14.00 (*0-449-00615-8*, Ballantine) Ballantine Pub Grp.

Busch, Frederick. The Night Inspector: A Novel. LC 99-11890. 288p. 1999. 23.00 (*0-609-60235-7*) Harmony Bks.

— The Talking Cure. 1998. write for info. (*0-609-60314-0*) Harmony Bks.

— War Babies. LC 89-35209. 128p. 1989. 15.95 (*0-8112-1103-7*, Pub. by New Directions) Norton.

Busch, Frederick, intro. Billy Budd & Other Stories. (Classics Ser.). 416p. 1986. pap. 7.95 (*0-14-039053-7*) Viking Penguin.

Busch, Fritz. Pages from a Musician's Life. Strachey, Marjorie, tr. LC 71-106715. (Illus.). 223p. 1971. reprint ed. lib. bdg. 59.50 (*0-8371-3445-5*, BUML, Greenwood Pr) Greenwood.

Busch, Gladys & Dillon, Tony. The Australian Historical Doll Collection. (C). 1990. pap. 30.00 (*0-86439-056-4*, Pub. by Boolarong Pubns) St Mut.

Busch, Gladys M., jt. auth. see Busch, John A.

Busch, Gladys M., jt. ed. see Busch, John A.

Busch, Glenn. You Are My Darling Zita. (Visual Studies). (C). 1991. 49.95 (*0-87722-791-8*) Temple U Pr.

Busch, Gunter, ed. see Modersohn-Becker, Paula.

Busch, H., ed. Mikrofiltration und Andere Tranfusions-Probleme in der Intensivmedizin. (Beitraege zur Infusionstherapie und Klinische Ernaehrung Ser.: Band 3). (Illus.). 1979. pap. 15.00 (*3-8055-3057-9*) S Karger.

Busch, Hans. Verdi's Aida: The History of an Opera in Letters & Documents. LC 76-11495. 743p. reprint ed. pap. 200.00 (*0-7837-2974-X*, 205748000006) Bks Demand.

Busch, Hans, ed. see Verdi, Giuseppe.

Busch, Harris, et al, eds. Methods in Cancer Research, Vols. 1-13. write for info. (*0-318-50296-8*) Acad Pr.

Busch, Heather & Silver, Burton. Cat Artists & Their Work. (Illus.). 48p. 1994. pap. 8.95 (*0-89815-611-4*) Ten Speed Pr.

— Why Cats Paint. LC 94-217523. (Illus.). 96p. 1994. pap. 16.95 (*0-89815-612-2*) Ten Speed Pr.

Busch, Heather, jt. auth. see Silver, Burton.

Busch, Hermann J., ed. see Palestrina, Pierluigi D., et al.

Busch, Jeffrey, jt. auth. see Irving, Washington.

Busch, Jeffrey, jt. auth. see Kipling, Rudyard.

*__Busch, Jeffrey A.__ Christians in Truth. LC 00-100533. 487p. 2000. 25.00 (*0-7388-1482-2*); pap. 18.00 (*0-7388-1483-0*) Xlibris Corp.

Busch, Jennifer, ed. The Gold Book: 1995 Edition. 900p. (Orig.). 1995. pap. 17.95 (*0-932053-17-3*) Prime Pubns.

Busch, Jennifer A., ed. The Gold Book - Twin Cities. 18th ed. 852p. 1996. pap. 17.95 (*0-932053-19-X*) Prime Pubns.

— The Gold Book - Twin Cities. 19th ed. 731p. 1999. pap. 17.95 (*0-932053-21-1*) Prime Pubns.

— The Gold Book - Twin Cities. 20th ed. 900p. 2000. pap. 19.95 (*0-932053-22-X*) Prime Pubns.

— The Silver Book - Twin Cities. 3rd ed. 384p. 1999. pap. 19.95 (*0-932053-23-8*) Prime Pubns.

— The Telecom Book - Twin Cities. 250p. 2000. pap. 19.95 (*0-932053-24-6*) Prime Pubns.

Busch, John A. & Busch, Gladys M. Sociocybernetics: A Perspective for Living in Complexity. 291p. (C). 1992. pap. 15.80 (*0-935563-24-5*) Social Sys Pr.

Busch, John A. & Busch, Gladys M., eds. Issues in Sociocybernetics: Current Perspectives. (Systems Inquiry Ser.). 139p. 1984. pap. text 16.95 (*0-914105-31-0*) Intersystems Pubns.

— Sociocybernetics: Rethinking Social Organization. (Systems Inquiry Ser.). 139p. 1988. pap. text 16.95 (*0-318-37715-2*) Intersystems Pubns.

Busch, John C., jt. ed. see Goldman, Bert A.

Busch, Julia. A Decade of Sculpture. (Illus.). 1974. 50.00 (*0-87982-007-1*) Art Alliance.

Busch, Julia & Davidson, Hollye. Powerful Prayer Secrets! How to Get What You Need Every Day! LC 95-94783. 128p. 1996. pap. 9.95 (*1-886369-00-3*, Kosmic Kurrents) Anti Aging Pr.

Busch, Julia M. Facelift Naturally: The At-Home or Anywhere, Painless, Natural Facelift for Men & Women That Really Works! LC 92-72331. (Illus.). 60p. 1992. 59.98 incl. audio (*0-9632907-6-2*) Anti Aging Pr.

Busch, Julia M. Facelift Naturally: The At-Home or Anywhere, Painless, Natural Facelift for Men & Women That Really Works! rev. ed. LC 93-90243. (Illus.). 128p. 1993. pap., per. 14.95 (*0-9632907-9-7*) Anti Aging Pr.

Busch, Julia M. The Fat Cat Shat! For Anyone with a Cat & a Litterbox. LC 94-78113. (Illus.). 128p. 1995. per. 9.95 (*0-9632907-7-0*) Anti Aging Pr.

— Love Poems with an After-Bite! For Bitter & Battered Lovers. LC 94-94645. (Illus.). 128p. (Orig.). 1996. pap. 9.95 (*0-9632907-0-3*) Anti Aging Pr.

— My Secret Life with an Angel: Earth in the Seventh Circle. LC 96-79343. (Illus.). 208p. (Orig.). 1997. pap. 14.95 (*1-886369-16-X*, SAN297-6986, Kosmic Kurrents) Anti Aging Pr.

— Positively Young! The How-to Live, Love, Laugh, Let Go & Erase Inner Wrinkles at Any Age Game Book for Men & Women. LC 93-90244. (Illus.). 144p. (Orig.). 1993. per. 9.95 (*0-9632907-2-X*) Anti Aging Pr.

— Treat Your Face Like a Salad! Skin Care Naturally, Blemish & Wrinkle-Free, Recipes & Gourmet Hints for a Fabu-lishous Face. LC 93-90245. (Illus.). 256p. (Orig.). 1993. per. 14.95 (*0-9632907-8-9*) Anti Aging Pr.

Busch, Julia M. & Davidson, Hollye. Power Color! How to Attract Romance, Wealth, Youth, Vitality, & More! LC 94-75321. (Illus.). 256p. (Orig.). 1994. pap. 14.95 (*0-9632907-1-1*, Kosmic Kurrents) Anti Aging Pr.

*__Busch, Julie A.__ Building Broad-Based Partnerships, Vol. 2. Ries, Eric, ed. (Illus.). 36p. 2000. pap. 6.50 (*0-89514-006-3*) ACTE.

Busch, K. F., et al. Geohydraulik, Band 3. (Lehrbuch der Hydrogeologie Ser.). xiv, 497p. 1993. 99.00 (*3-443-01004-0*, Pub. by Gebruder Borntraeger) Balogh.

Busch, K. L., et al. Mass Spectrometry - Mass Spectrometry: Techniques & Applications of Tandem. 333p. 1989. 139.00 (*0-471-18699-6*) Wiley.

Busch, Kenneth L. & Lehman, Thomas A. An Encyclopedia of Mass Spectrometry Terms. (Illus.). 400p. 1996. 49.95 (*1-56081-670-8*, Wiley-VCH) Wiley.

Busch, Kenneth L., et al. Mass Spectrometry - Mass Spectrometry: Techniques & Applications of Tandem Mass Spectrometry. LC 88-33755. 333p. 1989. 90.00 (*0-89573-275-0*, Wiley-VCH) Wiley.

Busch, Kenneth L., jt. auth. see Smith, R. Martin.

Busch, Kenneth W. & Busch, Marianna A. Multielement Detection Systems for Spectrochemical Analysis. LC 89-30004. 688p. 1990. 210.00 (*0-471-81974-3*) Wiley.

Busch, Kenneth W. & Busch, Marianna A., eds. Cavity-Ringdown Spectroscopy: An Ultratrace-Absorption Measurement Technique. LC 98-32088. (ACS Symposium Ser.: No. 720). (Illus.). 288p. 1999. text 95.00 (*0-8412-3600-3*) OUP.

Busch, Kristen. Golden Boy. LC PN2287.D255B87 1998. 1998. mass mkt. 5.99 (*0-345-42816-1*) Ballantine Pub Grp.

Busch, Lawrence. The Eclipse of Morality: Science, State & Market. LC 99-49622. (Sociological Imagination & Structural Change Ser.). 256p. 2000. pap. text 21.95 (*0-202-30622-4*); lib. bdg. 43.95 (*0-202-30621-6*) Aldine de Gruyter.

Busch, Lawrence, ed. Science & Agricultural Development. LC 81-65005. 198p. 1981. text 48.00 (*0-86598-022-5*) Rowman.

Busch, Lawrence, et al. Making Nature, Shaping Culture: Plant Biodiversity in Global Context. LC 95-10244. (Our Sustainable Future Ser.). (Illus.). xv, 261p. 1995. text 50.00 (*0-8032-1256-9*) U of Nebr Pr.

Busch, Marc L. Trade Warriors: States, Firms & Strategic Policy in High Technology Competition. LC 98-42612. (Illus.). 224p. 1999. 49.95 (*0-521-63340-0*) Cambridge U Pr.

Busch, Marianna A., jt. auth. see Busch, Kenneth W.

Busch, Marianna A., jt. ed. see Busch, Kenneth W.

Busch, Marie, tr. Selected Austrian Short Stories. LC 70-37260. (Short Story Index Reprint Ser.). 1977. reprint ed. 20.95 (*0-8369-4071-7*) Ayer.

Busch, Marie & Pick, Otto. Selected Czech Tales. LC 73-13412. (Short Story Index Reprint Ser.). 1977. reprint ed. 18.95 (*0-8369-3669-8*) Ayer.

Busch, Marlies. Friendship Bands: Braiding, Weaving, Knotting. LC 97-24985. (Illus.). 64p. 1997. 6.95 (*0-8069-0309-0*) Sterling.

Busch, Monica J. Over Forty Dinners in under Thirty Minutes: Recipe Book & Meal Planner. Ashe, Harold & Ashe, Suzanne, eds. LC 90-85201. (Illus.). 80p. 1990. ring bd. 18.95 (*0-9627669-0-9*) Ashford Pr IL.

Busch, Moritz. Bismarck: Some Secret Pages of His History. LC 70-144925. (Illus.). 1971. reprint ed. 49.00 (*0-403-00815-8*) Scholarly.

— Bismarck: Some Secret Pages of His History, 3 vols., Set. 1988. reprint ed. lib. bdg. 225.00 (*0-7812-0455-0*) Rprt Serv.

— Bismarck, Some Secret Pages of His History, 2 vols., Set. LC 76-112347. (BCL Ser. I). reprint ed. 155.00 (*0-404-01242-6*) AMS Pr.

— Our Chancellor: Sketches for a Historical Picture, 2 Vols, Set. Beatty-Kingston, W., tr. LC 76-109615. (Select Bibliographies Reprint Ser.). 1977. 54.95 (*0-8369-5225-1*) Ayer.

Busch, Niven. Duel in the Sun. 22.95 (*0-8488-0934-3*) Amereon Ltd.

— Duel in the Sun. 1993. reprint ed. lib. bdg. 18.95 (*1-56849-192-1*) Buccaneer Bks.

— Twenty-One Americans. LC 72-99686. (Essay Index Reprint Ser.). 1977. 26.95 (*0-8369-1552-6*) Ayer.

Busch, Noel F. Briton Hadden: A Biography of the Co-Founder of Time. LC 75-25253. 236p. 1975. reprint ed. lib. bdg. 59.50 (*0-8371-8395-2*, BUBH, Greenwood Pr) Greenwood.

Busch, Paul, et al. Operational Quantum Physics. Beigbock, W. et al, eds. (Lecture Notes in Physics Ser.: Vol. M31). 230p. 1997. 49.95 (*3-540-59358-6*) Spr-Verlag.

— The Quantum Theory of Measurement. 2nd ed. LC 96-26743. (Lecture Notes in Physics Ser.). 181p. 1996. 46.00 (*3-540-61355-2*) Spr-Verlag.

Busch, Phylis S. Wild Flowers. 1977. 10.00 (*0-684-14820-X*) S&S Trade.

Busch, Phyllis. Cactus in the Desert. LC 78-4771. (Let's-Read-&-Find-Out Science Bks.). (Illus.). (J). (gr. k-3). 1979. lib. bdg. 12.89 (*0-690-01336-1*) HarpC Child Bks.

*__Busch, Phyllis S.__ Autumn. LC 98-53295. (Year of Science & Nature Activities Ser.). (J). (gr. 2-5). 1999. 24.21 (*0-7614-0988-2*) Marshall Cavendish.

Busch, Phyllis S. Backyard Safaris: 52 Year-Round Science Adventures. (J). 1995. mass mkt. 8.95 (*0-689-80617-5*) Aladdin.

— Backyard Safaris: 52 Year-Round Science Adventures. LC 93-48410. (Illus.). 160p. (J). (gr. 1-5). 1995. 16.00 (*0-689-80302-8*, Mac Bks Young Read) S&S Childrens.

*__Busch, Phyllis S.__ Nature Projects for Every Season, 4 vols. (Illus.). 48p. (YA). (gr. 2 up). 2000. boxed set 96.86 (*0-7614-0985-8*, Benchmark NY) Marshall Cavendish.

— Spring. LC 98-49413. (gr. 2-5). 1999. 24.21 (*0-7614-0986-6*) Marshall Cavendish.

*__Busch, Phyllis S. & Halsey, Megan.__ Summer. LC 98-53326. (Nature Projects for Every Season Ser.). (gr. 2-5). 1999. 24.21 (*0-7614-0987-4*) Marshall Cavendish.

Busch, Richard M. Investigating Earth History. 512p. (C). 2000. pap. 52.00 (*0-02-317440-4*, Macmillan Coll) P-H.

Busch, Robert. The Cougar Almanac: An Exploration of the American Mountain Lion. LC 96-22399. (Illus.). 176p. 1996. 25.00 (*1-55821-403-8*) Lyons Pr.

— The Wolf Almanac. (Illus.). 224p. 1995. 27.95 (*1-55821-351-1*) Lyons Pr.

Busch, Robert, ed. Wolf Song. 1998. 22.75 (*0-8446-6935-0*) Peter Smith.

— Wolf Songs: The Classic Collection of Writings about Wolves. 208p. 1997. pap. 14.00 (*0-87156-911-6*, Pub. by Sierra) Random.

Busch, Robert, text. Loons. (Illus.). 120p. 1999. 24.95 (*1-55110-928-X*) Whitecap Bks.

*__Busch, Robert H.__ Grizzly Almanac. 2000. 29.95 (*1-58574-143-4*) Lyons Pr.

— Salmon Country: A History of Pacific Salmon. (Illus.). 160p. 2000. pap. 17.95 (*1-55263-162-1*, Pub. by Key Porter) Firefly Bks Ltd.

Busch, Robert H. The Wolf Almanac. rev. ed. (Illus.). 240p. 1998. reprint ed. pap. 18.95 (*1-55821-557-3*) Lyons Pr.

Busch, Robert L. Humor in the Major Novels of F. M. Dostoevsky. 168p. (Orig.). 1987. pap. 17.95 (*0-89357-176-8*) Slavica.

Busch, Robert L., tr. see Pirozhkova, A. N.

*__Busch, Sylvia.__ Die Entstehung der Allgemeinen Gerichtsordnung Fur die Preussischen Staaten Von, 1793/95: Ein Beitrag Zur Geschichte der Kodifikationsbewegung und der Reform des Zivilprozesses in Preussen im 18. Jahrhundert. XVI, 220p. 1999. 45.95 (*3-631-34505-4*) P Lang Pubng.

Busch, Ted & Thompson, Harlow. Fundamentals of Dimensional Metrology. 3rd ed. LC 97-15807. (Mechanical Technology Ser.). 704p. (C). 1997. mass mkt. 60.95 (*0-8273-7126-8*) Delmar.

Busch, Thomas W. Circulating Being: From Embodiment to Incorporation Essays in Late Existentialism. LC 99-31411. (Perspectives in Continental Philosophy Ser.: Vol. 7). 192p. 1999. pap. 19.00 (*0-8232-1929-1*, Pub. by Fordham) BookMasters.

*__Busch, Thomas W.__ Circulating Being: From Embodiment to Incorporation Essays in Late Existentialism. LC 99-31411. (Perspectives in Continental Philosophy Ser.: Vol. 7). 192p. 1999. 35.00 (*0-8232-1928-3*, Pub. by Fordham) BookMasters.

Busch, Thomas W. The Power of Consciousness & the Force of Circumstances in Sartre's Philosophy. LC 89-45191. (Studies in Continental Thought). 128p. 1990. 8.95 (*0-253-31283-3*) Ind U Pr.

Busch, Thomas W. & Gallagher, Shaun, eds. Merleau-Ponty, Hermeneutics, & Postmodernism. LC 91-33857. 263p. (C). 1992. text 21.50 (*0-7914-1139-7*) State U NY Pr.

Busch, Tony. Trout Fishing: A Guide to New Zealand's South Island. (Fly Fishing International Ser.). (Illus.). 232p. 1995. pap. 29.95 (*0-8117-2583-9*) Stackpole.

Busch, Ulrich. Lexikon Angiologie, Kardiologie. (GER.). 312p. 1992. 75.00 (*0-7859-8423-2*, 3541171413) Fr & Eur.

Busch, Ursula. Gestaltung Computergestutzter Lernprogramme unter Berucksichtigung der Padagogischen Konzeption Maria Montessoris. (Freiburger Beitrage Zur Erziehungwissenschaft und Fachdidaktik Ser.: Bd. 6). (GER., Illus.). XI, 179p. 1998. 37.95 (*3-631-33198-3*) P Lang Pubng.

Busch-Vishniac, I. Electromechanical Sensors & Actuators. LC 98-11966. (Mechanical Engineering Ser.). (Illus.). 420p. 1999. 59.00 (*0-387-98495-X*) Spr-Verlag.

Busch-Vishniac, Ilene J., ed. Noise-Con, '90: National Conference on Noise Control Engineering 1990 Proceedings. xviii, 494p. 1990. 60.00 (*0-931784-21-2*) Noise Control.

Busch, W. Dieter N. Development - Aquatic Habitat Classification System for Lakes. 240p. 1992. lib. bdg. 129.00 (*0-8493-0148-3*, SH329) CRC Pr.

Busch, Werner. Bonsai: From Native Trees & Shrubs. (Illus.). 144p. 1995. 24.95 (*0-7153-0336-8*, Pub. by D & C Pub) Sterling.

— Bonsai from Native Trees & Shrubs. (Illus.). 144p. 1998. pap. 17.95 (*0-7153-0537-9*, Pub. by D & C Pub) Sterling.

— Indoor Bonsai for Beginners. LC 97-158077. (Illus.). 112p. 1997. pap. 14.95 (*0-7063-7583-1*, Pub. by WrLock) Sterling.

Busch, Werner & Kohl, Hannah. The Passage of Time: Caspar David Friedrich & Philipp Otto Runge. (Illus.). 128p. 1996. 60.00 (*90-400-9838-7*, Pub. by Waanders) U of Wash Pr.

Busch, Wilhelm. Max & Moritz. Klein, H. Arthur, ed. 216p. (J). (gr. 3-6). 1962. pap. 6.95 (*0-486-20181-3*) Dover.

— Max & Moritz. Arndt, Walter, tr. LC 85-1241. (Illus.). (J). (gr. 4 up). 1985. 9.95 (*0-915361-19-1*) Lambda Pubs.

— Das Max & Moritz Buch. (GER., Illus.). 104p. 1994. pap. 10.63 (*0-8442-2252-6*, 22526, Natl Textbk Co) NTC Contemp Pub Co.

Busch, Wilhelm, et al. German Satirical Writings. Lotze, Wilhelm & Sander, Volkmar, trs. from GER. LC 82-18263. (German Library: Vol. 50). 320p. 1984. 27.50 (*0-8264-0284-4*); pap. 19.95 (*0-8264-0285-2*) Continuum.

Buscha, et al. Modalverben. 55p. 1989. 13.00 (*3-324-00511-6*) Langenscheidt.

Buscha, jt. auth. see Helbig.

Buscha, Annerose & Friedrich, Kirsten. Deutsches Ubungsbuch. 237p. 1995. 23.50 (*3-324-00703-8*) Langenscheidt.

Buscha, J. & Zoch, I. Der Konjunktiv. 95p. 1988. 73.00 (*3-324-00341-5*) Langenscheidt.

Buscha, Joachim. Lexikon Deutscher Konjunktionen. 159p. 1986. 21.00 (*3-324-00486-1*) Langenscheidt.

Buscha, Joachim & Zoch, Irene. Der Infinitiv. 126p. 1992. 11.25 (*3-324-00309-1*) Langenscheidt.

Buscha, Joachim, jt. auth. see Helbig, Gerhard.

Buschardt, A. Zur Fletchtenflora der Inneralpinen Trockentaeler unter Besonderer Beruecksichtinhung des Vinschgaus. (Bibliotheca Lichenologica Ser.: Vol. 10). 1979. lib. bdg. 80.00 (*3-7682-1226-2*) Lubrecht & Cramer.

Buschart, W. David, jt. ed. see Clendenin, Daniel B.

Buschbacher, Ralph. Musculoskeletal Disorders: A Practical Guide for Diagnosis & Rehabilitation. LC 93-36959. (Illus.). 416p. 1993. text 89.00 (*1-56372-077-9*) Buttrwrth-Heinemann.

Buschbacher, Ralph & Braddom, Randall L., eds. Sports Medicine & Rehabilitation: A Sport-Specific Approach. 400p. 1994. 52.00 (*1-56053-133-9*) Hanley & Belfus.

*__Buschbacher, Ralph M.__ Manual of Nerve Conduction Studies. (Illus.). 304p. 1999. pap. text 49.95 (*1-888799-36-6*, Pub. by Demos Medical) SCB Distributors.

Busche, jt. auth. see Bergerud.

Busche-Baumann, Maria. Rechtsextremismus und die Presse. (Hildesheimer Schriftenreihe Zur Sozialpadagogik und Sozialarbeit Ser.: Vol. 7). (GER.). 276p. 1994. write for info. (*3-487-09900-4*) G Olms Pubs.

Busche, Don. Desktop Publishing Using PageMaker on the Macintosh. 1991. pap. 30.00 incl. disk (*0-685-53443-X*) P-H.

— Microcomputer Business Applications & Projects. 1987. pap. text 188.95 (*0-471-84451-9*) P-H.

— Microcomputer Business Applications & Projects. 1988. pap. text 5.95 (*0-471-50073-9*) P-H.

Busche, Don & Bergerud, Marly. Microsoft Windows 98: Complete Course. LC 97-48423. 1998. mass mkt. 53.95 (*0-538-72054-9*) S-W Pub.

Busche, Don & Glenn, Bernice. The Desktop Design Workbook. 336p. 1992. pap. text, wbk. ed. 42.60 (*0-13-202425-X*, 220301) P-H.

Busche, Don, jt. auth. see Begerud, Marly.

Busche, Don, jt. auth. see Bergerud, Marly.

Busche, Don, jt. auth. see Bergerud, Marly K.

Busche, Robert M., ed. Opportunities for Innovation Biotechnology. 273p. 1994. pap. 44.95 (*1-56676-253-7*, 762537) Technomic.

*__Buschek, Alfred.__ In Sickness & in Health. 520p. 1999. mass mkt. 7.99 (*0-9671953-0-6*) A B Pubg.

Buschemeyer, Robin Q. Alphabet Pal. (Professor Elly Fun's Back to Basics Ser.). (Illus.). 64p. (Orig.). (J). (ps-3). 1986. pap. 2.99 (*0-935609-01-6*) Eduplay.

— Number Pal. (Professor Elly Fun's Back to Basics Ser.). (Illus.). 40p. (Orig.). (J). (ps-3). 1986. pap. 2.99 (*0-935609-02-4*) Eduplay.

— Word Pal. (Professor Elly Fun's Back to Basics Ser.). (Illus.). 40p. (Orig.). (J). (ps-3). 1986. pap. 2.99 (*0-935609-00-8*) Eduplay.

Buschenfelde, K. H., ed. Immunology & Liver. LC 93-23189. 480p. (C). 1993. text 164.50 (*0-7923-8830-5*) Kluwer Academic.

Buscher, Frank M. The U. S. War Crimes Trial Program in Germany, 1946-1955. 86. LC 88-24706. (Contributions in Military Studies Ser.: No. 86). 197p. 1989. 49.95 (*0-313-26471-6*, BUW, Greenwood Pr) Greenwood.

Buscher, Fred K. & McClure, Susan A. All about Pruning. Roth, Susan A., ed. LC 88-63844. (Illus.). 112p. Date not set. 14.95 (*0-89721-352-1*, Ortho Bks) Meredith Bks.

Buscher, Ludger. Integrated Rural Development: The Case of Sierra Leone. (Studies on Integrated Rural Development). 238p. 1985. pap. 24.95 (*3-87895-261-9*) Transaction Pubs.

Buscher, Michael, jt. auth. see Hopkins, Martha E.

Buscher, Sarah, jt. auth. see Ling, Bettina.

Buscher, Sherri, ed. see Arquette, Cliff.

Busching. Civil Engineering Materials. (C). 2001. text. write for info. (*0-06-041091-4*) Addson-Wesley Educ.

Busching, Thilo. Unabhangigkeit und Zinspolitik der Deutschen Bundesbank im Prozeb der Deutschen Vereinigung (1989-1992) (Europaische Hochschulschriften: Reihe 5: Bd. 2023). (GER., Illus.). 235p. 1997. pap. 44.95 (*3-631-30671-7*) P Lang Pubng.

Buschini, Henny & Buschini, Luciano. The Ship in the Field. LC 77-174719. (Illus.). 32p. (J). (gr. k-3). 1973. 12.95 (*0-87592-045-4*) Scroll Pr.

Buschini, Joseph. Communicating in Business, 001. (C). 1985. pap. 38.36 (*0-395-36005-6*) HM.

Buschini, Luciano, jt. auth. see Buschini, Henny.

Buschkiel, Alfred L. Fischereiwirtschaft Band IV: Geschichte der Binnenfischerei, Teichwirtschaft und Kunstliche Fischzucht. (Handbuch der Binnenfischerei Mitteleuropas Ser.: Lieferung 2). (GER., Illus.). v, 188p. 1931. 25.00 (*3-510-41017-3*, Pub. by E Schweizerbartsche) Balogh.

Buschkoetter, Wilhelm & Schaefer, Hansjuergen. Handbuch der Internationalen Konzertliteratur - Manual of International Concert Literature: Instrumental & Vokalmusik - Instrumental & Vocal Music. 2nd expanded rev. ed. (GER.). lxxviii, 1008p. (C). 1996. lib. bdg. 149.95 (*3-11-013905-7*) De Gruyter.

Buschl, Kay, jt. auth. see Narrow, Barbara W.

Buschlinger, Wolfgang. Wider Das Verbot Der Semantischen Geschlossenheit Einer Sprache: Der Wert Unliebsamer Sprachlicher Strukturen Fur Die Reduktion Von Graphentheorie Auf Logik. (Europaische Hochschulschriften, Reihe 20: No. 541). (GER., Illus.). 284p. 1997. 54.95 (*3-631-31918-5*) P Lang Pubng.

Buschman, Isabel. Handweaving: An Annotated Bibliography. LC 91-7153. 258p. 1991. 32.50 (*0-8108-2403-5*) Scarecrow.

An Asterisk (*) at the beginning of an entry indicates that the title is appearing for the first time.

Buschman, John, ed. Critical Approaches to Information Technology in Librarianship: Foundations & Applications, 74. LC 93-17866. (Contributions in Librarianship & Information Science Ser.: No. 74). 248p. 1993. 55.00 (*0-313-28415-6*, BTN/, Greenwood Pr) Greenwood.

Buschman, Penelope, et al, eds. The Pediatric Nurse & the Life-Threatened Child. LC 86-82710. (Current Thanatology Ser.). 100p. 1987. pap. 14.95 (*0-930194-39-X*) Ctr Thanatology.

Buschman, R. G. Integral Transformations, Operational Calculus, & Generalized Functions. LC 96-30331. (MAIA Mathematics & Its Applications Ser.: Vol. 377). 231p. (C). 1996. text 132.50 (*0-7923-4183-X*) Kluwer Academic.

Buschman, R. G., jt. auth. see Scrivastava, H. M.

Buschmann. Pattern-Oriented Software Architecture. text. write for info. (*0-471-48907-7*) Wiley.

Buschmann, Frank, et al. Pattern-Oriented Software Arch. LC 96-196873. 476p. 1996. 64.99 (*0-471-95869-7*) Wiley.

Buschmann, Gerd. Martyrium Polycarpi - Eine Formkritische Studie: Ein Beitrag zur Frage Nach der Entstehung der Gattung Maertyrerakte. (Beiheft zur Zeitschrift fuer die Neuetestamentliche Wissenschaft Ser.: Band 70). (GER.). xiv, 366p. (C). 1993. lib. bdg. 118.70 (*3-11-014199-X*) De Gruyter.

Buschmann, Silke. Literarische Zensur in der BRD Nach, 1945. (GER.). 139p. 1997. 32.95 (*3-631-31923-1*) P Lang Pubng.

Buschmohle, Michael, jt. auth. see Nelson, Stephen L.

Buschner, Craig A. Teaching Children Movement Concepts. (Becoming a Master Teacher Ser.). 160p. 1994. pap. text 31.95 incl. VHS (*0-87322-703-4*, ATMP0307) Human Kinetics.

— Teaching Children Movement Concepts & Skills: Becoming a Master Teacher. LC 93-33577. (Illus.). 160p. 1994. pap. text 16.00 (*0-87322-480-9*, BBUS0480) Human Kinetics.

***Buscho, Jayne.** Tales of Fact & Fantasy from Nature. LC 99-65728. (Illus.). 112p. 2001. pap. 15.00 (*0-88739-308-X*) Creat Arts Bk.

Buschow, K. H. Permanent-Magnet Materials & Their Applications. (Materials Science Foundations Ser.: Vol. 5). (Illus.). 88p. (C). 1999. text 48.00 (*0-87849-796-X*, Pub. by Trans T Pub) Enfield Pubs NH.

Buschow, K. H., ed. Handbook of Magnetic Materials. 732p. 1998. 316.00 (*0-444-82956-3*, North Holland) Elsevier.

— Handbook of Magnetic Materials, Vol. 6. xii, 654p. 1991. 276.00 (*0-444-88952-3*, North Holland) Elsevier.

— Handbook of Magnetic Materials, Vol. 7. (Illus.). 676p. 1993. 273.50 (*0-444-89853-0*) Elsevier.

— Handbook of Magnetic Materials, Vol. 8. 542p. 1995. 234.50 (*0-444-81974-6*, North Holland) Elsevier.

— Handbook of Magnetic Materials, Vol. 9. 708p. 1995. 301.00 (*0-444-82232-1*) Elsevier.

— Handbook of Magnetic Materials, Vol. 10. (Illus.). 682p. 1997. 301.50 (*0-444-82599-1*, North Holland) Elsevier.

Buschow, K. H., et al, eds. High Density Digital Recording. LC 92-40898. 1992. text 359.50 (*0-7923-2081-6*) Kluwer Academic.

Buschow, K. H. & Wohlfarth, E. P., eds. Handbook of Magnetic Materials Vol. 5: A Handbook on the Properties of Magnetically Ordered Substances. xii, 590p. 1990. 250.50 (*0-444-87477-1*, North Holland) Elsevier.

***Buschow, K. H. J.** Handbook of Magnetic Materials, Vol. 12. 586p. 1999. 215.50 (*0-444-50249-1*, North Holland) Elsevier.

Buschsbaum, Walter H. & Genn, Robert C., Jr. Buschsbaum's Complete Handbook of Practical Electronic Reference Date. 3rd ed. 672p. 1987. pap. 16.95 (*0-317-65985-5*) P-H.

Buschsel, Patricia, jt. auth. see Miaskowski, Christine.

***Buscis, Gerry & Somerville, Barbara.** Training Your Pet Rat. (Complete Pet Owner's Manual Ser.). (Illus.). 112p. 2000. pap. 6.95 (*0-7641-1208-2*) Barron.

Buscombe, Charles G. Television & Video Systems: Operation, Maintenance, Troubleshooting & Repair. 2nd ed. LC 97-39663. 451p. 1998. 105.00 (*0-13-442088-8*) P-H.

***Buscombe, Edward.** British Television: A Reader. LC 99-58400. 2000. write for info. (*0-19-874265-7*) OUP.

Buscombe, Edward. Stagecoach: BFI Film Classics. (Illus.). 96p. 1992. pap. 9.95 (*0-85170-299-6*, Pub. by British Film Inst) Ind U Pr.

Buscombe, Edward & Pearson, Roberta E., eds. Back in the Saddle Again: New Essays on the Western. LC 98-210526. (Illus.). 256p. 1998. 60.00 (*0-85170-660-6*, Pub. by British Film Inst); pap. 22.50 (*0-85170-661-4*, Pub. by British Film Inst) Ind U Pr.

Buscombe, Edward, ed. see Collins, Richard L., et al.

Buscombe, Eve. The Blomfield Letters Covering the Period 1799 to 1845. rev. ed. (Illus.). 70.00 (*0-646-08235-3*, Pub. by Eureka Res); pap. 25.00 (*0-646-08236-1*, Pub. by Eureka Res) Continental Bk.

— Maryborough, Queensland: Spirit of Place Album. (Practising History Ser.: No. 3). (Illus.). 80p. 1992. 50.00 (*0-646-08237-X*, Pub. by Eureka Res); pap. 20.00 (*0-646-08238-8*, Pub. by Eureka Res) Continental Bk.

Buscombe, John R., jt. auth. see Cox, Peter H.

Buscombe, William. MK Spectral Clasifications: 5th General Catalogue. LC 81-9555. 250p. (Orig.). 1981. pap. text 10.00 (*0-939160-03-X*) NWU Astro.

Buscombe, William & Foster, Bruce E. MK Spectral Classifications: 13th General Catalogue. 213p. (Orig.). (C). 1998. pap. 30.00 (*0-939160-10-2*) NWU Astro.

Buse, D. K., jt. auth. see Black, J. L.

Buse, Dieter K., et al, eds. Modern Germany: An Encyclopedia of History, People, & Culture, 1871-1990, 2 vols. LC 97-13829. (Canadian Review of Studies on Nationalism Ser.). (Illus.). 1158p. 1998. text 160.00 (*0-8153-0503-6*, H1520) Garland.

Buse, John J. In His Own Hand: A Historical Scrapbook of St. Charles County, Missouri. unabridged ed. Poelker, Greg, ed. LC 98-86784. (Illus.). 152p. 1998. pap. 20.00 (*0-9665338-0-1*) J Buse.

Buse, Melanie R., ed. Drug Store Market Guide, 1998. 1998. pap. 299.00 (*1-879463-07-5*) Melnor Pub.

— Drug Store Market Guide, 1991. 674p. 1990. pap. 239.00 (*1-879463-00-8*) Melnor Pub.

— Drug Store Market Guide, 1992. (Orig.). 1991. pap. 249.00 (*1-879463-01-6*) Melnor Pub.

— Drug Store Market Guide, 1995. 1995. pap. 285.00 (*1-879463-04-0*) Melnor Pub.

— Drug Store Market Guide, 1996. 1996. pap. 299.00 (*1-879463-05-9*) Melnor Pub.

Buse, Peter & Stott, Andrew. Ghosts: Deconstruction, Psychoanalysis, History. LC 98-34810. 272p. 1999. text 49.95 (*0-312-21739-0*) St Martin.

Buse, Rueben C. Rural Information Systems: New Directions in Data Collection & Retrieval. LC 92-13228. (Illus.). 468p. 1992. text 59.95 (*0-8138-0932-0*) Iowa St U Pr.

Buse, Rueben C. & Bromley, Daniel W. Applied Economics: Resource Allocation in Rural America. LC 74-19097. (Illus.). 633p. 1975. reprint ed. pap. 196.30 (*0-608-00117-1*, 206088200006) Bks Demand.

Buseck, P., ed. Minerals & Reactions at the Atomic Scale: Transmission Electron Microscopy. (Reviews in Mineralogy Ser.: Vol. 27). 1992. per. 28.00 (*0-939950-32-4*) Mineralogical Soc.

Buseck, Peter, et al, eds. High-Resolution Transmission Electron Microscopy: And Associated Techniques. (Illus.). 672p. 1992. reprint ed. pap. text 65.00 (*0-19-507262-6*) OUP.

— High-Resolution Transmission Electron Microscopy & Associated Techniques. (Illus.). 670p. 1989. text 115.00 (*0-19-504275-1*) OUP.

Buselle, A., Jr., ed. see Caffin, Charles H.

Buseman, Alan. Tutorial for AMPLE & STAMP. 150p. (Orig.). 1991. pap. text 5.00 (*1-878606-01-8*) JAARS Inc.

Busemann, H. Recent Synthetic Differential Geometry. LC 13-120381. (Ergebnisse der Mathematik und Ihrer Grenzgebiete Ser.: Vol. 54). 1970. 64.95 (*0-387-04810-3*) Spr-Verlag.

Busenbark, Ernest. Symbols, Sex & the Stars: An Outline of the Origins of Moon & Sun Worship, Astrology, Sex Symbolism, Mystic Meaning of Numbers, the Cabala, & Many Popular Customs, Myths, Superstitions & Religious Beliefs. 2nd ed. (Illus.). 396p. 1997. reprint ed. pap. 22.95 (*1-885395-19-1*) Book Tree.

Busenbark, R., jt. auth. see Bates, Henry.

Busenbark, Robert I., jt. auth. see Bates, Henry J.

Busenberg, Bonnie. Vanilla, Chocolate, & Strawberry: The Story of Your Favorite Flavors. LC 93-15101. (YA). (gr. 5 up). 1993. lib. bdg. 23.95 (*0-8225-1573-3*, Lerner Publctns) Lerner Pub.

Busenberg, Stavros N. Delay Differential Equations & Dynamical Systems: Proceedings of a Conference Held in Claremont, California, Jan. 13-16, 1990. Martelli, Maurizio, ed. (Lecture Notes in Mathematics Ser.: Vol. 1475). viii, 249p. 1991. 41.00 (*0-387-54120-9*) Spr-Verlag.

Busenberg, Stavros N. & Cooke, Kenneth. Vertically Transmitted Diseases. LC 92-49541. (Biomathematics Ser.: Vol. 23). 1993. write for info. (*3-540-52004-X*); 126.95 (*0-387-52004-X*) Spr-Verlag.

Busenberg, Stavros N., et al. Differential Equations Models in Biology, Epidemiology & Ecology: Proceedings of a Conference Held in Claremont, California, January 13-16, 1990. Martelli, Maurizio & Levin, S. A., eds. (Lecture Notes in Biomathematics Ser.: Vol. 92). ix, 267p. 1991. pap. 43.00 (*0-387-54283-3*) Spr-Verlag.

— Mathematical Modelling of Industrial Processes: Lectures Given at the 3rd Session of the Centro Internazionale Matematico Estive Held in Bari, Italy, Sept. 24-29, 1990. Capasso, Vincenzo & Fasano, A. P., eds. LC 92-16917. 1992. 40.95 (*0-387-55595-1*) Spr-Verlag.

Buser, Christella. Flowers from the Ark: True Stories from the Homes of lArche. LC 95-49270. 112p. 1996. pap. 7.95 (*0-8091-3639-2*, 3639-2) Paulist Pr.

***Buser, Cyndi.** College Bound: The Essential Guide to Life after High School. 40p. 2000. 1.99 (*1-57748-707-9*) Barbour Pub.

Buser, Daniel, et al. Guided Bone Regeneration in Implant Dentistry. LC 94-242. (Illus.). 270p. 1994. text 120.00 (*0-86715-249-4*) Quint Pub Co.

***Buser, David, et al.** Beginning Active Server Pages 3.0. 3rd ed. 550p. 2000. pap. 39.99 (*1-86100-338-2*) Wrox Pr Inc.

— Beginning ASP Databases. (Beginning Ser.). (Illus.). 800p. 1999. pap. 39.99 (*1-86100-272-6*) Wrox Pr Inc.

Buser, Hugo. Paleostructures of Nigeria & Adjacent Countries. (Geotektonische Forschungen Ser.: Vol. 24). (GER.). ii, 90p. 1966. pap. 20.00 (*3-510-50915-3*, Pub. by E Schweizerbartsche) Balogh.

Buser, Michael B. Auschwitz As Revelation. LC 74-83300. 61p. reprint ed. pap. 30.00 (*0-7837-6308-5*, 204602300010) Bks Demand.

Buser, Peter. Geometry & Spectra of Compact Riemann Surfaces. LC 92-23803. (Progress in Mathematics Ser.: Vol. 106). (Illus.). xiv, 454p. 1993. 78.50 (*0-8176-3406-1*) Birkhauser.

Buser, Pierre & Imbert, Michel. Audition. Kay, Roy H., tr. (Illus.). 280p. 1992. 49.50 (*0-262-02331-8*, Bradford Bks) MIT Pr.

— Vision. Kay, Roy H., tr. from FRE. (Illus.). 576p. 1992. 49.50 (*0-262-02336-9*, Bradford Bks) MIT Pr.

Busette, Cedric. La Familia de Pascual Duarte & el Tunel: Correspondences & Divergencies in the Exercise of Craft. LC 94-27152. 170p. (C). 1994. lib. bdg. 38.00 (*0-8191-9647-9*) U Pr of Amer.

Busev, A. I., et al. Handbook of the Analytical Chemistry of Rare Elements. LC 75-104379. (GER.). xi, 402 p. 1970. write for info. (*0-250-39960-1*) Buttrwrth-Heinemann.

Busey, Andrew & Lurie, Marc. VR Internet. (Illus.). 400p. 1995. 35.00 (*1-57521-008-8*) Sams.

Busey, James L. Latin American Political Guide. 20th ed. 113p. 1995. 8.50 (*0-912188-08-1*) Juniper Edit.

— Political Aspects of the Panama Canal: The Problem of Location. LC 73-84606. (Arizona University, Institute of Government Research, Comparative Government Studies: No. 5). 55p. reprint ed. pap. 30.00 (*0-608-13643-3*, 205524900011) Bks Demand.

Busey, John W. The Last Full Measure: Burials in the Soldiers' National Cemetery at Gettysburg. Martin, David G., ed. (Illus.). 277p. (C). 1988. text 20.00 (*0-944413-12-9*) Longstreet Hse.

— These Honored Dead: The Union Casualties at Gettysburg. 2nd ed. LC 97-168199. (Illus.). 490p. 1996. 30.00 (*0-944413-40-4*) Longstreet Hse.

Busey, John W. & Martin, David G. Regimental Strengths & Losses at Gettysburg. 3rd ed. 351p. 1994. 20.00 (*0-944413-32-3*) Longstreet Hse.

Busey, John W., jt. auth. see Harrison, Kathleen G.

Busey, Loure. Most of All. 288p. 1997. mass mkt. 4.99 (*0-7860-0456-8*, Pinncle Kensgtn) Kensgtn Pub Corp.

Busey, Samuel C. Immigration: Its Evils & Consequences. LC 69-18762. (American Immigration Collection. Series 1). 1969. reprint ed. 11.95 (*0-405-00510-5*) Ayer.

***Busfield, Buck.** Not in the Stars. 44p. 1998. pap. 5.60 (*0-87129-897-X*, N48) Dramatic Pub.

Busfield, Joan. Managing Madness. 406p. 1989. text 49.95 (*0-318-42465-7*) Routledge.

— Men, Women & Madness. (C). 1996. pap. text 19.00 (*0-8147-1281-9*) NYU Pr.

— Men, Women & Madness: Understanding Gender & Mental Disorder. Campling, Jo, ed. LC 95-42253. 296p. (C). 1996. text 50.00 (*0-8147-1278-9*) NYU Pr.

Busfield, Joan & Paddon, Michael. Thinking about Children: Sociology & Fertility in Post-War England. LC 76-22986. 324p. reprint ed. pap. 92.40 (*0-608-15698-1*, 2031625) Bks Demand.

Busfield, Roger M. Playwright's Art: Stage, Radio, Television, Motion Pictures. LC 78-139125. 260p. (C). 1971. reprint ed. lib. bdg. 65.00 (*0-8371-5741-2*, BUPA, Greenwood Pr) Greenwood.

Bush. Abracadabra Recorders, Bk. 1. (J). (gr. k-5). 1998. pap. 4.50 (*0-7136-2158-3*, Pub. by A & C Blk) Midpt Trade.

— Abracadabra Recorders, Bk. 1A. (J). (gr. k-5). 1998. pap. 4.50 (*0-7136-2374-8*, Pub. by A & C Blk) Midpt Trade.

— Abracadabra Recorders, Bk. 2. (J). (gr. k-5). 1998. pap. 4.50 (*0-7136-2159-1*, Pub. by A & C Blk) Midpt Trade.

— Abracadabra Recorders, Bk. 3. (J). (gr. k-5). 1998. pap. 4.50 (*0-7136-2165-6*, Pub. by A & C Blk) Midpt Trade.

— Abracadabra Recorders, Bk. 4. (J). (gr. k-5). 1998. pap. 4.50 (*0-7136-2166-4*, Pub. by A & C Blk) Midpt Trade.

— Abracadabra Recorders: Hymns, Bk. 6. (J). (gr. k-5). 1998. pap. 4.50 (*0-7136-2375-6*, Pub. by A & C Blk) Midpt Trade.

— Abracadabra Recorders: Treble, Bk. 7. (J). (gr. k-5). 1998. pap. 4.50 (*0-7136-2376-4*, Pub. by A & C Blk) Midpt Trade.

***Bush.** Dollars & Sense: Owning & Operating a Child Care Business. 2000. pap. 19.95 (*0-7668-2236-2*) Delmar.

Bush. Ecology of Changing Planet. 2nd ed. LC 99-24607. 498p. (C). 1999. pap. text 77.33 (*0-13-011202-X*) P-H.

— Finance Tutor IBM. (C). 1990. text 15.00 (*0-06-041071-X*) HarperTrade.

Bush. From the Command Economy to the Market. 1991. 57.95 (*1-85521-230-7*) Ashgate Pub Co.

Bush. Hey Presto! Abradacabra Recorder: Abracadabra Recorder Book. 80p. (J). 1998. pap. 13.95 (*0-7136-2302-0*, Pub. by A & C Blk) Midpt Trade.

— Marketing Research. LC 99-27710. 1999. 65.00 (*0-256-19555-2*) McGraw.

— Modern Physics with Quantum Mechanics. (C). 1999. text 81.00 (*0-03-047173-7*) Harcourt Coll Pubs.

— Social Orders & Social Classes since 1500. 1991. text. write for info. (*0-582-08344-3*, Pub. by Addison-Wesley) Longman.

Bush & Stetina, T. Speed & Thrash Metal Drum Method. 48p. 1992. pap. 17.95 (*0-7935-1854-7*, 06621762) H Leonard.

Bush & Stetina, T. Speed & Thrash Metal Drum Method. 1992. pap. 14.95 incl. audio (*0-7935-1855-5*, 06621761) H Leonard.

Bush, et al. Living with the Puerto Rico Shore. (Living with the Shore Ser.). (Illus.). 216p. 1995. pap. 17.95 (*0-8477-0239-1*) U of PR Pr.

Bush, Alan, ed. see Belza, Igor F.

Bush, Alan, ed. see Boelza, Igor F.

Bush, Alan W. Perturbation Methods for Engineers & Scientists. 320p. 1992. per. 72.95 (*0-8493-8614-4*) CRC Pr.

— Perturbation Methods for Engineers & Scientists. 320p. 1992. boxed set 104.95 (*0-8493-8608-X*, QA871) CRC Pr.

Bush, ALan W., et al. Flow Modelling in Industrial Processes. 1989. text 59.95 (*0-470-21498-8*) P-H.

Bush, Albert J., III & Baladi, Gilbert, eds. Nondestructive Testing of Pavements & Backcalculation of Moduli STP 1026. LC 89-38726. (Special Technical Publication Ser.). (Illus.). 725p. 1989. text 99.00 (*0-8031-1260-2*, STP1026) ASTM.

Bush, Alfred L. & Mitchell, Lee C. The Photograph & the American Indian. LC 94-12178. 352p. 1994. text 85.00 (*0-691-03489-3*, Pub. by Princeton U Pr) Cal Prin Full Svc.

***Bush, Alison M.** Bertram Pickard of Geneva. 176p. 1999. pap. 59.95 (*1-85072-206-4*, Pub. by W Sessions) St Mut.

Bush, Anita. Of Lovers & Madmen. Zagury, Carolyn S., ed. LC 95-60425. 240p. 1995. pap. 10.95 (*1-880254-26-3*) Vista.

Bush, Anita, ed. see Kotarski, Beth R.

Bush, Anita M. The Enemy Within. LC 93-60314. 176p. 1993. pap. 10.95 (*1-880254-07-7*) Vista.

Bush, Ann H., jt. auth. see Smith, Karlene R.

Bush, Anne K. The Misbegotten King. 368p. (Orig.). 1997. mass mkt. 5.99 (*0-446-60331-7*, Pub. by Warner Bks) Little.

Bush, Anne Kelleher. The Knight, the Harp & the Maiden. 327p. (Orig.). 1999. mass mkt. 6.99 (*0-446-60496-8*, Pub. by Warner Bks) Little.

Bush, B. M. Interpretation of Laboratory Results for Small Animal Clinicians. (Illus.). 528p. 1991. 92.95 (*0-632-03259-6*) Blackwell Sci.

Bush, B. M., jt. ed. see Roberts, Alan.

Bush, Barbara. Barbara Bush: A Memoir. (Illus.). 592p. 1994. 25.00 (*0-02-519635-9*) Macmillan.

— Barbara Bush: A Memoir. 1995. mass mkt. 6.99 (*0-312-95664-9*) St Martin.

— Barbara Bush Vol. 1: A Memoir, No. 1. large type ed. (Niagara Large Print Ser.). 459p. 1995. 29.50 (*0-7089-5807-9*) Ulverscroft.

— Barbara Bush Vol. 2: A Memoir, No. 2. large type ed. 448p. 1995. 29.50 (*0-7089-5808-7*) Ulverscroft.

— Heart Trouble: A Woman's Workshop on Christian Character. Kobobel, Janet, ed. (Woman's Workshop Ser.). 144p. (Orig.). 1985. mass mkt. 5.99 (*0-310-29431-2*, 12016P) Zondervan.

— Imperialism, Race, & Resistance: Africa & Britain, 1919-1945 LC 98-55761. 1999. pap. write for info. (*0-415-15973-3*) Routledge.

***Bush, Barbara.** Imperialism, Race & Resistance: Africa & Britain, 1919-1945. LC 98-55761. 1999. write for info. (*0-415-15972-5*) Routledge.

Bush, Barbara. Slave Women in Caribbean Society, 1650-1832. (Illus.). 198p. 1990. pap. 14.95 (*0-253-21251-0*) Ind U Pr.

— Walking in Wisdom: A Woman's Workshop on Ecclesiastes. (Woman's Workshop Ser.). 128p. (Orig.). 1982. pap. 2.95 (*0-310-43041-0*, 12014P) Zondervan.

— A Woman's Workshop on Mastering Motherhood. (Women's Workshop Ser.). 176p. 1981. mass mkt. 6.99 (*0-310-43031-3*, 12013P) Zondervan.

Bush, Betsy H., jt. auth. see Perlman, Seth.

Bush, Betsy Hills, jt. auth. see Perlman, Seth.

Bush, Betty J., ed. Quality Teaching in Higher Education: Reflections of Award-Winning Missouri Professors. 137p. (C). 1994. pap. 19.95 (*0-9633819-7-0*) Prescott Pub.

***Bush, Betty L.** Expect Sunshine. 240p. 2000. 23.95 (*0-9679646-2-8*, 132112) Muse Charity Pubng.

Bush, Beverly. Evidence of Things Unseen. LC 97-10953. 350p. 1997. pap. 12.99 (*0-8499-4040-0*) Word Pub.

Bush, Brian, et al. A Guide to the Reptiles & Frogs of the Perth Region. (Illus.). 240p. (C). 1995. pap. 19.95 (*1-875560-42-4*, Pub. by New South Wales Univ Pr) Intl Spec Bk.

Bush-Brown, Albert, et al, eds. Hospitable Design for Healthcare & Senior Communities. LC 91-8445. (Illus.). 320p. 1992. text 66.95 (*0-442-23959-9*, VNR) Wiley.

Bush-Brown, Albert & Davis, Dianne. Hospitable Design for Healthcare & Senior Communities. (Interior Design Ser.). 263p. 1991. 90.00 (*0-471-28922-1*, VNR) Wiley.

Bush-Brown, James & Bush-Brown, Louise. America's Garden Book. 4th ed. LC 96-18752. (Illus.). 1042p. 1996. 65.00 (*0-02-860995-6*) Macmillan USA.

— America's Garden Book. 4th rev. ed. New York Botanical Garden Staff, ed. (Illus.). 832p. 1980. 32.95 (*0-684-16270-9*, Scribners Ref) Mac Lib Ref.

Bush-Brown, Louise, jt. auth. see Bush-Brown, James.

***Bush, Bryan S.** Civil War Battles of the Western Theatre. LC 98-60774. 204 p. 1998. write for info. (*1-56311-434-8*) Turner Pub KY.

Bush, C. Allen, ed. Advances in Biophysical Chemistry, Vol. 1. 247p. 1990. 112.50 (*1-55938-159-0*) Jai Pr.

— Advances in Biophysical Chemistry, Vol. 2. 180p. 1992. 112.50 (*1-55938-396-8*) Jai Pr.

— Advances in Biophysical Chemistry, Vol. 3. 263p. 1993. 112.50 (*1-55938-425-5*) Jai Pr.

— Advances in Biophysical Chemistry, Vol. 4. 248p. 1995. 112.50 (*1-55938-708-4*) Jai Pr.

— Advances in Biophysical Chemistry, Vol. 5. 262p. 1995. 112.50 (*1-55938-978-8*) Jai Pr.

— Advances in Biophysical Chemistry, Vol. 6. 1997. 112.50 (*0-7623-0060-4*) Jai Pr.

— Advances in Biophysical Chemistry, Vol. 7. Date not set. 112.50 (*0-7623-0343-3*) Jai Pr.

Bush, C. Dana. Compact Guide to Wildflowers of the Rockies. 1990. pap. 7.95 (*0-919433-57-X*) Lone Pine.

Bush, Casey. Blessings of Madness. 26p. 1994. 5.00 (*0-614-30116-5*) Skydog OR.

Bush, Catharine S. 150 Skill-Building Reference Lists: Language Remediation & Expansion. (Illus.). 268p. 1989. pap. text 29.00 (*0-7616-7559-0*) Commun Skill.

Bush, Catherine. Elizabeth I. (World Leaders Past & Present Ser.). (Illus.). 120p. (YA). (gr. 5 up). 1987. lib. bdg. 19.95 (*0-87754-579-0*) Chelsea Hse.

— Minus Time. 2nd ed. (High Risk Ser.). 320p. 1995. pap. 12.99 (*1-85242-408-7*, High Risk Bks) Serpents Tail.

— Minus Time: A Novel. LC 92-32822. 352p. 1993. 19.45 (*1-56282-881-9*, Pub. by Hyperion) Time Warner.

— Mohandas K. Gandhi. (World Leaders Past & Present Ser.). (Illus.). 120p. (YA). (gr. 5 up). 1985. lib. bdg. 19.95 (*0-87754-555-3*) Chelsea Hse.

***Bush, Catherine.** The Rules of Engagement. 272p. 2000. 24.00 (*0-374-25280-7*) FS&G.

An Asterisk (*) at the beginning of an entry indicates that the title is appearing for the first time.

Bush, Charles W. How to Hear God Speak. 128p. (Orig.). 1975. pap. text 1.50 (0-89228-028-X) Impact Christian.

Bush, Chilton R. Editorial Thinking & Writing: A Textbook with Exercises. LC 74-98826. 453p. 1970. reprint ed. lib. bdg. 65.00 (0-8371-3078-6, BUET, Greenwood Pr) Greenwood.

Bush, Chilton R. Newswriting & Reporting Public Affairs. 2nd ed. LC 71-127596. x, 576p. 1970. write for info. (0-8019-6002-9) NP-Chilton.

Bush, Chilton R., ed. see Siebert, Fredrick S., et al.

Bush, Christine. Whisper a Warning. LC 98-96341. 192p. 1998. lib. bdg. 18.95 (0-8034-9319-3, Avalon Bks) Bouregy.

Bush, Clara N. Phonetic Variation & Acoustic Distinctive Features. (Janua Linguarum, Ser. Practica: No. 12). (Orig.). 1964. pap. text 47.70 (90-279-0631-9) Mouton.

Bush, Clifton. Third Prophecy. LC 94-90648. 1995. pap. 14.95 (0-9643612-0-5) FABCO Pubng.

Bush, Clive. Halfway to Revolution: Investigation & Crisis in the Work of Henry Adams, William James, & Gertrude Stein. 512p. (C). 1991. 60.00 (0-300-04729-0) Yale U Pr.

***Bush, Crystal.** Linda Goodman's Star Cards. (Illus.). 2000. 24.95 (1-57174-185-2) Hampton Roads Pub Co.

Bush, David M., et al. Living by the Rules of the Sea. LC 95-50855. (Living with the Shore Ser.). (Illus.). 208p. 1996. pap. 17.95 (0-8223-1796-6); text 49.95 (0-8223-1801-6) Duke.

— Living with the Puerto Rico Shore. Pilkey, Orrin H., Jr., ed. LC 94-42437. (Living with the Shore Ser.). (Illus.). 216p. 1995. pap. 17.95 (0-8223-1590-4); text 49.95 (0-8223-1575-0) Duke.

Bush, David V. How to Put the Subconscious Mind to Work (1924) 460p. 1998. reprint ed. pap. 33.00 (0-7661-0288-2) Kessinger Pub.

Bush, David V. & Waugh, W. Character Analysis: How to Read People at Sight (1923) 608p. 1998. reprint ed. pap. 45.00 (0-7661-0287-4) Kessinger Pub.

***Bush, Dawn.** Growing Healthy Babies: The Growing Family's Guide to Nutrition & Wellness. 259p. 1999. pap. 12.95 (0-9675154-0-8) Baby Cottag.

Bush, Donald J. The Streamlined Decade: Design in the 1930s. LC 75-10868. (Illus.). 192p. 1975. pap. 17.95 (0-8076-0793-2) Braziller.

Bush, Donald W. How to Edit Technical Documents Workbook. LC 95-9705. 1995. pap. text, wbk. ed. 10.00 (0-89774-964-2) Oryx Pr.

Bush, Donald W. & Campbell, Charles P. How to Edit Technical Documents. LC 95-9705. (Illus.). 384p. 1995. pap., student ed. 38.50 (0-89774-870-0) Oryx Pr.

Bush, Douglas. Engaged & Disengaged. LC 66-23462. 259p. reprint ed. pap. 80.30 (0-7837-2231-1, 205732100004) Bks Demand.

— Science & English Poetry: A Historical Sketch, 1590-1950. LC 80-18161. (Patten Lectures Ser., 1949, Indiana Univ.). 166p. 1980. reprint ed. lib. bdg. 49.75 (0-313-22654-7, BUSC, Greenwood Pr) Greenwood.

Bush, Douglas, ed. see Baptista Mantuanus.

Bush, Douglas, ed. see Keats, John.

Bush, Douglas, ed. see Milton, John.

Bush, Douglas, ed. see Shakespeare, William.

Bush, Douglas, ed. & intro. see Milton, John.

Bush, Douglas E., ed. Encyclopedia of Keyboard Instruments Vol. II: The Organ. 750p. 95.00 (0-8240-4549-1, H1227) Garland.

Bush, Duncan. The Hook. LC 99-216336. 140p. 1997. pap. 19.95 (1-85411-203-1, Pub. by Seren Bks) Dufour.

Bush, Edward F. Engine Houses & Turntables on Canadian Railways, 1850-1950. (Illus.). 160p. 1991. 35.00 (1-55046-002-1, Pub. by Boston Mills) Genl Dist Srvs.

Bush, Ellis M., Jr. Did Jesus Use a Modem at the Sermon on the Mount? LC 97-61852. 123p. 1997. pap. 9.95 (1-57921-066-X, Pub. by WinePress Pub) BookWorld.

Bush, Elsie R. Jungletown Lane. (Illus.). 96p. (J). (gr. 5-6). 1997. pap. 7.95 (0-9609440-1-X) E R Pub.

— Rhonda Raccoon. (Illus.). 32p. (J). (ps-1). 1997. pap. 7.95 (0-9609440-3-6) E R Pub.

Bush, Florence C. Dorie: Woman of the Mountains. LC 91-12875. (Illus.). 254p. (YA). (gr. 6 up). 1992. reprint ed. pap. 14.95 (0-87049-726-X); reprint ed. text 26.00 (0-87049-725-1) U of Tenn Pr.

— If Life Gives You Scraps, Make a Quilt: Short Stories of the Smoky Mountains. (Illus.). 180p. (Orig.). 1993. pap. 9.95 (0-9634680-0-6) Misty Cove Pr.

Bush, Francis M. & Dolwick, M. Franklin. The Temporomandibular Joint & Related Orofacial Disorders. LC 94-33796. (Illus.). 416p. 1994. text 69.50 (0-397-50982-0) Lppncott W & W.

— The Temporomandibular Joint & Related Orofacial Disorders. LC 94-33796. (Illus.). 432p. reprint ed. pap. 134.00 (0-608-09720-9, 206988600007) Bks Demand.

Bush, Fred W., compiled by. The Centennial Atlas of Athens County, Ohio. LC 75-23393. (Illus.). 166p. 1996. reprint ed. pap. text 21.95 (0-8214-1172-1) Ohio U Pr.

Bush, Frederic. Ruth, Esther. (Biblical Commentary Ser.: Vol. 9). 450p. 29.99 (0-8499-0208-8) Word Pub.

Bush, Friedrich T., et al. Constantin Brancusi, 1876-1957. LC 95-33184. (Illus.). 408p. 1995. pap. 36.00 (0-87633-097-9) Phila Mus Art.

Bush, G. P., jt. auth. see Hattery, L. H.

Bush, Geneva L., jt. ed. see Shearer, Barbara S.

***Bush, George.** All the Best, George Bush: My Life in Letters & Other Writings. 2000. pap. 16.00 (0-7432-0041-1, Touchstone) S&S Trade Pap.

— Building a Better America. (Illus.). 193p. (C). 1999. reprint ed. pap. text 25.00 (0-7881-8221-8) DIANE Pub.

Bush, George. Commentary on Exodus. LC 92-39337. 608p. 1993. pap. 20.99 (0-8254-2181-0, Kregel Class) Kregel.

— Commentary on Exodus. deluxe ed. LC 92-39337. 608p. 1993. 26.99 (0-8254-2182-9, Kregel Class) Kregel.

Bush, George, jt. auth. see Kopper, Philip.

Bush, George Herbert Walker. All the Best, George Bush: My Life in Letters & Other Writings. LC 99-40440. 640p. (YA). (gr. 9-12). 1999. 30.00 (0-684-83958-X) Scribner.

***Bush, George Herbert Walker.** All the Best, George Bush: My Life in Letters & Other Writings. limited aut. ed. 448p. 1999. 300.95 (0-684-86812-1) S&S Trade.

Bush, George Herbert Walker & Scowcroft, Brent. A World Transformed. 624p. 1999. pap. 16.00 (0-679-75259-5) Knopf.

— A World Transformed: The Collapse of the Soviet Empire, the Unification of Germany, Tiananmen Square, the Gulf War. LC 98-13499. (Illus.). 576p. 1998. 30.00 (0-679-43248-5) Knopf.

Bush, George P., ed. Technology & Copyright: Annotated Bibliography & Source Materials. LC 72-87129. 454p. 1972. 28.50 (0-912338-03-2); pap. 14.50 (0-685-03093-8); fiche 9.50 (0-912338-04-0) Lomond.

Bush, George P. & Dreyfuss, Robert, eds. Technology & Copyright: Sources & Materials. rev. ed. 552p. 1979. fiche 15.50 (0-912338-18-0) Lomond.

— Technology & Copyright: Sources & Materials. 2nd rev. ed. 552p. 1979. 32.50 (0-912338-17-2) Lomond.

Bush, George P., jt. auth. see Hattery, Lowell H.

Bush, George S. An American Harvest: The Story of Weil Brothers-Cotton. LC 82-9797. 495p. 1983. 25.00 (0-13-027458-5, Busn) P-H.

Bush, George S., ed. The Genius Belt: A History of the Arts in Bucks County, Pennsylvania. LC 96-78366. (Illus.). 192p. 1997. 45.00 (0-271-01672-8); pap. 24.95 (0-271-01673-6) Pa St U Pr.

Bush, George S., ed. see Reed, Cleota, et al.

***Bush, George W. & Herskowitz, Mickey.** A Charge to Keep. LC 99-52155. (Illus.). 256p. 1999. 23.00 (0-688-17441-8, Wm Morrow) Morrow Avon.

Bush, George W. & Scowcroft, Brent. American Foreign Policy. 1996. 30.00 (0-614-96908-5) Knopf.

Bush, Grace A., jt. auth. see Young, John E.

Bush, Graham. Local Government & Politics in New Zealand. 2nd ed. 336p. 1996. pap. 29.95 (1-86940-126-3, Pub. by Allen & Unwin Pty) Paul & Co Pubs.

Bush, Gregory, jt. auth. see McCabe, Arva M. P.

Bush, Gregory W. Lord of Attention: Gerald Stanley Lee & the Crowd Metaphor in Industrializing America. LC 90-37499. (Illus.). 240p. (C). 1991. lib. bdg. 30.00 (0-87023-724-1) U of Mass Pr.

Bush, Harold H. Flashbacks of a Forest Ranger. 128p. 1999. pap. 12.50 (0-87012-600-8) McClain. FLASHBACKS OF A FOREST RANGER gives a unique inside look into the world of the U.S. Forest Service from a veteran forest ranger. From personnel to government bureaucracy, Harold H. Bush tells of his own experiences in the national forests & the people who made his career with the greatest conservation movement in our history-the Civilian Conservation Corps when millions of young men, in helping America recover from the Great Depression, went to work in "Roosevelt's Tree Army" to create national, state & local parks to build roads, trails, bridges, dams, recreation area & new forests. FLASHBACK OF A FOREST RANGER is filled with humor, story telling & even suspense & is a must for anyone who has ever worked for the government.** ***Publisher Paid Annotation.

Bush, Harold K., Jr. American Declarations: Repentance & Rebellion in American Cultural History. LC 98-9009. 280p. (C). (gr. 13 up). 1998. text 49.94 (0-252-02428-1) U of Ill Pr.

— American Declarations: Repentance & Rebellion in American Cultural History. LC 98-9009. (Illus.). 280p. (C). (gr. 13 up). 1998. text 19.95 (0-252-06735-5) U of Ill Pr.

Bush, J. P. & Harkins, S. W., eds. Children in Pain: Clinical & Research Issues from a Developmental Perspective. xvii, 476p. 1991. 96.95 (0-387-97501-2) Spr-Verlag.

***Bush, James.** Encyclopedia of Northwest Music: From Classical Recordings to Classic Rock Performances, Your Guide to the Best of the Region. LC 99-16791. (Illus.). 340p. 1999. pap. 21.95 (1-57061-141-6) Sasquatch Bks.

Bush, James W. Ward's Automotive Yearbook, 1992. 1992. 205.00 (0-614-10586-2) Wards Comm.

Bush, James W., ed. Ward's Automotive Yearbook, 1991. 1991. 190.00 (0-614-10585-4) Wards Comm.

Bush, James W. & Stark, Harry A., eds. Ward's Automotive Yearbook, 1990. 1990. 175.00 (0-614-10584-6) Wards Comm.

Bush, Jan. Marks of the Maker. 256p. 1997. pap. 9.95 (1-896836-09-7) NStone Publ.

Bush, Jane. Spectra for the Identification of Monomers in Food Packaging. LC 93-25450. 448p. (C). 1993. text 285.50 (0-7923-2400-5) Kluwer Academic.

Bush, Janet. The Handbook of School Art Therapy: Introducing Art Therapy into a School System. LC 96-48444. (Illus.). 206p. 1997. text 48.95 (0-398-06740-6); pap. text 35.95 (0-398-06741-4) C C Thomas.

Bush, Janet, ed. see Delaware Art Museum Staff, et al.

Bush, Jeb & Yablonski, Brian. Profiles in Character. LC 95-83319. 288p. (Orig.). 1996. pap. 15.00 (0-9650912-0-1) J M Inst.

Bush, Jim & Johnston, Daniel. International Oil Company Financial Management in Nontechnical Language. LC 98-34042. xvi, 327 p. 1999. 64.95 (0-87814-597-4) PennWell Bks.

Bush, Jim, jt. auth. see Bergmann, Barbara R.

***Bush, Joe.** Gamma Radiation Safety Study Guide. (Illus.). 104p. 1999. pap. 58.00 (1-57117-031-6) Am Soc Nondestructive.

Bush, John. The Fish Who Could Wish. (Illus.). 32p. (J). (ps-3). 1991. 13.95 (0-916291-35-9) Kane-Miller Bk.

— The Fish Who Could Wish. LC 90-46667. (J). 1991. 12.15 (0-606-06379-X, Pub. by Turtleback) Demco.

— The Fish Who Could Wish. (Illus.). 32p. (J). 1994. reprint ed. pap. 6.95 (0-916291-48-0) Kane-Miller Bk.

Bush, John C. A New Reformed Catechism: A Shorter Catechism for Today. 64p. 1997. pap. 4.99 (1-882547-14-4, Viaticum) Kash Literary.

Bush, John C. & Tiemann, William H. Right to Silence. 3rd ed. 1989. pap. 15.95 (0-687-36314-4) Abingdon.

Bush, John R. John's Project Manual: Short Form Specification Workbook for Architects, Designers & Builders. 260p. 1997. wbk. ed. 135.00 (0-931481-50-3) Rosebush Pub.

Bush, John W. Venetia Redeemed: Franco-Italian Relations, 1864-1866. LC 67-26918. 176p. reprint ed. pap. 54.60 (0-8357-3978-3, 203667600005) Bks Demand.

Bush, Jonathan & Wijffels, Alain A. Learning the Law: Teaching & the Transmission of Law in England, 1150-1900. LC 99-32558. 1999. 65.00 (1-85285-184-8) Hambledon Press.

***Bush, JoShanna & Virbick, Diane.** Magicians of the Millennium: Traveling the Rainbow Bridge. large type ed. (Illus.). 168p. 1999. pap. 12.95 (0-9672888-0-0) Souls Sng.

Bush, JoShanna, et al. Golden Key: Book of Light. LC 98-65933. 174p. 1998. pap. 14.95 (0-9664094-5-0, 501) Key Pub Co.

Bush, Julia. Organizing for Empire: Edwardian Ladies & Imperial Power. LC 99-12380. (Women, Power & Politics Ser.). 242p. 1999. 75.00 (0-7185-0061-X) Bks Intl VA.

Bush, K. G. Electrical Variable Drives. Reeves, E. A., ed. LC 94-38727. 1995. 75.00 (0-632-02226-4) Blackwell Sci.

Bush, Karem. 201 More Hints for Horse Persons. (Illus.). 72p. Date not set. 13.95 (1-872119-12-3, Pub. by Kenilworth Pr) Half Halt Pr.

Bush, Karen. Curing Bad Habits. (Crowood Equestrian Guides Ser.). (Illus.). 96p. 1995. pap. 17.95 (1-85223-788-0, Pub. by Cro1wood) Trafalgar.

— The Problem Horse: An Owner's Guide. (Illus.). 160p. 1996. pap. 29.95 (1-85223-916-6) Cro1wood.

***Bush, Karen.** 201 Handy Hints for Horse Persons. (Illus.). 72p. 1998. 13.95 (1-872119-00-X, Pub. by Kenilworth Pr) Half Halt Pr.

***Bush, Karen & Colvin, Claire.** Pony Hobby Book. 2000. pap. 8.95 (0-85131-639-5, Pub. by J A Allen) Trafalgar.

Bush, Kathleen, jt. auth. see Rayburn, Rosalie.

Bush, Keith. Project Nirvana. Date not set. 12.95 (1-881542-62-9) Book World Inc.

Bush, Ken, ed. see Wycherley, William.

Bush, L. P. & Bucker, R. C., eds. Tall Fescue. (Agronomy Monograph Ser.: No. 20). (Illus.). 351p. 1979. 18.75 (0-89118-057-5) Am Soc Agron.

Bush, L. Russ. Psalms, Vol. 13. (The New American Commentary Ser.). 2000. 29.99 (0-8054-0113-X) Broadman.

Bush, L. Russ & Nettles, Tom J. Baptists & the Bible. expanded rev. ed. LC 99-17533. 448p. 1999. pap. 24.99 (0-8054-1832-6) Broadman.

Bush, Lawrence. American Torah Toons: 54 Illustrated Commentaries. LC 96-47020. 136p. 1997. pap. 24.95 (0-7657-5972-1) Aronson.

— Emma Ansky-Levine & Her Mitzvah Machine. LC 90-24491. (Do-It-Yourself Jewish Adventure Ser.). (Illus.). (J). (gr. 4-7). 1991. pap. 7.95 (0-8074-0458-6, 123933) UAHC.

— Rooftop Secrets: And Other Stories of Anti-Semitism. LC 86-1362. (Illus.). 144p. (J). (gr. 7-9). 1986. pap. 8.95 (0-8074-0314-8, 121720) UAHC.

Bush, Lawrence & Dekro, Jeffrey. Jews, Money & Social Responsibility: Developing a "Torah of Money" for Contemporary Life. 208p. 1993. pap. 18.00 (0-9635684-1-8) Shefa Fund.

Bush, Lawson, jt. auth. see African American Images Staff.

Bush, Lee O. & Hershey, Richard F. Conneaut Lake Park: The First One Hundred Years of Fun. LC 92-71229. (Illus.). 176p. 1992. 24.95 (0-935408-04-5) Amusement Pk Bks.

Bush, Lee O., et al. Euclid Beach Park - A Second Look. LC 79-55562. (Illus.). 229p. 1991. reprint ed. 24.95 (0-935408-01-0) Amusement Pk Bks.

Bush, Lee O., ed. see Munch, Richard W.

Bush, Louis F. Two-Thousand Ten, the American System: Resurrection or Revolution? LC 92-96824. 69p. (Orig.). (C). 1992. pap. text 6.00 (0-9633936-0-X) Scorpio OR.

Bush, Luis. Move of the Holy Spirit in the 10/40 Window. 1999. pap. 8.99 (1-57658-151-9) YWAM Pub.

Bush, M. B., ed. Discontinuous Materials & Structures. LC 98-86665. (Advances in Boundary Elements Ser.: Vol. 5). 280p. 1998. 155.00 (1-85312-534-2) Computational Mech MA.

Bush, M. L. The European Nobility Vol. 1: Noble Privilege. LC 83-4350. 294p. (C). 1983. 44.50 (0-8419-0873-7) Holmes & Meier.

— The Government Policy of Protector Somerset. LC 76-366433. 192p. reprint ed. pap. 59.60 (0-7837-6917-2, 204674600003) Bks Demand.

***Bush, M. L.** Servitude in Modern Times. 2000. 59.95 (0-7456-1729-8, Pub. by Polity Pr); pap. 26.95 (0-7456-1730-1, Pub. by Polity Pr) Blackwell Pubs.

Bush, M. Lloyd. Red Gold. LC 93-87293. 262p. (Orig.). 1994. pap. 10.00 (0-9636845-6-6) Senior Pr.

Bush, Mark. How to Get the Money to Make Money. LC 99-61560. (Orig.). 1999. pap. 10.95 (0-9663393-4-7) Truman Publ.

Bush, Martin, ed. see Cavaliere, Barbara.

Bush, Martin H. Ben Shahn: The Passion of Sacco & Vanzetti. LC 68-54903. (Illus.). 85p. 1968. reprint ed. pap. 30.00 (0-608-07599-X, 205991400010) Bks Demand.

— Sculptures by Duane Hanson. LC 84-82245. (Illus.). 128p. 1985. 25.00 (0-317-01521-4) Edwin Ulrich.

Bush, Max. The Boy Who Left Home to Find Out about the Shivers. (J). 1999. pap. 7.00 (0-87602-372-3) Anchorage.

— Chest of Dreams. 47p. (J). (gr. 1-5). 1981. reprint ed. pap. 3.95 (0-87129-037-5, C72) Dramatic Pub.

— The Emerald Circle. 59p. 1998. pap. 5.50 (0-87129-766-3, E37) Dramatic Pub.

— The Ghost of the River House. (J). 1997. pap. 6.50 (0-87602-354-5) Anchorage.

— Hansel & Gretel, the Little Brother & the Little Sister. 46p. (J). (gr. 1-7). 1995. pap. 6.00 (0-87602-334-0) Anchorage.

— Plays for Young Audiences by Max Bush: An Anthology of Selected Plays for Young Audiences. Ellis, Roger, ed. LC 95-2382. 392p. (Orig.). (J). (gr. 4-12). 1995. pap. 16.95 (1-56608-011-8, B131) Meriwether Pub.

Bush, Max. Sarah. 87p. Date not set. pap. 5.60 (1-58342-017-7, SE8) Dramatic Pub.

Bush, Max. Thirteen Bells of Boglewood. (J). (gr. k-3). 1987. pap. 6.00 (0-87602-272-7) Anchorage.

— The Troll & the Elephant Prince. (J). (gr. 4 up). 1985. pap. 6.00 (0-87602-254-9) Anchorage.

— The Voyage of the Dragonfly. (J). 1990. 6.00 (0-87602-287-5) Anchorage.

Bush, Michael, ed. Serfdom Slavery. 368p. (C). 1996. pap. 29.06 (0-582-29185-2) Addison-Wesley.

Bush, Michael D. & Terry, Robert M., eds. Defining & Developing Proficiency. (ACTFL Foreign Language Education Ser.). 1998. pap. 16.90 (0-8442-9385-7, VF9385-7) NTC Contemp Pub Co.

— Developing Language: Teachers for a Changing World. (ACTFL Foreign Language Education Ser.). 1998. pap. 16.90 (0-8442-9391-1, VF9391-1) NTC Contemp Pub Co.

— Foreign Language Learning: The Journey of a Lifetime. (ACTFL Foreign Language Education Ser.). 1998. pap. 16.90 (0-8442-9394-6, VF9394-6) NTC Contemp Pub Co.

— Foreign Language Proficiency in the Classroom & Beyond. (ACTFL Foreign Language Education Ser.). 1998. pap. 16.90 (0-8442-9384-9, VF9384-9) NTC Contemp Pub Co.

— International Perspectives on Foreign Language Teaching. (ACTFL Foreign Language Education Ser.). 1998. pap. 16.90 (0-8442-9390-3, VF9390-3) NTC Contemp Pub Co.

— Modern Media in Foreign Language Education. (ACTFL Foreign Language Education Ser.). 1998. pap. 16.90 (0-8442-9386-5, VF9386-5) NTC Contemp Pub Co.

— New Perspectives, New Directions in Foreign Language Education. (ACTFL Foreign Language Education Ser.). 1998. pap. 16.90 (0-8442-9388-1, VF9388-1) NTC Contemp Pub Co.

— Research in Language Learning. (ACTFL Foreign Language Education Ser.). 1998. pap. 16.90 (0-8442-9393-8, VF9393-8) NTC Contemp Pub Co.

— Teaching for Proficiency: The Organizing Principle. (ACTFL Foreign Language Education Ser.). 1998. pap. 16.90 (0-8442-9383-0, VF9383-0) NTC Contemp Pub Co.

— Technology-Enhanced Language Learning. LC 97-116795. (ACTFL Foreign Language Education Ser.). 378p. 1998. pap. 16.90 (0-8442-9396-2, VS9396-2) NTC Contemp Pub Co.

Bush, Michael L. The Pilgrimage of Grace: A Study of the Rebel Armies of October 1536. LC 95-1037. (Illus.). 280p. 1996. text 99.95 (0-7190-4696-3, Pub. by Manchester Univ Pr) St Martin.

— Social Orders & Social Classes in Europe Since 1500: Studies in Social Stratification. (Studies in Social Stratification). 320p. (C). 1991. pap. text 30.50 (0-582-08343-5, 78916) Longman.

Bush, Nancy. Folk Knitting in Estonia: A Garland of Symbolism, Tradition, & Technique. LC 99-22927. 120p. 1999. pap. 21.95 (1-883010-43-8, Pub. by Interweave) IPG Chicago.

— Folk Socks: The History & Techniques of Handknitted Footwear, with 18 Exceptional Patterns Adapted from Cultures Around the World. (Illus.). 112p. 1994. pap. 16.95 (0-934026-97-1) Interweave.

— Scandal's Darling. Tolley, Carolyn, ed. 320p. (Orig.). 1993. mass mkt. 4.99 (0-671-75177-8) PB.

Bush, Nancy J. Chemotherapy Certification Program: Self-Learning Module. 220p. 1993. pap. 500.00 (0-9638351-0-6) Valentine & Assocs.

Bush, Neil L. & Nicholl, Boyd. Bisbee, Arizona: A Comparative View of the Queen of the Copper Camps. LC 92-90267. (Illus.). 64p. 1992. pap. 9.95 (0-9633014-0-3) Bisbee Image.

***Bush, Perry.** Dancing with the Kobzar: Bluffton College & Mennonite Higher Education, 1899-1999. LC 99-86312. (Studies in Anabaptist & Mennonite History Ser.: Vol. 38). 320p. 2000. 34.95 (0-9665021-8-3); pap. 19.95 (0-9665021-3-2) Pandora PA.

Bush, Perry. Two Kingdoms, Two Loyalties: Mennonite Pacifism in Modern America. LC 97-44233. (Illus.). 376p. 1998. 39.95 (0-8018-5827-5) Johns Hopkins.

An Asterisk (*) at the beginning of an entry indicates that the title is appearing for the first time.

Bush, Peter & Malmkjaer, Kirsten, eds. Rimbaud's Rainbow: Literary Translation in Higher Education. LC 98-48939. (Benjamins Translation Library: Vol. 21). x, 200p. 1998. 65.00 (*1-55619-705-5*) J Benjamins Pubng Co.

Bush, Peter, tr. see Almodovar, Pedro.

Bush, Peter, tr. see Goytisolo, Juan.

Bush, Peter, tr. see Sepulveda, Luis.

Bush, Peter R., ed. The Voice of the Turtle: An Anthology of Cuban Stories. LC 97-38169. 400p. 1998. 14.00 (*0-8021-3555-2*, Grove) Grove-Atltic.

Bush, R. H., jt. ed. see Sanders, Charles L.

Bush, Randall B. Recent Ideas of Divine Conflict: The Influences of Psychological & Sociological Theories of Conflict upon the Trinitarian Theology of Paul Tillich & Jurgen Moltmann. LC 91-24962. 340p. 1991. lib. bdg. 99.95 (*0-7734-9949-0*) E Mellen.

Bush, Ray. Economic Crisis & the Politics of Reform in Egypt. LC 99-41454. 184p. 1999. 55.00 (*0-8133-3676-7*) HarpC.

Bush, Ray, ed. see Burgess, Doris.

Bush, Richard. A Parents' Guide to Child Therapy. LC 94-72054. 352p. 1994. pap. 40.00 (*1-56821-315-8*) Aronson.

Bush, Richard A., ed. Exporting to Japan. rev. ed. 57p. 1989. pap. text 15.00 (*0-317-02787-5*, Pub. by Am Chmbr Commerce) Transaction Pubs.

Bush, Richard C., et al. The Religious World: Communities of Faith. 3rd ed. (Illus.). 454p. (C). 1993. 73.00 (*0-02-317529-X*, Macmillan Coll) P-H.

Bush, Richard J. Reindeer, Dogs, & Snow-Shoes: A Journal of Siberian Travel & Explorations Made in the Years 1865, 1866 & 1867. LC 72-115514. (Russia Observed Ser., No. 1). (Illus.). 1970. reprint ed. 29.95 (*0-405-03011-8*) Ayer.

Bush, Rita, et al. Can You Come Here Where I Am? The Poetry & Prose of Seven Breast Cancer Survivors. LC 98-14173. 233p. (Orig.). 1998. pap. 21.95 (*1-880664-25-9*) E M Pr.

Bush, Robert. Grace King: A Southern Destiny. LC 83-9849. (Southern Literary Studies). 335p. 1983. pap. 103.90 (*0-7837-8448-1*, 204925300010) Bks Demand.

Bush, Robert A., et al. The Promise of Mediation: Responding to Conflict Through Empowerment & Recognition. LC 94-27217. (Management Ser.). 336p. 1994. text 34.95 (*0-7879-0027-3*) Jossey-Bass.

Bush, Robert G. Bird Stencil Designs. (Pictorial Archive Ser.). (Illus.). 64p. (Orig.). 1991. pap. 5.95 (*0-486-26704-0*) Dover.

— Designs for Glass Etching. (Illus.). 48p. 1989. pap. 4.95 (*0-486-26000-3*) Dover.

Bush, Robert G., jt. auth. see Capp, Robert A.

Bush, Robert H. Gray Whales, Wandering Giants. LC 97-81071. (Illus.). 144p. 1998. pap. 19.95 (*1-55143-114-9*) Orca Bk Pubs.

Bush, Robert K. Handbook of Allergy & Rhinitis. LC 96-42504. (Illus.). 304p. 1997. pap. text 34.95 (*0-86542-433-0*) Blackwell Sci.

Bush, Roderick D. We Are Not What We Seem: Black Nationalism & Class Struggle in the American Century. LC 98-25483. 272p. 1998. text 32.50 (*0-8147-1317-3*) NYU Pr.

***Bush, Roderick D.** We Are Not What We Seem: Black Nationalism & Class Struggle in the American Century. 2000. pap. text 19.00 (*0-8147-1318-1*) NYU Pr.

***Bush, Roger.** FAU: The Third Generation. 156p. 1999. pap. 38.00 (*1-85072-211-0*, Pub. by W Sessions) St Mut.

Bush, Ronald. American Voice/American Voices: An Inaugural Lecture Delivered Before the University of Oxford on 27 May 1999. LC 99-57697. write for info. (*0-19-951393-7*) OUP.

Bush, Ronald. The Genesis of Ezra Pound's Cantos. LC 76-3245. (Illus.). 346p. 1989. reprint ed. pap. 107.30 (*0-608-02528-3*, 206317200004) Bks Demand.

Bush, Ronald, ed. T. S. Eliot: The Modernist in History. (Cambridge Studies in American Literature & Culture: No. 51). 192p. (C). 1991. text 49.95 (*0-521-39074-5*) Cambridge U Pr.

Bush, Ronald, jt. ed. see Barkan, Elazar.

Bush, Ronald F., jt. auth. see Burns, Alvin C.

Bush, Rosemary, ed. see Cline, Catherine C.

Bush, Russell, jt. auth. see Lieberman, Ron.

Bush, Sam. Carving Techniques & Projects. 1986. pap. text 19.95 incl. VHS (*0-918804-59-0*, 60017) Taunton.

— Sam Bush Teaches Bluegrass Mandolin Repertoire, Level 4. 40p. 1999. pap. 19.95 incl. audio compact disk (*0-7935-9950-4*) H Leonard.

Bush, Sarah. The Silk Industry. 1989. pap. 25.00 (*0-85263-706-3*, Pub. by Shire Pubns) St Mut.

Bush, Sarah L. The Book of Pizzas & Italian Breads. (Book of...Ser.). (Illus.). 120p. (Orig.). 1989. pap. 12.00 (*0-89586-788-5*, HP Books) Berkley Pub.

Bush, Sargent. The Writings of Thomas Hooker: Spiritual Adventure in Two Worlds. LC 79-5404. 399p. 1980. reprint ed. pap. 123.70 (*0-608-01976-3*, 206263100003) Bks Demand.

Bush, Spencer H. Interpretive Report on Nondestructive Examination Techniques, Procedure A vs., B vs., C, Etc., for Piping & Heavy Section. 1997. pap. 130.00 (*0-9656164-4-4*, 420) Welding Res Coun.

Bush, Susan. Chinese Literati on Painting: Su Shih, 1037-1101 to Tung Ch'i-Ch'ang, 1555-1636. LC 78-152698. (Harvard-Yenching Institute Studies: No. 27). (Illus.). 239p. 1971. pap. 9.50 (*0-674-12425-1*) HUP.

Bush, Susan & Murck, Christian F., eds. Theories of the Arts in China. LC 83-42551. (Illus.). 474p. reprint ed. pap. 147.00 (*0-8357-4203-2*, 203698200006) Bks Demand.

Bush, Susan & Shih, Hsio-Yen. Early Chinese Texts on Painting. (Harvard Yenching Institute Ser.). (Illus.). 416p. 1985. pap. 20.00 (*0-674-22025-0*) HUP.

Bush, T. L. The Official Barbecue Cookbook. LC 95-45904. 70p. 1996. pap. 13.95 (*0-88415-593-5*, 5593) Gulf Pub.

— Official Tex-Mex Cookbook. LC 96-29844. 74p. (Orig.). 1997. pap. 14.95 (*0-88415-592-7*, 5592) Gulf Pub.

Bush, Thomas E. Social Security Disability Practice, 2 vols. 2nd ed. 304p. 1992. ring bd. 159.00 incl. disk (*0-938065-07-6*) James Pub Santa Ana.

Bush, Timothy. Benjamin McFadden & the Robot Babysitter. 1998. lib. bdg. 18.99 (*0-517-79985-5*, Crown) Crown Pub Group.

— Benjamin McFadden & the Robot Babysitter. LC 97-52589. (J). (gr. k-3). 1998. 17.00 (*0-517-79984-7*) Crown Pub Group.

***Bush, Timothy.** Ferocious Girls, Steamroller Boys & Other Poems in Between. LC 99-31532. 64p. (J). (gr. 1-4). 2000. lib. bdg. 17.99 (*0-531-33250-0*) Orchard Bks Watts.

— Ferocious Girls, Steamroller Boys & Other Poems in Between. LC 99-31532. (Illus.). 64p. (J). (gr. 1-4). 2000. 16.95 (*0-531-30250-4*) Orchard Bks Watts.

Bush, Timothy. Grunt! The Primitive Cave Boy. LC 94-27703. (Illus.). 32p. (J). (ps-3). 1995. 15.00 (*0-517-79967-7*, Pub. by Crown Bks Yng Read) Random.

— James in the House of Aunt Prudence. 1996. 12.19 (*0-606-10853-X*, Pub. by Turtleback) Demco.

Bush, Tony. Theories of Educational Management, Second Edition. 2nd ed. (One-Off Ser.). (Illus.). 176p. 1995. pap. (*1-85396-283-X*) Corwin Pr.

Bush, Tony, ed. Managing Education: Theory & Practice. (Management in Education Ser.). 176p. 1989. pap. 34.95 (*0-335-09242-X*) OpUniv Pr.

Bush, Tony & Middlewood, David, eds. Managing People in Education. (Educational Management Ser.). (Illus.). 240p. 1997. pap. (*1-85396-336-4*) Corwin Pr.

Bush, Tony & West-Burnham, John, eds. The Principles of Education Management. 288p. 1994. pap. 57.50 (*0-582-23904-4*, Pub. by Addison-Wesley) Trans-Atl Phila.

Bush, Tony, et al. Directors of Education: Facing Reform. 240p. 1989. pap. write for info. (*1-85302-506-2*, Pub. by Jessica Kingsley) Taylor & Francis.

— Managing Autonomous Schools: The Grant-Maintained Experience. 241p. 1993. pap. 33.00 (*1-85396-202-3*, Pub. by P Chapman) Taylor & Francis.

Bush, Vanessa T., jt. auth. see Banks, Tyra.

Bush, Vannevar. Endless Horizons. LC 74-26253. (History, Philosophy & Sociology of Science Ser.). 1975. reprint ed. 21.95 (*0-405-06581-7*) Ayer.

— Modern Arms & Free Men: A Discussion of the Role of Science in Preserving Democracy. LC 85-14840. 273p. 1985. reprint ed. lib. bdg. 65.00 (*0-313-24985-7*, BMOA, Greenwood Pr) Greenwood.

— Science the Endless Frontier: A Report to the President. Cohen, I. Bernard, ed. LC 79-7953. (Three Centuries of Science in America Ser.). 1980. reprint ed. lib. bdg. 28.60 (*0-405-12534-8*) Ayer.

Bush, W. M. Antarctica & International Law: A Collection of Inter-State & National Documents, 3 vols. LC 82-12408. 1991. ring bd. 645.00 (*0-379-01255-3*) Oceana.

Bush, W. Meiggs, jt. auth. see Tapley, George H.

Bush, William. The Mystery of the Church: The Pilgrimage of an Orthodox Convert. 158p. 1999. pap. 22.95 (*0-9649141-7-4*) Regina Orthodox.

— To Quell the Terror: The True Story of the Carmelite Martyrs of Compiegne. LC 98-33217. 244p. 1999. pap. 11.95 (*0-935216-67-7*) ICS Pubns.

***Bush, William H., et al.** Radiology Life Support (rad-ls) A Practical Approach. (Illus.). 208p. 1999. pap. text 35.00 (*0-340-74158-9*) OUP.

***Bush, William S. & Greer, Anja S., eds.** Mathematics Assessment: A Practical Handbook for Grades 9-12. LC 99-45423. (Classroom Assessment for School Mathematics Ser.). (Illus.). 144p. (YA). (gr. 9-12). 1999. pap. 20.95 (*0-87353-476-X*) NCTM.

Bush, William S., tr. & intro. see Bernanos, Georges.

Busha, Charles H. & Harter, Stephen P., eds. Research Methods in Librarianship: Techniques & Interpretation. LC 79-8864. (Library & Information Science Ser.). 432p. 1980. text 55.00 (*0-12-147550-6*) Acad Pr.

Busha, Gary, ed. see Hammond, Liz.

Busha, Gary C. Willowdown. 34p. 1995. pap. 5.00 (*1-891725-01-7*) Wolfsong Pubns.

Busha, Gary C., ed. see Halla, Chris.

Busha, Gary C., ed. see Koehler, Michael.

Busha, Mary. Devotions to Build up Your Relationships. (Proverbs for Busy Women Ser.: Vol. 3). 128p. 1995. pap. 7.99 (*0-8054-5387-3*, 4253-87) Broadman.

Busha, Mary, ed. Devotions to Refresh You in Your Work. LC 94-36448. (Proverbs for Busy Women Ser.: Vol. 2). 128p. 1995. 7.99 (*0-8054-5388-1*, 4253-88) Broadman.

— Devotions to Strengthen Your Walk with God. (Proverbs for Busy Women Ser.: Vol. 1). 128p. 1985. pap. text 7.99 (*0-8054-5386-5*, 4253-86) Broadman.

Busha, William J. 25 Mountain Bike Tours in Vermont: Scenic Tours Along Dirt Roads, Forest Trails, & Forgotten Byways. LC 89-32132. (25 Mountain Bike Tours Ser.). (Illus.). 176p. (Orig.). 1989. pap. 12.00 (*0-88150-130-1*, Pub. by Countryman) Norton.

Bushart, Howard. Soldiers of God. 384p. 1999. mass mkt. 5.99 (*0-7860-0649-8*) Pinnacle Books.

Bushart, Howard, et al. Soldiers of God: White Supremacists & Their Holy War for America. 320p. 1998. 22.95 (*1-57566-206-X*, Knsington) Kensgtn Pub Corp.

***Bushart, Howard L.** Soldiers of God. 2000. pap. 13.00 (*1-57566-659-6*, Knsington) Kensgtn Pub Corp.

Bushberg, Jerrold T. The Essential Physics of Medical Imaging. 2nd ed. 760p. text 89.00 (*0-683-30118-7*) Lppncott W & W.

Bushberg, Jerrold T., et al. The Essential Physics of Medical Imaging. LC 93-34268. 575p. 1993. 75.00 (*0-683-01140-5*) Lppncott W & W.

Bushby, Alex, jt. auth. see Lee.

Bushby, Katherine M. D. & Anderson, Louise V. B., eds. Muscular Dystrophy: Methods & Protocols. (Methods in Molecular Medicine Ser.: Vol. 43). (Illus.). 300p. 2000. 99.50 (*0-89603-695-2*) Humana.

Bushe, Gervase R. Estructuras de Aprendizaje Paralelo: La Innovacion de la Burocracia. (SPA.). (C). 1992. pap. text 11.33 (*0-201-51870-8*) Addison-Wesley.

Bushe, K. A., et al, eds. Stabilizing Cardiocervical Operations, Calcium Antagonists in SAH: Current Legal Issues. (Advances in Neurosurgery Ser.: Vol. 18). (Illus.). 384p. 1990. pap. 86.00 (*0-387-51967-X*) Spr-Verlag.

Bushee, Frederick A. Ethnic Factors in the Population of Boston. LC 76-129393. (American Immigration Collection. Series 2). 1970. reprint ed. 16.95 (*0-405-00548-2*) Ayer.

Bushell, Agnes. Days of the Dead. LC 94-68038. 290p. 1995. pap. 9.00 (*0-9639050-8-2*) J Brown Bks.

— Death by Crystal. LC 92-41202. (Illus.). 160p. (Orig.). 1993. pap., per. 8.95 (*0-9624626-5-9*) Astarte Shell Pr.

— The Enumerator, Vol. 1. LC 96-70960. (Mask Noir Ser.). 256p. (Orig.). 1997. pap. 13.99 (*1-85242-554-7*) Serpents Tail.

— Local Deities. LC 88-43569. 306p. (Orig.). 1990. pap. 11.95 (*0-915306-82-4*) Curbstone.

Bushell, Anthony. Austria, 1945-1955: Studies in Political & Cultural Re-Emergence. ix, 133p. 1996. write for info. (*0-7083-1339-6*, Pub. by Univ Wales Pr) Paul & Co Pubs.

Bushell, Brenda. Greening. 160p. 1995. pap. text 26.27 (*0-13-150096-1*) P-H.

Bushell, Chris. Jane's Urban Transport Systems, 1997-98: Transport Systems, Manufacturers & Products on an International Scale. 16th ed. 1997. 350.00 (*0-7106-1562-0*) Janes Info Group.

Bushell, Chris, ed. Jane's Urban Transport Systems, 98-99. 1998. pap. text 380.00 (*0-7106-1812-3*) Janes Info Group.

Bushell, Frank W., Sr. Driveways, Entries, Patios & Decks. (Landscape by Owner Ser.: Vol. 2). (Illus.). 352p. 1996. spiral bd. 39.95 (*0-9650695-4-0*) One Leaf.

— A Landscape Architect's Consultation. (Landscape by Owner Ser.: Vol. 1). (Illus.). 382p. 1996. spiral bd. 45.00 (*0-9650695-0-8*) One Leaf.

Bushell, Garvin & Tucker, Mark. Jazz from the Beginning. LC 98-7966. (Illus.). 196p. (Orig.). 1998. reprint ed. pap. 14.95 (*0-306-80848-X*) Da Capo.

Bushell, Isobel. Rudolph the Red-Nosed Reindeer: Musical Board Book. 12p. (J). (ps up). 1999. bds. 5.95 (*0-694-00564-9*) HarpC Child Bks.

— Santa Claus Is Coming to Town Board Book. (Musical Board Bk.). 12p. (J). (ps up). 1993. 5.95 (*0-694-00563-0*, HarpFestival) HarpC Child Bks.

Bushell, John J. Bermuda Handbook. 1976. lib. bdg. 59.95 (*0-8490-1492-1*) Gordon Pr.

Bushell, Keith. Papuan Epic. LC 75-35276. reprint ed. 32.50 (*0-404-14106-4*) AMS Pr.

Bushell, M. E., ed. Computers in Fermentation Technology: Progress in Industrial Microbiology, 25 1988. x, 98p. 1988. 123.00 (*0-444-42979-4*) Elsevier.

Bushell, Michael. The Songs of Zion: A Contemporary Case for Exclusive Psalmody. 240p. 1993. pap. 14.00 (*1-884527-04-3*) Crown & Covenant.

Bushell, R. Netsuke Masks. LC 84-48693. (Illus.). 208p. 1995. reprint ed. 80.00 (*0-8348-0341-0*) Weatherhill.

Bushell, Raymond. Collectors' Netsuke: An In-Depth Study of Japanese Miniature Sculptures. LC 70-139687. (Illus.). 200p. 1971. 47.50 (*0-8348-0056-X*) Weatherhill.

— The INRO Handbook: Studies of Netsuke, Inro & Lacquer. LC 78-32054. (Illus.). 264p. 1979. 75.00 (*0-8348-0135-3*) Weatherhill.

— Introduction to Netsuke. LC 78-147176. (Illus.). 80p. 1971. 12.95 (*0-8048-0905-4*) Tuttle Pubng.

— Netsuke Familiar & Unfamiliar: New Principles for Collecting. LC 75-22420. (Illus.). 260p. 1976. 75.00 (*0-8348-0115-9*) Weatherhill.

— The Wonderful World of Netsuke. 72p. 1995. pap. 12.95 (*0-8048-2022-8*) Tuttle Pubng.

Bushell, Raymond, tr. see Reikichi, Ueda.

Bushell, S. W. Chinese Art, 2 vols., Set. (C). 1988. 400.00 (*0-7855-0058-8*, Pub. by Print Hse) St Mut.

Bushell, S. W., tr. see Tichane, Robert.

***Bushell, Sandrajeanne.** Emergency Supplies. (Illus.). 150p. 1999. 25.00 (*1-58499-005-8*, 180) Full Spectrums.

— Family Medical Care. (Illus.). 258p. 1999. ring bd. 30.00 (*1-58499-002-3*, 130) Full Spectrums.

— Is Your Pet Ready for This? Be Prepared to Take Care of Your Pet During an Emergency. (Illus.). 200p. 1999. 25.00 (*1-58499-000-7*, 100) Full Spectrums.

— Last Minute Lists: If You Had Only 15 Minutes to Evacuate, What Would You Take With You? (Illus.). 46p. 1999. 10.00 (*1-58499-006-6*, 190) Full Spectrums.

— My Medical Records. 208p. 1999. ring bd. 25.00 (*1-58499-003-1*, 150) Full Spectrums.

— Pet Medical Records. 154p. 1999. 15.00 (*1-58499-001-5*, 120) Full Spectrums.

— Preparing Your Family Records & Finances for an Emergency. (Illus.). 234p. 1999. 25.00 (*1-58499-004-X*, 170) Full Spectrums.

Bushell, Tony. Key Geography: Basics Pupils' Book. (Illus.). 112p. (YA). (gr. 6-9). 1999. pap., student ed. 19.95 (*0-7487-4310-3*, Pub. by S Thornes Pubs) Trans-Atl Phila.

***Bushell, Tony.** Key Geography Basics: Activity Masters. (Illus.). 112p. 2000. pap., teacher ed. 59.50 (*0-7487-5199-8*, Pub. by S Thornes Pubs) Trans-Atl Phila.

Bushell, Tony & Smith, John. Key Geography Teacher Resource Pack, No. 2. 128p. 1998. pap., teacher ed. 195.00 (*0-7487-3710-3*) St Mut.

Bushell, Tony, jt. auth. see Waugh, David.

Bushell, Tony, jt. auth. see Wough, David.

Bushenkov, Vladimir A. & Smirnov, Georgi V. Stabilization Problems with Constraints: Analysis & Computational Aspects. 304p. 1998. text 62.00 (*90-5699-141-8*) Gordon & Breach.

Busher, Peter & Baublitz, Millard. Physical Science, Vols. 101-102. 2nd ed. 152p. (C). 1996. text, lab manual ed. 32.80 (*0-536-58601-2*) Pearson Custom.

Busher, Peter & Baublitz, Millard. Physical Science 101-102. 3rd ed. 162p. (C). 1995. text, lab manual ed. 35.60 (*0-536-59094-X*) Pearson Custom.

***Busher, Peter E. & Dziweciolowski, Ryszard.** Beaver Protection, Management & Utilization in Europe & North America. LC 99-30049. 182p. 1999. write for info. (*0-306-46121-8*, Kluwer Plenum) Kluwer Academic.

Bushev, Michael. Synergetics: Chaos, Order, Self-Organization. LC 95-115787. 252p. 1994. text 53.00 (*981-02-1286-0*) World Scientific Pub.

Bushey, Galen, ed. Prayer Book Concordance. 977p. 1988. 49.95 (*0-89869-150-8*) Church Pub Inc.

Bushey, Jeanne. Holiday Hang-Ups! A Step-by-Step Guide to Making 3-D Arts & Crafts. Britt, Leslie, ed. (Illus.). 64p. (Orig.). (J). (gr. k-3). 1995. pap. text 7.95 (*0-86530-308-8*, IP308-8) Incentive Pubns.

— A Sled Dog for Moshi. LC 93-13568. (Illus.). 40p. (J). (gr. 3-7). 1994. lib. bdg. 14.89 (*1-56282-632-8*, Pub. by Hyprn Child) Little.

— A Sled Dog for Moshi. large type ed. (Illus.). 40p. (J). (ps-3). 1994. write for info. (*0-920534-85-6*) Hyperion Pr.

Bushfield, Deborah & Bushfield, James. Things They Never Taught You in Seminary: Practical Tips for Dealing with the Nitty-Gritty Issues of Pastoral Life. LC 93-36050. 160p. 1994. pap. 9.99 (*0-8361-3649-7*) Herald Pr.

Bushfield, James, jt. auth. see Bushfield, Deborah.

Bushing, David. Sports Equipment Price Guide. LC 95-79728. (Illus.). 336p. 1995. pap. 16.95 (*0-87341-349-0*, SEP01) Krause Pubns.

Bushinsky, David A., ed. Renal Osteodystrophy. LC 97-46074. (Illus.). 424p. 1998. text 107.00 (*0-397-51836-6*) Lppncott W & W.

Bushkin, Estitta, jt. auth. see Bushkin, Gary.

Bushkin, Gary & Bushkin, Estitta. All about Green Food Supplements. (FAQs All about Health Ser.). 1999. mass mkt. 2.99 (*0-89529-963-1*, Avery) Penguin Putnam.

Bushko, Andrew. Introduction to Algebra with Applications for a Variety of Technologies. 324p. (C). 1998. spiral bd. 31.95 (*0-7872-5365-0*, 41536501) Kendall-Hunt.

Bushko, David, ed. Dartnell's Advertising Manager's Handbook. 4th ed. 484p. 1997. pap. 89.95 (*0-85013-312-2*) Dartnell Corp.

— Dartnell's Advertising Manager's Handbook. 4th rev. ed. LC 96-71225. 484p. 1997. 89.95 (*0-85013-249-5*) Dartnell Corp.

Bushkoff, Leonard, jt. auth. see Engelbourg, Saul.

Bushkovitch. History of Russia. (C). Date not set. pap. write for info. (*0-669-35381-7*) HM.

Bushkovitch, Paul. The Merchants of Moscow, Fifteen-Eighty to Sixteen-Fifty. LC 79-14491. 224p. reprint ed. pap. 63.90 (*0-608-15699-X*, 2031626) Bks Demand.

Bushkovitch, Paul, tr. see Jansson, Maija & Rogozhin, Nikolai.

Bushkowsky, Aaron. Ed & Mabel Go to the Moon. 94p. 1994. pap. text 11.95 (*0-88982-137-2*, Pub. by Oolichan Bks) Genl Dist Srvs.

***Bushkowsky, Aaron.** Strangers among Us. 96p. 2000. pap. 13.95 (*0-88754-584-X*) Theatre Comm.

Bushman, A. V., et al. Intense Dynamic Loading of Condensed Matter. 275p. 1992. 142.00 (*1-56032-003-6*) Hemisp Pub.

Bushman, Claudia L. America Discovers Columbus: How an Italian Explorer Became an American Hero. LC 91-50809. (Illus.). 232p. 1992. reprint ed. pap. 72.00 (*0-608-20673-3*, 207178000002) Bks Demand.

Bushman, Claudia L. A Good Poor Man's Wife: Being a Chronicle of Harriet Hanson Robinson & Her Family in Nineteenth Century New England. LC 80-54470. (Illus.). 300p. 1998. reprint ed. pap. 17.95 (*0-87451-883-0*) U Pr of New Eng.

Bushman, Claudia L., ed. Mormon Sisters: Women in Early Utah. LC 97-13396. (Illus.). 336p. 1997. pap. 17.95 (*0-87421-233-2*) Utah St U Pr.

Bushman, Claudia L., et al, eds. Proceedings of the Assembly of the Lower Counties on the Delaware, 1770-1776: The Constitutional Convention of 1776, & of the House of Assembly of the Delaware State, 1776-1781. LC 85-40510. 616p. 1986. 60.00 (*0-685-47145-4*) U Delaware Pr.

Bushman, Claudia L. & Bushman, Richard L. Mormons in America. (Religion in America Ser.). (Illus.). 144p. (J). 1999. text 22.00 (*0-19-510677-6*) OUP.

Bushman, Claudia L., et al. Proceedings of the Assembly of the Lower Counties on the Delaware 1770-1776, the Constitutional Convention of 1776 & of the House of Assembly of the Delaware State 1776-1781. LC 86-30791. (Illus.). 1024p. 1988. 75.00 (*0-87413-309-2*) U Delaware Pr.

Bushman, Eva M. Biology. 205p. (Orig.). (C). 1980. pap. text 12.95 (*0-89420-110-7*, 238040); audio 242.20 (*0-89420-203-0*, 238000) Natl Book.

B

An Asterisk (*) at the beginning of an entry indicates that the title is appearing for the first time.

— First Aid: Student Syllabus. (YA). (gr. 9-12). 1979. text 84.95 incl. audio (*0-89420-207-3*, 380000); pap. text 8.95 (*0-89420-075-5*, 380020) Natl Book.
— Introductory Chemistry. 130p. (C). pap. text 10.95 (*0-89420-217-0*, 236025); audio 165.95 (*0-89420-216-2*, 236000) Natl Book.
Bushman, John H. Teaching the English Language. (Illus.). 156p. (C). 1988. pap. text 30.95 (*0-398-05466-5*) C C Thomas.
***Bushman, John H.** Teaching the English Language. 2nd ed. LC 00-32611. 2000. write for info. (*0-398-07093-8*) C C Thomas.
Bushman, John H. & Bushman, Kay P. Teaching English Creatively. 2nd ed. LC 94-7069. (Illus.). 254p. (C). 1994. text 50.95 (*0-398-05911-X*) C C Thomas.
***Bushman, John H. & Haas, Kay P.** Using Young Adult Literature in the English Classroom. 3rd ed. LC 99-86306. 320p. 2000. pap. 44.00 (*0-13-026455-5*) P-H.
Bushman, Kay P., jt. auth. see Bushman, John H.
Bushman, Richard L. From Puritan to Yankee: Character & the Social Order in Connecticut, 1690-1765. 352p. 1980. pap. 17.95 (*0-674-32551-6*) HUP.
— Joseph Smith & the Beginnings of Mormonism. LC 84-2451. 270p. 1984. text 24.95 (*0-252-01143-0*) U of Ill Pr.
— Joseph Smith & the Beginnings of Mormonism. LC 84-2451. 270p. 1988. 14.95 (*0-252-06012-1*) U of Ill Pr.
— King & People in Provincial Massachusetts. LC 84-10383. (Institute of Early American History & Culture Ser.). x, 280p. (C). 1992. pap. text 24.95 (*0-8078-4398-9*) U of NC Pr.
— Making Space for the Mormons. (Leonard J. Arrington Mormon History Lecture Ser.: Vol. 2). 40p. (Orig.). 1997. pap. 5.95 (*0-87421-230-8*) Utah St U Pr.
— The Refinement of America: Persons, Houses, Cities. LC 93-13118. 1993. reprint ed. pap. 18.00 (*0-679-74414-2*) Vin Bks.
Bushman, Richard L., ed. The Great Awakening: Documents on the Revival of Religion, 1740-1745. LC 74-108821. (Institute of Early American History & Culture Ser.). xiv, 174p. (C). 1989. reprint ed. pap. 17.95 (*0-8078-4260-5*) U of NC Pr.
Bushman, Richard L., jt. auth. see Bushman, Claudia L.
Bushman, Tanisse, ed. see Leonard, Anne & Terrell, John.
Bushnaq, Inea, ed. Arab Folktales. LC 85-9569. 416p. 1987. pap. 18.00 (*0-394-75179-5*) Pantheon.
Bushnaq, Inea, tr. see Jiryis, Sabri.
Bushnell, jt. auth. see Cohen.
Bushnell, Amy T. Establishing Exceptionalism: Historiography & the Colonial Americas. (An Expanding World Ser.). 400p. 1995. 124.95 (*0-86078-504-1*, Pub. by Variorum) Ashgate Pub Co.
— Situado & Sabana: Spain's Support System for the Presido & Mission Provinces of Florida. 1995. pap. text 26.95 (*0-8203-1712-8*) U of Ga Pr.
Bushnell, Brooks. Directors & Their Films: A Comprehensive Reference, 1895-1990. LC 92-56633. 1045p. 1993. lib. bdg. 155.00 (*0-89950-766-2*) McFarland & Co.
***Bushnell, Candace.** Four Blondes. 192p. 2000. 24.00 (*0-87113-819-0*, Atlntc Mnthly) Grove-Atltic.
— Sex & the City. LC 97-15901. 240p. 1997. mass mkt. 13.95 (*0-446-67354-4*, Pub. by Warner Bks) Little.
Bushnell, Chris. High Tech Trains. 1992. 9.98 (*1-55521-777-X*) Bk Sales Inc.
Bushnell, Colin J. & Kutzko, Philip C. The Admissible Dual of GL(N) Via Compact Open Subgroups. LC 92-33614. (Annals of Mathematics Studies: No. 129). 313p. (C). 1993. text 75.00 (*0-691-03256-4*, Pub. by Princeton U Pr); pap. text 35.00 (*0-691-02114-7*, Pub. by Princeton U Pr) Cal Prin Full Svc.
Bushnell, D. Computerized Buckling Analysis of Shells. (Mechanics of Elastic Stability Ser.). 1985. text 293.00 (*90-247-3099-6*) Kluwer Academic.
Bushnell, D. & Hefner, J., eds. Viscous Drag Reduction in Boundary Layers. (PAAS Ser.: Vol. 123). 530p. 1990. 75.95 (*0-930403-66-5*, V-123) AIAA.
Bushnell, D. I., Jr. Cahokia & Surrounding Mound Groups. (Harvard University Peabody Museum of Archaeology & Ethnology Papers: Vol. 3, No. 1). 1972. reprint ed. pap. 25.00 (*0-527-01192-4*) Periodicals Srv.
Bushnell, Dana E., ed. "Nagging" Questions: Feminist Ethics in Everyday Life. LC 94-32590. (New Feminist Perspectives Ser.). 376p. 1995. lib. bdg. 24.95 (*0-8476-8006-1*) Rowman.
— "Nagging" Questions: Feminist Ethics in Everyday Life. LC 94-32590. (New Feminist Perspectives Ser.). 414p. 1995. pap. text 27.95 (*0-8476-8007-X*) Rowman.
Bushnell, David. Eduardo Santos & the Good Neighbor, 1938-1942. LC 67-65496. (Latin American Monographs: Ser. 2, No. 4). 136p. reprint ed. pap. 42.20 (*0-7837-4984-8*, 204465100004) Bks Demand.
— Making of Modern Colombia: A Nation in Spite of Itself. 384p. 1994. pap. 22.50 (*0-520-08289-3*, Pub. by U CA Pr) Cal Prin Full Svc.
— Santander Regime in Gran Colombia. No. 5--5. LC 78-100248. 381p. 1970. reprint ed. lib. bdg. 35.00 (*0-8371-2981-8*, BUSR, Greenwood Pr) Greenwood.
Bushnell, David & MacAulay, Neill. The Emergence of Latin America in the Nineteenth Century. 2nd ed. LC 93-2844. (Illus.). 352p. (C). 1994. text 60.00 (*0-19-508401-2*); pap. text 25.95 (*0-19-508402-0*) OUP.
Bushnell, David I., Jr. Burials of the Algonquian, Siouan & Caddoan Tribes West of the Mississippi. (Bureau of American Ethnology Bulletins Ser.). 103p. 1995. lib. bdg. 79.00 (*0-7812-4083-2*) Rprt Serv.
— Choctaw of Bayou Lacomb, St. Tammany Parish, Louisiana. (Bureau of American Ethnology Bulletins Ser.). 99p. 1995. lib. bdg. 69.00 (*0-7812-4048-4*) Rprt Serv.
Bushnell, David I. Evidence of Indian Occupancy in Albemarle County, Virginia, Pt. 7. fac. ed. (Smithsonian Miscellaneous Collections: No. 89). (Illus.). 38p. 1933. reprint ed. pap. text 4.38 (*1-55567-851-3*) Coyote Press.
Bushnell, David I., Jr. Native Cemeteries & Forms of Burial East of the Mississippi. (Bureau of American Ethnology Bulletins Ser.). 160p. 1995. lib. bdg. 79.00 (*0-7812-4071-9*) Rprt Serv.
Bushnell, David I. Native Cemeteries & Forms of Burial East of the Mississippi. 1988. reprint ed. lib. bdg. 49.00 (*0-7812-0095-4*) Rprt Serv.
Bushnell, David I., Jr. Native Villages & Village Sites East of the Mississippi. 1988. reprint ed. lib. bdg. 49.00 (*0-7812-0092-X*) Rprt Serv.
— Villages of the Algonquian, Siouan & Caddoan Tribes West of the Mississippi. (Illus.). 211p. 1991. reprint ed. 59.00 (*1-878592-24-6*); reprint ed. pap. 39.00 (*1-878592-23-8*) Native Amer Bk Pubs.
Bushnell, David I., Jr., ed. Native Villages & Village Sites East of the Mississippi. (Bureau of American Ethnology Bulletins Ser.). 111p. 1995. lib. bdg. 79.00 (*0-7812-4069-7*) Rprt Serv.
— Villages of the Algonquian, Siouan, & Caddoan Tribes West of the Mississippi. (Bureau of American Ethnology Bulletins Ser.). 211p. 1995. lib. bdg. 89.00 (*0-7812-4077-8*) Rprt Serv.
Bushnell, David L. Villages of the Algonquian, Siouan & Caddoan Tribes West of the Mississippi. 1988. reprint ed. lib. bdg. 39.00 (*0-7812-0742-8*) Rprt Serv.
Bushnell, Henry. History of Granville, Licking County, Ohio. (Illus.). 372p. 1993. reprint ed. lib. bdg. 41.50 (*0-8328-2928-5*) Higginson Bk Co.
Bushnell, Holly W., ed. see Cook, Harvey A. & Pederson, Duane E.
Bushnell, Horace. God in Christ. LC 76-39568. reprint ed. 47.50 (*0-404-01245-0*) AMS Pr.
— Nature & the Supernatural As Together Constituting the One System of God. LC 70-39569. reprint ed. 52.50 (*0-404-01246-9*) AMS Pr.
— Views of Christian Nurture & Subjects Related Thereto. LC 74-23297. 264p. 1975. reprint ed. lib. bdg. 50.00 (*0-8201-1147-3*) Schol Facsimiles.
— Women's Suffrage: The Reform Against Nature. LC 75-33280. 1976. reprint ed. 23.95 (*0-89201-000-2*) Zenger Pub.
Bushnell, Howard. Maria Malibran: A Biography of the Singer. LC 79-14880. (Illus.). 1979. 35.00 (*0-271-00222-0*) Pa St U Pr.
Bushnell, Ian. The Captive Court: A Study of the Supreme Court of Canada. 624p. 1992. 95.00 (*0-7735-0851-1*, Pub. by McG-Queens Univ Pr) CUP Services.
— The Federal Court of Canada: A History, 1875-1992. LC 98-115027. 476p. 1997. text 75.00 (*0-8020-4207-4*) U of Toronto Pr.
Bushnell, Ian W. & Mullin, Jim T. Experimental Psychology: A Computerized Laboratory Course. 272p. 1988. pap. text, student ed. 24.50 (*0-86377-058-4*) L Erlbaum Assocs.
Bushnell, Jack. Circus of the Wolves. LC 93-8092. (Illus.). (J). 1994. 15.00 (*0-688-12554-9*); lib. bdg. 14.93 (*0-688-12555-7*) Lothrop.
— Sky Dancer. LC 94-24577. (Illus.). 32p. 1996. lib. bdg. 15.93 (*0-688-05289-4*) Lothrop.
— Sky Dancer. LC 94-24577. (Illus.). 32p. (J). (ps). 1996. 16.00 (*0-688-05288-6*) Lothrop.
Bushnell, James W. Precious Metals Trade Guide - Adventure in Noble Metals: A to Z Reference Source. Bushnell, Lieselotte, ed. (Illus.). 248p. (Orig.). (C). 1993. per. 22.50 (*0-9632771-0-3*) Trident Pubns.
Bushnell, Joan L., jt. auth. see Randall, Charles H.
Bushnell, John. Mutiny Amid Repression: Russian Soldiers in the Revolution of 1905-1906. LC 84-48849. (Indiana-Michigan Series in Russian & East European Studies). 346p. reprint ed. pap. 107.30 (*0-7837-3693-2*, 205787100009) Bks Demand.
Bushnell, Lieselotte, ed. see Bushnell, James W.
Bushnell, Michael L., jt. auth. see Chen, Xionghao.
Bushnell, O. A. The Gifts of Civilization: Germs & Genocide in Hawai'i. 352p. (Orig.). (C). 1993. pap. text 20.00 (*0-8248-1457-6*) UH Pr.
— Ka'a'awa: A Novel about Hawaii in the 1850s. LC 72-83490. 520p. 1980. pap. 14.95 (*0-8248-0729-4*) UH Pr.
— Molokai. LC 74-31402. 540p. 1982. reprint ed. pap. 14.95 (*0-8248-0287-X*) UH Pr.
— The Return of Lono: A Novel of Captain Cook's Last Voyage. 300p. 1979. reprint ed. pap. 14.95 (*0-87022-931-1*) UH Pr.
Bushnell, O. A., jt. auth. see Daws, Gavan.
Bushnell, O. A., jt. auth. see Hanley, Mary L.
Bushnell, P. Timothy. Transformation of the American Manufacturing Paradigm. LC 94-487. (Studies on Industrial Productivity). 296p. 1994. text 15.00 (*0-8153-1530-9*) Garland.
Bushnell, Paul E., jt. ed. see Bray, Robert C.
Bushnell, Rebecca W. A Culture of Teaching: Early Modern Humanism in Theory & Practice. (Illus.). 232p. 1996. text 39.95 (*0-8014-3235-9*); pap. text 16.95 (*0-8014-8356-5*) Cornell U Pr.
— Prophesying Tragedy: Sign & Voice in Sophocles' Theban Plays. LC 87-47857. 155p. reprint ed. pap. 48.10 (*0-608-20879-5*, 207197800003) Bks Demand.
— Tragedies of Tyrants: Political Thought & Theater in the English Renaissance. LC 89-77175. 216p. 1990. text 37.50 (*0-8014-2271-X*) Cornell U Pr.
Bushnell, Rebecca W. & Nochimson, Richard, eds. King Lear & Macbeth. (Pegasus Shakespeare Bibliographies Ser.: Vol. 2). 115p. 1997. pap. 9.95 (*1-889818-00-3*, P33) Pegasus Pr.
***Bushnell, Richard & Dooley, James.** Bar Code Compliance Labeling for the Supply Chain: How to Do It. Kilbane, Doris, ed. Orig. Title: Compliance Labeling: How to Do It. (Illus.). 112p. 2000. pap. 39.95 (*0-941668-11-8*, Pub. by Tower Hill Pr) Quad II.
Bushnell, Richard, jt. auth. see Pearce, Stephen.
***Bushnell, Rick B.** Using Industry-Compliant Bar Codes. (Illus.). 41p. 2000. pap. 19.00 (*0-9700394-0-9*) Quad II.
Bushnell, Sheridan. Exquisite Torture - The Poetry of Passion, Longing & Obsession. 85p. 1998. pap. 12.00 (*0-9656392-3-1*) Sonorous Pr.
Bushnell, Sheridan. Stepping into the Circle - Healing Parables for a New Century. 4th ed. 96p. 1995. reprint ed. pap. 12.00 (*0-9656392-0-7*) Sonorous Pr.
Bushnell, Sheridan. Where Imagination Meets Infinity. 4th ed. xi, 91p. 1996. reprint ed. pap. 12.00 (*0-9656392-1-5*) Sonorous Pr.
Bushnell, Wayne M. Sunshine & Shadows Through Time: A Book of Poems. 64p. 1992. boxed set 8.95 (*0-87770-561-5*) Ye Galleon.
Bushong. Bright Landscapes. (C). 1992. mass mkt. 19.75 (*0-538-83199-5*) S-W Pub.
Bushong, Carolyn. The 7 Dumbest Relationship Mistakes Smart People Make. 1999. pap. 11.95 (*0-449-00569-0*) Fawcett.
Bushong, Joe G. Accounting & Auditing of Small Businesses. rev. ed. LC 94-32962. (Studies in Entrepreneurship). (Illus.). 144p. 1995. text 20.00 (*0-8153-1935-5*) Garland.
Bushong, Millard K. History of Jefferson County, West Virginia. (Illus.). 438p. 1997. reprint ed. lib. bdg. 46.00 (*0-8328-7185-0*) Higginson Bk Co.
Bushong, Steward C., ed. Radiation Protection. (Essentials of Medical Imaging Ser.). (Illus.). 264p. 1998. pap. text 26.95 (*0-07-012013-7*) McGraw-Hill HPD.
***Bushong, Stewart C.** Computed Tomography. (Essentials of Medical Imaging Ser.). (Illus.). 160p. 2000. pap. text 19.95 (*0-07-134354-7*) McGraw-Hill Prof.
— Diagnostic Ultrasound: Essentials of Medical Imaging Series. LC 99-10455. (Essentials of Medical Imaging Ser.). (Illus.). 150p. 1999. pap. text 26.95 (*0-07-012017-X*) McGraw-Hill HPD.
Bushong, Stewart C. Magnetic Resonance Imaging: Physical & Biological Principles. 2nd ed. LC 95-3071. (Illus.). 512p. (C). (gr. 13). 1995. text 56.00 (*0-8151-1342-0*, 24166) Mosby Inc.
— MRI Study Guide & Exam Review. (Illus.). 256p. (C). (gr. 13). 1995. pap. text, student ed. 27.95 (*0-8151-1340-4*, 26666) Mosby Inc.
— The Radiographic Image & Its Evaluation. (Illus.). 160p. 1999. pap. 19.95 (*0-07-012015-3*) McGraw.
Bushong, Stewart C. Radiologic Science for Technologists. 6th ed. (Illus.). 1997. wbk. ed., lab manual ed. write for info. (*0-8151-1580-6*) Mosby Inc.
Bushong, Stewart C. Radiologic Science for Technologists. 6th ed. LC 96-29488. (Illus.). 608p. (C). (gr. 13). 1997. text 59.00 (*0-8151-1579-2*, 30086) Mosby Inc.
Bushong, Stewart C., ed. see Burns, Evelyn F.
Bushong, Stewart C., ed. see Schubert, Mark J.
Bushong, Stewart C., ed. see Williams, Erica K.
Bushong, William. Uncle Sam's Architects: Builders of the Capitol. LC 94-60547. (Illus.). 64p. (Orig.). (YA). 1994. pap. 7.95 (*0-614-00693-7*) US Capitol Hist.
Bushoven, Neal. Traveling Notes. (Illus.). 128p. 1998. pap. 12.00 (*1-879934-54-X*) St Andrews NC.
Bushrui & Kuzbari, eds. Blue Flame: The Love Letters of Kahlil Gibran to May Ziadah. (Illus.). 118p. 1983. 25.00 (*0-86685-387-1*, LSL0780, Pub. by Librairie du Liban) Intl Bk Ctr.
Bushrui, S. B. & Prentki, Tim, eds. An International Companion to the Poetry of W. B. Yeats. 250p. (C). 1990. text 64.50 (*0-389-20905-8*) B&N Imports.
Bushrui, S. B., ed. see Smith, Byron P.
Bushrui, Suhbil B. Centenary Tribute to J. M. Synge. 356p. 1979. pap. 14.95 (*0-901072-78-8*, Pub. by Smyth) Dufour.
— Kahlil Gibran of Lebanon: A Reevaluation of the Life & Works of Kahlil Gibran. 98p. 1989. 19.95 (*0-86140-279-0*, Pub. by Smyth) Dufour.
Bushrui, Suhbil B., ed. Sunshine & the Moon's Delight: A Centenary Tribute to J. M. Synge. 356p. 1979. 50.00 (*0-900675-55-1*, Pub. by Smyth) Dufour.
Bushrui, Suheil. Gibran of Lebanon. 1986. 15.00 (*0-86685-008-2*) Intl Bk Ctr.
Bushrui, Suheil & Al-Kuzbari, Salma H., trs. Love Letters: Gibran. (Illus.). 136p. 1995. pap. 11.95 (*1-85168-106-X*, Pub. by Onewrld Pubns) Penguin Putnam.
Bushrui, Suheil & Jenkins, Joseph. Kahlil Gibran: Man & Poet. 384p. 1998. 28.95 (*1-85168-177-9*, Pub. by Onewrld Pubns) Penguin Putnam.
Bushrui, Suheil, ed. & tr. see Gibran, Kahlil.
Bushrui, Suheil B. The Style of the Kitab-I-Aqdas: Aspects of the Sublime. LC 94-40159. 74p. (C). 1995. 16.00 (*1-883053-08-0*) Univ Pr MD.
Bushrui, Suheil B., jt. ed. see Welch, Robert.
Bushrui, Suheil Badi & Benstock, Bernard, eds. James Joyce: An International Perspective. (Irish Literary Studies: Vol. #9). 302p. 1981. 59.95 (*0-86140-084-4*, Pub. by Smyth) Dufour.
Bushuk, W. Rye: Chemistry, & Technology. LC 76-29382. 181p. 1976. text 99.00 (*0-913250-11-2*) Am Assn Cereal Chem.
Bushuk, W., jt. ed. see Tkachuk, R.
Bushuyeva, Tatjana S., jt. auth. see Djakov, Yuri L.
Bushway, Stephen. The New Woodburner's Handbook: A Guide to Safe, Healthy & Efficient Woodburning. Twitchell, Mary, ed. LC 91-51125. (Illus.). 168p. 1992. pap. 12.95 (*0-88266-788-2*, Garden Way Pub) Storey Bks.
Bushwich, Nathan. El Calendario Judio. C. M., tr.Tr. of Understanding the Jewish Calendar. (ENG & SPA.). Illus.). 135p. 1992. 11.00 (*1-885220-12-X*) Moznaim.
Bushwich, Nathan, tr. see Yerushalm, Shmuel.
Bushwich, Nathan, tr. & intro. see Yerushalmi, Shmuel.
Bushwick, N., tr. see Yerushalmi, Shmuel.
Bushwick, Nathan. Understanding the Jewish Calendar. 114p. (YA). (gr. 9-12). 1989. 11.00 (*0-940118-17-3*) Moznaim.
Bushwick, Nathan, tr. & adapted by see Yerushalmi, Shmuel.
***Bushy, Angeline.** Orientation to Nursing in the Rural Community. LC 00-8364. 2000. pap. write for info. (*0-7619-1157-X*) Sage.
Bushy, Angeline. Rural Nursing, Vol. 1. (Illus.). 404p. 1991. text 58.00 (*0-8039-3834-9*); pap. text 28.00 (*0-8039-3835-7*) Sage.
— Rural Nursing, Vol. 1. LC 91-83. (Illus.). 424p. reprint ed. pap. 131.50 (*0-608-09627-X*, 205278500001) Bks Demand.
— Rural Nursing, Vol. 2. (Illus.). 358p. 1991. text 52.00 (*0-8039-4240-0*); pap. text 25.00 (*0-8039-4241-9*) Sage.
Bushy, Angeline, ed. Rural Nursing, Vol. 2. LC 91-83. (Illus.). 348p. reprint ed. pap. 107.90 (*0-608-09628-8*, 205278500002) Bks Demand.
Bushy, Angeline, jt. auth. see Sebastian, Juliann G.
Bushy, Thomas L., jt. auth. see Monroe, Jeffrey W.
Busi, F., jt. auth. see Baxendale, J.
Busi, Frederick. The Transformations of Godot. LC 79-4002. 160p. 1980. 19.00 (*0-8131-1392-X*) U Pr of Ky.
Busia, Abena P. Testimonies of Exile. LC 90-81310. (Illus.). 90p. (C). 1990. 19.95 (*0-86543-160-4*); pap. 7.95 (*0-86543-161-2*) Africa World.
Busia, Abena P., jt. ed. see James, Stanlie M.
Busia, Akosua. The Seasons of Beento Blackbird. 1997. per. 12.00 (*0-671-01409-9*) PB.
Busia, Kofi A. The Position of the Chief in the Modern Political System of Ashanti: A Study of the Influence of Contemporary Social Changes on Ashanti Political Institutions. LC 51-13932. 244p. reprint ed. pap. 75.70 (*0-8357-3220-7*, 205709200011) Bks Demand.
Busic, Karen M., ed. see Cleland, David I. & Vlasak, A. Yaroslav.
Busic-Snyder, Cynthia, jt. auth. see Wallschleager, Charles.
Busic, Valerie. Billy's New Home: For Foster Children Everywhere. (Illus.). 40p. (J). (gr. 2-6). 1998. pap. 9.95 (*1-882021-15-0*) Summer.
Busick, Bonnie S. & Gorman, Martha. Ill, Not Insane. (Illus.). 311p. (Orig.). 1986. pap. 12.95 (*0-9617099-0-1*) New Idea Pr.
Busick, Chris, jt. auth. see Baker, Ed.
***Busick, Joan.** Surviving Beyond: Happily Ever After. (Illus.). 139p. 1999. pap. 16.95 (*0-9627836-3-3*) James-Robert Pub Co.
Busick, Joan. Surviving Beyond Happily Ever After. LC 99-233773. (Illus.). x, 139p. 1999. pap. 16.95 (*1-888540-50-8*) James-Robert Pub Co.
Busick, John D., jt. auth. see Siuru, Bill.
Busick, Kathy & Stiggins, Richard J. Making Connections: Case Discussions for Student-Centered Classroom Assessment. 2nd ed. LC 96-79211. (Illus.). 160p. (Orig.). 1996. pap. text 16.00 (*0-9655101-0-7*) Assessmnt Trning.
Busiek, Ann Huntington. Kurt Busiek's Astro City: Family Album. (Illus.). 220p. 1999. pap. 19.95 (*1-58240-034-2*) Image Comics.
***Busiek, Kurt.** Astro City: Confession. (Illus.). 192p. 2000. pap. 19.95 (*1-56389-550-1*, Pub. by DC Comics) Time Warner.
— Astro City: Life in Big City. 192p. pap. 19.95 (*1-56389-551-X*, Pub. by DC Comics) Time Warner.
— Astro City: Life in the Big City. Orig. Title: Kurt Busick's Astro City. 192p. 39.95 (*1-56389-583-8*) DC Comics.
Busiek, Kurt. Astro City: Life in the Big City. Orig. Title: Kurt Busick's Astro City. (Illus.). 192p. 1996. reprint ed. pap. 19.95 (*0-9653290-1-1*) Aegis Ent.
***Busiek, Kurt.** Goblin Moon. (Spider-Man Ser.). (J). 2000. mass mkt. 6.99 (*0-425-17403-4*) Berkley Pub.
Busiek, Kurt. Heroes Return: The Avengers. (Illus.). 112p. 2000. reprint ed. pap. 14.95 (*0-7851-0728-2*, Pub. by Marvel Entrprs) LPC Group.
— Kurt Busiek's Astro City: Family Album. (Illus.). 224p. 1999. 29.95 (*1-56389-537-4*, Pub. by DC Comics) Diamond Comic Distributors Inc.
***Busiek, Kurt.** Kurt Busiek's Astro City: Tarnished Angel. (Illus.). 256p. (J). 2000. 29.95 (*1-56389-653-2*, Pub. by DC Comics) Time Warner.
Busiek, Kurt. Marvels. (Illus.). 216p. 1994. pap. 19.95 (*0-7851-0049-0*) Marvel Entrprs.
— Untold Tales of Spider-Man. 176p. 1997. pap. text 16.95 (*0-7851-0263-9*) Marvel Entrprs.
Busiek, Kurt & Archer, Nathan. Spider-Man: Goblin Moon. LC 99-21555. (Illus.). 304p. 1999. 24.95 (*0-399-14512-5*, G P Putnam) Peng Put Young Read.
Busiek, Kurt & Dini, Paul. Elvira, Mistress of the Dark Vol. 1: Comic Milestones--Comics Format. (Illus.). 152p. (Orig.). 1996. pap. 12.95 (*0-9653109-0-6*, Claypool Comics) Boffin Bks.
Busiek, Kurt, jt. ed. see Lee, Stan.
Busiello, G., et al, eds. Advances of Phase Transitions & Disorder Phenomena: Proceedings of the International Conference, Amalfi, Salerno, June 25-27, 1987. 588p. 1987. pap. 62.00 (*9971-5-0173-2*); text 144.00 (*9971-5-0168-6*) World Scientific Pub.
Businache, Jose L. Bolivar: Visto Por Sus Contemporaneos (As Seen by His Contemporaries) (SPA.). 339p. 1960. pap. 22.99 (*968-16-0898-4*, Pub. by Fondo) Continental Bk.

An Asterisk (*) at the beginning of an entry indicates that the title is appearing for the first time.

Busine, Laurent. Beyond Reason: Art & Psychosis. (Illus.). 196p. 1998. pap. 35.00 (*0-520-21740-3*, Pub. by U CA Pr) Cal Prin Full Svc.

Business & Commercial Aviation Magazine. Cause & Circumstance. 320p. 1996. 29.95 (*0-07-003171-1*) McGraw.

Business & Legal Reports Staff. The BLR Encyclopedia of Performance Appraisal. rev. ed. 440p. 1981. ring bd. 149.95 (*1-55645-536-4*, 536) Busn Legal Reports.

— The Effective Supervisor: How to Discipline. 177p. 1985. per. 29.95 (*1-55645-423-6*, 423) Busn Legal Reports.

— Employer's Handbook of Hazardous Waste Training Programs. 1982. pap. 29.95 (*1-55645-201-2*) Busn Legal Reports.

— Handbook of Hazardous Waste Regulation: How to Protect Employees During Environmental Incident Response, Vol. II. 1985. ring bd. 59.95 (*1-55645-312-4*) Busn Legal Reports.

— Hazardous Waste Compliance Checklists for Supervisors. 1985. pap. 24.95 (*1-55645-304-3*) Busn Legal Reports.

— How to Analyze Jobs: A Step by Step Approach. rev. ed. 82p. 1982. per. 27.95 (*1-55645-402-3*, 402) Busn Legal Reports.

— How to Write Job Descriptions the Easy Way. 1983. per. 27.95 (*1-55645-403-1*, 403) Busn Legal Reports.

— Supervisor's Guide to On-the-Job Alcoholism & Drug Problems. 1986. pap. 9.95 (*1-55645-432-5*) Busn Legal Reports.

Business & Legal Reports Staff, jt. auth. see Thompson, Sue Ellen.

Business & Professional Publishing. 360' Feedback Manual. 169p. (Orig.). 1999. pap. text 175.00 (*1-875680-50-0*) Woodslane.

***Business & Research Associates Staff.** Review of the U. K. Domestic Furniture Industry. LC 99-33818. (Illus.). 75p. 1999. spiral bd. 499.00 (*0-921577-98-2*) AKTRIN.

— The U. K. Market for Pine Furniture. LC 99-59028. (Illus.). 70p. 1999. pap. text 499.00 (*1-894330-07-2*) AKTRIN.

Business & Science of Special Forest Product Staff. Dancing with an Elephant: Proceedings: the Business & Science of Special Forest Products, a Conference & Exposition: January 26-27, 1994, Washington County Fairplex, Hillsboro, Oregon. Schnepf, Chris, ed. LC SD0387.M8B87. (Illus.). 223p. 1994. pap. 69.20 (*0-608-04877-1*, 206556900004) Bks Demand.

Business Communications Co., Inc. Staff. Advanced Building Control Systems & Devices. 158p. 1990. 1950.00 (*0-89336-743-5*, G089R) BCC.

— Advanced Materials for Air Frames, No. GB-122. 338p. 1990. 2950.00 (*0-89336-703-6*) BCC.

— Advanced Optical Material - Update, No. GB-103R. 235p. 1990. 2950.00 (*0-89336-786-9*) BCC.

— Advanced Optical Thin Films, No. GB-141. 330p. 1991. 2950.00 (*0-89336-811-3*) BCC.

— Aerospace Engine Materials, No. GB-124. 365p. 1990. 2950.00 (*0-89336-705-2*) BCC.

— Affinity Technology, No. C-130. 180p. 1991. 2650.00 (*0-89336-800-8*) BCC.

— Agriculture Chemicals Industry: Regulating LISA & the Future for Ag Chemicals. 186p. 1991. 1950.00 (*0-89336-771-0*, C119) BCC.

— Amino Acid Products & Technology. 120p. 1991. pap. 1750.00 (*0-89336-448-7*, C-056R) BCC.

— Bio-Immobilization Technology. (Illus.). 174p. 1994. pap. 2850.00 (*0-89336-429-0*, C-066R) BCC.

— Biocompatible Materials for the Human Body, No. GB-072R. 104p. 1990. 1950.00 (*0-89336-625-0*) BCC.

— Biohazard Testing, No. C-126. 335p. 1990. 2850.00 (*0-89336-787-7*) BCC.

— Biopesticides & Alternative Agriculture. 125p. 1990. 1850.00 (*0-89336-741-9*, C-082B) BCC.

— The Blood Industry (Update) 135p. 1991. 2250.00 (*0-89336-763-X*, C-071R) BCC.

— Blow Molded Plastic Containers - Update, No. P-029X. 164p. 1990. 1950.00 (*0-89336-781-8*) BCC.

— Ceramic Matrix Composites, No. GB-110R. 240p. 1990. 2850.00 (*0-89336-791-5*) BCC.

— The Changing Bag Market, No. P-082. 221p. 1990. 2350.00 (*0-89336-618-8*) BCC.

— Changing Bioreactor Business. 173p. 1990. pap. 2650.00 (*0-89336-580-7*, C-086) BCC.

— The Changing Plastics Film Business. 168p. 1990. 2450.00 (*0-89336-756-7*, P063U) BCC.

— Chlorobluorocarbons: Alternatives to CFC's, No. C-134. 199p. 1991. 2150.00 (*0-89336-804-0*) BCC.

— Coatings & Liners for Pipes & Tanks, No. GB-143. 177p. 1991. 2350.00 (*0-89336-838-5*) BCC.

— The Competitive U. S. Market for Auto Parts. 154p. 1990. 1800.00 (*0-89336-565-3*, GB-008R) BCC.

— Controlled & Modified Atmosphere Packing, No. GA-067. 215p. 1991. 2450.00 (*0-89336-821-0*) BCC.

— Diagnosis & Treatment Product for Immune Diseases, No. C-141. 162p. 1991. 2750.00 (*0-89336-832-6*) BCC.

— The Dynamic Media, Sera & Reagent Markets in Biotechnology (Update) 253p. 1995. pap. 2750.00 (*0-89336-588-2*, C-083R) BCC.

— Environmental Services & Remediation for Indoor Air Pollution. 150p. 1990. 1950.00 (*0-89336-779-6*, E052) BCC.

— Environmentally Acceptable Coatings: The Industry, No. C-136. 176p. 1991. 2250.00 (*0-89336-825-3*) BCC.

— Flavor Development for Generic & Custom-Specialty Market, No. GA-070. 120p. 1991. 2150.00 (*0-89336-815-6*) BCC.

— Growth Opportunities in Wire, Cable & Fiber Optics. 180p. 1991. 2450.00 (*0-89336-808-3*, G-070N) BCC.

— Hazardous Waste Control. 394p. 1992. pap. 2550.00 (*0-89336-585-8*, C-059R) BCC.

— The Impact of Recycling on Plastics Packaging, No. P-126. 194p. 1991. 2650.00 (*0-89336-843-1*) BCC.

— Industrial Hollow Plastic Parts: Markets by Technology, No. P-102. 129p. 1990. 1950.00 (*0-89336-553-X*) BCC.

— Ionic & Molecular Surface Modifications. 152p. 1990. 2850.00 (*0-89336-754-0*, GB-134) BCC.

— LAN Connectivity Technology. 179p. 1991. 1950.00 (*0-89336-759-1*, G129) BCC.

— Materials for Siding, Windows & Roofing. 141p. 1994. 2850.00 (*0-89336-748-6*, P-209R) BCC.

— Mold Release Agents. 133p. 1990. 2450.00 (*0-89336-777-X*, C125) BCC.

— Multichip Modules. 139p. 1990. 2650.00 (*0-89336-750-8*, GB138) BCC.

— New Abrasive Materials. 236p. 1991. 2650.00 (*0-89336-753-2*, GB-135) BCC.

— New Directions in Pharmaceutical Tablet Manufacture, No. C-135. 156p. 1991. 2250.00 (*0-89336-816-4*) BCC.

— New Fluorocarbon Compound Alternatives, No. C-134. 199p. 1991. 2150.00 (*0-89336-764-8*) BCC.

— New Horizons in the Pharmaceutical Industry. 245p. 1990. 2450.00 (*0-89336-566-1*, C-072) BCC.

— New Olefin Resins Via New Polymerization & Compounding, No. P-124. 129p. 1991. 2150.00 (*0-89336-841-5*) BCC.

— New Protein Technologies. 313p. 1991. 2850.00 (*0-89336-769-9*, C-117) BCC.

— Non-Invasive, Semi-Invasive Surgical Procedures, No. C-140. 189p. 1991. 2250.00 (*0-89336-831-8*) BCC.

— Opportunities for Transferring Defence Related Advanced Optics, No. GB-144. 280p. 1991. 2950.00 (*0-89336-839-3*) BCC.

— Opportunities in Plastics for the 1990's, No. P-2000. 250p. 1991. 1950.00 (*0-89336-814-8*) BCC.

— Pat Tap Technology Reviews: TAP-1, Superconductors. 1990. 450.00 (*0-89336-819-9*) BCC.

— Pat Tap Technology Reviews: TAP-10, Supercritical Fluids. 1991. 350.00 (*0-89336-850-4*) BCC.

— Pat Tap Technology Reviews: TAP-2, High Performance Diamond. 1991. 350.00 (*0-89336-818-0*) BCC.

— Pat Tap Technology Reviews: TAP-4, Chromatography. 1991. 550.00 (*0-89336-844-X*, TAP-04) BCC.

— Pat Tap Technology Reviews: TAP-6, Non-Linear Optics. 1991. 350.00 (*0-89336-846-6*) BCC.

— Pat Tap Technology Reviews: TAP-8, Polymers & Alloys. 1993. 1000.00 (*0-89336-848-2*, TAP-08R) BCC.

— Pat Tap Technology Reviews: TAP-9, Electrophoresis. 1991. 350.00 (*0-89336-849-0*, TAP-09) BCC.

— Patent Technology Review: Flame-Retardant Chemicals & Compositions, No. 3R. 306p. 1993. 1250.00 (*0-89336-820-2*) BCC.

— Physical Vapor Deposition. 179p. 1990. 2850.00 (*0-89336-746-X*, GB-133) BCC.

— Plant-Derived Chemicals, No. C-102. 176p. 1990. 2850.00 (*0-89336-639-0*) BCC.

— Plastics in Aircraft Interiors P-117. 218p. 1990. 2950.00 (*0-89336-765-6*) BCC.

— Plastics in ESD Applications. 198p. 1992. 2450.00 (*0-89336-575-0*, P-099R) BCC.

— Plastics vs. Paper & Paperboard. 302p. 1994. 2650.00 (*0-89336-757-5*, P027U) BCC.

— Point of Use Water Devices, No. GB-140. 1992. 1950.00 (*0-89336-810-5*) BCC.

— Printed Circuit Board Technologies. 173p. 1994. 2650.00 (*0-89336-760-5*, G-067X) BCC.

— Protective-Safety Clothing Materials-Markets, No. GB-142. 149p. 1991. 2250.00 (*0-89336-812-1*) BCC.

— Reagents for Food Testing: Impact of New Regulations & Biotechnology. 217p. 1992. 2850.00 (*0-89336-773-7*, C121) BCC.

— The Secondary Recycling Plastics Business, No. P-125. 245p. 1991. 2650.00 (*0-89336-842-3*) BCC.

— The Smart Card - Update, No. G-100R. 175p. 1991. 2350.00 (*0-89336-809-1*) BCC.

— Solar Thermal & Photovoltaics, No. E-036R. 175p. 1996. 2750.00 (*0-89336-806-7*, E-036N) BCC.

— Sorbent Materials for Spills & Other Liquid Pickups, No. C-133. 270p. 1991. 2850.00 (*0-89336-803-2*) BCC.

— Sorbents Materials for Non-Spill Applications, No. C-132A. 1992. 2850.00 (*0-89336-802-4*) BCC.

— Structural & Specialty Adhesives: Update, No. C-009X. 197p. 1991. 1950.00 (*0-89336-797-4*) BCC.

— Technologies for Management of Hazardous Waste. 394p. 1992. 2550.00 (*0-89336-827-X*, C-059R) BCC.

— Telecommunications' Retail Opportunities, No. G-133. 178p. 1991. 1950.00 (*0-89336-824-5*) BCC.

— Thick & Thin Films in Microelectronics. 151p. 1990. 2650.00 (*0-89336-729-X*, GB-128) BCC.

— Transformation of the Banking Industry. 214p. 1990. 2450.00 (*0-89336-661-7*, G-113B) BCC.

— The U. S. Energy Future: Environmental/Social Costs, No. E-007U. 1992. 2450.00 (*0-89336-805-9*) BCC.

— Waste to Energy: Impact, Directions & Trends, No. E-053. 155p. 1990. 1950.00 (*0-89336-785-0*) BCC.

— Water Soluble Polymers. 212p. 1991. 2250.00 (*0-89336-761-3*, C-012N) BCC.

— What's New in Barrier Packaging for Food & Non-Food Packaging, No. P-085N. 213p. 1990. 2650.00 (*0-89336-793-1*) BCC.

— Wire, Cable, & Fiber Optics. 131p. 1991. pap. 2450.00 (*0-89336-514-9*, G-070N) BCC.

— Wireless Communications, No. G-131. iv, 78p. 1993. 2250.00 (*0-89336-782-6*) BCC.

Business Communications Co Staff, jt. auth. see Hilton, Richard D.

Business Communications Co Staff, jt. auth. see Innes, George L.

Business Communications Company, Inc. Staff. BCC Diamond Directory, 1992: A Comprehensive Directory of the Companies Involved in Industrial Diamond & CBN Technology. 1992. 575.00 (*0-685-62470-6*) BCC.

— Directory of Companies Involved in the Conventional & Hazardous Waste Business. 1993. 175.00 (*0-685-62471-4*, DND92) BCC.

— Industrial Diamonds & CBN: Materials, Films & Products - U. S. Directory & Market Guide. 1992. 575.00 (*0-685-62467-6*, DDD) BCC.

— Proceedings from the Annual Conference - Recent Advances in Flame Retardancy of Polymeric Materials, 1992. 1992. 275.00 (*0-89336-894-6*, DFR-92) BCC.

— Recent Advances in Flame Retardancy of Polymeric Materials, 1991: Annual Conference Proceedings. 1992. pap. 275.00 (*0-685-62464-1*) BCC.

Business Communications Company, Inc. Staff & Filterex, Inc. Staff. Proceedings from the Ninth Annual Membrane Technology-Planning Conference, 1991. 1992. 350.00 (*0-89336-817-2*, DMC-91) BCC.

— Proceedings from the Tenth Annual Membrane Technology-Planning Conference, 1992. 1993. 350.00 (*0-89336-968-3*, DMC-92) BCC.

Business Communications Company Staff, jt. auth. see Favreau, Marc.

Business Development Systems, Inc. Staff. Advertising - And the Winner Is You or Is It Your Competition? How to Develop an Advertising Program from a Common Sense Approach. (Self-Improvement Business Ser.). 35p. 1995. pap. text 8.95 (*1-884392-11-3*) Busn Develop.

— Embarking on Entrepreneurship: Are You Ready to Go into Business for Yourself. (Down to Business Ser.). 9p. 1994. pap. text 4.95 (*1-884392-04-0*) Busn Develop.

— How to Compensate, Train, & Delegate Responsibility to Your Employees or Create Organizational Chaos: How to Open the Door to Success by Assigning Responsibility & Authority. (Self-Improvement Business Ser.). 32p. 1994. pap. text 8.95 (*1-884392-05-9*) Busn Develop.

— How to Find & Hire the High Performer & Terminate the Uncooperative Employee: How to Hire the Best People for Your Business & Terminate the Dead Wood. (Self-Improvement Business Ser.). 29p. 1993. pap. text 8.95 (*1-884392-03-2*) Busn Develop.

— To Plan Or Not to Plan Is the Question - The Answer Is Found in Your Desire to Succeed: How to Create a Winning Plan for Business Growth & Goal Setting for Small Business. (Self-Improvement Business Ser.). 40p. 1994. pap. text 8.95 (*1-884392-09-1*) Busn Develop.

— Why Record Keeping & Financial Feedback Is Not an Option but a Requirement of Success: How to Conquer the Financial Side of Your Business. (Self-Improvement Business Ser.). 37p. 1994. pap. text 8.95 (*1-884392-08-3*) Busn Develop.

— You Either Know What's Going on in Your Marketplace or You Lose: How to Identify & Develop a Powerful Market Awareness Program. (Self-Improvement Business Ser.). 30p. 1993. pap. 8.95 (*1-884392-02-4*) Busn Develop.

— Your Customers Must Come in Second Place to Your Employees If Your Objective Is Total Customer Satisfaction: How to Rate, Praise, Recognize, & Motivate Your Employees to Provide the Best Customer Service. (Self-Improvement Business Ser.). 27p. 1994. pap. text 8.95 (*1-884392-07-5*) Busn Develop.

Business Facts Press Editors. Your Complete Real Estate Game Plan & Playbook. LC 91-73124. 130p. (Orig.). 1991. pap. 24.00 (*0-9630224-0-7*) Busn Facts.

Business Information International Staff. Doing Business in Atlanta (Fulton Co.) 600p. Date not set. pap., spiral bd. 299.95 (*1-890631-00-0*) Busn Info Intl.

— Doing Business in Cleveland. 450p. Date not set. pap., spiral bd. 99.95 (*1-890631-01-9*) Busn Info Intl.

— Doing Business in Columbia. 250p. Date not set. pap., spiral bd. 139.95 (*1-890631-02-7*) Busn Info Intl.

— Doing Business in Dayton. 400p. Date not set. pap., spiral bd. 199.95 (*1-890631-04-3*) Busn Info Intl.

— Doing Business in Detroit. Date not set. pap., spiral bd. 350.00 (*1-890631-03-5*) Busn Info Intl.

— Doing Business in Phoenix. 450p. 1997. pap., spiral bd. 349.00 (*1-890631-05-1*) Busn Info Intl.

— Doing Business in Wichita. 450p. Date not set. pap., spiral bd. 279.00 (*1-890631-06-X*) Busn Info Intl.

— Doing Business in Youngstown. 300p. Date not set. pap., spiral bd. write for info. (*1-890631-07-8*) Busn Info Intl.

Business Kids Staff. The Business Kit. (Illus.). 129p. (YA). (gr. 8-12). 1989. teacher ed. 14.95 (*0-9625075-1-2*); student ed. 49.95 (*0-9625075-0-4*) Lemonade Kids.

Business of Your Own Staff. So You're Thinking about Starting a Business: A Comprehensive General Start up Manual. 240p. 1998. reprint ed. 49.95 (*0-943267-00-5*) Busn Your Own.

— Starting a Business to Sell Your Art Work. 240p. 1998. reprint ed. 59.95 (*0-943267-11-0*) Busn Your Own.

— Starting a Business to Sell Your Craft Items. 230p. 1998. reprint ed. 59.95 (*0-943267-08-0*) Busn Your Own.

— Starting a Clothing Boutique. 230p. 1998. reprint ed. 59.95 (*0-943267-07-2*) Busn Your Own.

— Starting a Day Care Center. 240p. 1998. reprint ed. 59.95 (*0-943267-06-4*) Busn Your Own.

— Starting a Flower Shop. 240p. 1998. reprint ed. 59.95 (*0-943267-05-6*) Busn Your Own.

— Starting a Franchise. 240p. 1998. reprint ed. 59.95 (*0-943267-09-9*) Busn Your Own.

— Starting a Gift Shop. 240p. 1998. reprint ed. 59.95 (*0-943267-01-3*) Busn Your Own.

— Starting a Home Based Business. 240p. 1998. reprint ed. 59.95 (*0-943267-03-X*) Busn Your Own.

— Starting a Mail Order Business. 240p. 1998. reprint ed. 59.95 (*0-943267-10-2*) Busn Your Own.

— Starting a Secretarial Service. Miller, Emily, ed. 230p. 1998. reprint ed. 59.95 (*0-943267-12-9*) Busn Your Own.

— Starting an Antique Business. 240p. 1998. reprint ed. 59.95 (*0-943267-02-1*) Busn Your Own.

Business Owners & Managers Association (BOMA) International Staff & ULI-Urban Land Institute Staff. What Office Tenants Want: Building Features, Amenities & Services. LC 98-83051. x, 102 p. 1999. pap. 79.95 (*0-87420-866-1*, OT1) Urban Land.

***Business Resources, Inc. Staff.** The One Page Financial Statement. 180p. 1999. pap. 15.95 (*1-880394-94-4*) Thomson Learn.

Business Travel Staff, ed. Passport's Guide to the Business Capitals of the World. 320p. 1986. 29.95 (*0-8442-9491-8*, Passprt Bks) NTC Contemp Pub Co.

— Passport's Guide to the Business Capitals of the World. 320p. 1994. pap. 14.95 (*0-8442-9492-6*, Passprt Bks) NTC Contemp Pub Co.

Business Trend Analysts, Inc. Staff. The Market for Pleasure Boats & Related Products. (Illus.). 270p. 1998. spiral bd. 1195.00 (*0-685-24423-7*) Busn Trend.

***Business Trend Analysts, Inc. Staff & Wichert, J.** The U. S. Market for Dental Equipment & Supplies. (Illus.). 200p. 2000. spiral bd. 1995.00 (*0-685-24421-0*) Lead Edge Reports.

Business Week Editors. Business Week Guide: The Information Revolution. 1994. pap. text 12.95 (*0-07-009423-3*) McGraw.

Business Week Staff. Bus Wk Gde Best Bus Sch (book) 6th ed. 1999. pap. 16.95 (*0-07-135148-5*) McGraw.

— Preparing Your Business for the Global Economy. LC 97-7418. (Illus.). 120p. 1997. pap. 14.95 (*0-07-009438-1*) McGraw.

***Business Week Staff & Laderman, Jeffrey M.** Business Week's Guide to Mutual Funds. (Illus.). 229p. 1999. pap. 14.95 (*0-07-134261-3*) McGraw.

Business Writers' Group (Practical Publications). Two-minute Thoughts: What Really Motivates Employees & Others Today. LC 97-218774. 1997. write for info. (*0-912914-63-7*) Practical Pubns.

Business Writers' Group (Practical Publications), contrib. by. Two-Minute Thoughts: How to Improve Any Product or Service You Already Have. LC 97-214417. 369p. 1997. pap. 49.95 (*0-912914-47-5*) Practical Pubns.

Busing, William R., ed. Intermolecular Forces & Packing in Crystals. (Transactions of the American Crystallographic Association Ser.: Vol. 6). 155p. 1970. pap. 25.00 (*0-686-60377-X*) Polycrystal Bk Serv.

Businger, A. PORTAL Language Description. (Lecture Notes in Computer Science Ser.: Vol. 198). viii, 186p. 1985. pap. 14.50 (*0-387-15682-8*) Spr-Verlag.

— PORTAL Language Description. (Lecture Notes in Computer Science Ser.: Vol. 198). viii, 197p. 1988. 33.00 (*0-387-18960-2*) Spr-Verlag.

Businger, J. A., ed. Meteorological Studies at Plateau Station, Antarctica. (Antarctic Research Ser.: Vol. 25). (Illus.). 155p. 1977. 38.00 (*0-87590-125-5*, AR2500) Am Geophysical.

— Meteorological Studies at Plateau Station, Antarctica: Mini Book, Papers 6-8. (Antarctic Research Ser.: Vol. 25). (Illus.). 51p. 1977. 38.00 (*0-87590-140-9*) Am Geophysical.

Businger, Joost A., jt. auth. see Kraus, Eric B.

Businger, Joost A., ed. see Kuhn, M., et al.

Busk, Rachel H. The Folk-Songs of Italy: Specimens with Translations & Notes from Each Province & Prefatory Treatise. Dorsen, Richard M., ed. LC 77-70588. (International Folklore Ser.). 1977. reprint ed. lib. bdg. 25.95 (*0-405-10085-X*) Ayer.

— The Valleys of Tirol: Their Traditions & Customs, & How to Visit Them. LC 77-87725. 488p. reprint ed. 54.50 (*0-404-16513-3*) AMS Pr.

Busk, Robert De, see De Busk, Robert.

Busk, Robert S. Magnesium Products Design. (Mechanical Engineering Ser.: Vol. 53). (Illus.). 560p. 1986. text 199.00 (*0-8247-7576-7*) Dekker.

Buskens, Joy C. Well, I've Never Met a Native: Stories of the Coastal People of Alabama. LC 86-90380. (Illus.). 330p. 1986. 19.95 (*0-9616351-1-8*); pap. 14.95 (*0-9616351-0-X*) J C Buskens.

Buskes, Gerard & Van Rooij, A. C. Topological Spaces: From Distance to Neighborhood. LC 97-3756. (Undergraduate Texts in Mathematics Ser.). 320p. 1997. text 39.95 (*0-387-94994-1*) Spr-Verlag.

Buskin, David. Outdoor Games. (Illus.). (J). (gr. k-4). 1966. lib. bdg. 13.95 (*0-87460-090-1*) Lion Bks.

Buskin, John, jt. ed. see Gingold, Alfred.

Buskin, Judith, jt. auth. see Singer, Laura J.

Buskin, Richard. Complete Idiot's Guide to British Royalty. (Complete Idiot's Guide Ser.). (Illus.). 352p. 1997. pap. text 18.95 (*0-02-862346-0*) Macmillan Gen Ref.

— Complete Idiot's Guide to the Beatles. LC 97-80970. 384p. 1997. 18.95 (*0-02-862130-1*) Macmillan Gen Ref.

— Days in the Life: The Lost Beatles Archives. 1999. 75.00 (*0-9669481-3-0*) Star Pubg.

***Buskin, Richard.** Days in the Life: The Lost Beatles Archives. (Illus.). 1999. 45.00 (*0-9669481-2-2*) Star Pubg.

Buskin, Richard. The Films of Marilyn Monroe. (Illus.). 96p. 1993. 9.98 (*1-56173-277-X*, 3110100) Pubns Intl Ltd.

— Inside Tracks: A First-Hand History of Popular Music from the World's Greatest Record Producers. 384p. 1999. pap. 14.00 (*0-380-80745-9*, Avon Bks) Morrow Avon.

— John Lennon: His Life & Legend. (Illus.). 256p. 1993. 29.95 (*1-56173-270-2*, 3110300) Pubns Intl Ltd.

— Prince William, Born to Be King, 1 vol. 1998. mass mkt. 6.99 (*0-451-19927-8*) NAL.

— Princess Diana, 1961-1997. rev. ed. (Illus.). 224p. 1997. mass mkt. 5.99 (*0-451-19711-9*, Sig) NAL.

Buskirk, Bruce, jt. auth. see Brown, Herbert.

Buskirk, E. Michael Van, see Van Buskirk, E. Michael.

B

B

Buskirk, Elsworth R. & Puhl, Susan M., eds. Body Fluid Balance: Exercise & Sport. LC 95-53970. 352p. 1996. boxed set 104.95 (0-8493-7918-0) CRC Pr.

Buskirk, Jim Van, see Stryker, Susan & Van Buskirk, Jim.

Buskirk, Kathleen Van, see Van Buskirk, Kathleen.

Buskirk, Luegenia Van, see Van Buskirk, Luegenia.

Buskirk, Martha. Richard Serra: Intersection. (Illus.). 192p. 1996. 60.00 (3-928762-52-4, 620791, Pub. by Richter Verlag) Dist Art Pubs.

Buskirk, Martha & Nixon, Mignon, eds. The Duchamp Effect. LC 95-46162. (Illus.). 232p. (C). 1996. pap. text 16.50 (0-262-52217-9) MIT Pr.

Buskirk, Martha, jt. ed. see Weyergraf-Serra, Clara.

Buskirk, Michael Van, see Minckler, Don S. & Van Buskirk, Michael.

Buskirk, Richard, Jr., et al. Management of a Sales Force International. 9th ed. (C). 1994. pap. text, student ed. 34.50 (0-256-18460-7, Irwn McGrw-H) McGrw-H Hghr Educ.

Buskirk, Richard H., et al. The Entrepreneur's Planning Handbook. 223p. 1997. pap. 25.00 (0-944303-18-8) Entre Ed Fndtn.

— Program for Writing Winning Business Plans. 88p. 1991. pap. 9.95 (0-944303-04-8) Entre Ed Fndtn.

Buskirk, Steven W., et al, eds. Martens, Sables, & Fishers: Biology & Conservation. (Comstock Bk.). (Illus.). 512p. 1994. text 67.50 (0-8014-2894-7) Cornell U Pr.

Buskirk, Velma Van, see Van Buskirk, Velma.

Buskirk, William R. Van, see Van Buskirk, William R.

Buskirk, William R. Van, see Frauchiger, Fritz & Van Buskirk, William R.

Buskist, William & Gerbing, David. Psychology Boundries & Froniters. LC 93-22902. (C). 1989. reprint ed. text 83.44 (0-673-38023-8) Addson-Wesley Educ.

Buskist, William & Mixon, Amy. Allyn & Bacon Guide to Master's Programs in Psychology & Counseling Psychology. 256p. 1997. pap. text 26.00 (0-205-27436-6) Allyn.

Buskist, William & Sherburne, Thomas R. Preparing for Graduate Study in Psychology: 101 Questions & Answers. LC 96-185889. 128p. (C). 1995. pap. text 16.00 (0-205-19858-9) Allyn.

Buskist, William, jt. auth. see Carlson, Neil H.

Buskist, William, jt. auth. see Carlson, Neil R.

Buskohl, Esther E. Honey: Story of a Little Brown Mule. LC 85-80216. (Illus.). 80p. (Orig.). (J). (gr. 3-5). 1985. 9.95 (0-9614991-0-9); pap. 4.95 (0-9614991-1-7) EEBART.

— Townline Road: Lines from the Beginning - the Place - the Time. (Illus.). 1996. pap. write for info. (0-9614991-2-5) EEBART.

***Busky, Donald F.** Democratic Socialism: A Global Survey. LC 99-59849. 248p. 2000. 65.00 (0-275-96886-3, Praeger Pubs) Greenwood.

Buslaev, V., et al. Differential Operators & Spectral Theory: M. Sh. Birman's 70th Anniversary Collection. LC 99-206508. 285p. 1999. 99.00 (0-8218-1387-0) Am Math.

Buslaev, Y., ed. Electron Structure & High Temperature Chemistry of Coordination Compounds. 356p. 1996. lib. bdg. 94.00 (0-614-16645-4) Nova Sci Pubs.

Buslaev, Y., ed. Electron Structure & High Temperature Chemistry of Coordination Compounds. 356p. 1996. write for info. (1-56072-187-1) Nova Sci Pubs.

Buslaev, Yu, ed. Complex Formation & Stereochemistry of Coordination Compounds. 388p. 1996. 145.00 (1-56072-186-3) Nova Sci Pubs.

Buslig, Bela, jt. ed. see Manthey, John.

Buslik, Gary. The Missionary's Position. LC 98-60334. 312p. 1999. pap. 12.95 (0-9665513-0-3) Sunny Bk.

Busman, Denise, jt. auth. see Davidson, Robert C.

Busman, Gloria. Union Representative's Guide to NLRB RC & CA Cases. (Policy & Practice Publication). 112p. 1984. 10.00 (0-89215-089-0) U Cal LA Indus Rel.

Busman, Gloria, ed. Union Strategies for a High Tech Era. (Current Issues Ser.: No. 10). 106p. 1993. reprint ed. 15.00 (0-89215-150-1) U Cal LA Indus Rel.

Busmann, Johannes, ed. RKW-Architects: Architecture, 1950-2000. (Illus.). 384p. 1999. 65.00 (3-7757-0735-2, Pub. by Gerd Hatje) Dist Art Pubs.

Busnaina, Ahmed A. & Rangan, Ravi, eds. Proceedings of the 1995 International Computers in Engineering Conference & 1995 ASME Database Symposium: September 17-20, 1995 Boston, Massachusetts. LC 95-80498. 1264p. 1995. 380.00 (0-7918-1701-6, H009) ASME.

Busnar, Gene, jt. auth. see Putnam, Howard D.

Busnar, Gene, ed. see Carson, Nancy & Fawcett, Allen.

Busnoys, Antoine. The Collected Works Parts 2 & 3: The Latin-Texted Works. Taruskin, Richard F., ed. (Masters & Monuments of the Renaissance Ser.: Vol. 5). (Illus.). 1989. pap. 150.00 (0-8450-7305-2) Broude.

Busolt, Georg. Griechische Geschichte Bis Zur Schlacht Bei Chaeroneia, 3 vols. in 4. (GER.). lxxx, 3170p. 1967. reprint ed. 720.00 (0-318-70885-X) G Olms Pubs.

Buson, et al. Born of a Dream: Fifty Haiku by Basho, Buson, Taigi, Issa, Shiki. Corman, Cid, tr. from JPN. & intro. by. LC 88-81708. 72p. (Orig.). 1989. pap. text 10.00 (0-917788-37-0) Gnomon Pr.

Busoni, Ferruccio. Complete Elegies 6 Sonatinas & Other. 240p. 1996. 14.95 (0-486-29386-6, 277911Q) Dover.

— Letters to His Wife. Ley, Rosamond, tr. LC 74-34378. (Music Reprint Ser.). (Illus.). 319p. 1975. reprint ed. lib. bdg. 37.50 (0-306-70732-2) Da Capo.

— Toccata & Fugue in D Minor & the Other Bach Transcriptions for Solo Piano. 128p. 1996. pap. 8.95 (0-486-29050-6) Dover.

Busoni, Ferruccio B. Letters to His Wife. (Music Book Index Ser.). 319p. 1992. reprint ed. lib. bdg. 89.00 (0-7812-9489-4) Rprt Serv.

Busool, A. N. Forty Ahadith: Asqalani. 95p. 1981. 4.95 (1-56744-012-6) Kazi Pubns.

Busool, Assad. Shape & Forms of Arabic Letters. 2nd ed. (J). (ps-4). 1991. reprint ed. pap. 4.00 (1-56316-001-3) Iqra Intl Ed Fdtn.

Busool, Assad, ed. see Abdallah, Fadel.

Busool, Assad N. Animals Rights & Nature in Islam. v, 50p. (Orig.). 1994. pap. write for info. (0-9639925-3-8) Am Islamic Educ.

— Guide for the Young Muslim Bk. 1: Tawhid, Fiqh, Akhlaq. Date not set. pap. 4.50 (1-56744-568-3) Kazi Pubns.

— Islamic Fundamentalism? 31p. (Orig.). 1993. pap. write for info. (0-9639925-1-1) Am Islamic Educ.

— Islam's Relationship to Christianity & Judaism. vii, 55p. (Orig.). 1994. pap. write for info. (0-9639925-0-3) Am Islamic Educ.

— Wise Judge Stories of Wit, Wisdom & Islamic: The Justice. (J). 1996. pap. 3.95 (1-871031-78-8) Kazi Pubns.

Busool, Assad N., ed. see Abdallah, Fadel I.

Busool, Assad N., tr. see Ghazi, Abidullah & Ghazi, Tasneema, eds.

Busool, Assad N., tr. see Taimiyah, Sheikh A.

Busqueta, Pere E. Diccionari Illustrat Catala-Castella i Castella-Catala. (CAT & SPA.). 740p. 1989. 31.95 (0-7859-5889-4, 8430310967) Fr & Eur.

Busquets, Juan, et al, contrib. by. Exploring the River: Seven Studies for a New Cross River Connection in Rotterdam. (Illus.). 112p. 1999. pap. 25.00 (90-5662-098-3, 910702, Pub. by NAi Uitgevers) Dist Art Pubs.

Buss. Evolutionary Psychology: The New Science of the Mind. LC 98-28483. (Illus.). 456p. 1998. 53.00 (0-205-19358-7) Allyn.

***Buss, Erik.** Freely Give: Evangelization & the New Church. 2000. 14.00 (0-945003-23-4) General Church.

Buss, Erik, ed. see Swedenborg, Emanuel.

Buss, Andreas. Societe, Politique, Individu: Les Formes Elementaires de la Vie Sociale en Inde Ancienne. fac. ed. LC JQ0200.B87. (FRE.). 129p. reprint ed. pap. 40.00 (0-7837-6952-0, 204678100003) Bks Demand.

Buss, Arnold H. Personality: Evolutionary Heritage & Human Distinctiveness. 280p. (C). 1988. text 49.95 (0-8058-0298-3) L Erlbaum Assocs.

— Social Behavior & Personality. 244p. (C). 1986. text 49.95 (0-89859-812-5) L Erlbaum Assocs.

Buss, Arnold H. & Plomin, Robert. Temperament: Early Developing Personality Traits. 200p. (C). 1984. text 39.95 (0-89859-415-4) L Erlbaum Assocs.

Buss, Carolyn. Moms, How Are You Doing? 1998. pap. text 8.99 (1-884369-94-4, EBED Pubns) McDougal Pubng.

Buss, Carolyn, jt. auth. see Buss, Scott.

Buss, Claude. Cory Aquino & the People of the Philippines. (Portable Stanford Bks.). (Illus.). 189p. 1987. 16.95 (0-916318-25-7); pap. 10.95 (0-916318-24-9) Stanford Alumni Assn.

Buss, D. M. & Cantor, Nancy, eds. Personality Psychology. (Illus.). 335p. 1989. 80.95 (0-387-96993-4) Spr-Verlag.

***Buss, Dale.** How to Think Like the World's Greatest New Media Moguls. (Leader's Edge Ser.). 2000. 18.95 (0-07-136069-7) McGraw.

Buss, David M. The Dangerous Passions: Why Jealousy Is As Necessary As Love & Sex. LC 99-59067. 272p. 2000. 25.00 (0-684-85081-8) Free Pr.

Buss, David M. & Malamuth, Neil M., eds. Sex, Power, Conflict: Evolutionary & Feminist Perspectives. LC 95-15685. (Illus.). 352p. 1996. pap. 35.00 (0-19-510357-2) OUP.

Buss, Dietrich G. Henry Villard: A Study of Transatlantic Investment & Interests, 1870-1895. LC 77-14757. (Dissertations in American Economic History Ser.). 1977. 28.95 (0-405-11027-8) Ayer.

Buss, Eugen. Lehrbuch der Wirtschaftssoziologie. (GER.). xii, 272p. 1985. pap. 34.65 (3-11-008897-5) De Gruyter.

Buss, Fran L. Journey of the Sparrows. 160p. (J). (gr. 4-7). 1993. pap. 4.50 (0-440-40785-0) Dell.

— Journey of the Sparrows. (J). 1993. 9.60 (0-606-05389-1, Pub. by Turtleback) Demco.

Buss, Fran L. The Moisture of the Earth: An Oral History of Mary Robinson. (Illus.). (C). text. write for info. (0-472-09587-0); pap. text. write for info. (0-472-06587-4) U of Mich Pr.

Buss, Fran L. La Partera: Story of a Midwife. 152p. 1980. pap. text 14.95 (0-472-06322-7, 06322) U of Mich Pr.

Buss, Fran Leeper. Dignity: Lower Income Women Tell of Their Lives & Struggles. (Illus.). 304p. 1985. pap. text 17.95 (0-472-06357-X, 06357) U of Mich Pr.

***Buss, Fran Leeper.** La Partera: Story of a Midwife. (Ann Arbor Paperbacks Ser.). (SPA., Illus.). 184p. (C). 2000. pap. 16.95 (0-472-08712-6) U of Mich Pr.

Buss, Gerald. The Bear's Hug: Christian Belief & the Soviet State, 1917-86. LC 87-19639. 223p. reprint ed. pap. 69.20 (0-8357-4359-4, 203718700007) Bks Demand.

Buss, Helen M. Mapping Our Selves: Canadian Women's Autobiography. 248p. 1993. 65.00 (0-7735-0975-5, Pub. by McG-Queens Univ Pr) CUP Services.

— Mapping Our Selves: Canadian Women's Autobiography. (Illus.). 252p. 1994. pap. 24.95 (0-7735-1244-6, Pub. by McG-Queens Univ Pr) CUP Services.

Buss, Helen M. & Clarke, Margaret. Memoirs from Away: A New Found Land Girlhood. 169p. 1999. pap. write for info. (0-88920-314-8) W Laurier U Pr.

***Buss, Helen M. & Clarke, Margaret.** Memoirs from Away: A New Found Land Girlhood. (Life Writing Ser.). 169p. 1999. pap. 21.95 (0-88920-350-4) Wilfrid Laurier.

Buss, Janice E., jt. ed. see Casey, Patrick J.

Buss, Jerry. A War of Their Own: The Krueger Affair. Kirsch, J. Allen, ed. (Heritage Ser.). (Illus.). 200p. 1998. pap. 12.95 (1-878569-52-X) Badger Bks Inc.

Buss, K. Studies in the Chinese Drama. 1977. lib. bdg. 59.95 (0-8490-2704-7) Gordon Pr.

Buss, Katherine. Big Book of Knitting. LC 99-20386. (Illus.). 240p. 1999. 29.95 (0-8069-6203-8) Sterling.

***Buss, Kathleen & Karnowski, Lee.** Reading & Writing Literary Genres. LC 99-59011. 208p. 2000. pap. 22.95 (0-87207-257-6, 257) Intl Reading.

Buss, Kathleen, jt. auth. see McClain-Ruelle, Leslie.

Buss, Leo W. The Evolution of Individuality. LC 87-45514. (Illus.). 219p. reprint ed. pap. 67.90 (0-608-06395-9, 206675600008) Bks Demand.

Buss, Leo W., ed. see Jackson, Jeremy B.

Buss, Martin J. Biblical Form Criticism in Its Context. LC 99-190630. (J. S. O. T. S. Ser.: Vol. 274). 512p. 1999. 85.00 (1-85075-876-X, Pub. by Sheffield Acad) CUP Services.

— The Prophetic Words of Hosea: A Morphological Study. (Beiheft zur Zeitschrift fuer die Alttestamentliche Wissenschaft Ser.: No. 111). (C). 1969. 66.15 (3-11-002579-5) De Gruyter.

Buss, Martin J., ed. Encounter with the Text: Form & History in the Hebrew Bible. LC 78-31182. (Society of Biblical Literature. Semeia Supplements Ser.: No. 8). 232p. (Orig.). reprint ed. pap. 72.00 (0-7837-5448-5, 204521300005) Bks Demand.

Buss, Nigel. Artforus: A Visual Arts Curriculum to Develop Fine & Gross Motor Skills in Handicapped Students. 87p. 1986. teacher ed. 10.00 (1-878276-37-9) Educ Systs Assocs Inc.

Buss, Robin. French Film Noir. LC 93-28651. (Illus.). 240p. 1994. 35.00 (0-7145-2963-X) M Boyars Pubs.

— French Film Noir: Film Writings. 1999. pap. text 16.95 (0-7145-3036-0) M Boyars Pubs.

— Taking a Second Look: The Changing Face of the Literary Past in European Cinema. LC 99-24958. 256p. 1999. 29.95 (0-7145-3039-5) M Boyars Pubs.

— Taking a Second Look: The Changing Face of the Literary Past in European Cultures. rev. ed. (Illus.). 256p. 1999. 19.95 (0-7145-3043-3) M Boyars Pubs.

Buss, Robin, tr. see Cocteau, Jean.

Buss, Robin, tr. see Green, Julian.

Buss, Robin, tr. see Liaut, Jean-Noel.

Buss, Robin, tr. & intro. see De Lafayette, Madame.

Buss, Robin, tr. & intro. see Dumas, Alexandre.

Buss, S. R., ed. see Miller, Arnold W.

***Buss, Sam, et al, eds.** Logic Colloquium '98. LC 99-51335. (Lecture Notes in Logic Ser.: No. 13). (Illus.). 550p. 2000. 85.00 (1-56881-113-6); pap. 40.00 (1-56881-114-4) AK Peters.

Buss, Samuel R. Handbook of Proof Theory. LC 98-18922. (Studies in Logic & the Foundations of Mathematics). 812p. 1998. write for info. (0-444-89840-9) Elsevier.

Buss, Samuel R. & Scott, Phillip J. Feasible Mathematics. (Progress in Control Systems Ser.: Vol. 9). 350p. 1990. 58.00 (0-8176-3483-5) Birkhauser.

Buss, Samuel R., jt. ed. see Beame, Paul W.

Buss, Scott & Buss, Carolyn. Heart Throb: Releasing the Musical & Artistic Potential Within God's People. 112p. 1993. pap. 6.00 (0-9637311-1-4) Genesis Comm Inc.

Buss, Terry, et al, eds. Economic Revitalization of America. (C). 1983. pap. 15.00 (0-918592-62-3) Pol Studies.

Buss, Terry, jt. auth. see Redburn, F. Stevens.

Buss, Terry F. & Redburn, F. Stevens. Hidden Unemployment: Discouraged Workers & Public Policy. LC 88-11760. 155p. 1988. 57.95 (0-275-92612-5, C2612, Praeger Pubs) Greenwood.

— Mass Unemployment: Plant Closings & Community Mental Health. LC 83-4450. (Sage Studies in Community Mental Health: No. 6). (Illus.). 224p. reprint ed. pap. 69.50 (0-8357-8481-9, 203474800091) Bks Demand.

— Shutdown at Youngstown: Public Policy for Mass Unemployment. LC 82-5686. (SUNY Series in Urban Public Policy). 219p. (C). 1983. text 20.50 (0-87395-646-X) State U NY Pr.

Buss, Terry F. & Vaughn, Roger J. On the Rebound: Helping Workers Cope with Plant Closings. LC 88-38398. 1989. 14.95 (0-934842-57-4) CSPA.

Buss, Terry F., jt. auth. see Redburn, F. Stevens.

Buss, Terry F., jt. auth. see Vaughan, Roger J.

***Bussagli, Marco.** Rome: Art & Architecture. (Illus.). 440p. 1999. 39.95 (3-8290-2259-X) Konemann.

Bussagli, Mario. Oriental Architecture I: India, Indonesia, Indochina. LC 88-43458. (History of World Architecture Ser.). (Illus.). 224p. 1989. reprint ed. pap. 29.95 (0-8478-1056-9, Pub. by Rizzoli Intl) St Martin.

— Oriental Architecture II: China, Korea, Japan. LC 88-43458. (History of World Architecture Ser.). (Illus.). 224p. 1989. reprint ed. pap. 29.95 (0-8478-1055-0, Pub. by Rizzoli Intl) St Martin.

Bussanich, J. The One & Its Relation to Intellect in Plotinus. vii, 258p. 1988. pap. 71.00 (90-04-08996-9, PHA, 49) Brill Academic Pubs.

— The Philosophy Of Late Antiquity. (History of Ancient & Medieval Philosophy Ser.). 256p. 2001. pap. 55.00 (0-8133-2523-4) Westview.

Bussanich, John. Philosophy of Late Antiquity. 2000. pap. text 21.95 (0-8133-2524-2) Westview.

Bussar-Maatz, Roswitha, jt. ed. see Weissbach, L.

Bussard, June E. Skinny Scotty: The Adventurous Life of Rosa Ellen Scott. LC 96-94290. (Illus.). 200p. (Orig.). 1996. pap. 10.95 (0-9652014-0-6) J&J Books.

Bussard, Lee. More Alike Than Different: An Inspiring Message for Anyone Coping with Life's Difficulties. 136p. 1997. 19.95 (1-890009-02-4) Exec Excell.

Bussard, Paula. Bug Beepers for Promise Keepers: Critter County Activity Book. (Nineteen Ninety-Nine 50-Day Spiritual Adventure Ser.). (Illus.). 64p. (J). 1998. pap. 7.00 (1-57849-109-6) Mainstay Church.

***Bussard, Paula.** Come to a Critter County Party: Children Critter County Activity Book - Discover How You Can Honor Jesus. Kenney, Cindy, ed. (Celebrate Jesus! Ser.). (Illus.). 64p. (J). 1999. 7.00 (1-57849-176-2) Mainstay Church.

— Critter County Clubhouse: Children's Activity Book. (Nineteen Ninety-Seven 50-Day Spiritual Adventure Ser.). (Illus.). 64p. (Orig.). (J). (gr. k-2). 1996. pap., wbk. ed. 6.00 (1-57849-003-0) Chapel of Air.

— Critter County Power Buddies: Children's Activity Book. Hieberti, Charlene & Washington, Linda, eds. (Nineteen Ninety-Eight Fifty-Day Spiritual Adventure Ser.). (Illus.). 64p. (J). (gr. k-2). 1997. wbk. ed. 6.00 (1-57849-042-1) Mainstay Church.

Bussard, Paula. Facing the Fearigators with Critter County Friends: Activity Book. (1995 50-Day Spiritual Adventure Ser.). (Illus.). 64p. (Orig.). (J). (gr. k-2). 1994. pap. text, student ed. 4.95 (1-879050-50-1) Chapel of Air.

Bussard, Paula. Pack up My Backpack for a Critter County Fieldtrip: Children's Activity Book. Gillespie, Judy & Walker, Cathy, eds. (Nineteen Ninety-Six 50-Day Spiritual Adventure Ser.). (Illus.). 64p. (Orig.). (J). (gr. k-2). 1995. pap., wbk. ed. 6.00 (1-879050-74-9) Chapel of Air.

Bussard, Paula & Wyrtzen, Christine. Children's Church Leader's Guide: A Critter County Camping Trip. (1993 50-Day Spiritual Adventure Ser.). (Illus.). 96p. (Orig.). (J). (gr. k-2). 1992. pap. text, student ed. 12.99 (1-879050-11-0) Chapel of Air.

— Children's Church Leader's Guide: The Critter County Dream Team. (1994 50-Day Spiritual Adventure Ser.). (Illus.). 80p. (Orig.). (J). (gr. k-2). 1993. pap. text 19.99 incl. audio (1-879050-40-4); pap. text, student ed. 12.99 (1-879050-20-X) Chapel of Air.

— A Critter County Camping Trip. (1993 50-Day Spiritual Adventure Ser.). (Illus.). 64p. (Orig.). (J). (ps-2). 1992. pap. text, student ed. 4.99 (1-879050-10-2) Chapel of Air.

— The Critter County Dream Team: Coming Soon to a Town Near You Activity Book. (1994 50-Day Spiritual Adventure Ser.). (Illus.). 64p. (Orig.). (J). (ps-2). 1993. pap. text, student ed. 4.99 (1-879050-17-X) Chapel of Air.

Bussard, Paula, et al. 1996 50-Day Spiritual Adventure: Grades 1-6 Leader's Guide & Sing-Along Tape. (Illus.). 128p. (Orig.). (J). (gr. k-2). 1995. pap. 30.00 incl. audio (1-879050-93-5) Chapel of Air.

Bussas, R., et al. Progress in the Chemistry of Aza-Analogs of SO-2, Vol. 2. 162p. 1983. pap. text 277.00 (3-7186-0153-2) Gordon & Breach.

Bussche, J. Vanden. Ignatius (George) Spencer, Passionist (1799-1864) Crusader of Prayer for England & Pioneer of Ecumenical Prayer. (Annua Nuntia Lovaniensia Ser.: No. 33). 283p. (Orig.). 1991. pap. 57.50 (90-6186-446-1, Pub. by Leuven Univ) Coronet Bks.

Bussche, Willy Van De, see Van De Bussche, Willy.

Busschen, Albert T. Micromechanical Modelling of the Transverse Strengths of Unidirectional Glass Fibre Reinforced Polyester. (Illus.). 246p. (Orig.). 1996. pap. 57.50 (90-407-1354-5, Pub. by Delft U Pr) Coronet Bks.

Busscher, H. J. Bacterial Adhesion & Its Prevention in Dentistry. 86p. 1991. pap. text 123.00 (3-7186-5188-2, Harwood Acad Pubs) Gordon & Breach.

***Busscher, H. J. & Evans, L. V., eds.** Oral Biofilms & Plaque Control. (Illus.). 480p. 1999. text 125.00 (90-5702-391-1, Harwood Acad Pubs) Gordon & Breach.

Busscher, Pierre-Olivier De, see De Busscher, Pierre-Olivier, ed.

Busse, et al. German Health Care System. 70.95 (1-84014-406-8) Ashgate Pub Co.

Busse, Chris, jt. auth. see Pike, Bob.

Busse, Ewald W. & Blazer, Dan G., eds. The American Psychiatric Press Textbook of Geriatric Psychiatry. 2nd ed. 560p. 1996. text 92.95 (0-88048-713-5, 8713) Am Psychiatric.

— Geriatric Psychiatry. LC 88-7432. 739p. 1989. reprint ed. pap. 200.00 (0-608-02024-9, 206268000003) Bks Demand.

Busse, Ewald W. & Maddox, George L. The Duke Longitudinal Studies of Normal Aging 1955-1980: Overview of History, Design & Findings. 192p. 1985. 26.95 (0-8261-4150-1) Springer Pub.

Busse, Ewald W. & Pfeiffer, Eric. Behavior & Adaptation in Late Life. 2nd ed. 1977. 24.50 (0-316-11833-8, Little Brwn Med Div); pap. 18.50 (0-316-11834-6, Little Brwn Med Div) Lppncott W & W.

***Busse, F. H.** Evolution of Spontaneous Structures in Dissipative Continuous Systems. LC 98-47923. (Lecture Notes in Physics Ser.). 1998. 89.95 (3-540-65154-3) Spr-Verlag.

Busse, F. H. & Kramer, L., eds. Nonlinear Evolution of Spatio-Temporal Structures in Dissipative Continuo. (NATO ASI Ser.: Vol. 225). (Illus.). 582p. (C). 1990. text 174.00 (0-306-43603-5, Kluwer Plenum) Kluwer Academic.

Busse, F. H. & Soward, A. M., eds. Dynamo Theory of Planetary Magnetism: A Special Issue of the Journal Geophysical & Astrophysical Fluid Dynamics. 272p. 1988. pap. text 157.00 (0-677-25790-2) Gordon & Breach.

Busse, Heribert. Islam, Judaism & Christianity: Theological & Historical Affiliations. Brown, Allison, tr. from GER. LC 97-40190. (Princeton Series on the Middle East). 260p. (C). 1998. text 49.95 (1-55876-143-8); pap. text 18.95 (1-55876-144-6) Wiener Pubs Inc.

Busse, J. G., jt. ed. see Appleman, Bernard R.

Busse, Kay, jt. auth. see Roegdke, Soren.

Busse, Laird R. I am Victory. 103p. (Orig.). 1993. pap. 10.95 (0-929385-41-1) Light Tech Pubng.

An Asterisk (*) at the beginning of an entry indicates that the title is appearing for the first time.

Busse, Mark, et al. The People of Lake Kutubu & Kikori: Changing Meanings of Daily Life. (Illus.). 96p. 1995. pap. text 17.00 (*9980-85-513-4*, Pub. by Papua New Guinea) UH Pr.

Busse, Rodger. Planning for Success on the Job. Harris, Valerie, ed. LC 93-71674. (Illus.). 264p. 1993. pap. 16.95 (*0-89262-220-2*); teacher ed., ring bd. 80.00 (*0-89262-221-0*) Career Pub.

Busse, Roger. Business Profiles. LC 98-90279. 150p. (C). 1998. pap. 49.95 (*0-9629242-5-3*) WKB Enterp.

Busse, Roger S. Ping Saves Earth. LC 95-90113. 128p. (Orig.). 1995. pap. 10.00 (*0-9629242-4-5*) WKB Enterp.

Busse, Ronald A. Into the Retrospectrum. 1997. pap. write for info. (*1-57553-543-2*) Watermrk Pr.

Busse, Thomas V. The Professor's Book of First Names. LC 83-80773. (Illus.). 120p. (Orig.). 1984. pap. 5.95 (*0-9610950-1-6*) Green Ball Pr.

Busse, Ulrich, ed. see Haenchen, Ernst.

Busse, W., jt. auth. see Holgate, Stephen T.

Busse, W. D., et al, eds. Antibacterial Therapy: Achievements, Problems & Future Perspectives. LC 97-22632. (Illus.). 80p. 1997. pap. 59.95 (*3-540-62896-7*) Spr-Verlag.

Busse, W. E., et al, eds. Dihydropyridines: Progress in Pharmacology & Therapy. LC 93-21268. 1993. 51.95 (*0-387-57308-9*) Spr-Verlag.

Busse, W. W., jt. auth. see Gern, James E.

Busse, W. W., jt. auth. see Holgate, Stephen T.

***Busse, William W. & Holgate, Stephen T.** Asthma & Rhinitis, 2 vols., Set. 2nd ed. LC 99-32708. (Illus.). 2304p. 2000. 450.00 (*0-632-04175-7*) Blackwell Sci.

Busse, Winfried & Trabant, Juergen, eds. Les Ideologues: Semiotique, Philosophie du Langage et Linguistique Pendant la Revolution Francaise Proceedings of the Conference, Berlin, Oct. 1983. LC 86-7863. (Foundations of Semiotics Ser.: Vol. 12). xvi, 404p. 1986. 124.00 (*90-272-3282-2*) J Benjamins Pubng Co.

Busse, Winfried & Varol-Bornes, Marie C., eds. Hommage a Haim Vidal Sephiha. (Sephardica Ser.: Vol. 1). (FRE.). 646p. 1996. 63.95 (*3-906755-91-6*, Pub. by P Lang) P Lang Pubng.

***Bussel, Abby.** SOM Evolutions: Recent Works of Skidmore, Owings & Merrill. (Illus.). 192p. 2000. 75.00 (*3-7643-6072-0*, Pub. by Birkhauser) Princeton Arch.

***Bussel, Robert.** From Harvard to the Ranks of Labor: Powers Hapgood & the American Working Class. LC 98-41426. 584p. 1999. 57.50 (*0-271-01897-6*) Pa St U Pr.

— From Harvard to the Ranks of Labor: Powers Hapgood & the American Working Class. LC 98-41426. (Illus.). 464p. 1999. pap. 19.95 (*0-271-01898-4*) Pa St U Pr.

Bussell. Black & White Photography. 1998. 19.95 (*2-88046-327-0*, Rotovision) Watsn-Guptill.

— Neonatal Immune Thrombocytopenia. 1991. write for info. (*0-8493-6469-8*, CRC Reprint) Franklin.

***Bussell, Daniel J.** Insights for the New Millennium. 12.95p. 1998. mass mkt. 12.95 incl. disk (*0-9669722-0-1*) C Bks Co.

Bussell, Daniel J., jt. auth. see Warren, William D.

***Bussell, Darcey.** Young Dancer. (Young Enthusiast Ser.). (J). 2000. 9.95 (*0-7894-5429-7*) DK Pub Inc.

Bussell, Darcy & Linton, Patricia. The Young Dancer: Royal Ballet School. LC 93-367901. (Illus.). 64p. (J). (gr. 2-6). 1994. 15.95 (*1-56458-468-2*) DK Pub Inc.

***Bussell, F. W.** The Roman Empire: Essays on the Constitutional History from the Accession, 2 vols., Set. LC 99-87026. 2000. write for info. (*1-58477-082-1*) Lawbk Exchange.

Bussell, F. W. The School of Plato: Its Origin, Development, & Revival under the Roman Empire (1896) 361p. 1996. reprint ed. pap. 29.95 (*1-56459-633-8*) Kessinger Pub.

Bussell, Frederick W. Marcus Aurelius & the Later Stoics. 1976. lib. bdg. 59.95 (*0-8490-2207-X*) Gordon Pr.

Bussell, Harold L. Lord, I Can Resist Anything but Temptation. (Orig.). 1985. pap. 4.70 (*0-310-37271-2*, 12389P) Zondervan.

— Unholy Devotion: Why Cults Lure Christians. 160p. 1983. pap. 6.95 (*0-310-37251-8*, 12388P) Zondervan.

***Busselle, Julien.** Processing & Printing. LC 99-40277. (B & W Photo-Lab Ser.). 128p. 2000. 29.95 (*1-883403-67-7*, Silver Pixel Pr) Saunders Photo.

— Processing & Printing Black & White for Effect. 1999. pap. 29.95 (*2-88046-427-7*) Watsn-Guptill.

Busselle, Michael. The Art of Photographic Lighting. (Illus.). 192p. 1995. pap. 21.95 (*0-7153-0282-5*, Pub. by D & C Pub) Sterling.

***Busselle, Michael.** Discovering the Country Vineyard. 1999. pap. 24.95 (*1-86205-285-9*, Pub. by Pavilion Bks Ltd) Trafalgar.

— Discovering the Country Vineyards of France. 2000. 31.50 (*0-8446-7113-4*) Peter Smith.

Busselle, Michael. Discovering the Villages of France. (Illus.). 192p. 1994. pap. 18.45 (*1-55970-248-6*, Pub. by Arcade Pub Inc) Time Warner.

— French Vineyards: The Complete Guide & Companion. (Illus.). 288p. 1998. 24.95 (*1-85793-598-5*, Pub. by Pavilion Bks Ltd) Trafalgar.

***Busselle, Michael.** French Vineyards: The Complete Guide & Companion. (Illus.). 288p. 1999. pap. 24.95 (*1-86205-205-0*, Pub. by Pavilion Bks Ltd) Trafalgar.

Busselle, Michael. Gardens & Flowers Photography. (Better Picture Guide Ser.). (Illus.). 124p. 1997. pap. 19.95 (*2-88046-326-2*, Rotovision) Watsn-Guptill.

— Landscape Photography: Better Picture Guides. (Better Picture Guide Ser.). (Illus.). 128p. 1998. pap. 19.95 (*2-88046-370-X*, Rotovision) Watsn-Guptill.

— Photographic Assignments: The Expert Approach. (Illus.). 192p. 1997. pap. 19.95 (*0-7153-0179-9*) Sterling.

— Photographing People. (Better Picture Guide Ser.). (Illus.). 128p. 1999. pap. 19.95 (*2-88046-393-9*, Rotovision) Watsn-Guptill.

***Busselle, Michael.** Still Life & Close-Up Photography: Better Picture Guides. 1999. pap. 19.95 (*2-88046-426-9*) Watsn-Guptill.

Busselle, Michael. Travel Photography. (Better Picture Guide Ser.). (Illus.). 124p. 1997. pap. 19.95 (*2-88046-325-4*, Rotovision) Watsn-Guptill.

— Using Colour Photography: Better Picture Guides. 120p. 1999. pap. 21.95 (*2-88046-493-5*) Watsn-Guptill.

***Busselle, Michael.** Vacation Photography. (Better Picture Guide Ser.). (Illus.). 2000. pap. 21.95 (*2-88046-443-9*, Rotovision) Watsn-Guptill.

Busselle, Michael, photos by. England: The Four Seasons. (Illus.). 160p. 1993. 29.95 (*1-55859-649-6*) Abbeville Pr.

Busselle, Rebecca. Bathing Ugly. (J). 1991. mass mkt. 4.99 (*0-440-80266-0*) Dell.

Bussemaker, Jet. Citizenship & Welfare State Reform in Europe. LC 98-51214. 1999. text. write for info. (*0-415-18927-6*) Routledge.

Bussemaker, Jet & Voet, Rian, eds. Gender, Participation, & Citizenship in the Netherlands. LC 97-78096. (Illus.). 151p. 1998. text 59.95 (*1-85972-680-1*, Pub. by Ashgate Pub) Ashgate Pub Co.

Busser, Fritz. Die Prophezei: Humanismus und Reformation in Zurich Ausgewahlte Aufsatze und Vortrage Zu Seinem 70. Geburtstag Am 12. Februar 1993. Schindler, Alfred, ed. (Zurcher Beitrage Zur Reformationsgeschichte Ser.: Bd. 17). (GER.). 241p. 1994. 48.95 (*3-906752-60-7*, Pub. by P Lang) P Lang Pubng.

Busser, Fritz, ed. see Biel, Pamela.

Busser, James A., jt. auth. see Bannon, Joseph J.

Busser, Marianne & Schroder, Ron. King Bobble. James, J. Alison, tr. LC 95-52224. (Illus.). 64p. (J). (gr. 2-4). 1996. 13.95 (*1-55858-591-5*, Pub. by North-South Bks NYC); lib. bdg. 13.88 (*1-55858-592-3*, Pub. by North-South Bks NYC) Chronicle Bks.

***Busser, Marianne & Schroder, Ron.** King Bobble. LC 95-52224. (Illus.). 64p. (J). (gr. 2-4). 1999. pap. 5.95 (*0-7358-1202-0*, Pub. by North-South Bks NYC) Chronicle Bks.

Busser, Marianne & Schroder, Ron. On the Road with Poppa Whopper. LC 94-40590. (Illus.). 64p. (J). (gr. 1-4). 1997. pap. 5.95 (*1-55858-776-4*, Pub. by North-South Bks NYC) Chronicle Bks.

Busser, Robert A., jt. ed. see Miller, Iris.

Bussey, Alex W. Webs Solidly Woven. 150p. 1999. pap. 9.95 (*1-891929-26-7*) Four Seasons.

Bussey, Charles M. Firefight at Yechon: Courage & Racism in the Korean War. (Association of the U. S. Army Book Ser.). 304p. 1991. 21.95 (*0-08-037448-4*, 3817M) Brasseys.

— Firefight at Yechon: Courage & Racism in the Korean War. (Illus.). 264p. 1998. text 24.00 (*0-7881-5733-7*) DIANE Pub.

Bussey, Eliza. Madam Wongs Guide to Men & Other Difficulties. 128p. (Orig.). 1996. pap. 13.00 (*0-9652626-1-8*) Orge Blossom.

Bussey, Ellen M., ed. Federal Civil Service Law & Procedures: A Basic Guide. 2nd ed. LC 89-23996. 628p. reprint ed. pap. 194.70 (*0-608-04265-X*, 206502000012) Bks Demand.

Bussey, G. Wireless: The Crucial Decade, 1924-34. (History of Technology Ser.: No. 13). 121p. 1990. 39.00 (*0-86341-188-6*, HT013) INSPEC Inc.

Bussey, H. J. Familial Polyposis Coli: Family Studies, Histopathology, Differential Diagnosis, & Results of Treatment. LC 74-24392. (Illus.). 120p. 1975. reprint ed. pap. 37.20 (*0-608-04073-8*, 206480500011) Bks Demand.

Bussey, Holly, jt. auth. see Swartzburg, Susan G.

Bussey-Jackson, Loure. Nightfall. 304p. 1996. mass mkt. 4.99 (*0-7860-0332-4*, Pinncle Kensgtn) Kensgtn Pub Corp.

***Bussey, Loure.** Images of Ecstasy. (Arabesque Ser.). 2000. mass mkt. 5.99 (*1-58314-115-4*) BET Bks.

Bussey, Loure. Love So True. 256p. 1999. mass mkt. 4.99 (*0-7860-0608-0*) Kensgtn Pub Corp.

— Taste of Love, 1. (Arabesque Ser.). 1999. mass mkt. 4.99 (*1-58314-029-8*) BET Bks.

— Twist of Fate. (Arabesque Ser.). 304p. 1998. pap. 4.99 (*0-7860-0513-0*, Pinncle Kensgtn) Kensgtn Pub Corp.

Bussey, M. T., ed. see Hale, Duane K.

Bussey, M. T., ed. see Otto, Simon.

Bussey, Melody, jt. auth. see Baggett, Shirley.

Bussey, P. J. & Knowles, I. G., eds. Proceedings of the XXVII International Conference on High Energy Physics, 21-27 July 1994, Glasgow, Scotland, U. K., Vol. 2. LC 95-6174. (Illus.). 1528p. 1995. 670.00 (*0-7503-0125-2*) IOP Pub.

Bussey, Sherrey, ed. see Kratz, Karl.

Bussgang, Julian F., tr. see Sliwowska, Wiktoria.

Bussi, Cathy. Pressed Flowers: A Creative Guide. 72p. (C). 1988. 75.00 (*1-85368-010-9*, Pub. by New5 Holland) St Mut.

Bussi, Gail, et al. Country Cross Stitch. (Illus.). 142p. 1996. write for info. (*1-57215-197-8*) World Pubns.

Bussi, L. & Cognazzo, M. T. New English-Italian Dictionary of the Medical Sciences: Nuovo Dizionario Inglese-Italiano delle Scienze Mediche. 864p. 1987. 150.00 (*0-8288-1846-0*, M14387) Fr & Eur.

Bussi, Rolando, jt. ed. see Settis, Salvatore.

Bussiere, Alice, et al. Sharing Information: A Guide to Federal Laws on Confidentiality & Disclosure of Information for Child Welfare Agencies. LC 97-25093. 1997. write for info. (*1-57073-464-X*) Amer Bar Assn.

Bussiere, Elizabeth. (Dis)Entitling the Poor: The Warren Court, Welfare Rights & the American Political Tradition. LC 96-6451. 1997. 26.50 (*0-271-01601-9*) Pa St U Pr.

Bussiere, J., jt. ed. see Holbrook, J.

Bussiere, J. F., et al, eds. Nondestructive Characterization of Materials II. LC 87-16609. (Illus.). 804p. 1987. 145.00 (*0-306-42610-2*, Plenum Trade) Perseus Pubng

Bussiere, Ronald L. Principles of Electrosurgery: Practical Overview of R. F. Electrosurgical Generators. (Illus.). 33p. 1997. 45.00 (*0-9661128-0-6*) Tektran.

Bussigel, Margaret N., et al. Innovation Processes in Medical Education. LC 87-27391. 170p. 1988. 62.95 (*0-275-92369-X*, C2369, Praeger Pubs) Greenwood.

***Bussing-Burks, Maire.** The Young Zillionaire's Guide to Taxation & Government Spending. LC 99-86074. (Be a Zillionaire Ser.). 2000. lib. bdg. 17.95 (*0-8239-3258-3*) Rosen Group.

Bussing, Charles E., et al. Laboratory Exercises for Environmental Geography. 3rd ed. 144p. 1996. spiral bd. 24.95 (*0-8403-8276-6*) Kendall-Hunt.

Bussing, Irvin. Public Utility Regulation & the So-Called Sliding Scale: A Study of the Sliding Scale As a Means of Encouraging & Rewarding Efficiency in the Management of Regulated Monopolies. LC 68-58552. (Columbia University. Studies in the Social Sciences: No. 415). reprint ed. 20.00 (*0-404-51415-4*) AMS Pr.

Bussing, Sabine. Aliens in the Home: The Child in Horror Fiction, 4. LC 86-19389. (Contributions to the Study of Childhood & Youth Ser.: No. 4). 224p. 1987. 57.95 (*0-313-25420-6*, BGL/, Greenwood Pr) Greenwood.

Bussink, Gerrit. Nice People: A Collection of Dutch Short Stories. (Prose Ser.: No. 23). 195p. 1993. pap. 12.00 (*0-920717-89-6*) Guernica Editions.

Bussink, Gerrit, ed. Bittersweet Pieces: A Collection of Dutch Short Stories. 110p. 1991. pap. 10.00 (*0-920717-48-9*) SPD-Small Pr Dist.

Bussino, Giovanni R., tr. see Bonaviri, Giuseppe.

Bussino, Giovanni R., tr. see Pirandello, Luigi.

Bussino, Giovanni R., tr. & intro. see Pirandello, Luigi.

Bussler, C., jt. auth. see Jablonski, Stefan.

Bussler, Darrol, et al. Introducing Educational Reconstruction: The Philosophy & Practice of Transforming Society Through Education. LC 97-3138. 136p. 1997. pap. 14.95 (*1-880192-22-5*) Caddo Gap Pr.

Bussler, Rod, ed. see McCaig, Barbara.

Bussmann, H. Lexicon of Scientific Terms: Lexikon der Sprachwissenschsft. (GER.). 603p. 1983. 49.95 (*0-8288-1973-4*, M15150) Fr & Eur.

Bussmann, Hadumod. Routledge Dictionary of Language & Linguistics. 1999. pap. 40.00 (*0-415-20319-8*) Routledge.

Bussmann, Hadumod, jt. auth. see Trauth, Gregory.

Bussmann, Hans. Mathematik Lernen - Lehrbar? Die Mathematiklernende Person Im Zyklus Ihrer Lebensumwelt. (GER., Illus.). 491p. 1997. 82.95 (*3-631-31201-6*) P Lang Pubng.

Bussmann, Kai-D., jt. ed. see Karstedt, Susanne.

Bussmann, W. D., et al, eds. Controlled Release Nitroglycerin in Buccal & Oral Form. (Advances in Pharmacotherapy Ser.: Vol. 1). (Illus.). xii, 220p. 1982. 101.00 (*3-8055-3507-4*) S Karger.

Busso, Maurizio, et al. Nuclei in the Cosmos: Third International Symposium on Nuclear Astrophysics. (AIP Conference Proceedings Ser.: No. 327). (Illus.). 650p. 1995. boxed set 135.00 (*1-56396-436-8*, AIP Pr) Spr-Verlag.

Bussoletti, E., et al, eds. Experiments on Cosmic Dust Analogues. (C). 1988. text 206.50 (*90-277-2777-5*) Kluwer Academic.

Bussoletti, E. & Vittone, Alberto A., eds. Dusty Objects in the Universe. (C). 1990. text 166.50 (*0-7923-0863-8*) Kluwer Academic.

Bussolin, Veronique. France. LC 94-13802. (Country Fact Files Ser.). (J). 1995. lib. bdg. 24.26 (*0-8114-2784-6*) Raintree Steck-V.

Busson, Georges & Schreiber, B. Charlotte. Sedimentary Deposition in Rift & Foreland Basins in France & Spain (Paleogene & Lower Neogene) LC 96-32223. 1997. 210.00 (*0-231-06786-0*) Col U Pr.

Busson, Terry & Coulter, Philip, eds. Policy Evaluation for Local Government. (Orig.). 1983. pap. 15.00 (*0-918592-69-0*) Pol Studies.

Busson, Terry & Coulter, Phillip, eds. Policy Evalution for Local Government, 182. LC 87-7532. (Contributions in Political Science Ser.: No. 182). 286p. 1987. 65.00 (*0-313-25953-4*, BEV/, Greenwood Pr) Greenwood.

Bussow, Conrad. The Disturbed State of the Russian Realm. Orchard, G. Edward, ed. & tr. by. (Illus.). 288p. 1994. 65.00 (*0-7735-1165-2*, Pub. by McG-Queens Univ Pr) CUP Services.

***Busst, Alan J. L.** L' Orphee de Ballanche Vol. 4: Genese et Signification. (Le Romantisme et Apres en France Ser.). 343p. 1999. 52.95 (*3-906763-81-1*, Pub. by P Lang) P Lang Pubng.

Bussy. Kraftwerk: Man, Machine & Music. 1999. pap. 17.95 (*0-946719-09-8*) Interlink Pub.

Bussy, Carvel De. Conferences de Litterature Francaise: XVIIIe Siecle. LC 78-66098. (FRE.). (C). 1984. pap. text 20.00 (*0-9602260-0-1*) C de Bussy.

Bussy, Carvel De, see De Bussy, Carvel.

Bussy, Dorothy, tr. see Gide, Andre.

Bust, Alyssa F., jt. auth. see Van Patten, George F.

Busta, William. Howling at the Edge of a Renaissance: Spaces & Alternative Art in Cleveland, 1978-1998. (Illus.). 80p. 1998. pap. 7.00 (*0-9667008-0-5*) SPACES.

Bustad, Leo K. Animals, Aging, & the Aged. LC 80-24415. (Wesley W. Spink Lectures on Comparative Medicine: No. 5). 245p. reprint ed. pap. 76.00 (*0-8357-2589-8*, 205236900013) Bks Demand.

— Compassion: Our Last Great Hope. 2nd ed. (Illus.). 152p. 1996. pap. 12.00 (*1-889785-00-8*) Delta Soc.

Bustad, Leo K., jt. ed. see Goldman, Marvin.

Bustafson, B. A. & Hanner, Martin S., eds. Physics, Chemistry & Dynamics of Interplanetary Dust Vol. 104: Iau Colloquium 150. (ASP Conference Series Proceedings). 538p. 1996. 34.00 (*1-886733-24-4*) Astron Soc Pacific.

Bustamante, Antonio R., ed. see Reimers, David M.

Bustamante, Cecilia. Flora Tristan: A Woman of Vision: Paul Gaugin's Astonishing Grandmother: Forerunner of Feminism & Workers' Organization. McGee, May L., tr. from FRE. (Seagreen Ser.). (Illus.). 200p. (C). 1990. pap. text 12.95 (*0-944181-00-7*) Extramares Edit.

— Lines & Paper Works: A Selection in English of Name of Things, New Poems, Love in Lima, Discernment, Legend Noa Noa - Poetry Collection. Ahern, Maureen et al, trs. from SPA. 56p. (C). 1990. teacher ed. 10.80 (*0-685-33318-3*) Extramares Edit.

Bustamante, Cecilia, jt. auth. see Reedy, Daniel.

Bustamante, Cecilia, jt. ed. see Coyne, Andre.

***Bustamante, Cruz M. & Fresno Chamber of Commerce Staff.** Fresno: Heartbeat of the Valley. LC 00-36449. (Urban Tapestry Ser.). (Illus.). 240p. 2000. 49.95 (*1-881096-80-7*) Towery Pub.

Bustamante, Eduardo. Parenting & the AD/HD Child: A New Approach. Robbins, Carroll, ed. LC 97-62018. 160p. 1997. pap. 12.95 (*0-9633007-4-1*) Whitcomb MA.

Bustamante, Eduardo M. Treating the Defiant Adolescent: Finding the Real Self Behind Oppositional Defiant Disorders. LC 99-37817. 1999. 65.00 (*0-7657-0235-5*) Aronson.

Bustamante, Georgina, tr. see Vega, Monica, et al.

Bustamante, I. D., jt. auth. see Lacasa, R.

Bustamante, I. Diaz De, see Navarro, R. Lacasa & De Bustamante, I. Diaz.

Bustamante, Ines S. Behavior Problems in Children: And Their Aftermath in Adult Age. De Varona, Carlos, ed. & tr. by. from ENG. (SPA.). 268p. (Orig.). 1988. pap. 9.95 (*0-9619497-0-8*) ISB Edns.

Bustamante, Jean-Marc. Bitter Almonds. 80p. 1997. pap. 19.95 (*0-7148-3707-5*, Pub. by Phaidon Press) Phaidon Pr.

Bustamante, Jorge A., et al, eds. U. S. - Mexico Relations: Labor Market Interdependence. LC 91-42423. (U. S. - Mexican Relations Ser.). 516p. (C). 1992. 55.00 (*0-8047-2020-7*) Stanford U Pr.

Bustamante, Jorge A., jt. auth. see Glazer, Nathan.

Bustamante, Jorge A., jt. ed. see Cornelius, Wayne A.

Bustamante, Jose M. Diccionario Tematico Ingles-Espanol, Espanol-Ingles. 2nd ed. (ENG & SPA.). 448p. 1990. pap. 35.00 (*0-7859-3698-X*, S31559) Fr & Eur.

***Bustamante, M. C.** Si Si Puede. (SPA.). 68p. 1999. write for info. (*92-806-3490-9*) U N I C E.

Bustamante, Nao, et al. New Langton Arts, 1991-1997. LC 99-177303. (Illus.). 160p. 1998. pap. 20.00 (*0-9627010-1-7*) New Langton Arts.

Bustamante, Rafael C., tr. see Flamming, Peter J.

Bustamante, Rafael C., tr. see Hybels, Bill.

Bustamante y Sirven, Antonio De Sanchez, see De Sanchez Bustamante y Sirven, Antonio.

Bustamente, C. P., ed. see Menendez Pidal, Ramon.

Bustani, Butros. Arabic Dictionary: Muhit al-Muhit. (ARA.). 997p. 1983. 65.00 (*0-86685-096-1*, LDL0961, Pub. by Librairie du Liban) Intl Bk Ctr.

Bustanoby, Andre. Being a Success at Who You Are. 1985. pap. 2.95 (*0-310-45381-X*, 9172P) Zondervan.

— But I Didn't Want a Divorce. 174p. 1978. pap. 9.99 (*0-310-22171-4*, 9207P) Zondervan.

— Eight Keys to Communicate Better. LC 85-14199. 64p. (Orig.). 1985. pap. 2.70 (*0-310-46242-8*, 9266P) Zondervan.

— Just Friends? 160p. (Orig.). 1985. pap. 6.99 (*0-310-45431-X*, 9254P) Zondervan.

— The Readymade Family: How to Be a Stepparent & Survive. 160p. (Orig.). 1982. pap. 5.70 (*0-310-45361-5*, 9212P) Zondervan.

— Single Parenting. Orig. Title: Being a Single Parent. 272p. 1992. pap. 9.99 (*0-310-57451-X*) Zondervan.

Bustanoby, Andre & Bustanoby, Fay. Just Talk to Me. 192p. (Orig.). 1981. pap. text 7.95 (*0-310-22181-1*, 9211P) Zondervan.

Bustanoby, Fay, jt. auth. see Bustanoby, Andre.

Bustard, Anne. T Is for Texas. LC 89-35633. (Illus.). 32p. (J). (ps-2). 1990. 12.95 (*0-89658-113-6*) Voyageur Pr.

Bustard, Bruce I. A New Deal for the Arts. LC 96-31607. 1997. write for info. (*1-880875-14-4*) Natl Archives VCSG.

— A New Deal for the Arts. LC 96-31607. (Illus.). 144p. 1997. pap. 24.95 (*0-295-97600-4*) U of Wash Pr.

— Picturing the Century: One Hundred Years of Photography from the National Archives. LC 98-44102. (Illus.). 144p. 1999. pap. 24.95 (*0-295-97772-8*) U of Wash Pr.

***Bustard, Bruce I., et al.** Treasures of Congress. LC 99-52775. (Illus.). 1999. pap. 15.00 (*1-880875-20-9*) National Archives & Recs.

***Bustard, Dave.** Systems Modeling for Business Process Improvement. LC 00-27445. 264p. 2000. 69.00 (*1-58053-050-8*) Artech Hse.

***Bustard, Ned, ed.** It Was Good: Making Art to the Glory of God. LC 00-105398. (Illus.). 256p. 2000. pap. 17.99 (*0-9658798-2-8*) Square Halo Bks.

***Busteed, H. E., contrib. by.** Echoes from Old Calcutta: Reminiscences of the Days of Warren Hastings, Francis & Impey H. E. Busteed. 2nd ed. 2000. pap. 17.50 (*81-7167-427-5*, Pub. by Rupa) S Asia.

Busteed, M. A. Voting Behaviour in the Republic of Ireland: A Geographical Perspective. (Illus.). 264p. 1991. 75.00 (*0-19-823276-4*) OUP.

Busteed, Marilyn & Wergin, Dorothy. Phases of the Moon. LC 82-73123. 219p. 1996. 18.95 (*0-86690-345-3*, W2644-014) Am Fed Astrologers.

Busteed, Tiffany. The Phases of the Moon. 1974. mass mkt. 7.95 (*0-394-49518-7*) Random.

B

Bustelo, Gabriela, tr. see Cleary, Beverly.

Bustelo, Mara R. & Alston, Philip, eds. Whose New World Order? What Role for the United Nations? xiv, 157p. 1991. pap. 32.50 (*1-86287-067-5*, Pub. by Federation Pr) Gaunt.

Buster, Dave. Basic Construction Math Review: A Manual of Basic Construction Mathematics for Contractor & Tradesman License Exams. 104p. 1973. pap. 18.95 (*0-935715-06-1*, 0083) Construct Bkstore.

Buster, Dave, jt. ed. see Rola, Fatima.

***Buster, Larry Vincent.** The Art & History of Black Memorabilia. LC 99-86917. (Illus.). 176p. 2000. 34.95 (*0-609-60425-2*) C Potter.

***Buster, R. Dalton.** The Walking Dead. 2nd rev. ed. 194p. 1999. spiral bd. 20.00 (*0-9676552-0-7*) R D Buster.

Busterna, John C. & Picard, Robert G. Joint Operating Agreements: The Newspaper Preservation Act & Its Application. LC 93-11299. (Communication & Information Science Ser.). 184p. 1993. pap. 39.50 (*1-56750-001-3*); text 73.25 (*0-89391-994-2*) Ablx Pub.

Busti, Kathryn M. Stage Production Handbook: Job Responsibilities for All Technical Backstage Crews. (Illus.). 178p. 1994. 40.00 (*0-9642913-0-4*) Theatre Things.

Bustin, Dillon. If You Don't Outdie Me: The Legacy of Brown County. LC 82-47784. 154p. reprint ed. pap. 47.80 (*0-7837-3694-0*, 205787200009) Bks Demand.

Bustin, Edouard. Lunda under Belgian Rule: The Politics of Ethnicity. (Illus.). 302p. 1975. 37.95 (*0-674-53953-2*) HUP.

Bustin, G. T. The Man Christ Jesus. 1987. pap. 9.99 (*0-88019-226-7*) Schmul Pub Co.

Busto, Graciela. Baba Is Here: Conversations with God on His Omnipresence. LC 97-76043. 1998. pap. text 12.00 (*1-887906-01-0*) Leela Pr.

Bustock, Anna, tr. see Fischer, Ernst & Marek, Franz.

***Bustos, Maria C.** Sedimentation & Thickening: Phenomenological Foundation & Mathematical Theory. LC 99-43422. (Mathematical Modelling--Theory & Applications Ser.). 1999. write for info. (*0-7923-5960-7*) Kluwer Academic.

Bustos, Roxann, compiled by. Interlibrary Loan in College Libraries. (CLIP Note Ser.: No. 16). 148p. 1993. pap. 34.50 (*0-8389-7652-2*) Assn Coll & Res Libs.

Bustos Tovar, Jesus. Universal Dictionary of Literature: Diccionario de Literatura Universal. (SPA.). 657p. 1985. 49.50 (*0-8288-1576-3*, S60726) Fr & Eur.

Busturia, Daniel, et al. Terminological Dictionary of the European Community: Diccionario Terminologico de las Comunidades Europeas. (SPA.). 680p. 1982. 85.00 (*0-7859-4969-0*) Fr & Eur.

Busutil, Ronald W. & Klintmalm, Goran B. Transplantation of the Liver. Bralow, Lisette, ed. (Illus.). 784p. 1996. text 275.00 (*0-7216-4942-4*, W B Saunders Co) Harcrt Hlth Sci Grp.

Busuttil, James, jt. auth. see Blackburn, Robert.

Busuttil, James J. Naval Weapons Systems & the Contemporary Law of War. (Oxford Monographs in International Law). 270p. 1998. text 90.00 (*0-19-826574-3*) OUP.

Busuttil, Joelle. Behind the Wall of China. (Young Discovery Library). (Illus.). 40p. (J). (gr. k-6). 1993. lib. bdg. 2.99 (*1-56674-057-6*, HTS Bks) Forest Hse.

— Behind the Wall of China. Bogard, Vicki, tr. from FRE. LC 92-969. (Illus.). (J). (gr. k-5). 1992. 5.95 (*0-944589-42-1*) Young Discovery Lib.

Busuttil, Salvino, jt. ed. see Agius, Emmanuel.

Busvine, James R. Disease Transmission by Insects: Its Discovery & 90 Years of Effort to Prevent It. LC 92-48241. 1993. 86.00 (*0-387-55457-2*); pap. write for info. (*3-540-55457-2*) Spr-Verlag.

Buswell, Barbara, jt. auth. see Schaffner, C. Beth.

***Buswell, Barbara E., et al, eds.** Opening Doors: Connecting Students to Curriculum, Classmates & Learning. 2nd ed. (Connecting Students Ser.). Orig. Title: Opening Doors: Strategies for Including All Student in Regular Education. 52p. 1999. pap. 13.00 (*1-884720-12-9*) PEAK Parent.

***Buswell, Barbara E., et al.** An Introductory Workshop Kit on Friendship Building Strategies. 2nd ed. (Illus.). 1999. 89.00 (*1-884720-11-0*) PEAK Parent.

Buswell, Barbara E., jt. auth. see Schaffner, C. Beth.

Buswell, Henry F. Civil Liability for Personal Injuries Arising Out of Negligence. LC 97-3619. lxxxv, 463p. 1997. reprint ed. 75.00 (*0-8377-1985-2*, Rothman) W S Hein.

— Statute of Limitations & Adverse Possession: With an Appendix Containing the English Acts of Limitation. lxvi, 623p. 1991. reprint ed. 65.00 (*0-8377-1951-8*) W S Hein.

Buswell, James O., Jr. Systematic Theology of the Christian Religion. 1969. 25.95 (*0-310-22190-0*, 9364) Zondervan.

Buswell, Richard S. Echoes: A Visual Reflection. (Illus.). 84p. (Orig.). 1997. pap. 29.95 (*1-56037-125-0*) Am Wrld Geog.

Buswell, Robert C., ed. see Greenlee, J. Harold.

Buswell, Robert E., Jr. The Formation of Ch'an Ideology in China & Korea: The Vajrasamadhi-Sutra, A Buddhist Apocryphon. (Library of Asian Translations). 288p. (C). 1989. text 55.00 (*0-691-07336-8*, Pub. by Princeton U Pr) Cal Prin Full Svc.

— Tracing Back the Radiance: Chinul's Korean Way of Zen. abr. ed. LC 91-28980. (Classics in East Asian Buddhism Ser.). (C). 1991. pap. text 18.00 (*0-8248-1427-4*) UH Pr.

Buswell, Robert E. The Zen Monastic Experience: Buddhist Practice in Contemporary Korea. 288p. (C). 1992. pap. text 16.95 (*0-691-03477-X*, Pub. by Princeton U Pr) Cal Prin Full Svc.

Buswell, Robert E., Jr., ed. Chinese Buddhist Apocrypha. LC 89-20614. 376p. 1990. text 40.00 (*0-8248-1253-0*) UH Pr.

Buswell, Robert E., Jr. & Gimello, Robert M., eds. Paths to Liberation: The Marga & Its Transformations in Buddhist Thought. LC 91-29277. (Studies in East Asian Buddhism: No. 7). (Illus.). 536p. (C). 1992. text 45.00 (*0-8248-1417-7*) UH Pr.

Busza, Andrew, ed. see Conrad, Joseph.

Busza, Andrzej, tr. see Bialoszewski, Miron.

Buszek, Beatrice R. Apple Connection. (Illus.). 210p. 1991. pap. 11.95 (*0-920852-48-3*) Nimbus Publ.

— Blueberry Connection. (Illus.). 228p. 1991. pap. 12.95 (*0-920852-32-7*) Nimbus Publ.

— Cranberry Connection. (Illus.). 214p. 1991. pap. 12.95 (*0-920852-30-0*) Nimbus Publ.

— Strawberry Connection. (Illus.). 232p. 1991. pap. 12.95 (*0-920852-31-9*) Nimbus Publ.

— Sugar Bush Connection. (Illus.). 204p. 1991. pap. 12.95 (*0-920852-33-5*) Nimbus Publ.

Buszkowski, W., et al, eds. Categorial Grammar. LC 88-338. (Linguistic & Literary Studies in Eastern Europe: Vol. 25). viii, 365p. (C). 1988. 133.00 (*90-272-1530-8*) J Benjamins Pubng Co.

Buszynski, Leszek. Russian Foreign Policy after the Cold War. LC 96-551. 256p. 1996. 65.00 (*0-275-95585-0*, Praeger Pubs) Greenwood.

— Seato: The Failure of an Alliance Strategy. 276p. 1983. 44.50 (*9971-69-060-8*, Pub. by Sngapore Univ Pr) Coronet Bks.

But, P. P-H., jt. ed. see Chang, H. M.

Buta, R., et al, eds. Barred Galaxies: IAU Colloquium 157. (ASP Conference Series Proceedings: Vol. 91). 585p. 1996. 34.00 (*1-886733-12-0*) Astron Soc Pacific.

***Butala, Sharon.** Country of the Heart. 2000. pap. 16.00 (*0-00-648158-2*) HarpC.

— Luna. 246p. 2000. pap. 18.95 (*0-00-648540-5*) HarpC.

Butala, Sharon. Perfection of the Morning: A Woman's Awakening in Nature. LC 96-78758. 194p. 1997. reprint ed. pap. 14.00 (*1-886913-16-1*) Ruminator Bks.

— Queen of the Headaches. 198p. 1985. reprint ed. mass mkt. 7.95 (*0-919926-48-7*, Pub. by Coteau) Genl Dist Srvs.

Butala, Tony, et al. The Lettermen-Backstage-Onstage! LC 94-71316. (Illus.). 28p. (Orig.). 1994. pap. 12.95 (*0-9634122-7-2*) Feather Fables.

Butala, Tony, jt. auth. see Fullerton, Patrick S.

Butalia, R. C. The Evolution of the Artillery in India: From the Battle of Plassey (1757) to the Revolt of 1857. LC 98-915587. xvii, 388 p. 1998. write for info. (*81-7023-872-2*) Allied Pubs.

Butalia, Urashi, ed. In Other Words: New Writing by Indian Women. (C). 1992. text 10.00 (*81-85107-48-3*, Pub. by Kali for Women) S Asia.

***Butalia, Urvashi.** The Other Side of Silence: Voices from the Partition of India. LC 99-50297. (Illus.). 278p. 2000. pap. 17.95 (*0-8223-2494-6*) Duke.

— The Other Side of Silence: Voices from the Partition of India. LC 99-921581. 1999. write for info. (*0-19-579054-5*) OUP.

— The Other Side of Silence: Voices from the Partition of India. LC 98-905436. xi, 278 p. 1998. 24.00 (*0-670-87892-8*) Viking Penguin.

Butalia, Urvashi, jt. ed. see Sarkar, Tanika.

Butani, D. The Third Sikh War? Towards or Away from Khalistan? 150p. 1987. text 90.00 (*0-7201-1893-X*) Continuum.

Butani, D. H. Baba Hariram: Saint of Sind. (C). 1981. 6.00 (*0-8364-2371-2*, Pub. by Promilla) S Asia.

— The Incredible Bhagat Wadhuram: Saint of Sind. 1986. 8.00 (*81-85882-01-0*, Pub. by Promilla) S Asia.

— The Third Sikh War? Towards or Away from Khalistan? 137p. 1986. 25.00 (*81-85002-02-9*, Pub. by Promilla) S Asia.

Butani, D. K. Insect Pests of Vegetables. (C). 1983. 185.00 (*81-7136-002-5*, Pub. by Periodical Expert) St Mut.

— Insects & Fruits. 415p. (C). 1989. text 260.00 (*0-89771-573-X*, Pub. by Intl Bk Distr) St Mut.

— Insects & Fruits. (C). 1979. 200.00 (*81-7136-000-9*, Pub. by Periodical Expert) St Mut.

— Insects & Fruits. 415p. 1979. reprint ed. 225.00 (*0-7855-3066-5*, Pub. by Intl Bk Distr) St Mut.

Butazzo, G., ed. see Serrin, J.

Butch, Dorothy. New York State Documents: An Introductory Manual. 138p. 1987. 10.00 (*0-318-22980-3*) NYS Library.

Butch, Suzanne H. & Tiehen, Ann, eds. Blood Irradiation: A User's Guide. (Illus.). 124p. 1996. pap. 69.00 (*1-56395-057-X*, PC97-PR9605) Am Assn Blood.

Butchart. Anatomy of Power, Vol. 1. LC 98-9749. 220p. 1998. text. write for info. (*1-85649-539-6*, Pub. by Zed Books); text 25.00 (*1-85649-540-X*) Zed Books.

Butchart, David S., ed. see Striggio, Alessandro & Merulo, Claudio.

Butchart, Duncan. Wild about Cape Town. LC 96-222258. 128p. 1998. pap. 14.95 (*1-86812-597-1*) Menasha Ridge.

— Wild about Johannesburg. 128p. pap. 14.95 (*1-86812-595-5*) Menasha Ridge.

— Wild about the Lowveld. 128p. pap. 14.95 (*1-86812-596-3*) Menasha Ridge.

— Wild about the Okavango. 128p. pap. 14.95 (*1-86812-594-7*) Menasha Ridge.

Butchart, Harvey. Grand Canyon Treks: 12,000 Miles Through the Grand Canyon. rev. ed. Benti, Wynne, ed. LC 97-36947. (Illus.). 288p. 1998. pap. 16.95 (*0-9647530-2-2*) Spotted Dog CA.

Butchart, M. Money in the English Tradition, 1640-1936. 1973. 59.95 (*0-8490-0661-9*) Gordon Pr.

Butchart, Ronald E. Local Schools: Exploring Their History. LC 86-22276. (Nearby History Ser.). (Illus.). 124p. 1986. reprint ed. pap. 17.95 (*0-910050-82-1*) AltaMira Pr.

— Northern Schools, Southern Blacks, & Reconstruction: Freedmen's Education, 1862-1875, 87. LC 79-8949. (Contributions in American History Ser.: No. 87). (Illus.). 309p. 1980. 38.50 (*0-313-22073-5*, BNS/) Greenwood.

Butchart, Ronald E. & McEwan, Barbara, eds. Classroom Discipline in American Schools: Problems & Possibilities for Democratic Education. LC 97-10600. 287p. (C). 1997. pap. text 19.95 (*0-7914-3618-7*) State U NY Pr.

Butchbaker, A. F. Electricity & Electronics for Agriculture. LC 76-25995. (Illus.). 399p. reprint ed. pap. 123.70 (*0-8357-8113-5*, 205680100087) Bks Demand.

Butcher. Psychogenic Voice Disorders. 186p. 1993. pap. 47.50 (*1-56593-238-2*, 0557) Singular Publishing.

Butcher, jt. auth. see Carson.

Butcher, Arona, ed. The Year in Trade (1997) Operation of the Trade Agreements Program, 49th Report. (Illus.). 204p. (C). 1999. pap. text 40.00 (*0-7881-7792-3*) DIANE Pub.

***Butcher, Bernard L.** Genealogical & Personal History of the Upper Monongahela Valley, West Virginia, 2 vols. 1762p. 1999. reprint ed. pap. 70.00 (*0-8063-4849-6*) Clearfield Co.

Butcher, Betty, jt. auth. see Romine, Andrea.

***Butcher, Bruce S.** Directors' Duties: A New Millennium, a New Approach? LC 00-24919. (Studies in Comparative Corporate & Financial Law). 416p. 2000. 132.50 (*90-411-9788-5*) Kluwer Law Intl.

Butcher, Clyde. Clyde Butcher: Portfolio I: Florida Landscapes. 2nd ed. Reding, Malcolm E., ed. LC 94-65397. (Illus.). 65p. 1994. reprint ed. 45.00 (*0-9638703-2-7*) Shade Tree Pr.

— Clyde Butcher, Portfolio I: Florida Landscapes. 2nd deluxe limited ed. Reding, Malcolm E., ed. (Illus.). 100p. 1994. reprint ed. boxed set 125.00 (*0-9638703-3-5*) Shade Tree Pr.

Butcher, D. W. On-Line Monitoring of Continuous Process Plant. 326p. 1983. text 107.00 (*0-470-27504-9*) P-H.

Butcher, David J. & Sneddon, Joseph. A Practical Guide to Graphite Furnace Atomic Absorption Spectrometry. LC 97-29336. (Chemical Analysis). 272p. 1998. 79.95 (*0-471-12553-9*, Wiley-Interscience) Wiley.

Butcher, Dennis. Developing the Caring Community: A 10-Week Course in Pastoral Care Ministry for Laity. pap. 15.95 (*1-56699-128-5*, OD105) Alban Inst.

Butcher, Devercuy, ed. see Collingwood, G. H. & Brush, Warren D.

Butcher, Devereux. Exploring Our National Parks & Monuments. 9th rev. ed. 478p. 1995. pap. 16.95 (*1-57098-025-X*) Roberts Rinehart.

Butcher, Edith L. The Story of the Church of Egypt, 2 vols., Set. LC 75-41459. reprint ed. 175.00 (*0-404-56231-0*) AMS Pr.

Butcher, G., jt. ed. see Fernandez, N.

Butcher, G. A. Lower Columbia River, Hugh Keenleyside Dam to Birchbank: Water Quality Assessment & Objectives : Technical Appendix LC 93-206922. 1992. write for info. (*0-7726-1650-7*) GovofBC.

Butcher, Geoff, jt. ed. see Fernandez, Nelson.

Butcher, Grace. Before I Go Out on the Road. (Cleveland Poets Ser.: No. 20). (Orig.). 1979. pap. 6.00 (*0-914946-15-3*) Cleveland St Univ Poetry Ctr.

Butcher, H. J., jt. auth. see Cattell, Raymond B.

***Butcher, H. Maxwell.** I, Adam. 2nd large type ed. (Illus.). (J). 1999. pap. 7.95 (*1-894303-08-3*) RRP.

Butcher, Hugh, et al, eds. Community & Public Policy. LC 93-36730. 1994. pap. 50.00 (*0-7453-0801-5*) Westview.

Butcher, Hugh, et al. Community & Public Policy. LC 93-36730. (C). 59.95 (*0-7453-0800-7*) Pluto GBR.

Butcher, James, ed. Personality Assessment in Managed Health Care: Using the MMPI-2 in Treatment Planning. LC 96-9456. (Illus.). 264p. (C). 1997. text 40.00 (*0-19-511160-5*) OUP.

Butcher, James & Spielberger, Charles D., eds. Advances in Personality Assessment, Vol. 6. 176p. 1987. text 39.95 (*0-89859-660-2*) L Erlbaum Assocs.

— Advances in Personality Assessment, Vol. 8. 296p. (C). 1990. text 69.95 (*0-8058-0503-6*) L Erlbaum Assocs.

Butcher, James, jt. auth. see American Legislative Exchange Council Staff.

Butcher, James, jt. ed. see Spielberger, Charles D.

Butcher, James N. A Beginner's Guide to the MMPI-2. LC 98-41100. 225p. 1999. 34.95 (*1-55798-564-2*, 431-615A) Am Psychol.

— The MMPI-2 in Psychological Treatment. (Illus.). 208p. (C). 1990. text 32.95 (*0-19-506344-9*) OUP.

Butcher, James N., ed. Clinical Personality Assessment: Practical Approaches. (Illus.). 576p. (C). 1995. text 67.95 (*0-19-508569-8*) OUP.

— International Adaptations of the MMPI-2: Research & Clinical Applications. 1996. 75.00 (*0-8166-2632-4*) U of Minn Pr.

Butcher, James N. & Spielberger, Charles D., eds. Advances in Personality Assessment, Vol. 2. 208p. (C). 1983. text 49.95 (*0-89859-216-X*) L Erlbaum Assocs.

— Advances in Personality Assessment, Vol. 4. 288p. (C). 1985. text 69.95 (*0-89859-341-7*) L Erlbaum Assocs.

— Advances in Personality Assessment, Vol. 10. (Advances in Personality Assessment Ser.). 192p. 1995. text 49.95 (*0-8058-1804-9*) L Erlbaum Assocs.

Butcher, James N. & Williams, Carolyn L. Essentials of MMPI-2 & MMPI-A Interpretation. 384p. (C). 1992. 44.95 (*0-8166-2100-4*) U of Minn Pr.

— Essentials of MMPI-2 & MMPI-A Interpretation. 2nd ed. 392p. 1999. 49.95 (*0-8166-3552-8*) U of Minn Pr.

Butcher, James N., et al. Development & Use of the MMPI-2 Content Scales. 200p. 1990. 29.95 (*0-8166-1817-8*) U of Minn Pr.

Butcher, James N., jt. auth. see Carson, Robert C.

Butcher, James N., jt. auth. see Carson, Robert S.

Butcher, James N., jt. auth. see Keller, Laura S.

Butcher, James N., jt. auth. see Spielberger, Charles D.

Butcher, James N., jt. ed. see Spielberger, Charles D.

***Butcher, Jim.** Storm Front: Book One of the Dresden Files. 2000. mass mkt. 6.99 (*0-451-45781-1*, ROC) NAL.

***Butcher, Jonathan B. & Water Environment Research Foundation Staff.** Watershed-Scale Ecological Risk Assessment: Project 93-IRM-4(a), 1998 LC 98-85201. 1998. write for info. (*0-9662553-4-8*) Wtr Environ Res.

Butcher, Judith. Copy-Editing: The Cambridge Handbook for Authors, Editors & Indexers. 3rd ed. (Illus.). 483p. (C). 1992. text 54.95 (*0-521-40074-0*) Cambridge U Pr.

Butcher, Kenneth S. Uniform Laws & Regulations in the Areas of Legal Metrology & Engine Fuel Quality, as Adopted by the 81st National Conference on Weights & Measures, 1996. 223p. 1996. per. 20.00 (*0-16-048921-0*) USGPO.

Butcher, Kennth S. Uniform Laws & Regulations in the Areas of Legal Metrology & Engine Fuel Quality, as Adopted by the 82d National Conference on Weights & Measures, 1997. 229p. 1997. per. 20.00 (*0-16-049333-1*) USGPO.

Butcher, Kevin. Roman Provincial Coins: An Introduction to the Greek Imperials. (Illus.). 138p. 1988. lib. bdg. 45.00 (*1-85264-010-3*) S J Durst.

Butcher, Kristin. The Runaways. (J). 1997. pap. 4.95 (*1-55074-379-1*) Kids Can Pr.

Butcher, Kristin. The Runaways. 168p. (J). (gr. 5-9). 1998. 16.95 (*1-55074-413-5*, Pub. by Kids Can Pr) Genl Dist Srvs.

Butcher, Lee. For a Mother's Love. (Illus.). 384p. 1992. mass mkt. 4.99 (*1-55817-665-9*, Pinncle Kensgtn) Kensgtn Pub Corp.

— Sex, Money & Murder in Daytona Beach. 1991. mass mkt. 4.99 (*1-55817-555-5*, Pinncle Kensgtn) Kensgtn Pub Corp.

— Sex, Money & Murder in Daytona Beach. 416p. 1999. mass mkt. 5.99 (*0-7860-0656-0*) Kensgtn Pub Corp.

Butcher, M. A. Before the Divorce, Read This! (Illus.). 48p. 1998. reprint ed. pap. text 5.00 (*0-9622939-0-3*) Yamoo Pubs.

Butcher, Marc A. Positive Messages: For Young Men Growing up Without Their Fathers. 96p. (YA). (gr. 3-12). 1999. pap. 9.00 (*0-9622939-1-1*) Yamoo Pubs.

Butcher, Marjorie V. & Nesbitt, Cecil J. Mathematics of Compound Interest. 6th ed. (Illus.). xii, 324p. (C). 1991. reprint ed. text 22.50 (*0-9603000-1-5*) Butcher & Nesbitt.

***Butcher, Mary.** Contemporary International Basketmaking. 1999. pap. 22.95 (*1-85894-078-8*) Merrell Holberton.

Butcher, Melissa, jt. auth. see Brosius, Christians.

Butcher, Nancy. Creepy Sleepaway. (Ghost Writer - Camp at Your Own Risk Ser.). 1995. 8.60 (*0-606-07571-2*, Pub. by Turtleback) Demco.

— Daycamp Nightmare. (Ghost Writer - Camp at Your Own Risk Ser.). 1995. 8.60 (*0-606-07569-0*, Pub. by Turtleback) Demco.

— Dr. Jekyll & Mr. Dog. LC 98-84971. (Adventures of Wishbone Ser.: Vol. 15). (Illus.). 143p. (J). (gr. 3-7). 1998. pap. 3.99 (*1-57064-388-1*, Big Red) Lyrick Pub.

— Lights! Camera! Action Dog! Ryan, Kevin, ed. LC 98-84944. (Wishbone Mysteries Ser.: Vol. 11). (Illus.). 144p. (J). (gr. 3-7). 1998. mass mkt. 3.99 (*1-57064-289-3*, Big Red) Lyrick Pub.

***Butcher, Nancy.** The Perfect Plan, No. 3. (Illus.). 132p. (J). (gr. 3-7). 2000. pap. 3.99 (*0-375-80339-4*, Pub. by Random Bks Yng Read) Random.

Butcher, Nancy. The Secret Pony Club: A Mystery Jigsaw Puzzle Thriller. (Spider Tales Ser.). (Orig.). (J). (gr. 3-7). 1996. pap. 13.50 (*1-57561-009-4*, 00807SPC) Bepuzzled.

Butcher, Nicholas. The Festive Food of Spain. (Illus.). 60p. 1994. 9.95 (*1-85626-045-3*) Trafalgar.

Butcher, P., et al. Physics of Low-Dimensional Semiconductor Structures. (Physics of Solids & Liquids Ser.). (Illus.). 606p. (C). 1992. text 130.00 (*0-306-44170-5*, Kluwer Plenum) Kluwer Academic.

Butcher, P. N. & Lu, Yu, eds. Superconductivity: From Basic Physics to the Latest Developments: Lecture Notes of the ICTP Spring College in Condensed Matter on "Superconductivity", Trieste, Italy 27 April - 19 June 1992. 352p. 1995. text 78.00 (*981-02-2456-7*, Pc-P2928) World Scientific Pub.

Butcher, Patricia S. Education for Equality: Women's Rights Periodicals & Women's Higher Education, 1849-1920, 111. LC 89-11874. (Contributions in Women's Studies: No. 111). 133p. 1989. 47.95 (*0-313-25940-2*, BQY/, Greenwood Pr) Greenwood.

Butcher, Paul N., et al, eds. Crystalline Semiconducting Materials & Devices. LC 86-9458. (Physics of Solids & Liquids Ser.). (Illus.). 664p. (C). 1986. text 174.00 (*0-306-42154-2*, Kluwer Plenum) Kluwer Academic.

Butcher, Paul N. & Cotter, David. The Elements of Nonlinear Optics. (Cambridge Studies in Modern Optics: No. 9). (Illus.). 358p. (C). 1991. pap. text 39.95 (*0-521-42424-0*) Cambridge U Pr.

Butcher, Philip. George Washington Cable. LC 62-16819. (Twayne's United States Authors Ser.). 1962. pap. 4.25 (*0-89197-988-3*); lib. bdg. 17.95 (*0-89197-769-4*) Irvington.

Butcher, Philip, ed. The Ethnic Image in Modern American Literature: 1900-1950, 2 vols., 1. 1984. 24.95 (*0-88258-119-8*) Howard U Pr.

— The Ethnic Image in Modern American Literature: 1900-1950, 2 vols., 2. 1984. 24.95 (*0-88258-120-1*) Howard U Pr.

— The Ethnic Image in Modern American Literature: 1900-1950, 2 vols., Set. 1984. 45.95 (*0-88258-110-4*) Howard U Pr.

— The Minority Presence in American Literature, 1600-1900, 2 vols., 1. LC 77-5687. 1977. pap. 12.95 (*0-88258-061-2*) Howard U Pr.

An Asterisk (*) at the beginning of an entry indicates that the title is appearing for the first time.

— The Minority Presence in American Literature, 1600-1900, 2 vols., 2. LC 77-5687. 1977. pap. 12.95 (*0-88258-100-7*) Howard U Pr.

— The Minority Presence in American Literature, 1600-1900, 2 vols., Set. LC 77-5687. 1977. pap. 20.50 (*0-88258-104-X*) Howard U Pr.

Butcher, Ralph L. Instrument Pilot Flight Training Manual. LC 93-92816. 342p. 1992. per. 34.95 (*1-881688-02-X*) Skyroamers.

— Private Pilot Flight Training Manual. LC 93-92817. 304p. 1996. pap., per. 34.95 (*1-881688-00-3*) Skyroamers.

Butcher, Ray L., ed. Manual of Ornamental Fish. (Illus.). 200p. 1994. pap. text 64.95 (*0-905214-18-8*, Pub. by BSAVA) Iowa St U Pr.

Butcher, Ronald, jt. ed. see Merrett, Patricia.

Butcher, Russel D. Exploring Our National Historic Parks & Sites. (Illus.). 496p. 1997. pap. 18.95 (*1-57098-125-6*) Roberts Rinehart.

***Butcher, Russell D.** Guide to National Parks in Alaska. Whitaker, Lynn P., ed. LC 99-31046. (NPCA National Park Guide Ser.). (Illus.). 96p. 2000. pap. text 11.95 (*0-7627-0570-1*) Globe Pequot.

Butcher, Russell D., jt. auth. see National Parks & Conservation Association Staff.

Butcher, S. H. & Lang, A., eds. The Odyssey of Homer. 25.00 (*0-8196-2881-6*) Biblo.

Butcher, S. H., ed. see Aristotle.

Butcher, S. H., tr. see Aristotle.

Butcher, Sally K., ed. see Adams, Azel.

Butcher, Sam. My First Book of Catholic Bible Stories. 1999. 9.95 (*0-88271-752-9*) Regina Pr.

— Precious Moments Nursery Rhymes. LC PZ8.3.P88935 1999. (Precious Moments Ser.). (Illus.). 32p. (J). (ps-3). 1999. 9.99 (*0-8010-4426-X*) Baker Bks.

Butcher, Sam. Precious Moments Bible Promises. 2nd rev. ed. LC 97-27093. 32p. (J). (ps-2). 1997. 10.99 (*0-8499-1463-9*) Tommy Nelson.

— A Precious Moments Christmas. 2nd rev. ed. LC 97-22769. 32p. (J). (ps-2). 1997. 10.99 (*0-8499-1517-1*) Tommy Nelson.

— A Precious Moments Gift of Love. 2nd rev. ed. LC 97-22774. 32p. (J). (ps-2). 1997. 10.99 (*0-8499-1523-6*) Tommy Nelson.

— Precious Moments, Prayers for Boys & Girls. 2nd rev. ed. LC 97-27093. 32p. (J). (ps-2). 1997. 10.99 (*0-8499-1476-0*) Tommy Nelson.

Butcher, Samuel H. Aristotle's Theory of Poetry & Fine Art. 4th ed. 497p. (C). 1951. pap. 12.95 (*0-486-20042-6*) Dover.

Butcher, Samuel J. Christmas. (Itty Bitty Books Precious Moments Ser.). (Illus.). (J). 1992. 4.99 (*0-8407-4264-9*) Nelson.

***Butcher, Samuel J.** Precious Moments Bible Stories. LC 00-29737. (Illus.). (J). 2000. write for info. (*0-8010-4447-2*) Baker Bks.

Butcher, Samuel J. Precious Moments Bible Stories: Old Testament. LC BS551.2.P75 1999. (Precious Moments for Children Ser.). (Illus.). 32p. (J). (ps-2). 1999. 9.99 (*0-8010-4427-8*) Baker Bks.

***Butcher, Samuel J.** Precious Moments Storybook Treasury. (Precious Moments for Children Ser.). 384p. (J). (gr. k-7). 2000. text 24.99 (*0-8010-4458-8*, Precious Moment) Baker Bks.

Butcher, Samuel S., et al, eds. Global Biogeochemical Cycles. (International Geophysics Ser.: Vol. 50). (Illus.). 379p. 1992. pap. text 70.00 (*0-12-147686-3*) Acad Pr.

Butcher, Solomon D. Pioneer History of Custer County. 15.50 (*0-931068-05-3*); pap. 10.00 (*0-685-04190-5*) Purcells.

Butcher, Susan, frwd. North Country Christmas. (Illus.). (J). (gr. 1-6). 1992. 15.95 (*0-934007-18-7*); pap. 8.95 (*0-934007-14-4*) Paws Four Pub.

***Butcher, T. Michael.** Earthforce: Race to Save the Earth. LC 99-91221. 1998. 25.00 (*0-7388-0678-1*); pap. 18.00 (*0-7388-0679-X*) Xlibris Corp.

Butcher, T. W. The Common Sense Spelling Book, Vol. 1. vi, 92p. (J). (gr. 1-8). 1998. reprint ed. pap. text 19.95 (*0-9654296-3-6*) Republic Policy.

— The Common Sense Spelling Book, Vol. 2. vi, 106p. (YA). (gr. 9-12). 1998. reprint ed. pap. text 19.95 (*0-9654296-2-8*) Republic Policy.

Butcher, Tina G. Specifications, Tolerances & Other Technical Requirements for Weighing & Measuring Devices: As Adopted by the 82d National Conference on Weights & Measures, 1997. 287p. 1997. per. 24.00 (*0-16-049313-7*) USGPO.

***Butcher, Tina G.** Specifications, Tolerances & Other Technical Requirements for Weighing & Measuring Devices: As Adopted by the 84th National Conference on Weights & Measures, 1999. 323p. 2000. per. 29.00 (*0-16-050258-6*) USGPO.

Butcher, Tina G., et al, eds. Specifications, Tolerances & Other Technical Requirements for Weighing & Measuring Devices: As Adopting by the 83rd National Conference on Weights & Measures, 1998. (NIST Handbook Ser.: No. 44). 295p. 1998. 24.00 (*0-16-049825-2*) USGPO.

Butcher, Tina G., jt. ed. see Opperman, Henry V.

Butcher, Tom, jt. auth. see Ellis, Dawn.

Butcher, Tony. Delivering Welfare: The Governance of the Social Services in the 1990s. LC 94-43713. (Public Policy & Management Ser.). 192p. 1995. pap. 34.95 (*0-335-15710-6*) OpUniv Pr.

Butcher, Tony, jt. auth. see Drewry, Gavin.

Butcher, William, tr. see Verne, Jules.

Butcher, William, tr. & intro. see Verne, Jules.

Butcher, Williams, tr. & intro. see Verne, Jules.

Butchins, Larry. The Kvetchit: A Hanukkah Tale. (Illus.). 32p. (J). (gr. k-3). 1994. 14.95 (*965-483-004-3*) Pitspopany.

Butchko, Thomas R., ed. Martin County Architectural Heritage: The Historic Structures of a Rural North Carolina County. LC 97-76490. 500p. 1999. 45.00 (*0-9626609-3-0*) MCH Soc NC.

Butchvarov, Panayot. Resemblance & Identity: An Examination of the Problem of Universals. LC 66-22437. 222p. reprint ed. pap. 68.90 (*0-8357-9239-0*, 20158110097) Bks Demand.

— Skepticism about the External World. LC 97-14104. 192p. 1998. text 45.00 (*0-19-511719-0*) OUP.

— Skepticism in Ethics. LC 88-45103. 238p. 1989. 37.50 (*0-253-35321-1*); pap. 15.95 (*0-253-20522-0*, MB-522) Ind U Pr.

Bute, Evangeline & Harmer, Harry. The Black Handbook: The People, History & Politics of Africa & the African Diaspora. 416p. 1997. pap. 24.95 (*0-304-33543-6*) Continuum.

Bute, Ruby. Golden Voices of S'maatin. LC 88-63794. (Illus.). 64p. (Orig.). 1989. pap. text 8.00 (*0-913441-08-2*) Hse of Nehesi.

Butel, Jane. Chili Madness. LC 80-51617. (Passionate Cookbook Ser.). (Illus.). 96p. 1980. pap. 6.95 (*0-89480-134-1*, 435) Workman Pub.

— Fiestas for Four Seasons Gift Pack: Southwest Entertaining. (Illus.). 192p. 1998. 29.95 (*1-57416-015-X*) Clear Light.

— Fiestas for the Four Seasons: Southwest Entertaining. LC 95-34069. (Illus.). 192p. 1997. pap. 14.95 (*0-940666-72-3*) Clear Light.

— Finger Lickin', Rib Stickin', Great Tastin' Hot & Spicy Barbecue. LC 81-43785. (Passionate Cookbook Ser.). (Illus.). 96p. 1982. pap. 6.95 (*0-89480-208-9*, 482) Workman Pub.

— Jane Butel's Hotter Than Hell. rev. ed. LC 94-10380. (Illus.). 208p. (Orig.). 1994. pap. 14.95 (*1-55788-096-4*, HP Books) Berkley Pub.

— Jane Butel's Quick & Easy Southwestern Cookbook. LC 98-28909. (Illus.). 256p. 1999. 23.00 (*0-609-60228-4*) Harmony Bks.

— Jane Butel's Southwestern Kitchen. LC 93-51013. (Illus.). 352p. (Orig.). 1994. pap. 17.00 (*1-55788-090-5*, HP Books) Berkley Pub.

— Jane Butel's Tex-Mex Cookbook. 192p. 1993. pap. 12.00 (*0-517-88014-8*) C Potter.

Butel, Jane & McMeen, Gordon. Jane Butel's Southwestern Grill. LC 95-37879. 266p. (Orig.). 1996. pap. 15.00 (*1-55788-242-8*, HP Books) Berkley Pub.

Butel, Paul. Atlantic. LC 98-38974. (Seas in History Ser.). 352p. (C). 1999. 58.00 (*0-415-10690-7*) Routledge.

***Buten, Howard.** When I Was Five I Killed Myself. LC 00-26887. 192p. 2000. 23.95 (*1-58567-039-1*, Pub. by Overlook Pr) Penguin Putnam.

Butenandt, O., jt. ed. see Laron, Z.

Butenhof, David. Programming with Posix Threads. LC 97-6635. 400p. (C). 1997. pap. text 39.95 (*0-201-63392-2*) Addison-Wesley.

Butenhoff, Linda. Social Movements & Political Reform in Hong Kong. LC 98-33608. 152p. 1999. 55.00 (*0-275-96293-8*, Praeger Pubs) Greenwood.

Butenhoff, Lisa K. Nina's Magic. Thatch, Nancy R., ed. LC 92-18293. (Books for Students by Students). (Illus.). 26p. (J). (gr. 3-4). 1992. lib. bdg. 15.95 (*0-933849-40-0*) Landmark Edns.

Butenhoff, Tom. Free Enterprise - Midwest Style. 256p. 1991. 19.95 (*0-929682-02-5*) Perin Pr.

***Butenschon, Nils, et al, eds.** Citizenship & the State in the Middle East: Approaches & Applications. LC 00-21079. (Illus.). 400p. 2000. pap. text 39.95 (*0-8156-2829-3*) Syracuse U Pr.

Buter, Clemens. Das Handwerk in der Wirschaftlichen Entwicklung der Ehemaligen DDR und im Ubergang zur Sozialen Marktwirtschaft. (Europaische Hochschulschriften: Reihe 5: Bd. 1978). (GER., Illus.). 239p. 1997. pap. 44.95 (*3-631-49140-9*) P Lang Pubng.

***Buter, Margaret.** War & Health: Crossing the Bridge to Peace. Hess, Gregory, ed. (Illus.). 46p. 1999. reprint ed. pap. text 20.00 (*0-7881-8076-2*) DIANE Pub.

Butera, Virginia F. Jim Jacobs: Screens. LC 88-60583. 32p. (Orig.). 1988. pap. write for info. (*0-942461-05-3*) Mus Art Fl.

Buterin, Leslie. Outrageous Temp Stories. 57p. 1998. pap. 7.00 (*0-9658697-1-7*) Lead Edge.

— Secrets to Scheduling the Executive Level Sales Call: How to Win over the Million-Dollar Decision Maker. McBride, Kirsten, ed. LC 97-93812. (Illus.). 249p. 1998. pap. 90.00 (*0-9658697-0-9*) Lead Edge.

Butfoy, Andrew. Common Security & Strategic Reform: A Critical Analysis. LC 96-46164. 224p. 1997. text 65.00 (*0-312-17248-6*) St Martin.

Buth. Verdades de la Vida. (SPA.). 1.50 (*0-685-74985-1*, 497420) Editorial Unilit.

Buth, G. M. Central Asia & Kashmir: Himalaya a Forgotten Links. (C). 1986. text 25.00 (*81-85046-94-8*, Pub. by Scientific Pubs) St Mut.

Buth, Leonor. Ensenando a Sus Hijos Sobre el Sexo. (Serie Enfoque a la Familia - Focus on the Family Ser.).Tr. of How to Talk Confidently with Your Child about Sex. (SPA.). 29p. 1995. 1.99 (*1-56063-710-2*, 497446) Editorial Unilit.

Buth, Manfred. Einfuhrung in die Formale Logik: Unter der Besonderen Fragestellung: Was Ist Wahrheit Allein Aufgrund der Form? (GER., Illus.). 209p. 1996. 31.95 (*3-631-30624-5*) P Lang Pubng.

Buthe, Julia-K. & Riis, Thomas L., eds. Studien Zur Geschichte des Ostseeraumes II: Die Stadte des Ostseeraumes Als Vermittler Von Kultur 1240-1720. (Odense University Studies in History & Social Sciences: Vol. 202). (Illus.). 148p. 27.75 (*87-7838-083-9*) Odense Univ.

Butherus, Cindy. Give Reading a Chance: A Read-at-Home Program. McClean, Cheryl, ed. (Illus.). 119p. 1988. lib. bdg. 21.95 (*0-945557-01-9*) Hug Bk Pubns.

***Buthiau, D. & Khayat, D.** Virtual Endoscopy. 220p. 2000. 105.00 (*2-287-59658-5*) Spr-Verlag.

Buthiau, D. & Khayat, David. CT Scan & MRI in Oncology. LC 97-45146. 1998. write for info. (*3-540-62750-2*) Spr-Verlag.

Buthle, Mari Jo, jt. auth. see Faragher, John M.

Buti, B. Cometary & Solar Plasma Physics, 1987. 372p. (C). 1988. pap. 53.00 (*9971-5-0448-0*); text 121.00 (*9971-5-0447-2*) World Scientific Pub.

Buti, B., ed. Advances in Space Plasma Physics: Proceedings of the ICTP College on Plasma Physics, Trieste, Itlay, 1985. 500p. 1985. 115.00 (*9971-5-0016-7*) World Scientific Pub.

— Solar & Planetary Plasma Physics: Papers Presented at the Spring College on Plasma Physics. 240p. (C). 1990. text 92.00 (*981-02-0155-9*) World Scientific Pub.

Buti, Bruno. Jackass Brandy. (Illus.). 380p. 1999. 23.95 (*0-9648960-1-X*) B Buti.

— Rumbling Wine Barrels. 356p. 1995. 19.95 (*0-9648960-0-1*) B Buti.

Buti, Marco & Sapir, Andre, eds. Economic Policy in EMU: A Study by the European Commission Services. LC 98-30961. 274p. 1998. text 65.00 (*0-19-829478-6*); pap. text 24.95 (*0-19-829477-8*) OUP.

Butigan, Ken. From Violence to Wholeness: A Ten Part Program in the Spirituality & Practice of Active Nonviolence. 176p. 1999. pap. 15.00 (*0-9669723-0-7*) Pace e Bene.

Butilerrez-Vasquez, J. M. Microorganismos. 3rd ed. OAS General Secretariat Staff, ed. (Serie de Biologia: No. 6). (SPA., Illus.). 79p. (C). 1981. pap. 3.50 (*0-685-03621-9*) OAS.

Butin. The Ten Nequdoth of the Torah. 1969. 15.00 (*0-87068-043-9*) Ktav.

— Woerterbuch Deutsch-Esperanto-Deutsch. (ESP & GER.). 420p. 1989. 95.00 (*0-7859-7446-6*, 3487070820) Fr & Eur.

Butin, Gitte Wernaa, tr. see Cain, David.

Butin, Heinz. Tree Diseases & Disorders: Causes, Biology, & Control in Forest & Amenity Trees. Lonsdale, D., ed. Strouts, R. G., tr. (Illus.). 262p. 1995. text 75.00 (*0-19-854932-6*) OUP.

Butin, Heinz & Peredo, Hernan L. Hongos Parasitos en Coniferas de America Del sur, Con Especial Referencia a Chile. (Bibliotheca Mycologica: Vol. 101). (SPA., Illus.). 1986. 24.00 (*3-443-59002-0*, Pub. by Gebruder Borntraeger) Balogh.

Butin, Max, et al. Esperanto-Worterbuch, 2 vols. (ESP.). 475p. 1992. reprint ed. 50.00 (*3-487-07082-0*) G Olms Pubs.

Butin, Philip W. Revelation, Redemption & Response: Calvin's Trinitarian Understanding of the Divine-Human Relationship. LC 93-43173. 248p. (C). 1995. text 55.00 (*0-19-508600-7*) OUP.

***Butin, Phillip W.** The Trinity: Why This Three-Person God? (Foundations of Christian Faith Ser.). (Illus.). xxxp. 2000. pap. 11.95 (*0-664-50140-0*) Geneva Press.

Butker, Burton, jt. auth. see Butker, Mabel.

Butker, Mabel & Butker, Burton. Track Talk. rev. ed. Duquette-May, Christy, ed. (Illus.). 64p. 1987. reprint ed. pap. 4.95 (*0-944012-02-7*) D M Communications.

Butkiewicz, James L., et al, eds. Keynes Economic Policy. LC 85-9508. 238p. 1985. 55.00 (*0-275-90038-X*, C0038, Praeger Pubs) Greenwood.

***Butkins, P. Robert.** Online Trading for Beginners: Secrets You Need to Know. (Illus.). 64p. 1999. pap. 19.95 (*0-9678230-0-5*) InkManager.

Butko, Brian A. The Lincoln Highway. (Pennsylvania Traveler's Guide Ser.). (Illus.). 352p. 1996. pap. 16.95 (*0-8117-2495-6*) Stackpole.

Butko, Brian A. & Patrick, Kevin Joseph. Diners of Pennsylvania. LC 99-18350. (Illus.). 208p. 1999. pap. 19.95 (*0-8117-2878-1*) Stackpole.

Butkoff, Paul N. Our Fight for Russia. LC 98-26933. 256p. 1998. 45.00 (*1-56072-554-0*) Nova Sci Pubs.

Butkov, E. Mathematical Physics. 35p. (C). 1968. 75.00 (*0-201-00727-4*) Addison-Wesley.

Butkova, Karla, et al. Moravian Tales: Legends & Myths. 3rd rev. ed. (Illus.). 209p. (YA). 1992. text 34.50 (*0-930329-51-1*) Kabel Pubs.

Butkovskiy, A. G. Characteristics of Distributed-Parameter Systems: Handbook of Equations of Mathematical Physics & Distributed-Parameter Systems. LC 93-30135. (Mathematics & Its Applications Ser.). 408p. (C). 1993. text 254.00 (*0-7923-2499-4*) Kluwer Academic.

— Structural Theory of Distributed Systems. LC 83-10727. (Mathematics & Its Applications Ser.). 314p. 1983. text 114.00 (*0-470-27469-7*) P-H.

Butkovskiy, Anatoliy G. Phase Portraits of Control Dynamical Systems. (Mathematics & Its Applications, Soviet Ser.). 184p. (C). 1991. text 139.00 (*0-7923-1057-8*) Kluwer Academic.

Butkovskiy, Anatoliy G. & Samoilenko, Y. I. Control of Quantum-Mechanical Processes & Systems. (C). 1990. text 182.50 (*0-7923-0689-9*) Kluwer Academic.

Butkovsky, A. G. & Pustyl'nikov, A. M. Mobile Control of Distributed Parameter Systems. (Engineering Science Ser.). 310p. 1987. text 94.95 (*0-470-20817-1*) F-H.

Butkowski, Joel & Van Kempen, Andra. Using Digital Cameras: A Comprehensive Guide to Digital Image Capture. LC 97-34329. (Illus.). 144p. 1997. 29.95 (*0-8174-3790-8*, Amphoto) Watsn-Guptill.

Butkus, D., jt. auth. see Styra, B.

Butkus, Michael J. Blackjack Beginner to Blackjack Winner in 10 Days. (Illus.). 136p. 1996. 19.95 (*0-9655571-0-3*) Flash Jack Casino.

— Winning Craps for the Gambling Impaired. (Illus.). 101p. (Orig.). 1996. 19.95 (*0-9655571-1-1*) Flash Jack Casino.

Butkus, Raymond T., jt. auth. see Green, Thad B.

Butkus, Sue N., ed. Caring Families: Food Choices. (Illus.). 206p. 1997. reprint ed. pap. text 35.00 (*0-7881-4584-3*) DIANE Pub.

***Butland, Charles.** Charlie's Thoughts. LC 98-74811. 1999. 24.95 (*0-9657536-2-X*) Creat Alternat.

Butland, Gilbert J. Chile: An Outline of Its Geography, Economics & Politics. LC 81-13237. 128p. 1981. reprint ed. lib. bdg. 55.00 (*0-313-23193-1*, BUCL, Greenwood Pr) Greenwood.

Butler. Biophysics Progression, ser. vol. 35. (Progress in Biophysics & Molecular Biology Ser.). 1980. pap. 26.00 (*0-08-026047-0*, no. 3, Pergamon Pr) Elsevier.

— British General Election 1997. LC 97-27660. 1997. text 55.00 (*0-312-21079-5*) St Martin.

— Business Research Sources. LC 98-21172. 480p. 1998. pap. 34.06 (*0-256-23003-X*) McGraw.

— Computer Aided Instruction for General Chemistry Set TRS 80 Model III. 1969. text. write for info. (*0-471-89732-9*) Wiley.

— Democracy & Apartheid. LC 98-28376. 212p. 1998. text 59.95 (*0-312-21696-3*) St Martin.

— Early Intervention II: Working with Parents & Families. 240p. 1994. 36.00 (*0-8342-0585-8*) Aspen Pub.

***Butler.** Multinational Finance. 2nd ed. LC 99-29724. 682p. 1999. pap. 97.95 (*0-324-00450-8*) Sth-Wstrn College.

Butler. New Orleans Times: Receptionist. 3rd ed. (Office Procedures Ser.). 1993. text 18.50 (*0-538-60950-8*) S-W Pub.

— Les Parlers Dialectaux et Populaires dans l'Oeuvre de Guy de Maupassant. (Publ. Romanes et Franc.). 15.50 (*0-685-34943-8*, F67900) Fr & Eur.

— Les Parlers Dialectaux et Populaires Dans l'Oeuvre de Guy de Maupassant. 15.50 (*0-8288-7636-3*, F67900) Fr & Eur.

— Progress in Biophysics, Vol. 19 1/2. (Progress in Biophysics & Molecular Biology Ser.). 1969. 98.00 (*0-08-006523-6*) Elsevier.

— Progress in Biophysics & Molecular Biology. (Progress in Biophysics & Molecular Biology Ser.: 30). 1975. pap. 24.00 (*0-08-019972-0*, Pergamon Pr) Elsevier.

— Progress in Biophysics & Molecular Biology, Vol. 1. 1950. 125.00 (*0-08-009001-X*, Pergamon Pr) Elsevier.

— Progress in Biophysics & Molecular Biology, 29 vols., Vol. 1. 1975. pap. 24.00 (*0-08-019719-1*, Pergamon Pr) Elsevier.

— Progress in Biophysics & Molecular Biology, Vol. 5. 1955. 185.00 (*0-08-009026-5*, Pergamon Pr) Elsevier.

— Progress in Biophysics & Molecular Biology, Vol. 6. 1956. 175.00 (*0-08-009034-6*, Pergamon Pr) Elsevier.

— Progress in Biophysics & Molecular Biology, Vol. 7. 1957. 175.00 (*0-08-009065-6*, Pergamon Pr) Elsevier.

— Progress in Biophysics & Molecular Biology, Vol. 8. 1958. 175.00 (*0-08-009096-6*, Pergamon Pr) Elsevier.

— Progress in Biophysics & Molecular Biology, Vol. 9. 1959. 165.00 (*0-08-009176-8*, Pergamon Pr) Elsevier.

— Progress in Biophysics & Molecular Biology, Vol. 10. 1960. 105.00 (*0-08-009293-4*, Pergamon Pr) Elsevier.

— Progress in Biophysics & Molecular Biology, Vol. 15. 1965. 76.00 (*0-08-011041-X*, Pergamon Pr) Elsevier.

— Progress in Biophysics & Molecular Biology, Vol. 17. 1967. 100.00 (*0-08-012046-6*, Pergamon Pr) Elsevier.

— Progress in Biophysics & Molecular Biology, Vol. 19. 1969. 48.00 (*0-08-006522-8*, Pergamon Pr) Elsevier.

— Progress in Biophysics & Molecular Biology, Vol. 20. 1970. 94.50 (*0-08-006627-5*, Pergamon Pr) Elsevier.

— Progress in Biophysics & Molecular Biology, Vol. 22. 1971. 100.00 (*0-08-016348-3*, Pergamon Pr) Elsevier.

— Progress in Biophysics & Molecular Biology, Vol. 24. 1972. 76.00 (*0-08-016868-X*, Pergamon Pr) Elsevier.

— Progress in Biophysics & Molecular Biology, Vol. 25. 1972. 100.00 (*0-08-016935-X*, Pergamon Pr) Elsevier.

— Progress in Biophysics & Molecular Biology, Vol. 26. 1973. 100.00 (*0-08-017048-X*, Pergamon Pr) Elsevier.

— Progress in Biophysics & Molecular Biology, Vol. 27. 1973. 100.00 (*0-08-017142-7*, Pergamon Pr) Elsevier.

— Progress in Biophysics & Molecular Biology, Vol. 28. 1974. 100.00 (*0-08-018005-1*, Pergamon Pr) Elsevier.

— Progress in Biophysics & Molecular Biology, Vol. 29. 1976. 100.00 (*0-08-020201-2*, Pergamon Pr) Elsevier.

— Progress in Biophysics & Molecular Biology, Vol. 30. 1976. 100.00 (*0-08-020207-1*, Pergamon Pr) Elsevier.

— Ready Notes-Multinational Finance. (Orig.). 1999. pap. 18.75 (*0-538-88568-8*) Thomson Learn.

— Social Change & the Middle Class. 352p. 1995. 85.00 (*1-85728-271-X*, Pub. by UCL Pr Ltd); pap. 29.95 (*1-85728-272-8*, Pub. by UCL Pr Ltd) Taylor & Francis.

***Butler.** StressBusters. 1998. pap. 53.70 (*1-56561-154-3*, Pub. by Chronimed) Natl Bk Netwk.

Butler. Tahoe Times - the Receptionist Office Job. 2nd ed. (KM - Office Procedures Ser.). 1985. 24.95 (*0-538-25820-9*) S-W Pub.

— Teeline Shorthand Made Simple. 320p. Date not set. pap. text 19.95 (*0-7506-0550-2*) Buttrwrth-Heinemann.

Butler & Binion. Environmental Law Simplified: A Practical Guide for Oil & Gas Operations. LC 92-33142. 120p. 1993. 25.00 (*0-87814-387-4*) PennWell Bks.

Butler & Livingston. Virginia Tidal & Coastal Law. 913p. 1988. 85.00 (*0-87473-319-7*, 60715-10, MICHIE) LEXIS Pub.

Butler & Oberlink. Promise of Productive Aging. 176p. 1990. 38.95 (*0-8261-6270-3*) Springer Pub.

Butler & Rohnke, Karl E. Quicksilver. 286p. 1996. pap. text 23.50 (*0-7872-2103-1*) Kendall-Hunt.

— Quicksilver: Adventure Games, Initiative Problems, Trust Activities & a Guide to Effective Leadership. 304p. 1995. 23.50 (*0-7872-0032-8*) Kendall-Hunt.

Butler & Smith. Tahoe Times, the Receptionist Office. 2nd ed. (Office Procedures Ser.). 1984. teacher ed. 5.50 (*0-538-27752-1*) S-W Pub.

B

An Asterisk (*) at the beginning of an entry indicates that the title is appearing for the first time.

Butler & Taber. Biology: The Science of Life. 4th ed. (C). Date not set. pap., teacher ed., suppl. ed. write for info. (*0-673-55614-X*) Addson-Wesley Educ.

***Butler.** The 50 Minute Essay. (C). 2000. pap. text. write for info. (*0-15-506965-9*) Harcourt.

Butler, Keith L. Internal Affairs: Making Room for Psychosemantic Internalism. LC 98-36790. 262p. 1998. 99.00 (*0-7923-5261-0*) Kluwer Academic.

Butler, A. J. Police Management. 2nd ed. 300p. (Orig.). 1992. pap. text 43.95 (*1-85521-215-3*, Pub. by Dartmth Pub) Ashgate Pub Co.

Butler, A. R. & Perkins, M. John, eds. Organic Reaction Mechanisms, 1974: An Annual Survey Covering the Literature Dated December 2973 Through November 1974. LC 66-23143. 668p. reprint ed. pap. 200.00 (*0-608-14051-1*, 202401700035) Bks Demand.

— Organic Reaction Mechanisms, 1973: An Annual Survey Covering the Literature Dated December 1972 Through November 1973. LC 66-23143. 587p. reprint ed. pap. 182.00 (*0-608-14050-3*, 202401600035) Bks Demand.

— Organic Reaction Mechanisms, 1975: An Annual Survey Covering the Literature Dated December 1974 Through November 1975. LC 66-23143. 630p. reprint ed. pap. 195.30 (*0-608-14052-X*, 202401800035) Bks Demand.

— Organic Reaction Mechanisms, 1976: An Annual Survey Covering the Literature Dated December 1975 Through November 1976. LC 66-23143. 695p. reprint ed. pap. 200.00 (*0-608-14053-8*, 202401900035) Bks Demand.

Butler, A. S. The Domestic Architecture of Sir Edward Lutyens. (Illus.). 110p. 1992. 175.00 (*1-85149-100-7*) Antique Collect.

***Butler, Alan.** The Bronze Age Computer Disc LC 99-203537. 190p. 1998. write for info. (*0-572-02217-4*, Pub. by Foulsham UK) Assoc Pubs Grp.

Butler, Alan, et al. Sheltered Housing for the Elderly. 1983. 80.00 (*0-7855-1307-8*, Pub. by Natl Inst Soc Work) St Mut.

— Sheltered Housing for the Elderly: Policy, Practice & the Consumer. (National Institute Social Services Library: No. 44). 1983. text 34.95 (*0-04-362055-8*) Routledge.

Butler, Alban. Lives of the Saints. 428p. 1995. pap. 18.00 (*0-89555-530-1*) TAN Bks Pubs.

Butler, Alfred J. The Arab Conquest of Egypt. (C). 1988. 135.00 (*1-85077-205-3*, Pub. by Darf Pubs Ltd) St Mut.

— The Arab Conquest of Egypt & the Last Thirty Years of the Roman Dominion. LC 72-180327. reprint ed. 67.50 (*0-404-56219-1*) AMS Pr.

— The Arab Invasion of Egypt: And the Last 30 Years of the Roman Dominion. LC 98-11658. 600p. 1992. pap. text 15.95 (*1-881316-06-8*) A&B Bks.

— The Arab Invasion of Egypt & the Last 30 Years of the Roman Dominion. LC 98-11658. 600p. 1998. 15.95 (*1-881316-51-3*) A&B Bks.

Butler, Andrea. Jeb's Barn. (Let Me Read Ser.). (Illus.). 16p. (J). (ps-1). 1995. 2.95 (*0-673-36279-5*, GoodYrBooks) Addson-Wesley Educ.

— El Senor Sol y el Senor Mar. Ada, Alma F., tr. (Dejame Leer Ser.).Tr. of Mr. Sun & Mr. Sea. (SPA., Illus.). 16p. (J). (ps-2). 1995. 2.95 (*0-673-36302-3*, GoodYrBooks) Addson-Wesley Educ.

— Whose List Is This? (Let Me Read Ser.). (J). 1996. 2.95 (*0-673-36334-1*, GoodYrBooks) Addson-Wesley Educ.

Butler, Andrea & Turbill, Jan. Towards a Reading-Writing Classroom. LC 87-29663. (Illus.). 90p. (Orig.). (C). 1987. reprint ed. pap. 16.00 (*0-435-08461-5*, 08461) Heinemann.

Butler, Andrew, tr. see De Schoutheete, Philippe.

Butler, Andy, ed. see PBS Engineering Department Staff.

Butler, Anita M. Virginia Family Law Manual. 360p. 1991. ring bd. 80.00 (*0-409-27224-8*, MICHIE) LEXIS Pub.

Butler, Ann B. & Hodos, William. Comparative Vertebrate Neuroanatomy: Evolution & Adaptation. 9th ed. LC 95-49380. 544p. 1996. 109.95 (*0-471-88889-3*) Wiley.

Butler, Anne & Henderson, C. Murray. Angola: Louisiana State Penitentiary, a Half-Century of Rage & Reform. LC 90-82517. 180p. 1990. pap. 15.00 (*0-940984-61-X*) Univ LA Lafayette.

— Dying to Tell: Angola: Crime, Consequence, Conclusion at Louisiana State Penitentiary. LC 91-77530. (Illus.). 181p. 1992. pap. 15.00 (*0-940984-72-5*) Univ LA Lafayette.

Butler, Anne M. Daughters of Joy, Sisters of Misery: Prostitutes in the American West, 1865-90. LC 84-195. (Illus.). 208p. 1987. pap. text 14.95 (*0-252-01466-9*) U of Ill Pr.

— Gendered Justice in the American West: Women Prisoners in Men's Penitentiaries. LC 96-45886. 304p. 1997. 29.95 (*0-252-02281-5*) U of Ill Pr.

***Butler, Anne M.** Gendered Justice in the American West: Women Prisoners in Men's Penitentiaries. 2000. pap. 18.95 (*0-252-06879-3*) U of Ill Pr.

— United States Senate Election, Expulsion & Censure Cases, 1793-1990. 516p. 1995. per. 26.00 (*0-16-063264-1*) USGPO.

Butler, Anne M., et al, eds. The Frontiers & Catholic Identities. LC 99-41112. (American Catholic Identities Ser.). 256p. 1999. 50.00 (*1-57075-270-2*) Orbis Bks.

— The Frontiers & Catholic Identities. LC 99-41112. (American Catholic Identities Ser.). 256p. 1999. pap. 20.00 (*1-57075-269-9*) Orbis Bks.

Butler, Anne M. & Siporin, Ona. Uncommon Common Women: Ordinary Lives of the West. LC 96-10025. (Illus.). 144p. 1996. pap. 21.95 (*0-87421-210-3*) Utah St U Pr.

Butler, Anne M. & Wolff, Wendy. Unites States Senate: Election, Expulsion & Censure Cases, 1793-1990. (Illus.). 486p. (C). 1998. pap. text 50.00 (*0-7881-7143-7*) DIANE Pub.

***Butler, Anthony.** Book of Blarney. 2000. pap. 6.99 (*0-517-16190-7*) Random Hse Value.

Butler, Arlene K., compiled by. Desolation & Destruction in the Last Days: Warnings from the Prophets. 1997. pap. 19.95 (*0-9660284-2-2*) Nelson Bk.

— Preparing & Protecting the Saints in the Last Days: Words from the Prophets to Inspire & Warn. 1997. pap. 19.95 (*0-9660284-1-4*) Nelson Bk.

— Zion Established the Second Coming & Millennium: Instruction & Inspiration from the Prophets. 1997. pap. 24.95 (*0-9660284-3-0*) Nelson Bk.

Butler, Arthur J. Dante: His Times & His Work. 1977. 15.95 (*0-8369-7156-6*, 7988) Ayer.

Butler, Arthur J., ed. The Forerunners of Dante: A Selection from Italian Poetry Before 1300. 1977. lib. bdg. 59.95 (*0-8490-1857-9*) Gordon Pr.

Butler, Audrey. Radical Perversions: Black Friday?/Claposis. (Illus.). 120p. pap. 9.95 (*0-88961-156-4*, Pub. by Womens Pr) LPC InBook.

Butler, Ava S. Team Think: 72 Ways to Make Good, Smart, Quick Decisions In Any Meeting. (Illus.). 218p. 1996. 29.95 (*0-07-009432-2*) McGraw.

— Team Think: 72 Ways to Make Good, Smart, Quick Decisions In Any Meeting. (Illus.). 218p. 1996. pap. 14.95 (*0-07-009433-0*) McGraw.

Butler, Ave S. The Trainer's Guide to Running Effective Team Meetings. 288p. 1996. 69.95 (*0-07-913129-8*) McGraw.

***Butler, B.** Official Illustrated History of the FA Cup. 1998. text 55.00 (*0-7472-2276-2*, Pub. by Headline Bk Pub) Trafalgar.

Butler, B. C. Interpretation of Geological Maps. (C). 1992. pap. text 59.75 (*0-582-30169-6*, Pub. by Addison-Wesley) Longman.

Butler, B. F. Bering Sea Controversy. (Shorey Historical Ser.). 24p. reprint ed. pap. 10.00 (*0-8466-0035-8*, S35) Shoreys Bkstore.

Butler, B. Robert. The Quest for the Historic Fremont & a Guide to the Prehistoric Pottery of Southern Idaho. (Occasional Papers of the Idaho Museum of Natural History: No. 33). 25p. 1983. pap. 4.00 (*0-317-11776-9*) Idaho Mus Nat Hist.

— When Did the Shoshoni Begin to Occupy Southern Idaho: Essays on Late Prehistoric Cultural Remains from the Upper Snake & Salmon River Countries. (Occasional Papers of the Idaho Museum of Natural History: No. 32). 27p. 1981. pap. 5.00 (*0-686-30007-6*) Idaho Mus Nat Hist.

Butler, Barbara. Wilderness Tracks. (Illus.). 216p. 1997. pap. 14.95 (*0-88839-410-1*) Hancock House.

— Wildhaunts: Reflections on Central Oregon Enchantments. (Illus.). 50p. (Orig.). 1989. spiral bd. 8.95 (*0-9614105-1-5*) B Butler.

Butler, Barbara, ed. Museum Studies Programs: A Guide to Evaluation. (Professional Practice Ser.). 37p. (Orig.). 1987. reprint ed. pap. text 14.50 (*0-931201-38-1*) Am Assn Mus.

Butler, Barbara & Turner, Diane M., eds. Children & Anthropological Research. LC 86-30517. 174p. 1987. 59.50 (*0-306-42499-1*, Plenum Trade) Perseus Pubng.

Butler, Barbara, jt. auth. see Feiler, Jesse.

Butler, Barbara H. & Sussman, Marvin B., eds. Museum Visits & Activities for Family Life Enrichment. LC 89-37694. (Marriage & Family Review Ser.: Vol. 13, Nos. 3-4). (Illus.). 191p. 1989. text 49.95 (*0-86656-758-5*) Haworth Pr.

Butler, Becky, ed. Ceremonies of the Heart: Celebrating Lesbian Unions. 2nd ed. LC 90-8721. (Illus.). 320p. (Orig.). 1997. pap. text 16.95 (*1-878067-87-7*) Seal Pr WA.

Butler, Benjamin F. The Law School Papers of Benjamin F. Butler: New York University School of Law in the 1830's, 39. LC 87-11891. (Contributions in Legal Studies: No. 39). 257p. 1987. 65.00 (*0-313-25917-8*, BWL/) Greenwood.

— Private & Official Correspondence, 5 vols. LC 74-39570. reprint ed. 225.00 (*0-404-01310-4*) AMS Pr.

Butler, Beverley, jt. auth. see Littlewood, Kevin.

***Butler-Biggs, Jane.** The Feng Shui Directory. (Illus.). 208p. 2000. 19.95 (*0-8230-1657-9*) Watsn-Guptill.

Butler-Biggs, Jane. Feng Shui in 10 Simple Lessons. LC 99-64427. (Illus.). 144p. 1999. pap. 19.95 (*0-8230-1656-0*) Watsn-Guptill.

Butler, Bill. The Versatile Trophy Hunter. LC 94-219752. 208p. 1993. pap. 12.95 (*0-9637553-0-7*) Bill Butler.

Butler, Brad. A World Flight over Russia. 2nd rev. ed. (Illus.). 216p. 1998. pap. 26.95 (*1-891118-31-5*, Wind Canyon Bks) Wind Canyon.

Butler, Brenda A., ed. Are You Hungry Tonight? Elvis' Favorite Recipes. (Illus.). 64p. 1992. 11.99 (*0-517-08242-X*) Random Hse Value.

Butler, Bret W. & Reynolds, Timothy D. Wildlife Case Study: Butte City Fire, Southeastern Idaho, July 1, 1994. (Illus.). 20p. 1997. reprint ed. pap. 2.50 (*0-89904-696-7*, Bear Meadows Resrch Grp) Crumb Elbow Pub.

Butler, Brett. Knee Deep in Paradise. (Illus.). 304p. (J). 1996. 22.95 (*0-7868-6136-3*, Pub. by Hyperion) Time Warner.

— Knee Deep in Paradise. (Illus.). 408p. (J). 1997. mass mkt. 5.99 (*0-7868-8914-4*, Pub. by Hyperion) Time Warner.

Butler, Brian. DC for Free: Hundreds of Free Things to Do in Washington, D.C. 3rd rev. ed. LC 96-49221. (Illus.). 96p. 1997. pap. 9.95 (*0-914457-84-5*) Mustang Pub.

— Europe for Free: Hundreds of Free Things to Do in Europe. 4th rev. ed. LC 96-49220. (Illus.). 320p. 1997. pap. 10.95 (*0-914457-85-3*) Mustang Pub.

— London for Free: Hundreds of Free Things to Do in London. 3rd rev. ed. LC 96-49222. (Illus.). 128p. 1997. pap. 9.95 (*0-914457-86-1*) Mustang Pub.

***Butler, Brian.** An Undergrowth of Folly: Public Order, Race Anxiety & the 1903 Evansville, Indiana Riot. LC 00-26981. 2000. write for info. (*0-8153-3722-1*) Garland.

Butler, Brian, jt. auth. see Kaufer, David S.

Butler, Brian E., jt. auth. see Bowen, Michael A.

Butler, Brian M., ed. Archaeological Investigations on the North Coast of Rota, Mariana Islands. LC 88-70301. (Center for Archaeological Investigations Occasional Paper Ser.: No. 8). (Illus.). xxxii, 504p. (Orig.). 1988. pap. 18.00 (*0-88104-066-5*) Center Archaeol.

Butler, Brian S., jt. auth. see Kaufer, David S.

Butler, C. Western Mysticism: Neglected Chapters in the History of Religion. 1973. 250.00 (*0-87968-244-2*) Gordon Pr.

Butler, C. J. & Doyle, J. G., eds. Solar & Stellar Activities - Similarities & Differences: Astronomical Society of the Pacific Meeting on Solar & Stellar Activity - Similarities & Differences (1998: Armagh, N. Ireland) LC 99-60528. (Conference Series Proceedings: Vol. 158). 415p. 1999. text 52.00 (*1-886733-78-3*) Astron Soc Pacific.

Butler, C. J. & Elliott, I. Stellar Photometry - Current Techniques & Future Developments. (Illus.). 393p. (C). 1994. text 74.95 (*0-521-41866-6*) Cambridge U Pr.

Butler, C. T. Lawrence & McHenry, Keith. Food Not Bombs. (Illus.). 116p. 2000. pap. 8.95 (*1-884365-21-3*) See Sharp Pr.

Butler, C. Woody, et al. Visual Basic Controls Desk Reference. 750p. 1995. pap. 44.95 (*1-878739-87-5*) Sams.

Butler, Carol A. & Walker, Dolores D. The Divorce Mediation Answer Book. LC 98-34008. 288p. 1999. pap. 16.00 (*1-56836-252-8*) Kodansha.

***Butler, Carolyn, ed.** Faith, Hope & Chastity: Honest Reflections on the Catholic Priesthood. 176p. 2000. pap. 16.95 (*0-00-628136-2*, Pub. by HarpC) Trafalgar.

Butler, Carolyn H., et al. Typetronics II: Applied Professional Typewriting. LC 88-83269. xvi, 185p. 1989. 30.80 (*0-02-830561-2*) Glencoe.

Butler, Carroll B. Treasures of the Longleaf Pines: Naval Stores. (Illus.). xx, 380p. 1998. 40.00 (*0-9660620-0-0*) Tarkel Pub.

***Butler, Cathy.** I Can Do That! 100+ Ways to Be on Mission. Smith, Joe, ed. (Illus.). 123p. 1999. pap. 6.99 (*1-56309-289-1*) Womans Mission Union.

Butler, Cathy. Servants of the Banquet: Stories & Ideas about Fighting Hunger. Nelson, Becky, ed. (Illus.). 100p. (Orig.). 1994. pap. text 6.95 (*1-56309-101-1*, N943118, New Hope) Womans Mission Union.

Butler, Cathy, ed. see Anderson, Monnie.

Butler, Cathy, ed. see Cummings, Margaret A.

Butler, Cathy, ed. see George, Timothy F.

Butler, Cathy, ed. see Madaris, Don.

Butler, Cctavia E., jt. auth. see Butler, Octavia E.

Butler, Charles. The Darkling. LC 97-30232. 176p. (YA). (gr. 7-12). 1998. per. 16.00 (*0-689-81796-7*, 870383) McElderry Bks.

— The Principles of Musik, in Singing & Setting. LC 74-25439. (English Experience Ser.: No. 284). 136p. 1971. reprint ed. 20.00 (*90-221-0284-X*) Walter J Johnson.

***Butler, Charles.** Timon's Tide. LC 99-19085. (Illus.). 192p. (J). (gr. 7-12). 2000. 16.00 (*0-689-82593-5*) McElderry Bks.

Butler, Charles, jt. auth. see Caudill, Maureen.

Butler, Charles, jt. auth. see Fearne, Charles.

Butler, Charles E. Cut Is the Branch. LC 73-144749. (Yale Series of Younger Poets: No. 43). reprint ed. 18.00 (*0-404-53843-6*) AMS Pr.

Butler, Charles F., jt. auth. see Addicott, James P.

Butler, Charles L., Jr. Golden Moments. (Orig.). 1996. pap. write for info. (*1-57553-431-2*) Watermrk Pr.

***Butler, Charlotte & Keary, John.** Managers & Mantras: One Company's Struggle for Simplicity. LC 99-43202. 250p. 2000. 29.95 (*0-471-83558-7*) Wiley.

Butler, Chris. Reincarnation Explained. unabridged ed. LC 83-61000. (Illus.). 288p. 1984. 12.95 (*0-88187-000-5*) Science Identity.

— Who Are You? Discovering Your Real Identity. unabridged ed. LC 83-80825. (Who Are You? Ser.: Vol. 1). (Illus.). 489p. 1984. 11.95 (*0-912093-00-5*) Identity Inst.

***Butler, Christine.** Powerful Program Keys: Successful Church Programs for All Occasions. 132p. 1998. reprint ed. pap. text 6.95 (*0-940955-47-4*) Urban Ministries.

Butler, Christopher. Early Modernism: Literature Music & Painting in Europe, 1900-1916. LC 93-26945. (Illus.). 332p. 1994. pap. 21.00 (*0-19-818252-X*, Clarendon Pr) OUP.

— Early Modernism: Literature Music & Painting in Europe, 1900-1916. LC 93-26945. (Illus.). 336p. (C). 1994. text 55.00 (*0-19-811746-9*, Clarendon Pr) OUP.

— Interpretation, Deconstruction, & Ideology. LC 84-5526. 170p. 1984. pap. text 21.00 (*0-19-815791-6*) OUP.

Butler, Christopher & Joyce, Victoria. Counselling Couples in Relationships: An Introduction to the Relate Approach. LC 97-17405. (Wiley Series in Brief Therapy & Counselling). 208p. 1998. pap. 36.50 (*0-471-97778-0*) Wiley.

Butler, Christopher, ed. & intro. see James, Henry.

Butler, Clark. Hegel's Logic: Between Dialectic & History. LC 96-35414. (Studies in Phenomenology & Existential Philosophy). 368p. 1997. 69.95 (*0-8101-1426-7*) Northwestern U Pr.

Butler, Clark, tr. see Hegel, Georg Wilhelm Friedrich.

***Butler, Cornelia H.** Afterimage: Drawing Through Process. LC 98-43473. (Illus.). 156p. 1999. pap. text 35.00 (*0-262-52262-4*) MIT Pr.

Butler, Cornelia H. Iowa Artists, 1988. LC 88-71450. (Illus.). 40p. (Orig.). 1988. pap. 10.00 (*0-9614615-5-1*) Edmundson.

— Peter Shelton: Waxworks. LC 88-70611. (Illus.). 44p. (Orig.). 1988. pap. 15.00 (*0-9614615-4-3*) Edmundson.

Butler, Cornelia H. & Museum of Contemporary Art (Los Angeles, Calif.) S. Afterimage: Drawing Through Process. LC 98-43473. 1999. pap. write for info. (*0-914357-66-2*) Los Angeles Mus Contemp.

Butler, Cuthbert. The Lausiac History of Palladius: A Critical Discussion Together with Notes on early Egyptian Monachism, 2 vols. 575p. reprint ed. lib. bdg. 150.00 (*0-685-13766-X*, 05101497) G Olms Pubs.

Butler, D. & Finsen, E. Arbitration in South Africa: Law & Practice. 336p. 1993. pap. 42.50 (*0-7021-2986-0*, Pub. by Juta & Co) Gaunt.

***Butler, D. & Maksimovic, C., eds.** Developments in Urban Drainage Modelling. (Water Science & Technology Ser.: Vol. 39/9). 294p. 1999. pap. 163.00 (*0-08-042811-8*, Pergamon Pr) Elsevier.

Butler, D. Martin. Financial Fitness. (Christian Living Ser.). 44p. 1988. pap. 3.50 (*0-8341-1244-2*) Beacon Hill.

Butler, D. W., jt. auth. see Van Der Merwe, C. G.

Butler, Dale. Blossom. LC 92-34265. (Voyages Ser.). (Illus.). (J). 1993. 14.00 (*0-383-03620-8*) SRA McGraw.

Butler, Dan. The Only Thing Worse You Could Have Told Me . . . 1997. pap. 5.25 (*0-8222-1613-2*) Dramatists Play.

Butler, Dan, jt. auth. see Oliver, Donald.

***Butler, Daniel.** Americas Dumbest Criminals. LC 99-48971. 2000. 9.99 (*0-517-20890-3*) Random Hse Value.

Butler, Daniel. Crimes & Misdumbmeanors. LC 98-34682. 240p. 1998. pap. 7.95 (*1-55853-673-6*) Rutledge Hill Pr.

Butler, Daniel & Ray, Alan. These Aren't My Pants - The Dumbest & Dimmest from the Files of America's Dumbest Criminals. LC 99-34842. 1999. pap. 16.95 (*1-55853-772-4*) Rutledge Hill Pr.

— Wanted! Dumb or Alive. LC 96-32030. (America's Dumbest Criminals Ser.: No. 2). 240p. (Orig.). 1996. pap. 7.95 (*1-55853-421-0*) Rutledge Hill Pr.

— The World's Dumbest Criminals: Based on True Stories from Law Enforcement Officials Around the World. LC 97-30695. (Illus.). 239p. 1997. pap. 7.95 (*1-55853-541-1*) Rutledge Hill Pr.

Butler, Daniel A. Unsinkable: The Full Story of the Titanic. LC 98-9294. (Illus.). 320p. 1998. 19.95 (*0-8117-1814-X*) Stackpole.

***Butler, Daniel Allen.** The Lusitania: The Life & Legacy of an Ocean Legend. 2000. 29.95 (*0-8117-0989-2*) Stackpole.

Butler, Daniel L. The Last Generation of Truth. (Illus.). 128p. (Orig.). 1989. pap. 7.00 (*0-932581-58-7*) Word Aflame.

Butler, Daniel R., et al. America's Dumbest Criminals. LC 96-12866. 224p. 1995. pap. 7.95 (*1-55853-372-9*) Rutledge Hill Pr.

— America's Dumbest Criminals. large type ed. LC 96-12866. 244p. 1996. lib. bdg. 23.95 (*0-7862-0714-0*) Thorndike Pr.

Butler, Daphne. Caring for Young. LC 95-8811. (Patterns of Life Ser.). (Illus.). 32p. (J). 1995. lib. bdg. 5.00 (*0-8172-4201-5*) Raintree Steck-V.

— Finding Shelter. LC 95-10785. (Patterns of Life Ser.). (Illus.). 32p. (J). 1995. lib. bdg. 21.40 (*0-8172-4203-1*) Raintree Steck-V.

— Fire Burns? LC 95-13658. (What Happens When? Ser.). (Illus.). 32p. (J). 1995. lib. bdg. 5.00 (*0-8172-4156-6*) Raintree Steck-V.

— Food Cooks? LC 95-13659. (What Happens When? Ser.). (Illus.). 32p. (J). 1995. lib. bdg. 5.00 (*0-8172-4155-8*) Raintree Steck-V.

— France. LC 92-16648. (On the Map Ser.). (Illus.). 32p. (J). (gr. 2-4). 1992. lib. bdg. 22.83 (*0-8114-3675-6*) Raintree Steck-V.

— Gathering Food. LC 95-16626. (Patterns of Life Ser.). (Illus.). 32p. (J). 1995. lib. bdg. 5.00 (*0-8172-4200-7*) Raintree Steck-V.

— Getting Around. LC 95-15547. (Patterns of Life Ser.). (Illus.). 32p. (J). 1995. lib. bdg. 5.00 (*0-8172-4202-3*) Raintree Steck-V.

— Italy. LC 92-16649. (On the Map Ser.). (Illus.). 32p. (J). (gr. 2-4). 1992. lib. bdg. 22.83 (*0-8114-3677-2*) Raintree Steck-V.

— Spain. LC 92-17032. (On the Map Ser.). (Illus.). 32p. (J). (gr. 2-4). 1992. lib. bdg. 22.83 (*0-8114-3678-0*) Raintree Steck-V.

— U. S. A. LC 92-13647. (On the Map Ser.). (Illus.). 32p. (J). (gr. 2-4). 1992. lib. bdg. 22.83 (*0-8114-3676-4*) Raintree Steck-V.

— What Happens When Flowers Grow? LC 95-10520. (What Happens When? Ser.). (Illus.). 32p. (J). 1995. lib. bdg. 5.00 (*0-8172-4150-7*) Raintree Steck-V.

— What Happens When People Talk? LC 95-12060. (Illus.). 32p. (J). 1996. lib. bdg. 5.00 (*0-8172-4154-X*) Raintree Steck-V.

— What Happens When Rain Falls? LC 95-12061. (What Happens When? Ser.). (Illus.). 32p. (J). 1996. lib. bdg. 5.00 (*0-8172-4151-5*) Raintree Steck-V.

— What Happens When Volcanoes Erupt? LC 95-10519. (What Happens When? Ser.). (Illus.). 32p. (J). 1995. lib. bdg. 5.00 (*0-8172-4157-4*) Raintree Steck-V.

— What Happens When Wheels Turn? LC 95-11782. (What Happens When? Ser.). (Illus.). 32p. (J). 1995. lib. bdg. 5.00 (*0-8172-4152-3*) Raintree Steck-V.

— What Happens When Wind Blows? LC 95-13660. (Illus.). 32p. (J). 1995. lib. bdg. 5.00 (*0-8172-4153-1*) Raintree Steck-V.

Butler, Daren. The Cure: On Record. (Illus.). 128p. 1995. pap. 24.95 (*0-7119-3867-9*, OP 47600) Omnibus NY.

***Butler, Darren J.** Abbie, Girl Spy - The Case of the Missing Locket. Greer, Margaret, ed. (Abbie, Girl Spy Mysteries Ser.). (Illus.). 140p. (J). (gr. 3-9). 2000. 12.99 (*0-9700752-1-9*); pap. 5.99 (*0-9700752-0-0*) Onstage Pubng.

Butler, David. Britain & the Information Society. LC P 0091.B7. (British Computer Society Workshop Ser.: Vol. 3). 38p. reprint ed. pap. 30.00 (*0-8357-7408-2*, 203267600080) Bks Demand.

***Butler, David.** The British General Elections, 1945-1992, 15 vols. 5500p. 2000. lib. bdg. write for info. (*0-333-77863-4*) Macmillan.

Butler, David. British General Elections since 1945. 2nd ed. (Making Contemporary Britain Ser.). (Illus.). 132p. (C). 1995. pap., per. 29.95 (*0-631-19828-8*) Blackwell Pubs.

***Butler, David.** British Politics & European Elections. 2000. pap. 72.00 (*0-312-23377-9*) St Martin.

— Business Planning: A Guide to Small Business Start-Up. (Illus.). 288p. 2000. pap. 34.95 (*0-7506-4706-X*) Buttrwrth-Heinemann.

Butler, David. David Butler: Interviewed by Irene Khan Atkins. LC 93-29551. (Directors Guild of American Oral History Ser.: No. 5). (Illus.). 337p. 1993. 47.50 (*0-8108-2705-0*) Scarecrow.

— Redistricting. LC 91-23487. 100p. 1991. pap. 22.60 (*0-02-317585-0*, Macmillan Coll) P-H.

— The Trouble with Reporting Northern Ireland. 176p. 1995. 68.95 (*1-85628-909-5*, Pub. by Avebry) Ashgate Pub Co.

***Butler, David.** Twentieth-century British Politic. LC 00-20047. 610p. 2000. text 79.95 (*0-312-22947-X*) St Martin.

Butler, David, ed. Hazards Research & Applications Workshop (1996) Proceedings. 194p. (C). 1999. reprint ed. pap. text 40.00 (*0-7881-7769-9*) DIANE Pub.

***Butler, David, et al, eds.** The Law, Politics & the Constitution: Essays in Honor of Geoffrey Marshall. LC 99-21477. (Illus.). 328p. 1999. text 85.00 (*0-19-829585-5*) OUP.

Butler, David & Butler, Gareth. British Political Facts, 1900-1994. 7th ed. LC 94-23030. 1994. text 59.95 (*0-312-12147-4*) St Martin.

***Butler, David & Davies, John W.** Urban Drainage. LC 99-35421. 352p. 2000. pap. 49.99 (*0-419-22340-1*, E & FN Spon) Routledge.

Butler, David & Rammey, Austin. Referendums Around the World: The Growing Use of Direct Democracy. LC 94-13296. 100p. 1994. pap. 19.95 (*0-8447-3853-0*) Am Enterprise.

Butler, David & Stokes, Donald E. Political Change in Britain, 1963-1970, 2 vols. 1972. write for info. (*0-89138-055-8*) ICPSR.

— Political Change in Britain, 1963-1970, 2 vols., 1. 1972. write for info. (*0-89138-056-6*) ICPSR.

— Political Change in Britain, 1963-1970, 2 vols., 2. 1972. write for info. (*0-89138-057-4*) ICPSR.

Butler, David & Westlake, Martin, eds. British Politics & European Elections, 1994. LC 95-8226. (Illus.). 432p. 1995. text 69.95 (*0-312-12641-7*) St Martin.

Butler, David, et al. Failure in British Government: The Politics of the Poll Tax. (Illus.). 352p. 1995. pap. 14.95 (*0-19-827876-4*) OUP.

Butler, David, ed. see Cox, Bette Y.

Butler, David, jt. ed. see McLean, Iain.

Butler, David A. Does "Independent" Mean "Free from Influence?" Escape Clause Decision-Making at the United States International Trade Commission. LC 94-45050. (Foreign Economic Policy of the United States Ser.). 950302p. 1995. text 58.00 (*0-8153-1941-X*) Garland.

Butler, David E. The Electoral System in Britain since 1918. 2nd ed. LC 85-30593. (Illus.). 246p. 1986. reprint ed. lib. bdg. 85.00 (*0-313-25118-5*, BUES, Greenwood Pr) Greenwood.

Butler, David E. Musician's Guide to Perception & Cognition. 265p. 1992. 63.00 incl. cd-rom (*0-02-870341-3*, Schirmer Books) Mac Lib Ref.

— Seasons of Hope: Readings for the Liturgical Year. 144p. 1998. pap. 15.95 (*0-8298-1236-9*) Pilgrim OH.

Butler, David E. & Ranney, Austin, eds. Electioneering: A Comparative Study of Continuity & Change. (Illus.). 304p. 1992. text 65.00 (*0-19-827375-4*) OUP.

Butler, David E., jt. auth. see Merton, Don.

Butler, David R. Zoogeomorphology: Animals As Geomorphic Agents. (Illus.). 239p. (C). 1995. text 54.95 (*0-521-43343-6*) Cambridge U Pr.

Butler, David S. Mobilisation of the Nervous System. (Illus.). 265p. 1991. text 83.00 (*0-443-04400-7*) Church.

Butler, Deborah, jt. auth. see Liner, Tom.

Butler, Deborah A. American Women Writers on Vietnam: Unheard Voices; A Selected Annotated Bibliography. LC 89-11963. (Reference Library of the Humanities: Vol. 1278). 328p. 1989. text 15.00 (*0-8240-3528-3*, H1278) Garland.

Butler, Deborah A. & Liner, Tom. Rooms to Grow: Natural Language Arts in the Middle School. 2nd ed. LC 98-87687. viii, 440 p. 1998. write for info. (*0-89089-697-6*) Carolina Acad Pr.

Butler, Deborah A. & Manning, M. Lee. Addressing Gender Differences in Young Adolescents. LC 98-22352. 133p. 1998. pap. 18.00 (*0-87173-144-4*) ACEI.

Butler, Deborah A., et al. On Site: Preparing Middle Level Teachers Through Field Experiences. 76p. 1991. 9.00 (*1-56090-059-8*) Natl Middle Schl.

Butler, Derek. Canterbury Cathedral. (Best of Britain in Old Photographs Ser.). (Illus.). 128p. 1997. pap. 17.95 (*0-7509-1541-2*, Pub. by Sutton Pub Ltd) Intl Pubs Mktg.

***Butler, Des & Rodrick, Sharon.** Australian Media Law. 569p. 1999. pap. 60.00 (*0-455-21675-4*, 18654, Pub. by LBC Info Servs) Gaunt.

Butler, Diana H. Standing Against the Whirlwind: Evangelical Episcopalians in Nineteenth-Century America. LC 93-34323. (Religion in America Ser.). 288p. (C). 1995. text 60.00 (*0-19-508542-6*) OUP.

Butler-Diaz, Jacqueline, ed. New Laos, New Challenges. (Illus.). xxvii, 356p. (C). 1998. pap. 19.95 (*1-881044-18-1*) ASU Prog SE Asian.

Butler, Dixie L. How to Get a Mortgage: A Complete, No-Nonsense Guide to Finding the Money to Buy, Refinance or Remodel Your Home. 240p. 1991. pap. 12.95 (*1-55738-193-3*, Irwn Prfssnl) McGraw-Hill Prof.

***Butler, Dom C., ed.** Western Mysticism: The Teaching of Saint Augustine & Saint Bernard on Contemplation & the Contemplative Life. rev. ed. 250p. 1999. 110.00 (*0-7103-0662-8*, Pub. by Kegan Paul Intl) Col U Pr.

***Butler, Don.** Guide to Ship Repair Estimates. 128p. 2000. 59.95 (*0-7506-4834-1*) Buttrwrth-Heinemann.

Butler, Don, jt. auth. see Bennett, Chuck.

Butler, Donald F. The History of Hudson. LC 92-26169. (Crestline Ser.). (Illus.). 336p. 1982. 44.95 (*0-87938-696-7*, Crestline Pub) MBI Pubg.

— 10-Minute Yoga: 100 Personal Programs for Daily Practice. (Illus.). 144p. 1999. pap. text 17.95 (*0-7063-7814-8*) Ward Lock Ltd UK.

Butler, Dori H. The Great Tooth Fairy Rip-Off. LC 96-38687. (Illus.). 32p. (J). (gr. k-4). 1997. 14.95 (*1-57749-023-1*) Fairview Press.

— M Is for Minnesota. LC 98-13074. (Illus.). 32p. (J). (gr. 1-6). 1998. 16.95 (*0-8166-3041-0*) U of Minn Pr.

— W Is for Wisconsin. McBride, Elizabeth, ed. LC 98-60163. (Illus.). 30p. (J). (gr. 4 up). 1998. 14.95 (*0-915024-62-4*) Trails Media.

***Butler, Dori Hillestad.** F Is for Firefighting. (Alpha Flight Bks.). (Illus.). 60p. (ps-3). 2000. 17.95 (*1-892920-20-4*) G H B Pubs.

Butler, Dorothy. Another Happy Tale. LC 91-23133. (Illus.). 32p. (J). (ps-3). 1991. 12.95 (*0-940793-88-1*, Crocodile Bks) Interlink Pub.

— Babies Need Books: Sharing the Joy of Books with Children from Birth to Six. rev. ed. 288p. 1998. pap. 15.95 (*0-435-08154-3*) Heinemann.

— Babies Need Books: Sharing the Joy of Books with Your Child from Birth to Six. 288p. 1998. reprint ed. pap. 15.95 (*0-435-08144-6*) Heinemann.

— A Happy Tale. LC 90-34500. (Illus.). 32p. (J). (ps-5). 1990. 11.95 (*0-940793-61-X*, Crocodile Bks) Interlink Pub.

— My Brown Bear Barney. LC 88-21199. (Illus.). 32p. (J). (ps up). 1989. 15.95 (*0-688-08567-9*, Grenwillow Bks) HarpC Child Bks.

***Butler, Dorothy.** My Brown Bear Barney. 2000. pap. 4.95 (*0-688-17723-9*, Wm Morrow) Morrow Avon.

— My Brown Bear Barney at the Party. (J). 2000. lib. bdg. 15.89 (*0-688-17549-X*, Grenwillow Bks) HarpC Child Bks.

— My Brown Bear Barney at the Party. (J). 2001. 15.95 (*0-688-17548-1*, Grenwillow Bks) HarpC Child Bks.

Butler, Dorothy & Clay, Marie M. Reading Begins at Home: Preparing Children for Reading Before They Go to School. 2nd rev. ed. LC 87-326. (Illus.). 48p. (C). 1987. pap. 13.50 (*0-435-08443-7*, 08443) Heinemann.

Butler, Doug. Farrier Science: Study Guide & Workbook. (Illus.). 162p. 1997. reprint ed. pap., student ed. 29.95 (*0-916992-05-5*) Btler Pub.

— Horse Foot Care. rev. ed. LC 93-248306. (Illus.). 1999. pap. text 7.95 (*0-916992-15-2*) Btler Pub.

— The Principles of Horseshoeing II: An Illustrated Textbook of Farrier Science & Craftsmanship. (Illus.). 567p. 1985. text 79.95 (*0-916992-02-0*) Btler Pub.

— Shoeing in Your Right Mind: How to Assess Conformation, Achieve Balance & Shoe Fit & Increase Your Efficiency in Horseshoeing. (Illus.). 160p. 1998. 49.95 (*0-916992-20-9*) Btler Pub.

***Butler, E. A.** Atrial Fibrillation - My Heart, the Doctors & Me: An Investigative Report by an Inquisitive Patient. LC 99-91049. 220p. 2000. 22.95 (*0-9675203-0-4*) King of Hearts.

Butler, E. J. Fungi & Disease in Plants. (C). 1973. text 250.00 (*0-89771-574-8*, Pub. by Intl Bk Distr) St Mut.

Butler, E. M. The Myth of the Magus. (Canto Book Ser.). 296p. (C). 1993. pap. 11.95 (*0-521-43777-6*) Cambridge U Pr.

— The Saint-Simonian Religion in Germany. 1968. reprint ed. 49.50 (*0-86527-177-1*) Fertig.

Butler, E. Sonny. Using Microsoft Access: A How-to-Do-It Manual for Librarians. LC 97-27406. (How-to-Do-It Manuals Ser.). 118p. 1997. pap. 38.50 (*1-55570-268-6*) Neal-Schuman.

Butler, E. Sonny & Scanio, Barbara. Using dBASE Version 5 for Windows: A-How-to-Do-It Manual for Librarians. (Illus.). 105p. (Orig.). 1995. pap. 38.50 (*1-55570-079-9*) Neal-Schuman.

Butler, Eamonn & Pirie, Madsen. The Sherlock Holmes IQ Book. LC 96-20656. 208p. 1996. pap. 9.95 (*0-7867-0330-X*) Carroll & Graf.

Butler, Eamonn F., jt. auth. see Schuettinger, Robert L.

Butler, Earl. Zero Bonding. (Bloody Twin Press Ser.). (Illus.). 32p. (Orig.). 1987. pap. 90.00 (*1-886350-37-X*) Bloody Twin Pr.

Butler, Edgar, et al. Mexico & Mexico City in the World Economy. (Illus.). 400p. 2000. text 65.00 (*0-8133-3542-6*) Westview.

Butler, Edgar W. & Kinnear, Karen L. Childhood Sexual Abuse: A Reference Handbook. LC 95-40065. (Contemporary World Issues Ser.). 333p. 1995. lib. bdg. 45.00 (*0-87436-691-7*) ABC-CLIO.

Butler, Edgar W. & Pick, James B. Geothermal Energy Development: Problems & Prospects in the Imperial Valley of California. LC 81-23402. 382p. 1982. 85.00 (*0-306-40772-8*, Plenum Trade) Perseus Pubng.

Butler, Edgar W., jt. auth. see Pick, James B.

Butler, Edgar W., jt. ed. see Gutknecht, Douglas B.

Butler, Edward B., jt. auth. see McElhone, Alice P.

Butler, Elaine. Attracting Birds. Kennedy, Phillip, ed. 1991. pap. 5.95 (*0-919433-87-1*) Lone Pine.

— Poodle Collectibles of the 50's & 60's. (Illus.). 151p. (Orig.). 1995. pap. 19.95 (*0-89538-038-2*) L-W Inc.

Butler, Elaine, ed. see Kavanaugh, James.

Butler, Elaine, ed. see Schalkwyk-Barendsen, Helene M.

Butler, Eliza M. Heinrich Heine: A Biography. LC 70-106684. 1970. reprint ed. lib. bdg. 69.50 (*0-8371-3607-5*, BUHH, Greenwood Pr) Greenwood.

***Butler, Elizabeth.** The Colonel's Widow. 250p. 1999. pap. 12.95 (*0-9675767-0-9*) B&E Pubng.

Butler, Elizabeth. The Fortunes of Faust. LC 99-182120. 840p. 1999. pap. 19.95 (*0-271-01844-5*) Pa St U Pr.

— Ritual Magic. LC 99-191883. 762p. 1999. pap. 19.95 (*0-271-01846-1*) Pa St U Pr.

***Butler, Elizabeth.** Trailboss. 250p. 2000. pap. 12.95 (*0-9675767-1-7*) B&E Pubng.

Butler, Elizabeth B. Women & the Trades. LC 70-89757. (American Labor, from Conspiracy to Collective Bargaining Ser., No. 1). 440p. 1972. reprint ed. 26.95 (*0-405-02108-9*) Ayer.

Butler, Elmer E. Butler: Butlers & Kinsfolk. (Illus.). 362p. 1991. reprint ed. pap. 56.00 (*0-8328-2109-8*); reprint ed. lib. bdg. 66.00 (*0-8328-2108-X*) Higginson Bk Co.

Butler, Elvie. Celebrate Easter. (Illus.). (J). (gr. k-3). 1990. pap. 3.95 (*0-590-43414-4*) Scholastic Inc.

Butler, Eugenia W., et al. An Auto-Instructional Text in Correct Writing, Form B. 2nd ed. 476p. (C). 1980. pap. text 36.76 (*0-669-02484-8*); pap. text, teacher ed. 2.66 (*0-669-02486-4*) HM Trade Div.

— Correct Writing. 4th ed. LC 86-81265. 405p. (C). 1987. 2.66 (*0-669-11771-4*) HM Trade Div.

— Correct Writing. 5th ed. 494p. (C). 1991. pap. text 36.36 (*0-669-20474-9*); teacher ed. 37.56 (*0-669-24714-6*) HM Trade Div.

Butler, Eva M. & Hadlock, Wendell S. Dogs of the Northeastern Woodland Indians. (Robert Abbe Museum Bulletin Ser.: No. XIII). 54p. 1994. reprint ed. pap. write for info. (*1-885410-02-6*) R Abbe Museum.

Butler, F. Coit. Instructional Systems Development for Vocational & Technical Training. LC 70-168490. 384p. 1972. 39.95 (*0-87778-027-7*) Educ Tech Pubns.

— Practical Electricity & Electronics: Electronics Fundamentals for Career Preparation. (Illus.). 178p. (Orig.). 1982. pap. text 8.00 (*0-86657-006-3*) Lab-Volt.

Butler, Fannie. There's Hope for the Child That Says, "If I Grow Up . . ." 146p. (Orig.). 1997. pap. 10.95 (*0-9656774-2-7*) Choice Pubng CA.

Butler, Fay E. Called to Be Saints. 140p. 1993. pap. 10.00 (*1-883483-00-X*) Ellis-Butler Minist.

— Called to Be Warriors. 160p. (Orig.). 1993. pap. 10.00 (*1-883483-02-6*) Ellis-Butler Minist.

— The Destruction of Our Children: Why Our Children Must Become Warriors. 130p. (Orig.). 1994. pap. 7.00 (*1-883483-05-0*) Ellis-Butler Minist.

Butler, Fiona, jt. auth. see Archer, Clive.

Butler, Francelia. Children's Literature, 23. Vol. 23. 1995. pap. 18.00 (*0-300-06236-2*) Yale U Pr.

— Children's Literature, Vol. 15. LC 79-66588. Vol 15. 256p. 1987. 50.00 (*0-300-03812-7*); pap. 18.00 (*0-300-03813-5*) Yale U Pr.

— Children's Literature, Vol. 17. LC 79-66588. 256p. (C). 1989. pap. 18.00 (*0-300-04422-4*) Yale U Pr.

— Children's Literature, Vol. 17. LC 79-66588. Vol 17. 256p. (C). 1989. 50.00 (*0-300-04421-6*) Yale U Pr.

— Sharing Literature with Children: A Thematic Anthology. (Illus.). 492p. (C). 1989. reprint ed. pap. text 32.95 (*0-88133-463-4*) Waveland Pr.

Butler, Francelia, ed. Children's Literature, Vol. 16. LC 79-66588. Vol. 16. 256p. (C). (ps up). 1988. pap. 18.00 (*0-300-04193-4*) Yale U Pr.

Butler, Francelia, et al, eds. Children's Literature, Vol. 10. LC 79-66588. Vol. 10. 272p. (C). 1982. 50.00 (*0-300-02805-9*) Yale U Pr.

— Children's Literature: Annual of the Modern Language Association Division on Children's Literature & the Children's Literature Association, No. 13. LC 79-66588. Vol. 13. 240p. 1985. 50.00 (*0-300-03319-2*) Yale U Pr.

— Children's Literature No. 19: Annual of the Modern Language Association Division on Children's Literature & the Children's Literature. (Illus.). 240p. (Orig.). (C). 1991. pap. 18.00 (*0-300-04973-0*) Yale U Pr.

— Children's Literature No. 22: Annual of the Modern Language Association Division on Children's Literature & the Children's Literature Association. (Illus.). 212p. 1994. pap. 18.00 (*0-300-05875-6*) Yale U Pr.

— Children's Literature Vol. 14: Annual of the Modern Language Association Division on Children's Literature & the Children's Literature Association. rev. ed. LC 79-66588. 224p. 1986. 50.00 (*0-300-03564-0*) Yale U Pr.

— Children's Literature Vol. 21: Annual of the Modern Language Association Division on Children's Literature & the Children's Literature Association. LC 72-181256. (Illus.). 264p. (C). 1993. 50.00 (*0-300-05423-8*) Yale U Pr.

Butler, Francelia, et al, eds. Children's Literature Vol. 21: Annual of the Modern Language Association Division on Children's Literature & the Children's Literature Association. (Illus.). 264p. (C). 1993. pap. 18.00 (*0-300-05424-6*) Yale U Pr.

Butler, Francelia, et al, eds. Children's Literature, Twenty: Annual of the Modern Language Association Division on Children's Literature & the Children's Literature Association. (Illus.). 265p. (Orig.). (C). 1992. 50.00 (*0-300-05173-5*); pap. 18.00 (*0-300-05172-7*) Yale U Pr.

— Children's Literature, 24. 304p. 1996. 50.00 (*0-300-06628-7*); pap. 18.00 (*0-300-06629-5*) Yale U Pr.

Butler, Francelia & Rees, Compton. Children's Literature, Vol. 12. LC 79-66588. Vol. 12. (Illus.). 264p. 1984. 50.00 (*0-300-03144-0*) Yale U Pr.

Butler, Francelia, et al. Children's Literature, No. 18. Vol. 18. 240p. (C). 1990. pap. 18.00 (*0-300-04645-6*) Yale U Pr.

— Children's Literature: Annual of the Modern Language Association Division on Children's Literature & the Children's Literature Association, No. 11. LC 79-66588. Vol. 11. (Illus.). 224p. (ps up). 1983. 50.00 (*0-300-02991-8*) Yale U Pr.

Butler, Francelia, ed. see Silvette, Herbert.

Butler, Frances, et al. Living Arrangements: Frances Butler, Diane Neumaier, Anton van Dalen. (Illus.). 32p. 1989. pap. 5.00 (*0-930495-07-1*) San Fran Art Inst.

— Trance & Recalcitrance: The Private Voice in the Public Realm. (Illus.). 48p. (Orig.). 1995. pap. 15.00 (*0-918395-16-X*) Poltroon Pr.

Butler, Francis G. History of Farmington, Franklin Co., from the Earliest Explorations to the Present Time, 1776-1885. (Illus.). 683p. 1997. reprint ed. lib. bdg. 69.00 (*0-8328-5837-4*) Higginson Bk Co.

— A History of Farmington, Franklin Co., Maine, from the Earliest Explorations to the Present Time, 1776-1885. (Illus.). 683p. 1992. reprint ed. lib. bdg. 44.00 (*0-8328-2527-1*) Higginson Bk Co.

— History of Farmington, Maine. LC 83-62057. (Illus.). 752p. 1983. reprint ed. 55.00 (*0-89725-042-7*, 1208) Picton Pr.

Butler, Francis J., ed. American Catholic Identity: Essays in an Age of Change. LC 94-25511. 272p. (Orig.). 1994. pap. 12.95 (*1-55612-707-3*) Sheed & Ward WI.

Butler, Frank. The Concertina. (Illus.). 64p. 1976. pap. 10.95 (*0-8256-0192-4*, OK63677, Oak) Music Sales.

Butler, Frank A. Improvement of Teaching in Secondary Schools. 3rd ed. LC 54-10718. 1993. lib. bdg. 17.50 (*0-226-08513-9*) U Ch Pr.

— The Improvement of Teaching in Secondary Schools. 3rd ed. LC 54-10718. (Illus.). 433p. Date not set. reprint ed. pap. 134.30 (*0-608-20620-2*, 205458800003) Bks Demand.

***Butler, Frank K.** Navy Seal Physical Fitness Guide. 298p. 1998. per. 25.00 (*0-16-061339-6*) USGPO.

Butler, G. Fundamental Algorithms for Permutation Groups. (Lecture Notes in Computer Science Ser.: Vol. 559). xii, 238p. 1991. 28.95 (*0-387-54955-2*) Spr-Verlag.

Butler, G. H. Thomas Butler & His Descendants, 1674-1886: A Genealogy of the Descendants of Thomas & Elizabeth Butler of Butler's Hill. 199p. 1989. reprint ed. pap. 30.00 (*0-8328-1295-1*); reprint ed. lib. bdg. 38.00 (*0-8328-1294-3*) Higginson Bk Co.

Butler, Gail. Recreation Gold Prospecting for Fun & Profit. Morrison, Paul D., ed. LC 97-77186. (Illus.). 208p. 1998. pap. 12.95 (*0-935182-98-5*) Gem Guides Bk.

Butler, Gail A. Rockhounding California. rev. ed. (Illus.). 200p. pap. 12.95 (*1-56044-639-0*) Falcon Pub Inc.

Butler, Gareth, jt. auth. see Butler, David.

Butler, Gathorne V. Organization & Management Theory & Practice. 464p. (C). 1986. 90.00 (*0-13-641754-X*, Pub. by IPM Hse) St Mut.

Butler, Geoff. The Hangashore. LC 97-62179. (Illus.). 32p. (YA). (gr. 4 up). 1998. 15.95 (*0-88776-444-4*) Tundra Bks.

— The Killick: A Newfoundland Story. LC 95-60982. (Illus.). 32p. (J). (gr. 4 up). 1995. 14.95 (*0-88776-336-7*) Tundra Bks.

— The Killick: A Newfoundland Story. (Illus.). 32p. (J). (gr. 5 up). 1998. reprint ed. pap. 6.95 (*0-88776-449-5*) Tundra Bks.

Butler, George, ed. County Parks. 1982. 18.95 (*0-8434-0445-0*, Pub. by McGrath NH) Ayer.

Butler, George & Kresta, Jiri E., eds. Cyclopolymerization & Polymers with Chain-Ring Structures. LC 82-11331. (ACS Symposium Ser.: No. 195). 455p. 1982. lib. bdg. 54.95 (*0-8412-0731-3*) Am Chemical.

Butler, George, jt. auth. see Gaines, Charles.

Butler, George B., ed. Cyclopolymerization & Cyclocopolymerization. (Illus.). 560p. 1992. text 245.00 (*0-8247-8625-4*) Dekker.

Butler, George B., et al, eds. Reviews in Macromolecular Chemistry, Vol. 3. LC 66-9971. (Illus.). 450p. 1968. reprint ed. pap. 139.50 (*0-608-08359-3*, 202799000003) Bks Demand.

— Reviews in Macromolecular Chemistry, Vol. 4. LC 66-9971. (Illus.). 427p. 1970. reprint ed. pap. 132.40 (*0-608-08360-7*, 202799100004) Bks Demand.

— Reviews in Macromolecular Chemistry, Vol. 5, Pt. 2. LC 66-9971. (Illus.). 242p. 1970. reprint ed. pap. 75.10 (*0-608-08361-5*, 202798900005) Bks Demand.

— Reviews in Macromolecular Chemistry, Vol. 6. LC 66-9971. (Illus.). 498p. 1971. reprint ed. pap. 154.40 (*0-608-08362-3*, 202799200006) Bks Demand.

— Reviews in Macromolecular Chemistry, Vol. 7. LC 66-9971. (Illus.). 313p. 1972. reprint ed. pap. 97.10 (*0-608-08363-1*, 202798800007) Bks Demand.

— Reviews in Macromolecular Chemistry, 1972, Vol. 8. LC 66-9971. (Illus.). 345p. reprint ed. pap. 107.00 (*0-7837-0921-8*, 204122600008) Bks Demand.

— Reviews in Macromolecular Chemistry, 1973, Vol. 9. LC 67-27715. (Illus.). 377p. reprint ed. pap. 116.90 (*0-7837-0777-0*, 204109100009) Bks Demand.

— Reviews in Macromolecular Chemistry, 1974, Vol. 11. LC 67-27715. (Illus.). 389p. reprint ed. pap. 120.60 (*0-7837-0779-7*, 204109300011) Bks Demand.

— Reviews in Macromolecular Chemistry, 1975, Vol. 12. LC 67-27715. (Illus.). 406p. reprint ed. pap. 125.90 (*0-7837-0780-0*, 204109400012) Bks Demand.

Butler, George B. & Berlin, K. Darrell. Fundamentals of Organic Chemistry: Theory & Application. LC 79-128351. 1125p. reprint ed. pap. 200.00 (*0-608-30445-X*, 201244900081) Bks Demand.

Butler, George B. & Kresta, Jiri E., eds. Cyclopolymerization & Polymers with Chain-Ring Structures. LC 82-11331. (ACS Symposium Ser.: Vol. 195). 471p. 1982. reprint ed. pap. 146.10 (*0-608-03118-6*, 206357100007) Bks Demand.

B

Butler, George D. Recreation Areas, Their Design & Equipment. 2nd ed. LC 57-11288. 192p. 1958. reprint ed. pap. 59.60 (0-7837-3433-6, 205775400008) Bks Demand.

Butler, George P., ed. Best Sermons, Nineteen Forty-Nine to Nineteen Fifty. LC 74-134065. (Essay Index Reprint Ser.). 1977. reprint ed. 25.95 (0-8369-2488-6) Ayer.

— Best Sermons, 1946. LC 74-134065. (Essay Index Reprint Ser.). 1977. reprint ed. 22.95 (0-8369-2757-5) Ayer.

— Best Sermons, 1947. LC 74-134065. (Essay Index Reprint Ser.). 1977. reprint ed. 25.95 (0-8369-2487-8) Ayer.

Butler, George V. Shuttle-Spacelab - The New Transportation System & Its Utilization, (3rd DGLR/AASSymposium), Spr. 28-30, 1980, Hannover, Germany: The New Transportation System & Its Utilization. Koelle, Dietrich E., ed. LC 57-43769. (Advances in the Astronautical Sciences Ser.: Vol. 43). (Illus.). 342p. 1981. 45.00 (0-87703-144-4, Am Astronaut Soc); pap. 35.00 (0-87703-146-0, Am Astronaut Soc) Univelt Inc.

Butler, George V., ed. The 21st Century in Space, 35th AAS Annual Meeting, Oct. 24-26, 1988, St. Louis, MO. LC 57-43769. (Advances in the Astronautical Sciences Ser.: Vol. 70). (Illus.). 446p. 1990. 90.00 (0-87703-314-5, Am Astronaut Soc); pap. 75.00 (0-87703-315-3, Am Astronaut Soc) Univelt Inc.

***Butler, Gerald.** Inquiry into Crown Prosecution Service Decision-making in Relation to Deaths in Custody & Related Matters. LC 99-494975. 1999. write for info. (0-11-341236-3) Statnry Office.

— Military History of Boston's Harbor Islands: Massachusetts. LC 00-104053. (Images of America Ser.). (Illus.). 128p. 2000. pap. 18.99 (0-7385-0464-5) Arcadia Publng.

Butler, Gerald J. Fielding's Unruly Novels. LC 96-140967. 200p. 1995. text 79.95 (0-7734-4216-2) E Mellen.

— Henry Fielding & Lawrence's Old Adam: A Reading of Restoration & Eighteenth-Century British Literature. LC 92-22672. 168p. 1992. text 79.95 (0-7734-9604-1) E Mellen.

— Love & Reading: An Essay in Applied Psychoanalysis. (American University Studies: Comparative Literature: Ser. III, Vol. 25). X, 192p. (C). 1988. text 32.95 (0-8204-0763-1) P Lang Pubng.

Butler, Gillian & Hope, Tony. Managing Your Mind: The Mental Fitness Guide. (Illus.). 384p. 1995. pap. 2.00 (0-19-262383-4) OUP.

— Managing Your Mind: The Mental Fitness Guide. (Illus.). 448p. 1997. reprint ed. pap. 12.95 (0-19-511125-7) OUP.

Butler, Glenn R. The Butler's Choice. (Illus.). 192p. 1995. write for info. (0-9644735-0-X) Butlers Choice.

Butler, Gold J. Holmes. Descendants of George Holmes-in American. (Illus.). 122p. 1997. reprint ed. pap. 21.00 (0-8328-9192-4); reprint ed. lib. bdg. 31.00 (0-8328-9191-6) Higginson Bk Co.

Butler, Grant C. Bali to Bahrein. 1969. 12.95 (0-8159-5100-0) Devin.

— Kings & Camels. 1960. 24.95 (0-8159-6000-X) Devin.

— Kings & Camels: An American in Saudi Arabia. LC 60-7601. (Illus.). 231p. reprint ed. pap. 71.70 (0-608-11636-X, 202270800029) Bks Demand.

Butler, Gregory G. J. S. Bach's Clavier-Ubung 111: The Making of a Print, with a Companion Study of the Canonic Variations on Vom Himmel hoch BWV 769. LC 89-23650. (Sources of Music & Their Interpretation; Duke Studies in Music). 154p. (C). 1990. text 47.95 (0-8223-1009-0) Duke.

Butler, Gregory S. In Search of the American Spirit: The Political Thought of Orestes Brownson. LC 91-35736. 296p. (C). 1992. 36.95 (0-8093-1796-6) S Ill U Pr.

Butler, Gregory S. & Slack, James D. U. S. Educational Policy Interest Groups: Institutional Profiles. LC 93-44516. 256p. 1994. lib. bdg. 75.00 (0-313-27292-1, Greenwood Pr) Greenwood.

Butler, Gwendoline. The Brides of Friedberg. large type ed. 1979. 12.00 (0-7089-0292-8) Ulverscroft.

— Butterfly. large type ed. LC 96-52559. 498p. 1997. pap. 21.95 (0-7862-1020-6) Thorndike Pr.

— Coffin & the Paper Man. (Worldwide Library Mysteries). 1993. mass mkt. 3.99 (0-373-26133-0, 1-26133-8) Harlequin Bks.

— A Coffin for Charley. (Worldwide Library Mysteries). 1996. per. 5.50 (0-373-26200-0, 1-26200-5, Wrldwide Lib) Harlequin Bks.

— Coffin in the Museum of Crime. (Mystery Ser.). 1993. per. 3.99 (0-373-26121-7, 1-26121-3) Harlequin Bks.

— Coffin on Murder Street. (Mystery Ser.). 1994. per. 3.99 (0-373-26147-0, 1-26147-8) Harlequin Bks.

— The Coffin Tree. 1997. per. 4.99 (0-373-26250-7, 1-26250-0, Wrldwide Lib) Harlequin Bks.

— Coffin Underground. 1992. per. 3.99 (0-373-26110-1, 1-26110-6) Harlequin Bks.

***Butler, Gwendoline.** Coffin's Game. (WWL Mystery Ser.: Bk. 353). 256p. 2000. mass mkt. 5.99 (0-373-26353-8, 1-26353-2, Wrldwide Lib) Harlequin Bks.

Butler, Gwendoline. Coffin's Game. LC 99-27590. 1999. text 21.95 (0-312-20512-0) St Martin.

— Cracking Open a Coffin. large type ed. 390p. 1994. lib. bdg. 17.95 (0-7862-0118-5) Thorndike Pr.

— A Dark Coffin. (WWL Mystery Ser.). 1998. per. 5.50 (0-373-26265-5, 1-26265-8, Wrldwide Lib) Harlequin Bks.

— Death Lives Next Door. large type ed. (Popular Ser.). 242p. 1993. reprint ed. lib. bdg. 17.95 (1-56054-630-1) Thorndike Pr.

— Death Next Door. (WWL Mystery Ser.). 1994. mass mkt. 3.99 (0-373-26157-8, 1-26157-7) Harlequin Bks.

— A Double Coffin. (WWL Mystery Ser.: No. 313). 1999. per. 4.99 (0-373-26313-9, 1-26313-6, Wrldwide Lib) Harlequin Bks.

— A Double Coffin. LC 98-3223. 240p. 1998. text 21.95 (0-312-18569-3) St Martin.

— A Double Coffin. large type ed. LC 98-3738. 1998. pap. text 22.95 (0-7862-1481-3) Mac Lib Ref.

***Butler, Gwendoline.** A Grave Coffin. 2000. 22.95 (0-312-26167-5, Minotaur) St Martin.

— A Nameless Coffin. large type ed. LC 99-49108. 2000. pap. 23.95 (0-7862-2302-2) Mac Lib Ref.

Butler, H. Coordination of Building Services. (C). 1977. 85.00 (0-86022-043-5, Pub. by Build Servs Info Assn) St Mut.

— Electrical Fire Alarms - Sources of Information. 1977. 75.00 (0-86022-040-0, Pub. by Build Servs Info Assn) St Mut.

— The Embryology of the Lesser Galago (Galago senegalensis) (Contributions to Primatology Ser.: Vol. 19). (Illus.). vi, 158p. 1983. pap. 66.25 (3-8055-3749-2) S Karger.

Butler, H., ed. Approximation of the Electrical Load of Lighting Installations. (C). 1976. 65.00 (0-86022-038-9, Pub. by Build Servs Info Assn) St Mut.

Butler, H. & Cary, M., eds. Suetonius: Divus Julius. 186p. 1983. reprint ed. 22.95 (0-86292-026-4, Pub. by Brist Class Pr) Focus Pub-R Pullins.

Butler, H. & Juurlink, B. H. An Atlas for Staging Mammalian & Chick Embryos. LC 86-9552. 224p. 1987. 132.00 (0-8493-6629-1, QL959, CRC Reprint) Franklin.

Butler, H., et al. Locating Fire Alarm Sounders for Audibility. (C). 1981. pap. 95.00 (0-86022-100-8, Pub. by Build Servs Info Assn) St Mut.

Butler, H. E., tr. Training of an Orator, 4 vols., 1. (Loeb Classical Library: No. 124-127). 568p. 1920. 18.95 (0-674-99138-9) HUP.

— Training of an Orator, 4 vols., 2. (Loeb Classical Library: No. 124-127). 538p. 1921. 18.95 (0-674-99139-7) HUP.

— Training of an Orator, 4 vols., 3. (Loeb Classical Library: No. 124-127). 504p. 1921. 18.95 (0-674-99140-0) HUP.

— Training of an Orator, 4 vols., 4. (Loeb Classical Library: No. 124-127). 556p. 1922. 18.95 (0-674-99141-9) HUP.

Butler, H. E., ed. see International Astronomical Union Staff.

Butler, H. E., tr. see Apuleius, Madaurensis.

Butler, H. E., tr. see Stephen, William F.

Butler, H. L. Tales of Our Kinsfolk Past & Present: The Story of Our Butler Ancestry for Ten Generations, from 1602 to 1919. (Illus.). 552p. 1993. reprint ed. pap. 84.50 (0-8328-6582-6) Higginson Bk Co.

Butler, H. Lee, jt. auth. see Spaulding, Malcolm L.

Butler, Harold E. The Elegies of Propertius. lxxxiv, 407p. 1964. reprint ed. 105.00 (0-318-71083-8) G Olms Pubs.

— Post-Augustan Poetry from Seneca to Juvenal. LC 70-99656. (Select Bibliographies Reprint Ser.). 1977. 30.95 (0-8369-5085-2) Ayer.

Butler, Harold E. & Barber, Eric A. The Elegies of Propertius. lxxxiv, 407p. 1996. reprint ed. 105.00 (3-487-00619-7) G Olms Pubs.

Butler, Helen, ed. see Rogers, Evelyn C.

Butler, Henry. Henry Butler: Collected Works. Phillips, Elizabeth V., ed. Worth, Jack A., tr. (Recent Researches in Music of the Baroque Era Ser.: Vol. RRB66). (Illus.). xx, 122p. 1991. pap. 45.00 (0-89579-263-X, RRB66) A-R Eds.

Butler, Henry N. Economic Analysis for Lawyers. 2nd ed. LC 97-35249. 958p. 1998. 75.00 (0-89089-698-4) Carolina Acad Pr.

— Unhealthy Alliances: Bureaucrats, Interest Groups, & Politicians in Health Reform. (Special Studies in Health Reform). 100p. (Orig.). 1994. pap. 9.95 (0-8447-7022-1, AEI Pr) Am Enterprise.

Butler, Henry N. & Macey, Jonathan R. Using Federalism to Improve Environmental Policy. 100p. Date not set. pap. 12.95 (0-8447-3963-4) Am Enterprise.

Butler, Henry N. & Ribstein, Larry E. The Corporation & the Constitution. 1994. pap. 17.95 (0-8447-3865-4, AEI Pr) Am Enterprise.

Butler, Henry W. & Ribstein, Larry E. The Corporation & the Constitution. 1994. 34.95 (0-8447-3864-6, AEI Pr) Am Enterprise.

Butler, Herbert J., ed. Antique Auto Body Leather Work for the Restorer. LC 82-62713. (Vintage Craft Ser.: No. 3). (Illus.). 1969. pap. 6.95 (0-911160-03-5) Post Group.

Butler, Hilda. Cosmetic Raw Material Analysis & Quality Vol. 1: Hydrocarbons, Glycerides, Waxes, & Other Esters. 156p. 1994. pap. text 42.00 (1-870228-11-1) Micelle Pr.

— Poucher's Perfumes, Cosmetics & Soaps. 10th ed. 800p. 2000. 260.00 (0-7514-0479-9) Kluwer Academic.

Butler, Hiram E. Narrow Way of Attainment. 144p. 1998. reprint ed. pap. 16.95 (0-7661-0458-3) Kessinger Pub.

— The Seven Creative Principles (1913) 170p. 1998. reprint ed. pap. 16.95 (0-7661-0242-4) Kessinger Pub.

— Solar Biology. 288p. 1996. pap. 25.00 (0-89540-234-3, SB-234, Sun Bks) Sun Pub.

Butler, Hiram E., ed. Revised Esoteric: A Magazine of Advanced & Practical Esoteric Thought (1895) 408p. 1998. reprint ed. pap. 29.95 (0-7661-0234-3) Kessinger Pub.

Butler, Hubert. Independent Spirit: Essays. LC 95-47240. 588p. 1996. text 35.00 (0-374-17551-9) FS&G.

Butler, Ian & Roberts, Gwenda. Social Work with Children & Families. LC 97-198780. 224p. 1997. pap. 26.95 (1-85302-365-5, Pub. by Jessica Kingsley) Taylor & Francis.

Butler, Ian & Shaw, Ian, eds. Case of Neglect? Children's Experience & the Sociology of Childhood. LC 96-83222. (Cardiff Papers in Qualitative Research: Vol. 9). 192p. 1996. 69.95 (1-85972-048-X, Pub. by Avebry) Ashgate Pub Co.

Butler, J. Import-Export. 161p. (C). 1988. 220.00 (0-7855-5719-9, Pub. by Inst Pur & Supply) St Mut.

Butler, J. A. Modern Biology & Its Human Implications. LC 76-27619. 119p. 1976. pap. 12.00 (0-8448-1007-X, Crane Russak) Taylor & Francis.

Butler, J. D. Butler: Butleriana, Genealogica et Biographica, or Genealogical Notes Concerning Mary Butler & Her Descendants, As Well As the Bates, Harris, Sigourney & Other Families with Which They Have Intermarried. 162p. 1994. reprint ed. pap. 25.00 (0-8328-4304-0); reprint ed. lib. bdg. 35.00 (0-8328-4303-2) Higginson Bk Co.

Butler, J. Douglas & Walbert, David F., eds. Abortion, Medicine, & the Law. LC 85-16137. 811p. reprint ed. pap. 200.00 (0-7837-2676-7, 204304700006) Bks Demand.

Butler, J. George. Simpler Times: Stories of Early Twentieth Century City Life. 208p. 1996. 19.95 (0-918339-25-1) Vandamere.

Butler, J. N. Carbon Dioxide Equilibria & Their Applications. 1982. pap. write for info. (0-201-10100-9) Addison-Wesley.

Butler, J. N., jt. ed. see Cheung, H. W.

Butler, Jack. Dreamers. LC 97-49478. 413p. 1998. 25.00 (0-679-44665-6) McKay.

— Jack's Skillet: Plain Talk & Some Recipes from a Guy in the Kitchen. LC 97-15925. 272p. 1997. 19.95 (1-56512-149-X, 72149) Algonquin Bks.

Butler, James. Market Relations. 241p. 1996. pap. 43.50 (0-273-62203-X, Pub. by F T P-H) Trans-Atl Phila.

Butler, James. Sword of the Dales. 1995. 6.95 (0-7869-0126-8, Pub. by TSR Inc) Random.

Butler, James, ed. see Wordsworth, William.

Butler, James E. & Taylor, Arthur. Penobscot River Renaissance: Restoring America's Premier Atlantic Salmon Fishery. deluxe limited ed. LC 92-90314. (Illus.). 160p. 1992. 50.00 (0-89272-325-4, Silver Quill Pr) Down East.

Butler, James J. The Design, Performance, & Analysis of Slug Tests. LC 97-24597. 252p. 1997. lib. bdg. 69.95 (1-56670-230-5) Lewis Pubs.

Butler, James N. Carbon Dioxide Equilibria & Their Applications. 250p. 1991. lib. bdg. 99.95 (0-87371-624-8, L624) Lewis Pubs.

— Solubility & PH Calculations. LC 64-15563. (Chemistry Ser.). (Orig.). (gr. 9 up). 1964. pap. write for info. (0-201-00733-9) Addison-Wesley.

Butler, James N. & Cogley, David R. Ionic Equilibrium: Solubility & pH Concentration. LC 97-13435. 559p. 1998. 84.95 (0-471-58526-2, Wiley-Interscience) Wiley.

Butler, James R. Hospital Cost Analysis. LC 94-41366. (Developments in Health Economics & Public Policy Ser.: Vol. 3). 1995. lib. bdg. 118.00 (0-7923-3247-4) Kluwer Academic.

Butler, James T. Isaac Roop: Pioneer & Political Leader of Northeastern California. LC 94-78246. (Illus.). 112p. (Orig.). 1994. pap. 9.95 (0-936029-40-4) Western Bk Journ.

Butler, Jan, jt. auth. see Bianchi, Susan.

Butler, Jane B. A Force Unfamiliar to Me: A Cautionary Tale. LC 99-168486. (Orig.). 1998. pap. 10.95 (0-9663825-0-1) Hamlet Bks.

Butler, Jane M., jt. auth. see Parramore, Barbara M.

***Butler, Jane Palsgrove.** Loan Liquidation & Acquired Property. 154p. 1998. pap. 14.00 (0-16-061941-6) USGPO.

— Small Business Administration Standard Operating Procedure, National: Loan Servicing. 142p. 1999. per. 13.00 (0-16-061940-8) USGPO.

***Butler, Janet.** Winning the Outsourcing Game: Making the Best Deals & Making Them Work. (Auerbach Best Practices Ser.). 2000. write for info. (0-8493-0875-5) Auerbach.

Butler, Janet, jt. auth. see Vacca, John.

Butler, Janet A., et al. Clinical Radiology of the Horse. (Illus.). 560p. (C). 1992. 268.95 (0-8464-4162-4) Beekman Pubs.

Butler, Janet A., ed. see Colles, Christopher M., et al.

Butler, Janet G. Contingency Planning & Disaster Recovery: Protecting Your Organization's Resources. LC 96-50424. (Illus.). 229p. 1998. pap. 270.00 (1-56607-986-1) Comput Tech Res.

— Enterprisewide Network Management. LC 95-2242. (Illus.). 186p. 1996. pap. 285.00 (1-56607-044-9) Comput Tech Res.

— Enterprisewide Systems Management. LC 95-31353. (Illus.). 245p. 1995. pap. 275.00 (1-56607-956-X) Comput Tech Res.

— Information Technology: Converging Strategies & Trends for the 21st Century. LC 97-33997. (Illus.). 238p. (Orig.). 1999. pap. 290.00 (1-56607-994-2) Comput Tech Res.

— Mainframe to Client/Server Migration: Strategic Planning Issues & Techniques. LC 96-14045. (Illus.). 210p. 1996. pap. 290.00 (1-56607-967-5) Comput Tech Res.

***Butler, Janet G.** Managing IT in an E-Commerce Environment. (Illus.). 180p. 2000. pap. 280.00 (1-56607-086-4) Comput Tech Res.

Butler, Janet G. Managing the Year 2000 Crisis: Strategies & Solutions. LC 98-6661. (Illus.). 225p. 1999. pap. 280.00 (1-56607-056-2) Comput Tech Res.

— Securing the Enterprise Network. LC 96-50426. (Illus.). 250p. (Orig.). 1997. pap. 280.00 (1-56607-984-5) Comput Tech Res.

— The Year 2000 Crisis: Developing a Successful Plan for Information Systems. LC 96-27631. (Illus.). 237p. (Orig.). 1997. pap. 290.00 (1-56607-978-0) Comput Tech Res.

Butler, Jeanne F. Competition 1792: Designing a Nation's Capitol. 2nd ed. (Illus.). 96p. (YA). (gr. 7-12). 1993. reprint ed. pap. 4.95 (0-916200-11-6) US Capitol Hist.

Butler, Jeffrey, et al, eds. Democratic Liberalism in South Africa: Its History & Prospect. LC 87-6071. (Illus.). 440p. 1987. pap. 25.00 (0-8195-6197-5, Wesleyan Univ Pr) U Pr of New Eng.

Butler, Jeffrey, et al. The Black Homelands of South Africa: The Political & Economic Development of Bophuthatswana & Kwa-Zulu. LC 76-7755. (Perspectives on Southern Africa Ser.: No. 21). 1977. pap. 14.95 (0-520-03716-2, Pub. by U CA Pr) Cal Prin Full Svc.

***Butler, Jeremy G.** Writing Sports Stories That Sell: How to Make Money from Writing about Your Favorite Pastime. (Illus.). 144p. (Orig.). 1999. pap. 19.95 (1-85703-442-2, Pub. by How To Bks) Trans-Atl Phila.

Butler, Jerry. A Drawing in the Sand: The Story of African American Art. LC 98-4139. (Illus.). 64p. (YA). (gr. 3 up). 1998. 24.95 (1-55933-216-6) Zino Pr.

— Raw Talent: The Adult Film Industry As Seen by Its Most Popular Male Star. Rimmer, Robert H. & Tavel, Catherine, eds. LC 89-42532. (Illus.). 323p. (Orig.). (C). 1990. 26.95 (0-87975-642-X); pap. 17.95 (0-87975-625-X) Prometheus Bks.

Butler, Jerry & Smith, Earl. Only the Strong Survive: Memoirs of a Soul Survivor. xviii, 380p. 1999. 19.95 (1-893731-00-6) Mandolin Hse.

***Butler, Jerry & Smith, Earl.** Only the Strong Survive: Memoirs of a Soul Survivor/Jerry Butler, with Earl Smith. LC 00-32002. 2000. 24.95 (0-253-33796-8) Ind U Pr.

Butler, Jessie. Mom Mission Accomplished: The Life of Anna Lola Swinford. 158p. 1998. pap. write for info. (1-57502-915-4, PO2525) Morris Pubng.

Butler, Jill. Paintbrush in Paris: The Artistic Adventures of an American Cat in Paris. LC 94-6228. (Illus.). 96p. 1994. 9.95 (1-56305-524-4, 3524) Workman Pub.

Butler, Jim. Alberta Wildlife Viewing Guide. (Watchable Wildlife Ser.). 96p. 1990. pap. 5.95 (0-919433-78-2) Lone Pine.

— Alberta Wildlife Viewing Guide. (Illus.). 96p. 1997. 15.95 (0-919433-79-0) Lone Pine.

Butler, Joan M. Fit & Pregnant: The Pregnant Woman's Guide to Exercise. LC 95-32263. (Illus.). 180p. 1996. pap. 16.00 (0-937921-55-6) Acorn Pub.

Butler, John. Cybersearch: Research Techniques in the Electronic Age. LC 97-44756. xvii, 204p. 1998. pap. 12.95 (0-14-051387-6) Viking Penguin.

— The Economics of Historic Country Houses LC 81-213322. viii, 138 p. 1981. write for info. (0-85374-186-7) Pol Studies Inst.

— Lord Herbert of Chirbury (1582-1648) An Intellectual Biography. (Studies in British History: Vol. 16). 592p. 1990. write for info. (0-88946-467-7) E Mellen.

***Butler, John.** Model - Escort. (Illus.). 285p. 1999. pap. 12.95 (1-891855-07-7, STARbks Pr) FL Lit Foundation.

Butler, John. Patients, Policies, & Politics: Before & after "Working for Patients" LC 92-18762. (State of Health Ser.). 160p. 1992. 118.95 (0-335-15648-7); pap. 35.95 (0-335-15647-9) OpUniv Pr.

— The Quest for Becket's Bones. LC 94-30026. (Illus.). 192p. 1995. 32.50 (0-300-06115-3) Yale U Pr.

— The Quest for Becket's Bones: The Mystery of the Relics of St. Thomas Becket of Canterbury. (Illus.). 192p. 1996. pap. 18.00 (0-300-06895-6) Yale U Pr.

***Butler, John.** WanderLUST. (Illus.). 500p. 2000. pap. 15.95 (1-891855-13-1, STARbks Pr) FL Lit Foundation.

— While You Were Sleeping. LC 99-46812. (Illus.). 32p. (J). (ps). 1999. 15.95 (1-56145-211-4, Peachtree) Peachtree Pubs.

Butler, John, ed. The Bronchial Circulation. (Lung Biology in Health & Disease Ser.: Vol. 57). (Illus.). 832p. 1992. text 285.00 (0-8247-8443-X) Dekker.

Butler, John & Hirsch, Allan. A Commitment to Watershed Protection: A Review of the Clean Lakes Program. (Illus.). 52p. (C). 1998. pap. text 25.00 (0-7881-4887-7) DIANE Pub.

Butler, John, tr. see Herbert of Chirbury.

Butler, John A. A Biography of Richard Cromwell, 1626-1712, the Second Protector. LC 93-44167. (Studies in British History: Vol. 33). (Illus.). 260p. 1994. text 89.95 (0-7734-9417-0) E Mellen.

***Butler, John A.** Sailing on Friday: A History of the U. S. Merchant Marine. 2000. reprint ed. pap. 19.95 (1-57488-299-6) Brasseys.

Butler, John A. Sailing on Friday: The Perilous Voyage of America's Merchant Marine. LC 97-20850. (Illus.). 320p. 1997. 28.95 (1-57488-124-8) Brasseys.

— Strike Able-Peter: The Stranding & Salvage of the USS Missouri. LC 95-18391. (Illus.). 246p. 1995. 31.95 (1-55750-094-0) Naval Inst Pr.

Butler, John B. The Bankruptcy Handbook, 2 vols. LC 97-154247. 1996. 195.00 (1-878337-48-3) Knowles Pub Inc.

Butler, John C. Historical Record of Macon & Central Georgia: Containing Many Interesting & Valuable Reminscences connected with the Whole State, Including Numerous Incidents & Facts Never Before Published & of Great Historic Value. (Illus.). 380p. 1997. reprint ed. lib. bdg. 42.50 (0-8328-6626-1) Higginson Bk Co.

Butler, John E. Immunochemistry of Solid-Phase Immunoassay. (Illus.). 336p. 1991. boxed set 292.95 (0-8493-5394-7, QR183) CRC Pr.

— Sewage Treatment Using Plants: Crop Protection from Sewage. 180p. (C). 1996. text 64.95 (0-13-807041-5) P-H.

Butler, John G. Abraham: The Father of the Jews. 381p. 1993. 19.50 (1-889773-09-3) LBC Publns.

— David: The King of Israel. 1025p. 1999. 34.50 (1-889773-15-8) LBC Publns.

— Elijah: The Prophet of Confrontation. 260p. 1994. 16.50 (1-889773-03-4) LBC Publns.

An Asterisk (*) at the beginning of an entry indicates that the title is appearing for the first time.

— Elisha: The Miracle Prophet. 338p. 1994. 18.50 (*1-889773-04-2*) LBC Publns.

— Gideon: The Mighty Man of Valor. 186p. 1992. 14.50 (*1-889773-05-0*) LBC Publns.

— Hezekiah: The King of Survival. 263p. 1999. 16.50 (*1-889773-18-2*) LBC Publns.

— Jacob: The Sower & Reaper. 415p. 1999. 19.50 (*1-889773-17-4*) LBC Publns.

— John the Baptist: The Herald of Christ. 214p. 1992. 14.50 (*1-889773-07-7*) LBC Publns.

— Jonah: The Parochial Prophet. 208p. 1994. 14.50 (*1-889773-02-6*) LBC Publns.

— Joseph: The Patriarch of Character. (Illus.). 209p. 1993. 14.50 (*1-889773-01-8*) LBC Publns.

— Joshua: The Conqueror of Canaan. LC 97-121116. 325p. 1996. 18.50 (*1-889773-13-1*) LBC Publns.

— Lot: The Wordly Christian. 224p. 1994. 15.50 (*1-889773-10-7*) LBC Publns.

***Butler, John G.** Mordecai: The Defender of the Jews. 273p. 1999. 16.50 (*1-889773-19-0*) LBC Publns.

Butler, John G. Moses: The Emancipator of Israel. 810p. 1996. 29.50 (*1-889773-12-3*) LBC Publns.

— Nehemiah: The Wall Builder. LC 99-180558. 327p. 1998. 18.50 (*1-889773-16-6*) LBC Publns.

— Paul: The Missionary Apostle. 806p. 1995. 29.50 (*1-889773-11-5*) LBC Publns.

— Peter: The Illustrious Disciple. 394p. 1993. 19.50 (*1-889773-08-5*) LBC Publns.

***Butler, John G.** Ruth: The Ancestress of Christ. 175p. 2000. 14.50 (*1-889773-20-4*) LBC Publns.

Butler, John G. Samson: The Weak Strong Man. 179p. 1992. 14.50 (*1-889773-06-9*) LBC Publns.

— Samuel: The Prophet of Transition. LC 97-148865. 243p. 1997. 16.50 (*1-889773-14-X*) LBC Publns.

Butler, John K. At the Stroke of Midnight. Wooley, John, ed. & intro. by. (Pulp Reprint Ser.). (Illus.). 256p. (C). 1998. pap. 15.95 (*1-886937-25-7*) Adventure Hse.

Butler, John L. First Highways of America: A Pictorial History of Early Roads for Automobiles. LC 93-80094. (Illus.). 320p. 1994. 29.95 (*0-87341-280-X*, HR01) Krause Pubns.

Butler, John L., Jr., ed. & frwd. see Williamson, James R. & Fossler, Linda A.

Butler, John P., compiled by. Index: The Papers of the Continental Congress, 1774-1789, 5 vols., Set. LC 78-23783. 6615p. (C). 1978. text 25.00 (*0-911333-56-8*, 100024) National Archives & Recs.

Butler, John P., ed. Index, the Papers of the Continental Congress 1774-1789, 5 vols. LC 78-23783. 1982. reprint ed. lib. bdg. 275.00 (*0-89941-233-5*, 201430) W S Hein.

Butler, John R. & Vaile, Michael S. Health & Health Services: An Introduction to Health Care in Britain. LC 83-27031. 256p. (Orig.). 1984. 15.95 (*0-7100-9902-9*, Routledge Thoemms) Routledge.

Butler, John S. Entrepreneurship & Self-Help among Black Americans: A Reconsideration of Race & Economics. LC 90-10329. (SUNY Series in Ethnicity & Race in American Life). 390p. (C). 1991. pap. text 23.95 (*0-7914-0736-5*) State U NY Pr.

— Entrepreneurship & Self-Help among Black Americans: A Reconsideration of Race & Economics. LC 90-10329. (SUNY Series in Ethnicity & Race in American Life). 390p. (C). 1991. text 64.50 (*0-7914-0735-7*) State U NY Pr.

Butler, John S., jt. auth. see Moskos, Charles.

Butler, John W. Butler Family of Northwestern New Jersey: Their Ancestors & Descendents & Related Families, Including McMurtrie, Howell, Allen, Cole, Barton, Clark, Underhill, Glingles & Green. (Illus.). 157p. 1996. pap. 22.00 (*0-8328-5470-0*); lib. bdg. 32.00 (*0-8328-5469-7*) Higginson Bk Co.

Butler, Johnnella E. & Walter, John C., eds. Transforming the Curriculum: Ethnic Studies & Women's Studies. LC 90-37670. 416p. (C). 1991. pap. text 21.95 (*0-7914-0587-7*) State U NY Pr.

— Transforming the Curriculum: Ethnic Studies & Women's Studies. LC 90-37670. 416p. (C). 1991. text 64.50 (*0-7914-0586-9*) State U NY Pr.

Butler, Jon. Awash in a Sea of Faith: Christianizing the American People. (Studies in Cultural History). (Illus.). 368p. 1992. pap. text 18.50 (*0-674-05601-9*) HUP.

— Awash in a Sea of Faith: The Christianization of the American People 1550-1865. (Studies in Cultural History). (Illus.). 376p. 1990. text 32.50 (*0-674-05600-0*) HUP.

— The Day the Rainbow Lost Its Color. large type ed. (Rainbow Chubs Bks.: Vol. 1). (Illus.). (J). (ps-5). 1997. pap. 4.35 (*0-9657505-1-5*) Staircase Pub.

— The Huguenots in America: A Refugee People in New World Society. (Historical Monographs: No. 72). (Illus.). 280p. 1984. 34.50 (*0-674-41320-2*) HUP.

— The Huguenots in America: A Refugee People in New World Society. (Illus.). 280p. 1992. pap. 16.50 (*0-674-41321-0*) HUP.

***Butler, Jon, ed.** Religion in Colonial America. LC 99-46294. (Religion in American Life Ser.). (Illus.). 160p. 2000. lib. bdg. 22.00 (*0-19-511998-3*) OUP.

Butler, Jon & Stout, Harry S., eds. Religion in American History: A Reader. LC 96-39446. 528p. (C). 1997. pap. text 33.95 (*0-19-509776-9*) OUP.

Butler, Jonathan L. Latin-inus, -ina, -inus, & -ineus: From Proto-Indo-European to the Romance Languages. LC 73-631070. (U. C. Publ. in Linguistics Ser.: Vol. 68). 154p. reprint ed. pap. 47.80 (*0-8357-9633-7*, 201509900092) Bks Demand.

Butler, Jonathan M., ed. The Disappointed: Millerism & Millenarianism in the Nineteenth Century. 2nd ed. LC 92-42469. (Illus.). 280p. (C). 1993. pap. 17.95 (*0-87049-793-6*) U of Tenn Pr.

Butler, JoNett & Farwell, Bea. America's Best Appetizers. (Illus.). 220p. (Orig.). 1985. pap. 11.95 (*0-9614834-0-7*) Butler-Farwell.

Butler, Joseph. The Analogy of Religion. 3rd ed. 1986. reprint ed. pap. 27.95 (*0-935005-41-2*); reprint ed. lib. bdg. 43.95 (*0-935005-40-4*) Lincoln-Rembrandt.

— Fifteen Sermons. 1986. reprint ed. pap. 24.95 (*0-935005-45-5*); reprint ed. lib. bdg. 40.95 (*0-935005-44-7*) Lincoln-Rembrandt.

— Five Sermons. Darwall, Stephen, ed. LC 83-12577. (HPC Classics Ser.). 86p. (C). 1983. pap. text 5.95 (*0-915145-61-8*); lib. bdg. 21.95 (*0-915144-00-X*) Hackett Pub.

Butler, Joseph C. An Educational Approach to Modern Jazz Orchestration: Methods & Techniques. (Orig.). 1985. 42.00 (*0-932315-01-1*) Butler Pub Hse.

— How to Think Positive & Achieve Great Success. (Orig.). 1984. 25.00 (*0-932315-00-3*) Butler Pub Hse.

Butler, Joseph G., Jr. History of Youngstown & the Mahoning Valley, 3 vols. in 2. (Illus.). 1652p. 1997. reprint ed. lib. bdg. 165.00 (*0-8328-6372-6*) Higginson Bk Co.

Butler, Joseph T. The American Eagle: Spirit & Symbol, 1782-1882. (Illus.). 16p. 1988. 5.00 (*0-915171-11-2*) Katonah Gal.

— Field Guide to American Antique Furniture: A Unique Visual System for Identifying the Style of Virtually Any Piece of American Antique Furniture. LC 86-12099. (Illus.). 400p. 1995. pap. 19.95 (*0-8050-0124-7*, Owl) H Holt & Co.

— Sleepy Hollow Restorations: A Cross-Section of the Collection. LC 82-16774. (Illus.). 344p. 1983. 39.95 (*0-912882-57-3*) Sleepy Hollow.

***Butler, Joy R.** The Musician's Guide Through the Legal Jungle: Answers to Frequently Asked Questions about Music Law. unabridged ed. (Guide Through the Legal Jungle Audiobook Ser.). (Orig.). 2000. pap. 29.95 incl. audio (*0-9672940-0-2*) Sashay Commns.

Butler, Joyce. Kennebunkport Scrapbook, Vol. I. 2nd ed. (Illus.). 100p. 1998. reprint ed. pap. 14.95 (*0-9613275-2-9*) Rosemary Hse.

— Kennebunkport Scrapbook, Vol. II. (Illus.). 110p. 1989. pap. 14.95 (*0-9613275-1-0*) Rosemary Hse.

— Pages from a Journal. LC 76-685. (Illus.). 171p. 1976. 11.95 (*0-89080-006-5*) Rosemary Hse.

— Wildfire Loose: The Week Maine Burned. 3rd ed. LC 97-65236. (Illus.). 304p. 1997. reprint ed. pap. 14.95 (*0-89272-409-9*) Down East.

Butler, Joyce, jt. auth. see Barry, William E.

***Butler, Judith.** Antigone's Claim: Kinship Between Life & Death. LC 00-30321. (Wellek Library Lectures). 2000. 19.95 (*0-231-11894-5*) Col U Pr.

Butler, Judith. Bodies that Matter: On the Discursive Limits of "Sex" LC 93-7667. 288p. (gr. 13). 1993. pap. 18.99 (*0-415-90366-1*, A4972) Routledge.

— Excitable Speech: Contemporary Scenes of Politics. 192p. 1997. pap. 17.99 (*0-415-91588-0*) Routledge.

— Excitable Speech: Contemporary Scenes of Politics. 192p. (C). 1997. 60.00 (*0-415-91587-2*) Routledge.

— Gender Trouble: Feminism & the Subversion of Identity. Nicholson, Linda J., ed. (Thinking Gender Ser.). 240p. 1989. 32.50 (*0-415-90042-5*, A1572) Routledge.

***Butler, Judith.** Gender Trouble: Tenth Anniversary Edition. 10th anniversary ed. LC 99-29349. 224p. 1999. pap. 19.95 (*0-415-92499-5*) Routledge.

Butler, Judith. The Psychic Life of Power: Theories in Subjection. LC 96-40851. 1997. pap. write for info. (*0-8047-2812-7*) Stanford U Pr.

***Butler, Judith.** Subjects of Desire: Hegelian Reflections in Twentieth-Century France. LC 99-462501. 268p. 1998. pap. 18.50 (*0-231-06451-9*) Col U Pr.

Butler, Judith & Scott, Joan W., eds. Feminists Theorize the Political. 432p. (gr. 13). 1992. pap. 20.99 (*0-415-90274-6*, A4266) Routledge.

***Butler, Judith, et al.** Contingency, Hegemony, Universality: Contemporary Dialogues on the Left. 300p. (C). 2000. 70.00 (*1-85984-757-9*, Pub. by Verso); pap. 20.00 (*1-85984-278-X*, Pub. by Verso) Norton.

Butler, Judith P. The Psychic Life of Power: Theories in Subjection. LC 96-40851. 1997. write for info. (*0-8047-2811-9*) Stanford U Pr.

***Butler, Judith P.** What's Left of Theory? New Work on the Politics of Literary Theory. (Essays from the English Institute Ser.). (Illus.). 304p. 2000. 85.00 (*0-415-92118-X*); pap. 21.00 (*0-415-92119-8*) Routledge.

Butler, Judith P., ed. see Singer, Linda.

Butler, Judy, tr. see Vilas, Carlos M.

Butler, Julie Ilkanic. Shadows on the Mountains. LC 99-95232. 216p. 1999. pap. 12.95 (*0-9672695-0-4*) Irisa Pubg.

Butler, K. T. Tools of the Trade. (Orig.). 1996. mass mkt. 5.95 (*1-56333-420-8*, Rosebud) Masquerade.

Butler, Karen T. Nantucket Lights: An Illustrated History of the Island's Legendary Beacons. LC 96-94744. 1996. 44.95 (*0-9638910-6-5*) Mill Hill Pr.

Butler, Katharine & Cheng, Li-Rong L., eds. Child Language. (Folia Phoniatrica et Logopaedica Ser.: Vol. 50, No. 5). (Illus.). 56p. 1998. pap. 37.50 (*3-8055-6796-0*) S Karger.

Butler, Katharine G. Assessment Across Disorders: Perspectives, Practices & Procedures. LC 93-34702. (Topics in Language Disorders Ser.). 240p. 1994. 36.00 (*0-8342-0593-9*) Aspen Pub.

— Language Disorders in Children. LC 86-15119. (PRO-ED Studies in Communicative Disorders). 72p. (Orig.). 1986. pap. text 9.00 (*0-89079-098-1*, 1387) PRO-ED.

— Prospering in Private Practice: A Handbook for Speech-Language Pathology & Audiology. LC 86-10828. 320p. (C). 1986. 75.00 (*0-87189-368-1*) Aspen Pub.

Butler, Katharine G., ed. Best Practices I: The Classroom As an Assessment Arena, 2. LC 93-36264. (Topics in Language Disorders Ser.). 240p. 1994. 36.00 (*0-8342-0586-6*, 20586) Aspen Pub.

— Best Practices II: The Classroom As an Intervention Context. LC 93-36264. (Topics in Language Disorders Ser.). 240p. 1994. 36.00 (*0-8342-0587-4*, 20587) Aspen Pub.

— Cross-Cultural Perspectives in Language Assessment & Intervention. 240p. 1994. pap. 38.00 (*0-8342-0594-7*) Aspen Pub.

— Early Intervention I: Working with Infants & Toddlers. LC 93-36266. 240p. 1994. 36.00 (*0-8342-0584-X*) Aspen Pub.

— Hearing Impairment & Language Disorders: Assessment & Intervention. LC 93-31105. 244p. 1994. 36.00 (*0-8342-0588-2*) Aspen Pub.

— Severe Communication Disorders: Intervention Strategies. LC 93-36267. 240p. 1993. 36.00 (*0-8342-0589-0*) Aspen Pub.

— Topics in Language Disorders Series, 8 vols., Set. 1900p. 1994. 216.00 (*0-8342-0590-4*) Aspen Pub.

Butler, Katherine. StressBusters: Tips to Feel Healthy, Alive & Energized. 192p. 1996. pap. 8.95 (*0-471-34706-X*) Wiley.

Butler, Katherine. StressBusters: Tips to Feel Healthy, Alive & Energized. 192p. 1998. pap. 8.95 (*1-56561-142-X*) Wiley.

Butler, Katherine G., jt. ed. see Wallach, Geraldine P.

Butler, Kathleen A. Learning & Teaching Style: In Theory & Practice. 2nd ed. (Illus.). 318p. (Orig.). 1988. pap. text 32.95 (*0-945852-00-2*, 10) Learners Dimension.

— Learning Styles: Personal Exploration & Practical Applications. 2nd rev. ed. (Illus.). 118p. (YA). (gr. 7-12). 1995. pap. text, student ed. 16.95 (*0-945852-07-X*) Learners Dimension.

— Teacher's Guide to Learning Styles; A Companion to the Student's Guide: Personal Exploration & Practical Applications. 2nd rev. ed. (Illus.). 94p. 1995. pap. text, teacher ed. 16.95 (*0-945852-08-8*) Learners Dimension.

Butler, Kathleen A., jt. auth. see Cardamone, Stevie.

Butler, Kathleen A., jt. auth. see Prewitt, Bobby W.

Butler, Kathleen M. The Economics of Emancipation: Jamaica & Barbados, 1823-1843. LC 94-36129. 240p. 1995. pap. text 19.95 (*0-8078-4501-9*); lib. bdg. 45.00 (*0-8078-2194-2*) U of NC Pr.

Butler, Kathryn R., ed. see Martin, Harvey J., III.

Butler, Ken. Derek Jarman. (Out Lines Ser.). 1997. pap. text 9.95 (*1-899791-50-7*) Stewart Tabori & Chang.

— Oklahoma Renegades: Their Deeds & Misdeeds. LC 96-44302. (Illus.). 160p. 1997. pap. 10.95 (*1-56554-231-2*) Pelican.

Butler, Kenneth G. The Concept of Objectivity: An Approximation. LC 90-34652. (American University Studies: Philosophy: Ser. V, Vol. 98). (Illus.). XXIII, 332p. (C). 1991. text 55.95 (*0-8204-1334-8*) P Lang Pubng.

Butler, Kenneth M. & Mercer, M. Ray. Assessing Fault Model & Test Quality. 160p. (C). 1991. text 98.00 (*0-7923-9222-1*) Kluwer Academic.

Butler, Kim D. Freedoms Given, Freedoms Won: Afro-Brazilians in Post-Abolition Sao Paolo & Salvador. LC 97-43478. (Illus.). 306p. (C). 1998. text 52.00 (*0-8135-2503-9*); pap. text 22.00 (*0-8135-2504-7*) Rutgers U Pr.

Butler, Kirk Charles. Multinational Finance. LC 95-34787. (FV - International Finance Ser.). 1996. mass mkt. 70.95 (*0-538-85385-9*) S-W Pub.

***Butler, Kristi T.** Rip's Secret Spot. LC 99-50802. (Illus.). 20p. (ps-3). 2000. 10.95 (*0-15-202640-1*, Harcourt Child Bks); pap. 3.95 (*0-15-202646-0*, Harcourt Child Bks) Harcourt.

Butler, Kurt. A Consumer's Guide to Alternative Medicine: A Close Look at Homeopathy, Acupuncture, Faith-Healing & Other Unconventional Treatments. LC 92-19859. 299p. (Orig.). (C). 1992. pap. 19.95 (*0-87975-733-7*) Prometheus Bks.

***Butler, Kurt.** Lying for Fun & Profit: The Truth about the Media. 304p. 1999. pap. 22.95 (*0-9673281-0-1*) Hlth Wise Prods.

Butler, Kurt & Rayner, Lynn. The New Handbook of Health & Preventive Medicine. rev. ed. LC 90-32513. (Illus.). 450p. 1990. reprint ed. pap. 21.95 (*0-87975-581-4*) Prometheus Bks.

Butler, L. J. & Ekboir, Javier. Dairying in California's Imperial Valley: Is It Feasible. Coppock, Ray, ed. 54p. (Orig.). (C). 1995. pap. text 13.00 (*1-885976-01-1*) U CA Agricult Issues.

Butler, L. Rick, jt. auth. see Jankowski, Dennis A.

Butler, Lance S. Critical Essays on Samuel Beckett. LC 93-18344. (Critical Thoughts Ser.: Vol. 4). 376p. 1993. 69.95 (*0-85967-871-7*, Pub. by Scolar Pr) Ashgate Pub Co.

— Victorian Doubt: Literary & Cultural Discourses. 240p. (C). 1990. text 75.00 (*0-389-20938-4*) B&N Imports.

Butler, Lance S., jt. ed. see Davis, Robin J.

Butler, Lance St John. Registering The Difference. LC 99-39980. 220p. 1999. 69.95 (*0-7190-5613-6*, Pub. by Manchester Univ Pr); pap. text 19.95 (*0-7190-5614-4*, Pub. by Manchester Univ Pr) St Martin.

Butler, Larry & Gorst, Anthony. Modern British History: A Guide to Study & Research. LC 97-178046. 288p. 1997. pap. 19.95 (*1-86064-208-X*, Pub. by I B T) St Martin.

Butler, Lawrence J. Industrialisation & the British Colonial State: West Africa 1939-1951. LC 97-189476. 320p. (C). 1997. 49.50 (*0-7146-4703-9*, Pub. by Irish Acad Pr) Intl Spec Bk.

Butler, Lee, jt. auth. see Zheutlin, Peter.

Butler, Lillian, ed. see Carella, C. J.

Butler, Lillian, ed. see McCoy, Elizabeth L. & Milliken, Walter.

Butler, Linda. The House on Mango Street, Vol. 3. (ESOL Companion Guide Ser.). 128p. (C). 1996. pap. 12.19 (*0-07-009429-2*) McGraw.

— The Light in the Forest, Vol. 1. (The ESOL Companion Guide Ser.). 128p. (C). 1996. pap. 12.19 (*0-07-009428-4*) McGraw.

— Of Mice & Men, Vol. 2. (ESOL Companion Guide Ser.). 128p. (C). 1996. pap. 12.19 (*0-07-009427-6*) McGraw.

— Rural Japan: Radiance of the Ordinary. LC 91-17090. (Illus.). 144p. 1992. pap. 26.95 (*1-56098-141-5*) Smithsonian.

Butler, Linda, photos by. Inner Light: The Shaker Legacy. LC 95-75677. (Illus.). 96p. 1995. pap. 24.95 (*0-917788-57-5*) Gnomon Pr.

— Italy: In the Shadow of Time. LC 98-66625. (Illus.). 120p. 1998. 50.00 (*0-8478-5784-0*, Pub. by Rizzoli Intl) St Martin.

Butler, Linda, jt. auth. see Bearden, Jim.

***Butler, Lindley S.** Pirates, Privateers & Rebel Raiders of the Carolina Coast. LC 99-86288. (Illus.). 296p. 2000. 29.95 (*0-8078-2553-0*); pap. 15.95 (*0-8078-4863-8*) U of NC Pr.

Butler, Lindley S. Rockingham County: A Brief History. (Illus.). xiv, 101p. 1997. reprint ed. pap. 6.00 (*0-86526-198-9*) NC Archives.

Butler, Lindley S., ed. The Papers of David Settle Reid, Vol. I, 1829-1852. (Illus.). lxii, 495p. (C). 1993. 45.00 (*0-86526-249-7*) NC Archives.

— The Papers of David Settle Reid Vol. II: 1853-1913. (Papers of David Settle Reid Ser.). (Illus.). xxv, 408p. (C). 1997. 35.00 (*0-86526-269-1*) NC Archives.

Butler, Lindley S. & Watson, Alan D., eds. The North Carolina Experience: An Interpretive & Documentary Approach. LC 83-27357. (Illus.). 475p. 1984. pap. 19.95 (*0-8078-4124-2*) U of NC Pr.

Butler, Lisa. Abnormal Psychology. 3rd ed. (C). Date not set. pap. text, teacher ed., suppl. ed. write for info. (*0-393-96660-7*, Norton Paperbks) Norton.

Butler, Lollie, jt. auth. see Cabat, Erni.

Butler, Luther. Preacher: A Novel. Ware, Laura, ed. LC 91-42294. 212p. (Orig.). 1992. pap. 14.95 (*0-86534-171-0*) Sunstone Pr.

Butler, Lynda L. & Livingston, Margit. Virginia Tidal & Coastal Law. 913p. 1988. 85.00 (*0-614-05993-3*, MICHIE) LEXIS Pub.

Butler, Lyndel, tr. see Baur, Hans.

Butler, Lynn. Planting the Voice: Poems from Poems. (University of Central Florida Contemporary Poetry Ser.). 104p. 1989. 17.95 (*0-8130-0921-9*); pap. 10.95 (*0-8130-0937-5*) U Press Fla.

— Planting the Voice: Poems from Poems. LC 88-32407. (Contemporary Poetry Ser.). 103p. 1989. reprint ed. pap. 32.00 (*0-608-04480-6*, 206522500001) Bks Demand.

Butler, Lynn B. Forever Is Easy. LC 93-7828. Orig. Title: Dream Thief. 64p. (Orig.). 1993. pap. 9.00 (*0-933532-92-X*) BkMk.

Butler, Lynne B. Sunday Afternoons with Tolstoy: Poems. LC 98-54957. 1999. write for info. (*0-89924-103-4*); pap. write for info. (*0-89924-102-6*) Lynx Hse.

Butler, Lynne M. Subgroup Lattices & Symmetric Functions. LC 94-26457. (Memoirs of the American Mathematical Society Ser.: Vol. 539). 160p. 1994. pap. 36.00 (*0-8218-2600-X*, MEMO/112/539) Am Math.

Butler, M., ed. Mammalian Cell Biotechnology: A Practical Approach. (Practical Approach Ser.). (Illus.). 264p. 1991. pap. text 45.00 (*0-19-963209-X*) OUP.

Butler, M., et al, eds. Proceedings of the Symposium on Chemical Sensors II. LC 93-70059. (Proceedings Ser.: Vol. 93-7). 864p. 1993. 77.00 (*1-56677-030-0*) Electrochem Soc.

Butler, M. & Dawson, M., eds. Cell Culture Labfax. (Labfax Ser.). (Illus.). 250p. 1992. text 63.00 (*0-12-148060-7*) Acad Pr.

Butler, M., jt. auth. see Alarcon, R.

Butler, M. Christina. Archie the Ugly Dinosaur. LC 96-86388. (Illus.). 32p. (J). 1997. pap. 5.95 (*0-7641-0092-0*) Barron.

Butler, M. Christina. Archie the Ugly Dinosaur. 1997. 11.15 (*0-606-11055-0*, Pub. by Turtleback) Demco.

Butler, M. Christina. Too Many Eggs: A Counting Book. LC 83-49007. (Illus.). 24p. (J). (gr. k-12). 1988. 15.95 (*0-87923-741-4*) Godine.

Butler, M. Christine. The Dinosaur Egg Mystery. (Illus.). 28p. (J). (ps-3). 1992. pap. 5.95 (*0-8120-1379-4*) Barron.

Butler, Manley C., Jr. How to Get an FAA TSO for Parachutes. 112p. 1984. pap. text 34.95 (*0-930747-00-3*) Tech Info Pubn.

Butler, Margaret. The Lion of Justice LC 75-326959. 280p. (J). 1975. write for info. (*0-333-14769-3*) Macmillan.

Butler, Marguerite L., ed. see Darkins, Claudia M.

Butler, Marian. Canadian Books in Print 1996: Subject Index. annuals 700p. 1996. text 135.00 (*0-8020-4988-5*) U of Toronto Pr.

— Canadian Books in Print 1998. 98th ed. 1300p. 1998. text 155.00 (*0-8020-4909-5*) U of Toronto Pr.

— Canadian Books in Print 1998: Subject Index. 98th ed. 750p. 1998. text 135.00 (*0-8020-4910-9*) U of Toronto Pr.

Butler, Marian, ed. Canadian Books in Print: Subject Index. LC 73-76124. 698p. 1993. text 125.00 (*0-8020-4668-1*) U of Toronto Pr.

— Canadian Books in Print, 1999: Author & Title Index. 1300p. 1999. text 165.00 (*0-8020-4924-9*) U of Toronto Pr.

***Butler, Marian, ed.** Canadian Books in Print, 1999: Quarterly Service, 2 vols. 1300p. 1999. 220.00 incl. fiche (*0-8020-4926-5*) U of Toronto Pr.

Butler, Marian, ed. Canadian Books in Print, 1999: Subject Index. 750p. 1999. text. write for info. (*0-8020-4925-7*) U of Toronto Pr.

An Asterisk (*) at the beginning of an entry indicates that the title is appearing for the first time.

— Canadian Books in Print 1993: Author & Title Index. LC 70-418272. 1235p. 1993. 145.00 (0-8020-4667-3) U of Toronto Pr.
— Canadian Books in Print 1994: Author - Title Index. 1235p. 1994. text 150.00 (0-8020-4674-6) U of Toronto Pr.
— Canadian Books in Print 1994: Subject Index. 698p. 1994. text 130.00 (0-8020-4675-4) U of Toronto Pr.
— Canadian Books in Print 1995: Author - Title Index. 1250p. (C). 1995. text 150.00 (0-8020-4682-7) U of Toronto Pr.
— Canadian Books in Print 1995: Subject Index. 700p. (C). 1995. text 130.00 (0-8020-4683-5) U of Toronto Pr.
— Canadian Books in Print 1996: Author/Title Index. annuals 1250p. 1996. 155.00 (0-8020-4987-7) U of Toronto Pr.
Butler, Marilyn. Jane Austen & the War of Ideas. 350p. 1988. pap. text 24.95 (0-19-812968-8) OUP.
— Romantics, Rebels, & Reactionaries: English Literature & Its Background, 1760 to 1830. (Opus Ser.). 220p. 1985. pap. text 19.95 (0-19-289132-4) OUP.
Butler, Marilyn, ed. Burke, Paine, Godwin & the Revolution Controversy. LC 83-15324. (English Prose Texts Ser.). 272p. 1984. pap. text 19.95 (0-521-28656-5) Cambridge U Pr.
Butler, Marilyn, ed. see Austen, Jane.
Butler, Marilyn, ed. see Shelley, Mary Wollstonecraft.
Butler, Marilyn, ed. & intro. see Edgeworth, Maria.
Butler, Marilyn, ed. & intro. see Shelley, Mary Wollstonecraft.
Butler, Marilyn S., jt. auth. see Hendrick, Judith C.
Butler, Martin, ed. see Jonson, Ben.
Butler, Mary. Piedras Negras Pottery. LC 36-19557. (Piedras Negras Preliminary Papers: No. 4). 100p. reprint ed. pap. 31.00 (0-608-12381-1, 205212400037) Bks Demand.
Butler, Mary & Ernest, Richard. The Listening Heart: Create Your Own Space, Lose the Weight of Your Past, Vol. 1. 1997. mass mkt. 12.50 incl. audio (1-929990-01-4) Listening Heart.
— The Listening Heart: Guided Meditations That Help You Take Charge of Your Life. 11p. 1999. pap. 5.00 (1-929990-00-6) Listening Heart.
— The Listening Heart: Relax on the Great Salt Lake, Step into the Spotlight, Vol. 3. 1998. mass mkt. 12.50 incl. audio (1-929990-03-0) Listening Heart.
Butler, Mary E. Oakland Welcomes the World. 136p. 1996. 45.00 (1-885352-27-1) Community Comm.
Butler, Mary K. Papa's Old Trunk. LC 81-68812. (Illus.). (J). (gr. 6-12). 1981. 10.00 (0-934530-03-3) Buck Pub.
***Butler, Mary Nyegard.** Fantasy Marsh. (Illus.). 20p. (J). (ps-2). 2000. per. 6.95 (0-9701497-0-0) Bay Tree.
Butler, Marya, jt. auth. see Butler, Paul.
Butler, Matilda & Paisley, William, eds. Women & the Mass Media: Sourcebook for Research & Action. LC 79-16271. 432p. 1980. 52.00 (0-87705-409-6, Kluwer Acad Hman Sci) Kluwer Academic.
Butler, Maureen, ed. see Emig, Janet.
Butler, Melvin A. & Committee on CCCC Language Statement Staff. Students' Rights to Their Own Language. 32p. 1974. pap. 3.95 (0-8141-4806-9) NCTE.
Butler, Meredith A., ed. Libraries As User-Centered Organizations: Imperatives for Organizational Change. LC 93-49814. (Journal of Library Administration). (Illus.). 256p. 1994. lib. bdg. 49.95 (1-56024-616-2) Haworth Pr.
Butler, Meredith A. & Kingma, Bruce R., eds. The Economics of Information in the Networked Environment. LC 98-54100. 313p. 1998. 69.95 (0-7890-0659-6) Haworth Pr.
— The Economics of Information in the Networked Environment: Proceedings of the Conference: Challenging Marketplace Solutions to Problems in the Economics of Information, Washington, D. C., September 18-19, 1995. LC 96-21222. (Illus.). 217p. 1996. pap. 40.00 (0-918006-29-5) Assn Res Lib.
Butler, Merlin G. Prader-Willi Syndrome: A Guide for Parents & Professionals. (Prader-Willi Syndrome Information Ser.: No. 4). (Illus.). 53p. (Orig.). 1995. pap. text 7.50 (0-9646533-0-3) P-W Perspect.
Butler, Michael. Australian Federal Company Taxation. 300p. 1994. pap. 97.00 (0-409-49209-4, Austral, MICHIE) LEXIS Pub.
***Butler, Michael & Evans, Robert.** The Challenge of the German Culture: Essays Presented to Wilfried Van Der Will. LC 00-41509. (New Perspectives in German Studies Ser.). 2000. write for info. (0-333-80090-7, Pub. by Macmillan) St Martin.
Butler, Michael & Pender, Malcolm, eds. Rejection & Emancipation: Contemporary Writing in German-Speaking Switzerland: Literature in Context, 1945-1991. 262p. 1991. 59.95 (0-85496-748-6) Berg Pubs.
***Butler, Michael, et al.** The Making of Modern Switzerland, 1848-1998. LC 00-27824. 2000. write for info. (0-312-23459-7) St Martin.
Butler, Michael, ed. & tr. see Lenz, J. M.
Butler, Michael A. Cautious Visionary: Cordell Hull & Trade Reform, 1933-1937. LC 97-36182. 258p. 1998. 39.00 (0-87338-596-9) Kent St U Pr.
Butler, Michael Alan, ed. see Electrochemical Society. Sensor Division.
Butler, Michael J. Animal Cell Culture & Technology. LC 96-26618. (The Basics). 1997. pap. write for info. (0-01-996341-6) Collins.
Butler, Mike. Colorado - Mile by Mile. 36p. (J). (gr. 3-8). 1991. pap. 6.95 (1-880372-12-6) Mile By Mile.
Butler, Mimi J., et al, eds. Cobb County, Georgia, Cemeteries Vol. 3: Marietta National Cemetery. LC 94-72040. (Illus.). 450p. 1994. lib. bdg. 45.00 (1-879768-01-1) Cobb Cnty Geneal.
Butler, Montagu C. Step by Step in Esperanto. 9th ed. 281p. 1991. text 13.00 (0-939785-01-3, STE001) Esperanto League North Am.
Butler-Moore, Nylea L. Come, O Long-Expected Jesus. 1.25 (0-687-50342-6) Abingdon.
— Grant Us Peace. 1.75 (0-687-07175-5) Abingdon.
— How Will We Know Messiah? 1.25 (0-687-08210-2) Abingdon.
— Light the Candle. 1.25 (0-687-08194-7) Abingdon.
Butler-Moore, Nylea L. Lost & Found: A Musical Story Based on the Parables of the Lost Coin, the Lost Sheep, & the Prodigal Son: PreviewPak. 1996. pap. 6.00 incl. audio (0-687-06514-3) Abingdon.
— Lost & Found: Intro Pak. 1994. audio 29.95 (0-687-22774-7); audio 10.95 (0-687-22775-5) Abingdon.
— Lost & Found: Leader/Accompanist Edition. 1994. 14.95 (0-687-22771-2) Abingdon.
— Lost & Found: Singer's Edition. 1994. 2.95 (0-687-22776-3) Abingdon.
Butler-Moore, Nylea L. & Krau, Carol F. Lost & Found: Intro Pak. Miller, Sandy & Smith, Gary, eds. 1994. 19.95 (0-687-22773-9) Abingdon.
***Butler, N. N.** The Eavesdropper. (Short Stories Ser.). 22p. 2000. pap. 3.95 (1-86092-027-6, Pub. by Travelman Pub) IPG Chicago.
Butler, Nancy. The Rake's Retreat. 224p. 1999. mass mkt. 4.99 (0-451-19789-5, Sig) NAL.
***Butler, Nancy.** Ramshackle Suitor. (Regency Romance Ser.). 2000. mass mkt. 4.99 (0-451-19975-8, Sig) NAL.
— Regency Christmas Eve. (Regency Romance Ser.). 2000. mass mkt. 6.99 (0-451-20167-1, Sig) NAL.
Butler, Narda & Beckman, Barbara. Main Dish Soups & Stews . . . And Breads: A Family Primer. (Family Primer Ser.). 56p. 1995. pap. text 4.95 (0-9648494-2-9) Dreamspnnrs.
Butler, Neville, et al. Enciclopedia de la Vida, 5 vols., Set. 6th ed. (SPA.). 2100p. 1978. 195.00 (0-8288-5217-0, S50570) Fr & Eur.
Butler, Nicholas M. The Effect of the War of 1812 Upon the Consolidation of the Nation. LC 78-63773. (Johns Hopkins University. Studies in the Social Sciences. Thirtieth Ser. 1912: 7). reprint ed. 32.50 (0-404-61039-0) AMS Pr.
— Is America Worth Saving? Addresses on National Problems & Party Policies. LC 76-37772. (Essay Index Reprint Ser.). 1977. reprint ed. 24.95 (0-8369-2583-1) Ayer.
— Meaning of Education: Contributions to a Philosophy of Education. enl. rev. ed. LC 72-142611. (Essay Index Reprint Ser.). 1977. reprint ed. 23.95 (0-8369-2219-0) Ayer.
— Scholarship & Service: The Policies & Ideals of a National University in a Modern Democracy. LC 78-134066. (Essay Index Reprint Ser.). 1977. reprint ed. 23.95 (0-8369-2220-4) Ayer.
— True & False Democracy. LC 78-93323. (Essay Index Reprint Ser.). 1977. 17.95 (0-8369-1278-0) Ayer.
— Why Should We Change Our Form of Government? Studies in Practical Politics. LC 73-167321. (Essay Index Reprint Ser.). 1977. reprint ed. 19.95 (0-8369-2758-3) Ayer.
Butler, Nicholas M., ed. Education in the United States: A Series of Monographs, 2 vols., Set. LC 79-89159. (American Education: Its Men, Institutions, & Ideas. Series 1). 1970. reprint ed. 42.95 (0-405-01396-5) Ayer.
Butler, Nicholas M., intro. The Wisdom of the East, Vol. 1. Date not set. 30.95 (0-8369-4792-4) Ayer.
Butler, Nick, jt. auth. see Kaldor, Nicholas.
Butler, Octavia E. Adulthood Rites. 304p. 1997. mass mkt. 6.50 (0-446-60378-3, Pub. by Warner Bks) Little.
— Bloodchild: And Other Stories. LC 96-41587. 144p. 1997. pap. 10.00 (1-888363-36-3) Seven Stories.
— Clay's Ark. 224p. 1996. reprint ed. mass mkt. 6.50 (0-446-60370-8, Pub. by Warner Bks) Little.
— Dawn. 1988. mass mkt. 3.95 (0-445-20516-4, Pub. by Warner Bks) Little.
— Dawn. 256p. 1997. mass mkt. 6.50 (0-446-60377-5, Pub. by Warner Bks) Little.
— Imago. 224p. 1997. mass mkt. 6.50 (0-446-60363-5, Pub. by Warner Bks) Little.
— Kindred. LC 87-47879. (Black Women Writers Ser.). 264p. 1998. reprint ed. pap. 13.00 (0-8070-8305-4) Beacon Pr.
***Butler, Octavia E.** Lilith's Brood. LC 00-25057. 752p. 2000. mass mkt. 13.95 (0-446-67610-1, Aspect) Warner Bks.
Butler, Octavia E. Mind of My Mind. 224p. 1994. reprint ed. mass mkt. 5.99 (0-446-36188-7, Pub. by Warner Bks) Little.
— Parable of the Sower. LC 93-8703. 352p. 1993. 19.95 (1-888363-25-8) Seven Stories.
— Parable of the Sower. LC 99-46567. 336p. 2000. reprint ed. mass mkt. 13.95 (0-446-67550-4, Pub. by Warner Bks) Little.
— Parable of the Talents. LC 98-35863. 365p. 1998. 24.95 (1-888363-81-9) Seven Stories.
***Butler, Octavia E.** Parable of the Sower. LC 99-46566. 384p. 2000. mass mkt. 13.95 (0-446-67578-4, Pub. by Warner Bks) Little.
Butler, Octavia E. Patternmaster. 208p. 1995. reprint ed. mass mkt. 6.50 (0-446-36281-6, Pub. by Warner Bks) Little.
— Wild Seed. 288p. 1999. reprint ed. mass mkt. 6.50 (0-446-60672-3, Pub. by Warner Bks) Little.
Butler, Octavia E. & Butler, Cctavia E. Parable of the Sower. 304p. 1995. reprint ed. mass mkt. 6.50 (0-446-60197-7, Pub. by Warner Bks) Little.
Butler, Orville R., jt. auth. see Adams, Stephen B.
Butler, Ovid, jt. auth. see Schenck, Carl A.
Butler, Ovid, ed. see Schenck, Carl A.
Butler, P. J., et al, eds. Imaging of the Nervous System. (Clinical Medicine & the Nervous System Ser.). 288p. 1990. 225.00 (0-387-19522-X) Spr-Verlag.
Butler, P. J., et al. Frcr Part 1, Pt. I. (Brainscan MCQs Ser.). 192p. 1991. 30.95 (0-387-19620-X) Spr-Verlag.
Butler, P. J., jt. ed. see Bridges, E. R.
***Butler, P. M.** The Mystery of the 13th Volume. LC 99-91731. 2000. 25.00 (0-7388-1210-2); pap. 18.00 (0-7388-1211-0) Xlibris Corp.
Butler, Pam, ed. see Florsheim, Peter & Florsheim, Fran.
Butler, Pamela E. Self-Assertion for Women. LC 90-84723. 288p. (Orig.). 1992. reprint ed. pap. 15.00 (0-06-250125-9, Pub. by Harper SF) HarpC.
Butler, Patricia. An ERISA Primer for State Legislators. 12p. 1995. 15.00 (1-55516-093-X, 7302-2008) Natl Conf State Legis.
***Butler, Patricia.** Three Hundred Years of Irish Watercolors & Drawings. (Illus.). 224p. 1999. pap. 24.95 (0-7538-0206-6) Phoenix Hse.
Butler, Patricia, jt. auth. see National Library of Ireland Staff.
Butler, Patricia A. Public Oversight of Managed Health Care Entities: Issues for State Policymakers. 31p. 1996. pap. 33.00 (1-55877-254-5) Natl Governor.
— Roadblock to Reform: ERISA Implications for State Health Care Initiatives. Glass, Karen, ed. 94p. (Orig.). 1994. pap. text 20.00 (1-55877-185-9) Natl Governor.
— Too Poor to Be Sick: Access to Medical Care for the Uninsured. 128p. 1988. 17.50 (0-87553-151-2) Am Pub Health.
***Butler, Patrick.** Develop the Power to Heal. 160p. 2000. pap. 15.95 (0-572-02516-5) W Foulsham.
Butler, Paul. Approaching the New Millennium: An Amillennial View of A. D. 2000. LC 98-35233. 315p. 1998. pap. 17.99 (0-89900-812-7) College Pr Pub.
***Butler, Paul, ed.** Endovascular Neurosurgery: A Multidisciplinary Approach. LC 99-32914. x, 166p. 1999. 139.00 (1-85233-620-X, Pub. by Spr-Verlag) Spr-Verlag.
Butler, Paul, et al, eds. Applied Radiological Anatomy. (Illus.). 1000p. (C). 1998. text 200.00 (0-521-48110-4) Cambridge U Pr.
Butler, Paul & Butler, Marya. Fine Boat Finishes. 160p. 1991. pap. 17.95 (0-87742-311-3) Intl Marine.
— Pine Boat Finishes. 160p. 1991. pap. 18.95 (0-07-009403-9) McGraw.
Butler, Perry. Gladstone: Church, State & Tractarianism, a Study of His Religious Ideas & Attitudes, 1809-1859. (Oxford Historical Monographs). 1982. 55.00 (0-19-821890-7) OUP.
Butler, Peter, ed. see Wagner, Richard.
***Butler, Petra.** Medical Misadventure Im Neuseelandischen Accident Compensation Scheme: Eine Antwort Auf die Unzulanglichkeiten des Tort Law Oder ein Fehlgeschlagener Versuch? (Europaische Hochschulschriften Ser: Bd. 2628). 190p. 1999. 37.95 (3-631-33879-1) P Lang Pubng.
Butler, Phil. War Prizes. (Illus.). 320p. 1994. 49.95 (0-904597-86-5) Specialty Pr.
Butler, Philip. A Student's Guide to Racine. (Student's Guides to European Literature Ser.). 106p. (C). 1978. pap. text 7.50 (0-435-37582-2, 37582) Heinemann.
Butler, Philip H. Point Group Symmetry Applications: Methods & Tables. LC 80-17947. 578p. 1981. 125.00 (0-306-40523-7, Plenum Trade) Perseus Pubng.
Butler, Philippa. Pawprints in Time. (Illus.). 32p. 1998. 14.99 (0-670-87177-X) Viking Penguin.
Butler, Phyllis F. Old Santa Clara Valley: A Guide to Historic Buildings from Palo Alto to Gilroy. rev. ed. LC 91-23254. (Illus.). 192p. 1991. pap. 9.95 (0-933174-81-0) Wide World-Tetra.
Butler, Pierce. Materials for the Life of Shakespeare. LC 71-113568. reprint ed. 34.50 (0-404-01248-5) AMS Pr.
***Butler, Pierce.** A Riddle of Stars. LC 99-29877. 287p. 1999. pap. 13.00 (1-58195-007-1, Pub. by Zoland Bks) SPD-Small Pr Dist.
Butler, Pierce. Sean O'Faolain. LC 93-18676. (Studies in Short Fiction: No. 50). 170p. 1993. 23.95 (0-8057-0860-X) Macmillan.
— Unhurried Years. (American Autobiography Ser.). 198p. 1995. reprint ed. lib. bdg. 69.00 (0-7812-8470-8) Rprt Serv.
— Women of Medieval France. 1978. 300.00 (0-87968-269-8) Gordon Pr.
Butler, Pierce, et al. Women in All Ages & All Nations, 10 vols. 1975. lib. bdg. 3000.00 (0-8490-1322-4) Gordon Pr.
Butler-Por, Nava. Underachievers in School: Issues & Intervention. fac. ed. LC 87-8295. (Illus.). 205p. 1987. reprint ed. pap. 63.60 (0-608-00963-6, 206181100011) Bks Demand.
Butler, R. F. Paleomagnetism: Magnetic Domains to Geologic Terranes. (Illus.). 336p. 1991. pap. 59.95 (0-86542-070-X) Blackwell Sci.
***Butler, R. M.** Bars & Walls of York. 1999. pap. 21.00 (0-9503519-0-3, Pub. by Yorkshire Architectural) St Mut.
Butler, R. M. Horizontal Wells for the Recovery of Oil, Gas & Bitumen No. 2: Petroleum Society of CIM Monograph. 228p. 1996. 75.00 (0-9697990-1-2, 99012) Gulf Pub.
Butler, R. M., ed. Medieval York. 1999. pap. 21.00 (0-900657-69-3, Pub. by W Sessions) St Mut.
Butler, R. Will. God Speaks: What the Bible Teaches about Itself. 2nd rev. ed. Bogue, Carl, ed. Date not set. pap. 6.95 (0-9658804-4-3) Deo Volente.
Butler, Ralph. Out of the Silence. 142p. 1978. pap. 6.50 (0-7050-0059-1) Attic Pr.
Butler, Reg. Amsterdam: A New Look. (City Breaks Ser.). 96p. 1997. pap. 6.95 (1-872876-50-1, Pub. by Settle Pr) Assoc Pubs Grp.
— Florence: A New Look. (City Breaks Ser.). 96p. 1997. pap. 6.95 (1-872876-54-4, Pub. by Settle Pr) Assoc Pubs Grp.
— Madrid, Barcelona, Seville & Granada. (Illus.). 100p. 1996. pap. 6.95 (1-872876-46-3, Pub. by Settle Pr) Assoc Pubs Grp.
— Paris: A New Look. (City Breaks Ser.). 96p. 1997. pap. 6.95 (1-872876-49-8, Pub. by Settle Pr) Assoc Pubs Grp.
— Rome: A New Look. (City Breaks Ser.). 96p. 1997. pap. 6.95 (1-872876-53-6, Pub. by Settle Pr) Assoc Pubs Grp.
— Venice: A New Look. (City Breaks Ser.). 96p. 1997. pap. 6.95 (1-872876-52-8, Pub. by Settle Pr) Assoc Pubs Grp.
Butler, Richard. The Buffalo Hook. large type ed. (Dales Large Print Ser.). 288p. 1996. pap. 18.99 (1-85389-667-5, Dales) Ulverscroft.
***Butler, Richard.** The Greatest Threat: Iraq, Weapons of Mass Destruction, & the Growing Crisis of Global Security. 304p. 2000. 26.00 (1-891620-53-3, Pub. by PublicAffairs NY) HarpC.
Butler, Richard. Lift-off at Satan. large type ed. 1996. pap. 18.99 (1-85389-571-7, Dales) Ulverscroft.
— Sharkbait. large type ed. (Dales Large Print Ser.). 1995. pap. 18.99 (1-85389-570-9, Dales) Ulverscroft.
***Butler, Richard & Boyd, Stephen.** Tourism & National Parks: Issues & Implications. 352p. 2000. 95.00 (0-471-98894-4) Wiley.
Butler, Richard & Hinch, Tom. Tourism & Indigenous Peoples. 448p. 1997. pap. 55.00 (1-86152-209-6) Thomson Learn.
Butler, Richard & Wilson, David C. Managing Voluntary & Non-Profit Organizations: Strategy & Structure. LC 89-20437. 204p. reprint ed. pap. 63.30 (0-608-20406-4, 207165900002) Bks Demand.
Butler, Richard, et al. Tourism & Recreation in Rural Areas. LC 97-25520. 274p. 1998. 100.00 (0-471-97680-6) Wiley.
Butler, Richard, jt. auth. see Pearce, Douglas G.
Butler, Richard J. Nocturnal Enuresis: The Child's Experience. LC 94-32797. (Illus.). 192p. 1995. pap. text 39.00 (0-7506-2132-X) Buttrwrth-Heinemann.
— Sports Psychology in Action. (Illus.). 224p. 1996. pap. text 37.50 (0-7506-2436-1) Buttrwrth-Heinemann.
Butler, Richard J. & Green, David. The Child Within: The Exploration of Personal Construct Theory with Young People. LC 98-6243. 144p. 1998. pap. text 32.50 (0-7506-2903-7) Buttrwrth-Heinemann.
Butler, Richard J., et al. Strategic Investment Decisions: Theory, Practice, & Process. LC 92-21100. 240p. (C). 1996. pap. 28.95 (0-415-07508-4, B0186) Thomson Learn.
— Strategic Investment Decisions: Theory, Practice, & Process. LC 92-21100. 240p. (C). (gr. 13). 1996. pap. 66.95 (0-415-07507-6, B0182) Thomson Learn.
Butler, Robert. Contemporary African American Fiction: The Open Journey. LC 98-11452. 168p. 1998. 32.50 (0-8386-3787-6) Fairleigh Dickinson.
***Butler, Robert.** The Gospel Unrevealed. 16p. 1999. pap. 1.50 (0-9674440-0-4, Pub. by Agape & Praise) Double Bless.
Butler, Robert. Native Son: The Emergence of a New Black Hero. LC 91-8827. (Twayne's Masterwork Studies: No. 77). 168p. (C). 1991. 25.95 (0-8057-8086-6, Twyne); per. 14.95 (0-8057-8148-X, Twyne) Mac Lib Ref.
— Porsche: Off-Road & Rally. (Illus.). 60p. (Orig.). (C). 1989. pap. write for info. (0-318-65901-8) Butler & Assocs.
***Butler, Robert & Sonesh Kedar, Eva.** A Naturalist's Guide for Mountain Bikers, Hikers & Drivers to the Seven Mountains. (Illus.). 152p. 1999. pap. Price not set. (0-9657934-2-7) Purple Lizard.
Butler, Robert, jt. intro. see Hakutani, Yoshinobu.
Butler, Robert A. Family Records of Revolutionary War Pension Applicants Vol. 1: Butler. LC 83-82119. vi, 102p. (Orig.). 1983. pap. 11.95 (0-914769-00-6) Heritage Tech Serv.
— Handbook of Practical Writing. 1978. text 22.74 (0-07-009341-5) McGraw.
***Butler, Robert Brown.** Standard Handbook Architectural Engineering. 1069p. 1999. 225.00 (0-07-135550-2) McGraw.
Butler, Robert Brown. Standard Handbook of Architectural Engineering. LC 98-159756. (Illus.). 1008p. 1998. 125.00 (0-07-913692-3) McGraw.
— Standard Handbook of Architectural Engineering. 1999. cd-rom 149.95 (0-07-134751-8) McGraw.
Butler, Robert E. & Rappaport, Donald. A Complete Guide to Money & Your Business. 1986. 37.50 (0-13-600073-8) P-H.
***Butler, Robert J.** The Critical Response to Ralph Ellison, 35. LC 00-20767. (Critical Responses in Arts & Letters Ser.: Vol. 35). 296p. 2000. lib. bdg. 79.50 (0-313-30285-5) Greenwood.
Butler, Robert J. The Critical Response to Richard Wright, 16. LC 94-40142. (Critical Responses in Arts & Letters Ser.: Vol. 15). 240p. 1995. lib. bdg. 57.95 (0-313-28860-7, Greenwood Pr) Greenwood.
Butler, Robert N., ed. Older & Wiser: Public Policy Issues for an Aging America. 240p. 1998. 24.95 (0-87078-424-2) Century Foundation.
Butler, Robert N. & Brody, Jacob A., eds. Delaying the Onset of Late-Life Dysfunction. (Illus.). 272p. 1995. 39.95 (0-8261-8880-X) Springer Pub.
Butler, Robert N. & Kiikuni, Kenzo, eds. Who Is Responsible for My Old Age? LC 92-25181. 288p. 1992. 36.95 (0-8261-8140-6) Springer Pub.
Butler, Robert N. & Lewis, Myrna I. Love & Sex after Forty: A Guide for Men & Women for Their Mid & Later Years. large type ed. (Illus.). 322p. 1987. reprint ed. lib. bdg. 19.95 (1-55736-008-1) BDD LT Grp.
— Love & Sex after Sixty. (Illus.). 320p. 1993. pap. 11.50 (0-345-38034-7) Ballantine Pub Grp.

— Love & Sex after Sixty. 2nd large type ed. LC 96-45183. (Spec-Hall Ser.). 375p. 1996. lib. bdg. 21.95 (*0-7838-2027-5*, G K Hall Lrg Type) Mac Lib Ref.
— Sex after Sixty: A Guide for Men & Women for Their Later Years. large type ed. (Illus.). 1977. 18.95 (*0-8161-6507-6*, G K Hall Lrg Type) Mac Lib Ref.
Butler, Robert N., et al. Aging & Mental Health: Positive Psychosocial & Biomedical Approaches. 5th ed. LC 97-30861. 530p. 1998. pap. 58.00 (*0-205-19336-6*) P-H.
Butler, Robert Olen. The Alleys of Eden. 256p. 1995. 25.00 (*0-8050-3199-5*); pap. 11.00 (*0-8050-3141-3*, Owl) H Holt & Co.
— Countrymen of Bones. LC 93-37099. 217p. 1995. pap. 11.00 (*0-8050-3142-1*) H Holt & Co.
— The Deep Green Sea. 288p. 1999. pap. 13.00 (*0-8050-6001-4*, Owl) H Holt & Co.
— The Deep Green Sea. LC 97-28239. 240p. 1998. text 23.00 (*0-8050-3130-8*) St Martin.
— The Deep Green Sea. large type ed. LC 97-51195. 215p. 1998. 25.95 (*0-7838-8431-1*, G K Hall Lrg Type) Mac Lib Ref.
— The Deuce: A Novel. LC 93-6303. 1995. pap. 11.00 (*0-8050-3139-1*, Owl) H Holt & Co.
— A Good Scent from a Strange Mountain: Stories. 256p. 1995. 19.95 (*0-8050-1986-3*) H Holt & Co.
— A Good Scent from a Strange Mountain: Stories. 272p. 1993. pap. 12.95 (*0-14-017664-0*, Penguin Bks) Viking Penguin.
***Butler, Robert Olen.** Mr. Spaceman. LC 99-46822. 224p. 2000. 24.00 (*0-8021-1660-4*, Pub. by Grove-Atltic) Publishers Group.
Butler, Robert Olen. On Distant Ground. 1995. 25.00 (*0-8050-3198-7*); pap. 11.00 (*0-8050-3140-5*, Owl) H Holt & Co.
— Sun Dogs. 1995. 25.00 (*0-8050-3201-0*); pap. 11.00 (*0-8050-3143-X*) H Holt & Co.
— Tabloid Dreams: Stories. 89p. 1995. 22.50 (*0-8050-3131-6*) H Holt & Co.
— Tabloid Dreams: Stories. 288p. 1997. pap. text 12.00 (*0-8050-5589-4*, Owl) H Holt & Co.
— They Whisper. 352p. 1995. 22.50 (*0-8050-1985-5*) H Holt & Co.
— They Whisper. 352p. 1995. pap. 10.95 (*0-14-024393-3*, Penguin Bks) Viking Penguin.
— Wabash: A Novel. 1995. 25.00 (*0-8050-3200-2*); pap. 11.00 (*0-8050-3138-3*) H Holt & Co.
— Wabash: A Novel. 15.95 (*0-317-57588-0*) Knopf.
***Butler, Robert W.** The Great Blue Heron. (Illus.). 184p. 1999. pap. 14.95 (*0-7748-0634-6*, Pub. by UBC Pr) U of Wash Pr.
***Butler, Roberta.** Sweden. (Nations of the World Ser.). (Illus.). 2000. 31.40 (*0-8172-5784-5*) Raintree Steck-V.
Butler, Robin. The Book of Wine Antiques. (Illus.). 288p. 1995. 45.00 (*1-85149-227-5*) Antique Collect.
Butler, Roger. The History of Australian Prints. LC 96-60304. (Illus.). 300p. (Orig.). 1996. pap. 39.95 (*0-500-97439-X*) Thames Hudson.
Butler, Rohan & Pelly, M. E., eds. The Conference at Potsdam, July-Aug. 1945. (Documents on British Policy Overseas Ser.). 1278p. 1984. 141.00 (*0-11-591682-2*, Pub. by Statnry Office) Balogh.
Butler, Rohan D. The Roots of National Socialism, 1783-1933. LC 78-63657. (Studies in Fascism: Ideology & Practice). 312p. reprint ed. 41.50 (*0-404-16917-1*) AMS Pr.
***Butler, Ron.** Dancing Alone in Mexico: From the Border to Baja & Beyond. LC 99-50478. 220p. 2000. 40.00 (*0-8165-2022-4*); pap. 17.95 (*0-8165-2023-2*) U of Ariz Pr.
Butler, Roy F. The Meaning of Agapao & Phileo in the Greek New Testament. 1977. pap. 7.50 (*0-87291-089-X*) Coronado Pr.
Butler, Rupert. Hitler's Jackals. 1998. 39.95 (*0-85052-593-4*, Pub. by Leo Cooper) Trans-Atl Phila.
— An Illustrated History of the Gestapo. LC 92-41018. (MBI Rights Ser.). (Illus.). 240p. 1993. 24.95 (*0-87938-801-3*) MBI Pubg.
Butler, Ruth. Rodin: The Shape of Genius. (C). 1996. pap. 20.00 (*0-614-12572-3*) Yale U Pr.
— Rodin: The Shape of Genius. LC 92-43552. (Illus.). 1996. pap. 20.00 (*0-300-06498-5*) Yale U Pr.
***Butler, Ruth.** Rodin's Monument to Victor Hugo. LC 98-68130. 2000. pap. 29.95 (*1-85894-071-0*) Merrell Holberton.
***Butler, Ruth & Parr, Hester, eds.** Mind & Body Spaces: Geographies of Illness Impairment & Disability. (Critical Geographies Ser.). (Illus.). 320p. (Orig.). (C). 1999. pap. 29.99 (*0-415-17903-3*); text 90.00 (*0-415-17902-5*) Routledge.
Butler, Ruth, et al. Rodin's Monument to Victor Hugo. LC 98-68130. (Illus.). 120p. 1998. 40.00 (*1-85894-070-2*, Pub. by Merrell Holberton) U of Wash Pr.
***Butler, Ruth A.** Trade Cases Adjudged in the United States Court of Appeals for the Federal Circuit, October 1993 To September 1994, October 1994 to September 1995 Parts 1 & 2, 2, Vols. 12 & 13. 441p. 2000. per. 13.00 (*0-16-061744-8*) USGPO.
***Butler, Ruth C., ed.** Answers to Potter's Questions II. 220p. 1998. mass mkt. 7.95 (*1-57498-085-8*, CA15) Am Ceramic.
— Great Ideas for Potters II. (Illus.). 194p. 1998. mass mkt. 7.95 (*1-57498-068-8*, CA13) Am Ceramic.
Butler, Ruth L., jt. auth. see Du Ru, Paul.
Butler, Samuel. Ainsi Va Toute Chair, Vol. 1. Orig. Title: Way of all Flesh. (FRE.). 237p. 1977. pap. 11.95 (*0-7859-1845-0*, 2070369145) Fr & Eur.
— Ainsi Va Toute Chair, Vol. 2. Orig. Title: Way of all Flesh. (FRE.). 1977. pap. 11.95 (*0-7859-1846-9*, 2070369153) Fr & Eur.
Butler, Samuel. Characters & Passages from Note-Books. (BCL1-PR English Literature Ser.). 489p. 1992. reprint ed. lib. bdg. 99.00 (*0-7812-7328-5*) Rprt Serv.
Butler, Samuel. Characters & Passages from Notebooks. 489p. reprint ed. 69.00 (*0-403-08911-5*) Somerset Pub.
— Erewhon. Mudford, Peter, ed. (English Library). 272p. 1970. pap. 10.95 (*0-14-043057-1*, Penguin Classics) Viking Penguin.
— Erewhon. (Classics Library). 1998. pap. 3.95 (*1-85326-284-6*, 2846WW, Pub. by Wrdsworth Edits) NTC Contemp Pub Co.
— Erewhon. LC 98-14269. (Literary Classics Ser.). 320p. 1998. reprint ed. pap. 8.95 (*1-57392-204-8*) Prometheus Bks.
— Hudibras, Pt. 2: A Facsimile Reproduction. LC 93-42232. 148p. 1993. 50.00 (*0-8201-1469-3*) Schol Facsimiles.
— Humour of Homer, & Other Essays. Streatfeild, Richard A., ed. LC 67-30178. (Essay Index Reprint Ser.). 1977. 20.95 (*0-8369-0268-8*) Ayer.
— The Note Books of Samuel Butler. 1988. reprint ed. lib. bdg. 75.00 (*0-7812-0347-3*) Rprt Serv.
***Butler, Samuel.** Odyssey. 2000. pap. write for info. (*1-930142-21-8*) Write Together.
Butler, Samuel. Prose Observations. De Quehen, Hugh, ed. (Oxford English Texts Ser.). (Illus.). 470p. 1980. text 110.00 (*0-19-812728-6*) OUP.
Butler, Samuel. Satires & Miscellaneous Poetry & Prose. Lamar, Rene, ed. LC 76-29457. (BCL Ser. II). reprint ed. 42.50 (*0-404-15301-1*) AMS Pr.
— The Shrewsbury Edition of the Works of Samuel Butler, 20 vols. Incl. Alps & Sanctuaries. 316p. 1999. reprint ed. lib. bdg. 88.00 (*1-58201-007-2*); Authoress of the Odyssey. 293p. 1999. reprint ed. lib. bdg. 88.00 (*1-58201-012-9*); Erewhon: or Over the Range. 242p. 1999. reprint ed. lib. bdg. 88.00 (*1-58201-002-1*); Erewhon Revisited. 266p. 1999. reprint ed. lib. bdg. 88.00 (*1-58201-016-1*); Evolution, Old & New. 393p. 1999. reprint ed. lib. bdg. 88.00 (*1-58201-005-6*); Ex Voto. 230p. 1999. reprint ed. lib. bdg. 88.00 (*1-58201-009-9*); Fair Haven. 259p. 1999. reprint ed. lib. bdg. 88.00 (*1-58201-003-X*); First Year in Canterbury Settlement & Other Early Essays. 259p. 1999. reprint ed. lib. bdg. 88.00 (*1-58201-001-3*, c0001); Iliad of Homer (Rendered into English Prose) 411p. 1999. reprint ed. lib. bdg. 88.00 (*1-58201-013-7*); Life & Habit. 263p. 1999. reprint ed. lib. bdg. 88.00 (*1-58201-004-8*, c0004); Luck or Cunning? 256p. 1999. reprint ed. lib. bdg. 88.00 (*1-58201-008-0*); Note-Books of Samuel Butler. 493p. 1999. reprint ed. lib. bdg. 88.00 (*1-58201-020-X*); Odyssey (Rendered into English Prose) 379p. 1999. reprint ed. lib. bdg. 88.00 (*1-58201-015-3*); Shakespeare's Sonnets. 380p. 1999. reprint ed. lib. bdg. 88.00 (*1-58201-014-5*); Unconscious Memory. 218p. 1999. reprint ed. lib. bdg. 88.00 (*1-58201-006-4*); Way of All Flesh. 414p. 1999. reprint ed. lib. bdg. 88.00 (*1-58201-017-X*); Vol. I. Collected Essays. 267p. 1999. reprint ed. lib. bdg. 88.00 (*1-58201-018-8*); Vol. I. Life & Letters of Dr. Samuel Butler. 468p. 1999. reprint ed. lib. bdg. 88.00 (*1-58201-010-2*); Vol. II. Collected Essays. 335p. 1999. reprint ed. lib. bdg. 88.00 (*1-58201-019-6*); Vol. II. Life & Letters of Dr. Samuel Butler. 487p. 1999. reprint ed. lib. bdg. 88.00 (*1-58201-011-0*); 1999. reprint ed. Set lib. bdg. 1760.00 (*1-58201-000-5*) Classic Bks.
Butler, Samuel. The Shrewsbury Edition of the Works of Samuel Butler, 20 vols., Set. (BCL1-PR English Literature Ser.). 1992. reprint ed. lib. bdg. 1500.00 (*0-7812-7469-9*) Rprt Serv.
— Way of All Flesh. 24.95 (*0-88411-788-X*) Amereon Ltd.
— The Way of All Flesh. LC 92-52916. 400p. 1992. 17.00 (*0-679-41718-4*) Everymns Lib.
— The Way of All Flesh. LC 98-21241. (Modern Library Ser.). 1998. pap. 9.95 (*0-375-75249-8*) Modern Lib NY.
— The Way of All Flesh. 416p. 1993. pap. 7.95 (*0-460-87240-0*, Everyman's Classic Lib) Tuttle Pubng.
— The Way of All Flesh. Hogart, Richard & Cochrane, James, eds. (English Library). 446p. 1966. pap. 10.95 (*0-14-043012-1*, Penguin Classics) Viking Penguin.
— The Way of All Flesh. (Classics Library). 400p. pap. 3.95 (*1-85326-228-5*, 2285WW, Pub. by Wrdsworth Edits) NTC Contemp Pub Co.
***Butler, Samuel.** The Way of All Flesh. large type ed. LC 99-26431. 1999. pap. 25.95 (*0-7838-8641-1*) Mac Lib Ref.
Butler, Samuel. The Way of All Flesh. 345p. 1983. reprint ed. lib. bdg. 17.95 (*0-89966-310-9*) Buccaneer Bks.
***Butler, Samuel.** The Way of All Flesh, Set. unabridged ed. (C). 1999. 65.95 incl. audio (*1-55685-582-6*) Audio Bk Con.
Butler, Samuel. Works of Samuel Butler, 20 vols. Jones, Henry F. & Bartholomew, A. T., eds. LC 77-181920. (BCL Ser. II). reprint ed. 800.00 (*0-404-01320-1*) AMS Pr.
Butler, Samuel, ed. & intro. see Shakespeare, William.
Butler, Sandra. Conspiracy of Silence: The Trauma of Incest. LC 78-1975. 215p. 1996. pap. 13.95 (*1-884244-12-2*) Volcano Pr.
— Conspiracy of Silence: The Trauma of Incest. 208p. 1978. 12.00 (*0-318-17075-2*) Kempe Nat Ctr.
— Feminist Groupwork. (Gender & Psychology Ser.: Vol. 3). 208p. (C). 1991. text 42.50 (*0-8039-8209-7*); pap. text 14.99 (*0-8039-8210-0*) Sage.
Butler, Sandra & Rosenblum, Barbara. Cancer in Two Voices. 2nd ed. LC 91-18052. 256p. (Orig.). 1996. pap. 12.95 (*1-883523-16-8*) Spinsters Ink.
***Butler, Sandra L.** The Bible Decoded: A Spiritual Understanding of God's Word. 236p. 2000. pap. 12.00 (*0-9677296-0-2*) Gilead Pubng.
— Judging the Twelve Tribes of Israel: The Spiritual Journey- a Supplement to The Bible Decoded. 150 p. 2000. pap. 10.00 (*0-9677296-1-0*) Gilead Pubng.
Butler, Sandra L., ed. see Ziegler, J. F.
Butler, Sandra S. Middle-Aged, Female & Homeless: The Stories of a Forgotten Group. LC 93-34143. (Children of Poverty Ser.). 184p. 1993. text 20.00 (*0-8153-1544-9*) Garland.
Butler, Sandy. Train Your Dog in One Hour. Keene, James A., ed. LC 98-72111. (Illus.). 200p. 1998. 21.95 (*0-944435-45-9*) Glenbridge Pub.
Butler, Sarah, jt. auth. see Wilson, Richard G.
Butler, Sarah A. Caring Ministry: A Contemplative Approach to Pastoral Care. LC 81-3357. 144p. 1999. 19.95 (*0-8264-1159-2*) Continuum.
Butler, Scott, et al. Jesus, Peter & the Keys: Scriptural Handbook on the Papacy. LC 96-70129. 432p. 1996. pap. text 14.95 (*1-882972-54-6*, 3541) Queenship Pub.
Butler, Sharon & Stoneman, William P., eds. Editing, Publishing, & Computer Technology: Papers Given at the Twentieth Annual Conference on Editorial Problems, University of Toronto, 2-3 November, 1984. LC 87-45815. (Conference on Editorial Problems Ser.: No. 20). 1988. 42.50 (*0-404-63670-5*) AMS Pr.
Butler, Sharon, jt. auth. see Hieatt, Constance B.
Butler, Sharon J. Conquering Carpal Tunnel Syndrome: And Other Repetitive Strain Injuries. LC 94-96893. 160p. 1996. pap. text 17.95 (*1-57224-039-3*) New Harbinger.
Butler, Shelley & Kratz, Deb. The Field Guide to Parenting: A Comprehensive Handbook of Great Ideas, Advice, Tips & Solutions for Parenting Children Ages One to Five. 400p. 2000. pap. 25.00 (*1-886284-21-0*, Pub. by Chandler Hse) Natl Bk Netwk.
***Butler, Shelly R.** Contested Representations: Revisiting into the Heart of Africa. 136p. 1999. pap. 19.50 (*90-5700-523-9*, Harwood Acad Pubs) Gordon & Breach.
— Contested Representations: Revisiting into the Heart of Africa. 136p. 1999. text 35.00 (*90-5700-522-0*, Harwood Acad Pubs) Gordon & Breach.
Butler-Sloss, Elizabeth & Levy, A. E. Legal Aspects of Child Abuse. (Waterlow Practitioner's Library). 256p. 1991. 40.01 (*0-08-036906-5*) Macmillan.
Butler, Smedley. War Is a Racket. 1973. 250.00 (*0-87700-153-7*) Revisionist Pr.
Butler, Stanley. Guide to the Best in Contemporary Piano Music: An Annotated List of Graded Solo Piano Music Published Since 1950, 2 vols. Incl. Vol. 1. Levels 1-5. LC 73-5693. 1973. 21.00 (*0-8108-0628-2*); Vol. 2. Levels 6-8. LC 73-5693. 1973. 21.00 (*0-8108-0669-X*); LC 73-5693. 368p. 1973. 34.50 (*0-8108-2027-7*) Scarecrow.
Butler, Stella. Science & Technology Museums. 256p. (C). 1992. text 54.00 (*0-7185-1357-6*, Pub. by Leicester U Pr) Cassell & Continuum.
Butler, Stephen D., jt. auth. see Cushman, Robert Frank.
Butler, Stephen J. 401 (K) Today: Designing, Maintaining, & Maximizing Your Company's Plan. 2nd rev. abr. ed. LC 99-31554. 250p. 1999. pap. text 27.95 (*1-57675-063-9*) Berrett-Koehler.
Butler, Steve. Promotionals, 1934-1983: Dealership Vehicles in Miniature. LC 97-185823. (Illus.). 1997. write for info. (*0-89538-090-0*) L-W Inc.
Butler, Stuart & Kondratas, Anna. Out of the Poverty Trap: A Conservative Strategy for Welfare Reform. LC 87-14640. 275p. 1987. text 35.00 (*0-02-905061-8*) Free Pr.
Butler, Stuart Lee. A Guide to Virginia Militia Units in the War of 1812. LC 88-34594. (Illus.). 405p. 1988. pap. 22.00 (*0-935931-41-4*) Iberian Pub.
— Virginia Soldiers in the United States Army, 1800-1815. 215p. (Orig.). 1986. pap. 17.00 (*0-935931-25-2*) Iberian Pub.
Butler, Stuart M. & Holmes, Kim R., eds. Issues 1996. LC 96-218255. 580p. (Orig.). Date not set. 25.95 (*0-89195-063-X*) Heritage Found.
— Mandate for Leadership Vol. 4: Turning Ideas into Action. (Illus.). 759p. (Orig.). (C). 1997. 29.95 (*0-89195-064-8*); pap. 24.95 (*0-89195-065-6*) Heritage Found.
Butler, Sue. Australian Phrasebook: Language Survival Kit. 2nd ed. LC 99-169462. (Lonely Planet Phrasebooks). 192p. 1998. pap. text 5.95 (*0-86442-576-7*) Lonely Planet.
Butler, Susan. Ana: Stroke. Date not set. mass mkt. write for info. (*0-380-80521-9*) Morrow Avon.
Butler, Susan. East of Dawn: The Life of Amelia Earhart. LC 98-47717. (Illus.). 512p. 1999. reprint ed. mass mkt. 17.95 (*0-306-80887-0*, Pub. by Da Capo) HarpC.
— East to the Dawn: The Life of Amelia Earhart. LC 97-19123. (Illus.). 489p. 1997. 27.50 (*0-201-31144-5*) Addison-Wesley.
***Butler, Susan.** The Hermit Thrush Sings. (YA). 2001. mass mkt. 5.50 (*0-440-22896-4*) BDD Bks Young Read.
Butler, Susan. The Hermit Thrush Sings. LC 98-22893. 282p. (YA). (gr. 5 up). 1999. 16.95 (*0-7894-2489-4*, D K Ink) DK Pub Inc.
— Non-Competitive Games for People of All Ages. LC 85-28644. 28p. (Orig.). 1986. pap. 9.99 (*0-87123-812-8*) Bethany Hse.
— A Trip to the Jungle. (Illus.). 40p. (Orig.). (J). (ps-2). 1978. pap. 3.95 (*0-931416-00-0*) Open Books.
***Butler, Susan P.** Ebusiness Legal Kit for Dummies. (For Dummies Ser.). 384p. 2000. pap. 24.99 (*0-7645-5265-1*) IDG Bks.
Butler, Susan S. Scenic Driving Yellowstone & Grand Teton National Parks. LC 98-13445. (Illus.). 200p. 1999. pap. 15.95 (*1-56044-633-1*) Falcon Pub Inc.
Butler, T. Eastern Promise. pap. text 23.00 (*0-85315-898-3*) Lawrence & Wishart.
Butler, T. R. & Garsia, Marston. Archbold Pleading, Evidence & Practice in Criminal Cases, 2 vols., Set. 36th ed. 1864p. 1995. reprint ed. 225.00 (*1-56169-109-7*) Gaunt.
Butler, Tajuana. The Desires of a Woman. large type ed. LC 97-94203. 68p. 1997. 7.95 (*0-9659254-0-4*) Lavelle Pub.
***Butler, Tajuana.** Sorority Sisters. LC 99-88342. 224p. 2000. 19.95 (*0-375-50415-X*) Villard Books.
Butler, Tajuana. Sorority Sisters: A Novel. LC 98-91633. 301p. 1998. 17.00 (*0-9659254-3-9*) Lavelle Pub.
Butler, Thomas. Monumenta Bulgarica: A Bilingual Anthology of Bulgarian Texts from the 9th to the 19th Century. LC 96-25043. (Michigan Slavic Materials Ser.: No. 41). 1998. 36.00 (*0-930042-80-8*) Mich Slavic Pubns.
Butler, Thomas A., jt. ed. see Knapp, Fern F.
Butler, Thomas A., jt. ed. see Knapp, Furn F., Jr.
Butler, Thomas C. Plague & Other Yersinia Infections. LC 83-17467. (Current Topics in Infectious Disease Ser.). 232p. 1983. 59.50 (*0-306-41414-7*, Plenum Trade) Perseus Pubng.
Butler, Thomas G., ed. see American Society of Mechanical Engineers Staff.
Butler, Thomas I. & Veazey, Earl W., eds. Film Extrusion Manual: Process, Materials, Properties. LC 92-11053. 792p. 1992. 145.00 (*0-89852-250-1*, 0101R186) TAPPI.
Butler, Thomas J., et al. Laboratory Exercises for Competency in Respiratory Care. LC 97-41975. (Illus.). 577p. 1998. pap. 47.95 (*0-8036-0248-0*) Davis Co.
Butler, Thomas W. Let Her Keep It Vol. 1: Jesus' Ordination of Mary of Bethany. large type unabridged ed. Hope, Barbara, ed. LC 98-65357. (Illus.). 360p. 1998. pap. 22.00 (*0-9627161-1-1*) QLP CA.
Butler, Thomas W., jt. auth. see Bacon, Frank R.
Butler, Thomas W., Jr., jt. auth. see Bacon, Frank R., Jr.
Butler, Tim. Gentrification & the Middle Classes. LC 97-72666. (Illus.). 208p. 1997. text 59.95 (*1-85972-371-3*, Pub. by Ashgate Pub) Ashgate Pub Co.
Butler, Tim & Rustin, Michael, eds. Rising in the East? The Regeneration of East London. 320p. 1996. pap. 25.00 (*0-85315-844-4*, Pub. by Lawrence & Wishart) NYU Pr.
***Butler, Timothy & Waldroop, James.** Maximum Success: Changing the 12 Behavior Patterns That Keep You from Getting Ahead. 320p. 2000. 24.95 (*0-385-49849-7*) Doubleday.
Butler, Timothy, jt. auth. see Waldroop, James.
Butler, Timothy P. The History of Formerly Salty Areas: Drawings of Timothy Patrick Butler. LC 95-222310. (Illus.). 76p. (Orig.). (C). 1994. pap. 12.00 (*0-9644469-0-1*) Cat Box Prods.
Butler, Tom. The Badger Game. 1990. pap. 5.00 (*1-878569-08-2*) Badger Bks Inc.
— Changing Mental Health Services: The Politics & Policy. LC 92-30606. 206p. 1992. pap. 41.50 (*1-56593-035-5*, 0283) Thomson Learn.
— Handbook of Metaphysics. LC 92-71612. (Illus.). 1994. 22.95 (*0-8158-0485-7*) Chris Mass.
***Butler, Tom.** Thirty-Five Years Later: Bruno Zupan & the Columbus Museum. Young, Becky, ed. 12p. (C). 2000. pap. Price not set. (*1-882650-09-3*) Colmbs Mus GA.
— Two Worlds, One Heart. 320p. mass mkt. 4.99 (*1-55197-053-8*) Picasso Publ.
***Butler, Tom & Reker, Les.** Motherwell at the Columbus Museum. (Illus.). 16p. 2000. pap. write for info. (*1-882650-10-7*) Colmbs Mus GA.
Butler, Traci L., jt. auth. see Karp, Cheryl L.
Butler, Trent C. Joshua. (Biblical Commentary Ser.: Vol. 7). 29.99 (*0-8499-0206-1*) Word Pub.
***Butler, Trent C.** Luke. (Holman New Testament Commentary Ser.: Vol. 3). 2000. 16.99 (*0-8054-0203-9*) Broadman.
Butler, Trent C. Points for Emphasis 1999-2000. (Points for Emphasis Ser.). 224p. 1999. pap. 6.99 (*0-8054-1269-7*); pap. 5.99 (*0-8054-1270-0*) Broadman.
Butler, Trent C., ed. Holman Bible Dictionary. (Illus.). 1450p. 1991. 32.99 (*1-55819-053-8*) Broadman.
Butler University Staff. Change & Tradition. 554p. (C). 1998. per. 37.95 (*0-7872-5294-8*) Kendall-Hunt.
Butler, Vera M. Education As Revealed by New England Newspapers Prior to 1850. LC 73-89160. (American Education: Its Men, Institutions, & Ideas. Series 1). 1974. reprint ed. 23.95 (*0-405-01397-3*) Ayer.
Butler, Vic, et al. Uganda: Long Term Observation of 1996 Presidential & Legislative Elections, May-July 1996. Cooper, Laurie, ed. vi, 262p. 1996. pap. text 28.00 (*1-879720-36-1*) Intl Fndt Elect.
Butler, Vincent. Casting for Sculptors. (Illus.). 96p. 1997. pap. text. write for info. (*90-5703-901-X*, Harwood Acad Pubs) Gordon & Breach.
Butler, W. D., et al. The Butler Family in America. (Illus.). 306p. 1989. reprint ed. pap. 48.50 (*0-8328-0357-X*); reprint ed. lib. bdg. 58.50 (*0-8328-0356-1*) Higginson Bk Co.
Butler, W. E. How to Read the Aura & Practice Psychometry, Telepathy, & Clairvoyance. LC 97-50030. 240p. 1998. pap. 12.95 (*0-89281-705-4*, Destiny Bks) Inner Tradit.
— How to Read the Aura, Practice Psychometry, Telepathy, & Clairvoyance. 235p. 1987. pap. 10.95 (*0-89281-161-7*, Destiny Bks) Inner Tradit.
— Lords of Light: The Path of Initiation in the Western Mysteries. Geikie, Toni, ed. 160p. (Orig.). 1990. pap. 10.95 (*0-89281-308-3*) Inner Tradit.
— Magician - His Training & Work. 175p. 1979. pap. 7.00 (*0-87980-212-X*) Wilshire.
Butler, W. E., ed. Russian Legal Theory. (The International Library of Essays in Law & Theory, Areas Ser.). 500p. (C). 1996. lib. bdg. 150.00 (*0-8147-1183-9*) NYU Pr.
Butler, W. E., tr. Securities & Banking Law of the Republic Kazakhstan. 202p. 1995. pap. 55.00 (*1-898029-21-0*, Pub. by Simmonds & Hill Pubng) Gaunt.
Butler, W. E., tr. Civil Code of the Republic Kazakhstan Adopted by the Supreme Soviet on 27 December, 1994, as Amended 31 August, 1995, 5 October, 1995, 27 January, 1996, 15 July, 1995, 7 December, 1996, 21

B

January, 1997, 5 March, 1997, 19 June, 1997, 2 July, 1997 & 11 July, 1997. 3rd ed. LC 99-196140. xxxviii, 223 p. 1997. write for info. (*1-898029-32-6*, Pub. by Simmonds & Hill Pubng) Gaunt.

Butler, W. E. & Murjas, Jolanta, eds. Russian Law Books: Books on Russian Law & Private & Public International Law Published in Russia. 260p. 1997. 78.00 (*1-898029-28-8*, Pub. by Simmonds & Hill Pubng) Gaunt.

Butler, W. H., et al, eds. Application of Multiple Scattering Theory to Materials Science. (Symposium Proceedings Ser.: Vol. 253). 533p. 1992. text 30.00 (*1-55899-147-6*) Materials Res.

Butler, W. H., jt. auth. see Gonis, A.

Butler, Walter. Marked for Life: The Crime & Redemption of Todd Ice. 1998. mass mkt. write for info. (*0-345-41252-4*) Ballantine Pub Grp.

Butler, Wayne, jt. auth. see Condon, William.

Butler, Wilford A., ed. see American Society of Association Executives Staff.

Butler, William. Butterfly Revolution. LC 67-10948. 224p. 1986. mass mkt. 5.99 (*0-345-33182-6*) Ballantine Pub Grp.

— House at Akiya. 135p. 1963. 29.95 (*0-7206-4173-X*, Pub. by P Owen Ltd) Dufour.

— How to Read the Aura, Practice Psychometry, Telepathy & Clairvoyance. (Warner Destiny Bks.). (Orig.). 1985. mass mkt. 4.95 (*0-446-34168-1*, Pub. by Warner Bks) Little.

— Man in a Net. 160p. 1971. 16.95 (*0-8464-0586-5*) Beekman Pubs.

— Ring in Meiji. 464p. 1965. 29.00 (*0-7206-7450-6*, Pub. by P Owen Ltd) Dufour.

Butler, William, jt. auth. see Krans, Horatio S.

Butler, William, jt. auth. see Strode, William.

Butler, William, ed. see Cowgill, Judy.

Butler, William, ed. see Martin, Mike & Valentine, Don.

Butler, William, ed. see Oefinger, Judy F.

Butler, William, jt. ed. see Strode, William.

Butler, William A. Mrs. Limber's Raffle: or A Church Fair & Its Victims. LC 71-137724. (American Fiction Reprint Ser.). 1977. 17.95 (*0-8369-7023-3*) Ayer.

— Our Last Chance: Sixty-Six Deadly Days Adrift. LC 92-81605. (Illus.). 312p. 1992. 22.50 (*0-9632519-0-2*); pap. 14.50 (*0-9632519-2-9*) Exmart Assocs.

***Butler, William Allen & Association of the Bar of the City of New York.** The Revision of the Statutes of the State of New York & the Revisers: An Address Delivered Before the Association of the Bar of the City of New York, January 22, 1889. LC 99-73242. (Illus.). 100p. 1999. 45.00 (*1-56169-541-6*) Gaunt.

Butler, William B. My Hurt Is Over: The Miserable Experience of a Combat Infantryman in the Vietnam War. 128p. 1997. pap. 12.95 (*0-89896-395-8*) Larksdale.

Butler, William E. Intellectual Property Law in Russia. 192p. 1998. 78.00 (*1-898029-37-7*, Pub. by Simmonds & Hill Pubng) Gaunt.

— International Law & the International System. LC 87-12210. 1987. lib. bdg. 99.00 (*90-247-3534-3*) Kluwer Academic.

— International Law in Comparative Perspective. 324p. 1980. lib. bdg. 98.50 (*90-286-0089-2*) Kluwer Academic.

— The Mongolian Legal System. 1982. lib. bdg. 452.50 (*90-247-2685-9*) Kluwer Academic.

— Perestroika & the Rule of Law: Soviet & Anglo-American Perspectives. 1991. text 64.50 (*1-85043-316-X*, Pub. by I B T) St Martin.

***Butler, William E.** Requeil des Cours/Collected Courses, Vol. 270. 416p. 1999. 129.00 (*90-411-1331-2*) Kluwer Law Intl.

Butler, William E. Russian Law. 736p. 1999. text 165.00 (*0-19-826032-6*) OUP.

— Russian Law of Treaties. LC 99-196165. 170p. 1997. 55.00 (*1-898029-29-6*, Pub. by Simmonds & Hill Pubng) Gaunt.

***Butler, William E., ed.** Civil Code of the Republic Uzbekistan. 576p. 1999. text 145.00 (*90-411-9482-7*) Kluwer Law Intl.

Butler, William E., ed. Control over Compliance with International Obligations. 216p. (C). 1991. lib. bdg. 114.00 (*0-7923-1025-X*) Kluwer Academic.

***Butler, William E., ed.** Criminal Code of the Russian Federation. 3rd ed. 256p. 1999. text 75.00 (*90-411-9502-5*) Kluwer Law Intl.

Butler, William E., ed. Perestroika & the Rule of Law: Soviet & Anglo-American Perspectives. 300p. 1991. 35.00 (*0-685-52915-0*, Pub. by I B T) St Martin.

— Russian Company Law: Basic Legislation. 328p. 1998. pap. 70.00 (*1-898029-35-0*, Pub. by Simmonds & Hill Pubng) Gaunt.

— A Sourcebook on Socialist International Organizations. 1168p. 1979. lib. bdg. 277.50 (*90-286-0798-6*) Kluwer Academic.

***Butler, William E., ed.** Tax Code of the Russian Federation, Pt. 1. 188p. 1999. text 50.00 (*90-411-9522-X*) Kluwer Law Intl.

— Turkmenistan Civil Code of Saparmurat Turkmenbashi. 458p. 1999. text 125.00 (*90-411-9552-1*) Kluwer Law Intl.

Butler, William E., ed. from RUS. Civil Code of the Republic of Uzbekistan. LC 97-192685. 494p. 1997. pap. 70.00 (*1-898029-30-X*, 14622, Pub. by Simmonds & Hill Pubng) Gaunt.

— Civil Code of the Russian Federation, Pts. 1 & 2. LC 97-136120. 514p. 1997. pap. 70.00 (*1-898029-25-3*, Pub. by Simmonds & Hill Pubng) Gaunt.

— Company Law in the Republic of Uzbekistan: Basic Legislation. 321p. 1996. 81.00 (*1-898029-24-5*) Gaunt.

— The Criminal Code of the Russian Federation. LC 98-156041. 248p. 1997. pap. 55.00 (*1-898029-31-8*, Pub. by Simmonds & Hill Pubng) Gaunt.

— Labour Code of the Republic Uzbekistan. LC 99-196148. 136p. 1996. pap. 55.00 (*1-898029-26-1*, Pub. by Simmonds & Hill Pubng) Gaunt.

***Butler, William E., ed.** Russian Family Law: The Family Code of the Russian Federation & Federal Law on Acts of Civil Status. LC 99-196152. xxv, 165 p. 1998. write for info. (*1-898029-39-3*, Pub. by Simmonds & Hill Pubng) Gaunt.

Butler, William E., tr. Civil Code of the Republic Belarus. 211p. 1998. 78.00 (*1-898029-38-5*, Pub. by Simmonds & Hill Pubng) Gaunt.

— Russian-English Legal Dictionary. (ENG & RUS.). 200p. 1996. 55.00 (*1-898029-20-2*, Pub. by Simmonds & Hill Pubng) Gaunt.

Butler, William E., tr. Civil Code of the Republic of Kazakhstan: General Part. 250p. 1995. pap. 62.00 (*1-898029-14-8*, Pub. by Simmonds & Hill Pubng) Gaunt.

— Labour Code of the Kazakh SSR. LC 99-196147. 168p. 1995. pap. 55.00 (*1-898029-18-0*, Pub. by Simmonds & Hill Pubng) Gaunt.

— Russian Joint-Stock Societies: Basic Legislation. LC 96-176942. 175p. 1996. 56.00 (*1-898029-23-7*, Pub. by Simmonds & Hill Pubng) Gaunt.

Butler, William E. & Hepple, B. A. Comparative Labour Law: Anglo-Soviet Perspectives. LC 86-25695. 200p. 1987. 87.95 (*0-566-05387-X*) Ashgate Pub Co.

Butler, William E. & Murjas, Jolanta, eds. Russian Law Books: Books on Russian Law & Private & Public International Law Published in Russia. 271p. 1998. 78.00 (*1-898029-34-2*, Pub. by Simmonds & Hill Pubng) Gaunt.

***Butler, William E. & Murjas, Jolanta, eds.** Russian Law Books 1998: Books Published on Russian Law & Private & Public International Law in Russia During 1998. 275p. 1999. pap. text 75.00 (*90-411-9472-X*) Kluwer Law Intl.

Butler, William E., et al. Russian Legal Texts: The Foundations of a Rule-of-Law State & a Market Economy. LC 98-11552. 1998. 150.00 (*90-411-0625-1*); 150.00 (*1-898029-33-4*) Kluwer Law Intl.

Butler, William E., ed. see Vinogradoff Institute (University College, London).

Butler, William E., ed. & tr. see Grabar, V. E.

Butler, William E., tr. see Kuznetsov, Anatolii.

Butler, William E., tr. see Tunkin, G. I.

Butler, William Elliott. Justice & Comparative. 1986. lib. bdg. 99.00 (*90-247-3375-8*, Pub. by M Nijhoff) Kluwer Academic.

— Tadzhikistan Legal Texts: The Foundations of Civic Accord & a Market Economy. LC 98-55941. 1999. 150.00 (*90-411-0649-9*) Kluwer Law Intl.

***Butler, William Elliott & Vinogradoff Institute (University College, London).** Uzbekistan Legal Texts: The Foundations of Civic Accord & a Market Economy. LC 99-37235. (CIS Legal Texts Ser.: Vol. 3). 990p. 1999. 195.00 (*90-411-9402-9*) Kluwer Law Intl.

Butler, William Elliott, jt. auth. see Pustogarov, V. V.

Butler, William Elliott, jt. auth. see Uzbekistan Republic Staff.

Butler, William F. Lombard Communes. LC 68-25226. (World History Ser.: No. 48). 1969. lib. bdg. 75.00 (*0-8383-0923-2*) M S G Haskell Hse.

— The Wild Northland, Being the Story of a Winter Journey, with Dogs, Across Northern North America. LC 72-2824. (American Explorers Ser.). reprint ed. 59.50 (*0-404-54904-7*) AMS Pr.

Butler, William J. The New South Africa: The Dawn of Democracy: Report of a Mission on Behalf of the International Commission of Jurists & the American Association for the International Commission of Jurists. LC 94-21392. 1994. 20.00 (*0-916265-06-4*) Am Assn Intl Comm Jurists.

Butler, William J., ed. United Nations World Conference on Human Rights. LC 93-10785. 1993. write for info. (*0-916265-05-6*) Am Assn Intl Comm Jurists.

Butler, William T., ed. see Institute of Medicine Staff.

Butlin, A. G. & D'Oyly-Watkins, C., eds. Gas Chromatography Abstracts: Cumulative Indexes, 1958-1963, Inclusive. LC 63-22896. 315p. reprint ed. pap. 97.70 (*0-608-13893-2*, 202368400033) Bks Demand.

Butlin, Jan. The Legacy. large type ed. 1994. 27.99 (*0-7089-3144-8*) Ulverscroft.

Butlin, Martin & Hamlin, Robin, texts. William Blake: Paintings, Drawings & Watercolors. (Illus.). 81p. 1992. pap. 45.00 (*1-58821-004-9*) Salander OReilly.

Butlin, Martin & Joll, Evelyn. The Paintings of J. M. W. Turner. rev. ed. LC 84-40182. (Studies in British Art). (Illus.). 944p. 1984. 325.00 (*0-300-03276-5*) Yale U Pr.

Butlin, Martin, et al. William Blake & His Circle: Papers Delivered at a Huntington Symposium. LC 85-10689. (Illus.). 204p. 1989. pap. 12.95 (*0-87328-084-9*) Huntington Lib.

Butlin, N. G. Forming a Colonial Economy, Australia, 1810-1850. (Illus.). 256p. (C). 1995. text 64.95 (*0-521-44006-8*) Cambridge U Pr.

Butlin, Noel G. Economics & the Dreamtime: A Hypothetical History. (Illus.). 264p. (C). 1993. text 64.95 (*0-521-43236-7*); pap. text 25.95 (*0-521-43820-9*) Cambridge U Pr.

Butlin, Noel G., jt. ed. see Gregory, R. G.

Butlin, R. A. & Dodgshon, Robert, eds. An Historical Geography of Europe. (Illus.). 390p. 1999. text 90.00 (*0-19-874179-0*) OUP.

Butlin, Robin. Historical Geography: Through the Gates of Space & Time. (Arnold Publicatons). (Illus.). 320p. 1993. pap. text 39.95 (*0-340-48969-3*, A3667) OUP.

Butlin, Robin & Dodgshon, Robert, eds. An Historical Geography of Europe. (Illus.). 390p. 1999. pap. text 35.00 (*0-19-874178-2*) OUP.

Butlin, Robin A., jt. ed. see Dodgshon, Robert A.

Butlin, Ron. Histories of Desire. 64p. 1996. pap. 16.95 (*1-85224-339-2*, Pub. by Bloodaxe Bks) Dufour.

— Night Visits. 128p. 1990. pap. text 21.00 (*1-84017-000-X*) St Mut.

Butlin, Ron, ed. Mauritian Voices: New Writing in English. (Illus.). 192p. 1997. pap. 15.95 (*1-873226-24-1*, Pub. by Flambard Pr) Firebird Dist.

Butling, Pauline. Seeing in the Dark: The Poetry of Phyllis Webb. xiv, 184p. 1997. pap. 24.95 (*0-88920-271-0*) W Laurier U Pr.

Butman, A. M., et al. Comprehensive Guide to Prehospital Skills: Comprehensive Guide to Pre-Hospital Skills. (Illus.). 904p. (Orig.). (C). 1995. pap. text 38.95 (*0-940432-09-9*, ET-2475, Emerg Training Inst) Educ Direction.

Butman, Alexander M. Responding to the Mass Casualty Incident: A Guide for EMS Personnel. 1982. 14.50 (*0-940432-02-1*) Educ Direction.

Butman, Alexander M. & Pendagast, Edward L., Jr. The First Minutes: What to Do until the Ambulance Arrives. 3rd rev. ed. Vomacka, Richard W., ed. 148p. 1994. pap. 10.50 (*0-940432-10-2*, ET-2483) Educ Direction.

Butman, Alexander M., et al. Advanced Skills in Emergency Care: A Text for the Intermediate EMT. 1982. 18.50 (*0-940432-01-3*) Educ Direction.

Butman, Alexander M., ed. see National Association of EMT's Pre-Hospital Life Su, et al.

Butman, Boris S., jt. auth. see Hunt, Everett C.

Butman, Harry R. Brown Boy: An Essay on Animal Immortality. (Illus.). 80p. (Orig.). 1989. pap. 7.95 (*0-914598-06-6*) Padre Prods.

— The Desert Face of God: Including Valley of the Valleys: Death Valley Experiences & Desert Flowers: A Sermonic Harvest. rev. ed. (Illus.). 168p. 1985. pap. 10.95 (*0-914598-56-2*) Padre Prods.

Butman, John. FlyingFox: A Business Adventure in Teams & Teamwork. 214p. 1994. pap. 14.95 (*0-8144-7868-9*) AMACOM.

— Juran: A Lifetime of Influence. LC 97-14194. (Illus.). 272p. 1997. 29.95 (*0-471-17210-3*) Wiley.

Butman, Richard E., jt. auth. see Jones, Stanton L.

Butman, Steve, photos by. Landmark Entertaining Vol. 1: Party Traditions & Favorite Recipes from the Junior League of Abileno. (Illus.). 224p. 1996. 24.95 (*0-9611620-0-7*) Jr Leag Abilene.

***Butnariu, Dan & Iusem, Alfredo N.** Totally Convex Functions for Fixed Points Computation. 220p. 2000. 95.00 (*0-7923-6287-X*, Kluwer Plenum) Kluwer Academic.

Butnariu, Dan & Klement, Erich P. Triangular Norm-Based Measures & Games with Fuzzy Coalitions. LC 93-24820. (Theory & Decision Library, Series C, Game Theory, Mathematical Programming, & Operations Research: Vol. 10). 212p. (C). 1993. lib. bdg. 160.50 (*0-7923-2369-6*) Kluwer Academic.

Butnaru, I. C. The Silent Holocaust: Romania & Its Jews, 31. LC 91-21181. (Contributions to the Study of World History Ser.: No. 31). 264p. 1992. 65.00 (*0-313-27985-3*, BFK, Greenwood Pr) Greenwood.

— Waiting for Jerusalem: Surviving the Holocaust in Romania, 37. LC 92-31755. (Contributions to the Study of World History Ser.: No. 37). 280p. 1993. 62.95 (*0-313-28798-8*, GM8798, Greenwood Pr) Greenwood.

Butner, Richard. Mindsnakes: Solving the N-Queen's Problem with One Pawn. (Illus.). 32p. (Orig.). 1988. pap. 4.95 (*0-929133-01-3*) Barefoot Pr.

Butnik, Samuel. Samuel Butnik's Europe: Drawing & Recollections, 1955-56. (Illus.). 56p. Date not set. pap. 10.00 (*1-893023-56-7*) Ohio Artists.

Butola, B. S. Political Economy of Underdevelopment. (C). 1992. text 27.50 (*0-7069-6024-6*, Pub. by Vikas) S Asia.

Butor, Michel. Degres. (FRE.). 1978. pap. 19.95 (*0-7859-2748-4*) Fr & Eur.

— Degres. (Imaginaire Ser.). (FRE.). 1960. 18.95 (*2-07-029734-9*) Schoenhof.

— Emploi du Temps. 1956. pap. 34.95 (*0-7859-0920-6*, F89850) Fr & Eur.

— Essais sur le Roman. (FRE.). 1992. pap. 23.95 (*0-7859-2949-5*) Fr & Eur.

— Essais sur les Modernes. (FRE.). 1992. pap. 30.95 (*0-7859-2948-7*) Fr & Eur.

— Frontiers. Miller, Elinor, tr. from FRE. LC 89-60481. 132p. 1989. pap. 17.95 (*0-917786-67-X*) Summa Pubns.

— Le Genie du Lieu. pap. 17.50 (*0-7859-0638-X*, F89910) Fr & Eur.

— Une Histoire Extraordinaire. (Folio Essais Ser.: No. 87). (FRE.). pap. 11.95 (*2-07-032471-0*) Schoenhof.

— Intervalle. 1973. pap. 8.95 (*0-7859-0656-8*, F60219) Fr & Eur.

— Mobile. (FRE.). 1991. pap. 24.95 (*0-7859-2951-7*) Fr & Eur.

— Mobile. (Imaginaire Ser.). (FRE.). pap. 19.95 (*2-07-072530-8*) Schoenhof.

— La Modification. 1957. pap. 12.95 (*0-7859-0602-9*, F89970) Fr & Eur.

— La Modification. (FRE.). 1980. reprint ed. pap. 16.95 (*0-7859-3299-2*) Fr & Eur.

— Les Mots Dans le Peinture. (Coll. Les Sentiers de la Creation). 14.50 (*0-685-37255-3*, F89980) Fr & Eur.

— Passage de Milan. 1954. pap. 14.95 (*0-7859-0657-6*, F89990) Fr & Eur.

— Portrait of the Artist As a Young Ape. LC 94-36953. 1995. pap. 10.95 (*1-56478-089-9*) Dalkey Arch.

— Portrait of the Artist As a Young Ape. Di Bernardi, Dominic, tr. from FRE. LC 94-36953. 128p. 1995. 19.95 (*1-56478-077-5*) Dalkey Arch.

— La Rose des Vents: 32 Rhumbs pour Charles Fournier. (Coll. Le Chemin). pap. 9.95 (*0-685-37258-8*) Fr & Eur.

— The Spirit of Mediterranean Places. Davis, Lydia, tr. from FRE. LC 97-29552. (Marlboro Travel Ser.). 147p. 1997. pap. 13.95 (*0-8101-6052-8*, Marlboro) Northwestern U Pr.

— Travaux d'Approche. 1972. pap. 10.95 (*0-7859-2771-9*, F90050) Fr & Eur.

***Butorac, George J.** A Better Me, a Better World. LC 98-91008. 1999. 19.50 (*0-533-13018-2*) Vantage.

— Larger Than Life. LC 00-40929. 2000. write for info. (*1-885590-83-0*) Golden West Pub.

Butorac, Yvonne. Great Exits: The 401. LC 95-216389. (Illus.). 160p. 1995. pap. 11.95 (*1-55046-137-0*) Boston Mills.

Butorin, Pavel. Dictionary of Development: Third World Economy, Environment, Society, 2 vols. Welsh, Brian W., ed. LC 90-3051. 1194p. 1990. text 45.00 (*0-8240-1447-2*, SS487) Garland.

Butovsky, M., tr. see Zipper, Jacob.

Butovsky, Mervin, jt. ed. see Robinson, Ira.

Butow, Kurt W. Treatment of Facial Cleft Deformities: An Illustrated Guide. LC \\ (Illus.). xiii, 146p. 1995. pap. 30.00 (*1-56386-032-5*, Ishiyaku EuroAmerica) Med Dent Media.

***Butowski, Piotr & Miller, Jay.** OKB MiG: A History of the Design Bureau & Its Aircraft. (Illus.). 250p. 2000. 39.95 (*0-904597-80-6*, Pub. by Midland Pubng) Specialty Pr.

Butrica, Andrew J. Out of Thin Air: A History of Air Products & Chemicals, Inc., 1940-1990. LC 90-39618. 344p. 1990. 75.00 (*0-275-93765-8*, C3765, Praeger Pubs) Greenwood.

Butrica, James L. The Manuscript Tradition of Propertius. LC 84-225780. (Phoenix Supplementary Ser.: No. 17). (Illus.). 383p. reprint ed. pap. 118.80 (*0-8357-3658-X*, 203638500003) Bks Demand.

Butrick, Lyn M. If This . . . And That . . . Then What. Cooper, William R., ed. LC 83-50783. (My Read & Think Ser.: Set). (Illus.). 27p. (J). (gr. 1-3). 1983. pap. 15.80 (*0-914127-13-6*) Univ Class.

— If This... & That.. Then What, 1. Cooper, William R., ed. LC 83-50783. (My Read & Think Ser.). (Illus.). 27p. (J). (gr. 1-3). 1983. 4.38 (*0-914127-04-7*) Univ Class.

— Logic for Space Age Kids. Cooper, William H., ed. LC 84-50892. (My Read & Think Ser.: Vol. II). (Illus.). 32p. (J). (gr. 3-6). 1984. pap. 5.27 (*0-914127-16-0*) Univ Class.

— Thinking Makes a Difference. Tate, Baird, ed. LC 86-50146. (My Read & Think Ser.: Vol. III). (Illus.). 160p. (J). (gr. 4-8). 1986. student ed. 6.60 (*0-914127-19-5*) Univ Class.

Butrick, Richard, Jr. Carnap on Meaning & Analyticity. LC 78-106469. (Janua Linguarum, Ser. Minor: No. 85). (Orig.). 1970. pap. text 9.25 (*3-11-000277-9*) Mouton.

Butron, Gloria, et al. Lengua Practica y Procesamiento Electronico de Texto. (SPA.). 114p. 1991. pap. 8.25 (*0-8477-3673-3*) U of PR Pr.

Butruille, Susan G. Women's Voices from the Mother Lode, Tales from the California Gold Rush. LC 99-173204. (Women's Voices Ser.). 286p. 1998. pap. text 16.95 (*1-886609-14-4*) Tamarack Bks.

— Women's Voices from the Oregon Trail: The Times That Tried Women's Souls. 2nd ed. LC 96-129516. (Illus.). 253p. (Orig.). 1994. pap. 14.95 (*0-9634839-8-6*) Tamarack Bks.

— Women's Voices from the Western Frontier. 323p. 1995. pap. 16.95 (*1-886609-00-4*) Tamarack Bks.

Butrum, R. R., jt. ed. see Simopoulos, A. P.

Butrum, Ray. I Saw a Slimeball Wiggle. LC 97-46881. (Our Amazing World--Making Science Fun Ser.). (Illus.). (J). (ps-3). 1998. 7.99 (*1-57673-309-2*, Gold n Honey) Zondervan.

— I'm Sorry You Can't Hatch an Egg. LC 97-46882. (God's Amazing World Ser.). (Illus.). (J). (ps-3). 1998. 7.99 (*1-57673-312-2*, Gold n Honey) Zondervan.

— I've Never Seen a Worm Like You. LC 97-46880. (God's Amazing World Ser.). (Illus.). (J). (ps-3). 1998. 7.99 (*1-57673-311-4*, Gold n Honey) Zondervan.

Butrum, Ray & Chapman, Jim. A Raindrop Hit My Nose. (God's Amazing World Ser.). (Illus.). (J). (ps-3). 1998. 7.99 (*1-57673-310-6*, Gold n Honey) Zondervan.

Butrymowicz, Sarah. World So Different. LC 98-37739. (Publish-a-Book Ser.). (gr. 4-7). 1999. pap. text 8.50 (*0-7398-0053-1*) Raintree Steck-V.

Buts, Jean-Paul & Sokal, Etienne M., eds. Management of Digestive & Liver Disorders in Infants & Children. LC 92-48383. 688p. 1993. 329.50 (*0-444-81456-6*) Elsevier.

Butsch, Albert F. Handbook of Renaissance Ornament: 1290 Designs from Decorated Books. Werner, Alfred, ed. & intro. by. LC 68-13685. Orig. Title: Die Bucherornamentik Der Renaissance. (Illus.). 231p. 1969. reprint ed. pap. 13.95 (*0-486-21998-4*) Dover.

Butsch, Charlotte A. American Labor Movement, Student Syllabus. 30p. 1976. pap. text 6.95 (*0-89420-078-X*, 330011); audio 25.60 (*0-89420-206-5*, 330000) Natl Book.

Butsch, Charlotte A., jt. auth. see Salser, Carl W.

Butsch, Charlotte A., ed. see Salser, Carl W., et al.

***Butsch, Richard.** The Making of American Audiences: From Stage to Television, 1750-1990. (Cambridge Studies in the History of Mass Communications). (Illus.). 448p. (C). 2000. 64.95 (*0-521-66253-2*); pap. 24.95 (*0-521-66483-7*) Cambridge U Pr.

Butsch, Richard, ed. For Fun & Profit: The Transformation of Leisure into Consumption. 288p. 1990. 49.95 (*0-87722-676-8*) Temple U Pr.

— For Fun & Profit: The Transformation of Leisure into Consumption. 288p. 1990. pap. 22.95 (*0-87722-740-3*) Temple U Pr.

Butsch, Richard A. Fields of Vision (Writing) A Coherent Approach to Writing as Process Across the Curriculum. 560p. (C). 1991. per. 49.95 (*0-8403-6856-9*) Kendall-Hunt.

Butscher, Berthold, et al, eds. Interactive Distributed Multimedia Systems & Services: European Workshop IDMS '96, Berlin, Germany, March 4-6, 1996: Proceedings. LC 96-10639. (Lecture Notes in Computer Science Ser.: Vol. 1045). xi, 333p. 1996. pap. 56.00 (*3-540-60938-5*) Spr-Verlag.

Butscher, Edward. Amagansett Cycle. LC 79-2525. (Poetry Ser.). (Illus.). 64p. (Orig.). 1979. 15.00 (*0-89304-033-9*, CCC121); pap. 7.50 (*0-89304-034-7*) Cross-Cultrl NY.

— Amagansett Cycle. deluxe limited ed. LC 79-2525. (Poetry Ser.). (Illus.). 64p. (Orig.). 1979. 25.00 (*0-89304-035-5*) Cross-Cultrl NY.

— Child in the House. 87p. (Orig.). 1994. pap. 10.00 (*0-9630164-9-0*) Canios Edit.

— Peter Wild. LC 92-52531. (Western Writers Ser.: No. 106). (Illus.). 53p. (Orig.). 1992. pap. 4.95 (*0-88430-105-2*) Boise St U W Writ Ser.

— Unfinished Sequence. Barkan, Stanley H., ed. (Cross-Cultural Review Chapbook Ser.: No. 6). 20p. 1980. 15.00 (*0-89304-849-6*, CCC131) Cross-Cultrl NY.

— Unfinished Sequence. Barkan, Stanley H., ed. (Cross-Cultural Review Chapbook Ser.: No. 6: American Poetry 3). 20p. 1980. pap. 5.00 (*0-89304-805-4*); audio 10.00 (*0-89304-830-5*) Cross-Cultrl NY.

Butscher, Edward, ed. Sylvia Plath: The Woman & the Work. 242p. 1979. 30.00 (*0-7206-0545-8*, Pub. by P Owen Ltd) Dufour.

Butscher, Edward, jt. ed. see Trachtman, Paula.

Butscher, Stephan A. Customer Clubs & Loyalty Programmes: A Practical Guide. LC 97-48985. 225p. 1998. 86.95 (*0-566-08024-9*, Pub. by Gower) Ashgate Pub Co.

Butson, Denver, et al. Ikons. 156p. 1997. pap. 12.00 (*1-879934-49-3*) St Andrews NC.

Butson, Thomas. Mikhail Gorbachev. (World Leaders Past & Present Ser.). (Illus.). 120p. (Orig.). (YA). (gr. 5 up). 1989. pap. 8.95 (*0-7910-0571-2*) Chelsea Hse.

— Mikhail Gorbachev. (World Leaders Past & Present Ser.). (Illus.). 112p. (Orig.). (YA). (gr. 5 up). 1990. lib. bdg. 19.95 (*1-55546-200-6*) Chelsea Hse.

Butson, Thomas G. The Tsar's Lieutenant: The Soviet Marshall. LC 84-4741. 281p. 1984. 29.95 (*0-275-91735-5*, C1735, Praeger Pubs) Greenwood.

Butt, Betty, jt. auth. see Ford, Mary.

Butt, C. R. & Zeegers, H., eds. Regolith Exploration Geochemistry in Tropical & Subtropical Terrains. (Handbook of Exploration Geochemistry Ser.: 4). xxii,608p. 1992. 267.00 (*0-444-89095-5*) Elsevier.

Butt, David. The English Country Lad. 64p. 1996. 24.95 (*0-85449-239-9*, Pub. by Gay Mens Pr) LPC InBook.

— Talking & Thinking: The Patterns of Behavior. (Language Education Ser.). 120p. 1989. pap. text 12.95 (*0-19-437151-4*) OUP.

— Talking & Thinking: The Patterns of Behaviour. 103p. (C). 1985. pap. 45.00 (*0-7300-0344-2*, ECS806, Pub. by Deakin Univ) St Mut.

— Young & Hairy. 1999. pap. text 25.00 (*0-85449-292-5*) Gay Mens Pr.

***Butt, Gerald.** The Lion in the Sand: The British in the Middle East. (Illus.). 215p. 2000. reprint ed. 27.00 (*0-7881-9378-3*) DIANE Pub.

***Butt, Graham.** Continuum Guide to Geographical Education. 2000. pap. text 26.95 (*0-8264-4793-7*) Continuum.

Butt, Heather, jt. auth. see Washburn, Donna.

Butt, Herbert W. Tests of Eternal Life: Studies in First John. pap. 0.99 (*0-87377-034-X*) GAM Pubns.

Butt, Howard E. Renewing America's Soul: A Spiritual Psychology for Home, Work & Nation. LC 80-5338. 288p. 1996. 19.95 (*0-8264-0880-X*) Continuum.

Butt, Irene, et al, eds. Bibliographie Bildende Kunst: Deutschsprachige Hochschulschriften & Veroffentlichungen Ausserhalb des Buchandels 1966-1980, 6 vols., Set. (GER.). 440p. 1992. lib. bdg. 1135.00 (*3-598-22380-3*) K G Saur Verlag.

Butt, Irene & Eichler, Monika, eds. Bibliographie Medizin: Deutschsprachige Hochschulschriften & VerNffentlichungen Ausserhalb des Buchhandels 1966-1980, 34 vols. (GER.). 420p. 1993. lib. bdg. 4730.00 (*3-598-22499-0*) K G Saur Verlag.

— Bibliographie Religion und Philosophie: Deutschsprachige Hochschulschriften & Veroffentlichungen Ausserhalb des Buchhandels 1966-1980, 5 vols. (GER.). 2091p. 1993. lib. bdg. 925.00 (*3-598-22485-0*) K G Saur Verlag.

— Bibliographie Sprach und Literatur: Deutschsprachige Hochschulschriften & Veroffentlichungen Ausserhalb des Buchhandels 1966-1980, 8 vols., Set. (GER.). 430p. 1992. lib. bdg. 1650.00 (*3-598-22470-2*) K G Saur Verlag.

— Bibliographie Veterinarmedizin: Deutschsprachige Hochschulschriften & Veroffentlichungen Ausserhalb des Buchhandels 1966-1980, 3 vols., Set. (GER.). 330p. 1992. lib. bdg. 295.00 (*3-598-22494-X*) K G Saur Verlag.

Butt, J., ed. Scottish Textile History. (Illus.). 256p. 1987. text 42.00 (*0-08-034511-5*, Pub. by Aberdeen U Pr) Macmillan.

Butt, J. A., et al, eds. Characterization of Spilled Oil Samples: Purpose, Sampling, Analysis & Interpretation. fac. ed. LC 85-17955. (Illus.). 105p. 1994. pap. 32.60 (*0-7837-7662-4*, 204741500007) Bks Demand.

Butt, John. The Age of Johnson, 1740-1789. Carnall, Geoffrey, ed. (Oxford History of English Literature Ser.: Vol. 10). 688p. 1990. 70.00 (*0-19-812236-5*) OUP.

Butt, John. Bach: "Mass in B Minor" (Cambridge Music Handbooks Ser.). (Illus.). 126p. (C). 1991. pap. text 12.95 (*0-521-38716-7*) Cambridge U Pr.

— Music Education & the Art of Performance in the German Baroque. (Cambridge Musical Texts & Monographs). (Illus.). 257p. (C). 1994. text 64.95 (*0-521-43327-4*) Cambridge U Pr.

— Pope's Taste in Shakespeare. LC 74-100736. 1970. reprint ed. pap. 39.95 (*0-8383-0011-1*) M S G Haskell Hse.

— Writers & Politics in Modern Spain. LC 78-18704. (Writers & Politics Ser.). 75p. 1978. pap. 10.50 (*0-8419-0415-4*) Holmes & Meier.

Butt, John, ed. The Cambridge Campanion to Bach. (Cambridge Companions to Music Ser.). (Illus.). 342p. (C). 1997. text 64.95 (*0-521-45350-X*); pap. text 19.95 (*0-521-58780-8*) Cambridge U Pr.

— Oxford Minireference Spanish Grammar. (Minireference Ser.). (SPA.). 364p. 1996. pap. 5.95 (*0-19-864521-X*) OUP.

— Spanish Grammar. 368p. 1997. pap. 7.95 (*0-19-860043-7*) OUP.

— Spanish Verbs: Oxford Minireference. LC 96-10585. 294p. 1997. pap. 6.95 (*0-19-860036-4*) OUP.

Butt, John & Benjamin, Carmen. A New Reference: Grammar of Modern Spanish. 448p. 1989. pap. 32.95 (*0-7131-6612-6*, Pub. by E A) Routldge.

— A New Reference Grammar of Modern Spanish. 2nd ed. 1994. write for info. (*0-340-58390-8*, Pub. by E A) Routldge.

***Butt, John & Benjamin, Carmen.** A New Reference Grammar of Modern Spanish. 3rd ed. LC 99-47014. 540p. 2000. pap. 32.95 (*0-658-00873-0*, 008730) NTC Contemp Pub Co.

Butt, John & Donnachie, Ian, eds. Industrial Archaeology Vol. 6, 1969: The Journal of the History of Industry & Technology, Nos. 1-4. LC 68-23828. (Illus.). 1970. 29.95 (*0-678-05674-9*) Kelley.

Butt, John, et al. The Sacred Choral Music of J. S. Bach: A Handbook. LC 97-29730. 66p. 1997. pap. 11.95 (*1-55725-197-5*, 930-039, Pub. by Paraclete MA) BookWorld.

Butt, John, jt. auth. see Benjamin, Carmen.

Butt, John, ed. see Pope, Alexander.

Butt, John, tr. see Voltaire.

Butt, John B. Reaction Kinetic & Reactor Design. 1980. text 75.00 (*0-13-753335-7*) P-H.

Butt, John E., jt. auth. see Dyson, Henry V.

Butt, M. Munawar. Psychology, Sin, & Society: An Essay on the Triumvirate of Psychology, Religion, & Democracy. 268p. (C). 1992. lib. bdg. 52.00 (*0-8191-8606-6*) U Pr of Amer.

Butt, Malcolm. None Too Fragile: Pearl Jam & Eddie Vedder. 1997. pap. text 16.95 (*0-85965-257-2*, Pub. by Plexus) Publishers Group.

— Sid: Sid Vicious, Rock 'n' Roll Star. (Illus.). 160p. 1996. pap. 15.95 (*0-85965-234-3*, Pub. by Plexus) Publishers Group.

— Special Agent Scully: The Gillian Anderson Files. (Illus.). 112p. 1997. pap. 15.95 (*0-85965-254-8*, Pub. by Plexus) Publishers Group.

Butt, Martha H. Anti-Fanaticism, a Tale of the South. LC 78-39571. reprint ed. 38.50 (*0-404-04575-8*) AMS Pr.

Butt, Miriam & Geuder, Wilhem, eds. The Projection of Arguments: Lexical & Compositional Factors. LC 97-45090. (Lecture Notes Ser.: Vol. 83). 360p. (C). 1998. text 64.95 (*1-57586-111-9*); pap. text 24.95 (*1-57586-110-0*) CSLI.

Butt, Miriam, et al. A Grammar Writer's Cookbook. LC 99-13457. (Lecture Notes Ser.: No. 95). 256p. (C). 1999. pap. text 22.95 (*1-57586-170-4*, Pub. by CSLI) Cambridge U Pr.

— A Grammar Writer's Cookbook. LC 99-13457. (Lecture Notes Ser.: No. 95). 256p. (C). 1999. text 59.95 (*1-57586-171-2*, Pub. by CSLI) Cambridge U Pr.

Butt, Miriam, jt. auth. see King, Tracy.

Butt, Miriam J. The Structure of Complex Predicates in Urdu. (Dissertations in Linguistics Ser.). 1995. 49.95 (*1-881526-59-3*); pap. 22.95 (*1-881526-58-5*) CSLI.

Butt, Miriam J., et al, eds. Theoretical Perspectives on Word Order in South Asian Languages. (CSLI Lecture Notes Ser.). 1995. pap. 22.95 (*0-521-52649-3*) Cambridge U Pr.

Butt, P. Butterworths Statutes - Property Law New South Wales. LC 94-238126. 504p. 1994. pap. write for info. (*0-409-31003-4*, MICHIE) LEXIS Pub.

Butt, P. J. The Standard Contract for Sale of Land in N. S. W. lxxxiv, 948p. 1985. suppl. ed. 168.50 (*0-455-20697-X*, Pub. by LawBk Co) Gaunt.

Butt, Paul D. The Successful Organized Stockbroker, 2 vols., Set. (Illus.). 83p. (Orig.). pap. 125.00 (*0-9635346-0-2*) Buttonwd Pub.

Butt, Peter. Land Law. 2nd ed. liii, 668p. 1988. pap. 61.50 (*0-455-20789-5*, Pub. by LawBk Co) Gaunt.

— Land Law. 3rd ed. 790p. 1996. 125.00 (*0-455-21358-5*, Pub. by LawBk Co); pap. 90.00 (*0-455-21359-3*, Pub. by LawBk Co) Gaunt.

Butt, Peter & Eagleson, Robert. Mabo: What the High Court Said. 128p. 1993. pap. 21.00 (*1-86287-118-3*, Pub. by Federation Pr) Gaunt.

— Mabo Vol. 1: What the High Court Said & What the Government Did. 2nd ed. 99p. 1996. pap. 24.00 (*1-86287-207-4*, Pub. by Federation Pr) Gaunt.

Butt, Sheila K. If Thine Heart Be Wise: A Practical Manual for Christian Mothers. (Practical Family Ser.). (Illus.). 160p. (Orig.). 1992. pap. 6.95 (*0-9632021-0-3*) Heart Wise.

Butt, Stephen, jt. auth. see Gee, Paul.

***Butt, T., et al, eds.** Fungal Biocontrol Agents: Progress, Problems & Potential. (CABI Publishing Ser.). 350p. 2000. text 100.00 (*0-85199-356-7*) OUP.

Butt-Thompson, Frederick W. West African Secret Societies: Their Organizations, Officials & Teaching. 1969. reprint ed. 20.00 (*0-87266-003-6*) Argosy.

— West African Secret Societies, Their Organizations, Officials & Teaching. LC 70-109320. (Illus.). 320p. 1970. reprint ed. lib. bdg. 52.50 (*0-8371-3585-0*, BWA&, Greenwood Pr) Greenwood.

Butt, Wilfrid. Practical Immunoassay. (Clinical & Biochemical Analysis Ser.: Vol. 14). (Illus.). 328p. 1984. text 175.00 (*0-8247-7094-3*) Dekker.

Butt, William. Churchill Downs Museum Book. (Illus.). 40p. (Orig.). 1986. pap. 4.95 (*0-916509-05-2*) Harmony Hse Pub.

Butta, Phyllis. Informed Consent & Voluntary Sterilization: An Implementation Guide for Program Managers. rev. ed. 26p. 1994. reprint ed. pap. text 5.00 (*1-885063-03-2*) AVSC Int.

Buttaci, Sal St. John, see St. John Buttaci, Sal.

Buttaci, Salvatore A. A Family of Sicilians: Stories & Poems. LC 98-96208. 125p. 1998. pap. 12.95 (*0-917398-21-1*) A M Buttaci.

— Promising the Moon. 100p. 1998. pap. 9.95 (*0-917398-20-3*) A M Buttaci.

Buttaci, Salvatore S. & Gerstle, Susan L., eds. Reflections of the Inward Silence. LC 76-19240. 1976. pap. 7.95 (*0-917398-04-1*) A M Buttaci.

Buttaci, Salvatore St. John. Coming-Home Poems: Stops & Pauses on the Scrapbook Express. 64p. 1974. pap. 2.00 (*0-917398-00-9*) A M Buttaci.

***Buttafuoco, Grazia & Varetto, Dede.** Great Book of Egg Decorating. 128p. 1999. 24.95 (*0-8069-5911-8*) Sterling.

***Buttaro, Peter J.** Legal Guide for Long-Term Care Administrators. LC 99-32771. (Long Term Care Administration Ser.). 240p. 1999. pap. 59.00 (*0-8342-1370-2*) Aspen Pub.

Buttaro, Peter J. Principles of Long-Term Health Care Administration. LC 99-14786. 300p. 1999. pap. text 99.00 (*0-8342-1371-0*) Aspen Pub.

***Buttaro, Raymond A.** Step-by-Step Guide to a Higher Score on the Nab Exam. LC 98-32393. 128p. 1999. pap. 55.00 (*0-8342-1314-1*) Aspen Pub.

Buttaro, Terry Mahan, et al, eds. Primary Care: A Collaborative Approach. LC 99-26596. (Illus.). 1450p. 1999. text 84.95 (*0-8151-3823-7*, 31844) Mosby Inc.

Buttarovoli. Minor Emergencies. LC 99-40670. 1999. pap. text 34.95 (*0-323-00756-2*) Mosby Inc.

Buttazzo, G., et al. Developments in Partial Differential Equations & Applications to Mathematical Physics. (Illus.). 252p. (C). 1993. text 85.00 (*0-306-44311-2*, Kluwer Plenum) Kluwer Academic.

Buttazzo, G., ed. see Ambrosio, L., et al.

Buttazzo, Giorgio C. Hard Real-Time Computing Systems: Predictable Scheduling Algorithms & Applications. LC 97-26718. (The Kluwer International Series in Engineering & Computer Science: No. 416). 379p. 1997. text 96.50 (*0-7923-9994-3*) Kluwer Academic.

Buttazzo, Giuseppe & Visintin, Augusto, eds. Motion by Mean Curvature & Related Topics: Proceedings of the International Conference Held at Trento, July 20-24, 1992. LC 94-680. viii, 219p. (C). 1994. lib. bdg. 104.95 (*3-11-013881-6*) De Gruyter.

Buttazzo, Giuseppe, et al. One-Dimensional Variational Problems Vol. 15: An Introduction. LC 99-214744. (Oxford Lecture Series in Mathematics & Its Applications: 15). (Illus.). 270p. 1999. text 65.00 (*0-19-850465-9*) OUP.

Butte, Charles D. Grampa: A Memoir. LC 98-107557. 1997. write for info. (*0-9656022-3-0*) SPUMC.

Butte County, California Pen Women Staff. Ripples along Chico Creek: Perspectives on People & Times. LC 91-73882. (Illus.). 250p. 1992. pap. 22.95 (*0-9631582-2-8*) NL Am Pen Women.

Buttel, Frederick H. & Newby, Howard, eds. The Rural Sociology of the Advanced Societies: Critical Perspectives. LC 79-5177. 538p. 1980. pap. text 29.00 (*0-916672-34-4*) Rowman.

Buttel, Frederick H., et al. The Sociology of Agriculture, 88. LC 89-17099. (Contributions in Sociology Ser.: No. 88). 283p. 1990. 59.95 (*0-313-26444-9*, BUT/, Greenwood Pr) Greenwood.

Buttel, Robert. Seamus Heaney. Carens, James F., ed. (Irish Writers Ser.). 1990. pap. 1.95 (*0-8387-1568-0*) Bucknell U Pr.

Buttel, Robert, jt. ed. see Doggett, Frank.

Buttenfield, B. P. Map Generalization: Making Rules for Knowledge Representation. 1991. 115.32 (*0-582-08062-2*, Pub. by Addison-Wesley) Longman.

Buttenheim, Alison. Nonprofit Consultants: How to Choose Them, How to Use Them. 20p. 1998. pap. 10.00 (*1-892233-02-9*) SCCNM.

***Buttenwieser, Ann L.** Manhattan Water-Bound: Manhattan's Waterfront from the Seventeenth Century to the Present. 2nd ed. LC 98-55154. (New York City History & Culture Ser.). 296p. 1999. pap. 19.95 (*0-8156-2801-3*) Syracuse U Pr.

Buttenwieser, Moses. The Psalms: Chronologically Treated with a New Translation. rev. ed. (Library of Biblical Studies). 1969. 79.50 (*0-87068-044-7*) Ktav.

Butter, Anton J. An Introduction to Mini-Economics. 142p. (Orig.). 1985. pap. 27.00 (*90-6032-263-0*, Pub. by B R Gruner) Humanities.

— A Road to Full Employment: An Essay on Regulation, Deregulation, Enterprise Zones & the Producibility of Jobs. 108p. (Orig.). 1982. pap. 21.00 (*90-6032-239-8*, Pub. by B R Gruner) Humanities.

Butter, E. & Brown, M. A Gendering Skill Conversations Around Women Work & Skill: An Australian Perspective. 1992. pap. 45.00 (*0-7300-1714-1*, Pub. by Deakin Univ) St Mut.

Butter, Francis J. Locks & Lockmaking. (Illus.). 142p. 1985. pap. 15.00 (*0-87556-724-X*) Saifer.

Butter, Irene, ed. see Simmons, Ruth J.

Butter, P. H., ed. Shelley--Alastor & Other Poems, Prometheus Unbound with Other Poems, Adonais. (Illus.). 368p. 1980. reprint ed. pap. 13.95 (*0-7121-0145-4*) Trans-Atl Phila.

Butter, P. H., ed. see Blake, William.

Butter, Peter. Shelley's Idols of the Cave. LC 68-24118. (Studies in Shelley: No. 25). 1969. reprint ed. lib. bdg. 75.00 (*0-8383-0781-7*) M S G Haskell Hse.

Butter, Peter, ed. William Blake. (Everyman's Poetry Ser.). 116p. 1997. pap. 1.95 (*0-460-87800-X*, Everyman's Classic Lib) Tuttle Pubng.

Butter, Peter H. Edwin Muir: Man & Poet. LC 76-11018. 314p. 1977. reprint ed. lib. bdg. 38.50 (*0-8371-8169-0*, BUEM, Greenwood Pr) Greenwood.

— The Truth of Imagination: Essays & Reviews by Edwin Muir. 274p. (C). 1988. text 29.90 (*0-08-036392-X*, Pub. by Aberdeen U Pr) Macmillan.

Butter, Stephen, jt. auth. see Spurgeon, Charles H.

Butterfass, T. Patterns of Chloroplast Reproduction. (Cell Biology Monographs: Vol. 6). (Illus.). 1980. 106.95 (*0-387-81541-4*) Spr-Verlag.

Butterfield. Art for Children: How to Do Creative Crafts. 96p. (J). 1995. 12.98 (*0-7858-0464-1*) Bk Sales Inc.

— Excellence in Advertising. 256p. 2000. pap. text 37.95 (*0-7506-3129-5*) Buttrwrth-Heinemann.

***Butterfield, Andrew.** Masterpieces of Renaissance Sculpture. (Illus.). (C). 1999. 45.00 (*1-58821-001-4*) Salander OReilly.

Butterfield, Andrew. The Sculptures of Andrea del Verrocchio. LC 97-13650. 288p. 1997. 65.00 (*0-300-07194-9*) Yale U Pr.

Butterfield, Arthur. Spanish-English - English-Spanish Practical Dictionary. enl. rev. ed. (Practical Dictionaries Ser.). 338p. 1993. pap. 9.95 (*0-7818-0179-6*) Hippocrene Bks.

Butterfield, Arthur S. Diccionario Bolsillo Cuyas Ingles-Espanol, Espanol-Ingles. (ENG & SPA.). 464p. 1985. pap. 14.95 (*0-7859-6248-4*, 8476400268) Fr & Eur.

Butterfield, B. G., jt. auth. see Meylan, B. A.

Butterfield, Barbara, et al. Incentive Pay: A Plan to Recognize Major Contributions by Individuals, Teams, or Departmental Units. 16p. 1995. 7.50 (*1-878240-43-9*) Coll & U Personnel.

— Workplace Alternatives: How to Make Them Work for Your Institution. 39p. 1993. 20.00 (*1-878240-22-6*) Coll & U Personnel.

***Butterfield, Barbara S., et al, eds.** Process & Organizational Redesign: Leading Change in Colleges & Universities. 132p. 1998. pap. 29.99 (*1-878240-68-4*) Coll & U Personnel.

Butterfield, Barbara S. & Wolfe, Susan. You Can Get There from Here: The Road to Downsizing in Higher Education. 136p. 1994. 20.00 (*1-878240-38-2*) Coll & U Personnel.

Butterfield, Bruce. The Mill. 2001. 25.00 (*0-06-019103-1*) HarpC.

***Butterfield, Bruce.** The Mill. 2002. pap. 13.00 (*0-06-093057-8*, Perennial) HarperTrade.

Butterfield, Bruce, jt. ed. see Kleist, Jurgen.

Butterfield, Bruce A., jt. ed. see Kleist, Jurgen.

Butterfield, C. W. An Historical Account of the Expedition Against Sandusky under Col. William Crawford. (Illus.). 403p. 1993. reprint ed. lib. bdg. 43.00 (*0-8328-2993-5*) Higginson Bk Co.

— An Historical Account of the Expedition Against Sandusky under Col. William Crawford in 1782. (Ohio History, Historic Indians, Revolutionary War Ser.). 419p. (C). 1990. reprint ed. pap. 47.00 (*1-56651-004-X*); reprint ed. lib. bdg. 64.10 (*1-56651-005-8*); reprint ed. fiche 3.35 (*1-56651-006-6*) A W McGraw.

Butterfield, Catherine. Joined at the Head. rev. ed. LC 99-205462. 1998. pap. 5.25 (*0-8222-1659-0*) Dramatists Play.

— Snowing at Delphi. 1994. pap. 5.25 (*0-8222-1377-X*) Dramatists Play.

Butterfield, Clare & Johnston, L. Recognitions. William, Johnston et al, eds. (Chapbook Ser.: No. 11). 18p. 1983. pap. 3.00 (*0-932884-10-5*) Red Herring.

Butterfield, Consul W. History of Lt. Col. George Rogers Clark's Conquest of the Illinois & Wabash Towns. LC 72-8729. (American Revolutionary Ser.). reprint ed. lib. bdg. 62.00 (*0-8398-0188-2*) Irvington.

— History of Seneca County, Containing a Detailed Narrative of the Principal Events That Have Occured since Its First Settlement...with Biographical Sketches. 252p. 1995. reprint ed. lib. bdg. 35.00 (*0-8328-4727-5*) Higginson Bk Co.

— History of the Girtys. 1993. reprint ed. lib. bdg. 89.00 (*0-7812-5348-9*) Rprt Serv.

Butterfield, Consul W., ed. see Savage, James W. & Bell, John T.

Butterfield, Cousul W. Girty. History of the Girtys, Being a Concise Account of the Girty Brothers - Thomas, Simon, James, & George, & Their Half-Brother John Turner - Also of the Part Taken by Them in Lord Dunsmore's War, the Western Border War of the Revolution, & the Indian War, 1790-95. 425p. 1995. reprint ed. pap. 42.50 (*0-8328-4874-3*); reprint ed. lib. bdg. 52.50 (*0-8328-4873-5*) Higginson Bk Co.

Butterfield, D. Allen, ed. Biofunctional Membranes. (Illus.). 306p. (C). 1996. text 89.50 (*0-306-45281-2*, Kluwer Plenum) Kluwer Academic.

Butterfield, Deb. Showdown with Diabetes. LC 99-19651. 256p. 1999. text 23.95 (*0-393-04753-9*) Norton.

***Butterfield, Deb.** Showdown with Diabetes. 282p. 2000. reprint ed. pap. 14.95 (*0-393-32083-9*) Norton.

Butterfield, E. C., jt. ed. see Carlson, Jerry.

Butterfield, Fox. All God's Children: The Bosket Family & the American Tradition of Violence. LC 95-1540. (Illus.). 416p. 1995. 30.00 (*0-394-58286-1*) Knopf.

— All God's Children: The Bosket Family & the American Tradition of Violence. LC 95-1540. 416p. 1996. pap. 15.00 (*0-380-72862-1*, Avon Bks) Morrow Avon.

Butterfield, Herbert. The Origins of Modern Science. 1997. 16.95 (*0-684-83637-8*) Free Pr.

— The Origins of Modern Science. rev. ed. 1965. pap. 16.95 (*0-02-905070-7*) Free Pr.

— The Whig Interpretation of History. LC 75-41043. (BCL Ser. II). reprint ed. 32.50 (*0-404-14515-9*) AMS Pr.

Butterfield, I., jt. auth. see Cribb, P. J.

Butterfield, Isabel. Manhattan Tales 1920-1945. (Illus.). 182p. 1999. 29.50 (*1-85776-367-X*, Pub. by Book Guild Ltd) Trans-Atl Phila.

Butterfield, Jan. The Art of Light & Space. (Illus.). 272p. 1996. 65.00 (*1-55859-272-5*); pap. 39.95 (*0-7892-0171-2*) Abbeville Pr.

Butterfield, Jan, jt. auth. see Albright, Thomas.

Butterfield, Jeremy, ed. The Arguments of Time. (Illus.). 272p. 2000. 49.95 (*0-19-726207-4*) OUP.

***Butterfield, Jeremy & Pagonis, Constantine, eds.** From Physics to Philosophy. LC 99-11531. (Illus.). 248p. (C). 1999. 59.95 (*0-521-66025-4*) Cambridge U Pr.

Butterfield, Jeremy, et al. Spacetime. (International Research Library of Philosophy). (Illus.). 500p. 1996. text 173.95 (*1-85521-640-X*, Pub. by Dartmth Pub) Ashgate Pub Co.

Butterfield, Jim. Driving the Amish. LC 96-49840. (Illus.). 112p. (Orig.). 1997. pap. 14.99 (*0-8361-9063-7*) Herald Pr.

Butterfield, Jody, jt. auth. see Savory, Allan.

Butterfield, L. H., ed. see Adams, Abigail S. & Adams, John.

Butterfield, L. H., ed. see Adams, Abigail & Adams, John.

Butterfield, L. H., ed. see Adams, John.

***Butterfield, Leslie & Institute of Practitioners in Advertising Staff.** Excellence in Advertising: The IPA Guide to Best Practice. 2nd ed. LC 99-43468. 304p. 1999. pap. text 37.95 (*0-7506-4479-6*) Buttrwrth-Heinemann.

Butterfield, Lindsay P. Roses & Other Flower Designs. LC 96-36599. (Illus.). 48p. 1997. pap. 5.95 (*0-486-29417-X*) Dover.

Butterfield, Lyman, jt. auth. see Lumpkin, William L.

Butterfield, M. Air Travel Games. (Travel Games Ser.). (Illus.). 32p. (J). (gr. 2 up). 1986. pap. 4.95 (*0-86020-997-0*) EDC.

— Art for Children: Papercraft. 96p. 1996. 12.98 (*0-7858-0635-0*) Bk Sales Inc.

— How to Draw Machines. (Young Artist Ser.). 32p. (J). (gr. 4 up). 1988. pap. 4.95 (*0-7460-0175-4*); lib. bdg. 12.95 (*0-88110-316-0*) EDC.

Butterfield, M., jt. auth. see Peach, S.

Butterfield, M., jt. auth. see Potter, T.

***Butterfield, Maria.** Oceans. (On the Spot Ser.). 16p. (gr. 4-6). 2000. 7.99 (*1-57584-377-3*) Rdrs Digest.

Butterfield, Moira. Amazon Rainforest. (Wildlife World Ser.). (Illus.). 16p. (J). 1992. pap. 7.95 (*0-8249-8566-4*, Ideals Child) Hambleton-Hill.

— Animals in Cold Places. LC 99-11583. (Looking at Ser.). 32p. (J). 1999. 22.83 (*0-7398-0111-2*) Raintree Steck-V.

— Animals in Cold Places. 32p. (J). (gr. k-3). 1999. pap. 5.95 (*0-7398-0714-5*) Raintree Steck-V.

— Animals in Hot Places. LC 99-10180. (Looking at Ser.). 32p. (J). 1999. 22.83 (*0-7398-0112-0*) Raintree Steck-V.

— Animals in Hot Places. 32p. (J). (gr. k-3). 1999. pap. 5.95 (*0-7398-0715-3*) Raintree Steck-V.

***Butterfield, Moira.** Animals in Rivers & Lakes. LC 98-53204. 32p. (J). 1999. lib. bdg. 22.83 (*0-7398-0108-2*) Raintree Steck-V.

Butterfield, Moira. Animals in the Oceans. LC 98-51599. (Looking at Ser.). 32p. (J). 1999. lib. bdg. 22.83 (*0-7398-0107-4*) Raintree Steck-V.

— Animals in the Oceans. 1999. pap. 5.95 (*0-7398-0717-X*) Raintree Steck-V.

***Butterfield, Moira.** Animals in Trees. LC 99-17902. (Looking at Ser.). (J). 1999. lib. bdg. 22.83 (*0-7398-0110-4*) Raintree Steck-V.

— Animals in Trees. 32p. (J). (gr. k-3). 1999. pap. 5.95 (*0-7398-0716-1*) Raintree Steck-V.

Butterfield, Moira. Animals on Plains & Prairies. LC 99-17901. (Looking at Ser.). 32p. (J). 1999. lib. bdg. 22.83 (*0-7398-0109-0*) Raintree Steck-V.

***Butterfield, Moira.** Arctic. (Where Am I? Ser.). (Illus.). 32p. (J). (gr. 2-6). 1999. lib. bdg. 15.95 (*1-929298-34-X*, Pub. by Thameside Pr) Smart Apple.

Butterfield, Moira. Art for Children: How to Do Creative Crafts. 96p. (J). 1995. 12.98 (*0-7858-0463-3*) Bk Sales Inc.

— Art for Children: Imaginative Craft Techniques, Practical Printing Ideas & Fantastic Paper Projects. (Illus.). (J). 1998. 19.99 (*0-7858-0747-0*) Bk Sales Inc.

— Big, Rough, & Wrinkly. LC 96-32109. (What Am I? Ser.). (Illus.). 32p. (J). (ps-3). 1997. lib. bdg. 19.97 (*0-8172-4584-7*) Raintree Steck-V.

— Big, Rough & Wrinkly. (What Am I? Ser.). 1998. pap. 5.95 (*0-8172-7232-1*) Raintree Steck-V.

— Book of London. (City Guide Ser.). (Illus.). 64p. (J). (gr. 5 up). 1987. pap. 8.95 (*0-7460-0050-2*) EDC.

— Bouncy, Big, & Furry. (What Am I? Ser.). (Illus.). 32p. (J). (gr. k-3). 1997. pap. 5.95 (*0-8172-7228-3*) Raintree Steck-V.

— Bouncy, Big, & Furry. LC 97-5404. (What Am I? Ser.). (Illus.). 32p. (J). (ps-3). 1998. lib. bdg. 19.97 (*0-8172-4589-8*) Raintree Steck-V.

— Bright, Lively & Loud. (What Am I? Ser.). (Illus.). 32p. (J). (gr. k-3). 1997. pap. 5.95 (*0-8172-7227-5*) Raintree Steck-V.

— Brown, Fierce & Furry. LC 96-32111. (What Am I? Ser.). (Illus.). 32p. (J). (ps-3). 1997. lib. bdg. 19.97 (*0-8172-4586-3*) Raintree Steck-V.

— Brown, Fierce & Furry. (What Am I? Ser.). 1998. pap. 5.95 (*0-8172-7230-5*) Raintree Steck-V.

— Bulldozers & Other Construction Machines. (Illus.). (J). pap. 8.99 (*0-590-24556-2*) Scholastic Inc.

— Creative Crafts. (Crafts for Children Ser.). (Illus.). 32p. (YA). (gr. 3 up). 1997. pap. 4.95 (*1-56010-212-8*, CC02) W Foster Pub.

***Butterfield, Moira.** Desert. (Where Am I? Ser.). 32p. (J). (gr. 2-6). 1999. lib. bdg. 15.95 (*1-929298-35-8*, Pub. by Thameside Pr) Smart Apple.

Butterfield, Moira. The Earth. LC 92-53101. (One-Thousand Facts about . . . Ser.). (Illus.). 48p. (J). (gr. 3-8). 1992. pap. 8.95 (*1-85697-808-7*, Kingfisher) LKC.

— Fast, Strong & Striped. LC 96-32110. (What Am I? Ser.). (Illus.). 32p. (J). (ps-3). 1997. lib. bdg. 19.97 (*0-8172-4583-9*) Raintree Steck-V.

— Fast, Strong & Striped. (What Am I? Ser.). 1998. pap. 5.95 (*0-8172-7229-1*) Raintree Steck-V.

— Fierce, Strong, & Snappy. (What Am I? Ser.). (Illus.). 32p. (J). (gr. k-3). 1997. pap. 4.95 (*0-8172-7225-9*) Raintree Steck-V.

— Fierce, Strong, & Snappy. LC 96-54493. (What Am I? Ser.). (Illus.). 32p. (J). (ps-3). 1998. lib. bdg. 19.97 (*0-8172-4588-X*) Raintree Steck-V.

— Goldilocks & the Three Bears. LC 97-42685. (Puppet Play Ser.). (J). 1998. (*1-57572-720-X*) Heinemann Lib.

— Hansel & Gretel. LC 97-24134. (Playtales Ser.). (J). 1998. 19.92 (*1-57572-648-3*) Heinemann Lib.

— How to Draw & Paint the Outdoors. 96p. (J). 1994. 12.98 (*1-55521-912-8*) Bk Sales Inc.

— How to Draw & Paint the Outdoors. (Art for Children Ser.). (Illus.). 32p. (YA). (gr. 3 up). 1997. pap. 4.95 (*1-56010-253-5*, AC03) W Foster Pub.

— Jumpy, Green, & Croaky. (What Am I? Ser.). (Illus.). 32p. (J). (gr. k-3). 1997. pap. 4.95 (*0-8172-7226-7*) Raintree Steck-V.

— Jumpy, Green, & Croaky. LC 97-8049. (What Am I? Ser.). (Illus.). 32p. (J). (ps-3). 1998. lib. bdg. 19.97 (*0-8172-4591-X*) Raintree Steck-V.

— Look Inside Cross-Sections: Jets. (Look Inside Cross-Sections Ser.). (Illus.). 32p. (J). 1996. pap. 6.95 (*0-7894-0767-1*) DK Pub Inc.

— Nature Cross-Section. LC 94-44798. (Illus.). 32p. (J). (gr. 5-8). 1995. 17.95 (*0-7894-0147-9*, 5-70599) DK Pub Inc.

***Butterfield, Moira.** Ocean. (Where Am I? Ser.). (Illus.). 32p. (J). (gr. 2-6). 1999. lib. bdg. 15.95 (*1-929298-36-6*, Pub. by Thameside Pr) Smart Apple.

— Pet of My Own: A Caring Guide to Pets. (Illus.). 2000. pap. 4.95 (*1-902618-22-X*, Pub. by Element Childrns) Penguin Putnam.

Butterfield, Moira. Pizza, Fries & a Slice of Pie. LC 97-22348. (Can You Find? Ser.). (Illus.). (J). 1998. pap. write for info. (*0-382-39988-9*) Silver Burdett Pr.

— Puss in Boots. LC 97-27966. (Playtales Ser.). (J). 1998. 19.92 (*1-57572-649-1*) Heinemann Lib.

— Quick, Quiet & Feathered. LC 96-30860. (What Am I? Ser.). (Illus.). 32p. (J). (ps-3). 1997. lib. bdg. 19.97 (*0-8172-4585-5*) Raintree Steck-V.

— Quick, Quiet & Feathered. (What Am I? Ser.). 1998. pap. 5.95 (*0-8172-7233-X*) Raintree Steck-V.

***Butterfield, Moira.** Rainforest. (Where Am I? Ser.). (Illus.). 32p. (J). (gr. 2-6). 1999. lib. bdg. 15.95 (*1-929298-37-4*, Pub. by Thameside Pr) Smart Apple.

— Sea Life: Four Exciting Information Board Books. LC 98-183801. (Carry Cases Ser.). (Illus.). 10p. (J). (ps-1). 1998. bds. 7.98 (*0-7651-0701-5*) Smithmark.

Butterfield, Moira. Sleeping Beauty. LC 97-27967. (Playtales Ser.). (J). 1998. 19.92 (*1-57572-651-3*) Heinemann Lib.

— Space. LC 94-18480. (Look Inside Cross-Sections Ser.). (Illus.). 32p. (J). (gr. 1-4). 1994. pap. 5.95 (*1-56458-682-0*) DK Pub Inc.

— Space. (Illus.). 32p. (J). pap. 8.99 (*0-590-24424-8*) Scholastic Inc.

— Switches, Doors, Knobs, & Drawers. LC 97-18466. (Can You Find It Ser.). (Illus.). (J). 1998. write for info. (*0-382-39991-9*); pap. write for info. (*0-382-39990-0*) Silver Press.

— The Three Little Pigs. LC 97-42680. (Puppet Play Ser.). (J). 1998. (*1-57572-719-6*) Heinemann Lib.

— The Tortoise & the Hare. LC 97-42679. (Puppet Play Ser.). (J). 1998. (*1-57572-721-8*) Heinemann Lib.

— The Ugly Duckling. LC 97-42684. (Puppet Play Ser.). (J). 1998. (*1-57572-722-6*) Heinemann Lib.

— Undersea. (Wildlife World Ser.). (Illus.). 16p. (J). (gr. 1-5). 1992. pap. 6.95 (*0-8249-8589-3*, Ideals Child) Hambleton-Hill.

***Butterfield, Moira.** Where Am I?, 4 vols. 32p. (J). 1999. lib. bdg. 63.80 (*1-929298-38-2*, Pub. by Thameside Pr) Smart Apple.

— Why? (J). 2000. 17.95 (*1-902618-93-9*, Pub. by Element Childrns) Penguin Putnam.

Butterfield, Moira. Wild Animals. LC 92-53114. (One-Thousand Facts about . . . Ser.). (Illus.). 48p. (J). (gr. 3-8). 1992. pap. 8.95 (*1-85697-809-5*, Kingfisher) LKC.

Butterfield, Moira & Ford, Wayne. Bright, Lively & Loud. LC 96-54599. (What Am I? Ser.). (Illus.). 32p. (J). (ps-3). 1998. lib. bdg. 19.97 (*0-8172-4590-1*) Raintree Steck-V.

Butterfield, Moira & Howe, Christine. Learning Clock. (J). 4.98 (*1-57717-128-4*) Todtri Prods.

Butterfield, Moira & Jenssen, Hans. Jets. (Illus.). 32p. (J). 1996. pap. 8.99 (*0-590-24939-8*) Scholastic Inc.

Butterfield, Moira & Lewis, Jan. Buttons, Buckles, Belts & Bows. LC 97-19795. (Can You Find? Ser.). (J). 1999. write for info. (*0-382-39984-6*); pap. write for info. (*0-382-39985-4*) Silver Burdett Pr.

— Pizza, Fries & a Slice of Pie. LC 97-22348. (Can You Find? Ser.). (Illus.). (J). 1998. lib. bdg. write for info. (*0-382-39989-7*) Silver Burdett Pr.

— Wheels, Wings, & Moving Things. LC 97-19102. (Can You Find? Ser.). (J). 1999. write for info. (*0-382-39987-0*) Silver Burdett Pr.

Butterfield, Moira & Wright, Nicola. Getting to Know Britain: People, Places. LC 93-29716. (Getting to Know Ser.). (Illus.). 32p. (J). (gr. 3-7). 1994. 12.95 (*0-8120-6392-9*); pap. 5.95 (*0-8120-1854-0*) Barron.

Butterfield, Moira, et al. Record Breakers & Other Speed Machines. (Illus.). 32p. (J). pap. 8.99 (*0-590-24653-4*) Scholastic Inc.

Butterfield, Moira, jt. auth. see Potter, Tony.

Butterfield, Moria. Little Red Riding Hood. LC 97-27965. (Playtales Ser.). (J). 1998. 19.92 (*1-57572-650-5*) Heinemann Lib.

Butterfield, Moria, jt. auth. see Edom, Helen.

Butterfield, Nancy, et al. Partners in Everyday Communicative Exchanges: A Guide to Promoting Interaction Involving People with Severe Intellectual Disability. 1995. 43.00 (*1-55766-241-X*) P H Brookes.

Butterfield, Nancy, ed. see Barrett, John P.

Butterfield, Oliver M. Sex Life in Marriage. (Illus.). 12.95 (*0-87523-035-0*) Emerson.

Butterfield, Perry M., jt. auth. see Dolezal, Sue.

Butterfield, Ralph, ed. Patton's GI Photographers. LC 92-5229. (Illus.). 192p. 1992. 39.95 (*0-8138-0216-4*) Iowa St U Pr.

Butterfield, Ron. Woodcarving: A Complete Course. (Illus.). 128p. 1992. pap. 14.95 (*0-946819-04-1*, Pub. by Guild Master) Sterling.

Butterfield, Sherri M. I'm Following Directions. (Skill Builders Ser.). (Illus.). 32p. (J). (gr. 1-3). 1995. pap. 4.95 (*0-88160-266-3*, LW815) Learning Wks.

Butterfield, Stephen. Amway: The Cult of Free Enterprise. LC 85-2133. 187p. 1985. 30.00 (*0-89608-254-7*); pap. 14.00 (*0-89608-253-9*) South End Pr.

— Amway: The Cult of Free Enterprise. LC 86-90130. (Black Rose Bks.: Vol. O95). 191p. 1986. reprint ed. pap. 59.30 (*0-608-00463-4*, 206128200007) Bks Demand.

— The Double Mirror: A Skeptical Journey into Buddhist Tantra. LC 93-39497. 270p. (Orig.). (C). 1994. pap. 14.95 (*1-55643-176-7*) North Atlantic.

Butterfield, Stephen, ed. see Burton, Bruce A.

Butterfield, Stephen, ed. see Pohl, Frederick J.

Butterfield, Sue. Educational Objectives & National Assessment. LC 94-23672. (Assessing Assessment Ser.). 256p. 1995. pap. 31.95 (*0-335-19418-4*) Taylor & Francis.

Butterfield, Suzanne K., et al. Color Palettes: Painted Rooms for Particular Places. LC 97-20914. 1998. 40.00 (*0-609-60144-X*) C Potter.

Butterick, Crim & George, Keith. Interpreters Dictionary of the Bible, Vol. 01. 1966. pap. 44.95 (*0-687-19270-6*) Abingdon.

— Interpreters Dictionary of the Bible, Vol. 02. 1966. pap. 44.95 (*0-687-19271-4*) Abingdon.

— Interpreters Dictionary of the Bible, Vol. 04. 1966. pap. 44.95 (*0-687-19273-0*) Abingdon.

Butterick, Crim, et al. Interpreters Dictionary of the Bible, Vol. 3. LC 62-9387. Vol. 3. (Illus.). 1966. pap. 44.95 (*0-687-19272-2*) Abingdon.

***Butterick Editors.** 101 Crafts under L6: Easy to Make Ideas for Gifts & Home. (Illus.). 160p. 2000. write for info. (*1-57389-025-1*) Butterick Co.

Butterick, George. The Collected Poems of George Butterick. Blevins, Richard W., ed. 256p. (Orig.). (C). 1988. pap. 8.00 (*0-922668-00-0*) SUNYB Poetry Rare Bks.

— Editing the Maximus Poems. (Illus.). 125p. 1983. pap. 10.00 (*0-917590-09-0*) Univ Conn Lib.

Butterick, George F. The Collected Poems of George F. Butterick. Blevins, Richard W., ed. 240p. (Orig.). (C). 1988. pap. 8.00 (*0-685-44372-8*) SUNYB Poetry Rare Bks.

Butterick, George F., ed. A Guide to the Maximus Poems of Charles Olson. LC 75-27921. 1978. pap. 32.50 (*0-520-04270-0*, Pub. by U CA Pr) Cal Prin Full Svc.

Butterick, George F., jt. ed. see Allen, Donald.

Butterick, George F., ed. see Olson, Charles.

Butterick, George F., ed. see Olson, Charles & Creeley, Robert.

Butterick, George F., ed. see Olson, Charles, et al.

Butterick, George F., ed. & intro. see Ferrini, Vincent.

Butterick Patterns Editors, jt. auth. see Vogue Magazine Editors.

***Butterick Patterns Staff, ed.** 101 Crafts under $10: Easy-to-Make Ideas for Gifts & Home. (Illus.). 160p. 2000. pap. 14.95 (*1-57389-024-3*) Butterick Co.

Butterick Publishing Co., Staff. Butterick's 1892 Metropolitan Fashions. LC 94-13379. (Illus.). 160p. 1994. reprint ed. pap. 11.95 (*0-486-27983-9*) Dover.

Butterick Publishing Co. Staff. Metropolitan Fashions of the 1880s: From the 1885 Butterick Catalog. LC 97-13138. (Illus.). 144p. 1997. reprint ed. pap. text 8.95 (*0-486-29706-3*) Dover.

Butterick Publishing Company Staff. The Art of Drawn Work. Kliot, Kaethe, ed. 128p. (C). 1989. reprint ed. pap. 18.00 (*0-916896-29-3*) Lacis Pubns.

Butteriss, Margaret. Re-Inventing Hr: Changing Roles In The High-Performance Organization. 288p. 1998. 54.95 (*0-471-64247-9*) Wiley.

Butterly, Daniel R. The Reckless Heart: Meleager & Atalanta. LC 86-71503. 64p. (Orig.). 1986. 25.00 (*0-86516-172-0*); pap. 15.00 (*0-86516-173-9*) Bolchazy-Carducci.

Butterman, Steve. Bicycle Touring: How to Prepare for Long Rides. LC 94-26226. 96p. (Orig.). 1994. pap. 6.95 (*0-89997-174-1*) Wilderness Pr.

Butterman, Steve, jt. auth. see Leib, Kurt.

Buttermore, Gregg, ed. see Sauer, Lee P.

Butters, Christopher. The Propaganda of a Seed. 72p. 1990. pap., per. 6.00 (*0-943594-10-3*) Cardinal Pr.

Butters, Cynthia R. Math-Pro: Preparation for Real World Medical Administration. 129p. 1992. pap. 17.95 (*0-397-54904-0*) Lppncott W & W.

Butters, Dorothy G. The Bells of Freedom. (Illus.). (J). (gr. 4-8). 1984. 16.00 (*0-8446-6162-7*) Peter Smith.

Butters, G. The Genealogical Registry of the Butters Family, Descendants of William Butter of Woburn, Mass., 1665, & Others in America. (Illus.). 476p. 1989. reprint ed. pap. 71.00 (*0-8328-0359-6*); reprint ed. lib. bdg. 79.00 (*0-8328-0358-8*) Higginson Bk Co.

Butters, H. C. Governors & Government in Early Sixteenth-Century Florence, 1502-1519. 368p. 1985. text 75.00 (*0-19-822593-8*) OUP.

Butters, J. A., jt. auth. see Sjut, Volker.

Butters, J. Keith, jt. auth. see Smith, Dan T.

Butters, J. Keith, jt. ed. see Smith, Dan T.

Butters, John N. Holography & Its Technology. LC 73-179369. (Institution of Electrical Engineers, IIE Monograph Ser.: No. 8). (Illus.). 236p. reprint ed. pap. 73.20 (*0-8357-8911-X*, 201759200007) Bks Demand.

Butters, Nancy, illus. see Pies, Ronald M.

Butters, Nelson, jt. ed. see Squire, Larry R.

Butters, Ronald R., et al, eds. Displacing Homophobia: Gay Male Perspectives in Literature & Culture. LC 89-27584. 315p. (C). 1989. pap. text 17.95 (*0-8223-0970-X*) Duke.

— Displacing Homophobia: Gay Male Perspectives in Literature & Culture. LC 89-27584. 315p. (C). 1989. text 49.95 (*0-8223-0962-9*) Duke.

Butterss, Philip. Southwords: Essays on South Australian Writing. LC 95-214579. xvi, 215 p. 1995. write for info. (*1-86254-354-2*, Pub. by Wakefield Pr) BHB Intl.

Butterweck, Joseph S. The Problem of Teaching High School Pupils How to Study. LC 75-176620. (Columbia University. Teachers College. Contributions to Education Ser.: No. 237). reprint ed. 37.50 (*0-404-55237-4*) AMS Pr.

Butterwick, Richard. Poland's Last King & English Culture: Stanislaw August Poniatowski, 1732-1792. (Oxford Historical Monographs). (Illus.). 400p. 1998. text 95.00 (*0-19-820701-8*) OUP.

Butterworth. Jake Again. (Illus.). (J). mass mkt. 7.95 (*0-340-68728-2*, Pub. by Hodder & Stought Ltd) Trafalgar.

Butterworth, jt. auth. see Inkpen.

Butterworth, A. Jake in Trouble. (Illus.). (J). text 22.95 (*0-340-69982-5*, Pub. by Hodder & Stought Ltd) Trafalgar.

— Jake in Trouble. (Illus.). (J). 1998. mass mkt. 7.95 (*0-340-69981-7*, Pub. by Hodder & Stought Ltd) Trafalgar.

Butterworth, A. The Southlands of Siva: Some Reminiscences of Life in Southern India. 1990. reprint ed. 20.00 (*81-206-0337-0*, Pub. by Asian Educ Servs) S Asia.

Butterworth, A. & Butterworth, D. Jake. 1996. mass mkt. 7.95 (*0-340-66749-4*, Pub. by Hodder & Stought Ltd) Trafalgar.

Butterworth, A., et al. Collection of the Inscriptions on Copper Plates & Stones in the Nellore District, 3 vols., Set. 1990. reprint ed. 140.00 (*81-206-0279-X*, Pub. by Asian Educ Servs) S Asia.

Butterworth, Annette & Butterworth, Nick. Jack in Trouble! (Illus.). 208p. (J). text 22.95 (*0-340-72292-4*, Pub. by Hodder & Stought Ltd) Trafalgar.

Butterworth, B. & Hutchinson, Martha L. Language Production: Development, Writing & Other Language Processes, Vol. 2. 1984. text 138.00 (*0-12-147502-6*) Acad Pr.

Butterworth, Bernard B. Laboratory Anatomy of the Human Body. 4th ed. 208p. (C). 1991. text. write for info. (*0-697-05141-2*, WCB McGr Hill) McGrw-H Hghr Educ.

Butterworth, Bill. When Life Doesn't Turn Out Like You Planned. LC 95-37259. 252p. 1996. pap. 16.99 (*0-7852-7561-4*) Nelson.

Butterworth, Bill, jt. auth. see Bates, Bill.

Butterworth, Brian. What Counts: How Every Brain Is Hardwired for Math. LC 99-17314. (Illus.). 432p. 1999. 26.00 (*0-684-85417-1*) Free Pr.

Butterworth, Brian, et al, eds. Explanations for Language Universals. viii, 292p. 1984. pap. 38.50 (*3-11-009797-4*) Mouton.

Butterworth, Bryon & Slaga, Thomas J., eds. Nongenotoxic Mechanisms in Carcinogenesis. (Banbury Reports: No. 25). 385p. 1987. text 70.00 (*0-87969-225-1*) Cold Spring Harbor.

Butterworth, Byron, et al. Chemically Induced Cell Proliferation: Implications for Risk Assessment. LC 91-15296. (Progress in Clinical & Biological Research Ser.). 582p. 1991. 335.00 (*0-471-56111-8*, Wiley-Interscience) Wiley.

Butterworth, Byron E. Strategies for Short-Term Testing for Mutagens-Carcinogens. 160p. 1979. 87.00 (*0-8493-5661-X*, QH465, CRC Reprint) Franklin.

Butterworth, C. E. & Haridi, Ahmad A., eds. Averroes' Middle Commentary on Aristotle's Poetics. (American Research Center in Egypt, Publications Ser.: No. 9). (ARA & ENG.). 152p. 1986. text 22.50 (*0-936770-08-2*, Pub. by Amer Res Ctr Egypt) Eisenbrauns.

— Averroes's Middle Commentary on Aristotle's Topics. (American Research Center in Egypt, Publications Ser.: Vol. 4). (ARA & ENG.). 247p. (Orig.). 1979. pap. text 10.50 (*0-936770-03-1*, Pub. by Amer Res Ctr Egypt) Eisenbrauns.

Butterworth, C. E., jt. ed. see Bendich, Adrianne.

Butterworth, Charles, tr. see Rousseau, Jean-Jacques.

Butterworth, Charles E. Essays on Islamic Political Philosophy. 1999. pap. 17.00 (*1-883058-45-7*, Nur) Global Pubns.

An Asterisk (*) at the beginning of an entry indicates that the title is appearing for the first time.

Butterworth, Charles E., ed. Averroes's Three Short Commentaries on Aristotle's Topic, Rhetoric, & Poetics. LC 75-4900. 206p. (C). 1977. text 29.50 (*0-87395-208-1*) State U NY Pr.

Butterworth, Charles E. & Kessel, Blake Andree, eds. The Introduction of Arabic Philosophy into Europe. LC 93-2402. (Studien und Texte zur Geistesgeschichte des Mittelalters Ser.). 1993. 67.00 (*90-04-09842-9*) Brill Academic Pubs.

***Butterworth, Charles E. & Zartman, I. William, eds.** Between the State & Islam. (Woodrow Wilson Center Press Ser.). 288p. (C). 2000. 49.95 (*0-521-78352-6*); pap. 19.95 (*0-521-78972-9*) Cambridge U Pr.

Butterworth, Charles E., tr. & intro. see Rushdj, Averroes E.

Butterworth, Charles E., tr. & notes see Rousseau, Jean-Jacques.

Butterworth, Christine. Alligators. LC 90-9927. (Animal World Ser.). (Illus.). 32p. (J). (gr. 2-3). 1990. pap. 4.95 (*0-8114-4608-5*) Raintree Steck-V.

Butterworth Co. of Cape Cod Staff. Cape Cod & Islands Atlas & Guide Book, Vol. 11. (Illus.). 96p. 1996. spiral bd. 15.95 (*0-937338-10-9*) Buttrwrth of Cape Cod.

Butterworth, D., jt. auth. see Butterworth, A.

Butterworth, E. A. Some Traces of the Pre-Olympian World in Greek Literature & Myth. LC 85-21959. (Illus.). (C). 1966. 62.35 (*3-11-005010-2*) De Gruyter.

Butterworth, Edward J. The Identity of Anselm's Proslogion Argument for the Existence of God with the Via Quarta of Thomas Aquinas. LC 90-45650. (Studies in the History of Philosophy: Vol. 8). 384p. 1990. lib. bdg. 99.95 (*0-88946-276-3*) E Mellen.

Butterworth, Elizabeth. Parrots, Macaws & Cockatoos. (Illus.). 64p. 1994. pap. 19.95 (*0-8109-2585-0*, Pub. by Abrams) Time Warner.

Butterworth, Emma M. As the Waltz Was Ending. 262p. (YA). (gr. 7 up). 1991. reprint ed. teacher ed. 1.25 (*0-590-40665-5*, Point) Scholastic Inc.

Butterworth, Eric. Celebrate Yourself: And Other Inspirational Messages. 4th ed. LC 84-51318. 190p. 1997. reprint ed. pap. 9.95 (*0-87159-207-X*, 40) Unity Bks.

— The Concentric Perspective: What's in It from Me? LC 88-51451. 114p. 1989. 5.48 (*0-87159-022-0*) Unity Bks.

— Descubre Tu Poder Interno. 2nd rev. ed. Sarraga, Hilda, tr. from ENG. LC 98-11515.Tr. of Discover the Power Within You. (SPA.). 370p. 1999. pap. 10.95 (*0-87159-221-5*, 266) Unity Bks.

— Discover the Power Within You: A Guide to the Unexplored Depths Within. LC 91-58166. 256p. 1992. reprint ed. pap. 15.00 (*0-06-250115-1*, Pub. by Harper SF) HarpC.

Butterworth, Eric. Economia Espiritual.Tr. of Spiritual Economics. (SPA.). 240p. Date not set. pap. 11.95 (*0-87159-237-1*, 298) Unity Bks.

Butterworth, Eric. In the Flow of Life. rev. ed. LC 82-50121. 178p. 1994. pap. 9.95 (*0-87159-066-2*) Unity Bks.

— MetaMorality. LC 87-82241. 137p. 1988. 4.48 (*0-87159-092-1*) Unity Bks.

— Positrends or Negatrends? Dealing Positively with the 3rd Millennium. LC 98-72264. 120p. 1998. pap. 9.95 (*0-87516-721-7*) DeVorss.

— Spiritual Economics: The Principles & Process of True Prosperity. 2nd abr. rev. ed. LC 97-26302. 232p. 1998. pap. 10.95 (*0-87159-211-8*) Unity Bks.

— Unity: A Quest for Truth. 1965. pap. 5.00 (*0-8315-0020-4*) Speller.

— Unity: A Quest for Truth. rev. ed. LC 85-50997. 108p. 1994. pap. 9.95 (*0-87159-177-4*) Unity Bks.

Butterworth, Eric. Unity: Una Busqueda de la Verdad.Tr. of Search for Truth. (SPA.). 162p. Date not set. pap. 11.95 (*0-87159-249-5*, 280, Unity Hse) Unity Bks.

Butterworth, Eric. The Universe Is Calling: Opening to the Divine Through Prayer. LC 91-59028. 192p. 1994. pap. 13.00 (*0-06-250094-5*, Pub. by Harper SF) HarpC.

Butterworth, F. Edward. Divine Origin of the Restoration. 1989. 12.00 (*0-941227-01-4*) Cosmic Pr Chico.

Butterworth, F. Edward. Locks & Lockmaking. (Illus.). 135p. 1926. 20.00 (*0-87556-392-9*) Saifer.

Butterworth, F. Edward. Return of the Ancients. (Orig.). 1987. pap. 12.00 (*0-941227-00-6*) Cosmic Pr Chico.

Butterworth, Francis A. Alexander. Records of a Family of the House of Lexander, 1640-1909. (Illus.). 89p. 1997. reprint ed. pap. 17.50 (*0-8328-7227-X*); reprint ed. lib. bdg. 27.50 (*0-8328-7226-1*) Higginson Bk Co.

Butterworth, Frank M., et al, eds. Biomonitors & Biomarkers As Indicators of Environmental Change: A Handbook. LC 95-39331. (Environmental Science Research Ser.: Vol. 50). (Illus.). 358p. (C). 1995. 105.00 (*0-306-45190-5*, QH541, Plenum Trade) Perseus Pubng.

Butterworth, G. W., tr. Exhortation to the Greeks, the Rich Man's Salvation, to the Newly Baptized. (Loeb Classical Library: No. 92). 432p. 1919. 18.95 (*0-674-99103-6*) HUP.

Butterworth, G. W., tr. see Origen.

Butterworth, George & Bryant, Peter, eds. Causes of Development: Interdisciplinary Perspectives. 288p. 1990. 59.95 (*0-8058-0796-9*) L Erlbaum Assocs.

Butterworth, George & Light, Paul, eds. Social Cognition: Studies of the Development of Understanding. LC 81-24075. (Illus.). 281p. reprint ed. pap. 87.20 (*0-608-09274-6*, 205414800004) Bks Demand.

Butterworth, George, jt. ed. see Light, Paul.

Butterworth, George, jt. ed. see Nadel, Jacqueline.

Butterworth, George E., et al, eds. The Child's Theory of Mind. (Illus.). 376p. 1991. text 65.00 (*0-19-852252-5*) OUP.

Butterworth, George E. & Light, Paul Charles. Social Cognition & Development: Studies of the Development of Understanding. LC 81-24075. 282p. (C). 1997. 24.00 (*0-226-08609-7*) U Ch Pr.

Butterworth, H. E., jt. auth. see Hooker, Richard.

Butterworth, Hezekiah. Story of Hymns & Tunes. 1988. reprint ed. lib. bdg. 89.00 (*0-685-55955-6*) Rprt Serv.

— Story of Hymns & Tunes. 1981. reprint ed. lib. bdg. 95.00 (*0-403-00107-2*) Scholarly.

— The Story of the Hymns. (Works of Hezekiah Butterworth). 1989. reprint ed. lib. bdg. 79.00 (*0-7812-0605-7*) Rprt Serv.

— Traveller Tales of the Pan-American Countries. LC 71-130986. (Illus.). reprint ed. 37.50 (*0-404-01255-8*) AMS Pr.

— The Works of Hezekiah Butterworth. 1989. reprint ed. lib. bdg. 63.00 (*0-685-74128-1*) Rprt Serv.

— Zig Zag Journeys. (Works of Hezekiah Butterworth). 1989. reprint ed. lib. bdg. 79.00 (*0-7812-2230-3*) Rprt Serv.

Butterworth, Ian, ed. The Impact of Electronic Publishing on the Academic Community. (Wenner Gren International Ser.: No. 73). 191p. (C). 1998. text. write for info. (*1-85578-122-0*, Pub. by Portland Pr Ltd) Ashgate Pub Co.

Butterworth, J. The Contra Noetum of Hippolytus. 1990. pap. 38.00 (*0-905764-01-3*) St Mut.

***Butterworth, Jez.** Birthday Girl: A Screenplay. 2000. pap. 10.95 (*0-7868-8588-2*, Pub. by Talk Miramax Bks) Time Warner.

Butterworth, Jez. Mojo. LC 99-462448. 1999. pap. 5.25 (*0-8222-1661-2*) Dramatists Play.

— Mojo. 96p. 1996. pap. text 14.95 (*1-85459-366-8*, Pub. by N Hern Bks) Theatre Comm.

— Mojo & a Filmmaker's Diary. (Illus.). 144p. 1999. pap. 14.95 (*0-571-19218-1*) Faber & Faber.

Butterworth, John. The Theory of Price Control & Black Markets. 233p. 1994. 77.95 (*1-85628-601-0*, Pub. by Avebry) Ashgate Pub Co.

Butterworth, John, jt. auth. see Hutson, Thomas G.

Butterworth, John F., IV. Atlas of Procedures in Anesthesia & Critical Care. (Illus.). 251p. 1991. text 41.00 (*0-7216-2916-4*, W B Saunders Co) Harcrt Hlth Sci Grp.

***Butterworth, John Mark.** Brightness Springs. (Illus.). 115p. 1999. pap. 9.95 (*0-9676429-0-6*) M Butterworth.

Butterworth, Keen. A Critical & Textual Study of Faulkner's "A Fable" Litz, A. Walton, ed. LC 83-5030. (Studies in Modern Literature: No. 11). 134p. reprint ed. pap. 41.60 (*0-8357-1420-9*, 207043300089) Bks Demand.

Butterworth, Keen & Butterworth, Nancy, annos. A Fable. 280p. 1990. text 23.00 (*0-8240-4392-8*) Garland.

Butterworth, Lena. Words from the Heart. (Illus.). 188p. 1998. pap. 13.95 (*1-57502-973-1*, PO2664) Morris Pubng.

Butterworth, Michael. Queens of Deliria: 19977 Sci-Fi Novel - Sequel to the Time of the Hawklords. 1995. pap. 12.95 (*1-896522-07-6*) CN06.

Butterworth, Michael, ed. see Birtton, David.

Butterworth, Mike. Structure & the Book of Zechariah. (JSOT Supplement Ser.: No. 130). 328p. (C). 1992. 85.00 (*1-85075-293-1*, Pub. by Sheffield Acad) CUP Services.

Butterworth, MyLinda. Just 24 Days Till Christmas: Act 1: Old & New. (Illus.). 224p. 1997. pap. 14.95 (*1-890905-00-3*) Day to Day.

— Just 24 Days Till Christmas: Act 1: Old & New. 2nd rev. ed. LC 97-77079. (Illus.). 224p. (YA). (gr. 6 up). 1998. pap. 14.95 (*1-890905-10-0*) Day to Day.

Butterworth, N. Un Dia Libre Ajetreodo. 1996. 15.95 (*84-233-2335-8*) Destino.

Butterworth, Nancy, jt. anno. see Butterworth, Keen.

Butterworth, Neil. The American Symphony. LC 98-14764. (Illus.). 338p. 1998. text 59.95 (*1-85928-459-0*, ML1255.B985, Pub. by Ashgate Pub) Ashgate Pub Co.

— Dvoirbak: His Life & Times LC 80-146552. 135 p. 1980. 7.50 (*0-85936-142-X*) The Baton Pr.

— Dvorak. (Illustrated Lives of the Great Composers Ser.). (Illus.). 136p. 1996. 17.95 (*0-7119-0256-9*, OP 42423) Omnibus NY.

Butterworth, Nick. The Good Stranger. (Illus.). (J). (ps-3). 1989. 4.99 (*0-310-55940-5*) Zondervan.

— I Wonder at the Zoo. (Illus.). 10p. (J). 1994. bds. 3.99 (*1-56476-359-5*, 6-3359, Victor Bks) Chariot Victor.

— I Wonder in the Country. (Illus.). 10p. (J). 1994. bds. 3.99 (*1-56476-362-5*, 6-3362, Victor Bks) Chariot Victor.

— Jasper's Beanstalk. LC 92-14886. (Illus.). 32p. (J). (ps-1). 1997. mass mkt. 5.99 (*0-689-81540-9*) Aladdin.

Butterworth, Nick. Jasper's Beanstalk. LC 92-14886. (J). 1997. 11.19 (*0-606-11518-8*, Pub. by Turtleback) Demco.

Butterworth, Nick. Jingle Bells. LC 98-15436. (Illus.). 32p. (J). (ps-2). 1998. 15.95 (*0-531-30124-9*) Orchard Bks Watts.

— The Little Gate. (Illus.). (J). (ps-3). 1989. 4.99 (*0-310-55970-7*) Zondervan.

Butterworth, Nick. My Dad Is Awesome. LC 91-71832. (Illus.). 24p. (J). (ps up). 1992. pap. 4.99 (*1-56402-033-9*) Candlewick Pr.

Butterworth, Nick. My Grandma Is Wonderful. LC 91-58747. (Illus.). 32p. (J). (ps up). 1992. pap. 4.99 (*1-56402-100-9*) Candlewick Pr.

— My Grandpa Is Amazing. LC 91-58746. (Illus.). 32p. (J). (ps up). 1992. pap. 4.99 (*1-56402-099-1*) Candlewick Pr.

— My Mom Is Excellent. LC 92-43769. (Illus.). 32p. (J). (ps up). 1994. pap. 4.99 (*1-56402-289-7*) Candlewick Pr.

***Butterworth, Nick.** Percy's Bumpy Ride. (Illus.). 28p. (J). 2000. write for info. (*1-58048-091-8*) Sandvik Pub.

Butterworth, Nick. The Puffin Book of Nursery Rhymes. (J). 1995. 10.19 (*0-606-08045-7*, Pub. by Turtleback) Demco.

— Rescue Party, Vol. 1. (J). (ps-3). 1993. 14.95 (*0-316-11923-7*) Little.

— The Rich Farmer. (Illus.). (J). (ps-3). 1989. 4.99 (*0-310-55960-X*) Zondervan.

— The Ten Silver Coins. (Illus.). (J). (ps-3). 1989. 4.99 (*0-310-55950-2*) Zondervan.

— A Year in Percy's Park. (Illus.). (J). 1997. pap. 14.98 (*1-58048-014-4*) Sandvik Pub.

Butterworth, Nick & Inkpen, Mick. The Fox's Story: Jesus Is Born. (Animal Tales Ser.). (J). (gr. 3-7). 1988. pap. 4.99 (*0-310-55790-9*) Zondervan.

— I Wonder at the Zoo. (I Wonder Ser.). 14p. (J). (ps). 1987. pap. 1.95 (*0-310-55411-X*, 19041P) Zondervan.

— I Wonder in the Country. (I Wonder Ser.). 14p. (J). (ps). 1987. pap. 1.95 (*0-310-55431-4*, 19043P) Zondervan.

— I Wonder in the Garden. (I Wonder Ser.). 14p. (J). (ps). 1987. pap. 1.95 (*0-310-55401-2*, 19040P) Zondervan.

— I Wonder on the Farm. (I Wonder Ser.). 14p. (J). (ps). 1987. pap. 1.95 (*0-310-55421-7*, 19042P) Zondervan.

— The Mouse's Story: Jesus & the Storm. (Animal Tales Ser.). (J). (gr. 3-7). 1988. 4.99 (*0-310-55810-7*) Zondervan.

— Stories Jesus Told. 224p. (J). (ps-k). 1994. 10.99 (*0-88070-633-3*, Gold n Honey) Zondervan.

— Wonderful Earth! LC 97-47411. 28p. (J). 1998. 14.99 (*0-8499-5832-6*) Tommy Nelson.

Butterworth, Nick, jt. auth. see Butterworth, Annette.

Butterworth, Oliver. The Enormous Egg. (Illus.). (J). (gr. 4). 1995. 9.00 (*0-395-73249-2*) HM.

Butterworth, Oliver. The Enormous Egg. 188p. (J). (gr. 3-5). pap. 4.95 (*0-8072-1393-4*) Listening Lib.

— Enormous Egg. (J). 1984. 10.05 (*0-606-05721-8*, Pub. by Turtleback) Demco.

Butterworth, Oliver. The Enormous Egg. large type ed. (Illus.). 214p. (J). (gr. 4). 53.50 (*0-614-20587-5*, L-38188-00 APHB) Am Printing Hse.

— The Enormous Egg: You Won't Believe Your Eyes. LC 56-5622. (Illus.). 188p. (J). (gr. 4-7). 1993. pap. 4.95 (*0-316-11920-2*) Little.

Butterworth, P. J., jt. auth. see Moss, D. W.

Butterworth, Rod R. The Perigee Visual Dictionary of Signing: An A-to-Z Guide to Over 1,250 Signs of American Sign Language. 3rd expanded rev. ed. Flodin, Mickey, ed. LC 95-1380. 512p. (Orig.). 1995. pap. 15.95 (*0-399-51952-1*, Perigee Bks) Berkley Pub.

— Pocket Dictionary of Signing. 1992. 12.05 (*0-606-02844-7*, Pub. by Turtleback) Demco.

Butterworth, Rod R. & Flodin, Mickey. The Pocket Dictionary of Signing. rev. ed. LC 91-30462. (Illus.). 224p. (YA). 1992. pap. 6.95 (*0-399-51743-X*, Perigee Bks) Berkley Pub.

— Signing Made Easy. LC 88-23878. (Illus.). 224p. 1989. pap. 12.00 (*0-399-51490-2*, Perigee Bks) Berkley Pub.

Butterworth, Roger. A Color Atlas of Forefoot Surgery. (Illus.). 264p. (gr. 13). 1992. text 108.00 (*0-8151-1387-0*, 21710) Mosby Inc.

Butterworth, Roger F., et al, eds. Hepatic Encephalopathy: Pathophysiology & Treatment. LC 89-20039. (Experimental Biology & Medicine Ser.: Vol. 22). 640p. 1989. 129.50 (*0-89603-164-0*) Humana.

Butterworth Staff. Alaska Administrative Code, 6 vols. 9000p. 1993. suppl. ed. 125.00 (*0-685-75306-9*, MICHIE); ring bd. 528.00 (*0-87473-454-1*, MICHIE) LEXIS Pub.

— Australian Company Law Reports, 13 vols., Set. 655.00 (*0-409-49009-1*, MICHIE) LEXIS Pub.

— The Blue Book. 550p. 1993. boxed set 83.00 (*0-406-02419-7*, UK, MICHIE) LEXIS Pub.

— Butterworth Landlord & Tenant Handbook. 4th ed. 949p. 1992. pap. text 66.00 (*0-406-01028-5*, UK, MICHIE) LEXIS Pub.

— Butterworths Court Tariffs & Fees. pap. write for info. (*0-409-01562-8*, SA, MICHIE) LEXIS Pub.

— Butterworth's Family Law Act, Rules & Regulations Student Edition. 1989. ring bd. 43.00 (*0-409-30322-4*, MICHIE) LEXIS Pub.

— Butterworth's Guide to the Council Tax in Scotland. 260p. 1993. pap. text 53.00 (*0-406-02453-7*, UK, MICHIE) LEXIS Pub.

— Butterworth's Handbook of Singapore Land Law. 917p. 1986. pap. 109.00 (*0-409-99516-9*, MICHIE) LEXIS Pub.

— Butterworth's Law Diary & Directory 1995. (Illus.). 1995. write for info. (*0-614-05466-4*, MICHIE) LEXIS Pub.

— Catalogo de Leyes del Ano. (SPA.). 1992. 150.00 (*0-685-75307-7*, MICHIE) LEXIS Pub.

— Catalogo de Reglamentos de Puerto Rico, 2 vols., Set. 1992. 525.00 (*0-685-75308-5*, MICHIE) LEXIS Pub.

— Connecticut Real Property Statutes, 1991-1992. 2nd ed. 720p. 1991. 35.00 (*1-56257-266-0*, MICHIE) LEXIS Pub.

— Connecticut Real Property Statutes, 1991-1992. 2nd ed. 720p. 1992. ring bd. 55.00 (*0-88063-008-6*, MICHIE) LEXIS Pub.

— Connecticut Time Limitations, 1991. 2nd ed. 390p. 1994. 56.00 (*1-56257-265-2*, MICHIE); ring bd. 65.00 (*0-88063-002-7*, MICHIE) LEXIS Pub.

— Corporate Law: The European Dimension. 220p. 1991. pap. 144.00 (*0-406-00296-7*, U.K., MICHIE) LEXIS Pub.

— Dunnell Minnesota Digest, 1978, 56 vols., Set. 4th ed. 1978. 1350.00 (*0-86678-002-5*, 80050-10, MICHIE) LEXIS Pub.

— Fiber Optic Cabling: Theory, Design, & Installation Practice. 1996. 14.95 (*0-614-18451-7*, B25004) Info Gatekeepers.

— Florida Rules of Court Service. 1994. ring bd., suppl. ed. 45.00 (*0-685-11435-X*, MICHIE) LEXIS Pub.

— Florida Rules of Court Service, 3 vols., Set. 1300p. 1991. ring bd. 120.00 (*0-409-26038-X*, MICHIE) LEXIS Pub.

— Florida Workers' Compensation Manual, 1979-1994, 2 vols. 1994. suppl. ed. 40.00 (*0-685-73807-8*, MICHIE) LEXIS Pub.

— Formularios Juridicos Para Puerto Rico. (SPA.). 1992. 110.00 incl. 5.25 hd (*1-56257-125-7*, 82921-10, MICHIE) LEXIS Pub.

— Haydn: The Illustrated Lives of the Great Composers. (Illustrated Lives of the Great Composers Ser.). (Illus.). 144p. 1983. pap. 17.95 (*0-7119-0249-6*, OP 42357) Music Sales.

— Illinois Limitations Manual 1989. 2nd ed. 350p. 1991. suppl. ed. 38.00 (*0-685-45479-7*, MICHIE) LEXIS Pub.

— Illinois Limitations Manual 1989. 2nd ed. 350p. 1993. spiral bd. 65.00 (*0-86678-152-8*, MICHIE) LEXIS Pub.

— Iowa Limitations Manual, 1989-1993. 2nd ed. 370p. 1993. ring bd. 50.00 (*0-86678-049-1*, MICHIE); suppl. ed. 45.00 (*0-250-40776-0*, MICHIE) LEXIS Pub.

— Is It in Force?, 1994. 615p. 1994. pap. text 62.00 (*0-406-02567-3*, UK, MICHIE) LEXIS Pub.

— Lawyer's Pocketbook 1993. 1993. pap. 45.00 (*0-409-03471-1*, SA, MICHIE) LEXIS Pub.

— Leyes del Trabajo Anotadas, 1986: Edicion Especial. 1994. ring bd., suppl. ed. 30.00 (*0-614-03736-0*, MICHIE) LEXIS Pub.

— Maine Probate Forms. rev. ed. 290p. 1991. suppl. ed. 20.00 (*0-685-59038-0*, MICHIE) LEXIS Pub.

— Maine Probate Series, 3 vols., Set. 1991. ring bd. 195.00 (*0-250-40780-9*, MICHIE) LEXIS Pub.

— Mallal's Digest, 3. 4th rev. ed. 805p. 1994. 400.00 (*0-409-99679-3*, MICHIE) LEXIS Pub.

— Mallal's Digest, Vol. 2. 4th ed. 1133p. 1994. write for info. (*0-409-99717-X*, MICHIE) LEXIS Pub.

— Mallal's Digest Case & Legislation Citator, 1932 to 1991, 2 vols., Set. 1994. write for info. (*0-409-99739-0*, ASIA, MICHIE) LEXIS Pub.

— Mallal's Digest Case & Legislation Citator, 1932 to 1991: Case Citator. 647p. 1994. write for info. (*0-409-99696-3*, ASIA, MICHIE) LEXIS Pub.

— Mallal's Digest Case & Legislation Citator, 1932 to 1991: Legislation Citator. 211p. 1994. write for info. (*0-409-99738-2*, ASIA, MICHIE) LEXIS Pub.

— Minnesota Crimes & Defenses. 300p. 1993. ring bd., suppl. ed. 37.00 (*0-614-03154-0*, MICHIE) LEXIS Pub.

— Minnesota Limitations Manual, 1989-1992. 1994. ring bd., suppl. ed. 42.00 (*0-614-03160-5*, MICHIE) LEXIS Pub.

— Minnesota Limitations Manual, 1989-1992. 2nd ed. 350p. 1994. spiral bd. 85.00 (*0-86678-040-8*, MICHIE) LEXIS Pub.

— Nebraska Limitations Manual, 1989-1990. 2nd ed. 370p. 1992. ring bd. 50.00 (*0-86678-056-4*, MICHIE) LEXIS Pub.

— New Hampshire Annotation Service. 130p. 1994. pap. 26.00 (*0-614-03163-X*, MICHIE) LEXIS Pub.

— New Hampshire Insurance Laws. 650p. 1993. pap. 35.00 (*1-56257-506-6*, MICHIE) LEXIS Pub.

— The Ontario Family Law Act & Related Statutes: 1994 Consolidation. 858p. 1994. pap. 65.00 (*0-433-39137-5*, CN, MICHIE) LEXIS Pub.

— Oregon Rules of Civil Procedure Annotated. 500p. 1994. pap. 68.00 (*0-250-44848-3*, MICHIE) LEXIS Pub.

— Servicio Legislativo de Puerto Rico (1989) (SPA.). 300p. 1989. pap. 85.00 (*0-88063-516-9*, MICHIE) LEXIS Pub.

— Texas Rules of Appellate Procedure, 1986-1992. 130p. 1992. ring bd. 39.50 (*0-409-25255-7*, MICHIE) LEXIS Pub.

— Washington Statutory Time Limitations: Washington State. 2nd ed. 650p. 1994. ring bd. 85.00 (*0-250-40722-1*, MICHIE) LEXIS Pub.

— Washington Tax Decisions: Index. 100p. 1992. ring bd. 50.00 (*1-56257-738-7*, MICHIE) LEXIS Pub.

— Wills, Trusts, & Estates. (Florida Paralegals Ser.). 250p. 1991. ring bd. 60.00 (*0-409-26086-X*, MICHIE) LEXIS Pub.

— Wills, Trusts & Estates. 250p. 1993. suppl. ed. 50.00 (*0-250-42172-0*, MICHIE) LEXIS Pub.

Butterworth Staff, ed. The Digest: Annotated British, Commonwealth & European Cases, 75 vols., Set. 1942. boxed set 4700.00 (*0-406-02500-2*, UK, MICHIE) LEXIS Pub.

— Informes Semanales Sobre Contribuciones. (Illus.). ring bd. 1800.00 (*0-614-05853-8*, MICHIE) LEXIS Pub.

— Informes Semanales Sobre Seguros. (Illus.). ring bd. 1620.00 (*0-614-05854-6*, NewStar Pr) NewStar Media.

— Informes Semanales Sobre Toda Legislacion. ring bd. 1500.00 (*0-614-05855-4*, MICHIE) LEXIS Pub.

— LARMAC Index to California Laws. 960p. 1994. pap. 85.00 (*0-250-47276-7*, MICHIE) LEXIS Pub.

— LARMAC Index to California Laws: 1994 Edition. 960p. 1993. pap. 85.00 (*0-250-47211-2*, MICHIE) LEXIS Pub.

— Ley de Vehiculos y Transito, 1993. 310p. 1993. pap. 30.00 (*0-88063-534-7*, MICHIE) LEXIS Pub.

— Ley Uniforme de Instrumentos Negociables - Uniform Negotiable Instruments Act: Edicion Especial. (ENG & SPA.). 180p. 1990. pap. 20.00 (*0-88063-675-0*, 31819-10, MICHIE) LEXIS Pub.

— Leyes de Corporaciones Anotadas: Edicion Especial. 170p. 1986. pap. 25.00 (*0-88063-498-7*, 31817-10, MICHIE) LEXIS Pub.

— Leyes de Puerto Rico. 24th ed. 1990. 85.00 (*0-614-05883-X*, MICHIE) LEXIS Pub.

— Leyes del Trabajo Anotadas, 1986: Edicion Especial. 740p. 1986. 45.00 (*0-88063-533-9*, MICHIE) LEXIS Pub.

— Leyes Selladas Del Ano. 1992. 140.00 (*0-685-66876-2*, MICHIE) LEXIS Pub.

— Mallal's Digest, Vol. 5. 4th ed. 703p. 1994. write for info. (*0-409-99716-1*, SI, MICHIE) LEXIS Pub.

— New England Rules of Court (CT, MA, ME, NH, RI, VT), 2 vols., Set. 1300p. 1992. ring bd. 140.00 (*1-56257-651-8*, MICHIE) LEXIS Pub.

B

An Asterisk (*) at the beginning of an entry indicates that the title is appearing for the first time.

— New Hampshire Actions & Proceedings. 690p. 1994. pap. 39.50 (*1-56257-148-6*, 21801-10, MICHIE); pap. 35.00 (*0-250-44435-6*, MICHIE) LEXIS Pub.
— New Hampshire Code of Administrative Rules Annotated, 1984-1991, 4 vols., Set. annot. ed. 1994. ring bd. 275.00 (*0-88063-471-5*, MICHIE) LEXIS Pub.
— New Hampshire Consolidated Index, 1994. 380p. 1994. 45.00 (*0-685-74750-6*, MICHIE) LEXIS Pub.
— New Hampshire Corporations, Partnerships & Associations. 300p. 1994. pap. 30.00 (*0-88063-474-X*, MICHIE); pap. 30.00 (*0-250-44733-9*, MICHIE); pap. 40.00 (*0-250-44766-5*, MICHIE) LEXIS Pub.
— New Hampshire Court Rules Annotated, 2 vols. annot. ed. 1000p. 1993. ring bd. 61.00 (*0-88063-475-8*, 45650-10, MICHIE) LEXIS Pub.
— New Hampshire Criminal Code. 300p. 1994. pap. 33.00 (*0-88063-472-3*, MICHIE); pap. 30.00 (*0-250-44736-3*, MICHIE) LEXIS Pub.
— New Hampshire Fish & Game Laws. (New Hampshire Statutes Ser.). 200p. 1994. pap. 30.00 (*0-250-44734-7*, MICHIE) LEXIS Pub.
— New Hampshire Juvenile Laws. 500p. 1994. pap. 37.50 (*0-250-44827-0*, MICHIE) LEXIS Pub.
— New Hampshire Juvenile Laws, Annual. 500p. 1993. pap. 35.00 (*1-56257-505-8*, MICHIE) LEXIS Pub.
— New Hampshire Planning & Land Use Regulation. (New Hampshire Statutes Ser.). 275p. 1994. pap. 30.00 (*0-250-44735-5*, MICHIE); pap. 35.00 (*0-614-05921-6*, MICHIE) LEXIS Pub.
— New Hampshire Reports, Vols. 1-138. 900p. 1979. boxed set 41.00 (*0-88063-492-8*, 45750-10, MICHIE) LEXIS Pub.
— New Hampshire Revised Statutes Annotated, 23 vols. annot. rev. ed. 1994. boxed set 500.00 (*0-88063-491-X*, 45605-10, MICHIE) LEXIS Pub.
— New Hampshire Rules of Evidence Deskbook, 1994. 150p. 1994. pap. 20.00 (*0-88063-465-0*, 91185-10, MICHIE) LEXIS Pub.
— Opiniones del Secretario de Justicia de Leyes de Puerto Rico. 1992. 50.00 (*0-88063-522-3*, MICHIE) LEXIS Pub.
— Opinions of the Attorney General of the Virgin Islands, 1965-1991, 9 vols., Set, Vols. 1, 3-10 (1935-1986) 2000p. 1965. boxed set 315.00 (*0-88063-540-1*, 48973-10, MICHIE) LEXIS Pub.
— Oregon Uniform Trial Court Rules & Supplementary Local Rules, 1985-1993. 460p. 1995. ring bd. 80.00 (*0-409-24951-3*, 82297-10, MICHIE) LEXIS Pub.
— Parker's California Corporations Code, 1994. 220p. 1993. pap. 39.50 incl. disk (*0-250-47212-0*, MICHIE) LEXIS Pub.
— Parker's California Family Code, 1994. 190p. 1993. pap. 39.50 incl. disk (*0-250-47213-9*, MICHIE) LEXIS Pub.
— Parker's 1995 California Civil Code. 1020p. 1994. pap. 25.00 incl. disk (*0-250-44768-1*, MICHIE) LEXIS Pub.
— Parker's 1995 California Code of Civil Procedure. 840p. 1994. pap. 25.00 incl. disk (*0-250-44767-3*, MICHIE) LEXIS Pub.
— Parker's 1995 California Evidence Code. 270p. 1994. pap. 17.50 incl. disk (*0-250-44770-3*, MICHIE) LEXIS Pub.
— Parker's 1995 California Family Code. 1994. pap. 28.00 incl. disk (*0-250-44771-1*, MICHIE) LEXIS Pub.
— Parker's 1995 California Insurance Code. 1150p. 1994. pap. 32.00 incl. disk (*0-250-44772-X*, MICHIE) LEXIS Pub.
— Parker's 1995 California Labor Code. 620p. 1994. pap. 28.00 incl. disk (*0-250-44773-8*, MICHIE) LEXIS Pub.
— Parker's 1995 California Probate Code. 600p. 1994. pap. 24.00 incl. disk (*0-250-44774-6*, MICHIE) LEXIS Pub.
— Parker's 1995 California Uniform Commercial Code. 270p. 1994. pap. 19.50 incl. disk (*0-250-44800-9*, MICHIE) LEXIS Pub.
— Parker's 1995 California Vehicle Code. 830p. 1994. pap. 32.00 incl. disk (*0-250-44801-7*, MICHIE) LEXIS Pub.
— Parker's 1995 California Business & Professions Code, 2 vols., Set. 1720p. 1994. pap. 55.00 incl. disk (*0-614-05941-0*, MICHIE) LEXIS Pub.
— Practica Forense Federal. 390p. 1992. 40.00 (*0-88063-506-1*, MICHIE) LEXIS Pub.
— Practica Forense Puertorriquena: Evidencia, Tomo 3. 380p. 1993. 35.00 (*0-614-05947-X*, MICHIE) LEXIS Pub.
— Practica Forense Puertorriquena: Procedimiento Civil, Tomo 1. 880p. 1993. 35.00 (*0-614-05948-8*, MICHIE) LEXIS Pub.
— Practica Forense Puertorriquena: Procedimiento Criminal, Tomo 2. 510p. 1993. 35.00 (*0-614-05949-6*, MICHIE) LEXIS Pub.
— Register of Regulations. ring bd. 255.00 (*0-614-05955-0*, MICHIE) LEXIS Pub.
— Registro de Reglamentos. ring bd. 255.00 (*0-614-05956-9*, MICHIE) LEXIS Pub.
— Reglamentos Por Agencia. ring bd. 60.00 (*0-614-05957-7*, MICHIE) LEXIS Pub.
— Regulations by Agency. ring bd. 60.00 (*0-614-05958-5*, MICHIE) LEXIS Pub.
— Servicio de Notas (Advanced Digesto Case Service) 100p. 1993. pap. 25.00 (*0-250-44701-0*, MICHIE) LEXIS Pub.
— Texas Business Statutes & Securities Rules. 500p. 1994. pap. 35.00 (*0-250-44807-6*, MICHIE) LEXIS Pub.
— Texas Uniform Commercial Code. 150p. 1994. pap. 25.00 (*0-250-44763-0*, MICHIE) LEXIS Pub.
— Vermont Court Rules Annotated, 1981-1991, 2 vols., Set. annot. ed. 1000p. 1989. ring bd. 98.00 (*0-88063-547-9*, 48940-10, MICHIE) LEXIS Pub.
— Vermont Family Law. 420p. 1993. pap. 39.00 (*0-88063-617-3*, MICHIE) LEXIS Pub.
— Vermont Planning, Development & Land Use Regulation. 290p. 1994. pap. 35.00 (*0-88063-551-7*, MICHIE) LEXIS Pub.
— Vermont Rules of Evidence. 200p. 1993. pap. 40.00 (*0-88063-548-7*, MICHIE) LEXIS Pub.
— Vermont Statutes Annotated, 28 vols. annot. ed. 1994. boxed set 800.00 (*0-88063-546-0*, 48905-10, MICHIE) LEXIS Pub.
— Virgin Island Reports: The Official Law Reports of the U. S. Virgin Islands, 1959-1994, 37 vols., Set. 420p. 1959. boxed set 1000.00 (*0-88063-542-8*, 88000-10, MICHIE) LEXIS Pub.
— Virgin Islands Code Annotated, 1964-1993, 19 vols. annot. ed. 1993. boxed set 675.00 (*0-88063-539-8*, 48953-10, MICHIE) LEXIS Pub.
— Virgin Islands Corporation Laws. 200p. 1985. pap. 21.00 (*0-88063-538-X*, MICHIE) LEXIS Pub.
— Virgin Islands Court Rules Annotated, 1993. 600p. 1993. pap. 65.00 (*1-56257-101-X*, MICHIE) LEXIS Pub.
— Virgin Islands Digest, 6 vols., Set. 450p. 1992. boxed set 300.00 (*1-56257-104-4*, 48982-10, MICHIE) LEXIS Pub.
— Virgin Islands Election Laws. 200p. 1988. pap. 21.00 (*0-88063-554-1*, MICHIE) LEXIS Pub.
— Virgin Islands Rules & Regulations, 4 vols., Set. 2000p. 1980. boxed set 275.00 (*0-88063-541-X*, MICHIE) LEXIS Pub.
— Virgin Islands Session Laws, 28 vols., Set. 600p. 1958. boxed set 772.00 (*0-88063-543-6*, 48980-10, MICHIE) LEXIS Pub.
— Virgin Islands Zoning, Building & Housing Laws & Regulations. 280p. 1984. pap. 20.00 (*0-88063-545-2*, MICHIE) LEXIS Pub.
— Washington Tax Decisions Excise Tax Bulletin. 840p. 1993. ring bd. 160.00 (*0-614-05996-8*, MICHIE) LEXIS Pub.
— Weekly Reports on All Legislation. ring bd. 1500.00 (*0-614-05997-6*, MICHIE) LEXIS Pub.
— Weekly Reports on Banking. ring bd. 1620.00 (*0-614-05998-4*, MICHIE) LEXIS Pub.
— Weekly Reports on Commerce & Consumer Affairs. ring bd. 1500.00 (*0-614-05999-2*, MICHIE) LEXIS Pub.
— Weekly Reports on Insurance. ring bd. 1620.00 (*0-614-06000-1*, MICHIE) LEXIS Pub.
— Weekly Reports on Labor-Management. ring bd. 1620.00 (*0-614-06001-X*, MICHIE) LEXIS Pub.
— Weekly Reports on Taxes. ring bd. 1800.00 (*0-614-06002-8*, MICHIE) LEXIS Pub.

Butterworth Staff & Sutton, Alastair, eds. Butterworth's Annual European Review, 1993. 600p. 1994. 300.00 (*0-406-03617-9*, U.K., MICHIE) LEXIS Pub.

Butterworth Staff, jt. auth. see Hoague, Eleanor C.

Butterworth, Stephen J., jt. auth. see Denny, Hamish.

Butterworth, Taia, ed. The Directory of Human Services of Morris County. rev. ed. 240p. 1998. pap. 19.95 (*0-925133-53-1*) Volt Directory.
— Human Care Services Directory of Metropolitan Chicago. 38th rev. ed. 700p. 1998. pap. 54.90 (*0-925133-52-3*) Volt Directory.
— The Human Services Directory for Broome County. 240p. 1998. pap. 23.90 (*0-925133-55-8*) Volt Directory.
— Salt Lake Area Human Services Directory. 200p. 1997. spiral bd. 29.95 (*0-925133-50-7*) Volt Directory.
— Salt Lake Area Self Help Support Group Directory. 5th ed. 160p. 1998. spiral bd. 9.95 (*0-925133-51-5*) Volt Directory.
— Utah Nonprofits Directory. 240p. 1997. pap. 54.90 (*0-925133-49-3*) Volt Directory.

Butterworth, Taia & Dunn, Maritza O., eds. CFIDS Resource Directory: A Comprehensive Guide to Chronic-Fatigue Related Services. 242p. (Orig.). 1997. pap. 34.90 (*0-925133-48-5*) Volt Directory.

Butterworth, Taia K., jt. ed. see Southern, Carol.

Butterworth, Tony, et al. Clinical Supervision & Mentorship in Nursing. 1998. pap. 42.50 (*0-7487-3304-3*, Pub. by S Thornes Pubs) Trans-Atl Phila.

Butterworth, W. E., jt. auth. see Hooker, Richard.

Butterworth, W. E., pseud. Leroy & the Old Man. 168p. (YA). (gr. 7-9). 1989. pap. 3.99 (*0-590-42711-3*) Scholastic Inc.
— Leroy & the Old Man. (Point Ser.). (J). 1980. 9.09 (*0-606-01139-0*, Pub. by Turtleback) Demco.

Butterworth, W. Walton, jt. auth. see Schmitt, Hans A.

Butterworths Asia Editors. Butterworths Annotated Statutes of Singapore - Statute Referencer. LC 97-945807. Date not set. write for info. (*0-409-99841-9*, MICHIE) LEXIS Pub.

Butterworths Editorial Staff. Butterworths Survey of South African Law, 1993. 412p. 1994. write for info. (*0-409-00445-6*, MICHIE) LEXIS Pub.
— Legiserve: Botswana. write for info. (*0-7021-1743-9*, R177,84, Pub. by Juta & Co) Gaunt.
— Legiserve: Lesotho. write for info. (*0-7021-1745-5*, R177,84, Pub. by Juta & Co) Gaunt.
— Legiserve: Namibia. write for info. (*0-7021-1750-1*, R238,26, Pub. by Juta & Co) Gaunt.
— Legiserve: Swaziland. write for info. (*0-7021-1746-3*, R238,26, Pub. by Juta & Co) Gaunt.

Butterworths Editorial Staff, compiled by. Labour Legislation Service. write for info. (*0-409-03783-4*, R270,18) Buttrwrth-Heinemann.
— Zimbabwe Income Tax Service. ring bd. write for info. (*0-7021-1037-X*, R220,00, Pub. by Juta & Co) Gaunt.

Butterworths Editors. The Blue Book 1996-97: The Directory of the Law Society of Scotland. 1996. write for info. (*0-406-99291-6*, BBDL1997, MICHIE) LEXIS Pub.
— Code of Advertising Practice & Procedural Guide. Date not set. ring bd. write for info. (*0-409-01010-3*, MICHIE) LEXIS Pub.
— Mallal's Digest 1989. anniversary ed. ix, 393p. 1992. suppl. ed. write for info. (*0-409-99626-2*, MICHIE) LEXIS Pub.
— Mallal's Digest 1995. annuals 4th ed. xliv, 632p. 1996. suppl. ed. write for info. (*0-409-99825-7*, MICHIE) LEXIS Pub.
— Mallal's Digest 1991. annuals ix, 539p. 1993. suppl. ed. write for info. (*0-409-99623-8*, MICHIE) LEXIS Pub.
— Mallal's Digest 1993. anniversary ed. ix, 578p. 1994. suppl. ed. write for info. (*0-409-99711-0*, MICHIE) LEXIS Pub.
— Mallal's Digest 1992. annuals ix, 543p. 1993. suppl. ed. write for info. (*0-409-99647-5*, MICHIE) LEXIS Pub.

Butterworths Editors, compiled by. Butterworths Guide to the Statutes of South Africa/Butterworths Gids tot die Wette Van Suid-Afrika, 1910-1995. annuals (AFR & ENG.). 1996. pap. write for info. (*0-409-01571-7*, MICHIE) LEXIS Pub.
— Butterworths Legislation Service: Administration of Estates Act 66 of 1965. Date not set. write for info. (*0-409-01404-4*, MICHIE) LEXIS Pub.
— Butterworths Legislation Service: Constitutional Court. Date not set. write for info. (*0-409-01463-X*, MICHIE) LEXIS Pub.
— Butterworths Legislation Service: Credit Agreements Act 75 of 1980. Date not set. write for info. (*0-409-01414-1*, MICHIE) LEXIS Pub.
— Butterworths Legislation Service: Criminal Procedure Act 51 of 1977. Date not set. write for info. (*0-409-01408-7*, MICHIE) LEXIS Pub.
— Butterworths Legislation Service: Deeds Registries Act 47 of 1937. Date not set. write for info. (*0-409-01409-5*, MICHIE) LEXIS Pub.
— Butterworths Legislation Service: Estate Duty Act 45 of 1955. Date not set. write for info. (*0-409-01411-7*, MICHIE) LEXIS Pub.
— Butterworths Legislation Service: Insolvency Act 24 of 1936. Date not set. write for info. (*0-409-01417-6*, MICHIE) LEXIS Pub.
— Butterworths Legislation Service: Insurance Act 27 of 1943. Date not set. write for info. (*0-409-01420-6*, MICHIE) LEXIS Pub.
— Butterworths Legislation Service: Land Survey Act 9 of 1927. Date not set. write for info. (*0-409-01452-4*, MICHIE) LEXIS Pub.
— Butterworths Legislation Service: Liquor Act 27 of 1989. Date not set. write for info. (*0-409-01460-5*, MICHIE) LEXIS Pub.
— Butterworths Legislation Service: Magistrates' Courts Act 32 of 1944. Date not set. write for info. (*0-409-01426-5*, MICHIE) LEXIS Pub.
— Butterworths Legislation Service: Motor Vehicle Accidents Act 84 of 1986. Date not set. write for info. (*0-409-01433-8*, MICHIE) LEXIS Pub.
— Butterworths Legislation Service: Multilateral Motor Vehicle Accidents Fund Act 93 of 1989. Date not set. write for info. (*0-409-01434-6*, MICHIE) LEXIS Pub.
— Butterworths Legislation Service: National Building Regulations & Building Standards Act 103 of 1977. Date not set. write for info. (*0-409-01440-0*, MICHIE) LEXIS Pub.
— Butterworths Legislation Service: Pension Funds Act 24 of 1956. Date not set. write for info. (*0-409-01436-2*, MICHIE) LEXIS Pub.
— Butterworths Legislation Service: Restitution of Land Rights Act & Expropriation Act. Date not set. write for info. (*0-409-01461-3*, MICHIE) LEXIS Pub.
— Butterworths Legislation Service: Road Transportation Act 74 of 1977. Date not set. write for info. (*0-409-01429-X*, MICHIE) LEXIS Pub.
— Butterworths Legislation Service: Sectional Titles Act 95 of 1986. Date not set. write for info. (*0-409-01471-0*, MICHIE) LEXIS Pub.
— Butterworths Legislation Service: Share Blocks Control Act 59 of 1980. Date not set. write for info. (*0-409-01468-0*, MICHIE) LEXIS Pub.
— Butterworths Legislation Service: Stamp Duties Act 77 of 1968. Date not set. write for info. (*0-409-01435-4*, MICHIE) LEXIS Pub.
— Butterworths Legislation Service: Supreme Court Act 59 of 1959. Date not set. write for info. (*0-409-01438-9*, MICHIE) LEXIS Pub.
— Butterworths Legislation Service: Transfer Duty Act 40 of 1949. Date not set. write for info. (*0-409-01441-9*, MICHIE) LEXIS Pub.
— Butterworths Legislation Service: Usury Act 73 of 1968. Date not set. write for info. (*0-409-01442-7*, MICHIE) LEXIS Pub.
— Consitutional Legislation Service. Date not set. ring bd. write for info. (*0-409-02009-5*, MICHIE) LEXIS Pub.
— Is It in Force? 1981-1995. 1996. pap. write for info. (*0-409-03394-4*, MICHIE) LEXIS Pub.
— Juridata Property Laws/Eiendomswette, 10 vols. (AFR & ENG.). Date not set. write for info. (*0-409-03434-7*, MICHIE) LEXIS Pub.

Butterworths European Information Services Staff, ed. Butterworths Annual European Review 1995. 1995. write for info. (*0-406-06508-X*, BAER1995, MICHIE) LEXIS Pub.

Butterworths Inhouse Editors. Australian Quantum of Damages, 1991-1994. 145p. 1995. pap. write for info. (*0-409-31188-X*, MICHIE) LEXIS Pub.
— Australian Sentencing Decisions, 1991-1994. 330p. 1995. pap. write for info. (*0-409-31186-3*, MICHIE) LEXIS Pub.
— Taxation Laws of Australia, 1936-1990. Date not set. write for info. (*0-409-30704-1*, MICHIE) LEXIS Pub.

Butterworths Legislation Service Staff. The Competition Act & Related Legislation: 1997 Consolidation. LC 98-1447. v, 171p. 1996. write for info. (*0-433-40192-3*) BUT.

Butterworths Redaksionele Personeel Staff. Suid-Afrikaanse Inkomstebelastingdiens (SAIB) write for info. (*0-409-03968-3*, R199,50) Buttrwrth-Heinemann.

Butterworths Staff. Nebraska Limitations Manual, 1989-1990. 2nd ed. 370p. 1992. suppl. ed. 47.00 (*1-56257-802-2*, MICHIE) LEXIS Pub.
— Oregon Uniform Trial Court Rules & Supplementary Local Rules, 1985-1993. 460p. 1993. suppl. ed. 32.50 (*1-56257-283-0*, MICHIE) LEXIS Pub.
— Statutory Time Limitations, 1981-1991: Colorado. LC 81-66550. 265p. 1991. ring bd. 50.00 (*0-409-20218-5*, MICHIE) LEXIS Pub.
— Statutory Time Limitations, 1981-1991: Colorado. LC 81-66550. 265p. 1992. suppl. ed. 45.00 (*1-56257-806-5*, MICHIE) LEXIS Pub.
— Texas Rules of Civil Procedure, 1984-1990. 430p. 1993. suppl. ed. 25.00 (*1-56257-970-3*, MICHIE) LEXIS Pub.
— Victorian Statutes, Annotations. 6th ed. ring bd. 127.00 (*0-409-48827-5*, MICHIE) LEXIS Pub.
— Virgin Islands Code - Interim Annotation Service. 1993rd ed. 60p. 1993. pap. 25.00 (*1-56257-092-7*, MICHIE) LEXIS Pub.

Butterworths Staff, ed. Butterworths Company Law Service/Butterworths Maatskappyeregdiens. (AFR & ENG.). 1977. ring bd. write for info. (*0-409-01544-X*, 89140-10, MICHIE) LEXIS Pub.
— Butterworths Tax Tables, 1993-94. 30th ed. 12p. 1994. pap. 10.00 (*0-406-03661-6*, U.K., MICHIE) LEXIS Pub.
— Missouri Court Rules Handbook: Local Rules of the 44 Judicial Circuit Courts of Missouri. 1994. ring bd., suppl. ed. 49.50 (*0-614-03774-3*, MICHIE) LEXIS Pub.
— Puerto Rico Sessions Laws: English Edition of Leyes de Puerto Rico. 1990. boxed set 70.00 (*0-88063-447-2*, MICHIE) LEXIS Pub.
— U. S. District Court of Puerto Rico: Local Rules. 157p. 1994. pap. 25.00 (*0-614-03768-9*, MICHIE) LEXIS Pub.

Butterworths Staff & Washington State Dept. of Revenue Staff, eds. Washington Tax Decisions, 1987-1993, 10 vols. 70.00 (*0-318-65031-2*, MICHIE) LEXIS Pub.

Butterworths Staff, ed. see Freedman, Warren.

Buttery, C. M. Handbook for Health Directors. (Illus.). 224p. 1991. text 35.00 (*0-19-506449-6*) OUP.

Buttery, P. J., et al, eds. The Control of Fat & Lean Deposition. 377p. 1992. 140.00 (*0-7506-0354-2*) Buttrwrth-Heinemann.

***Buttfield, Helen.** Posta Frutta. (Illus.). 30p. 2000. pap. 10.95 (*1-55670-997-8*) Stewart Tabori & Chang.
— Posta Verdura. (Illus.). 30p. 2000. pap. 10.95 (*1-55670-998-6*) Stewart Tabori & Chang.

Buttfield, Helen. The Secret Life of Fishes: From Angels to Zebras on the Coral Reef. LC 99-10892. 72p. 1999. 19.95 (*0-8109-3933-9*, Pub. by Abrams) Time Warner.

Buttfield, Helen. Posta Anamalia. 30p. 1996. pap. 10.95 (*1-55670-526-3*) Stewart Tabori & Chang.
— Posta Botanica. 30p. 1996. pap. 10.95 (*1-55670-525-5*) Stewart Tabori & Chang.
— Posta Insecta. 30p. 1996. pap. 10.95 (*1-55670-527-1*) Stewart Tabori & Chang.
— Traveler: A Voyager's Notebook. 160p. 1996. spiral bd. 17.95 (*1-55670-475-5*) Stewart Tabori & Chang.

Butti, Ken & Perlin, John. A Golden Thread: 2500 Years of Solar Architecture & Technology. 2nd rev. ed. (Illus.). Date not set. write for info. (*0-937948-12-8*); pap. write for info. (*0-937948-13-6*) aatec Pubns.

Buttigieg, Joseph A., ed. & tr. see Gramsci, Antonio.

Buttigieg, Ray. Apocraphasis. pap. 5.50 (*0-932436-07-2*) Cykx.
— Pastorale. 1978. pap. 4.99 (*0-685-63585-6*) Cykx.
— Pellrigunagg Ghas-Santwarjutal-Qalb. (MLT.). 3.99 (*0-932436-03-X*) Cykx.
— Rubaiyat Is-Cykx. (MLT.). 1978. pap. 3.99 (*0-932436-00-5*) Cykx.
— Windrhythm. 1983. pap. 5.50 (*0-932436-06-4*) Cykx.

Buttiglione, Rocco. Karol Wojtyla: The Thought of the Man Who Became Pope John Paul II. Guietti, Paolo & Murphy, Francesco, trs. from ITA. LC 97-23188. 424p. 1997. 35.00 (*0-8028-3848-0*) Eerdmans.

Buttiker, Urs. Louis I. Kahn: Light & Space. Bean, David, tr. from GER. LC 93-17933.Tr. of Licht & Raum. (ENG & GER.). 1993. 69.00 (*0-8176-2297-7*) Birkhauser.
— Louis I. Kahn: Light & Space.Tr. of Licht & Raum. (ENG & GER., Illus.). 192p. 1998. 68.00 (*3-7643-2297-7*) Birkhauser.

Buttiker, Wilhelm. The Wildlife of Saudi Arabia & It's Neighbors. (Illus.). 96p. 1995. 49.95 (*0-86685-547-5*, Pub. by Stacey Intl) Intl Bk Ctr.

Buttiker, William. The Wildlife of Saudi Arabia & Its Neighbors. (Illus.). 96p. 1980. boxed set 35.00 (*0-905743-62-8*, Pub. by Stacey Intl) Intl Bk Ctr.

Buttimer, Anne. Geography & the Human Spirit. LC 92-25972. (Illus.). 304p. 1993. text 44.00 (*0-8018-4338-3*) Johns Hopkins.
— Practice Geograph. LC 82-13091. (Illus.). (C). 1984. text 31.95 (*0-582-30087-8*) Longman.

Buttimer, Anne & Wallin, Luke. Nature, Culture, Identity. LC 99-18814. (Geojournal Library). 1999. write for info. (*0-7923-5651-9*) Kluwer Academic.

Buttimer, Annette. Values in Geography. 1987. reprint ed. 75.00 (*0-7855-1990-4*, Pub. by Scientific) St Mut.

Buttimer, Cornelius, jt. ed. see O'Flanagan, Patrick.

Buttimer, S. A. Values in Geography. (C). 1987. text 30.00 (*81-85046-54-9*, Pub. by Scientific Pubs) St Mut.

Buttimore, Jonathan. Holiday Law in Ireland. LC 99-195162. 250p. 1998. pap. 38.25 (*1-901657-24-8*) Gaunt.
— Holiday Law in Ireland LC 99-195162. xxv, 216 p. 1998. write for info. (*1-901657-04-3*, Pub. by Blackhall Pub) Gaunt.
— Security for Costs. 192p. 1998. pap. 38.25 (*1-901657-25-6*) Gaunt.

An Asterisk (*) at the beginning of an entry indicates that the title is appearing for the first time.

Buttinger, Joseph. Smaller Dragon. (WV Encore Edition Ser.). (C). 1996. pap. text 52.50 (*0-8133-7104-X*) Westview.

Buttino, Louis, Jr. Principles & Practice of Medical Therapy in Pregnancy. 3rd ed. 200p. 1998. pap., student ed. 55.00 (*0-8385-6296-5*, Apple Lange Med) McGraw.

Buttitta, Tony & Witham, Barry B. Uncle Sam Presents: A Memoir of the Federal Theatre, 1935-1939. LC 81-43517. (Illus.). 265p. 1982. reprint ed. pap. 82.20 (*0-608-03632-3*, 206445900009) Bks Demand.

Buttjes, Dieter & Byram, Michael, eds. Mediating Languages & Cultures. (Multilingual Matters Ser.: No. 60). 302p. 1990. 99.00 (*1-85359-071-1*); pap. 39.95 (*1-85359-070-3*) Taylor & Francis.

Buttkus, Burkhard. Spectral Analysis & Filter Theory in Applied Geophysics. (Illus.). xvi, 690p. 2000. 94.00 (*3-540-62674-3*) Spr-Verlag.

Buttlar, Johannes Von, see Von Buttlar, Johannes.

Buttlar, Lois J. & Wynar, Lubomyr R., compiled by. Guide to Information Resources in Ethnic Museum, Library, & Archival Collections in the United States, 7. LC 95-39038. (Bibliographies & Indexes in Ethnic Studies: Vol. 7). 384p. 1996. lib. bdg. 82.95 (*0-313-29846-7*, Greenwood Pr) Greenwood.

Buttle, Francis, ed. Relationship Marketing: Theory & Practice. LC 96-223102. 240p. 1996. pap. 34.95 (*1-85396-313-5*, Pub. by P Chapman) Taylor & Francis.

Buttler, H. & Petts, C., eds. Reliability of Boiler Plant. (C). 1980. 100.00 (*0-86022-090-7*, Pub. by Build Servs Info Assn) St Mut.

Buttler, H. J., et al. Estimation of Disequilibrium Models. (Lecture Notes in Economics & Mathematical Systems Ser.: Vol. 279). vi, 114p. 1986. 26.60 (*0-387-16817-6*) Spr-Verlag.

Buttler, Karl P. Field Guide to Orchids of Britain & Europe. (Illus.). 288p. 1992. pap. 22.95 (*1-85223-591-8*, Pub. by Cro1wood) Trafalgar.

***Buttler, Tony.** British Secret Projects. (Illus.). 176p. 2000. 39.95 (*1-85780-095-8*, Pub. by Midland Pubng) Specialty Pr.

Buttler, W. W. The Art & Science of Basic Handgun Accuracy. LC 91-71671. (Illus.). 72p. 1991. pap. 11.95 (*0-939427-74-5*, 07076) Alpha Pubns OH.

Buttler, Warren W. The Armed Option: Zen in the Art of Combat Pistolcraft. LC 93-70315. 160p. 1993. pap. 17.00 (*0-939427-75-3*) Alpha Pubns OH.

Buttles, Arlene. From Dream to Reality. 2nd ed. LC 82-81059. (Illus.). 192p. (Orig.). 1984. pap. 7.95 (*0-9606240-5-8*) Pearl-Win.

Buttles, Catherine, jt. auth. see Scott, John A.

Buttles, Janet R. The Queens of Egypt. (African Heritage Classical Research Studies). 250p. reprint ed. 35.00 (*0-938818-32-5*) ECA Assoc.

Buttmann, Philipp K. Lexilogus Oder Beitrage Zur Griechischen Worterklarung Hauptsachlich Fur Homer und Hesiod, 2 vols. in 1. xvi, 542p. 1968. reprint ed. 120.00 (*0-318-72004-3*) G Olms Pubs.

***Buttner, Brenda.** Pregnant Pauses. 2000. 22.00 (*0-8129-3257-9*, Times Bks) Random.

Buttner, Carl G. Anthologie aus der Suaheli-Literatur (Gedichte und Geschichten der Suaheli) (B. E. Ser.: No. 44). (GER.). 1894. 40.00 (*0-8115-2995-9*) Periodicals Srv.

Buttner, E. Holly, jt. auth. see Moore, Dorothy P.

Buttner, Gottfried. Lady & the Unicorn. Everett, Roland, tr. (Illus.). 128p. 1995. 34.95 (*1-869890-52-3*, Pub. by Hawthorn Press) Anthroposophic.

— Samuel Beckett's Novel "Watt" Dolan, Joseph, tr. LC 84-7234. (Illus.). 144p. 1985. 35.95 (*0-8122-7932-8*) U of Pa Pr.

Buttner, J., ed. History of Clinical Chemistry. LC 83-1968. (Illus.). 91p. 1983. 89.25 (*3-11-008912-2*) De Gruyter.

Buttner-Janz, Karin. The Development of the Artificial Disc: SB Charite. Rocky Mountain Translators Staff, tr. from GER. 200p. 1993. text. write for info. (*0-9635430-0-8*) Hundley & Assocs.

Buttner, Judi, ed. see Caddy, Eileen.

Buttner, Manfred. Geisteshaltung und Stadtgestaltung: Referate, Gehalten auf dem Geographentag in Potsdam, 1995. (Geographie Im Kontext Ser.: Bd. 1). (GER., Illus.). XIV, 374p. 1997. 57.95 (*3-631-32019-1*) P Lang Pubng.

— Geographie und Theologie: Zur Geschichte einer engen Beziehung Mit einem Geleitwort von Frank Richter. (Geographie Im Kontext Ser.: Vol. 2). (GER., Illus.). XIII, 161p. 1998. 37.95 (*3-631-33253-X*) P Lang Pubng.

Buttner, Manfred & Erdmann, Karl-Heinz. Geisteshaltung Und Umwelt - Stadt Und Land. Teil 1: Beitrage Zum Geographentag In Bonn 1997. (Illus.). XII, 150p. 1998. 31.95 (*3-631-33731-0*) P Lang Pubng.

***Buttner, Manfred & Richter, Frank.** Beziehungen Zwischen Religion (Geisteshaltung) und Wissenschaftlicher Umwelt (Theologie, Naturwissenschaft und Musikwissenschaft) eine Standortbestimmung: Festschrift Zum Zehnjahrigen Bestehen der Gesellschaft Zur Forderung der Religion/Umwelt-Forschung und Zum 75. Geburtstag von Manfred Buttner Referate, Gehalten Auf Dem Festsymposium Vom 3. Bis 5. Juli 1998 in Bochum. (Geographie im Kontext Ser.). Xvi, 389p. 1999. 62.95 (*3-631-35289-1*) P Lang Pubng.

Buttner, Manfred & Richter, Frank. Geisteshaltung Und Umwelt - Stadt Und Land. Teil 2: Beitrage Zum Geographentag In Bonn 1997. (Illus.). XVIII, 150p. 1998. 37.95 (*3-631-33629-2*) P Lang Pubng.

***Buttner, T.** Agglomeration, Growth, & Adjustment: A Theoretical & Empirical Study of Regional Labor Markets in Germany. LC 98-32343. (Illus.). 206p. 1999. pap. 63.00 (*3-7908-1160-2*) Spr-Verlag.

Buttner, Ulrich, ed. Vestibular Dysfunction & Its Therapy. (Advances in OtoRhinoLaryngology Ser.: Vol. 55). (Illus.). viii, 248p. 1998. 216.50 (*3-8055-6702-2*) S Karger.

Buttny, Richard. Social Accountability in Communication. 208p. (C). 1993. text 59.95 (*0-8039-8306-9*); pap. text 19.95 (*0-8039-8307-7*) Sage.

Buttolph, Ken, jt. auth. see Kowalke, Ron.

Buttolph, Ken, ed. see Lenzke, James T.

Buttolph, Ken, jt. ed. see Sieber, Mary.

Buttolph, Philip, tr. see Dibelius, Martin & Conzelmann, Hans.

***Button, Beth.** Classical Composers. Rogers, Kathy, ed. (Famous Faces Ser.). (Illus.). 8p. 2000. 6.95 (*1-56472-280-5*) Edupress Inc.

— Early Modern Artists. Rogers, Kathy, ed. (Famous Faces Ser.). (Illus.). 8p. 2000. 6.95 (*1-56472-282-1*) Edupress Inc.

— Notable Black Americans. Rogers, Kathy, ed. (Famous Faces Ser.). (Illus.). 8p. 2000. 6.95 (*1-56472-279-1*) Edupress Inc.

— Presidents Who Shaped the Nation. Rogers, Kathy, ed. (Famous Faces Ser.). (Illus.). 8p. 2000. 6.95 (*1-56472-275-9*) Edupress Inc.

Button, C. Lloyd. Una Vida Solitaria. Meyer, Richard, ed. (Adult Sunday School Ser.). (SPA.). 90p. 1991. 4.40 (*1-879892-03-0*) Editorial Bautista.

***Button, Chris.** Wings of Angels. Maginnis, John H., Jr. et al, eds. (Illus.). 104p. 1999. pap. 19.95 (*0-9675573-0-5*) Bl Cr & Bl Shld LA.

Button, D., jt. auth. see Hearn, P. M.

Button, Eric, ed. Personal Construct Theory & Mental Health: Theory, Research & Practice. 404p. 1985. 20.00 (*0-914797-15-8*) Brookline Bks.

Button, Graham, et al. Computers, Minds & Conduct. 240p. (C). 1995. text 58.95 (*0-7456-1287-3*); pap. text 24.95 (*0-7456-1571-6*) Blackwell Pubs.

Button, Graham, jt. auth. see Lee, John.

Button, James W. Black Violence: Political Impact of the Nineteen-Sixties Riots. LC 78-51158. (Illus.). 263p. reprint ed. pap. 81.60 (*0-8357-4122-2*, 205233300005) Bks Demand.

— Blacks & Social Change: Impact of the Civil Rights Movement in Southern Communities. 340p. 1989. pap. text 20.95 (*0-691-02105-8*, Pub. by Princeton U Pr) Cal Prin Full Svc.

Button, James W., et al. Private Lives, Public Conflicts: Battles over Gay Rights in American Communities. LC 96-53442. 223p. 1997. pap. 14.97 (*1-56802-278-6*) Congr Quarterly.

— Private Lives, Public Conflicts: Battles over Gay Rights in American Communities. LC 96-53442. 223p. (YA). (gr. 11). 1997. text 22.77 (*1-56802-279-4*) Congr Quarterly.

Button, John. A Dictionary of Green Ideas: Vocabulary for a Sane & Sustainable Future. LC 88-4325. 534p. reprint ed. pap. 165.60 (*0-608-20324-6*, 207157700002) Bks Demand.

Button, John, compiled by. The Radicalism Handbook: Radical Activists, Groups & Movements of the Twentieth Century. LC 95-15213. 460p. 1995. lib. bdg. 49.50 (*0-87436-838-3*) ABC-CLIO.

Button, K. High-Technology. (Progress in Planning Ser.: 29). 1988. pap. 30.50 (*0-08-036876-X*, Pergamon Pr) Elsevier.

Button, K. J. & Pearman, A. D. Applied Transport Economics: A Practical Case Studies Approach, Vol. 4. (Transportation Studies). x, 146p. 1985. text 98.00 (*2-88124-061-5*) Gordon & Breach.

Button, K. J. & Pitfield, D. E., eds. International Railway Economics. 384p. 1985. text 63.95 (*0-566-00854-8*, Pub. by Avebry) Ashgate Pub Co.

Button, Kenneth. Transport Economics. 2nd ed. (Illus.). 288p. (Orig.). 1993. 90.00 (*1-85278-521-7*); pap. text 30.00 (*1-85278-523-3*) E Elgar.

— Transport, the Environment & Economic Policy. 184p. 1993. 95.00 (*1-85278-443-1*) E Elgar.

Button, Kenneth, et al, eds. Transport Networks in Europe: Concepts, Analysis & Policies. LC 97-35406. 384p. 1998. 95.00 (*1-85898-582-X*) E Elgar.

***Button, Kenneth & Pentecost, Eric J.** Regional Economic Performance Within the European Union. LC 99-21831. 224p. 1999. 80.00 (*1-85898-064-X*) E Elgar.

Button, Kenneth & Stough, Roger R., eds. Transport Policy. LC 98-27153. (International Library of Comparative Public Policy). 672p. 1998. 240.00 (*1-85898-618-4*) E Elgar.

Button, Kenneth, et al. Academic Links & Communications. (European Science Foundation Ser.). 128p. 1993. 66.95 (*1-85628-546-4*, Pub. by Avebry) Ashgate Pub Co.

— Flying into the Future: Air Transport Policy in the European Union. LC 97-43525. 224p. 1998. 75.00 (*1-85898-799-7*) E Elgar.

— The Future of International Air Transport Policy: Responding to Global Change. LC 97-163288. 156p. (Orig.). 1997. pap. 45.00 (*92-64-15403-5*, 03-97-01-1, Pub. by Org for Econ) OECD.

Button, Kenneth J., ed. The Collected Essays of Harvey Leibenstein Vol. I: Population, Development & Welfare. 384p. 1989. 95.00 (*1-85278-151-3*) E Elgar.

— The Collected Essays of Harvey Leibenstein Vol. II: X-Efficiency & Micro-Micro Theory. 400p. 1989. 95.00 (*1-85278-163-7*) E Elgar.

Button, Kenneth J. & Banister, David, eds. Transport, the Environment & Sustainable Development. LC 92-39738. 1993. mass mkt. 88.95 (*0-419-17870-8*, E & FN Spon) Routledge.

Button, Kenneth J. & Gillingwater, David. Future Transport Policy. 240p. 1986. 59.95 (*0-7099-3225-1*, Pub. by C Helm) Routldge.

Button, Kenneth J. & Pearce, David W., eds. Improving the Urban Environment: How to Adjust National & Local Government Policy for Sustainable Urban Growth. (Progress in Planning Ser.: No. 32). (Illus.). 56p. 1989. pap. 31.00 (*0-08-040166-X*, Pergamon Pr) Elsevier.

Button, Kenneth J. & Swann, Dennis, eds. The Age of Regulatory Reform. (Illus.). 352p. 1989. 79.00 (*0-19-828601-5*) OUP.

Button, Kenneth J. & Verhoef, Erik T., eds. Road Pricing, Traffic Congestion & the Environment: Issues of Efficiency & Social Feasibility. LC 97-52044. 336p. 1998. 95.00 (*1-85898-365-7*) E Elgar.

***Button, Kenneth John & Stough, Roger.** Air Transport Networks: Theory & Policy Implications. LC 00-34827. (Transport Economics, Management & Policy Ser.). 2000. write for info. (*1-84064-429-X*) E Elgar

Button, Lue. Practical Scent Dog Training. LC 90-184. (Illus.). 160p. 1990. pap. 11.95 (*0-931866-47-2*) Alpine Pubns.

Button, Margot. The Unhinging of Wings. 104p. 1996. pap. text 12.95 (*0-88982-162-3*, Pub. by Oolichan Bks) Genl Dist Srvs.

Button, Marilyn Demarest & Reed, Toni, eds. The Foreign Woman in British Literature: Exotics, Aliens & Outsiders, 171. LC 98-41421. (Contributions in Women's Studies: Vol. 171). 224p. 1999. 57.95 (*0-313-30928-0*, Greenwood Pr) Greenwood.

Button, Robert. Managing Publications. 52p. 1982. 5.00 (*0-318-16332-2*) Quill & Scroll.

Button, Robert C. & Bleything, Dennis. The Handbook of Workplace Ergonomics. Date not set. 89.95 (*1-56670-247-X*) Lewis Pubs.

Button, Stuart W. Julian Bream: The Foundations of a Musical Career. LC 96-49287. 180p. 1997. 61.95 (*1-85928-390-X*, ML419.B74B87, Pub. by Scolar Pr) Ashgate Pub Co.

Button, Virginia & Searle, Adrian. The Turner Prize. (Illus.). 104p. 1997. pap. 35.00 (*1-85437-221-1*, Pub. by Tate Gallery) U of Wash Pr.

Buttonware. PC Calc & a Spreadsheet Program. 1986. pap. 21.95 (*0-256-05749-4*, Irwn McGrw-H) McGrw-H Hghr Educ.

Buttonwood, Betsy. Rockets. (Let Me Read Ser.). (J). 1996. 2.95 (*0-673-36333-3*, GoodYrBooks) Addson-Wesley Educ.

Buttram, Harold & Piccola, Richard. Our Toxic World: Who Is Looking after Our Kids?: A Guide for Parents to Protect Their Children from Environmental Chemicals & Other Toxic Substances. LC 96-86207. 200p. (Orig.). 1996. pap. 14.95 (*0-9653616-0-8*) Foresight Am Fnd.

Buttram, Harold E. Dangers of Immunization. 72p. (Orig.). 1987. pap. 4.00 (*0-916285-27-8*) Humanitarian.

— For Tomorrow's Children. 208p. 1991. pap. 12.00 (*0-916285-49-9*) Humanitarian.

— Freedom of Choice in the Healing Arts. 52p. (Orig.). 1971. pap. 2.00 (*0-916285-28-6*) Humanitarian.

— The Immune Trio: Dangers of Immunization, How to Legally Avoid Immunization, & Vaccinations & Immune Malfunction. 192p. 1996. pap. 10.00 (*0-916285-38-3*) Humanitarian.

— A Naturalist's View of the Healing Arts. 32p. 1969. pap. 2.00 (*0-916285-53-7*) Humanitarian.

— Today's Health Movement & the Future of America. 72p. 1982. pap. 4.00 (*0-916285-31-6*) Humanitarian.

— Your Health Habits Checkup. 28p. 1968. pap. 2.00 (*0-916285-59-6*) Humanitarian.

Buttram, Harold E. & Hoffman, John C. Vaccinations & Immune Malfunction. 3rd ed. 75p. (Orig.). 1987. pap. 4.00 (*0-916285-36-7*) Humanitarian.

Buttram, Harold E. & Ricchio, Paul P. Love, Sex & Marriage. 64p. (Orig.). 1983. pap. 2.95 (*0-916285-42-1*) Humanitarian.

Buttram, Harold E., et al. Hidden Influences of Love, Touch & Affection. 124p. (Orig.). 1981. pap. 2.00 (*0-916285-29-4*) Humanitarian.

Buttram, Joan L., et al. Sizing up Your School System: The District Effectiveness Audit. 219p. 1989. reprint ed. pap. 35.95 (*1-56602-028-X*) Research Better.

Buttram, Nora. Gone Are the Days: The Family Farm As It Was & Is. Lowe, Mark & Caturano, Terry, eds (Illus.). 144p. (Orig.). 1990. pap. write for info. (*0-9627057-0-5*) Shalom Pub KY.

Buttress, G. A. & Heaney, Henry J., eds. World Guide to Abbreviations of Organizations. 8th ed. 777p. 1987. 125.00 (*0-8103-2048-7*, Pub. by B & Sons) Gale.

***Buttress, Rob.** Boatowner's Guide to Using PCs on Board. (Illus.). 160p. 2000. pap. 19.95 (*0-07-136446-2*) McGraw.

Buttrey, John. When Storms Come. LC 98-93226. 130p. 1998. pap. 7.95 (*1-57502-943-X*, PO2595) Morris Pubng.

Buttrey, June, jt. auth. see Jones, Anthony.

Buttrey, T. V. & McPhee, Ian. The Extramural Sanctuary of Demeter & Persephone at Cyrene, Libya Vol. VI: Part I: The Coins; Part II: Attic Pottery. (University Museum Monographs: No. 97). (Illus.). xxi, 124p. 1998. 40.00 (*0-924171-48-0*) U Museum Pubns.

Buttrey, Theodore V., Jr., ed. Coinage of the Americas. LC 73-75064. (Illus.). 139p. reprint ed. pap. 43.10 (*0-7837-6999-7*, 204681200004) Bks Demand.

Buttrick, David. Preaching the New & the Now. LC 98-6848. 176p. 1998. pap. 15.00 (*0-664-25789-5*) Westminster John Knox.

***Buttrick, David.** Speaking Parables: A Homiletic Guide. (Illus.). 336p. 2000. pap. 24.95 (*0-664-22191-2*, Pub. by Westminster John Knox) Presbyterian Pub.

Buttrick, David G. A Captive Voice: The Liberation of Preaching. LC 93-31034. 176p. (Orig.). 1994. pap. 17.95 (*0-664-25540-X*) Westminster John Knox.

— Homiletic Moves & Structure. LC 86-45208. 512p. 1987. pap. 24.00 (*0-8006-2096-8*, 1-2096) Augsburg Fortress.

— Preaching As a Theological Task: World, Gospel, Scripture. Long, Thomas G. & Farley, Edward, eds. LC 96-8619. 216p. (Orig.). 1996. pap. 26.95 (*0-664-25617-1*) Westminster John Knox.

Buttrick, George A. The Interpreter's Bible, 12 vols., Set. Incl. Vol. 1. General Articles, Genesis, Exodus. LC 51-12276. 1952. 44.95 (*0-687-19207-2*); Vol. 5. Ecclesiastes - Jeremiah. LC 51-12276. 1956. 44.95 (*0-687-19211-0*); Vol. 8. Luke, John. LC 51-12276. 1952. 44.95 (*0-687-19214-5*); LC 51-12276. 1958. 425.00 (*0-687-19206-4*) Abingdon.

— So We Believe, So We Pray. (Abingdon Classics Ser.). 256p. 1992. reprint ed. pap. 1.79 (*0-687-39049-4*) Abingdon.

Buttrick, George A. & Crim, Keith R., eds. The Interpreter's Dictionary of the Bible, 5 vols., Set. LC 62-9387. 1976. 199.95 (*0-687-19268-4*) Abingdon.

***Buttrick, Robert.** Project Workout: A Toolkit for Reaping the Rewards of All You. 2nd ed. 450p. 2000. pap. text 34.00 (*0-273-64436-X*) F T P H.

Buttrick, Robert. Project Workout: A Toolkit to Drive Change & Improve the Health of Your Business. (Illus.). 250p. (Orig.). 1997. pap. text 25.00 (*0-273-62680-9*) F T P-H.

Buttrick, Shirley, ed. Research on Children. 66p. 1992. 14.95 (*0-87101-223-5*) Natl Assn Soc Wkrs.

Buttriss, J., jt. ed. see Saltmarsh, M.

Buttrose, Larry. The Blue Man: Tales of Travel, Love & Coffee. 264p. 1999. pap. 12.95 (*1-86450-000-X*) Lonely Planet.

***Buttross, Peter, Jr.** Songs from a Star: A Book of Poems. (Illus.). vi, 55p. 1999. pap. 10.00 (*0-9676242-0-7*) Red Dawn Pr.

Buttry, Daniel L. Bringing Your Church Back to Life: Beyond Survival Mentality. 160p. (Orig.). 1988. pap. 13.00 (*0-8170-1143-9*) Judson.

— Christian Peacemaking: From Heritage to Hope. 240p. 1994. pap. 16.00 (*0-8170-1213-3*) Judson.

— First-Person Preaching: Bringing New Life to Biblical Stories. LC 97-53070. 1998. pap. 14.00 (*0-8170-1275-3*) Judson.

— Peace Ministry: A Handbook for Local Churches. LC 94-42198. 240p. 1995. pap. 16.00 (*0-8170-1214-1*) Judson.

Butts, A. John Butts, His Ancestors & Some Descendants. (Illus.). 153p. 1989. reprint ed. pap. 24.50 (*0-8328-1297-8*); reprint ed. lib. bdg. 32.50 (*0-8328-1296-X*) Higginson Bk Co.

Butts, Allison, ed. Silver: Economics, Metallurgy, & Use. LC 74-34002. 498p. 1975. reprint ed. 57.50 (*0-88275-278-2*) Krieger.

Butts, Barbara, et al. Men, Women, & God: German Renaissance Prints from St. Louis Collections. Steiner, Mary A., ed. (Illus.). 84p. (Orig.). 1997. pap. 19.95 (*0-89178-046-7*) St Louis Art Mus.

***Butts, Barbara, et al.** Painting on Light: Drawings & Stained Glass in the Age of Dhurer & Holbein. LC 99-59416. (Illus.). 328p. 2000. 125.00 (*0-89236-578-1*, J P Getty Museum) J P Getty Trust.

Butts, Barbara, jt. auth. see Koerner, Joseph L.

Butts, Carrol M. The High School Band Clinic: Drills & Exercises That Improve Performance. (Illus.). 1978. 17.95 (*0-13-387621-7*, Parker Publishing Co) P-H.

Butts, Dennis, ed. see Hunt, Peter.

Butts, Dennis, ed. see Marryat, Frederick.

Butts, Dennis, ed. & intro. see Burnett, Frances Hodgson.

Butts, Dennis, ed. & intro. see Haggard, H. Rider.

Butts, Diana C. & Wright, Carol. Sugarbaker's Cookie-Cutter Cookbook: Baking & Decorating Beautiful Cookies for Every Holiday. LC 97-30673. (Illus.). 256p. 1997. 24.50 (*0-684-83318-2*) Simon & Schuster.

Butts, Diana C., jt. auth. see Eckhardt, Linda W.

Butts, Ed, jt. auth. see Horwood, Harold.

***Butts, Ellen R. & Schwartz, Joyce R.** Carl Sagan. LC 99-35583. (A & E Biography Ser.). (Illus.). 128p. (gr. 4-7). 2000. lib. bdg. 25.26 (*0-8225-4986-7*, Lerner Publctns) Lerner Pub.

Butts, Ellen R. & Schwartz, Joyce R. Eugenie Clark: Adventures of a Shark Scientist. LC 99-44957. (Illus.). 100p. (YA). (gr. 4-7). 1999. 18.50 (*0-208-02440-9*, Linnet Bks) Shoe String.

Butts, H. Daniel & Glaubinger, Jane. The Art of Phyllis Sloane. (Women's Ser.). 55p. 1996. pap. text 20.00 (*1-893023-54-0*) Ohio Artists.

Butts, Hugh F. The Blackness of Darkness Vol. 1: A Psychohistorical Study of Nineteenth & Twentieth Century American Authors & Their Use of Unconscious Symbolism, Emphasizing Their Depiction of Black Characters & Blackness. 140p. 1994. 21.95 (*0-9623987-3-X*) Clementine Pub Co.

Butts, Hugh F., ed. see Butts, Sydney C.

Butts, Jeffrey A., et al. Juvenile Court Statistics, 1991. (Illus.). 214p. (Orig.). (C). 1995. pap. text 45.00 (*0-7881-2434-X*) DIANE Pub.

— Juvenile Court Statistics (1994) (Illus.). 95p. (C). 1998. reprint ed. pap. text 25.00 (*0-7881-4558-4*) DIANE Pub.

Butts, Jeffrey A., jt. auth. see Poe-Yamagata, Eileen.

Butts, Jeffrey A., ed. see Bilchik, Shay.

Butts, Joe. Pricing for Profit. 46p. 1995. pap. 19.50 (*0-934420-19-X*) Studio Pr NE.

Butts, Joseph L. Crime & Other Critical Social Ills As Seen from Behind the Badge. LC 95-94436. 280p. (Orig.). 1995. pap. text 14.95 (*0-9648215-0-8*) J Butts.

Butts, Karen R. Breathing Exercises for Asthma. 3rd ed. LC 87-71059. (Illus.). 57p. (Orig.). 1999. pap. text, teacher ed. 12.95 (*0-9618671-0-8*) CKRB Pub.

Butts, L., ed. Process Engineering Handbook. 168p. (Orig.). 1991. pap. 72.00 (*0-89852-421-0*, 0101R184) TAPPI.

B

***Butts, Lauren.** Okay, So Now You're a Vegetarian: Advice & 100 Recipes from One Teenager to Another. LC 99-86652. 240p. 2000. pap. 12.95 (*0-7679-0527-X*) Broadway BDD.

Butts, Laurie, et al. Basic Training. Crane, Carla, ed. (Next Level Preteen Electives Ser.). (Illus.). 128p. 1996. teacher ed. 14.99 (*0-7847-0504-6*, 42104) Standard Pub.

Butts, Mary. ASHE of Rings & Other Writings. LC 97-49604. 384p. 1998. 24.00 (*0-929701-53-4*) McPherson & Co.

— The Classical Novels: The Macedonian & Scenes from the Life of Cleopatra. 385p. 1994. 24.00 (*0-929701-43-7*); pap. 14.00 (*0-929701-42-9*) McPherson & Co.

— From Altar to Chimney-Piece: Selected Stories of Mary Butts. LC 91-32692. (Recovered Classics Ser.). 295p. (Orig.). 1992. 22.00 (*0-929701-19-4*); pap. 12.00 (*0-929701-20-8*) McPherson & Co.

— Scenes from the Life of Cleopatra. (Sun & Moon Classics Ser.: No. 72). 288p. (Orig.). 1994. pap. 13.95 (*1-55713-140-6*) Sun & Moon CA.

— The Taverner Novels: Armed with Madness & Death of Felicity Taverner. LC 91-32693. (Recovered Classics Ser.). 384p. (Orig.). 1992. 25.00 (*0-929701-17-8*); pap. 15.00 (*0-929701-18-6*) McPherson & Co.

Butts, Miriam & Heard, Patricia. The Early Industrialization of America: "From Wharf to Waterfall" 39.00 (*1-56696-052-5*) Jackdaw.

Butts, Nancy. Cheshire Moon. LC 95-50377. 105p. (J). (gr. 5 up). 1996. 14.95 (*1-886910-08-1*, Front Street) Front Str.

Butts, Nancy. The Door in the Lake. LC 97-9372. 159p. (J). (gr. 4-7). 1997. 15.95 (*1-886910-27-8*) Front Str.

***Butts, Nancy.** The Door in the Lake. LC 00-29093. (Illus.). 160p. (J). (gr. 3-7). 2000. pap. 5.99 (*0-14-130978-4*, PuffinBks) Peng Put Young Read.

Butts, Nancy K., et al, eds. The Elite Athlete. LC 87-22860. (La Crosse Exercise & Health Ser.). (Illus.). 303p. 1985. reprint ed. pap. 94.00 (*0-608-04292-7*, 206507100012) Bks Demand.

Butts, R. Freeman. The Civic Mission in Educational Reform: Perspectives for the Public & the Profession, P-377. (Publication Series: Education & Society: No. 377). 361p. 1989. text 32.95 (*0-8179-8771-1*); pap. text 22.35 (*0-8179-8772-X*) Hoover Inst Pr.

— College Charts Its Course: Historical Conceptions & Current Proposals. LC 73-165710. (American Education, Ser, No. 2). 1978. reprint ed. 26.95 (*0-405-03699-X*) Ayer.

— In the First Person Singular: The Foundations of Education. LC 92-74545. 110p. (Orig.). 1993. pap. 12.95 (*1-880192-05-5*) Caddo Gap Pr.

— Morality of Democratic Citizenship: Goals for Civic Education in the Republics Third Century. 233p. (Orig.). 1988. pap. 14.95 (*0-89818-132-1*) Ctr for Civic Educ.

— Teacher Education & the Revival of Civic Learning. (DeGarmo Lectures: No. 7). 1982. 10.00 (*0-933669-31-3*) Soc Profs Ed.

Butts, R. Freeman, et al. Civic Learning in Teacher Education. (SPE Monographs). 1983. 3.00 (*0-933669-21-6*) Soc Profs Ed.

Butts, Rick. The Safari Adventure Company: Unlocking the 3 Treasures of Courage. 176p. (Orig.). 1997. pap. 14.98 (*0-9652991-4-7*) Safari Adventure.

— The Safari Chronicles, Vol. 1. 2nd rev. ed. 201p. 1998. 25.00 (*0-9660981-1-0*) Safari Adventure.

— The Safari Chronicles Vol. 2: The Ancient Library. 224p. Date not set. 19.95 (*0-9660981-2-9*) Safari Adventure.

Butts, Robert E. Historical Pragmatics: Philosophical Essays. LC 93-6004. (Boston Studies in the Philosophy of Science: Vol. 155). 374p. (C). 1993. lib. bdg. 174.50 (*0-7923-2498-6*, Pub. by Kluwer Academic) Kluwer Academic.

— Kant & the Double Government Methodology. 355p. 1984. lib. bdg. 122.50 (*90-277-1760-5*, D Reidel) Kluwer Academic.

— Kant & the Double Government Methodology. 355p. (C). 1987. pap. text 65.50 (*90-277-2384-2*, D Reidel) Kluwer Academic.

Butts, Robert E., ed. Kant's Philosophy of Physical Science. 376p. 1986. lib. bdg. 131.00 (*90-277-2309-5*, D Reidel) Kluwer Academic.

— Kant's Philosophy of Physical Science. 375p. 1986. pap. text 65.50 (*90-277-2310-9*, D Reidel) Kluwer Academic.

Butts, Robert E. & Brown, James R., eds. Constructivism & Science. 304p. (C). 1989. lib. bdg. 196.50 (*0-7923-0251-6*, Pub. by Kluwer Academic) Kluwer Academic.

Butts, Robert E. & Hintikka, Jaakko, eds. Basic Problems in Methodology & Linguistics. (Western Ontario Ser.: No. 11). 331p. 1977. text 177.50 (*90-277-0829-0*, D Reidel) Kluwer Academic.

— Historical & Philosophical Dimensions of Logic, Methodology & Philosophy of Science. (Western Ontario Ser.: No. 12). 346p. 1977. text 182.50 (*90-277-0831-2*, D Reidel) Kluwer Academic.

Butts, Robert E. & Pitt, Joseph C., eds. New Perspectives on Galileo. (Western Ontario Ser.: No. 14). 278p. 1978. pap. text 58.50 (*90-277-0891-6*, D Reidel); lib. bdg. 112.00 (*90-277-0859-2*, D Reidel) Kluwer Academic.

Butts, Robert F. American Education in International Development. LC 73-117763. (Essay Index Reprint Ser.). 1977. 19.95 (*0-8369-1786-3*) Ayer.

Butts, Russell, jt. ed. see Balakrishnan, A. V.

Butts, Sydney C. African-American & Hispanic Children's Concept of Death. Butts, Hugh F., ed. LC 90-84289. 56p. (C). 1991. 19.95 (*0-9623987-1-3*) Clementine Pub Co.

Butts, Terry L., et al, eds. Alabama Evidentiary Foundations. LC 99-61005. 386p. 1999. 65.00 (*0-327-00982-9*, 6300110) LEXIS Pub.

Butts, Thomas L. Tigers in the Dark: A Call to Courage & Christian Maturity. 110p. 1994. reprint ed. pap. text 7.95 (*0-940882-19-1*) HB Pubns.

Butts, W. E. The Inheritance. (Illus.). 32p. (J). (gr. 7-9). 1981. pap. 5.00 (*0-939622-27-0*) Four Zoas Night Ltd.

— Movies in a Small Town: Poems. LC 96-45641. 68p. 1997. pap. 14.95 (*0-7734-2705-8*, Mellen Poetry Pr) E Mellen.

— The Required Dance. LC 90-85369. (Orig.). 1990. pap. 7.00 (*0-9627891-0-0*) Igneus Pr.

Butts, William, ed. Conversations with Richard Wilbur. LC 89-28839. (Literary Conversations Ser.). 288p. 1990. text 39.50 (*0-87805-424-3*) U Pr of Miss.

Buttweiler, Robert T. Buttweiler's Guide to Ammunition Prices: The Complete Handbook of Values for the Collector. 224p. (Orig.). 1988. pap. 14.95 (*0-685-24539-X*) R T Buttweiler.

Buttwinick, Marty. Chord Chart Symbols & Abbreviations. Lamont, Daveda, ed. (Musician's How-To Ser.). 24p. 1998. pap. text 5.00 (*0-9642529-0-2*) Sonata Pubng.

— How to Make a Living As a Musician: So You Never Have to Have a Day Job Again. Evans, Marcia, ed. 272p. (Orig.). 1994. pap. 29.95 (*0-9642529-6-1*) Sonata Pubng.

Buttz, John A., jt. auth. see Daigger, Glen T.

Butusova, N. N., Physicochemical Aspects of Medicine Reviews Vol. 2, Pt. 5.4: Life As the Existence & Reproduction of Ordered Nucleotide & Amino-Acid Sequences, Vol. 2. (Soviet Medical Reviews Ser.: Section B). 145p. 1991. text 128.00 (*3-7186-5175-0*, Harwood Acad Pubs) Gordon & Breach.

Butweiku, Nana E., 1st. 500 Years of European Behavior: Its Effect on Afrika & Afrikan Behavior, Smart Weapons. 345p. (Orig.). 1994. pap. 14.00 (*1-56411-104-0*) Untd Bros & Sis.

***Butweitu, Nana Ekow.** Afrikan Theology, Cosmogony & Philosophy: Field Study of African Religions in the Villages. 416p. 1999. 20.00 (*1-56411-196-2*) Untd Bros & Sis.

Butwell, Ann, ed. see Russell, Grahame.

Butwin, Robert. Street-Smart Network Marketing: A No-Nonsense Guide for Creating the Most Richly Rewarding. LC 97-27234. 208p. 2000. pap. 14.95 (*0-7615-1000-1*) Prima Pub.

Butyagin, P. Y. Chemistry Reviews: Active States in Mechanochemical Reactions, Vol. 14. Vol'pin, M. E., ed. (Soviet Scientific Reviews Ser.: Vol. 14, Pt. 1). ii, 146p. 1989. pap. text 123.00 (*3-7186-4987-X*) Gordon & Breach.

Butykai, Istvan, tr. see Berecz, Janos.

Butykai, Istvan, tr. see Lukovich, Istvan.

Butykai, Istvan, tr. see Vass, Imre.

Butylkin, V. S., et al. Resonant Nonlinear Interactions of Light with Matter. (Illus.). 360p. 1989. 158.95 (*0-387-12109-9*) Spr-Verlag.

Butyn, Rene. Formwork for Contractors Exams: Based on Tables in ACI's Formwork for Concrete. 63p. (Orig.). (C). 1990. pap. text, student ed. 9.95 (*0-935715-15-0*, 4099) Construct Bkstore.

***Butz, Andreas, et al, eds.** Smart Graphics: Papers from the AAAI Spring Symposium. (Technical Reports: Vol. SS-00-04). (Illus.). 188p. 2000. spiral bd. 25.00 (*1-57735-110-X*) AAAI Pr.

Butz, Arthur R. The Hoax of the Twentieth Century: The Case Against the Presumed Extermination of European Jewry. rev. ed. LC 77-78964. (Illus.). 397p. (C). 1997. pap. 11.95 (*0-939484-46-3*, 0301) Legion Survival.

Butz, Ellen, jt. auth. see Butz, Rick.

Butz, Geneva M. Christmas Comes Alive. LC 88-19587. (Illus.). 94p. (Orig.). 1988. pap. 10.95 (*0-8298-0787-X*) Pilgrim OH.

— Christmas in All Seasons. LC 95-16995. 136p. (Orig.). 1995. pap. 10.95 (*0-8298-1068-4*) Pilgrim OH.

— Color Me Well. (Looking up Ser.). 24p. 1986. pap. 1.95 (*0-8298-0742-X*) Pilgrim OH.

Butz, George, jt. auth. see DeRisi, William J.

Butz, Isabelle. Diary of a Caregiver, a Love Story. 178p. 1998. pap. text 10.00 (*0-9641529-1-6*) R Edwards Pub.

Butz, Michael R. Chaos & Complexity: Implications for Psychological Theory & Practice. LC 97-19038. 1997. pap. 27.95 (*1-56032-419-8*); boxed set 59.95 (*1-56032-418-X*) Taylor & Francis.

Butz, Michael R. & Chamberlain, Linda L. Clinical Chaos: A Therapist's Guide to Nonlinear Dynamics & Therapeutic Change. LC 98-25958. 1998. write for info. (*0-87630-925-2*) Brunner-Mazel.

Butz, Michael R., et al. Strange Attractors: Chaos, Complexity, & the Art of Family Therapy. LC 96-1600. (Couples & Family Dynamics & Treatment Ser.). 267p. 1996. 69.95 (*0-471-07951-0*) Wiley.

Butz, Richard. How to Carve Wood: A Book of Projects & Techniques. LC 83-50680. (Illus.). 224p. 1985. pap. 19.95 (*0-918804-20-5*, 70030) Taunton.

Butz, Rick & Butz, Ellen. American Eagles. LC 96-18239. (Woodcarving Step by Step with Rick Butz Ser.). (Illus.). 128p. 1996. pap. 14.95 (*0-8117-2995-8*) Stackpole.

— How to Sharpen Tools. LC 96-38436. (Woodcarving Step by Step with Rick Butz Ser.). (Illus.). 96p. 1997. pap. 14.95 (*0-8117-2996-6*) Stackpole.

— Santas. LC 95-3763. (Woodcarving Step by Step with Rick Butz Ser.). (Illus.). 128p. 1995. pap. 14.95 (*0-8117-2566-9*) Stackpole.

— Woodcarving Step-by-Step with Rick Butz: Woodland Warblers. (Woodcarving Step by Step with Rick Butz Ser.). (Illus.). 128p. 1996. pap. 18.95 (*0-8117-2990-7*) Stackpole.

— Woodcarving with Rick Butz. LC 97-36759. (Illus.). 128p. 1998. pap. 19.95 (*0-8117-2994-X*) Stackpole.

— Woodland Creatures. LC 95-3762. (Woodcarving Step by Step with Rick Butz Ser.). (Illus.). 128p. 1995. pap. 14.95 (*0-8117-3064-6*) Stackpole.

***Butz, Steve.** Computer Projects for Middle Schools. 144p. 2000. pap., teacher ed. 19.95 (*1-57690-709-0*, TCM 2709) Tchr Create Mat.

Butz, Tilman, ed. Nuclear Spectroscopy on Charge Density Wave Systems. LC 92-12827. (Physics & Chemistry of Materials with Low-Dimensional Structures Ser.: Vol. 15). 332p. (C). 1992. text 208.00 (*0-7923-1779-3*) Kluwer Academic.

Butz, William. Building the Six-Hour Canoe. (Illus.). 64p. 1996. pap. 15.00 (*0-9610396-7-1*) Tiller.

Butz, William, jt. auth. see Montague, John.

Butzel, Henry M. Genetics in the Courts. LC 86-21725. (Studies in Health & Human Services: Vol. 9). 802p. 1986. lib. bdg. 149.95 (*0-88946-134-1*) E Mellen.

Butzel, Marsha. Mediating the National. 136p. 1994. pap. text 6.00 (*3-7186-0570-8*, Harwood Acad Pubs) Gordon & Breach.

***Butzel, Sandra S. & Knox, Deborah L.** Life Work Transitions.Com: Putting Your Spirit Online. LC 99-31481. 248p. 1999. pap. text 19.95 (*0-7506-7160-2*) Buttrwrth-Heinemann.

Butzen, Fred & Hilton, Christopher. The Linux Network. 552p. 1998. 39.99 incl. cd-rom (*1-55828-589-X*, M&T Bks) IDG Bks.

Butzer, Karl W. Early Hydraulic Civilization in Egypt: A Study in Cultural Ecology. LC 75-36398. (Prehistoric Archeology & Ecology Ser.). (Illus.). 150p. Date not set. reprint ed. pap. 46.50 (*0-608-20621-0*, 205458900003) Bks Demand.

— Geomorphology of the Lower Illinois Valley As a Spatial-Temporal Context for the Koster Archaic Site. (Reports of Investigations: No. 34). (Illus.). 60p. 1977. pap. 3.50 (*0-89792-067-8*) Ill St Museum.

— Recent History of an Ethiopian Delta: The Omo River & the Level of Lake Rudolf. LC 70-184080. (University of Chicago Department of Geography Research Paper Ser.: No. 136). 220p. 1971. reprint ed. pap. 68.20 (*0-608-02236-5*, 206279600004) Bks Demand.

Butzer, Karl W., ed. Dimensions of Human Geography: Essays on Some Familiar & Neglected Themes. LC 77-27874. (Research Papers: No. 186). (Illus.). 1978. pap. text 14.50 (*0-89065-093-4*) U Ch Pr.

Butzer, Karl W. & Freeman, Leslie G., eds. Early Hydraulic Civilization in Egypt: A Study in Cultural Ecology. LC 75-36398. (Prehistoric Archeology & Ecology Ser.). (Illus.). 1997. pap. text 10.00 (*0-226-08635-6*) U Ch Pr.

Butzer, Karl W. & Hansen, Carl L. Desert & River in Nubia: Geomorphology & Prehistoric Environments at the Aswan Reservoir. LC 67-20761. 584p. 1968. reprint ed. pap. 181.10 (*0-608-01917-8*, 206256900003) Bks Demand.

Butzer, Karl W. & Isaac, Glynn L., eds. After the Australopithecines: Stratigraphy, Ecology, & Culture Change in the Middle Pleistocene. (World Anthropology Ser.). xvi, 912p. 1975. 103.85 (*90-279-7629-5*) Mouton.

Butzer, Paul L., ed. Linear Spaces & Approximation: Proceedings. (International Series of Numerical Mathematics: No. 40). 688p. 1980. 111.00 (*0-8176-0979-2*) Birkhauser.

Butzer, Paul L., et al, eds. Approximation Theory & Functional Analysis: Anniversary Volume. (International Series of Numerical Mathematics: Vol. 65). 632p. 1984. 117.00 (*0-8176-1574-1*) Birkhauser.

— Linear Operators & Approximation, 2 vols., Vol. 1. (International Series of Numerical Mathematics: Nos. 20 & 25). 506p. 1980. 97.00 (*0-8176-0590-8*) Birkhauser.

— Linear Operators & Approximation, 2 vols., Vol. 2. (International Series of Numerical Mathematics: Nos. 20 & 25). 608p. 1980. 118.00 (*0-8176-0760-9*) Birkhauser.

Butzer, Paul L. & Feher, Ferenc, eds. E. B. Christoffel: The Influence of His Work in Mathematics & the Physical Sciences. (Illus.). 656p. (C). 1981. 49.00 (*0-8176-1162-2*) Birkhauser.

Butzer, Paul L. & Lohrmann, Dietrich, eds. Science in Western & Eastern Civilization in Carolingian Times. LC 93-20519. xii, 609p. 1993. 81.50 (*0-8176-2863-0*) Birkhauser.

Butzer, Paul L. & Szokefalvi-Nagy, B., eds. Abstract Spaces & Approximation. (International Series of Numerical Mathematics: No. 10). 423p. 1980. 105.00 (*0-8176-0194-5*) Birkhauser.

Butzlaff, Joachim, ed. Karl Rosenkranz: Briefe 1827 bis 1850. (Quellen und Studien zur Philosophie: Bd. 37). (GER.). viii, 539p. (C). 1994. lib. bdg. 200.00 (*3-11-014373-9*, 103-94) De Gruyter.

Butzler, Jean-Paul, ed. Campylobacter Infection in Man & Animals. 256p. 1984. 147.00 (*0-8493-5446-3*, QR201, CRC Reprint) Franklin.

Butzmann, Gerhard. Taschenlexikon Technik. (GER.). 1993. 59.95 (*0-7859-8501-8*, 3816909728) Fr & Eur.

Butzow, Carol M. & Butzow, John W. Exploring the Environment Through Children's Literature: An Integrated Approach. LC 98-43477. (Illus.). 160p. 1999. pap. 22.00 (*1-56308-650-6*) Teacher Ideas Pr.

— Intermediate Science Through Children's Literature: Over Land & Sea. LC 94-13769. 193p. 1994. pap. text 23.00 (*0-87287-946-1*) Teacher Ideas Pr.

— More Science Through Children's Literature: An Integrated Approach. LC 98-2734. (Illus.). 250p. (J). (gr. k-3). 1998. pap. 26.00 (*1-56308-266-7*) Libs Unl.

— Science Through Children's Literature: An Integrated Approach. 200p. 1989. pap. text 24.50 (*0-87287-667-5*) Teacher Ideas Pr.

***Butzow, Carol M. & Butzow, John W.** Science Through Children's Literature: An Integrated Approach. 2nd ed. LC 99-88098. 240p. 2000. pap. 27.50 (*1-56308-651-4*) Libs Unl.

Butzow, John W., jt. auth. see Butzow, Carol M.

Buultjens, Ralph. The Decline of Democracy: Essays on an Endangered Political Species. LC 77-13276. 160p. reprint ed. pap. 49.60 (*0-8357-8856-3*, 203348200086) Bks Demand.

— Rebuilding the Temple: Tradition & Change in Modern Asia. LC 73-85288. 256p. reprint ed. pap. 79.40 (*0-8357-7004-4*, 203353200086) Bks Demand.

Buunk, Bram & Van Driel, Barry. Variant Lifestyles & Relationships. LC 89-4309. (Family Studies Text: No. 11). 160p. 1989. reprint ed. pap. 49.60 (*0-7837-9897-0*, 206062300006) Bks Demand.

Buunk, Bram P. & Gibbons, Frederick X., eds. Health, Coping, & Well-Being: Perspectives from Social Comparison Theory. LC 96-54802. 392p. 1997. 99.95 (*0-8058-1858-8*) L Erlbaum Assocs.

Buunk, Bram P. & Van Driel, Barry. Variant Lifestyles & Relationships. (Family Studies Text Ser.: Vol. 11). 160p. (C). 1989. text 42.00 (*0-8039-3059-3*); pap. text 18.95 (*0-8039-3060-7*) Sage.

Buurman, P., et al. Manual of Soil & Water Analysis. 314p. 1996. pap. 53.00 (*90-73348-58-7*, Pub. by Backhuys Pubs) Balogh.

Buurman, P., jt. auth. see Van Breemen, N.

Buurman, Wim A., ed. see International Conference on Tumor Necrosis Factor.

Buursma, Kathryn & Stickney, Mary. Official Special Olympics Celebrity Cook Book. 1980. 15.00 (*0-87832-046-6*) Piper.

Buus, Jens. Single Frequency Semiconductor Lasers. 112p. 1991. pap. 20.00 (*0-8194-0535-3*, TT05) SPIE.

Buvac, Sasa, ed. Formalizing Context: Papers from the 1995 Fall Symposium. (Technical Reports). (Illus.). 119p. 1995. spiral bd. 25.00 (*0-929280-96-2*) AAAI Pr.

***Buvat, Colette.** Open up Words & Understand the World (Decouvrons les Mots et Nous Comprendrons le Monde) LC 99-54. 134p. 1999. spiral bd. 12.96 (*1-55212-303-0*) Trafford Pub.

Buvat, R. Ontogeny, Cell Differentiation & Structure of Vascular Plants. (Illus.). 600p. 1989. 281.95 (*0-387-19213-1*) Spr-Verlag.

***Buvens, Norma O.** Just Inside the Gate. 1999. pap. 14.95 (*1-57168-924-9*, Eakin Pr) Sunbelt Media.

Buvinic, Mayra, et al, eds. Women & Poverty in the Third World. LC 82-8992. (Johns Hopkins Studies in Development). 343p. reprint ed. pap. 106.40 (*0-8357-6752-3*, 203540800095) Bks Demand.

Buvinic, Mayra & Yudelman, Sally W. Women, Poverty & Progress in the Third World. LC 89-84292. (Headline Ser.: No. 289). (Illus.). 64p. (Orig.). 1989. pap. 5.95 (*0-87124-127-7*) Foreign Policy.

Buvinic, Mayra, et al. Investing in Women: Progress & Prospects for the World Bank. LC 96-13453. (Overseas Development Council Ser.: Vol. 19). 128p. (Orig.). 1996. pap. text 13.95 (*1-56517-018-0*) Overseas Dev Council.

Buvinic, Mayra, jt. ed. see Berger, Marguerite.

***Buvoli, Luca.** Flying: Practical Training for Beginners. 2000. 20.00 (*0-938437-61-5*) MIT List Visual Arts.

Buwalda, Piet. They Did Not Dwell Alone: Jewish Emigration from the Soviet Union, 1967-1990. LC 96-29951. 1997. 38.00 (*0-8018-5616-7*) Johns Hopkins.

Bux & Clark, J. Data Entry Activities for the Microcomputer. 2nd ed. (DF - Computer Applications Ser.). 1987. pap. 17.75 (*0-538-10060-5*) S-W Pub.

Bux & Gorman. Data Entry Activities for Microcomputers. 3rd ed. (DF - Computer Applications Ser.). (C). 1994. pap. 22.95 (*0-538-61432-3*) S-W Pub.

Bux, William E. Data Entry Activities for Microcomputer. 2nd ed. text, wbk. ed. 34.75 (*0-538-51083-8*) Thomson Learn.

Buxbaum, A. & Schierau, K. Design of Control Systems for DC Drives. Kassakian, John G. & Naunin, D. H., eds. Straughen, Alan, tr. from GER. (Electric Energy Systems & Engineering Ser.). 288p. 1991. 114.95 (*0-387-51864-9*) Spr-Verlag.

Buxbaum, David C., ed. Chinese Family Law & Social Change in Historical & Comparative Perspective. LC 76-7781. (Asian Law Ser.: No. 3). 582p. 1978. 50.00 (*0-295-95448-5*) U of Wash Pr.

Buxbaum, Edith. Troubled Children in a Troubled World. LC 79-128623. 341p. (Orig.). 1970. 50.00 (*0-8236-6653-0*) Intl Univs Pr.

— Your Child Makes Sense: A Guidebook for Parents. 204p. (Orig.). 1961. pap. 24.95 (*0-8236-8350-8*, 027040) Intl Univs Pr.

Buxbaum, Edwin C. The Greek American Group of Tarpon Springs, Florida: A Study of Ethnic Identification & Acculturation. Cordasco, Francesco, ed. LC 80-843. (American Ethnic Groups Ser.). 1981. lib. bdg. 54.95 (*0-405-13407-X*) Ayer.

***Buxbaum, Gerda.** Icons of Fashion: The Twentieth Century. (Illus.). 192p. 1999. 29.95 (*3-7913-2161-7*, Pub. by Prestel) te Neues.

Buxbaum, Gunter. Industrial Inorganic Pigments. 2nd ed. 306p. 1998. 205.00 (*3-527-28878-3*, Wiley-VCH) Wiley.

Buxbaum, Hannah L., jt. auth. see Shreve, Gene R.

Buxbaum, James M. The Corporate Politeia: A Conceptual Approach to Business, Government & Society. LC 81-40313. (Illus.). 96p. (Orig.). 1981. pap. text 16.00 (*0-8191-1764-1*) U Pr of Amer.

Buxbaum, Katherine. Iowa Outpost. (American Autobiography Ser.). 253p. 1995. reprint ed. lib. bdg. 79.00 (*0-7812-8471-6*) Rprt Serv.

Buxbaum, Melvin H. Benjamin Franklin: A Reference Guide, 1907-1983. 1988. 65.00 (*0-8161-8673-1*, Hall Reference) Macmillan.

— Critical Essays on Benjamin Franklin. (Critical Essays on American Literature Ser.). 208p. 1987. 48.00 (*0-8161-8699-5*, G K Hall & Co) Mac Lib Ref.

Buxbaum, Richard M., et al, eds. European Business Law: Legal & Economic Analyses on Integration & Harmonization. xxiv, 414p. (C). 1991. lib. bdg. 144.65 (*3-11-011648-0*) De Gruyter.

An Asterisk (*) at the beginning of an entry indicates that the title is appearing for the first time.

— European Economic & Business Law: Legal & Economic Analyses on Integration & Harmonization. LC 96-10972. xxii, 374p. (C). 1996. lib. bdg. 168.90 (3-11-014242-2) De Gruyter.

Buxbaum, Richard M. & Hendley, Kathryn, eds. The Soviet Sobranie of Laws: Problems of Codification & Non-Publication. LC 91-6393. (Research Ser.: No. 78). (Illus.). xii, 226p. (Orig.). (C). 1991. pap. text 16.95 (0-87725-178-9) U of Cal IAS.

Buxbaum, Richard M. & Hopt, Klaus J., eds. Integration Through Law - Europe & the American Federal Experience Vol. 4: Legal Harmonization & the Business Enterprise. (European University Institute, Series A (Law): Nos. 2-4). 347p. (C). 1988. lib. bdg. 123.10 (3-11-010742-2) De Gruyter.

***Buxbaum, Richard M., et al.** Corporations, Capital Markets & Business in the Law. LC 00-21885. 704p. 2000. 212.00 (90-411-1354-1) Kluwer Law Intl.

Buxbaum, Tim. Icehouses. (Album Ser.: No. 278). (Illus.). 32p. 1998. pap. 6.25 (0-7478-0150-9, Pub. by Shire Pubns) Parkwest Pubns.

***Buxbaum, Tim.** Pargeting. 1999. pap. 25.00 (0-7478-0414-1, Pub. by Shire Pubns) St Mut.

Buxbaum, Tim. Scottish Doocots. (Handbook Ser.: No. 190). (Illus.). 32p. 1989. pap. 6.25 (0-85263-848-5, Pub. by Shire Pubns) Parkwest Pubns.

— Suffolk. (Country Guide Ser.: No. 37). (Illus.). 128p. 1996. pap. 12.50 (0-7478-0319-6, Pub. by Shire Pubns) Parkwest Pubns.

Buxbaum, Yitzhak. Jewish Spiritual Practices. LC 89-35141. 774p. 1994. pap. 40.00 (1-56821-206-2) Aronson.

— An Open Heart: The Mystic Path of Loving People. (Jewish Spirit Booklet Ser.: Vol. 2). 96p. (Orig.). 1997. pap. 9.95 (0-9657112-2-6) Jewish Spirit.

***Buxbaum, Yitzhak.** A Person Is Like a Tree: A Sourcebook for Tu BeShvat. LC 99-48147. 1999. 25.00 (0-7657-6128-9) Aronson.

Buxbaum, Yitzhak. Real Davvening: Jewish Prayer As a Spiritual Practice & a Form of Meditation for Beginning & Experienced Davveners. (Jewish Spirit Booklet Ser.: No. 1). 50p. (Orig.). 1996. pap. 7.95 (0-9657112-1-8) Jewish Spirit.

— A Tu BeShvat Seder: The Feast of Fruits from the Tree of Life. (Jewish Spirit Booklet Ser.: Vol. 3). 85p. (Orig.). 1998. pap. 9.95 (0-9657112-3-4) Jewish Spirit.

Buxeda, Aline F., ed. Puerto Rico en America Latina. (SPA., Illus.). 400p. 1994. 25.00 (0-9623590-5-X) Libros-Ediciones.

Buxman, Annarie. Homophones: An Illustrated Dictionary. 176p. 1995. pap. 15.95 (0-937673-10-2) Peacock Ent LA.

***Buxmann, Peter & Konig, W.** Inter-Organizational Cooperation with SAP Systems: Perspectives on Logistics & Service Management. (SAP Excellence Ser.). 200p. 2000. 44.95 (3-540-66983-3) Spr-Verlag.

Buxtehude, Dieterich. Instrumental Works for Strings & Continuo. Linfield, Eva, ed. (The Collected Works: Vol. 14). (Illus.). 1994. lib. bdg. 200.00 (0-8450-7514-4) Broude.

— 9 Kantaten fur 4 Singstimmen & Instrumente, Pt. 1. Kilian, Dietrich, ed. (Dietrich Buxtehudes Werke Ser.: Vol. 8). (Illus.). 1978. reprint ed. pap. 85.00 (0-89371-018-0) Broude Intl Edns.

***Buxtehude, Dieterich.** Preludes, Toccatas & Ciacconas for Organ (Pedaliter) Belotti, Michael, ed. (Collected Works: No. 15, Pt. 1). (Illus.). 341p. 1998. lib. bdg. 200.00 (0-8450-7515-2, Broud Trust) Broude.

Buxtehude, Dieterich. Sacred Works for Four Voices with Instruments, Pt. 2. Snyder, Kerala, ed. (Collected Works: Vol. 9). (Illus.). 1987. lib. bdg. 200.00 (0-8450-7509-8) Broude.

Buxtehude, Dietrich. Organ Works. 320p. 1988. pap. 14.95 (0-486-25682-0) Dover.

Buxton. Alabama Criminal Code: 1993 Edition. annot. ed. 30.00 (0-614-05772-8, MICHIE) LEXIS Pub.

Buxton, A., jt. auth. see Llines, Salvador O.

Buxton, A., jt. auth. see Oliva, S.

Buxton, A. G. The Buxton Technological Course in Painless Chiropractic. 127p. 1996. reprint ed. spiral bd. 15.50 (0-7873-0136-1) Hlth Research.

Buxton, Amity P. The Other Side of the Closet: The Coming-Out Crisis for Straight Spouses & Families. expanded rev. ed. 352p. 1994. pap. 17.95 (0-471-02152-0) Wiley.

Buxton, Barry, et al, eds. The Great Forest: An Appalachian Story. 2nd rev. ed. (Illus.). 59p. (Orig.). 1985. pap. 4.00 (0-913239-38-0) Appalach Consortium.

Buxton, Barry, ed. see Lovingood, Paul & Reiman, Robert.

Buxton, Barry M., ed. The Cratis Williams Symposium Proceedings. 1989. pap. 5.95 (0-913239-61-5) Appalach Consortium.

Buxton, Ben. Mingulay: An Island & Its People. LC 96-140549. (Illus.). 200p. pap. 21.95 (1-874744-24-6, Pub. by Birlinn Ltd) Dufour.

Buxton, Bernard & Cipolla, Roberto, eds. Computer Vision, ECCV '96: Fourth European Conference on Computer Vision, Cambridge, UK, April 14-18, 1996 Proceedings, Vol. 1. LC 96-16950. (Lecture Notes in Computer Science Ser.: Vol. 1064). xxi, 725p. 1996. pap. 106.00 (3-540-61122-3) Spr-Verlag.

— Computer Vision, ECCV '96: Fourth European Conference on Computer Vision, Cambridge, UK, April 14-18, 1996 Proceedings, Vol. 2. LC 96-16950. (Lecture Notes in Computer Science Ser.: Vol. 1065). xix, 723p. 1996. pap. 106.00 (3-540-61123-1) Spr-Verlag.

Buxton, Bernard F., jt. auth. see Murray, David W.

Buxton, Bruce E., ed. Geostatistical, Sensitivity & Uncertainty Methods for Ground-Water Flow & Radionuclide Transport Modeling. LC 88-7376. 680p. 1989. 75.00 (0-935470-45-X) Battelle.

Buxton, C. R. Russian Composition & Conversation. (RUS & ENG., Illus.). 184p. 1994. pap. 14.95 (0-8442-4221-7, 42217, Natl Textbk Co) NTC Contemp Pub Co.

Buxton, Charles R. Prophets of Heaven & Hell. LC 78-100796. 1970. reprint ed. pap. 75.00 (0-8383-0086-3) M S G Haskell Hse.

Buxton, Claude E. Adolescents in School. LC 72-91290. 190p. reprint ed. pap. 58.90 (0-8357-5114-7, 202198600024) Bks Demand.

Buxton, Clyne W. End Times. 153p. 1993. pap. 9.99 (0-87148-293-2) Pathway Pr.

— Minister's Service Manual. 1985. text 11.99 (0-87148-584-2) Pathway Pr.

Buxton, D. R. & Baenziger, R. Stephen, eds. International Crop Science I. LC 93-40026. 928p. 1993. 50.00 (0-89118-538-0) Am Soc Agron.

Buxton, David, jt. auth. see Stubbs, Kendon L.

Buxton, David, tr. see Mattelart, Armand & Schmucler, Hector.

Buxton, Dickson C. You've Built a Successful Business, Now What? 1996. pap. text 19.95 (1-882180-62-3) Griffin CA.

Buxton, Ed, jt. auth. see Fulton, Sue.

Buxton, Edward. Creative People at Work. LC 73-37245. 292p. 1983. reprint ed. pap. 9.95 (0-917168-04-6) Executive Comm.

Buxton, Edward & Fulton, Susan. More New Business for Ad Agencies. 358p. 1991. pap. 35.00 (0-917168-13-5) Executive Comm.

Buxton, Frank & Owen, Bill. The Big Broadcast 1920-1950. 2nd ed. LC 96-41051. 320p. 1996. 59.50 (0-8108-2957-6) Scarecrow.

Buxton, Gail. Craft Making for Love & Money. LC 83-81742. (Illus.). 144p. 1983. pap. 12.50 (0-917168-08-9) Executive Comm.

Buxton, H. W. Memoir of the Life & Labours of the Late Charles Babbage Esq., F. R. S. (Charles Babbage Institute Reprint Series for the History of Computing). (Illus.). 425p. 1987. 65.00 (0-262-02269-9) MIT Pr.

Buxton, I. L., et al. Cargo Access Equipment for Merchant Ships. 366p. (C). 1978. 110.00 (0-7855-6170-6, Pub. by ICHCA) St Mut.

— Cargo Access Equipment for Merchant Ships. (C). 1989. 160.00 (0-7855-5074-7, Pub. by ICHCA) St Mut.

Buxton, J. Case Studies in Latin American Political Economy. LC 99-491026. 208p. 1999. 79.95 (0-7190-5457-5, Pub. by Manchester Univ Pr) St Martin.

***Buxton, J.** Developments in Latin American Political Economy: States, Markets & Actors. 1999. text 69.95 (0-7190-5458-3, Pub. by Manchester Univ Pr) St Martin.

Buxton, J. Developments in Latin American Political Economy: States, Markets & Actors. 1999. pap. text 24.95 (0-7190-5459-1, Pub. by Manchester Univ Pr) St Martin.

Buxton, Jane H., ed. Playful Pandas. (Pop-Up Bks.: No. 6). (Illus.). (J). (ps-3). 1998. 16.00 (0-87044-840-4) Natl Geog.

Buxton, John, ed. see Walton, Izaak & Cotton, Charles.

Buxton, Judith. Selected Canadian Spinning Wheels in Perspective: An Analytical Approach. (Mercury Ser.: History No. 30). (Illus.). 340p. 1992. pap. 24.95 (0-660-14000-4, Pub. by CN Mus Civilization) U of Wash Pr.

Buxton, Julie M. & Godfrey, Kelly B. Living Skills for the Brain Injured Child & Adolescent: A Rehabilitation Workbook. 400p. 1999. wbk. ed. 39.95 (0-937857-80-7, 1350) Speech Bin.

Buxton, Julie M., jt. auth. see Angle, Deborah K.

Buxton, Kathryn, jt. auth. see Ackermann, Rick.

Buxton, Kathryn, jt. auth. see Coleman, Loren.

Buxton, Laurie. Math Panic. LC 90-28874. 260p. (C). (gr. 9). 1991. pap. text 22.50 (0-435-08313-9, 08313) Heinemann.

Buxton, Maria. Antarctic Diary. (C). 1988. 50.00 (0-86138-024-X, Pub. by T Dalton) St Mut.

Buxton, Mary W. The Great Rappahannock River Race: A Battle of the Sexes. 133p. (Orig.). 1993. pap. 9.95 (1-880902-06-0) Rappahannock Pr.

— Sunrise on the Rappahannock: A River-Lover's Guide to Peace & Happiness. LC 92-93891. (Illus.). 83p. (Orig.). 1992. pap. 6.50 (1-880902-05-2) Rappahannock Pr.

— To Love a Virginian. 200p. 1991. pap. 9.95 (1-880902-03-6) Rappahannock Pr.

***Buxton, Mary Wakefield.** Bringing in the Wood: The Way It Was at Chesapeake Corporation. (Illus.). 200p. 1999. text. write for info. (1-880902-12-5); pap. text. write for info. (1-880902-13-3) Rappahannock Pr.

Buxton, Meriel. The World of Hunting. (Illus.). 128p. 1991. 34.95 (0-948253-53-3, Pub. by Sportmans Pr) Trafalgar.

Buxton, P. K., ed. ABC of Dermatology. 2nd ed. 104p. (C). 1993. pap. text 32.00 (0-7279-0777-8, Pub. by BMJ Pub) Login Brothers Bk Co.

— ABC of Dermatology. 3rd ed. (Illus.). 114p. 1998. pap. text 32.00 (0-7279-1150-3, Pub. by BMJ Pub) Login Brothers Bk Co.

Buxton, Paul. Two Chains. 1997. pap. 3.00 (1-57514-293-7, 3075) Encore Perform Pub.

***Buxton, Paul K., et al.** Keeping Score. Adams, Alison, ed. (Early Connections Ser.). 16p. (J). (gr. k-2). 1999. pap. 4.50 (1-58344-068-2) Benchmark Educ.

Buxton, Richard. From Myth to Reason? Studies in the Development of Greek Thought. LC 98-50450. 384p. 1999. text 75.00 (0-19-815234-5) OUP.

— Imaginary Greece: The Contents of Mythology. LC 93-27412. (Illus.). 266p. (C). 1994. pap. text 22.95 (0-521-33865-4) Cambridge U Pr.

Buxton, Shelia. Organic Stereochemistry. (C). 1996. pap. text 32.81 (0-582-23932-X, Pub. by Addison-Wesley) Longman.

Buxton, Suzanne. How to Improve Your Child's Reading. (C). 1988. 50.00 (0-7223-2231-3, Pub. by A H S Ltd) St Mut.

Buxton, Sydney C. Finance & Politics: An Historical Study, 1783-1885 2 Vols, Set. LC 66-21367. (Reprints of Economic Classics Ser.). 1966. reprint ed. 95.00 (0-678-00164-2) Kelley.

***Buxton, Ted.** Soccer Skills: For Young Players. LC GV943.B89 2000. (Illus.). 128p. (J). 2000. pap. 14.95 (1-55209-329-8) Firefly Bks Ltd.

Buxton, Thomas H., et al, eds. The Many Faces of Teaching. LC 86-26648. 504p. (Orig.). 1987. pap. text 34.00 (0-8191-5764-3); lib. bdg. 62.00 (0-8191-5763-5) U Pr of Amer.

Buxton, Tony & Chapman, Paul, eds. Britain's Economic Performance. 2nd ed. 448p. (C). 1997. 115.00 (0-415-14873-1); pap. 32.99 (0-415-14874-X) Routledge.

Buxton, Wally, jt. auth. see Canning, Jeff.

Buxton, William. Talcott Parsons & the Capitalist Nation State: Political Sociology As a Strategic Vocation. 344p. 1985. pap. 17.95 (0-8020-6531-7) U of Toronto Pr.

***Buxton, William & ACland, Charles R.** Harold Innis in the New Century: Reflections & Refractions. (ENG & FRE.). 456p. 2000. pap. 27.95 (0-7735-1738-5, Pub. by McG-Queens Univ Pr) CUP Services.

Buxton, William, jt. ed. see Baecker, Ronald.

Buxton, William J., jt. ed. see Acland, Charles R.

Buxton, Willis G., compiled by. History of Boscawen - Webster, Fifty Years, 1883-1933. (Illus.). 502p. 1997. reprint ed. lib. bdg. 53.50 (0-8328-5979-6) Higginson Bk Co.

Buxtorf, Johannes. De Abbreviaturis Hebraicis Liber Novus et Copiosus. 559p. 1985. reprint ed. 110.00 (3-487-07529-6) G Olms Pubs.

Buyana, T. Molecular Physics. 300p. 1997. text 55.00 (981-02-0830-8); pap. text 28.00 (981-02-0831-6) World Scientific Pub.

Buydens, Lutgarde M. & Schoenmakers, Peter J., eds. Intelligent Software for Chemical Analysis. LC 93-28143. (Data Handling in Science & Technology Ser.: Vol. 13). 366p. 1993. 237.50 (0-444-89207-9) Elsevier.

Buydens, Lutgarde M., jt. auth. see Kateman, G.

Buyens, Jim. Building Net Apps with Microsoft Internet Information Server. 512p. (C). 1997. pap. text 42.95 (0-201-87370-2) Addison-Wesley.

— Building Net Sites with Windows NT: An Internet Services Handbook. LC 96-11363. 640p. (C). 1996. pap. text 39.95 (0-201-47949-4) Addison-Wesley.

— Running Microsoft FrontPage. LC 97-33680. 864p. 1997. pap. 34.99 (1-57231-645-4) Microsoft.

— Running Microsoft FrontPage 97. 500p. 34.99 (1-57231-426-5) Microsoft.

***Buyens, Jim.** Running Microsoft FrontPage 2000. LC 98-43585. 800p. 1999. pap. text 44.99 (1-57231-947-X) Microsoft.

Buyens, Jim. Stupid Web Tricks. LC 98-19055. 252p. 29.99 incl. cd-rom (1-57231-922-4) Microsoft.

Buyer, Laurie W. Glass-Eyed Paint in the Rain: Poetry of the American West. LC 96-32611. 72p. 1996. pap. 10.95 (0-931271-40-1) Hi Plains Pr.

— Red Colt Canyon. 77p. 1999. pap. 12.95 (0-965126-8-6) Music Mtn Pr.

Buyer, Robert L. Blue Whale & Family. (Carving Sea Life Ser.). (Illus.). 48p. 1996. pap. 7.95 (0-8117-2467-0) Stackpole.

— Bottlenose Dolphin. LC 94-28505. (Carving Sea Life Ser.). (Illus.). 32p. 1995. pap. 12.95 (0-8117-2523-5) Stackpole.

— Humpback Cow & Calf. LC 95-6055. (Carving Sea Life Ser.). (Illus.). 32p. 1995. pap. 7.95 (0-8117-2465-4) Stackpole.

— Killer Whale & Pilot Whales. LC 95-6385. (Carving Sea Life Ser.). (Illus.). 32p. 1995. pap. 17.95 (0-8117-2466-2) Stackpole.

— Mackerel Sharks. (Carving Sea Life Ser.). (Illus.). 40p. 1996. pap. 7.95 (0-8117-2468-9) Stackpole.

— Sperm Whale. LC 94-26514. (Illus.). 1995. pap. 12.95 (0-8117-2521-9) Stackpole.

Buyer, Robert L. & Gilbert, Thomas E. Sea Turtles. LC 96-13622. (Carving Sea Life Ser.). (Illus.). 48p 1996. pap. 7.95 (0-8117-2470-0) Stackpole.

Buyer, Robert L. & Towers, Martha M. Seashells LC 96-13623. (Carving Sea Life Ser.). (Illus.). 40p 1996. pap. 7.95 (0-8117-2469-7) Stackpole.

***Buyer's Guide Staff.** Edmund's New Cars Prices & Reviews, Fall 1999. (Edmund's New Cars Ser.). 576p. 2000. mass mkt. write for info. (0-87759-654-9) Edmund Pubns.

— Edmunds New Trucks Includes Vans, Pickups & Sport Utilties: 1999 Edition. (New Trucks Ser.). 592p. 2000. mass mkt. write for info. (0-87759-655-7) Edmund Pubns.

Buys, Alain. Decomaster: Decorating with a Paper Cone, 120 Practice Sheets & Decorating with a Paper Cone. 192p. 94.95 (0-470-34555-1) Halsted Pr.

Buys, Alain. Decorating with a Paper Cone. (Illus.). 192p. 1996. 55.00 (0-471-16065-2) Wiley.

Buys, Alain & Decluzeau, Jean-Luc. Decomaster: Decorating with a Paper Cone, 120 Practice Sheets. 120p. 1998. pap. 59.95 (0-470-25011-9) Wiley.

Buys, Christian J. Historic Leadville in Rare Photographs & Drawings. LC 97-60564. (Illus.). 244p. 1997. 34.95 (1-890437-08-5) Western Reflections.

— Historic Telluride: In Rare Photographs. LC 98-87115. (Illus.). 307p. 1998. 39.95 (1-890437-02-6) Western Reflections.

***Buys, Christian J.** Illustrations of Historic Colorado. LC 99-66926. (Illus.). 256p. 1999. 34.95 (1-890437-42-5) Western Reflections.

Buys, Kathy. Invest with Confidence: A No-Nonsense Guide for Women & Their Money. LC 98-74419. (Illus.). 224p. 1999. pap. 15.95 (1-886284-20-2, Pub. by Chandler Hse) Natl Bk Netwk.

— Investment Basics for Women. LC 96-78159. 224p. 1996. 16.95 (0-02-861175-6, Pub. by Macmillan) S&S Trade.

Buys, William De, see De Buys, William.

Buyse, G., jt. ed. see De Cuyper, H.

Buyse, I. Association of HLA Class II Antigens with Insulin-Dependent Diabetes Mellitus: Development of an HLA Class II DNA Typing Method. No. 65. 134p. (Orig.). 1993. pap. 49.50 (90-6186-548-4, Pub. by Leuven Univ) Coronet Bks.

Buyse, M. Birth Defects Encyclopedia, 2 vols., Set. 1992. 275.00 (0-86542-228-1) Blackwell Sci.

Buyssen, Huub. Traumatic Experiences of Nurses: When Your Profession Becomes a Nightmare. LC 96-164781. 112p. 1996. pap. 16.95 (1-85302-377-9, Pub. by Jessica Kingsley) Taylor & Francis.

Buyst, E. An Economic History of Residential Building in Belgium Between 1890 & 1961. (Studies in Social & Economic History: No. 23). 307p. (Orig.). 1993. pap. 84.00 (90-6186-517-4, Pub. by Leuven Univ) Coronet Bks.

Buytaert, E., ed. Peter Abelard. No. 2. 195p. (Orig.). 1974. pap. 34.50 (90-6186-005-9, Pub. by Leuven Univ) Coronet Bks.

Buytaert, Elgius M., ed. Gregorii Ariminensis, O.E.S.A., Super Primum et Secundum Sententiarum. 656p. 1955. pap. 21.00 (1-57659-058-5) Franciscan Inst.

— Henry of Ghent, Summa Quaestionum Ordinariarum, 2. (Henry of Ghent Ser.). 1953. pap. 46.00 (1-57659-048-8) Franciscan Inst.

Buytaert, Elgius M., ed. see Hooper, M. Rachel.

Buytaert, Eligius M., ed. Peter Aureoli: Scriptum Super Primum Sententiarum, 2 vols., Vol. 2. (Text Ser.). 1956. 23.00 (1-57659-119-0) Franciscan Inst.

Buytaert, Eligius M., jt. auth. see Boehner, Philotheus.

Buytendijk, F. J. The Mind of the Dog. LC 73-2964. (Classics in Psychology Ser.). 1977. reprint ed. 20.95 (0-405-05137-9) Ayer.

Buytendijk, Frederik J. Pain: Its Modes & Functions. O'Shiel, Eda, tr. LC 72-12494. 189p. 1973. reprint ed. lib. bdg. 55.00 (0-8371-6741-8, BUPM, Greenwood Pr) Greenwood.

Buytendijk, Jacobus J. Wesen und Sinn des Spiels: The Essence & Meaning of Games. LC 75-35064. (Studies in Play & Games). (GER., Illus.). 1976. reprint ed. 19.95 (0-405-07915-X) Ayer.

Buyukataman, Kayaalp. Dynamic Responses of Aircraft Gears. (Nineteen Ninety Fall Technical Meeting Ser.: Vol. 90FTM6). (Illus.). 18p. 1990. pap. text 30.00 (1-55589-558-1) AGMA.

— A New Approach for the Derivation of Dynamic Loads of Heavily Loaded (d-e) High Speed Aircraft Gearing. (Nineteen Eighty-Eight Fall Technical Meeting Ser.: Vol. 88FTM5). (Illus.). 13p. 1988. pap. text 30.00 (1-55589-510-7) AGMA.

Buyukataman, Kayaalp & Calkins, S. C. Design Criteria of Advanced Technology Gearbox Gears for Aircraft Use. (Nineteen Eighty-Nine Fall Technical Meeting Ser.: Vol. 89FTM1). (Illus.). 12p. 1989. pap. text 30.00 (1-55589-540-9) AGMA.

Buyukataman, Kayaalp & Kazerounian, K. High Speed, Heavily Loaded & Precision Aircraft Type Epicyclic Gear System Dynamic Analysis by Using AGMA Gear Design Guidelines Enhanced by Exact Definition of Dynamic Loads. (1993 Fall Technical Meeting Ser.: Vol. 93FTM10). (Illus.). 19p. 1993. pap. text 30.00 (1-55589-622-7) AGMA.

Buyukmichi, Hope S., jt. auth. see Richards, Dorothy.

Buyya, Rajkumar. High Performance Cluster Computing: Programming & Applications, Vol. 2. LC 99-17906. Vol. 2. (Illus.). 700p. (C). 1999. 57.00 (0-13-013785-5) P-H.

— High Performance Cluster Computing Vol. 1, Vol. 1. LC 99-17906. (High Performance Cluster Computing Ser.: Vol. 1). (Illus.). 881p. 1999. 57.00 (0-13-013784-7) P-H.

***Buyya, Rajkumar, ed.** Cluster Computing: Proceedings International Workshop, Melbourne, Australia, 1999. LC 99-64613. 358p. 1999. 115.00 (0-7695-0343-8) IEEE Comp Soc.

Buza, P. Budapest Danube. 174p. (C). 1991. 80.00 (0-89771-848-8, Pub. by Collets) St Mut.

— One Week in Budapest. (Illus.). 146p. (C). 1990. 55.00 (0-7855-5220-0, Pub. by Collets) St Mut.

Buza, Peter. Budapest. (Illus.). 312p. 1999. 19.95 (3-8290-1553-4, 520597) Konemann.

— One Week in Budapest. 144p. 1989. 30.00 (963-13-3587-9, Pub. by Corvina Bks) St Mut.

Buzan, Barry. Anticipating the Future. 320p. 2000. 24.50 (0-684-86831-8) S&S Trade.

— People, States, & Fear: An Agenda for International Security Studies in the Post-Cold War Era. 2nd ed. LC 91-2097. 393p. (C). 1991. pap. text 22.00 (1-55587-282-4) L Rienner.

Buzan, Barry & Herring, Eric. The Arms Dynamic in World Politics. LC 97-48486. 320p. 1998. pap. 22.50 (1-55587-596-3); lib. bdg. 59.95 (1-55587-573-4) L Rienner.

***Buzan, Barry & Little, Richard.** International Systems in World History: Remaking the Study of International Relations. (Illus.). 380p. 2000. pap. 24.95 (0-19-878065-6) OUP.

Buzan, Barry, et al. Security: A New Framework for Analysis. LC 97-21300. 240p. 1997. pap. 19.95 (1-55587-784-2) L Rienner.

— Security: A New Framework for Analysis. LC 97-21300. 240p. 1997. 55.00 (1-55587-603-X) L Rienner.

Buzan, Barry, jt. auth. see Buzan, Tony.

B

Buzan, Barry G., et al. The Logic of Anarchy: Neorealism to Structural Realism. LC 92-31656. (New Directions in World Politics Ser.). (Illus.). 256p. (C). 1993. pap. 20.50 (*0-231-08041-7*) Col U Pr.

— Remaking the European Security Order: Scenarios for the Post-Cold War Era. 224p. 1990. text 14.50 (*0-86187-143-X*, Pub. by P P Pubs) Cassell & Continuum.

— Remaking the European Security Order: Scenarios for the Post-Cold War Era. 224p. 1990. text 49.00 (*0-86187-142-1*) St Martin.

Buzan, Norma S. Bed & Breakfast North America: A Directory of Small Urban Hotels, Historic Victorian Inns, Country Inns, Guesthouses & Reservation Services. 5th ed. (Illus.). 670p. 1989. 15.95 (*0-943232-06-6*) Betsy Ross Pubns.

— Bed & Breakfast Northwest - Pacific Rim - Alaska, Hawaii, Idaho, Montana, Oregon, Washington, Wyoming, British Columbia: A Guide to Historic Victorian Inns, Scenic Country Inns, Individual Guesthouses, Ranches, Working Farms, & Reservation Services. (Illus.). 190p. (Orig.). 1993. pap. 13.95 (*0-943232-07-4*) Betsy Ross Pubns.

Buzan, Tony. Brain Power: How to Unleash Your Extraordinary Range of Mental Skills. unabridged ed. 1991. 79.95 incl. audio (*0-924967-23-4*) Intl Ctr Creat Think.

***Buzan, Tony.** Crucible. (Literature Made Easy Ser.). 96p. 2000. pap. text 6.95 (*0-7641-1531-6*) Barron.

Buzan, Tony. Make the Most of Your Mind. 1986. 11.00 incl. audio (*0-671-61856-3*) S&S Bks Yung.

— Make the Most of Your Mind. 157p. 1984. per. 11.00 (*0-671-49519-4*) S&S Trade.

— Speed Reading. rev. ed. (Illus.). 1991. pap. 11.95 (*0-452-26604-1*, Plume) Dutton Plume.

***Buzan, Tony.** Tempest. (Literature Made Easy Ser.). 2000. pap. text 6.95 (*0-7641-1532-4*) Barron.

Buzan, Tony. Use Both Sides of Your Brain. 3rd ed. (Illus.). 1991. pap. 12.95 (*0-452-26603-3*, Plume) Dutton Plume.

— Use Your Perfect Memory. 3rd ed. (Illus.). 1991. pap. 12.95 (*0-452-26606-8*, Plume) Dutton Plume.

Buzan, Tony & Buzan, Barry. The Mind Map Book: How to Use Radiant Thinking to Maximize Your Brain's Untapped Potential. 320p. 1996. pap. 22.95 (*0-452-27322-6*, Plume) Dutton Plume.

Buzan, Tony & Israel, Richard. Brain Sell. rev. ed. 284p. 1995. 54.95 (*0-566-07658-6*); pap. 25.95 (*0-566-07667-5*) McGraw.

***Buzan, Tony, et al.** The BrainSmart Leader. LC 98-37054. 250p. 1999. 35.00 (*0-566-07962-3*, Pub. by Ashgate Pub) Ashgate Pub Co.

— Sales Genius: A Masterclass in Successful Selling. LC 99-11289. (Illus.). 250p. 1999. pap. 29.95 (*0-566-08209-8*, Pub. by Ashgate Pub) Ashgate Pub Co.

Buzan, Tony, jt. auth. see Hunt, Rikki.

Buzard, James. The Beaten Track: European Tourism, Literature & the Ways to "Culture" 1800-1918. (Illus.). 370p. 1993. pap. text 22.00 (*0-19-812276-4*) OUP.

***Buzard, Kurt A. & Friedlander, Miles H.** Blue Line Incision & Refractive Cataract Surgery. 250p. (C). 2000. text 130.00 (*1-55642-481-7*) SLACK Inc.

Buzas, I., jt. auth. see Pungor, E.

Buzas, I., ed. see International Conference on Thermal Analysis Staff.

Buzas, Martin A. & Culver, Stephen. The Distribution of Recent Benthic Foraminifera off the North American Pacific Coast from Oregon to Alaska. LC 85-600001. (Smithsonian Contributions to the Marine Sciences Ser.: No. 26). 238p. reprint ed. pap. 73.80 (*0-608-14834-2*, 202617600048) Bks Demand.

Buzas, Martin A., jt. auth. see Smith, Roberta K.

Buzas, Martin A., jt. ed. see Hayek, Lee-Ann C.

Buzawa, Carl G., jt. auth. see Buzawa, Eve S.

Buzawa, Carl G., jt. ed. see Buzawa, Eve S.

Buzawa, Eve S. & Buzawa, Carl G. Do Arrests & Restraining Orders Work? LC 95-41792. 184p. 1996. 45.00 (*0-8039-7072-2*); pap. 19.95 (*0-8039-7073-0*) Sage.

— Domestic Violence: The Criminal Justice Response. (Studies in Crime, Law, & Justice: Vol. 6). (Illus.). 160p. (C). 1990. 52.00 (*0-8039-3575-7*); pap. 21.95 (*0-8039-3576-5*) Sage.

— Domestic Violence: The Criminal Justice Response. 1995. pap. 21.95 (*0-7619-0116-7*) Sage.

— Domestic Violence: The Criminal Justice Response. 2nd ed. LC 95-32524. 285p. 1996. 48.00 (*0-7619-0115-9*) Sage.

Buzawa, Eve S. & Buzawa, Carl G., eds. Domestic Violence: The Changing Criminal Justice Response. LC 91-31937. 336p. 1992. 55.00 (*0-86569-001-4*, T001, Auburn Hse) Greenwood.

Buzbee, Bruce. Getting the Most Out of Family Origins. (Illus.). x, 175p. 1997. pap. 11.95 (*0-9661713-0-6*) FormalSoft.

— Getting the Most Out of Family Origins. 2nd ed. (Illus.). 214p. 1998. pap. 14.95 (*0-9661713-1-4*) FormalSoft.

***Buzbee, Bruce.** Getting the Most Out of Family Origins. 3rd ed. (Illus.). 230p. 1999. pap. 14.95 (*0-9661713-2-2*) FormalSoft.

Buzby, Beth M. & Locke, Kathy. Data Entry: Concepts & Applications. 3rd ed. LC 94-25812. 1994. teacher ed. 14.00 (*1-56118-591-4*) Paradigm MN.

— Data Entry: Concepts & Applications. 3rd ed. LC 94-25812. 1995. 27.95 (*1-56118-590-6*) Paradigm MN.

***Buzby, Jonathan H.** Coaching Kids: It's More Than X's & O's. (Illus.). vi, 35p. 1998. pap. text. write for info. (*0-9663553-0-X*) Kids-n-Sports.

— Raising a Sports Fanatic. (Illus.). 64p. 1999. pap. 5.00 (*0-9663553-1-8*) Kids-n-Sports.

***Buzcek, Greg.** Instant ASP Scripts. LC 99-28914. (Enterprise Computing Ser.). 800p. 1999. pap. 49.99 (*0-07-135205-8*) Osborne-McGraw.

Buzdugan, Gh., et al. Vibration Measurement. LC 84-25523. 1986. text 206.50 (*90-247-3111-9*) Kluwer Academic.

Buzek, C. Tertiary Flora of the Northern Part of the Petipsy Area. (Transactions of the Geological Survey of Czechoslovakia Ser.: Vol. 36). (Illus.). 118p. 1971. pap. 15.00 (*3-510-99103-6*, Pub. by E Schweizerbartsche) Balogh.

Buzek, F. J. & Holdert, H. M. Collision Cases: Judgments & Diagrams. 2nd ed. 328p. 1990. 115.00 (*1-85044-298-3*) LLP.

Buzelin, J., ed. Une Plume dans L'Alambic. 88p. 1993. text 23.00 (*2-906077-40-2*) Elsevier.

***Buzenberg, Bill & Buzenberg, Susan, eds.** Salant, CBS & the Battle for the Soul of Broadcast Journalism: The Memoirs of Richard S. Salant. LC 98-23296. 275p. 1998. text 29.00 (*0-8133-9091-5*, Pub. by Westview) HarpC.

Buzenberg, Bill & Buzenberg, Susan, eds. Salant, CBS & the Battle for the Soul of Broadcast Journalism: The Memoirs of Richard S. Salant. 352p. 1999. pap. 17.00 (*0-8133-3703-8*, Pub. by Westview) HarpC.

Buzenberg, Susan, jt. ed. see Buzenberg, Bill.

Buzescu, Radu. America Can Be Number One in Education: The Structural Biodynamic Approach. (Illus.). 160p. (Orig.). 1993. pap. 25.00 (*0-9624144-2-5*) Transdacia Co.

Buzgalin, Alexander & Kolganov, Andre. Bloody October in Moscow. Clarke, Renfrey, tr. from RUS. (Illus.). 224p. 1994. pap. 18.00 (*0-85345-896-0*, Pub. by Monthly Rev) NYU Pr.

Buzhardt, Gail & Hawthorne, Margaret. Recontres sur le Missisipi, 1682-1763. LC 93-14053. (Illus.). 280p. (YA). (gr. 10-12). 1993. text 28.00 (*0-87805-665-3*) U Pr of Miss.

***Buzinkay, Geza.** An Illustrated History of Budapest. (Illus.). 132p. 1999. 63.00 (*963-13-4474-6*, Pub. by Corvina Bks) St Mut.

Buzkirk, Stewart. WebServer Construction Kit for Mac. 1996. 45.00 incl. cd-rom (*0-614-14448-5*) Macmillan.

Buznikov, G. A. Analytical Aspects of Atomic Laser Spectrochemisty. (Laser Science & Technology Ser.). viii, 44p. 1989. pap. text 64.00 (*3-7186-4890-3*) Gordon & Breach.

Buznova, Viktoria, jt. auth. see Dratva, Tomas.

***Buzo, Adrian.** The Guerilla Dynasty: Politics & Leadership in North Korea. 320p. 1999. pap. 30.00 (*0-8133-3659-7*, Pub. by Westview); text 75.00 (*0-8133-3660-0*, Pub. by Westview) HarpC.

Buzo, Adrian & Prince, Tony, trs. from KOR. Kyunyo-jon: The Life, Times, & Songs of a Tenth-Century Korean Monk. (University of Sydney East Asian Ser.: No. 6). 150p. (C). 1993. pap. text 20.00 (*0-646-14772-2*, Pub. by Wild Peony Pty) UH Pr.

Buzsaki, G., et al, eds. Temporal Coding in the Brain. LC 94-12945. (Research & Perspectives in Neurosciences Ser.). 1994. 99.00 (*0-387-58074-3*) Spr-Verlag.

Buzsaki, G. & Vanderwolf, C. H. Electrical Activity of the Archicortex. 414p. (C). 1985. 132.00 (*963-05-4159-9*, Pub. by Akade Kiado) St Mut.

Buzsaki, G., jt. ed. see Haas, H. L.

Buzuloiu, V. Image Processing for Future High Energy Physics Detectors. 232p. 1993. text 81.00 (*981-02-1119-8*) World Scientific Pub.

Buzura, Augustin. Refugees. 460p. 1994. 68.50 (*0-88033-296-4*, 399, Pub. by East Eur Monographs) Col U Pr.

Buzz Boxx Staff, ed. see Graham, John & Ough, Stuart.

Buzz, Professor. Recreational Drugs. LC 88-46125. (Illus.). 168p. (Orig.). 1989. pap. 21.95 (*0-915179-88-1*, 85102) Loompanics.

Buzzacott & Wymore. Bi-Sexual Man: Evolution of the Sexes. 83p. 1996. reprint ed. spiral bd. 14.00 (*0-7873-0137-X*) Hlth Research.

***Buzzacott, Francis H.** Complete Sportsman's Encyclopedia. 2000. pap. 16.95 (*1-58574-127-2*) Lyons Pr.

Buzzacott, Francis H. The Mystery of the Sexes: Secrets of Past & Future Human Creationism. 183p. 1996. reprint ed. spiral bd. 16.50 (*0-7873-0138-8*) Hlth Research.

***Buzzanco.** Vietnam In America. 422p. 1999. pap. text 35.00 (*0-536-02678-5*) Pearson Custom.

Buzzanco, Robert. Masters of War: Military Dissent & Politics in the Vietnam Era. 400p. (C). 1996. text 39.95 (*0-521-48046-9*) Cambridge U Pr.

— Masters of War: Military Dissent & Politics in the Vietnam Era. 384p. 1997. pap. 18.95 (*0-521-59940-7*) Cambridge U Pr.

— Vietnam & the Transformation of American Life. LC 98-45677. (Problems in American History Ser.). (Illus.). 200p. 1999. 52.95 (*1-57718-093-3*); pap. 22.95 (*1-57718-094-1*) Blackwell Pubs.

Buzzanco, Robert & Ismi, Asad. Informed Dissent: Three Generals & the Vietnam War. (Vietnam Generation Ser.). 58p. (Orig.). (C). 1991. pap. text 10.00 (*0-9628524-4-9*) Burning Cities Pr.

***Buzzanell, Patrice M.** Rethinking Organizational & Managerial Communication from Feminist Perspectives. LC 00-8077. 2000. pap. write for info. (*0-7619-1279-7*) Sage.

Buzzard, A. J., et al. Medicine & Surgery for Lawyers. xxi, 675p. 1986. 121.00 (*0-455-20675-9*, Pub. by LawBk Co) Gaunt.

Buzzard, Anthony & Hunting, Charles F. The Doctrine of the Trinity: Christianity's Self-Inflicted Wound. LC 98-3870. 365p. 1998. pap. 24.95 (*1-57309-309-2*, Christ Univ Pr) Intl Scholars.

— The Doctrine of Trinity: Christianity's Self-Inflicted Wound. LC 98-3870. 184p. 1998. 74.95 (*1-57309-310-6*, Christ Univ Pr) Intl Scholars.

***Buzzard, Anthony F.** The Coming Kingdom of the Messiah: A Solution to the Riddle of the New Testament. 3rd rev. ed. 94p. 1999. pap. 6.00 (*0-9673249-0-4*) Restora Fello.

Buzzard, Karen. Electronic Media Ratings. (Electronic Media Guide Ser.). (Illus.). 128p. 1992. pap. 22.95 (*0-240-80066-4*, Focal) Buttrwrth-Heinemann.

Buzzard, Karen S. Chains of Gold: Marketing the Ratings & Rating the Markets. LC 90-19487. 226p. 1990. 35.00 (*0-8108-2356-X*) Scarecrow.

Buzzard, Lynn R. & Edwards, Susan M. Church Hiring & Volunteer Selection: A Legal & Policy Guide. 300p. (C). 1995. pap. text 24.50 (*0-614-09967-6*) U Pr of Amer.

— Risky Business: Church Hiring & Volunteer Recruitment. LC 96-169497. 280p. (Orig.). 1994. pap. text 19.95 (*1-886569-00-2*) J W Edwards.

Buzzard, Lynn R. & Kraybill, Ronald. Mediation - Arbitration: A Reader. 140p. (Orig.). (C). 1982. pap. text 7.50 (*0-944561-08-X*) Chr Legal.

Buzzard, Lynn R., et al. Readiness for Reconciliation. rev. ed. 32p. (Orig.). 1988. pap. text 4.00 (*0-944561-18-7*) Chr Legal.

Buzzard, Rod. Dad's Don't Die: In the Valley of the Shadow of Death. 115p. 1993. pap. 5.95 (*0-9638378-0-X*) Lght for Life.

Buzzard, Shirley & Edgcomb, Elaine, eds. Monitoring & Evaluating Small Business Projects: A Step by Step Guide for Private Development Organizations. (Illus.). 200p. (Orig.). 1987. pap. text 15.00 (*0-942127-00-5*) PACT Inc.

Buzzati, Dino. La boutique del mistero Level C. text 8.95 (*0-88436-746-0*) EMC-Paradigm.

Buzzati, Dino. L' Ecroulementde la Baliverna. (FRE.). 340p. 1978. pap. 11.95 (*0-7859-1872-8*, 2070370275) Fr & Eur.

— The Giro d'Italia: An Account of the Historic 1949 Giro. (Illus.). 200p. 1998. pap. 17.95 (*1-884737-51-X*) VeloPress.

— The Tartar Steppe. Hood, Stuart, tr. 208p. 1995. pap. 13.95 (*0-87923-992-1*) Godine.

***Buzzell.** Eliot. (Images of America Ser.). 128p. 1999. pap. 18.99 (*0-7385-0082-8*) Arcadia Publng.

Buzzell. Marketing in an Electronic Age. 1985. 39.95 (*0-07-103217-7*) McGraw.

— School & Family Partnerships: Parent/Teacher Relationship I. (Teaching Methods Ser.). 64p. 1996. pap., teacher ed. 8.50 (*0-8273-7164-0*) Delmar.

Buzzell, Allyn, ed. Consumer Bankruptcy. 129p. 1991. pap. 39.00 (*0-685-50411-5*, 630500) Am Bankers.

Buzzell, Allyn C., ed. see American Bankers Association Staff.

Buzzell, David. Bank Card Business (1996) Date not set. 52.00 (*0-89982-447-1*) Am Bankers.

Buzzell, Judith. Case Studies on Parent-Teacher Relationships. (Teaching Methods Ser.). (Illus.). 160p. (C). 1996. mass mkt. 35.95 (*0-8273-7163-2*) Delmar.

Buzzell, Judith B. & Piazza, Robert. Case Studies for Teaching Special Needs & At-Risk Students. LC 93-17633. 268p. (C). 1994. pap. 48.95 (*0-8273-5298-0*) Delmar.

— Case Studies for Teaching Special Needs & At-Risk Students. 77p. 1994. teacher ed. 16.95 (*0-8273-5299-9*) Delmar.

***Buzzell, Keith.** The Children of Cyclops: The Influence of Television Viewing on the Developing Human Brain. Mitchell, David, ed. (Illus.). 129p. 1998. pap. 10.00 (*1-888365-20-X*) Assn Waldorf Schls.

Buzzell, Linda. How to Make it in Hollywood: Second Edition. 2nd ed. LC 91-58469. 416p. 1996. pap. 15.00 (*0-06-273243-9*, Harper Ref) HarpC.

Buzzell, Robert D. & Gale, Bradley T. The PIMS Principles: Linking Strategy to Performance. 352p. 1987. 40.00 (*0-02-904430-8*) Free Pr.

Buzzell, Robert D., et al. Global Marketing Management. 2nd ed. (Illus.). 464p. (C). 1991. pap. text 41.66 (*0-201-54280-3*) Addison-Wesley.

— Global Marketing Management. 3rd ed. (Illus.). 704p. (C). 1994. pap. 70.00 (*0-201-53972-1*) Addison-Wesley.

Buzzell, Rolfe G., ed. & intro. see Morgan, Albert W.

Buzzelli, Buzz. Harley-Davidson Sportster Performance Handbook. 2nd ed. LC 97-44431. (Performance Handbook Ser.). (Illus.). 256p. 1997. pap. 21.95 (*0-7603-0307-X*, 124430AP) MBI Pubg.

Buzzelli, Buzz, et al. How to Get Water Smart: Products & Practices for Saving Water in the Nineties. LC 91-65066. 128p. 1991. pap. 9.95 (*0-9628895-0-4*) Terra Fir Pub.

Buzzelli, David T. & Lash, Jonathan. Building on Consensus: A Progress Report on Sustainable America. 57p. (Orig.). (C). 1997. pap. text 30.00 (*0-7881-4004-3*) DIANE Pub.

Buzzelli, Rich. Garden of the Gods: A Photographic Masterpiece of Garden of the Gods Park & Pike's Peak. (Illus.). 32p. (Orig.). 1994. pap. write for info. (*0-9644212-0-8*) R Buzzelli Photograph.

Buzzeo, Ronald W., et al. Pharmacist's Controlled Substances Regulatory Guide & Compliance Manual: A Complete Prescription Department Guide for Practicing Pharmacists. 130p. 1995. 130.00 (*0-9648291-0-X*) Regulatory Info Ctr.

Buzzeo, Toni & Kurtz, Jane. Terrific Author Connections: Real Space & Virtual Links with Authors, Illustrators & Storytellers. LC 99-28468. 175p. 1999. pap. 26.50 (*1-56308-744-8*) Teacher Ideas Pr.

Buzzetti, Dino & Ferriani, Maurizio, eds. Speculative Grammar, Universal Grammar, Philosophical Analysis: Papers in the Philosophy of Language. LC 87-8081. (Studies in the History of the Language Sciences: No. 42). x, 269p. (C). 1987. 59.00 (*90-272-4525-8*) J Benjamins Pubng Co.

Buzzi, Aldo. Journey to the Land of the Flies: And Other Travels. abr. ed. Goldstein, Anne T., tr. from ITA. LC 99-43515. (Steerforth Italia Ser.). 125p. 1999. pap. 10.00 (*1-883642-83-3*) Steerforth Pr.

***Buzzi, Aldo.** A Weakness for Almost Everything: Notes on Life, Gastronomy & Travel. Goldstein, Ann, tr. from ITA. LC 99-47313. (Sterrforth Italia Ser.). 100p. 1999. pap. 9.50 (*1-883642-70-1*) Steerforth Pr.

Buzzi-Ferraris, Guido. Scientific C++ Building Numerical Libraries the Object Oriented Way. 471p. (C). 1993. pap. text 42.19 (*0-201-63192-X*) Addison-Wesley.

Buzzi, Ruth Ann. Chemical Hazards at Water & Wastewater Treatment Plants. 160p. 1992. lib. bdg. 95.00 (*0-87371-491-1*, L491) Lewis Pubs.

Buzzoni, Alberto, et al, eds. Fresh View of Elliptical Galaxies. (ASP Conference Series Proceedings: Vol. 86). 352p. 1995. 34.00 (*1-886733-07-4*) Astron Soc Pacific.

Buzzota, V. R., et al. Making Common Sense Common Practice: A Leaders Guide to Using What You Already Know. LC 96-71404. (Illus.). 230p. 1996. 24.95 (*1-886710-01-5*) New Leaders.

Buzzotta, V. R. & Cheney, Alan. Making Common Sense Common Practice: A Leader's Guide to Using What You Already Know. (Illus.). 175p. 1996. write for info. (*0-614-13045-X*) Psy Assocs.

Buzzotta, V. R., et al. Effective Selling Through Psychology: Dimensional Sales & Sales Management Strategies. LC 82-16308. 334p. 1991. reprint ed. text 25.00 (*0-9630421-0-6*) Psy Assocs.

— Making Common Sense Common Practice: Achieving High Performance Using What You Already Know. LC 97-29039. 230p. 1997. reprint ed. lib. bdg. 24.95 (*1-57444-194-9*) CRC Pr.

Buzzworm Magazine Editors. Ecotravel. 240p. 1992. pap. 9.95 (*0-9603722-8-8*) Buzzworm.

BVMA Staff. Technical Reference Book on Valves for Control of Fluids. 2nd ed. 1966. 156.00 (*0-08-012268-X*, Pub. by Pergamon Repr) Franklin.

Bwalwel, Jean Pierre. Famille et Habitat: Implications Ethiques de l'Eclatement Urbain Cas de la Ville de Kinshasa Preface du Prof. Ferdinand Ngoma Ngambu. Friedli, Richard et al, eds. (Etudes d'Histoire Interculturelle du Christianisme Ser.: Vol. 112). (Illus.). xxiv, 407p. 1999. 55.95 (*3-906761-96-7*, Pub. by P Lang) P Lang Pubng.

Bwengye, Francis A. The Agony of Uganda: From Idi Amin to Obote. 1986. 60.00 (*0-7212-0717-0*, Pub. by Regency Pr GBR) St Mut.

BWI Staff. The Internet & Beyond. (C). 1999. pap. 69.95 (*0-13-861097-5*) P-H.

Byakutaga, Shirley C., jt. auth. see Musere, Jonathan.

Byalick. Whose Eyes Are These? 1997. 11.00 (*0-15-201430-6*); pap. 5.00 (*0-15-201431-4*) Harcourt.

Byalick, Marcia. It's a Matter of Trust. LC 94-49733. 192p. (YA). (gr. 7 up). 1995. 11.00 (*0-15-276660-X*, Harcourt Child Bks); pap. 5.00 (*0-15-200240-5*, Harcourt Child Bks) Harcourt.

— It's a Matter of Trust. LC 94-49733. 1995. 10.10 (*0-606-09480-6*, Pub. by Turtleback) Demco.

Byalick, Marcia & Saslow, Linda. How Come I Feel So Disconnected If This Is Such a User-Friendly World? Reconnecting with Your Family, Friends...& Your Life. LC 94-44125. 208p. 1995. pap. 9.95 (*1-56079-395-3*) Petersons.

— The Three-Career Couple. LC 93-360. (Illus.). 248p. 1993. pap. 12.95 (*1-56079-239-6*) Petersons.

Byalick, Marcia, jt. auth. see Ruden, Ronald A.

Byalko, Alexei V. Nuclear Waste Disposal: Geophysical Safety. 304p. 1994. lib. bdg. 159.00 (*0-8493-4469-7*, TD868) CRC Pr.

Byalobzhteskii, K. V. High Temperature Corrosion & Methods of Its Control. (C). 1987. 24.00 (*0-8364-2119-1*, Pub. by Oxford IBH) S Asia.

Byam, L. Dale. Community in Motion: Theatre for Development in Africa: Theatre for Development in Africa. LC 98-51216. (Critical Studies in Education & Culture). 240p. 1999. 59.95 (*0-89789-581-9*, Bergin & Garvey) Greenwood.

***Byam, Michele.** Arms & Armor. (Eyewitness Books). (Illus.). (J). (gr. 4-7). 2000. 19.99 (*0-7894-6553-1*) DK Pub Inc.

***Byam, Michelle.** Arms & Armor. (Eyewitness Books). (J). (gr. 4-7). 2000. 15.95 (*0-7894-5836-5*) DK Pub Inc.

Byam Shaw, Christina, ed. Pigeon Holes of Memory: The Life & Times of Dr. John Mackenzie (1803-1886) LC 87-63257. (Illus.). 436p. 1988. 36.00 (*0-930664-07-8*) SPOSS.

Byan, Rebecca, jt. auth. see Riosley, Lane.

Byard, Paul. The Architecture of Additions: Design & Regulation. LC 98-10361. 192p. 1998. 40.00 (*0-393-73021-2*) Norton.

Byard, Roger W. & Cohle, Stephen D. Sudden Death in Infancy, Childhood & Adolescence. LC 93-43607. (Illus.). 561p. (C). 1994. text 125.00 (*0-521-42031-8*) Cambridge U Pr.

***Byars, Betsy.** Death's Door. (Illus.). (J). 2000. 10.34 (*0-606-18400-7*) Turtleback.

— Disappearing Acts. (Illus.). (J). 1999. 10.34 (*0-606-18401-5*) Turtleback.

— El Verano de los. (SPA.). 1998. pap. 11.95 (*84-246-8609-8*) Gibson.

Byars, Betsy C. After the Goat Man. 1995. 19.25 (*0-8446-6802-8*) Peter Smith.

— After the Goat Man. (J). 1982. 9.60 (*0-606-01995-2*, Pub. by Turtleback) Demco.

— The Animal, the Vegetable, & John D. Jones. (Illus.). 160p. (YA). (gr. 5 up). 1983. pap. 3.99 (*0-440-40356-1*, YB BDD) BDD Bks Young Read.

Byars, Betsy C. The Animal, the Vegetable, & John D. Jones. 150p. (J). (gr. 4-6). pap. 3.50 (*0-8072-1414-0*) Listening Lib.

An Asterisk (*) at the beginning of an entry indicates that the title is appearing for the first time.

Byars, Betsy C. The Animal, the Vegetable, & John D. Jones. (J). 1982. 8.60 (*0-606-03121-9*, Pub. by Turtleback) Demco.
— The Animal, the Vegetable, & John D. Jones. large type ed. 166p. (J). (gr. 3-6). 1984. reprint ed. 47.64 (*0-317-01868-X*, 4-00950-00) Am Printing Hse.
— Ant Plays Bear. 1999. pap. 3.99 (*0-14-130351-4*, PuffinBks) Peng Put Young Read.
***Byars, Betsy C.** Ant Plays Bear. unabridged ed. (J). (gr. k-3). 1999. pap. 15.95 incl. audio (*0-87499-541-8*) Live Oak Media.
Byars, Betsy C. Ant Plays Bear, No. 2. LC 96-48278. (Illus.). 32p. (J). 1997. 13.99 (*0-670-86776-4*) Viking Penguin.
— Beans on the Roof. 80p. (J). 1990. pap. 3.99 (*0-440-40314-6*, YB BDD) BDD Bks Young Read.
— Beans on the Roof. (J). 1990. 9.19 (*0-606-03054-9*, Pub. by Turtleback) Demco.
— Bingo Brown & the Language of Love. LC 90-42257. (Illus.). 144p. (J). (gr. 3-7). 1991. pap. 4.99 (*0-14-034141-2*, PuffinBks) Peng Put Young Read.
Byars, Betsy C. Bingo Brown & the Language of Love. 1989. 9.60 (*0-606-04872-3*, Pub. by Turtleback) Demco.
Byars, Betsy C. Bingo Brown, Gypsy Lover. (Illus.). 128p. (J). (gr. 3-7). 1992. pap. 4.99 (*0-14-034518-3*, PuffinBks) Peng Put Young Read.
— Bingo Brown, Gypsy Lover. 1992. 10.09 (*0-606-00862-4*, Pub. by Turtleback) Demco.
— Bingo Brown's Guide to Romance. 160p. (J). (gr. 3-7). 1992. 14.99 (*0-670-84491-8*, Viking Child) Peng Put Young Read.
— Bingo Brown's Guide to Romance. (Illus.). 128p. (J). (gr. 3-7). 1994. pap. 4.99 (*0-14-036080-8*, PuffinBks) Peng Put Young Read.
Byars, Betsy C. Bingo Brown's Guide to Romance. 1992. 10.09 (*0-606-06936-4*, Pub. by Turtleback) Demco.
— A Blossom Promise. (Blossom Series). 145p. (J). (gr. 4-6). pap. 4.50 (*0-8072-1444-2*) Listening Lib.
— A Blossom Promise. (J). 1987. 9.09 (*0-606-04064-1*, Pub. by Turtleback) Demco.
Byars, Betsy C. A Blossom Promise. LC 87-5367. (Illus.). 160p. (J). (gr. 4-7). 1989. reprint ed. pap. 4.50 (*0-440-40137-2*, YB BDD) BDD Bks Young Read.
Byars, Betsy C. A Blossom Promise. unabridged ed. (J). (gr. 4-6). 1990. pap. 28.98 incl. audio Listening Lib.
— A Blossom Promise, Set. unabridged ed. (J). (gr. 4-6). pap. write for info. incl. audio (*0-8072-7322-8*, YA826SP) Listening Lib.
— A Blossom Promise, Set. unabridged ed. (J). (gr. 4-6). 1990. pap. 23.98 incl. audio (*0-8072-7292-2*, YA826CX) Listening Lib.
— Blossoms & the Green Phantom. 146p. (J). (gr. 4-6). pap. 3.99 (*0-8072-1443-4*) Listening Lib.
Byars, Betsy C. Blossoms & the Green Phantom. LC 86-19617. (J). 1987. 8.60 (*0-606-03734-9*, Pub. by Turtleback) Demco.
— The Blossoms & the Green Phantom. (Illus.). 160p. (J). (gr. k-6). 1988. reprint ed. pap. 3.99 (*0-440-40069-4*) Dell.
— The Blossoms Meet the Vulture Lady. 144p. (J). (gr. k-6). 1987. pap. 4.50 (*0-440-40677-3*, YB BDD) BDD Bks Young Read.
— The Blossoms Meet the Vulture Lady. (J). 3.99 (*0-385-40667-3*) Doubleday.
— The Blossoms Meet the Vulture Lady. (J). 1986. 9.09 (*0-606-03551-6*, Pub. by Turtleback) Demco.
Byars, Betsy C. The Blossoms Meet the Vulture Lady, Set. (J). (gr. 4-6). pap. 21.98 incl. audio (*0-8072-7323-6*, YA824SP) Listening Lib.
— The Blossoms Meet the Vulture Lady, Set. unabridged ed. (J). (gr. 4-6). 1995. 16.98 incl. audio (*0-8072-7286-8*, LL 3071, Chivers Child Audio) Chivers N Amer.
Byars, Betsy C. Bolas Locas.Tr. of Pinballs. (SPA.). 1996. pap. text 7.95 (*84-279-3168-9*) Lectorum Pubns.
— Bolas Locas.Tr. of Pinballs. 1985. 13.05 (*0-606-10382-1*, Pub. by Turtleback) Demco.
— The Burning Question of Bingo Brown. (Illus.). 176p. (J). (gr. 3-7). 1990. pap. 4.99 (*0-14-032479-8*, PuffinBks) Peng Put Young Read.
— The Burning Question of Bingo Brown. (J). 1988. 9.60 (*0-606-03141-3*, Pub. by Turtleback) Demco.
— The Burning Question of Bingo Brown. large type ed. 232p. (J). (gr. 3-7). 1989. lib. bdg. 14.95 (*0-8161-4770-1*, G K Hall Lrg Type) Mac Lib Ref.
Byars, Betsy C. Cartoonist. (J). 1978. 9.09 (*0-606-03743-8*, Pub. by Turtleback) Demco.
Byars, Betsy C. The Cartoonist. (Illus.). (J). (gr. 3-7). 1987. reprint ed. pap. 3.99 (*0-14-032309-0*, PuffinBks) Peng Put Young Read.
— Coast to Coast. 176p. (J). (gr. 4-7). 1994. pap. 3.99 (*0-440-40926-8*) Dell.
— Coast to Coast. LC 91-46451. 1992. 9.09 (*0-606-06285-8*, Pub. by Turtleback) Demco.
— The Computer Nut. 1992. pap. text. write for info. (*0-582-09557-3*, Pub. by Addison-Wesley) Longman.
— The Computer Nut. (Novels Ser.). (Illus.). 144p. (J). (gr. 3-7). 1986. pap. 4.99 (*0-14-032086-5*, PuffinBks) Peng Put Young Read.
— Computer Nut. (J). 1986. 9.60 (*0-606-01544-2*, Pub. by Turtleback) Demco.
— Cracker Jackson. LC 84-24684. 168p. (J). (gr. 5-7). 1985. 15.99 (*0-670-80546-7*, Viking Child) Peng Put Young Read.
— Cracker Jackson. (Novels Ser.). (Illus.). 160p. (J). (gr. 3-7). 1986. pap. 4.99 (*0-14-031881-X*, PuffinBks) Peng Put Young Read.
Byars, Betsy C. Cracker Jackson. (J). 1986. 9.60 (*0-606-01248-6*, Pub. by Turtleback) Demco.
Byars, Betsy C. Cybil War. (Illus.). 144p. (J). (gr. 3-7). 1990. pap. 4.99 (*0-14-034356-3*, PuffinBks) Peng Put Young Read.
Byars, Betsy C. Cybil War. (J). 1981. 9.09 (*0-606-03178-2*, Pub. by Turtleback) Demco.
Byars, Betsy C. The Dark Stairs: A Herculeah Jones Mystery. LC 94-14012. 128p. (J). (gr. 3-7). 1994. 13.99 (*0-670-85487-5*, Viking Child) Peng Put Young Read.
— The Dark Stairs: A Herculeah Jones Mystery, No. 1. (Illus.). 160p. (J). (gr. 3-7). 1997. pap. 4.99 (*0-14-036996-1*, Viking) Viking Penguin.
— Dead Letter. (Hurculeah Jones Mystery Ser.). 1998. 9.09 (*0-606-13320-8*, Pub. by Turtleback) Demco.
— Dead Letter: A Herculeah Jones Mystery. 128p. (J). (gr. 3-7). 1996. 14.99 (*0-670-86860-4*, Viking Child) Peng Put Young Read.
— Death's Door. (Herculeah Jones Mystery Ser.). 144p. (gr. 3-7). 1999. pap. 4.99 (*0-14-130288-7*, PuffinBks) Peng Put Young Read.
— Death's Door. LC 96-34425. (J). (gr. 3-7). 1997. 14.99 (*0-670-87423-X*, Viking) Viking Penguin.
***Byars, Betsy C.** Disappearing Acts. 2000. pap. 4.99 (*0-14-130287-9*, PuffinBks) Peng Put Young Read.
Byars, Betsy C. Disappearing Acts: A Herculeah Jones Mystery. LC 97-29434. 128p. (J). 1998. 14.99 (*0-670-87735-2*, Viking Child) Peng Put Young Read.
***Byars, Betsy C.** The 18th Emergency. (J). (gr. 5-8). 1999. 18.75 (*0-8446-7026-X*) Peter Smith.
Byars, Betsy C. The Eighteenth Emergency. (Illus.). 1128p. (J). (gr. 3-7). 1981. pap. 4.99 (*0-14-031451-2*, PuffinBks) Peng Put Young Read.
— 18th Emergency. (Camelot Bks.). (J). 1974. 9.60 (*0-606-03132-4*, Pub. by Turtleback) Demco.
— The Glory Girl. (Illus.). 160p. (J). (gr. 3-7). 1985. pap. 4.99 (*0-14-031785-6*, PuffinBks) Peng Put Young Read.
Byars, Betsy C. The Glory Girl. 1985. 9.09 (*0-606-12311-3*, Pub. by Turtleback) Demco.
Byars, Betsy C. The Golly Sisters Go West. (I Can Read Bks.). (Illus.). 64p. (J). (gr. 2-4). 1986. 11.95 (*0-06-020883-X*) HarpC Child Bks.
— The Golly Sisters Go West. LC 84-48474. (I Can Read Bks.). (Illus.). 64p. (J). (ps-3). 1986. lib. bdg. 15.89 (*0-06-020884-8*, HarpTrophy) HarpC Child Bks.
— The Golly Sisters Go West. LC 84-48474. (I Can Read Bks.). (Illus.). 64p. (J). (ps-3). 1989. pap. 3.95 (*0-06-444132-6*, HarpTrophy) HarpC Child Bks.
— The Golly Sisters Go West. (I Can Read Bks.). (J). (gr. 2-4). 1985. 8.95 (*0-606-04234-2*, Pub. by Turtleback) Demco.
Byars, Betsy C. The Golly Sisters Go West. unabridged ed. (I Can Read Bks.). (Illus.). 64p. (J). (gr. 2-4). 1995. pap. 8.95 incl. audio (*0-694-70027-4*) HarpC Child Bks.
Byars, Betsy C. The Golly Sisters Ride Again. (I Can Read Bks.). (Illus.). 64p. (J). (gr. 2-4). 1994. lib. bdg. 15.89 (*0-06-021564-X*) HarpC Child Bks.
— The Golly Sisters Ride Again. LC 92-23394. (I Can Read Bks.). (Illus.). 64p. (J). (ps-3). 1994. 14.95 (*0-06-021563-1*) HarpC Child Bks.
— The Golly Sisters Ride Again. LC 92-23394. (I Can Read Bks.). (SPA., Illus.). 64p. (J). (ps-3). 1996. pap. 3.95 (*0-06-444207-1*, HarpTrophy) HarpC Child Bks.
Byars, Betsy C. The Golly Sisters Ride Again. (I Can Read Bks.). (J). (gr. 2-4). 1996. 8.95 (*0-606-09340-0*, Pub. by Turtleback) Demco.
Byars, Betsy C. Good-Bye, Chicken Little. (J). 1979. 9.60 (*0-606-01254-0*, Pub. by Turtleback) Demco.
— Goodbye Chicken Little. LC 78-19829. 112p. (J). (gr. 5 up). 1979. lib. bdg. 14.89 (*0-06-020911-9*) HarpC Child Bks.
— Goodbye Chicken Little. LC 78-19829. (Trophy Bk.). 112p. (J). (gr. 4-7). 1990. pap. 4.95 (*0-06-440291-6*, HarpTrophy) HarpC Child Bks.
— Hooray for the Golly Sisters! LC 89-48147. (I Can Read Bks.). (Illus.). 64p. (J). (gr. k-3). 1990. lib. bdg. 15.89 (*0-06-020899-6*) HarpC Child Bks.
— Hooray for the Golly Sisters! LC 89-48147. (I Can Read Bks.). (Illus.). 64p. (J). (ps-3). 1992. pap. 3.95 (*0-06-444156-3*, HarpTrophy) HarpC Child Bks.
— Hooray for the Golly Sisters! (I Can Read Bks.). (J). (gr. 2-4). 1992. 8.95 (*0-606-02305-4*, Pub. by Turtleback) Demco.
— The House of Wings. (Illus.). 136p. (J). (gr. 3-7). 1982. pap. 4.99 (*0-14-031523-3*, PuffinBks) Peng Put Young Read.
— House of Wings. 1972. 10.09 (*0-606-00487-4*, Pub. by Turtleback) Demco.
— Human Resource Management. 6th ed. LC 99-15561. 528p. 1999. 78.44 (*0-07-229593-7*) McGraw.
— Human Resources Management. 5th ed. 1996. 14.68 incl. 3.5 hd (*0-256-24734-X*) McGraw.
— Human Resources Management. 5th ed. 1996. 15.31 (*0-256-24733-1*) McGraw.
— The Joy Boys. (J). 1996. pap. 4.99 (*0-440-91102-8*) BDD Bks Young Read.
— The Joy Boys. 48p. (J). (gr. 1-3). 1996. 13.95 (*0-385-32164-3*) Doubleday.
— Joy Boys. LC 94-33474. 1996. 9.19 (*0-606-09496-2*, Pub. by Turtleback) Demco.
***Byars, Betsy C.** Little Horse. 2000. text, pap. text 15.95 (*0-8050-6413-3*) St Martin.
Byars, Betsy C. McMummy. LC 93-16717. 160p. (J). (gr. 5-9). 1993. 14.99 (*0-670-84995-2*, Viking Child) Peng Put Young Read.
— McMummy. (Illus.). 160p. (J). (gr. 4-7). 1995. pap. 4.99 (*0-14-036439-0*, PuffinBks) Peng Put Young Read.
— McMummy. (J). 1995. 9.09 (*0-606-07854-1*, Pub. by Turtleback) Demco.
Byars, Betsy C. Me Tarzan. LC 99-34512. 96p. (gr. 2-5). mass mkt. 4.25 (*0-06-442119-8*) HarpC.
— Me Tarzan. LC 99-34512. 96p. (J). (gr. 2-5). 2000. lib. bdg. 14.89 (*0-06-028707-1*) HarpC Child Bks.
— Me Tarzan. LC 99-34512. (Illus.). 96p. (J). (gr. 2-5). 2000. 14.95 (*0-06-028706-3*) HarpC Child Bks.
Byars, Betsy C. The Midnight Fox. (Storybooks Ser.). (Illus.). 160p. (J). (gr. 3-7). 1981. pap. 4.99 (*0-14-031450-4*, PuffinBks) Peng Put Young Read.
— Midnight Fox. (J). 1981. 9.09 (*0-606-01689-9*, Pub. by Turtleback) Demco.
— The Moon & I. LC 95-53100. (Illus.). 112p. (YA). (gr. 7 up). 1996. mass mkt. 4.95 (*0-688-13704-0*, Wm Morrow) Morrow Avon.
Byars, Betsy C. The Moon & I. 1996. 10.05 (*0-606-11636-2*, Pub. by Turtleback) Demco.
Byars, Betsy C. The Moon & I. large type ed. 1994. 29.00 (*0-614-09808-4*, L-34134-00) Am Printing Hse.
— My Brother, Ant. LC 95-23725. (Easy-to-Read Classics Ser.). (Illus.). 31p. (J). (gr. k-3). 1996. 13.99 (*0-670-86664-4*, Viking Child) Peng Put Young Read.
— My Brother Ant. (Puffin Easy-to-Read Ser.). (J). 1998. 9.19 (*0-606-12996-0*, Pub. by Turtleback) Demco.
— My Brother Ant. 32p. (J). (ps-3). 1998. pap. 3.99 (*0-14-038345-X*) Viking Penguin.
***Byars, Betsy C.** My Brother Ant. unabridged ed. (J). (gr. k-3). 1999. 24.95 incl. audio (*0-87499-517-5*) Live Oak Media.
Byars, Betsy C. Night Swimmers. (J). 1980. 9.09 (*0-606-03873-6*, Pub. by Turtleback) Demco.
— The Night Swimmers. (Illus.). 144p. (J). (gr. 5-9). 1983. pap. 4.50 (*0-440-45857-9*, YB BDD) BDD Bks Young Read.
— The Not-Just-Anybody Family. 160p. (J). (gr. k-6). 1987. pap. 4.50 (*0-440-45951-6*, YB BDD) BDD Bks Young Read.
— The Not-Just-Anybody Family. (J). 1987. 9.09 (*0-606-03059-X*, Pub. by Turtleback) Demco.
Byars, Betsy C. Not-Just-Anybody Family. 149p. (J). (gr. 4-6). pap. 4.50 (*0-8072-1429-9*) Listening Lib.
Byars, Betsy C. The Pinballs. LC 76-41518. (Illus.). 144p. (YA). (gr. 4-7). 1977. lib. bdg. 15.89 (*0-06-020918-6*) HarpC Child Bks.
— The Pinballs. LC 76-41518. (Trophy Bk.). 144p. (YA). (gr. 5-9). 1993. pap. 4.95 (*0-06-440198-7*, HarpTrophy) HarpC Child Bks.
Byars, Betsy C. The Pinballs. 137p. (J). (gr. 4-6). pap. 4.95 (*0-8072-1383-7*); pap. 4.95 (*0-8072-1356-X*) Listening Lib.
Byars, Betsy C. The Pinballs. (J). 1987. 10.05 (*0-606-03346-7*, Pub. by Turtleback) Demco.
Byars, Betsy C. The Pinballs. unabridged ed. (J). (gr. 4-6). 1988. pap. 21.98 incl. audio (*0-8072-8536-6*, LB2SP) Listening Lib.
— The Pinballs. unabridged ed. (J). (gr. 4-6). 1999. pap. 15.98 incl. audio (*0-8072-1800-6*, JJRH100SP) Listening Lib.
Byars, Betsy C. The Seven Treasure Hunts. LC 90-32043. (Trophy Bk.). (Illus.). 80p. (J). (gr. 2-6). 1992. pap. 4.25 (*0-06-440435-8*, HarpTrophy) HarpC Child Bks.
— Seven Treasure Hunts. 1992. 9.70 (*0-606-01063-7*, Pub. by Turtleback) Demco.
— Summer of the Swans. LC 72-106919. (Illus.). 142p. (J). (gr. 4-7). 1970. 15.99 (*0-670-68190-3*, Viking Child) Peng Put Young Read.
— Summer of the Swans. (J). 1981. 9.60 (*0-606-01838-7*, Pub. by Turtleback) Demco.
— The Summer of the Swans. (Illus.). 144p. (J). (gr. 3-7). 1981. pap. 4.99 (*0-14-031420-2*, PuffinBks) Peng Put Young Read.
— The Summer of the Swans. (Scholastic Literature Guide Ser.). 16p. (J). 1997. pap. text 3.95 (*0-590-37363-3*) Scholastic Inc.
***Byars, Betsy C.** Summer of the Swans. large type ed. (LRS Large Print Cornerstone Ser.). (Illus.). 176p. (YA). (gr. 5-12). 2000. lib. bdg. 27.95 (*1-58118-060-8*, 23474) LRS.
Byars, Betsy C. Tarot Says Beware. (Herculeah Jones Mystery Ser.). (J). 1997. 9.09 (*0-606-12822-0*, Pub. by Turtleback) Demco.
— Tarot Says Beware. LC 95-12334. (Herculeah Jones Mystery Ser.). (Illus.). 128p. (J). (gr. 3-6). 1995. 13.99 (*0-670-85575-8*, Viking) Viking Penguin.
— Tarot Says Beware. (Illus.). 160p. (J). (gr. 3-7). 1997. pap. 3.99 (*0-14-036997-X*) Viking Penguin.
— Tornado. LC 95-41584. (Illus.). 64p. (J). (gr. 2-5). 1996. 14.95 (*0-06-026449-7*); lib. bdg. 14.89 (*0-06-026452-7*) HarpC Child Bks.
— Tornado. LC 95-41584. (Chapter Bks.). (Illus.). 64p. (J). (gr. 2-5). 1997. pap. 4.25 (*0-06-442063-9*, HarpTrophy) HarpC Child Bks.
— Tornado. (Trophy Chapter Bks.). (J). 1997. 9.15 (*0-606-11998-1*, Pub. by Turtleback) Demco.
— TR Strat Mgt Color Acetates. 1996. 136.87 (*0-256-23768-9*) McGraw.
Byars, Betsy C. Trouble River. 158p. (J). (gr. 3-5). pap. 4.99 (*0-8072-1388-8*) Listening Lib.
— Trouble River. (Illus.). 160p. (J). (gr. 3-7). 1989. pap. 4.99 (*0-14-034243-5*, PuffinBks) Peng Put Young Read.
— Trouble River. (J). (gr. 5-7). 1999. 18.75 (*0-8446-7024-3*) Peter Smith.
Byars, Betsy C. Trouble River. (J). 1989. 9.60 (*0-606-04396-9*, Pub. by Turtleback) Demco.
— TV Kid. (J). 1998. 9.60 (*0-606-03495-1*, Pub. by Turtleback) Demco.
— The TV Kid. 128p. (J). (gr. 3-7). 1998. pap. 4.99 (*0-14-038826-5*) Viking Penguin.
— The Two-Thousand-Pound Goldfish. LC 81-48652. 160p. (YA). (gr. 5 up). 1982. lib. bdg. 14.89 (*0-06-020890-2*) HarpC Child Bks.
***Byars, Betsy C.** The Two-Thousand-Pound Goldfish. LC 81-48652. 160p. (J). (gr. 3-7). 2000. mass mkt. 4.95 (*0-06-440855-8*, HarpTrophy) HarpC Child Bks.
Byars, Betsy C. Verano de los Cisnes (The Summer of the Swans) 1996. pap. 12.50 (*84-246-7831-1*) Lectorum Pubns.
— Wanted . . . Mud Blossom. (Illus.). 160p. (J). (gr. 4-7). 1993. pap. 4.99 (*0-440-40761-3*) Dell.
Byars, Betsy C. Wanted... Mud Blossom. (Blossom Series). 148p. (J). (gr. 4-6). pap. 4.99 (*0-8072-1470-1*) Listening Lib.
Byars, Betsy C. Wanted... Mud Blossom. (J). 1991. 9.60 (*0-606-02967-2*, Pub. by Turtleback) Demco.
— The Winged Colt of Casa Mia. (Illus.). 132p. (J). (gr. 3-7). 1981. pap. 2.95 (*0-380-00201-9*, Avon Bks) Morrow Avon.
— La Zorra Negra (The Midnight Fox) (SPA.). 1996. pap. text 7.95 (*84-320-6173-5*) Lectorum Pubns.
Byars, Betsy C., jt. auth. see Rue, Leslie W.
Byars, E. A. & McNulty, T., eds. Management of Concrete Structures for Long-Term Serviceability. LC 99-231241. 133p. 1997. 74.00 (*0-7277-2654-4*, 2654, Pub. by T Telford) RCH.
Byars, Ed. Coast to Coast in a Cab. (Illus.). 117p. 1988. 17.95 (*0-9619264-0-6*) E F Byars.
Byars, Edward F., et al. Engineering Mechanics of Deformable Bodies. 4th fac. ed. LC 82-15699. (Illus.). 564p. 1983. reprint ed. pap. 174.90 (*0-7837-8217-9*, 204791700008) Bks Demand.
***Byars, H. G.** Corrosion Control in Petroleum Production: TPC5. 2nd rev. ed. (Illus.). 350p. 1999. 87.00 (*1-57590-030-0*, 25022) NACE Intl.
***Byars, Harry G.** Corrosion Control in Petroleum Production. 2nd ed. LC 99-88824. (TPC Publication Ser.). 1999. write for info. (*0-8281-1274-6*) Forb Custom Pub.
Byars, J. C., Jr., ed. Black & White. LC 75-173602. (Black Heritage Library Collection). 1977. reprint ed. 19.95 (*0-8369-8914-7*) Ayer.
Byars, J. D. Dusty Memories. 100p. (Orig.). 1987. pap. 10.00 (*0-9619569-0-9*) J D Byars.
Byars, Jackie. All That Hollywood Allows: Re-reading Gender in 1950s Melodrama. LC 90-46738. (Gender & American Culture Ser.). (Illus.). x, 326p. (C). 1991. 60.00 (*0-8078-1953-0*); pap. 19.95 (*0-8078-4312-1*) U of NC Pr.
Byars, Lloyd & Rue, Leslie W. Gestion de Recursos Humanos. 4th ed. (SPA.). (C). 1996. text 28.00 (*84-8086-198-3*, Irwn McGrw-H) McGrw-H Hghr Educ.
Byars, Lloyd L. Strategic Management. 3rd ed. (C). 1991. pap. 60.50 (*0-06-500050-1*) Addson-Wesley Educ.
Byars, Lloyd L. & Rue, Leslie W. Human Resource Management. 2nd ed. (C). 1987. text 58.95 (*0-256-03630-6*, Irwn McGrw-H) McGrw-H Hghr Educ.
— Human Resource Management. 5th ed. 576p. (C). 1996. text 66.50 (*0-256-20193-5*, Irwn McGrw-H) McGrw-H Hghr Educ.
— Management. 7th ed. 312p. (C). 1995. text, student ed. 23.12 (*0-256-14483-4*, Irwn McGrw-H) McGrw-H Hghr Educ.
— Strategy in a Changing Environment. 384p. (C). 1995. text 43.75 (*0-256-22052-2*, Irwn McGrw-H) McGrw-H Hghr Educ.
— Supervision. 4th ed. 232p. (C). 1992. text, student ed. 22.50 (*0-256-12117-6*, Irwn McGrw-H) McGrw-H Hghr Educ.
Byars, Lloyd L., et al. Management & Recrafting America. 7th ed. (C). 1999. text 66.25 (*0-256-17860-7*, Irwn McGrw-H) McGrw-H Hghr Educ.
— Strategic Management. LC 95-38589. (Illus.). 1072p. (C). 1995. text 72.75 (*0-256-13619-X*, Irwn McGrw-H) McGrw-H Hghr Educ.
Byars, Lloyd L., jt. auth. see Rue, Leslie W.
Byars, Mel. The Design Encyclopedia. 612p. 1994. 60.00 (*0-471-02455-4*) Wiley.
***Byars, Mel.** 50 Beds: Innovations in Design & Materials. (Illus.). 2000. pap. 39.50 (*2-88046-449-8*, Rotovision) Watsn-Guptill.
— 50 Chairs: Innovations in Design & Materials. LC 98-160739. (Prodesign Ser.). 159p. 1999. pap. 35.00 (*2-88046-264-9*, Rotovision) Watsn-Guptill.
Byars, Mel. 50 Lights: Innovations in Design & Materials. (Illus.). 160p. 1997. pap. 39.50 (*2-88046-265-7*) Watsn-Guptill.
— 50 Products: Innovations in Design & Material. 1999. pap. 39.50 (*0-8230-6794-7*) Watsn-Guptill.
***Byars, Mel.** 50 Sports Wares. (Pro-Design Ser.). 160p. 1999. pap. 39.50 (*2-88046-418-8*) Watsn-Guptill.
Byars, Mel. 50 Tables: Innovations in Design & Materials. (Illus.). 160p. 1997. pap. 39.50 (*2-88046-311-4*, Rotovision) Watsn-Guptill.
— Less: Minimalist Design. (Pro-Design Ser.). 1998. pap. text 39.50 (*0-8230-6793-9*) Watsn-Guptill.
Byars, Merlene H. From My Scrapbook of the State of South Carolina. LC 98-67423. (Illus.). 305p. 1999. 49.95 (*1-57197-128-9*) Pentland Pr.
***Byars, Patti Wilson, ed.** Separate Fountains. LC 99-71546. 205p. 1999. pap. text 19.95 (*1-57736-132-6*, Hillsboro Pr) Providence Hse.
Byars, Rebecca L., jt. auth. see Riosley, Lane.
Byars, Robert S. & Love, Joseph L., eds. Quantitative Social Science Research on Latin America. LC 72-95001. (University of Illinois at Urbana-Champaign. Occasional Papers: No. 1). 280p. reprint ed. pap. 86.80 (*0-608-13890-8*, 202024500016) Bks Demand.
***Byars, Ronald P.** Christian Worship: Glorifying & Enjoying God. (Foundations of Christian Faith Ser.). (Illus.). xxxp. 2000. pap. 11.95 (*0-664-50136-2*) Geneva Press.
Byatt, A. S. Angels & Insects. Date not set. pap. 13.00 (*0-676-50318-7*) Coronet.
— Angels & Insects: Two Novellas. 1994. pap. 13.00 (*0-679-75134-3*) Vin Bks.
— Babel Tower. 1997. pap. 14.00 (*0-679-73680-8*) Vin Bks.
***Byatt, A. S.** The Biographer's Tale. 2001. 24.00 (*0-375-41114-3*) Knopf.

B

An Asterisk (*) at the beginning of an entry indicates that the title is appearing for the first time.

Byatt, A. S. The Djinn in the Nightingale's Eye: Five Fairy Stories. (Illus.). 288p. 1998. pap. 12.00 (*0-679-76222-1*) Vin Bks.

— Elementals: Stories of Fire & Ice. LC 99-10627. 240p. 1999. 21.95 (*0-375-50250-5*) Random.

***Byatt, A. S.** Elementals: Stories of Fire & Ice. (International Ser.). 240p. 2000. pap. 12.00 (*0-375-70575-9*) Vin Bks.

— Elementals: Stories of Fire & Ice. large type ed. 1999. pap. 21.95 (*0-7862-2004-X*, G K Hall Lrg Type) Mac Lib Ref.

Byatt, A. S. The Game. LC 92-53581. 1992. pap. 12.00 (*0-679-74256-5*) Vin Bks.

— The Matisse Stories. 1996. pap. 10.00 (*0-679-76223-X*) Random.

— The Matisse Stories. Date not set. 1.99 (*0-517-19704-9*) Random Hse Value.

— The Matisse Stories. 1996. pap. 10.00 (*0-614-99274-5*) Vin Bks.

***Byatt, A. S.** The Oxford Book of English Short Stories. 2000. pap. 18.95 (*0-19-288111-6*) OUP.

Byatt, A. S. Passions of the Mind: Selected Writings. LC 92-50586. 332p. 1993. pap. 12.00 (*0-679-73678-6*) Vin Bks.

B

***Byatt, A. S.** Possession: A Romance. LC 99-56297. 608p. 2000. 19.95 (*0-679-64030-4*) Modern Lib NY.

Byatt, A. S. Possession: A Romance. LC 91-50023. (Vintage International Ser.). 555p. 1991. pap. 14.00 (*0-679-73590-9*) Vin Bks.

— The Shadow of the Sun. 324p. 1993. pap. 10.95 (*0-15-681416-1*) Harcourt.

— Still Life. LC 96-28801. 1997. per. 13.00 (*0-684-83503-7*, Scribner Pap Fic) S&S Trade Pap.

— Sugar & Other Stories. LC 92-50003. 1992. pap. 12.00 (*0-679-74227-1*) Vin Bks.

— The Virgin in the Garden. 1992. pap. 13.00 (*0-679-73829-0*) Vin Bks.

Byatt, A. S., ed. The Oxford Book of English Short Stories. (Oxford Books of Prose). 470p. 1998. 30.00 (*0-19-214238-0*) OUP.

Byatt, A. S., intro. The Pocket Canons: Song of Solomon. (Pocket Canons Ser.). 48p. 1999. pap. 2.50 (*0-8021-3615-X*) Grove-Atltic.

Byatt, A. S., ed. see Eliot, George, pseud.

Bybee, Howard C. & L'Heureux, Conrad E. Bibliography of Syrian Archaeological Sites to 1980. LC 94-26074. 248p. 1995. text 89.95 (*0-7734-9040-X*) E Mellen.

Bybee, Jane. Guilt & Children. LC 97-80321. (Illus.). 296p. 1997. text 59.95 (*0-12-148610-9*) Morgan Kaufmann.

Bybee, Joan & Fleischman, Suzanne, eds. Modality in Grammar & Discourse. LC 95-17034. (Typological Studies in Language: No. 32). viii, 575p. 1995. pap. 37.95 (*1-55619-640-7*); lib. bdg. 125.00 (*1-55619-639-3*) J Benjamins Pubng Co.

Bybee, Joan, et al. The Evolution of Grammar: Tense, Aspect, & Modality in the Languages of the World. LC 93-43517. 420p. (C). 1994. pap. text 29.95 (*0-226-08665-8*) U Ch Pr.

— The Evolution of Grammar: Tense, Aspect, & Modality in the Languages of the World. LC 93-43517. 420p. (C). 1996. lib. bdg. 90.00 (*0-226-08663-1*) U Ch Pr.

Bybee, Joan, ed. see Givon, Talmy.

Bybee, Joan L. Morphology: A Study of the Relation Between Meaning & Form. LC 85-9021. (Typological Studies in Language Ser.: No. 9). xii, 235p. 1985. pap. 24.95 (*0-915027-38-0*) J Benjamins Pubng Co.

Bybee, Keith J. Mistaken Identity: The Supreme Court & the Politics of Minority Representation. LC 97-51799. 206p. 1998. text 35.00 (*0-691-01729-8*, Pub. by Princeton U Pr) Cal Prin Full Svc.

Bybee, R. Achieving Scientific Literacy: From Purposes to Practices. LC 96-45221. 1997. pap. text 32.50 (*0-435-07134-3*, 07134) Heinemann.

Bybee, Rodger W. Reforming Science Education: Social Perspectives & Personal Reflections. LC 93-17231. (Ways of Knowing in Science Ser.: Vol. 1). 216p. (C). 1993. 43.00 (*0-8077-3261-3*); pap. 19.95 (*0-8077-3260-5*) Tchrs Coll.

Bybee, Rodger W. & Sund, Robert B. Piaget for Educators. 2nd ed. (Illus.). 318p. (C). 1990. reprint ed. pap. text 24.95 (*0-88133-516-9*) Waveland Pr.

Bybee, Sandra. Common Knowledge: Finding a Place to Rent. Salazar, Yolanda L., ed. (Life Skills Ser.). 1991. 2.25 (*1-877709-09-3*) ADAPT Pub Co.

— Common Knowledge: Preparing for a Move. Cullen, Emily A. & Salazar, Yolanda L., eds. (Life Skills Ser.). 1991. 2.25 (*1-877709-12-3*) ADAPT Pub Co.

Bybee, Sandra, ed. see Teutsch, Austin.

Byber, Hazel E. Walking into December. LC 93-85257. (Illus.). 110p. 1993. pap. 10.00 (*1-881908-04-6*) PanPress.

Byce, Jonieta. Contemplations of the Spirit: A Collection of Contemplative Mood Poems. 82p. 1998. pap. write for info. (*1-57502-866-2*, PO2365) Morris Pubng.

Bychkov, Victor. The Aesthetic Face of Being: Art in the Theology of Pavel Florensky. Peeaver, Richard & Valokhonsky, Larissa, trs. LC 93-15303. 1993. pap. 7.95 (*0-88141-127-2*) St Vladimirs.

Bycina, David, jt. auth. see Richards, Jack.

Byckling, Eero & Kajantie, K. Particle Kinematics. LC 72-8595. (Illus.). 329p. reprint ed. pap. 102.00 (*0-608-18775-5*, 202979600065) Bks Demand.

Byczynski, Lynn. Flower Farmer: An Organic Grower's Guide to Raising & Selling Cut Flowers. LC 97-3553. 288p. 1998. pap. 24.95 (*0-930031-94-6*) Chelsea Green Pub.

Byczynski, Stuart J. Audrey Hepburn: A Secret Life. LC 98-11975. 288p. 1998. pap. 19.95 (*1-55618-168-X*) Brunswick Pub.

Bydder, Graeme, jt. auth. see Bradley, William G.

Bydder, Graeme M., jt. auth. see Bradley, William G., Jr.

Byden, Albert. Boyden: Here & There in the Family Tree. (Illus.). 294p. 1991. reprint ed. pap. 46.00 (*0-8328-2212-4*); reprint ed. lib. bdg. 56.00 (*0-8328-2211-6*) Higginson Bk Co.

Bye. Letters To Parents. (C). 1996. 58.00 (*0-13-459488-6*, Macmillan Coll) P-H.

Bye, A. E. Bye. (Illus.). 450p. 1991. reprint ed. pap. 69.00 (*0-8328-2056-3*); reprint ed. lib. bdg. 79.00 (*0-8328-2055-5*) Higginson Bk Co.

***Bye, A. E.** Moods in the Landscape. 1999. text 49.95 (*1-888931-18-3*) Spacemkr Pr.

Bye, Arthur E. Taylor, a Friendly Heritage along the Delaware: The Taylors of Washington Crossing & Some Allied Families in Bucks County. (Illus.). 258p. 1994. reprint ed. pap. 35.00 (*0-8328-4244-3*); reprint ed. lib. bdg. 45.00 (*0-8328-4243-5*) Higginson Bk Co.

Bye, Eric A. The Hair of the Bear. Knight, Denise E., ed. LC 90-82752. (Illus.). 192p. (Orig.). 1991. per. 9.95 (*0-943604-30-3*, BOO/20) Eagles View.

Bye, Eric A., tr. see Ludwig, Gerd.

Bye, Eric A., tr. see Weiss, Christof.

Bye, Holly, jt. auth. see Stone, Sylvia.

Bye, John E., jt. auth. see Strand, Mark.

Bye, K. L. Deadly Presents. LC 94-90346. (Illus.). 80p. (Orig.). 1994. pap. 13.00 (*0-9641945-3-8*) Turtle Run.

— A Step from Heaven. LC 96-90146. (Illus.). 88p. (Orig.). 1996. pap. 13.00 (*0-9641945-0-3*) Turtle Run.

— Tarnished Glory. LC 87-90740. (Illus.). 96p. 1998. pap. 13.00 (*0-9641945-4-6*) Turtle Run.

Bye, L. Dean. Hymns for Children. 32p. 1983. pap. 4.95 (*0-87166-116-0*, 93947) Mel Bay.

— Keyboard Guide & Practice. 6p. 1993. pap. 3.95 (*0-87166-896-3*, 93992) Mel Bay.

— Keyboard-Manuscript-Children. 32p. 1983. pap. 3.95 (*0-87166-923-4*, 93948) Mel Bay.

— Music Dictionary Pocketbook. 32p. 1994. pap. 0.95 (*0-7866-0060-8*, 95221) Mel Bay.

— Music Fundamentals. 32p. 1981. pap. 0.95 (*0-87166-549-2*, 93753) Mel Bay.

Bye, L. Dean. Piano Chords Pocketbook. 32p. 1981. pap. 0.95 (*0-87166-552-2*, 93749) Mel Bay.

Bye, L. Dean. Student's Complete Music Handbook. 80p. 1990. pap. 7.95 (*0-87166-988-9*, 94407) Mel Bay.

— Student's Guide to Music Theory. 48p. 1986. pap. 4.95 (*0-87166-312-0*, 94086) Mel Bay.

— Student's Guide to the Great Composers. 80p. 1988. pap. 4.95 (*0-87166-314-7*, 94230) Mel Bay.

— Student's Musical Dictionary. 64p. 1985. pap. 4.95 (*0-87166-313-9*, 94057) Mel Bay.

— Theory & Harmony for Everyone. 72p. 1981. pap. 8.95 (*0-87166-882-3*, 93790) Mel Bay.

— Trombone Pocketbook, Bk. 1. 32p. 1981. pap. 0.95 (*0-87166-558-1*, 93746) Mel Bay.

— You Can Teach Yourself about Music. 136p. 1989. pap. 9.95 (*0-87166-261-2*, 94300) Mel Bay.

Bye, Margaret G., jt. auth. see Iannone, Joan M.

Bye, Pamela C. Family Hymn Book. 148p. 1982. spiral bd. 12.95 (*0-87166-713-4*, 93830) Mel Bay.

Bye, Ranulph. Ranulph Bye's Bucks County: Today & Yesterday. LC 97-62245. (Illus.). 1997. write for info. (*0-911122-02-8*) Penn German Soc.

Bye, Ranulph. Ranulphbye's Bucks County. LC 88-63902. 120p. 1989. text 50.00 (*0-317-93487-2*) Bargeron Pub.

Bye, Raymond T. Capital Punishment in the United States. LC 82-45658. (Capital Punishment Ser.). 1983. reprint ed. 32.50 (*0-404-62405-7*) AMS Pr.

Bye, Reed. Heart's Bestiary. 72p. 1987. pap. 6.00 (*0-685-56974-8*) Rocky Ledge.

— Passing Freaks & Other Graces. 36p. (Orig.). 1996. pap. 5.00 (*1-887289-25-9*) Rodent Pr.

Bye, Tom. In the Middle. 1995. text 15.95 (*0-13-454380-7*) P-H.

— In the Middle, Bk. 1. LC 95-5232. (C). 1995. pap. text 18.60 (*0-13-454224-X*) P-H.

— In the Middle, Bk. 2. (C). 1995. text, student ed. 26.60 (*0-13-213802-6*); pap. text 18.60 (*0-13-454265-7*) P-H.

— In the Middle, Bk. 3. 1995. text 26.60 (*0-13-213810-7*) P-H.

— In the Middle, Bk. 3. LC 95-5232. (C). 1995. pap. text 18.60 (*0-13-454307-6*) P-H.

— In the Middle, Level 2 Bk. 2. 1995. pap. text, teacher ed. 53.27 (*0-13-454281-9*) P-H.

— In the Middle, Level 3 Bk. 3. 1995. pap. text, teacher ed. 53.27 (*0-13-454323-8*) P-H.

— In the Middle, Set. LC 95-5232. 112p. (C). 1995. pap. text 15.93 (*0-13-454398-X*) P-H.

— In the Middle: Newcomer Teacher's Resource Book. 1995. text 22.60 (*0-13-213794-1*) P-H.

— In the Middle: Newcomer Teacher's Resource Book. 1995. pap. text 45.67 (*0-13-454448-X*) P-H.

— In the Middle: Newcomer's Portfolio. (C). 1995. pap. text 10.00 (*0-13-454422-6*) P-H.

— In the Middle Bk. 2: Assessment Program. 1995. text 33.53 (*0-13-459232-8*) P-H.

— In the Middle Bk. 3: Assessment Program. 1995. text 33.53 (*0-13-459298-0*) P-H.

— Portfolio in the Middle, Bk. 1. 1995. pap. text 10.00 (*0-13-454232-0*) P-H.

— Portfolio in the Middle Student, Bk. 3. 1995. pap. text 10.00 (*0-13-454315-7*) P-H.

Byer. Dimensions in Human Sexuality. 5th ed. LC 97-52370. 672p. 1998. 70.63 (*0-697-26260-X*) McGraw.

Byer & Shainberg. Chapters from Dim. Human Sex. 4th ed. 1993. 30.25 (*0-697-24650-7*, WCB McGr Hill) McGrw-H Hghr Educ.

— Dimensions of Human Sexuality. 4th ed. 1993. student ed. 12.25 (*0-697-24423-7*, WCB McGr Hill) McGrw-H Hghr Educ.

— Dimensions of Human Sexuality, Test Item File/QIF. 4th ed. 1994. 13.43 (*0-697-12604-8*) McGraw.

Byer, et al. Living Well Workbook: Health in Your Hands. 2nd ed. (Health Science Ser.). (C). 1997. pap. text, student ed. 15.00 (*0-673-52396-9*) Jones & Bartlett.

Byer, Anders. The Music of Per Norgard: Fourteen Interpretative Essays. (Illus.). 300p. 1996. 56.95 (*1-85928-313-6*, Pub. by Scolar Pr) Ashgate Pub Co.

Byer, Carol. Henny Penny. LC 80-28146. 32p. (J). (gr. k-3). 1981. lib. bdg. 15.85 (*0-89375-490-0*) Troll Communs.

— Henny Penny. LC 80-28146. 32p. (J). (gr. k-3). 1997. pap. 3.95 (*0-89375-491-9*) Troll Communs.

Byer, Cu & Shainberg. Living Well. (C). 1991. pap. text 48.00 (*0-673-39885-4*) Addson-Wesley Educ.

Byer, Curtis O. & Shainberg, Louis W. Dimensions of Human Sexuality. 4th ed. 688p. (C). 1997. text. write for info. (*0-697-42192-9*, WCB McGr Hill) McGrw-H Hghr Educ.

Byer, Curtis O., et al. Course Kit: Dimensions of Human Sexuality/Taking Sides. (C). 1993. text. write for info. (*0-697-31640-8*) Brown & Benchmark.

— Dimensions of Human Sexuality. 4th ed. 208p. (C). 1993. text, student ed. write for info. (*0-697-12602-1*) Brown & Benchmark.

— Dimensions of Human Sexuality. 4th ed. 208p. (C). 1994. text, student ed. 21.25 (*0-697-12692-7*) Brown & Benchmark.

Byer, Dottie & Eckhardt, Su. Teaching Internet Basics. 25p. 1996. ring bd. 15.00 (*0-931510-64-3*) Hi Willow.

Byer, Doug. Northern Service. (Illus.). 160p. (Orig.). 1997. pap. write for info. (*1-55059-149-5*) Detselig Ents.

Byer, Glenn. Charlemagne & Baptism. LC 99-10372. 264p. 1999. 74.95 (*1-57309-370-X*); pap. 54.95 (*1-57309-369-6*) Intl Scholars.

Byer, Kathryn S. Black Shawl: Poems. LC 97-46082. 64p. 1998. pap. 11.95 (*0-8071-2251-3*); text 19.95 (*0-8071-2250-5*) La State U Pr.

— The Girl in the Midst of the Harvest. (Illus.). 73p. 1986. 13.95 (*0-89672-140-X*) Tex Tech Univ Pr.

— Wildwood Flower: Poems. LC 92-2519. 64p. 1992. pap. 8.95 (*0-8071-1771-4*); text 15.95 (*0-8071-1770-6*) La State U Pr.

Byer, Norman. The Peripheral Retina in Profile. (Illus.). 159p. 1982. 295.00 incl. digital audio, sl. (*0-9609428-0-7*) Criterion Pr.

Byer, R. L., et al, eds. Tunable Solid State Lasers for Remote Sensing. (Optical Sciences Ser.: Vol. 51). (Illus.). 160p. 1986. 72.95 (*0-387-16168-6*) Spr-Verlag.

Byer-Shainberg. Dimensions of Human Sexuality. 4th ed. 1993. teacher ed. 20.62 (*0-697-12603-X*, WCB McGr Hill) McGrw-H Hghr Educ.

Byerlee, Derek & Alex, Gary E. Strengthening National Agricultural Research Systems: Policy Issues & Good Practice. LC 97-51583. (Environmentally & Socially Sustainable Development Studies & Monographs). 100p. 1998. pap. 22.00 (*0-8213-4173-1*, 14173) World Bank.

Byerlee, Derek & Eicher, Carl K. Africa's Emerging Maize Revolution. LC 97-10662. 1997. pap. 29.95 (*1-55587-754-0*) L Rienner.

— Africa's Emerging Maize Revolution. LC 97-10662. 1997. 55.00 (*1-55587-776-1*) L Rienner.

Byerley, Donna. Census of Madison Co., Missouri, 1860. 98p. 1990. per. 7.00 (*1-55856-022-X*, 340) Closson Pr.

Byerley, Paul F., et al, eds. Computers, Communication, & Usability: Design Issues, Research & Methods for Integrated Services. LC 93-2340. (Studies in Telecommunication: Vol.19). 474p. 1993. 173.00 (*0-444-89974-X*, North Holland) Elsevier.

Byerley, Suzanne, ed. see Irwin, Elizabeth Mills.

Byerley, Timothy E. Saint John Neumann, Wonder-Worker of Philadelphia: Recent Miracles 1961-1991. Fehrenbach, Charles, ed. 211p. 1992. pap. write for info. (*0-9634825-0-5*) Nat Shrine.

***Byerly.** Many Faces of Science. 2000. 65.00 (*0-8133-6550-3*, Pub. by Westview) HarpC.

— Many Faces of Science. 2nd ed. 304p. 2000. pap. 25.00 (*0-8133-6551-1*, Pub. by Westview) HarpC.

Byerly, Alison. Realism, Representation, & the Arts in Nineteenth-Century Literature. LC 97-6958. (Studies in Nineteenth-Century Literature & Culture: Vol. 12). (Illus.). 246p. (C). 1998. text 59.95 (*0-521-58116-8*) Cambridge U Pr.

Byerly, Benjamin F. & Byerly, Catherine R., eds. Dearest Phylabe: Letters from Wartime England by Edith Base. 176p. 1996. 29.95 (*0-87081-421-4*) Univ Pr Colo.

Byerly, Catherine R., jt. ed. see Byerly, Benjamin F.

Byerly, Edwin & Deardoff, Kevin. National & State Population Estimates, 1990 to 1994. (Illus.). 86p. 1997. reprint ed. pap. text 30.00 (*0-7881-3845-6*) DIANE Pub.

Byerly, Henry, jt. auth. see Stevenson, Leslie.

Byerly, Robert D. Making Powder Horns, Bk. II. (Illus.). iv, 88p. (Orig.). 1996. mass mkt. 7.50 (*0-9653364-0-9*) Making Powder.

Byerly, Victoria. Hard Times Cotton Mill Girls: Personal Histories of Womanhood & Poverty in the South. 232p. 1987. pap. text 14.95 (*0-87546-129-8*, ILR Press) Cornell U Pr.

Byerly, W. G. Byerly. The Byerlys of Carolina. 69p. 1995. reprint ed. pap. 14.00 (*0-8328-4754-2*); reprint ed. lib. bdg. 24.00 (*0-8328-4753-4*) Higginson Bk Co.

Byerman. John Edgar Wideman. LC 97-43160. 1998. 25.95 (*0-8057-0870-7*) Macmillan.

Byerman, Keith, jt. auth. see Banks, Erma D.

Byerman, Keith E. Seizing the Word: History, Art, & Self in the Work of W. E. B. Du Bois. LC 93-30368. 256p. 1994. 40.00 (*0-8203-1624-5*) U of Ga Pr.

Byers. American Pronghorn. LC 97-14726. 288p. 1997. lib. bdg. 70.00 (*0-226-08698-4*) U Ch Pr.

Byers & Calter. Introduction to Algebra & Trigonometry with Applications, Vol. 2. (C). 1998. pap. text 43.00 (*0-536-01691-7*) Pearson Custom.

Byers, jt. auth. see Filby, P. William.

Byers, A. L. Birth of a Reformation: Life & Labours of D. S. Warner. (Illus.). 496p. reprint ed. 8.00 (*0-686-29104-2*) Faith Pub Hse.

— Moral Lessons of Yesterday. Wheeler, Richard & Wheeler, Noelle, eds. (Illus.). 168p. (C). 1995. 15.00 (*1-889128-30-9*) Mantle Ministries.

Byers, Alvah P., ed. The Byers Neurotherapy Reference Library. 2nd ed. 515p. 1998. pap. text 75.00 (*1-887114-04-1*) AAPB.

Byers, Ann. The Holocaust Camps. LC 97-37642. (Holocaust Remembered Ser.). (Illus.). 128p. (YA). (gr. 6 up). 1998. lib. bdg. 20.95 (*0-89490-995-9*) Enslow Pubs.

— The Holocaust Overview. LC 97-37637. (Holocaust Remembered Ser.). (Illus.). 128p. (YA). (gr. 6 up). 1998. lib. bdg. 20.95 (*0-7660-1062-7*) Enslow Pubs.

— Jaime Escalante: Sensational Teacher. LC 95-50071. (Hispanic Biographies Ser.). 128p. (YA). (gr. 6 up). 1996. lib. bdg. 20.95 (*0-89490-763-8*) Enslow Pubs.

***Byers, Ann.** Sexually Transmitted Diseases: A Hot Issue. LC 98-44420. (Hot Issues Ser.). 64p. (YA). (gr. 6 up). 1999. lib. bdg. 19.95 (*0-7660-1192-5*) Enslow Pubs.

— Teens & Pregnancy: A Hot Issue. LC 99-37357. (Hot Issues Ser.). (Illus.). 64p. (gr. 6 up). 2000. lib. bdg. 19.95 (*0-7660-1365-0*) Enslow Pubs.

Byers, Bob. Treasury of Carolers: Over 20 Years of Christmas Tradition & Remembrances. LC 99-19167. 1998. 35.00 (*1-56799-690-6*, Friedman-Fairfax) M Friedman Pub Grp Inc.

Byers, Brenda A., et al. Food Service Manual for Health Care Institutions, 1994. rev. ed. LC 94-7495. 574p. 1994. 44.95 (*1-55648-114-4*, 046172) AHPI.

Byers, Bryan, ed. Readings in Social Psychology: Perspective & Method. LC 92-26106. 336p. 1992. pap. text 30.00 (*0-205-13856-X*) Allyn.

Byers, Bryan & Mckean, Jerome. Data Analysis for the Social Sciences. LC 99-42598. 262p. (C). 2000. pap. text 21.00 (*0-205-27480-3*, Macmillan Coll) P-H.

Byers, Bryan, jt. auth. see Hendricks, James E.

Byers, Bryan, jt. ed. see Hendricks, James E.

Byers, C. H., jt. auth. see Holmes, J. M.

***Byers, C. Randall & Bettas, George A., eds.** Records of North American Big Game. 11th rev. ed. (Illus.). 700p. 1999. 49.95 (*0-940864-35-5*) Boone & Crockett.

Byers, C. Randall & Reneau, Jack, eds. Boone & Crockett Club's 23rd Big Game Awards, 1995-1997. LC 98-71413. (Illus.). 600p. 1998. 39.95 (*0-940864-34-7*) Boone & Crockett.

Byers, C. Randall, ed. see Nesbitt, William H. & Wright, Philip L.

Byers, Carla R. The Colors of Your Soul: Discover the Star You Are! Kepler, Kit & Hamme, Jeannie, eds. LC 97-92990. (Rainbow of Creation Ser.: Vol. 1). (Illus.). 158p. (Orig.). 1997. pap., wbk. ed. 20.00 (*0-9656124-1-4*) Heyokah Pub.

The Colors of Your Soul teaches you the ART OF DREAM WEAVING (RAINBOW OF CREATION ASTROLOGY) which dates back to the time of Atlantis when our Rainbow Star Teachers were still here. At the time you were born you were imprinted with Rainbow Lights of the Zodiac, YOUR PERSONAL BLUEPRINT. That Light Pattern is your SECRET KEY FOR SUCCESSFUL LIVING. Paint your Star Wheel the Colors of Your Soul. Discover your way of CONSCIOUSLY CREATING & INTENDING YOUR LIFE DREAMS. Learn the ORIGINAL SONG OF THE PLANETS. Restore your Personal Power. 15 Authentic Jewels of the Earth (Faery Stones) are included with the book. Cast the jewels on your Personal Painted Star Wheel for GUIDANCE FROM YOUR STAR TEACHERS. Metaphysical Reviews - Sept. 1997, Richard Fuller: "By discovering who we are, we can learn how to reclaim our personal power & direct our lives & that is the wonder of this first-in-a-series workbooks of transformation...is a treasure chest of discovery...If your interest is in your divine plan & personal pattern for creating the content of your life...you must read & use the Colors of Your Soul!" Heyokah Publishing Company, Box 45252, Boise, ID 83711. 1-208-465-5809. Ask for Carla Byers for more information. E-mail: hiheyokah@aol.com *Publisher Paid Annotation.*

–How to Have a Happy Heart! Walk the Rainbow Path of Creation "Bring Back Your Star Power!" Kepler, Kit & Hoch, Lana, eds. LC 97-93079. (Rainbow of Creation Ser.: Vol. 2). (Illus.). 120p. (Orig.). 1999. pap., wbk. ed. 20.00 (*0-9656124-2-2*) Heyokah Pub. How to Have a Happy Heart teaches you the Art of Directed Dreaming. It is a Soul Healing workbook. Guided Visualizations take the reader step by step on a Soul Healing Journey. Learn to use Rainbow Lights to heal your body, mind & Soul. Meet your Guardians & Guides. Find your Twin Flame. Find your Star Home & the Color of Your Bones. Reclaim the missing pieces of your Soul. Confront Shadow Self & Liberate Yourself From the Past. Follow the path of Human & Woman, when our Rainbow Star

An Asterisk (*) at the beginning of an entry indicates that the title is appearing for the first time.

Teachers were here. Transform your life with Love & Light so you can "Celebrate Beautiful Living." "Your Circle of Becoming" Star Wheel of the Soul in beautiful living colors is included in the book.The Book Reader 1999/2000 Fall issue--- "A Step by step guide that lets users optimize their talents & opportunities. With visualizations that share some of Byers' own "dreaming journeys" & releases a bonus that few constricted individuals ever find." Magical Blend Magazine, issue 69 page, 74 January through March 2000. ---"This extraordinary workbook is the guide to life that we've all been looking for. Take charge of your world & create a life that you love, using this work as an escort on your expedition. - Kimberly McCreen Heyokah Publishing Company, Box 45252, Boise, ID 83711. 1-208-465-5809. Ask for Carla Byers for more information. E-mail: heyokah@aol.com. *Publisher Paid Annotation.*

— Rainbow Lights of the Zodiac! Astrology for the New Age. (Rainbow of Creation Ser.). (Illus.). 120p. (Orig.). 2001. pap., wbk. ed. write for info. (*0-9656124-3-0*) Heyokah Pub.

— The Sacred Clowns of Wisdom Vol. 1: Star Wheel of the Wisdom Keepers. (Rainbow of Creation Ser.: \). (Illus.). 120p. (Orig.). 1998. pap., wbk. ed. write for info. (*0-9656124-4-9*) Heyokah Pub.

Byers, Carolyn. Forever Stories, 5 vols. (J). (ps-3). 1990. boxed set 49.99 (*0-8280-0898-1*) Review & Herald.

Byers, Chester. Cowboy Roping & Rope Tricks. xiii, 99p. 1988. reprint ed. pap. 3.95 (*0-486-25711-8*) Dover.

— Roping: Trick & Fancy Rope Spinning. 89p. 1986. pap. 7.95 (*0-918222-95-8*) Applewood.

— Trick Roping. (Buckaroos Ser.). 32p. (J). 1996. pap. 1.50 (*1-55709-368-7*) Applewood.

Byers, Cordia. Lady of the Night. 400p. 1998. mass mkt. 5.99 (*0-8439-4404-8*, Leisure Bks) Dorchester Pub Co.

Byers, Curtis & Johns, Helen. Life with God: First Steps. LC 96-85027. 64p. 1996. pap. 3.95 (*0-916035-67-0*) Evangel Indiana.

Byers, D. & Johnson, F. Two Sites on Martha's Vineyard, Vol. 1, No. 1. LC 40-3078. 1940. pap. 45.00 (*0-939312-00-X*) Peabody Found.

Byers, Dale A. I Left the Lodge. LC 88-31152. 128p. 1989. pap. 8.99 (*0-87227-127-7*, RBP5155) Reg Baptist.

— Suicide: How God Sustained a Family. LC 91-8836. 128p. (Orig.). 1991. reprint ed. pap. text 8.99 (*0-87227-146-3*, RBP5177) Reg Baptist.

Byers, David. Crapemyrtle. 1997. pap. text 27.95 (*1-885623-25-9*) Owl Bay Pubs.

***Byers, David.** The Federal Valley railroad Company & Its Ancestors, One. Pressler, Amy, ed. LC 00-26092. (Illus.). iv, 160p. 2000. 24.95 (*0-918048-14-1*) Integrity.

Byers, David, et al. The Catholic Way of Life. Huber, Monica T., ed. 100p. 1990. 9.95 (*0-918951-01-1*) Paulist Natl Catholic.

Byers, Dorie. Herbal Remedy Gardens. LC 98-29971. 192p. 1999. pap. 16.95 (*1-58017-095-1*, Storey Pub) Storey Bks.

— Natural Body Basics: Making Your Own Cosmetics. LC 96-94319. 1996. pap. 7.95 (*0-9652353-0-0*) Gooseberry.

Byers, Dorie, et al, eds. Taste Life! The Organic Choice. (Illus.). 164p. 1998. pap. 12.95 (*1-890612-08-1*) Vital Health.

Byers, Douglas, jt. auth. see La Farge, Oliver.

Byers, Douglas S. The Nevin Shellheap: Burial & Observations, Vol. 9. 1979. pap. 15.00 (*0-939312-10-7*) Peabody Found.

Byers, Dwight C. Better Health with Foot Reflexology. rev. ed. (Illus.). 263p. (Orig.). 1983. pap. 26.95 (*0-9611804-2-0*); pap. 18.95 (*0-9611804-4-7*) Ingham Pub.

— Better Health with Foot Reflexology. rev. ed. (Illus.). 263p. (Orig.). 1987. 26.95 (*0-9611804-8-X*) Ingham Pub.

Byers, E. Sandra & O'Sullivan, Lucia F., eds. Sexual Coercion in Dating Relationships. LC 96-7979. (Journal of Psychology & Human Sexuality: Vol. 8, Nos. 1/2). 179p. 1996. 39.95 (*1-56024-815-7*) Haworth Pr.

— Sexual Coercion in Dating Relationships. LC 96-7979. (Journal of Psychology & Human Sexuality: Vol. 8, Nos. 1/2). 179p. 1996. pap. 14.95 (*1-56024-844-0*) Haworth Pr.

Byers, Edward E. Ten Thousand Medical Words, Spelled & Divided for Quick Reference. 128p. 1972. text 10.24 (*0-07-009503-5*) McGraw.

Byers, Edward E., jt. auth. see Root, Kathleen B.

Byers, George H. Collaborative Discipline for At-Risk Students: Peer Support Activities Program for Grades 7-12. LC 94-23390. 1994. pap. text 29.95 (*0-87628-122-6*) Ctr Appl Res.

***Byers, Helen.** Kidding Around Boston: What to Do, Where to Go & How to Have Fun in Boston. 2nd ed. (Kidding Around Ser.). (Illus.). 144p. (J). (gr. 1-5). 2000. pap. 8.95 (*1-56261-586-6*) Avalon Travel.

Byers, Horace R. Elements of Cloud Physics. LC 65-17282. (Illus.). 1994. lib. bdg. 20.00 (*0-226-08697-6*) U Ch Pr.

— Elements of Cloud Physics. LC 65-17282. (Illus.). 201p. reprint ed. pap. 62.40 (*0-608-09275-4*, 205414900004); reprint ed. pap. 66.10 (*0-608-20622-9*, 205459000003) Bks Demand.

Byers, J. W. Parent & Child. 60p. pap. 1.50 (*0-686-29132-8*) Faith Pub Hse.

— Sanctification. 96p. 2.00 (*0-686-29140-9*) Faith Pub Hse.

Byers, James F., jt. ed. see Hansen, W. Lee.

Byers, James M. From Hippocrates to Virchow: Reflections on Human Disease. LC 87-18835. (Illus.). 160p. 1987. text 20.00 (*0-89189-257-5*) Am Soc Clinical.

Byers, Jeannette Q., tr. Brothers in Spirit: The Correspondence of Albert Schweitzer & William Larimer Mellon, Jr. 232p. (C). 1996. text 28.95 (*0-8156-0344-4*, BYBS) Syracuse U Pr.

Byers, Jerry P. Metalworking Fluids. (Manufacturing Engineering & Materials Processing Ser.: 41). (Illus.). 504p. 1994. text 150.00 (*0-8247-9201-7*) Dekker.

Byers, John A. American Pronghorn. LC 97-14726. 288p. 1997. pap. text 23.95 (*0-226-08699-2*) U Ch Pr.

Byers, John A., jt. ed. see Beckoff, Marc.

Byers, Kenneth. The Father & Son Survival Kit: A Journey into the Wilderness of Relationships. (YA). (gr. 9 up). 1988. 19.95 (*0-9619040-1-1*); student ed. 12.95 (*0-9619040-2-X*); pap. 12.95 (*0-9619040-0-3*) Journeys Together.

— Man in Transition . . . His Role As Father, Son, Friend & Lover. 216p. (gr. 9 up). 1990. pap. 9.95 (*0-9619040-3-8*) Journeys Together.

Byers, Kenneth F. WWTMMA? Who Was That Masked Man Anyway? 140p. (Orig.). 1993. pap. 12.95 (*0-685-55199-7*) Journeys Together.

— WWTMMA? Who Was That Masked Man Anyway? 1700p. (Orig.). 1993. pap. 12.95 (*0-9619040-4-6*) Journeys Together.

Byers, Laura T. Hortus Librorum: Early Botanical Books at Dumbarton Oaks. LC 83-5697. (Illus.). 48p. 1983. pap. 6.00 (*0-88402-118-1*) Dumbarton Oaks.

Byers, Louise. How to Catch a Man. Costa, Gwen, ed. LC 90-21756. (Illus.). (Orig.). 1992. 14.95 (*0-87949-347-X*) Ashley Bks.

Byers, Marvin. The Final Victory: The Year 2000. rev. ed. 384p. 1999. pap. 14.99 (*1-56043-824-X*, Treasure Hse) Destiny Image.

— Seis Dias y un Dia. (Orig.). 1996. pap. 11.95 (*0-9647871-1-3*, Hope of Israel) Hebron Minist.

— Six Days & a Day. 252p. (Orig.). 1996. pap. 14.99 (*1-56043-263-2*, Treasure Hse) Destiny Image.

— La Victoria Final del Ano 2.000. 2nd ed. 350p. (Orig.). 1995. pap. 11.95 (*0-9647871-0-5*) Hebron Minist.

— A Vitoria Final: O Ano 2000. (POR.). (Orig.). 1996. pap. 11.95 (*0-9647871-2-1*, Hope of Israel) Hebron Minist.

— Yasser Arafat - A Biblical Character? An Urgent Call to the Nation of Israel & the Body of Christ. 280p. (Orig.). 1996. pap. write for info. (*0-9647871-3-X*, Hope of Israel) Hebron Minist.

— Yasser Arafat - Un Personaje Biblico? Un Llamado Urgente a la Nacion de Israel y Al Cuerpo de Cristo. (ENG & SPA.). 280p. (Orig.). 1996. pap. write for info. (*0-9647871-4-8*, Hope of Israel) Hebron Minist.

— Yasser Arafat an Apocalyptic Character. rev. ed. 288p. 1996. pap. 12.98 (*0-9647871-5-6*, Hope of Israel) Hebron Minist.

Byers, Mary. Lake Simcoe: And Lake Couchiching. (Illus.). 1999. text 29.95 (*1-55046-269-5*, Pub. by Boston Mills) Genl Dist Srvs.

Byers, Mary & McBurney, Margaret. Atlantic Hearth: Early Homes & Families of Nova Scotia. (Illus.). 364p. 1994. text 60.00 (*0-8020-2935-3*); pap. text 24.95 (*0-8020-7762-5*) U of Toronto Pr.

— The Governor's Road: Early Buildings & Families from Mississauga to London. (Illus.). 336p. 1980. pap. 13.95 (*0-8020-6533-3*) U of Toronto Pr.

Byers, Mary, jt. auth. see McBurney, Margaret.

Byers, Michael. The Coast of Good Intentions. LC 97-49611. 176p. 1998. pap. 12.00 (*0-395-89170-1*, Mariner Bks) HM.

— Custom, Power & the Power of Rules: International Relations & Customary International Law. LC 99-207249. 224p. (C). 1998. text 54.95 (*0-521-63289-7*); pap. text 19.95 (*0-521-63408-3*) Cambridge U Pr.

***Byers, Michael, ed.** The Role of Law in International Politics: Essays in International Relations & International Law. LC 99-45592. 376p. 2000. write for info. (*0-19-826887-4*) OUP.

Byers, Michael, jt. auth. see Grewe, Wilhelm G.

Byers, Patricia, et al. The Kids' Money Book. LC 82-184275. (Illus.). 144p. (J). (gr. 2-6). 1983. pap. 4.95 (*0-89709-041-1*) Liberty Pub.

Byers, Paul, jt. auth. see Mead, Margaret.

Byers, Paula K. Ethnic Genealogy: Asian-American Searchbook. LC 95-31649. 1995. 69.00 (*0-8103-9228-3*) Gale.

Byers, Paula K., ed. African American Genealogical Sourcebook. LC 95-2263. (Genealogy Sourcebook Ser.). 250p. 1995. 75.00 (*0-8103-9226-7*) Gale.

— Hispanic American Genealogical Sourcebook. LC 94-37509. (Genealogy Sourcebook Ser.). 224p. 1994. 75.00 (*0-8103-9227-5*) Gale.

Byers, Paula K., ed. Native American Genealogical Sourcebook. (Genealogical Sourcebook Ser.). 250p. 1995. 75.00 (*0-8103-9229-1*) Gale.

Byers, Paula K., jt. auth. see Bourgoin, Suzanne M.

Byers, Peggy Y. Organizational Communication: Theory & Behavior: Instructor's Manual & Test Bank. (C). 1996. pap. text, teacher ed. write for info. (*0-205-26466-2*, T6466-1) Allyn.

Byers, Peggy Yunas. Organizational Communication. LC 96-24912. 382p. 1996. pap. text 50.00 (*0-205-17443-4*) Allyn.

Byers, R. A. Everyman's Database Primer Featuring dBASE II. 1985. pap. 19.95 (*0-685-17297-X*) McGraw.

Byers, R. B., ed. Canadian Annual Review of Politics & Public Affairs, 1979. 1981. text 55.00 (*0-8020-2407-6*) U of Toronto Pr.

— Canadian Annual Review of Politics & Public Affairs, 1980. 400p. 1982. text 55.00 (*0-8020-2462-9*) U of Toronto Pr.

— Canadian Annual Review of Politics & Public Affairs, 1981. 489p. 1984. text 55.00 (*0-8020-2500-5*) U of Toronto Pr.

— Canadian Annual Review of Politics & Public Affairs, 1982. (Canadian Annual Review Ser.). 368p. 1984. text 55.00 (*0-8020-2533-1*) U of Toronto Pr.

— Canadian Annual Review of Politics & Public Affairs, 1984. 344p. 1987. text 55.00 (*0-8020-2591-9*) U of Toronto Pr.

— Canadian Annual Review of Politics & Public Affairs, 1985. 428p. 1988. text 55.00 (*0-8020-5722-5*) U of Toronto Pr.

— Canadian Annual Review of Politics & Public Affairs 1987. 350p. 1991. text 60.00 (*0-8020-5851-5*) U of Toronto Pr.

Byers, R. K. Uptown Heads. 192p. 1996. pap. 9.95 (*1-874509-30-1*) LPC InBook.

Byers, R. McCulloch. The Hard Hat Girl - Power Engineer. LC 76-29554. 157p. (C). 1976. 5.95 (*0-9602048-0-6*) Fairfield Hse.

Byers, Richard L. Dark Kingdoms. (World of Darkness Ser.). 1998. pap. 11.99 (*1-56504-984-5*, 11049, Wrld of Darkness) White Wolf.

— Dead Time. 288p. 1992. mass mkt. 3.99 (*0-8217-3963-8*, Zebra Kensgtn) Kensgtn Pub Corp.

— The Tale of the Terrible Toys. (Are You Afraid of the Dark? Ser.: No. 21). (YA). (gr. 4-7). 1998. pap. 3.99 (*0-671-02113-3*, Minstrel Bks) PB.

— X-Men: Soul Killer. (X-Men Ser.). 1999. pap. 6.99 (*0-425-16737-2*) Blvd Books.

Byers, Richard M. Andromache Beneath the Loac of Life. LC 89-84139. (Illus.). 240p. 1989. 15.00 (*0-9602048-4-9*) Fairfield Hse.

— Andromache's Hector & Helenus. LC 89-83539 (Illus.). 279p. 1989. 16.00 (*0-9602048-3-0*) Fairfield Hse.

— The Return of Andromache. LC 89-84943. (Illus.). 122p. 1990. 12.00 (*0-9602048-5-7*) Fairfield Hse.

— The Winning of Andromache. LC 87-80719. (Illus.). 183p. 1987. 10.00 (*0-9602048-2-2*) Fairfield Hse.

***Byers, Robert, ed.** West Virginians Who Made a Difference. 1999. pap. write for info. (*0-941147-01-0*) Charleston Gazette.

Byers, Robert A., jt. auth. see Ratliff, Wayne.

Byers, Roger, tr. see Schnitzler, Arthur.

Byers, Roland O. Black Puff Polly: And Other Flights to Eternity. LC 90-92116. (Illus.). 288p. (Orig.). 1991. pap. text 15.95 (*0-9614563-2-9*) Pawpaw Pr.

— Flak Dodger. LC 85-60155. (Illus.). 256p. (Orig.). 1985. reprint ed. pap. 15.95 (*0-9614563-0-2*) Pawpaw Pr.

— To the Sundown Side. rev. ed. LC 86-90569. (Illus.). 216p. 1986. reprint ed. pap. 7.95 (*0-9614563-1-0*) Pawpaw Pr.

Byers, S. H. With Fire & Sword. LC 92-60389. (Illus.). 225p. 1992. reprint ed. 20.00 (*0-9628936-2-5*) Pr Camp Pope.

Byers, Sandra R. The Executive Nurse: Leadership for New Health Care Transitions. abr. rev. ed. (Professional Reference - Nursing Ser.). 320p. (C). 1996. mass mkt. 62.95 (*0-8273-6272-2*) Delmar.

***Byers, Stephen F.** Bent Coin. 331p. 1999. pap. 15.00 (*1-929663-01-3*) Books By Byers.

— The Naked Jaybird. 2nd ed. 282p. 1999. pap. 15.00 (*1-929663-00-5*) Books By Byers.

Byers, Stephen P. The Naked Jaybird. LC 98-89522. 375p. 1998. text 25.00 (*0-7388-0205-0*); pap. text 15.00 (*0-7388-0206-9*) Xlibris Corp.

Byers, Steve. Electronic Type Catalog. 1992. pap. 14.95 (*0-685-68957-3*) Random.

Byers, Steven N. A Reconstruction of the Skull of Gigantopithecus Blacki. (Illus.). viii, 87p. 1986. reprint ed. pap. text 10.63 (*1-55567-033-4*) Coyote Press.

Byers, T. J. Microprocessor Support Chips: Theory Design & Applications. 302p. (Orig.). 1982. 38.00 (*0-942412-05-2*) Micro Text Pubns.

— Solar Cells: Understanding & Using Photovoltaics. 256p. (Orig.). 1982. pap. 14.95 (*0-942412-04-4*) Micro Text Pubns.

Byers, Thomas B. What I Cannot Say: Self, Word, & World in Whitman, Stevens, & Merwin. 160p. 1989. text 24.95 (*0-252-01542-8*) U of Ill Pr.

Byers, Vera S. & Baldwin, R. W., eds. Immunology of Malignant Diseases. (Immunology & Medicine Ser.). (C). 1987. text 156.00 (*0-85200-964-X*) Kluwer Academic.

Byers, Virginia B. Nursing Observation. 2nd ed. LC 73-76772. 106p. 1973. write for info. (*0-697-05536-1*) Brown & Benchmark.

Byers, Walter. Unsportsmanlike Conduct: Exploiting College Athletes. 424p. (C). 1997. pap. 18.95 (*0-472-08442-9*, 08442) U of Mich Pr.

Byers, Walter & Hammer, Charles. Unsportsmanlike Conduct: Exploiting College Athletes. LC 95-15973. 424p. (C). 1995. 34.50 (*0-472-10666-X*, 10666) U of Mich Pr.

Byers, William. How to Implement Industrial Water Reuse: A Systematic Approach. LC 95-49252. 112p. 1996. 50.00 (*0-8169-0675-0*, C-5) Am Inst Chem Eng.

Byers, William N. & Kellom, John H. Handbook to the Gold Fields of Nebraska & Kansas. LC 72-9432. (Far Western Frontier Ser.). (Illus.). 122p. 1973. reprint ed. 13.95 (*0-405-04963-3*) Ayer.

Byfield, Barbara N. The Book of Weird: Being a Most Desirable Lexicon of the Fantastical... LC 94-6573. Orig. Title: Glass Harmonica. (Illus.). 160p. 1994. reprint ed. pap. 10.00 (*0-385-06591-4*) Doubleday.

Byfield, Bert. Brother Gregory: Rasputin Trilogy. (Father Gregory Trilogy: Bk. 2). 250p. 2000. pap. 9.00 (*1-887121-06-4*) Caravela Bks.

— Grisha. (Father Gregory Trilogy: Bk. 3). 250p. 1999. pap. 9.00 (*1-887121-05-6*) Caravela Bks.

— Last Stand at Perekop. (Russalka Trilogy Ser.). 1999. pap. 9.00 (*1-887121-03-X*) Caravela Bks.

— Rage of the Bear. LC 95-70527. (Russalka Trilogy Ser.: Vol. 1). 253p. (Orig.). 1996. per. 9.00 (*1-887121-01-3*) Caravela Bks.

— Scream of the Eagle. (Russalka Trilogy Ser.: Vol. 2). 255p. 1999. pap. 9.00 (*1-887121-02-1*) Caravela Bks.

Byfield, David. Chiropractic Manipulative Skills: The Fundamentals of Clinical Practice. (Illus.). 336p. 1995. pap. text 65.00 (*0-7506-0968-0*) Buttrwrth-Heinemann.

Byfield, Frederica J. The Belly up Curve: Who Is Michael? 286p. (Orig.). 1996. pap. 20.95 (*0-9651175-0-2*) F Byfield.

Byfield, John E., jt. ed. see Lokich, Jacob J.

Byfield, Ted & United Western Communications Staff. Alberta in the 20th Century: A Journalistic History of the Province in 12 Volumes. LC 93-173498. 1991. write for info. (*0-9695718-2-8*) UWC.

Byford, Jim. Close to the Land: Reflections on Re-Connecting. LC 98-25371. (Outdoor Tennessee Ser.). (Illus.). 192p. 1999. pap. 16.95 (*1-57233-029-5*, 9825371) U of Tenn Pr.

Byford, John, et al, eds. AACR, DDC, MARC & Friends: The Role of CIG in Bibliographic Control. 130p. 1993. 55.00 (*1-85604-023-2*, LAP0232, Pub. by Library Association) Bernan Associates.

Byford, Moyra. Decorative Picture Framing. 96p. 1995. 17.95 (*1-56799-255-2*, Friedman-Fairfax) M Friedman Pub Grp Inc.

— Picture Framing. 96p. 1996. pap. text 11.95 (*1-56799-262-5*, Friedman-Fairfax) M Friedman Pub Grp Inc.

Byford, Moyru. Framing: How to Frame Paintings, Prints, Photographs, Needlecrafts, Papercrafts, Models, Memorabilia & More. (Illus.). 80p. (Orig.). 1996. pap. 18.95 (*0-85532-805-3*, 805, Pub. by Srch Pr) A Schwartz & Co.

Byford-Ruth, Sharon. The Arabian: A Guide for New Owners. rev. ed. LC 99-26760. (Illus.). 174p. pap. write for info. (*1-57779-019-7*) Alpine Pubns.

Byg, Barton. Landscapes of Resistance: The German Films of Daniele Huillet & Jean-Marie Straub. LC 95-7214. (Illus.). 324p. 1995. 55.00 (*0-520-08908-1*, Pub. by U CA Pr); pap. 22.50 (*0-520-08910-3*, Pub. by U CA Pr) Cal Prin Full Svc.

Bygate, J. E. Aircraft Electrical Systems: Single & Twin Engine. IAP, Inc. Staff, ed. & illus. by. LC 92-24372. 128p. 1990. reprint ed. pap. text 14.50 (*0-89100-357-6*, JS312664) Jeppesen Sanderson.

Bygate, Martin. Speaking. Widdowson, H. G. & Candlin, C. N., eds. (Illus.). 136p. 1987. pap. text 14.95 (*0-19-437134-4*) OUP.

Bygrave, Bill. The Portable M B A in Entreprenevrship Case Studies. LC 98-136320. (Portable MBA Ser.). 336p. 1997. pap., student ed. 29.95 (*0-471-18229-X*) Wiley.

Bygrave, Stephen. Romantic Writings. 368p. (C). 1996. pap. 22.99 (*0-415-13578-8*) Routledge.

— Samuel Taylor Coleridge. Armstrong, Isobel & Loughrey, Bryan, eds. (Writers & Their Work Ser.). 1997. pap. 17.00 (*0-7463-0829-9*, Pub. by Northcote House) U Pr of Miss.

Bygrave, Stephen, ed. Romantic Writings: An Introductory Anthology. LC 96-7542. (Approaching Literature Ser.). 368p. (C). 1996. 90.00 (*0-415-13577-X*) Routledge.

Bygrave, William D. The Portable MBA in Entrepreneurship. 2nd ed. LC 96-43971. 528p. 1997. 34.95 (*0-471-16078-4*) Wiley.

Bygrave, William D., jt. auth. see Timmons, Jeffry A.

Byham, William & Pickett, Debra. Landing the Job You Want: How to Have the Best Job Interview of Your Life. LC 99-12529. (Illus.). 195p. 1999. pap. 14.00 (*0-609-80408-1*) Random Hse Value.

Byham, William C. Zapp! Empowerment in Health Care. 309p. 1993. pap. 11.00 (*0-449-90885-2*) Fawcett.

— Zapp! The Lightning of Empowerment. Cox, Jeff, ed. 224p. (C). 1989. pap. 9.95 (*0-9623483-1-7*) Dev Dimensions.

— Zapp! The Lightning of Empowerment. LC 97-97003. 208p. 1998. pap. 11.00 (*0-449-00282-9*) Fawcett.

— Zapp! In Education. 1992. pap. 11.00 (*0-449-90796-1*) Fawcett.

Byham, William C. & Cox, Jeff. Heroz: Empower Yourself, Your Coworkers, Your Company. 224p. 1995. pap. 11.00 (*0-449-90958-1*) Fawcett.

— Zapp! The Lightning of Empowerment. 208p. 1992. pap. 11.00 (*0-449-90705-8*, Columbine) Fawcett.

Byham, William C. & Dixon, George. Shogun Management: How to Thrive in Japanese Companies. LC 92-54747. 224p. 1993. 25.00 (*0-88730-630-6*, HarpBusn) HarpInfo.

Byham, William C. & Krauzer, Steven M. The Selection Solution: Solving the Mystery of Matching People to Jobs. (Illus.). 216p. 1996. 17.95 (*0-9623483-3-3*) Dev Dimensions.

Byham, William C. & Pickett, Debra. Landing the Job You Want: How to Have the Best Job Interview of Your Life. Matzen, Mary, ed. (Illus.). 196p. (Orig.). 1997. pap. 19.95 (*0-9623483-4-1*, BPLJYWPB) Dev Dimensions.

Byham, William C., et al. The Service Leaders Club: . Dazzling Your Customers Through Service. (Illus.). 200p. 1997. 17.95 (*0-9623483-7-6*, BPSLCHB) Dev Dimensions.

Byham, William C., jt. auth. see Thornton, George, III.

Byington, Cyrus. Dictionary of the Choctaw Language. (Bureau of American Ethnology Bulletins Ser.). (CHO & ENG.). 611p. 1995. lib. bdg. 149.00 (*0-7812-4046-8*) Rprt Serv.

— Dictionary of the Choctaw Language. Halbert, Henry S., ed. (CHO & ENG.). xii, 611p. 1990. reprint ed. pap. 39.00 (*1-878592-06-8*); reprint ed. lib. bdg. 59.00 (*1-878592-07-6*) Native Amer Bk Pubs.

Byington, Ele, jt. auth. see Gould, Christopher.

Byington, Ele, jt. ed. see Gould, Christopher.

B

An Asterisk (*) at the beginning of an entry indicates that the title is appearing for the first time.

Byington, Ezra H. The Puritan As a Colonist & Reformer. LC 75-31115. reprint ed. 34.50 (*0-404-13601-X*) AMS Pr.

***Byington, John.** Natural Alternatives to Viagra: How to Recharge Your Sexual Performance Without Surgery or Prescription. LC 99-41828. 1999. write for info. (*1-55972-527-3*) Carol Pub Group.

***Byington, Judy.** Behind Closed Eyes. 2000. 24.95 (*1-891400-18-5*) Champion Pr.

Byington, Margaret. Homestead: The Households of a Milltown. LC 70-89757. (American Labor, from Conspiracy to Collective Bargaining Ser., No. 1). 307p. 1976. reprint ed. 23.95 (*0-405-02109-7*) Ayer.

— Homestead: The Households of a Milltown. (Illus.). 292p. 1974. reprint ed. pap. 19.95 (*0-8229-8250-1*) U of Pittsburgh Pr.

Byington, Roy E. Byington, Bonyton, Baker Genealogy: With the Descendants of Cyrus Irving Byington of Norwalk, CT, 1865-1953. unabridged ed. (Illus.). vii, 180p. 1996. 50.00 (*0-9651129-0-X*) R E Byington.

Byington, Steven T., tr. see Eltzbacher, Paul.

Byington, Steven T., tr. see Stirner, Max.

Bykau, Vasil. Pack of Wolves. Solotaroff, Lynn, tr. from RUS. LC 80-2456. 192p. (YA). (gr. 7 up). 1981. 11.74 (*0-690-04114-4*); lib. bdg. 12.89 (*0-690-04115-2*) HarpC Child Bks.

— Sign of Misfortune. Myers, Alan, tr. from RUS. (Stebbins Ser.). 256p. 1990. 19.95 (*0-89864-049-0*) Allerton Pr.

Byker, Kathy, ed. see Hoskins, Bob & Benson, M. Wayne.

Bykerk, Loree, jt. auth. see Maney, Ardith L.

Bykhovsky, Bernard. Schopenhauer & the Ground of Existence. Moran, Philip, tr. from RUS. (Philosophical Currents Ser.: Vol. 30). vi, 194p. 1984. pap. write for info. (*90-6032-208-8*) B R Gruner.

Bykhovsky, Isidor I. Fundamentals of Vibration Engineering. 2nd ed. LC 77-20089. 384p. 1980. 38.50 (*0-88275-550-1*) Krieger.

Bykhovsky, Valery. Advanced Computer R&D in the U. S. S. R. 109p. (Orig.). 1989. teacher ed. 75.00 (*1-55831-092-4*) Delphic Associates.

Bykofsky, Sheree. The Complete Idiot's Guide to Getting Published. LC 98-86097. (Illus.). 352p. 1998. pap. text 16.95 (*0-02-862392-4*) Macmillan Gen Ref.

***Bykofsky, Sheree.** The 52 Most Romantic Dates in New York City. 96p. 2000. pap. 6.95 (*1-58062-462-6*) Adams Media.

Bykofsky, Sheree. 500 Terrific Ideas for Organizing Everything: The Best Techniques & Tools for Organizing Anything. 160p. 1997. 6.99 (*0-88365-994-8*) Galahad Bks.

— Me: Five Years from Now - The Life-Planning Book You Write Yourself. 224p. 1999. pap. 12.95 (*0-7868-8391-X*, Pub. by Hyperion) Time Warner.

Bykofsky, Sheree & Fargis, Paul, eds. The Big Book of Life's Instructions: Simple Solutions for Complicated Lives. 512p. 1999. 19.95 (*1-57866-078-5*) Galahad Bks.

Bykofsky, Sheree & Viera, Laurie. Popping the Question: Real-Life Stories of Marriage Proposals from the Romantic to the Bizarre. LC 96-28867. (Illus.). 128p. (Orig.). 1997. pap. 8.95 (*0-8027-7500-4*) Walker & Co.

Bykov, A., ed. English - Russian Traffic Dictionary. (ENG & RUS.). 212p. 1996. 32.95 (*0-8285-5466-8*) Firebird NY.

Bykov, V. A., ed. see Schroeter, A. L. & Panasiuk, V. A.

Bykov, V. I., et al. Elimination Methods in Polynomial Computer Algebra. LC 98-34670. 1998. 205.00 (*0-7923-5240-8*) Kluwer Academic.

Bykov, V. P. Radiation of Atoms in a Resonant Environment. (Optics & Photonics Ser.). 224p. 1994. text 48.00 (*981-02-1092-2*) World Scientific Pub.

Bykov, V. P. & Silichev, O. O. Laser Resonators. 350p. 1995. pap. 111.00 (*1-898326-28-2*, Pub. by CISP) Balogh.

Byl, John. Organizing Successful Tournaments. 2nd ed. LC 98-11714. (Illus.). 184p. 1998. pap. 19.95 (*0-88011-955-1*, PBYL0955) Human Kinetics.

Byle, Michael J. & Borden, Roy H., eds. Verification of Geotechnical Grouting: A Report from the ASCE Committee on Grouting of the Geotechnical Engineering Division & Papers Presented at the ASCE Convention in San Diego, California, October 23-27, 1995. 177p. 1995. 27.00 (*0-7844-0132-2*) Am Soc Civil Eng.

Bylebyl, Jerome J. Teaching the History of Medicine at a Medical Center. LC 82-148. 200p. 1982. 35.00 (*0-8018-2799-X*) Johns Hopkins.

Bylee Barnett, Ziegler. College Algebra. 7th ed. 2000. text 58.00 (*0-07-236868-3*) McGraw.

— College Algebra& Trigonometry. 7th ed. 2000. text 58.00 (*0-07-236869-1*) McGraw.

— Precalculus Funtions Graphs. 5th ed. (Barnett, Ziegler & Byleen's Precalculus Ser.). 2000. 58.00 (*0-07-236871-3*) McGraw.

Byleer. Looking Ahead, Level 3. (Global Esl/Elt Ser.). 304p. (J). 1998. pap. 29.95 (*0-8384-7902-2*) Heinle & Heinle.

— Looking Ahead Instructor's Manual, Bks. 1 & 2. (J). 1998. pap. 19.25 (*0-8384-7832-8*) Heinle & Heinle.

Bylen, Peter. Independent Ukraine, 1918-1920: A Catalog-Checklist of National Postage Stamp Issues as Well as Regional Trident Overprints & Occupational Issues. LC 96-61033. (Resources Ser.). 128 p. 1996. write for info. (*1-889581-04-6*) Ukrnian Phltlc.

Byler, Anna M. A Woman by God's Grace: "...Her Candle Goeth Not Out by Night." Prov. 31: 18. 146p. (Orig.). 1992. pap. 6.95 (*0-940883-04-X*) Calvary Pubns.

Byler, Dennis. Making War & Making Peace: Why Some Christians Fight & Some Don't. LC 89-2222. (Peace & Justice Ser.: Vol. 8). 104p. (Orig.). 1989. pap. 6.99 (*0-8361-3497-4*) Herald Pr.

Byler, Emma. Plain & Happy Living: Amish Recipes & Remedies. LC 92-6121. (Illus.). 160p. 1992. pap. 9.95 (*1-879863-71-5*, Pub. by Goosefoot Acres) Chelsea Green Pub.

Byles, A. T., ed. The Book of the Ordre of Chyualry. (EETS, OS Ser.: No. 168). 1972. reprint ed. 45.00 (*0-527-00165-1*) Periodicals Srv.

Byles, Daniel, jt. auth. see Talks, S. James.

Byles, Joan M. War, Women & Poetry, 1914-1945: British & German Writers & Activists. LC 94-48454. 200p. 1995. 34.50 (*0-87413-563-X*) U Delaware Pr.

Byles, Marie B. Footprints of Gautama the Buddha. LC 68-5855. (Illus.). 1967. pap. 7.95 (*0-8356-0399-7*, Quest) Theos Pub Hse.

Byles, Mather. Proteus Echo. LC 86-31375. 224p. 1987. 50.00 (*0-8201-1420-0*) Schol Facsimiles.

— The Works of Mather Byles. LC 78-6439. 560p. 1978. 75.00 (*0-8201-1309-3*) Schol Facsimiles.

Byles, Monica. Experiment with Plants. LC 92-43117. (Science Experiments Ser.). (Illus.). (J). (gr. 2-5). 1993. lib. bdg. 19.93 (*0-8225-2456-2*, Lerner Publctns) Lerner Pub.

— Experiment with Senses. LC 92-41110. (J). (gr. 2-5). 1993. lib. bdg. 19.93 (*0-8225-2455-4*, Lerner Publctns) Lerner Pub.

— Life in the Polar Lands. (Illus.). 32p. (J). (gr. 4-7). 1993. reprint ed. pap. 4.95 (*0-590-46130-3*) Scholastic Inc.

***Byles, Monica.** Senses. (Interfact Ser.). (Illus.). (J). (gr. 2-7). 2000. spiral bd. 14.95 (*1-58728-463-4*) Two Can Pub.

***Byles, Monica & World Book Staff.** Life in the Mountains. LC 97-62316. (Illus.). 32p. (J). (gr. 2-7). 1999. write for info. (*0-7166-5213-7*) World Bk.

— Life in the Woodlands. LC 97-62318. (Illus.). 32p. (J). (gr. 2-7). 1999. write for info. (*0-7166-5215-3*) World Bk.

Byles, Monica, jt. auth. see World Book Staff.

***Bylesna, Monica.** Life in the Polar Lands. World Book Staff, ed. LC 96-61735. (World Book Ecology Ser.). (Illus.). 32p. (J). (gr. 3-8). 1999. write for info. (*0-7166-5206-4*) World Bk.

Bylov, B. F., et al. Ten Papers on Analysis. LC 51-5559. (Translations Ser.: Series 2, Vol. 74). 260p. 1968. 49.00 (*0-8218-1774-4*, TRANS2/74) Am Math.

Bylsma, Dan & Bylsma, Jay. So Your Son Wants to Play in the NHL. LC 98-34926. (Illus.). 208p. 1998. 24.95 (*1-886947-39-2*) Sleepng Bear.

***Bylsma, Dan & Bylsma, Jay M.** So You Want yo Play in the NHL: A Guide for Young Players. LC 00-31410. (Illus.). 2001. 14.95 (*0-8092-9952-6*, Contemporary Bks) NTC Contemp Pub Co.

Bylsma, Jay, jt. auth. see Bylsma, Dan.

Bylsma, Jay M., jt. auth. see Bylsma, Dan.

Bylund, Duane A. Modern Tesla Coil Theory. (Illus.). 129p. (Orig.). 1991. 19.95 (*0-914119-09-5*) Tesla Bk Co.

Bylund, Stefan, jt. auth. see Jacobson, Ivar.

***Byman, Daniel.** Strengthening the Partnership: Improving Military Coordination with Relief Agencies & Allies in Humanitarian Operations. LC 00-41482. 2000. write for info. (*0-8330-2868-5*) Rand Corp.

***Byman, Daniel L. & Cliff, Roger.** China's Arms Sales: Motivations & Implications. (Illus.). xiii, 59p. (C). 1999. pap. 7.50 (*0-8330-2776-X*, MR-1119-AF) Rand Corp.

Byman, Daniel L. & Green, Jerrold D. Political Violence & Stability in the States of the Northern Persian Gulf. LC 99-25031. (Illus.). 116p. 1999. pap. 15.00 (*0-8330-2726-3*, MR-1021-OSD) Rand Corp.

***Byman, Daniel L. & Waxman, Matthew C.** Confronting Iraq: U. S. Policy & the Use of Force since the Gulf War. xxiii, 101p. (C). 2000. pap. 14.00 (*0-8330-2813-8*, MR-1146-OSD) Rand Corp.

***Byman, Daniel L., et al.** The Effectiveness of Air Power as a Coercive Instrument. LC 99-29409. (Illus.). xvii, 155p. 1999. pap. 15.00 (*0-8330-2743-3*, MR-1061-AF) Rand Corp.

Byman, Isabelle Y. Piano Teacher's Art (Guideline for Successful Piano Teaching) De Vito, Albert K., ed. LC 79-88361. 1979. pap. 15.95 (*0-934286-13-2*) Kenyon.

***Byman, Jeremy.** Andrew Grove & the Intel Corporation. LC 98-49120. (Notable Americans Ser.). 112p. (YA). (gr. 5 up). 1999. lib. bdg. 18.95 (*1-883846-38-2*) M Reynolds.

— Carl Sagan: In Contact with the Cosmos. (Great Scientists Ser.). (Illus.). 112p. (YA). (gr. 5 up). 2000. lib. bdg. 19.95 (*1-883846-55-2*) M Reynolds.

Byman, Jeremy. Madam Secretary: The Story of Madeleine Albright. LC 97-38397. (Notable Americans Ser.). (Illus.). 96p. (YA). (gr. 5 up). 1998. lib. bdg. 18.95 (*1-883846-23-4*) M Reynolds.

— Ted Turner: Cable Televison Tycoon. LC 98-5379. (Makers of the Media Ser.). (Illus.). 112p. (YA). (gr. 5 up). 1998. lib. bdg. 18.95 (*1-883846-25-0*) M Reynolds.

***Byman, Jeremy.** Tim Duncan. (Great Athletes Ser.). (Illus.). 64p. (YA). (gr. 3 up). 2000. lib. bdg. 19.95 (*1-883846-43-9*) M Reynolds.

Byman, Miriam, tr. see Vilkama, Kirsti.

Bynagle, BHans E. Philosophy: A Guide to Reference Literature. 2nd ed. LC 96-31379. (Reference Sources in the Humanities Ser.). 233p. 1996. lib. bdg. 38.50 (*1-56308-376-0*) Libs Unl.

Byne, M. The Sculptured Capital in Spain. 1976. lib. bdg. 59.95 (*0-8490-2577-X*) Gordon Pr.

— Spanish Gardens & Patios. 1976. lib. bdg. 75.00 (*0-8490-2649-0*) Gordon Pr.

Byne, Richard H. Confederate States of America Philatelic Subject Index & Bibliography, 1862-1984. Hartmann, Leonard H., ed. LC 85-70099. (Illus.). 352p. 1986. 45.00 (*0-917528-08-5*) L H Hartmann.

Byng, Edward J. The World of the Arabs. LC 74-869. (Essay Index Reprint Ser.). 1977. reprint ed. 21.95 (*0-518-10144-4*) Ayer.

Byng-Hall, John. Rewriting Family Scripts: Improvisation & Systems Change. LC 95-16208. (Family Therapy Ser.). 288p. 1995. lib. bdg. 36.95 (*0-89862-876-8*) Guilford Pubns.

— Rewriting Family Scripts: Improvisation & Systems Change. 288p. 1998. pap. text 21.00 (*1-57230-066-3*) Guilford Pubns.

Byng-Hall, John, jt. auth. see Papadoupoulos, Renos K.

Byng, Lucy M., tr. from RUM. Roumanian Stories. LC 73-169543. (Short Story Index Reprint Ser.). 1977. reprint ed. 20.95 (*0-8369-4004-0*) Ayer.

Byng, Sally. Aphasia Therapy File. 256p. 1999. 39.95 (*0-86377-566-7*) L Erlbaum Assocs.

Bynner, Edwin L. Chase of the Meteor, & Other Stories. LC 79-81264. (Short Story Index Reprint Ser.). (Illus.). 1977. 19.95 (*0-8369-3016-9*) Ayer.

***Bynner, J. M. & Silbereisen, R. K.** Adversity & Challenge in Life in the New Germany & in England. LC 99-25943. 1999. text 69.95 (*0-312-22427-3*) St Martin.

Bynner, John, et al, eds. Twenty Something in the 1990s: Getting on, Getting by, Getting Nowhere. LC 97-30130. (Illus.). 168p. 1997. text 55.95 (*1-84014-014-3*, Pub. by Ashgate Pub) Ashgate Pub Co.

Bynner, John, et al. Youth, Citizenship & Social Change in a European Context. LC 97-74457. 288p. 1997. text 69.95 (*1-85972-541-4*, Pub. by Ashgate Pub) Ashgate Pub Co.

Bynner, John M., jt. auth. see Romney, David M.

Bynner, Witter. Selected Poems. Wilbur, Richard, ed. 384p. 1978. 30.00 (*0-374-25863-5*) FS&G.

— Tiger. LC 77-70352. (One-Act Plays in Reprint Ser.). 1977. reprint ed. 16.00 (*0-8486-2013-5*) Roth Pub Inc.

Bynner, Witter, tr. Euripides: Four Tragedies, No. 2. LC 56-6639. (Illus.). 270p. 1956. pap. text 9.00 (*0-226-30781-6*, P309) U Ch Pr.

— Iphigenia in Tauris. LC 56-6639. write for info. U Ch Pr.

Bynon, James, ed. Current Progress in Afro-Asiatic Linguistics: Papers from the Third International Hamito-Semitic Congress, London, 1978. (Current Issues in Linguistic Theory Ser.: Vol. 28). xi, 505p. 1984. 103.00 (*90-272-3520-1*) J Benjamins Pubng Co.

Bynon, Theodora. Historical Linguistics. LC 76-62588. (Cambridge Textbooks in Linguistics Ser.). (Illus.). 280p. 1977. pap. text 22.95 (*0-521-29188-7*) Cambridge U Pr.

Bynon, Theodora, jt. ed. see Shibatani, Masayoshi.

Bynre, Randy. Optimum Home Designs: A105. National Plan Service Staff, ed. (Illus.). 32p. 1992. 4.95 (*0-934039-36-4*) Hme Dsgn Altntves.

Bynum. The Insulation Handbook. 2000. 59.95 (*0-07-134872-7*) McGraw.

Bynum, B. Brant. The Romantic Imagination in the Works of Gustavo Adolfo Becquer. LC 92-56386. (Studies in the Romance Languages & Literatures: No. 246). 150p. (C). 1993. pap. text 24.95 (*0-8078-9250-5*) U of NC Pr.

Bynum, Bill. Scents for Success. Boddington, Craig, ed. (Whitetail Secrets Ser.: No. 7). (Illus.). 194p. 1995. 19.95 (*1-56416-157-9*) Derrydale Pr.

— Teaching Youth with Confidence. 48p. 1983. pap. 4.25 (*0-910566-41-0*) Evang Trg Assn.

Bynum, Bill, jt. auth. see Weishuhn, Larry.

***Bynum, Caroline Walker.** Last Things: Death & the Apocalypse in the Middle Ages. LC 99-34223. 1999. pap. text 24.95 (*0-8122-1702-0*) U of Pa Pr.

Bynum, Caroline W. Fragmentation & Redemption: Essays on Gender & the Human Body in Medieval Religion. LC 90-12451. (Illus.). 426p. (C). 1990. 29.95 (*0-942299-63-9*) Zone Bks.

— Fragmentation & Redemption: Essays on Gender & the Human Body in Medieval Religion. LC 90-12451. (Illus.). 426p. (C). 1991. pap. 18.00 (*0-942299-62-0*) Zone Bks.

— Holy Feast & Holy Fast: The Religious Significance of Food to Medieval Women. LC 85-28896. (New Historicism: Studies in Cultural Poetics: No. 1). 300p. (C). 1987. pap. 18.95 (*0-520-06329-5*, Pub. by U CA Pr) Cal Prin Full Svc.

— Jesus As Mother: Studies in the Spirituality of the High Middle Ages. LC 81-13137. (Center for Medieval & Renaissance Studies, UCLA: Contribution: No. 16). 280p. 1982. pap. 17.95 (*0-520-05222-6*, Pub. by U CA Pr) Cal Prin Full Svc.

— The Resurrection of the Body in Western Christianity, 200-1336. LC 94-17299. (Lectures on the History of Religions Ser.: No. 15). 384p. 1995. 46.50 (*0-231-08126-X*) Col U Pr.

Bynum, David E., ed. Serbo-Croation Heroic Poems from Bihac, Cazin, & Kulen Vakuf. LC 93-16372. (Milman Parry Studies in Oral Tradition). (Illus.). 832p. 1993. text 10.00 (*0-8153-1236-9*) Garland.

Bynum, David E., jt. ed. see Lord, Albert B.

Bynum, David E., ed. see Parry, Milman.

Bynum, David E., ed. & tr. see Parry, Millman.

Bynum, Doris. Which Position Are You In? Pitt, Estella, ed. (Illus.). 40p. 1998. pap. 5.95 (*0-9642764-5-3*) E Pitt.

Bynum, Edward. African Unconscious: Roots of Ancient Mysticism & Modern Psychology, Vol. #5. LC 98-51477. 5. 384p. 1999. 70.00 (*0-8077-3775-5*) Tchrs Coll.

Bynum, Edward B. The African Unconscious: Roots of Ancient Mysticism & Modern Psychology. LC 98-51477. (Counseling & Development Ser.). 384p. 1999. pap. text 21.95 (*0-8077-3774-7*) Tchrs Coll.

— The Dreaming Skull. 76p. 1996. pap. write for info. (*1-57579-043-2*) Pine Hill Pr.

— Families & the Interpretation of Dreams: Awakening the Intimate Web. LC 92-17827. (Illus.). 252p. 1993. lib. bdg. 7.95 (*1-56024-336-8*) Haworth Pr.

— Godzillananda: His Life & Visions. 72p. 1996. pap. write for info. (*1-57579-042-4*) Pine Hill Pr.

— Transcending the Psychoneurotic Disturbances: New Approaches in Psychospirituality & Personality Development. LC 92-1577. (Illus.). 414p. 1994. lib. bdg. 49.95 (*1-56024-338-4*) Haworth Pr.

***Bynum, Edward Bruce, et al.** Legacy: Portrait of an Ancestor. unabridged ed. Axelson-Berry, Kitty, ed. (Illus.). 74p. 1999. write for info. (*0-9662602-2-8*) Modern Memoirs.

Bynum, Jack E. & Thompson, William E. Juvenile Delinquency: A Sociological Approach. 448p. 1989. text 43.00 (*0-205-11774-0*, H17742) Allyn.

— Juvenile Delinquency: A Sociological Approach. 4th ed. LC 98-10400. 522p. (C). 1998. 70.00 (*0-205-27612-1*) Allyn.

Bynum, Janie. Altoona Baboona. LC 98-15889. (Illus.). 32p. (J). 1999. 13.00 (*0-15-201860-3*) Harcourt.

— Altoona Baboona Sequel. 2001. write for info. (*0-15-202313-5*) Harcourt.

***Bynum, Janie.** Otis. LC 99-6087. 36p. (J). (ps-2). 2000. 14.00 (*0-15-202153-1*, Harcourt Child Bks) Harcourt.

Bynum, Josephine M., ed. see Ormsby, Waterman L.

Bynum, Juanita. Dont Get off the Train. 1997. pap. 7.99 (*1-56229-121-1*) Pneuma Life Pub.

— Juanita Bynum Topical Bible. LC 99-217440. 304p. 1998. pap. 24.99 (*1-56229-155-6*) Pneuma Life Pub.

***Bynum, Juanita.** Morning Glory Devotional. (Illus.). 1999. pap. 15.99 (*1-56229-150-5*) Pneuma Life Pub.

Bynum, Juanita. Morning Glory Prayer Journal. 1999. 19.99 (*1-56229-156-4*) Pneuma Life Pub.

— Morning Glory-Quote Book. 1998. pap. 6.99 (*1-56229-151-3*) Pneuma Life Pub.

— No More Sheets: The Truth About Sex. 1998. 19.99 (*1-56229-148-3*) Pneuma Life Pub.

— No More Sheets: Wholeness Through Holiness. 1999. 11.99 (*1-56229-126-2*) Pneuma Life Pub.

— No More Sheets - Quote Book. 1998. pap. 6.99 (*1-56229-154-8*) Pneuma Life Pub.

— No More Sheets Devotional: My Accident. 1998. pap. 11.99 (*1-56229-149-1*) Pneuma Life Pub.

— Planted Seed. LC 98-193799. 1997. pap. 6.99 (*1-56229-122-X*) Pneuma Life Pub.

Bynum, La Taunya & Jessup, Mary. Paul's Prison Letters. LC 96-84214. (Covenant Bible Studies). 70p. (Orig.). 1996. pap. 5.95 (*0-87178-007-0*, 8070) Brethren.

Bynum, M., et al. Goof-Proof Grammar. unabridged ed. (Smart Tapes Ser.). 32p. 1994. pap., pap. text 19.95 incl. audio (*1-55678-054-0*, 3230) Learn Inc.

Bynum, Margaret M. Corporate Grammar, Incl. cass. 72p. 1983. pap. text 39.95 incl. audio (*0-913286-75-3*) Learn Inc.

— Power English & Word Command, Bk. 3. 32p. (Orig.). (gr. 10-12). 1986. pap., student ed. 15.00 (*0-913286-99-0*) Learn Inc.

— Winning Vocabulary. (Smart Tapes Ser.). 28p. 1994. pap. text 19.95 incl. audio (*1-55678-050-8*) Learn Inc.

Bynum, Margaret M., ed. Power English & Word Command, Bk. 1. 64p. (Orig.). (YA). (gr. 10-12). 1986. student ed. 15.00 (*0-913286-97-4*) Learn Inc.

— Power English & Word Command, Bk. 2. 96p. (Orig.). (gr. 10-12). 1986. pap., student ed. 15.00 (*0-913286-98-2*) Learn Inc.

Bynum, Margaret M. & Giffen, Debra. Speed Learning Trainer's Guide. 1989. teacher ed. 75.00 (*1-55678-033-8*) Learn Inc.

Bynum, Margaret M. & Giffen, Debra, eds. Speed Learning. rev. ed. (Illus.). 275p. (YA). (gr. 10 up). 1997. pap. 129.00 incl. audio (*1-55678-059-1*, 4000) Learn Inc.

— Speed Learning: High Efficiency Reading, Bk. 1. rev. ed. (Illus.). 88p. (YA). (gr. 10 up). 1997. pap., wbk. ed. 25.00 (*1-55678-060-5*, 3276) Learn Inc.

— Speed Learning: High Efficiency Reading, Bk. 2. rev. ed. (Illus.). 115p. (YA). (gr. 10 up). 1997. pap., wbk. ed. 25.00 (*1-55678-061-3*, 3277) Learn Inc.

— Speed Learning: High Efficiency Reading, Bk. 3. rev. ed. (Illus.). 72p. (YA). (gr. 10 up). 1997. pap., wbk. ed. 25.00 (*1-55678-062-1*, 3278) Learn Inc.

Bynum, Mike. Pop Warner: Football's Greatest Teacher. (Illus.). 240p. 1992. pap. 9.95 (*1-878839-03-9*) Gridiron Football.

Bynum, Mike, ed. Woody Hayes: The Man & His Dynasty. LC 91-74093. (Illus.). 245p. 1991. text 19.95 (*1-878839-02-0*) Gridiron Football.

Bynum, Nora B. A Personal Creation. 42p. (Orig.). pap. 4.95 (*1-56411-033-8*) Untd Bros & Sis.

Bynum, R. Cary. Six Short Plays. LC 93-29396. 1993. pap. 12.95 (*1-878282-12-3*) St Johann Pr.

Bynum, Richard T., Jr., et al. Handbook of Alternative Materials in Residential Construction. LC 98-25182. (Illus.). 416p. 1998. 64.95 (*0-07-011978-3*) McGraw.

Bynum, Terrell W. & Moor, James, eds. The Digital Phoenix: How Computers Are Changing Philosophy. LC 98-5373. (Metaphilosophy Ser.). 256p. 1998. pap. 26.95 (*0-631-20352-4*) Blackwell Pubs.

Bynum, Thomas. Hecatomb. 128p. (Orig.). 1991. pap. 10.00 (*0-9628456-0-4*) Drogue Pr.

Bynum, Timothy S. & Grummon, Phyllis T., eds. Policy Choices: Framing the Debate for Michigan's Future. LC 93-31939. 211p. 1993. 19.95 (*0-87013-344-6*) Mich St U Pr.

Bynum, Tom. Ministry Gift Error. Stokes, Tanya C., ed. 62p. (Orig.). 1991. pap. 6.95 (*0-9627849-8-2*) Temperance Pub Hse.

Bynum, Victoria E. Unruly Women: The Politics of Social & Sexual Control in the Old South. LC 91-33851. (Gender & American Culture Ser.). (Illus.). xvi, 234p. (C). 1992. 45.00 (*0-8078-2016-4*); pap. 17.95 (*0-8078-4361-X*) U of NC Pr.

Bynum, W. F. Science & the Practice of Medicine in the Nineteenth Century. (Cambridge History of Science Ser.). (Illus.). 301p. (C). 1994. text 59.95 (*0-521-25109-5*); pap. text 19.95 (*0-521-27205-X*) Cambridge U Pr.

An Asterisk (*) at the beginning of an entry indicates that the title is appearing for the first time.

Bynum, W. F. & Porter, Roy, eds. Companion Encyclopedia of the History of Medicine, 2 vols. (Illus.). 1864p. (C). 1997. pap. 110.00 (*0-415-16418-4*) Routledge.

Bynum, William F., et al, eds. Dictionary of the History of Science. LC 81-47116. 528p. 1981. pap. text 24.95 (*0-691-02384-0*, Pub. by Princeton U Pr) Cal Prin Full Svc.

Bynum, William F. & Porter, R. S. Medical Fringe & Medical Orthodoxy, 1750-1850: A Volume in the Wellcome Institute. (History of Medicine Ser.). 288p. 1986. 57.50 (*0-7099-3959-0*, Pub. by C Helm) Routldge.

Bynum, William F. & Porter, Roy, eds. Companion Encyclopedia of the History of Medicine, 2 vols., 1. LC 92-26013. (Companion Encyclopedia Ser.). 1400p. 1994. write for info. (*0-415-09242-6*) Routledge.

— Companion Encyclopedia of the History of Medicine, 2 vols., 2. LC 92-26013. (Companion Encyclopedia Ser.). 1400p. 1994. write for info. (*0-415-09243-4*) Routledge.

— Companion Encyclopedia of the History of Medicine, 2 vols., Set. LC 92-26013. (Companion Encyclopedia Ser.). 1792p. (C). 1993. 305.00 (*0-415-04771-4*, B0377) Routledge.

— Medicine & the Five Senses. 349p. (C). 1993. text 69.95 (*0-521-36114-1*) Cambridge U Pr.

Byny, Richard L., jt. ed. see Thompson, Troy L.

BYO Staff. Build Your Own System-- Pentium II & Windows 98. 1998. pap. text 49.95 (*0-9662131-2-2*) BYOS Tech.

Byock, Arthur, jt. auth. see Byock, Ira.

Byock, Ira. Dying Well: Peace & Possibilities at the End of Life. 320p. 1998. pap. 14.00 (*1-57322-657-2*, Riverhd Trade) Berkley Pub.

Byock, Ira & Byock, Arthur. Dying Well: The Prospect for Growth at the End of Life. large type ed. LC 97-13225. 583p. 1997. 25.95 (*0-7862-1123-7*) Thorndike Pr.

Byock, Jesse, tr. The Saga of King Hrolf Kraki. 144p. 1999. pap. 11.95 (*0-14-043593-X*, Penguin Classics) Viking Penguin.

Byock, Jesse L. Feud in the Icelandic Saga. LC 82-40098. (Illus.). 300p. 1982. pap. 16.95 (*0-520-08259-1*, Pub. by U CA Pr) Cal Prin Full Svc.

— Medieval Iceland: Society, Sagas, & Power. (C). 1988. pap. 17.95 (*0-520-06954-4*, Pub. by U CA Pr) Cal Prin Full Svc.

Byock, Jesse L., ed. The Saga of the Volsungs: The Norse Epic of Sigurd the Dragon Slayer. 1990. pap. 15.95 (*0-520-06904-8*, Pub. by U CA Pr) Cal Prin Full Svc.

***Byock, Jesse L., tr.** The Saga of the Volsungs. (Penguin Classics Ser.). 160p. 2000. pap. 11.95 (*0-14-044738-5*, Penguin Classics) Viking Penguin.

Byong Man Ahn, jt. auth. see Boyer, William W.

***Byos Technology Inc.** Build Your Own System-- Pentium II & Windows 98: Handbook Edition. (Illus.). 172p. 1998. pap. 29.95 (*0-9662131-1-4*) BYOS Tech.

Byoung-Lo Philo Kim. Two Koreas in Development: A Comparative Study of Principles & Strategies of Capitalist & Communist Third World Development. 240p. (C). 1991. text 39.95 (*0-88738-437-4*) Transaction Pubs.

Byram, Daniel. Border of Vengeance. (Mason's Cavalry Ser.: No. 1). (Illus.). 188p. 1998. pap. 13.95 (*1-892798-00-X*) Sierra West.

— Crime Scenes. (Lieutenant Byram's Investigative Handbooks Ser.: Vol. 1). (Illus.). 1999. pap. 5.95 (*1-892798-05-0*) Sierra West.

— Legendary Peace Officers of Modern Arizona. (Legendary Peace Officers Ser.: No. 1). (Illus.). 120p. 1998. pap. 14.95 (*1-892798-04-2*) Sierra West.

— Narc in the Dark. (Illus.). 235p. 1998. pap. 14.95 (*1-892798-01-8*, 9801) Sierra West.

— Narcotics: Lieutenant Byram's Investigative Handbooks. (Illus.). 50p. 1999. pap. 5.95 (*1-892798-06-9*) Sierra West.

— Tall Tales of Queen Creek. (Illus.). 70p. 1998. pap. 6.95 (*1-892798-03-4*) Sierra West.

Byram, H. M. Some Problems in the Provision of Professional Education for College Teachers. LC 79-176621. (Columbia University. Teachers College. Contributions to Education Ser.: No. 576). reprint ed. 37.50 (*0-404-55576-4*) AMS Pr.

Byram, John D., Jr. & Madison, Olivia M., eds. Multi-script, Multi-lingual, Multi-character. Issues for the On-line Environment: Proceedings of a Workshop Sponsored by the IFLA Section on Cataloguing, Istanbul, Turkey - August 24, 1995. (IFLA Publications: 85). iv, 123p. 1998. write for info. (*3-598-21814-1*) K G Saur Verlag.

Byram, M., et al. Cultural Studies & Language Learning. 1990. pap. write for info. (*1-85359-088-6*, Pub. by Multilingual Matters) Taylor & Francis.

— Cultural Studies & Language Learning: A Research Report. (Multilingual Matters Ser.: No. 63). 350p. 1990. 95.00 (*1-85359-089-4*, Pub. by Multilingual Matters) Taylor & Francis.

Byram, Martin L. Theater for Development: A Guide to Training. (Illus.). 65p. (Orig.). (C). 1985. pap. text 4.00 (*0-932288-76-6*) Ctr Intl Ed U of MA.

Byram, Martin L., et al. Modules for Training Extension Workers with Handouts. (Curriculum Aid Ser.). 175p. 1986. ring bd. 15.00 (*0-932288-77-4*) Ctr Intl Ed U of MA.

Byram, Michael. Cultural Studies in Foreign Language Education. 176p. 1988. 69.00 (*1-85359-018-5*, Pub. by Multilingual Matters); pap. 24.95 (*1-85359-017-7*, Pub. by Multilingual Matters) Taylor & Francis.

— Language Teachers, Politics & Cultures. LC 98-31863. 1999. 39.95 (*1-85359-441-5*) Taylor & Francis.

— Minority Education & Ethnic Survival. 208p. 1986. 79.00 (*0-905028-55-4*, MM20, Pub. by Multilingual Matters); pap. 29.95 (*0-905028-54-6*, Pub. by Multilingual Matters) Taylor & Francis.

— Teaching & Assessing Intercultural Communicative Competence. LC 97-6559. 120p. 1997. 69.00 (*1-85359-378-8*, Pub. by Multilingual Matters); pap. 24.95 (*1-85359-377-X*, Pub. by Multilingual Matters) Taylor & Francis.

Byram, Michael, ed. Cultural & Language Learning in Higher Education. LC 93-50831. 108p. 1994. 29.95 (*1-85359-228-5*, Pub. by Multilingual Matters) Taylor & Francis.

***Byram, Michael & Brumfit, Christopher J.** The Encyclopedia of Language Teaching & Learning. LC 00-36626. 2001. write for info. (*0-415-12085-3*) Routledge.

Byram, Michael & Esarte-Sarries, Veronica. Investigating Cultural Studies in Foreign Language Teaching: A Book for Teachers. (Multilingual Matters Ser.: No. 62). 190p. 1991. 89.00 (*1-85359-087-8*, Pub. by Multilingual Matters); pap. 29.95 (*1-85359-086-X*, Pub. by Multilingual Matters) Taylor & Francis.

Byram, Michael & Fleming, Michael, eds. Language Learning in Intercultural Perspective: Approaches Through Drama & Ethnography. LC 97-47530. (Cambridge Language Teaching Library). (Illus.). 318p. (C). 1998. text 59.95 (*0-521-62376-6*); pap. text 21.95 (*0-521-62559-9*) Cambridge U Pr.

Byram, Michael & Leman. Bicultural & Trilingual Education: The Foyer Model in Brussels, No. 54. 250p. 1990. 89.00 (*1-85359-044-4*, Pub. by Multilingual Matters) Taylor & Francis.

— Bicultural & Trilingual Education: The Foyer Model in Brussels, No. 54. 250p. 1990. pap. 36.00 (*1-85359-043-6*) Taylor & Francis.

Byram, Michael & Morgan, Carol. Teaching-&-Learning Language-&-Culture. LC 93-30783. (Multilingual Matters Ser.: No. 100). 228p. 1994. 79.00 (*1-85359-212-9*, Pub. by Multilingual Matters); pap. 29.95 (*1-85359-211-0*, Pub. by Multilingual Matters) Taylor & Francis.

Byram, Michael, jt. ed. see Buttjes, Dieter.

Byran, Elizabeth M. Twin, Triplets & More. 160p. 1998. pap. 11.95 (*0-312-19533-8*) St Martin.

Byrand, Sherri. The Boulder Girl. (Illus.). 200p. (YA). 1999. pap. 11.00 (*1-886383-89-8*, Little Blue) Pride & Imprints.

***Byrappa, K.** Hydrothermal Technology for Crystal Growth. LC 00-21998. 2000. 155.00 (*0-8155-1445-X*) Noyes.

Byrd. Be in Control. (C). 1995. pap. 3.16 (*0-395-72049-4*) HM.

— Cardiology. 1999. pap. write for info. (*0-7216-5871-7*, W B Saunders Co) Harcrt Hlth Sci Grp.

— The Edicts of Vulcan. LC 84-70521. 213p. 1984. pap. 10.95 (*0-9613299-0-4*) Byrd SDI.

— Foreign Teaching Assistant's Manual. (J). 1989. mass mkt. 26.95 (*0-8384-3337-5*) Heinle & Heinle.

— Generations in Black & White. 1996. pap. 15.00 (*0-15-600236-1*) Harcourt.

***Byrd.** Interaction. 3rd ed. (C). 1999. pap. 22.33 (*0-13-022057-4*) P-H.

Byrd. Intracultural Communication Book. (C). 1993. pap. text 18.25 (*0-07-009559-0*) McGraw.

— Multicultural Communication. 2nd ed. 1998. 66.00 (*0-07-011663-6*) McGraw.

— Multicultural Communication & Pop Culture. 1996. text 30.00 (*0-07-011924-4*) McGraw.

— New Audio Program 2 & Spcetrum 2. 1994. 160.00 (*0-13-832882-X*) P-H.

— New Full Spectrum, Bk. 3. 1994. pap., teacher ed. 28.00 (*0-13-830092-5*) P-H.

— New Spectrum, Bk. 4. 1994. pap. text, teacher ed. 28.00 (*0-13-830175-1*) P-H.

— New Spectrum, Bk. 5. 1994. pap., teacher ed. 28.00 (*0-13-830217-0*) P-H.

— Operative Hip Arthroscopy. 179.00 incl. vdisk (*0-86577-783-7*) Thieme Med Pubs.

— Spectrum, Vol. 1. 1993. pap., teacher ed. 28.00 (*0-13-829920-X*) P-H.

— Spectrum 2B, Vol. 2B. (C). 1993. pap. text 9.27 (*0-13-830027-5*) P-H.

— Spectrum 2 Teacher's Edition, New Edition, Bk. 2. 1994. pap., teacher ed. 28.00 (*0-13-830001-1*) P-H.

Byrd & Gallingane. Write Away, Bk. 1. (J). 1991. mass mkt. 17.95 (*0-8384-2717-0*) Heinle & Heinle.

— Write Away, Bk. 2. (J). 1990. mass mkt. 17.95 (*0-8384-2719-7*) Heinle & Heinle.

— Write Away, Bk. 2. (J). 1992. teacher ed. 7.95 (*0-8384-2720-0*) Heinle & Heinle.

— Write Away, Bk. 3. (J). 1990. mass mkt. 17.95 (*0-8384-2721-9*); mass mkt., teacher ed. 7.95 (*0-8384-2722-7*) Heinle & Heinle.

Byrd, jt. auth. see Burden.

Byrd, A. Dean & Barlow, Sally H. Finding Wholeness & Happiness, after Divorce. LC 97-30919. viii, 245p. 1997. 15.95 (*1-57345-294-7*) Deseret Bk.

Byrd, A. Dean & Chamberlain, Mark D. Willpower Is Not Enough: Why We Don't Succeed at Change. LC 94-23989. x, 181p. (Orig.). 1995. pap. 11.95 (*0-87579-871-3*) Deseret Bk.

Byrd, Adrianne. Forget Me Note. 1998. 4.99 (*0-7860-0565-3*) Kensgtn Pub Corp.

— I Promise. 1999. mass mkt. 4.99 (*1-58314-019-0*) BET Bks.

***Byrd, Adrianne.** Love's Deception. (Arabesque Ser.). 288p. 2000. mass mkt. 5.99 (*1-58314-136-7*) BET Bks.

— Say You Love Me. (Arabesque Ser.). 2000. mass mkt. 5.99 (*1-58314-071-9*) BET Bks.

Byrd, Adrianne, et al. Man of the House. 384p. 1998. pap. 4.99 (*0-7860-0524-6*) Kensgtn Pub Corp.

Byrd, Adrienne. Defenseless. 304p. 1997. mass mkt. 4.99 (*0-7860-0454-1*, Pinncle Kensgtn) Kensgtn Pub Corp.

Byrd, Bobby. Get Some Fuses for the House: Householder Poems - El Paso Texas. 90p. (Orig.). 1987. 20.00 (*1-55643-006-X*); pap. 7.95 (*1-55643-004-3*) North Atlantic.

— Here: Poems. 60p. 1975. pap. 25.00 (*0-913028-37-1*) North Atlantic.

— On the Transmigration of Souls in El Paso: Poems. LC 92-54826. 96p. (Orig.). 1992. pap. 9.95 (*0-938317-19-9*) Cinco Puntos.

— The Price of Doing Business in Mexico. LC 98-27011. 131p. 1998. pap. 12.95 (*0-938317-40-7*) Cinco Puntos.

Byrd, Bobby & Byrd, Susannah M., eds. The Late Great Mexican Border: Reports from a Disappearing Line. LC 96-10507. (Illus.). 240p. 1998. pap. 13.95 (*0-938317-24-5*) Cinco Puntos.

Byrd-Bredbenner, Carol. Adventures in Food & Nutrition. LC 96-19155. 622p. (YA). (gr. 9-12). 1997. text 39.96 (*1-56637-324-7*) Goodheart.

***Byrd-Bredbenner, Carol.** Exploring Science in the Foods Lab. (Illus.). 2000. pap. text 26.60 (*1-56637-719-6*) Goodheart.

Byrd, Brian F., ed. The Natufian Encampment No. 1: Excavations at Beidha. (Jutland Archaeological Society Publications: No. 23). (Illus.). 126p. (C). 1989. 29.00 (*87-7288-054-6*, Pub. by Aarhus Univ Pr) David Brown.

Byrd, Brian F. & Serr, Carol. Multi-Component Archaic & Late Prehistoric Residential Camps Along the Sweetwater River, Rancho San Diego, California. (Brian F. Mooney Associates Anthropological Technical Ser.: No. 1). (Illus.). 431p. 1993. pap. write for info. (*0-9639458-0-7*) B Mooney Assocs.

Byrd, Brian F., et al. Prehistoric Settlement along the Eastern Margin of Rogers Dry Lake, Western Mojave Desert, California. (Brian F. Mooney Associates Anthropological Technical Ser.). (Illus.). 195p. 1994. pap. text 20.00 (*0-9639458-1-5*) B Mooney Assocs.

Byrd, Bridgette, ed. see Engstrand, Iris & Bullard, Anne.

Byrd, Byron K., jt. auth. see D'Agostino, Carla T.

Byrd, Caroline, jt. ed. see Hall, H. Palmer.

Byrd, Cecil K. A Bibliography of Illinois Imprints, 1814-58. LC 65-24423. 627p. reprint ed. pap. 194.40 (*0-8357-7192-X*, 202408600035) Bks Demand.

— Searching for Riches: The California Gold Rush. (Illus.). 95p. 1991. pap. 7.50 (*1-879598-02-7*) IN Univ Lilly Library.

— The Westbound Pioneer: Overland Emigration to Oregon. (Illus.). 1989. pap. 5.00 (*1-879598-06-X*) IN Univ Lilly Library.

Byrd, Cecil K., ed. Frank M. Hohenberger's Indiana Photographs. LC 93-9345. (Illus.). 142p. 1993. 35.00 (*0-253-31285-X*); pap. 19.95 (*0-253-31286-8*) Ind U Pr.

Byrd, Cecil K. & Moore, Ward W. Varsity Sports: A Pictorial History. LC 99-12930. 1999. 39.95 (*0-253-33578-7*) Ind U Pr.

Byrd, Cecil K. & Moore, Ward W., eds. Abraham Lincoln in Print & Photograph: A Picture History from the Lilly Library. LC 96-49731. (Illus.). 144p. (Orig.). 1997. pap. 13.95 (*0-486-29427-7*) Dover.

Byrd, Cecil K., jt. auth. see Dann, John C.

Byrd, Charles. The Christmas Stranger. 1992. pap. 3.95 (*1-55673-453-0*, 9248) CSS OH.

— If Only That Horse Were a Member of My Church. Sherer, Michael L., ed. 1988. pap. 8.75 (*1-55673-036-5*, 8821) CSS OH.

***Byrd, Charlie & Griggs, John.** Charlie Byrd Guitar Stylings. 48p. 1998. pap. 17.95 incl. audio compact disk (*0-7866-3848-6*, 97337BCD) Mel Bay.

***Byrd, Cheryl.** How to Survive the Pain. unabridged ed. 1999. mass mkt. 7.95 (*1-891371-10-X*) Angel Ministries.

Byrd-Clarke, Mary. Sothis: Star of Egypt. 254p. 1999. pap. 15.95 (*1-58444-007-4*, Looking Glass Pr) DiscUs Bks.

***Byrd, Daniel M., III & Cothern, C. Richard.** Introduction to Risk Analysis: A Systematic Approach to Science-Based Decision Making. 375p. 2000. text 89.00 (*0-86587-696-7*, 696) Gov Insts.

Byrd, David G. & Fleischel, Phyllis. Writing Effectively for Business & Government. (Illus.). 1986. pap. 10.00 (*0-917069-04-8*) Univ SC Inst Pub Affairs.

Byrd, David M. & McIntyre, D. John. Research on the Education of Our Nation's Teachers: Teacher Education Yearbook V. (ATE Ser.). (Illus.). 312p. 1997. 69.95 (*0-8039-6512-5*); pap. 32.95 (*0-8039-6513-3*) Corwin Pr.

Byrd, David M. & McIntyre, D. John, eds. Research on Professional Development Schools: Teacher Education Yearbook VII. (ATE Ser.). 288p. 1999. 65.95 (*0-8039-6829-9*) Corwin Pr.

Byrd, David M., jt. auth. see McIntyre, D. John.

Byrd, David M., jt. ed. see McIntyre, D. John.

Byrd, Dennis J. Slama Jama in the Jungle. 60p. (J). (gr. 4-5). 1994. pap. text 9.95 (*1-886114-00-5*) Arrow Pubns.

***Byrd, Dennis K.** Budget Survival Guide: A Revolutionary Approach to Home Budgeting. LC 99-96618. 2000. pap. 11.95 (*0-533-13329-7*) Vantage.

Byrd, Diana L. Love Is Straight from the Heart: A Collection of Poetry. 72p. (Orig.). 1997. pap. 7.00 (*0-8059-3993-8*) Dorrance.

Byrd, Don. Charles Olson's Maximus. LC 79-21738. 218p. 1980. text 24.95 (*0-252-00779-4*) U of Ill Pr.

***Byrd, Don.** Great Dime Store Centennial. 176p. 2000. pap. 15.95 (*1-58177-069-3*) Barrytown Ltd.

Byrd, Don. More Cupid's Coupons. 1998. pap. text 5.95 (*1-56352-549-6*) Longstreet.

— The Poetics of the Common Knowledge. LC 92-42637. (SUNY Series, The Margins of Literature). 404p. (C). 1993. pap. text 18.95 (*0-7914-1686-0*) State U NY Pr.

— The Poetics of the Common Knowledge. LC 92-42637. (SUNY Series, The Margins of Literature). 404p. (C). 1993. text 57.50 (*0-7914-1685-2*) State U NY Pr.

Byrd, Don & Aesop. Aesop's Garden. 1976. pap. 4.00 (*0-913028-42-8*) North Atlantic.

Byrd, Don & Wolfe, Leanna. Cupid Coupons. (Illus.). 96p. 1999. pap. 5.95 (*1-56352-548-8*) Longstreet.

***Byrd, Don & Wolfe, Leanna.** Cupid's Romance Coupons. (Illus.). 96p. 1998. pap. 5.95 (*1-56352-550-X*) Longstreet.

Byrd, Donald & Klosek. Can We Talk? A Multiskills Approach to Communication. 1991. pap. 10.50 (*0-685-40578-8*, 640106) P-H.

Byrd, Donald R. Spectrum 5. LC 94-5462. 144p. (C). 1994. pap. text 16.60 (*0-13-830191-3*) P-H.

— Spectrum 4. LC 93-40685. 176p. (C). 1994. pap. text 16.60 (*0-13-830159-X*) P-H.

— Spectrum 4b. (C). 1994. pap. text 9.27 (*0-13-832791-2*) P-H.

— Spectrum I. 176p. (C). 1992. pap. text 16.60 (*0-13-829862-9*) P-H.

— Spectrum 1A. 96p. (C). 1991. pap. text 9.27 (*0-13-829870-X*) P-H.

— Spectrum 1B. 96p. (C). 1992. pap. text 9.27 (*0-13-829888-2*) P-H.

— Spectrum VI. LC 94-5461. 144p. (C). 1994. pap. text 16.60 (*0-13-830233-2*) P-H.

— Spectrum 6. (C). 1994. pap. text, wbk. ed. 10.40 (*0-13-830258-8*) P-H.

— Spectrum III. LC 93-26881. 176p. (C). 1993. pap. text 16.60 (*0-13-830068-2*) P-H.

— Spectrum II. 176p. (C). 1993. pap. text 16.60 (*0-13-829979-X*) P-H.

— Spectrum 2A. (C). 1993. pap. text 9.27 (*0-13-829987-0*) P-H.

— Student Evaluation Package. 176p. (C). 1994. pap. 37.33 (*0-13-832593-6*) P-H.

Byrd, Donald R. & Cabetas, Isis C. React Interact. 2nd enl. rev. ed. 160p. (C). 1991. pap. text 25.00 (*0-13-753716-6*, 640201) P-H.

— React Interact: Situations for Communication. (Illus.). 100p. (YA). (gr. 10-12). 1987. pap. text 12.00 (*0-13-753377-2*, 18674) Prentice ESL.

Byrd, Donald R. & Zelinski, Stanley J., III. People Are Funny. (Pictures for Practice Ser.: Bk. 1). 80p. (Orig.). 1987. pap. text 16.91 (*0-582-79829-9*, 75079) Longman.

Byrd, Elizabeth. The Lady of Monkton. large type ed. 1990. 27.99 (*0-7089-2151-5*) Ulverscroft.

Byrd, Elizabeth L. Fonalfubet--Decoding the Sounds of American English. enl. rev. ed. LC 85-28964. 145p. (Orig.). (C). 1986. pap. text 25.00 (*0-9615393-1-3*) U Assocs.

— Fonalfubet--Sounds of American English: Names of Letters. (Illus.). 20p. (Orig.). 1985. pap. text 4.00 (*0-9615393-0-5*, F100) U Assocs.

— A Fonalfubet Pronunciation Dictionary of American English Words. (Orig.). (J). (gr. k up). 1986. pap. text 20.00 (*0-9615393-2-1*) U Assocs.

Byrd, Erick, jt. ed. see Abate, Frank.

Byrd, Erick P. NTC's Beginners German & English Dictionary. Abate, Frank R., ed. (Illus.). 496p. 1995. pap. 8.95 (*0-8442-2497-9*) NTC Contemp Pub Co.

— NTC's Beginners German & English Dictionary. Abate, Frank R., ed. (ENG & GER., Illus.). 496p. 1995. 12.95 (*0-8442-2496-0*) NTC Contemp Pub Co.

Byrd, Gary & Briggs, George. Street & Highway Maintenance Manual. (Illus.). 698p. 1985. ring bd. 65.00 (*0-917084-33-0*) Am Public Works.

Byrd, Gary W., jt. auth. see Alali, A. Odasuo.

***Byrd, Georgia.** Romantic Days & Nights in Savannah: Romantic Diversions in & Around the City. 2nd ed. 2001. pap. 15.95 (*0-7627-0841-7*) Globe Pequot.

Byrd, Georgia. Romantic Days & Nights in Savannah: Romantic Diversions in & Around the Port City. LC 98-32212. (Romantic Cities Ser.). (Illus.). 288p. 1998. pap. 15.95 (*0-7627-0292-3*) Globe Pequot.

Byrd, Georgie, et al. The History of Aviation in Savannah, Ga. (Illus.). 106p. 1998. mass mkt. 18.95 (*0-9661967-0-8*) Savannah Airport.

Byrd, Harold E. Cannot Plead Black Anymore. LC 78-67830. (Illus.). 1978. 9.95 (*0-9601972-0-6*); pap. 6.95 (*0-9601972-1-4*) Byrd.

Byrd, Harry F., Jr. Defying the Odds: An Independent Senator's Historic Campaign. LC 98-61532. (Illus.). 100p. 1998. 15.95 (*0-9666870-0-0*) H Byrd Jr.

Byrd, J. W. Operative Hip Arthroscopy. LC 97-30914. (Illus.). 232p. 1997. 129.00 (*0-86577-679-2*) Thieme Med Pubs.

— Operative Hip Arthroscopy. LC 97-30914. 1997. write for info. (*3-13-108621-1*) Thieme Med Pubs.

Byrd, Jack, Jr., et al. Simple Truths. LC 91-65108. (Illus.). 160p. 1991. pap. 14.95 (*1-879727-00-5*) Think About Pr.

***Byrd, James D. & Cheslik-DeMeyer, Steven.** The Good Book: The True Story of Y'All. Steele, Martha N., ed. LC 99-37120. (Illus.). 292p. 2000. 25.00 (*0-9672542-0-5*) Lucky Green Dress.

Byrd, James E. The Olde Bead Monger's Trade Bead Sketchbook. LC 92-81662. (Illus.). 68p. (Orig.). 1992. pap. 7.95 (*1-880655-02-0*) Scurlock Pub.

Byrd, Jason H. & Castner, James L. Forensic Entomology: Utility of Arthropods in Legal Investigations. 1999. 89.95 (*0-8493-8120-7*) CRC Pr.

Byrd, Jason H., jt. auth. see Castner, James L.

Byrd, Jerry. Louisiana Sports Legends: The Men & Women of the Louisiana Sports Hall of Fame. Cameron, Neill, ed. (Illus.). 336p. 1992. pap. 19.95 (*0-917898-18-4*) NSU Pr LA.

Byrd, Jerry, ed. see Kass-Annese, Barbara.

Byrd, Judie, jt. auth. see Peel, Kathy.

Byrd, Kathleen M., ed. The Poverty Point Culture: Local Manifestations, Subsistence Practices, & Trade Networks. LC 90-80205. (Geoscience & Man Ser.: Vol. 29). (Illus.). 206p. 1992. pap. 35.00 (*0-938909-50-9*) Geosci Pubns LSU.

B

An Asterisk (*) at the beginning of an entry indicates that the title is appearing for the first time.

Byrd, Kimberle. Jan Brett. (Favorite Authors Ser.). (Illus.). 112p. 1995. pap., teacher ed. 11.95 (1-55734-454-X) Tchr Create Mat.

Byrd, Larry C., jt. auth. see Henrickson, Charles H.

Byrd, Lee & Kranz, Yvonne. Listen to Women for a Change: Every Woman's Handbook. (Illus.). 250p. (Orig.). 1995. pap. 12.00 (0-9644942-0-5) Uppity Woman.

Byrd, Lee M. My Sister Disappears: Stories & a Novella. LC 93-19647. 200p. (Orig.). 1993. 22.50 (0-87074-351-1); pap. 10.95 (0-87074-359-7) SMU Press.

Byrd, Lori. Dreamcatcher. 192p. 1995. pap. 9.99 (1-883061-06-7) Rising AZ.

Byrd, M. L., jt. ed. see Ryder, O. A.

Byrd, Martha. Chennault: Giving Wings to the Tiger. LC 86-19238. 472p. reprint ed. pap. 146.40 (0-608-01662-4, 206231700002) Bks Demand.

Byrd, Martha. Kenneth N. Walker: Airpower's Untempered Crusader. (Illus.). 242p. 1997. pap. 15.00 (1-58566-020-5) Air Univ.

Byrd, Martha. A Shoebox of Violets. LC 95-41108. 1995. pap. 12.00 (0-9623388-5-0) Laney-Smith.

Byrd, Mary F. What the World Needs Now. 1998. 10.95 (0-533-12093-4) Vantage.

Byrd-Mauldin, Pamela. To Brighten All Our Future Days: The Life of F. M. Petree & the Story of Oklahoma City University's Miracle on 23rd Street. (Oklahoma Commerce & Industry Hall of Honor Ser.). (Illus.). 100p. (Orig.). (C). 1992. pap. text 12.95 (0-9623357-1-1) Okla City Univ Pr.

Byrd, Max. Grant. LC 99-56577. 384p. 2000. 23.95 (0-553-09633-8, Spectra) Bantam.

— Jackson: A Novel. 432p. 1998. pap. 13.95 (0-553-37935-6) Bantam.

— Jefferson. large type ed. (Niagara Large Print Ser.). 624p. 1997. 29.50 (0-7089-5870-2) Ulverscroft.

— Jefferson: A Novel. 432p. 1998. pap. 13.95 (0-553-37937-2) Bantam.

— London Transformed: Images of the City in the Eighteenth Century. LC 77-11875. 212p. reprint ed. pap. 65.80 (0-8357-8736-2, 203368900087) Bks Demand.

— Tristram Shandy. Rawson, Claude, ed. (Unwin Critical Library). 192p. 1985. text 34.95 (0-04-800033-7); pap. text 16.95 (0-685-09722-6) Routledge.

*Byrd, Nicole. Robert's Lady. 336p. 2000. mass mkt. 5.99 (0-515-12853-8, Jove) Berkley Pub.

Byrd, Patricia. Grammar in the Composition Classroom. LC 97-35676. (Miscellaneous/Catalogs Ser.). 176p. (J). 1997. mass mkt. 25.95 (0-8384-7210-9) Heinle & Heinle.

— Material Writer's Guide: Write for Publication. 240p. (J). 1994. mass mkt. 34.95 (0-8384-4270-6) Heinle & Heinle.

— Teaching Across Cultures in the University ESL Program (1986) 149p. 1986. pap. text 15.00 (0-912207-17-5) NAFSA Washington.

Byrd, Patricia & Benson, Beverly. Improving the Grammar of Written English: The Handbook & the Editing Process. 255p. (J). 1988. mass mkt. 23.95 (0-534-09654-9) Heinle & Heinle.

— Improving the Grammar of Written English: The Handbook & the Editing Process. 398p. (J). 1988. pap., teacher ed. 7.95 (0-534-09655-7) Heinle & Heinle.

— Problem-Solution: A Reference for Writers. LC 93-38194. 240p. (J). 1994. mass mkt. 26.95 (0-8384-4125-4) Heinle & Heinle.

*Byrd Reed, Dessa. The Butterfly Touch: Recovery Through Poetry, 1. LC 00-190689. 124p. 2000. pap. 12.95 (0-9678767-3-7, Pub. by Deer Pubng) ACCESS Pubs Network.

Byrd, Richard E. Alone. LC 96-84778. (Adventure Library: Vol. 8). 240p. 1996. reprint ed. lib. bdg. 32.50 (1-885283-07-5) Advent Library.

— Discovery: The Story of the Second Byrd Antarctic Expedition. LC 71-37874. (Select Bibliographies Reprint Ser.). 1977. reprint ed. 39.95 (0-8369-6711-9) Ayer.

— Discovery: The Story of the Second Byrd Antarctic Expedition. (American Biography Ser.). 397p. 1991. reprint ed. lib. bdg. 79.00 (0-7812-8055-9) Rprt Serv.

— A Guide to Personal Risk Taking. LC 74-75169. 256p. reprint ed. pap. 79.40 (0-608-14131-3, 205593600039) Bks Demand.

*Byrd, Richard E. Skyward: My Adventures As a Young American Flyer & Polar Explorer. LC 99-37617. (Illus.). 352p. 2000. reprint ed. pap. 14.95 (1-58542-010-7, Tarcher Putnam) Putnam Pub Group.

Byrd, Richard E. To the Pole: The Diary & Notebook of Richard E. Byrd, 1925-1927. Goerler, Raimund E., ed. LC 97-47148. (Illus.). 166p. 1998. text 22.95 (0-8142-0800-2, BYRTOX) Ohio St U Pr.

Byrd, Richard E. & Campbell, David G. Alone: The Classic Polar Adventure. Turner, Philip, ed. (Illus.). 320p. 1995. pap. 15.00 (1-56836-068-1, Kodansha Globe) Kodansha.

*Byrd, Robert. Saint Francis & the Christmas Donkey. LC 00-25415. (Illus.). 40p. (J). (ps-3). 2000. 15.99 (0-525-46480-8, Dutton Child) Peng Put Young Read.

Byrd, Robert, retold by. Finn MacCoul & His Fearless Wife: A Giant of a Tale from Ireland. LC 98-26132. (Illus.). 40p. (J). (ps-3). 1999. 16.99 (0-525-45971-5, Dutton Child) Peng Put Young Read.

Byrd, Robert C. Senate of the Roman Republic: Addresses on the History of Roman Constitutionalism. 207p. 1995. boxed set 18.00 (0-16-058996-7) USGPO.

— Senate, 1789-1989: Classic Speeches, 1830-1993, Vol. 3. 812p. 1995. boxed set 69.00 (0-16-063257-9) USGPO.

— Senate, 1789-1989: Historical Statistics, 1789-1992, Vol. 4. 760p. 1993. boxed set 47.00 (0-16-063256-0) USGPO.

Byrd, Robert O. Decision at Richmond, June 1788. A Documentry Drama of the Constitutional Ratification Convention in Virginia. 175p. 1987. pap. 14.95 (0-317-60739-1) World Without War.

Byrd, Robin. Australia's Home: Its Origins, Builders & Occupiers. 2nd ed. 256p. 1987. pap. 24.95 (0-522-84358-1, Pub. by Melbourne Univ Pr) Paul & Co Pubs.

Byrd, Rudolph P., ed. Generations in Black & White. LC 93-2684. (Illus.). 200p. 1997. pap. 24.95 (0-8203-1944-9) U of Ga Pr.

*Byrd, Rudolph P., ed. I Call Myself an Artist: Writings by & about Charles Johnson. LC 99-214697. (Illus.). 512p. 1999. text 35.00 (0-253-33541-8) Ind U Pr.

Byrd, Sandra. Accidental Angel. LC 99-462605. (Secret Sisters Ser.: Vol. 4). 112p. (J). (gr. 3-7). 1998. pap. 5.95 (1-57856-018-7) Waterbrook Pr.

*Byrd, Sandra. Camp Cowgirl. LC 99-47798. (Secret Sisters Ser.: Vol. 10). 112p. (J). (gr. 3-7). 2000. pap. 4.95 (1-57856-065-9) Waterbrook Pr.

Byrd, Sandra. Double Dare. LC 98-227916. (Secret Sisters Ser.: Vol. 5). 112p. (J). (gr. 3-7). 1998. pap. 5.95 (1-57856-019-5) Waterbrook Pr.

*Byrd, Sandra. First Place. LC 99-47797. (Secret Sisters Ser.: Vol. 9). 112p. (J). 2000. pap. 4.95 (1-57856-066-7) Waterbrook Pr.

— Heart to Heart. (The Secret Sisters Ser.: Bk. 1). 112p. (J). (gr. 3-7). 1998. pap. 5.95 (1-57856-015-2) Waterbrook Pr.

Byrd, Sandra. Heart to Heart. (Secret Sisters Ser.: Vol. 1). 112p. (J). (gr. 3-7). 1998. pap. 1.95 (1-57856-229-5) Waterbrook Pr.

*Byrd, Sandra. Heartbeats: Encouraging Words for New Moms. 96p. 2000. pap. 6.95 (1-57856-326-7) Waterbrook Pr.

Byrd, Sandra. Holiday Hero. (Secret Sisters Ser.: Vol. 7). 112p. (J). (gr. 3-7). 1999. pap. 5.95 (1-57856-114-0) Waterbrook Pr.

*Byrd, Sandra. Indian Summer. 12th ed. (Secret Sisters Ser.). 112p. (J). (gr. 3-7). 2000. 4.95 (1-57856-270-8) Waterbrook Pr.

Byrd, Sandra. Petal Power. (Secret Sisters Ser.: Vol. 8). 112p. (J). (gr. 4-7). 1999. pap. 5.95 (1-57856-115-9) Waterbrook Pr.

*Byrd, Sandra. Picture Perfect. (Secret Sisters Ser.: Vol. 11). 112p. (J). (gr. 3-7). 2000. pap. 4.95 (1-57856-063-2) Waterbrook Pr.

Byrd, Sandra. The Secret Sisters Handbook: 101 Cool Ideas for You & Your Best Friend. 160p. (J). (gr. 3-7). 1999. pap. 5.95 (1-57856-171-X) Waterbrook Pr.

*Byrd, Sandra. Twenty-One Ponies. (Secret Sisters Ser.: Bk. 2). 112p. (J). (gr. 3-7). 1998. pap. 5.95 (1-57856-016-0) Waterbrook Pr.

Byrd, Sandra. Twenty-One Ponies. (Secret Sisters Ser.: Vol. 2). 112p. (J). (gr. 3-7). 1998. pap. 4.95 (1-57856-230-9) Waterbrook Pr.

— War Paint. (Secret Sisters Ser.: Vol. 6). 112p. (J). (gr. 3-7). 1998. pap. 5.95 (1-57856-020-9) Waterbrook Pr.

*Byrd, Sandra. The White Pony: A Tale of Great Love. LC 99-37958. (Illus.). 32p. 1999. 14.95 (1-57856-192-2) Waterbrook Pr.

Byrd, Sandra E., jt. auth. see Van Reken, Randal S.

Byrd, Sigfridur, tr. see McIntyre, Sally.

Byrd, Susannah M., jt. auth. see Hayes, Joe.

Byrd, Susannah M., jt. ed. see Byrd, Bobby.

*Byrd, Syndey, et al, photos by. The Day the Music Stopped: The Biography of Raymond Anthony Myles, Sr. 175p. 2000. pap. 19.95 (0-9647689-0-9) Little Sistr Pubns.

— The Day the Music Stopped: The Biography of Raymond Anthony Myles, Sr. (Illus.). 175p. 2000. 24.95 (0-9647689-1-7) Little Sistr Pubns.

Byrd, Theresa, jt. auth. see Power, J. Gerald.

Byrd, Thomas. Lives Written in Sand: Addiction Awareness & Recovery Strategies. (Illus.). 354p. (Orig.). 1997. pap. text, per. 33.00 (0-9653658-0-8) Hallum Pub.

Byrd, Tim, et al. Liege, Lord, & Lackey. (Vampire Ser.). (Illus.). 96p. (Orig.). 1997. pap. 15.00 (1-56504-281-6, 2806) White Wolf.

Byrd, Toody. Toody Byrd Talks & Talks & Talks & Talks & Talks . . . (Illus.). 183p. 1999. reprint ed. pap. 12.50 (0-9667814-0-6) Toddy.

Byrd, Vernon B. Passing Gas: The History of Inflight Refueling. Heidelberg Graphics Staff & Kenedi, Aaron, eds. (Illus.). 288p. 1994. 39.95 (0-9639977-1-8) Byrd Pubng.

Byrd, W. A. A Song for My Mother. 129p. 1992. pap. 5.95 (0-9661927-1-0) Early Bird.

— 2 Black, 2 Strong, 2 Defeat. 200p. 1998. pap. 10.95 (0-9661927-0-2) Early Bird.

Byrd, W. G. A Guide to Medical School Admission. (Illus.). 122p. 1997. pap. text 16.95 (1-85070-796-0) Prthnon Pub.

Byrd, W. Michael & Clayton, Linda A. The American Health Dilemma: The Medical History of African Americans & the Problem of Race, Beginnings to 1900. LC 99-27882. 2000. 35.00 (0-415-92449-9) Routledge.

Byrd, Wade. The Only Thing That Really Matters. (Illus.). 180p. (Orig.). 1996. pap. 5.95 (0-9654192-0-7) New Day Co.

Byrd, Walter & Warren, Paul. Counseling & Children. (Resources for Christian Counseling Ser.: Vol. 22). 231p. 22.99 (0-8499-0597-4) Word Pub.

Byrd, William. History of the Dividing Line, & Other Tracts: From the Papers of William Byrd, 2 vols., Set. (BCL1 - United States Local History Ser.). 1991. reprint ed. text 150.00 (0-7812-6294-1) Rprt Serv.

— London Diary, 1717-1721 & Other Writings. Wright, Louis B. & Tinglin, Marion, eds. LC 77-141208. (Research Library of Colonial Americana). (Illus.). 1972. reprint ed. 42.95 (0-405-03305-2) Ayer.

— My Ladye Nevells Booke. Andrews, Hilda & Terry, Richard, eds. (Illus.). 292p. 1948. reprint ed. lib. bdg. 30.00 (0-8450-0101-9) Broude.

— My Ladye Nevells Booke of Virginal Music. Andrews, Hilda, ed. LC 68-55532. 245p. 1969. reprint ed. pap. 13.95 (0-486-22246-2) Dover.

— Prose Works of William Byrd of Westover: Narratives of a Colonial Virginian. Wright, Louis B., ed. LC 66-11359. (Illus.). 450p. reprint ed. pap. 139.50 (0-7837-4456-0, 205798600012) Bks Demand.

— The Secret Diary of William Byrd of Westover. 49.95 (0-8488-0235-7) Amereon Ltd.

— The Secret Diary of William Byrd of Westover, 1709-1712. LC 72-141097. 1972. reprint ed. 42.95 (0-405-03304-4) Arno Press.

— The Westover Manuscripts. (Works of William Byrd). 1989. reprint ed. lib. bdg. 79.00 (0-7812-2233-8) Rprt Serv.

— William Byrd's Histories of the Dividing Line Betwixt Virginia & North Carolina. (Illus.). xi, 340p. 1988. reprint ed. pap. 11.95 (0-486-25553-0) Dover.

— The Works of William Byrd. 1989. reprint ed. lib. bdg. 63.00 (0-685-74127-3) Rprt Serv.

— The Writings of Colonel William Byrd. (Works of William Byrd). 1989. reprint ed. lib. bdg. 79.00 (0-7812-2234-6) Rprt Serv.

Byrd, William & Attalia, Joseph. The Wilderness Gourmet. (Illus.). 248p. 1999. 29.95 (0-9659845-1-6) Ravenhaus Pub.

Byrd, William, et al. Parthenia: or the Maydenhead of the First Musicke That Ever Was Printed for the Virginalls. Stone, Kurt, ed. (Illus.). 62p. 1952. pap. 17.50 (0-8450-6001-5) Broude.

Byrd, William A. The Market Mechanism & Economic Reforms in China. LC 90-8105. (Studies on Contemporary China). 264p. (C). (gr. 13). 1991. text 72.95 (0-87332-719-5, East Gate Bk) M E Sharpe.

Byrd, William J. Letters from a Young Shaker: William S. Byrd at Pleasant Hill. Stein, Stephen J., ed. LC 84-27014. 176p. 1985. 19.00 (0-8131-1542-6) U Pr of Ky.

*Byrd, William L. Bladen County, North Carolina Tax Lists: 1768-1774. LC 98-73646. 180p. 1998. pap. 23.50 (0-9667425-0-8) William L Byrd.

*Byrd, William L., III. Bladen County North Carolina Tax Lists 1775 Through 1789, Vol. II. 273p. 2000. pap. 33.50 (0-7884-1426-7, 1426) Heritage Bk.

*Byrd, William L., 3rd. In Full Force & Virtue: North Carolina Emancipation Records, 1713-1860. 374p. 1999. pap. 54.00 (0-7884-1241-8, B961) Heritage Bk.

Byrdcliffe Writers Group Staff. Woodstock Originals, Vol. III. LC 84-151442. 144p. (Orig.). 1990. pap. 7.95 (0-9625244-0-9) Byrdcliffe Writers.

Byrdsong, Ennis. This Is My Life: Never Give Up - There Is Hope in God.Tr. of 2. 112p. (Orig.). 1997. pap. 11.99 (0-9633356-8-5) Harvest Time.

*Byrdsong, Ricky, et al. Coaching Your Kids in the Game of Life. 224p. 2000. 17.99 (0-7642-2353-4) Bethany Hse.

Byre, Angela D., ed. Human Rights Law & the Commonwealth Caribbean. (C). 1991. lib. bdg. 104.00 (90-247-3785-0) Kluwer Academic.

Byren, John & Rich, Daniel, eds. The Politics of Energy Research & Development. (Energy Policy Studies: Vol. 3). 170p. 1986. pap. 24.95 (0-88738-653-9) Transaction Pubs.

Byres, T. J., ed. Sharecropping & Sharecroppers. (Illus.). 284p. 1983. 45.00 (0-7146-3223-6, Pub. by F Cass Pubs) Intl Spec Bk.

Byres, T. J., et al, eds. Rural Labour Relations in India. LC 99-19731. (Library of Peasant Studies: No. 18). 368p. 1999. 57.50 (0-7146-4983-X, Pub. by F Cass Pubs); pap. 27.50 (0-7146-8046-X, Pub. by F Cass Pubs) Intl Spec Bk.

Byres, T. J. & Mukhia, Harbans, eds. Feudalism & Non-European Societies. (Library of Peasant Studies: No. 8). 292p. 1985. 32.50 (0-7146-3245-7, Pub. by F Cass Pubs) Intl Spec Bk.

Byres, T. J., et al. Agrarian Questions: Essays in Appreciation of T. J. Byres. Bernstein, Henry & Brass, Tom, eds. LC 96-35835. (Library of Peasant Studies: No. 14). 262p. 1996. 45.00 (0-7146-4774-8, Pub. by F Cass Pubs); pap. 19.50 (0-7146-4332-7, Pub. by F Cass Pubs) Intl Spec Bk.

Byres, T. J., jt. ed. see Brass, Tom.

Byres, Terence J. Capitalism from above & Capitalism from Below: An Essay in Comparative Political Economy. LC 96-13149. 528p. 1996. text 79.95 (0-312-16241-3) St Martin.

— The State, Development Planning & Liberalisation in India. LC 98-132228. (Shool of Oriental & African Studies). 444p. 1997. 26.00 (0-19-563973-1) OUP.

Byres, Terence J. The State, Development Planning & Liberalisation in India. (SOAS Studies on South Asia). 442p. 1999. pap. text 14.95 (0-19-564792-0) OUP.

Byres, Terrence J., ed. The Indian Economy: Major Debates since Independence. LC 98-902982. (Illus.). 432p. 1998. text 35.00 (0-19-564460-3) OUP.

*Byrge, Duane. Private Screenings: Insiders Share a Century of Great Movie Moments. (Illus.). 189p. 1999. reprint ed. pap. text 20.00 (0-7881-6788-X) DIANE Pub.

Byrge, Duane & Miller, Robert M. The Screwball Comedy Films: A History & Filmography, 1934-1942. LC 90-52654. (Illus.). 156p. 1991. lib. bdg. 32.50 (0-89950-539-2) McFarland & Co.

Byrkit, D. R. Statistics Today. 850p. (C). 1987. text 54.95 (0-8053-0740-0); pap. text, student ed. 12.95 (0-8053-0741-9) Addison-Wesley.

Byrkit, James. The Palatkwapi Trail. (Plateau Ser.: Vol. 59, No. 1). 32p. 1988. pap. 4.95 (0-685-72095-0) Mus Northern Ariz.

Byrkit, James W. Forging the Copper Collar: Arizona's Labor-Management War of 1901-1921. fac. ed. LC 82-2075. 451p. reprint ed. pap. 128.60 (0-7837-6957-1, 2046907) Bks Demand.

Byrkit, James W., ed. see Ives, Ronald L.

Byrkit, James W., ed. see Lummis, Charles.

Byrkit, Rebecca. Zealand. (Illus.). 80p. 1995. 25.00 (0-933313-27-6); pap. 14.95 (0-933313-28-4) SUN Gemini Pr.

— Zealand. deluxe limited ed. (Illus.). 80p. 1995. 35.00 (0-933313-26-8) SUN Gemini Pr.

Byrkjedal, Ingvar & Thompson, Des. Tundra Plovers: The Eurasian, American & Pacific Golden Plovers & Grey Plover. LC 99-159351. (Poyser Popular Bird Bks.). (Illus.). 422p. (C). 1998. boxed set 39.95 (0-85661-109-3) Poyser.

Byrlat, Katherine & Nay, Tim. P. O. P. S. Polishing Our People Skills. 79p. (Orig.). 1990. pap. 15.00 (1-877592-18-8) GSH&MC.

Byrn, Anne. The Art of Cooking with Certified Angus Beef. Mitterer, Franz, ed. LC 89-61562. (Illus.). 80p. 1989. write for info. (0-9623729-0-0) Culinaire.

*Byrn, Anne. The Cake Mix Doctor. (Illus.). 384p. 1999. 23.95 (0-7611-1790-3); pap. 14.95 (0-7611-1719-9) Workman Pub.

Byrn, Anne. Cooking in the New South: A Modern Approach to Traditional Southern Fare. LC 94-2396. 224p. 1994. pap. 13.95 (1-56145-089-8) Peachtree Pubs.

— Food Gifts for All Seasons. LC 96-12492. (Illus.). 80p. 1996. 15.95 (1-56145-124-X) Peachtree Pubs.

Byrna, Jeff. Easy Access for Windows 95. (Illus.). 244p. (Orig.). 1995. 19.99 (0-7897-0607-5) Que.

*Byrne. Alien Joke Book. (J). 2000. pap. 6.95 (0-552-54562-7, Pub. by Transworld Publishers Ltd) Trafalgar.

Byrne. Basic Comprehension Passages. Date not set. pap. text. write for info. (0-582-79335-1, Pub. by Addison-Wesley) Longman.

— Byrne's Book of Great Pool Stories. 1995. 22.00 (0-15-100165-0) Harcourt.

*Byrne. The Complete Sql Server 7 Training Course. (C). 1999. pap., student ed. 71.93 (0-13-087415-9) P-H.

Byrne. Corrections. 2000. text 63.67 (0-13-733908-9) P-H.

— Effective Management of Private Health Care. 1990. pap. text. write for info. (0-582-04283-6, Pub. by Addison-Wesley) Longman.

— Gandhi. 1983. pap. text. write for info. (0-582-53345-7, Pub. by Addison-Wesley) Longman.

*Byrne. The Haunted Joke Book. (J). 2000. pap. 5.95 (0-552-54505-8, Pub. by Transworld Publishers Ltd) Trafalgar.

Byrne. Risk, Uncertainty & Decision-Making. 2nd ed. (Illus.). 176p. (C). 1996. pap. 37.99 (0-419-20030-4, E & FN Spon) Routledge.

— Workskills, Bk. 1,2,3. 1996. pap. text, teacher ed. 8.20 (0-13-954280-9) P-H.

Byrne & Holden. Insight. Date not set. pap. text. write for info. (0-582-55249-4, Pub. by Addison-Wesley) Longman.

Byrne, et al. Management & Supervision. 414p. (C). 1995. pap. text 49.95 (1-56226-247-5) CAT Pub.

— Papers on California Archaeology, Nos. 70-73. fac. ed. (Reports of the University of California Archaeological Survey: No. 48). (Illus.). 120p. 1959. reprint ed. pap. 13.13 (1-55567-365-1) Coyote Press.

Byrne, jt. auth. see Baron.

Byrne, Alexander & Hilbert, David R., eds. Readings on Color Vol. 1: The Philosophy of Color. LC 96-44539. (Illus.). 368p. 1997. pap. text 30.00 (0-262-52230-6, Bradford Bks) MIT Pr.

Byrne, Alexander & Hilbert, David R., eds. Readings on Color Vol. 1: The Philosophy of Color. LC 96-44539. Vol. 1. (Illus.). 368p. 1997. 60.00 (0-262-02424-1, Bradford Bks) MIT Pr.

— Readings on Color Vol. 2: The Science of Color. LC 96-44539. (Illus.). 368p. 1997. 64.00 (0-262-02425-X, Bradford Bks); pap. text 32.00 (0-262-52231-4, Bradford Bks) MIT Pr.

Byrne, Andrew. Bedford Square: An Architectural Study. LC 89-48598. (Illus.). 160p. (C). 1990. text 70.00 (0-485-11386-4, Pub. by Athlone Pr) Humanities.

Byrne, Ann, jt. auth. see Johnson, Hilda.

Byrne, Anne & Byrne, Donald. Counselling Skills for Health Workers. 256p. 1995. 64.95 (0-7329-1938-X, Pub. by Macmill Educ); pap. 32.95 (0-7329-1937-1, Pub. by Macmill Educ) Paul & Co Pubs.

Byrne, Anne & Leonard, Madeleine, eds. Women & Irish Society: A Sociological Reader. LC 97-212647. 600p. 1997. pap. 33.95 (1-900960-03-6, Pub. by Beyond the Pale) Irish Bks Media.

Byrne, Anne, jt. ed. see Leonard, Madeleine.

Byrne, Art & McMahon, Sean. Great Northerners. 230p. (Orig.). 1991. pap. 15.95 (1-85371-106-3, Pub. by Poolbeg Pr) Dufour.

— Lives: 113 Great Irishwomen & Irishmen. (Illus.). 220p. (Orig.). (YA). (gr. 9-12). 1990. pap. 15.95 (1-85371-094-6, Pub. by Poolbeg Pr) Dufour.

Byrne, B. M. A Primer of LISREL. (Illus.). 225p. 1989. 72.95 (0-387-96972-1) Spr-Verlag.

Byrne, Barbara. Structural Equation Modeling with Lisrel, Prelis, & Simplis: Basic Concepts, Applications, & Programming. LC 97-49492. 424p. 1998. 55.00 (0-8058-2924-5) L Erlbaum Assocs.

Byrne, Barbara M. Measuring Self-Concept Across the Life Span: Issues & Instrumentation. LC 95-45591. (Measurement & Instrumentation in Psychology Ser.). 297p. 1996. 39.95 (1-55798-332-1); pap. text 29.95 (1-55798-346-1) Am Psychol.

Byrne, Barbara M. Structural Equation Modeling with EQS & EQS-Windows: Basic Concepts, Applications & Programming. LC 93-38513. 288p. (C). 1994. pap. text 21.95 (*0-8039-5092-6*) Sage.

Byrne, Barbara M. Structural Equation Modeling with EQS & EQS-Windows: Basic Concepts, Applications & Programming. LC 93-38513. 288p. (C). 1994. text 48.00 (*0-8039-5091-8*) Sage.

Byrne, Bill. Habits of Wealth: One Hundred Eleven Proven Strategies That Will Change the Way You Do Business Forever. 1993. pap. 12.00 (*0-425-13819-4*) Berkley Pub.

Byrne, Brendan. Bullying: A Community Approach. LC 95-101033. 96p. (Orig.). 1995. pap. 8.95 (*1-85607-103-0*, Pub. by Columba Press) Whitecap Bks.

***Byrne, Brendan.** The Hospitality of God: A Reading of Luke's Gospel. 208p. 2000. pap. 19.95 (*0-8146-2390-5*) Liturgical Pr.

Byrne, Brendan. Paul & the Christian Woman. 128p. (C). 1988. 60.00 (*0-7855-2323-5*, Pub. by St Paul Pubns) St Mut.

— Romans. Harrington, Daniel J., ed. (Sacra Pagina Ser.: Vol. 6). 528p. 1996. 29.95 (*0-8146-5808-3*, M Glazier) Liturgical Pr.

Byrne, Brendan J. Inheriting the Earth: The Pauline Basis of a Spirituality for Our Time. LC 91-9527. 114p. (Orig.). 1990. pap. 5.95 (*0-8189-0603-0*) Alba.

Byrne, Brian. The Foundation of Literacy: The Child's Acquisition of the Alphabetic Principle. (Essays in Developmental Psychology Ser.). 162p. 1998. 34.95 (*0-86377-818-6*, Pub. by Psychol Pr) Taylor & Francis.

Byrne, Christopher, ed. see Cohen, Mark H.

Byrne, Claire J., et al. Laboratory Tests: Implications for Nursing Care. 1981. write for info. (*0-201-00088-1*, Health Sci) Addison-Wesley.

— Laboratory Tests: Implications for Nursing Care. 2nd ed. 756p. (C). 1986. pap. text 34.69 (*0-201-12670-2*, Health Sci) Addison-Wesley.

Byrne, D. & Fisher, W. A., eds. Adolescents, Sex & Contraception. 336p. 1983. 59.95 (*0-89859-217-8*) L Erlbaum Assocs.

Byrne, D. & Heydon, J. D. Cross on Evidence. 4th ed. 1295p. 1991. pap. 94.00 (*0-409-30156-6*, Austral, MICHIE); boxed set 149.00 (*0-409-30651-7*, Austral, MICHIE) LEXIS Pub.

Byrne, D., jt. auth. see Dejavu.

Byrne, D. G. Behavioral Management of the Cardiac Patient. Caddy, Glenn R., ed. LC 87-1324. (Developments in Clinical Psychology Ser.: Vol. 7). 224p. 1987. text 73.25 (*0-89391-386-3*) Ablx Pub.

Byrne, D. G., et al, eds. Psychosomatic Medicine: New Facts & Old Controversies: Proceedings of the World Congress of the International College of Psychosomatic Medicine Held in Sydney-Australia, 9th, August-September, 1987, Pt. 1. (Journal: Psychotherapy & Psychosomatics: Vol. 47, No. 3-4, 1987). (Illus.). iv, 108p. 1988. pap. 99.25 (*3-8055-4845-1*) S Karger.

Byrne, D. G. & Rosenman, Ray H., eds. Anxiety & the Heart. (Series in Health Psychology & Behavioral Medicine). 325p. 1990. 79.95 (*0-89116-860-5*) Hemisp Pub.

Byrne, D. S. Complexity Theory & the Social Sciences: An Introduction. LC 98-23769. 224p. (C). 1998. 75.00 (*0-415-16295-5*) Routledge.

— Complexity Theory & the Social Sciences: An Introduction. LC 98-23769. 224p. (C). 1998. pap. 24.99 (*0-415-16296-3*) Routledge.

— Social Exclusion. LC 98-55527. (Issues in Society Ser.). 1999. 26.95 (*0-335-19974-7*) Taylor & Francis.

Byrne, Daniel W. Publishing Your Medical Research Paper: What They Don't Teach in Medical School. LC 97-29896. 298p. 1997. pap. 23.95 (*0-683-30074-1*) Lppncott W & W.

***Byrne, Danny.** The Complete Cartooning Course. LC 99-35139. (Illus.). 2000. write for info. (*0-7641-1318-6*) Barron.

***Byrne, David.** Your Action World: Winners Are Losers with a New Attitude. LC 99-39937. (Illus.). 128p. 1999. pap. 29.95 (*0-8118-2623-6*) Chronicle Bks.

Byrne, David, jt. auth. see Peterson, Gary.

Byrne, David, jt. auth. see Waters, John.

Byrne, Dawson. Story of Ireland's National Theatre. LC 70-119093. (Studies in Drama: No. 39). 1970. reprint ed. lib. bdg. 75.00 (*0-8383-1089-3*) M S G Haskell Hse.

Byrne, Deborah J. MARC Manual: Understanding & Using MARC Records. 2nd ed. LC 97-35961. (Illus.). 263p. 1998. pap. 45.00 (*1-56308-176-8*) Libs Unl.

Byrne, Desmond J. The Talbots of Malahide, 1630-1680. (Maynooth Studies in Local History). 64p. 1997. pap. 9.95 (*0-7165-2629-8*, Pub. by Irish Acad Pr) Intl Spec Bk.

Byrne, Don G. & Caddy, Glenn R. Behavioral Medicine Vol. 1: International Perspectives. 430p. (C). 1991. text 78.50 (*0-89391-620-X*) Ablx Pub.

— Behavioral Medicine Vol. 2: International Perspectives. 432p. (C). 1992. text 78.50 (*0-89391-680-3*) Ablx Pub.

Byrne, Donald, jt. auth. see Byrne, Anne.

Byrne, Donn. Down River Long Original. 1997. pap. text 7.35 (*0-582-27396-X*) Addison-Wesley.

— Messer Marco Polo. 19.95 (*0-8488-0074-5*) Amereon Ltd.

— Messer Marco Polo. LC 79-10460. 1979. reprint ed. lib. bdg. 16.00 (*0-8376-0437-0*) Bentley Pubs.

— Sargasso Sea & Other Stories. 344p. 1977. 21.95 (*0-8369-4144-6*) Ayer.

— Teaching Writing Skills: Longman Handbooks for Language Teachers. (Handbooks for Language Teachers Ser.). (Illus.). 1988. pap. text 21.95 (*0-582-74651-5*, 78275) Longman.

Byrne, Donn & Kelley, Kathryn. Alternative Approaches to the Study of Sexual Behavior. 240p. (C). 1986. text 49.95 (*0-89859-677-7*) L Erlbaum Assocs.

Byrne, Donn, jt. auth. see Baron, Robert A.

Byrne, Donn, ed. see Livingstone, Carol.

Byrne, Donn B., pseud. Alley of Flashing Spears & Other Stories. LC 70-103501. (Short Story Index Reprint Ser.). 1977. 19.95 (*0-8369-3243-9*) Ayer.

— Daughter of the Medici, & Other Stories. LC 73-125207. (Short Story Index Reprint Ser.). 1977. 19.95 (*0-8369-3574-8*) Ayer.

— Hound of Ireland, & Other Stories. LC 70-116942. (Short Story Index Reprint Ser.). 1977. 19.95 (*0-8369-3444-X*) Ayer.

— Island of Youth, & Other Stories. LC 74-116943. (Short Story Index Reprint Ser.). 1977. 20.95 (*0-8369-3445-8*) Ayer.

— Rivers of Damascus & Other Stories. LC 72-106253. (Short Story Index Reprint Ser.). 1977. 20.95 (*0-8369-3290-0*) Ayer.

— Stories Without Women & a Few with Women. LC 74-103502. (Short Story Index Reprint Ser.). 1977. 21.95 (*0-8369-3370-2*) Ayer.

Byrne, Edmund F. Work, Inc. A Philosophical Inquiry. 360p. 1990. 59.95 (*0-87722-688-1*) Temple U Pr.

— Work, Inc. A Philosophical Inquiry. 360p. 1992. pap. 24.95 (*0-87722-957-0*) Temple U Pr.

Byrne, Edmund F. & Pitt, Joseph C., eds. Technological Transformation: Contextual & Conceptual Implications. 325p. (C). 1989. pap. text 68.50 (*90-277-2827-5*, D Reidel); lib. bdg. 154.50 (*90-277-2826-7*, D Reidel) Kluwer Academic.

Byrne, Edward. Along the Dark Shore. (New Poets of America Ser.: No. 3). 53p. 1977. pap. 7.00 (*0-918526-10-8*) BOA Edns.

— East of Omaha. 74p. 1997. pap. 10.00 (*1-877603-44-9*) Pecan Grove.

Byrne, Edward, jt. ed. see Watts, Charles.

Byrne, Edward J. Words Spoken, Words Unspoken. 72p. 1995. pap. write for info. (*0-9627300-1-7*) Chimney Hill.

Byrne, Edward M. Military Crimes: Desertion & Desertion Quickfinder. Incl. Military Crimes: Desertion. LC 97-92897. 427p. 1997. Not sold separately (*0-9656899-0-5*); Military Crimes: Desertion Quickfinder. LC 97-92898. 1171p. 1997. Not sold separately (*0-9656899-1-3*); 249.00 (*0-9656899-2-1*) LawQuest Pub.

Byrne, Eileen M. Women in Science: The Snark Syndrome. 208p. 1993. 95.00 (*1-85000-654-7*, Falmer Pr); pap. 27.00 (*1-85000-655-5*, Falmer Pr) Taylor & Francis.

Byrne, Eileen M., jt. ed. see Wilson, Brian G.

Byrne, Eleanor J. Confusional States in Older People. 172p. 1994. pap. text 25.00 (*0-340-56298-6*, Pub. by E A) OUP.

Byrne, Eleanor J., jt. auth. see McQuillan, Martin.

Byrne, Elizabeth, et al. Families & Their Children with Down's Syndrome. 160p. 1988. text 47.50 (*0-415-00607-4*) Routledge.

Byrne, Elizabeth, ed. see Kronau-Sorensen, Barbara & Sorensen, Paul.

Byrne, Eugene, jt. auth. see Newman, Kim.

Byrne, F. J. Celtic Kingdoms. 240p. 1996. 49.50 (*1-85182-195-3*, Pub. by Four Cts Pr) Intl Spec Bk.

— Irish Kings & High Kings. (Illus.). 352p. 1999. pap. 29.95 (*1-85182-196-1*, Pub. by Four Cts Pr) Intl Spec Bk.

Byrne, F. L. Prophet of Prohibition: Neal Dow & His Crusade. 1990. 16.50 (*0-8446-0533-6*) Peter Smith.

Byrne, Francis. Grammatical Relations in a Radical Creole: Verb Complementation in Saramaccan. LC 87-865. (Creole Language Library: Vol. 3). xiv, 293p. 1987. 62.00 (*0-915027-96-8*) J Benjamins Pubng Co.

Byrne, Francis & Holm, John, eds. Atlantic Meets Pacific: A Global View of Pidginization & Creolization. LC 92-37121. (Creole Language Library: No. 11). ix, 465p. 1992. 97.00 (*1-55619-165-0*) J Benjamins Pubng Co.

Byrne, Francis & Huebner, Thom, eds. Development & Structures of Creole Languages: Essays in Honor of Derek Bickerton. LC 90-23249. (Creole Language Library: Vol. 9). x, 222p. 1991. 50.00 (*1-55619-162-6*) J Benjamins Pubng Co.

Byrne, Francis & Winford, Donald, eds. Focus & Grammatical Relations in Creole Languages: Papers from the University of Chicago Conference on Focus & Grammatical Relations in Creole Languages. LC 93-11700. (Creole Language Library: Vol. 12). xvi, 329p. 1993. 59.00 (*1-55619-166-9*) J Benjamins Pubng Co.

Byrne, Francis J. & Herity, Michael. The Irish. 1999. 26.95 (*0-631-16737-4*) Blackwell Pubs.

Byrne, Frank L., ed. The View from Headquarters: Civil War Letters of Harvey Reid. LC 65-63010. (Illus.). 258p. 1965. 7.50 (*0-87020-004-6*) State Hist Soc Wis.

Byrne, Frank L. & Weaver, Andrew T., eds. Haskell of Gettysburg: His Life & Civil War Papers. LC 88-30599. (Illus.). 278p. 1989. pap. 14.00 (*0-87338-386-9*) Kent St U Pr.

Byrne, Frank L., ed. see Spiegel, Marcus M.

Byrne, G. D., jt. ed. see Schiesser, William E.

Byrne, Gabriel. Pictures in My Head. (Illus.). 168p. 1995. 19.95 (*1-57098-046-2*) Roberts Rinehart.

— Pictures in My Head. (Illus.). 168p. 1997. pap. 12.95 (*1-57098-152-3*) Roberts Rinehart.

Byrne, Gary. Transfer of Undertakings. LC 99-194637. 300p. 1998. 127.50 (*1-901657-15-9*); pap. 76.50 (*1-901657-14-0*) Gaunt.

Byrne, Gary C. & Marx, Paul. The Great American Convention: A Political History of Presidential Elections. LC 76-14102. 168p. 1977. 17.95 (*0-87015-220-3*) Pacific Bks.

Byrne, Geraldine. Shakespeare's Use of the Pronoun of Address. LC 72-121150. (Studies in Shakespeare: No. 24). 1970. reprint ed. lib. bdg. 75.00 (*0-8383-1097-4*) M S G Haskell Hse.

Byrne, Gerard I. Interferon & Nonviral Pathogens. Turco, Jenifer, ed. (Immunology Ser.: Vol. 42). (Illus.). 336p. 1988. text 155.00 (*0-8247-7973-8*) Dekker.

Byrne, Gerry. Ruby. (Illus.). 192p. 1998. pap. 10.95 (*0-575-60233-3*, Pub. by V Gollancz) Trafalgar.

Byrne, Gerry, contrib. by. Coastal & Ocean Engineering Conference, 12th Australasian, 1995 & Port & Harbor Conference, 5th Australasian, 1995. (National Conference Proceedings 95 Ser.: Vol. 5). (Illus.). 510p. 1995. pap. 74.50 (*0-85825-639-8*, Pub. by Inst Engrs Aust-EA Bks) Accents Pubns.

Byrne, H. Richad, jt. auth. see Fetterman, Roger L.

Byrne, Herbert W. Education & Divine Revelation. (Illus.). 267p. (Orig.). 1998. pap. 19.95 (*0-9663098-1-2*) ACTS Multi-Ministries.

Byrne, Herbert W. John Wesley & Learning. 224p. 1997. pap. 13.99 (*0-88019-361-1*) Schmul Pub Co.

Byrne, Hugh. El Salvador's Civil War: A Study of Revolution. LC 96-14147. 242p. 1996. 52.00 (*1-55587-606-4*, 876064) L Rienner.

***Byrne, Hugh, et al.** Rescuing Police Reform: A Challenge to the New Guatemalan Government. Armento, Amira, tr.Tr. of Rescatar la Reforma Policial: Un Reto para el Nuevo Gobiemo Guatemalteco. (SPA & ENG.). (C). 2000. pap. text 9.00 (*0-929513-45-2*) WOLA.

Byrne, Iaine. The Human Rights of Street & Working Children: A Practical Manual for Advocates. 320p. 1999. pap. 47.50 (*1-85339-449-1*, Pub. by Intermed Tech) Stylus Pub VA.

Byrne, J. Darkseid vs. Galactus: The Hunger. Kahan, Bob, ed. (Illus.). 48p. 1995. pap. 5.95 (*1-56389-182-4*) DC Comics.

— A Family Apart: A Study Guide. Friedland, J. & Kessler, R., eds. (Novel-Ties Ser.). (J). (gr. 5-7). 1997. pap. text 15.95 (*0-7675-0163-2*) Lrn Links.

— Neutrons, Nuclei & Matter: An Exploration of the Physics of Slow Neutrons. LC 95-46493. (Illus.). 788p. 1996. pap. 90.00 (*0-7503-0366-2*) IOP Pub.

Byrne, J. V. & Guglielmi, G. Endovascular Treatment of Intracranial Aneurysms. LC 97-28768. (Illus.). 300p. 1997. 124.00 (*3-540-62764-2*) Spr-Verlag.

***Byrne, James E.** ISP 98 & UPC 500 Compared. 2000. pap. 89.00 (*1-888870-23-0*) Inst Intl Bnking.

Byrne, James E. Negotiability: The Doctrine & Its Application in U. S. Commercial Law. 416p. 1995. pap. 45.00 (*1-888870-06-0*) Inst Intl Bnking.

— 1996 Annual Survey of Letter of Credit Law & Practice. 768p. 1996. 149.00 (*1-888870-11-7*) Inst Intl Bnking.

Byrne, James E. The Official Commentary on the International Standby Practice. Barnes, James G., ed. xx, 353p. Date not set. 129.00 (*1-888870-17-6*) Inst Intl Bnking.

— The Original Documents Controversy: From Glencoe to the ICC Decision. viii, 160p. 1999. pap. 49.95 (*1-888870-21-4*) Inst Intl Bnking.

Byrne, James E. The Phantom Sugar Trade. iii, 223p. 1995. pap. 45.00 (*1-888870-05-2*) Inst Intl Bnking.

Byrne, James E., ed. 1998 Annual Survey of Letter of Credit Law & Practice. 677p. 1998. 175.00 (*1-888870-16-8*) Inst Intl Bnking.

***Byrne, James E., ed.** The 1999 Annual Survey of Letter of Credit Law Practice, 4 vols. vi, 486p. 1999. 99.00 (*1-888870-19-2*) Inst Intl Bnking.

— Standby LC Rules & Laws: Critical Texts. 378p. 1999. pap. 49.95 (*1-888870-20-6*) Inst Intl Bnking.

— The 2000 Annual Survey of Letter of Credit Law & Practice. 2000. 129.00 (*1-888870-24-9*) Inst Intl Bnking.

Byrne, James E., et al, eds. 1995 Annual Survey of Letter of Credit Law & Practice: Survey Handbook. vi, 686p. 1995. pap. 99.00 (*1-888870-03-6*) Inst Intl Bnking.

— 1994 Annual Survey of Letter of Credit Law & Practice: Survey Handbook. xv, 549p. 1994. pap. 99.00 (*1-888870-02-8*) Inst Intl Bnking.

— 1997 Annual Survey of Letter of Credit Law & Practice Survey Handbook. 635p. 1997. 149.00 (*1-888870-15-X*) Inst Intl Bnking.

— 1993 Annual Survey of Letter of Credit Law & Practice: Survey Handbook. 439p. 1993. pap. 99.00 (*1-888870-01-X*) Inst Intl Bnking.

— 1992 Letter of Credit Case Law Survey. 439p. 1992. pap. 75.00 (*1-888870-00-1*) Inst Intl Bnking.

Byrne, James M. Religion & the Enlightenment: From Descartes to Kant. LC 97-20355. 1997. pap. text 24.95 (*0-664-25760-7*) Westminster John Knox.

Byrne, James M., et al, eds. Smart Sentencing: The Emergence of Intermediate Sanctions. (Illus.). 320p. (C). 1992. 49.95 (*0-8039-4164-1*); pap. 26.00 (*0-8039-4165-X*) Sage.

Byrne, James M. & Sampson, Robert J. The Social Ecology of Crime. LC 85-27823. (Research in Criminology Ser.). (Illus.). 216p. 1986. 77.95 (*0-387-96231-X*) Spr-Verlag.

Byrne, Janet, ed. Key Issues: Issues & Events of 1979. LC 80-1717. (News in Print Ser.). (Illus.). 1980. lib. bdg. 30.95 (*0-405-12877-0*) Ayer.

— The Middle East: Issues & Events of 1979. LC 80-1718. (News in Print Ser.). (Illus.). 1980. lib. bdg. 30.95 (*0-405-12878-9*) Ayer.

Byrne, Jeffrey. MCSE: System Administrator for SQL Server 7. LC 98-42435. (MCSE Ser.). 352p. 1998. pap. text 49.99 (*0-13-010795-6*) P-H.

***Byrne, Jeffrey.** SQL Server 7 Interactive Training Course. (C). 2000. pap. 49.33 (*0-13-026543-8*) P-H.

Byrne, Jeffrey L. Building Microsoft SQL Server Websites. LC 99-23837. 458p. (C). 1999. pap. text 44.95 (*0-13-079763-4*, Prentice Hall) P-H.

— Easy Microsoft Access 2000. (Easy ... / Que Ser.). (Illus.). 256p. 1999. pap. 19.99 (*0-7897-1902-9*) Que.

***Byrne, Jeffry L.** The Complete Sql Server 7 Training Course. 2000. pap. text 99.99 (*0-13-086863-9*) P-H.

Byrne, Jeffry L. Easy Microsoft Access 97. 2nd ed. LC 98-86623. 250p. 1998. 19.99 (*0-7897-1822-7*) Que.

— In Business with Access. LC 95-18453. 384p. (C). 1995. pap. text 27.95 (*0-13-437690-0*) P-H.

Byrne, Jeffry L. & Gertler, Nat. Easy Microsoft Network. (Illus.). 246p. (Orig.). 1995. 21.99 (*0-7897-0682-2*) Que.

Byrne, John. Danger Unlimited, Bk. 1. (Illus.). 108p. 1995. pap. 14.95 (*1-56971-058-9*) Dark Horse Comics.

— Danger Unlimited, Bk. 1. limited ed. (Illus.). 108p. 1995. 59.95 (*1-56971-111-9*) Dark Horse Comics.

— Fantastic Four: Trial of Galactus. (Illus.). 176p. 1989. pap. 14.95 (*0-87135-575-2*) Marvel Entrprs.

***Byrne, John.** From the Cooking School at la Campagne: Provencal Recipes from the Famed Country Farmhouse. Fisher, Connie C., ed. LC 99-66020. (Illus.). 320p. 1999. pap. 16.95 (*0-9661200-3-5*) Small Potatoes.

— JAVA for COBOL Programmers. (Illus.). 2000. pap. 49.95 (*1-886801-84-3*) Chrles River Media.

Byrne, John. John Byrne's Next Men Bk. 5: Power. (Illus.). 120p. 1995. pap. 16.95 (*1-56971-061-9*) Dark Horse Comics.

— John Byrne's Next Men, Bk. 1. (Illus.). 184p. 1993. pap. 16.95 (*1-878574-70-1*) Dark Horse Comics.

— John Byrne's Next Men Bk. 3: Fame. (Illus.). 160p. 1994. pap. 16.95 (*1-56971-025-2*) Dark Horse Comics.

— John Byrne's Next Men Bk. 4: Faith. (Illus.). 104p. 1995. pap. 14.95 (*1-56971-055-4*) Dark Horse Comics.

— John Byrne's Twenty One-Twelve. rev. ed. (Illus.). 64p. (Orig.). 1992. pap. 9.95 (*1-878574-07-8*) Dark Horse Comics.

***Byrne, John.** Learn to Draw Cartoons. (Learn to Draw Ser.). (Illus.). 64p. 1999. pap. 14.95 (*0-00-413354-4*, Pub. by HarpC) Trafalgar.

— Mad Mag's Woof. (Illus.). 80p. (J). pap. 7.95 (*0-14-130043-4*, Pub. by Pnguin Bks Ltd) Trafalgar.

Byrne, John. Mirthful Kombat. 128p. 1995. 2.50 (*0-09-941471-6*) Random.

— Slab Boys. 128p. 1997. pap. 13.95 (*0-571-19254-8*) Faber & Faber.

— Superman: The Earth Steelers. O'Neil, Dennis, ed. (Illus.). 48p. 1995. mass mkt. 2.95 (*1-56389-067-4*, Pub. by DC Comics) Time Warner.

***Byrne, John.** Superman & Batman: Generations. Crain, Dale, ed. (Illus.). 192p. (YA). 2000. pap. 14.95 (*1-56389-605-2*, Pub. by DC Comics) Time Warner.

Byrne, John. Wonder Woman: Gods & Goddesses. 320p. 1998. per. 12.95 (*0-7615-1713-8*) Prima Pub.

— Wonder Woman: Gods & Goddesses - A Novel. LC 96-67541. 320p. 1997. boxed set 20.00 (*0-7615-0483-4*) Prima Pub.

— Wonder Woman: Lifelines. Kahan, Bob, ed. (Illus.). 160p. 1998. pap. text 9.95 (*1-56389-403-3*, Pub. by DC Comics) Time Warner.

— Wonder Woman: Second Genesis. Kahan, Bob, ed. LC 99-232463. (Illus.). 128p. 1997. pap. text 9.95 (*1-56389-318-5*, Pub. by DC Comics) Time Warner.

***Byrne, John.** Writing Comedy. 1999. pap. text 12.95 (*0-7136-4950-X*) A & C Blk.

Byrne, John. X-Men: The Coming of Bishop. (Illus.). 96p. 1995. pap. 12.95 (*0-7851-0099-7*) Marvel Entrprs.

Byrne, John, et al, eds. Families & the Energy Transition. LC 85-17706. (Marriage & Family Review Ser.: Vol. 9, Nos. 1-2). 307p. 1985. text 9.95 (*0-86656-451-9*); pap. text 29.95 (*0-86656-494-2*) Haworth Pr.

Byrne, John & Giordano, Dick. The Man of Steel. (Illus.). 152p. 1991. mass mkt. 7.50 (*0-930289-28-5*, Pub. by Warner Bks) Little.

Byrne, John & Hoffman, Steve, eds. Governing the Atom: The Politics of Risk. (Energy Policy Studies: Vol. 7). 313p. (C). 1996. pap. text 24.95 (*1-56000-834-2*) Transaction Pubs.

Byrne, John & Rich, Daniel, eds. Energy & Cities. (Energy Policy Studies: Vol. 2). 171p. (C). 1985. pap. 24.95 (*0-87855-813-6*) Transaction Pubs.

— Energy & Environment, Vol. 6: The Policy Challenge-Energy Policy Studies. (Energy Policy Studies). 300p. (C). 1992. pap. text 29.95 (*1-56000-573-4*) Transaction Pubs.

— Planning for Changing Energy Conditions. (Energy Policy Studies: Vol. 4). 196p. 1987. pap. 24.95 (*0-88738-713-6*) Transaction Pubs.

Byrne, John, jt. auth. see Lee, Stan.

Byrne, John, jt. auth. see Niven, Larry.

Byrne, John A. Business Week Guide to the Best Business Schools. 5th ed. LC 97-11436. 1997. pap. 16.95 (*0-07-009472-1*) McGraw.

— Chainsaw: The Notorious Career of Al Dunlap in the Era of Profit-at-Any-Price. LC 99-34634. 416p. 1999. 26.00 (*0-06-661980-7*) HarpC.

***Byrne, John A.** Chainsaw: The Notorious Career of Al Dunlap in the Era of Profit-at-Any-Price. 2000. pap. 15.00 (*0-06-661981-5*, HarpBusn) HarpInfo.

Byrne, John A. Informed Consent. 288p. 1997. pap. 12.95 (*0-07-011784-5*) McGraw.

Byrne, John H. & Schultz, Stanley G. An Introduction to Membrane Transport & Bioelectricity. 2nd ed. (Illus.). 208p. 1994. text 75.00 (*0-7817-0181-3*); pap. text 39.00 (*0-7817-0201-1*) Lppncott W & W.

Byrne, John H., jt. ed. see Koester, John.

Byrne, Johnny, jt. auth. see Fabian, Jenny.

Byrne, Josefa H. Mrs. Byrne's Dictionary of Unusual, Obscure, & Preposterous Words. Byrne, Robert, ed. & intro. by. LC 93-45370. 1974. 18.95 (*1-55972-233-9*, Birch Ln Pr) Carol Pub Group.

— Mrs. Byrne's Dictionary of Unusual, Obscure, & Preposterous Words. Byrne, Robert, ed. & intro. by. 1976. pap. 10.95 (*0-8065-0498-6*, Citadel Pr) Carol Pub Group.

***Byrne, Joseph J.** I-Net + Certification Study System. 480p. 2000. pap. text 39.99 (*0-7645-4655-4*) IDG Bks.

B

An Asterisk (*) at the beginning of an entry indicates that the title is appearing for the first time.

***Byrne, Judith.** How to Talk to the Media: Make the Most of Every Media Opportunity in Press, Radio & Television. 144p. 2000. pap. 14.95 (*1-85703-604-4*, Pub. by How To Bks) Midpt Trade.

Byrne, Julia. Gentle Conqueror. (Historical Ser.: No. 20). 1999. per. 4.99 (*0-373-30329-7*, 1-30329-6, Harlequin) Harlequin Bks.

***Byrne, Julia.** An Independent Lady. 320p. 2000. 26.99 (*0-263-16472-1*, Pub. by Mills & Boon) Ulverscroft.

Byrne, Julia. Mistress of Her Fate. large type ed. 350p. 1996. 23.99 (*0-263-14521-2*, Pub. by Mills & Boon) Ulverscroft.

***Byrne, Julia.** Ravensdene's Bride. 1999. per. 4.99 (*0-373-30338-6*) Harlequin Bks.

Byrne, Julia. Ravensdene's Bride. large type ed. (Mills & Boon Large Print Ser.). 350p. 1997. 23.99 (*0-263-14898-X*) Ulverscroft.

— Scandal & Miss Smith. (Historical Ser.: Vol. 1). 1998. mass mkt. 4.99 (*0-373-30310-6*, 1-30310-6) Harlequin Bks.

***Byrne, Julia.** Scandal & Miss Smith. (Readers Choice Ser.). 2000. mass mkt. 4.50 (*0-373-51117-5*, 1-51117-9, Harlequin) Harlequin Bks.

Byrne, Julia. Scandal & Miss Smith. large type ed. 350p. 1998. 24.99 (*0-263-15414-9*, Pub. by Mills & Boon) Ulverscroft.

Byrne, Justin, tr. see Maravall, Jose M.

***Byrne, Kate.** Painting on Ceramics. (Illus.). 2000. 24.95 (*1-57145-669-4*, Laurel Glen Pub) Advantage Pubs.

***Byrne, Kate, et al.** Painting on Ceramics. LC 00-32249. (Illus.). 2000. write for info. (*1-57145-670-8*, Laurel Glen Pub) Advantage Pubs.

Byrne, Katherine. A Parent's Guide to Anorexia & Bulimia: Understanding & Helping Self-Starvers & Binge - Purgers. 88p. 1995. pap. 9.95 (*0-8050-1037-8*, Owl) H Holt & Co.

Byrne, Kathleen. Paula Sandburg's Chikaming Goat Herd. 64p. 1993. pap. 4.50 (*0-915992-59-0*) Eastern National.

Byrne, Kathleen A., et al. Diagnostic Microbiology & Cytology of the Eye. LC 94-28598. 199p. 1995. spiral bd. 69.95 (*0-7506-9607-9*) Buttrwrth-Heinemann.

Byrne, Kevin P. Understanding & Managing Cholesterol: A Guide for Wellness Professionals. LC 90-5195. (Illus.). 344p. (Orig.). reprint ed. pap. 106.70 (*0-608-20821-3*, 207192000003) Bks Demand.

Byrne, L. S., tr. see Von Klarwill, Victor, ed.

Byrne, Lavinia. Life & Wisdom of Benedict. 1998. pap. 7.50 (*0-340-70974-X*, Pub. by Hodder & Stought Ltd) Trafalgar.

— Life & Wisdom of Catherine of Siena. 1998. pap. 7.50 (*0-340-70973-1*, Pub. by Hodder & Stought Ltd) Trafalgar.

— Life & Wisdom of Francis of Assisi. 1998. pap. 8.95 (*0-340-70968-5*, Pub. by Hodder & Stought Ltd) Trafalgar.

— Life & Wisdom of Francis Xavier. 1998. pap. 7.50 (*0-340-70975-8*, Pub. by Hodder & Stought Ltd) Trafalgar.

— Life & Wisdom of Helena, Mother of Constantine. 1998. pap. 4.99 (*0-340-70970-7*, Pub. by Hodder & Stought Ltd) Trafalgar.

— Life & Wisdom of Margaret of Scotland. 1998. pap. 4.99 (*0-340-70972-3*, Pub. by Hodder & Stought Ltd) Trafalgar.

— Life & Wisdom of Teresa of Avila. 1998. pap. 4.99 (*0-340-70969-3*, Pub. by Hodder & Stought Ltd) Trafalgar.

***Byrne, Lavinia.** Saints Alive Series. Incl. Life & Wisdom of Benedict. 83p. 1999. pap. text 4.95 (*0-8189-0868-8*); Life & Wisdom of Catherine of Siena. 88p. 1999. pap. text 4.95 (*0-8189-0867-X*); Life & Wisdom of Francis of Assisi. 85p. 1999. pap. text 4.95 (*0-8189-0865-3*); Life & Wisdom of Margaret of Scotland. 83p. 1999. pap. text 4.95 (*0-8189-0866-1*); 339p. 1999. Set pap. 17.95 (*0-8189-0869-6*) Alba.

Byrne, Lavinia. Traditions of Spiritual Guidance: Spiritual Direction in the Tradition Collected from "The Way" 213p. (Orig.). 1991. pap. 11.95 (*0-8146-2005-1*) Liturgical Pr.

— Woman at the Altar: The Ordination of Women in the Roman Catholic Church. 144p. 1999. pap. 16.95 (*0-8264-1143-6*) Continuum.

Byrne, Lee. Check List Materials for Public School Building Specifications, Covering the General Specifications. LC 71-178797. (Columbia University. Teachers College. Contributions to Education Ser.: No. 492). reprint ed. 37.50 (*0-404-55492-X*) AMS Pr.

Byrne, Lesley, jt. auth. see Fulford, Robert.

Byrne, M. St. Clare, ed. see Arts Council Of Great Britain.

Byrne, Malcolm. Pattern of Deceit: The Iran-Contra Affair. Date not set. pap. 55.00 (*0-8133-8175-4*); pap. 17.00 (*0-8133-8176-2*) Westview.

Byrne, Malcolm, jt. ed. see Kornbluh, Peter.

Byrne, Mary L., et al. Workskills, Bk. 1. LC 93-24766. 128p. 1993. pap. text 18.20 (*0-13-953076-2*) P-H.

— Workskills, Bk. 2. LC 93-14197. 144p. 1993. pap. text 19.13 (*0-13-953084-3*) P-H.

— Workskills, Bk. 3. LC 93-14196. 144p. 1994. pap. text 19.13 (*0-13-953092-4*) P-H.

— Workskills: Incls. 2 Cass., Bk. 1. 1994. 53.00 (*0-13-954298-1*) P-H.

Byrne, Michael. Setting Tile. LC 95-947. (Illus.). 244p. 1995. pap. 19.95 (*1-56158-080-5*, 070209) Taunton.

Byrne, Michael D. Dragons & Martinis: The Skewed Realism of John Cheever. LC 93-337. (Milford Series: Popular Writers of Today: Popular Writers of Today: Vol. 55). 136p. 1993. pap. 19.00 (*0-8095-3000-7*) Millefleurs.

***Byrne, Michelle.** The Collected Poems & Songs of George Campbell Hay. 584p. 1999. (*0-7486-1063-4*) Polygon.

Byrne, Monica & Bennett, F. J. Community Medicine in Developing Countries: A Manual for the Community Nurse. 2nd ed. (Illus.). 250p. 1986. 29.95 (*0-19-261453-3*) OUP.

Byrne, Muriel S., ed. The Lisle Letters, 6 vols., Set. LC 80-12019. 3982p. (C). 1981. lib. bdg. 400.00 (*0-226-08801-4*) U Ch Pr.

Byrne, Muriel S. & Boland, Bridget, eds. The Lisle Letters: An Abridgement. LC 82-15914. xxvi, 464p. 1983. reprint ed. 35.00 (*0-226-08800-6*) U Ch Pr.

— The Lisle Letters: An Abridgement. LC 82-15914. xxvi, 436p. 1995. reprint ed. pap. 12.95 (*0-226-08810-3*) U Ch Pr.

Byrne, P. B. & Mullan, D. J., eds. Surface Inhomogeneities on Late-Type Stars. (Lecture Notes in Physics Ser.: Vol. 397). 355p. 1992. 74.95 (*0-387-55310-X*) Spr-Verlag.

Byrne, Paddy, jt. auth. see Scott, David.

Byrne, Patrick. Les Liaisons Dangereuses: A Study of Motive & Moral. 186p. 1993. 59.00 (*0-85261-252-4*, Pub. by Univ of Glasgow) St Mut.

Byrne, Patrick, ed. see Prevost, Abbe.

Byrne, Patrick B. & Rodono, Marcello, eds. Activity in Red-Dwarf Stars. 1983. text 278.00 (*90-277-1601-3*) Kluwer Academic.

Byrne, Patrick H. Analysis & Science in Aristotle. LC 96-37783. (SUNY Series in Ancient Greek Philosophy). 303p. (C). 1997. text 59.50 (*0-7914-3321-8*); pap. text 19.95 (*0-7914-3322-6*) State U NY Pr.

Byrne, Patrick M., tr. see Lao-zi.

Byrne, Patrick P. Irish Ghost Stories of Sheridan Le Fanu. 112p. 1997. pap. 10.95 (*1-85635-187-4*, Pub. by Mercier Pr) Irish Amer Bk.

Byrne, Paul. The Campaign for Nuclear Disarmament. 256p. 1988. lib. bdg. 65.00 (*0-7099-5131-0*, A1793) Routledge.

— Social Movements in Britain. LC 97-226352. (Theory & Practice in British Politics Ser.). 208p. (C). 1997. 85.00 (*0-415-07122-4*); pap. 25.99 (*0-415-07123-2*) Routledge.

Byrne, Paula J. Criminal Law & Colonial Subject: New South Wales, 1810-1830. LC 92-11457. (Studies in Australian History). (Illus.). 315p. (C). 1993. text 69.95 (*0-521-40379-0*) Cambridge U Pr.

***Byrne, Peter.** Gone Are the Days. limited ed. (Illus.). 225p. 2000. 70.00 (*1-57157-130-2*) Safari Pr.

Byrne, Peter. The Moral Interpretation of Religion. LC 98-28239. 1998. pap. 26.00 (*0-8028-4554-1*) Eerdmans.

— Natural Religion & the Nature of Religion. 272p. 1989. 62.00 (*0-415-04104-X*, A3564) Routledge.

***Byrne, Peter.** Philosophical & Ethical Problems in Mental Handicap. LC 00-27830. 2000. write for info. (*0-312-23460-0*) St Martin.

Byrne, Peter. The Philosophical & Theological Foundations of Ethics: An Introduction to Moral Theory & Its Relation to Religious Belief. LC 91-44846. 192p. 1992. text 49.95 (*0-312-07937-0*) St Martin.

— Philosophical & Theological Foundations of Ethics: An Introduction to Moral Theory & Its Relation to Religious Belief. 2nd ed. LC 98-43030. 200p. 1999. pap. 19.95 (*0-312-22000-6*) St Martin.

— Philosophical & Theological Foundations of Ethics; An Introduction to Moral Theory & Its Rel. 2nd ed. LC 98-43030. 200p. 1999. text 59.95 (*0-312-21999-7*) St Martin.

— Prolegomena to Religious Pluralism: Reference & Realism. LC 95-10839. 265p. 1995. text 69.95 (*0-312-12843-6*) St Martin.

Byrne, Peter, ed. Ethics & Law in Health Care & Research, Vol. 5, Vol. 5. LC 90-13504. 204p. 1990. 189.95 (*0-471-92806-2*) Wiley.

Byrne, Peter, jt. ed. see Houlden, Leslie.

Byrne, Randy. Build Your Own Deck Manual. Sabotka, David, ed. & illus. by. Reed, Jim, illus. 64p. 1990. pap. 9.95 (*0-934039-28-3*, A200) Hme Dsgn Altntves.

— Build Your Own Shed Manual: A210. National Plan Service Staff, ed. (Illus.). 64p. 1992. per. 9.95 (*0-934039-38-0*) Hme Dsgn Altntves.

— Empty-Nester & Starter Homes: A106. National Plan Service Staff, ed. (Illus.). 32p. 1992. 4.95 (*0-934039-37-2*) Hme Dsgn Altntves.

— Superior Home Designs: A107. (Illus.). 32p. 1992. 4.95 (*0-934039-39-9*) Hme Dsgn Altntves.

Byrne, Raymond & McCutcheon, Paul. Byrne & McCutcheon: The Irish Legal System. 2nd ed. 1989. pap. 68.00 (*1-85475-131-X*, MICHIE) LEXIS Pub.

Byrne, Reneta & Williams, Docia S. Spirits of San Antonio & South Texas. LC 92-31559. (Illus.). 200p. 1992. pap. 16.95 (*1-55622-319-6*, Rep of TX Pr) Wordware Pub.

Byrne, Richard. The Thinking Ape: The Evolutionary Origins of Intelligence. (Illus.). 276p. (C). 1995. pap. text 31.95 (*0-19-852265-7*) OUP.

Byrne, Richard, ed. see Jerome, Judson.

Byrne, Richard H. Becoming a Master Counselor: Introduction to the Profession. LC 94-19530. 320p. 1994. 81.95 (*0-534-25110-2*) Brooks-Cole.

Byrne, Richard P., et al. California Trial Handbook, 2 Vols. 3rd ed. 120.00 (*0-327-13601-4*) LEXIS Pub.

Byrne, Richard P., et al. California Trial Handbook. 3rd ed. 1992. ring bd. write for info. (*0-327-00061-9*) LEXIS Pub.

— California Trial Handbook, 1998 Supplement. 401p. 1998. ring bd., suppl. ed. write for info. (*0-327-00739-7*, 6868712) LEXIS Pub.

Byrne, Richard W., jt. ed. see Whiten, Andrew.

Byrne, Robert. Byrne's Advanced Technique in Pool & Billiards. (Illus.). 256p. 1990. 22.95 (*0-15-115222-5*, Harvest Bks) Harcourt.

— Byrne's Advanced Technique in Pool & Billiards. (Illus.). 256p. (C). 1990. pap. 20.00 (*0-15-614971-0*, Harvest Bks) Harcourt.

— Byrne's New Standard Book of Pool & Billiards. 2nd ed. LC 98-14656. (Illus.). 416p. (C). 1998. 35.00 (*0-15-100325-4*, Harvest Bks); pap. 20.00 (*0-15-600554-9*, Harvest Bks) Harcourt.

— Byrne's Standard Book of Pool & Billiards: A Complete Guide to all Cue Games. (Illus.). 352p. 1987. pap. 12.95 (*0-317-64156-5*, Harvest Bks) Harcourt.

— Byrne's Treasury of Trick Shots in Pool & Billiards. LC 82-47676. (Illus.). 320p. 1982. 19.95 (*0-15-115224-1*) Harcourt.

— Byrne's Treasury of Trick Shots in Pool & Billiards. LC 83-8428. (Illus.). 320p. 1983. pap. 20.00 (*0-15-614973-7*, Harvest Bks) Harcourt.

— Byrne's Wonderful World of Pool & Billiards: A Cornucopia of Instruction, Strategy, Anecdote & Colorful Characters. 1996. 26.00 (*0-15-100166-9*) Harcourt.

— Byrne's Wonderful World of Pool & Billiards: A Cornucopia of Instruction, Strategy, Anecdote, & Colorful Characters. LC 96-22255. (Illus.). 240p. 1996. pap. 18.00 (*0-15-600222-1*) Harcourt.

— Death Train. large type ed. 1990. 27.99 (*0-7089-2308-9*) Ulverscroft.

***Byrne, Robert.** McGoorty: A Pool Room Hustler. (Illus.). 240p. 2000. pap. 12.95 (*1-892129-49-3*) Total Sprts.

Byrne, Robert. New York Times Book of Great Chess Victories & Defeats. (Illus.). 1990. pap. 8.95 (*0-8129-1844-4*, Times Bks) Crown Pub Group.

— 1,911 Best Things Anybody Ever Said. (Illus.). 352p. 1988. pap. 12.00 (*0-449-90285-4*) Fawcett.

— Thrill. 224p. 1995. 19.95 (*0-7867-0199-4*) Carroll & Graf.

— 2548 Best Things Anybody Ever Said. 656p. 1996. 12.99 (*0-88365-960-3*) Galahad Bks.

Byrne, Robert, compiled by. Byrne's Book of Great Pool Stories. LC 95-12589. 320p. 1995. pap. 18.00 (*0-15-600223-X*, Harvest Bks) Harcourt.

Byrne, Robert, ed. Byrne's Book of Great Pool Stories. 1995. pap. 18.00 (*0-614-15515-0*, Harvest Bks) Harcourt.

Byrne, Robert, ed. see Rose, Louis J.

Byrne, Robert, ed. & intro. see Byrne, Josefa H.

Byrne, S. Strider: A Study Guide. Friedland, J. & Kessler, R., eds. (Novel-Ties Ser.). (J). (gr. 3-5). 1997. pap. text 15.95 (*0-7675-0159-4*) Lrn Links.

Byrne, Sandie. The Poetry of Tony Harrison. LC 97-47407. 240p. 2000. 74.95 (*0-7190-5294-7*, Pub. by Manchester Univ Pr); pap. 19.95 (*0-7190-5295-5*, Pub. by Manchester Univ Pr) St Martin.

Byrne, Sandie, ed. Tony Harrison: Loiner. 252p. 1997. text 48.00 (*0-19-818430-1*) OUP.

Byrne, Sandra F. A-Scan Axial Eye Length Measurements: A Handbook for Intraocular Lens Calculations. LC 95-78392. (Illus.). 150p. (Orig.). 1995. pap. text. write for info. (*0-9647899-2-1*) Grove Park Pubs.

Byrne, Sean. Growing up in a Divided Society: The Inluence of Conflict on Belfast Schoolchildren. LC 96-28842. 232p. 1997. 38.50 (*0-8386-3655-1*) Fairleigh Dickinson.

***Byrne, Sean & Irvin, Cynthia L., eds.** Reconcilable Differences: Turning Points in Ethnopolitical Conflict. LC 99-88100. (Illus.). 240p. 2000. 55.00 (*1-56549-109-2*); pap. 24.95 (*1-56549-108-4*) Kumarian Pr.

Byrne, Sherry. Preservation Planning Program Resource Guides: Collection Maintenance & Improvement. 195p. 1993. pap. 15.00 (*0-918006-62-7*) ARL.

Byrne, Sherry, jt. auth. see McKern, Debra.

Byrne, Stephen. Irish Immigration to the United States: What It Has Been & What It Is. LC 69-18763. (American Immigration Collection. Series 1). (Illus.). 1976. reprint ed. 16.95 (*0-405-00511-3*) Ayer.

Byrne, Sydns A., jt. auth. see Shaw, Maura D.

Byrne, T. Brian. Wing of the Manukau: Capt. Thomas Wing : His Life & Harbour, 1810-1888. LC 94-171252. xix, 470 p. 1991. write for info. (*0-473-01265-0*) The Bradbury Hse.

Byrne, T. C. Alberta's Revolutionary Leaders. (Illus.). 247p. 1991. pap. 17.95 (*1-55059-024-3*) Temeron Bks.

Byrne, Terry. Power in the Eye: An Introduction to Contemporary Irish Film. LC 97-5509. 1997. 34.00 (*0-8108-3296-8*) Scarecrow.

Byrne, Thomas, jt. auth. see Poling, Alan D.

Byrne, Vincent. Choices & Other Poems. 1981. pap. 6.95 (*0-8159-5223-6*) Devin.

— Enlightenment & Other Poems. LC 90-35777. 1990. 9.50 (*0-8159-5411-5*) Devin.

— Miracles & Other Poems. LC 78-65634. 1979. pap. 6.95 (*0-8159-6216-9*) Devin.

Byrne, Vincent & Gilbertie, James L. Principles of Economics. 548p. (C). 1996. pap. text 47.75 (*1-56226-319-6*) CAT Pub.

Byrne, W. E. Tale of the Elk. 456p. 1995. reprint ed. pap. 14.95 (*0-9646197-2-5*) Quarrier Pr.

Byrne, Wes. Reverse Osmosis: A Practical Guide for Industrial Users. LC 95-60061. 461p. 1995. 90.00 (*0-927188-03-1*) Tall Oaks Pub.

***Byrne, William A.** Hanna Boys Center: Haven of Hope. (Illus.). 155p. 2000. write for info. (*0-9676437-0-8*) Hanna Boys Ctr.

Byrne, William J. Dictionary of English Law. xliv, 942p. 1991. reprint ed. 97.50 (*0-8377-1952-6*, Rothman) W S Hein.

Byrne, William M. Habits of Wealth: 111 Proven Entrepreneurial Strategies for Achieving & Leading in the 90s. 312p. 1992. 21.95 (*0-9629975-6-0*) Perf One Pub.

Byrnes. Management & the Arts. 2nd ed. LC 98-31726. 336p. 1999. pap. text 44.95 (*0-240-80334-5*, Focal) Buttrwrth-Heinemann.

Byrnes & Fink. Wendepunkt. (C). 1987. pap., student ed. 24.95 (*0-8384-1652-7*) Heinle & Heinle.

Byrnes, Alice. The Child: An Archetypal Symbol in Literature for Children & Adults. LC 94-34710. (American University Studies: Vol. 53). 122p. (C). 1995. text 31.95 (*0-8204-2416-1*) P Lang Pubng.

Byrnes, Andrew, et al, eds. Hong Kong Public Law Reports, Vol. 1. 428p. 1995. 125.00 (*962-209-332-9*, Pub. by HK Univ Pr) Coronet Bks.

— Hong Kong Public Law Reports, Vol. 2. 836p. 1995. 150.00 (*962-209-351-5*, Pub. by HK Univ Pr) Coronet Bks.

— Hong Kong Public Law Reports, Vol. 3, Pt. 1. 184p. 1995. pap. 49.50 (*962-209-346-9*, Pub. by HK Univ Pr) Coronet Bks.

— Hong Kong Public Law Reports, Vol. 3, Pt. 2. 200p. 1995. pap. 49.50 (*962-209-347-7*, Pub. by HK Univ Pr) Coronet Bks.

— Hong Kong Public Law Reports, Vol. 3, Pt. 3. 240p. 1995. pap. 49.50 (*962-209-349-3*, Pub. by HK Univ Pr) Coronet Bks.

— Hong Kong Public Law Reports, Vol. 3, Pt. 4. 352p. 1995. pap. 49.50 (*962-209-350-7*, Pub. by HK Univ Pr) Coronet Bks.

— Hong Kong Public Law Reports, Vol. 4, Pt. 1. 292p. 1995. pap. 49.50 (*962-209-374-4*, Pub. by HK Univ Pr) Coronet Bks.

— Hong Kong Public Law Reports, Vol. 4, Pt. 2. 288p. 1995. pap. 49.50 (*962-209-377-9*, Pub. by HK Univ Pr) Coronet Bks.

Byrnes, Andrew, et al. Advancing the Human Rights of Women. 192p. 1997. pap. 27.50 (*0-85092-515-0*, Pub. by Comm Sec) Stylus Pub VA.

Byrnes, C. I. & Lin, W. Feedback Design for Discrete Time Nonlinear Control Systems. (Systems & Control Ser.). 200p. 1996. 49.50 (*0-8176-3747-8*) Birkhauser.

Byrnes, C. I., ed. see Bardi, M. & Dolcetta, I.

Byrnes, Christopher I. Modelling & Adaptive Control. Kurzhanski, Alexander B., ed. (Lecture Notes in Control & Information Sciences: Vol. 105). 390p. 1988. 68.95 (*0-387-19019-8*) Spr-Verlag.

Byrnes, Christopher I., ed. Partial Differential Equations & Geometry: Proceedings of the Park City Conference. LC 79-12725. (Lecture Notes in Pure & Applied Mathematics Ser.: No. 48). (Illus.). 339p. reprint ed. pap. 105.10 (*0-608-18015-7*, 202799300058) Bks Demand.

Byrnes, Christopher I., et al, eds. Output Regulation of Uncertain Nonlinear Systems. LC 97-5748. (Systems & Control Ser.). 120p. 1997. 36.50 (*0-8176-3997-7*) Birkhauser.

Byrnes, Christopher I. & Kurzansky, A., eds. Nonlinear Synthesis: Proceedings of a IIASA Workshop Held in Sopron, Hungary, June 1989. (Progress in Systems & Control Theory Ser.: Vol. 9). viii, 304p. 1991. 109.50 (*0-8176-3484-3*) Birkhauser.

Byrnes, Christopher I. & Martin, Clyde F., eds. Algebraic & Geometric Methods in Linear Systems Theory. LC 80-27354. (Lectures in Applied Mathematics: Vol. 18). 327p. 1981. text 44.00 (*0-8218-1118-5*, LAM/18) Am Math.

Byrnes, Christopher I., et al. Output Regulation of Uncertain Nonlinear Systems. LC 97-5748. (Systems & Control Ser.). 136p. 1997. write for info. (*3-7643-3997-7*) Birkhauser.

Byrnes, Christopher I., ed. see Faib, P.

Byrnes, Christopher I., ed. see NATO ASI & AMS Summer Seminar in Applied Mathemati.

***Byrnes, Colin P.** 112 Things Kids Should Be Taught Before the Age of 18. 1999. pap. 5.95 (*1-929342-03-9*) Olde Ridge Bk.

Byrnes, Deborah A. & Kiger, Gary, eds. Common Bonds: Anti-Bias Teaching in a Diverse Society. (Illus.). 112p. (Orig.). 1992. pap. 15.00 (*0-87173-125-8*) ACEI.

— Common Bonds: Anti-Bias Teaching in a Diverse Society. 2nd rev. ed. (Illus.). 112p. (Orig.). 1996. pap. 15.00 (*0-87173-137-1*) ACEI.

***Byrnes, Donn A., et al. Blackbird Rising: Birth of an Aviation Legend. (Illus.). 385p. 2000. pap. 17.00 (0-9673327-0-2, 0071-1299) Sage Mesa Pubns Inc. If you want to know how the SR-71 came about & who did what to whom, you need to read this book. The Blackbird was forged from 1950s & 60s components merged with aerodynamics & structural metallurgy from the cutting edge. An aircraft with capabilities like no other, capabilities unequaled even today. The authors lived with these machines & their technology. Blackbird Rising chronicles political & technical events that molded the SR-71. The story follows the airframe & engine, as well as sensor technology up to delivery of the first operational aircraft to Beale Air Force Base, California. The book explains the sensors & how they evolved. It describes feeder programs leading to major aircraft components as delivered in 1968. The authors explain the SR-71 flight test program & other events at Edwards AFB. This story highlights individuals & their unique contributions. It is peppered with personal experiences as everyone added their special talents to create the Blackbird's aviation legend. Today SR-71s inhabit museums but they still beckon us to the upper reaches of the atmosphere. Blackbirds consumed our lives then & still capture our hearts today. Join the authors & relive air-breathing aviation history. BLACKBIRD RISING Birth of an Aviation Legend Book cost $17.95 ea. +**

An Asterisk (*) at the beginning of an entry indicates that the title is appearing for the first time.

Byrnes, Edd & Terrill, Marshall. Edd Byrnes: Kookie No More: Televisions First Teen Idol Tells His Story. LC 96-27919. (Illus.). 240p. 1996. 22.50 (*1-56980-092-8*) Barricade Bks.

Byrnes, Edward. Monarch Notes on Ibsen's Plays. (Orig.). (C). 3.95 (*0-671-00562-6*, Arco) Macmillan Gen Ref.

Byrnes, Edward T., jt. ed. see Dunn, Charles W.

Byrnes, Elizabeth & Aikins, Jan, eds. Innovative Applications of Artificial Intelligence 6, No. 6. (Illus.). 168p. (Orig.). 1994. pap. text 25.00 (*0-929280-62-8*) AAAI Pr.

Byrnes, Elizabeth, jt. ed. see Klahr, Phil.

Byrnes, Heidi, ed. Languages for a Multi-Cultural World in Transition. (Reports of the Northeast Conference on the Teaching of Foreign Languages). 204p. 1992. pap. 12.95 (*0-915432-92-7*) NE Conf Teach Foreign.

— Learning Foreign & Second Languages: Perspectives in Research & Scholarship. LC 98-39497. (Teaching Languages, Literatures, & Cultures Ser.: No. 1). 300p. 1998. pap. 19.75 (*0-87352-801-8*, TL01P); lib. bdg. 37.50 (*0-87352-800-X*, TL01C) Modern Lang.

Byrnes, Heidi, ed. see Georgetown University Round Table on Languages & L.

Byrnes, Hilary. Motive, Means . . . & Marriage? Women to Watch. (Intimate Moments Ser.). 1998. per. 4.25 (*0-373-07888-9*, 1-07888-0) Harlequin Bks.

Byrnes, J. S., ed. Wavelets & Their Applications: Proceedings of the NATO Advanced Study Institute, Il Ciocco, Italy 16-29 August 1992. (NATO Advanced Science Institutes: C - Mathematical & Physical Sciences Ser.). 428p. (C). 1994. text 251.00 (*0-7923-3078-1*) Kluwer Academic.

Byrnes, J. S., et al, eds. Probabilistic & Stochastic Methods in Analysis, with Applications: Proceedings of the NATO Advanced Study Institute, Il Ciocco, Italy, July 14-27, 1991. LC 92-11225. (NATO Advanced Study Institutes Series C, Mathematical & Physical Sciences: Vol. 372). 712p. (C). 1992. text 374.00 (*0-7923-1804-8*) Kluwer Academic.

Byrnes, J. S. & Byrnes, Jennifer L., eds. Recent Advances in Fourier Analysis & Its Applications. (C). 1990. text 309.50 (*0-7923-0875-1*) Kluwer Academic.

Byrnes, James. Cognitive Development & Learning in Instructional Contexts. (C). 1995. teacher ed. write for info. (*0-205-19225-4*, H9225-7) Allyn.

Byrnes, James F. Speaking Frankly. LC 74-4657. (Illus.). 324p. 1974. reprint ed. lib. bdg. 35.00 (*0-8371-7480-5*, BYSF, Greenwood Pr) Greenwood.

***Byrnes, James P.** Cognitive Development & Learning in Instructional Contexts. 2nd ed. 416p. 2000. pap. 44.00 (*0-205-30858-9*) Allyn.

Byrnes, James P. The Nature & Development of Decision-Making: A Self-Regulation Model. 1997. write for info. (*0-614-26980-6*) L Erlbaum Assocs.

— The Nature & Development of Decision Making: A Self-Regulation Model. LC 97-49262. 1998. write for info. (*0-8058-2287-9*) L Erlbaum Assocs.

Byrnes, Jennifer L., jt. ed. see Byrnes, J. S.

Byrnes, John. Emil Marriot: A Re-Evaluation Based on Her Short Fiction. LC 82-84613. (American University Studies: Germanic Languages & Literature: Ser. I, Vol. 6). 289p. (Orig.). (C). 1983. pap. text 33.40 (*0-8204-0005-X*) P Lang Pubng.

***Byrnes, Joseph F.** Network & Certification Study Guide. 384p. 1999. pap. 39.99 (*0-7645-3344-4*) IDG Bks.

Byrnes, Joseph F. The Psychology of Religion. LC 84-47854. 320p. (C). 1984. 35.00 (*0-02-903580-5*) Free Pr.

— The Virgin of Chartres: An Intellectual & Psychological History of the Work of Henry Adams. LC 78-75174. 128p. 1970. 28.50 (*0-8386-2369-7*) Fairleigh Dickinson.

Byrnes, Laurence. History of the Ninety-Fourth Infantry Division in World War II. (Divisional Ser.: No. 22). (Illus.). 534p. 1982. reprint ed. 49.95 (*0-89839-064-8*) Battery Pr.

Byrnes, Lynne. The Three Little Pigs. (Happytime Storybks.). 24p. (J). (ps-1). 1991. pap. 1.25 (*0-7214-5305-8*, S9016-6 SER., Ladybrd) Penguin Putnam.

Byrnes, Margaret & Cornesky, Robert. Quality Fusion: Turning Total Quality Management into Classroom Practice. 290p. 1994. pap. text, teacher ed. 22.50 (*1-881807-05-3*) Cornesky & Assocs.

***Byrnes, Mark.** James K. Polk: A Biographical Companion. 2000. lib. bdg. 45.00 (*1-57607-056-5*) ABC-CLIO.

— Truman Years, 1945-1953. 144p. 2000. pap. 11.95 (*0-582-32904-3*) Longman.

Byrnes, Mark, jt. ed. see Vile, John R.

Byrnes, Mark E. Field Sampling Methods for Environmental Site Assessment. 272p. 1994. lib. bdg. 85.00 (*0-87371-698-1*, L698) Lewis Pubs.

— Politics & Space: Image Making by NASA. LC 94-13727. 224p. 1994. 59.95 (*0-275-94950-8*, Praeger Pubs) Greenwood.

Byrnes, Michael. Australia & the Asia Game. 288p. 1994. pap. 19.95 (*1-86373-662-X*, Pub. by Allen & Unwin Pty) Paul & Co Pubs.

Byrnes, Mike. How to Prepare for the CDL: Commercial Driver's License Bus Driver's Test. 486p. 1991. pap. 16.95 (*0-8120-4521-1*) Barron.

— How to Prepare for the Commercial Truck Driver's Examination. 1991. pap. 16.95 (*0-8120-4529-7*) Barron.

Byrnes, Mike & Fox, Devorah, eds. Bumper to Bumper: The Complete Guide to Tractor-Trailer Operations. 3rd rev. ed. LC 97-141477. (Illus.). 550p. 1997. pap. 36.95 (*0-9621687-5-0*, B2B3) M Byrnes & Assocs.

Byrnes, Mike & Associates Staff. Como Preparar el Examen de la CDL - Examen Para Obtener la Licencia que le Permitira Conducir un Vehiculo Comercial: (How to Prepare for the CDL - Commercial Driver's License Test) (SPA.). 486p. 1991. pap. 16.95 (*0-8120-4528-9*) Barron.

Byrnes, Ollie. Against The Wind: Memories of Clare Hurling. 200p. 1997. pap. 16.95 (*1-85635-157-2*) Irish Amer Bk.

Byrnes, Patricia. Environmental Pioneers. LC 97-30233. (Profiles Ser.). (Illus.). 160p. (J). (gr. 5-12). 1998. lib. bdg. 18.95 (*1-881508-45-5*) Oliver Pr MN.

Byrnes, Patricia & Krenz, Nancy. Southwestern Arts & Crafts Projects: A Workbook. rev. ed. LC 77-18988. (Illus.). (J). (gr. 1-8). 1979. pap. 9.95 (*0-913270-62-8*) Sunstone Pr.

Byrnes, Patricia, jt. ed. see Watkins, T. H.

***Byrnes, Philippe.** Protocol Management in Computer Networking. LC 99-53123. (Telecommunications Library). 464p. 2000. 89.00 (*1-58053-069-9*) Artech Hse.

Byrnes, Rita M. South Africa: A Country Study. 586p. 1997. boxed set 37.00 (*0-16-061206-3*) USGPO.

Byrnes, Rita M. South Africa: A Country Study. 3rd ed. LC 96-48983. (Area Handbook Ser.). 532p. 1997. 32.00 (*0-8444-0796-8*, DT766, Pub. by Lib Congress) Bernan Associates.

— Uganda: A Country Study. 336p. 1992. boxed set 23.00 (*0-16-040474-6*) USGPO.

***Byrnes, Rita M., ed.** South Africa: A Country Study. LC 96-48983. 532p. 1999. 0.00 (*1-57980-355-5*) Claitors.

Byrnes, Rita M., ed. see Library of Congress, Federal Research Div. Staff.

Byrnes, Robert F. Bibliography of American Publications on East Central Europe, 1945-1957. LC 69-106305. (Indiana University Publications Russian & East European: Vol. 12). 243p. reprint ed. pap. 75.40 (*0-8357-7175-X*, 205095400074) Bks Demand.

— A History of Russian & East European Studies in the United States: Selected Essays. LC 94-18999. 288p. (C). 1994. lib. bdg. 49.50 (*0-8191-9566-9*) U Pr of Amer.

— Pobedonostsev: His Life & Thought. LC 68-14598. 509p. reprint ed. 157.80 (*0-8357-9231-5*, 201302200083) Bks Demand.

— V. O. Kliuchevskii, Historian of Russia. LC 95-18202. 288p. 1995. 39.95 (*0-253-32940-X*) Ind U Pr.

Byrnes, Robert F., ed. After Brezhnev: Sources of Soviet Conduct in the 1980s. LC 82-48614. (CSIS Publication Series on the Soviet Union in the 1980's; Midland Bks.). 475p. reprint ed. pap. 147.30 (*0-8357-3939-2*, 205703400004) Bks Demand.

— The United States & Eastern Europe. LC 67-23502. 1967. pap. 1.95 (*0-936904-04-6*) Am Assembly.

Byrnes, Robert F., ed. see American Assembly Staff.

Byrnes, Ronald. Exploring the Developing World: Life in Africa & Latin America. (Illus.). 1993. pap. 14.95 (*0-943804-78-7*) U of Denver Teach.

Byrnes, Ronald, et al. Teaching about Africa: A Continent of Complexities. 1994. pap., teacher ed. 24.95 incl. sl. (*0-943804-88-4*) U of Denver Teach.

Byrnes, Stephen. Gut Bugs, Colon Critters, & Other Fun Things You Need for Good Digestion. (Illus.). 104p. 1999. pap. 11.95 (*1-891530-08-9*) Centaur Bks.

— Healthy Hearts: Natural Medicine for Your Ticker. (Illus.). 110p. 1999. pap. 11.95 (*1-891530-09-7*) Centaur Bks.

Byrnes, Stephen C. The Mind of Jung: An Explanation of Jungian Theosophy. (Illus.). v, 140p. 1998. pap. 8.95 (*1-891530-01-1*) Centaur Bks.

— Overcoming AIDS with Natural Medicine. LC 97-92719. (Illus.). ix, 224p. 1997. pap. 19.95 (*1-891530-04-6*) Centaur Bks.

Byrnes, Steven. An Easy Guide to Modern Spells: Practical Magick. Templar, Thorguard, ed. (Illus.). 128p. 1994. text 25.00 (*1-57179-000-4*) Intern Guild ASRS.

***Byrnes, Thomas.** 1886 Professional Criminals of America. 2000. pap. 19.95 (*1-58574-113-2*) Lyon Press.

Byrnes, Timothy A. Catholic Bishops in American Politics. 187p. 1991. pap. text 16.95 (*0-691-00094-8*, Pub. by Princeton U Pr) Cal Prin Full Svc.

Byrnes, Timothy A., jt. ed. see Segers, Mary C.

Byrnes, Tom. Writing Bestselling True Crime & Suspense: Break into the Exciting Field of Book, Screenplay & Television Crime Writing. LC 97-38391. 336p. 1997. pap. 17.00 (*0-7615-1026-5*) Prima Pub.

Byrnes, Trish. Bible People: Early Learning Bible Sticker Books. (Illus.). 20p. (J). 1998. pap. text 4.99 (*0-8054-1714-1*) Broadman.

— The Story of Christmas: Early Learning Bible Sticker Books. (J). 1998. pap. text 4.99 (*0-8054-1700-1*) Broadman.

***Byrnes, W. P.** The Marvelous Crucifixion on Twin Peaks. LC 99-91730. 2000. 25.00 (*0-7388-1206-4*); pap. 18.00 (*0-7388-1207-2*) Xlibris Corp.

Byrnes, William J. Management & the Arts. 210p. 1992. pap. text 44.95 (*0-240-80131-8*, Focal) Buttrwrth-Heinemann.

Byrns. Economics Box. 6th ed. 960p. (C). 1997. text 92.00 (*0-673-99674-3*) Addison-Wesley.

— Speaking of Principle. (C). 1994. pap. text. write for info. (*0-07-009624-4*) McGraw.

Byrns, ed. Economics. 4th ed. (C). 1989. pap. text, student ed. 22.00 (*0-673-38335-0*) Addison-Wesley Educ.

— Microeconomics. 4th ed. (C). 1989. pap. text 17.66 (*0-673-38337-7*) Addison-Wesley Educ.

— Special Supplement for Macroeconomic Policy Making. (C). 1993. text 7.66 (*0-673-99159-8*) Addison-Wesley.

Byrns & Stone. Macroeconomics. 7th ed. 540p. (C). 2001. pap. text. write for info. (*0-321-03067-2*) Addison-Wesley.

— Microeconomics. 7th ed. (C). 1999. pap. text. write for info. (*0-321-03066-4*) Addson-Wesley Educ.

Byrns, James H. Speak for Yourself: An Introduction to Public Speaking. 3rd ed. LC 93-26863. (C). 1994. text 18.74 (*0-07-009513-2*) McGraw.

— Speak for Yourself: An Introduction to Public Speaking. 4th ed. LC 96-19071. 352p. (C). 1996. pap. 27.50 (*0-07-009632-5*) McGraw.

Byrns, Ralph & Thorpe, Steve. An Electronic Companion to Principles of Microeconomics. 300p. (C). 1999. pap. text, wbk. ed. 34.95 (*1-58032-039-2*) Cogito Lrning.

Byrns, Ralph T. Economics. 7th ed. (C). 1999. text. write for info. (*0-321-02018-9*) Addson-Wesley Educ.

Byrns, Ralph T. & Stone. Homework Sets Macroecon. 6th ed. (C). 1995. pap. text 10.00 (*0-673-99344-2*) Addson-Wesley Educ.

Byrns, Ralph T. & Stone, Gerald. Macroeconomics. 6th ed. 496p. (C). 1997. pap. text 70.00 (*0-673-99329-9*) Addson-Wesley Educ.

Byrns, Ralph T. & Stone, Gerald W., Jr. Economics. 5th ed. (C). 1992. 24.33 (*0-673-46573-X*) Addson-Wesley Educ.

Byrns, Ralph T. & Stone, Gerald W. Economics. 5th ed. 872p. (C). 1997. 96.00 (*0-673-99316-7*) Addson-Wesley Educ.

— Homework Sets Microecon. 6th ed. (C). 1995. text 16.88 (*0-673-99342-6*) Addson-Wesley Educ.

Byrns, Ralph T. & Stone, Gerald W., Jr. Macroeconomics. (C). 1997. text 49.33 (*0-673-46567-5*) Addson-Wesley Educ.

Byrns, Ralph T. & Stone, Gerald W. Macroeconomics. 6th ed. (C). 1995. pap. text, student ed. 24.38 (*0-673-99345-0*) Addson-Wesley Educ.

— Micro Sftwr Win Microeco. 6th ed. (C). 1997. text, student ed. 27.40 incl. disk (*0-673-99363-9*) Addison-Wesley Educ.

Byrns, Ralph T. & Stone, Gerald W., Jr. Microeconomics. (C). 1997. text 48.33 (*0-673-46561-6*) Addson-Wesley Educ.

Byrns, Ralph T. & Stone, Gerald W. Microeconomics. 4th ed. (C). 1989. text 40.00 (*0-673-38339-3*, Scott Frsmn) Addison-Wesley Educ.

— Microeconomics. 6th ed. (C). 1997. pap. text, student ed. 31.00 (*0-673-99343-4*) Addson-Wesley Educ.

— Microeconomics. 6th ed. LC 95-129582. 505p. (C). 1997. pap. text 70.00 (*0-673-99328-0*) Addson-Wesley Educ.

Byrns, Ralph T., jt. auth. see Thorpe, Steve.

Byrnside, Ron. Music in Eighteenth-Century Georgia. LC 96-3280. 1997. 45.00 (*0-8203-1853-1*) U of Ga Pr.

Byrom, Thomas. Dhammapada: The Sayings of the Buddha. LC 93-535. (Pocket Classics Ser.). 144p. 1993. pap. 6.95 (*0-87773-966-8*, Pub. by Shambhala Pubns) Random.

Byron. Poetry of Byron: Power,&Tyrone. abr. ed. 1996. audio 12.00 (*0-694-51707-0*, CPN 1042) HarperAudio.

Byron. Spectral Readings. LC 98-52329. 256p. 1999. text 55.00 (*0-312-22223-8*) St Martin.

Byron, et al, eds. Sustainable Development on the North Atlantic Margin: Selected Contributions to the 13th International Seminar on Marginal Regions. LC 97-72670. 368p. 1997. text 78.95 (*1-85972-649-6*, Pub. by Ashgate Pub) Ashgate Pub Co.

Byron, jt. adapted by see Clark, I. E.

Byron, Brian. Loyalty in the Spirituality of St. Thomas More. 171p. 1972. text 57.50 (*90-6004-293-X*, Pub. by B De Graaf) Coronet Bks.

***Byron, Carl R.** Boston & Maine Trackside with A. Mitchell. (Illus.). 128p. 1999. 54.95 (*1-58248-025-7*) Morning NJ.

Byron, Carl R. A Pinprick of Light: The Troy & Greenfield Railroad & Its Hoosac Tunnel. rev. ed. 152p. 1995. pap. text 16.95 (*1-881535-17-7*) New Eng Pr VT.

***Byron, Carl R.** Trackside Around Boston, 1942-1962 with Lawson Hill. (Illus.). 128p. 2000. 54.95 (*1-58248-040-0*) Morning NJ.

***Byron, Christopher.** Delete Your Broker.com: Using the Internet to Beat the Pros on Wall Street. 288p. 2001. 26.00 (*0-684-85468-6*) S&S Trade.

Byron, Ellen. Election Year, & So When You Get Married... Two Short Plays. 1989. pap. 5.25 (*0-8222-0353-7*) Dramatists Play.

— Graceland & Asleep on the Wind. 1984. pap. 5.25 (*0-8222-0469-X*) Dramatists Play.

Byron, Eve. Deceive Me Not. 384p. (Orig.). 1997. mass mkt. 5.99 (*0-380-79310-5*, Avon Bks) Morrow Avon.

— My Lord Destiny. 384p. 1999. mass mkt. 5.99 (*0-380-80365-8*, Avon Bks) Morrow Avon.

— My Lord Stranger. 384p. 1999. mass mkt. 5.99 (*0-380-80364-X*, Avon Bks) Morrow Avon.

— Only in My Dreams. 384p. 1998. mass mkt. 5.99 (*0-380-79311-3*, Avon Bks) Morrow Avon.

— Tempt Me Not. (Orig.). 1995. mass mkt. 4.99 (*0-380-77624-3*, Avon Bks) Morrow Avon.

Byron, Frederick W., Jr. & Fuller, Robert W. Mathematics of Classical & Quantum Physics. (Illus.). xii, 665p. 1992. reprint ed. pap. 18.95 (*0-486-67164-X*) Dover.

Byron, Frederick W. & Fuller, Robert W. Mathematics of Classical & Quantum Physics, 2 vols., 1. LC 69-18006. (Addison-Wesley Advanced Physics Ser.). (Illus.). 320p. pap. 99.20 (*0-608-15550-0*, 205637800001) Bks Demand.

— Mathematics of Classical & Quantum Physics, 2 vols., 2. LC 69-18006. (Addison-Wesley Advanced Physics Ser.). (Illus.). 368p. pap. 114.10 (*0-608-15551-9*, 205637800002) Bks Demand.

Byron, G. T. The Geocubic Matrix Flashing in the Universe & the Cosmos of Energy - Matter Caught in Its Time-Flow. (Illus.). 128p. 1992. pap. text 10.95 (*1-879352-35-4*) Mini-Novel Pub.

Byron, George Gordon. Byron: Selected Poetry & Prose. Low, Donald A., ed. LC 94-46997. (English Texts Ser.). 416p. (C). (gr. 13). 1995. pap. 20.99 (*0-415-07317-0*) Routledge.

— Byron Poetical Works. (Poetry Library). 1998. pap. 7.95 (*1-85326-406-7*, 4067WW, Pub. by Wrdsworth Edits) NTC Contemp Pub Co.

— Byron's Letters & Journals, 12 vols. Marchand, Leslie A., ed. Incl. Vol. I. In My Hot Youth: Seventeen Ninety-Eight to Eighteen Ten. 288p. 1973. 29.00 (*0-674-08940-5*); Vol. IV. Wedlock's the Devil, 1814-1815. 369p. 1975. 35.95 (*0-674-08944-8*); Vol. V. So Late into the Night, 1816 to 1817. 320p. 1990. 29.00 (*0-674-08945-6*); Vol. VI. Flesh Is Frail: Eighteen Eighteen to Eighteen Nineteen. 289p. 1990. 29.00 (*0-674-08946-4*); Vol. VII. Between Two Worlds: Eighteen Twenty. 282p. 1990. 29.00 (*0-674-08947-2*); Vol. VIII. Born for Opposition: Eighteen Twenty-One. 384p. 1990. 35.95 (*0-674-08948-0*); Vol. IX. In the Wind's Eye: Eighteen Twenty One to Eighteen Twenty Two. 248p. 1990. 29.00 (*0-674-08949-9*); Vol. XI. For Freedom's Battle. 245p. 1990. 29.00 (*0-674-08953-7*); Vol. XII. Trouble of an Index. 176p. 1990. 25.00 (*0-674-08954-5*); write for info. (*0-318-53015-5*) HUP.

— Byron's Letters & Journals, Vol. 2: Famous in My Time, 1810-1812. Marchand, Leslie A., ed. LC 74-160825. 308p. 1973. reprint ed. pap. 95.50 (*0-7837-1680-X*, 205721200002) Bks Demand.

— Byron's Letters & Journals, Vol. 3: Alas! the Love of Women. Marchand, Leslie A., ed. LC 73-81853. 299p. 1974. reprint ed. pap. 92.70 (*0-7837-1681-8*, 205721200003) Bks Demand.

— Byron's Letters & Journals Vol. 10: A Heart for Every Fate, 1822-1823. Marchand, Leslie A., ed. LC 73-81853. 245p. 1973. reprint ed. pap. 76.00 (*0-7837-4085-9*, 205721200010) Bks Demand.

— Byron's Poetry. McConnell, Frank D., ed. (Critical Editions Ser.). 484p. (C). 1978. pap. text 14.75 (*0-393-09152-X*) Norton.

— Childe Harold's Pilgrimage, Canto 3: A Facsimile of the Autograph Fair Copy Found in the "Scrope Davies" Notebook. LC 87-29120. (Manuscripts of the Younger Romantics: Vol. VII). 880226p. 1988. text 83.00 (*0-8240-7026-7*) Garland.

— The Complete Poetical Works, Vol. VI. McGann, Jerome J. & Weller, Barry, eds. (Oxford English Texts Ser.). (Illus.). 766p. 1991. text 175.00 (*0-19-812758-8*) OUP.

— The Complete Poetical Works, Vol. VII. McGann, Jerome J. & Weller, Barry, eds. (Oxford English Texts Ser.). (Illus.). 460p. 1993. text 89.00 (*0-19-812328-0*) OUP.

— The Complete Poetical Works of Byron, Vol. I. McGann, Jerome J., ed. (Oxford English Texts Ser.). (Illus.). 514p. 1980. text 119.00 (*0-19-811890-2*) OUP.

— The Complete Poetical Works of Byron, Vol. 3. McGann, Jerome J., ed. (Oxford English Texts Ser.). (Illus.). 508p. (C). 1981. text 175.00 (*0-19-812755-3*) OUP.

— The Complete Poetical Works of Byron, Vol. 3. McGann, Jerome J., ed. (Oxford English Texts Ser.). (Illus.). 508p. (C). 1981. pap. text 95.00 (*0-19-812765-0*) OUP.

— The Complete Poetical Works of Byron, Vol. 2: Childe Harold's Pilgrimage, Vol. 2. McGann, Jerome J., ed. (Oxford English Texts Ser.). (Illus.). (C). 1981. pap. 74.00 (*0-19-812764-2*) OUP.

— The Complete Poetical Works of Byron, Vol. 2: Childe Harold's Pilgrimage, Vol. 2. McGann, Jerome J., ed. (Oxford English Texts Ser.). (Illus.). 342p. (C). 1981. text 145.00 (*0-19-812754-5*) OUP.

— The Complete Poetical Works of Byron, Vol. 4, Vol. 4. McGann, Jerome J., ed. (Oxford English Texts Ser.). (Illus.). (C). 1986. 135.00 (*0-19-812756-1*) OUP.

— The Complete Poetical Works of Byron, Vol. 5: Don Juan, Vol. 5. McGann, Jerome J., ed. (Oxford English Texts Ser.). (Illus.). 794p. 1986. text 145.00 (*0-19-812757-X*) OUP.

— A Concordance to Byron's "Don Juan" Hagelman, Charles W., Jr. & Barnes, Robert J., eds. (Cornell Concordances Ser.). 981p. 1967. text 89.95 (*0-8014-0169-0*) Cornell U Pr.

— Confessions of Lord Byron. Bettany, W. A., ed. LC 72-3739. (Studies in Byron: No. 5). 1972. reprint ed. lib. bdg. 75.00 (*0-8383-1578-X*) M S G Haskell Hse.

— Don Juan. 31.95 (*0-89190-660-6*) Amereon Ltd.

Byron, George Gordon. Don Juan. 001. Marchand, Leslie A., ed. LC 81-3011. (C). 1972. pap. 13.96 (*0-395-05138-X*, RivEd) HM.

Byron, George Gordon. Don Juan. Steffan, T. G. et al, eds. (English Poets Ser.). 760p. 1988. pap. 14.95 (*0-14-042216-1*, Penguin Classics) Viking Penguin.

— Don Juan. 1992. reprint ed. lib. bdg. 21.95 (*0-89966-999-9*) Buccaneer Bks.

— Don Juan Cantos X, XI, XII & XVII: A Facsimile of the Original Draft Manuscripts in the University of London Library. Nicholson, Andrew, tr. & intro. by. LC 92-35185. (Manuscripts of the Younger Romantics, Lord Byron Ser.: No. 9). 228p. 1993. text 143.00 (*0-8153-1146-X*) Garland.

— Don Juan, Cantos III-IV Manuscript: A Facsimile of the Fair Copy Manuscripts in the University of London Library. Nicholson, Andrew, ed. LC 92-19692. (Manuscripts of the Younger Romantics Ser.). 174p. 1992. text 55.00 (*0-8153-1145-1*) Garland.

— Don Juan, Cantos I & II, 1819. LC 92-37029. (Revolution & Romanticism Ser.). 246p. 1992. reprint ed. 105.00 (*1-85477-121-3*) Continuum.

— The Essential Byron. (Essential Poets Ser.: Vol. 9). 128p. 1999. pap. 8.00 (*0-88001-181-5*) HarpC.

— Essential Poets: Byron, Set. 1992. 6.98 (*0-88365-803-8*) Galahad Bks.

— Fugitive Pieces. LC 72-3567. (Studies in Byron: No. 5). 1972. reprint ed. lib. bdg. 75.00 (*0-8383-1553-4*) M S G Haskell Hse.

B

— The Life, Letters, & Journals of Lord Byron, by Thomas Moore. (BCL1-PR English Literature Ser.). 735p. 1992. reprint ed. lib. bdg. 109.00 (*0-7812-7473-7*) Rprt Serv.

— Lord Byron. (Poets Ser.). 146p. 1993. 5.95 (*0-7117-0440-6*, Pub. by JARR UK) Seven Hills Bk.

— Lord Byron: Selected Letters & Journals. 408p. 1982. 32.00 (*0-674-53915-X*) Belknap Pr.

— Lord Byron: The Complete Miscellaneous Prose. Nicholson, Andrew, ed. (Oxford English Texts Ser.). (Illus.). 616p. (C). 1991. text 160.00 (*0-19-818543-X*) OUP.

***Byron, George Gordon.** Lord Byron: The Major Works. McGann, Jerome J., ed. (Oxford World's Classics Ser.). 1080p. 2000. pap. 16.95 (*0-19-284040-1*) OUP.

Byron, George Gordon. Lord Byron Vol. X, Don Juan Cantos XIV & XV Manuscript: A Facsimile of the Original Draft Manuscripts in the Berg Collection at the New York Public Library. Nicholson, Andrew, ed. LC 94-42004. (Manuscripts of the Younger Romantics Ser.: Vol. 10). 192p. 1995. text 121.00 (*0-8153-1147-8*) Garland.

— Lord Byron in His Letters. Collins, V. H., ed. LC 72-3626. (Studies in Byron: No. 5). 1972. reprint ed. lib. bdg. 75.00 (*0-8383-1582-8*) M S G Haskell Hse.

— Lord Byron's Correspondence, 2 vols., Set. (BCL1-PR English Literature Ser.). 1992. reprint ed. lib. bdg. 150.00 (*0-7812-7474-5*) Rprt Serv.

— The Love Poems of Lord Byron: A Romantic's Passion. 8th ed. 75p. 1990. text 9.95 (*0-312-05124-7*) St Martin.

— Miscellaneous Poems. McGann, Jerome J. & Levine, Alice, eds. LC 89-29116. (Manuscripts of the Younger Romantics & the Bodleian Shelley Manuscripts: Vol. IV). 276p. 1988. text 50.00 (*0-8240-6253-1*) Garland.

— Passionate Romantic. (Illus.). 1999. 19.95 (*1-86019-308-0*) Brockhampton Pr Ltd.

— Poems: Lord Byron. 256p. 1994. 12.50 (*0-679-43630-8*) Everymns Lib.

— Poems 1807-1824 & Beppo: A Facsimile of the Original Manuscripts in the British Library & in the Pforzheimer Library at the New York Public Library. Nicholson, Andrew, ed. & intro. by. LC 36-3645. (Manuscripts of the Younger Romantics Ser.: Vol. 12). 324p. 1998. text 225.00 (*0-8153-1149-4*) Garland.

— Poems, 1816. LC 90-14257. (Revolution & Romanticism Ser.). 48p. 1990. reprint ed. 35.00 (*1-85477-039-X*) Continuum.

— Poems in the Autograph of Lord Byron: Once in the Possession of Teresa Guicciolo, Don Juan, Cantos I-V: A Facsimile of the Original Draft Manuscripts in the Pierpont Morgan Library, Vol. II. McGann, Jerome J. & Levine, Alice, eds. LC 88-2416. (Manuscripts of the Younger Romantics & the Bodleian Shelley Manuscripts). 376p. 1985. text 50.00 (*0-8240-6251-5*) Garland.

— Poems 1819-1822, Poems in the Autograph of Lord Byron: Facsimile of Manuscripts in Pierpont Morgan Library, Vol. III. McGann, Jerome J. & Levine, Alice, eds. LC 88-2416. (Manuscripts of the Younger Romantics & the Bodleian Shelley Manuscripts). 468p. 1988. text 90.00 (*0-8240-6252-3*) Garland.

— Poetical Works. 3rd rev. ed. Page, Frederick & Jump, John D., eds. (Oxford Standard Authors Ser.). (Illus.). 934p. 1961. pap. text 21.00 (*0-19-281068-5*) OUP.

— The Prisoner of Chillon & Don Juan Canto IX: A Facsimile of the Original Draft Manuscripts in the Beinecke Library of Yale University. fac. ed. Cochran, Peter, ed. & intro. by. LC 94-42004. (Manuscripts of the Younger Romantics Ser.: Vol. 13). 206p. 1995. text 105.00 (*0-8153-1962-2*) Garland.

— The Prisoner of Chillon, 1816. LC 93-17423. (Revolution & Romanticism Ser.). 80p. 1993. reprint ed. 35.00 (*1-85477-133-7*) Continuum.

— Selected Poems. Wolfson, Susan J., ed. 1996. pap. 14.95 (*0-14-042381-8*) Viking Penguin.

— Selected Poems. LC 93-1522. 112p. 1993. reprint ed. pap. text 1.50 (*0-486-27784-4*) Dover.

— Selected Poetry. McGann, Jerome J., ed. & intro. by. LC 98-223848. (Oxford World's Classics Ser.). 256p. 1998. pap. 9.95 (*0-19-283529-7*) OUP.

— Three Plays, 1821. LC 90-19523. (Revolution & Romanticism Ser.). 456p. 1990. reprint ed. 65.00 (*1-85477-038-1*) Continuum.

— Werner: A Tragedy. 232p. 1970. pap. 54.95 (*3-7705-0360-0*) Adlers Foreign Bks.

— What Comes Uppermost? Byron's Letters & Journals, Supplementary Volume. Marchand, Leslie A., ed. 128p. 1994. 29.50 (*0-87413-576-1*) U Delaware Pr.

— The Works of Lord Byron, 13 vols., Set. (BCL1-PR English Literature Ser.). 1992. reprint ed. lib. bdg. 1170.00 (*0-7812-7472-9*) Rprt Serv.

Byron, George Gordon, et al. Ode to Napoleon Buonaparte & Don Juan Canto VIII & Stanzas from III & IX: Illustrating Byron's Attitudes Toward Napoleon, Wellington, & War. Giuliano, Cheryl F., ed. LC 97-36880. (Manuscripts of the Younger Romantics Ser.: Vol. 11). 232p. 1998. text 125.00 (*0-8153-1148-6*) Garland.

Byron, George Gordon, jt. auth. see Looper, Travis.

Byron, Gilbert. Cove Dweller. (Illus.). 120p. (Orig.). 1983. pap. 7.95 (*0-9615275-2-8*) Unicorn Bkshop.

— Done Crabbin' Noah Leaves the River. 1990. 16.95 (*0-8018-3988-2*) Johns Hopkins.

***Byron, Gilbert.** Done Crabbin' Noah Leaves the River. 208p. 2000. pap. 14.95 (*0-8018-6528-X*) Johns Hopkins.

Byron, Gilbert. Gilbert Byron: Selected Poems. (Illus.). 74p. (Orig.). 1993. pap. 14.95 (*0-937692-10-7*) Litrary Hse Pr.

— The Lord's Oysters. LC 57-6442. (Maryland Paperback Bookshelf Ser.). 344p. 1977. reprint ed. pap. 11.95 (*0-8018-1959-8*) Johns Hopkins.

— Sight of a Marsh Hawk. (Illus.). 58p. (Orig.). 1985. pap. 5.95 (*0-9615275-4-4*) Unicorn Bkshop.

— Sunbathing with the Professors: Poems of the Eastern Shore. (Illus.). (Orig.). 1982. pap. 5.95 (*0-9615275-0-1*) Unicorn Bkshop.

***Byron, Glennis.** Dracula: Bram Stoker. LC 98-28419. (New Casebooks Ser.). 237p. 1999. text 49.95 (*0-312-21828-1*) St Martin.

Byron, Glennis, ed. see Stoker, Bram.

Byron, H. M. Native American Truths: Philosophy of Good Medicine. (Illus.). 72p. 1999. pap. 10.00 (*0-8059-4595-4*) Dorrance.

***Byron, James & Huggins.** Hunter. 1999. per. 6.99 (*0-671-01535-4*, Pocket Books) PB.

Byron, Janet. Assessing the Impact of California's Proposition 65. 56p. 1998. lib. bdg. 235.00 (*0-9661863-0-3*) FCN Pub DC.

— The Country Music Lover's Guide to the U. S. A. (Illus.). 256p. 1996. pap. 15.95 (*0-312-14300-1*) St Martin.

— Selection Among Alternates in Language Standardization: The Case of Albanian. (Contributions to the Sociology of Language Ser.: No. 12). 1976. pap. text 35.40 (*90-279-7542-6*) Mouton.

Byron, Joseph. New York Interiors at the Turn of the Century. (Illus.). 176p. (Orig.). 1976. pap. 14.95 (*0-486-23359-6*) Dover.

— New York Life at the Turn of the Century in Photographs. (New York City Ser.). (Illus.). 144p. 1985. pap. 12.95 (*0-486-24863-1*) Dover.

Byron, Judy. Competition Obedience: A Balancing Act. LC 98-91768. 396 p. 1998. write for info. (*0-9664574-0-4*) JABBY Prod.

Byron, Ken. Drama in the English Classroom. (Teaching Secondary English Ser.). 220p. 1986. 35.00 (*0-416-38030-1*, 9895); pap. 14.95 (*0-416-38040-9*, 9911) Routledge.

Byron, Lynn. Christmas Book. 1992. 19.98 (*1-55521-781-8*); 19.98 (*1-55521-821-0*) Bk Sales Inc.

Byron, Margaret. Post War Caribbean Migration to Britain: The Unfinished Cycle. (Research in Ethnic Relations Ser.). 233p. 1995. 72.95 (*1-85628-615-0*, Pub. by Avebry) Ashgate Pub Co.

Byron, May C., intro. Jams & Jellies. 320p. 1975. pap. 7.95 (*0-486-23130-5*) Dover.

Byron, Michael, jt. auth. see Barnbaum, Deborah R.

Byron, Mike & Modha, Sanjay. How to Pass Selection Tests. 2nd ed. 160p. 1998. pap. 17.95 (*0-7494-2697-7*) Kogan Page Ltd.

Byron, Peter, et al, eds. Respiratory Drug Delivery VI. (Illus.). 354p. 1998. 200.00 (*1-57491-076-0*) Interpharm.

Byron, Peter R., ed. Respiratory Drug Delivery. 3304p. 1989. 158.00 (*0-8493-5344-0*, RM161, CRC Reprint) Franklin.

***Byron, Peter R., et al, eds.** Respiratory Drug Delivery VII, Vol. 1. (Illus.). 274p. 2000. 150.00 (*1-930114-14-1*) Serentec Pr.

— Respiratory Drug Delivery VII, Vol. 2. (Illus.). 382p. 2000. 150.00 (*1-930114-16-8*) Serentec Pr.

Byron, Reginald. Economic Future on the North Atlantic Margin: Selected Contributions to the Twelfth International Seminar on Marginal Regions. LC 95-60401. 384p. 1995. 82.95 (*1-85972-006-4*, Pub. by Avebry) Ashgate Pub Co.

— Irish America. LC 99-19343. 328p. 2000. pap. 24.95 (*0-19-823355-8*) OUP.

***Byron, Reginald.** Irish America. LC 99-19343. (Oxford Studies in Social & Cultural Anthropology). 328p. 2000. text 70.00 (*0-19-823356-6*) OUP.

***Byron, Reginald & Hutson, John, eds.** Local Enterprise on the North Atlantic Margin: Selected Contributions to the Fourteenth International Seminar on Marginal Regions. LC 99-72974. 380p. 1999. text 78.95 (*1-84014-932-9*, Pub. by Ashgate Pub) Ashgate Pub Co.

Byron, Reginald, ed. see Blacking, John.

Byron, Robert. The Byzantine Achievement. 352p. 1988. 24.95 (*0-7102-1392-1*, Routledge Thoemms) Routledge.

— New Delhi LC 98-904962. 30 p. 1997. write for info. (*81-206-1286-8*) Asian Educ Servs.

Byron, Robert, Jr. The Road to Oxiana. (Illus.). 292p. 1982. pap. 15.95 (*0-19-503067-2*) OUP.

Byron, T., jt. auth. see Gilmore, Tom.

Byron, William J. Answers from Within. 1997. 15.95 (*0-614-28197-0*) Macmillan.

— Answers from Within: Spiritual Guidelines for Managing Setbacks in Work & Life. 290p. 1998. 16.95 (*0-02-861753-3*) Macmillan.

***Byron, William J.** Jesuit Saturdays: Sharing the Ignatian Spirit with Lay Colleagues & Friends. LC 99-55854. 2000. 21.95 (*0-8294-1468-1*) Loyola Pr.

Byron, William J. Take Courage: Psalms of Support & Encouragement. 192p. (Orig.). 1995. pap. 10.95 (*1-55612-751-0*) Sheed & Ward WI.

— The 365 Days of Christmas: Keeping the Wonder of It All Ever Green. LC 96-16618. 88p. 1996. 9.95 (*0-8091-0481-4*) Paulist Pr.

Byron, William J., et al. Ethics of Change: Conflicting Values in the Use of Cultural & Natural Resources. Murphy, James J. & Booth, Jay, eds. (Proceedings of the February Forum Ser.: Vol. 1). 104p. (Orig.). 1988. pap. text 10.00 (*1-882070-02-X*) Atlantic Ctr Arts.

Byron, Yvonne, jt. ed. see Brookfield, Harold.

***Byrski, Liz.** Spectacular Australian Sea Rescues. 1998. pap. text 12.95 (*1-86436-301-0*) New Holland.

— Western Australia: Land of Contrasts. 1999. 49.95 (*1-86436-321-5*) New Holland.

Byrskog, Samual. Jesus the Only Teacher: Didactic Authority & Transmission in Ancient Israel, Ancient Judaism & the Matthean Community. (Coniectanea Biblica New Testament Ser.: No. 24). 501p. (Orig.). 1994. pap. 69.50 (*91-22-01590-6*) Coronet Bks.

***Byrskog, Samuel.** Story As History - History As Story: The Gospel Tradition in the Context of Ancient Oral History. (Wissenschaftliche Untersuchungen zum Neuen Testament Ser.: Vol. 123). 386p. 2000. 137.50 (*3-16-147305-1*, Pub. by JCB Mohr) Coronet Bks.

Byrson, John, photos by. The Private World of Katharine Hepburn. (Illus.). 1996. 39.95 (*0-316-11332-8*) Little.

Byrt, G. W. John Clifford: A Fighting Free Churchman. 192p. 1947. reprint ed. 4.50 (*0-87921-011-7*) Attic Pr.

Byrum, Beverly, jt. auth. see Huckins, Wesley.

Byrum, C. Stephen. The Book of Revelation. (Controversial Biblical Texts Ser.). 129p. 1990. 11.95 (*0-924234-21-0*) Milton Pub.

— Genesis. (Controversial Biblical Texts Ser.). 131p. 1991. 11.95 (*1-879908-02-6*) Milton Pub.

— Gifts of the Spirit. (Controversial Biblical Texts Ser.). 144p. 1991. 11.95 (*1-879908-03-4*) Milton Pub.

— Miracles. (Controversial Biblical Texts Ser.). 133p. 1991. 11.95 (*0-924234-23-7*) Milton Pub.

— Successful Speaking Practice: A Nuts & Bolts Approach. 75p. (Orig.). 1991. write for info. (*0-924234-22-9*) Milton Pub.

Byrum, C. Stephen, jt. auth. see Matherson, Charles.

Byrum, C. Stephen, jt. auth. see Parvin, Samuel.

Byrum, E. E. The Secret of Salvation. 264p. pap. 5.00 (*0-686-29166-2*) Faith Pub Hse.

Byrum, Isabel. Harry the Newsboy & Other Stories. 32p. 1982. pap. 1.00 (*0-686-36266-7*) Faith Pub Hse.

— How John Became a Man. 64p. (YA). (gr. 7 up). pap. 1.50 (*0-686-29118-2*) Faith Pub Hse.

— The Pilot's Voice. (Illus.). 146p. pap. 3.50 (*0-686-29159-X*) Faith Pub Hse.

— The Poorhouse Waif & His Divine Teacher. 223p. pap. 4.00 (*0-686-29161-1*) Faith Pub Hse.

***Byrum, Jody.** Pinnipeds from Pole to Pole: Seals, Sea Lions & Walruses. (Illus.). 75p. (YA). (gr. 4 up). 2000. pap. 10.00 (*1-893698-07-6*, SeaWorld Educ) SeaWorld Inc.

— Whales, Dolphins & Porpoises: A World Beneath the Waves. Wlodarski, Loran & Wolf, Joy L., eds. (Education Department Publications). (Illus.). 82p. (YA). pap. 8.00 (*1-893698-01-7*) SeaWorld Inc.

Byrum, John. Conflatio. 26p. (Orig.). 1991. pap. 3.00 (*0-926935-40-2*) Runaway Spoon.

— E. (Chapbook Ser.). 15p. 1987. pap. 4.00 (*0-945112-01-7*) Generator Pr.

— Meant. (Chapbook Ser.). 31p. 1987. 5.00 (*0-945112-03-3*) Generator Pr.

— Rimage. 30p. 1990. pap. 4.00 (*0-921331-15-0*, Pub. by Tsunami Edits) SPD-Small Pr Dist.

— Text Blocks. 18p. (Orig.). 1995. pap. 5.00 (*1-57141-004-X*) Runaway Spoon.

— Text Blocks, Drawn. (Illus.). 24p. (Orig.). 1995. pap. 5.00 (*1-57141-010-4*) Runaway Spoon.

Byrum, John & Hartman, Arleen. Utter. limited ed. 60p. 1995. 18.00 (*0-937013-63-3*) Potes Poets.

Byrum, Oliver. Old Problems in New Times: Urban Strategies for the 1990s. LC 92-73811. (Illus.). 140p. 1993. reprint ed. 36.00 (*0-918286-80-8*, Planners Press); reprint ed. pap. 27.95 (*0-918286-79-4*, Planners Press) Am Plan Assn.

Byrum, R. R. Holy Spirit Baptism & the Second Cleansing. 108p. pap. 2.00 (*0-686-29114-X*); pap. 1.00 (*0-686-29115-8*) Faith Pub Hse.

— Shadows of Good Things: or The Gospel in Type. (Illus.). 144p. pap. 3.50 (*0-686-29141-7*) Faith Pub Hse.

Byrum, Russell R. Christian Theology. rev. ed. Newell, Arlo F., ed. 1989. 19.95 (*0-87162-252-1*, D3051) Warner Pr.

***Byshalieve, Anarata.** The Challenge of Regional Cooperation in Central Asia: Preventing Ethnic Conflict in the Ferghana Valley. 54p. (C). 2000. pap. text 20.00 (*0-7567-0048-5*) DIANE Pub.

Bysinger, Bill & Knight, Ken. Investing in Information Technology: A Decision-Making Guide for Business & Technical Managers. (Illus.). 300p. (C). 1997. text 30.95 (*0-442-02337-5*, VNR) Wiley.

Bysinger, Bill & Knight, Ken. Investing Information Technolo. 222p. 1996. 29.95 (*0-471-28788-1*, VNR) Wiley.

Bysouth, John S. Easy to Use Fitness Log. (Illus.). 80p. (Orig.). (C). 1990. pap. 4.95 (*0-9626028-0-9*) Bradwin Intl.

Bysouth, Kaye, jt. auth. see D'Silva, Emmanuel H.

Bystritskii, V. M. & Didenko, A. N., eds. High-Power Ion Beams. Agyei, Alfred, tr. (AIP Translation Ser.). 176p. 1990. 99.95 (*0-88318-621-7*) Spr-Verlag.

Bystrom, Dianne, jt. ed. see Kaid, Lynda L.

Bystrom, Robert. Nature's Special Moments. Batts, H. Lewis, Jr., ed. & illus. by. Black, Marvin et al, illus. 80p. 1975. 7.50 (*0-939294-01-X*, QH-71-K3-A7) Beech Leaf.

Bystrov, Peter I., ed. Philosophical Logic & Logical Philosophy: Essays in Honour of Vladimir A. Smirnov. LC 96-36289. (Synthese Library SYLI: No. 257). 288p. (C). 1996. text 133.50 (*0-7923-4270-4*) Kluwer Academic.

Bystrovetal, P. I. Liquid Metal Coolants for Heat Pipes & Power Plants. 1990. 160.00 (*0-89116-303-4*) Hemisp Pub.

Bystydziendki, Jill M. Women in Electoral Politics: Lessons from Norway. LC 94-42816. 256p. 1995. 62.95 (*0-275-95072-7*, Praeger Pubs) Greenwood.

Bystydzienski, Jill M. Women in Electoral Politics: Lessons from Norway. LC 94-42839. 144p. 1995. 55.00 (*0-275-95108-1*, Praeger Pubs) Greenwood.

Bystydzienski, Jill M., ed. Women Transforming Politics: Worldwide Strategies for Empowerment. LC 91-20126. 239p. 1992. pap. 74.10 (*0-608-05010-5*, 205967100004) Bks Demand.

Bystydzienski, Jill M. & Resnick, Estelle P. Women in Cross-Cultural Transitions. 104p. 1994. pap. 16.50 (*0-87367-478-2*) Phi Delta Kappa.

Bystydzienski, Jill M. & Sekhon, Joti, eds. Democratization & Women's Grassroots Movements. LC 98-48402. 528p. 1999. pap. 19.95 (*0-253-21279-0*); text 39.95 (*0-253-33445-4*) Ind U Pr.

Byth, D. E., jt. auth. see Wallis, E. S.

Byther, Ralph S. Landscape Plant Problems (Of the Pacific Northwest) A Pictorial Diagnostic Manual. (Illus.). 151p. 1998. pap. text 50.00 (*0-7881-7333-2*) DIANE Pub.

Bytheriver, Marylee, ed. see George, Llewellyn.

Bytheway, Bill. Ageism. LC 94-27686. 142p. 1994. pap. 30.95 (*0-335-19175-4*) OpUniv Pr.

Bytheway, Bill, et al, eds. Becoming & Being Old: Sociological Approaches to Later Life. 208p. (C). 1989. 18.95 (*0-8039-8171-6*); text 45.00 (*0-8039-8170-8*) Sage.

Bytheway, Bill & Johnson, Julia, eds. Welfare & the Ageing Experience: A Multidisciplinary Analysis. 221p. 1990. text 72.95 (*1-85628-102-7*, Pub. by Avebry) Ashgate Pub Co.

Bytheway, John. Out of the Mouths of Babes & Dudes. LC 97-14590. 96p. 1997. 5.95 (*1-57345-241-6*) Deseret Bk.

— What I Wish I'd Known Before My Mission. LC 96-34139. v, 121p. 1996. pap. 11.95 (*1-57345-207-6*) Deseret Bk.

***Bytheway, John.** What I Wish I'd Known In High School. LC 99-26399. 144p. 1999. pap. 12.95 (*1-57345-568-7*, Shadow Mount) Deseret Bk.

Bytheway, John. What I Wish I'd Known in High School: A Crash Course in Teenage Survival. LC 94-29540. x, 162p. (Orig.). (YA). (gr. 10-12). 1994. pap. 10.95 (*0-87579-921-3*) Deseret Bk.

— What I Wish I'd Known in High School: The Second Semester. LC 95-36686. 145p. (Orig.). (YA). (gr. 10-12). 1995. pap. 10.95 (*1-57345-095-2*) Deseret Bk.

— What I Wish I'd Known When I Was Single: How to Do Life as a Young Adult LC 99-26302. 1999. write for info. (*1-57345-540-7*) Deseret Bk.

— You're Gonna Make It! LC 97-18318. xiii, 97p. (J). 1997. 9.95 (*1-57345-301-3*) Deseret Bk.

***Bytheway, John & Bytheway, Kimberly.** What We Wish We'd Known When We Were Newlyweds. LC 00-23066. 2000. write for info. (*1-57345-649-7*) Deseret Bk.

Bytheway, John & Wilcox, Brad. Big Ideas for Little Budgets. pap. 11.95 (*1-55517-078-1*) CFI Dist.

Bytheway, Kimberly, jt. auth. see Bytheway, John.

Byttebier, K. & Verroken, A. Structuring International Co-Operation Between Companies. LC 94-38628. 1995. lib. bdg. 105.00 (*1-85966-106-8*) G & T Inc.

BYU Religious Studies Center Staff. The Book of Mormon Vol. 8: Three Nephi 9-30, This Is My Gospel. Nyman, Monte S. & Tate, Charles D., Jr., eds. 1993. 11.95 (*0-88494-913-3*) Bookcraft Inc.

Byun, B. S., ed. Velocity Analysis on Multichannel Seismic Data. (Geophysics Reprint Ser.: No. 12). 528p. 1990. pap. text 75.00 (*1-56080-006-2*, 187A) Soc Expl Geophys.

Byun, Yong-Ik & Ng, Kin-Wang, eds. Cosmic Microwave Background & Large Scale Structure of the Universe. LC 98-73463. (Conference Series Proceedings: Vol. 151). 184p. 1998. 52.00 (*1-886733-71-6*) Astron Soc Pacific.

Byung-Nak Song, jt. auth. see Mills, Edwin S.

Bywalec, Gloria L. & Rzeppa, Anna M. Betrayed. (Illus.). 200p. (Orig.). 1996. pap. 14.95 (*0-9652174-0-X*) JMJ Publng.

Bywater, Beth, ed. see Gundling, Dorothy.

Bywater, Hector C. Sea-Power in the Pacific: A Study of the American-Japanese Naval Problem. LC 75-111749. (American Imperialism: Viewpoints of United States Foreign Policy, 1898-1941 Ser.). 1970. reprint ed. 24.95 (*0-405-02006-6*) Ayer.

Bywater, Hector C. & Ferraby, H. C. Strange Intelligence: Memoirs of Naval Secret Service. LC 98-24846. (Classics of Espionage Ser.). 1998. write for info. (*0-7146-4858-2*, Pub. by F Cass Pubs) Intl Spec Bk.

— Strange Intelligence: Memoirs of Naval Secret Service. LC 98-24846. (Classics of Espionage Ser.). 1999. pap. write for info. (*0-7146-4415-3*, Pub. by F Cass Pubs) Intl Spec Bk.

Bywater, Ingram. Contributions to the Textual Criticism of Aristotle's Nicomachean Ethics. LC 72-9285. (Philosophy of Plate & Aristotle Ser.). 1974. reprint ed. 23.95 (*0-405-04835-1*) Ayer.

Bywater, Ingram, ed. Ethica Nicomachea. (Oxford Classical Texts Ser.). 272p. 1920. text 27.00 (*0-19-814511-X*) OUP.

Bywater, Ingram, tr. see Aristotle.

Bywater, Murray A. Airport Report: Salt Lake City Int'l Airport - It's Development. Milton, David, ed. LC 97-94192. (Illus.). 300p. 1998. pap. 25.00 (*0-9639575-1-1*) B Twenty Five.

Bywater, Tim & Sobchack, Thomas. An Introduction to Film Criticism: Major Critical Approaches to Narrative Film. 238p. (C). 1989. pap. text 59.00 (*0-582-28606-9*, 71632) Longman.

Bywater, Tim, jt. auth. see Olson, Linda L.

Bywater, William G. Clive Bell's Eye. LC 74-23853. (Illus.). 250p. reprint ed. pap. 77.50 (*0-608-16047-4*, 203317700084) Bks Demand.

Bywaters, David. Dryden in Revolutionary England. LC 90-38470. 208p. 1991. 42.50 (*0-520-07061-5*, Pub. by U CA Pr) Cal Prin Full Svc.

Bywaters, Lynn. Cinderella. 32p. (J). (ps-3). 1992. 6.95 (*0-8362-4905-4*) Andrews & McMeel.

— Sleeping Beauty. 32p. (J). (ps-3). 1992. 6.95 (*0-8362-4915-1*) Andrews & McMeel.

An Asterisk (*) at the beginning of an entry indicates that the title is appearing for the first time.

Bywaters, Paul & McLeod, Eileen. Social Work Health & Equality. LC 99-34097. (State of Welfare Ser.). 216p. 1999. pap. 25.99 (*0-415-16490-7*) Routledge.

***Bywaters, Paul & McLeod, Eileen.** Social Work Health & Equality. LC 99-34097. 232p. (C). 2000. text. write for info. (*0-415-16489-3*) Routledge.

Bywaters, Paul & McLeod, Eileen, eds. Working for Equality in Health. LC 95-25987. (State of Welfare Ser.). (Illus.). 240p. (C). 1996. 85.00 (*0-415-12465-4*); pap. 25.99 (*0-415-12466-2*) Routledge.

Byyny, Richard L. & Speroff, Leon. A Clinical Guide for the Care of Older Women. (Illus.). 384p. 1990. 68.00 (*0-683-01150-2*) Lppncott W & W.

— A Clinical Guide for the Care of Older Women: Primary & Preventive Care. 2nd ed. LC 95-49918. (Illus.). 560p. 1996. 69.00 (*0-683-01151-0*) Lppncott W & W.

Byzantius, Aristophanes. Aristophanis Byzantii Grammatici Alexandrini Fragmenta. viii, 337p. 1963. reprint ed. 90.00 (*0-318-70857-4*) G Olms Pubs.

Byzantius, Dionysius. Anaplus Bospori. Gungerich, Rudolf, ed. (GER.). xlvi, 45p. 1958. 25.00 (*3-296-12400-4*) G Olms Pubs.

BZ-Rights Stuff, Inc. Staff. The Mini-Encyclopedia of Public Domain Songs. annuals 126p. 1998. ring bd. 299.00 (*1-884286-00-3*) BZ-Rights Stuff.

***Bzdak, Meredith A.** Public Sculpture in New Jersey: Monuments to Collective Identiy. LC 98-55319. (Illus.). 220p. 1999. 55.00 (*0-8135-2699-X*) Rutgers U Pr.

Bzdega, A., et al. Podreczny Slownik Polsko-Niemiecki (Manual Dictionary Polish-German) (GER & POL.). 1018p. 1977. 49.95 (*0-8288-5510-2*, M9129) Fr & Eur.

***Bzdek, Jim.** How to Participate in Politics Effectively: A Step-by-Step Guide Every Citizen Can Use. 153p. 1999. pap. 20.00 (*0-9674131-0-9*) J Bzdek.

Bzdell, S. Morgan County. (Images of America Ser.). Date not set. pap. 18.99 (*0-7385-0011-9*) Arcadia Publng.

Bzdyl, Donald G., tr. Layamon's "Brut" A History of the Britons. (Medieval & Renaissance Texts & Studies: Vol. 65). 304p. 1989. 26.00 (*0-86698-049-0*, MR65) MRTS.

Bzoch, Kenneth R. & Givens-Ackerman, Janet. Communicative Disorders Related to Cleft Lip & Palate. 4th ed. LC 96-22641. 690p. 1997. pap. text 42.00 (*0-89079-701-3*, 7956) PRO-ED.

Bzowski, Frances D., compiled by. American Women Playwrights, 1900-1930: A Checklist, 15. LC 92-12301. (Bibliographies & Indexes in Women's Studies: No. 15). 448p. 1992. lib. bdg. 69.50 (*0-313-24238-0*, BZA/, Greenwood Pr) Greenwood.

B806, 67W. St Joseph Missal Set-wht. 1992. pap. text 8.25 (*0-89942-740-5*) Catholic Bk Pub.

C

C & C Publishing, Inc. Staff, ed. see Blacque, I. M.

C & M Associates Staff. One Hundred of the Best Real Estate Agents Northern Virginia: 1988 Guide. 111p. (Orig.). 1988. pap. 2.25 (*0-945927-00-2*) C & M Associates.

C & P Press, Inc. Staff. Crop Protection Chemicals Reference, 1994. 10th ed. LC 85-642883. 2200p. 1994. 130.00 (*1-57009-003-3*) Chem & Pharmac.

— MSDS Reference for Crop Protection Chemicals, 1994. 6th ed. LC 88-17211. 1500p. 1993. 170.00 (*1-57009-002-5*) Chem & Pharmac.

— MSDS Reference for Crop Protection Chemicals, 1994: Update 1. 6th ed. LC 88-17211. 306p. 1994. pap. write for info. (*1-57009-004-1*) Chem & Pharmac.

— MSDS Reference for Crop Protection Chemicals, 1994: Update 2. 6th ed. LC 88-17211. 306p. 1994. pap. write for info. (*1-57009-005-X*) Chem & Pharmac.

— MSDS Reference for Crop Protection Chemicals, 1994: Update 3. 5th ed. LC 88-17211. 300p. 1993. pap. write for info. (*1-57009-000-9*) Chem & Pharmac.

— MSDS Reference for Crop Protection Chemicals, 1994: Update 3. 6th ed. LC 88-17211. 306p. 1994. pap. write for info. (*1-57009-006-8*) Chem & Pharmac.

— Turf & Ornamental Chemicals Reference, 1994. 3rd ed. 1100p. 1993. 110.00 (*1-57009-001-7*) Chem & Pharmac.

C. E. C. Staff. Radiation Protection Progress Reports, 1978. (Commission of the European Communities Ser.). xvi, 854p. 1979. text 480.00 (*3-7186-0011-0*) Gordon & Breach.

— Radiation Protection Progress Reports, 1980. (Commission of the European Communities Ser.). xxvi, 1342p. 1981. text 864.00 (*3-7186-0062-5*) Gordon & Breach.

— Radiation Protection Progress Reports, 1979. (Commission of the European Communities Ser.). xvi, 910p. 1980. text 688.00 (*3-7186-0047-1*) Gordon & Breach.

— Research & Development on Radioactive Waste Management & Storage: Second Annual Progress Report of the European Community Programme 1980-1984, Vol. 2. 2nd ed. iv, 310p. 1983. text 179.00 (*3-7186-0148-6*) Gordon & Breach.

***C. E. F. Press Publishing Staff.** Precious Moments Seasons, Vol. 4. (Illus.). 1999. pap. text 19.95 (*1-55976-190-3*) CEF Press.

C. Flag, jt. auth. see Office of NAHB General Counsel Staff.

C., Gaston du, tr. see Vasari, Giorgio.

C. H. Fellows Staff. Tattoo Book: Fantasy. 1999. pap. text 14.95 (*1-55709-496-9*, Pub. by Applewood) Consort Bk Sales.

C. I. M. P. A. (Center) Staff. Integrability of Nonlinear Systems: Proceedings of the CIMPA School, Pondicherry University, India, 8-26 January 1996. Kosmann-Schwarzbach, Yvette et al, eds. LC 97-45868. (Lecture Notes in Physics Ser.: Vol. 495). viii, 380p. 1997. 95.00 (*3-540-63353-7*) Spr-Verlag.

C. I. R. P. Staff & Paulsen, P., eds. Dictionary of Production Engineering/Worterbuch der Fertigungstechnik/Dictionnair e des Techniques de Production Mechanique: Metal Forming 1/Umformtechnik 1/Formage 1. 2nd ed. (ENG, FRE & GER., Illus.). 400p. 1996. 149.00 (*3-540-60863-X*) Spr-Verlag.

C, Katie, et al, eds. Stepping Stones to Recovery from Codependency: From Codependency. LC 91-42366. 208p. pap. 7.95 (*0-934125-24-4*) Hazelden.

C. M., tr. see Bushwich, Nathan.

C of E Doctrine Commission. The Gift of God: Study Guide for Groups on "the Mystery of Salvation" 45p. (Orig.). 1996. pap. 7.95 (*0-7151-3793-X*) Morehouse Pub.

C Q Staff. State Staff Directory. 1997. pap. 99.00 (*0-87289-132-1*) C Q Staff.

C R Gibson Company, R Gibson Company. How Does Your Baby Grow. 1997. 22.00 (*0-8378-0511-2*) Gibson.

C. R. Gibson Company Staff. Antique Rose. 1997. 6.00 (*0-7667-2214-7*) Gibson.

— The Antique Rose. 1997. 6.00 (*0-7852-2868-3*) Gibson.

C. R. Gibson Company Staff. Ballet Slippers Diary. (Illus.). (J). 8.00 (*0-8378-1245-3*) Gibson.

C. R. Gibson Company Staff. A Bee Home. 1997. 6.00 (*0-7667-2216-3*) Gibson.

— A Call to Community. 1997. 6.00 (*0-7667-2196-5*) Gibson.

— Cherry Blossoms. 1997. 6.00 (*0-7667-2213-9*) Gibson.

— The Church Steeple. 1997. 6.00 (*0-7667-2217-1*) Gibson.

— A Classic Angel. 1997. 6.00 (*0-7667-2219-8*) Gibson.

— Collected Treasures. 1997. 6.00 (*0-7667-2209-0*) Gibson.

— An Edwardian Rose. 1997. 6.00 (*0-7667-2215-5*) Gibson.

— Fisherman. 1997. 6.00 (*0-7667-2210-4*) Gibson.

— The Garden Angel. 1997. 6.00 (*0-7852-3737-2*) Gibson.

— The Garden of Praise. 1997. 6.00 (*0-7852-3725-9*) Gibson.

— A Gilded Age. 1997. 6.00 (*0-7667-2211-2*) Gibson.

C. R. Gibson Company Staff. Introduction to Jazz History. 3rd ed. pap. 5.95 (*0-8378-1745-5*) Gibson.

C. R. Gibson Company Staff. Jesus Loves Me. 1997. 6.00 (*0-7667-2197-3*) Gibson.

— The Language of Flowers. 1997. 6.00 (*0-7667-2208-2*) Gibson.

C. R. Gibson Company, Staff. Lullaby Baby. 1997. 22.00 (*0-7667-0705-9*) Gibson.

C. R. Gibson Company Staff. The Magnolia Garden. 1997. 6.00 (*0-7852-3730-5*) Gibson.

— Majolica. 1997. 6.00 (*0-7667-2212-0*) Gibson.

— Natures Wonders. 1997. 6.00 (*0-7852-3719-4*); pap. text 9.99 (*0-7852-3718-6*) Gibson.

C. R. Gibson Company, Staff. Noah: The Promises of God are Everlasting. 1997. 6.95 (*0-7852-1553-0*) Gibson.

C. R. Gibson Company Staff. Noah's Promise. 1997. 6.00 (*0-7852-2773-3*) Gibson.

— Peace in the Country. 1997. 6.00 (*0-7852-2772-5*) Gibson.

— Royal Rosier. 1997. 6.00 (*0-7667-2206-6*) Gibson.

C. R. Gibson Company, Staff. School Days Memories. 1997. 37.00 (*0-7667-1245-1*) Gibson.

C. R. Gibson Company Staff. Story of Easter. (Illus.). (J). 9.95 (*0-8378-2838-4*) Gibson.

C. R. Gibson Company Staff. Sunflower Girl. 1997. 6.00 (*0-7852-2774-1*) Gibson.

C. R. Gibson Company Staff. True Love Wedding Memories. (Illus.). 13.00 (*0-8378-9099-3*) Gibson.

C. R. Gibson Company Staff. Woodland Picnic. 1997. 6.00 (*0-7667-1891-3*) Gibson.

***C. R. Gibson Company, Staff, contrib. by.** Flowers & Poems. 36p. 1999. 0.00 (*0-7667-0387-8*) Gibson.

C. R. Gibson Staff. Florescence. 1997. 6.00 (*0-7667-2205-8*) Gibson.

— Fruit Teapots. 1997. 6.00 (*0-7667-2207-4*) Gibson.

C. S. Ordnance Bureau Staff. The Confederate Field Manual with Photographic Supplement: The Field Manual for the Use of Officers on Ordnance Duty. (Illus.). 176p. (C). 1984. reprint ed. 14.95 (*0-939631-02-4*) Thomas Publications.

C-Soriguer Escofet, Federico J. Es la Clinica una Ciencia? (SPA.). 119p. 1993. pap. 17.50 (*84-7978-067-3*, Pub. by Ediciones Diaz) IBD Ltd.

C-Span Staff. Traveling Tocqueville's America. LC 98-9957. (Illus.). 256p. 1998. text 39.95 (*0-8018-5965-4*) Johns Hopkins.

— Traveling Tocqueville's America: A Tour Book. LC 98-9957. (Illus.). 256p. 1998. pap. 18.95 (*0-8018-5966-2*) Johns Hopkins.

***C-Span Staff & Lamb, Brian.** Who's Buried in Grant's Tomb? A Tour to Presidential Grave Sites. (Illus.). 305p. 2000. pap. 14.95 (*1-881846-07-5*) Johns Hopkins.

C., Stuart. A Reference Guide to the Big Book of Alcoholics Anonymous. 168p. (Orig.). (C). pap. 9.95 (*0-934125-01-5*) Hazelden.

C. T. Donovan Associates Staff. A Sourcebook of Woodwaste Recovery & Recycling in the Southeast. 235p. (Orig.). (C). 1995. pap. text 50.00 (*0-7881-1908-7*) DIANE Pub.

C. Th. Smit Sibinga, ed. Coagulation & Blood Transfusion. (Developments in Hematology & Immunology Ser.). (C). 1991. text 91.00 (*0-7923-1331-3*) Kluwer Academic.

C. Thomas Olivo & Associates Staff & Olivo, Thomas P. Blueprint Reading & Technical Sketching for Industry. 2nd ed. 464p. 1992. pap. text 50.95 (*0-8273-5077-5*) Delmar.

***C. V. Mosby Company Staff.** Maternity & Women's Healthcare. 6th ed. 1999. 66.00 (*0-323-01063-6*) Mosby Inc.

— Nursing Reflections: A Century of Caring. LC 00-29218. 176p. 2000. pap. 34.95 (*0-323-01173-X*) Mosby Inc.

C. W. C. Sports Staff. Green Bay Packers. (NFL Team Yearbooks Ser.). 1998. pap. text. write for info. (*1-891613-21-9*) Everett Sports.

— Kansas City Chiefs. (NFL Team Yearbooks Ser.). 1998. pap. text 9.99 (*1-891613-23-5*) Everett Sports.

— Pittsburgh Steelers. 1998. pap. text 9.95 (*1-891613-19-7*) Innov Futures.

— San Francisco 49ers. 1998. pap. text 9.99 (*1-891613-20-0*) Innov Futures.

C/Net Staff. C/Net Guide to Shareware.com. 500p. 1999. pap. 39.99 (*1-56276-481-0*, Ziff-Davis Pr) Que.

Ca da Mosto, Alvise. Questa e Una Opera Necessaria a Tutti Li Naviganti, 1940. LC 92-16473. (Scholars' Facsimiles & Reprints Ser.: Vol. 472). 216p. 1992. reprint ed. 75.00 (*0-8201-1472-3*) Schol Facsimiles.

Caadaev, Petr J. Socinenija i Pis'ma, 2 bande. (GER., Illus.). xv, 782p. 1972. reprint ed. write for info. (*3-487-04475-7*) G Olms Pubs.

***Caamono, Juan.** La Economia de Dios (Gods Economy) (SPA.). 1999. pap. 3.99 (*0-8297-2074-X*) Vida Pubs.

CAAS Inc. Staff. Starting a Small Business in Connecticut. 2nd ed. Purtill, John, Jr., ed. (Illus.). 264p. 1994. pap. text 24.95 (*0-9639309-0-7*) Commun Account.

CAB International Staff. International Union List of Agricultural Serials. 784p. 1990. text 205.00 (*0-85198-661-7*) OUP.

Caba, Randall L. Neon Principles: The Art of Shaping Light with Neon. Incl. Neon Principles Workbook: A Guide to Shaping Light with Neon. (Illus.). 63p. 1993. pap., student ed. Not sold separately (*0-9634219-1-3*); LC 92-90942. (Illus.). 248p. 1992. Set pap. 39.95 (*0-9634219-0-5*) Neon Pr.

Cabada, Juan De La, see De La Cabada, Juan.

Cabadas, Paloma, tr. see Vieira, Waldo.

Cabaj, Robert P. & Purcell, David W., eds. On the Road to Same Sex Marriage: A Supportive Guide to Psychological, Political & Legal Issues. LC 97-24507. 256p. 1997. mass mkt. 23.00 (*0-7879-0962-9*) Jossey-Bass.

Cabaj, Robert P. & Stein, Terry S., eds. Textbook of Homosexuality & Mental Health. 1022p. 1996. text 92.95 (*0-88048-716-X*, 8716) Am Psychiatric.

Cabakulu, Mwamba. Dictionnaire des Proverbes Africains. (FRE.). 302p. 1992. pap. 59.95 (*0-7859-8017-2*, 2738416853) Fr & Eur.

Cabal, A. Borrero. L'Universite Aujourdhui: Elements de Reflexion. (FRE., Illus.). xxiv, 300p. 1995. pap. 19.00 (*0-88936-729-9*, Pub. by IDRC Bks) Stylus Pub VA.

Cabal, Alfonso B. The University as an Institution Today. 262p. 1994. pap. write for info. (*0-88936-685-3*) IDRC Bks.

Cabal, Fermin. Passage. Halsey, Martha, ed. Hite, H. Rick, tr. from SPA. LC 97-60261. (Contemporary Spanish Plays Ser.: Vol. 13).Tr. of Travesia. (Illus.). 64p. 1998. pap. 8.00 (*1-888463-03-1*) Estreno.

***Caball, Marc.** Poets & Politics: Continuity & Reaction in Irish Poetry, 1558-1625. LC 98-42848. (Critical Conditions Ser.: 8). 280p. 1999. pap. 30.00 (*0-268-03856-2*, Pub. by U of Notre Dame Pr) Chicago Distribution Ctr.

Caballe, Ana, ed. see Unamuno, Miguel de.

Caballero, Alfredo A. & Schifini, Humberto A. The English-Spanish Real Estate Dictionary. (Illus.). 140p. (Orig.). (C). 1986. pap. text 25.50 (*0-8191-5589-6*) U Pr of Amer.

Caballero, Arturo. Flora Analitica de Espana. (Illus.). xiv, 617p. 1983. reprint ed. pap. 205.70 (*3-87429-214-2*, 002161, Pub. by Koeltz Sci Bks) Lubrecht & Cramer.

Caballero Carrizos, Esteban. Venezuela: Election Technical Assessment Report, 1993. ii, 136p. 1994. pap. text 15.00 (*1-879720-39-6*) Intl Fndt Elect.

Caballero, Ernesto G. Don Quijote Ante el Mundo: (y Ante Mi) LC 77-87981. (Illus.). 1979. 15.00 (*0-913480-37-1*); pap. 7.95 (*0-913480-38-X*) Inter Am U Pr.

Caballero, Fernan. Familia de Alvareda, No. 56. (SPA.). 139p. 1975. write for info. (*0-8288-8581-8*) Fr & Eur.

Caballero, Jane. Art Projects for Young Children. LC 79-65813. 142p. 1979. lib. bdg. 26.95 (*0-89334-166-5*) Humanics Ltd.

Caballero, Jane A. The Handbook of Learning Activities for Young Children. LC 80-81660. 208p. (J). (ps-3). 1980. lib. bdg. 28.95 (*0-89334-185-1*, 185-1) Humanics Ltd.

— Vanilla Manila Folder Games for Young Children. LC 80-83231. (Illus.). 114p. 1981. lib. bdg. 28.95 (*0-89334-182-7*, 182-7) Humanics Ltd.

Caballero, Jane A. & Whordley, Derek. Humanics National Infant & Toddler Assessment Handbook. LC 81-81660. (Illus.). 168p. (Orig.). 1981. lib. bdg. 28.95 (*0-89334-190-8*, 190-8) Humanics Ltd.

Caballero, Juan. Mensajes de la Princesa Diana Desde la Cuarta Dimension. Chia, Mabel, ed. (SPA., Illus.). 2p. 1997. pap. 20.00 (*0-9662251-0-4*) La Luz del Univ.

Caballero, Juan, ed. see Garcia Lorca, Federico.

Caballero Jurado, Carlos. Resistance Warfare, 1940-45. (Men-at-Arms Ser.: No. 169). (Illus.). 48p. pap. 11.95 (*0-85045-638-X*, 9101, Pub. by Ospry) Stackpole.

Caballero Jurado, Carlos & Thomas, Nigel. Central American Wars 1958-89. (Men-at-Arms Ser.: No. 221). (Illus.). 48p. 1990. pap. 11.95 (*0-85045-945-1*, 9178, Pub. by Ospry) Stackpole.

Caballero, Manuel Morillo, see Morillo Caballero, Manuel, notes.

Caballero, Rafael, et al, eds. Advances in Multiple Objective & Goal Programming: Proceedings of the Second International Conference on Multi-Objective Programming & Goal Programming, Torremolinos, Spain, May 16-18, 1996. LC 97-35600. (Lecture Notes in Economics & Mathematical Systems Ser.: Vol. 455). (Illus.). viii, 391p. 1997. pap. 79.00 (*3-540-63599-8*) Spr-Verlag.

Caballero, Romero R. Flores, see Flores Caballero, Romero R.

Caballero, Sebastian De La Nuez, see De la Nuez Caballero, Sebastian, ed.

Caballeros, Harold. De Victoria en Victoria (On Eternal Victory) (What You Need to Know about ... in 12 Lessons Ser.). (ENG & SPA.). 224p. 1999. 9.99 (*0-88113-541-0*) Caribe Betania.

Caballion, Invicta & Mercurius, Kether. The Journal of T. H. O. T. H. The Early Teachings of the Founders of the Hermetic Order of Thricegreatest Hermes. LC 99-213080. 102p. 1995. write for info. (*0-9627695-4-1*) J Lantiere Bks.

Caballo, V. E. International Handbook of Cognitive & Behavioural Treatments for Psychological Disorders. LC 98-42129. 1998. write for info. (*0-08-043433-9*, Pergamon Pr) Elsevier.

Caban, Janice, ed. & illus. see Lipton, Alfred.

***Caban, Pedro A.** Constructing a Colonial People: Puerto Rico & the United States, 1898-1932. LC 99-28134. 296p. 1999. 60.00 (*0-8133-3692-9*, Pub. by Westview) HarpC.

Caban, Vanessa. Bertie & Small & the Brave Sea Journey. LC 98-51830. (Illus.). 24p. (J). (ps). 1999. 12.99 (*0-7636-0878-5*) Candlewick Pr.

— Bertie & Small & the Fast Bike Ride. LC 98-51121. (Illus.). 24p. (J). (ps). 1999. 12.99 (*0-7636-0879-3*) Candlewick Pr.

Cabana, Donald A. Death at Midnight: The Confession of an Executioner. LC 95-44967. (Illus.). 224p. 1996. text 42.50 (*1-55553-264-0*) NE U Pr.

— Death at Midnight: The Confession of an Executioner. (Illus.). 200p. 1998. reprint ed. pap. text 16.95 (*1-55553-356-6*) NE U Pr.

Cabana, Steven, jt. auth. see Purser, Ronald.

Cabanac, Michael. Human Selective Brain Cooling. LC 95-20060. (Illus.). 114p. 1996. 105.00 (*3-540-59083-8*) Spr-Verlag.

Cabanellas, Guillermo. Antitrust & Direct Regulation of International Transfer of Technology Transactions. (IIC Studies Ser.: Vol. 7). 176p. 1984. pap. 55.00 (*3-527-26001-3*, Wiley-VCH) Wiley.

Cabanellas, Guillermo & Hoague, Eleanor C. Buterworth's Spanish/English Legal Dictionary, 2 vols., Set. 1500p. Date not set. pap. text 105.00 (*0-409-25669-2*, 82942, MICHIE) LEXIS Pub.

Cabanellas, Guillermo & Massaguer, J. Know-How Agreements & EEC Competition Law. (IIC Studies Ser.: Vol. 12). 260p. 1991. pap. 195.00 (*3-527-26005-6*, Wiley-VCH) Wiley.

Cabanes, Marc, ed. Finite Reductive Groups: Related Structures & Representations. LC 96-15820. (Progress in Mathematics Ser.: Vol. 141). (Illus.). 400p. 1996. 89.50 (*0-8176-3885-7*) Birkhauser.

Cabanillas, Berta. Puerto Rican Dishes. 3rd ed. 151p. 1971. 21.50 (*0-8477-2780-7*) Adlers Foreign Bks.

Cabanillas, Berta, et al. Cocine a Gusto. (Illus.). 326p. 1992. 9.50 (*0-8477-2779-3*) U of PR Pr.

Cabanillas, Fernando & Rodriguez, M. Alma, eds. Advances in Lymphoma Research. LC 96-4655. (Cancer Treatment & Research Ser.: Vol. 85). 184p. (C). 1997. text 214.50 (*0-7923-3929-0*) Kluwer Academic.

Cabanillas, Francisco. Escrito Sobre Severo. (SPA.). 1995. pap. 9.95 (*0-89729-764-4*) Ediciones.

Cabanis, Emmanuel A., jt. auth. see Duvernoy, Henri M.

***Cabanis, Jeannette, ed.** Speaking of Project Management: The PM Network Interviews. (Illus.). 175p. 1999. pap. 32.95 (*1-880410-60-5*) Proj Mgmt Inst.

Cabanis, Jose. L' Age Ingrat. (FRE.). 320p. 1974. pap. 10.95 (*0-7859-1788-8*, 2070366006) Fr & Eur.

— Le Bonheur Du Temps: Le Bonheur Du Jour - Les Cartes Du Temps. (FRE.). 1972. pap. 11.95 (*0-7859-1696-2*, 2070360997) Fr & Eur.

— Une Femme Dans la Ville (Juliette Bonviolle) (FRE.). 1979. pap. 10.95 (*0-7859-1889-2*, 2070371085) Fr & Eur.

— Les Jardins de la Nuit: Les Jeux de la Nuit-la Bataille . . . (FRE.). 256p. 1973. pap. 10.95 (*0-7859-1742-X*, 2070363678) Fr & Eur.

— Night Games. Briscoe, Peter, tr. from FRE. LC 92-62605. (Illus.). 92p. (Orig.). 1993. pap. 12.95 (*0-9634898-0-1*) Palo Verde Pr.

Cabanis, Pierre J. On the Relations Between the Physical & Moral Aspects of Man, Vol. 1. Saidi, Margaret D., tr. LC 80-21694. 448p. reprint ed. pap. 138.90 (*0-608-30801-3*, 201994900001) Bks Demand.

Cabaniss, Allen. Pattern in Early Christian Worship. LC 89-2254. 144p. (C). 1989. 17.50 (*0-86554-345-3*, MUPH283) Mercer Univ Pr.

Cabaniss, Allen, tr. & intro. see Radbertus, Paschasius.

Cabaniss, James R. & Waldrop, Stephen P. Fast Lawyers & Fading Justice: A Nation of Lawyer Dominance. 185p. (Orig.). 1994. pap. 15.95 (*0-9644885-0-7*) Richcrest Bks.

Cabaniss, Micki. Fetal Monitoring Interpretation. LC 65-9897. (Illus.). 500p. 1993. text 93.00 (*0-397-50824-7*, Lippnctt) Lppncott W & W.

Cabaniss, Micki L. Fetal Monitoring Interpretation. 2nd ed. 1998. text. write for info. (*0-397-51860-9*) Lppncott W & W.

Cabanne, Pierre. Degas: Dancers. (Rhythem & Color One Ser.). 1970. 9.95 (*0-8288-9506-6*) Fr & Eur.

— Dialogues with Marcel Duchamp. (Quality Paperbacks Ser.). (Illus.). 152p. 1987. reprint ed. pap. 9.95 (*0-306-80303-8*) Da Capo.

C

An Asterisk (*) at the beginning of an entry indicates that the title is appearing for the first time.

***Cabanne, Pierre.** Honore Daumier Paintings Sculpture Literature. 1999. 49.95 (*2-7191-0486-8*) La Manufacture.

Cabanne, Pierre. Le Siecle de Picasso Vol. 1: La Naissance du Cubisme, 1881-1912. (FRE.). 416p. 1992. pap. 18.95 (*0-7859-1681-4*, 2070326500) Fr & Eur.

Cabanne, Pierre, jt. auth. see Seghers, Pierre.

Cabanski, Tom. MWSS: Object - Oriented Design in Java. LC 97-46425. (Mitchell Waite Signature Ser.). 768p. 1999. 49.99 (*1-57169-134-0*) Sams.

Cabarga, Alex, jt. auth. see Cabarga, Leslie.

Cabarga, Leslie. The Designer's Guide to Color Combinations: 500+ Historic & Modern Color Formulas in CMYK. LC 98-33482. (Illus.). 144p. 1999. 27.99 (*0-89134-857-3*, 31206, North Lght Bks) F & W Pubns Inc.

— Easy-to-Duplicate Fax Forms. (Quick Copy Ser.). (Illus.). 48p. 1992. pap. text 5.95 (*0-486-27082-3*) Dover.

— Letterheads: 100 Years of Great Designs. 16.99 (*0-8118-2253-2*) Rockport Pubs.

— Talks with Trees: A Plant Psychic's Interviews with Vegetables, Flowers & Trees. (Illus.). 176p. 1997. 15.95 (*0-9657628-0-7*, 006270) Iconoclassics.

— A Treasury of German Trademarks, 1925-1950, Vol. 2. LC 81-71799. 156p. 1985. 24.75 (*0-88108-007-1*) Art Dir.

Cabarga, Leslie & Cabarga, Alex. Ready-to-Use Trade Symbols & Motifs: 88 Different Copyright-Free Designs Printed One Side. (Clip Art Ser.). (Illus.). 64p. 1993. pap. 5.95 (*0-486-27681-3*) Dover.

Cabarga, Leslie E. Advertising Spot Illustrations of the Twenties & Thirties. (Illus.). 112p. 1989. pap. 8.95 (*0-486-26098-4*) Dover.

— Art Deco Advertising, Vol. 6. LC 95-77687. 1988. pap. 7.95 (*0-88108-153-1*) Art Dir.

— Dynamic Black & White Illustrations. LC 93-71343. (Illus.). 192p. 1993. text 22.50 (*0-88108-113-2*); pap. text 16.95 (*0-88108-114-0*) Art Dir.

— The Fleischer Story: The Max Fleischer Cartoon Studio in the Golden Age of Animation. rev. ed. (Quality Paperbacks Ser.). (Illus.). 192p. 1988. reprint ed. pap. 16.95 (*0-306-80313-5*) Da Capo.

— Food Designs. 1998. pap. 1.00 (*0-486-27465-9*) Dover.

— The Lettering & Graphic Design of F. G. Cooper. LC 96-84614. (Illus.). 128p. 1996. pap. 16.95 (*0-88108-192-2*) Art Dir.

— Lively Advertising Cuts of the Twenties & Thirties: 1102 Illustrations. (Illus.). 112p. 1990. pap. 7.95 (*0-486-26418-1*) Dover.

— Popular Advertising Cuts of the Twenties & Thirties. LC 96-11365. (Pictorial Archive Ser.). 1996. pap. 8.95 (*0-486-29228-2*) Dover.

— Ready-to-Use Menu Illustrations. (Illus.). 1990. pap. 5.95 (*0-486-26417-3*) Dover.

Cabarga, Leslie E., compiled by. Borders, Vol. 3. LC 91-70262. 64p. 1991. pap. text 7.95 (*0-88108-085-3*) Art Dir.

Cabarga, Leslie E., ed. Art Deco Advertising, No. 1. LC 88-82915. 48p. 1988. 5.75 (*0-88108-061-6*) Art Dir.

— Art Deco Advertising, No. 2. LC 88-82915. 48p. 1988. 5.75 (*0-88108-062-4*) Art Dir.

— Art Deco Advertising, No. 3. LC 88-82915. 48p. 1988. 5.75 (*0-88108-063-2*) Art Dir.

— Art Deco Advertising, No. 4. LC 88-82915. 48p. 1990. 5.75 (*0-88108-078-0*) Art Dir.

— Art Deco Advertising, No. 5. LC 88-82915. 48p. 1990. 5.75 (*0-88108-079-9*) Art Dir.

— The Art of F. G. Cooper. LC 95-75684. (Illus.). 128p. 1992. pap. text 16.95 (*0-88108-097-7*) Art Dir.

— Borders Vol. 5. 64p. 1991. pap. text 7.95 (*0-88108-087-X*) Art Dir.

Cabarga, Leslie E., et al, eds. One Thousand One Advertising Cuts from the Twenties & Thirties. (Pictorial Archive Ser.). (Illus.). 112p. (Orig.). 1987. pap. 8.95 (*0-486-25490-9*) Dover.

Cabarga, Leslie E. & Cabarga, Marcie, eds. One Thousand Three Hundred Thirty-Seven Spot Illustrations of the Twenties & Thirties. LC 92-9524. (Illus.). 96p. 1992. 8.95 (*0-486-27232-X*) Dover.

— Trademark Designs of the '20s. (Illus.). 48p. (Orig.). 1991. pap. 3.95 (*0-486-26804-7*) Dover.

Cabarga, Leslie E. & Robbins, Casey, eds. Borders, Vol. 1. LC 91-70262. (Illus.). 64p. 1991. pap. text 7.95 (*0-88108-083-7*) Art Dir.

— Borders, Vol. 2. LC 91-70262. (Illus.). 64p. 1991. pap. 7.95 (*0-88108-084-5*) Art Dir.

Cabarga, Marcie, jt. ed. see Cabarga, Leslie E.

Cabasilas, Nicholas. A Commentary on the Divine Liturgy. Hussey, J. M. et al, trs. from GRE. LC 98-33519. 120p. (Orig.). 1974. pap. 10.95 (*0-913836-37-0*) St Vladimirs.

Cabasso, Jackie & Moon, Susan. Risking Peace: Why We Sat in the Road. (Illus.). 80p. (Orig.). 1985. pap. 7.00 (*0-931416-03-5*) Open Books.

Cabat, Erni. Erni Cabat's Magical ABC: Animals Around the Farm. LC 90-5242. (Illus.). 64p. (Orig.). (J). (ps-2). Date not set. 23.00 (*0-943173-73-6*) Cabat Studio Pubns.

— Father Eusebio Francisco Kino & His Missions of the Pimeria Alta Bk. 1: The Side Altars. Polzer, Charles W., ed. Prezelski, Carmen V. & Cardon, Charlotte M., trs. LC 82-50219. (Illus.). 36p. Date not set. pap. 9.50 (*0-915076-06-3*) SW Mission.

Cabat, Erni & Butler, Lollie. Erni Cabat's Magical World of Prehistoric Animals. LC 89-84487. (Illus.). 64p. (J). (ps-6). Date not set. 23.00 (*0-925263-02-8*) Cabat Studio Pubns.

Cabat, Erni & Cardon, Charlotte M. Life on the Tanque Verde: The History, Bk. 1. (Illus.). 1983. 9.50 (*0-913521-00-0*) Cabat Studio Pubns.

Cabat, Erni & Engard, Rodney G. Arizona & the Southwest: Cacti & Succulents, Bk. 1. LC 83-63523. (Illus.). 32p. 1984. 9.50 (*0-913521-01-9*) Cabat Studio Pubns.

— Arizona & the Southwest: Cacti & Succulents, Bk.2. LC 83-63523. (Illus.). 32p. 1985. 9.50 (*0-913521-04-3*) Cabat Studio Pubns.

— Arizona Wildflowers & the Southwest, Bk. 2. LC 84-72111. (Illus.). 1985. 9.50 (*0-913521-03-5*) Cabat Studio Pubns.

Cabat, Erni & Keremes, Constance A. Erni Cabat's Magical World of the Carousel. LC 89-26890. (Illus.). 32p. Date not set. 23.00 (*0-943173-60-4*) Cabat Studio Pubns.

Cabat, Erni & Polzer, Charles W. Father Eusebio Francisco Kino & His Missions of the Pimeria Alta Bk. 2: The Main Altars. Prezelski, Carmen V., tr. LC 82-50219. (Illus.). 36p. Date not set. pap. 9.50 (*0-915076-08-X*) SW Mission.

— Father Eusebio Francisco Kino & His Missions of the Pimeria Alta Bk. 3: Facing the Missions. Prezelski, Carmen V., tr. LC 82-50219. (Illus.). 36p. Date not set. pap. 9.50 (*0-915076-09-8*) SW Mission.

Cabat, Erni, jt. auth. see Engard, Rodcey G.

Cabaton, Antoine. Java, Sumatra & Other Islands of the Dutch East Indies. Miall, Bernard, tr. LC 77-86967. (Illus.). reprint ed. 31.00 (*0-404-16699-7*) AMS Pr.

Cabaud. Simone Weil a New York et a Londres. 15.95 (*0-685-36635-9*) Fr & Eur.

Cabaup. Act: For OOH Grades Five-Six. 1995. pap. 18.95 (*1-56191-379-0*, 3075); pap., teacher ed. write for info. (*1-56191-380-4*) Meridian Educ.

— Act: For OOH Grades Seven-Nine. 1995. pap. 18.95 (*1-56191-377-4*, 3076); pap., teacher ed. write for info. (*1-56191-378-2*) Meridian Educ.

— Act: For OOH Grades Ten-Twelve. 1995. teacher ed. write for info. (*1-56191-376-6*); pap. 18.95 (*1-56191-375-8*, 3077) Meridian Educ.

Cabbell, Sally, jt. auth. see Brock, Susan.

Cabbil, Lila, et al. Skills for Success: A Career Education Handbook for Children & Adolescents with Visual Impairments. LC 98-8121. 480p. 1998. 37.95 (*0-89128-943-7*) Am Foun Blind.

Cabeceiras, James. The Multimedia Library: Materials Selection & Use. 3rd ed. (Library & Information Science Ser.). (Illus.). 316p. 1991. text 69.95 (*0-12-153953-9*) Acad Pr.

***Cabeci, Anne.** The Case of the Cyber-Hacker. Ryan, Kevin, ed. Vol. 19. (Illus.). 144p. (J). (gr. 3-7). 2000. mass mkt. 3.99 (*1-57064-773-9*, Big Red) Lyrick Pub.

Cabeen, David C., et al, eds. Critical Bibliography of French Literature Vol. 3: The 17th Century. LC 47-3282. (C). 1961. 80.00 (*0-8156-2007-1*) Syracuse U Pr.

— Critical Bibliography of French Literature Vol. 4A: The 18th Century-Supplement. LC 47-3282. (C). 1951. text 75.00 (*0-8156-2008-X*) Syracuse U Pr.

Cabeen, David C. & Schutz, Alexander H., eds. Critical Bibliography of French Literature Vol. 2: The 16th Century. LC 47-3282. (C). 1956. 80.00 (*0-8156-2006-3*) Syracuse U Pr.

Cabeen, Richard M., jt. auth. see Chase, Carroll.

Cabel, Sandra. Microsoft Excel 7.0 for Windows 95: Tutorial & Applications Ser. (Tutorial & Applications Ser.). 1996. mass mkt., student ed. 37.95 (*0-538-71518-9*) S-W Pub.

— Microsoft Excel 7.0 for Windows 95: Tutorial & Applications Ser. LC 95-49657. (Tutorial & Applications Ser.). 1996. mass mkt. 37.95 (*0-538-71508-1*) S-W Pub.

Cabell, David W. Cabell's Directory of Publishing Opportunities in Education. 5th ed. (C). 1998. pap. text 89.95 (*0-911753-12-5*) Cabell Pub.

Cabell, David W., ed. Cabell's Directory of Publishing Opportunities in Accounting, Economics & Finance. 7th ed. 1500p. (C). 1997. pap. 89.95 (*0-911753-10-9*) Cabell Pub.

— Cabell's Directory of Publishing Opportunities in Management & Marketing. 7th ed. 2000p. (C). 1997. pap. 89.95 (*0-911753-11-7*) Cabell Pub.

Cabell, Hanna & Branch, A. J. Rivers of America - The St. Johns. Date not set. lib. bdg. 24.95 (*0-8488-1960-8*) Amereon Ltd.

Cabell, Harriet. Learning for Life: Unite 3. 80p. (C). 1995. pap. text, per. 16.95 (*0-7872-0333-5*) Kendall-Hunt.

Cabell, Harriett, jt. auth. see Willimon, William H.

Cabell, James. The Witch Woman. 17.95 (*0-89190-273-2*) Amereon Ltd.

Cabell, James Branch. Beyond Life. (Collected Works of James Branch Cabell). 358p. 1998. reprint ed. lib. bdg. 98.00 (*1-58201-550-3*) Classic Bks.

— Certain Hour. (Collected Works of James Branch Cabell). 253p. 1998. reprint ed. lib. bdg. 88.00 (*1-58201-551-1*) Classic Bks.

— Chivalry. LC 71-140326. (Short Story Index Reprint Ser.). 1977. 16.95 (*0-8369-3718-X*) Ayer.

***Cabell, James Branch.** Chivalry. (Collected Works of James Branch Cabell). 1999. reprint ed. (*1-58201-552-X*) Classic Bks.

Cabell, James Branch. Cords of Vanity. (Collected Works of James Branch Cabell). 341p. 1998. reprint ed. lib. bdg. 98.00 (*1-58201-553-8*) Classic Bks.

— The Cream of the Jest. Flora, Joseph M., ed. (Masterworks of Literature Ser.). 1973. pap. 12.95 (*0-8084-0396-6*) NCUP.

— Cream of the Jest. (Collected Works of James Branch Cabell). 280p. 1998. reprint ed. lib. bdg. 90.00 (*1-58201-554-6*) Classic Bks.

— The Devil's Own Dear Son. 238p. reprint ed. lib. bdg. 21.95 (*0-88411-570-4*) Amereon Ltd.

— Domnei. LC 75-133517. (Select Bibliographies Reprint Ser.). 1977. 18.95 (*0-8369-5549-8*) Ayer.

Cabell, James-Branch. The Eagle's Shadow. 1973. 250.00 (*0-87968-088-1*) Gordon Pr.

Cabell, James Branch. The Eagle's Shadow. (Collected Works of James Branch Cabell). 256p. 1998. reprint ed. lib. bdg. 88.00 (*1-58201-555-4*) Classic Bks.

— Figures of Earth. (Collected Works of James Branch Cabell). 356p. 1998. reprint ed. lib. bdg. 99.00 (*1-58201-556-2*) Classic Bks.

— From the Hidden Way. (Collected Works of James Branch Cabell). 187p. 1998. 88.00 (*1-58201-557-0*) Classic Bks.

— Gallentry. (Collected Works of James Branch Cabell). 342p. 1998. reprint ed. lib. bdg. 98.00 (*1-58201-968-1*) Classic Bks.

— The High Place. 24.95 (*0-88411-795-2*) Amereon Ltd.

— High Place. (Collected Works of James Branch Cabell). 234p. 1998. reprint ed. lib. bdg. 88.00 (*1-58201-558-9*) Classic Bks.

— Jewel Merchants. (Collected Works of James Branch Cabell). 63p. 1998. reprint ed. lib. bdg. 88.00 (*1-58201-559-7*) Classic Bks.

— Joseph Hergesheimer. (Collected Works of James Branch Cabell). 57p. 1998. reprint ed. lib. bdg. 88.00 (*1-58201-560-0*) Classic Bks.

— Jurgen. (Illus.). 1990. 24.00 (*0-8446-5561-9*) Peter Smith.

— Jurgen. 1990. reprint ed. lib. bdg. 21.95 (*0-89966-708-2*) Buccaneer Bks.

— Jurgen. (Collected Works of James Branch Cabell). 325p. 1998. reprint ed. lib. bdg. 98.00 (*1-58201-561-9*) Classic Bks.

— Jurgen: A Comedy of Justice. 287p. reprint ed. lib. bdg. 25.95 (*0-88411-794-4*) Amereon Ltd.

— Jurgen: A Comedy of Justice. LC 77-74612. (Illus.). 346p. 1977. reprint ed. pap. 7.95 (*0-486-23507-6*) Dover.

— Ladies & Gentlemen: A Parcel of Reconsiderations. LC 68-14897. (Essay Index Reprint Ser.). 1977. 20.95 (*0-8369-0269-6*) Ayer.

— Line of Love. (Collected Works of James Branch Cabell). 368p. 1998. reprint ed. lib. bdg. 98.00 (*1-58201-562-7*) Classic Bks.

— Line of Love, Dizain des Mariages. LC 79-996077. (Select Bibliographies Reprint Ser.). 1977. 26.95 (*0-8369-5106-9*) Ayer.

— The Nightmare Has Triplets: Smirt, Smith & Smire. LC 70-156179. 311p. 1972. reprint ed. lib. bdg. 52.50 (*0-8371-6122-3*, CANT, Greenwood Pr) Greenwood.

— Preface to the Past. (American Biography Ser.). 309p. 1991. reprint ed. lib. bdg. 79.00 (*0-7812-8056-7*) Rprt Serv.

— Quiet, Please. LC 52-7061. (Illus.). 143p. reprint ed. pap. 44.40 (*0-8357-4634-8*, 203756300008) Bks Demand.

— Rivet in Grandfather's Neck. (Collected Works of James Branch Cabell). 368p. 1998. reprint ed. lib. bdg. 98.00 (*1-58201-563-5*) Classic Bks.

Cabell, James-Branch. A Roundtable in Poictesme. 1973. 250.00 (*0-87968-234-5*) Gordon Pr.

Cabell, James Branch. Soul of Melicent. (Collected Works of James Branch Cabell). 216p. 1998. reprint ed. lib. bdg. 88.00 (*1-58201-564-3*) Classic Bks.

***Cabell, James Branch.** Straws & Prayer Books. (Collected Works of James Branch Cabell). 1999. reprint ed. 98.00 (*1-58201-565-1*) Classic Bks.

Cabello, Andrea, ed. see Moore, Burton M.

Cabello-Argandona, Roberto, ed. Bilindex: Supplement I, 1985-86. 334p. 1988. pap. text 129.95 (*0-915745-02-X*) Floricanto Pr.

— Bilindex: Supplement II, 1987-1990. 365p. 1990. pap. text 129.95 (*0-915745-22-4*) Floricanto Pr.

Cabello-Castellet, George, et al, eds. Cine-Lit III: Essays on Hispanic Film & Fiction. (SPA., Illus.). 200p. (C). 1998. pap. write for info. (*0-9631927-2-8*) G H Wood.

Cabello, F., et al. Biology of Salmonella. LC 93-4806. (NATO ASI Ser.: Vol. 245). (Illus.). 482p. (C). 1993. text 135.00 (*0-306-44492-5*, Kluwer Plenum) Kluwer Academic.

Cabello, F. C. & Pruzzo, C., eds. Bacteria, Complement & the Phagocytic Cell. (NATO ASI Series H: Vol. 24). 385p. 1988. 171.95 (*0-387-18549-6*) Spr-Verlag.

Cabello, Francisco. Total Physical Response in First Year English. unabridged ed. Asher, James J., ed. (Illus.). 144p. (Orig.). 1998. pap. text 15.95 (*0-940296-33-0*, 221) Sky Oaks Prodns.

Cabello, Francisco, et al. Total Physical Response in First Year French. (Illus.). 156p. (Orig.). 1997. pap. text 15.95 (*1-56018-493-0*) Sky Oaks Prodns.

Cabello, Francisco, tr. see Silvers, Stephen Mark.

Cabello, Francisco L. Total Physical Response in First Year Spanish. 2nd ed. (Illus.). 207p. (Orig.). 1995. pap. text 15.95 (*1-56018-499-X*) Sky Oaks Prodns.

Cabello, Gerardo, tr. see Walsh, Ellen S.

Cabena, Peter. Discovering Data Mining from Concept to Implementation. LC 97-18170. 224p. (C). 1997. pap. text 39.99 (*0-13-743980-6*) P-H.

Cabera, Guillermo. Memories of Che. Fried, Jonathan, tr. 224p. 1987. 14.95 (*0-8184-0385-3*) Carol Pub Group.

Cabestrero, Teofilo. Blood of the Innocent: Victims of the Contras' War in Nicaragua. Barr, Robert R., tr. from SPA. LC 85-13658.Tr. of Nicaragua: Cronica de Una Sangre Inocente la Guerra Sucia De "Los Paladines de la Libertad". 112p. (Orig.). reprint ed. pap. 34.80 (*0-8357-8541-6*, 203485000091) Bks Demand.

— Faith: Conversations with Contemporary Theologians. Walsh, Donald D., tr. LC 80-14131. Orig. Title: Coversationes sobre la fe. 209p. (Orig.). reprint ed. pap. 64.80 (*0-8357-4057-9*, 203674700005) Bks Demand.

— Mystic of Liberation: A Portrait of Pedro Casaldaliga. Walsh, Donald D., tr. from SPA. LC 80-25402. (Illus.). 222p. reprint ed. pap. 68.90 (*0-8357-4065-X*, 203675500005) Bks Demand.

Cabet, Etienne. History & Constitution of the Icarian Community. LC 72-2962. (Communal Societies in America Ser.). reprint ed. 22.50 (*0-404-10726-5*) AMS Pr.

Cabetas, Isis C., jt. auth. see Byrd, Donald R.

Cabeza de Baca, Fabiola. We Fed Them Cactus. 2nd ed. LC 93-11951. (Paso por Aqui Ser.). (Illus.). 186p. 1994. pap. 15.95 (*0-8263-1503-8*) U of NM Pr.

Cabeza de Vaca, Alvar Nunez, see Nunez Cabeza de Vaca, Alvar.

Cabeza de Vaca, Alvar Nunez, see Johnston, Lissa J. & Nunez Cabeza de Vaca, Alvar.

Cabeza, Rita. Lucha Contra Principados Demoniacos.Tr. of Fight Demonic Principalities. (SPA.). 99p. 1995. 3.50 (*1-56063-997-0*, 550170) Editorial Unilit.

***Cabeza, Roberto & Kingstone, Alan, eds.** Handbook of Functional Neuroimaging of Cognition. LC 00-22253. (Illus.). 412p. (C). 2000. 59.95 (*0-262-03280-5*, Bradford Bks) MIT Pr.

Cabezas, Carlos. Retrato de una Epoca. 212p. (Orig.). 1986. pap. 8.00 (*0-917049-07-1*) Saeta.

Cabezas, Juan A., jt. auth. see Ortiz-Aponte, Sally.

Cabezas, Rita. Desenmascarado.Tr. of Unmasked. (SPA.). 172p. (Orig.). 1986. pap. 4.50 (*0-945792-04-2*, 490239) Editorial Unilit.

— Guia de Liberacion, Influencia Demoniaca.Tr. of Liberation Guide, Demonic Influence. (SPA.). 110p. 1990. pap. 4.99 (*1-56063-374-3*, 498581) Editorial Unilit.

Cabezon. Antonio de Cabezon Gestamtausgabe 1969-1975, Pt. 2. Jacobs, Charles, ed. (Gesamtausgaben - Collected Works: Vol. IV). (ENG & GER.). 80p. 1983. lib. bdg. 43.00 (*0-912024-61-5*) Inst Mediaeval Mus.

— Antonio de Cabezon Gestamtausgabe 1969-1975, Pt. 3. Jacobs, Charles, ed. (Gesamtausgaben - Collected Works: Vol. IV). (ENG & GER.). 80p. 1983. lib. bdg. 43.00 (*0-912024-62-3*) Inst Mediaeval Mus.

— Antonio de Cabezon Gestamtausgabe 1969-1975, Pt. 5. Jacobs, Charles, ed. (Gesamtausgaben - Collected Works: Vol. IV). (ENG & GER.). 80p. 1983. lib. bdg. 43.00 (*0-912024-64-X*) Inst Mediaeval Mus.

— Antonio de Cabezon Gestamtausgabe 1969-1975, Pts. 1-5. Jacobs, Charles, ed. (Gesamtausgaben - Collected Works: Vol. IV). (ENG & GER.). 1983. lib. bdg. 43.00 (*0-912024-63-1*) Inst Mediaeval Mus.

Cabezon, Jose I. Buddhism & Language: A Study of Indo-Tibetan Scholasticism. LC 93-23903. (SUNY Series, Toward a Comparative Philosophy of Religions). 299p. (C). 1994. text 64.50 (*0-7914-1899-5*); pap. text 21.95 (*0-7914-1900-2*) State U NY Pr.

— A Dose of Emptiness: An Annotated Translation of the "sTong thun chen mo" of mKhas grub dGe legs dpal bzang. LC 90-45292. (SUNY Series in Buddhist Studies). 590p. (C). 1992. text 29.50 (*0-7914-0729-2*) State U NY Pr.

Cabezon, Jose I., ed. Buddhism, Sexuality & Gender. LC 90-46557. 241p. (C). 1991. pap. text 21.95 (*0-7914-0758-6*) State U NY Pr.

— Buddhism, Sexuality & Gender. LC 90-46557. 241p. (C). 1992. text 64.50 (*0-7914-0757-8*) State U NY Pr.

— Scholasticism: Cross-Cultural & Comparative Perspectives. LC 97-35199. (SUNY Series, Toward a Comparative Philosophy of Religions). 224p. (C). 1998. pap. text 19.95 (*0-7914-3778-7*) State U NY Pr.

— Scholasticism: Cross-Cultural & Comparative Perspectives. LC 97-35199. (SUNY Series, Toward a Comparative Philosophy of Religions). 224p. (C). 1998. text 59.50 (*0-7914-3777-9*) State U NY Pr.

Cabezon, Jose I. & Jackson, Roger R. Tibetan Literature: Studies in Genre. (Studies in Indo-Tibetan Buddhism). 552p. 1995. 45.00 (*1-55939-031-X*); pap. 29.95 (*1-55939-044-1*) Snow Lion Pubns.

Cabezon, Jose Ignacio, ed. & intro. see Dalai Lama XIV.

Cabezon, Rosalia F. Como Leer a Leandro Fernandez de Moratin. 43.50 (*0-685-69531-X*) Scripta.

Cabezut-Ortiz, Delores J. Robert L. Cooper: A Cattle Trader. (Illus.). 50p. 1989. 19.00 (*0-685-26990-6*); text 25.00 (*0-685-26991-4*) D J Cabezut-Ortiz.

CABI Staff. The Oxford System of Decimal Classification for Forestry. (Illus.). 118p. (Orig.). 1954. pap. text 35.00 (*0-85198-372-3*) OUP.

— Tobacco Economics Today. 78p. (Orig.). 1985. pap. text 63.00 (*0-85198-551-3*) C A B Intl.

***Cabib, Dario, et al, eds.** Three-Dimensional & Multidimensional Microscopy: Image Acquisition & Processing VI. 354p. 1999. pap. text 84.00 (*0-8194-3075-7*) SPIE.

Cabibbo, Nicola, ed. Lepton Physics at CERN & Frascati. (Series in 20th Century Physics: Vol. 8). 396p. 1995. text 86.00 (*981-02-2078-2*) World Scientific Pub.

Cabico, Regie & Swift, Todd. Poetry Nation: The North American Anthology of Fusion Poetry. LC 99-191799. 288p. 1999. pap. 17.95 (*1-55065-112-9*) Vehicule Pr.

Cabie, Honor B. Beyond Images: One Hundred Selected Sonnets. vii, 100p. (Orig.). (C). 1992. pap. 8.75 (*971-10-0481-X*, Pub. by New Day Pub) Cellar.

Cabie, Robert. History of the Mass. Johnson, Lawrence J., tr. (Orig.). 1992. pap. text 9.95 (*0-912405-97-X*, Pastoral Press) OR Catholic.

Cabie, Robert, et al. The Church at Prayer Vol. II: The Eucharist. Martimort, Aime G., ed. O'Connell, Matthew, tr. from FRE. Orig. Title: L'Eglise en Priere: L'eucharistie. 287p. 1986. pap. 15.95 (*0-8146-1364-0*) Liturgical Pr.

Cabiedes, E. G., jt. auth. see Cremades, Bernardo M.

Cabilly, Shmuel, ed. Combinatorial Peptide Library Protocols. LC 97-36646. (Methods in Molecular Biology Ser.: Vol. 87). (Illus.). 328p. 1997. 74.50 (*0-89603-392-9*) Humana.

Cabin, William D. & Pyles, James C. Legal Aspects of Home Health Care. LC 87-28974. 1987. write for info. (*0-87189-897-7*) Aspen Pub.

Cabiness, Patsy C. Boyd's Mark. LC 95-70420. 128p. 1995. pap. 10.95 (*1-881576-49-3*) Providence Hse.

Cabinet Office Staff, compiled by. Be Fair: An Equal Opportunities Resource Manual. 224p. (C). 1987. 150.00 (*0-85292-390-2*, Pub. by IPM Hse) St Mut.

***Cabinet Office Staff, ed.** National Intelligence Machinery. 2000. 25.00 (*0-11-430171-9*, Pub. by Statnry Office) Balogh.

C

Cabirac, Daniel & Dobert, Raymond, eds. Biotechnology: Risk Assessment: Bibliography, Jan. 1986-April 1994. 50p. (C). 1998. pap. text 20.00 (*0-7881-4912-1*) DIANE Pub.

Cabirac, Daniel & Warmbrodt, Robert D. Biotechnology & Bioethics: Bibliography January 1979-December 1992. 25p. (Orig.). (C). 1995. pap. text 15.00 (*0-7881-2194-4*) DIANE Pub.

Cabirac, Daniel, jt. auth. see Warmbrodt, Robert D.

Cabirac, Daniel, jt. ed. see Warmbrodt, Robert D.

Cabiroy. MCSE Testing Guide. 800p. 1997. pap. text 74.99 incl. cd-rom (*0-7821-2049-0*) Sybex.

Cabiroy, Frank. CNE Testing Guide: 200: Networking Technologies. 240p. 1996. pap. 19.95 (*1-888426-00-4*) Pisces Press.

— CNE Testing Guide: 508: 3.1x Administration. 240p. (C). 1996. pap. 19.95 (*1-888426-03-9*) Pisces Press.

— CNE Testing Guide: 518: 3.1x Advanced Administration. 200p. (C). 1996. pap. 19.95 (*1-888426-04-7*) Pisces Press.

— CNE Testing Guide: 520: 4.1 Administration. 240p. (C). 1996. pap., student ed. 19.95 (*1-888426-02-0*) Pisces Press.

— CNE Testing Guide: 525: 4.1 Advanced Administration. 200p. (C). 1996. pap. 19.95 (*1-888426-05-5*) Pisces Press.

— CNE Testing Guide: 532: 4.1 Design & Implementation. 200p. (C). 1996. pap. 19.95 (*1-888426-10-1*) Pisces Press.

— CNE Testing Guide: 540: Building Intranets with IntranetWare. 125p. (Orig.). (C). 1997. pap. 19.95 (*1-888426-11-X*) Pisces Press.

— CNE Testing Guide: 605: TCP/IP Transport. 200p. (C). 1996. pap. 19.95 (*1-888426-09-8*) Pisces Press.

— CNE Testing Guide: 801: Service & Support. 240p. (C). 1996. pap., student ed. 19.95 (*1-888426-01-2*) Pisces Press.

— CNE Testing Guide: 802: 3.x Install & Configuration. 200p. (C). 1996. pap. 19.95 (*1-888426-07-1*) Pisces Press.

— CNE Testing Guide: 804: 4.1 Install & Configuration. 200p. (C). 1996. pap. text 19.95 (*1-888426-08-X*) Pisces Press.

— CNE Testing Guide for Intranetware. LC 97-65360. 1056p. 1997. pap. text 69.99 incl. cd-rom (*0-7821-2048-2*) Sybex.

— Novell Certified Internet Professional Testing Guide. 1997. pap. text 69.99 incl. cd-rom (*0-7821-2107-1*) Sybex.

— Romance Recipes for the Soul: An Inspiring Collection of Romantic & Unique Real-Life Dating Stories. LC 98-68274. 224p. 1999. 19.95 (*1-888426-12-8*) Pisces Press.

Cable, Andrew. A Family Affair: The Sean Puffy Combs Story. LC 98-96119. 1998. mass mkt. write for info. (*0-345-42652-5*) Ballantine Pub Grp.

Cable, Carole. Cable on Academe. LC 93-48668. (Illus.). 128p. (C). 1994. pap. 8.95 (*0-292-71170-0*) U of Tex Pr.

Cable, Charles, jt. auth. see Cable, Sherry.

Cable, Christina S. Understanding the Foal: Your Guide to Horse Health Care & Management. Duke, Jacqueline, ed. (Horse Health Care Library). (Illus.). 108p. 1998. pap. text 14.95 (*1-58150-008-4*) Blood-Horse.

Cable, Doris B. & Trident Software Staff. A Programming Language for Today, Compiler: RPG. 544p. (C). 1992. lib. bdg., ring bd. 81.75 incl. disk (*0-697-20998-9*, Irwn McGrw-H) McGrw-H Hghr Educ.

Cable, George W. Bonaventure. (Works of George Washington Cable). 1990. reprint ed. lib. bdg. 79.00 (*0-7812-1138-7*) Rprt Serv.

— Bonaventure: A Prose Pastoral of Acadian Louisiana. 314p. 1972. reprint ed. lib. bdg. 12.00 (*0-8398-0250-1*) Irvington.

— Bonaventure: A Prose Pastoral of Acadian Louisiana. 314p. (C). 1986. reprint ed. pap. text 5.95 (*0-8290-1866-2*) Irvington.

— The Bust Mans Bible. (Works of George Washington Cable). 1990. reprint ed. lib. bdg. 79.00 (*0-685-29294-0*) Rprt Serv.

— Bylow Hill. LC 02-14684. 2002. 13.00 (*0-403-00106-4*) Scholarly.

— Bylow Hill. LC 75-80625. (BCL Ser. I). (Illus.). reprint ed. 29.50 (*0-404-01355-4*) AMS Pr.

— Bylow Hill. (Works of George Washington Cable). 1990. reprint ed. lib. bdg. 79.00 (*0-7812-1144-1*) Rprt Serv.

— The Cavalier. (Works of George Washington Cable). 1990. reprint ed. lib. bdg. 79.00 (*0-7812-1143-3*) Rprt Serv.

— The Collected Works of George W. Cable, 19 vols., Set. Incl. Amateur Garden. 1914. reprint ed. 89.00 Bonaventure. 1974. reprint ed. 10.00 (*0-403-02974-0*); Bylow Hill. 1902. reprint ed. 14.00 (*0-403-02297-5*); Cavalier. reprint ed. 14.00 (*0-403-02956-2*); Creoles of Louisiana. 1984. reprint ed. 69.00 (*0-403-04550-9*); Doctor Sevier. reprint ed. 19.00 Flower of the Chapdelaines. 1971. reprint ed. 69.00 (*0-403-02991-0*); Gideon's Band: A Tale of the Mississippi. 1914. reprint ed. 69.00 (*0-403-02959-7*); Grandissimes. 1974. reprint ed. 79.00 (*0-403-02979-1*); John March, Southerner. 1994. reprint ed. 69.00 (*0-403-04554-1*); Kinkaid's Battery. 1971. reprint ed. 49.00 (*0-403-04555-X*); Lovers of Louisiana. 1971. reprint ed. 69.00 (*0-403-04557-6*); Madame Delphine. 1981. reprint ed. 9.00 (*0-403-02287-8*); Negro Question. 1990. reprint ed. 59.00 (*0-403-04553-3*); Old Creole Days. 1974. reprint ed. 10.00 (*0-403-03056-0*); Posson Jone & Pere Raphael. 1909. reprint ed. 29.00 (*0-403-02950-3*); Silent South. 1985. reprint ed. 49.00 (*0-403-04551-7*); Strange True Stories of Louisiana. 1974. reprint ed. 69.00 (*0-403-02952-X*); Strong Hearts. 1974. reprint ed. 29.00 (*0-403-02990-2*); 995.00 (*0-686-01544-4*) Somerset Pub.

***Cable, George W.** Creoles of Louisiana. 312p. 2000. pap. text 6.99 (*1-56554-752-7*) Pelican.

Cable, George W. The Creoles of Louisiana. (Works of George Cable). 1988. reprint ed. 79.00 (*0-7812-1135-2*) Rprt Serv.

— Doctor Sevier. LC 76-104426. 473p. reprint ed. lib. bdg. 19.50 (*0-8398-0251-X*) Irvington.

— Dr. Sevier. (Works of George Washington Cable). 1990. reprint ed. lib. bdg. 79.00 (*0-7812-1136-0*) Rprt Serv.

— The Flower of the Chapdelaines. (Works of George Cable). 1988. reprint ed. 79.00 (*0-7812-1149-2*) Rprt Serv.

— Gideon's Band: The Works of George Washington Cable. 1990. reprint ed. lib. bdg. 79.00 (*0-7812-1147-6*) Rprt Serv.

— The Grandissimes. 384p. 1988. pap. 14.95 (*0-14-043322-8*, Penguin Classics) Viking Penguin.

— The Grandissimes. LC 88-4876. (Brown Thrasher Bks.). 360p. 1988. reprint ed. pap. 15.95 (*0-8203-1020-4*) U of Ga Pr.

— Grandissimes. (Works of George Washington Cable). 1990. reprint ed. lib. bdg. 79.00 (*0-7812-1133-6*) Rprt Serv.

— The Grandissimes: The Story of Creole Life. 25.95 (*0-88411-796-0*) Amereon Ltd.

— John March: Southerner. 1972. reprint ed. 21.50 (*0-8422-8019-7*) Irvington.

— John March, Southerner. LC 72-83933. (Black Heritage Library Collection). 1977. 38.95 (*0-8369-8529-X*) Ayer.

***Cable, George W.** John March, Southerner. 252p. 2000. pap. 9.95 (*0-594-00885-9*) Eightn Hundrd.

Cable, George W. John March, Southerner: The Works of George Cable. 1988. reprint ed. 79.00 (*0-7812-1141-7*) Rprt Serv.

— Kincaid's Battery. (Works of George Washington Cable). 1990. reprint ed. lib. bdg. 79.00 (*0-7812-1145-X*) Rprt Serv.

— Lovers of Louisiana. (Works of George Cable). 1988. reprint ed. 59.00 (*0-685-48944-2*) Rprt Serv.

— Madame Delphine. LC 04-22066. 1986. 11.50 (*0-403-00039-4*) Scholarly.

— Madame Delphine. (Works of George Cable). 1988. reprint ed. 59.00 (*0-685-48943-4*) Rprt Serv.

— The Negro Question. (Works of George Cable). 1988. reprint ed. 59.00 (*0-685-48942-6*) Rprt Serv.

— Old Creole Days. LC 89-26517. 312p. 1990. reprint ed. pap. 4.95 (*0-88289-780-2*) Pelican.

— Old Creole Days. (Works of George Washington Cable). 1990. reprint ed. lib. bdg. 79.00 (*0-7812-1132-8*) Rprt Serv.

— Old Creole Days, Set, Pts. 1 & 2. LC 79-83932. (Black Heritage Library Collection). 1977. 25.95 (*0-8369-8530-3*) Ayer.

— Posson Jone & Pere Raphael. (Works of George Cable). 1988. reprint ed. 59.00 (*0-685-48941-8*) Rprt Serv.

— The Silent South. (Works of George Cable). 1988. reprint ed. 59.00 (*0-685-48940-X*) Rprt Serv.

— The Silent South: Including the Freedman's Case in Equity, the Convict Lease System & to Which Has Been Added Eight Hitherto Uncollected Essays by Cable on Prison & Asylum Reform & an Essay on Cable by Arlin Turner. LC 69-14915. (Criminology, Law Enforcement, & Social Problems Ser.: No. 57). 1969. 25.00 (*0-87585-057-X*) Patterson Smith.

— Strange True Stories of Louisiana. LC 78-116944. (Short Story Index Reprint Ser.). 1977. 27.95 (*0-8369-3446-6*) Ayer.

— Strong Hearts. LC 76-106254. (Short Story Index Reprint Ser.). 1977. 19.95 (*0-8369-3291-9*) Ayer.

— Strong Hearts. 1972. reprint ed. lib. bdg. 19.00 (*0-8422-8020-0*) Irvington.

— Strong Hearts. (C). 1986. reprint ed. pap. text 8.95 (*0-8290-1865-4*) Irvington.

— Strong Hearts. (Works of George Washington Cable). 1990. reprint ed. lib. bdg. 79.00 (*0-7812-1142-5*) Rprt Serv.

— The Works of George Washington Cable. 1990. reprint ed. lib. bdg. 79.00 (*0-685-74151-6*) Rprt Serv.

Cable, Greg, jt. auth. see Macho, James.

Cable, Gudrun M. Quotidian Two. LC 89-62678. (Illus.). 256p. 1989. write for info. (*0-9624011-0-2*) Rimsky Copy Hse.

Cable, Gudrun M., ed. Quotidian, No. II. (Illus.). 250p. (C). 1989. write for info. (*0-318-65563-2*) Rimsky Copy Hse.

Cable, James. Gunboat Diplomacy 1919-1991: Political Applications of Limited Naval Force. 3rd ed. LC 93-48526. 1994. pap. 20.95 (*0-312-12141-5*) St Martin.

Cable, James, tr. from FRE. The Death of King Arthur. (Classics Ser.). 240p. 1972. pap. 12.95 (*0-14-044255-3*, Penguin Classics) Viking Penguin.

Cable, James C., tr. see Hartmann, Ursula.

Cable, James C., tr. see Nowarra, Heinz J.

Cable, James C., tr. see Spielberger, Walter J.

Cable, John L., jt. auth. see Nanney, J. Louis.

Cable, Jon, ed. Current Issues in Industrial Economics. LC 93-18909. (Current Issues in Economics Ser.). 1993. text 55.00 (*0-312-09664-X*) St Martin.

Cable, Kimberly, ed. see Nityanawda, Mahamandaleshwar Swami.

Cable, Lana. Carnal Rhetoric: Milton's Iconoclasm & the Poetics of Desire. LC 94-38249. 248p. 1995. text 49.95 (*0-8223-1560-2*); pap. text 17.95 (*0-8223-1573-4*) Duke.

Cable, Larry E. Conflict of Myths: The Development of American Counterinsurgency Doctrine & the Vietnam War. LC 86-2420. 320p. (C). 1988. pap. text 18.50 (*0-8147-1409-9*) NYU Pr.

Cable, M. & Parker, J. M., eds. High-Performance Glasses. (Illus.). 304p. 1992. mass mkt. 224.95 (*0-412-02981-2*, A6360, Chap & Hall NY) Chapman & Hall.

Cable, Mary B., jt. auth. see Burt, Mary E.

Cable, Maryjane. Reading to Success: A Complete Adult Literacy Handbook. 2nd rev. ed. 300p. 1998. pap. text, teacher ed. 30.00 (*0-9619050-1-8*) M Cable.

***Cable, S. & Cheek, M.** Plants of Mount Cameroon: A Conservation Checklist. 198p. 1998. pap. 60.00 (*1-900347-57-1*, Pub. by Royal Botnic Grdns) Balogh.

Cable, Sandra. Excel 5.0 for Windows: Easy Reference Guide. (DF - Computer Applications Ser.). 1996. mass mkt. 9.95 (*0-538-71461-1*) S-W Pub.

Cable, Sandra. Lotus for Windows 95: Tutorial & Applications. 1997. pap. 32.75 (*0-538-71712-2*) Sth-Wstrn College.

— Lotus 1-2-3 97 for Windows 95: Tutorial & Applications. 1997. pap., teacher ed. 34.95 (*0-538-71709-2*) Sth-Wstrn College.

Cable, Sandra. Microsoft Excel 5.0 for Windows: Standard Course. (DF - Computer Applications Ser.). (C). 1995. mass mkt. 34.95 (*0-538-64439-7*) S-W Pub.

— Microsoft Excel 97 for Windows. (DF - Computer Applications Ser.). 1997. mass mkt. 33.95 (*0-538-71930-3*) S-W Pub.

Cable, Sandra. Microsoft Excel 97 for Windows: Tutorial & Applications. 1997. pap. 32.75 (*0-538-71932-X*) Thomson Learn.

Cable, Sandra. Paradox 5.0 for Windows: Quick Course. (Quick Course Ser.). 192p. 1995. mass mkt. 15.95 (*0-538-65038-9*) S-W Pub.

— Quattro Pro 6.O for Windows: Easy Reference Guide. (DF - Computer Applications Ser.). 144-160p. 1996. mass mkt. 9.95 (*0-538-71460-3*) S-W Pub.

***Cable, Sandra & Lindsey, William.** Teach Yourself Office 97 Visually. (Teach Yourself (IDG) Ser.). (Illus.). 130p. 1999. pap., wbk. ed. 0.00 (*0-7645-3364-9*) IDG Bks.

— Teach Yourself Windows 95 Visually. (Teach Yourself (IDG) Ser.). (Illus.). 96p. 1999. pap., wbk. ed. 0.00 (*0-7645-3385-1*) IDG Bks.

***Cable, Sandra & Pasewark, William.** Microsoft Access 2000: Complete Tutorial. LC 99-23423. (Tutorial Ser.). 368p. 1999. pap. 40.95 (*0-538-68842-4*) Sth-Wstrn College.

Cable, Sandra, et al. Microsoft Office 2000: Advanced Course. LC 99-23145. (Computer Applications Ser.). 1999. pap. 52.95 (*0-538-68828-9*) S-W Pub.

Cable, Sandra, jt. auth. see Morrison, Connie.

Cable, Sandra, jt. auth. see Pasewark, William.

Cable, Sherry & Cable, Charles. Environmental Problems, Grassroots Solutions: The Politics of Grassroots Environmental Conflict. (New Horizons in Environmental Economics). 157p. (C). 1994. pap. text 18.95 (*0-312-08142-1*) St Martin.

Cable, Ted, jt. auth. see Beck, Larry.

***Cable, Ted T.** Odysseys in West Africa: Commitments in Conservation. (Illus.). 256p. 2000. pap. write for info. (*1-57167-456-X*) Coaches Choice.

Cable, Thomas. A Companion to Baugh & Cable's History of the English Language. 2nd ed. LC 93-14419. 1993. pap. text 29.20 (*0-13-395716-0*) P-H.

— The English Alliterative Tradition. LC 91-9184. (Middle Ages Ser.). 205p. 1991. pap. 63.60 (*0-608-04819-0*, 206546600004) Bks Demand.

— The English Alliterative Tradition. LC 91-9184. (Middle Ages Ser.). 192p. (C). 1991. text 27.95 (*0-8122-3063-9*) U of Pa Pr.

— The Meter & Melody of Beowulf. LC 72-97683. (Studies in Language & Literature: No. 64). 132p. reprint ed. 41.00 (*0-8357-9689-2*, 201493100094) Bks Demand.

Cable, Thomas, jt. auth. see Baugh, Albert C.

Cable, Vincent & Bressand, Albert, eds. Globalization: Rules & Standards for the World Economy. (Chatham House Papers). 160p. Date not set. 44.95 (*1-85567-350-9*); pap. 15.95 (*1-85567-351-7*) Bks Intl VA.

Cable, Vincent & Henderson, David, eds. Trade Blocs: The Future of Economic Regionalism. 208p. (C). 1994. pap. 18.95 (*0-905031-81-4*) Brookings.

Cable, Vincent & Persaud, Bishnodat, eds. Developing with Foreign Investment. Orig. Title: Mobilising Foreign Investment for Development. 352p. 1987. lib. bdg. 55.00 (*0-7099-4825-5*, Pub. by C Helm) Routldge.

Cabot, David. Ireland: The New Naturalist. LC 99-176159. 336p. 1998. pap. 24.95 (*0-00-220080-5*) Collins SF.

***Cabot, David.** Natural History of Ireland. LC 99-176159. 1999. 60.00 (*0-00-220079-1*, Pub. by HarpC) Trafalgar.

Cabot, Harriet R. Handbook of the Bostonian Society. 110p. 1979. 10.00 (*0-317-33893-5*); pap. 3.50 (*0-317-33892-7*) Bostonian Soc.

Cabot, Henry B., jt. auth. see Warner, Sam B.

Cabot, Hugh & Kahl, Joseph A. Human Relations Vol. 2: Concepts & Cases in Concrete Social Science. LC 52-12256. 283p. reprint ed. pap. 87.80 (*0-608-30715-7*, 201774400007) Bks Demand.

Cabot, James E. A Memoir of Ralph Waldo Emerson, 2 vols. LC 78-97164. reprint ed. 75.00 (*0-404-01357-0*) AMS Pr.

Cabot, John G. The George Cabots: Vermont Descendents of George Cabot (1678-1717) of Salem. xiv, 235p. 1997. 30.00 (*0-88082-057-8*) New Eng Hist.

Cabot, John M. Toward Our Common American Destiny. LC 72-90621. (Essay Index Reprint Ser.). 1977. 23.95 (*0-8369-1553-4*) Ayer.

Cabot, Laurie. Celebrate the Earth: A Year of Holidays in the Pagan Tradition. 288p. 1994. pap. 12.95 (*0-385-30920-1*, Delta Trade) Dell.

Cabot, Laurie & Cowan, Tom. Love Magic: The Way to Love Through Rituals, Spells, & Magical Life. 288p. 1992. pap. 12.95 (*0-385-30570-2*, Delta Trade) Dell.

— Power of the Witch: The Earth, the Moon, & the Magical Path to Enlightenment. 320p. 1990. pap. 12.95 (*0-385-30189-8*, Delta Trade) Dell.

Cabot, Laurie & Mills, Jean. The Witch in Every Woman: Reawakening the Magical Nature of the Feminine to Heal, Protect, Create, & Empower. LC 97-3175. 256p. 1997. pap. 12.95 (*0-385-31649-6*) Doubleday.

Cabot, Mary R., ed. Annals of Brattleboro, 1681-1895, 2 vols. (Illus.). 1104p. 1997. reprint ed. lib. bdg. 119.00 (*0-8328-6503-6*) Higginson Bk Co.

***Cabot, Meg.** The Princess Diaries. LC 99-46479. (Illus.). 240p. (J). (gr. 7 up). 2000. 14.95 (*0-380-97848-2*, Avon Bks) Morrow Avon.

— Princess Diaries. LC 99-46479. 224p. (J). (gr. 7 up). 2000. 14.89 (*0-06-029210-5*) Morrow Avon.

Cabot, Natalie H. You Can't Count on Dying. Stein, Leon, ed. LC 79-8662. (Growing Old Ser.). 1980. reprint ed. lib. bdg. 28.95 (*0-405-12779-0*) Ayer.

***Cabot, Patricia.** Improper Proposal. 368p. 1999. pap. 5.99 (*0-312-97190-7*, St Martins Paperbacks) St Martin.

— Lady of Skye. 2001. mass mkt. 6.50 (*0-7434-1027-0*, Sonnet Bks) PB.

— A Little Scandal. 352p. 2000. mass mkt. 5.99 (*0-312-97413-2*, St Martins Paperbacks) St Martin.

Cabot, Patricia. Portrait of My Heart. 352p. 1999. mass mkt. 5.99 (*0-312-96814-0*) St Martin.

— Where Roses Grow Wild. 1998. mass mkt. 5.99 (*0-312-96489-7*) St Martin.

Cabot, Philip. The Sense of Immortality (1924) 50p. 1998. reprint ed. pap. 12.95 (*0-7661-0304-8*) Kessinger Pub.

Cabot, Richard C. Social Service & the Art of Healing. LC 73-84257. (NASW Classics Ser.). 192p. 1973. reprint ed. pap. text 9.95 (*0-87101-062-3*) Natl Assn Soc Wkrs.

— Social Work: Essays on the Meeting-Ground of Doctor & Social Worker. LC 76-180561. (Medicine & Society in America Ser.). 224p. 1972. reprint ed. 18.95 (*0-405-03940-9*) Ayer.

Cabot, Robert. The Joshua Tree. 244p. 1988. pap. 9.95 (*1-55643-039-6*) North Atlantic.

***Cabot, Robert.** That Sweetest Wine: Three Novellas. deluxe ed. LC 99-40262. 264p. 1999. 25.00 (*0-929701-60-7*) McPherson & Co.

***Cabot, Sandra.** The Healthy Liver & Bowel Book. 304p. 2000. pap. text 19.95 (*0-9586137-4-5*) Celestial Arts.

— The Healthy Liver & Bowel Book. (Illus.). 304p. 1999. pap. 19.95 (*0-9673983-0-4*) S C B Int.

Cabot, Sandra. The Liver Cleansing Diet: Love Your Liver & Live Longer. 2nd rev. ed. (Illus.). 192p. (Orig.). 1997. pap. 19.95 (*0-646-27789-8*, Pub. by SCB Intl) Ten Speed Pr.

— Smart Medicine for Menopause. 208p. 1999. mass mkt. 6.95 (*0-89529-897-X*, Avery) Penguin Putnam.

— Smart Medicine for Menopause: Hormone Replacement Therapy & Its Natural Alternatives. (Illus.). 208p. pap. 9.95 (*0-89529-628-4*, Avery) Penguin Putnam.

Cabot, Stephen. Labor Relations Strategic Guidebook: Practical Techniques for Managing Workplace Issues. 1988. pap. 29.95 (*0-88057-868-8*) Exec Ent Pubns.

Cabot, Stephen J. Creating a Pro-Active Workforce Environment: The Employer's Quick Reference to Positive Employee Relations & Remaining Union-Free. 64p. (Orig.). 1990. pap. 15.00 (*0-932823-05-X*) Am Somerset.

Cabot, Susan M. & Rouse, Michael D. Boone County. (Images of America Ser.). (Illus.). 128p. 1998. pap. 16.99 (*0-7524-1262-0*) Arcadia Publng.

Cabot, Tracy. How to Make a Man Fall in Love with You. 256p. 1987. mass mkt. 6.50 (*0-440-14536-8*) Dell.

Cabot, Tracy, jt. auth. see Wanderer, Zev.

Cabott, Jack H. Human Psychology: Index of New Information with Authors, Subjects, Research Categories & References. 160p. 1998. 44.50 (*0-7883-1870-5*); pap. 39.50 (*0-7883-1871-3*) ABBE Pubs Assn.

Cabourdin, G. Lexique de l'Histoire de la France, Ancien Regine. (FRE.). 1998. 79.95 (*0-320-00146-6*) Fr & Eur.

Cabraal, Anil, et al. Best Practices for Photovoltaic Household Electrification Programs: Lessons from Experiences in Selected Countries. LC 96-32250. (Technical Papers: No. 324). 128p. 1996. pap. 22.00 (*0-8213-3728-9*, 13728) World Bank.

***Cabral & Hay.** Math Connections Excel. 220p. 1999. pap. text 13.75 (*0-536-02548-7*) Pearson Custom.

***Cabral, Adalino & Dias, Eduardo Mayone, eds.** Portugueses Na Guerra Do Vietname: Entrevistas. unabridged ed. (Documentos Ser.: Vol. 2). (POR., Illus.). 192p. 2000. boxed set 18.00 (*1-889358-15-0*, 19) Peregrinacao.

Cabral, Amilcar. Return to the Source: Selected Speeches by Amilcar Cabral. Africa Information Service Staff, ed. LC 74-7788. 110p. reprint ed. pap. 34.10 (*0-7837-3918-4*, 204376600010) Bks Demand.

— Revolution in Guinea: Selected Texts. LC 73-124084. 176p. reprint ed. pap. 54.60 (*0-608-15879-8*, 203075800070) Bks Demand.

— Unity & Struggle: Speeches & Writings. Wolfers, Michael, tr. LC 79-2337. 334p. 1979. reprint ed. pap. 103.60 (*0-7837-9602-1*, 206035900005) Bks Demand.

Cabral, Andrea J. Obtaining, Enforcing & Defending 209A Restraining Orders in Massachussetts. LC 97-70632. 570p. 1997. ring bd. 75.00 (*1-57589-067-4*, 97-10.24-BK) Mass CLE.

Cabral, Ceasar N. Instructional Guide to Surfing Quick Tips. LC TXU760-599. (Illus.). 25p. 1998. pap. 9.95 (*0-9665864-0-9*) Pacific Pleasure.

Cabral de Melo Neto, Joao. Selected Poetry, 1937-1990. Kadir, Djelal, ed. Bishop, Elizabeth et al, trs. LC 94-17252. (Wesleyan Poetry Ser.). (POR.). 214p. 1994. text 30.00 (*0-8195-2217-1*, Wesleyan Univ Pr) U Pr of New Eng.

Cabral De Melo Neto, Joao. Selected Poetry, 1937-1990. Kadir, Djelal, ed. Bishop, Elizabeth et al, trs. LC 94-17252. (Wesleyan Poetry Ser.). (ENG & POR.). 214p. 1994. pap. 15.95 (*0-8195-2231-7*, Wesleyan Univ Pr) U Pr of New Eng.

***Cabral, Fabio, photos by.** Anjos Proibidos.Tr. of Forbidden Angels. 72p. 2000. 60.00 (*1-888425-17-2*) Ophelia Edits.

C

Cabral, J. Religiones, Sectas y Herejias.Tr. of Religions, Sects & Heresies. (SPA.). 180p. 1982. pap. 7.99 (*0-8297-1282-8*) Vida Pubs.

Cabral, J. M., et al, eds. Applied Biocatalysis: From Product Request to Idea to Product. LC 93-10598. x, 478p. 1994. text 134.00 (*3-7186-5391-5*) Gordon & Breach.

Cabral, Joaquim M., jt. ed. see Kennedy, J. F.

Cabral, Joaquim S., jt. ed. see Costa, Carlos A.

Cabral, Len. La Cinturita de Anansi. 3rd ed. Ada, Alma F., tr. (Dejame Leer Ser.).Tr. of Anansi's Narrow Waist. (SPA., Illus.). 16p. (J). (ps-2). 1995. bds. 2.95 (*0-673-36294-9*, GoodYrBooks) Addson-Wesley Educ.

Cabral, Len & Manouca, Mia. Len Cabral's Storytelling Book. LC 96-30376. 275p. 1996. pap. 32.95 (*1-55570-253-8*) Neal-Schuman.

Cabral, Louise M. Looking Back & Writing Forward: A Unique Approach to Lifewriting. Orig. Title: Islands of Recall: Write Your Life Story with Guided Imagery. 1998. pap. write for info. (*1-891968-01-7*) Knowop Inc.

***Cabral, Luis M., ed.** A Reader in Industrial Organization. (Readings in Contemporary Economics Ser.). 350p. 1999. 69.95 (*0-631-21616-2*); pap. text 34.95 (*0-631-21617-0*) Blackwell Pubs.

***Cabral, Luis M. B.** Introduction to Industrial Organization. LC 00-38666. (Illus.). 292p. (C). 2000. 45.00 (*0-262-03286-4*) MIT Pr.

Cabral, Mario. Wind of Fir: The Music & Musicians of Goa. LC 96-906060. (Illus.). 373p. (C). 1997. 43.00 (*81-85002-19-3*, Pub. by Promilla) Nataraj Bks.

Cabral, Nola, jt. auth. see Day, Vicki.

Cabral, Olga. The Green Dream. (Illus.). 50p. (Orig.). (C). 1990. pap. 5.00 (*0-936556-21-8*) Contact Two.

— Voice-Over: Collected Poems. 122p. (Orig.). 1993. pap. 9.95 (*0-931122-73-2*) West End.

Cabral, Stephen L. Tradition & Transformation: Portuguese Feasting in New Bedford. LC 88-46205. (Immigrant Communities & Ethnic Minorities in the U. S. & Canada Ser.: No. 47). 1989. 45.00 (*0-404-19457-5*) AMS Pr.

Cabranes, Jose A., jt. auth. see Stith, Kate.

Cabre, Jaume. Libro de Preludios. Sordo Lamadrid, Enrique, tr. (Nueva Austral Ser.: No. 62). (SPA.). 1991. pap. text 24.95 (*84-239-1862-9*) Elliots Bks.

***Cabre, M. Teresa.** Terminology: Theory, Methods & Applications. Sager, Juan C., ed. DeCesaris, Janet Ann, tr. LC 98-44718. (Terminology & Lexicography Research & Practice Ser.: Vol. 1). xii, 248p. 1999. 75.00 (*1-55619-787-X*); pap. 29.95 (*1-55619-788-8*) J Benjamins Pubng Co.

Cabre, Miriam. Cerveri de Girona & His Poetic Traditions, Vol. 169. LC 98-8828. (Spanish, Portuguese, Latin American Studies). (SPA.). 224p. 1998. 60.00 (*1-85566-042-3*) Boydell & Brewer.

Cabre, S. J., ed. Geodynamics of the Eastern Pacific Region, Caribbean & Scotia Arcs. (Geodynamics Ser.: Vol. 9). 170p. 1983. 24.00 (*0-87590-502-1*) Am Geophysical.

Cabre, Xavier, jt. auth. see Roberts, Luis A.

Cabrer, Carlos, et al. La Musica en el Caribe, Vol. 1. (SPA.). 145p. 1990. pap. 5.00 (*0-8477-2505-7*) U of PR Pr.

Cabrera, Blas, ed. see William Little Symposium Staff.

Cabrera, E., et al. Drought Management Planning in Water Supply Systems : Proceedings from the UIMP International Course Held in Valencia, November 1997. LC 98-39843. (Water Science & Technology Library Ser.). 1998. write for info. (*0-7923-5294-7*) Kluwer Academic.

— Hydraulic Machinery & Cavitation: Proceedings of the XVIII IAHR Symposium on the Conference Held in Valencia, Spain, 16th-19th September, 1996, 2 vols. LC 96-27438. (Water Science & Technology Library). 1181p. 1996. lib. bdg. 499.00 (*0-7923-4210-0*) Kluwer Academic.

Cabrera, E., jt. ed. see Blain, W. R.

Cabrera, Enrique & Vela, Antonio F., eds. Improving Efficiency & Reliability in Water Distribution Systems. LC 95-17563. (Water Science & Technology Library: Vol. 14). 1995. text 202.50 (*0-7923-3536-8*) Kluwer Academic.

Cabrera, Frank, jt. ed. see Kristos, Malvin.

Cabrera, Gilberto R. Fundamentos del Comercio Internacional. (SPA.). 408p. 1969. 6.00 (*0-8477-2602-9*) U of PR Pr.

Cabrera-Infante, Guillermo. Ella Cantaba Boleros. 1996. pap. 14.95 (*0-679-76847-5*) Vin Bks.

Cabrera, J. G., ed. Performance & Durability of Bituminous Materials. (Illus.). 336p. (C). 1995. 150.00 (*0-419-19730-3*, E & FN Spon) Routledge.

Cabrera, James C., jt. auth. see Morin, William J.

***Cabrera, Jane.** Cat's Colors. (Picture Puffin Ser.). (Illus.). 32p. (J). (ps-3). 2000. pap. 5.99 (*0-14-056487-X*, PuffinBks) Peng Put Young Read.

— Cat's Colors. (Illus.). (J). 2000. 11.44 (*0-606-18835-5*) Turtleback.

— Dog's Day. LC 99-42662. (Illus.). 32p. (J). (ps-k). 2000. 12.95 (*0-531-30262-8*) Orchard Bks Watts.

Cabrera, Jane. Over in the Meadow. LC 99-22683. 32p. (J). 2000. 16.95 (*0-8234-1490-6*) Holiday.

— Panda Big & Panda Small. LC 98-28833. (Toddlers Storybook Ser.). 24p. (J). 1998. 9.95 (*0-7894-3485-7*) DK Pub Inc.

***Cabrera, Jane.** Rory & the Lion. LC 99-20836. (Dk Toddler Story Book Ser.). (Illus.). 24p. (J). (ps). 1999. 9.95 (*0-7894-4843-2*) DK Pub Inc.

Cabrera, Jose M. Optica Electromegentica Fundamentos. (SPA.). 272p. (C). 1992. pap. text 14.33 (*0-201-60132-X*) Addison-Wesley.

Cabrera, Lydia. Anago Vogabulario Lucmi: El Yoruba Que se Habla en Cuba. 2nd ed. LC 76-112426. (Coleccion del Chichereku). 326p. 1986. reprint ed. pap. 18.00 (*0-89729-395-9*) Ediciones.

— Los Animales en el Folklore y la Magia de Cuba. LC 86-83333. (Coleccion del Chichereku). (SPA.). 213p. (Orig.). 1988. pap. 16.00 (*0-89729-434-3*) Ediciones.

***Cabrera, Lydia.** Arere Mareken: Cuento Negro. (SPA., Illus.). 60p. 1999. 39.00 (*968-6533-92-3*) Ediciones.

Cabrera, Lydia. Consejos, Pensamientos y Notas de Lydia E. Pinban: (Copiados por P. Guayaba para la Benemerita America Villiarbinbin) Castellanos, Isabel, ed. LC 92-74928. (Coleccion del Chichereku). (SPA., Illus.). 95p. (Orig.). 1993. pap. 9.95 (*0-89729-654-0*) Ediciones.

— Cuentos Negros De Cuba. 3rd ed. (Coleccion del Chichereku). (SPA.). 175p. 1993. pap. 16.00 (*0-89729-671-0*) Ediciones.

— Cuentos para Adultos Ninos y Retrasados Mentales. LC 83-80058. (Coleccion del Chichereku). (SPA.). 233p. 1983. reprint ed. pap. 16.00 (*0-89729-763-6*) Ediciones.

— Koeko Iyawo: Aprende Novicia: Pequeno Tratado de Regla Lucumi. LC 80-68718. (Coleccion del Chichereku). (SPA.). 232p. 1980. pap. 19.95 (*0-89729-637-0*) Ediciones.

— La Laguna Sagrada de San Joaquin. 2nd ed. (Coleccion del Chichereku). (SPA., Illus.). 105p. 1993. pap. 19.95 (*0-89729-673-7*) Ediciones.

— La Lengua Sagrada de los Nanigos. LC 86-82213. (Coleccion del Chichereku). (SPA.). 530p. (Orig.). 1988. pap. 30.00 (*0-89729-488-2*) Ediciones.

— La Medicina Popular en Cuba: Medicos de Antano, Curanderos, Santeros y Paleros de Hogano. LC 84-81080. (Coleccion del Chichereku). (SPA.). 272p. 1984. reprint ed. pap. 19.95 (*0-89729-762-8*) Ediciones.

— Otan Iyebiye: Las Piedras Preciosas. (Coleccion del Chichereku). (SPA.). 113p. 1986. pap. 6.95 (*0-89729-397-5*) Ediciones.

— Paginas Sueltas. LC 94-71015. (Coleccion del Chichereku). (SPA., Illus.). 579p. (Orig.). 1994. pap. 29.00 (*0-89729-733-4*) Ediciones.

— La Regla Kimbisa del Santo Cristo del Buen Viaje. 2nd ed. (Coleccion del Chichereku). (SPA.). 85p. 1986. reprint ed. pap. 6.95 (*0-89729-396-7*) Ediciones.

— Reglas de Congo: Palo Monte-Mayombe. LC 79-50627. (Coleccion del Chichereku). (SPA.). 225p. (Orig.). 1986. pap. 18.00 (*0-89729-398-3*) Ediciones.

— Supersticiones y Buenos Consejos. LC 86-83335. (Coleccion del Chichereku). (SPA.). 62p. (Orig.). 1988. pap. 7.95 (*0-89729-433-5*) Ediciones.

— Vocabulario Congo (EL Bantu Que Se Habla en Cuba. 1999. pap. 19.95 (*0-89729-708-3*) Ediciones.

— Yemaya y Ochun: Kariocha, Iyalorichas y Olorichas. LC 79-90203. (Coleccion del Chichereku). (SPA.). 370p. (Orig.). 1996. reprint ed. pap. 25.00 (*0-89729-761-X*) Ediciones.

Cabrera, Marfa. Selecciones de Aliento Cotidiano.Tr. of Meditations for Daily Devotionals. (SPA.). 385p. 1990. pap. 9.99 (*1-56063-101-5*, 498409) Editorial Unilit.

— Sola en el Camino de la Fe. (Serie Actualidades - Actualities Ser.).Tr. of Alone in the Walk of Faith. (SPA.). 30p. 1992. pap. 2.29 (*1-56063-405-7*, 498180) Editorial Unilit.

Cabrera, Martha E. Los Pobladores Prehispanicos de Acapulco: Proyecto Arqueologico Renacimiento. 245p. 1990. pap. 9.00 (*968-6487-44-1*, IN014) UPLAAP.

Cabrera-Meza, Gerardo, jt. auth. see Schneider, Virginia.

Cabrera, Miguel A. La Reflexion de David Hume en Torno a la Religion. 420p. 1996. 14.95 (*0-8477-0198-0*) U of PR Pr.

Cabrera, Natasha J., ed. see National Research Council, Roundtable on Head Star & Institute of Medicine Staff.

Cabrera, Neonetta C., et al. Beginning Tagalog, Set. unabridged ed. Bowen, J. Donald, tr. (Illus.). 526p. 1968. pap. text 295.00 incl. audio (*0-88432-103-7*, AFTG10) Audio-Forum.

Cabrera, R. Escape del Infierno.Tr. of Escape from Hell. 9.99 (*0-7899-0350-4*, 498275) Editorial Unilit.

Cabrera, Roberto & Meyers, Patricia. Classic Tailoring Techniques: A Construction Guide for Men's Wear. (Illus.). 245p. (C). 1983. 46.00 (*0-87005-431-7*) Fairchild.

— Classic Tailoring Techniques: A Construction Guide for Women's Wear. (Illus.). 307p. (C). 1984. 46.00 (*0-87005-435-X*) Fairchild.

Cabrera, Rosa M., jt. auth. see Zaldivar, Gladys.

Cabrera, Ruben, et al, eds. Teotihuacan, 1980-1982: Nuevas Interpretaciones. 400p. 1991. pap. 18.00 (*968-6487-48-4*, IN039) UPLAAP.

Cabrera, Sandra Z. & De Dueck, Elena R. La Alegria de Crear - Guia de Actividades Manuales: The Joy of Creating - Handwork Guide. (SPA., Illus.). 96p. 1991. pap. 8.99 (*0-311-26621-5*) Casa Bautista.

Cabrera, Segundina T. How to Read Musical Notes & Play the Piano, Organ & Electronic Keyboards. (Illus.). 98p. 1995. pap. 14.99 (*0-9651832-0-3*) S T Cabrera.

Cabrera, Vicente. La Noche del Te: El Gaban. LC 84-50238. (SPA.). 61p. 1984. pap. 10.00 (*0-89295-035-8*) Society Sp & Sp-Am.

Cabrera, Vicente & Boyer, Harriet, eds. Critical Views on Vicente Aleixandre's Poetry. LC 79-65008. 185p. reprint ed. pap. 57.40 (*0-608-14806-7*, 202561400045) Bks Demand.

Cabrera, Vicente, jt. auth. see Gonzalez Del Valle, L.

Cabrera, Yvette De Lourdes, see De Lourdes Cabrera, Yvette.

Cabrero C., Maria T. & Lopez C., Carlos. Catalogo de Piezas de Tumbas de Tiro del Canon de Bolanos. (SPA., Illus.). 100p. 1997. pap. 23.00 (*1-877812-70-6*, UN058) UPLAAP.

***Cabrero, Gabriel Ruiz.** The Modern in Spain: Architecture after 1948. (Illus.). 200p. (C). 2000. pap. 29.95 (*0-262-53172-0*) MIT Pr.

Cabrero, Maria T. Civilizacion en el Norte de Mexico: Arqueologia de la Canada del Rio Bolanos (Zacatecas y Jalisco) 360p. 1989. pap. 11.50 (*968-36-1092-7*, UN003) UPLAAP.

— La Muerte en el Occidente del Mexico Prehispanico. 190p. 1995. pap. 23.00 (*968-36-4286-1*, UN41) UPLAAP.

Cabrero, Maria T., ed. Il Coloquio Pedro Bosch-Gimpera. 510p. 1993. pap. 14.00 (*968-36-3128-2*, UN033) UPLAAP.

***Cabri, Louis J., et al, eds.** Analytical Technology in the Mineral Industries. LC 98-68633. (Illus.). 22p. 1999. 86.00 (*0-87339-418-6*, 4186) Minerals Metals.

***Cabri, Walter & Fabio, Romano Di.** From Bench to Market: The Evolution of Chemical Synthesis. (Illus.). 240p. 2000. text 100.00 (*0-19-850384-9*); pap. text 29.95 (*0-19-850383-0*) OUP.

Cabrillo, Francisco. The Economics of the Family & Family Policy. LC 98-18611. 208p. 1999. 80.00 (*1-85898-828-4*) E Elgar.

Cabrillo National Monument Foundation Staff, jt. auth. see Nauman, Jim.

***Cabrini, Massimo.** Psychology of Soccer. (Illus.). 137p. 1999. pap. 12.95 (*1-890946-25-7*) Reedswain.

***Cabrita, Jodao M.** Mozambique: The Tortuous Road to Democracy. LC 00-40457. 2000. write for info. (*0-333-92001-5*) Macmillan.

Cabu, Jean. Le Grand Duduche. (FRE.). 1978. pap. 11.95 (*0-7859-2214-8*, 207037002X) Fr & Eur.

— Le Journal de Catherine. (FRE.). 160p. 1974. pap. 10.95 (*0-7859-1773-X*, 2070365298) Fr & Eur.

Cabutan, Ross R. Sport of Bicycling-Helmet Law, Head & Body Injuries & Accident Prevention: Index & Reference Book of New Information. 173p. 1997. 47.50 (*0-7883-1404-1*); pap. 44.50 (*0-7883-1405-X*) ABBE Pubs Assn.

Caby, Errol. Improving Data Accuracy: The Data Tracking Technique. 2nd rev. ed. Grimes, Fran, ed. (AT&T Quality Library). (Illus.). 78p. (Orig.). 1992. pap. 22.45 (*0-932764-29-0*, 500-489) AT&T Customer Info.

Cacace, Philippe & Lamperti, Gainfranco. Advanced Relational Programming. LC 96-1966. (Mathematics & Its Applications Ser.). 416p. (C). 1996. text 206.00 (*0-7923-4081-7*) Kluwer Academic.

***Cacace, Vincent.** Loitering with Intent: Catholic Evangelization. 176p. 1999. pap. write for info. (*1-883520-18-5*) Jeremiah Pr.

Cacavas, John. The Art of Writing Music. LC 93-2594. 196p. 1993. 25.95 (*0-88284-619-1*, 4163) Alfred Pub.

— The Art of Writing Music. LC 93-2594. 196p. 1993. pap. 39.95 (*0-88284-618-3*, 4161) Alfred Pub.

Cacavas, John. Trios for Clarinets: 22 Distinctive Arrangements of Famous Music. 24p. 1993. pap. 5.95 (*0-7390-0841-2*, 4986) Alfred Pub.

Caccamise, Louise B. Echoes of Yesterday: A History of the DeLand Area Public Library 1912-1995. LC 95-52592. (Illus.). 304p. 1996. lib. bdg. 44.95 (*1-877633-31-3*) Luthers.

Caccamo, Carlo, et al. New Approaches to Old & New Problems in Liquid State Theory: Inhomogeneities & Phase Separation in Simple, Complex, & Quantum Fluids. LC 99-14205. (Nato Science Series, Series C, Mathematical & Physical Sciences). 1999. write for info. (*0-7923-5670-5*) Kluwer Academic.

***Caccamo, De Luca Rita.** Back to Middletown: Three Generations of Sociological Reflections. LC 99-16822. 1999. 45.00 (*0-8047-3493-3*) Stanford U Pr.

Caccamo, Domenico. Eretici Italiani in Moravia, Polonia, Transilvania (1558-1611) LC 72-3474. (Corpus Reformatorum Italicorum & Biblioteca Ser.). (ITA & LAT., Illus.). 286p. 1970. pap. 17.50 (*0-87580-511-6*) N Ill U Pr.

Caccamo, James F. Marriage Notices from the Ohio Observer Series, 1827-1855. LC 95-157023. 208p. 1995. per. 19.95 (*1-55856-189-7*, 191) Closson Pr.

Caccavale, Patricia. Revelations: A Poet in Search of God. 58p. (Orig.). 1995. pap. text 9.95 (*1-884707-12-2*) Lifestyles.

Caccavale, Salvatore. A Basic Guide to RCRA: Understanding Solid & Hazardous Waste Management. LC 98-3696. (Illus.). 78p. 1998. 29.95 (*1-885581-15-7*, 4372) ASSE.

Caccia, F. & D'Alfonso, A., eds. Quetes. (FRE.). 283p. 1982. pap. write for info. (*2-89135-006-5*) Guernica Editions.

Caccia, Fulvio. Aknos: Poisies, 1983-1991. 196p. 1994. pap. 18.00 (*2-89135-033-2*) Guernica Editions.

— Aknos & Other Poems. Sloate, Daniel, tr. from FRE. LC 97-72262. (Essential Poets Ser.: Vol. 76). 64p. 1998. pap. 8.00 (*1-55071-048-6*) Guernica Editions.

— Interview with the Phoenix. Sloate, Daniel, tr. from FRE. LC 97-72100. (Essay Ser.: Vol. 37). 224p. 1999. pap. 18.00 (*1-55071-064-8*) Guernica Editions.

***Caccia, Fulvio.** Selected Poems. Sloate, Daniel, tr. from FRE. (Essential Poets Ser.: No. 99). Orig. Title: Aknos. 128p. 2000. pap. 13.00 (*1-55071-110-5*, Pub. by Guernica Editions) Paul & Co Pubs.

Caccia, Fulvio. Sous le Signe du Phenix. (FRE.). 307p. 1985. pap. write for info. (*2-89135-010-3*) Guernica Editions.

Cacciabue, Peitro C. Modelling & Simulation of Human Behaviour in System Control. LC 97-51768. (Advances in Industrial Control Ser.). (Illus.). xxvi, 358p. 1998. 69.95 (*3-540-76233-7*) Spr-Verlag.

Cacciabue, Pietro C. & Papazoglou, Ioannis A. Probabilistic Safety Assessment & Management '96: ESREL '96--PSAM-III, 3 vols. LC 96-18476. 2352p. 1996. 269.50 (*3-540-76051-2*) Spr-Verlag.

***Cacciandra, Vittorio.** Fire Steels, 1. LC 97-154778. 1999. 85.00 (*88-422-0687-3*) Dist Art Pubs.

***Cacciapaglia, Bruce.** The Vision Managed Care Market. 17p. 1998. spiral bd. 47.00 (*0-929156-50-1*) Atlantic Info Services Inc.

Cacciari, C. & Clementini, G., eds. Confrontation Between Stellar Pulsation & Evolution. (ASP Conference Series Publications: Vol. 11). 597p. 1990. 34.00 (*0-937707-30-9*) Astron Soc Pacific.

Cacciari, Cristina & Tabossi, Patrizia, eds. Idioms: Processing, Structure, & Interpretation. 352p. 1993. text 69.95 (*0-8058-1038-2*) L Erlbaum Assocs.

Cacciari, E. & Prader, A., eds. Pathophysiology of Puberty. LC 80-40928. (Serono Symposia Ser.: No. 36). 1981. text 167.00 (*0-12-154160-6*) Acad Pr.

Cacciari, Massimo. Architecture & Nihilism: On the Philosophy of Modern Architecture. 1995. pap. 20.00 (*0-300-06304-0*) Yale U Pr.

— The Necessary Angel. Vatter, Miguel E., tr. from ITA. LC 93-50119. (SUNY Series, Intersections: Philosophy & Critical Theory). (Illus.). 124p. (C). 1994. text 14.50 (*0-7914-2189-9*) State U NY Pr.

— Posthumous People: Vienna at the Turning Point. Friedman, Rodger, tr. LC 96-14952. (Meridian: Crossing Aesthetics Ser.). 1979. 45.00 (*0-8047-2709-0*) Stanford U Pr.

— Posthumous People: Vienna at the Turning Point. Friedman, Rodger, tr. LC 96-14952. (Meridian: Crossing Aesthetics Ser.). 1997. pap. 16.95 (*0-8047-2710-4*) Stanford U Pr.

Cacciari, Massimo, jt. text see Celant, Germano.

Cacciatore, James D. I Celebrate Life: The Miracle Kid of Fort Collins, Colorado. 21p. (Orig.). pap. 4.95 (*0-9642546-7-0*) J D Cacciatore.

Cacciatore, Joanne. Dear Cheyenne: A Journal into Grief, a Collection of Angels & Miracles, a Celebration of Motherhood. rev. ed. 120p. 1996. reprint ed. 7.95 (*0-9663015-0-1*) Mothers Sympathy.

Caccini, Giulio. Giulio Caccini: Le Nuove Musiche (1602) Hitchcock, H. Wiley, ed. (Recent Researches in Music of the Baroque Era Ser.: Vol. RRB9). (Illus.). 140p. 1970. pap. 45.00 (*0-89579-028-9*) A-R Eds.

— Giulio Caccini: Nuove Musiche e Nuova Maniera Di Scriverle (1614) Hitchcock, H. Wiley, ed. (Recent Researches in Music of the Baroque Era Ser.: Vol. RRB28). (Illus.). xxiv, 97p. 1978. pap. 45.00 (*0-89579-105-6*) A-R Eds.

Cacciola, E., ed. Hemato-Oncology & Hemato-Immunology: Sicilian International Conference, Catania, Italy, 2nd, November 1986. (Journal: Acta Haematologica: Vol. 78, Suppl. 1). (Illus.). iv, 220p. 1988. pap. 68.00 (*3-8055-4727-7*) S Karger.

Cacciola, E., et al, eds. Hemopoietic Growth Factors, Oncogenes & Cytokines in Clinical Hematology: Current Aspects & Future Directions. LC 93-40874. (Illus.). viii, 306p. 1994. 216.75 (*3-8055-5842-2*) S Karger.

Cacciola, Elio, et al, eds. Adhesion Molecules in Hematology. (Journal Ser.: Vol. 97, Nos. 1-2, 1997). (Illus.). 126p. 1996. pap. 101.00 (*3-8055-6393-0*) S Karger.

***Cacek, P. D.** Canyons. 304p. 2000. text 23.95 (*0-312-87383-2*) Tor Bks.

Cacek, P. D. Leavings. LC 97-68713. 270p. 1997. mass mkt. 5.99 (*1-889120-10-3*) StarsEnd Creations.

— Night Prayers: A Vampire Novel. LC 98-70434. 240p. 1998. pap. 15.95 (*1-891946-01-3*) Design Image.

Cacek, P. D., jt. auth. see Hite, Ken.

Cacek, T. Solo Safari. 1994. 30.00 (*1-57157-058-6*) Safari Pr.

Caceres, Ana C. Introduccion a la Orientacion Individual. (UPREX, Pedagogia Ser.: No. 15). 181p. (C). 1978. pap. 1.50 (*0-8477-0015-1*) U of PR Pr.

— La Orientacion en Instituciones Educativas. LC 76-10359. 226p. (Orig.). 1976. pap. 3.50 (*0-8477-2737-8*) U of PR Pr.

Caceres, C. A., et al, eds. Medical Devices Measurements, Quality Assurance, & Standards - STP 800. LC 82-72890. 298p. 1983. text 38.00 (*0-8031-0235-6*, STP800) ASTM.

Caceres, Cesar A., et al, eds. Management & Clinical Engineering. LC 80-69068. (Artech Medical Library). 494p. reprint ed. pap. 153.20 (*0-8357-4187-7*, 203696500006) Bks Demand.

Caceres, Cesar A. & Williams, Jacqueline L., eds. The Management of Technology in Health & Medical Care. LC 80-1117. (Artech Medical Library). (Illus.). 542p. reprint ed. pap. 168.10 (*0-8357-4189-3*, 203696700006) Bks Demand.

Caceres de Fulleda, Carmen A., jt. auth. see De Hernandez, Cecilia.

Caceres Freire, Julian. Diccionario de Regionalismos de la Provincia de la Rioja. (SPA.). 75.00 (*0-7859-0705-X*, S33066) Fr & Eur.

Caceres, Javier N. Concordancias Lexicograficas de la Obra Poetica de Don Luis de Gongora. xxv, 489p. 1994. 35.00 (*1-56954-010-1*) Hispanic Seminary.

Caceres, Jose A. Sociologia y Educacion. 5th ed. LC 76-10842. 478p. 1989. pap. 12.95 (*0-8477-2736-X*) U of PR Pr.

Caceres, Milagros Rodriguez, see Pedraza Jimenez, Felipe B. & Rodriguez Caceres, Milagros.

Caceres, Raul S., intro. Del Cuerpo a las Palabras: La Narrativa de Antonio Skarmeta. 200p. 1983. 8.00 (*84-85594-05-3*, 3004) Ediciones Norte.

***Cach, Lisa.** Bewitching the Baron. 368p. 2000. pap. 4.99 (*0-505-52368-X*, Leisure Bks) Dorchester Pub Co.

— The Changeling Bride. 320p. 1999. mass mkt. 4.99 (*0-505-52342-6*, Love Spell) Dorchester Pub Co.

— Of Midnight Born. 368p. 2000. pap. 5.50 (*0-505-52399-X*, Love Spell) Dorchester Pub Co.

Cacha, Charles A. Ergonomics & Safety in Hand Tool Design. LC 98-45441. 128p. 1999. 59.95 (*1-56670-308-5*) Lewis Pubs.

An Asterisk (*) at the beginning of an entry indicates that the title is appearing for the first time.

— Research Design & Statistics for the Safety & Health Professional. 173p. 1997. 59.95 (*0-471-28697-4*, VNR) Wiley.

Cacha, Charles A. Research Design & Statistics for the Safety & Health Professional. LC 96-37475. (Industrial Health & Safety Ser.). (Illus.). 208p. 1997. text 49.95 (*0-442-02041-4*, VNR) Wiley.

Cachan, Manuel. Al Son del Tipley et Guiro . . . LC 86-83336. (Coleccion Caniqui). 59p. (Orig.). 1987. pap. 6.00 (*0-89729-423-8*) Ediciones.

Cache, Bernard. Earth Moves: The Furnishing of Territories. Speaks, Michael, ed. Boyman, Anne, tr. LC 95-17087. (Writing Architecture Ser.). (Illus.). 175p. (C). 1995. pap. text 20.00 (*0-262-53130-5*) MIT Pr.

***Cache, Dee.** Captain Tugalong. (Illus.). 30p. (J). (gr. 2-5). 1999. 12.95 (*0-87033-515-4*) Cornell Maritime.

Cachenmeyer, Charles. Organizational Politica. (Analysis Ser.). 74p. (Orig.). 1979. pap. text 18.00 (*0-938526-00-6*) Inst Analysis.

Cachera, J. P., ed. see European Society for Surgical Research Staff.

Cachey, Theodore, tr. see Pigafetta, Antonio.

Cachey, Theodore J., ed. Dante Now. (William & Katherine Devers Series in Dante Studies: Vol. 1). 1996. 32.95 (*0-268-00879-5*) U of Notre Dame Pr.

Cachey, Theodore J., Jr., ed. Dante Now: Current Trends in Dante Studies. LC 94-39220. (William & Katherine Devers Series in Dante Studies: Vol. 1). (C). 1995. pap. text 21.95 (*0-268-00875-2*) U of Notre Dame Pr.

Cachia, C., et al. Marine Mollusca of the Maltese Islands Pt. 2: Neotaenioglossa. (Illus.). 228p. 1996. pap. 48.00 (*90-73348-48-X*, Pub. by Backhuys Pubs) Balogh.

Cachia, Pierre. Al-Arif: A Dictionary of Grammatical Terms, Arabic-English, English-Arabic. (ARA & ENG.). 200p. 19.95 (*0-86685-119-4*, LDL1194, Pub. by Librairie du Liban) Intl Bk Ctr.

— Popular Narrative Ballads of Modern Egypt. 384p. 1989. text 86.00 (*0-19-826545-X*) OUP.

Cachia, Pierre, tr. see Haqqi, Yaha.

Cachia, Pierre A., jt. auth. see Watt, William M.

Cachia, Pierre A., tr. see Al-Hakim, Tawfiq.

Cachiaras, Dot. Sharing Makes Me Happy. Beegle, Shirley, ed. LC 82-80030. (Happy Day Bks.). (Illus.). 24p. (Orig.). (J). (ps). 1994. reprint ed. pap. 1.99 (*0-7847-0264-0*, 04214) Standard Pub.

Cachin, Charles. Watercolors by Paul Signac. Thompson, Lauri, ed. Balzer, Isabel, tr. from FRE. (Illus.). 42p. 1990. pap. text 15.00 (*0-942779-06-1*) Greenberg Van Doren.

***Cachin, Charles, et al.** Paul Signac: A Collection of Watercolors & Drawings. LC 99-44943. (Illus.). 128p. 2000. 39.95 (*0-8109-4366-2*, Pub. by Abrams) Time Warner.

Cachin, Francois, et al. Cezanne. Sanborn, Margaret, ed. 1996. 75.00 (*0-614-95665-X*) Abrams.

Cachin, Francoise. Gauguin: The Quest for Paradise. (Discoveries Ser.). (Illus.). 196p. 1992. pap. 12.95 (*0-8109-2800-0*, Pub. by Abrams) Time Warner.

— Manet: The Influence of the Modern. Kaplan, Rachel, tr. (Discoveries Ser.). (Illus.). 176p. 1995. pap. 12.95 (*0-8109-2892-2*, Pub. by Abrams) Time Warner.

Cachin, Francoise, ed. Arts of the 19th Century: 1850 to 1905, Vol. 2. (Illus.). 629p. 1999. 195.00 (*0-8109-1987-7*, Pub. by Abrams) Time Warner.

Cachin, Francoise, intro. Treasures of the Musee d'Orsay. (Tiny Folios Ser.). (Illus.). 320p. 1997. 11.95 (*0-7892-0408-8*) Abbeville Pr.

— Treasures of the Musee d'Orsay. rev. ed. LC 94-39367. (Illus.). 204p. 1995. 24.98 (*0-89660-054-8*, Artabras) Abbeville Pr.

Cachin, Francoise, et al. Cezanne. (Illus.). 600p. 1996. 45.00 (*0-87633-100-2*) Abrams.

— Cezanne. (Illus.). 600p. 1996. 75.00 (*0-8109-4039-6*, Pub. by Abrams) Time Warner.

Cachin, Francoise, ed. see Vaughan, William.

Cacho Blecva, Juan M., ed. see Berceo, Gonzalo D.

Cachola, Jean I. Kamehameha III: Kauikeaouli. LC 96-130368. (Kamehameha Schools Intermediate Reading Program Ser.). (Illus.). 136p. (Orig.). (J). (gr. 3-7). 1995. pap. 7.95 (*0-87336-033-8*) Kamehameha Schools.

CACI Marketing Systems Staff. The Sourcebook of County Demographics. 6th ed. 600p. 1993. 245.00 (*0-918417-04-X*) CACI Mktg Systs.

— The Sourcebook of County Demographics. 7th ed. 500p. 1994. 295.00 (*0-918417-51-1*) CACI Mktg Systs.

— The Sourcebook of Zip Code Demographics. 9th ed. 1750p. 1994. 295.00 (*0-918417-50-3*) CACI Mktg Systs.

— Zip Code Mapbook of Metropolitan Areas. 2nd ed. 360p. 1992. 195.00 (*0-918417-12-0*, 101845) CACI Mktg Systs.

Caci Staff. Sourcebook of County Demographics. 10th ed. 277p. 1997. pap. 395.00 (*0-918417-69-4*, 110577) CACI Mktg Systs.

— Sourcebook of Zip Code Demographics. 12th ed. 596p. 1997. pap. 495.00 (*0-918417-68-6*, 110578) CACI Mktg Systs.

Cacioppo, Carmen L. I Am: A Prophecy of the Christian Identity. 169p. 1998. pap. 7.00 (*0-9664560-0-9*) Alpha Omeg Min.

Cacioppo, John T. & Petty, Richard E., eds. Social Psychophysiology: A Sourcebook. LC 82-15575. (Illus.). 796p. reprint ed. pap. 200.00 (*0-7837-0688-X*, 204102100019) Bks Demand.

Cacioppo, John T. & Tassinary, Louis G., eds. Principles of Psychophysiology: Physical, Social & Inferential Elements. (Illus.). 926p. (C). 1990. pap. text 47.95 (*0-521-34885-4*) Cambridge U Pr.

Cacioppo, John T., jt. auth. see Petty, R. E.

Cacioppo, John T., jt. auth. see Petty, Richard E.

Cacioppo, Paul P. Health Care Fraud & Abuse: A Guide to Federal Sanctions, 2 vols. LC 90-23174. (Health Law Ser.). 1991. ring bd. 210.00 (*0-87632-806-0*) West Group.

Caclette, Walter M., jt. auth. see Levy, S. Jay.

Cacoullos, T. Exercise in Probability. (Problem Books in Mathematics). (Illus.). ix, 248p. 1988. 59.95 (*0-387-96735-4*) Spr-Verlag.

Cacoyannis, Michael, tr. see Euripides.

Cacucci, Pino. Tina Modotti: A Life. LC 98-31175. (Illus.). 240p. 1999. text 24.95 (*0-312-20036-6*) St Martin.

Cacuci, Dan G. Experimental Data, Uncertain Sensitivities & Adjustments. Date not set. 59.95 (*0-8493-9478-3*) CRC Pr.

— Sensitivity & Uncertainty Analysis: A Primer. Date not set. 30.00 (*0-8493-9408-2*) CRC Pr.

***Cacutt, Len.** The Big-Game Fishing Handbook. LC 99-42816. 160p. 2000. pap. 21.95 (*0-8117-2673-8*) Stackpole.

Cacutt, Len. Great Aircraft of the World. 1992. 22.98 (*1-55521-786-9*) Bk Sales Inc.

CAD-CAM Alert Editors. Manager's Guide to CAD-CAM Standards for Integration. Linden, Jonathan, ed. (Illus.). 88p. (Orig.). 1986. 99.00 (*0-932007-07-4*, B48) Mgmt Roundtable.

CAD-CIM Alert Editors, compiled by. Design for Manufacturability: Getting It Right the First Time. (Illus.). 400p. 1988. ring bd. 345.00 (*0-932007-15-5*) Mgmt Roundtable.

CAD Layer Guidelines Task Force Staff, ed. CAD Layer Guidelines: Recommended Designations for Architecture, Engineering, & Facility Management Computer Aided Design. (Illus.). 40p. 1990. pap. 20.00 (*1-55835-058-6*) AIA Press.

CAD Report Staff, jt. auth. see Wysack, Roy L.

Cadalso, Jose. Cartas Marruecas. Caso, Jose M., ed. (Nueva Austral Ser.: No. 94). (SPA.). 1991. pap. text 24.95 (*84-239-1894-7*) Elliots Bks.

Cadalso, Jose De, see De Cadalso, Jose.

Cadart, Nathalie. Dictionnaire de Votre Argent. (FRE.). 1989. 45.00 (*0-614-00411-X*, 2501012496) Fr & Eur.

Cadava, Eduardo. Emerson & the Climates of History. LC 96-3197. 1997. write for info. (*0-8047-2813-5*); pap. 17.95 (*0-8047-2814-3*) Stanford U Pr.

— Words of Light: Theses on the Photography of History. 204p. 1997. pap. text 15.95 (*0-691-00268-1*, Pub. by Princeton U Pr) Cal Prin Full Svc.

— Words of Light: Theses on the Photography of History. LC 96-17708. 224p. 1997. text 29.95 (*0-691-03450-8*, Pub. by Princeton U Pr) Cal Prin Full Svc.

Cadaval, Olivia. Creating a Latino Identity in the Nation's Capital: The Latino Festival. LC 98-41067. (Latino Communities Ser.). (Illus.). 288p. 1998. 68.00 (*0-8153-3221-1*) Garland.

Cadaver, Cliff. A Basic Guide to Body Piercing. (Illus.). 60p. 1996. 13.00 (*0-9700450-0-X*) Cadaver.

Cadavid, Carolina A. Desviacion y Verdad. La Re-Escritura en Arenas y la Avellaneda. LC 98-75143. (SPA.). 269p. 1999. pap. 30.00 (*0-89295-094-3*) Society Sp & Sp-Am.

Cadavid, Gilberto & Ordonez, Hernan. Arqueologia de Salvamento en la Vereda de Tajumbina, Municipio de la Cruz (Narino) (SPA., Illus.). 140p. 1992. pap. 8.50 (*1-877812-14-5*, BR004) UPLAAP.

Cadbury, Adrian. Company Chairman. 2nd ed. 200p. 1995. 26.00 (*0-13-434150-3*) P-H.

Cadbury, Deborah. Altering Eden. LC 99-33066. 304p. 1999. text 23.95 (*0-312-24396-0*) St Martin.

***Cadbury, Deborah.** Altering Eden. 2000. pap. write for info. (*0-312-26707-X*) St Martin.

Cadbury, Edward, Jr. Experiments in Industrial Organization. Chandler, Alfred D., ed. LC 79-7534. (History of Management Thought & Practice Ser.). 1980. reprint ed. lib. bdg. 31.95 (*0-405-12316-7*) Ayer.

Cadbury, Henry J. Behind the Gospels. LC 68-8591. (Orig.). 1968. pap. 4.00 (*0-87574-160-6*) Pendle Hill.

— The Character of a Quaker. LC 59-10262. (C). 1959. pap. 4.00 (*0-87574-103-7*) Pendle Hill.

— Eclipse of the Historical Jesus. LC 64-12998. (Orig.). 1964. 4.00 (*0-87574-133-9*) Pendle Hill.

— The Making of Luke - Acts. 386p. 1999. pap. 24.95 (*1-56563-453-5*) Hendrickson MA.

— Quaker Relief During the Siege of Boston. (C). 1983. pap. 4.00 (*0-686-43965-1*, 004) Pendle Hill.

***Cadbury, Henry J., ed.** George Fox's 'Book of Miracles' 3rd rev. ed. 176p. (C). 2000. 17.00 (*1-888305-16-9*) Friends Genl Conf.

Cadbury, Matheson S. Women's Work & Wages. 1976. lib. bdg. 59.95 (*0-8490-2836-1*) Gordon Pr.

Cadbury, Warder H. & Marsh, Henry F. Arthur Fitzwilliam Tai: Artist in the Adirondacks. LC 82-40437. (American Art Ser.). (Illus.). 344p. 1986. 95.00 (*0-87413-224-X*) U Delaware Pr.

Cadbury, William & Poague, Leland. Film Criticism: A Counter Theory. LC 82-9896. (Illus.). 338p. 1982. reprint ed. pap. 104.80 (*0-608-00171-6*, 206095300006) Bks Demand.

Cadby, Peter A., tr. see Teisseire, Paul Jose.

***Caddel, Richard.** Underwriter. (Poetry New York Pamphlet Ser.: No. 22). 16p. 1999. pap. 5.00 (*0-923389-35-0*) Meet Eyes Bind.

Caddel, Richard & Quartermain, Peter, eds. Other: British & Irish Poetry since 1970. LC 98-39557. (Wesleyan Poetry Ser.). 312p. 1999. pap. 19.95 (*0-8195-2258-9*, Wesleyan Univ Pr) U Pr of New Eng.

Caddell, Bill, ed. The Woodcuts of Harlan Hubbard: From the Collection of Bill Caddell. LC 94-13331. (Illus.). 192p. 1994. 25.00 (*0-8131-1879-4*) U Pr of Ky.

Caddell, Robert M. & Hosford, William F. Metal Forming: Mechanics & Metallurgy. (Illus.). 352p. (C). 1983. text 66.00 (*0-13-577700-3*) P-H.

Cadden, David. Chrysler Fuel Injection Systems: Diagnosis & Repair. 312p. (Orig.). 1992. student ed. 39.95 (*1-881483-02-9*) HyperGraphics.

— Ford Fuel Injection Systems: Diagnosis & Repair. 416p. (Orig.). 1992. student ed. 39.95 (*1-881483-01-0*) HyperGraphics.

— General Motors Fuel Injection Systems: Diagnosis & Repair. 348p. (Orig.). 1992. student ed. 39.95 (*1-881483-00-2*) HyperGraphics.

Cadden, Joan. The Meanings of Sex Difference in the Middle Ages: Medicine, Science, & Culture. (History of Medicine Ser.). (Illus.). 326p. (C). 1995. pap. text 20.95 (*0-521-48378-6*) Cambridge U Pr.

Cadden, John P. The Historiography of the American Catholic Church, 1785-1943. 1978. 17.95 (*0-405-10812-5*) Ayer.

Cadden, Michael & Jensen, Mary A. Oscar Wilde: A Writer for the Nineties. (Illus.). 76p. 1995. pap. 10.00 (*0-87811-039-9*) Princeton Lib.

***Cadden, Toni.** Good Form: Equestrian Etiquette. (Compass Points for Riders Ser.). 2000. pap. 13.95 (*1-900667-23-1*, Pub. by Compass Equestrian Ltd) Trafalgar.

Caddeo, R. & Tricerri, F. Differential Geometry & Topology. 300p. 1993. text 105.00 (*981-02-1401-4*) World Scientific Pub.

Caddick, Brian, jt. auth. see Brown, Allan.

Caddick, M. X., et al, eds. Microbial Responses to Light & Time. LC 98-172807. (Society for General Microbiology Symposium Ser.: No. 56). (Illus.). 330p. (C). 1998. 115.00 (*0-521-62286-7*) Cambridge U Pr.

Caddies, Kelvin. Kevin Costner: Prince of Hollywood. rev. ed. (Illus.). 160p. 1995. pap. text 14.95 (*0-85965-239-4*, Pub. by Plexus) Publishers Group.

Caddy, Caroline. Editing the Moon. 80p. 1999. pap. 16.95 (*1-86368-246-5*, Pub. by Fremantle Arts) Intl Spec Bk.

— The Working Temple. 94p. 1997. pap. 19.95 (*1-86368-190-6*) Intl Spec Bk.

***Caddy, David.** Smash. (Illus.). 120p. (J). 2000. pap. 10.95 (*1-86368-271-6*, Pub. by Fremantle Arts) Intl Spec Bk.

Caddy, David, jt. auth. see Morgan, David R.

Caddy, Douglas. Exploring America's Future. LC 86-23072. 192p. 1987. 21.50 (*0-89096-271-5*) Tex A&M Univ Pr.

— Legislative Trends in Insurance Regulation. LC 84-40562. 256p. 1986. 19.95 (*0-89096-222-7*) Tex A&M Univ Pr.

— Understanding Texas Insurance. LC 83-40499. 180p. 1984. 16.95 (*0-89096-179-4*) Tex A&M Univ Pr.

Caddy, Douglas & Dethloff, Henry C. Insurance Is Everybody's Business. (Series on Public Issues: No. 15). 26p. 1985. pap. 2.00 (*0-86599-051-4*) PERC.

Caddy, Eileen. The Dawn of Change. 2nd rev. ed. 192p. 1993. pap. 10.95 (*0-905249-87-9*, Pub. by Findhorn Pr) Words Distrib.

— Footprints on the Path. 3rd rev. ed. 192p. 1991. pap. 10.95 (*0-905249-80-1*, Pub. by Findhorn Pr) Words Distrib.

— God Spoke to Me. 144p. 1992. pap. 10.95 (*0-905249-81-X*) Findhorn Pr.

— The Living Word. 2nd ed. 112p. 1991. pap. 6.95 (*0-905249-69-0*, Pub. by Findhorn Pr) Words Distrib.

— Opening Doors Within: 365 Daily Meditations. Platts, David E., ed. (Illus.). 204p. 1987. reprint ed. 17.95 (*0-905249-66-6*, Pub. by Findhorn Pr); reprint ed. pap. 12.95 (*0-905249-68-2*, Pub. by Findhorn Pr) Words Distrib.

— The Spirit of Findhorn. rev. ed. 144p. 1994. pap. 10.95 (*0-905249-97-6*, Pub. by Findhorn Pr) Words Distrib.

— Waves of Spirit: Practical Ways to Face Today's Life Challenges. Buttner, Judi, ed. (Guidebooks for Growth Together). 128p. (Orig.). 1996. pap. 10.95 (*1-899171-75-4*, Pub. by Findhorn Pr) Words Distrib.

Caddy, Eileen & Hollingshead, Lisa. Flight into Freedom: The Autobiography of the Co-Founder of the Findhorn Foundation. (Illus.). 228p. 1993. pap. 14.95 (*1-85230-021-3*, Pub. by Element MA) Penguin Putnam.

Caddy, Eileen & Platts, David E. Bringing More Love into Your Life: The Choice Is Yours. 288p. (Orig.). 1992. pap. text 19.95 (*0-905249-75-5*, Pub. by Findhorn Pr) Words Distrib.

— Choosing to Love: A Practical Guide for Bringing More Love into Your Life. 128p. (Orig.). 1993. pap. 10.95 (*0-905249-90-9*, Pub. by Findhorn Pr) Words Distrib.

Caddy, Glenn, ed. see Keat, Donald B., II.

Caddy, Glenn R., jt. auth. see Byrne, Don G.

Caddy, Glenn R., ed. see Byrne, D. G.

Caddy, Glenn R., ed. see Colligan, Robert C. & Offord, Kenneth P.

Caddy, Glenn R., ed. see Haskell, Robert E. & University of New England Staff.

Caddy, Glenn R., ed. see Latimer, Paul R., et al.

Caddy, Glenn R., ed. see Newman, Frederick L. & Sorenson, James E.

Caddy, Glenn R., ed. see Nirenberg, Ted D. & Maisto, Stephen A.

Caddy, Glenn R., ed. see Spiegel, Allen D. & Hyman, Herbert H.

Caddy, Glenn R., ed. see Surwillo, Walter W.

Caddy, Glenn R., ed. see Tryon, Georgiana S.

Caddy, Glenn R., ed. see Vincent, Ken R.

Caddy, Glenn R., ed. see Vincent, Ken R., et al.

Caddy, Joanne, jt. ed. see Vari, Anna.

Caddy, John. The Color of Mesabi Bones: Poems & Prose Poems. LC 89-36393. (Illus.). 136p. 1989. pap. 8.95 (*0-915943-40-9*) Milkweed Ed.

— Eating the Sting: Poems. LC 86-62393. (Illus.). 112p. (Orig.). 1986. pap. 7.50 (*0-915943-19-0*) Milkweed Ed.

Caddy, John, ed. A Box of Night Mirrors. (Illus.). 120p. (Orig.). (J). 1980. pap. 5.00 (*0-927663-11-2*) COMPAS.

— Three Magics. (Illus.). 176p. (Orig.). 1987. pap. 7.50 (*0-927663-03-1*) COMPAS.

Caddy, John, jt. ed. see Altman, Amry.

Caddy, John F., ed. Marine Invertebrate Fisheries: Their Assessment & Management. LC 87-32436. 768p. 1989. 190.00 (*0-471-83237-5*) Wiley.

Caddy, Joyce. The Complete English Cocker Spaniel. (Book of the Breed). (Illus.). 160p. 1996. 24.95 (*1-86054-060-0*, Pub. by Ringpr Bks) Seven Hills Bk.

Caddy, Peter. In Perfect Timing: Memoirs of a Man for the New Millennium. 2nd ed. Slocombe, Jeremy & Caddy, Renata, eds. LC 96-204208. (Illus.). 464p. 1998. reprint ed. 28.00 (*1-899171-26-6*, Pub. by Findhorn Pr); reprint ed. pap. 15.95 (*1-899171-31-2*, Pub. by Findhorn Pr) Words Distrib.

Caddy, Renata, ed. see Caddy, Peter.

Cade, Alan, et al. An Aid to the Pediatric MRCP. 1995. pap. text 24.00 (*0-443-05246-8*, W B Saunders Co) Harcrt Hlth Sci Grp.

Cade, Blane. Twisted Justice. Martin, Doug, ed. (Greyhorse Ser.: Vol. 1). 128p. 1998. pap. 2.99 (*0-9658418-0-4*, G-1) CTN-WILDCO.

Cade, Brian & O'Hanlon, William H. A Brief Guide to Brief Therapy. 280p. (C). 1993. 25.00 (*0-393-70143-3*) Norton.

Cade, C. Maxwell. Awakened Mind: Biofeedback & the Development of Higher States of Awareness. 1993. pap. 14.95 (*1-85230-004-3*, Pub. by Element MA) Penguin Putnam.

Cade, Cathy. A Lesbian Photo Album: The Lives of Seven Lesbian Feminists. LC 87-50503. (Illus.). 144p. (Orig.). 1987. pap. 14.95 (*0-9618453-2-5*) Waterwomen Bks.

***Cade, Eddie.** Managing Banking Risks. 237p. 1999. 65.00 (*1-888998-63-6*) Glenlake Pub.

Cade, Eddie. Managing Banking Risks. (Gresham Bks.). 256p. 1997. boxed set 155.00 (*1-85573-206-8*, Pub. by Woodhead Pubng) Am Educ Systs.

Cade, Eddie. Managing Banking Risks: Reducing Uncertainty to Improve Bank Performance. LC 00-551058. (Illus.). 237p. 1999. 65.00 (*0-8144-0506-1*) AMACOM.

***Cade, Eddie.** Managing Banking Risks: Reducing Uncertainty to Improve Bank Performance. 250p. 1999. 65.00 (*1-57958-098-X*) Fitzroy Dearborn.

Cade, J. F. Uncommon Problems in Intensive Care. (Illus.). 600p. 1998. write for info. (*0-443-05104-6*) Church.

Cade, Jared. Agatha Christie & the Eleven Missing Days. LC 99-211620. 1999. 39.95 (*0-7206-1055-9*) P Owen Ltd.

***Cade, Jared.** Agatha Christie & the Eleven Missing Days. 2000. pap. 27.95 (*0-7206-1112-1*, Pub. by P Owen Ltd) Dufour.

Cade, Steven. Barrington's Women. large type ed. 352p. 1984. 27.99 (*0-7089-8210-7*, Charnwood) Ulverscroft.

— Slade's Marauder. large type ed. 352p. 1983. 11.50 (*0-7089-8150-X*) Ulverscroft.

Cade, W. Eurvin. The White Right of Heritage, an Affirmative Action Program for White Americans. v, 64p. 1998. pap. 16.00 (*0-9662460-0-4*) W E Cade.

Cade, Will. The Gallowsman. 208p. 1998. mass mkt. 4.50 (*0-8439-4452-8*, Leisure Bks) Dorchester Pub Co.

***Cade, Will.** Larimont. 240p. 1999. mass mkt. 4.50 (*0-8439-4618-0*, Leisure Bks) Dorchester Pub Co.

Cadek, J. Creep in Metallic Materials. (Materials Science Monographs: Vol. 48). (Illus.). 372p. 1988. 239.00 (*0-444-98916-1*) Elsevier.

Cadell, Ava. Confessions to a Sexologist: Peeking into the Sexual Secrets of America. Ross, Andrew, ed. 326p. 1999. pap. 19.95 (*0-9662623-2-8*) Peters Publishing.

— Love Around the House: Helpful Household Tips You Won't Find in Any Martha Stewart Book. Ross, Andrew S., ed. (Illus.). 160p. 1998. pap. 12.95 (*0-9662623-0-1*, 40001) Peters Publishing.

— The Stock Market Orgasm. Ross, Andrew, ed. (Illus.). 169p. 1999. pap. 14.95 (*0-9662623-1-X*) Peters Publishing.

— Twelve Steps to Everlasting Love. Larsen, Donna, ed. (Illus.). 200p. 1999. pap. 14.95 (*0-9662623-3-6*) Peters Publishing.

***Cadell, Elizabeth.** Any Two Can Play. large type ed. LC 99-54770. 2000. 30.00 (*0-7838-8837-6*, G K Hall Lrg Type) Mac Lib Ref.

Cadell, Elizabeth. Around the Rugged Rock. 22.95 (*0-88411-390-6*) Amereon Ltd.

— Be My Guest. large type ed. LC 97-12433. 280p. 1997. 23.95 (*0-7862-1107-5*) Thorndike Pr.

— Canary Yellow. 22.95 (*0-88411-391-4*) Amereon Ltd.

— Canary Yellow. 1990. reprint ed. lib. bdg. 18.95 (*0-89968-488-2*) Buccaneer Bks.

— The Cuckoo in Spring. 214p. 1976. reprint ed. lib. bdg. 22.95 (*0-89244-067-8*, Queens House) Amereon Ltd.

— The Cuckoo in Spring. 1990. reprint ed. lib. bdg. 19.95 (*0-89968-489-0*) Buccaneer Bks.

— Enter Mrs. Belchamber. 22.95 (*0-88411-392-2*) Amereon Ltd.

***Cadell, Elizabeth.** Game in Diamonds. large type ed. LC 99-43737. (Thorndike Romance Ser.). 1999. 25.95 (*0-7862-2238-7*) Thorndike Pr.

Cadell, Elizabeth. Gay Pursuit. 22.95 (*0-88411-393-0*) Amereon Ltd.

— Home for the Wedding. 21.95 (*0-8488-0693-X*) Amereon Ltd.

— I Love a Lass. 22.95 (*0-88411-394-9*) Amereon Ltd.

— The Lark Shall Sing. 21.95 (*0-88411-395-7*) Amereon Ltd.

— Money to Burn. 1976. 21.95 (*0-88411-396-5*, Queens House) Amereon Ltd.

— My Dear Aunt Flora. large type ed. 448p. 1996. 27.99 (*0-7089-3512-5*) Ulverscroft.

— Parson's House. large type ed. LC 98-34389. 280 p. 1999. write for info. (*0-7540-3478-X*) Chivers N Amer.

— Parson's House. large type ed. LC 98-34389. 1999. pap. text 22.95 (*0-7862-1608-5*) Thorndike Pr.

C

*__Cadell, Elizabeth.__ Past Tense of Love. large type ed. 243p. 1999. 27.95 (*0-7838-8593-8*, G K Hall & Co) Mac Lib Ref.

Cadell, Elizabeth. Royal Summons. LC 73-2724. 359p. 1973. write for info. (*0-8161-6092-9*, G K Hall & Co) Mac Lib Ref.

— Royal Summons. LC 99-10055. 1999. 26.95 (*0-7862-1956-4*) Thorndike Pr.

— Shadow on the Water. 21.95 (*0-88411-397-3*) Amereon Ltd.

— Six Impossible Things. 22.95 (*0-88411-398-1*) Amereon Ltd.

— The Toy Sword. large type ed. LC 94-22015. 270p. 1995. pap. 19.95 (*0-7862-0291-2*) Thorndike Pr.

— The Yellow Brick Road. 21.95 (*0-88411-399-X*) Amereon Ltd.

Cadell, H. M. Klondike & Yukon Goldfield in 1913. (Shorey Historical Ser.). 11p. reprint ed. pap. 10.00 (*0-8466-0027-7*, S27) Shoreys Bkstore.

Cadell, James, tr. see Bosi, Roberto.

Cadell, Simon. The Right Vintage: A Wine Lover's Companion. 1996. 24.95 (*0-86051-962-7*, Robson-Parkwest) Parkwest Pubns.

— The Right Vintage: A Wine Lover's Companion. (Illus.). 224p. 1997. pap. 10.95 (*1-86105-069-0*, Robson-Parkwest) Parkwest Pubns.

*__Cadena, Enrique.__ A Quest for Freedom: The Bird in the Cage & the Bird in the Forest. (ENG & SPA., Illus.). 222p. 1999. pap. 14.95 (*1-929342-00-4*) Olde Ridge Bk.

Cadena, Gilbert R., jt. ed. see Stevens, Anthony M.

Cadena, Josep M., jt. text see Gualdoni, Flaminio.

*__Cadena, Marisol de.__ Indigenous Mestizos: The Politics of Race & Culture, Place in Cuzco, 1919-1991. LC 99-37470. (Latin America Otherwise Ser.). 424p. 2000. pap. 21.95 (*0-8223-2420-2*) Duke.

*__Cadena, Marisol de la.__ Indigenous Mestizos: The Politics of Race & Culture in Cuzco, 1919-1991. LC 99-37470. 384p. 2000. text 64.95 (*0-8223-2385-0*) Duke.

Cadena y Almeida, Luis F. A Spanish Mystic in Quito: Sor Mariana de Jesus Torres. Foundation for a Christian Civilization Staff, ed. & tr. by. from SPA. De Zayas, Jose L., tr. from SPA. LC 90-82119. (Illus.). 159p. (Orig.). 1990. pap. 13.95 (*1-877905-18-6*) Am Soc Defense TFP.

C

Cadenas, Enrique & Forman, Henry Jay, eds. Oxidative Stress & Signal Transduction. LC 96-47089. (Illus.). 576p. 1997. write for info. (*0-412-07681-0*) Kluwer Academic.

*__Cadenas, Enrique & Packer, Lester.__ Understanding the Process of Aging: The Roles of Mitochondria, Free Radicals & Antioxidants. LC 98-55663. (Antioxidants in Health & Disease Ser.). (Illus.). 392p. 1999. text 175.00 (*0-8247-1723-6*) Dekker.

Cadenas, Enrique & Packer, Lester, eds. Handbook of Antioxidants. LC 95-47546. (Antioxidants in Health & Disease Ser.: No. 3). (Illus.). 624p. 1996. text 150.00 (*0-8247-9298-X*) Dekker.

Cadenas, Enrique, jt. ed. see Packer, Lester.

Cadenat, J. & Blache, J. Requins de Mediterranee et d'Atlantique (Plus Particulierement de la Cote Occidentale D'Afrique) (Sharks of the Mediterranean & the Atlantic (In Particular Off the West Coast of Africa)) (Faune Tropicale Ser.: Vol. XXI).Tr. of Sharks of the Mediterranean & the Atlantic (In Particular off the West Coast of Africa). (FRE., Illus.). 330p. 1981. pap. 44.00 (*2-7099-0576-0*, Pub. by LInstitut Francais) Balogh.

Cadene, Philippe & Holmstrom, Mark. Decentralized Production in India: Industrial Districts, Flexible Specialization & Employment. LC 98-24647. 1998. write for info. (*0-7619-9258-8*); write for info. (*81-7036-716-6*) Sage.

Cadenhead, Al, Jr. The Minister's Manual for Funerals. LC 87-14616. 208p. 1987. 16.99 (*0-8054-2317-6*, 4223-17) Broadman.

— My First Last Day at School: Daily Devotions for Living in the Real World. 192p. 1995. pap. 15.00 (*1-57312-011-1*) Smyth & Helwys.

Cadenhead, George M. Cadenhead: Family of Cadenhead. 57p. 1997. reprint ed. pap. 12.00 (*0-8328-7813-8*); reprint ed. lib. bdg. 22.00 (*0-8328-7812-X*) Higginson Bk Co.

Cadenhead, Roger, jt. auth. see Omax, Paul.

Cadenhead, Rogers. Sams Teach Yourself to Create a Home Page in 24 Hours. 2nd ed. LC 98-85218. 428p. 1999. 24.99 (*0-672-31346-4*) Sams.

*__Cadenhead, Rogers.__ Teach Yourself ICQ in 24 Hours. (Teach Yourself Today Ser.). 400p. 2000. pap. 19.99 (*0-672-31910-1*) Sams.

Cadenhead, Rogers. Teach Yourself Java 1.1 Programming in 24 Hours. LC 96-72266. 416p. 1997. 24.99 (*1-57521-270-6*) Sams.

— Teach Yourself Java 2 in 24 Hours. 1999. pap. text 19.99 (*0-672-31630-7*) Sams.

Cadenhead, Rogers, jt. auth. see Lemay, Laura.

Cader. That's Funny Mini Edition: A Little Book of Jokes from Today's Hottest Comedians. 1999. 4.95 (*0-8362-7855-0*) Andrews & McMeel.

Cader Books Staff. The Hanukkah Book. 80p. 1999. 4.95 (*0-7407-0214-9*) Andrews & McMeel.

*__Cader Books Staff.__ Happy Book for Birthdays: 501 Happy Thoughts. (Illus.). (J). 2001. pap. 4.95 (*0-7407-1037-0*) Andrews & McMeel.

— Happy Book for Friends: 501 Happy Thoughts. (Illus.). (J). 2001. pap. 4.95 (*0-7407-1038-9*) Andrews & McMeel.

Cader Books Staff. Mug Shots: Arresting Photos & Felonious Facts for Hundreds of Stars Behind Bars. LC 96-83356. 144p. (Orig.). 1996. pap. 7.95 (*0-8362-1503-6*, Cader Books) Andrews & McMeel.

*__Cader Books Staff.__ That's Really Funny: Over 1,000 More Great Jokes from Today's Hottest Comedians. LC 99-55766. 2000. pap. 9.95 (*0-7407-0469-9*) Andrews & McMeel.

Cader Books Staff, prod. People Entertainment Almanac: 1999 Edition. 5th ed. (Illus.). 608p. 1998. pap. 10.95 (*1-883013-48-8*, Pub. by Tme Inc) Natl Bk Netwk.

Cader, Michael. Meditations for Cats Who Do Too Much: Learning to Take Things One Life at a Time. LC 92-38347. (Illus.). 96p. (Orig.). 1993. pap. 5.95 (*0-14-017799-X*, Penguin Bks) Viking Penguin.

*__Cader, Michael.__ The Name Book. 2000. 8.99 (*0-517-16217-2*) Crown Pub Group.

Cader, Michael. That's Funny. 128p. 1996. pap. text 9.95 (*0-8362-1502-8*, Cader Bks) Andrews & McMeel.

Cader, Michael, jt. auth. see Glossbrenner, Alfred.

Cader, Michael, jt. auth. see Karp, Susan.

Cader, Teresa. The Paper Wasp. LC 98-34132. 80p. 1998. 39.95 (*0-8101-5083-2*); pap. 14.95 (*0-8101-5084-0*) Northwestern U Pr.

Cadere, R. French & Rumanian Dictionary of Geology, Mining & Petroleum: Dictionar de Geologie, Mine, Petrol, Francez-Roman. (FRE & RUM.). 1983. write for info. (*0-8288-0362-5*, M15849) Fr & Eur.

Cadet, Guichard. Lonewolf's Cry: Episodes of an Haimeri Poetic Lifetime. 1996. pap. 8.00 (*0-9647635-0-8*) La Caille-Nous.

— The Masks of Flipside: A Novel Collection. LC 97-52641. 1998. pap. 15.00 (*0-9647635-4-0*) La Caille-Nous.

Cadet, Jean-Robert. Restavec: From Haitian Slave Child to Middle-Class American. LC 97-4832. 193p. 1998. 25.00 (*0-292-71202-2*, CADRES); pap. 12.95 (*0-292-71203-0*, CADREP) U of Tex Pr.

Cadet, Nancy, tr. see Thorez, Paul.

*__Cadette, Walter M.__ Financing Long-Term Care. (Public Policy Brief Highlights Ser.: No. 59A). 6p. 2000. pap. write for info. (*0-941276-89-9*) J Levy.

— Financing Long-Term Care: Replacing a Welfare Model with an Insurance Model. (Public Policy Brief Ser.: No. 59). 36p. 2000. pap. write for info. (*0-941276-88-0*) J Levy.

Cadette, Walter M. Prescription for Health Care Policy. (Public Policy Brief Highlights Ser.: Vol. 30A). 8p. 1997. pap. write for info. (*0-941276-25-2*) J Levy.

— Prescription for Health Care Policy: The Case for Retargeting Tax Subsidies to Health Care. (Public Policy Briefs Ser.: Vol. 30). (Illus.). 40p. (Orig.). 1997. pap. text 3.00 (*0-941276-23-6*) J Levy.

— Regulating HMO's. (Public Policy Brief Highlights Ser.: Vol. 47A). 6p. 1998. pap. write for info. (*0-941276-60-0*) J Levy.

— Regulating HMO's: An Ethical Framework for Cost-Effective Medicine. (Public Policy Briefs Ser.: Vol. 47). 44p. 1998. pap. write for info. (*0-941276-59-7*) J Levy.

— Safeguarding Social Security. (Public Policy Brief Highlights Ser.: Vol. 34A). (Illus.). 6p. 1997. pap. text. write for info. (*0-941276-30-9*) J Levy.

— Safeguarding Social Security: The Challenge of Financing the Baby Boom's Retirement. (Public Policy Briefs Ser.: Vol. 34). (Illus.). 48p. 1997. pap. text 3.00 (*0-941276-29-5*) J Levy.

Cadette, Walter M., jt. auth. see Levy, S. Jay.

*__Cadham, Joan Eyolfson.__ Red Right Returning. (Illus.). 160p. 1998. pap. (*1-896754-06-6*) Shloreline.

Cadiau, Paul. Lexiwine - Lexivin: French - English, English - French Wine Dictionary. (ENG & FRE.). 198p. 1987. pap. 29.95 (*0-7859-3656-4*, 2907080008) Fr & Eur.

Cadick, John. Electrical Power Systems Safety Handbook. 384p. 1992. 69.95 (*0-07-009514-0*) McGraw.

*__Cadick, John.__ Electrical Safety Handbook. 2nd ed. (Illus.). 544p. 2000. 69.95 (*0-07-012071-4*) McGraw-Hill Prof.

*__Cadick, John & AVO International Staff.__ Cables & Wiring. 2nd ed. LC 98-40832. 256p. 1998. text 40.95 (*0-7668-0270-1*) Delmar.

Cadick, John & Hageman, Roderic L. Handbook of Electrical Equipment Inspection, Testing, & Maintenance. (Illus.). 864p. 1998. 89.95 (*0-07-009626-0*) McGraw-Hill Prof.

Cadieux, Charles L. Great RV Trips. rev. ed. LC 98-19086. (Illus.). 208p. 1998. pap. 16.95 (*1-55591-327-X*) Fulcrum Pub.

— The New Mexico Guide. 2nd ed. LC 91-58487. (Illus.). 304p. (Orig.). 1995. pap. 15.95 (*1-55591-219-2*) Fulcrum Pub.

Cadieux, Randy E. Bye Bye Dad: My Dad the Marine & Why He Deploys. (Illus.). 28p. (J). (ps-4). 1997. pap. 5.95 (*0-9662412-0-7*) Full Circle Creat.

Cadigan, Pat. Dirty Work. 1993. 29.95 (*0-929480-27-9*) Mark Ziesing.

— Dirty Work. limited ed. 1993. 65.00 (*0-929480-28-7*) Mark Ziesing.

— Home by the Sea. (Illus.). 306p. 1992. 65.00 (*0-9621725-3-7*) Washington Sci Fiction.

— Lost in Space: Promised Land. large type ed. LC 99-15812. 1999. pap. 30.00 (*0-7838-8675-6*) Mac Lib Ref.

*__Cadigan, Pat.__ Patterns. LC 98-32220. 1999. pap. 13.95 (*0-312-86837-5*) St Martin.

Cadigan, Pat. Promised Land. (Lost in Space (Digest) Ser.). 208p. 1999. mass mkt. 5.99 (*0-06-105909-9*) HarpC.

— Resurrecting the Mummy: The Making of the Movie. 1999. pap. 17.95 (*0-09-186830-0*) Random.

— Tea From an Empty Cup. LC 98-19409. 256p. 1998. 22.95 (*0-312-86665-8*, Pub. by Tor Bks) St Martin.

*__Cadigan, Pat.__ Tea From an Empty Cup, Vol. 1. 1999. mass mkt. 6.99 (*0-8125-4197-9*, Pub. by Tor Bks) St Martin.

Cadigan, Robert T., jt. auth. see Soreff, Stephen M.

Cadigan, Sean T. Hope & Deception in Conception Bay: Merchant-Settler Relations in Newfoundland, 1785-1855. (Illus.). 240p. 1995. pap. text 18.95 (*0-8020-7568-1*) U of Toronto Pr.

— Hope & Deception in Conception Bay: Merchant-Settler Relations in Newfoundland, 1785-1855. (Illus.). 242p. 1995. text 45.00 (*0-8020-0469-5*) U of Toronto Pr.

Cadilla De Martinez, Maria. Raices de la Tierra. LC 78-67694. (Folktale Ser.). reprint ed. 37.50 (*0-404-16065-4*) AMS Pr.

Cadillac Area Genealogical Society Staff. Wexford County Michigan Cemeteries - Colfax Township. 76p. (Orig.). 1989. pap. 8.00 (*0-940133-22-9*) Kinseeker Pubns.

Cadillac Area Genealogy Society Staff. Wexford County Michigan Cemeteries - Wexford Township. (Illus.). 390p. 1989. pap. 20.00 (*0-940133-24-5*) Kinseeker Pubns.

Cadiot, Olivier. Art Poetic. Swensen, Cole, tr. (Green Integer Bks.: No. 36). 222p. 1999. pap. text 12.95 (*1-892295-22-9*, Pub. by Green Integer) Consort Bk Sales.

Cadiot, Olivier, jt. auth. see Bernstein, Charles.

Cadiou, Jean-Marie, jt. auth. see Kitching, Ian J.

Cadisch, G. & Giller, K. E., eds. Driven by Nature: Plant Litter Quality & Decomposition. LC 97-158287. (CAB International Publication). 434p. (C). 1997. text 115.00 (*0-85199-145-9*) OUP.

Cadish, J. & Bartholet, E. J. The Manufacture of Precision Parallel Axis Gears. (1984 Fall Technical Meeting Ser.: Vol. 84FTM5). 10p. 1984. pap. text 30.00 (*1-55589-087-3*) AGMA.

Caditz, Judith. Diabetes, Visual Impairment, & Group Support: A Guidebook. LC 89-90678. (Illus.). 77p. 1989. pap. text 12.95 (*0-9622368-1-0*) Ctr Partially.

— Diabetes, Visual Impairment & Group Support: A Guidebook. large type ed. LC 89-90678. (Illus.). 114p. 1989. pap. text 12.95 (*0-9622368-0-2*) Ctr Partially.

— Large Print Recipes for a Healthy Life: Low Cholesterol, Low Fat, Low Sodium, No Added Sugar. large type ed. 283p. 1992. 19.95 (*0-9622368-2-9*) Ctr Partially.

Caditz, Mary H. Wandering & Feasting: A Washington Cookbook. LC 96-13943. (Illus.). 352p. (Orig.). (C). 1996. pap. 22.95 (*0-87422-138-2*) Wash St U Pr.

Cadivec, Edith. Eros: The Meaning of My Life. Gaspari, Hugo, tr. 192p. 1999. mass mkt. 7.95 (*1-56201-128-6*) Blue Moon Bks.

Cadiz, J. Lost in the Wilds of Canada. (Illus.). 96p. pap. 9.95 (*0-7710-1828-2*, 867297Q) McCland & Stewart.

Cadiz, John. The Wilds of Canada. LC 96-141877. (Illus.). 96p. 1995. pap. 12.95 (*0-385-25537-3*) Doubleday.

*__Cadjan, Nancy.__ Administering NDS 8. 1999. pap. 44.99 (*0-07-212208-0*) Osborne-McGraw.

Cadjan, Nancy & Cady, Dorothy L. Network+ Certification: Success Guide for Network Administrators. LC 99-12459. (Illus.). 262p. 1999. pap. 24.99 (*0-07-135018-7*) McGraw.

Cadle, Farris W. Georgia Land Surveying History & Law. LC 90-40785. (Illus.). 688p. 1991. 80.00 (*0-8203-1257-6*) U of Ga Pr.

Cadle, John E. Phylogenetic Relationships among Advanced Snakes: A Molecular Perspective. (Publications in Zoology: Vol. 119). 88p. (Orig.). (C). 1988. pap. 19.95 (*0-520-09956-7*, Pub. by U CA Pr) Cal Prin Full Svc.

Cadle, Terry & Narasimhan, K. S., eds. Advances in Powder Metallurgy & Particulate Materials, 1996, Vol. 6. (Illus.). 5000p. 1996. 840.00 (*1-878954-59-8*) Metal Powder.

Cadman. Dog Beside Me: Recollections of a Shooting Man. 1993. 29.95 (*0-948253-63-0*) Sportsmans Pr.

— Property Development. 1997. 39.95 (*0-419-14850-7*, E & FN Spon) Routledge.

— Summer Visitor. 1992. pap. text. write for info. (*0-17-555979-1*) Addison-Wesley.

*__Cadman, Dana L.__ Beacon & Eggs: A Vactioner's Guide to Inns, Resorts & Hostels in or Near a Lighthouse. (Vacation America Ser.). (Illus.). 52p. 1999. mass mkt. 12.95 (*0-9672993-0-6*, VAL001) Ft To Print.

Cadman, John. COM/DCOM Primer Plus. LC 98-88868. 1998. pap. text 39.99 (*0-672-31492-4*) Sams.

— Hockey: Skills of the Game. (Illus.). 128p. 1994. pap. 19.95 (*1-85223-767-8*, Pub. by Crolwood) Trafalgar.

— Hockey Rules Illustrated. (Illus.). 112p. 1980. 18.00 (*0-7207-1112-6*) Transatl Arts.

Cadman, S. Parkes. The Parables of Jesus. 1999. 6.99 (*0-517-20546-7*) Random Hse Value.

Cadman, Samuel P. Charles Darwin & Other English Thinkers. LC 76-142612. (Essay Index Reprint Ser.). 1977. 20.95 (*0-8369-2040-6*) Ayer.

Cadmium Pigments Subcommittee. Cadmium Pigments: An Encouraging Outlook. 21p. 1983. write for info. (*0-318-61698-X*) Dry Color Mfrs.

Cadmus, Bell S. Cadmus - Cole Genealogy. 165p. 1997. reprint ed. pap. 26.00 (*0-8328-7815-4*); reprint ed. lib. bdg. 36.00 (*0-8328-7814-6*) Higginson Bk Co.

— Davis-Adams Genealogy. 120p. 1997. reprint ed. pap. 19.50 (*0-8328-8226-7*); reprint ed. lib. bdg. 29.50 (*0-8328-8225-9*) Higginson Bk Co.

Cadmus, Paul, et al. Collaboration. (Illus.). 96p. 1992. 45.00 (*0-942642-41-4*) Twelvetrees Pr.

Cadmus, Robert R. Caring for Your Aging Parents. 253p. 1984. 17.95 (*0-13-114786-2*) P-H.

*__Cadnum, Michael.__ Book of the Lion. LC 99-39370. (YA). 2000. 15.99 (*0-670-88386-7*, Viking) Viking Penguin.

Cadnum, Michael. By Evening. 64p. 1992. pap. 12.00 (*0-937669-47-4*) Owl Creek Pr.

— The Cities We Will Never See. 80p. 1993. pap. 8.50 (*1-880286-16-5*) Singular Speech Pr.

— Edge. LC 96-44561. 256p. (J). (gr. 7-12). 1997. 15.99 (*0-670-87335-7*) Viking Penguin.

— Edge. (J). 1999. pap. 4.99 (*0-14-038714-5*) Viking Penguin.

— Ghostwright. 320p. 1993. mass mkt. 5.95 (*0-7867-0048-3*) Carroll & Graf.

— Heat. LC 97-40938. 176p. (J). (gr. 7-12). 1998. 15.99 (*0-670-87886-3*) Viking Penguin.

— The Horses of the Night. 320p. 1993. 19.95 (*0-88184-930-8*) Carroll & Graf.

— In a Dark Wood: A Novel. LC 97-24780. 246p. (YA). (gr. 9 up). 1998. 17.95 (*0-531-30071-4*); lib. bdg. 18.99 (*0-531-33071-0*) Orchard Bks Watts.

*__Cadnum, Michael.__ In a Dark Wood: A Novel. 256p. (J). (gr. 3-6). 1999. pap. 4.99 (*0-14-130638-6*, PuffinBks) Peng Put Young Read.

Cadnum, Michael. Invisible Mirror. (Offset Offshoot Ser.: No. 8). 1987. 5.00 (*0-941240-11-8*) Ommation Pr.

— The Judas Glass. 320p. 1996. 22.95 (*0-7867-0239-7*) Carroll & Graf.

*__Cadnum, Michael.__ Redhanded. LC 99-87652. (Illus.). 160p. (J). (gr. 7 up). 2000. 15.99 (*0-670-88775-7*, Viking Child) Peng Put Young Read.

Cadnum, Michael. Rundown. LC 98-49554. 160p. (YA). (gr. 7-12). 1999. 15.99 (*0-670-88377-8*) Viking Penguin.

— Saint Peter's Wolf. 432p. 1993. mass mkt. 4.99 (*0-8217-4183-7*, Zebra Kensgtn) Kensgtn Pub Corp.

— Skyscape. 368p. 1994. 21.95 (*0-7867-0135-8*) Carroll & Graf.

— Zero at the Bone. LC 95-50145. 202p. (YA). (gr. 7 up). 1996. 15.99 (*0-670-86725-X*, Viking Child) Peng Put Young Read.

— Zero at the Bone. (Illus.). 192p. (YA). (gr. 7 up). 1998. pap. 4.99 (*0-14-038628-9*, PuffinBks) Peng Put Young Read.

— Zero at the Bone. 1998. 10.09 (*0-606-13943-5*, Pub. by Turtleback) Demco.

Cado, Ernsto-Hernado. West African Economic & Monetary Union: Recent Developments & Policy Issues. 170. 1998. write for info. (*1-55775-755-0*) Intl Monetary.

Cadogan. Principles of Free Radical Chemistry. 1989. 9.00 (*0-85186-829-0*) CRC Pr.

Cadogan, Alan. Environment & Ecology. (UK - Science Ser.). 1992. pap. 22.95 (*0-17-448215-9*) S-W Pub.

*__Cadogan Books Staff.__ Britain's Top Tourist Attractions: A Guide to Great Days Out. 1999. text 12.95 (*1-86011-703-1*) Cadgn Bks.

— London's Markets for Collectors: A Guide to Finding Antiques, Bric-a-brac & Collectibles. 64p. 1999. text 12.95 (*1-86011-702-3*) Cadgn Bks.

— The River Thames: A Guide From Hampton Court to the Millennium Dome. 64p. 1999. text 12.95 (*1-86011-701-5*) Cadgn Bks.

— Steam Railways: A Guide to Great Days Out. 64p. 1999. text 12.95 (*1-86011-700-7*) Cadgn Bks.

Cadogan, Gerald. The End of the Early Bronze Age in the Aegean. (Cincinnati Classical Studies: No. 6). (Illus.). xiii, 196p. 1986. 62.00 (*90-04-07309-4*) Brill Academic Pubs.

— Palaces of Minoan Crete. (Illus.). 168p. 1980. pap. 12.95 (*0-416-73160-0*, 2878) Routledge.

Cadogan, Jean, ed. see Guarino, Sergio.

*__Cadogan, Jean K.__ Domenico Ghirlandaio: Artist & Artisan. (Illus.). 384p. 2000. 70.00 (*0-300-08720-9*) Yale U Pr.

Cadogan, Jean K., et al. Wadsworth Atheneum Paintings II: Italy & Spain, Fourteenth Through Nineteenth Centuries. LC 77-82219. (Paintings Ser.). (Illus.). 376p. 1992. 50.00 (*0-918333-09-1*) Hudson Hills.

Cadogan, Mary. Women with Wings: Female Flyers in Fact & Fiction. (Illus.). 280p. 1993. 25.00 (*0-89733-385-3*) Academy Chi Pubs.

Cadogan, Susan, ed. The Community Cooks. (Illus.). 216p. (Orig.). 1990. pap. text. write for info. (*0-9627566-0-1*) Amazon Pubns.

Cadoli, Marco. Tractable Reasoning in Artificial Intelligence. LC 95-23193. (Lecture Notes in Computer Science Ser.: Vol. 941). 1995. 49.00 (*3-540-60058-2*) Spr-Verlag.

Cadora, Frederic J. Bedouin, Village, & Urban Arabic: An Ecolinguistic Study. LC 92-10032. (Studies in Semitic Languages & Linguistics: Vol. 18). xiv, 168p. 1992. 72.00 (*90-04-09627-2*) Brill Academic Pubs.

Cadora, Frederic J., ed. see Straley, Dona S.

Cadora, Karen. Stardust Bound. LC 94-29814. 152p. 1994. pap. 8.95 (*1-56341-052-4*); lib. bdg. 18.95 (*1-56341-053-2*) Firebrand Bks.

Cadorette, Curt, et al, eds. Liberation Theology: An Introductory Reader. LC 92-15666. 1992. 18.00 (*0-88344-801-7*) Orbis Bks.

Cadorni, Elisa. English & Italian Commercial Correspondence. (ENG & ITA.). 292p. 1996. pap. 49.95 (*0-7859-9598-6*) Fr & Eur.

Cadotte, Ernest R. Marketplace Operating Manual Vol. III: A Guide to Marketplace Decisions. 182p. 1997. pap. 18.00 (*1-891622-01-3*) Univ TN Div.

Cadotte, Ernest R. & Bruce, Harry J. Marketplace Vol. II: The Management of Strategy in the Marketplace. (Illus.). 398p. 1997. pap. text 25.00 (*1-891622-00-5*) Univ TN Div.

Cadoux, Cecil John. The Early Christian Attitude Toward War. 1974. 250.00 (*0-87968-198-5*) Gordon Pr.

— The Historic Mission of Jesus: A Constructive Re-Examination of the Eschatological Teaching in the Synoptic Gospels with an Extensive Bibliography. 1977. lib. bdg. 59.95 (*0-8490-1955-9*) Gordon Pr.

Cadoux-Hudson, James & Heywood, Ian, eds. Association for Geographic Information Yearbook 1991. 420p. 1991. pap. 60.00 (*0-7484-0028-1*, Pub. by Tay Francis Ltd) Taylor & Francis.

— Geographic Information, 1992-93: The Yearbook of the AGI. 400p. 1992. pap. 65.00 (*0-7484-0046-X*, Pub. by Tay Francis Ltd) Taylor & Francis.

Cadoux, Remunda. L' Envolee, Vol. 3. (FRE.). 1972. write for info. (*0-02-268660-6*) Macmillan.

An Asterisk (*) at the beginning of an entry indicates that the title is appearing for the first time.

— Invitation Au Francais: Vous et Moi, Vol. 1. (FRE.). 1970. write for info. (*0-02-268500-6*) Macmillan.
— Notre Monde, Level 2. (FRE.). 1971. write for info. (*0-02-268580-4*) Macmillan.
— Vous et Moi: En Avant. (FRE.). 1970. 23.36 (*0-02-268400-X*) Macmillan.
— Vous et Moi: Premier Pas. (FRE.). 1970. write for info. (*0-02-268300-3*) Macmillan.
Cadrain, Linda A., adapted by. Guadalcanal Diary. LC 78-50958. (Contemporary Motivators Ser.). (Illus.). (J). (gr. 4-12). 1978. pap. text 2.25 (*0-88301-303-7*) Pendulum Pr.
***Cadre, Adam.** Ready, Okay! A Novel. LC 99-58863. 400p. 2000. 25.00 (*0-06-019558-4*, HarpCollins) HarperTrade.
***Caduto, Michael.** Remains Unknown Teacher's Guide: Exploring the Circle of Life & Death. 50p. 2000. pap., teacher ed. 9.95 (*1-884592-28-7*, Pub. by Images from the Past) Koen Bk Distributors.
Caduto, Michael J. All One Earth: Songs for the Generations - Songbook. unabridged ed. (Illus.). 32p. 1999. pap. 15.00 (*0-9670141-2-3*, Pub. by LunaBlu) Commn Ground Dist.
***Caduto, Michael J.** Crimson Elf: Italian Tales of Wisdom. (Illus.). 64p. (J). (gr. 3 up). 1999. pap. 12.95 (*1-55591-995-2*) Fulcrum Pub.
Caduto, Michael J. Earth Tales from Around the World. LC 97-7892. (Illus.). 208p. (Orig.). (J). (gr. 3 up). 1997. pap. 17.95 (*1-55591-968-5*) Fulcrum Pub.
Caduto, Michael J. Keepers of the Night: Native American Stories & Nocturnal Activities for Children. LC 94-2602. 1994. 20.05 (*0-606-06511-3*, Pub. by Turtleback) Demco.
— Long River Waltzes. 20p. 2000. pap. 15.00 (*0-9670141-3-1*) LunaBlu.
Caduto, Michael J. Pond & Brook: A Guide to Nature in Freshwater Environments. LC 89-38056. (Illus.). 288p. 1990. reprint ed. pap. 19.95 (*0-87451-509-2*) U Pr of New Eng.
— Remains Unknown: The Final Journey of a Human Spirit. LC 99-43621. (Illus.). 96p. 1999. 15.00 (*1-884592-24-4*) Images from the Past.
Caduto, Michael J. & Bruchac, Joseph. Keepers of Life: Discovering Plants Through Native American Stories & Earth Activities for Children. LC 97-22409. (Illus.). 288p. (J). (gr. 1-12). 1997. reprint ed. pap. 19.95 (*1-55591-387-3*) Fulcrum Pub.
— Keepers of Life Teacher's Guide. 66p. 1994. pap., teacher ed. 9.95 (*1-55591-187-0*) Fulcrum Pub.
— Keepers of the Animals: Native American Stories & Wildlife Activities for Children. LC 97-22401. (Illus.). 286p. (J). (gr. 1-7). 1997. reprint ed. pap. 19.95 (*1-55591-386-5*) Fulcrum Pub.
— Keepers of the Animals: Teacher's Guide. LC 91-71364. (Illus.). 66p. 1991. pap., teacher ed. 9.95 (*1-55591-107-2*) Fulcrum Pub.
— Keepers of the Earth: Native American Stories, & Environmental Activities for Children. LC 97-22411. (Illus.). 234p. (J). (gr. 1-6). 1997. reprint ed. pap. 19.95 (*1-55591-385-7*) Fulcrum Pub.
— Keepers of the Earth Teacher's Guide. 52p. 1988. pap. 9.95 (*1-55591-040-8*) Fulcrum Pub.
— Keepers of the Night: Native American Stories & Nocturnal Activities for Children. LC 94-2602. (Illus.). 160p. 1994. pap. 15.95 (*1-55591-177-3*) Fulcrum Pub.
— Native American Gardening: Stories, Projects & Recipes for Families. (Keepers of the Earth Ser.). (Illus.). 176p. (Orig.). 1996. pap. 15.95 (*1-55591-148-X*) Fulcrum Pub.
Caduto, Michael J., et al. Native Plant Stories. (Illus.). 140p. 1995. pap. 12.95 (*1-55591-212-5*) Fulcrum Pub.
Cadwalader, George. Castaways: The Penikese Island Experiment. LC 87-17891. 208p. 1988. reprint ed. pap. 64.50 (*0-608-00546-0*, 206142500008) Bks Demand.
Cadwallader, Allen, ed. Trends in Schenkerian Research. 168p. 1990. text 45.00 (*0-02-870551-3*, Schirmer Books) Mac Lib Ref.
Cadwallader, Allen & Gagne, David. Analysis of Tonal Music: A Schenkerian Approach. LC 97-5752. (Illus.). 432p. (C). 1998. text 47.95 (*0-19-510232-0*) OUP.
Cadwallader, Carole & Sutton, Anna. Lebanon. (Travellers Survival Kit Ser.). 256p. 1999. pap. 18.95 (*1-85458-217-8*, Pub. by Vac Wrk Pubns) Seven Hills Bk.
Cadwallader, Donald E. Biopharmaceutics & Drug Interactions. 3rd ed. LC 83-3278. (Illus.). 161p. 1983. reprint ed. pap. 50.00 (*0-608-07262-1*, 206749000009) Bks Demand.
Cadwallader, Helen A., jt. auth. see Martin, Dorothy R.
Cadwallader, Keith R., jt. ed. see Shahidi, Fereidoon.
Cadwallader, Martin. Migration & Residential Mobility: Macro & Micro Approaches. LC 92-50246. (Illus.). 292p. (Orig.). (C). 1993. pap. text 19.95 (*0-299-13494-6*); lib. bdg. 45.00 (*0-299-13490-3*) U of Wis Pr.
Cadwallader, Martin. Urban Geography: An Analytical Approach. LC 95-4904. 406p. (C). 1995. 56.00 (*0-13-341637-2*) P-H.
Cadwallader, Sharon. Cookie McCorkle & the Case of the Crooked Key. 112p. (Orig.). (J). 1993. pap. 3.50 (*0-380-76896-8*, Avon Bks) Morrow Avon.
— Cookie McCorkle & the Case of the Emerald Earrings. 128p. (Orig.). (J). (gr. 3-4). 1991. pap. 2.95 (*0-380-76098-3*, Avon Bks) Morrow Avon.
— Cookie McCorkle & the Case of the King's Ghost. 112p. (Orig.). (J). 1991. pap. 2.99 (*0-380-76350-8*, Avon Bks) Morrow Avon.
— Cookie McCorkle & the Case of the Missing Castle. 128p. (J). 1991. pap. 2.99 (*0-380-76348-6*, Avon Bks) Morrow Avon.
— Cookie McCorkle & the Case of the Mystery Map. 128p. (Orig.). (YA). 1993. pap. 3.50 (*0-380-76895-X*, Avon Bks) Morrow Avon.
— Cookie McCorkle & the Case of the Polka-Dot Safecracker. 128p. (Orig.). (J). (gr. 3-4). 1991. pap. 2.95 (*0-380-76099-1*, Avon Bks) Morrow Avon.
— Easy Vegetarian Cooking. LC 99-184711. (Illus.). 176p. 1998. pap. 8.95 (*1-55867-210-9*) Bristol Pub Ent CA.
***Cadwallader, Sharon.** Savoring Mexico: A Cookbook & Travel Guide to the Recipes & Regions of Mexico. LC 99-52408. 1999. pap. 14.95 (*0-9628236-9-4*) Ironwood AZ.
— Sofia's Heart. (American Dreams Ser.). 1996. 9.09 (*0-606-10302-3*, Pub. by Turtleback) Demco.
Cadwallader, Sharon. Sofia's Heart: American Dreams. 192p. (Orig.). (YA). 1996. mass mkt. 3.99 (*0-380-78322-3*, Avon Bks) Morrow Avon.
Cadwallader, Sylvanus. Three Years with Grant: As Recalled by War Correspondent Sylvanus Cadwallader. Thomas, Benjamin P., ed. & intro. by. Simpson, Brooks D., intro. LC 96-30286. xxxi, 362p. 1996. pap. 15.00 (*0-8032-6369-4*, Bison Books) U of Nebr Pr.
Cadway, Richard P. The 12 Inch Baby That Fried an Omlet: And Other Crazy Dreams. 160p. 1996. pap. 7.95 (*0-9644434-1-4*) RPC Intl.
Cadwell, Charles. The Human Touch Performance Appraisal. LC 97-3105. (AMI How-to Ser.). 95p. (Orig.). 1994. pap. 12.95 (*1-884926-23-1*, HUMAN) Amer Media.
— New Employee Orientation: A Practical Guide for Supervisors. Crisp, Michael G., ed. LC 87-73558. (Fifty-Minute Ser.). (Illus.). 76p. 1988. pap. 10.95 (*0-931961-46-7*) Crisp Pubns.
— Training That Works. Sanford, Bonnie, ed. LC 95-75606. (AMI How-to Ser.). 101p. 1995. per. 12.95 (*1-884926-36-3*, OJT) Amer Media.
Cadwell, Charles M. Team up for Success: Building Teams in the Workplace. Miller, Karen M., ed. LC 97-77104. (How-To Book Ser.). 118p. 1997. pap. 12.95 (*1-884926-82-7*, TEAM2) Amer Media.
Cadwell, Donald H., ed. The Wisconsinan Stage of the First Geological District, Eastern New York. (Bulletin Ser.: No. 455). 192p. (Orig.). 1986. pap. 12.00 (*1-55557-001-1*) NYS Museum.
Cadwell, Karin. Diabetic Sweet Treats. LC 97-13977. 160p. 1997. pap. 10.95 (*0-8069-5968-1*) Sterling.
— Great International Diabetic Desserts. LC 99-20752. 160p. 1999. pap. 11.95 (*0-8069-1889-6*) Sterling.
Cadwell, Karin & White, Edith. Great Diabetic Desserts & Sweets. LC 95-20036. (Illus.). 160p. 1995. pap. 10.95 (*0-8069-3845-5*) Sterling.
— The Natural Laxative Cookbook. LC 95-1230. (Illus.). 160p. 1995. pap. 10.95 (*0-8069-1344-4*) Sterling.
Cadwell, Louise B. Bringing Reggio Emilia Home: An Innovative Approach to Early Childhood Education. LC 97-17760. (Early Childhood Education Ser.). 1997. 43.00 (*0-8077-3661-9*); pap. 19.95 (*0-8077-3660-0*) Tchrs Coll.
Cadwell, Michael. Small Buildings. (Pamphlet Architecture Ser.: No. 17). (Illus.). 64p. (Orig.). 1996. pap. 12.95 (*1-56898-055-8*) Princeton Arch.
Cadwell, Stephen A., et al, eds. Therapists on the Front Line: Psychotherapy with Gay Men in the Age of AIDS. LC 93-46269. 608p. 1994. text 24.95 (*0-88048-558-2*, 8558) Am Psychiatric.
Cady. Administering Netware 5. LC 99-39936. 600p. 1999. pap. 44.99 (*0-07-135593-6*) McGraw.
Cady, Annie Cole, see Cole Cady, Annie.
Cady, Barbara. Icons of the Twentieth Century: 200 Men & Women Who Have Made a Difference. Naudet, Jean-Jaques & McGrath, Raymond, eds. LC 98-16615. (Illus.). 418p. 1998. 60.00 (*0-87951-893-6*, Pub. by Overlook Pr) Penguin Putnam.
Cady, Blake, jt. auth. see Bland, Kirby I.
Cady, Blake, jt. ed. see Daly, John M.
Cady, Casey W., jt. ed. see Shu Geng.
Cady, Dale R. Pilot's Bahamas & Caribbean Aviation Guide, 1990. 12th rev. ed. Jones, Tom & Strong, Brian, eds. (Illus.). 500p. 1989. pap. 24.95 (*0-938923-03-X*) Pilot Pubns.
— Pilot's Bahamas & Caribbean Aviation Guide, 1991. 13th rev. ed. Jones, Tom, ed. (Illus.). 500p. 1990. pap. 24.95 (*0-938923-04-8*) Pilot Pubns.
— Pilot's Bahamas Aviation Guide, 1988. 10th rev. ed. Strong, Brian & Pfaff, Donn, eds. (Illus.). 500p. 1987. pap. 19.95 (*0-938923-01-3*) Pilot Pubns.
Cady, Deborah, ed. see Whitney, William.
Cady, Denise A. Good Seats: Seating Diagrams of Thirty-Eight Chicago Area Theatres & Stadiums. rev. ed. (Illus.). 62p. 1993. pap. 8.50 (*0-9606976-2-4*) Clearview Pr Chi.
Cady, Denise A., compiled by. Good Seats: Seating Diagrams of Los Angeles Area Theatres & Stadiums. (Illus.). 62p. 1993. pap. 10.00 (*0-9606976-0-8*) Clearview Pr Chi.
Cady, Dorothy. CNE Netware 5: Accelerated CNE Study Guide. 360p. 1998. pap. text 24.99 (*0-07-134531-0*) McGraw.
— Designing & Implementing Netware 4 Networks. 513p. 1996. pap. text 50.00 (*1-56205-581-X*) New Riders Pub.
Cady, Dorothy, jt. auth. see Nance, Barry.
Cady, Dorothy L. CNA NetWare 5: Accelerated CNA Study Guide. 360p. 1998. pap. text 24.99 (*0-07-134532-9*) McGraw.
— The More Than Complete NetWare Command Reference. 2nd ed. 688p. 1995. 35.00 (*1-56205-451-1*) New Riders Pub.
Cady, Dorothy L., jt. auth. see Cadjan, Nancy.
Cady, Duane & Werner, Rick, eds. Just War, Non-Violence & Nuclear Deterrence. LC 91-27150. 1991. pap. 18.50 (*0-89341-676-2*, Longwood Academic) Hollowbrook.
Cady, Duane, jt. ed. see Warren, Karen J.
Cady, Duane L. From Warism to Pacifism: A Moral Continuum. LC 88-29547. 174p. (C). 1989. 34.95 (*0-87722-603-2*) Temple U Pr.
— From Warism to Pacifism: A Moral Continuum. 174p. 1990. pap. 22.95 (*0-87722-779-9*) Temple U Pr.
Cady, Duane L. & Beanblossom, Ronald E., eds. Natural Reason: Essays in Honor of Joseph Norio Uemura. LC 92-72687. 192p. (Orig.). 1992. text. write for info. (*0-9633686-1-3*); pap. text. write for info. (*0-9633686-0-5*) Hamline Univ.
Cady, Duane L., jt. auth. see Phillips, Robert L.
Cady, Duane L., jt. ed. see Warren, Karen S.
Cady, E. B. Clinical Magnetic Resonance Spectroscopy. (Illus.). 290p. (C). 1990. text 95.00 (*0-306-43449-0*, Kluwer Plenum) Kluwer Academic.
Cady, Edwin, jt. ed. see Budd, Louis J.
Cady, Edwin, ed. see Howells, William Dean.
Cady, Edwin H. The Big Game: College Sports & American Life. LC 78-6794. 266p. reprint ed. pap. 82.50 (*0-7837-3030-6*, 204291000006) Bks Demand.
— The Realist at War: The Mature Years 1885-1920 of William Dean Howells. LC 86-3174. 308p. 1986. reprint ed. lib. bdg. 96.00 (*0-313-25205-X*, CARE, Greenwood Pr) Greenwood.
— The Road to Realism: The Early Years 1837-1885 of William Dean Howells. LC 86-4633. 293p. 1986. reprint ed. lib. bdg. 75.00 (*0-313-25206-8*, CARO, Greenwood Pr) Greenwood.
— Stephen Crane. rev. ed. (United States Authors Ser.). 184p. 1980. 32.00 (*0-8057-7299-5*) Macmillan.
— Young Howells & John Brown: Episodes in a Radical Education. LC 85-5013. 128p. reprint ed. pap. 39.70 (*0-608-09659-8*, 206977400006) Bks Demand.
Cady, Edwin H. & Budd, Louis J., eds. On Dickinson. LC 89-17004. (Best from American Literature Ser.). 240p. (C). 1990. text 49.95 (*0-8223-1014-7*) Duke.
— On Emerson. LC 88-3750. (Best from American Literature Ser.). 296p. 1988. text 49.95 (*0-8223-0861-4*) Duke.
— On Frost: The Best from American Literature. LC 91-7885. 271p. 1991. text 49.95 (*0-8223-1159-3*) Duke.
— On Hawthorne. LC 89-25696. (Best from American Literature Ser.). 282p. (C). 1990. text 49.95 (*0-8223-1032-5*) Duke.
— On Howells. LC 92-23839. (Best from American Literature Ser.). 288p. 1993. text 49.95 (*0-8223-1300-6*) Duke.
— On Mark Twain: The Best from American Literature. LC 87-9020. x, 303p. 1987. text 49.95 (*0-8223-0759-6*) Duke.
Cady, Edwin H. & Cady, Norma W. Critical Essays on W. D. Howells, 1866-1920 LC 83-6089. (Critical Essays on American Literature Ser.). xxxii, 267 p. 1983. write for info. (*0-8161-8651-0*, G K Hall & Co) Mac Lib Ref.
Cady, Edwin H., jt. ed. see Budd, Louis J.
Cady, Edwin H., ed. see Howells, William Dean.
Cady, Foster, jt. ed. see Adams, Norma.
Cady, Frank. Poems on a White Page. (Flowering Quince Poetry Ser.: No. 4). (Illus.). 24p. (Orig.). 1982. pap. 7.50 (*0-940592-13-4*) Heyeck Pr.
Cady, Frederick M. Instructor's Manual for Software & Hardware Engineering: Motorola M68HC11. 56p. 1998. pap. text. write for info. (*0-19-511718-2*) OUP.
— Microcontrollers & Microcomputers: Principles of Software & Hardware Engineering. LC 96-234 0. (Illus.). 272p. (C). 1997. text 49.95 (*0-19-511008-0*) OUP.
— Software & Hardware Engineering: The Motorola M68HC11. LC 96-23409. (Illus.). 336p. (C). 1997. pap. text 41.95 (*0-19-511046-3*) OUP.
Cady, Fredrick M. Instructor's Manual to Accompany Microcomputers & Microcontrollers: Principles of Software & Hardware Engineering. 40p. 1998. pap. text. write for info. (*0-19-511178-8*) OUP.
***Cady, Fredrick M. & Sibigtroth, James M.** Software & Hardware Engineering: Motorola M68HC12. LC 99-35430. (Illus.). 592p. (C). 2000. pap. text 59.95 (*0-19-512469-3*) OUP.
Cady, H. Emilie. Como Use la Verdad. rev. ed. (SPA.). 128p. 1995. pap. 9.95 (*0-87159-068-9*, 265) Unity Bks.
— Complete Works of H. Emilie Cady: Lessons in Truth, How I Used Truth, & God a Present Help. Maday, Michael, ed. LC 95-5147. 290p. 1995. pap. 13.95 (*0-87159-029-8*) Unity Bks.
— Lecciones Acerca de la Verdad. 195p. 1986. pap. 6.95 (*0-87159-081-6*) Unity Bks.
— Lessons in Truth. rev. ed. LC 95-6534. 194p. 2000. 12.95 (*0-87159-108-1*) Unity Bks.
Cady, Harrison, jt. auth. see Burgess, Thornton W.
Cady, Henry L., jt. auth. see Scott Cady, Priscilla
***Cady, Jack.** American Writer. 384p. 2000. pap. 15.95 (*0-312-26709-6*) St Martin.
— The American Writer: Shaping a Nation's Mind. LC 99-15928. 352p. 1999. text 27.95 (*0-312-20274-1*) St Martin.
Cady, Jack. The Burning & Other Stories. LC 72-76304. (Iowa Short Fiction Award Ser.). 157p. 1972. 5.00 (*0-87745-030-7*) U of Iowa Pr.
— The Night We Buried Road Dog. 204p. 1998. 27.00 (*1-892058-00-6*) Dreamhaven.
Cady, Jack & McElroy, Colleen, intros. Tattoo. 1978. pap. 6.25 (*0-931594-01-4*) Circinatum Pr.
Cady, Jeff, jt. auth. see Barnard, Roger.
Cady, John F. Contacts with Burma, 1935-1949: A Personal Account. LC 81-22544. (Papers in International Studies: Southeast Asia Ser.: No. 61). 130p. 1983. reprint ed. pap. 40.30 (*0-7837-6476-6*, 204648100001) Bks Demand.
— The Southeast Asian World. LC 76-53353. (World of Asia Ser.). (Illus.). 1977. pap. text 6.95 (*0-88273-502-0*) Forum Pr IL.
— The United States & Burma. LC 75-22256. (American Foreign Policy Library). 315p. 1976. reprint ed. pap. 97.70 (*0-7837-6081-7*, 205912700007) Bks Demand.
***Cady, John Hutchins.** Civic & Architectural Development of Providence, 1636-1950. fac. ed. (Illus.). 320p. 2000. reprint ed. 49.00 (*0-8328-7030-7*) Higginson Bk Co.
Cady, John W. Magnetic & Gravity Anomalies in the Great Valley & Western Sierra Nevada Metamorphic Belt, California. LC 75-19540. (Geological Society of America, Special Paper: No. 168). 80p. reprint ed. pap. 30.00 (*0-608-14462-2*, 202503100041) Bks Demand.
Cady, L. B., ed. see Davenport, Marge.
Cady, Lanore. Houses & Letters: A Heritage in Architecture & Calligraphy. (Illus.). 70p. 1977. 55.00 (*0-87027-184-9*) Kennebec River.
Cady, Lee D., Jr., ed. Computer Techniques in Cardiology. LC 78-9860. (Biomedical Engineering & Instrumentation Ser.: No. 4). (Illus.). 478p. reprint ed. pap. 148.20 (*0-7837-3366-6*, 204332400008) Bks Demand.
Cady, Lew. They've Got Rockies in Their Heads! The Colorado Rockies' First Season...from the Fans' Point of View. (Illus.). 296p. (Orig.). 1993. pap. 10.00 (*0-9639257-0-9*) Hindsight Hist.
Cady, Linell E. Religion, Theology, & American Public Life. LC 92-3097. 202p. (C). 1993. pap. text 21.95 (*0-7914-1304-7*) State U NY Pr.
— Religion, Theology, & American Public Life. LC 92-3097. (SUNY Series in Religious Studies). 202p. (C). 1993. text 64.50 (*0-7914-1303-9*) State U NY Pr.
***Cady, M. P. & Trapp, C. A.** A MathCAD Primer for Physical Chemistry. LC 99-15225. 1999. write for info. (*0-19-850359-8*) OUP.
Cady, Norma W., jt. auth. see Cady, Edwin H.
Cady, Rebecca F. The Advanced Practice Nurse's Legal Handbook. 320p. pap. text 39.95 (*0-7817-2337-X*) Lppncott W & W.
Cady, Richard A. Marine Damage Survey Guide. (Illus.). 157p. (Orig.). 1977. pap. text 26.00 (*0-934114-68-4*, BK-121) Marine Educ.
— Marine Hawser Towing Guide. (Illus.). 123p. (Orig.). 1985. reprint ed. pap. text 26.00 (*0-934114-65-X*, BK-120) Marine Educ.
— Marine Survey Practice Compendium. (Illus.). 362p. (Orig.). 1980. pap. text 54.00 (*0-934114-69-2*, BK-134) Marine Educ.
Cady, Roger & Farmer, Kathleen. Headache Free. 208p. 1995. mass mkt. 6.50 (*0-553-57000-5*) Bantam.
— Headache Free. (Illus.). 110p. 1993. pap. text. write for info. (*0-9636528-0-X*) Moray Pr.
Cady, Roger K. & Fox, Anthony W., eds. Treating the Headache Patient. LC 94-25658. (Illus.). 384p. 1994. text 150.00 (*0-8247-9109-6*) Dekker.
Cady, Roslynn W. Really: Know Love for All-That-Is. Bryant, Kathleen M., ed. LC 98-65761. (Illus.). 306p. 1998. pap. 17.00 (*0-9663123-6-8*) Roster Pubns.
Cady, Sharmaine, jt. auth. see Gebelein, Charles G.
Cady, Steve & Stenlund, Vern K. High-Performance Skating for Hockey. LC 98-15931. (Illus.). 200p. 1998. pap. 15.95 (*0-88011-773-7*, PCAD0773) Human Kinetics.
Cady, Wallace M. Regional Tectonic Synthesis of Northwestern New England & Adjacent Quebec. LC 77-98020. (Geological Society of America, Memoir Ser.: No. 120). 248p. reprint ed. pap. 76.90 (*0-608-13559-3*, 202546600044) Bks Demand.
Caedel, Martin. The Origins of War Prevention: The British Peace Movement & International Relations, 1730-1854. 598p. 1996. text 110.00 (*0-19-822674-8*) OUP.
CAEL Staff. Best Practices of College Business & Industry Centers. 76p. 1998. ring bd. 79.95 (*0-7872-5579-3*, 41557901) Kendall-Hunt.
— Prior Learning Assessment. 208p. 1999. per. 24.95 (*0-7872-5589-0*, 41558901) Kendall-Hunt.
CAEL Staff. Your Hidden Credentials: The Value of Personal Learning Outside College. 181p. 1996. per. 7.95 (*0-7872-3346-3*) Kendall-Hunt.
CAEL Staff, jt. auth. see Lamdin, Lois.
Caelli, T. & Bischof, W. F. Machine Learning & Image Interpretation. LC 97-36803. (Advances in Computer Vision & Machine Intelligence Ser.). 448p. (C). 1997. 115.00 (*0-306-45761-X*, Kluwer Plenum) Kluwer Academic.
Caelli, T., jt. auth. see Liu, Z. Q.
Caelli, Terrence M., jt. ed. see Dodwell, Peter C.
Caelli, Terry. An Introduction to Modern Approaches in Visual Perception. LC 80-40167. (Illus.). 200p. 1981. 98.00 (*0-08-024420-3*, Pub. by Pergamon Repr) Franklin.
Caemmerer, Alex. The Houses of Key West. LC 91-42369. (Illus.). 112p. 1992. pap. 18.95 (*1-56164-009-3*) Pineapple Pr.
Caemmerer, H. Paul. Life of Pierre Charles l'Enfant. LC 71-87546. (Architecture & Decorative Art Ser.: Vol. 33). 1970. reprint ed. lib. bdg. 65.00 (*0-306-71381-0*) Da Capo.
Caemmerer, R. R. Preaching for the Church. 353p. 1976. pap. 19.00 (*0-570-03735-2*, 12-2639) Concordia.
Caen, Herb. Baghdad-by-the-Bay. 288p. 1987. reprint ed. 3.95 (*0-89174-047-3*) Comstock Edns.
— The Cable Car & the Dragon. LC 85-32004. (Illus.). 40p. (J). (ps-3). 1986. 12.95 (*0-87701-390-X*) Chronicle Bks.
— The Cable Car & the Dragon. (Illus.). 40p. (J). (ps-3). 1995. pap. 5.95 (*0-8118-1054-2*) Chronicle Bks.
— One Man's San Francisco. LC 75-14808. 1978. reprint ed. pap. 3.95 (*0-89174-031-7*) Comstock Edns.
Caen, Herb, et al. San Francisco. 2nd rev. ed. (Illus.). 226p. 1993. 49.50 (*0-8109-3834-0*, Pub. by Abrams) Time Warner.
Caenegem, R. C. Van, see Van Caenegem, R. C.

C

Caenepeel, Stefaan. Brauer Groups, Hopf Algebras, & Galois Theory. LC 97-31694. (K-Monographs in Mathematics Ser.). 7p. 1997. lib. bdg. 345.00 (*0-7923-4829-X*, D Reidel) Kluwer Academic.

Caenepeel, Stefaan & Van Oystaeyen, F. Brauer Groups & the Cohomology of Graded Rings. (Pure & Applied Mathematics Ser.: Vol. 121). (Illus.). 280p. 1988. text 155.00 (*0-8247-7978-9*) Dekker.

***Caenepeel, Stefaan & Verschoren, A.** Rings, Hopf Algebras, & Brauer Groups. LC 97-44125. (Lecture Notes in Pure & Applied Mathematics Ser.). (Illus.). 352p. 1998. pap. text 175.00 (*0-8247-0153-4*) Dekker.

Caerwyn Williams, J. E. & Ford, Patrick K. The Irish Literary Tradition. xii, 355p. 1997. reprint ed. pap. write for info. (*0-7083-1094-X*, Pub. by Univ Wales Pr) Paul & Co Pubs.

Caes, Charles J. Introduction to the Arguments for God. LC 82-82548. 1983. 10.95 (*0-87212-162-3*) Libra.

— Natural U. Learning from Nature. 256p. (Orig.). (C). 1995. pap. text 32.00 (*0-8191-9754-8*); lib. bdg. 52.00 (*0-8191-9753-X*) U Pr of Amer.

***Caes, Charles J.** Sign of the Souix. 370p. 2000. pap. 14.95 (*1-891929-35-6*) Four Seasons.

Caes, Charles J. Studies in Starlight: Understanding Our Universe. LC 87-33515. (Illus.). 256p. 1988. pap. 12.95 (*0-8306-2946-7*) McGraw-Hill Prof.

— Tools of the Bear: How Any Investor Can Make Money When Stocks Go Down. 225p. 1992. text 24.95 (*1-55738-419-3*, Irwn Prfssnl) McGraw-Hill Prof.

— Tools of the Bull: How to Make Money in Bull Markets. 225p. 1994. text 24.95 (*1-55738-563-7*, Irwn Prfssnl) McGraw-Hill Prof.

Caesar. Caesar: Civil War, Bk. III. Carter, ed. 1993. 59.99 (*0-85668-582-8*, Pub. by Aris & Phillips); pap. 28.00 (*0-85668-583-6*, Pub. by Aris & Phillips) David Brown.

— Caesar: Civil War, Vol. I-II. Carter, J. M., ed. (Classical Texts Ser.). 256p. (C). 1991. 59.99 (*0-85668-461-9*, Pub. by Aris & Phillips) David Brown.

— Caesar: Civil war I & II, Vol. I-II. Carter, J. M., ed. (Classical Texts Ser.). 256p. (C). 1991. pap. 28.00 (*0-85668-462-7*, Pub. by Aris & Phillips) David Brown.

— Commentarii De Bello Civili. Kraner, Friedrich et al, eds. xvi, 430p. 1968. 90.00 incl. 3.5 hd (*3-296-11000-3*) G Olms Pubs.

— Commentarii de Bello Gallico, Bd. 1, Buch 1-4. Kraner, Friedrich et al, eds. vii, 536p. 1980. 95.00 incl. 3.5 hd (*3-296-11101-8*) G Olms Pubs.

Caesar, A. D., jt. auth. see Rivise, Charles W.

Caesar, Adrian. Kenneth Slessor. (Australian Writers Ser.). 144p. (C). 1995. pap. text 22.00 (*0-19-553421-2*) OUP.

Caesar, Ann. Quality of Light: Modern Italian Short Stories. (Modern European Short Stories Ser.). 212p. 1994. pap. 13.99 (*1-85242-188-6*) Serpents Tail.

Caesar, Ann, ed. see Serao, Mathilde.

Caesar, Ann H. Characters & Authors in Luigi Pirandello. 226p. (C). 1998. text 77.00 (*0-19-815176-4*) OUP.

Caesar, Bishop & Coleman, David. The Methodist Way & Responsible Discipleship Leadership. LC 93-80658. 100p. (Orig.). 1993. pap. text 6.00 (*1-883667-06-2*) Christian Meth.

Caesar, C. Julius. Commentaries of Caesar, Translated into English, 2 vols. LC 77-161798. (Augustan Translators Ser.). reprint ed. 135.00 (*0-404-54104-6*) AMS Pr.

Caesar, Caius Julius. Egypt Books of Caius Julius Caesar Conteyning His Martiall Exployes in Gallia. Goldinge, Arthur, tr. LC 68-54623. (English Experience Ser.: No. 36). 1968. reprint ed. 42.00 (*90-221-0036-7*) Walter J Johnson.

Caesar, Fred. Love Thine Enemy. 190p. 1984. 8.95 (*0-89697-147-3*) Intl Univ Pr.

Caesar, Germanicus. Aratea Cum Scholiis. Breysig, A., ed. xxxvi, 260p. 1967. reprint ed. 65.00 (*0-318-71128-1*) G Olms Pubs.

Caesar, Judith. Crossing Borders: An American Woman in the Middle East. LC 97-3686. (Contemporary Issues in the Middle East Ser.). 280p. 1997. 34.95 (*0-8156-2735-1*) Syracuse U Pr.

***Caesar, Judith.** Crossing Borders: An American Woman in the Middle East Socioreligious Thought in Qajar Iran. 186p. 1999. pap. text 19.95 (*0-8156-2854-4*) Syracuse U Pr.

Caesar, Julius. Alexandrian, African, & Spanish Wars. Way, A. G., tr. from LAT. (Loeb Classical Library: No. 402). 440p. 1955. text 15.50 (*0-674-99443-4*) HUP.

— The Ancient State of the Court of Requests. LC 76-57367. (English Experience Ser.: No. 785). 1977. reprint ed. lib. bdg. 25.00 (*90-221-0785-X*) Walter J Johnson.

— C. Iuli Caesaris de Bello Gallico, 7 vols. Connor, W. R., ed. LC 78-67135. (Latin Texts & Commentaries Ser.). (ENG & LAT.). 1979. reprint ed. lib. bdg. 63.95 (*0-405-11607-1*) Ayer.

— Caesar: Gallic War I. (Bristol Latin Texts Ser.). (LAT.). 166p. (C). 1985. reprint ed. pap. 16.95 (*0-86292-177-5*, Pub. by Brist Class Pr) Focus Pub-R Pullins.

— Caesar: Gallic War V. (Bristol Latin Texts Ser.). (LAT.). 112p. (C). 1984. reprint ed. pap. 16.95 (*0-86292-136-8*, Pub. by Brist Class Pr) Focus Pub-R Pullins.

— The Civil War. Gardner, Jane F., tr. (Classics Ser.). 360p. 1976. pap. 10.95 (*0-14-044187-5*, Penguin Classics) Viking Penguin.

— The Civil War: With the Anonymous Alexandrian, African & Spanish Wars. Carter, John, tr. & intro. by. (Oxford World's Classics Ser.). (Illus.). 432p. 1999. pap. 9.95 (*0-19-283923-3*) OUP.

— Civil Wars. (Loeb Classical Library: No. 39). 382p. 1914. 19.95 (*0-674-99043-9*) HUP.

— Commentarii, 2 vols., 1. Du Pontet, R. L., ed. (Oxford Classical Texts Ser.). 239p. 1968. text 22.00 (*0-19-814602-7*) OUP.

— Commentarii, 2 vols., 2. Du Pontet, R. L., ed. (Oxford Classical Texts Ser.). 304p. 1922. text 22.00 (*0-19-814603-5*) OUP.

— Conquest of Gaul. 1976. 23.95 (*0-8488-0439-2*) Amereon Ltd.

— Gallic War. (Loeb Classical Library: No. 72). 15.50 (*0-674-99080-3*) HUP.

— The Gallic War. (Great Commanders Ser.). 363p. 1996. reprint ed. 30.00 (*1-56515-009-0*) Collect Reprints.

— Seven Commentaries on the Gallic War. Hammond, Carolyn, tr. (Oxford World's Classics Ser.). (Illus.). 310p. 1999. pap. 8.95 (*0-19-283582-3*) OUP.

— War Commentaries of Caesar. 1976. 25.95 (*0-8488-0344-2*) Amereon Ltd.

Caesar, Julius, et al. Classic of Latin. unabridged ed. LC 74-751028. (LAT.). 1977. audio 14.00 (*0-694-50201-4*, SWC 1296, Caedmon) HarperAudio.

Caesar, Kurt, jt. auth. see Lucas, James S.

Caesar, Michael. Dante. (Critical Heritage Ser.). 624p. 1989. 139.50 (*0-415-02822-1*) Routledge.

— Dante. 678p. (C). 1996. 160.00 (*0-415-13397-1*) Routledge.

— Umberto Eco: Philosophy, Semiotics & the Work of Fiction. LC 99-14108. (Key Contemporary Thinkers Ser.). 206p. 1999. 54.95 (*0-7456-0849-3*, Pub. by Polity Pr); pap. 22.95 (*0-7456-0850-7*, Pub. by Polity Pr) Blackwell Pubs.

Caesar, Michael, tr. see Della Volpe, Galvano.

Caesar, Neil B. Medicare Compliance. 1997. 60.00 (*0-7863-1242-4*, Irwn Prfssnl) McGraw-Hill Prof.

***Caesar, Nick.** Dr. Carabieni. 126p. 1999. pap. 4.75 (*0-9671150-0-0*) Seagriff Bks.

Caesar, P. Lynn & Hamberger, L. Kevin, eds. Treating Men Who Batter: Theory, Practice, & Programs. (Focus on Men Ser.: Vol. 5). 288p. 1989. 39.95 (*0-8261-6340-8*) Springer Pub.

Caesar, Shirley. The Lady, the Melody & the Word: The Inspirational Story of the First Lady of Gospel Music. LC 97-51908. (Illus.). 256p. 1998. 16.99 (*0-7852-7155-4*, J Thoma Bks) Nelson.

Caesar-Sutherland, Lillian. The Unrelenting Power of Words. 75p. 1995. 10.95 (*0-932831-14-1*) Eastern Caribbean Inst.

Caesar, Terry. Forgiving the Boundaries: Home As Abroad in American Travel Writing. LC 94-15274. 256p. 1995. 40.00 (*0-8203-1673-3*) U of Ga Pr.

***Caesar, Terry.** Traveling through the Boondocks: In & Out of Academic Hierarchy. LC 99-53741. (C). 2000. text 59.50 (*0-7914-4659-X*) State U NY Pr.

— Traveling Through the Boondocks: In & Out of Academic Hierarchy. LC 99-53741. 2000. pap. 19.95 (*0-7914-4660-3*) State U NY Pr.

Caesar, Terry. Writing in Disguise: Academic Life in Subordination. LC 97-30432. 177p. 1998. pap. 25.00 (*0-8214-1220-5*) Ohio U Pr.

Caesar, Terry, jt. ed. see Bueno, Eva.

Caesarea, Bishop. Exegetic Homilies. LC 63-12483. (Fathers of the Church Ser.: Vol. 46). 394p. 1963. reprint ed. pap. 122.20 (*0-7837-9145-3*, 204994500004) Bks Demand.

Caesariensis, Eusebius. Das Onomastikon der Biblischen Ortsnamen. (GER.). xxxvi, 207p. 1986. reprint ed. 65.00 (*3-487-01172-7*) G Olms Pubs.

Caesarius of Arles, Saint. Sermons, Vol. I, Nos. 1-80. Mueller, Mary M., tr. LC 56-3628. (Fathers of the Church Ser.: Vol. 31). 375p. 1956. 36.95 (*0-8132-0031-8*) Cath U Pr.

— Sermons, Vol. II, Nos. 81-186. Mueller, Mary M., tr. LC 56-3628. (Fathers of the Church Ser.: Vol. 47). 495p. 1964. 27.95 (*0-8132-0047-4*) Cath U Pr.

— Sermons, Vol. III, Nos. 187-238. Mueller, Mary M., tr. LC 56-3628. (Fathers of the Church Ser.: Vol. 66). 312p. 1973. 19.95 (*0-8132-0066-0*) Cath U Pr.

***Caestecker, Frank & Bade, Klaus J.** Alien Policy in Belgium, 1840-1940: The Creation of Guest Workers, Refugees & Illegal Immigrants. LC 99-85996. 2000. 59.95 (*1-57181-986-X*) Berghahn Bks.

Caetano, Ana, ed. Membrane Technology: Applications to Industrial Wastewater Treatment. 208p. (C). 1994. text 119.00 (*0-7923-3209-1*) Kluwer Academic.

Caetano-Anolles, Gustavo & Gresshof, Peter M. DNA Markers: Protocols, Applications & Overviews. LC 97-22138. 364p. (Orig.). 1997. pap. 74.95 (*0-471-16067-9*, Wiley-Liss) Wiley.

Cafagna, Albert C., et al, eds. Child Nurturance Vol. 1: Philosophy, Children, & the Family. LC 82-3701. 392p. 1982. 75.00 (*0-306-41003-6*, Plenum Trade) Perseus Pubng.

Cafagna, Marcus. The Broken World: Poems. LC 95-41769. (National Poetry Ser.). 80p. 1996. 10.95 (*0-252-06550-6*) U of Ill Pr.

Cafarchio, Pete, ed. Network Security & Firewalls Conference 4 (1997) Proceedings. (Illus.). 115p. (C). 1998. pap. text 50.00 (*0-7881-7156-9*) DIANE Pub.

***Cafaro, Nancy J., et al.** The Path Back Home. large type ed. Cafaro, Richard, ed. LC 99-94317. (Illus.). 725p. 1999. pap. 50.00 (*0-9671894-0-3*) Jo Pubg.

Cafaro, Richard, ed. see Cafaro, Nancy J., et al.

***Cafe İbanoğlu & Gosling, J. T.** Variable Stars As Essential Astrophysical Tools. 844p. 1999. pap. 104.00 (*0-7923-6084-2*) Kluwer Academic.

Cafe Pasqual's (Santa Fe, N.M.) Staff, jt. auth. see Kagel, Katharine.

Cafe, Sonia. Transforming Dragons. LC 97-52601. (Illus.). 160p. (Orig.). 1998. mass mkt. 16.95 (*1-57863-012-6*) Weiser.

Cafe, Sonia & Innecco, Neide. Attitude Adjustments: Affirmations for Inner Ecology: Includes Cards. LC 98-53593. (Illus.). 160p. 1999. pap. 16.95 (*1-57863-025-8*) Weiser.

— Meditating with the Angels. LC 94-17190. (Illus.). 96p. (Orig.). 1994. pap. 7.00 (*0-87728-812-7*) Weiser.

Cafeo, Marie H., et al. Who Dunnit? (Illus.). 109p. 1998. spiral bd. 5.00 (*0-9667395-1-5*) In the BAG.

***Caferra, Ricardo & Salzer, Gernot, eds.** Automated Deduction in Classical & Non-Classical Logics: Selected Papers. LC 00-28492. (Lecture Notes in Computer Science Ser.: Vol. 1761). viii, 299p. 2000. pap. 56.00 (*3-540-67190-0*) Spr-Verlag.

Caferro, William. Mercenary Raids & the Decline of Siena, Vol. 116. LC 97-38339. (Johns Hopkins University Studies in Historical & Political Science Ser.). (Illus.). 252p. 1998. text 39.95 (*0-8018-5788-0*) Johns Hopkins.

Caferro, William & Fisher, Duncan G., eds. The Unbounded Community: Papers in Christian Ecumenism in Honor of Jaroslav Pelikan. LC 95-19418. (Garland Reference Library of the Humanities: Vol. 1822). 264p. 1996. text 43.00 (*0-8153-1596-1*, H1822) Garland.

Caferro, William, jt. auth. see Jacks, Philip Joshua.

Caffarel, Henri. Being Present to God: Letters on Prayer. LC 83-15459. 202p. (Orig.). 1983. pap. 6.95 (*0-8189-0462-3*) Alba.

Caffarella, C. & O'Donnell, O. Self Directed Learning. (C). 1989. pap. 32.00 (*1-85041-029-1*, Pub. by Univ Nottingham) St Mut.

Caffarella, Rosemary S. Planning Programs for Adult Learners: A Practical Guide for Educators, Trainers & Staff Developers. LC 94-21355. (Higher & Adult Education Ser.). 276p. 1994. pap. text 34.95 (*0-7879-0033-8*) Jossey-Bass.

Caffarella, Rosemary S., jt. auth. see Merriam, Sharan B.

Caffarella, Rosemary S., jt. ed. see Jackson, Lewis.

Caffarelli, Luis, ed. Hyperbolic Equations & Frequency Interactions. LC 98-30060. (IAS-Park City Mathematics Ser.: Vol. 5). 466p. 1998. 69.00 (*0-8218-0592-4*) Am Math.

Caffarelli, Luis A. & Milman, Mario. Monge AMPERE Equation: Applications to Geometry & Optimization: NSF-CBMS Conference on the Monge AMP ERE Equation, Applications to Geometry & Optimization, July 9-13, 1997, Florida Atlantic University. LC 98-38822. (Contemporary Mathematics Ser.: Vol. 226). 1998. write for info. (*0-8218-0917-2*) Am Math.

Caffaro, John V. & Conn-Caffaro, Allison. Sibling Abuse Trauma: Assessment & Intervention Strategies for Children, Families & Adults. LC 98-8166. (Illus.). 303p. 1998. 49.95 (*0-7890-6007-8*, Maltreatment & Trauma Pr) Haworth Pr.

— Sibling Abuse Trauma: Assessment & Intervention Strategies for Children, Families, & Adults. LC 98-8166. (Illus.). 303p. 1998. pap. 24.95 (*0-7890-0491-7*, Maltreatment & Trauma Pr) Haworth Pr.

Caffary, Brian & Marwood, Des. Skilful Judo. pap. write for info. (*0-7136-3604-1*, 92779, Pub. by A & C Blk) Midpt Trade.

Caffee, Claude E. Introduction to Speech Communication, SPCH 1311. 1996. pap. text 12.24 (*1-56870-236-1*) RonJon Pub.

Caffee, Gabrielle L. The Story of a Mustard Seed. (Illus.). 184p. (Orig.). 1990. pap. 10.00 (*0-685-48817-9*) Coffeetable.

Caffee, Gabrielle L., tr. see Van Gennep, Arnold.

Caffell, Colin. In Search of the Rainbow's End: The Inside Story the Bamber Murders. (Illus.). 277p. 1995. 34.95 (*0-340-61745-4*, Pub. by Hodder & Stought Ltd) Trafalgar.

Caffentzis, Constantine G. Clipped Coins, Abused Words & Civil Government: John Locke's Philosophy of Money. 250p. 1989. pap. 10.00 (*0-936756-27-6*) Autonomedia.

***Caffentzis, Constantine George.** Exciting the Industry of Mankind: George Berkley's Philosophy. (Archives Internationales d'Histoire des Idees Ser.). 462p. 2000. 196.00 (*0-7923-6297-7*) Kluwer Academic.

Cafferkey, Mary, ed. Methicillin-Resistant Staphylococcus Aureus. (Illus.). 224p. 1992. text 125.00 (*0-8247-8604-1*) Dekker.

Cafferky, Michael. Managed Care & You: The Consumer Guide to Managing Your Healthcare. 3rd rev. ed. LC 98-113154. 234p. 1997. pap. 12.95 (*1-885987-04-8*, ME083, Health Info Pr) Practice Mgmt Info.

Cafferky, Michael E. Deja Que la Gente Hable/Let Your Customers Do the Talking. 1997. pap. text 19.95 (*0-7931-2542-1*) Dearborn.

— Managed Care & You: The Consumer Guide to Managing Your Health Care. 2nd ed. (Illus.). 224p. (Orig.). 1995. pap. 14.95 (*0-07-600759-6*, ME104) Practice Mgmt Info.

— Patients Build Your Practice: Word of Mouth Marketing for Healthcare Practitioners. 170p. (Orig.). 1994. pap. text 29.95 (*0-07-600676-X*, ME114) Practice Mgmt Info.

Cafferty, B., tr. see Ilyin-Genevsky, A.

Cafferty, Bernard & Hooper, David. A Complete Defence to 1d4: A Study of the Queen's Gambit Accepted. LC 79-41623. (Chess Ser.). 144p. 1981. 19.50 (*0-08-024103-4*, Pergamon Pr); pap. 13.95 (*0-08-024102-6*, Pergamon Pr) Elsevier.

— A Complete Defence to 1e4. 3rd ed. (Chess Ser.). 115p. 1986. 29.90 (*0-08-032036-8*, P115, Pergamon Pr); pap. 17.90 (*0-08-032035-X*, Pergamon Pr) Elsevier.

Cafferty, Bernard & Taimanov, Mark. The Soviet Championships. 1997. text 29.95 (*1-85744-201-6*) S&S Trade.

Cafferty, Bernard, jt. auth. see Harding, Tim.

Cafferty, Helen, jt. ed. see Clausen, Jeanette.

Cafferty, P., et al. The Dilemma of American Immigration: Beyond the Golden Door. LC 83-543. 230p. 1983. 39.95 (*0-87855-481-5*); pap. 24.95 (*0-87855-935-3*) Transaction Pubs.

Cafferty, Pastora & McCready, William, eds. Hispanics in the United States: A New Social Agenda. 330p. (C). 1991. 39.95 (*0-88738-018-2*); pap. 24.95 (*0-87855-975-2*) Transaction Pubs.

Cafferty, Pastora S. & Chestang, Leon, eds. The Diverse Society: Implications for Social Policy. LC 76-43633. 176p. 1976. pap. 18.95 (*0-87101-072-0*) Natl Assn Soc Wkrs.

Cafferty, Pastora S. J. & Spangenberg, Gail. Backs Against the Wall: Urban-Oriented Colleges & Universities & the Urban Poor & Disadvantaged. LC 82-25124. (Ford Foundation Report Series on Higher Education in the Cities). 76p. (Orig.). 1983. pap. write for info. (*0-916584-22-4*) Ford Found.

Cafferty, Patrick J. & Stillson, Linford J. Appleton & Lange's Review for the Physician Assistant. 2nd ed. (Illus.). 312p. (C). 1994. pap. text 34.95 (*0-8385-0065-X*, A0065-1) Appleton & Lange.

Cafferty, Thomas, jt. ed. see Medway, Frederic.

Cafferty, Tom, ed. Butch Boys. 1997. mass mkt. 6.50 (*1-56333-523-9*, Badboy) Masquerade.

***Caffery, James J.** Wireless Location in CDMA Cellular Radio Systems. LC 99-48309. (Series in Engineering & Computer Science). 1999. write for info. (*0-7923-7703-6*) Kluwer Academic.

Caffey, David L. Land of Enchantment, Land of Conflict: New Mexico in English-Language Fiction. LC 98-55985. (Tarleton State University Southwestern Studies in the Humanities: Vol. 11). (Illus.). 240p. 1999. 29.95 (*0-89096-891-8*) Tex A&M Univ Pr.

Caffey, Donna. Yikes-Lice! LC 97-30679. (Illus.). 24p. (J). (ps-5). 1998. lib. bdg. 13.95 (*0-8075-9374-5*) A Whitman.

Caffey, Jacquelyn S. Little Martin Coloring Book. large type ed. Scarbough, Ron & Houston, Lenora, eds. (Illus.). 32p. (Orig.). (J). (gr. 1-5). 1983. pap. 5.00 (*1-888587-01-6*) Write to Teach.

Caffey, Jacquelyn S., ed. see Buckingham, Maggie A.

Caffey, Marion J. My Estate Planner: Information for My Family. 92p. (Orig.). 1990. pap. 9.95 (*0-9622993-9-1*) Sunshine Pubns.

— Surviving in the Sunshine: An Entertainment Industry Guide & Date Book for Florida. 350p. 1989. write for info. (*0-318-65038-X*) Sunshine Pubns.

Caffi, Francesco. Storia della Musica Sacra, 2 vols. in 1. 775p. 1982. reprint ed. 190.00 (*3-487-07174-6*) G Olms Pubs.

Caffin, Caroline & Caffin, Charles H. Dancing & Dancers of Today. LC 78-2847. (Series in Dance). (Illus.). 1978. reprint ed. lib. bdg. 35.00 (*0-306-77579-4*) Da Capo.

Caffin, Charles H. American Masters of Painting. LC 73-128217. (Essay Index Reprint Ser.). 1977. 21.95 (*0-8369-1868-1*) Ayer.

— American Masters of Sculpture. LC 75-84301. (Essay Index Reprint Ser.). 1977. 18.95 (*0-8369-1253-5*) Ayer.

— American Masters of Sculpture. 1980. lib. bdg. 65.00 (*0-8490-3156-7*) Gordon Pr.

— How to Study Pictures. Buselle, A., Jr., ed. LC 68-58776. (Essay Index Reprint Ser.). 1977. 35.95 (*0-8369-0104-5*) Ayer.

— Story of Spanish Painting. LC 72-100521. (BCL Ser. I). (Illus.). reprint ed. 37.50 (*0-404-01361-9*) AMS Pr.

Caffin, Charles H., jt. auth. see Caffin, Caroline.

Caffo, Michele, et al, eds. Astronomy, Cosmology & Fundamental Physics. (C). 1989. text 234.50 (*0-7923-0258-3*) Kluwer Academic.

Caffrey, Debbie. An Alaskan Sampler. (Illus.). (Orig.). 1995. pap. 13.00 (*0-9645777-0-4*) Debbies Creat.

— Blocks & Quilts Everywhere. (Illus.). 88p. 1997. pap. 19.99 (*0-9645777-1-2*) Debbies Creat.

***Caffrey, Debbie.** Open a Can of Worms. 76p. 2000. pap. 23.95 (*0-9645777-4-7*) Debbies Creat.

— Quilting Season. (Illus.). 56p. 1999. pap. 19.00 (*0-9645777-3-9*) Debbies Creat.

Caffrey, Deborah J. Scraps to You, Too. (Illus.). 80p. 1998. pap. 21.95 (*0-9645777-2-0*) Debbies Creat.

Caffrey, J. M., et al, eds. Management & Ecology of Freshwater Plants: Proceedings of the 9th International Symposium on Aquatic Weeds, European Weed Research Society, Dublin, Ireland, 1994. LC 96-54609. (Development in Hydrobiology Ser.: Vol. 120). 354p. 1997. text 234.00 (*0-7923-4433-2*) Kluwer Academic.

Caffrey, J. M., jt. auth. see International Symposium on Aquatic Weeds Staff.

Caffrey, Jaye A. First Star I See. (Illus.). 150p. (Orig.). (J). (gr. 3-6). 1997. pap. 9.95 (*1-884281-17-6*) Verbal Images Pr.

Caffrey, Joanne Taylor. Veteran Soldiers of Montgomery County, Ohio, 1862-1885. 2nd rev. ed. LC 86-174221. 120p. 1986. pap. 8.00 (*1-887665-16-1*) MCC OGS.

Caffrey, Larry, ed. Information Sharing Between & Within Governments. 72p. pap. 18.95 (*0-85092-555-X*, Pub. by Comm Sec) Stylus Pub VA.

***Caffrey, Larry & Okut-Uma, Rogers W.** Government Secure Intranets. 60p. 2000. pap. 16.95 (*0-85092-611-4*, Pub. by Comm Sec) Stylus Pub VA.

Caffrey, Margaret M. Ruth Benedict: Stranger in This Land. LC 88-20589. (American Studies). (Illus.). 448p. 1989. 19.95 (*0-292-74655-5*) U of Tex Pr.

Caffrey, Martin. LIPIDAT: A Cent. Database for Therm Data on Lipid Mesmo Etc. 320p. 1993. lib. bdg. 159.00 (*0-8493-8924-0*, QP751) CRC Pr.

Caffrey, Matt, jt. auth. see Chadwick, Frank A.

Caffrey, Susan & Mundy, Gary, eds. The Sociology of Crime & Deviance: Selected Issues. 516p. (C). 1996. pap. 45.00 (*1-874529-52-3*, Pub. by Greenwich Univ Pr) NYU Pr.

Caffrey, Tom. Hitting Home. (Orig.). 1994. mass mkt. 4.95 (*1-56333-222-1*, Badboy) Masquerade.

***CAFH Foundation Staff.** Walking with Contemplation. rev. ed. LC 96-86226. 215 p. 1998. write for info. (*0-9609102-3-9*) CAFH Found Inc.

Cafiero, Renee V., tr. see Broger, Achim.

Cafiero, Renee V., tr. see Sommer-Bodenburg, Angela.

An Asterisk (*) at the beginning of an entry indicates that the title is appearing for the first time.

***Cafkey, Morris & Haney, John A.** Pueblo Steel Town Trollies. LC 98-73843. (Illus.). 144p. 1999. pap. 29.95 (*0-918654-57-2*) CO RR Mus.

Caflisch, Jacob, Sr. Issues in Russian Linguistics. 264p. (Orig.). (C). 1995. pap. text 29.50 (*0-8191-9843-9*) U Pr of Amer.

— Issues in Russian Linguistics. (Illus.). 264p. (Orig.). (C). 1995. lib. bdg. 52.00 (*0-8191-9842-0*) U Pr of Amer.

Caflisch, Lucius, jt. auth. see Zacklin, Ralph.

Caflisch, Russell E., ed. Mathematical Aspects of Vortex Dynamics. LC 89-6182. (Proceedings in Applied Mathematics Ser.: No. 37). xii, 220p. 1989. pap. 34.00 (*0-89871-235-1*) Soc Indus-Appl Math.

Caflisch, Russell E. & Papanicolaou, George C., eds. Singularities in Fluids, Plasmas, & Optics: Proceedings of a NATO Advanced Research Workshop July 6-10, 1992, Herkalion, Greece. LC 93-1726. (NATO Advanced Study Institutes Series C, Mathematical & Physical Sciences: Vol. 403). 356p. (C). 1993. text 236.00 (*0-7923-2333-5*) Kluwer Academic.

Cafolla, Ray, et al. Internet for Educators. 240p. 1996. pap. text 30.00 (*0-205-19814-7*) P-H.

Caforio. Slovensko-Anglicky Vedecko-Technicky Slovnik. (SLO.). 928p. 1996. write for info. (*80-08-01105-X*, Pub. by Slov Pegagog Naklad) IBD Ltd.

Caforio, A. English & Slovak Technical Dictionary. (ENG & SLO.). 1996. 95.00 (*0-7859-9366-5*) Fr & Eur.

— Slovak & English Technical Dictionary. (ENG & SLO.). 919p. 1996. 95.00 (*0-7859-9368-1*) Fr & Eur.

***Caforio, Giuseppe.** The Sociology of the Military. LC 97-35418. (International Library of Critical Writings in Sociology). 1998. 255.00 (*1-85898-619-2*) E Elgar.

Cafritz, Robert C., et al. Places of Delight: The Pastoral Landscape. LC 88-18028. (Illus.). 256p. 1988. pap. 19.95 (*0-943044-12-X*) Phillips Coll.

Cafruny, Alan & Peters, Patrick, eds. Union & the World. LC 97-38508. 320p. 1998. lib. bdg. 120.00 (*90-411-0500-X*) Kluwer Law Intl.

Cafruny, Alan W. & Lankowski, Carl, eds. Europe's Ambiguous Unity: Conflict & Concensus in the Post-Maastricht Era. 290p. 1997. lib. bdg. 55.00 (*1-55587-224-7*, 872247) L Rienner.

Caga, Gillian, jt. auth. see Caga, Tayfun.

Caga, Tayfun. Conversational Turkish in Seven Days. LC 97-52745. (TUR., Illus.). 96p. 1994. pap. 8.95 (*0-8442-4565-8*, 45658, Passprt Bks) NTC Contemp Pub Co.

Caga, Tayfun & Caga, Gillian. Conversational Turkish in Seven Days. (Language in 7 Days Ser.). (TUR.). 96p. 1995. pap. 14.95 incl. audio (*0-8442-9144-7*, Natl Textbk Co) NTC Contemp Pub Co.

Cagala, George. Coastal California: A Camping Guide. (Camping Guide Ser.). (Illus.). 288p. (Orig.). 1995. pap. 11.95 (*1-55650-679-1*) Hunter NJ.

— Hawaii - A Camping Guide. (Illus.). 224p. (Orig.). 1995. pap. 11.95 (*1-55650-641-4*) Hunter NJ.

Cagan, Andrea, jt. auth. see Jackson, Victoria.

Cagan, Andrea, jt. auth. see Lunden, Joan.

Cagan, Andrea, jt. auth. see Slick, Grace.

Cagan, Beth & Cagan, Steve. The Promised Land, El Salvador. (Illus.). 220p. (C). 1991. 24.95 (*0-8135-1679-X*) Rutgers U Pr.

Cagan, Penny. City Poems. Wessling, Suki, ed. (Illus.). 32p. 1997. pap. 15.00 (*0-9661452-0-8*) Chatoyant.

Cagan, Phillip. Changes in the Cyclical Behavior of Interest Rates. (Occasional Papers: No. 100). 40p. 1966. reprint ed. 20.00 (*0-87014-414-6*) Natl Bur Econ Res.

— The Channels of Monetary Effects on Interest Rates. (General Ser.: No. 97). 143p. 1972. 37.20 (*0-87014-235-6*) Natl Bur Econ Res.

— The Demand for Currency Relative to Total Money Supply. (Occasional Papers: No. 62). 37p. 1958. reprint ed. 20.00 (*0-87014-376-X*) Natl Bur Econ Res.

— Determinants & Effects of Changes in the Stock of Money, 1875-1960. (Business Cycles Ser.: No. 13). 408p. 1965. 106.10 (*0-87014-097-3*) Natl Bur Econ Res.

— The Effect of Pension Plans on Aggregate Saving: Evidence from a Sample Survey. (Occasional Papers: No. 95). 119p. 1965. reprint ed. 31.00 (*0-87014-409-X*) Natl Bur Econ Res.

Cagan, Phillip & Lipsey, Robert E. The Financial Effects of Inflation. LC 78-13124. (National Bureau of Economic Research. General Ser.: No. 103). 105p. reprint ed. pap. 32.60 (*0-608-16244-2*, 205217100049) Bks Demand.

Cagan, Phillip & Moore, Geoffrey H. The Consumer Price Index: Issues & Alternatives. LC 81-3621. (AEI Studies: No. 325). 75p. reprint ed. pap. 30.00 (*0-8357-4454-X*, 203729200008) Bks Demand.

Cagan, Phillip, jt. auth. see Haraf, William S.

Cagan, Phillip, jt. ed. see Guttentag, Jack M.

Cagan, Rebecca E., jt. auth. see DeLuca, Joseph M.

Cagan, Robert H., ed. Neural Mechanisms in Taste. 224p. 1989. lib. bdg. 159.00 (*0-8493-5834-5*, QP456) CRC Pr.

***Cagan, Steve.** Steve Cagan: No es Facil (It's Not Easy) (Contact Sheet Ser.: Vol. 104). (Illus.). 32p. 1999. pap. 10.00 (*0-935445-11-0*) Light Work.

Cagan, Steve, jt. auth. see Cagan, Beth.

Cagann, Robert A. Rehabilitating Apartments: A Recycling Process. LC 93-27771. (Illus.). 194p. 1993. pap. 44.95 (*0-944298-90-7*, 800) Inst Real Estate.

Cagdell, J. R. Foundations of Electric Circuits. LC 98-47447. 300p. 1998. pap. 38.40 (*0-13-907742-1*) P-H.

Cage, Bob N., jt. auth. see Wattenbarger, James L.

Cage, Cheryl A. Can You Start Monday? A 9-Step Job Search Guide - Resume to Interview. Ryan, Pam & Koneghi, Marsha, eds. LC 96-97012. (Illus.). 124p. 1998. pap. 14.95 (*0-9642839-1-3*) Cage Consult.

— Checklist for Success: A Pilot's Guide to the Successful Airline Interview. 3rd rev. ed. Ryan, Pam, ed. LC 94-92311. (Illus.). 118p. 1994. pap. 31.00 (*0-9642839-0-5*) Cage Consult.

Cage, Cheryl A., jt. auth. see Bock, Becky S.

Cage, Cheryl A., jt. ed. see Tarver, Judy A.

Cage, Dianne. Cooking & Gardening with Dianne. (Illus.). ix, 300p. 1996. lib. bdg. 17.95 (*0-9654648-0-6*) Garden District.

Cage, Elizabeth. Dial V for Vengeance. (Spy Girls Ser.: No. 5). (YA). (gr. 7 up). 1999. mass mkt. 4.50 (*0-671-03565-7*) S&S Trade.

— If Looks Could Kill. (Spy Girls Ser.: No. 6). (YA). (gr. 7 up). 1999. mass mkt. 4.50 (*0-671-03566-5*) S&S Trade.

— License to Thrill. (Spy Girls Ser.: No. 1). (YA). (gr. 7 up). 1998. mass mkt. 4.50 (*0-671-02286-5*, Minstrel Bks) PB.

— Live & Let Spy. (Spy Girls Ser.: No. 2). (YA). (gr. 7 up). 1998. mass mkt. write for info. (*0-671-02287-3*, Minstrel Bks) PB.

— Nobody Does It Better. (Spy Girls Ser.: No. 3). (YA). (gr. 7 up). 1999. mass mkt. 4.50 (*0-671-02288-1*, Minstrel Bks) PB.

— Spy Girls are Forever. (Spy Girls Ser.: No. 4). (YA). (gr. 7 up). 1999. per. 4.50 (*0-671-02289-X*, Minstrel Bks) PB.

Cage, Gary T. Clothed with Power: A Brief Study of the Indwelling of the Holy Spirit. abr. ed. 128p. (Orig.). 1996. pap. 8.95 (*0-9654828-0-4*, 572) Charlotte Mus.

— The Holy Spirit: A Sourcebook with Commentary. 640p. 1995. 29.95 (*0-9654828-1-2*, 993) Charlotte Mus.

Cage, John. Empty Words: Writings, '73 -'78. LC 78-27212. (Illus.). 199p. 1981. pap. 17.95 (*0-8195-6067-7*, Wesleyan Univ Pr) U Pr of New Eng.

— M: Writings '67-'72. LC 72-11051. (Illus.). 233p. 1974. pap. 18.95 (*0-8195-6035-9*, Wesleyan Univ Pr) U Pr of New Eng.

— Musicage: Cage Muses on Words * Art * Music. LC 95-9497. (Illus.). 408p. 1996. pap. 22.95 (*0-8195-6311-0*, Wesleyan Univ Pr); text 40.00 (*0-8195-5285-2*, Wesleyan Univ Pr) U Pr of New Eng.

— X: Writings '79-'82. LC 83-18275. (Illus.). 199p. 1986. pap. 17.95 (*0-8195-6098-7*, Wesleyan Univ Pr) U Pr of New Eng.

— A Year from Monday: New Lectures & Writings. LC 67-24105. (Illus.). 179p. 1969. reprint ed. pap. 17.95 (*0-8195-6002-2*, Wesleyan Univ Pr) U Pr of New Eng.

Cage, John, et al. The Guests Go in to Supper. Carnahan, Melody Sumner, ed. (Illus.). 384p. (C). 1986. pap. 30.00 (*0-936050-05-5*) Burning Bks.

Cage, John M. The Charles Eliot Norton Lectures, Nos. I-IV. deluxe ed. (Charles Eliot Norton Lectures). (Illus.). 464p. 1990. 165.00 (*0-674-44008-0*) HUP.

— Composition in Retrospect. 184p. 1993. pap. 13.95 (*1-878972-11-1*) Exact Change.

— First: Sixth. (Charles Eliot Norton Lectures). (Illus.). 464p. 1990. text 42.00 incl. audio (*0-674-44007-2*) HUP.

— For the Birds: John Cage in Conversation with Daniel Charles. 240p. 1996. pap. 19.95 (*0-7145-2691-6*) M Boyars Pubs.

— Silence: Lectures & Writings. LC 61-14238. 288p. 1973. pap. 19.95 (*0-8195-6028-6*, Wesleyan Univ Pr) U Pr of New Eng.

— Silence: Lectures & Writings. 276p. reprint ed. lib. bdg. 39.00 (*0-685-14865-3*) Rprt Serv.

— Themes & Variations. LC 81-13626. (Illus.). 150p. 1982. 34.00 (*0-930794-22-2*); pap. 35.00 (*0-930794-23-0*) Station Hill Pr.

Cage, John M., ed. Notations. reprint ed. lib. bdg. 49.00 (*0-685-14864-5*) Rprt Serv.

Cage, John M. & Ginsberg, Allen. The Poets' Encyclopedia. Andre, Michael & Rothenberg, Erika, eds. (Illus.). 1979. 35.00 (*0-934450-02-1*) Unmuzzled Ox.

Cage, John M. & Long, Lois. Mud Book: How to Make Pies & Cakes. (Illus.). 46p. 1988. 16.95 (*0-8109-1533-2*, Pub. by Abrams) Time Warner.

Cage, John M., et al. Aerial Six - Seven: Art Is Either a Complaint or Do Something Else. Smith, Rod, ed. 224p. (Orig.). 1991. pap. 15.00 (*0-9619097-3-0*) Edge Bks.

— The Poets' Encyclopedia. (Illus.). 1980. pap. 17.00 (*0-934450-03-X*) Unmuzzled Ox.

Cage, John M., jt. auth. see Hoover, Kathleen O.

Cage, N. L. & Berliner, David C. Educational Psychology. LC 87-80578. 672p. 1987. teacher ed. 2.36 (*0-318-32628-0*); student ed. 13.96 (*0-318-32627-2*) HM.

Cage, Patricia. The Gift of Life. (Heartbeats Ser.). 112p. (YA). (gr. 7 up). 1994. pap. 5.95 (*0-7910-2930-1*) Chelsea Hse.

Cage, R. A. Tramp Shipping Dynasty - Burrell & Son of Glasgow, 1850-1939: A History of Ownership, Finance & Profit, 184. LC 96-43408. (Contributions in Economics & Economic History Ser.: Vol. 184). 275p. 1997. 69.50 (*0-313-30346-0*, Greenwood Pr) Greenwood.

— The Working Class in Glasgow, 1750-1914. LC 86-24059. 192p. (C). 1987. 57.50 (*0-7099-3415-7*, Pub. by C Helm) Routldge.

Caggiano, Biba. From Biba's Italian Kitchen. LC 94-40010. 1995. 23.00 (*0-688-13865-9*, Hearst) Hearst Commns.

— Italy al Dente: The Glories of Italian Cooking. LC 97-6623. (Illus.). 368p. 1998. 25.00 (*0-688-14877-8*, Hearst) Hearst Commns.

— Modern Italian Cooking. (Illus.). 336p. 1992. per. 14.00 (*0-671-75445-9*, Fireside) S&S Trade Pap.

— Northern Italian Cooking. rev. ed. (Illus.). 192p. 1992. pap. 15.95 (*1-55788-051-4*, HP Books) Berkley Pub.

— Trattoria Cooking. 352p. 1992. 25.00 (*0-02-520252-9*) Macmillan.

***Caggiano, Biba.** Unti Italian Cookbook. 2001. write for info. (*0-688-15815-3*, Wm Morrow) Morrow Avon.

Caggiano, Rosemary & Martinez, Larry. The Circus. 48p. (J). (gr. k-6). 1978. pap. 14.95 (*0-86704-000-9*) Clarus Music.

Caggiano, Rosemary, jt. auth. see Fass, Bernie.

Caggiano, Rosemary, jt. auth. see Young, Roger.

Cagiano, Judi. The AmbuQual Data Guide: A System for Collecting, Organizing & Scoring Data. (AmbuQual Ser.). 1993. pap. 78.00 (*1-884742-00-9*) Clariar Hlth.

Cagidemetrio, Alide. Fictions of the Past: Hawthorne & Melville. LC 92-39609. 216p. (C). 1993. pap. 16.95 (*0-87023-861-2*) U of Mass Pr.

Caglar, Huguette. La Psciologia Escolar. (Breviarios Ser.). (SPA.). pap. 6.99 (*968-16-4076-4*, Pub. by Fondo) Continental Bk.

Caglayan, A., jt. auth. see Harrison, Colin G.

Cagle, Cheryl, jt. ed. see Witzleben, Donna.

***Cagle, Daryl.** True! The Complete Cartoon Encyclopedia of Human Knowledge. (Illus.). 144p. 1999. pap. 12.95 (*0-9660676-8-1*) Plan Nine Publ.

Cagle, Gerry. Payola! 300p. 1989. 17.95 (*0-8283-1925-1*) Branden Bks.

***Cagle, Gerry.** Sheet Music. Caso, Adolph, ed. LC 99-57416. 304p. 2000. 21.95 (*0-8283-2051-9*) Branden Bks.

Cagle, Gretchen. Decorative Painting with Gretchen Cagle. LC 95-26069. (Illus.). 144p. (Orig.). 1996. pap. 24.99 (*0-89134-733-X*, North Lght Bks) F & W Pubns Inc.

— Gretchen Cagle's Decorative Painting Keepsakes. LC 97-1899. (Illus.). 144p. 1997. pap. 24.99 (*0-89134-835-2*, North Lght Bks) F & W Pubns Inc.

Cagle, J. C. Sound Church Growth & Christian Development. 85p. (Orig.). 1989. pap. 3.95 (*0-685-34665-X*, 5556) White Wing Pub.

— Spanish Last Days Awareness.Tr. of Concientizacion de los Ultimos Dias. (Illus.). 118p. 1998. pap. text. write for info. (*1-889505-27-7*) White Wing Pub.

Cagle, J. C., ed. see McClure, John R.

Cagle, Jess. Home Cookin' with Dave's Mom. 176p. 1997. per. 12.00 (*0-671-00061-6*) PB.

Cagle, Jess & Letterman, Dorothy. Home Cookin' with Dave's Mom. (Illus.). 256p. 1996. 20.00 (*0-671-00060-8*) PB.

Cagle, Jess, jt. auth. see Letterman, Dorothy.

Cagle, Keith M. The Basics of Teaching American Sign Language. 12p. 24.95 incl. VHS (*0-915035-68-3*) Dawn Sign.

Cagle, Keith M. & Newell, William. The ASLTA Evaluation & Certification System: How to Achieve Certification as a Teacher of American Sign Language. 24p. 29.95 incl. VHS (*0-915035-69-3*) Dawn Sign.

Cagle, Keith M., jt. auth. see Cagle, Sharon J.

***Cagle, Kurt.** XML Developer's Handbook. (Illus.). 2000. pap. 49.99 (*0-7821-2704-5*) Sybex.

Cagle, Laurence T., jt. auth. see Wadsworth, Bruce.

***Cagle, Malcolm W. & Manson, Frank A.** The Sea War in Korea. (Illus.). 640p. 2000. 39.95 (*1-55750-216-1*) Naval Inst Pr.

Cagle, Malcolm W. & Manson, Frank A. The Sea War in Korea. LC 79-6104. (Navies & Men Ser.). (Illus.). 1980. reprint ed. lib. bdg. 41.95 (*0-405-13033-3*) Ayer

Cagle, Mary Branson, see Branson Cagle, Mary.

Cagle, Phillip, ed. Diagnostic Pulmonary Pathology. (Illus.). 792p. 2000. text 215.00 (*0-8247-0168-2*) Dekker.

Cagle, Ray. Teasers, Ticklers, & Tests. (Illus.). 88p. 1998. pap. text 9.95 (*1-889668-08-7*) S & D.

Cagle, Sandra & Shepard, Susan. Cooking is a Celebration. 120p. 1985. pap. 7.95 (*0-9615572-0-6*) Food Trends.

Cagle, Sharon J. & Cagle, Keith M. GA & SK Etiquette: Guidelines for Telecommunications in the Deaf Community. (Illus.). 60p. 1991. teacher ed., spiral bd. 11.95 (*0-9614621-7-5*) Bowling Gr Pr.

Cagle, Van M. Reinventing Pop-Subculture: The Impact of Andy Warhol. 260p. 1995. text 48.00 (*0-8039-5743-2*) Sage.

— Reinventing Pop-Subculture: The Impact of Andy Warhol. LC 94-48049. 240p. 1995. pap. 22.95 (*0-8039-5744-0*) Sage.

Cagle, William R., pref. The Lilly Library: The First Quarter Century, 1960-1985. (Illus.). 157p. (Orig.). (C). 1985. pap. 15.00 (*1-879598-04-3*) IN Univ Lilly Library.

Cagle, William R. & Gossy, Dorian. Two Hundred & Fifty Years of the British Novel, 1740-1989. (Illus.). 1990. pap. 10.00 (*1-879598-07-8*) IN Univ Lilly Library.

Cagle, William R. & Stafford, Lisa K. American Books on Food & Drink: A Bibliographical Catalog of the Gernon Collection Housed in the Lilly Library at the University of Indiana. LC 98-29889. 862p. 1998. 95.00 (*1-884718-67-1*) Oak Knoll.

— A Matter of Taste. rev. ed. LC 99-19304. (Gernon Collection on Food & Drink). (Illus.). 1205p. (C). 1999. 95.00 (*1-884718-86-8*, 53908RB) Oak Knoll.

Cagley-Knight, Joan. Alzheimer's: Things a Nurse Needs to Know. Halliburton, Barbara, ed. 78p. 1997. pap. write for info. (*1-57801-012-8*) Western Schls.

— Nursing Care of the Elderly. 4th rev. ed. Lantz, John, ed. (Illus.). 277p. 1998. pap. 39.95 (*1-57801-031-4*) Western Schls.

Cagli, Bruno, tr. see Rossini, Gioachino.

Caglioti, G. The Dynamics of Ambiguity. (Illus.). 192p. 1992. 104.95 (*0-387-52020-1*) Spr-Verlag.

Caglioti, Luciano & Giacconi, Mirella. The Two Faces of Chemistry. LC 82-12706. 240p. (C). 1983. 27.50 (*0-262-03088-8*) MIT Pr.

Cagnacci, Schwicker Angelo. International Dictionary of Building Construction: Civil Engineering-Architecture-Hydraulics in four languages:English-French-German-Italian. 1262p. 1972. 250.00 (*0-7859-8875-0*) Fr & Eur.

Cagnardi, Augusto, jt. text see Fuchs, Rudi.

Cagnat, jt. auth. see Stewart.

Cagnat, R., et al, eds. Inscriptiones Graecae Ad Res Romanas Pertinentes (IGRR), Set, Vols. I-IV. 150.00 (*0-89005-073-2*) Ares.

Cagnat, R., et al. Inscriptiones Graecae Ad Res Romanas Pertinentes, 3 vols. 1975. 150.00 (*0-89005-072-4*) Ares.

Cagnat, Rene L. L' Armee Romaine d'Afrique et l'Occupation Militaire de lAfrique sous les Empereurs. LC 75-7306. (Roman History Ser.). (FRE., Illus.). 1975. reprint ed. 66.95 (*0-405-07187-6*) Ayer.

Cagnati, Ines. Genie la Folle. (FRE.). 1979. pap. 10.95 (*0-7859-2217-2*, 2070307114X) Fr & Eur.

— Jour De Conge. (FRE.). 1980. pap. 10.95 (*0-7859-1916-3*, 2070372006) Fr & Eur.

— Mose Ou le Lezard Qui Pleurait. (FRE.). 256p. 1984. pap. 11.95 (*0-7859-2227-X*, 207037582X) Fr & Eur.

Cagney, J. Kenneth. How to Design & Conduct Retirement Planning Programs. Bruce, Stephen D., ed. 274p. 1989. ring bd. 79.95 (*1-55645-425-2*, 425) Busn Legal Reports.

Cagney, Lawrence K. Compensation Committees. (Corporate Practice Ser.: No. 73). 1998. 95.00 (*1-55871-367-0*) BNA.

Cagniant, D., ed. Complexation Chromatography. (Chromatographic Science Ser.: Vol. 57). (Illus.). 312p. 1991. text 150.00 (*0-8247-8577-0*) Dekker.

Cagno, Michael. Exercise Book for Italian: Level II. (C). 1984. pap. 3.95 (*0-913298-00-X*) S F Vanni.

— Exercise Book for Italian: Level III. 1984. pap. 3.95 (*0-913298-01-8*) S F Vanni.

Cagno, Michael & D'Arlon, Ben. Rapid Italian for Students & Tourists. (C). 1993. pap. 10.95 (*0-913298-05-0*) S F Vanni.

Cagnon, Maurice, ed. Ethique et Esthetique dans la Litterature Francaise du XXe Siecle. (Stanford French & Italian Studies: No. 10). vi, 214p. 1978. pap. 56.50 (*0-915838-38-9*) Anma Libri.

Cagnon, Maurice, et al. Analyse de Texte: Theorie et Pratique. (FRE.). XV, 151p. (C). 1996. pap. text 24.95 (*0-8204-3034-X*) P Lang Pubng.

Cagnone, Nanni. The Book of Giving Back: A Poem. LC 96-61926. (Illus.). 64p. 1997. pap. 10.00 (*0-9646466-4-1*) Edgewise Pr.

— What's Hecuba to Him or He to Hecuba? Verzoni, David, tr. LC 75-4969. (ENG & ITA.). 183p. 1975. 7.95 (*0-915570-01-7*) Oolp Pr.

Cagnoni, Stefano, ed. see EvoWorkshops 2000 Staff.

Cagon, Joanna & De Mause, Neil. Field of Schemes: The Great Stadium Swindle. LC 97-48625. 272p. 1999. pap. 12.71 (*1-56751-138-4*) Common Courage.

Caha, J. English-Czech Dictionary. (CZE & ENG.). 880p. 1982. 35.00 (*0-8288-0534-2*, M14849) Fr & Eur.

Caha, Jan & Kramsky, J. English-Czech Dictionary. (CZE & ENG.). 878p. 1980. 60.00 (*0-569-00405-5*, Pub. by Collets) St Mut.

Caha, Jan & Kramsky, J. R. English-Czech Dictionary. 6th ed. 877p. (C). 1988. 100.00 (*0-569-19831-3*, Pub. by Collets) St Mut.

Caha, Jan & Kramsky, Jiri. English-Czech Dictionary. 878p. 1982. 55.00 (*0-7855-1750-2*, Pub. by Collets) St Mut.

Cahagnet, Louis A. The Celestial Telegraph: Or, Secrets of the Life to Come Revealed Through Magnetism... LC 75-36832. (Occult Ser.). 1976. reprint ed. 36.95 (*0-405-07944-3*) Ayer.

Cahalan, Don. Digging for Irish Roots: How to Search for Your Ancestors. (Illus.). 220p. 1989. 17.95 (*0-915474-10-7*) Decalogue Bks.

— Problem Drinkers: A National Survey. LC 73-133617. (Jossey-Bass Behavioral Science Ser.). (Illus.). 220p. reprint ed. pap. 68.20 (*0-608-15165-3*, 205216300045) Bks Demand.

Cahalan, Don & Room, Robin. Problem Drinking Among American Men. 1974. 25.95 (*0-8084-0380-X*) NCUP.

— Problem Drinking Among American Men. LC 72-619570. (Monographs: No. 7). 1974. 8.25 (*0-911290-38-9*) Rutgers Ctr Alcohol.

Cahalan, Don, et al. American Drinking Practices. 1969. 19.95 (*0-8084-0412-1*) NCUP.

— American Drinking Practices: A National Study of Drinking Behavior & Attitudes. LC 70-626701. (Monographs: No. 6). 1969. pap. 10.95 (*0-911290-37-0*) Rutgers Ctr Alcohol.

Cahalan, James M. Double Visions: Women & Men in Modern & Contemporary Irish Fiction. LC 99-20984. (Irish Studies). 232p. 1999. 29.95 (*0-8156-2804-8*) Syracuse U Pr.

— Liam O'Flaherty: A Study of the Short Fiction. (Twayne's Studies in Short Fiction: No. 23). 184p. (C). 1991. 24.95 (*0-8057-8312-1*, Twyne) Mac Lib Ref.

— Modern Irish Literature: A Chronology. LC 92-15105. (G. K. Hall Reference Ser.). 250p. 1992. 50.00 (*0-8161-7264-1*, Hall Reference) Macmillan.

Cahalan, John C. Causal Realism: An Essay on Philosophical Method & the Foundations of Knowledge. Deely, John & Williams, Brooke, eds. LC 85-3309. (Sources in Semiotics Ser.: Vol. II). 516p. (Orig.). 1985. pap. 41.00 (*0-8191-4622-6*); lib. bdg. 75.50 (*0-8191-4621-8*) U Pr of Amer.

Cahalan, M. D. & Lepple-Wienhues, A., eds. Ion Channels in Lymphocyte Function. (Cellular Physiology & Biochemistry Ser.: Vol. 7, No. 3-4, 1997). (Illus.). 114p. 1997. pap. 23.50 (*3-8055-6591-7*) S Karger.

***Cahalan, Margaret W.** Academic Libraries: 1994. 60p. 1998. pap. 5.50 (*0-16-063652-3*) USGPO.

— Academic Libraries: 1996. 80p. 2000. pap. 7.50 (*0-16-050244-6*) USGPO.

Cahalan, Margaret W. & Parsons, Lee A. Historical Corrections Statistics in the U. S., 1850-1984. (Illus.). 248p. 1996. reprint ed. pap. text 40.00 (*0-7881-3198-2*) DIANE Pub.

Cahalan, Margaret Werner & Justh, Natalie M. The Status of Academic Libraries in the United States: Results from the 1994 Academic Library Survey with Historical Comparisons. (Education Department Publication Ser.: No. 98-311). (Illus.). 100p. 1998. pap. 12.00 (*0-16-049720-5*) USGPO.

C

Cahalane, Cornelius F. Policeman. LC 75-112529. (Rise of Urban America Ser.). 1974. reprint ed. 25.95 (*0-405-02440-1*) Ayer.

Cahall, Raymond D. The Sovereign Council of New France: A Study in Canadian Constitutional History. LC 15-13350. (Columbia University. Studies in the Social Sciences: No. 156). reprint ed. 36.50 (*0-404-51156-2*) AMS Pr.

Cahall, Raymond Du Bois. The Sovereign Council of New France. 276p. 1998. reprint ed. pap. 31.95 (*1-58211-062-X*, 097650) Quintin Pub RI.

***Cahall, Raymond Du Bois.** The Sovereign Council of New France. 274p. 1998. reprint ed. pap. 31.95 (*1-886560-63-3*) Quintin Pub RI.

***Cahan & Associates Staff.** I Am Almost Always Hungry. LC 99-36134. (Illus.). 224p. 1999. 45.00 (*1-56898-199-6*) Princeton Arch.

Cahan, Abraham. The Imported Bridegroom & Other Stories of the New York Ghetto. 1972. reprint ed. 36.50 (*0-8422-8021-9*) Irvington.

— The Rise of David Levinsky. Chametzky, Jules, ed. & intro. by. LC 92-34783. 544p. 1993. pap. 13.95 (*0-14-018687-5*, Penguin Classics) Viking Penguin.

— The Rise of David Levinsky. large type ed. LC 99-19811. 685p. 1999. 29.95 (*1-56000-496-7*) Transaction Pubs.

— The White Terror & the Red: A Novel of Revolutionary Russia. LC 74-27969. (Modern Jewish Experience Ser.). 1975. reprint ed. 37.95 (*0-405-06699-6*) Ayer.

— Yekl & the Imported Bridegroom & Other Stories of the New York Ghetto. 240p. 1970. pap. 6.95 (*0-486-22427-9*) Dover.

— Yekl & the Imported Bridegroom & Other Stories of the New York Ghetto. 1990. 15.50 (*0-8446-0048-2*) Peter Smith.

Cahan, Anthony C., jt. auth. see Ariel, I. M.

Cahan, David, ed. Hermann von Helmholtz & the Foundations of Nineteenth-Century Science. LC 93-16285. (California Studies in the History of Science: Vol. 12). 1993. 80.00 (*0-520-08334-2*, Pub. by U CA Pr) Cal Prin Full Svc.

Cahan, David & Rudd, M. Eugene. Science at the American Frontier: A Biography of DeWitt Bristol Brace. LC 99-49720. (Illus.). 256p. 2000. text 45.00 (*0-8032-1508-8*) U of Nebr Pr.

Cahan, David, ed. & intro. see Helmholtz, Hermann.

Cahan, Emily D. Past Caring: A History of U. S. Preschool Care & Education for the Poor, 1820-1965. LC 89-3425. (Illus.). 60p. (Orig.). 1989. pap. 7.95 (*0-926582-00-3*) NCCP.

Cahan, Leonard, ed. see Rabbinical Assembly Staff.

Cahan, Rich, jt. auth. see McNamee, Tom.

***Cahan, Richard.** Chicago: Rising from the Prairie. LC 00-103659. (Illus.). 500p. (C). 2000. 49.95 (*1-886483-46-9*) Heritge Media.

Cahan, Richard. They All Fall Down: Richard Nickel's Struggle to Save America's Architecture. LC 93-7613. (Illus.). 288p. 1995. 34.95 (*0-471-14426-6*) Wiley.

Cahan, Richard & Jacob, Mark. The Game That Was. (Illus.). 256p. 1996. 50.00 (*0-8092-3200-6*, 320060, Contemporary Bks) NTC Contemp Pub Co.

Cahan, Susan & Kocur, Zoya, eds. Contemporary Art in Multicultural Education. LC 95-10979. (Illus.). 423p. (C). 1996. pap. 36.99 (*0-415-91190-7*) Routledge.

— Contemporary Art in Multicultural Education. LC 95-10979. (Illus.). 423p. (C). (gr. 13). 1996. 85.00 (*0-415-91189-3*) Routledge.

Cahanko, Pamela, jt. auth. see Chessen, Bestey.

***Cahay, M., et al, eds.** Advanced Luminescent Materials & Quantum Confinement. 504p. 1999. 84.00 (*1-56677-245-1*, PV 99-22) Electrochem Soc.

Cahay, M., et al, eds. Proceedings of the International Symposium on Quantum Confinement, 2nd: Physics & Applications. LC 94-70849. (Proceedings Ser.: Vol. 94-17). 427p. 1994. 78.00 (*1-56677-049-1*) Electrochem Soc.

Cahay, M., et al, eds. Quatum Confinement V: Nanostructures. 690p. 90.00 (*1-56677-213-3*, PV 98-19) Electrochem Soc.

Cahell, Marjorie, jt. auth. see Simko, Joan.

***Cahen, Alfred.** Dynamic Technical Analysis. 175p. 2000. 69.95 (*0-471-89947-X*) Wiley.

Cahen, Alfred. The Western European Union & NATO: Building a European Defence Identity Within the Context of Atlantic Solidarity, No. 2. (Atlantic Commentaries Ser.). 150p. 1989. pap. 16.50 (*0-08-037340-2*, Pub. by Brasseys) Brasseys.

Cahen, Claude. La Regime Feodal de l'Italie Normande. LC 80-1995. reprint ed. 25.00 (*0-404-18555-X*) AMS Pr.

Cahen, L., et al. The Geochronology & Evolution of Africa. (Illus.). 526p. 1984. 175.00 (*0-19-857544-0*) OUP.

Cahen, M. & Flato, Moshe, eds. Differential Geometry & Relativity. (Mathematical Physics & Applied Mathematics Ser: No. 3). 1976. text 199.00 (*90-277-0745-6*) Kluwer Academic.

— Quantum Theories & Geometry. (C). 1988. text 140.50 (*90-277-2803-8*) Kluwer Academic.

Cahen, Michel. Pseudo-Riemannian Symmetric Spaces. LC 79-27541. (American Mathematical Society Ser.: No. 229). 117p. reprint ed. pap. 36.30 (*0-608-20156-1*, 205280100011) Bks Demand.

Cahen, Michel & Parker, Monique. Pseudo-Riemannian Symmetric Spaces. LC 79-27541. (Memoirs Ser.: No. 24/229). 108p. 1992. pap. 17.00 (*0-8218-2229-2*, MEMO/24/229) Am Math.

Cahen, Paul-Jean, ed. Commutative Ring Theory: Proceedings of the II International Conference. LC 96-41106. (Lecture Notes in Pure & Applied Mathematics Ser.: Vol. 185). (Illus.). 488p. 1996. pap. text 185.00 (*0-8247-9815-5*) Dekker.

Cahen, Paul-Jean, et al, eds. Commutative Ring Theory. LC 93-35648. (Lecture Notes in Pure & Applied Mathematics Ser.: Vol. 153). (Illus.). 280p. 1993. pap. text 150.00 (*0-8247-9170-3*) Dekker.

Cahen, Paul-Jean & Chabert, Jean-Luc. Integer-Valued Polynomials. LC 96-35954. (Mathematical Surveys & Monographs Ser.: Vol. 48). 322p. 1996. text 75.00 (*0-8218-0388-3*, SURV/48) Am Math.

Caher, James P. & Caher, John M. Debt Free! Your Guide to Personal Bankruptcy Without Shame. 288p. 1995. pap. 14.95 (*0-8050-4276-8*, Owl) H Holt & Co.

Caher, John M. King of the Mountain: The Rise, Fall & Redemption of Chief Judge Sol Wachtler. LC 97-49303. (Illus.). 391p. 1998. 26.95 (*1-57392-197-1*) Prometheus Bks.

Caher, John M., jt. auth. see Caher, James P.

Cahier, Charles & Martin, Arthur. Three Hundred Seventy-Six Decorative Allover Patterns from Historic Tilework & Textiles. (Illus.). 256p. 1989. pap. 12.95 (*0-486-26146-8*) Dover.

Cahill. Nixon Man. 240p. 1999. pap. 12.95 (*0-312-24488-6*) St Martin.

Cahill, jt. auth. see Mandava.

Cahill, Ann J. Women on the Hill: Alumnae Reflect on Twenty Years of Coeducation, 1972-1992. 263p. 1993. pap. text 20.00 (*0-9636118-0-1*) Coll Holy Cross.

Cahill, Ann J., jt. ed. see Bell, Diane.

Cahill, Anne. The Community Music Handbook. 204p. (Orig.). pap. 24.95 (*0-86819-567-7*, Pub. by Currency Pr) Accents Pubns.

Cahill, Bernard R. & Pearl, Arthur J., eds. Intensive Participation in Children's Sports. (Illus.). 240p. 1996. reprint ed. pap. text 25.00 (*0-88011-698-6*, BCAH0698) Human Kinetics.

Cahill, Bette. Butterbox Babies. 256p. (J). 1992. mass mkt. 7.99 (*0-7704-2517-8*) Bantam.

Cahill, Billie, et al, eds. Backroads Tour: Northern Kentucky Historic Road Tour. (Illus.). 32p. (Orig.). 1992. pap. 5.00 (*0-9624673-9-1*) Picture This Bks.

Cahill, Bob & Stephenson, John G. Microcomputer Troubleshooting & Repair. 368p. 1988. 24.95 (*0-672-22629-4*) Sams.

Cahill, Chris. Bear Magic. LC 89-61636. (Rhyme-Fingerplay-Puppet Bk.). (Illus.). 12p. (J). (ps-1). 1990. bds. 5.95 (*1-877779-00-8*) Schneider Educational.

— Bunny Magic. LC 89-61633. (Rhyme-Fingerplay-Puppet Bk.). (Illus.). 12p. (J). (ps-1). 1990. bds. 5.95 (*1-877779-02-4*) Schneider Educational.

— Un Conejito Encantador - Bunny Magic. LC 90-62627. (Finger Magic Bk.). (Illus.). 12p. (J). 1991. bds. 5.95 (*1-877779-20-2*) Schneider Educational.

— Un Osito Encantador - Bear Magic. LC 90-62628. (Finger Magic Bk.). (Illus.). 12p. (J). 1991. bds. 5.95 (*1-877779-19-9*) Schneider Educational.

Cahill, Dan L., III. Utopia Now: The Ultimate Success Story. LC 99-60410. 175p. 1999. pap. 11.95 (*0-9664536-7-0*) Chiyoko.

Cahill, David, jt. auth. see Bradley, Peter T.

Cahill, Denise & Cahill, Kevin. Ten Easy Steps to Selling Your Home: A Complete for Sale by Owner Kit (Multi State Version) (Illus.). 75p. 1998. mass mkt. 29.95 (*0-9666231-1-8*) Innovative Business Systems.

Cahill, Dennis J. How Consumers Pick a Hotel: Strategic Segmentation & Target Marketing. LC 96-41430. (Illus.). 164p. (C). 1997. 39.95 (*0-7890-0139-X*); pap. 19.95 (*0-7890-0184-5*) Haworth Pr.

Cahill, Dennis J. Internal Marketing: Your Company's Next Stage of Growth. LC 95-35020. (Illus.). 164p. (C). 1996. 29.95 (*0-7890-6005-1*) Haworth Pr.

Cahill, Dennis J. Squeezing a New Service into a Crowded Market. LC 94-45865. 175p. 1995. lib. bdg. 39.95 (*1-56024-939-0*) Haworth Pr.

Cahill, Donald & Cahill, Maureen. Goal Mine - Prospector, No. 3. 1998. spiral bd. 39.95 (*0-941457-10-9*) IEP.

***Cahill, Donald & Cahill, Maureen.** Goal Mine Prospector. 4th ed. 2000. pap. text 39.95 (*0-941457-19-2*) IEP.

Cahill, Donald R., rev. Lachman's Case Studies in Anatomy. 4th ed. (Illus.). 432p. 1996. pap. text 22.95 (*0-19-510297-5*) OUP.

Cahill, Donald R., et al. Atlas of Human Cross-Sectional Anatomy: With CT & MR Images. 3rd ed. LC 94-42877. 328p. 1995. 249.95 (*0-471-59165-3*) Wiley.

Cahill, E. The Framework of a Christian State: An Introduction to Social Science. 736p. 1997. reprint ed. text 49.95 (*0-912141-32-8*) Roman Cath Bks.

Cahill, E. D., jt. auth. see Cushman, J. A.

Cahill, Eileen M., jt. auth. see Adelman, Marilyn M.

Cahill, Emmett. The Shipmans of East Hawai'i. LC 95-47621. (Illus.). 296p. 1996. pap. 24.95 (*0-8248-1680-3*) UH Pr.

— Yesterday at Kalaupapa. 115p. 1991. pap. 18.95 (*0-915013-16-9*) Editions Ltd.

Cahill, George, Jr., ed. Peripatetic Club, 1933-1993. (Illus.). 211p. (Orig.). 1994. pap. write for info. (*0-9641132-0-1*) Peripat Club.

Cahill, George F., ed. see McDonald, Forrest.

Cahill, Heather. Day Surgery: Principles-Nursing. 1997. pap. text 36.95 (*0-7020-2028-1*) Bailliere Tindall.

Cahill, Heather, ed. Everything You Need to Know about Diseases. (Illus.). 928p. 1997. pap. 24.95 (*0-87434-945-1*) Springhouse Corp.

Cahill, Holger. American Folk Art: The Art of the Common Man in America 1750-1900. LC 71-86427. (Museum of Modern Art Publications in Reprint). (Illus.). 1969. reprint ed. 23.95 (*0-405-01530-5*) Ayer.

— American Painting & Sculpture: 1862-1932. LC 79-86429. (Museum of Modern Art Publications in Reprint). (Illus.). 1969. reprint ed. 21.95 (*0-405-01531-3*) Ayer.

— American Sources of Modern Art. LC 78-86426. (Museum of Modern Art Publications in Reprint). (Illus.). 1969. reprint ed. 18.95 (*0-405-01532-1*) Ayer.

— New Horizons in American Art. LC 75-86428. (Museum of Modern Art Publications in Reprint). (Illus.). 1969. reprint ed. 24.95 (*0-405-01533-X*) Ayer.

Cahill, Holger & Barr, Alfred H., Jr., eds. Art in America in Modern Times. LC 69-17569. (Essay Index Reprint Ser.). 1977. 38.95 (*0-8369-0067-7*) Ayer.

Cahill, Holger, et al. Masters of Popular Painting. LC 66-26120. (Museum of Modern Art Publications in Reprint). 1967. reprint ed. 20.95 (*0-405-01524-0*) Ayer.

Cahill, Hope L. Old Age - A Balance Sheet. LC 80-54452. (Illus.). 102p. 1981. pap. 3.95 (*0-933174-13-6*) Wide World-Tetra.

***Cahill, Jack.** Forgotten Patriots: Canadian Rebels on Australia's Convict Shores. 431p. 2000. pap. 16.95 (*1-896941-07-9*, Pub. by RBST) Midpt Trade.

Cahill, James. The Art of Southern Sung China. LC 74-27411. (Asia Society Ser.). (Illus.). 1976. reprint ed. lib. bdg. 26.95 (*0-405-06560-4*) Ayer.

— The Compelling Image: Nature & Style in Seventeenth-Century Chinese Painting. (Charles Eliot Norton Lectures). (Illus.). 262p. 1986. pap. 32.50 (*0-674-15281-6*) HUP.

— The Distant Mountains: Chinese Painting of the Late Ming Dynasty, 1570-1644. (History of Later Chinese Painting Ser.: Vol. 3). (Illus.). 336p. (C). 1982. 49.95 (*0-8348-0174-4*) Weatherhill.

— Fantastics & Eccentrics in Chinese Paintings. LC 74-27412. (Asia Society Ser.). (Illus.). 1976. reprint ed. lib. bdg. 36.95 (*0-405-06561-2*) Ayer.

— The Lyric Journey: Poetic Painting in China & Japan. LC 95-23906. (Edwin O. Reischauer Lectures). (Illus.). 296p. 1996. 45.00 (*0-674-53970-2*) HUP.

— New Dimensions in Chinese Ink Painting: Works from the Collection of John & Alice Z. Berninghausen. LC 91-11813. (Illus.). 56p. 1992. pap. 15.00 (*0-9625262-3-1*) Middlebury Coll Mus.

— The Painter's Practice: How Artists Lived & Worked in Traditional China. (Bampton Lectures in America). (Illus.). 208p. 1995. pap. 26.50 (*0-231-08181-2*) Col U Pr.

— Scholar Painters of Japan: The Nanga School. LC 74-27413. (Asia Society Ser.). (Illus.). 1976. reprint ed. lib. bdg. 36.95 (*0-405-06562-0*) Ayer.

— Three Alternative Histories of Chinese Painting. (Franklin D. Murphy Lectures: No. 9). (Illus.). 112p. 1990. 12.00 (*0-913689-28-9*) Spencer Muse Art.

Cahill, James, et al. Chen Chi Kwan Paintings, 1940-1980. (Illus.). 128p. 1981. 54.50 (*0-906610-14-1*, Pub. by Bamboo Pub) Antique Collect.

Cahill, James, ed. see Block, Lawrence.

Cahill, James, ed. see Bova, Ben, et al.

Cahill, Jane. Her Kind: Women from Greek Mythology. LC 96-138750. 275p. (C). 1995. pap. 19.95 (*1-55111-042-3*) Broadview Pr.

Cahill, Jean H., ed. see Cahill, Robert E.

Cahill, John J., jt. auth. see Kasavana, Michael L.

Cahill, Kathleen. The Nobel Peace Prize, 1989. (Monograph Ser.). 113p. (C). 1990. 25.00 (*0-8161-7253-6*, Hall Reference) Macmillan.

Cahill, Kathleen, jt. auth. see Cahill, Kent.

Cahill, Kent & Cahill, Kathleen. When an Angel Dies. Moog, Bob, ed. (Murder Mystery Parties Ser.). (Illus.). 50p. 1986. 8.00 (*0-935145-05-2*) Univ Games.

Cahill, Keri, ed. see Cahill, Robert E.

Cahill, Keri M., ed. see Cahill, Robert E.

Cahill, Kevin, jt. auth. see Cahill, Denise.

Cahill, Kevin, jt. auth. see Slafer, Anna.

Cahill, Kevin M. Framework for Survival: Health, Human Rights, & Humanitarian Assistance in Conflicts & Disasters. LC 99-20511. 1999. 75.00 (*0-415-92234-8*); pap. 24.99 (*0-415-92235-6*) Routledge.

— Irish Essays. LC 80-80550. 140p. 1980. 9.00 (*0-89444-028-4*) John Jay Pr.

Cahill, Kevin M., ed. Famine. LC 81-19034. (Illus.). 173p. (Orig.). reprint ed. pap. 53.70 (*0-8357-8542-4*, 203485300091) Bks Demand.

***Cahill, Kevin M., ed.** Preventive Diplomacy: Stopping Wars Before They Start. 2nd ed. 384p. 2000. 80.00 (*0-415-92284-4*); pap. 24.99 (*0-415-92285-2*) Routledge.

Cahill, Laura. Hysterical Blindness. pap. 5.95 (*0-8222-1715-5*) Dramatists Play.

— Mercy. 5.95 (*0-8222-1716-3*) Dramatists Play.

Cahill, Lawrence B. Environmental Audits. 7th ed. LC 96-180607. 727p. 1996. pap. text 79.00 (*0-86587-525-1*) Gov Insts.

Cahill, Lisa S. Between the Sexes: Foundations for a Christian Ethics of Sexuality. LC 84-48717. 106p. 1985. pap. 14.00 (*0-8006-1834-3*, 1-1834, Fortress Pr) Augsburg Fortress.

— Love Your Enemies: Discipleship, Pacifism, & Just War Theory. LC 93-35461. 288p. 1994. pap. 20.00 (*0-8006-2700-8*, 1-2700, Fortress Pr) Augsburg Fortress.

— Sex, Gender & Christian Ethics. (New Studies in Christian Ethics: No. 9). 344p. (C). 1996. pap. text 19.95 (*0-521-57848-5*) Cambridge U Pr.

Cahill, Lisa S. & Childress, James F., eds. Christian Ethics: Problems & Prospects. LC 96-39058. 416p. (Orig.). 1996. pap. 18.95 (*0-8298-1136-2*) Pilgrim OH.

Cahill, Lisa S. & Farley, Margaret A., eds. Embodient, Morality, & Medicine. LC 94-46674. (Theology & Medicine Ser.: Vol. 6). 236p. (C). 1995. lib. bdg. 154.50 (*0-7923-3342-X*, Pub. by Kluwer Academic) Kluwer Academic.

Cahill, Lisa S. & Mieth, Dietmar, eds. The Family. 150p. (Orig.). 1995. pap. 15.00 (*0-88344-885-8*) Orbis Bks.

Cahill, Lisa S., jt. ed. see Junker-Kenny, Maureen.

Cahill, Lisa S., jt. ed. see Mieth, Dietmar.

Cahill, Marie. Christmas in Texas. LC 94-24483. (Illus.). 120p. 1994. ring bd. 9.95 (*0-914846-86-8*) Golden West Pub.

— Marilyn. (Illus.). 64p. 1994. write for info. (*1-57215-031-9*) World Pubns.

Cahill, Marilyn. Elvis Presley. (Illus.). 64p. 1994. write for info. (*1-57215-032-7*) World Pubns.

Cahill, Marion C. Shorter Hours: A Study of the Movement since the Civil War. LC 68-54258. (Columbia University. Studies in the Social Sciences: No. 380). 1971. reprint ed. 34.50 (*0-404-51380-8*) AMS Pr.

Cahill, Mary & Grant, Gary. Victorian Danville: Fifth-Two Landmarks, Their Architecture & History. 2nd rev. ed. (Illus.). 130p. 1996. reprint ed. write for info. (*0-933571-10-0*) Ure Pr.

Cahill, Mary Jane. Lebanon: Major World Nations. LC 98-4315. (Major World Nations Ser.). (Illus.). 144p. (YA). (gr. 5 up). 1999. lib. bdg. 19.95 (*0-7910-4981-7*) Chelsea Hse.

— Northern Ireland: Major World Nations. LC 99-13780. (Major World Nations Ser.). (Illus.). 144p. (YA). (gr. 5 up). 1998. 19.95 (*0-7910-4764-4*) Chelsea Hse.

Cahill, Matt. Professional Handbook of Diagnostic Tests. LC 94-39918. (Illus.). 704p. 1995. 32.95 (*0-87434-775-0*) Springhouse Corp.

Cahill, Maureen, jt. auth. see Cahill, Donald.

Cahill, Michael. Nixon Man. LC 98-13706. 224p. 1998. text 22.95 (*0-312-18749-1*) St Martin.

Cahill, Michael, ed. The First Commentary on Mark: An Annotated Translation. LC 97-1306. 168p. 1998. text 39.95 (*0-19-511601-1*) OUP.

Cahill, Michele, et al. In School Together: School-based Child Care Serving Student Mothers. 135p. (Orig.). 1987. pap. 13.00 (*0-89492-061-8*) Acad Educ Dev.

Cahill, R. N., jt. ed. see Trnka, Z.

Cahill, Richard A. Collisions & Their Causes. 2nd rev. ed. LC 96-72387. (Illus.). 262p. 1997. 59.95 (*0-9630018-7-6*) Nautical TX.

— Disasters at Sea: Titantic to Exxon Valdez. 288p. 1992. pap. 19.95 (*0-9630018-8-4*) Nautical TX.

Cahill, Rick. Arizona Wilderness Guide. Frantz, Ilena, ed. (Illus.). 214p. (Orig.). 1994. pap. text 13.95 (*0-9630853-1-X*) West Imports.

— The Story of Casas Grandes Pottery. Carson, Carrie, ed. Gates, Julia, tr. from ENG. (SPA., Illus.). (Orig.). 1991. pap. 14.95 (*0-9630853-0-1*) West Imports.

Cahill, Robert B. & Herbic, Herbert. How to Take an Essay Exam: Stack the Deck Writing Program Ser. 48p. 1981. pap. 2.50 (*0-933282-06-0*) Stack the Deck.

Cahill, Robert B. & Hrebic, Herbert J. Cut the Deck. rev. ed. Barry, Jimi, ed. (Writing Program Ser.). (J). (gr. 8-9). 1985. text 15.95 (*0-933282-16-8*); pap. text 9.95 (*0-933282-15-X*) Stack the Deck.

— Fan the Deck. (Writing Program Ser.). (YA). (gr. 9-12). 1978. pap. text 15.95 (*0-933282-12-5*) Stack the Deck.

— Stack the Deck. (Writing Program Ser.). (YA). (gr. 9-12). 1973. text 15.95 (*0-933282-11-7*); pap. text 11.95 (*0-933282-25-7*) Stack the Deck.

— Stack the Deck. rev. ed. (Illus.). 1980. reprint ed. pap. 11.95 (*0-933282-00-1*) Stack the Deck.

Cahill, Robert E. Amazing Fish Stories. Thompson, Beth, ed. (Undersea Classics Ser.: No. 1-C). (Illus.). 112p. (Orig.). 1996. pap. 6.95 (*1-889193-00-3*) Old Salt Box.

— Finding New England's Shipwrecks & Treasures. (Collectible Classics Ser.: No. 6). (Illus.). 54p. (Orig.). 1984. pap. 3.95 (*0-916787-05-2*) Chandler-Smith.

— Haunted Happenings: With New Photos of Old Ghosts. (Old New England Ser.: Vol. 4). (Illus.). (Orig.). 1995. pap. 6.95 (*0-9626162-3-0*) Old Salt Box.

— Haunted Ships of the North Atlantic. (Old New England Ser.: Vol. 8A). 1997. 6.95 (*1-889193-03-8*) Old Salt Box.

— The Horrors of Salem's Witch Dungeon. (Collectible Classics Ser.: No. 9). (Illus.). 50p. (Orig.). 1986. pap. 3.95 (*0-916787-08-7*) Chandler-Smith.

— Lighthouse Mysteries of the North Atlantic, No. 7-A. Scanlon, Stacey, ed. (Illus.). 104p. 1998. pap. 6.95 (*1-889193-02-X*) Old Salt Box.

— New England's Ancient Mysteries. (Old New England Ser.: Vol. 5). (Illus.). 88p. (Orig.). 1993. pap. 6.95 (*0-9626162-4-9*) Old Salt Box.

— New England's Christmas Memories. Cahill, Jean H., ed. (Old Salt Box Ser.: No. 3B). 48p. (Orig.). 1993. pap. 5.50 (*0-9626162-6-5*) Old Salt Box.

— New England's Cruel & Unusual Punishments. Cahill, Keri, ed. (Old New England Ser.: Vol. 6). (Illus.). 88p. 1994. pap. 6.95 (*0-9626162-9-X*) Old Salt Box.

— New England's Ghostly Haunts. (Collectible Classics Ser.: No. 2). (Illus.). 50p. (Orig.). 1983. pap. 3.95 (*0-916787-01-X*) Chandler-Smith.

— New England's Mad & Mysterious Men. (Collectible Classics Ser.: No. 4). (Illus.). 50p. (Orig.). 1984. pap. 3.95 (*0-916787-03-6*) Chandler-Smith.

— New England's Marvelous Monsters. (Collectible Classics Ser.: No. 3). (Illus.). 50p. 1983. pap. 3.95 (*0-916787-02-8*) Chandler-Smith.

— New England's Mountain Madness. (Collectible Classics Ser.: No. 15). (Illus.). 48p. (Orig.). 1989. pap. 3.95 (*0-916787-14-1*) Chandler-Smith.

— New England's Naughty Navy. (Collectible Classics Ser.: No. 11). (Illus.). 60p. (Orig.). 1987. pap. 4.95 (*0-916787-10-9*) Chandler-Smith.

— New England's Pirates & Lost Treasures. (Collectible Classics Ser.: No. 14). 60p. (Orig.). 1987. pap. 4.95 (*0-916787-13-3*) Chandler-Smith.

— New England's Riotous Revolution. (Collectible Classics Ser.: No. 13). (Illus.). 68p. (Orig.). 1987. pap. 4.95 (*0-916787-12-5*) Chandler-Smith.

— New England's Strange Sea Sagas. (Collectible Classics Ser.: No. 5). (Illus.). 54p. 1984. pap. 3.95 (*0-916787-04-4*) Chandler-Smith.

— New England's Things That Go Bump in the Night. (Collectible Classics Ser.: No. 16). (Illus.). 48p. (Orig.). 1989. pap. 3.95 (*0-916787-15-X*) Chandler-Smith.

C

— New England's Viking & Indian Wars. (Collectible Classics Ser.: No. 12). (Illus.). 56p. (Orig.). 1986. pap. 3.95 (*0-916787-11-7*) Chandler-Smith.

— New England's Visitors from Outer Space. (Collectible Classics Ser.: No. 8). (Illus.). 54p. (Orig.). 1985. pap. 3.95 (*0-916787-07-9*) Chandler-Smith.

— New England's War Wonders. (Collectible Classics Ser.: No. 7). (Illus.). 50p. (Orig.). 1984. pap. 3.95 (*0-916787-06-0*) Chandler-Smith.

— New England's Witches & Wizards. (Collectible Classics Ser.: No. 1). (Illus.). 50p. (Orig.). 1983. pap. 3.95 (*0-916787-00-1*) Chandler-Smith.

— The Old Irish of New England. (Collectible Classics Ser.: No. 10). (Illus.). 50p. (Orig.). 1985. pap. 3.95 (*0-916787-09-5*) Chandler-Smith.

— Old New England's Curious Customs & Cures, Vol. 1. (Illus.). 48p. 1990. per. 4.95 (*0-9626162-0-6*) Old Salt Box.

— Olde New England's Sugar & Spice & Everything... America's First Cookbook & Food History. Cahill, Keri M., ed. (Olde New England Ser.). (Illus.). 63p. (YA). 1991. pap. 6.50 (*0-9626162-2-2*) Old Salt Box.

***Cahill, Robert E. & Story, William L.** Salem's Secret: Fiction Based on Fact. (Helen Highwaters Mystery Ser.). (Illus.). 144p. 1999. pap. 7.95 (*1-889193-05-4*) Old Salt Box.

Cahill, S. J. Designing Microprocessor-Based Digital Circuitry. (Illus.). 192p. (C). 1985. pap. text 16.95 (*0-685-09683-1*) P-H.

Cahill, S. J. & McCrum, I. Digital & Microprocessor Engineering. 2nd ed. LC 93-6499. (Ellis Horwood Series in Electrical & Electronic Engineering). 576p. 1993. write for info. (*0-13-217928-8*, Pub. by Tavistock-E Horwood) Routldge.

Cahill, Sid. Essence of Microprocessor-Based Engineering. LC 97-43886. (Essence of Engineering Ser.). 240p. (C). 1998. pap. text 19.95 (*0-13-244708-8*, Prentice Hall) P-H.

Cahill, Spencer E., ed. Inside Social Life: Readings in Sociological Psychology & Microsociology. 2nd rev. ed. LC 97-30472. (Illus.). 310p. (C). 1998. pap. text. write for info. (*0-935732-89-6*) Roxbury Pub Co.

***Cahill, Spencer E., ed.** Inside Social Life: Readings in Sociological Psychology & Microsociology. 3rd ed. LC 00-20821. 335p. (C). 2000. pap. text. write for info. (*1-891487-42-6*) Roxbury Pub Co.

Cahill, Sue, jt. auth. see Cahill, Tom.

Cahill, Susan. Desiring Italy. LC 97-3973. 1997. pap. 12.00 (*0-449-91080-6*) Fawcett.

— Wise Women: Over Two Thousand Years of Spiritual Writing by Women. 428p. 1997. pap. 15.95 (*0-393-31679-3*) Norton.

Cahill, Susan, ed. Wise Women: Over 2000 Years of Spiritual Writing by Women. LC 95-40575. 416p. 1996. 27.50 (*0-393-03946-3*) Norton.

— Women & Fiction: Short Stories by & about Women. 400p. 1975. mass mkt. 6.99 (*0-451-62729-6*, Ment) NAL.

— Writing Women's Lives: An Anthology of Autobiographical Narratives by Twentieth-Century Women Writers. annuals LC 93-41136. 528p. (Orig.). 1994. pap. 18.00 (*0-06-096998-9*, Perennial) HarperTrade.

Cahill, Suzanne E. Transcendence & Divine Passion: The Queen Mother of the West in Medieval China. LC 92-26835. (Illus.). 326p. 1995. 45.00 (*0-8047-2112-2*); pap. 16.95 (*0-8047-2584-5*) Stanford U Pr.

***Cahill, Thomas.** Desire of the Everlasting Hill. 2001. pap. 14.00 (*0-385-48372-4*) Doubleday.

— Desire of the Everlasting Hills: The World Before & after Jesus. LC 99-16560. (Hinges of History Ser.: Vol. III). (Illus.). 353p. 1999. 24.95 (*0-385-48251-5*) Doubleday.

— Desire of the Everlasting Hills: The World Before & After Jesus. large type ed. LC 99-36511. 480p. 1999. 24.95 (*0-375-40852-5*) Wheeler Pub.

— The Gifts of the Jews: How a Tribe of Desert Nomads Changed the Way Everyone Thinks, Set. abr. ed. 1998. audio 23.00 (*0-671-57686-0*, 493623, Pub. by S&S Audio) Lndmrk Audiobks.

Cahill, Thomas. The Gifts of the Jews: How a Tribe of Desert Nomads Changed the Way Everyone Thinks & Feels. LC 97-45139. (Illus.). 304p. 1998. 23.50 (*0-385-48248-5*, N A Talese) Doubleday.

— The Gifts of the Jews: How a Tribe of Desert Nomads Changed the Way Everyone Thinks & Feels. 291p. 1999. pap. 14.00 (*0-385-48249-3*) Doubleday.

— How the Irish Saved Civilization: The Untold Story of Ireland's Heroic Role from the Fall of Rome to the Rise of Medieval Europe. LC 94-28130. 256p. 1995. 24.95 (*0-385-41848-5*, N A Talese) Doubleday.

— How the Irish Saved Civilization: The Untold Story of Ireland's Heroic Role from the Fall of Rome to the Rise of Medieval Europe. (Hinges of History Ser.). (Illus.). 246p. 1996. pap. 12.95 (*0-385-41849-3*, Anchor NY) Doubleday.

Cahill, Thomas, compiled by. Jesus' Little Instruction Book: His Words to Your Heart. LC 94-15752. 256p. 1994. pap. 8.95 (*0-553-37433-8*) Bantam.

Cahill, Thomas, jt. auth. see McCray, James A.

Cahill, Tim. Jaguars Ripped My Flesh. (Orig.). 1996. pap. 13.00 (*0-679-77079-8*) Vin Bks.

— Pass the Butterworms: Remote Journeys Oddly Rendered. 283p. 1998. pap. 13.00 (*0-375-70111-7*) Vin Bks.

— Pecked to Death by Ducks. LC 93-6328. (Vintage Departures Ser.). 377p. 1994. pap. 13.00 (*0-679-74929-2*) Vin Bks.

— Pecked to Death by Ducks. large type ed. LC 93-7804. 545p. 1993. lib. bdg. 22.95 (*0-8161-5771-5*, G K Hall Lrg Type) Mac Lib Ref.

— Road Fever: A High-Speed Travelogue. 1992. 10.00 (*0-685-51847-7*); pap. 12.00 (*0-394-75837-4*) Vin Bks.

— A Wolverine Is Eating My Leg. (Departures Original Ser.). (Orig.). 1989. pap. 13.00 (*0-679-72026-X*) Vin Bks.

***Cahill, Tim, et al, eds.** Not So Funny When It Happened: The Best of Travel Humor & Misadventure. 224p. 2000. pap. 12.95 (*1-885211-55-4*) Trvlers Tale.

Cahill, Timothy. Johnny Tractor & Friends: Taking Over. Linden, Pat, ed. (John Deere Storybook for Little Folks Ser.). (Illus.). 20p. (J). (gr. 2 up). 1998. boxed set 6.95 (*1-887327-19-3*) Ertl Co.

— Johnny Tractor & Friends: Working Together. Linden, Pat, ed. (John Deere Storybook for Little Folks Ser.). (Illus.). 20p. (J). (gr. 2 up). 1998. boxed set 6.95 (*1-887327-20-7*) Ertl Co.

***Cahill, Timothy, et al.** Muses in Arcadia: Cultural Life in the Berkshires. LC 99-58282. (Illus.). 320p. 2000. pap. 19.95 (*1-58157-016-3*, Pub. by Berkshire Hse) Natl Bk Netwk.

Cahill, Timothy P. Profiles in the American Dream. LC 94-71215. (Illus.). 1994. 16.95 (*0-8158-0501-2*) Chris Mass.

***Cahill, Tina.** Are You Ready for the Journey in the Next Millennium? (Illus.). 10p. 1999. pap. 4.95 (*0-9671672-0-5*) Step-Up Prods.

Cahill, Tom & Cahill, Sue. Big City Stories by Modern American Writers. 1976. 28.95 (*0-8488-0440-6*) Amereon Ltd.

Cahill, V., et al, eds. The Comandos Distributed Application Platform. (Research Reports ESPRIT, Project 2071, COMANDOS, Coed: Commission of the European Communities: Vol. 1). xviii, 312p. 1993. 50.95 (*0-387-56660-0*) Spr-Verlag.

Cahill, Willy. Self-Defense for Women. LC 96-72480. Orig. Title: Kick & Run. (Illus.). 96p. 1978. pap. 10.95 (*0-89750-061-X*, 209) Ohara Pubns.

Cahimite. Don't Git Hit by a Coconut. LC ND0237.R87C3. 200p. reprint ed. pap. 62.00 (*0-608-12397-8*, 205557000030) Bks Demand.

Cahir, Linda C. Solitude & Society in the Works of Herman Melville & Edith Wharton, 3. LC 98-26435. (Contributions to the Study of American Literature: Vol. 1). 176p. 1999. 55.00 (*0-313-30407-6*, Greenwood Pr) Greenwood.

Cahlander, Adele. Bolivian Tubular Edging & Crossed-Warp Techniques. 1994. 9.50 (*0-932394-22-1*) Dos Tejedoras.

— Double Woven Treasures from Old Peru. LC 85-70065. 1985. 30.00 (*0-932394-08-6*); pap. 28.00 (*0-932394-05-1*) Dos Tejedoras.

Cahm, Eric. Dreyfus Affair in French. 232p. (C). 1996. text 59.25 (*0-582-27679-9*, Pub. by Addison-Wesley) Longman.

Cahn. Rethinking California. 1999. pap. text. write for info. (*0-13-467912-1*) P-H.

Cahn & Lassen. New Brain Imaging Techniques in Cerebrovascular Disease. (Current Problems in Neurology Ser.: Vol. 2). 136p. 1985. 54.95 (*0-86196-060-2*, Pub. by J Libbey Med) Bks Intl VA.

Cahn, Ann, ed. see Florence, Robert.

Cahn, Ann F., ed. Women in the U. S. Labor Force. LC 78-22130. (Praeger Special Studies). 309p. 1979. 69.50 (*0-275-90337-0*, C0337, Praeger Pubs) Greenwood.

Cahn, Anne H. Killing Detente: The Right Attacks the CIA. LC 97-49346. 1998. 35.00 (*0-271-01790-2*); pap. 17.95 (*0-271-01791-0*) Pa St U Pr.

***Cahn, Arno, ed.** Proceedings of the 4th World Conference on Detergents: Strategies for the 21st Century. LC 99-26240. (Illus.). 360p. 1999. text 160.00 (*1-893997-01-4*, PC131) Am Oil Chemists.

Cahn, Arno, ed. Proceedings of the 3rd World Conference on Detergents: Global Perspectives. LC 94-8065. (Illus.). vii, 279 p. 1994. lib. bdg. 120.00 (*0-935315-52-7*, PCWC93) Am Oil Chemists.

Cahn, Charles H., tr. see Leonhard, K.

Cahn, Dudley D. Conflict in Intimate Relationships. LC 92-1556. (Series on Intimate Relationships). 148p. 1992. pap. text 21.00 (*0-89862-982-9*); lib. bdg. 45.00 (*0-89862-975-6*) Guilford Pubns.

Cahn, Dudley D., Jr. Letting Go: A Practical Theory of Relationship Disengagement & Re-engagement. LC 86-14549. (SUNY Series, Human Communication Processes). 243p. (C). 1987. text 64.50 (*0-88706-452-3*); pap. text 21.95 (*0-88706-454-X*) State U NY Pr.

Cahn, Dudley D., ed. Conflict in Personal Relationships. (LEA's Communication Ser.). 248p. 1994. pap. 27.50 (*0-8058-1278-4*); text 59.95 (*0-8058-1277-6*) L Erlbaum Assocs.

— Intimates in Conflict: A Communication Perspective. (Communication Ser.). 272p. (C). 1990. pap. 39.95 (*0-8058-1169-9*) L Erlbaum Assocs.

Cahn, Dudley D. & Lloyd, Sally A., eds. Family Violence from a Communication Perspective. LC 95-50233. 339p. (C). 1996. 52.00 (*0-8039-5982-6*); pap. 25.00 (*0-8039-5983-4*) Sage.

Cahn, Dudley D., jt. ed. see Cushman, Donald P.

***Cahn, Edgar.** Time Dollars: How to Build Community Through Social Capital. 2000. pap. write for info. (*1-885429-23-1*) Family Resource.

Cahn, Edgar S. & Rowe, Jonathan. Time Dollars: The New Currency That Enables Americans to Turn Their Hidden Resource - Time - Into Personal Security & Community Renewal. LC 98-21296. 1998. 17.99 (*1-885429-20-7*) Family Resource.

Cahn, Edmond. The Moral Decision. xii, 342p. 1993. reprint ed. 42.50 (*0-8377-2050-8*, Rothman) W S Hein.

Cahn, Edmond N. Confronting Injustice: The Edmond Cahn Reader. Cahn, Lenore L., ed. LC 72-8525. (Essay Index Reprint Ser.). 1977. reprint ed. 33.95 (*0-8369-7308-9*) Ayer.

— The Predicament of Democratic Man. LC 78-16399. 194p. 1979. reprint ed. lib. bdg. 55.00 (*0-313-20597-3*, CAPR, Greenwood Pr) Greenwood.

Cahn, Edmond N., ed. Supreme Court & Supreme Law. LC 68-55629. (Illus.). 250p. 1968. reprint ed. lib. bdg. 65.00 (*0-8371-0335-5*, CASC, Greenwood Pr) Greenwood.

Cahn, Eric & Saltzman, Marilyn. Maybe Tomorrow: A Hidden Child of the Holocaust. (Illus.). 210p. (Orig.). 1995. pap. 11.95 (*0-9645410-0-9*) Casan Pub.

Cahn, Frances. Federal Employees in War & Peace: Selection, Placement, & Removal. LC 78-16400. 253p. 1978. reprint ed. lib. bdg. 55.00 (*0-313-20602-3*, CAFE, Greenwood Pr) Greenwood.

Cahn, Frances & Bary, Valeska. Welfare Activities of Federal, State, & Local Governments in California, 1850-1934. LC 75-17212. (Social Problems & Social Policy Ser.). 1976. reprint ed. 36.95 (*0-405-07484-0*) Ayer.

Cahn, Isabelle. Paul Cezanne: A Life in Art. 144p. 1996. 39.95 (*0-304-34777-9*, Pub. by Cassell) Sterling.

— Renoir Nudes. (Illus.). 80p. 1996. text 18.95 (*0-7893-0062-1*) St Martin.

Cahn, Jean-Paul. Le Parti Social-Democrate Allemand et la Fin de la Quatrieme Republique Francaise (1954-1958) (Contacts Ser.: Series II, Vol. 18). (FRE.). 522p. 1996. 62.95 (*3-906754-69-3*, Pub. by P Lang) P Lang Pubng.

Cahn, Julie. Spotlight on Love. (Dream Your Own Romance Ser.: No. 3). (J). (gr. 2-7). 1984. pap. 2.95 (*0-671-52625-1*) S&S Trade.

Cahn, Karen, ed. see Schweid, Richard.

Cahn, Katharine & Johnson, Paul, eds. Children Can't Wait: Reducing Delays in Out-of-Home Care. 1993. pap. 9.95 (*0-87868-510-3*) Child Welfare.

Cahn, Lenore L., ed. see Cahn, Edmond N.

Cahn, Marilyn. Our Bodies, Our Cells: Children's Activities in Body Systems. LC 92-15985. (Children's Activity Ser.). (Illus.). 1992. 14.95 (*1-56071-087-X*) ETR Assocs.

Cahn, Matthew A. Environmental Deceptions: The Tension Between Liberalism & Environmental Policymaking in the United States. LC 94-6017. (SUNY Series in International Environmental Policy & Theory). (Illus.). 179p. (C). 1994. pap. text 19.95 (*0-7914-2264-X*) State U NY Pr.

— Environmental Deceptions: The Tension Between Liberalism & Environmental Policymaking in the United States. LC 94-6017. (SUNY Series in International Environmental Policy & Theory). (Illus.). 179p. (C). 1995. text 59.50 (*0-7914-2263-1*) State U NY Pr.

Cahn, Matthew A. & O'Brien, Rory, eds. Thinking about Environment: Readings on Politics, Property & the Physical World. LC 96-10749. 312p. (C). (gr. 13). 1996. text 74.95 (*1-56324-795-X*) M E Sharpe.

— Thinking about the Environment: Readings on Politics, Property, & the Physical World. LC 96-10749. 312p. (C). (gr. 13). 1996. pap. text 34.95 (*1-56324-796-8*) M E Sharpe.

Cahn, Matthew A. & Schockman, H. Eric. California: An Owner's Manual. LC 96-48098. 56p. 1996. pap. text 17.60 (*0-13-741778-0*) P-H.

Cahn, Matthew A., jt. ed. see Theodoulou, Stella Z.

Cahn, Miranda. How Compatible Are You? Reveal the Secrets of Your Relationship Using Handwriting & Analysis. LC 98-18470. 256p. 1999. pap. 14.00 (*1-56836-259-5*) Kodansha.

Cahn, Naomi, jt. auth. see Michie, Helena.

Cahn, Peter & Heimer, Anne-Katrin, eds. De Musica et Cantu: Studien Zur Geschichte der Kirchenmusik und der Oper. (Musikwissenschaftliche Publikationen Ser.: Vol. 2). (GER.). 642p. 1995. write for info. (*3-487-09793-1*) G Olms Pubs.

Cahn, R. W. Artifice & Artefacts: 100 Essays in Materials Science. (Illus.). 384p. 1992. 54.00 (*0-7503-0152-X*) IOP Pub.

Cahn, R. W., et al, eds. Materials Science & Technology: Comprehensive Treatment, Index of Vol. 1-18. (Materials Science & Technology). 412p. 1998. 398.00 (*3-527-29504-6*) Wiley.

Cahn, R. W., et al. Materials Science & Technology: A Comprehensive Treatment, 18 Vols. LC 90-21936. 999p. 1997. 7349.00 (*3-527-26813-8*) Wiley.

Cahn, R. W., jt. auth. see Fujita, F. E.

Cahn, Robert. Wide Area Network Design: Concepts & Tools for Optimization. 441p. 1998. 64.95 (*1-55860-458-8*) Morgan Kaufmann.

Cahn, Robert, ed. see Adams, John H., et al.

Cahn, Robert N., ed. Ete-Annihilation: New Quarks & Leptons. (Annual Reviews Special Collections Program Ser.). 1984. 43.25 (*0-8053-1610-8*) Addison-Wesley.

Cahn, Robert W. Encyclopedia in Materials Science & Engineering: Series Supplement 1. 1988. 245.00 (*0-08-036192-7*, Pergamon Pr) Elsevier.

— Encyclopedia in Materials Science & Engineering: Series Supplement 2. 1990. 245.00 (*0-08-036197-8*, Pergamon Pr) Elsevier.

Cahn, Robert W., ed. Encyclopedia of Materials Science & Engineering, Supplementary Vol. 1. 650p. 1988. 295.00 (*0-262-03142-6*) MIT Pr.

— Encyclopedia of Materials Science & Engineering Supplementary, Vol. 2. (Illus.). 831p. 1990. 379.25 (*0-08-036196-X*, Pergamon Pr) Elsevier.

— Encyclopedia of Materials Science & Engineering Supplementary, Vol. 2. (Advances in Materials Science & Engineering Ser.). (Illus.). 842p. 1990. 295.00 (*0-262-03173-6*) MIT Pr.

Cahn, Robert W. & Bever, Michael B. Encyclopedia of Materials Science & Engineering, Vol. 3. 770p. pap., suppl. ed. 300.00 (*0-08-040591-6*, Pergamon Pr) Elsevier.

Cahn, Robert W. & Bever, Michael B., eds. Encyclopedia of Materials Science & Engineering, Supplementary, Vol. 1. (Advances in Materials Science & Engineering Ser.: 1). (Illus.). 670p. 1988. 346.50 (*0-08-032521-1*, Pergamon Pr) Elsevier.

Cahn, Robert W. & Haasen, Peter, eds. Physical Metallurgy 4th Revised & Enhanced Edition, 3 vols. 4th rev. ed. 2888p. 1996. 883.50 (*0-444-89875-1*, North Holland) Elsevier.

Cahn, Robert W. & Lifshin, Eric, eds. Concise Encyclopedia of Materials Characterization. LC 92-10673. (Advances in Materials Science & Engineering Ser.: II). 666p. 1992. 272.25 (*0-08-040603-3*, Pergamon Pr) Elsevier.

Cahn, Robert W., jt. ed. see Bever, Michael B.

Cahn, R.W. The Coming of Materials Science. 1999. write for info. (*0-08-042679-4*, Pergamon Pr) Elsevier.

***Cahn, Sammy.** New Sammy Cahn Song Book. (Illus.). 1999. pap. 24.95 (*1-57623-763-X*) Wrner Bros.

Cahn, Sidney B. & Nadgorny, Boris E. A Guide to Physics Problems: Mechanics, Relativity & Electrodynamics, Pt. 1. LC 94-5210. (Illus.). 350p. (C). 1994. pap. text 27.50 (*0-306-44679-0*, Kluwer Plenum) Kluwer Academic.

Cahn, Sidney B., et al. A Guide to Physics Problems Pt. 2: Thermodynamics, Statistical Physics & Quantum Mechanics, Pt. 2. 374p. (C). 1997. pap. text 27.50 (*0-306-45291-X*, Kluwer Plenum) Kluwer Academic.

Cahn-Speyer, P., tr. see Allianz Versicherungs-AG Staff & Muenchner Rueckversicherungs-Gesellschaft Staff, eds.

Cahn, Stephen M. & Shatz, David, eds. Contemporary Philosophy of Religion. 320p. (C). 1982. pap. text 23.95 (*0-19-503009-5*) OUP.

Cahn, Steven M. Affirmative Action & the University: A Philosophical Inquiry. LC 92-18787. 320p. (C). 1995. pap. text 24.95 (*1-56639-399-X*) Temple U Pr.

— Classics of Modern Political Theory: Machiavelli to Mill. 1040p. (C). 1996. pap. text 39.95 (*0-19-510173-1*) OUP.

— Fate, Logic & Time. LC 67-24491. 160p. reprint ed. pap. 49.60 (*0-8357-8716-8*, 203369000087) Bks Demand.

— Fate, Logic & Time. viii, 150p. 1982. reprint ed. pap. text 12.00 (*0-917930-62-2*) Ridgeview.

— Morality, Responsibility, & the University: Studies in Academic Ethics. 1992. pap. 24.95 (*0-87722-959-7*) Temple U Pr.

— Reason at Work. 3rd ed. LC 95-77374. (C). 1995. text 51.50 (*0-15-502096-X*, Pub. by Harcourt Coll Pubs) Harcourt.

— Reason at Work. 4th ed. (C). 2000. text. write for info. (*0-15-506868-7*) Harcourt.

— Saints & Scamps: Ethics in Academia. rev. ed. LC 94-233952. 136p. (C). 1993. pap. text 9.95 (*0-8226-3028-1*) Littlefield.

Cahn, Steven M., compiled by. Classic & Contemporary Readings in the Philosophy of Education. expanded ed. LC 96-5368. Orig. Title: The Philosophical Foundations of Education. 544p. (C). 1996. pap. 37.19 (*0-07-009619-8*) McGraw.

Cahn, Steven M., ed. The Affirmative Action Debate. LC 95-38816. 224p. (C). 1995. pap. 19.99 (*0-415-91493-0*) Routledge.

— Classics of Western Philosophy. 5th rev. ed. LC 98-47547. 1328p. (C). 1999. pap. 32.00 (*0-87220-436-7*); lib. bdg. 55.00 (*0-87220-437-5*) Hackett Pub.

***Cahn, Steven M., ed.** Exploring Philosophy: An Introductory Anthology. LC 99-29797. (Illus.). 448p. (C). 2000. pap. text 29.95 (*0-19-513352-8*) OUP.

— Exploring Philosophy: An Introductory Anthology. LC 99-29797. (Illus.). 448p. 2000. 35.00 (*0-19-513619-5*) OUP.

Cahn, Steven M., ed. New Studies in the Philosophy of John Dewey. LC 76-62914. 223p. reprint ed. pap. 69.20 (*0-7837-0374-0*, 204069400018) Bks Demand.

— Scholars Who Teach: The Art of College Teaching. LC 78-944. 258p. 1978. pap. text 30.95 (*0-88229-598-5*) Burnham Inc.

Cahn, Steven M. & Haber, Jeram G. Twentieth Century Ethical Theory. 736p. (C). 1994. pap. text 57.00 (*0-02-318031-5*, Macmillan Coll) P-H.

Cahn, Steven M. & Markie, Peter, eds. Ethics: History, Theory & Contemporary Issues. LC 97-14435. 896p. (C). 1998. pap. text 39.95 (*0-19-510453-6*) OUP.

Cahn, Steven M., et al. Reason at Work: Introductory Readings in Philosophy. 2nd ed. 740p. (C). 1989. text 28.75 (*0-15-575991-4*) Harcourt Coll Pubs.

Cahn, Susan K. Coming on Strong: Gender & Sexuality in Twentieth-Century Women's Sport. 358p. 1994. 22.95 (*0-02-905075-8*) Free Pr.

— Coming on Strong: Gender & Sexuality in Twentieth-Century Women's Sports. (Illus.). 384p. (C). 1995. pap. 14.95 (*0-674-14434-1*) HUP.

— Industry of Devotion: The Transformation of Women's Work in England, 1500-1660. 288p. 1987. text 50.00 (*0-231-06500-0*) Col U Pr.

***Cahn, Victor L.** The Plays of Shakespeare: A Thematic Guide. LC 00-22337. 296p. 2000. 50.00 (*0-313-30981-7*, GR0981, Greenwood Pr) Greenwood.

Cahn, Victor L. Shakespeare the Playwright: A Companion to the Complete Tragedies, Histories, Comedies & Romances. LC 90-34319. 888p. 1991. lib. bdg. 75.00 (*0-313-27493-2*, CSO, Greenwood Pr) Greenwood.

— Shakespeare the Playwright: A Companion to the Complete Tragedies, Histories, Comedies, & Romances. LC 95-42501. 888p. 1996. pap. 30.95 (*0-275-95522-2*, Praeger Pubs) Greenwood.

— A Thinking Student's Guide to College. LC 87-71926. 1988. pap. 6.95 (*0-8158-0445-8*) Chris Mass.

Cahn, Walter. Romanesque Bible Illumination. LC 82-71593. (Illus.). 308p. 1982. text 135.00 (*0-8014-1446-6*) Cornell U Pr.

— Romanesque Manuscripts. LC 96-176010. (Survey of Manuscripts Illuminated in France Ser.: Vol. 1). (Illus.). 224p. 1996. text 200.00 (*1-872501-60-5*, Pub. by Harvey Miller) Gordon & Breach.

C

— The Romanesque Wooden Doors of Auvergne. LC 74-15391. (College Art Association Monographs: Vol. 30). (Illus.). 225p. 1985. reprint ed. 35.00 (*0-271-00400-2*) Pa St U Pr.

Cahn, William L. Performing Live with MIDI: A Percussionist's (& Anybody Else's) Guide to the Fundamentals. 100p. 1993. spiral bd. 15.00 (*0-9634060-1-9*) HoneyRock.

Cahn, Yehudah. An Ancient Tale of Rags & Riches. LC 91-61773. (Illus.). 126p. (J). (gr. 5-8). 12.95 (*1-56062-073-0*); pap. 9.95 (*1-56062-074-9*) CIS Comm.

Cahn, Yoel T. Links Beyond Time: The Book of Esther in Light of the Life of Yosef. 279p. 1995. 19.95 (*1-56871-074-7*, Pub. by Targum Pr); 19.95 (*0-568-71074-6*) Targum Pr.

Cahn, Zilla G. Suicide in French Thought from Montesquieu to Cioran. LC 97-39227. (Studies in the Humanities: Vol. 41). 438p. (C). 1999. 65.95 (*0-8204-4003-5*) P Lang Pubng.

Cahnano, W., et al, eds. Sediments & Toxic Substances: Environmental Effects & Ecotoxicity. (Environmental Science Ser.). (Illus.). 350p. 1996. 115.00 (*3-540-60051-5*) Spr-Verlag.

Cahnman, Werner J. & Imber, Jonathan B. Constructive Sociological Theory: The Forgotten Legacy of Thomas G. Masarykj. Woolfolk, Alan, ed. 350p. (C). 1994. text 54.95 (*1-56000-134-8*) Transaction Pubs.

Cahoon, Cecil, II. A Chosen Vessel: The Luke H. Wetherington Story. (Illus.). 117p. (Orig.). 1992. pap. 8.95 (*1-880994-02-X*) Mt Olive Coll Pr.

Cahoon, Cecil, 2nd. Unquiet Waters. (Illus.). 83p. (Orig.). 1994. pap. text 10.00 (*1-880994-21-6*) Mt Olive Coll Pr.

Cahoon, H., ed. The Mary Flagler Cary Music Collection. LC 73-133290. (Illus.). 108p. 1970. pap. 6.00 (*0-87598-009-0*) Pierpont Morgan.

Cahoon, Harold P. & Cahoon, Priscilla J. Utah's "Dixie" Birthplace, Vol. III. 2nd large type rev. ed. LC 96-60234. (Illus.). 282p. 1996. pap. 25.95 (*1-888106-20-4*) Agreka Bks.

Cahoon, Heather. Word Play ABC. LC 98-39614. (Illus.). 32p. (J). (ps). 1999. 15.95 (*0-8027-8683-9*) Walker & Co.

— Word Play ABC. LC 98-39614. (Illus.). 32p. (J). (ps-2). 1999. lib. bdg. 16.85 (*0-8027-8684-7*) Walker & Co.

Cahoon, Herbert, et al. American Literary Autographs from Washington Irving to Henry James. LC 77-89415. (Illus.). (Orig.). 1977. pap. 16.95 (*0-486-23548-3*) Dover.

— American Literary Autographs from Washington Irving to Henry James. (Orig.). 1990. 19.50 (*0-8446-5655-0*) Peter Smith.

Cahoon, James P. & Davidson, Jack W. C++ Program Design: An Introduction to Programming & Object-Oriented Design. 2nd ed. LC 98-26288. 1998. pap. 40.00 (*0-07-012135-4*) McGraw.

Cahoon, Priscilla J., jt. auth. see Cahoon, Harold P.

Cahoone, Lawrence E. The Dilemma of Modernity: Philosophy, Culture, & Anti-Culture. LC 86-30195. (SUNY Series in Philosophy). 325p. (C). 1987. text 59.50 (*0-88706-549-X*); pap. text 19.95 (*0-88706-550-3*) State U NY Pr.

— The Ends of Philosophy. LC 94-11683. (SUNY Series in Philosophy). 418p. (C). 1995. text 59.50 (*0-7914-2321-2*); pap. text 19.95 (*0-7914-2322-0*) State U NY Pr.

Cahoone, Lawrence E., ed. Modernism to Postmodernism: An Anthology. 768p. (C). 1995. pap. 34.95 (*1-55786-603-1*) Blackwell Pubs.

Cahow, Clark R. People, Patients & Politics. Grob, Gerald N., ed. LC 78-22554. (Historical Issues in Mental Health Ser.). (Illus.). 1980. lib. bdg. 23.95 (*0-405-11908-9*) Ayer.

Cahpel of the Air Ministries Staff. The Family God Wants Us to Be: Your Rx for Healthier Church Relationships Leader's Manual. (1992 50-Day Spiritual Adventure Ser.). (Illus.). 98p. 1991. teacher ed., ring bd. 34.95 (*1-879050-06-4*) Chapel of Air.

Cahse, Marlene J. Pictures from the Word. LC 98-70855. (Illus.). 240p. 1998. pap. 6.00 (*0-9657601-3-8*, Crest Books) SANP.

Cahsmore, Chris. Parties to a Contract of Carriage. 252p. 1990. 130.00 (*1-85044-329-7*) LLP.

Cai, C. Q. & Lin, Y. K. Probabilistic Structural Dynamics: Advanced Theory & Applications. (C). 1994. pap. text, teacher ed. 20.31 (*0-07-038039-2*) McGraw.

Cai, Camilla, jt. auth. see Haugen, Einar.

Cai, Camilla, ed. see Hensel, Fanny.

Cai, G. Q., jt. auth. see Lin, Y. K.

Cai, Jack & Yu, Emma. The Analects of Confucius: A Standard English Version with a Chinese Study Text. unabridged ed. LC 97-73847. (CHI & ENG., Illus.). 300p. 1997. 20.95 (*1-58075-500-3*, 1010); pap. 15.95 (*1-58075-501-1*, 1010) AmeriCD-ROM.

Cai, Jin-Yi. Advances in Computational Complexity Theory. LC 93-25900. (DIMACS Series in Discrete Mathematics & Theoretical Computer Science: No. 13). 209p. 1993. text 84.00 (*0-8218-6597-8*, DIMACS/13) Am Math.

Cai, Jin-Yi & Wong, Chak Huen. Computing & Combinatorics: Second Annual International Conference, Cocoon '96, Hong Kong, June 17-19, 1996 Proceedings, Vol. 109. LC 96-21907. (Lecture Notes in Computer Science Ser.). 421p. 1996. pap. 68.00 (*3-540-61332-3*) Spr-Verlag.

Cai, Jinfa. A Cognitive Analysis of U. S. & Chinese Students' Mathematical Performance on Tasks Involving Computation, Simple Problem Solving, & Complex Problem Solving. LC 95-50590. (JRME Monographs: No. 7). (Illus.). 151p. 1995. pap. 11.95 (*0-87353-424-7*) NCTM.

Cai, Kai-Yuan. Introduction to Fuzzy Reliability. LC 96-21647. (International Series in Engineering & Computer Science, Natural Language Processing & Machine Translation: Vol. 363). 336p. (C). 1996. text 139.00 (*0-7923-9737-1*, D Reidel) Kluwer Academic.

— Software Defect & Operational Profile Modeling. LC 98-28057. (International Series in Software Engineering). 1998. write for info. (*0-7923-8259-5*) Kluwer Academic.

Cai, Sean X. The Martial Arts: An Introduction to Self-Defense. (Illus.). 200p. (C). 1999. pap. text 34.00 (*1-893435-07-5*) Lakeshore Comm.

Cai, Shenglin. Trilingual Agricultural Dictionary: Chinese, English, French. (CHI, ENG & GER.). 324p. 1995. 195.00 (*0-7859-9934-5*) Fr & Eur.

Cai, Zhi-Xiong & Zhu, Yimei. Microstructures & Structural Defects in High-Temperature Superconductors. 400p. 1998. 68.00 (*981-02-3285-3*) World Scientific Pub.

Cai, Zong-qi. The Matrix of Lyric Transformation: Poetic Modes & Self-Presentation in Early Chinese Pentasyllabic Poetry. LC 96-9730. (Michigan Monographs in Chinese Studies: No. 75). 320p. 1997. text 50.00 (*0-89264-111-8*) Ctr Chinese Studies.

Caiaccia, Laura, ed. see Anderson, Kristin.

Caianiello, E. R. Neural Nets: Proceedings of the 5th Italian Workshop. LC 92-21204. 384p. 1993. text 100.00 (*981-02-1302-6*) World Scientific Pub.

— Neural Nets, Wirn Vietri: Proceedings of the 6th Italian Workshop, 1993. 420p. 1994. text 109.00 (*981-02-1700-5*) World Scientific Pub.

Caianiello, E. R., ed. Advances in Theoretical Physics. 240p. (C). 1991. text 74.00 (*981-02-0717-4*) World Scientific Pub.

— Parallel Architectures & Neural Network: Third Italian Workshop, Vietri Sul Mare, Salerno, 15-18 May 1990. 440p. (C). 1990. text 91.00 (*981-02-0308-X*) World Scientific Pub.

— Parallel Architectures & Neural Networks: 1st Italian Workshop. 212p. (C). 1989. text 77.00 (*9971-5-0905-9*) World Scientific Pub.

— Parallel Architectures & Neural Networks: 2nd Italian Workshop. 380p. (C). 1990. text 113.00 (*981-02-0146-X*) World Scientific Pub.

— Parallel Architectures & Neural Networks: 4th Italian Workshop. 350p. (C). 1991. text 89.00 (*981-02-0763-8*) World Scientific Pub.

— Physics of Cognitive Processes: Proceedings of the International Symposium. 480p. (C). 1987. pap. 46.00 (*9971-5-0327-1*); text 148.00 (*9971-5-0255-0*) World Scientific Pub.

Caianiello, E. R. & Aizerman, M. A., eds. Topics in the General Theory of Structures. (C). 1987. text 147.00 (*90-277-2451-2*) Kluwer Academic.

Caiati, Carl. Customizing Your Harley. (Illus.). 304p. 1992. 29.95 (*0-8306-4118-1*, 4223); pap. 19.95 (*0-8306-4117-3*, 4223) McGraw-Hill Prof.

— Fly Fishing Collectibles. (Instant Expert Ser.). (Illus.). 130p. 1997. pap. text 14.00 (*1-887110-11-9*) Allian Pubng.

— Hopped-up Harleys & Performance Street Machines. 1994. pap. 19.95 (*0-8306-4394-X*) McGraw-Hill Prof.

— Instant Expert: Collecting Harley Davidson. (Illus.). 130p. 1997. pap. 14.00 (*1-887110-14-3*) Allian Pubng.

— Real-Life Scenic Techniques for Model Railroaders. (Illus.). 144p. 1987. pap. 14.95 (*0-8306-2765-0*, NO. 2765) McGraw-Hill Prof.

***Caiazza, John C.** Can Religious Believers Accept Evolution: 25 Questions Answered Regarding the Conflict Between Evolution & Revealed Religion. 2000. 34.00 (*1-56072-660-1*, Nova Troitsa Bks) Nova Sci Pubs.

Caicedo, Xavier & Montenegro, Carlos H., eds. Models, Algebras & Proofs: Proceedings Latin-American Symposium on Mathematical Logic,1996, Bogota, Colombia. LC 98-45734. (Illus.). 472p. 1998. pap. text 165.00 (*0-8247-1970-0*) Dekker.

Caiden, Gerald, ed. Public Policy & Administrative Reform. (Orig.). (C). 1981. pap. 15.00 (*0-918592-47-X*) Pol Studies.

Caiden, Gerald E. Administrative Reform Comes of Age. (Studies in Organization: No. 28). xii, 347p. (C). 1991. pap. 29.95 (*3-11-012645-1*); lib. bdg. 54.95 (*3-11-012895-0*) De Gruyter.

— Public Employment Compulsory Arbitration in Australia. LC 79-634392. (Comparative Studies in Public Employment Labor Relations Ser.). 1971. 10.00 (*0-87736-001-4*); pap. 5.00 (*0-87736-002-2*) U of Mich Inst Labor.

Caiden, Gerald E., ed. International Handbook of the Ombudsman: Evolution & Present Function, 2 vols., Set. LC 81-20190. (Illus.). 190p. 1983. lib. bdg. 195.00 (*0-313-22685-7*, COM/) Greenwood.

— International Handbook of the Ombudsman: Evolution & Present Function, 2 vols., Vol. 1. LC 81-20190. (Illus.). 1983. lib. bdg. 125.00 (*0-313-23715-8*, COM/01) Greenwood.

— International Handbook of the Ombudsman: Evolution & Present Function, 2 vols., Vol. 2. LC 81-20190. (Illus.). 1983. lib. bdg. 125.00 (*0-313-23716-6*, COM/02) Greenwood.

Caiden, Gerald E. & Kim, Bun W., eds. A Dragon's Progress: Development Adminstration in Korea. LC 90-21333. (Kumarian Press Library of Management for Development Ser.). 302p. Date not set. reprint ed. pap. 93.70 (*0-608-20738-1*, 205449700003) Bks Demand.

Caiden, Martin. Buck Rogers: Life in the Future. 1996. pap. 5.99 (*0-7869-0527-1*, Pub. by TSR Inc) Random.

Caiden, Naomi & White, Joseph, eds. Budgeting, Policy, Politics: An Appreciation of Aaron Wildavsky. 148p. (C). 1994. 34.95 (*1-56000-192-5*) Transaction Pubs.

Caiden, Naomi & Wildavsky, Aaron. Planning & Budgeting in Poor Countries. 371p. (Orig.). 1979. pap. text 21.95 (*0-87855-707-5*) Transaction Pubs.

Caiden, Naomi, jt. auth. see Wildavsky, Aaron.

Caidin, Martin. Ghosts of the Air: True Stories of Aerial Hauntings. enl. expanded rev. ed. LC 94-23741. (Illus.). 288p. 1995. 24.95 (*1-880090-11-2*); pap. 14.95 (*1-880090-10-4*) Galde Pr.

— Golden Wings: Pictorial History of the U. S. Navy & Marine Corps in the Air. LC 72-169410. (Literature & History of Aviation Ser.). 1972. reprint ed. 30.95 (*0-405-03755-4*) Ayer.

— Indiana Jones & the Sky Pirates. 320p. 1993. mass mkt. 5.50 (*0-553-56192-8*) Bantam.

— Indiana Jones & the White Witch. 336p. 1994. mass mkt. 5.50 (*0-553-56194-4*) Bantam.

— A Life in the Future. (Buck Rogers Ser.). 1995. 19.95 (*0-7869-0144-6*, Pub. by TSR Inc) Random.

Caidin, Martin & Gilbert, James B., eds. Air Force: A Pictorial History of American Airpower. LC 79-7233. (Flight: Its First Seventy-Five Years Ser.). (Illus.). 1980. reprint ed. lib. bdg. 27.95 (*0-405-12149-0*) Ayer.

Caidin, Martin, jt. auth. see Barbree, Jay.

***Caie, Graham D., ed.** The Old English Poem "Judgement Day II" A Critical Edition with Editions of Bede's "De Die Iudich" & the Hatton 113 "Be Domes Daege" LC 99-52815. (Anglo-Saxon Texts Ser.). 192p. 2000. 75.00 (*0-85991-570-0*, DS Brewer) Boydell & Brewer.

Caie, James, jt. ed. see Kaminski, Mike.

***Caieco, Keith, et al, eds.** Association Meeting Planners & Conference Convention Directors. 1188p. 2000. write for info. (*0-87228-135-3*) Douglas Pubns.

***Caiedo, Keith.** RN & WPL Encyclopedia 2000. 2000. 343.75 (*0-87228-139-6*) Douglas Pubns.

***Caiedo, Keith, et al, eds.** Gift, Housewares & Home Textiles Buyers 2000. 872p. 1999. 195.00 (*0-87228-133-7*) Douglas Pubns.

— The Hospital Phone Book. 485p. 1999. 129.95 (*0-87228-127-2*) Douglas Pubns.

— Insurance Phone Book, 1999. 240p. 1999. 129.95 (*0-87228-126-4*) Douglas Pubns.

— Major Mass Markets, 1999. 802p. 1999. 179.95 (*0-87228-128-0*, Salesmn Gde) Douglas Pubns.

— RN & WPL Encyclopedia 1999. 1370p. 1999. 259.95 (*0-87228-125-6*, Salesmn Gde) Douglas Pubns.

— Sporting Goods Buyers, 1999. 958p. 1998. pap. 199.00 (*0-87228-132-9*, Salesmn Gde) Douglas Pubns.

Caig, John. Topper Sailing. (C). 1990. text 59.00 (*0-906754-04-6*, Pub. by Fernhurst Bks) St Mut.

Caiger, Andrew. Cause Lawyering in South Africa: Lawyers & the Law in the Struggle Against Apartheid. 287p. 1998. 69.95 (*1-57292-015-7*); pap. 49.95 (*1-57292-014-9*) Austin & Winfield.

Caiger, George, ed. Australian Way of Life. LC 69-18921. (Essay Index Reprint Ser.). 1977. 19.95 (*0-8369-1026-5*) Ayer.

Caiger, J. G., jt. auth. see Mason, R. H.

Caiger-Smith, Alan. Lustre Pottery. (Illus.). 246p. (Orig.). 1985. pap. 38.00 (*0-9650786-5-5*) Gentle Br.

— Pottery, People & Time: A Workshop in Action. (Illus.). 216p. 1995. 60.00 (*0-903685-39-6*, Pub. by R Dennis) Antique Collect.

Caignon, P. Biotechnology Dictionary Fre-Eng/Eng-Fre. LC 95-940433. Orig. Title: Dictionnaire des Biotechnologies. 185p. 1995. pap. 42.50 (*2-7430-0034-1*, Pub. by Technique et Documentation) IBD Ltd.

— French/English-English/French Dictionary of Biotechnology. (ENG & FRE.). 188p. 1995. 95.00 (*0-7859-9278-2*) Fr & Eur.

Cailac, Jean, jt. auth. see Delteil, Loys.

***Cailingold, Asher.** An Unlikely Heroine: Esther Cailingold's Fight for Jerusalem. (Illus.). 264p. 2000. 34.95 (*0-85303-409-5*, Pub. by M Vallentine & Co); pap. 19.95 (*0-85303-408-7*, Pub. by M Vallentine & Co) Intl Spec Bk.

Caillat, Carleen, jt. auth. see Marko-Geenen, Suzette.

Caillavet, France, et al, eds. Agricultural Household Modelling & Family Economics. LC 94-37299. (Developments in Agricultural Economics Ser.: Vol. 10). 326p. 1994. 228.00 (*0-444-81969-X*) Elsevier.

Caille, Alain, jt. auth. see Godbout, Jacques T.

Caille, Julie. A Family for Ronnie. (Special Edition Ser.). 1995. per. 3.75 (*0-373-09966-5*, 1-09966-2) Silhouette.

— The Scandalous Marquis. 384p. 1993. mass mkt. 3.99 (*0-8217-4203-5*, Zebra Kensgtn) Kensgtn Pub Corp.

Caillemer, Exupere. Etudes Sur les Antiquites Juridiques D'athenes, 10 pts., 1 bk. LC 78-15859. (Morals & Law in Ancient Greece Ser.). (FRE.). 1979. reprint ed. lib. bdg. 28.95 (*0-405-11532-6*) Ayer.

Caillens, Nicolas. Nicaragua. (Illus.). 46p. 1994. 40.00 (*1-880515-52-0*) Schl Mus Fine.

Cailler, Bernadette, et al. Toward Defining the African Aesthetic. Johnson, Lemuel et al, eds. LC 82-40408. (Annual Selected Papers of the African Literature Association). 140p. 1983. 22.00 (*0-89410-356-3*); pap. 14.00 (*0-89410-357-1*) Cornell AS&RC.

Caillet, Albert. Manual Bibliographique des Science Physiques ou Occultes, 3 vols. (Illus.). 1907p. 1997. reprint ed. 195.00 (*1-57898-004-6*) Martino Pubng.

— Manuel Bibliographique des Sciences Psychiques Ou Occultes, 3 vols., Set. (FRE.). 1831p. 1964. text 325.00 (*90-6004-024-4*, Pub. by B De Graaf) Coronet Bks.

Caillet, Gregor, jt. auth. see Ferguson, Ava.

Caillet, Marie. Louisiana Iris History & Culture. 1988. 23.95 (*0-914641-09-3*) TX Gardener Pr.

Caillet, Marie & Mertzweiller, Joseph K., eds. The Louisiana Iris: The History & Culture of Five Native American Species & Their Hybrids. (Illus.). 1988. 23.95 (*0-317-65674-0*) TX Gardener Pr.

***Caillet, Marie & Society for Louisiana Irises Staff.** The Louisiana Iris: The Taming of a Native American Wildflower. 2nd ed. LC 99-57037. (Illus.). 272p. 2000. 34.95 (*0-88192-477-6*) Timber.

Cailleteau, Thierry & Vatine, Olivier. Aquablue, Bk. 1. Richardson, Mike, ed. Lofficier, Randy & Lofficier, Jean-marc, trs. from FRE. (Illus.). 48p. 1988. reprint ed. pap. 6.95 (*1-878574-00-0*) Dark Horse Comics.

— Aquablue, Bk. 2: The Blue Planet. Richardson, Mike, ed. Lofficier, Randy & Lofficier, Jean-Marc, trs. from FRE. (Illus.). 48p. 1990. reprint ed. pap. 8.95 (*1-878574-04-3*) Dark Horse Comics.

Cailleux, E. Elements de Geologie en Six Langues. (ENG, FRE, GER, RUS & SPA.). 191p. 1965. pap. 49.95 (*0-8288-6744-5*, M6055) Fr & Eur.

***Cailliau, Robert & Gillies, James.** How the Web Was Born: The Story of the World Wide Web. (Illus.). 2000. pap. 15.95 (*0-19-286207-3*) OUP.

Caillie, Rene. Travels Through Central Africa to Timbuctoo, 1. 483p. (C). 1992. 125.00 (*1-85077-196-0*, Pub. by Darf Pubs Ltd) St Mut.

— Travels Through Central Africa to Timbuctoo, 2. 515p. (C). 1992. 125.00 (*1-85077-199-5*, Pub. by Darf Pubs Ltd) St Mut.

Cailliet, Emile. Pascal: The Emergence of Genius. 2nd ed. LC 75-94602. 383p. 1970. reprint ed. lib. bdg. 22.50 (*0-8371-2537-5*, CAP, Greenwood Pr) Greenwood.

Cailliet, Gregor, et al. Fishes: A Field & Laboratory Manual on Their Structure, Identification & Natural History. (Illus.). 202p. (C). 1996. reprint ed. pap. text 21.95 (*0-88133-908-3*) Waveland Pr.

Cailliet, Gregor M., jt. ed. see Simenstad, Charles A.

Cailliet, Rene. Foot & Ankle Pain. 3rd ed. LC 96-46127. (Pain Ser.). (Illus.). 287p. (C). 1996. pap. text 24.95 (*0-8036-0216-2*) Davis Co.

— Hand Pain & Impairment. 4th ed. LC 93-46466. (Pain Ser.). 311p. 1994. pap. 24.95 (*0-8036-1619-8*) Davis Co.

— Head & Face Pain Syndromes. (Pain Ser.). (Illus.). 229p. (C). 1992. pap. text 19.95 (*0-8036-1625-2*) Davis Co.

— Knee Pain & Disability. 3rd ed. LC 91-28232. (Pain Ser.). (Illus.). 287p. (C). 1991. pap. 23.95 (*0-8036-1622-8*) Davis Co.

— Neck & Arm Pain. 3rd ed. LC 90-13849. (Pain Ser.). (Illus.). 226p. 1990. pap. 21.95 (*0-8036-1610-4*) Davis Co.

— Pain: Mechanisms & Management. LC 93-9422. (Pain Ser.). (Illus.). 299p. (C). 1993. pap. text 24.95 (*0-8036-1635-X*) Davis Co.

— Scoliosis: Diagnosis & Management. LC 75-6709. (Illus.). 121p. 1975. text 22.95 (*0-8036-1640-6*) Davis Co.

— The Shoulder in Hemiplegia. LC 79-18598. (Illus.). 130p. 1980. text 15.95 (*0-8036-1602-3*) Davis Co.

— Shoulder Pain. 3rd ed. (Pain Ser.). (Illus.). 277p. 1991. pap. 21.95 (*0-8036-1614-7*) Davis Co.

— Soft Tissue Pain & Disability. 3rd ed. LC 95-39159. (Pain Ser.). (Illus.). 545p. (C). 1996. pap. text 32.97 (*0-8036-0110-7*) Davis Co.

— Understand Your Backache: A Guide to Prevention, Treatment, & Relief. LC 83-24071. (Illus.). 194p. 1984. pap. 13.95 (*0-8036-1647-3*) Davis Co.

Cailliet, Renee. Low Back Pain Syndrome. 5th ed. LC 94-22969. (Pain Ser.). (Illus.). 381p. 1994. pap. text 25.95 (*0-8036-1607-4*) Davis Co.

Caillods, F., et al, eds. Science Education & Development: Planning & Policy Issues at Secondary Level. LC 97-212352. 140p. 1997. 65.00 (*0-08-042789-8*, Pergamon Pr) Elsevier.

Caillois, Roger. A la Gloire de l'Image et Art Poetique Con Quince Litografias de Zao Wou-Ki. deluxe limited ed. (Ediciones Especiales y de Bibliofilo Ser.). (FRE., Illus.). 128p. 1993. 7500.00 (*84-343-0241-1*) Elliots Bks.

— Jeux et Sports. 1848p. 1968. 130.00 (*0-7859-5608-5*, 2070104257) Fr & Eur.

Caillois, Roger, ed. see De Montesquieu, Charles-Louis.

Caillot, Auguste C. Histoire de l'Ile Oparo ou Rapa. LC 75-35179. reprint ed. 18.50 (*0-404-14207-9*) AMS Pr.

Caillot, M., ed. Learning Electricity & Electronics with Advanced Educational Technology. (NATO ASI Series F: Computer & Systems Sciences, Special Programme AET: Vol. 115). vii, 329p. 1993. 93.95 (*0-387-56654-6*) Spr-Verlag.

Caillot, Simonne, jt. auth. see Nail, Simonne.

Caillou, A. Assault on Fellawi. 1976. pap. 1.50 (*0-380-00718-5*, Avon Bks) Morrow Avon.

Caillou, Aliza, ed. see Lawrence, Linda & Thorne, Kate.

Caillou, Aliza, ed. see Rodda, Jeanette & Smith, Nancy.

Caillou, Aliza, ed. see Ruland-Thorne, Kate.

Caillou, Aliza, ed. see Thorne, Kate R.

Caillou, Aliza, ed. see Thorne, V. Keith.

Caimans, Andrew C., jt. ed. see Seymour-Smith, Martin.

Caimey, Trevor H. Pathways to Literacy. (Children, Teachers & Learning Ser.). (Illus.). 208p. 1996. 100.00 (*0-304-32721-2*); pap. 33.95 (*0-304-32723-9*) Continuum.

Caimi, Frank M., ed. Selected Papers on Underwater Optics. LC 95-45446. (Milestone Ser.: Vol. MS118). 1996. 118.00 (*0-8194-2098-0*) SPIE.

Caimi, Gina. Betrayals. 384p. (Orig.). 1989. mass mkt. 3.95 (*0-445-20836-8*, Pub. by Warner Bks) Little.

Caimo, Gioseppe. Gioseppe Caimo: Madrigali & Canzoni for Four & Five Voices. Miller, Leta E., ed. (Recent Researches in Music of the Renaissance Ser.: Vol. RRR84-85). (Illus.). xxxvii, 246p. 1990. pap. 85.00 (*0-89579-246-X*, RRR84-85) A-R Eds.

Cain. Simon & Schuster Rough Drafts Activity Book. 4th ed. 1995. pap. text, student ed. 10.00 (*0-13-438441-5*) P-H.

Cain. Simon & Schuster's Answer Key, Workbook, & Handbook. 4th ed. 1996. pap. text, wbk. ed. write for info. (*0-13-456245-3*) Allyn.

An Asterisk (*) at the beginning of an entry indicates that the title is appearing for the first time.

Cain. William Lloyd Garrinson. 1997. pap. 17.95 (*0-312-14991-3*) St Martin.

Cain, jt. auth. see Duquette.

Cain, A. J. Animal Species & Their Evolution. LC 92-35149. (Science Library). (Illus.). 196p. 1993. reprint ed. pap. 16.95 (*0-691-02098-1*, Pub. by Princeton U Pr) Cal Prin Full Svc.

Cain, Albane, jt. auth. see Morgan, Carol.

Cain, Andrew W. History of Lumpkin County for the First Hundred Years, 1832-1932. LC 78-12902. 1999. reprint ed. 40.00 (*0-87152-277-2*) Reprint.

Cain, Ann & Buchanan, Melisa. Bubblin' Over: Simple Ideas for Spectacular Parties. (Illus.). 160p. (Orig.). 1991. pap. write for info. (*1-879129-01-9*) Oak Plantation.

Cain, Annette, jt. auth. see Cortopassi, Joan.

***Cain, Anthony B.** David Duval. LC 99-28122. (Illus.). 24P32p. (J). 1999. lib. bdg. 21.36 (*1-56766-659-0*) Childs World.

Cain, Anthony B. Jeff Gordon. LC 99-19753. (Illus.). 24P32p. 1999. lib. bdg. 21.36 (*1-56766-660-4*) Childs World.

Cain, B. Edward. The Basics of Technical Communicating. LC 88-3325. (Professional Reference Book Ser.). (Illus.). xiii, 200p. 1988. 24.95 (*0-8412-1452-2*) Am Chemical.

— The Basics of Technical Communicating. LC 88-3325. (Professional Reference Book Ser.). (Illus.). xiii, 200p. 1988. 38.00 (*0-8412-1451-4*, Pub. by Am Chemical) OUP.

— The Basics of Technical Communicating. LC 88-3325. (ACS Professional Reference Bk.). 216p. 1988. reprint ed. pap. 67.00 (*0-608-03839-3*, 206428600008) Bks Demand.

Cain, Barbara S. Double-Dip Feelings: A Book to Help Children Understand Emotions. LC 89-49382. (Illus.). 32p. (J). (ps-3). 1990. pap. 8.95 (*0-945354-20-7*) Am Psychol.

— Double-Dip Feelings: A Book to Help Children Understand Emotions. LC 89-49382. (Illus.). 32p. (J). (ps-5). 1990. 11.95 (*0-945354-23-1*) Am Psychol.

***Cain, Barbara S.** I Don't Know Why... I Guess I'm Shy. LC 99-20916. (Illus.). 32p. (J). (ps-3). 1999. 14.95 (*1-55798-596-0*, 441-5960, Magination Press) Am Psychol.

Cain, Barbara T., et al, eds. Guide to Private Manuscript Collections in the North Carolina State Archives. x, 706p. 1999. pap. 25.00 (*0-86526-142-3*) NC Archives.

Cain, Betty. Beyond Outlining: New Approaches to Rhetorical Form. 218p. (C). 1991. pap. text 19.50 (*0-8191-8416-0*); lib. bdg. 44.00 (*0-8191-8415-2*) U Pr of Amer.

Cain, Betty S. American from Sweden: The Story of A. V. Swanson. LC 86-33029. 99p. 1987. text 17.95 (*0-8093-1362-6*) S Ill U Pr.

Cain, Bonnie & Comings, John. The Participatory Process: Producing Photo-Literature. (Illus.). 40p. (Orig.). (C). 1977. pap. 4.00 (*0-932288-45-6*) Ctr Intl Ed U of MA.

Cain, Bruce, et al. The Personal Vote: Constituency Service & Electoral Independence. LC 86-22839. (Illus.). 288p. 1987. 41.00 (*0-674-66317-9*) HUP.

— The Personal Vote: Constituency Service & Electoral Independence. 280p. 1990. pap. 18.50 (*0-674-66318-7*) HUP.

Cain, Bruce E. & Noll, Roger G., eds. Constitutional Reform in California: Making State Government More Effective & Responsive. LC 95-38514. 514p. (Orig.). 1995. pap. 19.95 (*0-87772-365-6*) UCB IGS.

***Cain, Bruce E., et al.** Ethnic Context, Race Relations & California Politics. LC 00-40312. 2000. write for info. (*1-58213-051-5*) Pub Policy Inst.

Cain, Bruce E., jt. ed. see Lubenow, Gerald C.

Cain, Chelsea. Dharma Girl: A Road Trip Across the American Generations. LC 96-23697. 171p. 1996. pap. 12.00 (*1-878067-84-2*) Seal Pr WA.

***Cain, Chelsea, ed.** Wild Child: Girlhoods in the Counterculture. LC 99-44610. (Illus.). 220p. 1999. pap. 16.00 (*1-58005-031-X*, Pub. by Seal Pr WA) Publishers Group.

***Cain, Christine.** Dead or Alive 2: Prima's Official Strategy Guide. LC 99-69665. (Official Strategy Guides Ser.). (Illus.). 118p. (YA). 2000. pap. 14.99 (*0-7615-2741-9*) Prima Pub.

Cain, Christine. GranStream Saga: Prima's Official Strategy Guide. LC 98-65945. (Illus.). 96p. 1998. per. 14.99 (*0-7615-1640-9*) Prima Pub.

— Lunar: Silver Star Story Complete: Unauthorized Strategy. LC 98-65941. (Illus.). 126p. 1999. pap. 12.99 (*0-7615-1642-5*) Prima Pub.

— Mega Man Legends: Prima's Official Strategy Guide. (Games Ser.). 96p. 1998. per. 12.99 (*0-7615-1871-1*) Prima Pub.

***Cain, Christine.** The Misadventures of Tron Bonne. LC 99-66299. (Official Strategy Guides Ser.). (Illus.). 96p. 2000. pap. 14.99 (*0-7615-2579-3*) Prima Pub.

— Monkey Hero: Official Strategy Guide. LC 98-67307. (Secrets of the Game Ser.). (Illus.). 132p. 1998. pap. 14.99 (*0-7615-1807-X*) Prima Pub.

Cain, Christine. Official Guide to Chaos Island. 192p. 1997. pap. 14.99 (*1-56686-740-1*) Brady Pub.

***Cain, Christine.** Rocket. LC 99-67472. (Prima's Official Strategy Guides). (Illus.). 95p. 1999. pap. 12.99 (*0-7615-2681-1*) Prima Pub.

— Space Channel 5: Prima's Official Strategy Guide. 2000. pap. 12.99 (*0-7615-3001-0*) Prima Pub.

— Super Magnetic Neo: Prima's Official Strategy Guide. 2000. pap. 14.99 (*0-7615-3038-X*) Prima Pub.

— Super Mario Bros. deluxe ed. LC 99-62470. (Prima's Official Strategy Guides Ser.). (Illus.). 109p. 1999. pap. 12.99 (*0-7615-2190-9*, Prima Games) Prima Pub.

Cain, Christine. Totally Unauthorized Guide to Resident Evil 2. 112p. 1997. pap. 11.99 (*1-56686-685-5*) Brady Pub.

— Totally Unauthorized Super Mario 64 Guide. 112p. 1996. 9.99 (*1-56686-561-1*) Brady Pub.

Cain, Christine, jt. auth. see Brady Games Staff.

Cain, Christine, jt. auth. see Brady Publishing Staff.

Cain, Christopher S. Road Map to Your Vacation Property Dream. Stoddard, Sarah W., ed. LC 98-92667. (Illus.). 224p. 1998. pap. 16.95 (*0-914895-01-X*) Chrstophr Comm.

Cain, Cyril E. Four Centuries on the Pascagoula, 2 Vols., Set. LC 83-17812. 1999. reprint ed. 65.00 (*0-87152-383-3*) Reprint.

— Four Centuries on the Pascagoula, Vol. I. LC 83-17812. 228p. 1999. reprint ed. 32.50 (*0-87152-384-1*) Reprint.

— Four Centuries on the Pascagoula, Vol. II. LC 83-17812. 255p. 1999. reprint ed. 32.50 (*0-87152-385-X*) Reprint.

Cain, Dana. Collecting Japanese Movie Monsters: Starring Gamera, Ghidrah, Godzilla & Other Terrifying Beasts from the East. LC 98-89044. (Illus.). 176p. 1998. pap. 26.95 (*0-930625-55-2*, Antique Trader) Krause Pubns.

— Collecting Monsters of Film & TV: Identification & Value Guide. LC 97-73777. (Illus.). 192p. (Orig.). 1997. pap. 22.95 (*0-87341-515-9*, CTM) Krause Pubns.

— Dinosaur Collectibles. (Illus.). 208p. 1999. pap. 26.95 (*0-930625-99-4*, Antique Trader) Krause Pubns.

— Film & TV Animal Star Collectibles. LC 98-71060. (Illus.). 208p. 1998. pap. 26.95 (*0-930625-98-6*, Antique Trader) Krause Pubns.

***Cain, Dana.** Saturday Morning TV Collectibles: '60s '70s '80s. (Illus.). 288p. 2000. pap. 24.95 (*0-87341-801-8*, TOON) Krause Pubns.

Cain, Dana. UFO & Alien Collectibles Price Guide. LC 99-63753. (Illus.). 160p. 1999. per. 19.95 (*0-87341-690-2*) Krause Pubns.

Cain, Dana, jt. auth. see Lindenberger, Jan.

Cain, Danny & Russell, Bob. Blessed are the Caregivers: Practical Advice & Encouragement for Those Providing Care to Others. Shaw, Barrett, ed. 120p. (Orig.). 1995. pap. 9.95 (*0-9646630-0-7*) NB Pub.

Cain, David. An Evocation of Kierkegaard. Butin, Gitte Wernaa, tr.Tr. of En Fremkaldelse af Kierkegaard. (ENG & DAN.). 131p. 1997. 45.00 (*87-7876-010-0*, Pub. by C A Reitzel) D Cain.

Cain, Del. Lawmen of the Old West: The Good Guys. LC 99-46989. 1999. pap. 16.95 (*1-55622-677-2*) Wordware Pub.

Cain, Doreyl A. Greatness in a Nutshell: Principles of Logo Design for Print Media & Web Page. 2nd rev. ed. Garza, Amy A., ed. Orig. Title: How to Create Your Logo & Use It. (Illus.). 100p. 1999. per., wbk. ed. 18.99 (*0-9668900-2-7*) Seat Pants Vis.

— "How to Create Your Logo & Use It" For Business Owners & Entreprenuers. Garza, Amy A., ed. Cain, Jerry, tr. (Illus.). 96p. 1999. per., wbk. ed. 18.99 (*0-9668900-1-9*) Seat Pants Vis.

Cain, Elna. Fulfilled Parents: A Guide to Inform, Stimulate, Enrich, & Entertain Throughout the Parenting Years. LC 88-90715. (Illus.). 190p. (Orig.). 1988. pap. 11.95 (*0-929043-00-6*) Nanel Unlimited.

Cain, Errol Le, see Miles, Sally.

Cain, Eulalia. The ABCs of Taxes: A Poor Man's Primer. 1978. pap. 9.95 (*0-89420-051-8*, 481000); audio 23.95 (*0-89420-197-2*, 481004) Natl Book.

Cain, Frank. The Australian Security Intelligence Organization: An Unofficial History. LC 92-38419. (Cass Series, Studies in Intelligence). (Illus.). 292p. (C). 1994. 49.50 (*0-7146-3477-8*, Pub. by F Cass Pubs); pap. 24.50 (*0-7146-4124-3*, Pub. by F Cass Pubs) Intl Spec Bk.

— Menzies in War & Peace. LC 98-142725. 192p. 1998. pap. 24.95 (*1-86448-573-6*, Pub. by Allen & Unwin Pty) Paul & Co Pubs.

Cain, Frazier & Findley, Nigel. GURPS Talislanta. (Talislanta Ser.). 180p. 1993. pap. 16.95 (*1-880992-17-5*) Wizards Coast.

Cain, G. F., jt. auth. see Andrew, Alfred D.

Cain, George. Blueschild Baby. 1994. pap. 11.00 (*0-88001-349-4*) HarpC.

Cain, George H. & American Bar Association Staff. Law Partnership: Its Rights & Responsibilities. 2nd ed. LC 98-53814. (Illus.). 1999. write for info. (*1-57073-648-0*) Amer Bar Assn.

Cain, George L. An Introduction to General Topology. LC 92-43576. 216p. (C). 1993. 93.00 (*0-201-57698-8*) Addison-Wesley.

Cain, Glen G., et al. Labor Market Analysis of Engineers & Technical Workers. LC 73-8136. (Policy Studies in Employment & Welfare: No. 18). 96p. reprint ed. pap. 30.00 (*0-608-06041-0*, 206637300008) Bks Demand.

Cain, Gordon. Everybody Wins! A Life in Free Enterprise. LC 96-48448. (Chemical Heritage Foundation in Innovation & Entrepreneurship Ser.). (Illus.). 348p. 1997. 24.95 (*0-941901-14-9*) Chem Heritage Fnd.

Cain, Gordon & Curran, J. B. Dobbie: Probate & Administration Practice. 4th ed. 463p. 1986. boxed set 108.00 (*0-409-70215-3*, NZ, MICHIE) LEXIS Pub.

Cain, H. J., jt. auth. see Walmsley, R. N.

Cain, H. Thomas. Pima Indian Basketry: Illustrated with Photographs from the Collection of the Heard Museum. LC 62-20907. (Heard Museum Research Project Ser.: No. 2). (Illus.). 40p. (Orig.). 1962. pap. 5.00 (*0-934351-17-1*) Heard Mus.

Cain, Harvey D. Flint's Emergency Treatment & Management. 7th ed. (Illus.). 842p. 1985. text 65.00 (*0-7216-2313-1*, W B Saunders Co) Harcrt Hlth Sci Grp.

Cain, Herman. Leadership Is Common Sense. LC 98-40000. (Illus.). 196p. 1999. pap. 12.95 (*0-86730-750-1*, Pub. by Lebhar Friedman) Natl Bk Netwk.

Cain, Herman. Leadership Is Common Sense. 224p. 1996. 25.95 (*0-471-28796-2*, VNR) Wiley.

Cain, Herman. Leadership Is Common Sense. LC 96-31822. (Culinary Arts Ser.). 199p. (C). 1996. 25.95 (*0-442-02368-5*, VNR) Wiley.

— Speak As a Leader: Develop the Better Speaker in You. LC 99-30476. 176p. 1999. 24.95 (*0-86730-782-X*) Lebhar Friedman.

Cain, J. B., jt. auth. see Clark, G. C., Jr.

Cain, Jack & Carman, Robert A. Mathematics for Business Careers. 4th ed. LC 96-49152. 895p. 1997. pap. text 80.00 (*0-13-849258-1*) P-H.

— Mathematics for Business Careers. 5th ed. 816p. 2000. pap. 72.00 (*0-13-019749-1*) P-H.

Cain, Jack A. & Hulse, Ray. Structural Mechanics. 1997. text 29.95 (*0-333-48078-3*, Pub. by Macmillan) St Martin.

Cain, Jackson. Hell Hound. 304p. (Orig.). 1984. mass mkt. 2.75 (*0-446-32100-1*, Pub. by Warner Bks) Little.

— Hellbreak Country. 320p. (Orig.). 1984. mass mkt. 2.75 (*0-446-30621-5*, Pub. by Warner Bks) Little.

— Savage Blood. 336p. (Orig.). 1984. mass mkt. 2.75 (*0-446-30622-3*, Pub. by Warner Bks) Little.

Cain, James Hallie & Joliff, Barry. Teamwork & Teamplay. LC 98-224238. 512p. 1997. per. 39.95 (*0-7872-4532-1*) Kendall-Hunt.

Cain, James M. Assurances Sur la Mort. Orig. Title: Double Indemnity. (FRE.). pap. 11.95 (*0-7859-1966-X*, 2070374327) Fr & Eur.

Cain, James M. Au-Dela du Deshonneur. (FRE.). 183p. 1985. pap. 11.95 (*0-7859-2024-2*, 2070377016) Fr & Eur.

— Career in C Major & Other Fiction. Hoopes, Roy, ed. 288p. 1987. pap. 6.95 (*0-07-009594-9*) McGraw.

— Cloud Nine. LC 83-63036. 178p. 1999. 14.45 (*0-89296-079-5*, Pub. by Mysterious Pr) Little.

— Dette De Coeur. (FRE.). 245p. 1986. pap. 11.95 (*0-7859-2044-7*, 2070377636) Fr & Eur.

— Double Indemnity. Date not set. lib. bdg. 14.95 (*0-8488-1754-0*) Amereon Ltd.

— Double Indemnity. 1992. pap. 8.00 (*0-679-74096-1*) Random.

— Double Indemnity. (Vintage Crime Ser.). 1989. pap. 8.00 (*0-679-72322-6*) Vin Bks.

— Double Indemnity. 1992. pap. 8.00 (*0-394-23901-6*) Vin Bks.

— Le Facteur Sonne Toujours Deux Fois. (FRE.). 150p. 1979. pap. 10.95 (*0-7859-1885-X*, 2070370887) Fr & Eur.

— Jealous Woman. large type ed. 198p. 1992. pap. 14.95 (*0-8161-5461-9*, G K Hall Lrg Type) Mac Lib Ref.

Cain, James M. Magicians Wife. 1986. pap. 9.95 (*0-88748-018-7*) Carnegie-Mellon.

Cain, James M. Mildred Pierce. 1976. 15.95 (*0-8488-1259-X*) Amereon Ltd.

— Mildred Pierce. (FRE.). 438p. 1977. pap. 11.95 (*0-7859-1848-5*, 2070369226) Fr & Eur.

— Mildred Pierce. (Vintage Crime Ser.). 1989. pap. 12.00 (*0-679-72321-8*) Vin Bks.

— Mildred Pierce. large type ed. 544p. 1988. 27.99 (*0-7089-1829-8*) Ulverscroft.

— Mildred Pierce. 489p. 1981. reprint ed. lib. bdg. 14.95 (*0-89968-233-2*, Lghtyr Pr) Buccaneer Bks.

— The Postman Always Rings Twice. 20.95 (*0-89190-815-3*) Amereon Ltd.

— The Postman Always Rings Twice. 1992. pap. 8.00 (*0-679-74097-X*) Random.

— The Postman Always Rings Twice. (Crime Ser.). 1989. pap. 9.00 (*0-679-72325-0*) Vin Bks.

— The Postman Always Rings Twice. 1992. pap. 8.00 (*0-394-23899-0*) Vin Bks.

— The Postman Always Rings Twice. large type ed. LC 94-28140. 188p. 1995. pap. 18.95 (*0-7862-0279-3*) Thorndike Pr.

— The Postman Always Rings Twice. 457p. 1981. reprint ed. lib. bdg. 27.95 (*0-89968-234-0*, Lghtyr Pr) Buccaneer Bks.

— The Postman Always Rings Twice. 200p. 1995. reprint ed. 35.00 (*1-883402-18-2*) S&S Trade.

— The Root of His Evil. large type ed. LC 93-697. (Large Print Bks.). 256p. 1993. pap. 17.95 (*0-8161-5715-4*, G K Hall Lrg Type) Mac Lib Ref.

— Serenade. (FRE.). 256p. 1983. pap. 11.95 (*0-7859-1976-7*, 2070374750) Fr & Eur.

— Sinful Woman. large type ed. LC 92-27528. (Nightingale Ser.). 160p. 1993. pap. 15.95 (*0-8161-5462-7*, G K Hall Lrg Type) Mac Lib Ref.

— Sixty Years of Journalism by James M Cain. Hoopes, Roy, ed. & intro. by. LC 85-70856. 240p. 1986. 30.95 (*0-87972-327-0*) Bowling Green Univ Popular Press.

Cain, James M., jt. auth. see MacDougall, Ranald.

***Cain, Janan.** The Way I Feel. LC 00-32690. 2000. write for info. (*1-884734-71-5*) Parenting Pr.

Cain, Janet, jt. auth. see Burke, Betty.

Cain, Janet, ed. see Burke, Betty.

Cain, Janet, ed. see Friedman, Pamela.

Cain, Janet, ed. see Robbins, Mari L.

Cain, Jerry, ed. see Francis, Jack & Bouvier, Jacques.

Cain, Jerry, tr. see Cain, Doreyl A.

Cain, Joan, tr. see De la Harpe, Jean-Baptiste.

Cain, Joanna M., jt. auth. see Stenchever, Morton A.

Cain, Joe. Capcom's Fighter's Edge. LC 98-67871. 1998. pap. 12.99 (*0-7615-1917-3*) Prima Pub.

Cain, Joe, jt. auth. see Hartmann, William K.

Cain, John. The BBC: 70 Years of Broadcasting. LC 95-83726. (Illus.). 160p. 1996. 24.95 (*0-563-36750-4*, BBC-Parkwest) Parkwest Pubns.

— John Cain's Years: Power, Parties & Politics. 344p. 1995. pap. 19.95 (*0-522-84615-7*, Pub. by Melbourne Univ Pr) Paul & Co Pubs.

— John Cain's Years: Power, Parties & Politics. (Illus.). 340p. 1996. pap. 16.95 (*0-522-84707-2*, Pub. by Melbourne Univ Pr) Paul & Co Pubs.

Cain, Jonathan. Code Zero. (Saigon Commandos Ser.: No. 2). 1984. mass mkt. 2.50 (*0-8217-1329-9*, Zebra Kensgtn) Kensgtn Pub Corp.

— Saigon Commandos: Dinky-Dau Death, No. 3. 1984. mass mkt. 2.50 (*0-317-02894-4*, Zebra Kensgtn) Kensgtn Pub Corp.

— Saigon Commandos: You Die, du Ma, No. 8. 320p. 1987. mass mkt. 2.50 (*0-317-56089-1*, Zebra Kensgtn) Kensgtn Pub Corp.

Cain, Joseph A. Totally Unauthorized Donkey Kong Country 2. (Illus.). (Orig.). Date not set. pap. 9.99 (*0-614-10338-X*) Brady Pub.

Cain, Katherine. Change Begins with Me. 7th ed. (Illus.). (Orig.). 1976. pap. 3.95 (*0-9603188-0-1*) K Tolson.

— Now Is the Time. 2nd ed. Cain, Kay, ed. (Illus.). 40p. (Orig.). 1979. reprint ed. pap. 3.95 (*0-9603188-1-X*) K Tolson.

Cain, Kathleen. The Mercury Reader. (C). 2000. pap. text. write for info. (*0-321-07499-8*) Addson-Wesley Educ.

Cain, Kathleen S. Leon Uris: A Critical Companion. LC 97-52324. (Critical Companions to Popular Contemporary Writers Ser.). 232p. 1998. 29.95 (*0-313-30231-6*, Greenwood Pr) Greenwood.

Cain, Kay, ed. see Cain, Katherine.

Cain, Louis, jt. auth. see Harmon, George.

Cain, Louis P. Sanitation Strategy for a Lakefront Metropolis: The Case of Chicago. LC 76-14711. 173p. 1978. 28.00 (*0-87580-064-5*) N Ill U Pr.

Cain, M. & Kulcsar, Kalman. Disputes & the Law. 286p. (C). 1983. 81.00 (*963-05-3379-0*, Pub. by Akade Kiado) St Mut.

Cain, Madelyn. First Time Mothers Last Chance Babies: Parenting at 35. 1993. 23.95 (*0-88282-086-9*); pap. 13.95 (*0-88282-083-4*) New Horizon NJ.

***Cain, Marvin Fay.** Jesus the Man: An Introduction for People at Home in the Modern World. LC 99-49449. 1999. 18.00 (*0-944344-79-8*) Polebridge Pr.

Cain, Mary. The Historical Development of State Normal Schools for White Teachers in Maryland. LC 72-176622. (Columbia University. Teachers College. Contributions to Education Ser.: No. 824). reprint ed. 37.50 (*0-404-55824-0*) AMS Pr.

Cain, Mary, jt. auth. see Mittman, Robert.

Cain, Mary A. Revisioning Writers' Talk: Gender & Culture in Acts of Composing. LC 94-8007. (SUNY Series, Literacy, Culture, & Learning: Theory & Practice). 215p. (C). 1995. text 49.50 (*0-7914-2075-2*); pap. text 16.95 (*0-7914-2076-0*) State U NY Pr.

Cain, Maureen, ed. Growing up Good: Policing the Behaviour of Girls in Europe. 246p. (C). 1989. text 45.00 (*0-8039-8021-3*); pap. text 18.95 (*0-8039-8022-1*) Sage.

Cain, Maureen & Harrington, Christine B. Lawyers in a Postmodern World: Translation & Transgression. Sumner, Colin, ed. (New Directions in Criminology Ser.). 336p. 1994. pap. 2.00 (*0-335-09694-8*) OpUniv Pr.

Cain, Maureen & Harrington, Christine B., eds. Lawyers in a Postmodern World: Translation & Transgression. LC 93-35979. (C). 1994. text 50.00 (*0-8147-1504-4*) NYU Pr.

— Lawyers in a Postmodern World: Translation & Transgression. LC 93-35979. (C). 1994. pap. text 18.50 (*0-8147-1503-6*) NYU Pr.

Cain, Mead, jt. ed. see McNicholl, Geoffrey.

Cain, Mead T. The World on Paper: A Celebration of the Mapmaker's Art Catalogue of an Exhibition, March 3-June 3, 1994, Rare Book & Manuscript Library. Ellenbogen, Rudolph & Funke, Claudia, eds. LC 95-164338. (Illus.). 56p. 1994. pap. 20.00 (*0-9607862-7-9*) Columbia U Libs.

Cain, Melinda, jt. ed. see Dauber, Roslyn.

Cain, Michael. The Legend of Sir Miguel. Thatch, Nancy R., ed. LC 90-5927. (Books for Students by Students). (Illus.). 26p. (J). (gr. 3-6). 1990. lib. bdg. 15.95 (*0-933849-26-5*) Landmark Edns.

Cain, Michael S. Co-Op Publishing Handbook. 1978. 8.95 (*0-913218-76-6*) Dustbooks.

***Cain, Michael S.** The Community College in the Twenty-First Century: A Systems Approach. LC 99-12586. 168p. 1999. 32.00 (*0-7618-1357-8*) U Pr of Amer.

Cain, Mike. Autos of Interest. 1977. pap. 6.50 (*0-9601458-1-8*) M Cain.

Cain, Nancy. Healing the Child: A Mother's Story. 288p. 1997. per. 14.00 (*0-671-01001-8*) PB.

— Healing the Child: A Mother's Story. 288p. 1996. 21.50 (*0-684-80169-8*) S&S Trade.

Cain, Nancy Woodard & Cain, Thomas. Structured Programming with Lotus 1-2-3. (Illus.). 352p. 1989. pap. 29.95 (*0-13-853540-X*) Brady Pub.

***Cain, P. J.** Empire & Imperialism: The Debate of the 1870's. LC 99-38503. (Key Issues Ser.). 1999. pap. 30.00 (*1-890318-24-8*) St Augustines Pr.

***Cain, P. J. & Harrison, Mark.** Imperialism: Critical Concepts in Historical Studies, 3 vols. LC 00-32314. 2000. write for info. (*0-415-20630-8*) Routledge.

Cain, P. J. & Hopkins, A. G. BRIT IMPERIALISM 1914 90. LC 92-18672. (C). 1993. text 68.95 (*0-582-20966-8*, 79757) Longman.

— British Imperialism: Crisis & Deconstruction 1914-1990, Vol.2. LC 92-18672. (C). 1999. pap. text 44.00 (*0-582-20965-X*, 79756) Longman.

Cain, P. J. & Hopkins, A. G. British Imperialism Vol. 1: Innovation & Expansion 1688-1914. LC 92-21715. 576p. (C). 1995. pap. 53.00 (*0-582-49176-2*, 79754) Longman.

Cain, Pamela V., jt. auth. see Ulrich, Larry.

C

An Asterisk (*) at the beginning of an entry indicates that the title is appearing for the first time.

Cain, Patricia A. Lesbian & Gay Rights: The Legal Controversies. (New Perspectives on Law, Culture & Society Ser.). 288p. 2000. pap. text 24.00 (0-8133-2617-6) Westview.

Cain, Patrick. The Touchstone: A Transcendent Adventure. 188p. 1997. pap. 14.00 (0-9659223-0-8) Lifestream Pub.

Cain, Paul. Seven Slayers. 194p. 1987. 14.95 (0-940941-03-1) Blood & Guts Pr.

— Seven Slayers. limited ed. 194p. 1987. 35.00 (0-940941-04-X) Blood & Guts Pr.

Cain, Paul, et al, eds. Community Nursing: Dimensions & Dilemmas. 192p. 1995. pap. 34.95 (1-56593-612-4, 1270) Singular Publishing.

***Cain, Paul & Kendall, R. T.** The Word & the Spirit. LC 98-27452. 1998. pap. 8.99 (0-88419-544-9) Creation House.

Cain, Peter. Free Trade & Protectionism, 4 vols., Set. (Wellesley Ser.). 1600p. (C). 1996. text, boxed set 655.00 (0-415-13325-4) Routledge.

— The Social & Economic Works of John Ruskin, 6 vols., Set. (Modern Economics Ser.). 1540p. (C). (gr. 13 up). 1994. text, boxed set 620.00 (0-415-11350-4) Routledge.

Cain, Peter, ed. Empire & Its Critics, 1899-1939: Classics of Imperialism, 8 vols., Set. 3100p. (C). (gr. 13). 1998. 905.00 (0-415-17945-9) Routledge.

— Richard Cobden: Political & Economic Works, 6 vols., Set. 2nd ed. 3185p. (C). (gr. 13 up). 1996. 745.00 (0-415-12742-4) Routledge.

Cain, Peter, ed. Empire & Imperialism: The Debate of the 1870s. (Key Issues Ser.: No. 20). 250p. 1999. 72.00 (1-85506-580-0); pap. 24.95 (1-85506-581-9) Thoemmes Pr.

Cain, Peter, intro. Collected Works of Thorstein Veblen, 10 vols. 4270p. 1994. boxed set 695.00 (0-415-10502-1) Routledge.

***Cain, Robert J., ed.** The Colonial Records of North Carolina Second Series, Vol. 10: The Church of England in North Carolina: Documents, 1699-1741. (Illus.). lxix, 615p. 1999. 75.00 (0-86526-283-7) NC Archives.

Cain, Robert J., ed. North Carolina Higher-Court Minutes, 1724-1730. (Colonial Records of North Carolina Ser.: Vol. 6). lxi, 791p. 1981. 30.00 (0-86526-027-3) NC Archives.

— Records of the Executive Council, 1664-1734. (Colonial Records of North Carolina Ser.: Vol. 7). 1984. 25.00 (0-86526-210-1) NC Archives.

— Records of the Executive Council, 1735-1754. (Colonial Records of North Carolina Ser.: Vol. 8). lxxvii, 723p. 1988. 45.00 (0-86526-251-9) NC Archives.

— Records of the Executive Council, 1755-1775. LC 94-66892. (Colonial Records of North Carolina Ser.: Vol. 9). lxxix, 870p. 1994. 75.00 (0-86526-261-6) NC Archives.

Cain, Robert L. RV Air Conditioning Preventive Maintenance & Service Manual. (Illus.). 66p. 1991. pap. 12.95 (0-9628736-0-8) Cain Bks.

***Cain, Sandra & Maxwell, Michelle.** When What You've Got Is Not What You Want: Using NLP to Create the Life You Want & Live It to the Full. (Pathways Ser.). 208p. 2000. pap. 15.95 (1-85703-501-1, Pub. by How To Bks) Midpt Trade.

Cain, Sandra E. & Evans, Jack M. Sciencing: An Involvement Approach to Elementary Science Methods. 3rd ed. 432p. (C). 1990. pap. text 35.20 (0-675-20869-6, Merrill Coll) P-H.

Cain, Seymour. Gabriel Marcel. LC 79-50156. 128p. 1979. pap. 4.50 (0-89526-905-8) Regnery Pub.

— Gabriel Marcel's Theory of Religious Experience, Vol. 182. LC 94-22423. (American University Studies: Series VII). XV, 206p. (C). 1995. text 42.95 (0-8204-2595-8) P Lang Pubng.

***Cain, Sheridan.** Goodnight, Little Hare. (Illus.). 14p. (J). 1998. pap. 16.98 (1-58048-044-6) Sandvik Pub.

— Little Turtle & the Song of the Sea. LC 99-53456. (Illus.). (J). (gr. k-3). 2000. 15.95 (1-56656-355-0, Pub. by Interlink Pub) Kane-Miller Bk.

Cain, Sheridan. Why So Sad, Brown Rabbit? LC 97-26756. (Illus.). 32p. (J). 1998. 14.99 (0-525-45963-4, Dutton Child) Peng Put Young Read.

Cain, Stephen. Dyslexicon. 171p. 1998. pap. 22.95 (1-55245-027-9) Coach Hse Bks.

Cain, Suzy. A Ghostly Experience Vol. 1: Tales of Saint Augustine Florida. (Illus.). 50p. 1997. pap. 5.00 (0-9661203-0-2) Tour Saint.

Cain, T. G., jt. ed. see Thornton, R. K.

Cain, Thomas, jt. auth. see Cain, Nancy Woodard.

Cain, Thomas H. Praise in "The Faerie Queene" LC 78-8962. 245p. reprint ed. pap. 76.00 (0-7837-0227-2, 204053500017) Bks Demand.

Cain, Tim. Peck's Beach: A Pictorial History of Ocean City, New Jersey. Travers, Gail, ed. (Illus.). 96p. 1988. reprint ed. 27.00 (0-945582-04-8) Down the Shore Pub.

***Cain, Tubal.** Building Simple Model Steam Engines. 1999. reprint ed. 13.95 (1-85486-104-2, Pub. by Nexus Special Interests) Trans-Atl Phila.

Cain, Tubal. Building Simple Model Steam Engines, Bk. 2. (Illus.). 106p. 1998. pap. 16.95 (1-85486-147-6, Pub. by Nexus Special Interests) Trans-Atl Phila.

— Drills, Taps & Dies. (Workshop Practice Ser.: No. 12). (Illus.). 104p. (Orig.). 1987. pap. 18.50 (0-85242-866-9, Pub. by Nexus Special Interests) Trans-Atl Phila.

— Milling Operations in the Lathe. (Workshop Practice Ser.: No. 5). (Illus.). 128p. (Orig.). 1984. pap. 18.50 (0-85242-840-5, Pub. by Nexus Special Interests) Trans-Atl Phila.

Cain, Tubal. The Model Engineer's Handbook. 3rd ed. (Illus.). 250p. 1996. pap. 22.50 (1-85486-134-4, Pub. by Nexus Special Interests) Trans-Atl Phila.

Cain, Tubal. Simple Workshop Devices. 2nd ed. (Workshop Practice Ser.: No. 28). (Illus.). 140p. 1998. pap. 19.95 (1-85486-150-6) Nexus Special Interests.

— Soldering & Brazing. (Workshop Practice Ser.: No. 9). (Illus.). 136p. (Orig.). 1985. pap. 18.50 (0-85242-845-6, Pub. by Nexus Special Interests) Trans-Atl Phila.

— Workholding in the lathe. (Workshop Practice Ser.: No. 15). (Illus.). 112p. (Orig.). 1986. pap. 18.50 (0-85242-908-8, Pub. by Nexus Special Interests) Trans-Atl Phila.

Cain, William & Fried, Lewis L. B. Paul de Man. (Wellesley Studies in Critical Theory). 700p. Date not set. text 105.00 (0-8153-1783-2) Garland.

Cain, William & Ross, Charles L. Authority & Textual Critical Theory. (Wellesley Studies in Critical Theory). 200p. Date not set. text 27.00 (0-8153-0833-7) Garland.

Cain, William, ed. see Baker, Harold.

Cain, William, jt. ed. see Brown, Julie.

Cain, William, ed. see Childress, Rennie.

Cain, William, ed. see DiSalvo, Jacqueline, et al.

Cain, William, ed. see Fried, Lewis L.

Cain, William, jt. ed. see Jeffreys, Mark.

Cain, William, jt. ed. see Jordan, David M.

Cain, William, ed. see Paananen, Victor N.

Cain, William, jt. ed. see Rado, Lisa.

Cain, William, ed. see Sellers, Roy.

Cain, William E. The Crisis in Criticism: Theory, Literature, & Reform in English Studies. LC 83-49197. 336p. 1984. 49.95 (0-8018-3191-1) Johns Hopkins.

— F. O. Matthiessen & the Politics of Criticism. LC 88-40188. 288p. (C). 1988. pap. text 19.95 (0-299-11914-9) U of Wis Pr.

— F. O. Matthiessen & the Politics of Criticism. LC 88-17275. (Wisconsin Project on American Writers). 252p. 1988. reprint ed. pap. 78.20 (0-608-07459-4, 206768600009) Bks Demand.

***Cain, William E.** A Historical Guide to Henry David Thoreau. (Historical Guide to American Authors). (Illus.). 272p. 2000. pap. 15.95 (0-19-513863-5); text 39.95 (0-19-513862-7) OUP.

Cain, William E. Making Feminist History: The Literary Scholarship of Sandra M. Gilbert & Susan Gubar. LC 93-3787. (Wellesley Studies in Critical Theory, Literary History & Culture: Vol. 1). li, 325p. 1994. text 25.00 (0-8153-1467-1) Garland.

— Reconceptualizing American Literary/Cultural Studies: Rhetoric, History, & Politics in the Humanities. LC 96-14419. (Wellesley Studies in Critical Theory, Literary History & Culture: Vol. 12). 248p. 1996. text 60.00 (0-8153-2391-3, H2000) Garland.

— William Lloyd Garrison: Selections from the Liberator & the Fight Against Slavery. 224p. 1994. pap. text 12.95 (0-312-10386-7) St Martin.

Cain, William E., ed. Philosophical Approaches to Literature: New Essays on Nineteenth & Twentieth Century Texts. LC 82-48652. 256p. 1984. 38.50 (0-8387-5055-9) Bucknell U Pr.

— Teaching the Conflicts: Gerald Graff, Curricular Reform, & the Culture Wars. LC 93-29157. (Wellesley Studies in Critical Theory: Vol. 2). 280p. 1993. text 20.00 (0-8153-1466-3, H1782) Garland.

Cain, William E., jt. ed. see Cudjoe, Selwyn R.

Cain, William E., ed. see Philip, Maxwell, et al.

Cain, William E., jt. ed. see Sadoff, Dianne F.

Cainainn, Tomas. Traditional Music in Ireland. 148p. 1994. 14.95 (0-946005-73-7, OS00048) Omnibus NY.

Caine, Barbara. Destined to be Wives: The Sisters of Beatrice Webb. (Illus.). 292p. 1987. text 39.95 (0-19-820054-4) OUP.

— English Feminism, 1780-1980. LC 96-51166. 354p. 1997. text 85.00 (0-19-820686-0); pap. text 19.95 (0-19-820434-5) OUP.

Caine, Barbara. Victorian Feminists. (Illus.). 298p. (C). 1993. reprint ed. pap. text 22.00 (0-19-820433-7, 14328) OUP.

Caine, Barbara, et al, eds. Australian Feminism: A Companion. LC 98-200084. (Illus.). 600p. 1999. 72.00 (0-19-553818-8) OUP.

Caine, Barbara & Grosz, E. A., eds. Crossing Boundries. 1988. pap. text 16.95 (0-04-305004-2, Pub. by Allen & Unwin Pty) Paul & Co Pubs.

Caine, Barbara & Pringle, Rosemary, eds. Transitions: New Australian Feminism. LC 94-47582. 1995. pap. 16.95 (0-312-12548-8); text 55.00 (0-312-12547-X) St Martin.

***Caine, Barbara & Sluga, Glenda.** Gendering European History LC 99-28935. 192p. 2000. 26.95 (0-7185-0132-2) Continuum.

Caine, Carolyn. On Your Own in San Francisco: An Entry Plan with Shops, Cafes, Public Transit & Restrooms. rev. ed. Gardiner, Ann, ed. (Illus.). 160p. 1995. pap. 16.00 (0-9621246-1-3) Blue Pearl Pr.

Caine, Dennis J., et al, eds. Epidemiology of Sports Injuries. LC 95-39000. (Illus.). 472p. 1996. text 69.00 (0-87322-466-3, BCAI0466) Human Kinetics.

Caine, Dona & Caine, Michael. When Benjamin Wants to Know: Family Conversations about the Facts of Life. McCormick, Love & Rosenberg, Love, eds. LC 97-155814. (Illus.). 61p. 1996. spiral bd. 9.95 (1-880849-07-0) Chapel Hill NC.

Caine, Donald B. Neurodegenerative Diseases. LC 93-13286. (Illus.). 992p. 1994. text 220.00 (0-7216-4349-3, W B Saunders Co) Harcrt Hlth Sci Grp.

Caine, Geoffrey, et al. Mindshifts: A Brain-Based Process for Restructuring Schools & Renewing Education. rev. ed. LC 98-34855. 1998. 37.00 (1-56976-091-8) Zephyr Pr AZ.

— MindShifts: Brain-Based Process for Restructuring Schools & Renewing Education. LC 94-27925. 280p. 1995. pap. 35.00 (1-56976-007-1) Zephyr Pr AZ.

Caine, Geoffrey, jt. auth. see Caine, Renate N.

Caine, Hall. Christian. 1976. 22.95 (0-8488-0255-1) Amereon Ltd.

— Cobwebs of Criticism. LC 71-39879. reprint ed. 39.50 (0-404-07287-9) AMS Pr.

— The Manxman. LC 79-8243. reprint ed. 44.50 (0-404-61801-4) AMS Pr.

— Recollections of Rossetti. LC 72-6285. (English Literature Ser.: No. 33). 267p. 1972. reprint ed. lib. bdg. 75.00 (0-8383-1634-4) M S G Haskell Hse.

— The Scapegoat: A Romance, 2 vols., 1 bk. LC 79-8244. reprint ed. 44.50 (0-404-61802-2) AMS Pr.

***Caine, K. Winston.** Lose Your Gut Now! Drop Your Weight & Get in Shape Fast. LC 00-23906. 2000. write for info. (1-57954-277-8) Rodale Pr Inc.

Caine, K. Winston & Garfinkel, Perry. The Male Body: An Owner's Manual: The Ultimate Guide to Staying Healthy & Fit for Life. Men's Health Books Staff, ed. LC 96-18195. (Illus.). 432p. 1996. pap. 19.95 (0-87596-401-X); text 31.95 (0-87596-297-1) St Martin.

Caine, Kenneth W., compiled by. The Positive Bible: From Genesis to Revelation: Scripture that Inspires, Nurtures & Heals. 320p. 1999. pap. 12.00 (0-380-79180-3, Avon Bks) Morrow Avon.

***Caine, Kenneth Winston & Kaufman, Brian Paul.** Prayer, Faith & Healing: Cure Your Body, Heal Your Mind & Restore Your Soul. 544p. 2000. pap. 19.95 (1-57954-265-4) Rodale Pr Inc.

Caine, Kenneth Winston, et al. Prayer, Faith & Healing: Cure Your Body, Heal Your Mind & Restore Your Soul. LC 98-31577. (Illus.). 512p. 1999. 29.95 (1-57954-006-6) Rodale Pr Inc.

Caine, Lynn. Being a Widow. 264p. 1990. pap. 12.95 (0-14-013025-X, Penguin Bks) Viking Penguin.

Caine, M., ed. The Pharmacology of the Urinary Tract: Clinical Practice in Urology. (Illus.). 180p. 1984. 111.00 (0-387-13238-4) Spr-Verlag.

***Caine, Mary.** Celtic Saints & the Glastonbury Zodiac. 1998. pap. 19.95 (1-86163-022-0, Pub. by Capall Bann Pubng) Holmes Pub.

Caine, Michael. Acting in Film: An Actor's Take on Movie Making. Aitken, Maria, ed. (Acting Series & BBC Master Class). (Illus.). 154p. 1989. 14.95 (0-936839-86-4) Applause Theatre Bk Pubs.

— Acting in Film: An Actor's Take on Moviemaking. 2nd rev. expanded ed. (Illus.). 192p. 1997. pap. text 14.95 (1-55783-277-3) Applause Theatre Bk Pubs.

Caine, Michael, jt. auth. see Caine, Dona.

Caine, Nel. The Mountains of Northeastern Tasmania: A Study of Alpine Geomorphology. 208p. (C). 1983. text 110.00 (90-6191-289-X, Pub. by A A Balkema) Ashgate Pub Co.

Caine, Philip D. Aircraft Down! Evading Capture in WWII Europe. LC 97-19667. 298p. 1997. 24.95 (1-57488-086-1) Brasseys.

***Caine, Philip D.** Aircraft Down! Evading Capture in WWII Europe. 2000. pap. 16.95 (1-57488-234-1) Brasseys.

Caine, Philip D. American Pilots in the RAF: The WWII Eagle Squadrons. (Brassey's WWII Commemorative Ser.). (Illus.). 417p. 1993. 25.00 (0-02-881070-8) Brasseys.

— American Pilots in the RAF: The WWII Eagle Squadrons. LC 98-24964. (Illus.). 432p. 1998. pap. 23.95 (1-57488-137-X) Brasseys.

— Eagles of the RAF: The World War II Eagle Squadrons. (Illus.). 417p. (Orig.). (C). 1994. pap. text 45.00 (0-7881-1114-0) DIANE Pub.

Caine, Philip D., II. Spitfires, Thunderbolts, & Warm Beer: An American Fighter Pilot over Europe. (World War II Commemorative Ser.). (Illus.). 248p. 1995. 23.95 (0-02-881115-1) Brasseys.

***Caine, Philip D.** Spitfires, Thunderbolts & Warm Beer: An American Fighter Pilot over Europe. 2000. pap. 17.95 (1-57488-232-5) Brasseys.

Caine, Philip D. Spitfires, Thunderbolts, & Warm Beer: An American Fighter Pilot over Europe. (World War II Commemorative Ser.: Vol. 2). (Illus.). 248p. 1999. reprint ed. pap. 19.95 (1-57488-116-7) Brasseys.

Caine, Philip D., jt. auth. see Folkman, David I., Jr.

Caine, Renate N. & Caine, Geoffrey. Education on the Edge of Possibility. LC 97-4604. 1997. pap. 20.95 (0-87120-282-4) ASCD.

— Making Connections: Teaching & the Human Brain. fac. ed. LC 91-7631. (Illus.). 203p. (Orig.). 1991. reprint ed. pap. 63.00 (0-608-01024-3, 2082500) Bks Demand.

— Unleashing the Power of Perceptual Change: The Potential of Brain-Based Teaching. LC 97-33743. 1997. pap. 18.95 (0-87120-287-5) ASCD.

Caine, Renate N., jt. ed. see Blair, Billie G.

Caine, Shulamith W. Love Fugue. Moody, Rodger, ed. 80p. (Orig.). 1997. pap. 10.00 (1-878851-10-1) Silverfish Rev Pr.

Caine, Stanley P. The Myth of a Progressive Reform: Railroad Regulation in Wisconsin, 1903-1910. LC 75-630131. (Illus.). 250p. 1970. 7.95 (0-87020-110-7) State Hist Soc Wis.

Caine, Stanley P., ed. see Philipp, Emanuel L.

Cainelli, G. & Cardillo, G. Chromium Oxidations in Organic Chemistry. (Reactivity & Structure, Concepts in Organic Chemistry Ser.: Vol. 19). (Illus.). 290p. 1984. 158.95 (0-387-12834-4) Spr-Verlag.

Cainer, Jonathan. The Complete Book of the Zodiac. LC 99-14065. 1999. pap. 14.95 (0-8069-5922-3) Sterling.

— Phychic Explorer: A Down-to-Earth Guide to Six Magical Arts. 1998. pap. text 16.95 (0-7499-1685-0, Pub. by Piatkus Bks) London Brdge.

Caines, Arthur & Haycock, Roger. Automotive Lubricants Reference Book. LC 96-22048. 1996. 125.00 (1-56091-525-0, R-145) Soc Auto Engineers.

Caines, Jeanette. I Need a New Lunch Box. (J). 1988. pap. text 5.95 (0-590-47262-3) Scholastic Inc.

Caines, Jeannette F. Abby. (Illus.). (J). (ps-3). 1996. 7.66 (0-06-020921-6, 180875) HarpC.

— Abby. LC 73-5480. (Trophy Picture Bk.). (Illus.). 32p. (J). (ps-3). 1984. pap. 5.95 (0-06-443049-9, HarpTrophy) HarpC Child Bks.

— Abby. (J). 1984. 10.15 (0-606-03369-6, Pub. by Turtleback) Demco.

— Chilly Stomach. LC 85-45250. (Illus.). 32p. (J). (ps-2). 1986. 11.95 (0-06-020976-3) HarpC Child Bks.

— I Need a Lunch Box. LC 85-45829. (Trophy Picture Bk.). (Illus.). 32p. (J). (ps-1). 1993. pap. 5.95 (0-06-443341-2, HarpTrophy) HarpC Child Bks.

— I Need a Lunchbox. LC 85-45829. (Illus.). 32p. (J). (ps-3). 1988. lib. bdg. 16.89 (0-06-020985-2) HarpC Child Bks.

— Just Us Women. LC 81-48655. (Trophy Picture Bk.). (Illus.). 32p. (J). (ps-3). 1984. pap. 5.95 (0-06-443056-1, HarpTrophy) HarpC Child Bks.

— Just Us Women. (J). 1982. 11.15 (0-606-01885-9, Pub. by Turtleback) Demco.

Caines, Joseph E., jt. auth. see McElroy, Jerome L.

Caines, Peter B. & Hermann, Robert. Geometry & Identification: Proceedings of APSM Workshop - On System Geometry, System Identification, Parameter Identification. (LIE Groups Ser.: Vol. 1; Pt. B). 1983. 30.00 (0-915692-33-3) Math Sci Pr.

Caiola, Marcello. A Manual for Country Economists. 1995. write for info. (1-55775-460-8) Intl Monetary.

Caipora Women's Group Staff. Women in Brazil. 160p. pap. 12.00 (0-85345-883-9, Pub. by Monthly Rev) NYU Pr.

Cair, Angela. How to Draw & Paint People. (Art for Children Ser.). (Illus.). 32p. (YA). (gr. 3 up). 1997. pap. 4.95 (1-56010-252-7, AC02) W Foster Pub.

***Caira, Alma.** Ceramic & Glassware Style: Paint Your Own Tableware, Glassware & Decorative Objects. (Illus.). 244p. 2000. pap. 24.95 (0-8230-0588-7) Watsn-Guptill.

Caira, Janine. Principles of Biology: Laboratory Manual. (C). 1993. student ed. 20.52 (1-56870-077-6) RonJon Pub.

Caird, Edward. Collected Works of Edward Caird, 12 Vol. Tyler, Colin, ed. & intro. by. 5524p. 1999. 1300.00 (1-85506-591-6) Thoemmes Pr.

— Evolution of Theology in the Greek Philosophers, the Gifford Lectures, 1900-1902, 2 vols., Set. 1968. 39.00 (0-403-00116-1) Scholarly.

— Hegel. LC 71-181924. (BCL Ser. I). reprint ed. 32.50 (0-404-01362-7) AMS Pr.

Caird, Edward, jt. ed. see Miller, William L.

Caird, F. I. Rehabilitation in Parkinson's Disease. 144p. 1991. pap. 54.50 (1-56593-561-6, 0707) Singular Publishing.

Caird, F. I. & Brewin, T. B., eds. Cancer in the Elderly. (Illus.). 295p. 1990. text 185.00 (0-7236-0972-1) Buttrwrth-Heinemann.

Caird, F. I. & Scott, P. J. Drug Safety in Pregnancy. (Drug Induced Disorders Ser.: No. C1). xxii,520p. 1990. 311.50 (0-444-90362-3, Excerpta Medica) Elsevier.

Caird, G. B. The Language & Imagery of the Bible. 308p. 1997. pap. 24.00 (0-8028-4221-6) Eerdmans.

— New Testament Theology. Hurst, L. D., ed. 518p. 1995. reprint ed. pap. text 26.00 (0-19-826388-0) OUP.

Caird, George B. The Revelation of Saint John. (Black's New Testament Commentary Ser.: No. 19). 316p. 1993. 22.95 (1-56563-018-1) Hendrickson MA.

Caird, James. English Agriculture in 1850-51. 2nd ed. 550p. 1968. reprint ed. 35.00 (0-7146-1281-2, Pub. by F Cass Pubs) Intl Spec Bk.

— The Landed Interest & the Supply of Food. 4th ed. LC 67-16346. (Reprints of Economic Classics Ser.). xx, 184p. 1967. reprint ed. 25.00 (0-678-05034-1) Kelley.

— Landed Interest & the Supply of Food. 5th rev. ed. 184p. 1967. 26.00 (0-7146-1042-9, Pub. by F Cass Pubs) Intl Spec Bk.

— Prairie Farming in America: With Notes by the Way on Canada & the United States. LC 72-89090. (Rural America Ser.). 1973. reprint ed. 16.00 (0-8420-1479-9) Scholarly Res Inc.

Caird, John. The Fundamental Ideas of Christianity, 2 vols., Set. LC 77-27231. (Gifford Lectures: 1892-93, 1895-96). reprint ed. 74.50 (0-404-60460-9) AMS Pr.

— An Introduction to the Philosophy of Religion. LC 75-113569. (BCL Ser. I). reprint ed. 27.50 (0-404-01363-5) AMS Pr.

— Spinoza. LC 75-164593. (Select Bibliographies Reprint Ser.). 1977. reprint ed. 23.95 (0-8369-5877-2) Ayer.

Caird, Kenneth A. Cameraready. (Illus.). 400p. 1973. ring bd. 60.00 (0-87703-066-9) Univelt Inc.

Caird, Mona. The Daughters of Danaus. LC 89-11627. 544p. 1989. 35.00 (1-55861-014-6); pap. 13.95 (1-55861-015-4) Feminist Pr.

Cairl, R. Somebody Tell Me Who I Am! Reshaping Thoughts on Care & Management of Confused & Memory Impaired Older Adults. 300p. (Orig.). (C). pap. text 29.95 (1-887454-00-4) Caremore Pubns.

***Cairn, North T.** By Monomoy Light: Nature & Healing in an Island Sanctuary. (Illus.). 264p. 2000. 22.95 (1-55553-448-1) NE U Pr.

Cairncross. Costing the Earth. 300p. 1992. 29.95 (0-07-103367-X) McGraw.

Cairncross. Economics & Economic Policy. 240p. 1993. 61.95 (0-7512-0227-4) Ashgate Pub Co.

Cairncross, Alec. Austin Robinson: The Life of an Economic Adviser. LC 92-36201. viii, 198 p. 1993. write for info. (0-333-59477-0) Macmillan.

— The British Economy since 1945: Economic Policy & Performance, 1945-1995. 2nd ed. LC 95-17554. (Making Contemporary Britain Ser.). (Illus.). 368p. (C). 1995. pap. 29.95 (0-631-19961-6) Blackwell Pubs.

— A Country to Play With: Level of Industry Negotiations in Berlin, 1945-46. LC 87-63151. 72p. (Orig.). 1987. pap. 14.95 (0-86140-274-X, Pub. by Smyth) Dufour.

An Asterisk (*) at the beginning of an entry indicates that the title is appearing for the first time.

— Economic Ideas & Government Policy: Contributions to Contemporary Economic History. LC 95-21622. 296p. (C). (gr. 13). 1995. 90.00 (*0-415-13245-2*) Routledge.

— Essays in Economic Management. (Modern Revivals in Economics Ser.). 224p. 1993. text 49.95 (*0-7512-0226-6*, Pub. by Gregg Revivals) Ashgate Pub Co.

— Home & Foreign Investment, 1870-1913: Studies in Capital Accumulation. (Modern Revivals in Economic & Social History Ser.). 268p. 1993. 63.95 (*0-7512-0111-1*, Pub. by Gregg Pub) Ashgate Pub Co.

— Snatches. 44p. 1980. pap. 6.95 (*0-86140-051-8*, Pub. by Smyth) Dufour.

— Years of Recovery: British Economic Policy, 1945-1951. LC 85-18541. 544p. 1985. text 59.95 (*0-416-37920-6*, 9522) Routledge.

Cairncross, Alec & Foudatio, Ditcley. Britain's Economic Prospects Reconsidered. LC 70-860682. 244p. 1971. write for info. (*0-04-330180-0*) Routledge.

Cairncross, Alec & Watts, Nitta. The Economic Section Nineteen Thirty-Nine to Sixty-One: A Study in Economic Advising. 352p. 1989. 56.00 (*0-415-03173-7*, A3240) Routledge.

Cairncross, Alec, jt. auth. see Burk, Kathleen.

Cairncross, Alec, jt. auth. see Devons, Ely.

Cairncross, Alec, jt. auth. see Hall, R. L.

Cairncross, Alec, ed. see Clarke, Richard.

Cairncross, Alec, ed. see Singer, Hans W.

Cairncross, Alex, ed. The Robert Hall Diaries, 1947-1953, Vol. I. 326p. 1989. text 90.00 (*0-04-445273-X*) Routledge.

Cairncross, Alexander K. Control of Long-Term International Capital Movement. LC 73-12634. (Brookings Institution Staff Papers). 118p. reprint ed. pap. 36.60 (*0-608-12154-1*, 202536700043) Bks Demand.

Cairncross, Andrew S., ed. see Shakespeare, William.

Cairncross, Frances. Costing the Earth: The Challenge for Governments, the Opportunities for Business. LC 91-33750. 368p. 1992. 24.95 (*0-87584-315-8*) Harvard Busn.

— Costing the Earth: The Challenge for Governments, the Opportunities for Business. 368p. 1993. pap. 14.95 (*0-87584-410-3*) Harvard Busn.

— The Death of Distance: How the Communications Revolution Will Change Our Lives. LC 97-17612. 320p. 1997. 24.95 (*0-87584-806-0*, HBS Pr) Harvard Busn.

— Green, Inc. A Guide to Business & the Environment. LC 95-77352. 287p. 1995. 27.00 (*1-55963-445-6*) Island Pr.

— Green Ink. 1995. 17.95 (*1-85383-250-2*, Pub. by Escan Pubns) Island Pr.

Cairncross, Frances & Keeley, Phil. Guide to the Economy. LC 87-138822. viii, 161p. 1987. 2.95 (*0-416-39600-3*) Routledge.

Cairncross, John. After Polygamy Was Made a Sin: The Social History of Christian Polygamy. 236p. 1974. 29.95 (*0-7100-7730-0*) Dufour.

— After Polygamy Was Made a Sin: The Social History of Christian Polygamy. 236p. 1974. 17.95 (*0-318-39996-2*, Pub. by Smyth) Dufour.

— La Fontaine Fables & Other Poems. 108p. 11.95 (*0-317-54261-3*) Dufour.

— La Fontaine Fables & Other Poems. 108p. 1982. pap. 15.95 (*0-86140-122-0*) Dufour.

— La Fontaine Fables & Other Poems. 108p. 11.95 (*0-317-57939-8*, Pub. by Smyth) Dufour.

Cairncross, John, tr. see Racine, Jean.

Cairncross, John, tr. & intro. see Corneille, Pierre.

Cairncross, Liz, et al. Housing Management, Consumers, & Citizens. LC 96-7569. 224p. (C). 1996. 75.00 (*0-415-07066-X*); pap. 25.99 (*0-415-07067-8*) Routledge.

Cairncross, S. & Mara, D. Duncan. Guidelines for the Safe Use of Wastewater & Excreta in Agriculture & Aquaculture: Measures for Public Health Protection. (CHI, ENG, FRE, RUS & SPA.). vii, 187p. 1989. pap. text 35.00 (*92-4-154248-9*, 1150324) World Health.

Cairncross, Sandy & Kochar, Vijay, eds. Studying Hygiene Behaviour: Methods, Issues, & Experiences. LC 93-44528. (Illus.). 1994. 36.00 (*0-8039-9159-2*) Sage.

Cairncross, Sandy & Reachem, Richard G. Environmental Health Engineering in the Tropics: An Introductory Text. 2nd ed. LC 92-41230. 320p. 1993. pap. 80.00 (*0-471-93885-8*) Wiley.

Cairnes, John E. Essays in Political Economy. LC 65-20923. (Reprints of Economic Classics Ser.). x, 371p. 1965. reprint ed. 45.00 (*0-678-00105-7*) Kelley.

— An Examination into the Principles of Currency Involved in the Bank Charter Act of 1844. LC 88-35764. (Reprints of Economic Classics Ser.). 78p. 1989. reprint ed. 25.00 (*0-678-00106-5*) Kelley.

— Political Essays. LC 66-22615. viii, 350p. 1967. reprint ed. 45.00 (*0-678-00206-1*) Kelley.

— Some Leading Principles of Political Economy Newly Expounded. LC 66-22617. (Reprints of Economic Classics Ser.). 421p. 1967. reprint ed. 49.50 (*0-678-00205-3*) Kelley.

*__Cairnes, Margot.__ Approaching the Corporate Heart. 230p. 2000. per. 11.00 (*0-684-87207-2*) S&S Trade.

Cairnes, Margot. Approaching the Corporate Heart: Breaking Through to New Horizons of Personal & Professional Success. 1998. pap. text. write for info. (*0-7318-0655-7*) Simon & Schuster.

Cairnes, William E., ed. see Bonaparte, Napoleon.

*__Cairney, J. W. & Chambers, S. M., eds.__ Ectomycorrhizal Fungi: Key Genera in Profile. LC 99-15545. (Illus.). 350p. 1999. 219.00 (*3-540-65609-X*) Spr-Verlag.

*__Cairney, John.__ On the Trail of Robert Burns. 2000. pap. 14.95 (*0-946487-51-0*) Luath Pr Ltd.

Cairney, T. & Fairhurst, W. A., eds. Contaminated Land: Problems & Solutions. 1992. 109.00 (*0-87371-870-4*, BSL870) Lewis Pubs.

Cairney, Tom. Contaminated Land: Problems & Solutions. 2nd ed. 1997. pap. write for info. (*0-7514-0386-5*) Thomson Learn.

Cairney, Tom. The Re-Use of Contaminated Land: A Handbook of Risk Assessement. 228p. 1995. 155.00 (*0-471-94893-4*) Wiley.

Cairney, Tom & Hobson, David M., eds. Contaminated Land: Problems & Solutions. 2nd ed. LC 98-166787. (Illus.). 392p. (C). (gr. 13). 1998. 150.00 (*0-419-23090-4*, D5738, E & FN Spon) Routledge.

Cairney, Trevor. Balancing the Basics: A Handbook for Teachers of Reading (K through Eight) 2nd ed. 127p. (C). (gr. k). 1990. pap. text 22.00 (*0-86896-545-6*, 00674) Heinemann.

Cairney, Trevor H. Other Worlds: The Endless Possibilities of Literature. LC 90-30709. (Illus.). 152p. (Orig.). (C). 1990. pap. 15.00 (*0-435-08531-X*, 08531) Heinemann.

Cairney, Trevor H. & Munsie, Lynne. Beyond Tokenism: Parents As Partners in Literacy. LC 94-31882. 95p. 1995. pap. text 16.50 (*0-435-08832-7*, 08832) Heinemann.

Cairns. Renaissance Theatre, Vol.2. 157.95 (*0-7546-0008-4*) Ashgate Pub Co.

Cairns, Jr., jt. ed. see Buikema, Jr.

Cairns, Adrian. The Making of the Professional Actor. 224p. 1996. 45.00 (*0-7206-1002-8*, Pub. by P Owen Ltd) Dufour.

Cairns, Al. Nothing Sacred. 1998. mass mkt. 6.99 (*0-7704-2766-9*) Bantam.

Cairns, Alan. The Dictionary of Theological Terms: Theological Terms in a Readable & Cross Referenced Form. 2nd rev. ed. 455p. (Orig.). 1998. reprint ed. pap. 24.99 (*1-84030-039-6*) Ambassador Prodns Ltd.

*__Cairns, Alan.__ Eagle's Wings: Daily Devotional. 374p. 1999. pap. 14.99 (*0-907927-73-4*) Emerald House Group Inc.

Cairns, Alan. Sure Foundation. 1997. pap. text 15.99 (*1-898787-80-8*) Emerald House Group Inc.

— Throned in Highest Bliss. 174p. 1990. pap. 7.99 (*0-907927-61-0*) Emerald House Group Inc.

Cairns, Alan, jt. auth. see Burnside, Scott.

Cairns, Alan C. Charter vs. Federalism: The Dilemmas of Constitutional Reform. 160p. 1992. 60.00 (*0-7735-0891-0*, Pub. by McG-Queens Univ Pr); pap. 22.95 (*0-7735-0892-9*, Pub. by McG-Queens Univ Pr) CUP Services.

*__Cairns, Alan C.__ Citizens Plus: Aboriginal Peoples & the Canadian State. 280p. 2000. 39.95 (*0-7748-0767-9*, Pub. by UBC Pr) U of Wash Pr.

— Citizenship, Diversity & Pluralism: Canadian & Comparative Perspectives. 368p. 1999. 65.00 (*0-7735-1888-6*) McG-Queens Univ Pr.

Cairns, Bernard C. Australian Civil Procedure. 4th ed. LC 97-179883. 766p. 1996. 145.00 (*0-455-21415-8*, Pub. by LawBk Co); pap. 110.00 (*0-455-21412-3*, Pub. by LawBk Co) Gaunt.

Cairns, Beverley D., jt. auth. see Cairns, Robert B.

Cairns, Bill. The Trout Unlimited Book of Basic Trout Fishing. LC 82-50368. (Illus.). 128p. 1990. pap. 9.95 (*0-913276-37-5*) Stone Wall Pr.

*__Cairns, Bill.__ The Trout Unlimited Book of Basic Trout Fishing. (Illus.), 122p. 1999. reprint ed. pap. text 10.00 (*0-7881-6672-7*) DIANE Pub.

Cairns, C., ed. see Jack, R. D.

*__Cairns, Carol.__ Verify & Comply: A Quick Reference Guide to the JCAHO & NCQA Standards for Credentialing. Dorman, Steve, ed. (Illus.). 176p. 2000. pap. text. write for info. (*1-57839-075-3*) Opus Communs.

Cairns, Christopher. Domenico Bollani, Bishop of Brescia: Devotion to Church & State in the Republic of Venice in the 16th Century. 306p. 1976. 87.50 (*90-6004-346-4*, Pub. by B De Graaf) Coronet Bks.

Cairns, Christopher, ed. The Commedia dell'arte from the Renaissance to Dario Fo: The Italian Origins of European Theatre VI. LC 89-13576. (Illus.). 472p. 1989. lib. bdg. 109.95 (*0-88946-080-9*) E Mellen.

— The Renaissance Theatre - Texts, Performance & Design Vol. 1: English & Italian Theatre. (Illus.). 200p. 1999. text 70.95 (*0-7546-0006-8*, Pub. by Ashgate Pub) Ashgate Pub Co.

— Scenery, Set & Staging in the Italian Renaissance: Studies in the Practice of Theatre. LC 96-3909. (Illus.). 340p. 1996. text 99.95 (*0-7734-8814-6*) E Mellen.

Cairns, Christopher, ed. see Ariosto, Ludovico & Aretino, Pietro.

Cairns, Christopher, ed. see Machiavelli, Niccolo, et al.

*__Cairns, Christpher, ed.__ The Renaissance Theatre Vol. 2: Texts, Performance, & Design, Image & Acting. LC 99-29487. 130p. 1999. text 70.95 (*0-7546-0007-6*, Pub. by Ashgate Pub) Ashgate Pub Co.

Cairns, Conrad. Medieval Castles. (Cambridge Introduction to World History Topic Bks.). (Illus.). 48p. 1987. pap. 12.95 (*0-521-31589-1*) Cambridge U Pr.

Cairns, D. Conversations with Husserl & Fink. (Phaenomenologica Ser.: No. 66). 127p. 1976. lib. bdg. 99.50 (*90-247-1793-0*, Pub. by M Nijhoff) Kluwer Academic.

Cairns, David. Advocacy & the Making of the Adversarial Criminal Trial, 1800-1865: Passioned for the Hour. 230p. 1999. text 68.00 (*0-19-826284-1*) OUP.

*__Cairns, David.__ Berlioz Vol. I: The Making of an Artist, 1803-1832. LC 99-53825. 616p. 2000. 40.00 (*0-520-22199-0*, Pub. by U CA Pr) Cal Prin Full Svc.

— Berlioz Vol. I: The Making of an Artist, 1803-1832. (Illus.). 648p. 2000. text 40.00 (*0-7139-9385-5*, A Lane) Viking Penguin.

— Berlioz Vol. II: Servitude & Greatness. LC 99-53825. 780p. 2000. 40.00 (*0-520-22200-8*, Pub. by U CA Pr) Cal Prin Full Svc.

— Berlioz Vol. II: Servitude & Greatness. 2nd ed. (Illus.). 896p. 2000. text 40.00 (*0-7139-9386-3*, A Lane) Viking Penguin.

Cairns, David. A Guide to Applying International Accounting Standards. 2nd ed. 1998. pap. 54.95 (*1-86012-722-3*, GAIAS, Pub. by Tolley Pubng) St Mut.

— Responses. LC 80-18152. (Music Ser.). 1980. reprint ed. 32.50 (*0-306-76047-9*) Da Capo.

Cairns, David, jt. ed. see Johnson, Toni O.

Cairns, David, tr. see Ohler, Annemarie.

Cairns, Donald, jt. auth. see Schmieder, June H.

Cairns, Dorion, tr. see Husserl, Edmund.

Cairns, Douglas L. Aidos: The Psychology & Ethics of Honour & Shame in Ancient Greek Literature. LC 92-12131. 490p. 1993. text 95.00 (*0-19-814684-1*, Clarendon Pr) OUP.

Cairns, Earle E. Christianity Through the Centuries: A History of the Christian Church. 3rd rev. ed. LC 96-3255. (Illus.). 560p. 1996. 29.99 (*0-310-20812-2*) Zondervan.

Cairns, Ed. Caught in the Crossfire: Children & the Northern Ireland Conflict. (Irish Studies). 192p. 1987. text 37.95 (*0-8156-2421-2*) Syracuse U Pr.

— Children & Political Violence. Dunn, Judy, ed. & pref. by. (Understanding Children's Worlds Ser.). (Illus.). 256p. 1996. pap. 27.95 (*1-55786-351-2*) Blackwell Pubs.

— A Safer Future: Reducing the Human Cost of Conflict. (Oxfam Insight Ser.). 128p. 1997. pap. 11.95 (*0-85598-386-8*, Pub. by Oxfam Pub) Stylus Pub VA.

Cairns, Edith M., jt. auth. see University of Reading, UK, Multilingual Resources.

Cairns, Elizabeth. Raising Funds for Charity. 200p. (C). 1994. 175.00 (*0-85459-760-3*, Pub. by Tolley Pubng) St Mut.

Cairns, Elizabeth, ed. All the Time in the World. LC 97-180554. 143p. 1996. pap. 17.95 (*0-949142-33-6*, Pub. by Stirling Pr) Intl Spec Bk.

Cairns, George F., et al, eds. Healing & the Healer. LC 96-83837. 264p. 1996. 32.95 (*0-913552-60-7*) Exploration Pr.

Cairns, George F., jt. ed. see Teasdale, Wayne.

Cairns, Helen S. The Acquisition of Language. 2nd ed. LC 86-423. (PRO-ED Studies in Communicative Disorders). (Illus.). 197p. 1996. pap. text 27.00 (*0-89079-672-6*, 7319) PRO-ED.

*__Cairns, Helen S.__ Psycholinguistics: An Introduction. LC 98-45758. 1999. pap. write for info. (*0-89079-807-9*) PRO-ED.

Cairns, Huntington. Legal Philosophy from Plato to Hegel. LC 49-7752. 599p. reprint ed. pap. 185.70 (*0-608-10103-6*, 200495700048) Bks Demand.

— Legal Philosophy from Plato to Hegel. LC 79-12703. 583p. 1980. reprint ed. lib. bdg. 47.50 (*0-313-21499-9*, CALP, Greenwood Pr) Greenwood.

Cairns, Huntington, ed. The Limits of Art. 1500p. 1996. 19.98 (*1-56731-162-8*, MJF Bks) Fine Comms.

Cairns, Huntington, jt. ed. see Hamilton, Edith.

Cairns, J., Jr., et al, eds. Environmental Biomonitoring, Assessment, Prediction & Management-Certain Case Studies & Related Quantitative Issues. (Statistical Ecology Ser.: Vol. 11). 1979. 45.00 (*0-89974-008-1*) Intl Co-Op.

Cairns, J., et al, eds. Estimating the Hazard of Chemical Substances to Aquatic Life - STP 657. 283p. 1981. pap. 19.50 (*0-8031-0336-0*, STP657) ASTM.

Cairns, J., jt. ed. see Dickson, K. L.

Cairns, J., Jr., ed. see International Symposium on the Recovery of Damaged.

Cairns, JoAnn. Welcome, Stranger: Welcome Friend. LC 87-82531. 144p. 1988. pap. 3.95 (*0-88243-626-0*, 02-0626) Gospel Pub.

Cairns, John. Community Toxicity Testing, STP 920. LC 86-20568. (Special Technical Publication (STP) Ser.). (Illus.). 345p. 1986. text 48.00 (*0-8031-0488-X*, STP920) ASTM.

— Matters of Life & Death. LC 96-18026. 260p. 1997. text 29.95 (*0-691-02872-9*, Pub. by Princeton U Pr) Cal Prin Full Svc.

— Matters of Life & Death: Perspectives on Public Health, Molecular Biology, Cancer, & the Prospects for the Human Race. 272p. 1997. pap. text 14.95 (*0-691-00250-9*, Pub. by Princeton U Pr) Cal Prin Full Svc.

Cairns, John, Jr., ed. Rehabilitating Damaged Ecosystems. LC 94-15305. 448p. 1994. lib. bdg. 95.00 (*1-56670-043-4*, L1043) Lewis Pubs.

— Rehabilitating Damaged Ecosystems, Vol. I. 192p. 1988. lib. bdg. 202.95 (*0-8493-4391-7*) CRC Pr.

— Rehabilitating Damaged Ecosystems, Vol. II. 224p. 1988. lib. bdg. 203.00 (*0-8493-4392-5*) CRC Pr.

Cairns, John, ed. The Structure & Function of Fresh-Water Microbial Communities. LC 75-30823. (Research Division Monographs: No. 3). 309p. reprint ed. pap. 95.80 (*0-8357-3278-9*, 203950100013) Bks Demand.

Cairns, John, et al, eds. Cancer Incidence in Defined Populations. LC 80-7676. (Banbury Reports: Vol. 4). (Illus.). 458p. 1980. 52.00 (*0-87969-203-0*) Cold Spring Harbor.

— Phage & the Origins of Molecular Biology. LC 92-15934. 384p. 1992. 40.00 (*0-87969-407-6*) Cold Spring Harbor.

Cairns, John, Jr. & Crawford, Todd V. Integrated Environmental Management. (Illus.). 232p. 1990. lib. bdg. 89.95 (*0-87371-279-X*, L279) Lewis Pubs.

Cairns, John, Jr & Dickson, K. L., eds. Biological Methods for the Assessment of Water Quality - STP 528. 262p. 1981. 16.25 (*0-8031-0114-7*, STP528) ASTM.

Cairns, John, Jr. & Dickson, Kenneth L., eds. The Environment: Costs, Conflicts, Action. LC 73-86818. (Illus.). 166p. reprint ed. pap. 51.50 (*0-7837-0658-8*, 204099400019) Bks Demand.

Cairns, John, Jr. & Patrick, Ruth, eds. Managing Water Resources. LC 86-18215. (Environmental Regeneration Ser.). 144p. 1986. 49.95 (*0-275-92200-6*, C2200, Praeger Pubs) Greenwood.

Cairns, John, Jr. & Pratt, J. R., eds. Functional Testing of Aquatic Biota for Estimating Hazards of Chemicals. LC 88-31528. (Special Technical Publication Ser.: No. STP 988). (Illus.). 231p. 1989. text 45.00 (*0-8031-1165-7*, STP988) ASTM.

Cairns, John, Jr., et al. Biological Monitoring of Water & Effluent Quality-STP 607. 242p. 1977. 24.25 (*0-8031-0190-2*, STP607) ASTM.

— Fresh Water Pollution III: Problems & Control. (Illus.). 220p. (C). 1973. text 29.00 (*0-8422-7103-1*) Irvington.

— Predicting Ecosystem Risk, Vol. XX. (Advances in Modern Environmental Toxicology Ser.: Vol. 20). (Illus.). 345p. (Orig.). 1992. 65.00 (*0-911131-27-2*) Specialist Journals.

Cairns, John, Jr., jt. auth. see Niederlehner, B. R.

Cairns, Julia, jt. auth. see Unobagha, Uzoamaka Chinyelu.

Cairns, Julie. The Golden Retriever: All That Glitters. LC 98-22869. 224p. 1998. 27.95 (*0-87605-041-0*) Howell Bks.

— The Golden Retriever: An Owner's Guide to a Happy, Healthy Pet. LC 95-15668. (Owner's Guide to a Happy, Healthy Pet Ser.). (Illus.). 160p. 1995. 12.95 (*0-87605-380-0*) Howell Bks.

Cairns, Kathleen. Last Wishes: A Psychologist's Guide to Living Life Prepared for Death. 300p. 1998. pap. 14.95 (*1-891409-01-8*) Life Goes On.

— The Psychotherapy Workbook: A Home-Study Guide for Growth & Change. 255p. 1997. pap. 19.95 (*1-891409-00-X*) Life Goes On.

Cairns, Kathleen, et al. The Bald & the Beautiful: Surviving Breast Cancer. 1999. pap. 6.95 (*1-891409-07-7*) Life Goes On.

Cairns, Lucille. Marie Cardinal: Motherhood & Creativity. 296p. 1993. 60.00 (*0-85261-339-3*, Pub. by Univ of Glasgow) St Mut.

— Privileged Pariahdom: Homosexuality in the Novels of Dominique Fernandez. 178p. 1996. pap. 31.95 (*3-906756-16-5*, Pub. by P Lang) P Lang Pubng.

Cairns, Lynne & Henderson, Graeme. Unfinished Voyages Vol. 3: Western Australian Shipwrecks 1881-1900. 383p. (C). 1995. 45.00 (*1-875560-24-6*, Pub. by Univ of West Aust Pr) Intl Spec Bk.

Cairns, Marion. Jupiter Descends. 55p. 1984. 4.95 (*0-89697-210-0*) Intl Univ Pr.

Cairns, Peter, ed. see Eliot, George, pseud.

Cairns, R. A. Generation & Application of Highpower Microwaves. 1997. 209.00 (*0-7503-0451-0*); pap. text 63.00 (*0-7503-0474-X*) IOP Pub.

*__Cairns, Robert B., et al, eds.__ Development Science. (Studies in Social & Emotional Development). 313p. (C). 2001. pap. Price not set. (*0-521-79459-5*) Cambridge U Pr.

Cairns, Robert B., et al, eds. Developmental Science. (Studies in Social & Emotional Development). (Illus.). 308p. (C). 1996. text 44.95 (*0-521-49585-7*) Cambridge U Pr.

Cairns, Robert B. & Cairns, Beverley D. Lifelines & Risks: Pathways of Youth in Our Time. 325p. (C). 1995. text 59.95 (*0-521-48112-0*) Cambridge U Pr.

— Lifelines & Risks: Pathways of Youth in Our Time. 300p. (C). 1995. pap. text 19.95 (*0-521-48570-3*) Cambridge U Pr.

Cairns, Robert B. & Stoff, David M., eds. Aggression & Violence: Genetic, Neurobiological, & Biosocial Perspectives. 416p. 1996. text 79.95 (*0-8058-1755-7*) L Erlbaum Assocs.

— Aggression & Violence: Genetic, Neurobiological, & Biosocial Perspectives. 376p. 1996. pap. 39.95 (*0-8058-2504-5*) L Erlbaum Assocs.

Cairns, Robert B., et al. Methods & Models for Studying the Individual. LC 98-19777. 308p. 1998. 58.00 (*0-7619-1451-X*); pap. 27.95 (*0-7619-1452-8*) Sage.

Cairns, S., ed. Biology of the Antarctic Seas Thirteen. (Antarctic Research Ser.: Vol. 63). 99p. 1994. 33.00 (*0-87590-844-6*, AR0638446) Am Geophysical.

Cairns, S. D. & Wells, J. W. Bulletins of American Paleontology Vol. 93: Neogene Paleontology in the Northern Dominican Republic: 5. The Suborders Caryophylliina & Dendrophylliina (Anthozoa: Scleractinia), Issue 328. 74p. 1987. 30.00 (*0-614-17837-1*) Paleo Res.

Cairns, S. D., et al. Common & Scientific Names of Aquatic Invertebrates from the United States & Canada: Cnidaria & Ctenophora. LC 91-73763. (Special Publication Ser.: No. 22). 75p. 1991. pap. 33.00 (*0-913235-74-1*, 510.18P) Am Fisheries Soc.

Cairns, Scott. Recovered Body. LC 98-22741. 75p. 1998. pap. 12.95 (*0-8076-1437-8*) Braziller.

— The Theology of Doubt. (CSU Poetry Ser.: No. XVIII). 58p. (Orig.). 1985. pap. 6.00 (*0-914946-52-8*) Cleveland St Univ Poetry Ctr.

Cairns, Scott, ed. see Merritt, Constance.

Cairns, Scott, jt. ed. see Olsen, W. Scott.

Cairns-Smith, A. G. Evolving the Mind: On the Nature of Matter & the Origin of Consciousness. (Illus.). 337p. (C). 1996. text 29.95 (*0-521-40220-4*) Cambridge U Pr.

— Evolving the Mind: On the Nature of Matter & the Origin of Consciousness. (Illus.). 336p. (C). 1998. reprint ed. pap. 15.95 (*0-521-63755-4*) Cambridge U Pr.

— Secrets of the Mind: A Tale of Discovery & Mistaken Identity. LC 99-14663. 130p. 1999. 24.00 (*0-387-98692-8*, Copernicus) Spr-Verlag.

— Seven Clues to the Origin of Life: A Scientific Detective Story. (Canto Book Ser.). (Illus.). 143p. (C). 1990. pap. 10.95 (*0-521-39828-2*) Cambridge U Pr.

Cairns, Stephen, ed. Biology of the Antarctic Seas Twenty-Two. (Antarctic Research Ser.: Vol. 58). 1993. 38.00 (*0-87590-826-8*) Am Geophysical.

C

Cairns, Stephen D. A Revision of the Ahermatypic Scleractinia of the Philippine Islands & Adjacent Waters, Pt. 1. LC 89-600214. (Smithsonian Contributions to Zoology Ser.: No. 486). (Illus.). 142p. reprint ed. pap. 44.10 (*0-8357-7906-8*, 203633400001) Bks Demand.
— Stylasteridae: Hydrozoa: Hydroida, of the Galapagos Islands. LC 85-600176. (Smithsonian Contributions to Zoology Ser.: No. 426). 46p. reprint ed. pap. 30.00 (*0-608-16205-1*, 202713900054) Bks Demand.
Cairns, Stephen D., ed. Biology of the Antarctic Seas XXIV - Antarctic & Subantarctic Pycnogonida: Nymphonidae, Colossendeidae, Phynchothoraxidae, Pycnogonidae, Endeididae, & Callipallenidae. LC 86-647920. (Antarctic Research Ser.: Vol. 69). 165p. 1996. 45.00 (*0-87590-885-3*, 70998) Am Geophysical.
Cairns, Stewart S. Introductory Topology. LC 68-8995. (Illus.). 256p. reprint ed. 79.40 (*0-8357-9917-4*, 201245000081) Bks Demand.
***Cairns, Thomas.** Modern Roses XI. 2000. 99.95 (*0-12-155053-2*) Acad Pr.
Cairns, Thomas, intro. Modern Roses 10: The Comprehensive List of Roses of International & Botanical Importance Including All Modern International Rose Registrations. 760p. (C). 1993. 50.00 (*0-9636340-0-3*) Am Rose Soc.
Cairns, Tommy. All about Roses. LC 98-66913. (Ortho's All about Ser.). (Illus.). 96p. 1998. pap. 11.95 (*0-89721-428-5*, Ortho Bks) Meredith Bks.
Cairns, Trevor. Medieval Knights. (Cambridge Introduction to World History Topic Bks.). (Illus.). 64p. (YA). (gr. 7 up). 1992. pap. 13.95 (*0-521-38953-4*) Cambridge U Pr.
Cairns, W. J., ed. North Sea Oil & the Environment: Developing Oil & Gas Resources Environmental Impacts & Responses. (Illus.). 712p. (C). (gr. 13). 1992. 375.00 (*1-85166-704-0*) Elsevier Applied Sci.
Cairns, Walter. Introduction to European Union Law. LC 98-138796. 345p. 1997. pap. 23.50 (*1-85941-205-X*, Pub. by Cavendish Pubng) Gaunt.
Cairns, Walter & McKeon, Robert. Introduction to French Law. 241p. 1995. pap. 32.00 (*1-85941-112-6*, Pub. by Cavendish Pubng) Gaunt.
Cairns, William B. British Criticisms of American Writing. 1988. reprint ed. lib. bdg. 79.00 (*0-7812-0169-1*) Rprt Serv.
Cairns, William T. Religion of Dr. Johnson. LC 71-93324. (Essay Index Reprint Ser.). 1977. 19.95 (*0-8369-1279-9*) Ayer.
Cairo, Gabriel J., et al. New Voices in Latin American Literature. Monge-Rafuls, Pedro R., ed. & intro. by. LC 93-85756. (Literature/Conversation Ser.: Vol. III). (ENG & SPA.). 260p. 1993. pap. 17.00 (*0-9625127-0-2*) Ollantay Pr.
Cairo, Jim. Motivation & Goal Setting: How to Set & Achieve Goals & Inspire Others. LC 98-10412. 128p. 1998. pap. 10.99 (*1-56414-364-3*) Career Pr Inc.
Cairo, Joel. Everything I Know about Wall Street I Learned from My Cat. (Illus.). 72p. 1998. pap. text 6.00 (*0-7881-5119-3*) DIANE Pub.
Cairo, Osvaldo, ed. see Intelligence Mexican International Conference on Artificial Intelligence Staff.
Cairo, Peter C., jt. auth. see Dotlich, David L.
Cairo Roots Society Staff. Cairo Community Heritage. (Illus.). 317p. 1986. 42.00 (*0-88107-055-6*) Curtis Media.
Cairo, Shelly, et al. Our Brother Has Down's Syndrome. (Illus.). 24p. (J). (ps-3). 1985. pap. 5.95 (*0-920303-31-5*, Pub. by Annick); lib. bdg. 15.95 (*0-920303-30-7*, Pub. by Annick) Firefly Bks Ltd.
Cairol, Julie C., ed. see Capp, Al.
Cairoli, R. & Dalang, Robert C. Sequential Stochastic Optimization. LC 94-39134. (Probability & Mathematical Ser.). 352p. 1996. 94.95 (*0-471-57754-5*) Wiley.
***CAiSE '2000 Staff, et al.** Advanced Information Systems Engineering: Proceedings of the 12th International Conference, CAiSE 2000, Stockholm, Sweden, June, 2000. LC 00-41041. (Lecture Notes in Computer Science Ser.). 2000. pap. write for info. (*3-540-67630-9*) Spr-Verlag.
Caiserman-Roth, Ghitta & Cohen, Rhoda. Insights, Discoveries, Surprises: Drawing from the Model. (Illus.). 120p. 1993. 39.95 (*0-7735-0993-3*, Pub. by McG-Queens Univ Pr) CUP Services.
Caisley, Raewyn. Hannah & Her Dad. LC 93-28997. (Voyages Ser.). (Illus.). (J). 1994. 4.25 (*0-383-03787-5*) SRA McGraw.
— The Leaf Raker. LC 93-26218. (Voyages Ser.). (Illus.). (J). 1994. 4.25 (*0-383-03756-5*) SRA McGraw.
— Raewyn's Got the Writing Bug Again. LC 93-24529. (Voyages Ser.). (J). 1994. 4.25 (*0-383-03734-4*) SRA McGraw.
Caisley, Robert. Letters to an Alien. 39p. 1996. pap. 5.50 (*0-87129-682-9*, L58) Dramatic Pub.
***Caison, Charles Crawford, Jr., et al.** Professional ADO 2.5 RDS Programming with ASP 3.0. 700p. 1999. pap. 49.99 (*1-86100-324-2*) Wrox Pr Inc.
Caisse, Arthur J., Jr. Electric Motors. (C). 2001. 63.00 (*0-13-362971-6*, Macmillan Coll) P-H.
Caisse, Arthur J., Jr., jt. auth. see Richardson, Donald V.
Caissy, G. A. Early Adolescence: Understanding the 10 to 15 Year Old. (Illus.). 280p. (C). 1994. 26.95 (*0-306-44762-2*, Plen Insight) Perseus Pubng.
Caistor, Nick. Argentina in Focus. (In Focus Ser.). (Illus.). 80p. Date not set. pap. 12.00 (*0-85345-978-9*, Pub. by Lat Am Bur) Monthly Rev.
— Chile in Focus: A Guide to the People, Politics & Culture. (In Focus Guides Ser.). (Illus.). 100p. 1998. pap. 12.95 (*1-56656-231-7*) Interlink Pub.
— Mexico City: A Cultural & Literary Companion. LC 99-56320. (Cities of the Imagination Ser.). 256p. 2000. pap. 15.00 (*1-56656-349-6*) Interlink Pub.
— Rainstick Pack. (Illus.). 96p. 1997. text 25.00 (*0-7893-0092-3*, Pub. by Universe) Universe.
Caistor, Nick, tr. see Aira, Cesar.
Caistor, Nick, tr. see Arlt, Roberto.
Caistor, Nick, tr. see Ramirez, Sergio.
Caistor, Nick, tr. see Soriano, Osvaldo.
***Caiti, A.** Experimental Acoustic Inversion Methods for Exploration of the Shallow Environment. LC 00-35407. 2000. write for info. (*0-7923-6305-1*) Kluwer Academic.
Caitlin, Stephen. Amazing World of Birds. LC 89-4968. (Illus.). 32p. (J). (gr. 2-4). 1990. lib. bdg. 17.25 (*0-8167-1747-8*) Troll Communs.
— Amazing World of Birds. LC 89-4968. (Illus.). 32p. (J). (gr. 2-4). 1996. pap. 3.50 (*0-8167-1748-6*) Troll Communs.
— Discovering Reptiles & Amphibians. LC 89-4972. (Illus.). 32p. (J). (gr. 2-4). 1990. pap. 3.50 (*0-8167-1754-0*); lib. bdg. 17.25 (*0-8167-1753-2*) Troll Communs.
— Skateboard Fun. LC 87-19179. (First-Start Easy Readers Ser.). (J). (ps-1). 1988. lib. bdg. 13.05 (*0-8167-1233-6*) Troll Communs.
— Skateboard Fun. LC 87-19179. (First-Start Easy Readers Ser.). (J). (ps-1). 1997. pap. 2.50 (*0-8167-1234-4*) Troll Communs.
— Wonders of Swamps & Marshes. LC 89-4967. (Illus.). 32p. (J). (gr. 7-11). 1996. pap. 3.50 (*0-8167-1766-4*) Troll Communs.
— You Dirty Dog. LC 87-19182. (Giant First Start Reader Ser.). (Illus.). (J). (gr. k-2). 1996. pap. 3.95 (*0-8167-1104-6*) Troll Communs.
Caius, Jean F. The Medicinal & Poisonous Plants of India. 493p. 1986. 500.00 (*81-85046-30-1*, Pub. by Scientific) St Mut.
— The Medicinal & Poisonous Plants of India. 528p. (C). 1986. 160.00 (*0-7855-2273-5*, Pub. by Scientific) St Mut.
Caius, John. Of Englishe Dogges: The Diversities & the Properties. Fleming, A., tr. LC 73-26240. (English Experience Ser.: No. 110). 44p. 1969. reprint ed. 15.00 (*90-221-0110-X*) Walter J Johnson.
Caivollelo, Massimo. Rose By Any Other Name: Pre-Shakespearian Accounts of Romeo & Juliet. 200p. 2000. 24.95 (*1-56886-074-9*) Marsilio Pubs.
Caiwei, Ouyang, tr. see Baishi, Qi.
Cajal, S. R. Texture of the Nervous System of Man & the Vertebrates. Pasik, P. & Pasik, T., eds. & trs. by. LC 99-12316. (Illus.). 750p. 1998. 189.00 (*3-211-83057-X*) Spr-Verlag.
***Cajal, S. R.** Texture of the Nervous System of Man & the Vertebrates, Vol. II. annot. ed. Pasik, P. & Pasik, T., eds. & trs. by. from SPA. (Illus.). 600p. 2000. 175.00 (*3-211-83201-7*) Spr-Verlag.
Cajal, S. Ramon y. Cajal's Histology of the Nervous System, 2 vols. Swanson, Larry W., ed. Swanson, Neely, tr. from FRE. LC 93-35437. (History of Neuroscience Ser.: No. 6). (Illus.). 1672p. 1995. text 195.00 (*0-19-507401-7*) OUP.
Cajal, Santiago R. El Mundo Visto a los Ochenta Anos: Impresiones de un Arteriosclerotico. Kastenbaum, Robert J., ed. LC 78-22214. (Aging & Old Age Ser.). (SPA.). 1979. reprint ed. lib. bdg. 21.95 (*0-405-11827-9*) Ayer.
— Recollections of My Life. Craigie, E. Horne & Cano, Juan, trs. from SPA. (Illus.). 664p. 1989. reprint ed. pap. text 23.00 (*0-262-68060-2*) MIT Pr.
Cajal, Santiago R. & FIDIA Research Foundation Staff. Cajal on the Cerebral Cortex: An Annotated Translation of the Complete Writings. DeFelipe, Javier & Jones, Edward G., eds. & trs. by. (History of Neuroscience Ser.: No. 1). (Illus.). 672p. 1988. text 79.50 (*0-19-505280-3*) OUP.
Cajape, Freddy G. De Frederias y Otros Poemas. (SPA.). 56p. 1984. pap. 5.00 (*0-9606758-7-6*) SLUSA.
Cajetanus, Thomas De Vio. Cajetan: Commentary on St. Thomas Aquinas on Being & Essence. Kendzierski, Lottie H. & Wade, S. J., trs. LC 64-7794. (Medieval Philosophical Texts in Translation Ser.). 1965. pap. 20.00 (*0-87462-214-X*) Marquette.
— Opuscula Omnia. (GER.). 307p. 1995. reprint ed. 210.00 (*3-487-10034-7*) G Olms Pubs.
Cajete, Gregory. Look to the Mountain: An Ecology of Indigenous Education. LC 94-175203. (Illus.). 248p. (Orig.). (C). 1993. pap. 19.95 (*1-882308-65-4*) Kivaki Pr.
— Native Science: Natural Laws of Interdependence. LC 99-54279. (Illus.). 256p. 1999. 24.95 (*1-57416-035-4*); pap. 14.95 (*1-57416-041-9*) Clear Light.
Cajete, Gregory A. Igniting the Sparkle: An Indigenous Science Education Model. (Illus.). 230p. 1999. pap. write for info. (*1-882308-66-2*) Kivaki Pr.
Cajio, Linda. Bachelor Daddy. (Holiday Heart Ser.). 1997. per. 3.75 (*0-373-16678-8*, 1-16678-4) Harlequin Bks.
— Boss Man. 1997. per. 3.75 (*0-373-16694-X*, 1-16694-1) Harlequin Bks.
— Diamond Daddies. (American Romance Ser.: No. 779). 1999. per. 3.99 (*0-373-16779-2*, 1-16779-0, Harlequin) Harlequin Bks.
— Doctor Valentine. (American Romance Ser.). 1997. per. 3.75 (*0-373-16667-2*, 1-16667-7) Harlequin Bks.
— Doorstep Daddy: The Holiday Heart. (American Romance Ser.: No. 752). 1998. per. 3.99 (*0-373-16752-0*, 0-16752-8) Harlequin Bks.
— Family to Be. (American Romance Ser.: Bk. 805). 2000. per. 3.99 (*0-373-16805-5*, 1-16805-3) Harlequin Bks.
— House Husband. (American Romance Ser.: No. 715). 1998. per. 3.99 (*0-373-16715-6*, 1-16715-4) Harlequin Bks.
— Knight's Song. 352p. 1996. mass mkt. 4.99 (*0-8217-5194-8*, Zebra Kensgtn) Kensgtn Pub Corp.
— Mister Christmas. 251p. 1997. per. 3.75 (*0-373-16704-0*, 1-16704-8) Harlequin Bks.
— Rescuing Diana. 1995. mass mkt. 2.95 (*0-553-55034-9*) Bantam.
— A Tender Masquerade. 1997. mass mkt. 4.99 (*0-8217-5752-0*) Kensgtn Pub Corp.
Cajkler, Wasyl & Addelman, Ron. The Practice of Foreign Language Teaching. 160p. 1992. pap. 29.95 (*1-85346-205-5*, Pub. by David Fulton) Taylor & Francis.
Cajolet-Laganiere, H. French at the Office: Le Francais au Bureau. (FRE.). 197p. 1982. pap. 22.95 (*0-8288-0987-9*, M9037) Fr & Eur.
Cajori, Florian. The Chequered Career of Ferdinand Rudolph Hassler: First Superintendent of the U. S. Coast Survey. Cohen, I. Bernard, ed. LC 79-7954. 1980. reprint ed. lib. bdg. 23.95 (*0-405-12535-6*) Ayer.
— History of Mathematical Notations, 2 vols. Incl. Vol. 1. Notations in Elementary Mathematics. 467p. 1951. pap. 10.95 (*0-87548-154-X*); Vol. 2. Notations Mainly in Higher Mathematics. 384p. 1952. 24.95 (*0-87548-172-8*); (Illus.). write for info. (*0-318-54785-6*) Open Court.
— A History of Mathematical Notations, Vols. 1-2, 2 vols., Set. (Illus.). xxviii, 820p. 1993. reprint ed. pap. text 19.95 (*0-486-67766-4*) Dover.
— A History of Mathematics. 5th rev. ed. Nim, A., ed. LC 70-113120. xi, 524p. 1985. text 29.50 (*0-8284-1303-7*, 303) Chelsea Pub.
— A History of the Logarithmic Slide Rule & Allied Instruments. (Illus.). 178p. 1994. reprint ed. 24.95 (*1-879335-52-2*) Astragal Pr.
Cakanac, Chris J. & Ajamian, Paul C. Cornea & Conjunctiva: Clinical Procedures. LC 95-17809. (Optometric Procedures Ser.). (Illus.). 118p. 1995. spiral bd. 42.00 (*0-7506-9582-X*) Buttrwrth-Heinemann.
Cakanac, Chris J., ed. see Johnston, Robert L.
Cakavell, Frank, jt. auth. see Kaye, Dorris.
Cake, J. C. Good (K)night Stories. Strickler, Ruth, ed. 190p. (J). (gr. 1 up). 1967. 7.95 (*0-932785-49-2*) Philos Pub.
Cake, Patrick. The Pro-Am Murders. LC 78-70580. (Illus.). 1979. 8.95 (*0-932864-00-7*) Proteus Calif.
Cakes, Patti & Hunt, Tammy. Snake Stew. 32p. (J). 1995. pap. 9.95 (*0-9649800-0-2*) Cozy Bks.
Cakir, A., et al. Visual Display Terminals: A Manual Covering Ergonomics, Workplace Design, Health & Safety, Task Organization. LC 80-40070. (Illus.). 335p. reprint ed. pap. 103.90 (*0-608-17582-X*, 203042000069) Bks Demand.
Cakmak, A. S., ed. Ground Motion & Engineering Seismology. LC 87-70780. (SDEE Ser.: Vol. 3). 632p. 1987. 154.00 (*0-931215-87-0*, 1899) Computational Mech MA.
— Soil Dynamics & Earthquake Engineering III: Soil Dynamics & Liquefaction. LC 87-70778. (SDEE Ser.: Vol. 3). 386p. 1987. 112.00 (*0-931215-57-9*) Computational Mech MA.
— Soil Dynamics & Earthquake Engineering III: Soil-Structure Interaction. LC 87-70779. (SDEE Ser.: Vol. 3). 382p. 1987. 105.00 (*0-931215-86-2*) Computational Mech MA.
— Soil Dynamics & Earthquake Engineering III: Structures & Stochastic Methods. LC 87-70781. (SDEE Ser.: Vol. 3). 500p. 1987. 134.00 (*0-931215-88-9*) Computational Mech MA.
— Soil Dynamics & Earthquake Engineering IV: Soil Dynamics & Liquification, Vol. 2. LC 89-85630. (SDEE Ser.: Vol. 4). 1989. 103.00 (*0-945824-35-1*) Computational Mech MA.
— Soil Dynamics & Earthquakes Engineering IV Vol. 1: Structural Dynamics & Soil Structure Interaction. LC 89-85630. (SDEE Ser.: Vol. 4). 498p. 1989. 152.00 (*0-945824-36-X*) Computational Mech MA.
— Soils Response Spectrum. LC 90-82732. (Progress in Engineering Ser.: Vol. 10). 1990. pap. 54.00 (*0-945824-63-7*) Computational Mech MA.
— Stochastic Methods in Earthquake Engineering. (Progress in Engineering Ser.). 170p. 1985. pap. 46.00 (*0-931215-08-0*) Computational Mech MA.
Cakmak, A. S., et al, eds. Soil Dynamics & Earthquake Engineering: Proceedings of the Conference, Southampton, 13-15 July 1982, 2 vols., Set. 1017p. (C). 1982. text 427.00 (*90-6191-253-9*, Pub. by A A Balkema) Ashgate Pub Co.
Cakmak, A. S. & Botha, J. F. Applied Mathematics for Engineers. 320p. 1995. 101.00 (*1-85312-275-0*) Computational Mech MA.
Cakmak, A. S. & Botha, J. F. Applied Mathematics for Engineers. LC 94-70415. 320p. (C). 1995. text 101.00 (*1-56252-199-3*, 2750); pap. text 34.00 (*1-56252-306-6*, 382X) Computational Mech MA.
Cakmak, A. S. & Brebbia, C. A., eds. Soil Dynamics & Earthquake Engineering VII. LC 95-67975. 680p. 1995. 302.00 (*1-56252-239-6*, 3153) Computational Mech MA.
— Soil Dynamics & Earthquake Engineering VII. 680p. 1995. 302.00 (*1-85312-315-3*, Pub. by WIT Pr) Computational Mech MA.
Cakmak, A. S. & Brebbia, C. A., eds. Soil Dynamics & Earthquake Engineering VI. 960p. 1993. 337.00 (*1-85312-231-9*) Computational Mech MA.
Cakmak, A. S. & Brebbia, Carlos A., eds. Soil Dynamics & Earthquake Engineering VI. LC 92-75802. (SDEE Ser.: Vol. 6). 960p. 1993. 337.00 (*1-56252-154-3*, 2319) Computational Mech MA.
Cakmak, A. S., et al. Computational & Applied Mathematics for Engineering Analysis. LC 87-70949. 390p. (C). 1987. text 75.00 (*0-931215-17-X*) Computational Mech MA.
— Computational & Applied Mathematics for Engineering Analysis. (Illus.). 415p. 1987. 114.95 (*0-387-17505-9*) Spr-Verlag.
Cakouros, Jeanette K. & Flowers, Ruth K., eds. Cats' Meow! An Anthology of Cat Tales. LC 95-75502. (Illus.). 208p. (Orig.). 1996. pap. 13.50 (*0-9620600-1-1*) Maine Rhode Pubs.
Cakouros, Jeanette K., ed. see Kinney, Lila G.
CAL Staff. English-Czech Phrasebook with Useful Wordlist. 140p. 1985. pap. 5.00 (*0-685-16927-8*) Ctr Appl Ling.
— English-Hungarian Phrasebook with Useful Wordlist. 140p. 1985. pap. 5.00 (*0-685-16931-6*) Ctr Appl Ling.
— English-Polish Phrasebook with Useful Wordlist. 140p. 1985. pap. 5.00 (*0-685-16933-2*) Ctr Appl Ling.
— English-Romanian Phrasebook with Useful Wordlist. 140p. 1985. pap. 5.00 (*0-685-16934-0*) Ctr Appl Ling.
***Cal State University Staff.** Biology Labs Online Manual. 96p. (C). 1999. pap. 28.60 (*0-8053-7443-4*) Benjamin-Cummings.
Cal-Vidal, Jose, jt. auth. see Chandra, Prabir K.
Cala, F. R. & Winston, A. E. Handbook of Aqueous Cleaning Technology for Electronic Assemblies. 295p. 1997. pap. 252.00 (*0-901150-31-2*) St Mut.
Calab, Silvio. Trout & Salmon of the World. 1990. 34.98 (*1-55521-665-X*) Bk Sales Inc.
Calabi, Silvio. The Illustrated Encyclopedia of Fly-Fishing: A Complete A-Z of Terminology, Tackle & Techniques. LC 92-34565. (Illus.). 352p. 1995. 45.00 (*0-8050-1989-8*); pap. 19.95 (*0-8050-3809-4*, Owl) H Holt & Co.
Calabnese, Edward J. Biological Effects of Low Level Exposures to Chemicals. 156p. 1992. lib. bdg. 71.95 (*0-87371-665-5*, L665) Lewis Pubs.
***Calabrese, Adrian.** How to Get Everything You Ever Wanted: Complete Guide to Using Your Psychic Common Sense. LC 00-30934. 2000. 14.95 (*1-56718-119-8*) Llewellyn Pubns.
Calabrese, Andrew & Burgelman, Jean-Claude. Communication, Citizenship, & Social Policy: Rethinking the Limits of the Welfare State. LC 98-35374. 352p. 1999. 69.00 (*0-8476-9107-1*) Rowman.
Calabrese, Andrew & Burgelman, Jean-Claude, eds. Communication, Citizenship, & Social Policy: Rethinking the Limits of the Welfare State. LC 98-35374. 352p. 1999. pap. 24.95 (*0-8476-9108-X*) Rowman.
Calabrese, E. J., ed. Biological Effects of Low Level Exposure. 127p. 1996. pap. text 45.00 (*2-88449-188-0*) Gordon & Breach.
Calabrese, Edward J. Alcohol Interactions with Drugs & Chemicals. 96p. 1991. lib. bdg. 79.95 (*0-87371-403-2*, L403) Lewis Pubs.
— ATSDR Public Health Assessment Guidance Manual. 336p. 1992. lib. bdg. 75.00 (*0-87371-857-7*, L857) Lewis Pubs.
— Multiple Chemical Interactions. (Illus.). 736p. 1990. lib. bdg. 139.00 (*0-87371-146-7*, L146) Lewis Pubs.
— Nutrition & Environmental Health: The Influence of Nutritional Status on Pollutant Toxicity & Carcinogenicity. LC 79-21089. (Illus.). 607p. reprint ed. pap. 188.20 (*0-8357-6238-6*, 205644800001) Bks Demand.
— Nutrition & Environmental Health: The Influence of Nutritional Status on Pollutant Toxicity & Carcinogenicity, Vol. 2. LC 79-21089. (Illus.). 488p. reprint ed. pap. 151.30 (*0-8357-6239-4*, 205644800002) Bks Demand.
— Principles of Animal Extrapolation. 616p. 1991. lib. bdg. 119.00 (*0-87371-410-5*, L410) Lewis Pubs.
— Principles of Petroleum Contaminated Soils. 672p. 1992. lib. bdg. 110.00 (*0-87371-394-X*, L394) Lewis Pubs.
— Principles of Risk Assessment. Date not set. 59.95 (*1-56670-016-7*) Lewis Pubs.
— Risk Assessment - Environmental Fate Methodologies. 192p. 1992. boxed set 104.95 (*0-87371-711-2*) CRC Pr.
Calabrese, Edward J., ed. Biological Effects of Low Level Exposures: Dose-Response Relationships. LC 93-50076. 320p. 1994. lib. bdg. 95.00 (*1-56670-093-0*, L1093) Lewis Pubs.
Calabrese, Edward J., et al, eds. Contaminated Soils, Vol. 3. 400p. 1998. text 59.95 (*1-884940-22-6*) Amherst Sci Pubs.
— Drinking Water & Cardiovascular Disease, Vol. 1. LC 80-81669. 327p. 1980. 47.00 (*0-930376-16-1*) Chem-Orbital.
— Inorganics in Drinking Water & Cardiovascular Disease. LC 85-62107. (Advances in Modern Environmental Toxicology Ser.: Vol. 9). (Illus.). 340p. 1985. 65.00 (*0-911131-10-8*) Specialist Journals.
— Ozone Risk Communication & Management. (Illus.). 216p. 1990. lib. bdg. 95.00 (*0-87371-130-0*, L130) Lewis Pubs.
— Safe Drinking Water Act. (Illus.). 240p. 1989. lib. bdg. 99.95 (*0-87371-138-6*, L138) Lewis Pubs.
Calabrese, Edward J. & Kenyon, Elaina. Air Toxics & Risk Assessment. (Illus.). 688p. 1991. lib. bdg. 110.00 (*0-87371-165-3*, L165) Lewis Pubs.
Calabrese, Edward J. & Kostecki, Paul T., eds. Hydrocarbon Contaminated Soils & Groundwater, Vol. 4. (Illus.). 307p. 1994. text 59.95 (*1-884940-16-1*) Amherst Sci Pubs.
— Petroleum Contaminated Soils: Remediation Techniques, Environmental Fate & Risk Assessment, Vol. II. (Illus.). 532p. 1989. lib. bdg. 99.95 (*0-87371-226-9*, L226) Lewis Pubs.
Calabrese, Edward J. & Scherr, George H., eds. Advances in Human Nutrition, Vol. 2. LC 81-82478. 300p. 1985. 35.00 (*0-930376-35-8*) Chem-Orbital.
Calabrese, Edward J., jt. auth. see Kostecki, Paul T.
Calabrese, Edward J., jt. ed. see Kostecki, Paul T.
Calabrese, John. China's Changing Relations with the Middle East. 224p. 1991. text 49.00 (*0-86187-138-3*, Pub. by P P Pubs) Cassell & Continuum.

An Asterisk (*) at the beginning of an entry indicates that the title is appearing for the first time.

— Revolutionary Horizons: Regional Foreign Policy in Post-Khomeini Iran. LC 93-44096. (International Political Economy Ser.). 1994. text 55.00 (*0-312-12095-8*) St Martin.

Calabrese, John, ed. The Future of Iraq. 141p. (C). 1997. pap. 5.00 (*0-916808-46-7*) Mid East Inst.

Calabrese, Joseph. The Comstock Reader. 2nd ed. LC 97-61023. 186p. (C). 1997. per. 32.95 (*0-7872-3957-7*) Kendall-Hunt.

Calabrese, Joseph R., jt. ed. see Joffe, Russell T.

Calabrese, Michael, ed. see Goodwin, Robert.

Calabrese, Michael, jt. ed. see Goodwin, Robert.

Calabrese, Michael A. Chaucer's Ovidian Arts of Love. LC 94-8387. 184p. 1994. 49.95 (*0-8130-1301-1*) U Press Fla.

*__Calabrese, Omar, ed.__ Italian Style: Forms of Creativity. (Illus.). 232p. 1999. 55.00 (*88-8118-522-9*, Pub. by Skira IT) Abbeville Pr.

Calabrese, Omar, jt. auth. see Versace, Gianni.

*__Calabrese, Prudence.__ Intentions: The Intergalactic Bathroom Enlightenment Guide. 184p. 2000. pap. 19.95 (*0-9701826-7-8*) Twelve-oh-seven.

*__Calabrese, Raymond L.__ Leadership for Safe Schools: A Community-Based Approach. LC 00-44546. 2000. write for info. (*0-8108-3898-2*) Scarecrow.

Calabrese, Raymond L. & Zepeda, Sally J. The Reflective Supervisor: A Practical Guide for Educators. LC 97-3483. (Illus.). 250p. 1997. 39.95 (*1-883001-38-2*) Eye On Educ.

Calabrese, Raymond L., et al. Hands-on Leadership Tools for Principals. 256p. (C). 1996. 39.95 (*1-883001-15-3*) Eye On Educ.

Calabrese, Richard J., jt. auth. see Holli, Betsy B.

Calabrese, Ronald, et al. Essentials of Neural Science: A Behavior Study Guide/Problem Book. (Illus.). 364p. (C). 1997. pap. text, student ed. 34.95 (*0-8385-2221-1*, A2221-8, Apple Lange Med) McGraw.

Calabrese, Salvatore. Classic After-Dinner Drinks. LC 99-12492. (Illus.). 176p. 1999. 14.95 (*0-8069-5940-1*) Sterling.

— Classic Cocktails. LC 97-22145. (Illus.). 192p. 1997. 14.95 (*0-8069-0507-7*) Sterling.

Calabresi, Guido. A Common Law for the Age of Statutes. LC 81-6747. (Oliver Wendell Holmes Lectures). 331p. 1982. 40.00 (*0-674-14604-2*) HUP.

— A Common Law for the Age of Statutes. (Holmes Lectures). 331p. 1986. pap. 23.95 (*0-674-14605-0*) HUP.

*__Calabresi, Guido.__ A Common Law for the Age of Statutes. LC 99-44889. 2000. 85.00 (*1-58477-040-6*) Lawbk Exchange.

Calabresi, Guido. Costs of Accidents: Legal & Economic Analysis. 1970. pap. 20.00 (*0-300-01115-6*) Yale U Pr.

— Ideals, Beliefs, Attitudes, & the Law: Private Law Perspectives on a Public Law Problem. LC 85-2590. (Frank W. Abrams Lectures). 224p. 1985. pap. 17.95 (*0-8156-2310-0*) Syracuse U Pr.

— Ideals, Beliefs, Attitudes, & the Law: Private Law Perspectives on a Public Law Problem. LC 85-2590. (Frank W. Abrams Lectures). 227p. 1985. reprint ed. pap. 70.40 (*0-608-06957-4*, 206716500009) Bks Demand.

Calabresi, Guido & Bobbitt, Philip. Tragic Choices. (C). 1978. pap. text 13.25 (*0-393-09085-X*) Norton.

Calabresi, Paul & Schein, Philip S., eds. Medical Oncology: Basic Principles & Clinical Management of Cancer. 2nd ed. (Illus.). 1408p. 1993. text 139.00 (*0-07-105408-1*) McGraw-Hill HPD.

Calabretta, Brenda. Phonics, Phonemic Awareness, & Word Recognition Activities. (Phonics Ser.). 320p. 1997. pap. 24.95 (*1-57690-316-8*) Tchr Create Mat.

Calabretta, Fred. Guide to Oral History Collections at Mystic Seaport Museum. vi, 74p. 1992. pap. 12.00 (*0-913372-63-3*) Mystic Seaport.

Calabria, Antonio & Marin, John A. Good Government in Spanish Naples. (American University Studies: History: Ser. IX, Vol. 71). XIII, 320p. (C). 1989. text 49.95 (*0-8204-0929-4*) P Lang Pubng.

Calabria, Don G., jt. auth. see Lewis, C. S.

Calabria, Frank M. Dance of the Sleepwalkers: The Dance Marathon Fad. LC 92-73976. 1993. 39.95 (*0-87972-569-9*) Bowling Green Univ Popular Press.

Calabria, Jane. Microsoft Windows NT Workstation 6 in 1. 600p. 1997. 29.99 (*0-7897-1386-1*) Que.

— Microsoft Works 4.5: 6-in-1. LC 97-68088. 648p. 1997. 29.99 (*0-7897-1357-8*) Que.

— MOUS Essentials Excel 97 Proficient. LC 98-66766. 350p. (C). 1998. pap. text 31.00 incl. audio compact disk (*1-58076-054-6*) Que Educ & Trng.

*__Calabria, Jane.__ Mouse Essentials Excel 97 Proficient. (C). 1999. pap. 29.33 (*0-13-018053-X*) P-H.

— Mouse Essentials Excel 97 Expert. 350p. (C). 1999. pap. 29.33 (*0-13-018040-8*) P-H.

Calabria, Jane. Teach Yourself Lotus Notes & Domino 5 Development in 24 Hours. (Teach Yourself . . . Ser.). 600p. 1999. pap. 39.99 (*0-672-31416-9*) Sams.

— Sams Teach Yourself Lotus Notes 5 in 24 Hours. (Teach Yourself . . . Ser.). 1998. pap. 19.99 (*0-672-31417-7*) Sams.

— Sams Teach Yourself Lotus Notes 5 in 10 Minutes. (Teach Yourself . . . Ser.). 1998. pap. 12.99 (*0-672-31419-3*) Sams.

— 10 Minute Guide to Lotus Notes Mail 4.5. LC 96-70544. 1996. pap. 14.99 (*0-7897-0974-0*) Que.

— Using Microsoft Word 97. 3rd ed. LC 98-84534. (Using... Ser.). 617p. 1998. pap. text 29.99 (*0-7897-1568-6*) Que.

— Word 97, 1. LC 98-66779. 1998. pap. text 29.33 (*1-58076-052-X*) Que Educ & Trng.

Calabria, Jane & Burke, Dorothy. Microsoft Office User Specialist Microsoft Word 97 Exam Guide. LC 97-81449. 352p. 1998. pap. 29.99 (*0-7897-1507-4*) Que.

*__Calabria, Jane & Burke, Dorothy.__ Mouse Essentials Excel 97 Expert. 350p. (C). 1998. pap. text 29.33 incl. audio compact disk (*1-58076-055-4*) Que Educ & Trng.

Calabria, Jane & Burke, Dorothy. Ten Minute Guide to Lotus Notes Mail 4.6. LC 97-80539. (10 Minute Guide Ser.). 226p. 1997. pap. text 14.99 (*0-7897-1534-1*) Que.

Calabria, Jane, et al. Microsoft Office User Specialist Microsoft Word 97 Exam Guide. LC 97-80541. 430p. 1997. pap. 29.99 (*0-7897-1290-3*) Que.

*__Calabria, Jane, et al.__ Mouse Essentials Powerpoint 97 Expert. 350p. (C). 1998. pap. text 29.33 incl. audio compact disk (*1-58076-056-2*) Que Educ & Trng.

— Mouse Essentials Word 97 Expert. 350p. (C). 1998. pap. text 29.33 incl. audio compact disk (*1-58076-053-8*) Que Educ & Trng.

Calabria, Jane, jt. auth. see Burke, Dorothy.

Calabria, Michael D. Florence Nightingale in Egypt & Greece: Her Diary & "Visions" LC 96-6296. (SUNY Series in Western Esoteric Traditions). 128p. (C). 1996. text 44.50 (*0-7914-3115-0*) State U NY Pr.

— Florence Nightingale in Egypt & Greece: Her Diary & "Visions" LC 96-6296. (Series in Western Esoteric Traditions). (Illus.). 128p. (C). 1996. pap. text 14.95 (*0-7914-3116-9*) State U NY Pr.

Calabria, Michael D. & Macrae, Janet A., eds. Suggestions for Thought by Florence Nightingale: Selections & Commentaries. LC 93-37576. (Studies in Health, Illness, & Caregiving). 218p. (Orig.). (C). 1994. text 39.95 (*0-8122-3174-0*); pap. text 16.95 (*0-8122-1501-X*) U of Pa Pr.

Calabro, John J. & Dick, W. Carson, eds. Infections & Arthritis. (New Clinical Applications Rheumatology Ser.). 1989. lib. bdg. 139.00 (*0-7462-0052-8*, Pub. by Kluwer Academic) Kluwer Academic.

— Infections & Arthritis. (New Clinical Applications Rheumatology Ser.). (C). 1989. lib. bdg. 62.00 (*0-685-25560-3*) Kluwer Academic.

Calabro, Marian. Great Courtroom Lawyers: Fighting the Cases That Made History. LC 96-5107. (American Profiles Ser.). 176p. 1996. 19.95 (*0-8160-3323-4*) Facts on File.

— Operation Grizzly Bear. LC 88-37497. (Illus.). 112p. (J). (gr. 5 up). 1989. text 13.95 (*0-02-716241-9*, Four Winds Pr) S&S Childrens.

— The Perilous Journey of the Donner Party. LC 98-29610. (Illus.). 192p. (YA). (gr. 5 up). 1999. 20.00 (*0-395-86610-3*, Clarion Bks) HM.

Calabro, Rose L. Living in the Raw: Recipes for a Healthy Lifestyle. 192p. 1999. pap. 17.95 (*0-9666816-0-6*, LTR7101) Rose Pubg.

Calabro, Tony. Bertolt Brecht's Art of Dissemblance. LC 90-5995. 125p. 1990. 25.00 (*0-89341-606-1*, Longwood Academic) Hollowbrook.

Calado, Jorge, ed. Waterproof: Water in Photography since 1852. (Illus.). 567p. 1998. 75.00 (*3-908161-26-6*) Abbeville Pr.

Calaf, Dolores. Exploring Forts of Old San Juan: A Discovery Book. Johnson, Mark, tr. from SPA. (Illus.). 32p. (J). (gr. 5-7). 1995. pap. 3.75 (*0-915992-75-2*) Eastern National.

Calaferte, Louis. C'est la Guerre: A Novel. Wainhouse, Austryn, tr. from FRE. LC 99-13415. 130p. 1999. 59.95 (*0-8101-6032-3*, Marlboro); pap. 14.95 (*0-8101-6068-4*, Marlboro) Northwestern U Pr.

— Septentrion. (FRE.). 440p. 1990. pap. 16.95 (*0-7859-2137-0*, 2070382273) Fr & Eur.

— The Way It Works with Women. Harrison, Sarah, tr. LC 98-23814. 150p. 1998. text 24.95 (*0-8101-6033-1*, Marlboro) Northwestern U Pr.

Calagione, John, et al, eds. Workers' Expressions: Beyond Accommodation & Resistance. LC 90-26178. (SUNY Series in the Anthropology of Work). 233p. (C). 1992. text 74.50 (*0-7914-0835-3*); pap. text 24.95 (*0-7914-0836-1*) State U NY Pr.

Calahan, David. Snow Camp Lookout: View with a Room Mouse Included. LC 96-76155. (Illus.). 169p. (Orig.). 1996. pap. 14.00 (*0-9619808-1-8*) In-Forms Pub Hse.

Calahan, H. A. Learning to Sail. LC 99-50132. 370p. 2000. text 9.95 (*0-486-40728-4*) Dover.

Calais-Germain, Blandine. Anatomy of Movement. LC 93-71669. (Illus.). 289p. (C). 1993. pap. text 28.50 (*0-939616-17-3*) Eastland.

Calais-Germain, Blandine & Lamotte, Andree. Anatomy of Movement: Exercises. Anderson, Stephen, ed. Commarmond, Nicole, tr. from FRE. LC 94-61964. (Illus.). 282p. (C). 1996. pap. text 29.95 (*0-939616-22-X*) Eastland.

Calais, J. L. & Kryachko, Eugene S., eds. Structure & Dynamics of Atoms & Molecules: Conceptual Trends. 288p. (C). 1995. text 136.00 (*0-7923-3388-8*) Kluwer Academic.

Calais, J. L., jt. ed. see Kryachko, Eugene S.

Calais, Jean. Villon. 1981. pap. 4.95 (*0-915008-18-1*) Duende.

Calais, Jean-Louis. Quantum Chemistry Workbook: Basic Concepts & Procedures in the Theory of the Electronic Structure of Matter. 216p. 1994. pap. 49.95 (*0-471-59435-0*) Wiley.

*__Calais, Marguerite.__ Ganga Gita. LC 99-90815. 1999. 25.00 (*0-7388-0518-1*); pap. 18.00 (*0-7388-0519-X*) Xlibris Corp.

— Purity: A Love Story. LC 99-90814. 124p. 1999. 25.00 (*0-7388-0520-3*); pap. 18.00 (*0-7388-0521-1*) Xlibris Corp.

Calalano, Gary. The Empire of Grass. 1991. pap. 14.95 (*0-7022-2321-2*, Pub. by Univ Queensland Pr) Intl Spec Bk.

Calaluce, Robert, jt. auth. see Dix, Jay.

Calam, C. T. Process Development in Antibiotic Fermentations. (Cambridge Studies in Biotechnology: No. 4). (Illus.). 228p. 1987. text 69.95 (*0-521-30490-3*) Cambridge U Pr.

Calam, J. Clinicians' Guide to Helicobacter Pylori. (Clinicians' Guide Ser.). (Illus.). 192p. 1995. pap. 39.50 (*0-412-74000-1*, Pub. by E A) OUP.

Calam, John, ed. Alex Lord's British Columbia: Recollections of a Rural School Inspector, 1915-1936. (Pioneers of British Columbia Ser.). (Illus.). 212p. 1992. pap. 15.95 (*0-7748-0385-1*) U of Wash Pr.

Calamandrei, Piero, Jr. Eulogy of Judges: Written by a Lawyer. 50th anniversary ed. Adams, John C. & Phillips, C. Abbott, Jr., trs. from ITA. LC 92-75443. xxxii, 121p. 1992. reprint ed. text 12.00 (*0-8318-0693-1*, B693) Am Law Inst.

Calamari, Andrew M., jt. auth. see Stengel, James L.

Calamari, Barbara. Novena: The Power of Prayer. (Illus.). 156p. 1999. text 24.95 (*0-670-88444-8*) Penguin Books.

Calamari, Davide, ed. Chemical Exposure Predictions. 256p. 1992. lib. bdg. 95.00 (*0-87371-852-6*, L852) Lewis Pubs.

Calamari, John D. Contracts: Adaptable to Courses Utilizing Materials by Calamari. write for info. (*0-318-57016-5*) Harcourt.

Calamari, John D. & Perillo, Joseph M. Contracts. 2nd ed. (Black Letter Ser.). 462p. (C). 1990. reprint ed. pap. text 24.50 (*0-314-73305-1*) West Pub.

— Contracts. 3rd ed. (Hornbook Ser.). 1049p. (C). 1987. reprint ed. text 34.00 (*0-314-34698-8*) West Pub.

— Hornbook on Contracts. 4th ed. LC 98-4458. (Paralegal). 1100p. 1998. text 40.00 (*0-314-21167-5*) West Pub.

Calamari, John D., et al. Contracts, Cases & Problems. 2nd ed. (American Casebook Ser.). 905p. (C). 1989. reprint ed. 62.50 (*0-314-51814-2*) West Pub.

— Contracts, Cases & Problems on, Teacher's Edition to Accompany. 2nd ed. (American Casebook Ser.). 184p. 1989. pap. text. write for info. (*0-314-56510-8*) West Pub.

Calamaro, Emanuel. Trois Ours: The Three Bears. 2nd ed. (Interlingo Ser.). (FRE., Illus.). 19p. (Orig.). (J). (gr. k-12). 1995. reprint ed. pap. 2.95 (*0-922852-07-3*) Another Lang Pr.

Calamaro, Emanuel, tr. Le Flutiste de Jamelin.Tr. of Pied Piper of Hamlin. (FRE., Illus.). 20p. (Orig.). (J). (gr. 1-2). 1992. pap. 2.95 (*0-922852-11-1*, E014) Another Lang Pr.

— Le Petit Chaperon Rouge.Tr. of Little Red-Riding-Hood. (FRE., Illus.). 20p. (Orig.). (J). (gr. 1-2). 1989. pap. 2.95 (*0-922852-02-2*, E007) Another Lang Pr.

Calamaro, Emanuel, tr. see Hutchinson, Hanna.

Calambokidis, John & Steiger, Gretchen. Blue Whales. LC 96-39848. (WorldLife Library). (Illus.). 72p. (Orig.). (YA). (gr. 5 up). 1997. pap. 16.95 (*0-89658-338-4*) Voyageur Pr.

Calame, Claude. Choruses of Young Women in Ancient Greece: Their Morphology, Religious Role & Social Function. Orion, Janice & Collins, Derek, trs. LC 97-110468. 352p. 1997. 62.50 (*0-8226-3062-1*); pap. 24.95 (*0-8226-3063-X*) Rowman.

— The Craft of Poetic Speech in Ancient Greece. Orion, Janice, tr. (Myth & Poetics Ser.). (Illus.). 240p. 1995. text 42.50 (*0-8014-2743-6*); pap. text 16.95 (*0-8014-8022-1*) Cornell U Pr.

Calame, Claude & Lloyd, Janet. The Poetics of Eros in Ancient Greece. LC 98-37129. 1999. 35.00 (*0-691-04341-8*, Pub. by Princeton U Pr) Cal Prin Full Svc.

Calame, J., contrib. by. Financing Cultural/Natural Heritage & Sustainable Development: International Conference. 1996. pap. 15.00 (*0-9627931-8-3*) World Monuments.

Calame, J., ed. see Sanday, J., et al.

Calame, O., ed. High-Precision Earth Rotation & Earth-Moon Dynamics. 1982. text 176.50 (*90-277-1405-3*) Kluwer Academic.

Calamos, John P. Convertible Securities: The Latest Instruments, Portfolio Strategies, &... 2nd ed. LC 97-51242. 1998. 65.00 (*1-55738-921-7*, Irwn Prfssnl) McGraw-Hill Prof.

*__Calamug, Christine & Calamug, Cynthia, photos by.__ Monkey & Turtle Philippine Folktale. (Illus.). 18p. (J). 1999. pap. write for info. (*1-929416-00-8*) Magner Pubg.

Calamug, Cynthia, jt. photos by see Calamug, Christine.

Calandra, Denis. All's Well That Ends Well & the Merry Wives of Windsor Notes. (Cliffs Notes Ser.). 71p. (Orig.). (C). 1985. pap. text 4.50 (*0-8220-0004-0*, Cliff) IDG Bks.

Calandra, Denis M. The Comedy of Errors. (Cliffs Notes Ser.). 88p. 1982. pap. text 4.95 (*0-8220-0010-5*, Cliff) IDG Bks.

— Lord of the Flies Notes. (Cliffs Notes Ser.). 72p. 1971. pap. 4.95 (*0-8220-0754-1*, Cliff) IDG Bks.

— Richard II Notes. (Cliffs Notes Ser.). 80p. 1982. pap. 4.95 (*0-8220-0068-7*, Cliff) IDG Bks.

Calandra, Denis M. & Roberts, James L. Fathers & Sons Notes. (Cliffs Notes Ser.). 72p. 1966. pap. 4.95 (*0-8220-0470-4*, Cliff) IDG Bks.

— Tartuffe, Misanthrope & the Bourgeois Gentleman Notes. (Cliffs Notes Ser.). 112p. 1968. pap. 4.95 (*0-8220-1265-0*, Cliff) IDG Bks.

Calandra, Denis M., et al. The Crucible, Notes. (Cliffs Notes Ser.). 80p. 1968. pap. 4.95 (*0-8220-0337-6*, Cliff) IDG Bks.

Calandra, Denis M., ed. see Fassbinder, Rainer Werner.

Calandra, Denis M., ed. see Shakespeare, William.

Calandro, Ed. The Fourth Estate Murders. Pierpont Publishing, Inc. Staff, ed. LC 93-85173. 218p. 1994. 17.95 (*1-884520-00-6*) Pierpont Pubng.

— Skiriki. Moore, Carolyn, ed. 386p. 1994. 22.00 (*1-884520-02-2*); pap. write for info. (*1-884520-03-0*) Pierpont Pubng.

Calantone, Roger, jt. ed. see Droge, Cornelia.

Calaprice, Alice, ed. The Quotable Einstein. LC 96-3543. 310p. 1996. 16.95 (*0-691-02696-3*, Pub. by Princeton U Pr) Cal Prin Full Svc.

Calaprice, Alice, jt. auth. see Einstein, Albert.

Calaprice, F. P., jt. ed. see Dunford, R. W.

Calarco, Joe. Shakespeare's R & J. 1998. pap. 5.25 (*0-8222-1679-5*) Dramatists Play.

Calarco, Tom. Hi-Doh Hi-Dee Ha-Ha! (Illus.). 200p. (Orig.). 1996. pap. 15.95 (*0-9651922-0-2*) Nordel Pubng.

Calas, A. & Eugene, D., eds. Neurocytochemical Methods. (NATO ASI Series H: Cell Biology: Vol. 58). xvi, 335p. 1991. 216.95 (*0-387-53148-3*) Spr-Verlag.

Calas, Elena, ed. see Miro, Joan.

Calas, Marta B., jt. ed. see Smircich, Linda.

Calas, Nicolas. Transfigurations, Art Critical Essays, on the Modern Period. LC 85-16353. (Contemporary American Art Critics Ser.: No. 7). 291p. reprint ed. pap. 90.30 (*0-8357-1690-2*, 207053500001) Bks Demand.

Calas, Nicolas, ed. see Miro, Joan.

Calas, Terrington, et al. Louisiana Contemporaries: Selections from the ARCO Collection. (Illus.). 32p. (Orig.). 1992. 7.00 (*0-936819-06-5*) USL Art Museum.

Calasibetta, Charlotte. Essential Terms of Fashion: A Collection of Definitions. (Illus.). 244p. 1985. 39.00 (*0-87005-519-4*) Fairchild.

Calasibetta, Charlotte Mankey, see Mankey Calasibetta, Charlotte.

Calasso, M. G. Business Correspondence. (ENG & SPA.). 247p. 1980. pap. 20.75 (*0-8288-1548-8*, S35380) Fr & Eur.

Calasso, M. G. & Mirak, M. L. A Reader in Electronics & Telecommunications, English-Italian. 470p. 1978. pap. 49.95 (*0-7859-0911-7*, M9194) Fr & Eur.

*__Calasso, Roberto.__ Ka. Parks, Tim, tr. from ITA. (Illus.). 464p. 1998. 27.50 (*0-679-45131-5*) Knopf.

Calasso, Roberto. Ka. 1999. pap. 15.00 (*0-679-77547-1*) Knopf.

— The Marriage of Cadmus & Harmony. 416p. 1994. pap. 14.00 (*0-679-73348-5*) Random.

— The Ruin of Kasch. Weaver, William & Sartorelli, Stephen, trs. from ITA. LC 94-5383. Orig. Title: Rovina di Kasch. 400p. 1996. pap. text 24.95 (*0-674-78026-4*) Belknap Pr.

— The Ruin of Kasch. Weaver, William & Sartarelli, Stephen, trs. Orig. Title: Rovina di Kasch. 400p. 1996. pap. 14.95 (*0-674-78029-9*) HUP.

Calatayud, Emma, tr. see Green, Julien.

Calatayud, Ernesto V. Diccionario Alcoyano De Musica y Musicos. (SPA.). 460p. 1988. pap. 59.95 (*0-7859-6368-5*, 8485878094) Fr & Eur.

Calatayud, J. Martinez. Flow Injection Analysis of Pharmaceuticals: Automation in the Laboratory. LC 97-116588. 250p. 1996. 150.00 (*0-7484-0445-7*, Pub. by Tay Francis Ltd) Taylor & Francis.

Calatchi, R. & Rosenberg, S., eds. World Property Finance Atlas. 545p. 1996. 170.00 (*1-85564-439-8*, Pub. by Euromoney) Am Educ Systs.

Calati, Carl. Instant Expert: Fly Fishing Collectibles. (Illus.). 130p. (Orig.). 1997. pap. 14.00 (*1-887110-10-0*) Allian Pubng.

— Instant Expert-Fishing Collectibles. (Illus.). 130p. (Orig.). 1997. pap. 14.00 (*1-887110-12-7*) Allian Pubng.

Calatrava, Santiago. Santiago Calatrava: Secret Sketchbook. Zardini, Mirko, ed. LC 95-81809. (Illus.). 96p. 1996. 40.00 (*1-885254-33-4*, Pub. by Monacelli Pr) Penguin Putnam.

— Stadelhofen Train Station, Zurich. (Opus Ser.: Vol. 10). (ENG & GER., Illus.). 64p. 1993. 45.00 (*3-8030-2710-1*, Pub. by E J Wasmuth) Dist Art Pubs.

Calavita, Kitty. Big Money Crime: Fraud & Politics in The Savings & Loan Crisis. 259p. 1999. pap. 17.95 (*0-520-21947-3*, Pub. by U CA Pr) Cal Prin Full Svc.

— California's "Employer Sanctions" The Case of the Disappearing Law. (Research Reports: No. 39). 64p. (Orig.). (C). 1982. ring bd. 5.00 (*0-935391-38-X*, RR-39) UCSD Ctr US-Mex.

Calavita, Kitty, et al. Big Money Crime: Fraud & Politics in the Savings & Loan Crisis. LC 96-53295. 281p. 1997. 27.50 (*0-520-20856-0*, Pub. by U CA Pr) Cal Prin Full Svc.

Calaway, Bernie L. Revealing the Revelation: A Guide to the Literature of the Apocalypse. LC 98-19158. 486p. 1998. 74.95 (*1-57309-156-1*); pap. 54.95 (*1-57309-155-3*) Intl Scholars.

Calayayud, contrib. by. Guitar Music of Spain, Vol. 1. 1994. 24.95 (*0-7119-3303-0*, AM90240) Omnibus NY.

Calbert, Cathleen. Bad Judgment. LC 98-19571. 72p. 1999. 20.95 (*1-889330-23-X*, Pub. by Sarabande Bks); pap. 12.95 (*1-889330-24-8*, Pub. by Sarabande Bks) Consort Bk Sales.

— Lessons in Space. LC 96-49005. (Contemporary Poetry Ser.). 88p. 1997. 19.95 (*0-8130-1502-2*); pap. 10.95 (*0-8130-1503-0*) U Press Fla.

— My Summer As a Bride. 26p. 1995. pap. 5.00 (*1-890044-05-9*) Riverstone PA.

Calbi, Evan, jt. ed. see Vangelisti, Paul.

Calbo, Leonard J. Handbook of Coatings Additives, Vol. 1. (Illus.). 568p. 1987. text 225.00 (*0-8247-7561-9*) Dekker.

Calbo, Leonard J., ed. Handbook of Coatings Additives, Vol. 2. (Illus.). 328p. 1992. text 155.00 (*0-8247-8710-2*) Dekker.

Calboli, Gualtiero, ed. Subordination & Other Topics in Latin: Proceedings of the Third Colloquium on Latin Linguistics, Bologna, 1-5 April 1985. LC 89-247. (Studies in Language Companion: Vol. 17). (FRE.). xxix, 691p. 1989. 127.00 (*90-272-3018-8*) J Benjamins Pubng Co.

Calboli-Montefusco, Lucia. La Dottrina Degli "Status" Nella Retorica Greca e Romana. viii, 218p. 1986. 50.00 (*3-487-07783-3*) G Olms Pubs.

Calbom, Cheri. The Juice Lady's Juicing for Health & Healing: Recipes for Longevity, Energy, Weight-Loss, & Relief from Common Ailments. LC 98-35517. 272p. 1999. pap. 12.00 (*0-609-80349-2*) Harmony Bks.

Calbom, Cherie. The Healthy Gourmet. 256p. 1996. pap. 18.00 (*0-517-88664-2*) C Potter.

***Calbom, Cherie.** The Juice Lady's Guide to Juicing for Health: Unleashing the Healing Power of Whole Fruits & Vegetables. 224p. 2000. pap. 12.95 (*0-89529-999-2*, Avery) Penguin Putnam.

Calbom, Cherie & Keane, Maureen. Jugos para una Vida Saludable: Una Guia para Obtener el Maximo Beneficio de las Frutas y los Vegetales Frescos.Tr. of Juicing for Life. (SPA.). 384p. 1999. pap. 15.95 (*0-89529-955-0*, Avery) Penguin Putnam.

Calbom, Cherie & Keane, Maureen B. Juicing for Life: A Guide to the Health Benefits of Fresh Fruit & Vegetable Juicing. LC 91-39423. 350p. (Orig.). 1992. pap. 12.95 (*0-89529-512-1*, Avery) Penguin Putnam.

Calbom, Cherie, jt. auth. see Foreman, George.

Calbom, Linda M., ed. Federal Electricity Activities Vol. 1: The Federal Government's Net Cost & Potential for Future Losses. (Illus.). 47p. (C). 1999. reprint ed. pap. text 20.00 (*0-7881-7717-6*) DIANE Pub.

Calbom, Linda M., et al, eds. Depository Institutions: Divergent Loan Loss Methods Undermine Usefulness of Financial Reports. (Illus.). 80p. 1998. pap. text 20.00 (*0-7881-4175-9*) DIANE Pub.

***Calbon, Charlie.** Zumos Para Su Salud. 1998. pap. text 9.95 (*84-8327-006-4*) E Martinez Roca.

Calbreath, Donald F. Clinical Chemistry. 2nd ed. 1991. text 50.00 (*0-7216-2621-1*, W B Saunders Co) Harcrt Hlth Sci Grp.

— Clinical Chemistry: A Fundamental Textbook. (Illus.). 490p. 1992. teacher ed. write for info. (*0-7216-2622-X*, W B Saunders Co) Harcrt Hlth Sci Grp.

Calbris, Genevieve. The Semiotics of French Gestures. LC 88-46027. (Advances in Semiotics Ser.). (Illus.). 256p. 1990. 14.95 (*0-253-31297-3*) Ind U Pr.

Calcada, Leticia, tr. see Palau, Luis.

Calcagnino, Steve, jt. auth. see Rotner, Shelley.

Calcagno, Anne. Pray for Yourself & Other Stories. (TriQuarterly Bks.). 104p. 1993. 26.95 (*0-8101-5000-X*); pap. 12.95 (*0-8101-5003-4*) Northwestern U Pr.

Calcagno, Anne, ed. Italy. (Travelers' Tales Guides Ser.). 463p. 1998. pap. 17.95 (*1-885211-16-3*, 16-3) Trvlers Tale.

Calcagno, Antonio. Giordano Bruno & the Logic of Coincidence: Unity & Multiplicity in the Philosophical Thought of Giordano Bruno. LC 97-14972. (Renaissance & Baroque: Vol. 23). XIII, 233p. (C). 1998. text 46.95 (*0-8204-3869-3*) P Lang Pubng.

Calcagno, P. L., jt. ed. see Pascual, J. F.

Calce, Fiorella D. Toni. 96p. 1990. pap. 8.00 (*0-920717-42-X*) Guernica Editions.

— Vinnie & Me. (Prose Ser.: No. 31). 90p. (C). 1995. pap. 10.00 (*1-55071-017-6*) Guernica Editions.

Calchman, J. B. Vampire Heart. (Illus.). 288p. (J). pap. 9.95 (*0-14-038627-0*, Pub. by Pnguin Bks Ltd) Trafalgar.

Calciano, Joan. Love, Hope & Tragedy: A Brooklyn Memoir. Gabor, Don & Cowell, Eileen, eds. 204p. 1998. pap. 12.00 (*1-879834-06-5*) Convstn Arts.

Calciati, Romola. Corpus Nummorum Siculorum Vol. III: The Bronze Coinage, 3 vols., Set. (Illus.). 400p. 1988. lib. bdg. 180.00 (*0-317-01701-2*, Pub. by R Calciati) Parkwest Pubns.

Calciu, George. Christ Is Calling You: A Course in Catacomb Pastorship. St. Herman of Alaska Brotherhood Staff, ed. LC 97-67548. (St. Paisius Missionary School Ser.: No. 3). (Illus.). 223p. 1997. pap. 9.95 (*1-887904-52-2*) St Herman Pr.

Calcote, P. M. Spicy, Spicy & Spicy. 88p. 1997. pap. 5.50 (*0-9647104-1-2*) M Calcote.

Calcott, M. V., ed. see Couper, Greta E.

Calcott, Peter H. Continuous Cultures of Cells, 2 vols. 208p. 1981. 79.00 (*0-8493-5377-7*, QH585, CRC Reprint); 77.00 (*0-8493-5378-5*, QH585, CRC Reprint) Franklin.

Calcraft, ed. see Guerrero.

Calculator, Stephen N. & Jorgensen, Cheryl M. Including Students with Severe Disabilities in Schools - Fostering Communication, Interaction & Participation. LC 94-10002. (School-Age Children Ser.). (Illus.). 284p. (Orig.). (C). 1994. pap. 39.95 (*1-56593-080-0*, 0385) Thomson Learn.

Calcutt, Andrew. White Noise: An A-Z of the Contradictions in Cyberculture. LC 98-17748. 1998. pap. 18.95 (*0-312-21661-0*); text 49.95 (*0-312-21660-2*) St Martin.

Calcutt, Andrew & Shephard, Richard. Cult Fiction: A Reader's Guide. LC 99-22281. 320p. 1999. pap. 16.95 (*0-8092-2506-9*, 250690, Contemporary Bks) NTC Contemp Pub Co.

Calcutt, D. M., et al. 8051 Microcontrollers: Hardware, Software & Applications. LC 98-216291. 320p. 1998. pap. 41.95 (*0-471-31426-9*) Wiley.

Calcutt, D. M., jt. auth. see Maddock, R. J.

Calcutt, David. Satellite Communications. (Electrical Engineering Ser.). 1995. pap. 40.95 (*0-340-61448-X*, VNR) Wiley.

***Calcutt, Ian.** Matt Damon: An Illustrated Story. (Illustrated Story Ser.). (Illus.). 80p. 2000. pap. 9.95 (*0-600-59750-4*, Pub. by P HM) Trafalgar.

Caldara, Jon. RTD's Competitive Contracting Program: Cost Savings Produce More Service, Attract More Passengers. (Two-99 Ser.). 6p. 1999. pap. 8.00 (*1-57655-172-5*) Independ Inst.

Caldara, Jon C. Nothing Is Funny: The True Costs of Political Corrections. 11p. 1993. pap. text 8.00 (*1-57655-101-6*) Independ Inst.

Caldarera, Claudio M., et al, eds. Advances in Polyamine Research, Vol. 3. fac. ed. LC 77-83687. (Illus.). 511p. pap. 158.50 (*0-7837-7149-5*, 204714700003) Bks Demand.

Caldarini, E., jt. auth. see Du Bellay, Joachim.

Caldarola, Carlo, ed. Religion & Societies: Asia & the Middle East. (Religion & Society Ser.: No. 22). 688p. 1982. text 96.15 (*90-279-3259-X*) Mouton.

— Religion & Societies: Asia & the Middle East. (Religion & Society Ser.: No. 22). 688p. 1984. pap. 69.25 (*3-11-010021-5*) Mouton.

Caldart, Charles C., jt. auth. see Ashford, Nicholas A.

Caldas-Coulthard, Carmen R. & Coulthard, Malcolm, compiled by. Texts & Practices: Readings in Critical Discourse Analysis. LC 95-10857. 312p. (C). 1995. pap. 27.99 (*0-415-12143-4*) Routledge.

— Texts & Practices: Readings in Critical Discourse Analysis. LC 95-10857. 312p. (C). (gr. 13). 1995. 90.00 (*0-415-12142-6*) Routledge.

Caldas, Ricardo W. Brazil in the Uruguay Round of the GATT: The Evolution of Brazil's Position in the Uruguay Round, with Emphasis on the Issue of Services. LC 97-37028. (Strategies & Policies for the Global Political Economy Ser.). 304p. 1997. text 68.95 (*1-84014-040-2*, Pub. by Ashgate Pub) Ashgate Pub Co.

Caldecott, J. O. An Ecological & Behavioural Study of the Pig-Tailed Macaque. (Contributions to Primatology Ser.: Vol. 21). (Illus.). xiv, 262p. 1985. 101.00 (*3-8055-4212-7*) S Karger.

***Caldecott, Julian.** Deep Water. 1999. pap. 25.00 (*1-899858-79-2*, Pub. by Ellipsis) Norton.

Caldecott, Julian. Designing Conservation Projects. (Illus.). 321p. (C). 1996. text 74.95 (*0-521-47328-4*) Cambridge U Pr.

Caldecott, Julian, jt. ed. see Lutz, Ernst.

Caldecott, Moyra. Emily's Rainbow. LC 80-105683. (Illus.). 1978. pap. 10.95 (*0-914676-20-2*, Green Tiger S&S) S&S Childrens.

— Guardians of the Tall Stones. LC 86-12900. 540p. (Orig.). 1995. pap. 16.95 (*0-89087-463-8*) Celestial Arts.

— Mythical Journeys, Legendary Quests: The Spiritual Search - Traditional Stories from World Mythology. LC 96-229518. (Illus.). 176p. 1996. 27.95 (*0-7137-2546-X*, Pub. by Blandford Pr) Sterling.

— Myths of the Sacred Tree. (Illus.). 224p. (Orig.). 1993. pap. 12.95 (*0-89281-414-4*, Destiny Bks) Inner Tradit.

— Women in Celtic Myth: Tales of Extraordinary Women from Ancient Celtic Tradition. 224p. (Orig.). 1992. pap. 12.95 (*0-89281-357-1*) Inner Tradit.

Caldecott, Randolph, jt. illus. see Crane, Walter.

Caldecott, Stratford, ed. Beyond the Prosaic: Renewing the Liturgical Movement. 176p. 1998. 43.95 (*0-567-08613-5*, Pub. by T & T Clark) Bks Intl VA.

***Caldecott, Stratford, ed.** Beyond the Prosaic: Renewing the Liturgical Movement. 176p. 2000. pap. 24.95 (*0-567-08636-4*) T&T Clark Pubs.

Caldecott, Stratford & Morrill, John, eds. Eternity in Time: Christopher Dawson & the Catholic Idea of History. 224p. 43.95 (*0-567-08548-1*, Pub. by T & T Clark) Bks Intl VA.

Caldecott, W. Shaw. Solomon's Temple, Its History & Its Structure. 358p. 1998. reprint ed. pap. 21.50 (*0-7873-0139-6*) Hlth Research.

Caldecott, William. The Cotswolds. (Illus.). (C). 1988. 55.00 (*1-85368-034-6*, Pub. by New5 Holland) St Mut.

— Stratford Upon-Avon & Shakespeare Country. (C). 1989. 30.00 (*1-85368-029-X*, Pub. by New5 Holland) St Mut.

Caldeira, Edward & NAHB Research Center, Inc. Staff. Quality Management: Best Practices for Home Builders. LC 96-46804. (National Housing Quality Best Practices Ser.: Vol. 1). 64p. (Orig.). 1997. pap. 20.63 (*0-86718-426-4*) Home Builder.

***Caldeira, Teresa Pires do Rio.** City of Walls: Crime, Segregation & Citizenship in Sdao Paulo. LC 00-28713. 2000. write for info. (*0-520-22143-5*) U CA Pr.

***Caldenbury, Claes & Architektur Forlag, Olaf.** Architecture in Sweden, 1995-1999. (Illus.). 160p. 2000. 45.00 (*91-86050-47-8*, Pub. by Arkitektur Forlag) Gingko Press.

Caldenby, Claes, et al, eds. Sweden: 20th-Century Architecture. LC 98-206482. (Illus.). 400p. 1998. 85.00 (*3-7913-1936-1*) te Neues.

Calder. Insertion Reactions. pap. write for info. (*0-471-08809-9*) Wiley.

Calder, Alex, et al, eds. Voyages & Beaches: Pacific Encounters, 1769-1840. LC 98-42426. (Illus.). 344p. (C). 1999. 45.00 (*0-8248-2039-8*) UH Pr.

Calder, A. A. Coleoptera - Elateroidea. (Zoological Catalogue of Australia Ser.: Vol. 29.6). (Illus.). 264p. 74.95 (*0-643-06353-6*, Pub. by CSIRO) Accents Pubns.

Calder, A. A. Monographs on Invertebrate Taxonomy 2: Click Beetles. Genera of the Australian Elateriade (Coleoptera) LC 97-123634. (Illus.). 142p. 1996. 130.00 (*0-643-05671-8*, Pub. by CSIRO) Accents Pubns.

Calder, A. A., jt. ed. see Drife, J. O.

Calder, Alexander. Animal Sketching. (Illus.). 62p. 1973. reprint ed. pap. 3.50 (*0-486-20129-5*) Dover.

Calder, Alexander. Fables of Aesop According to Sir Roger L'Estrange. 124p. (J). (gr. k-6). 1967. pap. 5.95 (*0-486-21780-9*) Dover.

Calder, Alexander, jt. auth. see La Fontaine, Jean de.

Calder, Andrew. Moliere: The Theory & Practice of Comedy. LC 92-30595. 180p. (C). 1993. text 65.00 (*0-485-11427-5*, Pub. by Athlone Pr) Humanities.

— Moliere: The Theory & Practice of Comedy. 244p. 1996. pap. 25.00 (*0-485-12127-1*, Pub. by Athlone Pr) Humanities.

Calder, Andrew, jt. auth. see Wallace, Evan.

Calder, Angus. The Myth of the Blitz. (Illus.). 320p. 1996. pap. 24.95 (*0-7126-9820-5*, Pub. by Pimlico) Trafalgar.

— Revolving Culture: Notes from the Scottish Republic. 256p. 1994. text 15.95 (*1-85043-647-9*, Pub. by I B T) St Martin.

Calder, Angus, ed. Byron. 96p. 1987. 102.50 (*0-335-15095-0*); pap. 27.95 (*0-335-15086-1*) OpUniv Pr.

— Byron & Scotland: Radical or Dandy? 256p. (C). 1989. text 50.50 (*0-389-20873-6*) B&N Imports.

Calder, Angus, et al, eds. Hugh MacDiarmid: The Rancle Tongue, Vol. I. LC 97-172673. 320p. 1997. text 45.00 (*1-85754-234-7*, Pub. by Carcanet Pr) Paul & Co Pubs.

Calder, Angus, ed. see Stevenson, Robert Louis.

Calder, Ann, jt. auth. see Watt, Jill.

Calder, Bruce J. The Impact of Intervention: The Dominican Republic During the U. S. Occupation of 1916-1924. LC 83-23447. (Texas Pan American Ser.). (Illus.). 376p. 1984. pap. 116.60 (*0-7837-8957-2*, 204967000002) Bks Demand.

Calder, C., jt. auth. see Biswas, K.

Calder, C. C. List of Species & Genera & Indian Planerograms Not Included in Sir J. D. Hooker's Flora of British India. (C). 1978. text 250.00 (*0-89771-576-4*, Pub. by Intl Bk Distr) St Mut.

Calder, Clare Evans, jt. text see Larrimore, Don.

Calder, Clarence A., ed. Mechanics of Materials Exam File. LC 84-24702. (Exam File Ser.). 378p. (C). 1985. pap. 20.50 (*0-910554-46-3*) Engineering.

Calder, Daniel G., jt. auth. see Greenfield, Stanley B.

Calder, G. A Gaelic Grammar. pap. 29.95 (*0-8288-3338-9*, F139650) Fr & Eur.

Calder, George, ed. see Virgil.

Calder, Isabel M., ed. see Davenport, John, Jr.

Calder, J. Kent & Neville, Susan, eds. Falling Toward Grace: Images of Religion & Culture from the Heartland. LC 98-4045. (Illus.). 176p. 1998. 24.95 (*0-253-33453-5*) Ind U Pr.

Calder, J. Kent, ed. see Slutz, Ted.

Calder, J. William. All Aboard, Vol. 1. (Illus.). 139p. 1974. pap. 5.95 (*0-88780-006-8*, Pub. by Formac Publ Co) Formac Dist Ltd.

***Calder, James D.** Intelligence, Espionage, & Related Topics: An Annotated Bibliography of Serial, Journal, & Magazine Scholarship, 1844-1998, 11. LC 99-39950. (Bibliographies & Indexes in Military Studies). 1368p. 1999. lib. bdg. 150.00 (*0-313-29290-6*) Greenwood.

Calder, James D. The Origins & Development of Federal Crime Control Policy: Herbert Hoover's Initiatives. LC 93-20298. 328p. 1993. 65.00 (*0-275-94284-8*, C4284, Praeger Pubs) Greenwood.

Calder, Jeanie. Break Free: And Never Diet Again. 1998. pap. 13.95 (*1-86950-271-X*) HarpC.

Calder, Jenni. Animal Farm & Nineteen Eighty-Four. (Open Guides to Literature Ser.). 112p. 1987. 102.50 (*0-335-15266-X*) OpUniv Pr.

***Calder, Jenni.** French. (Illus.). 64p. 1999. pap. 7.95 (*1-901663-33-7*) Natl Mus Scotland.

— Gaelic. (Illus.). 64p. 1999. pap. 7.95 (*1-901663-32-9*) Natl Mus Scotland.

— German. (Illus.). 64p. 1999. pap. 7.95 (*1-901663-37-X*) Natl Mus Scotland.

— Italian. (Illus.). 64p. 1999. pap. 7.95 (*1-901663-34-5*) Natl Mus Scotland.

— Japanese. (Illus.). 64p. 1999. pap. 7.95 (*1-901663-36-1*) Natl Mus Scotland.

Calder, Jenni. Present Poets. (Illus.). 64p. 1998. pap. 6.95 (*1-901663-14-0*, 3140, Pub. by Natl Mus Scotland) A Schwartz & Co.

***Calder, Jenni.** Spanish. (Illus.). 64p. 1999. pap. 7.95 (*1-901663-35-3*) Natl Mus Scotland.

Calder, Jenni. The Story of the Scottish Soldier, 1600-1914: Bonny Fighters. (Illus.). 36p. 1992. pap. 2.95 (*0-11-493386-3*, 3863, Pub. by Natl Mus Scotland) A Schwartz & Co.

— Treasure Islands: A Robert Louis Stevenson Centenary Anthology. (Illus.). 88p. 1995. 14.95 (*0-948636-59-9*, 6599) A Schwartz & Co.

Calder, Jenni, ed. R. L. Stevenson. (Everyman's Poetry Ser.). 128p. 1997. pap. 3.50 (*0-460-87809-3*, Everyman's Classic Lib) Tuttle Pubng.

***Calder, Jenni, ed.** Translated Kingdoms Scottish Poems of the Sea. 72p. 1999. pap. 5.99 (*1-901663-04-3*, Pub. by Natl Mus Scotland) A Schwartz & Co.

Calder, Jenni, ed. The Wealth of a Nation in the National Museums of Scotland. (Illus.). 208p. 1995. pap. 29.95 (*0-86267-265-1*, 2651, Pub. by Natl Mus Scotland) A Schwartz & Co.

***Calder, Jenni, ed.** Who's Who in the Museum of Scotland. 72p. 1999. pap. 8.95 (*1-901663-23-X*, Pub. by Natl Mus Scotland) A Schwartz & Co.

Calder, Jenni, ed. & intro. see Stevenson, Robert Louis.

Calder, John, ed. Anthology of Absurdist Drama. 450p. (Orig.). pap. 18.95 (*0-7145-4222-9*) Riverrun NY.

— As No Other Dare Fail: Festschrifft for Samuel Beckett's 80th Birthday. LC 86-13961. (Illus.). 224p. (C). 1986. 16.95 (*0-7145-4077-3*) Riverrun NY.

Calder, John & Fletcher, John, eds. The Nouveau Roman Reader. LC 85-18353. 256p. (Orig.). 1986. pap. 11.95 (*0-7145-3720-9*) Riverrun NY.

Calder, Judith, ed. Disaffection & Diversity: Overcoming Barriers for Adult Learners. LC 92-27883. 224p. 1992. 110.00 (*0-7507-0117-X*, Falmer Pr); pap. 39.95 (*0-7507-0118-8*, Falmer Pr) Taylor & Francis.

Calder, Judith & McCollum, Ann. Open & Flexible Learning in Vocational Education & Training. 192p. 1998. pap. 29.95 (*0-7494-2172-X*, Kogan Pg Educ) Stylus Pub VA.

***Calder, Julian.** New 35mm Photographers Handbook, Vol. 1. 3rd ed. 1999. pap. 19.95 (*0-609-80422-7*) Crown Pub Group.

Calder, K. Professional Chiller System Monitoring. (C). 1994. pap. 60.00 (*0-86022-369-8*, Pub. by Build Servs Info Assn) St Mut.

Calder, Kate, jt. auth. see Kalman, Bobbie.

Calder, Kent E. Asia's Deadly Triangle: How Arms, Energy, & Growth Threaten to Destabilize Asia-Pacific. LC 97-9102. 1997. pap. 16.00 (*1-85788-161-3*) Nicholas Brealey.

— Japan's Changing Role in Asia: Emerging Co-Prosperity? 48p. 1992. 12.00 (*0-685-70368-1*) Japan Soc.

— Strategic Capitalism: Private Business & Public Purpose in Japanese Industrial Finance. 395p. (C). 1993. pap. text 19.95 (*0-691-04475-9*, Pub. by Princeton U Pr) Cal Prin Full Svc.

Calder, Lendol G. Financing the American Dream: Debt, Credit & the Making of American Consumer Culture. LC 98-34875. 377p. 1999. 29.95 (*0-691-05827-X*, Pub. by Princeton U Pr) Cal Prin Full Svc.

Calder, Loren D. The Political Thought of Yu F. Samarin, 1840-1864. (Modern European History Ser.). 358p. 1987. text 15.00 (*0-8240-8052-1*) Garland.

Calder, Lyn. Blue-Ribbon Friends. LC 90-85433. (Minnie 'n Me Ser.). (Illus.). 32p. (J). (gr. k-3). 1991. 5.95 (*1-56282-034-6*) Disney Pr.

— Gold-Star Homework. LC 90-85434. (Minnie 'n Me Ser.). (Illus.). 32p. (J). (gr. k-3). 1991. 5.95 (*1-56282-035-4*) Disney Pr.

— Walt Disney's Alice's Tea Party. LC 91-73810. (Illus.). 48p. (J). (gr. k-4). 1992. 12.95 (*1-56282-145-8*, Pub. by Disney Pr); lib. bdg. 12.89 (*1-56282-199-7*, Pub. by Disney Pr) Little.

— Walt Disney's Alice's Tea Party. LC 91-73810. (Illus.). 48p. (J). (gr. k-4). 1994. pap. 5.95 (*1-56282-648-4*, Pub. by Disney Pr) Time Warner.

***Calder, M. & Magill, E., eds.** Feature Interactions in Telecommunications & Software Systems IV. 340p. 2000. 89.00 (*1-58603-065-5*) IOS Press.

Calder, Martin C. & Horwath, Jan. Working for Children on the Child Protection Register: An Inter-Agency Practice Guide. LC 98-35471. 320p. (C). 1999. text 43.95 (*1-85742-367-4*, HV751.A6W66, Pub. by Arena) Ashgate Pub Co.

Calder, Michael. Yachtsman's Fiji. 249p. (C). 1989. 115.00 (*0-7855-5903-5*, Pub. by Laurie Norie & Wilson Ltd) St Mut.

— Yachtsman's Fiji. 249p. 1994. pap. 125.00 (*0-646-14682-3*, Pub. by Laurie Norie & Wilson Ltd) St Mut.

Calder, Niegel. Cuba: A Cruising Guide. (Illus.). 300p. (C). 1997. pap. 159.95 (*0-85288-370-6*, Pub. by Laurie Norie & Wilson Ltd) Bluewater Bks.

Calder, Nigel. Boatowner's Mechanical & Electrical Manual: How to Maintain, Repair, & Improve Your Boat's Essential Systems. 2nd ed. (Illus.). 604p. 1995. 49.95 (*0-07-009618-X*) Intl Marine.

— Comets: Speculation & Discovery. (Illus.). 176p. 1994. reprint ed. pap. text 8.95 (*0-486-27879-4*) Dover.

— The Cruising Guide to the Northwest Caribbean: The Yucatan Coast of Mexico, Belize, Guatemala, Honduras & the Bay Islands. 288p. 1991. 29.95 (*0-87742-303-2*, 0303) Intl Marine.

— The Cruising Guide to the Northwest Caribbean: The Yucatan Coast of Mexico, Belize, Guatemala, Honduras & the Bay Islands. 272p. 1991. 29.95 (*0-07-158016-6*) McGraw.

***Calder, Nigel.** Cuba: A Cruising Guide. 260p. 1999. pap. 125.00 (*0-85288-413-3*, Pub. by Laurie Norie & Wilson Ltd) St Mut.

Calder, Nigel. Einstein's Universe. 1980. pap. 12.95 (*0-14-013516-2*) Viking Penguin.

— Marine Diesel Engines: Maintenance, Troubleshooting, & Repair. 2nd ed. 1991. 24.95 (*0-07-009612-0*) McGraw.

— Marine Diesel Engines: Maintenance, Troubleshooting & Repair. 2nd ed. 224p. 1991. 24.95 (*0-87742-313-X*) Intl Marine.

— Refrigeration for Pleasureboats: Installation, Maintenance & Repair. (Illus.). 192p. 1990. text 24.95 (*0-87742-286-9*) Intl Marine.

— Refrigeration for Pleasureboats: Installation, Maintenance & Repair. 192p. 1990. 25.95 (*0-07-157998-2*) McGraw.

Calder, Nigel & Newell, John. On the Frontiers of Science: How Scientists See Our Future. (Illus.). 256p. (J). 1989. 35.00 (*0-8160-2205-4*) Facts on File.

Calder, Paul & Thomas, Bruce, eds. Computer Human Interaction Conference (Ozchi '98), 1998 Australasion, 1 Vol. LC 98-88396. 350p. 1998. pap. 120.00 (*0-8186-9206-5*) IEEE Comp Soc.

Calder, Richard. Dead Girls. 1996. mass mkt. 4.99 (*0-312-95717-3*) St Martin.

— Dead Girls: Dead Boys, Dead Things. LC 97-53082. 400p. 1998. pap. 15.95 (*0-312-18078-0*) St Martin.

— Dead Things. LC 96-34271. 208p. 1996. 21.95 (*0-312-15103-9*) St Martin.

Calder, Richard, et al. Leviathan: The Legacy of Boccacio. Vandermeer, Jeff & Secrest, Rose, eds. (Leviathan Anthology Ser.: Vol. II). 192p. 1998. pap. 10.99 (*1-890464-03-1*) Ministry of Whimsy.

Calder, Ritchie. Living with the Atom. LC 62-13562. (Illus.). 284p. reprint ed. pap. 88.10 (*0-608-09276-2*, 205415000004) Bks Demand.

Calder, Robert R., ed. see Abenheimer, Karl M.

Calder, Robert W., jt. auth. see Walker, Dan.

Calder, S. J. First Facts, 8 bks., Set. (Illus.). (J). (ps-1). 1989. pap. 23.60 (*0-382-24601-2*, Julian Messner); lib. bdg. 83.40 (*0-671-94107-0*, Julian Messner) Silver Burdett Pr.

— If You Were a Bird. Brook, Bonnie, ed. (First Facts Ser.). (Illus.). 32p. (J). (ps-1). 1989. pap. 4.95 (*0-671-24404-3*, Silver Pr NJ) Silver Burdett Pr.

— If You Were a Bird. Brook, Bonnie, ed. (First Facts Ser.). (Illus.). 32p. (J). (ps-1). 1989. lib. bdg. 6.95 (*0-671-68595-3*, Silver Pr NJ) Silver Burdett Pr.

— If You Were a Bird. 32p. 1996. pap. 2.95 (*0-382-24404-4*) Silver Burdett Pr.

C

An Asterisk (*) at the beginning of an entry indicates that the title is appearing for the first time.

— If You Were a Cat. Brook, Bonnie, ed. (First Facts Ser.). (Illus.). 32p. (J). (ps-1). 1989. pap. 4.95 (*0-382-24405-2*); lib. bdg. 6.95 (*0-671-68598-8*, Silver Pr NJ) Silver Burdett Pr.
— If You Were a Fish. Brook, Bonnie, ed. (First Facts Ser.). (Illus.). 32p. (J). (ps-1). 1989. pap. 4.95 (*0-382-24406-0*); lib. bdg. 6.95 (*0-671-68596-1*, Silver Pr NJ) Silver Burdett Pr.
— If You Were an Ant. Brook, Bonnie, ed. (First Facts Ser.). (Illus.). 32p. (J). (ps-1). 1989. pap. 4.95 (*0-382-24403-6*) Silver Burdett Pr.
— If You Were an Ant. Brook, Bonnie, ed. LC 89-6411. (First Facts Ser.). (Illus.). 32p. (J). (ps-1). 1989. lib. bdg. 8.99 (*0-671-68597-X*, Silver Pr NJ) Silver Burdett Pr.
— If You Were An Ant. LC 89-6411. (First Facts Ser.). (Illus.). (J). 1989. 4.95 (*0-671-68603-8*, Silver Pr NJ) Silver Burdett Pr.
Calder, Sharon, jt. auth. see Griffith, Susan.
***Calder, Simon.** Panamericana: On the Road Through Mexico & Central America. (Illus.). 2000. pap. 19.95 (*1-85458-234-8*) Vac Wrk Pubns.
Calder, Simon. U. S. A. & Canada Travellers Survival Kit. (Travellers Survival Kit Guides Ser.). 480p. (Orig.). 1997. pap. 17.95 (*1-85458-089-2*, Pub. by Vac Wrk Pubns) Seven Hills Bk.
— U. S. A. & Canada TSK. 4th ed. (Travellers Survival Kit Ser.). 480p. 1997. pap. 17.95 (*1-85458-179-1*, Pub. by Vac Wrk Pubns) Seven Hills Bk.
Calder, Simon & Hatchwell, Emily. Cuba. (Travellers Survival Kit Ser.). 352p. 1999. pap. 18.95 (*1-85458-221-6*, Pub. by Vac Wrk Pubns) Seven Hills Bk.
— Cuba Travellers Survival Kit. (Travellers Survival Kit Guides Ser.). 352p. (Orig.). 1997. pap. 17.95 (*1-85458-144-9*, Pub. by Vac Wrk Pubns) Seven Hills Bk.
Calder, Simon, jt. auth. see Hatchwell, Emily.
Calder, William & Magison, Ernest C. Electrical Safety in Hazardous Locations: Instructor's Guide. LC 83-169373. (Instructional Resource Package Ser.). 72p. reprint ed. pap. 30.00 (*0-7837-5139-7*, 204486700004) Bks Demand.
Calder, William A. Size Biological Diversity & Conservation. 2nd ed. 1999. 59.95 (*0-8493-9484-8*, 9484) CRC Pr.
Calder, William A., 3rd. Size, Function & Life History. unabridged ed. LC 83-22815. (Illus.). 448p. 1996. reprint ed. pap. 14.95 (*0-486-69191-8*) Dover.
Calder, William M., III. Men in Their Books. Harris, John P. & Smith, R. Scott, eds. (Studies in the Modern History of Classical Scholarship). (GER.). xlvi, 324p. 1998. write for info. (*3-487-10686-8*) G Olms Pubs.
Calder, William M., III, ed. Ulrich Von Wilamowitz-Moellendorff: Further Letters of Ulrich von Wilamowitz-Moellendorff (1869-1930) (GER.). xii, 262p. 1994. 68.00 (*3-615-00099-4*, Pub. by Weidmann) Lubrecht & Cramer.
Calder, William M., et al, eds. Hypatia: Essays in Classics, Comparative Literature, & Philosophy: Presented to Hazel E. Barnes on Her Seventieth Birthday. LC 85-72021. (Illus.). 319p. reprint ed. pap. 98.90 (*0-608-18778-X*, 202981700065) Bks Demand.
Calder, William M., III & Demandt, Alexander, eds. Eduard Meyer: Leben und Leistung Eines Universalhistorikers. LC 90-38588. (Mnemosyne Ser.: Supplement 112). (ENG, GER & ITA.). ix, 537p. 1990. pap. 162.00 (*90-04-09131-9*) Brill Academic Pubs.
Calder, William M., III & Huss, Bernhard, eds. Der Briefwechsel Zwischen Ulrich v. Wilamowitz-Moellendorff und Eduard Norden. LC 98-118137. 1997. 60.00 (*3-615-00188-5*, Pub. by Weidmann) Lubrecht & Cramer.
Calder, William M., III & Kramer, Daniel J. An Introductory Bibliography to the History of Classical Scholarship Chiefly in the Nineteenth & Twentieth Centuries. (GER.). xii, 410p. 1992. lib. bdg. 80.00 (*3-487-09643-9*) G Olms Pubs.
Calder, William M., III & Trzaskoma, Stephen, eds. George Grote Reconsidered: A 200th Birthday Celebration with a First Edition of His Essay of the Athenian Government. x, 98p. 1996. 29.80 (*3-615-00180-X*, Pub. by Weidmann) Lubrecht & Cramer.
***Caldera Incorporated Staff, et al.** Openlinux 2.2: Putting Linux to Work for You. 3rd ed. 1999. pap. text 59.99 (*0-13-015824-0*) P-H.
Caldera Press Staff. OpenLinux Web Publishing ToolKit. 1997. pap. text 69.95 (*0-13-913088-8*) P-H.
Caldera Staff. Caldera DR-Dos Complete. 416p. 1998. pap. 29.95 incl. audio compact disk (*1-889492-03-5*) Caldera Pr.
***Caldera Systems Staff.** Caldera Openlinux Three Point O. 4th ed. 2000. pap. 69.99 (*0-13-088247-X*) P-H.
— Linux Enterprise Administration Certification Handbook. (Open Source Technology Ser.). 520p. 2000. pap. text 44.99 (*0-13-019314-3*) P-H.
— Linux Network Administration Certification Handbook. (Open Source Technology Ser.). 500p. 2000. pap. text 44.99 (*0-13-019315-1*) P-H.
— Linux System Administration Certification Handbook. (Open Source Technology Ser.). 490p. 2000. pap. text 44.99 (*0-13-019317-8*) P-H.
Calderaro, M. A. A Silent New World: Ford Madox Ford's Parade's End. 136p. 1995. pap. 12.95 (*88-8091-132-5*) Paul & Co Pubs.
Calderazzo, John. One Hundred One Questions about Volcanoes. Jorgen, Randolph, ed. LC 93-84875. (Illus.). 32p. (Orig.). (J). 1994. pap. 6.95 (*1-877856-33-9*) SW Pks Mnmts.
— Writing from Scratch: Freelancing. 168p. 1990. pap. 10.95 (*0-8226-3007-9*) Littlefield.
— Writing from Scratch: Freelancing. 168p. 1990. 24.95 (*0-8476-7633-1*) Rowman.
Calderbank, Robert, ed. Different Aspects of Coding Theory: Proceedings of the American Mathematical Society Short Course (1995: San Francisco, CA) LC 95-35165. (Proceedings of Symposia in Applied Mathematics Ser.: Vol. 50). 239p. 1995. text 49.00 (*0-8218-0379-4*, PSAPM/50) Am Math.
Calderbank, Robert, et al, eds. Coding & Quantization: DIMACS - IEEE Workshop, October 19-21, 1992. LC 93-29283. (DIMACS Series in Discrete Mathematics & Theoretical Computer Science). 263p. 1993. text 69.00 (*0-8218-6603-6*, DIMACS/14) Am Math.
Calderbank, V. J. Programming in FORTRAN 77. 3rd ed. 1989. 55.00 (*0-412-30500-3*, A3298) Chapman & Hall.
***Calderbon, Alberto P., et al.** Harmonic Analysis & Partial Differential Equations: Essays in Honor of Alberto Calderbon. LC 99-20385. (Chicago Lectures in Mathematics). 384p. 2000. 50.00 (*0-226-10456-7*) U Ch Pr.
Calderbon, Margarita, jt. auth. see Slavin, Robert E.
Calderhead, James, ed. Educational Research in Europe. LC 94-30160. (BERA Dialogues Ser.). 94p. 1994. 69.00 (*1-85359-256-0*); pap. 29.95 (*1-85359-255-2*) Taylor & Francis.
— Teachers' Professional Learning. 225p. 1988. pap. 34.95 (*1-85000-389-0*, Falmer Pr) Taylor & Francis.
Calderhead, James & Gates, Peter, eds. Conceptualising Reflection in Teacher Development. LC 92-2724. 192p. 1993. 89.95 (*0-7507-0123-4*, Falmer Pr); pap. 34.95 (*0-7507-0124-2*, Falmer Pr) Taylor & Francis.
Calderhead, James & Shorrock, Susan. Understanding Teacher Education: Case Studies in the Professional Development of Beginning Teachers. LC 97-175062. 240p. 1995. 85.00 (*0-7507-0398-9*, Falmer Pr); pap. 29.95 (*0-7507-0399-7*, Falmer Pr) Taylor & Francis.
Calderhead, R. G., jt. ed. see Ohshiro, Toshio.
Calderhead, Richard, jt. ed. see Pedersen, B. Martin.
Calderini, G. & Toffano, Gino, eds. Development & Regeneration of Nervous System. (Journal: Developmental Neuroscience: Vol. 5, No. 1). (Illus.). 116p. 1982. pap. 50.50 (*3-8055-3524-4*) S Karger.
Caldero, Michael A., jt. auth. see Crank, John P.
Calderon, A. P., ed. see Pure Mathematics Symposium Staff.
Calderon De La Barca & Frances, E. Life in Mexico During a Residence of Two Years in That Country. LC 75-41046. reprint ed. 67.50 (*0-404-14517-5*) AMS Pr.
Calderon de la Barca, Frances. Life in Mexico. (Illus.). 550p. (C). 1982. reprint ed. pap. 18.95 (*0-520-04662-5*, Pub. by U CA Pr) Cal Prin Full Svc.
Calderon de la Barca, Pedro. A Secreto Agravio, Secreta Venganza: La Dama Duende. 5th ed. 168p. 1983. pap. 11.95 (*0-7859-5168-7*) Fr & Eur.
— El Alcalde de Zalamea. Ruano De La Haza, Jose M., ed. (Nueva Austral Ser.: Vol. 50). (SPA.). 1991. pap. text 12.95 (*84-239-1850-5*) Elliots Bks.
— El Alcalde de Zalamea. (SPA.). 134p. 1977. 11.95 (*0-8288-7150-7*, S8830) Fr & Eur.
— El Alcalde de Zalamea. unabridged ed. (SPA.). pap. 5.95 (*84-410-0044-1*, Pub. by Bookking Intl) Distribks Inc.
— El Alcalde de Zalamea. 2nd ed. 192p. 1990. pap. 11.95 (*0-7859-5178-4*) Fr & Eur.
— La Aurora en Copacabana. Engling, Ezra S., ed. (Textos Ser.: Series B, No. 36). (SPA., Illus.). 264p. (C). 1995. 63.00 (*1-85566-015-6*, Pub. by Tamesis Bks Ltd) Boydell & Brewer.
— Autos Sacramentales. 257p. reprint ed. write for info. (*0-318-71617-8*) G Olms Pubs.
— Autos Sacramentales, Alegoricos, y Historiales. 459p. reprint ed. write for info. (*0-318-71616-X*) G Olms Pubs.
— Autos Sacramentales J. (SPA.). 195p. 1972. 15.95 (*0-8288-7183-3*, S20289) Fr & Eur.
— Autos Sacramentales 2. (SPA.). 213p. 1967. 15.95 (*0-8288-7037-3*, S20289) Fr & Eur.
— Bertolt Brecht: Poems 1913-1956. Raine, Kathleen & Nadal, R. M., trs. 1986. pap. 1.95 (*0-87830-072-4*) Routledge.
— Calderon: Plays One. Edwards, Gwynne, tr. from SPA. & intro. by. (Methuen World Dramatists Ser.). 304p. (Orig.). (C). 1991. pap. 14.95 (*0-413-63460-4*, A0538, Methuen Drama) Methn.
— Casa con Dos Puertas, Mala es de Guardar Planeta 1989. (SPA.). 304p. 1978. pap. 16.95 (*0-7859-5134-2*) Fr & Eur.
— Comedias Religiosas. (SPA.). 229p. 1970. 15.95 (*0-8288-7180-9*, S8839) Fr & Eur.
— Conference on Harmonic Analysis, Vol. 1. (C). 1982. ring bd. 110.95 (*0-534-98040-6*, Chap & Hall CRC) CRC Pr.
— Conference on Harmonic Analysis, Vol. 2. (C). 1982. ring bd. 110.95 (*0-534-98041-4*, Chap & Hall CRC) CRC Pr.
— La Devocion de la Cruz. 9th ed. (SPA.). 148p. 1986. pap. 6.40 (*0-7859-5154-7*) Fr & Eur.
Calderon de la Barca, Pedro. Dream Life. abr. ed. (SPA.). 1970. audio 22.00 (*0-694-50366-5*, SWC 2001) HarperAudio.
Calderon de la Barca, Pedro. En la Vida Todo Es Verdad Y Todo Mentira. Cruickshank, Don W., ed. (Textos B Ser.: Vol. X). (Illus.). 255p. (Orig.). (C). 1971. pap. 51.00 (*0-900411-14-7*, Pub. by Tamesis Bks Ltd) Boydell & Brewer.
— Una Fiesta Sacramental Barroca. (SPA.). 218p. 1984. 9.95 (*0-8288-7157-4*) Fr & Eur.
— Four Comedies. Muir, Kenneth, tr. LC 80-14570. 304p. 1980. 32.50 (*0-8131-1409-8*) U Pr of Ky.
— El Gran Duque de Gandia. (SPA.). 167p. 1963. pap. write for info. (*0-7859-5132-6*) Fr & Eur.
— The Great Theatre of the World. 1994. pap. 3.50 (*0-87129-292-0*, G57) Dramatic Pub.
— Konkordanz zu Calderon Pt. I: Konkordanz der Autos Sacramentales, Vols. 1-V. 7180p. 1983. 1100.00 (*3-487-06895-8*) G Olms Pubs.
— Life a Dream. Fitzgerald, Edward, tr. from SPA. LC 92-53872. 70p. (Orig.). 1992. pap. 7.00 (*0-88734-254-X*) Players Pr.
— Life Is a Dream. Clifford, John, tr. 96p. 1998. pap. 6.95 (*1-85459-188-6*, Pub. by Theatre Comm) Consort Bk Sales.
— Life's a Dream. adapted ed. Mitchell, Adrian, ed. 1994. pap. 5.50 (*0-87129-295-5*, L77) Dramatic Pub.
— Love Is No Laughing Matter. (Hispanic Classics Ser.). 1986. 59.95 (*0-85668-365-5*, Pub. by Aris & Phillips); pap. 25.00 (*0-85668-366-3*, Pub. by Aris & Phillips) David Brown.
— El Magico Prodigioso. Sese, Bernard, ed. (Nueva Austral Ser.: Vol. 88). (SPA.). 1991. pap. text 12.95 (*84-239-1888-2*) Elliots Bks.
— El Magico Prodigioso. 9th ed. (SPA.). 160p. 1989. pap. write for info. (*0-7859-5133-4*) Fr & Eur.
Calderon de la Barca, Pedro. El Magico Prodigioso: A Composite Edition & Study of the Manuscript & Printed Versions. McKendrick, Melveena, ed. (Illus.). 288p. 1992. text 79.00 (*0-19-815867-X*) OUP.
Calderon de la Barca, Pedro. El Mayor Monstruo del Mundo. Ruano De La Haza, Jose M., ed. (Nueva Austral Ser.: Vol. 81). (SPA.). 1991. pap. text 12.95 (*84-239-1881-5*) Elliots Bks.
— El Mayor Monstruo del Mundo. Valbuena-Briones, Angel J., ed. (Ediciones Criticas Ser.: Vol. 8). (SPA., Illus.). 176p. 1995. pap. 16.00 (*0-936388-74-9*) Juan de la Cuesta.
— Mayor Monstruo del Mundo - Principe Constante. 284p. 1989. pap. write for info. (*0-7859-5164-4*) Fr & Eur.
— The Mayor of Zalamea. adapted ed. 1994. pap. 5.50 (*0-87129-296-3*, M83) Dramatic Pub.
— No Hay Burlas Con el Amor. 7th ed. 232p. 1985. pap. 12.95 (*0-7859-5165-2*) Fr & Eur.
— The Painter of Dishonour. Johnston, David & Boswell, Laurence, trs. 128p. (Orig.). 1996. pap. 12.95 (*0-948230-88-6*, Pub. by Absolute Classics) Theatre Comm.
— Painter of His Dishonour. (Hispanic Classics Ser.). 1991. pap. 25.00 (*0-85668-347-7*, Pub. by Aris & Phillips) David Brown.
— The Painter of His Dishonour. (Hispanic Classics Ser.). 1991. 59.95 (*0-85668-346-9*, Pub. by Aris & Phillips) David Brown.
— The Physician of His Honour. Fox, Dian & Hindley, Donald, eds. & trs. by. from SPA.Tr. of Medico de su Honra. 1996. 59.95 (*0-85668-639-5*, Pub. by Aris & Phillips); pap. 25.00 (*0-85668-640-9*, Pub. by Aris & Phillips) David Brown.
— Pintor de Su Deshonra. (SPA.). 236p. 1969. 8.95 (*0-8288-7065-9*, S8849) Fr & Eur.
— El Postrer Duelo de Espana. Rossetti, Guy, ed. (Textos B Ser.: Vol. XXIII). 218p. (C). 1977. 51.00 (*0-7293-0045-5*, Pub. by Tamesis Bks Ltd) Boydell & Brewer.
— The Schism in England: La Cisma de Inglaterra. (Hispanic Classics Ser.). 1990. 59.95 (*0-85668-331-0*, Pub. by Aris & Phillips); pap. 25.00 (*0-85668-332-9*, Pub. by Aris & Phillips) David Brown.
***Calderon de la Barca, Pedro.** Sueno. 75p. 1999. pap. 5.60 (*0-87129-935-6*, SD7) Dramatic Pub.
Calderon de la Barca, Pedro. The Surgeon of His Honour. Campbell, Roy & Hesse, Everett W., trs. from SPA. LC 77-13711. 1978. reprint ed. lib. bdg. 52.50 (*0-8371-9871-2*, CASU, Greenwood Pr) Greenwood.
— Three Comedies. Muir, Kenneth & MacKenzie, Ann L., trs. LC 85-5369. (Studies in Romance Languages: Vol. 31). 256p. 1985. 32.50 (*0-8131-1546-9*) U Pr of Ky.
— La Vida es Sueno. 3rd ed. (SPA.). 128p. 1997. pap. text 4.00 (*1-56328-060-4*) Edit Plaza Mayor.
— La Vida es Sueno, No. 31. Rodriguez Cuadros, Evangelina, ed. (SPA.). pap. 10.95 (*84-239-1831-9*) Elliots Bks.
— Vida es Sueno - Alcalde de Zalamea. 3rd ed. 1963. 1986. pap. 10.95 (*0-7859-5161-X*) Fr & Eur.
— La Vida Es Sueno, el Alcalde de Zalamea. (SPA.). pap. 8.95 (*968-432-195-3*, Pub. by Porrua) Continental Bk.
***Calderon de la Barca, Pedro.** La Vida es Suero. (SPA.). 1999. 13.00 (*84-481-0942-2*, McGrw-H College) McGrw-H Hghr Educ.
Calderon de la Barca, Pedro, jt. auth. see Oppenheimer, Max, Jr.
Calderon, Frank. Como Pescar Marido por Primera, Segunda, y Tercera Vez. (SPA.). 112p. (Orig.). 1987. pap. 2.95 (*0-939193-16-7*) Edit Concepts.
— Conflictos Emocionales del Nino.Tr. of Children's Emotional Problems & Conflicts. (SPA.). 192p. 1998. pap. 5.95 (*0-939193-21-3*) Edit Concepts.
— Cual Es Su Color? (SPA.). 80p. (Orig.). 1985. pap. 2.25 (*0-939193-09-4*) Edit Concepts.
— Curas y Remedios Naturales. (SPA.). 320p. 1987. pap. text 4.95 (*0-939193-13-2*) Edit Concepts.
— La Dieta Definitiva. (SPA.). 128p. (Orig.). 1986. pap. 2.95 (*0-939193-06-X*) Edit Concepts.
— Diez Sistemas para Averiguar Su Destino. (SPA., Illus.). 208p. (Orig.). 1985. pap. 4.95 (*0-939193-01-9*) Edit Concepts.
— Estrategias para Bajar de Peso Comiendo! (Strategies to Lose Weight by Eating!) (SPA.). 192p. 1998. per. 5.95 (*0-939193-23-X*) Edit Concepts.
— Etiqueta Hoy, en la Oficina. (SPA.). 160p. (Orig.). 1987. pap. 4.95 (*0-939193-17-5*) Edit Concepts.
— Etiqueta Hoy, para el Hombre. (SPA.). 160p. (Orig.). 1987. pap. text 4.95 (*0-939193-18-3*) Edit Concepts.
— Etiqueta Hoy, para los Ninos. (SPA.). 160p. (Orig.). 1987. pap. text 4.95 (*0-939193-19-1*) Edit Concepts.
— Ingle's Esencial.Tr. of Essential English. (SPA., Illus.). 192p. 1998. pap. 7.95 (*0-939193-26-4*) Edit Concepts.
— Lo Mejor de la Vida Sexual de la Pareja.Tr. of Best of the Sexual Life of Couples. (SPA.). 192p. 1998. pap. 5.95 (*0-939193-27-2*) Edit Concepts.
— Re Encarnacion, los Muertos Estan Vivos. (SPA.). 96p. (Orig.). 1987. pap. 2.95 (*0-939193-15-9*) Edit Concepts.
— So Piel & Como Debe Cuidarla? (SPA.). 192p. 1998. pap. 5.95 (*0-939193-28-0*) Edit Concepts.
— Su Salud en Peligro... Y No Lo Sabe? Date not set. pap. 5.95 (*0-939193-31-0*) Edit Concepts.
— Suene y Gane en la Loto, Vol. 1. large type ed. (SPA.). 200p. 1999. pap. 5.95 (*0-939193-30-2*) Edit Concepts.
— Terapia Celular, una Nueva Dimension, en la Medicina. (SPA.). 192p. (Orig.). 1987. pap. text 4.95 (*0-939193-14-0*) Edit Concepts.
— Todo Sobre el Embarazo. (SPA., Illus.). 192p. 1998. pap. 5.95 (*0-939193-25-6*) Edit Concepts.
— Trastornos Digestivos (Digestive System Problems) Como Controlarlos. (SPA.). 192p. 1998. pap. 5.95 (*0-939193-22-1*) Edit Concepts.
Calderon, Frank, ed. Diccionario de Sinonimos Con Antonimos y Paronimos. 2nd rev. ed. (SPA.). 432p. (Orig.). 1992. pap. 5.00 (*1-56259-021-9*) Editorial Amer.
— Horoscopo Prenatal. deluxe ed. 336p. 1998. pap. 5.95 (*0-939193-52-3*) Edit Concepts.
— Ingles Facil. (ENG & SPA., Illus.). 416p. (Orig.). 1992. pap. 5.00 (*1-56259-022-7*) Editorial Amer.
— Sexo Total. (SPA.). pap. 4.95 (*1-56259-011-1*) Editorial Amer.
— Washington Irving's Pilgrim of Love: From the Tales of the Alhambra. 2nd ed. (Illus.). 64p. (J). (gr. 4 up). 1990. text 19.95 (*0-939193-20-5*) Edit Concepts.
Calderon, Frank. Amor y Sexo, Eres Compatible? deluxe ed. (SPA.). 192p. 1999. pap. 5.95 (*0-939193-35-3*) Edit Concepts.
— Analice, Numeros, Colores, Velas y Auras (How to Interpret Numbers, Colors, Candles & Auras) deluxe ed. (SPA.). 192p. 1999. pap. 5.95 (*0-939193-36-1*) Edit Concepts.
Calderon, George. Eight One-Act Plays. LC 79-50020. (One-Act Plays in Reprint Ser.). 1980. reprint ed. 25.00 (*0-8486-2044-5*) Roth Pub Inc.
Calderon, German. A Bilingual Introduction to Personal Computers Bk. 1: Hardware. LC 95-75139. (ENG & SPA., Illus.). 192p. 1995. pap. 14.95 (*0-9645037-1-9*) BilinguaTec.
Calderon, Hector & Saldivar, Jose D., eds. Criticism in the Borderlands: Studies in Chicano Literature, Culture, & Ideology. LC 90-25853. (Post-Contemporary Interventions Ser.). 312p. 1991. text 54.95 (*0-8223-1137-2*); pap. text 19.95 (*0-8223-1143-7*) Duke.
***Calderon, Javier.** J. S. Bach Transcriptions for Classic Guitar. 72p. 1999. pap. 17.95 incl. audio compact disk (*0-7866-2893-6*, 96683BCD) Mel Bay.
— Johannes Brahms Arranged for Guitar. 64p. 1999. pap. 17.95 (*0-7866-5264-0*, 98144BCD) Mel Bay.
***Calderon, Jose.** LA Blue Girl, Vol. 1. 3rd ed. (Illus.). ii, 150p. 1999. reprint ed. pap. 16.95 (*1-56219-906-4*, CMX 06041) Central Pk Media.
— LA Blue Girl, Vol. 2. 2nd ed. (Illus.). ii, 158p. 2000. reprint ed. pap. 16.95 (*1-56219-911-0*, CMX 06042) Central Pk Media.
Calderon-Madrid, Angel. The Role of Private Financial Wealth in a Portfolio Model: A Study of the Effects of Fiscal Deficits on the Real Exchange Rate. LC 94-45746. 1995. text 79.95 (*0-312-12605-0*) St Martin.
***Calderon, Margarita.** TLCs: Teachers' Learning Communities. 100p. 2000. pap. 25.95 (*1-58237-038-9*) Creat Think.
Calderon, Moshe, ed. Food Preservation by Modified Atmospheres. 416p. 1990. lib. bdg. 295.00 (*0-8493-6569-4*, TP371) CRC Pr.
***Calderon, Roberto R.** Mexican Coal Mining Labor in Texas & Coahuila, 1880-1930. LC 99-34596. 1999. 39.95 (*0-89096-884-5*) Tex A&M Univ Pr.
Calderon, Sara L. The Two Mujeres. Kaufer, Gina, tr. from SPA. LC 91-21444. 204p. 1991. pap. 9.95 (*1-879960-00-1*) Aunt Lute Bks.
Calderon, T. Rey. Introduction to Oilwell Service & Workover. 2nd ed. (Well Servicing & Workover Ser.: Lesson 1). 111p. 1991. pap. text 16.00 (*0-88698-150-6*, 3.70120) PETEX.
Calderon, W. Liderazgode la Mujer en la Iglesia.Tr. of Leadership & Church Administration. (SPA.). 176p. 1982. pap. 7.99 (*0-8297-1354-9*) Vida Pubs.
Calderon, W. Frank. Animal Painting & Anatomy. LC 72-75583. (Illus.). 336p. 1975. reprint ed. pap. 11.95 (*0-486-22523-2*) Dover.
Calderon, Wilfredo. ESTO Aprendimos Vivimos Predicamos: Manual de Doctrina Cristiana. (SPA.). 112p. 1992. pap. 2.50 (*0-938127-14-4*) Publ Senda de Vida.
— Orientatcion Basica Para Recien Convertidos. (SPA.). 116p. 1986. pap. 2.50 (*0-938127-00-4*) Publ Senda de Vida.
Calderon, Wilfredo, jt. auth. see Carcamo, Otila.
Calderon-Young, Estelita & Mebane, Rodney M. Mas Facil: A Concise Review of Spanish Grammar. LC 92-35386. 256p. 1993. pap. text 27.40 (*0-13-178336-X*) P-H.
***Calderone, J., et al, eds.** The NAEP Guide (1997 Edition) A Description of the Contents & Methods of the 1997 & 1998 Assessments. rev. ed. (Illus.). 72p. (C). 1999. pap. text 20.00 (*0-7881-8359-1*) DIANE Pub.
Calderone, Mary S. Family Book about Sexuality. 1981. 15.95 (*0-397-01377-9*) Lppncott W & W.
Calderone-Stewart, Lisa M. In Touch with the Word: Cycle A for Ordinary Time. (Lectionary-Based Prayer Reflections Ser.). (Illus.). 136p. 1998. pap. 15.95 (*0-88489-545-9*) St Marys.

C

An Asterisk (*) at the beginning of an entry indicates that the title is appearing for the first time.

— In Touch with the Word: Cycle A for Ordinary Time. Stamschror, Robert, ed. (Lectionary-Based Prayer Reflections Ser.). (Illus.). 136p. 1998. spiral bd. 18.95 (*0-88489-576-9*) St Marys.

Calderone-Stewart, Lisa-Marie. Faith Works for Junior High: Scripture & Tradition-Based Sessions for Faith Formation. 132p. 1994. spiral bd. 22.95 (*0-88489-324-3*) St Marys.

— Faith Works for Senior High: Scripture & Tradition-Based Sessions for Faith Formation. 144p. 1993. spiral bd. 24.95 (*0-88489-297-2*) St Marys.

— In Touch with the Word: Advent, Christmas, Lent & Easter. 208p. 1996. spiral bd. 14.95 (*0-88489-399-5*) St Marys.

— In Touch with the Word: Advent, Christmas, Lent & Easter. Stamschror, Robert P., ed. (Illus.). 208p. 1996. pap. 12.95 (*0-88489-375-8*) St Marys.

— In Touch with the Word: Cycle B for Ordinary Time. (Lectionary-Based Prayer Reflections Ser.). (Illus.). 120p. 1999. pap. 15.95 (*0-88489-577-7*) St Marys.

— In Touch with the Word: Cycle C for Ordinary Time, Cycle C. LC 98-139451. (Lectionary-Based Prayer Reflections Ser.). (Illus.). 136p. 1997. pap. 15.95 (*0-88489-513-0*); spiral bd. 17.95 (*0-88489-533-5*) St Marys.

— In Touch with the Word: Cycle fo Ordinary Time. (Lectionary-Based Prayer Reflections Ser.). (Illus.). 152p. 1999. spiral bd. 18.95 (*0-88489-578-5*) St Marys.

***Calderone-Stewart, Lisa-Marie.** Know It! Pray It! Live It! A Family Guide to the Catholic Youth Bible. LC 00-8246. 92p. 2000. pap. 9.95 (*0-88489-648-X*) St Marys.

— Life Works & Faith Fits: True Stories for Teens. 112p. (YA). 1999. pap. 9.95 (*0-88489-547-5*) St Marys.

Calderone-Stewart, Lisa-Marie. Lights for the World: Training Youth Leaders for Peer Ministry. 120p. (YA). (gr. 9 up). 1995. spiral bd. 15.95 (*0-88489-350-2*) St Marys.

— Prayer Works for Teens, Bk. 1. Samschror, Robert, ed. (Resources for Parishes, Schools & Families Ser.: Vol. 1). (Illus.). 72p. (YA). 1997. pap. 12.95 (*0-88489-432-0*) St Marys.

— Prayer Works for Teens, Bk 2. Samschror, Robert, ed. Vol. 2. (Illus.). 64p. (YA). 1997. pap. 12.95 (*0-88489-433-9*) St Marys.

— Prayer Works for Teens, Bk. 3. (Resources for Parishes, Schools & Families Ser.: Vol. 3). (Illus.). 72p. (YA). 1997. pap. 12.95 (*0-88489-434-7*) St Marys.

— Prayer Works for Teens, Bk. 4. (Resources for Parishes, Schools & Families Ser.: Vol. 4). (Illus.). 72p. (YA). 1997. pap. 12.95 (*0-88489-435-5*) St Marys.

***Calderone-Stewart, Lisa-Marie.** Vibrant Worship with Youth: Keys for Implementing from Age to Age. Singer-Towns, Brian, ed. LC 99-50936. (Illus.). 216p. (YA). 2000. pap. 24.95 (*0-88489-488-6*) St Marys.

***Calderone-Stewart, Lisa-Marie & Kunzman, Ed.** Better Than Natural & Other Stories. (Stories for Teens Ser.: Vol. 3). (YA). 1999. pap. 4.95 (*0-88489-591-2*) St Marys.

— Meeting Frankenstein & Other Stories. (Stories for Teens Ser.: Vol. 5). 72p. (YA). 1999. pap. 4.95 (*0-88489-593-9*) St Marys.

— My Wish List & Other Stories. (Stories for Teens Ser.: Vol. 2). 72p. (YA). 1999. pap. 4.95 (*0-88489-590-4*) St Marys.

— Straight from the Heart & Other Stories. (Stories for Teens Ser.: Vol. 4). 72p. (YA). 1999. pap. 4.95 (*0-88489-592-0*) St Marys.

— That First Kiss & Other Stories. (Stories for Teens Ser.). 96p. (YA). 1999. pap. 4.95 (*0-88489-589-0*) St Marys.

Calderone, Tony. City of Rocks. 1998. pap. 20.00 (*1-57540-116-9*) Falcon Pub Inc.

— Climbs of the Northern Wasatch: A Supplement. Blumental, Joshua, ed. (Orig.). Date not set. pap. 12.95 (*0-9650455-0-1*) Pika Mntneerng.

Calderonello. The Teaching of Writing. (C). 2000. 28.00 (*0-205-27254-1*) Allyn.

Calderonello, Alice, et al. Perspectives on Academic Writing. 144p. (C). 1996. pap., teacher ed. write for info. (*0-02-318296-2*) Macmillan.

Calders, Pere. Brush. Feitlowitz, Marguerite, tr. from SPA.Tr. of Cepillo. (Illus.). 32p. (J). (ps-3). 1988. reprint ed. pap. 6.95 (*0-916291-16-2*) Kane-Miller Bk.

— The Virgin of the Railway & Other Stories. Bath, Amanda, ed. 220p. (C). 1991. 59.95 (*0-85668-546-1*, Pub. by Aris & Phillips); pap. 22.00 (*0-85668-547-X*, Pub. by Aris & Phillips) David Brown.

***Calderwood, David.** The Dragonslayer's Apprentice. (Blue-Ribbon Listen-&-Read Ser.). (Illus.). 160p. (YA). (gr. 6-12). 1998. mass mkt. 4.50 (*0-590-63093-8*) Scholastic Inc.

Calderwood, David. A Solution of Doctor Resolutus, His Resolutions for Kneeling. LC 79-84093. (English Experience Ser.: No. 913). 60p. 1979. reprint ed. lib. bdg. 15.00 (*90-221-0913-5*) Walter J Johnson.

— The True History of the Church of Scotland: From the Beginnings of the Reform to the End of the Reign of King James VI, 8 vols. Thomson, Thomas, ed. LC 83-45577. reprint ed. write for info. (*0-404-19894-5*) AMS Pr.

Calderwood, James. A Midsummer Night's Dream. LC 92-22796. (Twayne's New Critical Introduction to Shakespeare Ser.: No. 14). 224p. 1992. pap. 13.95 (*0-8057-8734-8*, Twyne) Mac Lib Ref.

Calderwood, James L. Metadrama in Shakespeare's Henriad: Richard II to Henry V. LC 77-93467. 235p. reprint ed. pap. 72.90 (*0-7837-4757-8*, 20445040003) Bks Demand.

— The Properties of "Othello" LC 88-27767. 176p. 1989. 25.00 (*0-87023-666-0*) U of Mass Pr.

— Shakespeare & the Denial of Death. LC 87-5922. 248p. (Orig.). (C). 1988. pap. text 17.95 (*0-87023-583-4*) U of Mass Pr.

— Shakespearean Metadrama: The Argument of the Play in Titus Andronicus, Love's Labour's Lost, Romeo & Juliet, a Midsummer Night's Dream & Richard II. LC 71-141839. 202p. 1971. reprint ed. pap. 62.70 (*0-7837-2973-1*, 205748100006) Bks Demand.

Calderwood, Michael. Mexico: A Higher Vision. (Illus.). 192p. 1995. 35.00 (*1-883051-06-1*) ALTI Pub.

***Calderwood, Patricia E.** Learning Community: Finding Common Ground in Difference. LC 00-24926. 2000. pap. write for info. (*0-8077-3952-9*) Tchrs Coll.

Calderwood-Schonrr, Veronika. Collins Gem German Dictionary. (ENG & GER.). 628p. 1991. write for info. (*0-7859-7414-8*, 0004589769) Fr & Eur.

Calderwood, Simone. Clothes. LC 92-27086. (Voyages Ser.). (Illus.). (J). 1993. 2.50 (*0-383-03560-0*) SRA McGraw.

Caldes, Marlene F. Inner Voices: How Listening to Yourself Empowers You to Realize Your Hopes & Dreams! 88p. (Orig.). 1990. pap. 7.95 (*0-9622313-2-0*) Prosper Natural.

Caldes, Sarah. Neighborhood Commercial Revitalization. Sampson, Stephanie, ed. 32p. (Orig.). 1983. pap. 13.00 (*0-317-04851-1*) Natl Coun Econ Dev.

***Caldewey, Jeffrey & Home, Chuck.** Icon: Art of Wine Label. (Illus.). 228p. 2000. 85.00 (*1-891267-30-2*) Wine Appreciation.

***Caldewey, Jeffrey & Howie, Mildred.** Mendocino - Lake Counties. (California Wine Tour Ser.). 128p. 2000. pap. 11.95 (*1-891267-26-4*) Wine Appreciation.

— Napa Valley. (California Wine Tour Ser.). 128p. 2000. pap. 11.95 (*1-891267-08-6*) Wine Appreciation.

— Sonoma. (California Wine Tour Ser.). 128p. 2000. pap. 11.95 (*1-891267-09-4*) Wine Appreciation.

Caldi, D., jt. ed. see Mostow, G.

Caldi, D. G., et al, eds. Storrs Meeting: Proceedings of the 1988 Division of Particles & Fields of the American Physical Society. 952p. (C). 1989. pap. 48.00 (*9971-5-0797-8*); text 166.00 (*9971-5-0777-3*) World Scientific Pub.

***Caldicott, Chris.** World Food Cafe: Global Vegetarian Cooking. LC 99-39829. (Illus.). 192p. 1999. 28.00 (*1-57959-060-8*, SOMA) BB&T Inc.

Caldicott, D. A., jt. auth. see Langley, F. P.

Caldicott, Helen. A Desperate Passion. (Illus.). 384p. 1997. pap. 13.95 (*0-393-31680-7*) Norton.

— A Desperate Passion: An Autobiography. (Illus.). 320p. 1996. 27.50 (*0-393-03947-1*) Norton.

— If You Love This Planet: A Plan to Heal the Earth. 224p. 1992. pap. 12.95 (*0-393-30835-9*) Norton.

— Nuclear Madness: What You Can Do! rev. ed. LC 94-5016. 1994. pap. 10.95 (*0-393-31011-6*) Norton.

***Caldicott, Lawrence, et al.** Vascular Anesthesia: A Practical Handbook. 288p. 2000. text 52.00 (*0-7506-3468-5*) Buttrwrth-Heinemann.

Caldiero, Alex. Various Atmospheres: Poems & Drawings. LC 97-45947. (Illus.). 64p. (Orig.). 1998. pap. 10.95 (*1-56085-101-5*) Signature Bks.

Caldon, C. Christopher. Concrete Hotel. 254p. 1998. pap. 8.95 (*0-9666693-0-4*, 32465A) Tiras Bks.

Calduch-Benages, N., jt. auth. see Vermeylen, J.

Caldwall, Bishop R. History of Tinnevelly. 312p. 1986. 30.00 (*0-8364-1728-3*, Pub. by Manohar) S Asia.

Caldwell. Beyond Self Manage School. LC 99-160208. 1998. pap. text 26.95 (*0-7507-0448-9*, Falmer Pr) Taylor & Francis.

— How You Can Stop Smoking Permanently. 1975. pap. 5.00 (*0-87980-074-7*) Wilshire.

— Product, Music Gallery, Business Simulation. 9th ed. (GB - Basic Business Ser.). 1990. 20.95 (*0-538-60196-5*) S-W Pub.

Caldwell & Testa. Biological Regulation & Consequences. 600p. 1998. write for info. (*0-12-155065-6*) Acad Pr.

Caldwell, Linda & Mou, Shela. Integrating Social Science & Ecosystem Management: A National Challenge. (Illus.). 213p. 1999. pap. text 35.00 (*0-7881-7677-3*) DIANE Pub.

Caldwell, A. & Kimball, S. John Caldwell & Sarah (Dillingham) Caldwell, His Wife, Ipswich Mass., 1654: Genealogical Records of Their Descendants, Eight Generations, 1654-1900. (Illus.). 318p. 1989. reprint ed. pap. 48.00 (*0-8328-0363-4*); reprint ed. lib. bdg. 56.00 (*0-8328-0362-6*) Higginson Bk Co.

Caldwell, Aaron. The Contemporary Agnostic Believer. 2nd rev. ed. (Illus.). 88p. 1999. lib. bdg. 19.95 (*0-9621639-7-X*) Grand Natl Pr.

Caldwell, Anne. Scandal's Darling. 400p. 1991. mass mkt. 4.50 (*0-380-76110-6*, Avon Bks) Morrow Avon.

Caldwell, B. E., et al. Intellectual Property Rights Associated with Plants. (ASA Special Publications: No. 52). 206p. 1989. 10.00 (*0-89118-101-6*) Am Soc Agron.

Caldwell, Benjamin H., Jr. Tennessee Silversmiths. LC 88-63431. (Frank L. Horton Ser.). (Illus.). 228p. 1989. 49.95 (*0-945578-01-6*) Mus South Deco.

Caldwell, Bettie D. Founders & Builders of Greensboro, 1808-1908: Fifty Sketches. (Illus.). 356p. 1997. reprint ed. lib. bdg. 39.00 (*0-8328-6899-X*) Higginson Bk Co.

Caldwell, Bettye & Stedman, Donald, eds. Infant Education. 1977. pap. 9.95 (*0-8027-7267-6*) Walker & Co.

Caldwell, Bettye M. & Ricciuti, Henry N. Review of Child Development Research, Vol. 3. 600p. 1976. pap. text 10.00 (*0-226-09044-2*, P680) U Ch Pr.

Caldwell, Bettye M., jt. ed. see Gunzenhauser, Nina.

Caldwell, Brian & Spinks, Jim. Policy Formation & Resource Allocation. 121p. (C). 1986. 48.00 (*0-7300-0378-7*, Pub. by Deakin Univ) St Mut.

Caldwell, Brian, jt. auth. see Hayward, Don.

Caldwell, Brian J. Creating a High Performing School of the Future. 208p. 1995. 79.00 (*0-7507-0451-9*, Falmer Pr); pap. 26.95 (*0-7507-0452-7*, Falmer Pr) Taylor & Francis.

Caldwell, Brian J. & Cater, Earl M., eds. The Return of the Mentor: Strategies for Workplace Learning. LC 93-2874. (Education Policy Perspectives Ser.). 1993. pap. 34.95 (*0-7507-0167-6*, Falmer Pr) Taylor & Francis.

Caldwell, Brian J. & Spinks, Jim M. Beyond the Self Managing School: Student Outcomes & the Reform of the Education Series. LC 99-160208. 9p. 1998. text 85.00 (*0-7507-0447-0*, Falmer Pr) Taylor & Francis.

— Leading the Self-Managing School. (Education Policy Perspectives Ser.). 250p. 1992. 89.95 (*1-85000-656-3*, Falmer Pr); pap. 34.95 (*1-85000-657-1*, Falmer Pr) Taylor & Francis.

Caldwell, Brian J. & Spinks, Jim M. The Self-Managing School. 260p. 1988. pap. 37.95 (*1-85000-331-9*, Falmer Pr) Taylor & Francis.

Caldwell, Bruce. Auto Upholstery & Interiors: A Do-It-Yourself, Basic Guide to Repairing, Replacing or Customizing Automotive Interiors. LC 96-44793. 144p. 1997. pap. 17.95 (*1-55788-265-7*, HP Books) Berkley Pub.

— Beyond Positivism: Economic Methodology in the Twentieth Century. 2nd rev. ed. LC 93-48811. 304p. (C). 1994. pap. 29.99 (*0-415-10911-6*, B3703) Routledge.

— Jajmani System: An Investigation. (C). 1991. text 12.00 (*0-685-50095-0*, Pub. by Hindustan) S Asia.

***Caldwell, Bruce.** Marriage in Sri Lanka: A Century of Change. LC 99-931663. (Studies in Sociology & Social Anthropology). xvi, 233p. 1999. write for info. (*81-7075-048-2*) S Asia.

Caldwell, Bruce, ed. see Hayek, Friedrich A.

Caldwell, Bruce J. Beyond Positivism: Economic Methodology in the Twentieth Century. 288p. 1984. pap. text 18.95 (*0-04-330342-0*) Routledge.

— Fuel Gas Energy Metering. (Gas Measurement Committee Reports: No. 5). 58p. 1970. pap. 2.00 (*0-318-12618-4*, XQ0776) Am Gas Assn.

Caldwell, Bruce J., ed. Carl Menger & His Legacy in Economics. 407p. (C). 1990. text 49.95 (*0-8223-1087-2*) Duke.

— The Philosophy & Methodology of Economics, 3 vols. (International Library of Critical Writings in Economics). 1512p. 1993. 510.00 (*1-85278-385-0*) E Elgar.

Caldwell, Bruce J. & Boehm, Stephan, eds. Austrian Economics: Tensions & Directions. LC 92-22611. (Recent Economic Thought Ser.). 304p. (C). 1993. lib. bdg. 134.00 (*0-7923-9262-0*) Kluwer Academic.

Caldwell, C. E., ed. see Waldecki, Michael.

Caldwell, C. Max, jt. auth. see Otten, Leaun G.

Caldwell, Carol. Fields of Fire. 384p. 1995. mass mkt. 4.99 (*0-8217-0088-X*, Zebra Kensgtn) Kensgtn Pub Corp.

— Opportunities in Nutrition Careers. (Opportunities In . . . Ser.). (Illus.). 160p. pap. 12.95 (*0-8442-8188-3*, 2970INT, VGM Career) NTC Contemp Pub Co.

— Sea of Fire. 352p. 1997. mass mkt. 4.99 (*0-7860-0363-4*, Pinncle Kensgtn) Kensgtn Pub Corp.

Caldwell, Carol C. Nutrition. (Illus.). 160p. 14.95 (*0-8442-8187-5*) NTC Contemp Pub Co.

— Opportunities in Nutrition Careers. (Illus.). 160p. 1988. 13.95 (*0-8442-6172-6*, VGM Career) NTC Contemp Pub Co.

— Opportunities in Nutrition Careers. (Illus.). 160p. 1993. pap. 10.95 (*0-8442-6173-4*, VGM Career) NTC Contemp Pub Co.

Caldwell, Carol Coles. Opportunities in Nutrition Careers. (Opportunities in... Ser.). 160p. 1999. 14.95 (*0-8442-3240-8*) NTC Contemp Pub Co.

— Opportunities in Nutrition Careers. rev. ed. LC 99-34064. (Opportunities in... Ser.). 160p. 1999. pap. 11.95 (*0-8442-3251-3*, 32513) NTC Contemp Pub Co.

Caldwell, Charles. Autobiography of Charles Caldwell, M.D. (American Biography Ser.). 454p. 1991. reprint ed. lib. bdg. 89.00 (*0-7812-8057-5*) Rprt Serv.

Caldwell, Charles F. Head & Glory: Sacred Order or Secular Chaos. LC 96-29118. 140p. (Orig.). 1996. pap. 12.95 (*1-886412-04-9*) Preserv Press.

Caldwell, Chip. Mentoring Strategic Change in Healthcare: An Action Guide. (Illus.). 262p. 1995. 32.00 (*0-87389-224-0*, H0787) ASQ Qual Pr.

Caldwell, Chip, ed. The Handbook for Managing Change in Health Care. LC 97-2861. (Illus.). 735p. 1998. 75.00 (*0-87389-403-0*, H0943) ASQ Qual Pr.

Caldwell, Chris. Alsek's ABC Adventure. (Illus.). 32p. 1996. pap. 7.95 (*1-896758-00-2*, Pub. by Lost Moose) Genl Dist Srvs.

Caldwell, Christine, ed. Getting in Touch: The Guide to New Body-Centered Therapies. LC 97-17060. 288p. (Orig.). 1997. pap. 14.00 (*0-8356-0761-5*, Quest) Theos Pub Hse.

Caldwell, Claire. Surf's Up for Laney. 187p. (YA). (gr. 7 up). 1995. pap. 49.95 (*0-671-53390-8*) PB.

Caldwell, Clay. Ask Ol' Buddy. 1995. mass mkt. 5.95 (*1-56333-346-5*, Badboy) Masquerade.

— Jock Studs. (Orig.). 1997. mass mkt. 6.50 (*1-56333-472-0*, Badboy) Masquerade.

— Queers Like Us. (Orig.). 1995. mass mkt. 4.95 (*1-56333-262-0*, Badboy) Masquerade.

— Service, Stud. 5.95 (*0-15-633336-8*) Masquerade.

— Service, Stud. 1995. mass mkt. 5.95 (*1-56333-336-8*, Badboy) Masquerade.

— Some Like It Rough. (Orig.). 1998. mass mkt. 6.95 (*1-56333-544-1*, Badboy) Masquerade.

— Stud Shorts. (Orig.). 1995. mass mkt. 5.95 (*1-56333-320-1*, Badboy) Masquerade.

— Tag Team Studs. (Orig.). 1996. mass mkt. 6.50 (*1-56333-465-8*, Badboy) Masquerade.

— Tailpipe Trucker. 1995. mass mkt. 5.95 (*1-56333-296-5*, Badboy) Masquerade.

Caldwell, Clay, jt. auth. see Eighner, Lars.

Caldwell, Clifton, ed. see Tippitt, John Allen.

Caldwell, Clyde. The Vampire Players Guide. 2nd ed. (Vampire Ser.). 1994. 22.00 (*1-56504-053-8*, 2206) White Wolf.

Caldwell, D. G., jt. ed. see Gray, J. O.

Caldwell, D. O. & Paar, H. P. Photon-Photon Collisions, 1992: 9th International Workshop. 532p. 1992. text 106.00 (*981-02-1053-1*) World Scientific Pub.

Caldwell, D. W. Roadside Geology of Maine. Ort, Kathleen, ed. LC 98-17184. (Roadside Geology Ser.). (Illus.). 320p. 1998. pap. 18.00 (*0-87842-375-3*) Mountain Pr.

Caldwell, Dan. American-Soviet Relations: From Nineteen Forty-Seven to the Nixon-Kissinger Grand Design, 61. LC 80-27333. (Contributions in Political Science Ser.: No. 69). (Illus.). 283p. 1981. 65.00 (*0-313-22538-9*, CCC/, Greenwood Pr) Greenwood.

— Missiles in Cuba: A Decision-Making Game. (CISE Learning Packages in International Studies). (Illus.). 38p. (Orig.). 1979. pap. text 3.50 (*0-936876-35-2*) LRIS.

— Permissive Action Links (PAL) A Description & Proposal. (CISA Working Papers: No. 56). 27p. (Orig.). 1986. pap. 15.00 (*0-86682-073-6*) Ctr Intl Relations.

— World Politics & You. LC 99-27555. 360p. 1999. pap. 41.00 (*0-13-954728-2*) P-H.

Caldwell, Dan, jt. ed. see Krepon, Michael.

***Caldwell, Daniel.** The Esoteric World of Madame Blavatsky. 360p. 2000. 28.95 (*0-8356-0794-1*, Pub. by Theos Pub Hse) Natl Bk Netwk.

Caldwell, Daniel, compiled by. Esoteric She. (Tributes to H. P. Blavatsky Ser.). 1992. pap. 6.00 (*0-913004-72-3*) Point Loma Pub.

Caldwell, Daniel H., ed. The Occult World of Madame Blavatsky: Reminiscences & Impressions by Those Who Knew Her. (Illus.). 336p. (Orig.). 1991. pap. 13.95 (*0-941657-04-3*) Impossible Dream.

Caldwell, Daniel R. Microbial Physiology & Metabolism. 384p. (C). 1994. text 50.00 (*0-697-17192-2*, WCB McGr Hill) McGrw-H Hghr Educ.

— Microbial Physiology & Metabolism. 2nd rev. ed. LC 98-53183. (Illus.). 11p. 1999. 69.95 (*0-89863-208-0*) Star Pub CA.

Caldwell, David. Contracting Your Own Home: A Step-by-Step Guide. (Illus.). 256p. (Orig.). 1996. pap. 24.95 (*0-7737-5801-1*) Stoddart Publ.

— Layman's Guide to Contracting Your Own Home. (Illus.). 220p. 1994. pap. 16.95 (*0-9698056-0-8*) Lone Pine.

— Renovating Your Own Home: A Step-by-Step Guide. (Illus.). 240p. (Orig.). 1996. pap. 24.95 (*0-7737-5802-X*) Stoddart Publ.

Caldwell, David E., jt. auth. see Boland, Jack.

Caldwell, David H. Scotland's Wars & Warriors: Winning Against the Odds. (Discovering Historic Scotland Ser.). (Illus.). 104p. 1998. pap. 26.00 (*0-11-495786-X*, Pub. by Statnry Office) Balogh.

Caldwell, David O., ed. Cosmo - 98. (AIP Conference Proceedings Ser.: No. 478). (Illus.). 496p. 1999. 125.00 (*1-56396-853-3*) Am Inst Physics.

Caldwell, Delmar R., ed. Cataracts. LC 87-42928. (Transactions of the New Orleans Academy of Ophthalmology Ser.). 379p. 1988. reprint ed. pap. 117.50 (*0-608-00349-2*, 206106500007) Bks Demand.

Caldwell, Donald. JG 26 War Diary, 1939-1942, Vol. 1. 416p. 1997. 44.95 (*1-898697-52-3*, Pub. by Grub St) Seven Hills Bk.

Caldwell, Donald H. U. S. Health Law & Policy: A Guide to the Current Literature. LC 98-18221. 1998. 100.00 (*1-55648-236-1*) AHPI.

Caldwell, Donald L. JG 26: Top Guns of the Luftwaffe. 1993. mass mkt. 5.99 (*0-8041-1050-6*) Ivy Books.

— JG 26 War Diary, 1939-1942, Vol. 2. 1999. 44.95 (*1-898697-86-8*, Pub. by Grub St) Seven Hills Bk.

Caldwell, Dondeena. If Quetzals Could Cry: A Guatemalan Scrapbook with Designs for Worship. 1990. pap. 4.95 (*0-377-00206-2*) Friendship Pr.

Caldwell, Dorothy J., ed. Missouri Historic Sites Catalogue. LC 63-63854. (Illus.). 199p. 1963. 15.00 (*0-614-14522-8*) SHS MO.

Caldwell, E. The Complete Stories of Eskine Caldwell. 36.95 (*0-88411-455-4*) Amereon Ltd.

Caldwell, E., jt. auth. see Bourke-White, Margaret.

Caldwell, E. K., contrib. by. Dreaming the Dawn: Conversations with Native Artists & Activists. LC 98-51490. (American Indian Lives Ser.). (Illus.). 136p. 1999. 22.50 (*0-8032-1500-2*) U of Nebr Pr.

Caldwell, E. S. The New Youth Pastor's Handbook: Guidelines for the 1990's & Beyond. rev. ed. Peterson, Alan H., ed. 200p. 1992. pap. text 34.95 (*1-877858-08-0*, TNYPH2) Amer Focus Pub.

Caldwell, Earl. Black American Witness: Reports from the Front by Earl Caldwell. Walker, Kenneth & Rackley, Lurma, eds. 279p. 1994. write for info. (*1-886446-10-5*) Lion Hse Pub.

Caldwell, Elizabeth. Teenagers: A Bewildered Parent's Guide. 176p. 1996. pap. 11.95 (*0-9624945-0-X*) Silvercat Pubns.

Caldwell, Elizabeth F. Come unto Me: Rethinking the Sacraments for Children. LC 95-51064. 144p. (Orig.). 1996. pap. 12.95 (*0-8298-1119-2*) Pilgrim OH.

***Caldwell, Elwood F. & Fast, Rober B., eds.** Breakfast Cereals & How They Are Made. 2nd rev. ed. 400p. 2000. 139.00 (*1-891127-15-2*) Am Assn Cereal Chem.

Caldwell, Erskine. Bagarre De Juillet. (FRE.). 224p. 1985. pap. 11.95 (*0-7859-2008-0*, 2070376346) Fr & Eur.

— Call It Experience. 1976. 20.95 (*0-8488-0940-8*) Amereon Ltd.

— Call It Experience: The Years of Learning How to Write. LC 96-865. 248p. 1996. pap. 15.95 (*0-8203-1849-3*) U of Ga Pr.

— Deep South: Memory & Observation. LC 94-36671. (Brown Thrasher Bks.). 272p. (C). 1995. pap. 14.95 (*0-8203-1716-0*) U of Ga Pr.

— Le Doigt De Dieu. (FRE.). 1984. pap. 11.95 (*0-7859-1989-9*, 2070375358) Fr & Eur.

— Episode in Palmetto. 1976. 19.95 (*0-8488-0441-4*) Amereon Ltd.

***Caldwell, Erskine.** Erskine Caldwell: Selected Letters, 1929-1955. McDonald, Robert L., ed. LC 98-46975. (Illus.). 259p. 1999. lib. bdg. 48.50 (*0-7864-0108-7*) McFarland & Co.

Caldwell, Erskine. Georgia Boy. LC 95-13815. (Brown Thrasher Bks.). 248p. 1995. pap. 12.95 (*0-8203-1736-5*) U of Ga Pr.

— God's Little Acre. 18.95 (*0-88411-456-2*) Amereon Ltd.

— God's Little Acre. (Illus.). 212p. 1977. 25.00 (*0-88322-024-5*) Beehive GA.

— God's Little Acre. LC 94-25816. (Brown Thrasher Bks.). 232p. 1995. pap. 12.95 (*0-8203-1663-6*) U of Ga Pr.

— God's Little Acre. 300p. 1993. reprint ed. lib. bdg. 25.95 (*0-89966-869-0*) Buccaneer Bks.

— Humorous Side of Erskine Caldwell. 283p. Date not set. 23.95 (*0-8488-2580-2*) Amereon Ltd.

— In Search of Bisco. LC 95-14565. (Brown Thrasher Bks.). 1995. pap. 12.95 (*0-8203-1784-5*) U of Ga Pr.

— Jenny Toute Nue. (FRE.). pap. 10.95 (*0-7859-1840-X*, 2070369072) Fr & Eur.

— Journeyman. 144p. Date not set. 18.95 (*0-8488-2531-4*) Amereon Ltd.

— Journeyman. LC 96-4267. (Brown Thrasher Bks.). 216p. (C). 1996. pap. 14.95 (*0-8203-1848-5*) U of Ga Pr.

— Nous les Vivants. (FRE.). 1979. pap. 11.95 (*0-7859-1892-2*, 2070371131) Fr & Eur.

— Un Patelin Nomme Estherville. (FRE.). 213p. 1985. pap. 11.95 (*0-7859-2019-6*, 2070376850) Fr & Eur.

— Un Pauvre Type. (FRE.). 192p. 1980. pap. 10.95 (*0-7859-1906-6*, 2070371646) Fr & Eur.

— Le Petit Arpent du Bon Dieu. (FRE.). 1983. pap. 10.95 (*0-7859-1751-9*, 2070364194) Fr & Eur.

— Poor Fool: Novel. LC 94-11456. (Voices of the South Ser.). 155p. 1994. pap. 12.95 (*0-8071-1947-4*) La State U Pr.

— Un P'tit Gars de Georgie. (FRE.). 182p. 1978. pap. 10.95 (*0-7859-1881-7*, 2070370593) Fr & Eur.

— La Route au Tabac. (FRE.). 256p. 1973. pap. 10.95 (*0-7859-1753-5*, 2070364380) Fr & Eur.

— The Stories of Erskine Caldwell. LC 96-18365. (Brown Thrasher Bks.). 680p. 1996. reprint ed. pap. 24.95 (*0-8203-1694-6*) U of Ga Pr.

— The Stories of Erskine Caldwell. LC 96-18365. (Brown Thrasher Bks.). 680p. 1996. reprint ed. 55.00 (*0-8203-1693-8*) U of Ga Pr.

— Terre Tragique. (FRE.). 224p. 1986. pap. 10.95 (*0-7859-2049-8*, 2070377733) Fr & Eur.

— This Very Earth. 22.95 (*0-89190-164-7*) Amereon Ltd.

— Tobacco Road. large type ed. LC 95-14356. 236p. 1995. lib. bdg. 20.95 (*0-7838-1365-1*, G K Hall Lrg Type) Mac Lib Ref.

— Tobacco Road. LC 78-55752. 1978. reprint ed. lib. bdg. 14.00 (*0-8376-0422-2*) Bentley Pubs.

— Tobacco Road. LC 78-55752. 1993. reprint ed. lib. bdg. 35.95 (*0-89966-304-4*) Buccaneer Bks.

— Tobacco Road. LC 78-55752. (Brown Thrasher Bks.). 200p. 1995. reprint ed. pap. 12.95 (*0-8203-1661-X*) U of Ga Pr.

— Toute la Verite. (FRE.). 1984. pap. 11.95 (*0-7859-1997-X*, 2070375714) Fr & Eur.

— Tragic Ground. 1979. pap. 4.95 (*0-452-25204-0*, Z5204, Plume) Dutton Plume.

— Trouble in July. (Illus.). 160p. 1977. 25.00 (*0-88322-025-3*) Beehive GA.

— Trouble in July. LC 98-37958. 272p. 1999. pap. 14.95 (*0-8203-2105-2*) U of Ga Pr.

— Les Voies du Seigneur. (FRE.). 224p. 1981. pap. 10.95 (*0-7859-1942-2*, 2070373304) Fr & Eur.

— With All My Might: An Autobiography. deluxe limited ed. (Illus.). 344p. 1987. 175.00 (*0-934601-21-6*) Peachtree Pubs.

Caldwell, Erskine & Bourke-White, Margaret. You Have Seen Their Faces. McCurry, Dan C. & Rubenstein, Richard E., eds. LC 74-30622. (American Farmers & the Rise of Agribusiness Ser.). (Illus.). 1975. reprint ed. 23.95 (*0-405-06769-0*) Ayer.

— You Have Seen Their Faces. LC 74-30622. (Brown Thrasher Bks.). (Illus.). 136p. 1995. reprint ed. 40.00 (*0-8203-1691-1*); reprint ed. pap. 19.95 (*0-8203-1692-X*) U of Ga Pr.

Caldwell, Ester, jt. auth. see Hegner, Barbara R.

Caldwell, Esther & Hegner, Barbara R. Health Care Assistant. 4th ed. LC 84-26021. 352p. (C). 1985. teacher ed. 13.95 (*0-8273-2454-5*) Delmar.

Caldwell, Esther, jt. auth. see Hegner, B. R.

Caldwell, Esther, jt. auth. see Hegner, Barbara.

Caldwell, Esther, jt. auth. see Hegner, Barbara R.

Caldwell, Francis E. The Ebb & the Flood: A History of the Halibut Producers Cooperative. Matsen, Bradford, ed. LC 80-51978. (Illus.). 108p. (Orig.). 1980. 7.95 (*0-937288-00-4*) Anchor Pub.

— Land of the Ocean Mists: The Wild Ocean Coast West of Glacier Bay. DeArmond, Robert, ed. LC 86-3338. (Illus.). 209p. (Orig.). 1996. 7.95 (*0-88240-311-7*) Anchor Pub.

***Caldwell, Francis E.** Pacific Troller: Life on the Northwest Fishing Grounds. LC 99-34. (Illus.). 152p. 1999. pap. 16.00 (*1-55212-283-2*) Trafford Pub.

Caldwell, Fred G. Trials & Glory: Keeping Proper Prospective in Trying Times. Peacock, Jimmy, ed. 144p. 1997. pap. 12.00 (*0-9657706-1-3*) Phos Pub.

Caldwell, Gary. Mammoth Gold: The Ghost Towns of Lake District. LC 89-26340. (Illus.). 174p. (Orig.). 1990. pap. 8.95 (*0-931378-12-5*) Live Oak.

Caldwell, Gayle, ed. see Vogel, Thomas A.

Caldwell, George. Drama 160: Introduction to Theatre Handbook. 64p. (C). 1994. 10.95 (*0-8403-9851-4*) Kendall-Hunt.

Caldwell, H. M. History of the Elyton Land Company & Birmingham, Ala. The Origin & Development of an American City. reprint ed. pap. 3.75 (*0-87651-988-5*) Southern U Pr.

Caldwell, H. Stephen & Dixon, Stacey L. Projective Psychodiagnostic Assessment. 185p. (Orig.). 1992. pap. text 12.95 (*0-929240-49-9*) EMIS.

Caldwell, Hansonia. African American Music - A Chronology 1619-1995. LC 96-215402. 444p. 1996. 37.95 (*0-9650441-1-4*); pap. 27.95 (*0-9650441-0-6*) Ikoro Commns.

***Caldwell, Hansonia L.** African American Music-Spirituals: An Introduction to the Fundamental Folk Music of Black America. 110p. 2000. pap. 18.85 (*0-9650441-4-9*) Ikoro Commns.

Caldwell, Hansonia L. An Educator's Resource Manual Vol. 1: For African American Music, a Chronology 1619-1995. (C). 1997. ring bd. 18.95 (*0-9650441-3-0*, 0-9650441) Ikoro Commns.

Caldwell, Happy. Saving Our Cities: You Can Change Your City for God. LC 97-148678. 1997. pap. text 6.99 (*0-89274-698-X*) Harrison Hse.

Caldwell, Hardy. The Agile Manager's Guide to Hiring Excellence. LC 97-81353. (Agile Manager Ser.). (Illus.). 96p. 1998. pap. 9.95 (*1-58099-006-1*) Velocity Busn.

Caldwell, Harry B. & Middleton, David L. English Tragedy, 1370-1600: Fifty Years of Criticism. LC 72-153857. (Checklists in the Humanities & Education Ser.). 105p. reprint ed. pap. 32.60 (*0-8357-6347-1*, 203562100096) Bks Demand.

Caldwell, Harry M., et al. California Criminal Trialbook. 3rd ed. LC 95-47002. 250p. (C). 1995. ring bd. 85.00 (*0-314-08725-7*) West Pub.

Caldwell, Helen. Michio Ito: The Dancer & His Dances. LC 76-7756. (Illus.). 200p. reprint ed. pap. 62.00 (*0-7837-4671-7*, 204441700003) Bks Demand.

Caldwell, Helen, tr. see Machado de Assis, Joaquim Maria.

Caldwell, Henry B., frwd. Alfred Khouri Collection II. (Illus.). 1969. pap. 4.00 (*0-940744-06-6*) Chrysler Museum.

— Alfred Khouri Memorial Collection I. (Illus.). 50p. 1963. pap. 4.00 (*0-940744-05-8*) Chrysler Museum.

— The Melvin Gutman Collection of Antique Jewelry. (Illus.). 48p. 1966. 5.00 (*0-940744-07-4*) Chrysler Museum.

Caldwell, Howard. Tony Hinkle: Coach for All Seasons. LC 90-49194. (Illus.). 208p. 1991. 19.95 (*0-253-31298-1*) Ind U Pr.

Caldwell, Ian. Sumatra: Island of Adventure. (Regional Guides of Indonesia Ser.). 1994. pap. 15.95 (*0-8442-9907-3*, Passprt Bks) NTC Contemp Pub Co.

Caldwell, Ian & Volkman, Toby A., eds. Sulawesi: Celebes. Pessireron, Sylvia & Scargo, Lisa, trs. from ENG. (Indonesie Reisbibliotheek Ser.). (DUT.). 256p. 1991. pap. 19.95 (*0-945971-38-9*) Periplus.

Caldwell, J., et al, eds. ISSX European Meeting on Foreign Compound Metabolism. (Xenobiotica Ser.: Vol. 16, Nos. 10 & 11). 196p. 1986. 91.00 (*0-85066-937-5*) Taylor & Francis.

Caldwell, J. & Bradley, Raymond S., eds. Industrial Vibration Modelling. 1986. text 168.00 (*90-247-3423-1*) Kluwer Academic.

***Caldwell, J. & Ram, Y. M.** Mathematical Modelling: Concepts & Case Studies LC 99-29973. (Mathematical Modelling Ser.). 1999. write for info. (*0-7923-5820-1*) Kluwer Academic.

Caldwell, J. A. & Newton, J. H. History of Belmont & Jefferson Counties, & Incidentally Historical Collections Pertaining to Border Warfare & Early Settlement of the Adjacent Portion of the Ohio Valley. With Biographical Sketches. (Illus.). 641p. 1997. reprint ed. lib. bdg. 68.00 (*0-8328-6293-2*) Higginson Bk Co.

Caldwell, J. B. & Ward, G., eds. Practical Design of Ships, 2 vols., 2. LC 92-13190. 1992. write for info. (*1-85166-862-4*) Elsevier.

Caldwell, J. J., jt. ed. see Atreya, S. K.

Caldwell, J. Paul. Sleep: The Complete Guide to Sleep Disorders & a Better Night's Sleep. (Your Personal Health Ser.). (Illus.). 222p. 1997. pap. 14.95 (*1-55209-122-8*) Firefly Bks Ltd.

Caldwell, J. R. History of Tama County, 2 vols., Set. (Illus.). 1020p. 1995. reprint ed. lib. bdg. 105.00 (*0-8328-5026-8*) Higginson Bk Co.

Caldwell, Jack A. & Reith, Charles. Encapsulation Technologies. 448p. 1993. lib. bdg. 95.00 (*0-87371-992-1*, L992) Lewis Pubs.

Caldwell, James F. J. The History of a Brigade of South Carolinians: Known First As "Gregg's" & Subsequently As "McGowan's Brigade" rev. ed. Wallace, Lee A., Jr., ed. (Illus.). 326p. 1992. reprint ed. 35.00 (*0-89029-001-6*, Mrngside Press) Morningside Bkshop.

Caldwell, Jeanne. Learning to Trust God's Faithfulness. LC 96-145987. 160p. (Orig.). pap. 7.99 (*0-89274-929-6*, HH-929) Harrison Hse.

Caldwell, JoAnne & Ford, Michael P., eds. Where Have All the Bluebirds Gone? Transforming Ability-Based Reading Classrooms. 117p. (Orig.). 1996. pap. text 8.00 (*1-888714-01-8*) Wiscon St Rding.

Caldwell, Joanne & Richek, Margaret A. Reading Problems: Assessment & Teaching Strategies. 3rd ed. 416p. 1995. 68.00 (*0-205-16388-2*) Allyn.

Caldwell, JoAnne, jt. auth. see Leslie, Lauren.

Caldwell, JoAnne S., jt. auth. see Richek, Margaret A.

Caldwell, John C. Pakistan: Major World Nations. LC 99-11827. (Illus.). 144p. 1999. 19.95 (*0-7910-5392-X*) Chelsea Hse.

Caldwell, John C., et al. The Causes of Demographic Change: Experimental Research in South India. LC 88-40189. (Orig.). 1988. text 40.00 (*0-299-11610-7*) U of Wis Pr.

— The Causes of Demographic Change: Experimental Research in South India. LC 88-40189. (Social Demography Ser.). 297p. (Orig.). 1988. reprint ed. pap. 92.10 (*0-608-07458-6*, 206768500009) Bks Demand.

— Micro-Approaches to Demographic Research. 400p. 1988. lib. bdg. 75.00 (*0-7103-0297-5*) Routledge.

Caldwell, John M., jt. auth. see Goins, Charles R.

Caldwell, John R. Seven New Artists: Pittsburgh Today. 24p. (Orig.). 1984. pap. 4.00 (*0-88039-008-5*) Mus Art Carnegie.

Caldwell, John S. The Jumping Plant-Lice of Ohio (Homoptera: Chermidae) (Bulletin Ser.: No. 34). 1938. pap. text 5.00 (*0-86727-033-0*) Ohio Bio Survey.

Caldwell, John T. Televisuality: Performing Style in American Television. LC 94-39017. (Communication, Media & Culture Ser.). (Illus.). 475p. 1995. text 55.00 (*0-8135-2163-7*); pap. text 20.00 (*0-8135-2164-5*) Rutgers U Pr.

Caldwell, John T., ed. Electronic Media & Technoculture. LC 99-38182. (Depth of Field Ser.). (Illus.). 278p. 2000. text. write for info. (*0-8135-2733-3*); pap. text 21.00 (*0-8135-2734-1*) Rutgers U Pr.

Caldwell, John, pseud. American Paintings in the Metropolitan Museum of Art Vol. 1: A Catalogue of Works by Artists... 624p. (C). 1994. text 135.00 (*0-691-03795-7*, Pub. by Princeton U Pr) Cal Prin Full Svc.

— Amphetamines & Related Stimulants, Vol. 1. 216p. 1981. 121.00 (*0-8493-5347-5*, RM666, CRC Reprint) Franklin.

— China's Conventional Military Capabilities: An Assessment. LC 95-141342. (CSIS Panel Reports). 28p. (C). 1994. pap. 14.95 (*0-89206-257-6*) CSIS.

— Desperate Voyage. (Illus.). 324p. 1985. pap. 14.95 (*0-924486-20-1*) Sheridan.

— Editing Early Music. 2nd ed. (Early Music Ser.: No. 5). (Illus.). 150p. 1995. pap. text 28.00 (*0-19-816544-7*) OUP.

— English Keyboard Music Before the Nineteenth Century. (Music Bks.). 352p. 1985. reprint ed. pap. 11.95 (*0-486-24851-8*) Dover.

— Fax This Book: Over 100 Sit-Up-&-Take-Notice Cover Sheets for Better Business. (Illus.). 96p. (Orig.). 1990. pap. 10.95 (*0-89480-807-9*, 1807) Workman Pub.

— George R. Stewart. LC 81-67300. (Western Writers Ser.: No. 46). (Illus.). 51p. (Orig.). 1981. pap. text 4.95 (*0-88430-070-6*) Boise St U W Writ Ser.

— India: Major World Nations. LC 98-15265. (Major World Nations Ser.). (Illus.). 144p. (YA). (gr. 5 up). 1999. lib. bdg. 19.95 (*0-7910-4988-4*) Chelsea Hse.

— Intimacy with God: Christian Disciplines for Spiritual Growth. 319p. 1995. pap. 9.99 (*0-89900-697-3*) College Pr Pub.

— Joan Witek. LC 84-810. (Illus.). 36p. 1984. pap. 5.00 (*0-88039-007-7*) Mus Art Carnegie.

— The New Cross-Country Ski Book. (Illus.). 160p. 1987. 9.95 (*0-317-60384-1*, Penguin Bks) Viking Penguin.

— The New Cross-Country Ski Book. 1988. 9.95 (*0-317-67797-7*) Viking Penguin.

— The Oxford History of English Music: c. 1715 to the Present Day, Vol. 2. (Illus.). 648p. 1999. text 135.00 (*0-19-816288-X*) OUP.

— The Oxford History of English Music Vol. 1: From the Beginnings to c. 1715. (Oxford History of English Music Ser.). (Illus.). 708p. 1992. text 105.00 (*0-19-816129-8*) OUP.

— Ten Americans. (Illus.). 32p. (Orig.). 1987. pap. 5.95 (*0-88039-016-6*) Mus Art Carnegie.

— Top Priority: Building an Evangelistic Church. LC 95-17518. 1995. pap. 8.99 (*0-89900-739-2*) College Pr Pub.

***Caldwell, John, pseud.** William Findley from West of the Mountains: A Politician in Pennsylvania, 1783-1791. 350p. 1999. pap. 14.95 (*1-880222-36-1*) Red Apple Pub.

Caldwell, John, pseud, ed. The Manchester Concerto Partbooks, 2 vols., Set. LC 89-7887. (Outstanding Dissertations in Music from British Universities Ser.). 664p. 1990. text 10.00 (*0-8240-0194-X*) Garland.

Caldwell, John, pseud & Brady, Michael. Citizen Racing. (Orig.). 1983. 16.75 (*0-8446-6045-0*) Peter Smith.

Caldwell, John, pseud & Nill, Annegreth. Pittsburgh Photography: A New Generation. (Illus.). 1987. pap. 5.00 (*0-88039-015-8*) Mus Art Carnegie.

Caldwell, John, pseud, et al. American Paintings in the Metropolitan Museum of Art Vol. 1: A Catalogue of Works by Artists Born by 1815. Luhrs, Kathleen, ed. (Illus.). 672p. 1994. 110.00 (*0-87099-708-4*); pap. 75.00 (*0-87099-709-2*) Metro Mus Art.

— Richard Deacon. (Illus.). 96p. (Orig.). 1988. pap. 11.95 (*0-88039-018-2*) Mus Art Carnegie.

— Sean Scully. LC 85-4203. (Illus.). 36p. 1985. pap. 6.95 (*0-88039-010-7*) Mus Art Carnegie.

Caldwell, Joni, tr. see Bachelard, Gaston.

Caldwell, Joseph W. Sabbatical on Winifrede Hollow. 40p. (Orig.). 1992. pap. 4.95 (*1-881692-03-5*) Trillium WV.

Caldwell, Justin. The Sleeping Porch. LC 78-17912. (Lost Roads Poetry Ser.: No. 16). 1979. pap. 4.00 (*0-918786-17-7*) Lost Roads.

Caldwell, Kirbyjon & Seal, Mark. The Gospel of Good Success: A Six-Step Program to Spiritual, Emotional, & Financial Success. LC 98-43542. 256p. 1999. 22.50 (*0-684-83668-8*) Simon & Schuster.

***Caldwell, Kirbyjon H.** The Gospel of Good Success: A Road Map to Spiritual, Emotional & Financial Wholeness. 2000. pap. 12.00 (*0-684-86307-3*, Fireside) S&S Trade Pap.

***Caldwell, L. John, ed.** Incidents Associated with Oil & Gas Operations: Outer Continental Shelf 1995-1996. (Illus.). 122p. (C). 1999. pap. text 25.00 (*0-7881-7884-9*) DIANE Pub.

Caldwell, Lee A. Women on the Colonial Frontier: A Study of Frederica & Early Georgia. Spalding, Phirizy, ed. LC 96-111889. (Illus.). 60p. 1995. pap. 7.95 (*0-930803-02-7*) Fort Frederica.

Caldwell, Lesley, ed. Psychoanalysis & Culture. (New Formations Twenty-Six Ser.). 192p. (C). 1997. pap. 19.50 (*0-85315-813-4*, Pub. by Lawrence & Wishart) NYU Pr.

Caldwell, Lindsay. Don't Let Me Die. (gr. 8-12). 1998. pap. 4.99 (*0-590-56735-7*) Scholastic Inc.

Caldwell, Lise. Classic Bible Stories: A Family Treasury. LC 97-50562. (Illus.). 160p. (J). (ps-1). 1998. 12.99 (*0-7847-0713-8*, 24-03848) Standard Pub.

***Caldwell, Lise.** Donut Forget. (Illus.). 48p. (ps-2). 1999. pap. 2.49 (*0-7847-0993-9*, 22063, Bean Sprouts) Standard Pub.

— God Made Pets. (Illus.). 16p. (J). (ps). 1999. pap. 1.49 (*0-7847-0877-0*, 22069, Bean Sprouts) Standard Pub.

— God's Animal Friends. (Illus.). 16p. (ps). 1999. pap. 1.49 (*0-7847-0875-4*, 22067, Bean Sprouts) Standard Pub.

— God's Animals on the Farm. (Illus.). 24p. (ps-2). 1999. pap. 2.99 (*0-7847-1092-9*, 22076, Bean Sprouts) Standard Pub.

— Jesus Always Loves Me. (Illus.). 16p. (ps). 1999. pap. 1.49 (*0-7847-0878-9*, 22070, Bean Sprouts) Standard Pub.

Caldwell, Lise. The Life of Christ: Classic Bible Stories. LC 97-50563. (Illus.). 24p. (J). (ps-1). 1998. pap. 1.99 (*0-7847-0828-2*, 24-04258) Standard Pub.

— The Old Testament: Classic Bible Stories. LC 97-50564. (Illus.). 24p. (J). (ps-1). 1998. pap. 1.99 (*0-7847-0827-4*, 24-04257) Standard Pub.

***Caldwell, Lise.** Please & Thank-You. 2000. pap. text. write for info. (*0-7847-1109-7*) Standard Pub.

— Sharing Is Fun. (Illus.). 16p. (ps). 1999. pap. 1.49 (*0-7847-0876-2*, 22068, Bean Sprouts) Standard Pub.

***Caldwell, Lise, ed.** Around the World. (Illus.). 48p. (ps-2). 1999. pap. 2.49 (*0-7847-0994-7*, 22064, Bean Sprouts) Standard Pub.

Caldwell, Lise, ed. see Brewer, Karen & Rushing, Donna.

Caldwell, Lise, ed. see Clark, Laura S. & Shippe, Dave.

Caldwell, Lise, ed. see Cloninger, Curt.

Caldwell, Lise, ed. see Cosper, John, Jr.

Caldwell, Lise, ed. see Ferris, Audrey.

Caldwell, Lise, ed. see Harrast, Tracy.

Caldwell, Lise, ed. see Hartman, Robert & Hird, Nancy E.

Caldwell, Lise, ed. see Hayes, Wanda.

Caldwell, Lise, ed. see Jansen, Larry.

Caldwell, Lise, ed. see Major, Richard.

Caldwell, Lise, ed. see McConnaughhay, JoDee.

Caldwell, Lise, ed. see Mishica, Clare.

Caldwell, Lise, ed. see Nappa, Tony & Nappa, Mike.

Caldwell, Lise, ed. see Ring, Laura.

Caldwell, Lise, ed. see Ritz, Randy.

Caldwell, Lise, ed. see Sheppard, Sandy.

Caldwell, Lise, ed. see Shippe, Dave & Clark, Laura S.

Caldwell, Lise, ed. see Standard Publishing Staff.

Caldwell, Lise, ed. see Stevans, Joy.

Caldwell, Lise, ed. see Taylor, Mark A.

Caldwell, Lois, jt. auth. see Diou, Suzanne.

Caldwell, Louis O. After the Tassel Is Moved: Guidelines for High School Graduates. 2nd ed. LC 96-41988. 96p. (YA). (gr. 10). 1997. 9.99 (*0-8010-1133-7*) Baker Bks.

Caldwell, Luis. Tu Puedes Enfrentar el Sufrimiento. (Serie Tu Puedes - You Can Ser.).Tr. of You Can Face Suffering. (SPA.). 24p. 1982. pap. 1.79 (*1-56063-155-4*, 490489) Editorial Unilit.

***Caldwell, Lynn Borders.** Guide to Careers in Health Professions. 2000. pap. 23.00 (*0-375-76158-6*) Random.

Caldwell, Lynton K. The Administrative Theories of Hamilton & Jefferson. 2nd ed. LC 87-28535. 265p. (C). 1987. 35.00 (*0-8419-1049-9*) Holmes & Meier.

— Between Two Worlds: Science, the Environmental Movement & Policy Choice. (Environmental Policy Ser.: No. 1). 240p. (C). 1992. pap. text 24.95 (*0-521-33743-7*) Cambridge U Pr.

— Environment As a Focus for Public Policy. Bartlett, Robert V. & Gladden, James N., eds. LC 94-37751. 368p. 1995. 39.50 (*0-89096-643-5*) Tex A&M Univ Pr.

— International Environmental Policy: From the 20th Century to the 21st Century. 3rd ed. LC 96-20958. 504p. 1996. text 59.95 (*0-8223-1861-X*); pap. text 22.95 (*0-8223-1866-0*) Duke.

— The National Environmental Policy Act: An Agenda for the Future. LC 98-38666. 272p. 1998. text 29.95 (*0-253-33444-6*) Ind U Pr.

Caldwell, Lynton K., ed. Environmental Policymaking. 264p. (Orig.). 1993. pap. 15.00 (*0-944285-40-6*) Pol Studies.

— Perspectives on Ecosystem Management for the Great Lakes: A Reader. LC 87-24497. (SUNY Series in Environmental Public Policy). 365p. (C). 1988. pap. text 21.95 (*0-88706-766-2*) State U NY Pr.

Caldwell, Lynton K. & Bartlett, Robert V. Environmental Policy: Transnational Issues & National Trends. LC 96-26268. 256p. 1997. 65.00 (*1-56720-079-6*, Quorum Bks) Greenwood.

Caldwell, Lynton K., et al. Citizens & the Environment: Case Studies in Popular Action. LC 75-31422. 479p. reprint ed. pap. 148.50 (*0-608-17125-5*, 205622200056) Bks Demand.

C

Caldwell, Lynton K., jt. auth. see Shrader-Frechette, Kristin S.

Caldwell, M. L. & Taylor, R. L., eds. Prader-Willi Syndrome. (Illus.). 120p. 1988. 94.95 (0-387-96699-4) Spr-Verlag.

Caldwell, M. M., jt. ed. see Schulze, E. D.

Caldwell, M. M., jt. ed. see Worrest, R. C.

Caldwell, Margaret. Hair Design. LC 94-175170. 48p. (J). (gr. 4-7). 1993. pap. 7.95 (0-590-47144-9) Scholastic Inc.

Caldwell, Marianne D. Gone Without a Trace. LC 94-61037. 112p. (Orig.). 1995. pap. 10.95 (0-943873-24-X) Elder Bks.

Caldwell, Mark. Saranac Lake: Pioneer Health Resort. Parnass, Barbara et al, eds. (Illus.). 40p. (Orig.). 1993. pap. 11.95 (0-9615159-1-0) Hist Saranac.

***Caldwell, Mark.** A Short History of Rudeness: Manners, Morals & Misbehavior in Modern America. 288p. 2000. pap. 13.00 (0-312-26389-9) St Martin.

— A Short History of Rudeness: Manners, Morals & Misbehavior in Modern America. 2nd ed. LC 99-22051. 274p. 1999. 23.00 (0-312-20432-9, Picador USA) St Martin.

Caldwell, Martha B. Annals of Shawnee Methodist Mission & Indian Manual Labor School. 2nd ed. LC 39-28738. (Illus.). 120p. 1977. pap. 3.00 (0-87726-005-2) Kansas St Hist.

Caldwell, Martyn M. & Pearcy, Robert W., eds. Exploitation of Environmental Heterogeneity by Plants: Ecophysiological Processes Above- & Belowground. (Physiological Ecology Ser.). (Illus.). 429p. 1994. text 104.00 (0-12-155070-2) Acad Pr.

Caldwell, Martyn M., jt. ed. see Schulze, Ernst-Detlef.

Caldwell, Mary. Morning, Rabbit, Morning. LC 81-47724. (Illus.). 32p. (J). (ps-1). 1982. 10.95 (0-06-020939-9) HarpC Child Bks.

— Morning, Rabbit, Morning. LC 81-47724. (Trophy Picture Bk.). (Illus.). 32p. (J). (ps-1). 1987. pap. 2.95 (0-06-443131-2, HarpTrophy) HarpC Child Bks.

— Praying for Fishhooks: Understanding Intercessory Prayer. 108p. 1994. pap. 11.00 (1-880837-75-7) Smyth & Helwys.

Caldwell, Mary B. A is for Adobe. (Illus.). 60p. (J). (gr. k-3). 1998. 17.00 (0-944551-35-1) Sundance Pr TX.

Caldwell Messenger Staff. Sumner County, Kansas. (Illus.). 295p. 1987. 45.00 (0-88107-096-3) Curtis Media.

Caldwell, Michael D., jt. auth. see Rombeau, John L.

***Caldwell, Michael J.** Varietal Tendencies. (Crush Chronicles Ser.: Vol. 1). (Illus.). 252p. 1998. pap. 19.95 (0-9661486-0-6) Tannin Ink.

Caldwell, Nathanial F., Jr. Arctic Leverage: Canadian Sovereignty & Security. LC 90-31362. 144p. 1990. 47.95 (0-275-93453-5, C3453, Praeger Pubs) Greenwood.

***Caldwell, Niall, et al.** World Wide What? Understanding the Web for Health, Wealth, Friends & More!: Discover How the Web Will Change Your Life! LC 00-32548. 2000. write for info. (1-57243-362-0) Triumph Bks.

Caldwell, Norm. Here's a Thought. 160p. (Orig.). 1999. pap. 7.95 (1-56273-178-5) My Mothers Pub.

— Lunch Box Notes (From Those Who Care) LC 97-33611. 160p. (Orig.). 1997. pap. 7.95 (1-56273-177-7) My Mothers Pub.

Caldwell, Oliver, et al. Thomas Pradzynski: Collector's Edition Book I: Galerie Du Midi. Includes Serigraph (Deluxe Edition on Black Paper) deluxe ed. LC 93-72847. (Illus.). 176p. 1993. 1700.00 (1-884495-06-0) Caldwell Snyder.

— Thomas Pradzynski: Collector's Edition Book I: Galerie Du Midi Includes Serigraph (Deluxe Edition on White Paper) LC 93-72847. (Illus.). 176p. 1993. 1500.00 (1-884495-01-X) Caldwell Snyder.

— Thomas Pradzynski: Collector's Edition Book II: Le Bistrot Includes Serigraph (Deluxe Edition on White Paper) LC 93-72847. (Illus.). 176p. 1993. 850.00 (1-884495-02-8) Caldwell Snyder.

— Thomas Pradzynski: Collector's Edition Book II: Le Bistrot. Includes Serigraph(Deluxe Edition on Black Paper) deluxe ed. LC 93-72847. (Illus.). 176p. 1993. 1250.00 (1-884495-07-9) Caldwell Snyder.

— Thomas Pradzynski: Collector's Edition Book III: Librairie St. Germain. Includes Serigraph (Deluxe Edition on Black Paper) deluxe ed. (Illus.). 175p. 1993. 950.00 (1-884495-08-7) Caldwell Snyder.

— Thomas Pradzynski: Collector's Edition Book III: Librairie St. Germain Includes Serigraph (Deluxe Edition on White Paper) LC 93-72847. (Illus.). 176p. 1993. 850.00 (1-884495-03-6) Caldwell Snyder.

Caldwell, Otis W. & Courtis, Stuart A. Then & Now in Education, 1845-1923. LC 77-165711. (American Education Ser, No. 2). 1972. reprint ed. 21.95 (0-405-03700-7) Ayer.

Caldwell, Pamela. Runaway Bride. 1997. mass mkt. 4.99 (0-8217-5728-8) Kensgtn Pub Corp.

— Runaway Bride. 1998. pap. 4.99 (0-8217-5352-5) Kensgtn Pub Corp.

Caldwell, Patricia, ed. see Williams, Catherine.

Caldwell, Paul & Molloy, William. Alzheimer's Disease: Everything You Need to Know. (Illus.). 216p. 1998. pap. 14.95 (1-55209-241-0) Firefly Bks Ltd.

Caldwell, Peter. Adventurer's Hawaii. LC 92-80609. (Illus.). 144p. 1992. pap. 19.95 (0-9626124-1-3) Taote Pub.

— Bac-si: A Doctor Remembers Vietnam. LC 90-90086. (Illus.). 144p. 1991. pap. 9.95 (0-9626124-0-5) Taote Pub.

— Drawing Light & Shade, No. 8. (Understand How to Draw Ser.). (Illus.). 32p. pap. 4.95 (0-85532-612-3, 612-3, Pub. by Srch Pr) A Schwartz & Co.

— Popular Sovereignty & the Crisis of German Constitutional Law: The Theory & Practice of Weimar Constitutionalism. LC 97-17282. 300p. 1997. pap. text 17.95 (0-8223-1988-8); lib. bdg. 49.95 (0-8223-1979-9) Duke.

***Caldwell, Peter C. & Scheuerman, William E.** From Liberal Democracy to Fascism: Legal & Political Thought in the Weimar Republic. LC 99-98003. (Studies in Central European Histories). 2000. write for info. (0-391-04098-7) Humanities.

Caldwell, Randall B., ed. Nonlinear Financial Forecasting: Proceedings of the 1st INFFC. 320p. (Orig.). 1997. pap. 59.95 (0-9651332-1-4) Finance & Technol.

Caldwell, Randall B., ed. see Van Eyden, Robert J.

***Caldwell, Rex.** Wiring: Basic & Advanced Projects. (Illus.). 240p. 2001. pap. 19.95 (1-58011-062-2) Creative Homeowner.

Caldwell, Rhonda. Country Fixin's for All Seasons, Vol. 3. 63p. 1995. pap. 10.50 (1-56770-332-1) S Scheewe Pubns.

Caldwell, Richard S. The Origin of the Gods: A Psychoanalytic Study of Greek Theogonic Myth. (Illus.). 224p. (C). 1993. reprint ed. pap. text 19.95 (0-19-507266-9) OUP.

Caldwell, Richard S., tr. & intro. see Hesiod.

Caldwell, Robert. A Comparative Grammar of the Dravidian or South Indian Family of Languages. (C). 1987. reprint ed. 36.00 (0-8364-2398-4, Pub. by Asian Educ Servs) S Asia.

— A Comparative Grammar of the Dravidian or South Indian Family of Languages. 3rd rev. ed. LC 98-906401. xi, 640 p. 1998. write for info. (81-206-0117-3) Asian Educ Servs.

— The Performer Prepares. 158p. 1990. 19.95 (1-877761-26-5) Pst.

***Caldwell, Robert & Wall, Joan.** Advancing the Technique. (Excellence in Singing Ser.: Vol. 3). (C). 2000. pap. 39.95 (1-877761-18-4) Pst.

— Becoming an Artist. (Excellence in Singing Ser.: Vol. 4). (C). 2000. pap. 39.95 (1-877761-19-2) Pst.

— Beginning the Process. (Excellence in Singing Ser.: Vol. 1). (C). 2000. pap. 25.95 (1-877761-16-8) Pst.

— Mastering the Fundamentals. (Excellence in Singing Ser.: Vol. 2). (C). 2000. pap. 34.95 (1-877761-17-6) Pst.

Caldwell, Robert, jt. auth. see Wall, Joan.

Caldwell, Robert, ed. see Lavielle, Gail.

Caldwell, Robert G. Foundations of Law Enforcement & Criminal Justice. Nardini, William, ed. LC 76-46478. 1977. 16.95 (0-672-61412-X, Bobbs) Macmillan.

Caldwell, Rodney K., jt. auth. see White, Robert A.

Caldwell, Ronald J. The Era of Napoleon: A Bibliography of the History of Western Civilization, 1799-1815, 2 vols., Set. LC 89-37074. 1494p. 1990. text 60.00 (0-8240-5644-2, 1097) Garland.

Caldwell, Ronald J., jt. auth. see Caldwell, Sandra M.

Caldwell, Ruby J. Celebrity Chefs. 1992. 25.00 (0-9634042-0-2) R J Caldwell.

Caldwell, Russell H. Reelfoot Lake. (Illus.). 160p. (Orig.). 1989. pap. 9.95 (0-317-94051-1) Caldwells Office.

— Reelfoot Lake: History - Duck Call Makers - Hunting Tales. rev. ed. (Illus.). 270p. 1989. 24.95 (0-9623039-2-5) Caldwells Office.

— Reelfoot Lake: History-Duck Call Makers-Hunting Tales. LC 88-92272. (Illus.). 240p. 1988. 24.95 (0-9623039-0-9) Caldwells Office.

— Reelfoot Lake: The Tourists' Guide. (Illus.). 160p. (Orig.). 1989. pap. 9.95 (0-9623039-1-7) Caldwells Office.

Caldwell, S. Oh Terrifying Mother: Sexuality, Violence & Worship of the Goddess Kali. (Illus.). 320p. 2000. text 24.95 (0-19-564462-X) OUP.

— Playing Chess. (Usborne Guides Ser.). (Illus.). 64p. (J). (gr. 5-9). 1987. pap. 7.95 (0-7460-0135-5) EDC.

— Playing Chess. (Usborne Guides Ser.). (Illus.). 64p. (J). (gr. 5 up). 1999. lib. bdg. 15.95 (0-88110-288-1) EDC.

Caldwell, Sally. Romantic Deception. LC 99-31862. 240p. 1999. pap. 10.95 (1-58062-210-0) Adams Media.

Caldwell, Samuel T., jt. auth. see Schuman, Stanley H.

Caldwell, Sandra M. & Caldwell, Ronald J. The History of the Episcopal Church in America, 1607-1991: A Bibliography. LC 92-45272. (Religious Information Systems Ser.). 544p. 1993. text 30.00 (0-8153-0936-8, H1635) Garland.

***Caldwell, Sarah & Kielson, Marie-Eve.** So You Want to Be a Screenwriter: How to Face the Fears & Take the Risks. 224p. 2000. pap. 14.95 (1-58115-062-8, Pub. by Allworth Pr) Watsn-Guptill.

Caldwell, Stan R. & Crissman, Randy D., eds. Design for Ice Forces: A State of the Practice Report. LC 83-70400. (Illus.). 218p. 1983. reprint ed. pap. 67.60 (0-608-04430-X, 205966700012) Bks Demand.

Caldwell, Stephen A. A Banking History of Louisiana. Bruchey, Stuart, ed. LC 80-1137. (Rise of Commercial Banking Ser.). 1981. reprint ed. lib. bdg. 15.95 (0-405-13637-4) Ayer.

Caldwell, Stevhan & Richardsen, Cailen. Insights: An Adventure to Inner Happiness. LC 95-169563. (Illus.). 384p. (Orig.). 1995. pap., student ed. 22.00 (1-882765-03-6) ATI Pub.

Caldwell, T. Knowing God. 1995. pap. 8.00 (0-927936-62-3) Vincom Pubng Co.

***Caldwell, Tanya.** Time to Begin Anew: Dryden's Georgics & Aeneis. LC 99-89592. 264p. 2000. 44.00 (0-8387-5435-X) Bucknell U Pr.

Caldwell, Taylor. Answer As a Man. 1976. 29.95 (0-88411-143-1) Amereon Ltd.

— The Arm & the Darkness. 1974. reprint ed. lib. bdg. 34.95 (0-88411-151-2) Amereon Ltd.

— The Balance Wheel. 1974. reprint ed. lib. bdg. 31.95 (0-88411-153-9) Amereon Ltd.

— Captains & the Kings. 1983. mass mkt. 6.99 (0-449-20562-2, Crest) Fawcett.

— Dear & Glorious Physician. 1993. reprint ed. lib. bdg. 49.95 (1-56849-242-1) Buccaneer Bks.

— The Devil's Advocate. 1976. reprint ed. lib. bdg. 26.95 (0-88411-163-6) Amereon Ltd.

— Dialogues with the Devil. 22.95 (0-89190-279-1) Amereon Ltd.

— The Eagles Gather. 602p. reprint ed. lib. bdg. 30.95 (0-88411-165-2) Amereon Ltd.

— The Earth Is the Lord's: A Tale of the Rise of Genghis Kahn. 1974. reprint ed. lib. bdg. 32.95 (0-88411-154-7) Amereon Ltd.

— The Final Hour. 1974. reprint ed. lib. bdg. 33.95 (0-88411-152-0) Amereon Ltd.

— Glory & the Lightning. Date not set. lib. bdg. 25.95 (0-8488-1961-6) Amereon Ltd.

— Let Love Come Last. 1974. reprint ed. lib. bdg. 27.95 (0-88411-160-1) Amereon Ltd.

— The Listener. 1984. mass mkt. 3.95 (0-553-24483-3) Bantam.

— The Listener. 288p. reprint ed. lib. bdg. 22.95 (0-88411-166-0) Amereon Ltd.

— Maggie: Her Marriage. 204p. reprint ed. lib. bdg. 21.95 (0-88411-169-5) Amereon Ltd.

— Melissa. 1974. reprint ed. lib. bdg. 27.95 (0-88411-159-8) Amereon Ltd.

— Never Victorious, Never Defeated. 1976. reprint ed. lib. bdg. 32.95 (0-88411-162-8) Amereon Ltd.

— No One Hears but Him. 1976. 21.95 (0-8488-0442-2) Amereon Ltd.

— On Growing up Tough. 160p. Date not set. reprint ed. lib. bdg. 20.95 (0-88411-170-9, Aeonian Pr) Amereon Ltd.

— Romance of Atlantis. 1976. 22.95 (0-8488-0443-0) Amereon Ltd.

— Strong City. 1974. reprint ed. lib. bdg. 34.95 (0-88411-158-X) Amereon Ltd.

— Testimony of Two Men. 34.95 (0-88411-171-7) Amereon Ltd.

— There Was a Time. 1974. reprint ed. lib. bdg. 30.95 (0-88411-157-1) Amereon Ltd.

— This Side of Innocence. 1994. lib. bdg. 39.95 (1-56849-489-0) Buccaneer Bks.

— This Side of Innocence. 1976. reprint ed. lib. bdg. 31.95 (0-88411-164-4) Amereon Ltd.

— Time No Longer. Date not set. reprint ed. lib. bdg. 25.95 (0-88411-161-X, Aeonian Pr) Amereon Ltd.

— The Turnbulls. 1974. reprint ed. lib. bdg. 31.95 (0-88411-155-5) Amereon Ltd.

— Wicked Angel. 224p. reprint ed. lib. bdg. 19.95 (0-88411-167-9) Amereon Ltd.

— The Wide House. 1974. reprint ed. lib. bdg. 32.95 (0-88411-156-3) Amereon Ltd.

— Your Sins & Mine. 156p. reprint ed. lib. bdg. 19.95 (0-88411-168-7) Amereon Ltd.

Caldwell, Taylor, jt. auth. see Fernand, Ronald.

Caldwell, Terry H., et al. Special Health Care in the School. (Exceptional Children at Risk Ser.). 56p. 1991. pap. text 9.00 (0-86586-209-5, P352) Coun Exc Child.

***Caldwell, Thomas.** A Summer for a Lifetime! The Life & Times of George I. Purdy as Told to Thomas Caldwell. 200p. 2000. 24.95 (1-882897-45-5, Pub. by Lost Coast) Partners-West.

Caldwell, Thomas, et al. An Akkadian Grammar: A Translation of Lehrbuch Des Akkadischen. 3rd ed. (AKK.). 1978. pap. 20.00 (0-87462-444-4) Marquette.

Caldwell, Thomas A. Airland Combat: An Organization for Joint Warfare. LC 92-21120. (Illus.). 289p. 1992. pap. 13.00 (1-58566-045-0) Air Univ.

Caldwell, Timothy. Expressive Singing: Dalcroze Eurythmics for Voice. LC 94-2030. 177p. 1994. 41.00 (0-13-045295-5) P-H.

***Caldwell, V. M.** The Ocean Within. LC 99-13418. (Illus.). 236p. (J). (gr. 3-8). 1999. pap. 6.95 (1-57131-624-8) Milkweed Ed.

— The Ocean Within. LC 99-13418. (Illus.). 273p. (J). (gr. 6-9). 1999. 15.95 (1-57131-623-X) Milkweed Ed.

— Solar-Powered Sam. (Books for Young Learners). (Illus.). 12p. (J). (gr. k-2). 1999. pap. text 5.00 (1-57274-282-8, A2498) R Owen Pubs.

— Tides. LC 99-51671. (Illus.). (J). 2000. write for info. (1-57131-629-9) Milkweed Ed.

***Caldwell, Victoria.** Frommer's South Florida 2001. (Illus.). 2000. pap. 15.99 (0-7645-6090-5) IDG Bks.

Caldwell, W. G., ed. The Cretaceous System in the Western Interior of North America: The Proceedings of an International Symposium Organized by the Geological Association of Canada & Held at the University of Saskatchewan in Saskatoon, May 23-26, 1973. LC 76-370440. (Geological Association of Canada. Special Paper: No. 13). (Illus.). 675p. reprint ed. pap. 200.00 (0-608-18794-1, 203031600068) Bks Demand.

Caldwell, Wallace C., et al. Physics - The Root Science with Applications: Suggestions for the Teacher. 3rd rev. ed. (Illus.). vii, 404p. (YA). (gr. 10-13). 1996. text. write for info. (0-9663589-0-2) Archimedies Pubns.

— Physics - The Root Science with Applications Suppl. 1: Problem Solution Manual. 3rd rev. ed. (Illus.). 84p. (YA). (gr. 10-12). 1996. pap. write for info. (0-9663589-1-0) Archimedies Pubns.

Caldwell, Wallace E. Hellenic Conceptions of Peace. LC 19-18236. (Columbia University. Studies in the Social Sciences: No. 195). reprint ed. 20.00 (0-404-51195-3) AMS Pr.

Caldwell, Warren. Archaeological Investigations at the Coralville Reservoir, Iowa, Vol. 22. fac. ed. (Smithsonian Institution, Bureau of American Ethnology Ser.: Bulletin 179). (Illus.). 83p. (C). 1961. reprint ed. pap. text 9.70 (1-55567-700-2) Coyote Press.

Caldwell, Warren W., et al. Archaeological Investigation at the Hickey Brothers Site (39LM4), Big Bend Reservoir, Lyman County, South Dakota, Vol. 36. fac. ed. (Smithsonian Institution, Bureau of American Ethnology Ser.: Bulletin 189). (Illus.). 38p. (C). 1964. reprint ed. pap. text 4.38 (1-55567-705-3) Coyote Press.

Caldwell, Wayne E. Angels & Demons. Hale, D. Curtis, ed. 120p. 1997. pap. 7.99 (0-88019-369-7) Schmul Pub Co.

— The Fruit & Gifts of the Holy Spirit: Student Book. Peisker, Armor D., ed. 158p. 1979. pap., student ed. 8.95 (0-89827-005-7, BKM92) Wesleyan Pub Hse.

Caldwell, Wayne E. & Wesleyan Church, History Committee Staff, eds. Reformers & Revivalists: The History of the Wesleyan Church. (Wesleyan History Ser.). 718p. 1992. 17.95 (0-89827-095-2, BKJ09) Wesleyan Pub Hse.

Caldwell, Wayne E., jt. ed. see Carter, Charles W.

Caldwell, William. Tu Puedes Dejar de Sentirte Culpable. (Serie Tu Puedes - You Can Ser.).Tr. of You Can Stop Feeling Guilty. (SPA.). 1992. 1.79 (1-56063-154-6, 490488); pap. write for info. (0-614-27149-5) Editorial Unilit.

Caldwell, William L. Cancer of the Urinary Bladder: With Emphasis on Treatment by Irradiation. LC 72-96980. (Illus.). 128p. 1970. 12.50 (0-87527-003-4) Green.

Caldwell, Willie W. Stonewall Jim: A Biography of General James A. Walker, C. S. A. Savage, Lon K., ed. (Illus.). 280p. (YA). (gr. 10-12). 1990. 24.95 (0-9617256-4-8); pap. 12.95 (0-9617256-5-6) Northcross Hse.

***Caldwell, Wilma, ed.** Obesity Sourcebook: Basic Consumer Health Information about Diseases & Other Problems Associated with Obesity. (Health Reference Ser.). 400p. 2000. lib. bdg. 48.00 (0-7808-0333-7) Omnigraphics Inc.

Caldwell-Wilson, Marolyn. Whirlwind. (Judy Sullivan Romance Ser.). 1985. 14.95 (0-8027-0850-1) Walker & Co.

Caldwell-Wood, Naomi & Wood, Patrick W. Checklist of Bibliographies Appearing in the Bulletin of Bibliography, 1897-1987. 150p. 1989. lib. bdg. 79.50 (0-313-27668-4) Greenwood.

Cale, Emily & Coffee, Linda. The Diabetic Four Ingredient Cookbook. Date not set. pap. 9.95 (0-9628550-4-9, Pub. by Coffee & Cale) Bk Marketing Plus.

Cale, Emily & Coffee, Linda. Low Fat & Light Four Ingredient Cookbook. 144p. 1996. pap. 9.95 (0-9628550-2-2) Coffee & Cale.

Cale, Emily, jt. auth. see Coffee, Linda.

Cale, Hume H., jt. auth. see Smith, James H.

***Cale, John & Backris, Victor.** What's Welsh for Zen: The Autobiography of John Cale. (Illus.). 320p. 2000. pap. 24.95 (1-58234-068-4, Pub. by Bloomsbury Pubg) St Martin.

***Cale, Michelle.** Law & Society: An Introduction to Sources for Criminal & Legal History from 1800. (Readers' Guides Ser.: No. 14). 148p. 1999. pap. text 20.95 (1-873162-30-8, Pub. by PRO Pubns) Midpt Trade.

Cale, T. S. & Pintchovski, F. S., eds. Advanced Metallization for ULSI Applications 1992. (Conference Proceedings Ser.: Vol. V-8). 401p. 1993. text 65.00 (1-55899-192-1) Materials Res.

Caleb, A. & Slaton, D. E. Subpoena George Bush. 372p. 1993. pap. 18.95 (1-880365-60-X) Prof Pr NC.

Caledon Institute of Social Policy Staff, jt. auth. see Osberg, Lars.

Caleel, Richard T. & Littell, John. Surgeon! A Year in the Life of an Inner City Surgeon. 1988. pap. 3.95 (0-317-62245-5) St Martin.

Calef, Carol, jt. auth. see Smith, David.

Calef, John, ed. Siege of Penobscot by the Rebels & the Proceedings of the General Assembly & of the Council of the State of Massachusetts Bay Relating to the Penobscot Expedition. LC 78-140857. (Eyewitness Accounts of the American Revolution Ser.). (Illus.). 1971. reprint ed. 14.95 (0-405-01226-8) Ayer.

Calef, Richard T. New Cooks Almost Alone! A Gourmet Survival Manual. (Illus.). 113p. (Orig.). pap. text. write for info. (0-9634266-0-5) Calco Pub.

Calef, Wesley. Private Grazing & Public Lands. Bruchey, Stuart, ed. LC 78-56701. (Management of Public Lands in the U. S. Ser.). 1979. reprint ed. lib. bdg. 24.95 (0-405-11321-8) Ayer.

Caleff, George O. & Carter, Marion P. Holbrook Family, 1560-1800 Holbrook Family, Fifteen Sixty to Eighteen Hundred. 42p. 1997. reprint ed. pap. 8.50 (0-8328-9172-X); reprint ed. lib. bdg. 18.50 (0-8328-9171-1) Higginson Bk Co.

Calegari, Marc, tr. see Paul, VI, pseud.

Caleina Del Vecchio, Gloria. Patriarch Athenagoras - Man of Love. 1998. pap. 9.95 (1-887213-13-9) Blck Oak Pr.

Calella, John. Cooking Naturally. LC 78-54342. (Illus.). 1978. pap. 5.95 (0-915904-35-7) And-Or Bks.

Calendar, Carl, ed. see Kornbluth, Williams.

Calendar Marketing Association Staff, compiled by. Best Calendar Design & Graphics. (Illus.). 160p. 1995. 34.99 (1-56496-164-8) Rockport Pubs.

Calendar, R. The Bacteriophages, Vol. 1. LC 88-9770. (Viruses Ser.). (Illus.). 614p. (C). 1988. text 135.00 (0-306-42730-3, Kluwer Plenum) Kluwer Academic.

— The Bacteriophages, Vol. 2. LC 88-9770. (Viruses Ser.). (Illus.). 778p. (C). 1988. text 155.00 (0-306-42853-9, Kluwer Plenum) Kluwer Academic.

Calendar, Richard. Quality Living on a Tight Budget. large type ed. (Illus.). 300p. Date not set. pap. 24.95 (1-56559-915-2) HGI-Over Fifty.

Calender, June. Phantom Voices in Tibet. LC 98-83085. 256p. 2000. pap. 14.95 (0-88739-240-7) Creat Arts Bk.

Calenko, M. S., et al. Twelve Papers on Algebra, Number Theory & Topology. (Translations Ser.: Series 2, Vol. 58). 260p. 1967. 47.00 (0-8218-1758-2, TRANS2/58) Am Math.

An Asterisk (*) at the beginning of an entry indicates that the title is appearing for the first time.

— Twenty-Two Papers on Algebra, Number Theory, & Differential Geometry. LC 51-5559. (Translations Ser.: Series 2, Vol. 37). 429p. 1964. 47.00 (*0-8218-1737-X*, TRANS2/37) Am Math.

Calero, Henry H., jt. auth. see Morrison, William F.

Calero, Luis Fernando. Chiefdoms under Siege: Spain's Rule & Native Adaptation in the Southern Colombian Andes, 1535-1700. LC 96-25395. 234p. 1997. 50.00 (*0-8263-1772-3*) U of NM Pr.

Calero, Victor J. La Administracion de Inmuebles.Tr. of Property Management in Mexico. (SPA.). 208p. (Orig.). 1997. pap. 22.95 (*0-7931-2699-1*, 1700-0801, Real Estate Ed) Dearborn.

Calet. Deposition Process. 1992. text. write for info. (*0-442-01257-8*, VNR) Wiley.

Calet, Henri. Le Bouquet. (FRE.). 320p. 1983. pap. 12.95 (*0-7859-1974-0*, 2070374645) Fr & Eur.

Calev, Avraham, ed. Assessment of Neuropsychological Functions in Psychiatric Disorders. LC 98-29253. 1999. 74.95 (*0-88048-912-X*, 8912) Am Psychiatric.

Caley, Kevin, et al. Small Enterprise Development. 208p. 1993. 85.00 (*1-85396-215-5*, Pub. by P Chapman) Taylor & Francis.

***Caley, Matthew.** Thirst. 64p. 1999. pap. 14.95 (*1-871033-50-0*, Pub. by Slow Dancer) Dufour.

Caley, Michael T. & Sawada, Daiyo, eds. Mindscapes: The Epistemology of Magoroh Maruyama. 256p. 1994. text 48.00 (*2-88124-442-4*) Gordon & Breach.

Caley, Ray L. And the Shots Rang Out! A Musical Play about Harvey Milk, Incl. 17 Mus. Nos. 2nd rev. ed. (Illus.). 73p. 1990. reprint ed. spiral bd. 24.95 (*0-910987-06-8*) Dragons Lair.

Caley, Ray Leland. Lady of Sadness: A Play in 3 Acts. 57p. 1994. pap. text 14.95 (*0-910987-08-4*) Dragons Lair.

— The Little Blue Star Christmas Cantata. 37p. 1999. pap. text 14.95 (*0-910987-13-0*) Dragons Lair.

Caley, Ray Leland. New & Original Opera Librettos. LC 83-70679. (Illus.). 283p. (C). 1983. 20.00 (*0-910987-03-3*) Dragons Lair.

Caley, Ray Leland. The Song of Ramona. 45p. 1995. pap. text 14.95 (*0-910987-07-6*) Dragons Lair.

Calfee, Barbara E. Lawsuit Prevention Techniques for Mental Health Professionals, Chemical Dependency Specialists & Clergy. 135p. (Orig.). 1992. pap. 19.95 (*0-9633540-1-9*) ARC Pub.

— Nurses in the Courtroom: Cases & Commentary for Concerned Professionals. 250p. (Orig.). 1992. pap. text 25.00 (*0-9633540-2-7*) ARC Pub.

— Staying Out of Court: A Self-Assessment Guide for Nurses. 4th ed. 90p. 1994. pap. text, per., ring bd. 19.95 (*0-9633540-3-5*) ARC Pub.

Calfee, Barbara E. & Calfee, David A. What Do I Do? Who Do I Call? Resources for Health Care Professionals Seeking Information Related to the Legal Profession. 115p. (Orig.). 1995. pap. text 10.00 (*0-9633540-4-3*) ARC Pub.

Calfee, Carol, et al. Building a Full-Service School: A Step-by-Step Guide. LC 98-25318. (Education Ser.). 320p. 1998. pap. text 34.95 (*0-7879-4058-5*) Jossey-Bass.

Calfee, David A., jt. auth. see Calfee, Barbara E.

Calfee, John E. Fear of Persuasion: A New Perspective on Advertising. LC 97-37977. (Focus on Issues Ser.). 128p. 1997. pap. 19.95 (*2-940124-02-7*, Pub. by Agora Assn) Am Enterprise.

***Calfee, John E.** Prices, Markets & the Pharmaceutical Revolution. 87p. 2000. pap. 9.95 (*0-8447-7147-3*, Pub. by Am Enterprise) Pub Resources Inc.

Calfee, Robert & Bruning, Roger H. Rethinking the Teaching of Literacy. (C). 2002. pap. 27.00 (*0-13-462383-5*, Macmillan Coll) P-H.

Calfee, Robert C. & Patrick, Cynthia L. Teach Our Children Well: Bringing K-12 Education into the 21st Century. Goldman, Bruce, ed. (Portable Stanford Bks.). (Illus.). 234p. (Orig.). 1995. pap. 14.95 (*0-916318-55-9*) Stanford Alumni Assn.

Calfee, Robert C. & Perfumo, Pamela, eds. Writing Portfolios in the Classroom: Policy & Practice, Promise & Peril. LC 96-22692. 384p. 1996. text 79.95 (*0-8058-1835-9*); pap. text 34.00 (*0-8058-1836-7*) L Erlbaum Assocs.

Calfee, Robert C., jt. auth. see Chambliss, Marilyn J.

Calfee, Robert C., jt. ed. see Spivey, Nancy N.

Calfior, Fred J. Aerodynamics for Naval Aviators. 1994. pap. text, wbk. ed. 15.50 (*0-89100-433-5*, JS322707) Jeppesen Sanderson.

Calfior, Fred J. & Miller, Douglas W. Airienteering with "13MIKE" A Microsoft Flight Simulator Action Book, Bk. 3, Level A. LC 94-72676. 280p. 1995. 19.95 (*0-9639052-3-6*) CalMil Pubng.

— Flights of "13MIKE" A Microsoft Flight Simulator Companion, Bk. 1, Level A. LC 93-90850. 270p. (Orig.). 1994. 19.95 (*0-9639052-2-8*) CalMil Pubng.

— IFR Flights of "13MIKE" A Microsoft Flight Simulator Action Book, Bk. 2, Level B. LC 94-94166. 320p. 1994. 19.95 (*0-9639052-1-X*) CalMil Pubng.

Calgin, M. G. Lagrangian & Hamiltonian Mechanics: Solutions to the Exercises. 240p. 1999. 28.00 (*981-02-3782-0*) World Scientific Pub.

Calhoon, F. D. California Gold & the Highgraders. (Illus.). 375p. (Orig.). 1988. pap. 10.00 (*0-945862-00-8*) F D Calhoon.

— Coolies, Kanakas, & Cousin Jacks. (Illus.). 359p. (Orig.). 1986. pap. 8.00 (*0-945862-01-6*) F D Calhoon.

— Forty-Niner Irish. LC 77-72534. (Illus.). 194p. (Orig.). 1981. pap. write for info. (*0-945862-03-2*) F D Calhoon.

— The Lassen Trail: Memoirs of James Eaton. (Illus.). 178p. (Orig.). 1987. pap. 6.00 (*0-945862-02-4*) F D Calhoon.

Calhoon, John A., jt. auth. see Reed, James B.

Calhoon, Kenneth S. Fatherland: Novalis, Freud & the Discipline of Romance. LC 91-39468. (Kritik: German Literary Theory & Cultural Studies). (Illus.). 192p. (C). 1992. 29.95 (*0-8143-2367-7*) Wayne St U Pr.

Calhoon, Kenneth S., jt. ed. see Schultz, Karla L.

Calhoon, Margaret & Speno, Lynn. Tallulah Falls, GA. LC 98-87319. (Images of America Ser.). (Illus.). 128p. 1998. pap. 16.99 (*0-7524-0941-7*) Arcadia Publng.

Calhoon, Robert M. Dominion & Liberty: Ideology in the Anglo-American World, 1660-1801. (Illus.). 160p. (C). 1994. pap. text 13.95 (*0-88295-913-1*) Harlan Davidson.

Calhoon, Robert M., et al. Loyalists & Community in North America, 158. LC 93-49539. (Contributions in American History Ser.: No. 158). 240p. 1994. 59.95 (*0-313-28947-6*, Greenwood Pr) Greenwood.

Calhoon, Tom S. Multimedia & Computer-Based Training: New Paradigms for Success. 150p. 1993. ring bd. 185.00 (*1-56909-008-4*) Info Systs Mgmt.

Calhoun. Perspectives Criminal Justice. 1996. 6.75 (*0-07-217377-7*) McGraw.

— Psychological Adjustments: Human Relationships. 3rd ed. 1990. 14.06 (*0-07-009769-0*) McGraw.

— Sociological Inquiry. 1998. 19.95 (*0-07-011507-9*) McGraw.

***Calhoun.** Spinout! 112p. (YA). 1999. mass mkt. 3.99 (*0-06-106560-9*) HarpC.

Calhoun. Vocational & Career Education. (Education Ser.). 1976. pap. 16.00 (*0-534-00437-7*) Wadsworth Pub.

Calhoun, jt. auth. see Townsley.

***Calhoun, Dia.** Aria of the Sea. 264p. (YA). (gr. 4-7). 2000. 15.95 (*1-890817-25-2*, Pub. by Winslow Pr) Publishers Group.

— Firegold. (Illus.). (J). 1999. 15.30 (*0-606-18341-8*) Turtleback.

Calhoun, Dia. Firegold. LC 98-89830. (Illus.). 196p. (YA). (gr. 7-12). 2000. 15.95 (*1-890817-10-4*, Pub. by Winslow Pr); pap. 9.95 (*1-890817-28-7*, Pub. by Winslow Pr) Publishers Group.

Calhoun, Linda M. Air Traffic Control: Improved Cost Information Needed to Make Billion Dollar Modernization Investment Decisions. (Illus.). 60p. (C). 1999. reprint ed. pap. text 20.00 (*0-7881-4379-4*) DIANE Pub.

Calhoun, Adele, jt. auth. see Mains, Karen.

***Calhoun, Ann.** The Arts & Crafts Movement in New Zealand, 1870-1940. (Illus.). 300p. 2000. 59.95 (*1-86940-229-4*, Pub. by Auckland Univ) Paul & Co Pubs.

Calhoun, Arthur W. A Social History of the American Family from Colonial Times to the Present. 1972. 60.95 (*0-405-03886-0*) Ayer.

Calhoun, B. B. His & Hers: Summer Dreams. 128p. (J). (gr. 6-8). 1998. mass mkt. 3.99 (*0-380-78471-8*, Avon Bks) Morrow Avon.

— Journal of the NGI (Winter, 1995) 176p. 1995. 50.00 (*0-614-05006-5*, NGW5) Capitol Publns.

— New in Town. (His & Hers Ser.). 128p. (Orig.). (YA). 1997. mass mkt. 3.99 (*0-380-78470-X*, Avon Bks) Morrow Avon.

Calhoun, Barbara Ann. Tale of Two Gardens. 1998. pap. text 15.99 (*0-9661138-0-2*) Tell the Wrld.

***Calhoun, Bruce.** Close Calls & Foolhardy Romances: The Maturation of an Environmentalist. 192p. 2000. pap. 12.95 (*1-882897-41-2*) Lost Coast.

Calhoun, Bruce & Calhoun, Dave. Cruising the San Juan Islands. 2nd ed. 208p. 1991. reprint ed. pap. 24.95 (*0-935727-07-8*) Weatherly Pr.

Calhoun, Calfrey C. & Robinson, Bettye W. Managing the Learning Process in Business Education. 756p. (C). 1995. pap. text 40.00 (*1-56883-058-0*) Colonial Pr AL.

Calhoun, Calfrey C., ed. see Rhodes, George S.

Calhoun, Catherine. Egyptian Designs. (International Design Library). (Illus.). 48p. 1983. pap. 6.95 (*0-88045-012-6*) Stemmer Hse.

Calhoun, Charles. Wisconsin. 2nd ed. LC 96-49821. (Compass American Guides Ser.). 320p. 1997. pap. 18.95 (*1-878867-49-0*, Compass Amrcn) Fodors Travel.

Calhoun, Charles C. A Small College in Maine: Two Hundred Years of Bowdoin. LC 93-79513. (Illus.). 275p. (Orig.). (C). 1994. pap. 21.95 (*0-916606-24-4*) Bowdoin Coll.

Calhoun, Charles H., et al. Ethics & the CPA: Building Trust & Value-Added Services. LC 98-17658. 257p. 1998. 89.95 (*0-471-18488-8*) Wiley.

Calhoun, Charles R. Tin Can Sailor: Life Aboard the USS Sterett, 1939-1945. LC 93-14743. (Illus.). 198p. 1993. 26.95 (*1-55750-108-4*) Naval Inst Pr.

Calhoun, Charles R. & Fulop, Laszlo G. The Hurricanes Are Coming: How to Retrofit Your Coastal Home to Prepare for Hurricanes. (Home Improvement & Construction Ser.). (Illus.). 79p. (Orig.). 1996. pap. 19.95 (*0-9658613-0-9*) Callaz Res.

Calhoun, Charles W. The Gilded Age: Essays on the Origins of Modern America. LC 95-17891. (Illus.). 348p. 1995. pap. 17.95 (*0-8420-2500-6*); text 45.00 (*0-8420-2499-9*) Scholarly Res Inc.

— Gilded Age Cato: The Life of Walter Q. Gresham. LC 87-24171. 288p. 1988. text 34.95 (*0-8131-1615-5*) U Pr of Ky.

Calhoun, Charles W., jt. ed. see Anderson, David L.

Calhoun, Charles W., jt. ed. see Woodworth, Steven E.

Calhoun, Cherlene, ed. Inspirational Moments from the Heart. 56p. 1993. pap. 7.50 (*0-9626735-6-0*) Rabeth Pub Co.

***Calhoun, Cheshire.** Feminism, the Family & the Politics of the Closet: Lesbian & Gay Displacement. 240p. 2000. 29.95 (*0-19-829559-6*) OUP.

Calhoun, Cheshire & Solomon, Robert C., eds. What Is an Emotion? Classic Readings in Philosophical Psychology. 368p. 1984. pap. text 23.95 (*0-19-503304-3*) OUP.

***Calhoun County Museum Staff.** Cemeteries of Families of Amelia Township & Calhoun County, South Carolina. LC 98-50016. 1998. write for info. (*0-87152-521-6*) Reprint.

Calhoun, Craig. Critical Social Theory: Culture, History & the Challenge of Difference. (Twentieth Century Social Theory Ser.). 280p. (C). 1995. pap. 25.95 (*1-55786-288-5*) Blackwell Pubs.

— Nationalism. LC 97-30511. (Concepts in Social Thought Ser.). 144p. 1998. pap. 14.95 (*0-8166-3121-2*); text 37.95 (*0-8166-3120-4*) U of Minn Pr.

— Neither Gods nor Emperors: Students & the Struggle for Democracy in China. 1997. pap. text 15.95 (*0-520-21161-8*, Pub. by U CA Pr) Cal Prin Full Svc.

— The Question of Class Struggle: The Social Foundation of Popular Radicalism During the Industrial Revolution. LC 81-2018. xiv, 322p. (C). 1994. reprint ed. pap. text 11.00 (*0-226-09091-4*) U Ch Pr.

— Social Theory & the Politics of Identity. LC 94-203937. 352p. 1994. pap. text 26.95 (*1-55786-473-X*) Blackwell Pubs.

Calhoun, Craig, ed. Business Institutions, Vol. 12. (Comparative Social Research Ser.). 379p. 1990. 78.50 (*1-55938-075-6*) Jai Pr.

— Comparative Social Research: Religion & Belief Systems, Vol. 15. 1996. 78.50 (*1-55938-649-5*) Jai Pr.

— Culture, Vol. 11. (Comparative Social Research Ser.). 342p. 1987. 78.50 (*0-89232-902-5*) Jai Pr.

— Religious Institutions, Vol. 13. (Comparative Social Research Ser.). 248p. 1992. 78.50 (*1-55938-239-4*) Jai Pr.

— Transcendence in Society Suppl. 1: Case Studies. (Comparative Social Research Ser.). 252p. 1990. 78.50 (*1-55938-070-5*) Jai Pr.

— The Transition from State Socialism in Eastern Europe Vol. 14: The Case of Hungary. (Comparative Social Research Ser.). 232p. 1994. 78.50 (*1-55938-527-8*) Jai Pr.

Calhoun, Craig, et al, eds. Bordieu: Critical Perspectives. LC 93-12631. 296p. 1993. pap. text 16.95 (*0-226-09093-0*); lib. bdg. 49.95 (*0-226-09092-2*) U Ch Pr.

Calhoun, Craig & Light, Donald. Sociology. 7th ed. LC 96-11433. 648p. (C). 1996. 65.00 (*0-07-038069-4*) McGraw.

Calhoun, Craig & McGowan, John, eds. Hannah Arendt & the Meaning of Politics. LC 97-10901. (Contradictions of Modernity Ser.: Vol. 6). 376p. 1997. pap. 21.95 (*0-8166-2917-X*); text 54.95 (*0-8166-2916-1*) U of Minn Pr.

Calhoun, Craig & Ritzer, George, eds. Social Problems. 1992. text. write for info. (*0-07-152746-X*) McGraw.

Calhoun, Craig & Thomasson, Richard, eds. Comparative Social Research: Annual, Vol. 3. 350p. (Orig.). 1980. 78.50 (*0-89232-150-4*) Jai Pr.

Calhoun, Craig & Tomasson, Richard F., eds. Comparative Social Research: Religion & Belief Systems, Vol. 5. 391p. 1982. 78.50 (*0-89232-295-0*) Jai Pr.

— Comparative Social Research: Welfare State, Vol. 6. 378p. 1984. 78.50 (*0-89232-329-9*) Jai Pr.

— Comparative Social Research Annual, Vol. 2. 347p. 1979. 78.50 (*0-89232-112-1*) Jai Pr.

— Comparative Social Research Annual, Vol. 4. 359p. 1981. 78.50 (*0-89232-188-1*) Jai Pr.

— Deviance. (Comparative Social Research Ser.: Vol. 8). 352p. 1986. 78.50 (*0-89232-520-8*) Jai Pr.

— Historical Studies, Vol. 9. (Comparative Social Research Ser.). 392p. 1986. 78.50 (*0-89232-574-7*) Jai Pr.

Calhoun, Craig, et al. Sociology. 6th ed. LC 93-25016. 1993. VHS. write for info. (*0-07-037943-2*) McGraw.

— Sociology. 6th ed. LC 93-25016. (C). 1993. text 55.25 (*0-07-037879-7*) McGraw.

Calhoun, Craig, ed. see Tomasson, R.

Calhoun, Craig J. The Question of Class Struggle: Social Foundations of Popular Radicalism During the Industrial Revolution. LC 81-2018. 335p. reprint ed. pap. 103.90 (*0-608-09277-0*, 205415100004) Bks Demand.

Calhoun, Craig J. & Ianni, Francis A., eds. The Anthropological Study of Education. (World Anthropology Ser.). xii, 360p. 1976. 39.25 (*90-279-7769-0*) Mouton.

Calhoun, Creighton L., Jr. Old Southern Apples. (Illus.). 336p. 1995. 49.95 (*0-939923-37-8*); pap. 39.95 (*0-939923-59-9*) M & W Pub Co.

Calhoun, Daniel F. The United Front: The TUC & the Russians, 1923-1928. LC 75-23486. (Soviet & East European Studies). 462p. reprint ed. pap. 131.70 (*0-608-12075-8*, 2024572) Bks Demand.

Calhoun, Daniel H. Professional Lives in America. Structure & Aspiration, 1750-1850. LC 65-22042. (Center for the Study of the History of Liberty in America Ser.). (Illus.). 247p. reprint ed. 76.60 (*0-8357-9174-2*, 201774500007) Bks Demand.

Calhoun, D'Ann, ed. see Farr, Naunerle C.

Calhoun, D'Ann, ed. see Verne, Jules.

Calhoun, Dave, jt. auth. see Calhoun, Bruce.

Calhoun, David B. History of Princeton Seminary. 495p. 1994. 35.99 (*0-85151-670-X*) Banner of Truth.

— History of Princeton Seminary Vol. 2: The Majestic Testimony 1869-1929, 2 vols. 560p. 1995. 32.99 (*0-85151-695-5*) Banner of Truth.

— A Place for Truth: The Bicentennial James Henley Thornwell Lectures. Berry, Stephen R., ed. 75p. 1998. pap. text 9.95 (*1-884416-16-0*) A Press.

Calhoun, Donald. Spirituality & Community: An Autobiographical Memoir. (Illus.). 200p. (Orig.). (C). 1995. pap. 14.95 (*0-87047-101-5*) Schenkman Bks Inc.

Calhoun, Donald W. Sport, Culture, & Personality. 2nd ed. LC 86-27196. (Illus.). 394p. reprint ed. pap. 122.20 (*0-608-07094-7*, 206732100009) Bks Demand.

Calhoun, Dorothy, ed. see Hardy, Thomas.

Calhoun, Emily F. How to Use Action Research in the Self-Renewing School. LC 94-8999. 1994. pap. 8.95 (*0-87120-229-8*, 194030) ASCD.

— Teaching Beginning Reading & Writing with the Picture Word Inductive Model. LC 98-58153. vii, 127 p. 1999. pap. 16.95 (*0-87120-337-5*, 199025) ASCD.

Calhoun, Emily F., jt. auth. see Joyce, Bruce R.

Calhoun, Emily F., jt. ed. see Joyce, Bruce R.

***Calhoun, Florence.** Choosing a Career in Teaching. LC 00-8772. (World of Work Ser.). (C). 2000. lib. bdg. write for info. (*0-8239-3247-8*) Rosen Group.

Calhoun Forecki, Marcia. Speak to Me. 2nd rev. ed. LC 84-28740. 160p. 1985. pap. 12.95 (*0-930323-68-8*) Gallaudet Univ Pr.

Calhoun, Frances B. Miss Minerva & William Green Hill. LC 75-20498. (Tennesseana Editions Ser.). (Illus.). 246p. 1976. 16.95 (*0-87049-182-2*) U of Tenn Pr.

Calhoun, Frederick S. Power & Principle: Armed Intervention in Wilsonian Foreign Policy. LC 85-24086. 345p. 1986. 28.00 (*0-87338-327-3*) Kent St U Pr.

— Uses of Force & Wilsonian Foreign Policy. LC 92-31632. (American Diplomatic History Ser.: No. 6). 184p. (Orig.). 1993. pap. 15.00 (*0-87338-464-4*) Kent St U Pr.

Calhoun, Frederick S., et al. Letters Received by the Attorney General, 1809-1870: Western Law & Order. LC 96-3287. (Research Collections in American Legal History). 1996. 1515.00 (*1-55655-634-9*) U Pubns Amer.

Calhoun, Fryar. Earthquake Survival Guide: Emergency Planning for Family, Home, Workplace & School. (Illus.). 1994. pap. 2.95 (*0-9625335-1-3*) Magnet Pr CA.

Calhoun, Fryar, jt. auth. see Cassady, Jim.

Calhoun, George. Digital Cellular Radio. (Telecommunications Applications Library). 450p. 1988. text 73.00 (*0-89006-266-8*) Artech Hse.

***Calhoun, George.** Third Generation Wireless Communications: Post Shannon Architectures. (Universal Personal Communications Ser.). 2000. 75.00 (*1-58053-043-5*) Artech Hse.

***Calhoun, George M.** The Growth of Criminal Law in Ancient Greece. LC 99-43132. 1999. 50.00 (*1-58477-037-6*) Lawbk Exchange.

Calhoun, George M. The Growth of Criminal Law in Ancient Greece. LC 73-10874. x, 149p. 1974. reprint ed. lib. bdg. 22.50 (*0-8371-7043-5*, CACL, Greenwood Pr) Greenwood.

Calhoun, George M., et al. A Working Bibliography of Greek Law. (Harvard Series of Legal Bibliographies: Vol. 1). xix, 144p. 1980. reprint ed. lib. bdg. 45.00 (*0-89941-132-0*, 300120) W S Hein.

Calhoun, Grace O., et al. Growing up Country & Liking It! (Illus.). 64p. (Orig.). 1996. pap. 6.95 (*1-57072-035-5*) Overmountain Pr.

Calhoun, Graig, ed. Habermas & the Public Sphere. (Studies in Contemporary German Social Thought). (Illus.). 512p. (C). 1993. pap. text 21.50 (*0-262-53114-3*) MIT Pr.

Calhoun, Jackie. Birds of a Feather. LC 98-46299. 192p. 1999. pap. 11.95 (*1-56280-240-2*) Naiad Pr.

— Changes. 208p. 1995. pap. 10.95 (*1-56280-083-3*) Naiad Pr.

— Lifestyles. 304p. 1990. pap. 10.95 (*0-941483-57-6*) Naiad Pr.

— Love or Money. 256p. (Orig.). 1996. pap. 10.95 (*1-56280-147-3*) Naiad Pr.

— Seasons of the Heart. LC 96-45489. 256p. (Orig.). 1997. pap. 11.95 (*1-56280-167-8*) Naiad Pr.

— Triple Exposure. LC 94-16240. 224p. 1994. pap. 10.95 (*1-56280-067-1*) Naiad Pr.

Calhoun, James, jt. ed. see Calhoun, Nancy H.

Calhoun, James F. & Acocella, Joan R. Psychology of Adjustment & Human Relations. 3rd ed. 512p. (C). 1990. 62.81 (*0-07-557738-0*) McGraw.

— Psychology of Adjustment & Human Relations. 3rd ed. (C). 1990. text, student ed. 22.74 (*0-07-009761-5*) McGraw.

Calhoun, Jeryn W. How to Buy a Business with No Money Down. 10th ed. 130p. 1999. pap. 19.50 (*1-56150-298-7*) Intl Wealth.

***Calhoun, Jeryn W.** How to Buy a Business with No Money Down. 11th ed. 130p. 2000. pap. 19.50 (*1-56150-358-4*) Intl Wealth.

Calhoun, Jeryn W. How to Buy a Business with No Money Down: The Complete Guide to Finding, & Buying, the Business You Want. 2nd ed. 130p. (Orig.). 1996. pap. 19.50 (*1-56150-197-2*) Intl Wealth.

— How to Buy a Business with No Money Down: The Complete Guide to Finding, & Buying, the Business You Want. 2nd ed. 130p. (Orig.). 1998. pap. 19.50 (*1-56150-247-2*) Intl Wealth.

***Calhoun, Jim.** Dare to Dream: Connecticut Basketball's Remarkable March to the National Championship, Vol. 1. 240p. 1999. 25.00 (*0-7679-0475-3*) Broadway BDD.

Calhoun, John & Post, C. Gordon. A Disquisition on Government & Selections from the Discourse. LC 95-79153. 139p. (C). 1995. reprint ed. pap. text 9.95 (*0-87220-293-3*); reprint ed. lib. bdg. 29.95 (*0-87220-294-1*) Hackett Pub.

Calhoun, John, ed. see Wommack, Andrew.

Calhoun, John A., et al. What, Me Evaluate? A Basic Evaluation Guide for Citizen Crime Prevention Programs / National Crime Prevention Council. LC 86-62890. 73 p. 1986. write for info. (*0-934513-01-5*) Natl Crime DC.

Calhoun, John B., ed. Environment & Population: Problems of Adaptation. LC 82-19086. (Illus.). 486p. 1983. 95.00 (*0-275-90955-7*, C0955, Praeger Pubs) Greenwood.

Calhoun, John C. Address to the People of the South. (Works of John Caldwell Calhoun). 1990. reprint ed. lib. bdg. 90.00 (*0-7812-2238-9*) Rprt Serv.

C

— Complete Works. (Works of John Calswell Calhoun). 1990. reprint ed. lib. bdg. 300.00 (0-7812-2240-0) Rprt Serv.

— Correspondence. (Works of John Calswell Calhoun). 1990. reprint ed. lib. bdg. 79.00 (0-7812-2241-9) Rprt Serv.

— Papers of John C. Calhoun, Vol. 4, 1819-1820. Hemphill, W. Edwin, ed. LC 59-10351. xxii, 820p. 1969. text 59.95 (0-87249-150-1) U of SC Pr.

— Papers of John C. Calhoun, Vol. 5, 1820-1821. Wilson, Clyde N. et al, eds. LC 59-10351. (Illus.). 791p. 1971. text 59.95 (0-87249-210-9) U of SC Pr.

— The Papers of John C. Calhoun, Vol. 7, 1822-1823. Hemphill, W. Edwin, ed. LC 59-10351. iiv, 663p. 1973. text 59.95 (0-87249-288-5) U of SC Pr.

— Papers of John C. Calhoun, Vol. 15. Wilson, Clyde N., ed. LC 59-10351. (Papers of John C. Calhoun Ser.). 902p. 1984. text 59.95 (0-87249-418-7) U of SC Pr.

— The Papers of John C. Calhoun Vol. 19: June 9 - September 30, 1844. Wilson, Clyde N., ed. LC 59-10351. (Papers of John C. Calhoun Ser.). 966p. 1990. text 59.95 (0-87249-677-5) U of SC Pr.

— The Papers of John C. Calhoun Vol. 20: October-December, 1844. Wilson, Clyde N., ed. LC 59-10351. 738p. 1991. text 59.95 (0-87249-769-0) U of SC Pr.

— The Papers of John C. Calhoun Vol. 21: January-June 1845. Wilson, Clyde N., ed. LC 59-10351. 667p. 1993. text 59.95 (0-87249-889-1) U of SC Pr.

— The Papers of John C. Calhoun, 1843-1844, Vol. 17. Wilson, Clyde N., ed. 988p. 1987. text 59.95 (0-87249-483-7) U of SC Pr.

— The Papers of John C. Calhoun, 1845-1846, 22 vols. , Vol. XXII. Wilson, Clyde N., ed. LC 59-10351. 856p. 1995. text 59.95 (1-57003-023-5) U of SC Pr.

— The Papers of John C. Calhoun, 1837-1839, Vol. 14. Wilson, Clyde N., ed. LC 59-10351. (Illus.). 713p. 1981. text 59.95 (0-87249-409-8) U of SC Pr.

— Union & Liberty: The Political Philosophy of John C. Calhoun. Lence, Ross M., ed. LC 92-10391. 656p. 1992. 25.00 (0-86597-102-1); pap. 9.50 (0-86597-103-X) Liberty Fund.

— Works, 4 vols., Set. (Works of John Calswell Calhoun). 1990. reprint ed. lib. bdg. 300.00 (0-7812-2239-7) Rprt Serv.

— The Works of John Calswell Calhoun. 1990. reprint ed. lib. bdg. 63.00 (0-685-27708-9) Rprt Serv.

Calhoun, John C., jt. auth. see Wilson, Clyde N.

Calhoun, Joseph H., et al. Atlas of Pediatric Ophthalmic Surgery. (Illus.). 320p. 1987. text 115.00 (0-7216-1104-4, W B Saunders Co) Harcrt Hlth Sci Grp.

Calhoun, Joseph H., jt. auth. see Simon, John W.

Calhoun, Julius C., jt. auth. see Fisk, Edward R.

Calhoun, K. & Stiernberg, C., eds. Surgery of the Lip. (American Academy of Facial Plastic & Reconstructive Surgery Monograph: Vol. 9). (Illus.). 112p. 1991. pap. text 82.00 (0-86577-409-9) Thieme Med Pubs.

Calhoun, Karen H., et al. Basic Head & Neck Pathology. LC 95-42455. (Monograph). (Illus.). 228p. (Orig.). 1996. pap. text 30.00 (1-56772-020-X) AAO-HNS.

Calhoun, Keith Benton, see Benton Calhoun, Keith.

***Calhoun, Kenneth G. & Nassar, Mark.** Advanced Online Day Trading - The NASDAQ Level 2 Workbook: How to Successfully Daytrade Nasdaq Stocks Online. (Illus.). 207p. 2000. pap., wbk. ed. 39.95 (0-9677855-0-2) Hawaii Business.

Calhoun, Laurie. Philosophy Unmasked: A Skeptic's Critique. LC 97-1484. 208p. 1997. 25.00 (0-7006-0833-8) U Pr of KS.

Calhoun, Lawrence G. & Tedeschi, Richard G. Facilitating Posttraumatic Growth: A Clinician's Guide. LC 99-18525. (Personality & Clinical Psychology Ser.). 176p. 1999. 24.95 (0-8058-2412-X) L Erlbaum Assocs.

Calhoun, Marcy. Are You Really Too Sensitive? How to Understand & Develop Your Sensitivity as the Strength It Is. LC 87-7983. 208p. 1987. pap. 12.95 (0-931892-10-4) B Dolphin Pub.

Calhoun, Margaret. Pioneers of the Mono Basin. (Illus.). 172p. 1984. reprint ed. pap. 7.95 (0-932347-07-X) Artemisia Pr.

***Calhoun, Mary.** Blue-Ribbon Henry. LC 97-6470. (Illus.). 40p. (J). 1999. 15.93 (0-688-14675-9, Wm Morrow) Morrow Avon.

Calhoun, Mary. Blue-Ribbon Henry. LC 97-6470. (Illus.). 40p. (J). (gr. k-3). 1999. 16.00 (0-688-14674-0, Wm Morrow) Morrow Avon.

— Cross-Country Cat. LC 78-31718. (Illus.). 40p. (J). (gr. k-3). 1979. 17.00 (0-688-22186-6, Wm Morrow) Morrow Avon.

Calhoun, Mary. Cross-Country Cat. LC 78-31718. (Illus.). 40p. (J). (gr. k-3). 1986. mass mkt. 5.95 (0-688-06519-8, Wm Morrow) Morrow Avon.

— Cross-Country Cat. (J). 1979. 10.15 (0-606-02478-6, Pub. by Turtleback) Demco.

— Flood. LC 96-14836. (Illus.). 40p. (J). 1997. 15.89 (0-688-13920-5, Wm Morrow) Morrow Avon.

Calhoun, Mary. Flood. LC 96-14836. (Illus.). 40p. (J). (gr. k up). 1997. 16.00 (0-688-13919-1, Wm Morrow) Morrow Avon.

— Henry the Sailor Cat. LC 92-29794. (Illus.). 40p. (J). (gr. k up). 1994. 16.00 (0-688-10840-7, Wm Morrow) Morrow Avon.

— Henry the Sailor Cat. (Illus.). 40p. (J). (gr. k-3). 1998. mass mkt. 4.95 (0-688-15846-3, Wm Morrow) Morrow Avon.

— Henry the Sailor Cat. 1998. 10.15 (0-606-13474-3, Pub. by Turtleback) Demco.

— Henry the X-Mas Cat. (J). Date not set. write for info. (0-688-16560-5, Wm Morrow) Morrow Avon.

— Henry the X-Mas Cat. (Illus.). (J). Date not set. lib. bdg. write for info. (0-688-16561-3, Wm Morrow) Morrow Avon.

Calhoun, Mary. High-Wire Henry. LC 89-35642. (Illus.). 40p. (J). (gr. k up). 1991. 15.95 (0-688-08983-6, Wm Morrow) Morrow Avon.

Calhoun, Mary. Hot-Air Henry. LC 80-26189. (Illus.). 40p. (J). (gr. k-3). 1981. 16.00 (0-688-00501-2, Wm Morrow) Morrow Avon.

Calhoun, Mary. Hot-Air Henry. LC 80-26189. (Illus.). 40p. (J). (ps-3). 1984. mass mkt. 5.95 (0-688-04068-3, Wm Morrow) Morrow Avon.

Calhoun, Mary. Hot-Air Henry. (Reading Rainbow Bks.). (J). 1981. 10.15 (0-606-02487-5, Pub. by Turtleback) Demco.

Calhoun, Mary. Hot-Air Henry. unabridged ed. (Picture Book Read-Alongs Ser.). (J). 1991. pap. text 15.98 incl. audio (0-8072-6037-1, MR 27SP) Listening Lib.

Calhoun, Mary. Julie's Tree. LC 87-45857. 160p. (J). (gr. 2-5). 1988. 11.95 (0-06-020995-X) HarpC Child Bks.

— Katie John. LC 60-5775. (Illus.). (J). (gr. 4-7). 1960. lib. bdg. 15.89 (0-06-020951-8) HarpC Child Bks.

— Katie John & Heathcliff. LC 80-7770. (I Can Read Bks.). 160p. (J). (ps-3). 1981. pap. 3.50 (0-06-440120-0, HarpTrophy) HarpC Child Bks.

— Tonio's Cat. LC 95-35386. (Illus.). 32p. (J). 1996. lib. bdg. 15.93 (0-688-13315-0, Wm Morrow) Morrow Avon.

— Tonio's Cat. LC 95-35386. (Illus.). 32p. (J). (gr. k up). 1996. 16.00 (0-688-13314-2, Wm Morrow) Morrow Avon.

Calhoun, Mary J. In My Father's Hands: A Book of Devotional Thoughts. 52p. 1997. pap. 10.00 (1-57502-602-3, P01735) Morris Pubng.

— On Angel's Wings. 58p. (Orig.). 1995. pap. write for info. (1-57502-019-X, P00406) Morris Pubng.

***Calhoun-Medlock, Nancy.** Echoes: Foundation of Eternity. LC 99-97448. 88p. 1999. pap. 8.99 (0-9656256-2-1) S M J.

Calhoun-Medlock, Nancy. Light: Finding the Way. 67p. 1998. pap. 3.99 (0-9656256-1-3) S M J.

Calhoun, Milburn. Louisiana Almanac, 2000-2001. (Illus.). 672p. 1997. pap. 16.95 (1-56554-771-3) Pelican.

Calhoun, Milburn, ed. Louisiana Almanac, 2000-2001. (Illus.). 704p. 1997. 26.00 (1-56554-770-5) Pelican.

Calhoun, Moses. Out of Control: The Addictive Behavioral Personality. (Illus.). 250p. 1993. 29.95 (0-9638949-0-0) Winning Artist.

Calhoun, Nancy H. & Calhoun, James, eds. Guia Pelican a las Casas de Plantaciones de Louisiana. Smith, Josie H., tr. LC 81-10646. (Pelican Guide Ser.). Orig. Title: Pelican Guide to Plantation Homes of Louisiana. (SPA., Illus.). 128p. 1982. pap. 8.95 (0-88289-292-4) Pelican.

Calhoun, Newell M. Litchfield County Sketches. 177p. 1997. reprint ed. pap. 22.00 (0-8328-5660-6) Higginson Bk Co.

Calhoun, Randall. Dorothy Parker: A Bio-Bibliography, 4. LC 92-30882. (Bio-Bibliographies in American Literature Ser.: No. 4). 192p. 1992. lib. bdg. 52.95 (0-313-26507-0, CDY, Greenwood Pr) Greenwood.

Calhoun, Ray. Pretty Faire Eats: Dr. Ray's Recipe Book of Pretty Faire Eats. 288p. 1991. pap. 11.95 (0-9630855-0-6) Pretty Faire.

Calhoun, Richard J. Galway Kinnell. (Twayne's United States Authors Ser.). 150p. 1992. 23.95 (0-8057-3955-6) Macmillan.

Calhoun, Russ. Lost Heritage: The People of Old Butler, Tennessee & the Watauga Valley. (Illus.). 387p. 1998. pap. 19.95 (1-57072-081-9) Overmountain Pr.

Calhoun, Sharon C. & English, Billy J. The Wisconsin Adventure. large type ed. (Illus.). 240p. (J). (gr. 4). 1997. text 24.95 (0-9619484-5-0) Apple Corps Pubs.

— The Wisconsin Story. 202p. (J). (gr. 4). 1987. 59.95 (0-9619484-1-8) Apple Corps Pubs.

— The Wisconsin Story. 202p. (J). (gr. 4). 1992. 18.95 (0-9619484-0-X, TXU-299476) Apple Corps Pubs.

Calhoun, Sharon C., jt. auth. see English, Billie J.

Calhoun, Susan & Bradley, Jane. Nutrition, Cancer & You: What You Need to Know, & Where to Start. McKenzie, Michael, ed. LC 96-85765. 192p. 1996. pap. 12.95 (1-886110-06-9, Pub. by Addax Pubng) Midpt Trade.

***Calhoun, T. B.** In the Groove. (NASCAR Pole Position Adventure Ser.: No. 2). 128p. (YA). (gr. 5-8). 1998. mass mkt. 3.99 (0-06-105937-4) HarpC.

— Race Ready. (NASCAR Pole Position Adventure Ser.: No. 3). 128p. (YA). (gr. 5-8). 1998. mass mkt. 3.99 (0-06-105959-5) HarpC.

— Rolling Thunder. (NASCAR Pole Position Adventure Ser.: No. 1). 128p. (YA). (gr. 5-8). 1998. mass mkt. 3.99 (0-06-105930-7) HarpC.

— Speed Demon. (NASCAR Pole Position Adventure Ser.: No. 4). 128p. (YA). (gr. 5-8). 1999. mass mkt. 3.99 (0-06-105964-1) HarpC.

Calhoun, Thomas C., jt. ed. see Thio, Alex.

Calhoun, Thomas O. Henry Vaughan: The Achievement of Silex Scintillans. LC 79-51851. 272p. 1981. 35.00 (0-87413-165-0) U Delaware Pr.

Calhoun, Thomas O., et al, eds. The Collected Works of Abraham Cowley Vol. 2: Poems (1656), Part I; the Mistress. LC 87-40005. (Illus.). 656p. 1993. 80.00 (0-87413-408-0) U Delaware Pr.

***Calhoun, Tom.** Africa's Rose: A Novel. 1999. 25.00 (0-7388-0548-3); pap. 18.00 (0-7388-0549-1) Xlibris Corp.

Calhoun, W. L. History of the Forty-Second Regiment Georgia Volunteers, Infantry - C. S. A. Perry, Phillip A., ed. 52p. 1993. reprint ed. pap. 12.95 (1-56869-045-2) Oldbuck Pr.

Calhoun, Wes. Texas Nighthawks. large type ed. (Linford Western Library). 256p. 1992. pap. 16.99 (0-7089-7174-1, Linford) Ulverscroft.

Calhoun, William G. Fort Scott: A Pictorial History. LC 77-93303. (Illus.). (Orig.). pap. 11.00 (0-9601568-1-X) Historic Pres Bourbon.

Calhoun, William P. The Caucasian & the Negro in the United States: They Must Separate, If Not, Then Extermination. a Proposed Solution : Colonization. Grob, Gerald N., ed. LC 76-46070. (Anti-Movements in America Ser.). 1977. reprint ed. lib. bdg. 19.95 (0-405-09944-4) Ayer.

Cali, Charlene & Fernandez, Wanda. Creatures of Character: A Complete Character Education Program. LC 98-87033. (Illus.). 136p. (J). (gr. k-1). 1998. pap. 44.95 (1-57543-066-5) Mar Co Prods.

— Creatures of Character: A Complete Character Education Program. (Illus.). 136p. (J). (gr. 2-3). 1998. pap. 44.95 (1-57543-067-3) Mar Co Prods.

— Creatures of Character: A Complete Character Education Program. LC 98-87033. (Illus.). 136p. (J). (gr. 4-5). 1998. pap. 44.95 (1-57543-068-1) Mar Co Prods.

Cali, Grace. Paul Tillich First-Hand: A Memoir of the Harvard Years. LC 95-61557. xv, 123p. 1996. 19.95 (0-913552-58-5) Exploration Pr.

Cali, James F. TQM for Purchasing Management. 223p. 1993. 29.95 (0-07-009623-6) McGraw.

Cali, John. Strategies for Getting Charge Card Merchant Status at Your Bank: Even If You're Running a Home-Based or Mail Order Business. rev. ed. 64p. 1990. pap. 27.95 (0-924033-22-3) Great West Pub.

Cali, Santo. Yossiph Shyryn. Scammacca, Nat, ed. (ENG & ITA.). 132p. 1980. 20.00 (0-89304-563-2); pap. 10.00 (0-89304-564-0) Cross-Cultrl NY.

Calia, Charles L. The Lazarus Man. 304p. 2001. 24.00 (0-688-16754-3, Wm Morrow) Morrow Avon.

Calia, Charles L. The Unspeakable. 1924. pap. write for info. (0-688-16642-3, Quil) HarperTrade.

Calia, Charles L. The Unspeakable. LC 97-36049. 224p. 1998. 23.00 (0-688-15119-1, Wm Morrow) Morrow Avon.

— The Unspeakable: A Novel. 224p. 1999. reprint ed. pap. 12.00 (0-688-16710-1, Quil) HarperTrade.

Calian, Carnegie S. Survival or Revival: Ten Keys to Church Vitality. LC 98-34781. 168p. 1999. 16.00 (0-664-25734-8) Westminster John Knox.

— Theology Without Boundaries: Encounters of Eastern Orthodoxy & Western Tradition. 144p. (Orig.). 1992. pap. 17.95 (0-664-25156-0) Westminster John Knox.

Caliandro, Arthur & Lenson, Barry. Simple Steps: Ten Things You Can Do to Create an Exceptional Life. 1999. 18.95 (0-07-134797-6) McGraw.

Caliandro, Gloria & Judkins, Barbara L. Primary Nursing Practice. 663p. (C). 1988. text 50.00 (0-673-39731-9) Lppncott W & W.

Calibration Interval Committee. Calibration System Specification: Recommended Practice RP-4. (RP Ser.). 10p. 1971. reprint ed. 15.00 (1-58464-012-X) Natl Conf Stds Labs.

— Establishment & Adjustment of Calibration Intervals: RP-1. 3rd ed. (RP Ser.: No. 1). 132p. 1996. reprint ed. 20.00 (1-58464-010-3) Natl Conf Stds Labs.

— Preparation of Specifications: RP-5. (RP Ser.: No. 5). (Illus.). 6p. 1980. reprint ed. 15.00 (1-58464-013-8) Natl Conf Stds Labs.

Calibration Procedures Committee. Calibration Procedures: Recommended Practice RP-3. 2nd ed. (RP Ser.). (Illus.). 32p. 1990. reprint ed. 15.00 (1-58464-011-1) Natl Conf Stds Labs.

Calibration Reports Subcomittee. Report & Certificates of Calibration: RP-11. (RP Ser.: No. 11). (Illus.). 23p. 1991. reprint ed. 15.00 (1-58464-019-7) Natl Conf Stds Labs.

Calibration Systems Committee. Calibration Laboratory Capability Documentation: Recommended Practice RP-9. (RP Ser.). 17p. 1989. reprint ed. 15.00 (1-58464-017-0) Natl Conf Stds Labs.

Calibration Systems Requirement Committee. Acronym List. unabridged ed. 18p. 1995. 10.00 (1-58464-002-2) Natl Conf Stds Labs.

Calicchio, David, tr. see Camon, Ferdinando.

Calico Museum, Ahmedabad Staff. Treasures of Indian Textiles. (Illus.). 148p. 1980. 49.95 (0-940500-44-2) Asia Bk Corp.

***Caliendo, Stephen M.** Teachers Matter: The Trouble with Leaving Political Education to the Coaches. LC 99-86109. 160p. 2000. 49.00 (0-275-96907-X, C6907, Praeger Pubs) Greenwood.

Calif. Dept. of Educ. Staff, et al. California's Gold, 1991 ("200" Series) (Two Hundred Ser.). 172p. (Orig.). 1992. pap. text, teacher ed. 15.00 (0-929722-54-X) CA State Library Fndtn.

***Califano, A., et al.** Shape & Pattern Matching in Computational Biology. 1998. write for info. (0-306-45138-7, Kluwer Plenum) Kluwer Academic.

Califano, Joseph A., Jr. Presidential Nation. 1975. pap. text 3.95 (0-393-09135-X) Norton.

Califano, Joseph A., Jr. Student Revolution: A Global Confrontation. (C). 1969. 3.95 (0-393-05391-1) Norton.

Califano, Joseph A., Jr. Student Revolution: A Global Confrontation. 96p. (C). 1970. pap. 1.50 (0-393-00519-4) Norton.

***Califano, Joseph A., Jr.** The Triumph & Tragedy of Lyndon Johnson: The White House Years. LC 00-36413. (Joseph V. Hughes, Jr. & Holly O. Hughes Presidency & Leadership Studies: Vol. 8). (Illus.). 416p. 2000. pap. 17.95 (0-89096-960-4) Texas A&M Univ.

Califano, S. Vibrational States. LC 75-19268. 347p. reprint ed. pap. 107.60 (0-608-18836-0, 203048600069) Bks Demand.

Califano, S., et al. Lattice Dynamics of Molecular Crystals. (Lecture Notes in Chemistry Ser.: Vol. 26). 309p. 1981. pap. 36.00 (0-387-10868-8) Spr-Verlag.

***Califf, Mary E., ed.** Machine Learning for Information Extraction: Papers from the AAAI Workshop. (Technical Reports: Vol. WS-99-11). (Illus.). 52p. 1999. spiral bd. 25.00 (1-57735-095-2) AAAI Pr.

Califf, Randy J., ed. see Samp, Ardyce H.

Califf, Robert M., et al, eds. Acute Coronary Care in the Thrombolytic Era. 2nd ed. (Illus.). 984p. (C). (gr. 13). 1994. text 108.00 (0-8016-6753-4, 06753) Mosby Inc.

Califf, Robert M. & Wagner, Galen S., eds. Acute Coronary Care, 1986. 1985. text 132.50 (0-89838-762-0) Kluwer Academic.

— Acute Coronary Care, 1987. 1986. text 177.00 (0-89838-842-2) Kluwer Academic.

Califf, Robert M., jt. ed. see Braunwald, Eugene.

Califia, Pat. Between Our Lips: Passionate Lesbian Verse. 1999. mass mkt. 7.95 (1-58419-009-4) Masq Bks.

— Diesel Fuel. LC 98-230631. (Orig.). 1997. pap. 12.95 (1-56333-535-2, R Kasak Bks) Masquerade.

Califia, Pat. Doc & Fluff: A Dystopian Tale of a Girl & Her Bike. rev. ed. 256p. 1996. pap. text 11.95 (1-55583-369-1) Alyson Pubns.

Califia, Pat. Macho Sluts. 296p. (Orig.). 1988. pap. 11.95 (1-55583-115-X) Alyson Pubns.

— Melting Point. 224p. 1996. pap. 11.95 (1-55583-380-2) Alyson Pubns.

***Califia, Pat.** No Mercy. LC 00-23866. 260p. 2000. pap. 14.95 (1-55583-542-2, Pub. by Alyson Pubns) Consort Bk Sales.

— Public Sex: The Culture of Radical Sex. 2nd rev. ed. 250p. 2000. pap. 16.95 (1-57344-096-5, Pub. by Cleis Pr) Publishers Group.

Califia, Pat. Sapphistry: The Book of Lesbian Sexuality. 3rd rev. ed. (Illus.). 208p. (Orig.). 1988. pap. 12.95 (0-941483-24-X) Naiad Pr.

— The Second Coming. Sweeney, Robin, ed. 392p. 1996. pap. 12.95 (1-55583-281-4) Alyson Pubns.

— Sensuous Magic. 2nd ed. (Orig.). 1996. pap. 12.95 (1-56333-458-5, R Kasak Bks) Masquerade.

— Sensuous Magic: A Guide for Adventurous Lovers. 1998. mass mkt. 7.95 (1-56333-610-3) Masquerade.

— Sex Changes: The Politics of Transgenderism. LC 97-19966. 250p. (Orig.). 1997. pap. 16.95 (1-57344-072-8) Cleis Pr.

Califia, Pat, ed. Doing It for Daddy: Short & Sexy Fiction about a Very Forbidden Fantasy. LC 95-179309. 240p. (Orig.). 1994. pap. 11.95 (1-55583-227-X) Alyson Pubns.

— The Lesbian S-M Safety Manual. 80p. 1988. pap. 7.95 (1-55583-301-2) Alyson Pubns.

Califia, Pat & Campbell, Drew, eds. Bitch Goddess: The Spiritual Path of the Dominant Women. (Illus.). 256p. 1998. pap. 15.95 (1-890159-04-2) Greenery Pr.

Califia, Pat & Fuller, Janine, eds. Forbidden Passages: Writings Banned in Canada. (Illus.). 200p. 1995. pap. 14.95 (1-57344-019-1) Cleis Pr.

***Califonia St. University Staff.** Media Writing Handbook: Guidelines for Radio, Tv & Film Scripts & Academic Papers. 42p. (C). 1999. spiral bd. 13.95 (0-7872-6375-3, 41637501) Kendall-Hunt.

California Academy of Sciences Staff, jt. auth. see San Francisco Zoological Gardens Staff.

California Afro-American Museum Foundation, Los An, jt. auth. see Turenne des Pres, Francois.

California Apartment Association Staff. California Rental Housing Reference Book. 5th ed. 431p. 1992. pap. 24.95 (1-882243-00-5) CA Apt Assn.

California Center for Wildlife Staff, et al. Living with Wildlife: How to Enjoy, Cope with & Protect North America's Wild Creatures Around Your Home & Theirs. LC 93-33982. (Illus.). 352p. (Orig.). 1994. pap. 15.00 (0-87156-547-1, Pub. by Sierra) Random.

California Chamber of Commerce Staff & California Trade & Commerce Agency Staff, eds. European Community & Europe: A Legal Guide to Business Development. 375p. (Orig.). (C). 1993. pap. text 29.50 (1-878630-48-2) CA Chamber Commerce.

California Coastal Commission. The California Coastal Access Guide. 5th ed. LC 96-35486. (Illus.). (Orig.). 1997. pap. 18.95 (0-520-20859-5, Pub. by U CA Pr) Cal Prin Full Svc.

California Coastal Commission, ed. The California Coastal Resource Guide. 384p. 1987. pap. 19.95 (0-520-06186-1, Pub. by U CA Pr) Cal Prin Full Svc.

California College for Health Sciences Staff. Administration of an Early Childhood Education Center: ECE 121 Course. 300p. (C). 1992. ring bd. write for info. (0-933915-40-3) CA College Health Sci.

— Behavior Modification: HP 612. 346p. (C). 1992. student ed., spiral bd. write for info. (0-933195-68-0) CA College Health Sci.

— Business Communications: BUS 320. 95p. (C). 1995. student ed. write for info. (0-933195-61-3) CA College Health Sci.

— Curriculum for Early Childhood Education. 142p. (C). 1992. ring bd. Price not set. (0-933195-05-2) CA College Health Sci.

— Dealing with Death & Dying: HP560, Health Promotions Version. 176p. (C). 1989. spiral bd. write for info. (0-933195-29-X) CA College Health Sci.

— Dealing with Death & Dying: SOC 110, Sociology Version. 176p. (C). 1990. spiral bd. write for info. (0-933195-28-1) CA College Health Sci.

— Early Childhood Education Internship: ECE 140. 243p. (C). 1994. student ed. write for info. (0-933195-77-X) CA College Health Sci.

— Effective Communication Through Technical Writing. 124p. (C). 1990. student ed., ring bd. write for info. (0-933195-19-2) CA College Health Sci.

— Effective Management: BUS 110 Course Study Guide. rev. ed. 308p. (C). 1992. ring bd. write for info. (0-933195-18-4) CA College Health Sci.

— English Essentials: ENG 101. 2nd rev. ed. 124p. (C). 1993. ring bd. write for info. (*0-933915-25-X*) CA College Health Sci.
— Fundamentals of Child Care Education: ECE 111 Course. 658p. (C). 1991. ring bd. write for info. (*0-933195-33-8*) CA College Health Sci.
— Health Psychology. 138p. (C). 1990. pap. text Price not set. (*0-933195-03-6*) CA College Health Sci.
— Infant & Toddler Care. 134p. (C). 1993. ring bd. Price not set. (*0-933195-06-0*) CA College Health Sci.
— Introduction to Biology. 147p. (C). 1992. pap. text Price not set. (*0-933195-10-9*) CA College Health Sci.
— Introduction to Early Childhood Education: ECE 105 Course. 235p. (C). 1995. ring bd. write for info. (*0-933195-45-1*) CA College Health Sci.
— Introduction to Psychology: PSY 101. rev. ed. 178p. (C). 1993. student ed., ring bd. write for info. (*0-933195-31-1*) CA College Health Sci.
— Issues in Death & Dying Nursing: CEU. 84p. (C). 1993. 49.95 (*0-933195-55-9*) CA College Health Sci.
— Issues in Negotiation. 250p. (C). 1993. spiral bd. Price not set. (*0-933195-12-5*) CA College Health Sci.
— Microcomputer Applications. 96p. (C). 1990. spiral bd. write for info. (*0-933195-27-3*) CA College Health Sci.
— The New Supervisor: BUS 101. 148p. (C). 1992. ring bd. write for info. (*0-933915-36-5*) CA College Health Sci.
— Nutrition: Concepts & Controversies. (Illus.). 226p. (C). 1993. spiral bd. 25.00 (*0-933195-04-4*) CA College Health Sci.
— Practicum in Healthcare Management: HSM 489. 10p. (C). 1994. pap., student ed. write for info. (*0-933195-56-7*) CA College Health Sci.
— Pre-Clinical Assessment Manual. 106p. (C). 1985. write for info. (*0-933195-52-4*) CA College Health Sci.
— Professional Leadership: HSM 465. 225p. (C). 1991. ring bd. write for info. (*0-933195-24-9*) CA College Health Sci.
— Psychological Aspects of Illness & Disease. 166p. (C). 1992. spiral bd. 155.00 (*0-933195-16-8*) CA College Health Sci.
— Respiratory Care Assistant: Performance Evaluation Guide. 60p. (C). 1992. write for info. (*0-933195-34-6*) CA College Health Sci.
— Speaking the Language of Respiratory Care. LC 85-4141. 48p. (C). 1991. pap. 22.95 incl. audio (*0-933195-00-1*) CA College Health Sci.
— Stress Management: HP 630. 23p. (C). 1990. student ed. write for info. (*0-933195-30-3*) CA College Health Sci.
— Theory & Practice in Social Services: SOC 120 Course Study Guide. 172p. (C). 1992. ring bd. write for info. (*0-933195-20-6*) CA College Health Sci.
— Theory & Practice of Counseling & Psychotherapy: HP 611. 22p. (C). 1991. spiral bd. write for info. (*0-933195-35-4*) CA College Health Sci.

California Continuing Education of the Bar Staff. California Attorney's Damages Guide. LC 74-620090. 449p. 1974. pap. 85.00 (*0-88124-036-2*, CP-31430) Cont Ed Bar-CA.
— California Corporate Securities Law Notebook. 356p. 1986. 50.00 (*0-88124-024-9*, BU-71010) Cont Ed Bar-CA.
— California Judicial Council Forms Manual, 3 vols. LC 81-65171. 350p. 1981. 80.00 (*0-88124-081-8*, CP-74000) Cont Ed Bar-CA.
— California Mechanics' Liens & Other Remedies. 2nd ed. LC 70-189671. 347p. 1988. 105.00 (*0-88124-192-X*, RE-30990) Cont Ed Bar-CA.
— California Probate Workflow Manual, 2 vols. rev. ed. Blaine, William L., ed. LC 79-53359. 1990. suppl. ed. 32.00 (*0-88124-314-0*, ES-31561) Cont Ed Bar-CA.
— California Probate Workflow Manual, 2 vols., Set. rev. ed. Blaine, William L., ed. LC 79-53359. 1989. 120.00 (*0-88124-072-9*, ES-31560) Cont Ed Bar-CA.
— California Uninsured Motorist Practice. LC 72-619679. 349p. 1973. 55.00 (*0-88124-028-1*, TO-30580) Cont Ed Bar-CA.
— Drafting Agreements for the Sale of Businesses. LC 88-62938. 350p. 1988. 110.00 (*0-88124-015-X*, BU-39670) Cont Ed Bar-CA.

California Continuing Education of the Bar Staff & Chuan, Victor L. California Breach of Contract Remedies: A Basic Guide for General Practitioners. LC 79-54861. ix, 235p. 1980. 75.00 (*0-88124-070-2*, CP-34460) Cont Ed Bar-CA.

California Continuing Education of the Bar Staff, et al. Advising California Employers. LC 81-65536. (Illus.). xiv, 635p. 1981. 100.00 (*0-88124-078-8*, BU-35510) Cont Ed Bar-CA.
— California Administrative Mandamus. 2nd ed. LC 66-64355. xxiv, 463p. 1989. 95.00 (*0-88124-003-6*, CP-38810) Cont Ed Bar-CA.

California Continuing Education of the Bar Staff, ed. see Dean, Michael A., et al.

California Continuing Education ot the Bar, jt. auth. see Hosack, John L.

California Culinary Academy Staff. Cooking at the Academy. LC 91-60965. (Illus.). 192p. (Orig.). 1991. pap. 17.95 (*0-912333-10-3*, KQED Bks) BB&T Inc.
— Festive Favorites: Entertaining with the California Culinary Academy. LC 95-52. (Illus.). 240p. (Orig.). 1995. pap. 18.95 (*0-912333-12-X*) BB&T Inc.
— Wrap & Roll. LC 97-38974. 224p. 1998. 14.95 (*0-02-862287-1*) Macmillan.

California Department of Education Staff. Adoption Recommendations of the Curriculum Development & Supplemental Materials Commission to the State Board of Education, 1988: California Basic Instructional Materials in English-Language Arts. 64p. 1988. pap. 4.00 (*0-8011-0795-4*) Calif Education.
— Adoption Recommendations of the Curriculum Development & Supplemental Materials Commission to the State Board of Education, 1990: California Basic Instructional Materials in History-Social Science. 88p. 1990. pap. 5.50 (*0-8011-0913-2*) Calif Education.
— Adoption Recommendations of the Curriculum Development & Supplemental Materials Commission to the State Board of Education, 1991: California Basic Instructional Materials in English As a Second Language & Foreign Language. 58p. 1991. pap. 6.00 (*0-8011-1013-0*) Calif Education.
— Adoption Recommendations of the Curriculum Development & Supplemental Materials Commission to the State Board of Education, 1992: California Basic Instructional Materials in Science. 60p. 1992. pap. 6.00 (*0-8011-1063-7*) Calif Education.
— Adoption Recommendations of the Curriculum Development & Supplemental Materials Commission to the State Board of Education, 1993: California Basic Instructional Materials in History-Social Science. 58p. 1993. pap. 6.00 (*0-8011-1103-X*) Calif Education.
— Adoption Recommendations of the Curriculum Development & Supplemental Materials Commission to the State Board of Education, 1994: California Basic Instructional Materials in Science, Follow-up. 16p. 1994. pap. 6.00 (*0-8011-1151-X*) Calif Education.
— The American Indian: Yesterday, Today, & Tomorrow. (Illus.). 88p. 1991. pap. 8.75 (*0-8011-0973-6*) Calif Education.
— Attendance Accounting & Reporting in California Public Schools. 192p. 1991. pap. 8.00 (*0-8011-1012-2*) Calif Education.
— California Private School Directory, 1996-97. 314p. 1997. pap. 17.50 (*0-8011-1331-8*) Calif Education.
— California School Accounting Manual. 240p. 1992. pap. 13.50 (*0-8011-1025-4*) Calif Education.
— California State Plan for Carl D. Perkins Vocational & Applied Technology Education Act Funds, 1994-1996. 770p. 1994. pap. 18.00 (*0-8011-1174-9*) Calif Education.
— California State Plan for Child Care & Development Services Funded under Federal Block Grant. 112p. 1994. pap. 10.00 (*0-8011-1176-5*) Calif Education.
— California Strategic Plan for Parental Involvement in Education. 52p. 1992. pap. 6.50 (*0-8011-1036-X*) Calif Education.
— Caught in the Middle: Education Reform for Young Adolescents in California Public Schools. (Illus.). 162p. 1987. pap. 9.25 (*0-8011-0488-2*) Calif Education.
— Celebrating the National Reading Initiative. (Illus.). 96p. 1989. pap. 8.50 (*0-8011-0760-1*) Calif Education.
— Choose Well, Be Well: A Curriculum for Junior High School. (Nutrition Education Ser.). (Illus.). 344p. 1984. pap. 7.00 (*0-8011-0229-4*) Calif Education.
— Choose Well, Be Well: A Curriculum Guide for High School. (Nutrition Education Ser.). (Illus.). 382p. 1984. pap. 7.00 (*0-8011-0228-6*) Calif Education.
— Choose Well, Be Well: Color Supplement to the Preschool & Kindergarten Curriculum Guide. (Nutrition Education Ser.). (Illus.). 48p. 1985. pap. 6.50 (*0-8011-0254-5*) Calif Education.
— Commodity Administrative Manual. 170p. 1993. ring bd. 14.00 (*0-8011-1072-6*) Calif Education.
— Course in Carpentry: Blueprint Reading, Commerical & Industrial, Workbook & Testbook. (Apprenticeship Instructional Materials Ser.). (Illus.). 22p. 1976. pap. 4.00 (*0-8011-0511-0*) Calif Education.
— Course in Carpentry: Blueprint Reading, Workbook & Testbook. (Apprenticeship Instructional Materials Ser.). (Illus.). 72p. 1986. pap. 5.75 (*0-8011-0510-2*) Calif Education.
— Course in Carpentry: Builder's Level & Transit Level, Workbook & Testbook. (Apprenticeship Instructional Materials Ser.). (Illus.). 64p. 1981. pap. 4.00 (*0-8011-0512-9*) Calif Education.
— Course in Carpentry: California Contemporary House Plans. (Apprenticeship Instructional Materials Ser.). (Illus.). 16p. 1975. pap. 4.25 (*0-8011-0513-7*) Calif Education.
— Course in Carpentry: Concrete, Workbook & Testbook. (Apprenticeship Instructional Materials Ser.). (Illus.). 72p. 1976. pap. 8.00 (*0-8011-0514-5*) Calif Education.
— Course in Carpentry: Exterior Finish, Workbook & Testbook. (Apprenticeship Instructional Materials Ser.). (Illus.). 64p. 1981. pap. 8.00 (*0-8011-0515-3*) Calif Education.
— Course in Carpentry: Form Detailing, Construction & Erection, Workbook & Testbook. (Apprenticeship Instructional Materials Ser.). (Illus.). 102p. 1976. pap. 9.00 (*0-8011-0516-1*) Calif Education.
— Course in Carpentry: Foundation & Floors, Workbook & Testbook. (Apprenticeship Instructional Materials Ser.). (Illus.). 86p. 1975. pap. 8.00 (*0-8011-0517-X*) Calif Education.
— Course in Carpentry: Heavy Timber Construction, Workbook & Testbook. (Apprenticeship Instructional Materials Ser.). (Illus.). 120p. 1977. pap. 9.00 (*0-8011-0518-8*) Calif Education.
— Course in Carpentry: Interior Finish, Workbook & Testbook. (Apprenticeship Instructional Materials Ser.). (Illus.). 86p. 1981. pap. 9.00 (*0-8011-0519-6*) Calif Education.
— Course in Carpentry: Materials of Construction, Workbook & Testbook. (Apprenticeship Instructional Materials Ser.). (Illus.). 48p. 1975. pap. 9.00 (*0-8011-0520-X*) Calif Education.
— Course in Carpentry: Mathematics, Workbook & Testbook. (Apprenticeship Instructional Materials Ser.). (Illus.). 108p. 1983. pap. 4.00 (*0-8011-0521-8*) Calif Education.
— Course in Carpentry: Precast & Prestressed Concrete, Workbook & Testbook. (Apprenticeship Instructional Materials Ser.). (Illus.). 64p. 1976. pap. 4.00 (*0-8011-0522-6*) Calif Education.
— Course in Carpentry: Roof Framing, Workbook & Testbook. (Apprenticeship Instructional Materials Ser.). (Illus.). 78p. 1976. pap. 4.00 (*0-8011-0523-4*) Calif Education.
— Course in Carpentry: Rough Framing, Workbook & Testbook. (Apprenticeship Instructional Materials Ser.). (Illus.). 58p. 1983. pap. 4.25 (*0-8011-0524-2*) Calif Education.
— Course in Carpentry: Safety, Workbook & Testbook. (Apprenticeship Instructional Materials Ser.). (Illus.). 38p. 1975. pap. 4.00 (*0-8011-0525-0*) Calif Education.
— Course in Carpentry: Site Work, Workbook & Testbook. (Apprenticeship Instructional Materials Ser.). (Illus.). 40p. 1983. pap. 4.25 (*0-8011-0526-9*) Calif Education.
— Course in Carpentry: Stair Building, Workbook & Testbook. (Apprenticeship Instructional Materials Ser.). (Illus.). 72p. 1982. pap. 4.00 (*0-8011-0527-7*) Calif Education.
— Course in Carpentry: The Apprentice Carpenter & the Trade, Workbook & Testbook. (Apprenticeship Instructional Materials Ser.). (Illus.). 64p. 1984. pap. 4.00 (*0-8011-0509-9*) Calif Education.
— Course in Carpentry: Welding, Workbook & Testbook. (Apprenticeship Instructional Materials Ser.). (Illus.). 54p. 1976. pap. 4.00 (*0-8011-0528-5*) Calif Education.
— Course Models for the History-Social Science Framework - World History & Geography: Ancient Civilizations. (Illus.). 128p. (J). (gr. 6). 1993. pap. 12.00 (*0-8011-1034-3*) Calif Education.
— Course Models for the History-Social Science Framework - World History & Geography: Medieval & Early Modern Times. (Illus.). 386p. (J). (gr. 7). 1994. pap. 15.25 (*0-8011-1132-3*) Calif Education.
— Culinary Arts: Testbook, Pt. 1. (Apprenticeship Instructional Materials Ser.). 76p. 1972. pap. 7.50 (*0-8011-0533-1*) Calif Education.
— Culinary Arts: Testbook, Pt. 2. (Apprenticeship Instructional Materials Ser.). 72p. 1975. pap. 7.50 (*0-8011-0536-6*) Calif Education.
— Culinary Arts: Workbook, Pt. 1. (Apprenticeship Instructional Materials Ser.). (Illus.). 168p. 1972. pap., wbk. ed. 8.75 (*0-8011-0532-3*) Calif Education.
— Culinary Arts, Pt. 2: Workbook. (Apprenticeship Instructional Materials Ser.). (Illus.). 144p. 1975. pap., wbk. ed. 8.75 (*0-8011-0535-8*) Calif Education.
— Desktop Publishing Guidelines for the California Department of Education. 48p. 1989. pap. 5.50 (*0-8011-0797-0*) Calif Education.
— Directory of Microcomputer Software for School Business Administration. 136p. 1990. pap. 9.00 (*0-8011-0833-0*) Calif Education.
— Drywall Construction: Testbook, Pt. 2. (Apprenticeship Instructional Materials Ser.). 104p. 1982. pap. 5.50 (*0-8011-0542-0*) Calif Education.
— Drywall Construction: Workbook, Pt. 2. (Apprenticeship Instructional Materials Ser.). (Illus.). 258p. 1982. pap., wbk. ed. 4.75 (*0-8011-0538-2*); pap., wbk. ed. 10.00 (*0-8011-0541-2*) Calif Education.
— Drywall Construction, Pt. 1: Testbook. (Apprenticeship Instructional Materials Ser.). 104p. 1982. pap. 7.00 (*0-8011-0539-0*) Calif Education.
— Economic Education Mandate: Handbook for Survival - a Practical Guide for Today's High School Economics Editors. 102p. 1991. ring bd. 8.50 (*0-8011-0976-0*) Calif Education.
— Electrical Wiring Pt. 1: Testbook. (Apprenticeship Instructional Materials Ser.). 96p. 1974. pap. 3.55 (*0-8011-0545-5*) Calif Education.
— Electrical Wiring Pt. 2: Testbook. (Apprenticeship Instructional Materials Ser.). 104p. 1969. pap. 3.55 (*0-8011-0548-X*) Calif Education.
— Electrical Wiring Pt. 2: Workbook. (Apprenticeship Instructional Materials Ser.). (Illus.). 212p. 1969. pap. 4.00 (*0-8011-0547-1*) Calif Education.
— Electrical Wiring Pt. 3: Testbook. (Apprenticeship Instructional Materials Ser.). 104p. 1979. pap. 3.50 (*0-8011-0551-X*) Calif Education.
— Electrical Wiring Pt. 3: Workbook. (Apprenticeship Instructional Materials Ser.). (Illus.). 280p. 1975. pap., teacher ed., wbk. ed. 4.25 (*0-8011-0550-1*) Calif Education.
— Electrical Wiring Pt. 4: Testbook. (Apprenticeship Instructional Materials Ser.). 96p. 1971. pap. 7.00 (*0-8011-0554-4*) Calif Education.
— Electrical Wiring Pt. 4: Workbook. (Apprenticeship Instructional Materials Ser.). (Illus.). 128p. 1971. pap., wbk. ed. 4.00 (*0-8011-0553-6*) Calif Education
— Electrical Wiring, Pt. 1: Workbook. (Apprenticeship Instructional Materials Ser.). (Illus.). 296p. 1974. pap., wbk. ed. 4.00 (*0-8011-0544-7*) Calif Education
— English As a Second Language: Implementing Effective Adult Education Programs. (English-As-a-Second Language Ser.). 48p. 1993. pap. 7.00 (*0-8011-1098-X*) Calif Education.
— English-Language Arts Model Curriculum Standards, 9-12. (Illus.). 56p. 1991. pap. 8.50 (*0-8011-0927-2*) Calif Education.
— Enrichment Opportunities Guide: A Resource for Teachers & Students in Math & Science. 230p. 1988. pap. 9.25 (*0-8011-0786-5*) Calif Education.
— ESEA, Chapter Two, Manual of Information. 180p. 1991. pap. 5.50 (*0-8011-0987-6*) Calif Education.
— Exemplary Program Standards for Child Development Programs Serving Preschool & School-Age Children. (Program for Infant - Toddler Caregivers Ser.). 74p. 1991. pap. 8.00 (*0-8011-1011-4*) Calif Education.
— Foreign Language Framework for California Public Schools. 46p. (J). (gr. k-12). 1989. pap. 7.25 (*0-8011-0804-7*) Calif Education.
— Greatest Hits of Environmental Education: The Environmental Education Grant Program. 82p. 1993. pap. 9.00 (*0-8011-1089-0*) Calif Education.
— Guide & Criteria for Program Quality Review - Elementary. 230p. 1997. pap. 13.50 (*0-8011-1343-1*) Calif Education.
— Guidelines & Procedures for Meeting the Specialized Physical Health Care Needs of Pupils. (Illus.). 212p. 1990. pap. 11.00 (*0-8011-0902-7*) Calif Education.
— Handbook for Contracting with Nonpublic Schools for Exceptional Individuals. 116p. 1990. pap. 9.50 (*0-8011-0875-6*) Calif Education.
— Handbook for Planning an Effective Foreign Language Program. (Illus.). 64p. 1985. pap. 8.00 (*0-8011-0249-9*) Calif Education.
— Handbook for Planning an Effective Writing Program, K-12. (Illus.). 80p. 1986. pap. 8.00 (*0-8011-0290-1*) Calif Education.
— Handbook for Teaching Cantonese-Speaking Students. 88p. 1989. pap. 8.00 (*0-8011-0824-1*) Calif Education.
— Handbook for Teaching Japanese-Speaking Students. 136p. 1987. pap. 8.00 (*0-8011-0680-X*) Calif Education.
— Handbook for Teaching Korean-American Students. 192p. 1992. pap. 8.00 (*0-8011-0986-8*) Calif Education.
— Handbook for Teaching Pilipino-Speaking Students. 96p. 1986. pap. 8.00 (*0-8011-0291-X*) Calif Education.
— Handbook for Teaching Portuguese-Speaking Students. 118p. 1989. pap. 8.00 (*0-8011-0825-X*) Calif Education.
— Handbook for Teaching Vietnamese-Speaking Students. 190p. 1994. pap. 8.00 (*0-8011-1083-1*) Calif Education.
— Handbook on California Education for Language-Minority Parents. (CHI.). 50p. 1985. pap. 5.00 (*0-8011-0250-2*) Calif Education.
— Handbook on California Education for Language-Minority Parents. (ARM.). 50p. 1986. pap. 5.00 (*0-8011-0292-8*); pap. 5.00 (*0-8011-0293-6*); pap. 5.00 (*0-8011-0294-4*); pap. 5.00 (*0-8011-0295-2*); pap. 5.00 (*0-8011-0296-0*); pap. 5.00 (*0-8011-0298-7*) Calif Education.
— Handbook on California Education for Language-Minority Parents. (JPN.). 50p. 1989. pap. 5.00 (*0-8011-0743-1*); pap. 5.00 (*0-8011-0826-8*) Calif Education.
— Handbook on California Education for Language Minority Parents. (ENG & POR.). 50p. 1990. pap. 5.00 (*0-8011-0909-4*) Calif Education.
— Health Framework for California Public Schools, K-12. (Illus.). 244p. 1994. pap. 10.00 (*0-8011-1064-5*) Calif Education.
— History-Social Science Framework for California Public Schools, K-12: 1997 Updated Edition. LC 97-142071. (Illus.). 136p. 1997. pap. 12.50 (*0-8011-1284-2*) Calif Education.
— Hope for the Future: The State Plan for Educating Homeless Children & Youth. (Illus.). 44p. 1991. pap. write for info. (*0-8011-1015-7*) Calif Education.
— Implementation of Middle Grade Reforms in California Public Schools, 1988-89 Through 1992-93. 56p. 1993. pap. 7.00 (*0-8011-1114-5*) Calif Education.
— Instructional Materials Approved for Legal Compliance. 200p. 1996. pap. 23.00 (*0-8011-1269-9*) Calif Education.
— Instructor's Manual for California's Bus Driver's Training Course. (Illus.). 600p. 1990. pap. 20.00 (*0-8011-0897-7*) Calif Education.
— It's Elementary! Elementary Grades Task Force Report. 104p. 1992. pap. 9.00 (*0-8011-1024-6*) Calif Education.
— Literature for History-Social Science, K-8. rev. ed. (Illus.). 128p. 1993. pap. 9.00 (*0-8011-1107-2*) Calif Education.
— Literature for Science & Mathematics, K-12. (Illus.). 152p. 1993. pap. 11.00 (*0-8011-1066-1*) Calif Education.
— Machine Shop Pt. 1: Testbook. (Apprenticeship Instructional Materials Ser.). 134p. 1973. pap. 6.25 (*0-8011-0567-6*) Calif Education.
— Machine Shop Pt. 1: Workbook. (Apprenticeship Instructional Materials Ser.). (Illus.). 192p. 1973. pap. 8.25 (*0-8011-0566-8*) Calif Education.
— Machine Shop Pt. 2: Testbook. (Apprenticeship Instructional Materials Ser.). 80p. 1977. pap. 6.25 (*0-8011-0570-6*) Calif Education.
— Machine Shop Pt. 2: Workbook. (Apprenticeship Instructional Materials Ser.). (Illus.). 112p. 1977. pap. 8.25 (*0-8011-0569-2*) Calif Education.
— Machine Shop Pt. 3: Testbook. (Apprenticeship Instructional Materials Ser.). 110p. 1976. pap. 6.25 (*0-8011-0572-2*) Calif Education.
— Machine Shop Pt. 3: Workbook. (Apprenticeship Instructional Materials Ser.). (Illus.). 136p. 1976. pap. 8.25 (*0-8011-0571-4*) Calif Education.
— Machine Shop Pt. 4: Testbook. (Apprenticeship Instructional Materials Ser.). 88p. 1969. pap. 3.75 (*0-8011-0575-7*) Calif Education.
— Machine Shop Pt. 4: Workbook. (Apprenticeship Instructional Materials Ser.). (Illus.). 176p. 1969. pap. 7.25 (*0-8011-0574-9*) Calif Education.
— Mathematics Framework for California Public Schools, K-12. (Illus.). 234p. 1992. pap. 8.00 (*0-8011-1033-5*) Calif Education.
— Mathematics Model Curriculum Guide, K-8. 112p. 1987. pap. 7.50 (*0-8011-0664-8*) Calif Education.
— Meat Cutting: Testbook, Pt. 1. (Apprenticeship Instructional Materials Ser.). 88p. 1981. pap. 3.50 (*0-8011-0578-1*) Calif Education.
— Meat Cutting: Testbook, Pt. 2. (Apprenticeship Instructional Materials Ser.). 96p. 1982. pap. 3.75 (*0-8011-0581-1*) Calif Education.
— Meat Cutting: Workbook, Pt. 1. (Apprenticeship Instructional Materials Ser.). (Illus.). 160p. 1981. pap. 4.75 (*0-8011-0577-3*) Calif Education.
— Meat Cutting: Workbook, Pt. 2. (Apprenticeship Instructional Materials Ser.). (Illus.). 144p. 1982. pap. 5.25 (*0-8011-0580-3*) Calif Education.

C

— Model Curriculum Standards, Program Framework, & Progress Guide for Industrial & Technology Education in California. 324p. 1990. pap. 16.00 (*0-8011-0864-0*) Calif Education.

— Model Standards for Adult Education Instructors. (English-As-a-Second Language Ser.). 88p. 1992. pap. 11.25 (*0-8011-1046-7*) Calif Education.

— Not Schools Alone: Guidelines for Schools & Communities to Prevent the Use of Tobacco, Alcohol, & Other Drugs among Children & Youth. 40p. 1990. pap. 5.25 (*0-8011-0969-8*) Calif Education.

— On Alert! Gang Prevention: School In-Service Guidelines. 96p. 1994. pap. 7.50 (*0-8011-1113-7*) Calif Education.

— Physical Education Framework for California Public Schools, K-12. LC 94-621237. (Illus.). 104p. 1994. pap. 7.75 (*0-8011-1065-3*) Calif Education.

— Physical Education Model Curriculum Standards, Grades 9-12. (Illus.). 40p. 1991. pap. 6.50 (*0-8011-0845-4*) Calif Education.

— Plastering: Testbook, Pt. 1. (Apprenticeship Instructional Materials Ser.). 80p. 1972. pap. 3.50 (*0-8011-0596-X*) Calif Education.

— Plastering: Testbook, Pt. 2. (Apprenticeship Instructional Materials Ser.). 68p. 1974. pap. 6.25 (*0-8011-0599-4*) Calif Education.

— Plastering: Workbook, Pt. 1. (Apprenticeship Instructional Materials Ser.). (Illus.). 144p. 1972. pap. 4.00 (*0-8011-0595-1*) Calif Education.

— Plastering: Workbook, Pt. 2. (Apprenticeship Instructional Materials Ser.). (Illus.). 148p. 1974. pap. 4.00 (*0-8011-0598-6*) Calif Education.

— Prelude to Performance Assessments in the Arts, K-12. (Illus.). 68p. 1994. pap. 8.50 (*0-8011-1119-6*) Calif Education.

— Program Guidelines for Hearing Impaired Individuals. 64p. 1986. pap. 10.00 (*0-8011-0309-6*) Calif Education.

— Program Guidelines for Individuals Who Are Deaf-Blind. 94p. 1990. pap. 10.00 (*0-8011-0886-1*) Calif Education.

— Program Guidelines for Individuals Who Are Severely Orthopedically Impaired. 112p. 1992. pap. 10.00 (*0-8011-1032-7*) Calif Education.

— Program Guidelines for Visually Impaired Individuals. 88p. 1997. pap. 10.00 (*0-8011-1289-3*) Calif Education.

— A Question of Thinking: A First Look at Students' Performance on Open-Ended Questions in Mathematics. (Illus.). 92p. 1989. pap. 7.00 (*0-8011-0815-2*) Calif Education.

— Read to Me: Recommended Literature for Children Ages Two Through Seven. (Illus.). 144p. 1992. pap. 9.00 (*0-8011-1048-3*) Calif Education.

— Recommended Literature, Grades 9-12. (Illus.). 118p. 1990. pap. 8.00 (*0-8011-0831-4*) Calif Education.

— Recommended Readings in Literature, K-8. annot. rev. ed. (Illus.). 176p. 1996. 10.00 (*0-8011-1171-4*, 1171) Calif Education.

— Recommended Readings in Spanish Literature, K-8. 64p. 1991. pap. 7.00 (*0-8011-0895-0*) Calif Education.

— Roads to the Future: Strategic Plan for Educational Options in the 21st Century, Final Report. 156p. 1994. pap. 11.00 (*0-8011-1118-8*) Calif Education.

— Roofing: Asphalt & Wood Shingling, Workbook & Testbook. (Apprenticeship Instructional Materials Ser.). (Illus.). 80p. 1982. pap. 9.50 (*0-8011-0601-X*) Calif Education.

— Roofing: Built-up Roofing, Workbook & Testbook. (Apprenticeship Instructional Materials Ser.). (Illus.). 94p. 1981. pap. 9.50 (*0-8011-0604-4*) Calif Education.

— Roofing: Cold-Applied Roofing Systems & Waterproofing & Dampproofing, Workbook & Testbook. (Apprenticeship Instructional Materials Ser.). (Illus.). 80p. 1982. pap. 9.50 (*0-8011-0607-9*) Calif Education.

— Roofing: Common Roofing & Waterproofing Materials & Equipment, Workbook & Testbook. (Apprenticeship Instructional Materials Ser.). (Illus.). 64p. 1993. pap. 8.00 (*0-8011-1105-6*) Calif Education.

— Roofing: Entering the Roofing & Waterproofing Industry, Workbook & Tests. (Apprenticeship Instructional Materials Ser.). (Illus.). 96p. 1991. pap. 6.50 (*0-8011-0971-X*) Calif Education.

— Roofing: First-Aid Training, Workbook & Testbook. (Apprenticeship Instructional Materials Ser.). (Illus.). 72p. 1982. pap. 8.75 (*0-8011-0616-8*) Calif Education.

— Roofing: Maintenance Repair, & Roofing, Workbook & Testbook. (Apprenticeship Instructional Materials Ser.). (Illus.). 72p. 1983. pap. 9.50 (*0-8011-0619-2*) Calif Education.

— Roofing: Plans & Specifications, Workbook & Testbook. (Apprenticeship Instructional Materials Ser.). (Illus.). 56p. 1983. pap. 9.50 (*0-8011-0622-2*) Calif Education.

— Roofing: Rigid Roofing, Workbook & Testbook. (Apprenticeship Instructional Materials Ser.). (Illus.). 88p. 1980. pap. 9.50 (*0-8011-0625-7*) Calif Education.

— Roofing: Single-Ply Roofing & Waterproofing Workbook & Tests. (Apprenticeship Instructional Materials Ser.). (Illus.). 88p. 1987. pap. 6.25 (*0-8011-0661-3*) Calif Education.

California Department of Education Staff. A Sampler of English-Language Arts Assessment, High School. (Illus.). 152p. 1992. pap. 6.50 (*0-8011-1062-9*) Calif Education.

— A Sampler of English-Language Arts Assessment, Middle Grades. (Illus.). 132p. 1992. pap. 6.50 (*0-8011-1061-0*) Calif Education.

California Department of Education Staff. A Sampler of Mathematics Assessment. (Illus.). 56p. 1991. pap. 6.00 (*0-8011-0972-8*) Calif Education.

— School Nutrition & Food Service Techniques: For Children with Exceptional Needs. 56p. 1982. pap. 4.50 (*0-8011-0261-8*) Calif Education.

— School Nutrition Facility Planning Guide. (Illus.). 106p. 1992. spiral bd. 10.00 (*0-8011-1042-4*) Calif Education.

— Schools for the Twenty-First Century. (Illus.). 48p. 1990. pap. 5.25 (*0-8011-0911-6*) Calif Education.

— Science Facilities Design for California Public Schools. (Illus.). 72p. 1992. pap. 8.25 (*0-8011-1038-6*) Calif Education.

— Science Framework for California Public Schools, K-12. (Illus.). 220p. 1990. pap. 9.50 (*0-8011-0870-5*) Calif Education.

— Science Safety Handbook for California High Schools. (Illus.). 184p. 1987. pap. 7.25 (*0-8011-0669-9*) Calif Education.

— Second to None: A Vision of the New California High School. (Illus.). 56p. 1992. pap. 9.50 (*0-8011-1040-8*) Calif Education.

— Secondary Textbook Review: Biology & Life Science, Grades 9-12. 418p. 1989. pap. 13.50 (*0-8011-0803-9*) Calif Education.

— Secondary Textbook Review: General Mathematics, Grades 9-12. 152p. 1987. pap. 7.00 (*0-8011-0677-X*) Calif Education.

— Secondary Textbook Review: Mathematical Analysis. 210p. 1993. pap. 12.50 (*0-8011-1087-4*) Calif Education.

— Seeing Fractions: A Unit for the Upper Elementary Grades. (Illus.). 130p. 1990. pap. 10.25 (*0-8011-0926-4*) Calif Education.

— Statement on Competencies in Languages Other Than English Expected of Entering Freshmen, Phase I: French, German, Spanish. 74p. 1986. pap. 5.50 (*0-8011-0807-1*) Calif Education.

— Statement on Competencies in Mathematics Expected of Entering Freshmen. 64p. 1989. pap. 5.50 (*0-8011-0836-5*) Calif Education.

— Stationary Engineers, Testbook. (Apprenticeship Instructional Materials Ser.). 174p. 1972. pap. 3.75 (*0-8011-0643-5*) Calif Education.

— Stationary Engineers, Workbook. (Apprenticeship Instructional Materials Ser.). (Illus.). 380p. 1972. pap. 5.25 (*0-8011-0642-7*) Calif Education.

— Survey of Basic Skills: Grade Six, Rationale & Content. 72p. 1982. pap. 6.00 (*0-8011-0267-7*) Calif Education.

— Tilesetting: Testbook. (Apprenticeship Instructional Materials Ser.). 104p. 1986. pap. 5.50 (*0-8011-0491-2*) Calif Education.

— Tilesetting: Workbook. (Apprenticeship Instructional Materials Ser.). (Illus.). 254p. 1986. pap. 16.00 (*0-8011-0490-4*) Calif Education.

— Visual & Performing Arts Framework for California Public Schools, K-12. (Illus.). 176p. 1996. pap. 15.00 (*0-8011-1261-3*) Calif Education.

— With History - Social Science for All: Access for Every Student. (Illus.). 74p. 1992. pap. 8.00 (*0-8011-1016-5*) Calif Education.

— Work Experience Education: Instructional Guide. 492p. 1987. pap. 13.50 (*0-8011-0670-2*) Calif Education.

— Writing Achievement of California Eighth Graders: A First Look. 58p. 1989. pap. 5.50 (*0-8011-0814-4*) Calif Education.

— Writing Assessment Handbook Grade 8. 170p. 1990. pap. 10.00 (*0-8011-0887-X*) Calif Education.

— Writing Assessment Handbook, High School. 224p. 1993. pap. 11.00 (*0-8011-1073-4*) Calif Education.

— Year-Round Education, Year-Round Opportunities: A Study of Year-Round Education in California. 134p. 1987. pap. 6.75 (*0-8011-0686-9*) Calif Education.

California Department of Education Staff, et al. California's Gold 1994 ("500" Series) (500 Ser.). 113p. 1995. pap. text, teacher ed. 15.00 (*0-929722-84-1*) CA State Library Fndtn.

— California's Gold 1995. (600 Ser.). 109p. 1996. pap. text, teacher ed. 15.00 (*0-929722-89-2*) CA State Library Fndtn.

California Deptartment of Education Staff, et al. California's Gold 1992 ("300" Series) 104p. (Orig.). 1993. pap. text, teacher ed. 15.00 (*0-929722-55-8*) CA State Library Fndtn.

California Design Publications Staff. Preferred Resources. 2nd ed. (Illus.). 144p. 1989. pap. 19.95 (*0-929374-02-9*) CA Design Pubns.

— Profiles, No. 2. 2nd ed. (Illus.). 288p. 1989. pap. 14.95 (*0-929374-00-2*) CA Design Pubns.

California Design Publications Staff, ed. Profiles: Architecture, 1990. 2nd ed. (Illus.). 136p. 1989. pap. 24.95 (*0-929374-04-5*) CA Design Pubns.

California Energy Commission. California Wind Atlas. (Illus.). 216p. 1985. pap. 39.95 (*0-88016-065-9*) WindBks.

California Energy Commission Staff. Advanced Lighting Guidelines. 2nd ed. (Illus.). 200p. (Orig.). (C). 1993. pap. text 45.00 (*0-941375-67-6*) DIANE Pub.

— California Wind Energy Projects, 1985-1994. 330p. 1997. pap. 125.00 (*0-88016-066-7*) WindBks.

California Fertilizer Association Staff. Western Fertilizer Handbook. 8th ed. (Illus.). 351p. 1995. pap. text 26.95 (*0-8134-2972-2*, 2490) Interstate.

— Western Fertilizer Handbook: Horticulture Edition. (Illus.). 290p. (C). 1998. pap. text 26.95 (*0-8134-3146-8*) Interstate.

California Heritage Museum Staff, jt. auth. see Congdon-Martin, Douglas.

***California Institute of Public Affairs Staff.** Trade & Professional Associations. 7th ed. LC 99-43206. (Information Guides Ser.). 1999. write for info. (*1-880028-09-3*) Cal Inst Public.

California Institute of Technology Staff, ed. see Wiersma, Cornelius G.

California Instructional Technology Clearinghouse Staff, contrib. by. Guidelines for the Evaluation of Instructional Technology Resources. (Illus.). 44p. 1997. pap. 14.95 (*1-56484-131-6*) Intl Society Tech Educ.

California Journal & State Net Staff. California Local Government Directory, 1995-96. rev. ed. 320p. 1995. pap. 60.00 (*0-930302-32-X*) Cal Journal.

— 50-State Legislative Directory 1996. rev. ed. 320p. 1996. pap., ring bd. 95.00 (*0-930302-35-4*) Cal Journal.

— 50-State Legislative Directory, 1997. rev. ed. 320p. 1997. 95.00 (*0-930302-43-5*) Cal Journal.

California Journal & State Net Staff, ed. The California Directory Vol. 3: Local Government. 348p. (Orig.). 1989. pap. 60.00 (*0-930302-67-2*) Cal Journal.

— California Journal Roster 1996 Pocket Edition. rev. ed. (Illus.). 144p. 1996. pap. 9.95 (*0-930302-37-0*) Cal Journal.

— California Lobbyists - PACS Directory, 1995. rev. ed. 240p. 1995. pap. 40.00 (*0-930302-31-1*) Cal Journal.

— California Lobbyists - Pacs Directory, 1996. rev. ed. 240p. 1996. pap. 40.00 (*0-930302-38-9*) Cal Journal.

— California Lobbyists/Pacs Directory, 1997. rev. ed. 240p. 1997. 40.00 (*0-930302-47-8*) Cal Journal.

— California Local Government Directory, 1996-1998. rev. ed. 320p. 1997. pap. 60.00 (*0-930302-40-0*) Cal Journal.

California Journal Staff, ed. California Journal Roster: 1998 Pocket Edition. rev. ed. (Illus.). 141p. 1998. pap. 9.95 (*1-891704-00-1*) Cal Journal.

— California Journal Roster 1992 Pocket Edition. (Illus.). 142p. (Orig.). 1992. pap. 9.95 (*0-930302-82-6*) Cal Journal.

— California Journal Roster 1993 Pocket Edition. (Illus.). 142p. (Orig.). 1993. pap. 9.95 (*0-930302-87-7*) Cal Journal.

— California Journal Roster 1994 Pocket Edition. rev. ed. (Illus.). 139p. 1994. pap. 9.95 (*0-930302-93-1*) Cal Journal.

— California Journal Roster 1995 Pocket Edition. rev. ed. (Illus.). 140p. 1995. pap. 9.95 (*0-930302-28-1*) Cal Journal.

California Journal Staff & State Net Staff, eds. California Lobbyists - PACS Directory, 1998. rev. ed. 250p. 1998. pap. 40.00 (*0-930302-49-4*) Cal Journal.

— California Lobbyists - PACS Directory, 1994. 239p. 1984. pap. 40.00 (*0-930302-94-X*) Cal Journal.

— California Local Government Directory, 1998. rev. ed. 360p. 1998. pap. 60.00 (*1-891704-01-X*) Cal Journal.

— California Local Government Directory, 1994-1995. rev. ed. 318p. 1994. pap. 60.00 (*0-930302-96-6*) Cal Journal.

— California State Government Directory. (Illus.). 170p. pap., ring bd. 125.00 (*0-930302-75-3*) Cal Journal.

— California State Government Directory, 1998. (Illus.). 170p. 1998. pap. 125.00 (*1-891704-02-8*) Cal Journal.

— 50-State Legislative Directory, 1998. rev. ed. 320p. 1998. pap. 95.00 (*0-930302-48-6*) Cal Journal.

— 50-State Legislative Directory 1995. rev. ed. 320p. 1995. pap., ring bd. 95.00 (*0-930302-92-3*) Cal Journal.

California Landscape Standards Committee Staff. California Landscape Standards. Fiske, Roger D., ed. (Illus.). 170p. (C). 1989. write for info. (*0-9624700-8-2*) CA Landscape.

California Law Review Staff, ed. Essays in Honor of Hans Kelsen: Celebrating the 90th Anniversary of His Birth, 8 vols. LC 70-178735. (Illus.). 256p. 1971. reprint ed. 25.00 (*0-8377-0528-2*, Rothman) W S Hein.

California MBA Staff. Quality Control Plan for Loan Origination Operations, Vol. 1. (C). 1997. ring bd. 100.00 (*1-57599-018-0*, Real Est Fin Pr) Mortgage Bankers.

California MBA Staff. Quality Control Plan for Loan Servicing Operations, Vol. 2. 1997. ring bd. 100.00 (*1-57599-017-2*, Real Est Fin Pr) Mortgage Bankers.

California Medical Association Staff, ed. see Thurber, Packard.

California Native Plant Society, Marin Chapter Sta, jt. auth. see Point Reyes National Seashore Association Staff.

California Poets in the Schools Staff, ed. On the Other Side of That Window. 1993. pap. 10.95 (*0-939927-10-1*) Calif Poets Schls.

California Project Lean Staff. Choose Health, Choose Lean: A Guide for a Supermarket Lean Meat Nutrition Education Program. Breitrose, Prudence, ed. 84p. (Orig.). 1992. pap. 19.50 (*1-879552-09-4*) SCRDP.

California Redevelopment Association Staff. California Affordable Housing Handbook. Carlson, William A. et al, eds. (Illus.). x, 202p. 1998. pap. text 39.00 (*1-893291-00-6*) Calif Redevelop.

— Citizen Guide to Redevelopment. 2nd ed. Carlson, William A., ed. Johnson, Carmen et al, trs. (Illus.). 22p. 1994. pap. 2.50 (*1-893291-02-2*); pap. 2.50 (*1-893291-03-0*) Calif Redevelop.

— Introduction to Redevelopment. Carlson, William A. et al, eds. (Illus.). xi, 180p. 1996. pap. 35.00 (*1-893291-01-4*) Calif Redevelop.

California School Library Association. From Library Skills to Information Literacy: A Handbook for the 21st Century. 2nd ed. 150p. 1997. pap. 22.00 (*0-931510-67-8*) Hi Willow.

California Spanish Language Data Base Staff. Bilindex: A Bilingual Spanish-English Subject Heading List: Spanish Equivalents to Library of Congress Subject Headings. LC 83-25285. 1983. 149.95 (*0-915745-00-3*) Floricanto Pr.

***California Staff.** Deskbook on the Management of Complex Civil Litigation. LC 00-23817. 2000. 50.00 (*0-8205-4391-8*) Bender.

California, State Board of Control Staff. California & the Oriental. Daniels, Roger, ed. LC 78-54809. (Asian Experience in North America Ser.). (Illus.). 1979. reprint ed. lib. bdg. 18.95 (*0-405-11265-3*) Ayer.

California State Coastal Conservancy Staff. San Francisco Bay Shoreline Guide. LC 94-17818. 1995. pap. 17.95 (*0-520-08878-6*, Pub. by U CA Pr) Cal Prin Full Svc.

California State Department of Health Staff. Leisure Time Activities for Deaf-Blind Children. LC 75-70071. 24.95 (*0-917002-06-7*) Joyce Media.

California State Department of Health Staff, et al. Sign Language for Everyone. LC 75-70066. (Illus.). 14.95 (*0-917002-02-4*) Joyce Media.

— Talk with Me: Communication with the Multi-Handicapped Deaf. LC 75-70066. 35.00 (*0-917002-05-9*) Joyce Media.

California State Grange Staff. California Gold. LC 92-32005. 1992. write for info. (*0-87197-355-3*) Favorite Recipes.

California State Staff. Computers in the Curriculum: Exercises for Integrating. LC 94-70871. 448p. (C). 1994. text 33.35 (*0-697-25065-2*, Irwn McGrw-H) McGrw-H Hghr Educ.

— Wings. 5th ed. 162p. (C). 1999. per. 20.95 (*0-7872-5763-X*, 41576301) Kendall-Hunt.

California State University at Northridge, Office. Computer Technology & Persons with Disabilities: Proceedings. Murphy, Harry J. & Dunnigan, J. A., eds. 327p. (Orig.). 1986. pap. 12.95 (*0-937475-00-9*) CSUN Disabled.

California State University, Fullerton Staff. Beatrice Wood Retrospective. (Illus.). 48p. (Orig.). 1983. pap. 12.00 (*0-935314-23-7*) CSU Art Gallery.

— Charles Arnoldi & Laddie John Dill. (Orig.). 1983. pap. write for info. (*0-935314-24-5*) CSU Art Gallery.

***California State University Sacramento Staff, Sacramento.** California Public Management Casebook. Keene, Barry, ed. LC 99-16521. 245p. 1999. pap. 21.95 (*0-87772-391-5*) UCB IGS.

California State University Staff. Constructing the Paragraph: The Ramblestones on the Road for Use with IBM-PC. 1984. 39.95 (*0-07-831013-X*) McGraw.

— Contestination: Developing Successful Estimating Abilities for Use with Apple II. 1984. 49.95 (*0-07-831021-0*) McGraw.

— Introduction to Language for Use with IBM PC. 1984. 49.95 (*0-07-831035-0*) McGraw.

— Ten Common Inferences: Oscar-The Big Escape for Use with IBM-PC, Pt. 2. 1984. 49.95 (*0-07-831015-6*) McGraw.

California Trade & Commerce Agency Staff, jt. ed. see California Chamber of Commerce Staff.

California Travel Association Staff. California Visitor's Guide. (Illus.). 1987. pap. 4.95 (*0-913290-23-8*) Camaro Pub.

California Travel Association Staff, ed. California Weekender: Northern California, Vol. 2. (Illus.). 1987. pap. 4.95 (*0-913290-74-2*) Camaro Pub.

— California Weekender: Southern California, Vol. 1. (Illus.). 1987. pap. 4.95 (*0-913290-73-4*) Camaro Pub.

California University, Center for Medieval & Renai. The Dawn of Modern Banking. LC 78-14022. 329p. reprint ed. pap. 102.00 (*0-8357-8703-6*, 203369900087) Bks Demand.

California University Committee on International R. Problems of Hemispheric Defense. LC 77-167322. (Essay Index Reprint Ser.). 1977. reprint ed. 18.95 (*0-8369-2759-1*) Ayer.

— Problems of War & Peace in the Society of Nations. LC 67-23188. (Essay Index Reprint Ser.). 1977. 19.95 (*0-8369-0270-X*) Ayer.

— Southwest Pacific & War. LC 74-3750. 168p. 1974. reprint ed. lib. bdg. 65.00 (*0-8371-7473-2*, CUSP, Greenwood Pr) Greenwood.

— United States among the Nations. LC 68-54336. (Essay Index Reprint Ser.). 1977. 18.95 (*0-8369-0271-8*) Ayer.

California University, Department of English Staff. Essays in Criticism. LC 67-22083. (Essay Index Reprint Ser.). 1977. 20.95 (*0-8369-0272-6*); 21.95 (*0-8369-1327-2*) Ayer.

California University Regents Staff. The Essential Handbook for Academic Success Skills. 156p. (C). 1997. per. 28.95 (*0-7872-4416-3*, 41441601) Kendall-Hunt.

California Urban Water Agencies Staff. Evaluating Urban Water Conservation Programs: A Procedures Manual. (Illus.). 308p. 1993. pap. 54.00 (*0-89867-676-2*, 20292) Am Water Wks Assn.

California Writers' Club, High Desert Branch Staff. Images: An Anthology. 192p. 1995. 8.00 (*0-9646728-0-4*) High Desert Branch.

California Writers' Club Staff. West Winds Four: An Anthology. LC 89-11401. 232p. (Orig.). 1990. pap. 9.95 (*0-89407-097-5*) Strawberry Hill.

California Year Book Print. Your Business Plan: A Workbook for Owners of Small Businesses. 118p. 1998. pap. text, wbk. ed. 20.00 (*0-536-01829-4*) Pearson Custom.

Caligaris-Cappio, Federico, jt. ed. see Ferrarini, Manlio.

Caligiuri, Paul & Herbst, Dan. High-Performance Soccer. LC 96-15783. (Illus.). 256p. (Orig.). 1996. pap. 15.95 (*0-88011-552-1*, PCAL0552) Human Kinetics.

Caligiuri, Tony, jt. auth. see Miller, Bill.

Caligor, Judith, et al. Combining Individual & Group Therapy. LC 93-73982. 234p. 1994. pap. 40.00 (*1-56821-169-4*) Aronson.

Caligor, L., et al. Clinical Perspectives on the Supervision of Psychoanalysis & Psychotherapy. (Critical Issues in Psychiatry Ser.). (Illus.). 302p. (C). 1984. text 75.00 (*0-306-41403-1*, Kluwer Plenum) Kluwer Academic.

***Caliguire, Jeff.** Write for Your Soul: The Whys & Hows of Journaling. 1998. pap. 9.95 (*1-929794-14-2*) Soul Care.

Calija, Marc, jt. auth. see Baugher, Robert.

Calimano, Ivan E. Index to Spanish Language Short Stories in Anthologies. 332p. (Orig.). 1994. pap. 52.95 (*0-917617-41-X*) SALALM.

Calin, Alex A. Mar Ratacit (Stray Apple) Poems. H & H Promotions Staff, ed. (ENG & RUM., Illus.). x, 158p. 1998. pap. 10.00 (*0-9664844-1-X*) H & H Promotions.

An Asterisk (*) at the beginning of an entry indicates that the title is appearing for the first time.

C

***Callaghan.** Physical Bases of Voice. LC 99-40616. 1999. pap. 57.95 (*0-7693-0044-8*) Thomson Learn.

Callaghan & Shakespeare, William. Romeo & Juliet: Texts & Contexts. pap. text. write for info. (*0-312-19192-8*) St Martin.

Callaghan, jt. auth. see Schwiebert, Ernest.

Callaghan, jt. auth. see Shakespeare, William.

Callaghan, Barry, tr. see Ziedonis, Imants.

Callaghan, Brent. Network File System Version 4. LC 99-56696. 448p. (C). 1999. 49.95 (*0-201-32570-5*) Addison-Wesley.

Callaghan, Catherine A. Northern Sierra Miwok Dictionary. 2nd ed. LC 86-28908. (University of California Publications in Linguistics: No. 110). 408p. 1987. reprint ed. pap. 126.50 (*0-7837-8129-6*, 204793600008) Bks Demand.

— Plains Miwok Dictionary. LC 83-18034. (University of California Publications in Linguistics: No. 105). 319p. pap. 98.90 (*0-7837-7474-5*, 204919600010) Bks Demand.

Callaghan, Charles, jt. photos by see Perloff, Stephen.

Callaghan, Christopher T., jt. ed. see Connors, Tracy D.

Callaghan, Dennis W., jt. auth. see Elkins, Arthur.

***Callaghan, Dympna.** The Duchess of Malfi. LC 99-45127. 2000. text 49.95 (*0-312-22861-9*) St Martin.

— Shakespeare Without Women LC 99-15659. (Accents on Shakespeare Ser.). 1999. pap. 27.99 (*0-415-20232-9*) Routledge.

— Shakespeare Without Women. LC 99-15659. (Accents on Shakespeare Ser.). 240p. (C). 1999. text. write for info. (*0-415-20231-0*) Routledge.

Callaghan, Dympna, ed. A Feminist Companion to Shakespeare. LC 99-56237. (Companions to Literature & Culture Ser.). 496p. 1999. 99.95 (*0-631-20806-2*) Blackwell Pubs.

Callaghan, Dympna, et al. The Weyward Sisters: Shakespeare & Feminist Politics. 192p. 1994. pap. 24.95 (*0-631-17798-1*) Blackwell Pubs.

Callaghan, Ed. Sell on Purpose, Not by Accident. 200p. 1998. pap. 12.95 (*1-57502-875-1*, PO2343) Morris Pubng.

Callaghan, Ed & Nauert, Peter W. TechnoSelling: How to Use Today's Technology to Increase Your Sales. 288p. 1995. 24.95 (*0-9645225-0-0*) Lone Str Pub.

Callaghan Editorial Staff. Plaintiff's Proof of a Prima Facie Case. 1988. 130.00 (*0-685-30210-5*) West Group.

Callaghan, Frank, ed. see Schuller, Robert H.

Callaghan, George S. Flexibility, Mobility & the Labour Market. LC 97-72669. (Illus.). 256p. 1997. text 64.95 (*1-85972-604-6*, Pub. by Ashgate Pub) Ashgate Pub Co.

Callaghan, H. Cambridge University. LC 99-233998. (Best of Britain in Old Photographs Ser.). (Illus.). 128p. 1998. pap. 17.95 (*0-7509-1698-2*, Pub. by Sutton Pub Ltd) Intl Pubs Mktg.

Callaghan, Hugh. Cruel Fate: One Man's Triumph over Injustice. 207p. 1993. 30.00 (*1-85371-258-2*, Pub. by Poolbeg Pr) Dufour.

Callaghan, Hugh & Mulready, Sally. Cruel Fate: One Man's Triumph over Injustice. 2nd ed. LC 95-23619. (Illus.). 272p. 1995. pap. 16.95 (*0-87023-987-2*) U of Mass Pr.

— Cruel Fate: One Man's Triumph over Injustice. 2nd ed. LC 95-23619. (Illus.). 304p. (C). 1995. text 35.00 (*0-87023-986-4*) U of Mass Pr.

Callaghan, Jean, jt. auth. see Kuhlmann, Jurgen.

Callaghan, John. Great Power Complex: British Imperialism, International Crises & National Decline, 1914-51. LC 96-48789. (Socialist History of Britain Ser.). 140p. 1997. 39.95 (*0-7453-1184-9*, Pub. by Pluto GBR); pap. 13.95 (*0-7453-1179-2*, Pub. by Pluto GBR) Stylus Pub VA.

— Rajani Palme Dutt: A Study in British Stalinism. 256p. (C). 1993. pap. 35.00 (*0-85315-779-0*, Pub. by Lawrence & Wishart) NYU Pr.

Callaghan, John. The Retreat of Social Democracy. pap. write for info. (*0-7190-5032-4*, Pub. by Manchester Univ Pr); text. write for info. (*0-7190-5031-6*, Pub. by Manchester Univ Pr) St Martin.

Callaghan, John. Yorkshire Cricket Greats. 180p. (C). 1989. text 35.00 (*0-85976-325-0*, Pub. by J Donald) St Mut.

Callaghan, John, et al, eds. The Adult Hip, 2 vols. LC 97-28141. (Illus.). 1600p. 1997. text 335.00 (*0-397-51704-1*) Lppncott W & W.

Callaghan, John C. & Wartak, Joseph, eds. Open Heart Surgery: Theory & Practice. 7. LC 86-5005. (Surgical Science Ser.: Vol. 7). (Illus.). 190p. 1986. 57.95 (*0-275-92088-7*, C2088, Praeger Pubs) Greenwood.

Callaghan, John J., ed. Orthopaedic Knowledge Update: Hip & Knee Reconstruction. LC 95-39517. 334p. 1995. pap. 115.00 (*0-89203-117-4*) Amer Acad Ortho Surg.

Callaghan, John J., et al. The Adult Hip. LC 97-28141. 1500p. 1997. text 475.00 (*0-7817-1429-X*) Lppncott W & W.

Callaghan, John J., ed. see Galante, Jorge O.

Callaghan, Karen A., ed. Ideals of Feminine Beauty: Philosophical, Social & Cultural Dimensions, 141. LC 93-39353. (Contributions in Women's Studies: No. 141). 200p. 1994. 55.00 (*0-313-26136-9*, Greenwood Pr) Greenwood.

***Callaghan, Linda Y.** InRage: Healing the Inner Rage of Child Sexual Abuse. 2000. 25.00 (*0-7388-0726-5*); pap. 18.00 (*0-7388-0727-3*) Xlibris Corp.

Callaghan, Linda Y. Inrage: Healing the Rage of Child Sexual Abuse. LC 91-60650. (Illus.). 150p. 1991. 25.00 (*0-943806-07-0*) Neahtawanta Pr.

Callaghan, M. R. The Awkward Girl. (C). 1990. 36.00 (*0-946311-95-1*) St Mut.

Callaghan, Margaret. Devlin's Desire. large type ed. (Magna Large Print Ser.). 368p. 1998. 29.99 (*0-7505-1278-4*, Pub. by Mgna Lrg Print) Ulverscroft.

— Devlin's Desire: Passionate Prisoner. 400p. (Orig.). 1996. mass mkt. 3.99 (*1-85487-708-9*, Pub. by Scarlet Bks) London Brdge.

— Marriott's Legacy. (Scarlet Ser.). 1999. mass mkt. 3.99 (*1-85487-557-4*, Pub. by Scarlet Bks) London Brdge.

— Scarlet Master of the House. 1997. mass mkt. 3.99 (*1-85487-928-6*) London Brdge.

— Temporary Arrangement. (Scarlet Ser.). 1998. mass mkt. 3.99 (*1-85487-570-1*, Pub. by Scarlet Bks) London Brdge.

— Wilde Affair. 1998. mass mkt. 3.99 (*1-85487-983-9*, Pub. by Scarlet Bks) London Brdge.

Callaghan, Mary R. Emigrant Dreams. 298p. 1996. pap. 12.95 (*1-85371-620-0*, Pub. by Poolbeg Pr) Dufour.

— Kitty O'Shea: A Life of Katherine Parnell. 210p. (Orig.). 1989. pap. 14.95 (*0-04-440360-7*) Routledge.

Callaghan, Morley. A Fine & Private Place. 213p. 1983. pap. 7.95 (*0-7715-9861-0*) Genl Dist Srvs.

— More Joy in Heaven. 200p. 1996. pap. text 6.95 (*0-7710-9956-8*) McCland & Stewart.

— Native Argosy. LC 70-106255. (Short Story Index Reprint Ser.). 1977. 20.95 (*0-8369-3292-7*) Ayer.

— Such Is My Beloved. 184p. 1996. pap. text 6.95 (*0-7710-9955-X*) McCland & Stewart.

— They Shall Inherit the Earth. 336p. 1996. pap. text 6.95 (*0-7710-9881-2*) McCland & Stewart.

***Callaghan, Patsy & Dobyns, Ann.** Literary Conversation: Thinking, Talking, & Writing about Literature. LC 95-34155. 260p. 2005. pap. text 28.00 (*0-205-16897-3*) Allyn.

Callaghan, Paul T. Principles of Nuclear Magnetic Resonance Microscopy. (Illus.). 510p. 1994. reprint ed. pap. text 55.00 (*0-19-853997-5*) OUP.

Callaghan, Polly & Hartmann, Heidi. Contingent Work: A Chart Book on Part-Time & Temporary Employment. 1992. 10.00 (*0-944826-45-8*) Economic Policy Inst.

Callaghan, Steven. Brainercise Mental Exercise Program: Arithmetic, Vol. 1, Bk. 7. large type ed. 25p. (J). (gr. k up). 1991. spiral bd. 5.00 (*0-925395-22-6*) SGC Biomedical.

— Brainercise Mental Exercise Program: Arithmetic, Vol. 1, Bk. 8. large type ed. 25p. (J). (gr. k up). 1991. spiral bd. 5.00 (*0-925395-23-4*) SGC Biomedical.

— Brainercise Mental Exercise Program: Arithmetic, Vol. 1, Bk. 9. large type ed. 25p. (J). (gr. k up). 1991. spiral bd. 5.00 (*0-925395-29-3*) SGC Biomedical.

— Brainercise Mental Exercise Program: Arithmetic, Vol. 1, Bk. 10. large type ed. 25p. (J). (gr. k up). 1991. spiral bd. 5.00 (*0-925395-30-7*) SGC Biomedical.

— Brainercise Mental Exercise Program: Arithmetic, Vol. 2, Bk. 1. large type ed. 25p. (J). (gr. k up). 1991. spiral bd. 5.00 (*0-925395-27-7*) SGC Biomedical.

— Brainercise Mental Exercise Program: Arithmetic, Vol. 2, Bk. 2. large type ed. 25p. (J). (gr. k up). 1991. spiral bd. 5.00 (*0-925395-31-5*) SGC Biomedical.

— Brainercise Mental Exercise Program: Arithmetic, Vol. 2, Bk. 3. large type ed. 25p. (J). (gr. k up). 1991. spiral bd. 5.00 (*0-925395-32-3*) SGC Biomedical.

— Brainercise Mental Exercise Program: Arithmetic, Vol. 3, Bk. 1. large type ed. 25p. (J). (gr. k up). 1991. spiral bd. 5.00 (*0-925395-28-5*) SGC Biomedical.

— Brainercise Mental Exercise Program Bk. 3: Arithmetic, Vol. 3. large type ed. 25p. 1991. spiral bd. 5.00 (*0-925395-16-1*) SGC Biomedical.

— Brainercise Mental Exercise Program Bk. 4: Arithmetic, Vol. 1. large type ed. 25p. 1991. spiral bd. 5.00 (*0-925395-17-X*) SGC Biomedical.

— Global Positioning System: Gold Code Balance-Run-Autocorrelation Properties Reference. 200p. 1994. 50.00 (*0-925395-98-6*) SGC Biomedical.

— Global Positioning System: Navigation Message Timing Reference. 158p. (C). 1992. 30.00 (*0-925395-99-4*) SGC Biomedical.

Callaghan, William. What's Right? What's Wrong? Director's Manual. Sawyer, Kieran, ed. LC 97-169764. (Developing Faith Ser.). 16p. 1997. pap. text, teacher ed. 16.95 (*0-87793-609-9*) Ave Maria.

— What's Right? What's Wrong? Participant Book. Sawyer, Kieran, ed. (Developing Faith Ser.). 80p. (YA). (gr. 9-12). 1997. pap. text 5.95 (*0-87793-608-0*) Ave Maria.

Callaghy, Thomas M. The State-Society Struggle: Zaire in Comparative Perspective. LC 84-5865. 515p. 1984. pap. text 32.50 (*0-231-05721-0*) Col U Pr.

Callaghy, Thomas M., ed. South Africa in Southern Africa: The Intensifying Vortex of Violence. 432p. 1983. 79.50 (*0-275-90956-5*, C0956, Praeger Pubs) Greenwood.

Callaghy, Thomas M. & Ravenhill, John, eds. Hemmed In: Global Responses to Africa's Economic Decline. LC 93-19692. 1994. 61.50 (*0-231-08228-2*); pap. 23.00 (*0-231-08229-0*) Col U Pr.

Callaham, L. I. Russian-English Dictionary of Science & Technology. 3rd ed. (ENG & RUS.). 852p. 1993. 150.00 (*0-7859-9081-X*) Fr & Eur.

Callahan. Corporate Dynamic Worship. 16.00 (*0-685-69292-2*) HarperTrade.

— Design Producing News Online. 2001. 25.74 (*0-07-234394-X*) McGraw.

— A Journalist's Guide to the Internet: The Net as a Reporting Tool. LC 98-39183. 126p. 1998. pap. 24.00 (*0-205-28215-6*) Allyn.

Callahan, jt. auth. see Corey.

Callahan, jt. auth. see Scheer.

Callahan & Associates, Inc. Staff, ed. 1998 CFO's Guide to Credit Union Investments: Including Detailed Information on Corporate Credit Unions. 4th ed. Orig. Title: Corporate Sourcebook. (Illus.). 188p. 1998. pap. 95.00 (*1-889265-11-X*) Callahan & Assocs.

— 1998 Credit Union Directory: The First Guide to All Credit Unions. 13th rev. ed. (Illus.). 578p. 1997. pap. 135.00 (*1-889265-06-3*) Callahan & Assocs.

— 1998 Credit Union Yearbook, 5 vols. 11th ed. (Illus.). 316p. 1998. pap. 555.00 (*1-889265-02-0*) Callahan & Assocs.

— The 1998 Defense Credit Union Council Directory. 2nd rev. ed. (Illus.). 178p. 1998. pap. 95.00 (*1-889265-08-X*) Callahan & Assocs.

— 1999 Budget & Planning Workbook. 10th ed. (Illus.). 71p. 1998. pap. 210.00 (*1-889265-10-1*) Callahan & Assocs.

— 1999 Credit Union Directory: The First Guide to All Credit Unions. 14th rev. ed. (Illus.). 578p. 1998. pap. 135.00 (*1-889265-07-1*) Callahan & Assocs.

Callahan, Alice A. The Osage Ceremonial Dance I'n-Lon-Schka. LC 90-50230. (C). 1993. pap. 11.95 (*0-8061-2486-5*) U of Okla Pr.

Callahan, Allen D. Embassy of Onesimus: The Letter of Paul to Philemon. LC 97-214. (New Testament in Context Ser.). 112p. (Orig.). 1997. pap. 11.00 (*1-56338-147-8*) TPI PA.

Callahan, Anne, jt. auth. see Furber, Donald.

Callahan, Annice. Evelyn Underhill: Spirituality for Daily Living. LC 97-17958. 264p. 1997. 47.50 (*0-7618-0849-3*) U Pr of Amer.

Callahan, Betsy N. Grief Counseling: A Manual for Social Workers. 96p. (C). 1999. pap. text 14.95 (*0-89108-268-9*, 9906) Love Pub Co.

Callahan, Betsy N., jt. auth. see Freeman, Vivian.

Callahan, Billy. Muckraker. LC 99-29501. 224p. 1999. pap. 12.75 (*1-892657-06-6*) Town Bk Pr.

Callahan, Bob, ed. The New Comics Anthology. (Illus.). 288p. (Orig.). 1991. pap. 19.95 (*0-02-009361-6*) Macmillan.

Callahan, Bob, ed. see Auster, Paul & Spiegelman, Art.

Callahan, Bob, ed. & intro. see Sauer, Carl Ortwin.

Callahan, C. M., jt. auth. see Renzulli, Joseph S.

Callahan, Carol, compiled by. Prairie Avenue Cookbook: Recipes & Recollections from Prominent 19th-Century Chicago Families. LC 92-23088. (Illus.). 224p. (C). 1993. 36.95 (*0-8093-1814-8*); pap. 18.95 (*0-8093-1815-6*) S Ill U Pr.

Callahan, Carol, et al. Chart Your Success on the COMPASS Test. 240p. (Orig.). 1997. pap. text 30.00 (*0-89892-153-8*) Contemp Pub Co of Raleigh.

***Callahan, Carolyn M.** Instruments & Evaluation Designs Used in Gifted Programs. 139p. 2000. reprint ed. pap. text 30.00 (*0-7881-8825-9*) DIANE Pub.

Callahan, Carolyn M., jt. auth. see Bear, George G.

Callahan, Charles. The American Classic Organ: A History in Letters. (Illus.). xxv, 531p. 1990. 34.00 (*0-913499-05-6*) Organ Hist Soc.

— Washington: The Man & the Mason (1913) 400p. 1998. reprint ed. pap. 49.95 (*0-7661-0245-9*) Kessinger Pub.

Callahan, Cheryl. Campbell's Port, a Family Memoir. LC 98-96737. (Illus.). 96p. 1998. pap. 9.95 (*0-9668059-5-X*) Calla Pubg.

Callahan, Collen & Gunter, Frank. Columbia: An Opening Economy, Vol. 3. LC 99-26283. (Contemporary Studies in Economic & Financial Analysis: Vol. 84). 1999. 78.50 (*0-7623-0418-9*) Jai Pr.

***Callahan, Cornelius P.** The Ringbear. (Illus.). 38p. (J). (ps-4). 2000. 14.99 (*0-9658769-2-6*) Sextant.

Callahan, Cornelius P. The Search for Truth: An Introduction to the Jury Trial Process. Fitzgerald, Kathleen & Burt, Patricia, eds. LC 97-92212. 283p. 1997. text 35.00 (*0-9658769-1-8*) Sextant.

Callahan, D. & Bok, S. Ethics Teaching in Higher Education. LC 80-24002. (Hastings Center Series in Ethics). (Illus.). 332p. (C). 1980. 56.00 (*0-306-40522-9*, Plenum Trade) Perseus Pubng.

Callahan, D. & Jennings, B. Ethics, the Social Sciences, & Policy Analysis. LC 82-22277. (Hastings Center Series in Ethics). (Illus.). 408p. (C). 1983. 60.00 (*0-306-41143-1*, Plenum Trade) Perseus Pubng.

Callahan, D., jt. auth. see Jennings, B.

Callahan, Daniel. False Hopes: Why America's Quest for Perfect Health Is a Recipe for Failure. LC 97-40541. 366p. 1998. 24.00 (*0-684-81109-X*, Scribner Pap Fic) S&S Trade Pap.

— Setting Limits: Medical Goals in An Aging Society, with "A Reponse to My Critics" LC 94-34439. 272p. 1995. pap. 16.95 (*0-87840-572-0*) Georgetown U Pr.

***Callahan, Daniel.** The Troubled Dream of Life: In Search of a Peaceful Death. LC 00-26365. 256p. 2000. reprint ed. pap. 15.95 (*0-87840-815-0*) Georgetown U Pr.

Callahan, Daniel. The Tyranny of Survival: And Other Pathologies of Civilized Life. LC 85-5316. (Illus.). 300p. 1985. reprint ed. pap. text 24.50 (*0-8191-4636-6*) U Pr of Amer.

— What Kind of Life? The Limits of Medical Progress. LC 94-34440. 320p. 1995. pap. 15.95 (*0-87840-573-9*) Georgetown U Pr.

***Callahan, Daniel, ed.** Promoting Healthy Behavior: How Much Freedom? Whose Responsibility? LC 99-38856. (Hastings Center Studies in Ethics). 192p. 2000. text 45.00 (*0-87840-762-6*) Georgetown U Pr.

Callahan, Daniel, ed. The Teaching of Ethics in Higher Education: A Report by the Hastings Center. LC 80-10294. (Teaching of Ethics Ser.). 103p. 1980. pap. 5.00 (*0-916558-09-6*) Hastings Ctr.

Callahan, Daniel, et al, eds. Applying the Humanities. LC 85-9479. (Hastings Center Series in Ethics). (Illus.). 346p. (C). 1985. 59.00 (*0-306-41968-8*, Plenum Trade) Perseus Pubng.

— A World Growing Old: The Coming Health Care Challenges. LC 95-6447. 190p. 1996. pap. 16.95 (*0-87840-632-8*) Georgetown U Pr.

Callahan, Daniel & Clark, Phillip G., eds. Ethical Issues of Population Aid: Culture, Economics & International Assistance. 1982. text 32.50 (*0-8290-0364-9*) Irvington.

Callahan, Daniel & Engelhardt, H. Tristram, eds. The Roots of Ethics: Science, Religion, & Values. (Hastings Center Series in Ethics). 464p. 1981. 60.00 (*0-306-40796-5*, Plenum Trade) Perseus Pubng.

Callahan, Daniel, et al. Congress & the Media: The Ethical Connection. LC 85-11965. 52p. pap. 7.00 (*0-916558-22-3*) Hastings Ctr.

Callahan, Daniel, jt. ed. see Callahan, Sidney.

Callahan, Daniel, jt. ed. see Caplan, Arthur L.

Callahan, Daniel, jt. ed. see Hanson, Mark J.

Callahan, David. False Hopes: Overcoming the Obstacles to a Sustainable, Affordable Medicine. LC 98-52987. 330p. 1999. pap. 17.00 (*0-8135-2674-4*) Rutgers U Pr.

— State of the Union. 1998. mass mkt. 6.99 (*0-451-19725-9*, Sig) NAL.

— Unwinnable Wars: American Power & Ethnic Conflict. (Twentieth Century Fund Book Ser.). 288p. 1998. pap. 13.00 (*0-8090-1610-9*) Hill & Wang.

— Unwinnable Wars: American Power & Ethnic Conflicts. LC 97-27912. (Twentieth Century Fund Book Ser.). 273p. 1998. 24.00 (*0-8090-3046-2*) Hill & Wang.

Callahan, Deborah L., intro. Proceedings of the International Conference on Spinal Manipulation, 1992. (Annual ICSM Proceedings Ser.). (Illus.). 210p. 1992. pap. 35.00 (*0-9631715-1-8*) Fnd Chiro Educ Res.

Callahan, Dolly M. Health Foods & Disease Avoidance: Index of New Information with References. (Illus.). 150p. 1999. 47.50 (*0-7883-2224-9*); pap. 44.50 (*0-7883-2225-7*) ABBE Pubs Assn.

Callahan, Dorothy M. Julie Krone: A Winning Jockey. (Illus.). 64p. (J). (gr. 3 up). 1990. write for info. (*0-685-31386-7*, Mac Bks Young Read) S&S Childrens.

— Julie Krone: A Winning Jockey. LC 89-26061. (Taking Part Ser.). (Illus.). 64p. (J). (gr. 3 up). 1990. lib. bdg. 13.95 (*0-87518-425-1*, Dillon Silver Burdett) Silver Burdett Pr.

Callahan, Edward E. Metal Plate Connected Wood Truss Handbook. Sabean, Pam, ed. (Illus.). 318p. (C). 1993. pap. text 39.95 (*0-9638738-0-6*) WoodTruss Coun.

Callahan, Edward L. Power Cookies: The Most Important Day in the Life of Wendy Johnson, Good Girl Extraordinaire. (Orig.). pap. 6.95 (*0-9637180-0-2*) Groth Pub.

Callahan, Edward W. List of Officers of the Navy of the U. S. & of the Marine Corps, 1775-1900. LC 68-31274. (Genealogy Ser.: No. 43). 1969. reprint ed. lib. bdg. 75.00 (*0-8383-0327-7*) M S G Haskell Hse.

— List of Officers of the Navy of the U. S. & the Marine Corps from 1775-1900. 750p. 1989. reprint ed. 35.00 (*0-942211-74-X*) Olde Soldier Bks.

Callahan, Evan. Microsoft Access 97/Visual Basic Step by Step. LC 96-37208. 416p. 34.95 incl. cd-rom (*1-57231-319-6*) Microsoft.

***Callahan, Evan.** Microsoft Access 2000 VBA Fundamentals/Mastering Solution Set. 1999. pap., boxed set 99.99 incl. cd-rom (*0-7356-0814-8*) Microsoft Pr.

Callahan, Evan. Microsoft Access 2000 Visual Basic Fundamentals. LC 99-13362. 475p. 1999. pap. 39.99 (*0-7356-0592-0*) Microsoft.

— Microsoft Access/Visual Basic Step by Step. (Step by Step Ser.). 368p. 1995. 29.95 incl. disk (*1-55615-890-4*) Microsoft.

— The Power of Intranets: Creating Workgroup Web Sites with Microsoft Office 2000 & FrontPage 2000. LC 99-21356. (Illus.). 300p. 1999. pap. 29.99 incl. cd-rom (*0-7356-0641-2*) Microsoft.

***Callahan, Evan.** Troubleshooting Your Web Page. 352p. 2000. pap. 19.99 (*0-7356-1164-5*) Microsoft Pr.

Callahan, Frank. Hampton Roads. LC 98-44367. (Illus.). 256p. 1998. 45.00 (*1-885352-82-4*) Community Comm.

Callahan, Gary L. Articulation. (Illus.). (Orig.). 1997. pap. 9.95 (*1-890471-03-8*) Charis Pubns.

— Contracting with Governments. (Orig.). 1997. pap., wbk. ed. 14.95 (*1-890471-02-X*) Charis Pubns.

— The Practical Child Support Collection Workbook. 65p. (Orig.). 1991. pap., wbk. ed. 10.00 (*1-890471-00-3*) Charis Pubns.

— The Practical Child Support Collection Workbook. rev. ed. 75p. (Orig.). 1997. pap., wbk. ed. 14.95 (*1-890471-01-1*) Charis Pubns.

Callahan, Genevieve, jt. auth. see Richardson, Louvice F.

Callahan, Genevieve A. & Richardson, Lou. Home Economics Show-How & Showmanship: With Accent on Visuals. LC 66-14369. (Illus.). 159p. 1966. reprint ed. pap. 49.30 (*0-608-00056-6*, 206082200006) Bks Demand.

Callahan, Gerald N. River Odyssey: A Story of the Colorado Plateau. LC 97-44141. (Illus.). 184p. 1998. 27.50 (*0-87081-469-9*) Univ Pr Colo.

Callahan, H. Dee. Mother's Day: From Surviving to Thriving. LC 97-7358. (Illus.). 144p. (Orig.). 1997. pap. 11.95 (*1-56474-220-2*) Fithian Pr.

Callahan, Harry & Johnson, Diana L. Callahan in New England. (Illus.). 52p. (Orig.). 1994. pap. 20.00 (*0-933519-28-1*) D W Bell Gallery.

Callahan, Harry & National Gallery of Art Staff. Harry Callahan. (Illus.). 220p. 1996. 50.00 (*0-8212-2313-5*, Pub. by Bulfinch Pr) Little.

Callahan, Harry M., ed. Ansel Adams in Color. LC 92-46502. (Illus.). 132p. 1993. 60.00 (*0-8212-1980-4*, Pub. by Bulfinch Pr) Little.

***Callahan, Helen.** Augusta: A Pictorial History. (Illus.). 258p. 1998. 45.00 (*0-937044-13-X*) Richmond Cty Hist Soc.

Callahan, Helen. Summerville: A Pictorial History. (Illus.). 174p. 1993. 45.00 (*0-937044-14-8*) Richmond Cty Hist Soc.

Callahan-Howell, Kathy. Spiritual Exercises for Couch Potatoes. LC 97-228554. 168p. 1997. pap. text 9.99 (*0-89367-209-2*) Light & Life Comm.

An Asterisk (*) at the beginning of an entry indicates that the title is appearing for the first time.

***Callahan, Ian.** Winter Skies: A Celtic Christmas. 1999. 14.95 incl. audio compact disk (*0-87946-210-8*, 774) ACTA Pubns.

Callahan, James. Calculus in Context. (C). pap. text, teacher ed. 24.00 (*0-7167-2683-1*) W H Freeman.

— Primitivist Piety: The Ecclesiology of the Early Plymouth Brethren. LC 96-614. 312p. 1996. 48.00 (*0-8108-3126-0*) Scarecrow.

Callahan, James, et al. Calculus in Context: The Five College Calculus Project. LC 94-45886. 816p. (C). 1995. pap. text 76.95 (*0-7167-2630-0*) W H Freeman.

Callahan, James F., jt. ed. see Cohen, Sidney.

Callahan, James J. Geometry of Spacetime. LC 98-48083. (Illus.). 320p. 1999. 42.95 (*0-387-98641-3*) Spr-Verlag.

— Walls. rev. ed. 176p. 1996. pap. 10.00 (*0-9636270-1-5*) Callahan Assocs.

Callahan, James J., Jr., ed. Aging in Place. LC 92-41721. (Generations & Aging Ser.). 145p. 1993. pap. text 23.95 (*0-89503-113-2*) Baywood Pub.

Callahan, James M. American Foreign Policy in Canadian Relations. 1937. 30.00 (*0-686-33257-1*) R S Barnes.

— American Foreign Policy in Canadian Relations. LC 66-30786. 1970. reprint ed. 71.00 (*0-8154-0044-6*) Cooper Sq.

— American Foreign Policy in Canadian Relations. (History - United States Ser.). 576p. 1993. reprint ed. lib. bdg. 129.00 (*0-7812-4929-5*) Rprt Serv.

— American Foreign Policy in Mexican Relations. LC 66-30787. 1970. reprint ed. 75.50 (*0-8154-0045-4*) Cooper Sq.

— Cuba & International Relations. LC 76-39880. reprint ed. 42.50 (*0-404-01364-3*) AMS Pr.

— Diplomatic History of the Southern Confederacy. (History - United States Ser.). 304p. 1992. reprint ed. lib. bdg. 89.00 (*0-7812-6182-1*) Rprt Serv.

Callahan, Janet A. Characteristics of Work-Related Injuries & Illnesses in Maine. (Illus.). 67p. (Orig.). (C). 1993. pap. text 20.00 (*1-56806-343-1*) DIANE Pub.

Callahan, Joan, ed. Menopause: A Midlife Passage. LC 92-41565. 240p. 1993. 31.95 (*0-253-31312-0*); pap. 13.95 (*0-253-20817-3*) Ind U Pr.

Callahan, Joan C. Reproduction, Ethics & the Law: Feminist Perspectives. LC 95-13722. 416p. 1995. 39.95 (*0-253-32938-8*); pap. 24.95 (*0-253-20996-X*) Ind U Pr.

Callahan, Joan C., ed. Ethical Issues in Professional Life. 496p. (C). 1988. pap. text 41.95 (*0-19-505026-6*) OUP.

Callahan, Joan R., ed. Recent Advances & Issues in Environmental Science. LC 99-50342. (Frontiers of Science Ser.). (Illus.). 344p. 2000. boxed set 44.95 (*1-57356-244-0*) Oryx Pr.

Callahan, Joanne, jt. auth. see Callahan, Roger J.

Callahan, John. Do Not Disturb Any Further. LC 89-48123. (Illus.). 104p. (Orig.). 1990. pap. 7.95 (*1-55710-011-X*, Quil) HarperTrade.

— Do What He Says! He's Crazy! LC 92-16272. 1992. pap. 8.00 (*0-688-11815-1*, Quil) HarperTrade.

— Don't Worry He Won't Get Far on Foot. LC 89-40488. 224p. 1990. pap. 12.00 (*0-679-72824-4*) Vin Bks.

— Will the Real John Callahan Please Stand Up?--A Quasi-Memoir: Lurid Revelations, Shocking Rejections & Irate Letters. LC 97-33327. 1998. 20.00 (*0-688-13339-8*, Wm Morrow) Morrow Avon.

Callahan, John A., et al, eds. Classics of Cardiology, 5 vols., Vol. 3. LC 82-7830. 640p. 1983. 80.00 (*0-89874-516-0*) Krieger.

Callahan, John A., et al. Classics of Cardiology, Pt. 1, Vol. 4. LC 82-7830. 600p. 1988. lib. bdg. 80.00 (*0-89874-872-0*) Krieger.

— Classics of Cardiology, Pt. 2, Vol. 4. LC 82-7830. 514p. 1988. lib. bdg. 75.00 (*0-89464-265-0*) Krieger.

Callahan, John C. The Fine Hardwood Veneer Industry in the United States: 1838-1990. LC 90-63376. (Illus.). xvi, 368p. 1990. 32.00 (*0-9628075-0-8*) Natl Woodlands Pub.

Callahan, John D. Science & Christianity. 2nd ed. (Illus.). 120p. 1986. pap. 9.95 (*0-9615767-0-7*) Callahan CA.

Callahan, John F. Four Views of Time in Ancient Philosophy. LC 69-13850. 212p. 1970. reprint ed. lib. bdg. 35.00 (*0-8371-0337-1*, Greenwood Pr) Greenwood.

— In the African-American Grain: Call-&-Response in Twentieth-Century Black Fiction. 280p. (C). 1998. pap. 15.00 (*0-7881-5282-3*) DIANE Pub.

— In the African-American Grain: The Pursuit of Voice in Twentieth-Century Black Fiction. LC 87-5888. 296p. 1988. text 24.95 (*0-252-01459-6*) U of Ill Pr.

Callahan, John F., ed. see Ellison, Ralph.

Callahan, John J. Needed: Professional Management in Data Processing. (Illus.). 240p. 1983. 40.00 (*0-13-610956-X*) P-H.

Callahan, John W. & Lowden, J. Alexander, eds. Lysosomes & Lysosomal Storage Diseases. fac. ed. LC 79-5315. (Advances in Pediatric Research Ser.). (Illus.). 456p. pap. 141.40 (*0-7837-7298-X*, 204700800005) Bks Demand.

Callahan, Joseph F., et al. Teaching in the Middle & Secondary Schools. 6th ed. LC 97-14079. 468p. 1997. pap. text 61.00 (*0-13-621004-X*, Merrill Coll) P-H.

Callahan, Juanita D. Journey Through a Metamorphosis. 300p. (Orig.). 1996. pap. 12.99 (*1-57502-174-9*, PO796) Morris Pubng.

Callahan, Kathe, et al, eds. Reinventing New Jersey: Innovative Approaches under Fiscal Pressure. 82p. (Orig.). (C). 1996. pap. text 9.95 (*1-57420-054-2*); VHS 9.95 (*1-57420-055-0*) Chatelaine.

Callahan, Kathe, jt. auth. see Hozler, Marc.

Callahan, Kathleen, ed. Our Best to You. (Illus.). 268p. (Orig.). 1984. pap. 7.50 (*0-9615563-0-7*) K J Callahan.

Callahan, Kathryn. The Crossword Quick-List: Three Thousand Words They Use All the Time, Plus One Thousand Names & Phrases Other Dictionaries Don't Include. 128p. (Orig.). 1988. pap. 8.95 (*0-9620018-9-9*) Newpenny Pr.

Callahan, Kathy L. Our Origin & Destiny: An Evolutionary Perspective on the New Millennium. LC 96-44801. 312p. 1997. pap. 14.95 (*0-87604-368-6*, 478) ARE Pr.

Callahan, Kennon L. Building for Effective Mission: A Complete Guide for Congregations on Bricks & Mortar Issues. LC 97-24749. (Twelve Keys to an Effective Church Ser.). 152p. 1997. 17.00 (*0-7879-3872-6*) Jossey-Bass.

— Dynamic Worship: Mission, Grace, Praise & Power. LC 94-1873. 160p. 1994. 18.00 (*0-06-061281-9*) Harper SF.

— Dynamic Worship: Mission, Grace, Praise, & Power. LC 97-17946. (Twelve Keys to an Effective Church Ser.). 176p. 1997. 18.00 (*0-7879-3866-1*) Jossey-Bass.

— Effective Church Finances: Fund-Raising & Budgeting for Church Leaders. LC 91-59051. 192p. 1992. 16.00 (*0-06-061288-6*) Harper SF.

— Effective Church Finances: Fund-Raising & Budgeting for Church Leaders. LC 97-24750. (Twelve Keys to an Effective Church Ser.). 176p. 1997. 17.00 (*0-7879-3869-6*) Jossey-Bass.

— Effective Church Leadership: Building on the Twelve Keys. 1990. 21.00 (*0-06-061299-1*) Harper SF.

— Effective Church Leadership: Building on the Twelve Keys. LC 97-24751. (Religion in Practice Ser.). 288p. 1997. 22.00 (*0-7879-3865-3*) Jossey-Bass.

— Giving & Stewardship in an Effective Church: A Guide for Every Member. LC 91-58893. 1992. 16.00 (*0-06-061327-0*) Harper SF.

— Giving & Stewardship in an Effective Church: A Guide for Every Member. LC 97-25584. (Twelve Keys to an Effective Church Ser.). 144p. 1997. 16.00 (*0-7879-3867-X*) Jossey-Bass.

***Callahan, Kennon L.** A New Beginning for Pastors & Congregations: Building on the Twelve Keys. LC 99-6345. 228p. 1999. 22.00 (*0-7879-4289-8*) Jossey-Bass.

Callahan, Kennon L. Preaching Grace: Possibilities for Growing Your Preaching & Touching People's Lives. LC 98-51232. 192p. 1999. 22.00 (*0-7879-4295-2*) Jossey-Bass.

***Callahan, Kennon L.** Strong, Small Congregations. 208p. 2000. 22.00 (*0-7879-4980-9*) Jossey-Bass.

Callahan, Kennon L. Twelve Keys for Living: Possibilities for a Whole, Healthy Life. LC 98-9092. (Religion in Practice Ser.). 208p. 1998. 20.00 (*0-7879-4140-9*) Jossey-Bass.

— Twelve Keys to an Effective Church. LC 83-47718. 1983. 19.00 (*0-06-061297-5*) Harper SF.

— Twelve Keys to an Effective Church. LC 86-45802. 1987. teacher ed. 15.00 (*0-06-061295-9*) Harper SF.

— Twelve Keys to an Effective Church. 1997. pap. text, student ed. 10.00 (*0-7879-3942-0*) Jossey-Bass.

— Twelve Keys to an Effective Church. LC 97-24748. 1997. 10.00 (*0-7879-3873-4*) Jossey-Bass.

— Twelve Keys to an Effective Church. LC 97-24760. 160p. 1997. 20.00 (*0-7879-3871-8*) Jossey-Bass.

— Twelve Keys to an Effective Church: The Leader's Guide. LC 97-24760. 126p. 1997. teacher ed. 15.00 (*0-7879-3870-X*) Jossey-Bass.

— Twelve Keys to an Effective Church: The Planning Workbook. rev. ed. 1991. pap. 9.95 (*0-06-061304-1*) Harper SF.

— Visiting in an Age of Mission: A Handbook for Person-to-Person Ministry. 176p. 1994. 16.00 (*0-06-061287-8*) Harper SF.

— Visiting in an Age of Mission: A Handbook for Person-to-Person Ministry. LC 97-24759. 160p. 1997. 16.00 (*0-7879-3868-8*) Jossey-Bass.

Callahan, Kennon L. & Tanner, Ian B. Twelve Keys: A Companion to Twelve Keys to an Effective Church. LC 91-55475. 64p. 1992. pap., student ed. 6.00 (*0-06-061305-X*) Harper SF.

Callahan, M. Mrs. M's Gratitude Journal: Helped Me Survive 18 Major Disasters Because I Still Believe in God, Prayers, Angels & Miracles. spiral bd. 12.00 (*0-915453-06-1*) Dollars Info Bks.

— Mrs. M.'s Quick & Easy Refund & Rebate System: Information in a Nutshell. 15p. 1982. reprint ed. spiral bd. 12.00 (*0-915453-00-2*) Dollars Info Bks.

— Mrs. M's Winning Sweepstakes System. 9p. (Orig.). 1982. pap. 12.00 (*0-915453-02-9*) Dollars Info Bks.

— Winning Slots Jackpots Collector First Edition: Help You See the Light to Win Money in Slots Jackpots. 52p. 1996. pap. 50.00 (*0-915453-04-5*) Dollars Info Bks.

Callahan, Mathew. Sex, Death & the Angry Young Man: Conversations with Riane Eisler & David Loye. (Illus.). 120p. (Orig.). 1993. pap. 8.50 (*0-87810-040-7*) Times Change.

***Callahan, Mathew.** Testimony. Kormann, Stefan, tr. (Illus.). 131p. 2000. pap. 29.95 (*0-915117-01-0*) Freedom Voices Pubns.

Callahan, Maureen. DHEA: The Miracle Hormone That Can Help You Boost Immunity, Increase Energy, Lighten Your Mood, Improve Your Sex Drive & Lenghten Your Lifespan. LC 97-151524. 256p. 1997. mass mkt. 5.99 (*0-451-19335-0*, Sig) NAL.

— The Healthy Weigh: A Practical Food Guide. 33p. 1991. pap. text 6.25 (*0-88091-085-2*, 0808) Am Dietetic Assn.

— Skimming the Fat: A Practical Food Guide. LC 92-40300. 1992. pap. 9.95 (*0-88091-112-3*) Am Dietetic Assn.

Callahan, Maureen, jt. auth. see Holt, Tamara.

Callahan, Maureen, ed. see Sonberg, Lynn.

Callahan, Maximillian S. Insider Secrets to Diamond Dealing: How Real Money Is Made. (Illus.). 168p. 1996. pap. 15.00 (*0-87364-876-5*) Paladin Pr.

Callahan, Michael. Discovery in Constitutional Litigation: 1991 Cumulative Supplement. 2nd ed. 154p. 1991. pap. text. write for info. (*0-87473-791-5*, 60634-10, MICHIE) LEXIS Pub.

***Callahan, Michael D.** Mandates & Empire: The League of Nations & Africa, 1914-1931. LC 99-20795. 304p. 1999. 75.00 (*1-902210-23-9*, Pub. by Sussex Acad Pr) Intl Spec Bk.

Callahan, Michael E. Defined Benefit Answer Book, 1. LC 99-168197. 976p. 1998. boxed set 118.00 (*1-56706-864-2*) Panel Pubs.

Callahan, Michael J. Keys to the Workplace: Skills & Supports. LC 96-37324. 1997. pap. text 29.95 (*1-55766-276-2*) P H Brookes.

Callahan, Michael T. Discovery in Construction Literature: 1990 Supplement. 2nd ed. 1990. write for info. (*0-87473-722-2*, 60633-10, MICHIE) LEXIS Pub.

***Callahan, Michael T. & Bramble, Barry B.** Construction Delay Claims. 3rd ed. 860p. 1999. pap. text 165.00 (*0-7355-0548-9*) Panel Pubs.

Callahan, Michael T. & Hohns, H. Murray. Construction Schedules: Analysis, Evaluation & Interpretation of Schedules in Litigation. 314p. 1983. 50.00 (*0-87215-642-7*, MICHIE) LEXIS Pub.

Callahan, Michael T., et al. Construction Project Scheduling. 576p. (C). 1991. 82.19 (*0-07-009701-1*) McGraw.

— Discovery in Construction Litigation. 3rd ed. LC 94-75441. 615p. 1994. 105.00 (*1-55834-148-X*, 60632-11, MICHIE) LEXIS Pub.

— Discovery in Construction Litigation: With 1991 Cumulative Supplement. 2nd ed. 685p. 1994. 135.00 (*0-87473-320-0*, MICHIE) LEXIS Pub.

Callahan, Michael T., Jr., jt. auth. see Connell, Lee R.

Callahan, Michael T., jt. auth. see Hohns, H. Murray.

Callahan, Mike. Oldies on CD: A Guide to Oldies on Compact Disc. 2nd ed. LC 94-71069. 480p. 1994. pap. 29.95 (*0-9641180-0-9*) Both Sides.

— Oldies on CD: A Guide to Oldies on Compact Disc. 2nd limited ed. LC 94-71069. 480p. 1994. 59.95 (*0-9641180-1-7*) Both Sides.

Callahan, Murray. The Pastor's Guide to Counseling Ministry. 150p. 1995. pap. text 45.00 (*1-888915-01-X*) Counselsource.

Callahan, Murray. Bundle of Joy: A Precious Gift. (Charming Petites Ser.). 80p. 1995. 4.95 (*0-88088-772-9*) Peter Pauper.

Callahan, Murray D. The Comprehensive Guide to Church-Based Counseling, 1997. (Illus.). 300p. (Orig.). 1997. pap. 45.00 (*1-888916-19-2*) Counselsource.

— Marriage Enrichment Workbook: A Workbook for Couples in Marital Therapy. (MARC Ser.). (Illus.). 200p. (Orig.). 1997. pap. 35.00 (*1-888916-05-2*) Counselsource.

Callahan, Nathan & Payton, William, eds. Shut up, Fag! Quotations from the Files of Congressman Bob Dornan. LC 94-76626. 120p. (Orig.). 1994. pap. 8.95 (*0-9641241-0-6*) Mainstreet Media.

Callahan, Nelson J., jt. auth. see Burtsell, Richard L.

Callahan, North. Carl Sandburg: His Life & Works. LC 86-43031. (Illus.). 320p. 1987. 29.75 (*0-271-00486-X*) Pa St U Pr.

— Daniel Morgan: Ranger of the Revolution. LC 71-161759. reprint ed. 29.50 (*0-404-09017-6*) AMS Pr.

— Daybreak. LC 85-442. 264p. 1986. 15.95 (*0-8453-4796-9*, Cornwall Bks) Assoc Univ Prs.

— Peggy. LC 83-45139. 248p. 1983. 14.95 (*0-8453-4717-9*, Cornwall Bks) Assoc Univ Prs.

— Thanks, Mr. President: The Trail-Blazing Second Term of George Washington. LC 90-84706. (Illus.). 256p. 1992. 19.95 (*0-8453-4835-3*, Cornwall Bks) Assoc Univ Prs.

Callahan, Philip S. Exploring the Spectrum. LC 93-72876. 150p. 1994. pap. 16.00 (*0-911311-44-0*) Acres USA.

— My Search for Traces of God. 204p. 1997. pap. 18.00 (*0-911311-54-8*) Acres USA.

— Nature's Silent Music. LC 91-76335. 194p. 1992. pap. 15.00 (*0-911311-33-5*) Acres USA.

— Paramagnetism: Rediscovering Nature's Secret Force of Growth. LC 95-78655. (Illus.). 140p. 1995. pap. 15.00 (*0-911311-49-1*) Acres USA.

— Soul of the Ghost Moth: Paths of a Naturalist. (Illus.). 1980. 12.00 (*0-8159-6840-X*) Devin.

— Tuning into Nature. (Illus.). 240p. 1976. 24.95 (*0-8159-6309-2*) Devin.

— A Walk in the Sun. LC 88-71244. (Illus.). 242p. 1988. pap. 11.00 (*0-911311-13-0*) Acres USA.

Callahan, Rachel & McDonnell, Rea. God Is Close to the Brokenhearted: Good News for Those Who Are Depressed. 192p. (Orig.). 1996. pap. 10.95 (*0-86716-254-6*, B2546) St Anthony Mess Pr.

***Callahan, Rachel & McDonnell, Rea.** Harvest Us Home: Good News as We Age. 2000. pap. 11.95 (*0-86716-372-0*) St Anthony Mess Pr.

Callahan, Rachel & McDonnell, Rea. Hope for Healing: Good News for Adult Children of Alcoholics. 2nd rev. ed. 112p. 1998. pap. 9.95 (*1-888461-08-X*) Islewest Pub.

Callahan, Rachel, jt. auth. see McDonnell, Rea.

Callahan, Raymond A. The East India Company & Army Reform, 1783-1798. LC 70-188351. (Historical Monographs: No. 67). (Illus.). 258p. 1972. 20.00 (*0-674-22410-8*) HUP.

— The Worst Disaster: The Fall of Singapore. LC 75-29730. 293p. 1977. 39.50 (*0-87413-112-X*) U Delaware Pr.

Callahan, Raymond A., pref. Churchill: Retreat from Empire. LC 83-20285. 293p. 1984. lib. bdg. 45.00 (*0-8420-2210-4*) Scholarly Res Inc.

Callahan, Raymond E. Education & the Cult of Efficiency. 288p. 1964. pap. text 17.00 (*0-226-09150-3*) U Ch Pr.

Callahan, Robert, jt. ed. see Eron, Leonard D.

Callahan, Roger & Perry, Paul J. Why Do I Eat When I'm Not Hungry? 240p. 1993. reprint ed. mass mkt. 5.99 (*0-380-71872-3*, Avon Bks) Morrow Avon.

***Callahan, Roger & Trubo, Richard.** Tapping the Healer Within: Using Thought Field Therapy to Conquer Your Fears, Anxieties & Emotional Distress. LC 00-31407. 2001. write for info. (*0-8092-9879-1*, Contemporary Bks) NTC Contemp Pub Co.

***Callahan, Roger J. & Callahan, Joanne.** Stop the Nightmares of Trauma: Thought Field Therapy - The Power of Therapy for the 21st Century. 334p. 2000. pap. 24.95 (*1-57087-505-7*) Prof Pr NC.

Callahan, S. Alice. Wynema: A Child of the Forest. Ruoff, A. LaVonne, ed. & intro. by. LC 96-28385. (Illus.). xlviii, 120p. 1997. pap. 9.95 (*0-8032-6378-3*, Bison Books); text 25.00 (*0-8032-1460-X*) U of Nebr Pr.

Callahan, Sally. My Mother's Voice. 357p. 2000. pap. 12.95 (*0-943873-49-5*, Pub. by Elder Bks) Midpt Trade.

Callahan, Scott B. Portraits of Love. Hogue, Wayne D., ed. (Illus.). 81p. (Orig.). 1996. pap. 9.95 (*0-9651766-5-7*) Star-Lit Pub.

Callahan, Sidney. Parents Forever. 228p. 1995. pap. 14.95 (*0-8245-1513-7*) Crossroad NY.

— A Retreat with Mary of Magdala & Augustine: Rejoicing in Human Sexuality. Hutchinson, Gloria, ed. LC 98-129487. 152p. 1997. pap. 8.95 (*0-86716-262-7*, B2627) St Anthony Mess Pr.

— With All Our Heart & Mind: The Spiritual Works of Mercy in a Psychological Age. LC 87-34574. 176p. (Orig.). 1988. pap. 8.95 (*0-8245-0971-4*) Crossroad NY.

Callahan, Sidney & Callahan, Daniel, eds. Abortion: Understanding Differences. LC 84-9965. (Hastings Center Series in Ethics). (Illus.). 360p. (C). 1984. text 65.00 (*0-306-41640-9*, Kluwer Plenum) Kluwer Academic.

Callahan, Sidney, ed. see Berger, Brigitte.

Callahan, Steven. Adrift: Seventy-Six Days Lost at Sea. 1996. pap. 11.00 (*0-345-41015-7*) Ballantine Pub Grp.

— Adrift: Seventy-Six Days Lost at Sea. 1987. 16.10 (*0-606-04011-0*, Pub. by Turtleback) Demco.

— Adrift: Seventy-Six Days Lost at Sea. rev. ed. LC 98-74469. (Adventure Library: Vol. 17). 1999. reprint ed. lib. bdg. 32.50 (*1-885283-16-4*) Advent Library.

Callahan, Thomas C. & Turner, Freda. Shadow of Death. LC 80-50008. (Illus.). 192p. 1980. 9.95 (*0-936354-01-1*) Val-Hse Pub.

Callahan, Tim. Biblical Prophecy: Failure or Fulfillment? LC 96-78367. (Illus.). 275p. 1997. 21.00 (*0-9655047-0-0*) Millennium Pr.

— Biblical Prophecy: Failure or Fulfillment? (Illus.). 274p. 1998. pap. 14.95 (*0-9655047-1-9*) Millennium Pr.

Callahan, Virginia Woods, tr. see St. Gregory of Nyssa.

***Callahan, Wanda L.** Straight Talk from a Brethren Sister. LC 00-22508. 112p. 2000. pap. 8.99 (*0-8361-9130-7*) Herald Pr.

***Callahan, William A.** Pollwatching, Elections & Civil Society in Southeast Asia. LC 99-46215. (Leeds Studies in Democratization). 218p. 1999. text 70.95 (*1-84014-474-2*, Pub. by Ashgate Pub) Ashgate Pub Co.

Callahan, William G. The Boulder Weather Log. (Illus.). 225p. (C). 1986. pap. 16.00 (*0-945527-00-4*) Upslope Pr.

— The Boulder Weather Log. 9th ed. (Illus.). 225p. (C). 1988. pap. 16.00 (*0-945527-08-X*) Upslope Pr.

***Callahan, William J.** The Church in Spain, 1875-1998. LC 99-37180. 2000. 49.95 (*0-8132-0961-7*) Cath U Pr.

Callahan, William J. Church, Politics, & Society in Spain, 1750-1874. (Historical Monographs: No. 73). (Illus.). 336p. 1984. 25.00 (*0-674-13125-8*) HUP.

— The Enneagram for Youth. LC 92-470. 156p. (Orig.). 1992. pap., teacher ed. 12.95 (*0-8294-0731-6*); pap., student ed. 8.95 (*0-8294-0730-8*) Loyola Pr.

Callahan, William T., Jr. & Banaszak, Ronald A., eds. Citizenship for the Twenty-First Century. 354p. (Orig.). 1990. pap. 15.00 (*0-941339-10-6*) Ind U SSDC.

Callahan, Xavier, tr. see Henaff, Marcel.

Callahan-Young, Sheila, jt. auth. see O'Connor, Anna T.

Callam, Daniel, tr. see Ambrose of Milan.

Callan. Environmental Economics & Management. LC 99-74295. (C). 1999. text 59.00 (*0-03-025631-3*) Harcourt Coll Pubs.

Callan, Lyndall, jt. auth. see Rappaport, Doreen.

***Callan, Annette, ed.** All about Skin Care. (Illus.). 207p. 2000. pap. 19.95 (*0-19-551303-7*) OUP.

Callan, Annette, ed. Skin Wise: A Guide to Healthy Skin for Women. (Illus.). 208p. (C). 1996. pap. 22.95 (*0-19-553745-9*) OUP.

Callan, Annie. The Back Door: Poems. 1995. pap. 7.00 (*0-932264-10-7*) Trask Hse Bks.

Callan, Benedicte. Pirates on the High Seas: Why the Unites States Cares about Global Intellectual Property Rights & What It Can Do about Them. 1998. pap. 5.00 (*0-87609-219-9*) Coun Foreign.

Callan, Benedicte & Costigan, Sean. Exporting U. S. High-Tech: Facts & Fiction about the Globalization of Industrial R & D. LC 98-186470. 1998. pap. 5.00 (*0-87609-227-X*) Coun Foreign.

Callan, Charles J. Your Soul's Gentle Shepherd: Why You Can Have Absolute Trust in Jesus Christ. LC 99-18651. Orig. Title: Sheperd of My Soul. 226p. 1999. reprint ed. pap. 15.95 (*0-918477-93-X*) Sophia Inst Pr.

Callan, Charles J. & Callan, Frank H. Excellence in English. 1924. 14.50 (*0-8159-5402-6*) Devin.

Callan, Dawn. Awakening the Warrior Within: Secrets of Personal Safety & Inner Security. 2nd rev. ed. LC 98-61698. 212p. 1999. pap. 12.95 (*0-9686086-9-8*) Tenacity Pr.

Callan, Eamonn. Autonomy & Schooling. 176p. (C). 1988. text 60.00 (*0-7735-0647-0*, Pub. by McG-Queens Univ Pr) CUP Services.

— Creating Citizens: Political Education & Liberal Democracy. LC 97-14447. (Oxford Political Theory Ser.). 272p. (C). 1997. 48.00 (*0-19-829258-9*) OUP.

Callan, Edward. Alan Paton. rev. ed. (World Authors Ser.: No. 40). 1982. 24.95 (*0-8057-6512-3*, Twyne) Mac Lib Ref.

— Cry, the Beloved Country: A Novel of South Africa. (Twayne's Masterwork Studies: No. 69). 136p. (C). 1991. 25.95 (*0-8057-8063-7*, Twyne); pap. 18.00 (*0-8057-8109-9*, Twyne) Mac Lib Ref.

***Callan, F. Mary.** Christmas Patchwork: Live Reports from Bethlehem. 96p. 1999. pap. 45.00 (*1-85072-232-3*, Pub. by W Sessions) St Mut.

Callan, Frank H., jt. auth. see Callan, Charles J.

Callan, Georgina, ed. Art of Shakespeare. (Illus.). 136p. 1989. write for info. (*0-318-64075-9*) Corky Inc.

Callan, Georgina O. The Thames & Hudson Dictionary of Fashion Design & Designers. LC 97-61609. (World of Art Ser.). (Illus.). 272p. 1998. pap. 16.95 (*0-500-20313-X*, Pub. by Thames Hudson) Norton.

Callan, Ginny. Beyond the Moon: From the Author of The Horn of the Moon Cookbook. LC 96-14268. 368p. 1996. pap. 18.00 (*0-06-095195-8*, Perennial) HarperTrade.

— Beyond the Moon Cookbook. 1996. pap. 17.00 (*0-614-20723-1*) HarpC.

— Beyond the Moon Cookbook. 1996. 27.75 (*0-8446-6920-2*) Peter Smith.

— Horn of the Moon Cookbook. 1987. 26.75 (*0-8446-6916-4*) Peter Smith.

— Horn of the Moon Cookbook: Recipes from Vermont's Renowned Vegetarian Restaurant. LC 86-45644. (Illus.). 304p. 1987. pap. 18.00 (*0-06-096038-8*, PL6038, Perennial) HarperTrade.

Callan, H. C. Lampbrush Chromosomes. (Molecular Biology, Biochemistry & Biophysics Ser.: Vol. 36). (Illus.). 290p. 1986. 199.95 (*0-387-16430-8*) Spr-Verlag.

Callan, James. Collaborative Computing with Delphi, 3. LC 97-41788. (Illus.). 600p. 1997. pap. 59.99 (*1-55622-554-7*) Wordware Pub.

— Object-Oriented Software Management. 1997. pap. text 44.95 (*1-55622-574-1*) Wordware Pub.

Callan, James R. Computer Literacy Made Easy...& Fun: Bits, Bytes, Apples & Mice. LC 95-69488. (Illus.). 128p. (Orig.). 1995. pap. 12.95 (*0-9646850-3-5*) Pennant Pubng.

Callan, K. Directing Your Directing Career: A Resource Book & Agent Guide for Directors. 210p. 1994. pap. 15.95 (*1-878355-01-5*) Sweden Pr.

***Callan, K.** Directing Your Directing Career, Support Book & Agent Guide for Directors. 2nd ed. 300p. 2000. pap. 17.95 (*1-878355-11-2*, Pub. by Sweden Pr) SCB Distributors.

Callan, K. How to Sell Yourself As an Actor. 4th ed. 250p. 1999. pap. 17.95 (*1-878355-10-4*) Sweden Pr.

— Los Angeles Agent Book: Get the Agent You Need for the Career You Want. 6th ed. 314p. 1998. pap. text 17.95 (*1-878355-09-0*) Sweden Pr.

***Callan, K.** The Los Angeles Agent Book: Get the Agent You Need for the Career You Want. 7th ed. 315p. 2001. pap. 18.95 (*1-878355-12-0*, Pub. by Sweden Pr) SCB Distributors.

Callan, K. New York Agent Book. 5th ed. 1998. pap. text 17.95 (*1-878355-07-4*) Sweden Pr.

***Callan, K.** The New York Agent Book: Get the Agent You Need for the Career You Want. 6th ed. Nolte, Kristi, ed. 290p. 2000. pap. 18.95 (*1-878355-13-9*, Pub. by Sweden Pr) SCB Distributors.

Callan, K. The Script Is Finished, Now What Do I Do? The Scriptwriter's Resource Book & Agent Guide. 300p. 1997. pap. 17.95 (*1-878355-08-2*) Sweden Pr.

Callan, Katherine, jt. auth. see Mittleman, Stuart.

Callan, Kevin. Brook Trout & Blackflies: A Paddler's Guide to Algonquin Park. LC 98-226133. 144p. 1997. pap. text 13.50 (*1-55046-211-3*, Pub. by Boston Mills) Genl Dist Srvs.

— Cottage Country Canoe Routes. Hudson, Noel, ed. (Illus.). 96p. pap. 15.95 (*1-55046-071-4*, Pub. by Boston Mills) Genl Dist Srvs.

— Further up the Creek: A Paddler's Guide to the Rivers of Ontario & Quebec. (Illus.). 1999. pap. 13.95 (*1-55046-275-X*, Pub. by Boston Mills) Genl Dist Srvs.

— Killarney. Hudson, Noel, ed. (Illus.). 80p. (Orig.). 1990. pap. 16.95 (*1-55046-018-8*, Pub. by Boston Mills) Genl Dist Srvs.

— Up the Creek: A Paddler's Guide to Ontario. (Illus.). 120p. (Orig.). 1996. pap. 13.50 (*1-55046-167-2*, Pub. by Boston Mills) Genl Dist Srvs.

— The Ways of the Wild: A Practical Guide to the Outdoors. 250p. 1993. pap. 16.95 (*1-55111-024-5*) Broadview Pr.

***Callan, Kristi, ed.** The Working Actor's Guide to Los Angeles 2001. 14th ed. 487p. 2000. spiral bd. 37.50 (*0-937609-18-8*, Pub. by Aaron Blake Pubs) SCB Distributors.

Callan, Kristi, ed. The Working Musician's Guide to Los Angeles 2001. 326p. 2000. spiral bd. 22.50 (*0-937609-16-1*, Pub. by Aaron Blake Pubs) SCB Distributors.

Callan, Leigh. Human Anatomy. 144p. (C). 1995. pap. text, student ed. 18.95 (*0-7872-0608-3*, 41060801) Kendall-Hunt.

— Laboratory Activities/Human Anatomy. 144p. (C). 1995. spiral bd. 17.95 (*0-7872-0607-5*) Kendall-Hunt.

— Laboratory Instruction for Introductory Medical Microbiology. 80p. (C). 1995. spiral bd. 14.95 (*0-8403-7846-7*) Kendall-Hunt.

***Callan, Lou.** Lonely Planet Dubai. Lonely Planet Publications Staff, ed. (Travel Guides Ser.). (Illus.). 176p. 2000. pap. text 14.95 (*1-86450-131-6*) Lonely Planet.

***Callan, Lou & Robinson, Gordon.** Lonely Planet Oman & the Untied Arab Emirates. (Travel Guides Ser.). (Illus.). 256p. 2000. pap. 15.99 (*1-86450-130-8*) Lonely Planet.

Callan, Michael F. Anthony Hopkins: In Darkness & Light. (Illus.). 361p. 1994. pap. 17.95 (*0-330-32889-1*, Pub. by Pan) Trans-Atl Phila.

— Sean Connery: The Untouchable Hero. 1995. mass mkt. 6.95 (*0-86369-755-0*) London Brdge.

***Callan, Michaila.** Love in Bloom. (Zebra Bouquet Ser.: Vol. 51). 256p. 2000. pap. 3.99 (*0-8217-6625-2*, Zebra Kensgtn) Kensgtn Pub Corp.

— Love Me Tender, Vol. 15. (Zebra Bouquet Ser.). 1999. mass mkt. 3.99 (*0-8217-6350-4*, Zebra Kensgtn) Kensgtn Pub Corp.

— Worth the Wait. (Zebra Bouquet Ser.: Vol. 52). 256p. 2000. pap. 3.99 (*0-8217-6626-0*, Zebra Kensgtn) Kensgtn Pub Corp.

Callan, Patrick M. & Finney, Joni E., eds. Public & Private Financing of Higher Education: Shaping Public Policy for the Future. LC 97-29457. (Ace/Oryx Series on Higher Education). 264p. (C). 1997. boxed set 39.95 (*1-57356-116-9*) Oryx Pr.

Callan, R. E. Building Object-Oriented Systems: An Introduction from Concepts to Implementation in C++. 304p. 1994. 80.00 (*1-85312-340-4*) Computational Mech MA.

***Callan, Richard J.** Jung, Alchemy & Josbe Donoso's Novel el Obsceno Pbajaro de la Noche. LC 00-32875. (Hispanic Literature Ser.: Vol. 58). 184p. 2000. 79.95 (*0-7734-7687-3*) E Mellen.

Callan, Robert. The Essence of Neural Networks. LC 98-27559. 1998. write for info. (*0-13-908732-X*) P-H.

Callan, Robert E. Building Object-Oriented Systems: An Introduction from Concepts to Implementation in C Plus Plus. LC 94-68194. 304p. (C). 1994. text 80.00 (*1-56252-264-7*, 3404) Computational Mech MA.

Callan, Scott & Thomas, Janet. Environmental Economics & Management: Theory, Policy, & Applications. 672p. (C). 1995. text 66.95 (*0-256-13254-2*, Irwn Prfssnl) McGraw-Hill Prof.

Callan, Terrance. The Origins of Christian Faith. LC 93-23465. 160p. (Orig.). 1994. pap. 9.95 (*0-8091-3459-4*) Paulist Pr.

Callan, Terrence. Psychological Perspectives on the Life of Paul: An Application of the Methodology of Gerd Theissen. LC 90-33278. (Studies in the Bible & Early Christianity: Vol. 22). 172p. 1990. lib. bdg. 79.95 (*0-88946-622-X*) E Mellen.

Callan, Tim & Economic & Social Research Institute Staff. Budget Perspectives: Proceedings of a Conference Held on 27 October 1998. LC 98-229365. 84p. 1998. write for info. (*0-7070-0176-5*) Econ & Soc Res.

***Callanan, Brian.** Ireland's Shannon Story: Leaders, Visions & Networks: A Case Study in Local & Regional Development. LC 99-10073. 260p. 1999. 49.50 (*0-7165-2710-3*, Pub. by Irish Acad Pr); pap. 24.50 (*0-7165-2643-3*, Pub. by Irish Acad Pr) Intl Spec Bk.

Callanan, Frank. The Parnell Split, 1890-91. LC 92-32592. (Irish Studies). (Illus.). 320p. 1993. 42.50 (*0-8156-2597-9*); pap. 19.95 (*0-8156-2598-7*) Syracuse U Pr.

— T. M. Healy: The Rise & Fall of Parnell & the Establishment of the Irish Free State. 320p. 1996. 32.95 (*1-85918-009-4*, Pub. by Cork Univ) Intl Spec Bk.

— T. M. Healy: The Rise & Fall of Parnell & the Establishment of the Irish Free State. 754p. 1998. pap. 26.95 (*1-85918-172-4*, Pub. by Cork Univ) Intl Spec Bk.

Callanan, Geraldene, jt. auth. see Hames, Richard David.

Callanan, Gerard A., jt. auth. see Greenhaus, Jeffrey H.

Callanan, John. Dreaming With Tony De Mello: A Handbook of Meditation Exercise. 144p. 1998. pap. 13.95 (*1-85635-192-0*, Pub. by Mercier Pr) Irish Amer Bk.

Callanan, Maggie & Kelley, Patricia. Final Gifts. large type ed. 320p. 1995. pap. 15.95 (*0-8027-2692-5*) Walker & Co.

— Final Gifts: Understanding the Special Awareness, Needs, & Communications of the Dying. 256p. 1997. reprint ed. pap. 12.95 (*0-553-37876-7*) Bantam.

Callanan, Michael I. & Wusinich, Bill. Electrical Systems: Based on the 1996 NEC. LC 96-42422. (Illus.). 432p. (Orig.). 1996. pap. text 32.96 (*0-8269-1690-2*) Am Technical.

— Electrical Systems: Based on the 1999 NEC. LC 99-192158. (Illus.). 424p. 1998. pap. text 36.96 (*0-8269-1692-9*) Am Technical.

Callander, Don. Aeromancer. 304p. 1997. mass mkt. 5.99 (*0-441-00472-5*) Ace Bks.

— Aquamancer. 304p. (Orig.). 1993. mass mkt. 5.50 (*0-441-02816-0*) Ace Bks.

— Dragon Companion. 336p. (Orig.). 1994. mass mkt. 5.99 (*0-441-00115-7*) Ace Bks.

— Dragon Rescue. 240p. (Orig.). 1995. mass mkt. 5.50 (*0-441-00263-3*) Ace Bks.

— Dragon Tempest. (Callander's Dragon Ser.: Bk. 3). 243p. 1998. mass mkt. 5.99 (*0-441-00555-1*) Ace Bks.

— Marbleheart. 1998. mass mkt. 5.99 (*0-441-00538-1*) Ace Bks.

— Pyromancer. 1992. mass mkt. 5.50 (*0-441-69222-2*) Ace Bks.

Callander, Imogene A. Joe O'Malley & Us: A Powerful Biography in Celebration of the Canadian/American/ Irish Family. Grebe, Marie et al, eds. LC 95-92654. (Illus.). 200p. (Orig.). 1996. pap. 12.00 (*0-9648867-0-7*) Straw Hat Pubng.

Callander, Joan. Second Time Around: Help for Grandparents Who Raise Their Children's Kids. LC 98-74183. 1999. pap. 15.95 (*1-58151-021-7*) BookPartners.

Callander, John. Deformities of Dr. Samuel Johnson: Selected from His Works. 2nd ed. LC 92-23649. (Augustan Reprints Ser.: No. 147-148). 1971. reprint ed. 21.50 (*0-404-70147-7*, PR3534) AMS Pr.

Callander, Marilyn B. Willa Cather & the Fairy Tale. Litz, A. Walton, ed. LC 88-27775. (Studies in Modern Literature: No. 97). 108p. reprint ed. 30.50 (*0-8357-1929-4*, 2070702) Bks Demand.

Callander, Meryn G., jt. auth. see Travis, John W.

Callander, R. A., jt. auth. see Stephenson, John.

Callander, Robert J. Liberal Learning & the World: A Banker's Perspective. 7p. (Orig.). 1986. pap. text 2.00 (*0-911696-39-3*) Assn Am Coll.

Callander, Robin, jt. auth. see Mackenna, B. R.

Callander, Robin, jt. auth. see McNaught, Ann B.

Callao, David P. & Rowland, Benjamin M. America & the World Political Economy: Atlantic Dreams & National Realities. LC 73-173390. 383p. reprint ed. pap. 118.80 (*0-8357-5348-4*, 205602500044) Bks Demand.

Callard, David, et al. The Case of Anna Kavan: A Biography. (Illus.). 168p. 1994. 32.00 (*0-7206-0867-8*, Pub. by P Owen Ltd) Dufour.

***Callard, Judith & Germantown Historical Society Staff.** Germantown, Mount Airy & Chestnut Hill: Pennsylvania. LC 00-100870. (Images of America Ser.). (Illus.). 128p. 2000. pap. 18.99 (*0-7385-0416-5*) Arcadia Publng.

Callard, Lloyd & Pallot, William. Business Valuation Practice. 420p. 1994. pap. 75.00 (*0-455-21213-9*, Pub. by LawBk Co) Gaunt.

Callard, Lucille. Aquarius. (Astro-Pups: Your Sign, Your Dogs Ser.). (Illus.). 60p. 1991. pap. 9.95 (*1-881038-10-6*) Penzance Pr.

— Aries. (Astro-Pups: Your Sign, Your Dogs Ser.). (Illus.). 60p. (Orig.). 1991. pap. 9.95 (*1-881038-00-9*) Penzance Pr.

— Cancer. (Astro-Pups: Your Sign, Your Dogs Ser.). (Illus.). 60p. 1991. pap. 9.95 (*1-881038-03-3*) Penzance Pr.

— Capricorn. (Astro-Pups: Your Sign, Your Dogs Ser.). (Illus.). 60p. 1991. pap. 9.95 (*1-881038-09-2*) Penzance Pr.

— Gemini. (Astro-Pups: Your Sign, Your Dogs Ser.). (Illus.). 60p. 1991. pap. 9.95 (*1-881038-02-5*) Penzance Pr.

— Leo. (Astro-Pups: Your Sign, Your Dogs Ser.). (Illus.). 60p. 1991. pap. 9.95 (*1-881038-04-1*) Penzance Pr.

— Libra. (Astro-Pups: Your Sign, Your Dogs Ser.). (Illus.). 60p. 1991. pap. 9.95 (*1-881038-06-8*) Penzance Pr.

— Pisces. (Astro-Pups: Your Sign, Your Dogs Ser.). (Illus.). 60p. 1991. pap. 9.95 (*1-881038-11-4*) Penzance Pr.

— Sagittarius. (Astro-Pups: Your Sign, Your Dogs Ser.). (Illus.). 60p. 1991. pap. 9.95 (*1-881038-08-4*) Penzance Pr.

— Scorpio. (Astro-Pups: Your Sign, Your Dogs Ser.). (Illus.). 60p. 1991. pap. 9.95 (*1-881038-07-6*) Penzance Pr.

— Taurus. (Astro-Pups: Your Sign, Your Dogs Ser.). (Illus.). 60p. 1991. pap. 9.95 (*1-881038-01-7*) Penzance Pr.

— Virgo. (Astro-Pups: Your Sign, Your Dogs Ser.). (Illus.). 60p. 1991. pap. 9.95 (*1-881038-05-X*) Penzance Pr.

Callard, Robin. The Cytokine Factsbook. 2nd ed. 448p. 1999. pap. text 42.00 (*0-12-155142-3*) Acad Pr.

Callard, Robin, ed. Cytokines & B Lymphocytes. 274p. 1990. text 83.00 (*0-12-155145-8*) Acad Pr.

Callard, Robin & Gearing, Andrew J. The Cytokine Factsbook, 3 vols., Set. (Factsbooks Ser.). (Illus.). 272p. 1994. pap. text 53.00 (*0-12-155143-1*) Acad Pr.

Callari & Wolff. How Economics Was Invented. 55.95 (*1-84014-943-4*) Ashgate Pub Co.

Callari, Antonio, et al, eds. Marxism in the Postmodern Age: Confronting the New World Order. LC 93-49636. (Critical Perspectives Ser.). 560p. 1994. pap. text 21.95 (*0-89862-424-X*); lib. bdg. 49.95 (*0-89862-423-1*, C2423) Guilford Pubns.

Callarman. Operations Management. (C). 1997. pap. text, teacher ed. write for info. (*0-03-029394-4*); pap. text, student ed. write for info. (*0-03-029398-7*) Harcourt Coll Pubs.

— Operations Managment. (C). 1997. pap. text. write for info. (*0-03-029393-6*) Harcourt Coll Pubs.

Callarman, Ruth. California Guide to Motel-Hotel Discounts. 104p. (Orig.). 1985. pap. 6.98 (*0-9613087-1-0*) Potter Pubns.

— California Guide to Restaurant Discounts. 160p. (Orig.). 1985. pap. 8.98 (*0-9613087-2-9*) Potter Pubns.

— Seniors Living It up on a Budget: California Edition. 212p. (Orig.). 1983. pap. 10.00 (*0-9613087-0-2*) Potter Pubns.

***Callary, Edward.** Place Names in the Midwestern United States. LC 00-33951. 208p. 2000. 89.95 (*0-7734-7723-3*) E Mellen.

Callas, Evangelia & Blochman, Lawrence G. My Daughter Maria Callas. Farkas, Andrew, ed. LC 76-29928. (Opera Biographies Ser.). (Illus.). 1979. reprint ed. lib. bdg. 21.95 (*0-405-09671-2*) Ayer.

Callas, Gerald. Manual for Human Dissection: Photographs with Clinical Applications. (Illus.). 203p. (C). 1994. pap. text 34.95 (*0-8385-6133-0*, A6133-1, Apple Lange Med) McGraw.

***Callaway.** Comprehensive Review of Radiography. 2nd rev. ed. 2000. text. write for info. (*0-323-01191-8*) Mosby Inc.

Callaway. I Still Know What You Did Last Summer: The Screenplay. (J). 1998. mass mkt. 4.99 (*0-671-03456-1*) PB.

Callaway, Alison. Deaf Children in China. LC 99-88446. 256p. 1999. 49.95 (*1-56368-085-8*) Gallaudet Univ Pr.

***Callaway, Anita.** Visual Ephemera: Theatrical Arts in Nineteenth Century Australia. 272p. 2000. 49.95 (*0-86840-634-1*, Pub. by NSW U Pr) Intl Spec Bk.

Callaway, Archibald, et al. The Nigerian Political Scene. Tilman, Robert O. & Cole, Taylor, eds. LC 62-18315. (Duke University Commonwealth-Studies Center Publication Ser.: No. 17). 352p. reprint ed. pap. 109.20 (*0-608-13805-3*, 201793900010) Bks Demand.

Callaway, Barbara & Creevey, Lucy. The Heritage of Islam: Women, Religion, & Politics in West Africa. LC 93-35396. 221p. 1993. pap. text 19.95 (*1-55587-414-2*) L Rienner.

Callaway, Barbara J. Muslim Hausa Women in Nigeria: Tradition & Change. LC 87-6464. (Illus.). 264p. 1987. text 39.95 (*0-8156-2406-9*) Syracuse U Pr.

Callaway, Buzz. Specimen Tank. 256p. (Orig.). 1993. pap. 10.95 (*0-916397-20-3*) Manic D Pr.

Callaway, Colin G. Indians of the Northeast. (First Americans Ser.). (Illus.). 96p. (J). (gr. 5-9). 1991. lib. bdg. 23.95 (*0-8160-2389-1*) Facts on File.

Callaway, Dorothy J. The World of Magnolias. LC 93-2793. (Illus.). 308p. 1994. 49.95 (*0-88192-236-6*) Timber.

***Callaway, Dorothy J. & Callaway, M. Brett.** Breeding Ornamental Plants. LC 99-87325. (Illus.). 372p. 2000. 34.95 (*0-88192-482-2*) Timber.

***Callaway, Dustin.** Inside Servlets: Server-Side Programming for the Java Platform. LC 99-20222. 464p. (C). 1999. pap. text 39.95 (*0-201-37963-5*) Addison-Wesley.

Callaway, Edgar H., Jr., et al. Ssri Probl Dist Serv DES. LC 92-46898. (Six Sigma Research Institute Ser.). 1993. pap. text 27.95 (*0-201-63438-4*) Addison-Wesley.

Callaway, Erin. Enterprise Resource Planning: Integrating Applications & Business Processes Across the Enterprise. LC 99-13885. (Illus.). 179p. 1999. pap. 295.00 (*1-56607-068-6*) Comput Tech Res.

***Callaway, Erin.** ERP-The Next Generation: ERP Is Web Enabled for E-business. (Illus.). 2000. pap. 290.00 (*1-56607-075-9*) Comput Tech Res.

Callaway Gardens Staff. American Garden Guides: Vegetable Gardening. 224p. 1994. pap. 25.00 (*0-679-41434-7*) Pantheon.

Callaway, Gloria & Kear, Mary. Improving Learning & Teaching in the Arts. LC 99-36832. 224p. 1999. pap. 26.95 (*0-7507-0799-2*, Falmer Pr) Taylor & Francis.

***Callaway, H. G. & Del Caro, Adrian, frwds.** Thomas Mann & Friedrich Nietzsche: Eroticism, Death, Music & Laughter. (Value Inquiry Book Ser.: Vol. 85). xxii, 151p. 1999. pap. 30.50 (*90-420-0557-2*) Editions Rodopi.

Callaway, Helen. Gender, Culture & Empire: European Women in Colonial Nigeria. LC 86-19225. (Illus.). 296p. 1987. text 29.95 (*0-252-01393-X*) U of Ill Pr.

Callaway, Helen, jt. ed. see Okely, Judith.

Callaway, Henri. Nursery Tales, Traditions, & Histories of the Zulus: In Their Own Words, with a Translation into English & Notes, Vol. 1. (B. E. Ser.: No. 36). 1868. 40.00 (*0-8115-2987-8*) Periodicals Srv.

Callaway, Jack M. & Nicholls, Elizabeth L., eds. Ancient Marine Reptiles. LC 96-41835. (Illus.). 501p. 1997. text 72.00 (*0-12-155210-1*) Morgan Kaufmann.

Callaway, John. Thing of It Is. 292p. 1994. 25.00 (*0-915463-65-2*) Jameson Bks.

Callaway, Joseph. Quantum Theory of the Solid State. 2nd ed. 954p. (C). 1991. text 82.00 (*0-12-155203-9*) Acad Pr.

Callaway, Joseph A. The Early Bronze Age Citadel & Lower City at AI (Et-Tell) LC 79-23011. (Report of the Joint Archaeological Expedition to Ai Ser.: Vol. 2). 295p. 1980. text 80.00 (*0-89757-202-5*, Pub. by Sheffield Acad) CUP Services.

— Faces of the Old Testament. LC 94-27687. (Illus.). 216p. (C). 1995. pap. 17.00 (*1-880837-56-0*) Smyth & Helwys.

Callaway, Lew L., Jr. Montana's Righteous Hangmen: The Vigilantes in Action. Burlingame, Merrill G., ed. & frwd. by. LC 81-40282. (Illus.). 256p. 1997. pap. 12.95 (*0-8061-2912-3*) U of Okla Pr.

Callaway, Lew L. Montana's Righteous Hangmen: The Vigilantes in Action. Callaway, Lew L., Jr., ed. LC 81-40282. (Illus.). 240p. 1982. 21.95 (*0-8061-1728-1*) U of Okla Pr.

Callaway, Lew L., Jr., ed. see Callaway, Lew L.

Callaway, M. Brett & Francis, Charles A., eds. Crop Improvement for Sustainable Agriculture. LC 93-18567. (Our Sustainable Future Ser.: Vol. 4). xiv, 262p. 1993. text 45.00 (*0-8032-1462-6*) U of Nebr Pr.

Callaway, M. Brett, jt. auth. see Callaway, Dorothy J.

Callaway, Merrill. The ARexx Cookbook: A Tutorial Guide to the ARexx Language on the Commodore Amiga Personal Computer. LC 92-81371. (Illus.). 251p. (Orig.). 1992. pap. 24.95 (*0-9632773-0-8*); pap. 49.95 incl. disk (*0-9632773-2-4*); disk 9.95 (*0-9632773-1-6*) Whitestone NM.

— The Rexx Cookbook: A Tutorial Guide to the Rexx Language in OS-2 & Warp on the IBM Personal Computer. LC 94-62030. (Illus.). 320p. (Orig.). 1995. 3.5 hd 14.95 (*0-9632773-5-9*) Whitestone NM.

— The REXX Cookbook: A Tutorial Guide to the REXX Language in OS-2 & Warp on the IBM Personal Computer. LC 94-62030. (Illus.). 320p. (Orig.). 1995. pap. 27.95 (*0-9632773-4-0*) Whitestone NM.

Callaway, Nicholas & Bry, Doris, eds. Georgia O'Keefe: In the West. (Illus.). 1989. 100.00 (*0-685-26633-8*) Knopf.

Callaway, Nicholas, ed. see O'Keeffe, Georgia.

***Callaway, Phil.** Como Enriquecer Suvida Sin Dinero. (SPA.). 1999. pap. 8.99 (*0-7899-0616-3*) Spanish Hse Distributors.

— I Used to Have Answers, Now I Have Kids: What It's Really Like at My House. LC 99-88440. 200p. 2000. pap. 9.99 (*0-7369-0229-5*) Harvest Hse.

Callaway, Phil. Making Life Rich Without Any Money. LC 98-15495. 160p. 1998. pap. 8.99 (*1-56507-899-3*) Harvest Hse.

Callaway, Redman. White Captain, Black Troops: Stories of World War II. LC 93-79330. 144p. 1993. 19.95 (*0-932845-60-6*) Lowell Pr.

Callaway, Rolland, ed. Satire & Humor in Education: Selected Readings. 284p. (Orig.). (C). 1990. pap. text 26.00 (*0-8191-7871-3*); lib. bdg. 50.00 (*0-8191-7870-5*) U Pr of Amer.

An Asterisk (*) at the beginning of an entry indicates that the title is appearing for the first time.

Callaway, Royce L. The Realities of Management: A View from the Trenches. LC 99-10386. 240p. 1999. 59.95 (*1-56720-315-9*, Q315, Quorum Bks) Greenwood.
Callaway, Tucker N. Zen Way - Jesus Way. 264p. 1993. pap. 12.95 (*0-8048-1885-1*) Tuttle Pubng.
***Callaway, Vincent F.** Between Earth & Sky. LC 99-97454. 2000. pap. 7.95 (*0-533-13431-5*) Vantage.
Callaway, William J. Mosby's Comprehensive Review of Radiography. 2nd ed. LC 97-41998. (Illus.). 336p. (C). (gr. 13). 1998. pap. text 32.95 (*0-8151-2900-9*, 31811) Mosby Inc.
Callaway, William J., jt. auth. see Gurley, LaVerne T.
Callaway, William J., jt. ed. see Gurley, LaVerne T.
Callcott, George H. History in the United States, 1800-1860: Its Practice & Purpose. LC 74-88115. 250p. 1970. reprint ed. pap. 77.50 (*0-608-05931-5*, 206626700008) Bks Demand.
— Maryland & America, 1940-1980. LC 85-166. (Illus.). 392p. 1985. 39.95 (*0-8018-2492-3*) Johns Hopkins.
— Maryland Political Behavior: Four Centuries of Political Culture. (Illus.). 64p. (Orig.). 1986. pap. 8.95 (*0-938420-42-9*) MD Hist.
Callcott, Margaret L. Mistress of Riversdale: The Plantation Letters of Rosalie Stier Calvert, 1795-1821. (Maryland Paperback Bookshelf Ser.). (Illus.). 432p. 1992. reprint ed. pap. 16.95 (*0-8018-4399-5*) Johns Hopkins.
— The Negro in Maryland Politics, 1870-1912. LC 69-15395. (Johns Hopkins University Studies in Historical & Political Science: Ser. 87, No. 1). 215p. reprint ed. pap. 66.70 (*0-608-14669-2*, 202583500046) Bks Demand.
Callcott, W. H. South Carolina: Economic & Social Conditions in 1944. LC 74-34437. 248p. 1975. reprint ed. 25.00 (*0-87152-189-X*) Reprint.
Callcott, Wilfrid H. Liberalism in Mexico, 1857-1929. 1976. lib. bdg. 59.95 (*0-8490-2157-X*) Gordon Pr.
— Santa Anna: The Story of an Enigma Who Once Was Mexico. LC 36-37514. 405p. reprint ed. pap. 125.60 (*0-608-13723-5*, 205550900023) Bks Demand.
Calle-Grubar, Mireille, jt. auth. see Cixous, Helen.
Calle-Grubar, Mireille, jt. auth. see Cixous, Helene.
Calle, Mireille, ed. On the Feminine. McGann, Catherine, tr. LC 95-49878. 200p. 1996. 49.95 (*0-391-03968-7*); pap. 15.00 (*0-391-03969-5*) Humanities.
***Calle, Ramiro A.** Superar la Depresion. 2000. pap. 16.95 (*84-270-2526-2*) E Martinez Roca.
Calle, Sophie. La Distance/Die Entfernung: A Berlin Travel Guide. (Illus.). 48p. 1997. pap. text 39.00 (*90-5705-046-3*) Gordon & Breach.
— Double Game & the Gotham Handbook, 2 vols. 1998. pap. text 65.00 (*1-900828-06-5*, Pub. by Violette) Dist Art Pubs.
— La Visite Guide E. 48p. 1996. 35.00 (*90-6918-158-4*, Pub. by Boymans Mus) Dist Art Pubs.
Calle, Sophie & Baudrillard, Jean. Suite Venitienne (Please Follow Me) Barash, Dany & Hatfield, Danny, trs. from FRE. LC 87-73233.Tr. of Please Follow Me. (FRE., Illus.). 96p. (Orig.). 1998. reprint ed. pap. 13.95 (*0-941920-09-7*) Bay Pr.
Calle, Sophie, et al. Sophie Calle: Absence. (FRE., Illus.). 72p. 1995. pap. 25.00 (*90-6918-131-2*) Dist Art Pubs.
Calle, Stuart C. The American Children's Museum Guidebook: Over 400 Places Just for Kids. LC 98-90322. (Illus.). 360p. 1998. pap. 17.95 (*0-9664599-0-3*) Samuel Press.
Callea, Olivia & Willan, Anne. Burgundy Gastronomique. (Illus.). 144p. 1996. 29.95 (*0-7892-0075-9*) Abbeville Pr.
Callear, Brian & Pinches, Michael. Power Pneumatics. 368p. 1997. pap. 67.00 (*0-13-489790-0*) P-H.
Callear, D. H. Prolog Programming for Students. 256p. 1994. pap. 59.95 (*1-85805-093-6*, Pub. by DP Publns) St Mut.
Callebat, L., ed. see Vitruvius.
Callebat, Louis, ed. Actes Du Ive Colloque International Sur le Latin Vulgaire et Tardif. (GER.). 748p. 1995. write for info. (*3-487-10045-2*) G Olms Pubs.
Callebat, Louis & Fleury, Philippe, eds. Vitruvius: Dictionnaire des Termes Techniques du De Architectura de Vitruve. (GER.). 1995. write for info. (*3-487-09398-7*) G Olms Pubs.
Callebat, Louis, ed. see Vitruvius.
Callebaut, D. K. & Malfliet, W. Nonlinear Stability & Waves: Sixth Workshop. 1994. text 75.00 (*981-02-1060-4*) World Scientific Pub.
Callebaut, Werner. Taking the Naturalistic Turn: or How Real Philosophy of Science Is Done. (Science & Its Conceptual Foundations Ser.). (Illus.). 576p. 1993. pap. text 29.95 (*0-226-09187-2*); lib. bdg. 85.00 (*0-226-09186-4*) U Ch Pr.
Callebaut, Werner & Pinxten, Rik, eds. Evolutionary Epistemology. 468p. (C). 1987. text 186.00 (*90-277-2582-9*, D Reidel) Kluwer Academic.
Callegari, Dennis. Cook's Cannon & Anchor. (Illus.). 96p. 1995. 24.95 (*0-86417-644-9*) Seven Hills Bk.
Callegari-Jacques, Sidia M., jt. auth. see Salzano, Francisco M.
Calleghan, William, ed. see Isenberg, Arnold.
Calleiro, Mary. Distancia de un Espacio Prometido. LC 84-73242. (Coleccion Espejo de Paciencia). (SPA., Illus.). 78p. (Orig.). 1985. pap. 6.95 (*0-89729-365-7*) Ediciones.
Calleja, Betty R. Come Play with the Angels: A Playbook in Self Discovery & Spirit Recovery. LC 96-72418. (Illus.). 208p. (Orig.). 1997. pap. 35.00 incl. audio (*1-882792-39-4*) Proctor Pubns.
***Calleja, Francisco Jose Balta & Fakirov, Stoyko.** Microhardness of Polymers. (Illus.). 350p. 2000. write for info. (*0-521-64218-3*) Cambridge U Pr.
***Calleja, Gina.** Bloor & Christie: The Mystery of the Bright Red Ribbon. (Illus.). 40p. (J). (ps-k). 1998. pap. 7.95 (*0-929141-58-X*) Napoleon Publ.
— Wizzo & the Cookie Babies. (Illus.). 48p. 1994. pap. 7.95 (*0-929141-21-0*) Napoleon Publ.
Calleja, Gode B. Microbial Aggregation. 288p. 1984. 163.00 (*0-8493-5708-X*, QR73, CRC Reprint) Franklin.
Calleja, James, et al, eds. International Education & the University. LC 94-49580. 272p. 1995. pap. 49.50 (*1-85302-274-8*) Taylor & Francis.
Callejas, Juan, ed. see Cosby, Bill, et al.
Callejas, Juan, ed. see Schimmels, Cliff & Resnik, Hank.
Callejas, Roger F., tr. see Roberts, Allen E.
Callejo, Alfonso & Pajares, Maria T., eds. Textos y Concordancias: Fabula de Polyfemo y Galathea, y las Soledades. (Spanish Ser.: No. 25). iv, 128p. 1985. 15.00 (*0-942260-67-8*) Hispanic Seminary.
***Callejo, Cabo Jesus.** Historia Magica de las Flores. 1999. 24.95 (*84-270-2445-2*) E Martinez Roca.
Callejo, Fernando. Music & Musicians of Puerto Rico. (Puerto Rico Ser.). 1979. lib. bdg. 59.95 (*0-8490-2974-0*) Gordon Pr.
Callela, Trisha, et al. Barney Bear, World Traveler, Vol. 3901. Williams, Rozanne L., ed. (Social Studies Learn to Read Ser.). (Illus.). 8p. (J). (ps-2). 1996. pap. 1.75 (*1-57471-120-2*, 3901) Creat Teach Pr.
Callella-Jones, Trisha. I Try to Be a Good Person, Vol. 4414. Kupperstein, Joel, ed. (Learn to Read Social Studies). (Illus.). 16p. (J). (ps-2). 1998. pap. 2.75 (*1-57471-337-X*, 4414) Creat Teach Pr.
— Numbers All Around Me, Vol. 4470. Kupperstein, Joel, ed. (Learn to Read Math Ser.). (Illus.). 16p. (J). 1998. pap. 2.75 (*1-57471-377-9*, 4470) Creat Teach Pr.
— Patterns All Around Me, Vol. 4471. Kupperstein, Joel, ed. (Learn to Read Math Ser.). (Illus.). 16p. (J). 1998. pap. 2.75 (*1-57471-378-7*, 4471) Creat Teach Pr.
***Callella-Jones, Trisha & Jordano, Kimberly.** Fall Phonemic Awareness Songs & Rhymes Vol. 2340: Fun Lyrics Sung to Familiar Tunes. Johnson, Kristine, ed. (Illus.). 96p. 1998. pap. 9.98 (*1-57471-692-1*, 2340) Creat Teach Pr.
— Spring Phonemic Awareness Songs & Rhymes Vol. 2342: Fun Lyrics Sung to Familiar Tunes. Johnson, Kristine, ed. (Illus.). 96p. 1998. pap. 9.98 (*1-57471-694-8*, 2342) Creat Teach Pr.
— Winter Phonemic Awareness Songs & Rhymes Vol. 2341: Fun Lyrics Sung to Familiar Tunes. Johnson, Kristine, ed. (Illus.). 96p. 1998. pap. 9.98 (*1-57471-693-X*) Creat Teach Pr.
Callella-Jones, Trisha, jt. auth. see Jordano, Kimberly.
Callella, Trisha. What Do We Need?, Vol. 3910. Williams, Rozanne L., ed. (Social Studies Learn to Read Ser.). (Illus.). 8p. (J). (ps-2). 1996. pap. 1.75 (*1-57471-129-6*, 3910) Creat Teach Pr.
— What Do We Need?, Vol. 3967. Williams, Rozanne L., ed. (Social Studies Big Bks.). (Illus.). 8p. (J). (ps-2). 1997. pap. 8.98 (*1-57471-175-X*, 3967) Creat Teach Pr.
***Callella, Trisha & Jordano, Kimberly.** Interactive Writing Vol. 2291: Sharing the Pen to Create Meaningful Text. Johnson, Kristine, ed. (Illus.). 96p. (J). (gr. k-2). 2000. pap. text 9.98 (*1-57471-687-5*) Creat Teach Pr.
Callella, Trisha, et al. Barney Bear, World Traveler, Vol. 3958. Williams, Rozanne L., ed. (Social Studies Big Bks.). (Illus.). 8p. (J). (ps-2). 1997. pap. 8.98 (*1-57471-166-0*, 3958) Creat Teach Pr.
— Celebrate the Months Vol. 2377: October. Thrall Cicciarelli, Joellyn, ed. (Illus.). 96p. (J). (gr. k-3). 1998. pap. 9.98 (*1-57471-351-5*) Creat Teach Pr.
— Celebrate the Months Vol. 2378: November. Johnson, Kristine, ed. (Illus.). 96p. (J). (gr. k-3). 1998. pap. 9.98 (*1-57471-352-3*) Creat Teach Pr.
Callen. Color Atlas Dermatology. 1994. 1100.00 (*0-7216-3757-4*) Harcourt.
Callen, Anna T. Food & Memories of Abruzzo: Italy's Pastoral Land. LC 96-5553. (Illus.). 352p. 1998. 35.00 (*0-02-520915-9*) Macmillan.
***Callen, Anthea.** The Art of Impressionism: Painting Technique & the Making of Modernity. (Illus.). 304p. 2000. 65.00 (*0-300-08402-1*) Yale U Pr.
Callen, Anthea. The Spectacular Body: Science, Method, & Meaning in the Work of Degas. LC 94-30122. 1995. 57.00 (*0-300-05443-2*) Yale U Pr.
— Techniques of the Impressionists. 192p. 1997. 17.98 (*0-89009-545-0*) Bk Sales Inc.
Callen, Barry L. Contours of a Cause: Theological Vision of the Church of God Movement (Anderson, Indiana) (Illus.). 230p. 1995. pap. text 4.00 (*0-9646682-0-3*) Anderson Univ.
— Faithful in the Meantime: A Biblical View of Final Things & Present Responsibilities. LC 97-60625. 285p. 1997. pap. 12.00 (*0-916035-74-3*) Evangel Indiana.
— God As Loving Grace: The Biblically Revealed Nature & Work of God. LC 95-61999. 356p. (Orig.). 1996. pap. 14.00 (*0-916035-65-4*) Evangel Indiana.
— Journeying Together. Harman, Dan, ed. LC 97-200310. (Record of Actions of the General Assembly of the Church of God Ser.: Vol. 3). (Illus.). 1996. pap. write for info. (*0-87162-684-5*) Warner Pr.
— Seeking the Light: America's Modern Quest for Peace, Justice, Prosperity & Faith. LC 98-70165. (Illus.). 382p. 1998. 24.95 (*0-916035-79-4*, Pub. by Evangel Indiana) BookWorld.
— She Came Preaching. 1992. pap. 3.99 (*0-87162-601-2*, D1390) Warner Pr.
Callen, Barry L., ed. Sharing Heaven's Music: The Heart of Christian Preaching. 272p. 1995. 18.95 (*0-687-01108-6*) Abingdon.
Callen, Barry L. & North, James B. Coming Together in Christ: Pioneering a New Testament Way to Christian Unity: Christian Churches Churches of Christ & the Church of God (Anderson) LC 97-3137. 1997. pap. 9.99 (*0-89900-783-X*) College Pr Pub.
Callen, Gayle. The Darkest Knight. 384p. 1999. mass mkt. 5.99 (*0-380-80493-X*, Avon Bks) Morrow Avon.
***Callen, Gayle.** My Lady's Guardian. 384p. 2000. mass mkt. 5.99 (*0-380-81376-9*, Avon Bks) Morrow Avon.
Callen, Herbert B. Thermodynamics Level 4. 2nd ed. LC 85-6387. 512p. 1985. text 102.95 (*0-471-86256-8*) Wiley.
***Callen, Jeffrey P.** Color Atlas of Dermatology. 2nd ed. LC 99-42915. (Illus.). (C). 1999. text 145.00 (*0-7216-8256-1*, W B Saunders Co) Harcrt Hlth Sci Grp.
Callen, Jeffrey P. Current Practice of Dermatology. (Illus.). 200p. 1995. text 95.00 (*1-85922-801-1*) Current Med.
— Current Practice of Dermatology. 188p. (C). 1995. pap. 110.00 (*0-8385-1505-3*, A-1505-5, Apple Lange Med) McGraw.
— Current Practice of Medicine: Dermatology. (Illus.). 200p. 1995. text 39.95 (*1-85922-688-4*) Current Med.
— Current Practice of Medicine Vol. 2: Dermatology. (Illus.). 200p. 1995. text 39.95 (*0-443-07891-2*) Current Med.
Callen, Jeffrey P., ed. Cutaneous Aspects of Internal Disease. LC 80-14099. (Illus.). 697p. reprint ed. pap. 200.00 (*0-8357-7609-3*, 205692200096) Bks Demand.
Callen, Jeffrey P., et al. Color Atlas of Dermatology. (Illus.). 368p. 1993. text 175.00 (*0-7216-3756-6*, W B Saunders Co) Harcrt Hlth Sci Grp.
— Dermatological Signs of Internal Disease. 2nd ed. LC 94-30224. (Illus.). 436p. 1994. text 110.00 (*0-7216-5454-1*, W B Saunders Co) Harcrt Hlth Sci Grp.
— A Manual of Dermatology: An Introduction to Diagnosis & Treatment. LC 79-19865. (Illus.). 306p. reprint ed. pap. 94.90 (*0-8357-8577-7*, 203494300091) Bks Demand.
Callen, Karena, jt. auth. see Cochrane, Amanda.
Callen, Larry. Who Kidnapped the Sheriff? (Illus.). 176p. (J). (gr. 4 up). 1985. 14.95 (*0-316-12499-0*, Joy St Bks) Little.
Callen, Paulette. Charity. LC 96-45020. 1997. 21.50 (*0-684-82942-8*) S&S Trade.
***Callen, Paulette.** Charity. 1998. reprint ed. pap. 6.99 (*0-425-16516-7*) Berkley Pub.
Callen, Peter W. Ultrasonography in Obstetrics & Gynecology. 4th ed. (Illus.). 925p. (C). 2000. text. write for info. (*0-7216-8132-8*, W B Saunders Co) Harcrt Hlth Sci Grp.
Callen, Peter W., ed. Ultrasonography in Obstetrics & Gynecology. 3rd ed. LC 93-6621. (Illus.). 736p. 1993. text 89.95 (*0-7216-6712-0*, W B Saunders Co) Harcrt Hlth Sci Grp.
Callen, Richard M. Become a 911 Dispatcher: Your Personal Career Guide. (Illus.). 156p. 1996. pap. text 15.95 (*0-89262-494-9*) Career Pub.
Callen, Tony, jt. auth. see Meudell, Karen.
Callenbach, A. Ernest & Phillips, Michael. A Citizen Legislature. LC 84-28377. 96p. (Orig.). 1985. pap. 6.00 (*0-9604320-5-1*) Banyan Tree.
Callenbach, Ernest. Bring Back the Buffalo! A Sustainable Future for America's Great Plains. LC 95-4864. 280p. 1995. 25.00 (*1-55963-440-5*) Island Pr.
***Callenbach, Ernest.** Bring Back the Buffalo! A Sustainable Future for America's Great Plains. LC 99-44965. 285p. 2000. 16.95 (*0-520-22407-8*, Pub. by U CA Pr) Cal Prin Full Svc.
Callenbach, Ernest. Ecology: A Pocket Guide. LC 98-4728. (Illus.). 176p. 1998. pap. 9.95 (*0-520-21463-3*, Pub. by U CA Pr) Cal Prin Full Svc.
— Ecotopia. LC 74-84366. 168p. 1975. pap. 8.75 (*0-9604320-1-9*) Banyan Tree.
— Ecotopia: The Notebooks & Reports of William Weston. 192p. 1990. pap. 12.95 (*0-553-34847-7*) Bantam.
— Ecotopia Emerging. LC 81-10821. 320p. (Orig.). 1981. pap. 10.95 (*0-9604320-3-5*) Banyan Tree.
***Callenbach, Ernest.** Living Cheaply with Style. 2nd rev. ed. 196p. 2000. pap. 11.95 (*1-57951-014-0*, Pub. by Ronin Pub) Publishers Group.
Callenbach, Ernest & Leefeldt, Christine. Humphrey the Wayward Whale. (Illus.). 24p. (Orig.). (J). (gr. k-6). 1986. pap. 4.95 (*0-930588-23-1*) Heyday Bks.
Callenbach, Ernest, et al. EcoManagement: The Elmwood Guide to Ecological Auditing & Sustainable Business. LC 93-17285. (Illus.). 224p. 1993. 27.95 (*1-881052-27-3*) Berrett-Koehler.
Callender. The Eye of Horus: A History of Ancient Egypt. 1992. pap. text. write for info. (*0-582-87682-6*, Pub. by Addison-Wesley) Longman.
Callender, Ann B. How Shall We Govern India? A Controversy among British Administrators, 1800-1882. McNeill, William H. & Stansky, Peter, eds. (Modern European History Ser.). 368p. 1987. text 15.00 (*0-8240-7801-2*) Garland.
— Pathways Through Pain: Women's Journeys. LC 98-54172. 176p. 1999. 16.95 (*0-8298-1306-3*) Pilgrim OH.
Callender, C., et al. Employers & Family Credit. (DSS Research Report Ser.). 1995. write for info. (*0-11-762272-9*, Pub. by Statnry Office) Bernan Associates.
Callender, Christine. Education for Empowerment. 1997. pap. 22.00 (*1-85856-072-1*, Trentham Bks) Stylus Pub VA.
***Callender, Craig & Huggett, Nick, eds.** Physics Meets Philosophy at the Planck Scale: Contemporary Theories in Quantum Gravity. (Illus.). 340p. 2001. write for info. (*0-521-66280-X*); pap. write for info. (*0-521-66445-4*) Cambridge U Pr.
Callender, Dale. Sexual Harassment Claims Step-by-Step. LC 97-43902. (Legal-Ease Ser.). 240p. 1998. pap. 14.95 (*0-7641-0113-7*) Barron.
***Callender, Dexter E.** Adam in Myth & History: Ancient Israelite Perspectives on the Primal Human. LC 00-32135. (Semitic Studies). 2000. write for info. (*1-57506-902-4*) Eisenbrauns.
Callender, Edward B. Thaddeus Stevens, Commoner. LC 70-39881. reprint ed. 34.00 (*0-404-00011-8*) AMS Pr.
Callender, G., ed. see Southey, Robert.
Callender, Guy S. Selections from the Economic History of the United States 1765-1860: With Introductory Essays. LC 65-19646. (Reprints of Economic Classics Ser.). xviii, 809p. 1965. reprint ed. 57.50 (*0-678-00080-8*) Kelley.
Callender, J. F., ed. Ash-Flow Tuffs: Their Origin, Geologic Relations & Identification Zones & Zonal Variations in Welded Ash Flows. (Special Publications: No. 9). (Illus.). 104p. 1980. reprint ed. pap. 15.00 (*1-58546-008-7*) NMex Geol Soc.
Callender, J. F., et als, eds. Land of Cochise: Southwestern Arizona. (Guidebook Ser.: No. 29). (Illus.). 348p. 1978. 35.00 (*1-58546-059-1*); pap. 17.00 (*1-58546-060-5*) NMex Geol Soc.
Callender, J. F., jt. ed. see Chapin, C. E.
Callender, J. F., jt. ed. see Epis, R. C.
Callender, J. F., jt. ed. see Ingersol, R. V.
Callender, J. L., jt. auth. see Jackson, R.
Callender, Jeff. Factoring Small Receivables: How to Make Money in Little Deals the Big Guys Brush Off. 4th large type rev. ed. (Illus.). 201p. 1998. ring bd. 59.95 (*1-889095-08-7*) Coastlne Fin.
Callender, John. Historical Discourse on the Civil & Religious Affairs of the Colony of Rhode Island. LC 79-150172. (Select Bibliographies Reprint Ser.). 1977. 20.95 (*0-8369-5685-0*) Ayer.
Callender, John B. Studies in the Nominal Sentence in Egyptian & Coptic. fac. ed. LC 83-17961. (University of California Publications: No. 24). 231p. 1984. reprint ed. pap. 71.70 (*0-7837-8134-2*, 204794100008) Bks Demand.
Callender, John H., et al. Time-Saver Standards for Architectural Design Data. 7th rev. ed. LC 97-18390. (Illus.). 1072p. 1997. 150.00 (*0-07-068506-1*) McGraw.
Callender, Melanie, jt. auth. see Jones-Lee, Anita.
Callender, Norma A. Anthony Plays Ball. large type ed. (Beginning Reader Comprehension Ser.: Vol. 6). (Illus.). 12p. (Orig.). (J). (ps-2). 1997. pap. 4.95 (*1-890274-06-2*) BATA Bks.
— Hear Drew Play. large type ed. (Beginning Reader Comprehension Ser.: Vol. 4). (Illus.). 12p. (Orig.). (J). (ps-2). 1997. pap. 4.95 (*1-890274-04-6*) BATA Bks.
— Jenny & the Hat. large type ed. (Beginning Reader Comprehension Ser.: Vol. 5). (Illus.). 12p. (Orig.). (J). (ps-2). 1997. pap. 4.95 (*1-890274-05-4*) BATA Bks.
— Parker Hides. large type ed. (Beginning Reader Comprehension Ser.: Vol. 3). (Illus.). 12p. (Orig.). (J). (ps-2). 1997. pap. 4.95 (*1-890274-03-8*) BATA Bks.
— See Amber. large type ed. (Beginning Reader Comprehension Ser.: Vol. 2). (Illus.). 12p. (Orig.). (J). (ps-2). 1997. pap. 4.95 (*1-890274-02-X*) BATA Bks.
— Zach Reads. large type ed. (Beginning Reader Comprehension Ser.: Vol. 1). (Illus.). 12p. (Orig.). (J). (ps-2). 1997. pap. 4.95 (*1-890274-01-1*) BATA Bks.
Callender, Rosheen, ed. Equality in Law Between Men & Women in the European Community: Ireland. LC 94-17848. 294p. (C). 1994. lib. bdg. 80.50 (*0-7923-1834-X*); lib. bdg. 99.00 (*0-7923-1828-5*) Kluwer Academic.
Callender, Timothy. It So Happen. (Caribbean Writers Ser.). 128p. (Orig.). (C). 1991. pap. 8.95 (*0-435-98926-X*, 98926) Heinemann.
Callender, Vesta, ed. see Mayer, Margarita.
Callender, Willard D., Jr. Reflections of a Fanatical Learner: Memories, Meanings, & Musings. LC 94-26462. 318p. (C). 1994. pap. text 36.50 (*0-8191-9672-X*); lib. bdg. 49.50 (*0-8191-9671-1*) U Pr of Amer.
Callens, Johan. From Middleton & Rowley's "Changeling" to Sam Shepard's "Bodyguard" A Contemporary Appropriation of a Renaissance Drama. LC 97-1767. (Studies in Comparative Literature Ser.). 177 p. 1997. write for info. (*0-88946-393-X*) E Mellen.
— From Middleton & Rowley's "Changeling" to Sam Shepard's "Bodyguard" A Contemporary Appropriation of a Renaissance Drama. LC 97-1767. (Studies in Comparative Literature: Vol. 19). 182p. 1997. text 79.95 (*0-7734-8653-4*) E Mellen.
Callens, Johan, ed. American Literature & the Arts. (Illus.). 128p. 1994. pap. 29.95 (*90-70289-83-0*, Pub. by VUB Univ Pr) Paul & Co Pubs.
— Re-Discoveries of America: The Meeting of Cultures. (Illus.). 144p. 1994. pap. 19.95 (*90-5487-050-8*) Paul & Co Pubs.
— Sam Shepard: Between the Margin & the Center 1. 98p. 1998. pap. text 14.00 (*90-5702-151-X*, Harwood Acad Pubs) Gordon & Breach.
— Sam Shepard: Between the Margin & the Center 2, Vol. 2. 96p. 1998. pap. text 14.00 (*90-5702-152-8*, Harwood Acad Pubs) Gordon & Breach.
Calleo, David P. American Political System. LC 69-17194. (Background Ser.). 1969. 18.95 (*0-8023-1210-1*) Dufour.
— The Atlantic Fantasy: The U. S., NATO, & Europe. LC 75-128823. (Studies in International Affairs: No. 13). 192p. 1970. reprint ed. pap. 59.60 (*0-608-04080-0*, 206481200011) Bks Demand.
— The Bankrupting of America: How the Federal Budget Is Impoverishing the Nation. 304p. 1993. reprint ed. pap. 12.00 (*0-380-71033-1*, Avon Bks) Morrow Avon.
— Europe's Future: The Grand Alternatives. (C). 1967. pap. 2.00 (*0-393-00406-6*) Norton.
— The Imperious Economy. LC 81-20066. (Illus.). 304p. 1982. 37.95 (*0-674-44522-8*) HUP.
Calleo, David P. & Gordon, Philip H., eds. From the Atlantic to the Urals: National Perspectives on the New Europe. LC 92-18291. 187p. 1992. pap. 13.95 (*0-929765-11-7*) Seven Locks Pr.
Calleo, David P. & Morgenstern, Claudia, eds. Recasting Europe's Economies: National Strategies in the 1980s. 228p. (C). 1990. pap. text 23.50 (*0-8191-7651-6*); lib. bdg. 42.00 (*0-8191-7650-8*) U Pr of Amer.

C

Calleo, David P. & Staal, Eric R., eds. Europe's Franco-German Engine. LC 97-80644. 145p. 1998. pap. 18.95 (*0-8157-1279-0*) Brookings.

Caller & Ober. Genealogy of the Descendants of Lawrence & Cassandra Southwick of Salem, Massachusetts. (Illus.). 616p. 1989. reprint ed. pap. 92.00 (*0-8328-1089-4*); reprint ed. lib. bdg. 100.00 (*0-8328-1088-6*) Higginson Bk Co.

Callero, Monti D., et al. Enhancing Weapon System Analysis: Issues & Procedures for Integrating a Research & Development Simulator with a Distributed Simulation Network. LC 94-13928. 1994. pap. text 13.00 (*0-8330-1539-7*, MR-340-ARPA) Rand Corp.

— Light Helicopter Trade-Off Assessments. LC 93-19286. 1993. pap. 13.00 (*0-8330-1373-4*, MR-198-A) Rand Corp.

Callero, Monti D., jt. auth. see Veit, Clairice T.

Callero, Peter J., jt. ed. see Howard, Judith A.

Callero, Peter L., jt. auth. see Piliavin, Jane A.

Calleros. Legal Method Writing. 1990. 22.00 (*0-316-12502-4*, Aspen Law & Bus) Aspen Pub.

Calleros, Charles R. Legal Method & Writing. 2nd ed. 576p. 1994. teacher ed. write for info. (*0-316-13280-2*, 32802) Aspen Law.

— Legal Method & Writing. 2nd ed. LC 94-75305. 576p. 1994. pap. 26.50 (*0-316-12505-9*, Aspen Law & Bus) Aspen Pub.

— Legal Method & Writing. 3rd ed. LC 97-51907. 1998. pap. text 32.95 (*1-56706-647-X*) Aspen Law.

Callery, B. G. & Mosimann, E. A., compiled by. The Tradition of Fine Bookbinding in the Twentieth Century. (Illus.). 120p. 1979. 5.00 (*0-913196-28-2*) Hunt Inst Botanical.

Callery, Emma. The Complete Book of Herbs: A Practical Guide to Cultivating, Drying & Cooking with More Than 50 Herbs. LC 93-85549. (Illus.). 128p. 1994. 14.98 (*1-56138-351-1*, Courage) Running Pr.

— The Complete Calligrapher. 1994. 17.98 (*0-7858-0032-8*) Bk Sales Inc.

— Hot & Spicy Cookbook. 1991. 19.98 (*1-55521-753-2*) Bk Sales Inc.

— New Riders Companion. 1994. 19.98 (*0-7858-0165-0*) Bk Sales Inc.

— Quilting, Patchwork & Samplers. 1995. write for info. (*0-7858-0248-7*) Bk Sales Inc.

— Quilts, Patchwork & Samplers. 1995. 14.98 (*0-7858-0249-5*) Bk Sales Inc.

Callery, Marjana F., jt. auth. see Nevalainen, David E.

Callery, Michael. Learning Lingo: The Art & Science of Programming with Macromedia Directories. 352p. 1995. pap. text 34.95 (*0-201-87043-6*) Addison-Wesley.

Callery, Michael, jt. auth. see Schwartz, Roberta.

Callery, Nancy. Mares, Mud & Manure: Poems for Horse Lovers. unabridged ed. (Illus.). 80p. 1996. 14.95 (*0-9656068-0-5*) N Callery.

Callery, Sean. Family Matters: Card Games for Two. rev. ed. (Family Matters Ser.). (Illus.). 96p. 1994. pap. 6.95 (*0-7063-7223-9*, Pub. by WrLock) Sterling.

— London. (Illus.). 24p. 1996. pap. text 6.95 (*0-19-422801-0*) OUP.

Callery, Terence, jt. auth. see McIntyre, Cindy.

Callesen, Gerd & Logue, John. Social-Demokraten & Internationalism: The Copenhagen Social Democratic Newspaper's Coverage of International Labor Affairs, 1871-1958. LC 79-121967. (University of Gothenburg (Sweden), Research Section Post-War History Publications Ser.: No. 8). (Illus.). 73p. 1979. pap. 4.95 (*0-933522-00-2*) Kent Popular.

Callesen, Gerd, ed. see Bryld, Claus, et al.

Callewaert, Denis M. & Genyea, Julien. Basic Chemistry: General, Organic, Biological. 1980. text 49.95 (*0-87901-130-0*) Worth.

— Fundamentals of College Chemistry. 1980. text 34.95 (*0-87901-125-4*) Worth.

— Fundamentals of Organic & Biological Chemistry. 1980. text 35.95 (*0-87901-129-7*) Worth.

Callewaert, Winand & Lath, Mukund. The Hindi Padavali of Namdev: A Critical Edition of Namdev's Hindi Songs with Translation & Annotation. (C). 1989. 42.50 (*81-208-0607-7*) S Asia.

Callewaert, Winand M. Gods & Temples in South India. LC 95-905809. (C). 1995. 32.00 (*81-7304-107-5*, Pub. by Manohar) S Asia.

— The Hindi Biography of Dadu Dayal. (C). 1988. 18.00 (*81-208-0490-2*, Pub. by Motilal Bnarsidass) S Asia.

— Sarvagi of Gopaldas: A Seventeenth Century Anthology of Bhakti Literature. (C). 1993. 80.00 (*0-685-69769-X*, Pub. by Manohar) S Asia.

— Sri Guru Granth Sahib with Complete Index, 2 vols., Set. (C). 1996. 200.00 (*81-208-1379-0*, Pub. by Motilal Bnarsidass) S Asia.

Callewaert, Winand M. & Op De Beeck, Bart. Devotional Hindi Literature, 2 vol. (C). 1991. 88.00 (*81-85425-65-5*, Pub. by Manohar) S Asia.

— Devotional Hindi Literature, 2 vol., 1. (C). 1991. 50.00 (*81-85425-66-3*, Pub. by Manohar) S Asia.

— Devotional Hindi Literature, 2 vol., 2. (C). 1991. 50.00 (*81-85425-67-1*, Pub. by Manohar) S Asia.

Callewaert, Winand M., et al. E.E.C. India, Towards A Common Perspective: Proceedings of The Ec-india Seminar, Leuven, 11-12th Nov. 1984. LC 88-111638. xvi, 214 p. 1985. write for info. (*90-6831-032-1*) Peeters Pub.

Calley, Karin & Pearson, Noel. Caden Walaa! (Jam Roll Picture Bks.). 32p. (J). 1995. 19.95 (*0-7022-2704-8*, Pub. by Univ Queensland Pr) Intl Spec Bk.

Calleya, Stephen C. Navigating Regional Dynamics in the Post-Cold War World: Patterns of Relations in the Mediterranean Area. LC 96-43126. (Illus.). 288p. 1997. text 83.95 (*1-85521-850-X*, Pub. by Dartmth Pub) Ashgate Pub Co.

Calleya, Stephen C. Regionalism in the Post-Cold World War. 70.95 (*1-84014-417-3*) Ashgate Pub Co.

Callian, Carnegie S., jt. auth. see Goslin, Thomas S.

Callick, E. B. Metres to Microwaves. (History of Technology Ser.: No. 11). 240p. 1990. 85.00 (*0-86341-212-2*, HT011) INSPEC Inc.

Callick, Rowan. Comrades & Capitalists: Hong Kong since the Takeover. 213p. 1998. pap. 16.95 (*0-86840-728-3*, Pub. by New South Wales Univ Pr) Intl Spec Bk.

Callicott, J. Baird. Beyond the Land Ethic: More Essays in Environmental Philosophy. LC 98-53504. (SUNY Series in the Philosophy & Biology). 368p. (C). 1999. text 74.50 (*0-7914-4083-4*); pap. text 24.95 (*0-7914-4084-2*) State U NY Pr.

— Earth's Insights. 1997. pap. text 17.95 (*0-520-08560-4*, Pub. by U CA Pr) Cal Prin Full Svc.

— In Defense of the Land Ethic: Essays in Environmental Philosophy. LC 88-7039. (SUNY Series in Philosophy & Biology). 325p. (C). 1989. text 59.50 (*0-88706-899-5*); pap. text 21.95 (*0-88706-900-2*) State U NY Pr.

Callicott, J. Baird, ed. Companion to a Sand County Almanac: Interpretive & Critical Essays. LC 87-10396. 310p. (C). 1987. text 27.95 (*0-299-11230-6*); pap. text 15.95 (*0-299-11234-9*) U of Wis Pr.

Callicott, J. Baird & Ames, Roger T., eds. Nature in Asian Traditions of Thought: Essays in Environmental Philosophy. LC 88-16003. (SUNY Series in Philosophy & Biology). 335p. (C). 1989. pap. text 22.95 (*0-88706-951-7*) State U NY Pr.

Callicott, J. Baird & Da Rocha, Fernando J., eds. Earth Summit Ethics: Toward a Reconstructive Postmodern Philosophy of Environmental Education. LC 95-42277. (SUNY Series in Constructive Postmodern Thought). 256p. (C). 1996. pap. text 19.95 (*0-7914-3054-5*) State U NY Pr.

— Earth Summit Ethics: Toward a Reconstructive Postmodern Philosophy of Environmental Education. LC 95-42277. (SUNY Series in Constructive Postmodern Thought). 256p. (C). 1996. text 59.50 (*0-7914-3053-7*) State U NY Pr.

Callicott, J. Baird & Nelson, Michael P. The Great New Wilderness Debate. LC 97-47023. 1998. pap. 30.00 (*0-8203-1984-8*) U of Ga Pr.

Callicott, J. Baird & Nelson, Michael P., eds. The Great New Wilderness Debate. LC 97-47023. 696p. 1998. text 70.00 (*0-8203-1983-X*) U of Ga Pr.

Callicott, J. Baird, jt. auth. see Overholt, Thomas W.

Callicott, J. Baird, ed. see Leopold, Aldo.

***Callicott, Nick.** Computer Aided Manufacture in Architecture Changing the Craft of Design. (Illus.). 288p. 2000. pap. 49.95 (*0-7506-4647-0*, Architectural Pr) Buttrwrth-Heinemann.

Callicutt, James W., jt. ed. see Watkins, Ted R.

Callier, Billue, jt. ed. see Monroe, Barbara.

Callier, F. M. & Desoer, C. A. Linear System Theory. (Texts in Electrical Engineering Ser.). (Illus.). xiv, 509p. 1994. 79.95 (*0-387-97573-X*) Spr-Verlag.

— Multivariable Feedback Systems. (Texts in Electrical Engineering Ser.). (Illus.). 275p. 1982. 116.95 (*0-387-90768-8*) Spr-Verlag.

Callier, Pierre. Denis: Etchings & Lithographs, Catalogue Raisonne. (FRE., Illus.). 1999. 150.00 (*1-55660-299-5*) A Wofsy Fine Arts.

Callies, David L. Preserving Paradise: Why Regulation Won't Work. LC 93-28244. (C). 1994. pap. 16.95 (*0-8248-1576-9*) UH Pr.

Callies, David L., et al. Cases & Materials on Land Use. 2nd ed. (American Casebook Ser.). 729p. (C). 1994. text. write for info. (*0-314-03253-3*) West Pub.

— Land Use to Accompany Cases & Materials On. 2nd ed. (American Casebook Ser.). 200p. 1994. pap. text, teacher ed. write for info. (*0-314-04263-6*) West Pub.

California College for Health Sciences Staff. Healthcare Planning & Marketing. 246p. (C). 1994. spiral bd. Price not set. (*0-933195-13-3*) CA College Health Sci.

Calligaris, G., et al, eds. Indices Chronologici Ad Scriptores Rerum Italicarum Quos L. A. Muratorius Collegit. xvi, 189p. 1976. reprint ed. 40.00 (*3-487-06317-4*) G Olms Pubs.

***Calligaro, Julie A.** Arranging Your Financial & Legal Affairs: A Step-by-Step Guide to Getting Your Affairs in Order. 112p. 1998. 14.00 (*1-890117-07-2*) Womens Source.

Calligaro, Julie A. The Widow's Resource: How to Solve the Financial & Legal Problems That Occur Within the First Six to Nine Months of Your Husband's Death. LC 96-61700. 124p. 1997. pap. 12.95 (*1-890117-03-X*) Womens Source.

Calligaro, Keith. Management of Extracranial Cerebrovascular Disease. LC 96-33256. 190p. 1996. text 100.00 (*0-397-51655-X*) Lppncott W & W.

Calligaro, Keith, et al, eds. Modern Management of Renovascular Hypertension & Renal Salvage. (Illus.). 313p. 1996. 89.00 (*0-683-01357-2*) Lppncott W & W.

Calligaro, Keith D. & Veith, Frank J., eds. Management of Infected Arterial Grafts. LC 94-7228. (Illus.). 243p. 1994. 75.00 (*0-942219-57-0*) Quality Med Pub.

Calligaro, Keith D., et al. Diagnosis & Treatment for Aortic & Peripheral Arterial Aneurysms. Lambert, Richard, ed. LC 98-5823. (Illus.). 336p. (C). 1998. text 98.00 (*0-7216-7675-8*, W B Saunders Co) Harcrt Hlth Sci Grp.

Callighan, Cheryl L. How to Teach Spelling Without Going Crazy. (Illus.). 128p. 1999. pap., teacher ed. 14.95 (*1-57612-080-5*, MM2094) Monday Morning Bks.

— How to Teach Vocabulary Without Going Crazy. (Illus.). 128p. (J). (gr. 4-8). 1999. pap. 14.95 (*1-57612-081-3*, MM2095) Monday Morning Bks.

Callighan, Donna, jt. auth. see Failla, Kathy.

Callihan, Steven E. Create Your First Web Page in a Weekend: Mac/Imac. LC 99-64746. (In a Weekend Ser.). 1999. pap. 24.99 (*0-7615-2135-6*) Prima Pub.

***Callihan, David & Callihan, Laurie.** The Guidance Manual for the Christian Home School: A Parent's Guide to Preparing Home School Students for College Or Career. 264p. 2000. pap. 22.99 (*1-56414-452-6*) Career Pr Inc.

Callihan, Laurie, jt. auth. see Callihan, David.

***Callihan, Steve.** Create Web Animations in a Weekend. LC 98-67578. (Computer Bks.). 358p. 1998. per. 24.99 (*0-7615-1822-3*) Prima Pub.

Callihan, Steve. Create Your First Web Page in a Weekend. LC 96-68058. 432p. 1996. per. 24.99 incl. cd-rom (*0-7615-0692-6*) Prima Pub.

***Callihan, Steve.** Create Your First Web Page in a Weekend. 1999. pap. 24.99 (*0-7615-2482-7*) Prima Pub.

Callihan, Steve. Learn HTML in a Weekend. LC 97-69599. (Computer Bks.). 432p. 1997. per. 24.99 (*0-7615-1293-4*) Prima Pub.

— Learn HTML in a Weekend. rev. ed. LC 98-67613. (In a Weekend Ser.). 350p. 1998. per. 24.99 (*0-7615-1800-2*) Prima Pub.

Callihan, Steve, jt. auth. see Wagner, Lisa D.

***Callil, Carmen & Toibin, Colm.** The Modern Library: The Best 200 Novels in English since 1950. 287p. 1999. 27.50 (*0-330-34182-0*, Pub. by Picador) Trans-Atl Phila.

Callimachus. Aetia, Iambi, Lyric Poems, Hecale, Minor Epic & Elegiac Poems, Fragments of Epigrams, Fragments of Uncertain Location. (Loeb Classical Library: No. 421). 440p. 1958. 19.95 (*0-674-99463-9*) HUP.

— Callimachus, 2 vols. Pfeiffer, Rudolfus & Connor, W. R., eds. LC 78-18592. (Greek Texts & Commentaries Ser.). 1979. reprint ed. lib. bdg. 71.95 (*0-405-11433-8*) Ayer.

— Hecale. Hollis, Adrian S., ed. (Illus.). 414p. 1990. text 74.00 (*0-19-814044-4*) OUP.

— Hymni et Epigrammata. Von Wilamowitz-Moellendorff, Ulrich, ed. 62p. 1985. write for info. (*3-296-13000-4*) G Olms Pubs.

***Callimachus.** The Poems of Callimachus. 300p. 2000. pap. text 24.95 (*0-19-815224-8*) OUP.

— The Poems of Callimachus. Nisetich, Frank, tr. 300p. 2000. text 70.00 (*0-19-814760-0*) OUP.

Callimachus. Works, 2 vols. Pfeiffer, Rudolph, ed. 316p. 1985. text 82.00 (*0-19-814116-5*) OUP.

— Works, 2 vols. Pfeiffer, Rudolph, ed. 536p. 1986. text 110.00 (*0-19-814115-7*) OUP.

Callimahos, Lambros D. Traffic Analysis & the Zendian Problem. 259p. (Orig.). (C). 1989. pap. 32.80 (*0-89412-161-8*) Aegean Park Pr.

Callimahos, Lambros D., jt. auth. see Friedman, William F.

Callinan, David, jt. auth. see Rawson, Gloria.

Callinan, Ian. The Lawyer & the Libertine. 1997. pap. 19.95 (*1-875998-36-5*, Pub. by Central Queensland) Accents Pubns.

Callinan, Paul. Family Homeopathy. Bensen, Don R., ed. 344p. 1995. 24.95 (*0-87983-687-3*, 36873K, Keats Publng) NTC Contemp Pub Co.

Callinan, Tom & Shapiro, Ann. Let's Clean up Our Act: Songs for the Earth. (gr. 1-6). 1990. 3.50 (*1-879305-06-2*, AM-B-106) Am Melody.

Callingham, Glyn, jt. auth. see Marsh, Graham.

Callingham, Glyn, jt. ed. see Marsh, Graham.

Callinicos, Alex. Against Post-Modernism: A Marxist Critique. 200p. 1990. pap. 19.95 (*0-312-04225-6*) St Martin.

***Callinicos, Alex.** Equality. 2000. 56.95 (*0-7456-2324-7*, Pub. by Polity Pr); pap. 21.95 (*0-7456-2325-5*, Pub. by Polity Pr) Blackwell Pubs.

Callinicos, Alex. Making History: Agency, Structure, & Change in Social Theory. LC 87-47766. 276p. 1988. text 49.95 (*0-8014-2121-7*) Cornell U Pr.

— The Revenge of History: Marxism & the East European Revolutions. 161p. 1991. 35.00 (*0-271-00767-2*); pap. 15.95 (*0-271-00768-0*) Pa St U Pr.

— Social Theory: A Historical Introduction LC 99-12809. 1999. pap. text 20.00 (*0-8147-1594-X*) NYU Pr.

***Callinicos, Alex.** Social Theory: A Historical Introduction. LC 99-12809. 356p. 1999. text 60.00 (*0-8147-1593-1*) NYU Pr.

Callinicos, Alex. Theories & Narratives: Reflections on the Philosophy of History. LC 94-24970. (Post-Contemporary Interventions Ser.). 264p. 1995. text 49.95 (*0-8223-1631-5*); pap. text 17.95 (*0-8223-1645-5*) Duke.

— Trotskyism. Parkin, Frank, ed. (Concepts in the Social Sciences Ser.). 112p. 1990. 32.50 (*0-335-15624-X*); pap. 9.99 (*0-335-15623-1*) OpUniv Pr.

— Trotskyism. (Concepts in Social Thought Ser.). 128p. (C). 1990. pap. 12.95 (*0-8166-1905-0*) U of Minn Pr.

Callinicos, Alex, et al, eds. Marxist Theory. (Oxford Readings in Politics & Government Ser.). 288p. (C). 1989. 49.95 (*0-19-827294-4*); pap. text 15.95 (*0-19-827295-2*) OUP.

Callinicos, Constance. American Aphrodite: Becoming Female in Greek America. (Illus.). 298p. (Orig.). 1991. pap. text 14.00 (*0-918618-44-4*) Pella Pub.

Callinicos, Constantine. Beyond the Grave. Dimopoulos, George & Newville, Leslie J., trs. from GRE. 175p. (C). reprint ed. 14.95 (*1-878997-07-6*) St Tikhons Pr.

Callinicos, Luli. Gold & Workers, 1886-1924. (People's History of South Africa Ser.: Vol. 1). 112p. 1990. reprint ed. pap. 14.95 (*0-86975-119-0*, Pub. by Ravan Pr) Ohio U Pr.

— A Place in the City. (People's History of South Africa Ser.: Vol. 3). (Illus.). 150p. (Orig.). (C). 1993. pap. text 19.95 (*0-86975-424-6*) Ohio U Pr.

— Working Life: Factories, Townships, & Popular Culture on the Rand, 1886-1940. (People's History of South Africa Ser.: Vol. 2). 263p. 1987. pap. 22.95 (*0-86975-278-2*, Pub. by Ravan Pr) Ohio U Pr.

Callinus, et al. Greek Elegy, Iambus, & Anacreontea, 2 vols., 1. (Loeb Classical Library: No. 258-259). 15.50 (*0-674-99284-9*) HUP.

Calliope, Tami, tr. see Moravia, Alberto, pseud.

Calliope, Tami, tr. see Ramotti, Ottavio C.

Calliope, Tami, tr. see Rito, Daniele L.

Callis, Helmut G. Foreign Capital in Southeast Asia. LC 75-30051. (Institute of Pacific Relations Ser.). reprint ed. 39.50 (*0-404-59514-6*) AMS Pr.

— Foreign Capital in Southeast Asia. Bruchey, Stuart & Bruchey, Eleanor, eds. LC 76-4998. (American Business Abroad Ser.). (Illus.). 1976. reprint ed. 19.95 (*0-405-09267-9*) Ayer.

Callis, Jeannie. Temple Talk. 120p. (Orig.). 1997. pap. write for info. (*0-9659640-0-0*) Temple Talk.

Callis, Robert. Housing Vacancies & Homeownership: Annual Statistics, 1993. (Illus.). 59p. (Orig.). (C). 1994. pap. text 30.00 (*0-7881-0868-9*) DIANE Pub.

Callis, Stephen, et al. The Big Sweep.Tr. of La Gran Limpieza. (SPA & ENG.). 64p. 1993. pap. 6.00 (*1-879395-10-X*, Pub. by Blue Heron OR) Consort Bk Sales.

— Murder in My Suite: Bienvenidos al Hotel California. LC 97-74316. (ENG & SPA., Illus.). 70p. 1998. pap. 6.00 (*0-9639050-0-7*, Pub. by Blue Heron OR) Consort Bk Sales.

Callis, Stephen, jt. auth. see Spall, Bob.

Callisch, Richard. Somehow These Things Are All Connected. 74p. 1988. pap. 7.95 (*0-941363-03-1*) Lake Shore Pub.

Callison, Barbara. Swim for Life. LC 99-163867. (Illus.). 140p. 1998. pap., per. 22.95 (*0-9665297-0-7*) Barcal.

Callison, Charles H., ed. America's Natural Resources. LC 67-14482. 229p. reprint ed. pap. 71.00 (*0-8357-5408-1*, 205509200008) Bks Demand.

Callison, Charles S. Land-to-the-Tiller in the Mekong Delta: Economic, Social & Political Effects of Land Reform in Four Villages of South Vietnam. LC 83-6745. (Monographs: No. 23). (Illus.). 418p. (Orig.). (C). 1983. pap. text 36.00 (*0-8191-3253-5*); lib. bdg. 63.00 (*0-8191-3252-7*) U Pr of Amer.

Callison, Dudley. For Seniors Only: Student Workbook. 200p. 1998. pap. text 14.95 (*1-887002-74-X*) Cross Trng.

Callison, Frank. Find God In The Crowd. 1999. pap. text. write for info. (*1-878898-21-3*) Christian Pub.

Callison, J. William. Limited Liability Companies: A State-by-State Guide to Law & Practice, 1996 Supplement. Sullivan, Maureen A., ed. 338p. 1996. pap. text. write for info. (*0-314-20430-X*) West Pub.

— Limited Liability Companies: State Statutes & Federal Materials, 1997 LC 99-159713. 1744 p. 1997. write for info. (*0-314-22806-3*) West Pub.

Callison, J. William & Sullivan, Maureen A. Limited Liability Companies: A State-by-State Guide to Law & Practice. 558p. text. write for info. (*0-314-02422-0*) West Pub.

— Limited Liability Companies: A State-by-State Guide to Law & Practice, 1995 Supplement. 268p. (C). 1995. pap. text. write for info. (*0-314-06536-9*) West Pub.

— Limited Liability Companies: State Statutes & Federal Materials, 1995. 1000p. (C). 1995. pap. text. write for info. (*0-314-06672-1*) West Pub.

— Limited Liability Companies: A State-by-State Guide: 1997 Supplement. annuals (Practice Ser.). 414p. 1997. pap. text, suppl. ed. write for info. (*0-314-21468-2*) West Pub.

Callison, William & McAllister, Carol H. Elementary School Principal's Handbook. LC 98-88324. 240p. 1998. ring bd. 49.95 (*1-56676-700-8*) Scarecrow.

Callison, William, et al. Substance Abuse Prevention Handbook. LC 95-60050. 387p. 1995. pap. text 39.95 (*1-56676-238-3*) Scarecrow.

Callister. Solutions Manual to Accompany Material Science & Engineering. 560p. 1994. pap. text 27.95 (*0-471-30901-X*) Wiley.

Callister, J. Herbert. Dress from Three Centuries. LC 76-14506. (Illus.). 86p. 1976. pap. 7.00 (*0-317-13585-6*) Wadsworth Atheneum.

***Callister, Jeffrey C.** Brief Review in Earth Science. LC 99-214859. (Illus.). 1999. write for info. (*0-13-436111-3*) P-H.

Callister, Jeffrey C. & Stroud, Sharon M. Earth at Hand: A Collection of Articles from NSTA's Journals. (Illus.). 176p. 1993. pap. text 19.95 (*0-87355-112-5*) Natl Sci Tchrs.

Callister, Reed R., jt. auth. see Strong, William J.

***Callister, Tad R.** The Infinite Atonement. LC 99-55571. 2000. write for info. (*1-57345-623-3*) Deseret Bk.

Callister, Thomas, jt. auth. see Burbules, Nicholas C.

Callister, William D. Materials Science & Engineering: An Introduction. LC 96-18784. 880p. 1996. text 105.95 (*0-471-13459-7*) Wiley.

Callister, William D. Materials Science & Engineering: An Introduction. 5th ed. LC 99-17182. 896p. 1999. text 109.95 (*0-471-32013-7*) Wiley.

***Callister, William D.** Materials Science & Engineering: An Introduction. 5th ed. 86p. 2000. pap., student ed. 26.95 (*0-471-38912-9*) Wiley.

Callman, Ellen. Family Pride: The Italian Renaissance House & Its Furnishings. LC 84-80552. 54p. 1984. pap. text 3.00 (*0-9606718-2-X*) Hyde Collect.

Callman, Rudolf, jt. auth. see Altman, Louis.

Callmer, Johan, et al, eds. The Archaeology of the Cultural Landscape: Field Work & Research in a South Swedish Rural Region. (Acta Archaeologica Lundensia Ser.: Vol. 4.0, No. 19). (Illus.). 498p. 1993. 120.00 (*91-22-01550-7*) Coronet Bks.

Callner & Portnov. Georgia Domestic Relations Case Finder: 1991 Supplement. 45p. 1991. pap. text. write for info. (*0-87473-761-3*, 60762-10, MICHIE) LEXIS Pub.

C

An Asterisk (*) at the beginning of an entry indicates that the title is appearing for the first time.

Callner & Portnoy. Georgia Domestic Relations Case Finder: 1992 Supplement. 73p. 1992. write for info. (*0-87473-869-5*, 60763-10, MICHIE) LEXIS Pub.
— Georgia Domestic Relations Case Finders. 2nd ed. 795p. 1996. text 90.00 (*1-55834-394-6*, 60761-11, MICHIE) LEXIS Pub.
Callner, Bruce W. & Portnoy, Kathy L. Georgia Domestic Relations Case Finder. 704p. 1994. suppl. ed. 90.00 (*0-87473-640-4*, MICHIE) LEXIS Pub.
— Georgia Domestic Relations Case Finder: 1998 Cumulative Supplement. 150p. 1998. write for info. (*0-327-00300-6*, 6076414) LEXIS Pub.
Callo, Joseph F. Legacy of Leadership: Lessons from Admiral Lord Nelson. LC 99-47211. 154p. 2000. 17.95 (*1-55571-510-9*) PSI Resch.
Callon, David & Seward, Melea L., eds. Rockhurst Review, 1996: A Fine Arts Journal, Vol. IX. 100p. 1996. pap. 6.00 (*1-886761-08-6*) Rockhurst Col.
Callon, Gordon J., ed. see Colman, Charles, et al.
Callon, Jack D. Business Strategy & Information Systems. LC 95-81166. 370p. (C). 1995. 71.88 (*0-07-011250-9*) McGraw.
Callon, Michael, ed. The Laws of the Markets. (Sociological Review Monographs). 270p. 1998. pap. 33.95 (*0-631-20608-6*) Blackwell Pubs.
Callon, Ross W. Multiprotocol Routing over ATM: Bringing Internet Protocols to ATM. (C). 1998. 46.95 (*0-201-57165-X*) Addison-Wesley.
Callon, Scott. Divided Sun: MITI & the Breakdown of Japanese High Tech Industrial Policy, 1975-1993. LC 95-11675. (Studies in International Policy). 256p. 1995. 39.50 (*0-8047-2505-5*) Stanford U Pr.
— Divided Sun: MITI & the Breakdown of Japanese High-Tech Industrial Policy, 1975-1993. (Studies in International Policy). 256p. 1997. pap. 16.95 (*0-8047-3154-3*) Stanford U Pr.
Callori, B. Robert, jt. auth. see Omura, George.
Callow, Alexander B., Jr. The Tweed Ring. LC 81-6528. (Illus.). 351p. 1981. reprint ed. lib. bdg. 35.00 (*0-313-22761-6*, CATR, Greenwood Pr) Greenwood.
Callow, Alexander B., Jr., ed. American Urban History: An Interpretive Reader with Commentaries. 3rd ed. (Illus.). 576p. (C). 1982. pap. text 29.95 (*0-19-502981-X*) OUP.
Callow, Allan. Surgery of the Carotoid & Vertebral Arteries: For the Prevention of Stroke. LC 95-15498. (Illus.). 448p. 1996. 150.00 (*0-683-01369-6*) Lppncott W & W.
Callow, Allan & Ernst, Calvin B. Vascular Surgery: Theory & Practice. 1776p. (C). 1996. 235.00 (*0-8385-9384-4*, A9384-7, Apple Lange Med) McGraw.
Callow, Edward. The Phynodderree & Other Legends of the Isle of Man. LC 75-174441. (Illus.). 134p. 1972. reprint ed. 23.95 (*0-405-08336-X*, Pub. by Blom Pubns) Ayer.
Callow, J., ed. Advances in Botanical Research, Vol. 20. (Illus.). 256p. 1994. text 104.00 (*0-12-005920-7*) Acad Pr.
***Callow, J. A., ed.** Advances in Botanical Research. (Advances in Botanical Research Ser.: Vol. 33). 272p. 2000. 139.95 (*0-12-005933-9*) Acad Pr.
Callow, J. A., ed. Advances in Botanical Research, Vol. 12. (Serial Publication Ser.). 304p. 1986. text 104.00 (*0-12-005912-6*) Acad Pr.
— Advances in Botanical Research, Vol. 14. (Serial Publication Ser.). 198p. 1988. text 104.00 (*0-12-005914-2*) Acad Pr.
— Advances in Botanical Research, Vol. 15. (Serial Publication Ser.). 211p. 1989. text 104.00 (*0-12-005915-0*) Acad Pr.
— Advances in Botanical Research, Vol. 17. (Serial Publication Ser.). 303p. 1990. text 104.00 (*0-12-005917-7*) Acad Pr.
— Advances in Botanical Research, Vol. 19. (Illus.). 344p. 1993. text 104.00 (*0-12-005919-3*) Acad Pr.
— Advances in Botanical Research, Vol. 22. (Illus.). 352p. 1996. text 89.95 (*0-12-005922-3*) Acad Pr.
— Advances in Botanical Research Vol. 29: Incorporating Advances in Plant Pathology. (Illus.). 240p. (C). 1998. boxed set 99.95 (*0-12-005929-0*) Acad Pr.
***Callow, J. A., ed.** Advances in Botanical Research Vol. 30. 300p. 1999. 99.00 (*0-12-005930-4*) Acad Pr.
Callow, J. A., ed. Advances in Botanical Research Incorporating Advances in Plant Pathology, Vol. 27. (Illus.). 464p. 1997. text 99.95 (*0-12-005927-4*) Morgan Kaufmann.
— Advances in Botanical Research Incorporating Advances in Plant Pathology, Vol. 28. (Illus.). 352p. 1998. text 99.95 (*0-12-005928-2*) Morgan Kaufmann.
— Biochemical Plant Pathology. fac. ed. LC 82-19963. 496p. 1983. reprint ed. pap. 153.80 (*0-7837-8265-9*, 204904600009) Bks Demand.
***Callow, J. A., ed.** Plant Trichomes Vol. 31. (Advances in Botanical Research Ser.). 900p. 2000. 99.95 (*0-12-005931-2*) Acad Pr.
Callow, J. A., et al, eds. Advances in Botanical Research: Incorporating Advances in Plant Pathology, Vol. 21. (Illus.). 256p. 1995. text 89.95 (*0-12-005921-5*) Acad Pr.
— Biotechnology & Plant Genetic Resources: Conservation & Use. LC 97-13545. (Biotechnology in Agriculture Ser.: No. 19). 320p. 1997. text 90.00 (*0-85199-142-4*) OUP.
Callow, J. A. & Green, J. R., eds. Perspectives in Plant Cell Recognition. (Society for Experimental Biology Seminar Ser.: No. 48). (Illus.). 318p. (C). 1992. text 100.00 (*0-521-40445-2*) Cambridge U Pr.
Callow, J. A. & Woolhouse, Harold W., eds. Advances in Botanical Research, Vol. 11. (Serial Publication Ser.). 1985. text 104.00 (*0-12-005911-8*) Acad Pr.
Callow, John. A Semantic & Structural Analysis of 2 Thessalonians. Kopesec, Michael F., ed. 118p. 1982. pap. 6.30 (*0-88312-923-X*) S I L Intl.
Callow, John, jt. auth. see Beekman, John.
Callow, John, ed. see Banker, John.
Callow, Kathleen. Man & Message: A Guide to Meaning-Based Text Analysis. LC 98-6629. 400p. (C). 1998. 64.00 (*0-7618-1127-3*); pap. 44.50 (*0-7618-1128-1*) U Pr of Amer.
Callow, Maureen E. 9th International Congress on Marine Corrosion & Biofouling. 274p. 1997. pap. text 206.00 (*90-5702-110-2*, Harwood Acad Pubs) Gordon & Breach.
Callow, Philip. Chekhov: The Hidden Ground. LC 97-46679. 448p. 1998. 30.00 (*1-56663-187-4*) I R Dee.
— From Noon to Starry Night: A Life of Walt Whitman. (Illus.). 416p. 1992. text 28.50 (*0-929587-95-2*) I R Dee.
— From Noon to Starry Night: A Life of Walt Whitman. 408p. 1996. pap. 14.95 (*1-56663-133-5*, Pub. by I R Dee) Natl Bk Netwk.
— Lost Earth: A Life of Cezanne. LC 95-10065. (Illus.). 416p. 1995. 30.00 (*1-56663-084-3*) I R Dee.
— The Magnolia. LC 97-111589. 208p. (Orig.). 1996. pap. write for info. (*0-7490-0168-2*) Allison & Busby.
— Son & Lover: The Young D. H. Lawrence. 324p. 1991. reprint ed. pap. text 11.95 (*0-929587-52-9*, Elephant Paperbacks) I R Dee.
— Vincent Van Gogh: A Life. (Illus.). 320p. 1990. text 24.95 (*0-929587-37-5*) I R Dee.
— Vincent Van Gogh: A Life. 312p. 1996. pap. 12.95 (*1-56663-134-3*, Pub. by I R Dee) Natl Bk Netwk.
Callow, Phillip. Cave Light. 1989. 25.00 (*0-904524-32-9*, Pub. by Rivelin Grapheme Pr) St Mut.
Callow, R. S., jt. auth. see Cook, L. M.
Callow, Simon. Acting in Restoration Comedy. Aitken, Maria, ed. (Acting Series & BBC Master Class). (Illus.). 128p. 1991. pap. 14.95 (*1-55783-119-X*) Applause Theatre Bk Pubs.
— Being an Actor. 1995. pap. 12.95 (*0-312-13433-9*) St Martin.
— Charles Laughton: A Difficult Actor. LC 97-881. (Illus.). 368p. 1997. pap. 15.95 (*0-88064-180-0*) Fromm Intl Pub.
— Love Is Where It Falls. LC 99-26551. 208p. 1999. 23.00 (*0-88064-239-4*) Fromm Intl Pub.
***Callow, Simon.** Love Is Where It Falls. 2001. reprint ed. pap. 13.00 (*0-88064-257-2*) Fromm Intl Pub.
Callow, Simon. National: The Theatre & Its Work 1963-97. (Nick Hern Books, Drama Classics). 1998. pap. 26.95 (*1-85459-323-4*, Pub. by N Hern Bks) Theatre Comm.
— Orson Welles: The Road to Xanadu. (Illus.). 680p. 1997. pap. 14.95 (*0-14-025456-0*) Viking Penguin.
***Callow, Simon.** Shakespeare on Love. (Illus.). 128p. 2000. 19.95 (*0-7112-1535-9*, Pub. by F Lincoln) Antique Collect.
Callow, Simon. Snowdon on Stage: A Personal View of the British Theatre. LC 96-71419. (Illus.). 158p. 1997. text 55.00 (*0-8478-2026-2*) St Martin.
Calloway. Native American History. LC 98-87523. 574p. 1999. pap. text 42.95 (*0-312-15003-2*) St Martin.
— Our Hearts Fell to the Ground. 226p. 1996. pap. text 11.95 (*0-312-13354-5*) St Martin.
Calloway, et al. Intercultural Communication. LC 98-34367. 273p. 1998. pap. text 47.00 (*0-205-29263-1*) Allyn.
Calloway, Bertha W. & Smith, Alonzo N. Visions of Freedom on the Great Plains: An Illustrated History of African Americans in Nebraska. LC 98-25659. 1998. write for info. (*1-57864-027-X*) Donning Co.
Calloway, Brenda. America's First Western Frontier: East Tennessee. (Illus.). 198p. 1989. 17.95 (*0-932807-34-8*) Overmountain Pr.
Calloway, Burt & FitzSimons, Jennifer. Triad Hauntings: Ghost Stories from Winston-Salem, Greensboro, High Point, & Surrounding Areas. LC 90-83941. (Illus.). 96p. (Orig.). 1990. pap. 5.95 (*1-878177-00-1*) Bandit Bks.
Calloway, Colin G. The American Revolution in Indian Country: Crisis & Diversity in Native American Communities. (Cambridge Studies in North American Indian History). (Illus.). 353p. (C). 1995. text 69.95 (*0-521-47149-4*); pap. text 18.95 (*0-521-47569-4*) Cambridge U Pr.
— New Worlds for All: Indians, Europeans, & the Remaking of Early America. LC 96-20625. (Illus.). 216p. 1997. 24.95 (*0-8018-5448-2*) Johns Hopkins.
— New Worlds for All: Indians, Europeans, & the Remaking of Early America. LC 96-20625. (The American Moment Ser.). (Illus.). 256p. 1998. reprint ed. pap. text 14.95 (*0-8018-5959-X*) Johns Hopkins.
— The Western Abenakis of Vermont, 1600-1800: War, Migration & the Survival of an Indian People. LC 89-40736. (Civilization of the American Indian Ser.: No. 197). (Illus.). 352p. 1990. 34.95 (*0-8061-2274-9*) U of Okla Pr.
— The Western Abenakis of Vermont, 1600-1800: War, Migration, & the Survival of an Indian People. LC 89-40736. (Civilization of the American Indian Ser.: Vol. 197). (Illus.). 346p. 1994. pap. 15.95 (*0-8061-2568-3*) U of Okla Pr.
— The World Turned Upside Down: Indian Voices from Early America. 160p. 1994. text 39.95 (*0-312-10281-X*) St Martin.
Calloway, Colin G., ed. Dawnland Encounters: Indians & Europeans in Northern New England. LC 90-38192. (Illus.). 311p. 1991. pap. 19.95 (*0-87451-594-7*) U Pr of New Eng.
— New Directions in American Indian History. LC 88-5424. (D'Arcy McNickle Center Bibliographies in American Indian History Ser.: Vol. 1). 272p. 1992. pap. text 14.95 (*0-8061-2233-1*) U of Okla Pr.
— North Country Captives: Selected Narratives of Indian Captivity from Vermont & New Hampshire. LC 91-50810. (Illus.). 176p. 1992. pap. 16.95 (*0-87451-582-3*) U Pr of New Eng.
— Our Hearts Fell to the Ground: Plains Indian Views of How the West was Lost. 1997. pap. text 21.15 (*0-312-19123-5*) St Martin.
— The World Turned Upside Down: Indian Voices from Early America. 6th ed. 224p. 1994. pap. text 11.95 (*0-312-08350-5*) St Martin.
Calloway, Colin G., ed. After King Philip's War: Presence & Persistence in Indian New England. LC 96-51813. (Reencounters with Colonialism Ser.). (Illus.). 278p. 1997. pap. 19.95 (*0-87451-819-9*) U Pr of New Eng.
— Our Hearts Fell to the Ground: Plains Indians Views of How the West Was Lost. (Bedford Series in History & Culture). 224p. 1996. text 39.95 (*0-312-16050-X*) St Martin.
Calloway County Library Volunteers Staff. Photographic Pot-Pourri of Calloway County, Kentucky. LC 37-71192. 200p. 1988. 49.95 (*0-938021-22-2*) Turner Pub KY.
Calloway, Jan. The Trapnall Legacy. LC 81-67266. (Illus.). 112p. (Orig.). 1981. 9.95 (*0-9606278-0-4*); pap 5.95 (*0-9606278-1-2*) AR Commemorative.
Calloway, Jane, jt. auth. see Thornton, Kim C.
***Calloway, Joe.** Focus on the Customer: Winning & Keeping Today's Tough New Customer. 80p. 1999. pap. write for info. (*0-9675911-0-4*) Busn Resources.
— Market Leadership: Managing the Customer Focused Team. 80p. 1999. pap. write for info. (*0-9675911-1-2*) Busn Resources.
— Revival: Just When the Caterpillar Thought the World Was Ended, It Became a Butterfly. 100p. 1999. pap. write for info. (*0-9675911-2-0*) Busn Resources.
Calloway, Kate. Fifth Wheel: A Cassidy James Mystery. LC 98-13220. (Cassidy James Mystery Ser.: No. 5). 256p. 1998. pap. 11.95 (*1-56280-218-6*) Naiad Pr.
— First Impressions: A Cassidy James Mystery. LC 95-51025. 208p. (Orig.). 1996. pap. 11.95 (*1-56280-133-3*) Naiad Pr.
— Fourth Down: A Cassidy James Mystery. LC 97-40430. 240p. (Orig.). 1998. pap. 11.95 (*1-56280-193-7*) Naiad Pr.
— Second Fiddle: A Cassidy James Mystery. LC 96-47130. 224p. (Orig.). 1996. pap. 11.95 (*1-56280-161-9*) Naiad Pr.
***Calloway, Kate.** Seventh Heaven: A Cassidy James Mystery. LC 99-58810. (Cassidy James Mystery Ser.). 224p. 1999. pap. 11.95 (*1-56280-262-3*) Naiad Pr.
Calloway, Kate. Sixth Sense: A Cassidy James Mystery. LC 98-44746. (Cassidy James Mystery Ser.). 208p. 1999. pap. 11.95 (*1-56280-228-3*) Naiad Pr.
— Third Degree: A Cassidy James Mystery. LC 97-10811. 256p. (Orig.). 1997. pap. 11.95 (*1-56280-185-6*) Naiad Pr.
***Calloway, Phil.** Who Put the Skunk in the Trunk? Learning to Laugh When Life Stinks. LC 99-40423. 230p. 1999. pap. 10.99 (*1-57673-576-1*) Multnomah Pubs.
***Calloway, Stephen.** Baroque Baroque: The Culture of Excess. 240p. 1999. pap. 29.95 (*0-7148-3860-8*) Phaidon Pr.
Calloway, Stephen. Baroque Baroque: The Culture of Excess. (Illus.). 240p. (C). 1994. text 59.95 (*0-7148-2985-4*, Pub. by Phaidon Press) Phaidon Pr.
— Elements of Style. 568p. 1997. 70.00 (*0-684-83521-5*) S&S Trade.
— Elements of Style: A Practical Encyclopedia of Interior Architectural Details. 1991. 65.00 (*0-671-73981-6*) S&S Trade.
Calloway, Stephen, ed. Liberty of London: Masters of Style & Decoration. LC 92-53855. (Illus.). 224p. 1992. 60.00 (*0-8212-1974-X*) Little.
Calloway, Stephen & Beardsley, Aubrey. Aubrey Beardsley. LC 97-27611. (Illus.). 224p. 1998. 39.95 (*0-8109-4009-4*, Pub. by Abrams) Time Warner.
***Calloway, Stephen & Colvin, David.** Oscar Wilde: An Exquisite Life. (Illus.). 112p. 1999. pap. 19.95 (*1-56649-074-X*) Welcome Rain.
Calloway, Sue D. Ohio Nursing Law. 536p. 1991. pap. text 48.50 (*0-8322-0371-8*) Banks-Baldwin.
Calloway-Thomas, Carolyn & Lucaites, John L., eds. Martin Luther King, Jr., & the Sermonic Power of Public Discourse. LC 92-21236. (Studies in Rhetoric & Communication). 256p. (C). 1993. text 34.95 (*0-8173-0689-7*) U of Ala Pr.
Calloway, Warren L., jt. auth. see Withers, Paul K.
Callu, Florence, et al. Delaunay (Sonia & Robert) Collection to the Bibliotheque Nationale. (FRE., Illus.). 186p. 1977. pap. 50.00 (*2-7177-1388-3*, Pub. by Biblio Natio) Wittenborn Art.
Callus, D. A., ed. Robert Grosseteste: Scholar & Bishop. 1969. 22.50 (*0-19-821387-5*) OUP.
Callus, D. A. & Hunt, R. W. Johannes Blund: Tractatus de Anima. (Auctores Britannici Medii Aevi Ser.: Vol. II). 1970. 14.98 (*0-19-725635-X*) David Brown.
Callwell, C. E. Military Operations & Maritime Preponderance: Their Relations & Interdependence. Gray, Colin S., ed. & intro. by. LC 97-102933. (Classics of Sea Power Ser.). (Illus.). 512p. 1996. 39.95 (*1-55750-341-9*) Naval Inst Pr.
— Small Wars: Their Principles & Practices. 3rd ed. LC 95-25837. xviii, 579p. 1996. pap. 25.00 (*0-8032-6366-X*, Bison Books) U of Nebr Pr.
***Calman, Kenneth.** Potential for Health. LC 97-51536. (Illus.). 304p. 1998. text 36.00 (*0-19-262585-3*) OUP.
Calman, Kenneth, jt. ed. see Bennett, Peter.
Calman, Kenneth C. The Potential for Health. (Illus.). 292p. 1998. pap. text 32.50 (*0-19-262944-1*) OUP.
Calman, Kenneth C., jt. auth. see Downie, R. S.
Calman-Levy, Louis C. Assassin of Paris. 276p. 1994. 29.95 (*0-226-10360-9*) U Ch Pr.
Calmann & King Staff. British Design & Art. 36th ed. (Illus.). 1999. 85.00 (*0-688-16485-4*, Wm Morrow) Morrow Avon.
— British Design & Art Directory. 35th ed. 1998. 79.95 (*0-688-15725-4*, Wm Morrow) Morrow Avon.
***Calmann, Marianne.** Avignon: An Historical Novel. 448p. 1999. pap. text 14.95 (*0-7490-0446-0*) Allison & Busby.
Calmano, W., et al, eds. Contaminated Sediments. 454p. 1998. pap. 318.00 (*0-08-043383-9*, Pergamon Pr) Elsevier.
Calmano, W. & Forstner, U., eds. Sediments & Toxic Substances: Environmental Effects & Ecotoxity. LC 95-52310. (Environmental Science Ser.: No. 3234). 1996. write for info. (*0-387-60051-5*) Spr-Verlag.
Calmbach, Walter L. Musculoskeletal Conditions (aafp) The Academy Collection--Quick Reference Guides for Family Physicians. pap. text 29.95 (*0-683-30422-4*) Lppncott W & W.
Calmeil, Louis-Florentin. De la Folie: Consideree Sous le Point de Vue Pathologique, Philosophique, Historique et Judiciai Re, 2 vols. LC 75-16695. (Classics in Psychiatry Ser.). (FRE.). 1976. reprint ed. 87.95 (*0-405-07423-9*) Ayer.
— De la Paralysie Consideree chez les Alienes. LC 75-16696. (Classics in Psychiatry Ser.). (FRE.). 1976. reprint ed. 37.95 (*0-405-07424-7*) Ayer.
Calmels, ed. see Pagnol, Marcel.
Calmenson, Cole. Ready Set Read, Laugh. (J). 1995. 24.95 (*0-385-44635-7*) BDD Bks Young Read.
Calmenson, Staphanie. Welcome, Baby. write for info. (*0-688-17736-0*, Wm Morrow) Morrow Avon.
Calmenson, Stephanie. Dinner at Panda Palace. LC 90-33720. (Illus.). 32p. (J). (ps-3). 1991. 15.00 (*0-06-021010-9*); lib. bdg. 14.89 (*0-06-021011-7*) HarpC Child Bks.
— Dinner at the Panda Palace. (Trophy Picture Bk.). (Illus.). 32p. (J). (ps-3). 1995. pap. 6.95 (*0-06-443408-7*, HarpTrophy) HarpC Child Bks.
— Dinner at the Panda Palace. 1991. 11.15 (*0-606-07433-3*, Pub. by Turtleback) Demco.
Calmenson, Stephanie. Dinner at the Panda Palace Book & Tape. (Tell Me a Story Book Ser.). (Illus.). 32p. (J). (ps-3). 1996. pap. 8.95 incl. audio (*0-694-70054-1*) HarpC.
Calmenson, Stephanie. Engine, Engine, Number Nine! LC 95-7478. (Illus.). 32p. (J). (ps-2). 1997. 13.95 (*0-7868-0155-7*, Pub. by Hyprn Child) Time Warner.
— Engine, Engine, Number Nine! LC 95-7478. (Illus.). 32p. (J). (ps-2). 1997. lib. bdg. 13.89 (*0-7868-2127-2*, Pub. by Hyprn Child) Little.
— The Frog Principal. LC 97-51168. (Illus.). (J). 1999. 15.95 (*0-590-37070-7*) Scholastic Inc.
— Gator Girls. (Gator Girls Ser.). 1997. 10.15 (*0-606-11359-2*, Pub. by Turtleback) Demco.
— The Gator Girls. 1. LC 94-20110. (Gator Girls Ser.). (Illus.). 64p. 1997. pap. 4.95 (*0-688-15297-X*, Wm Morrow) Morrow Avon.
— It Begins with an A. LC 92-72016. (Illus.). 32p. (J). (ps-2). 1994. pap. 4.95 (*1-56282-689-1*, Pub. by Hyprn Child) Time Warner.
— Kinderkittens Show & Tell. (Read with Me Paperback Ser.). (Illus.). 32p. (J). (ps-1). 1994. pap. 2.50 (*0-590-46349-7*, Cartwheel) Scholastic Inc.
— Kinderkittens Show & Tell: Who Took the Cookie from the Cookie Jar? LC 95-182787. (Read with Me Paperback Ser.). (Illus.). 32p. (J). (ps-2). 1995. pap. 2.50 (*0-590-46350-0*, Cartwheel) Scholastic Inc.
— The Little Bunny. (Chubby Shape Bks.). (Illus.). 16p. (J). (ps-k). 1985. pap. 3.50 (*0-671-53110-7*) Litle Simon.
— The Little Bunny. (Illus.). (J). (gr. 2-6). 1986. 4.95 (*0-671-62079-7*) Litle Simon.
— The Little Chick. (Chubby Shape Bks.). 16p. (J). (ps-1). 1985. 3.50 (*0-671-53111-5*) Litle Simon.
— Marigold & Grandma on the Town. (I Can Read Bks.). (Illus.). 64p. (J). (gr. 1-3). 1994. lib. bdg. 15.89 (*0-06-020813-9*) HarpC Child Bks.
— Marigold & Grandma on the Town. (I Can Read Bks.). (J). (gr. 1-3). 1997. 8.95 (*0-606-10871-8*, Pub. by Turtleback) Demco.
— My Dog's the Best. LC 97-9726. (Hello Reader! Ser.). (Illus.). (J). (ps-1). 1997. 3.50 (*0-590-33072-1*) Scholastic Inc.
— My Dog's the Best. 1997. 9.44 (*0-606-11655-9*) Turtleback.
— My Summer Camp Diary. 96p. (J). (ps-3). 1995. pap. 2.99 (*0-590-48398-6*) Scholastic Inc.
— One Hundred One Silly Summertime Jokes. 96p. (J). (gr. 4-6). 1989. pap. 1.95 (*0-590-42556-0*) Scholastic Inc.
— The Principal's New Clothes. (Illus.). (J). (ps-3). 1989. pap. 13.95 (*0-590-41822-X*) Scholastic Inc.
— The Principal's New Clothes. LC 88-30314. (Illus.). 40p. (J). (ps-3). 1991. pap. 4.95 (*0-590-44778-5*, Blue Ribbon Bks) Scholastic Inc.
— The Principal's New Clothes. 1991. 10.15 (*0-606-12490-X*, Pub. by Turtleback) Demco.
— Rockin' Reptiles Vol. 2: The Gator Girls. (Gator Girls Ser.). 1998. 10.15 (*0-606-13416-6*, Pub. by Turtleback) Demco.
— Roller Skates! LC 92-3857. (Hello Reader! Ser.). 32p. (J). (ps-3). 1992. pap. 3.50 (*0-590-45716-0*, Cartwheel) Scholastic Inc.
Calmenson, Stephanie. Roller Skates. (Hello, Reader! Ser.). (J). 1992. 8.70 (*0-606-01935-9*, Pub. by Turtleback) Demco.
Calmenson, Stephanie. Rosie: A Visting Dog's Story. LC 93-21243. (Illus.). 48p. (J). (ps-2). 1998. pap. 5.95 (*0-395-92722-6*, Clarion Bks) HM.
— Rosie, a Visiting Dog's Story. LC 93-21243. (Illus.). 48p. (J). (gr. k up). 1994. 16.00 (*0-395-65477-7*, Clarion Bks) HM.
— Shaggy, Waggy Dogs (And Others) LC 97-33094. (Illus.). 48p. (ps-4). 1998. 15.00 (*0-395-77605-8*) HM.
— The Teeny Tiny Teacher: A Teeny Tiny Ghost Story. LC 97-23070. (Illus.). 32p. (J). (ps-3). 1998. 15.95 (*0-590-37123-1*) Scholastic Inc.
— What Am I? Very First Riddles. LC 87-22959. (Illus.). 32p. (J). (ps-2). 1989. 11.95 (*0-06-020997-6*) HarpC Child Bks.

C

An Asterisk (*) at the beginning of an entry indicates that the title is appearing for the first time.

— Where Is Grandma Rabbit? (Rabbit Tales Ser.: No. S899-2). (J). 1989. pap. 3.95 (0-7214-5231-0, Ladybrd) Penguin Putnam.

— Who Am I? LC 95-23465. (J). 2000. write for info. (0-7868-0156-5); lib. bdg. write for info. (0-7868-2128-0) Hyprn Child.

— Winnie the Pooh & Tigger Too. LC 93-73813. (Many Adventures of Winnie the Pooh Ser.). (Illus.). 48p. (J). (ps-4). 1994. 12.95 (1-56282-630-1, Pub. by Disney Pr) Time Warner.

***Calmenson, Stephanie, et al.** What's My Job? LC 00-20343. (Hello Reader! Ser.). 2000. pap. write for info. (0-439-20473-9) Scholastic Inc.

Calmenson, Stephanie & Cole, Joanna. Rockin Reptiles. (Illus.). 80p. (J). 1998. pap. 5.95 (0-688-15633-9, Wm Morrow) Morrow Avon.

— Rockin' Reptiles. LC 96-16067. (Gator Girls Ser.). (Illus.). 80p. (J). 1997. 15.00 (0-688-12739-8, Wm Morrow) Morrow Avon.

— Rockin' Reptiles Vol. 2: The Gator Girls. LC 96-16067. (Illus.). 80p. (J). (ps-3). 1997. lib. bdg. 14.93 (0-688-12740-1, 707272, Wm Morrow) Morrow Avon.

Calmenson, Stephanie, jt. auth. see Cole, Joanna.

Calmenson, Stephenia, jt. auth. see Cole, Joanna.

Calmes, Anne M., ed. Community Association Leadership: A Guide for Volunteers. LC 96-48977. 32p. (C). 1997. 3.00 (0-941301-36-2) CAI.

Calmes, Leslie S., contrib. by. The Letters Between Edward Weston & Willard Van Dyke. (Illus.). 76p. 1992. pap. 15.00 (0-938262-23-8) Ctr Creat Photog.

Calmet, Dom A. Treatise on Vampires & Revenants: The Phantom World. rev. ed. Leatherdale, Clive, ed. Christmas, Henry, tr. 192p. 1993. 29.95 (1-874287-06-6, Pub. by Desert Island Bks) Firebird Dist.

Calmet, J., ed. Algebraic Algorithms & Error-Correcting Codes. (Lecture Notes in Computer Science Ser.: Vol. 229). vii, 416p. 1986. 45.00 (0-387-16776-5) Spr-Verlag.

— Computer Algebra: EUROCAM 82, Marseille, France 1982. (Lecture Notes in Computer Science Ser.: Vol. 144). 301p. 1982. 31.00 (0-387-11607-9) Spr-Verlag.

Calmet, Jacques, et al, eds. Integrating Symbolic Mathematical Computation & Artificial Intelligence: Cambridge, United Kingdom, August 3-5, 1994, Vol. X. LC 95-24613. (Lecture Notes in Computer Science Ser.: Vol. 958). 275p. 1995. 49.00 (3-540-60156-2) Spr-Verlag.

Calmet, Jacques & Campbell, John A., eds. Artificial Intelligence & Symbolic Mathematical Computing: International Conference, Karlsruhe, Germany, August 1992, Proceedings, AISMC-1. LC 93-36465. (Lecture Notes in Computer Science Ser.: Vol. 737). 1993. 50.95 (0-387-57322-4) Spr-Verlag.

Calmet, Jacques & Limongelli, Carla. Design & Implementation of Symbolic Computation Systems: International Symposium, Disco '96, Karlsruhe, Germany, September 18-20, 1996: Proceedings. LC 96-38259. (Lecture Notes in Computer Science Ser.: Vol. 1128). 356p. 1996. pap. 62.00 (3-540-61697-7) Spr-Verlag.

Calmet, Jacques & Plaza, Jan. Artificial Intelligence & Symbolic Computation: International Conference AISC'98, Plattsburgh, New York, USA, September 16-18, 1998, Proceedings, Vol. 147. Carbonell, J. G. et al, eds. LC 98-41662. (Lecture Notes in Artificial Intelligence Ser.: Vol. 1476). xi, 309p. 1998. pap. 55.00 (3-540-64960-3) Spr-Verlag.

Calmet, Jacques, et al. Artificial Intelligence & Symbolic Mathematical Computation: International Conference, AISMC-3, Steyr, Austria, September 23-25, 1996, Proceedings, Vol. 113. LC 96-41752. (Lecture Notes on Computer Science Ser.). viii, 381p. 1996. 62.00 (3-540-61732-9) Spr-Verlag.

Calmette, Joseph L. La Societe Feodale. LC 80-1994. reprint ed. 30.00 (0-404-18556-8) AMS Pr.

Calmeyn, Toni. Allie the Angel. LC 96-92174. (Illus.). 16p. (Orig.). (J). (ps). 1996. pap. write for info. (0-9651176-0-X) Pop Pubng.

— Blessings from Heaven. LC 96-92175. (Allie the Angel Ser.: Bk. 2). (Illus.). 16p. (Orig.). (J). (ps-2). 1996. pap. write for info. (0-9651176-1-8) Pop Pubng.

Calmfors, Lars. EMU: A Swedish Perspective. LC 97-27413. 1997. lib. bdg. 135.00 (0-7923-9990-0) Kluwer Academic.

— Wage Formation & Macroeconomic Policy in the Nordic Countries. 448p. 1990. 115.00 (91-7150-368-4) OUP.

Calmfors, Lars, jt. ed. see Layard, Richard.

Calmon, Paulo Du Pin, see Galbraith, James K. & Du Pin Calmon, Paulo.

Calmour, Alfred C. Fact & Fiction About Shakespeare. LC 70-39876. reprint ed. 41.50 (0-404-01365-1) AMS Pr.

Calmunson, Stephanie. Chubby Snowman. (Chubby Shape Bks.). (Illus.). 16p. (J). (ps-k). 1984. pap. 2.95 (0-671-50948-9) Litle Simon.

Calmus, Lawrence. The Business Guide to Small Computers. LC 82-10080. 240p. reprint ed. pap. 74.40 (0-8357-3249-5, AU0041100013) Bks Demand.

Calnan, Alan L. Justice & Tort Law. LC 96-20114. 412p. (C). 1997. 45.00 (0-89089-701-8) Carolina Acad Pr.

Calnan, Charles. The Life & Times of Geoffrey Dowling. (Illus.). 304p. 1992. 85.00 (0-632-03505-6) Blackwell Sci.

Calnan, H. E. The Mass Is a Sacrifice. (Compact Study Ser.). 20p. (Orig.). 1993. pap. 1.95 (0-935952-91-8) Angelus Pr.

Calnan, Michael W. Health & Illness: The Lay Perspective. LC 87-1534. 192p. 1987. pap. 19.95 (0-422-79420-1, Pub. by Tavistock) Routldge.

Calnan, Michael W., et al. Going Private: Changing Expectations about Health Care? LC 92-40057. (State of Health Ser.). 1993. 80.00 (0-335-09981-5); pap. 23.00 (0-335-09980-7) OUP.

Calnan, T. R. Molluscan Distribution in Copano Bay, Texas. (Reports of Investigations: RI 103). (Illus.). 71p. 1980. pap. 2.50 (0-318-03236-8) Bur Econ Geology.

Calne. Parkinsonism. (Pharmacology & Therapeutics Ser.). Date not set. pap. write for info. (0-08-034187-X, Pergamon Pr) Elsevier.

Calne, D. B., ed. Drugs for the Treatment of Parkinson's Disease. (Handbook of Experimental Pharmacology Ser.: Vol. 88). (Illus.). 555p. 1989. 415.00 (0-387-50041-3, 2034) Spr-Verlag.

***Calne, Donald.** Within Reason: Rationality & Human Behavior. 352p. 2000. pap. 14.00 (0-375-70322-5) Vin Bks.

Calne, Donald B. Parkinsonism: Physiology, Pharmacology & Treatment. LC 74-500723. xii, 136 p. 1970. write for info. (0-7131-4175-1) St Martin.

— Within Reason: Rationality & Human Behavior. LC 98-38230. 352p. 1999. 26.00 (0-375-40351-5) Pantheon.

Calne, Donald B., ed. Progress in the Treatment of Parkinsonism. fac. ed. LC 73-180269. (Advances in Neurology Ser.: No. 3). (Illus.). 342p. pap. 106.10 (0-7837-7356-0, 204716500005) Bks Demand.

Calne, Donald B., et al, eds. Lisuride & Other Dopamine Agonists: Basic Mechanisms & Endocrine & Neurological Effects. fac. ed. LC 82-42592. (Illus.). 575p. pap. 178.30 (0-7837-7507-5, 204699900005) Bks Demand.

Calne, Donald B., jt. ed. see Tsui, Joseph King Ching.

Calne, Roy. Art, Surgery, & Transplantation. (Illus.). 227p. 1996. write for info. (0-683-23094-8) Lppncott W & W.

— Too Many People: A Radical Solution to the Population Explosion & a Survey of What Has Led to It. LC 94-16384. (World in Crisis Ser.: No. 1). (Illus.). 150p. pap. 15.95 (0-7145-4269-5) Riverrun NY.

Calne, Roy Y., ed. Liver Transplantation. 2nd ed. 576p. 1987. text 115.00 (0-8089-1858-3, 790768, Grune & Strat) Harcrt Hlth Sci Grp.

***Calne, S.** Sharp Compassion. 1998. text 40.00 (0-7472-2043-3, Pub. by Headline Bk Pub) Trafalgar.

Calnek, Anthony, ed. see Guggenheim Museum Staff.

Calnek, B. W. Diseases of Poultry. 10th ed. LC 97-2161. (Illus.). 1146p. 1997. 139.95 (0-8138-0427-2) Iowa St U Pr.

***Calnek, W. A. & Savary, A. W.** History of the County of Annapolis: Including Old Port Royal & Acadia, with Memoirs of Its Representatives in the Provincial Parliament & Biographical Sketches of Its Early English Settlers & Their Families. (Illus.). 718p. 1999. pap. 47.00 (0-7884-1321-X, C045) Heritage Bk.

Calnek, W. A. & Savary, A. W. History of the County of Annapolis, Including Old Port Royal & Acadia, with Genealogical Sketches of Its Early English Settlers & Their Families. (Illus.). 682p. 1989. reprint ed. lib. bdg. 69.50 (0-8328-0580-7) Higginson Bk Co.

Calo. Art History, Vol. 1. 1996. pap. text, student ed. 18.20 (0-13-507021-X) P-H.

— Writing about Art: Viewpoints. 2nd ed. (C). 2000. write for info. (0-13-959396-9, Macmillan Coll) P-H.

Calo, Carole G. Writings about Art. LC 92-47106. 367p. (C). 1993. pap. text 42.00 (0-13-761701-1) P-H.

Calo, Joseph M., jt. ed. see Li, Norman N.

Calo, Mary A. Bernard Berenson & the Twentieth Century. LC 93-15584. (Illus.). 288p. 1994. pap. text 22.95 (1-56639-117-2) Temple U Pr.

Calo, Mary A., ed. Critical Issues in American Art: A Book of Readings. LC 97-23797. 336p. (C). 1997. pap. text 29.00 (0-06-430987-8, Pub. by Westview) HarpC.

Calof & Simons. The Couple Who Became Each Other: And Other Tales of Healing & Transformation from a Master Hypnotherapist. 1997. pap. 12.95 (0-440-37992-X) Dell.

Calof, Rachel. Rachel Calof's Story: Jewish Homesteader on the Northern Plains. LC 95-5742. (Illus.). 176p. 1995. 25.00 (0-253-32942-6) Ind U Pr.

Calogeras, Meagan, ed. see Higginson, William J.

Calogeras, Meagan, ed. see Leigh, Michelle D.

Calogeras, Meagan, ed. see Reid, T. R.

Calogero, F., ed. see Zakharov, V. E., et al.

Calogero, Francesco, jt. auth. see De Andreis, Marco.

Calogero, Guido. Studien Uber Den Eleatismus. viii, 327p. 1970. reprint ed. 70.00 (0-318-70888-4) G Olms Pubs.

Caloia, Philip E. Open Says-a-Me. LC 94-92059. (Illus.). 1024p. 1994. pap. 55.00 (0-9640814-0-7) Philications.

Calomino, Salvatore. From Verse to Prose: The Barlaam & Josaphat Legend in Fifteenth-Century Germany. (GER.). 1990. 37.50 (0-916379-68-X) Scripta.

Calomino, Salvatore, ed. Helyas or Lohengrin: Late Medieval Transformations of the Swan Knight Legend. (Library of Medieval Literature: No. 83A). 400p. 50.00 (0-8240-3714-6) Garland.

Calomiris. Banking in Three Countries. 1994. pap. text 1.80 (0-201-76509-8) Addison-Wesley.

— Budget Deficit. (Readings Money Financial Systems & Economy). 1993. pap. text 2.00 (0-201-67248-0) Addison-Wesley.

— Controlling Inflation. 1994. pap. text 1.80 (0-201-76515-2) Addison-Wesley.

— Deposit Insurance Savings. 1994. pap. text 1.80 (0-201-76507-1) Addison-Wesley.

— Discrinination Credit. 1994. pap. text 1.80 (0-201-76510-1) Addison-Wesley.

— Exchanging Rates in the Economy. 1994. pap. text 1.80 (0-201-76516-0) Addison-Wesley.

— Federal Independent Secrecy. 1993. pap. text 1.80 (0-201-76511-X) Addison-Wesley.

— Fixed Versus Flexible. 1994. pap. text 1.80 (0-201-76517-9) Addison-Wesley.

— Globalization in Financial Markets. 1994. pap. text 1.80 (0-201-76505-5) Addison-Wesley.

— Information on Interest Rates. (Readings Money Financial Systems & Economy). 1994. pap. text 1.80 (0-201-76502-0) Addison-Wesley.

— Managing Interest. 1994. pap. text 1.80 (0-201-76503-9) Addison-Wesley.

— Monetry Policy Operations. 1993. pap. text 2.00 (0-201-76513-6) Addison-Wesley.

Calomiris. The Postmodern Bank Safety Net: Lessons from Developed & Developing Economies. LC 98-137537. 1997. pap. 9.95 (0-8447-7100-7) Am Enterprise.

Calomiris. Readings Money Financial Systems & Economy Tax Policy. 1994. pap. text 1.80 (0-201-76501-2) Addison-Wesley.

— Recent Innovation. 1994. pap. text 1.80 (0-201-76508-X) Addison-Wesley.

— Should Discount Win. 1994. pap. text 1.80 (0-201-76512-8) Addison-Wesley.

— Stock Market Efficient. 1993. pap. text 1.80 (0-201-76504-7) Addison-Wesley.

— Uniqueness Intermediate. 1994. pap. text 1.80 (0-201-76506-3) Addison-Wesley.

***Calomiris, Charles W.** U. S. Bank Deregulation in Historical Perspective. (Illus.). 376p. (C). 2000. text 54.95 (0-521-58362-4) Cambridge U Pr.

***Calomiris, Charles W. & Mason, Joseph R.** High Loan-to-Value Mortgage Lending: Problem or Cure? LC 99-218017. 75p. 1999. pap. 9.95 (0-8447-7125-2, Pub. by Am Enterprise) Pub Resources Inc.

Calomiris, Charles W., et al. Is the Bank Merger Wave of the 1990s Efficient? Lessons from Nine Case Studies. LC 99-163545. (Studies on Financial Market Deregulation). 117p. 1998. pap. 9.95 (0-8447-7119-8, AEI Pr) Am Enterprise.

Calonge, F. Gasteromycetes No. 1: Lycoperdales, Nidulariales, Phallales, Sclerodermatales, Tulostomatales. (Flora Mycologica Iberica Ser.: Vol. 3). (GER.). 270p. 1998. 83.00 (3-443-65008-2, Pub. by Gebruder Borntraeger) Balogh.

Calonico, James M., jt. auth. see Nash, Jeffrey E.

Calonja, J. Ruiz, jt. auth. see Estrany, Santiago P.

Calonne, David S. William Saroyan, My Real Work Is Being. LC 83-1184. 200p. reprint ed. pap. 62.00 (0-8357-3908-2, 203664200004) Bks Demand.

Calore, Paul. Land Campaigns of the Civil War. (Illus.). 272p. 2000. lib. bdg. 39.95 (0-7864-0323-3) McFarland & Co.

Caloren, Fred, ed. Is the Canadian Economy Closing Down? 174p. 1978. 38.99 (0-919618-81-2, Pub. by Black Rose); pap. 9.99 (0-919618-80-4, Pub. by Black Rose) Consort Bk Sales.

Calori, Roland & Lawrence, Peter, eds. The Business of Europe: Managing Change. 224p. (C). 1991. 49.95 (0-8039-8492-8); pap. text 24.95 (0-8039-8746-3) Sage.

Caloroso, Elizabeth, et al. Clinical Management of Strabismus. LC 92-49704. 367p. 1993. pap. text 57.50 (0-7506-9047-X) Buttrwrth-Heinemann.

Calos, Michele. Molecular Evolution of Chromosomes. (Illus.). 300p. 2000. 50.00 (0-19-509957-5) OUP.

Calos, Michele P., jt. ed. see Miller, Jeffrey H.

***Calosso, Jo-Anne.** Street Smarts: or School's Out, Time to Begin the Rest of Your Life. (Illus.). 106p. (YA). (gr. 11 up). 1998. spiral bd. 9.95 (0-9666947-0-8) Wibsstem Pubg.

Calotta, Charles, ed. Designing for High Technology Use. (Sessions Proceedings Ser.). 44p. 1986. 3.00 (0-87262-561-3) Am Soc Civil Eng.

Calotychos, Vangelis, ed. Cyprus & Its People: Nation, Identity & the Experience in an Unimaginable Community, 1955-1997. LC 98-19812. 344p. (C). 1998. text 65.00 (0-8133-3515-9, Pub. by Westview) HarpC.

Calow, P. Handbook of Ecotoxicology Vol. 2, Vol. 2. LC 92-39663. (Illus.). 500p. 1994. 145.00 (0-632-02989-7, Pub. by Blckwll Scitfc UK) Blackwell Sci.

Calow, P. & Petts, G. E. River's Handbook: Hydrological & Ecological Processes, Vol. 1. (Illus.). 544p. 1992. 195.00 (0-632-02832-7) Blackwell Sci.

Calow, P., jt. auth. see Maltby, L.

Calow, P., jt. auth. see Petts, G.

Calow, P., jt. auth. see Sibly, R.

Calow, Peter. Blackwell's Concise Encyclopedia of Ecology. LC 99-12177. (Illus.). 1999. pap. 24.95 (0-632-04872-7) Blackwell Sci.

— Blackwell's Concise Encyclopedia of Environmental Management. LC 99-12178. (Illus.). 1999. pap. 29.95 (0-632-04951-0) Blackwell Sci.

— Controlling Environmental Risks from Chemicals: Principles & Practice. LC 96-39526. 150p. 1997. 72.00 (0-471-96995-8) Wiley.

— The Encyclopedia of Ecology & Environmental Management. LC 97-43092. (Illus.). 1998. 199.95 (0-86542-838-7) Blackwell Sci.

Calow, Peter. Handbook of Ecotoxicology. (Illus.). 1997. pap. text 295.00 (0-632-04933-2) Blackwell Sci.

Calow, Peter. Handbook of Ecotoxicology, Vols. 1 & 2. 1994. 295.00 (0-86542-849-2) Blackwell Sci.

Calow, Peter. Handbook of Environmental Risk Assessment & Management. (Illus.). 1997. 175.00 (0-86542-732-1) Blackwell Sci.

Calow, Peter, ed. Handbook of Ecotoxicology Vol. 2, Vol. 1. LC 92-39663. 1993. 175.00 (0-632-03573-0) Blackwell Sci.

Calow, Peter & Petts, Geoffrey E., eds. River Biota: Selected Extracts from the Rivers Handbook. LC 96-6929. 1996. 49.95 (0-86542-716-X) Blackwell Sci.

Calow, Peter, jt. ed. see Tytler, Peter.

Caloz, Masseo. Etude Sur la LXX Origenienne du Psautier. (Orbis Biblicus et Orientalis Ser.: Vol. 19). 1978. text 86.25 (2-8271-0138-6, Pub. by Ed Univ Fri) Eisenbrauns.

Calpe, Espasa. Enciclopedia del Hoger, 8 vols. 8000p. 1993. 1600.00 (0-7859-9878-0) Fr & Eur.

Calre, Val, et al. Reaction & Responses to High Serum Cholesterol Results (DINROO) (Research Monographs: No. 6). 90p. 1992. pap. 45.00 (0-7300-2010-X, Pub. by Deakin Univ) St Mut.

Calsat, H. J. Dictionary of Space Management: French-English-German-Spanish. (ENG, FRE, GER & SPA.). 703p. 1993. 225.00 (0-7859-8766-5) Fr & Eur.

— Dictionnaire d'Amenagement d'Espace: French-English-German-Spanish. (ENG, FRE, GER & SPA.). 703p. 1993. 225.00 (0-7859-7474-1, 2853192458) Fr & Eur.

Calsat, H. J., et al. Dictionary of Space Management: French-English-German-Spanish. (ENG, FRE, GER & SPA.). 703p. 1993. 210.00 (2-85319-245-8) IBD Ltd.

Calta, Marialisa. Fresh from Vermont: The Vermont Life Book of Seasonal Vermont Cooking. 1992. pap. 14.95 (0-936896-24-8) VT Life Mag.

Caltabiano, Maria C. La Monetazione di Messana: Con le Emissioni di Rhegion Dell'eta Della Tirannide. German Archeological Institute Staff, ed. (Antike Muenzen & Geschnittene Steine Ser.: Band XIII). (GER.). xix, 383p. (C). 1993. lib. bdg. 232.00 (3-11-013527-2) Mouton.

Caltagirone, C., jt. ed. see Gainotti, G.

Caltagirone, Carmen L. Friendship As Sacrament. LC 88-3404. 99p. 1988. pap. 5.95 (0-8189-0532-8) Alba.

Caltagirone, Dennis. Theatre Arts: The Dynamics of Acting. (Illus.). teacher ed., ring bd. 53.32 (0-8442-5164-X) NTC Contemp Pub Co.

— Theatre Arts: The Dynamics of Acting. 4th rev. ed. LC 95-51220. (J). 1995. write for info. (0-8442-5165-8) NTC Contemp Pub Co.

— Theatre Arts: The Dynamics of Acting: Actor's Logbook. 4th ed. (Illus.). 352p. 1997. pap. 21.12 (0-8442-5124-0) NTC Contemp Pub Co.

— Theatre Arts: The Dynamics of Acting: Actor's Playbook. 4th ed. (Illus.). 352p. 1997. pap. 18.33 (0-8442-5141-0) NTC Contemp Pub Co.

Calter. Technical Math. 3rd annot. ed. 1995. text 69.79 (0-471-36882-2) Wiley.

***Calter.** Technical Math. 4th ed. 928p. 1999. text 96.95 (0-471-36903-9) Wiley.

— Technical Math with Calculus. 3rd ed. 1376p. 1995. text 108.95 (0-471-36884-9) Wiley.

Calter. Technical Math with Calculus. 3rd annot. ed. 1995. text 44.60 (0-471-36885-7) Wiley.

***Calter.** Technical Math with Calculus. 4th ed. LC 98-43766. 1328p. 1999. text 108.95 (0-471-36887-3) Wiley.

Calter, jt. auth. see Bayers.

Calter, jt. auth. see Byers.

Calter, Paul. Mathematics for Computer Technology. (Illus.). 608p. (C). 1986. text 47.00 (0-13-562190-9) P-H.

— Practical Math Handbook for the Building Trades. (Illus.). 288p. 1983. pap. 17.25 (0-13-692228-7) P-H.

— Technical Calculus. 2nd ed. LC 98-20379. 1998. text 70.00 (0-13-617788-3) P-H.

***Calter, Paul.** Technical Calculus. 2nd ed. 1999. pap. 96.95 (0-471-37344-3) Wiley.

Calter, Paul. Technical Mathematics. (Illus.). 688p. (C). 1983. 26.95 (0-13-598714-8) P-H.

— Technical Mathematics. 3rd ed. (C). 1995. text 91.00 (0-13-898883-8) P-H.

***Calter, Paul.** Technical Mathematics Student Solutions Manual. 4th ed. 2000. pap. text 36.95 (0-471-37345-1) Wiley.

Calter, Paul. Technical Mathematics with Calculus. 3rd ed. (C). 1995. text 100.00 (0-13-898875-7) P-H.

***Calter, Paul & Rogers, Carol Felsinger.** Introductory Algebra & Trigonometry with Applications. 768p. (C). 1999. text 96.95 (0-471-36876-8) Wiley.

Calthorpe, Charles. The Relation Between the Lord of a Mannor & the Coppy-Holder His Tenent, Etc. LC 74-38163. (English Experience Ser.: No. 440). 100p. 1972. reprint ed. 15.00 (90-221-0440-0) Walter J Johnson.

Calthorpe, Peter. The Next American Metropolis: Ecology, Community & the American Dream. LC 93-10170. (Illus.). 160p. (Orig.). 1993. pap. 24.95 (1-878271-68-7) Princeton Arch.

***Calthorpe, Peter & Fulton, William.** The Regional City: New Urbanism & the End of Sprawl. (Illus.). 260p. 2000. 55.00 (1-55963-783-8, Shearwater Bks); pap. 35.00 (1-55963-784-6, Shearwater Bks) Island Pr.

Calthorpe, Peter, jt. auth. see Van der Ryn, Sim.

Calton, Vicki L. You Can Be All That! A Guide to Beauty & Success. LC 99-26600. 2000. 12.95 (1-56825-046-0) Rainbow Books.

Caltrider, Sue, ed. see Appel, John & Appel, Selma.

Caltrider, Sue, ed. see MacDowell, Marsha.

Caltrider, Sue, ed. see Marston, Gwen & Cunningham, Joe.

Caltrider, Suzanne, ed. see McClurken, James M.

Calucci, G., jt. auth. see Costa, G.

Calude, C. S., et al, eds. Unconventional Models of Computation: Proceedings of the 1st International Conference - UMC'98. LC 97-49031. (Springer Series in Discrete Mathematics & Theoretical Computer Science). 260p. 1998. pap. 59.95 (981-3083-69-7, Pub. by Spr-Verlag) Spr-Verlag.

***Calude, C. S. & Dinneen, M. J., eds.** Combinatorics, Computation & Logic: Proceedings of DMTCS '99 & CATS '99. (Discrete Mathematics & Theoretical Computer Science Ser.). 380p. 1999. pap. text 69.95 (981-4021-56-3, Pub. by Spr-Verlag) Spr-Verlag.

Calude, Cristian. Information & Randomness: An Algorithmic Perspective. LC 94-33125. (Monographs on Theoretical Computer Science). 1995. 49.00 (0-387-57456-5) Spr-Verlag.

Calugareanu, Grigore & Hamburg, Peter. Exercises in Basic Ring Theory. LC 97-46746. 198p. 1998. lib. bdg. 90.00 (0-7923-4918-0) Kluwer Academic.

An Asterisk (*) at the beginning of an entry indicates that the title is appearing for the first time.

***Caluggero, Lynne.** New Home, New School. (Illus.). 40p. (J). (ps-3). 2000. 6.50 (*0-9700250-0-9*) L Lemon O'Pea.

Calumpong, H. P. The Giant Clam: An Ocean Culture Manual. 68p. 1992. pap. 96.00 (*1-86320-070-3*, Pub. by ACIAR) St Mut.

***Caluori.** Frame & Focus. 2nd ed. 448p. 1999. pap. text 27.75 (*0-536-02272-0*) Pearson Custom.

***Caluori & Renick, Butera.** Frame & Focus: Anthology Investigative Reading. 160p. (C). 1998. pap. text 28.00 (*0-536-00975-9*) Pearson Custom.

Caluori, Eleanor. The Cantatas of Luigi Rossi: Analysis & Thematic Index, 2 vols., Vol. 1. Buelow, George, ed. LC 81-4749. (Studies in Musicology: No. 41). 311p. reprint ed. pap. 96.50 (*0-8357-1191-9*, 207006700001) Bks Demand.

— The Cantatas of Luigi Rossi: Analysis & Thematic Index, 2 vols., Vol. 2. Buelow, George, ed. LC 81-4749. (Studies in Musicology: No. 41). 218p. reprint ed. pap. 67.60 (*0-8357-1192-7*, 207006700002) Bks Demand.

Calus, Irene M. & Fairley, J. A. Fourier Series & Partial Differential Equations: A Programmed Course for Students of Science & Technology. LC 72-140893. (Programmes on Differential Equations Ser.). 111p. reprint ed. pap. 34.50 (*0-608-15665-5*, 203193500077) Bks Demand.

Caluwe, Rita De, see De Caluwe, Rita.

Calvaer, A. J., ed. Power Systems: Modelling & Control Applications. LC 89-31106. (IFAC Proceedings Ser.: IFPS 8909). (Illus.). 548p. 1989. 135.01 (*0-685-26444-0*) Elsevier.

Calvan, Rita A., compiled by. Selected Theses & Dissertations on the Washington, D. C. Region, Vol. CA. 1982. 4.00 (*1-888028-27-0*) GWU Ctr WAS.

Calvan, Rita A., jt. auth. see Greene, Sherwin.

Calvani, Terry & Siegfried, John J. Economic Analysis & Antitrust Law. 2nd ed. 448p. 1988. pap. 30.00 (*0-316-12501-6*, Aspen Law & Bus) Aspen Pub.

Calvarese, Thomas. Whispers in the Wind: Songs from the Silence. LC 98-75146. (Illus.). 110p. 1998. pap. 14.95 (*1-57502-980-4*, PO2680) Morris Pubng.

***Calvary Temple Church Women's Ministry Staff.** Heartstrings. (Illus.). 428p. 1999. pap. 12.95 (*0-9676455-0-6*, PO3879) Cal Temp Gospel Ch.

Calvasina. Chopstick Co. A Bus Simulation. 2nd ed. (C). 1991. 26.00 (*0-03-033107-2*) Harcourt Coll Pubs.

— Chopstick Co. Bus Simulation. (C). 1993. 26.00 (*0-03-097213-2*) Harcourt Coll Pubs.

Calve, Emma. My Life. Farkas, Andrew, ed. Gilder, Rosamond, tr. LC 76-29929. (Opera Biographies Ser.). (Illus.). 1977. reprint ed. lib. bdg. 33.95 (*0-405-09672-0*) Ayer.

***Calvel.** Flavor of Bread. 1999. 49.00 (*0-8342-1660-4*) Aspen Pub.

Calver, Stephen, et al. Marketing Management. (Resource Based Series for Hospitality & Tourism). 60p. 1994. pap. 23.95 (*0-304-32926-6*) Continuum.

Calver, William L. & Bolton, Reginald P. History Written with Pick & Shovel: Military Buttons, Belt-Plates, Badges & Other Relics Excavated from Colonial, Revolutionary, & War of 1812 Camp Sites by the Field Exploration Committee of the New York Historical Society. LC 50-10740. 334p. reprint ed. pap. 103.60 (*0-608-15439-3*, 202928800059) Bks Demand.

Calvera, Elizabeth C., ed. see Fugate, Clara T.

Calvera, Elizabeth C., ed. see Hartman, Fran.

Calverhall, Randolph D. Serpent's Walk. 449p. (Orig.). 1991. pap. 7.95 (*0-937944-05-X*) Natl Vanguard.

Calverley, Charles S., tr. see Theocritus.

Calverley, E. E. The Mysteries of Worship in Islam. 1981. 6.95 (*1-56744-166-1*) Kazi Pubns.

Calverley, John. Country Risk Analysis. (C). 1986. 390.00 (*0-7855-4190-X*, Pub. by Witherby & Co) St Mut.

— Country Risk Analysis. 2nd ed. 215p. 1990. boxed set 130.00 (*0-406-10937-0*, U.K., MICHIE) LEXIS Pub.

— Pocket Guide to Economics for the Global Investor. 1996. 19.95 (*1-55738-924-1*, Irwn Prfssnl) McGraw-Hill Prof.

Calverley, John & O'Brien, Richard, eds. Finance & the International Economy: The AMEX Bank Review Prize Essays. 216p. 1988. 38.00 (*0-19-828643-0*) OUP.

Calverley, P. M. & Pride, N. B., eds. Chronic Obstructive Pulmonary Disease. LC 93-71830. (An Arnold Publication). (Illus.). 600p. 1994. text 99.00 (*0-412-46450-0*, Pub. by E A) OUP.

Calvert. Evil Eye. 2000. 25.00 (*0-8133-6627-5*) HarpC.

Calvert, A. Spain, 2 vols., Set. 1976. lib. bdg. 500.00 (*0-8490-2634-2*) Gordon Pr.

Calvert, Albert F. The Cameroons. 1976. lib. bdg. 59.95 (*0-8490-1564-2*) Gordon Pr.

— Nigeria & Its Tin Fields. Wilkins, Mira, ed. LC 76-29763. (European Business Ser.). (Illus.). 1977. reprint ed. lib. bdg. 35.95 (*0-405-09778-6*) Ayer.

Calvert, Catherine. Coffee: The Essential Guide to the Essential Bean. LC 94-8503. 1994. 20.00 (*0-688-13328-2*, Hearst) Hearst Commns.

Calvert, Catherine, jt. auth. see Foley, Tricia.

Calvert, Catherine, jt. auth. see Hart, Cynthia.

Calvert, Cecil & Baron Baltimore. A Relation of the Successful Beginnings of the Lord Baltimore's Plantation in Mary-Land. LC 77-6864. (English Experience Ser.: No. 857). 1977. reprint ed. lib. bdg. 15.00 (*90-221-0857-0*) Walter J Johnson.

Calvert, Charlie. Charlie Calvert's Borland C++ Builder Unleashed. 1320p. 1997. 59.99 (*0-672-31022-8*) Sams.

***Calvert, Charlie.** Charlie Calvert's C++ Builder 3 Unleashed. LC 98-84228. (Unleashed Ser.). 1216p. 1998. pap. text 59.99 (*0-672-31265-4*) Sams.

Calvert, Charlie. Charlie Calvert's Delphi 4 Unleashed. LC 98-84929. 1000p. 1998. 49.99 (*0-672-31285-9*, Bobbs) Macmillan.

— Sams Teach Yourself Delphi 4 in 21 Days. 850p. 1998. 39.99 (*0-672-31286-7*, Pub. by Macmillan) S&S Trade.

Calvert, Christiane R., jt. auth. see Wielkieqicz, Richard M.

Calvert, Donald R. Descriptive Phonetics: Transcription Workbook. 2nd rev. ed. LC 92-457. 1992. pap. text 39.00 (*0-86577-452-8*) Thieme Med Pubs.

Calvert, Donald R. & Silverman, S. Richard. Speech & Deafness: A Text for Learning & Teaching. rev. ed. LC 83-71360. 300p. 1983. reprint ed. pap. 93.00 (*0-7837-9095-3*, 204984500003) Bks Demand.

Calvert, E. Roy. Capital Punishment in the 20th Century & the Death Penalty Enquiry, Being a Review of the Evidence Before the Select Committee on Capital Punishment, 1930: With Intro. & Index Added. 5th rev. ed. LC 73-172571. (Criminology, Law Enforcement & Social Problems Ser.: Vol. 153). 404p. 1975. reprint ed. lib. bdg. 31.50 (*0-87585-153-3*) Patterson Smith.

Calvert, G. C. A Little Bit of History Series Bk. 1: Tribute to G. C. Dude Calvert, Mr. Michigan City. 40p. 1987. 2.00 (*0-935549-10-2*) MI City Hist.

Calvert, G. H. Spanish Dictionary. (Routledge Pocket Dictionaries Ser.). 560p. 1980. pap. 9.95 (*0-415-05913-5*, 0558X) Routledge.

Calvert, Gene. Highwire Management: Risk-Taking Tactics for Leaders, Innovators, & Trailblazers. LC 93-5385. (Management Ser.). 249p. 1993. 29.50 (*1-55542-553-4*) Jossey-Bass.

Calvert, Gregory N. Democracy from the Heart: Spiritual Values, Decentralism, & Democratic Idealism in the Movement of the 1960s. 302p. (Orig.). (C). 1991. pap. 14.95 (*0-9628800-0-0*); lib. bdg. 29.95 (*0-9628800-1-9*) Communitas Oregon.

Calvert, Gwalter, jt. auth. see Kitchell, Edna P.

Calvert, H. G. An Introduction to British Constitutional Law. 226p. 1985. pap. 28.00 (*0-906322-68-5*, Pub. by Blackstone Pr) Gaunt.

Calvert, Hilary. Chameleon Ware Art Pottery: A Collector's Guide to George Clews. LC 98-84397. 144p. 1998. pap. 29.95 (*0-7643-0577-8*) Schiffer.

Calvert, Hugh. Shakespeare's Sonnets & Problems of Autobiography. (C). 1989. 45.00 (*0-86303-302-4*, Pub. by Merlin Bks) St Mut.

Calvert, J. Roger. Mechanics for Electrical & Electronic Engineers. LC 92-18185. (Ellis Horwood Series in Mechanical Engineering). 150p. 1993. pap. 40.00 (*0-13-569922-3*, Pub. by Tavistock-E Horwood) Routldge.

Calvert, Jack G. The Chemistry of the Atmosphere: Its Impact on Global Change, a Chemistry for the 21st Century Monograph. LC 93-20857. xxi, 394p. 1994. 125.00 (*0-632-03779-2*) Blackwell Sci.

Calvert, Jack G. & Teasley, John I., eds. SO2, NO, & NO2 Oxidation Mechanisms: Atmospheric Considerations. (Acid Precipitation Ser.: Vol. 3). 326p. 1984. 79.95 (*0-250-40568-7*) Buttrwrth-Heinemann.

Calvert, Jack G., et al. The Mechanisms of Atmospheric Oxidation of the Alkenes. LC 98-50026. (Illus.). 560p. 2000. text 105.00 (*0-19-513177-0*) OUP.

Calvert, Jack M. & McCausland, M. A. Electronics. LC 78-4113. (Manchester Physics Ser.). (Illus.). 637p. reprint ed. pap. 197.50 (*0-8357-7543-7*, 203626500001) Bks Demand.

Calvert, Jacquelyn, jt. auth. see Noonan, Janet.

Calvert, James & Voxman, William. Finite Mathematics with Computer-Supported Applications. 1995. text 60.63 incl. disk (*0-07-832907-8*, WCB McGr Hill) McGrw-H Hghr Educ.

Calvert, James, jt. auth. see Williams, Thomas.

Calvert, James E. & Voxman, William L. Linear Programming. 655p. (C). 1989. text 77.50 (*0-15-551027-4*) SCP.

— Linear Programming. 655p. (C). 1989. pap. text 28.00 (*0-15-551028-2*) SCP.

— Linear Programming. 655p. (C). 1989. 7.00 (*0-15-551029-0*) SCP.

Calvert, James F. Silent Running: My Years on a World War II Attack Submarine. LC 95-15447. 304p. 1995. 27.95 (*0-471-12778-7*) Wiley.

— Silent Running: My Years on a World War II Attack Submarine. LC 95-15447. (Illus.). 304p. 1997. pap. 16.95 (*0-471-19705-X*) Wiley.

— Surface at the Pole: The Extraordinary Voyages of the USS Skate. LC 95-46460. (Bluejacket Bks.). (Illus.). 236p. 1996. pap. 14.95 (*1-55750-119-X*) Naval Inst Pr.

Calvert, Jerry W. The Gibraltar: Socialism & Labor in Butte, Montana, 1895-1920. LC 88-1629. (Illus.). 198p. (C). 1988. 16.95 (*0-917298-14-4*) MT Hist Soc.

Calvert, Joan M., jt. auth. see Pevac, Irena.

Calvert, John C., jt. auth. see Longe, R. Leon.

***Calvert, Ken, ed.** Human Genome Project: How Private Sector Developments Affect the Government Program: Congressional Hearing. (Illus.). 429p. 2000. reprint ed. pap. text 50.00 (*0-7881-8844-5*) DIANE Pub.

Calvert, L. D., jt. ed. see Villars, Pierre.

Calvert, M. Dawn over the Kennebec. LC 83-91227. (Illus.). xxiv, 452p. 1984. 22.95 (*0-9609914-3-3*) M Calvert.

— Technology Contracts - A Handbook for Law & Business. LC 95-184684. 612p. 1995. pap. write for info. (*0-409-30769-6*, MICHIE) LEXIS Pub.

Calvert, Mary. Children. LC 88-70829. (Illus.). 160p. 1990. 23.50 (*0-9609914-5-X*) M Calvert.

— The Kennebec Wilderness Awakens. (Illus.). 584p. 1986. 19.95 (*0-9609914-4-1*) M Calvert.

— Maine Captured in Color. rev. ed. (Illus.). 1983. 16.95 (*0-9609914-1-7*) M Calvert.

— Nature Trails Captured in Color. (Illus.). iv, 144p. 1983. 18.95 (*0-9609914-2-5*) M Calvert.

Calvert, Mary R. Black Robe on the Kennebec. LC 91-91754. (Illus.). 328p. 1991. 22.95 (*0-9609914-6-8*) Monmouth Pr.

— The First Maine Cavalry. LC 97-73352. (Illus.). 336p. 1997. 25.00 (*0-9609914-7-6*) M Calvert.

Calvert, Melodie, jt. ed. see Terry, Jennifer.

Calvert, Michael. Prisoners of Hope. (Illus.). 310p. 1996. pap. 17.95 (*0-85052-492-X*, Pub. by Leo Cooper) Trans-Atl Phila.

Calvert, Mike & Henderson, Jenny. Managing Pastoral Care. LC 98-218268. 1998. 69.95 (*0-304-70067-3*); pap. 24.95 (*0-304-70068-1*) Continuum.

Calvert, Mike, jt. auth. see Fletcher, Sarah.

Calvert, Monte A. The Mechanical Engineer in America, 1830-1910: Professional Cultures in Conflict. LC 66-26683. 317p. reprint ed. pap. 98.30 (*0-608-15004-5*, 202588700046) Bks Demand.

Calvert, Patricia. Bigger. LC 93-14415. 144p. (J). (gr. 4-6). 1994. mass mkt. 16.00 (*0-684-19685-9*) Atheneum Yung Read.

— Bigger. (J). (gr. 3-7). 1995. pap. 3.95 (*0-8167-3741-X*) Troll Communs.

— Bigger. 1994. 9.05 (*0-606-07287-X*, Pub. by Turtleback) Demco.

— Glennis, Before & After. LC 96-2017. 160p. (J) (gr. 3-7). 1996. 16.00 (*0-689-80641-8*) Atheneum Yung Read.

— Glennis, Before & After. 144p. (J). (gr. 3-7). 1999. mass mkt. 3.99 (*0-380-73132-0*, Avon Bks) Morrow Avon.

— Great Lives: The American Frontier. LC 96-48519. 400p. (J). (gr. 4-9). 1997. 25.00 (*0-689-80640-X*) S&S Childrens.

— Michael, Wait for Me. LC 99-19104. (Illus.). 160p. (J). 2000. 16.00 (*0-689-82102-6*) Atheneum Yung Read.

— Picking up the Pieces. 176p. (J). 1999. per. 4.50 (*0-689-82451-3*) S&S Childrens.

— Picking up the Pieces. LC 92-27909. 192p. (YA). (gr. 7 up). 1993. 15.00 (*0-684-19558-5*) Scribner.

— Sooner. LC 97-28007. 166p. (J). (gr. 4-7). 1998. 16.00 (*0-689-81114-4*) S&S Childrens.

***Calvert, Patricia.** Stand-Off at Standing Rock. LC 00-24729. 2000. lib. bdg. write for info. (*0-7613-1360-5*) TFC Bks NY.

Calvert, Patricia. Stranger, You & I. 160p. (YA). (gr. 7 up). 1988. pap. 2.50 (*0-380-70600-8*, Avon Bks) Morrow Avon.

— When Morning Comes. 160p. 1992. pap. 3.50 (*0-380-71186-9*, Avon Bks) Morrow Avon.

— Writing to Richie. LC 94-14458. 128p. (J). 1994. 13.95 (*0-684-19764-2*) S&S Trade.

— Yesterday's Daughter. (YA). 1988. pap. 2.75 (*0-380-70470-6*, Avon Bks) Morrow Avon.

***Calvert, Patricia, ed.** The Communicator's Handbook: Tools, Techniques & Technology. 4th ed. LC 99-56129. (Illus.). 178p. 2000. pap. 37.95 (*0-929895-32-0*) Maupin Hse.

Calvert, Peter. The International Politics of Latin America. LC 93-50581. 1994. text 27.95 (*0-7190-3496-5*, Pub. by Manchester Univ Pr) St Martin.

— Revolution & Counter-Revolution. Parkin, Frank, ed. (Concepts in the Social Sciences Ser.). 96p. 1990. 32.50 (*0-335-15398-4*); pap. 9.99 (*0-335-15397-6*) OpUniv Pr.

— Revolution & International Politics. 2nd ed. LC 96-17189. 192p. 1997. 79.50 (*1-85567-396-7*); pap. 24.95 (*1-85567-395-9*) Bks Intl VA.

— Study of Revolution. 1970. 29.50 (*0-19-827177-8*) OUP.

Calvert, Peter, ed. The Central American Security System. 224p. (C). 1989. text 64.95 (*0-521-35132-4*) Cambridge U Pr.

Calvert, Peter & Calvert, Susan. Latin America in the Twentieth Century. LC 90-31061. 256p. 1991. text 49.95 (*0-312-04759-2*) St Martin.

— Latin America in the Twentieth Century. 2nd ed. LC 92-44989. 240p. 1993. pap. 18.95 (*0-312-09103-6*) St Martin.

— The South, the North & the Environment. LC 98-50607. (Illus.). 224p. 1999. 65.00 (*1-85567-535-8*); pap. 21.95 (*1-85567-536-6*) Continuum.

Calvert, Peter, jt. auth. see Burnell, Peter J.

Calvert, Peter, jt. auth. see Calvert, Susan.

Calvert, Peter, jt. ed. see Burnell, Peter J.

Calvert, R. E. Introduction to Building Management. 6th ed. LC 95-3604. (Illus.). 495p. 1995. pap. 39.95 (*0-7506-0510-3*) Buttrwrth-Heinemann.

Calvert, Randall L. Models of Imperfect Information in Politics, Vol. 6. (Fundamentals of Pure & Applied Economics Ser.: Volume 6). viii, 62p. 1986. pap. text 35.00 (*3-7186-0321-7*) Gordon & Breach.

Calvert, Randall L., ed. see Riker, William H.

Calvert, Robert & Abildgaard, Noel. International Massage & Bodywork Resource Guide. 114p. 1991. pap. 12.95 (*1-879933-03-9*) Noah Pub.

Calvert, Robert A. & De Leon, Arnold. The History of Texas. 2nd rev. ed. (Illus.). 500p. (C). 1995. pap. text 38.95 (*0-88295-926-3*) Harlan Davidson.

Calvert, Robert A., jt. auth. see Forman, Maury B.

Calvert, Robert A., jt. ed. see Barr, Alwyn.

Calvert, Robert A., jt. ed. see Buenger, Walter L.

Calvert, Robert A., jt. ed. see Wooster, Ralph A.

Calvert, Robert E., ed. The Constitution of the People: Reflections on Citizens & Civil Society. LC 90-48987. xii, 172p. 1991. 27.50 (*0-7006-0476-6*) U Pr of KS.

— The Constitution of the People: Reflections on Citizens & Civil Society. LC 90-48987. xii, 172p. 1991. pap. 14.95 (*0-7006-0478-2*) U Pr of KS.

Calvert, Robert N. The Hundredth Monkey Conspiracy. 100p. (Orig.). 1995. pap. 12.95 (*1-879933-06-3*) Noah Pub.

Calvert, Roz. Zora Neale Hurston: Storyteller of the South. LC 91-42231. (Junior Black Americans of Achievement Ser.). (Illus.). 76p. (J). (ps-3). 1993. lib. bdg. 15.95 (*0-7910-1766-4*) Chelsea Hse.

Calvert, Sandra L. Children's Journeys Through the Information Age. LC 98-28385. (Series in Developmental Psychology). 322p. 1998. pap. 34.38 (*0-07-011664-4*) McGraw.

Calvert, Sherry, et al. Track & Field Drills for Women, 4 bks. 66p. (Orig.). 1983. pap. 25.95 (*0-932741-94-0*) Championship Bks & Vid Prodns.

Calvert, Stephen, ed. see Connors, Dean & Duppler, Dana.

Calvert, Stephen, ed. see Loeffelholz, John.

Calvert, Stephen J., ed. Best Books for Young Adult Readers: Grades 7-12. LC 97-478. 744p. (YA). (gr. 7-12). 1997. 59.95 (*0-8352-3832-6*) Bowker.

Calvert, Stuart. Prisms: Being God's Light for Missionaries Through Prayer & Ministry. Hansen, Susan, ed. 96p. 1996. pap. text 7.95 (*1-56309-167-4*, N964104, New Hope) Womans Mission Union.

— Transformed: Shaped by the Hand of God. (Illus.). 134p. 1998. pap. text 7.95 (*1-56309-232-8*, W983107) Womans Mission Union.

Calvert, Susan & Calvert, Peter. Argentina: Political Culture & Instability. LC 89-40048. (Illus.). 342p. 1991. pap. 19.95 (*0-8229-6097-4*) U of Pittsburgh Pr.

— Politics & Society in the Third World: An Introduction. LC 95-37428. 256p. (C). 1996. pap. text 31.50 (*0-13-355231-4*) P-H.

Calvert, Susan, jt. auth. see Calvert, Peter.

Calvert, Thomas H. Regulation of Commerce under the Federal Constitution. (Studies in Constitutional Law). xiv, 380p. 1981. reprint ed. 47.50 (*0-8377-0429-4*, Rothman) W S Hein.

Calvert, Trish. The Essence of Mertie: Mertie Willigar Buckman. Jones-Cornwell, Ilene, ed. (Illus.). 80p. 1998. pap. text 10.00 (*0-9667740-0-0*) Womens Found Grtr Memphis.

Calvert, Trudie, ed. see Birckmayer, Jennifer & Westendorf, Bonnie J.

Calvert, Trudie, ed. see Cherry, Florence.

Calvert, Trudie, ed. see Edelstein, Karen.

Calvert, Trudie, ed. see Mackin, Jeanne.

Calvert, Trudy L., jt. auth. see Rice, David L.

Calvert, W. Uji Lectures on the Aurora. (Illus.). 116p. 1997. pap. text 24.95 (*0-9661349-0-7*) W Calvert.

Calvert, W. E., tr. see Birket-Smith, Kaj.

Calvert, W. E., tr. see Fischer-Moller, Knud.

Calvert, William S. & Ma, J. Meimei. Concepts & Case Studies in Data Management. LC 96-170413. 176p. (C). 1996. pap. 21.95 (*1-55544-761-9*, BR55220) SAS Publ.

Calverton, V. F. Bankruptcy of Marriage. LC 76-169403. (Family in America Ser.). 344p. 1977. reprint ed. 29.95 (*0-405-03852-6*) Ayer.

Calverton, V. F. & Schmalhausen, Samuel D., eds. New Generation: The Intimate Problems of Modern Parents & Children. LC 70-165712. (American Education, Ser, No. 2). (Illus.). 1978. reprint ed. 42.95 (*0-405-03701-5*) Ayer.

Calverton, Victor F. Where Angels Dared to Tread. 381p. 1977. 24.95 (*0-8369-0009-X*) Ayer.

Calverton, Victor F. & Schmalhausen, Samuel D., eds. Sex in Civilization. LC 72-9630. reprint ed. 75.00 (*0-404-57429-7*) AMS Pr.

Calves, Marcus Gon, see Gon Calves, Marcus.

Calves, Maurizio. Piero della Francesca. (Illus.). 248p. 1998. 75.00 (*0-8478-2148-X*, Pub. by Rizzoli Intl) St Martin.

***Calvesi, Maurizio.** Rejoice! 700 Years of the Papal Jubilees. (Illus.). 240p. 1999. 75.00 (*0-8478-2236-2*, Pub. by Rizzoli Intl) St Martin.

Calvet De Magalhaes, Jose. The Pure Concept of Diplomacy, 214. Pereira, Bernardo F., tr. LC 88-3109. (Contributions in Political Science Ser.: No. 214). 150p. 1988. 49.95 (*0-313-26259-4*, CPT/, Greenwood Pr) Greenwood.

Calvet, Koala. Forked Tongue Poetry: Pirate's Laughter, Suenode Nomede. Le Blanc, Daird, ed. (ENG & SPA., Illus.). 162p. 1992. pap. text 10.00 (*0-9635498-4-7*) Aroma Images.

Calvet, Louis-Jean. Language Wars & Linguistic Politics. Petheram, Michel, tr. (Illus.). 232p. 1998. text 90.00 (*0-19-823598-4*); pap. text 29.95 (*0-19-870021-0*) OUP.

Calvey, Phyllis. The House of the Lord: Stories from the Family Room. LC 92-64035. (Illus.). 112p. (Orig.). 1993. pap. 7.95 (*1-55612-550-X*, LL1550) Sheed & Ward WI.

— The Journey Home: How to Be Church. LC 95-137137. 176p. (Orig.). 1994. pap. 9.95 (*1-55612-702-2*) Sheed & Ward WI.

Calvey, Robert W. Name, Rank & Number: A POW's Indomitable Will to Survive. 112p. 1998. 42.50 (*1-85776-207-X*, Pub. by Book Guild Ltd) Trans-Atl Phila.

Calvey, T. N. & Williams, N. E. Principles & Practice of Pharmacology for Anaesthetists. 3rd ed. LC 96-20973. (Illus.). 608p. 1997. 165.00 (*0-632-04156-0*) Blackwell Sci.

Calvez, Daniel. Le Langage Proverbial de Voltaire dans Sa Correspondance (1704-1769) (American University Studies: Romance Languages & Literature: Ser. II, Vol. 103). VIII, 312p. (C). 1988. text 20.95 (*0-8204-0868-9*) P Lang Pubng.

Calvez, Daniel J. French Reference Grammar. LC 98-13388. (FRE., Illus.). 424p. 1995. pap. 17.95 (*0-8442-1497-3*, 14973, Natl Textbk Co) NTC Contemp Pub Co.

Calvez, J. Y., et al. Conferences on the Chief Decrees of the Jesuit General Congregation XXXII: A Symposium by Some of Its Members. LC 76-2977. (Studies on Jesuit Topics IV: No. 4). xii, 161p. 1976. pap. 1.75 (*0-912422-17-3*) Inst Jesuit.

Calvez, Jacques-Yves. A Stone Inheritance. LC 92-61730. 140p. (Orig.). 1993. pap. 16.95 (*0-9635239-0-2*) Presse-Gauloise.

Calvez, Jean-Paul. Embedded Real-Time Systems: A Specification & Design Methodology. LC 00-92. 672p. 1993. 285.00 (*0-471-93563-8*) Wiley.

C

Calvez, Jean Y. Politics & Society in the Third World. O'Connell, M. J., tr. LC 72-85792.Tr. of Aspects Politiques et Sociaux des Pays en Voie de Developpment. 333p. (Orig.). reprint ed. pap. 103.30 (*0-8357-8990-X*, 203352500086) Bks Demand.
— The Social Thought of John Twenty-Third: Mater et Magistra. McKenzie, George J., tr. LC 75-40992. 121p. 1977. reprint ed. lib. bdg. 49.75 (*0-8371-8711-7*, CASCJ, Greenwood Pr) Greenwood.

Calvez, Jean-Yves. Faith & Justice: The Social Dimension of Evangelization. Blewett, John E., tr. from FRE. LC 91-75164. (Studies on Jesuit Topics IV: No. 14). vi, 193p. 1991. pap. 17.95 (*0-912422-49-1*) Inst Jesuit.

Calvi, jt. auth. see Coleman.

Calvi, Giulia. Histories of a Plague Year: The Social & the Imaginary in Baroque Florence. Biocca, Dario & Ragin, Bryant T., Jr., trs. (Studies on the History of Society & Culture: No. 8). 1989. 55.00 (*0-520-05799-6*, Pub. by U CA Pr) Cal Prin Full Svc.

***Calvi, James V. & Coleman, Susan E.** American Law & Legal Systems. 4th ed. LC 98-43816. 356p. 1999. pap. text 48.00 (*0-13-083336-3*) P-H.

Calvi, Licia & Geerts, Walter, eds. CALL, Culture & the Language Curriculum. LC 98-4819. xviii, 166p. 1998. pap. 49.95 (*3-540-76192-6*) Spr-Verlag.

Calvie, Lucien, ed. see Furet, Francois & Marx, Karl.

Calvin, Allen D., ed. Programmed Instruction: Bold New Venture. LC 69-15993. 260p. reprint ed. pap. 80.60 (*0-608-30289-9*, 205012100059) Bks Demand.

Calvin, Clyde L., jt. auth. see Briggs, George B.

Calvin, Donna. Good Works: A Guide to Careers in Social Change. 5th ed. LC 93-15886. 704p. 1994. pap. 24.00 (*0-9623032-8-3*) Barricade Bks.

Calvin, Dorothy. The DOS Primer & More. 2nd ed. LC 97-149801. 540p. (Orig.). (C). 1996. pap. text 46.21 (*1-881991-30-X*) Scott Jones Pubng.

Calvin, Jack. Sitka: A Short History. 2nd rev. ed. (Illus.). 48p. 1983. pap. 10.00 (*0-9615529-0-5*) Old Harbor Pr.

Calvin, James E., jt. auth. see Klein, Lloyd W.

Calvin, James N. Tax Return Preparer's Guide 1991. (C). 1991. 132.50 (*0-13-886425-X*, Macmillan Coll) P-H.

Calvin, Jean. Rallying to Win. (Illus.). 1974. 8.95 (*0-393-60002-5*) Norton.
— Sermons on Jeremiah by Jean Calvin. Reynolds, Blair, tr. from FRE. LC 90-31837. (Texts & Studies in Religion: Vol. 46). 312p. 1990. lib. bdg. 99.95 (*0-88946-835-4*) E Mellen.
— Sermons on Micah by Jean Calvin. Reynolds, Blair, tr. from FRE. LC 90-30841. (Texts & Studies in Religion: Vol. 47). 468p. 1990. lib. bdg. 109.95 (*0-88946-839-7*) E Mellen.

***Calvin, Jim T.** Educational Jollies 101. LC 99-94970. 2000. pap. 9.95 (*0-533-13247-9*) Vantage.

***Calvin, John.** Abridgement of the Institutions of Christian Religion. 1999. 90.00 (*1-57074-384-3*) Greyden Pr.

Calvin, John. Acts. LC 95-6664. (Classic Commentaries Ser.). 384p. 1995. pap. 19.99 (*0-89107-725-1*) Crossway Bks.
— Acts 1-14-28. (Calvin's New Testament Commentaries Ser.: Vol. 7). 1995. pap. 22.00 (*0-8028-0807-7*) Eerdmans.
— Acts 1-13. (Calvin's New Testament Commentaries Ser.: Vol. 6). 1995. pap. 22.00 (*0-8028-0806-9*) Eerdmans.

Calvin, John. Calvin's Calvinism: Treatises on "The Eternal Predestination of God" & "The Secret Providence of God" Cole, Henry, tr. LC 87-90436. 354p. 1987. reprint ed. pap. 17.95 (*0-916206-32-7*) Refrd Free Pub Assn.

Calvin, John. Calvin's Commentaries, 22. 22224p. (gr. 10). 1974. reprint ed. 763.00 (*0-8010-2440-4*) Baker Bks.
— Calvin's Ecclesiastical Advice. Beaty, M. & Farley, B. W., trs. 180p. 1998. pap. 24.95 (*0-567-29196-0*, Pub. by T & T Clark) Bks Intl VA.
— Calvin's Institutes. 703p. 1959. pap. 35.00 (*0-8028-8166-1*) Eerdmans.
— Calvin's Institutes: 1536 Edition. 396p. 1995. pap. text 20.00 (*0-8028-4167-8*) Eerdmans.
— Calvin's Institutes of the Christian Religion, 2 vols., Set. McNeill, John T., ed. LC 60-5379. (Library of Christian Classics). 1812p. 1960. 64.95 (*0-664-22028-2*) Westminster John Knox.
— Calvin's New Testament Commentaries Series: Torrance Edition, 12 vols. pap. 264.00 (*0-8028-0800-X*) Eerdmans.
— Comentarios a Kas Epistolas Pastorales. (SPA.). 455p. 1994. pap. 12.95 (*0-939125-09-9*) CRC Wrld Lit.
— Commentaries on the Minor Prophets, 5 vols., Set. (Hosea Through Malachi Ser.). 1990. 105.99 (*0-85151-569-X*) Banner of Truth.
— Commentaries on the Minor Prophets: Hosea, Vol. 1. Owen, John, tr. from LAT. (Geneva Series of Commentaries). 530p. (C). 1986. reprint ed. 22.99 (*0-85151-473-1*) Banner of Truth.
— Commentaries on the Minor Prophets: Joel, Amos & Obadiah, Vol. 2. Owen, John, tr. from LAT. (Geneva Series of Commentaries). 513p. (C). 1986. reprint ed. 22.99 (*0-85151-474-X*) Banner of Truth.
— Commentaries on the Minor Prophets: Jonah, Micah & Nahum, Vol. 3. Owen, John, tr. from LAT. (Geneva Series of Commentaries). 534p. 1986. reprint ed. 22.99 (*0-85151-475-8*) Banner of Truth.
— Commentaries on the Minor Prophets: Zechariah & Malachi, Vol. 5. Owen, John, tr. from LAT. (Geneva Series of Commentaries). 668p. 1986. reprint ed. 26.99 (*0-85151-476-6*) Banner of Truth.
— A Commentary on Jeremiah, Vol. 1. Owens, John, tr. from LAT. (Geneva Series Commentary on Jeremiah & Lamentations). 508p. (C). 1989. reprint ed. 22.99 (*0-85151-547-9*) Banner of Truth.
— A Commentary on Jeremiah, Vol. 2. Owens, John, tr. from LAT. (Geneva Series Commentary on Jeremiah & Lamentations). 496p. (C). 1989. reprint ed. 22.99 (*0-85151-548-7*) Banner of Truth.
— A Commentary on Jeremiah, Vol. 3. Owens, John, tr. from LAT. (Geneva Series Commentary on Jeremiah & Lamentations). 480p. (C). 1989. reprint ed. 22.99 (*0-85151-549-5*) Banner of Truth.
— A Commentary on Jeremiah, Vol. 4. Owens, John, tr. from LAT. (Geneva Series Commentary on Jeremiah & Lamentations). 647p. (C). 1989. reprint ed. 22.99 (*0-85151-550-9*) Banner of Truth.
— A Commentary on Jeremiah & Lamentations, Vol. 5. Owen, John, tr. from LAT. (Geneva Series Commentary on Jeremiah & Lamentations). 576p. (C). 1989. reprint ed. 22.99 (*0-85151-551-7*) Banner of Truth.
— Concerning Scandals. Fraser, John W., tr. LC 78-8675. 131p. reprint ed. 40.70 (*0-8357-9126-2*, 201280200083) Bks Demand.
— Concerning the Eternal Predestination of God. Reid, J. K., tr. from LAT. LC 96-49120. 192p. 1997. pap. 19.95 (*0-664-25684-8*) Westminster John Knox.
— The Covenant Enforced: Sermons on Deuteronomy 27 & 28. Jordan, James B., ed. LC 90-32836. 290p. 1990. 14.95 (*0-930464-33-8*) Inst Christian.
— Daniel. Myers, Thomas, ed. (Geneva Commentaries Ser.). 806p. 1995. reprint ed. 35.99 (*0-85151-092-2*) Banner of Truth.
— A Defense of the Orthodox: Doctrine of Human CHoice Against Pighius. Lane, A. N. S., ed. Davies, G. I., tr. LC 96-25635. (Texts & Studies in Reformation & Post-Reformation Thought). 272p. (YA). (gr. 10). 1996. pap. 17.99 (*0-8010-2076-X*, Labyrinth) Baker Bks.
— Ezekiel One, Chapters 1-12. Foxgrover, David & Martin, Donald, trs. (Calvin's Old Testament Commentaries Ser.). 334p. (C). 1994. text 35.00 (*0-8028-2468-4*); pap. text 25.00 (*0-8028-0751-8*) Eerdmans.

***Calvin, John.** 1 & 2 Timothy & Titus. LC 98-34828. (Crossway Classic Commentaries Ser.). 1998. pap. 14.99 (*1-58134-021-4*) Crossway Bks.

Calvin, John. I Corinthians: Torrance Ed. (Calvin's New Testament Commentaries Ser.: Vol. 9). 1996. pap. 22.00 (*0-8028-0809-3*) Eerdmans.
— Galatians, Ephesians, Philippians & Colossians: Torrance Edition. (Calvin's New Testament Commentaries Ser.: Vol. 11). 1996. pap. 22.00 (*0-8028-0811-5*) Eerdmans.
— Genesis. (Geneva Commentaries Ser.). 523p. 1992. reprint ed. 39.99 (*0-85151-093-0*) Banner of Truth.
— Golden Booklet of the True Christian Life. LC 55-12085. 96p. (gr. 10). 1995. reprint ed. mass mkt. 5.99 (*0-8010-2366-1*) Baker Bks.
— Great Sermons, Vol. 1. (Essential Christian Library Ser.). 322p. 1998. 9.97 (*1-57748-346-4*) Barbour Pub.
— Heart Aflame: Daily Readings from Calvin on the Psalms. LC 98-50430. 384p. 1999. pap. 14.99 (*0-87552-458-3*) P & R Pubng.
— Hebrews, 1 & 2 Peter: Torrance Edition. (Calvin's New Testament Commentaries Ser.: Vol. 12). 1994. pap. 22.00 (*0-8028-0812-3*) Eerdmans.
— Human Nature in Its Fourfold State. 506p. 1997. reprint ed. 29.99 (*0-85151-559-2*) Banner of Truth.
— The Institutes of Christian Religion. abr. ed. Lane, Tony & Osborne, Hilary, eds. 272p. 1987. pap. 11.99 (*0-8010-2524-9*) Baker Bks.
— Instruction in Faith (1537) Fuhrmann, Paul T., ed. & tr. by. 212p. 1992. reprint ed. pap. 13.95 (*0-664-25314-8*) Westminster John Knox.

***Calvin, John.** Isaiah. LC 99-53547. (Classic Commentaries Ser.). 384p. 2000. pap. 19.99 (*1-58134-156-3*) Crossway Bks.
— Jeremiah & Lamentations. LC 99-53548. (Classic Commentaries Ser.). 288p. 2000. 17.99 (*1-58134-157-1*) Crossway Bks.

Calvin, John. Jeremiah & Lamentations, 5 vols., Set. 2500p. 1989. 109.99 (*0-85151-552-5*) Banner of Truth.
— John. abr. ed. LC 94-2284. (Classic Commentaries Ser.). 544p. 1994. pap. 17.99 (*0-89107-778-2*) Crossway Bks.
— John 11-21: 1 John: Torrance Edition. (Calvin's New Testament Commentaries Ser.: Vol. 5). 1994. pap. 22.00 (*0-8028-0805-0*) Eerdmans.
— John 1-10: Torrance Edition. (Calvin's New Testament Commentaries Ser.: Vol. 4). 1995. pap. 22.00 (*0-8028-0804-2*) Eerdmans.
— Letters of John Calvin. 1980. pap. 10.99 (*0-85151-323-9*) Banner of Truth.
— Matthew, Mark & Luke: Torrance Edition. (Calvin's New Testament Commentaries Ser.: Vol. 1). 1994. pap. 22.00 (*0-8028-0801-8*) Eerdmans.
— Matthew, Mark & Luke: Torrance Edition. (Calvin's New Testament Commentaries Ser.: Vol. 2). 1995. pap. 22.00 (*0-8028-0802-6*) Eerdmans.
— Matthew, Mark, Luke, James & Jude: Torrance Edition. (Calvin's New Testament Commentaries Ser.: Vol. 3). 1995. pap. 22.00 (*0-8028-0803-4*) Eerdmans.
— Old Testament Commentary: Daniel 1-6. LC 93-206. 1993. 35.00 (*0-8028-2451-X*); pap. 25.00 (*0-8028-0750-X*) Eerdmans.

Calvin, John. Providence. 27p. pap. 2.99 (*0-9652883-1-5*) Audubon Pr.

Calvin, John. Romans & Thessalonians: Torrance Edition. (Calvin's New Testament Commentaries Ser.: Vol. 8). 1995. pap. 22.00 (*0-8028-0808-5*) Eerdmans.
— 2 Corinthians: Torrance Edition. (Calvin's New Testament Commentaries Ser.: Vol. 10). 1996. pap. 22.00 (*0-8028-0810-7*) Eerdmans.
— Senecae Libri Duo de Clementia Commentariis Illustrati (1532) Battles, Ford L. & Hugo, Andre M., eds. No. 3. 1969. write for info. (*0-318-59381-5*) Renaiss Society Am.
— Sermones Sobre la Obra Salvadora de Cristo. Kratzig, Guillermo, tr. from ENG. (SPA.). 250p. 1988. 15.00 (*0-939125-11-0*) CRC Wrld Lit.
— Sermons on Deuteronomy. Golding, Arthur, tr. from FRE. (Sixteenth-Seventeenth Century Facsimile Editions Ser.). 1408p. 1987. 99.99 (*0-85151-511-8*) Banner of Truth.
— Sermons on Election & Reprobation. unabridged ed. 370p. 1996. 36.95 (*0-9632557-9-7*) Old Paths Pubns.
— Sermons on Ephesians. 1979. 35.99 (*0-85151-170-8*) Banner of Truth.
— Sermons on Job. 752p. 1993. reprint ed. 69.99 (*0-85151-644-0*) Banner of Truth.
— Sermons on Psalm 119. unabridged ed. 500p. 1996. 41.95 (*1-889058-00-9*) Old Paths Pubns.
— Sermons on Second Samuel. Kelly, Douglas, tr. (Illus.). 520p. 1992. 46.99 (*0-85151-578-9*) Banner of Truth.
— Sermons on the Deity of Christ. unabridged ed. 325p. 1997. 34.95 (*1-889058-02-5*) Old Paths Pubns.
— Thessalonians, Vols. 1-2. abr. ed. LC 99-29562. (Crossway Classic Commentaries Ser.). 112p. 1999. pap. 12.99 (*1-58134-117-2*) Crossway Bks.

***Calvin, John.** Truth for All Time. Olyott, Stuart, tr. 90p. 1998. pap. 5.99 (*0-85151-749-8*) Banner of Truth.

Calvin, John & Gilby, Anthony, trs. The Geneva Bible 1599: Breeches Bible. (Illus.). 1200p. 1990. reprint ed. lthr. 150.00 (*0-9629888-4-7*); reprint ed. lthr. 150.00 (*0-9629888-3-9*) L L Brown Pub.

Calvin, John & Henry, Matthew. 1, 2 & 3 John. LC 98-7752. (Crossway Classic Commentaries Ser.). 128p. 1998. pap. 12.99 (*0-89107-993-9*) Crossway Bks.

Calvin, June. My Lady Ghost. 224p. 1998. mass mkt. 4.99 (*0-451-19541-8*, Sig) NAL.
— Siege of Hearts. (Signet Regency Romance Ser.). 1999. mass mkt. 4.99 (*0-451-19542-6*) NAL.

Calvin, Larry. The Best of Family Forum. 86p. 1995. pap. 5.95 (*0-89137-712-3*) Quality Pubns.
— No Fear! The Calling of Angels. LC 95-68829. (Faith Focus Adult Studies). 1995. pap. 9.95 (*0-8344-0245-9*) Sweet Pub.
— The Power Zone: Jesus' Model for a New Humanity. Crowley, Patty, ed. LC 95-67132. (Faith Focus Ser.). 181p. (Orig.). 1995. pap. 9.95 (*0-8344-0242-4*, FFSBH) Sweet Pub.

Calvin, Linda & Strait, Sandy. What Was It Like in Vietnam? Honest Answers from Those Who Were There. 160p. (YA). (gr. 7 up). 1994. pap. 14.99 (*0-88092-049-1*) Royal Fireworks.

Calvin, Madeleine. Section 28: A Practical Guide to the Law & Its Implications. (C). 1988. 21.00 (*0-946088-32-2*, Pub. by NCCL) St Mut.

Calvin, Margaret. An Alaskan A B C Coloring Book. (Illus.). 32p. (Orig.). (J). (ps-4). 1986. pap. 3.95 (*0-9615529-3-X*) Old Harbor Pr.

Calvin, Margaret, ed. Famous Russian Recipes. rev. ed. Kashevaroff, Sasha, tr. from RUS. (Illus.). 48p. 1985. pap. 5.95 (*0-9615529-2-1*) Old Harbor Pr.

Calvin, Martin. Our Father's Before Us. 305p. (Orig.). 1983. pap. 4.95 (*0-914397-00-1*) Cornell Des.

Calvin, Melvin. Melvin Calvin: Following the Trail of Light, a Scientific Odyssey. LC 92-3989. (Profiles, Pathways, & Dreams Ser.). 175p. 1992. text 36.00 (*0-8412-1828-5*, Pub. by Am Chemical) OUP.

Calvin, Robert J. Profitable Sales Management & Marketing for Growing Businesses. 326p. (C). reprint ed. pap. 15.00 (*0-685-29363-7*) Mgmt Dimensions.

Calvin, Robert M. CDL Air Brakes Test: Study Book. Martin, Marilyn M., ed. 1999. pap. text 5.95 (*0-89262-238-5*); pap. text 5.95 (*0-89262-281-4*) Thomson Learn.
— CDL Basic Control Skills Test: Study Book. Martin, Marilyn M., ed. 1999. pap. 6.95 (*0-89262-245-8*); pap. 6.95 (*0-89262-284-9*) Thomson Learn.
— CDL Combination Vehicles Test: Study Book. Martin, Marilyn M., ed. (Illus.). 42p. 1991. pap. 5.95 (*0-89262-239-3*); pap. text 5.95 (*0-89262-282-2*) Career Pub.
— CDL Doubles - Triples Test: Study Book. Martin, Marilyn M., ed. (SPA., Illus.). 42p. 1991. pap. text 5.95 (*0-89262-285-7*); spiral bd. 5.95 (*0-89262-243-1*) Career Pub.
— CDL General Knowledge Test: Study Book. Martin, Marilyn M., ed. 1999. pap. text 8.95 (*0-89262-237-7*); pap. text 8.95 (*0-89262-279-2*) Thomson Learn.
— CDL Hazardous Materials Test: Study Book. Martin, Marilyn M., ed. (SPA., Illus.). 88p. 1991. pap. text 7.95 (*0-89262-287-3*); spiral bd. 7.95 (*0-89262-241-5*) Career Pub.

Calvin, Robert M. CDL Passenger Transport Test: Study Book. Martin, Marilyn, ed. (Illus.). 42p. 1990. spiral bd. 5.95 (*0-89262-242-3*) Career Pub.
— CDL Passenger Transport Test: Study Book. Martin, Marilyn, ed. (SPA., Illus.). 42p. 1991. pap. text 5.95 (*0-89262-280-6*) Career Pub.

Calvin, Robert M. CDL School Bus Pre-Trip Inspection Test: Study Book. Martin, Marilyn M., ed. (Illus.). 90p. 1991. pap. text 7.95 (*0-89262-377-2*); pap. text 7.95 (*0-89262-425-6*) Career Pub.
— CDL Straight Truck Pre-Trip Inspection Test: Study Book. Martin, Marilyn M., ed. (SPA.). 1999. pap. 7.95 (*0-89262-408-6*); pap. 7.95 (*0-89262-400-0*) Thomson Learn.
— CDL Tank Vehicles Test: Study Book. Martin, Marilyn M., ed. (SPA., Illus.). 39p. 1991. pap. text 5.95 (*0-89262-286-5*); spiral bd. 5.95 (*0-89262-240-7*) Career Pub.
— CDL Tractor-Trailer Pre-Trip Inspection Test: Study Book. Martin, Marilyn M., ed. 1999. pap. 7.95 (*0-89262-392-6*); pap. 7.95 (*0-89262-422-1*) Thomson Learn.
— CDL Transit Coach Bus Pre-Trip Inspection Test: Study Book. Martin, Marilyn M., ed. (SPA., Illus.). 90p. 1991. spiral bd. 7.95 (*0-89262-409-4*); spiral bd. 7.95 (*0-89262-404-3*) Career Pub.

Calvin, Ross. Sky Determines: An Interpretation of the Southwest. LC 48-6466. (Illus.). 350p. 1993. reprint ed. pap. 13.95 (*0-944383-19-X*) High-Lonesome.

Calvin, Samuel L. Ultimate Crappie Techniques. 1994. pap. 9.95 (*1-878175-84-X*) F Amato Pubns.

Calvin, Scott, ed. see Orsay, Jonathan.

***Calvin, Stephanie.** Young Wife. 2000. mass mkt. 6.95 (*0-352-33502-5*) Nexus.

Calvin, Thomas W. How & When to Perform Bayesian Acceptance Sampling, Vol. 7. rev. ed. (How to Ser.). (Illus.). 51p. 1990. pap. 21.00 (*0-87389-097-3*, T3507) ASQ Qual Pr.

Calvin, William H. The Ascent of Mind: Ice Age Climate & the Evolution of Intelligence. 1991. 19.95 (*0-685-38866-2*) Bantam.
— Cerebral Code: Thinking a Thought in the Mosaics of the Mind. (Illus.). 248p. 1996. 28.00 (*0-262-03241-4*, Bradford Bks) MIT Pr.
— The Cerebral Code: Thinking a Thought in the Mosaics of the Mind. (Illus.). 264p. 1998. pap. text 14.00 (*0-262-53154-2*, Bradford Bks) MIT Pr.
— How Brains Think: Evolving Intelligences, Then & Now. 1997. pap. 12.00 (*0-465-07278-X*, Pub. by Basic) HarpC.
— How Brains Think: Evolving Intelligences, Then & Now, Vol. 7. (Illus.). 176p. 1996. 20.00 (*0-465-07277-1*, Pub. by Basic) HarpC.

***Calvin, William H. & Bickerton, Derek.** Lingua Ex Machina: Reconciling Darwin & Chomsky with the Human Brain. LC 99-33464. (Illus.). 304p. 2000. 26.95 (*0-262-03273-2*) MIT Pr.

Calvin, William H. & Ojemann, George A. Conversations with Neil's Brain: Searching for the Narrator of Consciousness. LC 93-23661. 1994. 23.08 (*0-201-63217-9*) Addison-Wesley.
— Conversations with Neil's Brain: The Neural Nature of Thought & Language. (Illus.). 352p. 1995. pap. 13.00 (*0-201-48337-8*) Addison-Wesley.

Calvine, Angella M. Psychology, Parapsychology & Clairvoyance: Index of New Information & Research. rev. ed. LC 94-24770. 125p. 1995. 47.50 (*0-7883-0460-7*); pap. 44.50 (*0-7883-0461-5*) ABBE Pubs Assn.

Calvino, Giuseppe M. Poesie Scherzevoli: Italian Poetry. 251p. 1990. pap. 10.00 (*0-89304-665-5*) Cross-Cultrl NY.

Calvino, Italo. The Baron in the Trees. Colquhoun, Archibald, tr. LC 76-39704. 226p. (C). 1977. reprint ed. pap. 11.00 (*0-15-610680-9*, Harvest Bks) Harcourt.
— The Castle of Crossed Destinies. Weaver, William, tr. LC 78-23588. 132p. 1979. pap. 12.00 (*0-15-615455-2*, Harvest Bks) Harcourt.
— Cosmicomics. Weaver, William, tr. LC 76-14795. 168p. (C). 1976. pap. 11.00 (*0-15-622600-6*, Harvest Bks) Harcourt.
— Difficult Loves. Weaver, William et al, trs. from ITA. LC 84-685. (Helen & Kurt Wolff Bk.). 300p. 1985. pap. 12.00 (*0-15-626055-7*, Harvest Bks) Harcourt.
— Fantastic Tales. 1998. pap. 15.00 (*0-679-75544-6*) Vin Bks.
— If on a Winter's Night a Traveler. LC 92-54302. 1993. 17.00 (*0-679-42025-8*) Everymns Lib.
— If on a Winter's Night a Traveler. Weaver, William, tr. LC 80-8741. 276p. (C). 1982. reprint ed. pap. 13.00 (*0-15-643961-1*, Harvest Bks) Harcourt.
— Invisible Cities. Weaver, William, tr. LC 77-16002. (Helen & Kurt Wolff Bk.). 180p. (C). 1978. pap. 11.00 (*0-15-645380-0*, Harvest Bks) Harcourt.
— Invisible Cities. limited ed. Weaver, William, tr. from ITA. (Illus.). 164p. 1999. 750.00 (*0-910457-40-9*) Arion Pr.
— Italian Folktales. (Illus.). 763p. 1992. pap. 24.00 (*0-15-645489-0*, Harvest Bks) Harcourt.

***Calvino, Italo.** Italo Calvino - Le Litta Invisibili. Falyhera, Maurizio & Grocometti, Cristiana, eds. (Audio Anthology of Italian Literature Ser.). (ITA.). 1999. 19.95 incl. audio (*1-58214-124-X*); 14.95 incl. audio compact disk (*1-58214-149-5*) Mltilingl Bks.
— Marcovaldo: Level B. text 8.95 (*0-88436-993-5*) EMC-Paradigm.

Calvino, Italo. Marcovaldo: The Seasons in the City. Weaver, William, tr. from ITA. LC 83-4372. (Helen & Kurt Wolff Bk.). 128p. 1983. pap. 9.00 (*0-15-657204-4*, Harvest Bks) Harcourt.
— Mr. Palomar. Weaver, William, tr. 144p. 1986. pap. 11.00 (*0-15-662780-9*, Harvest Bks) Harcourt.
— Mr. Palomar. Weaver, William, tr. from ITA. LC 85-5490. (Helen & Kurt Wolff Bk.). 144p. 1985. reprint ed. 12.95 (*0-15-162835-1*) Harcourt.
— The Nonexistent Knight & the Cloven Viscount. Ferrone, J. & Wolff, H., eds. LC 76-39699. 264p. 1977. pap. 11.00 (*0-15-665975-1*, Harvest Bks) Harcourt.
— Numbers in the Dark. 288p. 1996. pap. 12.00 (*0-679-74353-7*) Random.

***Calvino, Italo.** The Path to the Spiders' Nests: Revised Edition. rev. ed. LC 00-28150. Orig. Title: The Path to the Nest of Spiders. 192p. 2000. pap. 12.00 (*0-06-095658-5*, Ecco Press) HarperTrade.

Calvino, Italo. Path To The Spiders' Nests, The Revised Ed. rev. ed. McLaughlin, Martin, ed. Colquhoun, Archibald, tr. from ITA. LC 98-18174. 192p. 1998. 23.00 (*0-88001-621-3*) HarpC.
— Road to San Giovanni.Tr. of ITA. 1994. pap. 11.00 (*0-679-74348-0*) Vin Bks.
— The Road to San Giovanni. 1995. 21.50 (*0-8446-6873-7*) Peter Smith.
— Six Memos for the Next Millennium. Creagh, Patrick, tr. LC 87-26025. (Charles Eliot Norton Lectures). (Illus.). 134p. 1988. text 17.95 (*0-674-81040-6*) HUP.
— Six Memos for the Next Millennium. LC 92-50641. 1993. pap. 11.00 (*0-679-74237-9*) Vin Bks.

— T-Zero. Weaver, William, tr. LC 76-14789. (Helen & Kurt Wolff Bk.). 168p. 1976. pap. 10.00 (*0-15-692400-5*, Harvest Bks) Harcourt.

— Under the Jaguar Sun. Weaver, William, tr. 96p. 1988. 12.95 (*0-15-192820-7*) Harcourt.

— Under the Jaguar Sun. Weaver, William, tr. 96p. (C). 1990. pap. 10.00 (*0-15-692794-2*) Harcourt.

— The Uses of Literature. Creagh, Patrick, tr. 348p. 1987. pap. 14.00 (*0-15-693250-4*, Harvest Bks) Harcourt.

— The Uses of Literature: Essays. Creagh, Patrick & Weaver, William, trs. from ITA. 352p. 1986. 17.95 (*0-15-193205-0*) Harcourt.

— The Watcher & Other Stories. Weaver, William & Colquhoun, Archibald, trs. from ITA. LC 75-9829. 192p. 1975. pap. 10.00 (*0-15-694952-0*, Harvest Bks) Harcourt.

— Why Read the Classics? McLaughlin, Martin, tr. from ITA. LC 99-21535. 288p. 1999. 26.00 (*0-679-41524-6*) Pantheon.

Calvino, Italo, ed. Fantastic Tales: Visionary & Everyday. LC 92-12824.Tr. of Racconti Fantastici dell'Ottocento. 608p. 1997. 30.00 (*0-679-41526-2*) Pantheon.

Calvino, J. Dictionary Nicois/Francais/Nicois. (FRE.). 332p. 1993. 95.00 (*0-320-00904-1*) Fr & Eur.

Calvino, Juan. Epistola a los Hebreos. (SPA.). 369p. pap. 12.00 (*1-55883-062-6*, 6703-1510C) Libros Desafio.

— Epistola a los Romanos. (SPA.). 394p. pap. 12.00 (*1-55883-061-8*, 6703-1520C) Libros Desafio.

Calvo, Alex. The Craft of Windows 95 Interface Design: A Practical Guide to Windows 95 Software Design. LC 96-19946. 185p. 1996. pap. 34.95 (*0-387-94814-7*) Spr-Verlag.

Calvo, Andrea. News of the Islands & the Mainland Newly Discovered in India by the Captain of His Imperial Majesty's Fleet. Tuttle, Edward F., ed. (Illus.). 1985. pap. 10.00 (*0-911437-29-0*) Labyrinthos.

Calvo Bruzos, Socorro. Educacion Para la Salud en la Escuela. (SPA.). 762p. 1992. pap. 44.00 (*84-7978-012-6*, Pub. by Ediciones Diaz) IBD Ltd.

Calvo, Cesar. The Three Halves of Ino Moxo: Teachings of the Wizard of the Upper Amazon. Symington, Kenneth, tr. LC 94-30522. (Illus.). 160p. 1994. pap. 14.95 (*0-89281-519-1*) Inner Tradit.

Calvo, Clara & Weber, Jean J. Literature. LC 97-47183. (Illus.). 176p. (C). 1998. wbk. ed. 70.00 (*0-415-16986-0*) Routledge.

— The Literature Workbook. LC 97-47183. 176p. (C). 1998. pap. 20.99 (*0-415-16987-9*) Routledge.

Calvo, Emily & Minsky, Lawrence. How to Succeed in Advertising When All You Have Is Talent: Today's Creatives Show You How. LC 93-9210. 256p. 1994. 35.00 (*0-8442-3474-5*, NTC Business Bks) NTC Contemp Pub Co.

Calvo, Emily Thornton & Minsky, Laurence. 25 Words or Less. LC 97-43788. 224p. 1998. pap. 12.95 (*0-8092-2878-5*, 287850, Contemporary Bks) NTC Contemp Pub Co.

Calvo, Gabriel. Face to Face: Becoming a Happier Married Couple. 166p. 1988. pap. 5.00 (*0-936098-57-0*) Intl Marriage.

Calvo, Gabriel & Sauppe, Eberhard. Diccionario de Biblioteconomia (Dictionary of Librarianship) (ENG, GER & SPA.). 430p. 1997. write for info. (*3-598-11269-6*) K G Saur Verlag.

Calvo, Guillermo. Money, Exchange Rates, & Output. (Illus.). 532p. 1996. 60.00 (*0-262-03236-8*) MIT Pr.

Calvo, Guillermo A. Reform, Distortions, & Credibility. 24p. 1991. 8.00 (*0-940602-42-3*) IADB.

***Calvo, Guillermo A., et al, eds.** Money, Capital Mobility & Trade: Essays in Honor of Robert A. Mundell. 538p. (C). 2000. 55.00 (*0-262-03282-1*) MIT Pr.

Calvo, Guillermo A., et al, eds. Private Capital Flows to Emerging Markets after the Mexican Crisis. LC 96-35399. 320p. (Orig.). 1996. pap. 18.95 (*0-88132-232-6*) Inst Intl Eco.

Calvo, Guillermo A., et al. The Capital Inflows Problem: Concepts & Issues. LC 94-33340. (Occassional Papers: Vol.56). 1994. pap. 9.95 (*1-55815-344-6*) ICS Pr.

— Financial Sector Reforms & Exchange Arrangements in Eastern Europe, Pt. 2: Exchange Arrangements of Previously Centrally Planned Economies. LC 92-45213. (Occasional Paper - International Fund: No. 102). 59p. 1993. pap. 15.00 (*1-55775-279-6*) Intl Monetary.

***Calvo, Hernando.** Cuban Exile Movement: Dissidents or Mercenaries? 200p. 1999. pap. text 16.95 (*1-876175-15-X*) Ocean Pr NJ.

Calvo, L. Martinez. Spanish-Russian Dictionary: Diccionario Espanol-Ruso. (RUS & SPA.). 1916p. 1982. 125.00 (*0-8288-0797-3*, S50411) Fr & Eur.

Calvo, Lorena, tr. see Domroese, Margret C. & Sterling, Eleanor J.

Calvo, M. D. Legislation on Women's Employment in Latin America: A Comparative Study. LC 97-109125. (Occasional Papers: Vol. 11). iv, 57p. 1996. pap. 13.50 (*92-2-109509-6*) Intl Labour Office.

Calvo, Michel A. The SALT Agreements. 1987. lib. bdg. 107.00 (*90-247-3547-5*, Pub. by M Nijhoff) Kluwer Academic.

Calvo, Randolph R. & Klinger, Nevin J., eds. Clergy Procedural Handbook. 283p. 1992. 18.00 (*0-943616-57-3*) Canon Law Soc.

Calvo Sanz, Roberto, ed. see Zorrilla, Jose.

Calvocoressi, M. D. The Principles & Methods of Musical Criticism. LC 79-9864. (Music Reprint Ser.). 1979. reprint ed. pap. 29.50 (*0-306-79557-4*) Da Capo.

Calvocoressi, M. D., tr. see Bartok, Bela.

Calvocoressi, M. D., tr. see Scherchen, Hermann.

Calvocoressi, Michel D. Moussorgsky: Music Book Index. 216p. 1993. reprint ed. lib. bdg. 79.00 (*0-7812-9612-9*) Rprt Serv.

— Music & Ballet. LC 74-24053. reprint ed. 37.50 (*0-404-12877-7*) AMS Pr.

— A Survey of Russian Music: Music Book Index. 142p. 1993. reprint ed. lib. bdg. 69.00 (*0-7812-9567-X*) Rprt Serv.

Calvocoressi, Peter. The British Experience, 1945-75 LC 78-316140. 252 p. 1978. write for info. (*0-370-30100-5*) Bodley Head.

— Fall Out: World War II & the Shaping of Postwar Europe. LC 97-17733. (C). 1997. text 60.00 (*0-582-30908-5*, Pub. by Addison-Wesley) Longman.

***Calvocoressi, Peter.** Fall Out: World War II & the Shaping of Postwar Europe. LC 97-17733. 203p. (C). 1998. pap. text 20.20 (*0-582-30907-7*) Addison-Wesley.

Calvocoressi, Peter. Independent Africa & the World. (Illus.). 160p. (C). 1985. pap. text 17.95 (*0-582-29654-4*, 71831) Longman.

— Resilient Europe: A Study of the Years, 1870-2000. 240p. (C). 1991. text 66.50 (*0-582-07853-9*, 78917) Longman.

— Who's Who in the Bible. 1988. 19.95 (*0-670-81188-2*) Grossman.

***Calvocoressi, Peter.** Who's Who in the Bible. (Illus.). 224p. 2000. pap. 19.95 (*0-14-051426-0*) Viking Penguin.

Calvocoressi, Peter. World Politics since Nineteen Forty-Five. 5th ed. 546p. (C). 1987. pap. text 22.95 (*0-582-29713-3*, 71838) Longman.

— World Politics since 1945. 6th ed. (Illus.). 754p. (C). 1991. pap. text 30.50 (*0-582-07379-0*, 79013) Longman.

— World Politics since Nineteen Forty-Five. 7th ed. LC 96-21988. 754p. (C). 1996. pap. text 32.81 (*0-582-27796-5*) Longman.

Calvocoressi, Peter, ed. Who's Who in the Bible. 304p. 1988. pap. 20.99 (*0-14-051212-8*, Penguin Bks) Viking Penguin.

Calvocoressi, Richard. Early Works: Lucian Freud. (Illus.). 60p. 1997. pap. 19.95 (*0-903598-66-3*, Pub. by Natl Galleries) Antique Collect.

— Magritte. (Color Library). (Illus.). 128p. (C). 1993. reprint ed. pap. 14.95 (*0-7148-2760-6*, Pub. by Phaidon Press) Phaidon Pr.

— Oskar Kokoschka. (Illus.). 1986. 38.00 (*0-89207-060-9*); pap. 26.00 (*0-89207-059-5*) S R Guggenheim.

***Calwell, Margaret. Speak to the Past: A Memoir Fat with Words. 232p. 2000. pap. 19.95 (*0-87012-612-1*) McClain.**

More than a simple collection of personal remembrances. Speak to the Past artfully blends beautifully described personal experiences with straightforward historical & cultural observation. West Virginia native Margaret Calwell captures well the values, diversities & inner workings of the people of Appalachia. Not one to shy away from controversy, Mrs. Calwell intelligently interjects her well-developed views on many topics, from politics & religion to education, feminism & war. Speak To The Past is both entertaining & thought provoking, challenging its readers to live life to its fullest, observing, thinking & contributing. *Publisher Paid Annotation.*

Calyx Editorial Collective Staff, ed. Florilegia: A Retrospective of Calyx, a Journal of Art & Literature by Women, 1976-1986. LC 87-6395. 252p. (C). 1986. pap. 12.00 (*0-934971-06-4*) Calyx Bks.

Calyx Editorial Collective Staff, et al, eds. Women & Aging: An Anthology by Women. (Illus.). 262p. (C). 1986. 28.95 (*0-934971-07-2*); pap. 15.95 (*0-934971-00-5*) Calyx Bks.

Calyx Editorial Collective Staff & Donnelly, Margarita, eds. Florilegia: A Retrospective of Calyx, a Journal of Art & Literature by Women, 1976-1986. LC 87-6395. 252p. (C). 1986. 24.95 (*0-934971-09-9*) Calyx Bks.

Calza, Gian C. Ikko Tanaka. (Illus.). 256p. 1997. 49.95 (*0-7148-3716-4*, Pub. by Phaidon Press) Phaidon Pr.

***Calzado, Jorge Sierra, ed.** Flora de La Republica de Cuba Fasc. 3, Series A: Plantas Vasculares-Begoniaceae, Chloranthaceae, Elaeocarpaceae, Sterculiaceae, Tiliaceae. (Illus.). 38p. 2000. text 50.00 (*3-87429-415-3*, Pub. by Koeltz Sci Bks) Lubrecht & Cramer.

Calzaretta, William A., jt. auth. see Geist, Chrisann S.

Calzetti, Daniela, et al, eds. Extragalactic Background Radiation. (Space Telescope Science Institute Symposium Ser.: No. 7). (Illus.). 307p. (C). 1995. text 69.95 (*0-521-49558-X*) Cambridge U Pr.

Calzonetti, Frank J. & Solomon, Barry D., eds. Geographical Dimensions of Energy. 1985. lib. bdg. 178.50 (*90-277-2061-4*) Kluwer Academic.

Calzonetti, Frank J., et al. Power from the Appalachians: A Solution to the Northeast's Electricity Problems?, 89. LC 88-28399. (Contributions in Economics & Economic History Ser.: No. 89). 249p. 1989. 59.95 (*0-313-25797-3*, CZW, Greenwood Pr) Greenwood.

Cam, Helen M. Law-Finders & Law Makers in Medieval England: Collected Studies in Legal & Constitutional History. LC 79-13344. 240p. 1979. reprint ed. lib. bdg. 35.00 (*0-678-08062-3*) Kelley.

— Liberties & Communities in Medieval England: Collected Studies in Local Administration & Topography. (C). 1963. text 17.00 (*0-85036-042-0*, Pub. by MRLN) Paul & Co Pubs.

Cam, Helen M. & Ehrlich, Ludwik. Studies in the Hundred Rolls: Some Aspects of Thirteenth-Century Administration: Proceedings Against the Crown (1216-1377) LC 73-22295. x, 198p. 1974. write for info. (*0-374-96165-4*) FS&G.

CAM-I Activity Based Management Group, jt. auth. see White, Timothy.

CAM-I Cost Management Integration Team Staff, jt. auth. see McNair, C. J.

CAM-I Service Process Interest Group Staff. Service Process Measurement: Breaking the Code: Applying Activity Based Performance Measures to Service Processes. 1998. pap. 20.00 (*1-890783-02-1*) CAM-I.

Cam, Lucien M. Le, see Le Cam, Lucien M.

Cama, H. R., jt. ed. see Bourne, Geoffrey H.

Camacho, A. A Model of Societies & Social Decision Functions. 1982. lib. bdg. 112.50 (*90-277-1407-X*) Kluwer Academic.

Camacho, Antonio. Division of Labor, Variability, Coordination, & the Theory of Firms & Markets. LC 95-45692. (Theory & Decision Library - A: Series A, No. 22). 196p. (C). 1996. lib. bdg. 118.00 (*0-7923-3832-4*) Kluwer Academic.

***Camacho, Austin S.** Blood & Bone. 178p. 1999. pap. 13.95 (*0-7414-0144-4*) Buy Books.

Camacho, Cesar & Neto, A. Lins. Geometric Theory of Foliations. 1986. 60.50 (*0-8176-3139-9*) Birkhauser.

Camacho, David. U. S. Politics & Democracy: A Supplement Reader & Workbook. 2nd ed. 176p. (C). 1998. spiral bd., suppl. ed., wbk. ed. 30.95 (*0-7872-5324-3*) Kendall-Hunt.

Camacho De Rodas, Isabel, ed. see Donn, Elizabeth R.

Camacho, E. F. & Bordons, C. Model Predictive Control. Grimble, M. & Johnson, M., eds. LC 98-42055. (Advanced Textbooks in Control & Signal Processing Ser.). 300p. 1999. pap. text 54.95 (*3-540-76241-8*) Spr-Verlag.

— Model Predictive Control in the Process Industry. LC 94-47060. (Advances in Industrial Control Ser.). (Illus.). 239p. 1995. 54.50 (*3-540-19724-9*) Spr-Verlag.

Camacho, E. F., et al. Advanced Control of Solar Plants. LC 97-4493. (Advances in Industrial Control Ser.). 290p. 54.95 (*3-540-76144-6*) Spr-Verlag.

Camacho, E. F., jt. ed. see Ollero, A.

Camacho, Enrique Lavin, see Lavin Camacho, Enrique.

Camacho-Gingerich, Alina. La Cosmovision Poetica De Jose Lezama Lima En "Paraiso" y "Oppiano Licario" LC 88-82892. (SPA.). 169p. (Orig.). 1991. pap. 19.95 (*0-89729-511-0*) Ediciones.

Camacho, J. Juventud en Revolucion (Youth in Rebellion) (SPA.). 1.00 (*0-685-74948-7*, 540380) Editorial Unilit.

Camacho, Jario. Mitos y Leyendas Latino Americanas. 2nd ed. 1992. 10.15 (*0-606-10486-0*, Pub. by Turtleback) Demco.

Camacho, Jose, et al, eds. The Proceedings of the Fourteenth West Coast Conference on Formal Linguistics. 600p. (C). 1996. 74.95 (*1-57586-043-0*) CSLI.

— Proceedings of the 14th West Coast Conference on Formal Linguistics. 600p. (C). 1996. pap. 28.95 (*1-57586-042-2*) CSLI.

Camacho, Jose D. El Ministerio de los Santos.Tr. of Ministry of the Saints. (SPA.). 224p. 1992. pap. 6.99 (*1-56063-390-5*, 498544) Editorial Unilit.

Camacho, Juana, tr. see Stemper, David M.

Camacho, Loida C., ed. Como Nave de Mercader. (SPA.). 47p. 1974. pap. 2.00 (*0-87148-180-4*) Pathway Pr.

Camacho, Panfilo D. Marta Abreu, una Mujer Comprendida. (SPA.). 1995. pap. 16.00 (*0-89729-743-1*) Ediciones.

***Camacho, Patricia Garrido.** El Tema del Reconocimiento en el Teatro Espanol del Siglo XVI: La Teoria de la Anagnorisis. (Monografias A Ser.). (Illus.). 150p. 1999. 60.00 (*1-85566-048-2*, Pub. by Tamesis Bks Ltd) Boydell & Brewer.

Camacho, Terry, jt. auth. see Stoynoff, Stephen.

Camacho, Vicki. Tell the Truth & Shame the Devil. LC 97-62019. 64p. 1997. pap. 9.95 (*1-56664-125-X*) WorldComm.

Camagay, M. Luisa. Working Women of Manila in the 19th Century. LC 95-947529. 208p. 1996. pap. text 18.00 (*971-542-059-1*, Pub. by U of Philippines Pr) UH Pr.

Camagay, Maria L., ed. French Consular Dispatches on the Philippine Revolution. LC 97-946681. 228p. 1999. pap. text 23.00 (*971-542-172-5*, Pub. by U of Philippines Pr) UH Pr.

Camagni, Roberto, ed. Innovation Networks: Spatial Perspectives. LC 90-27696. 224p. 1999. 200.00 (*0-471-94502-1*) Wiley.

Camaioni, Luigia & De Lemos, Claudia, eds. Questions on Social Explanation: Piagetian Themes Reconsidered. LC 85-26727. (Pragmatics & Beyond Ser.: VI-4). viii, 141p. (Orig.). 1986. pap. 49.00 (*0-915027-66-6*) J Benjamins Pubng Co.

Camaj, Martin, tr. see Gjecovi, Shtjefen & Logoreci, Anton, eds.

Camak, Carole H. There Came a Lion. LC 97-61741. 224p. 1997. pap. 10.95 (*1-57921-056-2*) WinePress Pub.

Caman, David & Young, Trevor. Principles of Agricultural Economics: Markets & Prices in Less Developed Countries. (Wye Studies in Agricultural & Rural Development). (Illus.). 336p. 1989. pap. text 33.95 (*0-521-33664-3*) Cambridge U Pr.

Camandone de Cohen, Mirta. Escritura Sin Fronteras: Poesia Espanola en Castellano Desde 1936. (American University Studies: Romance Languages & Literature: Ser. II, Vol. 192). (SPA.). XVIII, 287p. (C). 1993. text 49.95 (*0-8204-1840-4*) P Lang Pubng.

Camara, Evandro. The Cultural One or the Racial Many: Religion, Culture & the Interethnic Experience. LC 97-74508. (Research in Ethnic Relations Ser.). 294p. 1998. text 78.95 (*1-84014-119-0*, Pub. by Ashgate Pub) Ashgate Pub Co.

Camara, Helder. The Desert Is Fertile. Livingstone, Dinah, tr. LC 73-89315.Tr. of Le/Desert est Fertile. (Illus.). 85p. reprint ed. pap. 30.00 (*0-7837-5519-8*, 204528900005) Bks Demand.

— It's Midnight, Lord. Gallagher, Joseph et al, trs. (Illus.). (Orig.). 1984. pap. 7.95 (*0-912405-02-3*, Pastoral Press) OR Catholic.

— Sister Earth: Creation, Ecology, & the Spirit. LC 95-16784. (Illus.). 112p. 1995. pap. 7.95 (*1-56548-031-7*) New City.

Camara, J. A. 101 Solved Nuclear Engineering Problems. 168p. 1999. pap. 52.95 (*1-888577-30-4*, NESP) Prof Pubns CA.

Camara, J. Mattoso, Jr. The Portuguese Language. Naro, Anthony J., tr. LC 79-167939. (History & Structure of Languages Ser.). 208p. 1993. lib. bdg. 22.00 (*0-226-51121-9*) U Ch Pr.

Camara, Joaguim M. A Forma Verbal Portuguesa Em -Ria. LC 67-22854. 104p. reprint ed. pap. 32.30 (*0-7837-6309-3*, 204602400010) Bks Demand.

Camara, Joaquim M. The Portuguese Language: With an Analytical Bibliography of the Writings of Joaquim Mattoso Camara, Jr. Naro, Anthony J., tr. from POR. & compiled by by. Reighard, John, compiled by. LC 79-167939. (History & Structure of Languages Ser.). 284p. reprint ed. pap. 88.10 (*0-608-09278-9*, 205415200004) Bks Demand.

Camara, Madeline, jt. auth. see Fernandez, Damian J.

Camara, Mary. Enjoy Cooking with Mary Camara. Aced, Dan, ed. (Illus.). 192p. 1997. 15.95 (*0-9656996-0-9*) M Camara.

Camarao, P. C. & Serra, M. A. Great Technical Dictionary: Dicionario Tecnico English-Portuguese. (ENG & POR.). 462p. 1979. pap. 49.95 (*0-8288-4810-6*, M9214) Fr & Eur.

Camarata, Stephen M. Manual of Child Language Disorders. 300p. 2000. 60.95 (*1-56593-842-9*, 1644) Thomson Learn.

Camard, Jean Pierre & Belfort, Anne Marie. Dictionnaire des Peintres et Sculpteurs Provencaux. (FRE.). 444p. 1974. pap. 19.95 (*0-8288-6021-1*, M6636) Fr & Eur.

Camarda, Bill. The Cheapskate's Guide to Bargain Computing. LC 97-26393. 528p. (C). 1997. pap. text 34.95 incl. cd-rom (*0-13-756404-X*) P-H.

— Inside Word for Windows 95. (Illus.). 1248p. (Orig.). 1995. pap. 40.00 incl. cd-rom (*1-56205-355-8*) New Riders Pub.

— Microsoft Office 2000 Administrator's Desk Reference. 1000p. 2000. 49.99 (*0-7897-1931-2*) Que.

***Camarda, Bill.** Upgrading & Fixing Networks for Dummies. 2nd ed. LC 99-62839. (For Dummies Ser.). 408p. 1999. pap. 29.99 incl. cd-rom (*0-7645-0542-4*) IDG Bks.

Camarda, Bill. Using Micro Soft Word 97: Best-Seller Edition. 2nd ed. LC 97-68762. 1080p. 1997. 34.99 (*0-7897-1398-5*) Que.

Camarda, Bill, et al. Using Microsoft Word 2000 With CDROM: Special Edition. LC 98-86980. (Special Edition Using... Que Ser.). (Illus.). 1402p. 1999. pap. 39.99 (*0-7897-1852-9*) Que.

Camarda, Jeff. The Sensible Cigar Connoisseur: A Keen & Irreverent Look at How to Make the Most of One of Life's Richest Pleasures. Jones, Carrie B., ed. LC 98-86586. (Illus.). 230p. 1999. pap. 19.95 (*0-9665495-7-0*, Brainware) Frank Multi Inc.

Camargo, Edmar. Design of FET Frequency Multipliers & Harmonic Oscillators. LC 98-33848. 216p. 1998. 93.00 (*0-89006-481-4*) Artech Hse.

Camarillo, Albert. Chicanos in a Changing Society. LC 97-143791. (Illus.). 344p. 1996. pap. text 18.50 (*0-674-11397-7*) HUP.

— Chicanos in a Changing Society: From Mexican Pueblos to American Barrios in Santa Barbara & Southern California, 1848-1930. LC 79-10687. (Illus.). 338p. 1980. pap. 16.95 (*0-674-11396-9*) HUP.

— Chicanos in California. Hundley, Norris, Jr. & Schutz, John A., eds. (Golden State Ser.). (Illus.). 152p. 1990. pap. 12.00 (*0-929651-08-1*) MTL.

Camarillo, Albert, compiled by. Mexican Americans in Urban Society: A Selected Bibliography. LC 86-22741. 296p. 1990. pap. 29.95 (*0-915745-12-7*) Floricanto Pr.

Camarillo, Albert, jt. auth. see Gomez-Quinones, Juan.

Camarillo, Leo. Team Roping. Witte, Randy, tr. (Illus.). 144p. (Orig.). 1982. pap. 12.95 (*0-911647-00-7*) Western Horseman.

Camarillo, Sharon. Barrel Racing. Witte, Randy, ed. (Illus.). 144p. (Orig.). 1985. pap. 12.95 (*0-911647-06-6*) Western Horseman.

***Camarinha-Matos, Luis M. & Afsarmanesh, Hamideh.** Infrastructures for Virtual Enterprises: Networking Industrial Enterprises: IFIP TC5 WG5.3/Prodnet Working Conference on Infrastructures for Virtual Enterprises (PTO-VE '99), October 27-28, 1999, Porto, Portugal. LC 99-40811. 1999. pap. write for info. (*0-7923-8639-6*) Kluwer Academic.

Camarinha-Matos, Luis M., et al. Intelligent Systems for Manufacturing: Multi-Agent Systems & Virtual Organizations: Proceedings of the BASYS '98 - 3rd IEEE IFIP International Conference on Information Technology for Balanced Automation Systems in Manufacturing, Prague, Czech Republic, August, 1998. LC 98-33567. 1998. 210.00 (*0-7923-8233-1*) Kluwer Academic.

Camaro Editors. California Events Annual. (Illus.). 1987. pap. 4.95 (*0-913290-80-7*) Camaro Pub.

— California Food, Wine & Travel. (Illus.). 1987. pap. 4.95 (*0-913290-68-8*) Camaro Pub.

— Food, Wine, Travel Handbook. (Illus.). 1988. pap. 9.95 (*0-913290-93-9*) Camaro Pub.

— Historical California Touring Guidebook. (Illus.). 1985. pap. 5.95 (*0-913290-64-5*) Camaro Pub.

— Little Restaurants of San Francisco. LC 73-85631. (Illus.). 1985. 4.95 (*0-913290-06-8*) Camaro Pub.

— Los Angeles Little Restaurant Guide. (Illus.). 1985. pap. 4.95 (*0-913290-85-8*) Camaro Pub.

— Master Chef Cookbook. (Illus.). 1985. pap. 10.95 (*0-913290-63-7*) Camaro Pub.

— Official Visitors Guide: Los Angeles. 1982. 4.95 (*0-913290-30-0*) Camaro Pub.

C

— Official Visitors Guide: San Francisco. 1988. 4.95 (0-913290-32-7) Camaro Pub.
— Old California: Almanac of Fairs & Festivals. (Old California Ser.: No. 1). (Illus.). 1988. pap. 4.95 (0-913290-43-2) Camaro Pub.
— Old California: Art, Theater, & Museums. (Old California Ser.: No. 10). (Illus.). 1983. pap. 3.95 (0-913290-51-3) Camaro Pub.
— Old California: Camping Sites & Campgrounds. (Old California Ser.: No. 7). (Illus.). 1985. pap. 3.95 (0-913290-48-3) Camaro Pub.
— Old California: Christmas Time & Mountain Recreation. (Old California Ser.: No. 12). (Illus.). 1984. pap. 3.95 (0-913290-53-X) Camaro Pub.
— Old California: Cooking, Recipes, & Menus. (Old California Ser.: No. 11). (Illus.). 1983. pap. 3.95 (0-913290-52-1) Camaro Pub.
— Old California: Country Inns & Historic Hotels. (Old California Ser.: No. 4). (Illus.). 1983. pap. 3.95 (0-913290-45-9) Camaro Pub.
— Old California: Gold Mines & Gold Mining Towns. (Old California Ser.: No. 8). (Illus.). 1985. pap. 3.95 (0-913290-49-1) Camaro Pub.
— Old California: Historical Landmarks & Scenic Backroads. (Old California Ser.: No. 9). (Illus.). 1984. pap. 4.95 (0-913290-50-5) Camaro Pub.
— Old California: Historical Restaurants, Wineries, & Wine Tasting. (Old California Ser.: No. 3). (Illus.). 1983. pap. 3.95 (0-913290-44-0) Camaro Pub.
— Old California: Visitors Guide. (Old California Ser.: No. 5). (Illus.). 1983. pap. 3.95 (0-913290-46-7) Camaro Pub.
— Old California for Children: Picnic Spots, Haunted Houses, & Ghost Towns. (Old California Ser.: No. 6). (Illus.). 1983. pap. 3.95 (0-913290-47-5) Camaro Pub.
— Phone Book for Small Hotels & Country Inns, Vol. I. (Illus.). 1987. pap. 3.95 (0-913290-35-1) Camaro Pub.
— Phone Book for Small Hotels & Country Inns, Vol. II. (Illus.). 1987. pap. 3.95 (0-913290-40-8) Camaro Pub.
— Restaurant Five Hundred: All-American Restaurant & Chef Yearbook. (Illus.). 1988. pap. 6.95 (0-913290-71-8) Camaro Pub.
— San Diego Little Restaurant Guide. (Illus.). 1985. pap. 4.95 (0-913290-87-4) Camaro Pub.
— San Francisco Little Restaurant Guide. (Illus.). 1985. pap. 4.95 (0-913290-86-6) Camaro Pub.
— See the World Passport. 1988. pap. 4.95 (0-913290-70-X) Camaro Pub.
Camarota, Steven. The Wages of Immigration Vol. 12: The Effect on the Low-Skilled Labor Market. 62p. 1998. pap. 12.00 (1-881290-09-3) Ctr Immigrat.
Camas, Nick. The Pop Vocabulary Book. Quinn, Robin, ed. (Illus.). 246p. (Orig.). 1996. reprint ed. pap. 9.95 (0-9645851-1-1) Pennhills.
Camasso, Michael, jt. auth. see Geismar, Ludwig L.
Camatte, Jacques. This World We Must Leave. 256p. Date not set. 8.00 (1-57027-020-1) Autonomedia.
— The Wandering of Humanity. 1975. pap. 1.25 (0-934868-06-9) Black & Red.
Camayd-Freixas, Eric. Relismo Magico y Primitivismo: Relecturas de Crpentier, Asturias, Rulfo y Gracia Marquez. (SPA.). 372p. (C). 1998. pap. 36.50 (0-7618-1102-8) U Pr of Amer.
***Camayd-Freixas, Erik & Gonzalez, Jose Eduardo, eds.** Primitivism & Identity in Latin America: Essays on Art, Literature & Culture. LC 00-8340. (Illus.). 285p. 2000. 50.00 (0-8165-2045-3) U of Ariz Pr.
Camayd-Freixas, Yohel. Crisis in Miami: Community Context & Institutional Response in the Adaptation of 1980 Mariel Boatlift Cubans & Undocumented Haitian Entrants in South Florida. LC 88-72214. 186p. (Orig.). 1988. pap. 25.00 (0-923206-00-0) Boston UR & DG.
Camayd-Freixas, Yohel, et al, eds. The Other Boston: A Vision for the Future. LC 88-51167. 180p. (Orig.). 1988. pap. 25.00 (0-923206-01-9) Boston UR & DG.
Camazine, Scott. Velvet Mites & Silken Webs: Wonderful Details of Nature in Photographs & Essays. LC 91-2395. (Science Editions Ser.). (Illus.). 192p. 1991. 24.95 (0-471-61485-8) Wiley.
Cambanis, S., et al. Stochastic Processes & Related Topics: In Memory of Stamatis Cambanis, 1943-1995. LC 98-16658. (Trends in Mathematics Ser.). 1998. 89.50 (3-7643-3998-5) Birkhauser.
Cambanis, Stamatis, et al, eds. Stable Processes & Related Topics: A Selection of Papers from the Mathematical Sciences Institute Workshop, January 9-13, 1990. (Progress in Probability Ser.: Vol. 25). 330p. 1991. 86.50 (0-8176-3485-1) Birkhauser.
Cambanis, Stamatis & Weron, A., eds. Probability Theory on Vector Spaces, Vol. 4. viii, 424p. 1989. 56.95 (0-387-51548-8) Spr-Verlag.
Cambanis, Stamatis, et al. Stochastic Processes: A Festschrift in Honor of Gopinath Kallianpur. LC 92-31111. 392p. 1992. 69.95 (0-387-97921-2) Spr-Verlag.
Cambeira, Alan. Quisqueya la Bella: The Dominican Republic in Historical & Cultural Perspective. LC 96-32355. (Perspectives on Latin American & the Caribbean Ser.). 286p. (C). 1996. text 74.95 (1-56324-935-9); pap. text 30.95 (1-56324-936-7) M E Sharpe.
Cambel, A. B., ed. Energy Devices & Processes: Proceedings of a Workshop on the Second Law of Thermodynamics, Held at the George Washington University, Wash. D. C., 14-16 Aug. 1979. 300p. 1980. pap. 73.00 (0-08-026704-1, Pergamon Pr) Elsevier.
Cambel, A. B., et al, eds. The Solar Energy-Utility Interface. 190p. 1982. pap. 26.00 (0-08-028695-X, Pergamon Pr) Elsevier.
Cambel, Ali B. Applied Chaos Theory: A Paradigm for Complexity. (Illus.). 246p. 1992. text 49.00 (0-12-155940-8) Acad Pr.
Cambel, Ali B. & Anderson, Thomas P., eds. Magnetohydrodynamics: Proceedings of Magnetohydrodynamics Conference, Northwestern University, Evanston, Ill. LC TK2970.N6. 403p. reprint ed. pap. 125.00 (0-608-11020-5, 200637400058) Bks Demand.
Cambel, Ali B., et al. Dissipative Strukturen in Integrierten Systemen. (GER.). 351p. 1989. 85.00 (3-7890-1711-6, Pub. by Nomos Verlags) Intl Bk Import.
Cambel, Halet. The Hieroglyphic Luwian Inscriptions of the Iron Age Vol. 4: The Inscriptions of Karatepe-Aslantas. LC 98-38764. 136p. 1999. 290.35 (3-11-014870-6) De Gruyter.
Cambell. Introduction to News Writing. 2002. pap. text. write for info. (0-312-17985-5) St Martin.
— Media & Society. 2002. pap. text. write for info. (0-312-17986-3) St Martin.
Cambell, Angus Peter. One Road. LC 98-189657. 1994. write for info. (0-9520010-1-2) Fountain Publ.
Cambell, Brian, et al, eds. Nor Meekly Serve My Time: The H Block Struggle, 1976-1981. (Illus.). 264p. 1994. pap. 20.95 (0-9514229-5-2, Pub. by Beyond the Pale) Irish Bks Media.
Cambell, David L. Learn Multimedia Programming with Visual Basic 5.0. LC 97-20679. (Illus.). 450p. 1997. pap. 39.95 (1-55622-541-5) Wordware Pub.
Cambell, Janet, ed. see Canright, David.
Cambell, John, jt. auth. see Zeigler, Earle F.
Cambell, Josephine. J. C.'s Favorite Rhymes. 60p. (Orig.). 1988. pap. 5.00 (0-9622712-0-9) J Cambell.
Cambell, Kurt M. & MacFarlane, S. Neil, eds. Gorbachev's Third World Dilemmas. 352p. 1989. 49.95 (0-415-00487-X, A3437) Routledge.
Cambell, Nina. The Art of Decoration. LC 96-1141. (Illus.). 160p. 1996. 40.00 (0-517-70466-8) C Potter.
Cambell, Patty G., et al, eds. Conducting Research in Business Communication. 303p. (Orig.). 1988. pap. 13.00 (0-931874-19-X) Assn Busn Comm.
Cambell, Suzann, et al, eds. Physical Therapy for Children. 2nd ed. (Illus.). 1055p. Date not set. text. write for info. (0-7216-8316-9, W B Saunders Co) Harcrt Hlth Sci Grp.
Cambers, Gillian & Magoon, Orville T., eds. Coastlines of the Caribbean. (Coastlines of the World Ser.). 196p. 1991. pap. text 25.00 (0-87262-836-1) Am Soc Civil Eng.
Cambi, Vincenzo, ed. Short Dialysis. (Topics in Renal Medicine Ser.). (C). 1987. text 183.50 (0-89838-858-9) Kluwer Academic.
Cambiaggio, M. C., et al. Nuclear Physics: Proceedings of the 12th Workshop. 396p. (C). 1990. text 113.00 (981-02-0158-3) World Scientific Pub.
Cambiaire, Celestin P. The Influence of Edgar Allan Poe in France. (BCL1-PS American Literature Ser.). 332p. 1992. reprint ed. lib. bdg. 89.00 (0-7812-6834-6) Rprt Serv.
Cambiare, C. P. Influence of Poe in France. LC 71-92954. (Studies in Comparative Literature: No. 35). 1970. reprint ed. lib. bdg. 75.00 (0-8383-0963-1) M S G Haskell Hse.
Cambias, James. Gurps Planet Krishna: From the Classic Viagens Books by L. Sprauge de Camp: Swashbuckling Adventure in Space. Barrett, Sean, ed. (Illus.). 128p. 1997. pap. 19.95 (1-55634-263-2, 6080, Pub. by S Jackson Games) BookWorld.
Cambias, James, et al. In Nomine Fall of the Malakim: Revelations Cycle Vol. 4, 4. Sellers, Janice, ed. (Revelations Cycle Ser.: 4). (Illus.). 128p. 1998. pap. 19.95 (1-55634-341-8, 3308, Pub. by S Jackson Games) BookWorld.
— In Nomine Heaven & Hell. Hite, Kenneth, ed. (Revelations Cycle Ser.: 3). (Illus.). 128p. 1997. pap. 19.95 (1-55634-339-6, 3306, Pub. by S Jackson Games) BookWorld.
Cambias, James L., ed. see Neumeier, Craig & Schiffer, Michael S.
Cambias, Terrence, tr. see Galilea, Segundo.
Cambie, R. C. & Ash, J. Fijian Medicinal Plants. LC 94-117116. 356p. 1994. 95.00 (0-643-05404-9, Pub. by CSIRO) Accents Pubns.
Cambie, R. C. & Brewis, A. A. Anti-Fertility Plants of the Pacific. (Illus.). 192p. 1997. 120.00 (0-643-05986-5, Pub. by CSIRO) Accents Pubns.
Cambie, R. C., jt. auth. see Cooper, R. C.
Cambier, John C., ed. B-Lymphocyte Differentiation. 208p. 1986. 106.00 (0-8493-5172-3, QR185, CRC Reprint) Franklin.
— Ligands, Receptors, & Signal Transduction in Regulation of Lymphocyte Function. (Illus.). 440p. 1990. 49.00 (1-55581-021-7) ASM Pr.
Cambini, A., et al, eds. Generalized Convexity & Fractional Programming with Economic Applications: Proceedings of the International Workshop on "Generalized Concavity, Fractional Programming & Economic Applications", Pisa, Italy, May 30-June 1, 1988. (Lecture Notes in Economics & Mathematical Systems Ser.: Vol. 345). (Illus.). viii, 361p. 1990. 50.95 (0-387-52673-0) Spr-Verlag.
Cambini, Andrea. Two Very Notable Commentaries, of the Originall of Turcks, Etc. Shute, J., tr. LC 75-25772. (English Experience Ser.: No. 235). 1970. reprint ed. 45.00 (90-221-0235-1) Walter J Johnson.
Cambitoglou, A., jt. auth. see Trendall, Arthur D.
Cambon, Glauco. Dante's Craft: Studies in Language & Style. LC 70-88564. 225p. reprint ed. pap. 69.80 (0-608-16069-5, 203320900084) Bks Demand.
— Eugenio Montale's Poetry: A Dream in Reason's Presence. LC 82-47584. 287p. 1982. reprint ed. pap. 89.00 (0-608-02891-6, 206395500007) Bks Demand.
Cambon, J., et al. Foreign Policy of the Powers. LC 77-111831. (Essay Index Reprint Ser.). 1977. 19.95 (0-8369-1804-5) Ayer.
Cambon, Marlis, tr. see Blickensdorfer, Hans.
Cambone, Joseph. Teaching Troubled Children: A Case Study in Effective Classroom Practice. 224p. (C). 1994. pap. text 18.95 (0-8077-3303-2) Tchrs Coll.
Cambone, Stephen A. A New Structure for National Security Policy Planning: Revisiting the National Security Act of 1947. LC 98-37026. (Significant Issue Ser.). 272p. 1998. pap. text 23.95 (0-89206-345-9) CSIS.
Cambone, Stephen A., ed. NATO's Role in European Stability. LC 95-16089. (CSIS Panel Reports). 70p. (C). 1995. pap. text 14.95 (0-89206-324-6) CSIS.
Cambor, Kathleen. The Book of Mercy. LC 95-47729. 288p. 1996. text 22.00 (0-374-11550-8) FS&G.
— The Book of Mercy. LC 97-24442. 1997. pap. 12.00 (0-15-600519-0, Harcourt Child Bks) Harcourt.
***Cambor, Kathleen.** In Sunlight, in a Beautiful Garden. 256p. 2001. 23.00 (0-374-16537-8) FS&G.
Cambou, B., ed. Behaviour of Granular Materials. ((Cism International Centre for Mechanical Sciences. Courses & Lectures. Supplement: No. 385)). (Illus.). 247p. 1998. pap. 87.00 (3-211-82920-2) Spr-Verlag.
Cambournac, Pascal. Dictionnaire du Transport Aerien. (FRE.). 136p. 1993. pap. 65.00 (0-7859-5669-7, 2908537087) Fr & Eur.
Cambourne, Brian. The Whole Story: Natural Learning & the Acquisition of Literacy in the Classroom. pap. 17.50 (0-908643-49-7) Scholastic Inc.
— The Whole Story: Natural Learning & the Acquisition of Literacy in the Classroom. 1993. pap. 19.95 (0-590-21976-6) Scholastic Inc.
Cambourne, Brian & Turbill, Jan. Coping with Chaos. LC 90-27029. 71p. (Orig.). (C). 1991. pap. 17.50 (0-435-08584-0, 08584) Heinemann.
Cambourne, Brian & Turbill, Jan, eds. Responsive Evaluation: Making Valid Judgments About Student Literacy. LC 94-29683. 144p. 1995. pap. text 19.00 (0-435-08829-7, 08829) Heinemann.
Cambourne, Brian, jt. auth. see Brown, Hazel.
Cambra, Ronald E., jt. auth. see Klopf, Donald W.
Cambras, Trinitat, jt. ed. see Diez-Noguera, Antoni.
Cambray, C. K. Programmed for Peril. 336p. (Orig.). 1993. mass mkt. 4.99 (0-671-73540-3) PB.
— Where Is Crystal Martin? large type ed. 1989. 27.99 (0-7089-2186-8) Ulverscroft.
Cambray, Joan M., jt. auth. see Hansen, Charles A.
Cambre, Dale. Daytona Beach, Florida: A Postcard Tour. LC 98-88059. (Postcard History Ser.). (Illus.). 128p. 1998. pap. 18.99 (0-7524-1323-6) Arcadia Publng.
Cambre, Suzanne. Lady Killer: Heart Disease: Women at Risk. Hollingsworth, Anna, ed. LC 35-3309. (Illus.). 24p. 1995. pap. text 5.95 (0-939838-38-9) Pritchett & Hull.
— The Sensuous Heart: Guidelines for Sex after a Heart Attack or Heart Surgery. Hoffman, Faye & Hull, Nancy, eds. LC 90-8192. (Illus.). 20p. (Orig.). 1990. pap. text 5.75 (0-939838-28-1) Pritchett & Hull.
Cambrell, Herbert P. Mirabeau Buonaparte Lamar, Troubadour & Crusader. 1993. reprint ed. lib. bdg. 75.00 (0-7812-5930-4) Rprt Serv.
Cambrensis, Giraldus. The History & Topography of Ireland. O'Meara, John J., tr. (Illus.). 136p. 1982. 22.00 (0-85105-311-4, Pub. by Smyth) Dufour.
Cambridge. Basic Reading Skill. 1988. pap. text 6.30 (0-8428-9328-8) P-H.
— Building a Portfolio. LC 97-22725. 372p. 1997. pap. text 38.60 (0-13-299819-X) P-H.
— The Cambridge Pre-Ged Program in Math. 2nd ed. 1988. pap. text 9.00 (0-13-113762-X) P-H.
— Exercise Book for Interpreting Literature & the Arts: Cambridge GED Program. rev. ed. 1993. pap. 7.75 (0-13-701774-X) P-H.
— Exercise Book for Science Cambridge Program. 1993. pap. 6.33 (0-13-701962-9) P-H.
— Exercise Book for Writing Skills Pt. 1: Cambridge GED Program. rev. ed. 1993. pap. 7.75 (0-13-600685-X) P-H.
— GED High School Equivalency. 1988. pap. 16.00 (0-8428-8700-8) P-H.
— GED Math Test. 1988. pap. text 10.00 (0-8428-8705-9) P-H.
— Get Hired! Finding Job Opportunities: The Janus Employability Skills Program. 1996. pap. text 19.95 (0-8359-1410-0) P-H.
— Know Your Government. text 8.25 (0-8359-0691-4) Globe Fearon.
Cambridge, Ada. Thirty Years in Australia. 251p. 1989. pap. 19.95 (0-86840-020-3, Pub. by New South Wales Univ Pr) Intl Spec Bk.
— A Woman's Friendship. Morrison, Elizabeth, ed. (Colonial Text Ser.). 314p. 1989. pap. 31.95 (0-86840-163-3, Pub. by New South Wales Univ Pr) Intl Spec Bk.
Cambridge Adult Education Staff. Cambridge GED Program: Comprehensive Teacher's Guide. 2nd ed. 1996. pap. text, teacher ed. 10.85 (0-13-388919-X) P-H.
Cambridge, Alrick, et al. Where You Belong: Government & Black Culture. 160p. 1992. 66.95 (1-85628-394-1, Pub. by Avebry) Ashgate Pub Co.
Cambridge, Barbara S. And This I Know. 2nd ed. (Illus.). 24p. (J). 1987. pap. write for info. (0-9621018-1-8) CBridge Pubns.
— And This I Know: Affirmations for Children. rev. ed. (Illus.). 28p. (J). 1987. reprint ed. pap. 6.95 (0-317-91380-8) CBridge Pubns.
***Cambridge, Christine R.** Forgive Us Our Trespasses. 1999. pap. write for info. (1-928781-12-8) Hollis Bks.
Cambridge Communication, Ltd. Staff. Anatomy & Physiology: A Self Instructional Course, 5 vols. 2nd ed. LC 84-4977. (Illus.). 1997. text 16.00 (0-443-03170-3); text 16.00 (0-443-03206-8); text 16.00 (0-443-03207-6); text 16.00 (0-443-03208-4); text 16.00 (0-443-03209-2) Church.
***Cambridge, E. Bobby.** A Rose by Another Name. 177p. 2000. pap. 11.95 (0-533-13087-5) Vantage.
Cambridge Educational Services Staff. Arco's Teach Yourself the SAT in 24 Hours. 416p. 1998. pap. 16.95 (0-02-862689-3, Pub. by Macmillan) S&S Trade.
***Cambridge, Fam.** Cambridge Family Bible, Vol. 1. 1999. 150.00 (0-521-51298-0) Cambdge U Bibles.
***Cambridge, Gerry.** Nothing but Heather: Scottish Nature in Poems, Photographs & Prose. 2000. pap. 24.95 (0-946487-49-9) Luath Pr Ltd.
Cambridge Historical Commission Staff. Survey of Architectural History in Cambridge. Incl. Report Three: Cambridgeport. 1971. 12.95 (0-262-53013-9); pap. write for info. (0-318-54342-7) MIT Pr.
Cambridge Historical Commission Staff, photos by. East Cambridge. 2nd ed. (Survey of Architectural History in Cambridge Ser.: No. 1). (Illus.). 272p. (Orig.). 1989. pap. text 16.95 (0-262-53078-3) MIT Pr.
***Cambridge International Reference on Current Affairs Staff.** People of Consequence. 150p. 1999. pap. (0-11-702657-3, Pub. by Statnry Office) Balogh.
Cambridge, Joan. Clarise Cumberbatch Want to Go Home. 224p. 1987. 15.45 (0-89919-403-6, Pub. by Ticknor & Fields) HM.
Cambridge, Paul & Brown, Hilary, eds. HIV & Learning Disability. 250p. 1996. pap. 39.95 (1-873791-91-7, Pub. by Brit Inst Lrning) Taylor & Francis.
Cambridge, Paul, et al. Care in the Community: Five Years On: Life in the Community for People with Learning Disabilities. 3rd ed. 128p. 1994. 55.95 (1-85742-282-1, Pub. by Arena) Ashgate Pub Co.
Cambridge Physics Outlet Staff. Electric Motor. (Illus.). 120p. 1997. text 99.95 (1-58100-009-X) Beckley Cardy.
— Simple Machines & Motion. (Illus.). 120p. 1997. text 99.95 (1-58100-014-6) Beckley Cardy.
Cambridge-Pickard, A. W. Demosthenes & the Last Days of Greek Freedom: 384-322 B. C. Vlastos, Gregory, ed. LC 78-19377. (Morals & Law in Ancient Greece Ser.). 1979. reprint ed. lib. bdg. 42.95 (0-405-11566-0) Ayer.
***Cambridge Review Staff.** Teach Yourself the TOEFL in 24 Hours. 416p. 1999. pap. 16.95 incl. cd-rom (0-02-863241-9, Arco) Macmillan Gen Ref.
Cambridge Review Staff. Arco Teach Yourself the TOEFL in 24 Hours: Teach Yourself in 24 Hours. 416p. 1999. pap. 14.95 incl. cd-rom (0-02-863240-0) Macmillan.
— Arco's Teach Yourself to Beat the GMAT CAT in 24 Hours. LC 99-162331. 416p. 1998. pap. 17.95 (0-02-862692-3, Arco) Macmillan Gen Ref.
— Arco's Teach Yourself to Beat the GRE in 24 Hours. LC 99-162333. 416p. 1998. pap. 17.95 (0-02-862690-7, Arco) Macmillan Gen Ref.
— Arco's Teach Yourself to Beat the LSAT in 24 Hours. 416p. 1998. pap. 17.95 (0-02-862691-5, Arco) Macmillan Gen Ref.
— GMAT Power. 384p. 1996. 17.95 (0-02-861076-8) Macmillan.
— GMAT Power. 1997. pap. text 29.95 incl. disk (0-02-861515-8, Arco) Macmillan Gen Ref.
— GRE Power. LC 97-121418. 384p. 1996. 16.95 (0-02-861075-X) Macmillan.
— LSAT Power. 384p. 1996. 16.95 (0-02-861077-6) Macmillan.
— SAT Power. 384p. 1996. 16.95 (0-02-861074-1) Macmillan.
Cambridge Review Staff & Vedral, Joyce L. GRE Power. 1997. pap. text 29.95 incl. disk (0-02-861517-4, Arco) Macmillan Gen Ref.
— LSAT Power. 1997. pap. text 29.95 incl. disk (0-02-861516-6, Arco) Macmillan Gen Ref.
Cambridge School Classics Project Foundation Staff. Cambridge Latin Course, 3 bklts, Unit 5, Pupils Books. Incl. Dido et Aeneas. 1974. Nero et Agrippina. 1974. Words & Phrases. 1974. (Illus.). 1974. Set pap. 5.95 (0-521-08545-4) Cambridge U Pr.
Cambridge School Classics Project Foundation Staff, ed. Athens: City & Empire. (Illus.). 80p. (C). 1990. pap. text 12.95 (0-521-38874-0) Cambridge U Pr.
Cambridge Songs Staff. The Cambridge Songs, a Goliard's Song Book of the 11th Century. Breul, Karl, ed. LC 77-178517. reprint ed. 29.50 (0-404-56529-8) AMS Pr.
Cambridge Staff. Cambridge GED Program: Science. 2nd rev. ed. 448p. (C). 1992. pap. text 7.65 (0-13-116427-9) P-H.
— Cambridge GED Program: Social Science. 2nd rev. ed. 384p. (C). 1992. pap. text 7.65 (0-13-116435-X) P-H.
— Cambridge GED Program Interpreting Literature & the Arts. 1995. pap. 9.75 (0-13-116443-0) P-H.
— Cambridge Pre-GD Exercise in Reading. 1988. pap. text 3.50 (0-13-114273-9) P-H.
— The Cambridge Pre-Ged Program in Reading. 1988. pap. text 9.00 (0-13-114265-8) P-H.
— New Revised Cambridge GED Program: Comprehensive Book. 2nd ed. 912p. (C). 1992. pap. text 9.45 (0-13-388752-9) P-H.
— New Revised Cambridge GED Program: Social Studies Workbook. rev. ed. 1995. pap. 6.95 (0-13-702101-1) P-H.
— New Revised Cambridge GED Program: Writing. 2nd ed. 1993. pap. text 7.65 (0-13-116963-7) P-H.
— Threshold: Cambridge Pre-GED Program in Interpreting Literature & the Arts. 2nd ed. 224p. (C). 1992. pap. text 7.25 (0-13-111097-7) P-H.
— Threshold: Cambridge Pre GED Program in Math Two. 288p. 1993. pap. text 7.25 (0-13-917600-4, 640803) P-H.
— Threshold: Cambridge Pre-GED Program in Mathematics. 256p. 1992. pap. text 7.25 (0-13-110966-9) P-H.
— Threshold: Cambridge Pre-GED Program in Science. 256p. (C). 1992. pap. text 7.25 (0-13-116419-8) P-H.
— Threshold: Cambridge Pre-GED Program in Social Studies. LC 93-49665. 224p. 1994. pap. text 7.25 (0-13-111089-6) P-H.

C

An Asterisk (*) at the beginning of an entry indicates that the title is appearing for the first time.

— Threshold: Cambridge Pre-GED Program in Writing. LC 93-5349. (C). 1993. pap. text 7.25 (*0-13-110958-8*) P-H.

Cambridge Staff, ed. Reading: Kentucky Educational Television Study Guide. rev. ed. (GED Program Ser.). 206p. 1988. pap. text. write for info. (*0-8428-9370-9*, 893-709) Cambridge Bk.

Cambridge University, Fitzwilliam Museum Staff. Catalogue of Paintings, Vol. 3: British School by J. W. Goodison. LC 61-19559. 385p. reprint ed. pap. 109.80 (*0-608-12506-7*, 2024455) Bks Demand.

***Cambridge University Press.** Cambridge International Dictionary of Idioms. LC 98-36963. 1998. write for info. (*0-521-62364-2*) Cambridge U Pr.

— Cambridge International Dictionary of Phrasal Verbs, Anglais-Francais. LC 98-36962. 1998. pap. write for info. (*0-521-56557-X*) Cambridge U Pr.

***Cambridge University Publishing Staff.** Double-Column Bible. 2000. 15.99 (*0-521-50358-2*) Cambridge U Pr.

— English Bible: Leather Blue. rev. ed. 45.00 (*0-521-50724-3*) Cambdge U Bibles.

Cambridge University Publishing Staff. New Revised Cambridge GED Program: Exercise Book for Mathematics. LC 93-7573. (Illus.). 160p. (C). 1994. pap. text 5.55 (*0-13-701897-5*) P-H.

Cambron, Beverly, ed. see Olsen, Brad.

Cambron, Mark. Come, Lord Jesus. pap. 1.45 (*0-686-12745-5*) Grace Pub Co.

— Doktriny Bibliyi. Slavic Christian Publishing Staff & Michka, Vitaly, trs. from ENG. (RUS.). 290p. (C). 1994. write for info. (*0-9641805-0-2*) Baptist Intl.

Cambron-McCabe, Nelda, ed. Case Citations No. 12: Employment Issues. 69p. 1992. pap. 30.00 (*1-56534-075-2*) Ed Law Assn.

Cambron-McCabe, Nelda H., jt. auth. see McCarthy.

Cambrosio, Alberto & Keating, Peter. Exquisite Specificity: The Monoclonal Antibody Revolution. (Illus.). 272p. 1995. text 59.95 (*0-19-509741-6*) OUP.

Cambrosio, Alberto, ed. see Lock, Margaret.

Camburn, Eric M., jt. auth. see Sebring, Penny A.

Camburn, Herbert, jt. auth. see Gaughenbaugh, Michael.

Camburn, K. E., et al. The Haptobenthic Diatom Flora of Long Branch Creek, South Carolina. (Offprint from Nova Hedwigia Ser.: No. 30). (Illus.). 1979. 50.00 (*3-7682-1197-5*) Lubrecht & Cramer.

Camby, P. Petit Dictionary Licencieux des Bretons. (FRE.). 208p. 1996. 45.00 (*0-320-00902-5*) Fr & Eur.

Camden Arts Centre Exhibition Staff. Contemporary African Art. LC 70-108670. 40p. 1970. pap. 8.95 (*0-8419-0040-X*, Africana) Holmes & Meier.

Camden, Carroll. The Elizabethan Woman. 333p. 1975. reprint ed. pap. 35.00 (*0-911858-30-X*) Appel.

Camden, Nancy. The True Story of Jimmy Trueberry. 194p. 1998. pap. 13.95 (*0-9664930-0-1*) Raspberry MI.

Camden, Patricia. Scarlet Kisses. 384p. (Orig.). 1992. mass mkt. 4.50 (*0-380-76825-9*, Avon Bks) Morrow Avon.

— Surrender in Scarlet. 400p. (Orig.). 1991. mass mkt. 4.50 (*0-380-76262-5*, Avon Bks) Morrow Avon.

Camden Society, London Staff. Camden Society Publications, 1838 to 1872, 105 vols. reprint ed. 5780.00 (*0-404-50100-1*) AMS Pr.

Camden Society Staff. Camden Miscellany, 6 vols. LC 66-80313. (First Ser). reprint ed. 315.00 (*0-404-50212-1*) AMS Pr.

Camden, Vera J. John Bunyan & Modern Criticism. (Studs in English & American Literature Ser.). 2002. 55.00 (*1-57113-134-5*) Camden Hse.

Camden, Vera J., ed. Compromise Formations: Current Directions in Psychoanalytic Criticism. LC 88-28464. 272p. 1989. 21.00 (*0-87338-380-X*); pap. 12.50 (*0-87338-381-8*) Kent St U Pr.

Camden, William. Britannia, 4 vols. (Illus.). reprint ed. 15.00 (*3-487-05492-2*) Adlers Foreign Bks.

— History of Elizabeth I: The History of the Renowned & Victorious Princess Elizabeth. 4th ed. LC 70-113570. reprint ed. 215.00 (*0-404-01366-X*) AMS Pr.

— History of the Most Renowned & Victorious Princess Elizabeth Late Queen of England: Selected Chapters. MacCaffrey, Wallace T., ed. LC 74-115682. (Classics of British Historical Literature Ser.). 1993. pap. text 3.45 (*0-226-09219-4*, P399) U Ch Pr.

— Remaines Concerning Britain. LC 77-113572. (Illus.). reprint ed. 84.50 (*0-404-01367-8*) AMS Pr.

— Remains Concerning Britain. Dunn, R. D., ed. 632p. 1984. text 80.00 (*0-8020-2457-2*) U of Toronto Pr.

Camden, William & Mertner, Edgar. Remains Concerning Britain. (Anglistica & Americana Ser.: No. 74). ix, 446p. 1970. reprint ed. 120.00 (*0-685-66440-6*, 05102523) G Olms Pubs.

Camealy, John B., jt. auth. see Anderson, Jerry W., Jr.

Cameeb, Inc. Staff. Boston Terrier Champions, 1988-1994. LC 98-138573. (Illus.). 90p. 1997. pap. 32.95 (*1-55893-051-5*) Camino E E & Bk.

— Pekingese Champions, 1987-1999. (Illus.). 2000. pap. 32.95 (*1-55893-052-3*) Camino E E & Bk.

Camejo, Peter. Racism, Revolution, Reaction, 1861-1877: The Rise & Fall of Radical Reconstruction. LC 76-24184. (Illus.). 266p. 1976. pap. 17.95 (*0-87348-821-0*) Pathfinder NY.

— Racism, Revolution, Reaction 1861-1877: The Rise & Fall of Radical Reconstruction. LC 76-24184. (Illus.). 269p. 1976. lib. bdg. 50.00 (*0-913460-49-4*) Pathfinder NY.

Cameli, A. P., ed. The Information Superhighway: Issues & Challenges. 177p. (C). 1996. lib. bdg. 95.00 (*1-56072-304-1*) Nova Sci Pubs.

Camell, Dennis G. Uncertainty Assessment for Standard Antenna Measurements on the Open Area Test Site. 19p. 1998. pap. 3.50 (*0-16-056809-9*) USGPO.

Camelot Research Committee Staff, jt. auth. see Alcock, Leslie.

Camenisch, Paul. Grounding Professional Ethics in a Pluralistic Society. LC 83-83297. (Professional Ethics Ser.). 160p. (Orig.). 1983. text 50.00 (*0-614-13737-3*); pap. text 21.00 (*0-930586-11-5*) Haven Pubns.

Camenisch, Paul F., ed. Religious Methods & Resources in Bioethics. LC 93-24817. (Theory & Medicine Ser.: Vol. 2). 356p. (C). 1993. lib. bdg. 205.50 (*0-7923-2102-2*, Pub. by Kluwer Academic) Kluwer Academic.

Camenson, Blyth & Goldberg, Jan. Real People Working in Education. LC 96-45455. (On the Job Ser.). (Illus.). 144p. 1997. 17.95 (*0-8442-4734-0*, 47340, Natl Textbk Co) NTC Contemp Pub Co.

***Camenson, Blythe.** Anthropology Majors. LC 99-23598. 1999. pap. text 11.95 (*0-658-00022-5*, NTC Business Bks) NTC Contemp Pub Co.

— Careers for Aquatic Types & Others Who Want to Make a Splash. LC 99-29187. (Careers for You Ser.). 192p. 1999. pap. 9.95 (*0-658-00216-3*, 002163) NTC Contemp Pub Co.

— Careers for Aquatic Types & Others Who Want to Make a Splash. (Careers for You Ser.). 192p. 2000. 14.95 (*0-658-00215-5*, 002155) NTC Contemp Pub Co.

Camenson, Blythe. Careers for Born Leaders: And Other Decisive Types. LC 97-50253. (Careers for You Ser.). 144p. 1998. pap. 9.95 (*0-8442-2293-3*, 22933, VGM Career) NTC Contemp Pub Co.

— Careers for Born Leaders & Other Decisive Types: And Other Decisive Types. LC 97-50253. (Careers for You Ser.). (Illus.). 144p. 1998. 14.95 (*0-8442-2292-5*, 22925, VGM Career) NTC Contemp Pub Co.

— Careers for Health Nuts & Others Who Like to Stay Fit. (Careers for You Ser.). (Illus.). 160p. 1996. 14.95 (*0-8442-4117-2*, 41172, VGM Career); pap. 9.95 (*0-8442-4118-0*, 41180, VGM Career) NTC Contemp Pub Co.

— Careers for History Buffs: And Others Who Learn from the Past. LC 93-46827. (Illus.). 160p. 1994. 14.95 (*0-8442-4108-3*, 41083, VGM Career) NTC Contemp Pub Co.

— Careers for History Buffs: And Others Who Learn from the Past. (Illus.). 160p. 1994. pap. 9.95 (*0-8442-4109-1*, 41091, VGM Career) NTC Contemp Pub Co.

— Careers for Legal Eagles & Other Law-&-Order Types: And Other Law - & - Order Types. LC 97-46614. (Careers for You Ser.). (Illus.). 152p. 1998. 14.95 (*0-8442-2288-7*, 22887, VGM Career); pap. 9.95 (*0-8442-2289-5*, 22895, VGM Career) NTC Contemp Pub Co.

— Careers for Mystery Buffs: And Other Snoops & Sleuths. LC 96-2034. (Illus.). 160p. 1996. 14.95 (*0-8442-4331-0*, 43310, VGM Career); pap. 9.95 (*0-8442-4332-9*, 43329, VGM Career) NTC Contemp Pub Co.

— Careers for Perfectionists & Other Meticulous Types. LC 98-37298. (Careers for You Ser.). 192p. 1999. 14.95 (*0-8442-2061-2*, 20612, VGM Career); pap. 9.95 (*0-8442-2059-0*, 20590, VGM Career) NTC Contemp Pub Co.

— Careers for Plant Lovers & Other Green Thumb Types. LC 95-3224. (Careers for You Ser.). (Illus.). 160p. 1995. pap. 9.95 (*0-8442-4120-2*, 41202, Natl Textbk Co) NTC Contemp Pub Co.

— Careers for Plant Lovers & Other Green Thumb Types. (Careers for You Ser.). (Illus.). 160p. 1995. 14.95 (*0-8442-4119-9*, 41199, Natl Textbk Co) NTC Contemp Pub Co.

— Careers for Romantics & Other Dreamy Types. LC 99-28740. (Careers for You Ser.). 160p. 1999. 14.95 (*0-8442-2962-8*); pap. 9.95 (*0-8442-2963-6*) NTC Contemp Pub Co.

***Camenson, Blythe.** Careers for Scholars & Other Deep Thinkers. (Careers for You Ser.). 2000. 14.95 (*0-658-00191-4*, VGM Career); pap. 9.95 (*0-658-00192-2*) NTC Contemp Pub Co.

Camenson, Blythe. Careers for Self-Starters & Other Entrepreneurial Types. LC 96-27791. 160p. 1997. 14.95 (*0-8442-4329-9*, 43299); pap. 9.95 (*0-8442-4330-2*, 43302) NTC Contemp Pub Co.

— Careers in Art. LC 99-19985. (VGM Professional Ser.). 144p. 1999. pap. 13.95 (*0-658-00028-4*, 000284) NTC Contemp Pub Co.

***Camenson, Blythe.** Careers in Art. LC 99-19985. (VGM Professional Ser.). 144p. 1999. 17.95 (*0-658-00027-6*, 000276, NTC Business Bks) NTC Contemp Pub Co.

— Careers in Writing. (Professional Careers Ser.). 2000. 17.95 (*0-658-00103-5*, VGM Career); pap. 13.95 (*0-658-00104-3*, VGM Career) NTC Contemp Pub Co.

Camenson, Blythe. Firefighting. (VGM Career Portraits Ser.). (Illus.). 96p. (J). 1995. 13.95 (*0-8442-4374-4*, 43744, VGM Career) NTC Contemp Pub Co.

— Great Jobs for Biology Majors. LC 98-45285. (Great Jobs for... Ser.). 272p. 1999. pap. 11.95 (*0-8442-1917-7*, 19177, VGM Career) NTC Contemp Pub Co.

— Great Jobs for Communications Majors. Kennedy, Sarah, ed. (Illus.). 224p. (Orig.). (C). 1995. pap. 11.95 (*0-8442-4355-8*, 43558, VGM Career) NTC Contemp Pub Co.

***Camenson, Blythe.** Great Jobs for Economics Majors. LC 99-44167. (Great Jobs Ser.). (Illus.). 192p. 2000. pap. 11.95 (*0-658-00222-8*, 002228, VGM Career) NTC Contemp Pub Co.

— Great Jobs for Geology Majors. LC 99-26993. 1999. 11.95 (*0-658-00021-7*) NTC Contemp Pub Co.

Camenson, Blythe. Introverts & Other Solitary Types. LC 98-29474. (Careers for... Ser.). 136p. 1998. 14.95 (*0-8442-6385-0*, 63850, VGM Career); pap. 9.95 (*0-8442-6386-9*, 63869, VGM Career) NTC Contemp Pub Co.

— Landscape Architecture, Botanical Gardens, & Arboreta. LC 98-18216. (Opportunities in... Ser.). 160p. 1998. 14.95 (*0-8442-6483-0*, 64830); pap. 11.95 (*0-8442-6534-9*, 65349) NTC Contemp Pub Co.

— Nursing. LC 94-42628. (VGM Career Portraits Ser.). (Illus.). 96p. (J). (gr. 7 up). 1995. 13.95 (*0-8442-4369-8*, 43698, VGM Career) NTC Contemp Pub Co

***Camenson, Blythe.** Opportunities in Adult Education Careers. LC 99-37763. (Opportunities in...Ser.). 160p. 1999. pap. 11.95 (*0-658-00109-4*, 001094) NTC Contemp Pub Co.

— Opportunities in Education Careers. LC 99-37763. (Opportunities in... Ser.). 160p. 2000. 14.95 (*0-658-00108-6*, 001086) NTC Contemp Pub Co.

Camenson, Blythe. Opportunities in Museums Careers. (Opportunities in...Ser.). (Illus.). 160p. 1996. 14.95 (*0-8442-4593-3*, 45933, Natl Textbk Co) NTC Contemp Pub Co.

— Opportunities in Overseas Careers: Blythe Camenson. LC 97-41354. (Opportunities in...Ser.). (Illus.). 160p. 1998. 14.95 (*0-8442-2342-5*, 23425, VGM Career); pap. 11.95 (*0-8442-2343-3*, 23433, VGM Career) NTC Contemp Pub Co.

— Opportunities in Summer Camp Careers. LC 97-41353. (Opportunities in...Ser.). (Illus.). 160p. 1998. 14.95 (*0-8442-2344-1*, 23441, VGM Career); pap. 11.95 (*0-8442-2345-X*, 2345X, VGM Career) NTC Contemp Pub Co.

— Opportunities in Teaching English to Speakers of Other Languages. LC 94-49617. (Opportunities In . . Ser.). (Illus.). 160p. pap. 11.95 (*0-8442-4428-7*, 44287, VGM Career) NTC Contemp Pub Co.

— Opportunities in Zoo Careers. LC 97-21798. (Opportunities in...Ser.). (Illus.). 160p. 1997. 14.95 (*0-8442-2312-3*, 23123, VGM Career); pap. 11.95 (*0-8442-2313-1*, 23131, VGM Career) NTC Contemp Pub Co.

— Real People Working in Building & Construction. LC 98-46769. (On the Job Ser.). 160p. 1999. 17.95 (*0-8442-1927-4*, 19274, VGM Career); pap. 12.95 (*0-8442-1932-0*, 19320) NTC Contemp Pub Co.

— Real People Working in Business. LC 98-25044. (On the Job Ser.). 192p. 1998. 17.95 (*0-8442-6559-4* 65594, VGM Career) NTC Contemp Pub Co.

— Real People Working in Finance. LC 98-45625. (On the Job Ser.). 144p. 1999. 17.95 (*0-8442-1920-7* 19207, VGM Career); pap. 12.95 (*0-8442-1926-6*, 19266) NTC Contemp Pub Co.

— Real People Working in Government. LC 97-35169. (On the Job Ser.). (Illus.). 192p. 1998. 17.95 (*0-8442-4710-3*, 47103, Natl Textbk Co) NTC Contemp Pub Co.

— Real People Working in Law. LC 96-45454. (On the Job Ser.). (Illus.). 160p. 1997. 17.95 (*0-8442-4738-3*, 47383, Natl Textbk Co) NTC Contemp Pub Co.

***Camenson, Blythe.** Real People Working in Mechanics, Installation & Repair. (On the Job Ser.). 192p. 1999. 17.95 (*0-658-00017-9*, 000179); pap. 12.95 (*0-658-00018-7*, 000187, NTC Business Bks) NTC Contemp Pub Co.

Camenson, Blythe. Real People Working in Transportation. LC 99-25387. (On the Job Ser.). 160p. 1999 pap. 12.95 (*0-658-00107-8*, 001078) NTC Contemp Pub Co.

***Camenson, Blythe.** Real People Working in Transportation. (On the Job Ser.). 192p. 1999. 18.95 (*0-658-00019-5*); 17.95 (*0-658-00105-1*, 001051, NTC Business Bks); pap. 12.95 (*0-658-00020-9*) NTC Contemp Pub Co.

Camenson, Blythe. Travel. LC 94-43362. (VGM Career Portraits Ser.). (Illus.). 96p. (gr. 7 up). 1995. 13.95 (*0-8442-4365-5*, 43655) NTC Contemp Pub Co.

— Writing. (VGM Career Portraits Ser.). (Illus.). 96p. (J). 1995. 13.95 (*0-8442-4372-8*, 43728, VGM Career) NTC Contemp Pub Co.

Camenson, Blythe & Cook, Marshall J. Your Novel Proposal: From Creation to Contract. LC 99-23558. 256p. 1999. 18.99 (*0-89879-875-2*, 10628, Wrtrs Digest Bks) F & W Pubns Inc.

Camenson, Blythe & Goldberg, Jan. Real People Working in Business. LC 98-25044. (On the Job Ser.). 192p. 1998. pap. 12.95 (*0-8442-6563-2*, 65632, VGM Career) NTC Contemp Pub Co.

— Real People Working in Communications. LC 96-28072. (On the Job Ser.). (Illus.). 144p. 1996. 17.95 (*0-8442-4730-8*, 47308, Natl Textbk Co); pap. 12.95 (*0-8442-4731-6*, 47316, Natl Textbk Co) NTC Contemp Pub Co.

— Real People Working in Education. LC 96-45455. (On the Job Ser.). (Illus.). 144p. 1997. pap. 12.95 (*0-8442-4735-9*, 47359, Natl Textbk Co) NTC Contemp Pub Co.

— Real People Working in Engineering. LC 97-21515. (On the Job Ser.). (Illus.). 160p. 1997. 17.95 (*0-8442-4741-3*, 47413, Natl Textbk Co); pap. 12.95 (*0-8442-4742-1*, 47421, Natl Textbk Co) NTC Contemp Pub Co.

***Camenson, Blythe & Goldberg, Jan.** Real People Working in Entertainment. LC 98-17060. (On the Job Ser.). 192p. 1998. 17.95 (*0-8442-6569-1*, 65691); pap. 12.95 (*0-8442-6570-5*, 65705) NTC Contemp Pub Co.

Camenson, Blythe & Goldberg, Jan. Real People Working in Government. LC 97-35169. (On the Job Ser.). (Illus.). 192p. 1998. pap. 12.95 (*0-8442-4711-1*, 47111, Natl Textbk Co) NTC Contemp Pub Co.

— Real People Working in Health Care. LC 96-26671. (On the Job Ser.). (Illus.). 144p. 1996. pap. 12.95 (*0-8442-4727-8*) NTC Contemp Pub Co.

— Real People Working in Helping Professions. LC 97-23005. (On the Job Ser.). (Illus.). 160p. 1997. 17.95 (*0-8442-4721-9*, 47219, Natl Textbk Co); pap. 12.95 (*0-8442-4722-7*, 47227, Natl Textbk Co) NTC Contemp Pub Co.

— Real People Working in Law. LC 96-45454. (On the Job Ser.). (Illus.). 160p. 1997. pap. 12.95 (*0-8442-4739-1*, 47391, Natl Textbk Co) NTC Contemp Pub Co.

— Real People Working in Sales & Marketing. LC 96-28073. (On the Job Ser.). (Illus.). 144p. 1996. 17.95 (*0-8442-4728-6*, 47286, Natl Textbk Co); pap. 12.95 (*0-8442-4729-4*, 47294, Natl Textbk Co) NTC Contemp Pub Co.

— Real People Working in Service Businesses. LC 96-27790. (On the Job Ser.). (Illus.). 144p. 1996. 17.95 (*0-8442-4732-4*, 47324, Natl Textbk Co); pap. 12.95 (*0-8442-4733-2*, 47332, Natl Textbk Co) NTC Contemp Pub Co.

Camenson, Blythe, et al. Great Jobs for Art Majors. LC 96-47309. (Great Jobs for... Ser.). (Illus.). 208p. 1997. pap. 11.95 (*0-8442-4747-2*, 47472, Natl Textbk Co) NTC Contemp Pub Co.

— Great Jobs for Liberal Arts Majors. LC 96-45456. (Great Jobs for... Ser.). (Illus.). 240p. 1997. pap. 11.95 (*0-8442-4748-0*, 47480, Natl Textbk Co) NTC Contemp Pub Co.

Camenson, Blythe, jt. auth. see Edelfelt, Roy A.

Camenson, Blythe, jt. auth. see Goldberg, Jan.

Camenzind, Jane T., ed. Jackson Hole a la Carte: Fabulous Food for Sharing with Friends. LC 86-81363. (Illus.). 128p. 1986. spiral bd. 11.95 (*0-9617014-0-4*) JHAFRP.

***Camera, Austria.** Camera Austria International #65. 1999. pap. text 18.50 (*3-900508-25-9*) Forum Stadt.

Camera, Austria. Camera Austria International #66. 1999. pap. text 18.50 (*3-900508-26-7*) Forum Stadt.

— Camera Austria International #67. 1999. pap. text 18.50 (*3-900508-27-5*) Forum Stadt.

Camera Offical de Comercio Staff. Diccionari d'Informatica. 2nd ed. (CAT.). 1982. 12.95 (*0-7859-5039-7*) Fr & Eur.

Cameraрix Staff, ed. Spectrum Guide to Ethiopia. (Illus.). 364p. 1999. pap. 22.95 (*1-56656-350-X*) Interlink Pub.

— Spectrum Guide to India. (Spectrum Guides Ser.). (Illus.). 364p. 1998. pap. 22.95 (*1-56656-268-6*) Interlink Pub.

— Spectrum Guide to Maldives. LC 98-38997. 320p. 1999. pap. 22.95 (*1-56656-290-2*) Interlink Pub.

— Spectrum Guide to Mauritius. (Spectrum Guides Ser.). (Illus.). 364p. 1997. pap. 19.95 (*1-56656-271-6*) Interlink Pub.

— Spectrum Guide to Nepal. LC 99-41838. 364p. 2000. pap. 22.95 (*1-56656-332-1*) Interlink Pub.

— Spectrum Guide to Pakistan. LC 98-12460. (Spectrum Guides Ser.). (Illus.). 364p. 1998. pap. 22.95 (*1-56656-240-6*, Interlink Bks) Interlink Pub.

— Spectrum Guide to the United Arab Emirates. (Spectrum Guides Ser.). (Illus.). 364p. 1998. pap. 21.95 (*1-56656-272-4*) Interlink Pub.

— Spectrum Guide to Uganda. (Spectrum Guides Ser.). (Illus.). 364p. 1998. pap. 19.95 (*1-56656-270-8*) Interlink Pub.

***Camerapix Staff, ed.** Spectrum Guide to Zimbabwe. (Illus.). 2000. pap. 22.95 (*1-56656-367-4*) Interlink Pub.

Camerawork Ltd. Staff. Bodies of Experience: Stories about Living with HIV. (C). 1990. 50.00 (*1-871103-02-9*, Pub. by Camerawork) St Mut.

— Sense of Self. (C). 1990. 50.00 (*1-871103-01-0*, Pub. by Camerawork) St Mut.

— Silent Health: Women, Health & Representation. (Illus.). 96p. (C). 1990. 59.00 (*1-871103-03-7*, Pub. by Camerawork) St Mut.

— Turning the Map: Images from the Americas. 90p. (C). 1990. 75.00 (*1-871103-04-5*, Pub. by Camerawork) St Mut.

Camerer, Colin, ed. Making Decisions about Liability & Insurance. 144p. (C). 1993. lib. bdg. 134.00 (*0-7923-9393-7*) Kluwer Academic.

Camerer, M. C. & Capps, Emerson. Raising Other People's Kids: A Guide for Houseparents, Foster Parents & Direct Care Staff. LC 94-48371. 186p. (C). 1995. text 38.95 (*0-398-05985-3*); pap. text 24.95 (*0-398-05986-1*) C C Thomas.

Camerer, T. P. The Camerer Cuss Book of Antique Watches. (Illus.). 336p. 1976. 69.50 (*0-902028-33-2*) Antique Collect.

Camerford, B., et al. Federal Tax Deductions. 1992. 155.00 (*0-7913-1091-4*) Warren Gorham & Lamont.

Camerini-Davalos, R. A. & Cole, H. S., eds. Prediabetes. (Illus.). 418p. 1989. 110.00 (*0-306-43105-X*, Plenum Trade) Perseus Pubng.

Camerius, James W., jt. ed. see Klein, Hans E.

Cameron. Advanced Surgery, Vol. 34. 2000. text 69.95 (*0-323-00343-5*) Harcourt Coll Pubs.

— Advances in Surgery, 32. 32nd ed. (Illus.). 432p. 1998. text 73.00 (*0-8151-8407-7*, 25068) Mosby Inc.

— Atlas of Surgery: Soft Tissue, Endocrine Glands. (gr. 13). 1992. 250.00 (*1-55664-253-9*) Mosby Inc.

— Cases in International Law. LC 98-74477. (SWC-Business Law). 1999. pap. 24.95 (*0-87393-811-9*) Dame Pubns.

***Cameron.** Odontologia Pediatrica. (C). 1998. text 42.50 (*84-8174-337-2*) Mosby Inc.

Cameron. On Track - Antonio. (J). 1992. mass mkt., teacher ed. 7.95 (*0-8384-2935-1*) Heinle & Heinle.

— On Track Julio-intructors Manual. (Adult ESL). (J). 1992. teacher ed. 5.95 (*0-8384-2929-7*) Heinle & Heinle.

— Pediatric Dentistry. 1997. text 44.95 (*0-7234-3068-3*) Mosby Inc.

— Personal Finance. write for info. (*0-534-92254-6*) Wadsworth Pub.

— SHELLEY POETRY PROS* 49* (C). 1951. pap. text 31.00 (*0-03-008100-9*) Harcourt Coll Pubs.

Cameron, ed. A Common Sense Handbook & Guide for Writers. (C). 1998. text. write for info. (*0-321-01187-2*) Addson-Wesley Educ.

— Modern Times: Life, Labor & Leisure in America, 1890-1930. (C). 1998. text. write for info. (*0-321-01119-8*) Addson-Wesley Educ.

Cameron & Walker. The Paired Writing Handbook. 1994. pap. text. write for info. (*0-582-86075-X*, Pub. by Addison-Wesley) Longman.

C

An Asterisk (*) at the beginning of an entry indicates that the title is appearing for the first time.

Cameron & Wilson. Film Review 1998-99. 1998. text 24.95 (*1-85227-767-X*) Virgin Pr.

Cameron, et al. Business Law & Regulatory Environments. 5th ed. 1996. 74.95 (*0-87393-304-4*); pap., student ed., wbk. ed. 31.95 (*0-87393-305-2*) Dame Pubns.

Cameron, jt. auth. see Field.

Cameron, jt. auth. see Saunders.

Cameron, jt. auth. see Scaletta.

Cameron, jt. auth. see Whetten.

Cameron, ed. see Loti.

Cameron, ed. see Meigret.

Cameron, A. & Herrin, J., eds. Constantinople in the Early Eighth Century. 1984. 49.00 (*90-04-07010-9*, CSCT, 10) Brill Academic Pubs.

Cameron, A. Colin & Trivedi, Pravin K. Regression Analysis of Count Data. LC 98-15184. (Econometric Society Monographs: No. 30). (Illus.). 430p. (C). 1998. text 64.95 (*0-521-63201-3*); pap. text 24.95 (*0-521-63567-5*) Cambridge U Pr.

Cameron, A. Colin, et al. The Effects of Unemployment Compensation on the Employment of Youths. (Illus.). 106p. (C). 1998. reprint ed. pap. text 30.00 (*0-7881-3914-2*) DIANE Pub.

Cameron, A. D. The Caledonian Canal. 169p. (C). 1988. 65.00 (*0-906664-15-2*, Pub. by Mercat Pr Bks) St Mut.

— Discover Scotland's History. LC 98-188440. 256p. 1997. pap. 30.00 (*1-898218-76-5*) St Mut.

Cameron, A. E., ed. see AEC Technical Information Center Staff.

Cameron, A. G., ed. Astrophysics Today. LC 84-70879. (Readings from Physics Today Ser.). (Illus.). 348p. 1984. pap. 49.95 (*0-88318-446-X*) Spr-Verlag.

Cameron, A. G., ed. see Cosmochemistry Symposium Staff.

Cameron, A. G. W., ed. see Greisen, Kenneth.

Cameron, Ailsa, ed. see Rinpoche, Lama Thubten Zopa.

Cameron, Ailsa, ed. see Yeshe, Lama Thubten.

Cameron, Alan. Bank of Scotland 1695-1995: A Very Singular Institution. (Illus.). 256p. 1996. 35.00 (*1-85158-691-1*, Pub. by Mainstream Pubng) Trafalgar.

— Callimachus & His Critics. LC 95-2674. 533p. 1995. text 55.00 (*0-691-04367-1*, Pub. by Princeton U Pr) Cal Prin Full Svc.

— The Greek Anthology from Meleager to Planudes. 432p. (C). 1993. 78.00 (*0-19-814023-1*) OUP.

Cameron, Alan & Long, Jacqueline. Barbarians & Politics at the Court of Arcadius. LC 91-16486. (Transformation of the Classical Heritage Ser.: Vol. XIX). (C). 1993. 65.00 (*0-520-06550-6*, Pub. by U CA Pr) Cal Prin Full Svc.

C

Cameron, Alastair. The Principles of Lubrication. LC 67-70366. 625p. reprint ed. pap. 193.80 (*0-608-18645-7*, 205594300040) Bks Demand.

Cameron, Alex D. Go Listen to the Crofters. (C). 1989. 53.70 (*0-86152-063-7*, Pub. by Acair Ltd) St Mut.

***Cameron, Alex J.** Vocabulary Workshop Level C: Interactive Audio Pronunciation Program. 2p. (YA). (gr. 8-9). 1998. pap. 33.00 incl. audio (*0-8215-0688-9*) Sadlier.

— Vocabulary Workshop Level D: Interactive Audio Pronunciation Program. 2p. (YA). (gr. 9-10). 1998. pap. 33.00 incl. audio (*0-8215-0689-7*) Sadlier.

— Vocabulary Workshop Level A: Interactive Audio Pronunciation Program. 2p. (YA). (gr. 6-7). 1998. pap. 33.00 incl. audio (*0-8215-0686-2*) Sadlier.

— Vocabulary Workshop Level B: Interactive Audio Pronunciation Program. 2p. (YA). (gr. 7-8). 1998. pap. 33.00 incl. audio (*0-8215-0687-0*) Sadlier.

— Vocabulary Workshop Level E: Interactive Audio Pronunciation Program. 2p. (YA). (gr. 10-11). 1998. pap. 33.00 incl. audio (*0-8215-0690-0*) Sadlier.

— Vocabulary Workshop Level F: Interactive Audio Pronunciation Program. 2p. (YA). (gr. 11-12). 1998. pap. 33.00 incl. audio (*0-8215-0691-9*) Sadlier.

Cameron, Alexander. Poultry in the Pulpit. large type ed. LC 90-29321. 433p. 1991. reprint ed. lib. bdg. 19.95 (*1-56054-126-1*) Thorndike Pr.

— Reliquiae Celticae, 2 vols. MacBain, Alexander & Kennedy, John K., eds. LC 78-72621. (Celtic Language & Literature Ser.: Goidelic & Brythonic). reprint ed. 84.50 (*0-404-17543-0*) AMS Pr.

— Vet in the Vestry. large type ed. LC 90-10793. 451p. 1990. lib. bdg. 17.95 (*0-89621-993-3*) Thorndike Pr.

Cameron, Alison S. Chinese Painting Techniques. LC 99-36978. (Illus.). 226p. 1999. reprint ed. pap. text 22.95 (*0-486-40708-X*) Dover.

Cameron, Allan, tr. see Camporesi, Piero.

***Cameron, Andrew.** Express Newspapers: The Inside Story of a Turbulent Decade. (Illus.). 2000. 26.95 (*1-902809-44-0*, London House) Allison & Busby.

Cameron, Andrew, ed. The Man Who Loved to Draw Horses: James Howe, 1780-1836. 96p. 1986. pap. text 10.00 (*0-08-032466-5*, Pub. by Aberdeen U Pr) Macmillan.

***Cameron, Andy.** Stereolab: One Note Samba. 128p. 2000. pap. write for info. (*1-58754-004-5*, Pub. by Olmstead Pr) LPC Group.

Cameron, Angus, et al, eds. Old English Word Studies: A Preliminary Author & Word Index. (McMaster Old English Studies & Texts). 208p. 1983. text 65.00 (*0-8020-5526-5*) U of Toronto Pr.

Cameron, Angus & Jones, Judith B. The L. L. Bean Game & Fish Cookbook. (Illus.). 475p. 1983. 25.95 (*0-394-51191-3*) Random.

Cameron, Angus, ed. see Frank, Roberta.

Cameron, Ann. Gloria's Way. LC 99-12104. (Illus.). 112p. (J). (ps-3). 2000. 15.00 (*0-374-32670-3*) FS&G.

— Julian, Dream Doctor. (Illus.). (J). (gr. 3). 1995. 8.60 (*0-395-73237-9*) HM.

— Julian, Dream Doctor. LC 89-37562. (Stepping Stone Bks). (Illus.). 64p. (J). (ps-3). 1990. lib. bdg. 11.99 (*0-679-90524-3*, Pub. by Random Bks Yng Read) Random.

— Julian, Dream Doctor. LC 89-37562. (Stepping Stone Bks). (Illus.). 64p. (J). (gr. 4-7). 1993. pap. 3.99 (*0-679-80524-9*, Pub. by Random Bks Yng Read) Random.

— Julian, Dream Doctor. LC 89-37562. (Stepping Stone Bks.). 1990. 9.19 (*0-606-09497-0*, Pub. by Turtleback) Demco.

— Julian, Dream Doctor. large type ed. (Illus.). 76p. (J). (gr. 3). 19.00 (*0-614-20599-9*, L-38178-00 APHB) Am Printing Hse.

Cameron, Ann. Julian, Secret Agent. LC 88-4428. (Stepping Stone Bks). (Illus.). 64p. (J). (gr. 4-7). 1988. pap. 0.03 (*0-394-81949-7*, Pub. by Random Bks Yng Read) Random.

Cameron, Ann. Julian, Secret Agent. (Stepping Stone Bks.). (J). 1988. 9.19 (*0-606-03835-3*, Pub. by Turtleback) Demco.

— Julian's Glorious Summer. LC 86-33828. (Stepping Stone Bks). (Illus.). 64p. (J). (ps-3). 1987. pap. 3.99 (*0-394-89117-1*, Pub. by Random Bks Yng Read) Random.

— Julian's Glorious Summer. LC 86-33828. (Stepping Stone Bks.). 1987. 9.19 (*0-606-10235-3*, Pub. by Turtleback) Demco.

— Julian's Glorious Summer. large type ed. (Illus.). 1993. 17.50 (*0-614-09833-5*, L-34086-00) Am Printing Hse.

— The Kidnapped Prince: The Life of Olaudah Equiano. 160p. 2000. pap. 4.99 (*0-375-80346-7*) Vin Bks.

— More Stories Huey Tells. LC 96-18420. (Illus.). 128p. (J). (gr. 3-5). 1997. 13.00 (*0-374-35065-5*) FS&G.

— More Stories Huey Tells. LC 98-26989. (J). 1999. pap. 4.99 (*0-679-88363-0*) Knopf.

— More Stories Huey Tells. (J). 1998. pap. 4.99 (*0-679-88576-5*, Pub. by Knopf Bks Yng Read) Random.

— More Stories Julian Tells. (J). 1986. 10.09 (*0-606-04278-4*, Pub. by Turtleback) Demco.

— More Stories Julian Tells. LC 84-10095. (Illus.). 96p. (J). (gr. k-3). 1989. reprint ed. pap. 4.99 (*0-394-82454-7*, Pub. by Knopf Bks Yng Read) Random.

— The Most Beautiful Place in the World. (J). 1993. 9.19 (*0-606-05475-8*, Pub. by Turtleback) Demco.

— The Secret Life of Amanda K. Woods. LC 97-24132. 208p. (J). (gr. 5-9). 1998. 16.00 (*0-374-36702-7*) FS&G.

— The Secret Life of Amanda K. Woods. LC 99-25547. (Illus.). (YA). (gr. 5-9). 1999. pap. 4.99 (*0-14-130642-4*, PuffinBks) Peng Put Young Read.

***Cameron, Ann.** The Secret Life of Amanda K. Woods. LC 00-41185. (Illus.). 2000. write for info. (*0-7862-2777-X*) Thorndike Pr.

Cameron, Ann. The Stories Huey Tells. LC 94-6221. (Illus.). 112p. (J). (gr. k-4). 1995. 16.00 (*0-679-86732-5*, Pub. by Knopf Bks Yng Read) Random.

— The Stories Huey Tells. 1997. 10.09 (*0-606-13042-X*, Pub. by Turtleback) Demco.

— The Stories Huey Tells. (Illus.). 112p. (J). (gr. 1-5). 1997. reprint ed. pap. 4.99 (*0-679-88559-5*, Pub. by Knopf Bks Yng Read) Random.

— The Stories Julian Tells. (J). 1995. pap. text 13.10 (*0-15-305580-4*) Harcourt.

***Cameron, Ann.** The Stories Julian Tells. (J). 1999. 9.95 (*1-56137-671-X*) Novel Units.

Cameron, Ann. The Stories Julian Tells. LC 80-18023. (Illus.). 96p. (J). (gr. k-5). 1981. lib. bdg. 15.99 (*0-394-94301-5*) Pantheon.

— The Stories Julian Tells. (J). 1996. pap. 3.99 (*0-679-88125-5*, Pub. by Random Bks Yng Read) Random.

— The Stories Julian Tells. (J). 1981. 10.19 (*0-606-03480-3*, Pub. by Turtleback) Demco.

— The Stories Julian Tells. LC 80-18023. (Illus.). 88p. (J). (gr. k-3). 1989. reprint ed. pap. 4.99 (*0-394-82892-5*, Pub. by Knopf Bks Yng Read) Random.

Cameron, Ann, adapted by. The Kidnapped Prince: The Life of Olaudah Equiano. LC 93-29914. (Illus.). 144p. (J). (gr. 4-9). 1995. 16.00 (*0-679-85619-6*, Pub. by Knopf Bks Yng Read) Random.

***Cameron, Anne.** Aftermath. 400p. 1999. pap. 18.95 (*1-55017-193-3*) Harbour Pub Co.

Cameron, Anne. Child of Her People. LC 87-62315. 204p. (Orig.). 1987. pap. 10.95 (*0-933216-28-9*) Spinsters Ink.

— Daughters of Copper Woman. large type ed. 256p. 1981. pap. 19.95 (*0-88974-055-0*, Pub. by Press Gang Pubs) LPC InBook.

— Daughters of Copper Woman. large type ed. 152p. 1981. pap. 12.95 (*0-88974-022-4*, Pub. by Press Gang Pubs) LPC InBook.

***Cameron, Anne.** Dreamspeaker. (J). 2000. pap. 6.99 (*0-7736-7482-9*, Stoddart Kids) Stoddart Publ.

Cameron, Anne. Dzelarhons: Mythology of the Northwest Coast. 160p. (Orig.). 1987. pap. text 10.95 (*0-920080-89-8*) Harbour Bks.

— The Journey. LC 86-62137. 314p. 1986. reprint ed. pap. 9.95 (*0-933216-24-6*) Spinsters Ink.

Cameron, Anne. Kick the Can. 176p. (Orig.). 1997. pap. text 15.95 (*1-55017-039-2*) Harbour Pub Co.

Cameron, Archie. Bare Feet & Tackety Boots. LC 99-185050. 164p. (C). 1989. 14.95 (*0-946487-17-0*) Luath Pr Ltd.

Cameron, Ardis. Radicals of the Worst Sort: Laboring Women in Lawrence, Massachusetts, 1860-1912. LC 92-39119. (Working Class in American History - Women in American History Ser.). 240p. 1993. 36.95 (*0-252-02013-8*) U of Ill Pr.

— Radicals of the Worst Sort: Laboring Women in Lawrence, Massachusetts, 1860-1912. (Illus.). 260p. (C). 1995. pap. text 16.95 (*0-252-06318-X*) U of Ill Pr.

Cameron, Averil. Changing Cultures in Early Byzantium. (Variorum Collected Studies: No. CS536). 350p. 1996. 109.95 (*0-86078-587-4*, Pub. by Variorum) Ashgate Pub Co.

— Christianity & the Rhetoric of Empire: The Development of Christian Discourse. 1991. pap. 16.95 (*0-520-08923-5*, Pub. by U CA Pr) Cal Prin Full Svc.

— Christianity & the Rhetoric of Empire: The Development of Christian Discourse. LC 90-39376. (Sather Classical Lectures: No. 55). (Illus.). 275p. 1991. 50.00 (*0-520-07160-3*, Pub. by U CA Pr) Cal Prin Full Svc.

— The Later Roman Empire, AD 284-430. LC 92-41000. 256p. 1993. 36.50 (*0-674-51193-X*); pap. 16.00 (*0-674-51194-8*) HUP.

— The Mediterranean World in Late Antiquity, AD 395-600. LC 92-34600. (History of the Ancient World Ser.). (Illus.). 264p. (C). (gr. 13). 1993. pap. 24.99 (*0-415-01421-2*) Routledge.

— Procopius. 312p. (C). 1996. pap. 27.99 (*0-415-14294-6*) Routledge.

Cameron, Averil, ed. The Byzantine & Early Islamic Near East: States, Resources & Armies. (Studies on Late Antiquity & Early Islam: No. 1, Vol. III). xvi, 491p. 1995. 35.00 (*0-87850-107-X*) Darwin Pr.

***Cameron, Averil, et al, eds.** Late Antiquity: Empire & Successors, AD 425-600, Vol. 14. (The Cambridge Ancient History Ser.). (Illus.). 1152p. (C). 2001. Price not set. (*0-521-32591-9*) Cambridge U Pr.

Cameron, Averil & Conrad, Lawrence I., eds. The Byzantine & Early Islamic Near East: Problems in the Literary Source Material. LC 92-352. (Studies in Late Antiquity & Early Islam: No. 1, Vol. I). (Illus.). xiv, 428p. 1992. 29.95 (*0-87850-080-4*) Darwin Pr.

Cameron, Averil & Garnsey, Peter, eds. The Cambridge Ancient History Vol. 13: The Late Empire, A. D. 337-425. 905p. (C). 1998. text 150.00 (*0-521-30200-5*) Cambridge U Pr.

Cameron, Averil, ed. see Eusebius.

Cameron, Averil, jt. ed. see King, G. R.

Cameron-Bandler, Leslie. Solutions: Practical & Effective Antidotes for Sexual & Relationship Problems. rev. ed. LC 85-70138. 259p. (C). 1985. pap. 11.95 (*0-932573-01-0*) Real People.

Cameron-Bandler, Leslie & Lebeau, Michael. The Emotional Hostage: Rescuing Your Emotional Life. LC 85-81627. 221p. 1986. pap. 13.50 (*0-932573-03-7*) Real People.

Cameron-Bandler, Leslie, et al. The Emprint Method: A Guide to Reproducing Competence. LC 85-80457. 335p. (C). 1985. pap. 13.50 (*0-932573-02-9*) Real People.

— Know How: Guided Programs for Inventing Your Own Best Future. LC 85-80006. 270p. 1985. pap. 11.95 (*0-932573-00-2*) Real People.

Cameron, Barbara. Predictive Planetary Periods. LC 82-73122. 158p. 1984. 17.00 (*0-86690-235-X*, C2645-014) Am Fed Astrologers.

— Turning the Tables. LC 84-71622. 128p. 1984. 15.00 (*0-86690-282-1*, C2559-014) Am Fed Astrologers.

Cameron, Barbara, ed. A Gift of Dreams: Creative Grief. (Illus.). 36p. 1993. pap. 3.00 (*0-927663-20-1*) COMPAS.

Cameron, Barry. John Metcalf. (Twayne's World Authors Ser.: No. 771). 1986. 22.95 (*0-8057-6622-7*) Macmillan.

Cameron, Barry, ed. Clark Blaise & His Works. (Canadian Author Studies). 69p. (C). 1985. pap. text 9.95 (*0-317-05854-1*, Pub. by ECW) Genl Dist Srvs.

Cameron, Barry L. First Steps. (Orig.). 1990. pap., student ed. 2.00 (*0-9625248-0-8*) First Christian Ch.

Cameron, Beverly J. & Cameron, Norman E. Economics in Action. 192p. (C). 1983. teacher ed. write for info. (*0-318-57727-5*); pap. text 9.00 (*0-312-23656-5*) St Martin.

Cameron, Bradley J., jt. auth. see Reed, Thomas W.

Cameron, Brenda & Cameron, Brian. Making Bent Willow Furniture. LC 98-12990. (Rustic Home Ser.). (Illus.). 139p. 1998. pap. 19.95 (*1-58017-048-X*) Storey Bks.

Cameron, Brian, jt. auth. see Cameron, Brenda.

Cameron, Bruce W. Police Cars: A Graphic History. LC 96-71797. (Illus.). 216p. 1997. write for info. (*0-7853-2196-9*) Pubns Intl Ltd.

Cameron, Bunny. Breakfast with Bunny. 1993. pap. 15.95 (*0-9636411-0-7*) Bombay Hse.

Cameron, Burgess. Input-Output Analysis & Resource Allocation. LC 68-21188. 117p. reprint ed. pap. 33.40 (*0-608-10724-7*, 2050791) Bks Demand.

Cameron, C. & MacDonald, W. A. A Review of Driver-Rider Licensing in Relation to Road Safety. LC 76-354283. (Expert Group on Road Safety Ser.). iv, 54p. 1973. write for info. (*0-642-00322-X*, Pub. by Aust Inst Criminology) Lib Res.

Cameron, Caryn. Freedom Flame. (Harlequin Historical Ser.: No. 49). 1990. per. 3.25 (*0-373-28649-X*) Harlequin Bks.

Cameron, Caryn, et al. Harlequin Historical Christmas Stories. 1991. 384p. (Orig.). 1991. per. 4.99 (*0-373-83225-7*) Harlequin Bks.

***Cameron, Catherine.** Resolving Childhood Trauma: A Long Term Study of Abuse Survivors. LC 99-50448. 340p. 2000. 65.00 (*0-7619-2128-1*) Sage.

Cameron, Catherine M. Dialectics in the Arts: The Rise of Experimentalism in American Music. LC 96-14784. 184p. 1996. 55.00 (*0-275-95610-5*, Praeger Pubs) Greenwood.

— Hopi Houses: Architectural Change at Orayvi LC 98-40105. 1999. 39.95 (*0-8165-1781-9*) U of Ariz Pr.

Cameron, Catherine M. & Tomka, Steve A., eds. Abandonment of Settlements & Regions: Ethnoarchaeological & Archaeological Approaches. (New Directions in Archaeology). (Illus.). 217p. 1996. pap. text 20.95 (*0-521-57469-2*) Cambridge U Pr.

Cameron, Charles. Veto Bargaining: Presidents & the Politics of Negative Power. LC 99-12886. (Political Economy of Institutions & Decisions Ser.). (Illus.). 288p. 2000. 59.95 (*0-521-62391-X*); pap. 18.95 (*0-521-62550-5*) Cambridge U Pr.

Cameron, Charles M. The Problem of Polarization: An Approach Based on the Writings of G. C. Berkouwer. LC 92-34398. (Rutherford Studies in Contemporary Theology: Vol. 2). 616p. 1992. text 129.95 (*0-7734-1633-1*) E Mellen.

Cameron, Chris & Ledford, Cawood. Basketball Pitino Style. Kromer, Ed & Rutledge, J. D., eds. 144p. 1990. pap. 14.95 (*1-879688-05-0*) Host Comns Inc.

Cameron, Christina. Charles Baillairg[00e9]: Architect & Engineer. (Illus.). 236p. (C). 1988. 70.00 (*0-7735-0638-1*, Pub. by McG-Queens Univ Pr) CUP Services.

***Cameron, Christine.** Christmas Kisses. 1999. mass mkt. 5.99 (*0-8217-6299-0*, Zebra Kensgtn) Kensgtn Pub Corp.

Cameron, Christine. Wild Highland Rose. 352p. 1999. mass mkt. 4.99 (*0-8217-6102-1*) Kensgtn Pub Corp.

Cameron, Clark T. & Cameron, Sharon M. Controlling the Game: Controlling Your Attitude in Sales. 100p. 1993. pap. 10.00 (*0-9635820-0-3*) Watershed CA.

Cameron, Colleen, et al. Economics & Microeconomics: Principles & Policy. 7th ed. 672p. (C). 1997. pap. text, teacher ed. 35.00 (*0-03-011737-2*) Dryden Pr.

Cameron, Constance. Archaeological Investigations on the Rancho San Clemente, Orange County, California. (Archives of California Prehistory Ser.: Vol. 27). (Illus.). 270p. (Orig.). (C). 1989. pap. text 28.13 (*1-55567-063-6*) Coyote Press.

Cameron, Constance, ed. Agriculture: Origins & Impacts of a Technological Revolution. LC 90-61361. (Occasional Papers of the Archaeological Research Facility). (Illus.). 83p. (Orig.). (C). 1990. pap. 10.00 (*0-938217-01-1*) CSU Mus Anthrop.

— The Great Apes: A Collection of Papers Presented at the 14th Annual Anthropology Symposium. LC 92-60323. (Occasional Papers of the Archaeological Research Facility: No. 6). (Illus.). 61p. (Orig.). 1992. pap. 10.00 (*0-938217-02-X*) CSU Mus Anthrop.

— Museums & Anthropology: Acquisitions, Curation, Research. LC 86-60694. (Occasional Papers of the Archaeological Research Facility: No. 3). (Illus.). 90p. 1986. pap. 10.00 (*0-938217-00-3*) CSU Mus Anthrop.

Cameron, Craig & Fair, Terry. Buying Your First Computer? This Simple Step by Step Approach Teaches You How to Understand Software, Hardware, & Computer Jargon. Bransom, Christine, ed. (Illus.). 85p. 1995. 24.95 (*1-887760-00-8*) Acad Pubng.

Cameron, Craig M. American Samurai: Myth, Imagination, & the Conduct of Battle in the First Marine Division, 1941-1951. 315p. (C). 1994. 39.95 (*0-521-44168-4*) Cambridge U Pr.

Cameron, Cyril T. Public Relations in the Emergency Department. LC 80-15894. 126p. 1980. text 18.95 (*0-87619-746-2*) P-H.

Cameron, D. A. Arabic-English Dictionary. (ARA & ENG.). 322p. 1979. 24.00 (*0-86685-084-8*, LDL0848, Pub. by Librairie du Liban) Intl Bk Ctr.

Cameron, D. C., jt. ed. see Kramer, J. F.

Cameron, D. Y. Conflicting Tides. large type ed. 320p. 1989. 27.99 (*0-7089-2005-5*) Ulverscroft.

— Enchanting Adventure. large type ed. 290p. 1989. 27.99 (*0-7089-1940-5*) Ulverscroft.

— The Happy Awakening. large type ed. 288p. 1989. 27.99 (*0-7089-2021-7*) Ulverscroft.

— Moonlight & March Roses. large type ed. 1990. 27.99 (*0-7089-2280-5*) Ulverscroft.

— Night Scented Air. large type ed. 1990. pap. 16.99 (*0-7089-6915-1*, Linford) Ulverscroft.

— A Puzzled Heart. large type ed. 320p. 1988. 27.99 (*0-7089-1909-X*) Ulverscroft.

— Twisting Paths. large type ed. 1990. pap. 16.99 (*0-7089-6873-2*) Ulverscroft.

Cameron, Dan. Lewis DeSoto. (Illus.). 36p. 1998. pap. 10.00 (*1-889195-19-7*) Smart Art Pr.

***Cameron, Dan.** Pierre et Gilles. (Illus.). 2000. 35.00 (*1-85894-113-X*, Pub. by Merrell Holberton) Rizzoli Intl.

Cameron, Dan. William Kentridge. (Contemporary Artists Ser.). 1999. 29.95 (*0-7148-3829-2*) Phaidon Pr.

— Willie Doherty. LC 93-79935. (Illus.). 64p. 1994. 20.00 (*0-934349-11-8*) Grey Art Gallery Study Ctr.

Cameron, Dan & Merewether, Charles. Unland: The Work of Doris Salcedo. LC 97-75682. (Illus.). 80p. 1998. pap. 22.95 (*0-915557-81-9*) New Mus Contemp Art.

Cameron, Dan, et al. Carolee Schneemann: Up to & Including Her Limits. LC 96-71007. (Illus.). 68p. (Orig.). (C). 1996. pap. 21.95 (*0-915557-80-0*) New Mus Contemp Art.

— Investigations 1985. (Illus.). 1985. pap. 7.50 (*0-88454-039-1*) U of Pa Contemp Art.

— Investigations 1987. 21p. 1988. pap. 7.50 (*0-88454-045-6*) U of Pa Contemp Art.

— Marcel Odenbach. LC 98-66517. (Illus.). 56p. 1998. pap. 22.00 (*0-915557-82-7*) New Mus Contemp Art.

Cameron, Dan, jt. auth. see Grachos, Louis.

Cameron, Dan, jt. auth. see Louver Gallery New York Staff.

Cameron, Dan, ed. see New Museum of Contemporary Art Staff (New York, N. & Akron Art Museum Staff.

Cameron, Dan, ed. see New Museum of Contemporary Art Staff (New York, N., et al.

Cameron, Dana, ed. see Ricketts, Marijane G.

Cameron, Darrell L., ed. see Malone, Raven.

Cameron, David, ed. The Referendum Papers: Essays on Secession & National Unity. 544p. 1999. text 65.00 (*0-8020-4449-2*); pap. text 29.95 (*0-8020-8238-6*) U of Toronto Pr.

An Asterisk (*) at the beginning of an entry indicates that the title is appearing for the first time.

Cameron, David K. The Cornkister Days: A Portrait of a Land & Its Rituals. (Illus.). 264p. pap. 17.95 (*1-874744-18-1*, Pub. by Birlinn Ltd) Dufour.
— The English Fair. LC 98-234215. (Illus.). 265p. 1998. 35.00 (*0-7509-1772-5*, Pub. by Sutton Pub Ltd) Intl Pubs Mktg.
— Willie Gavin, Crofter Man: A Portrait of a Vanished Lifestyle. (Illus.). 222p. pap. 17.95 (*1-874744-17-3*, Pub. by Birlinn Ltd) Dufour.
Cameron, David M. More Than an Academic Question: Universities, Government & Public Policy in Canada. 471p. 1991. pap. 35.95 (*0-88645-134-5*, Pub. by Inst Res Pub) Ashgate Pub Co.
Cameron, Deborah. Feminism & Linguistic Theory. 2nd ed. LC 92-8906. 257p. 1992. pap. 19.95 (*0-312-08376-9*) St Martin.
— The Feminist Critique of Language: A Reader. 2nd ed. LC 97-23068. 392p. (C). 1998. pap. 24.99 (*0-415-16400-1*) Routledge.
— The Feminist Critique of Language: A Reader. 2nd ed. LC 97-23068. 392p. (C). 1998. 75.00 (*0-415-16399-4*) Routledge.
— Verbal Hygiene. LC 94-39801. (Politics of Language Ser.). 278p. (C). 1995. pap. 21.99 (*0-415-10355-X*, C0119) Routledge.
Cameron, Deborah, jt. ed. see Coates, Jennifer.
***Cameron, Debra.** Business-to-Business E-Commerce Strategies. 200p. 2000. pap. 290.00 (*1-56607-084-8*) Comput Tech Res.
Cameron, Debra. E-Commerce Security Strategies: Protecting the Enterprise. LC 98-24938. (Illus.). 243p. 1998. pap. 285.00 (*1-56607-057-0*) Comput Tech Res.
— Electronic Commerce: The New Business Platform for the Internet. LC 96-50425. (Illus.). 226p. 1999. pap. 295.00 (*1-56607-985-3*) Comput Tech Res.
***Cameron, Debra.** Global Network Security: Threats & Countermeasures. LC 99-43207. (Illus.). 208p. 2000. pap. 290.00 (*1-56607-077-5*) Comput Tech Res.
Cameron, Debra. GNU Emacs Pocket Reference. Estabrook, Gigi, ed. (Illus.). 62p. 1998. reprint ed. pap. 8.95 (*1-56592-496-7*) OReilly & Assocs.
— Implementing Next-Generation E-Business Strategies. LC 99-16330. (Illus.). 190p. 1999. pap. 295.00 (*1-56607-073-2*) Comput Tech Res.
— Implementing the Internet for Business. LC 95-16295. (Illus.). 301p. (Orig.). 1996. pap. 275.00 (*1-56607-952-7*) Comput Tech Res.
— The Internet: A Global Business Opportunity. LC 94-25076. (Illus.). 223p. 1996. pap. 290.00 (*1-56607-035-X*) Comput Tech Res.
— Internet 2: The Future of the Internet & Next-Generation Initiatives. LC 98-46356. (Illus.). 150p. 1999. pap. 290.00 (*1-56607-064-3*) Comput Tech Res.
— Intranet Security. LC 97-24165. (Illus.). 218p. (Orig.). 1997. pap. 295.00 (*1-56607-990-X*) Comput Tech Res.
— Intranets: Technical Issues & Business Applications. LC 96-34308. (Illus.). 196p. (Orig.). 1998. pap. 290.00 (*1-56607-976-4*) Comput Tech Res.
— Java Strategies: High-Performance Application Development for the Internet & Intranets. LC 98-4498. (Illus.). 196p. 1998. pap. 280.00 (*1-56607-051-1*) Comput Tech Res.
— Security Issues for the Internet & the World Wide Web. LC 96-15422. (Illus.). 219p. 1997. pap. 290.00 (*1-56607-973-X*) Comput Tech Res.
— The World Wide Web: Strategies & Opportunities for Business. LC 95-50704. (Illus.). 243p. 1996. pap. 290.00 (*1-56607-959-4*) Comput Tech Res.
***Cameron, Del.** Call of the Hounds. LC 99-96522. (Illus.). 269p. 1999. 14.95 (*0-912299-90-8*) Stoneydale Pr Pub.
Cameron, Don. Keeper of the Town. (Illus.). 128p. (Orig.). 1996. pap. 11.95 (*1-886028-15-X*) Savage Pr.
Cameron, Don, jt. auth. see Finger, Bill.
Cameron, Doug. Liberating Solutions to Alcohol Problems: Treating Problem Drinkers Without Saying No. LC 94-47466. 1995. reprint ed. 50.00 (*1-56821-462-6*) Aronson.
Cameron, E., et al. The New Labour Relations Act - The Law after the 1988 Amendments. 305p. 1989. pap. write for info. (*0-7021-2235-1*, Pub. by Juta & Co) Gaunt.
Cameron, E., jt. auth. see Honore, A. M.
Cameron, E. C., ed. see Laser Tech Staff.
Cameron, E. E., jt. ed. see Cogger, H. G.
Cameron, Edwin, ed. Juta's Index & Annotations to the South African Law Reports Vols. 1-10: Cumulative Index, 1980-1989. 183p. 1990. pap. write for info. (*0-7021-2517-2*, Pub. by Juta & Co) Gaunt.
Cameron, Edwin & Gevisser, Mark, eds. Defiant Desire: Gay & Lesbian Lives in South Africa. LC 94-22150. 374p. (C). (gr. 13). 1995. 80.00 (*0-415-91060-9*, B4485); pap. 21.99 (*0-415-91061-7*, B4489) Routledge.
Cameron, Eleanor. The Court of the Stone Children. 192p. (J). (gr. 4 up). 1990. pap. 4.99 (*0-14-034289-3*, PuffinBks) Peng Put Young Read.
— The Court of the Stone Children. (J). 1994. 18.75 (*0-8446-6757-9*) Peter Smith.
Cameron, Eleanor. Court of the Stone Children. (J). 1968. 10.09 (*0-606-03169-3*, Pub. by Turtleback) Demco.
Cameron, Eleanor. Mr. Bass's Planetoid. (Illus.). (J). (gr. 3-7). 1958. 14.95 (*0-316-12525-3*, Joy St Bks) Little.
— A Spell Is Cast. 1992. 23.25 (*0-8446-6560-6*) Peter Smith.
— The Wonderful Flight to the Mushroom Planet. (Illus.). 195p. (J). (gr. 4-6). 1988. pap. 7.95 (*0-316-12540-7*, Joy St Bks) Little.
***Cameron, Eleanor.** The Wonderful Flight to the Mushroom Planet. (J). (gr. 4-8). 2000. 21.00 (*0-8446-7139-8*) Peter Smith.
Cameron, Eleanor. The Wonderful Flight to the Mushroom Planet. 1988. 12.05 (*0-606-12581-7*, Pub. by Turtleback) Demco.
Cameron, Elisabeth & Lewis, Philippa. Potters on Pottery. (Illus.). 1976. 11.95 (*0-312-63280-0*) St Martin.
Cameron, Elisabeth L. & Ross, Doran H. Isn't She a Doll? Play & Ritual in African Sculpture. LC 96-43304. (Illus.). 124p. 1996. 45.00 (*0-930741-54-4*) UCLA Fowler Mus.
Cameron, Elisabeth L & Ross, Doran H. Isn't She a Doll? Play & Ritual in African Sculpture. LC 96-43304. (Illus.). 124p. 1996. pap. 24.00 (*0-930741-55-2*) UCLA Fowler Mus.
Cameron, Elizabeth R., tr. see Lusseyran, Jacques.
Cameron, Ellen. Understanding Graphology. 1987. 5.95 (*0-85030-818-6*, Pub. by Aqrn Pr) Harper SF.
Cameron, Elsa, ed. Airport Cafe. (Illus.). 80p. 1986. write for info. (*0-9617165-0-9*) Cmnty Arts.
— Chairs: An Exhibition. (Illus.). 36p. 1986. write for info. (*0-9617165-1-7*) Cmnty Arts.
Cameron, Elspeth. Hugh MacLennan: A Writer's Life. 421p. 1981. mass mkt. 5.95 (*0-88780-104-8*, Pub. by Formac Publ Co) Formac Dist Ltd.
Cameron, Elspeth. Hugh MacLennan: A Writer's Life. 424p. 1981. text 30.00 (*0-8020-5556-7*) U of Toronto Pr.
— Hugh MacLennan: An Annotated Bibliography. 153p. (C). 1979. pap. 9.00 (*0-920763-58-8*, Pub. by ECW) Genl Dist Srvs.
***Cameron, Esther.** Facilitation Made Easy. 160p. 1998. pap. 24.95 (*0-7494-2756-6*, Kogan Pg Educ) Stylus Pub VA.
Cameron, Esther, tr. see Mendes-Flohr, Paul R., ed.
Cameron, Euan. The European Reformation. (Illus.). 580p. 1991. pap. text 27.50 (*0-19-873093-4*) OUP.
— The Reformation of the Heretics: The Waldenses of the Alps, 1480-1580. (Oxford Historical Monographs). (Illus.). 291p. 1984. 59.00 (*0-19-822930-5*) OUP.
Cameron, Euan, ed. Early Modern Europe. LC 98-26115. (Illus.). 434p. 1999. 39.95 (*0-19-820528-7*) OUP.
Cameron, Eugene N. At the Crossroads: The Mineral Problems of the United States. LC 85-29587. (Wiley-Interscience Publications). 344p. reprint ed. pap. 106.70 (*0-7837-2389-X*, 204007400006) Bks Demand.
— The Mineral Position of the United States, 1975-2000. LC 72-7983. 181p. 1973. reprint ed. pap. 56.20 (*0-608-01924-0*, 206257900003) Bks Demand.
Cameron, Eugene N., et al. Internal Structure of Granitic Pegmatites. LC QE0462.P4. (Economic Geology, Monograph: No. 2). 172p. reprint ed. pap. 53.40 (*0-608-13792-8*, 202033600017) Bks Demand.
Cameron, Evan W., tr. see Green, Julian.
Cameron, Ewan & Pauling, Linus. Cancer & Vitamin C: A Discussion of the Nature, Causes, Prevention, & Treatment of Cancer, with Special Reference to the Value of Vitamin C. rev. ed. LC 93-12150. (Illus.). 278p. 1993. pap. 13.95 (*0-940159-21-X*) Camino Bks.
Cameron, Faye. Moneyblocks: How to Let Go & Get Going Financially. 150p. 1991. pap. 7.95 (*0-9630261-0-0*) Dunbar CO.
Cameron, Frank. Cottrell: Samaritan of Science. 416p. 1993. reprint ed. pap. 19.95 (*0-9633504-2-0*) Res Corp.
***Cameron, Fraser.** The Foreign & Security Policy of the European Union: Past, Present & Future. (Contemporary European Studies: No. 7). 160p. 1999. pap. 16.95 (*1-84127-001-6*, Pub. by Sheffield Acad) CUP Services.
Cameron, G., jt. ed. see Rothery, M.
Cameron, Gary & Vanderwoerd, Jim R. Protecting Children & Supporting Families: Promising Programs & Organizational Realities. LC 96-33570. (Modern Applications of Social Work Ser.). 301p. 1997. pap. text 22.95 (*0-202-36106-3*); lib. bdg. 45.95 (*0-202-36105-5*) Aldine de Gruyter.
Cameron, Gay. The Defendant. 1997. per. 3.75 (*0-373-22404-4*, 1-22404-7) Silhouette.
— His Brother's Keeper. (Intrigue Ser.). 1994. per. 2.99 (*0-373-22264-5*, 1-22264-5) Harlequin Bks.
Cameron, George & Scaletta, Phillip J., Jr. Business Law: Text & Cases. 3rd ed. (C). 1989. student ed. 21.95 (*0-256-07245-0*, Irwn McGrw-H) McGrw-H Hghr Educ.
Cameron, George C. History of Early Iran. 1976. lib. bdg. 69.95 (*0-8490-1972-9*) Gordon Pr.
Cameron, George D. The Soviet Lawyer & His System: A Historical & Bibliographic Study. LC 78-9652. (Michigan International Business Studies: No. 14). 210p. reprint ed. pap. 65.10 (*0-608-15385-0*, 205635900060) Bks Demand.
Cameron, George G. History of Early Iran. LC DS0275.C3. (Midway Reprint Ser.). 273p. reprint ed. pap. 84.70 (*0-608-16533-6*, 202676800052) Bks Demand.
Cameron, George G. Persepolis Treasury Tablets. 1997. lib. bdg. 7.50 (*0-226-09227-5*) U Ch Pr.
Cameron, George G., ed. see Chiera, Edward.
Cameron, Glenn & Momen, Wendi. A Basic Baha'i Chronology. LC 97-100926. (Illus.). 550p. (Orig.). 1996. pap. 29.95 (*0-85398-404-2*) G Ronald Pub.
Cameron, Gloria. Mango Spice. (J). pap. write for info. (*0-7136-2107-9*, 93118, Pub. by A & C Blk) Midpt Trade.
Cameron, Gordon C. Regional Economic Development: The Federal Role. LC 77-86390. (Resources for the Future Ser.). reprint ed. 37.50 (*0-404-60329-7*) AMS Pr.
— Regional Economic Development: The Federal Role. LC 70-142108. 225p. reprint ed. pap. 69.80 (*0-7837-3576-6*, 204343500009) Bks Demand.
Cameron, Gregory N., ed. Anthology of Contemporary Poetry. (Illus.). 208p. 1988. 24.95 (*0-944653-00-6*) Silver State Pub.
Cameron, Greta, jt. ed. see Danson, Mike.
Cameron, I. R. Nuclear Fission Reactors. LC 82-18128. 398p. 1982. 85.00 (*0-306-41073-7*, Plenum Trade) Perseus Pubng.
Cameron, I. T., et al, eds. Clinical Disorders of the Endometrium & Menstrual Cycle. (Illus.). 462p. 1998. text 149.50 (*0-19-262724-4*) OUP.
Cameron, Iain. The Protective Principle of International Criminal Jurisdiction. 412p. 1993. 87.95 (*1-85521-366-4*, Pub. by Dartmth Pub) Ashgate Pub Co.
Cameron, Iain A. Crime & Repression in the Auvergne & the Guyenne, 1720-1790. LC 80-841953. 299p. reprint ed. pap. 85.30 (*0-608-15701-5*, 2031628) Bks Demand.
Cameron, Ian. Island at the Top of the World. 1976. 20.95 (*0-8488-0445-7*) Amereon Ltd.
— Kingdom of the Sun God: A History of the Andes & Their People. LC 90-37627. (Illus.). 240p. 1990. reprint ed. pap. 74.40 (*0-7837-8152-0*, 204785700008) Bks Demand.
— One Hundred Twenty-Five Years of State Public Works, 1895-1984. 324p. (C). 1990. 90.00 (*0-86439-083-1*, Pub. by Boolarong Pubns) St Mut.
Cameron, Ian, ed. The Jimmy Shand Story. 208p. 1994. 45.00 (*1-84017-019-0*) St Mut.
Cameron, Ian & Pye, Douglas, eds. The Book of Westerns. LC 94-25280. (Illus.). 320p. 1996. 27.95 (*0-8264-0818-4*) Continuum.
Cameron, J. & Dodd, W. A. Society, Schools & Progress in Tanzania. 1970. 127.00 (*0-08-015564-2*, Pub. by Pergamon Repr) Franklin.
Cameron, J. A., jt. auth. see Sheridan, M. B.
Cameron, J. D. Omega Sub, No. 1. 256p. 1991. pap. 2.95 (*0-380-76049-5*, Avon Bks) Morrow Avon.
— Omega Sub No. 2: Command Decision. 240p. 1991. pap. 2.95 (*0-380-76206-4*, Avon Bks) Morrow Avon.
— Omega Sub No. 3: City of Fear. 192p. (Orig.). 1991. pap. 2.95 (*0-380-76050-9*, Avon Bks) Morrow Avon.
— Omega Sub No. 4: Blood Tide. 224p. (Orig.). 1991. pap. 3.50 (*0-380-76321-4*, Avon Bks) Morrow Avon.
— Omega Sub No. 5: Death Dive. 224p. (Orig.). 1992. pap. 3.50 (*0-380-76492-X*, Avon Bks) Morrow Avon.
— Omega Sub No. 6: Raven Rising. 224p. (Orig.). 1992. pap. 3.50 (*0-380-76493-8*, Avon Bks) Morrow Avon.
Cameron, J. M., et al, eds. New Frontiers in Particle Physics: Proceedings of the 1st Lake Louise Winter Institute, Lake Louise, Canada, February 16-22, 1986. 650p. 1986. text 124.00 (*9971-5-0135-X*) World Scientific Pub.
Cameron, J. M., tr. see Picard, Max.
Cameron, J. Stewart. Kidney Failure: The Facts. 2nd ed. (The Facts Ser.). (Illus.). 248p. 1996. pap. text 19.95 (*0-19-262643-4*) OUP.
Cameron, J. Stewart & Glassock, Richard J. The Nephrotic Syndrome. (Kidney Disease Ser.: Vol. 8). (Illus.). 1080p. 1987. text 299.00 (*0-8247-7361-6*) Dekker.
***Cameron, James.** James Cameron's Titanic Holiday. 1998. 39.95 (*0-06-019347-6*) HarpC.
Cameron, James. A Time of Terror. 207p. 1994. 22.00 (*0-933121-45-8*); pap. 14.95 (*0-933121-44-X*) Black Classic.
— Titanic: James Cameron's Illustrated Screenplay. LC 99-194412. (Illus.). 368p. 1999. pap. 30.00 (*0-06-095307-1*, Perennial) HarperTrade.
Cameron, James, et al, eds. Trade & the Environment: The Search for Balance, 2 vols. LC 96-120920. (Environmental Law Ser.). 1200p. 1994. 275.00 (*1-874698-55-4*, Pub. by Cameron May) Gaunt.
***Cameron, James, et al, eds.** Trade & the Environment--Law & Policy: Introduction, Cases & Materials. 1999. pap. 320.00 (*1-874698-18-X*, Pub. by Cameron May) Gaunt.
Cameron, James & Campbell, Karen, eds. Dispute Resolution in the WTO. (International Law Ser.). 421p. 1998. 136.00 (*1-874698-51-1*, Pub. by Cameron May) Gaunt.
Cameron, James & Fijalkowski, Agata, eds. Trade & the Environment: Bridging the Gap. 1998. 65.00 (*1-874698-17-1*) Gaunt.
Cameron, James & O'Riordan, Timothy. Interpret Precaution Principle. 1993. 32.00 (*1-85383-200-6*, Pub. by Escan Pubns) Island Pr.
Cameron, James & Wisher, William. Terminator 2: Judgment Day: The Book of the Film. (Screenplay Ser.). (Illus.). 336p. (Orig.). 1991. pap. 17.95 (*1-55783-097-5*) Applause Theatre Bk Pubs.
Cameron, James, jt. ed. see O'Riordan, Tim.
Cameron, James B. Life in Advertising & at War. (C). 1989. text 80.00 (*1-85821-020-8*, Pub. by Pentland Pr) St Mut.
Cameron, James D. For the People: A History of St Francis Xavier University. LC 96-222627. (Illus.). 576p. 1996. 55.00 (*0-7735-1385-X*, Pub. by McG-Queens Univ Pr) CUP Services.
Cameron, James M. Images of Authority: A Consideration of the Concepts of "Regnum" & "Sacerdotium" LC 66-12489. 97p. reprint ed. pap. 30.10 (*0-8357-9261-7*, 201676900006) Bks Demand.
— Nuclear Catholics & Other Essays. LC 89-28096. 277p. reprint ed. pap. 85.90 (*0-7837-3184-1*, 204278800006) Bks Demand.
— On the Idea of a University. LC 78-318149. 106p. reprint ed. pap. 32.90 (*0-8357-4135-4*, 203690700006) Bks Demand.
Cameron, James N. The Respiratory Physiology of Animals. (Illus.). 368p. 1989. text 70.00 (*0-19-506019-9*) OUP.
Cameron, Jane. Without Issue: New Zealanders Who Choose Not to Have Children. LC 97-221508. 240 p. 1997. pap. 29.95 (*0-908812-66-3*, Pub. by Canterbury Univ) Accents Pubns.
Cameron, Jane, jt. auth. see Layman, C. H.
Cameron, Janet E. Double-Crostics, Vol. 6. 1982. pap. 5.00 (*0-8317-2415-3*) Smithmark.
— Double-Crostics, Vol. 7. 1982. pap. 5.00 (*0-8317-2416-1*) Smithmark.
— Double-Crostics, Vol. 8. 1982. pap. 5.00 (*0-8317-2417-X*) Smithmark.
— Double-Crostics, Vol. 9. 1982. pap. 5.00 (*0-8317-2418-8*) Smithmark.
— Double-Crostics, Vol. 10. 1982. pap. 5.00 (*0-8317-2419-6*) Smithmark.
— Double-Crostics, Vol. 11. 1982. pap. 5.00 (*0-8317-2420-X*) Smithmark.
— Double-Crostics, Vol. 12. 1982. pap. 5.00 (*0-8317-2421-8*) Smithmark.
— Double-Crostics, Vol. 13. 1982. pap. 5.00 (*0-8317-2422-6*) Smithmark.
— Double-Crostics, Vol. 14. 1982. pap. 5.00 (*0-8317-2411-0*) Smithmark.
Cameron, Jean. Anne Hutchinson, Guilty or Not? A Closer Look at Her Trials. LC 93-17290. (American University Studies: History: Ser. IX, Vol. 146). VIII, 240p. (C). 1994. text 45.95 (*0-8204-2227-4*) P Lang Pubng.
Cameron, Jean W. The Orchids of Maine. 1976. pap. 8.95 (*0-89101-001-7*) U Maine Pr.
Cameron, Jenks. The Bureau of Biological Survey: Its History, Activities & Organization. LC 72-3071. (Brookings Institution. Institute for Government Research. Service Monographs of the U. S. Government: No. 54). reprint ed. 42.50 (*0-404-57154-9*) AMS Pr.
— The Bureau of Biological Survey: Its History, Activities, & Organization. LC 73-17805. (Natural Sciences in America Ser.). 354p. 1974. reprint ed. 26.95 (*0-405-05722-9*) Ayer.
— The Bureau of Dairy Industry: Its History, Activities & Organization. LC 72-3072. (Brookings Institution. Institute for Government Research. Service Monographs of the U. S. Government: No. 55). reprint ed. 21.50 (*0-404-57155-7*) AMS Pr.
— The Development of Governmental Forest Control in the United States. (Brookings Institution Reprint Ser.). reprint ed. lib. bdg. 32.00 (*0-697-00153-9*) Irvington.
— The National Park Service: Its History, Activities & Organization. LC 72-3024. (Brookings Institution. Institute for Government Research. Service Monographs of the U. S. Government: No. 11). reprint ed. 25.00 (*0-404-57111-5*) AMS Pr.
Cameron, Jenny, jt. auth. see Richardson, Nohel.
Cameron, Jerry D. Kings of the Road. Halgerson, Alison, ed. LC 85-90693. 220p. (C). 1985. 12.50 (*0-317-19555-7*) Lyman Co Herald.
Cameron, Jody. Brand Name Supermarket Cookbook. 1990. pap. 4.50 (*0-425-12312-X*) Berkley Pub.
Cameron, Jody, compiled by. The Brand Name Supermarket Cookbook. pap. 4.50 (*0-425-12757-5*) Berkley Pub.
— The Money-Savers Cookbook. 256p. (Orig.). 1992. mass mkt. 4.99 (*0-380-76642-6*, Avon Bks) Morrow Avon.
Cameron, John. The Development of Education in East Africa. LC 68-9320. (Columbia University, Center for Education in Asia, Publications). 158p. reprint ed. pap. 49.00 (*0-608-14966-7*, 202599700048) Bks Demand.
***Cameron, John, ed.** Advances in Surgery. (Illus.). 500p. 2001. write for info. (*0-323-01529-8*) Mosby Inc.
Cameron, John, et al, eds. Poverty & Power: The Role of Institutions & the Market in Development. (Illus.). 304p. 1995. text 24.95 (*0-19-563654-6*) OUP.
***Cameron, John, et al.** Physics of the Body. 2nd ed. LC 99-26114. (Illus.). 410p. 1999. text 53.95 (*0-944838-90-1*); pap. text 45.95 (*0-944838-91-X*) Med Physics Pub.
Cameron, John, jt. ed. see Keeton, G. W.
Cameron, John G., Jr. Michigan Real Estate Forms, 3 vols. 1988. disk 75.00 (*0-685-74624-0*, MICHIE) LEXIS Pub.
— Michigan Real Estate Forms, 3 vols. 1993. suppl. ed. 85.00 (*0-685-74623-2*, MICHIE) LEXIS Pub.
— Michigan Real Estate Forms, Issue 8. LC 93-39800. 300p. 1998. ring bd. write for info. (*0-327-00563-7*, 8172514) LEXIS Pub.
— Michigan Real Estate Forms, 3 vols., Set. 1990p. 1994. spiral bd. 299.00 (*0-8342-0032-5*, 81720-10, MICHIE) LEXIS Pub.
— Michigan Real Property Law, 2 vols. 2nd ed. LC 93-77009. 1900p. 1993. 165.00 (*0-685-65991-7*, 93-020) U MI Law CLE.
Cameron, John H., tr. see Girard, Paul F.
Cameron, John Home, tr. see Girard, Paul Frederic.
Cameron, John L. Current Surgical Therapy, Vol. 6. 6th ed. (Illus.). 1300p. (C). (gr. 13). 1998. text 135.00 (*0-8151-2835-5*, 30964) Mosby Inc.
Cameron, John L., ed. Atlas of Biliary Tract Surgery. LC 93-9302. (Surgical Practice Illustrated Ser.). (Illus.). 240p. 1993. text 175.00 (*0-443-08742-3*) Church.
Cameron, John L., jt. auth. see Gordon, Toby.
Cameron, John R. & Suntharalingam, N. Thermoluminescent Dosimetry. LC 68-16061. 256p. reprint ed. pap. 79.40 (*0-608-11656-4*, 201263100082) Bks Demand.
Cameron, Judy. Fishing in My Blood. (Stories We Tell Ser.). 29p. 1993. pap. 4.00 (*1-884983-02-2*) Homegrown Bks.
Cameron, Julia. The Artist's Date Book: A Companion Volume to the Artist's Way. LC 99-29066. (Illus.). 384p. 1999. pap. 14.95 (*0-87477-653-8*, Tarcher Putnam) Putnam Pub Group.
— The Artist's Way. deluxe ed. (Inner Work Bks.). 256p. 1995. 24.95 (*0-87477-821-2*, Tarcher Putnam) Putnam Pub Group.
— The Artist's Way Morning Pages Journal: A Companion Volume to the Artist's Way. LC 95-23431. 304p. 1995. pap., wbk. ed. 20.00 (*0-87477-820-4*, Tarcher Putnam) Putnam Pub Group.
— The Artist's Way Morning Pages Journal: A Companion Volume to the Artist's Way. 1997. pap. 14.95 (*0-87477-886-7*, Tarcher Putnam) Putnam Pub Group.
— Blessings: Prayers & Declarations for a Heartful Life. LC 97-36670. 1998. pap. 9.95 (*0-87477-906-5*, Tarcher Putnam) Putnam Pub Group.
— The Dark Room. LC 98-234084. 448p. 1998. 25.00 (*0-7867-0564-7*) Carroll & Graf.

***Cameron, Julia.** God Is Dog Spelled Backwards. (Illus.). 144p. 2000. pap. 9.95 (*1-58542-062-X*, Tarcher Putnam) Putnam Pub Group.
— God Is No Laughing Matter. 240p. 2000. 19.95 (*1-58542-065-4*, Tarcher Putnam) Putnam Pub Group.
Cameron, Julia. Heart Steps: Prayers & Declarations for a Creative Life. LC 97-19438. 112p. 1997. pap. 9.95 (*0-87477-899-9*, Tarcher Putnam) Putnam Pub Group.
***Cameron, Julia.** Popcorn: Hollywood Stories. 256p. 2000. pap. 14.95 (*1-893329-12-7*, Pub. by Really Great Bks) SCB Distributors.
Cameron, Julia. Prayers for the Little Ones. LC 98-51023. 112p. 1999. 11.95 (*1-58063-048-0*, Pub. by Renaissance) St Martin.
— Prayers to the Nature Spirits. LC 98-51022. 112p. 1999. 11.95 (*1-58063-047-2*, Pub. by Renaissance) St Martin.
— The Right to Write: An Invitation & Initiation into the Writing Life. LC 98-22242. 256p. 1998. 19.95 (*0-87477-937-5*, Tarcher Putnam) Putnam Pub Group.
— The Right to Write: An Invitation & Initiation into the Writing Life. LC 98-22242. 256p. 1999. pap. 12.95 (*1-58542-009-3*, Tarcher Putnam) Putnam Pub Group.
***Cameron, Julia.** The Right to Write: An Invitation & Initiation into the Writing Life. abr. ed. 1999. 16.95 incl. audio (*1-55927-523-5*) Audio Renaissance.
— Supplies: A Companion Volume to the Artist's Way. (Illus.). 128p. 2000. pap. 12.95 (*1-58542-066-2*, Tarcher Putnam) Putnam Pub Group.
Cameron, Julia. Transitions: Prayers & Declarations for a Changing Life. LC 99-15573. 160p. 1999. pap. 9.95 (*0-87477-995-2*, Tarcher Putnam) Putnam Pub Group.
— The Vein of Gold: A Journey to Your Creative Heart. LC 96-13593. (Inner Work Bks.). 304p. 1996. 23.95 (*0-87477-836-0*, Tarcher Putnam) Putnam Pub Group.
Cameron, Julia & Bryan, Mark. The Artist's Way: A Spiritual Path to Higher Creativity. LC 92-5906. 240p. 1992. pap. 15.95 (*0-87477-694-5*, Tarcher Putnam) Putnam Pub Group.
Cameron, Julia & Wheater, Tim. This Earth. unabridged ed. 1997. audio 10.95 (*1-56455-549-6*, W368) Sounds True.
Cameron, Julia, jt. auth. see Bryan, Mark.
Cameron, Julia Margaret. Whisper of the Muse: The Overstone Album & Other Photographs by Julia Margaret Cameron. LC 86-20939. (Illus.). 104p. 1986. 49.95 (*0-89236-088-7*, Pub. by J P Getty Trust) OUP.
Cameron, June. Destination Cortez Island: A Sailor's Life Along the B.C. Coast. LC 98-32225. (Illus.). 224p. (Orig.). 1999. pap. 17.95 (*0-938665-60-X*) Fine Edge Prods.
Cameron, K. & McLaren, R. G. Soil Science: Sustainable Production & Environmental Protection. 2nd ed. (Illus.). 314p. 1996. pap. text 65.00 (*0-19-558345-0*) OUP.
Cameron, K. C., et al. Computers & Modern Language Studies. 1986. text 46.95 (*0-470-20343-9*) P-H.
Cameron, Karen, jt. auth. see Schmidt, Diane.
***Cameron, Kate.** Under the Wolf's Head. 1999. 24.95 (*0-9661879-3-8*, SKP98-44) St Kitts.
Cameron, Katherine. The Artist As Teacher: William Merritt Chase & Irving R. Wiles. (Illus.). 48p. 1994. pap. 15.00 (*0-933793-30-8*) Guild Hall.
Cameron, Katherine & Korn, Henry. The Moran Family Legacy. 1997. pap. 20.00 (*0-933793-45-6*) Guild Hall.
Cameron, Kay. A la Rose. 84p. 1988. pap. 4.95 (*1-879945-02-9*) Katydid Pubns.
— Breakfasts Ozark Style. 150p. 1986. pap. 7.95 (*1-879945-00-2*) Katydid Pubns.
— Grandma's Ozark Legacy. 100p. 1989. pap. 5.95 (*1-879945-01-0*) Katydid Pubns.
Cameron, Keith. Agrippa d'Aubigne. LC 77-540. (Twayne's World Authors Ser.). 169p. (C). 1977. 20.95 (*0-8057-6280-9*) Irvington.
— Computer Assisted Language Learning: Trials & Tests. 92p. (Orig.). 1990. pap. text 14.95 (*1-871516-22-6*, Pub. by Intellect) Cromland.
— Evaluation of Call Programs. 128p. (Orig.). 1990. pap. text 29.95 (*1-871516-18-8*, Pub. by Intellect) Cromland.
***Cameron, Keith, ed.** Call: Media, Design & Applications. 322p. 1999. 84.00 (*90-265-1543-X*) Swets.
Cameron, Keith, ed. From Valois to Bourbon: Dynasty, State, & Society in Early Modern France. 186p. 1989. pap. text 15.95 (*0-85989-310-3*, Pub. by Univ Exeter Pr) Northwestern U Pr.
— The Literary Portrayal of Passion Through the Ages: An Interdisciplinary View. LC 95-47647. (Illus.). 144p. 1996. 69.95 (*0-7734-8786-7*) E Mellen.
Cameron, Keith & Woodrough, Elizabeth, eds. Ethics & Politics in Seventeenth-Century France. 240p. 1996. 69.95 (*0-85989-466-5*, Pub. by Univ Exeter Pr) Northwestern U Pr.
Cameron, Keith, ed. see De Larivey, Pierre.
Cameron, Kenneth. Papp. 1969. pap. 5.25 (*0-8222-0872-5*) Dramatists Play.
Cameron, Kenneth M. America on Film: Hollywood & American History. LC 98-8470. (Illus.). 272p. 1997. 29.50 (*0-8264-1033-2*) Continuum.
— Ralph Waldo Emerson's Reading: Guide for Source-Hunters & Scholars. (BCL1-PS American Literature Ser.). 144p. 1993. reprint ed. lib. bdg. 69.00 (*0-7812-6961-X*) Rprt Serv.
Cameron, Kenneth M. & Gillespie, Patti P. The Enjoyment of the Theatre. 5th ed. LC 99-35230. 454p. (C). 1999. pap. text 54.00 (*0-205-29590-8*, Longwood Div) Allyn.
Cameron, Kenneth M., ed. & intro. see Eastman, George.
Cameron, Kenneth N. Dialectical Materialism & Modern Science. (Orig.). 1994. pap. 10.95 (*0-7178-0708-8*) Intl Pubs Co.
— Marxism, a Living Science. 264p. 1993. pap. 9.95 (*0-7178-0707-X*) Intl Pubs Co.
— Shelley: The Golden Years. LC 73-80566. 681p. reprint ed. pap. 200.00 (*0-7837-3865-X*, 204368700010) Bks Demand.
— Stalin: Man of Contradiction. 200p. 1990. text 21.95 (*0-920053-97-1*, Pub. by NC Ltd) U of Toronto Pr.
Cameron, Kenneth N., ed. Romantic Rebels: Essays on Shelley & His Circle. LC 72-97087. (Carl H. Pforzheimer Library). 330p. 1973. 30.50 (*0-674-77937-1*) HUP.
Cameron, Kenneth W. Emerson the Essayist: An Outline of His Philosophical Development Through 1836, 2 vols., Set. LC 80-2529. reprint ed. 92.00 (*0-404-19280-7*) AMS Pr.
— Ralph Waldo Emerson's Reading. LC 72-10872. (American Biography Ser.: No. 32). 1969. reprint ed. lib. bdg. 75.00 (*0-8383-0518-0*) M S G Haskell Hse.
Cameron, Kevin. Sportbike Performance Handbook. LC 97-46054. (Cyclepro Ser.). (Illus.). 176p. 1998. pap. 21.95 (*0-7603-0229-4*) MBI Pubg.
Cameron, Kim S., et al, eds. Readings in Organizational Decline: Frameworks, Research, & Prescriptions. LC 87-27136. 352p. 1988. text 39.95 (*0-88730-223-8*, HarpBusn); pap. text 22.95 (*0-88730-270-X*, HarpBusn) HarpInfo.
Cameron, Kim S. & Quinn, Robert E. Diagnosing & Changing Organizational Culture: Based on the Competing Values Framework. LC 98-22049. (Organization Development Ser.). (Illus.). 160p. (C). 1999. pap. 40.00 (*0-201-33871-8*) Addison-Wesley.
Cameron, Kim S., jt. auth. see Whetten, David A.
Cameron, Kim S., jt. ed. see Quinn, Robert E.
Cameron, Kirk & White, Graham. Northern Governments in Transition: Political & Constitutional Development in the Yukon, Nunavut & the Western Northwest Territories. LC 96-111285. (Illus.). 152p. 1995. pap. 14.95 (*0-88645-177-9*, Pub. by Inst Res Pub) Ashgate Pub Co.
Cameron, Laura. Openings: A Meditation on History, Method & Sumas Lake. (Illus.). 160p. 1997. text 34.95 (*0-7735-1666-2*, Pub. by McG-Queens Univ Pr) CUP Services.
***Cameron, Layne.** Indiana: An Atlas of Indiana's Greatest Off-Road Bicycle Rides. 2nd ed. (Mountain Bike America Guidebks.). (Illus.). 256p. 2000. pap. 17.95 (*0-7627-0703-8*) Globe Pequot.
Cameron, Layne S. Kidding Around Indianapolis: What to Do, Where to Go & How to Have Fun in Indianapolis. LC 00-503367. (Kidding Around Ser.). (Illus.). 144p. (J). (ps-3). 1997. pap. 7.95 (*1-56261-346-4*) Avalon Travel.
Cameron, Lewis. Opportunity My Ally. (Illus.). 253p. 1965. 7.50 (*0-227-67706-4*) Attic Pr.
Cameron, Lindsley. The Music of Light. LC 97-49506. 240p. 1998. 24.00 (*0-684-82409-4*) Free Pr.
— The Music of Light. large type ed. LC 98-28957. 1998. 23.95 (*0-7838-0286-2*, G K Hall Lrg Type) Mac Lib Ref.
— The Prospect of Detachment. 1991. pap. 8.95 (*0-312-05496-3*) St Martin.
Cameron, Loren. Body Alchemy: Transsexual Portraits. (Illus.). 100p. 1996. pap. 24.95 (*1-57344-062-0*) Cleis Pr.
***Cameron, Lou.** The Spirit Horses. large type ed. LC 99-89076. (Thorndike Western Ser.). 2000. 20.95 (*0-7862-2424-X*) Thorndike Pr.
Cameron, Louisa P. The Private Gardens of Charleston. (Illus.). 96p. 1992. 39.95 (*0-941711-14-5*) Wyrick & Co.
Cameron, Lucille W., ed. Labor & Industrial Relations Journals & Serials: An Analytical Guide, 14. LC 89-11887. (Annotated Bibliographies of Serials: A Subject Approach Ser.: No. 14). 248p. 1989. lib. bdg. 65.00 (*0-313-25986-0*, CLR/) Greenwood.
***Cameron, Lynne & Low, Graham.** Researching & Applying Metaphor. (Applied Linguistics Ser.). (Illus.). 311p. (C). 1999. 59.95 (*0-521-64022-9*); pap. 22.95 (*0-521-64964-1*) Cambridge U Pr.
Cameron, Lynne, jt. ed. see Coleman, Hywel.
Cameron, M. Coleoptera - Staphylinidae: Staphylinidae, Vol. I. (Fauna of British India Ser.). (Illus.). xviii, 478p. 1978. reprint ed. 30.00 (*0-88065-026-5*) Scholarly Pubns.
— Coleoptera - Staphylinidae: Staphylinidae, Vol. II. (Fauna of British India Ser.). (Illus.). vii, 260p. 1978. reprint ed. 30.00 (*0-88065-027-3*) Scholarly Pubns.
— Coleoptera - Staphylinoidea: Staphylinidae, Vol. 4, Pt. 2. (Fauna of British India Ser.). (Illus.). 691p. 1977. reprint ed. 40.00 (*0-88065-030-3*) Scholarly Pubns.
— Coleoptera-Staphylinoidea: Staphy-linoidea, Vol. 3. (Fauna of British India Ser.). (Illus.). 1978. reprint ed. 30.00 (*0-88065-028-1*) Scholarly Pubns.
— Coleoptera-Staphylinoidea: Staphylinodea, Vol. 4, Pt. 1. (Fauna of British India Ser.). (Illus.). reprint ed. 30.00 (*0-88065-029-X*) Scholarly Pubns.
Cameron, Marcia. Broken Child. 384p. 1995. 20.00 (*0-8217-4826-2*, Zebra Kensgtn) Kensgtn Pub Corp.
Cameron, Marcia. Broken Child. 448p. 1996. mass mkt. 5.99 (*1-57566-000-8*) Kensgtn Pub Corp.
Cameron, Margaret. Four Decades & a Baby. 240p. 1995. pap. 40.00 (*0-7855-2705-2*, Pub. by Argyll Pubng) St Mut.
— Life Begins . . . Later! 240p. 1995. pap. write for info. (*1-874640-06-8*, Pub. by Argyll Pubng) St Mut.
Cameron, Margaret E. & Van Staveren, Wija A., eds. Manual on Methodology for Food Consumption Studies. (Illus.). 284p. 1988. 70.00 (*0-19-261577-7*) OUP.
Cameron, Margaret M., tr. see Lanctot, Gustave.
Cameron, Marvin. Meandering Streams. (Illus.). 108p. (Orig.). 1994. pap. 7.95 (*0-944653-02-2*) Silver State Pub.
Cameron, Marvin N. Colorado Remembrances. (Illus.). 8p. 1988. pap. 2.00 (*0-944653-01-4*) Silver State Pub.
Cameron, Mary M. On the Edge of the Auspicious: Gender & Caste in Nepal. LC 97-45408. 376p. 1998. text 49.95 (*0-252-02412-5*); text 24.95 (*0-252-06716-9*) U of Ill Pr.
Cameron, Matt. Tear from a Glass Eye. pap. 14.95 (*0-86819-559-6*, Pub. by Currency Pr) Accents Pubns.
Cameron, Maxwell A. Democracy & Authoritarianism in Peru: Political Coalitions & Social Change. LC 94-9119. 1994. text 49.95 (*0-312-12153-9*) St Martin.
Cameron, Maxwell A., et al, eds. Deadly Legacy: The International Movement to Ban Anti-Personnel Mines. LC 99-177812. (Illus.). 508p. 1998. pap. text 24.95 (*0-19-541414-4*) OUP.
Cameron, Maxwell A. & Mauceri, Philip, eds. The Peruvian Labyrinth. LC 96-42209. 288p. 1997. 55.00 (*0-271-01660-4*); pap. 19.95 (*0-271-01661-2*) Pa St U Pr.
***Cameron, Maxwell A. & Tomlin, Brian W.** The Making of NAFTA: How the Deal Was Done. LC 00-8915. 2000. write for info. (*0-8014-3800-4*) Cornell U Pr.
Cameron, Maxwell A., jt. ed. see Grinspun, Ricardo S.
Cameron, Meribeth E., et al. China, Japan & the Powers: A History of the Modern Far East. 2nd ed. LC 60-7761. 726p. reprint ed. 200.00 (*0-8357-9857-7*, 201247300081) Bks Demand.
Cameron, Michael J., jt. ed. see Luiselli, James K.
Cameron, Michelle H. Instructor's Manual for Physical Agents. Williams, Adrianne, ed. 135p. 1998. pap. text. write for info. (*0-7216-6245-5*, W B Saunders Co) Harcrt Hlth Sci Grp.
— Physical Agents in Rehabilitation: From Research to Practice. Kuhn, Shirley, ed. LC 98-21395. (Illus.). 480p. (C). 1998. pap. text 39.00 (*0-7216-6244-7*, W B Saunders Co) Harcrt Hlth Sci Grp.
— Study Guide for Physical Agents. Allen, Andrew, ed. 105p. 1999. student ed. write for info. (*0-7216-6246-3*, W B Saunders Co) Harcrt Hlth Sci Grp.
Cameron, Miriam. Living with AIDS: Experiencing Ethical Problems. (Illus.). 256p. (C). 1993. text 48.00 (*0-8039-4778-X*); pap. text 19.95 (*0-8039-4779-8*) Sage.
Cameron, Morag, ed. see International Union for the Scientific Study of Po.
Cameron, Moven, ed. Voices of Our Kind: An Anthology of Contemporary Scottish Verse. 80p. 1975. 25.00 (*0-85411-000-3*, Pub. by Saltire Soc) St Mut.
***Cameron, Myra.** Enciclopedia de Remedios Caseros Naturales. (SPA.). 2000. pap. 14.00 (*0-7352-0211-7*) PH Pr.
— Instructor's Manual With Tests. 2nd ed. 1999. pap. text 13.95 (*0-13-020827-2*, Prentice Hall) P-H.
Cameron, Myra. Lifetime Treasury of Home Remedies. LC 93-1957. 448p. (C). 1993. pap. text 12.95 (*0-13-535212-6*) P-H.
— Mother Nature's Guide to Vibrant Beauty & Health. 1990. pap. 9.95 (*0-685-33309-4*) P-H.
— Mother Nature's Guide to Vibrant Beauty & Health. 251p. (C). 1990. text 24.95 (*0-13-603119-6*) P-H.
Cameron, Myra & DiGeronimo, Theresa. Mother Nature's Guide to Vibrant Beauty & Health. 2nd ed. LC 96-52951. 288p. (C). 1997. text 24.95 (*0-13-845314-4*) P-H.
— Mother Nature's Guide to Vibrant Beauty & Health. 2nd rev. expanded ed. LC 96-52951. 288p. (C). 1997. pap. text 13.95 (*0-13-845018-8*) P-H.
Cameron, N., et al, eds. The Oil & Gas of the South Atlantic. (Geological Society Special Publication Ser.: No. 153). 400p. 1999. 149.00 (*1-86239-030-4*, Pub. by Geol Soc Pub Hse) AAPG.
Cameron, N. D. Selection Indices & Prediction & Genetic Merit in Animal Breeding. LC 97-13555. (A CAB International Publication). 216p. 1997. pap. text 42.50 (*0-85199-169-6*) OUP.
Cameron, N. E. The Evolution of the Negro, Vol. 1. 254p. 1998. reprint ed. pap. 18.95 (*1-58073-012-4*) BCP Bks.
***Cameron, Nancy Scott.** Kate Felt Confident at School: A Guide to Dealing with Everyday Stress. (Illus.). 128p. (J). (gr. 4-7). 2000. pap. text 5.95 (*1-902618-15-7*, Pub. by Element Childrns) Penguin Putnam.
Cameron, Neil. The Running & Stamping Book. 96p. (C). 1995. pap. 19.95 (*0-86819-410-7*, Pub. by Currency Pr) Accents Pubns.
— The Running & Stamping Book. 96p. 1995. pap. 9.95 (*0-435-08681-2*, 08681) Heinemann.
Cameron, Neill, ed. see Babb, Arthur.
Cameron, Neill, ed. see Byrd, Jerry.
Cameron, Neill, ed. see Dollar, Susan E.
Cameron, Nigel. Barbarians & Mandarins. (Illus.). 448p. 1990. text 35.00 (*0-19-585005-X*) OUP.
— Barbarians & Mandarins: Thirteen Centuries of Western Travellers in China. (Illus.). 448p. 1999. pap. text 19.95 (*0-19-590373-0*) OUP.
Cameron, Nigel & Hase, Patrick. The Hong Kong Collection: Memorabilia of a Colonial Era. (Illus.). 100p. 1998. 26.00 (*962-7283-19-3*, Pub. by FormAsia) Weatherhill.
Cameron, Nigel, jt. pref. see Goodrich, L. Carrington.
Cameron, Nigel de S. Biblical Higher Criticism & the Defense of Infallibilism in 19th Century Britain. LC 87-7924. (Texts & Studies in Religion: Vol. 33). 440p. 1987. lib. bdg. 109.95 (*0-88946-821-4*) E Mellen.
Cameron, Nigel M. Are Christians Human? An Exploration of True Spirituality. 1989. pap. 8.95 (*0-310-51611-0*) Zondervan.
Cameron, Nigel M., et al, eds. The Dictionary of Scottish Church History & Theology. LC 93-3838. (Illus.). 800p. 1993. 79.99 (*0-8308-1407-8*, 1407) InterVarsity.
***Cameron, Nigel M. de S., et al, eds.** BioEngagement: Making a Christian Difference Through Bioethics Today. (Horizons in Bioethics Ser.). 280p. 2000. pap. 22.00 (*0-8028-4793-5*) Eerdmans.
Cameron, Nonnie & Phillips, Diane. Easy & Elegant: Hors d'Oeuvres. 56p. (Orig.). 1984. pap., per. 3.95 (*0-942320-10-7*) Am Cooking.
Cameron, Norman. Guianese Poetry. (B. E. Ser.: No. 22). 1931. 30.00 (*0-8115-2973-8*) Periodicals Srv.
Cameron, Norman & Rychlak, Joseph F. Personality Development & Psychopathology: A Dynamic Approach. 2 vols. 2nd ed. LC 84-80710. 816p. (C). 1984. text 78.36 (*0-395-34387-9*) HM.
Cameron, Norman, et al. Collected Poems: And Selected Translations. 160p. 1990. 34.95 (*0-85646-202-0*, Pub. by Anvil Press) Dufour.
Cameron, Norman, tr. see Baudelaire, Charles.
Cameron, Norman, tr. see Ivanov, Vyacheslav I.
Cameron, Norman, tr. see Stendhal, pseud.
Cameron, Norman E., jt. auth. see Cameron, Beverly J.
Cameron, P. J. Oligomorphic Permutation Groups. (London Mathematical Society Lecture Note Ser.: No. 152). 168p. (C). 1990. pap. text 38.95 (*0-521-38836-8*) Cambridge U Pr.
Cameron, P. J. & Van Lint, J. H. Designs, Graphs, Codes & Their Links. (London Mathematical Society Student Texts Ser.: No. 22). (Illus.). 250p. (C). 1991. pap. text 28.95 (*0-521-42385-6*) Cambridge U Pr.
Cameron, P. J., et al. A Review of Biological Control of Invertebrate Pest & Weeds in New Zealand 1874-1987. 424p. 1989. text 115.00 (*0-85198-645-5*) OUP.
Cameron, Pam. Mesa: More Than a Spiritual Adventure. LC 99-162957. 320p. 1999. pap. 14.95 (*0-9657104-0-8*) Luminaria Pr.
Cameron, Pat. Crete. 6th ed. (Blue Guide Ser.). (Illus.). 320p. 1993. pap. 22.95 (*0-393-30969-X*) Norton.
Cameron, Patience. Beyond Cleveland on Foot: 57 Hikes in Northeast Ohio's Lake, Geauga, Portage, Summit, Medina, Lorain & Erie Counties. LC 96-25254. (Illus.). 320p. 1996. pap. 14.95 (*1-886228-07-8*) Gray & Co Pubs.
Cameron, Patience. Cleveland on Foot: 50 Hikes & Walks in Cleveland & Vicinity. 3rd ed. LC 97-53763. (Illus.). 320p. 1998. pap. 14.95 (*1-886228-15-9*) Gray & Co Pubs.
Cameron, Patricia, ed. Guide to the American Law Institute Publications. LC 94-87587. xii, 254p. 1995. ring bd. 75.00 (*0-89941-904-6*, 308760) W S Hein.
Cameron, Paul, et al, eds. Standards & Guidelines for the Psychotherapies. LC 99-166523. (Illus.). 496p. 1998. text 70.00 (*0-8020-0804-6*); pap. text 24.95 (*0-8020-7166-X*) U of Toronto Pr.
Cameron, Penny. Larger Than Life: Folk Heroes of the United States. LC 93-47027. 176p. (C). 1994. pap. text 19.53 (*0-13-299470-4*) P-H.
Cameron, Penny, ed. Tales from Many Cultures, Bk. 1. LC 94-37550. 112p. 1995. pap. text, student ed. 16.55 (*0-201-82521-X*) Addison-Wesley.
Cameron, Peter. Andorra. LC 97-39782. 272p. 1998. pap. 12.95 (*0-452-27944-5*, Plume) Dutton Plume.
— Andorra. LC 96-27928. 256p. 1997. text 23.00 (*0-374-10505-7*) FS&G.
— Andorra. large type ed. (Niagara Large Print Ser.). 304p. 1997. 29.50 (*0-7089-5873-7*) Ulverscroft.
— Good Pharmaceutical Freeze-Drying Practice. LC 96-39290. 350p. 1996. 195.00 (*1-57491-031-0*) Interpharm.
— The Half You Don't Know: Selected Stories. LC 96-26346. 256p. 1997. pap. 11.95 (*0-452-27732-9*) NAL.
— Leap Year. LC 98-10532. 256p. 1998. pap. 12.95 (*0-452-27985-2*, Plume) Dutton Plume.
— Necessary Heresies: Alternatives to Fundamentalism. 175p. 1996. reprint ed. pap. 24.95 (*0-86840-293-1*, Pub. by New South Wales Univ Pr) Intl Spec Bk.
— Permutation Groups. LC 98-45456. (London Mathematical Society Student Texts Ser.: No. 45). (Illus.). 232p. (C). 1999. text 64.95 (*0-521-65302-9*); pap. text 24.95 (*0-521-65378-9*) Cambridge U Pr.
— Textbook of Adult Emergency Medicine. LC 99-23408. 2000. text. write for info. (*0-443-06280-3*) Church.
— The Weekend. LC 93-37428. 184p. 1994. 17.00 (*0-374-28739-2*) FS&G.
— The Weekend. LC 94-43823. 1995. pap. 11.95 (*0-452-27411-7*) NAL.
Cameron, Peter, jt. ed. see International Bar Association Staff.
Cameron, Peter J. Combinatorics: Topics, Techniques, Algorithms. (Illus.). 365p. (C). 1995. pap. text 29.95 (*0-521-45761-0*) Cambridge U Pr.
— Introduction to Algebra. LC 98-2555. (Illus.). 306p. 1998. text 65.00 (*0-19-850195-1*); pap. text 32.00 (*0-19-850194-3*) OUP.
***Cameron, Peter J.** Sets, Logic & Categories. LC 98-29309. (Undergraduate Mathematics Ser.). x, 180 p. 1999. pap. text 39.95 (*1-85233-056-2*) Spr-Verlag.
— To Praise, to Bless, to Preach: Spiritual Reflections on the Sunday Gospels. LC 99-70508. 176p. 1999. pap. 15.95 (*0-87973-822-7*) Our Sunday Visitor.
***Cameron, Peter J. & Cessario, Romanus, eds.** The Magnificat Pilgrim's Guide to the Great Jubilee: A Spiritual Manual. (Illus.). 304p. 1999. lib. bdg. 4.50 (*0-9676186-1-4*) Magnificat.
— The Magnificat Pilgrim's Guide to the Great Jubilee: Boston Archdiocese. (Illus.). 304p. 1999. lib. bdg. 4.50 (*0-9676186-4-9*) Magnificat.
— The Magnificat Pilgrim's Guide to the Great Jubilee: Brooklyn Diocese. (Illus.). 304p. 1999. lib. bdg. 4.50 (*0-9676186-3-0*) Magnificat.
— The Magnificat Pilgrim's Guide to the Great Jubilee: New York Archdiocese. (Illus.). 340p. 1999. 0.85 (*0-9676186-0-6*) Magnificat.
— The Magnificat Pilgrim's Guide to the Great Jubilee: Norwich Diocese. (Illus.). 304p. 1999. lib. bdg. 4.50 (*0-9676186-2-2*) Magnificat.

C

— The Magnificat Pilgrim's Guide to the Great Jubilee: Washington Archdiocese. (Illus.). 304p. 1999. lib. bdg. 4.50 (*0-9676186-6-5*) Magnificat.

Cameron, Peter John. The Classics of Catholic Spirituality: An Introduction to Proven Patterns of Holiness. LC 95-50963. 160p. 1996. pap. 5.95 (*0-8189-0743-6*) Alba.

***Cameron, Peter John.** To Praise, To Bless, To Preach: Spiritual Reflections on the Sunday Gospels, Cycle C. LC 00-130351. 176p. 2000. pap. 15.95 (*0-87973-823-5*) Our Sunday Visitor.

Cameron, Philip. How to Get All Your Family Saved. 128p. (Orig.). 1996. pap. 7.99 (*0-9656008-0-7*) P Cameron Minist.

Cameron, R. A., et al. A Field Key to the Slugs of the British Isles. (Illus.). 17p. 1983. pap. 12.55 (*0-916422-60-7*) Mad River.

***Cameron, R. G. & Feuer, G., eds.** Apoptosis & Its Modulation by Drugs. LC QH671.A654 2000. (Handbook of Experimental Pharmacology Ser.: Vol. 142). (Illus.). 550p. 2000. 350.00 (*3-540-66121-2*) Spr-Verlag.

Cameron, R. G., jt. auth. see Barnett, S.

Cameron, R. G., ed. see Feuer, George.

Cameron, R. H. & Storvick, A. A Simple Definition of the Feynman Integral, with Applications. LC 83-15605. (Memoirs Ser.: No. 46/288). 48p. 1983. pap. 16.00 (*0-8218-2288-8*, MEMO/46/288) Am Math.

Cameron, Randolph W. Minority Executives' Handbook. 20th rev. ed. LC 94-12488. (Illus.). 282p. 1997. reprint ed. pap. 11.95 (*1-56743-021-X*, Amistad) HarperTrade.

***Cameron, Rebecca Hancock.** Training to Fly: Military Flight Training, 1907-1945. 691p. 2000. boxed set 58.00 (*0-16-050181-4*) USGPO.

***Cameron, Richard.** Cameron Plays, No. 1. 2000. pap. 14.95 (*0-413-71660-0*) Methn.

Cameron, Richard. Strugglers. 112p. (C). 1995. pap. 9.95 (*0-413-65690-X*, A0619) Heinemann.

Cameron, Richard & Rattner, Ronald, eds. City & Garden. (Classicist Ser.: 3). 112p. (Orig.). 1996. pap. text 34.95 (*1-56000-936-5*) Transaction Pubs.

Cameron, Richard W., jt. ed. see Rattner, Donald M.

Cameron, Rita G. Let's Learn about Maryland. 5th rev. ed. (Illus.). 96p. (J). (gr. 4). 1995. pap. text 9.99 (*1-55596-166-5*, 00092) Learning Well.

Cameron, Robert. Above Chicago. LC 92-93090. (Illus.). 159p. 1992. 29.50 (*0-918684-27-7*) Cameron & Co.

— Above Tahoe & Reno: A New Collection of Historical & Original Aerial Photographs of Tahoe & Reno. LC 95-92422. (Illus.). 108p. 1995. 24.50 (*0-918684-52-8*); pap. 14.50 (*0-918684-51-X*) Cameron & Co.

— Above Washington: A Collection of Nostalgic & Contemporary Aerial Photographs of the District of Columbia. LC 79-89078. 158p. 1979. 29.50 (*0-918684-08-0*) Cameron & Co.

— The Last Pew on the Left. LC 94-68048. 224p. 1995. pap. 11.99 (*0-933451-28-8*) Prescott Pr.

Cameron, Robert & Cooke, Alistair. Above London. LC 80-80944. 160p. 1980. 29.50 (*0-918684-10-2*) Cameron & Co.

Cameron, Robert & Gilliam, Harold. Above Carmel, Monterey & the Big Sur. LC 94-94170. 96p. 1994. pap. 14.50 (*0-918684-44-7*) Cameron & Co.

Cameron, Robert & Hoppe, Arthur. Above San Francisco. LC 98-93262. (Illus.). 3p. 1998. 29.50 (*0-918684-73-0*) Cameron & Co.

Cameron, Robert & Porter, Phil. Above Mackinac. LC 94-94165. 96p. 1994. pap. 14.50 (*0-918684-38-2*) Cameron & Co.

Cameron, Robert & Salinger, Pierre. Above Paris: A New Collection of Aerial Photographs of Paris, France. LC 84-71415. (Illus.). 160p. 1984. 29.50 (*0-918684-19-6*) Cameron & Co.

Cameron, Robert & Sheehan, Jack. Above Las Vegas, Its Canyons & Mountains: A New Collection of Historical & Original Aerial Photographs. LC 96-85987. (Illus.). 160p. 1996. 29.50 (*0-918684-54-4*) Cameron & Co.

Cameron, Robert & Watson, Emmett. Above Seattle. LC 94-94006. 160p. 1994. 29.50 (*0-918684-41-2*) Cameron & Co.

Cameron, Robert B. Practical Oncology. (Illus.). 720p. (C). 1995. pap. text 34.95 (*0-8385-1326-3*, A1326-6, Apple Lange Med) McGraw.

Cameron, Robert W. Above Los Angeles. LC 90-81499. 160p. 1990. 29.50 (*0-918684-48-X*) Cameron & Co.

— Above San Diego. 160p. 1990. 29.50 (*0-918684-24-2*) Cameron & Co.

— Alcatraz. 1983. 9.95 (*0-918684-39-0*) Cameron & Co.

Cameron, Robert W. & Gilliam, Harold. Above Yosemite. LC 83-90192. 160p. 1983. 29.50 (*0-918684-20-X*) Cameron & Co.

Cameron, Robert W., et al. Above New York. LC 87-73037. (Illus.). 160p. 1988. 29.50 (*0-918684-42-0*) Cameron & Co.

— The Howells of New Jersey, Virginia, Ohio, & Points West. LC 95-111040. (Illus.). 191p. (Orig.). 1994. pap. text 23.00 (*0-7884-0052-5*) Heritage Bk.

Cameron, Roderick. Preparing for Y2K & Beyond: A Comprehensive Resource Guide. 4th rev. ed. LC 99-70207. 256p. (Orig.). 1999. pap. 19.95 (*0-9644958-1-3*) One Wrld Press.

Cameron, Roger. PCs to Corporate America: From Military Tactics to Corporate Interviewing Strategy. 2nd ed. LC 92-21911. 288p. (Orig.). 1992. pap. 19.95 (*0-9623216-5-6*) Odenwald Pr.

***Cameron, Roger.** PCS to Corporate America: From Military Tactics to Corporate Interviewing Strategy. 3rd rev. ed. 240p. 2000. pap. 19.95 (*1-884363-18-0*) Odenwald Pr.

Cameron, Ron, ed. The Other Gospels: Non-Canonical Gospel Texts. LC 82-8662. 192p. 1982. pap. 19.95 (*0-664-24428-9*) Westminster John Knox.

Cameron, Ron, tr. see Cologne Mani Codex, English & Greek Staff.

Cameron, Rondo. A Concise Economic History of the World: From Paleolithic Times to the Present. 3rd ed. (Illus.). 480p. (C). 1997. text 59.95 (*0-19-510781-0*); pap. text 34.95 (*0-19-510782-9*) OUP.

Cameron, Rondo, ed. Financing Industrialization, 2 vols. (International Library of Macroeconomic & Financial History: Vol. 4). 760p. 1992. 280.00 (*1-85278-433-4*) E Elgar.

Cameron, Rondo E. & Schnore, Leo F., eds. Cities & Markets: Studies in the Organization of Human Space. LC 96-41461. 384p. 1997. pap. text 37.50 (*0-7618-0523-0*); lib. bdg. 64.50 (*0-7618-0522-2*) U Pr of Amer.

Cameron, S. & Probert, P. Advanced Guided Vehicles: Aspects of the Oxford AGV Project. (Robotics & Automated Systems Ser.). 280p. 1994. text 48.00 (*981-02-1393-X*) World Scientific Pub.

Cameron, S., jt. auth. see Yovits, M.

***Cameron, Samuel & Collins, Ian.** Playing the Love Market: Dating, Romance & the Real World. 280p. 2000. 30.00 (*1-85343-494-9*, Pub. by Free Assoc Bks) Intl Spec Bk.

Cameron, Sandi, ed. see Jorgenson, Cathleen.

Cameron, Sandra J. & Nesbit, Jan. Ready-to-Use Math Games Activities Kit: Games for Meeting Math Curriculum Grades 3-8. LC 97-16632. 350p. 1997. pap. text, teacher ed. 28.95 (*0-87628-717-8*) Ctr Appl Res.

— Ready-To-Use Math Games Activities Kit: Games for Meeting Math Curriculum Standards. LC 97-16632. 350p. 1997. pap. text, teacher ed. 27.50 (*0-87628-552-3*) Ctr Appl Res.

Cameron, Sarah. Caribbean Islands Handbook, 1999: With the Bahamas. 10th ed. (Footprint Handbooks Ser.). (Illus.). 1008p. 1998. 24.95 (*0-8442-4963-7*) NTC Contemp Pub Co.

***Cameron, Sarah.** Caribbean Islands Handbook 2000. 11th ed. (Footprints Bks.). 1008p. 1999. pap. 22.95 (*0-8442-4629-8*, 46298, Natl Textbk Co) NTC Contemp Pub Co.

Cameron, Sarah. Caribbean Islands Handbook, 1998. 9th ed. (Footprint Handbks.). (Illus.). 1008p. 1997. 24.95 (*0-8442-4785-5*, Passprt Bks) NTC Contemp Pub Co.

— Cuba Handbook. LC 97-76425. (Footprint Handbooks Ser.). (Illus.). 272p. 1998. 19.95 (*0-8442-4948-3*, 49483, Natl Textbk Co) NTC Contemp Pub Co.

***Cameron, Sarah.** Footprint Cuba Handbook. 2nd ed. (Footprint Handbooks Ser.). 416p. 2000. pap. 17.95 (*0-658-00658-4*, 006584) NTC Contemp Pub Co.

— Footprint Mexico Handbook. (Footprint Handbks.). (Illus.). 832p. 2000. pap. 19.95 (*0-658-00657-6*, 006576) NTC Contemp Pub Co.

Cameron, Sarah. Mexico & Central American Handbook, 1999. 9th ed. (Footprint Handbooks Ser.). (Illus.). 1344p. 1998. 27.95 (*0-8442-4962-9*) NTC Contemp Pub Co.

Cameron, Sarah & Box, Ben, eds. 1997 Caribbean Island Handbook. 8th rev. ed. (Footprint Handbks.). (Illus.). 1024p. 1996. 21.95 (*0-8442-4907-6*, Passprt Bks) NTC Contemp Pub Co.

Cameron, Sarah, jt. ed. see Box, Ben.

***Cameron, Sharon.** Beautiful Work: A Meditation on Pain. LC 99-59146. 128p. 2000. 18.95 (*0-8223-2508-X*) Duke.

Cameron, Sharon. Choosing Not Choosing: Dickinson's Fascicles. LC 92-15544. (Illus.). 272p. 1993. pap. text 18.95 (*0-226-09234-8*); lib. bdg. 49.50 (*0-226-09232-1*) U Ch Pr.

— The Corporeal Self: Allegories of the Body in Melville & Hawthorne. 1991. text 46.00 (*0-231-07568-5*); pap. text 18.00 (*0-231-07569-3*) Col U Pr.

— Lyric Time: Dickinson & the Limits of Genre. LC 78-9983. 292p. reprint ed. pap. 90.60 (*0-608-06275-8*, 206660400008) Bks Demand.

— Thinking in Henry James. LC 89-4707. 208p. 1989. 35.95 (*0-226-09230-5*) U Ch Pr.

— Thinking in Henry James. (Illus.). 208p. 1991. pap. text 14.95 (*0-226-09231-3*) U Ch Pr.

— Writing Nature: Henry Thoreau's Journal. LC 88-25163. 186p. 1989. pap. 14.50 (*0-226-09228-3*) U Ch Pr.

Cameron, Sharon M. Designing Your Heart's Desire: The Releasing Strategy for Personal Power & Peace of Mind. rev. ed. 144p. 1995. pap. 12.95 (*0-9635820-7-0*) Watershed CA.

— The Releasing Strategy: For Personal Power & Peace of Mind. LC 93-93813. 133p. (Orig.). 1993. pap. 11.95 (*0-9635820-6-2*) Watershed CA.

Cameron, Sharon M., jt. auth. see Cameron, Clark T.

***Cameron, Sheila.** The Business Student's Handbook: Developing Transferable Skills. (Illus.). 381p. 1999. pap. 42.50 (*0-273-63083-0*, Pub. by F T P-H) Trans-Atl Phila.

Cameron, Sheila. The MBA Handbook: Study Skills for Managers. 3rd ed. vii, 337p. 1997. 57.50 (*0-273-62346-X*, Pub. by Pitman Pub) Trans-Atl Phila.

Cameron, Sheila K. Balancing the Request to Be Good: An Account of a Visit to the Outskirts of Child Psychotherapy. 200p. (C). 1995. 55.00 (*1-85343-323-3*, Pub. by Free Assoc Bks) NYU Pr.

— Balancing the Request to Be Good: An Account of a Visit to the Outskirts of Child Psychotherapy. LC 97-194514. (C). 1995. pap. 24.95 (*1-85343-324-1*, Pub. by Free Assoc Bks) NYU Pr.

Cameron, Sheila M., jt. auth. see NM Magazine Staff.

Cameron, Shelia. Against the Grain: Tools & Techniques for the Thinking Manager. LC 97-144554. 251p. 1997. pap. text 29.95 (*0-7506-2779-4*) Buttrwrth-Heinemann.

Cameron, Silver D. The Baitchopper. (Illus.). 167p. (YA). (gr. 5 up). 1995. pap. 6.95 (*0-88862-598-7*) Formac Dist Ltd.

— Once upon a Schooner. (Illus.). 146p. 1995. 24.95 (*0-88780-226-5*, Pub. by Formac Publ Co); pap. 14.95 (*0-88780-225-7*, Pub. by Formac Publ Co) Formac Dist Ltd.

Cameron, Simon. Silent Witnesses: Adelaide's Statues & Monuments. LC 97-159488. 163 p. 1997. write for info. (*1-86254-402-6*, Pub. by Wakefield Pr) BHB Intl.

Cameron-Smith, Marye. Complete Book of Preserving. LC 76-3976. 1976. 18.95 (*0-672-52241-1*, Bobbs) Macmillan.

Cameron, Stella. All Smiles. 448p. 2000. per. 5.99 (*1-55166-615-4*, 1-66615-5, Mira Bks) Harlequin Bks.

— Beloved. 416p. (Orig.). 1996. reprint ed. mass mkt. 6.50 (*0-446-60176-4*, Pub. by Warner Bks) Little.

— The Best Revenge. 448p. 1998. mass mkt. 6.50 (*0-8217-5842-X*, Zebra Kensgtn) Kensgtn Pub Corp.

— The Best Revenge. large type ed. LC 98-6952. 1998. 25.95 (*1-57490-142-7*, Beeler LP Bks) T T Beeler.

— Breathless. 384p. 1994. mass mkt. 5.50 (*0-380-77286-8*, Avon Bks) Morrow Avon.

— Bride. 416p. (Orig.). 1995. reprint ed. mass mkt. 6.50 (*0-446-60175-6*, Pub. by Warner Bks) Little.

— Charmed. 384p. (Orig.). 1995. mass mkt. 5.99 (*0-380-77075-X*, Avon Bks) Morrow Avon.

— Dear Stranger. 400p. (Orig.). 1997. reprint ed. mass mkt. 6.50 (*0-446-60429-1*, Pub. by Warner Bks) Little.

— Fascination. 416p. (Orig.). 1993. mass mkt. 5.99 (*0-380-77074-1*, Avon Bks) Morrow Avon.

— French Quarter. LC 97-76039. 384p. 1998. text 16.95 (*1-57566-312-0*, Knsington) Kensgtn Pub Corp.

— French Quarter. 445p. 1999. mass mkt. 6.99 (*0-8217-6251-6*) Kensgtn Pub Corp.

— French Quarter. LC 99-10597. 1999. 26.95 (*1-56895-643-6*) Wheeler Pub.

***Cameron, Stella.** Glass Houses. 384p. 2000. 24.00 (*1-57566-586-7*) Kensgtn Pub Corp.

Cameron, Stella. Guilty Pleasures. 432p. 1997. mass mkt. 5.99 (*0-8217-5624-9*, Zebra Kensgtn) Kensgtn Pub Corp.

— Guilty Pleasures. large type ed. LC 98-5509. (Core Ser.). 524p. 1998. 27.95 (*0-7838-0114-9*, G K Hall Lrg Type) Mac Lib Ref.

— His Magic Touch. 416p. (Orig.). 1993. mass mkt. 4.50 (*0-380-76607-8*, Avon Bks) Morrow Avon.

***Cameron, Stella.** Key West, Vol. 1. 1999. 23.00 (*1-57566-454-2*) Kensgtn Pub Corp.

— Key West. 479p. 2000. mass mkt. 6.99 (*0-8217-6595-7*, Zebra Kensgtn) Kensgtn Pub Corp.

— Key West. large type ed. 2000. 26.95 (*1-56895-851-X*) Wheeler Pub.

Cameron, Stella. A Man for Easter. (American Romance Ser.: No. 433). 1992. per. 3.39 (*0-373-16433-5*, 1-16433-4) Harlequin Bks.

— Moontide. (Mira Bks.). 1998. per. 5.50 (*1-55166-463-1*, 1-66463-0, Mira Bks) Harlequin Bks.

— More & More. 408p. 1999. mass mkt. 6.99 (*0-446-60613-8*, Pub. by Warner Bks) Little.

***Cameron, Stella.** More & More. large type ed. LC 99-43302. (Thorndike Basic Ser.). 600p. 1999. 28.95 (*0-7862-2212-3*) Thorndike Pr.

Cameron, Stella. No Stranger. 1993. per. 5.50 (*0-373-20091-9*, 1-20091-4) Harlequin Bks.

— Once & for Always. 2000. per. 5.99 (*1-55166-580-8*) Harlequin Bks.

— Only by Your Touch. 384p. (Orig.). 1992. mass mkt. 4.50 (*0-380-76606-X*, Avon Bks) Morrow Avon.

— Pure Delights. 432p. 1995. mass mkt. 5.99 (*0-8217-4798-3*, Zebra Kensgtn) Kensgtn Pub Corp.

— Pure Delights. large type ed. LC 97-34967. (ROMC-Hall Ser.). 488p. 1997. lib. bdg. 24.95 (*0-7838-8325-0*, G K Hall Lrg Type) Mac Lib Ref.

— Sheer Pleasures. 1995. mass mkt. 5.99 (*0-8217-5093-3*, Zebra Kensgtn) Kensgtn Pub Corp.

— True Bliss. 384p. 1996. mass mkt. 5.99 (*0-8217-5369-X*, Zebra Kensgtn) Kensgtn Pub Corp.

— Undercurrents. 1999. per. 5.99 (*1-55166-495-X*, 1-66495-2, Mira Bks) Harlequin Bks.

— Wait for Me. 432p. (Orig.). 1997. mass mkt. 6.50 (*0-446-60430-5*, Pub. by Warner Bks) Little.

— The Wish Club. 432p. 1998. mass mkt. 6.50 (*0-446-60431-3*, Pub. by Warner Bks) Little.

Cameron, Stella, et al. Avon Books Presents: A Christmas Collection. 400p. (Orig.). 1992. mass mkt. 4.99 (*0-380-76833-X*, Avon Bks) Morrow Avon.

— Avon Books Presents: To Love & to Honor. 384p. (Orig.). 1993. mass mkt. 4.99 (*0-380-77159-4*, Avon Bks) Morrow Avon.

Cameron, Stephen. Titanic: Belfast's Own. LC 99-165702. 160p. 1998. write for info. (*0-86327-685-7*) Wolfhound Press.

Cameron, Stephen V., jt. auth. see Aaronson, Stephanie.

Cameron, Steve. Brett Favre: Huck Finn Grows Up. rev. ed. LC 97-201834. (Illus.). 256p. 1997. pap. 12.00 (*1-57028-145-9*, 81459H, Mstrs Pr) NTC Contemp Pub Co.

— Feeding Frenzy: The Wild New World of the San Jose Sharks. 1994. 29.95 (*0-87833-102-6*) Taylor Pub.

— Moments, Memories, Miracles: A Quarter Century with the Kansas City Royals LC 95-140490. xxv, 238 p. 1992. write for info. (*0-87833-040-2*) Taylor Pub.

— 101 Ways to Enjoy Baseball. LC 99-21239. (Illus.). 144p. 1999. 9.95 (*1-886110-73-5*, Pub. by Addax Pubng) Midpt Trade.

— Packers. 1996. pap. text 23.95 (*0-87833-133-6*) Taylor Pub.

— Pappy: The Gentle Bear: A Coach Who Changed Football... And the Men Who Played It. LC 99-51514. (Illus.). 256p. 1999. 24.95 (*1-886110-80-8*, Pub. by Addax Pubng) Midpt Trade.

— Rip City: A Quarter Century with the Portland Trail Blazers. limited ed. 240p. 1994. 75.00 (*0-87833-090-9*) Taylor Pub.

Cameron, Steve & Brett, George. George Brett: Last of a Breed. LC 95-127573. 190 p. 1993. write for info. (*0-87833-081-X*) Taylor Pub.

Cameron, Steve, jt. auth. see Brett, George.

Cameron, Steve, jt. auth. see Harmon, Dick.

Cameron, Steve, ed. see Carlson, Chuck.

Cameron, Steve, ed. see Lazenby, Roland.

Cameron, Stevie. Blue Trust: The Author, the Lawyer, His Wife & Her Money. LC 98-226874. (Illus.). 328p. 1999. text 20.95 (*1-55199-027-X*) Genl Dist Srvs.

— On the Take. LC 96-110133. 592p. 1995. pap. 8.99 (*0-7704-2708-1*) Bantam.

Cameron, Stevie. On the Take: Crime, Corruption & Greed in the Mulroney Years. (Illus.). 528p. 1995. 29.95 (*0-921912-73-0*) MW&R.

Cameron, Stuart C. Buddhism--Nature, Culture, Philosophy & Practices: Index of New Information. 160p. 1998. 47.50 (*0-7883-1696-6*); pap. 44.50 (*0-7883-1697-4*) ABBE Pubs Assn.

— Buddhism--Nature, Culture, Philosophy & Practices: Index of New Information. rev. ed. 135p. 1999. pap. 44.50 (*0-7883-2149-8*) ABBE Pubs Assn.

***Cameron, Stuart C.** Buddhism--Nature, Culture, Philosophy & Practices: Index of New Information. 2nd rev. ed. 135p. 1999. 47.50 (*0-7883-2148-X*) ABBE Pubs Assn.

Cameron, Sue. Love, Sex, & Murder. 416p. 1997. mass mkt. 6.99 (*0-446-60438-0*, Pub. by Warner Bks) Little.

Cameron, Susan. The Bible Cookbook: Nourishment for the Body & Soul. 150p. 1996. 12.95 (*1-55874-389-8*, 3898) Health Comm.

— Lleonard, the Llama That Lied. 32p. (Orig.). (J). (ps-1). 1997. pap. 6.95 (*0-8091-6636-4*) Paulist Pr.

Cameron, Susan, jt. auth. see Sherman, Ed.

Cameron, T., jt. auth. see Breen, Dale H.

Cameron, T. D., et al. Geology of the Southern North Sea. (British Geological Survey United Kingdom Offshore Regional Report Ser.). (Illus.). 160p. 1993. pap. 60.00 (*0-11-884492-X*, Pub. by Statnry Office) Balogh.

Cameron, Theresa. A Bibliography for the Housing of Children with AIDS. LC 92-10380. (CPL Bibliographies Ser.: No. 278). 1992. 10.00 (*0-86602-278-3*, Sage Prdcls Pr) Sage.

Cameron, Thomas W. The Parasites of Man in Temperate Climates. LC 43-17056. 227p. reprint ed. pap. 70.40 (*0-608-30219-8*, 201608200098) Bks Demand.

Cameron, Verne L. Map Dowsing. (Dowser's Hdbk. Ser.: No. 1). 40p. 1970. pap. 5.75 (*0-88234-003-4*) Life Understanding.

— Oil Locating. (Dowser's Hdbk. Ser.: No. 2). 40p. 1970. pap. 7.00 (*0-88234-004-2*) Life Understanding.

Cameron, Verne L., et al. The Original Cameron Aurameter Book: Dowsing Auras, Invisible Energies & Thoughtforms. 2nd abr. rev. ed. Cox, Bill & Cox, Davina, eds. Orig. Title: The Cameron Aurameter. (Illus.). 68p. 1997. pap. 17.50 (*0-88234-014-X*) Life Understanding.

Cameron, Vicki. That Kind of Money. 203p. 1999. mass mkt. 5.99 (*1-58365-004-0*, Timeless Romance) BT Pub.

Cameron, Viola R. Emigrants from Scotland to America, 1774-1775. LC 61-40562. 117p. 1999. reprint ed. pap. 15.00 (*0-8063-0066-3*) Clearfield Co.

Cameron, W. J. Covenant People. 3.00 (*0-685-08801-4*) Destiny.

***Cameron, Ward.** Mountain Bike! Southwestern British Columbia. Coello, Dennis, ed. LC 99-29363. (North America by Mountain Bike Ser.). (Illus.). 400p. 1999. pap. 15.95 (*1-55068-094-3*, Pub. by Vanwell Publ) Howell Pr VA.

Cameron, Ward. Mountain Bike! The Canadian Rockies. LC 98-1235. (Illus.). 250p. 1997. pap. text 14.95 (*0-89732-250-9*) Menasha Ridge.

Cameron-Webb, Ian M., jt. auth. see Harri-Augstein, Sheila.

***Cameron, Wendy.** Assisting Emigration to Upper Canada: The Petworth Project, 1832-1837. 568p. 2000. text 65.00 (*0-7735-2034-1*) McG-Queens Univ Pr.

— English Immigrant Voices: Labourers' Letters from Upper Canada in the 1830s. 696p. 2000. text 65.00 (*0-7735-2035-X*) McG-Queens Univ Pr.

Cameron, William E. Great Dramas of the Bible. LC 81-71560. 288p. 1982. 4.48 (*0-87159-047-6*) Unity Bks.

Cameron, William J., ed. Poems on Affairs of State Vol. 5: Augustan Satirical Verse, 1660-1774. LC 63-7983. (Illus.). 1972. 80.00 (*0-300-01190-3*) Yale U Pr.

Cameron, William J. & WHSTC Project. A Bibliography in Short-title Catalog Form of Bell's British Theatre, 1791-1797. LC 85-109166. (Whstc Bibliography Ser.). iv, 87p. 1984. write for info. (*0-7714-0555-3*) UWO2.

Cameron, William T. The Cameron Story. limited ed. LC 90-81754. (Illus.). 200p. 1990. 39.95 (*0-9626599-1-6*) Aztex.

***Cameron-Wilson, James.** The Film Review 1999-2000: The Definitive Film Yearbook. annuals 55th ed. (Illus.). 192p. 2000. 29.95 (*1-903111-00-5*, Pub. by Reynolds & Hearn) Firefly Bks Ltd.

Cameron-Wilson, James. Film Review, 1997-98. rev. ed. (Illus.). 192p. 1997. pap. text 19.95 (*0-7535-0108-2*, Pub. by Virgin Bks) London Brdge.

— Hollywood: The New Generation. (Illus.). 224p. 1998. pap. text 24.95 (*0-7134-8119-6*, Pub. by B T B) Branford.

— Young Hollywood. LC 94-19583. 1995. 34.95 (*1-56833-038-3*) Madison Bks UPA.

Cameron-Wilson, James & Speed, F. Maurice. Film Review 1995-96. (Illus.). 192p. (Orig.). 1996. pap. 19.95 (*0-86369-928-6*, Pub. by Virgin Bks) London Brdge.

— Film Review 1996-97. (Illus.). 192p. (Orig.). 1996. pap. 19.95 (*0-7535-0012-4*, Pub. by Virgin Bks) London Brdge.

Camerson, Blythe. Opportunities in Museums Careers. (Opportunities In . . . Ser.). (Illus.). 160p. pap. 11.95 (*0-8442-4594-1*, 45941, Natl Textbk Co) NTC Contemp Pub Co.

Camery-Hoggatt, Jerry. Irony in Mark's Gospel: Text & Subtext. (Society for New Testament Studies Monographs: No. 72). 231p. (C). 1992. text 75.00 (*0-521-41490-3*) Cambridge U Pr.

— Speaking of God: Reading & Preaching the Word of God. 278p. (C). 1995. pap. 16.95 (*1-56563-172-2*) Hendrickson MA.

Camerzpix Staff, ed. Spectrum Guide to Tanzania. LC 98-12591. (Spectrum Guides Ser.). (Illus.). 364p. 1998. pap. 22.95 (*1-56656-234-1*) Interlink Pub.

Camesasca, Ettore. Mantegna. (Grandes Maestros del Arte Ser.). (SPA., Illus.). 80p. (Orig.). 1992. pap. 12.99 (*1-878351-25-7*) Riverside NY.

— Mantegna. Lister, Susan M., tr. from ITA. LC 98-158629. (Library of Great Masters). (Illus.). 80p. (Orig.). 1992. pap. 12.99 (*1-878351-16-8*) Riverside NY.

C

Cametti, Alberto. Palestrina. LC 74-24055. reprint ed. 44.50 (*0-404-12878-5*) AMS Pr.

Camfferman, Kees. Voluntary Annual Report Disclosure by Listed Dutch Companies, 1945-1983. LC 97-17768. (New Works in Accounting History Ser.). (Illus.). 400p. 1997. text 75.00 (*0-8153-3011-1*) Garland.

Camfield & Rowe. Exploring United States History Vol. II: A Reader. 2nd ed. 304p. 1992. pap. text 17.95 (*0-8403-7106-3*) Kendall-Hunt.

Camfield, Gregg. Necessary Madness: The Humor of Domesticity in Nineteenth-Century American Literature. LC 96-26019. (Illus.). 256p. 1997. text 55.00 (*0-19-510040-9*) OUP.

— Sentimental Twain: Samuel Clemens in the Maze of Moral Philosophy. LC 94-5007. (New Cultural Studies). 296p. (C). 1994. text 37.50 (*0-8122-3285-2*) U of Pa Pr.

Camfield, Thomas M. & Rowe, Joseph M. Exploring United States History: A Reader, Vol. 1. 2nd ed. 304p. (C). 1992. per. 21.95 (*0-8403-7900-5*, 40790001) Kendall-Hunt.

Camfield, William. Max Ernst: Dada & the Dawn of Surrealism. (Illus.). 376p. 1998. pap. text 35.00 (*3-7913-1944-2*) Prestel.

Camfield, William, et al. Max Ernst: Dada & the Dawn of Surrealism. (Illus.). 376p. 1993. 75.00 (*3-7913-1260-X*, Pub. by Prestel) te Neues.

Camfield, William A. & Museum of Fine Arts Staff. More Than a Constructive Hobby: The Paintings of Frank Freed. LC 96-19437. (Illus.). 108p. (C). 1997. pap. 19.95 (*0-89090-073-6*) Tex A&M Univ Pr.

Camhi, Betty. Sunyata: The Recollections of a Rare-Born Mystic. Isenberg, Elliott, ed. 120p. 1990. pap. 12.95 (*1-55643-096-5*) North Atlantic.

Camhi, Elaine, ed. Aerospace America, Vol. 32. 1994. 70.00 (*0-685-63109-5*) AIAA.

Camhi, Jane J. Women Against Women: American Anti-Suffragism, 1880-1920. LC 94-20242. (Scholarship in Women's History Ser.: Vol. 4). 330p. 1994. 60.00 (*0-926019-65-1*) Carlson Pub.

Camhi, Leslie. Portia Munson: Paintings & Pink. (Illus.). 8p. (Orig.). 1994. pap. 5.00 (*0-9626731-8-8*) Yoshii Gallery.

Camhi, Morrie, photos by. Faces & Facets: The Jews of Greece. (Illus.). 144p. 1993. text 60.00 (*0-89241-533-9*) Caratzas.

Camhy, Sherry. Art of the Pencil: A Revolutionary Look at Drawing, Painting, & the Pencil. LC 97-22486. (Illus.). 144p. 1997. pap. 19.95 (*0-8230-1373-1*, 755239) Watsn-Guptill.

Cami, Pierre. Drames De la Vie Courante. (FRE.). 110p. 1991. pap. 10.95 (*0-7859-2171-0*, 2070384128) Fr & Eur.

Camic, Charles. Experience & Enlightenment: Socialization for Cultural Change in Eighteenth-Century Scotland. LC 83-4992. 314p. 1996. 33.00 (*0-226-09238-0*) U Ch Pr.

Camic, Charles, ed. Reclaiming the Sociological Classics. LC 97-20349. 320p. (C). 1997. text 62.95 (*1-57718-030-5*) Blackwell Pubs.

Camic, Charles, ed. Reclaiming the Sociological Classics. LC 97-20349. 320p. (C). 1997. pap. text 27.95 (*1-57718-031-3*) Blackwell Pubs.

Camic, P. & Knight, S., eds. Clinical Handbook of Health Psychology. LC 97-77702. (Illus.). 658p. 1998. text 49.50 (*0-88937-177-6*) Hogrefe & Huber Pubs.

Camic, P. M. & Brown, F. D., eds. Assessing Chronic Pain. (Contributions to Psychology & Medicine Ser.). (Illus.). 250p. 1989. 96.95 (*0-387-96942-X*) Spr-Verlag.

Camicas, Jean-Louis, et al. Les Tiques du Monde (The Ticks of the World) (FRE.). 233p. 1998. 70.00 (*2-7099-1418-2*, Pub. by LInstitut Francais) Balogh.

Camici, Alberto, jt. auth. see Gentili, Antonio.

Camico. CPA's Guide to Loss Prevention Practices. 98th ed. 1998. pap. text 65.00 (*0-15-606236-4*) Harcourt Coll Pubs.

Camille, Alice. Seven Last Words: Lenten Reflections for Today's Believers. 96p. 1999. pap. 6.95 (*0-87946-191-8*, 266) ACTA Pubns.

— Seven Last Words: Lenten Reflections for Today's Believers. abr. ed. 96p. 1998. pap. 9.95 incl. audio, VHS (*0-87946-192-6*, 341) ACTA Pubns.

Camille, Alice L. God's Word Is Alive! Entering the Sunday Readings. LC 98-60276. 416p. 1998. pap. 19.95 (*0-89622-926-2*) Twenty-Third.

Camille, C. & Dehaine, M. Harrap's French & English Data Processing Dictionary. (ENG & FRE.). 320p. 1985. 75.00 (*0-8288-0230-0*, M6058) Fr & Eur.

Camille, Michael. Gothic Art: Glorious Visions. (The Perspectives Ser.). (Illus.). 176p. 1996. 16.95 (*0-8109-2701-2*, Pub. by Abrams); pap. text. write for info. (*0-13-570177-5*) Abrams.

— Image on the Edge: The Margins of Medieval Art. (Essays in Art & Culture Ser.). (Illus.). 176p. (C). 1993. pap. 21.00 (*0-674-44362-4*) HUP.

— Master of Death: The Lifeless Art of Pierre Remiet, Illuminator. LC 95-9088. (Illus.). 286p. 1996. 45.00 (*0-300-06457-8*) Yale U Pr.

— The Medieval Art of Love: Objects & Subjects of Desire. LC 98-17485. (Illus.). 182p. 1998. 35.00 (*0-8109-1544-8*, Pub. by Abrams) Time Warner.

— Mirror in Parchment: The Luttrell Psalter & the Making of Medieval England. annuals LC 98-13986. (Illus.). 416p. 1998. 40.00 (*0-226-09240-2*) U Ch Pr.

Camille, Pamela. Getting Older, Getting Fleeced: The National Shame of Financial Elder Abuse. 208p. (Orig.). 1996. pap. 12.95 (*1-56474-172-9*) Fithian Pr.

Camiller, Patrick, jt. ed. see Anderson, Perry.

Camiller, Patrick, tr. see Beck, Ulrich.

Camiller, Patrick, tr. see Corvi, Roberta.

Camiller, Patrick, tr. see Manea, Norman.

Camiller, Patrick, tr. see Martin, Hans-Peter & Schuman, Harald.

Camiller, Patrick, tr. see Popper, Karl R.

Camiller, Patrick, tr. see Poulantzas, Nicos.

Camiller, Patrick, tr. see Sebastian, Mihail.

Camiller, Patrick, tr. see Virilio, Paul.

Camilleri, Albert, jt. auth. see Srivas, Mandayam.

Camilleri, Anna, et al. Boys Like Her: Transfictions. LC PR9194.5.L47T37 1998. (Illus.). 224p. 1998. pap. 14.95 (*0-88974-086-0*, Pub. by Press Gang Pubs) LPC InBook.

Camilleri, J. P., et al, eds. Diseases of the Arterial Wall. (Illus.). 730p. 1989. 477.00 (*0-387-17492-3*) Spr-Verlag.

***Camilleri, Joseph A.** States, Markets & Civil Society in Asia-Pacific. LC 00-34816. 2000. write for info. (*1-85898-838-1*) E Elgar.

Camilleri, Joseph A., et al, eds. The State in Transition: Reimagining Political Space. LC 94-38877. (Critical Perspectives on World Politics Ser.). 250p. 1995. lib. bdg. 49.95 (*1-55587-538-6*) L Rienner.

Camilleri, Juanito, jt. ed. see Melham, Thomas F.

Camilleri, Nazareno. The Pope Speaks: Pope Plus XII on Purity. 79p. 1985. pap. 1.25 (*0-911988-18-1*, 44808) AMI Pr.

Camilleri, Patrick. Capillary Electrophoresis. 2nd ed. LC 97-22491. (New Directions in Organic & Biological Chemistry Ser.). 1997. lib. bdg. 129.95 (*0-8493-9127-X*) CRC Pr.

— Capillary Electrophoresis: Theory & Practice. 512p. 1993. boxed set 136.95 (*0-8493-7862-1*, QP519) CRC Pr.

Camilleri, Peter J. (Re)Constructing Social Work: Exploring Social Work Through Text & Talk. 188p. 1996. text 68.95 (*1-85972-480-9*, Pub. by Avebry) Ashgate Pub Co.

Camilleri, Rosemary. Advanced Writing. 146p. (C). 1995. ring bd. 50.00 (*0-9649117-8-7*) R Camilleri.

— The Well Written Paper. 2nd ed. 28p. (C). 1995. pap. text 5.00 (*0-9649117-9-5*) R Camilleri.

Camilleri, Stephanie. The House Book: Keys to Planetary Influence. LC 99-20578. (Illus.). 288p. 1999. pap. 12.95 (*1-56718-108-2*, K108) Llewellyn Pubns.

Camilleri, Tony. Carnivorous Plants. (Illus.). 96p. 1999. pap. 16.95 (*0-86417-917-0*, Pub. by Kangaroo Pr) Seven Hills Bk.

***Camilleri, Tony.** Carnivorous Plants. 104p. 2000. per. 16.00 (*0-684-87199-8*) S&S Trade.

Camilli, Camillo. Impressions of Famous Men: Imprese Illustri Di Diversi, 1586, 3 Vols. (Printed Sources of Western Art Ser.). (LAT., Illus.). 1981. reprint ed. boxed set 55.00 (*0-915346-66-4*) A Wofsy Fine Arts.

Camilli, Eileen, et al. Archeological Investigations in West-Central New Mexico, Vol. 1: Report of the First Field Season Bureau of Land Management, New Mexico State Office. Daniels, Barbara L. & Waybourn, Marilu, eds. (Cultural Resources Ser.: No. 3). (Illus.). 269p. (Orig.). 1988. pap. write for info. (*1-878178-04-0*) Bureau of Land Mgmt NM.

Camilli, Gregory & Shepard, Lorrie A. Methods for Identifying Biased Test Items. (Measurement Methods for the Social Sciences Ser.: Vol. 4). 184p. (C). 1994. text 44.00 (*0-8039-4415-2*); pap. text 19.95 (*0-8039-4416-0*) Sage.

Camilli, Ivan, jt. auth. see Veray, Amaury.

Camilli, Thomas. Calculator Puzzles: Basic Mathematics Skills. Evans, Marilyn, ed. (Illus.). 32p. (J). (gr. 4-6). 1995. pap., wbk. ed. 2.50 (*1-58610-095-5*, Learn on the Go) Learn Horizon.

Camilli, Thomas. Calculator Puzzles (Math) (Mathematics Ser.). (Illus.). 32p. (J). (gr. 4-6). 1996. pap., teacher ed. 2.95 (*1-55799-474-9*, 4076) Evan-Moor Edu Pubs.

Camilli, Thomas. A Case of Red Herrings A1: Solving Mysteries Through Critical Questioning. 37p. (YA). (gr. 4 up). 1992. pap. 12.95 (*0-89455-462-X*) Crit Think Bks.

— A Case of Red Herrings A2: Solving Mysteries Through Critical Questioning. 37p. (YA). (gr. 4 up). 1993. pap. 12.95 (*0-89455-483-2*) Crit Think Bks.

— A Case of Red Herrings B1: Solving Mysteries Through Critical Questioning. 38p. (YA). (gr. 7 up). 1992. pap. 12.95 (*0-89455-463-8*) Crit Think Bks.

— A Case of Red Herrings B2: Solving Mysteries Through Critical Questioning. 37p. (YA). (gr. 7 up). 1993. pap. 12.95 (*0-89455-484-0*) Crit Think Bks.

— Geometry: Basic Mathematics Skills. DeWeese, Bob, ed. (Illus.). 32p. (J). (gr. 5-6). 1995. pap., wbk. ed. 2.50 (*1-58610-101-3*, Learn on the Go) Learn Horizon.

Camilli, Thomas. Hands on Science/Brains on Math. (Illus.). 128p. (J). (gr. k-6). 1994. pap., teacher ed. 12.95 (*1-55799-283-5*, 985) Evan-Moor Edu Pubs.

— Make It Metric. (Illus.). 72p. (Orig.). 1982. pap. text 9.95 (*0-9607366-7-0*, KP111) Kino Pubns.

— Make It Metric. 66p. (Orig.). 1982. pap. 9.99 (*0-89824-421-8*) Trillium Pr.

— Math & Money Management. (Math Is Everywhere Ser.). 48p. (J). (gr. 4-6). 1994. pap. text 6.45 (*1-55799-328-9*, EMC 101) Evan-Moor Edu Pubs.

Camilli, Thomas. Math Brain Teasers: Basic Mathematics Skills. DeWeese, Bob, ed. (Illus.). 32p. (J). (gr. 4-6). 1995. pap., wbk. ed. 2.50 (*1-58610-093-9*, Learn on the Go) Learn Horizon.

Camilli, Thomas. Math Brainbusters Grades 3-4. (Daily Problem Solving Ser.). (Illus.). 44p. (J). (gr. 3-4). 1994. pap. text 14.95 (*1-55799-281-9*, EMC 385) Evan-Moor Edu Pubs.

— Math Brainbusters Grades 5-6. (Daily Problem Solving Ser.). (Illus.). 44p. (J). (gr. 5-6). 1994. pap. text 14.95 (*1-55799-282-7*, EMC 386) Evan-Moor Edu Pubs.

— Math in Space. (Math Is Everywhere Ser.). (Illus.). 48p. (J). (gr. 4-6). 1994. pap. text, teacher ed. 6.45 (*1-55799-330-0*, EMC 114) Evan-Moor Edu Pubs.

Camilli, Thomas. Measuring & Calculating: Basic Mathematics Skills. DeWeese, Bob, ed. (Illus.). 32p. (J). (gr. 4-6). 1995. pap., wbk. ed. 2.50 (*1-58610-096-3*, Learn on the Go) Learn Horizon.

Camilli, Thomas. Pre-Algebra. (Mathematics Ser.). (Illus.). 32p. (J). (gr. 4-6). 1997. pap., teacher ed. 2.95 (*1-55799-481-1*, 4083) Evan-Moor Edu Pubs.

Camilli, Thomas. Pre-Algebra: Basic Mathematics Skills. DeWeese, Bob, ed. (Illus.). 32p. (J). (gr. 5-6). 1995. pap., wbk. ed. 2.50 (*1-58610-102-1*, Learn on the Go) Learn Horizon.

— Problem Solving with Time & Money: Basic Mathematics Skills. DeWeese, Bob, ed. (Illus.). 31p. (J). (gr. 4-6). 1995. pap., wbk. ed. 2.50 (*1-58610-097-1*, Learn on the Go) Learn Horizon.

— Real World Math: Basic Mathematics Skills. DeWeese, Bob, ed. (Illus.). 32p. (J). (gr. 4-6). 1995. pap., wbk. ed. 2.50 (*1-58610-098-X*, Learn on the Go) Learn Horizon.

— Using Graphs & Charts: Basic Mathematics Skills. Evans, Marilyn, ed. (Illus.). 32p. (J). (gr. 4-6). 1995. pap., wbk. ed. 2.50 (*1-58610-089-0*, Learn on the Go) Learn Horizon.

Camillo, Kevin Di, see Di Camillo, Kevin.

Camillo, Kevin T. Patrick di, see Patrick di Camillo, Kevin T.

***Camillus, Joe, et al.** Technology-Based Training: Global Strategies for Learning. Elliott, Susan, ed. 83p. 1999. spiral bd. 395.00 (*1-928593-13-5*) Am Prodtv Qual.

***Camillus, John, et al.** Turning Strategy into Action: Tools & Techniques for Implementing Strategic Plans. Henderson, Craig, ed. (Illus.). 81p. 1999. ring bd. 295.00 (*1-928593-16-X*) Am Prodtv Qual.

Camillus, John C. Strategic Planning & Management Control Systems for Survival & Success. LC 85-40001. 331p. 1986. 37.00 (*0-669-10315-2*) Lxngtn Bks.

Camilo, Jose, jt. auth. see Trulock, Cela.

Camin, Aguilar & Meyer, Lorenzo. In the Shadow of the Mexican Revolution: Contemporary Mexican History, 1910-1989. Fierro, Luis A., ed. LC 93-5168. (Translations from Latin America Ser.). 297p. (C). 1993. pap. 16.95 (*0-292-70451-8*) U of Tex Pr.

Camin, Hector A. La Guerra de Galio (Galio's War) 552p. 1995. pap. 16.95 (*0-679-76319-8*) Vin Bks.

Caminada, David A. Food I Was Forced to Eat as a Child: (Or Mom's Great Italian Recipes) 6th ed. (Illus.). viii, 114p. 1996. spiral bd. 12.99 (*0-9672286-0-3*, 131-96) D A Caminda.

Caminals-Heath, Roser. Once Remembered, Twice Lived. LC 92-31509. (Catalan Studies: Translations & Criticism: Vol. 4). 258p. (Orig.). (C). 1993. pap. text 32.95 (*0-8204-1969-9*) P Lang Pubng.

Caminals-Heath, Roser, ed. see Riera, Carme.

Caminer, David, et al. Leo: The Incredible Story of the World's First Business Computer. LC 97-37095. 392p. 1997. 22.95 (*0-07-009501-9*) McGraw.

— User-Driven Innovation: The World's First Business Computer. 1995. write for info. (*0-07-709236-8*) McGraw.

Caminero-Santangelo, Marta. The Madwoman Can't Speak: or Why Insanity Is Not Subversive. LC 98-4027. (Reading Women Writing Ser.). (Illus.). 224p. 1998. 39.95 (*0-8014-3514-5*); pap. text 14.95 (*0-8014-8514-2*) Cornell U Pr.

Caminha, Adolfo. Bom-Crioulo: The Black Man & the Cabin Boy. Lacey, E. A., tr. from POR. 144p. 1982. 25.00 (*0-917342-89-5*); pap. 14.95 (*0-917342-88-7*) Gay Sunshine.

Caminiti, R., et al, eds. Control of Arm Movement in Space: Neurophysical & Computational Approaches. LC 92-2264. (Experimental Brain Research Ser.: Vol. 22). (Illus.). xii, 338p. 1992. 123.00 (*0-387-55054-2*) Spr-Verlag.

Camino, E. E. & B. K. Co., Staff. Doberman Pinscher Champions, 1986-1987. (Illus.). 90p. (Orig.). 1988. pap. 24.95 (*0-940808-83-8*) Camino E E & Bk.

Camino E. E. & Bk. Co. Staff. Afghan Champions, 1982-1986. (Illus.). 75p. 1988. pap. 28.95 (*0-940808-51-X*) Camino E E & Bk.

— Airedale Terrier Champions, 1952-1986. (Illus.). 187p. 1987. pap. 36.95 (*0-940808-45-5*) Camino E E & Bk.

— Akita Champions, 1982-1986. (Illus.). 82p. 1987. pap. 28.95 (*0-940808-54-4*) Camino E E & Bk.

— Akita Champions, 1987-1993. (Illus.). 145p. 1994. pap. 32.95 (*1-55893-028-0*) Camino E E & Bk.

— Alaskan Malamute Champions, 1981-1986. (Illus.). 95p. 1988. pap. 28.95 (*0-940808-59-5*) Camino E E & Bk.

— American Staffordshire Terrier Champions, 1952-1986. (Illus.). 190p. 1988. pap. 36.95 (*0-940808-74-9*) Camino E E & Bk.

— Australian Cattle Dog Champions, 1980-1986. (Illus.). 103p. 1987. pap. 36.95 (*0-940808-42-0*) Camino E E & Bk.

— Basenji Champions, 1982-1986. (Illus.). 95p. 1988. pap. 28.95 (*0-940808-60-9*) Camino E E & Bk.

— Bearded Collie Champions, 1977-1986. (Illus.). 110p. 1988. pap. 36.95 (*0-940808-69-2*) Camino E E & Bk.

— Bichon Frise Champions, 1973-1986. (Illus.). 113p. 1988. pap. 36.95 (*0-940808-71-4*) Camino E E & Bk.

— Bloodhound Champions: 1952-1986. (Illus.). 210p. 1988. pap. 36.95 (*0-940808-46-3*) Camino E E & Bk.

— Borzoi Champions, 1982-1986. (Illus.). 73p. 1987. pap. 28.95 (*0-940808-50-1*) Camino E E & Bk.

— Boston Terrier Champions, 1952-1987. (Illus.). 372p. 1988. pap. 36.95 (*0-940808-76-5*) Camino E E & Bk.

— Boxer Champions, 1952-1988. 175p. 1997. reprint ed. pap. 36.95 (*0-940808-91-9*) Camino E E & Bk.

— Brittany Champions, 1987-1994. LC 97-210019. (Illus.). 125p. 1996. pap. 32.95 (*1-55893-036-1*) Camino E E & Bk.

— Brussels Griffon Champions, 1952-1991. (Illus.). 175p. 1993. pap. 36.95 (*1-55893-000-0*) Camino E E & Bk.

— Bull Terrier Champions, 1982-1986. (Illus.). 62p. 1987. pap. 28.95 (*0-940808-58-7*) Camino E E & Bk.

— Bulldog Champions, 1952-1987. (Illus.). 320p. 1988. pap. 36.95 (*0-940808-78-1*) Camino E E & Bk.

— Bulldog Champions, 1988-1994. (Illus.). 104p. 1998. pap. 32.95 (*1-55893-047-7*) Camino E E & Bk.

— Cairn Terrier Champions: 1952-1986. (Illus.). 229p. 1987. pap. 36.95 (*0-940808-47-1*) Camino E E & Bk.

— Chesapeake Bay Retriever Champions, 1952-1987. (Illus.). 170p. 1988. pap. 36.95 (*0-940808-77-3*) Camino E E & Bk.

— Chow Chow Champions, 1983-1986. (Illus.). 85p. 1988. pap. 28.95 (*0-940808-67-6*) Camino E E & Bk.

— Curly Coated Retriever Champions, 1952-1987. 86p. 1988. pap. 36.95 (*0-940808-87-0*) Camino E E & Bk.

— Curly-Coated Retriever Champions, 1988-1993. (Illus.). 60p. 1995. pap. 32.95 (*1-55893-033-7*) Camino E E & Bk.

— Dalmatian Champions, 1983-1986. (Illus.). 104p. 1988. pap. 28.95 (*0-940808-68-4*) Camino E E & Bk.

— Doberman Pinscher Champions, 1981-1985. (Illus.). 221p. 1986. pap. 28.95 (*0-940808-26-9*) Camino E E & Bk.

— Doberman Pinscher Champions, 1988-1991. (Illus.). 150p. 1992. pap. 32.95 (*1-55893-026-4*) Camino E E & Bk.

— English Springer Spaniel Champions: 1982-1986. (Illus.). 113p. 1987. pap. 28.95 (*0-940808-49-8*) Camino E E & Bk.

— English Toy Spaniel Champions: 1982-1986. (Illus.). 48p. 1987. pap. 28.95 (*0-940808-55-2*) Camino E E & Bk.

— Field Spaniel Champions, 1952-1989. (Illus.). 150p. 1992. pap. 36.95 (*1-55893-009-4*) Camino E E & Bk.

— Flat-Coated Retriever Champions, 1952-1987. (Illus.). 112p. 1988. pap. 36.95 (*0-940808-80-3*) Camino E E & Bk.

— French Bulldog Champions, 1952-1988. (Illus.). 185p. 1990. pap. 36.95 (*0-940808-95-1*) Camino E E & Bk.

— German Shepherd Champions, 1981-1986. (Illus.). 96p. 1987. pap. 28.95 (*0-940808-27-7*) Camino E E & Bk.

— German Shorthaired Pointer Champions, 1981-1986. (Illus.). 98p. 1987. pap. 28.95 (*0-940808-48-X*) Camino E E & Bk.

— Giant Schnauzer Champions, 1952-1987. (Illus.). 102p. 1988. pap. 36.95 (*0-940808-82-X*) Camino E E & Bk.

— Golden Retriever Champions, 1983-1986. (Illus.). 95p. 1988. pap. 28.95 (*0-940808-61-7*) Camino E E & Bk.

— Gordon Setter Champions, 1952-1990. (Illus.). 175p. 1995. pap. 36.95 (*1-55893-002-7*) Camino E E & Bk.

Camino, E. E. & Bk. Co. Staff. Great Dane Champions, 1983-1986. (Illus.). 93p. 1987. pap. 28.95 (*0-940808-52-8*) Camino E E & Bk.

Camino E. E. & Bk. Co. Staff. Greyhound Champions, 1952-1986. (Illus.). 111p. 1987. pap. 36.95 (*0-940808-44-7*) Camino E E & Bk.

— Greyhound Champions, 1987-1993. (Illus.). 95p. 1995. pap. 32.95 (*1-55893-037-X*) Camino E E & Bk.

— Irish Setter Champions, 1876-1951 & 1982-1989. (Illus.). 95p. 1994. pap. 32.95 (*0-940808-62-5*) Camino E E & Bk.

— Irish Wolfhound Champions, 1952-1987. (Illus.). 166p. 1988. pap. 36.95 (*0-940808-79-X*) Camino E E & Bk.

— Irish Wolfhound Champions, 1988-1993. LC 96-225194. (Illus.). 95p. 1996. pap. 32.95 (*1-55893-039-6*) Camino E E & Bk.

— Italian Greyhound Champions, 1988-1992. (Illus.). 155p. 1994. pap. 32.95 (*1-55893-029-9*) Camino E E & Bk.

An Asterisk (*) at the beginning of an entry indicates that the title is appearing for the first time.

— Italian Greyhound Champions, 1952-1987. (Illus.). 244p. 1988. pap. 36.95 (*0-940808-75-7*) Camino E E & Bk.
— Keeshond Champions, 1983-1994. (Illus.). 125p. 1999. pap. 32.95 (*0-940808-98-6*) Camino E E & Bk.
— Komondor Champions, 1952-1990. (Illus.). 150p. 2001. pap. 36.95 (*0-940808-99-4*) Camino E E & Bk.
Camino, E. E. & Bk. Co. Staff. Kuvasz Champions, 1952-1990. 175p. 1993. pap. 28.95 (*0-940808-93-5*) Camino E E & Bk.
Camino E. E. & Bk. Co. Staff. Labrador Retriever Champions, 1952-1988. (Illus.). 200p. 1993. pap. 36.95 (*0-940808-96-X*) Camino E E & Bk.
— Lakeland Terrier Champions, 1934-1990. (Illus.). 310p. 1991. pat. 36.95 (*1-55893-023-X*) Camino E E & Bk.
— Lhasa Apso Champions, 1981-1986. (Illus.). 75p. 1988. pap. 28.95 (*0-940808-64-1*) Camino E E & Bk.
— Maltese Champions, 1952-1990. (Illus.). 200p. 1992. pap. 36.95 (*1-55893-012-4*) Camino E E & Bk.
— Maltese Champions, 1990-1994. (Illus.). 130p. 1995. pap. 36.95 (*1-55893-040-X*) Camino E E & Bk.
— Mastiff Champions, 1952-1988. (Illus.). 175p. 1990. pap. 36.95 (*1-55893-004-3*) Camino E E & Bk.
— Mastiff Champions, 1989-1993. LC 95-136174. (Illus.). 138p. 1995. pap. 32.95 (*1-55893-032-9*) Camino E E & Bk.
— Miniature Schnauzer Champions, 1952-1987. (Illus.). 200p. 1989. pap. 36.95 (*0-940808-84-6*) Camino E E & Bk.
— Old English Sheepdog Champions, 1952-1987. 175p. 1989. pap. 36.95 (*0-940808-88-9*) Camino E E & Bk.
— Otter Hound Champions, 1952-1994. LC 96-212446. (Illus.). 70p. 1992. pap. 36.95 (*1-55893-020-5*) Camino E E & Bk.
— Pekingese Champions, 1982-1986. (Illus.). 76p. 1987. pap. 28.95 (*0-940808-57-9*) Camino E E & Bk.
— Pointer Champions, 1981-1986. (Illus.). 145p. 1987. pap. 28.95 (*0-940808-43-9*) Camino E E & Bk.
— Pointer Champions, 1987-1992. (Illus.). 150p. 1993. pap. 32.95 (*1-55893-031-0*) Camino E E & Bk.
— Pomeranian Champions, 1987-1994. (Illus.). 115p. 1997. pap. 32.95 (*1-55893-044-2*) Camino E E & Bk.
— Pug Champions, 1987-1994. (Illus.). 120p. 1998. pap. 32.95 (*1-55893-046-9*) Camino E E & Bk.
— Pug Champions, 1983-1986. (Illus.). 115p. 1989. pap. 28.95 (*1-55893-021-3*) Camino E E & Bk.
— Pulik Champions, 1952-1990. 175p. 1993. pap. 28.95 (*0-940808-94-3*) Camino E E & Bk.
— Rhodesian Ridgeback Champions, 1981-1986. (Illus.). 132p. 1988. pap. 28.95 (*0-940808-65-X*) Camino E E & Bk.
— Rhodesian Ridgeback Champions, 1987-1991. (Illus.). 150p. 1993. pap. text 32.95 (*1-55893-027-2*) Camino E E & Bk.
— Rottweiler Champions, 1982-1986. (Illus.). 128p. 1987. pap. 28.95 (*0-940808-53-6*) Camino E E & Bk.
— Saint Bernard Champions, 1952-1989. (Illus.). 200p. 1994. pap. 36.95 (*1-55893-001-9*) Camino E E & Bk.
— Saluki Champions, 1952-1989. (Illus.). 180p. 1991. pap. 36.95 (*0-940808-97-8*) Camino E E & Bk.
— Samoyed Champions, 1952-1987. (Illus.). 309p. 1988. pap. 36.95 (*0-940808-85-4*) Camino E E & Bk.
— Schipperke Champions, 1988-1993. (Illus.). 90p. 1994. pap. 32.95 (*1-55893-035-3*) Camino E E & Bk.
— Schipperke Champions, 1952-1987. 242p. 1989. pap. 36.95 (*0-940808-86-2*) Camino E E & Bk.
— Scottish Terrier Champions, 1952-1990. (Illus.). 175p. 1992. pap. 36.95 (*1-55893-005-1*) Camino E E & Bk.
— Sealyham Terrier Champions, 1911-1987. 144p. 1988. pap. 36.95 (*0-940808-90-0*) Camino E E & Bk.
— Siberian Husky Champions, 1981-1986. (Illus.). 114p. 1988. pap. 28.95 (*0-940808-66-8*) Camino E E & Bk.
— Skye Terrier Champions, 1952-1987. 175p. 1989. pap. 36.95 (*0-940808-92-7*) Camino E E & Bk.
— Soft-Coated Wheaten Terrier Champions, 1973-1986. (Illus.). 131p. 1988. pap. 36.95 (*0-940808-73-0*) Camino E E & Bk.
— Staffordshire Bull Terrier Champions, 1988-1993. (Illus.). 85p. 1996. pap. 32.95 (*1-55893-038-8*) Camino E E & Bk.
— Staffordshire Bull Terrier Champions, 1975-1986. (Illus.). 128p. 1988. pap. 36.95 (*0-940808-72-2*) Camino E E & Bk.
— Tibetan Spaniel Champions, 1984-1986. (Illus.). 46p. 1987. pap. 24.95 (*0-940808-41-2*) Camino E E & Bk.
— Tibetan Terrier Champions, 1988-1994. (Illus.). 90p. 1998. pap. 32.95 (*1-55893-045-0*) Camino E E & Bk.
— Tibetan Terrier Champions, 1973-1986. (Illus.). 119p. 1988. pap. 36.95 (*0-940808-70-6*) Camino E E & Bk.
— Vizsla Champions, 1985-1994. (Illus.). 65p. 1998. pap. 32.95 (*0-940808-63-3*) Camino E E & Bk.
— Weimaraner Champions, 1952-1987. (Illus.). 338p. 1988. pap. 36.95 (*0-940808-81-1*) Camino E E & Bk.
— Welsh Springer Spaniel Champions, 1952-1989. (Illus.). 125p. 1990. pap. 36.95 (*1-55893-013-2*) Camino E E & Bk.
— Whippet Champions, 1981-1986. (Illus.). 158p. 1984. pap. 32.95 (*0-940808-29-3*) Camino E E & Bk.
— Whippet Champions, 1987-1995. (Illus.). 118p. 1998. pap. 32.95 (*1-55893-048-5*) Camino E E & Bk.
— Yorkshire Terrier Champions, 1981-1986. (Illus.). 129p. 1987. pap. 28.95 (*0-940808-28-5*) Camino E E & Bk.
— Yorkshire Terrier Champions, 1987-1993. (Illus.). 105p. 1994. pap. 32.95 (*1-55893-034-5*) Camino E E & Bk.
Camino E. E. & Bk. Co. Staff & Johnson, Dorothy L. Ibizan Hound Champions, 1978-1986. (Illus.). 67p. 1987. pap. 28.95 (*0-940808-38-2*) Camino E E & Bk.
— Pharaoh Hound Champions, 1983-1986. (Illus.). 36p. 1987. pap. 24.95 (*0-940808-39-0*) Camino E E & Bk.
— Portuguese Water Dog Champions, 1983-1986. (Illus.). 49p. 1987. pap. 28.95 (*0-940808-40-4*) Camino E E & Bk.
Camino E. E. & Bk. Co. Staff, jt. auth. see Freund, Jan L.
Camino, Linda, ed. Reconstructing Lives, Recapturing Meaning. 253p. 1994. text 49.00 (*2-88449-109-0*); pap. text 25.00 (*2-88449-110-4*) Gordon & Breach.
Camino, Lisa. Treating Sexually Abused Boys: A Guide for Therapists & Counselors. LC 99-16647. 288p. 1999. pap. 34.95 (*0-7879-4793-8*) Jossey-Bass.
Camino, Mercedes M. The Stage Am I? Raping Lucrece in Early Modern England. LC 96-140957. 228p. 1996. 89.95 (*0-7734-4220-0*) E Mellen.
Camino Staff, jt. auth. see Linzy, Jan.
***Caminos.** Law of the Sea. 570p. 2000. 180.00 (*1-84014-090-9*) Ashgate Pub Co.
Caminos. A Tale of Woe Vol. 127: Papyrus Pushkin. (Illus.). 110p. 1977. 45.00 (*0-900416-09-2*, Pub. by Aris & Phillips) David Brown.
Caminos, Horacio & Goethert, Reinhard. Urbanization Primer: Project Assessment, Site Analysis, Design Criteria for Site & Services or Similar Dwelling Environments in Developing Areas, with a Documentary Collection of Photographs on Urbanization. (Illus.). 1978. 45.00 (*0-262-03066-7*) MIT Pr.
Caminos, Ricardo & Fischer, Henry G. Ancient Egyptian Epigraphy & Paleography. (Illus.). 62p. 1976. pap. 5.00 (*0-87099-197-3*) Metro Mus Art.
Camins, Martin B. & O'Leary, Patrick F. Disorders of the Cervical Spine. (Illus.). 656p. 1992. 155.00 (*0-683-01401-3*) Lppncott W & W.
Camins, Martin B. & O'Leary, Patrick F., eds. The Lumbar Spine. LC 86-24862. (Illus.). 511p. 1987. reprint ed. pap. 158.50 (*0-608-05799-1*, 205976400007) Bks Demand.
Camion, Arlette & Lajarrige, Jacques, eds. Religion(s) et Litterature en Autriche au XXe Siecle: Actes du Colloque d'Orleans (Octobre 1995) (FRE.). 259p. 1997. 39.95 (*3-906754-59-6*, Pub. by P Lang) P Lang Pubng.
Camion, G. F. & Davies, P. J. Reefs & Carbonate Platforms in the Pacific & Indian Oceans. LC 97-28586. (Special Publication Number 27 of the International Association of Sedimentologists Ser.). 1998. write for info. (*0-06-324954-5*) HarpC.
Camion, Jean. Dictionnaire des Homonymes de la Langue Francaise. (FRE.). 683p. 1986. lib. bdg. 135.00 (*0-8288-2588-2*, 2906444006) Fr & Eur.
Camion, P. & Charpin, P., eds. Eurocode '92: International Symposium on Coding Theory & Applications. (CISM International Centre for Mechanical Sciences Ser.: Vol. 339). (Illus.). xi, 403p. 1994. pap. 74.00 (*0-387-82519-3*) Spr-Verlag.
Camire, Bernard. Living Bread: Reflections for Eucharistic Prayer. 88p. 1998. pap. 4.50 (*0-8198-4485-3*) Pauline Bks.
***Camisa, Charles.** The Handbook of Psoriasis. LC 97-45689. (Illus.). 321p. 1999. pap. 45.00 (*0-86542-558-2*) Blackwell Sci.
Camisa, Charles. Psoriasis. LC 93-11762. (Illus.). 368p. 1993. 99.95 (*0-86542-247-8*) Blackwell Sci.
Camlin, Jill. Sixty-Five Miles. 48p. 1998. pap. 8.00 (*0-8059-4414-1*) Dorrance.
***Camm.** Electrophysiological Disorders. 2001. text. write for info. (*0-443-06570-5*) Harcrt Hlth Sci Grp.
Camm. Space, People, Place. 1981. pap. text. write for info. (*0-582-68214-2*, Pub. by Addison-Wesley) Longman.
Camm & Evans. Management Science & Decision Technology. (SWC-Management). 1999. pap. text 45.00 (*0-324-02015-5*) Sth-Wstrn College.
Camm, A. John & Ward, David E., eds. Clinical Aspects of Cardiac Arrhythmias. (Current Status of Clinical Cardiology Ser.). (C). 1988. text 235.50 (*0-85200-972-0*) Kluwer Academic.
Camm, A. John, ed. see Janse, Michiel J.
Camm, A. John, jt. ed. see Malik, Marek.
Camm, A. John, jt. ed. see Martin, Anthony.
Camm, A. John, jt. ed. see Murgatroyd, Francis D.
Camm, Elizabeth, ed. see Fetscher, Elmar.
Camm, Frank, jt. auth. see Drezner, Jeffrey A.
Camm, Frank A. Expanding Private Production of Defense Services. LC 96-19536. (Illus.). 65p. 1996. pap. 15.00 (*0-8330-2388-8*, MR-734-CRMAF) Rand Corp.
— Regulatory Rulemaking to Implement Congressional Legislation: Lessons from the Powerplant & Industrial Fuel Use Act of 1978. LC 83-11010. 1983. pap. 7.50 (*0-8330-0510-3*, R-2982-DOE/RC) Rand Corp.
Camm, Frank A. & Lachman, Beth E. Energy Effects of Ending the Department of Defense's Use of Chemicals that Deplete Stratospheric Ozone. LC 93-16004. 1993. pap. text 13.00 (*0-8330-1390-4*, MR-223-P&L) Rand Corp.
Camm, Frank A. & Shulman, H. L. When Internal Transfer Prices & Costs Differ: How Stock Funding of Depot-Level Reparables Affects Decision Making in the Air Force. LC 93-23292. 1993. pap. 13.00 (*0-8330-1440-4*, MR-307-AF) Rand Corp.
Camm, Jeffrey D. Management Science. (MB - Business/Vocational Math Ser.). (C). 1995. mass mkt., student ed. 24.95 (*0-538-82739-4*) S-W Pub.
Camm, John, jt. auth. see Waktare, Johan.
Camm, John, jt. ed. see Murgatroyd, Francis D.
Camm, Sue. Daisy is Lost. (Read to Me Ser.). 10p. (J). (ps). 1994. bds. 3.98 (*1-85854-136-0*) Brimax Bks.
— The Hungry Puppy. (Read to Me Ser.). 10p. (J). (ps). 1994. bds. 3.98 (*1-85854-137-9*) Brimax Bks.
— A New Nest. (Read to Me Ser.). 10p. (J). (ps). 1994. bds. 3.98 (*1-85854-139-5*) Brimax Bks.
— Rosie's Day Out. (Read to Me Ser.). 10p. (J). (ps). 1994. bds. 3.98 (*1-85854-138-7*) Brimax Bks.
Cammack, Diana. The Rand at War, 1899-1902: The Witwatersrand & Anglo-Boer War. (Illus.). 240p. 1990. pap. 28.00 (*0-86980-729-3*, Pub. by Univ Natal Pr) Intl Spec Bk.
Cammack, Diane. The Rand at War, 1899-1902: The Witwatersrand & Anglo-Boer War. 1990. 55.00 (*0-520-06852-1*, Pub. by U CA Pr) Cal Prin Full Svc.
Cammack, John. Basic Accounting for Small Groups. (Illus.). 64p. (C). 1992. pap. 9.95 (*0-85598-148-2*, Pub. by Oxfam Pub) Stylus Pub VA.
Cammack, Nell, jt. auth. see Creadick, Jean P.
Cammack, Paul A. Capitalism & Democracy in the Third World: The Doctrine for Political Development. LC 96-34462. (Critical Political Studies). 192p. 1997. 75.00 (*0-7185-0088-1*); pap. 21.95 (*0-7185-0089-X*) Bks Intl VA.
Cammack, Paul A., et al. Third World Politics: A Comparative Introduction. 2nd ed. LC 93-13687. 320p. (C). 1993. text 48.00 (*0-8018-4750-8*); pap. text 18.95 (*0-8018-4751-6*) Johns Hopkins.
Cammack, Phyllis. Missionary Moments. LC 66-30364. (Illus.). 134p. 1966. 6.50 (*0-913342-09-2*) Barclay Pr.
Cammack, Raymond & Steely, Arthur W. Building Bridges into Algebra. LC 87-70828. (Basic Math Ser.: Bk. II). 332p. (C). 1987. pap. text 14.95 (*0-938991-12-4*) Colonial Pr AL.
Cammack, Raymond, jt. auth. see Steely, Arthur W.
Cammack, Richard, jt. ed. see Sykes, A. G.
Cammack, Shirley & Eisenberg, Myron G., eds. Key Words in Physical Rehabilitation: A Guide to Contemporary Usage. LC 94-23159. 152p. 1995. 25.95 (*0-8261-8740-4*) Springer Pub.
Cammaerts, Judy. Dressage Test Technique. (Threshold Picture Guides Ser.). (Illus.). 24p. 1994. pap. 12.00 (*1-872082-51-3*, Pub. by Kenilworth Pr) Half Halt Pr.
Camman, Karl. Working with Ion-Selective Electrodes. Schroeder, A. H., tr. from GER. (Chemical Laboratory Practice Ser.). (Illus.). 1979. 59.00 (*0-387-09320-6*) Spr-Verlag.
Camman, Schuyler. Trade Through the Himalayas. LC 74-90477. 186p. 1970. reprint ed. lib. bdg. 75.00 (*0-8371-3260-6*, CAHI, Greenwood Pr) Greenwood.
Cammann, Peter F. Fishing Vermont's Streams & Lakes: A Guide to the Green Mountain State's Best Trout & Bass Waters. LC 92-26300. (Illus.). 206p. (Orig.). 1992. pap. 15.00 (*0-88150-239-1*, Pub. by Countryman) Norton.
— Ultralight Spin-Fishing: A Practical Guide for Freshwater & Saltwater Anglers. LC 94-26283. (Illus.). 150p. (Orig.). 1994. pap. 12.00 (*0-88150-301-0*, Pub. by Countryman) Penguin Books.
Cammarano, James J. Lessons to Be Learned Just in Time. LC 97-18858. (Illus.). 290p. 1997. 34.95 (*0-89806-162-8*, LESSON) Eng Mgmt Pr.
***Cammarano, Jewell.** Beach Cuisine: A Collection of Recipes from the Coastal Carolinas. 204p. 2000. pap. 10.95 (*0-942407-47-4*) Father & Son.
Cammarano, Joseph, jt. ed. see Reeher, Grant.
Cammarano, Nicholas & Klink, James J. Real Estate Accounting & Reporting: A Guide for Developers, Investors, & Lenders. 3rd ed. LC 94-48266. 352p. 1995. 150.00 (*0-471-51069-6*) Wiley.
Cammarano, Roy F. Entrepreneurial Transitions: From Inspired Genius to Visionary Leader. 1993. pap. 16.95 (*1-882180-15-1*) Griffin CA.
Cammarata, Antonio. Unraveling on the Old Silk Road: Hitchhiking China & Beyond. (Illus.). 450p. 1998. pap. 21.95 (*1-889534-24-2*) Jay St Pubs.
Cammarata, Charles. Lighting the Flame: A Resource Book for Worship. LC 96-38669. 96p. (Orig.). 1997. pap. 10.95 (*0-7880-0870-6*) CSS OH.
Cammarata, John. A Physician's Guide to Herbal Wellness: Safe & Effective Remedies for Achieving & Maintaining Health. LC 96-12822. (Illus.). 192p. (Orig.). 1996. pap. 14.95 (*1-55652-273-8*) Chicago Review.
Cammarata, R. C., et al, eds. Structure & Evolution of Surfaces. LC 97-28343. (Materials Research Society Symposium Proceedings Ser.: No. 440). 509p. 1997. text 68.00 (*1-55899-344-4*) Materials Res.
— Thin Films - Structure & Morphology. LC 97-21318. (Materials Research Society Symposium Proceedings Ser.: No. 441). 793p. 1997. text 68.00 (*1-55899-345-2*) Materials Res.
— Thin Films--Stresses & Mechanical Properties VII Vol. 505: Materials Research Society Symposium Proceedings. 646p. 1998. text 71.00 (*1-55899-410-6*) Materials Res.
Cammarata, R. C., jt. ed. see Edelstein, A. S.
Cammarata, R. C., ed. see Suhir, Ephraim.
Cammarata, Stephanie, et al. The RAND Metadata Management System (RMMS) A Metadata Storage Facility to Support Data Interoperability, Reuse & Sharing. LC 94-6663. 52p. 1995. pap. text 7.50 (*0-8330-1515-X*, MR-163-OSD/A/AF) Rand Corp.
Cammarota, Marianne, ed. More Practice Questions for the Registered Professional Reporter Exam. 16p. 1998. pap. 19.95 (*1-881859-24-X*) Natl Ct Report.
Cammayo, Ines T. Hear the Wind Turning & Other Stories. 84p. (Orig.). (C). 1992. pap. 6.50 (*971-10-0431-3*, Pub. by New Day Pub) Cellar.
***Cammelli, Antonio, et al, eds.** Database & Expert Systems Applications: Proceedings International Workshop on Database & Expert Systems Applications, Florence, Italy, 1999. LC 99-64235. 937p. 1999. 180.00 (*0-7695-0281-4*) IEEE Comp Soc.
Cammenga, Ronald & Hanko, Ronald. Saved by Grace: A Study of the Five Points of Calvinism. LC 95-68231. 257p. 1995. pap. 13.25 (*0-916206-54-8*) Refrd Free Pub Assn.
— Saved by Grace (Study Guide) A Study of the Five Points of Calvinism. LC 95-68230. 30p. 1995. pap., student ed. 4.75 (*0-916206-55-6*) Refrd Free Pub Assn.
Cammer, Leonard. Up from Depression. 1990. mass mkt. 5.99 (*0-671-73482-2*) PB.
Cammermeyer, Margarethe & Appeldorn, Claudia, eds. Core Curriculum for Neuroscience Nursing. 3rd rev. ed. (Illus.). 326p. 1990. 49.95 (*0-9625729-1-8*) Am Assoc Neuroscience.
Cammett, John M., ed. The Italian American Novel. 1969. 5.00 (*0-934675-02-3*) Am Italian.
Cammick, Stephen P. Last Breath: Space Station Rescue. (Illus.). 328p. 1999. pap. 12.95 (*0-9671200-0-4*) Palm Coast Pubg.
***Cammisa, Anne M.** From Rhetoric to Reform? Welfare Policy in American Politics. LC 97-49311. (Dilemmas in American Politics Ser.). 192p. (C). 1998. pap. text 17.00 (*0-8133-2996-5*, Pub. by Westview) HarpC.
Cammisa, Anne M. Governments As Interest Groups: Intergovernmental Lobbying & the Federal System. LC 95-14428. 176p. 1995. 55.00 (*0-275-94962-1*, Praeger Pubs) Greenwood.
Cammisa, Anne M., jt. auth. see Manuel, Paul C.
Cammock-Elliott, Bede. Get a Life! A Success Guide for Young People. 104p. 1998. pap. 13.95 (*1-85835-515-X*, Indust Soc) Stylus Pub VA.
Cammuso, Frank. Below the Belt: Cartoons from the Syracuse Herald Journal, Herald American. LC 93-37909. 1993. write for info. (*0-9629159-5-5*) Pine Tree NY.
***Cammuso, Frank & Seely, Hart.** 2007-Eleven: And Other American Comedies. LC 99-44112. 208p. 2000. 19.95 (*0-375-50412-5*) Villard Books.
Camner, James. Great Composers in Historic Photographs. 144p. 1981. pap. 14.95 (*0-486-24132-7*) Dover.
— The Great Instrumentalists in Historic Photographs: 275 Portraits from 1850 to 1950. (Illus.). 1980. pap. 8.95 (*0-486-23907-1*) Dover.
Camner, James, ed. The Great Opera Stars in Historic Photographs: 343 Portraits from the 1850's to the 1940's. LC 77-86260. (Illus.). 199p. 1978. pap. 14.95 (*0-486-23575-0*) Dover.
— Stars of the Opera, 1950-1985, in Photographs. (Illus.). 128p. 1987. pap. 12.95 (*0-486-25240-X*) Dover.
Camner, James & Edwards, Carl R., eds. Opera Stars, 1970s-1990s: 200 Photographs by Winnie Klotz. LC 98-52669. (Illus.). 128p. 1998. pap. 12.95 (*0-486-40153-7*) Dover.
Camner, James, jt. auth. see Appelbaum, Stanley.
Camnitzer, Luis. Juan Francisco Elso Padillo. (Illus.). 15p. 1991. pap. 5.00 (*0-938437-36-4*) MIT List Visual Arts.
— New Art of Cuba. LC 92-43116. (Illus.). 448p. (C). 1993. text 45.00 (*0-292-71149-2*) U of Tex Pr.
Camnitzer, Luis, et al. The Hybrid State. (Illus.). 108p. (Orig.). 1992. pap. 25.00 (*0-913263-40-0*) Exit Art.
***Camnitzer, Luis, et al.** Wim Delvoye: Pigs. (Illus.). 125p. 2000. 45.00 (*90-5779-012-2*, Pub. by Exhibitions Intl) Dist Art Pubs.
Camo, Pierre. Dufy. (FRE., Illus.). 153p. 1947. pap. 17.95 (*0-8288-3982-4*) Fr & Eur.
Camoin, Francois. The End of the World Is Los Angeles: Stories. LC 81-69838. 104p. 1982. pap. 12.95 (*0-8262-0365-5*) U of Mo Pr.
— Like Love, but Not Exactly: Stories. 120p. (C). 1992. 19.95 (*0-8262-0845-2*) U of Mo Pr.
Camoin, G. F. & Davies, P. J. Reefs & Carbonate Platforms in the Pacific & Indian Oceans. LC 97-28586. (Special Publication Number 25 of the International Association of Sedimentologists). 1998. pap. 95.00 (*0-632-04778-X*) Blackwell Sci.
Camon Aznar, Jose. La Arquitectura y la Orfebreria Espanolas del siglo XVI. (Summa Artis Ser.: Vol. 17). 600p. 1989. 295.00 (*84-239-5217-7*) Elliots Bks.
— Arte Espanol del Siglo XVIII. (Summa Artis Ser.: Vol. 27). 600p. 1989. 295.00 (*84-239-5227-4*) Elliots Bks.
— La Escultura y la Rejeria Espanolas del Siglo XVI. (Summa Artis Ser.: Vol. 18). (SPA.). 600p. 1989. 295.00 (*84-239-5218-5*) Elliots Bks.
— La Pintura Espanola del Siglo XVII. (Summa Artis Ser.: Vol. 25). 600p. 1989. 295.00 (*84-239-5225-8*) Elliots Bks.
— La Pintura Espanola del Siglo XVI. (Summa Artis Ser.: Vol. 24). 600p. 1989. 295.00 (*84-239-5224-X*) Elliots Bks.
— Pintura Medieval Espanola. (Summa Artis Ser.: Vol. 22). 600p. 1989. 295.00 (*84-239-5222-3*) Elliots Bks.
Camon, Ferdinando. Conversations with Primo Levi. Shepley, John, tr. from ITA. LC 88-64143. Orig. Title: Autoritratto Di Primo Levi. 88p. (Orig.). 1989. pap. 9.95 (*0-910395-48-9*) Marlboro Pr.
— The Fifth Estate. Shepley, John, tr. from ITA. 176p. 1987. 29.95 (*0-910395-29-2*); pap. 9.95 (*0-910395-30-6*) Marlboro Pr.
— Life Everlasting. Shepley, John, tr. from ITA. 192p. 1987. 29.95 (*0-910395-31-4*); pap. 10.95 (*0-910395-32-2*) Marlboro Pr.
— La Maladie Humaine. (FRE.). 215p. 1987. pap. 10.95 (*0-7859-2062-5*, 2070378306) Fr & Eur.
— Memorial. Calicchio, David, tr. 122p. 1996. pap. 13.95 (*0-8101-6013-7*, Marlboro) Northwestern U Pr.
— The Sickness Called Man. Shepley, John, tr. from ITA. LC 92-60850. 180p. 1992. 18.95 (*0-910395-90-X*) Marlboro Pr.
— The Sickness Called Man. Shepley, John, tr. 177p. 1996. pap. 14.95 (*0-8101-6015-3*, Marlboro) Northwestern U Pr.
— The Story of Sirio. Bertea, Cassandra, tr. from ITA. LC 84-63123. Orig. Title: Storia Di Sirio. 131p. (Orig.). 1985. pap. 9.95 (*0-910395-12-8*) Marlboro Pr.
Camoriano, David, ed. see Canfield, Patrick M.
Camou, Fernando. Chemistry 230 LL Lab Manual. 1996. pap. text 12.05 (*1-56870-231-0*) RonJon Pub.
Camou, Mario, jt. auth. see Couwenberghe, Aaron.
Camozzi, Anne, jt. auth. see Tower, Julie.

Camp. Environmental Science CTB. (Agriculture Ser.). 1994. 105.95 (*0-8273-6130-0*) Delmar.
— Managing Our Natural Resources. 3rd ed. (Agriculture Ser.). 48p. (C). 1996. text, teacher ed. 12.75 (*0-8273-6717-1*) Delmar.
— Managing Our Natural Resources CTB. 3rd ed. (Agriculture Ser.). 1996. 100.00 (*0-8273-7492-5*) Delmar.
***Camp & Daugherty.** Managing Our Natural Resources. 4th ed. (C). 2000. text 36.00 (*0-7668-1554-4*); text, wbk. ed. 18.00 (*0-7668-1556-0*) Delmar.
Camp & Hehn, Darold. Managing Our Natural Resources. 3rd ed. (Agriculture Ser.). 144p. (C). 1995. mass mkt., wbk. ed. 17.00 (*0-8273-6926-3*) Delmar.
— Managing Our Natural Resources. 3rd ed. (Agriculture Ser.). 32p. 1996. pap. text, teacher ed. 12.75 (*0-8273-6927-1*) Delmar.
***Camp, David N.** History of New Britain: With Sketches of Farmington & Berlin, Connecticut 1640-1889. (Illus.). 572p. 2000. pap. 37.54 (*0-7884-1485-2*, 1485) Heritage Bk.
Camp, A. Cinema Mexicain. 1976. lib. bdg. 59.95 (*0-8490-1634-7*) Gordon Pr.
Camp, Ann. Pen Lettering. (Illus.). pap. 6.95 (*0-8008-6272-4*) Taplinger.
Camp, Anthony J. Everyone Has Roots: An Introduction to English Genealogy. LC 78-62818. 189p. 9.50 (*0-8063-0828-1*) Clearfield Co.
— My Ancestors Came with the Conqueror: Those Who Did & Some of Those Who Probably Did Not. 89p. 1998. reprint ed. pap. 9.50 (*0-8063-1390-0*, 878) Genealog Pub.
***Camp, Ashby L.** Feet Firmly Planted: A Theological Handbook for the Church of Christ. LC 99-73772. 258p. 1999. pap. 12.95 (*0-9642076-3-X*) Ktisis Pubng.
Camp, Ashby L. The Myth of Natural Origins: How Science Points to Divine Creation. LC 94-77024. 136p. (Orig.). 1994. pap. 9.95 (*0-9642076-2-1*) Ktisis Pubng.
Camp, Beth. Effective Workplace Writing. 1997. teacher ed. 11.77 (*0-256-25744-2*, Irwn McGrw-H) McGrw-H Hghr Educ.
Camp, Beth. Writing for the Workplace. 352p. (C). 1996. text 25.50 (*0-256-22016-6*, Irwn McGrw-H) McGrw-H Hghr Educ.
Camp, C. L., ed. see White, Philo.
Camp, C. V. & Gipson, G. Steven. Boundary Element Analysis of Nonhomogeneous Biharmonic Phenomena. Brebbia, Carlos A. & Orszag, S. A., eds. (Lecture Notes in Engineering Ser.: Vol. 74). (Illus.). xii, 246p. 1992. 72.95 (*0-387-55020-8*) Spr-Verlag.
***Camp, Cameron J.** Montessori Based Activities for Persons with Dementia, Vol. 1. 76p. 1999. pap. 46.50 (*0-9676343-1-8*) Myers Resear Inst.
Camp, Cameron J., jt. illus. see Brush, Jennifer A.
Camp, Candace. Impetuous. 1998. per. 5.99 (*1-55166-450-X*) Harlequin Bks.
— Impulse. 408p. 1997. per. 5.99 (*1-55166-264-7*, 1-662642, Mira Bks) Harlequin Bks.
***Camp, Candace.** Impulse. 2000. mass mkt. 3.99 (*1-55166-634-0*, 1-66634-6, Mira Bks) Harlequin Bks.
Camp, Candace. Indiscreet. 408p. 1999. mass mkt. write for info. (*1-55166-297-3*, 0-66297-3, Mira Bks) Harlequin Bks.
***Camp, Candace.** Indiscreet. 2000. mass mkt. 3.99 (*1-55166-633-2*, 1-66633-8, Mira Bks) Harlequin Bks.
— No Other Love. 2001. mass mkt. 6.50 (*1-55166-788-6*, Mira Bks) Harlequin Bks.
— Promise Me Tomorrow. 408p. 2000. mass mkt. 6.50 (*1-55166-607-3*, 1-66607-2, Mira Bks) Harlequin Bks.
Camp, Candace. Satan's Angel. (Promo Ser.). 1998. mass mkt. 5.99 (*0-373-83404-7*, 1-83404-3) Harlequin Bks.
— Scandalous. 1996. mass mkt. 5.99 (*1-55166-166-7*, 0-66166-0, Mira Bks) Harlequin Bks.
— A Stolen Heart. 402p. 2000. per. 5.99 (*1-55166-552-2*, Mira Bks) Harlequin Bks.
— Suddenly. 1996. per. 5.99 (*1-55166-035-0*, 1-66035-6, Mira Bks) Harlequin Bks.
— Suddenly. 408p. 1996. mass mkt. 5.99 (*0-614-96285-4*) Mira Pubns.
— Swept Away. (Mira Bks.). 1999. mass mkt. 5.99 (*1-55166-508-5*, 1-66508-2, Mira Bks) Harlequin Bks.
Camp, Candace, et al. Maternity Leave: Tabloid Baby; The Nine-Month Knight; The Paternity Test. 1998. per. 5.99 (*0-373-48366-X*) Harlequin Bks.
Camp, Carole A. American Astronomers: Searchers & Wonderers. LC 95-14472. (Collective Biographies Ser.). (Illus.). 104p. (YA). (gr. 6 up). 1996. lib. bdg. 20.95 (*0-89490-631-3*) Enslow Pubs.
— Sally Ride: First American Woman in Space. LC 97-9339. (People to Know Ser.). (Illus.). 104p. (YA). (gr. 6 up). 1997. lib. bdg. 20.95 (*0-89490-829-4*) Enslow Pubs.
Camp, Carole A., ed. From Flicker to Flame: Clergywomen's Sermons, Vol. I. LC 94-73462. (Illus.). (Orig.). 1995. pap. 15.95 (*1-886172-13-7*) Ash Grove Pr.
— From Flicker to Flame: Clergywomen's Sermons, Vol. II. LC 94-73462. (Illus.). (Orig.). 1995. pap. 15.95 (*1-886172-15-3*) Ash Grove Pr.
Camp, Carole Ann, jt. auth. see Schaper, Donna.
Camp, Catherine C. De, see De Camp, L. Sprague & De Camp, Catherine C.
***Camp, Charles.** Encyclopedia of American Foodways. 2001. lib. bdg. 50.00 (*1-57607-152-9*) ABC-CLIO.
Camp, Charles L. & Allison, H. J. Bibliography of Fossil Vertebrates, 1949-1953. LC 61-65012. (Geological Society of America, Memoir Ser.: No. 84). 570p. reprint ed. 176.70 (*0-8357-7184-9*, 203179600077) Bks Demand.
Camp, Charles L., et al. Bibliography of Fossil Vertebrates, 1954-1958. LC 64-19064. (Geological Society of America, Memoir Ser.: No. 92). 675p. reprint ed. pap. 200.00 (*0-8357-7185-7*, 203179600077) Bks Demand.
— Bibliography of Fossil Vertebrates, 1959-1963. LC 68-54218. (Geological Society of America, Memoir Ser.: No. 117). 688p. reprint ed. pap. 200.00 (*0-8357-7186-5*, 203181600077) Bks Demand.
— Bibliography of Fossil Vertebrates, 1964-1968. LC 79-190170. (Geological Society of America, Memoir Ser.: No. 134). 1183p. reprint ed. pap. 200.00 (*0-8357-7187-3*, 202502800041) Bks Demand.
Camp, Charles L., jt. auth. see Doble, John.
Camp, Charlie. Traces of the Light. (Illus.). 344p. (Orig.). 1996. pap. 14.95 (*0-89896-154-8*) Larksdale.
Camp, Christopher. Beginning Ragtime Guitar. LC 75-16976. (Illus.). (Orig.). 1976. pap. 12.95 (*0-8256-2351-0*, AM35221) Music Sales.
Camp County Genealogical Society Staff. Camp County Texas Marriages, 1874-1978. LC 95-72838. (Illus.). 496p. 1996. write for info. (*0-89725-252-7*, 1722, Penobscot Pr) Picton Pr.
Camp, Deborah. Black-Eyed Susan. 400p. 1990. pap. 3.95 (*0-380-75742-7*, Avon Bks) Morrow Avon.
— Cheyenne's Shadow. 400p. (Orig.). 1994. mass mkt. 4.99 (*0-380-76739-2*, Avon Bks) Morrow Avon.
— Fallen Angel. 384p. (Orig.). 1989. pap. 3.95 (*0-380-75741-9*, Avon Bks) Morrow Avon.
— Fire Lily. 384p. (Orig.). 1991. mass mkt. 4.50 (*0-380-76394-X*, Avon Bks) Morrow Avon.
— Lady Legend. 416p. (Orig.). 1992. mass mkt. 4.50 (*0-380-76735-X*, Avon Bks) Morrow Avon.
— Lonewolf's Woman. 384p. (Orig.). 1995. mass mkt. 4.99 (*0-380-77757-6*, Avon Bks) Morrow Avon.
— Master of Moonspell. 416p. (Orig.). 1993. mass mkt. 4.50 (*0-380-76736-8*, Avon Bks) Morrow Avon.
— My Wild Rose. 416p. (Orig.). 1992. mass mkt. 4.50 (*0-380-76738-4*, Avon Bks) Morrow Avon.
— Primrose. 384p. (Orig.). 1988. pap. 3.95 (*0-380-75435-5*, Avon Bks) Morrow Avon.
— Too Tough to Tame. 1996. mass mkt. 5.50 (*0-380-78251-0*, Avon Bks) Morrow Avon.
— Tough Man's Woman. 384p. 1997. mass mkt. 5.99 (*0-380-78252-9*, Avon Bks) Morrow Avon.
— Tough Talk & Tender Kisses. 384p. (Orig.). 1997. mass mkt. 5.99 (*0-380-78250-2*, Avon Bks) Morrow Avon.
Camp, Deborah L. Doing Business in Memphis: A Directory of Business & Industry. 350p. 1996. write for info. (*1-888868-00-7*) Delta Cnslting.
Camp, Delayne. Taming the Wild Man. 1995. per. 3.50 (*0-373-16598-6*) Harlequin Bks.
Camp, Dennis, ed. The Poetry of Vachel Lindsay, Vol. 3. 190p. 1986. 14.95 (*0-933180-77-2*) Spoon Riv Poetry.
Camp, Dennis, ed. see Lindsay, Vachel.
Camp, Doug. Turkey Hunting: Spring & Fall. Taylor, Buck, ed. (Illus.). 176p. (Orig.). 1983. pap. 12.95 (*0-940022-01-X*) Outdoor Skills.
Camp, Glen D., Jr., ed. Berlin in the East-West Struggle, 1958-61. LC 70-159689. (Interim History Ser.). 258p. reprint ed. pap. 80.00 (*0-8357-7141-5*, 202289700031) Bks Demand.
Camp, Gregory S. Selling Fear: Conspiracy Theories & End-Times Paranoia. LC 96-18779. 288p. 1997. pap. 15.99 (*0-8010-5721-3*) Baker Bks.
Camp, Helen B., jt. auth. see Bradley, Robert L.
Camp, Helen C. Iron in Her Soul: Elizabeth Gurley Flynn & the American Left. (Illus.). 396p. 1995. 40.00 (*0-87422-105-6*); pap. 28.00 (*0-87422-106-4*) Wash St U Pr.
Camp, Henry R. Sequatchie County: A Story of a Place & Its People. LC 97-29666. (THL Ser.). 1997. 19.95 (*1-57736-055-9*, Hillsboro Pr) Providence Hse.
Camp, James. Carnal Refreshment: Poems. (Burning Deck Poetry Ser.). 1975. 15.00 (*0-930900-02-2*); pap. 4.00 (*0-930900-03-0*) Burning Deck.
Camp, Jeffery. Draw: How to Master the Art. LC 93-34251. (Illus.). 256p. 1994. reprint ed. pap. 14.95 (*1-56458-526-3*) DK Pub Inc.
Camp, John. Discovering Bells & Bellringing. 1989. pap. 25.00 (*0-85263-913-9*, Pub. by Shire Pubns) St Mut.
— Discovering Bells & Bellringing. (Handbook Ser.: No. 29). (Illus.). 64p. 1999. pap. 8.50 (*0-7478-0326-9*, Pub. by Shire Pubns) Parkwest Pubns.
Camp, John, see Sandford, John, pseud.
Camp, John F., Jr. & Parke, N. Grier, II. Camp: Ancestry & Descendants of Frederick Tracy Camp & His Wife Marion Fee. Jacobus, Donald L., ed. 171p. 1997. reprint ed. pap. 25.00 (*0-8328-7825-1*); reprint ed. lib. bdg. 35.00 (*0-8328-7824-3*) Higginson Bk Co.
Camp, John M., II. The Athenian Agora: A Guide to the Excavation & Museum. 4th ed. LC 91-226122. (Illus.). 292p. 1990. pap. 15.00 (*960-7067-00-2*) Am Sch Athens.
Camp, John M. The Athenian Agora: Excavations in the Heart of Classical Athens. LC 85-51469. (Illus.). 232p. 1998. reprint ed. pap. 24.95 (*0-500-27683-8*, Pub. by Thames Hudson) Norton.
Camp, John M., II. Gods & Heroes in the Athenian Agora. (Excavations of the Athenian Agora Picture Bks.: No. 19). (Illus.). 32p. 1980. pap. 3.00 (*0-87661-623-6*) Am Sch Athens.
— Horses & Horsemanship in the Athenian Agora. LC 98-191575. (Athenian Agora Picture Bks.: Vol. 24). (Illus.). 40p. 1998. pap. 5.00 (*0-87661-639-2*) Am Sch Athens.
Camp, John M., II & Dinsmoor, William B., Jr. Ancient Athenian Building Methods. (Excavations of the Athenian Agora Picture Bks.: No. 21). (Illus.). 32p. 1984. pap. 3.00 (*0-87661-626-0*) Am Sch Athens.
Camp, John R., ed. see Crawford, William R., et al.
***Camp, Justin J.** The Heart & Soul of Venture Capital: An Early-Stage Venture Capital Due Diligence Framework. LC 00-190660. 255p. 2000. 25.00 (*0-7388-1916-6*); pap. 18.00 (*0-7388-1917-4*) Xlibris Corp.
***Camp, Kim.** Fit to Be a Lady. (EZ Lesson Plan Ser.). (Illus.). 2000. pap., student ed. 7.99 (*0-8499-8828-4*) Word Pub.
Camp, Kim. Twelve Going on Twenty. LC 99-59373. 160p. 1999. pap. 12.99 (*0-8499-3759-0*) Word Pub.
Camp, L. Jean. Trust & Risk in Internet Commerce. (Illus.). 283p. 2000. 32.95 (*0-262-03271-6*) MIT Pr.
Camp, L. Raymond. Roger Williams, God's Apostle of Advocacy: Biography & Rhetoric. LC 88-26708. (Studies in American Religion: Vol. 36). 240p. 1989. lib. bdg. 89.95 (*0-88946-679-3*) E Mellen.
Camp, L. Raymond, jt. auth. see Kell, Carl L.
Camp, L. Sprague De, see Sprague De Camp, L.
Camp, L. Sprague De, see Turtledove, Harry & Sprague De Camp, L.
Camp, L. Sprague De, see Sprague De Camp, L.
Camp, LaVonne T. Lingering Fever: A World War II Nurse's Memoir. LC 96-48855. (Illus.). 184p. 1997. lib. bdg. 25.00 (*0-7864-0322-5*) McFarland & Co.
Camp, Linda, jt. auth. see Graham, Terry L.
Camp, Lindsay. The Biggest Bed in the World. LC 99-61184. (Illus.). 40p. (J). (ps-1). 2000. 14.95 (*0-06-028687-3*) HarpC.
— Keeping up with Cheetah. (ARA & ENG., Illus.). 28p. (J). (ps-2). pap. 12.95 (*1-85269-145-X*); pap. 12.95 (*1-85269-147-6*); pap. 12.95 (*1-85269-150-6*) Writers & Readers.
— Why? LC 98-34382. (Illus.). 32p. (J). (ps-3). 1999. 15.99 (*0-399-23396-2*, G P Putnam) Peng Put Young Read.
***Camp, Marcia.** You Can't Leave Till You Do the Paperwork: Matters of Life & Death. LC 99-91899. 184p. 1999. 25.00 (*0-7388-1356-7*); pap. 18.00 (*0-7388-1357-5*) Xlibris Corp.
Camp, Mark J. & Richardson, Graham T. Roadside Geology of Indiana. LC 99-24724. (Roadside Geology Ser.: Vol. 20). (Illus.). 326p. 1999. pap. 18.00 (*0-87842-396-6*) Mountain Pr.
Camp, Martin. Life on the High Wire: Faith & a Man's Search for Balance. LC 96-39503. 160p. 1997. pap. 12.00 (*0-687-05239-4*) Dimen for Liv.
— Why Alligators Don't Have Wings. (Illus.). 32p. (J). (ps-5). 1994. 13.95 (*1-880092-06-9*) Bright Bks TX.
Camp, Max W. Developing Piano Performance: A Teaching Philosophy. 228p. (Orig.). (C). 1990. reprint ed. pap. text 24.95 (*0-88284-617-5*, 11133) Alfred Pub.
— Teaching Piano: Synthesis of Mind, Ear & Body. 224p. (C). 1992. 39.95 (*0-88284-526-8*, 6518); pap. 24.95 (*0-88284-527-6*, 6032) Alfred Pub.
Camp, Maxime Du, see Du Camp, Maxime.
Camp, Melanie, ed. see Camp, Steven C.
Camp, Melanie, ed. see Opera Society of Fort Lauderdale Staff.
Camp, Mildred, jt. auth. see Camp, Shelby.
Camp, Nancy, jt. auth. see Iyer, Patricia W.
Camp, Norma C. George Washington: Man of Prayer & Courage. LC 76-3084. (Sower Ser.). (Illus.). 169p. (YA). (gr. 5-9). 1977. pap. 7.99 (*0-915134-25-X*) Mott Media.
Camp, Norman M., et al. Stress, Strain, & Vietnam: An Annotated Bibliography of Two Decades of Psychiatric & Social Sciences Literature Reflecting the Effect of the War on the American Soldier, 1. LC 88-30138. (Bibliographies & Indexes in Military Studies). 334p. 1988. lib. bdg. 85.00 (*0-313-26272-1*, CSN) Greenwood.
Camp, P. E. Van, see Devreese, Jozef T., ed.
Camp, P. E. Van, see Devreese, Jozef T. & Van Camp, P. E., eds.
Camp, P. E. Van, see Devreese, J. T., ed.
Camp, P. E. Van, see Devreese, J. T. & Van Camp, P. E., eds.
Camp, P. E. Van, see Devreese, J. T., ed.
Camp, P. E. Van, see Devreese, J. T. & Van Camp, P. E., eds.
Camp, Pamela S., et al. Exploring Biology. 2nd ed. (C). 1984. pap. text, student ed. 45.00 (*0-03-063373-7*, Pub. by SCP) Harcourt.
Camp, Peggy, et al. JCAHO Education Standards: From Challenge to Implementation. 98p. (Orig.). 1996. pap. write for info. (*0-939583-96-8*) Assn Oper Rm Nurses.
Camp, Piet Van, see Devreese, Josef T., ed.
Camp, Piet Van, see Devreese, Josef T. & Van Camp, Piet, eds.
***Camp, Priscilla, et al.** Capacity & Undue Influence: Assessing, Challenging & Defending, Fall 1999 Action Guide. Gerber, Mary, ed. 52p. 1999. 58.00i (*0-7626-0383-6*, ES-11920) Cont Ed Bar-CA.
Camp, R. D. Lima-6: A Marine Company Commander in Vietnam. McCarthy, Paul, ed. 360p. 1990. reprint ed. per. 4.99 (*0-671-70436-2*) PB.
Camp, Raymond. Game Cookery in America & Europe. rev. ed. LC 58-10599. (Illus.). 192p. 1983. reprint ed. 29.95 (*0-318-00146-2*) Wild Duck Pr.
Camp, Richard D. & Hammel, Eric. Lima-6: A Marine Company Commander in Vietnam. LC 99-19185. (Illus.). 295p. 1999. reprint ed. pap. 19.95 (*0-935553-36-3*) Pacifica Military.
Camp, Richard Van, see Van Camp, Richard.
Camp, Robert. Destiny Cards: Your Birth Card & What It Reveals about Your Past, Present & Future. LC 98-41430. 368p. 1997. pap. 24.95 (*1-57071-189-5*) Sourcebks.
— Love Cards: What Your Birthday Reveals about You & Your Personal Relationships. 3rd ed. LC 97-1800. 384p. 1997. otabind 24.95 (*1-57071-145-3*) Sourcebks.
Camp, Robert C. Benchmarking: The Search for Industry Best Practices That Lead to Superior Performance. (Illus.). 299p. 1989. 34.95 (*0-87389-058-2*, H0575) ASQ Qual Pr.
— Benchmarking: The Search for Industry Best Practices That Lead to Superior Performance. (Illus.). 299p. 1989. text 34.95 (*0-527-91635-8*, 916358) Productivity Inc.
— Business Process Benchmarking: Finding & Implementing Best Practices. LC 94-34028. (Illus.). 464p. 1994. text 44.00 (*0-87389-296-8*, H0852) ASQ Qual Pr.
Camp, Robert C., ed. Global Cases in Benchmarking: Best Practices from Organizations Around the World. LC 97-50315. 640p. 1998. 51.75 (*0-87389-388-3*, H0949) ASQ Qual Pr.
Camp, Roderic A. Crossing Swords: Politics & Religion in Mexico. 352p. 1997. text 70.00 (*0-19-510784-5*) OUP.
— Entrepreneurs & Politics in Twentieth-Century Mexico. 320p. 1989. text 65.00 (*0-19-505719-8*) OUP.
— Intellectuals & the State in Twentieth-Century Mexico. (Latin American Monographs: No. 65). (Illus.). 293p. (C). 1985. pap. 12.95 (*0-292-73839-0*) U of Tex Pr.
— The Making of a Government: Political Leaders in Modern Mexico. LC 84-8811. 237p. 1984. 34.00 (*0-8165-0871-2*) U of Ariz Pr.
— Memoirs of a Mexican Politician. LC 87-30244. (Illus.). 248p. 1988. reprint ed. pap. 76.90 (*0-608-04128-9*, 206486100011) Bks Demand.
— Mexican Political Biographies, 1884-1934. 490p. 1991. text 80.00 (*0-292-75119-2*) U of Tex Pr.
— Mexican Political Biographies, 1935-1993. 652p. (C). 1995. text 55.00 (*0-292-71174-3*) U of Tex Pr.
— Mexican Political Biographies, 1935-1993. 3rd ed. 652p. (C). 1995. pap. 24.95 (*0-292-71181-6*) U of Tex Pr.
— Mexico's Leaders, Their Education & Recruitment. LC 79-19836. 277p. 1980. pap. 85.90 (*0-608-05648-0*, 206610200006) Bks Demand.
— Political Recruitment Across Two Centuries: Mexico, 1884-1991. 304p. (Orig.). (C). 1995. pap. 17.95 (*0-292-71173-5*); text 40.00 (*0-292-71172-7*) U of Tex Pr.
— Politics in Mexico: The Decline of Authoritarianism. 3rd ed. LC 98-29058. (Illus.). 288p. (C). 1999. pap. 22.95 (*0-19-512412-X*) OUP.
— Successor. LC 92-34656. 300p. 1993. 11.95 (*0-8263-1420-1*) U of NM Pr.
— Who's Who in Mexico Today. 2nd ed. LC 92-35773. 206p. 1993. pap. 85.00 (*0-8133-8452-4*, Pub. by Westview) HarpC.
Camp, Roderic A., et al, eds. Polling for Democracy: Public Opinion & Political Liberalization in Mexico. (Latin American Silhouettes Ser.). 180p. (C). 1996. 45.00 (*0-8420-2583-9*) Scholarly Res Inc.
Camp, Roderic Ai, see Ai Camp, Roderic, ed.
Camp, Scott D. Worker Response to Plant Closings: Steelworkers in Johnstown & Youngstown. rev. ed. LC 94-47515. (Garland Studies in the History of American Labor). (Illus.). 324p. 1995. text 25.00 (*0-8153-2017-5*) Garland.
Camp, Shelby & Camp, Mildred. Louisiana Gumbo: A Cajun Cookbook. 256p. (Orig.). 1986. pap. 10.00 (*0-935687-00-9*, 186) Best Cookbks.
Camp-Sorrell, Dawn, jt. ed. see Liebman, Marcia C.
Camp, Steven C. Money: 127 Answers to Your Most-Asked Financial Questions: The Q & A Reference for Everything from Asset Allocation to Zero-Coupon Bonds. Trunkey, Melanie, ed. (Illus.). 118p. (Orig.). 1995. pap. 12.95 (*1-887620-00-1*) Trunkey Pub.
— Money Matters Made Easy: The Q & A Reference on Everything from Asset Allocation to Zero-Coupon Bonds. Camp, Melanie et al, eds. LC 97-61406. 179p. 1997. pap. 12.95 (*1-887620-01-X*) Trunkey Pub.
Camp, Sue C. Developing Editing Skill. 176p. 1985. text 9.56 (*0-07-009638-4*) McGraw.
— Developing Proofreading Skill. Tinervia, Joseph, ed. LC 80-12596. (Illus.). 128p. (YA). (gr. 11-12). 1980. text 6.96 (*0-07-009635-X*) McGraw.
— Developing Proofreading Skill. 2nd ed. 1987. pap. 12.25 (*0-07-009727-5*) McGraw.
— Developing Proofreading Skill: With Editing Applications. 3rd ed. LC 92-36771. 1993. 12.50 (*0-02-800897-9*) Glencoe.
***Camp, Sue C. & Satterwhite, Marilyn L.** College Communication. 448p. 1998. text 46.56 (*0-02-802171-1*) Glencoe.
— College Communication. annot. ed. 1998. teacher ed. 53.22 (*0-02-802172-X*) Glencoe.
Camp, Sue C. & Satterwhite, Marilyn L. College Communication. 7th ed. 1998. teacher ed., student ed. 27.75 (*0-02-802184-3*); student ed., wbk. ed. 23.59 (*0-02-802183-5*) Glencoe.
***Camp, Sue C. & Satterwhite, Marilyn L.** College English & Communication. 7th annot. ed. 1998. teacher ed. 65.25 (*0-02-802169-X*) Glencoe.
Camp, Sue C., et al. College English & Communication. 7th ed. LC 97-29555. 1997. write for info. (*0-02-802168-1*) Glencoe.
Camp, Sylvia. I Wonder from Job. 1989. pap. 3.95 (*0-89315-127-0*) Lambert Bk.
Camp, Sylvia L. Obscure Voices from the Past. 1990. pap. 5.80 (*0-89137-458-2*) Quality Pubns.
— Welcome to My World. 1985. pap. 6.15 (*0-89137-435-3*) Quality Pubns.
***Camp, Terri.** The Greatest Mom Ever. 2000. pap. 10.99 (*1-929125-08-9*, Pub. by Loyal Pubng) BookWorld.
Camp, Thomas. With Both Eyes Shut Everything Looks the Same. 300p. 1992. 19.95 (*1-878208-16-0*) Guild Pr IN.
Camp, Victoria. Making Music on Your PC. LC 97-11569. 1997. 29.95 incl. cd-rom (*1-55755-327-0*) Abacus MI.
Camp, W. The New Mexico Showdown. 1989. pap. 2.95 (*1-55817-194-0*) Kensgtn Pub Corp.
Camp, Walter. American Football. LC 74-15732. (Popular Culture in America Ser.). 248p. 1975. reprint ed. 25.95 (*0-405-06367-9*) Ayer.
— Custer in 1976: Walter Camp's Notes on the Custer Fight. Hammer, Kenneth, ed. LC 89-70512. (Illus.). 318p. 1990. pap. 15.95 (*0-8061-2279-X*) U of Okla Pr.

An Asterisk (*) at the beginning of an entry indicates that the title is appearing for the first time.

Camp, Wesley D. Camp's Unfamiliar Quotations from 2,000 BC to the Present 496p. (C). 1998. pap. 3.98 (*0-13-619081-2*) P-H.
— Roots of Western Civilization, 2 vols. Incl. Vol. 1. From Ancient Times to 1715. (C). 1983. pap. text 26.50 (*0-07-554669-8*); Vol. 2. From the Enlightenment to the 1980's. (C). 1983. pap. text 26.50 (*0-07-554670-1*); (Illus.). (C). 1983. pap. text. write for info. (*0-318-57752-6*) McGraw.

***Camp, Wesley D.** Word Lover's Book of Unfamiliar Quotations. LC 99-223303. 496p. 1999. pap. 18.00 (*0-7352-0098-X*) PH Pr.

Camp, Wesley D., tr. see Egret, Jean.

Camp, Will. Comanche Trail. (Tony Hillerman's Frontier Ser.). 272p. 1999. mass mkt. 5.99 (*0-06-101293-9*) HarpC.
— Tarnished Badge. 1990. mass mkt. 2.95 (*1-55817-390-0*, Pinncle Kensgtn) Kensgtn Pub Corp.

Camp, William. Managing Our National Resources. 2nd ed. 1991. pap., teacher ed. 12.00 (*0-8273-4067-2*) Delmar.
— Managing Our Natural Resources. 2nd ed. 1991. pap. 33.95 (*0-8273-4066-4*) Delmar.

Camp, William, jt. auth. see Stoff, Joshua.

Camp, William E., et al, eds. The Principal's Legal Handbook. rev. ed. 320p. 1993. text 35.00 (*1-56534-056-6*) Ed Law Assn.

Camp, William G. & Daugherty, Thomas B. Managing Our Natural Resources. 3rd ed. LC 95-15154. 368p. (J). 1995. mass mkt. 55.95 (*0-8273-6716-3*) Delmar.

Camp, William G. & Donahue, Roy L. Environmental Science for Agriculture & the Life Sciences. LC 92-43120. 423p. 1993. mass mkt. 55.95 (*0-8273-5025-2*) Delmar.
— Environmental Science for Agriculture & the Life Sciences. 487p. 1994. teacher ed. 89.95 (*0-8273-6128-9*) Delmar.
— Environmental Science for Agriculture & the Life Sciences: Instructor's Guide. 48p. 1994. pap., teacher ed. 12.75 (*0-8273-5026-0*) Delmar.

Camp, William G., jt. auth. see Heath, Betty.

Campa, Arthur. Hispanic Folklore Studies of Arthur Campa: An Original Anthology. Cortes, Carlos E., ed. & intro. by. LC 76-1475. (Chicano Heritage Ser.). (Illus.). 1977. 46.95 (*0-405-09536-8*) Ayer.

Campa, Arthur L. Hispanic Culture in the Southwest. LC 78-58135. (Illus.). 328p. (C). 1993. pap. 27.95 (*0-8061-2569-1*) U of Okla Pr.
— Hispanic Culture in the Southwest. LC 78-58135. (Illus.). 328p. reprint ed. pap. 101.70 (*0-8357-8897-0*, 203329500085) Bks Demand.
— Treasure of the Sangre De Cristos: Tales & Traditions of the Spanish Southwest. LC 94-8093. (Illus.). 223p. 1994. pap. 13.95 (*0-8061-1176-3*) U of Okla Pr.

Campa, M., et al. Pseudomonas Aeruginosa As an Opportunistic Pathogen. (Infectious Agents & Pathogenesis Ser.). (Illus.). 440p. (C). 1993. text 110.00 (*0-306-44265-5*, Kluwer Plenum) Kluwer Academic.

Campa, Pedro F. Emblemata Hispanica: An Annotated Bibliography of Spanish Emblem Literature to the Year 1700. LC 90-2847. 170p. (C). 1990. text 49.95 (*0-8223-1031-7*) Duke.

Campa, Ricardo. New Aspects of Renaissance Art. 1998. pap. 24.00 (*1-883058-69-4*) Global Pubns.

Campa, Roman de La, see De la Campa, Roman.

Campadonica, Carol. How to Build a California Mission: San Juan Capistiano, 20 vols. Mueller, Bondell et al, eds. (How to Build a California Mission Ser.). (Illus.). (J). (gr. 4-5). 1998. pap. write for info. (*0-9648488-8-0*) Buzzard Pr.

Campagna, Ann B., jt. auth. see Campagna, Daniel S.

Campagna, Anthony S. The Economic Consequences of the Vietnam War. LC 90-45296. 176p. 1991. 39.95 (*0-275-93816-6*, C3816, Praeger Pubs); pap. 18.95 (*0-275-93388-1*, B3388, Praeger Pubs) Greenwood.
— Economic Policy in the Carter Administration, 171. LC 95-22981. (Contributions in Economics & Economic History Ser.: Vol. 171). 232p. 1995. 65.00 (*0-313-29568-9*, Greenwood Pr) Greenwood.
— The Economy of the Reagan Years: The Economic Consequences of the Reagan Administration, 150. LC 93-14125. (Contributions in Economics & Economic History Ser.: No. 150). 240p. 1994. 65.00 (*0-313-28866-6*, GM8866, Greenwood Pr) Greenwood.

Campagna, Anthony S. U. S. National Economic Policy, 1917-1985. LC 86-30316. 662p. 1987. 55.00 (*0-275-92426-2*, C2426, Praeger Pubs) Greenwood.
— U. S. National Economic Policy, 1917-1985. LC 86-30316. (Illus.). 662p. 1988. pap. 24.95 (*0-275-92907-8*, B2907, Praeger Pubs) Greenwood.

Campagna, Daniel S. & Campagna, Ann B. Democracy, Law, & Justice. (Illus.). 80p. (YA). (gr. 5). 1996. pap. text 9.95 (*1-58037-006-3*, Pub. by M Twain Media) Carson-Dellos.

Campagna, Daniel S. & Poffenberger, Donald L. The Sexual Trafficking in Children: An Investigation of the Child Sex Trade. LC 87-1242. 264p. 1987. 45.00 (*0-86569-154-1*, T154, Auburn Hse); pap. 17.95 (*0-86569-155-X*, R155, Auburn Hse) Greenwood.

Campagna, Don, jt. auth. see Campagna, Joyce.

Campagna, Jeff, ed. see McIntosh, Anne.

Campagna, Joyce & Campagna, Don. Cooking Contest Cookbook: More Than 100 Prize Winning Recipes. LC 99-57592. 304p. 2000. per. 12.00 (*0-684-84447-8*, Fireside) S&S Trade Pap.

Campagna, Palmiro. Storms of Controversy: The Secret Avro Arrow Files Revealed. (Illus.). 176p. 1992. 26.95 (*0-7737-2649-7*) Genl Dist Srvs.
— Storms of Controversy: The Secret Avro Arrow Files Revealed. 1999. pap. 14.95 (*0-7737-5990-5*) Genl Dist Srvs.
— Storms of Controversy: The Secret Avro Arrow Files Revealed. rev. ed. (Illus.). 272p. 1997. pap. 16.95 (*0-7737-5861-5*) Stoddart Publ.
— The UFO Files: The Canadian Connection Exposed. LC 97-164879. (Illus.). 8p. 1997. pap. 21.95 (*0-7737-3015-X*) Stoddart Publ.
— The UFO Files: The Canadian Connection Exposed. rev. ed. LC 99-182831. (Illus.). 224p. 1998. pap. 14.95 (*0-7737-5973-5*) Stoddart Publ.

***Campagna, Phil.** The Liberty Circle. 248p. (YA). (gr. 9-12). 2000. pap. 7.95 (*0-929141-69-5*) Napoleon Publ.

Campagnari, F., et al, eds. Scientific-Technical Backgrounds for Biotechnology Regulations: Based on the Lectures Given During the Eurocourse on 'Scientific-Technical Backgrounds for Biotechnology Regulations' Held at the Joint Research Centre Ispra, Italy, June 4-7, 1991. LC 94-1388. (Eurocourses: Technological Innovation Ser.: Vol. 2). 196p. (C). 1994. text 127.50 (*0-7923-1587-1*) Kluwer Academic.

Campagnoni, A. T., ed. Expression of Developmentally Regulated Genes in the Nervous System. (Journal: Developmental Neuroscience: Vol. 12, No. 4-5, 1990). (Illus.). 128p. 1990. pap. 81.00 (*3-8055-5313-7*) S Karger.

Campaign for Human Development Staff. Novena for Justice & Peace. LC 98-191022. 13 p. 1998. 1.00 (*1-57455-237-6*) US Catholic.

***Campaign for Labor Rights Staff & Essential Action Staff, eds.** False Profits: Who Wins, Who Loses When the IMF, World Bank & WTO Come to Town. (Illus.). 24p. 2000. 1.00 (*0-9679024-0-1*) Allil Global Justice.

Campaign, Jessica E. The Path of the Tiger. (Illus.). 160p. (J). (gr. 4-8). 1994. pap., per. 10.95 (*0-9644299-1-8*) Tora Prods.

Campaigne, Barbara & Lampman, Richard M. Exercise in the Clinical Management of Diabetes. LC 93-43321. (Illus.). 224p. 1994. text 36.00 (*0-87322-634-8*, BCAM0634) Human Kinetics.

Campaigne, Carol, ed. see Benson, Seymour.

Campaigne, Carol, ed. see Hicks, William M.

Campaigne, Carol, ed. see Hilfiker, Alan F., et al.

Campaigne, E. Adventures in Organic Sulfur Chemistry, Vol. 10. (Sulfur Reports). 102p. 1990. text 185.00 (*3-7186-5057-6*, Harwood Acad Pubs) Gordon & Breach.

Campaigne, R. J. Who Am I? Find Yourself & Your Perfect Mate. 1999. pap. 8.95 (*0-533-12863-3*) Vantage.

Campaigns & Elections Staff. The Road to Victory 2000. 2nd ed. LC 98-101705. 669p. 1997. per. 39.96 (*0-7872-4389-2*) Kendall-Hunt.

Campana, A. M. Teacher of Picture Frame Finishing. (Illus.). 12.95 (*0-939608-12-X*) Campana Art.

Campana, D. M. Amateur Artist' Encyclopedia. (Illus.). 13.95 (*0-939608-17-0*) Campana Art.
— The Artist & the Decorator. (Illus.). 14.95 (*0-939608-16-2*) Campana Art.
— Beginner in China Painting. Date not set. 4.00 (*0-939608-32-4*) Campana Art.
— Beginner in Oil Printing. (Illus.). Date not set. 4.00 (*0-939608-31-6*) Campana Art.
— Beginner in Water Color. (Illus.). 4.00 (*0-939608-30-8*) Campana Art.
— Book of Monograms. (Illus.). 10.00 (*0-939608-06-5*) Campana Art.
— Decorative Design, No. 4. (Illus.). 10.50 (*0-939608-22-7*) Campana Art.
— Decorative Designs, No. 5. (Illus.). Date not set. 17.50 (*0-939608-23-5*) Campana Art.
— Decorative Designs, No. 6. (Illus.). 10.50 (*0-939608-24-3*) Campana Art.
— Decorative Designs: No. 7. (Illus.). 17.50 (*0-939608-19-7*) Campana Art.
— Enamel & Raised Paste: For the China Painter. rev. ed. reprint ed. 4.50 (*0-939608-45-6*) Campana Art.
— Enamel Decorations for Porcelain & Glass. 4.50 (*0-939608-05-7*) Campana Art.
— Fifty-Five Full Color Designs. (Illus.). 65.00 (*0-939608-37-5*) Campana Art.
— Glass Decorating & Firing. rev. ed. 4.50 (*0-939608-46-4*) Campana Art.
— Gold Formula. (Illus.). 1999. 19.95 (*0-939608-41-3*) Campana Art.
— Leather Craft & Patterns. (Illus.). 1997. 4.50 (*0-939608-49-9*) Campana Art.
— New Transparent Decorations. 9.95 (*0-939608-27-8*) Campana Art.
— 100 Lustre Color Effects. Date not set. 4.50 (*0-939608-04-9*) Campana Art.
— 1000 Design & Ideas. 1200p. 1998. 17.00 (*0-939608-39-1*) Campana Art.
— Picture Painting Self Taught. 16.95 (*0-939608-28-6*) Campana Art.
— Roses & How to Paint Them. (Illus.). 9.95 (*0-939608-40-5*) Campana Art.
— Self-Taught China Printing. 1997. 4.50 (*0-939608-47-2*) Campana Art.
— Teacher of Advertising & Lettering. (Illus.). 12.95 (*0-939608-29-4*) Campana Art.
— Teacher of Animal Painting. (Illus.). 9.95 (*0-939608-14-6*) Campana Art.
— Teacher of China Painting. (Illus.). 17.95 (*0-939608-00-6*) Campana Art.
— Teacher of Drawing. (Illus.). 12.00 (*0-939608-13-8*) Campana Art.
— Teacher of Flower & Fruit Painting. (Illus.). 17.95 (*0-939608-03-0*) Campana Art.
— The Teacher of Jesso-Craft. (Illus.). 9.50 (*0-939608-21-9*) Campana Art.
— Teacher of Linoleum Block Painting. 7.50 (*0-939608-25-1*) Campana Art.
— Teacher of Oil Painting. (Illus.). 15.95 (*0-939608-07-3*) Campana Art.
— Teacher of Pastel Painting. (Illus.). 9.95 (*0-939608-09-X*) Campana Art.
— Teacher of Pottery, Clay Modeling, Casting, Sculpturing, Wood Carving. (Illus.). 9.50 (*0-939608-10-3*) Campana Art.
— Teacher of Pottery Made at Home. (Illus.). 9.50 (*0-939608-11-1*) Campana Art.
— Teacher of Rose Painting. (Illus.). 17.95 (*0-939608-01-4*) Campana Art.
— Teacher of Textile Painting. (Illus.). 5.50 (*0-939608-15-4*) Campana Art.
— Teacher of Water Color Painting. (Illus.). 9.95 (*0-939608-08-1*) Campana Art.

Campana, Dino. Canti Orphici: Orphic Songs & Other Poems. Bonaffini, Luigi, tr. from ITA. LC 91-34869. (Studies in Southern Italian & Italian American Culture: Vol. 3). (ENG & ITA.). 277p. (C). 1992. text 56.95 (*0-8204-1738-6*) P Lang Pubng.
— Orphic Songs. Salomon, I. L., tr. from ITA. LC 98-9893. (Pocket Poets Ser.: Vol. 54).Tr. of Canti Orfici. 176p. 1998. pap. 12.95 (*0-87286-340-9*) City Lights.
— Orphic Songs. Wright, Charles, tr. from ITA. LC 83-63448. (Field Translation Ser.).Tr. of Canti Orfici. 130p. 1984. 11.50 (*0-932440-16-9*); pap. 6.50 (*0-932440-17-7*) Oberlin Coll Pr.

Campana, Manny. Things That Go: Paint Box Fun. 32p. (J). (ps-3). 1993. pap. 1.95 (*0-590-46290-3*) Scholastic Inc.

***Campana, Richard J.** Arboriculture: History & Development in North America. LC 99-6658. 443p. 1999. 39.95 (*0-87013-497-3*) Mich St U Pr.

***Campanacci, M.** Bone & Soft Tissue Tumors: Clinical Features, Imaging, Pathology & Treatment. 2nd ed. (Illus.). 1300p. 1999. 379.00 (*3-211-83235-1*) Spr-Verlag.

Campanaro, Michael. The United States & Europe: Jobs, Trade & Investment. (Illus.). 118p. (C). 1998. pap. text 35.00 (*0-7881-3116-8*) DIANE Pub.

Campanella. It's Good to Be Alive. 1976. 29.95 (*0-8488-1548-3*) Amereon Ltd.

***Campanella, Jack.** Principles of Quality Costs: Principles, Implementation & Use. 3rd ed. LC 98-46411. 175p. 2000. 49.50 (*0-87389-443-X*) ASQ Qual Pr.

Campanella, Jack, ed. see ASQ Quality Costs Committee.

Campanella, Marina, jt. auth. see Campanella, Richard.

Campanella, Richard & Campanella, Marina. New Orleans Then & Now. LC 98-47016. (Illus.). 400p. 1999. 39.95 (*1-56554-347-5*) Pelican.

Campanella, Roy. It's Good to Be Alive. LC 94-39776. (Illus.). xviii, 314p. 1995. pap. 10.95 (*0-8032-6363-5*, Bison Books) U of Nebr Pr.

Campanella, Tommaso. The City of the Sun: A Poetical Dialogue. Donno, Daniel J., ed. LC 80-20133. (Biblioteca Italiana Ser.: No. 2).Tr. of La/Citta del Sol: Dialogo Poetico. 1981. pap. 14.95 (*0-520-04036-8*, Pub. by U CA Pr) Cal Prin Full Svc.
— The Defense of Galileo. LC 74-26254. (History, Philosophy & Sociology of Science Ser.). 1978. reprint ed. 17.95 (*0-405-06582-5*) Ayer.
— The Defense of Galileo of Thomas Campanella. McColley, Grant, tr. from ITA. LC 76-1114. (Smith College Studies in History). 93p. 1976. reprint ed. lib. bdg. 16.00 (*0-915172-20-8*) Richwood Pub.
— A Defense of Galileo, the Mathematician from Florence. Blackwell, Richard J., tr. from LAT. & intro. by. LC 93-8497.Tr. of Apologia pro Galileo. (C). 1994. text 32.50 (*0-268-00869-8*) U of Notre Dame Pr.
— The Lusiads. White, Landeg, tr. LC 97-19376. (The World's Classics Ser.). (Illus.). 286p. 1998. pap. 7.95 (*0-19-283191-7*) OUP.
— Os Lusiadas. (POR.). 378p. 1985. reprint ed. lib. bdg. 97.50 (*3-487-07486-9*) G Olms Pubs.
— Sonnets. enl. ed. Draghici, Simona, ed. Symonds, John A., tr. from ITA. LC 98-50408. 223p. 1999. pap. text 9.95 (*0-943045-13-4*) Plutarch Pr OR.
— Spanish Conquest. 1972. 59.95 (*0-8490-1101-9*) Gordon Pr.

Campanelli, Dan & Campanelli, Pauline. Halloween Collectables. (Illus.). 168p. (Orig.). 1995. pap. 24.95 (*0-89538-027-7*) L-W Inc.
— Romantic Valentines - A Price Guide. (Illus.). 160p. (Orig.). 1996. pap. 14.95 (*0-89538-078-1*) L-W Inc.

Campanelli, Dan, jt. auth. see Campanelli, Pauline.

Campanelli, Jeanne F. & Price, Jonathan L. Write in Time: Essay Exam Strategies. LC 90-49875. (Illus.). 167p. (C). 1991. pap. text 22.50 (*0-03-032593-5*, Pub. by Harcourt Coll Pubs) Harcourt.

***Campanelli, Michele W.** Margarita: The Case of the Numbers Kidnapper. 1999. pap. write for info. (*1-928781-19-5*) Hollis Bks.

Campanelli, Pauline. Ancient Ways: Reclaiming Pagan Traditions. LC 91-26543. (Practical Magick Ser.). (Illus.). 256p. (Orig.). 1999. pap. 14.95 (*0-87542-090-7*) Llewellyn Pubns.
— Pagan Rites of Passage. 2nd ed. LC 97-53320. (Illus.). 288p. 1999. pap. 14.95 (*1-56718-111-2*) Llewellyn Pubns.
— Wheel of the Year: Living the Magical Life. LC 89-38809. (Practical Magick Ser.). (Illus.). 176p. (Orig.). 1989. pap. 12.95 (*0-87542-091-5*) Llewellyn Pubns.

Campanelli, Pauline & Campanelli, Dan. Holiday Collectables: A Price Guide. LC 97-212557. (Illus.). 226p. 1997. 34.95 (*0-89538-092-7*) L-W Inc.

Campanelli, Pauline, jt. auth. see Campanelli, Dan.

Campaniello, Mickey. Mr. Mick Visits Our School. large type ed. (Illus.). (J). (ps-2). 1999. 12.95 (*0-9673179-0-8*) Someone Special.

Campanile. Campanile Workshop Notes. 68p. 1997. spiral bd. 12.00 (*1-891803-00-X*, 1CWN97) Above The Line.

Campanile. Il Segreto e Altri Racconti: B Level. text 7.95 (*0-8219-1066-3*) EMC-Paradigm.

Campanile, Achille. The Inventor of the Horse. Loriggio, Francesco, tr. from ITA. (Drama Ser.: No. 7). 128p. 1995. pap. 13.00 (*0-920717-97-7*) Guernica Editions.

***Campano, Miguel Angel.** Miguel Angel Campano. (Illus.). 212p. 2000. pap. 50.00 (*84-8026-126-9*) Dist Art Pubs.

Campany, Richard C., Jr. Turkey & the United States: The Arms Embargo Period. LC 86-9303. 154p. 1986. 47.95 (*0-275-92141-7*, C2141, Praeger Pubs) Greenwood.

Campany, Robert F. Strange Writing: Anomaly Accounts in Early Medieval China. LC 94-45736. 524p. (C). 1996. text 74.50 (*0-7914-2659-9*); pap. text 24.95 (*0-7914-2660-2*) State U NY Pr.

Campardon, Emile. L' Academie Royale de Musique au 18e Siecle, 2 vols., Set. LC 73-141152. (Music Ser.). 1971. reprint ed. lib. bdg. 110.00 (*0-306-70090-5*) Da Capo.

***Campargue, R., ed.** Atomic & Molecular Beams: The State of the Art, 2000. xii, 600p. 2000. 109.00 (*3-540-67378-4*) Spr-Verlag.

Campari, Irene, jt. ed. see Frank, Andrew U.

Campari, Joao S., jt. auth. see De Almeida, Anna.

***Campbel, Kimberly.** Funny Mystery: True Graffiti Club, Bk. 2. (Illus.). 80p. (J). 2000. 4.99 (*0-7868-3276-2*, Pub. by Disney Pr) Time Warner.

Campbell. Approach to College Writing: Easy Writer: Process & Sentence Combining. 3rd ed. 1997. teacher ed. 13.00 (*0-06-361157-0*) Longman.

Campbell. Audit Judgement Applications: An Integrated Case. 5th ed. (SWC-Accounting). 1998. pap. 30.95 (*0-324-00886-4*) Thomson Learn.

***Campbell.** Barra's Angel. 2000. pap. 13.95 (*1-85702-977-1*, Pub. by Fourth Estate) Trafalgar.

Campbell. Biochemistry. 2nd ed. (C). 1995. pap. text, student ed. 29.50 (*0-03-001874-9*) Harcourt Coll Pubs.
— Biochemistry. 2nd ed. (C). 1995. pap. text, teacher ed. 47.75 (*0-03-001873-0*) Harcourt Coll Pubs.
— Biochemistry. 3rd ed. 206p. 1998. 75.00 (*0-03-021183-2*) SCP.

***Campbell.** Biology. 5th ed. 1999. 132.50 (*0-201-50340-9*); 85.31 (*0-201-50342-5*) Benjamin-Cummings.

Campbell. Calculus. 2nd ed. (Mathematics Ser.). Date not set. suppl. ed. 6.75 (*0-87150-264-X*) PWS Pubs.
— Calculus with Analytic Geometry. 2nd ed. (Mathematics Ser.). 1978. 28.75 (*0-87150-244-5*) PWS Pubs.
— The Chocolate War. 1997. 26.95 (*0-8057-8808-5*, Twyne); pap. 13.95 (*0-8057-8809-3*, Twyne) Mac Lib Ref.
— Choosing Democracy: A Practial Guide to Multicultural Education. 2nd ed. LC 99-51550. (Illus.). 410p. 1999. pap. text 55.00 (*0-13-096102-7*) P-H.
— Comparative Law Yearbook. 1998. lib. bdg. 122.00 (*90-411-0740-1*) Kluwer Law Intl.
— Computer Application - Techknowledge Reference Series. (TP - Technology Education Ser.). 176p. (J). (gr. k-12). 1996. pap. 21.95 (*0-538-64476-1*) S-W Pub.
— Cust Redctn Bio Concpts. (C). 1997. pap. text 74.00 (*0-201-32630-2*) Addison-Wesley.
— Deaths & Pretty Cousins. (Australian National University Press Ser.). 1975. pap. text 8.75 (*0-08-032837-7*, Pergamon Pr) Elsevier.
— Differential Equations. (C). 1996. pap. 17.16 (*0-395-74632-9*) HM.
— Do's & Don'ts for Publications. 1998. 2.00 (*0-318-19217-9*) Quill & Scroll.
— Easy Writer 1. 3rd ed. (C). Date not set. text, teacher ed. write for info. (*0-321-40620-6*) Addson-Wesley Educ.
— English Santhali Dictionary. 1984. 59.95 (*0-8288-8424-2*) Fr & Eur.
— Experiments in Biochemistry. (C). 1999. pap. text. write for info. (*0-03-097862-9*); pap. text, teacher ed. write for info. (*0-03-097863-7*) Harcourt.

***Campbell.** Forged Metal. 2000. pap. 8.95 (*0-552-14570-X*, Pub. by Transworld Publishers Ltd) Trafalgar.

Campbell. Friendships in Dark, Vol. 1. 1998. 5.99 (*0-312-96634-2*, Pub. by Tor Bks) St Martin.

Campbell. Fundamental Legal Conceptions. 68.95 (*1-85521-668-X*) Ashgate Pub Co.

Campbell. Garden, Dreams & Plans. (Illus.). 160p. 1998. pap. 22.50 (*1-55670-837-8*) Stewart Tabori & Chang.
— Genocide & the Global Village. 1999. text 45.00 (*0-312-21890-7*) St Martin.
— Guide to Teaching & Writing. LC 98-113900. (C). 1997. pap. text 20.00 (*0-15-508153-5*, Pub. by Harcourt Coll Pubs) Harcourt.

***Campbell.** Humankind Emerging. 8th ed. LC 99-12135. 679p. (C). 1999. pap. text 67.00 (*0-321-02274-2*) Allyn.

Campbell. Improving Your Soil. (Country Wisdom Bulletins Ser.: Vol. A-20). 1983. pap. 2.95 (*0-88266-194-9*) Storey Bks.
— Introductory Electronics. (Electronics Technology Ser.). 1995. pap., teacher ed. 14.00 (*0-8273-5600-5*); pap., lab manual ed. 24.95 (*0-8273-5601-3*); text 43.50 (*0-8273-5514-9*) Delmar.
— Laser. (Techknowledge Reference Ser.). (J). (gr. k-12). 1998. pap. 18.95 (*0-538-66139-9*) S-W Pub.

Campbell. Lloyd George: The Goat in the Wilderness. 408p. 1993. 69.95 (*0-7512-0138-3*) Ashgate Pub Co.
— Mastering Harvard Graphics 2.3. 1993. teacher ed. write for info. incl. disk (*0-02-802580-6*) Glencoe.
— Media. 5th ed. 1999. student ed. 20.00 (*0-8053-6571-0*) Benjamin-Cummings.

Campbell. Media & Culture. 1998. pap. text 10.00 (*0-312-19061-1*) St Martin.
— Media & Culture Introduction. 1997. pap. text, teacher ed. 10.00 (*0-312-11959-3*) St Martin.

***Campbell.** Medical Statistics: A Commonsense Approach. 3rd ed. LC 99-13004. 218p. 1999. pap. 34.95 (*0-471-98721-2*) Wiley.

Campbell. Non Disclosure. 1993. 19.95 (*0-07-881940-7*) McGraw.

— Operating System Principles: With Multiprocessors & Object Oriented Design. 448p. (C). 2002. write for info. (*0-02-318585-6*, Macmillan Coll) P-H.
— Our Awesome God. 1997. pap. 9.99 (*1-85792-318-9*, Pub. by Christian Focus) Spring Arbor Dist.
— Pigeon Pie. 296p. 1998. 20.00 (*0-7862-1527-5*) Thorndike Pr.
— The Place of Lions. 1995. pap. 5.00 (*0-15-201031-9*) Harcourt.
— Power to Learn. 1992. mass mkt., teacher ed. 11.50 (*0-534-19406-0*) Wadsworth Pub.
— The Prairie Schoolhouse. LC 95-4357. (Illus.). 151p. 1996. pap. 29.95 (*0-8263-1660-3*) U of NM Pr.
— Principles of Writing for Teacher Source. LC 98-143975. (Adult ESL Ser.). 112p. (J). 1998. mass mkt. 22.95 (*0-8384-7892-1*) Heinle & Heinle.
— Program Guide to Calculus. 2nd ed. (Mathematics Ser.). 1979. 6.75 (*0-87150-271-2*) PWS Pubs.
— Regionalization & Labour Market. LC 97-18984. 1997. text 69.95 (*0-312-17703-8*) St Martin.
— Santhali-English Dictionary. 1988. 95.00 (*0-8288-8425-0*) Fr & Eur.
— School Newspaper Management. 2.00 (*0-318-19222-5*) Quill & Scroll.
— Science Animals Serve Humanity. 4th ed. 2001. 81.50 (*0-07-366175-9*) McGraw.
— The Shark Callers. 101. pap. 4.95 (*0-15-200803-9*, Harcourt Child Bks) Harcourt.
— Solid-State AC Motor Controls: Selection & Application. (Mechanical Engineering Ser.: Vol. 56). (Illus.). 248p. 1987. text 135.00 (*0-8247-7728-X*) Dekker.
— Survival Strategies for the New Workplace. 1995. pap. 11.00 (*0-671-87584-1*, Fireside) S&S Trade Pap.
— Transnational Person. 1992. pap. text 96.00 (*90-6544-604-4*) Kluwer Academic.
— Trusts & Estates. (American Casebook Ser.). Date not set. text. write for info. (*0-314-06780-9*) West Pub.
— Turnip Blues. large type ed. LC 98-42041. 1999. 25.95 (*0-7862-1673-5*) Thorndike Pr.
Campbell, ed. Myths, Dreams & Religion. 256p. 1999. 6.98 (*1-56731-340-X*, MJF Bks) Fine Comms.
Campbell & Brodie, eds. Biology of the Pit Vipers. 75.00 (*0-9630537-0-1*) Serpents Tale.
Campbell & Brody. Whole Lotta Shakin' Goin' On. LC 99-10095. 1999. 33.00 (*0-02-864727-0*) Mac Lib Ref.
Campbell & Dierker. Calculus. 2nd ed. (Mathematics Ser.). Date not set. teacher ed. 6.75 (*0-87150-579-7*) PWS Pubs.
Campbell & Garcia. Organisation of Maternity Care: A Guide to Evaluation. 160p. 1997. pap. text 30.00 (*1-898507-37-6*) Buttrwrth-Heinemann.
Campbell & Kennedy. Space & Equipment Guidelines for Student Publications. 2.00 (*0-318-19223-3*) Quill & Scroll.
Campbell & Lack. A Dictionary of Birds. 700p. 1985. 94.00 (*0-85661-039-9*) Acad Pr.
***Campbell & Mitchell.** Biology: Concepts & Connections. 3rd ed. 2000. 87.00 (*0-8053-6625-3*) Benjamin-Cummings.
Campbell & Ricchiute, David N. Audit Judgement Applications: An Integrated Case. 4th ed. (Accounting Principles Ser.). (C). 1994. pap. 24.95 (*0-538-83884-1*) S-W Pub.
Campbell, et al. Financial Management in a Managed Care Environment - IML. 94p. 1998. teacher ed. 16.00 (*0-8273-8134-4*) Delmar.
Campbell, jt. auth. see Bowman.
Campbell, jt. auth. see Delaune.
Campbell, jt. auth. see Mitchell.
Campbell, jt. compiled by see Mitchell.
***Campbell, Brian.** Clanbook: Gangrel. (Vampire Ser.). 2000. pap. 14.95 (*1-56504-265-4*) White Wolf.
— Nosferatu. (Clan Novel Ser.). 2000. pap. 14.95 (*1-56504-266-2*) White Wolf.
— Order of Reason. (Mage Ser.). 2000. pap. 22.00 (*1-56504-469-X*) White Wolf.
Campbell, Brian. Ratkin. (Werewolf Ser.). (Illus.). 128p. 1999. pap. 19.95 (*1-56504-342-1*, 3080) White Wolf.
***Campbell, Brian.** Transylvania Chronicles Iv: The Dragon Ascendant, Iv. (Transylvania Chronicles Ser.). 2000. pap. text 15.95 (*1-56504-293-X*) White Wolf.
Campbell, Brian & Sellers, Janice. Price of Freedom. 1999. 25.00 (*0-671-04003-0*) S&S Trade.
Campbell, A. Charters of Rochester. (Anglo-Saxon Charters Ser.: Vol. I). 1973. 27.00 (*0-19-725936-7*) David Brown.
— Der Kosmos-Strandfuehrer (The Kosmos Beach Guide) (Kosmos Naturfuehrer (Nature Guides) Ser.). (GER., Illus.). 320p. 1987. pap. 40.00 (*3-440-04355-X*, Pub. by Franckh-Kosmos) Balogh.
— Santal Folk Tales. LC 78-67700. (Folktale Ser.). reprint ed. 29.50 (*0-404-16066-2*) AMS Pr.
Campbell, A., et al, eds. Annual Review of Genetics, Vol. 25. LC 67-29891. 1991. text 40.00 (*0-8243-1225-2*) Annual Reviews.
Campbell, A., jt. ed. see Jamieson, G. S.
Campbell, A. D. A Grammar of the Telugu Language. (ENG & TEL.). 204p. 1991. 49.95 (*0-8288-8426-9*) Fr & Eur.
Campbell, A. E., ed. see Taft, William Howard.
Campbell, A. G. & McIntosh, N., eds. Forfar & Arneil's Textbook of Pediatrics. 5th ed. (Illus.). 2000p. 1997. write for info. (*0-443-05393-6*) Church.
Campbell, A. H., ed. see Del Vecchio, Giorgia.
Campbell, A. J. Classic & Antique Fly-Fishing Tackle: A Guide for Collectors & Anglers. LC 96-53509. (Illus.). 360p. 1997. 50.00 (*1-55821-400-3*) Lyons Pr.
Campbell, A. M. Monoclonal Antibody & Immunosensor Technology. (Laboratory Techniques in Biochemistry & Molecular Biology Ser.: Vol. 23). xvii,428p. 1991. 213.00 (*0-444-81413-2*); pap. 76.50 (*0-444-81412-4*) Elsevier.
Campbell, Ada M., jt. auth. see Penfield, Marjorie P.
Campbell, Adrian, jt. ed. see Batley, Richard.
Campbell, Aidan. Privileging the Primitive: African Ethnicity & the Rehabilitation of the West. LC 97-607. 1997. 89.95 (*0-304-70076-2*); pap. 29.95 (*0-304-70077-0*) Continuum.
Campbell, Aileen. The Wee Scot Book: Scottish Poems & Stories. LC 93-28728. 64p. (J). (ps-3). 1994. 19.95 (*1-56554-018-2*) Pelican.
***Campbell, Alan, et al, eds.** British Trade Unions & Industrial Politics: The High Tide of Trade Unionism, 1964-79. LC 99-67214. (Studies in Labour History: Vol. 2). 335p. 2000. text 86.95 (*0-7546-0018-1*, Pub. by Ashgate Pub) Ashgate Pub Co.
— British Trade Unions & Industrial Politics: The Post-War Compromise, 1945-64. LC 99-67212. (Studies in Labour History: Vol. 1). 335p. 2000. text 86.95 (*0-7546-0017-3*, Pub. by Ashgate Pub) Ashgate Pub Co.
Campbell, Alan, et al, eds. Miners, Unions & Politics, 1910-1947. (Illus.). 320p. 1996. 78.95 (*1-85928-269-5*, Pub. by Scolar Pr) Ashgate Pub Co.
Campbell, Alan, tr. see Dyer, Constance E., ed.
Campbell, Alan K., et al, eds. Improving the Recruitment, Retention, & Utilization of Federal Scientists & Engineers. 136p. (Orig.). (C). 1993. pap. text 24.00 (*0-309-04849-4*) Natl Acad Pr.
Campbell, Alan T. Getting to Know Waiwai: An Amazonian Ethnography. LC 94-42515. (Illus.). 264p. (C). 1995. pap. 22.99 (*0-415-12557-X*, B4895) Routledge.
— Getting to Know Waiwai: An Amazonian Ethnography. LC 94-42515. (Illus.). 264p. (C). (gr. 13). 1995. 85.00 (*0-415-12556-1*, B4891) Routledge.
***Campbell, Alastair.** The Designer's Lexicon: The Illustrated Dictionary of Design, Printing & Computer Terms. (Illus.). 320p. 2000. spiral bd. 22.95 (*0-8118-2625-2*) Chronicle Bks.
— A History of Clan Campbell Vol. 1: From Origins to the Battle of Flodden. 420p. 2000. pap. text 30.00 (*1-902930-17-7*) Col U Pr.
Campbell, Alastair. The New Macdesigner's Handbook. 2nd ed. (Illus.). 192p. 1997. spiral bd. 27.50 (*0-7624-0206-7*) Running Pr.
Campbell, Alastair, ed. see Charlesworth, Max, et al.
Campbell, Alastair V. Health As Liberation: Medicine, Theology & the Quest for Justice. LC 94-40930. 112p. (Orig.). 1995. 14.95 (*0-8298-1022-6*) Pilgrim OH.
— Professionalism & Pastoral Care. Browning, Don S., ed. LC 84-48710. (Theology & Pastoral Care Ser.). 119p. reprint ed. pap. 36.90 (*0-608-18363-6*, 203304700083) Bks Demand.
Campbell, Albert H. Report on the Pacific Wagon Roads. 1969. 24.95 (*0-87770-003-6*) Ye Galleon.
Campbell, Alexander. The Christian System. LC 73-83412. (Religion in America, Ser.). 1975. reprint ed. 46.54 (*0-405-00233-5*) Ayer.
— The Covenant Story of the Bible. 102p. 1994. pap. 14.95 (*1-877871-69-9*, 6750) Ed Ministries.
***Campbell, Alexander & Chapman, Michael.** Handbook of Poisoning in Dogs & Cats. LC 99-54108. 272p. 2000. pap. text 42.95 (*0-632-05029-2*, Pub. by Blckwell Science) Iowa St U Pr.
Campbell, Alexander & Haff, Gerry. Live with Jesus. 90p. (Orig.). (J). (gr. 1-6). 1984. pap. 12.95 (*0-940754-20-7*) Ed Ministries.
— Live with Moses. 90p. (Orig.). (J). (gr. 1-6). 1982. pap. 12.95 (*0-940754-13-4*) Ed Ministries.
Campbell, Alexandra. Spaces for Living: How to Create Multifunctional Rooms for Today's Homes. LC 98-26900. 160p. 1999. pap. 24.95 (*0-609-80355-7*) Crown Pub Group.
Campbell, Alexandra, tr. see Blot, Jean-Yves.
Campbell, Alexandra, tr. see Bonafoux, Pascal.
Campbell, Alexandra, tr. see Hugon, Anne.
Campbell, Alexandra, tr. see Laroque, Francois.
Campbell, Alice. Short History of Rosalia, Washington. 10p. 1970. reprint ed. pap. 2.95 (*0-87770-037-0*) Ye Galleon.
Campbell, Alistair. The Frigate Bird. 142p. (Orig.). (C). 1990. pap. 9.95 (*0-7900-0046-6*, A0428, Pub. by Heinemnn) Musson Publ.
— Old English Grammar. 3rd ed. 440p. (C). 1983. pap. text 24.95 (*0-19-811943-7*) OUP.
— Tia. LC 93-114384. (Pacific Writers Series). 190 p. 1993. write for info. (*0-7900-0282-5*) Reed Pubng.
Campbell, Alistair, ed. Encomium Emmae Reginae. LC 97-40934. (Camden Classic Reprints Ser.: No. 4). (Illus.). 208p. (C). 1998. text 64.95 (*0-521-62307-3*); pap. text 22.95 (*0-521-62655-2*) Cambridge U Pr.
Campbell, Alistair, ed. see Brunanburh.
Campbell, Alistair, jt. ed. see Toller, T. Northcote.
Campbell, Alister. Battle of Brunanburh. 1988. reprint ed. lib. bdg. 59.00 (*0-7812-0211-6*) Rprt Serv.
Campbell, Allan. Ten Sails in the Sunrise. 200p. 1986. 14.95 (*0-317-39595-5*) C I L Inc.
— Voodoo: Treasure in Bootle Bay, Vol. 1. (Illus.). 200p. 1985. 14.95 (*0-9613326-0-3*) C I L Inc.
Campbell, Allan, ed. Annual Review of Genetics, Vol. 29. LC 67-29891. 1995. text 47.00 (*0-8243-1229-5*) Annual Reviews.
— Annual Review of Genetics, Vol. 30. LC 67-29891. 1996. text 52.00 (*0-8243-1230-9*) Annual Reviews.
— Annual Review of Genetics, Vol. 31. LC 67-29891. 1997. text 60.00 (*0-8243-1231-7*) Annual Reviews.
Campbell, Allan, et al, eds. Annual Review of Genetics, Vol. 19. LC 67-29891. (Illus.). 1985. text 40.00 (*0-8243-1219-8*) Annual Reviews.
— Annual Review of Genetics, Vol. 21. LC 67-29891. (Illus.). 1987. text 40.00 (*0-8243-1221-X*) Annual Reviews.
— Annual Review of Genetics, Vol. 22. LC 67-29891. (Illus.). 1988. text 40.00 (*0-8243-1222-8*) Annual Reviews.
— Annual Review of Genetics, Vol. 24. 1990. text 40.00 (*0-8243-1224-4*) Annual Reviews.
— Annual Review of Genetics, Vol. 26. LC 67-29891. (Illus.). 1992. text 44.00 (*0-8243-1226-0*) Annual Reviews.
— Annual Review of Genetics, Vol. 27. LC 67-29891. (Illus.). 1993. text 44.00 (*0-8243-1227-9*) Annual Reviews.
— Annual Review of Genetics, 1994, Vol. 28. LC 67-29891. (Illus.). 1994. text 47.00 (*0-8243-1228-7*) Annual Reviews.
Campbell, Allan & Niel, Tim. A Life in Pieces: Reflections on Alexander Trocchi LC 97-220379. xi, 307p. 1997. write for info. (*0-86241-680-9*, Pub. by Canongate Books) Interlink Pub.
Campbell, Allan N. The Railroad Sirens. 1979. 8.95 (*0-533-03906-1*) C I L Inc.
Campbell, Allen. Man Defined. (Illus.). 286p. (Orig.). 1992. pap. text 10.00 (*0-9634502-0-4*) RACY Pub.
Campbell, Allen D. Concrete Structures. (C). 1996. 173.95 (*0-582-05067-7*, Pub. by Addison-Wesley) Longman.
***Campbell, Andrea.** Bringing up Ziggy. LC 99-36199. 208p. 1999. 21.95 (*1-58063-085-5*) Renaissance.
Campbell, Andrea. Great Games for Great Parties: How to Throw a Perfect Party. (Illus.). 160p. (J). (gr. 3-10). 1992. pap. 7.95 (*0-8069-8319-1*) Sterling.
***Campbell, Andrea.** Legal-Ease. 2001. pap. 18.95 (*0-936085-67-3*) Blue Heron OR.
Campbell, Andrea. Unauthorized Guide to Ziggy Collectibles. (Illus.). 160p. 1999. pap. 16.95 (*0-7643-0931-5*) Schiffer.
***Campbell, Andrea Mandell.** Passport Argentina: Your Pocket Guide to Argentine Business, Customs & Etiquette. Szerlip, Barbara, ed. LC 99-16124. 1999. pap. text 6.95 (*1-885073-21-6*) Wrld Trade Pr.
***Campbell, Andrew.** Collaborative Enterprise: Why Links Between Business Units Often Fail & How to Make Them Work. 240p. 2000. pap. text 17.00 (*0-7382-0310-6*) Perseus Pubng.
Campbell, Andrew. Core Competency Based Strategy. (ITBP Textbooks Ser.). 327p. 1997. pap. 19.99 (*1-86152-273-8*) Thomson Learn.
— Landcare. (Illus.). 356p. 1995. pap. 17.95 (*1-86373-555-0*, Pub. by Allen & Unwin Pty) Paul & Co Pubs.
— Managing the Andrew File System. LC 97-43581. 496p. (C). 1998. pap. text 44.99 (*0-13-802729-3*) P-H.
— Synergy: Why Links Between Business Units So Often Fail & How to Make Them Work LC 98-186145. 256p. 1998. write for info. (*1-900961-57-1*) Capstone Pub NH.
Campbell, Andrew & Goold, Michael. The Collaborative Enterprise: Why Links Across the Corporation Often Fail & How to Make Them Work. LC 99-61219. (British Commonwealth, United States, United Nations, 1993 Ser.). (Illus.). 240p. 1999. text 27.50 (*0-7382-0089-1*, Pub. by Perseus Pubng) HarpC.
Campbell, Andrew & Luchs, Kathleen. Strategic Synergy. 2nd rev. ed. 224p. 1998. pap. 20.99 (*1-86152-222-3*) Thomson Learn.
Campbell, Andrew & Tawadey, Kiran. La Mision de los Negocios. (SPA.). 411p. 1992. pap. 34.00 (*84-7978-035-5*, Pub. by Ediciones Diaz) IBD Ltd.
— Mission & Business Philosophy. 242p. 1993. pap. text 47.95 (*0-7506-0509-X*) Buttrwrth-Heinemann.
Campbell, Andrew, jt. auth. see Campbell, Marti.
Campbell, Andrew, jt. ed. see Banister, Keith.
Campbell, Angus. Surge & Decline: A Study of Electoral Change. (Reprint Series in Social Sciences). (C). 1993. reprint ed. pap. text 1.00 (*0-8290-3655-5*, PS-38) Irvington.
Campbell, Angus & Converse, Philip E., eds. Human Meaning of Social Change. LC 75-169837. 548p. 1972. 55.00 (*0-87154-193-9*) Russell Sage.
Campbell, Angus & Converse, Phillip E. Quality of American Life, 1978. LC 80-84081. 1980. write for info. (*0-89138-951-2*) ICPSR.
Campbell, Angus, et al. American National Election Study, 1956. 1974. write for info. (*0-89138-066-3*) ICPSR.
— American National Election Study, 1960. 1974. write for info. (*0-89138-067-1*) ICPSR.
— The American Voter. LC 76-21115. (Midway Reprint Ser.). 576p. 1980. pap. text 39.00 (*0-226-09254-2*) U Ch Pr.
— The Quality of American Life: Perceptions, Evaluations & Satisfactions. LC 75-7176. 600p. 1976. 55.00 (*0-87154-194-7*) Russell Sage.
— The Voter Decides. LC 73-138211. 242p. 1971. reprint ed. lib. bdg. 79.50 (*0-8371-5566-5*, CAVD, Greenwood Pr) Greenwood.
Campbell, Angus L., ed. see Coates, John M. & Williamson, Brian J.
Campbell, Ann. Once upon a Princess & a Pea. LC 92-30526. (Illus.). 32p. (J). (gr. 1 up). 1993. 14.95 (*1-55670-289-2*) Stewart Tabori & Chang.
***Campbell, Ann.** Wolf at the Door. (Annie O'Hara & Claudius Mysteries Ser.). 247p. 2000. mass mkt. 5.99 (*0-451-20021-7*, Sig) NAL.
Campbell, Ann, jt. auth. see Iacono, Joan.
Campbell, Ann, ed. see Null, Gary.
Campbell, Ann-Jeanette. Dora's Box. LC 97-6992. (Illus.). (J). 1998. 18.99 (*0-679-97642-6*) Knopf.
— The New York Public Library Amazing Space: A Book of Answers for Kids. LC 96-29785. 192p. (J). 1997. pap. 12.95 (*0-471-14498-3*) Wiley.
Campbell, Ann O. Archibald the Horse: A Children's Illustrated Story Book. (Illus.). 1982. 4.95 (*0-938686-25-9*) H Spriggle.
Campbell, Anna M. Black Death & Men of Learning. LC 31-29792. reprint ed. 37.50 (*0-404-01368-6*) AMS Pr.
— In True Love, 1. 1998. pap. text 14.95 (*1-881116-93-X*) Black Forest Pr.
Campbell, Anne. Crafts Throughout the Year: Projects That Help Kids Learn, Vol. 1. 1999. pap. 6.95 (*0-88347-411-5*) T More.
***Campbell, Anne.** Social Child. 432p. 1999. pap. 29.95 (*0-86377-823-2*) L Erlbaum Assocs.
Campbell, Anne. Social Child. 1998. 54.95 (*0-86377-822-4*, Pub. by Psychol Pr) Taylor & Francis.
— Vocational Education in an Information Age: Society at Risk? 20p. 1984. 3.00 (*0-318-22242-6*, OC99) Ctr Educ Trng Employ.
Campbell, Anne, et al. Assessing Literacy: The Framework for the National Adult Literacy Survey. (Illus.). 43p. (C). 1996. reprint ed. pap. text 20.00 (*0-7881-3374-8*) DIANE Pub.
***Campbell, Anne, et al.** Faith-Filled Classroom: Top 10 Ideas That Really Work. 94p. 1999. pap. 6.95 (*0-88347-405-0*) T More.
Campbell, Anne J. Dora's Box. LC 97-6992. (Illus.). 32p. (J). (gr. k-3). 1998. 17.00 (*0-679-87642-1*) Random.
Campbell, Annejet. Listen to the Children: Parents Tell Their Stories. 2nd ed. LC 87-81505. (Yes (with Listen for a Change) Ser.). (Illus.). 112p. 1987. pap. 7.50 (*1-85239-006-9*) Grosvenor USA.
Campbell, Annejet, ed. Listen for a Change. LC 86-81348. (Illus.). 116p. 1987. 7.50 (*1-85239-001-8*) Grosvenor USA.
Campbell, Anneke, jt. auth. see Marston, Elsa.
Campbell, Annie. The New York Coloring Book. (Illus.). 32p. (Orig.). 1996. pap. 6.95 (*0-935526-26-9*); pap. 6.95 (*0-935526-27-7*); pap. 6.95 (*0-935526-28-5*); pap. 6.95 (*0-935526-29-3*) McBooks Pr.
Campbell, Annily. Childfree & Sterilized: Women's Decisions & Medical Responses. LC 99-18201. 196p. 1999. pap. 17.95 (*0-304-33747-1*) Continuum.
***Campbell, Annily.** Childfree & Sterilized: Women's Decisions & Medical Responses. LC 99-18201. 160p. 1999. 45.00 (*0-304-33746-3*) Continuum.
Campbell, Anson. A Matter of Degree: Playscript. rev. ed. 1985. pap. 6.00 (*0-88734-203-5*) Players Pr.
Campbell, Anthony. Getting the Best for Your Bad Back. large type ed. 167p. 1995. 22.95 (*1-85695-056-5*, Pub. by ISIS Lrg Prnt) Transaction Pubs.
***Campbell, Anthony F. & O'Brien, Mark.** Unfolding the Deuteronomistic History: Origins, Upgrades, Present Text. 2000. pap. 37.00 (*0-8006-2878-0*, Fortress Pr) Augsburg Fortress.
Campbell, Anthony F. & O'Brien, Mark A. Sources of the Pentateuch: Texts, Introductions, Annotations. LC 92-20894. 288p. 1993. 29.00 (*0-8006-2701-6*, 1-2701) Augsburg Fortress.
***Campbell, Antony F.** God First Loved Us: The Challenge of Accepting Unconditional Love. 2001. pap. 8.95 (*0-8091-3977-4*) Paulist Pr.
Campbell, Antony F. Of Prophets & Kings: A Late Ninth Century Document (1 Samuel 1-2 Kings 10 No. 17) Karris, Robert J., ed. LC 85-12791. (Catholic Biblical Quarterly Monographs: No. 17). vii, 240p. (Orig.). 1986. pap. 7.50 (*0-915170-16-7*) Catholic Bibl Assn.
Campbell, Archibald. Journal of an Expedition Against the Rebels of Georgia in North America under the Orders of Archibald Campbell, Esquire, Lieut. Colonel of His Majesty's 71 Regiment, 1778. LC 80-52940. 1981. pap. 15.00 (*0-937044-08-3*) Richmond Cty Hist Soc.
— Journal of an Expedition Against the Rebels of Georgia in North America under the Orders of Archibald Campbell, Esquire, Lieut. Colonel of His Majesty's 71 Regiment, 1778. LC 80-52940. 1981. 25.00 (*0-937044-07-5*) Richmond Cty Hist Soc.
— Scottish Swords from the Battlefield at Culloden. Mowbray, Andrew, ed. (Illus.). 63p. 1971. 15.00 (*0-917218-04-3*) A Mowbray.
Campbell, Archibald, ed. Craignish Tales & Others. LC 78-144454. (Waifs & Strays of Celtic Tradition: Argyllshire Ser.: No. 1). reprint ed. 29.50 (*0-404-53531-3*) AMS Pr.
— Waifs & Strays of Celtic Tradition. (Argyllshire Ser.). reprint ed. 198.00 (*0-404-53530-5*) AMS Pr.
Campbell, Archibald Y. Horace, a New Interpretation. LC 70-109714. 303p. 1970. reprint ed. lib. bdg. 38.50 (*0-8371-4204-0*, CAHO, Greenwood Pr) Greenwood.
Campbell, Arthur. John Day River Drift & Historical Guide. (Illus.). 90p. (Orig.). 1995. pap. 19.95 (*0-936608-11-0*) F Amato Pubns.
Campbell, Arthur R. Expert Advisor: Xywrite III Plus. 400p. 1989. pap. text 21.95 (*0-201-51721-3*) Addison-Wesley.
Campbell, Arthur W. Entertainment Law: Cases & Materials. 4th ed. LC 97-18267. 523p. 1997. 85.00 (*1-57292-085-8*); pap. 64.95 (*1-57292-084-X*) Austin & Winfield.
— Law of Sentencing. 2nd ed. LC 91-77224. 1991. 120.00 (*0-685-59851-9*) West Group.
Campbell, B. & McCandless, W. Introduction to Space Sciences. 344p. 1996. 45.00 (*0-88415-411-4*, 5411) Gulf Pub.
Campbell, B. A., et al, eds. Particle Physics, the Factory Era: Proceedings of the Sixth Lake Louise Winter Institute Chateau Lake Louise, Canada, 17-23 February 1991. 600p. (C). 1991. text 118.00 (*981-02-0733-6*) World Scientific Pub.
— Quantum Chromodynamics, Theory & Experiment: Proceedings of the Third Lake Louise Winter Institute, Chateau Lake Louis, Canada, Maryc 6-12, 1988. 656p. 1988. text 125.00 (*9971-5-0657-2*) World Scientific Pub.
Campbell, B. A., et al. Spin & Symmetry in the Standard Model. 600p. 1992. text 121.00 (*981-02-1034-5*) World Scientific Pub.
Campbell, B. M. A Classification of the Mountain Vegetation of the Fynbos Biome. (Memoirs of the Botanical Survey of South Africa Ser.: No. 50). (Illus.). 121p. 1985. 15.00 (*0-621-08862-5*, Pub. by Natl Botanical Inst) Balogh.

 An Asterisk (*) at the beginning of an entry indicates that the title is appearing for the first time.

Campbell, Ballard. The Good Roads Movement in Wisconsin Eighteen Ninety to Nineteen Eleven. (Wisconsin Stories Ser.). 24p. pap. 1.75 (*0-87020-201-4*) State Hist Soc Wis.

Campbell, Ballard C. The Growth of American Government: From the Cleveland Era to the Present. LC 94-40804. (Interdisciplinary Studies in History). 304p. 1995. text 35.00 (*0-253-32871-3*); pap. text 14.95 (*0-253-20962-5*) Ind U Pr.

— Representative Democracy: Public Policy & Midwestern Legislatures in the Late Nineteenth Century. 267p. 1980. 37.95 (*0-674-76275-4*) HUP.

***Campbell, Ballard C., ed.** The Human Tradition in the Gilded Age & Progressive Era. LC 99-29786. (Human Tradition in America Ser.). 304p. 1999. pap. 18.95 (*0-8420-2735-1*) Scholarly Res Inc.

— Human Tradition in the Gilded Age & Progressive Era. LC 99-29786. (Human Tradition in America Ser.). 304p. 1999. 50.00 (*0-8420-2734-3*) Scholarly Res Inc.

Campbell, Barbara. Gabriella Gordini. 1999. text 13.99 (*0-670-84279-6*) NAL.

— Taking Care of Yoki. LC 85-26040. (Trophy Bk.). (Illus.). 176p. (J). (gr. 3-7). 1986. reprint ed. pap. 4.95 (*0-06-440173-1*, HarpTrophy) HarpC Child Bks.

Campbell, Barbara, ed. see McKinley, Robert.

Campbell, Barbara A., jt. auth. see Kennedy, Daniel W.

Campbell, Barbara-Ann. Paris. (Architecture Guides Ser.). (Illus.). 320p. 1998. pap. 5.95 (*3-89508-642-8*, 520200) Konemann.

Campbell, Barbara E., tr. see Richard, Pablo.

Campbell, Barry R., ed. The Impact of the Freeze of Kuwaiti & Iraqi Assets on Financial Institutions & Financial Transactions. (C). 1990. pap. text 169.00 (*1-85333-558-4*, Pub. by Graham & Trotman) Kluwer Academic.

Campbell, Beatrix. Diana, Princess of Wales: How Sexual Politics Shook the Monarchy. LC 99-232667. 259p. 1999. pap. 17.95 (*0-7043-4585-4*) Womens Press.

Campbell, Bebe Moore. Brothers & Sisters. LC 96-208545. 560p. 1995. mass mkt. 6.99 (*0-425-14940-4*) Berkley Pub.

***Campbell, Bebe Moore.** Brothers & Sisters. 2000. pap. 13.95 (*0-425-17267-8*) Berkley Pub.

Campbell, Bebe Moore. Brothers & Sisters. 1997. 4.98 (*0-681-56088-6*) Waldenbooks Co Inc.

— Brothers & Sisters. large type ed. LC 95-5418. (Large Print Bks.). 1995. 26.95 (*1-56895-211-2*) Wheeler Pub.

— Singing in the Comeback Choir. LC 97-31649. 320p. 1998. 24.95 (*0-399-14298-3*, G P Putnam) Peng Put Young Read.

— Singing in the Comeback Choir. large type ed. LC 98-25159. (Large Print Book Ser.). 1998. 26.95 (*1-56895-613-4*) Wheeler Pub.

— Singing in the Comeback Choir. 381p. 1999. reprint ed. mass mkt. 7.50 (*0-425-16662-7*) Berkley Pub.

— Sweet Summer: Growing up with & Without My Dad. 272p. 1990. pap. 12.00 (*0-345-36694-8*) Ballantine Pub Grp.

— Sweet Summer: Growing up with & Without My Dad. 1996. mass mkt. write for info. (*0-449-14984-6*) Fawcett.

***Campbell, Bebe Moore.** Sweet Summer: Growing up with & Without My Dad. 272p. 2000. reprint ed. pap. 12.95 (*0-425-17474-3*) Berkley Pub.

Campbell, Bebe Moore. Your Blues Ain't Like Mine. 1995. mass mkt. 6.99 (*0-345-40112-3*) Ballantine Pub Grp.

— Your Blues Ain't Like Mine. 336p. 1993. pap. 12.00 (*0-345-38395-8*) One Wrld.

— Your Blues Ain't Like Mine. 352p. 1992. 23.95 (*0-399-13746-7*, G P Putnam) Peng Put Young Read.

— Your Blues Ain't Like Mine. large type ed. LC 95-8920. (Large Print Bks.). 1995. 24.95 (*1-56895-221-X*) Wheeler Pub.

***Campbell, Ben Nighthorse, ed.** Gaming Regulatory Improvement Act: Congressional Hearing. 179p. 2000. reprint ed. pap. text 30.00 (*0-7881-8510-1*) DIANE Pub.

— Indian Provisions Contained in the Tobacco Settlement: Congressional Hearing. 66p. 2000. reprint ed. pap. text 20.00 (*0-7881-8738-4*) DIANE Pub.

Campbell, Ben Nighthorse, jt. ed. see Smith, Christopher H.

Campbell, Bernard. Human Ecology. 2nd ed. (Evolutionary Foundations of Human Behavior Ser.). (Illus.). 230p. 1995. pap. text 19.95 (*0-202-02035-5*); lib. bdg. 34.95 (*0-202-02034-7*) Aldine de Gruyter.

Campbell, Bernard G. Human Evolution: An Introduction to Man's Adaptations. 4th ed. LC 98-8760. (Evolutionary Foundations of Human Behavior Ser.). 1998. pap. text 32.95 (*0-202-02042-8*); lib. bdg. 59.95 (*0-202-02041-X*) Aldine de Gruyter.

Campbell, Bernard G. & Loy, James D., eds. Humankind Emerging. 7th ed. (Illus.). (C). 1996. pap. text, student ed. 13.50 (*0-673-52530-9*) Addson-Wesley Educ.

Campbell, Bernard G., ed. see Clark, W. E.

Campbell, Bethany. Add a Little Spice. (Romance Ser.). 1993. per. 2.89 (*0-373-03260-9*, 1-03260-6) Harlequin Bks.

— Amarillo by Morning. (Crystal Creek Ser.). 1993. per. 3.99 (*0-373-82515-3*, 82515-7) Harlequin Bks.

— Child's Play. (Intrigue Ser.). 1992. per. 2.89 (*0-373-22196-7*, 1-22196-9) Harlequin Bks.

— The Cloud Holders. (Romance Ser.: No. 133). 1991. per. 2.75 (*0-373-03133-5*) Harlequin Bks.

— Don't Talk to Strangers. 320p. 1996. mass mkt. 5.50 (*0-553-56973-2*) Bantam.

— Every Kind of Heaven. (Romance Ser.: No. 163). 1991. per. 2.79 (*0-373-03163-7*) Harlequin Bks.

— Gentle on My Mind. LC 97-10614. (Crystal Creek Ser.: Vol. 20). 298p. 1994. per. 3.99 (*0-373-82532-3*, 1-82532-2) Harlequin Bks.

— Guardian, 837. (Harlequin Super Romance Ser.). 1999. per. 4.25 (*0-373-70837-8*) Harlequin Bks.

— Hear No Evil. 384p. 1998. mass mkt. 5.99 (*0-553-57688-7*) Bantam.

— Heartland. (Romance Ser.). 1991. per. 2.79 (*0-373-15155-1*) Harlequin Bks.

— The Lady & the Tomcat. (Romance Ser.). 1993. per. 2.99 (*0-373-03277-3*, 1-03277-0) Harlequin Bks.

— Lone Star State of Mind. LC 95-4585. (Crystal Creek Ser.). 299p. 1995. mass mkt. 3.99 (*0-373-82536-6*, 1-82536-3) Harlequin Bks.

— The Man Who Came for Christmas: Back to the Ranch. (Romance Ser.). 1993. per. 2.99 (*0-373-03293-5*, 1-03293-7) Harlequin Bks.

***Campbell, Bethany.** P. S. Love You Madly. (Superromance Ser.). 2000. mass mkt. 4.50 (*0-373-70931-5*, 1-70931-0) Harlequin Bks.

Campbell, Bethany. Pros & Cons. 1994. per. 3.59 (*0-373-45171-7*) Harlequin Bks.

— Rhinestone Cowboy. 1994. mass mkt. 3.99 (*0-373-82527-7*) Harlequin Bks.

— Sand Dollar. (Romance Ser.: No. 211). 1992. pap. 2.89 (*0-373-03211-0*) Harlequin Bks.

— See How They Run. LC 98-48910. (Large Print Bks). 1998. 22.95 (*1-56895-591-X*) Wheeler Pub.

— Spellbinder. (Romance Ser.: No. 187). 1992. per. 2.89 (*0-373-03187-4*, 1-03187-1) Harlequin Bks.

— The Thunder Rolls. (Crystal Creek Ser.). 1993. per. 3.99 (*0-373-82520-X*, 1-82520-7) Harlequin Bks.

— Whose Little Girl Are You? 448p. 2000. mass mkt. 5.99 (*0-553-57691-7*) Bantam Dell.

Campbell, Bethany, et al. With This Ring. 1991. mass mkt. 4.95 (*0-373-83228-1*) Harlequin Bks.

Campbell, Bethany J., ed. see Graham, Cary D.

Campbell, Bill. The Campbell Machine Shorthand Dictionary. 2nd ed. 558p. (C). 1989. spiral bd. 29.95 (*1-881069-00-1*) Obsidian Pub.

***Campbell, Bill.** Install, Configure & Customize. 1999. pap. 34.99 (*0-7615-2307-3*) Prima Pub.

***Campbell, Bill.** The Lavender Bear of Oz. 160p. (J). 1998. 34.95 (*0-929605-83-7*) Books of Wonder.

Campbell, Bill. The Lavender Bear of Oz. (Illus.). 160p. (J). 1998. pap. 9.95 (*0-929605-77-2*) Books of Wonder.

Campbell, Bill & Terry, Irwin. Masquerade in Oz. (Illus.). 125p. (J). (gr. 2 up). 1995. 34.95 (*0-929605-34-9*); pap. 9.95 (*0-929605-33-0*) Books of Wonder.

Campbell, Bobbi A. Kendra: A Story of God's Providence. LC 97-21603. 112p. (Orig.). 1997. pap. 12.00 (*1-888683-16-3*) Wooster Bk.

Campbell, Bonita J. Wendell August Forge. LC 98-66660. 192p. 1998. 34.95 (*0-944933-07-6*) Dragonflyer Pr.

Campbell, Bonnie, jt. ed. see Hall, Bob.

Campbell, Bonnie Jo. Women & Other Animals. LC 99-15159. 208p. 1999. 25.00 (*1-55849-219-4*) U of Mass Pr.

Campbell, Bonnie K., jt. ed. see Bernstein, Henry.

Campbell, Brad & Fields, Jay. The Craft Heritage Trials of Western North Carolina: Back Roads & Scenic Byways to Some of the Most Beautiful Handmade Objects in the World. 2nd rev. ed. Harrmann, Laura, ed. LC 96-76105. (Illus.). 144p. 1998. pap. 13.95 (*0-9651905-1-X*) HandMade Amer.

Campbell, Brad, jt. auth. see Fields, Jay.

Campbell, Brian. The Roman Army, 31 B.C.-A.D. 337: A Sourcebook. LC 93-9032. (Illus.). 288p. (C). 1994. pap. 25.99 (*0-415-07173-9*) Routledge.

— Transylvania Chronicles I: Dark Tides Rising, Vol. 1. (Vampire Ser.). 1998. pap. 15.00 (*1-56504-290-5*) White Wolf.

Campbell, Brian & Rea, Nicky. Transylvania Chronicles: Son of the Dragon. (Vampire Ser.). (Illus.). 1998. pap. 15.00 (*1-56504-291-3*, 2812) White Wolf.

Campbell, Brian, et al. Litany of the Tribes, Vol. 3. (Werewolf Ser.). (Illus.). 1998. reprint ed. pap. 20.00 (*1-56504-304-9*, 3382) White Wolf.

Campbell, Brian, jt. auth. see Brucato, Phil.

***Campbell, Bruce.** Listening to Your Donors. 208p. 2000. pap. 27.95 (*0-7879-5037-8*, Pfffr & Co) Jossey-Bass.

Campbell, Bruce. The SA Generals & the Rise of Nazism. LC 98-5266. (Illus.). 288p. 1998. 34.95 (*0-8131-2047-0*) U Pr of Ky.

Campbell, Bruce & Campbell, Linda. Washington: A State of Learning. (Illus.). 140p. Date not set. pap. text 20.00 (*0-9642037-1-5*) Campbell & Assocs.

Campbell, Bruce & Cooper, M. J. Surgical Signs. 2nd ed. LC 99-27852. (Colour Guide Ser.). 2000. write for info. (*0-443-06145-9*) Harcrt Hlth Sci Grp.

Campbell, Bruce & Cooper, Martin. Surgical Signs. LC 93-3750. (Colour Guide Ser.). 1994. pap. text 16.95 (*0-443-04005-2*) Harcrt Hlth Sci Grp.

Campbell, Bruce & Lack, Elizabeth, eds. A Dictionary of Birds. LC 84-72101. (Illus.). 700p. 1985. 75.00 (*0-931130-12-3*) Harrell Bks.

Campbell, Bruce, jt. auth. see Campbell, Linda.

Campbell, Bruce, tr. see Lindsley, Margaret H.

***Campbell, Bruce B.** Death Squads in Global Perspective: Murder with Deniability. 1999. text 45.00 (*0-312-21365-4*) St Martin.

Campbell, Bruce B. & Koninklijk Instituut voor de Tropen Staff. Health Management Information Systems in Lower Income Countries: An Analysis of System Design, Implementation & Utilization in Ghana & Nepal. LC 98-112359. viii, 219 p. 1997. write for info. (*90-6832-113-7*, Pub. by Royal Tropical) Eiron.

***Campbell, Bruce M. S.** English Seignorial Agriculture, 1250-1450. LC 99-39384. (Cambridge Studies in Historical Geography: No. 31). (Illus.). 562p. (C). 2000. 85.00 (*0-521-30412-1*) Cambridge U Pr.

Campbell, Bruce M. S., jt. ed. see Britnell, Richard.

***Campbell, Burkholder.** Critiques of Contemporary Rhetoric. 3rd ed. 2002. pap. text 28.25 (*0-534-54904-7*) Thomson Learn.

Campbell, Burnham O., et al, eds. The Economic Impact of Demographic Change in Thailand, 1980-2015: An Application of the HOMES Household Forecasting Model. 240p. (C). 1993. pap. text 19.00 (*0-86638-135-X*) EW Ctr HI.

Campbell, Byron A., et al, eds. Attention & Information Processing in Infants & Adults: Perspectives from Human & Animal Research. 368p. 1991. text 79.95 (*0-8058-0782-9*) L Erlbaum Assocs.

Campbell, C., et al, eds. Groups: St. Andrews, 1997 in Bath I. LC 98-31985. (London Mathematical Society Lecture Note Ser.: No. 260). 350p. (C). 1999. pap. text 44.95 (*0-521-65588-9*) Cambridge U Pr.

Campbell, C. A. Moral Intuition & the Principle of Self-Realization. 1970. reprint ed. pap. 39.95 (*0-8383-0114-2*) M S G Haskell Hse.

Campbell, C. Blaine. A Student's Guide to Practical Interviewing in the Corporate World. Murphy, Amy, ed. (C). 1998. text. write for info. (*0-9666616-0-5*) Quantum Busn Solns.

Campbell, C. G. Magnetohydrodynamics in Binary Stars. LC 97-20159. (Astrophysics & Space Science Library). 306p. 1997. lib. bdg. 148.00 (*0-7923-4606-8*) Kluwer Academic.

Campbell, C. J. The Golden Century of Oil, 1950-2050: The Depletion of a Resource. 388p. 1991. lib. bdg 153.50 (*0-7923-1442-5*) Kluwer Academic.

Campbell, C. Jean. The Game of Courting & the Art of the Commune of San Gimignano, 1290-1320. LC 97-20230. 352p. 1998. text 55.00 (*0-691-01210-5*, Pub. by Princeton U Pr) Cal Prin Full Svc.

Campbell, C. L. & Benson, D. M., eds. Epidemiology & Management of Root Diseases. LC 94-14991. 1994. 174.95 (*0-387-57579-0*) Spr-Verlag.

Campbell, C. Lee. The Fischer-Smith Controversy: Are There Bacterial Diseases of Plants? LC 80-85458. (Phytopathological Classics Ser.). 65p. 1981. 22.00 (*0-89054-014-4*) Am Phytopathol Soc.

***Campbell, C. Lee, et al, eds.** The Formative Years of Plant Pathology in the United States. LC 99-61684. (Illus.). 448p. 1999. 53.00 (*0-89054-233-3*) Am Phytopathol Soc.

Campbell, C. Lee & Madden, Laurence V. Introduction to Plant Epidemiology Disease. LC 89-34349. 560p. 1990. 150.00 (*0-471-83236-7*) Wiley.

Campbell, C. M. Destiny & Disease in Mental Disorders. 1977. lib. bdg. 59.95 (*0-8490-1710-6*) Gordon Pr.

Campbell, C. M., et al, eds. Groups '93 Galway - St. Andrews, Vol. 1. (London Mathematical Society Lecture Note Ser.: No. 211). 316p. (C). 1995. pap. text 47.95 (*0-521-47749-2*) Cambridge U Pr.

— Groups '93 Galway - St. Andrews, Vol. 2. (London Mathematical Society Lecture Note Ser.: No. 212). 316p. (C). 1995. pap. text 47.95 (*0-521-47750-6*) Cambridge U Pr.

Campbell, C. M. & Robertson, E. F., eds. Groups: St. Andrews, 1989, 2 vols., Vol. 1. (London Mathematical Society Lecture Note Ser.: Nos. 159 & 160). 253p. (C). 1991. pap. text 49.95 (*0-521-39849-5*) Cambridge U Pr.

— Groups: St. Andrews, 1989, 2 vols., Vol. 2. (London Mathematical Society Lecture Note Ser.: Nos. 159 & 160). 247p. (C). 1991. pap. text 49.95 (*0-521-40669-2*) Cambridge U Pr.

Campbell, Calvin L. Balloons Are for Chasing. (Illus.). 155p. (Orig.). 1985. pap. 5.95 (*0-9615404-0-0*) Zia Enter.

— Balloons Are for Chasing. limited ed. (Illus.). 155p. (Orig.). 1985. 15.00 (*0-9615404-1-9*) Zia Enter.

Campbell, Cameron, jt. auth. see Lee, James.

Campbell, Camilla. After the Peewits. (C). 1988. 60.00 (*0-7855-2249-2*, Pub. by Granary) St Mut.

Campbell, Carl. Economic Growth, Capital Gains & Income Distribution: 1897-1956 (Doctoral Dissertation University of California, Berkley, 1964) LC 76-39824. (Illus.). 1977. lib. bdg. 54.95 (*0-405-09904-5*) Ayer.

Campbell, Carlos C. Birth of a National Park in the Great Smoky Mountains. rev. ed. LC 60-12223. (Illus.). 184p. (C). 1978. pap. 14.95 (*0-87049-815-0*) U of Tenn Pr.

Campbell, Carlos C., et al. Great Smoky Mountains Wildflowers. 4th ed. LC 94-61451. (Illus.). 112p. 1994. pap. 5.95 (*0-9643417-4-3*) Windy Pines.

— Great Smoky Mountains Wildflowers. 4th ed. LC 77-126938. 115p. 1970. reprint ed. pap. 35.70 (*0-608-01435-4*, 206219700002) Bks Demand.

— Great Smoky Mountains Wildflowers: When & Where to Find Them. 5th ed. LC 95-61682. (Illus.). 144p. 1996. pap. 10.95 (*0-9643417-3-5*) Windy Pines.

Campbell, Carmen & Nolet, Andree. English - French Lexicon of Microelectronics. (ENG & FRE.). 48p. 1987. pap. 24.95 (*0-8288-9399-3*) Fr & Eur.

Campbell, Carol A. Wildflower Field Guide & Press for Kids. LC 91-50963. (Illus.). 64p. (J). (gr. 1-7). 1993. pap. 13.95 (*1-56305-242-3*, 3242) Workman Pub.

Campbell, Carol Anne. Wildflower Field Guide & Press. (Hand in Hand with Nature Ser.). (Illus.). 64p. (J). (gr. k-7). 1998. pap. 13.95 (*0-921051-56-5*) Somerville Hse.

Campbell, Carol O. & Campbell, Griffin O. Views from a Pier: Visions of Hope, Dreams, Awareness, & Peace. Potter, Janet, ed. LC 95-74760. (Illus.). 181p. (Orig.). 1995. pap. 16.00 (*1-880439-05-0*) PERQ Pubns.

Campbell, Carol R. The Powder Monkey. LC 99-21655. (Young Americans Ser.: Vol. 4). (Illus.). 116p. (J). (gr. 4-12). 1999. pap. 5.99 (*1-57249-170-1*, WM Kids) White Mane Pub.

Campbell, Carole A. Women, Men, the Family & HIV/AIDS: A Sociological Perspective on the Epidemic in America. LC 98-29607. (Illus.). 256p. (C). 1999. text 49.95 (*0-521-56211-2*); pap. text 18.95 (*0-521-56679-7*) Cambridge U Pr.

Campbell, Carole R. Window of Time Teacher's Guide. 76p. 1997. pap. 8.95 (*1-57249-060-8*) White Mane Pub.

Campbell, Caroline & Page, Patty. The Austin Handbook. (Illus.). 200p. (Orig.). 1996. pap., spiral bd. 14.95 (*0-9655483-7-6*) Hill Cnty Welcome Serv.

***Campbell, Carolyn.** Love Lost & Found. 2000. mass mkt. 7.50 (*0-425-17627-4*) Berkley Pub.

— Together Again: True Stories of Birth Parents & Adopted Children Reunited. 342p. 1999. mass mkt. 6.99 (*0-425-16454-3*) Berkley Pub.

Campbell, Carolyn E. Reflections of a White Bear & Other Poems. 61p. 1992. lib. bdg. 8.95 (*0-9631703-1-7*) Fireweed Pr.

— Soiled Doves of Colorado & the Old West: Poems & Ballads. (Illus.). 68p. 1997. pap. 9.95 (*0-9631703-2-5*) Fireweed Pr.

— Tattooed Woman. 128p. (Orig.). 1996. pap. 11.95 (*1-888219-05-X*) Pearl Edit.

— Waiting for the Conder, Vol. 1. 91p. 1992. pap. write for info. (*0-9631703-0-9*) Fireweed Pr.

Campbell, Catherine. Social Psychology: Forging Social Identities in a Changing Society. (International Series in Experimental Social Psychology: Vol. 34). 250p. 1995. text 68.01 (*0-08-042401-5*, Pergamon Pr) Elsevier.

Campbell, Catherine, jt. auth. see Phillips, Michael.

Campbell, Catherine G. A Tree Is Special. 1992. pap. 2.95 (*0-87813-537-5*) Christian Light.

Campbell, Charles. The Backpacker's Photography Handbook: How to Take Great Wilderness Pictures While Hiking, Climbing, & Skiing. LC 94-9027. (Illus.). 144p. 1994. pap. 19.95 (*0-8174-3609-X*, Amphoto) Watsn-Guptill.

— The Intolerable Hulks: British Shipboard Confinement, 1776-1857. rev. ed. (Illus.). 1994. pap. 22.00 (*0-7884-0014-2*) Heritage Bk.

***Campbell, Charles, et al.** SQL Programmer's Reference. 400p. 2000. pap. 29.99 (*1-86100-317-X*) Wrox Pr Inc.

Campbell, Charles, ed. see Brueggemann, Walter.

Campbell, Charles A. & Quinlan, Hamid, trs. from PER. Peshawar Nights. rev. ed. 630p. Date not set. pap. 14.95 (*1-890847-00-3*) Texas Islam.

— Peshawar Nights. 2nd rev. ed. 630p. Date not set. reprint ed. 24.95 (*1-890847-01-1*) Texas Islam.

C

Campbell, Charles E., jt. auth. see Odell, Mark.

Campbell, Charles G. Tales from the Arab Tribes. Dorson, Richard M., ed. LC 80-790. (Folklore of the World Ser.). (Illus.). 1981. reprint ed. lib. bdg. 25.95 (*0-405-13329-4*) Ayer.

Campbell, Charles I., tr. see Muhammad & Ali, Hazrat.

Campbell, Charles L. Preaching Jesus: New Directions for Homiletics in Hans Frei's Post-Liberal Theology. LC 96-53633. 272p. 1997. pap. 28.00 (*0-8028-4156-2*) Eerdmans.

Campbell, Charles L., jt. auth. see Saunders, Stanley P.

Campbell, Charles M. Sun Son Song: Songs of Light, Life & Love. unabridged ed. 105p. 1999. per. 11.95 (*0-9651080-7-4*) St George MI.

Campbell, Charles P., jt. auth. see Bush, Donald W.

Campbell, Charles S., Jr. Anglo-American Understanding: 1898-1903. LC 79-25199. (Illus.). 385p. 1980. reprint ed. lib. bdg. 75.00 (*0-313-22162-6*, CAAA, Greenwood Pr) Greenwood.

Campbell, Chris. No Guarantees. large type ed. LC 93-42933. (J). 1994. lib. bdg. 15.95 (*0-7862-0146-0*) Thorndike Pr.

— No Guarantees: A Young Woman's Fight to Overcome Drug & Alcohol Addiction. LC 92-25183. (Illus.). 192p. (YA). (gr. 6 up). 1993. lib. bdg. 19.00 (*0-02-716445-4*, Mac Bks Young Read) S&S Childrens.

Campbell, Christian. International Media Liability: Civil Liability in the Information Age. LC 97-28574. 458p. 1997. 174.95 (*0-471-96578-2*) Wiley.

Campbell, Christian, ed. International Civil Procedures. 850p. 1995. 170.00 (*1-85044-863-9*) LLP.

***Campbell, Christian & Dowling, Donald, eds.** International Employment Law: The Multinational Employer & the Global Workforce. LC 99-57991. (International Business Law Practice Ser.). 450p. 2000. text 125.00 (*1-57105-105-8*) Transnatl Pubs.

***Campbell, Christian & Wouters, Mia, eds.** Deregulation in the International Market. 300p. 2000. 125.00 (*1-57105-108-2*) Transnatl Pubs.

Campbell, Christian, jt. ed. see Breidenbach, Stephan.

Campbell, Christian, jt. ed. see Campbell, Dennis.

Campbell, Christian X. & El-Rahaiby, Said K. Databook on Mechanical & Thermophysical Properties of Fiber-Reinforced Ceramic Matrix Composites. LC 96-40244. 1997. write for info. (*0-931682-62-2*) Purdue U Pubns.

— Databook on Mechanical & Thermophysical Properties of Particulate-Reinforced Ceramic Matrix Composites. LC 95-48874. (C). 1995. write for info. (*0-931682-57-6*) Purdue U Pubns.

— Databook on Mechanical & Thermophysical Properties of Whisker-Reinforced Ceramic Matrix Composites. LC 95-48873. 1995. write for info. (*0-931682-56-8*) Purdue U Pubns.

Campbell, Christiana M. The Farm Bureau & the New Deal: A Study of the Making of National Farm Policy, 1933 to 1940. LC 62-13210. 225p. reprint ed. 69.80 (*0-8357-9676-0*, 201502600096) Bks Demand.

***Campbell, Christine E., ed.** Coat-Tails of Empire: The ADFA Letters. 120p. 1999. pap. 19.95 (*0-7317-0370-7*, Pub. by ADFA) Intl Spec Bk.

Campbell, Christopher. Commercial Aircraft Markings & Profiles LC 93-151143. 192p. 1991. write for info. (*0-600-57288-9*, Pub. by Hamlyn Publishing Group Ltd) Sterling.

— The Hamlyn Guide to Commercial Aircraft & Airline Markings LC 93-135909. 159p. 1992. write for info. (*0-600-57450-4*, Pub. by Hamlyn Publishing Group Ltd) Sterling.

Campbell, Christopher P. Race, Myth & the News. 170p. 1995. text 45.00 (*0-8039-5871-4*); pap. text 21.50 (*0-8039-5872-2*) Sage.

Campbell, Christopher S. & Hyland, Fay. Winter Keys to Woody Plants of Maine. rev. ed. LC 74-30438. (Illus.). 1978. pap. 14.95 (*0-89101-034-3*) U Maine Pr.

Campbell, Civardi. Viking Raiders. (Time Travelers Bks.). (J). (gr. 4-9). 1977. pap. 6.95 (*0-86020-085-X*, Usborne); lib. bdg. 14.95 (*0-88110-102-8*, Usborne) EDC.

Campbell, Clare & Underdown, Brian. Corporate Insolvency in Practice: An Analytical Approach. 208p. (C). 1991. pap. text 36.00 (*1-85396-085-3*, Pub. by P Chapman) Taylor & Francis.

Campbell, Clarice T. Civil Rights Chronicle: Letters from the South. LC 96-17995. 264p. 1997. 45.00 (*0-87805-952-0*); pap. 17.00 (*0-87805-953-9*) U Pr of Miss.

***Campbell, Claude A.** A Tennessee Jar. LC 00-190925. 340p. 2000. pap. 18.00 (*0-7388-2100-4*) Xlibris Corp.

Campbell, Claudia, et al. Financial Management in a Managed Care Environment. LC 98-3061. 432p. (C). 1998. text 60.95 (*0-8273-8133-6*) Delmar.

Campbell, Clifton P. Education & Training for Work Vol. 1: Planning Programs. LC 96-60623. 295p. 1996. text 44.50 (*1-56676-417-3*) Scarecrow.

— Education & Training for Work Vol. 2: Delivering Instruction. LC 96-60623. 300p. 1996. text 44.50 (*1-56676-418-1*) Scarecrow.

Campbell, C.M., et al, eds. Groups: St. Andrews, 1997 in Bath II. LC 98-31985. (London Mathematical Society Lecture Note Ser.: No. 261). 350p. (C). 1999. pap. text 44.95 (*0-521-65576-5*) Cambridge U Pr.

Campbell, Colin. Beggarstaff Poster. (Illus.). 128p. 1993. 12.98 (*1-55859-545-7*, Cross Riv Pr) Abbeville Pr.

— Diana in Private: The Princess Nobody Knows. large type ed. LC 92-30414. (General Ser.). 471p. 1993. 21.95 (*0-8161-5608-5*, G K Hall Lrg Type) Mac Lib Ref.

— Governments under Stress: Political Executives & Key Bureaucrats in Washington, London, & Ottawa. 400p. 1983. 32.50 (*0-8020-5622-9*); pap. text 17.95 (*0-8020-6572-4*) U of Toronto Pr.

— Instrumental Book Vol. 1: Canntaireachd by Campbell. (GAE.). 194p. 1992. pap. 35.00 (*0-9621754-2-0*) A MacRaonuill.

— Instrumental Book Vol. 2: Canntaireachd by Campbell. (GAE.). 188p. 1992. pap. 34.00 (*0-9621754-7-1*) A MacRaonuill.

— Jobscape: Career Survival in the New Global Economy. LC 97-28978. (Illus.). 272p. 1997. pap. 16.95 (*1-56370-316-5*) Park Ave.

— Managing the Presidency: Carter, Reagan & the Search for Executive Harmony. LC 86-4069. (Policy & Institutional Studies). (Illus.). 352p. (Orig.). (C). 1986. pap. 15.95 (*0-8229-5412-5*) U of Pittsburgh Pr.

— The Myth of Social Action. 207p. (C). 1996. text 54.95 (*0-521-55079-3*) Cambridge U Pr.

— The Myth of Social Action. 230p. (C). 1998. pap. text 19.95 (*0-521-64636-7*) Cambridge U Pr.

— New Directions in Suspension Design: Making the Fast Car Faster. LC 80-24348. (Illus.). 224p. 1981. 21.95 (*0-8376-0150-9*) Bentley Pubs.

— Real Diana. 360p. 1999. mass mkt. 6.99 (*0-312-96943-0*) St Martin.

— Sports Car: Its Design & Performance. 4th ed. LC 77-94089. (Illus.). 306p. 1979. 21.95 (*0-8376-0158-4*) Bentley Pubs.

— Surface Acoustic Wave Devices for Mobile & Wireless Communications. LC 97-40551. (Applications of Modern Acoustics Ser.). (Illus.). 631p. 1998. text 120.00 (*0-12-157340-0*) Acad Pr.

— The U. S. Presidency in Crisis: A Comparative Perspective. 272p. (C). 1998. pap. text 21.95 (*0-19-509144-2*) OUP.

Campbell, Colin & Halligan, John. Political Leadership in an Age of Restraint: The Australian Experience. LC 92-27355. (Series in Policy & Institutional Studies). 284p. (C). 1993. text 29.95 (*0-8229-1170-1*) U of Pittsburgh Pr.

Campbell, Colin & Kryszewska, Hanna. Learner Based Teaching. Maley, Alan, ed. (Illus.). 136p. 1992. pap. text 13.95 (*0-19-437163-8*) OUP.

Campbell, Colin & Rockman, Bert A. The Clinton Presidency: First Appraisals. LC 95-22611. (Illus.). 416p. (C). 1995. 34.95 (*1-56643-013-5*, Chatham House Pub) Seven Bridges.

***Campbell, Colin & Rockman, Bert A., eds.** The Clinton Legacy. LC 99-6299. (Illus.). 368p. 2000. pap. 24.95 (*1-889119-14-8*, Pub. by Seven Bridges) Stylus Pub VA.

Campbell, Colin & Rockman, Bert A., eds. The Clinton Presidency: First Appraisals. LC 95-22611. (Illus.). 416p. (C). 1995. pap. text 24.95 (*1-56643-014-3*, Chatham House Pub) Seven Bridges.

Campbell, Colin & Wilson, Graham K. The End of Whitehall: Death of a Paradigm? (Comparative Politics Ser.). 304p. 1995. pap. 31.95 (*1-55786-140-4*) Blackwell Pubs.

Campbell, Colin, et al. Politics & Government in Europe Today, 2 vols. 2nd ed. 658p. (C). 1994. text 57.56 (*0-395-66128-5*) HM.

Campbell, Colin, jt. ed. see Falk, Pasi.

Campbell, Colin A., ed. see Weaver, Betsy & Frederick, Gary E.

Campbell, Colin D. Alternative Monetary Regimes. Dougan, William R., ed. LC 85-30034. (Illus.). 267p. reprint ed. pap. 82.80 (*0-608-06116-6*, 206644900008) Bks Demand.

Campbell, Colin D., ed. Financing Social Security. LC 78-21683. (AEI Symposia Ser.: No. 78H). 364p. reprint ed. pap. 112.90 (*0-8357-4481-7*, 203733200008) Bks Demand.

— Income Redistribution. LC 77-6342. 276p. reprint ed. pap. 85.60 (*0-8357-4492-2*, 203734500008) Bks Demand.

Campbell, Collier A. & Moncla, Susie M. Texas City: Images of the Twentieth Century. LC 99-20985. 1999. 32.00 (*1-57864-071-7*) Donning Co.

Campbell, Colm. Emergency Law in Ireland, 1918-1925. (Illus.). 456p. 1994. 75.00 (*0-19-825675-2*) OUP.

Campbell, Colm, et al, eds. Nationalism, Minorities, & Diasporas: Identity & Rights in the Middle East. 266p. 1996. text 65.00 (*1-86064-052-4*, Pub. by I B T) St Martin.

Campbell, Colton C. & Rae, Nicol C., eds. New Majority or Old Minority? The Impact of the Republicans on Congress. LC 98-54157. 256p. 1999. 65.00 (*0-8476-9168-3*); pap. 19.95 (*0-8476-9169-1*) Rowman.

Campbell, Courtney, ed. What Price for Parenthood? Ethics & Assisted Reproduction. 120p. 1992. text 78.95 (*1-85521-224-2*, Pub. by Dartmth Pub) Ashgate Pub Co.

Campbell, Courtney S. & Lustig, B. Andrew, eds. Duties to Others. LC 93-40310. (Theology & Medicine Ser.: Vol. 4). 332p. (C). 1994. lib. bdg. 148.50 (*0-7923-2638-5*, Pub. by Kluwer Academic) Kluwer Academic.

Campbell, Craig & Crull, Anna. Non-Cryogenic Gas Separations: Technologies & Markets. LC 98-120615. (Report Ser.: No. C-128R). 171p. 1997. 2950.00 (*1-56965-387-9*) BCC.

Campbell, Craig & Crull, Anna, contrib. by. Electrophoresis: What's New. 114p. 1995. 2350.00 (*1-56965-044-6*, C-191) BCC.

Campbell, Craig & Ogden, Michael. Constructed Wetlands in the Sustainable Landscape. LC 99-24352. 288p. 1999. pap. 59.95 (*0-471-10720-4*) Wiley.

Campbell, Craig G. History of Loves Park, Illinois. LC 97-77090. (Illus.). 200p. 1998. 30.00 (*0-9661357-4-1*) C G Campbell.

***Campbell-Crystal, Vicki.** Midnight Journeys. 1999. pap. write for info. (*1-58235-229-1*) Watermrk Pr.

Campbell, Cynthia J., jt. auth. see Campbell, William E.

***Campbell, Cynthia M.** Renewing the Vision: Reformed Faith & Life for the Twenty-First Century. 160p. 2000. pap. 14.95 (*0-664-50124-9*, Pub. by Geneva Press) Presbyterian Pub.

Campbell, D., ed. Transnational Legal Practice: A Guide to Selected Countries, 2 vols. 410p. 122.50 (*90-6544-028-3*) Kluwer Academic.

Campbell, D., jt. auth. see Ellen, E.

Campbell, D., jt. auth. see Hulsenbek, R.

Campbell, D. A. Greek Lyric Poetry: A Selection of Early Greek Lyric, Elegiac & Iambic Poetry. (GRE.). 500p. 1982. reprint ed. 33.95 (*0-86292-008-6*, Pub. by Brist Class Pr) Focus Pub-R Pullins.

Campbell, D. H., ed. see Muntz, E. P., et al.

Campbell, D. J. Business for Non-Business Students. 342p. 1994. pap. 59.95 (*1-85805-082-0*, Pub. by DP Publns) St Mut.

Campbell, D. K., ed. Chaos - XAOC. 512p. 1990. 79.95 (*0-88318-777-9*); pap. 39.95 (*0-88318-778-7*) Spr-Verlag.

***Campbell, D. M.** My Miserable Mother-in-Law: The Big Nightmare. 2000. pap. 5.95 (*0-533-13467-6*) Vantage.

Campbell, D. M. & Kleinpoppen, H. Selected Topics on Electron Physics: Proceedings of the Peter Farago Symposium on Electron Physics Held As a Satellite Symposium to the Fifth European Conference on Atomic & Molecular Physics, March 31-April 1, 1995, Edinburgh, Scotland. LC 96-43717. (Physics of Atoms & Molecules Ser.). (Illus.). 501p. (C). 1996. text 155.00 (*0-306-45484-X*, Kluwer Plenum) Kluwer Academic.

Campbell, D. S. Capacitive & Resistive Electronic Components. (Electrocomponent Science Monographs). 374p. 1994. pap. text 47.00 (*2-88124-999-X*) Gordon & Breach.

Campbell, D. S. & Hayes, J. A. Capacitive & Resistive Electronic Components. LC 93-23721. (Electrocomponent Science Monographs: Vol. 8). 374p. 1994. text 134.00 (*2-88124-845-4*) Gordon & Breach.

Campbell, Dale. Jogging: A Successful Guide to Aerobics. (Illus.). 124p. (C). 1994. pap. text 11.95 (*0-89641-264-4*) American Pr.

Campbell, Dan. Edgar Cayce on the Power of Color, Stones, & Crystals. Cayce, Charles T., ed. 222p. (Orig.). 1989. mass mkt. 6.50 (*0-446-34982-8*, Pub. by Warner Bks) Little.

***Campbell, Daniel.** Bad to the Bone. (Funnie Mysteries Ser.: No. 6). 80p. (J). (gr. 2-7). 2000. pap. 4.99 (*0-7868-4412-4*) Disney Pr.

Campbell, D'Ann. Women at War with America: Private Lives in a Patriotic Era. (Illus.). 320p. 1984. 34.95 (*0-674-95475-0*) HUP.

Campbell, Darlene. Proper Care of Rabbits. 256p. 1992. 16.95 (*0-86622-196-4*, TW110) TFH Pubns.

Campbell, Dave & Campbell, Mary. The Student's Guide to Doing Research on the Internet. LC 95-13498. 368p. (C). 1995. pap. text, student ed. 14.95 (*0-201-48916-3*) Addison-Wesley.

***Campbell, David.** Business Strategy An Introduction. 352p. 1999. pap. text 34.95 (*0-7506-4207-6*) Buttrwrth-Heinemann.

Campbell, David. Evening under Lamplight. 193p. 1987. pap. 14.95 (*0-7022-2106-6*, Pub. by Univ Queensland Pr) Intl Spec Bk.

— The Failure of Marxism: The Concept of Inversion in Marx's Critique of Capitalism. (Socio-Legal Studies). (Illus.). 344p. 1996. 91.95 (*1-85521-692-2*, Pub. by Dartmth Pub) Ashgate Pub Co.

— If You Don't Know Where You're Going, You'll Probably End up Somewhere Else. (Illus.). 136p. 1974. reprint ed. pap. 9.95 (*0-88347-327-5*, 7327) Res Christian Liv.

— Learning Consultation: A Systematic Framework. 176p. 1995. pap. text 30.00 (*1-85575-117-8*, Pub. by H Karnac Bks Ltd) Other Pr LLC.

— National Deconstruction: Violence, Identity, & Justice in Bosnia. LC 98-17006. 382p. 1998. 62.95 (*0-8166-2936-6*); pap. 24.95 (*0-8166-2937-4*) U of Minn Pr.

***Campbell, David.** The Socially Constructed Organisation. 256p. 2000. pap. 30.50 (*1-85575-245-X*, Pub. by H Karnac Bks Ltd) Other Pr LLC.

Campbell, David. Tales to Tell, Vol. 2. 128p. 1993. pap. 24.00 (*0-7855-7033-0*, Pub. by St Andrew) St Mut.

— Writing Security: United States Foreign Policy & the Politics of Identity. 266p. (C). 1992. text 49.95 (*0-8166-2221-3*) U of Minn Pr.

— Writing Security: United States Foreign Policy & the Politics of Identity. LC 98-14152. 312p. 1998. 19.95 (*0-8166-3144-1*) U of Minn Pr.

Campbell, David, ed. Tales to Tell. 88p. (C). 1989. pap. 39.00 (*0-7855-7005-5*, Pub. by St Andrew) St Mut.

***Campbell, David & Lewis, N. Douglas, eds.** Promoting Participation: Law or Politics? 420p. 1999. pap. 63.00 (*1-85941-483-4*, Pub. by Cavendish Pubng) Gaunt.

Campbell, David & Spence, Alastair A. Norris & Campbell's Anaesthetics, Resuscitation & Intensive Care. 8th ed. LC 96-26056. 1998. pap. text 35.95 (*0-443-04886-X*) Church.

Campbell, David & Van Velsor, Ellen. The Use of Personality Measures in the Leadership Development Program. (Special Reports: No. 308G). 72p. pap. 45.00 (*0-912879-57-2*) Ctr Creat Leader.

Campbell, David & Vincent-Jones, Peter, eds. Contract & Economic Organisation: Socio-Legal Initiatives. LC 95-48248. (Socio-Legal Studies). (Illus.). 288p. 1996. text 87.95 (*1-85521-694-9*, Pub. by Dartmth Pub) Ashgate Pub Co.

Campbell, David, et al. Second Thoughts on the Theory & Practice of the Milan Approach to Family Therapy. 96p. 1992. pap. text 22.00 (*1-85575-014-7*, Pub. by H Karnac Bks Ltd) Other Pr LLC.

— Systemic Work with Organizations: A New Model for Managers & Change Agents. (Systemic Thinking & Practice Ser.). 206p. 1994. pap. text 30.00 (*1-85575-100-3*, Pub. by H Karnac Bks Ltd) Other Pr LLC.

— Teaching Systemic Thinking. 88p. 1992. pap. text 22.00 (*1-85575-015-5*, Pub. by H Karnac Bks Ltd) Other Pr LLC.

Campbell, David, jt. auth. see Campbell, Mary.

Campbell, David, jt. auth. see Gere, Don.

Campbell, David, jt. auth. see Sienkiewicz, Teresa.

Campbell, David, jt. ed. see Duerk, Donna.

Campbell, David A. Greek Lyric Vol. V: The New School of Poetry & Anonymous Songs & Hymns. 464p. 1993. 19.95 (*0-674-99559-7*) HUP.

Campbell, David A., ed. Greek Lyric Vol. III: Stesichorus, Ibycus, Simonides & Others. (Loeb Classical Library: No. 476). 652p. 1992. 18.95 (*0-674-99525-2*) HUP.

— Greek Lyric Vol. 4: Bacchylides, Corinna, & Others. (Loeb Classical Library: No. 461). 428p. 1992. text 19.95 (*0-674-99508-2*) HUP.

Campbell, David A., tr. Greek Lyric, Vol. I. (Loeb Classical Library: No. 142). (GRE.). 510p. 1982. text 18.95 (*0-674-99157-5*) HUP.

— Greek Lyric, Vol. II. (Loeb Classical Library: No. 143). (Illus.). 547p. 1989. text 18.95 (*0-674-99158-3*) HUP.

Campbell, David G. & Hammond, H. David, eds. Floristic Inventory of Tropical Countries: The Status of Plant Systematics, Collections, & Vegetation, Plus Recommendations for the Future. LC 88-26058. (Illus.). 545p. (C). 1989. text 85.00 (*0-89327-333-3*) NY Botanical.

Campbell, David G., jt. auth. see Byrd, Richard E.

Campbell, David K., et al, eds. Nonlinear Science: The Next Decade. (Physica D Ser.). (Illus.). 592p. 1992. pap. text 40.00 (*0-262-53109-7*, Bradford Bks) MIT Pr.

Campbell, David K., jt. auth. see Baeriswyl, D.

Campbell, David L. Learn Multimedia with Visual Basic. (Illus.). 700p. 1997. 15.00 (*1-57914-029-7*) Campbell-Smith.

Campbell, David L., jt. auth. see Smith, Larry W.

***Campbell, David P.** The Complete Inklings: Columns on Leadership & Creativity. LC 99-23297. 265p. 1999. pap. text 30.00 (*1-882197-48-8*) Ctr Creat Leader.

Campbell, David P. If I'm in Charge Here: Why Is Everybody Laughing? 164p. 1980. pap. 9.95 (*0-912879-90-4*) Ctr Creat Leader.

— Inklings: Collected Columns on Leadership & Creativity. 173p. pap. text 15.00 (*0-912879-67-X*) Ctr Creat Leader.

— Take the Road to Creativity & Get off Your Dead End. 136p. 1977. pap. 9.95 (*0-912879-91-2*) Ctr Creat Leader.

Campbell, David P., jt. auth. see Reddy, Allan C.

Campbell, David R. Quicken 7 Made Easy. 1993. pap. 19.95 (*0-07-881971-7*) McGraw.

— Quicken 3 for Windows Made Easy. 1993. pap. 19.95 (*0-07-881972-5*) McGraw.

Campbell, David R. & Campbell, Mary V. Mastering Microcomputer Applications: WordPerfect 6.0, Lotus 1-2-3 Release 2.4, dBase IV 2.0, & DOS 6. LC 93-12424. (Glencoe-Osborne Ser.). 1994. write for info. (*0-02-800419-1*) Glencoe.

— Mastering Microcomputer Applications: WordPerfect 6.0, Lotus 1-2-3 Release 2.4, dBase IV 2.0, & DOS 6. large type ed. 1994. 209.50 (*0-614-09807-6*, L-31412-00) Am Printing Hse.

Campbell, David R. & Rose, Harvey, eds. Order in Chaos: Proceedings of the International Conference, Los Alamos, NM, U. S. A., 24-28 May, 1982. x, 362p. 1983. reprint ed. 111.50 (*0-444-86727-9*, I-299-84, North Holland) Elsevier.

Campbell, David R., jt. auth. see Campbell, Mary.

Campbell, David R., jt. auth. see Campbell, Mary V.

Campbell, Dawn L. The Tea Book. LC 94-31638. (Illus.). 224p. 1995. text 19.95 (*1-56554-074-3*) Pelican.

Campbell, Dawn V. & Smith, Janet. The Coffee Book. LC 92-45038. (Illus.). 176p. 1993. 19.95 (*0-88289-950-3*) Pelican.

Campbell, Dee A., ed. see Dorsey, Jason.

Campbell, Denele P. Notes of a Piano Tuner. LC 96-49856. 160p. 1997. 16.95 (*1-56164-127-8*) Pineapple Pr.

Campbell, Dennis. Business Transactions in Germany, 4 vols. (Illus.). 1983. ring bd. 510.00 (*0-8205-1394-6*) Bender.

— Campbell Comparative Law Yearbook. 1982. lib. bdg. 150.00 (*90-247-2563-1*, Pub. by M Nijhoff) Kluwer Academic.

— Comparative Law. (Comparative Law Yearbook Ser.). 1993. lib. bdg. 139.00 (*1-85333-788-9*) Kluwer Academic.

— Comparative Law. (Comparative Law Yearbook Ser.). 1994. lib. bdg. 152.00 (*1-85966-063-0*) Kluwer Academic.

— Comparative Law Index. (Comparative Law Yearbook Ser.). 1993. lib. bdg. 82.50 (*1-85333-936-9*) Kluwer Academic.

— Comparative Law Yearbook. (Coly Ser.). 1992. lib. bdg. 161.50 (*1-85333-717-X*) Kluwer Academic.

— Comparative Law Yearbook. 1996. lib. bdg. 140.00 (*90-411-0940-4*) Kluwer Academic.

— Comparative Law Yearbook, Vol. III. 294p. 1980. lib. bdg. 96.00 (*90-286-0340-9*) Kluwer Academic.

— International Employment Law, 2 vols. annuals LC 96-45746. 1997. ring bd. 405.00 (*0-8205-2485-9*) Bender.

— International Environmental Law & Regulations, Vol. 1. LC 96-179183. (Environmental Law Library). 326p. 1996. 194.95 (*0-471-95229-X*) Wiley.

— International Execution Against Judgement Debtors, 2 vols. (International Business & Law Ser.). 1993. ring bd. 250.00 (*0-87632-973-3*) West Group.

— International Immigration & Nationality Law. LC 93-16497. (YA). (gr. 7 up). 1993. write for info. (*0-7923-2204-5*) Kluwer Academic.

— International Immigration & Nationality Law. LC 93-16497. (YA). (gr. 7 up). 1993. write for info. (*0-7923-2203-7*, Pub. by M Nijhoff) Kluwer Academic.

— International Information Tech. LC 97-1636. (Intellectual Property Law Ser.). 446p. 1997. 174.95 (*0-471-96871-4*) Wiley.

***Campbell, Dennis.** International Insurance Law & Regulation. Center for International Legal Studies Staff, ed. LC 99-87833. 1999. ring bd. 325.00 (*0-379-01285-5*) Oceana.

Campbell, Dennis. Lawyer's Guide. 1991. lib. bdg. 153.50 (*90-6544-602-8*) Kluwer Academic.

— Serving Process & Obtaining Evidence Abroad. LC 99-192033. 540p. 1998. 177.00 (*90-411-9710-9*) Kluwer Law Intl.

— Technology Transfer. 1900. pap. text 143.00 (*90-6544-609-5*) Kluwer Academic.

— The U. S. Legal System: A Practice Handbook. 1983. lib. bdg. 130.50 (*90-247-2782-0*) Kluwer Academic.

Campbell, Dennis, ed. Approaching 2000: The Corporation in Transition. LC 94-42391. 1994. write for info. (*90-411-0007-5*) Kluwer Law Intl.

— Attacking Foreign Assets. 512p. 1992. 170.00 (*1-85044-467-6*) LLP.

— Commercial Alliances in the Information Age. LC 96-221252. 442p. 1996. 177.00 (*0-471-96552-9*) Wiley.

— Comparative Law Yearbook, Vol. 8. 1985. lib. bdg. 144.50 (*90-247-3178-X*) Kluwer Academic.

— Comparative Law Yearbook, Vol. 11. 248p. (C). 1992. lib. bdg. 131.00 (*0-7923-1701-7*) Kluwer Academic.

— Comparative Law Yearbook of International Business Vol. 16, 1994. 400p. (C). 1994. lib. bdg. 134.00 (*90-247-3002-3*, Pub. by Graham & Trotman) Kluwer Academic.

— Comparative Law Yearbook of International Business: Cumulative Index Vols. 1-18: 1977-1996. (Comparative Law Yearbook Ser.: Vol. 19). 348p. 1998. 113.00 (*90-411-0747-9*) Kluwer Law Intl.

— Comparative Law Yearbook of International Business, 1991, Vol. 13. 320p. 1991. lib. bdg. 163.50 (*1-85333-588-6*) Kluwer Law Intl.

— Comparative Law Yearbook of International Business,1990, Vol. 12. (C). 1991. lib. bdg. 163.00 (*1-85333-484-7*, Pub. by Graham & Trotman) Kluwer Academic.

— Environmental Hazards & Duties of Disclosure: An International Survey. LC 94-35270. 400p. (C). 1994. lib. bdg. 134.50 (*1-85966-061-4*) Kluwer Law Intl.

— Environmental Regulation & Its Impact on Foreign Investment. LC 92-28236. 640p. (C). 1992. lib. bdg. 183.50 (*1-85333-726-9*, Pub. by Graham & Trotman) Kluwer Academic.

— Europe & Nineteen Ninety-Two: The Challenge for American Enterprise. 104p. 1989. pap. 56.00 (*90-6544-452-1*) Kluwer Law Intl.

— International Consumer Protection. LC 95-5769. 1995. pap. 427.50 (*0-7923-3391-8*, Pub. by M Nijhoff); write for info. (*0-7923-3390-X*, Pub. by M Nijhoff) Kluwer Academic.

— International Franchising Law, 2 vols., Set. LC 92-38917. 1993. ring bd. 405.00 (*0-8205-1927-8*) Bender.

— International Liability of Corporate Directors. 824p. 1993. 190.00 (*1-85044-545-1*) LLP.

An Asterisk (*) at the beginning of an entry indicates that the title is appearing for the first time.

— International Product Liability. 639p. 1993. 190.00 (*1-85044-520-6*) LLP.

— International Tax Planning. LC 95-17309. 1995. 142.00 (*90-411-0853-X*) Kluwer Law Intl.

— Legal Aspects of Doing Business in Africa. (International Business Ser.: Vol. 4). 1992. 146.00 (*90-6544-932-9*) Kluwer Law Intl.

— Legal Aspects of Doing Business in Asia & the Pacific. (International Business Ser.: Vol. 3). 1992. ring bd. 203.00 (*90-6544-982-5*) Kluwer Law Intl.

— Legal Aspects of Doing Business in Europe. (International Business Ser.: Vol. 1). 1992. ring bd. 260.00 (*90-6544-970-1*) Kluwer Law Intl.

— Legal Aspects of Doing Business in Latin America. (International Business Ser.: Vol. 2). 1992. 212.00 (*90-6544-930-2*) Kluwer Law Intl.

— Legal Aspects of Doing Business in North America & Canada, Set. (International Business Ser.: Vols. 6 & 7). 1992. ring bd. 206.00 (*90-6544-999-X*) Kluwer Law Intl.

— Legal Aspects of Doing Business in the Middle East. LC 92-9683. (International Business Ser.: Vol. 5). 1992. 146.00 (*90-6544-917-5*) Kluwer Law Intl.

***Campbell, Dennis, ed.** Legal Implications of the Millennium Bug. (Comparative Law Yearbook of International Business Ser.: Vol. 21A). 480p. 1999. text 165.00 (*90-411-9776-1*) Kluwer Law Intl.

Campbell, Dennis, et al, eds. Consumer Protection Two Thousand: Public Interest & Corporate Priorities in the 1990s. LC 93-32027. 1993. write for info. (*90-6544-776-8*) Kluwer Law Intl.

— Trademarks: Legal & Business Aspects. LC 94-27720. 1994. 203.00 (*90-6544-859-4*) Kluwer Law Intl.

***Campbell, Dennis & Birkeland, Brian, eds.** Lawyering in the International Market. LC 99-42141. (International Business Law Practice Ser.). 450p. 2000. text 125.00 (*1-57105-104-X*) Transnatl Pubs.

Campbell, Dennis & Campbell, Christian, eds. Professional Liability of Lawyers. 400p. 1995. 175.00 (*1-85044-869-8*) LLP.

Campbell, Dennis & Center for International Legal Studies Staff. International Joint Ventures, 2 vols. annuals LC 96-20979. 1996. ring bd. 405.00 (*0-8205-2474-3*) Bender.

***Campbell, Dennis & Center for International Legal Studies Staff, eds.** World Intellectural Property Rights & Remedies. LC 99-75931. 1999. ring bd. 325.00 (*0-379-01284-7*) Oceana.

Campbell, Dennis & Collins, Anthony E., eds. Corporate Insolvency & Rescue: The International Dimension. LC 92-45136. 1993. 94.00 (*90-6544-685-0*) Kluwer Law Intl.

***Campbell, Dennis & Cotter, Susan, eds.** Comparative Law Yearbook of International Business Vol. 20: 1998. (Comparative Law Yearbook Ser.: Vol. 21). 432p. 1998. 135.00 (*90-411-9694-3*) Kluwer Law Intl.

Campbell, Dennis & Cotter, Susan, eds. Copyright Infringement: Comparative Law Yearbook of International Business Special Issue, 1997. LC 98-158247. (Comparative Law Yearbook Ser.: No. 21). 472p. 1998. 143.00 (*90-411-9654-4*) Kluwer Law Intl.

— International Intellectual Property Law: European Jurisdictions, Vol. 1. (Intellectual Property Library Ser.). 556p. 1996. 194.50 (*0-471-94086-0*) Wiley.

— International Intellectual Property Law, New Development, Vol. 3. 418p. 1996. 194.95 (*0-471-96081-0*) Wiley.

***Campbell, Dennis & Dadge, David, eds.** Remedies for International Sellers of Goods, 2 vols. 1282p. 1999. ring bd. 297.00 (*90-411-0788-6*) Kluwer Law Intl.

Campbell, Dennis & Fisher, Joy, eds. Data Transmission & Privacy. LC 94-969. 532p. (C). 1994. lib. bdg. 222.50 (*0-7923-2713-6*) Kluwer Academic.

Campbell, Dennis & Fisher, Joy, eds. International Immigration & Nationality Law Vols. 1-3: Basic Work, 3 vols. 1995. ring bd. 540.00 (*0-7923-2228-2*) Kluwer Academic.

Campbell, Dennis & Flint, Charles, eds. 1993, the European Market: Myth or Reality? LC 94-4588. 1994. 107.00 (*90-6544-822-5*) Kluwer Law Intl.

Campbell, Dennis & Lafili, Louis, eds. Distributorships, Agency & Franchising in an International Arena: Europe, the United States, Japan & Latin America. 230p. 1990. pap. 64.00 (*90-6544-504-8*) Kluwer Law Intl.

***Campbell, Dennis & Meek, Susan, eds.** Comparative Law Yearbook of International Business 1999. (Comparative Law Yearbook Ser.: Vol. 21). 544p. 1999. text 195.00 (*90-411-9768-0*) Kluwer Law Intl.

Campbell, Dennis & Meroni, Rudolf, eds. Bankers' Liability: Risks & Remedies. LC 93-14368. 1993. write for info. (*90-6433-728-4*) Kluwer Law Intl.

Campbell, Dennis & Moore, Mickela, eds. Financial Services in the New Europe: Comparative Law Yearbook of International Business - Special Issue. LC 92-42623. 376p. (C). 1993. lib. bdg. 154.00 (*1-85333-878-8*, Pub. by Graham & Trotman) Kluwer Academic.

Campbell, Dennis & Pombo, Fernando, eds. Penetrating International Markets: From Sales & Licensings to Subsidiaries & Acquisitions. 340p. 1991. pap. 76.00 (*90-6544-550-1*) Kluwer Law Intl.

Campbell, Dennis & Powers, Jennifer, eds. Shareholders' Liability: The Comparative Law Yearbook of International Business Special Issue, 1993. LC 93-46209. (Comparative Law Yearbook Ser.). 528p. (C). 1994. lib. bdg. 177.00 (*1-85966-048-7*, Pub. by Graham & Trotman) Kluwer Academic.

Campbell, Dennis & Proksch, Reinhard, eds. International Business Transactions, 2 vols. 1989. disk. write for info. (*0-318-68483-7*) Kluwer Law Intl.

— International Business Transactions, 2 vols., Set. 1989. ring bd. 340.00 (*90-6544-981-7*) Kluwer Law Intl.

***Campbell, Dennis & Siefarth, Christof, eds.** International Distribution Law. 350p. 2000. 125.00 (*1-57105-140-6*) Transnatl Pubs.

Campbell, Dennis & Solomon, Robert, eds. International Securities Law & Regulation. (International Business Law Practice Ser.). 350p. Date not set. text 115.00 (*1-57105-106-6*) Transnatl Pubs.

Campbell, Dennis & Summerfield, Peter. Effective Dispute Resolution for the International Commercial Lawyer. LC 89-2643. 240p. 1989. pap. 66.00 (*90-6544-415-7*) Kluwer Law Intl.

Campbell, Dennis & Swart, Marilise, eds. International Environmental Law & Regulations, Vol. 2. 386p. 1997. 174.95 (*0-471-97611-3*) Wiley.

***Campbell, Dennis, et al.** International Asset Securitization & Other Financing Tools. LC 00-44346. (International Business Law Practice Ser.). 2000. write for info. (*1-57105-110-4*) Transnatl Pubs.

Campbell, Dennis, et al. International Intellectual Property Law: Global Jurisdictions, Vol. 2. LC 96-22599. 350p. 1996. 194.95 (*0-471-95329-6*) Wiley.

— Offshore Trust. LC 96-23270. 1996. 200.00 (*90-411-0921-8*) Kluwer Law Intl.

— Structuring International Transactions. LC 97-14653. 1997. pap. 99.00 (*90-411-0404-6*) Kluwer Law Intl.

— A Survey of the Commercial Agency. 1984. lib. bdg. 95.00 (*90-6544-181-6*) Kluwer Law Intl.

— Unfair Trading Practices. LC 97-31122. 440p. 1997. 171.00 (*90-411-0721-5*) Kluwer Law Intl.

Campbell, Dennis, ed. see Center for International Legal Studies Staff.

Campbell, Dennis M. Who Will Go for Us? An Invitation to Ordained Ministry. LC 93-23623. 128p. (Orig.). 1994. pap. 7.95 (*0-687-46775-6*) Abingdon.

***Campbell, Dennis M., et al, eds.** Doctrines & Discipline: Methodist Theology & Practice. LC 99-15044. (United Methodism & American Culture Ser.: Vol. 3). 320p. 1999. pap. 19.95 (*0-687-02139-1*) Abingdon.

Campbell, Dennis M., et al, eds. Questions for the Twenty-First-Century Church. LC 99-17834. (United Methodism & American Culture Ser.: Vol. 4). 320p. 1999. pap. 19.95 (*0-687-02146-4*) Abingdon.

Campbell, Diana. Skill Builders: Sentence Writing Workout. 176p. (C). 1997. pap. text 16.80 (*0-06-501401-4*) Addson-Wesley Educ.

— Teaching Guide for Indian Literature, 2 vols., Set. 69p. (gr. 6 up). 1983. 16.00 (*0-685-42638-6*) Rough Rock Pr.

Campbell, Diane. Step-by-Step to Natural Food. LC 79-84548. 224p. 1979. spiral bd. 7.95 (*0-9603766-0-7*) C C Pubs.

Campbell, Diane, jt. auth. see Cripe, Helen.

Campbell, Dianna. Better Sentence-Writing in 30 Minutes a Day. (Better English Ser.). 224p. (Orig.). (YA). 1995. pap. 9.99 (*1-56414-203-5*) Career Pr Inc.

***Campbell, Don.** Mozart Effect. 2000. pap. 14.00 (*0-380-79013-0*, Quil) HarperTrade.

Campbell, Don. The Mozart Effect: Tapping the Power of Music to Heal the Body, Strengthen the Mind & Unlock the Creative Spirit. LC 97-27570. 352p. 1998. 24.00 (*0-380-97418-5*, Avon Bks) Morrow Avon.

***Campbell, Don.** The Mozart Effect (R) for Children: Awakening Your Child's Mind, Health & Creativity With Music. 288p. 2000. 25.00 (*0-380-97782-6*, Wm Morrow) Morrow Avon.

Campbell, Don. Music: Physician for Times to Come. Orig. Title: Music as Physician. 318p. 1995. pap. 15.00 (*0-8356-0668-6*, Quest) Theos Pub Hse.

***Campbell, Don.** Music: Physician for Times to Come. 2nd rev. ed. Orig. Title: Music as Physician. 365p. 2000. pap. 15.95 (*0-8356-0788-7*, Pub. by Theos Pub Hse) Natl Bk Netwk.

Campbell, Don. The Roar of Silence: Healing Powers of Breath, Tone & Music. LC 89-40173. (Illus.). 174p. 1989. pap. 9.95 (*0-8356-0645-7*, Pub. by Theos Pub Hse) Natl Bk Netwk.

Campbell, Don, ed. Music & Miracles: A Companion to Music: Physician for Times to Come. LC 92-50145. 280p. 1992. pap. 14.00 (*0-8356-0683-X*, Quest) Theos Pub Hse.

Campbell, Don & Wilson, Tim. Healing Powers of Tone & Chant. 1994. audio 18.95 (*0-8356-1906-0*, Quest) Theos Pub Hse.

Campbell, Don G. Introduction to the Musical Brain. (Illus.). 176p. 1983. pap. 14.95 (*0-918812-28-3*) MMB Music.

— 100 Ways to Improve Teaching Using Your Voice & Music: Pathways to Accelerate Learning. 112p. 1992. pap. 27.00 incl. audio (*0-913705-74-8*) Zephyr Pr AZ.

Campbell, Don G., jt. auth. see Brewer, Chris B.

Campbell, Donal, jt. auth. see McArt, Pat.

Campbell, Donald. Playing for Scotland: A History of the Scottish Stage, 1715-1965. LC 96-172387. 168p. 1996. pap. 40.00 (*1-873644-57-4*, Pub. by Mercat Pr Bks) St Mut.

***Campbell, Donald.** Theological Wordbook: While the Bible Teaches on Two Hundred Theological Terms & Their Relevance for Today. (Swindoll Leadership Library). 2000. 29.99 (*0-8499-1381-0*) Word Pub.

Campbell, Donald & Spence, Alistair A. Norris & Campbell's Anaesthetics, Resuscitation & Intensive Care. 7th ed. (Illus.). 254p. 1990. pap. text 29.95 (*0-443-04067-2*) Church.

Campbell, Donald, et al. Polymer Characterization. 2nd rev. ed. (Illus.). 400p. 2000. pap. 67.50 (*0-7487-4005-8*, Pub. by S Thornes Pubs) Trans-Atl Phila.

Campbell, Donald E. Arabian Medicine & Its Influence on the Middle Ages, 2 vols., Set. LC 74-180330. reprint ed. 84.50 (*0-404-56235-3*) AMS Pr.

— Design & Operation of Smallholder Irrigation in South Asia. LC 94-29953. (Technical Paper, 256, Irrigation & Drainage Ser.: Vol. 256). 134p. 1995. pap. 22.00 (*0-8213-2995-2*, 12995) World Bank.

— Equity, Efficiency, & Social Choice. 200p. 1992. 55.00 (*0-19-828708-9*) OUP.

— Incentives: Motivation & the Economics of Information. (Illus.). 367p. (C). 1995. text 69.95 (*0-521-47264-4*); pap. text 25.95 (*0-521-47857-X*) Cambridge U Pr.

***Campbell, Donald G.** Steam Locomotives of the Kansas City Southern. (Illus.). 48p. 2000. pap. 14.95 (*0-942035-54-2*) South Platte.

Campbell, Donald H. Microscopical Examination & Interpretation of Portland Cement & Clinker. LC 85-63563. (Illus.). 48p. 1985. 55.00 (*0-89312-084-7*, SP030T) Portland Cement.

— Microscopical Examination & Interpretation of Portland Cement & Clinker. rev. ed. LC 85-63563. (Illus.). 48p. 1999. pap. 55.00 (*0-89312-179-7*, SPO30.T) Portland Cement.

Campbell, Donald K. Daniel, God's Man in a Secular Society. LC 96-29450. 192p. 1988. pap. 10.99 (*0-929239-05-9*) Discovery Hse Pubs.

— No Time for Neutrality: A Bible Study on Joshua. LC 94-2716. 264p. 1994. pap. 12.99 (*0-929239-84-9*) Discovery Hse Pubs.

Campbell, Donald K. & Townsend, Jeffrey L. The Coming Millennial Kingdom: A Case for Premilennial Interpretation. LC 97-30808. 288p. 1997. 12.99 (*0-8254-2352-X*) Kregel.

Campbell, Donald P. Sunday's Warriors: The Philadelphia Eagles' Games. Hope, Barbara, ed. LC 92-29011. (Illus.). 672p. 1994. pap. 24.95 (*0-9627161-5-4*) QLP CA.

— Sunday's Warriors: The Philadelphia Eagles' History. 2nd rev. ed. Hope, Barbara, ed. LC 95-70751. (Illus.). 669p. 1995. pap. 24.95 (*0-9627161-6-2*) QLP CA.

Campbell, Donald T. Methodology & Epistemology for Social Sciences: Selected Papers. Overman, E. Samuel, ed. 630p. 1988. 75.00 (*0-226-09248-8*) U Ch Pr.

***Campbell, Donald T.** Variations in Organization Science In Honor of Donald T. Campbell. 5p. 1999. write for info. (*0-7619-1125-1*); write for info. (*0-7619-1126-X*) Sage.

***Campbell, Donald T. & Kenny, David A.** A Primer on Regression Artifacts. LC 99-23003. (Methodology in the Social Sciences Ser.). 202p. 1999. lib. bdg. 32.00 (*1-57230-482-0*, CO482) Guilford Pubns.

Campbell, Donald T. & Russo, Jean M. Social Experimentation. LC 98-25447. 407p. 1998. 58.00 (*0-7619-0404-2*); pap. 26.95 (*0-7619-0405-0*) Sage.

Campbell, Donald T. & Stanley, Julian C. Experimental & Quasi-Experimental Designs for Research, 001. LC 81-80806. (C). 1966. pap. 29.56 (*0-395-30787-2*) HM.

Campbell, Donald T., jt. auth. see Cook, Thomas H.

***Campbell, Donna.** Pale as the Moon. LC 99-32229. (Carolina Young People Ser.). (Illus.). 104p. (J). (gr. 4-8). 1999. pap. 10.95 (*1-928556-02-7*) Coastal NC.

Campbell, Donna. Resisting Regionalism: Gender & Naturalism in American Fiction, 1885-1915. LC 96-45666. 200p. 1997. text 36.95 (*0-8214-1177-2*) Ohio U Pr.

Campbell, Donna, jt. auth. see Campbell, John.

Campbell, Donna, jt. auth. see Campbell, John M.

Campbell, Doris. Sanddollars: A Story of California's Pacific Valley. LC 97-68999. 301p. 1998. pap. 14.50 (*0-88739-166-4*) Creat Arts Bk.

***Campbell, Dorothy.** Tuning into Your Intuition: Introduction to Dowsing. (Illus.). 16p. 1998. pap. write for info. (*0-9658996-6-7*) Positive Pr MA.

***Campbell, Dorothy M.** Portfolio & Performance Assessment in Teacher Education. LC 99-23805. 154p. 1999. pap. text 27.95 (*0-205-30850-3*) Allyn.

***Campbell, Dorothy M. & Cignetti, Pamela B.** How to Develop a Professional Portfolio. 2nd ed. 116p. 2000. pap. text 21.33 (*0-205-31979-3*) Allyn.

Campbell, Dorothy M., et al. How to Develop Professional Teaching Portfolio. 96p. 1996. pap. text 22.00 (*0-205-26153-1*) Allyn.

Campbell, Douglas, ed. Carolina Indians. LC 98-92904. (Illus.). 230p. 1998. pap. 10.95 (*1-890238-49-X*) Golden Age Pr.

Campbell, Douglas, ed. see Day, Jean.

Campbell, Douglas A. Rhetoric of Righteousness in Romans 3:21-26. (Journal for the Study of the New Testament, Supplement Ser.: No. 66). 272p. (C). 1992. 60.00 (*1-85075-350-4*, Pub. by Sheffield Acad) CUP Services.

— The Rhetoric of Righteousness in Romans 3.21-26. (JSNT Supplement Ser.: No. 65). 272p. (C). 1992. 75.00 (*1-85075-294-X*, Pub. by Sheffield Acad) CUP Services.

Campbell, Douglas A., ed. The Call to Serve: Biblical & Theological Perspectives on Ministry in Honour of Bishop Penny Jamieson. (Sheffield Academic Press Ser.). 299p. 1996. 85.00 (*1-85075-625-2*, Pub. by Sheffield Acad) CUP Services.

Campbell, Douglas G. Free Press vs. Fair Trial: Supreme Court Decisions since 1807. LC 93-18241. 264p. 1993. 65.00 (*0-275-94277-5*, C4277, Praeger Pubs) Greenwood.

Campbell, Douglas S. The Supreme Court & the Mass Media: Selected Cases, Summaries, & Analyses. LC 89-26567. 248p. 1990. 55.00 (*0-275-93421-7*, C3421); pap. 18.95 (*0-275-93549-3*, B3549) Greenwood.

Campbell, Douglas S., et al. Mass Communication Law in Pennsylvania. 104p. 1996. pap. 12.95 (*0-913507-68-7*) New Forums.

***Campbell, Drew.** The Bride Wore Black Leather... And He Looked Fabulous! An Etiquette Guide for the Rest of Us. (Illus.). 176p. 2000. pap. 11.95 (*1-890159-17-4*) Greenery Pr.

Campbell, Drew. Technical Theater for Nontechnical People. LC 98-74538. (Illus.). 256p. 1999. pap. 18.95 (*1-58115-020-2*) Allworth Pr.

Campbell, Drew, jt. ed. see Califia, Pat.

Campbell, Dudley M. History of Oneonta, from Its Earliest Settlement to the Present Time. (Illus.). 190p. 1997. reprint ed. lib. bdg. 28.50 (*0-8328-6188-X*) Higginson Bk Co.

Campbell, Dugald. In the Heart of Bantuland. LC 70-79271. 313p. 1969. reprint ed. lib. bdg. 59.50 (*0-8371-4835-9*, CAB&) Greenwood.

Campbell, Duncan. Nature of a God-Sent Revival. 28p. 1993. pap. 2.50 (*0-942889-05-3*) Christ Life Pubns.

— Sinners in the Hands of an Angry God. rev. ed. 19p. (C). 1992. pap. text 0.95 (*0-942889-06-1*) Christ Life Pubns.

Campbell, Duncan C. & Rowan, Richard L. Multinational Enterprises & the OECD Industrial Relations Guidelines. LC 83-81083. (Multinational Industrial Relations Ser.: No. 11). (Illus.). 308p. 1983. reprint ed. pap. 95.50 (*0-608-04371-0*, 206515200001) Bks Demand.

Campbell, Dwight P. A Primer on Divine Revelation: Scripture & Tradition. 78p. 1998. pap. 4.95 (*1-890177-06-7*) Midwest Theol.

Campbell, E. The Place of Lions. LC 91-8037. 160p. (J). (gr. 3-7). 1995. pap. 6.00 (*0-15-200371-1*) Harcourt.

Campbell, E. F., jt. ed. see Freedman, D. N.

Campbell, E. Michael, jt. ed. see Miley, George H.

***Campbell, Earl & Ruane, John.** The Earl Campbell Story: A Football Great's Battle with Panic Disorder. (Illus.). 220p. 1999. pap. 17.95 (*1-55022-391-7*, ECWR & EC) Evangel Concern Wstrn.

Campbell, Earl V. Confessions of Some Lonely Housewives: A Book on Marriage Problems. 106p. 1973. 4.95 (*0-686-02488-5*) Dade Variety Pr.

Campbell, Earline. Giving Cookies & Love. 46p. 1998. pap. text 6.95 (*1-56309-249-2*, N983118, New Hope) Womans Mission Union.

Campbell, Edmund D., Jr. Letting Go: From the Writings of the Rev. Dr. Edmund D. Campbell, Jr. 1998. pap. 1.95 (*0-88028-201-0*, 1488) Forward Movement.

Campbell, Edward. Some Unusual Aspects of Communication. 12p. 1971. pap. 4.00 (*0-9500029-3-3*, Pub. by Octagon Pr) ISHK.

Campbell, Edward D., Jr. & Rice, Kym S., eds. Before Freedom Came: African-American Life in the Antebellum South. (Illus.). 300p. 1991. pap. 25.00 (*0-8139-1332-2*) U Pr of Va.

— A Woman's War: Southern Women, Civil War & the Confederate Legacy. LC 96-29648. (Illus.). 236p. 1997. pap. 25.00 (*0-8139-1739-5*) U Pr of Va.

Campbell, Edward D., Jr., jt. ed. see Salmon, Emily J.

Campbell, Edward F. Ruth. LC 74-18785. (Anchor Bible Ser.: Vol. 7). (Illus.). 208p. 1975. 32.50 (*0-385-05316-9*, Anchor NY) Doubleday.

Campbell, Edward F., Jr. Schechem II: Portrait of a Hill Country Vale, the Shechem Regional Survey. (Archaeological Reports: No. 2). (Illus.). 123p. (C). 1992. reprint ed. 45.00 (*1-55540-639-4*, 85 00 02, Pub. by Am Sch Orient Res) David Brown.

Campbell, Edward O. The Encyclopedia of Palmistry. LC 95-21732. 320p. (Orig.). 1996. pap. 15.00 (*0-399-51977-7*, Perigee Bks) Berkley Pub.

Campbell, Eileen. Body, Mind, & Spirit: A Dictionary of New Age Ideas, People, Places, & Terms. (Alternative Health Ser.). 256p. 1994. pap. 14.95 (*0-8048-3010-X*) Tuttle Pubng.

***Campbell, Eileen.** The Company of Strangers. large type ed. 408p. 1999. 31.99 (*0-7089-4142-7*) Ulverscroft.

Campbell, Eileen. A Dancing Star: Inspirations to Guide & Heal. LC 95-2459. 256p. 1995. pap. 10.00 (*0-06-251272-2*, Pub. by Harper SF) HarpC.

— A Guide to the World of Jellyfish. (Illus.). 16p. 1992. pap. 5.95 (*1-878244-08-6*) Monterey Bay Aquarium.

***Campbell, Eileen.** Time to Be: Reflections on Facing the Future. 2000. 19.95 (*0-00-710309-3*) Thorsons.

Campbell, Eileen. The Unknown Region: Inspirations on Living & Dying. 1993. 14.00 (*1-85538-304-7*, Pub. by Aqrn Pr) Harper SF.

Campbell, Eileen, jt. auth. see Silberstein, Mark.

Campbell, Elaine. The Childless Marriage: An Exploratory Study of Couples Who Do Not Want Children. 200p. 1986. text 33.00 (*0-422-60060-1*, 9777, Pub. by Tavistock); pap. text 14.95 (*0-422-60070-9*, 9780, Pub. by Tavistock) Routldge.

— ESL Resource Book for Engineers & Scientists. LC 96-12349. 336p. 1995. 59.99 (*0-471-12171-1*) Wiley.

Campbell, Elaine. ESL Resource Book for Engineers & Scientists. LC 96-12349. 336p. 1995. pap. 24.95 (*0-471-12172-X*) Wiley.

Campbell, Elaine & Frickey, Pierrette, eds. The Whistling Bird: Women Writers of the Caribbean. LC 97-46089. 280p. 1998. pap. 19.95 (*0-89410-410-1*, Three Contnts) L Rienner.

Campbell, Elisabeth, ed. see McKinzie, Harry & Tindimwebwa, Issy K.

Campbell, Elizabeth. Castle Hopping in the U. K. with Elizabeth. (Illus.). 60p. (Orig.). (YA). (gr. 9-12). 1988. pap. 12.95 (*0-9618324-0-1*) EFC Pub.

Campbell, Elizabeth A., jt. auth. see Brown, Jennifer M.

Campbell, Elizabeth W. & Campbell, William H. The Archeology of Pleistocene Lake Mohave. 118p. 1963. reprint ed. pap. 5.00 (*0-916561-09-7*) Southwest Mus.

— The Pinto Basin Site. 51p. 1963. reprint ed. pap. 5.00 (*0-916561-55-0*) Southwest Mus.

Campbell, Ellen, ed. see Derricott, Betty A.

Campbell, Elsie, ed. see Meunier, Christiane.

Campbell, Emily A. Publications Based on Project TALENT: An Annotated Bibliography. 1979. pap. 10.00 (*0-89785-628-7*) Am Inst Res.

Campbell, Enid, et al. Legal Research: Materials & Methods. 3rd ed. xii, 326p. 1988. pap. 38.50 (*0-455-20803-4*, Pub. by LawBk Co) Gaunt.

— Legal Research: Materials & Methods. 4th ed. LC 97-136079. 400p. 1996. pap. 60.00 (*0-455-21411-5*, Pub. by Cavendish Pubng) Gaunt.

— Student's Guide to Legal Writing. 57p. 1998. pap. 15.00 (*1-86287-277-5*, Pub. by Federation Pr) Gaunt.

Campbell, Eric. Papa Tembo. LC 97-45808. 288p. (J). (gr. 8 up). 1998. 16.00 (*0-15-201727-5*, Harcourt Child Bks) Harcourt.

— The Place of Lions. LC 91-8037. 160p. (J). (gr. 3 up). 1991. 17.00 (*0-15-262408-2*, Harcourt Child Bks) Harcourt.

— Place of Lions. (J). 1991. 11.35 (*0-606-08019-8*) Turtleback.

— The Shark Callers. LC 93-44881. 224p. (YA). (gr. 5 up). 1994. 10.95 (*0-15-200007-0*); pap. 4.95 (*0-15-200010-0*) Harcourt.

— The Year of the Leopard Song. (J). 1995. 10.10 (*0-606-08406-1*, Pub. by Turtleback) Demco.

*__Campbell, Eric, ed.__ A Grand Terrible Dramma: From Gettysburg to Petersburg the Civil War Letters of Charles Wellington Reed. (North's Civil War Ser.: No. 14). (Illus.). 384p. 2000. 49.95 (*0-8232-1971-2*) Fordham.

Campbell, Eric A., jt. auth. see Reed, Charles Wellington.

Campbell, Ewing. Raymond Carver: A Study of the Short Fiction. (Twayne's Studies in Short Fiction: No. 31). 200p. (C). 1992. 23.95 (*0-8057-8300-8*, Twyne) Mac Lib Ref.

Campbell, F., et al. Extinction in Paradise: Protecting Our Hawaiian Species. 1989. pap. 5.00 (*0-317-01841-8*) Natl Resources Defense Coun.

Campbell, F. C. Small Bowel Enterocyte Culture & Transplantation. (Medical Intelligence Unit Ser.). 116p. 1994. 99.00 (*1-57059-004-4*, LN9004) Landes Bioscience.

Campbell, Farragher J., jt. auth. see Bender's Editors.

Campbell, Federico. Pretexta. (SPA.). pap. 10.99 (*968-16-4855-2*, Pub. by Fondo) Continental Bk.

— Tijuana: Stories on the Border. Castillo, Debra A., tr. LC 94-9498. (ENG & SPA.). 1995. 45.00 (*0-520-08946-4*, Pub. by U CA Pr); pap. 14.95 (*0-520-08603-1*, Pub. by U CA Pr) Cal Prin Full Svc.

— Tijuanenses (Tijuana) (SPA.). 1996. pap. 12.50 (*0-679-76846-7*) Vin Bks.

Campbell, Ferdinand. Jamaica, the Land We Love. 32p. 1983. pap. 5.00 (*0-912444-26-6*) DARE Bks.

— A Profile of Love. LC 78-62758. 96p. reprint ed. 10.95 (*0-912444-16-9*) DARE Bks.

Campbell, Ffyona. The Whole Story: A Walk Around the World. (Illus.). 280p. 1998. 35.00 (*0-7528-0109-0*, Pub. by Orion Pubng Grp) Trafalgar.

Campbell, Fiona. Calligraphy. (Arts & Crafts Skills Ser.). (Orig.). 1999. lib. bdg. 6.95 (*0-516-26450-8*) Childrens.

— The Construction of Environmental News: A Study of Scottish Journalism. LC 98-74204. (Illus.). 11p. (C). 1999. text 61.95 (*1-84014-348-7*, Pub. by Ashgate Pub) Ashgate Pub Co.

— Flight. (Information Ser.). (Illus.). 32p. (J). 3.50 (*0-7214-1748-5*, Ladybrd) Penguin Putnam.

Campbell, Flann. The Dissenting Voice: Protestant Democracy in Ulster from Plantation to Partition. 513p. (Orig.). 1991. pap. 29.00 (*0-85640-457-8*, Pub. by Blackstaff Pr) Dufour.

Campbell, Florence. Your Days Are Numbered. 21st ed. 255p. 1980. reprint ed. pap. 10.95 (*0-87516-422-6*) DeVorss.

Campbell, Florence & Randall, Edith L. Sacred Symbols of the Ancients. (Illus.). 200p. 1982. reprint ed. pap. 24.95 (*0-87516-487-0*) DeVorss.

Campbell, Frances, jt. auth. see Daley, Dennis C.

Campbell, Francis D. Numismatic Bibliography & Libraries. 39p. 1994. pap. 4.00 (*1-889172-19-7*) Numismatic Intl.

Campbell, Francis S. The Menace of the Herd. Von Kuehnelt-Leddihn, Erik, ed. 1976. lib. bdg. 300.00 (*0-87968-372-4*) Gordon Pr.

Campbell, Francis W. & Cohen, Jerry. Trademarks & Related Unfair Competition: Selection & Protection. 2nd ed. (Corporate Practice Ser.: No. 18). 1991. ring bd. 95.00 (*1-55871-106-6*) BNA.

Campbell, Frank. Canada Post Offices, 1755-1895. LC 72-77023. (Illus.). 191p. 1972. 35.00 (*0-88000-008-2*) Quarterman.

Campbell, Frank D., Jr. John D. MacDonald & the Colorful World of Travis McGee. LC 77-773. (Milford Series: Popular Writers of Today: Vol. 5). 63p. 1977. pap. 13.00 (*0-89370-208-0*) Millefleurs.

Campbell, Frederick C. & Dube, Richard L. Landscaping Makes Cents: A Homeowner's Guide to Adding Value & Beauty to Your Property. LC 96-30159. 176p. (Orig.). 1997. pap. 16.95 (*0-88266-948-6*) Storey Bks.

Campbell, Frederick C., jt. auth. see Dube, Richard L.

Campbell, G., jt. auth. see Eckbreth, Alan C.

Campbell, G. A., et al. The Management of Common Metabolic Bone Disorders. (Illus.). 180p. (C). 1994. text 80.00 (*0-521-43037-2*); pap. text 29.95 (*0-521-43623-0*) Cambridge U Pr.

*__Campbell, G. Douglas.__ Contemporary Diagnosis & Management of Community-Acquired Pneumonia. LC 99-67668. (Illus.). 155p. 2000. pap. 29.95 (*1-884065-60-0*, Hndbks Hlth Care) Assocs in Med.

Campbell, G. S. An Introduction to Environmental Biophysics. LC 76-43346. (Heidelberg Science Library). 1989. pap. 32.00 (*0-387-90228-7*) Spr-Verlag.

— Soil Physics with Basic: Transport Models for Soil-Plant Systems. (Developments in Soil Science Ser.: No. 14). xvi,150p. 1985. 145.50 (*0-444-42557-8*) Elsevier.

Campbell, Gabriel. Saints & Householders: A Study of Hindu Ritual & Myth among the Kangra Rajputs. 1976. 80.00 (*0-7855-0321-8*, Pub. by Ratna Pustak Bhandar) St Mut.

— Saints & Householdes: A Study of Hindu Ritual & Myth among the Kangra Rajputs. 1976. 80.00 (*0-7855-0235-1*, Pub. by Ratna Pustak Bhandar) St Mut.

Campbell, Gabriel, ed. Saints & Householdes: A Study of Hindu Ritual & Myth among the Kangra Rajputs. 175p. (C). 1976. 65.00 (*0-89771-121-1*, Pub. by Ratna Pustak Bhandar) St Mut.

Campbell, Gary. Expansions: A Method for Developing New Material for All Instruments. (Illus.). 80p. (Orig.). (C). 1988. pap. 12.00 (*1-56516-057-6*) H Leonard.

— Hank Mobley's Transcribed Solos for Tenor Sax. (Illus.). 38p. (Orig.). (C). 1989. pap. 7.95 (*1-56516-058-4*) H Leonard.

Campbell, Gavin, jt. auth. see Stewart, Dougals.

Campbell, Gaylon S. & Norman, John M. An Introduction to Environmental Biophysics. 2nd ed. LC 97-15706. 304p. (C). 1997. pap. write for info. (*0-387-94937-2*) Spr-Verlag.

*__Campbell, Genie & Martell, Chris.__ The Insiders' Guide to Madison. 3rd ed. (Insiders' Guide Travel Ser.). (Illus.). 456p. 1999. pap. 15.95 (*1-57380-136-4*, The Insiders Guide) Falcon Pub Inc.

*__Campbell, Geoffrey A.__ The Pentagon Papers: National Security versus the Public's Right to Know. LC 00-8083. (Famous Trials Ser.). 128p. (YA). (gr. 4-12). 2000. 18.96 (*1-56006-692-X*) Lucent Bks.

Campbell, George. Concise Compendium of the World's Languages. LC 94-31294. 640p. (C). (gr. 13). 1994. 110.00 (*0-415-11392-X*, B4069) Routledge.

— Concise Compendium of the World's Languages. 680p. (C). 1998. pap. 32.99 (*0-415-16049-9*) Routledge.

Campbell, George, Jr. Engineering & Affirmative Action: Crisis in the Making, Special Edition, 8 vols. (Research Letter Ser.). (Illus.). 22p. 1997. write for info. (*0-9662172-0-9*) NACME Inc.

Campbell, George. The Philosophy of Rhetoric. Bitzer, Lloyd F., ed. & intro. by. LC 87-13108. (Landmarks in Rhetoric & Public Address Ser.). 512p. (C). 1988. text 16.95 (*0-8093-1417-7*) S Ill U Pr.

— The Philosophy of Rhetoric. LC 91-46681. 424p. 1992. 50.00 (*0-8201-1460-X*) Schol Facsimiles.

Campbell, George, Jr., et al, eds. Access Denied: Race, Ethnicity, & the Scientific Enterprise. LC 99-10024. (Illus.). 352p. 2000. text 65.00 (*0-19-510774-8*) OUP.

Campbell, George A. The Knights Templars, Their Rise & Fall. LC 78-63330. (Crusades & Military Orders Ser.: Second Series). reprint ed. 47.50 (*0-404-17005-6*) AMS Pr.

— Strindberg. LC 71-163501. (Studies in Drama: No. 39). 1971. reprint ed. lib. bdg. 75.00 (*0-8383-1320-5*) M S G Haskell Hse.

Campbell, George F., ed. Health Education & Youth: A Review of Research & Developments. 460p. 1984. write for info. (*0-318-66778-9*) Taylor & Francis.

Campbell, George L. Compendium of the World's Languages LC 90-35827. xxiv, 1574 p. 1991. write for info. (*0-415-06979-3*) Routledge.

— Compendium of the World's Languages. 2nd ed. (Illus.). 1920p. 2000. 410.00 (*0-415-20298-1*) Routledge.

— Compendium of the World's Languages 2nd ed. LC 99-15194. 2000. write for info. (*0-415-20297-3*) Routledge.

— Handbook of Scripts & Alphabets. LC 96-5765. 144p. 1997. pap. 18.99 (*0-415-13715-2*) Routledge.

— Handbook of Scripts & Alphabets. 144p. (C). (gr. 13). 1997. 60.00 (*0-415-18344-8*) Routledge.

Campbell, George R. Nature of Things on Sanibel. 2nd rev. ed. LC 87-36112. (Illus.). 174p. 1988. reprint ed. pap. 16.95 (*0-910923-47-7*) Pineapple Pr.

Campbell, George R. & Winterbotham, Ann L. Jaws, Too! The Natural History of Crocodillians with Emphasis on Sanibel Island's Alligators. LC 85-50388. (Illus.). 267p. 1986. 41.95 (*0-930942-06-X*) Sutherland IA.

Campbell, George V. Days of the North Shore Line. (Illus.). 256p. 1986. 38.00 (*0-933449-01-1*) Transport Trails.

Campbell, Georgina. The Best of Irish Breads & Baking: Traditional, Contemporary & Festive. (Shamrock Ser.). (Illus.). 144p. 1997. pap. 15.95 (*0-86327-500-1*, Pub. by Wolfhound Press) Irish Amer Bk.

— Classic Irish Recipes. LC 91-43520. (Illus.). 128p. 1992. pap. 6.95 (*0-8069-8444-9*) Sterling.

Campbell, Georgina. Irish Country House Cooking. (Illus.). 110p. 1997. pap. 16.95 (*0-86327-519-2*, Pub. by Wolfhound Press) Irish Amer Bk.

Campbell, Georgina. Meals for All Seasons. LC 92-253154. (Illus.). 250p. 1997. 24.95 (*0-86327-322-X*, Pub. by Wolfhound Press) Irish Amer Bk.

Campbell, Gini M., ed. see Burke, Bob.

Campbell, Gini Mooie, ed. see Stewart, Roy P. & Shank, Judith Stewart.

Campbell, Gini Moore, ed. see Burke, Bob.

Campbell, Gini Moore, ed. see Burke, Bob & Franks, Kenny.

Campbell, Gini Moore, ed. see Burke, Bob & Miles-LaGrange, Vicki.

Campbell, Gini Moore, ed. see Burke, Bob & Monson, Angela.

Campbell, Gini Moore, ed. see Burke, Bob & Parr, Royse.

Campbell, Gini Moore, ed. see Burke, Bob, et al.

Campbell, Gini Moore, ed. see Franks, Kenny A. & Lambert, Paul F.

Campbell, Gini Moore, ed. see Lambert, Paul F., et al.

Campbell, Gini Moore, ed. see Lambert, Paul, et al.

Campbell, Gini Moore, ed. see Thompson, Ralph G. & Burke, Bob.

Campbell, Glen, ed. Kentucky Motor Vehicle Laws Annotated: 1992 Edition. Savoie, Paul, tr. 151p. 25.00 (*0-614-05873-2*, MICHIE) LEXIS Pub.

Campbell, Glenn. Rhinestone Cowboy: An Autobiography. 1995. mass mkt. 5.99 (*0-312-95679-7*) Tor Bks.

Campbell, Glester. Remember Me. 1989. write for info. (*0-318-65486-5*) Tri Cor.

Campbell, Gloria & Gerhard, Molly. The Accidental Editor. (Illus.). 82p. (Orig.). pap. text. write for info. (*0-9631679-1-X*) GR Comm Col Edu TC.

Campbell, Gloria, ed. see Braman, James D.

Campbell, Gordon. An Analysis of Austin's Lectures on Jurisprudence or the Philosophy of Positive Law. xiv, 198p. 1997. reprint ed. 64.50 (*1-56169-319-7*, 14649) Gaunt.

— Compendium of Roman Law: Founded on the Institutes of Justinian Together with Questions Set in the University & Bar Examiniations (with Solutions) & Definitions of Leading Terms in the Words of Principal Authorities. 2nd ed. LC 93-79710. 302p. 1994. reprint ed. 85.00 (*1-56169-068-6*) Gaunt.

— Environmental Liability. LC 96-143932. 106p. 1995. pap. 36.50 (*1-85811-033-5*, Pub. by CLT Prof) Gaunt.

— Environmental Liability Issues for Corporate & Property Professionals. 2nd ed. 148p. 1998. pap. 49.50 (*1-85811-137-4*, Pub. by CLT Prof) Gaunt.

— Famous American Athletes of Today. 9th ed. (Essay Index Reprint Ser.). 1977. reprint ed. 31.95 (*0-8369-7313-5*) Ayer.

*__Campbell, Gordon.__ Heritage Law: Listed Buildings & Conservation Areas. 230p. 2000. pap. 92.00 (*1-902558-27-8*, Pub. by Palladian Law) Gaunt.

Campbell, Gordon, ed. Andrew Marvell. (Everyman's Poetry Ser.). 1997. pap. 3.50 (*0-460-87812-3*, Everyman's Classic Lib) Tuttle Pubng.

— John Milton. (Everyman's Poetry Ser.). 116p. 1997. pap. 1.95 (*0-460-87813-1*, Everyman's Classic Lib) Tuttle Pubng.

— Oliver Goldsmith. (Everyman's Poetry Ser.). 1997. pap. 3.50 (*0-460-87827-1*, Everyman's Classic Lib) Tuttle Pubng.

— The Renaissance, 1550-1660, Vol. 2. LC 89-70174. (St. Martin's Anthologies of English Literature Ser.: Vol. No. 2). 443p. 1990. text 20.00 (*0-312-04478-X*) St Martin.

Campbell, Gordon, ed. see Milton, John.

Campbell, Gordon, ed. & intro. see Johnson, Ben.

Campbell, Gordon, ed. & intro. see Jonson, Ben.

Campbell, Gordon M., ed. Crime & Probation... And Other Things. (Illus.). 269p. (Orig.). (C). 1989. pap. text 10.00 (*0-9625340-0-5*) Campbell Enter.

Campbell, Gordon R., jt. ed. see Campbell, Julie H.

Campbell, Grace. La Synphore Dans "la Jeune Parque" De Paul Valery. LC 74-28038. (Romance Monographs: No. 12). 1975. 13.00 (*84-399-3510-2*) Romance.

Campbell, Graham, jt. auth. see Goolsby, Elaine.

*__Campbell, Grant M., et al, eds.__ Bubbles in Food. LC 99-61672. (Illus.). 348p. 1999. 119.00 (*1-891127-08-X*) Am Assn Cereal Chem.

Campbell, Grant M., et al, eds. Cereals: Novel Uses & Processes. LC 97-1547. (Illus.). 306p. (C). 1997. text 114.00 (*0-306-45583-8*, Kluwer Plenum) Kluwer Academic.

Campbell, Greg. The Road to Kosovo. LC DR2086.C36 1999. 256p. 1999. 25.00 (*0-8133-3589-2*, Pub. by Westview) HarpC.

*__Campbell, Greg.__ Road to Kosovo: A Balkan Diary. LC 99-88252. 2000. pap. 16.00 (*0-8133-3767-4*, Pub. by Westview) HarpC.

Campbell, Gregory, ed. see Nityanawda, Mahamandaleshwar Swami.

Campbell, Gregory A., jt. auth. see Kanai, Toshitaka.

Campbell, Gregory R. Many Americas: Critical Perspectives on Race, Racism, & Ethn. LC 98-73129. 432p. (C). 1998. per. 69.95 (*0-7872-4987-4*) Kendall-Hunt.

Campbell, Griffin O., jt. auth. see Campbell, Carol O.

Campbell, Gwyn, jt. ed. see Whitenack, Judith A.

Campbell, H. D. & Fried, Katrina. Fat Cats. Suares, J. C., ed. LC 97-60493. (Illus.). 80p. 1997. 15.95 (*1-55670-682-0*) Stewart Tabori & Chang.

Campbell, H D R. Good Dog Journal: A Record Keeper for Your Pet. (Illus.). 160p. 1999. 15.95 (*1-55670-950-1*) Stewart Tabori & Chang.

— Pretty Kitty Journal: A Record Keeper for Your Pet. (Illus.). 160p. 1999. text 15.95 (*1-55670-951-X*) Stewart Tabori & Chang.

— Restaurants: A Dining Journal. (Illus.). 160p. 1999. text 15.95 (*1-55670-910-2*) Stewart Tabori & Chang.

Campbell, H. F. & Owen, A. D. The Economics of Paua New Guinea Tuna Fisheries. 269p. 1994. pap. 180.00 (*1-86320-114-9*, Pub. by ACIAR) St Mut.

Campbell, H. S. Darkness & Daylight: Or, Lights & Shadows of New York Life. 1972. 59.95 (*0-87968-997-8*) Gordon Pr.

Campbell-Harding, Valerie. Beaded Tassels, Braids & Fringes. LC 98-46795. 1999. 27.95 (*0-8069-4891-4*) Sterling.

— Strip Patchwork. (Illus.). 144p. 1988. pap. 8.95 (*0-486-25729-0*) Dover.

Campbell-Harding, Valerie, ed. Textile Artistry. 128p. 1996. pap. 17.95 (*0-8019-8780-6*) Krause Pubns.

Campbell-Harding, Valerie & Watts, Pamela M. Bead Embroidery. (Illus.). 124p. 1993. 35.00 (*0-916896-50-1*) Lacis Pubns.

Campbell-Harding, Valerie, et al. Goldwork. (Illus.). 48p. 1994. pap. 25.00 (*0-85532-778-2*, Pub. by Srch Pr) St Mut.

Campbell, Harriet. Children's Literature. (Illus.). 64p. 1981. 24.00 (*0-88014-032-1*) Mosaic Pr OH.

*__Campbell, Harry.__ Supernatural Scotland. (Scottish Collection Ser.). (Illus.). 64p. 2000. 8.95 (*0-00-472325-2*, Pub. by HarpC) Trafalgar.

Campbell, Heather & Masser, Ian. GIS & Organizations: How Effective Are GIS in Practice? 208p. 1995. 76.00 (*0-7484-0204-7*, Pub. by Tay Francis Ltd); pap. 35.95 (*0-7484-0205-5*, Pub. by Tay Francis Ltd) Taylor & Francis.

Campbell, Helen. Turnip Blues. LC 98-5390. 256p. 1998. pap. 10.95 (*1-883523-23-0*) Spinsters Ink.

— Women Wage-Earners: Their Past, Their Present, & Their Future. LC 72-2594. (American Women Ser.: Images & Realities). 324p. 1978. reprint ed. 23.95 (*0-405-04451-8*) Ayer.

Campbell, Helene D., ed. Fat Cats. (Illus.). 80p. 1997. reprint ed. write for info. (*0-941807-04-5*) Welcome Enterprises.

*__Campbell, Henry & Black.__ Blacks Law Dictionary. 7th deluxe ed. 1999. 69.00 (*0-314-24130-2*) West Pub.

Campbell, Hilary. Designing Patterns: A Fresh Approach to Pattern Cutting. (Illus.). 128p. (Orig.). 1988. pap. 49.50 (*0-85950-404-2*, Pub. by S Thornes Pubs) Trans-Atl Phila.

Campbell, Hilbert H., ed. The Sherwood Anderson Diaries, 1936-1941. LC 86-19311. (Illus.). 1987. 24.95 (*0-8203-0908-7*) U of Ga Pr.

Campbell Hill, Bonnie, et al. Classroom Based Assessment. LC 98-71523. (Illus.). 328p. 1998. pap. text 48.95 (*0-926842-84-6*) CG Pubs Inc.

Campbell, Hollis A., et al. Seymour: Past & Present. (Illus.). 613p. 1995. reprint ed. lib. bdg. 64.00 (*0-8328-4990-1*) Higginson Bk Co.

Campbell, Honor J. The Foodwatch Alternative Cookbook. 2nd ed. (Illus.). 256p. (Orig.). 1997. pap. 12.50 (*1-85398-040-4*, Pub. by Ashgrove Pr) Words Distrib.

Campbell, Hope. Managing Technology in the Early Childhood Classroom. LC 99-180853. 256p. 1998. pap. 24.95 (*1-57690-434-2*) Tchr Create Mat.

Campbell, Horace. Rasta & Resistance: From Marcus Garvey to Walter Rodney. LC 85-73332. 240p. (Orig.). 1987. 32.95 (*0-86543-034-9*); pap. 14.95 (*0-86543-035-7*) Africa World.

Campbell, Howard. Zapotec Renaissance: Ethnic Politics & Cultural Revivalism in Southern Mexico. LC 93-46953. (Illus.). 327p. 1994. 27.00 (*0-8263-1537-2*) U of NM Pr.

*__Campbell-Howe, Rebecca & Wilkins-Crowder, B., eds.__ Proceedings of the Solar 99 Conference: Including Proceedings of ASES Annual Conference - Proceedings of the 24th National Passive Solar Conference. (Proceedings of the American Solar Energy Society Conference Ser.). (Illus.). 766p. 1999. pap. 150.00 (*0-89553-171-2*) Am Solar Energy.

Campbell-Howe, Rebecca, ed. 21st National Passive Solar Conference Proceedings. (Illus.). 400p. (Orig.). 1996. pap. 100.00 (*0-614-11336-9*) Am Solar Energy.

Campbell-Howe, Rebecca, et al, eds. Annual Conference Proceedings, 1998. (Illus.). 597p. 1998. pap. 100.00 (*0-89553-170-4*) Am Solar Energy.

Campbell-Howe, Rebecca & Wilkins-Crowder, Barbara, eds. Annual Conference Proceedings, 1997. (Illus.). 359p. 1997. pap. 100.00 (*0-89553-169-0*) Am Solar Energy.

— Annual Conference Proceedings, 1996: Asheville, NC. (Illus.). 432p. 1996. pap. 100.00 (*0-89553-168-2*) Am Solar Energy.

*__Campbell, Hugh.__ Lightning's Tale. (Illus.). 38p. (YA). (gr. 3 up). 2000. reprint ed. pap. 12.95 (*1-57188-199-9*) F Amato Pubns.

Campbell, Hugh, et al. Voice Speech & Gesture. LC 72-5589. (Granger Index Reprint Ser.). 1977. reprint ed. 57.95 (*0-8369-6381-4*) Ayer.

Campbell, Hugh D. & Bauer, Camille. Programmed French Readers, 4 bks. Incl. Bk. 1. Contes pour Debutants., 001 (C). 1972. pap. 25.56 (*0-395-04258-5*); (C). pap. write for info. (*0-318-53416-9*) HM.

Campbell, Huxman. The Rhetorical Act. 3rd ed. (Speech & Theater Ser.). 2000. 34.75 (*0-534-56097-0*) Wadsworth Pub.

Campbell, I. Heart of the Gospel. 14.99 (*1-85792-182-8*, Pub. by Christian Focus) Spring Arbor Dist.

Campbell, I. & Priest, F. G. Brewing Microbiology. 2nd ed. 306p. 1995. 130.00 (*0-8342-1353-2*) Aspen Pub.

Campbell, I. A. & Giovannella, C., eds. Relaxation in Complex Systems & Related Topics. (NATO ASI Ser.: Vol. 222). (Illus.). 348p. (C). 1990. text 132.00 (*0-306-43600-0*, Kluwer Plenum) Kluwer Academic.

Campbell, I. C. "Gone Native" in Polynesia: Captivity Narratives & Experiences from the South Pacific. 63. LC 98-13973. (Contributions to the Study of World History Ser.: Vol. 63). 208p. 1998. 55.00 (*0-313-30787-3*, Greenwood Pr) Greenwood.

— A History of the Pacific Islands. 1994. pap. 19.95 (*0-7022-2291-7*, Pub. by Univ Queensland Pr) Intl Spec Bk.

Campbell, I. D. Biological Spectroscopy. 1984. text 45.25 (*0-8053-1847-X*) Benjamin-Cummings.

Campbell, I. G. Mental Disorder & Criminal Law in Australia & New Zealand. 270p. 1989. 69.00 (*0-409-49482-8*, AT, MICHIE) LEXIS Pub.

Campbell, Iain D. The Doctrine of Sin: In Reformed & Neo-Orthodox Thought. 272p. 1999. pap. 17.99 (*1-85792-438-X*) Christian Focus.

Campbell, Ian. A History of the Pacific Islands. 1990. 50.00 (*0-520-06900-5*, Pub. by U CA Pr); pap. 16.95 (*0-520-06901-3*, Pub. by U CA Pr) Cal Prin Full Svc.

— Thomas Carlyle. (C). 1993. pap. 40.00 (*0-85411-052-6*, Pub. by Saltire Soc) St Mut.

— The U. S. A., 1917-1941. LC 98-150118. (History Program Ser.). (Illus.). 64p. (J). 1998. pap. 13.95 (*0-521-56864-1*) Cambridge U Pr.

Campbell, Ian, ed. see Carlyle, Thomas.

Campbell, Ian, ed. see Ryals, Clyde D., et al.

Campbell, Ian, tr. see Poupard, Paul, ed.

Campbell, Ian C., ed. Mayflies & Stoneflies: Proceedings of the 5th International Epheropters Conference & the 9th International Plecopters Conference. (C). 1990. text 320.50 (*0-7923-0289-3*) Kluwer Academic.

Campbell, Ian M. Catalysis at Surfaces. (Illus.). 200p. (C). 1988. text 65.00 (*0-412-31880-6*) Chapman & Hall.

An Asterisk (*) at the beginning of an entry indicates that the title is appearing for the first time.

— Introduction to Synthetic Polymers. (Oxford Chemistry Ser.). (Illus.). 222p. (C). 1994. pap. text 31.95 (*0-19-855398-6*) OUP.

*__Campbell, Ian M.__ Introduction to Synthetic Polymers. 2nd ed. (Illus.). 260p. 2000. pap. text 40.00 (*0-19-856470-8*) OUP.

Campbell, Ian R., jt. ed. see Dunne, Kerry.

Campbell, Ivor E. & Sherwood, Edwin M., eds. High Temperature Materials & Technology. LC 67-13541. (Electrochemical Society Proceedings Ser.). 1034p. reprint ed. pap. 200.00 (*0-608-11255-0*, 205163000004) Bks Demand.

Campbell, J. The Mythic Dimension: A Course on Mythology. LC 96-46156. 272p. 1997. pap. 15.00 (*0-06-096612-2*) HarpC.

— The Mythic Image. (Illus.). 552p. 1996. reprint ed. 10.98 (*1-56731-122-9*, MJF Bks) Fine Comms.

— Mythic Imagination. 2000. pap. 14.95 (*0-06-096610-6*) HarpC.

— Mythic Imagination. 2000. 30.00 (*0-06-055309-X*) HarperTrade.

— Psyche & Symbol. pap. 15.00 (*0-06-092478-0*) HarpC.

— Western Religions. 1997. pap. 12.00 (*0-06-092476-4*) HarpC.

Campbell, J. & McGuire. The Confessions of Saint Augustine. 1984. reprint ed. pap. 18.00 (*0-86516-058-9*) Bolchazy-Carducci.

Campbell, J., jt. auth. see Lansdown, A. V.

Campbell, J., jt. ed. see Cross, M.

Campbell, J., ed. see King, J. E. & Oakes, M.

Campbell, J. A. & Cuena, J., eds. Perspectives in Artificial Intelligence: Expert Systems, Applications & Technical Foundations, Vol. 1. 1989. text 64.95 (*0-470-21434-1*) P-H.

— Perspectives in Artificial Intelligence: Machine Translation, Nlp, Databases & Computer-Aided Instruction. 1989. text 74.95 (*0-470-21435-X*) P-H.

Campbell, J. B. Mapping the Land: Aerial Imagery for Land Use Information. (C). 1987. text 49.00 (*81-85046-51-4*, Pub. by Scientific Pubs) St Mut.

Campbell, J. B. & Charlton, K. M., eds. Rabies. (Developments in Veterinary Virology Ser.). (C). 1988. text 249.50 (*0-89838-390-0*) Kluwer Academic.

Campbell, J. Douglas, tr. see Pirandello, Luigi.

Campbell, J. Duncan, jt. auth. see O'Donnell, Michael J.

Campbell, J. F. More West Highland Tales, Vol. 1. 562p. pap. 25.95 (*1-874744-22-X*, Pub. by Birlinn Ltd) Dufour.

— More West Highland Tales, Vol. 2. 400p. pap. 25.95 (*1-874744-23-8*, Pub. by Birlinn Ltd) Dufour.

— Popular Tales of the West Highlands, Vol. 1. 572p. pap. 25.95 (*1-874744-15-7*, Pub. by Birlinn Ltd) Dufour.

— Popular Tales of the West Highlands, Vol. 2. 612p. pap. 25.95 (*1-874744-16-5*, Pub. by Birlinn Ltd) Dufour.

Campbell, J. Gary. Automatic Transaxles & Transmissions. 2nd ed. LC 94-36828. (C). 1995. pap. text 48.80 (*0-13-291147-7*) Prntice Hall Bks.

— Shop Manual. (C). 1990. 17.00 (*0-13-053257-6*, Macmillan Coll) P-H.

*__Campbell, J. J.__ Just Add Water. 24p. 2000. pap. 3.95 (*1-930935-04-8*, Pick Pocket Pr) Phony Lid Pubns.

Campbell, J. K. Honour, Family & Patronage: A Study of Institutions & Moral Values in a Greek Mountain Community. (Illus.). 406p. (C). 1973. reprint ed. pap. text 26.95 (*0-19-519756-9*) OUP.

Campbell, J. L. Canna: The Story of a Hebridean Island. (Illus.). 1985. 48.00 (*0-19-920137-4*) OUP.

Campbell, J. M., jt. auth. see Deferrari, Roy J.

*__Campbell, J. McLeod.__ The Nature of the Atonement. 304p. 1999. pap. 28.00 (*1-57910-320-0*) Wipf & Stock.

Campbell, J. R. The Sportplane Resource Guide. 2nd ed. (Illus.). 1100p. pap. (*1-886743-14-2*) Kindrd Sprt Pr.

Campbell, J. Scott & Hartnell, Andy. Danger Girl: The Dangerous Collection, No. 1. (Illus.). 56p. 1998. pap. 5.95 (*1-58240-023-7*) Image Comics.

— Danger Girl: The Dangerous Collection, No. 2. (Illus.). 56p. 1998. pap. 5.95 (*1-58240-042-3*) Image Comics.

Campbell, Jack. Individualizing Instruction for the Educationally Handicapped: Teaching Strategies in Remedial & Special Education. (Illus.). 186p. 1998. 41.95 (*0-398-06901-8*); pap. 28.95 (*0-398-06892-5*) C C Thomas.

— Over My Shoulder: A Collection of Warmth. 110p. 1991. pap. text 9.95 (*0-942761-10-3*) JONopher Pub.

— Silent Heroes. 276p. (Orig.). 1987. pap. text 9.95 (*0-942761-42-1*) JONopher Pub.

*__Campbell, Jack.__ Student Discipline & Classroom Management: Preventing & Managing Discipline Problems in the Classroom. LC 99-37869. (Illus.). 126p. 1999. 29.95 (*0-398-07003-2*); pap. 18.95 (*0-398-07004-0*) C C Thomas.

Campbell, Jack. Who Is a Campbell? More Than Most Campbells Ever Learn about Their Famous (and Infamous) Scottish Family. LC 88-42581. (Illus.). 144p. (Orig.). 1988. 17.00 (*0-945508-00-X*); pap. 12.00 (*0-945508-01-8*) Deertrail Bks.

*__Campbell, Jack.__ A Word for Scotland. (Illus.). 256p. 1999. pap. 14.95 (*0-946487-48-0*, Pub. by Luath Pr Ltd) Midpt Trade.

Campbell, Jacquelyn. Empowering Survivors of Abuse: Health Care, Battered Women & Their Children. LC 98-25308. (Series on Violence Against Women). 1998. 57.95 (*0-7619-1121-9*); pap. 25.95 (*0-7619-1122-7*) Sage.

— Nursing Care of Survivors of Family Violence. (Illus.). 416p. (C). (gr. 13). 1993. pap. text 35.00 (*0-8016-6378-4*, 06378) Mosby Inc.

Campbell, Jacquelyn, et al. To Have & to Hit: Cultural Perspectives on Wife Beating. 2nd ed. LC 98-58070. 344p. 1999. pap. 18.95 (*0-252-06797-5*) U of Ill Pr.

Campbell, Jacquelyn C., ed. Assessing Dangerousness: Violence by Sexual Offenders, Batterers & Child Abusers, Vol. IV. (Interpersonal Violence: the Practice Ser.: Vol. 8). 160p. 1994. 48.00 (*0-8039-3746-6*) Sage.

— Assessing the Risk of Dangerousness: Potential for Further Violence of Sexual Offenders, Batterers & Child Abusers, Vol. IV. (Interpersonal Violence: the Practice Ser.: Vol. 8). 160p. 1994. pap. 21.50 (*0-8039-3747-4*) Sage.

Campbell, James. The Bombing of Nuremberg. (World at War Ser.: No. 5). 1978. mass mkt. 2.25 (*0-89083-356-7*, Zebra Kensgtn) Kensgtn Pub Corp.

— The Community Reconstructs: The Meaning of Pragmatic Social Thought. 160p. 1992. text 27.50 (*0-252-01842-7*); pap. text 12.95 (*0-252-06207-8*) U of Ill Pr.

— Essays in Anglo-Saxon History, 400-1200. 220p. (C). 1986. 55.00 (*0-907628-32-X*) Hambledon Press.

— Exiled in Paris: Richard Wright, James Baldwin, Samuel Beckett & Others on the Left Bank. 288p. 1995. 24.50 (*0-689-12172-5*) Atheneum Yung Read.

— Greek Fathers. LC 63-10279. (Our Debt to Greece & Rome Ser.). 167p. 1963. reprint ed. 44.00 (*0-8154-0046-2*) Cooper Sq.

— Invisible Country. (Illus.). 163p. (Orig.). (C). 1990. pap. 11.95 (*0-941533-94-8*, NAB) I R Dee.

— Recovering Benjamin Franklin. LC 98-38063. 312p. 1998. 69.95 (*0-8126-9386-8*); pap. 26.95 (*0-8126-9387-6*) Open Court.

— Weapons of Mass Destruction & Terrorism. (Illus.). 600p. (Orig.). 1967. pap. text 29.95 (*0-9628700-3-X*) Inter Pact Pr.

Campbell, James, ed. The Anglo-Saxons. (Illus.). 272p. 1991. pap. 26.95 (*0-14-014395-5*, Penguin Bks) Viking Penguin.

Campbell, James, intro. Selected Writings of James Hayden Tufts. LC 91-3193. 496p. (C). 1992. 47.00 (*0-8093-1714-1*) S Ill U Pr.

Campbell, James, jt. auth. see Emery, Gary.

Campbell, James, ed. see Todd, Malcolm.

Campbell, James, ed. see Wilkes, John.

Campbell, James A. Christmas Stories & the Christmas Story. 48p. 1992. pap. 3.50 (*0-687-07820-2*) Abingdon.

— The Secret Places: The Story of a Child's Adventure with Grief. (Illus.). 45p. (Orig.). (J). (gr. 2 up). 1992. pap. 4.95 (*1-56123-051-0*, SEPC) Centering Corp.

Campbell, James B. Introduction to Remote Sensing. 2nd ed. LC 96-15196. 622p. 1996. lib. bdg. 70.00 (*1-57230-041-8*, 0041) Guilford Pubns.

Campbell, James B., jt. auth. see Hole, Francis D.

Campbell, James C. Achieving Company Goals: Strategy for Success. rev. ed. (Skill Centered Leadership Ser.). 15p. 1997. pap., wbk. ed. 12.95 incl. audio (*1-891161-54-7*) ClamShell Pub.

— Achieving Standards of Excellence: Measuring High Performance. rev. ed. (Skill Centered Leadership Ser.). 8p. 1997. pap., wbk. ed. 12.95 incl. audio (*1-891161-68-7*) ClamShell Pub.

— Data Analysis & Decision. rev. ed. (Skill Centered Leadership Ser.). 26p. 1997. pap., wbk. ed. 24.95 incl. audio (*1-891161-06-7*) ClamShell Pub.

— Data Collection. rev. ed. (Skill Centered Leadership Ser.). (Illus.). 28p. 1997. pap., wbk. ed. 24.95 incl. audio (*1-891161-73-3*) ClamShell Pub.

— Dealing with Problem People. (Illus.). 18p. 1997. pap., wbk. ed. 12.95 incl. audio (*1-891161-10-5*) ClamShell Pub.

*__Campbell, James C.__ Deciding What to Pay People: Motivating with Compensation. (Learning to Lead Ser.). (Illus.). 8p. 1999. reprint ed. pap., wbk. ed. 12.95 incl. audio (*1-891161-23-7*) ClamShell Pub.

Campbell, James C. Developing a Win/Win Team (for Managers) rev. ed. (Skill Centered Leadership Ser.). 8p. 1997. pap., wbk. ed. 12.95 incl. audio (*1-891161-67-9*) ClamShell Pub.

— Developing Leadership Style: Strengthening Your Team. rev. ed. (Skill Centered Leadership Ser.). 6p. 1997. pap., wbk. ed. 12.95 incl. audio (*1-891161-52-0*) ClamShell Pub.

— Effective Delegation: Strengthening Individual Initiative. rev. ed. (Skill Centered Leadership Ser.). 12p. 1997. pap., wbk. ed. 12.95 incl. audio (*1-891161-58-X*) ClamShell Pub.

— The Fine Art of Training. rev. ed. (Skill Centered Leadership Ser.). 8p. 1997. pap., wbk. ed. 12.95 incl. audio (*1-891161-64-4*) ClamShell Pub.

*__Campbell, James C.__ Getting the Best from Your People: Setting Expectation. (Learning to Lead Ser.). (Illus.). 8p. 1999. reprint ed. 12.95 incl. audio (*1-891161-24-5*) ClamShell Pub.

Campbell, James C. How Motivation Works to Increase Productivity Pt. 1: Eliminating Things That Demotivate People. rev. ed. (Skill Centered Leadership Ser.). 8p. 1997. pap., wbk. ed. 12.95 incl. audio (*1-891161-62-8*) ClamShell Pub.

— How Motivation Works to Increase Productivity Pt. 2: Boosting People to Higher Productivity. rev. ed. (Skill Centered Leadership Ser.). 8p. 1997. pap., wbk. ed. 12.95 incl. audio (*1-891161-63-6*) ClamShell Pub.

— Keeping Clients & Customers. (Illus.). 12p. 1997. pap., wbk. ed. 12.95 incl. audio (*1-891161-34-2*) ClamShell Pub.

— Keys to Productive Meetings: Team Building in Action. rev. ed. (Skill Centered Leadership Ser.). 6p. 1997. pap., wbk. ed. 12.95 incl. audio (*1-891161-65-2*) ClamShell Pub.

— Leading a Winning Team (for Supervisors) rev. ed. (Skill Centered Leadership Ser.). 31p. 1997. pap., wbk. ed. 12.95 incl. audio (*1-891161-66-0*) ClamShell Pub.

— Making Good Decisions. rev. ed. (Skill Centered Leadership Ser.). 12p. 1997. pap., wbk. ed. 12.95 incl. audio (*1-891161-60-1*) ClamShell Pub.

— Managing Problem Behavior: Creating Harmony in the Workplace. rev. ed. (Skill Centered Leadership Ser.). 10p. 1997. wbk. ed. 12.95 incl. audio (*1-891161-69-5*) ClamShell Pub.

— Managing Time for Sales. rev. ed. (Skill Centered Leadership Ser.). 4p. 1997. pap., wbk. ed. 12.95 incl. audio (*1-891161-72-5*) ClamShell Pub.

— The Pre Employment Interview: Hiring the Right People. rev. ed. (Skill Centered Leadership Ser.). 30p. 1997. pap., wbk. ed. 12.95 incl. audio (*1-891161-53-9*) ClamShell Pub.

— Problem Identification: Statistical Process Control. rev. ed. (Skill Centered Leadership Ser.). (Illus.). 32p. 1997. pap., wbk. ed. 24.95 incl. audio (*1-891161-74-1*) ClamShell Pub.

— Professional Communication Skills Pt. 1: Getting Your Ideas Across. rev. ed. (Skill Centered Leadership Ser.). 8p. 1997. pap., wbk. ed. 12.95 incl. audio (*1-891161-50-4*) ClamShell Pub.

— Professional Communication Skills Pt. 2: Leading by Listening. rev. ed. (Skill Centered Leadership Ser.). 8p. 1997. pap., wbk. ed. 12.95 incl. audio (*1-891151-51-2*) ClamShell Pub.

— Profitable Time Management. rev. ed. (Skill Centered Leadership Ser.). 5p. 1997. pap., wbk. ed. 12.95 incl. audio (*1-891161-71-7*) ClamShell Pub.

— The Role & Tasks of the Supervisor: Leading Others to Accept Responsibility. rev. ed. (Skill Centered Leadership Ser.). 12p. 1997. pap., wbk. ed. 12.95 incl. audio (*1-891161-59-8*) ClamShell Pub.

— Setting Company Objectives: Setting Expectations. rev. ed. (Skill Centered Leadership Ser.). 12p. 1997. pap., wbk. ed. 12.95 incl. audio (*1-891161-56-3*) ClamShell Pub.

Campbell, James C. The Successful Facilitator: Developing Leadership Through Training. (Learning to Lead Ser.). (Illus.). 48p. 1988. reprint ed. ring bd. 9.95 (*1-891161-01-6*) ClamShell Pub.

Campbell, James C. The Synergestic Leader in the New Millennium: Skill Centered Leadership in Action. rev. ed. 129p. 1998. mass mkt. 24.95 (*1-891161-00-8*) ClamShell Pub.

— Understanding Personalities. rev. ed. (Skill Centered Leadership Ser.). 8p. 1997. pap., wbk. ed. 12.95 incl. audio (*1-891161-70-9*) ClamShell Pub.

— Using Job Descriptions to Increase Performance. rev. ed. (Skill Centered Leadership Ser.). 8p. 1997. pap., wbk. ed. 12.95 incl. audio (*1-891161-57-1*) ClamShell Pub.

— Working with New People: Setting Expectation up Front. rev. ed. (Skill Centered Leadership Ser.). 8p. 1997. pap., wbk. ed. 12.95 incl. audio (*1-891161-55-5*) ClamShell Pub.

— Your Professional Image. rev. ed. (Skill Centered Leadership Ser.). (Illus.). 4p. 1997. pap., wbk. ed. 12.95 incl. audio (*1-891161-08-3*) ClamShell Pub.

Campbell, James D. After Geometry: The Abstract Art of Claude Tousignant. LC 95-193814. (Illus.). 178p. 1995. 65.00 (*1-55022-245-7*, Pub. by ECW) Genl Dist Srvs.

— Depth Markers: Selected Art Writings 1985-1994. LC 95-183715. 397p. 1995. pap. 25.00 (*1-55022-244-9*, Pub. by ECW) Genl Dist Srvs.

— The Thought from Outside: The Art & Artefacts of John Heward. LC 96-156207. (Illus.). 160p. 1996. pap. 20.00 (*1-55022-276-7*, Pub. by ECW) Genl Dist Srvs.

*__Campbell, James E.__ The American Campaign: U. S. Presidential Campaigns & the National Vote. LC 99-52762. 320p. 2000. 34.95 (*0-89096-939-6*); pap. 18.95 (*0-89096-940-X*) Tex A&M Univ Pr.

Campbell, James E. Cheap Seats: The Democratic Party's Advantage in U. S. House Elections. LC 96-36122. (Parliaments & Legislatures Ser.). 1996. pap. text 23.95 (*0-8142-0709-X*) Ohio St U Pr.

— The Presidential Pulse of Congressional Elections. 2nd ed. LC 97-18724. 312p. 1997. pap. 24.95 (*0-8131-0926-4*) U Pr of Ky.

Campbell, James E., et al, eds. Application of Fracture Mechanics for Selection of Metallic Structural Materials. LC 82-71791. (Illus.). 384p. reprint ed. pap. 119.10 (*0-7837-1859-4*, 204206000001) Bks Demand.

*__Campbell, James E. & Garand, James C., contrib. by.__ Before the Vote: Forecasting American National Elections. LC 99-6921. 224p. 2000. write for info. (*0-7619-1636-9*) Sage.

Campbell, James F. Hostage: Terror & Triumph, 19. LC 92-14354. (Contributions in Psychology Ser.: No. 19). 176p. 1992. 47.95 (*0-313-28486-5*, CTT, Greenwood Pr) Greenwood.

Campbell, James J. Abortion: Applying Objective Reason to the Debate. 83p. 1999. pap. 7.50 (*0-9669893-0-5*, 10199801) Eudaimonia Pubns.

Campbell, James K., et al, eds. Kaulana na Pua: A Hawaiian Album, 1890-1930. LC 77-156041. (Illus.). 1977. pap. 6.95 (*0-917850-01-7*) Pueo Pr.

Campbell, James K., ed. see Liliuokalani.

Campbell, James M. Muslim & Parsi Castes & Tribes of Gujarat. 1990. reprint ed. 41.00 (*81-85326-29-0*, Pub. by Vintage) S Asia.

Campbell, James M., jt. auth. see Deferrari, Roy J.

Campbell, James N., jt. ed. see Cohen, Mitchell J.

Campbell, James P. The Third Millennium: A Catholic Perspective. 76p. (Orig.). 1996. pap. 8.00 (*1-55833-173-5*) Natl Cath Educ.

— Understanding Scripture: The Genesis Creation Story. 1998. pap. 3.95 (*0-8294-0977-7*) Loyola Pr.

Campbell, James P., jt. auth. see Cowgill, Carol.

Campbell, James R. Air of Injustice: The True Story of the Injustice Done to R. A. "Bob" Hoover. (Illus.). 336p. 1999. 29.95 (*1-886743-15-0*) Kindrd Sprt Pr.

— Festival Fever: The Ultimate Guide to Musical Celebrations in the Northeast (TM) LC 95-90446 (Illus.). 854p. (Orig.). 1996. pap. 49.95 (*0-9647309-9-5*) FestPress.

— Raising Your Child to Be Gifted: Successful Parents Speak. 196p. 1995. pap. 15.95 (*1-57129-000-1*) Brookline Bks.

— SportPlane Resource Guide, 1995-1996. rev. ed. LC 94-74268. (Illus.). 736p. (Orig.). 1995. pap. 39.95 (*1-886743-13-4*) Kindrd Sprt Pr.

Campbell, James T. Songs of Zion: The African Methodist Episcopal Church in the United States & South Africa. (Illus.). 448p. 1995. text 65.00 (*0-19-507892-6*) OUP.

— Songs of Zion: The African Methodist Episcopal Church in the United States & South Africa. LC 97-35030. (Illus.). 448p. (C). 1998. pap. 19.95 (*0-8078-4711-9*) U of NC Pr.

Campbell, James W., ed. see Stryker, William S.

Campbell, Jamie I., ed. The Nature & Origins of Mathematical Skills. LC 92-18326. (Advances in Psychology Ser.: 91). x,570p. 1992. 185.00 (*0-444-89014-9*, North Holland) Elsevier.

Campbell, Jan. Arguing with the Phallus Feminist Queer & Postcolonial Theory: A Psychoanalytic Contribution. LC 99-86750. (C). 1998. pap. 22.50 (*1-85649-444-6*, Pub. by Zed Books); text 59.95 (*1-85649-443-8*, Pub. by Zed Books) St Martin.

— Psycho-Politics & Cultural Desires. 1998. pap. text 24.95 (*1-85728-807-6*) Taylor & Francis.

*__Campbell, Jan.__ Psycho-Politics & Cultural Desires. 240p. 1998. 75.00 (*1-85728-806-8*) Taylor & Francis.

Campbell, Jan. Sexual Interactions. 4th ed. (C). 1995. pap. text, student ed. 22.36 (*0-669-33338-7*) HM Trade Div.

*__Campbell, Jane.__ Becoming an Effective Supervisor: A Workbook for Counselors & Therapists. (Illus.). 2000. pap. 19.95 (*1-56032-847-9*) Taylor & Francis.

Campbell, Jane. Mythic Black Fiction: The Transformation of History. LC 86-6909. 200p. (C). 1986. text 28.00 (*0-87049-508-9*) U of Tenn Pr.

Campbell, Jane, jt. auth. see Middleton, John.

Campbell, Janet W., jt. ed. see Erickson, Cynthia B.

Campbell, Jay R. NAEP 1994 Trends in Academic Progress: Achievement of United States Students in Science, 1969 to 1994; Mathematics, 1973 to 1994; Reading, 1971 to 1994 & Writing, 1984 to 1994. 582p. 1996. pap. 46.00 (*0-16-048918-0*) USGPO.

— Report in Brief: NAEP 1996 Trends in Academic Progress. 29p. 1997. pap. 4.50 (*0-16-063640-X*) USGPO.

— Students Selecting Stories, the Effects of Choice in Reading Assessment: Results from the NAEP Reader Special Study of the 1994 National Assessment of Educational Progress. 104p. 1997. pap. 10.00 (*0-16-063636-1*) USGPO.

Campbell, Jay R., et al. Interviewing Children about Their Literacy Experiences. (Illus.). 92p. (C). 1998. pap. text 25.00 (*0-7881-7181-X*) DIANE Pub.

*__Campbell, Jean.__ Art Therapy: Race & Culture. 1998. pap. 24.95 (*1-85302-578-X*) Jessica Kingsley.

Campbell, Jean. Art Therapy, Race & Culture. LC 99-193490. 1998. 71.95 (*1-85302-579-8*) Taylor & Francis.

— Australian Watercolour Painters: 1780-Present Day. (Illus.). 384p. 1989. text 52.00 (*0-947131-28-0*) Gordon & Breach.

Campbell, Jean, jt. auth. see Durant, Judith.

Campbell, Jean, ed. see Ridley, Gustave.

Campbell, Jean M. The Adventures of Wally Walnut. unabridged ed. (Illus.). iii, 24p. (J). (gr. k-6). 1996. pap. write for info. (*0-9651833-0-0*) J Campbell.

Campbell, Jeanine & Bloom, Lora. Raping the Muse. (Illus.). 64p. 1998. pap. 10.00 (*1-892494-03-5*) Repossessed Head.

Campbell, Jeff. Good As New. LC 97-47285. 208p. 1998. pap. 9.95 (*0-440-50791-X*) Dell.

— Shivers II: Harvest of Souls: The Official Strategy Guide. LC 97-65551. 288p. 1997. per. 19.99 (*0-7615-1072-9*) Prima Pub.

Campbell, Jeff & Clean Team Staff, The. Clutter Control. 176p. 1992. pap. 9.99 (*0-440-50339-6*, Dell Trade Pbks) Dell.

— Speed Cleaning. 2nd rev. ed. 208p. (Orig.). 1991. pap. 9.95 (*0-440-50374-4*, Dell Trade Pbks) Dell.

Campbell, Jeff, et al. Raiders of the Lost Ark. LC 98-13786. (Mighty Chronicles Ser.). (Illus.). 320p. 1999. 9.95 (*0-8118-2209-5*) Chronicle Bks.

— Terminator 2: Judgment Day. LC 98-16834. (Mighty Chronicles Ser.). (Illus.). 320p. 1999. 9.95 (*0-8118-2208-7*) Chronicle Bks.

Campbell, Jeff, jt. auth. see Clean Team Staff, The.

Campbell, Jeff H. Updike's Novels: Thorns Spell a Word. 250p. 1987. 17.50 (*0-915323-02-8*) Midwestern St U Pr.

Campbell, Jesse H. Georgia Baptists: Historical & Biographical. Sperry, Phillip A., ed. 307p. 1993. reprint ed. 32.95 (*1-56869-043-6*); reprint ed. pap. 24.95 (*1-56869-044-4*) Oldbuck Pr.

Campbell, Jill. Natural Masques: Gender & Identity in Fielding's Plays & Novels. LC 94-33011. 378p. (C). 1994. pap. 16.95 (*0-8047-2520-9*) Stanford U Pr.

— Natural Masques: Gender & Identity in Fielding's Plays & Novels. LC 94-33011. i, 326p. 1995. 45.00 (*0-8047-2391-5*) Stanford U Pr.

Campbell, Jim. Joe Louis. Jones, Mary E., ed. LC 96-47849. (Importance of Ser.). (Illus.). (J). (gr. 4-12). 1997. lib. bdg. 22.45 (*1-56006-085-9*) Lucent Bks.

Campbell, Jim & Chelsea House Publishing Staff. Cal Ripken, Jr. LC 97-610. (Baseball Legends Ser.). (Illus.). 64p. (J). (gr. 3 up). 1997. 15.95 (*0-7910-4380-0*) Chelsea Hse.

Campbell, Jim & Little, eds. Humanities in the Primary School. (Contemporary Analysis in Education Ser.). 250p. 1989. 85.00 (*1-85000-544-3*, Falmer Pr); pap. 34.95 (*1-85000-545-1*, Falmer Pr) Taylor & Francis.

C

An Asterisk (*) at the beginning of an entry indicates that the title is appearing for the first time.

Campbell, Jim & Manktelow, Roger, eds. Mental Health Social Work in Ireland: Comparative Issues in Policy & Practice. LC 98-70982. 200p. 1998. text 59.95 (*1-85972-694-1*, Pub. by Ashgate Pub) Ashgate Pub Co.

***Campbell, Jo.** Ashleigh: A Dangerous Ride, No. 6. (Ashleighs Ser.: No. 6). 192p. (J). (gr. 3-7). 1999. mass mkt. 4.50 (*0-06-106559-5*) HarpC.

— Ashleigh: Derby Day, No. 7. 176p. 1999. mass mkt. 4.50 (*0-06-106606-0*) HarpC.

— Ashleigh: Goodbye, Midnight Wanderer, No. 4. (Ashleighs Ser.: No. 4). 176p. 1999. mass mkt. 4.50 (*0-06-106557-9*) HarpC.

— Ashleigh: Lightning's Last Hope, No. 1. (Ashleighs Ser.: No. 1). 176p. 1998. mass mkt. 4.50 (*0-06-106540-4*) HarpC.

— Ashleigh: Waiting for Stardust, No. 3. (Ashleighs Ser.: No. 3). 176p. 1999. mass mkt. 4.50 (*0-06-106544-7*) HarpC.

— Thoroughbred: Racing Parker, No. 33. (Thoroughbred Ser.: No. 33). 176p. 1999. mass mkt. 4.50 (*0-06-106562-5*) HarpC.

Campbell, Joan. The German Werkbund: The Politics of Reform in the Applied Arts. LC 77-71974. (Illus.). 373p. 1978. reprint ed. pap. 115.70 (*0-608-02522-4*, 206316600004) Bks Demand.

— Joy in Work, German Work: The National Debate, 1800-1945. LC 88-37120. 443p. reprint ed. pap. 137.40 (*0-608-06318-5*, 206668000008) Bks Demand.

— The Ministry to the Imprisoned. (Ministry Ser.). 48p. 1989. pap. 2.95 (*0-8146-1789-1*) Liturgical Pr.

— North American Wildlife. LC 87-63429. 1988. 8.95 (*0-916809-22-6*) Scott Pubns MI.

Campbell, Joan & Polk, David P., eds. Bread Afresh, Wine Anew: Sermons by Disciples Women. 168p. (Orig.). 1991. pap. 13.99 (*0-8272-0218-0*) Chalice Pr.

Campbell, Joanie, et al. Patterns for Manipulatives: Basic Skills - Grades K-3. Rogers, Kathy, ed. (Illus.). 192p. 1995. pap., wbk. ed. 15.95 (*1-56472-065-9*) Edupress Inc.

Campbell, Joann, ed. Toward a Feminist Rhetoric: The Writing of Gertrude Buck. (Series in Composition, Literacy, & Culture). (Illus.). 287p. (C). 1996. pap. 19.95 (*0-8229-5573-3*); text 49.95 (*0-8229-3900-2*) U of Pittsburgh Pr.

***Campbell, Joanna.** Ashleigh: A Horse for Christmas, No. 2. (Thoroughbred Ser.). 176p. 1998. mass mkt. 4.50 (*0-06-106542-0*) HarpC.

— Ashleigh: Holiday Homecoming, No. 9. 176p. 2000. 4.50 (*0-06-105876-9*) HarpC.

— Ashleigh: The Forbidden Stallion, No. 5. 176p. (J). (gr. 3-7). 1999. mass mkt. 4.50 (*0-06-106558-7*, Pub. by Harper SF) HarpC.

Campbell, Joanna. Ashleigh's Christmas Miracle. LC 94-242053. Vol. 1. 256p. (J). (gr. 3-7). 1994. mass mkt. 4.50 (*0-06-106249-9*) HarpC Child Bks.

— Ashleigh's Diary. (Thoroughbred Super Ser.: No. 2). 256p. (J). 1995. mass mkt. 4.50 (*0-06-106292-8*, Harp PBks) HarpC.

— Ashleigh's Diary. (Thoroughbred Super Edition Ser.). (J). 1995. 9.09 (*0-606-08297-2*, Pub. by Turtleback) Demco.

— Ashleigh's Dream. (Thoroughbred Ser.). (J). 1993. 9.09 (*0-606-08292-1*, Pub. by Turtleback) Demco.

Campbell, Joanna. Ashleigh's Dream Special Edition. 192p. (J). 1993. boxed set 2.50 (*0-06-106222-7*) HarpC.

Campbell, Joanna. Ashleigh's Hope. (Thoroughbred Ser.: 3). 192p. 1996. mass mkt. 4.50 (*0-06-106395-9*, Harp PBks) HarpC.

— Battlecry Forever. 192p. (YA). (gr. 7 up). 1992. mass mkt. 3.50 (*0-06-106771-7*, Harp PBks) HarpC.

— Battlecry Forever! 192p. (J). (gr. 4-7). 1998. mass mkt. 4.50 (*0-06-106482-3*, Harp PBks) HarpC.

— Cindy's Glory. (Thoroughbred Ser.). (J). 1995. 9.85 (*0-606-08642-0*) Turtleback.

— Cindy's Runaway Colt. (Thoroughbred Ser.). (J). 1995. 9.09 (*0-606-08291-3*, Pub. by Turtleback) Demco.

— A Horse Called Wonder. (Thoroughbred Ser.). (J). 1991. 9.60 (*0-606-01148-X*, Pub. by Turtleback) Demco.

Campbell, Joanna. A Horse Called Wonder Special Edition. 192p. 1993. boxed set 2.50 (*0-06-106217-0*) HarpC.

— The Lost Foal. (Ashleighs Ser.: No. 8). 176p. 2000. mass mkt. 4.50 (*0-06-106632-X*) HarpC.

Campbell, Joanna. Pride's Challenge. (Thoroughbred Ser.). (J). 1994. 8.60 (*0-606-08296-4*, Pub. by Turtleback) Demco.

— Pride's Last Race. (Thoroughbred Ser.). (J). 1994. 9.09 (*0-606-08288-3*, Pub. by Turtleback) Demco.

— Samantha's Journey, No. 24. (Thoroughbred Super Ser.: No. 4). 208p. (J). (gr. 3-7). 1997. mass mkt. 4.50 (*0-06-106494-7*) HarpC Child Bks.

— Samantha's Pride. (Thoroughbred Ser.). (J). 1993. 9.09 (*0-606-08294-8*, Pub. by Turtleback) Demco.

— Shining's Orphan. (Thoroughbred Ser.). (J). 1995. 8.60 (*0-606-08290-5*, Pub. by Turtleback) Demco.

— Sierra's Steeplechase. (Thoroughbred Ser.). (J). 1993. 8.60 (*0-606-08295-6*, Pub. by Turtleback) Demco.

— Star of Shadowbrook Farm. 192p. (J). (gr. 3-7). 1998. mass mkt. 4.50 (*0-06-106483-1*, Harp PBks) HarpC.

***Campbell, Joanna.** Thoroughbred: A Home for Melanie, No. 31. LC 98-226175. (Thoroughbred Ser.: Vol. 31). 176p. (J). (gr. 3-7). 1998. mass mkt. 4.50 (*0-06-106541-2*) HarpC.

— Thoroughbred: A Horse Called Wonder, No. 1. (Thoroughbred Ser.: No. 1). 192p. (J). (gr. 3-7). 1991. mass mkt. 4.50 (*0-06-106120-4*, Harp PBks) HarpC.

— Thoroughbred: Ashleigh's Dream, No. 5. (Thoroughbred Ser.: No. 05). 192p. (J). (gr. 4-7). 1993. mass mkt. 4.50 (*0-06-106737-7*, Harp PBks) HarpC.

— Thoroughbred: Ashleigh's Farewell, No. 17. LC 49-122630. (Thoroughbred Ser.: Vol. 17). 192p. (J). (gr. 4-7). 1996. mass mkt. 4.50 (*0-06-106397-5*) HarpC.

— Thoroughbred: Camp Saddlebrook, No. 28. (Thoroughbred Ser.: No. 28). 192p. (J). 1998. mass mkt. 4.50 (*0-06-106530-7*) HarpC.

— Thoroughbred: Cassidy's Secret, No. 32. (Thoroughbred Ser.: Vol. 32). 176p. 1999. mass mkt. 4.50 (*0-06-106543-9*) HarpC.

— Thoroughbred: Christina's Courage, No. 27. (Thoroughbred Ser.). 176p. (J). 1998. mass mkt. 4.50 (*0-06-106529-3*) HarpC.

— Thoroughbred: Cindy's Glory, No. 14. (Thoroughbred Ser.: No. 14). 192p. (J). 1995. mass mkt. 4.50 (*0-06-106325-8*, Harp PBks) HarpC.

— Thoroughbred: Cindy's Heartbreak, No. 19. (Thoroughbred Ser.: No. 19). 192p. (J). (gr. 3-7). 1997. mass mkt. 4.50 (*0-06-106489-0*, Harp PBks) HarpC.

— Thoroughbred: Cindy's Honor, No. 23. (Thoroughbred Ser.: No. 23). 176p. (J). 1997. mass mkt. 4.50 (*0-06-106493-9*) HarpC Child Bks.

— Thoroughbred: Cindy's Runaway Colt, No. 13. (Thoroughbred Ser.: No. 13). 192p. (J). 1995. mass mkt. 4.50 (*0-06-106303-7*, Harp PBks) HarpC.

— Thoroughbred: Close Call, No. 41. (Thoroughbred Ser.: No. 41). 192p. (J). (gr. 3-7). 2000. mass mkt. 4.50 (*0-06-106635-4*, HarpEntertain) Morrow Avon.

— Thoroughbred: Dead Heat, 35 vols., No. 35. (Thoroughbred Ser.). 176p. 1999. mass mkt. 4.50 (*0-06-106564-1*) HarpC.

— Thoroughbred: Down to the Wire, No. 38. (Thoroughbred Ser.: No. 38). 176p. 1999. mass mkt. 4.50 (*0-06-106609-5*, Pub. by Harper SF) HarpC.

— Thoroughbred: Dylan's Choice, No. 30. LC 99-188027. (Thoroughbred Ser.). 176p. 1998. mass mkt. 4.50 (*0-06-106539-0*) HarpC.

— Thoroughbred: Fallen Star, Vol. 43. Vol. 43. 176p. (gr. 3-7). 2000. 4.50 (*0-06-105874-2*, HarpEntertain) Morrow Avon.

— Thoroughbred: Glory in Danger, No. 16. (Thoroughbred Ser.: No. 16). 192p. (J). (gr. 4-7). 1996. mass mkt. 4.50 (*0-06-106396-7*, Harp PBks) HarpC.

— Thoroughbred: Glory's Rival, No. 18. (Thoroughbred Ser.: No. 18). 208p. (J). (gr. 5-7). 1997. mass mkt. 4.50 (*0-06-106398-3*, Harp PBks) HarpC.

— Thoroughbred: Glory's Triumph, No. 15. (Thoroughbred Ser.: No. 15). 208p. 1996. mass mkt. 4.50 (*0-06-106277-4*) HarpC.

— Thoroughbred: Living Legend, No. 39. (Thoroughbred Ser.: No. 39). 192p. (J). (gr. 4-7). 2000. mass mkt. 4.50 (*0-06-106633-8*, HarpEntertain) Morrow Avon.

— Thoroughbred: Melanie's Last Ride, No. 29. LC 99-199903. (Thoroughbred Ser.: No. 29). 192p. (J). 1998. mass mkt. 4.50 (*0-06-106531-5*) HarpC.

— Thoroughbred: Melanie's Treasure, No. 25. (Thoroughbred Ser.: Vol. 25). 160p. (J). 1998. mass mkt. 4.50 (*0-06-106798-9*) HarpC.

— Thoroughbred: On the Track, No. 34. (Thoroughbred Ser.: No. 34). 176p. (J). (gr. 3-7). 1999. mass mkt. 4.50 (*0-06-106563-3*) HarpC.

— Thoroughbred: Perfect Image, Vol. 44. (Thoroughbred Ser.: No. 44). 176p. 2000. 4.50 (*0-06-105854-8*) HarpC.

— Thoroughbred: Pride's Challenge, No. 9. (Thoroughbred Ser.: No. 9). 192p. (J). (gr. 4-7). 1994. mass mkt. 4.50 (*0-06-106207-3*, Harp PBks) HarpC.

— Thoroughbred: Pride's Last Race, No. 10. (Thoroughbred Ser.: No. 10). 192p. (YA). 1994. mass mkt. 4.50 (*0-06-106765-2*) HarpC.

— Thoroughbred: Samantha's Pride, No. 7. (Thoroughbred Ser.: No. 7). 192p. (J). (gr. 4-7). 1993. mass mkt. 4.50 (*0-06-106163-8*, Harp PBks) HarpC.

— Thoroughbred: Shining's Orphan, No. 12. (Thoroughbred Ser.: No. 12). 192p. (J). (gr. 4-7). 1995. mass mkt. 4.50 (*0-06-106281-2*) HarpC Child Bks.

— Thoroughbred: Sierra's Steeplechase, No. 8. (Thoroughbred Ser.: No. 8). 192p. (J). (gr. 4-7). 1993. mass mkt. 4.50 (*0-06-106164-6*, Harp PBks) HarpC.

— Thoroughbred: Sterling's Second Chance, No. 26. (Thoroughbred Ser.: Vol. 26). 176p. (J). (gr. 3-7). 1998. mass mkt. 4.50 (*0-06-106799-7*) HarpC.

— Thoroughbred: The Bad Luck Filly, Vol. 42. (Thoroughbred Ser.: No. 42). 176p. (J). (gr. 4-7). 2000. mass mkt. 4.50 (*0-06-105873-4*, HarpEntertain) Morrow Avon.

— Thoroughbred: The Horse of Her Dreams, No. 24. (Thoroughbred Ser.: Vol. 24). 176p. (J). 1998. mass mkt. 4.50 (*0-06-106797-0*) HarpC.

— Thoroughbred: Ultimate Risk, No. 40. (Thoroughbred Ser.: No. 40). 176p. (J). (gr. 3-7). 2000. mass mkt. 4.50 (*0-06-106634-6*) HarpC.

— Thoroughbred: Without Wonder, No. 36. (Thoroughbred Ser.: No. 36). 176p. (J). (gr. 4-7). 1999. mass mkt. 4.50 (*0-06-106607-9*, Pub. by Harper SF) HarpC.

— Thoroughbred: Wonder's First Race, No. 3. (Thoroughbred Ser.: No. 3). 192p. (J). (gr. 6-9). 1991. mass mkt. 4.50 (*0-06-106082-8*, Harp PBks) HarpC.

— Thoroughbred: Wonder's Promise, No. 2. (Thoroughbred Ser.: No. 2). 192p. (J). 1991. mass mkt. 4.50 (*0-06-106085-2*, Harp PBks) HarpC.

— Thoroughbred: Wonder's Sister, No. 11. (Thoroughbred Ser.: No. 11). 192p. (J). (gr. 4-7). 1994. mass mkt. 4.50 (*0-06-106250-2*) HarpC Child Bks.

— Thoroughbred: Wonder's Victory, No. 4. (Thoroughbred Ser.: No. 4). 192p. (J). (gr. 7-9). 1991. mass mkt. 4.50 (*0-06-106083-6*, Harp PBks) HarpC.

— Thoroughbred: Wonder's Yearling, No. 6. (Thoroughbred Ser.: No. 6). 192p. (J). (gr. 4-7). 1993. mass mkt. 4.50 (*0-06-106747-4*, Harp PBks) HarpC.

Campbell, Joanna. The Wild Mustang. 144p. (J). (gr. 3-5). 1989. pap. 3.50 (*0-553-15698-5*, Skylark BDD) BDD Bks Young Read.

— Wonder's First Race. (Thoroughbred Ser.). (J). 1991. 9.09 (*0-606-01153-6*, Pub. by Turtleback) Demco.

Campbell, Joanna. Wonder's First Race Special Edition. 192p. 1993. boxed set 2.50 (*0-06-106220-0*) HarpC.

Campbell, Joanna. Wonder's Promise. (Thoroughbred Ser.). (J). 1991. 9.09 (*0-606-01152-8*, Pub. by Turtleback) Demco.

Campbell, Joanna. Wonder's Promise Special Edition. 208p. 1993. boxed set 2.50 (*0-06-106218-9*) HarpC.

Campbell, Joanna. Wonder's Sister. (Thoroughbred Ser.). (J). 1994. 9.09 (*0-606-08289-1*, Pub. by Turtleback) Demco.

— Wonder's Victory. (Thoroughbred Ser.). (J). 1991. 8.60 (*0-606-01156-0*, Pub. by Turtleback) Demco.

Campbell, Joanna. Wonder's Victory Special Edition. 192p. 1993. boxed set 2.50 (*0-06-106219-7*) HarpC.

Campbell, Joanna. Wonder's Yearling. (Thoroughbred Ser.). (J). 1993. 8.60 (*0-606-08293-X*, Pub. by Turtleback) Demco.

Campbell, Joanna. Wonder's Yearling Special Edition. 192p. 1993. boxed set 2.50 (*0-06-106221-9*) HarpC.

Campbell, Joanna, creator. Thoroughbred: Arabian Challenge, No. 22. 208p. (J). (gr. 4-7). 1997. mass mkt. 4.50 (*0-06-106492-0*, Harp PBks) HarpC.

— Thoroughbred: Champion's Spirit, No. 20. 208p. (J). (gr. 4-7). 1997. mass mkt. 4.50 (*0-06-106490-4*, Harp PBks) HarpC.

— Thoroughbred: Wonder's Champion, No. 21. 208p. (J). (gr. 4-7). 1997. mass mkt. 4.50 (*0-06-106491-2*, Harp PBks) HarpC.

Campbell, Joanna, ed. European Labor Unions. LC 92-12281. 672p. 1992. lib. bdg. 139.50 (*0-313-26371-X*, CEL/, Greenwood Pr) Greenwood.

Campbell, Joe. C Programmer's Guide to Serial Communications. 2nd ed. 952p. (Orig.). 1993. 39.95 (*0-672-30286-1*) Sams.

— California Funicular Railway. 1994. pap. 5.50 (*0-87505-406-4*) Borden.

Campbell, Joe B. & Campbell, June M. Laboratory Mathematics: Medical & Biological Applications. 5th ed. (Illus.). 496p. (C). (gr. 13). 1996. pap. text 33.00 (*0-8151-1397-8*, 25633) Mosby Inc.

— Thank You, God, for Who I Am. (Illus.). viii, 36p. (J). Date not set. 8.95 (*0-9665389-1-9*) Sprng Hollow Bks.

— To Sarah, with Love, from Maw: Daily Living Guides from the Ages, for a Happier, Healthier Life. (Illus.). xii, 208p. 1998. pap. 16.95 (*0-9665389-0-0*) Sprng Hollow Bks.

Campbell, John. An Account of the Spanish Settlements in America. LC 73-2680. (Illus.). reprint ed. 55.00 (*0-404-00276-5*) AMS Pr.

***Campbell, John.** Asiatic Tribes in North America. (LC History-America-E). 38p. 1999. reprint ed. lib. bdg. 69.00 (*0-7812-4316-5*) Rprt Serv.

Campbell, John. Campbell's on U. S. History 1866 to 1960 Quiz Book. 233p. (YA). (gr. 9-12). 2000. pap. 13.95 (*0-944322-28-X*) Patricks Pr.

— Castings. 2nd ed. 288p. 1993. pap. text 52.95 (*0-7506-1696-2*) Buttrwrth-Heinemann.

***Campbell, John.** Castings Problems & Solutions. (Illus.). 220p. 2002. pap. 37.95 (*0-7506-4842-2*) Buttrwrth-Heinemann.

— Castings Processes. (Illus.). 320p. 2003. 85.95 (*0-7506-4841-4*) Buttrwrth-Heinemann.

Campbell, John. Cobra Dane. 352p. (Orig.). 1995. mass mkt. 4.99 (*0-380-77686-3*, Avon Bks) Morrow Avon.

— Dieppe Revisited: A Documentary Investigation. LC 92-19265. (Studies in Intelligence). 1992. 49.50 (*0-7146-3496-4*, Pub. by F Cass Pubs) Intl Spec Bk.

— GMDSS Handbook: Understanding the Global Maritime Distress & Safety System. 1998. 24.95 (*1-84037-010-6*, Pub. by Waterline) Motorbooks Intl.

— In Darwin's Wake: Revisiting Beagle's South American Anchorages. LC 96-49604. (Illus.). 296p. 1997. 27.50 (*1-57409-025-9*) Sheridan.

— Jutland: An Analysis of the Fighting. LC 99-174877. (Illus.). 440p. 1997. pap. 22.95 (*1-55821-759-2*, 17592) Lyons Pr.

— Map Use & Analysis. 2nd ed. 448p. (C). 1993. text. write for info. (*0-697-13579-9*, WCB McGr Hill) McGrw-H Hghr Educ.

— Map Use & Analysis. 3rd ed. LC 96-78490. 464p. (C). 1997. text. write for info. (*0-697-22969-6*, WCB McGr Hill) McGrw-H Hghr Educ.

— Map Use & Analysis. 4th ed. 384p. 2000. pap. 59.38 (*0-07-303748-6*) McGraw.

— Past, Space & Self. (Representation & Mind Ser.). 282p. 1995. pap. text 16.00 (*0-262-53131-3*) MIT Pr.

— Speak for Yourself: A Practical Guide to Giving Successful Presentations, Speeches & Talks. (Illus.). 144p. 1992. pap. 9.95 (*0-563-21511-9*, BBC-Parkwest) Parkwest Pubns.

— Sub Zero. 352p. (Orig.). 1996. mass mkt. 5.99 (*0-380-78061-5*, Avon Bks) Morrow Avon.

— The Winchester Single-Shot: A History & Analysis. LC 94-73342. (Illus.). 272p. 1996. 55.00 (*0-917218-68-X*) A Mowbray.

— A Yachtsman's Guide to the Collision Rules. (Illus.). 96p. 1998. 24.95 (*1-84037-013-0*) Airlife.

Campbell, John, ed. Basic Trauma Life Support for Paramedics & Advanced EMS Providers. 4th ed. LC 99-34895. (Illus.). 364p. (C). 1999. pap. text 50.00 (*0-13-084584-1*) P-H.

Campbell, John & Campbell, Donna. P-51 Mustang: Nose Art Gallery. LC 93-37242. (Illus.). 96p. 1994. pap. text 7.98 (*0-87938-782-3*) MBI Pubg.

Campbell, John, et al. The Flying Wings of Jack Northrop: A Photo Chronicle. LC 94-66966. (Illus.). 80p. (Orig.). 1994. pap. 9.95 (*0-88740-597-5*) Schiffer.

Campbell, John, jt. auth. see Skocpol, Theda.

Campbell, John, jt. auth. see Stock, Gregory B.

Campbell, John, ed. see Dietrich, Ann Marie & Shaner, Steven.

Campbell, John, ed. see Robinson, Robert A.

Campbell, John A., Jr., ed. Campbell's List: A Directory of Selected Lawyers Since 1879. annuals LC 34-11733. 260p. 1998. pap. 10.00 (*0-933089-00-7*) Campbells List.

Campbell, John A., ed. Implementation of Prolog. LC 83-26578. (Artificial Intelligence Ser.: I-381). 391p. 1984. text 94.95 (*0-470-20044-8*); pap. text 39.95 (*0-470-20045-6*) P-H.

Campbell, John A., jt. ed. see Calmet, Jacques.

Campbell, John C. American Policy Toward Communist Eastern Europe: The Choices Ahead. LC 65-15982. 150p. reprint ed. pap. 46.50 (*0-8357-5390-5*, 205584600039) Bks Demand.

— French Influence & the Rise of Roumanian Nationalism, Generation of 1848: 1830-1857. LC 73-135839. (Eastern Europe Collection). 1971. reprint ed. 25.95 (*0-405-02781-8*) Ayer.

— How Policies Change: The Japanese Government & the Aging Society. 420p. 1992. text 49.50 (*0-691-07884-X*, Pub. by Princeton U Pr) Cal Prin Full Svc.

— Lives of the Lord Chancellors & Keepers of the Great Seal of England, 10 vols. 5th ed. LC 74-39877. reprint ed. 765.00 (*0-404-01380-5*) AMS Pr.

— Shakespeare's Legal Acquirements Considered. LC 79-39811. reprint ed. 32.50 (*0-404-01369-4*) AMS Pr.

— Two Dogs Plus. (Illus.). 95p. (Orig.). (J). (gr. 8 up). 1984. pap. 7.95 (*0-685-09160-0*); pap. text 9.95 (*0-9613596-0-9*) Deer Creek Pr.

Campbell, John C., ed. The Middle East. 1976. 27.95 (*0-405-06660-0*) Ayer.

— Parties, Candidates, & Voters in Japan: Six Quantitative Studies. LC 81-6190. (Michigan Papers in Japanese Studies: No. 2). viii, 169p. 1981. pap. 8.25 (*0-939512-07-6*) U MI Japan.

— Successful Negotiation: Trieste 1954: An Appraisal by the Five Participants. LC 75-2981. 192p. reprint ed. pap. 59.60 (*0-7837-1940-X*, 204215500001) Bks Demand.

Campbell, John C. & Ikegami, Naoki, eds. Long-Term Care for Frail Older People: Reaching for the Ideal System. LC 99-17631. (Keio University Symposia for Life Science & Medicine Ser.). 270p. 1999. 139.00 (*4-431-70250-4*) Spr-Verlag.

Campbell, John C., jt. ed. see Ikegami, Naoki.

Campbell, John D. Uptime: Strategies for Excellence in Maintenance Management. (Illus.). 250p. 1994. 35.00 (*1-56327-053-6*) Productivity Inc.

***Campbell, John E.** BTLS: Basic Trauma Life Support for the EMT-B & First Responder. 3rd ed. LC 99-35610. 324p. 2000. write for info. (*0-13-084581-7*) P-H.

— Words of Wisdom, Vol. III. LC 98-91092. 1999. pap. 7.95 (*0-533-13049-2*) Vantage.

Campbell, John E., et al. Basic Trauma Life Support for Paramedics & Advanced EMS Providers. 3rd rev. ed. LC 97-16013. 384p. 1997. pap. text 43.00 (*0-8359-5159-6*) P-H.

Campbell, John E., jt. auth. see Alabama ACEP Staff.

Campbell, John Emory. Basic Trauma Life Support para Paramedicos y Proveedores Avanzados de SME: Primera Edicion en Espanol. Hicks, Eduardo Romero, tr. from ENG. (SPA.). (C). Date not set. pap. text 12.00 (*0-9647418-2-2*) Basic Trauma.

Campbell, John F. Campbell: The Campbells of Drumaboden on the River Lyennon, New Rathmelton, County Donegal, North of Ireland. 147p. 1997. reprint ed. pap. 24.00 (*0-8328-7829-4*); reprint ed. lib. bdg. 34.00 (*0-8328-7828-6*) Higginson Bk Co.

— More West Highland Tales, 2 vols., Set. Watson, W. J. et al, eds. McKay, John G., tr. LC 78-67695. (Folktale Ser.). reprint ed. 90.00 (*0-404-16070-0*) AMS Pr.

Campbell, John G. Clan Traditions & Popular Tales of the Western Highlands & Islands. Wallace, Jessie & MacIsaac, Duncan, eds. LC 72-144458. (Waifs & Strays of Celtic Tradition: Argyllshire Ser.: No. 5). reprint ed. 29.50 (*0-404-53535-6*) AMS Pr.

— Fians. LC 79-144457. (Waifs & Strays of Celtic Tradition: Argyllshire Ser.: No. 4). reprint ed. 45.00 (*0-404-53534-8*) AMS Pr.

— Superstitions of the Highlands & Islands of Scotland. LC 71-173104. (Illus.). 1972. reprint ed. 20.95 (*0-405-08337-8*, Pub. by Blom Pubns) Ayer.

Campbell, John H. Logistics: Concepts & Applications. Nishi, Masao & O'Neill, William J., Jr., eds. LC 82-84389. 328p. (Orig.). 1982. pap. 15.45 (*0-9610146-0-1*) Leaseway Trans Corp.

— Logistics: Issues for the Eighties. Nishi, Masao, ed. LC 81-86565. 211p. 1981. pap. 15.45 (*0-685-07934-1*) Leaseway Trans Corp.

Campbell, John H. & Schopf, J. William. Creative Evolution. (Life Science Ser.). 128p. (C). 1994. pap. text 40.00 (*0-86720-961-5*) Jones & Bartlett.

Campbell, John J., jt. auth. see Zimmerman, Carolyn M.

Campbell, John L. Canna: The Story of a Hebridean Island. (Illus.). 352p. 1991. pap. 18.95 (*0-86241-430-X*, Pub. by Canongate Books) Interlink Pub.

— Collapse of an Industry: Nuclear Power & the Contradictions of U. S. Policy. LC 87-47856. (Cornell Studies in Political Economy). 1988. pap. 17.95 (*0-8014-9500-8*) Cornell U Pr.

— Highland Songs of the Forty-Five. LC 75-173105. 362p. 1979. reprint ed. 30.95 (*0-405-08338-6*, Pub. by Blom Pubns) Ayer.

— Inside OS-2: The Complete Programmer's Reference. (Illus.). 224p. 1988. 39.95 (*0-8306-1319-6*, 3019); pap. 24.95 (*0-8306-9319-X*) McGraw-Hill Prof.

— The Lives of the Chief Justices of England: From the Norman Conquest till the Death of Lord Mansfield, 2 vols. 1997. reprint ed. 245.00 (*1-56169-312-X*) Gaunt.

— The Lives of the Chief Justices of England: From the Norman Conquest till the Death of Lord Tenterden, 3 Vols., Set. LC 70-152976. (Select Bibliographies Reprint Ser.). 1977. reprint ed. 114.95 (*0-8369-5728-8*) Ayer.

C

An Asterisk (*) at the beginning of an entry indicates that the title is appearing for the first time.

— Negro-Mania: Examination of the Falsely Assumed Equality of the Various Races of Men. LC 79-89420. (Black Heritage Library Collection). 1977. 40.95 (*0-8369-8532-X*) Ayer.

— Songs Remembered in Exile: Traditional Gaelic Songs from Nova Scotia Recorded in Cape Breton & Antigonish County Mostly in 1937. (Illus.). 260p. 1990. text 60.00 (*0-08-037977-X*, Pub. by Aberdeen U Pr) Macmillan.

***Campbell, John L.** A Very Civil People: Hebridean Folk History & Tradition. Cheape, Hugh, ed. & intro. by. (Illus.). 256p. 1999. 39.95 (*1-84158-015-5*, Pub. by Birlinn Ltd) Dufour.

Campbell, John L., ed. The Experience of World War II. (Illus.). 256p. 1989. 40.00 (*0-19-520792-0*) OUP.

Campbell, John L., et al, eds. Governance of the American Economy. (Structural Analysis in the Social Sciences Ser.). (Illus.). 474p. (C). 1991. text 85.00 (*0-521-40257-3*); pap. text 32.95 (*0-521-40827-X*) Cambridge U Pr.

Campbell, John L. & Collinson, Francis, eds. Hebridean Folksongs, Vol. 3. 1981. 74.00 (*0-19-815215-9*) OUP.

Campbell, John L. & Pedersen, Ove K., eds. Legacies of Change: Transformations of Postcommunist European Economies. (Sociology & Economics Ser.). 270p. 1996. pap. text 26.95 (*0-202-30559-7*); lib. bdg. 52.95 (*0-202-30558-9*) Aldine de Gruyter.

Campbell, John L., jt. ed. see De Pina-Cabral, Joao.

Campbell, John L., ed. & intro. see Rea, F. G.

Campbell, John L., tr. see MacLellan, Angus.

***Campbell, John Lorne.** Songs Remembered in Exile: Traditional Gaelic Songs from Nova Scotia. 246p. 2000. pap. 29.95 (*1-84158-010-4*, Pub. by Birlinn Ltd) Dufour.

Campbell, John M. American Bomber Aircraft in World War II Vol. II: Boeing B-29 Superfortress. LC 97-66913. 264p. 1997. 45.00 (*0-7643-0272-8*) Schiffer.

— Few & Far Between: Moments in the North American Desert. LC 97-12607. (Illus.). 176p. 1997. 40.00 (*0-89013-315-8*); pap. 29.95 (*0-89013-322-0*) Museum NM Pr.

— North Alaska Chronicle: Notes from the End of Time. LC 97-44708. (Illus.). 160p. 1998. 45.00 (*0-89013-353-0*); pap. 29.95 (*0-89013-354-9*) Museum NM Pr.

— North American XB-70 in Color. LC 97-80704. (Illus.). 112p. 1998. pap. 19.95 (*0-7643-0507-7*) Schiffer.

Campbell, John M. & Campbell, Donna. Allied Aircraft Art. (Illus.). 64p. 1992. pap. 12.95 (*0-88740-444-8*) Schiffer.

— American Bomber Aircraft Vol. I: Consolidated B-24 Liberator. LC 92-62298. (Illus.). 256p. 1993. 39.95 (*0-88740-452-9*) Schiffer.

— Talisman: A Collection of Nose Art. LC 92-60358. (Illus.). 256p. 1992. text 49.95 (*0-88740-414-6*) Schiffer.

Campbell, John M. & Hill, Michael. Roll Call: Thud--A Photographic Record of the Republic F-105 Thunderchief. LC 96-67102. (Illus.). 176p. 1996. 59.95 (*0-7643-0062-8*) Schiffer.

Campbell, John M., jt. auth. see Hill, Michael.

Campbell, John M., jt. auth. see Pape, Garry R.

Campbell, John N. Gator the Cowpony Goes to School. (Illus.). 72p. (J). (gr. 4-7). 1990. 9.95 (*0-89015-699-9*) Sunbelt Media.

— Gator the Cowpony Goes to School. 72p. (J). 1997. pap. 6.95 (*1-57168-138-8*, Eakin Pr) Sunbelt Media.

Campbell, John P., Jr. Campbell's Accent Cubed: Humanities, Math & Science. (J). (gr. 9 up). 1998. pap. 19.95 (*0-944322-25-5*) Patricks Pr.

Campbell, John P. Campbell's Accent on the Alphabet Quiz Book. 190p. 1999. pap. 14.95 (*0-944322-27-1*) Patricks Pr.

— Campbell's Elementary Quiz Book, No. 1. rev. ed. (Elementary School Ser.). 161p. (J). 1989. pap., per. 13.95 (*0-944322-00-X*) Patricks Pr.

— Campbell's Elementary Quiz Book, No. 2. (Elementary School Ser.). 247p. (J). 1983. pap. 15.95 (*0-944322-15-8*) Patricks Pr.

— Campbell's Explorations/U. S. History Quiz Book to 1865. 279p. (YA). (gr. 9 up). 1997. pap. 13.95 (*0-944322-24-7*) Patricks Pr.

— Campbell's High School/College Quiz Book: The Quiz Contestant's Vade Mecum. expanded rev. ed. LC 84-19012. 524p. (YA). (gr. 9 up). 1984. pap. 15.95 (*0-9609412-3-1*) Patricks Pr.

— Campbell's Mastering the Myths in a Giant Nutshell Quiz Book. 559p. 1995. pap. 19.95 (*0-944322-29-8*) Patricks Pr.

— Campbell's Middle School Quiz Book. rev. ed. (Middle School Ser.). 327p. (YA). (gr. 5-8). 1995. pap. 15.95 (*0-9609412-4-X*) Patricks Pr.

— Campbell's Middle School Quiz Book, No. 2. rev. ed. 332p. (YA). (gr. 5-8). 1996. pap. 15.95 (*0-9609412-6-6*) Patricks Pr.

— Campbell's Middle School Quiz Book, No. 3. rev. ed. (Middle School Ser.). 269p. (YA). 1996. pap., per. 15.95 (*0-944322-05-0*) Patricks Pr.

— Campbell's 175 Lightning Rounds. rev. ed. (Lightning Rounds Ser.). 181p. 1992. pap. 15.95 (*0-944322-08-5*) Patricks Pr.

— Campbell's 176 Lightning Rounds. (Lightning Rounds Ser.). 180p. (Orig.). 1994. pap., per. 15.95 (*0-944322-18-2*) Patricks Pr.

— Campbell's Potpourri V of Quiz Bowl Questions. (Quiz Bowl Questions Ser.: Vol. V). 351p. 1995. pap., per. 15.95 (*0-944322-21-2*) Patricks Pr.

— Campbell's Potpourri III of Quiz Bowl Questions. (Campbell's Potpourri Ser.). 288p. (YA). (gr. 9 up). 1993. reprint ed. pap. 15.95 (*0-9609412-5-8*) Patricks Pr.

— Campbell's Potpourri II of Quiz Bowl Questions. rev. ed. LC 84-61238. (Campbell's Potpourri Ser.). 349p. (YA). (gr. 9 up). 1997. pap. 15.95 (*0-944322-04-2*) Patricks Pr.

— Campbell's 3001 Quiz Questions. 290p. (YA). (gr. 9-12). 1996. pap. 17.95 (*0-944322-22-0*) Patricks Pr.

— Campbell's 2701 Quiz Questions. 279p. (J). (gr. 6-8). 1996. pap. 17.95 (*0-944322-23-9*) Patricks Pr.

— Campbell's 213 Lightning Rounds. (Lightning Rounds Ser.: No. 213). 219p. (Orig.). 1994. pap., per. 15.95 (*0-944322-19-0*) Patricks Pr.

— Campbell's 2004 Quiz Questions. (Two Thousand Ser.). 232p. (Orig.). 1993. pap., per. 15.95 (*0-944322-13-1*) Patricks Pr.

— Campbell's 2003 Quiz Questions. (Two Thousand Ser.). 229p. (Orig.). 1992. pap., per. 15.95 (*0-944322-10-7*) Patricks Pr.

— Campbell's 2002 Quiz Questions. (Two Thousand Ser.). 253p. (Orig.). 1991. pap., per. 15.95 (*0-944322-06-9*) Patricks Pr.

— Campbell's 212 Lightning Rounds. (Lightning Rounds Ser.). 217p. (Orig.). 1993. pap., per. 15.95 (*0-944322-14-X*) Patricks Pr.

— Omniscience: The Basic Game of Knowledge in Book Form. rev. ed. 392p. 2000. pap. 16.95 (*0-944322-12-3*) Patricks Pr.

— What to Study: Generating & Developing Research Questions. LC 82-10720. (Studying Organizations Ser.: No. 6). 168p. 1982. reprint ed. pap. 52.10 (*0-608-02988-2*, 205962800006) Bks Demand.

Campbell, John P., et al. Productivity in Organizations: New Perspectives from Industrial & Organizational Psychology. LC 88-42780. (Management Ser.). 477p. 1988. text 43.95 (*1-55542-100-8*) Jossey-Bass.

***Campbell, John Quincy Adams, et al.** The Union Must Stand: The Civil War Diary of John Quincy Adams Campbell, Fifth Iowa Volunteer Infantry. Grimsley, Mark & Miller, Todd D., eds. LC 99-6744. (Voices of the Civil War Ser.). 296p. 2000. 38.00 (*1-57233-069-4*) U of Tenn Pr.

Campbell, John R. Dealing with Disaster: Hurricane Response in Fiji. 209p. 1984. pap. 9.00 (*0-86638-058-2*) EW Ctr HI.

***Campbell, John R.** Dry Rot in the Ivory Tower: A Case for Fumigation, Ventilation & Renewal of the Academic Sanctuary. LC 99-462211. 200p. 2000. pap. 24.50 (*0-7618-1646-1*) U Pr of Amer.

Campbell, John R. Reclaiming a Lost Heritage: Land-Grant & Other Higher Education Initiatives. 269p. 1998. pap. 19.95 (*0-87013-499-X*) Mich St U Pr.

Campbell, John R. & Chung, Joseph. Post-Disaster Assessment, 2 vols., Vol. 1. (Pacific Disaster Preparedness Project Ser.). 40p. 1991. 3.00 (*0-86638-073-6*) EW Ctr HI.

— Post-Disaster Assessment, 2 vols., Vol. 2. (Pacific Disaster Preparedness Project Ser.). 40p. 1991. 3.00 (*0-86638-075-2*) EW Ctr HI.

Campbell, John R. & Rew, Alan. Identity & Affect: Experiences of Identity in a Globalising World. LC 98-42633. (Anthropology, Culture & Society Ser.). 240p. 1999. 59.50 (*0-7453-1428-7*, Pub. by Pluto GBR) Stylus Pub VA.

***Campbell, John R. & Rew, Alan.** Identity & Affect: Experiences of Identity in a Globalising World. 240p. 1999. pap. 22.50 (*0-7453-1423-6*, Pub. by Pluto GBR) Stylus Pub VA.

Campbell, John T. Our Twentieth Century's Greatest Poems. 700p. 1982. 59.95 (*0-910147-00-0*) World Poetry Pr.

— Our World's Best Loved Poems. 608p. 1983. 69.95 (*0-910147-03-5*) World Poetry Pr.

— Raid on Truman. 336p. 1992. mass mkt. 4.99 (*0-380-71816-2*, Avon Bks) Morrow Avon.

— Today's Greatest Poems. 665p. 1983. 59.95 (*0-910147-01-9*) World Poetry Pr.

Campbell, John T., ed. Our Western World's Greatest Poems. 450p. 1983. 69.95 (*0-317-03222-4*); text 69.95 (*0-685-42659-9*) World Poetry Pr.

***Campbell, John W.** Antarktos Cycle. 1999. pap. 19.95 (*1-56882-146-8*) Chaosium.

Campbell, John W., Jr. The John W. Campbell Letters, Vol. I. Chapdelaine, Perry A., Sr. et al, eds. LC 84-71553. (Illus.). 610p. 1985. 35.00 (*0-931150-15-9*); pap. 5.95 (*0-931150-16-7*) AC Projects.

— The Moon Is Hell! 256p. 1990. mass mkt. 3.95 (*0-88184-674-0*) Carroll & Graf.

— Who Goes There? 236p. Date not set. 21.95 (*0-8488-2225-0*) Amereon Ltd.

— Who Goes There? 152p. 1997. reprint ed. lib. bdg. 31.95 (*0-89966-734-1*) Buccaneer Bks.

Campbell, John W., Jr., et al. The John W. Campbell Letters with Isaac Asimov & A. E. van Vogt, Vol. 2. Chapdelaine, Perry A., Sr. et al, eds. LC 84-71553. (Illus.). 600p. 1991. 45.00 (*0-931150-19-1*) AC Projects.

Campbell, John Y. A Solution Manual to the Econometrics of Financial Markets. LC 97-18350. 1997. write for info. (*0-691-01569-4*) Princeton U Pr.

***Campbell, John Y. & Feldstein, Martin S.** Risks Aspects of Investment-Based Social Security Reform. LC 00-41798. (National Bureau of Economic Research Conference Report Ser.). 2000. write for info. (*0-226-09255-0*) U Ch Pr.

Campbell, John Y., et al. The Econometrics of Financial Markets. LC 96-27868. 320p. 1997. text 49.50 (*0-691-04301-9*, Pub. by Princeton U Pr) Cal Prin Full Svc.

Campbell, Jon, ed. see Stearn, Marshall B.

Campbell, Jonathan. Dead Sea Scrolls: The Complete Story. LC 97-37220. 240p. 1998. pap. 12.95 (*1-56975-092-0*) Ulysses Pr.

Campbell, Jonathan A. Amphibians & Reptiles of Northern Guatemala, the Yucatan & Belize. LC 98-13121. (Animal Natural History Ser.). (Illus.). 400p. 1998. 100.00 (*0-8061-3064-4*) U of Okla Pr.

— Amphibians & Reptiles of Northern Guatemala, the Yucatan & Belize, 4. 1999. pap. text 29.95 (*0-8061-3066-0*) U of Okla Pr.

Campbell, Jonathan A. & Ford, Linda S. Phylogenetic Relationships of the Colubrid Snakes of the Genus Adelphicos in the Highlands of Middle America. (Occasional Papers: No. 100). 22p. 1982. 1.00 (*0-317-04838-4*) U KS Nat Hist Mus.

Campbell, Jonathan A. & Lamar, William W. The Venomous Reptiles of Latin America. LC 88-47934. (Comstock Bk.). (Illus.). 440p. 1989. text 69.95 (*0-8014-2059-8*) Cornell U Pr.

Campbell, Jonathan G. The Use of Scripture in the Damascus Document 1-8, 19-20. LC 95-5898. (Beiheft zur Zeitschrift fuer die Alttestamentliche Wissenschaft Ser.: No. 228). 230p. 1995. lib. bdg. 85.50 (*3-11-014240-6*) De Gruyter.

Campbell, Jorge R. Las Radiaciones: Reto y Realidades. (Ciencia para Todos Ser.). (SPA.). pap. 6.99 (*968-16-2395-9*, Pub. by Fondo) Continental Bk.

— Las Radiaciones II: El Manejo de las Rad. (Ciencia para Todos Ser.). (SPA.). pap. 6.99 (*968-16-3545-0*, Pub. by Fondo) Continental Bk.

Campbell, Joseph. Erotic Irony: And Mythic Forms in the Art of Thomas Mann. (Broadside Editions Ser.). 34p. (C). 1988. reprint ed. pap. 4.95 (*0-931191-09-2*) Rob Briggs.

— Hero with a Thousand Faces. (Illus.). 416p. 1996. reprint ed. 9.98 (*1-56731-120-2*, MJF Bks) Fine Comms.

— Hero with a Thousand Faces. rev. ed. LC 49-8590. (Bollingen Ser.: No. XVII). (Illus.). 464p. (C). 1949. pap. 14.95 (*0-691-01784-0*, Pub. by Princeton U Pr) Cal Prin Full Svc.

— The Historical Atlas of World Mythology. 1988. write for info. (*0-318-63661-1*) HarperTrade.

— Joseph Campbell Audio Collection: Inward Journey: East & West. 1997. pap. 34.95 incl. audio (*1-56511-188-5*, Pub. by Penguin-HghBrdg) Penguin Putnam.

— The Masks of God, 4 vols. 1991. reprint ed. pap. 12.95 (*0-685-72477-8*, Arkana) Viking Penguin.

— The Masks of God, 4 vols., Vol. I: Primitive Mythology. 520p. 1991. reprint ed. pap. 16.95 (*0-14-019443-6*, Arkana) Viking Penguin.

— The Masks of God, 4 vols., Vol. II: Oriental Mythology. 576p. 1992. reprint ed. pap. 23.99 (*0-14-019442-8*, Arkana) Viking Penguin.

— The Masks of God, 4 vols., Vol. III: Occidental Mythology. 576p. 1991. reprint ed. pap. 16.95 (*0-14-019441-X*, Arkana) Viking Penguin.

— The Masks of God, 4 vols., Vol. IV: Creative Mythology. 752p. 1991. reprint ed. pap. 16.95 (*0-14-019440-1*, Arkana) Viking Penguin.

Campbell, Joseph. The Masks of God: Occidental Mythology. (Illus.). 564p. 1976. pap. 9.95 (*0-14-004306-3*, Penguin Bks) Viking Penguin.

Campbell, Joseph. The Mountainy Singer by Seosamh MacCathmhaoil. LC 74-64007. (Des Imagistes: Literature of the Imagist Movement Ser.). 88p. reprint ed. 29.50 (*0-404-17078-1*) AMS Pr.

— Mythos: The Shaping of Our Mythic Tradition. (Illus.). 256p. 1999. text 39.95 (*1-86204-527-5*, Pub. by Element MA) Penguin Putnam.

— Myths to Live By. 304p. 1993. pap. 14.95 (*0-14-019461-4*, Arkana) Viking Penguin.

Campbell, Joseph. The Power of Myth. 320p. 1991 pap. 12.95 (*0-385-41886-8*) Doubleday.

Campbell, Joseph. Transformations of Myth Through Time. LC 89-45788. 272p. 1990. pap. 20.00 (*0-06-096463-4*, Perennial) HarperTrade.

— The Way of Myth: Talking with Joseph Campbell. LC 94-6186. (Pocket Classics Ser.). 240p. 1994. reprint ed. pap. 6.00 (*1-57062-042-3*, Pub. by Shambhala Pubns) Random.

— The Way of the Seeded Earth, 2 vols. 1989. 50.00 (*0-685-74089-7*, Perennial) HarperTrade.

— Wings of Art: Joseph Campbell on James Joyce. 1995. 34.95 incl. audio (*1-56511-113-3*, Pub. by HighBridge) Penguin Putnam.

***Campbell, Joseph, ed.** Marching Orders: The Civil War Diary of Alex Crawford Gwin. 87p. 1999. 8.75 (*0-9670553-1-8*) Daisy Pubg.

Campbell, Joseph, ed. Upanishads, Vol. I. Nikhilananda, Swami, tr. LC 49-9558. 333p. 1990. 18.00 (*0-911206-15-9*) Ramakrishna.

— Upanishads, Vol. II. Nikhilananda, Swami, tr. LC 49-9558. 400p. 1990. 18.00 (*0-911206-16-7*) Ramakrishna.

— Upanishads, Vol. III. Nikhilananda, Swami, tr. LC 49-9558. 408p. 1990. 18.00 (*0-911206-17-5*) Ramakrishna.

— Upanishads, Vol. IV. Nikhilananda, Swami, tr. LC 49-9558. 424p. 1994. 15.00 (*0-911206-18-3*) Ramakrishna.

Campbell, Joseph & Abadie, M. J. The Mythic Image. LC 79-166363. (Bollingen Ser.: No. C). (Illus.). 560p. 1981. pap. 39.50 (*0-691-01839-1*, Pub. by Princeton U Pr) Cal Prin Full Svc.

Campbell, Joseph & Hull, R. F. C., eds. Papers from Eranos Yearbooks, 6 vols. Manheim, Ralph, tr. Incl. Vol. 1. Spirit & Nature. (Illus.). 498p. 1982. pap. text 22.95 (*0-691-01841-3*, Pub. by Princeton U Pr); Vol. 2. Mysteries. 496p. 1955. pap. text 22.95 (*0-691-01823-5*, Pub. by Princeton U Pr); Vol. 3. Man & Time. (Illus.). 440p. 1957. pap. text 24.95 (*0-691-01857-X*, Pub. by Princeton U Pr); Vol. 4. Spirtual Disciplines. (Illus.). 528p. 1960. pap. text 22.95 (*0-691-01863-4*, Pub. by Princeton U Pr); Vol. 5. Man & Transformation. (Illus.). 413p. 1964. pap. text 22.95 (*0-691-01834-0*, Pub. by Princeton U Pr); (Bollingen Ser.: No. 30). 508p. 1969. Set pap. text 22.95 (*0-691-01842-1*, Pub. by Princeton U Pr) Cal Prin Full Svc.

Campbell, Joseph & Moyers, Bill. The Power of Myth. LC 88-4218. (Illus.). 256p. 1988. pap. 29.95 (*0-385-24774-5*) Doubleday.

Campbell, Joseph & Roberts, Richard. Tarot Revelations. 2nd ed. LC 81-86684. (Illus.). 308p. 1982. pap. 10.95 (*0-942380-00-2*) Vernal Equinox.

Campbell, Joseph & Robinson, Henry M. A Skeleton Key to Finnegans Wake. 1993. reprint ed. 38.95 (*1-56849-168-9*) Buccaneer Bks.

Campbell, Joseph, jt. auth. see Toms, Michael.

Campbell, Joseph, ed. see Jung, C. G.

Campbell, Joseph, ed. see King, J. E. & Oakes, Maud.

Campbell, Joseph, ed. see Zimmer, Heinrich.

Campbell, Joseph, ed. see Zimmer, Heinrich R.

Campbell, Josie P. John Irving: A Critical Companion. LC 98-9349. (Critical Companions to Popular Contemporary Writers Ser.). 224p. 1998. 29.95 (*0-313-30222-7*, Greenwood Pr) Greenwood.

Campbell, Josie P., ed. Popular Culture in the Middle Ages. LC 86-71408. 157p. 1986. 20.95 (*0-87972-339-4*) Bowling Green Univ Popular Press.

Campbell, Joy. Batik. (Start a Craft Ser.). 1994. 7.98 (*0-7858-0063-8*) Bk Sales Inc.

Campbell, Joy, jt. auth. see Engen, Barbara.

Campbell, Judith. Let's Talk About It: Stories about Sensitive Issues, Dilemmas & Ethical Decision Making, Vol. I. large type ed. Howard, Joanne, ed. (Illus.). 64p. (J). (gr. 2-6). 1998. pap. 10.00 (*1-891180-51-7*) Campbell & Lockwood.

— Police Horses. 1975. pap. 2.00 (*0-87980-199-9*) Wilshire.

— The Stuff of Life Vol. 1: Poems Prayers & Meditations on the Gift of Life (As We Really Live It!) (Illus.). 96p. 1997. pap. 9.00 (*1-891180-50-9*) Campbell & Lockwood.

— Watercolor Painting on the Trail: A Hiking Artist's Handbook. LC 93-11461. (Illus.). 160p. (Orig.). 1993. pap. 18.95 (*1-878239-29-5*) AMC Books.

Campbell, Judith, ed. see Belford, Fontaine M.

Campbell, Judith, ed. see Stang, Jennifer.

Campbell, Julie A. Studies in Arizona History. (Illus.). 304p. 1998. text 32.00 (*0-910037-38-8*); pap. text 23.00 (*0-910037-39-6*) AZ Hist Soc.

Campbell, Julie H. Vascular Smooth Muscle in Culture, Vol. I. 200p. 1987. 114.00 (*0-8493-4326-7*, CRC Reprint) Franklin.

Campbell, Julie H. & Campbell, Gordon R., eds. Vascular Smooth Muscle in Culture, 2 vols. 1987. 212.00 (*0-8493-4325-9*, QP110, CRC Reprint) Franklin.

— Vascular Smooth Muscle in Culture, 2 vols., I. 168p. 1987. 98.00 (*0-8493-4327-5*, CRC Reprint) Franklin.

Campbell, June. Traveller in Space: In Search of Female Identity in Tibetan Buddhism. 225p. 1998. text 27.00 (*0-7881-5623-3*) DIANE Pub.

Campbell, June M. Mosby's Survival Guide to Medical Abbreviations, Acronyms, Symbols, Prefixes & Suffixes. LC 95-119665. 608p. (C). (gr. 13). 1994. text 24.95 (*0-8151-1398-6*, 25635) Mosby Inc.

Campbell, June M., jt. auth. see Campbell, Joe B.

Campbell, K. S. & Day, M. F., eds. Rates of Evolution. (Illus.). 384p. (C). 1987. text 85.00 (*0-04-575030-0*) Routledge.

Campbell, Kamin. Dos 5.0. 1995. pap. text 22.95 (*0-201-62248-3*) Addison-Wesley.

Campbell, Karen & Miner, Colleen. Crafts All Together. (Illus.). 366p. 1993. spiral bd. 7.50 (*1-879127-26-1*) Lighten Up Enter.

Campbell, Karen, jt. ed. see Cameron, James.

Campbell, Karen J., ed. German Mystical Writings: Hildegard of Bingen, Meister Eckhart, Jacob Boehme & Others. (German Library: Vol. 5). 342p. 1991. 19.95 (*0-8264-0347-6*) Continuum.

Campbell, Karlyn K. Critiques of Contemporary Rhetoric. 217p. (C). 1972. pap. 20.95 (*0-534-00135-1*) Wadsworth Pub.

— Man Cannot Speak for Her: A Critical Study of Early Feminist Rhetoric, 2 vols. (Contributions in Women's Studies). 1989. 104.95 (*0-313-26668-9*, CMK/, Greenwood Pr) Greenwood.

— Man Cannot Speak for Her: A Critical Study of Early Feminist Rhetoric, Vol. 1. LC 88-37438. 224p. 1989. pap. 21.95 (*0-275-93269-9*, B32661, Praeger Pubs) Greenwood.

— Man Cannot Speak for Her: A Critical Study of Early Feminist Rhetoric, Vol. 1. LC 88-32825. (Contributions in Women's Studies: No. 101). 220p. 1989. 49.95 (*0-313-25649-7*, CMK01, Greenwood Pr) Greenwood.

— Man Cannot Speak for Her: A Critical Study of Early Feminist Rhetoric, Vol. 2. LC 88-37378. (Contributions in Women's Studies: No. 102). 587p. 1989. 65.00 (*0-313-25650-0*, CMK02, Greenwood Pr) Greenwood.

— The Rhetorical Act. 310p. (C). 1982. 24.25 (*0-534-01008-3*) Wadsworth Pub.

— The Rhetorical Act. 2nd ed. LC 95-5414. 398p. 1995. pap. 50.95 (*0-534-16752-7*) Wadsworth Pub.

— Women Public Speakers in the United States, 1925-1993: A Bio-Critical Sourcebook. LC 93-21145. 520p. 1994. lib. bdg. 85.00 (*0-313-27535-1*, Greenwood Pr) Greenwood.

Campbell, Karlyn K., compiled by. Man Cannot Speak for Her: A Critical Study of Early Feminist Rhetoric, Vol. 2. LC 88-37438. 587p. 1989. pap. 27.95 (*0-275-93267-2*, B32662, Praeger Pubs) Greenwood.

Campbell, Karlyn K., ed. Women Public Speakers in the United States, 1800-1925: A Bio-Critical Sourcebook. LC 92-14615. 544p. 1993. lib. bdg. 85.00 (*0-313-27533-5*, CAG, Greenwood Pr) Greenwood.

Campbell, Karlyn K. & Burkholder, Thomas R. Critiques of Contemporary Rhetoric. 2nd ed. (Speech & Theater Ser.). 335p. (C). 1996. 41.95 (*0-534-19500-8*) Wadsworth Pub.

Campbell, Karlyn K. & Jamieson, Kathleen H. Deeds Done in Words: Presidential Rhetoric & the Genres of Governance. LC 89-20579. 286p. 1990. 29.95 (*0-226-09241-0*) U Ch Pr.

C

An Asterisk (*) at the beginning of an entry indicates that the title is appearing for the first time.

Campbell, Karlyn K., jt. auth. see Jamieson, Kathleen H.

Campbell, Kate. Critical Feminism Argument in the Disciplines. (Ideas & Production Ser.). 192p. 1992. pap. 34.95 (*0-335-09757-X*) OpUniv Pr.

***Campbell, Kate.** Journalism, Literature & Modernity: From Hazlitt to Modernism. 288p. 2000. text 65.00 (*1-85331-175-8*) Col U Pr.

Campbell, Katherine N. & Ellis, Susan J. The Help! I-Don't-Have-Enough-Time Guide to Volunteer Management. (Illus.). 120p. (Orig.). 1995. pap. 14.95 (*0-940576-16-3*) Energize.

Campbell, Kathleen. Essential Audiology for Physicians. LC 97-34544. (Illus.). 300p. (Orig.). 1997. pap. 33.95 (*1-56593-691-4*, 1352) Thomson Learn.

— Poems on Several Occasions Written in the Eighteenth Century. (BCL1-PR English Literature Ser.). 212p. 1992. reprint ed. lib. bdg. 79.00 (*0-7812-7139-8*) Rprt Serv.

Campbell, Kathleen, ed. An Anthology of English Poetry: Dryden to Blake. LC 75-168777. (Granger Index Reprint Ser.). 1977. reprint ed. 23.95 (*0-8369-6297-4*) Ayer.

Campbell, Kathy, jt. auth. see Elder, Terri.

Campbell, Katie, ed. see Task Force of Parents.

Campbell, Kay, et al. Developing Individualized Activities for Language. 146p. 1995. pap. text 32.50 (*0-930951-98-0*) Acad Comm.

Campbell, Kay, jt. auth. see Miller, Constance.

Campbell, Kay H. Dhahran's American Consulate: The History of the United States Consulate General Dhahran, Saudi Arabia. (Illus.). 82p. (Orig.). 1991. pap. 12.95 (*0-9615945-3-5*) Chiefton Pub.

Campbell, Keith. Body & Mind. 2nd ed. LC 80-10126. 160p. 1980. pap. 7.00 (*0-268-00673-3*) U of Notre Dame Pr.

Campbell, Keith O. Food for the Future: How Agriculture Can Meet the Challenge. LC 78-23982. 190p. reprint ed. pap. 58.90 (*0-7837-1817-9*, 204201700001) Bks Demand.

Campbell, Kelly, jt. auth. see Brain, Marshall.

Campbell-Kelly, Martin. Computer: A History of the Information Machine. 1997. pap. 17.00 (*0-465-02990-6*, Pub. by Basic) HarpC.

— ICL: A Business & Technical History. (Illus.). 460p. 1990. 65.00 (*0-19-853918-5*) OUP.

Campbell-Kelly, Martin, ed. Babbage: Passages from the Life of a Philosopher. LC 93-43903. 390p. (Orig.). (C). 1994. pap. 18.95 (*0-8135-2066-5*) Rutgers U Pr.

Campbell-Kelly, Martin & Williams, M. R., eds. The Moore School Lectures. (Charles Babbage Institute Reprint Series for the History of Computing). (Illus.). 616p. 1985. 65.00 (*0-262-03109-4*) MIT Pr.

Campbell-Kelly, Martin, ed. see Babbage, Charles.

Campbell-Kelly, Martin, jt. ed. see Williams, M. R.

Campbell, Ken. The Bald Trilogy. LC 95-194483. (Methuen Plays Ser.). 1995. pap. 16.95 (*0-413-69080-6*, Methuen Drama) Methn.

— Credible Church. LC 99-6800. 1999. pap. 15.95 (*0-941037-72-X*, BIBAL Press) D & F Scott.

— The Furtive Nudist. (Illus.). 98p. (Orig.). (C). 1992. pap. 15.95 (*0-413-66100-8*, A0614, Methuen Drama) Methn.

— Pigspurt. 112p. 1995. pap. write for info. (*0-413-68100-9*, A0710, Methuen Drama) Methn.

— Skungpoomery. 47p. (J). 1988. pap. write for info. (*0-413-33910-6*, A0263, Methuen Drama) Methn.

— Those Ugly Emotions. 1996. mass mkt. 9.99 (*1-85792-244-1*, Pub. by Christian Focus) Spring Arbor Dist.

— Violin Time: Or the Lady from Montsequr. 1996. pap. 13.95 (*0-413-70960-4*, Methuen Drama) Methn.

Campbell, Ken, jt. auth. see Waechter, F. K.

Campbell, Kenneth E., Jr. The Non-Passerine Pleistocene Avifauna of the Talara Tar Seeps, Northwestern Peru. (Illus.). 208p. pap. 20.57 (*0-88854-230-5*) Brill Academic Pubs.

Campbell, Kenneth L. The Intellectual Struggle of the English Papists in the Seventeenth Century: The Catholic Dilemma. LC 86-23893. (Texts & Studies in Religion: Vol. 30). 256p. 1986. lib. bdg. 89.95 (*0-88946-818-4*) E Mellen.

Campbell, Kenneth L., ed. Versatility of Wetlands in the Agricultural Landscape. LC 96-84439. (Illus.). 760p. 1995. pap. 52.00 (*0-929355-69-5*, P0995) Am Soc Ag Eng.

Campbell, Kenneth L. & Wood, James W., eds. Human Reproductive Ecology: Interactions of Environment, Fertility, & Behavior. LC 94-697. (Annals Ser.: Vol. 709). 429p. 1994. pap. 115.00 (*0-89766-842-1*) NY Acad Sci.

Campbell, Kerry S. & Colonna, Marco, eds. Natural Killer Cell Protocols: Cellular & Molecular Methods. LC 99-12944. (Methods in Molecular Biology Ser.: Vol. 121). (Illus.). 408p. 2000. 99.50 (*0-89603-683-9*) Humana.

***Campbell, Kim.** Invasion of the Judy Snatchers. (Funnie Mysteries Ser.: No. 1). 80p. (J). 2000. pap. 4.99 (*0-7868-4382-9*, Pub. by Disney Pr) Time Warner.

Campbell, Kim, jt. auth. see Fontes.

Campbell, Kim S. Coherence, Continuity & Cohesion: Theoretical Foundations for Document Design. 128p. 1995. 29.95 (*0-8058-1301-2*); pap. 17.95 (*0-8058-1703-4*) L Erlbaum Assocs.

Campbell, Kim S., jt. auth. see Campbell, Danny.

Campbell, Kimberlee A. The Protean Text: A Study of the Versions of the Medieval French Legend of "Doon & Olive" LC 88-25078. (Garland Monographs in Medieval Literature: Vol. 1). 881028p. 1988. text 12.00 (*0-8240-4786-9*, 865) Garland.

Campbell, Kimo, ed. see Speakman, Cummins E.

Campbell, Kit, jt. auth. see John, Geraint.

Campbell, Kumari. New Brunswick. LC 96-33931. (Hello Canada Ser.). (Illus.). 76p. (J). 1996. lib. bdg. 19.95 (*0-8225-2764-2*, Lerner Publctns) Lerner Pub.

— Prince Edward Island. LC 95-4221. (Hello Canada Ser.). (Illus.). 76p. (J). 1996. lib. bdg. 19.95 (*0-8225-2762-6*, Lerner Publctns) Lerner Pub.

Campbell, Kurt N. & Falk, Pamela. The United States, Soviet Union, Cuba & South Africa in Angola: The Quagmire of Four Party Negotiations, 1981-88. (Pew Case Studies in International Affairs). 50p. (C). 1988. pap. text 3.50 (*1-56927-429-0*) Geo U Inst Dplmcy.

Campbell, L. A. Campbell: Earliest Campbell Families in Maine. 77p. 1994. reprint ed. pap. 15.00 (*0-8328-4180-3*); reprint ed. lib. bdg. 25.00 (*0-8328-4179-X*) Higginson Bk Co.

Campbell, L. D. & Spencer, R. S. Bulletins of American Paleontology Vol. 92: The Fauna & Paleoecology of the Late Pleistocene Marine Sediments of Southeastern Virginia, Vol. 327. 124p. 1987. 30.00 (*0-87710-407-7*) Paleo Res.

Campbell, L. J. Fairbanks. Rennick, Penny, ed. LC 72-92087. (Alaska Geographic Ser.: Vol. 22, No. 1). (Illus.). 96p. 1995. pap. 19.95 (*1-56661-025-7*) Alaska Geog Soc.

— Native Cultures of Alaska: Traditions Through Time. Rennick, Penny, ed. LC 72-92087. (Alaska Geographic Ser.: Vol. 23-2). (Illus.). 112p. (Orig.). 1996. pap. 19.95 (*1-56661-031-1*) Alaska Geog Soc.

— North Slope Now. Rennick, Penny, ed. LC 75-79112. (Alaska Geographic Ser.: Vol. 16, No. 2). (Illus.). 96p. 1989. pap. 9.95 (*0-88240-189-0*) Alaska Geog Soc.

— People of Alaska. Rennick, Penny, ed. LC 72-92087. (Alaska Geographic Ser.: Vol. 21, No. 3). (Illus.). 96p. 1994. pap. 19.95 (*1-56661-022-2*) Alaska Geog Soc.

— Skagway: A Legacy of Gold. Rennick, Penny, ed. LC 72-92087. (Illus.). 96p. lib. bdg. 24.95 (*1-56661-001-X*) Alaska Geog Soc.

— Skagway: A Legacy of Gold. Rennick, Penny, ed. LC 72-92087. (Illus.). 96p. 1992. pap. 9.95 (*1-56661-000-1*) Alaska Geog Soc.

Campbell, L. J. & Rennick, Penny. Admiralty Island: Fortress of the Bears. LC 72-92087. (Alaska Geographic Ser.: Vol. 18, No. 3). (Illus.). 96p. 1991. pap. 21.95 (*0-88240-198-X*) Alaska Geog Soc.

— Unalaska - Dutch Harbor. LC 72-92087. (Alaska Geographic Ser.: Vol. 18, No. 4). (Illus.). 96p. 1991. pap. 19.95 (*0-88240-199-8*) Alaska Geog Soc.

Campbell, L. J., jt. auth. see Rennick, Penny.

Campbell, L. J., ed. see Alaska Geographic Society Staff.

Campbell, L. J., & Staff & Alaska Geographic Society Staff. The Aleutian Islands. Rennick, Penny, ed. LC 72-92087. (Alaska Geographic Society Ser.: Vol. 22-2). (Illus.). 96p. (Orig.). 1995. pap. 19.95 (*1-56661-026-5*) Alaska Geog Soc.

Campbell, Lance K. Prisoner of War & Concentration Camp Money. 2nd ed. (Illus.). 220p. 1992. 25.00 (*0-931960-31-2*); pap. 35.00 (*0-931960-32-0*) BNR Pr.

Campbell-Lange, Barbara. John Lautner. (Illus.). 180p. 1999. 29.99 (*3-8228-6621-0*) Taschen Amer.

Campbell, Larry, ed. see Braman, James D.

***Campbell, Laura K.** Storybooks for Tough Times. LC 99-16278. (Illus.). 160p. 1999. pap. 15.95 (*1-55591-964-2*) Fulcrum Pub.

Campbell, Laurence, tr. from SLA. The All-Night Vigil Service for Choir & Laity. 144p. 1993. 15.00 (*0-912927-88-7*, Y005) St John Kronstadt.

Campbell, Laurence, tr. see Clader, Timothy.

Campbell, Laurence, tr. see Clader, Timothy, ed.

Campbell, Laurence A. Hawaiian Papaya Booklet. 1991. write for info. (*1-883950-00-7*) L A Campbell.

Campbell, Laurie. And Father Makes Three. 1995. per. 3.75 (*0-373-09990-8*, 1-09990-2) Silhouette.

— Bird & Nature Photography. (Illus.). 160p. 1990. 29.95 (*0-7153-9470-3*, Pub. by D & C Pub) Sterling.

***Campbell, Laurie.** Good Morning, Stranger. (Special Edition Ser.). 2000. per. 4.50 (*0-373-24314-6*) Silhouette.

Campbell, Laurie. Guide to Bird & Nature Photography. (Illus.). 152p. 1993. pap. 19.95 (*0-7153-0127-6*, Pub. by D & C Pub) Sterling.

— Unexpected Family. 1999. per. 4.25 (*0-373-24230-1*, Harlequin) Harlequin Bks.

Campbell, Laurie & Dennis, Roy. Golden Eagles. (Illus.). 96p. 1996. 39.95 (*0-948661-55-0*, Pub. by Colin Baxter Ltd) Voyageur Pr.

Campbell, Lawrence. Wolf Kahn, New Landscapes. Maxon, Gayle & Hancock, Diana, eds. LC 88-80230. (Illus.). 44p. 1988. 12.00 (*0-935037-19-5*) G Peters Gallery.

Campbell, Lawrence, et al. Elaine de Kooning. Bledsoe, Jane K., ed. LC 91-45232. (Illus.). 120p. 1992. pap. 30.00 (*0-915977-09-5*) Georgia Museum of Art.

***Campbell, Lee A., ed.** Auditing Investments. 74p. 1999. pap. 25.00 (*0-89413-427-2*) Inst Inter Aud.

— Contract Auditing. (Tool Kit Ser.). 141p. 1998. pap. 200.00 (*0-89413-401-9*) Inst Inter Aud.

— Electronic Commerce & the Internet. LC 97-172520. (Professional Practices Pamphlet Ser.: Vol. 97-1). 56p. 1997. pap. 15.00 (*0-89413-377-2*) Inst Inter Aud.

— The Internal Auditor Job Market, 1998: A Comprehensive Review of Salaries, Staff Sizes, Director... 260p. 1998. pap. 49.00 (*0-89413-418-3*) Inst Inter Aud.

Campbell, Lee A., ed. The Role of Internal Auditors in Environmental Issues: CH2M Hill, Commissioned by the Institute of Internal Auditors Research Foundation. 220p. 1993. pap. text 25.00 (*0-89413-284-9*, A863) Inst Inter Aud.

***Campbell, Lee A., ed.** A Vision for the Future: Professional Practices Framework for Internal Auditing. 116p. 1999. pap. 25.00 (*0-89413-424-8*) Inst Inter Aud.

Campbell, Lee A., ed. see Andersen, Arthur.

Campbell, Lee A., ed. see Apostolou, Barbara & Alleman, Francine.

Campbell, Lee A., ed. see Austin, Gary R.

Campbell, Lee A., ed. see Bank of Canada Staff & Institute of Internal Auditors Staff.

Campbell, Lee A., ed. see Blevins, Dallas R.

Campbell, Lee A., ed. see Carolus, Roger & Nelson, Donald.

Campbell, Lee A., ed. see Coopers & Lybrand LLP Staff.

Campbell, Lee A., ed. see Dittenhofer, Mortimer A. & Sennetti, J. T.

Campbell, Lee A., ed. see Dolenko, Marilyn.

Campbell, Lee A., ed. see Fargason, James S.

Campbell, Lee A., ed. see Felix, William L.

Campbell, Lee A., ed. see Fiorelli, Paul E. & Rooney, Cynthia J.

Campbell, Lee A., ed. see Flesher, Dale L.

Campbell, Lee A., ed. see Friedlob, G. Thomas & Institute of Internal Auditors Staff.

Campbell, Lee A., ed. see Frigo, Mark L. & Institute of Internal Auditors. Research Foundation.

Campbell, Lee A., ed. see Frigo, Mark L., et al.

Campbell, Lee A., ed. see Galloway, David.

Campbell, Lee A., ed. see Glover, H. D. & Flagg, J. C.

Campbell, Lee A., ed. see Glover, Hubert D. & Flagg, James C.

Campbell, Lee A., ed. see Gray, Glen L. & Gray, Maryann J.

Campbell, Lee A., ed. see Gupta, Praveen P. & Ray, Manash R.

Campbell, Lee A., ed. see Institute of Internal Auditors.

Campbell, Lee A., ed. see Institute of Internal Auditors Staff.

Campbell, Lee A., ed. see Jones, Laurie G.

Campbell, Lee A., ed. see Jordan, Glenda S.

Campbell, Lee A., ed. see Kaplan, James M.

Campbell, Lee A., ed. see Knowles, J. W. & Postel, J.

Campbell, Lee A., ed. see Ladd, W. H.

Campbell, Lee A., ed. see Langer, Maria.

Campbell, Lee A., ed. see Leech, Tim J.

Campbell, Lee A., ed. see Marcella, A. J., Jr., et al.

Campbell, Lee A., ed. see Marcella, Albert J.

Campbell, Lee A., ed. see Marcella, Albert J. & Sampias, William.

Campbell, Lee A., ed. see Marcella, Albert J., et al.

Campbell, Lee A., ed. see McIntosh, Elaine.

Campbell, Lee A., ed. see McKechnie, Gary.

Campbell, Lee A., ed. see McNamee, D.

Campbell, Lee A., ed. see McNamee, David.

Campbell, Lee A., ed. see McNamee, David W.

Campbell, Lee A., ed. see McNamee, David, et al.

Campbell, Lee A., ed. see Ramamoorti, Sridhar, et al.

Campbell, Lee A., ed. see Ratliff, R., et al.

Campbell, Lee A., ed. see Ridley, Jeffrey & Stephens, Krystyna.

Campbell, Lee A., ed. see Rittenberg, Larry E. & Institute of Internal Auditors. Research Foundation.

Campbell, Lee A., ed. see Roth, James P.

Campbell, Lee A., ed. see Tener, W. T.

Campbell, Lee A., ed. see Vanasco, Rocco R.

Campbell, Lee A., ed. see Wallace, Wanda A. & White, G. Thomas.

Campbell, Lee A., ed. see Waterhouse, Price.

Campbell, Leon G. The Military & Society in Colonial Peru, 1750-1810. LC 77-91650. (American Philosophical Society, Memoirs Ser.: No. 123). 272p. reprint ed. pap. 84.40 (*0-608-15297-8*, 202923400059) Bks Demand.

Campbell, Lesley, jt. auth. see Ryder, Judith.

Campbell, Leslie L. Dance Family in Virginia. (Illus.). 134p. 1993. reprint ed. pap. 22.50 (*0-8328-3162-X*); reprint ed. lib. bdg. 32.50 (*0-8328-3161-1*) Higginson Bk Co.

Campbell, Letha. When I Was Ten: Of McLoud, Oklahoma. Kuhn, Glenda P., ed. (Our Heritage Ser.: Vol. II). (Illus.). 29p. (J). 1995. pap. 4.99 (*0-9643029-2-6*) SpritSBo.

Campbell, Lewis. A Guide to Greek Tragedy for English Readers. 1980. lib. bdg. 75.00 (*0-8490-3200-8*) Gordon Pr.

— Paralipomena Sophoclea. xv, 287p. 1969. reprint ed. 95.00 (*0-685-66441-4*, 05102319) G Olms Pubs.

— Religion in Greek Literature: A Sketch in Outline. LC 79-148874. (Select Bibliographies Reprint Ser.). 1977. reprint ed. 24.95 (*0-8369-5645-1*) Ayer.

Campbell, Lewis, ed. see Plato.

Campbell, Lily B. Divine Poetry & Drama in Sixteenth-century England. LC 59-3609. 276p. reprint ed. pap. 78.70 (*0-608-12263-7*, 2024437) Bks Demand.

— Divine Poetry & Drama in 16th Century England. LC 79-148614. 276p. 1972. reprint ed. 75.00 (*0-87752-143-3*) Gordian.

— Shakespeare's Histories: Mirrors of Elizabethan Policy. LC 47-2108. (Huntington Library Publications). 356p. 1978. reprint ed. pap. 110.40 (*0-608-03172-0*, 206362500007) Bks Demand.

— Shakespeare's Tragic Heroes: Slaves of Passion. (BCL1-PR English Literature Ser.). 248p. 1992. reprint ed. lib. bdg. 79.00 (*0-7812-7299-8*) Rprt Serv.

Campbell, Lily B., ed. see Higgins, John & Blenerhasset, Thomas.

Campbell, Lily G. Shakespeare's Tragic Heroes: Slaves of Passion. 1960. 25.75 (*0-8446-1806-3*) Peter Smith.

Campbell, Linda. Endangered & Threatened Animals of Texas: Their Life History & Management. (Orig.). (C). 1996. pap. text 19.95 (*1-885696-04-3*) TX Prks & Wldlife.

— Teaching & Learning Through Multiple Intelligences. 2nd ed. 362p. 1998. pap. text 31.00 (*0-205-29348-4*, Longwood Div) Allyn.

***Campbell, Linda & Campbell, Bruce.** Multiple Intelligences & Student Achievement: Success Stories from 6 Schools. LC 99-6910. 109p. 1999. pap. 15.95 (*0-87120-360-X*, 199274) ASCD.

Campbell, Linda, et al. The SUM Program Beginning Medical Transcription. 300p. 1994. pap. text 840.00 incl. audio (*0-934385-60-2*) Hlth Prof Inst.

Campbell, Linda, jt. auth. see Campbell, Bruce.

Campbell, Linda C. & Turley, Susan M. Teacher's Manual: The SUM Program Curriculum in Medical Transcription. 2nd rev. ed. 177p. 1992. pap. 95.00 (*0-934385-53-X*) Hlth Prof Inst.

Campbell, Linda C., jt. auth. see Turley, Susan M.

Campbell, Linda E., jt. auth. see Johnston, Janet R.

***Campbell, Lisa.** Jumps, Etc. Jumps, Dressage Arenas & Stable Equipment You Can Build. (Illus.). 96p. 2000. 26.95 (*0-939481-56-1*) Half Halt Pr.

Campbell, Lisa. Michael Jackson: King of Pop. Caso, A., ed. (Illus.). 300p. 1993. reprint ed. 24.95 (*0-8283-1957-X*) Branden Bks.

— Michael Jackson - The King of Pop: His Darkest Hour. Caso, A., ed. (Illus.). 250p. 1994. 24.95 (*0-8283-2003-9*) Branden Bks.

***Campbell, Liz.** The Powwow Calendar: Guide to Native American Gatherings in the U. S. A. & Canada, 2000. 112p. 1999. pap. 9.95 (*1-57067-084-6*) Book Pub Co.

Campbell, Lorne. The Fifteenth-Century Netherlandish Schools. (Illus.). 128p. 1998. 75.00 (*0-300-07701-7*) Yale U Pr.

— Renaissance Portraits: European Portrait - Painting in the 14th, 15th, & 16th Centuries. LC 89-22686. 252p. (C). 1990. 70.00 (*0-300-04675-8*) Yale U Pr.

Campbell, Louis H. The Frightful Fate of Wilhelmina Worthington. 1984. pap. 1.75 (*0-912963-06-9*) Eldridge Pub.

Campbell, Louis W. & Gavin, Claire. The Marshes of Southwestern Lake Erie. LC 94-21052. (Illus.). 247p. 1994. pap. 24.95 (*0-8214-1094-6*) Ohio U Pr.

— The Marshes of Southwestern Lake Erie. LC 94-21052. (Illus.). 247p. 1995. 45.00 (*0-8214-1107-1*) Ohio U Pr.

Campbell, Louisa. A World of Holidays! Family Festivities All over the World. LC 93-22591. (Family Ties Ser.). (Illus.). 64p. (J). (gr. 4-7). 1993. lib. bdg. 14.95 (*1-881889-08-4*) Silver Moon.

Campbell, Louisa & Taylor, Bridget S. Phoebe's Fabulous Father. LC 95-34811. (Illus.). 32p. (J). 1996. 14.00 (*0-15-200996-5*) Harcourt.

Campbell, Louise. Coventry Cathedral: Art & Architecture in Post-War Britain. (Clarendon Studies in the History of Art). (Illus.). 306p. 1996. text 150.00 (*0-19-817519-1*) OUP.

Campbell, Lucile M. On Wings of Power. 35p. (Orig.). 1986. pap. 1.95 (*0-9607114-2-2*) L M Campbell.

— To God Be the Glory. (Orig.). 1981. pap. 1.95 (*0-9607114-0-6*) L M Campbell.

Campbell, Lucille C. Alien Logic. (J). (gr. 4-12). 1992. pap. text 7.97 (*0-937659-56-8*) GCT.

— Missing Pieces. (J). (gr. 4-12). 1992. pap. text 9.97 (*0-937659-55-X*) GCT.

Campbell, Luther & Miller, John R. As Nasty As They Wanna Be: The Uncensored Story of Luther Campbell of the 2 Live Crew. LC 91-42274. 1992. pap. 17.95 (*0-942637-43-7*) Barricade Bks.

***Campbell, Lydia.** London Fitness Guide: The Only Guide You Need to Sports & Fitness Facilities in London, 2000. 512p. 2000. pap. text 24.95 (*1-84000-210-7*) Mitchell Beazley.

Campbell, Lyla, ed. see Wright, Lloyd.

Campbell, Lyle. American Indian Language: The Historical Linguistics of Native America. (Oxford Studies in Anthropological Linguistics: No. 4). (Illus.). 528p. 1997. text 75.00 (*0-19-509427-1*) OUP.

***Campbell, Lyle.** American Indian Languages. (Oxford Studies in Anthropological Linguistics). (Illus.). 528p. 2000. pap. 35.00 (*0-19-514050-8*) OUP.

Campbell, Lyle. Historical Linguistics: An Introduction. LC 98-39549. (Illus.). 396p. 1999. pap. text 30.00 (*0-262-53159-3*) MIT Pr.

— The Pipil Language of El Salvador. (Grammar Library: No. 1). xiv, 957p. 1985. 106.15 (*0-89925-040-8*) Mouton.

Campbell, Lyle, jt. auth. see Harris, Alice C.

Campbell, Lyle, jt. ed. see Justeson, John S.

***Campbell, M.** Classical Greek Prose, a Basic Vocabulary. 120p. (C). 1998. pap. text 16.95 (*1-85399-559-2*, Pub. by Brist Class Pr) Focus Pub-R Pullins.

— Sensor Systems for Environmental Monitoring: Sensor Technologies, Vol. 1 384p. 1996. write for info. (*0-7514-0418-7*) Kluwer Academic.

Campbell, M., ed. Sensor Systems for Environmental Monitoring Vol. 2: Environmental Monitoring, Vol. 2. LC 96-83011. 359p. 1997. write for info. (*0-7514-0419-5*) Kluwer Academic.

Campbell, M. & Macmillan, J. D. Gleanings of Highland Harvest. 8.50 (*0-614-11437-3*, Pub. by Christian Focus) Spring Arbor Dist.

Campbell, M. & McMillan, J. D. Gleanings of Highland Harvest. 8.50 (*1-871676-10-X*, Pub. by Christian Focus) Spring Arbor Dist.

Campbell, M. C. Castle on the Hill. 112p. 1993. pap. 6.00 (*1-880365-50-2*) Prof Pr NC.

Campbell, M. J., ed. Technology & the Rural Community: The Social Impact. LC 87-30345. Orig. Title: New Technology & Rural Development. 432p. 1989. lib. bdg. 55.00 (*0-7099-4864-6*, Pub. by C Helm) Routldge.

Campbell, M. M. Light on the Dark Side of God. 120p. (Orig.). 1989. pap. 6.95 (*0-927022-00-1*) CHJ Pub.

Campbell, Magda, et al. Child & Adolescent Psychopharmacology. (Developmental Clinical Psychology & Psychiatry Ser.: Vol. 2). 1985. 42.00 (*0-8039-2463-1*); pap. 18.95 (*0-8039-2464-X*) Sage.

— Child & Adolescent Psychopharmacology. LC 85-2190. (Developmental Clinical Psychology & Psychiatry Ser.: No. 2). (Illus.). 168p. 1985. reprint ed. pap. 52.10 (*0-7837-9898-9*, 206062400006) Bks Demand.

Campbell, Malcolm. A Commentary of Apollonius Rhodius Argonautica III 1-471. LC 94-29384. (Mnemosyne, Bibliotheca Classica Batava Ser.: Vol. 141). 1994. 152.00 (*90-04-10158-6*) Brill Academic Pubs.

— The DK Pocket Guide to Golf Etiquette. LC 96-38304. (Illus.). 28p. 1998. pap. 18.95 (*0-7894-1467-8*) DK Pub Inc.

Campbell, Malcolm. Greek Prose Reading Course for Post-Beginners Bk. I: Forensic Oratory (Lysias: On the Murder of Eratosthenes) (GRE.). 70p. (C). 1997. pap. text 12.95 (*1-85399-537-1*, Pub. by Brist Class Pr) Focus Pub-R Pullins.

— Greek Prose Reading Course for Post-Beginners Bk. II: Philosophy (Plato: Crito) (GRE.). 74p. (C). 1997. pap. text 12.95 (*1-85399-538-X*, Pub. by Brist Class Pr) Focus Pub-R Pullins.

— Greek Prose Reading Course for Post-Beginners Bk. III: Political Oratory (Demosthenes: Third Philippic) (GRE.). 76p. (C). 1997. pap. text 12.95 (*1-85399-539-8*, Pub. by Brist Class Pr) Focus Pub-R Pullins.

— Greek Prose Reading Course for Post-Beginners Bk. IV: Historiography (Thycydides: Events at Pylos & Sphacteria) (GRE.). 98p. (C). 1997. pap. text 12.95 (*1-85399-540-1*, Pub. by Brist Class Pr) Focus Pub-R Pullins.

Campbell, Malcolm. Kingdom of the Ryans: The Irish in Southwest New South Wales 1816-1890. LC 97-170386. 208p. 1997. pap. 34.95 (*0-86840-191-9*, Pub. by New South Wales Univ Pr) Intl Spec Bk.

— Pietro da Cortona at the Pitti Palace: A Study of the Planetary Rooms & Related Projects. LC 76-3247. (Princeton Monographs in Art & Archaeology: Vol. 41). 426p. 1977. reprint ed. pap. 132.10 (*0-608-04637-X*, 206532400003) Bks Demand.

***Campbell, Malcolm.** The Scottish Golf Book. (Illus.). 224p. 1999. 34.95 (*1-58382-053-1*, Pub. by Sports Masters) Partners-West.

Campbell, Malcolm. Studies in Apollonius Rhodius Argonautica, Bk. III. (Altertumswissenschaftliche Texte und Studien: Vol. 9). (GER.). viii, 131p. 1983. 25.00 (*3-487-07436-2*) G Olms Pubs.

— Ultimate Golf Techniques. LC 95-44327. (Illus.). 216p. 1996. 34.95 (*0-7894-0442-7*) DK Pub Inc.

Campbell, Malcolm, ed. Apollonius Rhodius - Index Verborum of Apollonius Rhodius. (Alpha-Omega, Reihe A Ser.: Bd. LXII). (GER.). viii, 292p. 1983. 80.00 (*3-487-07342-0*) G Olms Pubs.

— Moschus et Bion - Index Verborum in Moschum et Bionem. (Alpha-Omega, Reihe A Ser.: Bd. LXXXIX). (GER.). vi, 96p. 1987. 50.00 (*3-487-07851-1*) G Olms Pubs.

Campbell, Malcolm, ed. see Aratus.

Campbell, Malcolm, ed. see Triphiodorus.

Campbell, Malcolm J. Business Information Services: Some Aspects of Structure, Organisation, & Problems. 2nd fac. ed. LC 82-125825. 179p. 1981. reprint ed. pap. 55.50 (*0-7837-8148-2*, 204795600008) Bks Demand.

— Case Studies in Business Information Provision. fac. ed. LC 83-21011. 126p. 1983. reprint ed. pap. 39.10 (*0-7837-8149-0*, 204795700008) Bks Demand.

Campbell, Malcolm J., ed. Manual of Business Library Practice. 2nd ed. LC 84-43215. 248p. 1985. reprint ed. pap. 76.90 (*0-608-02477-5*, 206312100004) Bks Demand.

***Campbell, Marcia.** An Assessment of the Opportunities for Developing a Mill Reuse Project in California. (Illus.). 250p. (C). 2000. reprint ed. pap. text 35.00 (*0-7881-8583-7*) DIANE Pub.

Campbell, Margaret. Family: A Celebration. LC 95-34486. (Illus.). 192p. 1995. 24.95 (*1-56079-468-2*) Petersons.

Campbell, Margaret, ed. see Stark, Raymond.

***Campbell, Margaret M.** Critical Theory & Liberation Theology: A Comparison of the Intial Work of Jurgen Habermas & Gustavo Gutierrez. LC 99-35082. (American University Studies: Vol. VII). 128p. 1999. 36.95 (*0-8204-2020-4*) P Lang Pubng.

Campbell, Margaret W. Paper Toy Making. LC 75-2570. 96p. 1975. reprint ed. pap. 4.95 (*0-486-21662-4*) Dover.

Campbell, Maria. Half-Breed. 184p. 1973. mass mkt. 8.95 (*0-88780-116-1*, Pub. by Formac Publ Co) Formac Dist Ltd.

— Halfbreed. LC 82-8382. 157p. 1982. reprint ed. pap. 7.95 (*0-8032-6311-2*, Bison Books) U of Nebr Pr.

— People of the Buffalo: How the Plains Indians Lived. (How They Lived Ser.). (Illus.). 48p. (J). (gr. 4-7). 1992. pap. 7.95 (*0-88894-329-6*) Firefly Bks Ltd.

Campbell, Maria, ed. Revolutionary Services & Civil Life of General William Hull. 1972. reprint ed. lib. bdg. 29.50 (*0-8422-8022-7*) Irvington.

Campbell, Maria, jt. auth. see Griffiths, Linda.

***Campbell, Marie.** Tales from the Cloud Walking Country. LC 99-35649. 1999. pap. 14.00 (*0-8203-2186-9*) U of Ga Pr.

Campbell, Marie. Tales from the Cloud Walking Country. LC 76-14944. (Illus.). 270p. 1976. reprint ed. lib. bdg. 38.50 (*0-8371-8607-2*, CATC, Greenwood Pr) Greenwood.

Campbell, Marilyn. Come into My Parlor. 320p. 1992. mass mkt. 4.50 (*0-8217-3933-6*, Zebra Kensgtn) Kensgtn Pub Corp.

— Come into My Parlor. 320p. 1997. mass mkt. 5.99 (*0-7860-0399-5*, Pinncle Kensgtn) Kensgtn Pub Corp.

— Pretty Maids in a Row. 416p. (Orig.). 1995. mass mkt. 5.99 (*0-451-40571-4*, Onyx) NAL.

— Pyramid of Dreams. 368p. 1994. pap. text 4.99 (*0-505-51993-3*, Love Spell) Dorchester Pub Co.

— See How They Run. 1996. pap. 5.99 (*0-614-98079-8*, Onyx) NAL.

— Stardust Dreams. 384p. (Orig.). 1993. mass mkt. 4.99 (*0-451-40413-0*, Topaz) NAL.

— Topaz Dreams. 368p. 1997. mass mkt. 5.50 (*0-505-52181-4*) Dorchester Pub Co.

Campbell, Marilyn, et al. Swept Away. 400p. 1998. mass mkt. 5.50 (*0-8439-4415-3*, Leisure Bks) Dorchester Pub Co.

***Campbell, Marion.** Prowler. 1999. 17.95 (*1-86368-251-1*, Pub. by Fremantle Arts) Intl Spec Bk.

***Campbell, Marjorie W.** The Silent Song: A Daughter's Tribute to a Reluctant Pioneer. (Western Canadian Classics Ser.). 143p. 1999. pap. 9.95 (*1-894004-36-1*) Fifth Hse Publ.

Campbell, Mark. The Art of Hair Work: Hair Braiding & Jewelry of Sentiment. Kliot, Kaethe, ed. 208p. (C). 1996. reprint ed. pap. 20.00 (*0-916896-31-5*) Lacis Pubns.

***Campbell, Mark.** Doctor Who. 2000. pap. 5.95 (*1-903047-19-6*, Pub. by Pocket Essentials) Trafalgar.

Campbell, Mark & Mallemont, A. The Techniques of Ladies' Hairdressing of the 19th Century. Kliot, Jules & Kliot, Kaethe, eds. (Illus.). 144p. 1996. pap. 16.00 (*0-916896-71-4*, LA24) Lacis Pubns.

Campbell, Marsha. About My Impotence or Sainthood. Volbrecht, Robert, ed. & intro. by. 64p. (Orig.). (C). 1995. pap. 8.95 (*0-9625153-7-X*) Freedom Voices Pubns.

— Reply of Our Lady Teresa to the Poet Crashaw on the Occasion of His Having Written a Hymn for Her Sake a Few Years after Her Death. (Illus.). 69p. (Orig.). 1996. pap. 12.00 (*0-9642457-0-1*) Goddesses We Aint.

Campbell, Marsha, et al. Goddesses We Ain't: Tenderloin Women Writers. (Poetry & Prose from San Francisco's Tenderloin District Ser.). (Illus.). 96p. (Orig.). 1992. per. 9.95 (*0-9625153-2-9*) Freedom Voices Pubns.

Campbell, Martha, jt. auth. see Moseley, Fred.

Campbell, Martha, jt. ed. see Moseley, Fred.

Campbell, Martha E. Focus: Writing Paragraphs & Essays. 2nd ed. LC 98-24400. 326p. (C). 1998. pap. text 42.00 (*0-13-896465-3*) P-H.

— Focus: Writing Sentences & Paragraphs. LC 99-11753. 432p. (C). 1999. pap. text 42.00 (*0-13-901141-2*, Macmillan Coll) P-H.

Campbell, Marti & Campbell, Andrew. Swinging Sporran. pap. 11.95 (*0-14-011995-7*, Pub. by Pnguin Bks Ltd) Trafalgar.

Campbell, Marty, ed. see Darklight, Senya.

Campbell, Marty, ed. see Darklight, Senya, et al.

Campbell, Marty, ed. see Gleckler, Walter E.

Campbell, Mary. The Best One Thousand One WordPerfect Tips Ever. 1993. pap., pap. text 39.95 incl. disk (*0-07-881819-2*) Osborne-McGraw.

— Excel at Work. (C). 1992. pap. text. write for info. (*0-201-60851-0*) Addison-Wesley.

— LOTUS GD 1 2 3 FUNCTION. 256p. 1988. pap. 21.95 (*0-201-12948-5*) Addison-Wesley.

— Lotus Guide to 1-2-3-G. 1990. pap. write for info. (*0-201-55068-7*) Addison-Wesley.

— Microsoft Access Answers: Certified Tech Support. (Certified Tech Support Ser.). 352p. 1994. pap. text 16.95 (*0-07-882069-3*) McGraw.

— Quickbooks for Profit. 1993. pap. 24.95 (*0-07-881934-2*) Osborne-McGraw.

— Teach Yourself WordPerfect 6. 2nd ed. 1993. pap. 24.95 (*0-07-881894-X*) Osborne-McGraw.

— Understanding DOS 6. LC 93-10838. 336p. (C). 1993. pap. text 38.67 (*0-13-098393-4*) Prntice Hall Bks.

— WordPerfect for Windows Answers: Certified Tech Support. (Certified Tech Support Ser.). 336p. 1994. pap. 16.95 (*0-07-882053-7*) Osborne-McGraw.

Campbell, Mary & Campbell, David. Quicken 4 for Windows Answers: Certified Tech Support. (Certified Tech Support Ser.). 304p. 1995. pap. text 19.95 (*0-07-882129-0*) Osborne-McGraw.

Campbell, Mary & Campbell, David R. Quicken 6 Made Easy. 478p. 1992. pap. 19.95 (*0-07-881890-7*, QA76.76) Osborne-McGraw.

Campbell, Mary & Lawrence, Gabrielle A. Microsoft Word for Windows 95: The Complete Reference. LC 96-135032. (The Complete Reference Ser.). 880p. 1995. pap. text 29.95 (*0-07-882150-9*) McGraw.

Campbell, Mary, jt. auth. see Campbell, Dave.

Campbell, Mary, ed. see Penner, Mil.

Campbell, Mary B. The Witness & the Other World: Exotic European Travel Writing, 400-1600. LC 88-47720. (Illus.). 312p. 1988. 42.50 (*0-8014-2137-3*); pap. text 16.95 (*0-8014-9933-X*) Cornell U Pr.

— Wonder & Science: Imagining Worlds in Early Modern Europe. LC 99-29103. 1999. 35.00 (*0-8014-3648-6*) Cornell U Pr.

Campbell, Mary B. & Rollins, Mark, eds. Begetting Images: Studies in the Art & Science of Symbol Production. (New Connections: Studies in Interdisciplinarity). XII, 249p. (C). 1989. text 46.95 (*0-8204-1045-4*) P Lang Pubng.

***Campbell, Mary Jane.** Strangers in the House. LC 99-62943. 192p. 1999. pap. 12.00 (*1-57921-199-2*) WinePress Pub.

Campbell, Mary K. Biochemistry. 2nd ed. LC 95-112709. (C). 1994. text 94.50 (*0-03-001872-2*) Harcourt Coll Pubs.

— Biochemistry. 3rd ed. 184p. (C). teacher ed. 26.75 (*0-03-025072-2*) SCP.

— Biochemistry. 3rd rev. ed. (Illus.). 832p. (C). 1998. text 63.00 (*0-03-024426-9*, Pub. by SCP) Harcourt.

— Biochemistry: Student Companion & Problems Book. 3rd ed. 302p. (C). 1998. pap. text, student ed. 29.50 (*0-03-025069-2*, W B Saunders Co) Harcrt Hlth Sci Grp.

Campbell, Mary S. The Well Formed Story: How to Use NLP Processes in a Fictional Format. 100p. 1997. pap. 19.95 (*0-9660177-0-6*) M S Campbell.

Campbell, Mary S., intro. Harlem Renaissance: Art of Black America. LC 93-20814. (Illus.). 200p. 1994. pap. 14.98 (*0-8109-8128-9*, Pub. by Abrams) Time Warner.

Campbell, Mary V. & Campbell, David R. Mastering Harvard Graphics 2.3. LC 92-42891. 1993. write for info. (*0-02-802578-4*) Glencoe.

— Mastering Harvard Graphics 2.3. large type ed. 1993. 158.50 (*0-614-09560-3*, L-31423-00) Am Printing Hse.

Campbell, Mary V., jt. auth. see Campbell, David R.

Campbell, MaryBelle, ed. see McLean, Clifton C.

Campbell, Matthew. Rhythm & Will in Victorian Poetry. LC 98-38095. (Studies in Nineteenth-Century Literature & Culture: No. 22). 288p. (C). 1999. text 59.95 (*0-521-64295-7*) Cambridge U Pr.

Campbell, Maurice. Four Australians at War: Letters to Argyl, 1914-1919. LC 96-162876. 1996. pap. text 16.95 (*0-86417-789-5*, Pub. by Kangaroo Pr) Seven Hills Bk.

Campbell, Mavis C. Back to Africa: George Ross & the Maroons: From Nova Scotia to Sierra Leone. LC 93-12742. 150p. 1993. 39.95 (*0-86543-383-6*); pap. 12.95 (*0-86543-384-4*) Africa World.

— The Dynamics of Change in a Slave Society: A Sociopolitical History of the Free Colored's of Jamaica, 1800-1865. LC 74-4968. 393p. (C). 1976. 38.50 (*0-8386-1584-8*) Fairleigh Dickinson.

— The Maroons of Jamaica. LC 88-70992. 225p. 1992. reprint ed. pap. 14.95 (*0-86543-096-9*) Africa World.

— The Maroons of Jamaica: A History of Resistance, Collaboration & Betrayal. LC 88-10413. 302p. 1988. 65.00 (*0-89789-148-1*, Bergin & Garvey) Greenwood.

Campbell, Meg. Solo Crossing. LC 99-70238. (Poetry Ser.). (Illus.). 96p. 1999. pap. 12.00 (*1-877675-31-8*) Midmarch Arts.

***Campbell, Meg & Duke, William, eds.** Split Verse: Poems to Heal Your Heart. LC 00-130315. (Poetry Ser.). (Illus.). 85p. 2000. pap. 14.00 (*1-877675-35-0*) Midmarch Arts.

Campbell, Michael. Lord Dismiss Us. LC 83-18173. (Phoenix Fiction Ser.). 384p. 1993. pap. 9.95 (*0-226-09244-5*) U Ch Pr.

***Campbell, Michael.** Nothing but Net: How I Generated $750,000 in Internet Revenues with Virtually No Advertising Costs. 97p. 1999. ring bd. 68.00 (*1-930336-04-7*) Adnet Intl.

Campbell, Michael D. Building Results: New Tolls for an Age of Discovery in Government. LC 94-19016. 1994. 15.95 (*0-934842-31-0*) CSPA.

Campbell, Michael D., jt. auth. see Brizius, Jack A.

Campbell, Michael H. & Brewer, Edward C., eds. Railway Labor Act of 1926: A Legislative History, 4 vols., Set. deluxe ed. LC 88-81073. 1988. 425.00 (*0-89941-641-1*, 305610) W S Hein.

Campbell, Michael J. John Martin: Visionary Printmaker. 212p. 1993. pap. 86.95 (*0-9519387-0-3*, Pub. by Scolar Pr) Ashgate Pub Co.

Campbell, Mike. Dandy the Chipbear's . . . Fun Day at Dad's. (Adventures of Dandy Ser.: No. 1). (Illus.). 28p. (J). (ps-1). 1997. pap. text. write for info. (*0-9660574-0-6*) Dandy Creations.

— Sightsinging: The Complete Method for Singers. 160p. 1998. otabind 16.95 (*0-7935-8191-5*) H Leonard.

Campbell, Mike & Duffy, Katherine. Local Labour Markets: Problems & Policies. LC 93-162543. ix, 202p. 1992. pap. 20.00 (*0-582-09103-9*) Longman.

Campbell, Mike, et al. Patterns of Social & Technological Change in Europe. 336p. 1994. 72.95 (*1-85628-608-8*, Pub. by Avebry) Ashgate Pub Co.

Campbell, Mildred. English Yeoman. (C). 1983. pap. 9.95 (*0-85036-289-X*, Pub. by MRLN) Paul & Co Pubs.

Campbell, Milton H., ed. High Level Radioactive Waste Management. LC 76-25020. (Advances in Chemistry Ser.: No. 153). 1976. 32.95 (*0-8412-0270-2*) Am Chemical.

— High-Level Radioactive Waste Management. LC 76-25020. (Advances in Chemistry Ser.: Vol. 153). 408p. 1976. reprint ed. pap. 126.50 (*0-608-03890-3*, 206433700008) Bks Demand.

Campbell, Mirian. Decorative Ironwork. (Illus.). 128p. 1998. 35.00 (*0-8109-3241-5*, Pub. by Abrams) Time Warner.

Campbell-Mohn, Celia, et al, eds. Hornbook on Environmental Law: From Resources to Recovery. (Hornbook Ser.). 994p. (C). 1993. text 39.50 (*0-314-02229-5*) West Pub.

Campbell, Molly. Rhode Island 1998 Advance Legislative Service, 3 vols. 1800p. 1998. pap. 80.00 (*0-327-06110-3*, 47795-14) LEXIS Pub.

Campbell, Molly, ed. Rhode Island, 1998 Advance Legislative Service Pamphlet, No. 1. 600p. 1998. pap. write for info. (*0-327-06111-1*, 47796-14) LEXIS Pub.

— Rhode Island, 1998 Advance Legislative Service Pamphlet, No. 2. 600p. 1998. pap. write for info. (*0-327-06112-X*, 47797-14) LEXIS Pub.

— Rhode Island, 1998 Advance Legislative Service Pamphlet, No. 3. 600p. 1998. pap. write for info. (*0-327-06113-8*, 47798-14) LEXIS Pub.

Campbell, Monty. How to Manage a Doctor's Office. 75p. (Orig.). (C). 1989. pap. 6.50 (*1-877718-02-5*) Archangel Pr.

— How to Start a Child-Care Center. 75p. (Orig.). (C). 1989. pap. 7.00 (*1-877718-01-7*) Archangel Pr.

— Injured Workers in California: The Injured Worker's Guidebook. 103p. (Orig.). (C). 1989. pap. 9.00 (*1-877718-00-9*) Archangel Pr.

— The Vocational Rehabilitation Business: A Case-Management & Business Start-Up. 136p. (Orig.). 1992. pap. 17.50 (*1-877718-04-1*) Archangel Pr.

Campbell, Monty & Gruppioni, Fabrizio. So, You Want to Own a Restaurant? The Dream, the Steps, the Reality. 110p. (C). 1989. pap. 7.50 (*1-877718-03-3*) Archangel Pr.

Campbell, Morag. Writing about Travel. 2nd ed. 112p. 1996. pap. write for info. (*0-7136-4174-6*, Pub. by A & C Blk) Midpt Trade.

Campbell, Mozelle J., et al. Plano, Texas: The Early Years. (Illus.). ix, 402p. 1986. 32.00 (*0-9651841-0-2*) Frnds Plano Public Lbry.

— Plano, Texas: The Early Years. (Illus.). 402p. 1986. reprint ed. lthr. 100.00 (*0-9651841-1-0*) Frnds Plano Public Lbry.

Campbell, N., et al. Biology: Concepts & Connections. 2nd ed. (C). 1996. 18.00 (*0-8053-2025-3*) Benjamin-Cummings.

***Campbell, Nancy.** Using Women: Gender, Drug Policy & Social Justice. LC 99-87644. 256p. 2000. write for info. (*0-415-92412-X*) Routledge.

Campbell, Nancy. Writing Effective Policies & Procedures: A Step-by-Step Resource for Clear Communication. LC 97-40744. 320p. 1997. spiral bd. 60.00 (*0-8144-7960-X*) AMACOM.

Campbell, Nancy, jt. auth. see Peterson, Christine E.

Campbell, Nancy C. The German Shorthaired Pointer: An Owner's Guide Happy Healthy Pet. LC 99-14625. (Illus.). 158p. 1999. 12.95 (*1-58245-058-7*) Howell Bks.

***Campbell, Nancy D.** Using Women: Gender, Drug Policy & Social Justice. LC 99-87644. 256p. 2000. pap. 19.95 (*0-415-92413-8*) Routledge.

Campbell, Nancy D., ed. see Technical Committee on Earnings Sharing Staff.

Campbell, Nancy R., jt. auth. see Lyman, Robert D.

Campbell, Naomi. Swan. 357p. 1994. pap. 20.00 (*0-434-00097-3*) Buttrwrth-Heinemann.

— Swan. 407p. 1996. pap. 5.99 (*0-7493-2208-X*) Buttrwrth-Heinemann.

Campbell, Neil. Biology: Concepts & Applications. 2nd ed. (C). 1996. student ed., lab manual ed. 110.75 (*0-8053-2102-0*) Benjamin-Cummings.

— Biology: Concepts & Connections. 2nd ed. LC 96-24104. (C). 1997. text 77.81 incl. disk (*0-8053-2022-9*) Addison-Wesley.

— Biology: Concepts & Connections. 2nd ed. 880p. (C). 1998. text 83.00 (*0-8053-6512-5*) Addison-Wesley.

— Biology - Interactive Guide. 5th ed. LC 98-45707. 1175p. (C). 1998. 102.00 (*0-8053-3044-5*) Benjamin-Cummings.

— Biology with the Interactive Study Guide. 4th ed. (C). 1996. pap. text, student ed. 81.57 incl. cd-rom (*0-8053-6678-4*) Benjamin-Cummings.

— Biology 5e School Edition. 5th ed. 1280p. (C). 1999. text 87.00 (*0-8053-6566-4*) Addison-Wesley.

— Interactive Study Guide to Biology Concepts & Connections. 2nd ed. (C). 1996. text 8.20 (*0-8053-2019-9*) Benjamin-Cummings.

— Internet Guide for Biology. 5th ed. (C). 1999. pap. text. write for info. (*0-8053-6694-6*) Benjamin-Cummings.

Campbell, Neil & Kean, Alasdair. American Cultural Studies: An Introduction to American Culture. LC 97-2113. (Illus.). 328p. (C). 1998. 80.00 (*0-415-12797-1*); pap. 24.99 (*0-415-12798-X*) Routledge.

Campbell, Neil A. Biology. LC 92-45736. (Series in the Life Sciences). (C). 1993. student ed., spiral bd. 38.44 (*0-8053-1830-5*) Benjamin-Cummings.

— Biology. 2nd ed. Williams, Robin, ed. (C). 1990. text 72.75 (*0-8053-1800-3*) Benjamin-Cummings.

— Biology. 3rd ed. LC 92-45736. (Series in the Life Sciences). (C). 1993. pap. text, student ed. 23.44 (*0-8053-1881-X*) Benjamin-Cummings.

***Campbell, Neil A.** Biology: Concepts & Connections. 3rd ed. LC 99-23620. 860p. (C). 1999. 87.00 incl. cd-rom (*0-8053-6585-0*) Benjamin-Cummings.

Campbell, Neil A. Biology Concepts & Connections. 2nd ed. (C). 1996. text 76.00 (*0-8053-2058-X*) Addison-Wesley.

— Biology Concepts & Connections. 2nd ed. (C). 1997. text 69.33 incl. cd-rom (*0-8053-2048-2*) Benjamin-Cummings.

***Campbell, Neil A.** Biology Concepts & Connections. 3rd unabridged ed. (C). 2000. text 83.00 (*0-8053-6599-0*) Benjamin-Cummings.

— Biology Concepts & Connections Study Guide. 3rd ed. 480p. (C). 2000. pap. text, student ed. 19.50 (*0-8053-6587-7*) Benjamin-Cummings.

Campbell, Neil A. Biology School Edition. 4th ed. 1296p. (C). 1996. text 91.00 (*0-8053-1957-3*) Addison-Wesley.

Campbell, Neil A., et al. Biology: Concepts & Connections. LC 93-30071. (C). 1994. pap. text, student ed. 23.44 (*0-8053-0921-7*) Benjamin-Cummings.

— Biology: Concepts & Connections. LC 93-30071. 544p. (C). 1994. spiral bd., lab manual ed. 60.00 (*0-8053-0922-5*) Benjamin-Cummings.

Campbell-Nelson, John. Indonesia in Shadow & Light. LC 97-37534. 1998. 9.45 (*0-377-00321-2*) Friendship Pr.

Campbell-Nelson, Karen. Leader's Guide to "Indonesia in Shadow & Light" (Illus.). 48p. 1998. pap., teacher ed. 6.95 (*0-377-00322-0*) Friendship Pr.

Campbell, Nick, ed. see Higuchi, Norio.

Campbell, Nicola, et al. International Network of Public Libraries, 6 vols. (Illus.). 832p. 1999. pap. 110.00 (*0-8108-3575-4*) Scarecrow.

— International Network of Public Libraries Vol. 1: Organizational Change in a Public Library: A Case Study: Strategic Management for Better Customer Service in Public Libraries. LC 99-12675. (Illus.). 160p. 1999. pap. 22.00 (*0-8108-3576-2*) Scarecrow.

Campbell, Nigel, ed. Advances in Chinese Industrial Studies, Vol. 6. 1998. 78.50 (*0-7623-0315-8*) Jai Pr.

— Advances in Chinese Industrial Studies Vol. 5: A Coming of Age: Developments in Sino-Foreign Joint Ventures. 372p. 1997. 78.50 (*1-55938-961-3*) Jai Pr.

Campbell, Nigel, et al, eds. Advances in Chinese Industrial Studies, Vol. 2. 267p. 1991. 78.50 (*1-55938-141-8*) Jai Pr.

— Advances in Chinese Industrial Studies: Changes in the Iron Rice Bowl, Vol. 3. 313p. 1993. 78.50 (*1-55938-478-6*) Jai Pr.

C

An Asterisk (*) at the beginning of an entry indicates that the title is appearing for the first time.

— Advances in Chinese Industrial Studies: Joint Ventures & Industrial Change in China, Vol. 1, Pt. B. 318p. 1989. 78.50 (*1-55938-056-X*) Jai Pr.

— Advances in Chinese Industrial Studies: Reform Policy & the Chinese Enterprise, Vol. 1, Pt. A. 367p. 1989. 78.50 (*1-55938-053-5*) Jai Pr.

— Advances in Chinese Industrial Studies Vol. 1: Joint Ventures & Industrial Change in China, 2 pts. 1989. 157.00 (*1-55938-048-9*) Jai Pr.

Campbell, Nigel A. Return to Kairi: A Trinidad & Tobago Journey. (Illus.). 136p. 1998. 40.00 (*976-8106-01-8*) Jett Samm.

***Campbell, Nina.** Nina Campbell's Decorating Secrets: 100 Ways to Achieve a Professional Look. (Illus.). 176p. 2000. 40.00 (*0-609-60675-1*) C Potter.

Campbell, Norine D. Patrick Henry: Patriot & Statesman. (Illus.). 1969. 24.95 (*0-8159-6501-X*) Devin.

Campbell, Olav P. My Sixty Years with Norwegian Elghunds. (Illus.). 124p. 1988. 27.95 (*0-9621512-0-3*) Show Quality Pet Prod.

***Campbell, Olav P.** Solving the Puzzle of Revelation. 132p. 1999. pap. 12.95 (*0-7880-0989-3*) CSS.

Campbell, Olivia, jt. auth. see Shevlin, Philip B.

Campbell, Olwen W. Shelley & the Unromantics. LC 68-1189. (Studies in Shelley: No. 25). 1969. reprint ed. lib. bdg. 75.00 (*0-8383-0652-7*) M S G Haskell Hse.

— Thomas Love Peacock. LC 73-157327. (Select Bibliographies Reprint Ser.). 1977. reprint ed. 17.95 (*0-8369-5787-3*) Ayer.

Campbell, Oscar & Quinn, George, eds. Reader's Encyclopedia of Shakespeare. LC 97-75620. 1014p. 1998. reprint ed. 14.98 (*1-56731-257-8*, MJF Bks) Fine Comms.

Campbell, Oscar J. The Comedies of Holberg. LC 68-20216. 1972. reprint ed. 24.95 (*0-405-08339-4*, Pub. by Blom Pubns) Ayer.

— Comicall Satyre & Shakespeare's Troilus & Cressida. LC 39-1295. (Huntington Library Publications). 256p. reprint ed. pap. 79.40 (*0-7837-6676-9*, 204629200011) Bks Demand.

— Shakespeare's Satire. LC 74-159036. 239p. (C). 1971. reprint ed. 50.00 (*0-87752-150-6*) Gordian.

Campbell, Oscar J. & Pyre, J. F., eds. Great English Poets. LC 77-152147. (Granger Index Reprint Ser.). 1977. reprint ed. 66.95 (*0-8369-6250-8*) Ayer.

Campbell, Oscar J. & Rice, Richard A., eds. Book of Narratives. LC 72-5901. (Short Story Index Reprint Ser.). 1977. reprint ed. 30.95 (*0-8369-4196-9*) Ayer.

Campbell, Oscar J., ed. see Alden, Raymond M.

Campbell, Oscar J., ed. see Bos, Lambert Van Den.

Campbell, P. G., jt. auth. see Coval, S. C.

Campbell, P. N. & Marshall, R. D., eds. Essays in Biochemistry, Vol. 20. (Serial Publication Ser.). 1985. pap. text 62.00 (*0-12-158120-9*) Acad Pr.

Campbell, Pam. The Church You've Always Longed For: Small Group Guide. (Orig.). 1996. pap., wbk. ed. 8.00 (*1-57849-012-X*) Chapel of Air.

Campbell, Pam. Hands Up Art Activities: Week-by-Week Projects Using Hand-Shaped Art. Mitchell, Judy, ed. (Illus.). 112p. (Orig.). (J). (gr. k-3). 1995. pap., teacher ed. 10.95 (*1-57310-028-5*) Teachng & Lrning Co.

Campbell, Pam. Untapped Miracles for Tapped-Out Christians: Small Group Leader's Guide. Davis, Brad & Oliver, Marian, eds. (Nineteen Ninety-Eight Fifty-Day Spiritual Adventure Ser.). (Illus.). 1997. wbk. ed. 8.00 (*1-57849-052-9*) Mainstay Church.

Campbell, Pam & Campbell, Stan. Let There Be Life. LC 92-487. (BibleLog Ser.). 180p. (Orig.). 1992. pap. 7.99 (*0-89693-871-9*, 6-1871, Victor Bks) Chariot Victor.

— Tunes, Tales, & Truths. (BibleLog Ser.). 180p. (Orig.). 1992. pap. 7.99 (*0-89693-873-5*, 6-1873, Victor Bks) Chariot Victor.

— Watchmen Who Wouldn't Quit. (BibleLog Ser.). 180p. (Orig.). 1992. pap. 8.99 (*0-89693-874-3*, 6-1874, Victor Bks) Chariot Victor.

— Who's Running This Kingdom? (BibleLog Ser.). 180p. (Orig.). 1992. pap. 7.99 (*0-89693-872-7*, 6-1872, Victor Bks) Chariot Victor.

Campbell, Pam & Gruben, Nancy. Adventuring with Friends & Family Pamphlet. (Nineteen Ninety-Seven 50-Day Spiritual Adventure Ser.). (Orig.). 1996. pap. 6.00 (*1-57849-021-9*) Chapel of Air.

Campbell, Pam, et al. Improving Social Competence: A Resource for Elementary School Teachers. LC 93-31685. 384p. (C). 1994. pap. text 60.00 (*0-205-13757-1*, Longwood Div) Allyn.

Campbell, Pam, jt. auth. see Burns, Ridge.

Campbell, Pamela T., jt. auth. see Hughes, Donna R.

Campbell, Pat. Blade of Grass. (C). 1988. 60.00 (*0-86236-102-8*, Pub. by Granary) St Mut.

***Campbell, Pat & Burnaby, Barbara, eds.** Participatory Practices in Adult Education. 320p. 2001. write for info. (*0-8058-3704-3*) L Erlbaum Assocs.

***Campbell, Pat & Burnaby, Barbara J., eds.** Participatory Practices in Adult Education. 320p. 2001. pap. write for info. (*0-8058-3705-1*) L Erlbaum Assocs.

***Campbell, Patricia B. & Ayars, Mimi.** The Best of Jacobean Applique Vol. 3: Includes Exotica & Romantica Patterns. Pyron, Cherry, ed. (Illus.). 176p. 2000. pap. 24.95 (*1-57432-738-0*, Am Quilters Soc) Collector Bks.

Campbell, Patricia B. & Ayars, Mimi. Theorem Applique Bk. I: Abundant Harvest. Johnson, Janice P., ed. LC 94-31563. (Illus.). 40p. (Orig.). 1994. pap. 11.95 (*0-9622565-9-5*) Chitra Pubns.

— Theorem Applique Bk. II: Summer Splendor. Johnson, Janice P., ed. LC 94-31563. (Illus.). 36p. (Orig.). 1995. pap. 11.95 (*1-885588-03-8*) Chitra Pubns.

Campbell, Patricia B. & Ayers, Mimi. Jacobean Rhapsodies: Composing with 28 Applique Designs. LC 98-6691. (Illus.). 160p. 1998. pap. 27.95 (*1-57120-049-5*, 10173) C & T Pub.

Campbell, Patricia B. & Jack, Michelle L. Red Hot Chili Peppers Quilting. (Illus.). 48p. 1994. 12.95 (*0-614-06711-1*) Tex Stars.

Campbell, Patricia J. Presenting Robert Cormier. rev. ed. (Twayne's United States Authors Ser.: No. 496). 142p. (C). 1989. 28.00 (*0-8057-8212-5*, Twayne) Mac Lib Ref.

Campbell, Patricia J. & Mahoney-Norris, Kathleen, eds. Democratization & the Protection of Human Rights: Challenges & Contradictions. LC 98-11128. 160p. 1998. 49.95 (*0-275-96231-8*, Praeger Pubs) Greenwood.

Campbell, Patricia S. Music in Cultural Context: Eight Views on World Music Education. (Illus.). 88p. (Orig.). 1996. pap. 16.50 (*1-56545-100-7*, 1634) MENC.

— Songs in Their Heads: Music & Its Meaning in Children's Lives. (Illus.). 264p. 1998. text 49.95 (*0-19-511100-1*) OUP.

— Songs in Their Heads: Music & Its Meanings in Children's Lives. (Illus.). 264p. 1998. pap. 18.95 (*0-19-511101-X*) OUP.

— Sounds of the World: Music of Eastern Europe (Teacher's Guide) (Sounds of the World Ser.). (Illus.). 5p. 1989. pap., teacher ed. write for info. incl. audio (*0-940796-70-8*, 3038) MENC.

Campbell, Patricia S. & McCarthy, Marie. Cross Currents: Setting an Agenda for Music Education in Community Culture. LC 96-45344. 1996. 12.00 (*0-9655233-0-6*) Univ MD Coll Pk.

Campbell, Patricia S. & Scott-Kassner, Carol. Music in Childhood: From Preschool Through the Elementary Grades. LC 94-30663. (Illus.). 384p. 1995. 38.00 (*0-02-870552-1*, Schirmer Books) Mac Lib Ref.

Campbell, Patricia S., et al. Roots & Branches: A Legacy of Multicultural Music for Children. LC 94-39274. (Illus.). 153p. (Orig.). 1994. pap. 24.95 incl. audio (*0-937203-52-1*); pap. 29.95 incl. audio compact disk (*0-937203-55-6*) World Music Pr.

Campbell, Patricia S., jt. auth. see Anderson, William M.

Campbell, Patricia S., jt. auth. see Han, Kuo-huana.

Campbell, Patricia S., jt. auth. see Kuo-huang Han.

Campbell, Patricia S., jt. auth. see Nguyen, Phong.

Campbell, Patricia S., jt. auth. see Sam, Sam-Ang.

Campbell, Patrick. My Life & Some Letters. LC 71-173104. (Illus.). 1972. reprint ed. 30.95 (*0-405-08340-8*, Pub. by Blom Pubns) Ayer.

— Siefgried Sassoon: A Study of the War Poetry. 237p. 1999. lib. bdg. 35.00 (*0-7864-0525-2*) McFarland & Co.

***Campbell, Patrick.** The Tides of Wight: A Sherlock Holmes Drama. (Sherlockian Scholarship Ser.). 1999. 25.00 (*1-55246-062-2*) Battered Silicon.

Campbell, Patrick. Travels in the Interior Inhabited Parts of North America in the Years 1791 & 1792, Vol. 23. Langton, H. H., ed. LC 68-28611. 326p. 1968. reprint ed. lib. bdg. 75.00 (*0-8371-5061-2*, CATI, Greenwood Pr) Greenwood.

Campbell, Patrick, ed. Analyzing Performance: Issues & Interpretations. LC 95-12859. (Illus.). 413p. 1996. text 79.95 (*0-7190-4249-6*); text 29.95 (*0-7190-4250-X*, Pub. by Manchester Univ Pr) St Martin.

***Campbell, Patrick H.** Tunnel Tigers. (Illus.). 200p. 2000. pap. 13.95 (*0-9637701-1-X*) P H Campbell.

Campbell, Patrick J. How to Share Christ with a Jehovah's Witness. (Illus.). 56p. (Orig.). 1991. pap. write for info. (*0-925703-30-3*) Crown MA.

Campbell, Patrick J. Shades of Sherlock. LC 98-108768. (Illus.). 230p. 1997. 25.00 (*1-896648-69-X*) Battered Silicon.

Campbell, Patrick L. Priceless Guide to the Antique Business. (Illus.). 128p. (Orig.). 1994. pap. 5.95 (*0-89538-066-8*) L-W Inc.

Campbell, Patrick T. Networking the Small Office. LC 95-72478. 384p. 1995. pap. 29.99 (*0-7821-1790-2*, Network Pr) Sybex.

Campbell, Patty. Two Pioneers of Young Adult Library Services. LC 98-34918. (VOYA Occasional Papers Ser.). 48p. 1998. pap. 14.00 (*0-8108-3423-5*) Scarecrow.

Campbell, Patty, jt. auth. see Shore, David.

Campbell, Patty G., jt. auth. see White, Jane F.

Campbell, Paul. Plastic Component Design. 1996. 40.95 (*0-8311-3065-2*) Indus Pr.

— Population Projections for States, by Age, Sex, Race & Hispanic Origin: 1993-2020. (Illus.). 105p. (Orig.). (C). 1994. pap. text 40.00 (*0-7881-1007-1*) DIANE Pub.

***Campbell, Paul.** Survival Skills of Native California. LC 99-24412. (Illus.). 448p. 1999. pap. 39.95 (*0-87905-921-4*) Gibbs Smith Pub.

Campbell, Paul. Tori Amos: Collectibles. LC 97-197636. (Illus.). 160p. 1997. pap. 29.95 (*0-8256-1578-X*, OP 47869) Omnibus NY.

Campbell, Paul & Howard, Peter. The Strategy of St. Paul. Orig. Title: A Story of Effective Statesmanship. 85p. (Orig.). 1985. reprint ed. pap. 2.95 (*0-901269-69-7*) Grosvenor USA.

Campbell, Paul, ed. see Hopkins, Stephen.

Campbell, Paul B. & Panzano, Phyllis. Toward Excellence in Secondary Vocational Education: Elements of Program Quality. 35p. 1985. 4.75 (*0-318-22217-5*, IN291) Ctr Educ Trng Employ.

Campbell, Paul D. Astronomy & the Maya Calendar Correlation. (Illus.). 127p. (Orig.). (C). 1992. pap. 30.80 (*0-89412-194-4*) Aegean Park Pr.

— Basic Fixture Design. LC 93-33165. 170p. 1994. text 31.50 (*0-8311-3052-0*) Indus Pr.

— The Humboldt Celt: Key to the Lost Olmec World. (Illus.). 192p. (Orig.). 1992. pap. 28.80 (*0-89412-190-1*) Aegean Park Pr.

— An Introduction to Measuration & Calibration. LC 94-31185. (Illus.). 208p. 1995. pap. 25.95 (*0-8311-3060-1*) Indus Pr.

Campbell, Paul G., Jr., ed. see Minerals, Metals & Materials Society Staff.

Campbell, Paul G., ed. see Zimmerman, D. Patrick.

Campbell, Paul J., ed. UMAP Modules: Tools for Teaching, 1990. (Illus.). 184p. 1991. pap. text 35.00 (*0-912843-19-5*) COMAP Inc.

— Umap Modules: Tools for Teaching, 1992. (Illus.). 230p. 1993. pap. text 35.00 (*0-912843-28-4*) COMAP Inc.

— UMAP Modules: Tools for Teaching, 1993. (Illus.). 208p. 1994. pap. text 35.00 (*0-912843-37-3*) COMAP Inc.

Campbell, Paul J., ed. see COMAP, Inc. Staff.

Campbell, Paul J., ed. see COMAP Inc. Staff.

Campbell, Paul J., jt. ed. see Grinstein, Louise S.

Campbell, Paul J., jt. ed. see Straffin, Philip D., Jr.

Campbell, Paul N. Form & the Art of Theatre. LC 84-71037. 136p. 1984. 17.95 (*0-87972-279-7*); pap. 9.95 (*0-87972-280-0*) Bowling Green Univ Popular Press.

Campbell, Paula H. Health Care & Peer Review: Index of New Information & Bibliography. 150p. 1996. 47.50 (*0-7883-0994-3*); pap. 44.50 (*0-7883-0995-1*) ABBE Pubs Assn.

***Campbell, Pauline.** I Can Touch a Rainbow. 1999. pap. write for info. (*1-58235-257-7*) Watermrk Pr.

***Campbell, Peg, ed.** Lightning Strikes Twice: Franklin: The Key to the New Millennium. (Illus.). 240p. 1999. pap. 13.95 (*1-891722-03-4*) Am Hist Co.

Campbell, Penelope. Maryland in Africa: The Maryland State Colonization Society, 1831-1857. LC 75-131058. 272p. reprint ed. pap. 84.40 (*0-608-14869-5*, 202591500047) Bks Demand.

Campbell, Persia. The Consumer Interest: A Study in Consumer Economics. LC 75-17213. (Social Problems & Social Policy Ser.). 1976. reprint ed. 54.95 (*0-405-07485-9*) Ayer.

Campbell, Persia C. Chinese Coolie Emigration to Countries Within the British Empire. 240p. 1971. reprint ed. 35.00 (*0-7146-2000-9*, Pub. by F Cass Pubs) Intl Spec Bk.

— Chinese Coolie Emigration to Countries Within the British Empire. LC 70-88402. 240p. 1969. reprint ed. lib. bdg. 59.50 (*0-8371-1751-8*, CCE&) Greenwood.

***Campbell, Peter.** Canadian Marxists & the Search for a Third Way. 312p. 1999. text 34.95 (*0-7735-1848-7*) McG-Queens Univ Pr.

Campbell, Peter. Launch Day. (Illus.). 32p. (J). (gr. 2-4). 1995. pap. 7.95 (*1-56294-190-9*); lib. bdg. 21.40 (*1-56294-611-0*) Millbrook Pr.

— Louis XIV. 184p. (C). 1995. pap. 15.00 (*0-582-01770-X*) Addison-Wesley.

Campbell, Peter, jt. auth. see Cole, Alistair.

Campbell, Peter A. Alien Encounters. LC 99-25360. 48p. (J). (gr. 4-8). 2000. lib. bdg. 23.90 (*0-7613-1402-4*) Millbrook Pr.

Campbell, Peter A. & McMahon, Edwin M. Bio-Spirituality: Focusing As a Way to Grow. 2nd ed. LC 96-39189. 213p. 1997. pap. 10.95 (*0-8294-0937-8*) Loyola Pr.

Campbell, Peter A., jt. auth. see McMahon, Edwin M.

***Campbell, Peter N.** Biochemistry Illustrated. 4th ed. 2000. text. write for info. (*0-443-06217-X*, W B Saunders Co) Harcrt Hlth Sci Grp.

Campbell, Peter N. & Smith, Anthony D. Biochemistry Illustrated. 2nd ed. (Illus.). 288p. 1988. pap. text 37.00 (*0-443-03454-0*) Church.

— Biochemistry Illustrated: An Illustrated Summary of the Subject for Medical & Other Students of Biochemistry. 3rd ed. LC 93-3365. (Illus.). 336p. 1994. pap. text 28.95 (*0-443-04573-9*) Church.

Campbell, Peter Scott, jt. auth. see Whiteman, Michael.

***Campbell, Phil & Smith, Bryson.** Old Testament: God's Unfolding Promise. (Faith Walk Bible Studies). 80p. 2000. 4.99 (*1-58134-145-8*) Crossway Bks.

Campbell, Phyllis. Friendships in the Dark: A Blind Woman's Story of the People & Pets Who Light up Her World. LC 96-2412. 216p. 1996. 18.95 (*0-9636620-4-X*) Brett Bks.

— Friendships in the Dark: A Blind Woman's Story of the People & Pets Who Light up Her World. large type ed. LC 99-18404. 267p. 1999. 25.95 (*0-7838-8587-3*, G K Hall & Co) Mac Lib Ref.

Campbell, Phyllis, jt. auth. see Burton, Stephanie K.

***Campbell-Platt, Geoffrey.** Fermented Foods of the World. 2nd ed. 376p. 2000. text 270.00 (*1-85573-502-4*, Pub. by Woodhead Pubng) Am Educ Systs.

Campbell, Praed. The Brother of the Shadow: A Mystery of Today. Reginald, R. & Menville, Douglas A., eds. LC 76-1539. (Supernatural & Occult Fiction Ser.). 1976. reprint ed. 17.95 (*0-405-08162-6*) Ayer.

Campbell, Previti. Teachers, Students Activities Are Newsmakers. 2.00 (*0-318-19220-9*) Quill & Scroll.

Campbell, R. Biological Control of Microbial Plant Pathogens. (Illus.). 228p. (C). 1989. text 69.95 (*0-521-34088-8*) Cambridge U Pr.

— Biological Control of Microbial Plant Pathogens. (Illus.). 228p. (C). 1989. pap. text 24.95 (*0-521-34900-1*) Cambridge U Pr.

— The Christian Home. pap. 4.95 (*0-88172-006-2*) Believers Bkshelf.

— Complete Guide & Descriptive Books of Mexico. 1976. lib. bdg. 59.95 (*0-8490-1654-1*) Gordon Pr.

— Hearing by Eye II: The Psychology of Speechreading & Auditory-Visual Speech. LC 98-136135. 319p. 1998. 64.95 (*0-86377-502-0*, Pub. by Psychol Pr) Taylor & Francis.

— Statistics for Biologists. 3rd ed. 464p. (C). 1989. pap. text 29.95 (*0-521-36932-0*) Cambridge U Pr.

Campbell, R. & Bagshaw, M. Human Performance & Limitations. 1991. pap. 34.95 (*0-632-02929-3*) Blackwell Sci.

Campbell, R., tr. see Allameh Sayyed Mohammad Hosayn Tabatabai.

Campbell, R., tr. see Mutahhari, Ayatullah M.

Campbell, R., tr. see Shariati, Ali.

Campbell, R., tr. see Taleghani, Sayyid M.

Campbell, R. Alastair. The Elders: Seniority Within Earliest Christianity. (Studies in the New Testament & Its World). 288p. 1994. text 49.95 (*0-567-09702-1*, Pub. by T & T Clark) Bks Intl VA.

***Campbell, R. D. & Bagshaw, M.** Human Performance & Limitations in Aviation. 2nd ed. LC 99-88747. 2000. pap. write for info. (*0-632-04986-3*) Blackwell Sci.

Campbell, R. D., jt. ed. see Hall, R. J.

Campbell, R. G. Scotch-Irish Family Research Made Simple. rev. ed. (Illus.). 65p. 1992. pap. 10.00 (*1-878311-14-X*, Heritge House) Ye Olde Genealogie Shoppe.

— State Supervision & Regulation of Budgetary Procedure in Public School Systems: An Evaluation of State Provisions for Budget-Making in Local School Systems. LC 73-176625. (Columbia University. Teachers College. Contributions to Education Ser.: No. 637). reprint ed. 37.50 (*0-404-55637-X*) AMS Pr.

Campbell, R. H. Owners & Occupiers: Changes in Rural Society in South-West Scotland Before 1914. (Aberdeen University Press Bks.). 192p. 1991. text 29.90 (*0-08-041218-1*, Pub. by Aberdeen U Pr) Macmillan.

— Scotland since 1707. 3rd ed. 288p. (C). 1996. pap. 45.00 (*0-85976-122-3*, Pub. by J Donald) St Mut.

Campbell, R. H. & Skinner, Andrew S. Adam Smith. LC 82-3308. 231p. 1982. 32.50 (*0-312-00423-0*) St Martin.

Campbell, R. H., ed. see Smith, Adam.

Campbell, R. J. The Story of Christmas. 1977. lib. bdg. 59.95 (*0-8490-2677-6*) Gordon Pr.

Campbell, R. J., ed. Breadth & Balance in the Primary Curriculum. 208p. 1993. 99.95 (*0-7507-0179-X*, Falmer Pr); pap. 34.95 (*0-7507-0180-3*, Falmer Pr) Taylor & Francis.

— The Routledge Compendium of Primary Education. LC 88-2731. (Education Bks.). 263p. reprint ed. pap. 81.60 (*0-608-20326-2*, 207157900002) Bks Demand.

Campbell, R. J. & Zimmerman, L. E. WHO-Histological Typing of Tumours of the Eye & Its Adnexa. 2nd rev. ed. LC 98-26176. (International Histological Classification of Tumors Ser.). (Illus.). 130p. 1998. pap. 75.00 (*3-540-64131-9*) Spr-Verlag.

Campbell, R. Joe. A Morphological Dictionary of Classical Nahuatl: A Morpheme Index to the Vocabulario en Lengua Mexicana y Castellana of Fray Alonso de Molinas. xxiv, 488p. 1985. 50.00 (*0-942260-52-X*) Hispanic Seminary.

Campbell, R. Joe, ed. see Linguistic Symposium on Romance Languages Staff.

Campbell, R. K. The Church of the Living God. pap. 6.95 (*0-88172-007-0*) Believers Bkshelf.

— Divine Principles of Gathering. 40p. pap. 0.45 (*0-88172-015-1*) Believers Bkshelf.

— Essentials of the Christian Life. 46p. pap. 0.95 (*0-88172-008-9*) Believers Bkshelf.

— Our Wonderful Bible. 417p. pap. 10.50 (*0-88172-010-0*) Believers Bkshelf.

— Outside the Camp. 16p. pap. 0.30 (*0-88172-157-3*) Believers Bkshelf.

— Parables in Matthew's Gospel. 1978. pap. 3.25 (*0-915374-42-0*, 42-0) Rapids Christian.

— Prophetic History of Christendom. 7.95 (*0-88172-012-7*) Believers Bkshelf.

— Woman's Role. 32p. pap. 0.60 (*0-88172-014-3*) Believers Bkshelf.

Campbell, R. L., jt. auth. see Bickhard, Mark H.

Campbell, R. M., jt. auth. see IFAC Symposium Staff.

Campbell, R. T. Bodies in a Bookshop. 192p. 1984. reprint ed. pap. 6.95 (*0-486-24720-1*) Dover.

— Unholy Dying. 128p. 1985. reprint ed. pap. 5.95 (*0-486-24977-8*) Dover.

Campbell, R. Thomas. Academy on the James: The Confederate Naval School. LC 98-20355. 300p. 1999. 39.95 (*1-57249-130-2*, Burd St Pr) White Mane Pub.

***Campbell, R. Thomas.** The CSS H. L. Hunley: Confederate Submarine. LC 99-35335. (Illus.). 185p. 1999. pap. text 14.95 (*1-57249-175-2*) White Mane Pub.

Campbell, R. Thomas. Fire & Thunder Vol. 4: Exploits of the Confederate States Navy. LC 97-38176. 294p. 1997. 24.95 (*1-57249-067-5*, Burd St Pr) White Mane Pub.

— Gray Thunder: Exploits of the Confederate States Navy. LC 95-47584. (Illus.). 211p. 1996. 19.95 (*0-942597-99-0*, Burd St Pr) White Mane Pub.

***Campbell, R. Thomas.** Hunters of the Night: Confederate Torpedo Boat in the War Between the States. (Illus.). 190p. 2000. pap. 14.95 (*1-57249-202-3*, Burd St Pr) White Mane Pub.

— Sea Hawk of the Confederacy: Lt. Charles W. Read & the Confederate Navy. LC 99-37551. (Illus.). 252p. 2000. 29.95 (*1-57249-178-7*) White Mane Pub.

Campbell, R. Thomas. Southern Fire: Naval Exploits of the Confederacy. LC 96-29725. 263p. 1997. 24.95 (*1-57249-046-2*, Burd St Pr) White Mane Pub.

— Southern Thunder: Exploits of the Confederate States Navy. LC 96-37062. (Illus.). 195p. 1997. 19.95 (*1-57249-029-2*, Burd St Pr) White Mane Pub.

Campbell, R. Thomas, ed. Beneath the Stainless Banner: John McIntosh Kell, CSN. LC 98-46744. (Illus.). 244p. 1999. 24.95 (*1-57249-147-7*, Burd St Pr) White Mane Pub.

— Midshipman in Gray. LC 97-23402. (Illus.). 220p. 1997. 24.95 (*1-57249-061-6*, Burd St Pr) White Mane Pub.

Campbell, R. W., jt. auth. see Green, David W.

Campbell, R. Wayne, et al. The Birds of British Columbia Vol. 1: Nonpasserines: Introduction, Loons Through Waterfowl. (Illus.). 532p. 1997. 80.00 (*0-7748-0618-4*) U of Wash Pr.

An Asterisk (*) at the beginning of an entry indicates that the title is appearing for the first time.

— The Birds of British Columbia Vol. 2: Nonpasserines: Diurnal Birds of Prey Through Woodpeckers. (Illus.). 642p. 1997. 80.00 (*0-7748-0619-2*) U of Wash Pr.
— The Birds of British Columbia Vol. 3: Passerines (Flycatchers through Vireos) (Illus.). 696p. 1997. 95.00 (*0-7748-0572-2*) U of Wash Pr.
Campbell, R. Wayne, jt. auth. see Gregory, Patrick T.
Campbell, R. Wright. Killer of Kings. LC 78-11198. 1979. 8.95 (*0-672-52583-6*, Bobbs) Macmillan.
— Pigeon Pie. large type ed. LC 98-22096. 1999. 27.95 (*0-7862-1528-3*) Thorndike Pr.
— Where Pigeons Go to Die. 154p. 1999. pap. 12.95 (*1-58444-054-6*) DiscUs Bks.
Campbell, Ramsey. The Count of Eleven. 416p. 1993. mass mkt. 4.99 (*0-8125-2169-2*) Tor Bks.
— Demons by Daylight. 192p. 1990. pap. 3.95 (*0-88184-610-4*) Carroll & Graf.
— The Face That Must Die. (Illus.). 256p. 1984. 12.95 (*0-910489-01-7*) Scream Pr.
— Far Away & Never. LC 96-69336. x, 116p. (Orig.). 1996. pap. 7.95 (*0-940884-86-0*) Necronomicon.
***Campbell, Ramsey.** Ghosts & Grisly Things. 320p. 2000. text 24.95 (*0-312-86758-1*) St Martin.
Campbell, Ramsey. Incarnate. 512p. 1984. reprint ed. pap. 3.95 (*0-8125-1650-8*) Tor Bks.
— Influence. 1989. mass mkt. 4.50 (*0-8125-1638-9*) Tor Bks.
***Campbell, Ramsey.** The Last Voice They Hear. 384p. 1999. pap. 6.99 (*0-8125-4194-4*, Pub. by Forge NYC) St Martin.
Campbell, Ramsey. The Last Voice They Hear. LC 98-10256. 384p. 1998. text 24.95 (*0-312-86611-9*) St Martin.
— The Long Lost. 448p. 1996. mass mkt. 6.99 (*0-8125-5086-2*, Pub. by Tor Bks) St Martin.
— Midnight Sun. 1992. mass mkt. 4.99 (*0-8125-1803-9*) Tor Bks.
— The Nameless. 288p. 1984. pap. 3.50 (*0-671-44489-1*) PB.
— Nameless. 1987. mass mkt. 4.99 (*0-8125-2243-5*) Tor Bks.
— Nazareth Hill. LC 96-6567. 384p. 1997. text 23.95 (*0-312-86344-6*) St Martin.
— Nazareth Hill: Gates of Hades. 1998. mass mkt. 5.99 (*0-8125-3930-3*, Pub. by Tor Bks) St Martin.
— Night of the Claw. 1992. mass mkt. 4.99 (*0-8125-1280-4*) Tor Bks.
— Obsession. 320p. 1986. reprint ed. pap. 3.95 (*0-8125-1656-7*) Tor Bks.
— The One Safe Place. 384p. 1996. 23.95 (*0-312-86035-8*) Forge NYC.
— The One Safe Place. 1997. mass mkt. 6.99 (*0-8125-4555-9*, Pub. by Tor Bks) St Martin.
— The Parasite. 352p. 1989. mass mkt. 4.95 (*0-8125-1668-0*) Tor Bks.
***Campbell, Ramsey.** Silent Children. 352p. 2000. 24.95 (*0-312-87056-6*) Forge NYC.
Campbell, Ramsey. Strange Things & Stranger Places. 256p. 1994. pap. 4.99 (*0-8125-2479-9*, Pub. by Tor Bks) St Martin.
Campbell, Ramsey & Peters, Sally, eds. Deathport. (Horror Writers of America Ser.). 368p. (Orig.). 1993. mass mkt. 4.99 (*0-671-69575-4*) PB.
Campbell, Ramsey, et al. Made in Goatswood: New Tales of Horror in the Severn Valley. Aniolowski, Scott D., ed. (Call of Cthulhu Fiction Ser.). (Illus.). 288p. (Orig.). 1995. pap. 10.95 (*1-56882-046-1*, 6009) Chaosium.
Campbell, Ramsey, et al. Shadows over Innsmouth. Jones, Stephen, ed. (Illus.). 450p. 1994. 29.00 (*1-878252-18-6*) Fedogan & Bremer.
— Shadows over Innsmouth. deluxe limited ed. Jones, Stephen, ed. (Illus.). 450p. 1994. boxed set 95.00 (*1-878252-19-4*) Fedogan & Bremer.
Campbell, Ramsey, jt. ed. see Jones, Stephen.
Campbell, Randolph B. An Empire for Slavery: The Peculiar Institution in Texas, 1821-1865. LC 88-31357. xvii, 344p. 1989. pap. text 14.95 (*0-8071-1723-4*) La State U Pr.
— Grass Roots Reconstruction in Texas, 1865-1880. LC 97-17335. (Illus.). 280p. 1997. text 35.00 (*0-8071-2194-0*) La State U Pr.
— Sam Houston & the American Southwest. LC 92-26949. (Library of American Biography). 178p. (C). 1997. pap. 21.20 (*0-06-500688-7*) Addson-Wesley Educ.
Campbell, Randolph B. Texas Voices: Documents from Texas History. 3rd ed. LC 97-208326. 1997. pap. text. write for info. (*1-57259-462-4*) Worth.
Campbell, Randolph B., jt. auth. see Lowe, Richard G.
Campbell, Randy, jt. auth. see Lutzker, John R.
Campbell-Reed, Eileen. What It Means to Be Human: Youth Study Guide. 1996. pap. 5.00 (*1-57312-089-8*) Smyth & Helwys.
***Campbell-Reed, Eileen R.** Being Baptist: A Resource for Individual & Group Study. LC 98-176996. 96p. 1998. pap. 6.00 (*1-57312-254-8*) Smyth & Helwys.
***Campbell, Regina.** Regina's New World Vegetarian Cuisine. (Cookbook Library). 2001. 24.50 (*0-688-17704-2*, Wm Morrow) Morrow Avon.
Campbell, Regina. Regina's Vegetarian Table. LC 96-39849. 224p. 1998. 27.95 (*0-7615-0697-7*) Prima Pub.
Campbell, Reginald J. Livingstone. LC 77-138212. (Illus.). 295p. (C). 1972. reprint ed. lib. bdg. 55.00 (*0-8371-5567-3*, CALI, Greenwood Pr) Greenwood.
Campbell, Reginald L. & Langford, R. Everett. Substance Abuse in the Workplace. 224p. 1995. lib. bdg. 65.00 (*0-87371-131-9*, L131) Lewis Pubs.
Campbell, Reginald L. & Langford, Roland E. Fundamentals of Hazardous Materials Incidents. (Illus.). 472p. 1990. lib. bdg. 110.95 (*0-87371-362-1*, L362BJ) Lewis Pubs.
Campbell, Rich. The Magic of Magic: A How-To Guide for Using Magic in Affective Education. rev. ed. (Illus.). 148p. 1990. pap., spiral bd. 23.95 (*0-9633284-1-7*); ring bd. 28.95 (*0-9633284-0-9*) Brougham Pr.
— More Magic of Magic: A How-To Guide for Using Magic in Affective Education. (Illus.). 160p. 1992. pap., spiral bd. 26.95 (*0-9633284-3-3*); ring bd. 29.95 (*0-9633284-2-5*) Brougham Pr.
Campbell, Rich, jt. auth. see Lewis, Robert.
Campbell, Richard. Hotel Rubio Print (Mt. Lowe) 1993. 56.00 (*0-87505-404-8*) Borden.
— Sixty Minutes & the News: A Mythology for Middle America. (Illinois Studies in Communications). (Illus.). 304p. 1991. 29.95 (*0-252-01777-3*) U of Ill Pr.
— Truth & Historicity. 474p. 1992. text 95.00 (*0-19-823927-0*) OUP.
Campbell, Richard, ed. A Guide to Mangoes in Florida. (Illus.). 200p. (Orig.). (C). 1992. pap. text. write for info. (*0-9632264-0-1*) Fairchild Trop.
Campbell, Richard. Las Flores Trestle (Mt. Lowe) limited ed. 1993. 40.00 (*0-87505-423-4*) Borden.
— Incline & Chalet (Mt. Lowe) limited ed. 1993. 40.00 (*0-87505-422-6*) Borden.
Campbell, Richard & St. David's University Press Staff. From Belief to Understanding: A Study of Anselm's Proslogion Argument on the Existence of God. 1987. lib. bdg. 99.95 (*0-88946-038-8*) E Mellen.
Campbell, Richard, jt. auth. see Reeves, Jimmie L.
Campbell, Richard, jt. auth. see Thompson, Mary J.
Campbell, Richard C. Two Eagles in the Sun: Your Questions Answered about Mexican Hispanics in the Border Southwest & Other Hispanics in the United States. Huntsberger, Paul E., ed. LC 94-61432. (Illus.). (Orig.). 1995. pap. 19.95 (*1-884512-74-7*) Two Eagles.
Campbell, Richard D. The People of the Land of Flint. (Illus.). 130p. (Orig.). 1985. pap. text 19.50 (*0-8191-4551-3*) U Pr of Amer.
Campbell, Richard H. & Pitts, Michael R. The Bible on Film: A Checklist 1897-1980. LC 81-13560. 224p. 1981. 24.00 (*0-8108-1473-0*) Scarecrow.
Campbell, Richard J. & Carlson, Victor. Visions of Antiquity: Neoclassical Figure Drawings. LC 93-15097. (Illus.). 368p. 1993. 75.00 (*0-295-97309-9*) U of Wash Pr.
Campbell, Richard J., jt. auth. see Sessa, Valerie I.
Campbell, Richard L. Historical Sketches of Colonial Florida. Dodson, Pat, ed. LC 75-14032. (Floridiana Facsimile & Reprint Ser.). 304p. 1975. reprint ed. 27.95 (*0-8130-0370-9*) U Press Fla.
Campbell, Richmond. Illusions of Paradox: A Feminist Epistemology Naturalized. LC 97-52358. (Studies in Epistemology & Cognitive Theory). 304p. 1998. 58.00 (*0-8476-8918-2*); pap. 24.95 (*0-8476-8919-0*) Rowman.
Campbell, Rick, ed. see Brock, Van K.
Campbell, Roald F. & Mazzoni, Tim L., Jr. State Policy Making for the Public Schools. LC 75-31311. 476p. 1976. 37.30 (*0-8211-0224-9*) McCutchan.
Campbell, Robert. Alice in La-La Land. 232p. 1999. pap. 17.95 (*1-58444-024-4*) DiscUs Bks.
— Alice in La-La Land. Chelius, Jane, ed. 1990. mass mkt. 4.95 (*0-671-73343-5*) PB.
— Boneyards. large type ed. (Cloak & Dagger Ser.). 549p. 1993. reprint ed. lib. bdg. 21.95 (*1-56054-627-1*) Thorndike Pr.
— Boneyards. Chelius, Jane, ed. 304p. 1993. reprint ed. mass mkt. 5.50 (*0-671-70320-X*) PB.
— The Chasm: The Life & Death of a Great Experiment in Ghetto Education. LC 85-31687. 271p. 1986. reprint ed. lib. bdg. 65.00 (*0-313-25119-3*, CALD, Greenwood Pr) Greenwood.
— The Earthly Recordings: A Sun Ra Discography. LC 95-194704. 256p. (Orig.). 1994. 25.00 (*1-881993-26-4*) Cadence Jazz.
***Campbell, Robert.** A Flannery Trilogy Vol. I: Featuring The Junkyard Dog, 600-Pound Gorilla & Hip-Deep in Alligators. rev. ed. (Jimmy Flannery Ser.: Vol. 1). 384p. 1999. pap. 24.95 (*1-58444-073-2*) DiscUs Bks.
Campbell, Robert. The Gift Horse's Mouth. large type ed. 267p. 1991. reprint ed. lib. bdg. 19.95 (*1-56054-163-6*) Thorndike Pr.
— In a Pig's Eye. large type ed. LC 91-45150. 309p. 1992. reprint ed. 17.95 (*1-56054-350-7*) Thorndike Pr.
— In a Pig's Eye. Chelius, Jane, ed. 224p. 1992. reprint ed. mass mkt. 4.99 (*0-671-70328-5*) PB.
— In La-La Land We Trust. 230p. 1999. pap. 17.95 (*1-58444-051-1*) DiscUs Bks.
— In La-La Land We Trust. 1987. mass mkt. 4.95 (*0-445-40596-1*, Pub. by Warner Bks) Little.
— Juice. Chelius, Jane, ed. 320p. 1990. mass mkt. 4.95 (*0-671-67454-4*) PB.
***Campbell, Robert.** The Master of the Sundown Shore. 208p. 1999. pap. 15.95 (*1-58444-055-4*) DiscUs Bks.
Campbell, Robert. A Narrative of Colonel Robert Campbell's Experiences in the Rocky Mountain Fur Trade from 1825 to 1835. Holloway, Drew A., ed. 67p. 1995. pap. 12.95 (*0-87770-510-0*) Ye Galleon.
— Nibbled to Death by Ducks. Chelius, Jane, ed. 288p. 1990. reprint ed. mass mkt. 4.99 (*0-671-67583-4*) PB.
— Pigeon Pie. LC 97-48921. Vol. 27. 240p. 1998. 21.50 (*0-89296-665-3*, Pub. by Mysterious Pr) Little.
— The Real Worlds of Canadian Politics. 3rd ed. 300p. 1994. pap. 12.95 (*1-55111-029-6*) Broadview Pr.
— Sauce for the Goose. 208p. 1996. mass mkt. 5.99 (*0-446-40463-2*, Pub. by Warner Bks) Little.
— Sauce for the Goose. large type ed. LC 95-35220. (Cloak & Dagger Ser.). 290p. 1995. 23.95 (*0-7862-0547-4*) Thorndike Pr.
— Sweet La-La Land. 232p. 1999. pap. 17.95 (*1-58444-050-3*) DiscUs Bks.
— Sweet La-La Land. Chelius, Jane, ed. 320p. 1991. reprint ed. mass mkt. 4.99 (*0-671-73236-6*) PB.
— The Wizard of La-La Land. 244p. 1999. pap. 17.95 (*1-58444-052-X*) DiscUs Bks.
— Worker's Compensation Fraud Control & Investigation: A Manual Covering the Whole Spectrum of Conducting Worker's Compensation Claims Investigations. 78p. (Orig.). (C). 1997. pap. 35.00 (*0-918487-96-X*) Thomas Investigative.
Campbell, Robert & Chelius, Jane, eds. Plugged Nickel. 1988. mass mkt. 4.99 (*0-671-64363-0*) PB.
Campbell, Robert & Collinson, Diane. Ending Lives. 208p. 1988. pap. text 26.95 (*0-631-15331-4*) Blackwell Pubs.
Campbell, Robert & Cruikshank, Jeffrey. Artists & Architects Collaborate: Designing the Wiesner Building. (Illus.). 94p. (Orig.). 1985. pap. 10.00 (*0-938437-12-7*) MIT List Visual Arts.
***Campbell, Robert & Trent, Christopher.** The Earthly Recordings of Sun Ra. 2nd ed. 848p. 2000. pap. 80.00 (*1-881993-35-3*, Pub. by Cadence Jazz) NorthCountry Distributors.
Campbell, Robert & Vanderwarker, Peter. Cityscapes of Boston. (Illus.). 240p. 1994. pap. 25.00 (*0-395-70065-5*, P Davison Bk) HM.
Campbell, Robert, jt. auth. see Palady, Paul.
Campbell, Robert, ed. see Austin, John.
Campbell, Robert, ed. see Deleveau, John.
Campbell, Robert, ed. see Palady, Paul.
Campbell, Robert A., et al, eds. Advances in Polyamine Research, Vol. 1. fac. ed. LC 77-83687. (Illus.). 300p. pap. 93.00 (*0-7837-7275-0*, 204703100001) Bks Demand.
Campbell, Robert A., ed. see Advances in Polyamine Research Staff.
***Campbell, Robert B.** The Abandoned. 272p. 2000. pap. 12.95 (*0-9700492-2-6*) Steel Pr Pubng.
Campbell, Robert B., ed. Contemporary Arab Writers: An Autobiographical Guide. (Three Continents Ser.). 625p. 2000. 75.00 (*0-89410-854-9*) L Rienner.
Campbell, Robert B., jt. auth. see Remmling, Gunter W.
Campbell, Robert C. Jesus Still Has Something to Say. LC 87-4169. 192p. 1987. pap. 13.00 (*0-8170-1114-5*) Judson.
***Campbell, Robert D.** Loch Lomond & the Trossachs. (Illus.). 208p. 1999. 19.95 (*1-84018-189-3*, Pub. by Mainstream Pubng) Trafalgar.
Campbell, Robert E. Ahab. 40p. (Orig.). (C). 1989. pap. 12.95 (*0-9621912-0-5*, TXV 324 342) Leviathan Bks.
Campbell, Robert E. & Sechler, Judith A. Adult Literacy: Programs & Practices. 94p. 1987. 8.75 (*0-318-23424-6*, RD 265A) Ctr Educ Trng Employ.
Campbell, Robert F. History of Basic Metals Price Control in World War Two. LC 77-76654. (Columbia University. Studies in the Social Sciences: No. 541). reprint ed. 29.50 (*0-404-51541-X*) AMS Pr.
***Campbell, Robert G.** Neutral Rights & Obligations in the Anglo-Boer War. 149p. 1999. reprint ed. 50.00 (*1-56169-452-5*) Gaunt.
Campbell, Robert G. The Panhandle Aspect of the Chaquaqua Plateau. (Graduate Studies: No. 11). (Illus.). 118p. (Orig.). 1976. pap. 5.00 (*0-89672-021-7*) Tex Tech Univ Pr.
Campbell, Robert J. Competitive Cost-Based Pricing Systems for Modern Manufacturing. LC 91-47561. 272p. 1992. 65.00 (*0-89930-653-5*, CSX, Quorum Bks) Greenwood.
— Mother Is Blessed: A Sermon & Order of Service for Mother's Day. 1992. pap. 3.95 (*1-55673-602-5*, 9322) CSS OH.
— Psychiatric Dictionary. 7th ed. 840p. (C). 1996. text 67.50 (*0-19-510259-2*) OUP.
Campbell, Robert J., III, jt. ed. see Edgerton, Jane E.
Campbell, Robert M. First Twenty-One: Life, History & Thoughts. 247p. (Orig.). (YA). (gr. 10-12). 1984. pap. 6.95 (*0-9613542-0-8*) R M Campbell.
— The Politics of the Post: Canada's Postal System from Public Service to Privatization. 500p. 1994. 49.95 (*1-55111-034-2*) Broadview Pr.
Campbell, Robert N. The New Science: Self-Esteem Psychology. LC 84-5085. 354p. (Orig.). 1984. lib. bdg. 52.00 (*0-8191-3892-4*) U Pr of Amer.
Campbell, Robert P. Uncovering & Investigating Insurance Healthcare Claims Fraud. 103p. (Orig.). (C). 1997. pap. 45.00 (*0-918487-97-8*) Thomas Investigative.
Campbell, Robert R. James Duncan Campbell: A Memoir by His Son, Robert R. Campbell. LC 72-123565. (East Asian Monographs: No. 38). 145p. 1970. pap. 20.00 (*0-674-47131-8*) HUP.
Campbell, Robert S., ed. see Palady, Paul.
Campbell, Robert W. The Economics of Soviet Oil & Gas. LC 68-22277. (Resources for the Future Ser.). (Illus.). 294p. 1968. 24.95 (*0-8018-0105-2*) Johns Hopkins.
— The Economics of Soviet Oil & Gas. LC 68-22277. (Illus.). 299p. reprint ed. pap. 92.70 (*0-608-18804-2*, 203019200067) Bks Demand.
— The Failure of Soviet Economic Planning: System, Performance, Reform. LC 91-39964. (Illus.). 204p. 1992. 5.00 (*0-253-31311-2*) Ind U Pr.
— The Socialist Economies in Transition: A Primer on Semi-reformed Systems. LC 91-8653. (Illus.). 256p. 1991. 35.00 (*0-253-31301-5*); pap. 13.95 (*0-253-20670-7*, MB-670) Ind U Pr.
— Soviet Energy Technologies: Planning, Policy, Research, & Development. LC 80-7562. 278p. reprint ed. pap. 86.20 (*0-8357-3958-9*, 205705400004) Bks Demand.
— Trends in the Soviet Oil & Gas Industry. LC 76-15940. (Resources for the Future Ser.). (Illus.). 144p. 1977. 12.00 (*0-8018-1870-2*) Johns Hopkins.
— Trends in the Soviet Oil & Gas Industry. LC 76-15940. 141p. reprint ed. pap. 43.80 (*0-608-17382-7*, 203019300067) Bks Demand.
Campbell, Robert W., ed. The Post-Communist Economic Transformation: Essays in Honor of Gregory Grossman. LC 94-16359. 320p. (C). 1994. text 79.00 (*0-8133-8856-2*, Pub. by Westview) HarpC.
Campbell, Robin. Hearing Children Read. LC 88-25143. (Illus.). 108p. reprint ed. pap. 33.50 (*0-608-20325-4*, 207157800002) Bks Demand.
***Campbell, Robin.** Literacy from Home to School: Reading with Alice. 182p. 1999. pap. 19.95 (*1-85856-166-3*, Trentham Bks) Stylus Pub VA.
— Literacy in Nursery Education. 72p. 1996. pap. 9.00 (*1-85856-064-0*, Trentham Bks) Stylus Pub VA.
Campbell, Robin. Reading in the Early Years Handbook. LC 94-40594. 192p. 1995. pap. 31.95 (*0-335-19309-9*) OpUniv Pr.
— Reading Real Books. (Rethinking Reading Ser.). 112p. 1992. 31.95 (*0-335-15793-9*); pap. 103.95 (*0-335-15794-7*) OpUniv Pr.
— Reading Together. (Rethinking Reading Ser.). 100p. 1990. pap. 30.95 (*0-335-09449-X*) OpUniv Pr.
Campbell, Robin, ed. Facilitating Preschool Literacy. LC 98-10386. 288p. 1998. pap. text 28.95 (*0-87207-187-1*) Intl Reading.
Campbell, Robin, tr. see Seneca, Lucius Annaeus.
Campbell, Robin D. It's My Turn. (Illus.). 32p. (J). (ps up). 1996. 12.95 (*0-9653688-1-5*) P & P Ent.
Campbell, Rod. Baby's First ABC Book. (Illus.). 12p. (J). (ps). 1992. pap. 7.50 (*1-881445-12-7*) Sandvik Pub.
— Baby's First Counting Book. (Illus.). 12p. (J). 1992. pap. 7.50 (*1-881445-13-5*) Sandvik Pub.
— Dear Zoo. (Classic Board Bks.). (Illus.). 18p. (J). (ps-k). 1999. bds. 6.99 (*0-689-82549-8*, 076714006997) Litle Simon.
— Dear Zoo. LC 82-83224. (Illus.). 20p. (J). (ps-1). 1986. pap. 10.95 (*0-02-716440-3*, Four Winds Pr) S&S Childrens.
— Dear Zoo. (J). 1987. reprint ed. pap. 4.95 (*0-317-62180-7*, PuffinBks) Peng Put Young Read.
***Campbell, Rod.** I Can Spell! With Consonants B C D F G H. (Illus.). 24p. (J). 2000. pap. 4.99 (*1-85292-172-2*) Campbell Bks Ltd.
— I Can Spell! With Consonants R S T V W Z. (Illus.). 24p. (J). 2000. pap. 4.99 (*1-85292-174-9*) Campbell Bks Ltd.
— I Can Spell! With Vowels A E I O U. (Illus.). 24p. (J). 2000. pap. 4.99 (*1-85292-171-4*) Campbell Bks Ltd.
— Little Bird. (Illus.). 20p. (J). (ps-k). 2000. 10.99 (*1-85292-234-6*) Campbell Bks Ltd.
— Little Bird. (J). 2000. pap. 4.99 (*0-333-63340-7*) Mcm Child Bks.
Campbell, Rod. Look, Touch, & Feel with Buster. (Illus.). 12p. (J). 1992. pap. 8.49 (*1-881445-06-2*) Sandvik Pub.
Campbell, rod. My Pop-Up Garden Friends. (J). 1993. 59.40 (*0-689-71650-8*) Litle Simon.
Campbell, Rod. My Pop-Up Garden Friends. LC 92-4382. (Illus.). 14p. (J). (ps). 1993. mass mkt. 4.95 (*0-689-71643-5*) Aladdin.
***Campbell, Rod.** Pop-Up Jungle. (Illus.). 8p. (J). (ps-k). 2000. 7.99 (*1-85292-247-8*) Campbell Bks Ltd.
— This Baby! (J). 2000. pap. 5.99 (*0-333-67488-X*) Mcm Child Bks.
Campbell, Roger. Let's Communicate. (Orig.). 1977. pap. 4.50 (*0-87508-060-X*) Chr Lit.
— Preach for a Year. LC 87-29400. (Preach for a Year Ser.: No. 2). 224p. 1993. pap. 11.99 (*0-8254-2330-9*) Kregel.
— Preach for a Year. (Preach for a Year Ser.: No. 3). 224p. 1995. pap. 11.99 (*0-8254-2321-X*) Kregel.
— Preach for a Year, No. 4. 224p. 1996. pap. 11.99 (*0-8254-2318-X*) Kregel.
— Predique por un Ano, No. 1. (SPA.). 224p. 1996. pap. 8.99 (*0-8254-1114-9*, Edit Portavoz) Kregel.
— Predique por un Ano (Preach for a Year), Vol. 3. (SPA.). 224p. 1998. pap. 8.99 (*0-8254-1116-5*, Edit Portavoz) Kregel.
— Predique por un Ano (Preach for a Year), Vol. 4. (SPA.). 224p. 1999. pap. 8.99 (*0-8254-1117-3*, Edit Portavoz) Kregel.
— Spurgeon's Daily Treasures in the Psalms. LC 96-47387. 1997. 14.99 (*0-7852-7536-3*) Nelson.
— Staying Positive in a Negative World: Biblical Alternatives to Attitudes That Steal the Joy of Life. LC 96-46391. 136p. 1997. pap. 8.99 (*0-8254-2346-5*) Kregel.
— Weight! a Better Way to Lose. LC 98-44657. 1999. pap. 9.99 (*0-8254-2349-X*) Kregel.
— You Can Win! No Losers in God's Family. LC 92-40958. 136p. 1993. pap. 8.99 (*0-8254-2323-6*) Kregel.
Campbell, Roger F. Preach for a Year. LC 87-29400. (Preach for a Year Ser.: No. 1). 224p. 1988. pap. 11.99 (*0-8254-2329-5*) Kregel.
— Preach for a Year No. 5: Two Complete Outlines for Every Sunday of the Year. (Preach for a Year Ser.). 224p. 1998. pap. 11.99 (*0-8254-2347-3*) Kregel.
— Predique por un Ano: 104 Bosquejos de Sermones, Vol. 2. (SPA.). 224p. 1997. pap. 8.99 (*0-8254-1115-7*, Edit Portavoz) Kregel.
— They Call Him the Walking Bible. 4th ed. 298p. 1977. pap. 9.00 (*0-934803-66-8*) J Van Impe.
Campbell, Ron. Plato's Garage. 272p. 2000. text 23.95 (*0-312-20569-4*) St Martin.
Campbell, Ron G. Free from Freemasonry: Understanding Freemasonry & Its Affects on Those We Love. LC 99-50376. 191p. 1999. pap. 10.99 (*0-8307-2383-8*, Renew) Gospel Lght.
***Campbell, Ronald.** Transpersonal Psychology: An Integral Encounter with Self-Awareness. LC 99-91219. 520p. 1999. 25.00 (*0-7388-0674-9*); pap. 18.00 (*0-7388-0675-7*) Xlibris Corp.
Campbell, Ronald, et al. Organization & Control of American Schools. 6th ed. 512p. (C). 1990. 125.00 (*0-675-21126-3*, Merrill Coll) P-H.
Campbell, Ronald W. International Handbook of Arrhythmia. (Illus.). 88p. 1997. text 25.00 (*0-8247-9819-8*) Dekker.

An Asterisk (*) at the beginning of an entry indicates that the title is appearing for the first time.

Campbell, Ronald W., ed. INTERFACE - International Forum for Action Cardiovascular Education. (Journal Ser.: Vol. 85, Suppl. 1, 1994). (Illus.). iv, 122p. 1995. pap. 38.50 (*3-8055-6144-X*) S Karger.
Campbell, Ronald W. & Janse, Michiel J., eds. Cardiac Arrhythmias: The Management of Atrial Fibrillation. LC 92-49869. 1992. write for info. (*3-540-55588-9*) Spr-Verlag.
Campbell, Ronald W., jt. ed. see Wren, Christopher.
Campbell, Rosamond. The Parlour Dulcimer. 104p. 1995. pap. 12.95 (*0-7866-0315-1*, 95377) Mel Bay.
Campbell, Rosamond. The Victorian Dulcimer. 68p. 1992. pap. 8.95 (*1-56222-315-1*, 94690) Mel Bay.
— The Victorian Dulcimer. 1997. audio compact disk 15.98 (*0-7866-2862-6*, 94690CD) Mel Bay.
Campbell, Ross. How to Really Love Your Child. rev. ed. LC 92-12130. 144p. 1992. pap. 9.99 (*0-89693-066-1*, 6-1066, Victor Bks) Chariot Victor.
— How to Really Love Your Children, 2 vols. in 1. 288p. 1996. 9.99 (*0-88486-135-X*) Arrowood Pr.
— How to Really Love Your Teenager. rev. ed. 132p. 1993. pap. 9.99 (*0-89693-067-X*, 6-1067, Victor Bks) Chariot Victor.
— Kids in Danger. 192p. 1995. pap. 9.99 (*1-56476-471-0*, 6-3471, Victor Bks) Chariot Victor.
— Relational Parenting. LC 99-58017. 2000. pap. 12.99 (*0-8024-6393-2*) Moody.
— Si Amas a Tu Adolescente. Araujo, Juan S., tr. from ENG.Tr. of How to Really Love Your Teenager. (SPA.). 144p. 1986. pap. 7.99 (*0-88113-030-3*) Caribe Betania.
— Si Amas a Tu Hijo. Araujo, Juan S., tr. from ENG.Tr. of How to Really Love Your Child. (SPA.). 144p. 1986. pap. 7.99 (*0-88113-031-1*) Caribe Betania.
***Campbell, Ross & Chapman, Gary.** Parenting Your Adult Child: How You Can Help Them Achieve Their Full Potential. 1999. pap. 11.99 (*0-8024-7312-1*) Moody.
— Parenting Your Adult Child: How You Can Help Them Achieve Their Full Potential. 1999. pap. 14.99 incl. audio (*0-8024-7389-X*) Moody.
Campbell, Ross & Chapman, Gary. Parenting Your Adult Child: How You Can Help Them Achieve Their Full Potential. LC 99-215576. 200p. 1999. pap. 11.99 (*1-881273-12-1*) Northfield Pub.
Campbell, Ross & Lambert, Dave. Getting a Clue in a Clueless World: Hope, Encouragement & Challenge for Students. LC 96-8621. (Illus.). 208p. (J). 1996. pap. 9.99 (*0-310-20817-3*) Zondervan.
Campbell, Ross, jt. auth. see Chapman, Gary.
Campbell, Ross D. How to Really Love Your Child. 1982. mass mkt. 4.99 (*0-451-16835-6*) NAL.
Campbell, Roy. Broken Record, Reminiscenses. LC 70-131657. 1971. reprint ed. 29.00 (*0-403-00544-2*) Scholarly.
— Flaming Terrapin. LC 74-131658. 1970. reprint ed. 29.00 (*0-403-00545-0*) Scholarly.
— Flowering Reeds: Poems. LC 78-131659. 1971. reprint ed. 29.00 (*0-403-00546-9*) Scholarly.
— Flowering Reeds: Poetry. 1988. reprint ed. lib. bdg. 49.00 (*0-7812-0036-9*) Rprt Serv.
— Lorca: An Appreciation of His Poetry. LC 76-137665. (Studies in Poetry: No. 38). (C). 1971. reprint ed. lib. bdg. 75.00 (*0-8383-1226-8*) M S G Haskell Hse.
— Mass at Dawn. 2nd rev. ed. 20p. (Orig.). 1991. pap. 20.00 (*0-930126-35-1*) Typographeum.
***Campbell, Roy.** Poems of St. John of the Cross. 96p. 2000. pap. 13.00 (*1-86046-589-7*) Harvill Press.
Campbell, Roy. Wayzgoose: A South African Satire. LC 72-131660. 1971. reprint ed. 29.00 (*0-403-00547-7*) Scholarly.
— Wyndham Lewis. Meyers, Jeffrey, ed. 80p. 1985. pap. 9.95 (*0-86980-412-X*, Pub. by Univ Natal Pr) Intl Spec Bk.
Campbell, Roy, et al. Voorslag 1-3 (1926) A Magazine of South African Life & Art. No. 5. (Illus.). 1985. reprint ed. 24.95 (*0-86980-423-5*, Pub. by Univ Natal Pr) Intl Spec Bk.
Campbell, Roy, tr. see Bentley, Eric, ed.
Campbell, Roy, tr. see Calderon de la Barca, Pedro.
Campbell, Roy, tr. see de Queiros, Eca.
Campbell, Russel N., ed. see Celce-Murcia, Marianne & Hilles, Sharon L.
Campbell, Russel N., ed. see Silberstein, Sandra.
Campbell, Russell. Cinema Strikes Back: Radical Filmmaking in the United States, 1930-1942. LC 82-4819. (Studies in Cinema: No. 20). 397p. 1982. pap. 123.10 (*0-8357-1330-X*, 207031900068) Bks Demand.
Campbell, Russell N., jt. auth. see King, Harold V.
Campbell, Ruth & Conway, Martin, eds. Broken Memories: Case Studies in Memory Impairment. (Illus.). 496p. 1995. 68.95 (*0-631-18722-7*) Blackwell Pubs.
— Broken Memories: Case Studies in Memory Impairment. (Illus.). 496p. 1995. pap. 33.95 (*0-631-18723-5*) Blackwell Pubs.
Campbell, Ruth, jt. ed. see Messing, Lynn S.
Campbell, Ruth, ed. see Thurston, Les.
Campbell, S. How to Be a Successful Student. (FreshmanOrient/College Success). (Orig.). pap. write for info. (*0-534-23448-8*) Wadsworth Pub.
Campbell, S. Looney Coon. 1980. pap. 3.00 (*0-933062-16-8*) R H Sommer.
— Sweet Sue's Adventure. 1980. pap. 3.00 (*0-933062-11-7*) R H Sommer.
Campbell, S., ed. Sampling & Analysis of Rain - STP 823. 96p. 1984. pap. 18.00 (*0-8031-0266-6*, STP823) ASTM.
Campbell, S. & Joint Nature Conservation Committee (Great Britain) Staff. Quaternary of South-West England. LC 97-78418. (The Geological Conservation Review Ser.). 1998. write for info. (*0-412-83220-8*, Chap & Hall NY) Chapman & Hall.
Campbell, S., jt. ed. see Walsh, F. C.
Campbell, S. A. & Lewerenz, H. J. Semiconductor Micromachining, Vol. 2. LC 97-26052. 406p. 1998. 225.00 (*0-471-96682-7*) Wiley.
***Campbell, S. A. & Lewerenz, H. J.** Semiconductor Micromachining: Fundamental Electrochemistry & Physics, Vol. 1. LC 97-26052. 330p. 1998. 225.00 (*0-471-96681-9*) Wiley.
Campbell, S. L. Generalized Inverses of Linear Transformations. 288p. 1991. pap. 8.95 (*0-486-66693-X*) Dover.
Campbell, Sabine, et al, eds. Fiddlehead Gold: 50 Years of the Fiddlehead Magazine. LC 96-146207. 248p. 1995. pap. 14.95 (*0-86492-177-2*, Pub. by Goose Ln Edits) Genl Dist Srvs.
***Campbell, Sally.** A Primer of Christianity: For Pew Sitters & Other People. LC 99-95092. 150p. 1999. pap. 10.00 (*0-9673650-0-7*) Springs.
Campbell, Sally & Liegel, Leon, eds. Disturbance & Forest Health in Oregon & Washington. (Illus.). 124p. 1997. reprint ed. 19.00 (*0-89904-561-8*, Bear Meadows Resrch Grp); reprint ed. pap. 14.00 (*0-89904-562-6*, Bear Meadows Resrch Grp) Crumb Elbow Pub.
***Campbell, Sally & Liegel, Leon, eds.** Disturbance & Forest Health in Oregon & Washington. (Illus.). 105p. (C). 1999. reprint ed. pap. text 30.00 (*0-7881-7867-9*) DIANE Pub.
Campbell, Sally R. The Confident Consumer. LC 99-11552. (Illus.). 541p. 2000. 47.96 (*1-56637-635-1*) Goodheart.
***Campbell, Sally Van Winkle.** But Always Fine Bourbon: Pappy Van Winkle & the Story of Old Fitzgerald. (Illus.). 220p. 1999. 29.95 (*0-9674208-0-6*) Limestone Ln.
Campbell, Sandy, ed. Mrs. Joyce of Zurich & Mr. Forster of King's. limited ed. (Illus.). 80p. 1989. 35.00 (*0-917366-09-3*) S Campbell.
Campbell, Sara, et al. Masterpieces from the Norton Simon Museum. (Illus.). 207p. (Orig.). 1989. 35.00 (*0-915776-05-7*); pap. 20.00 (*0-915776-04-9*) NS Mus.
Campbell, Sarah F., ed. see Piaget, Jean.
Campbell, Sarah K. Postcolumbian Culture History in the Northern Columbia Plateau A. D. 1500-1900. LC 90-48883. (Evolution of North American Indians Ser.). 246p. 1990. text 10.00 (*0-8240-2224-6*) Garland.
Campbell, Scott & Fainstein, Susan S., eds. Readings in Planning Theory. 380p. 1996. 82.95 (*1-55786-612-0*) Blackwell Pubs.
— Readings in Planning Theory. LC 95-36047. 380p. (C). 1996. pap. 31.95 (*1-55786-613-9*) Blackwell Pubs.
Campbell, Scott & Silverman, Phyllis R. Widower: When Men Are Left Alone. (Death, Value & Meaning Ser.). 247p. 1996. 36.95 (*0-89503-140-X*) Baywood Pub.
Campbell, Scott, jt. ed. see Fainstein, Susan S.
Campbell, Scott D. The Complete Book of Birdhouse Construction for Woodworkers. 40th ed. (Crafts Ser.). (Illus.). 48p. (Orig.). 1984. pap. 2.50 (*0-486-24407-5*) Dover.
— Making Birdhouses & Bird Feeders, 2 vols., Set. (Illus.). 1989. pap. 5.45 (*0-486-25917-X*) Dover.
Campbell, Scott O. Easy-to-Make Bird Feeders. (Illus.). 96p. 1989. pap. 2.95 (*0-486-25847-5*) Dover.
Campbell, Shane. Folk Carving with Shane Campbell. LC 97-80467. (Illus.). 64p. 1998. pap. 14.95 (*0-7643-0465-8*) Schiffer.
***Campbell, Shannon K.** Implementing HR & Payroll with SAP R/3. (Illus.). 400p. 2000. 49.99 (*0-7615-2439-8*, Prima Tech) Prima Pub.
Campbell, Shari, ed. Build a Better Staff: Developing & Keeping Top Notch Staff, 2 vols. 1996. 139.00 (*0-8342-0415-0*) Aspen Pub.
***Campbell, Sharon.** Friendship's Tapestry. 1999. pap. write for info. (*1-58235-371-9*) Watermrk Pr.
Campbell, Sheila D. Malcove Collection. (Illus.). 440p. 1998. reprint ed. pap. 39.95 (*0-8020-8169-X*) U of Toronto Pr.
Campbell, Shepherd. Presidential Lies: Illustrated History of White House Golf. LC 96-161800. (Illus.). 288p. 1996. 23.95 (*0-02-861258-2*) Macmillan.
— Presidential Lies: The Illustrated History of White House Golf. (Illus.). 288p. 1998. pap. text 14.95 (*0-02-862356-8*) Macmillan.
Campbell, Sheri. Down & Dirty. 1998. pap. 10.95 (*1-874509-71-9*, Pub. by X Pr) LPC InBook.
***Campbell, Sheri.** Up All Night. 1999. pap. text 10.95 (*1-874509-97-2*) XPress.
Campbell, Sheri. Wicked in Bed. 192p. 1996. pap. 9.95 (*1-874509-14-X*) LPC InBook.
Campbell, Sheri, jt. auth. see Struck, Darla.
Campbell, Sheri T. Rude Gal. 1997. pap. 9.95 (*1-874509-32-8*, Pub. by X Pr) LPC InBook.
Campbell, Shirley. Scribbling & More. 200p. 1996. pap. 10.95 (*0-941092-32-1*) Mtn St Pr.
***Campbell, Shirley.** Talking about Writing: A Sequential Programme of Sentence Stucture, Grammar, Punctuation & Usage for Grade 8 with Accompanying Answer Key. LC 99-14. 36p. (YA). (gr. 8). 1999. spiral bd. 10.40 (*1-55212-245-X*, Pub. by Tra3fford) Trafford Pub.
Campbell, Shirley. Talking about Writing Vol. 2: A Sequential Programme of Sentence Structure, Grammar, Punctuation & Usage for Grade 9 with Accompanying Answer Key. LC 99-15. 46p. (YA). (gr. 9). 1999. spiral bd. 10.40 (*1-55212-246-8*, 99-0015, Pub. by Tra3fford) Trafford Pub.
— Talking about Writing Vol. 3: A Sequential Programme of Sentence Structure, Grammar, Punctuation & Usage for Grade 10 with Accompanying Answer Key. 36p. 1999. spiral bd. 10.40 (*1-55212-247-6*, 99-0016) Trafford Pub.
— Talking about Writing Vol. 4: A Sequential Programme of Sentence Structure, Grammar, Punctuation & Usage for Grade 11 with Accompanying Answer Key. 42p. 1999. spiral bd. 10.40 (*1-55212-248-4*, 99-0017) Trafford Pub.
— Talking about Writing Vol. 5: A Sequential Programme of Sentence Structure, Grammar, Punctuation & Usage for Grade 12 with Accompanying Answer Key. 34p. 1999. spiral bd. 10.40 (*1-55212-249-2*, 99-0018) Trafford Pub.
— Talking about Writing - Answer Key: A Sequential Programme of Sentence Structure, Grammar, Punctuation & Usage for Grades 8 to 12, Vol. 6. LC 99-8. 116p. (YA). (gr. 8-12). 1999. spiral bd. 31.85 (*1-55212-240-9*, Pub. by Tra3fford) Trafford Pub.

— Sequel. (C). 1984. pap. write for info. (*0-943461-02-2*) Hill & Valley Pub.
Campbell, Sid. Ancient Fighting Secrets of the Yin-Yang: Martial Arts Combative Hand Sciences. (Audio Cassette Book). 1988. 29.95 incl. audio (*0-318-37594-X*) Gong Prods.
— Exotic Weapons of the Ninja. LC 98-52804. (Illus.). 200p. 1999. pap. 12.00 (*0-8065-2063-9*, Citadel Pr) Carol Pub Group.
— Exotic Weapons of the Ninja. (Illus.). 200p. 1994. pap. 25.00 (*0-87364-788-2*) Paladin Pr.
— Kobudo & Bugei: The Ancient Weapon Way of Okinawa & Japan. LC 99-174124. (Illus.). 96p. 1998. pap. 20.00 (*0-87364-988-5*) Paladin Pr.
— The Mercenary's Tactical HBK. (Illus.). 120p. (Orig.). 1990. pap. 12.00 (*0-918751-16-0*) Delta Pr.
— Self-Defense for Wimps (Yuppie Survival Guide of the 1990's) 1989. 29.95 incl. audio (*0-682-87113-3*) Gong Prods.
Campbell, Sid, et al. Balisong: The Lethal Art of Filipino Knife Fighting. (Illus.). 192p. 1986. pap. 16.00 (*0-87364-354-2*) Paladin Pr.
Campbell, Siobhan. The Permanent Wave. LC 96-140207. 86p. 1997. pap. 12.95 (*0-85640-572-8*, Pub. by Blackstaff Pr) Dufour.
Campbell, Siri. Inside Monaco. (Illus.). 224p. (Orig.). 1996. pap. 11.95 (*0-911445-08-0*) Page Prods.
Campbell-Smith, Ray. Drawing Landscapes, No. 9. (Illus.). 32p. 1990. pap. 4.95 (*0-85532-641-7*, 641-7, Pub. by Srch Pr) A Schwartz & Co.
Campbell Soup Company Staff & Time-Life Books Editors. Pace Family Recipe Round-Up: 100 Easy Recipes from Pace Picante Sauce. LC 96-28262. (Illus.). 112p. (gr. 11). 1999. 14.95 (*0-7835-4861-3*) Time-Life.
***Campbell, Spencer.** Leadership: A Comprehensive Guide to Understanding & Development. 250p. 2000. pap. 11.95 (*1-885003-56-0*, Pub. by R D Reed Pubs) Midpt Trade.
Campbell Staff, L. J. Prehistoric Alaska. Rennick, Penny, ed. LC 72-92087. (Alaska Geographic Ser.: Vol. 21, No. 4). (Illus.). 112p. 1994. pap. 19.95 (*1-56661-024-9*) Alaska Geog Soc.
Campbell Staff, L. J. & Alaska Geographic Society Staff. Kenai Peninsula. Rennick, Penny, ed. LC 72-92087. (Alaska Geographic Ser.: Vol. 21, No. 2). (Illus.). 124p. 1994. pap. 19.95 (*1-56661-020-6*) Alaska Geog Soc.
Campbell, Stan. Faith-Building Questions - Why Do You Ask? 12 Sessions for Small Groups or Personal Study. (Truthseed Ser.). 96p. 1997. pap. text 4.99 (*1-56476-545-8*, Victor Bks) Chariot Victor.
— Fear Not! Be Outrageously Courageous Student Leader's Guide. (1995 50-Day Spiritual Adventure Ser.). (Illus.). 48p. (Orig.). (YA). (gr. 7-12). 1994. pap. text, student ed. 6.99 (*1-879050-53-6*) Chapel of Air.
— Nobody Like Me. 96p. (YA). (gr. 7-9). 1986. teacher ed. 2.80 (*0-89693-188-9*, Victor Bks); pap., student ed. 0.60 (*0-89693-515-9*, Victor Bks) Chariot Victor.
— What's This World Coming To? (Biblelog Ser.: Bk. 4). 144p. (YA). (gr. 8 up). 1988. pap. text 6.50 (*0-89693-865-4*, 6-2865, Victor Bks) Chariot Victor.
Campbell, Stan & Vogel, Jane. Fun Nights & Faith Builders. Southern, Randy, ed. (Snap Sessions Ser.). (YA). (gr. 6-12). 1993. pap. 17.95 (*0-614-11717-8*, 84319) Cook.
Campbell, Stan, jt. auth. see Bell, Jim.
Campbell, Stan, jt. auth. see Campbell, Pam.
Campbell, Stanislaus. From Breviary to Liturgy of the Hours: The Structural Reform of the Roman Office, 1964-1971. 400p. (Orig.). 1995. pap. text 34.95 (*0-8146-6133-5*, Pueblo Bks) Liturgical Pr.
Campbell, Stanley W. The Slave Catchers: Enforcement of the Fugitive Slave Law. LC 79-109463. 246p. reprint ed. pap. 76.30 (*0-8357-3863-9*, 203659500004) Bks Demand.
Campbell, Stephen. Cosme Tura of Ferrara: Style, Politics, & the Renaissance City, 1450-1495. LC 97-46071. (Illus.). 240p. 1998. 60.00 (*0-300-07219-8*) Yale U Pr.
— The Great Irish Famine: Words & Images from the Famine Museum Strokestown Park, County Roscommon. (Illus.). 56p. 1994. pap. 11.95 (*0-9523541-1-X*, Pub. by Famine Museum) Irish Bks Media.
Campbell, Stephen A. The Science & Engineering of Semiconductor Fabrication. (Oxford Series in Electrical & Computer Engineering). (Illus.). 560p. (C). 1996. text 89.00 (*0-19-510508-7*) OUP.
Campbell, Stephen J. & Seekins, Sandra. The Body (Un)Veiled: Boundaries of the Figure in Early Modern Europe. (Illus.). 84p. 1997. pap. text 10.00 (*0-9660585-1-8*) U MI Dept Hist.
Campbell, Stephen L. & Haberman, Richard. Introduction to Differential Equations with Boundary Value Problems. 750p. (C). 1996. text 80.36 (*0-395-70828-1*) HM.
Campbell, Steuart. The Loch Ness Monster: The Evidence. rev. ed. (Illus.). 128p. 1991. reprint ed. pap. 11.90 (*0-08-041197-5*, Pub. by Aberdeen U Pr) Macmillan.
Campbell, Steve. Statistics You Can't Trust: A Friendly Guide to Clear Thinking about Statistics in Everyday Life. LC 98-90593. (Illus.). 272p. 1999. pap. 24.95 (*0-9666171-5-0*) Think Twice.
Campbell, Stewart. The Loch Ness Monster: The Evidence. LC 97-36148. (Illus.). 128p. 1997. pap. text 14.95 (*1-57392-178-5*) Prometheus Bks.
***Campbell, Stu.** Good Things to Know... about Gliding on Snow. (Illus.). 2000. pap. 9.95 (*0-9676747-0-0*) Mt Sports Pr.
Campbell, Stu. Home Water Supply: How to Find, Filter, Store & Conserve It. Griffith, Roger, ed. LC 83-1635. (Illus.). 240p. (Orig.). 1983. 14.95 (*0-88266-403-4*, Garden Way Pub) Storey Bks.
— Home Water Supply: How to Find, Filter, Store & Conserve It. Griffith, Roger, ed. LC 83-1635. (Illus.). 240p. (Orig.). 1983. pap. 18.95 (*0-88266-324-0*, Garden Way Pub) Storey Bks.
***Campbell, Stu.** Horsin' Around a Lot. (Illus.). 160p. 1999. pap. 12.95 (*0-9675164-0-4*) Stu Campbell.
— Improving Your Soil. rev. ed. LC 99-15835. 1999. pap. 3.95 (*1-58017-223-7*) Storey Bks.
Campbell, Stu. Let It Rot! The Gardener's Guide to Composting. rev. ed. Foster, Kim, ed. LC 90-50354. (Illus.). 160p. 1990. pap. 8.95 (*0-88266-635-5*) Storey Bks.
— Let It Rot! The Gardener's Guide to Composting. 3rd rev. ed. LC 97-36405. (Illus.). 1998. 11.95 (*1-58017-023-4*, Garden Way Pub) Storey Bks.
— The Mulch Book: A Complete Guide for Gardeners. rev. ed. Moore, Donna, ed. LC 90-50603. (Illus.). 160p. 1991. reprint ed. pap. 10.95 (*0-88266-659-2*) Storey Bks.
***Campbell, Stu.** Mulch It: A Homeowner's Guide to a Carefree Garden & a More Beautiful Landscape. rev. ed. 128p. 2001. pap. 11.95 (*1-58017-316-0*) Storey Bks.
Campbell, Stuart. Translation into the Second Language. LC 97-31003. (Applied Linguistics & Language Study Ser.). 1998. pap. text 23.01 (*0-582-30188-2*) Addison-Wesley.
Campbell, Stuart, ed. Russians on Russian Music, 1830-1880: An Anthology in Translation. 317p. (C). 1994. text 69.95 (*0-521-40267-0*) Cambridge U Pr.
Campbell, Stuart & Green, Anthony, eds. The Archaeology of Death in the Ancient Near East. (Oxbow Monographs in Archaeology: No. 51). (Illus.). 312p. 1995. pap. 60.00 (*0-946897-93-X*, Pub. by Oxbow Bks) David Brown.
Campbell, Stuart, jt. auth. see Watkins, Trevor.
Campbell, Stuart, jt. ed. see Harrington, Kevin P.
Campbell, Stuart L. The Second Empire Revisited: A Study in French Historiography. LC 77-20247. 246p. reprint ed. pap. 76.30 (*0-7837-5660-7*, 205908600005) Bks Demand.
Campbell, Sue. Interpreting the Personal: Expression & the Formation of Feelings. LC 97-26197. 232p. 1998. text 39.95 (*0-8014-3374-6*); pap. text 15.95 (*0-8014-8408-1*) Cornell U Pr.
Campbell, Sue, jt. auth. see Babbitt, Susan.
Campbell, SueEllen. Bringing the Mountain Home. LC 96-4466. 118p. 1996. 32.50 (*0-8165-1616-2*); pap. 15.95 (*0-8165-1617-0*) U of Ariz Pr.
— The Enemy Opposite: The Outlaw Criticism of Wyndham Lewis. LC 87-28330. 251p. 1988. text 29.95 (*0-8214-0887-9*) Ohio U Pr.
Campbell, Susan. Charleston Kedding: A History of Kitchen Gardening. (Illus.). 288p. 1996. 45.00 (*0-09-181385-9*, Pub. by Pavilion Bks Ltd) Trafalgar.
— Expanding Your Teaching Potential: A Role Clarification Guide for Educators & Human Service Workers. enl. ed. LC 76-58637. (Mandala Series in Education). 1983. reprint ed. pap. 15.95 (*0-8290-0349-5*) Irvington.
***Campbell, Susan.** Homelessness: Coordination & Evaluation of Programs Are Essential. (Illus.). 149p. (C). 1999. pap. text 30.00 (*0-7881-8161-0*) DIANE Pub.
Campbell, Susan. Walled Kitchen Gardens. (Album Ser.: No. 339). (Illus.). 32p. 1998. pap. 6.25 (*0-7478-0369-2*, Pub. by Shire Pubns) Parkwest Pubns.
Campbell, Susan, ed. see McQuilkin, Robert.
Campbell, Susan B. Behavior Problems in Preschool Children: Clinical & Developmental Issues. LC 89-16838. 270p. 1990. lib. bdg. 34.50 (*0-89862-395-2*) Guilford Pubns.
Campbell, Susan K. Decision Making in Pediatric Neurologic Physical Therapy. Allen, Andrew, ed. LC 98-38541. 335p. 1999. text. write for info. (*0-443-07923-4*) Church.
***Campbell, Susan Schuster.** Called to Heal: African Shamanic Healing. (Illus.). 179p. 2000. pap. 16.95 (*0-914955-91-8*) Lotus Pr.
Campbell, Susie. Is There Sex After 40? pap. 7.95 (*1-85479-768-9*, Pub. by M OMara) Trafalgar.
Campbell, Suzan. And There Is Only the Dance: The Photography of Chuck Venrick. (Illus.). 48p. 1997. pap. text 10.95 (*1-889921-04-1*, Pub. by Western Edge Pr) Mountain Pr.
Campbell, Suzann K. Physical Therapy for Children. Palisono, Robert & Vander Linden, Darl W., eds. LC 94-10990. (Illus.). 880p. 1994. text. write for info. (*0-7216-6503-9*, W B Saunders Co) Harcrt Hlth Sci Grp.
Campbell, Suzann K., ed. Pediatric Neurologic Physical Therapy. 2nd ed. (Clinics in Physical Therapy Ser.). (Illus.). 459p. 1991. text 60.00 (*0-443-08764-4*) Church.
Campbell, Suzann K. & Wilhelm, Irma J., eds. Meaning of Culture in Pediatric Rehabilitation & Health Care. LC 91-35397. (Physical & Occupational Therapy in Pediatrics Ser.). 72p. 1992. pap. text 19.95 (*1-56024-262-0*) Haworth Pr.

Campbell, Suzanne, jt. auth. see Jones, William N.

Campbell, T. Colin, jt. auth. see Roe, Daphne A.

Campbell, T. Colin, ed. see Chen, Junshi, et al.

Campbell, T. E. Colonial Caroline: A History of Caroline County, Virginia. 1974. reprint ed. 30.00 (*0-87517-039-0*) Dietz.

Campbell, T. J., jt. ed. see Williams, E. M.

Campbell, Tammie L. Honey Brown in Search of Her Identity, Vol. 1. (Illus.). 24p. (Orig.). (J). (gr. k-5). 1990. pap. 4.95 (*0-9623947-0-X*) T L Campbell.

Campbell, Ted. John Wesley & Christian Antiquity. (Kingswood Ser.). (Illus.). 256p. (Orig.). 1991. pap. 18.95 (*0-687-20432-1*) Abingdon.

Campbell, Ted A. Christian Confessions: A Historical Introduction. LC 95-46675. 352p. (Orig.). 1996. pap. 29.95 (*0-664-25650-3*) Westminster John Knox.

— Methodist Doctrine: The Essentials. LC 98-43793. 144p. 1999. pap. 12.00 (*0-687-03475-2*) Abingdon.

***Campbell, Ted A.** The Religion of the Heart. 230p. 2000. pap. 22.00 (*1-57910-433-9*) Wipf & Stock.

Campbell, Teresa B., et al. Lauderdale County, Alabama: Annotated Index to Chancery Court Records, 1827-1830. viii, 53p. (Orig.). 1985. pap. 7.00 (*0-933253-03-6*) Natchez Trace.

***Campbell, Terry.** Fat Chance. (Romance Ser.). 2000. 25.95 (*0-7862-2438-X*) Thorndike Pr.

— Mr. Wrong. LC 99-38418. (Romances Ser.). 1999. 24.95 (*0-7862-2154-2*) Five Star.

Campbell, Terry. A New Owner's Guide to Samoyeds. (Illus.). 160p. 1998. 12.95 (*0-7938-2790-6*, JG141) TFH Pubns.

Campbell, Terry, jt. auth. see Gleim, Irvin N.

Campbell, Terry L. Principles of Accounting, Vol. 1. 2nd rev. ed. 333p. (C). 1989. pap. text 14.50 (*0-15-601651-6*) Harcourt Coll Pubs.

Campbell, Terry L., jt. auth. see Gleim, Irvin N.

Campbell, Terry W. Avian Hematology & Cytology. 2nd ed. LC 94-36354. (Illus.). 112p. 1994. text 62.95 (*0-8138-2970-4*) Iowa St U Pr.

***Campbell-Thiebaud Gallery Staff.** Wayne Thiebaud: Pastels 1960-2000. (Illus.). 2000. pap. write for info. (*0-9701314-0-2*) Campbell Thbd.

Campbell, Thomas. Complete Poetical Works of Thomas Campbell. Robertson, J. Logie, ed. LC 68-24901. (Studies in Poetry: No. 38). 1969. reprint ed. lib. bdg. 75.00 (*0-8383-0924-0*) M S G Haskell Hse.

— The Complete Poetical Works of Thomas Campbell. (BCL1-PR English Literature Ser.). 376p. 1992. reprint ed. lib. bdg. 89.00 (*0-7812-7482-6*) Rprt Serv.

— Gertrude of Wyoming. LC 91-30187. 146p. 1991. reprint ed. 65.00 (*1-85477-061-6*) Continuum.

Campbell, Thomas, ed. see Shakespeare, William.

Campbell, Thomas F. & Miggins, Edward M., eds. The Birth of Modern Cleveland, 1865-1930. LC 86-50868. (Illus.). 405p. 1988. pap. 8.95 (*0-911704-36-1*) Western Res.

Campbell, Thomas G., et al, eds. Computational Electromagnetics & Its Applications. LC 97-33972. (ICASE/LARC Interdisciplinary Series in Science & Engineering: No. 5). 324p. 1997. text 167.00 (*0-7923-4733-1*) Kluwer Academic.

Campbell, Thomas H., jt. auth. see Rivers, D. Wayne.

Campbell, Thomas J., III. The Greenbelt Site: An Example of Variation among Prehistoric Plains Village Sites in the Texas Panhandle. (Illus.). 62p. 1996. pap., spiral bd. 7.95 (*1-885812-02-7*) Aquamarine.

Campbell, Thomas J. The Jesuits, 1534 to 1921, 2 vols. 1977. lib. bdg. 500.00 (*0-8490-2093-X*) Gordon Pr.

Campbell, Thomas L., jt. auth. see Doherty, William J.

Campbell, Thomas M. Masquerade Peace: America's U. N. Policy, 1944-1945. LC 72-93328. 236p. reprint ed. pap. 73.20 (*0-7837-5076-5*, 204477400004) Bks Demand.

— Movable School Goes to the Negro Farmer. Cremin, Lawrence A. & Barnard, Frederick A., eds. LC 78-101403. (American Education). 1974. reprint ed. 17.95 (*0-405-01398-1*) Ayer.

— The Poetical Works. Hill, Alfred, ed. LC 73-39665. (Select Bibliographies Reprint Ser.). 1977. reprint ed. 22.95 (*0-8369-9932-0*) Ayer.

Campbell, Thomas P. & Davidson, Clifford, eds. The Fleury Playbook. (Early Drama, Art & Music Monograph: No. 7). 1985. pap. 10.95 (*0-918720-66-4*); boxed set 19.95 (*0-918720-65-6*) Medieval Inst.

Campbell, Thorbjorn. Standing Witness. LC 97-115606. (C). 1993. pap. 68.00 (*0-85411-061-5*, Pub. by Saltire Soc) St Mut.

— Standing Witnesses. (Illus.). 200p. (C). 1993. text 35.00 (*0-85976-381-1*, Pub. by J Donald) St Mut.

Campbell Thorton, Kim & Parker Guidry, Virginia. For the Love of Dogs. LC 97-207940. (Illus.). 215p. 1997. write for info. (*0-7853-2441-0*) Pubns Intl Ltd.

Campbell, Thrane Lucille, ed. Correspondence Education Moves to the Year 2000: National Invitational Forum on Correspondence Education. 187p. 1984. 16.50 (*0-318-17783-8*, SN47) Ctr Educ Trng Employ.

Campbell-Thrane, Lucille, et al. Building Basic Skills: Models for Implementation. 43p. 1983. 5.75 (*0-318-22047-4*, SN41) Ctr Educ Trng Employ.

Campbell, Tim. Innovations & Risk Taking: The Engine of Reform in Local Government in Latin America & the Caribbean. LC 97-1945. (Discussion Paper Ser.: No. 357). 40p. 1997. pap. 22.00 (*0-8213-3882-X*, 13882) World Bank.

Campbell, Tim S. Money & Capital Markets. (C). 1988. text 67.50 (*0-673-18712-8*) Addson-Wesley Educ.

Campbell, Tim S. & Kracaw, William A. Financial Markets & Institutions. (C). 1994. text 73.95 (*0-673-46330-3*) Addson-Wesley Educ.

Campbell, Timothy A. The Gospel of Timothy: I Saw God & He Had Flesh. 70p. (Orig.). 1996. pap. 10.00 (*1-57502-150-1*) Morris Pubng.

***Campbell, Todd.** Above & Beyond Slickrock. 1999. pap. text 16.95 (*0-87480-627-5*) U of Utah Pr.

Campbell, Tom. Batman & Robin. Sahler, John, ed. (Magic Touch Talking Bks.). (Illus.). (J). (ps-2). 1997. 19.99 (*1-888208-34-1*) Hasbro.

— The Contemplative Stroller. (Illus.). 96p. 1982. pap. 4.95 (*0-9607506-1-4*) News Rev Pub.

— Mental Illness. (Medico-Legal Issues Ser.: Vol. 5). 1991. text 74.95 (*1-85521-028-2*, Pub. by Dartmth Pub) Ashgate Pub Co.

— The Old Man's Trail: A Novel about Vietcong. LC 95-18660. 256p. 1995. 25.95 (*1-55750-117-3*) Naval Inst Pr.

— Seven Theories of Human Society. 250p. (C). 1981. pap. text 23.95 (*0-19-876105-8*) OUP.

— Superman: The Lost Son of Krypton. Sahler, John, ed. (Magic Touch Talking Bks.). (Illus.). (J). (ps-2). 1997. 19.99 (*1-888208-36-8*) Hasbro.

— Windows & DOS File Formats. 1993. pap. write for info. (*0-201-62241-6*) Addison-Wesley.

***Campbell, Tom, ed.** Judicial Power, Democracy & Legal Positivism. LC 99-46651. (Applied Legal Philosophy Ser.). 450p. 2000. text 87.95 (*0-7546-2061-1*, Pub. by Ashgate Pub) Ashgate Pub Co.

Campbell, Tom D. Law & Enlightenment in Britain. (Enlightenment Rights & Revolution Ser.). 200p. 1990. pap. text 38.00 (*0-08-040921-0*, Pub. by Aberdeen U Pr) Macmillan.

— The Legal Theory of Ethical Positivism. (Applied Legal Philosophy Ser.). (Illus.). 304p. 1996. text 87.95 (*1-85521-171-8*, Pub. by Dartmth Pub) Ashgate Pub Co.

***Campbell, Tom D., ed.** Legal Positivism. LC 99-72416. (International Library of Essays in Law & Legal Theory). 500p. 1999. text 175.95 (*1-84014-732-6*, Pub. by Ashgate Pub) Ashgate Pub Co.

Campbell, Tom D. & Sadurski, W., eds. Freedom of Communication. (Applied Legal Philosophy). 315p. 1994. 87.95 (*1-85521-542-X*, Pub. by Dartmth Pub) Ashgate Pub Co.

Campbell, Tom D., jt. ed. see Arnheim, Michael.

Campbell, Tom D., ed. see Patterson, Dennis.

Campbell, Tom D., ed. see White, Patricia D.

Campbell, Tracy. The Politics of Despair: Power & Resistance in the Tobacco Wars. LC 92-47277. 240p. 1993. text 29.95 (*0-8131-1821-2*) U Pr of Ky.

— Short of the Glory: The Fall & Redemption of Edward F. Prichard, Jr. LC 98-29859. (Illus.). 360p. 1998. 29.95 (*0-8131-2073-X*) U Pr of Ky.

Campbell, Trini M. Simplemente Yo. 62p. (Orig.). 1993. pap. 7.00 (*0-913983-06-3*) M & A Edns.

Campbell, Tyrone, et al. Navajo Pictorial Weaving, 1880-1950. (Illus.). 128p. 1995. pap. 19.95 (*0-8263-1617-4*) U of NM Pr.

Campbell, Tyrone D. Fact, Fun & Fantasy: Navajo Pictorial Weavings from the Weber Collection. 32p. 1994. pap. 18.00 (*0-9639643-0-5*) UNA AZ.

Campbell, Vicki L. & Watkins, C. Edward, Jr. Testing in Counseling Practice. Walsh, W. Bruce & Osipow, Samuel H., eds. (Contemporary Topics in Vocational Psychology Ser.). 512p. 1993. reprint ed. pap. 39.95 (*0-8058-1439-6*) L Erlbaum Assocs.

Campbell, Vicki L., jt. ed. see Watkins, C. Edward, Jr.

Campbell, Victor. The Wicked Mate: The Antarctic Diary of Victor Campbell. King, Harry, ed. & intro. by. (Antarctic Classics Ser.). (Illus.). 192p. (C). 1989. 120.00 (*1-85297-030-8*, Pub. by Archival Facs) St Mut.

Campbell, Victor S. Junction - County Road 197: Mild Adventure for the Armchair Ruralist. LC 89-16209. (Illus.). 294p. 1992. 25.00 (*0-933776-32-2*) Xander Creek.

Campbell, Vincent. Noah's Ark. 184p. (Orig.). 1987. pap. 7.95 (*0-9617742-0-7*) Decision Syst.

Campbell, Vincent, et al. Decisions - Based on Science. LC 97-68383. (Illus.). 144p. 1997. pap. text 19.95 (*0-87355-165-6*, PB141X) Natl Sci Tchrs.

Campbell, Viola D. Juguemos.Tr. of Let's Play. (SPA., Illus.). 199p. 1960. reprint ed. pap. 9.50 (*0-311-11006-1*) Casa Bautista.

— Recreacion Cristiana.Tr. of Christian Recreation - Games & Programs. (SPA., Illus.). 160p. 1980. reprint ed. pap. 10.50 (*0-311-11037-1*) Casa Bautista.

Campbell, W., jt. auth. see Clark, S. H.

Campbell, W. A. Industrial Chemistry 1800-1900. (History of Chemistry Wallcharts Ser.). 1993. 17.00 (*0-85186-470-8*, R6470) CRC Pr.

— Milestones in 150 Years of the Chemical Industry, No. 96. Roberts, H. L., ed. 1991. 87.00 (*0-85186-456-2*) CRC Pr.

Campbell, W. B. Complications in Arterial Surgery. LC 96-162886. 224p. 1996. text 125.00 (*0-7506-0568-5*) Buttrwrth-Heinemann.

Campbell, W. C., ed. Ivermectin & Abanectin. (Illus.). 360p. 1994. 92.95 (*0-387-96944-6*) Spr-Verlag.

***Campbell, W. Cothran.** Lightning in a Jar: Catching Racing Fever: A Thoroughbred Owner's Guide. 256p. 2000. 29.95 (*1-58150-053-X*, Pub. by Blood-Horse) IPG Chicago.

Campbell, W. John. Lysistrata, the Birds, the Clouds, & the Frogs Notes. (Cliffs Notes Ser.). 80p. (C). 1983. pap. text 4.95 (*0-8220-0776-2*, Cliff) IDG Bks.

Campbell, W. Joseph. The Emergent Independent Press in Benin & Cote D'Ivoire: From Voice of the State to Advocate of Democracy. LC 98-15655. 152p. 1998. 55.00 (*0-275-96309-8*, Praeger Pubs) Greenwood.

Campbell, W. L., ed. see Nagarjuna.

Campbell, Wade. The Universe Phenomenon: The Meaning of Life. unabridged ed. (Illus.). 136p. 1998. write for info. (*0-9666308-0-7*) W Campbell.

Campbell, Wallace H. Earth Electrical Conductivity: PAGEOPH Ser., Vol. 134. 96p. 1991. 13.50 (*0-8176-2564-X*) Birkhauser.

— Introduction to Geomagnetic Fields. (Illus.). 302p. (C). 1997. text 69.95 (*0-521-57193-6*) Cambridge U Pr.

— Quiet Daily Geomagnetic Fields. 234p. 1989. 27.50 (*0-8176-2338-8*) Birkhauser.

Campbell, Wallace H., ed. Electrical Properties of the Earth's Mantle. 400p. 1987. 34.50 (*0-8176-1901-1*) Birkhauser.

Campbell, Wallace J. The History of CARE: A Personal Account. LC 90-31860. 256p. 1990. 57.95 (*0-275-93231-1*, C3231, Praeger Pubs) Greenwood.

Campbell, Walter E. Across Fortune's Tracks: A Biography of William Rand Kenan, Jr. LC 95-34702. (Illus.). 434p. (C). 1996. 39.95 (*0-8078-2268-X*) U of NC Pr.

Campbell, Walter S. Mountain Men. LC 77-99620. (Essay Index Reprint Ser.). 1977. 27.95 (*0-8369-1397-3*) Ayer.

Campbell, Wanda. Suicide: Reason for Living. 65p. (YA). (gr. 7-12). 1995. pap. 6.95 (*1-57515-049-2*) PPI Pubng.

Campbell, Wayne, jt. auth. see Bovey, Robin.

Campbell, Wendy L., jt. compiled by see Keeling, Brian.

Campbell, Wesley. Welcoming a Visitation of the Holy Spirit. LC 95-68308. 1995. pap. 10.99 (*0-88419-410-8*) Creation House.

Campbell, Wilbur, jt. auth. see Biasiotto, Judson.

Campbell, Wilfred. At the Mermaid Inn: Wilfred Campbell, Archibald Lampman, Duncan Campbell Scott in the Globe, 1892-93. LC 79-313103. (Literature of Canada, Poetry & Prose in Reprint Ser.: No. 21). 377p. reprint ed. pap. 116.90 (*0-8357-5828-1*, 202364200033) Bks Demand.

— The Scotsman in Canada Vol. 1: Eastern Canada, including Nova Scotia, Prince Edward Island, New Brunswick, Quebec & Ontario, 2. (Illus.). 432p. 1998. reprint ed. pap. 60.00 (*1-58211-067-0*, 097640) Quintin Pub RI.

Campbell, Will D. And Also with You: Duncan Gray & the American Dilemma. LC 97-73595. 288p. 1997. 26.95 (*1-57736-036-2*) Providence Hse.

— Brother to a Dragonfly. LC 63-20159. 268p. 1980. pap. 14.95 (*0-8264-0032-9*) Continuum.

***Campbell, Will D.** Brother to a Dragonfly. 25th anniversary ed. LC 00-31402. 2000. write for info. (*0-8264-1296-3*) Continuum.

Campbell, Will D. The Convention: A Parable. LC 88-61455. 414p. reprint ed. pap. 128.40 (*0-7837-6555-X*, 204612000011) Bks Demand.

***Campbell, Will D.** Forty Acres & a Goat: A Memoir. 286p. 2000. pap. 26.00 (*1-57910-121-6*) Wipf & Stock.

Campbell, Will D. The Pear Tree That Bloomed in the Fall. LC 96-70723. (Father Thyme Bks.). (Illus.). 32p. (J). (gr. 1-5). 1996. 14.95 (*1-57736-017-6*) Providence Hse.

— Providence. LC 91-77196. 336p. 1992. 19.95 (*1-56352-024-9*) Longstreet.

— Soul among Lions: Musings of a Bootleg Preacher. LC 98-53718. (Illus.). 96p. 1999. 14.95 (*0-664-22130-0*) Westminster John Knox.

— The Stem of Jesse: Costs of Community at a 1960s Southern School. LC 94-25708. 1994. 25.00 (*0-86554-449-2*, MUP/H356) Mercer Univ Pr.

Campbell, William, Jr. Formosa under the Dutch: Described from Contemporary Records. 629p. 1987. reprint ed. 40.00 (*0-89986-379-5*) Oriental Bk Store.

— Missionary Success in the Island of Formosa, 2 vols. 1000p. 1996. reprint ed. 75.00 (*957-638-299-8*) Oriental Bk Store.

— Sketches from Formosa. 394p. 1996. reprint ed. 40.00 (*957-638-377-3*) Oriental Bk Store.

— A Workingman Skiff. 112p. (Orig.). 1995. pap. 9.95 (*0-924771-51-8*, Covered Brdge Pr) Douglas Charles Ltd.

Campbell, William, Jr., ed. Materials for a History of the Reign of Henry VII from Original Documents Preserved in the Public Record Office, 2 vols. (Rolls Ser.: No. 60). 1969. reprint ed. 140.00 (*0-8115-1128-6*) Periodicals Srv.

Campbell, William, Jr., jt. auth. see Gravius, D.

Campbell, William A. Casting Your Vote in North Carolina. 2nd ed. 25p. (YA). (gr. 10-12). 1990. pap. text 6.00 (*1-56011-171-2*) Institute Government.

— Guidebook for North Carolina Property Mappers. 2nd ed. 64p. (C). 1995. pap. text 11.00 (*1-56011-232-8*) Institute Government.

***Campbell, William A.** North Carolina City & County Privilege License Taxes. 5th ed. (C). 2000. pap. 14.50 (*1-56011-365-0*) Institute Government.

Campbell, William A. North Carolina Guidebook for Registers of Deeds. 8th ed. 2000. pap. write for info. (*1-56011-353-7*) Institute Government.

***Campbell, William A.** Notary Public Guidebook for North Carolina. 7th rev. ed. LC 99-229796. (C). 1999. pap. text 10.00 (*1-56011-348-0*, 99.04) Institute Government.

— Notary Public Guidebook for North Carolina. 8th ed. (C). 2000. pap. write for info. (*1-56011-382-0*) Institute Government.

Campbell, William A. Property Tax Collection in North Carolina. 4th ed. LC 98-132171. 286p. 1998. pap. text 34.00 (*1-56011-302-2*, 97.04) Institute Government.

***Campbell, William A.** Property Tax Collection in North Carolina: 2000 Supplement. (C). 2000. pap. write for info. (*1-56011-375-8*) Institute Government.

Campbell, William A. Property Tax Lien Foreclosure: Forms & Procedures. 5th ed. (C). 1999. pap. text 19.00 (*1-56011-323-5*) Institute Government.

Campbell, William C., ed. Trichinella & Trichinosis. LC 82-2390. 606p. 1983. 125.00 (*0-306-41140-7*, Plenum Trade) Perseus Pubng.

Campbell, William C. & Rew, Robert S., eds. Chemotherapy of Parasitic Diseases. LC 85-19377. (Illus.). 684p. (C). 1986. text 174.00 (*0-306-42029-5*, Kluwer Plenum) Kluwer Academic.

***Campbell, William E.** Behavior Problems in Dogs. 3rd rev. ed. LC 98-93966. (Illus.). 328p. 1999. pap. 24.95 (*0-9668705-0-6*, BPD99) Behaviorx Systs.

— Dog Behavior Problems - The Counselor's Handbook. LC 99-96430. vii, 115p. 1999. pap. 19.95 (*0-9668705-1-4*, DBP99, Pub. by Behaviorx Systs) Dogwise Dog.

Campbell, William E. The New Better Behavior in Dogs: A Guide to Solving All Your Dog's Problems. LC 99-10974. (Illus.). 302p. 1999. pap. 16.95 (*1-57779-018-9*) Alpine Pubns.

— The Power to Learn: Helping Yourself to College Success. 2nd ed. LC 96-21479. (Freshman Orientation Ser.). 235p. (C). 1996. 31.95 (*0-534-26352-6*) Wadsworth Pub.

Campbell, William E. & Campbell, Cynthia J. Campbell's Guide to Cruising Texas. LC 96-85034. (Illus.). 384p. 1996. spiral bd. 29.95 (*0-9652635-0-9*) W Eden.

Campbell, William E. & Smith, Karl A., eds. New Paradigms for College Teaching. 285p. (Orig.). 1997. pap. text, teacher ed. 20.00 (*0-939603-26-8*) Interaction Bk Co.

Campbell, William F. The Qur'an & the Bible in the Light of History & Science. ix, 343p. 1986. pap. 12.00 (*1-881085-00-7*, 5007, Pub. by Middle E Res) Chr Lit.

Campbell, William H. Anthropology for the People: A Refutation of the Theory of the Adamic Origin of All Races. LC 72-6467. (Black Heritage Library Collection). 1977. reprint ed. 29.95 (*0-8369-9154-0*) Ayer.

Campbell, William H., jt. auth. see Campbell, Elizabeth W.

Campbell, William M., Jr. Born to Dream: How to Unlock the God-Given Dreams Inside You; Life-Changing Lessons from the Story of Joseph. 112p. 1998. pap. 7.95 (*1-58169-009-6*, WC101, Third Stry Window) Genesis Comm Inc.

Campbell, William P. Appalachian Gold. (Illus.). 52p. 1976. pap. 4.95 (*0-932807-04-6*) Overmountain Pr.

Campbell, William P. Focus on Adults: A Handbook for Teachers. (Focus On Ser.). 128p. 1993. pap. 4.50 (*0-88243-407-1*) Gospel Pub.

Campbell, William S. Paul's Gospel in an Intercultural Context: Jew & Gentile in the Letter to the Romans. 2nd ed. LC 92-20330. VII, 213p. 1992. 45.00 (*3-631-42981-9*) P Lang Pubng.

Campbell, William W. Annals of Tryon County, N.Y. 257p. 1993. reprint ed. lib. bdg. 29.50 (*0-8328-3075-5*) Higginson Bk Co.

— Annals of Tyron County, N.Y. 257p. 1993. reprint ed. lib. bdg. 79.00 (*0-7812-5169-9*) Rprt Serv.

— The Border Warfare of New York During the Revolution: The Annals of Tryon County. 406p. 1992. reprint ed. pap. 26.00 (*1-55613-612-9*) Heritage Bk.

— Essentials of Electrodiagnostic Medicine. LC 98-14102. 338p. 1998. 79.00 (*0-683-30239-6*) Lppncott W & W.

***Campbell, William W.** The Great Hoo-Hah. (Illus.). 48p. (J). (gr. k-4). 2000. pap. 6.95 (*1-58066-059-2*, Covered Brdge Pr) Douglas Charles Ltd.

Campbells Staff. Campbell's Back Label Recipes & More. 96p. 1996. 12.95 (*0-696-20505-X*) Meredith Bks.

***Campbell's Staff.** Campbell's Healthy Request Healthy Cooking Made Easy. LC 98-141876. 96p. 1998. 12.95 (*0-696-20842-3*) Meredith Bks.

Campden, Jan Van, see Jorg, Christiaan & Van Campden, Jan.

Campden-Main, Simon M. A Field Guide to the Snakes of South Vietnam. (Illus.). 1983. reprint ed. pap. 9.95 (*0-9612494-0-4*) Herpetological Search.

Campderros, Daniel. Bosquejos Biblicos Tomo I: Antiguo Testamento. 96p. 1966. reprint ed. pap. 6.50 (*0-311-43025-2*) Casa Bautista.

— Bosquejos Biblicos Tomo II: Biblical Sermon N.T. Outlines. 96p. 1966. reprint ed. pap. 6.50 (*0-311-43026-0*) Casa Bautista.

— Bosquejos Biblicos Tomo III: Biblical Sermon Outlines. 96p. 1974. reprint ed. pap. 6.50 (*0-311-43033-3*) Casa Bautista.

***Campe, K. M.** Evaluation of AP600 Containment Thermal-hydraulic Performance. 136p. 1998. per. 11.00 (*0-16-062748-6*) USGPO.

Campe, Petra. Case, Semantic Roles, & Grammatical Relations: A Comprehensive Bibliography. LC 94-4230. (Case & Grammatical Relations Across Languages Ser.: Vol. 1). vii, 644p. 1994. lib. bdg. 125.00 (*1-55619-675-X*) J Benjamins Pubng Co.

Campeanu, Pavel. Exit: Toward Post-Stalinism. LC 90-8853. 184p. 1990. text 70.95 (*0-87332-587-7*) M E Sharpe.

— The Genesis of the Stalinist Social Order. LC 88-26324. 172p. (gr. 13). 1988. text 70.95 (*0-87332-420-X*) M E Sharpe.

— The Origins of Stalinism: From Leninist Revolution to Stalinist Society. LC 84-18410. 200p. (gr. 13). 1986. text 70.95 (*0-87332-363-7*) M E Sharpe.

***Campeau.** Limited Radiography. 2nd ed. LC 98-27596. (Allied Health Ser.). 352p. 1998. text 45.95 (*0-7668-0205-1*) Delmar.

Campeau, Frances. Radiography: Technology, Environment, Professionalism. LC 98-24217. 350p. 1998. pap. text 29.95 (*0-397-55196-7*) Lppncott W & W.

Campeau, Frances E. & Phelps, Jeana. Limited Radiography. LC 92-49682. (C). 1992. mass mkt. 32.00 (*0-8273-3335-8*) Delmar.

Campeau, Frances E. & Phelps, M. Jeana. Limited Radiography: Instructor's Guide. 50p. 1993. 14.00 (*0-8273-3336-6*) Delmar.

Campeau, Joesph. Finding That Extra in the Ordinary: Discovering God on Ordinary Days, Serving God in Ordinary Wa. 1999. pap. text 8.99 (*0-87509-772-3*) Chr Pubns.

Campeau, Stephanie, et al. Diatoms from the Beaufort Sea Coast, Southern Arctic Ocean (Canada) (Bibliotheca Diatomologica Ser.: Band 42). (Illus.). vi, 244p. 1999. pap. 120.00 incl. cd-rom (*3-443-57033-X*) Gebruder Borntraeger.

C

Campell, Danny & Campbell, Kim S. Skeeter Loves Patti? (Doug Chronicles: no. 14). (Illus.). 64p. (J). (gr. 2-4). 2000. pap. 5.00 (*0-7868-4322-5*, Pub. by Disney Pr) Time Warner.

Campell, David L. Learn Visual Basic 5.0 in Three Days. LC 97-24327. (Illus.). 250p. 1997. pap. 19.95 incl. disk (*1-55622-542-3*) Wordware Pub.

***Campell, Dawn & Halderman, Karen.** Word Walls Activities. (Illus.). 208p. (J). (gr. k-3). 1999. pap., teacher ed. 15.95 (*1-57690-481-4*, TCM2481) Tchr Create Mat.

Campell, Giraud W. A Doctor's Proven New Home Cure for Arthritis. 224p. (C). 1989. pap. text 10.95 (*0-13-216375-6*) P-H.

Campell, James B. Mapping the Land: Aerial Imagery for Land Use Information. Knight, C. Gregory, ed. 85p. (Orig.). 1983. pap. 15.00 (*0-89291-167-0*) Assn Am Geographers.

Campell, James B. Mapping the Land: Aerial Imagery for Land Use Information. (Orig.). 1987. 75.00 (*0-7855-1973-4*, Pub. by Scientific) St Mut.

Campell, Ken. Old King Cole. (Oberon Bks.). 96p. 1997. pap. 12.95 (*1-870259-12-2*) Theatre Comm.

***Campell, Kumari.** Prince Edward Island. (Hello Canada Ser.). 1999. pap. 7.95 (*1-55041-267-1*) Fitzhenry & W Ltd.

Campell, M. A., et al. The Employment of Airpower in the Greek Guerrilla War, 1947-1949. (Air University Project Ser.: No. AU-411-62-ASI). 80p. 1964. reprint ed. pap. text 25.95 (*0-89126-158-3*) MA-AH Pub.

Campen, Alan D., ed. The First Information War: The Story of Communications, Computers, & Intelligence Systems in the Persian Gulf War. LC 92-33100. 195p. 1992. 18.95 (*0-916159-24-8*) AFCEA Intl Pr.

Campen, Alan D., et al, eds. Cyberwar: Security, Strategy & Conflict in the Information Age. LC 96-19365. (Illus.). 298p. 1996. 24.95 (*0-916159-26-4*) AFCEA Intl Pr.

***Campen, Alan D. & Dearth, Douglas H.** Cyberwar 3.0: Human Factors in Information Operations & Future Conflict. LC 00-41615. 2000. write for info. (*0-916159-29-9*) AFCEA Intl Pr.

Campen, Alan D. & Dearth, Douglas H. Cyberwar 2.0: Myths, Mysteries & Reality. 1998. 29.95 (*0-916159-27-2*) AFCEA Intl Pr.

Campen, James T. Benefit, Cost, & Beyond: The Political Economy of Benefit-Cost Analysis. LC 86-10718. 256p. 1986. text 34.95 (*0-88730-106-1*, HarpBusn) HarpInfo.

Campen, Richard N. Distinguished Homes of Shaker Heights: An Architectural Overview. LC 91-72012. (Illus.). 144p. 1992. write for info. (*0-9601356-7-7*) West Summit.

— Images of Sanibel-Captiva-Fort Myers. LC 95-60829. (Illus.). 1995. pap. 14.95 (*0-9601356-8-5*) West Summit.

Campen, S. I. Van, see Van Campen, S. I.

Campenhausen, Hans Von, see Von Campenhausen, Hans.

Camper, Anne K. Factors Limiting Microbial Growth in the Distribution System Pt. 1: Laboratory & Pilot - Scale Experiments. LC 97-106343. (Illus.). 146p. 1996. pap. 195.00 (*0-89867-876-5*) Am Water Wks Assn.

***Camper, Anne K. & AWWA Research Foundation Staff.** Investigation of the Biological Stability of Water in Treatment Plants & Distribution Systems. LC 00-32758. 2000. write for info. (*1-58321-072-5*) Am Water Wks Assn.

Camper, Anne K. & AWWA Research Foundation Staff. Pathogens in Model Distribution System Biofilms. LC 97-31828. 1997. write for info. (*0-89867-932-X*, 90738) Am Water Wks Assn.

***Camper, Anne K. & Jones, Warren L.** Factors Affecting Microbial Growth in Model Distribution Systems. LC 99-53761. 2000. write for info. (*1-58321-051-2*) Am Water Wks Assn.

Camper, Carol. Bugs Before Time. LC 98-22872. (J). 2001. per. 16.00 (*0-689-82092-5*) S&S Childrens.

Camper, Carol, ed. Miscegenation Blues: Voices of Mixed Race Women. LC 95-156038. (Illus.). 416p. 1994. per. 19.95 (*0-920813-95-X*) Sister Vis Pr.

Camper, Frank. High Seas Security. LC 93-77150. (Illus.). 80p. (Orig.). 1993. pap. 10.00 (*1-55950-102-2*, 17061) Loompanics.

***Camper, Jennifer.** SubGURLZ. (Illus.). 120p. 1999. pap. 10.95 (*1-57344-090-6*, Pub. by Cleis Pr) Publishers Group.

***Camper, L. W.** Source Disconnects Resulting from Radiography Drive Cable Failures: Final Report. 260p. 1998. per. 21.00 (*0-16-062749-4*) USGPO.

Campert, Remco. This Happened Everywhere: Selected Poems of Remco Campert. Wolf, Manfred, tr. from DUT. 84p. (Orig.). 1997. pap. 12.00 (*1-879594-20-X*) Androgyne Bks.

Campese, V. M. & Hsueh, W. A., eds. The Kidney in Hypertension. (Journal: American Journal of Nephrology Ser.: Vol. 3, No. 2-3). (Illus.). vi, 140p. 1983. pap. 88.75 (*3-8055-3648-8*) S Karger.

Campesino, Antonio, tr. see Weinberg, Steven L., ed.

***Campetella, Andrea, et al.** Defining the Nonprofit Sector: Argentina. (Working Papers of the Johns Hopkins Comparative Nonprofit Sector Project: Vol. 33). (Illus.). 30p. 1998. pap. text 6.00 (*1-886333-38-6*) JH Univ Inst Pol Studies.

Campfens, Hubert. Community Development Around the World: Practice, Theory, Research & Training. LC 97-133084. (Illus.). 520p. 1997. pap. text 24.95 (*0-8020-7884-2*) U of Toronto Pr.

Campfens, Hubert, ed. Community Development Around the World: Practice, Theory, Research, Training. (Illus.). 481p. 1997. text 60.00 (*0-8020-0903-4*) U of Toronto Pr.

Campfield. Estate Planning & Drafting. 2nd ed. LC 95-234170. 1128p. 1995. 89.00 (*0-8080-0067-5*, BLS-3421) CCH INC.

Campfield, Regis W., et al. Taxation of Estates, Gifts & Trusts. 12th ed. (American Casebook Ser.). 210p. 1997. pap. text, teacher ed., suppl. ed. write for info. (*0-314-22769-5*) West Pub.

— Taxation of Estates, Gifts & Trusts. 20th ed. LC 97-2351. (American Casebook Ser.). 863p. (C). 1997. text. write for info. (*0-314-21204-3*) West Pub.

Camphausen, Rufus C. The Divine Library: A Comprehensive Reference Guide to the Sacred Texts & Spiritual Literature of the World. LC 91-39547. (Illus.). 128p. (Orig.). 1992. pap. 12.95 (*0-89281-351-2*) Inner Tradit.

— The Encyclopedia of Sacred Sexuality: From Aphrodisiacs & Ecstasy to Yoni Worship & Zap-Lam Yoga. LC 98-23650. (Illus.). 288p. 1998. pap. 29.95 (*0-89281-719-4*) Inner Tradit.

— Return of the Tribal: A Celebration of Body Adornment. LC 97-17043. (Illus.). 160p. 1997. pap. 19.95 (*0-89281-610-4*) Inner Tradit.

— The Yoni: Sacred Symbol of Female Creative Power. (Illus.). 144p. 1996. pap. 19.95 (*0-89281-562-0*) Inner Tradit.

Camphor, Alexander P. Missionary Story Sketches: Folk-Lore from Africa. LC 79-173603. (Black Heritage Library Collection). 1977. reprint ed. 28.95 (*0-8369-8915-5*) Ayer.

Campi, Mario & Ciorra, Pippo. Young Italian Architects: Giovani Architetti Italiani. LC 98-14469. 1998. write for info. (*0-8176-5783-5*) Birkhauser.

Campi, Mario & Ciorra, Pippo, eds. Young Italian Architects. LC 98-14469. (ENG & ITA., Illus.). 149p. 1998. pap. 45.00 (*3-7643-5783-5*, Pub. by Birkhauser) Princeton Arch.

***Campi, Mario & Zurkirchen, Patrick.** Skyscrapers: An Urban Type. (Illus.). 240p. 2000. pap. write for info. (*3-7643-6130-1*, Pub. by Birkhauser) Spr-Verlag.

***Campiche, David.** Sometime Around Midnight. (Chapbooks Ser.: Vol. 6). 38p. 2000. pap. 8.00 (*1-930259-10-7*) Anabasis.

Campidonica, Mark. How to Find Agricultural Information on the Internet. Auburn, Jill S., ed. LC 97-61146. (Illus.). viii, 92p. 1997. pap. 12.00 (*1-879906-31-7*, 3387) ANR Pubns CA.

***Campiglia, James & Wells, Steve.** The Official US Casino Chip Price Guide. (Illus.). 320p. 2000. pap. 29.95 (*0-7643-1157-3*) Schiffer.

Campilho, A., jt. ed. see Barbosa, M. A.

Campillo, Anthony J., jt. ed. see Chang, Richard K.

Campilonga, Margaret S. Blue Frogs: The Second Adventure in John's Colorful World. LC 96-84399. (John's Colorful World Ser.: No. 2). (Illus.). 32p. (J). (ps-3). 1996. lib. bdg. 13.95 (*0-9646904-1-1*) Chicken Soup.

— The Green Giraffe: The Third Adventure in John's Colorful World. LC 97-69358. (John's Colorful World Ser.: No. 3). (Illus.). 32p. (J). (ps-3). 1997. lib. bdg. 13.95 (*0-9646904-4-6*) Chicken Soup.

— I Am the Flute. LC 91-62535. 1992. 15.00 (*0-87212-252-2*) Libra.

— Inland Wind: Poems of the Seashore. LC 94-5760. (Illus.). 52p. 1994. 7.95 (*0-912526-70-X*) Lib Res.

— The Yellow Lion: The First Adventure in John's Colorful World. LC 95-69561. (John's Colorful World Ser.: No. 1). (Illus.). 32p. (J). (ps-3). 1995. lib. bdg. 13.95 (*0-9646904-0-3*) Chicken Soup.

Camping, Harold. 1994? (POR.). 595p. 1994. pap. 14.95 (*1-885000-01-4*) Omega Pr Fmly Stat.

— 1994? (ARA.). 605p. 1994. pap. 14.95 (*1-885000-02-2*) Omega Pr Fmly Stat.

— 1994. Campins, Anaceli G., tr. (SPA.). 588p. (Orig.). (C). 1994. pap. 14.95 (*1-885000-00-6*) Omega Pr Fmly Stat.

Campins, Anaceli G., tr. see Camping, Harold.

Campio, jt. auth. see Kyriakou.

***Campion, Anna & Campion, Jane.** Holy Smoke: A Novel. 259p. (J). 1999. 18.45 (*0-7868-6349-8*, Pub. by Hyperion) Time Warner.

Campion, Charles, jt. auth. see Kyriakou, Theodore.

Campion, D. R., et al. Animal Growth Regulation. LC 88-31736. (Illus.). 424p. (C). 1989. text 125.00 (*0-306-42978-0*, Kluwer Plenum) Kluwer Academic.

Campion, Dan. Peter De Vries & Surrealism. LC 95-5571. 240p. 1995. 37.50 (*0-8387-5311-6*) Bucknell U Pr.

Campion, Daniel. Calypso. (Illus.). 40p. (Orig.). 1981. pap. 3.00 (*0-9603794-1-X*) Syncline.

Campion, Donald R. & Louapre, Albert C., eds. Documents of the Thirty-Third General Congregation of the Society of Jesus: An English Translation of the Official Latin Texts. LC 84-80080. (Jesuit Primary Sources in English Translation Ser.: No. 5). 115p. 1984. pap. 3.00 (*0-912422-64-5*) Inst Jesuit.

Campion, E., ed. see Du Ryer.

Campion, Edmund. A Historie of Ireland. LC 41-6539. 168p. 1977. reprint ed. 50.00 (*0-8201-1191-0*) Schol Facsimiles.

Campion, Edmund J. Montaigne, Rabelais, & Marot as Readers of Erasmus. LC 95-1894. 1995. write for info. (*0-7734-9029-9*) E Mellen.

Campion, James. Deep Tank Jersey. 1997. pap. 15.00 (*0-9635338-5-1*, Callaloo Pr) Vegetarian Dining.

***Campion, Jane.** Holy Smoke. (Illus.). 272p. 1999. pap. 14.00 (*0-7868-8563-7*, Pub. by Hyperion) Time Warner.

Campion, Jane. The Piano. (Illus.). 160p. (J). 1993. pap. 9.50 (*1-56282-703-0*, Pub. by Hyperion) Time Warner.

Campion, Jane & Pullinger, Kate. The Piano. large type ed. (Charnwood Large Print Ser.). 1995. 27.99 (*0-7089-8833-4*, Charnwood) Ulverscroft.

— The Piano: A Novel. 218p. (J). 1995. pap. 12.45 (*0-7868-8096-1*, Pub. by Hyperion) Time Warner.

Campion, Jane, jt. auth. see Campion, Anna.

Campion, Jane, jt. auth. see Lee, Gerard.

Campion, Jennifer, jt. auth. see Wissolik, Richard D.

Campion, Joan, et al. Smokestacks & Black Diamonds: A History of Carbon County, Pennsylvania. LC 98-9593. (Illus.). 286p. 1998. pap. 29.50 (*0-930973-19-4*) H M Historical.

Campion, Kitty. Holistic Woman's Herbal: How to Achieve Health & Well-Being at Any Age. LC 96-18750. 256p. 1996. pap. 16.95 (*1-885203-37-3*) Jrny Editions.

***Campion, L.** Liaison Pride & Prurience. 1998. mass mkt. 6.95 (*0-7472-5768-X*) Headline Bk Pub.

***Campion, Lynn H.** Training & Showing the Cutting Horse. 2000. pap. 19.95 (*1-58574-184-1*) Lyons Pr.

Campion, Mary, compiled by. Jupiter's Children. LC 99-187435. (Illus.). 192p. 1998. pap. 16.95 (*0-85323-753-0*, Pub. by Liverpool Univ Pr) Intl Spec Bk.

Campion, Michael, et al. Modern Colposcopy: A Practical Approach. (Illus.). 280p. (Orig.). (C). 1991. pap. text. write for info. (*0-9629655-0-2*) Educ Systems.

Campion, Mukti J. The Baby Challenge: A Handbook on Pregnancy for Women with a Physical Disability. LC 89-39067. 219p. (C). 1990. pap. text 15.95 (*0-415-04859-1*, A4697) Routledge.

— Good Parent Guide. LC 93-34167. 1994. pap. 10.95 (*1-85230-425-1*, Pub. by Element MA) Penguin Putnam.

— Who's Fit to Be A Parent? LC 94-8500. 336p. (C). 1995. pap. 27.99 (*0-415-06684-0*, A7822) Routledge.

Campion, Nardi R. Mother Ann Lee, Morning Star of the Shakers. LC 90-50305. (Illus.). 205p. (YA). (gr. 9-10). 1990. reprint ed. pap. 15.95 (*0-87451-527-0*) U Pr of New Eng.

Campion, Nicholas & Eddy, Steve. The New Astrology: The Art & Science of the Stars. (Illus.). 288p. 1999. 35.00 (*1-57076-152-3*, Trafalgar Sq Pub) Trafalgar.

Campion, Owen F. The Rosary on Tape. 7.95 incl. audio (*0-87973-188-5*, 188) Our Sunday Visitor.

Campion, Thomas. Campion's Work. 400p. 1990. reprint ed. lib. bdg. 79.00 (*0-7812-9056-2*) Rprt Serv.

— The Description of a Maske, in Honour of the Lord Hayes. LC 75-25214. (English Experience Ser.: No. 153). 20p. 1969. reprint ed. 15.00 (*90-221-0153-3*) Walter J Johnson.

— Observations in the Art of English Poesie. LC 78-38164. (English Experience Ser.: No. 441). 52p. 1972. reprint ed. 15.00 (*90-221-0441-9*) Walter J Johnson.

— Thomas Campion (1567-1620) Ayres & Observations. Hart, Joan, ed. 1976. pap. 7.50 (*0-85635-099-0*) Carcanet Pr.

Campione. Java Tutor Continued. LC 98-37595. 976p. (C). 1998. pap. text 39.95 (*0-201-48558-3*) Addison-Wesley.

Campione, Adele. Women's Hats: Il Cappello da Donna. Jensen, Jack, ed. LC 93-47971. (Bella Cosa Ser.). (ITA & ENG., Illus.). 144p. 1994. pap. 12.95 (*0-8118-0781-9*) Chronicle Bks.

Campione, Mary. The Java Tutorial. 2nd ed. LC 97-43574. (Java Tutorial Ser.). 992p. (C). 1998. pap. text 45.95 (*0-201-31007-4*) Addison-Wesley.

***Campione, Mary & Walrath, Kathy.** The Java Tutorial. 3rd ed. 560p. 2000. pap. text 39.95 incl. cd-rom (*0-201-70393-9*) Addison-Wesley.

Campione, Mary & Walrath, Kathy. The Java Tutorial: Object-Oriented Programming for the Internet. (Java Ser.). 864p. (C). 1996. pap. text 41.95 (*0-201-63454-6*) Addison-Wesley.

Campisano, Jim. American Muscle Cars. LC 94-34914. 128p. 1995. text 15.98 (*1-56799-164-5*, MetroBooks) M Friedman Pub Grp Inc.

— Modern Mustangs: Twenty Years of Muscle. LC 99-17647. 1999. 14.98 (*1-56799-697-3*) M Friedman Pub Grp Inc.

— Mustang. 1997. 16.98 (*1-56799-438-5*, MetroBooks) M Friedman Pub Grp Inc.

***Campisi, Dominic J., et al.** California Trust & Probate Litigation. Tom, Janette, ed. LC 99-62300. 814p. 1999. ring bd. 159.00 (*0-7626-0290-2*) Cont Ed Bar-CA.

Campisi, Jack. The Mashpee Indians: Tribe on Trial. (Iroquois & Their Neighbors Ser.). (Illus.). 176p. (C). 1991. pap. 17.95 (*0-8156-2595-2*) Syracuse U Pr.

Campisi, Jack & Hauptman, Laurence M., eds. The Oneida Indian Experience. 244p. 1988. pap. 18.95 (*0-8156-2453-0*) Syracuse U Pr.

— The Oneida Indian Experience: Two Perspectives. LC 88-20110. (Iroquois Book Ser.). (Illus.). 224p. 1988. reprint ed. pap. 69.50 (*0-608-06970-1*, 206717800009) Bks Demand.

Campisi, Judith, et al, eds. Perspectives on Cellular Regulation: From Bacteria to Cancer. LC 90-26568. (MBL Lectures in Biology: Vol. 11). 370p. 1991. 195.00 (*0-471-56090-1*, Wiley-Interscience) Wiley.

***Campisi, Mary.** Innocent Betrayal. (Splendor Historical Romances Ser.). 352p. 2000. mass mkt. 4.99 (*0-8217-6602-3*, Zebra Kensgtn) Kensgtn Pub Corp.

Campistol, J. R., ed. see Menendez Pidal, Ramon.

Campiti, Michele, jt. auth. see Altomare, Francesco.

***Campkin, Peter, et al.** Operating Environment. 256p. (Orig.). 1999. pap. 37.50 (*0-273-62876-3*, Pub. by F T P-H) Trans-Atl Phila.

Camplese, Virginia A. Journeys of Spirit. 48p. 1999. pap. 12.95 (*1-892668-06-8*) Prospect Pr.

Camplin, Paul. A New History of Muhlenberg County. LC 84-71350. (Illus.). 304p. 1985. 28.95 (*0-9613634-0-1*) Caney Station Bks.

Campling, Christopher. Food of Love: Reflections on Music & Faith. 1997. pap. 19.00 (*0-334-02691-1*) TPI PA.

***Campling, Frankie & Sharpe, Michael.** Chronic Fatigue Syndrome: The Facts. (The Facts Ser.). (Illus.). 176p. 2001. pap. 19.95 (*0-19-263049-0*) OUP.

Campling, Jo, jt. auth. see Bryson, Valerie.

Campling, Jo, jt. auth. see Crowther, Christy.

Campling, Jo, jt. auth. see Radcliffe, James.

Campling, Jo, jt. auth. see Rumgay, Judith.

Campling, Jo, jt. auth. see Thomas, Nigel.

Campling, Jo, ed. see Baker, Adrienne.

Campling, Jo, ed. see Burnard, Philip.

Campling, Jo, ed. see Busfield, Joan.

Campling, Jo, ed. see Cowburn, Will.

Campling, Jo, ed. see Dalglish, Carol.

Campling, Jo, jt. ed. see De Souza, Lorraine.

Campling, Jo, ed. see Ham, Rosalind & Cotton, Leonard.

Campling, Jo, ed. see Isaac, D.

Campling, Jo, ed. see Maczka, Kathleen.

Campling, Jo, ed. see Maslin, Zielfa.

Campling, Jo, ed. see Penso, Dorothy E.

Campling, Jo, ed. see Russell, Diana E.

Campling, Jo, ed. see Smyth, Lucinda, et al.

Campling, Jo, ed. see Thompson, Simon B. & Morgan, Maryanne.

***Campling, John & Gollan, Paul.** Bargained Out: Negotiating Without Unions in Australia. 143p. 1999. pap. 45.00 (*1-86287-346-1*, 18628, Pub. by Federation Pr) Gaunt.

Campling, Penelope, jt. auth. see Haigh, Rex.

Campo, Allan, jt. auth. see Bartlett, Lee.

Campo, Anna L. Anthropomorphic Representations in Prehistoric Cyprus: A Formal & Symbol Analysis of Figurines, C. 3500-1800 B. C. (Studies in Mediterranean Archaeology & Literature: No. 109). (Illus.). 257p. (Orig.). 1994. pap. 57.50 (*91-7081-069-9*, Pub. by P Astroms) Coronet Bks.

Campo, Carlos P. Del, see Del Campo, Carlos P.

Campo, John V., jt. ed. see Ammerman, Robert T.

Campo, Joseph J., jt. auth. see Tierney, Terence E.

Campo, Juana M. Del, see Del Campo, Juana M.

Campo, Mariano. Christiano Wolff E il Razionalismo Precritico, 2 vols. in 1. (Wolff, Christian, Gesammelte Werke, Materialien und Dokumente Ser.: No. III, Vol. 9). xxxii, 718p. 1980. reprint ed. 160.00 incl. 3.5 hd (*3-487-06968-7*) G Olms Pubs.

Campo, Rachel, et al. The Plantation Landscape: Slaves & Freedom at Seabrook Plantation, Hilton Head Island, South Carolina. LC 98-39805. (Research Ser.: No. 34). (Illus.). 197p. 1998. pap. 30.00 (*1-58317-003-0*) Chicora Found.

Campo, Rafael. The Desire to Heal: A Doctor's Education in Empathy, Identity, & Poetry. 272p. 1998. pap. 13.00 (*0-393-31771-4*) Norton.

***Campo, Rafael.** Diva. LC 99-18342. 112p. 1999. text 39.95 (*0-8223-2383-4*) Duke.

Campo, Rafael. The Other Man Was Me: A Voyage to the New World. LC 94-8659. 90p. 1994. pap. 8.00 (*1-55885-111-9*) Arte Publico.

— The Poetry of Healing: A Doctor's Education in Empathy, Identity, & Desire. LC 96-23121. 192p. 1997. 23.00 (*0-393-04009-7*) Norton.

— What the Body Told. LC 95-36519. 136p. 1996. pap. 13.95 (*0-8223-1742-7*); text 39.95 (*0-8223-1733-8*) Duke.

***Campo, Rafael & Garcia Lorca, Federico.** Diva. LC 99-18342. 98p. 1999. pap. 14.95 (*0-8223-2417-2*) Duke.

Campo, Renata S. El Planeta de los Ratonejos (The Planet of the Bunnyrats) (SPA.). 64p. (YA). 1992. pap. 5.99 (*968-16-3749-6*, Pub. by Fondo) Continental Bk.

Campo, Roberto. Ronsard's Contentious Sisters: The Paragone Between Poetry & Painting in the Works of Pierre de Ronsard. LC 98-29034. (North Carolina Studies in Romance Languages & Literatures: No. 257). 200p. 1998. pap. 28.50 (*0-8078-9261-0*) U of NC Pr.

Campo, Salustiano Del, see Del Campo, Salustiano.

Campo, Vincent, et al. The Middle of the Journey. (Illus.). 156p. write for info. (*0-318-56311-8*) V Campo.

Campoamor, Diana, et al, eds. Nuevos Senderos: Reflections on Hispanics & Philanthropy. LC 98-38439. 224p. 1998. pap. 19.95 (*1-55885-263-8*) Arte Publico.

Campoamor Y Campoosorio, Ramon De. Doloras - Cantares. 7th ed. (SPA.). 160p. 1981. pap. 9.95 (*0-7859-5139-3*) Fr & Eur.

— Poesia. (SPA.). 192p. 1983. pap. 10.95 (*0-7859-5140-7*) Fr & Eur.

Campobello, Nellie. Cartucho & My Mother's Hands. Meyer, Doris & Matthews, Irene, trs. LC 87-25462. (Texas Pan American Ser.). 143p. 1988. 19.95 (*0-292-71110-7*); pap. 10.95 (*0-292-71111-5*) U of Tex Pr.

Campodonica, Carol. How to Build a California Mission: San Juan Bautista, 20 vols. Weber, Francis J. et al, eds. (How to Build a California Mission Ser.: Vol. 2). (Illus.). 74p. (J). (gr. 4-5). 1997. pap. 14.95 (*0-9648488-1-3*) Buzzard Pr.

— How to Build a California Mission: Santa Barbara, 20 vols. Wardup, Shirley et al, eds. (How to Build a California Mission Ser.). (Illus.). (J). (gr. 4-5). Date not set. pap. write for info. (*0-9648488-3-X*) Buzzard Pr.

— How to Build a California Mission: Santa Cruz, 20 vols. Weber, Francis J. et al, eds. (How to Build a California Mission Ser.). (Illus.). (J). (gr. 4-5). Date not set. pap. write for info. (*0-9648488-5-6*) Buzzard Pr.

— How to Build the White House, Vol. 3. Scouten, Rex et al, eds. (Illus.). 40p. (J). (gr. 4-5). 1998. pap. 19.95 (*0-9648488-6-4*) Buzzard Pr.

— How to Build Washington D.C.'s Key Attractions: Jefferson Memorial, Lincoln Memorial, & Washington Monument. Ketchum, Sue, ed. (Illus.). 112p. (J). (gr. 4-5). 1997. pap. 19.95 (*0-9648488-7-2*) Buzzard Pr.

Campodonica, Carol A. How to Build a California Mission: San Carlos de Borromeo del Rio Carmelo, 20 vols. Weber, Francis J. & Warcup, Shirley, eds. LC 96-84482. (How to Build a California Mission Ser.: Vol. 1). (Illus.). 74p. (Orig.). (J). (gr. 4 up). 1996. pap. 14.95 (*0-9648488-2-1*) Buzzard Pr.

Campoli, John F. And the Miracle Is... 66p. (Orig.). 1990. pap. text 4.95 (*0-9625676-0-4*) His Love Pr.

Campolini, C. Dictionnaire Logopedie 2, Troubles Sphere ORL. (FRE.). 1998. 250.00 (*0-320-00266-7*) Fr & Eur.

C

An Asterisk (*) at the beginning of an entry indicates that the title is appearing for the first time.

Campolo, Anthony, Jr. El Engano del Poder, Vida Cristiana.Tr. of Power of Delusion, Christian Life. (SPA.). 174p. 1993. pap. 6.50 (*1-56063-440-5*, 498552) Editorial Unilit.

Campolo, Anthony. Growing up in America: A Sociology of Youth Ministry. 1989. 14.99 (*0-310-52470-9*) Zondervan.

***Campolo, Anthony.** Let Me Tell You a Story. LC 00-34985. 224p. 2000. pap. 12.99 (*0-8499-4205-5*) Word Pub.

Campolo, Anthony. Who Switched the Price Tags? 200p. 1987. pap. 10.99 (*0-8499-3088-X*) Word Pub.

Campolo, Anthony & Campolo, Tony. Carpe Diem. audio 15.99 (*0-8499-6082-7*, 6054) Word Pub.

Campolo, Anthony & Fraser, David A. Sociology Through the Eyes of Faith. LC 91-55337. 336p. 1992. pap. 13.00 (*0-06-061315-7*, Pub. by Harper SF) HarpC.

***Campolo, Bart.** The Kingdom Works. 2001. pap. 10.99 (*1-56955-195-2*) Servant.

Campolo, T. Fantasia del Exito.Tr. of Success Fantasy. (SPA.). 1996. pap. 8.99 (*0-8297-0477-9*) Vida Pubs.

Campolo, Tony. Can Mainline Denominations Make a Comeback? LC 95-18064. 224p. 1995. pap. 16.00 (*0-8170-1234-6*) Judson.

— Carpe Diem. 1995. pap. 10.99 (*0-8499-3680-2*) Word Pub.

— Como Ser Pentecostal Sin Hablar en Lenguas.Tr. of How to Be Pentecostal Without Speaking in Tongues. (SPA.). 185p. 1991. pap. 5.99 (*1-56063-262-3*, 498519) Editorial Unilit.

— Everything You've Heard is Wrong: The Surprising Secret to Business Success. 192p. 1992. 15.99 (*0-8499-0934-1*) Word Pub.

— Following Jesus Without Embarrassing God. LC 97-28505. 240p. 1997. pap. 12.99 (*0-8499-4068-0*) Word Pub.

— How to Be Pentecostal Without Speaking in Tongues. 1994. pap. 10.99 (*0-8499-3569-5*) Word Pub.

— Is Jesus a Republican or a Democrat? And 14 Other Polarizing Issues. write for info. (*0-614-21934-5*) Word Pubng.

— Partly Right. 1995. pap. 10.99 (*0-8499-3633-0*) Word Pub.

— A Reasonable Faith. 1995. pap. 10.99 (*0-8499-3634-9*) Word Pub.

***Campolo, Tony.** Revolution & Renewal: How Churches Are Saving Our Cities. LC 99-49161. 272p. 2000. pap. 16.95 (*0-664-22198-X*, Pub. by Westminster John Knox) Presbyterian Pub.

Campolo, Tony. Todo lo Que Han Oido es Erroneo.Tr. of Everything You've Heard Is Wrong. (SPA.). 192p. 1992. pap. 6.99 (*1-56063-380-8*, 490277) Editorial Unilit.

— Twenty Hot Potatoes Christians Are Afraid to Touch. 1993. pap. 10.99 (*0-8499-3505-9*) Word Pub.

Campolo, Tony, jt. auth. see Campolo, Anthony.

Campomar, Andreas. Uruguay: Open for Growth. 1999. 170.00 (*1-85564-675-7*, Pub. by Euromoney) Am Educ Systs.

Campondonica, Carol. How Congress Works. Miller, Bondell, ed. LC 99-95369. (Illus.). (J). (gr. 4-5). Date not set. pap. write for info. (*0-9648488-9-9*) Buzzard Pr.

Camponeschi, Eugene T., Jr., ed. Composite Materials Vol. 11: Testing & Design. (Special Technical Publication Ser.: No. STP 1206). (Illus.). 365p. 1993. text 100.00 (*0-8031-1879-1*, STP1206) ASTM.

Campoosorio, Ramon De Campoamor Y, see Campoamor Y Campoosorio, Ramon De.

Campora, Olga K. Saint Behind Enemy Lines. LC 97-12495. i, 248p. 1997. 15.95 (*1-57345-227-0*) Deseret Bk.

***Camporeale, Louis A.** The New York City Motorists' Parking Survival Guide: A Primer on How to Avoid & Deal with Parking Tickets Effectively. LC 98-91641. (Motorist Educational Bks.). (Illus.). 147p. 1998. pap. 11.95 (*0-9664678-0-9*) Park Pal Co.

Camporesi, Piero. The Anatomy of the Senses: Natural Symbols in Medieval & Early Modern Italy. Cameron, Allan, tr. from ITA. LC 94-36318. 230p. 1995. 60.95 (*0-7456-0506-0*, Pub. by Polity Pr) Blackwell Pubs.

— Bread of Dreams: Food & Fantasy in Early Modern Europe. Gentilcore, David, tr. vi, 212p. 1996. pap. 17.95 (*0-226-09258-5*) U Ch Pr.

— Bread of Dreams: Food & Fantasy in Early Modern Europe. Gentilcore, David, tr. LC 89-4689. 218p. 1996. 33.00 (*0-226-09257-7*) U Ch Pr.

— Exotic Brew: The Art of Living in the Age of Enlightenment. Woodall, Christopher, tr. 200p. 1994. 37.95 (*0-7456-0877-9*) Blackwell Pubs.

— Exotic Brew: The Art of Living in the Age of Enlightenment. Woodall, Christopher, tr. 200p. 1999. reprint ed. pap. 22.95 (*0-7456-2197-X*) Blackwell Pubs.

— The Fear of Hell. 230p. 1991. 40.00 (*0-271-00734-6*) Pa St U Pr.

— The Land of Hunger. Croft-Murray, Tania et al, trs. from ITA. 224p. (C). 1996. text 58.95 (*0-7456-0888-4*, Pub. by Polity Pr) Blackwell Pubs.

— The Magic Harvest: Food, Folklore & Society. Hall, Joan, tr. 260p. 1994. 55.95 (*0-7456-0835-3*) Blackwell Pubs.

— The Magic Harvest: Food, Folkore & Society. Hall, Joan, tr. 253p. 1999. reprint ed. pap. 22.95 (*0-7456-2196-1*) Blackwell Pubs.

Campos, A., jt. ed. see Ciges, M.

Campos, Anthony. Stock Market Illusionology: Block-Volume Reversal, the Stock Specialist Theory. LC 87-62182. 75p. (Orig.). 1990. pap. 24.95 (*0-944527-00-0*) Wall St Inquirer.

Campos, Anthony J. Mexican Folk Tales. (J). 1977. 14.05 (*0-606-04382-9*, Pub. by Turtleback) Demco.

Campos, Anthony J., ed. Mexican Folk Tales. LC 77-10603. 136p. 1977. reprint ed. pap. 10.95 (*0-8165-0560-8*) U of Ariz Pr.

Campos-Boralevi, Lea. Bentham & the Oppressed. LC 84-14951. (European University Institute, Series C (Political & Social Science): No. 1). xii, 248p. 1984. 80.00 (*3-11-009974-8*) De Gruyter.

***Campos, Carlos.** Salsa & Afro Cuban Montunos for Guitar. Gordon, Andrew D., ed. 104p. 1999. pap. 22.95 incl. audio compact disk (*1-882146-72-7*) A D G Prods.

Campos, Carlos. Salsa & Afro Cuban Montunos for Piano. Gordon, Andrew D., ed. 120p. 1996. 22.95 incl. audio compact disk (*1-882146-54-9*) A D G Prods.

— Salsa, Further Adventures in Afro Cuban Music for Piano. Gordon, Andrew D., ed. 145p. 1998. pap. 24.95 incl. audio compact disk (*1-882146-66-2*) A D G Prods.

Campos, Emilio C., ed. Sensory Evaluation of Strabismus & Amblyopia in a Natural Environment. (Documenta Ophthalmologica Proceedings Ser.). 1984. text 118.00 (*90-6193-508-3*) Kluwer Academic.

Campos, Guillermo, et al. Aqui No Mas. (C). 1994. pap. text 21.00 (*0-07-042037-8*) McGraw.

Campos, Guillermo, jt. auth. see Clarkson, William B.

Campos Guimaraes, J. P. De, see De Campos Guimaraes, J. P.

Campos, Hector. De la Oracion Simple A la Oracion Compuesta: Curso Superior De Gramatica Espanola. LC 92-45723. (SPA.). 232p. (Orig.). (C). 1993. pap. text 24.95 (*0-87840-240-3*) Georgetown U Pr.

— De la Oracion Simple A la Oracion Compuesta: Curso Superior De Gramatica Espanola: Clave De los Ejercicios. (SPA.). 94p. (Orig.). (C). 1993. pap. text, teacher ed. 5.00 (*0-87840-241-1*) Georgetown U Pr.

Campos, Hector, ed. Evolution & Revolution in Linguistic Theory. LC 95-1843. (Studies in Romance Linguistics). 608p. 1995. text 75.00 (*0-87840-248-9*) Georgetown U Pr.

Campos, Hector & Martinez-Gil, Fernando, eds. Current Studies in Spanish Linguistics. LC 91-25304. 656p. (C). 1992. pap. text 33.00 (*0-87840-234-9*) Georgetown U Pr.

Campos, Hector, jt. ed. see Silva-Corvalan, Carmen.

Campos, J. G. & Barella, A. Diccionario de Refranes. (SPA.). 432p. 1993. pap. 49.50 (*84-239-5984-8*) Elliots Bks.

Campos, John. Only a Little Planet. LC 84-90335. (Poems & Drawings of John Campos Ser.). (Illus.). 78p. (Orig.). 1984. pap. 4.95 (*0-917021-00-2*) Lighthouse Pr.

— Walk Slowly: Poems & Drawings. LC 86-83186. (Illus.). 80p. (Orig.). 1987. pap. 5.00 (*0-917021-02-9*) Lighthouse Pr.

Campos, Jorge, jt. tr. see Ferrara-Balanquet, Raul.

Campos, Jose E. & Root, Hilton L. The Key to the Asian Miracle: Making Shared Growth Credible. 198p. 1996. 26.95 (*0-8157-1360-6*) Brookings.

Campos, Julieta. Celina or the Cats. Miller, Yvette E., ed. Chambers, Leland H., tr. from SPA. LC 95-21118. (Discoveries Ser.). 144p. 1995. pap. 15.95 (*0-935480-72-2*) Lat Am Lit Rev Pr.

— The Fear of Losing Eurydice. Chambers, Leland H., tr. from SPA. LC 92-29130. 121p. 1993. 19.95 (*1-56478-020-1*) Dalkey Arch.

— The Fear of Losing Eurydice. Chambers, Leland H., tr. from SPA. LC 92-29130. 121p. 1994. reprint ed. pap. 8.95 (*1-56478-030-9*) Dalkey Arch.

— La Herencia Obstinada: Cuentos Nahuas. (SPA.). pap. 8.99 (*968-16-1091-1*, Pub. by Fondo) Continental Bk.

Campos, Lenora, jt. auth. see Lenn, Marjorie P.

Campos, Lenora, jt. ed. see Lenn, Marjorie P.

***Campos, M. & Cunha-Ribeiro, L. M., eds.** International Congress on Thrombosis: 16th International Congress, Porto, Portugal, May 2000: Abstracts. (Haemostasis Ser.: Vol. 30, Suppl. 1 (2000)). (Illus.). xxx, 206p. 2000. pap. 48.75 (*3-8055-7082-1*) S Karger.

Campos, Manuel, jt. auth. see Hughes, H. P.

Campos-Ortega, J. A. & Hartenstein, V. The Embryonic Development of Drosophila Melanogaster. 2nd ed. (Illus.). 352p. 1997. 199.00 (*0-387-57079-9*) Spr-Verlag.

Campos-Ortega, J. A. & Hartenstein, Volker. The Embryonic Development of Drosophila Melanogaster. (Illus.). 260p. 1985. 127.00 (*0-387-15867-7*) Spr-Verlag.

Campos-Ortega, Jose A. & Hartenstein, Volker. The Embryonic Development of Drosophila Melanogaster. 2nd ed. LC 96-46947. 1997. write for info. (*3-540-57079-9*) Spr-Verlag.

***Campos-Outcalt, Doug.** 20 Common Problems in Preventive Health Care. 512p. 2000. pap. 34.95 (*0-07-012044-7*) McGraw-Hill HPD.

Campos, Patricia, tr. see Day, Marlena & Nature Institute Staff.

Campos, Paul F. Jurismania: The Madness of American Law. LC 97-17940. 208p. 1998. 23.00 (*0-19-510785-3*) OUP.

— Jurismania: The Madness of American Law. 208p. 1999. pap. 13.95 (*0-19-513083-9*) OUP.

Campos, Paul F., et al. Against the Law. LC 96-22190. (Constitutional Conflicts Ser.). 360p. 1996. text 49.95 (*0-8223-1835-0*); pap. text 17.95 (*0-8223-1841-5*) Duke.

Campos, Ricardo, jt. auth. see Bonilla, Frank.

***Campos, Roger A.** Sleeping with an Angel. 288p. (YA). (gr. 10 up). 2000. pap. 24.95 (*0-9676067-5-6*) St Johns Pr.

Campos, Zella, et al. Pocket Atlas of MRI of the Pelvis. LC 92-49417. (Illus.). 128p. 1993. pap. text 16.95 (*0-88167-987-9*) Lppncott W & W.

Camposano, Raul & Wolf, Wayne H., eds. High-Level VLSI Synthesis. (C). 1991. text 133.50 (*0-7923-9159-4*) Kluwer Academic.

Camposano, Raul, jt. ed. see Walker, Robert A.

Camposeco, Jose B. El Maguey y Sus Usos en Guatemala: An Ch'ech, Sajchi' o ki' (SPA., Illus.). 54p. (Orig.). 1995. pap. 3.75 (*1-886502-00-5*, Ediciones Yax Te) Yax Te Found.

— La Marimba de Guatemala: Te' son, Chinab' o K'ojom. 2nd ed. (SPA., Illus.). 95p. 1995. pap. 4.75 (*1-886502-02-1*, Ediciones Yax Te) Yax Te Found.

Campoy, F. Isabel, tr. see Ehlert, Lois.

Campoy, F. Isabel, tr. see Wood, Audrey.

***Campoy, Renee W.** A Professional Development School Partnership: Conflict & Collaboration. LC 99-89268. 160p. 2000. 62.50 (*0-89789-705-6*, Bergin & Garvey) Greenwood.

Campra, Andre. Le Carnaval de Venise: Comedie Lyrique, Vol. XVII. LC 89-753010. (French Opera in the 17th & 18th Centuries Ser.: No. 5). (ENG & FRE., Illus.). 300p. 1990. lib. bdg. 86.00 (*0-945193-07-6*) Pendragon NY.

Camps & Conference Unit of Wamy Staff. Islamic Camps. 124p. 1990. pap. write for info. (*1-882837-15-0*) W A M Y Intl.

Camps, Anna & Milian, Marta, eds. Metalinguistic Activity in Learning to Write. (International Series on the Research of Learning & Instruction of Writing Ser.). 250p. 1999. pap. 44.50 (*90-5356-341-5*, Pub. by Amsterdam U Pr) U of Mich Pr.

Camps, Arnulf. Partners in Dialogue: Christianity & Other World Religions. LC 82-18798.Tr. of Christendom en godsdienstein der wereld. 272p. (Orig.). reprint ed. pap. 84.40 (*0-8357-8543-2*, 20348550091) Bks Demand.

***Camps, Arnulf.** Studies in Asian Mission History, 1956-1998. LC 99-59896. (Studies in Christian Mission). 2000. 88.50 (*90-04-11572-2*) Brill Academic Pubs.

Camps, Christian. Dictionnaire du Francais Regional du Languedoc. (FRE.). 160p. 1991. 50.00 (*0-8288-9483-3*) Fr & Eur.

— Dictionnaire du Francais Regional du Roussillon. (FRE.). 93p. 1991. 50.00 (*0-8288-9487-6*) Fr & Eur.

Camps, Janett, ed. see Aguirre Hectrano, Fidel.

Camps, Janett, ed. see Delgadillo, Leon C.

Camps, Janett, ed. see Hernandez, Roberto.

Camps, Janett, ed. see Medrano, Fidel A.

Camps, W. A. An Introduction to Homer. 116p. 1980. pap. text 15.95 (*0-19-872101-3*) OUP.

— An Introduction to Virgil's Aeneid. 174p. (Orig.). 1979. pap. text 17.95 (*0-19-872024-6*) OUP.

Camps, W. A., ed. Propertius: Elegies II, Bk. II. (Bristol Latin Texts Ser.). (LAT.). 255p. 1985. reprint ed. 25.95 (*0-86292-148-1*, Pub. by Brist Class Pr) Focus Pub-R Pullins.

— Propertius: Elegies III, Bk. III. (Bristol Latin Texts Ser.). (LAT.). 188p. 1986. reprint ed. 25.95 (*0-86292-116-3*, Pub. by Brist Class Pr) Focus Pub-R Pullins.

Camps, W. A., ed. see Propertius.

Campschreur, Willem & Divendal, Joost, eds. Culture in Another South Africa. LC 89-3243. (Illus.). 288p. 1989. 24.95 (*0-940793-35-0*, Olive Branch Pr); pap. 14.95 (*0-940793-36-9*, Olive Branch Pr) Interlink Pub.

Campsie, Jane. Hair & Make-Up. 1999. pap. 19.95 (*0-86411-805-8*) Gr Arts Ctr Pub.

— Inner Health, Outer Beauty. 1997. 19.95 (*0-86411-764-7*) Whitecap Bks.

Campton, David. The Cagebirds. 1977. pap. 3.50 (*0-87129-274-2*, C44) Dramatic Pub.

— Cards, Cups & Crystal Ball. 1987. pap. 3.50 (*0-87129-337-4*, C67) Dramatic Pub.

— The Life & Death of Almost Everybody. 1971. pap. 5.25 (*0-8222-0657-9*) Dramatists Play.

— Little Brother, Little Sister & Out of the Flying Pan: Two Plays. 1967. pap. 5.25 (*0-8222-0674-9*) Dramatists Play.

— A Point of View. 1967. pap. 3.50 (*0-87129-147-9*, P43) Dramatic Pub.

— Smell of Burning & Then: Two Plays. 1969. pap. 3.25 (*0-8222-1047-9*) Dramatists Play.

— Smile. 31p. 1991. pap. 3.50 (*0-87129-088-X*, S96) Dramatic Pub.

— Some of My Best Friends Are Smiths. 1974. pap. 3.50 (*0-87129-254-8*, S44) Dramatic Pub.

— Us & Them. 1982. 3.50 (*0-87129-426-5*, U15) Dramatic Pub.

— Who Calls? 28p. 1980. pap. 3.50 (*0-87129-177-0*, W46) Dramatic Pub.

— The Winter of 1917. 31p. 1990. pap. 3.50 (*0-87129-028-6*, W69) Dramatic Pub.

Campus Crusade for Christ Staff. Action Group Leader's Guide. (Discipleship Ser.: No. 3). 47p. Date not set. pap., teacher ed. 4.99 (*0-86605-133-3*) Integrtd Res.

— Discipleship Leader's Guide. (Discipleship Ser.: No. 2). 39p. Date not set. pap. 4.99 (*0-86605-137-6*) Integrtd Res.

Campus Crusade Staff. In Search of the Greatest Treasure. 28p. (J). 1999. 7.99 (*1-56399-120-9*) NewLife Pubns.

Campus Journal Staff. What's God Have to Do with It? LC 93-39921. 384p. (ps up). 1993. pap. 14.99 (*0-929239-76-8*) Discovery Hse Pubs.

Campus Life Editors, ed. Campus Guide to Christian Colleges, Universities & Seminaries. 1998. pap. text 14.99 (*0-8054-9038-8*) Broadman.

Campus Marketing Staff. Free Supplement Shelf Tag. pap. write for info. (*0-534-51396-4*) Thomson Learn.

— Inherent Value Shelf Tag. pap. write for info. (*0-534-51395-6*) Thomson Learn.

Campuzano Cifuentes, Marcela, jt. auth. see Llano Restrepo, Maria C.

Camrass, Roger & Smith, Ken. Wiring up the Workplace: A Practical Guide for Management. (Illus.). 167p. (Orig.). 1987. pap. 59.00 (*0-941723-00-3*) BCR Enterprises.

Camrbidge University Press Staff. Features in the Architecture of Physiological Function. (Genes Cells & Organisms Ser.). (Illus.). 380p. 1988. text 10.00 (*0-8240-1375-1*) Garland.

Camrud, Madelyn. This House Is Full of Cracks: Poems. LC 93-83976. (Minnesota Voices Project Ser.: Vol. 61). 68p. 1994. pap. 9.95 (*0-89823-153-1*) New Rivers Pr.

— Under the Whelming Tide: The 1997 Flood of the Red River of the North. Hylden, Eric & Reuter, Laurel, eds. (Illus.). 172p. 1998. pap. 38.00 (*0-943107-09-1*) ND Mus Art.

***Camsey, Terry.** Slightly off Center: Growth Principles for Thawing Frozen Paradigms. 96p. 2000. pap. write for info. (*0-9657601-8-9*, Crest Books) SANP.

Camsey, Terry, jt. auth. see Smart, Janette.

Camson, Glauco, ed. see Montale, Eugenio.

Camsong, Thidavadee & Luffe, Peter. Asian Vegetarian Cooking. LC 97-8228. (Illus.). 96p. 1997. pap. text 14.95 (*0-7641-0025-4*) Barron.

Camuffo, Dario. Microclimate for Cultural Heritage. LC 98-9287. (Developments in Atmospheric Science Ser.). 428p. 1998. 227.00 (*0-444-82925-3*) Elsevier.

Camuffo, Giorgio. Italian Graphic Designers. 1997. pap. text 40.00 (*88-86502-40-0*, Pub. by Canal & Stamperia) Antique Collect.

Camuffo, Giorgio, ed. Italian Graphic Design. (Illus.). 272p. 1997. pap. 175.00 (*88-86502-30-3*, Pub. by Canal & Stamperia) Antique Collect.

Camurati, Mireya. Poesia y Poetica de Vicente Huidobro. (SPA.). 210p. 1980. pap. 12.50 (*0-685-13896-8*, 3024) Ediciones Norte.

Camurati, Mireya & Rosenberg, Dorothy B. Enfoques: Temas De Comentario Oral y Escrito. (SPA.). 225p. (C). 1990. pap. text 29.16 (*0-669-01919-4*) HM Trade Div.

Camurati, Mireye, jt. ed. see Gracia, Jorge J.

Camurati, Paolo E. & Eveking, Hans, eds. Correct Hardware Design & Verification Methods: IFIP WG10.5 Advanced Research Working Conference, CHARME 95, Frankfurt, Germany, October 1995. LC 95-39591. 342p. 1995. 56.00 (*3-540-60385-9*) Spr-Verlag.

Camus, Albert. Actuelles: Ecrits Politiques. (FRE.). 1977. pap. 10.95 (*0-7859-2847-2*) Fr & Eur.

— Albert Camus: Konkordanz zu den Romanen und Erzahlungen von Albert Camus, 2 vols., Set. (Alpha-Omega, Reihe E Ser.). 1922p. 1988. 480.00 (*3-487-07966-6*) G Olms Pubs.

— American Journals. Levick, Hugh, tr. (Illus.). 153p. 1995. pap. 12.95 (*1-56924-823-0*) Marlowe & Co.

— Between Hell & Reason: Essays from the Resistance Newspaper, "Combat" 1944-1947. De Gramont, Alexandre, tr. from FRE. LC 87-21331. 189p. 1991. pap. 16.95 (*0-8195-5189-9*, Wesleyan Univ Pr) U Pr of New Eng.

— Caligula. Incl. Malentendu. write for info. (*0-318-63439-2*, M5895) Fr & Eur.

— Caligula: Suivi de Le Malentendu. (FRE.). (C). 1958. pap. 9.95 (*0-8442-1831-6*, VF1831-6) NTC Contemp Pub Co.

— Caligula & Malentendu. (FRE.). 1972. pap. 10.95 (*0-8288-3661-2*, F90651) Fr & Eur.

— Caligula & Malentendu. (Folio Ser.: No. 64). (FRE.). pap. 9.25 (*2-07-036064-4*) Schoenhof.

Camus, Albert. Caligula & Three Other Plays. Gilbert, Stuart, tr. Incl. Just Assassin. 1962. Misunderstanding. 1962. State of Siege. 1962. 1962. Set pap. 7.96 (*0-394-70207-7*, V-207) Random.

Camus, Albert. Carnets. Incl. I. Mai, 1935 a Fevrier 1942. 37.95 (*2-07-021219-X*); Tome II. Janvier 1942-Mars 1951. 44.95 (*2-07-021220-3*); (Gallimard Ser.). (FRE.). write for info. (*0-318-51941-0*) Schoenhof.

— Chute. (Folio Ser.: No. 10). (FRE.). 1956. pap. 6.95 (*2-07-036010-5*) Schoenhof.

— La Chute. (FRE.). 1972. pap. 10.95 (*0-8288-3662-0*, F90551) Fr & Eur.

— La Chute. (FRE.). (C). 1956. pap. 7.95 (*0-8442-1964-9*, VF1964-9) NTC Contemp Pub Co.

— La Chute. Bree, Germaine, ed. (ENG & FRE.). 135p. 1986. 3.95 (*0-88332-465-2*) Schoenhof.

— Discours de Suede. 1958. pap. 27.95 (*0-7859-0595-2*, F90560) Fr & Eur.

— L' Envers et 'Endroit. (Folio Essais Ser.: No. 41). 1958. pap. 8.95 (*2-07-032368-4*) Schoenhof.

— L' Envers et l'Endroit. (FRE.). 1986. pap. 8.95 (*0-7859-2835-9*) Fr & Eur.

— Essais. Quilliot, Roger, ed. (FRE.). 2000p. 1992. lib. bdg. 120.00 (*0-7859-3745-5*, 2070101053) Fr & Eur.

— Essais. (Pleiade Ser.). (FRE.). 1965. 93.95 (*2-07-010105-3*) Schoenhof.

— Etranger. 1942. write for info. (*0-318-63470-8*, F90602) Fr & Eur.

— Etranger. (Folio Ser.: No. 3). (FRE.). 1942. 6.95 (*0-685-11174-1*); pap. 6.95 (*2-07-036002-4*) Schoenhof.

— L' Etranger. (FRE.). 1972. pap. 10.95 (*0-8288-3663-9*, F90601); pap. 10.95 (*0-7859-1683-0*, 2070360024) Fr & Eur.

— L' Etranger. (FRE.). (C). 1942. pap. 7.95 (*0-8442-1756-5*, VF1756-5) NTC Contemp Pub Co.

Camus, Albert. L' Etranger. Bree, Germaine & Lynes, Carlos, Jr., eds. 182p. 1955. pap. text 21.00 (*0-13-530790-2*) P-H.

Camus, Albert. Exil et le Royaume. (Folio Ser.: No. 78). (FRE.). 1957. pap. 9.25 (*2-07-036078-4*) Schoenhof.

— L' Exil et le Royaume. (FRE.). 1972. pap. 10.95 (*0-8288-3664-7*, F90611); pap. 10.95 (*0-7859-1693-8*, 2070360784) Fr & Eur.

— Exile & the Kingdom. 1976. 21.95 (*0-8488-0444-9*) Amereon Ltd.

— Exile & the Kingdom. O'Brien, Justin, tr. LC 91-50021. (Vintage International Ser.). 224p. 1991. pap. 12.00 (*0-679-73385-X*) Vin Bks.

— The Fall. Date not set. lib. bdg. 17.95 (*0-8488-2135-1*) Amereon Ltd.

— The Fall. O'Brien, Justin, tr. LC 90-50475. 160p. 1991. pap. 10.00 (*0-679-72022-7*) Vin Bks.

— The First Man. Hagwood, David, tr. from FRE. LC 95-2668. 336p. 1995. 25.00 (*0-679-43937-4*) Knopf.

— Happy Death. Howard, Richard, tr. 208p. 1995. pap. 12.00 (*0-679-76400-3*) Random.

C

— A Happy Death: A Novel. LC 72-8028. 224p. 1973. pap. 8.00 (0-394-71865-8, V865) Vin Bks.

— L' Homme Revolte. (Folio Essais Ser.: No. 15). (FRE.). pap. 11.95 (2-07-032302-1) Schoenhof.

— Les Justes. (FRE.). 1973. pap. 10.95 (0-8288-3665-5, F90631) Fr & Eur.

— Les Justes. (Folio Ser.: No. 477). (FRE.). 1950. pap. 6.95 (2-07-036477-1) Schoenhof.

— Lettres a un Ami Allemand. (FRE.). 1945. pap. 10.95 (0-8288-3666-3, F90640) Fr & Eur.

— Lettres a un Ami Allemand. (FRE.). 1991. pap. 10.95 (0-7859-2924-X, 2070383261) Fr & Eur.

— Lettres a un Ami Allemand. (Folio Ser.: No. 2226). (FRE.). 1948. pap. 8.95 (2-07-038326-1) Schoenhof.

— Lyrical & Critical Essays. LC 67-18621. 384p. 1970. pap. 12.00 (0-394-70852-0, V626) Vin Bks.

— Le Malentendu. (Coll. Soleil Ser.). 6.95 (0-685-37267-7) Schoenhof.

— La Mort Heureuse. (Cahiers Albert Camus Ser.). 34.95 (0-685-37268-5, F90660) Fr & Eur.

— Music: An Appreciation. 6th ed. (C). 1995. pap., student ed., wbk. ed. 28.75 (0-07-034071-4) McGraw.

— Music-Brief. 3rd ed. 176p. 1997. pap., student ed. 12.81 (0-07-036527-X) McGraw.

— The Myth of Sisyphus & Other Essays. O'Brien, Justin, tr. LC 90-50476. 192p. 1991. pap. 12.00 (0-679-73373-6) Vin Bks.

— Mythe de Sisyphe. (Folio Essais Ser.: No. 11). (FRE.). 1942. pap. 8.50 (2-07-032288-2) Schoenhof.

— Neither Victims nor Executioners. MacDonald, Dwight, tr. (Modern Classics of Peace Ser.). 1968. pap. 2.95 (0-912018-04-6) World Without War.

— Noces et l'Ete. (FRE.). 1972. pap. 10.95 (0-8288-3667-1, F90682) Fr & Eur.

— Noces Suivi de l'Ete. (FRE.). 1972. pap. 10.95 (0-7859-1686-5, 2070360164) Fr & Eur.

— Notebooks, 1935-1942. Thody, Philip M. & O'Brien, Justin, trs. LC 98-162086. 225p. 1994. pap. 12.95 (1-56924-993-8) Marlowe & Co.

— Notebooks, 1935 to 1951. Thody, Philip M. & O'Brien, Justin, trs. LC 98-27433. 1998. 16.95 (1-56924-666-1) Marlowe & Co.

— Notebooks, 1942-1951. Thody, Philip M. & O'Brien, Justin, trs. LC 98-162086. 288p. 1994. pap. 12.95 (1-56924-967-9) Marlowe & Co.

— Noves et l'Ete. (Folio Ser.: No. 16). (FRE.). 1959. pap. 6.95 (2-07-036016-4) Schoenhof.

— La Peste. (FRE.). 1972. pap. 10.95 (0-8288-3668-X, F90691) Fr & Eur.

— La Peste. (FRE.). (C). 1947. pap. 9.95 (0-8442-1765-4, VF1765-4) NTC Contemp Pub Co.

— La Peste. (Folio Ser.: No. 42). (FRE.). pap. 9.25 (2-07-036042-3) Schoenhof.

— Peste. 1942. write for info. (0-318-63575-5, F90692) Fr & Eur.

— The Plague. 1948. 19.45 (0-07-541541-0) McGraw.

— The Plague. Gilbert, Stuart, tr. (Modern Library College Editions). 278p. (C). 1965. pap. 5.00 (0-07-553649-8, T69) McGraw.

— The Plague, 2 vols. 20.00 (0-614-30537-3) NAVH.

— The Plague. Gilbert, Stuart, tr. LC 90-50477. (Vintage International Ser.). 308p. 1991. pap. 12.00 (0-679-72021-9) Vin Bks.

— Plague. 1948. 16.10 (0-606-04321-7, Pub. by Turtleback) Demco.

— The Plague. large type ed. 400p. 1984. 27.99 (0-7089-8192-5, Charnwood) Ulverscroft.

— Le Premier Homme. 331p. 1994. 49.95 (0-7859-9876-4) Fr & Eur.

— Le Premier Homme. (FRE.). 1995. pap. 29.95 (2-07-073827-2) Schoenhof.

— The Rebel: An Essay on Man in Revolt. Bower, Anthony, tr. LC 91-50022. (Vintage International Ser.). 320p. 1991. pap. 12.00 (0-679-73384-1) Vin Bks.

— Resistance, Rebellion & Death. O'Brien, Justin, tr. & intro. by. 288p. 1995. pap. 13.00 (0-679-76401-1) Random.

— Resistance, Rebellion & Death. LC 73-14867. 1974. pap. 9.00 (0-394-71966-2, V-966) Vin Bks.

— Roman Roi. (FRE.). 1985. pap. 19.95 (0-7859-2699-2) Fr & Eur.

— Stranger. Ward, Matthew, tr. LC 92-54290. 1993. 15.00 (0-679-42026-6) Everymns Lib.

— Stranger. (Vintage International Ser.). 1989. 14.10 (0-606-01426-8, Pub. by Turtleback) Demco.

— The Stranger. 20.95 (0-89190-220-1) Amereon Ltd.

— The Stranger. (Barron's Book Notes Ser.). 1986. pap. 3.95 (0-8120-3543-7) Barron.

— The Stranger. Laredo, Joseph, tr. LC 83-48885. 1988. 25.00 (0-394-53305-4) Knopf.

— The Stranger. 1988. 16.45 (0-07-543227-7) McGraw.

— The Stranger. 1989. pap. 7.95 (0-07-547812-9) McGraw.

— The Stranger. Ward, Matthew, tr. (International Ser.). 144p. 1989. pap. 9.00 (0-679-72020-0) Vin Bks.

— The Stranger. 156p. 1988. reprint ed. lib. bdg. 24.95 (0-89966-623-X) Buccaneer Bks.

— Theatre, Recits et Nouvelles. Quilliot, Claude, ed. (FRE.). 2128p. 1962. lib. bdg. 125.00 (0-7859-3744-7, 207010103 7) Fr & Eur.

— Theatre, Recits et Nouvelles. (Pleiade Ser.). (FRE.). 1962. 87.95 (2-07-010103-7) Schoenhof.

— Tricks: Twenty-Five Encounters. (High Risk Ser.). 252p. 1996. pap. 13.99 (1-85242-414-1, High Risk Bks) Serpents Tail.

Camus, Albert & Viallaneix, Paul. Youthful Writings. Conroy, Ellen, tr. 279p. 1994. pap. 12.95 (1-56924-968-7) Marlowe & Co.

Camus, E. G. Les Bambusees, Set. 1979. reprint ed. 500.00 (0-7855-3065-7, Pub. by Intl Bk Distr) St Mut.

— Les Bambusees, Vols. 1-2. (C). 1979. text 750.00 (0-89771-577-2, Pub. by Intl Bk Distr) St Mut.

— Les Bambusees-Monographic-Biologie-Culture Principaus Usages: Text, Vol. 1. 215p. (C). 1978. 170.00 (0-7855-3250-1, Pub. by Scientific) St Mut.

Camus, Emmanuel, et al. Vector-Borne Pathogens: International Trade & Tropical Animal Diseases. LC 96-31285. (Annals of the New York Academy of Sciences). 1996. write for info. (0-89766-955-X); pap. 130.00 (0-89766-956-8) NY Acad Sci.

Camus, Jean-Pierre. A Spirituall Combat, 1632 LC 75-320788. (English Recusant Literature, 1558-1640 Ser.). (ENG.). 288 p. 1974. write for info. (0-85967-165-8) Ashgate Pub Co.

Camus, M. Bibliotheque Choisie des Livres de Droit. viii, 376p. 1976. reprint ed. 90.00 (3-487-05992-4) G Olms Pubs.

Camus, Nick. Think about It. 1996. pap. text 8.95 (0-9645851-7-0) Pennhills.

Camus, Raoul F. Military Music of the American Revolution. (Illus.). 231p. 1993. 16.95 (0-918048-10-9) Integrity.

— Three Centuries of American Music: A Collection of Sacred & Secular Music: Wind & Percussion, Vol. 12. 1992. 105.00 (0-8161-0553-7, G K Hall & Co) Mac Lib Ref.

Camus, Sebastien Le, see Green, Robert A.

Camus, Sebastien Le, see Le Camus, Sebastien.

Camuse, Ruth A., jt. auth. see Bitter, Gary G.

Camuti, Louis J. All My Patients Are Under the Bed. 222p. 1985. pap. 11.00 (0-671-55450-6, Fireside) S&S Trade Pap.

Camuto, Christopher. Another Country: Journeying Toward the Cherokee Mountains. LC 97-2794. 352p. 1995. 25.00 (0-8050-2694-0) H Holt & Co.

***Camuto, Christopher.** Another Country: Journeying Toward the Cherokee Mountains. LC 99-57974. 2000. pap. 16.95 (0-8203-2237-7) U of Ga Pr.

Camuto, Christopher. A Fly Fisherman's Blue Ridge. (Illus.). 256p. 1995. pap. 10.95 (0-8050-1857-3, Owl) H Holt & Co.

— Hunting from Home. 1995. 22.50 (0-8050-3772-1) H Holt & Co.

Can, Wu X. & Liu, X. Drew, eds. Issues in China's Political Reform, Vol. 01. (CHI.). 257p. 1997. pap. 15.00 (0-9660502-0-7) China Strat Inst.

Can Xue. Old Floating Cloud: Two Novellas. Janssen, Ronald J. & Jian Zhang, trs. from CHI. 269p. 1991. 32.95 (0-8101-0974-3); pap. 13.95 (0-8101-0988-3) Northwestern U Pr.

Canaan, Don. Horror in Hocking County. rev. ed. (Illus.). 100p. (Orig.). 1994. pap. 12.95 (0-9622875-0-4) Land Canaan.

Canaan, Garson. Rebuilding the Land of Israel. (Illus.). 221p. 1991. 24.50 (0-942655-05-2) Archit CT.

Canache, Damarys J. & Kulisheck, Michael R., eds. Reinventing Legitimacy: Democracy & Political Change in Venezuela, 11. LC 97-43934. (Contributions in Latin American Studies: Vol. 11). 264p. 1998. 59.95 (0-313-30668-0, Greenwood Pr) Greenwood.

Canache, George, et al. Kvaroble Kvaroble Kvar: 4 x (4 x 4) Rumanaj Poemoj. Onet, Ionel, tr. from RUM. & intro. by. (ESP.). 80p. 1990. pap. 5.00 (1-882251-00-8) Eldonejo Bero.

Canada. Occupational Injuries & Their Cost: Canada, 1988-1990 = Les accidents du travail et leur cocut : Canada, 1988-1990. LC 93-156749. (ENG.). ix, 114p. 1992. write for info. (0-662-59193-3) Stat Can Mktg.

— The Refugee Status Determination Pocess: A Report of the Task Force on Immigration Practices & Procedures. LC 82-138599. xxiii, 132 p. 1981. write for info. (0-662-11798-0) Stat Can Mktg.

Canada & Blais, Jean-Jacques. Supporting Democracy. LC 98-191018. 1998. write for info. (0-662-63315-6) Can7 Govern Pub.

Canada & United Nations Staff. Sustainable Development of Minerals & Metals LC 98-225916. (Sustainable Development in Canada Monograph Ser.). 1997. write for info. (0-662-62900-0) Can7 Govern Pub.

Canada BC Economic & Regional Development Agreement Staff, jt. auth. see Van den Driessche, R.

Canada Canadian Heritage Staff & Canada Citizen's Participation Directorate Human R. The International Covenant on Economic, Social & Cultural Rights: Third Report of Canada: Covering the Period for Articles 6-9 (December 1987 to September 1994), for Articles 10-15 (September 1992 to September 1994) LC 97-704426. 319p. 1997. write for info. (0-662-25889-4, Pub. by Can7 Govern Pub) Intl Spec Bk.

Canada, Carol, jt. auth. see Womach, Jasper.

Canada Citizen's Participation Directorate Human R, jt. auth. see Canada Canadian Heritage Staff.

Canada Communication Group Staff. Glossary of Health Services. (Glossary Ser.: No. 205). (ENG & FRE.). 1992. 39.95 (0-8288-7372-0, 660565331) Fr & Eur.

— Vocabulary of Educational Technology & Training. (Vocabulary Ser.: No. 196). (ENG & FRE.). 1992. 95.00 (0-8288-7362-3, 660557932) Fr & Eur.

Canada Department of Labour Staff. Two Reports on Japanese Canadians in World War II, 2 vols. Daniels, Roger, ed. LC 78-7079. (Asian Experience in North America Ser.). (Illus.). 1979. reprint ed. lib. bdg. 15.95 (0-405-11266-1) Ayer.

Canada Dry Editors, ed. see Logan, Shelly Kilander.

***Canada, Edward R., et al, compiled by.** Spiritual Diversity & Social Work: A Comprehensive Bibliography with Annotations. (Teaching Social Work Ser.). 48p. 1999. pap. text 10.00 (0-87293-069-6) Coun Soc Wk Ed.

***Canada Environment Staff.** Marine Weather Hazards Manual: West Coast Edition. 3rd ed. 1999. pap. 22.50 (0-660-17774-9) Can Mus Nature.

Canada, Eric P. Economic Development: Marketing for Results. (Orig.). 1995. pap. 100.00 (1-886094-24-1) Chicago Spectrum.

— Marketer's Planning Guide. (Illus.). 226p. (Orig.). 1995. wbk. ed. 30.00 (0-9650270-0-7) Blane Canada.

Canada Gazetteer Atlas Staff. The Canada Gazetteer Atlas. (Illus.). 174p. (C). 1980. lib. bdg. 90.00 (0-226-09259-3) U Ch Pr.

Canada, Geoffrey. Fist Stick Knife Gun: A Personal History of Violence in America. 224p. (Orig.). 1996. pap. 12.00 (0-8070-0423-5) Beacon Pr.

— Reaching up for Manhood: Transforming the Lives of Boys in America. LC 97-19919. 160p. 1998. 22.00 (0-8070-2316-7) Beacon Pr.

— Reaching up for Manhood: Transforming the Lives of Boys in America. 176p. 1999. pap. 12.50 (0-8070-2317-5) Beacon Pr.

Canada, John R., et al. Capital Investment Analysis for Engineering & Management. 2nd ed. LC 95-411. 566p. 1995. 100.00 (0-13-311036-2) P-H.

Canada Mortgage & Housing Corporation. A Comparison of Canadian & German Building Methods, Codes & Standards for Wood-frame Construction. LC 98-142270. (Illus.). i, 65 p. 1997. write for info. (0-662-26064-3) Can7 Govern Pub.

Canada, Ray, ed. Proceedings: MDS, 1986. 611p. 1986. pap. text 35.00 (0-933957-03-3) Marine Tech Soc.

Canada Royal Commission on Chinese & Japanese Immi. Report of the Royal Commission on Chinese & Japanese Immigration. Daniels, Roger, ed. LC 78-54812. (Asian Experience in North America Ser.). 1979. reprint ed. lib. bdg. 33.95 (0-405-11268-8) Ayer.

Canada Staff. The National Atlas of Canada. 4th rev. ed. LC 76-351950. 254p. 1974. write for info. (0-7705-1198-8) Trans-Atl Phila.

Canada Staff & McNairn, Colin H. H. Consolidated Insurance Companies Act of Canada & Regulations, 1994 LC 94-123141. xxxv, 566 p. 1993. write for info. (0-459-56803-5) Wrld Trade Pr.

Canada Staff, jt. auth. see Hawley, Donna Lea.

Canada Staff, jt. auth. see Langille, P. G.

***Canada Statistics Staff.** Canadian Social Trends. 288p. 1999. pap. 21.95 (1-55077-105-1) Thompson Educ.

Canada, Steve. Collected Published Poems by Steve Canada: Poems from Literary Journals in Five Countries, 1968-1990. 40p. (Orig.). 1997. pap. 4.95 (1-883424-56-9) Crop Circle Bks.

— Crop Circle Meanings: Understanding the Symbols: The Returning Goddess & Coming Transformations. (Illus.). 70p. (Orig.). 1995. pap. 8.95 (1-883424-37-2) Crop Circle Bks.

— Crop Circle Origins: Ancient Symbols Used Reveal Where Circlemakers Are From. rev. ed. 70p. 1993. pap. 6.95 (1-883424-10-0) Crop Circle Bks.

— Crop Circles: Deception - Methods & Implications. (National Security Ser.: Vol. 3). 76p. 1994. pap. 5.95 (1-883424-30-5) Crop Circle Bks.

— Crop Circles - A Convergence of Narrative: Making Sense of the Symbols. Closing the Loop of History. Answering the Question: "Why in England?" (Illus.). 117p. 1996. pap. 18.95 (1-883424-40-2) Crop Circle Bks.

— Crop Circles - A Vocabulary of the Symbols: How to Understand What Crop Formations Mean. (Illus.). 171p. (Orig.). 1998. pap. 16.95 (1-883424-54-2) Crop Circle Bks.

— Crop Circles - Allah's Daughter Returns to Earth. (Illus.). 150p. 1997. pap. 16.95 (1-883424-51-8) Crop Circle Bks.

— Crop Circles - Cracking the Code: Analysis of National Interest Implications. (National Security Ser.: No. 2). 68p. 1994. pap. 5.95 (1-883424-27-5) Crop Circle Bks.

— Crop Circles - How to Read the Mandala Formations: Author's Original Decipherment Methodology Identifies Ancient Rulers Returning to Earth from Nibiru. (Illus.). 78p. 1997. pap. 9.95 (1-883424-47-X) Crop Circle Bks.

— Crop Circles - Interplanetary Communication Begins: Interplanetary Communication Begins: Four Volumes of Communication Book Series Combined Between 2 Covers, 1997 Update. (Illus.). 125p. 1997. reprint ed. pap. 16.95 (1-883424-46-1) Crop Circle Bks.

— Crop Circles - Temple of Inanna/Ishtar: Returning Goddess Directs Us to Rebuild Her Temples. unabridged ed. (Inanna Bks.: Vol. 6). (Illus.). 88p. 1995. pap. 9.95 (1-883424-41-0) Crop Circle Bks.

— Crop Circles - The Theory That Works: Outline of Author's Original, Verifiable Translation Method. (Illus.). 135p. (Orig.). 1998. pap. 18.95 (1-883424-53-4) Crop Circle Bks.

— Crop Circles--Goddess Language: Archaeology of Imagery & Symbolism. (Inanna Bks.: No. 5). 86p. 1994. pap. 7.95 (1-883424-36-4) Crop Circle Bks.

— Crop Circles--Language of the Goddess: Meanings of Crop-Inscribed Ancient Symbols. (Inanna Bks.: No. 4). 84p. 1994. pap. 7.95 (1-883424-35-6) Crop Circle Bks.

— Crop Circles--Returning Rulers from Biblical Planet Olam: Ancient Astronauts Reveal Themselves, 1976-1996. (Illus.). 190p. 1998. pap. 18.95 (1-883424-55-0) Crop Circle Bks.

— Crop Circles & Genetics: Reproduction, Bioengineering & Immortality. rev. ed. 88p. 1993. pap. 10.95 (1-883424-07-0) Crop Circle Bks.

— Crop Circles & Isis, "Mistress of the Great Pyramid" at Giza: Ishtar Comes to the Fields of England - Includes the 1996 Spiral of Isis Crop Formation. unabridged ed. (Illus.). 90p. (Orig.). 1997. pap. 10.95 (1-883424-49-6) Crop Circle Bks.

— Crop Circles & National Security. (National Security Ser.: No. 1). 72p. 1993. pap. 5.95 (1-883424-23-2) Crop Circle Bks.

— Crop Circles & Quantum Physics: Hydrogen Atom Electron States. 52p. 1993. pap. 6.95 (1-883424-22-4) Crop Circle Bks.

— Crop Circles & the Mistresses of the Martian Pyramids: Stonehenge 1996 Spiral, Giza Plateau, & Mars Cydonia Structures. (Illus.). 140p. (Orig.). 1997. pap. 18.95 (1-883424-50-X) Crop Circle Bks.

— Crop Circles & the Returning Goddess Inanna, Queen of Heaven & Earth. (Inanna Bks.: No. 1). 64p. 1994. pap. 6.95 (1-883424-25-9) Crop Circle Bks.

— Crop Circles & the Returning Ruler Inanna, Great Lady of Heaven. (Inanna Bks.: No. 2). 72p. 1994. pap. 7.95 (1-883424-28-3) Crop Circle Bks.

— Crop Circles & the Tree of Life: The Earth Is Dying, the Garden of Eden Creators Are Returning. (Illus.). 125p. (Orig.). 1997. pap. 18.95 (1-883424-48-8) Crop Circle Bks.

***Canada, Steve.** Crop Circles 1999--Theory Confirmed: Season's Formations in England Decoded. (Illus.). 135p. 2000. 17.95 (1-883424-57-7) Crop Circle Bks.

Canada, Steve. Crop Circles, 1994 - The Returning "Bull of Heaven" More of the 1994 Season Deciphered. (Illus.). 96p. 1995. pap. 12.95 (1-883424-39-9) Crop Circle Bks.

— Crop Circles, UFOs, & Music: The Diatonic Scale Discovered in Crop Circles, UFO Notes Heard, Ancient Ratio Uncovered. 100p. (Orig.). 1994. pap. 16.95 (0-88342-433-9) Crop Circle Bks.

— Crop Circles, 1994: Interim Report on the English 1994 Summer Season: New Decoding Principles Discovered. (Illus.). 100p. (Orig.). 1995. pap. 12.95 (1-883424-38-0) Crop Circle Bks.

— Crop Circles...The End of Time: The Return to Earth of Allah, Quetzalcoatl, Ra, Vishnu, & Yahweh. unabridged ed. (Illus.). 112p. (Orig.). 1996. pap. 18.95 (1-883424-44-5) Crop Circle Bks.

— Crops Circles - Mission Colony Earth: Returning Colonizers from Ancient Astronauts' Planet Nibiru. (Illus.). 140p. (Orig.). 1998. pap. 18.95 (1-883424-52-6) Crop Circle Bks.

— Invasion: UFOs, ETs, & Crop Circle Warnings. (National Security Ser.: No. 4). 88p. 1994. 9.95 (0-88342-431-2) Crop Circle Bks.

— The Sphinx & Mars Face Identified: Crop Circle Analysis Leads to New Findings. (Inanna Bks.: No. 3). 76p. 1994. pap. 7.95 (1-883424-26-7) Crop Circle Bks.

— UFOs, Crop Circles, & Mars Structures: Their Common Origin. 59p. 1993. pap. 8.95 (1-883424-24-0) Crop Circle Bks.

***Canada Supreme Court Staff & Uukw, Delgam.** Delgamuukw: The Supreme Court of Canada Decision on Aboriginal Title. LC 99-59781. 142p. 2000. pap. 16.95 (0-295-97935-6) U of Wash Pr.

Canada Translation Services Staff & Public Works & Government Services Staff, eds. Employment Glossary. 2nd ed. 790p. 1997. pap. 59.95 (0-660-60166-4, Pub. by Canadian Govt Pub) Accents Pubns.

***Canada 21 Council Staff & Canadian Heritage Staff.** Je Parle Francais: Un Portrait de la Francophonie au Canada. (FRE., Illus.). 112p. 1999. pap. 24.95 (0-662-27895-X, Pub. by Canadian Govt Pub) Intl Spec Bk.

Canaday. What Is Art. 2nd ed. 1997. teacher ed. 46.95 (0-07-010921-4) McGraw.

Canaday, Bob & Canaday, Jackie. Franklin Vol. II: A Photographic Recollection. (Illus.). 100p. 1989. 70.00 (0-9655205-0-1) Canaday Photography.

— Franklin Vol. II: A Photographic Recollection. Crutchfield, James, ed. (Illus.). 224p. 1996. 75.00 (0-9655205-1-X) Canaday Photography.

Canaday, Cindi, jt. auth. see Canaday, Matt.

Canaday, Jackie, jt. auth. see Canaday, Bob.

Canaday, John. Late Gothic to Renaissance Paintings, 1. (C). 1969. 22.25 (0-393-02415-6) Norton.

— Mainstreams of Modern Art. 2nd ed. (C). 1981. pap. text 69.50 (0-03-057638-5, Pub. by Harcourt Coll Pubs) Harcourt.

— Neo-Classic Post Impressionist Painters: Lives of the Painters, Vol. 3. (C). 1969. 22.25 (0-393-02417-2) Norton.

***Canaday, John.** The Nuclear Muse: Literature, Physics & the First Atomic Bombs. LC 99-52229. (Illus.). 2000. pap. 22.95 (0-299-16854-9) U of Wis Pr.

Canaday, John E. Embattled Critic: Views on Modern Art. LC 72-8492. (Essay Index Reprint Ser.). 1977. reprint ed. 18.95 (0-8369-7309-7) Ayer.

— Lives of the Painters, 4 vols. LC 67-17666. (Illus.). (C). 1969. 83.50 (0-393-04231-6) Norton.

— What Is Art? An Introduction to Painting, Sculpture & Architecture. (C). 1980. 72.75 (0-07-554329-X) Knopf.

Canaday, Matt & Canaday, Cindi. Book of Mormon Circle a Word, Bk. 2. Griffin, Grace, ed. 51p. (Orig.). (YA). pap., student ed. 2.95 (1-56998-000-4) Gospel Puzzles.

Canadeo, Anne. Ralph Lauren: Master of Fashion. Young, Richard G., ed. LC 91-32777. (Wizards of Business Ser.). (Illus.). 64p. (J). (gr. 4-8). 1992. lib. bdg. 17.26 (1-56074-021-3) Garrett Ed Corp.

— Warren G. Harding: Twenty-Ninth President of the United States. Young, Richard G., ed. LC 89-39952. (Presidents of the United States Ser.). (Illus.). 128p. (J). (gr. 5-9). 1990. lib. bdg. 21.27 (0-944483-64-X) Garrett Ed Corp.

Canadian-American Committee. Bilateral Relations in an Uncertain World Context: Canada-U.S. Relations in 1978. LC 78-71435. (Canadian-American Committee Ser.). 112p. 1978. 4.00 (0-88806-044-0) Natl Planning.

— The New Environment for Canadian-American Relations. LC 72-86374. 80p. 1974. 1.50 (0-89068-018-3) Natl Planning.

Canadian Association of Oilwell Drilling Contracto. An Introduction to Oilwell Drilling & Servicing. LC 82-12027. 98p. (Orig.). 1982. pap. 9.95 (0-87201-202-6, 1202) Gulf Pub.

— Introduction to Oilwell Drilling & Servicing. LC 82-12027. (Illus.). 107p. 1982. reprint ed. pap. 33.20 (0-608-07943-X, 206791600012) Bks Demand.

— SI Drilling Manual. LC 82-15466. (Illus.). 869p. 1982. reprint ed. pap. 200.00 (*0-608-07936-7*, 206790900012) Bks Demand.

Canadian Bar Association Staff & Musgrove, James B. Competition Law for the 21st Century: Papers of the Canadian Bar Association Competition Law Section, 1997 Annual Conference. LC 98-3542. 1998. 60.00 (*1-57823-051-9*) Juris Pubng.

***Canadian Broadcasting Company cast.** Midnight Cab: The Mystery of the Lost Child. unabridged ed. 1999. audio 5.99 (*1-55204-615-X*, PAC-8615) Durkin Hayes Pub.

Canadian Broadcasting Company Staff. Thirty-Four Biographies of Canadian Composers. 1988. reprint ed. lib. bdg. 49.00 (*0-7812-0748-7*) Rprt Serv.

— Thirty-Four Biographies of Canadian Composers. LC 75-166224. 1964. reprint ed. 39.00 (*0-403-01351-8*) Scholarly.

Canadian Cancer Conference Staff. Proceedings, 5 vols. Begg, R. W., ed. Incl. 1st Conference, 1954. 1955. 75.00 (*0-12-149001-7*); 2nd Conference, 1956. 1957. 75.00 (*0-12-149002-5*); 3rd Conference, 1958. 1959. 75.00 (*0-12-149003-3*); 4th Conference, 1960. 1961. 75.00 (*0-12-149004-1*); 5th Conference, 1962. 1963. 75.00 (*0-12-149005-X*); write for info. (*0-318-50344-1*) Acad Pr.

Canadian Centre for Justice Statistics. Profile of Courts in Canada 1995. LC 96-151252. v, 227p. 1996. write for info. (*0-660-15593-1*) Can7 Govern Pub.

— Profile of Courts in Canada, 1987-1988. LC 90-110409. 161 p. 1989. write for info. (*0-660-12543-9*) Can7 Govern Pub.

***Canadian Centre for Justice Statistics Staff.** Juristat Reader: An Overview of the Canadian Justice System. 288p. 1999. 21.95 (*1-55077-106-X*) Thompson Educ.

Canadian Centre for Policy Alternatives Staff. Alternative Federal Budget Papers 1997. LC 97-157749. (Illus.). 403p. (Orig.). 1997. pap. 19.95 (*0-88627-159-2*, Pub. by J Lorimer) Formac Dist Ltd.

— Alternative Federal Budget Papers 1998: Fairer Taxes, Reinvesting in Health Care, Education & the Environment; Sustaining the Recovery & Job Creation. 379p. 1998. pap. 19.95 (*0-88627-942-9*, Pub. by J Lorimer) Formac Dist Ltd.

Canadian Centre for Policy Alternatives Staff & Coalition for Social Justice Staff. The 1997 Alternative Budget: The Canadian Centre for Policy Alternatives & Choices, a Coalition for Social Justice. (Illus.). 200p. 1997. pap. 19.95 (*1-55028-548-3*, Pub. by J Lorimer) Formac Dist Ltd.

***Canadian Corporation for Studies in Religion Staff.** Towards an Ethics of Community: Negotiations of Difference in a Pluralist Society. Olthuis, James H., ed. LC 99-932233. (Comparative Ethics Ser.: Vol. 5). 240p. 2000. pap. 29.95 (*0-88920-339-3*) Wilfrid Laurier.

Canadian Corporation for Studies in Religion Staff, jt. auth. see Donaldson, Terence L.

Canadian Corporation for Studies in Religion Staff, jt. auth. see Paleczny, Barbara.

Canadian Council for Southeast Asian Studies Staff. Poverty & Social Change in Southeast Asia: Selections from the Proceedings, Canadian Council for Southeast Asian Studies, 1978. Mehmet, Ozay, ed. LC 81-484905. 289p. 1979. reprint ed. pap. 89.60 (*0-608-02183-0*, 206285200003) Bks Demand.

***Canadian Council on International Law Staff.** Selected Papers in International Law (Textes Choisis en Droit International) (ENG & FRE.). 592p. 1999. text 150.00 (*90-411-9764-8*) Kluwer Law Intl.

Canadian Council on International Law Staff, ed. Treaty Compliance: Some Concerns & Remedies. LC 98-162705. 168p. 1998. pap. text 62.00 (*90-411-0732-0*) Kluwer Law Intl.

Canadian Diabetes Association Staff. Healthy & Hearty Diabetic Cooking. (Illus.). 356p. 1993. 26.92 (*0-9631701-2-0*) R A Rapaport.

Canadian Forest Service Staff. Biodiversity in the Forest: The Canadian Forest Service Three Year Action Plan. LC 97-224442. 38p. 1997. write for info. (*0-662-25736-7*, Pub. by Can7 Govern Pub) Intl Spec Bk.

Canadian Forestry Service Staff. Tree Diseases of Eastern Canada. LC 95-125730. 172p. (Orig.). 1994. pap. 51.95 (*0-660-14936-2*, Pub. by Canadian Govt Pub) Accents Pubns.

***Canadian Geographic Magazine Staff.** The Canadian Geographic Quiz Book. Wright, Ian, ed. (Illus.). 224p. 2000. pap. 11.95 (*1-55041-392-9*) Fitzhenry & W Ltd.

Canadian Government Staff. Never Say Die: The Canadian Air Force Survival Manual. (Illus.). 208p. 1979. pap. 20.00 (*0-87364-112-4*) Paladin Pr.

Canadian Healthcare Association Staff & Association for the Advancement of Medical Instrum. The Reuse of Single-Use Medical Devices: Guidelines for Healthcare Facilities. LC 97-209735. xii, 127p. 1996. write for info. (*1-57020-073-4*) Assn Adv Med Instrn.

Canadian Heritage Staff, jt. auth. see Canada 21 Council Staff.

Canadian Institute of Chartered Accountants Staff & AICPA Staff. Audit Implications of Electronic Document Management. 1997. pap. 31.50 (*0-87051-189-0*, 021066) Am Inst CPA.

Canadian Institute of Geomatics. Defence Geomatics, Then & Now: Celebrating the 50th Anniversary of Army Survey Establishment/Mapping & Charting Establishment, 1946-1996. LC 98-158940. (Illus.). 1996. write for info. (*0-919088-52-X*) Can Inst Sur.

Canadian International Development Agency, Briefin. Desertification: Meeting the Challenge. LC 98-157341. 28 p. 1997. write for info. (*0-662-62790-3*, Pub. by Can7 Govern Pub) Intl Spec Bk.

Canadian Mineral Processors Staff, jt. auth. see McDonald, G. W.

Canadian Museum of Contemporary Photography Staff. Anima Mundi: Still Life in Britain. (Illus.). 68p. 1992. pap. 29.95 (*0-88884-555-3*) U Ch Pr.

— Thirteen Essays on Photography. (Illus.). 258p. 1992. pap. 39.95 (*0-88884-557-X*) U Ch Pr.

Canadian Museum of Nature Staff. The Secret World of Animals - Below & Above the Ground. 1992. lib. bdg. 9.95 (*0-660-13062-9*) U Ch Pr.

— The Secret World of Animals - In the Air. 1992. lib. bdg. 9.95 (*0-660-13059-9*) U Ch Pr.

— The Secret World of Animals - On the Earth. 1992. lib. bdg. 9.95 (*0-660-13061-0*) U Ch Pr.

— The Secret World of Animals - Under the Water. 1996. lib. bdg. 9.95 (*0-660-13060-2*) U Ch Pr.

Canadian Nature Federation Staff & Patterson, Freeman. The Last Wilderness: Images of the Canadian Wild. 2nd ed. (Illus.). 180p. 1990. 50.00 (*1-55013-251-2*) Firefly Bks Ltd.

Canadian Networking Toxicology Center Staff. Manual of Immunological Methods. LC 98-3373. (Pharmacology & Toxicology Ser.). 160p. 1998. per. 64.95 (*0-8493-8558-X*) CRC Pr.

Canadian Number Theory Association Staff, et al. Proceedings of the 5th Conference of the Canadian Number Theory Association. LC 98-49282. (CRM Proceedings & Lecture Notes Ser.). 1999. write for info. (*0-8218-0964-4*) Am Math.

Canadian Parks Service Reconstruction Workshop Staff & Canadian Parks Service Staff. Proceedings of the Canadian Parks Service Reconstruction Workshop: Hull, Quebec, 11-13 March 1992. LC 94-182086. 107p. 1993. write for info. (*0-662-20364-X*, Pub. by Can7 Govern Pub) Intl Spec Bk.

Canadian Parks Service Staff, jt. auth. see Canadian Parks Service Reconstruction Workshop Staff.

Canadian Polish Millenium Fund Staff. Poland's Millenium of Christianity. (ENG & FRE.). 50p. 1966. 1.00 (*0-940962-29-2*) Polish Inst Art & Sci.

Canadian Press Association Staff. A History of Canadian Journalism in the Several Portions of the Dominion. LC 75-41047. reprint ed. 49.50 (*0-404-14745-3*) AMS Pr.

Canadian Red Cross Society Staff. Adapted Aquatics: Promoting Aquatic Opportunities for All. 186p. 1989. pap. text 37.00 (*0-921234-16-3*, R4163) AAHPERD.

— Let's Cook International. 189p. (Orig.). 1989. pap. 11.95 (*0-920581-02-1*) Gordon Soules Bk.

Canadian Reliability Engineers Staff. Reliability Engineering 1980: Proceedings of the 1980 Canadian SRE Reliability Symposium, Ottawa, Ontario, Canada May 15-16 1980. 170p. 1981. pap. 43.00 (*0-08-026163-9*, Pergamon Pr) Elsevier.

— Reliability Engineering 1975. 1976. pap. 35.00 (*0-08-019977-1*, Pergamon Pr) Elsevier.

— Reliability Engineering 1978: Proceedings of the SRE Reliability Symposium, Ottawa, Ontario, Canada, October, 1978. LC 78-10571. 1979. pap. 29.00 (*0-08-023228-0*, Pergamon Pr) Elsevier.

Canadian Research Committee on Taxation. Henry George & the End of Tax Commissions: An Evaluation of the Report of the Ontario Fair Tax Commission. LC 95-900614. 100p. 1995. pap. 6.00 (*0-9698812-1-5*, Pub. by Canadian Res Comm) Schalkenbach.

Canadian Society For Computational Studies Of Inte & Mccalla, Gordon. Advances in Artificial Intelligence: 11th Biennial Conference of the Canadian Society for Computational Studies of Intelligence, Ai'96 Toronto, Ontario, Canada, May 21-24, 1996 Proceedings, Vol. 108. LC 96-3028. (Lecture Notes in Artificial Intelligence Ser.). 459p. 1996. pap. 75.00 (*3-540-61291-2*) Spr-Verlag.

***Canadian Society for Computational Studies of Intelligence Staff & Hamilton, Howard J.** Advances in Artificial Intelligence: Proceedings of the 13th Biennial Conference of the Canadian Society for Computational Studies of Intelligence, AI 2000, Montreal, Quebec, Canada, May 14-17, 2000. LC 00-40013. (Lecture Notes in Computer Science Ser.). 2000. pap. write for info. (*3-540-67557-4*) Spr-Verlag.

Canadian Society for Immunology Staff. Biological Activities of Complement: Proceedings of the International Symposium of the Canadian Society for Immunology, 5th, Guleph, 1970. Ingram, D. G., ed. (Illus.). 1972. 73.25 (*3-8055-1310-0*) S Karger.

Canadian Standards Association Staff. Electric Clothes Dryers, UL 2158. 2nd ed. LC 96-7194. (FRE & ENG., Illus.). 94p. (J). 1997. pap. text 95.00 (*1-55989-506-3*) Underwrtrs Labs.

— Electric Clothes Washing Machines & Extractors, UL 2157. 2nd ed. LC 96-7195. (FRE & ENG., Illus.). 93p. (C). 1997. pap. text 95.00 (*1-55989-505-5*) Underwrtrs Labs.

— Household Refrigerators & Freezers, UL 250. 10th ed. LC 96-7197. (FRE & ENG., Illus.). 94p. (C). 1993. pap. text 95.00 (*1-55989-461-X*) Underwrtrs Labs.

— Vacuum Cleaners, Blower Cleaners, & Household Floor Finishing Machines, UL 1017. 5th ed. LC 97-5562. (Illus.). 116p. (C). 1996. pap. text 135.00 (*1-55989-191-2*) Underwrtrs Labs.

Canadian Standards Association Staff, contrib. by. Standard for Reinforced Thermosetting Resin Conduit (RTRC) & Fittings, UL 1684. 2nd ed. LC 97-15229. (Illus.). xii, 41p. (C). 1996. pap. text 135.00 (*1-55989-471-7*) Underwrtrs Labs.

Canadian Trade Committee Staff. Canadian Economic Policy since the War: A Series of Six Public Lectures in Commemoration of the Twentieth Anniversary of the "White paper" on Employment & Income of 1945, Delivered at Carleton University, September-November 1965. LC HC0115.C283. 161p. 1966. reprint ed. pap. 50.00 (*0-608-01375-7*, 206212000002) Bks Demand.

Canadian Transportation Agency Staff. Communication Barriers: A Look at Barriers to Communication Facing Persons with Disabilities Who Travel by Air. LC 98-141969. 75 p. 1997. write for info. (*0-662-25825-8*, Pub. by Can7 Govern Pub) Intl Spec Bk.

Canadian Transportation Safety Board Staff. Advancing Safety: Safety in the Sky, at Sea & on the Tracks. 246p. 1994. pap. 35.75 (*0-660-15406-4*, Pub. by Canadian Govt Pub) Accents Pubns.

Canadian-U. S. Conference on Communications Policy. Cultures in Collision: The Interaction of Canadian & U. S. Broadcasting Policies. LC 83-19232. 224p. 1984. 49.95 (*0-275-91136-5*, C1136, Praeger Pubs) Greenwood.

Canadian-U. S. Conference on Communications Policy. Cultures in Collision: The Interaction of Canadian & U. S. Broadcasting Policies. LC 83-19232. 224p. 1984. 49.95 (*0-275-91136-5*, C1136, Praeger Pubs) Greenwood.

Canadian Waste Management Conference Staff. Proceedings, 8th Canadian Waste Management Conference: September 3-5, 1986, Sheraton Hotel, Halifax Comptes Rendus, 8iaeme Conference Canadienne sur la Gestion des Dechets: Le 3, 4 et 5 Septembre 1986, Hotcel Sheraton, Halifax. LC 88-148814. ix, 377p. 1986. write for info. (*0-662-54631-8*) Can7 Govern Pub.

Canadian Wildlife Federation Staff, jt. auth. see Gregorich, L. J.

Canadian Wildlife Service Staff & Ontario. A Framework for Guiding Habitat Rehabilitation in Great Lakes Areas of Concern. LC 98-184265. viii, 76p. 1998. write for info. (*0-662-26577-7*) Can7 Govern Pub.

Canadian Workplace Automation Research Center, CWA. Thesaurus of Information Sciences & Technologies. (ENG & FRE.). 1991. pap. 95.00 (*0-8288-9441-8*) Fr & Eur.

***Canady, Charles T., ed.** The Applicaiton of the Americans with Disabilities Act to Medical Licensure & Judicial Officers: Congressional Hearing. 242p. (C). 2000. reprint ed. pap. text 35.00 (*0-7881-8695-7*) DIANE Pub.

Canady, John. Lives of the Painters. (C). 1969. 22.25 (*0-393-02418-0*) Norton.

***Canady, Pat.** Boots the World's Best Kid-Sitter: Springtime Adventures. (Illus.). 6p. (J). (ps-4). 2000. pap. 10.00 (*1-929889-02-X*) Canady SW.

— Tippy the Holiday Tree, 1. (Illus.). 9p. (J). (ps-4). 2000. pap. 10.00 (*1-929889-01-1*) Canady SW.

— Upside - Downside, Downside - Upside. (Illus.). 42p. (J). (ps-4). 2000. pap. 10.00 (*1-929889-00-3*) Canady SW.

Canady, Robert J., jt. auth. see Raines, Shirley C.

Canady, Robert L. & Rettig, Michael D. Block Scheduling: A Catalyst for Change in High Schools. (Illus.). 280p. 1995. 42.95 (*1-883001-14-5*) Eye On Educ.

Canady, Robert L. & Rettig, Michael D., eds. Teaching in the Block: Strategies for Engaging Active Learners. LC 96-12419. (Illus.). 320p. 1996. 42.95 (*1-883001-23-4*) Eye On Educ.

Canady, Robert Lynn, jt. auth. see Duke, Daniel L.

Canagarajah, R. Sudarshan, jt. auth. see CFNPP Staff.

Canainn, Tomas O. Tomas' Tunebook. 36p. 1998. pap. 9.95 (*0-946005-28-1*) Dufour.

— Traditional Slow Airs of Ireland. 1997. pap. text 9.95 (*0-946005-84-2*) Dufour.

Canak, William L. & Swanson, Laura. Modern Mexico. LC 97-38941. (Comparative Societies Ser.). 240p. 1997. pap. 14.69 (*0-07-034431-0*) McGraw.

Canak, William L., jt. auth. see Miller, Berkeley.

Canakis, Costas P., et al, eds. Papers from the 28th Regional Meeting of CLS, Vol. 1. 566p. 1992. pap. 16.00 (*0-914203-39-8*) Chicago Ling.

Canal & Stamperia Staff. Aldo Loris Rossi. 1999. pap. write for info. (*88-86502-82-6*, Pub. by Canal & Stamperia) Antique Collect.

— Fallingwater. 1999. pap. write for info. (*88-86502-81-8*, Pub. by Canal & Stamperia) Antique Collect.

— Frank O. Gehry. (Pocket Architecture Ser.). (Illus.). 96p. 1998. pap. 7.99 (*88-86502-84-2*, Pub. by Canal & Stamperia) Antique Collect.

— Luis Barragan. 1998. pap. write for info. (*88-86502-86-9*, Pub. by Canal & Stamperia) Antique Collect.

— Peter Eisenman. 1999. pap. write for info. (*88-86502-83-4*, Pub. by Canal & Stamperia) Antique Collect.

— Zaha Hadid. 1998. pap. 7.99 (*88-86502-85-0*) Canal & Stamperia.

Canal Corridor Association Staff. Historical Map & Guide to the Illinois & Michigan Canal National Heritage Corridor. 1998. pap. text 6.95 (*0-226-09260-7*) U Ch Pr.

Canal, Denis, ed. see De Chateaubriand, Rene.

***Canal, G. Orobitg.** Les Pume et Leurs Reves. (FRE.). 192p. 1998. pap. text 50.00 (*90-5709-008-2*) Craftsman House.

Canal, John. Silencing the Lone Assassin: The Murders of JFK & Lee Harvey Oshield. LC 99-45392. 208p. 2000. 24.95 (*1-55778-782-4*) Paragon Hse.

Canal, Nicola, et al, eds. Guidelines for Drug Trials in Memory Disorders. LC 93-24715. (Aging Ser.: No. 39). (Illus.). 380p. 1993. reprint ed. pap. 117.80 (*0-608-05842-4*, 205980800007) Bks Demand.

Canale, Fernando L. A Criticism of Theological Reason: Time & Timelessness as Primordial Presuppositions. (Andrews University Seminary Doctoral Dissertation Ser.: Vol. 10). 479p. 1987. pap. 19.99 (*0-943872-43-X*) Andrews Univ Pr.

Canale, Larry. Mickey Mantle, The Yankee Years: The Classic Photography of Ozzie Sweet. LC 98-87758. 224p. 1998. 39.95 (*0-930625-21-8*, Antique Trader) Krause Pubns.

Canale, Ray, jt. auth. see Chapra, Steve.

Canale, Raymond P., jt. auth. see Chapra, Steven

Canale, Raymond P., jt. auth. see Chapra, Steven C.

Canale, S. Terry. Campbell's Operative Orthopaedics. 9th ed. LC 97-33348. (Illus.). 4656p. (C). (gr. 13). 1997. text 450.00 (*0-8151-2087-7*, 28867) Mosby Inc.

Canale, S. Terry & Beaty, James H. Operative Pediatric Orthopaedics, No. 2. 1994. write for info. (*0-8016-7990-7*) Mosby Inc.

Canales, Isaac. Multi-Ethnicity. Hayner, Stephen & Aeschliman, Gordon, eds. (Global Issues Bible Study Ser.). 48p. 1990. wbk. ed. 4.99 (*0-8308-4905-X*, 4905) InterVarsity.

Canales, Luis. Contos Tristes. 2nd ed. (Illus.). 60p. 1988. pap. 3.95 (*0-933704-64-X*) Dawn Pr.

— Mishima. (Illus.). 40p. 1986. pap. 7.75 (*0-933704-55-0*) Dawn Pr.

Canales, Luis A. Imperial Gina. (Illus.). 1990. 19.95 (*0-8283-1932-4*) Branden Bks.

Canales, Maria C. & Morrissey, Jane F., eds. Gracias, Matiox, Thanks, Hermano Pedro: A Trilingual Anthology of Guatemalan Oral Tradition. LC 95-35357. (Albert Bates Lord Studies in Oral Tradition: Vol. 12). (Illus.). 448p. 1996. text 94.00 (*0-8153-1333-0*, H1731) Garland.

Canales, Nemesio. Antologia Nueva De Nemesio Canales, 4 bks., Set. Montana Palaez, Servando, ed. Incl. Bk. 21. Glosario. 1.50 (*0-8477-0021-6*); Bk. 22. Meditaciones Acres. 1.50 (*0-8477-0022-4*); Bk. 23. Boberias. 1.50 (*0-8477-0023-2*); Bk. 24. Hacia un Lejano Sol. 1.50 (*0-8477-0024-0*); (UPREX, Puerto Rico Ayer Ser.). (C). 6.00 (*0-8447-0000-2*) U of PR Pr.

Canales-Ruiz, R., ed. Control of Power Plants & Power Systems: SIPOWER '95. LC 96-49427. (IFAC Proceedings Ser.). 556p. 1996. pap. 92.50 (*0-08-042362-0*, Pergamon Pr) Elsevier.

Canaletto. Canaletto Drawings: Forty-Seven Works. (Illus.). 48p. 1991. pap. 4.95 (*0-486-26647-8*) Dover.

Canaletto, Antonio. Views of Venice by Canaletto. (Illus.). 90p. 1971. pap. 9.95 (*0-486-22705-7*) Dover.

***Canalis, Ernesto.** Skeletal Growth Factors. LC 99-52559. 2000. write for info. (*0-7817-2474-0*) Lppncott W & W.

Canalis, Rinaldo F. & Goodhill, Victor. Goodhill's Textbook of Otology. 2nd ed. (Illus.). 800p. 1997. text 125.00 (*0-397-51169-8*) Lppncott W & W.

Canalis, Rinaldo F. & Lambert, Paul R. The Ear: A Comprehensive Textbook of Otology & Neurotology. LC 99-16731. 822p. 2000. text 149.00 (*0-7817-1558-X*) Lppncott W & W.

Canalos, David, et al. Mad National Geogery. Richards, Brian & Smith, Larry, eds. (Wild Dog Ser.: No. 3). (Illus.). 40p. (Orig.). 1990. pap. 12.00 (*0-933087-16-0*) Bottom Dog Pr.

***Canals, Cuca.** Berta La Larga. 2000. pap. 10.95 (*1-86230-021-6*, Pub. by Transworld Publishers Ltd) Trafalgar.

— Llora, Alegria. 1999. 21.95 (*84-08-02947-9*) Planeta Edit.

Canals, Jordi. Competitive Strategies in European Banking. (Illus.). 304p. 1994. reprint ed. pap. text 24.95 (*0-19-877350-1*) OUP.

***Canals, Jordi.** Managing Corporate Growth. LC 99-42803. 200p. 2000. pap. 24.95 (*0-19-829668-1*); text 60.00 (*0-19-829667-3*) OUP.

Canals, Jordi. Universal Banking: International Comparisons & Theoretical Perspectives. LC 96-34856. (Illus.). 382p. 1997. text 85.00 (*0-19-877506-7*); pap. text 29.95 (*0-19-877505-9*) OUP.

Canals, Salvatore. Jesus As Friend. 176p. (Orig.). 1998. pap. 7.95 (*1-889334-03-0*) Scepter Pubs.

***Canals, Sonia.** Castanets. (Illus.). 8p. (J). (ps). 1999. 6.95 (*1-899607-75-7*) Levinson Bks.

— Drum. (J). 1999. pap. 6.95 (*1-899607-74-9*) Levinson Bks.

— Maraca. (J). 1999. pap. 6.95 (*1-899607-72-2*) Levinson Bks.

— Tambourine. (J). 1999. pap. 6.95 (*1-899607-73-0*) Levinson Bks.

Canamero, Dolores, ed. Emotional & Intelligent: The Tangled Knot of Cognition: Papers from the AAAI Fall Symposium. (Technical Reports: Vol. FS-98-03). (Illus.). 188p. 1998. spiral bd. 25.00 (*1-57735-077-4*) AAAI Pr.

Canan, Craig T. Progressive Periodicals Directory. 2nd ed. Orig. Title: U.S. Progressive Periodicals Directory. 52p. 1989. 16.00 (*0-935396-03-9*) Prog Educ.

— Southern Progressive Periodicals Directory. LC 80-644934. 1983. 8.00 (*0-935396-01-2*) Prog Educ.

***Canan, Janine.** Changing Woman. unabridged ed. Kuypers, Janet, ed. (Illus.). 176p. 2000. pap. write for info. (*1-891470-21-3*) Scars Pubns.

Canan, Janine. Of Your Seed. 1977. 2.00 (*0-685-80004-0*) Oyez.

Canan, Michael & Mitchell, William. Employee Fringe & Welfare Benefit Plans, 1997. (C). 1997. pap. text. write for info. (*0-314-21463-1*) West Pub.

Canan, Michael J. Interim Supplement to Qualified Retirement & Other Employee Benefit Plans, 1996 Edition. 100p. 1996. pap. text. write for info. (*0-314-21767-3*) West Pub.

— Qualified Retirement & Other Employee Benefit Plans. 1223p. 1991. pap. text. write for info. (*0-314-83467-2*) West Pub.

— Qualified Retirement & Other Employee Benefit Plans. 1992nd ed. 1218p. 1992. pap. text. write for info. (*0-314-00413-0*) West Pub.

— Qualified Retirement & Other Employee Benefit Plans, 1990. (Lawyers Practice Ser.). 1989. pap. text. write for info. (*0-314-69557-5*) West Pub.

— Qualified Retirement & Other Employee Benefit Plans, 1993. 1450p. 1993. pap. text. write for info. (*0-314-01726-7*) West Pub.

— Qualified Retirement & Other Employee Benefit Plans, 1996: Student Edition. 1405p. (C). 1996. pap. text. write for info. (*0-314-09883-6*) West Pub.

C

— Qualified Retirement & Other Employee Benefit Plans, 1996 Practitioner Edition, Vol. 1. (West's Employment Law Ser.). 1300p. 1996. pap. text. write for info. (*0-314-20330-3*) West Pub.

— Qualified Retirement & Other Employee Benefit Plans, 1996 Practitioner Edition, Vol. 2. (West's Employment Law Ser.). 550p. 1996. pap. text. write for info. (*0-314-20331-1*) West Pub.

— Qualified Retirement & Other Employee Benefit Plans, 1997. 7th ed. 1500p. (C). 1997. pap. text, student ed. write for info. (*0-314-22312-6*) West Pub.

Canan, Michael J. & Mitchell, Bill. Employee Fringe & Welfare Benefit Plans. 664p. 1994. pap. write for info. (*0-314-03654-7*) West Pub.

Canan, Michael J. & Mitchell, William B. Employee Fringe & Welfare Benefit Plans. 680p. 1993. pap. text. write for info. (*0-314-01922-7*) West Pub.

— Employee Fringe & Welfare Benefit Plans, 1996 Edition. 770p. 1996. pap. text. write for info. (*0-314-09728-7*) West Pub.

Canan, Michael J. & Mitchell, William D. Employee Fringe & Welfare Benefit Plans. 1992nd ed. (Handbook Ser.). 608p. 1992. pap. text. write for info. (*0-314-00475-0*) West Pub.

Canan, Penelope, jt. auth. see Pring, George W.

Canan, Syd, et al. Taigman's Advanced Cardiology: In Plain English. LC 94-48021. 256p. 1995. pap. text 51.00 (*0-89303-999-3*) P-H.

Cananaugh, Arthur. Rosemoore. 384p. 1989. mass mkt. 4.95 (*0-380-70484-6*, Avon Bks) Morrow Avon.

Canandian, Darshan S. Terrorism in Punjab: Selected Articles & Speeches. Dang, Satyapal, ed. 1987. 12.50 (*81-7050-040-0*, Pub. by Patriot Pubs) S Asia.

Canann, Scott A., ed. see ASME/ASCE/SES Summer Meeting on Trends in Unstruct.

Canape, Charlene. Adoption: Parenthood Without Pregnancy. 320p. 1988. mass mkt. 4.95 (*0-380-70505-2*, Avon Bks) Morrow Avon.

Canarache, A., et al. Dictionary of Soil Science: In English (with Definitions), French, German & Spanish. (ENG, FRE, GER & SPA.). 950p. write for info. (*0-444-82478-2*) Elsevier.

Canard, M., ed. see New, Tim R.

Canarina, John. Uncle Sam's Orchestra: Memories of the Seventh Army Symphony. LC 98-10520. (Illus.). 224p. 1998. 50.00 (*1-58046-019-4*) Univ Rochester Pr.

Canary. Interpersonal Communication. 1994. pap. text, teacher ed. 28.00 (*0-312-10837-0*) St Martin.

— Interpersonal Communication. 1994. pap. text, teacher ed. 5.00 (*0-312-03695-7*) St Martin.

***Canary & Cody.** Interpersonal Communication. 2nd ed. 2000. pap. text 48.95 (*0-312-19198-7*) St Martin.

Canary, Daniel J. & Cody, Michael J. Interpersonal Communication: A Goals-Based Approach. 432p. 1994. pap. text 48.95 (*0-312-03696-5*) St Martin.

Canary, Daniel J. & Dindia, Kathryn, eds. Sex & Gender Differences in Communication. LC 97-49098. (Communication Ser.). 300p. 1998. text 99.95 (*0-8058-2333-6*); pap. text. write for info. (*0-8058-2334-4*) L Erlbaum Assocs.

Canary, Daniel J. & Stafford, Laura, eds. Communication & Relational Maintenance. (Illus.). 313p. 1994. text 59.95 (*0-12-158430-5*) Acad Pr.

Canary, Daniel J., et al. Relationship Conflict: Conflict in Parent-Child, Friendship & Romantic Relationship. (Series on Close Relationships: Vol. 10). 200p. 1995. 42.00 (*0-8039-5129-9*); pap. 17.95 (*0-8039-5130-2*) Sage.

— Sex & Gender Differences in Personal Relationships. LC 97-37290. (Personal Relationships Ser.). 193p. 1997. lib. bdg. 30.00 (*1-57230-256-9*, C0256) Guilford Pubns.

— Sex & Gender Differences in Personal Relationships. (Personal Relationships Ser.). 193p. 1998. pap. text 21.00 (*1-57230-322-0*) Guilford Pubns.

Canary, Daniel J., jt. auth. see Cupach, William R.

Canary, Daniel J., jt. auth. see Siebold, David R.

Canary, Robert. The Cabell Scene. (James Branch Cabell Ser.). 300p. 1975. lib. bdg. 250.00 (*0-87700-236-3*) Revisionist Pr.

Canary, Robert H. George Bancroft. (Twayne's United States Authors Ser.). 1974. 15.95 (*0-8057-0034-X*) Irvington.

— T. S. Eliot: The Poet & His Critics. LC 81-20516. (Poet & His Critics Ser.). 407p. 1982. reprint ed. pap. 126.20 (*0-7837-9677-3*, 206040500005) Bks Demand.

Canary, Robert H. & Kozicki, Henry, eds. The Writing of History: Literary Form & Historical Understanding. LC 78-4590. 183p. 1978. reprint ed. pap. 56.80 (*0-608-06992-2*, 206720000009) Bks Demand.

Canary, Sarah. Karen Joy Fowler. 1995. pap. 11.00 (*0-8217-4991-9*, Zebra Kensgtn) Kensgtn Pub Corp.

Canas, Dionisio. Que Dice el Periodico. (Lecturas Faciles). (SPA.). 70p. 1983. pap. text 3.75 (*0-88345-522-6*, 21268); pap. text 7.00 (*0-13-748138-1*) Prentice ESL.

Canas, Jose, jt. auth. see Paris, Federico.

Canatella, Ray, et al. The Save Your Life Anti-Crime Guide for You & Your Family. large type ed. (Illus.). 100p. (YA). 1999. spiral bd. 10.00 (*0-940178-96-6*) Sitare.

Canaton, Frank M. Frontier Trails: Autobiography of Frank M. Canton. (American Biography Ser.). 236p. 1991. reprint ed. lib. bdg. 69.00 (*0-7812-8059-1*) Rprt Serv.

Canatsey, Kenneth. The Daimon Call: A Travel Journal in Verse & Other Poems. LC 98-53795. 56p. 1999. pap. text 14.95 (*0-7734-3126-8*) E Mellen.

Canaud, B. & Koch, K. M., eds. Treatment of Renal Anemia: Mini-Symposium on Recombinant Human Erythropoietin - Journal: Blood Purification, Vol. 8, No. 5, 1990. (Illus.). 76p. 1991. pap. 40.00 (*3-8055-5344-7*) S Karger.

Canault, Nina. Incredibly Small. LC 93-9337. (Frontiers of the Invisible Ser.). (Illus.). 48p. (YA). (gr. 6 up). 1993. lib. bdg. 14.95 (*0-02-716455-1*, New Dscvry Bks) Silver Burdett Pr.

Canavaggio, Jean. Cervantes. Jones, Joseph R., tr. from SPA. 1990. 25.00 (*0-393-02812-7*) Norton.

Canavaggio, Pierre. Dictionnaire des Superstitions et des Croyances. (FRE.). 353p. 1993. pap. 85.00 (*0-7859-5652-2*, 2850765546) Fr & Eur.

— Dictionnaire Raisonne des Superstitions et des Croyances Populaires.Tr. of Superstitions & Popular Belief. (FRE.). 247p. 1977. pap. 39.95 (*0-8288-5393-2*, M6059) Fr & Eur.

Canavan. Business Organization & Management. 2nd ed. 1998. 82.25 (*0-07-428684-6*) McGraw.

Canavan, Bernard. Economists for Beginners. 12.95 (*0-906495-51-2*) Writers & Readers.

Canavan, Bernard. Psychiatry for Beginners. (Writers & Readers Documentary Comic Bks.). 176p. 1986. pap. 6.95 (*0-86316-029-8*) Writers & Readers.

Canavan, Diane D. & Sanborn, LaVonne H. Using Children's Books in Reading Language Arts Programs: A How-to-Do-It Manual. (How-to-Do-It Ser.). 216p. 1992. 38.50 (*1-55570-101-9*) Neal-Schuman.

Canavan, Francis. Freedom of Expression: Purpose As Limit. LC 83-71826. 196p. 1986. reprint ed. lib. bdg. 25.00 (*0-89089-269-5*) Carolina Acad Pr.

— Pins in the Liberal Balloon. McFadden, Maria, ed. LC 90-62956. (Illus.). 192p. 1990. pap. 12.95 (*0-9627780-0-1*) Natl Comm of Cath Laymen.

— The Pluralist Game: Pluralism, Liberalism & the Moral Conscience. LC 95-4609. 192p. (C). 1995. pap. text 22.95 (*0-8476-8094-0*); lib. bdg. 56.50 (*0-8476-8093-2*) Rowman.

— The Political Economy of Edmund Burke: The Role of Property in His Thought. xi, 185p. (C). 1994. text 30.00 (*0-8232-1590-3*); pap. text 17.95 (*0-8232-1591-1*) Fordham.

***Canavan, John R., et al.** Family Support: Direction from Diversity. LC 00-28425. 2000. 27.95 (*1-85302-850-9*) Jessica Kingsley.

Canavan, Kim. Predict & Applications Development Guide. 1994. 55.00 (*1-878960-21-0*) WH&O Intl.

***Canavan, Marcia.** Woman's Law. LC 00-27885. 2000. write for info. (*0-8377-3100-3*, Rothman) W S Hein.

Canavan, P. Joseph. The Effective Writer's Companion. (C). 1981. 27.13 (*0-673-15449-1*) Addson-Wesley Educ.

Canavan, Paul K., ed. Rehabilitation in Sports Medicine. 10th ed. LC 97-17095. 600p. (C). 1999. 65.00 (*0-8385-8313-X*, A-8313-7, Apple Lange Med) McGraw.

Canavan, Richar W., IV & Siver, Peter A. Connecticut Lakes: A Study of the Chemical & Physical Properties of 56 Connecticut Lakes. (Illus.). 299p. 1995. pap. 9.95 (*1-878899-04-X*) CT Coll Arboretum.

Canavan, Rosemary. The Island. (Irish Literature Ser.). 116p. (Orig.). 1994. pap. 10.95 (*0-934257-56-6*) Story Line.

Canavan, Tony. Frontier Town: An Illustrated History of Newry. LC 89-81777. 240p. 1990. pap. 24.00 (*0-85640-430-6*, Pub. by Blackstaff Pr) Dufour.

Canaveral Council of Technical Societies Space Con. Space Congress Proceedings, Vol. 35. (Illus.). xix, 500p. 1998. pap. write for info. (*0-9659969-0-5*) CCTS.

Canavos. Introduction to Modern Business Statistics. (Business Statistics Ser.). 1993. pap. 49.00 (*0-534-16846-9*) Brooks-Cole.

— Introduction to Modern Business Statistics. (Business Statistics Ser.). 1993. pap., teacher ed. 88.25 (*0-534-16844-2*) Brooks-Cole.

— Introduction to Modern Business Statistics. 2nd ed. (Business Statistics Ser.). 1998. pap., student ed. 21.00 (*0-534-36202-8*) Wadsworth Pub.

Canavos & Miller. Introduction to Modern Business Statistics. (Business Statistics Ser.). 1993. pap., teacher ed. 44.25 (*0-534-16845-0*) Brooks-Cole.

Canavos, George C. & Miller, Don M. An Introduction to Modern Business Statistics. LC 92-42831. 797p. 1993. pap. 70.95 (*0-534-16842-6*) Wadsworth Pub.

— An Introduction to Modern Business Statistics. 2nd ed. LC 98-7637. 1998. pap. 86.95 (*0-534-35819-5*) PWS Pubs.

Canavos, George C. & Miller, Don M. Modern Business Statistics. LC 94-28751. 952p. 1994. pap. 110.95 (*0-534-16836-1*) Wadsworth Pub.

Canaway, W. H. Glory of the Seas. LC 74-21149. 192p. 1975. 5.95 (*0-672-52109-1*, Bobbs) Macmillan.

Canby, Courtlandt. A Guide to the Archaeological Sites of the British Isles. LC 88-25068. (Illus.). 368p. reprint ed. pap. 114.10 (*0-7837-6696-3*, 204631300011) Bks Demand.

Canby, Henry S. Alma Mater: The Gothic Age of the American College. LC 75-1835. (Leisure Class in America Ser.). (Illus.). 1975. reprint ed. 23.95 (*0-405-06904-9*) Ayer.

— The Brandywine. 2nd ed. (Illus.). 285p. 1977. pap. 12.95 (*0-916838-06-4*) Schiffer.

— College Sons & College Fathers. LC 68-16917. (Essay Index Reprint Ser.). 1977. reprint ed. 20.95 (*0-8369-0274-2*) Ayer.

— Definitions: Essays in Contemporary Criticism. (BCL1-PS American Literature Ser.). 308p. 1992. reprint ed. lib. bdg. 89.00 (*0-7812-6600-9*) Rprt Serv.

— Rivers of America: The Brandywine. Date not set. lib. bdg. 23.95 (*0-8488-1962-4*) Amereon Ltd.

— A Study of the Short Story. Dashiell, Alfred, ed. LC 83-45726. reprint ed. 33.00 (*0-404-20050-8*) AMS Pr.

— Turn West, Turn East: Mark Twain & Henry James. LC 65-23485. 1951. pap. 24.00 (*0-8196-0154-3*) Biblo.

Canby, Jeanny V. Ancient Near East in the Walters Art Gallery. LC 75-310215. (Illus.). 1974. pap. 1.50 (*0-911886-01-X*) Walters Art.

Canby, Jeanny V., et al. Ivory: The Sumptuous Art. (Illus.). 1983. pap. 5.00 (*0-911886-27-3*) Walters Art.

Canby, Jeanny V., ed. see Mellink, Machteld J.

Canby, Peter. The Heart of the Sky: Travels among the Maya. Turner, Philip, ed. LC 94-14939. (Illus.). 384p. 1994. pap. 13.00 (*1-56836-026-6*) Kodansha.

Canby, Sheila. Humayan's Garden Party: Princess of the House of Timur & Early Mughal Painting. LC 94-901413. (C). 1995. 53.00 (*81-85026-27-0*, Pub. by Marg Publns) Art Media Resources.

***Canby, Sheila R.** Golden Age of Persian Art, 1501-1722. (Illus.). 192p. 2000. 60.00 (*0-8109-4144-9*, Pub. by Abrams) Time Warner.

Canby, Sheila R. Rebellious Reformer: The Drawings & Paintings of Riza-Ya'Abbasi of Isafan. (Illus.). 248p. 1996. 200.00 (*1-898592-05-5*, Pub. by Art Bks Intl) Partners Pubs Grp.

***Canby, Sheila R.** Rebellious Reformer: The Drawings & Paintings of Riza-yi'abbasi of Isfahan. 1999. 149.50 (*1-85043-243-0*, Pub. by I B T) St Martin.

Canby, Thomas T. From Botswana to the Bering Sea: My Thirty Years with National Geographic. LC 98-5968. (Illus.). 288p. 1998. 24.95 (*1-55963-517-7*, Shearwater Bks) Island Pr.

Canby, Vincent, et al. The New York Times Guide to the Best 1,000 Movies Ever Made. LC 98-45289. (Illus.). 1024p. 1999. pap. 25.00 (*0-8129-3001-0*, Times Bks) Crown Pub Group.

Canby, William C., Jr. American Indian Law in a Nutshell. 2nd ed. (Nutshell Ser.). 336p. (C). 1988. reprint ed. pap. text 17.00 (*0-314-41160-7*) West Pub.

Canby, William C. American Indian Law in a Nutshell. 3rd ed. LC 98-7644. (Paralegal). 250p. 1998. pap. 20.95 (*0-314-22637-0*) West Pub.

Cancalon, Elaine D. & Spacagna, Antoine, eds. Intertextuality in Literature & Film: Selected Papers from the Thirteenth Annual Florida State University Conference on Literature & Film. (Florida State University Annual Conference on Literature & Film Ser.). 176p. (C). 1994. pap. 19.95 (*0-8130-1287-2*) U Press Fla.

Cancalon, Paul, jt. ed. see Elam, John S.

Cancel, Miguel, ed. see Aristotle.

Cancellieri, Giovanni, ed. Single-Mode Optical Fiber Measurement: Characterization & Sensing. LC 92-32247. (Artech House Optoelectronics Library). (Illus.). 348p. 1993. reprint ed. pap. 107.90 (*0-608-00568-1*, 206145100009) Bks Demand.

Cancellieri, Giovanni & Ravaioli, Umberto. Measurements of Optical Fibers & Devices: Theory & Experiments. LC 83-72775. (Artech House Telecommunications Library). 515p. reprint ed. pap. 159.70 (*0-7837-3016-0*, 204292400006) Bks Demand.

Cancelmo, Jesse. Diving Cayman Islands. LC 97-8606. (Illus.). 128p. (Orig.). 1997. pap. 18.95 (*1-881652-10-6*) Aqua Quest.

Cancelmo, Jesse & Strohofer, Michael. Diving Bermuda. 2nd ed. LC 90-82636. (Illus.). 128p. 2000. pap. 18.95 (*1-881652-20-3*, Pub. by Aqua Quest) Natl Bk Netwk.

Cancelmo, Joseph A. & Bandini, Carol. For Love or Money? The Paradox of Child Care: A Guide to the Relationship Between Parents & In-Home Caregivers. LC 98-20599. xxv, 258p. 1999. 30.00 (*0-7657-0178-2*) Aronson.

Cancer Care, Inc. Staff & National Cancer Foundation, Inc. Staff. Listen to the Children: A Study of the Impact on the Mental Health of Children of a Parent's Catastrophic Illness. LC 77-94376. 1977. 2.50 (*0-9606494-1-7*) Cancer Care.

Canche, Pablo. Semana Santa en Tierra Santa-bL-Alumno. (SPA.). 1989. pap. 1.00 (*1-55955-010-4*) CRC Wrld Lit.

— Semana Santa en Tierra Santa-bL-Maestro. (SPA.). 1990. pap. 1.00 (*1-55955-011-2*) CRC Wrld Lit.

— Semana Santa en Tierra Santa-C-Alumno. (SPA.). 1989. pap. 1.00 (*1-55955-006-6*) CRC Wrld Lit.

— Semana Santa en Tierra Santa-C-Maestro. (SPA.). 1990. pap. 1.00 (*1-55955-007-4*) CRC Wrld Lit.

— Semana Santa en Tierra Santa-Db-Alumno. (SPA.). 1989. pap. 1.00 (*1-55955-008-2*) CRC Wrld Lit.

Cancian, Francesca M. Love in America: Gender & Self-Development. (Illus.). 224p. 1987. text 59.95 (*0-521-34202-3*) Cambridge U Pr.

— What Are Norms? A Study of Beliefs & Action in a Maya Community. LC 74-77833. 222p. reprint ed. pap. 63.30 (*0-608-17064-X*, 2027284) Bks Demand.

***Cancian, Francesca M. & Olkier, Stacey.** Caring & Gender. LC 99-6311. (Gender Lens Ser.). 1999. write for info. (*0-8039-9096-0*) Pine Forge.

Cancian, Frank. The Decline of Community in Zinacantan: Economy, Public Life, & Social Stratification, 1960-1987. LC 92-5550. (Illus.). 328p. (C). 1992. 45.00 (*0-8047-2040-1*) Stanford U Pr.

— Decline of Community in Zinacantan: Economy, Public Life, & Social Stratification, 1960-1987. xxiv, 300p. 1994. pap. 15.95 (*0-8047-2362-1*) Stanford U Pr.

— The Innovator's Situation: Upper-Middle-Class Conservatism in Agricultural Communities. LC 78-65327. xvi, 159p. 1979. reprint ed. pap. 12.95 (*0-8047-1111-9*) Stanford U Pr.

Cancik, Hildegard. Untersuchungen Zu Senecas "Epistulae Morales" (GER.). x, 163p. 1967. 40.00 (*0-318-70622-9*) G Olms Pubs.

Cancik, Hubert. Untersuchungen zur Lyrischen Kunst des P. P. Statius. (GER.). 155p. 1965. 32.00 (*0-318-70486-2*) G Olms Pubs.

Cancik-Kirschbaum, Eva C., ed. see Bock, Barbara.

***Cancilla, Bob.** Getting Dow to E-Business with AS/400. 420p. 2000. 89.00 (*1-58347-010-7*) Midrange Comput.

— Getting down to E-Business with AS/400. (Illus.). 500p. 1999. pap. 89.00 (*0-9663375-4-9*) AS-Four Hundr Pr.

Cancilla, Dorothy Rose. Death by HMO: The Jennifer Gigliello Story. LC 98-41967. (Illus.). 156p. 2000. 19.95 (*0-9671922-0-X*, Pub. by Dedicated Pr) Midpt Trade.

Cancilla, P. A. & Vogel, F. Stephen. Neuropathology: Based on the 1989 IAP Annual Long Course. (Illus.). 160p. 1990. 69.00 (*0-683-01430-7*) Lppncott W & W.

Cancio-Gonzalez, Sylvia E., jt. auth. see Serrano-Gayls, Raul.

Canclini, A. Comentario Biblico Continente Nuevo: I Corintios.Tr. of New Continent Bible Commentary: I Corinthians. (SPA.). 276p. 9.99 (*0-7899-0159-5*, 498645) Editorial Unilit.

— Comentario Biblico Continente Nuevo: 1 Corintios.Tr. of New Continent Bible Commentary: I Corinthians. (SPA.). pap. 5.99 (*0-7899-0160-9*, 498646) Editorial Unilit.

— Instrucciones para una Nueva Vida en Cristo.Tr. of New Life in Christ. (SPA.). 100. pap. 4.50 (*1-56063-998-9*, 497481) Editorial Unilit.

Canclini, Arnoldo. Abuelos: Gran Experiencia en la Vida. (Serie Realidades - Realities Ser.).Tr. of Grandparents. (SPA.). 1991. pap. 1.99 (*1-56063-046-9*, 498118) Editorial Unilit.

— Apocalipsis: Vision del Triunfo Final. (Estudios Biblicos Basicos Ser.).Tr. of Revelations: Vision of the Final Triumph. (SPA.). 160p. (Orig.). 1989. pap. 7.99 (*0-311-04360-7*) Casa Bautista.

— Filemon 2, Pedro - Judas: Cuadros de la Experiencia Cristiana.Tr. of Philemon 2, Peter - Jude: Portraits of the Christian Experience. (SPA.). 160p. (Orig.). 1990. pap. 7.99 (*0-311-04366-6*) Casa Bautista.

— La Soledad: El Remedio Supremo. (Serie Realidades - Realities Ser.).Tr. of Loneliness. (SPA.). 88p. 1991. pap. 1.99 (*1-56063-047-7*, 498119) Editorial Unilit.

Canclini, Arnoldo, tr. see Drakeford, John W.

Canclini, Arnoldo, tr. see Edge, Findley B.

Canclini, Arnoldo, tr. see Humphreys, Fisher.

Canclini, Arnoldo, tr. see Jones, J. Estill.

Canclini, Arnoldo, tr. see Taylor, Preston.

Canclini, Nestor G. & Lopez, Silvia L. Hybrid Cultures: Strategies for Entering & Leaving Modernity. LC 94-47137.Tr. of Culturis Hibridas. (SPA.). 1995. pap. 19.95 (*0-8166-2315-5*) U of Minn Pr.

Canclini, Nestor Garcia, see Garcia Canclini, Nestor.

Cancogni, Anna, tr. see Eco, Umberto.

Cancogni, Annapaola, tr. see Pontiggia, Giuseppe.

Cancogni, Annapaola, tr. see Radiguet, Raymond.

Cancogni, Annapaola, tr. see Rossellini, Roberto.

Cancogni, Manlio. A Friendship. Magri, Iole F., tr. from ITA. LC 85-19273.Tr. of Azorin e Miro. 110p. 1986. 20.00 (*0-913993-03-4*) Paideia Pubs.

Cancro, Robert, et al, eds. Progress in Functional Psychoses. LC 78-31828. (Illus.). 250p. 1979. 44.95 (*0-88331-185-2*) R B Luce.

Cancro, Robert, jt. ed. see Georgotas, Anastasios.

Canda, Edward R., ed. Spirituality in Social Work: New Directions. LC 98-17375. (Social Thought Monograph Ser.: Vol. 18, No. 2). 112p. 1998. 29.95 (*0-7890-0515-8*) Haworth Pr.

***Canda, Edward R. & Furman, Leola D.** Spiritual Diversity in Social Work Practice: The Heart of Helping. LC 99-22123. (Illus.). 400p. 1999. 29.45 (*0-684-84411-7*) S&S Trade.

Candage, Mellen, ed. see Bader, Barry S. & Umbdenstock, Richard J.

Candage, Mellen, ed. see Falk, John H. & Dierking, Lynn D.

Candage, Mellen, ed. see Little, Carl.

Candage, R. G. Historical Sketches of Bluehill. (Illus.). 83p. 1997. reprint ed. pap. 16.50 (*0-8328-5813-7*) Higginson Bk Co.

Candan, Theodore K. The Many Seasons of Love. 100p. 1999. pap. 9.95 (*0-7392-0056-9*, 2869) Morris Pubng.

Candani, Yaakov. Hamilon Haivri Hechdash: Complete Hebrew Dictionary, 7 vols. 6th ed. (HEB.). 1998. reprint ed. 200.00 (*1-880880-29-6*) Israeli Trad.

Candappa, Beulah. The Bharunda Bird. (Myths & Legends Ser.). (Illus.). (J). 1998. (*1-57572-013-2*) Heinemann Lib.

***Candappa, Rohan.** Little Book of Stress: Calm Is for Whimps; Get Real, Get Stressed. 2000. pap. 4.95 (*0-7407-0474-5*) Andrews & McMeel.

— Little Book of Wrong Shui: How to Drastically Improve Your Life by Basically Moving Stuff Around. 160p. 2000. pap. 4.95 (*0-7407-0475-3*) Andrews & McMeel.

Candau de Cevallos, Maria del C. Historia de la Lengua Espanola. (SPA.). 1985. 33.00 (*0-916379-22-1*) Scripta.

Candau, Francoise & Ottewill, Ronald H., eds. Scientific Methods for the Study of Polymer Colloids & Their Applications: Proceedings of the NATO Advanced Study Institute on Polymer Colloids Held in Strasbourg, France, July 15, 1988. (C). 1990. text 298.50 (*0-7923-0599-X*) Kluwer Academic.

Cande, Roland de. Diccionari de la Musica. 2nd ed. (CAT.). 224p. 1985. pap. 10.95 (*0-7859-5875-4*, 8429705783) Fr & Eur.

— Dictionnaire des Musiciens. (FRE.). 288p. 1974. pap. 29.95 (*0-8288-6020-3*, F17742) Fr & Eur.

Cande, Roland De, see De Cande, Roland.

Candee, A. H. Gear Geometry: A New Approach to Gear Analysis. (Technical Papers: Vol. P29). (Illus.). 42p. 1929. pap. text 30.00 (*1-55589-173-X*) AGMA.

— Geometrical Determination of Tooth Form Factor. (Technical Papers: Vol. P223). (Illus.). 20p. 1941. pap. text 30.00 (*1-55589-189-6*) AGMA.

— Industrial Applications of Spiral Bevel Gears & Hypoid Gears. (Technical Papers: Vol. P202A). (Illus.). 12p. 1938. pap. text 30.00 (*1-55589-417-8*) AGMA.

— Involute Gear Calculations Simplified. (Technical Papers: Vol. P238). (Illus.). 7p. 1945. pap. text 30.00 (*1-55589-190-X*) AGMA.

An Asterisk (*) at the beginning of an entry indicates that the title is appearing for the first time.

— Large Spiral Bevel & Hypoid Gears. (Technical Papers: Vol. P57). (Illus.). 8p. 1929. pap. text 30.00 (*1-55589-415-1*) AGMA.

— Recent Developments in Bevel & Hypoid Gearing. (Technical Papers: Vol. P140). (Illus.). 17p. 1936. pap. text 30.00 (*1-55589-416-X*) AGMA.

— Symbols for Gear Terms. (Technical Papers: Vol. P96). (Illus.). 18p. 1930. pap. text 30.00 (*1-55589-148-9*) AGMA.

— Tooth Bearings in Bevel Gears. (Technical Papers: Vol. P205). (Illus.). 34p. 1940. pap. text 30.00 (*1-55589-418-6*) AGMA.

Candee, A. H. & Zamis, A. Oversize of Wormgear Hobs. (Technical Papers: Vol. P129.09). (Illus.). 12p. 1953. pap. text 30.00 (*1-55589-156-X*) AGMA.

Candee, A.H. Calculated Bending Stress in Spur Gear Teeth. (Technical Papers: Vol. P222). (Illus.). 28p. 1941. pap. text 30.00 (*1-55589-268-X*) AGMA.

Candee, Andrea & Andrusia, David. Gentle Healing for Baby & Child: A Parent's Guide to Child-Friendly Herbs & Other Natural Remedies for Common Ailments & Injuries. 288p. 2000. per. 12.95 (*0-671-03622-X*) PB.

Candee, Richard M. Atlantic Heights: A World War I Shipbuilders Community. LC 85-3644. (Portsmouth Marine Society Ser.: No. 7). (Illus.). 136p. 1985. 19.95 (*0-915819-06-6*) Portsmouth Marine Soc.

***Candel, Alberto & Conlon, Lawrence.** Foliations I. LC 99-45694. (Graduate Studies in Mathematics). 402p. 1999. write for info. (*0-8218-0809-5*) Am Math.

Candel, Danielle. Dictionnaire de Sigles Domaines Economique et Sociaux. (FRE.). 740p. 1992. 155.00 (*0-7859-8105-5*, 2856080456) Fr & Eur.

Candel, Gregory. A Hokum County Almanac. (Illus.). 104p. (Orig.). 1996. pap. 7.95 (*0-9648040-0-X*) Hen Hse Prods.

Candela, Antonio. Adventures of an Innocent in the Spanish Civil War. 224p. (C). 1988. 65.00 (*1-85200-020-1*, Pub. by United Writers Pubns) St Mut.

***Candela, Giuseppe.** Casistiche Ideologiche tra Politica e Letteratura. LC 98-44640. (Studies in Italian Culture: Vol. 26). (ITA.). 172p. (C). 1999. text 45.00 (*0-8204-4418-9*) P Lang Pubng.

Candela, Giuseppe. Manierismo e Condizione Della Scrittura in Anton Francesco Doni. LC 93-25226. (Studies in Italian Culture: Vol. 15). 190p. (C). 1994. text 41.95 (*0-8204-2271-1*) P Lang Pubng.

Candelaria, Cordelia. Chicano Poetry: A Critical Introduction. LC 85-10019. 276p. 1986. 49.95 (*0-313-23683-6*, CCH/, Greenwood Pr) Greenwood.

— Seeking the Perfect Game: Baseball in American Literature, 24. LC 89-2157. (Contributions to the Study of Popular Culture Ser.: No. 24). 175p. 1989. 49.95 (*0-313-25465-6*, CBA, Greenwood Pr) Greenwood.

Candelaria, Cordelia, jt. ed. see Keller, Gary D.

Candelaria, Cordelia C., jt. ed. see Brogan, Jacqueline V.

Candelaria, Frederick. Poems New & Selected. 84p. 1984. pap. 6.95 (*0-86492-029-6*, Pub. by Goose Ln Edits) Genl Dist Srvs.

Candelaria, Judith, jt. auth. see Fairbanks, Jo.

Candelaria, Michael R. Popular Religion & Liberation: The Dilemma of Liberation Theology. LC 89-4573. (SUNY Series in Religion, Culture, & Society). 194p. (C). 1990. text 21.50 (*0-7914-0229-0*) State U NY Pr.

Candelaria, Nash. The Day the Cisco Kid Shot John Wayne. LC 88-70125. 172p. 1990. pap. 15.00 (*0-916950-81-6*) Biling Rev-Pr.

— Inheritance of Strangers. LC 85-71527. 272p. 1985. pap. text 17.00 (*0-916950-59-X*); lib. bdg. 27.00 (*0-916950-58-1*) Biling Rev-Pr.

— Leonor Park. LC 91-20652. 168p. 1991. 25.00 (*0-927534-18-5*); pap. 15.00 (*0-927534-19-3*) Biling Rev-Pr.

— Memories of the Alhambra. LC 76-26410. 192p. 1977. 25.00 (*0-9601086-1-0*) Biling Rev-Pr.

— Memories of the Alhambra. LC 76-26410. 192p. 1982. reprint ed. pap. 15.00 (*0-916950-32-8*) Biling Rev-Pr.

— Not by the Sword. LC 81-71731. 235p. 1982. 26.00 (*0-916950-30-1*); pap. 16.00 (*0-916950-31-X*) Biling Rev-Pr.

— Uncivil Rights: And Other Stories. LC 98-35871. 128p. 1998. pap. 12.00 (*0-927534-83-5*) Biling Rev-Pr.

Candelario, Andres. La Vieja Furia de los Fusiles: Cuentos de la Revolucion Cubana. LC 90-83327. (Coleccion Caniqui). (SPA.). 96p. (Orig.). 1990. pap. 9.95 (*0-89729-255-3*) Ediciones.

Candell, Amy B., jt. auth. see Krepps, Matthew B.

Candell-Riera, J. & Ortega-Alcalde, D., eds. Nuclear Cardiology in Everyday Practice. LC 93-24826. (Developments in Cardiovascular Medicine Ser.: Vol. 146). 396p. (C). 1994. text 243.00 (*0-7923-2374-2*) Kluwer Academic.

Candelora, Deborah. Learning Center Activities: Science. (Illus.). 80p. (J). (gr. k-2). 1997. pap., teacher ed. 9.95 (*1-57690-072-X*, TCM2072) Tchr Create Mat.

Candelore, Craig. You Can Pass the Bar Examination. 1999. pap. 19.95 (*1-881116-99-9*, Pub. by Black Forest Pr) Epic Bk Promo.

***Candeloro, Dominic.** Italians in Chicago. (Images of America Ser.). 1999. pap. 16.99 (*0-7524-1317-1*) Arcadia Publng.

Candeloro, Dominic & Paul, Barbara. Chicago Heights. (Images of America Ser.). (Illus.). 128p. 1998. pap. 16.99 (*0-7524-1282-5*) Arcadia Publng.

***Candeloro, Dominic & Paul, Barbara.** Chicago Heights Revisited. (Images of America Ser.). (Illus.). 128p. 2000. pap. 18.99 (*0-7385-0129-8*) Arcadia Publng.

Candemil, Francisco, tr. see Yorde, Adele & George, Elizabeth M.

Cander, H. S., jt. auth. see Ruppel, S. C.

Candib, Lucy M. Medicine & the Family: A Feminist Perspective. LC 95-7114. 1995. 38.00 (*0-465-02374-6*, Pub. by Basic) HarpC.

Candida-Smith, Richard. Utopia & Dissent: Art, Poetry, & Politics in California. (Illus.). 560p. 1996. pap. 22.50 (*0-520-20699-1*, Pub. by U CA Pr) Cal Prin Full Svc.

Candido, Antonio. On Literature & Society. Becker, Howard S., ed. & tr. by. LC 94-32403. 248p. 1995. text 49.50 (*0-691-03629-2*, Pub. by Princeton U Pr); pap. text 17.95 (*0-691-03630-6*, Pub. by Princeton U Pr) Cal Prin Full Svc.

Candido, Jeane H. Levi: The Smartest Boy in the World. (Illus.). 30p. (J). (gr. 1-5). 1998. pap. 9.95 (*1-886383-34-0*) Pride & Imprints.

— The Redemption of Corporal Nolan Giles. 2nd ed. LC 96-51044. 250p. (Orig.). 1996. pap. 12.95 (*1-886383-14-6*) Pride & Imprints.

— Shepherd's Song. 300p. 2001. pap. 12.95 (*1-886383-59-6*, Keystone) Pride & Imprints.

***Candido, Joseph, ed.** Value & Vision in American Literature: Essays in Honor of Ray Lewis White. LC 99-30999. 288p. 2000. 45.00 (*0-8214-1291-4*) Ohio U Pr.

Candido, Joseph, ed. see Shakespeare, William.

Candido, Keith R. A. De, see De Candido, Keith R. A.

Candilis, Wray O., ed. United States Service Industries Handbook. LC 87-25865. 254p. 1988. 59.95 (*0-275-92367-3*, C2367, Praeger Pubs) Greenwood.

***Candis, Judy.** Colorblind. 1998. pap. 12.00 (*0-9669271-0-9*) Ishai Creat.

Candisky, Catherine, jt. auth. see Yocum, Robin.

Candland, Douglas K. Feral Children & Clever Animals: Reflections on Human Nature. LC 93-59. (Illus.). 432p. (C). 1993. text 35.00 (*0-19-507468-8*) OUP.

— Feral Children & Clever Animals: Reflections on Human Nature. (Illus.). 432p. 1995. reprint ed. pap. 16.95 (*0-19-510284-3*) OUP.

Candland, Elanor, jt. auth. see Bob.

Candler, Allen D., ed. see Georgia Colony Staff.

Candler, Allen D., ed. see Georgia General Assembly Staff.

Candler, Charles H. Asa Griggs Candler: Founder of Coca-Cola. 2nd ed. Watson, Casey, ed. LC 94-38325. (Illus.). 512p. 1999. pap. 19.95 (*1-57090-005-1*) Alexander Dist.

Candler, Edmund. Abdication. LC 92-63034. 280p. 1993. reprint ed. pap. 13.95 (*0-9627987-4-6*) Turtle Point Pr.

— The Unveiling of Lhasa. 3rd ed. (Illus.). 304p. 1987. reprint ed. 19.95 (*0-9617066-2-7*); reprint ed. pap. 12.95 (*0-9617066-1-9*) Snow Lion-SLG Bks.

Candler, John. Brief Notices of Hayti. 1977. 16.95 (*0-8369-9219-9*, 9074) Ayer.

Candler, Laura. Discovering Decimals Through Cooperative Learning. (Illus.). 170p. 1997. pap. text 20.00 (*1-879097-43-5*) Kagan Cooperative.

— Hands on Science! (Illus.). 200p. 1994. pap. text 25.00 (*1-879097-26-5*) Kagan Cooperative.

— Wee Science. (Illus.). 200p. 1994. pap. text 25.00 (*1-879097-25-7*) Kagan Cooperative.

Candler-Lotven, Ann C., jt. auth. see Tallent-Runnels, Mary K.

Candler, Wilfred C. & Kumar, Nalini. India: The Dairy Revolution : the Impact of Dairy Development in India & the World Bank's Contribution. LC 98-39156. (Oed Study Ser.). 96p. 1998. pap. 22.00 (*0-8213-4289-4*) World Bank.

Candlewick Press Staff. Numbers: Flip-&-Find. (Illus.). 24p. (J). (ps-1). 1999. 7.99 (*0-7636-0893-9*) Candlewick Pr.

— Opposites: Flip-&-Find. LC 98-87862. (Illus.). 24p. (J). (ps-1). 1999. 7.99 (*0-7636-0894-7*) Candlewick Pr.

Candlin, C. N., ed. see Anderson, Anne & Lynch, Tony.

Candlin, C. N., ed. see Batstone, Rob.

Candlin, C. N., ed. see Bygate, Martin.

Candlin, C. N., ed. see Cook, Guy.

Candlin, C. N., ed. see Dalton, Christiane & Seidhofer, Barbara.

Candlin, C. N., ed. see Malamah-Thomas, Ann.

Candlin, C. N., ed. see McCarthy, Michael.

Candlin, C. N., ed. see Nunan, David.

Candlin, C. N., ed. see Rea-Dickins, Pauline & Germaine, Kevin.

Candlin, C. N., jt. ed. see Riley, Philip.

Candlin, C. N., ed. see Wallace, Catherine.

Candlin, C. N., ed. see Wright, Tony.

Candlin, Christopher & Hyland, Ken. Writing: Texts, Processes & Practices. LC 98-46959. (Applied Linguistics & Language Study Ser.). 344p. 1999. 37.32 (*0-582-31750-9*) Longman.

Candlin, Christopher N. The Communicative Teachings of English Principles & an Exercise Typology. 230p. (C). 1981. pap. text 12.95 (*0-582-55064-5*) Longman.

Candlin, Christopher N., jt. ed. see Leech, Geoffrey N.

Candlin, Lillian. Memories of Old Sussex. 96p. 1987. 30.00 (*0-905392-78-7*) St Mut.

— Tales of Old Sussex. 96p. 1987. 30.00 (*0-905392-45-0*) St Mut.

Candlish, J. K. A Medical Biochemistry for the Tropics. 1977. text 30.00 (*0-7020-0619-X*) Bailliere Tindall.

Candlish, J. K. & Crook, M. J. Notes on Clinical Biochemistry. 272p. 1993. text 55.00 (*981-02-1065-5*); pap. text 28.00 (*981-02-1066-3*) World Scientific Pub.

Candlish, John. Dietary Imbalances, Metabolism & Disease: The Southeast Asian Perspective. 164p. (Orig.). 1990. pap. 38.50 (*9971-69-145-0*, Pub. by Sngapore Univ Pr) Coronet Bks.

Candlish, Patricia Ann Morgan. Not Deaf Enough: Raising a Child Who Is Hard of Hearing with Hugs, Humor & Imagination. (Illus.). 242p. (Orig.). 1996. pap. 22.95 (*0-88200-201-5*) Alexander Graham.

Candlish, Robert. First John. 577p. 1993. 28.99 (*0-85151-662-9*) Banner of Truth.

Candlish, Robert S. Commentary on First John. LC 79-14801. 608p. 1992. pap. 20.99 (*0-8254-2333-3*, Kregel Class) Kregel.

— Studies in First Corinthians 15: Life in a Risen Savior. LC 89-2564. 440p. 1989. reprint ed. pap. 18.99 (*0-8254-2331-7*, Kregel Class) Kregel.

— Studies in Romans 12: The Christian's Sacrifice & Service of Praise. LC 89-2660. 368p. 1989. reprint ed. pap. 15.99 (*0-8254-2332-5*, Kregel Class) Kregel.

Candole, James De, see De Candole, James.

Candoli, Carl I., et al. Superintendent Performance Evaluation: Current Practice & Directions for Improvement. LC 97-2392. (Evaluation in Education & Human Services Ser.). 1997. lib. bdg. 88.00 (*0-7923-9891-2*) Kluwer Academic.

Candoli, Conte, ed. The Greatest Jazz Solos-Trumpet. (Illus.). 1978. pap. 7.95 (*0-89705-000-2*) Almo Pubns.

Candoli, I. Carl. School System Administration: A Strategic Plan for Site-Based Management. LC 90-71213. 245p. 1994. 39.95 (*0-87762-728-2*) Scarecrow.

— Site-Based Management in Education: How to Make It Work in Your School. LC 94-62043. 235p. 1996. pap. text 34.95 (*1-56676-223-5*) Scarecrow.

Candoli, I. Carl, et al. School Business Administration: A Planning Approach. 3rd ed. 421p. 1984. text 42.95 (*0-205-08152-5*, H81524) Allyn.

Candolle, A. De. Memoires sur la Famille des Legumineuses. (Illus.). 1966. reprint ed. 220.00 (*3-7682-0299-2*) Lubrecht & Cramer.

Candolle, Alphonse De, see De Candolle, Alphonse.

Candolle, Augustin P. De, see De Candolle, Augustin P.

Candolle, Benedict De, see Peter, Wolfgang.

***Candoni, Jean-Francois.** La Genese du Drame Musical Wagnerien. xviii, 421p. 1998. 53.95 (*3-906760-18-9*, Pub. by P Lang) P Lang Pubng.

Candow, James E., jt. ed. see Corbin, Carol.

Candragomin. Joy for the World: A Buddhist Play by Candragomin. Hahn, Michael, tr. from TIB. LC 87-22257. (Tibetan Translation Ser.: Vol. 15). 133p. 1987. 25.00 (*0-89800-148-X*) Dharma Pub.

Candray, Carlena. Ceramics with an Old World Flavor. LC 98-84112. (ENG & SPA.). 90p. 1998. pap. 12.95 (*0-916809-23-4*) Scott Pubns MI.

Candrea, J. Mike, jt. auth. see Janssen, Jeffrey J.

Candreva, Ilene A., jt. auth. see Prenzlow, Linda.

Candreva, Ilene Allinger, jt. auth. see Prenzlow, Linda.

Candy, Catherine. Priestly Fictions: Popular Irish Novelists of The Early 20th Century. LC 96-140065. 240p. 1997. pap. 19.95 (*0-86327-334-3*, Pub. by Wolfhound Press) Irish Amer Bk.

Candy, F., jt. auth. see Casselberry, L.

Candy, James C. & Temes, Gabor C., eds. Oversampling Delta-Sigma Data Converters: Theory, Design, & Simulation. LC 91-19110. (Illus.). 512p. 1991. text 79.95 (*0-87942-285-8*, PC0274-1) Inst Electrical.

Candy, Philip C. Self-Direction for Lifelong Learning: A Comprehensive Guide to Theory & Practice. LC 90-47291. (Higher & Adult Education Ser.). 600p. 1991. text 45.00 (*1-55542-303-5*) Jossey-Bass.

Cane, Aleta F., jt. auth. see Shearer, Beth.

Cane, Andries C. Basic Arrest & Prisoner Control Tactics: Practical Techniques - Fast, Simple, Effective. (Illus.). 236p. 1989. pap., spiral bd. 55.95 (*0-398-05602-1*) C C Thomas.

Cane, Bill. Circles of Hope: Breathing Life & Spirit into a Wounded World. LC 92-10629. (Illus.). 160p. (Orig.). 1992. pap. 13.00 (*0-88344-816-5*) Orbis Bks.

Cane, Edric. Cap - Cash-On-Cash: A Program for the HP 17BII & HP 19BII Financial Calculators. 34p. (Orig.). 1991. pap. 25.00 incl. disk (*0-916785-10-6*) E Cane Sem.

— Hands-On Introduction to the HP 17BII & HP 19BII: Tape, Documentation, Practice Problems. 60p. (Orig.). 1991. pap. 14.95 (*0-916785-11-4*) E Cane Sem.

— The HP 12C Made Easy, Vol. I: Regular Compound Interest Functions. 260p. (Orig.). (C). 1984. pap. 19.95 (*0-916785-03-3*) E Cane Sem.

— The HP 12C Made Easy, Vol. II: Irregular Cash Flows, Statistics, Programming. 250p. (C). 1986. pap. text 19.95 (*0-916785-05-X*) E Cane Sem.

— Income Projection Cash Flow Analysis of Investment Real Estate: A Program for the HP 17BII & HP 19BII Financial Calculators. abr. ed. 28p. (Orig.). 1990. pap. text 14.95 incl. disk (*0-916785-06-8*) E Cane Sem.

— Loan Data - Qualifier: A Program for the HP 17BII Financial Calculator. 48p. (Orig.). 1991. pap. 14.95 incl. disk (*0-916785-12-2*) E Cane Sem.

— Ratios in Investment Real Estate. 125p. (Orig.). 1993. pap. 27.50 (*0-916785-14-9*) E Cane Sem.

Cane, Edric, ed. Property Analyzer: A Program for the HP 17BII & HP 19BII Financial Calculators. 54p. (Orig.). 1991. pap. text 14.95 incl. disk (*0-916785-08-4*) E Cane Sem.

Cane, Florence. The Artist in Each of Us. LC 83-14347. (Illus.). 380p. (C). 1983. reprint ed. pap. 20.95 (*0-9611462-0-6*) Art Therapy.

Cane, Harry, jt. auth. see Speck, Wieland.

Cane, Hugh. Atiyah's Accidents, Compensation, & the Law. 5th ed. (Law in Context Ser.). 428p. (C). 1994. pap. text 43.95 (*0-406-03146-0*) Northwestern U Pr.

Cane, Marilyn B. Securities Arbitration: Law & Procedure. LC 91-22848. 583p. 1991. reprint ed. pap. 180.80 (*0-608-00705-6*, 206147700009) Bks Demand.

Cane, Melville, et al, eds. Golden Year. LC 73-76941. (Granger Index Reprint Ser.). 1977. 25.95 (*0-8369-6004-1*) Ayer.

***Cane, Nancy.** Keeper of the Rings. 400p. 2000. pap. 5.99 (*0-505-52400-7*, Love Spell) Dorchester Pub Co.

Cane, Peter. The Anatomy of Tort Law. LC 98-104302. 288p. 1997. 70.00 (*1-901362-08-6*, Pub. by Hart Pub); pap. 25.00 (*1-901362-09-4*, Pub. by Hart Pub) Northwestern U Pr.

— Atiyah's Accidents, Compensation & the Law. (Law in Context Ser.). xxiii, 639p. 1987. 75.00 (*0-297-79052-8*) W S Hein.

— An Introduction to Administrative Law. 2nd ed. (Clarendon Law Ser.). 422p. 1992. pap. text. write for info. (*0-19-825690-6*, Clarendon Pr) OUP.

— An Introduction to Administrative Law. 3rd ed. (Clarendon Law Ser.). 448p. 1997. 69.00 (*0-19-876464-2*, Clarendon Pr) OUP.

Cane, Peter. An Introduction to Administrative Law. 3rd ed. 442p. 1997. pap. text 31.00 (*0-19-876465-0*) OUP.

Cane, Peter. The Law of Obligations: Essays in Celebration of John Fleming. LC 98-29125. 474p. 1999. text 90.00 (*0-19-826484-4*) OUP.

— Tort Law & Economic Interests. 2nd ed. LC 95-46834. 562p. (C). 1996. pap. text 48.00 (*0-19-876429-4*, Clarendon Pr) OUP.

Cane, Peter & Stapleton, Jane, eds. Essays for Patrick Atiyah. (Illus.). 400p. 1992. text 79.00 (*0-19-825410-5*) OUP.

Cane, Peter & Trindade, Francis A. The Law of Torts in Australia. 2nd ed. 826p. 1993. pap. text 85.00 (*0-19-553316-X*) OUP.

Cane, Peter, jt. auth. see Baldwin, Robert.

Cane, Shelia. Kaizen Strategies for Winning Through People. LC 96-144403. 240p. 1995. 24.95 (*0-273-61708-7*) F T P-H.

Cane, William. The Art of Hugging. LC 95-40764. 160p. 1996. pap. 7.95 (*0-312-14096-7*, St Martin Griffin) St Martin.

— Art of Kissing. rev. ed. 1994. pap. 8.95 (*0-312-11744-2*) St Martin.

— Art of Kissing Book of Questions & Answers: Everything You Ever Wanted to Know about Perfecting Your Kissing Technique. LC 98-46413. 176p. 1998. pap. 8.95 (*0-312-19830-2*) St Martin.

Cane, William, ed. The Book of Kisses: A Definitive Collection of the Most Passionate, Romantic, Outlandish, & Wonderful Quotations on the Intimate Art of Kissing. LC 92-39748. 1993. pap. 6.95 (*0-312-08710-1*) St Martin.

Caneda, Marion & Casner, Jan. The Inventive Thinking Resource Directory. (Illus.). 220p. (Orig.). (C). 1994. pap. text 35.00 (*0-7881-0622-8*) DIANE Pub.

Canedo, L., et al, eds. Cell Function & Disease. (Illus.). 534p. 1988. 125.00 (*0-306-43201-3*, Plenum Trade) Perseus Pubng.

Canedo, Lino G., ed. Cronica De los Colegios De Propaganda Fide De la Nueva Espana, De Fr. Isidro Felix De Espinosa. (Franciscan Historical Classics Ser.). (Illus.). 1964. 100.00 (*0-88382-153-2*); 100.00 (*0-88382-154-0*); pap. 50.00 (*0-88382-152-4*) AAFH.

— Cronica Franciscana De las Provincias Del Peru De Fr. Diego De Cordoba Salinas. (Franciscan Historical Classics Ser.). (SPA., Illus.). 1957. 100.00 (*0-88382-150-8*) AAFH.

Canedo, Marion. The Inventive Thinking Curriculum Project. (Illus.). 68p. (Orig.). (C). 1994. pap. text 25.00 (*0-7881-0647-3*) DIANE Pub.

Canedy, Susan. America's Nazis: A Democratic Dilemma. LC 88-63604. (Illus.). 240p. (C). 1990. 28.95 (*0-944109-07-1*); pap. 18.95 (*0-944109-06-3*) Margraf Pubns Grp.

***Caneiro.** Evolutionary Essays. 2000. 70.00 (*0-8133-3719-4*, Pub. by Westview) HarpC.

Canel, Fausto. Ni Tiempo para Pedir Auxilio. LC 90-84964. (Coleccion Caniqui). (SPA.). 202p. (Orig.). 1991. pap. 18.00 (*0-89729-587-0*) Ediciones.

Canelas, D. A., et al, contrib. by. Advances in Polymer Science Vol. 133: Metal Complex Catalysts - Supercritical Fluid Polymerisation - Supermolecular Architecture. LC 97-208968. (Illus.). viii, 208p. 1997. 250.00 (*3-540-62699-9*) Spr-Verlag.

***Canelias, Peter S.** Patent Law Handbook. LC 00-38098. 2000. pap. write for info. (*0-7355-1510-7*) Panel Pubs.

Canellos, George P., et al. The Lymphomas. Lampert, Richard, ed. LC 97-22034. 544p. 1997. text 175.00 (*0-7216-5030-9*, W B Saunders Co) Harcrt Hlth Sci Grp.

Canelo, David A. The Last Crypto Jews of Portugal. 1991. pap. 15.00 (*0-685-40182-0*) Inst Judaic Std.

Canemaker, John. Before the Animation Begins: The Art & Lives of Disney Inspirational Sketch Artists. LC 95-48200. (Illus.). 224p. (J). 1996. 60.00 (*0-7868-6152-5*, Pub. by Hyperion) Time Warner.

— Dreams in Motion: The Art of Windsor McCay. (Illus.). 16p. 1988. 5.00 (*0-915171-09-0*) Katonah Gal.

— Felix: The Twisted Tale of the World's Most Famous Cat. LC 96-13085. (Illus.). 192p. 1996. reprint ed. pap. 16.95 (*0-306-80731-9*) Da Capo.

— Paper Dreams: The Art & Artists of Disney Storyboards. LC 98-28884. (Illus.). 288p. 1999. text 60.00 (*0-7868-6307-2*, Pub. by Hyperion) Time Warner.

— Storytelling in Animation Vol. 2: The Art of the Animated Image. pap. 9.95 (*0-573-60697-8*) French.

***Canemaker, John.** Tex Avery: Artist, Animator, & Director from the Golden Age of Animated Cartoons. 224p. 1998. write for info. (*1-57215-270-2*) World Pubns.

Canemaker, John. Winsor McCay: His Life & Art. LC 86-28792. (Illus.). 224p. 1987. 65.00 (*0-89659-687-7*) Abbeville Pr.

***Canepa, G., et al.** Dysmorphic Syndromes & Constitutional Disease of the Skeleton, 2 vols. (Illus.). 2180p. 2000. write for info. (*88-299-1240-9*, Pub. by Piccin Nuova) Bristol-Myers Squibb.

Canepa, Horacio, et al. Paraguay: International Donor Conference Final Report, December 6, 1995. ii, 146p. 1996. pap. text 16.00 (*1-879720-24-8*) Intl Fndt Elect.

C

Canepa, Nancy, ed. Out of the Woods: The Origins of the Literary Fairy Tale in Italy & France. (Illus.). 448p. 1997. 39.95 (*0-8143-2687-0*) Wayne St U Pr.

Canepa, Nancy L. From Court to Forest: Giambattista Basile's Lo Cunto de Li Cunti & the Birth of the Literary F. LC 98-43947. 1999. 39.95 (*0-8143-2758-3*) Wayne St U Pr.

Canepari, Luciano. Manuale Di Pronuncia Italiana. (ITA.). 416p. 1993. 150.00 incl. audio (*0-8288-9429-9*) Fr & Eur.

Caner, George C., Jr. The History of the Essex County Club. 300p. 1994. pap. text. write for info. (*0-9641777-0-6*) Essex Cnty Club.

Canesso, Claudia. Cambodia: Major World Nations. LC 97-23524. (Major World Nations Ser.). (Illus.). 144p. (YA). (gr. 5 up). 1999. lib. bdg. 19.95 (*0-7910-4732-6*) Chelsea Hse.

Canesso, Claudia & Beneke, Jeff. South Africa: Major World Nations. (Major World Nations Ser.). (Illus.). 144p. (YA). (gr. 5 up). 1999. lib. bdg. 19.95 (*0-7910-4766-0*) Chelsea Hse.

***Canestrelli, E., ed.** Current Topics in Quantitative Finance. LC 99-42100. (Contributions to Management Science Ser.). (Illus.). viii, 139p. 1999. pap. 56.00 (*3-7908-1231-5*) Spr-Verlag.

Canet, D. Nuclear Magnetic Resonance: Concepts & Methods. LC 95-39900. 270p. 1996. pap. 79.95 (*0-471-96145-0*) Wiley.

Canetti, Elias. Agony of Flies: Notes & Notations. 236p. 1994. pap. 14.00 (*0-374-52410-6*) FS&G.

— Die Blendung. 29th ed. (GER.). 512p. 1996. pap. 18.00 (*3-596-20696-0*, Pub. by Fischer Tasch) Intl Bk Import.

— Crowds & Power. Stewart, Carol, tr. from GER. 496p. (C). 1984. pap. 17.00 (*0-374-51820-3*) FS&G.

— The Memoirs of Elias Canetti, 3 bks. in 1. LC 98-48752. 840p. 1999. 40.00 (*0-374-19950-7*) FS&G.

***Canetti, Elias.** The Memoirs of Elias Canetti, 3 bks. in 1. LC 98-48752. 840p. 2000. pap. 20.00 (*0-374-52714-8*) FS&G.

Canetti, Elias. Notes from Hampstead: The Writer's Notes, 1954-1971. Hargraves, John, tr. from GER. LC 97-26918. 224p. 1998. 23.00 (*0-374-22326-2*) FS&G.

— The Secret Heart of the Clock: Notes, Aphorisms, Fragments. Agee, Joel, tr. from GER. 158p. 1989. 19.95 (*0-374-25694-2*) FS&G.

— The Wedding. Honegger, Gitta, tr. 1986. pap. 8.95 (*1-55554-008-2*) PAJ Pubns.

Canetti-Mirabal, Ileana. Lengua, Literatura y Comunicacion: Antologia de Lecturas, Ejercicios Gramaticales y Destrezas Linguisticas. 8th ed. (Textbook Ser.). (SPA., Illus.). 260p. (Orig.). (C). 1991. reprint ed. pap. text 14.95 (*1-56328-008-6*) Edit Plaza Mayor.

Canetti, Veza. Die Gelbe Strasse. (GER.). 192p. 1993. pap. 13.50 (*3-596-10914-0*, Pub. by Fischer Tasch) Intl Bk Import.

— Yellow Street. Mitchell, Ian, tr. from GER. LC 90-22154. 144p. 1991. 18.95 (*0-8112-1159-2*, Pub. by New Directions); pap. 10.95 (*0-8112-1160-6*, NDP709, Pub. by New Directions) Norton.

Canetti, Veza, et al. Anthology of Contemporary Austrian Folk Plays. Dixon, Richard, tr. & afterword by. by. LC 93-18742. (Studies in Austrian Literature, Culture, & Thought. Translation Ser.). 397p. 1993. pap. 28.50 (*0-929497-67-8*) Ariadne CA.

Canetti, Yanitzia. The Mural. LC 96-27312. (Illus.). (J). 1996. write for info. (*1-56492-227-8*) Laredo.

— Novelita Rosa. rev. ed. (SPA.). 192p. 1997. pap. 16.00 (*1-58018-023-X*) Versal Ed Grp.

Canetti, Yanitzia, tr. see Allard, Harry.

Canetti, Yanitzia, tr. see Lachtman, Ofelia D.

Canetti, Yanitzia, tr. see Nikola-Lisa, W.

Canetti, Yanitzia, tr. see Nikola-Lisa, W.

Canetti, Yanitzia, tr. see Parish, Peggy.

Canetto, Silvia S. & Lester, David, eds. Women & Suicidal Behavior. LC 94-31918. (Focus on Women Ser.). (Illus.). 320p. 1995. 38.95 (*0-8261-8630-0*) Springer Pub.

***Caneva, Caterina, et al.** Crafting the Medici: Patrons & Artisans in Florence, 1537-1737. Conklin, Jo-Ann, ed. (Illus.). 48p. 1999. pap. 20.00 (*0-933519-39-7*) D W Bell Gallery.

Caneva, Caterina, et al. The Uffizi: Guide to the Collections & Catalogue of All Paintings. (Illus.). 192p. 1992. 24.95 (*0-8161-0607-X*, G K Hall & Co) Mac Lib Ref.

Caneva, Kenneth L. Robert Mayer & the Conservation of Energy. LC 92-25400. (Illus.). 496p. (C). 1993. text 55.00 (*0-691-08758-X*, Pub. by Princeton U Pr) Cal Prin Full Svc.

Caneva, Thomas, jt. auth. see Bailey, Wayne.

Canevari. Voices from Beyond. 1995. mass mkt. write for info. (*0-312-95581-2*) St Martin.

Canevari, P., jt. auth. see Blanco, D.

Caney-Peterson, Susan, ed. see Levin, Barry & Ferrier, David O.

Caney, Steven. Make Your Own Time Capsule. LC 89-40725. (Steven Caney's Kids' America Kits Ser.). (Illus.). 64p. (Orig.). (J). (gr. 2-6). 1991. pap. 14.95 (*0-89480-418-9*, 1418) Workman Pub.

— Steve Caney's Toy Book. LC 75-8814. (Illus.). 176p. (J). (ps-5). 1972. pap. 8.95 (*0-911104-17-8*, 023) Workman Pub.

— Steven Caney's Invention Book. 1985. 16.05 (*0-606-02581-2*, Pub. by Turtleback) Demco.

— Steven Caney's Invention Book. LC 84-40679. (Illus.). 208p. (J). (gr. 3-8). 1999. pap. 10.95 (*0-89480-076-0*, 406) Workman Pub.

— Steven Caney's Kids' America. LC 77-27465. (Illus.). 416p. (J). (ps-9). 1978. pap. 13.95 (*0-911104-80-1*, 114) Workman Pub.

— Steven Caney's Play Book. LC 75-9816. (Illus.). 240p. (J). (ps-5). 1975. pap. 9.95 (*0-911104-38-0*, 050) Workman Pub.

Canfield. Catorce Claves para una Exitosa Patertnidad. (Hombres de Integridad Ser.).Tr. of Fourteen Keys to Successful Fathering. (SPA.). 1995. 2.99 (*1-56063-575-4*, 495676) Editorial Unilit.

— Information Processing. 200p. 1997. pap. text 15.00 (*0-226-09261-5*) U Ch Pr.

— Kaleidoscope. 3rd ed. 1993. teacher ed. 28.12 (*0-07-047321-8*) McGraw.

Canfield, Andrea, ed. see Lugenbuchl, Michael.

Canfield, Anita. Remember, & Perish Not. 1998. 15.95 (*1-57008-420-3*) Bookcraft Inc.

— The Young Woman & Her Self-Esteem. 93p. (YA). (gr. 7-12). 1990. reprint ed. pap. 4.95 (*0-87579-365-7*) Deseret Bk.

Canfield, Anita, jt. auth. see Flynn, Johanna.

Canfield, Arthur G. The Reappearing Characters in Balzac's "Comedie Humaine" Ham, Edward B., ed. LC 77-14166. (Studies in Romance Languages & Literature: No. 37). 61p. 1977. reprint ed. lib. bdg. 45.00 (*0-8371-9836-4*, CARC, Greenwood Pr) Greenwood.

Canfield, Betty M. The Bible World Maps of the Old & New Testaments. (Illus.). 24p. (Orig.). 1983. pap. text 4.95 (*0-9611756-0-5*) Humble Pub Co.

Canfield, Bruce N. Bruce Canfield's Complete Guide to the M1 Garand & the M1 Carbine. LC 98-66754. (Illus.). 297p. 1998. 39.50 (*0-917218-83-3*) A Mowbray.

— A Collector's Guide to the '03 Springfield. LC 89-63274. 160p. 1989. pap. 22.00 (*0-917218-40-X*) A Mowbray.

— A Collector's Guide to United States Combat Shotguns. LC 92-60913. (Illus.). 184p. 1992. pap. 24.00 (*0-917218-53-1*) A Mowbray.

— A Collector's Guide to Winchester in the Service. LC 91-60416. (Illus.). 185p. 1997. pap. 22.00 (*0-917218-46-9*) A Mowbray.

***Canfield, Bruce N.** U. S. Infantry Weapons of the First World War. LC 99-85941. (Illus.). 296p. 2000. 39.95 (*0-917218-90-6*) A Mowbray.

Canfield, Bruce N. U. S. Infantry Weapons of World War II. 2nd ed. LC 94-78247. (Illus.). 303p. 1996. 35.00 (*0-917218-67-1*) A Mowbray.

Canfield Cass, Cass, ed. Masterworks of Latin American Short Fiction: Eight Novellas. 416p. (C). 1997. pap. 16.00 (*0-06-430984-3*, Pub. by Westview) HarpC.

Canfield, Chauncy L., ed. see Jackson, Alfred T.

Canfield, Cheryl, ed. see Churchill, Randal.

Canfield, Cheryl, ed. see Pilgrim, Peace.

Canfield, Christopher J., jt. auth. see Reisman, Rosemary M.

Canfield, Clarke. Now Hiring! Jobs in Eastern Europe: The Insider's Guide to Working & Living in the Czech Republic, Hungary, Poland & Slovakia. LC 94-74013. (Illus.). 260p. 1996. pap. 14.95 (*1-881199-62-2*) Perptual Pr.

Canfield, Clifford R. Canfield: Our Canfield Ancestors & Some Related Families. (Illus.). 131p. 1997. reprint ed. pap. 21.00 (*0-8328-7833-2*); reprint ed. lib. bdg. 31.00 (*0-8328-7832-4*) Higginson Bk Co.

Canfield, Craig. Never Open the Bottom of a Circus. (Illus.). 55p. (Orig.). 1998. pap. 5.50 (*1-880764-15-6*) Northwind NJ.

Canfield, Curtis, ed. Plays of the Irish Renaissance, 1880-1930. LC 73-4881. (Play Anthology Reprint Ser.). 1980. reprint ed. 34.95 (*0-8369-8248-7*) Ayer.

Canfield, D. Lincoln. Spanish Pronunciation in the Americas. LC 80-23664. 128p. 1981. pap. 14.00 (*0-226-09263-1*) U Ch Pr.

Canfield, Daniel E., jt. auth. see Hoyer, Mark V.

Canfield, David C., jt. auth. see Harvey, W. Proctor.

Canfield, De Los Lincoln. Spanish Literature in Mexican Languages As a Source for the Study of Spanish Pronunciation. 257p. 3.00 (*0-318-14306-2*) Hispanic Inst.

Canfield, Donna A. Honeymoon Mania: The Male Abuser's Best Weapon. Failes, Susan, ed. (Illus.). 168p. 1995. 22.00 (*0-9645596-0-9*) Morgan Meadow Enter.

Canfield, Dorothy. Bent Twig. 1976. 18.95 (*0-8488-1260-3*) Amereon Ltd.

— The Bent Twig. 340p. (J). 1981. reprint ed. lib. bdg. 13.95 (*0-89967-018-0*, Harmony Rain) Buccaneer Bks.

— The Bent Twig. LC 97-5678. 400p. 1997. reprint ed. pap. 16.95 (*0-8214-1185-3*) Ohio U Pr.

— The Home-Maker. rev. ed. 320p. 1996. pap. 14.00 (*0-89733-069-2*) Academy Chi Pubs.

— Understood Betsy. 1976. 17.95 (*0-8488-1261-1*) Amereon Ltd.

— Understood Betsy. 213p. (J). 1980. reprint ed. lib. bdg. 21.95 (*0-89967-016-4*, Harmony Rain) Buccaneer Bks.

— Understood Betsy. 219p. (J). 1981. reprint ed. lib. bdg. 25.95 (*0-89966-342-7*) Buccaneer Bks.

***Canfield, Elizabeth.** When the Heart Is Reached. 32p. 1999. pap. 7.00 (*0-9672078-0-0*) Feathermoon.

Canfield, F. A. A History of Thomas & Matthew Canfield with a Genealogy of Their Descendants in New Jersey. (Illus.). 228p. 1989. reprint ed. pap. 34.00 (*0-8328-1305-2*); reprint ed. lib. bdg. 42.00 (*0-8328-1304-4*) Higginson Bk Co.

Canfield, Gae W. Sarah Winnemucca of the Northern Paiutes. LC 82-40448. (Illus.). 336p. (Orig.). 1988. pap. 14.95 (*0-8061-2090-8*) U of Okla Pr.

Canfield, George L. & Dalzell, George W. Law of the Sea: A Manual of the Principles of Admiralty Law for Students, Mariners & Ship Operators. xvi, 315p. 1983. reprint ed. 42.50 (*0-8377-0442-1*, Rothman) W S Hein.

Canfield, J. Douglas. Cultural Readings of Restoration & Eighteenth-Century English Theater. LC 94-8524. 1995. pap. 30.00 (*0-8203-1751-9*) U of Ga Pr.

— Heroes & States: On the Ideology of Restoration Tragedy. LC 99-13693. 264p. (C). 1999. 39.95 (*0-8131-2125-6*) U Pr of Ky.

***Canfield, J. Douglas.** Mavericks on the Border: The Early Southwest in Historical Fiction & Films. LC 00-28310. 256p. (C). 2000. 27.50 (*0-8131-2180-9*) U Pr of Ky.

Canfield, J. Douglas. Tricksters & Estates: On the Ideology of Restoration Comedy. LC 96-48626. (Illus.). 352p. 1997. 44.95 (*0-8131-2012-8*) U Pr of Ky.

Canfield, J. Douglas & Hunter, J. Paul, eds. Rhetorics of Order-Ordering Rhetorics in English Neoclassical Literature. LC 88-40578. 200p. 1990. 36.50 (*0-87413-374-2*) U Delaware Pr.

***Canfield, Jack.** Chicken Soup for the Golfer's Soul: 101 Stories of Insight, Inspiration & Laughter on the Links. LC 98-54998. 1999. 24.00 (*1-55874-659-5*) Health Comm.

— Chicken Soup for the Kid's Soul. (Illus.). (J). 2000. 18.30 (*0-606-18203-9*) Turtleback.

— Chicken Soup for the Preteen Soul: 101 Stories of Changes, Choices & Growing Up. (Chicken Soup for the Soul Ser.). (Illus.). (J). 2000. 24.00 (*1-55874-801-6*) Health Comm.

— Chicken Soup for the Soul at Christmas. LC 99-62875. (Illus.). 80p. 1999. 4.95 (*0-7407-0118-5*) Andrews & McMeel.

— Chicken Soup for the Teenage Soul II: 101 More Stories of Life, Love & Learning. (Illus.). (J). 1998. 18.30 (*0-606-18204-7*) Turtleback.

— Chicken Soup for the Teenage Soul Letters: Letters of Life, Love & Learning. (Chicken Soup for the Soul Ser.). (Illus.). (J). 2000. 24.00 (*1-55874-805-9*) Health Comm.

— Chicken Soup for the Teenage Soul Letters: Letters of Life, Love & Learning. (Chicken Soup for the Soul Ser.). (Illus.). (J). 2000. pap. 12.95 (*1-55874-804-0*) Health Comm.

— Heartwarming Stories to Renew Your Faith. 1999. 4.95 (*0-7407-0121-5*) Andrews & McMeel.

— Little Sip of Chicken Soup for the Golfer's Soul. 2000. pap. 4.95 (*0-7407-1140-7*) Andrews & McMeel.

— Pet Lover's Collection of Chicken Soup for the Soul. 2000. pap. 4.95 (*0-7407-1141-5*) Andrews & McMeel.

Canfield, Jack. Spirited Sip of Chicken Soup for the Soul: In Celebration of Women. LC 98-181151. (Chicken Soup for the Soul Ser.). 1998. 4.95 (*0-8362-5090-7*) Andrews & McMeel.

— Stirring Sip of Chicken Soup for the Soul: Uplifting Moments from Everyday Heroes. LC 98-181158. (Chicken Soup for the Soul Ser.). 1998. 4.95 (*0-8362-5089-3*) Andrews & McMeel.

***Canfield, Jack.** Stories to Uplift the Spirit. 1999. 4.95 (*0-7407-0120-7*) Andrews & McMeel.

Canfield, Jack, et al, eds. Chicken Soup for the Soul at Work: 101 Stories of Courage, Compassion & Creativity in the Workplace. 352p. (Orig.). 1996. 24.00 (*1-55874-430-4*, 424X); pap. 12.95 (*1-55874-424-X*, 424X) Health Comm.

— Chicken Soup for the Teenage Soul: 101 Stories of Life, Love & Learning. LC 97-5378. 352p. (J). 1997. pap. 12.95 (*1-55874-463-0*) Health Comm.

— Chicken Soup for the Woman's Soul: 101 Stories to Open the Hearts & Rekindle the Spirits of Women. 352p. (Orig.). 1996. 24.00 (*1-55874-429-0*, 4150); pap. 12.95 (*1-55874-415-0*, 4150) Health Comm.

— Condensed Chicken Soup for the Soul. abr. ed. (Illus.). 208p. (Orig.). 1996. pap. 8.95 (*1-55874-414-2*) Health Comm.

— A Cup of Chicken Soup for the Soul. LC 96-32299. (Illus.). 214p. (Orig.). 1996. pap. 8.95 (*1-55874-421-5*, 4215) Health Comm.

— A 4th Course of Chicken Soup for the Soul: 101 More Stories to Open the Heart & Rekindle the Spirit. LC 96-52504. 376p. 1997. 24.00 (*1-55874-467-3*) Health Comm.

***Canfield, Jack & Hansen, Mark V.** A Little Spoonful of Chicken Soup for the Couple's Soul Gift Book. 64p. 1999. 6.99 (*1-58375-544-6*) Garborgs.

— A Little Spoonful of Chicken Soup for the Kid's Soul Gift Book. 64p. 1999. 6.99 (*1-58375-545-4*) Garborgs.

Canfield, Jack & Hansen, Mark V. Little Spoonful of Chicken Soup for the Soul: Just for friends Gift Book. 64p. 1998. 6.99 (*1-58375-436-9*) Garborgs.

— Little Spoonful of Chicken Soup for the Soul Gift Book. 64p. 1998. 6.99 (*1-58375-435-0*) Garborgs.

***Canfield, Jack & Hansen, Mark V.** Little Spoonful of Chicken Soup for the Soul Gift Book. 64p. 1998. 6.99 (*1-58375-434-2*); 6.99 (*1-58375-433-4*) Garborgs.

— A Little Spoonful of Chicken Soup for the Woman's Soul Gift Book. 64p. 1999. 6.99 (*1-58375-546-2*) Garborgs.

— A Second Helping: A Little Spoonful of Chicken Soup for the Soul Gift Book. 64p. 1999. 6.99 (*1-58375-543-8*) Garborgs.

Canfield, Jack & Hansen, Mark Victor. The Aladdin Factor. 256p. 1995. pap. 13.00 (*0-425-15075-5*) Berkley Pub.

— Best of Fifth Portion of Chicken Soup for the Soul. abr. ed. LC 97-46612. (Chicken Soup for the Soul Ser.: Vol. 5). 1998. 11.95 incl. audio compact disk (*1-55874-545-9*); 9.95 incl. audio (*1-55874-546-7*) Health Comm.

***Canfield, Jack & Hansen, Mark Victor.** Chicken Soup for the College Soul: Inspiring & Humorous Stories About College. abr. ed. LC 99-22238. (Chicken Soup for the Soul Ser.). (C). 1999. audio compact disk 11.95 (*1-55874-704-4*) Health Comm.

Canfield, Jack & Hansen, Mark Victor. Chicken Soup for the Soul: 101 Stories to Open the Heart & Rekindle the Spirit. 327p. 1993. 24.00 (*1-55874-291-3*, 2913) Health Comm.

— Chicken Soup for the Soul: 101 Stories to Open the Heart & Rekindle the Spirit. large type ed. 400p. 1996. pap. 16.95 (*1-55874-381-2*, 3812) Health Comm.

— Chicken Soup for the Surviving Soul. abr. ed. LC 97-40969. (Chicken Soup for the Soul Ser.). 1998. pap. 9.95 incl. audio (*1-55874-532-7*) Health Comm.

— Dare to Win. 224p. 1996. pap. 13.00 (*0-425-15076-3*) Berkley Pub.

— A 5th Portion of Chicken Soup for the Soul: 101 More Stories to Open the Heart & Rekindle the Spirit. LC 97-46612. 352p. 1998. pap. 12.95 (*1-55874-543-2*) Health Comm.

— A 5th Serving of Chicken Soup for the Soul: 101 More Stories to Open the Heart & Rekindle the Spirit. LC 97-46612. 352p. 1998. 24.00 (*1-55874-544-0*) Health Comm.

— My Chicken Soup for the Soul Personal Journal. 192p. 1997. 12.95 (*1-55874-484-3*) Health Comm.

— A 2nd Helping of Chicken Soup for the Soul: 101 More Stories to Open the Heart & Rekindle the Spirit. 349p. 1995. 24.00 (*1-55874-332-4*, 3324); pap. 12.95 (*1-55874-331-6*, 3316) Health Comm.

— A 2nd Helping of Chicken Soup for the Soul: 101 More Stories to Open the Heart & Rekindle the Spirit. large type ed. 480p. 1996. pap. 16.95 (*1-55874-382-0*, 3820) Health Comm.

— Un Segundo Plato de Sopa de Pollo Para el Alma: Nuevos Relatos que Conmueven el Corazon y Ponen Fuego en el Espiritu. (SPA.). 305p. 1997. pap. 12.95 (*1-55874-502-5*) Health Comm.

***Canfield, Jack & Hansen, Mark Victor.** A Sixth Bowl of Chicken Soup for the Soul, 6. abr. ed. LC 98-55214. (Chicken Soup for the Soul Ser.). 1999. audio 19.95 (*1-55874-665-X*); audio compact disk 11.95 (*1-55874-664-1*) Health Comm.

Canfield, Jack & Hansen, Mark Victor. A 6th Bowl of Chicken Soup for the Soul: 101 More Stories to Open the Heart & Rekindle the Spirit. LC 98-55214. 1999. 24.00 (*1-55874-663-3*) Health Comm.

***Canfield, Jack & Hansen, Mark Victor.** A 6th Bowl of Chicken Soup for the Soul: 101 More Stories to Open the Heart & Rekindle the Spirit. LC 98-55214. (Illus.). 384p. 1999. pap. 12.95 (*1-55874-662-5*) Health Comm.

Canfield, Jack & Hansen, Mark Victor. Sopa de Pollo para el Alma: Relatos que Conmueven el Corazon y Ponen Fuego en el Espiritu.Tr. of Chicken Soup for the Soul. (SPA.). 305p. 1995. pap. 12.95 (*1-55874-353-7*) Health Comm.

— Sopa de Pollo para el Alma de la Mujer: Relatos que Conmueven el Corazon y Ponen Fuego en el Espiritu de las Mujeres.Tr. of Chicken Soup for the Woman's Soul. (SPA.). 305p. 1997. pap. 12.95 (*1-55874-519-X*) Health Comm.

— Un Tercer Plato de Sopa de Pollo para el Alma: Nuevos Relatos que Conmueven el Corazon y Ponen Fuego en el Espiritu. (SPA.). 305p. 1997. pap. 12.95 (*1-55874-520-3*) Health Comm.

— A 3rd Serving of Chicken Soup for the Soul: 101 More Stories to Open the Heart & Rekindle the Spirit. large type ed. 376p. 1996. 24.00 (*1-55874-380-4*); pap. 16.95 (*1-55874-400-2*, 4002) Health Comm.

Canfield, Jack & Hansen, Mark Victor, eds. Chicken Soup for the Soul: 101 Stories to Open the Heart & Rekindle the Spirit. LC 94-178730. (Illus.). 327p. 1993. pap. 12.95 (*1-55874-262-X*, 262X) Health Comm.

— A 3rd Serving of Chicken Soup for the Soul: 101 More Stories to Open the Heart & Rekindle the Spirit. 376p. 1996. pap. 12.95 (*1-55874-379-0*, 3901) Health Comm.

Canfield, Jack & Miller, Jacqueline. Heart at Work: Stories & Strategies for Building Self-Esteem & Reawakening the Soul at Work. 320p. 1998. pap. 8.95 (*0-07-012030-7*) McGraw.

Canfield, Jack & Siccone, Frank. One Hundred One Ways to Develop Student Self-Esteem & Responsibility. LC 94-21227. 526p. 1994. pap. text 36.00 (*0-205-16884-1*, Longwood Div) Allyn.

— One Hundred One Ways to Develop Student Self-Esteem & Responsibility, Vol. I: The Teachers Coach. 288p. (C). 1992. pap. text 34.50 (*0-205-13368-1*) Allyn.

— One Hundred One Ways to Develop Student Self-Esteem & Responsibility, Vol. I: The Teachers Coach. 256p. (C). 1993. pap. text 63.95 (*0-205-13370-3*) Allyn.

***Canfield, Jack, et al.** Chicken Soup for the Cat & Dog Lover's Soul: Celebrating Pets as Family with Stories about Cats, Dogs & Other Critters. LC 99-33710. (Chicken Soup for the Soul Ser.). 350p. 1999. 24.00 (*1-55874-711-7*); pap. 12.95 (*1-55874-710-9*) Health Comm.

— Chicken Soup for the Christian Family Soul: 101 Stories to Open the Heart & Rekindle the Spirit. LC 99-57883. (Chicken Soup for the Soul Ser.). (Illus.). 350p. 2000. pap. 12.95 (*1-55874-714-1*) Health Comm.

Canfield, Jack, et al. Chicken Soup for the Christian Soul: 101 Stories to Open the Heart & Rekindle the Spirit. LC 97-19433. 352p. 1997. 24.00 (*1-55874-503-3*); pap. 12.95 (*1-55874-501-7*) Health Comm.

***Canfield, Jack, et al.** Chicken Soup for the College Soul: Inspiring & Humorous Stories about College. LC 99-22238. (Chicken Soup for the Soul Ser.). 340p. 1999. pap. 12.95 (*1-55874-702-8*) Health Comm.

— Chicken Soup for the College Soul: Inspiring & Humorous Stories about College. LC 99-22238. (Chicken Soup for the Soul Ser.). 350p. 1999. 24.00 (*1-55874-703-6*) Health Comm.

Canfield, Jack, et al. Chicken Soup for the Country Soul: Stories Served Up Country-Style & Straight from the Heart. LC 98-7072. 250p. 1998. pap. 14.95 incl. audio compact disk (*1-55874-562-9*) Health Comm.

— Chicken Soup for the Country Soul: Stories Served Up Country Style & Straight from the Heart. LC 98-7072. 250p. 1998. 24.95 (*1-55874-563-7*) Health Comm.

— Chicken Soup for the Couple's Soul: 101 Stories to Open the Heart & Rekindle the Spirit of Loving Relationships. LC 98-43069. 250p. 1999. 24.00 (*1-55874-645-5*); pap. 12.95 (*1-55874-646-3*) Health Comm.

C

An Asterisk (*) at the beginning of an entry indicates that the title is appearing for the first time.

***Canfield, Jack, et al.** Chicken Soup for the Expectant Mother's Soul: 101 Stories to Inspire & Warm the Hearts of Soon-to-Be-Mothers. LC 00-39543. 2000. 24.00 (*1-55874-797-4*); pap. 12.95 (*1-55874-796-6*) Health Comm.

— Chicken Soup for the Golden Soul: Heartwarming Stories for People 60 & Over. LC 99-51533. (Chicken Soup for the Soul Ser.). 350p. 2000. 24.00 (*1-55874-726-5*) Health Comm.

— Chicken Soup for the Golden Soul: Heartwarming Stories for People 60 & Over. LC 99-51533. (Chicken Soup for the Soul Ser.). (Illus.). 350p. 2000. pap. 12.95 (*1-55874-725-7*) Health Comm.

— Chicken Soup for the Golden Soul: Heartwarming Stories for People 60 & Over. large type ed. LC 99-51533. (Chicken Soup for the Soul Ser.). (Illus.). 350p. 2000. pap. 16.95 (*1-55874-733-8*) Health Comm.

— Chicken Soup for the Golfer's Soul: 101 Stories of Insight, Inspiration & Laughter on the Links. LC 98-54998. (Chicken Soup for the Soul Ser.). (Illus.). 328p. 1999. pap. 12.95 (*1-55874-658-7*) Health Comm.

Canfield, Jack, et al. Chicken Soup for the Kid's Soul: 101 Stories of Courage, Hope & Laughter. LC 98-16871. 352p. (J). 1998. 24.00 (*1-55874-608-0*); pap. 12.95 (*1-55874-609-9*) Health Comm.

— Chicken Soup for the Mother's Soul. abr. ed. audio 9.95 (*1-55874-528-9*) Health Comm.

— Chicken Soup for the Mother's Soul: 101 Stories to Open the Hearts & Rekindle the Spirits of Mothers. LC 97-17783. 352p. 1997. 24.95 (*1-55874-504-1*); pap. 12.95 (*1-55874-460-6*) Health Comm.

***Canfield, Jack, et al.** Chicken Soup for the Parent's Soul. (Chicken Soup for the Soul Ser.). 2000. 24.00 (*1-55874-748-6*) Health Comm.

— Chicken Soup for the Parent's Soul: 101 Stories of Loving, Learning & Parenting. (Chicken Soup for the Soul Ser.). 2000. pap. 12.95 (*1-55874-747-8*) Health Comm.

Canfield, Jack, et al. Chicken Soup for the Pet Lover's Soul: Stories about Pets as Teachers, Healers, Heroes & Friends. LC 97-50409. 403p. 1998. pap. text 12.95 (*1-55874-571-8*) Health Comm.

— Chicken Soup for the Pet Lover's Soul: Stories about Pets as Teachers, Healers, Heroes & Friends. LC 97-50409. 352p. 1998. 24.00 (*1-55874-572-6*) Health Comm.

***Canfield, Jack, et al.** Chicken Soup for the Preteen Soul: 101 Stories of Changes, Choices & Growing Up for Kids 9-13. (Chicken Soup for the Soul Ser.). 2000. pap. 12.95 (*1-55874-800-8*) Health Comm.

— Chicken Soup for the Single's Soul: 101 Stories of Love & Inspiration for the Single, Divorced & Widowed. (Chicken Soup for the Soul Ser.). 350p. 1999. 24.00 (*1-55874-707-9*); pap. 12.95 (*1-55874-706-0*) Health Comm.

Canfield, Jack, et al. Chicken Soup for the Soul Cookbook: 101 Stories with Recipes from the Heart. LC 95-32259. 476p. 1995. 29.95 (*1-55874-363-4*, 3634); pap. 16.95 (*1-55874-354-5*, 3545) Health Comm.

— Chicken Soup for the Surviving Soul: 101 Healing Stories of Courage & Inspiration. 352p. 1996. 24.00 (*1-55874-403-7*, 4037); pap. 12.95 (*1-55874-402-9*, 4029) Health Comm.

— Chicken Soup for the Teenage Soul: 101 Stories of Life, Love & Learning. LC 97-5378. 352p. (J). 1997. 24.00 (*1-55874-468-1*) Health Comm.

***Canfield, Jack, et al.** Chicken Soup for the Teenage Soul Vol. III: 101 More Stories of Life, Love & Learning. LC 99-87144. (Chicken Soup for the Soul Ser.). 400p. (J). (gr. 7-12). 2000. 24.00 (*1-55874-762-1*) Health Comm.

— Chicken Soup for the Teenage Soul Vol. III: 101 More Stories of Life, Love & Learning. LC 99-87144. (Chicken Soup for the Soul Ser.). (Illus.). 400p. (J). (gr. 7-12). 2000. pap. 12.95 (*1-55874-761-3*) Health Comm.

Canfield, Jack, et al. Chicken Soup for the Teenage Soul II: 101 More Stories of Life, Love & Learning. 2nd ed. LC 98-29642. 350p. 1998. 24.00 (*1-55874-615-3*); pap. 12.95 (*1-55874-616-1*) Health Comm.

— Chicken Soup for the Teenage Soul Journal. LC 98-36018. 300p. 1998. pap. 12.95 (*1-55874-637-4*) Health Comm.

***Canfield, Jack, et al.** Chicken Soup for the Unsinkable Soul: Stories of Triumph & Overcoming Life's Obstacles. 350p. 1999. 24.00 (*1-55874-699-4*) Health Comm.

— Chicken Soup for the Unsinkable Soul: Stories of Triumph & Overcoming Life's Obstacles. LC 99-28465. (Chicken Soup for the Soul Ser.). 350p. 1999. pap. 12.95 (*1-55874-698-6*) Health Comm.

— Chicken Soup for the Writer's Soul: 101 Stories to Open the Heart & Rekindle the Spirit of Writers. LC 00-24342. 400p. 2000. 24.00 (*1-55874-770-2*, Simcha Press); pap. 12.95 (*1-55874-769-9*, Simcha Press) Health Comm.

— More Chicken Soup for the Christian Family Soul: 101 Stories to Open the Heart & Rekindle the Spirit. (Chicken Soup for the Soul Ser.). 350p. 2000. 24.00 (*1-55874-715-X*) Health Comm.

— The Power of Focus: How to Hit Your Business, Personal & Financial Targets with Absolute Certainty. LC 99-89886. (Illus.). 300p. 2000. pap. 12.95 (*1-55874-752-4*) Health Comm.

Canfield, Jack, et al. A Second Chicken Soup for the Woman's Soul: 101 More Stories to Open the Hearts & Rekindle the Spirit. LC 98-27114. 328p. 1998. 24.00 (*1-55874-621-8*); pap. 12.95 (*1-55874-622-6*) Health Comm.

***Canfield, Jack, et al.** Sopa de Pollo Para el Alma del Cristiano: 101 Relatos Que Commueven el Corazon y Ponen Fuego en el Espiritu. (Chicken Soup for the Soul Ser.). (SPA.). 300p. 2000. pap. 12.95 (*1-55874-783-4*) Health Comm.

Canfield, Jack, jt. auth. see Chinmoy, Sri.

Canfield, Jack, ed. see Hansen, Mark Victor.

Canfield, James D., jt. auth. see Dethlefsen, Merle.

***Canfield, Jeff.** Life Isn't Rocket Science. 144p. 2000. pap. 9.99 (*1-930027-13-3*, 921-029, Pub. by Insght Pub) BookWorld.

Canfield, John. Routledge History of Philosophy Vol. 10: Philosophy of the English-Speaking World in the Twentieth Century, Vol. 10. 504p. (C). 1996. 90.00 (*0-415-05605-5*) Routledge.

Canfield, John D. Nicholas Rowe & Christian Tragedy. LC 76-39917. (Illus.). 224p. reprint ed. pap. 69.50 (*0-7837-4945-7*, 204461100004) Bks Demand.

Canfield, John V. The Looking-Glass Self: An Examination of Self-Awareness. LC 90-7143. 264p. 1990. 65.00 (*0-275-93586-8*, C3586, Praeger Pubs) Greenwood.

— Wittgenstein: Language & World. LC 81-4522. 240p. 1981. lib. bdg. 30.00 (*0-87023-318-1*) U of Mass Pr.

Canfield, Joy Elaine. Living in Retirement: And Helping Your Parents Enjoy Retirement. 209p. 1995. pap. 9.95 (*0-9639607-1-7*) Image Cascade.

Canfield, Joy Elaine, jt. ed. see Canfield, Merle L.

Canfield, K. Los Siete Secretos de los Padres Eficaces.Tr. of Seven Secrets of Effective Fatherhood. (SPA.). 260p. pap. 8.99 (*1-56063-940-7*, 497674) Editorial Unilit.

Canfield, K. 365 Promesas Biblicas para Padres Ocupados. (SPA.). 6.99 (*0-7899-0330-X*, 497555) Editorial Unilit.

Canfield, Ken. The Heart of a Father: How Dads Are Shaping the Destiny of America. 19.99 (*0-8024-7330-X*) Moody.

— The Heart of a Father: How Dads Are Shaping the Destiny of America. LC 96-203370. 253p. 1996. 19.99 (*1-881273-30-X*) Northfield Pub.

— 7 Secrets of Effective Fathers. 244p. 1993. pap. 9.99 (*0-8423-5918-4*) Tyndale Hse.

— Spiritual Secrets of Faithful Fathers. 56p. (Orig.). 1997. pap. 2.99 (*0-8341-1663-4*) Beacon Hill.

Canfield, Ken R. 365 Bible Promises for Busy Dads. (Living Bks.). 384p. 1996. mass mkt. 5.99 (*0-8423-2502-6*) Tyndale Hse.

Canfield, Leon H. The Early Persecutions of the Christians. LC 68-54259. (Columbia University. Studies in the Social Sciences: No. 136). reprint ed. 37.50 (*0-404-51136-8*) AMS Pr.

— The Presidency of Woodrow Wilson. LC 66-24796. (Illus.). 299p. 1975. 39.50 (*0-8386-6744-9*) Fairleigh Dickinson.

Canfield, Merle L. & Canfield, Joy Elaine, eds. A Collection of Psychological Scales. 118p. 1993. pap. 9.95 (*0-9639607-0-9*) Image Cascade.

Canfield, Michael, jt. auth. see Weberman, Alan J.

Canfield, Muriel. Anne. (Springsong Bks.). 176p. (J). (gr. 7-10). 1995. mass mkt. 4.99 (*1-55661-584-1*) Bethany Hse.

Canfield, Nancy, jt. auth. see Gilchrist, John.

Canfield, Patrick M. Growing up with Bootleggers, Gamblers & Pigeons. rev. ed. Abbate, Matthew, ed. 288p. (Orig.). 1993. pap. 7.95 (*0-9633952-1-1*) Interlude Ent.

— White Ebony. Abbate, Matthew & Camoriano, David, eds. LC 95-81060. 315p. (Orig.). 1998. pap. 12.95 (*0-9633952-2-X*) Interlude Ent.

Canfield Reisman, Rosemary M. & Booker-Canfield, Suzanne. Contemporary Southern Men Fiction Writers: An Annotated Bibliography. LC 97-53063. (Magill Bibliograhies Ser.). 448p. 1998. 55.00 (*0-8108-3195-3*) Scarecrow.

Canfield, Richard A. Blackjack Your Way to Riches. 1989. pap. 10.95 (*0-8184-0498-1*) Carol Pub Group.

Canfield, Robert L. Faction & Conversion in a Plural Society: Religious Alignments in the Hindu Kush. (Anthropological Papers Ser.: No. 50). 1973. 2.00 (*0-932206-48-4*) U Mich Mus Anthro.

Canfield, S. S. History of the Twenty-First Regiment, Ohio Volunteer Infantry, in the War of the Rebellion. (Illus.). 239p. 1995. reprint ed. lib. bdg. 32.50 (*0-8328-4716-X*) Higginson Bk Co.

Canfield, Sandra. The Hired Husband. (Just Married Ser.). 1993. mass mkt. 4.99 (*0-373-83258-3*, 1-83258-3) Harlequin Bks.

— Jericho. (Superromance Ser.). 1996. per. 3.99 (*0-373-70702-9*, 1-70702-5) Harlequin Bks.

— Mariah. (Calloway Corners Ser.). 1993. per. 3.50 (*0-373-83278-8*, 1-83278-1) Harlequin Bks.

— Snap Judgement. (Superromance Ser.). 1993. mass mkt. 3.39 (*0-373-70545-X*, 1-70545-8) Harlequin Bks.

— Tigers by Night. (Superromance Ser.: No. 419). 1990. per. 2.95 (*0-373-70419-4*) Harlequin Bks.

Canfield, Sandra, et al. Baby Beat, Someone' Baby, Come Home to Me. LC 96-7355. 635p. 1996. per. 5.99 (*0-373-20120-6*, 1-20120-1) Harlequin Bks.

Canfield, William W. At Seneca Castle. 274p. 1998. reprint ed. lib. bdg. 79.00 (*0-7812-4794-2*) Rprt Serv.

— Legends of the Iroquois. 1998. lib. bdg. 26.95 (*1-56723-131-4*) Yestermorrow.

— Legends of the Iroquois. 211p. 1993. reprint ed. lib. bdg. 79.00 (*0-7812-5157-5*) Rprt Serv.

— The Sign above the Door. 325p. 1998. reprint ed. lib. bdg. 75.00 (*0-7812-4792-6*) Rprt Serv.

— Spotter, the a Romance of the Oil Region. 360p. 1998. reprint ed. lib. bdg. 75.00 (*0-7812-4791-8*) Rprt Serv.

— Things Worth Knowing about Oneida County. 148p. 1998. reprint ed. lib. bdg. 75.00 (*0-7812-4793-4*) Rprt Serv.

Canfora, Luciano. The Vanished Library: A Wonder of the Ancient World. Ryle, Martin, tr. (Hellenistic Culture & Society Ser.). (Orig.). 1990. pap. 17.95 (*0-520-07255-3*, Pub. by U CA Pr) Cal Prin Full Svc.

Cangany, Harry. Great American Drums & the Companies That Made Them, 1920-1969. LC 97-118322. (Illus.). 72p. 1996. per. 19.95 (*0-7935-6356-9*, 06620010) H Leonard.

Cangelosi. Classroom Strategies. 3rd ed. 1997. pap. text, teacher ed. 25.00 (*0-471-36489-4*) Wiley.

Cangelosi. Monitoring Student Learning. LC 99-10749. 662p. (C). 1999. 81.00 (*0-321-02332-3*) Addson-Wesley Educ.

Cangelosi, Don & Carpini, Joe D. Italian Without Words. 96p. 1989. pap. 6.00 (*0-671-67743-8*) S&S Trade.

Cangelosi, Don & Corpini, Joe D. Italian Without Words. LC 88-31820. 100p. 1989. pap. 6.00 (*0-88166-156-2*) Meadowbrook.

Cangelosi, Donna. Saying Goodbye in Child Psychotherapy: Planned, Unplanned, & Premature Endings in Child Psychotherapy. LC 96-49473. 192p. 1997. 40.00 (*1-56821-677-7*) Aronson.

***Cangelosi, Drew.** 101 Ways to Make Things Worse: And Even More Ways to Make Them Better. LC 00-190191. 2000. 25.00 (*0-7388-1540-3*); pap. 18.00 (*0-7388-1541-1*) Xlibris Corp.

Cangelosi, James S. Classroom Management Strategies: Gaining & Maintaining Students Cooperation. 1997. pap., teacher ed. 46.95 (*0-471-36501-7*) Wiley.

Cangelosi, James S. Classroom Management Strategies: Gaining & Maintaining Students' Cooperation. 2nd ed. 352p. (C). 1993. teacher ed. write for info. (*0-8013-1090-3*, 79541) Longman.

— Cooperation in the Classroom: Students & Teachers Together. 2nd ed. 80p. 1990. pap. 9.95 (*0-8106-3072-9*) NEA.

— Designing Tests for Evaluating Student Achievement. 230p. (C). 1990. pap. text 33.50 (*0-8013-0263-3*, 75916) Longman.

— Systematic Teaching Strategies. (Orig.). (C). 1992. teacher ed. write for info. (*0-8013-0930-1*) Longman.

— Teaching Middle & Secondary School Math. 2nd ed. 480p. (C). 1995. pap. text 84.00 (*0-13-439233-7*) P-H.

Cangemi. America & Its Neighbors: Grade 5. 1986. 45.50 (*0-03-001802-1*) Harcourt Schl Pubs.

— Holt Social Studies Grade 1: People. (J). 1986. pap., teacher ed. 61.75 (*0-03-001779-3*) Harcourt Schl Pubs.

— Holt Social Studies Grade 2: Neighbors. (J). 1986. pap., teacher ed. 65.00 (*0-03-001783-1*) Harcourt Schl Pubs.

— Holt Social Studies Grade 3: Communities. (J). 1986. pap., teacher ed. 74.50 (*0-03-001787-4*) Harcourt Schl Pubs.

— Holt Social Studies Grade 5: America & Its Neighbors. (J). 1986. pap., teacher ed. 87.50 (*0-03-001803-X*) Harcourt Schl Pubs.

— Holt Social Studies Grade 6+ The World. (J). 1986. pap., teacher ed. 95.25 (*0-03-001812-9*) Harcourt Schl Pubs.

— Holt Social Studies Grade K: Me. (J). 1986. pap., teacher ed. 39.25 (*0-03-001777-7*) Harcourt Schl Pubs.

— Holt Social Studies Workbook Grade 5: America & Its Neighbors. (J). 1986. pap., student ed. 12.00 (*0-03-001804-8*) Harcourt Schl Pubs.

— Holt Social Studies Workbook Grade 6+ The World. (J). 1986. pap., student ed. 12.00 (*0-03-001813-7*) Harcourt Schl Pubs.

— Social Studies: The World, 1986. 1986. 46.25 (*0-03-001809-9*) Harcourt Schl Pubs.

— Social Studies Communities 3. 1988. 34.25 (*0-03-001784-X*) Harcourt Schl Pubs.

— Social Studies, 1986: Neighbor Grade 2. 1986. 28.75 (*0-03-001782-3*) Harcourt Schl Pubs.

— Social Studies Region 4. 1986. 45.50 (*0-03-001793-9*) Harcourt Schl Pubs.

Cangemi, Joseph P., et al, eds. Leadership Behavior. LC 97-40212. 196p. (C). 1997. text 49.00 (*0-7618-0940-6*) U Pr of Amer.

Cangemi, Joseph P. & Kowalski, Casimir J., eds. Andersonville Prison: Lessons in Organizational Failure. LC 92-16723. 134p. (C). 1992. 36.00 (*0-8191-8758-5*) U Pr of Amer.

Cangemi, Joseph P., et al. Leadership Behavior. LC 97-40212. 1997. pap. write for info. (*0-7618-0941-4*) U Pr of Amer.

Cangemi, Michael P. Managing the Audit Function: A Corporate Audit Department Procedures Guide. LC 95-42391. 272p. 1995. 145.00 (*0-471-01255-6*) Wiley.

Canger, Raffaele, ed. see Epilepsy International Symposium Staff.

Cangialosi, Karen, jt. auth, see Paffrath, Jim.

Cangiani, Michele & Mendell, Marguerite, eds. The Milano Papers: Essays in Societal Alternatives. (Critical Perspectives on Historic Issues Ser.: Vol. 7). 254p. 1995. 48.99 (*1-55164-023-6*, Pub. by Black Rose); pap. 19.99 (*1-55164-022-8*, Pub. by Black Rose) Consort Bk Sales.

Canguilhem, Georges. The Normal & the Pathological. Fawcett, Carolyn R. & Cohen, Robert S., trs. from FRE. LC 88-20626. 327p. 1989. reprint ed. 28.95 (*0-942299-58-2*) Zone Bks.

— The Normal & the Pathological. Fawcett, Carolyn R., tr. from FRE. LC 88-20626. 327p. 1989. reprint ed. pap. 16.95 (*0-942299-59-0*) Zone Bks.

— A Vital Rationalist: Selected Writings from Georges Canguilhem. Delaporte, Francois, ed. Goldhammer, Arthur, tr. LC 93-8613. 481p. 1994. 27.95 (*0-942299-72-8*) Zone Bks.

***Canguilhem, Georges.** A Vital Rationalist: Selected Writings from Georges Canguilhem. 482p. 2000. pap. text 21.00 (*0-942299-73-6*) Zone Bks.

Canham-Clyne, John. Capitol Gains: Congressional Votes, Campaign Cash & the Public Interest. 28p. (Orig.). 1996. pap. 10.00 (*0-937188-07-7*) Pub Citizen.

Canham-Clyne, John, et al. The Rational Option for a National Health Program. 112p. 1995. 17.95 (*0-9630587-2-X*); pap. 9.95 (*0-9630587-1-1*) Pamphleteers.

— Saving Money, Saving Lives: The Documented Benefits of Federal Health & Safety Protections. 40p. 1995. pap. text 15.00 (*0-937188-88-3*) Pub Citizen.

Canham, Donald B. & Paladino, Larry. From the Inside: A Half Century of Michigan Athletics. Stevens, Rita J., ed. (Illus.). 300p. (Orig.). 1996. pap. 18.95 (*0-9654263-0-0*) Olympia Sprts.

***Canham, Elizabeth.** Heart Whispers: Benedictine Wisdom for Today. Collett, Rita, ed. LC 99-21609. 176p. 1999. pap. 13.00 (*0-8358-0892-0*, UR892) Upper Room Bks.

— Heart Whispers: Leader's Guide. Collett, Rita, ed. 48p. 1999. pap., teacher ed. 5.00 (*0-8358-0893-9*, UR893) Upper Room Bks.

Canham, Elizabeth J. Journaling with Jeremiah. LC 92-16467. 160p. 1992. pap. 9.95 (*0-8091-3334-2*) Paulist Pr.

Canham, Erwin D., ed. see Christian Science Monitor Editors.

Canham, Hugh O. & Gray, John, eds. Federal Income Tax Change & the Private Forest Sector. (Breaking New Ground Ser.: No. 2). 36p. (Orig.). 1986. pap. 3.95 (*0-938549-01-4*) Grey Towers Pr.

Canham, L., ed. Properties of Porous Silicon. (EMIS Datareviews Ser.: No. 18). 424p. 1997. 245.00 (*0-85296-932-5*, EM018) INSPEC Inc.

Canham, L. T. & Bellet, D. New Developments in Porous Silicon: Relation with Other Nanostructured Porous Materials: Proceedings of Symposium L on New Developments in Porous Silicon: Relation with Other Nanostructured Porous Materials of the 1996 E-MRS Spring Conference, Strasbourg, France June 4-7, 1996. LC 98-149194. (European Materials Research Society Symposia Proceedings Ser.: Vol. 600). 340p. 1997. 201.00 (*0-444-20508-X*) Elsevier.

Canham, Leigh T., et al, eds. Microcrystalline & Nanocrystalline Semiconductors--1998, Vol. 536. LC 99-18521. (Symposium Proceedings Ser.). 569p. 1999. 83.00 (*1-55899-442-4*) Materials Res.

Canham, Marsha. Across a Moonlit Sea. 400p. 1996. mass mkt. 5.99 (*0-440-21785-7*) Dell.

— The Blood of Roses. 576p. 1998. mass mkt. 6.50 (*0-440-22455-1*) Doubleday.

— In the Shadow of Midnight. 416p. 1994. mass mkt. 6.50 (*0-440-20613-8*) Dell.

— The Last Arrow. 448p. (Orig.). 1997. mass mkt. 5.99 (*0-440-22257-5*) Dell.

— The Last Arrow. (Orig.). 1997. mass mkt. 5.99 (*0-614-27733-7*) Dell.

— Pale Moon Rider. 384p. 1998. mass mkt. 6.50 (*0-440-22259-1*) Dell.

— The Pride of Lions. 416p. 1997. mass mkt. 5.99 (*0-440-22457-8*, Dell Trade Pbks) Dell.

— Straight for the Heart. 448p. 1995. mass mkt. 6.50 (*0-440-21786-5*) Dell.

***Canham, Marsha.** Swept Away. 400p. 1999. mass mkt. 6.50 (*0-440-23521-9*) Dell.

Canham, Marsha. Through a Dark Mist. 480p. 1991. mass mkt. 5.99 (*0-440-20611-1*) Dell.

— Under the Desert Moon. 512p. 1992. mass mkt. 5.99 (*0-440-20612-X*) Dell.

Canham, Marsha M. Dark & Dangerous. rev. ed. (Temptation Ser.: No. 386). 1992. mass mkt. 2.99 (*0-373-25486-5*, 1-25486-1) Harlequin Bks.

Canham, Rod. Hawai'i Below: An Island by Island Guide. (Illus.). 235p. 1991. pap. 19.95 (*0-922769-21-4*) Aqua Quest.

Canicatti, C., jt. ed. see Scalera-Liaci, L.

***Caniels, Marjolein C. J.** Knowledge Spillovers & Economic Growth: Regional Growth Differentials Across Europe. LC 99-88520. (New Horizons in the Economics of Innovation Ser.). 224p. 2000. 90.00 (*1-84064-236-X*) E Elgar.

Canieso Dronila, Maria L. Landscapes of Literacy: An Ethnographic Study of Functional Literacy in Marginal Philippine Communities. 206p. 1997. pap. 22.95 (*1-898942-16-1*, Pub. by Luzac Oriental) Weatherhill.

Caniff, Milt. The Complete Dickie Dare. (Illus.). 160p. 1986. pap. 14.95 (*0-930193-21-0*) Fantagraph Bks.

Caniff, Milton. Now in My Day . . . (Illus.). 48p. 1992. 28.00 (*0-88014-083-6*) Mosaic Pr OH.

Canigo Staff. Canigo Diccionari Castella-Catala, Catala-Castella. (CAT & SPA.). 878p. pap. 59.95 (*0-8288-1757-X*, S31565) Fr & Eur.

Canin, Ethan. Blue River. 240p. 1992. reprint ed. mass mkt. 12.99 (*0-446-39447-5*, Pub. by Warner Bks) Little.

— Emperor of the Air. LC 88-45581. 192p. 1989. reprint ed. pap. 13.00 (*0-06-097208-4*, PL 7208, Perennial) HarperTrade.

***Canin, Ethan.** Emperor of the Air: Stories. LC 99-40640. 192p. 1999. pap. 13.00 (*0-618-00414-9*, Mariner Bks) HM.

Canin, Ethan. For Kings & Planets. 2nd ed. LC 99-42424. 334p. 1999. pap. 14.00 (*0-312-24125-9*, Picador USA) St Martin.

— The Palace Thief. large type ed. 261p. 1994. lib. bdg. 22.95 (*0-8161-7468-7*, G K Hall Lrg Type) Mac Lib Ref.

— The Palace Thief: Stories. LC 94-45087. 1994. pap. 11.00 (*0-312-11930-5*) St Martin.

Canin, Ethan, ed. Writers Harvest 2: A Collection of New Fiction. 1996. pap. 12.00 (*0-614-20734-7*, Harvest Bks) Harcourt.

Canine, Craig. Dream Reaper: The Story of an Old-Fashioned Inventor in the High-Tech, High-Stakes World of Modern Agriculture. LC 96-49988. 1997. pap. 14.95 (*0-226-09265-8*) U Ch Pr.

Canine, John. The Psychosocial Aspects of Death & Dying. 320p. (C). 1996. pap. 44.95 (*0-8385-8098-X*, A8098-4, Apple Lange Med) McGraw.

— What Am I Going to Do with Myself When I Die? LC 98-12718. 192p. 1999. pap. 34.95 (*0-8385-9710-6*, Apple Lange Med) McGraw.

C

*__Canino, Frank.__ The Angelina Project. (Drama Ser.: No. 19). 150p. 2000. pap. 13.00 (*1-55071-109-1*, , Pub. by Guernica Editions) Paul & Co Pubs.

Canino, Glorisa J., jt. auth. see Helzer, John E.

Canino, Ian A. & Spurlock, Jeanne. Culturally Diverse Children & Adolescents: Assessment, Diagnosis & Treatment. LC 93-50824. 196p. 1994. lib. bdg. 27.95 (*0-89862-409-6*, C2409) Guilford Pubns.

*__Canino, Ian A. & Spurlock, Jeanne.__ Culturally Diverse Children & Adolescents: Assessment, Diagnosis & Treatment. 2nd ed. 210p. 2000. lib. bdg. 28.95 (*1-57230-583-5*, C0583) Guilford Pubns.

Canino Salgado, Marcelino. Gozos Devocionales En la Tradicion De Puerto Rico. (UPREX, Folklore Ser.: No. 32). 145p. (C). 1974. pap. 1.50 (*0-8477-0032-1*) U of PR Pr.

Canino, Thomas L. Mountain Man Cookbook: Venison & Other Recipes. 2nd ed. (Illus.). 100p. (Orig.). 1989. spiral bd. 8.95 (*0-9614922-1-X*) TLC Enterprises.

Canion, Michael. Satan Is in Sales. 114p. (Orig.). 1997. pap. 10.00 (*1-57502-464-0*, PO1386) Morris Pubng.

Caniou, Joseph. Passive Infrared Detection: Theory & Applications LC 99-15354. 1999. write for info. (*0-7923-8532-2*) Kluwer Academic.

Canipe, Kenneth W. Between Earth & Sky. 48p. (Orig.). 1986. pap. 3.00 (*0-9616329-0-9*) K W Canipe.

Canis, Wayne F., et al. Living with the Alabama-Mississippi Shore. LC 84-24679. (Living with the Shore Ser.). 232p. 1985. text 39.95 (*0-8223-0510-0*); pap. text 17.95 (*0-8223-0511-9*) Duke.

Canitrot, Adolfo & Junco, Silvia, eds. Macroeconomic Conditions & Trade Liberalization. 224p. 1993. 14.50 (*0-940602-66-0*) IADB.

Canizares, Orlando. A Manual of Dermatology for Developing Countries. 2nd ed. LC 92-49991. (Illus.). 392p. 1993. 85.00 (*0-19-262293-5*); pap. 29.50 (*0-19-262294-3*) OUP.

Canizares, Rafael. On the Application of Data Assimilation in Regional Coastal Models. (IHE Thesis Ser.: Vol. 18). (Illus.). 144p. (C). 1999. pap. text 40.00 (*90-5410-416-3*) A A Balkema.

Canizares, Raul. Cuban Santeria: Walking with the Night. LC 99-11654. (Illus.). 160p. 1999. 12.95 (*0-89281-762-3*, Destiny Bks) Inner Tradit.

Canizares, Susan. All Kinds of Books. LC 98-54203. 1998. pap. 2.50 (*0-439-04607-6*) Scholastic Inc.

— Cactus Names. LC 98-8010. (Science Emergent Readers Ser.). (J). 1998. 3.25 (*0-590-63871-8*) Scholastic Inc.

— Dancing. LC 98-53541. 1998. pap. 2.50 (*0-439-04569-X*) Scholastic Inc.

— Evergreens Are Green. LC 97-34216. (Science Emergent Readers Ser.). (J). 1997. pap. 2.50 (*0-590-15582-2*) Scholastic Inc.

*__Canizares, Susan.__ Feelings. LC 98-54611. (Social Studies Emergent Readers Ser.). (J). 1998. 2.50 (*0-439-04555-X*) Scholastic Inc.

Canizares, Susan. Gravity. LC 98-53318. (Science Emergent Readers Ser.). 1999. pap. 10.01 (*0-439-08127-0*) Scholastic Inc.

— How a Butterfly Grows. LC 98-18819. (Science Emergent Readers Ser.). (J). 1998. pap. 2.50 (*0-590-76160-9*) Scholastic Inc.

— Jobs. LC 98-54176. 1998. pap. 2.50 (*0-439-04551-7*) Scholastic Inc.

— Little Raccoon Catches a Cold. LC 97-49177. (Side-by-Side Ser.). (Illus.). (J). 1997. write for info. (*0-590-10969-3*); pap. 3.50 (*0-590-02601-1*) Scholastic Inc.

— Make It Move. LC 98-53313. 1999. pap. 10.01 (*0-439-08121-1*) Scholastic Inc.

— The Northern Lights. LC 97-34210. (Science Emergent Readers Ser.). (J). 1998. lib. bdg. 2.50 (*0-590-76155-2*) Scholastic Inc.

— Push & Pull. LC 98-53316. (Science Emergent Readers Ser.). 1999. pap. 10.01 (*0-439-08119-X*) Scholastic Inc.

*__Canizares, Susan.__ Red, White & Blue. LC 98-47669. (Social Studies Emergent Readers Ser.). 1998. pap. 10.01 (*0-439-04564-9*) Scholastic Inc.

— Science, Tools & Magic, vol.12. LC 98-48546. (Learning Center Emergent Readers Ser.). (J). 1998. pap. write for info. (*0-439-04603-3*) Scholastic Services Publishing Co.

Canizares, Susan. Shelter. LC 98-53115. 1998. pap. write for info. (*0-439-04552-5*) Scholastic Inc.

— Spider Names. LC 97-29196. (Science Emergent Readers Ser.). (Illus.). (J). 1998. pap. 2.50 (*0-590-39795-8*) Scholastic Inc.

— Sun. LC 97-34213. (Science Emergent Readers Ser.). (J). 1997. pap. 2.50 (*0-590-10731-3*) Scholastic Inc.

*__Canizares, Susan.__ Tedd & Huggly. LC 98-48539. (Learning Center Emergent Readers Ser.). (J). 1998. 3.25 (*0-439-04610-6*) Scholastic Services Publishing Co.

Canizares, Susan. Tools. LC 98-53315. 1999. pap. 10.01 (*0-439-08128-9*) Scholastic Inc.

— Wheels. LC 98-53309. 1999. pap. 10.01 (*0-439-08123-8*) Scholastic Inc.

— Where Does It Park? LC 98-35584. 1998. pap. 2.50 (*0-439-04583-5*) Scholastic Inc.

*__Canizares, Susan & Berger, Samantha.__ At Home. LC 00-20639. 2000. write for info. (*0-439-15367-0*) Scholastic Inc.

Canizares, Susan & Berger, Samantha. Building Shapes. LC 98-34073. (J). 1998. pap. 3.25 (*0-439-04585-1*) Scholastic Inc.

— Canada. LC 98-53370. 1999. 2.50 (*0-439-04573-8*) Scholastic Inc.

— Meet Jim Henson. LC 99-14914. (Social Studies Emergent Readers Ser.). (J). 1999. 4.35 (*0-439-04575-4*) Scholastic Inc.

— Pele, the King of Soccer. LC 98-50493. (Social Studies Emergent Readers Ser.). (J). 1999. 2.50 (*0-439-04577-0*) Scholastic Inc.

*__Canizares, Susan & Berger, Samantha.__ Restaurant. LC 99-462013. (Placebook Ser.). 2000. pap. write for info. (*0-439-15366-2*) Scholastic Inc.

Canizares, Susan & Berger, Samantha. The Voyage of Mae Jemison. LC 98-53308. 1999. 2.50 (*0-439-04579-7*) Scholastic Inc.

— What Do Artists Use? LC 98-53182. (Learning Center Emergent Readers Ser.). 1998. 2.50 (*0-439-04591-6*) Scholastic Inc.

Canizares, Susan & Chanko, Pamela. Babies. LC 98-38325. (Learning Center Emergent Readers Ser.). (J). 1998. pap. 2.50 (*0-439-04588-6*) Scholastic Inc.

— Busy Beavers. LC 97-29199. (Science Emergent Readers Ser.). (Illus.). (J). 1997. pap. 2.50 (*0-590-76170-6*) Scholastic Inc.

— First Aid. LC 98-35283. (Learning Center Emergent Readers Ser.). 1998. pap. 2.50 (*0-439-04590-8*) Scholastic Inc.

— Look at This Tree. LC 97-34204. (Science Emergent Readers Ser.). (J). 1997. pap. 2.50 (*0-590-14998-9*) Scholastic Inc.

— Mexico. LC 98-53355. (Social Studies Emergent Readers Ser.). 1999. 2.50 (*0-439-04570-3*) Scholastic Inc.

— Ocean LC 98-23226. (Science Emergent Readers Ser.). 1998. 2.50 (*0-590-63886-6*) Scholastic Inc.

— Ready, Set, Go! LC 98-53543. 1998. 2.50 (*0-439-04565-7*) Scholastic Inc.

*__Canizares, Susan & Chanko, Pamela.__ Store. LC 99-462073. 2000. pap. write for info. (*0-439-15369-7*) Scholastic Inc.

Canizares, Susan & Chanko, Pamela. Up, Up, & Away: The Story of Amelia Earhart. LC 98-53334. (Social Studies Emergent Readers Ser.). 1999. 2.50 (*0-439-04578-9*) Scholastic Inc.

— Water. LC 97-34215. (Science Emergent Readers Ser.). (J). 1998. pap. 2.50 (*0-590-10727-5*) Scholastic Inc.

— What Do Insects Do? LC 97-29197. (Science Emergent Readers Ser.). (Illus.). (J). 1997. pap. 2.50 (*0-590-39794-X*) Scholastic Inc.

— Wheat. LC 98-53336. 1999. 2.50 (*0-439-04563-0*) Scholastic Inc.

— Who Lives in the Arctic? LC 97-34205. (Science Emergent Readers Ser.). (J). 1997. pap. 2.50 (*0-590-76150-1*) Scholastic Inc.

— Who's Hiding? LC 97-34238. (Science Emergent Readers Ser.). (Illus.). (J). 1997. pap. 2.50 (*0-590-76963-4*) Scholastic Inc.

Canizares, Susan & Chessen, Betsey. Colors in the Desert. LC 98-8009. (Science Emergent Readers Ser.). (J). 1998. 3.25 (*0-590-63870-X*) Scholastic Inc.

— From Egg to Robin. LC 98-18826. (Science Emergent Readers Ser.). (J). 1998. pap. 2.50 (*0-590-76162-5*) Scholastic Inc.

*__Canizares, Susan & Chessen, Betsey.__ In the Kitchen. LC 98-38323. (Learning Center Emergent Readers Ser.). 1998. pap. 2.50 (*0-439-04586-X*) Scholastic Inc.

Canizares, Susan & Chessen, Betsey. Italy. LC 98-53369. 1999. 2.50 (*0-439-04572-X*) Scholastic Inc.

— Numbers All Around. LC 98-54205. (Learning Center Emergent Readers Ser.). 1998. 2.50 (*0-439-04598-3*) Scholastic Inc.

— Rainforest Colors. LC 97-34201. (Science Emergent Readers Ser.). (Illus.). (J). 1997. pap. 2.50 (*0-590-76962-6*) Scholastic Inc.

— Storms. LC 97-34214. (Science Emergent Readers Ser.). (J). 1997. pap. 2.50 (*0-590-10729-1*) Scholastic Inc.

— Two Can Do It! LC 98-54254. (Social Studies Emergent Readers Ser.). 1998. 2.50 (*0-439-04559-2*) Scholastic Inc.

— What Comes in a Shell? LC 98-23224. (Science Emergent Readers Ser.). 1998. 3.95 (*0-590-63878-5*) Scholastic Inc.

— Who Lives in a Tree? LC 97-34239. (Science Emergent Readers Ser.). (Illus.). (J). 1997. pap. 2.50 (*0-590-15856-2*) Scholastic Inc.

— Wind. LC 97-34240. (Science Emergent Readers Ser.). (J). 1997. pap. 2.50 (*0-590-10726-7*) Scholastic Inc.

*__Canizares, Susan & Einhorn, Kama.__ Supermarket. LC 99-462074. 2000. pap. write for info. (*0-439-15368-9*) Scholastic Inc.

*__Canizares, Susan & McVeigh, Mark.__ Museum. LC 00-23933. (Illus.). (J). 2000. write for info. (*0-439-15375-1*) Scholastic Inc.

Canizares, Susan & Moreton, Daniel. Babies on the Move. LC 98-54251. (Social Studies Emergent Readers Ser.). (J). 1998. 2.50 (*0-439-04556-8*) Scholastic Inc.

— Bridges. LC 98-34072. 1998. pap. 3.25 (*0-439-04581-9*) Scholastic Inc.

*__Canizares, Susan & Moreton, Daniel.__ Construction Site. LC 00-26544. 2000. pap. write for info. (*0-439-15373-5*) Scholastic Inc.

Canizares, Susan & Moreton, Daniel. Frogs. LC 98-18822. (Science Emergent Readers Ser.). (J). 1998. 2.50 (*0-590-76159-5*) Scholastic Inc.

— In a Painting. LC 98-53177. 1998. 2.50 (*0-439-04593-2*) Scholastic Inc.

— In Our Country. LC 99-12153. 1999. 2.50 (*0-439-04562-2*) Scholastic Inc.

— This Bird Can't Fly. LC 98-18823. (Science Emergent Readers Ser.). (J). 1998. pap. 3.25 (*0-590-76968-5*) Scholastic Inc.

Canizares, Susan & Reid, Mary. Arctic Winter, Arctic Summer. LC 97-34207. (Science Emergent Readers Ser.). (J). 1997. pap. 2.50 (*0-590-76151-X*) Scholastic Inc.

— Coral Reef. LC 97-29184. (Science Emergent Readers Ser.). (Illus.). (J). 1997. pap. 2.50 (*0-590-76182-X*) Scholastic Inc.

— Homes in the Ground. LC 97-29200. (Science Emergent Readers Ser.). (Illus.). (J). 1997. pap. 3.25 (*0-590-76168-4*) Scholastic Inc.

— Nests, Nests, Nests. LC 97-29198. (Science Emergent Readers Ser.). (Illus.). (J). 1997. pap. 2.50 (*0-590-76183-8*) Scholastic Inc.

— Treats from a Tree. LC 97-34212. (Science Emergent Readers Ser.). (J). 1998. pap. 2.50 (*0-590-16137-7*) Scholastic Inc.

— What Is an Insect? LC 97-29203. (Science Emergent Readers Ser.). (Illus.). (J). 1997. pap. 2.50 (*0-590-39790-7*) Scholastic Inc.

— Where Do Insects Live? LC 97-29201. (Science Emergent Readers Ser.). (Illus.). (J). 1997. pap. 2.50 (*0-590-39793-1*) Scholastic Inc.

— Who Lives in the Rainforest? LC 97-34202. (Science Emergent Readers Ser.). (J). 1997. pap. 2.50 (*0-590-76961-8*) Scholastic Inc.

*__Canizares, Susan & Waugh, Betsey.__ Firehouse. LC 00-26370. 2000. pap. write for info. (*0-439-15370-0*) Scholastic Inc.

— On a Farm. LC 99-462012. (Illus.). (J). 2000. pap. write for info. (*0-439-15371-9*) Scholastic Inc.

*__Canizares, Susan & Weber, Arianne.__ Airport. LC 00-26369. 2000. pap. write for info. (*0-439-15374-3*) Scholastic Inc.

— At the Zoo. LC 00-26543. (Illus.). (J). 2000. pap. write for info. (*0-439-15377-8*) Scholastic Inc.

*__Canizares, Susan, et al.__ Aquarium. LC 00-26542. (Illus.). (J). 2000. pap. write for info. (*0-439-15372-7*) Scholastic Inc.

— Clay Art with Gloria Elliott. LC 98-48699. (Learning Center Emergent Readers Ser.). (Illus.). (J). 1998. 2.50 (*0-439-04595-9*) Scholastic Inc.

— Garden. LC 99-85711. (Placebook Ser.). (Illus.). (J). 2000. pap. write for info. (*0-439-15376-X*) Scholastic Inc.

Canizares, Susan, et al. Polar Bears. LC 97-34209. (Science Emergent Readers Ser.). (J). 1998. pap. 3.50 (*0-590-76153-6*) Scholastic Inc.

Canizares, Susan, jt. auth. see Chanko, Pamela.

*__Canja, Jeff.__ Collectible Paperback Books - 10,000 Prices Realized: A New Paperbakc Price Reference. (Illus.). 176p. 2000. pap. 29.95 (*0-9673639-2-6*) Glenmoor Pubg.

Canjar, Lawrence N. & Manning, Francis S. Thermodynamic Properties & Reduced Correlations for Gases. LC 66-30022. 258p. 1967. reprint ed. pap. 80.00 (*0-608-08480-8*, 205187400013) Bks Demand.

— Thermodynamic Properties & Reduced Correlations for Gases, Chpts. 1 & 22. LC 66-30022. 74p. 1967. reprint ed. pap. 30.00 (*0-8357-8347-2*, 203288300081) Bks Demand.

Cankaya, Birsen. English-Turkish Comprehensive Dictionary. (ENG & TUR.). 1293p. 1996. 90.00 (*0-7818-0469-8*) Hippocrene Bks.

Canler, Louis. Autobiography of a French Detective from 1818 to 1858: Most Curious Revelations of the French Detective Police System. LC 75-32738. (Literature of Mystery & Detection Ser.). 1976. reprint ed. 26.95 (*0-405-07866-8*) Ayer.

Canmer, Gibson L., ed. History of Wheeling City & Ohio County, & Representative Citizens. (Illus.). 853p. 1995. reprint ed. lib. bdg. 85.00 (*0-8328-4649-X*) Higginson Bk Co.

CANMET-ACI International Symposium on Superplastic. Superplasticizers in Concrete. LC 79-89813. (American Concrete Institute, ACI Publication: No. SP-62). (Illus.). 433p. reprint ed. pap. 134.30 (*0-608-17698-2*, 203003700067) Bks Demand.

Cann, Alan, ed. Principles of Molecular Virology. 2nd ed. LC 96-47478. (Illus.). 328p. 1997. pap. text 29.95 (*0-12-158532-8*) Morgan Kaufmann.

*__Cann, Alan J.__ RNA Viruses: A Practical Approach. LC 99-57577. 304p. 2000. write for info. (*0-19-963716-4*) OUP.

— Virus Culture: A Practical Approach. LC 99-19983. (The Practical Approach Ser.: Vol. 208). 304p. 2000. text 110.00 (*0-19-963715-6*); pap. text 55.00 (*0-19-963714-8*) OUP.

*__Cann, Alan J., ed.__ DNA Virus Replication. LC 99-46601. (Frontiers in Molecular Biology Ser.). 256p. 2000. write for info. (*0-19-963712-1*) OUP.

— DNA Virus Replication. (Illus.). 256p. 2000. text 110.00 (*0-19-963713-X*) OUP.

— DNA Viruses: A Practical Approach. LC 99-32190. (The Practical Approach Ser.: 214). (Illus.). 352p. 2000. 120.00 (*0-19-963719-9*); pap. 55.00 (*0-19-963718-0*) OUP.

— RNA Viruses: A Practical Approach. LC 99-57577. 304p. 2000. write for info. (*0-19-963717-2*) OUP.

Cann, Carroll C., ed. see Barragry, Thomas B.

Cann, Carroll C., ed. see Smith.

Cann, Helen. Animal Worlds. (J). 1997. pap. 9.99 (*1-58048-002-0*) Sandvik Pub.

*__Cann, Helen.__ A Calendar of Festivals. 80p. (J). (gr. 3-7). 2000. pap. 9.99 (*1-84148-244-7*) Barefoot Bks NY.

Cann, Helen. Mother & Daughter Tales. LC 97-146158. (Abbeville Anthology Ser.). 80p. (J). (ps-3). 1996. 19.95 (*0-7892-0281-6*, Abbeville Kids) Abbeville Pr.

Cann, Helen, jt. auth. see Pirotta, Saviour.

Cann, J. R., et al, eds. Mid-Ocean Ridges: Dynamics of Processes Associated with Creation of New Ocean Crust. LC 98-8322. (Illus.). 288p. (C). 1999. text 69.95 (*0-521-58522-8*) Cambridge U Pr.

Cann, John. The Stunt Guide. 1991. pap. 19.95 (*0-9629292-0-4*) Action P A C.

— The Stunt Guide: Comprehensive Stunt Reference Book for the Entertainment Industry. 3rd ed. Atteberry, Mark, ed. (Illus.). 348p. (C). 1992. spiral bd. 25.00 (*0-9629292-1-2*) Action P A C.

Cann, John P. Counterinsurgency in Africa: The Portuguese Way of War, 1961-1974, 167. LC 96-38260. (Contributions in Military Studies Ser.). 240p. 1997. 59.95 (*0-313-30189-1*, Greenwood Pr) Greenwood.

Cann, Jonathan. The Case of the Crooked Candles. (Publish-a-Book Ser.). (Illus.). 28p. (J). (gr. k-7). 1997. pap. 5.95 (*0-8172-7212-7*) Raintree Steck-V.

Cann, Jonathan V. The Case of the Crooked Candles. LC 96-44842. (Publish-a-Book Clippers Ser.). (Illus.). (J). (gr. 1-6). 1997. lib. bdg. 22.83 (*0-8172-4432-8*) Raintree Steck-V.

Cann, Kate. Caught in the Act. 144p. (J). 1997. pap. 6.95 (*0-09-926318-1*, Pub. by Random) Trafalgar.

Cann, Kate. Diving In. (Livewire Ser.). 238p. (YA). (gr. 7-11). 1997. pap. 7.95 (*0-7043-4937-X*, Pub. by Womens Press) Trafalgar.

Cann, Kate. Diving in. 256p. (gr. 7 up). mass mkt. 5.95 (*0-06-440869-8*) HarpC.

— Diving in. 256p. (YA). (gr. 7 up). 15.89 (*0-06-028938-4*) HarpC.

— In the Deep End. 256p. (J). (gr. 7 up). 15.89 (*0-06-028937-6*); mass mkt. 5.95 (*0-06-440870-1*) HarpC.

— Sink or Swim. 256p. (J). (gr. 7 up). 15.89 (*0-06-028939-2*); mass mkt. 5.95 (*0-06-440868-X*) HarpC.

— Too Hot to Handle. 144p. (J). 1997. pap. 6.95 (*0-09-925122-1*, Pub. by Random) Trafalgar.

Cann, Marjorie M. Cann's Keys to Better Meetings: An Authoritative New Guide to Parliamentary Procedure. 80p. 1990. pap. 7.95 (*0-940882-17-5*) HB Pubns.

— Point of Order: The Ready Reference for Simple Rules of Order & Parliamentary Procedure. 80p. (Orig.). 1993. pap. 7.95 (*0-399-51815-0*, Perigee Bks) Berkley Pub.

Cann, Richard Du, see Du Cann, Richard.

Cann, Ronnie. Formal Semantics: An Introduction. LC 92-8538. (Cambridge Textbooks in Linguistics Ser.). (Illus.). 362p. (C). 1993. text 80.00 (*0-521-37463-4*); pap. text 26.95 (*0-521-37610-6*) Cambridge U Pr.

Cann, Steve J. Administrative Law. LC 94-11312. 400p. 1994. 52.00 (*0-8039-5146-9*) Sage.

Cann, Steven J. Administrative Law. 2nd ed. LC 97-45281. 1998. 55.00 (*0-7619-0976-1*) Sage.

Cann, Susan A. Santa Barbara with Kids! Places to Go, Things to Do. LC 91-76064. (Illus.). 168p. (Orig.). 1992. pap. 10.95 (*0-9630810-0-4*) Chaparral.

*__Cannabich, Christian.__ Ballet Music from the Mannheim Court Pt. III: Christian Cannabich - "Renaud et Armide" & "Les Mariages Samnites" McClymonds, Marita P. & Marsh, Carol G., eds. (Recent Researches in the Music of the Classical Era Ser.: Vol. C57). xx, 118p. 1999. pap. 55.00 (*0-89579-419-5*) A-R Eds.

Cannabich, Christian & Vogler, Georg J. Ballet Music from the Mannheim Court, Pt. I. Grave, Floyd K., ed. (Recent Researches in Music of the Classic Era Ser.: Vol. RRC45). (Illus.). xliv, 144p. 1996. pap. 60.00 (*0-89579-330-X*) A-R Eds.

Cannabich, Christian, jt. auth. see Toeschi, Carl J.

Cannada, Robert C. & Williamson, W. Jack. PCA Polity: Documents Illustrative of Historic Presbyterian Church Government. 1997. 29.50 (*1-884416-19-5*) A Press.

Cannaday, Antoinette. Out of Me Went 43 Demons. 170p. (Orig.). 1994. pap. 6.95 (*0-89228-111-1*) Impact Christian.

Cannaday, Marilyn. Bigger Than Life: The Creator of Doc Savage. LC 89-85739. (Illus.). 200p. (C). 1990. 34.95 (*0-87972-471-4*); pap. 17.95 (*0-87972-472-2*) Bowling Green Univ Popular Press.

Cannaday, Marilyn E. Order Out of Chaos: How to Simplify Your Life & Housework. LC 97-92199. (Illus.). 128p. 1997. pap. 6.95 (*1-890826-02-2*) Rock Creek Pr.

Cannadine, David. Aspects of Aristocracy. 320p. 1995. pap. 15.95 (*0-14-024953-2*) Viking Penguin.

— Aspects of Aristocracy: Grandeur & Decline in Modern Britain. LC 93-40460. (Illus.). 352p. 1994. 37.50 (*0-300-05981-7*) Yale U Pr.

— Britain in "Decline"? LC 98-84644. (Charles Edmondson Historical Lectures). 62p. 1998. pap. 5.95 (*0-918954-67-3*) Baylor Univ Pr.

— The Decline & Fall of the British Aristocracy. LC 99-22542. 1999. pap. 20.00 (*0-375-70368-3*) Vin Bks.

— G. M. Trevelyan: A Life in History. LC 98-141600. (Illus.). xvi, 288p. 1998. pap. 15.95 (*0-14-026482-5*, Penguin Bks) Viking Penguin.

— History in Our Time. LC 98-86268. 288p. 1998. 25.00 (*0-300-07702-5*) Yale U Pr.

— Pleasures of the Past: Reflections in Modern British History. 1991. pap. 10.95 (*0-393-30749-2*) Norton.

*__Cannadine, David.__ The Rise & Fall of Class in Britain. LC 98-28611. 320p. 1999. pap. 29.95 (*0-231-09666-6*) Col U Pr.

— The Rise & Fall of Class in Britain. 2000. reprint ed. pap. 16.95 (*0-231-09667-4*) Col U Pr.

Cannadine, David, jt. ed. see Blanning, Timothy C. W.

Cannadine, David, ed. see Cunningham, Hugh.

Cannady, Criss, ed. see Felipe, Leon.

Cannady, James. Intrusion Detection. (C). 1999. pap. text. write for info. (*0-201-18386-2*) Addison-Wesley.

Cannain, Tomas O, see O Cannain, Tomas.

Cannam, Helen. Candle in the Dark. large type ed. (Magna Large Print Ser.). 575p. 1997. 27.99 (*0-7505-1164-8*, Pub. by Mgna Lrg Print) Ulverscroft.

*__Cannam, Helen.__ The Chieftain. large type ed. 386p. 2000. 31.99 (*0-7505-1443-4*, Pub. by Mgna Lrg Print) Ulverscroft.

Cannam, Helen. A Clouded Sky. 192p. 1999. 24.00 (*0-7278-2287-X*, Pub. by Severn Hse) Chivers N Amer.

*__Cannam, Helen.__ Family Business. 1999. 25.00 (*0-7278-5448-8*, Pub. by Severn Hse) Chivers N Amer.

Cannam, Helen. First Parish. 224p. 1998. 24.00 (*0-7278-5328-7*) Severn Hse.

An Asterisk (*) at the beginning of an entry indicates that the title is appearing for the first time.

Cannam, Helen. First Parish. large type ed. 336p. 31.99 (*0-7505-1356-X*, Pub. by Mgna Lrg Print) Ulverscroft.

Cannam, Helen. The Highwayman. 24.00 (*0-7278-5393-7*) Severn Hse.

***Cannam, Helen.** The Highwayman. large type ed. 336p. 1999. 31.99 (*0-7505-1427-2*, Pub. by Mgna Lrg Print) Ulverscroft.

— An Honourable Man. 192p. 25.00 (*0-7278-5478-X*) Severn Hse.

Cannam, Helen. The Last Ballad. large type ed. (Magna Large Print Ser.). 1994. 27.99 (*0-7505-0697-0*, Pub. by Mgna Lrg Print) Ulverscroft.

***Cannam, Helen.** Spy for Cromwell. large type ed. 352p. 1999. 31.99 (*0-7505-1442-6*, Pub. by Mgna Lrg Print) Ulverscroft.

Cannam, Helen. Stranger in the Land. large type ed. 1995. 27.99 (*0-7505-0696-2*, Pub. by Mgna Lrg Print) Ulverscroft.

Cannan, Denis, jt. auth. see Higgins, Colin.

Cannan, Edwin. A History of the Theories of Production & Distribution in English Political Economy from 1776 to 1848: 1891 Edition. 410p. 1996. reprint ed. 75.00 (*1-85506-332-8*) Bks Intl VA.

Cannan, Edwin, ed. Paper Pound of 1797-1812. 2nd ed. 72p. 1970. reprint ed. 35.00 (*0-7146-1210-3*, Pub. by F Cass Pubs) Intl Spec Bk.

Cannan, Edwin, intro. The Paper Pound of 1797-1812: The Bullion Report, 8th June, 1810. 2nd ed. LC 67-24748. (Reprints of Economic Classics Ser.). 1969. reprint ed. 35.00 (*0-678-00536-2*) Kelley.

Cannan, Edwin, ed. see Smith, Adam.

Cannan, G. Samuel Butler: A Critical Study. LC 70-133284. (English Biography Ser.: No. 31). 1970. reprint ed. lib. bdg. 75.00 (*0-8383-1183-0*) M S G Haskell Hse.

Cannan, Gilbert, tr. see Chekhov, Anton.

Cannan, Gilbert, tr. see Larbaud, Valery.

***Cannan, Joanna.** And Be a Villain. large type ed. 304p. 2000. pap. 18.99 (*0-7089-5676-9*, Linford) Ulverscroft.

Cannan, Joanna. Death at the Dog. Schantz, Tom & Schantz, Enid, eds. 1999. reprint ed. pap. 14.95 (*0-915230-23-2*) Rue Morgue.

***Cannan, Joanna.** Murder Included. large type ed. 344p. 2000. pap. 18.99 (*0-7089-5670-X*, Linford) Ulverscroft.

— They Rang up the Police. Schantz, Enid & Schantz, Tom, eds. 154p. 1999. pap. 14.00 (*0-915230-27-5*) Rue Morgue.

***Cannan, John.** The Angle: Spotsylvania. 2000. pap. 16.95 (*1-58097-051-6*) Combined Pub.

Cannan, John. The Atlanta Campaign: May-November 1864. (Great Campaigns Ser.). (Illus.). 176p. 1991. 24.95 (*0-938289-05-5*, 289055) Combined Pub.

***Cannan, John.** Burnside's Bridge: Antietam. 2000. pap. 16.95 (*1-58097-035-4*, 970354) Combined Pub.

— The Crater: Petersburg. 2000. pap. 16.95 (*1-58097-052-4*) Combined Pub.

Cannan, John. The Spotsylvania Campaign: May 7-19, 1864. LC 97-31902. (Great Campaigns Ser.). (Illus.). 256p. 1997. 24.95 (*0-938289-47-0*, 289470) Combined Pub.

— The Wilderness Campaign: March-May, 1864. (Great Campaigns Ser.). (Illus.). 240p. 1993. 19.95 (*0-938289-16-0*, 289160) Combined Pub.

Cannan, Stephen J. & Otten, Gerard A. SQL: The Standard Handbook. LC 92-28176. 1992. 29.95 (*0-07-707664-8*) McGraw.

***Cannandine, David.** The Decline & Fall of the British Aristocracy. 2000. 29.50 (*0-8446-7114-2*) Peter Smith.

Cannar, K. Essential Cases in Insurance Law. (C). 1985. 420.00 (*0-7855-4176-4*, Pub. by Witherby & Co) St Mut.

Cannar, Kenneth. Liability Insurance Claims. 600p. 1983. 280.00 (*0-900886-80-3*, Pub. by Witherby & Co) St Mut.

— Motor Insurance Theory & Practice. 410p. (C). 1979. 150.00 (*0-900886-24-2*, Pub. by Witherby & Co) St Mut.

— Motor Insurance Theory & Practice. 450p. (C). 1995. 120.00 (*1-85609-065-5*, Pub. by Witherby & Co) St Mut.

***Cannarella, Deborah.** Powers That Be: Discover the Amazing Powers of the Energies Around You. (Illus.). 120p. 1999. pap. 25.00 (*0-88363-931-9*, Pub. by H L Levin) Publishers Group.

***Cannarella, Deborah & Fournier, Jane.** Engineering. LC 99-30926. (Into the Next Millennium Ser.). 32p. 1999. lib. bdg. write for info. (*1-57103-272-X*) Rourke Pr.

— Exploration. LC 99-27214. (Into the Next Millennium Ser.). 32p. 1999. lib. bdg. write for info. (*1-57103-273-8*) Rourke Pr.

— Medicine. LC 99-25472. (Into the Next Millennium Ser.). 32p. 1999. lib. bdg. write for info. (*1-57103-271-1*) Rourke Pr.

— Sports. LC 99-31161. (Into the Next Millennium Ser.). 32p. 1999. lib. bdg. write for info. (*1-57103-275-4*) Rourke Pr.

Cannarella, Deborah, ed. see Dailey, Nils L.

Cannarella, Deborah, ed. see Verdet-Fierz, Bernard & Verdet-Fierz, Regula.

Cannarozzi, Sam. Part of the Only Of. Mycue, Edward, ed. (Took Modern Poetry in English Ser.: No. 24). (FRE., Illus.). 28p. (Orig.). 1992. pap. 4.00 (*1-879457-25-3*) Norton Coker Pr.

***Cannarozzi, Susan.** Sometimes the Dragon Wins. LC 99-91576. 1999. 25.00 (*0-7388-0896-2*); pap. 18.00 (*0-7388-0897-0*) Xlibris Corp.

***Cannarsa, Piermarco.** Semiconcave Functions & Optimal Control. 2000. 64.50 (*0-8176-4084-3*) Birkhauser.

Cannat, Guillaume & Locoste, Nathalie. Be Your Own Astronomy Expert. (Illus.). 48p. (J). 1996. 14.95 (*0-8069-6131-7*) Sterling.

Cannata, Benedene. New York Judge Reviews, Vol. 1. Millican-Glenn, Cynthia, ed. 540p. 1997. pap. 125.00 (*1-58012-004-0*) James Pub Santa Ana.

Cannata, F. & Ueberall, H. Giant Resonance Phenomena in Intermediate-Energy Nuclear Reactions. (Tracts in Modern Physics Ser.: Vol. 89). (Illus.). 112p. 1980. 38.95 (*0-387-10105-5*) Spr-Verlag.

Cannatella, David C. A Review of the Phyllomedusa Buckleyi Group: Anura: Hylidae. (Occasional Papers: No. 87). 40p. 1980. 1.00 (*0-317-04840-6*) U KS Nat Hist Mus.

Cannatella, Mary M. & Arnold, Rita E. Plants of the Texas Shore: A Beachcomber's Guide. LC 84-40553. (Illus.). 78p. 1985. pap. 5.95 (*0-89096-214-6*) Tex A&M Univ Pr.

Cannatello, Carmine. Advanced Assembler Language & MVS Interfaces for IBM Systems & Applications Programmers. 2nd ed. LC 99-30833. 848p. 1999. pap. 59.99 (*0-471-36176-3*) Wiley.

***Cannato.** John Lindsay's New York & the Crisis. 2000. 30.00 (*0-465-00843-7*, Pub. by Basic); pap. 16.00 (*0-465-00844-5*, Pub. by Basic) HarpC.

Cannavo, Marleen J. Free at Last: Galatians 5: 1. (Illus.). 1997. pap. 7.00 (*0-9661276-0-9*) Trans Pubns.

***Cannavo, Marlene.** Without Spot or Wrinkle. 192p. 2000. pap. 10.99 (*1-930027-12-5*, 921-024, Pub. by Insght Pub) BookWorld.

Cannavo, S. Think to Win: The Power of Logic in Everyday Life. LC 98-12719. 284p. 1998. pap. text 17.95 (*1-57392-211-0*) Prometheus Bks.

***Canne, Harriet.** Be My Angel. LC 98-52825. 1999. pap. 11.99 (*0-8163-1708-9*) Pacific Pr Pub Assn.

Cannelin, K. Finnish-Swedish Dictionary: Suomi-Ruotsi Suursanakirja. 4th ed. (FIN & SWE.). 1141p. 1986. 195.00 (*0-8288-1078-8*, M12069) Fr & Eur.

Cannell, Charles F., et al, eds. Experiments in Interviewing Techniques: Field Experiments in Health Reporting, 1971-1977. LC 79-53851. (Institute for Social Research, University of Michigan, Research Report Ser.). (Illus.). 448p. (Orig.). reprint ed. pap. 138.90 (*0-608-18490-X*, 203149100075) Bks Demand.

Cannell, Charles F., et al. A Technique for Evaluating Interviewer Performance: A Manual for Coding & Analyzing Interviewer Behavior from Tape Recordings of Household Interviews. LC 75-320702. 144p. reprint ed. pap. 44.70 (*0-7837-5242-3*, 204497600005) Bks Demand.

***Cannell, D. M.** George Green: Mathematician & Physicist, 1793-1841: The Background to His Life & Work. 2nd ed. LC 00-41938. (Illus.). 2000. write for info. (*0-89871-463-X*) Soc Indus-Appl Math.

Cannell, D. M. George Green - Mathematician & Physicist 1793-1841: The Background to His Life & Work. LC 92-45166. 240p. (C). 1993. text 70.00 (*0-485-11433-X*, Pub. by Athlone Pr) Humanities.

Cannell, Dinah, tr. see Janssen, Paul.

***Cannell, Dorothy.** Bridesmaids Revisited. 256p. 2000. 22.95 (*0-670-89205-X*, Viking) Viking Penguin.

Cannell, Dorothy. Down the Garden Path. LC 85-12520. 288p. 1998. pap. 5.99 (*0-14-026623-2*) Viking Penguin.

— Femmes Fatal. 304p. 1994. mass mkt. 6.50 (*0-553-29684-1*) Bantam.

— God Save the Queen. large type ed. LC 98-14668. 1998. pap. 23.95 (*1-56895-542-1*, Wheeler) Wheeler Pub.

— God Save the Queen. LC 96-25041. 272p. 1998. reprint ed. mass mkt. 6.50 (*0-553-57468-X*, Crimeline) Bantam.

— How to Murder the Man of Your Dreams. 304p. 1996. mass mkt. 6.50 (*0-553-57360-8*) Bantam.

— How to Murder the Man of Your Dreams. large type ed. 428p. 1996. 23.95 (*0-7838-1493-3*, G K Hall Lrg Type) Mac Lib Ref.

— How to Murder Your Mother-in-Law. 288p. 1995. mass mkt. 5.99 (*0-553-56951-1*) Bantam.

— How to Murder Your Mother-in-Law. large type ed. LC 93-43626. 385p. 1994. lib. bdg. 23.95 (*0-8161-5930-0*, G K Hall Lrg Type) Mac Lib Ref.

— Mum's the Word. 272p. 1991. mass mkt. 5.99 (*0-553-28686-2*) Bantam.

— The Spring Cleaning Murders: An Ellie Haskell Mystery. 288p. 1999. pap. 5.99 (*0-14-027615-7*) Viking Penguin.

***Cannell, Dorothy.** The Spring Cleaning Murders: An Ellie Haskell Mystery. large type ed. LC 98-38043. 1998. 25.95 (*1-57490-162-1*, Beeler LP Bks) T T Beeler.

— The Thin Woman. large type ed. 376p. 2000. lib. bdg. 28.95 (*1-58547-008-2*) Ctr Point Pubg.

Cannell, Dorothy. The Thin Woman: An Epicurean Mystery. 304p. 1992. mass mkt. 6.50 (*0-553-29195-5*) Bantam.

***Cannell, Dorothy.** The Trouble with Harriet. (Ellie Haskell Mysteries Ser.). 288p. 2000. pap. 5.99 (*0-14-029182-2*) Viking Penguin.

— The Trouble with Harriet. large type ed. LC 99-88116. 2000. pap. 22.95 (*1-56895-833-1*) Wheeler Pub.

— The Trouble with Harriet: An Ellie Haskell Mystery. LC 99-17376. (Ellie Haskell Mysteries Ser.). 256p. 1999. 21.95 (*0-670-88629-7*, Viking) Viking Penguin.

Cannell, Dorothy. The Widows' Club. 352p. 1989. mass mkt. 6.50 (*0-553-27794-4*) Bantam.

***Cannell, Fenella.** Power & Intimacy in the Christian Philippines. LC 98-24883. (Studies in Social & Cultural Anthropology: No. 109). (Illus.). 275p. (C). 1999. text 64.95 (*0-521-64147-0*); pap. text 24.95 (*0-521-64622-7*) Cambridge U Pr.

Cannell, G. H., et al, eds. Agriculture in Semi-Arid Environments. (Ecological Studies: Vol. 34). (Illus.). 1979. 106.95 (*0-387-09414-8*) Spr-Verlag.

Cannell, J. Secrets of Houdini. 7.95 (*0-685-47573-5*) Wehman.

Cannell, J. C. The Secrets of Houdini. LC 72-93609. (Illus.). 288p. 1973. reprint ed. pap. 7.95 (*0-486-22913-0*) Dover.

Cannell, M. G., et al, eds. Biophysical Research for Asian Agroforestry. 292p. (Orig.). (C). 1991. text 14.00 (*0-933595-32-8*) Winrock Intl.

— The Ecology of Mixed Species Stands of Trees. (Special Publication of the British Ecological Society Ser.: No. 11). (Illus.). 320p. 1991. 110.00 (*0-632-03148-4*) Blackwell Sci.

Cannell, Marian. Caregiver's Handbook. 1986. 46.50 (*0-939273-00-4*) Caregiving Resc.

Cannell, Michael & Wood, Stephen. Incentive Pay: Impact & Evolution. 150p. (C). 1992. pap. 90.00 (*0-85292-490-9*, Pub. by IPM Hse) St Mut.

Cannell, Michael T. & Zimmer, Judith. Free Weights. LC 84-4060. (At Home Gym Ser.). 64p. 1985. pap. 2.95 (*0-685-09965-2*) Villard Books.

Cannell, Richard J. P., ed. Natural Products Isolation: Methods & Protocols. LC 98-16651. (Methods in Biotechnology Ser.: No. 4). (Illus.). 480p. 1998. 89.50 (*0-89603-362-7*) Humana.

***Cannell, Stephen J.** Devil's Workshop. 2000. mass mkt. 6.99 (*0-380-73221-1*) Morrow Avon.

Cannell, Stephen J. The Devil's Workshop: A Novel. LC 99-24082. 432p. 1999. 25.00 (*0-688-16618-0*, Wm Morrow) Morrow Avon.

— Final Victim. 1995. 25.00 (*0-614-96267-6*, Wm Morrow) Morrow Avon.

— Final Victim. LC 96-16243. 380p. 1997. mass mkt. 6.99 (*0-380-72816-8*, Avon Bks) Morrow Avon.

— King Con. large type ed. LC 98-14662. 1998. 25.95 (*1-56895-536-7*, Wheeler) Wheeler Pub.

— King Con: A Novel. LC 96-52531. 432p. 1998. mass mkt. 6.99 (*0-380-72817-6*, Avon Bks) Morrow Avon.

— The Plan. LC 94-35145. 1995. 23.00 (*0-688-14046-7*, Wm Morrow) Morrow Avon.

— The Plan. 1996. mass mkt. 6.99 (*0-380-72754-4*, Avon Bks) Morrow Avon.

— Riding the Snake. LC 97-48564. 416p. 1999. mass mkt. 6.99 (*0-380-80016-0*, Avon Bks) Morrow Avon.

— Riding the Snake: A Novel. LC 97-49674. 416p. 1998. 25.00 (*0-688-15805-6*, Wm Morrow) Morrow Avon.

Cannell, William & Dankbaar, Ben, eds. Technology Management & Public Policy in the European Union. (Illus.). 212p. 1996. text 55.00 (*0-19-829028-4*) OUP.

Cannella, Frank, Jr., ed. Infomercial Insights. rev. ed. 256p. 1995. pap. 29.95 (*0-9645547-0-4*) Cannella Resp.

Cannella, Gaile. Deconstructing Early Childhood Education: Social Justice & Revolution. (Rethinking Childhood Ser.: Vol. 2). X, 224p. (C). 1997. pap. text 29.95 (*0-8204-3452-3*) P Lang Pubng.

Canner, Mark, jt. ed. see Collins, Dana.

Canner, W. H. The Air Transport Industry. (C). 1987. 100.00 (*0-85174-522-9*) St Mut.

— Flight Navigation. (C). 1987. 130.00 (*0-85174-496-6*) St Mut.

Canney, Don L. Lincoln's Navy: The Ships, Men & Organization, 1861-65. (Illus.). 240p. 1998. 49.95 (*1-55750-519-5*) Naval Inst Pr.

Canney, Donald L. The Old Steam Navy Vol. 1: Frigates, Sloops, & Gunboats, 1815-1885. LC 89-13675. (Illus.). 288p. 1990. 49.95 (*0-87021-004-1*) Naval Inst Pr.

— U. S. Coast Guard & Revenue Cutters, 1790-1935. LC 94-33326. (Illus.). 192p. 1995. 49.95 (*1-55750-101-7*) Naval Inst Pr.

Canney, J. C. Health & Fitness in the Martial Arts. (Illus.). 144p. 1992. pap. 14.95 (*0-8048-1861-4*) Tuttle Pubng.

Canney, Margaret, et al, eds. Catalogue of the Goldsmith's Library of Economic Literature, 4 vols., Set. (C). 1983. text 550.00 (*0-485-15016-6*, Pub. by Athlone Pr) Humanities.

— Catalogue of the Goldsmith's Library of Economic Literature, Vol. 2. 772p. (C). 1975. text 160.00 (*0-485-15015-8*) Humanities.

— Catalogue of the Goldsmith's Library of Economic Literature, Vol. 4. 449p. (C). 1983. text 190.00 (*0-485-15013-1*) Humanities.

— Catalogue of the Goldsmith's Library of Economic Literature Vol. 3: Additions to Printed Books 1840 Periodicals & Manuscripts. (C). 1982. text 160.00 (*0-485-15012-3*, Pub. by Athlone Pr) Humanities.

Canney, Robert S. Early Marriages of Strafford County New Hampshire, Supplement 1630-1870. LC 98-103374. iv, 245p. 1997. pap. 21.00 (*0-7884-0681-7*, C055) Heritage Bk.

— The Early Marriages of Strafford County, New Hampshire 1630-1850. 678p. (Orig.). 1991. pap. 39.50 (*1-55613-477-0*) Heritage Bk.

— The Early Marriages of Strafford County, NH, 1630-1860. rev. ed. LC 98-138558. 1766p. (Orig.). 1998. pap. 70.00 (*0-7884-0158-0*, C059) Heritage Bk.

Cannie, Joan K. & Caplin, Donald. Keeping Customers for Life. 288p. 1992. 14.95 (*0-8144-7812-3*) AMACOM.

Canniff, Kiki. NW Free/Historic Places OR/WA: The Best Free Historic Attractions in Oregon & Washington. 189p. 1995. pap. 5.95 (*0-941361-13-6*, KFH1) F Amato Pubns.

— The NW Golfer. rev. ed. 254p. 1996. pap. 9.95 (*0-941361-12-8*, KNWG) F Amato Pubns.

Canniff, Wendy J. Perfect Paper Beads. (Illus.). 16p. (J). (gr. 4-7). 1994. pap. 6.95 (*0-8167-3492-5*) Troll Communs.

Cannin, Jo-Ann, ed. see Kimbley, Laurel.

Canning. Self Discipline, No. 6. LC 96-49486. (Adventures from the Book of Virtues). (Illus.). 24p. (J). 1997. 3.25 (*0-689-81278-7*) S&S Childrens.

Canning, B. W. Raise the Speed, Reduce the Errors. (Pitman Secretarial Science Ser.). 96p. 1975. pap. 14.55 (*0-8464-0782-5*) Beekman Pubs.

Canning, Charlotte. Feminist Theaters in the U. S. A. Staging Women's Experience. LC 95-12132. (Gender & Performance Ser.). (Illus.). 288p. (C). 1995. pap. 25.99 (*0-415-09805-X*) Routledge.

— Feminist Theaters in the U. S. A. Staging Women's Experience. LC 95-12132. (Gender & Performance Ser.). (Illus.). 288p. (C). (gr. 13). 1995. 85.00 (*0-415-09804-1*) Routledge.

Canning, Elizabeth U. & Lom, Jiri. The Microsporida of Vertebrates. 1986. text 136.00 (*0-12-158790-8*) Acad Pr.

Canning, George & Frere, John H. Poetry of the Anti-Jacobin. LC 91-3943. 260p. 1991. reprint ed. 48.00 (*1-85477-067-5*) Continuum.

Canning House Library Editors. Catalogues of the Canning House Library: Author & Subject Catalogues, 2 pts. Incl. Pt. 2. Luso-Brazilian Catalogues. 1973. lib. bdg., suppl. ed. 120.00 write for info. (*0-318-52342-6*, G K Hall & Co) Mac Lib Ref.

Canning, Jane, jt. auth. see Cockcroft, James D.

Canning, Jane Carolina, jt. ed. see Cockcroft, James D.

Canning, Jeff & Buxton, Wally. History of the Tarrytowns: Westchester County New York, from Ancient Times to the Present. LC 75-22042. (Illus.). 348p. 1993. reprint ed. 24.95 (*0-916346-14-5*) Purple Mnt Pr.

Canning, Jeremiah W., ed. Values in an Age of Confrontation: A Symposium Sponsored by the Religion in Education Foundation. LC 72-109054. (Studies of the Person). 216p. reprint ed. pap. 67.00 (*0-608-10326-8*, 205523900011) Bks Demand.

Canning, John, ed. One Hundred Great Modern Lives. 36.95 (*0-88411-286-1*) Amereon Ltd.

Canning, John B. The Economics of Accountancy: A Critical Analysis of Accounting Theory. Brief, Richard P., ed. LC 77-16723. (Development of Contemporary Accounting Thought Ser.). 1980. reprint ed. lib. bdg. 35.95 (*0-405-10948-2*) Ayer.

Canning, Joseph. A History of Medieval Political Thought, 300-1450. LC 96-10821. 272p. (C). 1996. pap. 24.99 (*0-415-01350-X*) Routledge.

Canning, Kathleen. Languages of Labor & Gender: Female Factory Work in Germany, 1850-1914. LC 96-793. (Illus.). 352p. 1996. text 45.00 (*0-8014-3123-9*) Cornell U Pr.

Canning, Linda, jt. auth. see Francis, Peter.

Canning, Miles B., ed. Ready, Aim, Hire! How to Master the Hiring Process. (Illus.). 224p. (Orig.). 1992. pap. 19.95 (*0-9632704-0-0*) PerSysCo.

Canning, Nancy, compiled by. A Glenn Gould Catalog. 50. LC 92-24263. (Discographies Ser.: No. 50). 272p. 1992. lib. bdg. 55.00 (*0-313-27412-6*, CGC, Greenwood Pr) Greenwood.

Canning, Peter. Paramedic. 1998. mass mkt. 6.99 (*0-8041-1614-8*) Ivy Books.

— Paramedic: On the Front Lines of Medicine. LC 97-7397. 320p. 1997. 24.00 (*0-449-91276-0*) Fawcett.

***Canning, Peter.** Rescue 471: A Paramedic's Stories. 2000. mass mkt. 6.99 (*0-8041-1882-5*) Ivy Books.

Canning, Ray R. My Continuing Quest: Sociological Perspectives on Mormonism. Larson, Stan, ed. LC 96-29378. 160p. 1996. text 12.95 (*0-9634732-4-7*) Freethinker.

***Canning, Richard.** Gay Fiction Speaks: Conversations with Gay Novelists. 2001. pap. 18.95 (*0-231-11695-0*); text 49.50 (*0-231-11694-2*) Col U Pr.

Canning, Richard G. The Tuesday/Thursday Club. 217p. 1999. pap. 14.95 (*0-7414-0062-6*) Buy Books.

Canning, Shelagh. Adventures from the Book of Virtues, No. 5. LC 96-37542. (Illus.). 24p. (J). (ps-2). 1997. 3.25 (*0-689-81277-9*) S&S Childrens.

— Becoming a Witch. (Sabrina, the Teenage Witch Ser.: No. 1). (J). (gr. 2-4). 1998. pap. 3.99 (*0-689-82123-9*, Simon Spot) Litle Simon.

— Caring. LC 98-48389. (Doing the Right Thing Ser.). 32p. 1999. lib. bdg. write for info. (*1-55916-235-X*) Rourke Bk Co.

— Friendship, No. 7. LC 96-37541. (Adventures from the Book of Virtues). (Illus.). 24p. (J). (ps-2). 1997. 3.25 (*0-689-81279-5*) S&S Childrens.

— Horses & Ponies. (Illus.). 1997. pap. 2.25 (*1-56293-932-7*, McClanahan Book) Learn Horizon.

— Just Be Nice... And Get Ready for Bed. LC 96-77297. (Super Shape Bks.). (Illus.). (J). 1997. pap. text 3.29 (*0-307-10062-6*, 10062, Goldn Books) Gldn Bks Pub Co.

— Loyalty. (Illus.). 1997. pap. 3.25 (*0-614-27577-6*) S&S Childrens.

— Loyalty, Bk. 8. LC 96-29809. (Adventures from the Book of Virtues). (Illus.). 24p. (J). 1997. 3.25 (*0-689-81280-9*) S&S Childrens.

— Perserverence. (Adventures from the Book of Virtues). (J). 1997. pap. 3.25 (*0-689-81282-5*) Litle Simon.

— Respect. (Adventures from the Book of Virtues). (J). 1997. pap. text 3.25 (*0-689-81281-7*) Litle Simon.

— Self-Discipline & Loyalty. (Adventures from the Book of Virtues Ser.). (Illus.). (J). (ps-2). 1997. pap. 3.25 (*0-614-29076-7*) Aladdin.

— The Turkey Saves the Day. LC 97-228494. (Big Shape Bks.). (Illus.). (J). (ps-2). 1997. pap. 3.95 (*0-8167-4302-9*, Whistlstop) Troll Communs.

— Work & Friendship. (Adventures from the Book of Virtues Ser.). (Illus.). (J). (ps-2). 1997. pap. 3.25 (*0-614-29075-9*) Aladdin.

— Work, Self-Discipline, Friendship. (Illus.). 1997. pap. 3.25 (*0-614-27576-8*) S&S Childrens.

Canning, Victor. Birds of a Feather. large type ed. 304p. 1986. 27.99 (*0-7089-1428-4*) Ulverscroft.

— The Crimson Chalice. large type ed. 380p. 1980. 27.99 (*0-7089-0543-9*) Ulverscroft.

— The Immortal Wound. large type ed. 372p. 1981. 27.99 (*0-7089-0600-1*) Ulverscroft.

— Memory Boy. large type ed. Orig. Title: The Boy on Platform One. 320p. 1983. 27.99 (*0-7089-0926-4*) Ulverscroft.

— Table Number Seven. large type ed. 321p. 1989. 27.99 (*0-7089-1970-7*) Ulverscroft.

C

Canning, W., & Co., Ltd. Staff. The Canning Handbook: Surface Finishing Technology, Integrated Design. (Illus.). 1060p. 1982. 69.95 (*0-419-12900-6*, NO. 5031, E & FN Spon) Routledge.

Canning, Whitt. Doak Walker: More Than a Hero. limited ed. Jenkins, Dan, ed. (Texas College Football Legends Ser.). (Illus.). 160p. 1997. 99.95 (*1-57028-175-0*, Mstrs Pr) NTC Contemp Pub Co.

— Sam Baugh: Best There Ever Was. limited ed. Jenkins, Dan, ed. (Texas College Football Legends Ser.). (Illus.). 160p. 1997. 99.95 (*1-57028-174-2*, Mstrs Pr) NTC Contemp Pub Co.

Cannistraci, David. Apostles & the Emerging Apostolic Movement: A Biblical Look at Apostleship & How God is Using It to Bless His Church Today. 1998. pap. 11.99 (*0-8307-2338-2*, Renew) Gospel Lght.

***Cannistraci, David.** God's Vision for Your Church. Durham, Ron, ed. LC 99-49021. 2000. pap. 12.99 (*0-8307-2515-6*, Regal Bks) Gospel Lght.

Cannistrar. The Western Perspective. (C). 1998. pap. text, student ed. 26.50 (*0-03-045658-4*, Pub. by Harcourt Coll Pubs) Harcourt.

— The Western Perspective. alternate ed. (C). 1998. pap. text 72.50 (*0-03-022208-7*, Pub. by Harcourt Coll Pubs) Harcourt.

— The Western Perspective, Vol. 1. (C). 1998. pap. text 40.50 (*0-03-045644-4*, Pub. by Harcourt Coll Pubs) Harcourt.

— The Western Perspective, Vol. A. (C). 1998. pap. text 36.00 (*0-03-045647-9*, Pub. by Harcourt Coll Pubs) Harcourt.

— The Western Perspective: A History of Civilization in the West. LC 98-72301. (C). 1998. text 90.00 (*0-03-045643-6*) Harcourt.

— The Western Perspective: 1300 - 1815, Vol. B. (C). 1998. pap. text 36.00 (*0-03-045648-7*, Pub. by Harcourt Coll Pubs) Harcourt.

— The Western Perspective: 1789 - Present, Vol. C. (C). 1998. pap. text 51.50 (*0-03-045763-7*) Harcourt.

— The Western Perspective since 1500, Vol. 2. (C). 1998. pap. text 40.50 (*0-03-045649-5*, Pub. by Harcourt Coll Pubs) Harcourt.

Cannistraro. Benito Mussolini. 2000. 30.00 (*0-06-019394-8*); 17.00 (*0-06-093208-2*) HarpC.

***Cannistraro, Philip V.** Blackshirts in Little Italy: Italian Americans & Fascism: 1921-1929. LC 99-26528. (VIA Folios Ser.: Vol. 17). 115p. 1999. pap. 12.00 (*1-884419-27-5*, Pub. by Bordighera) SPD-Small Pr Dist.

Cannistraro, Philip V., ed. Historical Dictionary of Fascist Italy. LC 81-4493. (Illus.). 657p. 1982. lib. bdg. 85.00 (*0-313-21317-8*, CFA/, Greenwood Pr) Greenwood.

Cannito, Michael P., et al. Neuromotor Speech Disorders: Nature, Assessment, & Management. LC 97-33161. 1997. 44.95 (*1-55766-326-2*) P H Brookes.

Cannito, Michael P., jt. ed. see Vogel, Deanie.

Cannizzo, Jeanne. Into the Heart of Africa. (Illus.). 96p. 1989. pap. 19.95 (*0-88854-350-6*) U of Wash Pr.

Cannizzo, Karen, ed. see Amidei, Kathie, et al.

Cannizzo, Karen, ed. see Dotterweich, Kass P.

Cannizzo, Karen, ed. see Givens, Steve.

Cannizzo, Karen, ed. see Howard, Patrick.

Cannizzo, Karen, ed. see Olla, Debbie.

Cannizzo, Karen, ed. see Symonette, Craig.

***Cannold, Leslie.** The Abortion Myth: Feminism, Morality & the Hard Choices Women Make. LC 99-34374. 208p. 2000. 25.00 (*0-8195-6377-3*, Wesleyan Univ Pr) U Pr of New Eng.

***Cannon.** CCNA Guide to Cisco Routing. (C). 2000. pap., lab manual ed. 16.50 (*0-619-01553-5*) Course Tech.

— CCNA Test Prep. (Networking Ser.). (C). 2000. text 45.00 (*0-619-01574-8*) Course Tech.

Cannon. Lab Manual for Cisco Networking Fundamentals. (Networking Ser.). (C). 1999. pap. text 14.00 (*0-619-00091-0*) Course Tech.

***Cannon.** Mcse Guide to MS Windows 2000 Networking. (Networking Ser.). (C). 2000. pap. 45.00 (*0-619-01645-0*) Course Tech.

— Official Negligence. 2000. pap. 18.00 (*0-8133-6818-9*, Pub. by Westview) HarpC.

— Parliamentary Reform 1640-1832. 352p. 1994. 61.95 (*0-7512-0271-1*) Ashgate Pub Co.

Cannon. Understanding Solid State Electronics. 5th ed. 307p. (C). 1997. pap. text 21.40 (*0-13-649088-3*) P-H.

Cannon & Ball. Christianity for Beginners. 13.95 (*0-340-62146-X*, Pub. by Hodder & Stought Ltd) Trafalgar.

Cannon, jt. auth. see Elich.

Cannon, jt. auth. see Loveday.

Cannon, A. E. Great-Granny Rose & the Family Christmas Tree. LC 96-8466. (Illus.). 32p. (J). (ps-3). 1996. 13.95 (*1-57345-118-5*) Deseret Bk.

— Sam's Gift. LC 97-36739. 97p. (J). 1997. pap. 7.95 (*1-57345-289-0*, Shadow Mount) Deseret Bk.

— Shadow Brothers. 1992. mass mkt. 3.99 (*0-440-80328-4*) Bantam.

— Shadow Brothers. 192p. (YA). 1992. mass mkt. 3.99 (*0-440-21167-0*) Dell.

— Shadow Brothers. 1990. 9.09 (*0-606-00748-2*, Pub. by Turtleback) Demco.

Cannon, A.E. Amazing Gracie. 1991. 9.60 (*0-606-05115-5*, Pub. by Turtleback) Demco.

Cannon, Alexander. The Invisible Influence: A Story of the Mystic Orient with Great Truths Which Can Never Die. 168p. 1996. reprint ed. pap. 16.95 (*1-56459-584-6*) Kessinger Pub.

— Powers That Be (1935) 210p. 1998. reprint ed. pap. 19.95 (*0-7661-0376-5*) Kessinger Pub.

— The Science of Hypnotism (1936) 115p. 1998. reprint ed. pap. 14.95 (*0-7661-0127-4*) Kessinger Pub.

Cannon-Alfred, C., jt. auth. see Alfred, J. Tyrone.

Cannon, Alice. Sexuality Gods Gift. 1993. pap. text 7.99 (*0-8054-9968-7*) Broadman.

Cannon, Almon B. Cannon: Descendants of Samuel (Carnahan) Cannon of Ulster, Ireland, & Blandford, Massachusetts. (Illus.). 168p. 1997. reprint ed. pap. 26.50 (*0-8328-7835-9*); reprint ed. lib. bdg. 36.50 (*0-8328-7834-0*) Higginson Bk Co.

Cannon, Angus M., jt. auth. see Cannon, Martha H.

Cannon, Ann. The Guardian Lepraclone. LC 95-92713. (Illus.). 32p. (J). (gr. 1-4). 1998. lib. bdg. 14.95 (*0-9649539-1-9*) Star Chaser.

— The Legend of the Lepraclone. LC 95-92714. (Illus.). 32p. (J). (ps-3). 1998. lib. bdg. 14.95 (*0-9649539-0-0*) Star Chaser.

Cannon, Ann B. Somethin's Cookin' Fifty Easy-to-Do Youth Programs. LC 93-42361. (Essentials for Christian Youth Ser.). 112p. (Orig.). 1994. pap. 13.95 (*0-687-39076-1*) Abingdon.

Cannon, Ann B., ed. When God Scrambles Your Plans-- And 49 Other Complete Lessons for Youth Bible Study. LC 96-24114. (Essentials for Christian Youth Ser.). 224p. 1997. pap. 19.95 (*0-687-02599-0*) Abingdon.

Cannon, Ann E. I Know What You Do When I Go to School. LC 96-5219. (Illus.). 32p. (J). (ps-3). 1996. 14.95 (*0-87905-743-2*) Gibbs Smith Pub.

— What's a Mother to Do? LC 97-28908. (Illus.). 170p. 1997. pap. 12.95 (*1-56085-095-7*) Signature Bks.

Cannon, Annie. The Bat in the Boot. LC 95-20849. (Illus.). 32p. (J). (ps-2). 1996. 15.95 (*0-531-09495-2*) Orchard Bks Watts.

— The Bat in the Boot. LC 95-20849. (Illus.). 32p. (J). (ps-3). 1996. lib. bdg. 16.99 (*0-531-08795-6*) Orchard Bks Watts.

Cannon, Anthon S., et al. Popular Beliefs & Superstitions from Utah. Hand, Wayland D. & Talley, Jeannine E., eds. LC 84-5286. 530p. reprint ed. pap. 164.30 (*0-7837-5538-4*, 204531200005) Bks Demand.

Cannon, Ariel & Row, Matthew. Guide to Owning a Pug. (Illus.). 64p. 1997. pap. 6.95 (*0-7938-1894-X*, RE343) TFH Pubns.

Cannon, Aubrey, jt. auth. see Hayden, Brian.

Cannon, Betty. Sartre & Psychoanalysis: An Existentialist Challenge to Clinical Metatheory. LC 90-12993. xviii, 398p. 1991. 45.00 (*0-7006-0445-6*) U Pr of KS.

Cannon, Betty, ed. Gandhi in the Postmodern Age: Issues in War & Peace. LC 84-12720. 105p. 1984. pap. text 7.50 (*0-918062-59-4*) Colo Sch Mines.

***Cannon, Bill.** Treasury of Texas Humor. LC 99-49385. 1999. pap. 14.95 (*1-55622-693-4*) Wordware Pub.

Cannon, Bill. A Treasury of Texas Trivia. LC 96-40199. 224p. (Orig.). 1997. pap. 12.95 (*1-55622-526-1*, Rep of TX Pr) Wordware Pub.

***Cannon, Bill.** A Treasury of Texas Trivia II. LC 99-30025. 1999. 14.95 (*1-55622-699-3*, Rep of TX Pr) Wordware Pub.

Cannon-Bowers, Janis A., ed. Making Decisions under Stress: Implications for Individual & Team Training. LC 98-25041. (Illus.). 447p. 1998. 49.95 (*1-55798-525-1*) Am Psychol.

Cannon, Brian Q. Life & Land: Farm Security Administration Photographers in Utah, from 1936 to 1941. (Illus.). 64p. (Orig.). 1988. pap. 4.00 (*0-87421-132-8*) Utah St U Pr.

— Remaking the Agrarian Dream: New Deal Rural Resettlement in the Mountain West. 195p. 1996. 40.00 (*0-8263-1716-2*) U of NM Pr.

Cannon-Brookes, Peter, ed. The Painted Word: British History Painting, 1750-1830. (Illus.). 140p. (C). 1991. 75.00 (*0-85115-290-2*) Boydell & Brewer.

Cannon, Byron. Politics of Law & the Courts in Nineteenth-Century Egypt. LC 88-14315. 345p. reprint ed. pap. 107.00 (*0-7837-6872-9*, 204670200003) Bks Demand.

Cannon, Carol. Never Good Enough: Growing up Imperfect in a "Perfect" Family: How to Break the Cycle of Codependence & Addiction for the Next Generation. LC 92-43283. 1993. pap. 11.99 (*0-8163-1145-5*) Pacific Pr Pub Assn.

Cannon, Caroline C. & Hare, Elizabeth. Richardsons' Chartbook & Cruising Guide: Lake Michigan. 6th ed. LC 95-179779. (Illus.). 128p. 1995. spiral bd. 69.95 (*0-932647-15-4*, LM6) Rchrdsns Pubng.

— Richardsons' Chartbook & Cruising Guide: 1994 Lake Erie Edition. 4th ed. LC 94-675505. (Illus.). 140p. 1994. spiral bd. 69.95 (*0-932647-13-8*) Rchrdsns Pubng.

***Cannon, Casey.** Simply AIX 4.3. 2nd ed. LC 99-11803. 368p. 1999. pap. 47.00 (*0-13-021344-6*) P-H.

Cannon, Casey & Meyer, Don. Mine Your Own Business. LC 97-38980. 256p. (C). 1997. pap. text 41.99 (*0-13-890757-9*) P-H.

Cannon, Charles D. A Warning for Fair Women: A Critical Edition. LC 73-81080. (Studies in English Literature: No. 86). 241p. 1975. text 58.50 (*90-279-3134-8*) Mouton.

Cannon, Chris. Great Retreats for Youth Groups: Twelve Complete Faith-Building Weekends. LC 94-15086. 1994. pap. 10.99 (*0-310-49161-4*) Zondervan.

Cannon, Christopher. The Making of Chaucer's English: A Study of Words. LC 97-35262. (Cambridge Studies in Medieval Literature: No. 39). (Illus.). xiii, 435p. (C). 1998. 64.95 (*0-521-59274-7*) Cambridge U Pr.

Cannon, Christopher P. Management of Acute Coronary Syndromes. (Contemporary Cardiology Ser.: Vol. 1). 680p. 1998. 125.00 (*0-89603-552-2*) Humana.

Cannon, Christopher P., jt. auth. see Sharis, Peter J.

Cannon, Dale S., jt. ed. see Baker, Timothy B.

Cannon, Dale W. Six Ways of Being Religious: A Framework for Comparative Studies of Religion. LC 95-16047. 402p. 1995. 44.95 (*0-534-25332-6*) Wadsworth Pub.

Cannon, David, jt. auth. see Glover, John.

Cannon, David L. The Legend of Motley Mansion. (Appleseed Books for Children). (Illus.). 96p. (J). (gr. 4-5). 1994. 9.95 (*0-9631028-3-4*) Comm Just Foun TX.

— A Secret Prize in Every Box. (Appleseed Books for Children). (Illus.). 70p. (J). (gr. 3-4). 1993. 9.95 (*0-9631028-1-8*) Comm Just Foun TX.

Cannon, Devereaux D., Jr. Flags of Tennessee. LC 90-7679. (Illus.). 96p. (J). (gr. 6-8). 1990. 15.95 (*0-88289-794-2*) Pelican.

Cannon, Devereaux D. The Flags of the Confederacy: An Illustrated History. LC 94-28637. (Illus.). 128p. 1994. pap. 14.95 (*1-56554-109-X*) Pelican.

Cannon, Devereaux D., Jr. The Flags of the Union: An Illustrated History. LC 93-22570. (Illus.). 96p. 1994. pap. 14.95 (*0-88289-953-8*) Pelican.

Cannon, Dolores. Between Death & Life: Conversations with a Spirit. LC 92-83931. 241p. 1993. pap. 21.95 (*0-9632776-5-0*) Ozark Mountn.

— Conversations with Nostradamus, Vol. 2. rev. ed. LC 92-60547. 357p. 1992. pap. 23.95 (*0-9632776-1-8*) Ozark Mountn.

— Conversations with Nostradamus, Vol. 3. rev. ed. LC 92-60547. 365p. (C). 1992. pap. 24.95 (*0-9632776-3-4*) Ozark Mountn.

Cannon, Dolores. Conversations with Nostradamus: His Prophecies Explained, Vol. II. (Illus.). 345p. (Orig.). 1991. pap. 14.95 (*0-922356-02-5*) Amer West Pubs.

Cannon, Dolores. Conversations with Nostradamus: Revised Edition & Addendum, Vol. I. rev. ed. LC 96-92695. 371p. 1997. pap. 23.95 (*1-886940-00-2*) Ozark Mountn.

Cannon, Dolores. Conversations with Nostradamus Vol. 1: His Prophecies Explained. (Illus.). 322p. (Orig.). 1989. pap. 13.95 (*0-922356-01-7*) Amer West Pubs.

***Cannon, Dolores.** Custodians: Beyond Abduction. LC 98-68365. (Illus.). 556p. 1999. pap. 26.95 (*1-886940-04-5*) Ozark Mountn.

— Jesus & the Essenes: Fresh Insights into Christ's Ministry & the Dead Sea Scrolls. 271p. 1999. pap. text 14.50 (*1-886940-08-8*, Pub. by Ozark Mountn) Assoc Pubs Grp.

Cannon, Dolores. Jesus & the Essenes: Fresh Insights into Christ's Ministry & the Dead Sea Scrolls. 4th ed. 272p. 1992. pap. 14.95 (*0-946551-92-8*) ACCESS Pubs Network.

***Cannon, Dolores.** Jesus y los Esenios.Tr. of Jesus & the Essenes. (SPA.). 320p. 1999. 15.00 (*84-87232-74-4*, Pub. by Luciernaga) Ozark Mountn.

— Keepers of the Garden. LC 92-83930. 287p. 1993. pap. 23.95 (*0-9632776-4-2*) Ozark Mountn.

— Legacy from the Stars. LC 96-67899. 320p. (Orig.). 1996. pap. 23.95 (*0-9632776-9-3*) Ozark Mountn.

— Legend of Starcrash. LC 94-65021. 250p. 1994. pap. 21.95 (*0-9632776-7-7*) Ozark Mountn.

— A Soul Remembers Hiroshima. LC 92-83932. 167p. 1993. pap. 20.95 (*0-9632776-6-9*) Ozark Mountn.

— They Walked with Jesus: Past Life Experiences with Christ. 240p. 1999. pap. text 13.50 (*1-886940-09-6*, Pub. by Ozark Mountn) Assoc Pubs Grp.

Cannon, Dolores. They Walked with Jesus: Past Life Experiences with Christ. 2nd ed. (Illus.). 226p. 1994. pap. write for info. (*1-85860-007-3*) ACCESS Pubs Network.

Cannon, Don L. Understanding Digital Troubleshooting. 3rd ed. LC 91-60987. 296p. (C). 1997. pap. text 25.00 (*0-13-649096-4*) P-H.

Cannon, Donald & Whittaker, David, eds. Supporting Saints: Life Stories of Nineteenth-Century Mormons. (Specialized Monographs: Vol. 1). 12.95 (*0-88494-565-0*) Bookcraft Inc.

Cannon, Donald Q., jt. auth. see Dahl, Larry E.

Cannon, Doran W. Authorship: The Dynamic Principles of Creative Writing. 224p. (C). 1993. teacher ed. 19.95 (*1-883636-12-4*); pap. 15.95 (*1-883636-10-8*); lib. bdg. 24.95 (*1-883636-07-8*) Hannah Hse.

Cannon, Douglas F., et al. How Shall They Hear? A Handbook for Religion Communicators. Slack, R. Thomas, ed. LC 95-68198. (Illus.). 153p. (Orig.). 1995. pap. 12.95 (*0-9646110-0-7*) Relig Public Rel Coun.

Cannon, E. C., jt. auth. see Simmons, G. A.

Cannon, Elaine. Baptized & Confirmed Your Lifeline to Heaven. (J). 1986. 12.95 (*0-88494-617-7*) Bookcraft Inc.

— Boy of the Land, Man of the Lord. 1989. pap. 5.95 (*0-88494-722-X*) Bookcraft Inc.

— Choose the Right. 1996. pap. 3.95 (*1-57008-281-2*) Bookcraft Inc.

— Count Your Many Blessings. LC 95-80567. 1995. 12.95 (*1-57008-192-1*) Bookcraft Inc.

— Eight Is Great. (J). 1987. pap. 7.95 (*0-88494-612-6*) Bookcraft Inc.

***Cannon, Elaine.** Gatherings: Favorite Writings by Elaine Cannon. LC 00-20246. 2000. write for info. (*1-57008-708-3*) Bookcraft Inc.

Cannon, Elaine. Happy Baptism Day. 1994. pap. 1.95 (*0-88494-942-7*) Bookcraft Inc.

— I Know the Scriptures Are True. 1997. pap. 3.95 (*1-57008-342-8*) Bookcraft Inc.

— Love One Another. 1995. pap. 3.95 (*1-57008-194-8*) Bookcraft Inc.

— Mary's Child. 1997. 13.95 (*1-57008-359-2*) Bookcraft Inc.

— Merry, Merry Christmases. 1988. 8.95 (*0-88494-673-8*) Bookcraft Inc.

— Mighty Missionaries. 1994. pap. 1.95 (*0-88494-944-3*) Bookcraft Inc.

— Minerva! The Story of an Artist with a Mission. 1997. 19.95 (*1-57008-377-0*) Bookcraft Inc.

— The Truth about Angels. 1996. 14.95 (*1-57008-289-8*) Bookcraft Inc.

— Women Testify of Jesus Christ. LC 98-70868. 1998. 15.95 (*1-57008-418-1*) Bookcraft Inc.

Cannon, Elaine & Pinegar, Ed J. Called to Serve Him. pap. 12.95 (*1-55517-341-1*) CFI Dist.

Cannon, F. Feud at Sweetwater. 1987. 2.50 (*0-8217-2146-1*) Kensgtn Pub Corp.

Cannon, Frances A. Nutritional Therapy. Petz, Richard, ed. pap. write for info. (*0-318-62235-1*) RAPCOM Enter.

— A Picture Book. Petz, Rita K., ed. (Illus.). (J). (gr. 4-6). write for info. (*0-318-62234-3*) RAPCOM Enter.

Cannon, Frances A., ed. see Petz, Richard A.

Cannon, Frank. Texas Gunsmoke. 192p. 1988. mass mkt. 2.50 (*0-8217-2488-6*, Zebra Kensgtn) Kensgtn Pub Corp.

Cannon, Frank, ed. see Vincent, James E.

Cannon, Garland. The Life & Mind of Oriental Jones: Sir William Jones, the Father of Modern Linguistics. 431p. (C). 1991. text 64.95 (*0-521-39149-0*) Cambridge U Pr.

— Sir William Jones: A Bibliography of Primary & Secondary Sources. (Library & Information Sources in Linguistics: No. 7). xiv, 73p. 1979. 29.00 (*90-272-0998-7*) J Benjamins Pubng Co.

Cannon, Garland, intro. The Collected Works of Sir William Jones, 13 vols., Set. LC 93-3862. 6240p. (C). 1993. reprint ed. lib. bdg. 995.00 (*0-8147-4199-1*) NYU Pr.

Cannon, Garland & Brine, Kevin, eds. Objects of Enquiry: The Life, Contributions, & Influence of Sir William Jones (1746-1794) (Illus.). 176p. (C). 1995. text 45.00 (*0-8147-1517-6*) NYU Pr.

Cannon, Garland, jt. ed. see Pfeffer, J. Alan.

Cannon, George Q. Writings from the "Western Standard" reprint ed. 49.50 (*0-404-01379-1*) AMS Pr.

Cannon, Grant W. & Zimmerman. The Lung in Rheumatic Diseases. (Lung Biology in Health & Disease Ser.: Vol. 45). (Illus.). 576p. 1990. text 205.00 (*0-8247-8211-9*) Dekker.

Cannon, H. Graham. Lamarck & Modern Genetics. LC 75-10211. 152p. 1975. reprint ed. lib. bdg. 55.00 (*0-8371-8173-9*, CALA, Greenwood Pr) Greenwood.

Cannon, Hal, ed. Cowboy Poetry: A Gathering. (Illus.). 192p. 1985. pap. 10.95 (*0-87905-208-2*) Gibbs Smith Pub.

Cannon, Hal, ed. New Cowboy Poetry: A Contemporary Gathering. (Illus.). 176p. (Orig.). 1990. pap. 10.95 (*0-87905-243-0*) Gibbs Smith Pub.

Cannon, Harold C., jt. auth. see Banner, James M., Jr.

Cannon, Harold C., jt. auth. see Banner, James M.

Cannon, Helen L. & Hopps, Howard C., eds. Environmental Geochemistry in Health & Disease: American Association for Advancement of Science Symposium. LC 78-111440. (Geological Society of America, Memoir Ser.: No. 123). 240p. reprint ed. pap. 74.40 (*0-608-13558-5*, 202546500044) Bks Demand.

Cannon, J. P., jt. auth. see Trotsky, Leon.

Cannon, J. R. The One-Dimensional Heat Equation. 1984. 68.00 (*0-201-13522-1*) Cambridge U Pr.

Cannon, J. R., jt. auth. see Hornung, U.

Cannon, J. T. & Dostrovsky, S. The Evolution of Dynamics: Vibration Theory from 1687 to 1742. (Studies in the History of Mathematics & Physical Sciences: Vol. 6). (Illus.). 584p. 1981. 118.95 (*0-387-90626-6*) Spr-Verlag.

Cannon, James. Cost Effective Personnel Decisions. 250p. (C). 1979. 75.00 (*0-85292-253-1*) St Mut.

Cannon, James G. Clearing-Houses: Their History, Methods & Administration. Bruchey, Stuart, ed. LC 80-1138. (Rise of Commercial Banking Ser.). (Illus.). 1981. reprint ed. lib. bdg. 38.95 (*0-405-13638-2*) Ayer.

Cannon, James M. Time & Chance: Gerald Ford's Appointment with History. 528p. (C). 1998. reprint ed. pap. 21.95 (*0-472-08482-8*, 08482) U of Mich Pr.

Cannon, James P. America's Road to Socialism. LC 74-26234. 124p. 1975. reprint ed. pap. 11.95 (*0-87348-417-7*) Pathfinder NY.

— The Communist League of America, 1932-34. Taber, Michael & Stanton, Frederick, eds. LC 85-72188. (James P. Cannon: Writings & Speeches). 439p. (Orig.). 1985. pap. 22.95 (*0-913460-99-0*); lib. bdg. 60.00 (*0-913460-98-2*) Pathfinder NY.

— The First Ten Years of American Communism. LC 73-88411. (Illus.). 343p. 1973. reprint ed. pap. 19.95 (*0-87348-353-7*); reprint ed. lib. bdg. 55.00 (*0-87348-352-9*) Pathfinder NY.

— The Founding of the Socialist Workers Party: Minutes & Resolutions, 1938-1939. LC 82-82052. 395p. 1982. lib. bdg. 55.00 (*0-913460-90-7*) Pathfinder NY.

— The History of American Trotskyism: Report of a Participant. 3rd ed. LC 72-78439. 314p. 1995. pap. 18.95 (*0-87348-814-8*); lib. bdg. 55.00 (*0-87348-815-6*) Pathfinder NY.

— James P. Cannon & the Early Years of American Communism: Selected Writings & Speeches, 1920-1928. 624p. 1992. 22.50 (*0-9633828-0-2*); pap. 14.50 (*0-9633828-1-0*) Spartacist Pub.

— The Left Opposition in the U. S. Writings & Speeches, 1928 to 1931. Stanton, Frederick, ed. LC 81-83236. 446p. (C). 1981. pap. 22.95 (*0-913460-87-7*); lib. bdg. 60.00 (*0-913460-86-9*) Pathfinder NY.

— Letters from Prison: A Revolutionary Party Prepares for Post-World War II Labor Battles. Lavan, George, ed. LC 73-79781. 362p. 1973. lib. bdg. 55.00 (*0-87348-006-6*) Pathfinder NY.

— Letters from Prison: A Revolutionary Party Prepares for Post-World War II Labor Battles. 2nd ed. Weissman, George L., ed. LC 73-79781. (Illus.). 362p. 1973. pap. 21.95 (*0-87348-307-3*) Pathfinder NY.

— La Lutte pour un Parti Proletarien. 58p. 1997. pap. 8.00 (*0-87348-865-2*) Pathfinder NY.

— Notebook of an Agitator: From the Wobblies to the Fight Against the Korean War & McCarthyism. 2nd ed. LC 73-79782. (Illus.). 379p. 1974. lib. bdg. 55.00 (*0-87348-304-9*) Pathfinder NY.

— Notebook of an Agitator: From the Wobblies to the Fight

An Asterisk (*) at the beginning of an entry indicates that the title is appearing for the first time.

Against the Korean War & McCarthyism. 3rd ed. LC 93-84144. (Illus.). 379p. 1993. pap. 21.95 (*0-87348-770-2*) Pathfinder NY.
— The Revolutionary Party: Its Role in the Struggle. 1985. reprint ed. pap. 2.00 (*0-87348-346-4*) Pathfinder NY.
— The Revolutionary Perspective for the United States. 37p. pap. 6.00 (*0-87348-695-1*) Pathfinder NY.
— Socialism on Trial. 2nd ed. LC 73-86630. 192p. 1973. pap. 14.95 (*0-87348-317-0*) Pathfinder NY.
— The Socialist Workers Party in World War Two: Writings & Speeches, 1940-1943. Breitman, George & Evans, Les, eds. LC 75-20719. (Illus.). 446p. 1975. pap. 22.95 (*0-87348-457-6*); lib. bdg. 60.00 (*0-87348-456-8*) Pathfinder NY.
— Speeches for Socialism. Weissman, George L., ed. LC 72-92843. 462p. 1971. pap. 22.95 (*0-87348-198-4*); lib. bdg. 60.00 (*0-87348-196-8*) Pathfinder NY.
— Speeches to the Party. LC 73-86189. 431p. 1973. reprint ed. pap. 22.95 (*0-87348-321-9*); reprint ed. lib. bdg. 60.00 (*0-87348-320-0*) Pathfinder NY.
— The Struggle for a Proletarian Party. 2nd rev. ed. Wright, John G., ed. LC 73-133396. 302p. 1972. reprint ed. pap. 21.95 (*0-87348-260-3*) Pathfinder NY.
— The Struggle for Socialism in the "American Century" Writings & Speeches, 1945-1947. Evans, Les, ed. LC 75-20719. 480p. 1977. 60.00 (*0-87348-550-5*); pap. 22.95 (*0-87348-551-3*) Pathfinder NY.
— Wall Street Enjuicia al Socialismo (Socialism on Trial) 2nd ed. (SPA.). 188p. 1981. pap. 16.95 (*0-87348-617-X*) Pathfinder NY.
Cannon, James P. & Hansen, Joseph. What Is American Fascism? 47p. pap. 8.00 (*0-87348-721-4*) Pathfinder NY.
Cannon, James P., et al. Background to 'The Struggle for a Proletarian Party' 45p. pap. 6.00 (*0-87348-670-6*) Pathfinder NY.
— The Fight Against Fascism in the U. S. A. Forty Years of Struggle Described by Participants. 53p. pap. 8.00 (*0-87348-679-X*) Pathfinder NY.
— The Founding of the Socialist Workers Party: Minutes & Resolutions, 1938-1939. LC 82-82052. 395p. 1996. pap. 20.95 (*0-87348-837-7*) Pathfinder NY.
— James P. Cannon: A Political Tribute. 46p. pap. 7.00 (*0-87348-686-2*) Pathfinder NY.
— Revolutionary Strategy in the Fight Against the Vietnam War. 94p. pap. 10.00 (*0-87348-696-X*) Pathfinder NY.
Cannon, James S. A Clear View: Guide to Industrial Pollution Control. Halloran, Jean M., ed. LC 75-15321. 257p. reprint ed. pap. 79.70 (*0-7837-0325-2*, 204064400017) Bks Demand.
— Coal Conversion at New Jersey Utilities: A Study of the Conversion Prospects & Obstacles at Seven Power Plants. Stryker, Perrin, ed. LC 83-82880. (INFORM Report Ser.). 144p. reprint ed. pap. 44.70 (*0-7837-0326-0*, 204064500017) Bks Demand.
— Converting New York State Utilities to Coal: A Study of the Costs & Environmental Impacts of Conversion. LC TK1005.C22. (INFORM Report Ser.). 45p. reprint ed. pap. 30.00 (*0-7837-0327-9*, 204064600017) Bks Demand.
— The Drive for Clean Air: Natural Gas & Methanol Vehicles. LC 89-20007. 252p. reprint ed. pap. 78.20 (*0-7837-6409-X*, 204638900012) Bks Demand.
— Harnessing Hydrogen: The Key to Sustainable Transportation. (Illus.). 360p. (Orig.). 1995. pap. 30.00 (*0-918780-65-9*) INFORM NY.
***Cannon, Janell.** Crickwing. LC 99-50456. (Illus.). 48p. (J). (ps-3). 2000. 16.00 (*0-15-201790-9*, Harcourt Child Bks) Harcourt.
Cannon, Janell. Stelaluna. 1996. 9.05 (*0-606-13815-3*, Pub. by Turtleback) Demco.
— Stelaluna - Stellaluna. 1996. 16.95 (*84-261-2849-1*) Lectorum Pubns.
— Stellaluna. (J). Date not set. pap. write for info. (*0-15-201953-7*) Harcourt.
— Stellaluna. LC 92-16439. (Illus.). 48p. (J). (ps-3). 1993. 16.00 (*0-15-280217-7*) Harcourt.
— Stellaluna. LC 92-16439. (Illus.). 32p. (J). (ps-3). 1997. pap. 23.95 (*0-15-201540-X*) Harcourt.
— Stellaluna: A Pop-Up Book & Mobile. rev. ed. LC 96-47338. (Illus.). 12p. (J). (ps-3). 1999. 18.95 (*0-15-201530-2*) Harcourt.
— Trupp: A Fuzzhead Tale. LC 94-19765. (Illus.). 48p. (J). 1999. pap. 7.00 (*0-15-201695-3*, Harcourt Child Bks) Harcourt.
— Trupp: A Fuzzhead Tale. LC 94-19765. (Illus.). 48p. (J). (ps-3). 1999. 15.00 (*0-15-200130-1*) Harcourt.
— Trupp: A Fuzzhead Tale. (J). 1998. 12.20 (*0-606-13876-5*, Pub. by Turtleback) Demco.
— Verdi. LC 96-18442. (Illus.). 48p. (J). (ps-3). 1999. 16.00 (*0-15-201028-9*) Harcourt.
***Cannon, Jeff.** Make Your Website Work for You: How to Convert Your Online Content into Profits. 208p. 1999. pap. 19.95 (*0-07-135241-4*) McGraw.
Cannon, Jim, et al. The Contemporary World: Conflict or Co-Operation? 2nd ed. (Illus.). 128p. (Orig.). (YA). (gr. 9-12). 1979. pap. text 23.76 (*0-05-003734-X*, 70092) Longman.
— The Great Powers. 1987. pap. text 16.50 (*0-05-004042-1*, 70095) Longman.
Cannon, JoAnn. Postmodern Italian Fiction: The Crisis of Reason in Calvino, Eco, Sciascia, Malerba. LC 88-45733. 144p. 1989. 32.50 (*0-8386-3346-3*) Fairleigh Dickinson.
Cannon, Joanna & Vauchez, Andre. Margherita of Cortona & the Lorenzetti: Sienese Art & the Cult of a Holy Woman in Medieval Tuscany. LC 97-48436. 1998. 80.00 (*0-271-01756-2*) Pa St U Pr.
***Cannon, Joanna & Williamson, Beth, eds.** Art, Politics & Religion in Central Italy, 1261-1352. LC 99-55000. (Illus.). 208p. 2000. text 78.95 (*1-84014-635-4*, Pub. by Ashgate Pub) Ashgate Pub Co.
***Cannon, John.** The History of the Bronte Family: From Ireland to Wuthering Heights. (Illus.). 160p. 2000. pap. 16.95 (*0-7509-2406-3*) Sutton Publng.
Cannon, John. Samuel Johnson & the Politics of Hanoverian England. LC 94-9429. 334p. 1995. text 65.00 (*0-19-820452-3*, Clarendon Pr) OUP.
Cannon, John, ed. The Oxford Companion to British History. LC 97-27598. (Illus.). 1,056p. (C). 1997. 60.00 (*0-19-866176-2*) OUP.
Cannon, John & Griffiths, Ralph. The Oxford Illustrated History of the British Monarchy. (Illus.). 744p. 1988. 55.00 (*0-19-822786-8*) OUP.
— The Oxford Illustrated History of the Monarchy. LC 97-39075. (Oxford Paperback Reference Ser.). (Illus.). 738p. 1998. reprint ed. pap. 26.50 (*0-19-288073-X*) OUP.
Cannon, John R. The One-Dimensional Heat Equation. (Encyclopedia of Mathematics & Its Applications Ser.: No. 23). 576p. 1984. text 100.00 (*0-521-30243-9*, 30243-9) Cambridge U Pr.
Cannon, Joseph. Pharmacology for Chemists. LC 98-25069. (ACS Professional Reference Book Ser.). (Illus.). 288p. 1998. text 60.00 (*0-8412-3524-4*, Pub. by Am Chemical) OUP.
Cannon, Joseph G. The Memoirs of Joseph Gurney "Uncle Joe" Cannon. (Illus.). viii, 171p. 1996. pap. 10.75 (*0-9654976-0-7*) Vermil.
— Uncle Joe Cannon: The Story of a Pioneer American. (American Biography Ser.). 362p. 1991. reprint ed. lib. bdg. 79.00 (*0-7812-8058-3*) Rprt Serv.
Cannon, Joseph G., ed. Advances in CNS Drug-Receptor Interactions, Vol. 1. 178p. 1991. 109.50 (*1-55938-163-9*) Jai Pr.
***Cannon, K. L.** I Wonder Why? (Illus.). 60p. 1999. pap. 6.95 (*0-9675594-0-5*) K L Cannon.
Cannon, Katie G. Black Womanist Ethics. LC 87-38120. (American Academy of Religion Academy Ser.). 250p. 1988. pap. 16.95 (*1-55540-216-X*, 01 01 60) OUP.
— Katie's Canon: Womanism & the Soul of the Black Community. 192p. 1997. pap. 15.95 (*0-8264-1034-0*) Continuum.
Cannon, Kelly. Henry James & Masculinity: The Man At the Margins. LC 93-30200. 176p. 1994. text 45.00 (*0-312-10405-7*) St Martin.
— Henry James & Masculinity: The Man at the Margins. 176p. 1996. pap. 17.95 (*0-312-16456-4*) St Martin.
Cannon, Lawrence O. & Elich, Joseph. Precalculus. 2nd ed. LC 93-15109. 192p. (C). 1997. pap. text 23.50 (*0-673-46729-5*) Addison-Wesley.
— Precalculus. 2nd ed. LC 93-15109. (C). 1994. text 61.00 (*0-673-46728-7*) HarpC.
— Precalculus: Problem Solving with Technology. 2nd alternate ed. (C). 1996. teacher ed. write for info. (*0-673-97334-4*) Addson-Wesley Educ.
— Precalculus: Student's Solutions Manual. 2nd alternate ed. (C). 1996. pap. text, student ed. 12.00 (*0-673-99971-8*) Addson-Wesley Educ.
Cannon, Le Grand. Personal Reminiscences of the Rebellion, 1861-1866. LC 78-157363. (Black Heritage Library Collection). 1977. 25.95 (*0-8369-8801-9*) Ayer.
Cannon, Lee. Menu Celebrations: Meal Planning for the Family, Every Day of the Year. (Illus.). 416p. 1995. 23.95 (*0-9638568-9-8*) Owl Bay Pubs.
Cannon, LeGrand, Jr. Look to the Mountain. 416p. 1991. reprint ed. pap. 7.95 (*0-88150-215-4*, Pub. by Countryman) Norton.
Cannon, Lester R., ed. see International Symposium on the Biology of the Turb.
Cannon, Lou. Official Negligence: How Rodney King & the Riots Changed Los Angeles & the LAPD. 700p. 1999. pap. 19.00 (*0-8133-3725-9*, Pub. by Westview) HarpC.
***Cannon, Lou.** President Reagan: The Role of a Lifetime. LC 99-88017. 992p. 2000. pap. 18.00 (*1-891620-91-6*, Pub. by PublicAffairs NY) HarpC.
Cannon, Lou. Reporting: An Inside View. LC 77-79691. (C). 1977. 9.95 (*0-930302-12-5*); pap. 4.95 (*0-930302-13-3*) Cal Journal.
Cannon, L.R. & Silver, H. North Australian Sea Cucumbers. 1994. 86.95 (*3-540-14194-4*); 86.95 (*3-540-14193-6*) Spr-Verlag.
Cannon, Lynn W., jt. auth. see Vanneman, Reeve.
Cannon, M. Hamlin. United States Army in World War 2, War in the Pacific, Leyte, Return To The Philippines (clothbound) 440p. 1954. boxed set 26.00 (*0-16-061285-3*) USGPO.
Cannon, Margaret H., compiled by. Index to South Carolina Magazine of Ancestral Research: Volumes I-X, 1973-1982. LC 85-8314. 392p. 1985. 35.00 (*0-87152-408-2*) Reprint.
Cannon, Marian G. Robert E. Lee: Defender of the South. LC 93-415. (First Bks.). (Illus.). 64p. (J). (gr. 4-6). 1993. lib. bdg. 24.00 (*0-531-20120-1*) Watts.
Cannon, Mark, jt. auth. see Stone, Philip.
Cannon, Martha H. & Cannon, Angus M. Letters from Exile: The Correspondence of Martha Hughes Cannon & Angus M. Cannon, 1886-1888. limited ed. Lieber, Constance L. & Sillito, John, eds. LC 89-32696. (Significant Mormon Diaries Ser.: No. 3). (Illus.). 344p. 1989. 60.00 (*0-941214-77-X*) Signature Bks.
Cannon, Max. More Red Meat. LC 98-36215. 112p. 1998. pap. 9.95 (*0-312-19514-1*) St Martin.
— Red Meat: From the Secret Files of Max Cannon. LC 97-42220. (Illus.). 112p. (Orig.). 1997. pap. 9.95 (*0-312-18302-X*) St Martin.
Cannon, Melissa. Sister Fly Goes to Market. LC 80-21120. (Illus.). (Orig.). 1980. pap. 1.95 (*0-937212-01-6*) Truedog.
Cannon, Michael. The Borough. 192p. (Orig.). (C). 1997. pap. 13.99 (*1-85242-383-8*) Serpents Tail.
— A Conspiracy of Hope. 176p. (Orig.). 1996. pap. 13.99 (*1-85242-517-2*) Serpents Tail.
— The Land Boomers: The Complete Illustrated History. (Illus.). 420p. 1995. pap. 39.95 (*0-522-84663-7*, Pub. by Melbourne Univ Pr) Paul & Co Pubs.
***Cannon, Michael.** That Disreputable Firm: The Inside Story of Slater & Gordon. 464p. 1999. 39.95 (*0-522-84787-0*, Pub. by Melbourne Univ Pr) Paul & Co Pubs.
Cannon, Michael J. A Guide to Basic Health & Disease in Birds. (Illus.). 96p. (Orig.). 1996. pap. 23.95 (*0-646-23057-3*) Avian Pubns.
Cannon, Moya. Oar. 48p. 1995. reprint ed. pap. 11.95 (*1-897648-24-3*) Dufour.
— The Parchment Boat. LC 98-102742. 48p. 1998. 24.95 (*1-85235-202-7*, Pub. by Gallery Pr); pap. 14.95 (*1-85235-201-9*, Pub. by Gallery Pr) Dufour.
Cannon, Nancy A. & Cooney, Nancy H. Come to the Table. 64p. 1997. pap. 9.95 (*1-58051-029-9*, LL2029) Sheed & Ward WI.
Cannon, Noreen, jt. auth. see Au, Wilkie.
***Cannon, Otis A.** A Combat Infantryman in World War II. LC 99-96692. 1999. 15.95 (*0-533-13287-8*) Vantage.
Cannon, P. F. & Minter, D. W., eds. The Rhytismataceae of the Indian Subcontinent. (Mycological Papers: No. 155). 123p. (C). 1986. pap. text 31.50 (*0-00-000082-5*) C A B Intl.
Cannon, P. F., et al. The British Ascomycotina: Annotated Checklist. 302p. (Orig.). 1985. pap. text 135.00 (*0-85198-546-7*) OUP.
Cannon, P. H. Pulptime. LC 84-50724. (Illus.). 96p. 1985. reprint ed. 15.00 (*0-932445-07-1*) Necronomicon.
Cannon, P. H., jt. auth. see Eckhardt, Jason C.
Cannon, Patrick. Tolley's Stamp Duties & Stamp Duty Reserve Tax. 150p. 1993. 115.00 (*0-85459-796-4*, Pub. by Tolley Pubng) St Mut.
— Tolley's Stamp Duties & Stamp Duty Reserve Tax. 150p. 1995. 195.00 (*1-86012-071-7*, Pub. by Tolley Pubng) St Mut.
— Tolley's Stamp Duties & Stamp Duty Reserve Tax Sixth Edition. 6th rev. ed. 1998. pap. write for info. (*1-86012-594-8*, Pub. by Tolley Pubng) St Mut.
Cannon, Patrick D., ed. Accessibility Guidelines for Buildings & Facilities, State & Local Government Facilities, & Building Elements Designed for Children's Use. (Illus.). 81p. (C). 1998. pap. text 25.00 (*0-7881-7390-1*) DIANE Pub.
Cannon, Peter, ed. Lovecraft Remembered. LC 98-43006. (Illus.). 489p. 1998. 29.95 (*0-87054-173-0*) Arkham.
Cannon, Peter, ed. see Lovecraft, H. P.
Cannon, Peter W. Flowers of Hawaii. (Viewbook Ser.). (Illus.). 32p. (Orig.). 1996. pap. 6.96 (*1-886229-14-7*) Hawaiian Resources.
Cannon, Peter W., ed. see Lyon, Charles, et al.
Cannon, Phil & DaleCarter, Glenn. Tecumseh, Oklahoma: An Illustrated History of Its First Century. (Illus.). 115p. 1991. write for info. (*0-934188-36-X*) Evans Pubns.
Cannon, Poppy. Fast Gourmet Cookbook. 1981. pap. 2.50 (*0-87980-034-8*) Wilshire.
Cannon, Raymond & Peters & Peters Staff. Business Law of the European Union: A Practice Guide. text 68.00 (*0-8205-2495-6*) Bender.
Cannon, Raymond J., Jr. Calculus for Management, Social & Life Sciences. 2nd ed. 168p. (C). 1991. text, student ed. 20.00 (*0-697-10565-2*, WCB McGr Hill) McGrw-H Hghr Educ.
Cannon, Raymond J., Jr. & Williams, Gareth. Calculus for Management, Social & Life Sciences. 560p. (C). 1988. text 15.63 (*0-697-06993-1*, WCB McGr Hill) McGrw-H Hghr Educ.
Cannon, Richard O., jt. ed. see Panza, Julio A.
Cannon, Robert, jt. auth. see Newble, David I.
Cannon, Robert E., jt. auth. see Ang, Conny.
Cannon, Robert H. Dynamics of Physical Systems. 750p. (C). 1967. 124.38 (*0-07-009754-2*) McGraw.
Cannon, Robert K. Volunteer's for Union & Liberty: History of the 5th Tennessee Infantry, U. S. A. 1862-1865. LC 95-75454. (Illus.). 428p. 1995. 39.95 (*1-877791-06-7*) Bohemian Brigade.
Cannon, Robert L. & Banks, Michael A. The Rocket Book: A Guide to Building & Launching Model Rockets for Teachers & Students Of the Space Age. (Illus.). 240p. 1985. 22.95 (*0-13-782251-0*) P-H.
Cannon, Robin M. Under the Spell of God: Poems for the Lord's Pleasure. LC 95-16896. 72p. 1995. pap. 8.95 (*1-887089-02-0*) Torchlight Pub.
Cannon, Roderick D. A Bibliography of Bagpipe Music. 296p. (C). 1989. 65.00 (*0-85976-024-3*, Pub. by J Donald) St Mut.
— The Highland Bagpipe & Its Music. 280p. 1996. pap. 45.00 (*0-85976-416-8*, Pub. by J Donald) St Mut.
Cannon, Ronald B., frwd. Emerald Coast Review 1989 Vol. I: A Collection of Works of West Florida Writers. 1988. pap. 9.95 (*0-685-47850-5*) W FL Lit Fed.
— Emerald Coast Review 1990 Vol. II: A Collection of Works of West Florida Writers. 212p. (Orig.). 1989. pap. 9.95 (*0-685-40632-6*) W FL Lit Fed.
Cannon, Ronald B., ed. see Temme, Leonard A.
Cannon, Russell, jt. ed. see Whitelock, Patricia.
Cannon, Sara, et al. A Selection of British Paintings. 32p. 1988. 6.00 (*0-945192-00-2*) USC Fisher Gallery.
Cannon, Scott R. Understanding Programming: An Introduction Using C++ LC 96-27896. (C). 1996. mass mkt. 63.95 (*0-314-20410-5*) West Pub.
***Cannon, Scott R.** Understanding Programming: An Introduction Using C++ 2nd ed. LC 00-44458. (Illus.). 2001. write for info. (*0-534-37975-3*) Brooks-Cole.
Cannon, Sean, jt. ed. see Gallagher, Raphael.
Cannon, Sharol. Social Functioning Patterns in Families of Offspring Receiving Treatment for Drug Abuse. LC 75-42602. 1975. 10.95 (*0-87212-040-6*) Libra.
***Cannon, Sharyn.** Prince of Perfect. Wise, Noreen, ed. (Lemonade Collection). (Illus.). 48p. (YA). (ps up). 2000. pap. 5.95 (*1-58584-212-5*) Huckleberry CT.
Cannon, Steve. Groove, Bang & Jive Around. 1998. pap. 8.99 (*1-885478-53-4*, Pub. by Genesis Press) BookWorld.
Cannon, Steve, et al. David Hammons: Rousing the Rubble. LC 91-61578. (Illus.). 96p. 1991. 32.50 (*0-262-03184-1*) MIT Pr.
Cannon, Susan H. An Evaluation of the Travel-Distance Potential of Debris Flows. (Miscellaneous Publication Ser.: Vol. 89-2). (Illus.). 35p. 1989. pap. 4.00 (*1-55791-302-1*, MP-89-2) Utah Geological Survey.
Cannon, Susan W. Where Hearts Gather. 224p. 1999. 16.95 (*1-885620-03-9*) Special Delivery.
Cannon, Taffy. Guns & Roses: A Modern Mystery Set in Colonial Williamsburg. LC 99-42053. 240p. 2000. pap. 12.95 (*1-880284-34-0*, Pub. by J Daniel) SCB Distributors.
— Tangled Roots. Date not set. mass mkt. write for info. (*0-449-14950-1*, GM) Fawcett.
Cannon, Terence. Revolutionary Cuba. LC 77-26587. (Illus.). 368p. (YA). (gr. 9 up). 1981. 16.95 (*0-690-01307-8*) HarpC Child Bks.
Cannon, Teresa & Davis, Peter. Aliya: Stories of the Elephants of Sri Lanka. LC 96-200819. 192p. 1996. 39.95 (*0-646-21408-X*) B Dolphin Pub.
***Cannon, Teresa & Davis, Peter.** Kerala. (Illus.). 256p. 2000. pap. 15.95 (*0-86442-696-8*) Lonely Planet.
***Cannon, Terry.** China's Economic Growth & Transition: Macroeconomic, Environmental & Social - Regional Dimensions. LC 99-89961. 320p. 2000. text 69.95 (*0-312-23217-9*) St Martin.
Cannon, Terry & Jenkins, Alan, eds. The Geography of Contemporary China: The Impact of the Post-Mao Decade. (Illus.). 240p. (C). 1990. pap. 27.99 (*0-415-00103-X*) Routledge.
Cannon, Therese A. Ethics & Professional Responsibility for Legal Assistants. 3rd ed. LC 98-35788. 416p. 1995. pap. 26.50 (*0-316-12762-0*, Aspen Law & Bus) Aspen Pub.
— Ethics & Professional Responsibility for Legal Assistants. 3rd ed. LC 98-35788. xxiv, 424 p. 1998. pap. text 38.95 (*0-7355-0233-1*) Panel Pubs.
Cannon, Thomas C. Survival Routines for Professionals: Moving Toward Corporate Success. (Illus.). 176p. (C). 1988. text 29.20 (*0-13-879271-2*) P-H.
Cannon, Thomas H. History of the Lake & Calumet Region of Indiana, Embracing the Counties of Lake, Porter & LaPorte, 2 vols., Vol. I. Loring, H. H. & Robbins, Charles J., eds. (Illus.). 840p. 1992. reprint ed. lib. bdg. 84.00 (*0-8328-2545-X*) Higginson Bk Co.
— History of the Lake & Calumet Region of Indiana, Embracing the Counties of Lake, Porter & LaPorte, 2 vols., Vol. II. Loring, H. H. & Robbins, Charles J., eds. (Illus.). 827p. 1992. reprint ed. lib. bdg. 84.00 (*0-8328-2546-8*) Higginson Bk Co.
Cannon, Timothy L. & Whitmore, Nancy F. Ghosts & Legends of Fredrick County. LC 79-64285. (Illus.). (Orig.). 1979. pap. 5.95 (*0-9602816-0-6*) Ghosts & Legends.
Cannon, Tom. Basic Marketing: Principles & Practice. 4th ed. (Illus.). 489p. 1995. pap. 37.95 (*0-304-33221-6*) Continuum.
— Corporate Responsibility: Issues in Business Ethics, Governance & Responsibilities. 384p. (Orig.). 1994. pap. 53.50 (*0-273-60270-5*, Pub. by Pitman Pub) Trans-Atl Phila.
— Marketing: Principles & Practice. 512p. 1998. pap. 27.95 (*0-304-70294-3*) Continuum.
— Marketing: Principles & Practice. 5th ed. 512p. 1998. 60.00 (*0-304-70293-5*) Continuum.
— The Ultimate Book of Business Breakthroughs: Lessons From the 20 Greatest Business Decisions Ever Made. 1999. pap. 19.95 (*1-84112-028-6*) Capstone Pr.
— Welcome to the Revolution: Managing Paradox in the Information Age. (Illus.). 320p. 1996. 25.00 (*0-273-62049-5*) F T P-H.
Cannon, W. Dilworth, Jr., ed. Instructional Course Lectures, Vol. 47. (Illus.). 560p. 1998. 100.00 (*0-89203-173-5*) Amer Acad Ortho Surg.
Cannon, W. Dilworth, Jr., et al. Arthroscopic Meniscal Repair. LC 99-10909. (American Academy of Orthopaedic Surgeons Monograph Series). vii, 63p. 1999. write for info. (*0-89203-213-8*) Amer Acad Ortho Surg.
Cannon, W. Roger, jt. ed. see Blum, John B.
Cannon, Walter B. The Mechanical Factors of Digestion. LC 86-10161. 1987. 20.00 (*0-88135-082-6*) Watson Pub Intl.
— The Way of an Investigator: A Scientist's Experiences in Medical Research. LC 65-20089. 239p. reprint ed. pap. 74.10 (*0-608-16738-X*, 202639300049) Bks Demand.
Cannon, William A. How to Cast Small Metal & Rubber Parts. 2nd ed. (Illus.). 176p. 1986. pap. 14.95 (*0-07-157501-4*) McGraw.
— How to Cast Small Metal & Rubber Parts. 2nd ed. (Illus.). 176p. 1986. pap. 11.95 (*0-8306-0414-6*) McGraw-Hill Prof.
Cannon, William B. New Class Politics: The Polarization of America & What We Can Do About It. 138p. 1987. 7.95 (*0-89758-042-7*) Inst Policy Stud.
Cannon, William R. A Magnificent Obsession: The Autobiography of William Ragsdale Cannon. LC 98-55936. 400p. 1999. 25.00 (*0-687-08575-6*) Abingdon.
Cannon, Zander. Replacement God, Bk. 1. 216p. 1997. pap. 19.95 (*0-943151-18-X*) Slave Labor Bks.
Cannongate Staff. Master Weavers: Tapestry from the Dovecot Studios, 1912 to 1980. (Illus.). 144p. 1982. pap. 15.95 (*1-56554-620-2*) Pelican.
Cannoy-Bender, Tammy, jt. auth. see Bender, Robert.
Cannum. Deluxe on Farts. (Illus.). 8p. 1979. pap. 2.95 (*0-89708-032-7*) And Bks.

C

An Asterisk (*) at the beginning of an entry indicates that the title is appearing for the first time.

— On Farts. (Illus.). 8p. 1979. pap. 0.95 (*0-89708-002-5*) And Bks.

Canny, J. F., jt. ed. see Li, Zexiang.

Canny, John F. The Complexity of Robot Motion Planning, 1987. (ACM Doctoral Dissertation Award Ser.). 216p. 1988. 35.00 (*0-262-03136-1*) MIT Pr.

Canny, Nicholas, ed. The Oxford History of the British Empire: The Origins of Empire: British Overseas Enterprise to the Close of the Seventeenth Century, Vol. 1. (Illus.). 554p. 1998. 45.00 (*0-19-820562-7*) OUP.

Canny, Nicholas & Pagden, Anthony, eds. Colonial Identity in the Atlantic World, 1500-1800. (History of Rhetoric Ser.). 303p. 1987. pap. text 19.95 (*0-691-00840-X*, Pub. by Princeton U Pr) Cal Prin Full Svc.

Canny, Nicholas P. Kingdom & Colony: Ireland in the Atlantic World, 1560-1800. LC 87-46309. (Johns Hopkins Studies in Atlantic History & Culture). 159p. 1988. reprint ed. pap. 49.30 (*0-608-00810-9*, 206159800010) Bks Demand.

Cano, jt. auth. see Gomez.

Cano Ballesta, Juan, ed. see Hernandez, Miguel.

Cano, Carlos J., tr. see Henderson, Ann L. & Mormino, Gary R., eds.

Cano, Daniel. Shifting Loyalties. LC 95-13564. 311p. 1995. pap. 9.95 (*1-55885-144-5*) Arte Publico.

Cano, Elena, jt. auth. see Panos, Ingo Sanchez.

Cano, Fray A. Manche & Peten: The Hazards of Itza Deceit & Barbarity. Bowditch, Charles P. & Rivera, Guillermo, trs. from SPA. LC 83-83344. 32p. 1984. pap. 10.00 (*0-911437-02-9*) Labyrinthos.

Cano, Isabel, tr. see Cole, Joanna.

Cano, Jamie, et al. Discovering Learning Preferences & Learning Differences in the Classroom. Stuts, Jacqueline A., ed. (Illus.). 76p. (Orig.). 1995. pap. text, teacher ed. 18.95 (*1-56502-007-3*, 0312G) Ohio Agri Educ.

Cano, Jose L., intro. Antologia De los Poetas Del Veinte Siete. (Nueva Austral Ser.: No. 8). (SPA.). 1991. pap. text 34.95 (*84-239-1808-4*) Elliots Bks.

Cano, Juan, tr. see Cajal, Santiago R.

Cano, Pablo, jt. auth. see Franca, Lourdes G.

Cano, Percy. Una Carta para America Latina: Proyeccion Ecologica Hacia el Desarollo del Area Latinoamericana. (SPA., Illus.). 80p. (Orig.). 1992. pap. 8.00 (*0-9635754-0-6*) Percy Cano.

***Cano, Robin B.** Estamos Aqui Para la Fiesta! (SPA.). 2000. pap. 5.95 (*1-56492-274-X*) Laredo.

Cano, Robin B. Lucita Regresa a Oaxaca (Lucita Comes Home to Oaxaca) Ricardez, Rafael E., tr. LC 98-24323. (ENG & SPA., Illus.). 32p. (J). (gr. 3-6). 1998. 16.95 (*1-56492-111-5*) Laredo.

Cano, Robin B., et al. Ramona Viaja Al Norte (North with Ramona) LC 98-26936. (Tales in Two Languages, LS Ser.). (ENG & SPA.). (J). (gr. 3-6). 1998. 16.95 (*1-56492-254-5*) Laredo.

Cano, Ronnie M. Through the Eyes of Love. 112p. pap. 5.95 (*1-56236-979-2*, Pub. by Aspen Bks) Origin Bk Sales.

Cano, Tony & Sochat, Ann. Bandido: The True Story of Chico Cano, the Last Western Bandit. LC 97-66355. (Illus.). 256p. 1997. pap. 14.95 (*0-9639210-4-5*) Reata Pub.

— Chuck Wagon Heyday: The History & Color of the Chuck Wagon at Work. LC 96-92892. 128p. 1997. pap. 12.95 (*0-9639210-2-9*) Reata Pub.

— Dutch Oven Cooking with Tony Cano. LC 93-90742. 120p. 1993. pap. 14.95 (*0-9639210-0-2*) Reata Pub.

— Echoes in the Wind: Ranch Recollections & Poetry. LC 94-94609. (Illus.). 140p. 1994. pap. 12.95 (*0-9639210-1-0*) Reata Pub.

Cano, Tony, jt. auth. see Sochat, Ann.

Cano, Yvonne, et al, eds. Creating High Functioning Schools: Practice & Research. LC 98-9539. (Illus.). 302p. 1998. text 58.95 (*0-398-06858-5*); pap. text 45.95 (*0-398-06859-3*) C C Thomas.

***Canobbio, Mary M.** Handbook of Patient Teaching. 2nd ed. (Illus.). 2000. pap. text 29.95 (*0-323-01103-9*) Mosby Inc.

Canobbio, Mary M. Mosby's Handbook of Patient Teaching. LC 96-15637. (Illus.). 752p. (C). (gr. 13). 1996. text 26.95 (*0-8151-1537-7*, 24917) Mosby Inc.

Canon. Longman Political Pamplet. (Political Pampheleteer Ser.). (C). 1997. pap. text 8.00 (*0-673-99775-8*) Addson-Wesley Educ.

Canon & Howe, G. E. Stories from The Catechist: Nine Hundred Seven Traditional Catholic Stories Illustrating the Truths of the Catholic Catechism. LC 82-50589. 387p. (YA). 1989. reprint ed. pap. 17.50 (*0-89555-184-5*) TAN Bks Pubs.

Canon, Antonio, jt. auth. see Tarbin, Juan J.

Canon, Bradley C. & Johnson, Charles A. Judicial Policies: Implementation & Impact. 2nd ed. LC 98-34687. 200p. 1998. pap. text 24.95 (*1-56802-306-5*) Congr Quarterly.

***Canon Communications Staff, ed.** 2000 Consultants Directory: A Comprehensive Guide to Medical Device Industry Consultants. 170p. 2000. pap. 10.00 (*1-884551-07-6*) Canon Comns.

***Canon, David.** We the People 2nd ed. (C). 1999. pap. text 54.00 (*0-393-97323-9*) Norton.

Canon, David, et al. The Enduring Debate: Classic & Contemporary Readings in American Politics. LC 97-28414. (C). 1997. pap. text 22.50 (*0-393-97134-1*) Norton.

Canon, David T. Actors, Athletes & Astronauts: Political Amateurs in the United States Congress. LC 89-16765. (American Politics & Political Economy Ser.). (Illus.). 196p. 1990. pap. text 19.95 (*0-226-09268-2*); lib. bdg. 38.50 (*0-226-09267-4*) U Ch Pr.

— Race, Redistricting, & Representation: The Unintended Consequences of Black Majority Districts. LC 99-24134. 1999. pap. text 18.00 (*0-226-09271-2*) U Ch Pr.

— Race, Redistricting, & Representation: The Unintented Consequences of Black Majority Districts. LC 99-24134. 1999. lib. bdg. 50.00 (*0-226-09270-4*) U Ch Pr.

Canon, David T. & Mayer, Kenneth R. Dilemma of Congressional Reform: The Individual Roots of an Institutional Dilemma. LC 98-55277. (Dilemmas in American Politics Ser.). 192p. 1999. text 59.00 (*0-8133-2698-2*, Pub. by Westview); pap. text 17.00 (*0-8133-2699-0*, Pub. by Westview) HarpC.

Canon, Harry J. & Brown, Robert D., eds. Applied Ethics in Student Services. LC 84-82379. (New Directions for Student Services Ser.: No. SS 30). (Orig.). 1985. pap. 22.00 (*0-87589-768-1*) Jossey-Bass.

Canon, Jill. Civil War Heroines. (Illus.). (Orig.). (J). (gr. 7 up). 1989. pap. 4.95 (*0-88388-147-0*) Bellerophon Bks.

Canon, Jill & Archambault, Alan. Civil War Heroes. (Illus.). 48p. (Orig.). (J). (gr. 7). 1988. pap. 4.95 (*0-88388-130-6*) Bellerophon Bks.

Canon, Joel. Heroines of the American Revolution. (J). (gr. 1-9). 1993. pap. 4.95 (*0-88388-173-X*) Bellerophon Bks.

Canon, Lana, ed. see Dees, Mary R.

Canon Law Society of America Staff. CLSA Proceedings, 1987: 49th Annual Meeting. 385p. (Orig.). 1988. pap. 7.50 (*0-943616-39-5*) Canon Law Soc.

— CLSA Proceedings, 1988: 50th Annual Meeting. 371p. (Orig.). 1989. pap. 10.00 (*0-943616-44-1*) Canon Law Soc.

— CLSA Proceedings, 1989: 51st Annual Meeting. 276p. (Orig.). 1990. pap. 9.00 (*0-943616-46-8*) Canon Law Soc.

— CLSA Proceedings, 1992: 54th Annual Meeting. 289p. (Orig.). 1993. pap. 7.50 (*0-943616-60-3*) Canon Law Soc.

— CLSA Proceedings, 1993: 55th Annual Meeting. 304p. (Orig.). 1994. pap. 8.00 (*0-943616-63-8*) Canon Law Soc.

— CLSA Proceedings 1997: 59th Annual Meeting. 440p. 1998. pap. 20.00 (*0-943616-81-6*) Canon Law Soc.

— CLSA Proceedings 1996: 58th Annual Meeting. 536p. 1997. pap. 20.00 (*0-943616-76-X*) Canon Law Soc.

Canon Law Society of America Staff, ed. The Canonical Implications of Ordaining Women to the Permanent Diaconate. 55p. 1995. pap. 7.00 (*0-943616-71-9*) Canon Law Soc.

— CLSA Proceedings, 1980: 42nd Annual Meeting. 252p. 1981. pap. 4.00 (*0-943616-07-7*) Canon Law Soc.

— CLSA Proceedings, 1990: 52nd Annual Meeting. 337p. (Orig.). 1991. pap. 10.00 (*0-943616-49-2*) Canon Law Soc.

— CLSA Proceedings, 1991: 53rd Annual Meeting. 344p. 1992. pap. 8.00 (*0-943616-55-7*) Canon Law Soc.

Canon Law Society of America Staff, tr. Code of Canons of the Eastern Churches: Latin-English Edition. Orig. Title: Codex Canonum Ecclesiarum Orientalium. xlviii, 785p. 1992. pap. 25.00 (*0-943616-52-2*) Canon Law Soc.

Canon, Mary. The Defiant. (O'Hara Dynasty Ser.). 400p. 1988. pap. 3.95 (*0-373-97081-1*) Harlequin Bks.

Canon, Rachel. The Anniversary. 1995. 23.00 (*0-614-96237-4*) Random.

Canonoico, A. & Estevez, O. Advances in Medical Oncology, Research & Education: Proceedings of the 12th International Cancer Congress, Buenes Aires, 1978, 5 vols., Set. LC 79-40032. 1979. 978.00 (*0-08-023777-0*, Pub. by Pergamon Repr) Franklin.

CanoRico, Jose R. Legal Dictionary, English-Spanish-French. (ENG, FRE & SPA.). Date not set. 150.00 (*0-7859-9585-4*) Fr & Eur.

Canosa, C. A., et al, eds. Nutrition, Growth & Development: Proceedings of the International Symposium, Valencia, May, 1973. (Modern Problems in Pediatrics Ser.: Vol. 14). (Illus.). 1974. 85.25 (*3-8055-1757-2*) S Karger.

Canosa, Cipriano A., et al, eds. Changing Needs in Pediatric Education. LC 90-8708. (Nestle Nutrition Workshop Ser.: Vol. 20). (Illus.). 334p. 1990. reprint ed. pap. 103.60 (*0-608-07183-8*, 206740800009) Bks Demand.

Canoso, Juan J. Rheumatology in Primary Care. Kersey, Ray, ed. LC 96-40174. 432p. 1997. text 47.00 (*0-7216-6080-0*, W B Saunders Co) Harcrt Hlth Sci Grp.

Canouts, Veletta, et al. Cultural Frontiers in the Upper Cache Valley, Illinois. LC 82-72482. (Center for Archaeological Investigations Research Paper Ser.: No. 16). (Illus.). xviii, 240p. 1984. pap. 14.00 (*0-88104-004-5*) Center Archaeol.

***Canova, Patricia.** Tarot Sutra: An Intimate Guide to the Secret Language of Sex. 128p. 2000. 30.00 (*0-7894-5966-3*) DK Pub Inc.

Canovan, Margaret. Hannah Arendt: A Reinterpretation of Her Political Thought. 308p. (C). 1994. pap. text 21.95 (*0-521-47773-5*) Cambridge U Pr.

— Nationhood & Political Theory. LC 95-31939. 168p. 1996. 75.00 (*1-85278-852-6*) E Elgar.

***Canovan, Margaret.** Nationhood & Political Theory. 168p. 1998. pap. 20.00 (*1-84064-011-1*) E Elgar.

Canovas Sanchez, Francisco, et al. Historia de Espana Vol. 1, No. 29: La Epoca de los Primeros Borbones: La Nueva Monarquia y su Posicion en Europa (1700-1759) 778p. 1992. 189.50 (*84-239-4837-4*) Elliots Bks.

Canright, D. M. Life of Mrs. E. G. White, Seventh-Day-Adventist Prophet. 190p. 1998. reprint ed. pap. text 12.95 (*0-9664531-0-7*) UT State Installations.

Canright, David. Ships & the River. Cambell, Janet, ed. (Illus.). 32p. (J). (gr. 2-6). 1975. pap. 2.00 (*0-913344-22-2*) South St Sea Mus.

Cansbourg, Yitchok. Sefer Hamafteichos l'Sifrei Admor Hazoken, Vol. 2. (HEB.). 92p. (Orig.). 1981. pap. 3.00 (*0-8266-5302-2*) Kehot Pubn Soc.

Cansdale, Lena. Qumran & the Essenes: A Re-Evaluation of the Evidence. LC 97-214178. (Texte und Studien Zum Antiken Judentum Ser.: Vol. 60). 230p. 1997. 119.50 (*3-16-146719-1*, Pub. by JCB Mohr) Coronet Bks.

Canseco, Maria R. De Diez, see De Diez Canseco, Maria R.

Canseco, Maria Rostworowski de Diez, see Rostworowski de Diez Canseco, Maria.

Cansino, Cesar, jt. auth. see Gellner, Ernest.

Cansino, Cesar, jt. ed. see Gellner, Ernest.

Cansler, Philip T. Twentieth-Century Music for Trumpet & Organ: An Annotated Bibliography. LC 84-20422. (Research Ser.: No. 11). 1984. pap. 10.00 (*0-914282-30-1*) Brass Pr.

Canstantopoulos, E. Stories from Greek Mythology. (GRE., Illus.). (gr. 3-4). 4.00 (*0-686-79632-2*) Divry.

Canstatt, Carl. Die Krankheiten des Hoheren Alters unt Ihre Heilung, 2 vols. Kastenbaum, Robert J., ed. LC 78-22187. (Aging & Old Age Ser.). (GER., Illus.). 1979. reprint ed. lib. bdg. 53.95 (*0-405-11805-8*) Ayer.

Cant. Childrens World English Bk. 3. 1997. pap. text, teacher ed. write for info. (*0-582-30222-6*, Pub. by Addison-Wesley) Longman.

Cant, Bob, ed. Invented Identities? Lesbians & Gays Talk about Migration. (Sexual Politics Ser.). 192p. 1997. 69.95 (*0-304-33555-X*); pap. 17.95 (*0-304-33556-8*) Continuum.

Cant, Bob & Hemmings, Susan. Radical Records: Personal Perspectives on Lesbian & Gay History, 1957-87. 304p. 1988. pap. text 14.95 (*0-415-00201-X*) Routledge.

***Cant, Chris.** Writing Windows WDM Device Drivers: Master the New Windows Driver Model. 568p. 1999. pap. 49.95 incl. cd-rom (*0-87930-565-7*, Pub. by C M P Books) Publishers Group.

Cant, Douglas J. & Hein, Frances J. Approaches to Interpretation of Sedimentary Environments: Selected Papers Reprinted from Journal of Sedimentary Petrology & SEPM Special Publication Nos. 15, 16, 25, 31 & 35. LC 90-121760. (SEPM Reprint Ser.: No. 11). (Illus.). 267p. 1987. reprint ed. pap. 82.80 (*0-608-02975-0*, 206344300006) Bks Demand.

Cant, Jennifer, jt. auth. see Fritz, Anne.

Cant, Malcolm. Marchmont in Edinburgh. 176p. (C). 1989. pap. 23.00 (*0-85976-099-5*, Pub. by J Donald) St Mut.

— Sciennes & the Grange. 250p. (C). 1989. pap. 50.00 (*0-85976-253-X*, Pub. by J Donald) St Mut.

— Villages of Edinburgh: North Edinburgh. 252p. (C). 1989. pap. 40.00 (*0-85976-131-2*, Pub. by J Donald) St Mut.

— The Villages of Edinburgh Vol. 2: South Edinburgh. 80p. (C). 1989. pap. 40.00 (*0-85976-186-X*, Pub. by J Donald) St Mut.

Cant, Malcolm, ed. Yerbury: A Photographic Collection, 1850-1991: Photographs by Four Generations of the Yerbury Family. 200p. (C). 1992. text 120.00 (*0-85976-348-X*, Pub. by J Donald) St Mut.

Cant, R. C., jt. ed. see Aylmer, G. E.

Cant, Sarah. New Medical Pluralism: Alternative Medicine, Doctors, Patients & the State. 1998. 25.95 (*1-85728-511-5*) UCL Pr Ltd.

Cant, Sarah & Sharma, Ursula, eds. Complementary Medicine: Knowledge in Practice. 220p. (C). 1997. 50.00 (*1-85343-351-9*, Pub. by Free Assoc Bks) NYU Pr.

— Complementary Medicine: Knowledge in Practice. 220p. 1997. pap. 20.00 (*1-85343-352-7*) NYU Pr.

Cantabrica. Multilengua Diccionario de Cartas Comerciales en Cuatro Idiomas, 3 vols., Set. (ENG, FRE, GER & SPA.). 972p. 1975. 175.00 (*0-8288-5939-6*, S50102) Fr & Eur.

Cantabrica Staff. Diccionario de la Lengua Espanola Cantabrica. (SPA.). 1736p. 1985. 295.00 (*0-7859-3338-7*, 8422104687) Fr & Eur.

Cantacuzene, Princess. Revolutionary Days: Recollections of Romanoffs & Bolsheviki 1914-1917. LC 76-115515. (Russia Observed Ser., No. 1). 1970. reprint ed. 23.95 (*0-405-03012-6*) Ayer.

Cantaño, Leopold J. Space-Based Radar Handbook. (Radar Library). 686p. 1989. text. write for info. (*0-89006-281-1*) Artech Hse.

Cantaño, R. Whatever Happened to General Practitioners? 268p. 1997. lib. bdg. 75.00 (*1-56072-382-3*) Nova Sci Pubs.

***Cantaño, Ralph.** The Tyranny of the Common Man & the Perversion of American Liberties. 200p. 2000. 21.95 (*1-56311-476-3*) Turner Pub KY.

Cantalamessa, Raniero. Easter in the Early Church: An Anthology of Jewish & Early Christian Texts. 272p. (Orig.). 1993. pap. 19.95 (*0-8146-2164-3*) Liturgical Pr.

— The Eucharist, Our Sanctification. 96p. (Orig.). 1993. pap. 9.95 (*0-8146-2075-2*) Liturgical Pr.

— The Holy Spirit in the Life of Jesus: The Mystery of Christ's Baptism. Neame, Alan, tr. 63p. 1994. pap. 5.95 (*0-8146-2128-7*) Liturgical Pr.

— Jesus Christ: The Holy One of God. 166p. (C). 1996. pap. 39.95 (*0-85439-370-6*, Pub. by St Paul Pubns) St Mut.

— Jesus Christ, the Holy One of God. 172p. (Orig.). 1992. pap. 9.95 (*0-8146-2073-6*) Liturgical Pr.

— Mary, Mirror of the Church. Villa, Frances L., tr. 216p. (Orig.). 1992. pap. 11.95 (*0-8146-2059-0*) Liturgical Pr.

— The Mystery of Christmas. 80p. (C). 1989. pap. 6.95 (*0-8146-1813-8*) Liturgical Pr.

— The Mystery of Christmas: A Commentary on the Magnificat, Gloria & Nunc Dimittis. 127p. (C). 1996. pap. 39.95 (*0-85439-282-3*, Pub. by St Paul Pubns) St Mut.

— The Mystery of Easter. Neame, Alan, tr. 126p. (Orig.). 1994. pap. 9.95 (*0-8146-2129-5*) Liturgical Pr.

— The Mystery of God's Word. 96p. (Orig.). 1995. pap. 7.95 (*0-8146-2127-9*) Liturgical Pr.

— Poverty. Serignat, Charles, tr. from ITA. LC 97-2512.Tr. of Poverta. 96p. (Orig.). 1997. mass mkt. 5.50 (*0-8189-0788-6*) Alba.

— Virginity: A Positive Approach to Celibacy for the Sake of the Kingdom of Heaven. Serignat, Charles, tr. from ITA. LC 95-32603. 124p. (Orig.). (YA). (gr. 10 up). 1995. pap. 5.50 (*0-8189-0745-2*) Alba.

Cantalamessa, Raniero, ed. The Mystery of Christmas Reflections on the Magnificat, Gloria & Nunc Dimittis. 112p. (C). 1988. 39.00 (*0-7855-2321-9*, Pub. by St Paul Pubns) St Mut.

Cantalamessa, Raniero & Board of St. Paul Editorial Staff. Obedience. 78p. (C). 1996. pap. 39.95 (*0-85439-281-5*, Pub. by St Paul Pubns) St Mut.

Cantalamessa, Raniero, jt. auth. see Cordes, Paul J.

Cantalupo, Charles. A Literary Leviathan: Thomas Hobbes's Masterpiece of Language. LC 89-46576. 280p. 1991. 39.50 (*0-8387-5186-5*) Bucknell U Pr.

Cantalupo, Charles, ed. Ngugi Wa Thiong'o. 390p. 1995. pap. 19.95 (*0-86543-445-X*) Africa World.

— Ngugi Wa Thiong'o: Text & Contexts. LC 95-21818. 390p. 1995. 69.95 (*0-86543-444-1*) Africa World.

— The World of Ngugi Wa Thiong'o. 248p. 1995. pap. 16.95 (*0-86543-459-X*) Africa World.

— The World of Ngugi Wa Thiong'o. 248p. 1996. 49.95 (*0-86543-458-1*) Africa World.

Cantalupo, Charles, jt. auth. see Reesom Haile Staff.

Cantalupo, Michael, ed. see Henderson, C. J.

Cantaneo, David. Tony C: The Triumph & Tragedy of Tony Conigliaro. 268p. 1998. pap. text 12.95 (*1-55853-659-0*) Rutledge Hill Pr.

Cantar, Brenda, ed. see Greene, Robert.

Cantarella, Cara, jt. auth. see Slowik, Donald W.

Cantarella, Eva. Bisexuality in the Ancient World.Tr. of Secondo Natura. (C). 1994. pap. 17.00 (*0-300-05924-8*) Yale U Pr.

Cantarion. Civilizacion y Cultura de Espana. 4th ed. LC 98-47161. (SPA.). 490p. (C). 1998. 46.67 (*0-13-096149-3*) P-H.

Cantarow, Ellen, et al. Moving the Mountain: Women Working for Social Change. LC 79-11840. (Women's Lives - Women's Work Ser.). (Illus.). 208p. (YA). (gr. 11 up). 1998. pap. 12.95 (*0-912670-61-4*) Feminist Pr.

Cantarutti, Michael. United States Bar Review Multistate Questions. 500p. (Orig.). (C). 1996. reprint ed. pap. text 39.95 (*1-879563-37-1*) Lexicon CA.

Cantelay, Chuck, des. How Can They Possibly Think Like That? Professional Personality Index Resource Guide. 2nd ed. (Illus.). 1997. 29.95 (*0-9627859-6-2*) Elliott Bay Pub.

Cantell, K. & Schellekens, H., eds. Biology of the Interferon System 1986. 1987. text 278.50 (*90-247-3468-1*) Kluwer Academic.

Cantell, Kari. The Life of a Science: The Development of a New Medicine. LC 98-198486. 239p. 1997. text 15.00 (*981-02-3148-2*) World Scientific Pub.

***Cantell, Margaret.** Teach Yourself Latin American Dancing. (Teach Yourself Ser.). 192p. 2000. pap. 12.95 (*0-8442-2669-6*, Teach Yrslf) NTC Contemp Pub Co.

Cantella, Papa. The Ultimate Italian Sausage Cookbook. Cantella, Tom, ed. (Illus.). 108p. 1995. reprint ed. pap. 12.95 (*0-9649632-0-5*) Papa Cantellas.

Cantella, Tom, ed. see Cantella, Papa.

Cantelon, Hart & Gruneau, Richard, eds. Sport, Culture, & the Modern State. LC 83-143220. 332p. reprint ed. pap. 103.00 (*0-8357-6376-5*, 203573000096) Bks Demand.

— Sport, Culture, & the Modern State: Papers Presented at a Conference Held at Queen's University, Kingston, Ont., Oct. 1979. 315p. 1982. pap. text 15.95 (*0-8020-6493-0*) U of Toronto Pr.

Cantelon House Publishers Staff, ed. & intro. see Bunyan, John.

Cantelon, James. Theology for Non-Theologians. 288p. 1989. pap. 8.95 (*0-02-084280-5*) Macmillan.

Cantelon, Philip L., et al, eds. The American Atom: A Documentary History of Nuclear Policies from the Discovery of Fission to the Present. 2nd ed. LC 91-31676. 392p. (Orig.). (C). 1992. text 49.95 (*0-8122-3096-5*); pap. text 19.95 (*0-8122-1354-8*) U of Pa Pr.

Cantelon, Philip L., jt. ed. see Jones, Arnita A.

Cantelon, Robert L., ed. The Words: The Words of Jesus. (Orig.). 1990. 12.95 (*0-9626942-0-7*); pap. 6.95 (*0-9626942-1-5*) T Catelon Pub.

Cantempre, Thomas De, see De Cantempre, Thomas.

Cantempre, Thomas De, see De Vitry, Jacques & De Cantempre, Thomas.

***Canter, Andrea S. & Carroll, Servio A., eds.** Crisis Prevention & Response: A Collection of NASP Resources. 250p. 1999. ring bd. 40.95 (*0-932955-92-4*, N9908) Natl Assn Schl Psych.

— Helping Clhildren at Home & School: Handouts from Your School Psychologist. 1998. ring bd. 55.00 (*0-932955-95-9*, 6800) Natl Assn Schl Psych.

Canter, Bram D., jt. auth. see Hamann, Richard G.

Canter, D. V., jt. auth. see Alison, Laurence J.

Canter, David. Fires & Human Behaviour. 2nd ed. (C). 1989. 195.00 (*0-86108-126-9*, Pub. by Fuel Metallurgical Jrnl) St Mut.

— Readings in Environmental Psychology Series. 1995. pap. text 106.24 (*0-12-158810-6*) Acad Pr.

Canter, David, ed. Environmental Interaction. LC 75-37077. 374p. (Orig.). 1976. 55.00 (*0-8236-1685-1*) Intl Univs Pr.

— Psychology in Action. (Dartmouth Benchmark Ser.). (Illus.). 340p. 1995. text 77.95 (*1-85521-365-6*, Pub. by Dartmth Pub) Ashgate Pub Co.

Canter, David & Alison, Laurence J., eds. Profiling in Policy & Practice. LC 98-74579. (Offender Profiling Ser.). 280p. 1999. 30.95 (*1-84014-782-2*); text 74.95 (*1-84014-779-2*) Ashgate Pub Co.

C

***Canter, David & Alison, Laurence J., eds.** The Social Psychology of Crime: Groups, Teams & Networks. LC 99-44828. (Offender Profiling Ser.). 344p. 2000. pap. 30.95 (*1-84014-497-1*, Pub. by Ashgate Pub) Ashgate Pub Co.

Canter, David, et al. New Directions in Environmental Participation. 450p. 1988. text 78.95 (*0-566-05570-8*, Pub. by Avebry) Ashgate Pub Co.

— Traditional Vegetarian Cooking: Recipes from Europe's Famous Cranks Restaurants. (Illus.). 192p. 1991. reprint ed. pap. 14.95 (*0-89281-425-X*, Heal Arts VT) Inner Tradit.

Canter, David, jt. auth. see Alison, Laurence J.

Canter, David, jt. ed. see Canter, Sandra.

Canter, David, tr. see Levy-Leboyer, Claude.

Canter, David V., ed. Facet Theory: Approaches to Social Research. (Social Psychology Ser.). (Illus.). 330p. 1984. 71.00 (*0-387-96016-3*) Spr-Verlag.

Canter, David V., et al, eds. Environmental Social Psychology. 1988. lib. bdg. 185.00 (*90-247-3706-0*) Kluwer Academic.

Canter, David V. & Alison, Laurence J., eds. Criminal Detection & the Psychology of Crime. LC 97-6099. (International Library of Criminology, Criminal Justice & Penology). 510p. 1997. text 189.95 (*1-85521-454-7*, Pub. by Ashgate Pub) Ashgate Pub Co.

Canter, David V., jt. ed. see Breakwell, Glynis M.

Canter, John. Aran Song. LC 95-197900. 88p. pap. 8.95 (*1-874700-88-5*, Pub. by Clo Iar-Chonnachta) Dufour.

***Canter, Jonathan D.** Employment Termination Digest. 2000. write for info. (*1-58012-055-5*) James Pub Santa Ana.

Canter, K. F., jt. auth. see Mills, A.

Canter, L. W. River Water Quality Monitoring. (Illus.). 192p. 1985. 106.00 (*0-87371-011-8*, L011) Lewis Pubs.

Canter, Larry W. Environmental Impact Assessment. (McGraw-Hill Series in Environmental Engineering & Water Resources). (Illus.). (C). 1977. text 79.74 (*0-07-009764-X*) McGraw.

— Environmental Impact Assessment. 2nd ed. LC 95-935. 480p. (C). 1995. 108.44 (*0-07-009767-4*) McGraw.

— Nitrates in Groundwater. (Illus.). 320p. 1996. lib. bdg. 75.00 (*0-87371-569-1*, L569) Lewis Pubs.

Canter, Larry W. & Knox, R. C. Ground Water Pollution Control. LC 84-28927. (Illus.). 552p. 1985. lib. bdg. 95.00 (*0-87371-014-2*, L014) Lewis Pubs.

— Septic Tank System Effects on Ground Water Quality. (Illus.). 360p. 1985. lib. bdg. 89.00 (*0-87371-012-6*, L012) Lewis Pubs.

Canter, Larry W., et al. Ground Water Quality Protection. (Illus.). 592p. 1987. lib. bdg. 95.00 (*0-87371-018-5*, L018) Lewis Pubs.

Canter, Larry W., jt. ed. see Clark, E. Ray.

Canter, Larry W., jt. ed. see Fairchild, Deborah M.

Canter, Laurence A. & Siegel, Martha S. U. S. Immigration Made Easy: An Action Guide. LC 88-93057. 620p. (Orig.). 1989. pap. 79.00 (*0-9621876-4-X*) Sheridan Chandler.

Canter, Laurence A., jt. auth. see Siegel, Martha S.

Canter, Lee. Assertive Discipline Administrator Guide. (Illus.). 260p. 1986. 69.95 (*0-939007-25-8*) Canter & Assocs.

— Assertive Discipline Elementary Workbook. (Illus.). 128p. 1992. student ed. 9.95 (*0-939007-48-7*) Canter & Assocs.

— Assertive Discipline for Bus Drivers. (Illus.). 37p. 1987. student ed. 4.95 (*0-939007-01-0*) Canter & Assocs.

— Assertive Discipline for Paraprofessionals. (Illus.). 34p. student ed. 4.95 (*0-939007-06-1*) Canter & Assocs.

— Assertive Discipline for Parents, Revised Edition: A Proven, Step-by-Step Approach to Solving Everyday Behavior Problems. rev. ed. 144p. 1993. pap. 12.00 (*0-06-273279-X*, Perennial) HarperTrade.

— Assertive Discipline Middle School Workbook. (Illus.). 128p. 1992. student ed. 9.95 (*0-939007-49-5*) Canter & Assocs.

— Assertive Discipline Seasonal Motivators. (Illus.). 96p. (Orig.). 1992. pap. 7.95 (*0-939007-47-9*) Canter & Assocs.

— Assertive Discipline Secondary Workbook. (Illus.). 128p. 1992. student ed. 9.95 (*0-939007-50-9*) Canter & Assocs.

— Awards for Reinforcing Positive Behavior, Intermediate Grades 4-6. (Illus.). 31p. 1987. student ed. 5.95 (*0-939007-05-3*) Canter & Assocs.

— Awards for Reinforcing Positive Behavior, Primary Grades K-3. (Illus.). 31p. student ed. 5.95 (*0-939007-04-5*) Canter & Assocs.

— Back to School with Assertive Discipline. (Illus.). 174p. 1990. student ed. 9.95 (*0-939007-31-2*) Canter & Assocs.

— Bulletin Boards for Reinforcing Positive Behavior. (Illus.). 46p. 1986. student ed. 7.95 (*0-939007-00-2*) Canter & Assocs.

— Bulletin Boards for Reinforcing Positive Behavior: Primary Grades 1-3. (Illus.). 48p. 1986. student ed. 7.95 (*0-9608978-9-5*) Canter & Assocs.

— Caring Administrator Positive Resource Guide. (Illus.). 261p. 1988. 69.95 (*0-939007-22-3*) Canter & Assocs.

— Desktop Motivators. (Illus.). 32p. student ed. 5.95 (*0-939007-07-X*) Canter & Assocs.

— Help! It's Homework Time: Improving Your Child's Homework Habits. (Illus.). 48p. (Orig.). 1995. pap. 5.95 (*0-939007-75-4*) Canter & Assocs.

— The High Performing Teacher. LC 94-94161. 110p. (Orig.). 1996. pap. 10.95 (*0-939007-82-7*) Canter & Assocs.

— The High Performing Teacher: Inservice Video Package Leader's Manual. 76p. (Orig.). pap. write for info. (*0-939007-87-8*) Canter & Assocs.

— The High Performing Teacher: Inservice Video Package Video Booklet. 24p. (Orig.). pap. 2.95 (*0-939007-88-6*) Canter & Assocs.

— Homework Organizer. 32p. 1988. student ed. 3.95 (*0-939007-21-5*) Canter & Assocs.

***Canter, Lee.** Homework Without Tears. 176p. 2005. pap. 13.00 (*0-06-273132-7*) HarpC.

Canter, Lee. How to Study & Take Tests. (Illus.). 64p. 1989. student ed. 7.95 (*0-939007-29-0*) Canter & Assocs.

— How to Use the Library. (Illus.). 64p. 1989. student ed. 7.95 (*0-939007-30-4*) Canter & Assocs.

— How to Write a Research Paper Grades 5-8. (Illus.). 64p. 1989. student ed. 7.95 (*0-939007-28-2*) Canter & Assocs.

— How to Write Better Book Reports. (Illus.). 64p. 1989. student ed. 7.95 (*0-939007-36-3*) Canter & Assocs.

— Managing the Morning Rush. (Lee Canter Effective Parenting Bks.). (Illus.). 48p. (Orig.). 1995. pap. 5.95 (*0-939007-73-8*) Canter & Assocs.

— Monthly Citizen Slips. (Illus.). 80p. 1991. student ed. 6.95 (*0-939007-41-X*) Canter & Assocs.

— Parents on Your Side: A Comprehensive Parent Involvement Program for Teachers. (Illus.). 300p. 1991. pap. 14.95 (*0-939007-39-8*) Canter & Assocs.

— Parents on Your Side: Administrator Guide. (Illus.). 310p. 1993. student ed. 69.95 (*0-939007-51-7*) Canter & Assocs.

— Parents on Your Side: Resource Materials Workbook. (Illus.). 128p. (Orig.). 1991. pap. 9.95 (*0-939007-40-1*) Canter & Assocs.

— Plan Book Plus, No. 3. (Illus.). 104p. 1990. student ed. 6.95 (*0-939007-37-1*) Canter & Assocs.

— Positive Reinforcement Activities Grades K-6. (Illus.). 48p. 1983. student ed. 5.95 (*0-9608978-3-6*) Canter & Assocs.

— Positive Reinforcement Activities Grades 7-12. (Illus.). 40p. 1987. student ed. 5.95 (*0-939007-02-9*) Canter & Assocs.

— Record Book Plus. 158p. 1992. student ed. 6.95 (*0-939007-43-6*) Canter & Assocs.

— Succeeding with Difficult Students: Inservice Video Package Leader's Manual. pap. text. write for info. (*0-939007-81-9*) Canter & Assocs.

— Succeeding with Difficult Students Workbook. 144p. 1993. student ed. 9.95 (*0-939007-53-3*) Canter & Assocs.

— Surviving Sibling Rivalry. (Illus.). 48p. (Orig.). 1995. pap. 5.95 (*0-939007-77-0*) Canter & Assocs.

— Teacher's Planbook Plus, No. 1. (Illus.). 1994. student ed. 6.95 (*0-939007-17-7*) Canter & Assocs.

— Teacher's Planbook Plus, No. 2. (Illus.). 104p. 1987. student ed. 6.95 (*0-939007-18-5*) Canter & Assocs.

— Teacher's Planbook Plus, No. 4. (Illus.). 104p. 1992. student ed. 6.95 (*0-939007-44-4*) Canter & Assocs.

— Teacher's Post Office. (Illus.). 64p. 1988. student ed. 7.95 (*0-939007-11-8*) Canter & Assocs.

— Teaching Responsible Homework Habits Grades 1-3. (Illus.). 64p. 1993. student ed. 7.95 (*0-939007-54-1*) Canter & Assocs.

— Teaching Responsible Homework Habits Grades 4-6. (Illus.). 64p. 1993. student ed. 7.95 (*0-939007-55-X*) Canter & Assocs.

— Teaching Responsible Homework Habits Grades 6-8. (Illus.). 64p. 1993. student ed. 7.95 (*0-939007-56-8*) Canter & Assocs.

— What to Do When Your Child Hates to Read. (Illus.). 48p. (Orig.). 1995. pap. 5.95 (*0-939007-84-3*) Canter & Assocs.

— What to Do When Your Child Won't Behave. (Illus.). 48p. 1995. pap. 5.95 (*0-939007-85-1*) Canter & Assocs.

— What to Do When Your Child Won't Study. (Illus.). 48p. (Orig.). 1995. pap. 5.95 (*0-939007-83-5*) Canter & Assocs.

Canter, Lee & Canter, Marlene. Assertive Discipline: Positive Behavior Management for Today's Classroom. rev. ed. 263p. 1992. pap. 14.95 (*0-939007-45-2*) Canter & Assocs.

— Assertive Discipline Parent Resource Guide. (Illus.). 110p. 1985. pap., student ed. 9.95 (*0-9608978-7-9*, 1010) Canter & Assocs.

— Behavior Management in the Middle School Classroom: A Teacher's Guide to Meeting the Special Challenges of Early Adolescents. 149p. (Orig.). 1996. pap. text 14.95 (*1-57271-003-9*) Canter & Assocs.

— Couch Potato Kids: Teaching Kids to Turn off the TV & Tune in to Fun. (Illus.). 48p. (Orig.). 1996. pap. 5.95 (*0-939007-76-2*) Canter & Assocs.

— No More Bedtime Battles. (Lee Canter Effective Parenting Bks.). (Illus.). 48p. (Orig.). 1996. pap. 5.95 (*0-939007-78-9*) Canter & Assocs.

— Succeeding with Difficult Students: New Strategies for Reaching Your Most Challenging Students. 255p. (Orig.). pap. 14.95 (*0-939007-52-5*) Canter & Assocs.

— Winning the Chores Wars: How to Get Your Child to Do Household Chores. (Lee Canter Effective Parenting Bks.). (Illus.). 48p. (Orig.). 1996. pap. 5.95 (*0-939007-74-6*) Canter & Assocs.

Canter, Lee & Garrison, Ron. Scared or Prepared: Preventing Conflict & Violence in Your Classroom. 125p. (Orig.). 1994. pap. text 10.95 (*0-939007-97-5*) Canter & Assocs.

Canter, Lee & Hausner, Lee. Homework Without Tears: A Parent's Guide for Motivating Children to Do Homework & to Succeed in School. (Illus.). 157p. (Orig.). 1987. pap. 10.95 (*0-939007-12-6*) Canter & Assocs.

— Homework Without Tears for Parents (Tareas Escolares Sin Lagrimas) (SPA., Illus.). 169p. (Orig.). 1990. pap. 10.95 (*0-939007-38-X*) Canter & Assocs.

Canter, Lee & Peterson, Katia. Teaching Students to Get Along: Reducing Conflict & Increasing Corporation in K-6 Classrooms. LC 95-69590. 166p. 1996. pap. text 14.95 (*0-939007-99-1*) Canter & Assocs.

Canter-Lund, Hilda & Lund, J. W. Freshwater Algae: Their Microscopic World Explored. (Illus.). 360p. 1995. 130.00 (*0-948737-25-5*, Pub. by Biopress) Balogh.

Canter, Marlene. Teacher's Plan Book Plus, Vol. 6 (Illus.). 104p. 1998. pap. text 6.95 (*1-57271-019-5*) Canter & Assocs.

Canter, Marlene, jt. auth. see Canter, Lee.

Canter, Marlene, ed. see Rueben, Steven C.

Canter, Miriam. Dazzling Desserts: Over 100 Delicious Recipes. (Illus.). 40p. 1983. pap. 1.00 (*0-94106-08-0*) Penfield.

Canter, P., et al. Beyond TV Dinners: Three Levels of Recipes for Visually Handicapped Cooks. large type ed. 214p. 1979. reprint ed. 31.30 (*0-317-01874-4*, 4-02470-00) Am Printing Hse.

Canter, Patrick J., ed. see Good, Anthony.

Canter, Sandra & Canter, David, eds. Psychology in Practice: Perspectives on Professional Psychology. LC 82-2733. (Illus.). 369p. reprint ed. pap. 114.40 (*0-8357-7550-X*, 203627300001) Bks Demand.

Canter, Sandra, jt. auth. see Wilkinson, Jill.

Canter Staff. First Class Teacher: Success Strategies for New Teachers. 239p. 1998. 19.95 (*1-57271-028-4*) Canter & Assocs.

Canter, Stan, ed. see Dodd, Ed & Elrod, Jack.

Canter, Stan, ed. see Houk, Rose.

Canter, W. Horace & D'Angelo, Jimmy. Jimmy D'Angelo & Myrtle Beach Golf. LC 91-76705. (Illus.). 220p. 1992. pap. 9.95 (*0-937866-31-8*) Atlantic Pub Co.

Cantera, Jorge, jt. ed. see Carolina Hospital Staff.

Canterbery, E. Ray. Literate Economist: A Brief History of Economics. 2nd ed. 1999. pap. text 28.00 (*981-02-3849-5*) World Scientific Pub.

— Wall Street Capitalism: The Theory of the Bondholding Class. 210p. 1999. 36.00 (*981-02-3850-9*); pap. 18.00 (*981-02-3851-7*) World Scientific Pub.

***Canterbery, E.R.** Literate Economist: A Brief History of Economics. 2nd ed. 224p. 1999. 52.00 (*981-02-3848-7*) World Scientific Pub.

Canterbury. Making of Economics. 1976. pap. 10.50 (*0-534-00429-6*) Thomson Learn.

Canterbury, Gloria, jt. auth. see Parra, Mario.

Canterbury, Gloria, jt. illus. see Parra, Mario.

Canterbury, Janice L. Pay-As-You-Throw: Lessons Learned about Unit Pricing of Municipal Solid Waste. 86p. 1996. reprint ed. pap. text 30.00 (*0-7881-3175-3*) DIANE Pub.

Canterbury, Patricia E. The Secret of St. Gabriel's Tower. 117p. (J). (gr. 3-6). 1998. pap. 5.99 (*0-9639147-6-6*) ReGeJe Press.

Canterna. Introductory Astronomy. (C). 1997. pap. text 40.50 (*0-03-022764-X*); pap. text, teacher ed. 10.00 (*0-03-022767-4*); pap. text, student ed. 21.00 (*0-03-022768-2*) Harcourt Coll Pubs.

Canters, G. W. & Vijgenboom, E. Biological Electron Transfer Chains: Genetics, Composition & Mode of Operation: Proceedings of the NATO Advanced Research Workshop on Biological Electron Transfer Chains: Genetics, Composition, & Mode of Operation, Tomar, Portugal, May 3-7, 1997. LC 98-8193. (NATO ASI Ser.). 304p. 1998. 138.00 (*0-7923-5138-X*) Kluwer Academic.

Canti, John, tr. see Revel, Jean-Francois & Ricard, Matthieu.

Cantillon, Bea, jt. auth. see Berghman, Jos.

Cantillon, Eli. The Mysterious Pen Pal. (J). (ps-5). 1994. 16.95 (*0-938971-83-2*) JTG Nashville.

***Cantillon, Eli A.** Amadeus: Four Stories in One. 62p. (J). (ps). 1998. 12.98 (*1-58048-056-X*) Sandvik Pub.

— A New Home for Fab the Fox. (Illus.). 14p. (J). (ps-1). 1998. 14.98 (*1-58048-043-8*) Sandvik Pub.

Cantillon, Eli A. Noah's Ark. (Illus.). (J). 1997. 12.98 (*1-58048-017-9*) Sandvik Pub.

Cantillon, Richard. Essays on the Nature of Commerce in General. LC 99-21222. 194p. 1999. pap. 24.95 (*0-7658-0499-9*) Transaction Pubs.

Cantimpre, Thomas De, see De Cantimpre, Thomas.

Cantin, Candis, jt. auth. see Tierra, Michael.

Cantin, M., ed. Cell Biology of the Secretory Process. (Illus.). viii, 624p. 1983. 259.25 (*3-8055-3619-4*) S Karger.

Cantin, M. & Jasmin, G., eds. Stress Revisited: Neuroendocrinology of Stress. (Methods & Achievements in Experimental Pathology Ser.: Vol. 14). (Illus.). xii, 176p. 1991. 169.75 (*3-8055-5374-9*) S Karger.

Cantin, M., jt. ed. see Jasmin, G.

Cantin, Paul. Alanis Morissette: You Oughta Know. LC 97-50591. 208p. 1998. pap. 11.95 (*0-312-18035-7*) St Martin.

Cantin, Sadie, et al. Growing up Strong: Four North Country Women Recall Their Lives. Potter, Joan, ed. (Illus.). 200p. (Orig.). 1995. pap. 12.95 (*0-9632476-2-X*) Pinto Pr.

Cantine, John, et al. Shot by Shot: A Practical Guide to Filmmaking. 2nd ed. LC 96-165759. (Illus.). 156p. (Orig.). (C). 1995. pap. text 13.00 (*0-9637433-1-7*) Pittsbrgh Film.

Cantine, Marguerite J. The Patient's Daily Pain Journal: An Illustrative Reference & Identification Guide to Targeting Chronic Pain for Improved Communication Between Doctor & Patient. Kilpatrick, Elizabeth A., ed. (Illus.). 113p. 1996. write for info. (*0-614-13541-9*) Cantine & Kilpatrick.

Cantini, Andrea. Logical Frameworks for Truth & Abstraction: An Axiomatic Study. LC 96-4681. (Studies in Logic & the Foundations of Mathematics Ser.: Vol. 135). 474p. 1996. text 143.50 (*0-444-82306-9*, North Holland) Elsevier.

Cantino, E. C., jt. auth. see Myers, R. B.

Cantlay, Lynne. Detecting Child Abuse: Recognizing Children at Risk Through Drawings. LC 96-76093. 115p. 1996. pap. 19.95 (*0-9651068-2-9*) Holly Press.

Cantle, Gordon S. A Collection of Essays on Horse-Drawn Carriages & Carriage Parts. 1993. pap. 20.00 (*1-880499-02-9*) Carriage Museum.

Cantley, Charles, jt. auth. see Novick, Lee.

Cantlie, Hugh. Ancestral Castles of Scotland. (Illus.). 160p. 1997. pap. 19.95 (*1-85585-118-0*, Pub. by Collins & Br) Trafalgar.

Cantlon, John E., et al. U. S. Nuclear Waste Technical Review Board: Report to the U. S. Congress & the Secretary of Energy, January to December 1996. (Illus.). 72p. (C). 1998. pap. text 25.00 (*0-7881-4307-7*) DIANE Pub.

Cantlon, Marie. White Gloves & Raised Fists. 1999. text 29.95 (*0-670-86743-8*) Viking Penguin.

Cantlon, Teresa L. Structuring Your Classroom Successfully for Cooperative Team Learning. (Orig.). 1989. teacher ed. 22.00 (*0-9622312-0-7*) Prestige Portland.

Cantlupe, Joe & Petrillo, Lisa. Badge of Betrayal. 296p. (Orig.). 1991. mass mkt. 4.99 (*0-380-76009-6*, Avon Bks) Morrow Avon.

Cantly, Caroline, jt. auth. see Smith, Gilbert.

Cantner, E., et al. Animal Production: Technical Dictionary, English-German & German-English. (Agricultural Dictionaries Ser.). 137p. 1991. pap. 21.00 (*3-8236-1155-0*, VJM1550, Pub. by Backhuys Pubs) Balogh.

***Cantner, U., et al, eds.** Economic Evolution, Learning & Complexity. vi, 290p. 2000. (*3-7908-1275-7*) Spr-Verlag.

Canto, Estela. Borges a Contraluz. (Nueva Austral Ser.: Vol. 93). (SPA.). 1991. pap. text 24.95 (*84-239-1893-9*) Elliots Bks.

Canto, Julio P. Economic & Social Progress of the Republic of Chile. 1977. lib. bdg. 59.95 (*0-8490-1745-9*) Gordon Pr.

Canto, Muriel G. & Cantor, Joel M. Prime-Time Television: Content & Control. 2nd ed. LC 91-30889. (Sage Commtext Ser.: No. 3). 143p. 1992. reprint ed. pap. 44.40 (*0-608-04303-6*, 206508200012) Bks Demand.

Canto Rum of St Peters Scholar Staff. Light from the East: A Central & Eastern Europe Christmas CD. 1999. cd-rom 16.95 (*0-8146-7933-1*) Liturgical Pr.

Canto, Victor A. Currency Substitution. 1987. lib. bdg. 80.50 (*0-89838-195-9*) Kluwer Academic.

— The Determinants & Consequences of Trade Restrictions in the U. S. Economy. LC 85-12211. 218p. 1985. 55.00 (*0-275-90050-9*, C0050, Praeger Pubs) Greenwood.

Canto, Victor A., et al, eds. The Financial Analyst's Guide to Fiscal Policy. LC 85-19339. 240p. 1985. 59.95 (*0-275-90039-8*, C0039, Praeger Pubs) Greenwood.

— The Financial Analyst's Guide to Monetary Policy. LC 85-28315. 171p. 1986. 47.95 (*0-275-92023-2*, C2023, Praeger Pubs) Greenwood.

Canto, Victor A. & Dietrich, J. Kimball, eds. Industrial Policy & Industrial Trade. LC 92-6374. (Contemporary Studies in Economic & Financial Analysis: Vol. 62). 186p. 1992. 78.50 (*0-89232-840-1*) Jai Pr.

Canto, Victor A. & Laffer, Arthur B., eds. Monetary Policy, Taxation, & International Investment Strategy. LC 90-30017. 376p. 1990. 75.00 (*0-89930-534-2*, Quorum Bks) Greenwood.

— Supply-Side Portfolio Strategies. LC 87-13091. 192p. 1988. 55.00 (*0-89930-286-6*, LFP/, Quorum Bks) Greenwood.

Canto, Victor A., et al. Investment Strategy & State & Local Economic Policy. LC 91-48060. 219p. 1992. 52.95 (*0-89930-405-2*, CIV, Quorum Bks) Greenwood.

Canton, A. N. ComputerMoney: Making Serious Dollars in High-Tech Consulting. LC 93-71430. 320p. 1993. pap. 29.95 (*1-883422-01-9*) Adams-Blake.

Canton, Alan. Success from Home: The Writing Business. 300p. 1999. pap. 59.00 (*1-883422-22-1*) Adams-Blake.

Canton, Alan N. The Silver Pen: Starting a Profitable Writing Business from a Lifetime of Experience. LC 95-79412. 380p. (Orig.). 1996. pap. 22.95 (*1-883422-11-6*) Adams-Blake.

Canton, Antonio D., jt. ed. see Andreucci, Vittorio E.

Canton, Antonio Dal, see Andreucci, Vittorio E. & Dal Canton, Antonio, eds.

Canton, Beverly. All Things Possible. 128p. (J). (gr. 8). 1996. pap. 7.95 (*0-9644857-7-X*) Wrds & Pict Pr.

Canton-Delgado, Manuela. Bautizados en Fuego: Protestantes, Discursos de Conversion y Politica en Guatemala (1989-1993) LC 98-70879. (Monograph Ser.: No. 9). (SPA., Illus.). 370p. 1998. pap. 22.00 (*0-910443-14-9*) Plumsock Meso Studies.

Canton, Frank M. Frontier Trails: The Autobiography of Frank M. Canton. Dale, Edward E., ed. LC 66-13415. (Western Frontier Library: Vol. 30). 251p. reprint ed. 77.90 (*0-8357-9728-7*, 201620000002) Bks Demand.

Canton, James. Technofutures: How Leading-Edge Technology Will Transform Business in the 21st Century. LC 99-14182. 350p. 1999. text 23.00 (*1-56170-653-1*) Hay House.

Canton, Katia. The Fairy Tale Revisited: A Survey of the Evolution of the Tales, from Classical Literary Interpretations to Innovative Contemporary Dance Theatre Productions. LC 93-27277. (New Connections Ser.: Vol. 8). 186p. (C). 1994. text 23.95 (*0-8204-2309-2*) P Lang Pubng.

Canton, Lucien G. Guard Force Management. LC 95-32405. 256p. 1995. 34.95 (*0-7506-9299-5*) Buttrwrth-Heinemann.

C

An Asterisk (*) at the beginning of an entry indicates that the title is appearing for the first time.

Canton, Maj. Maj Canton's Reference Guide to Movies & Miniseries for TV & Cable, 1984-1994. LC 94-78089. 410p. (Orig.). 1994. pap. 115.00 (*1-883422-44-2*) Adams-Blake.

Canton, Maria P. & Sanchez, Julio. IBM Microcomputer COBOL in Ten Programming Lessons. 200p. (C). 2001. pap. 20.00 (*0-13-013830-4*) P-H.

— The Mcgraw-Hill PC Programmer's Desk Reference. 470p. 1996. 50.00 (*0-07-057203-8*) McGraw.

— McGraw-Hill's Programmer's Desk Reference. (Illus.). 452p. 1996. text 50.00 incl. disk (*0-07-912176-4*); pap. text 34.95 (*0-07-912177-2*) McGraw.

Canton, Maria P., jt. auth. see Sanchez, Julio.

Canton, Rolf J. The Moriarty Principle: An Irregular Look at Sherlock Holmes. LC 96-40346. (Illus.). 272p. 1997. pap. 19.95 (*1-880090-46-5*) Galde Pr.

Canton, Steve. Terminal Justice. 135p. 1994. 15.95 (*1-883114-04-7*) Waterview Pr.

Cantone, A., et al. Computable Set Theory, Vol. 1. (International Series of Monographs on Computer Science: No. 6). (Illus.). 360p. 1990. text 69.00 (*0-19-853807-3*) OUP.

Cantoni, Angelo. La Reference a Bach dans les Oeuvres Neo-Classiques de Stravinsky, Vol. 8. (GER.). iv, 358p. Date not set. write for info. (*3-487-10598-5*) G Olms Pubs.

Cantoni, Gabriella, ed. The Road to an Aging Policy for the 21st Century: 1995 White House Conference on Aging, Executive Summary. (Illus.). 149p. 1998. pap. text 30.00 (*0-7881-4635-1*) DIANE Pub.

Cantoni, Gina. Content-Area Language Instruction, Approaches & Strategies. LC 86-22287. 224p. 1987. pap. text 28.68 (*0-201-14097-7*) Addison-Wesley.

Cantoni, V. Human & Machine Vision: Analogies & Divergencies. LC 94-43083. (Illus.). 410p. (C). 1994. text 125.00 (*0-306-44902-1*, Kluwer Plenum) Kluwer Academic.

Cantoni, V. & Ferretti, M. Pyramidal Architectures for Computer Vision. LC 93-29212. (Advances in Computer Vision & Machine Intelligence Ser.). (Illus.). 356p. (C). 1994. 85.00 (*0-306-44453-4*, Kluwer Plenum) Kluwer Academic.

***Cantoni, Virginio, ed.** Human & Machine Perception Two: Emergence, Attention & Creativity. 222p. 1999. 125.00 (*0-306-46291-5*, Kluwer Plenum) Kluwer Academic.

C

Cantoni, Virginio, et al, eds. Artifical Vision: Image Description, Recognition & Communication. (Signal Processing Ser.). (Illus.). 320p. 1996. text 59.95 (*0-12-444816-X*) Acad Pr.

Cantoni, Virginio, et al, eds. Human & Machine Perception: Information Fusion: Proceedings of the Second International Workshop Held in Trabia, Italy 21-25, 1996. LC 97-33281. 340p. (C). 1997. 115.00 (*0-306-45708-3*, Plenum Trade) Perseus Pubng.

Cantoni, Virginio, et al, eds. Image Analysis & Processing II. LC 88-9416. (Illus.). 530p. 1988. 120.00 (*0-306-42901-2*, Plenum Trade) Perseus Pubng.

— Image Analysis & Processing, Vol. 1. LC 86-22668. 280p. 1986. 75.00 (*0-306-42391-X*, Plenum Trade) Perseus Pubng.

— Progress in Image Analysis & Processing II: Proceedings of the 6th International Conference. 600p. (C). 1992. text 143.00 (*981-02-0800-6*) World Scientific Pub.

— Recent Issues in Pattern Analysis & Recognition. (Lecture Notes in Computer Science Ser.: Vol. 399). vii, 400p. 1990. 44.95 (*0-387-51815-0*) Spr-Verlag.

Cantoni, Virginio, et al. Progress in Image Analysis & Processing: Proceedings of the 5th International Conference. 804p. 1990. text 147.00 (*981-02-0061-7*) World Scientific Pub.

***Cantonwine, Sheila Cullen.** Safety Training That Delivers: How to Design & Present Better Technical Training LC 99-41073. 1999. pap. write for info. (*1-885581-29-7*) ASSE.

Cantor. American Government. Date not set. pap. text. write for info. (*0-314-72629-2*) West Pub.

— Historic Black Landmarks. 2nd ed. 1999. 47.00 (*0-8103-8572-4*, 101387) Gale.

Cantor. In the Wake of the Plague: The World of the Black Death. Date not set. write for info. (*0-684-85735-9*) Free Pr.

Cantor, ed. Western Civilazition: Its Genesis & Destiny, Vol. I. (C). 1999. pap. text, student ed. write for info. (*0-673-98401-X*) Addison-Wesley.

— Western Civilization: Its Genesis & Destiny, Vol. I. (C). 1999. pap. text, wbk. ed. write for info. (*0-673-98403-6*) Addison-Wesley.

— Western Civilization: Its Genesis & Destiny, Vol. II. (C). 1999. pap. text, student ed. write for info. (*0-673-98402-8*); pap. text, wbk. ed. write for info. (*0-673-98404-4*) Addison-Wesley.

Cantor, Alan. Extending SAS Survival Analysis Techniques for Medical Research. LC 98-149814. 208p. (C). 1999. pap. 34.95 (*1-55544-954-9*, BR55504) SAS Publ.

Cantor, Andreas. Gooal! (SPA., Illus.). 256p. 1996. 22.50 (*0-684-81456-0*, Libros) S&S Trade Pap.

— Goooal! 1997. per. 12.00 (*0-684-83340-9*, Fireside) S&S Trade Pap.

***Cantor, Andres & Arcucci, Daniel.** Goooal! A Celebration of Soccer. (Illus.). 297p. 1999. reprint ed. text 23.00 (*0-7881-6618-2*) DIANE Pub.

***Cantor, Arthur & Little, Stuart W.** The Playmakers. 352p. 2000. pap. 20.95 (*1-58348-382-9*, Authors Guild Backinprint) iUniversecom.

Cantor, Aviv. Jewish Women - Jewish Men. pap. 12.00 (*0-685-68967-0*, Perennial) HarperTrade.

Cantor, Aviva, et al, compiled by. The Jewish Woman, 1900-1985: Bibliography. 2nd ed. 214p. 1987. pap. 9.95 (*0-930395-04-2*) Biblio NY.

Cantor, Barbara, ed. Chart Your Courses: Calvert Marine Museum 25th Anniversary Cookbook. 170p. 1995. ring bd. 9.00 (*0-941647-13-7*) Calvert MM Pr.

Cantor, Benjamin J. The Role of the Expert Witness in a Court Trial: A Guide for the Expert Witness. LC 96-85935. (Illus.). 160p. (Orig.). 1996. spiral bd. 22.00 (*0-9653897-0-7*) Legal Evidence.

Cantor, C. R., jt. auth. see Lim, H. A.

Cantor, Carla. Phantom Illness. 368p. 1997. pap. 15.00 (*0-395-85992-1*) HM.

***Cantor, Carla & Fallon, Brian A.** Phantom Illness: Shattering the Myth of Hypochondria. 351p. 2000. reprint ed. text 23.00 (*0-7881-9269-8*) DIANE Pub.

Cantor, Charles R. & Hwa A Lim. Electrophoresis, Supercomputing & the Human Genome: Proceedings of the 1st International Conference. 352p. 1991. text 130.00 (*981-02-0273-3*) World Scientific Pub.

Cantor, Charles R. & Schimmel, Paul R. Biophysical Chemistry Part I: The Conformation of Biological Macromolecules. LC 79-22043. (Illus.). 365p. (C). 1980. pap. text 62.95 (*0-7167-1188-5*) W H Freeman.

— Biophysical Chemistry Part II: Techniques for the Study of Biological Structure & Function. LC 79-24854. (Illus.). 365p. (C). 1980. pap. text 62.95 (*0-7167-1190-7*) W H Freeman.

— Biophysical Chemistry Part III: The Behavior of Biological Macromolecules. LC 79-27860. (Illus.). 597p. (C). 1980. pap. text 62.95 (*0-7167-1192-3*) W H Freeman.

Cantor, Charles R. & Smith, Cassandra L. Genomics: The Science & Technology Behind the Human Genome Project. LC 98-40448. (George Fisher Baker Non-Resident Lectureship in Chemistry at Cornell University). 624p. 1999. 125.00 (*0-471-59908-5*) Wiley.

Cantor, Charles R., ed. see Scopes, R. K.

Cantor, D., et al, eds. Selected Papers of Theodore S. Motzkin. 1983. 122.00 (*0-8176-3087-2*) Birkhauser.

***Cantor, David A., Sr.** Knowing Him: Discovering God Through His Names & Attributes. 2000. pap. 12.99 (*0-87148-484-6*) Pathway Pr.

Cantor, David S. Handbook of Gastroenterology. 1991. write for info. (*0-8151-1423-0*) Mosby Inc.

Cantor, Diane L. & Thomson, Jeani. What to Do about Personnel Problems in Your State, 2 vols., Set. rev. ed. 1983. ring bd. 295.00 (*1-55645-001-X*) Busn Legal Reports.

Cantor, Donald, jt. auth. see Black, James C.

Cantor, Donna. Sunnyside. LC 98-45224. 272p. 1999. pap. 12.00 (*0-380-79571-X*, Avon Bks) Morrow Avon.

Cantor, Dorothy & Thompson, Andrea. What Do You Want to Do When You Grow Up ? Starting the Next Chapters of Your Life. 208p. 2001. 22.95 (*0-316-12714-0*) Little.

Cantor, Dorothy W. Women in Power: The Secrets of Leadership. 336p. 1992. pap. 12.95 (*0-395-61860-6*) HM.

Cantor, Dorothy W., ed. Women As Therapists: A Multi-Theoretical Casebook. LC 92-21975. 264p. 1992. pap. 45.00 (*0-87668-313-8*) Aronson.

— Women As Therapists: A Multi-Theoretical Casebook. LC 90-35520. 272p. 1990. 33.95 (*0-8261-6910-4*) Springer Pub.

Cantor, Dorothy W., jt. ed. see Bernay, Toni.

Cantor, Eddie. Caught Short! 15.95 (*0-89190-984-2*) Amereon Ltd.

— Caught Short! A Saga of Wailing Wall Street. (Illus.). 48p. 1992. reprint ed. pap. 8.00 (*0-87034-108-1*) Fraser Pub Co.

***Cantor, Eddie.** My Life Is in Your Hands & Take My Life: The Autobiographies of Eddie Cantor. (Illus.). 2000. pap. 22.95 (*0-8154-1057-3*) Cooper Sq.

Cantor, Eddie & Freedman, David. Yoo Hoo Prosperity: The Eddie Cantor Five-Year Plan. LC 92-74295. (Illus.). 64p. 1992. reprint ed. pap. 8.00 (*0-87034-107-3*) Fraser Pub Co.

Cantor, Ellen. My Perversion is the Belief in True Love. (Illus.). 112p. 1999. pap. 29.95 (*3-908247-02-0*) Scalo Pubs.

Cantor, G. N. & Olby, Robert C., eds. Companion to the History of Modern Science. 1120p. (C). 1996. pap. 60.00 (*0-415-14578-3*) Routledge.

Cantor, Geoffrey, et al. Michael Faraday. (Illus.). 124p. (C). 1996. pap. 12.50 (*0-391-03982-2*) Humanities.

— Michael Faraday. (Illus.). 124p. (C). 1996. text 39.95 (*0-391-03981-4*) Humanities.

Cantor, Geoffrey, et al. Michael Faraday. 1996. pap. 18.00 (*1-57392-556-X*, Humanity Bks) Prometheus Bks.

Cantor, Geoffrey, jt. auth. see Brooke, John.

Cantor, Georg. Contributions to the Founding of the Theory of Transfinite Numbers. Jourdain, Philip E., tr. 211p. 1955. pap. 7.95 (*0-486-60045-9*) Dover.

Cantor, George. Back on Top: The University of Michigan's Odyssey to the National Championship. (Illus.). 256p. 1998. 22.95 (*0-87833-206-5*) Taylor Pub.

***Cantor, George.** Bad Guys in American History. LC 99-36031. 1999. pap. 19.95 (*0-87833-242-1*) Taylor Pub.

— Confederate Generals: Life Portraits. (Illus.). 2000. 29.95 (*0-87833-179-4*) Taylor Pub.

Cantor, George. The Great Lakes Guidebook: Lake Huron & Eastern Lake Michigan. (Illus.). 208p. 1985. pap. 17.95 (*0-472-06362-6*, 06362) U of Mich Pr.

— The Great Lakes Guidebook: Lakes Ontario & Erie. 2nd ed. 248p. 1985. pap. 17.95 (*0-472-06361-8*, 06361) U of Mich Pr.

— Historic Festivals: A Traveler's Guide. LC 95-36742. 392p. 1995. 55.00 (*0-8103-9150-3*, 101752) Gale.

— Historic Festivals: A Traveler's Guide. (Illus.). 392p. 1996. 17.95 (*0-7876-0824-6*) Visible Ink Pr.

— North American Indian Landmarks: A Traveler's Guide. (Illus.). 409p. 1999. reprint ed. pap. text 18.00 (*0-7881-6284-5*) DIANE Pub.

— Old Roads of the Midwest. LC 96-45829. 248p. (Orig.). 1997. pap. 17.95 (*0-472-08288-4*, 08288) U of Mich Pr.

— The Tigers of '68: Baseball's Last Real Champions. LC 96-29580. (Illus.). 256p. 1997. 22.95 (*0-87833-928-0*) Taylor Pub.

— Where to Gamble. LC 97-37392. (Illus.). 274p. 1997. 18.95 (*1-57859-022-1*, 00157352) Visible Ink Pr.

***Cantor, George.** Where to Gamble: A Guide to Casinos, Riverboats, Reservations, Racetracks & More. (Illus.). 259p. 2000. pap. text 20.00 (*0-7881-9035-0*) DIANE Pub.

Cantor, George, ed. Historic Landmarks of Black America. 408p. 1991. 47.00 (*0-8103-7809-4*, 100828-M94814) Gale.

— Pop Culture Landmarks: A Travelers Guide. LC 94-29924. 401p. 1994. 55.00 (*0-8103-9399-9*, 102250) Gale.

Cantor, George, jt. auth. see Johnson, Anne J.

Cantor, Gilbert M. The Lawyer's Complete Guide to the Perfect Will. 1984. pap. 47.50 (*0-916621-00-6*) Cato Pr.

Cantor, Gilbert M., jt. auth. see Rothkopf, Nancy.

Cantor, Gordon N. Race & Sex Effects in the Conformity Behavior of Children. (Augustana College Library Occasional Papers, Wallin Lecture: No. 14). 16p. 1978. pap. 1.00 (*0-910182-37-X*) Augustana Coll.

***Cantor, Harold.** Clifford Odets. 2nd ed. LC 99-46820. 192p. 2000. pap. 28.50 (*0-8108-3732-3*) Scarecrow.

— Clifford Odets: Playwright-Poet. LC 99-46820. 192p. 2000. 52.00 (*0-8108-3731-5*) Scarecrow.

Cantor, J. Winterthur: A Portrait. (Illus.). 64p. 1991. pap. 9.95 (*0-912724-21-8*) Winterthur.

Cantor, J. H., ed. Psychology at Iowa: Centennial Essays. 176p. (C). 1991. text 39.95 (*0-8058-0761-6*) L Erlbaum Assocs.

***Cantor-Jackson, Betty.** Live Sound Recording. 180p. 2001. pap. 29.95 (*0-87288-755-3*) Intertec Pub.

Cantor, Jay, et al. Masters of American Modernism: Vignettes from the Katz Collection. (Illus.). 48p. (Orig.). 1995. pap. 20.00 (*0-936270-34-9*) CA St U LB Art.

Cantor, Jay E. Winterthur. LC 97-4303. (Illus.). 264p. 1985. 60.00 (*0-8109-1785-8*, Pub. by Abrams) Time Warner.

Cantor, Jeffrey A. Apprenticeship & Community Colleges: Promoting Collaboration with Business, Labor & the Community for Workforce Training. 202p. (C). 1993. lib. bdg. 42.50 (*0-8191-9135-3*) U Pr of Amer.

— Cooperative Apprenticeships: A School-to-Work Handbook. LC 96-61085. 300p. 1996. pap. 39.95 (*1-56676-471-8*) Scarecrow.

— Experiential Learning in Higher Education: Linking Classroom & Community. Fife, Jonathan D., ed. LC 96-79653. (Illus.). 90p. 1995. pap. 24.00 (*1-878380-71-0*, 95-7) GWU Grad Schl E&HD.

— A Guide to Academic Writing. LC 93-564. 200p. 1993. pap. 16.95 (*0-275-94660-6*, B4660); lib. bdg. 59.95 (*0-313-29017-2*, GR9017) Greenwood.

Cantor, Jeffrey A. & Cantor, Ruth F. Parents' Guide to Special Needs Schooling: Early Intervention Years. LC 95-24262. 264p. 1995. 45.00 (*0-86569-243-2*, Auburn Hse) Greenwood.

Cantor, Jeffrey A., jt. auth. see Stabile, Donald R.

Cantor, Jerome O., ed. Handbook of Animal Models of Pulmonary Disease, 2 Vols. 1989. write for info. (*0-685-44645-X*) CRC Pr.

— Handbook of Animal Models of Pulmonary Disease, 2 Vols., Vol. I. 272p. 1989. lib. bdg. 210.00 (*0-8493-2978-7*, RC756) CRC Pr.

— Handbook of Animal Models of Pulmonary Disease, 2 Vols., Vol. II. 264p. 1989. lib. bdg. 210.00 (*0-8493-2979-5*) CRC Pr.

Cantor, Joan H., et al, eds. Child Behavior & Development: Training for Diversity. 288p. (C). 1988. text 73.25 (*0-89391-726-5*) Ablx Pub.

Cantor, Joanne. Mommy I'm Scared: How TV & Movies Frighten Children & What We Can Do to Protect Them. LC 98-17080. 320p. (C). 1998. pap. 13.00 (*0-15-600592-1*, Harvest Bks) Harcourt.

— Mommy I'm Scared: How TV & Movies Frighten Children & What We Can Do to Protect Them. LC 98-17080. 250p. 1998. 25.00 (*0-15-100402-1*, Harvest Bks) Harcourt.

Cantor, Joel M., jt. auth. see Canto, Muriel G.

Cantor, Joel M., jt. auth. see Cantor, Muriel B.

Cantor, Leonard. The Changing English Countryside. 1987. 47.50 (*0-7102-0501-5*, 05015, Routledge Thoemms) Routledge.

— Vocational Education & Training in the Developed World: A Comparative Study. 192p. 1989. 49.95 (*0-415-02541-9*, A3449) Routledge.

Cantor, Leonard, et al. A Guide to Further Education in England & Wales. (Cassell Education Ser.). (Illus.). 128p. 1996. 100.00 (*0-304-33132-5*) Continuum.

Cantor, M. Catherine, jt. auth. see Seward, Peter G.

Cantor, Marjorie A., ed. see Lewis, Christine L., et al.

Cantor, Marjorie H., ed. Family Caregiving: Agenda for the Future. (Critical Debates in an Aging Society Ser.). 149p. (Orig.). (C). 1994. pap. 19.95 (*0-9640387-0-6*) Am Soc Aging.

Cantor, Marjorie H. & Brennan, Mark. Social Care of the Elderly: The Effects of Ethnicity, Class & Culture. LC 99-38047. (Illus.). 288p. 1999. text 38.95 (*0-8261-1263-3*) Springer Pub.

Cantor, Milton. Max Eastman. LC 71-120012. (Twayne's United States Authors Ser.). 1970. lib. bdg. 20.95 (*0-89197-844-5*) Irvington.

Cantor, Milton, ed. American Working Class Culture: Explorations in American Labor & Social History, 7. LC 78-59260. (Contributions in Labor History Ser.: No. 7). 444p. 1979. 69.50 (*0-313-20611-2*, CAW/, Greenwood Pr) Greenwood.

— Black Labor in America, 2. LC 74-111265. (Contributions in Afro-American & African Studies: No. 2). (Illus.). 170p. 1970. 52.95 (*0-8371-4667-4*, CLM&) Greenwood.

Cantor, Moritz. Mathematische Beitrage Zum Kulturleben der Volker. xii, 432p. 1964. reprint ed. 110.00 (*0-318-70731-4*) G Olms Pubs.

Cantor, Morton B., jt. ed. see Silver, Ann-Louise S.

Cantor, Muriel B. & Cantor, Joel M. Prime-Time Television: Content & Control. 2nd ed. (CommText Ser.: Vol. 3). 160p. (C). 1991. text 42.00 (*0-8039-3169-7*); pap. text 18.95 (*0-8039-3170-0*) Sage.

Cantor, Muriel G. The Hollywood TV Producer: His Work & His Audience. 276p. 1987. 39.95 (*0-88738-165-0*) Transaction Pubs.

Cantor, Muriel G. & Pingree, Suzanne. The Soap Opera. LC 83-11057. (Sage Commtext Ser.: Vol. 12). 167p. 1983. reprint ed. pap. 51.80 (*0-608-02990-4*, 205963000006) Bks Demand.

Cantor, Muriel G., jt. ed. see Ball-Rokeach, Sandra J.

Cantor, Muriel G., jt. ed. see Stewart, Phyllis L.

Cantor, Murray. Object-Oriented Project Management with UML. LC 98-16413. 368p. 1998. 39.99 (*0-471-25303-0*) Wiley.

Cantor, N. & Kihlstrom, John F., eds. Personality, Cognition, & Social Interaction. LC 81-208. 384p. 1981. text 79.95 (*0-89859-057-4*) L Erlbaum Assocs.

Cantor, Nancy, jt. ed. see Buss, D. M.

Cantor, Norman. Civilization of the Ancient World. Date not set. 15.00 (*0-06-093098-5*) HarpC.

— Civilization of the Ancient World. 448p. 2000. pap. 35.00 (*0-06-017409-9*) HarpC.

— Imagining the Law: Common Law & the Foundations of the American Legal System. LC 97-8766. 432p. 1999. pap. 16.00 (*0-06-092953-7*) HarpC.

Cantor, Norman F. The American Century: Varieties of Culture in Modern Times. 672p. 1998. pap. 16.00 (*0-06-092876-X*, Perennial) HarperTrade.

— Civilization of the Middle Ages. rev. ed. LC 92-56237. 624p. 1994. pap. 18.00 (*0-06-092553-1*) HarpC.

— Inventing the Middle Ages: The Lives, Works, & Ideas of the Great Medievalists of the Twentieth Century. LC 92-26178. 477p. 1993. pap. 14.00 (*0-688-12302-3*, Quil) HarperTrade.

— Jewish Experience. 1999. 12.99 (*0-7858-1128-1*) Bk Sales Inc.

— Medieval Lives: Eight Charismatic Men & Women of the Middle Ages. 224p. 1995. pap. 12.00 (*0-06-092579-5*, Perennial) HarperTrade.

— The Sacred Chain: The History of the Jews. 512p. 1995. pap. 15.00 (*0-06-092652-X*) HarperTrade.

Cantor, Norman F., ed. Encyclopedia of the Middle Ages. LC 99-14265. 1999. 40.00 (*0-670-10011-0*, PuffinBks) Peng Put Young Read.

Cantor, Norman F. & Schneider, Richard I. How to Study History. LC 67-14303. 288p. (C). 1967. pap. text 14.95 (*0-88295-709-0*) Harlan Davidson.

Cantor, Norman F., ed. see Mandelbaum, Seymour J.

Cantor, Norman L. Advance Directives & the Pursuit of Death with Dignity. LC 92-46072. (Medical Ethics Ser.). 228p. 1993. 29.95 (*0-253-31304-X*) Ind U Pr.

— Legal Frontiers of Death & Dying. LC 86-45502. (Medical Ethics Ser.). 220p. 1987. reprint ed. pap. 68.20 (*0-608-01053-7*, 205936100001) Bks Demand.

Cantor, Norman R. Medieval Reader. 384p. 1995. pap. 19.50 (*0-06-272055-4*, Harper Ref) HarpC.

Cantor, Paul A. Shakespeare: "Hamlet" (Landmarks of World Literature Ser.). (Illus.). 128p. (C). 1989. pap. text 11.95 (*0-521-34983-4*) Cambridge U Pr.

Cantor, Robin, et al. Making Markets: An Interdisciplinary Perspective on Economic Exchange, 135. LC 91-42731. (Contributions in Economics & Economic History Ser.: No. 135). 208p. 1992. 55.00 (*0-313-26821-5*, CME/, Greenwood Pr) Greenwood.

Cantor, Ruth F., jt. auth. see Cantor, Jeffrey A.

Cantor, Sheila. Childhood Schizophrenia. LC 88-5180. 193p. 1988. lib. bdg. 32.50 (*0-89862-713-3*) Guilford Pubns.

Cantor, Steven L. Contemporary Trends in Landscape Architecture. 348p. 1996. 69.95 (*0-471-28791-1*, VNR) Wiley.

Cantor, Steven L. Contemporary Trends in Landscape Architecture. 2nd ed. LC 96-11733. (Illus.). 368p. 1997. text 59.95 (*0-442-02347-2*, VNR) Wiley.

— Innovative Design Solutions in Landscape Architecture. 300p. 1996. 69.95 (*0-471-28506-4*, VNR) Wiley.

Cantor, Steven L. Innovative Design Solutions in Landscape Architecture. LC 96-11734. (Illus.). 300p. 1996. text 59.95 (*0-442-01235-7*, VNR) Wiley.

Cantore, Jean A. & Gregory, James. Designing Communications with Confidence & Reliability. 2nd ed. 170p. (C). 1996. pap. text, per. 44.95 (*0-7872-2629-7*, 41262901) Kendall-Hunt.

***Cantos, Angel Lbopez.** Los Puertorriquednos: Mentalidad Y Actitudes, Siglo XVIII. LC 99-25123. 1999. write for info. (*0-8477-0375-4*) U of PR Pr.

Cantow, H. J., ed. Polydiacetylenes. (Advances in Polymer Science Ser.: Fortschritte der Hochpolymerenforschung: Vol. 63). (Illus.). 160p. 1984. 79.95 (*0-387-13414-X*) Spr-Verlag.

Cantow, H. J., et al, eds. Analysis-Reactions-Morphology. (Advances in Polymer Science Ser.: Vol. 71). (Illus.). 220p. 1985. 102.00 (*0-387-15482-5*) Spr-Verlag.

— Luminescence. (Advances in Polymer Science Ser.: Vol. 40). (Illus.). 200p. 1981. 57.00 (*0-387-10550-6*) Spr-Verlag.

— Specialty Polymers. (Advances in Polymer Science Ser.: Vol. 41). (Illus.). 186p. 1981. 67.00 (*0-387-10554-9*) Spr-Verlag.

— Synthesis & Degradation-Rheology & Extrusion. (Advances in Polymer Science Ser.: Vol. 47). (Illus.). 170p. 1982. 62.00 (*0-387-11774-1*) Spr-Verlag.

Cantow, H. J., et al. Behavior of Macromolecules. (Advances in Polymer Science Ser.: Vol. 46). (Illus.). 170p. 1982. 66.00 (*0-387-11640-0*) Spr-Verlag.

Cantrall, Janice, jt. ed. see Pence, Terry.

An Asterisk (*) at the beginning of an entry indicates that the title is appearing for the first time.

***Cantrell, Bambi & Cohen, Skip.** The Art of Wedding Photography: Professional Techniques with Style. (Illus.). 144p. 2000. pap. 29.95 (*0-8174-3325-2*) Watsn-Guptill.

Cantrell, Bernadine B. Bending the Twig. 240p. 1999. 16.95 (*0-9647028-6-X*) Sowers Press.

— Cpsq Portfolio Composition. 3rd ed. 1998. pap. text 9.25 (*0-07-229286-5*) McGraw.

— Her Husband is Known in the Gates: Helping Your Husband Succeed. LC 95-70737. 1995. 14.95 (*0-9647028-3-5*) Sowers Press.

— Her Husband Is Known in the Gates: Study Guide. 96p. (Orig.). 1996. pap., student ed. 6.95 (*0-9647028-0-0*) Sowers Press.

Cantrell, Bill H. Friends, Dear Friends, & Heroes. (Illus.). 441p. 1997. 25.00 (*0-9659136-0-0*) Freebooter Pub.

Cantrell, C. D. Modern Mathematical Methods for Physicists & Engineers. LC 98-24761. (Illus.). 700p. (C). 1999. text. write for info. (*0-521-59180-5*); pap. text. write for info. (*0-521-59827-3*) Cambridge U Pr.

Cantrell, C. G. The Cantrell Family: A Biographical Album & History of the Descendants of Zebulen Cantrell, the Immigrant, with Data Concerning the Families Who Have Allied Themselves by Marriage, 1700-1898. (Illus.). 156p. 1989. reprint ed. pap. 25.00 (*0-8328-1307-9*); reprint ed. lib. bdg. 35.00 (*0-8328-1306-0*) Higginson Bk Co.

Cantrell, Charles L. Oklahoma Criminal Law: Statutes & Rules Annotated LC 98-214959. 850 p. 1997. write for info. (*0-9648201-6-1*) Grail & Tucker.

Cantrell, Chris. Professionals Guide to Auto Repossession. 1997. pap. 35.00 (*1-891247-03-4*) Thomas Investigative.

***Cantrell, Debra Ann.** Changing Course: A Woman's Guide to Choosing the Cruising Life. 192p. 2000. 21.95 (*0-07-136087-5*) McGraw.

Cantrell, Gregg. Kenneth & John B. Rayner & the Limits of Southern Dissent. LC 92-14168. (Blacks in the New World Ser.). (Illus.). 384p. (C). 1993. text 47.50 (*0-252-01937-7*) U of Ill Pr.

— Stephen F. Austin: Empresario of Texas. LC 98-51176. (Illus.). 448p. 1999. 29.95 (*0-300-07683-5*) Yale U Pr.

Cantrell, Jacob. The Basics of Winning Chess. 2nd ed. LC 92-70773. (Illus.). 64p. 1993. mass mkt. 4.95 (*0-940685-28-0*, Gambling Res) Cardoza Pub.

Cantrell, James. Topical Child Development. 186p. 1994. student ed. 25.50 (*0-8273-6092-4*) Delmar.

Cantrell, John, jt. auth. see Kelly, Richard N.

Cantrell, John, jt. auth. see Wilkinson, Donald.

Cantrell, Karen & Wallen, Denise. Funding for Research, Study & Travel: Latin America & the Caribbean. LC 87-220653. 320p. 1997. pap. 32.50 (*0-89774-326-1*) Oryx Pr.

Cantrell, Krista. Catch Your Dog Doing Something Right: How to Train Any Dog in Five Minutes a Day. LC 97-29692. 1998. pap. 15.95 (*0-452-27755-8*, Plume) Dutton Plume.

***Cantrell, Krista.** Housetrain Your Dog Now. LC 99-43790. 2000. pap. 12.95 (*0-452-28160-1*, Plume) Dutton Plume.

Cantrell, Lana C. The Alternative vs. Orthodox Treatment of Leukemia. LC 98-93567. 214p. 1999. pap. write for info. (*0-9620749-1-8*) L C Cantrell.

— The Greatest Story Never Told: A Scientific Inquiry into the Evidence of the Fall of Man from a Higher Civilization in Antiquity. (Illus.). 1013p. (C). 1988. 15.00 (*0-9620749-0-X*) L C Cantrell.

Cantrell, Larry J. Mental Competency: Index of New Information with Authors, Subjects & References. 150p. 1996. 47.50 (*0-7883-1274-X*); pap. 44.50 (*0-7883-1275-8*) ABBE Pubs Assn.

— Mental Fatigue: Index of New Information with Authors, Subjects & References. 150p. 1996. 47.50 (*0-7883-1272-3*); pap. 44.50 (*0-7883-1273-1*) ABBE Pubs Assn.

Cantrell, Leon, ed. Writing of the Eighteen Nineties: Stories, Verses & Essays. (UQP Australian Authors Ser.). 1978. pap. 14.95 (*0-7022-2019-1*) Intl Spec Bk.

Cantrell, Lisa, jt. auth. see Porter, Lori.

Cantrell, Lisa W. Boneman. 256p. 1995. 4.99 (*0-8125-1970-1*, Pub. by Tor Bks) St Martin.

— The Manse. 352p. 1987. pap. 3.95 (*0-8125-1673-7*) Tor Bks.

— Ridge. 1989. mass mkt. 4.95 (*0-8125-0011-3*) Tor Bks.

— Torments. 1990. mass mkt. 4.95 (*0-8125-0668-5*) Tor Bks.

Cantrell, M. H., et al, eds. Bridging School & University. 250p. 1993. pap. text 40.00 (*90-5383-152-5*, Pub. by VU Univ Pr) Paul & Co Pubs.

***Cantrell, Mary Lynn, et al.** A Revisitation of the Ecological Perspectives on Emotional/Behavioral Disorders: Underlying Assumptions & Implications for Education & Treatment. (What Works for Children & Youth with Emotional/Behavior Disorders Ser.). 51p. 1999. pap. 11.40 (*0-86586-347-4*) Coun Exc Child.

Cantrell, Nancy T. Seeds of Hope. Kroitzsh, H. Donald et al, eds. 288p. 1999. pap. 9.95 (*1-886699-13-5*) Five Corners.

Cantrell, Patty, jt. auth. see Bredfeldt, Denise.

Cantrell, Will & Modderno, Francine. How to Find an Overseas Job with the U. S. Government: A Complete & Comprehensive Guide. vii, 421 p. (Orig.). 1992. pap. 28.95 (*0-941541-01-0*) Worldwise Bks.

— International Internships & Volunteer Programs: International Options for Students & Professionals. 233p. (Orig.). 1992. pap. 18.95 (*0-941541-02-9*) Worldwise Bks.

Cantrelle, P., et al. Estimation de la Mortalite de Juene Enfant (0-5 and) Pour Guider les Actions de Sante dans les Pays en Developpement. (Colloque de L'INSERM Ser.: No. 145). 570p. 1987. lib. bdg. 42.00 (*2-85598-306-1*) S M P F Inc.

Cantrick, Bob, tr. see Riddell, John, ed.

Cantril, Albert H. The Opinion Connection: Polling, Politics & the Press. 285p. 1991. 22.95 (*0-87187-583-7*) Congr Quarterly.

Cantril, Albert H., ed. Psychology, Humanism, & Scientific Inquiry: The Selected Essays of Hadley Cantril. 288p. 1987. 44.95 (*0-88738-176-6*) Transaction Pubs.

Cantril, Albert H. & Cantril, Susan D. Reading Mixed Signals: Ambivalence in American Public Opinion about Government. LC 99-16905. (Woodrow Wilson Center Press Ser.). 208p. 1999. 42.50 (*0-943875-92-7*, Pub. by W Wilson Ctr Pr); pap. 18.95 (*0-943875-91-9*, Pub. by W Wilson Ctr Pr) Johns Hopkins.

Cantril, H. The Invasion from Mars. 1976. 21.95 (*0-8488-0256-X*) Amereon Ltd.

Cantril, Hadley. The Invasion from Mars: A Study in the Psychology of Panic: With the Complete Script of the Famous Orson Welles Broadcast. LC 82-47626. (Illus.). 240p. reprint ed. pap. 74.40 (*0-7837-1947-7*, 204216200001) Bks Demand.

— Pattern of Human Concerns Data, 1957-1963. 1977. write for info. (*0-89138-115-5*) ICPSR.

Cantril, Hadley & Allport, Gordon W. Psychology of Radio. LC 72-161159. (History of Broadcasting: Radio & Television Ser.). 1980. reprint ed. 27.95 (*0-405-03574-8*) Ayer.

Cantril, Susan D., jt. auth. see Cantril, Albert H.

Cantrill, Dante. Adam's Apple: The Struggle Against Ourselves to Know, Vol. 161. LC 93-47399. (American University Studies: Philosophy: Ser. V, Vol. 161). XVII, 237p. (C). 1994. text 41.95 (*0-8204-2440-4*) P Lang Pubng.

Cantrill, James G. & Oravec, Christine L., eds. The Symbolic Earth: Discourse & Our Creation of the Environment. LC 96-5956. 486p. 1996. pap. 19.95 (*0-8131-0883-7*); text 45.00 (*0-8131-1973-1*) U Pr of Ky.

Cantrill, James G., jt. auth. see Honeycutt, James.

Cantu, Caesar C. Cortes & the Fall of the Aztec Empire. (Illus.). 1966. 12.95 (*0-685-16803-4*, 0-910978-1-3) Modern World.

— Mexico: All about the Country & Its People. (Illus.). 10.95 (*0-685-16804-2*, 0-910978-3-4) Modern World.

Cantu, Dean. Presidential Elections. LC 97-78307. (Perspectives on History Ser.: Pt. III). (Illus.). 66p. 1998. pap. 6.95 (*1-57960-023-9*) Disc Enter Ltd.

Cantu, Elizabeth. Natalia. Goodman, Jack, ed. LC 89-36803. (C). 1992. pap. 14.95 (*0-87949-307-0*) Ashley Bks.

Cantu, Gaston G. Las Invasiones Norteamericanas en Mexico (The North American Invasions into Mexico) (SPA.). 349p. 1996. pap. 13.99 (*968-16-5083-2*, Pub. by Fondo) Continental Bk.

Cantu, Marco. Delphi X Developer's Handbook. 1998. pap. text 54.99 (*0-7821-2348-1*) Sybex.

— Mastering Borland Latte. 848p. 1996. pap. text 49.99 (*0-7821-1989-1*) Sybex.

— Mastering Delphi 4. LC 98-86254. (Mastering Ser.). 1280p. 1998. pap. 49.99 (*0-7821-2350-3*) Sybex.

***Cantu, Marco.** Mastering Delphi X. 3rd ed. 1120p. 1999. 49.99 (*0-7821-2565-4*) Sybex.

Cantu, Marco, et al. Delphi Developers Handbook. LC 97-61715. (Illus.). 1168p. 1997. pap. text 49.99 incl. cd-rom (*0-7821-1987-5*) Sybex.

Cantu, Norma E. Canicula: Snapshots of a Girlhood en la Frontera. LC 94-27153. (Illus.). 132p. (C). 1995. pap. 12.95 (*0-8263-1828-2*) U of NM Pr.

Cantu, Norma E., ed. see Aguilar-Henson, Marcela.

Cantu-Ortiz, Francisco. Applications of Advanced Information Technologies: Fourth World Congress of Expert Systems, Mexico City, Mexico, March 1988. LC 97-51423. 1998. pap. 185.00 (*1-882345-22-3*) Cognizant Comm.

Cantu-Ortiz, Francisco J., ed. Operational Expert System Applications in Mexico. LC 91-17802. (Illus.). 217p. 1991. reprint ed. pap. 67.30 (*0-608-04554-3*, 206529600001) Bks Demand.

Cantu, R. C. Diabetes & Exercise. (Illus.). pap. 24.95 (*0-525-93236-4*) Mouvement Pubns.

Cantu, Rey G. Quiero ser Lider. Hdalgo, Javier, ed. (SPA.). 100p. 1998. pap. 10.00 (*0-9669489-0-4*) Nev Giv Up.

Cantu, Robert. Myofascial Manipulation. 190p. 1992. 75.00 (*0-8342-0310-3*) Aspen Pub.

***Cantu, Robert.** Myofascial Manipulation. 2nd ed. 2000. 75.00 (*0-8342-1779-1*) Aspen Pub.

— Neurologic Athletic Head & Spinal Injuries. (Illus.). 430p. Date not set. text. write for info. (*0-7216-8339-8*, W B Saunders Co) Harcrt Hlth Sci Grp.

Cantu, Robert. Toward Fitness: Guided Exercise for Those with Health Problems. LC 79-27686. 258p. 1980. 32.95 (*0-87705-496-7*, Kluwer Acad Hman Sci) Kluwer Academic.

Cantu, Robert C., ed. Boxing & Medicine. LC 94-33961. (Illus.). 224p. 1995. text 39.00 (*0-87322-797-2*, BCAN0797) Human Kinetics.

***Canturri, Miguel Angel, intro.** Andorran Memories: Photographs of Valenti Claverol. (Illus.). 144p. 2000. 49.95 (*1-885586-16-7*, Pub. by Turtle Point Pr) Dist Art Pubs.

CANTUS Staff, ed. Cambrai, Mediatheque Municipale, 38 & Impr. XVI C4. LC 96-103344. (Wissenschattliche Abhandluuzen Musicological Studies Ser.: Vol. 55, Pt. 4). 224p. 1996. 96.00 (*0-931902-98-3*) Inst Mediaeval Mus.

— An Utrecht Antiphoner: Utrecht Bibl. Der Rijksuniversiteit 406 (3. J. 7) LC 97-168457. (Musicological Studies Ser.: Vol. 55, Pt. 6). 232p. 1997. 82.00 (*1-896926-05-3*) Inst Mediaeval Mus.

Cantwell, Aileen, jt. auth. see Polon, Linda.

Cantwell, Alan, Jr. AIDS: The Mystery & the Solution. rev. ed. Highland, Jim, ed. LC 86-1210. (Illus.). 210p. 1984. pap. 9.95 (*0-917211-16-2*) Aries Rising.

— AIDS & the Doctors of Death: An Inquiry into the Origin of the AIDS Epidemic. Henig, Suzanne & Rappaport, Jon, eds. LC 87-37355. 239p. 1988. reprint ed. pap. 14.95 (*0-917211-25-1*) Aries Rising.

— The Cancer Microbe. Henig, Suzanne, ed. (Illus.). 281p. 1990. pap. 19.95 (*0-917211-01-4*) Aries Rising.

— Queer Blood: The Secret AIDS Genocide Plot. Fiske, Sallie, ed. 168p. (Orig.). 1993. pap. 12.95 (*0-917211-26-X*) Aries Rising.

Cantwell, Anne-Marie. Dickson Camp & Pond: Two Early Havana Tradition Sites in the Central Illinois Valley. (Reports of Investigations: No. 36). (Illus.). 174p. 1980. pap. 6.00 (*0-89792-086-4*) Ill St Museum.

Cantwell, Anne-Marie, ed. see Goodman, Claire G.

Cantwell, Aston. Tease for Two. 240p. (Orig.). 1983. mass mkt. 2.75 (*0-446-30293-7*, Pub. by Warner Bks) Little.

Cantwell, David. Liner Notes: George Strait. 128p. 1996. pap. 7.95 (*1-57297-121-5*) Blvd Books.

Cantwell, Dennis & Baker, Lorian. Developmental Speech & Language Disorders. LC 86-26989. (Child Psychopathology Ser.). 214p. 1987. lib. bdg. 30.00 (*0-89862-400-2*) Guilford Pubns.

Cantwell, Denton. Once upon an Earth. 2nd ed. LC 98-89362. 200p. (Orig.). 1998. pap. 6.99 (*1-893181-11-1*) Le Gesse Stevens.

Cantwell, Dick & Allen, Fal. Barley Wine: History, Brewing Techniques, Recipes. LC 97-47349. (Classic Beer Style Ser.). (Illus.). 144p. 1998. pap. 14.95 (*0-937381-59-4*) Brewers Pubns.

Cantwell, George E., ed. Insect Diseases, Vol. 1. LC 73-90772. (Illus.). 235p. reprint ed. pap. 72.90 (*0-8357-6158-4*, 203451800001) Bks Demand.

— Insect Diseases, Vol. 2. LC 73-90772. 310p. pap. 96.10 (*0-7837-0030-X*, 203451800002) Bks Demand.

Cantwell, Gerald T. Citizen Airmen: A History of the Air Force Reserve, 1944-1994. (Illus.). 563p. 1998. 38.00 (*0-16-049269-6*) AFH & MP.

***Cantwell, J. D.** The Second World War: A Guide to Sources. 3rd rev. ed. (PRO Handbks.: No. 15). 308p. 1999. pap. text 24.95 (*1-873162-60-X*, Pub. by PRO Pubns) Midpt Trade.

Cantwell, James R. Reforming Medicaid. 14p. 1995. pap. 10.00 (*1-56808-062-X*, 197) Natl Ctr Pol.

Cantwell, James R. & Armitage, Michael. Nevada Medicaid Vol. 1: Constructive Reform of the State System. 26p. 1996. spiral bd. 10.00 (*1-886306-15-X*) Nevada Policy.

Cantwell, John, ed. Foreign Direct Investment & Technological Change, 2 vols. LC 99-21905. 1007p. 1999. 175.00 (*1-85898-929-9*) E Elgar.

— Multinational Investment in Modern Europe: Strategic Interaction in the Integrated Community. (New Horizons in International Business Ser.). 416p. 1992. 100.00 (*1-85278-421-0*) E Elgar.

— Transnational Corporations: Technology Transfer. LC 93-15973. (United Nations Library on Transnational Corporations: Vol. 18). 1994. write for info. (*0-415-08545-4*) Routledge.

Cantwell, John D. The Public Record Office, 1838-1958. x, 631p. 1991. 115.00 (*0-11-440224-8*, Pub. by Statnry Office) Balogh.

Cantwell, Lee G. Finders Keepers. 1996. pap. 10.95 (*1-57008-224-3*) Bookcraft Inc.

***Cantwell, Mary.** Manhattan Memoir. LC 99-52553. 440p. 2000. pap. 17.95 (*0-14-029190-3*) Viking Penguin.

Cantwell, Mary. Manhattan, When I Was Young. 224p. 1996. pap. 12.95 (*0-14-023223-0*, Penguin Bks) Viking Penguin.

— Speaking with Strangers: A Memoir. LC 97-48292. 160p. 1998. 23.00 (*0-395-82751-5*) HM.

— Speaking with Strangers: A Memoir. 160p. 1999. pap. 11.95 (*0-14-028360-9*) Viking Penguin.

Cantwell, Mary A. Homosexuality: The Secret a Child Dare Not Tell. 150p. 1996. pap. 12.00 (*0-9649829-9-4*) Rafael Pr.

Cantwell, Robert. Bluegrass Breakdown: The Making of the Old Southern Sound. LC 83-4861. (Music in American Life Ser.). 328p. 1984. 24.95 (*0-252-01054-X*) U of Ill Pr.

— Bluegrass Breakdown: The Making of the Old Southern Sound. (Illus.). 334p. 1992. reprint ed. pap. 14.95 (*0-306-80495-6*) Da Capo.

— Ethnomimesis: Folklife & the Representation of Culture. LC 93-9681. xxii, 324p. (C). 1993. pap. 19.95 (*0-8078-4424-1*); text 55.00 (*0-8078-2112-8*) U of NC Pr.

Cantwell, Robert S. When We Were God: The Folk Revival. (Illus.). 432p. 1997. pap. text 15.95 (*0-674-95133-6*) HUP.

— When We Were Good: The Folk Revival. LC 95-20954. (Illus.). 416p. 1996. 24.95 (*0-674-95132-8*) HUP.

***Cantwell, Susan.** Mind over Matter: Personal Choices for a Lifetime of Fitness. 176p. 1999. 16.95 (*0-7737-3216-0*) Stoddart Publ.

Cantwell, Susan. Policies That Work for Personal Trainers. LC 97-76871. (Business Ser.: Vol. 1). 114p. 1997. per. 24.95 (*1-887781-02-1*, C899002) IDEA Pr.

***Cantwell, Susan & Laumann, Silken.** Mind over Matter: Personal Choices for a Lifetime of Fitness. 176p. 1999. pap. 16.95 (*0-7737-6059-8*, Pub. by Stoddart Publ) Genl Dist Srvs.

Canty, Carol S., jt. auth. see Guderjan, Thomas H.

Canty, Donald. Lasting Aalto Masterwork: The Library at Mount Angel Abbey. 1992. pap. 19.95 (*0-918941-04-0*) Mt Angel Abbey.

Canty, Donald J., jt. auth. see Smith, William S.

Canty, John. Shadows. LC 87-205. (Illus.). 24p. (J). (gr. k-3). 1987. 12.95 (*0-06-020988-7*) HarpC Child Bks.

Canty, Kevin. Into the Great Wide Open. LC 97-6672. 1997. pap. 12.00 (*0-679-77652-4*) Vin Bks.

— Nine Below Zero. LC 98-41402. 384p. 1999. 23.95 (*0-385-49160-3*, N A Talese) Doubleday.

***Canty, Kevin.** Nine Below Zero. (Contemporaries Ser.). 384p. 2000. pap. 13.00 (*0-375-70799-9*) Vin Bks.

Canty, Kevin. Rounders: A Novelization. LC 98-35291. 208p. 1998. pap. 11.95 (*0-7868-8398-7*, Pub. by Hyperion) Time Warner.

— A Stranger in This World. LC 95-6780. 192p. 1995. pap. 10.00 (*0-679-76394-5*) Vin Bks.

Canty, Laurence. How to Play Bass Guitar. 3rd ed. LC 92-7230. (How-to-Play Ser.). (Illus.). 100p. (Orig.). 1992. pap. 10.95 (*0-312-08211-8*) St Martin.

Canty, Laurence, jt. auth. see Bacon, Tony.

Canty, Morton J., jt. auth. see Avenhaus, Rudolf.

***Canty, T. J.** Dictionary of Literary Pseudonyms in the English Language. 2nd ed. 844p. 2000. 85.00 (*1-57958-209-5*) Fitzroy Dearborn.

Canty, Thomas. Monster at Christmas. (Illus.). 1986. 30.00 (*0-937986-67-4*) D M Grant.

Cantz. Documenta (Documents), Vol. 1. LC 96-227170. 1996. pap. text 12.95 (*3-89322-826-8*) Dist Art Pubs.

— Documenta (Documents), Vol. 2. 1996. pap. 12.95 (*3-89322-859-4*) Dist Art Pubs.

Cantz Publishing Staff. Art in the Center. 80p. 1998. pap. 14.95 (*3-89322-330-4*, Pub. by Edition Cantz) Dist Art Pubs.

Cantzlaar, George L., jt. auth. see Brussel, James A.

Canudas De Wit, Carlos A., et al, eds. Theory of Robot Control: The ZODIAC. LC 96-289. (Communications & Control Engineering Ser.). (Illus.). xvi, 392p. 89.50 (*3-540-76054-7*) Spr-Verlag.

Canull, Nancy, jt. auth. see March, Deborah.

Canup, John. The Cry of Sodom Enquired Into: Bestiality & the Wilderness of Human Nature in Seventeenth-Century New England. 21p. 1988. reprint ed. pap. 5.00 (*0-944026-06-0*) Am Antiquarian.

***Canup, Robin M.** Origin of the Earth & Moon. (Space Science Ser.). 2000. 50.00 (*0-8165-2073-9*) U of Ariz Pr.

Canuto, C., Jr., et al. Spectral Methods in Fluid Dynamics. (Computational Physics Ser.). (Illus.). 600p. 1987. 90.50 (*0-387-17371-4*) Spr-Verlag.

— Spectral Methods in Fluid Dynamics. Glowinski, Roland et al, eds. (Computational Physics Ser.). (Illus.). 591p. 1993. reprint ed. 53.95 (*0-387-52205-0*) Spr-Verlag.

Canuto, C., et al. Spectral Methods in Fluid Dynamics. 3rd ed. (Computational Physics Ser.). (Illus.). xv, 567p. 1996. pap. 59.95 (*3-540-52205-0*) Spr-Verlag.

Canuto, V. The Impact of Space Exploration on Mankind. Chagas, Carlos, ed. xv, 364p. 1987. text 264.00 (*2-88124-232-4*) Gordon & Breach.

Canuto, V., jt. auth. see Gordon, C. W.

Canuto, V. M. & Elmegreen, B. G. Galaxies & Cosmology. 885p. 1988. 140.00 (*0-677-21720-X*) Gordon & Breach.

— Handbook of Astronomy, Astrophysics & Geophysics, Vol. 2: Galaxies & Cosmology, Vol. 2. 480p. 1988. text 312.00 (*0-677-22150-9*) Gordon & Breach.

Canutt, Yakima & Drake, Oliver. Stunt Man: The Autobiography of Yakima Canutt. LC 96-41114. (Illus.). 288p. 1997. pap. 15.95 (*0-8061-2927-1*) U of Okla Pr.

Canwell, Albert & Frederick, Timothy, contrib. by. Albert F. Canwell: An Oral History. LC 97-196228. (Illus.). xiv, 429p. 1997. pap. write for info. (*1-889320-05-6*) WA St Oral Hist.

Canwell, Bruce. Batman Chronicles: The Gauntlet. Peterson, Scott, ed. (Illus.). 48p. 1997. pap. 4.95 (*1-56389-364-9*) DC Comics.

Canyon, A. M., ed. Assessment of China into the 21st Century. 215p. (C). 1997. lib. bdg. 75.00 (*1-56072-414-5*) Nova Sci Pubs.

Canyon Ranch Staff. Great Tastes: Healthy Cooking from Canyon Ranch. rev. ed. (Illus.). 288p. 1995. 27.00 (*0-9624102-2-5*) Canyon Ranch.

Canz, Gottlieb. Disciplinae Morales, 2 vols., Vol. 32. (GER.). xli, 1388p. 1994. reprint ed. write for info. (*3-487-09825-3*) G Olms Pubs.

— Meditationes Philosophiae. (GER.). 1016p. 1996. reprint ed. 198.00 (*3-487-10221-8*) G Olms Pubs.

— Philosophia Fundamentalis, Vol. 33. (GER.). 608p. 1997. reprint ed. 180.00 (*3-487-10153-X*) G Olms Pubs.

Canzius, Joe. Fast Road to Nowhere. 1998. pap. 10.95 (*0-575-60104-3*, Pub. by V Gollancz) Trafalgar.

Canzona, jt. auth. see Montross, C.

Canzona, Nicholas A., jt. auth. see Montross, Lynn.

Canzoneri, Matthew, et al, eds. Establishing a Central Bank for Europe: Issues in Europe & Lessons from the U. S. (Illus.). 325p. (C). 1992. text 59.95 (*0-521-42098-9*) Cambridge U Pr.

Canzoneri, Matthew & Henderson, Dale. Monetary Policy in Interdependent Economies: A Game-Theoretic Approach. 192p. 1991. 30.00 (*0-262-03178-7*) MIT Pr.

Canzoneri, Matthew B., et al, eds. The New Transatlantic Economy. LC 97-108427. 348p. (C). 1996. text 59.95 (*0-521-56205-8*) Cambridge U Pr.

Canzoniere, Petrarch, comment see Petrarca, Francesco.

Cao, Antonio. Lorca y las Vanguardias: Hacia el Teatro. (Monagrafias A Ser.: Vol. CXII). (SPA.). 106p. (C). 1984. 41.00 (*0-7293-0202-4*, Pub. by Tamesis Bks Ltd) Boydell & Brewer.

Cao, B. S., jt. ed. see He, Y. J.

Cao, C., ed. Investigation of the Ionosphere by Means of Beacon Satellite Measurement: Proceedings of the International Beacon Satellite Symposium, Beijing, China, 18-21 April, 1988. (International Academic Publishers Ser.). 300p. 1989. 92.00 (*0-08-037035-7*, Pergamon Pr) Elsevier.

Cao, Carlo, et al, eds. Urban Storm Drainage. 320p. 1993. text 45.00 (*0-918334-75-6*) WRP.

Cao Garcia, Ramon I., jt. auth. see Andic, Suphan.

Cao, Glen. Beijinger in New York. 220p. 1994. pap. 14.95 (*0-8351-2526-2*) China Bks.

C

Cao, Guanlong. The Attic: Memoir of a Chinese Landlord's Son. Moskin, Nancy, tr. from CHI. LC 95-38541. 255p. (C). 1996. 35.00 (*0-520-20405-0*, Pub. by U CA Pr) Cal Prin Full Svc.
— The Attic: Memoir of a Chinese Landlord's Son. 255p. 1998. pap. 15.95 (*0-520-20406-9*, Pub. by U CA Pr) Cal Prin Full Svc.
Cao, J., jt. ed. see Osaki, Shunji.
Cao, Lan. Everything You Need to Know about Asian American History. (Illus.). (J). 1996. 19.30 (*0-606-18362-0*) Turtleback.
Cao, Lan. Monkey Bridge. LC 96-52418. 260p. 1998. pap. 12.95 (*0-14-026361-6*) Viking Penguin.
Cao, Lan & Novas, Himilce. Everything You Need to Know about Asian-American History. LC 96-1942. 366p. 1996. pap. 13.95 (*0-452-27315-3*, Plume); pap. 12.95 (*0-614-97863-7*, Plume) Dutton Plume.
Cao, Ngoc-Phuong. Thu Tim Cau Chan Tren Cat: Ghi Chep Ve Tho Thay Nhat Hanh. (VIE.). 312p. 1988. pap. 12.00 (*1-891667-02-5*) La Boi Soc.
Cao, Tian Y. Conceptual Developments of 20th Century Field Theories. LC 96-25090. 453p. (C). 1997. text 59.95 (*0-521-43178-6*) Cambridge U Pr.
— Conceptual Developments of 20th Century Field Theories. 451p. (C). 1998. pap. text 39.95 (*0-521-63420-2*) Cambridge U Pr.
Cao, Tian Yu, ed. Conceptual Foundations of Quantum Field Theory. LC 98-24394. (Illus.). 500p. (C). 1998. 100.00 (*0-521-63152-1*) Cambridge U Pr.
Cao, Tiehua & Sanderson, A. C. Intelligent Task Planning Using Fuzzy Petri Nets. LC 96-290. (Series in Intelligent Control & Intelligent Automation). 208p. 1996. write for info. (*981-02-2556-3*) World Scientific Pub.
Cao Van Vien. Leadership. 201p. 1989. reprint ed. pap. 22.50 (*0-923135-08-1*) Dalley Bk Service.
Cao Van Vien & Dong Van Khuyen. Reflections on the Vietnam War. 165p. 1989. reprint ed. pap. 18.50 (*0-923135-06-5*) Dalley Bk Service.
Cao, X. H. Rings, Groups & Algebras. LC 96-22831. (Lecture Notes in Pure & Applied Mathematics Ser.: Vol. 181). (Illus.). 352p. 1996. pap. text 165.00 (*0-8247-9733-7*) Dekker.
Cao, Xi-Ren, jt. auth. see He, Yu-Chi.
Cao, Yi. Controllability Analysis & Control Structure Selection. (Engineering Systems Modelling & Control Ser.). 1999. 85.00 (*0-86380-211-7*) Research Studies Pr Ltd.
Cao, Zhen, jt. auth. see Ashmore, Rhea.
Cao, Zuoya. The Internal & the External: A Comparison of the Artistic Use of Natural Imagery in English Romantic & Chinese Classic Poetry. LC 97-13445. (Asian Thought & Culture Ser.: Vol. 32). 163p. (C). 1998. text 40.95 (*0-8204-3815-4*) P Lang Pubng.
Caoili, Manuel A. The Origins of Metropolitan Manila: A Political & Social Analysis. (Illus.). 299p. (Orig.). (C). 1989. pap. 18.75 (*971-10-0385-6*, Pub. by New Day Pub) Cellar.
Caola, S. Precontrol. 1997. text. write for info. (*0-442-01237-3*, VNR) Wiley.
Caole, Frances, jt. auth. see Michael, Veronica.
Caole, Francis & Michael, Veronica. Cameg Nertussia? (What Do I Eat?) large type ed. (ESK., Illus.). 8p. (J). (gr. k-3). 1999. pap. text 6.00 (*1-58084-149-X*) Lower Kuskokwim.
— Canek Nerlarcia? (What Do I Eat?) large type ed. (ESK., Illus.). 8p. (J). (gr. k-3). 1999. pap. text 6.00 (*1-58084-094-9*) Lower Kuskokwim.
— What Do I Eat? large type ed. (Illus.). 8p. (J). (gr. k-3). 1999. pap. text 6.00 (*1-58084-093-0*) Lower Kuskokwim.
Caolo, Alan. Fly Fisherman's Guide to Atlantic Baitfish & Other Food Sources. (Illus.). 48p. 1995. pap. 9.95 (*1-57188-017-8*) F Amato Pubns.
Caorsin, Gulielmus. To the Most Excellente Kyng, Kyng Edward 4th Cohan Kay Hys Humble Poete Lawreate, etc. LC 72-179. (English Experience Ser.: No. 236). 48p. 1970. reprint ed. 21.00 (*90-221-0236-X*) Walter J Johnson.
Caouette, Jack B. Managing Credit Risk: The Next Great Financial Challenge. LC 98-17660. (Frontiers in Finance Ser.). 464p. 1998. 79.95 (*0-471-11189-9*) Wiley.
Caoursin, Guillaume, jt. auth. see Aesop.
Caovilla, Paola B. Shoes: Objects of Art & Seduction. (Illus.). 200p. 1999. 60.00 (*88-8118-470-2*, Pub. by Skira IT) Abbeville Pr.
Cap, Biruta, ed. see Mann, Thomas.
Cap, Cydney, ed. see Marshall & Swift Staff.
Cap, F., ed. Waves & Instabilities in Plasmas. (CISM International Centre for Mechanical Sciences Ser.: Vol. 349). 282p. 1995. 81.95 (*3-211-82636-X*) Spr-Verlag.
Cap, Ferdinand, tr. see Karpman, V. I.
Cap, Jean-Pierre. Decadence of Freedom. 1985. text 51.00 (*0-88033-041-4*, 149, Pub. by East Eur Monographs) Col U Pr.
Cap, Reginald. Devotions for the Holy Souls. 1989. pap. 30.00 (*0-86217-299-3*, Pub. by Veritas Pubns) St Mut.
Cap, Roberta K. & Frederick, V. Ray, Jr., eds. Proceedings of the Conference on Changes in the Biota of Lakes Erie & Ontario, March 10-11, 1980. (Bulletin of the Buffalo Society of Natural Sciences Ser.: Vol. 25, No. 4). (Illus.). 120p. (Orig.). 1981. pap. 4.75 (*0-944032-32-X*) Buffalo SNS.
Capa, Cornell. Robert Capa: Photographs. LC 96-83976. (Illus.). 192p. 1996. 76.00 (*0-89381-675-2*) Aperture.
Capa, Cornell & Favrod, Charles-Henri. La Famille Deriaz: Five Generations of Swiss Photographers. 112p. 1995. 45.00 (*3-7231-0387-1*) Dist Art Pubs.
Capa, Cornell & Havel, Vaclav. Safe Conduct: The Photographs of Paul Ickovic. (Illus.). 96p. 1991. 29.95 (*0-933642-15-6*) Intl Ctr Photo.
Capa, Robert. Heart of Spain: Robert Capa. (Illus.). 228p. 1998. 76.00 (*0-89381-831-3*) Aperture.
— Robert Capa. 1999. pap. 19.95 (*3-570-19203-2*) Gruner & Jahr AG &.
— Running for Shelter During Air Raid. 1939. write for info. (*0-89381-706-6*) Aperture.
— Slightly Out of Focus. LC 99-24637. (Illus.). 240p. 1999. 24.95 (*0-679-60328-X*) Modern Lib NY.
— Slightly Out of Focus. (American Autobiography Ser.). 243p. 1995. reprint ed. lib. bdg. 79.00 (*0-7812-8472-4*) Rprt Serv.
Capablanca, Jose. Chess Fundamentals. 144p. 1994. pap. 15.95 (*1-85744-073-0*, Pub. by Cadgn Bks) Macmillan.
— A Primer of Chess. 160p. 1995. pap. 15.95 (*1-85744-165-6*, Pub. by Cadgn Bks) Macmillan.
Capablanca, Jose R. Chess Fundamentals. (Illus.). 1979. pap. 15.00 (*0-679-14004-2*, 27, Tarten) McKay.
— My Chess Career. (Illus.). 194p. 1966. pap. 7.95 (*0-486-21548-2*) Dover.
— Primer of Chess. LC 35-3374. (Illus.). 288p. 1977. pap. 12.00 (*0-15-673900-3*, Harvest Bks) Harcourt.
Capacchione, Lucia. The Creative Journal: The Art of Finding Yourself. 192p. 1989. pap. 12.95 (*0-87877-148-4*, 642) Newcastle Pub.
— The Creative Journal: The Art of Finding Yourself. LC 78-51590. (Illus.). 180p. 1979. pap. 12.95 (*0-8040-0798-5*) Swallow.
— The Creative Journal for Children: A Guide for Parents, Teachers, & Counselors. LC 89-42621. (Illus.). 144p. (Orig.). 1989. pap. 19.95 (*0-87773-497-6*, Pub. by Shambhala Pubns) Random.
***Capacchione, Lucia.** Creative Journal for Parents: A Guide to Unlocking Your Natural Parenting Wisdom. LC 99-44704. 240p. 2000. pap. 15.95 (*1-57062-399-6*, Pub. by Shambhala Pubns) Random.
Capacchione, Lucia. The Creative Journal for Teens: Making Friends with Yourself. (Illus.). 182p. 1992. pap. 12.95 (*0-87877-175-1*, 644) Newcastle Pub.
— The Picture of Health: Healing Your Life with Art. 2nd ed. (Illus.). 176p. (Orig.). 1996. pap. 12.95 (*0-87877-231-6*) Newcastle Pub.
— The Power of Your Other Hand: A Course in Channeling the Inner Wisdom of the Right Brain. 207p. (Orig.). 1988. pap. 12.95 (*0-87877-130-1*, 640) Newcastle Pub.
— The Recovery of Your Inner Child. (Illus.). 288p. (Orig.). 1991. per. 14.00 (*0-671-70135-5*, Fireside) S&S Trade Pap.
***Capacchione, Lucia.** Visioning: Ten Steps to Designing the Life of Your Dreams. LC 99-41035. (Illus.). 272p. 2000. 25.95 (*1-58542-012-3*, Tarcher Putnam) Putnam Pub Group.
Capacchione, Lucia. The Well-Being Journal: Drawing on Your Inner Power to Heal Yourself. 168p. (Orig.). 1989. pap. 12.95 (*0-87877-141-7*, 641) Newcastle Pub.
Capacchione, Lucia & Bardsley, Sandra. Creating a Joyful Birth: Awakening Your Inner Guidance & Creativity for Pregnancy, Labor & Early Parenting. (Illus.). 320p. 1994. pap. 13.00 (*0-671-87027-0*, Fireside) S&S Trade Pap.
Capacchione, Lucia & Van Pelt, Peggy. Putting Your Talent to Work: Identifying, Cultivating & Marketing Your Natural Talents. 200p. (Orig.). 1996. pap. 12.95 (*1-55874-406-1*, 4061) Health Comm.
Capacchione, Lucia, et al. Lighten up Your Body - Lighten up Your Life: Beyond Diet & Exercise - The Inner Path to Lasting Change. 92p. 1990. pap. 12.95 (*0-87877-150-6*, 643) Newcastle Pub.
Capaccioli, Massimo, ed. Astronomy with Schmidt-Type Telescopes. 1984. text 274.00 (*90-277-1756-7*) Kluwer Academic.
Capaccioli, Massimo & Corwin, H., Jr., eds. Gerard & Antoinette de Vaucouleurs: A Life for Astronomy. (Advanced Series in Astrophysics & Cosmology: Vol. 4). 400p. 1989. text 151.00 (*9971-5-0636-X*) World Scientific Pub.
Capachi, Nicholas E. Excavation & Grading Handbook. rev. ed. 380p. 1987. pap. 22.75 (*0-934041-29-6*) Craftsman.
Capacino, William F., et al. Modern Logistics Management: Integrating Marketing, Manufacturing & Physical Distribution. LC 85-6524. (Marketing Management Ser.). 430p. 1985. 152.95 (*0-471-81261-7*) Wiley.
Capalari, Steve, tr. see Heisenberg, Elisabeth.
***Capalbo, Carla.** La Cucina Italiana: Authentic Recipes from All over Italy. (Illus.). 1998. 11.98 (*1-84038-076-4*) Hermes Hse.
Capalbo, Carla. A Food Lover's Companion to Tuscany. LC 97-36633. (Illus.). 416p. 1998. pap. 14.95 (*0-8118-1209-X*) Chronicle Bks.
***Capalbo, Carla.** Italian Cooking Encyclopedia. 2000. 45.00 (*1-85967-851-3*) Anness Pub.
— The Ultimate Italian Cookbook: Over 200 Authentic Recipes from Italy Step-by-Step. rev. ed. (Ultimate Cookbook Ser.). (Illus.). 256p. 1998. 19.98 (*0-7651-0854-2*) Smithmark.
***Capalbo, Carla, et al.** The Italian Cooking Encyclopedia. (Illus.). 512p. 2000. reprint ed. 40.00 (*0-7881-9219-1*) DIANE Pub.
Capalbo, Susan M. & Antle, John M., eds. Agricultural Productivity: Measurement & Explanation. LC 87-27224. 404p. 1988. 32.00 (*0-915707-37-3*) Resources Future.
Capaldi, D. & Patterson, G. R. Psychometric Properties of Fourteen Latent Constructs from the Oregon Youth Society. (Recent Research in Psychology Ser.). (Illus.). 440p. 1988. 78.95 (*0-387-96845-8*) Spr-Verlag.
***Capaldi, E. John & Proctor, Robert W.** Contextualism in Psychological Research? A Critical Review. LC 99-6362. 193p. 1999. 69.95 (*0-7619-0997-4*) Sage.
Capaldi, E. John, jt. ed. see Boysen, Sarah T.
Capaldi, Elizabeth P., ed. Why We Eat What We Eat: The Psychology of Eating. LC 96-33870. (Illus.). 339p. 1996. 49.95 (*1-55798-366-6*, 4318500) Am Psychol.
***Capaldi, Gina.** Civil War Garments History Leg. (Illus.). 1999. pap. text. write for info. (*0-7682-0064-4*) Good Apple.
Capaldi, Nicholas. The Art of Deception. 1996. 17.95 incl. audio (*1-57392-057-6*) Prometheus Bks.
Capaldi, Nicholas. The Art of Deception. 3rd rev. ed. LC 87-62207. 222p. 1987. pap. 17.95 (*0-87975-424-9*) Prometheus Bks.
— The Enlightenment Project in the Analytic Conversation Vol. 4: Philosophical Studies in Contemporary Culture. LC 98-9777. 532p. 1998. text 173.00 (*0-7923-5014-6*) Kluwer Academic.
***Capaldi, Nicholas.** How to Win Every Argument: An Introduction to Critical Thinking. 224p. 1999. 7.98 (*1-56731-330-2*, MJF Bks) Fine Comms.
Capaldi, Nicholas. Hume's Place in Moral Philosophy. (Studies in Moral Philosophy: Vol. 3). XII, 393p. (C). 1992. text 54.50 (*0-8204-0858-1*) P Lang Pubng.
— Immigration: Debating the Issues. LC 97-6542. 324p. 1997. pap. 16.95 (*1-57392-142-4*) Prometheus Bks.
— Out of Order: Affirmative Action & the Crisis of Doctrinaire Liberalism. LC 84-43181. 211p. 1985. 30.95 (*0-87975-279-3*) Prometheus Bks.
Capaldi, Nicholas, ed. An Invitation to Philosophy. LC 81-81131. 295p. (Orig.). (C). 1981. pap. text 24.95 (*0-87975-162-2*) Prometheus Bks.
Capaldi, Nicholas, et al, eds. Journeys Through Philosophy. rev. ed. LC 81-85574. 484p. (C). 1982. pap. text 25.95 (*0-87975-171-1*) Prometheus Bks.
Capaldi, Nicholas & Livingston, Donald W., eds. Liberty in Hume's History of England. 240p. (C). 1990. lib. bdg. 155.00 (*0-7923-0650-3*, Pub. by Kluwer Academic) Kluwer Academic.
Capaldi, Nicholas, jt. auth. see Mosley, Albert G.
Capaldi, Roderick A., ed. Membrane Proteins & Their Interactions with Lipids. LC 76-58609. (Membrane Proteins Ser.: No. 1). (Illus.). 272p. reprint ed. pap. 84.40 (*0-7837-0607-3*, 204095500019) Bks Demand.
— Membrane Proteins in Energy Transduction. LC 79-17584. (Membrane Proteins Ser.: No. 2). (Illus.). 542p. reprint ed. pap. 168.10 (*0-7837-0821-1*, 204113500019) Bks Demand.
Capallen, Ric. CNE Guide to Windows NT 4.0. 600p. 1999. 39.99 (*0-7897-1293-8*) Que.
Capanna, Paloma, ed. Women & the Law in New York State. 2nd rev. ed. LC 94-71712. 1994. pap. 14.95 (*0-938588-12-5*) LWV NYS.
***Capano, Daniel E.** Contractor's Guide to Network Cabling. (Illus.). 448p. 2000. pap. text 39.95 (*0-07-012011-0*) McGraw.
Capano, Peter. Baseball Collectibles. LC 88-64081. (Illus.). 128p. 1989. pap. 14.95 (*0-88740-160-0*) Schiffer.
Caparatta, Paul. Merchants at War: Survival Tactics for Armed & Unarmed Merchants. LC 98-60175. (Illus.). 269p. 1998. pap. 19.95 (*1-888644-99-0*) Varro Pr.
***Caparros, Alonso.** El Arte del Beso. 1999. pap. 18.95 (*84-270-2456-8*) E Martinez Roca.
Caparros, Domingo. Diccionario de Gentilicos y Toponimos: Dictionary of Place Names & Proper Names. (SPA.). 1981. 49.95 (*0-8288-2031-7*, F107510) Fr & Eur.
CAPART (Council for Advancement of People's Action, jt. auth. see CENDIT (Centre for Development of Instructional Te.
Capart, Jean. Egyptian Art: Introductory Studies. Dawson, Warren R., tr. from FRE. (Select Bibliographies Reprint Ser.). 1977. reprint ed. 31.95 (*0-8369-6638-4*) Ayer.
Capasso, F., ed. Physics in Quantum Electron Devices. (Electronics & Photonics Ser.: Vol. 28). (Illus.). 425p. 1990. 74.50 (*0-387-51128-8*) Spr-Verlag.
Capasso, F. & Margaritondo, Giorgio, eds. Heterojunction Band Discontinuities: Physics & Device Applications. x, 652p. 1987. pap. 101.00 (*0-444-88090-9*, North Holland) Elsevier.
Capasso, Francesco & Gaginella, Timothy S. Laxatives: A Practical Guide. LC 97-3681. 1997. text. write for info. (*3-540-75037-1*) Spr-Verlag.
Capasso, Nicholas, jt. auth. see Lafo, Rachel R.
Capasso, Nick. Good-bye to Apple Pie: Contemporary Artists View the Family in Crisis. (Illus.). 64p. (Orig.). 1992. pap. 10.00 (*0-945506-09-0*) DeCordova Mus.
— John Van Alstine: Vessels & Voyages. LC 96-84241. 8p. (Orig.). Date not set. pap. write for info. (*0-945506-20-1*) DeCordova Mus.
Capasso, Nick & Wallace, Brian. The Computer in the Studio. LC 94-68746. 20p. (Orig.). Date not set. pap. write for info. (*0-945506-17-1*) DeCordova Mus.
Capasso, Nick, jt. auth. see Lafo, Rachel R.
Capasso, Paul F. Telecommunications & Information Assurance: America's Achilles' Heel?, Vol. P-97-1. unabridged ed. LC 98-129574. (Illus.). 58p. 1997. pap. text. write for info. (*1-879716-40-2*) Ctr Info Policy.
***Capasso, Ronald L. & Daresh, John C.** The School Administrator Internship Handbook: Leading, Mentoring & Participating in the Internship Program. LC 00-9507. 2000. pap. write for info. (*0-7619-7657-4*) Corwin Pr.
Capasso, V. & Caselli, R., eds. Mathematical Methods for Industrial Problems: Proceedings of the International Workshop, Bari, Italy, 1988. 344p. 1989. 199.00 (*90-6764-122-7*, Pub. by VSP) Coronet Bks.
Capasso, Vincenzo. Mathematical Structures of Epidemic Systems. LC 93-10042. (Lecture Notes in Biomathematics Ser.: Vol. 97). 1993. 64.95 (*0-387-56526-4*) Spr-Verlag.
Capasso, Vincenzo, ed. see Busenberg, Stavros N., et al.
Capazzoli, Tom, jt. auth. see Ludden, LaVerne.
Capco, David, et al, eds. Current Topics in Developmental Biology Vol. 31: Cytoskeletal Mechanisms During Animal Development, Vol. 31. (Illus.). 501p. (C). 1996. text 85.00 (*0-12-153131-7*) Acad Pr.
Capdevila, A. Amor de Schahrazada Zincali. (SPA.). 157p. 1957. 9.95 (*0-8288-7073-X*, S19906) Fr & Eur.
Capdevila, C. Coll, ed. see Creatsas, G. & European Society of Contraception Staff.
Capdevila Font, Juan. Diccionario Basico Escolar de la Lengua Espanola. 2nd ed. (SPA.). 398p. 1975. pap. 4.75 (*0-8288-5802-0*, S50255) Fr & Eur.
— Diccionario de la Literatura Universal: Universal Dictionary of Literature. (SPA.). 536p. 1977. 22.50 (*0-8288-5315-0*, S50261) Fr & Eur.
— Diccionario de la Vida Sexual. (SPA.). 200p. 1976. 14.95 (*0-8288-5594-3*, S50262) Fr & Eur.
— Diccionario de Matematicas. (SPA.). 160p. 1976. 14.95 (*0-8288-5596-X*, S50263) Fr & Eur.
— Moderna Enciclopedia Universal Distein. (SPA.). 600p. 1974. pap. 24.95 (*0-8288-6074-2*, S-50448) Fr & Eur.
Capdevila, I Valls Ro. La Escuela Que Aventura Roser. 1999. pap. text 15.95 (*84-261-3005-4*) Lectorum Pubns.
Capdevila, Luis A. El Anticristo Viene En un Ovni. (SPA.). 50p. 1999. pap. 6.96 (*0-7392-0152-2*, PO3099) Morris Pubng.
— La Eternidad. (SPA.). 78p. 1999. pap. 5.95 (*0-7392-0153-0*, PO3100) Morris Pubng.
***Capdevila, Luis A.** El Proximo Mover de Dios. 44p. 1999. mass mkt. write for info. (*0-7392-0218-9*, PO3245) Morris Pubng.
Cape, B. F. & Dobson, P. Dictionnaire Maloine de l'Infirmiere et Aide-Memoire des Pri. (FRE.). 1979. 49.95 (*0-7859-7816-X*, 2224005210) Fr & Eur.
Cape Cod Academy Staff, jt. ed. see Cookbook Committee Staff.
Cape Cod Bird Club Staff & Massachusetts Audubon Society Staff. Birding Cape Cod. LC 89-6883. (Illus.). 125p. 1990. pap. 12.95 (*0-9619485-1-5*, 101) MA Audubon Soc.
Cape Codder Staff. The Sea, the Land, the Life Through the Cameras of The Cape Codder. (Illus.). 120p. (Orig.). 1988. pap. 14.95 (*0-9619737-0-6*) Cape Codder Pr.
Cape, David, jt. auth. see Tenney, Tommy.
Cape, Diane, ed. see Anderson, Rachell N.
Cape, Edward M. The Economic Council & Its Fifth Annual Review. LC 79-552199. 67p. 1969. reprint ed. pap. 30.00 (*0-608-01367-6*, 206210600002) Bks Demand.
Cape, Elizabeth, jt. auth. see Albregts, Melisa.
Cape, J. N., jt. auth. see Sheppard, L. J.
Cape, Ronald D., et al, eds. Fundamentals of Geriatric Medicine. LC 81-48595. (Illus.). 479p. 1983. reprint ed. pap. 148.50 (*0-608-00647-5*, 206123500007) Bks Demand.
Cape, Stephen H. Changing Images: Nineteenth-Century British Book Illustration. (Illus.). 62p. 1991. pap. 6.00 (*1-879598-00-0*) IN Univ Lilly Library.
Cape, W. H. Public Employee Retirement Plans in South Dakota. 1956. 5.00 (*1-55614-099-1*) U of SD Gov Res Bur.
Cape, William H. Constitutional Revision in South Dakota. 1957. 5.00 (*1-55614-028-2*) U of SD Gov Res Bur.
Cape, William H. & Felt, F. O. Handbook for South Dakota Municipal Officials. 1970. 5.00 (*1-55614-046-0*) U of SD Gov Res Bur.
Cape, William H., jt. auth. see Farber, William O.
Capecchi, Mario, ed. Molecular Genetics of Early Drosophila & Mouse Development. (Current Communications in Molecular Biology Ser.). (Illus.). 141p. 1989. pap. 24.00 (*0-87969-339-8*) Cold Spring Harbor.
Capeci, Anne. The Halloween Joker. Ryan, Kevin, ed. LC 98-85453. (Wishbone Super Mysteries Ser.: No. 1). (Illus.). 255p. (J). (gr. 3-7). 1998. mass mkt. 3.99 (*1-57064-338-5*, Big Red) Lyrick Pub.
— Key to the Golden Dog, No. 8. LC 97-76053. (Illus.). 144p. (J). (gr. 3-7). 1998. mass mkt. 3.99 (*1-57064-284-2*, Big Red) Lyrick Pub.
***Capeci, Anne.** To Sniff a Thief. (Wishbone Mysteries Ser.: Vol. 21). (Illus.). 144p. (J). (gr. 3-7). 2000. mass mkt. 3.99 (*1-57064-841-7*, Big Red) Lyrick Pub.
Capeci, Dominic J., Jr. The Lynching of Cleo Wright. LC 98-5635. (Illus.). 352p. 1998. 29.95 (*0-8131-2048-9*) U Pr of Ky.
Capeci, Dominic J., Jr., ed. Detroit & the "Good War" The World War II Letters of Mayor Edward Jeffries & Friends. (Illus.). 336p. (C). 1996. text 34.95 (*0-8131-1974-X*) U Pr of Ky.
Capeci, Jerry. Gotti. 1996. mass mkt. 7.50 (*0-451-40681-8*, Onyx) NAL.
Capeci, Jerry & Mustain, Gene. Murder Machine: A True Story of Murder, Madness, & the Mafia. (Illus.). 496p. 1993. mass mkt. 6.99 (*0-451-40387-8*, Onyx) NAL.
Capecia, Mayotte. I Am a Martinican Woman & the White Negress. Clark, Beatrice S., tr. from FRE. LC 97-14262.Tr. of Je Suis Martiniquiase & La Negresse Blanche. 245p. (Orig.). (C). 1997. pap. 15.00 (*1-57889-001-2*) Passeggiata.
Capehart, B. L. & Hamza, M. H., eds. Energy '83: Proceedings, IASTED Symposium, Orlando, Florida, U. S. A., November 9-11, 1983. 105p. 1983. 65.00 (*0-88986-052-1*, 059) Acta Pr.
Capehart, B. L., et al. Guide to Energy Management. 2nd ed. LC 97-19050. 515p. 1997. 79.00 (*0-88173-282-6*) Fairmont Pr.
***Capehart, B. L., et al.** Guide to Energy Management. 3rd ed. LC 99-54995. 514p. 2000. 92.00 (*0-88173-336-9*) Fairmont Pr.
***Capehart, Barney L.** Electrical Engineering: Guide to Energy Management. 3rd ed. 544p. 2000. 92.00 (*0-13-019611-8*) P-H.

C

An Asterisk (*) at the beginning of an entry indicates that the title is appearing for the first time.

— Protectionism in the World Economy. (International Library of Macroeconomic & Financial History: Vol. 7). 584p. 1992. 240.00 (*1-85278-549-7*) E Elgar.

Capie, Robert M., ed. see UPCO's Review of Biology Staff & Alcabes, Sylvan.

Capiiolo, Paola. Floria Tosca. Heron, Liz, tr. from ITA. LC 95-71062. 224p. (Orig.). (C). 1997. pap. 12.99 (*1-85242-381-1*) Serpents Tail.

Capilano Computing Systems, Ltd., Staff. Logicworks 4. LC 98-36517. 448p. (C). 1998. pap. text, teacher ed. write for info. (*0-201-44488-7*) Addison-Wesley.

— LogicWorks Verilog Modeler: Interactive Circuit Simulation Software for Windows & Macintosh; Version 3. 102p. (C). 1996. 32.00 incl. audio compact disk (*0-201-49885-5*) Addison-Wesley.

— LogicWorks Verilog Modeler Manual. LC 96-25111. 112p. (C). 1996. pap. text. write for info. (*0-201-89585-4*) Addison-Wesley.

— Logicworks 3: Interactive Circuit Design Software for Windows & Macintosh with 3.5 Disk. 2nd ed. (C). 1996. pap. text 52.95 (*0-8053-1316-8*) Benjamin-Cummings.

Capilla, Ramiro Antonio Calle. Buda, el Principe de la Luz; Su Vide, Su Ensenanza. 1998. pap. text 11.95 (*84-7880-756-X*) E Temas de Hoy.

Capin de Aguilar, Marilu. Un Pincel en el Alba: Poemas Selectos. LC 92-71411. (Coleccion Espejo de Paciencia). (SPA.). 176p. (Orig.). 1992. pap. 15.00 (*0-89729-641-9*) Ediciones.

Capineri, Cristina & Rietveld, Piet, eds. Networks in Transport & Communications: A Policy Approach. LC 97-74509. (Illus.). 368p. 1998. text 83.95 (*1-85972-533-3*, Pub. by Ashgate Pub) Ashgate Pub Co.

Capinski, M. & Cutland, N. J. Nonstandard Methods for Stochastic Fluid Mechanics. (Series on Advances in Mathematics). 248p. 1995. text 61.00 (*981-02-1710-2*) World Scientific Pub.

Capinski, Marek & Kopp, P. E. Measure, Integral, & Probability. LC 98-34763. (Undergraduate Mathematics Ser.). 1999. pap. 29.95 (*3-540-76260-4*) Spr-Verlag.

***Capioppo, John T., et al, eds.** Handbook of Psychophysiology. 2nd ed. LC 99-36718. (Illus.). 1400p. (C). 2000. 120.00 (*0-521-62634-X*) Cambridge U Pr.

Capirola, Vincenzo. Vincenzo Capirola Lute Book. Gombosi, Otto, ed. (Music Ser.). 236p. (C). 1983. reprint ed. lib. bdg. 75.00 (*0-306-76100-9*) Da Capo.

***Capisani, Giampaolo R.** Handbook of Central Asia. 2000. text 75.00 (*1-86064-429-5*, Pub. by I B T) St Martin.

Capistrani, Angelo. Let's Eat Italian at Home! (Let's Eat...at Home! Ser.). 160p. 1995. pap. 5.95 (*0-572-01747-2*, Pub. by Foulsham UK) Assoc Pubs Grp.

Capistrano-Baker, Florina H. Art of Island Southeast Asia: The Fred & Rita Richman Collection in the Metropolitan Museum of Art. LC 93-51050. (Illus.). 156p. 1994. 39.95 (*0-87099-697-5*); pap. 19.95 (*0-87099-698-3*) Metro Mus Art.

Capistrano-Baker, Florina H., et al. Basketry of the Luzon Cordillera, Philippines. LC 98-4286. (Illus.). 136p. 1998. 45.00 (*0-930741-66-8*); pap. 24.00 (*0-930741-67-6*) UCLA Fowler Mus.

Capistrano de Abreu, Joao. Chapters in Brazil's Colonial History, 1500-1800. Scwartz, Stuart, ed. Brakel, Arthur, tr. LC 96-43461. (Library of Latin America). (Illus.). 272p. 1997. 30.00 (*0-19-510301-7*) OUP.

***Capital Access International Staff.** Capital Access International Mortgage & Asset-Backed Desk Reference, Summer 2000 Edition: U. S. Buyside & Sellside Profiles. 4th ed. (International Desk Reference Ser.). 896p. 2000. pap. 395.00 (*1-888815-18-3*) Capital Access.

***Capital Access International Staff, ed.** Capital Access International Derivatives Desk Reference, Winter 1999-2000 Edition: U. S. Buyside & Sellside Profiles Plus Top U. K. Investors. 4th ed. 626p. 1999. pap. 395.00 (*1-888815-16-7*) Capital Access.

***Capital Growth, Inc. Staff.** 1999 Guide to Entrepreneurial Venture Financing - South & Middle Atlantic. 120p. 1999. pap. 95.00 (*1-929744-09-9*) Penn Chamber of Bus.

Capital Movements & the Growth of International Indebtedness Study Group Staff. The Outlook for International Bank Lending. (Report Ser.). 51p. 1981. pap. 10.00 (*1-56708-054-5*) Grp of Thirty.

Capital Movements Study Group. Balance-of-Payments Problems of Developing Countries. (Report Ser.). 35p. 1981. pap. 10.00 (*1-56708-053-7*) Grp of Thirty.

Capital Research Center Staff, jt. auth. see Yablonski, Christopher.

***Capitan, William H.** The Ethical Navigator. LC 00-36446. 208p. 2000. pap. 29.50 (*0-7618-1700-X*) U Pr of Amer.

Capitein, Jacobus E. The Agony of Asar: A Thesis on Slavery by the Former Slave, Jacobus Eliza Johannes 1717-1747. Parker, Grant, tr. from LAT. & comment by. LC 95-48329. (Illus.). 160p. (C). 2000. text 34.95 (*1-55876-125-X*); pap. text 14.95 (*1-55876-126-8*) Wiener Pubs Inc.

***Capitelli, M.** Plasma Kinetics in Atmospheric Gases. LC 00-41961. (Series on Atomic, Optical & Plasma Physics). 2000. write for info. (*3-540-67416-0*) Spr-Verlag.

Capitelli, M. & Bardsley, J. N., eds. Nonequilibrium Processes in Partially Ionized Gases. (NATO ASI Ser.: Vol. 220). (Illus.). 706p. (C). 1990. text 186.00 (*0-306-43586-1*, Kluwer Plenum) Kluwer Academic.

Capitelli, M. & Gorse, C. Plasma Technology: Fundamentals & Applications. (Illus.). 232p. (C). 1992. text 75.00 (*0-306-44207-8*, Kluwer Plenum) Kluwer Academic.

Capitelli, Mario, ed. Molecular Physics & Hypersonic Flows. LC 96-13182. (NATO ASI Ser.: Series C, Vol. 482). 795p. 1996. text 364.50 (*0-7923-4055-8*) Kluwer Academic.

Capitman, Barbara. American Trademark Designs: A Survey of 732 Marks, Logos, & Corporate-Identity Symbols. 160p. 1976. pap. 9.95 (*0-486-23259-X*) Dover.

Capitman, Barbara B., et al. Rediscovering Art Deco U. S. A. A Nationwide Tour of Architectural Delights. (Illus.). 192p. 1994. pap. 25.00 (*0-525-48604-6*, Dutton Studio) Studio Bks.

***Capitman, Barbara Baer.** Deco Delights: Preserving the Beauty & Joy of Miami Beach Architecture. (Illus.). 116p. 2000. reprint ed. pap. 22.00 (*0-7881-9301-5*) DIANE Pub.

Capito, Diane & Willis, Mark. San Antonio on Foot. 2nd ed. LC 97-22289. (Illus.). 240p. 1997. pap. 13.95 (*0-89672-382-8*) Tex Tech Univ Pr.

***Capitol Brass Quintet.** Caroling with the Capitol Brass - Brass Quintet. 128p. 1998. pap. 19.95 (*0-7866-4412-5*, 98113) Mel Bay.

Capitol Communication Systems, Inc. Staff, ed. & illus. see American Correctional Association Staff.

Capitol Enquiry Staff, compiled by. Pocket Directory of the California Legislature, 1986. 64p. (Orig.). 1986. pap. 5.95 (*0-917982-32-0*) Capitol Enquiry.

Capitol Preservation Committee. Guidebook to the Tiled Pavement in the Capitol of Pennsylvania. (Illus.). 105p. 1997. pap. 9.95 (*0-9643048-6-4*, 0219) Penn Capitol Presrv.

Capitol Preservation Committee Staff. Advance the Colors! Pennsylvania Civil War Battle Flags, Vol. 1. (Illus.). 304p. 1987. 45.00 (*0-8182-0090-1*) Penn Capitol Presrv.

— Advance the Colors! Pennsylvania Civil War Battle Flags, Vol. 2. (Illus.). 304p. 1991. 45.00 (*0-8182-0155-X*) Penn Capitol Presrv.

Capizzi, Joseph, jt. auth. see Larew, Hiram.

Capkova, V. Cesko-Francouzsky-Cesky Slovnik na Cesty. (CZE & FRE.). 431p. 1981. 8.95 (*0-8288-1696-4*, M14021) Fr & Eur.

***Caplan.** Thinking Critically About Research on Sex & Gender. 2nd ed. LC 98-27621. 144p. (C). 1998. pap. text 24.00 (*0-321-04929-2*) Allyn.

***Caplan & Creps, Bob.** Encyclopedia of Artists' Signatures, Symbols & Monograms: North American, European Plus More. Old Masters to Modern. LC 99-235656. 1050p. 1999. lib. bdg. 245.00 (*0-9668526-0-5*) Dealers Choice.

Caplan, A. L. & Jennings, B. Darwin, Marx & Freud: Their Influence on Moral Theory. LC 84-1909. (Hastings Center Series in Ethics). (Illus.). 258p. (C). 1984. text 49.50 (*0-306-41530-5*, Kluwer Plenum) Kluwer Academic.

Caplan, A. Patricia. Choice & Constraint in a Swahili Community: Property, Hierarchy, & Cognatic Descent on the East African Coast. LC 76-353359. (Illus.). 182p. 1975. reprint ed. pap. 56.50 (*0-8357-3214-2*, 205708500010) Bks Demand.

Caplan, Ann P. Choice & Constraint in a Swahili Community: Property Hierarchy & Cognatic Descent on the East African Coast. (International African Institute Ser.). (Illus.). 1975. 29.95 (*0-19-724195-6*) OUP.

Caplan, Arthur. Due Consideration: Controversy in the Age of Medical Miracles. LC 97-29022. 296p. 1997. pap. 17.95 (*0-471-18344-X*) Wiley.

Caplan, Arthur L. Am I My Brother's Keeper? The Ethical Frontiers of Biomedicine. Smith, David H. & Veatch, Robert M., eds. LC 97-19268. (Medical Ethics Ser.). 232p. 1998. write for info. (*0-253-33358-X*) Ind U Pr.

Caplan, Arthur L. If I Were a Rich Man Could I Buy a Pancreas? And Other Essays on the Ethics of Health Care. LC 91-32112. (Medical Ethics Ser.). (Illus.). 372p. 1992. text 15.95 (*0-253-31307-4*) Ind U Pr.

Caplan, Arthur L. If I Were a Rich Man Could I Buy a Pancreas? And Other Essays on the Ethics of Health Care. LC 91-32112. (Medical Ethics Ser.). (Illus.). 372p. 1994. pap. 15.95 (*0-253-20868-8*) Ind U Pr.

Caplan, Arthur L., ed. When Medicine Went Mad: Bioethics & the Holocaust. LC 92-11687. (Contemporary Issues in Biomedicine, Ethics, & Society Ser.). 359p. 1992. 44.50 (*0-89603-235-3*) Humana.

Caplan, Arthur L., et al, eds. Compelled Compassion: Government Intervention in the Treatment of Critically Ill Newborns. LC 91-44190. (Contemporary Issues in Biomedicine, Ethics, & Society Ser.). 352p. 1992. 49.50 (*0-89603-224-8*) Humana.

Caplan, Arthur L. & Callahan, Daniel, eds. Ethics in Hard Times. LC 81-17728. (Hastings Center Series in Ethics). 312p. 1981. 49.50 (*0-306-40790-6*, Plenum Trade) Perseus Pubng.

Caplan, Arthur L. & Coelho, Daniel H., eds. The Ethics of Organ Transplants: The Current Debate. (Contemporary Issues Ser.). 358p. 1999. pap. 17.95 (*1-57392-224-2*) Prometheus Bks.

Caplan, Arthur L., et al. Concepts of Health & Disease: Interdisciplinary Perspectives. 608p. (C). 1981. pap. text. write for info. (*0-201-00973-0*, Health Sci) Addison-Wesley.

Caplan, Arthur L., jt. auth. see Rosen, Bernard.

Caplan, Arthur L., jt. ed. see Engelhardt, H. Tristram.

Caplan, Arthur L., jt. ed. see Kane, Rosalie A.

Caplan, Arthur L., jt. ed. see Murray, Thomas H.

Caplan, Basil. The Complete Manual of Organic Gardening. (Illus.). 406p. 1993. 49.95 (*1-55859-644-5*) Abbeville Pr.

Caplan, Bruce. Buster Boppington & His Talking Dog: In the Case of the Impossible Bank Robbery. 96p. (J). (gr. 2-6). 1994. pap. text 9.95 (*0-9644610-0-5*) Seattle Miracle.

Caplan, Bruce M., ed. see Marshall, Logan.

Caplan, Carl M. Dental Practice Management Encyclopedia. 280p. 1985. 10.00 (*0-87814-288-6*) PennWell Bks.

Caplan, D. I., jt. auth. see Sank, D.

Caplan, David. Como Beneficiarse de las Opciones Sobre Futures (Spanish Profiting with Futures Options) (SPA.). 52p. 1997. pap. 7.95 (*0-915513-88-9*) Ctr Futures Ed.

— Language: Structure, Processing & Disorders. (Issues in the Biology of Language & Cognition). (Illus.). 536p. 1996. reprint ed. pap. text 27.00 (*0-262-53138-0*, Bradford Bks) MIT Pr.

— Lucrar Com Opcoes de Futuros (Portuguese Profiting with Futures Options) (POR.). 52p. 1997. pap. 7.95 (*0-915513-86-2*) Ctr Futures Ed.

— The New Option Secret - Volatility. 310p. 1996. pap. 65.00 (*1-883272-18-1*) Traders Lib.

***Caplan, David L.** The New Option Secret: Volatility: The Weapon of the Professional Trader & the Most Important Indicator in Option Trading. (Illus.). 311p. 2000. pap. text 65.00 (*1-883272-33-5*) Traders Lib.

Caplan, David L. The New Options Advantage: Gaining a Trading Edge over the Markets, Revised Edition. 2nd rev. ed. 225p. 1995. text 45.00 (*1-55738-863-6*, Irwn Prfssnl) McGraw-Hill Prof.

— Options Advantage: Gaining a Trading Edge over the Markets. 250p. 1991. 40.00 (*1-55738-214-X*, Irwn Prfssnl) McGraw-Hill Prof.

— Profiting with Futures Options. 48p. (Orig.). 1994. pap. 7.95 (*0-915513-56-0*) Ctr Futures Ed.

Caplan, David N. Language: Structure, Processing & Disorders. (Illus.). 400p. 1992. 55.00 (*0-262-03189-2*) MIT Pr.

— Neurolinguistics & Linguistic Aphasiology: An Introduction. (Cambridge Studies in Speech Science & Communication). (Illus.). 512p. 1987. text 89.95 (*0-521-32420-3*); pap. text 34.95 (*0-521-31195-0*) Cambridge U Pr.

Caplan, David N., et al, eds. Biological Perspectives on Language. (Neuropsyche-Neurolinguistic Ser.). (Illus.). 432p. 1984. 52.00 (*0-262-03101-9*) MIT Pr.

Caplan, David N. & Hildebrandt, Nancy. Disorders of Syntactic Comprehension. (Issues in the Biology of Language & Cognition Ser.). 288p. 1988. 42.50 (*0-262-03132-9*, Bradford Bks) MIT Pr.

Caplan, David N., jt. ed. see Studdert-Kennedy, Michael.

Caplan, Deborah. Back Trouble: A New Approach to Prevention & Recovery. (Illus.). 224p. (Orig.). 1987. pap. 14.95 (*0-937404-26-8*) Triad Pub FL.

Caplan, Eric. Mind Games: American Culture & the Birth of Psychotherapy. LC 98-16999. (Medicine & Society Ser.). 246p. 1998. 35.00 (*0-520-21169-3*, Pub. by U CA Pr) Cal Prin Full Svc.

Caplan, Frank. First Twelve Months of Life: Your Baby's Growth Month by Month. rev. ed. 416p. 1995. mass mkt. 6.99 (*0-553-57406-X*) Bantam.

— The Quality System: A Sourcebook for Managers & Engineers. 2nd ed. LC 89-42860. 352p. 1990. lib. bdg. 49.95 (*0-8019-7975-7*) NP-Chilton.

— The Second Twelve Months of Life. LC 77-78748. (Illus.). 1983. reprint ed. pap. 15.95 (*0-399-50776-0*, Perigee Bks) Berkley Pub.

Caplan, Frank, ed. The Second Twelve Months of Life. 448p. 1982. mass mkt. 6.99 (*0-553-26438-9*) Bantam.

Caplan, Gayle & Teese, Mary K. Survivors: How to Keep Your Best People on Board after Downsizing. LC 96-20606. 288p. 1996. 25.95 (*0-89106-091-X*, 7893, Davies-Black Pub) Consulting Psychol.

Caplan, Gerald. Arab & Jew in Jerusalem: Explorations in Community Mental Health. LC 79-27832. 308p. 1980. 37.95 (*0-674-04315-4*) HUP.

— Population-Oriented Psychiatry. LC 87-30985. 244p. 1989. 38.95 (*0-89885-418-0*, Kluwer Acad Hman Sci) Kluwer Academic.

***Caplan, Gerald & Caplan, Ruth B.** Mental Health Consultation & Collaboration. 393p. 1999. pap. 27.95 (*1-57766-073-0*) Waveland Pr.

Caplan, Gerald M. Model Procedures for Police Interrogation. 27p. (Orig.). (C). 1995. pap. text 10.00 (*0-7881-2011-5*) DIANE Pub.

Caplan, H. H. The Classified Directory of Artists' Signatures, Symbols & Monograms. 2nd ed. 873p. 1982. 125.00 (*0-86043-658-6*, Pub. by P Grahame) Dealers Choice.

— The Classified Directory of Artists' Signatures, Symbols & Monograms: International & American Editions. 3rd ed. 608p. 1987. 128.00 (*0-9508893-1-8*) Edns Publisol.

Caplan, Harry, tr. see Cicero, Marcus Tullius.

Caplan, I. L., ed. see World Titanium Conference Staff.

Caplan, Jack. Memories of the Gorbals. 123p. (C). 1989. text 50.00 (*1-872795-17-X*, Pub. by Pentland Pr) St Mut.

— Memories of the Gorbals: Jewish Life in the Gorbals Section of Glasgow Between the Wars. large type ed. (Reminiscence Ser.). 21.95 (*1-85695-151-0*, Pub. by ISIS Lrg Prnt) Transaction Pubs.

Caplan, Jane. Government Without Administration: State & Civil Service in Weimar & Nazi Germany. (Oxford Historical Monographs). 400p. 1989. 72.00 (*0-19-822993-3*) OUP.

***Caplan, Jane.** Written on the Body: The Tattoo in European & American History. (Illus.). 304p. 2000. 65.00 (*0-691-05722-2*, Pub. by Princeton U Pr); pap. 19.95 (*0-691-05723-0*, Pub. by Princeton U Pr) Cal Prin Full Svc.

Caplan, Jane, jt. ed. see Childers, Thomas.

Caplan, Jane, ed. see Mason, Tim.

Caplan, Jay. Framed Narratives: Diderot's Genealogy of the Beholder. LC 84-24150. 141p. 1985. pap. 11.95 (*0-8166-1406-7*) U of Minn Pr.

— In the King's Wake: Post-Absolutist Culture in France. LC 99-40561. 208p. 2000. pap. text 19.00 (*0-226-09312-3*); lib. bdg. 45.00 (*0-226-09311-5*) U Ch Pr.

Caplan, Jeffrey H., jt. auth. see Inmon, William H.

Caplan, Jimmy & Caplan, Leslie. Recipes for Romance: 50 Ways to Sweeten Your Love Life. LC 95-35700. 128p. 1996. pap. 8.95 (*1-880032-78-3*) New Wrld Lib.

Caplan, Lawrence H., jt. ed. see Kaplan, Dorlene V.

Caplan, Leslie, jt. auth. see Caplan, Jimmy.

Caplan, Lincoln. Skadden: Legal Power Money & the Rise of a Empire. 1993. 25.00 (*0-374-26566-6*) FS&G.

— Up Against the Law: Affirmative Action & the Supreme Court. LC 97-13214. 75p. 1997. pap. 9.95 (*0-87078-409-9*) Century Foundation.

Caplan, Lionel. Administration & Politics in a Nepalese Town. (Illus.). 1975. 19.95 (*0-19-713585-4*) OUP.

— Class & Culture in Urban India: Fundamentalism in a Christian Community. 312p. 1988. text 75.00 (*0-19-823402-3*) OUP.

— Warrior Gentlemen: "Gurkhas" in the Western Imagination. LC 94-37858. 192p. 1995. 39.95 (*1-57181-852-9*) Berghahn Bks.

Caplan, Lionel, ed. Studies in Religious Fundamentalism. LC 86-30026. 216p. (C). 1988. text 24.50 (*0-88706-518-X*) State U NY Pr.

Caplan, Louis, jt. ed. see Bogousslavsky, Julien.

Caplan, Louis R. Posterior Circulation Disease: Clinical Findings, Diagnosis, & Management. (Illus.). 700p. 1996. 165.00 (*0-86542-298-2*) Blackwell Sci.

— Stroke: A Clinical Approach. 3rd ed. LC 92-49251. (Illus.). 562p. 2000. text 105.00 (*0-7506-9181-6*) Buttrwrth-Heinemann.

***Caplan, Louis R.** Stroke: A Clinical Approach. 3rd ed. LC 99-54757. (Illus.). 608p. 2000. 100.00 (*0-7506-9953-1*) Buttrwrth-Heinemann.

Caplan, Louis R., ed. Brain Ischemia: Basic Concepts & Clinical Relevance. LC 93-49746. (Illus.). 380p. 1995. 165.00 (*0-387-19850-4*) Spr-Verlag.

Caplan, Louis R., et al, eds. Brain-Stem Localization & Function. LC 93-5073. 1993. 95.00 (*0-387-56608-2*) Spr-Verlag.

Caplan, Louis R., et al. American Heart Association Family Guide to Stroke: Treatment, Recovery, & Prevention. LC 92-50500. 320p. 1994. 23.00 (*0-8129-2011-2*, Times Bks) Crown Pub Group.

***Caplan, Louis R., et al.** Clinical Neurocardiology. LC 99-26885. (Fundamental & Clinical Cardiology Ser.). (Illus.). 520p. 1999. text 195.00 (*0-8247-1991-3*) Dekker.

Caplan, Louis R., jt. auth. see Berguer, Ramon.

Caplan, Louis R., jt. auth. see Kase, Carlos S.

Caplan, Louis R., jt. ed. see Moskowitz, Michael A.

Caplan, Maria S., jt. auth. see Shapiro, Jack J.

Caplan, Mariana. Halfway up the Mountain: The Error of Premature Claims to Enlightenment. unabridged ed. LC 98-45837. 578p. 1999. pap. 24.95 (*0-934252-91-2*, Pub. by Hohm Pr) SCB Distributors.

— Untouched: The Need for Genuine Affection in an Impersonal World. LC 97-48934. (Illus.). 384p. 1998. pap. 19.95 (*0-934252-80-7*, Pub. by Hohm Pr) SCB Distributors.

— When Holidays Are Hell. . . ! A Guide to Surviving Family Gatherings. LC 97-2535. 144p. (Orig.). 1997. pap. 7.95 (*0-934252-77-7*, Pub. by Hohm Pr) SCB Distributors.

— When Sons & Daughters Choose Alternative Lifestyles. 264p. (Orig.). 1996. pap. 14.95 (*0-934252-69-6*, Pub. by Hohm Pr) SCB Distributors.

***Caplan, Marvin.** Farther Along: A Civil Rights Memoir. LC 98-50883. (Illus.). 272p. 1999. 29.95 (*0-8071-2352-8*) La State U Pr.

Caplan, Maurice. In the Shadow of the Workhouse: The Implementation of the New Poor Law Throughout Nottinghamshire, 1836-1846. (C). 1985. text 40.00 (*0-7855-3214-5*, Pub. by Univ Nottingham) St Mut.

Caplan, Michael & Levine, Mark. Lifescripts for Managers. LC 98-52415. 162p. 1999. pap. 14.95 (*0-02-862622-2*, Pub. by Macmillan) S&S Trade.

Caplan, Nathan, et al. Children of the Boat People: A Study of Educational Success. 176p. (C). 1991. pap. text 19.95 (*0-472-08162-4*, 08162) U of Mich Pr.

Caplan, Neil. Futile Diplomacy Vol. 1: Early Arab Zionist Negotiation Attempts 1913-31. (Illus.). 277p. 1983. 52.50 (*0-7146-3214-7*, Pub. by Irish Acad Pr) Intl Spec Bk.

— Futile Diplomacy Vol. 2: Arab-Zionist Negotiations & the End of the Mandate. 358p. 1986. 52.50 (*0-7146-3215-5*, Pub. by Irish Acad Pr) Intl Spec Bk.

— Futile Diplomacy Vol. 3: The United Nations, the Great Powers, & Middle East Peacemaking 1948-1954. LC 96-39814. (Futile Diplomacy Ser.).Tr. of Vol. III. 440p. (C). 1997. 62.50 (*0-7146-4756-X*, Pub. by Irish Acad Pr) Intl Spec Bk.

— Futile Diplomacy Vol. 4: Operation Alpha & the Failure of Anglo-American Coercive Diplomacy in the Arab-Israeli Conflict 1954-1956. 424p. (C). 1997. 62.50 (*0-7146-4757-8*, Pub. by Irish Acad Pr) Intl Spec Bk.

— Futile Diplomacy Vol. 5: 'Operation Alpha' & the Failure of Anglo-American Coercive Diplomacy in the Arab-Israeli Conflict 1954-1956. 1997. pap. 25.00 (*0-7146-4318-1*, Pub. by F Cass Pubs) Intl Spec Bk.

— The Lausanne Conference, 1949: A Case Study on Middle Eastern Peacemaking. 190p. (C). 1994. pap. text 14.95 (*0-8156-7056-7*, Pub. by Moshe Dayan Ctr) Syracuse U Pr.

— Palestine Jewry & the Arab Question, 1917-1925. 268p. 1978. 49.50 (*0-7146-3110-8*, Pub. by F Cass Pubs) Intl Spec Bk.

Caplan, Neil, jt. auth. see Eisenberg, Laura Z.

Caplan, Neil, jt. ed. see Zittrain Eisenberg, Laura.

Caplan, Pat. Cultural Construction of Sexuality. 320p. (C). 1987. pap. 25.99 (*0-415-04013-2*) Routledge.

— Feasts, Fasts, Famine: Food for Thought. (Berg Occasional Papers in Anthropology). 35p. 1994. pap. 7.00 (*0-85496-384-7*) Berg Pubs.

***Caplan, Pat.** Risk Revisited. (Anthropology, Culture & Society Ser.). 2000. pap. 22.50 (*0-7453-1463-5*) Pluto GBR.

C

An Asterisk (*) at the beginning of an entry indicates that the title is appearing for the first time.

Caplan, Patricia. Class & Gender in India: Women & Their Organization in a South Indian City. 264p. 1986. text 37.50 (*0-422-79970-X*, 9610, Pub. by Tavistock); pap. text 16.95 (*0-422-79980-7*, 9611, Pub. by Tavistock) Routldge.

— Food, Health & Identity. LC 96-51909. (Illus.). 296p. (C). 1997. 85.00 (*0-415-15679-3*); pap. 25.99 (*0-415-15680-7*) Routledge.

— Personal Narratives, Multiple Voices: The Worlds of a Swahili Peasant. LC 96-25693. (Illus.). 288p. (C). 1997. 80.00 (*0-415-13723-3*); pap. 24.99 (*0-415-13724-1*) Routledge.

***Caplan, Patricia.** Risk Revisited. LC 99-48076. (Anthropology, Culture & Society Ser.). 2000. write for info. (*0-7453-1468-6*) Pluto GBR.

Caplan, Patricia, et al, eds. Understanding Disputes: The Politics of Argument. LC 94-34791. (Explorations in Anthropology Ser.). (Illus.). 248p. 1995. 49.50 (*0-85496-924-1*, Pub. by Berg Pubs); pap. 19.50 (*0-85496-925-X*, Pub. by Berg Pubs) NYU Pr.

Caplan, Paula. Barriers Between Women. LC 80-12983. 167p. 1981. 24.95 (*0-88331-113-5*) R B Luce.

— Lifting a Ton of Feathers: A Woman's Guide to Surviving in the Academic World. LC 93-93082. 1993. pap. 18.95 (*0-8020-7411-1*); text 45.00 (*0-8020-2903-5*) U of Toronto Pr.

***Caplan, Paula.** The New Don't Blame Mother: Mending the Mother-Daughter Relationship. (Illus.). 320p. 2000. pap. 15.95 (*0-415-92630-0*) Routledge.

Caplan, Paula J. The Myth of Women's Masochism. 2nd ed. 280p. 1993. pap. 18.95 (*0-8020-7745-5*) U of Toronto Pr.

— They Say You're Crazy: How the World's Most Powerful Psychiatrists Decide Who's Normal. 384p. 1996. pap. 13.00 (*0-201-48832-9*) Addison-Wesley.

Caplan, Philip J. The Puzzle of the 613 Commandments & Why Bother. LC 96-6422. 272p. 1996. 40.00 (*1-56821-893-1*) Aronson.

Caplan, Rebekah. Writers in Training: A Guide to Developing a Composition Program. pap. text 11.25 (*0-86651-203-9*) Seymour Pubns.

Caplan, Richard & Feffer, John. Europe's New Nationalism: States & Minorities in Conflict. 256p. (C). 1996. pap. 23.95 (*0-19-509149-3*); text 47.00 (*0-19-509148-5*) OUP.

Caplan, Richard M. Dr. Watson, Mr. Sherlock Holmes. (Illus.). 172p. 1996. 24.00 (*1-896648-53-3*) Battered Silicon.

Caplan, Robert D. Adhering to Medical Regimens: Pilot Experiments in Patient Education & Social Support. LC 76-620035. (Illus.). 296p. reprint ed. pap. 91.80 (*0-7837-5281-4*, 204501900005) Bks Demand.

Caplan, Robert D., et al. Job Demands & Worker Health: Main Effects & Occupational Differences. LC 80-25067. (Institute for Social Research, Research Report). 360p. reprint ed. pap. 111.60 (*0-7837-5257-1*, 204499400005) Bks Demand.

— Tranquilizer Use & Well-Being: A Longitudinal Study of Social & Psychological Effects. LC 84-9116. (Institute for Social Research, Research Report). 440p. (Orig.). reprint ed. pap. 136.40 (*0-7837-5250-4*, 204498600005) Bks Demand.

Caplan, Ron, jt. ed. see Sinclair, John.

Caplan, Roy S., et al, eds. Bioelectrochemistry: General Introduction. LC 94-30062. (Biochemistry: Vol. 1). (Illus.). 1995. 111.00 (*3-7643-2687-5*) Birkhauser.

Caplan, Ruth B., jt. auth. see Caplan, Gerald.

Caplan, S. R., et al, eds. Bioelectrochemistry: General Introduction. LC 94-30062. (Bioelectrochemistry: Vol. 1). (Illus.). xi, 368p. 1995. 139.00 (*0-8176-2687-5*) Birkhauser.

Caplan, S. Roy & Essig, Alvin. Bioenergetics & Linear Nonequilibrium Thermodynamics: The Steady State. (Harvard Books in Biophysics: No. 3). (Illus.). 448p. 1983. 68.00 (*0-674-07352-5*) HUP.

Caplan, Sandi & Lang, Gordon. Grief's Courageous Journey. 160p. 1995. pap., wbk. ed. 12.95 (*1-57224-017-2*) New Harbinger.

Caplan, Suzanne. High Profit Financial Management for Your Small Business. LC 99-16668. 288p. 1999. pap. 22.95 (*1-57410-128-5*, 61014301) Dearborn.

— A Piece of the Action: How Women & Minorities Can Launch Their Own Successful Businesses. LC 93-42510. 160p. 1994. pap. 17.95 (*0-8144-7869-7*) AMACOM.

— Streetwise Finance & Accounting. LC 99-46256. 352p. 1999. pap. 17.95 (*1-58062-196-1*) Adams Media.

***Caplan, Suzanne.** Streetwise Small Business Success Kit: The Ultimate Source for Forms & Tools for Starting & Growing a Small Business - With CD-ROM for Windows. (Streetwise Ser.). (Illus.). 400p. 2000. pap. 24.95 incl. cd-rom (*1-58062-367-0*) Adams Media.

Caplan, Suzanne & Nunnally, Thomas M. Small Business Insiders Guide to Bankers. LC 97-13597. (Illus.). 163p. 1997. pap. 18.95 (*1-55571-400-5*, Oasis Pr) PSI Resch.

Caplan, Suzanne, jt. auth. see Cronin, Mary M.

Caplan, Theresa. Early Childhood Years. 560p. 1984. mass mkt. 6.99 (*0-553-26967-4*) Bantam.

— The First Twelve Months of Life: Your Baby's Growth Month by Month. rev. ed. (Illus.). 288p. (Orig.). 1993. reprint ed. pap. 15.95 (*0-399-51804-5*, Perigee Bks) Berkley Pub.

— Frank Caplan: Champion of Child's Play. LC 98-90862. xix, 567p. 1999. pap. 21.95 (*0-533-12955-9*) Vantage.

Caplan, Thomas. Grace & Favor. LC 97-15664. 336p. 1997. 24.95 (*0-312-17106-4*, Thomas Dunne) St Martin.

— Grace & Favor. 336p. 1998. pap. 14.95 (*0-312-19459-5*) St Martin.

Caplan, Usher & Steinberg, M. W., eds. A.M. Klein: Literary Essays & Reviews. 1987. pap. 19.95 (*0-8020-6607-0*); text 45.00 (*0-8020-5686-5*) U of Toronto Pr.

Caplan, Usher, ed. see Klein, A. M.

Caplar, R. & Greiner, Walter, eds. Heavy-Ion Physics: Today & Tomorrow. 400p. (C). 1991. text 104.00 (*981-02-0801-4*) World Scientific Pub.

Caplat, G. Dictionnaire Biographique des Inspecteurs de l'Academie de Paris, 1949-1939. (FRE.). 1998. 135.00 (*0-320-00403-1*) Fr & Eur.

Caple, C., jt. auth. see Giles, G. B.

***Caple, Chris.** Conservation Skills: Judgement, Method & Decision. LC 00-32183. 2000. pap. write for info. (*0-415-18881-4*) Routledge.

Caple, Jeremy N. The Bristol Riots of 1831 & Social Reform in Britain. LC 90-22628. (Studies in British History: Vol. 21). 312p. 1991. lib. bdg. 99.95 (*0-88946-224-0*) E Mellen.

Caple, Jim, jt. auth. see Allan, Ian.

Caple, Jim, jt. auth. see Buckley, Roger.

Caple, John. Ultimate Interview: How to Get It, Get Ready & Get the Job You Want. 192p. 1991. pap. 11.95 (*0-385-26583-2*) Doubleday.

Caple, Kathy. The Biggest Nose, 001. LC 84-19745. (Illus.). 32p. (J). (gr. k-3). 1985. 15.95 (*0-395-36894-4*) HM.

— The Biggest Nose. LC 84-19745. (Illus.). 32p. (J). (gr. k-3). 1988. pap. 5.95 (*0-395-47943-6*) HM.

***Caple, Kathy.** The Friendship Tree. LC 98-39043. (House Readers Ser.). 48p. (J). 2000. 14.95 (*0-8234-1376-4*) Holiday.

— Hillary to the Rescue. LC 00-8020. (Picture Bks.). (Illus.). 32p. (J). (gr. k-3). 2000. 15.95 (*1-57505-420-5*, Carolrhoda) Lerner Pub.

Caple, Kathy. The Purse. 32p. (J). (gr. k-3). 1992. pap. 6.95 (*0-395-62981-0*, Sandpiper) HM.

— Starring Hillary. LC 97-32209. (Picture Bks). 32p. (J). (gr. k-3). 1999. 14.95 (*1-57505-261-X*, Carolrhoda) Lerner Pub.

— The Wimp. LC 94-7121. (Illus.). 32p. (J). 1994. 14.95 (*0-395-63115-7*) HM.

***Caple, Kathy.** The Wimp. (Illus.). 32p. (J). 2000. pap. 5.95 (*0-618-05577-0*) HM.

— Wow, It's Worm! (Brand New Readers Ser.). (Illus.). (J). 2000. 10.99 (*0-7636-1152-2*); pap. 4.99 (*0-7636-1153-0*) Candlewick Pr.

Caple, Natalee. Heart Is Its Own Reason. 240p. 1998. pap. text 14.99 (*1-895837-25-1*) Insomniac.

Caple, Richard B. To Mark the Beginning: A Social History of College Student Affairs. LC 97-43939. 1998. 45.00 (*1-883485-11-8*); pap. 25.95 (*1-883485-12-6*) U Pr of Amer.

Caplen, Peter. Boat Owners Guide to Marine Engines I. 1997. 26.95 (*1-86126-090-3*, Pub. by Crolwood) Trafalgar.

***Caples, Garrett.** The Garrett Caples Reader. 104p. 2000. pap. 9.00 (*0-9675144-0-1*, Pub. by Neko Buildings) SPD-Small Pr Dist.

Caples, John. How to Make Your Advertising Make Money. LC 83-4455. (Illus.). 383p. (C). 1983. pap. 13.95 (*0-13-423590-8*) P-H.

— Making Ads Pay. 1966. pap. 6.95 (*0-486-21575-X*) Dover.

— Tested Advertising Methods. 5th ed. 320p. (C). 1998. pap. text 14.95 (*0-13-095701-1*) P-H.

— Tested Advertising Methods. 5th rev. ed. LC 96-47752. 320p. (C). 1997. text 29.95 (*0-13-244609-X*) P-H.

Caplin, Andrew, et al. Housing Partnerships: A New Approach to a Market at a Crossroads. LC 96-37852. (Illus.). 280p. 1997. 35.00 (*0-262-03243-0*) MIT Pr.

Caplin, Donald, jt. auth. see Cannie, Joan K.

Caplin, Elliot. Al Capp Remembered. LC 93-79503. (Illus.). 148p. (C). 1994. pap. 10.95 (*0-87972-630-X*) Bowling Green Univ Popular Press.

Caplin, Irvin. The Palm Springs Nutritional Plan: A Thin Book about Fat. Foote, Jim & Foote, Johnnie, eds. 150p. (Orig.). 1992. pap. 10.00 (*0-9628752-1-X*) Fifty-Six Palms.

Caplin, Lee E., ed. The Business of Art. 1986. 11.95 (*0-13-106500-9*, Busn); text 22.95 (*0-13-106518-1*, Busn) P-H.

Caplin, Mortimer M. Time Value of Money Rules under the 1984 Tax Act. LC 85-136473. 35.00 (*0-685-13481-4*) Harcourt.

— What Lawyers & Accountants Need to Know about the 1978 Tax Law. (Illus.). v, 413p. 1979. write for info. (*0-318-58245-7*) Harcourt.

Caplin, Mortimer M., et al. Real Estate & Leasing Transactions in the Shadow of Tax Reform. write for info. (*0-318-60226-1*) Harcourt.

Caplin, William E. Classical Form: A Theory of Formal Functions for the Instrumental Music of Haydn, Mozart & Beethoven. LC 97-25561. (Illus.). 320p. 1998. text 75.00 (*0-19-510480-3*) OUP.

Capling, M. Ann & Galligan, Brian. Beyond the Protective State: The Political Economy of Australia's Manufacturing Industry Policy. LC 92-17349. (Illus.). 256p. (C). 1993. pap. write for info. (*0-521-42629-4*); text 64.95 (*0-521-41626-4*) Cambridge U Pr.

Caplinger, Dennis. Gospel Banjo. (Illus.). 88p. 1999. pap. 9.95 (*1-57424-071-4*) Centerstream Pub.

Caplinger, Michael. Bridges over Time: A Technological Context for the Baltimore & Ohio Railroad Main Stem at Harpers Ferry, West Virginia. LC 97-11526. (Monograph Ser.: Vol. IV, 1997). (Illus.). (C). 1997. pap. 15.00 (*1-885907-04-4*) WV U Inst Hist of Tech.

Caplis, M. E., et al, eds. Drug Mechanisms. (Journal: Clinical Physiology & Biochemistry: Vol. 3, No. 2-3). (Illus.). 96p. 1985. pap. 73.25 (*3-8055-4051-5*) S Karger.

Caploe, Jamie, jt. auth. see Caploe, Roberta.

Caploe, Roberta & Caploe, Jamie. Melrose Confidential: An Unauthorized Guide to Hollywood's Hottest Address. LC 95-26389. (Illus.). 160p. 1996. pap. 14.95 (*0-8065-1743-3*, Citadel Pr) Carol Pub Group.

Caplovich, Judd. Blizzard! The Great Storm of Eighty-Eight. Westbrook, Wayne W., ed. LC 87-51196. (Illus.). 242p. 1987. 24.95 (*0-9619282-0-4*) Vero Pub.

Caplovitz, David. Student-Faculty Relations in Medical School: A Study of Professional Socialization. Zuckerman, Harriet & Merton, Robert K., eds. LC 79-8980. (Dissertations on Sociology Ser.). 1980. lib. bdg. 29.95 (*0-405-12956-4*) Ayer.

Caplovitz, David, jt. auth. see Bradburn, Norman M.

Caplow, Theodore. Perverse Incentives: The Neglect of Social Technology in the Public Sector. LC 94-2981. 176p. 1994. 52.95 (*0-275-94911-7*, Praeger Pubs); pap. 16.95 (*0-275-94933-8*, Praeger Pubs) Greenwood.

— The Sociology of Work. LC 77-18112. (Illus.). 330p. 1978. reprint ed. lib. bdg. 85.00 (*0-313-20111-0*, CASOW, Greenwood Pr) Greenwood.

Caplow, Theodore & Bahr, Howard M. Middletown Families: Fifty Years of Change & Continuity. LC 81-14757. 462p. 1982. reprint ed. pap. 131.70 (*0-608-00833-8*, 2061624) Bks Demand.

Caplow, Theodore & Hicks, Louis. Systems of War & Peace. LC 94-44517. 288p. (C). 1995. pap. text 28.50 (*0-8191-9858-7*); lib. bdg. 59.50 (*0-8191-9857-9*) U Pr of Amer.

Caplow, Theodore & McGee, Reece J. The Academic Marketplace. 2nd ed. 262p. 1999. pap. 27.95 (*0-7658-0609-6*) Transaction Pubs.

Caplow, Theodore, et al. All Faithful People: Change & Continuity in Middletown's Religion. LC 82-24759. 390p. reprint ed. pap. 120.90 (*0-7837-2972-3* 205748200006) Bks Demand.

***Caplow, Theodore, et al.** The First Measured Century: An Illustrated Guide to Trends in American, 1900-2000. (Illus.). 300p. 2000. 50.00 (*0-8447-4137-X*, Pub. by Am Enterprise); pap. 20.00 (*0-8447-4138-8*, Pub. by Am Enterprise) Pub Resources Inc.

Caplow, Theodore, et al. Recent Social Trends in the United States, 1960-1990. 608p. 1991. 75.00 (*0-7735-0872-4*, Pub. by McG-Queens Univ Pr) CUP Services.

— Recent Social Trends in the United States, 1960-1990. (Comparative Charting of Social Change Ser.). 608p. (C). 1994. pap. text 27.95 (*0-7735-1212-8*, Pub. by McG-Queens Univ Pr) CUP Services.

Caplow, Theodore, ed. see Metzger, Walter P. & Reece, J. McGee.

Capmany. Optical Telecommunications Network. text. write for info. (*0-471-81850-X*) Wiley.

***Capo, Fran.** It Happened in New York. LC 99-89601. (Illus.). 144p. 2000. pap. 9.95 (*1-56044-899-7*, Falcon) Falcon Pub Inc.

Capo, Hounkpati. A Comparative Phonology of Gbe. LC 91-33621. (Publications in African Languages & Linguistics: No. 14). xxiv, 238p. (C). 1991. lib. bdg. 106.15 (*3-11-013392-X*) Mouton.

Capobianco, Joseph P. Italy. (Pelham Guides Ser.). 47p. (Orig.). (C). 1996. 22.00 (*0-929851-92-7*) Am Assn Coll Registrars.

— Italy: A Study of the Educational System of Italy & a Guide to the Academic Placement of Students from Italy in Educational Institutions of the United States. LC 80-27851. (World Education Ser.). (Illus.). 108p. reprint ed. pap. 33.50 (*0-608-18370-9*, 203624500001) Bks Demand.

Capobianco, Michael, jt. auth. see Barton, William.

Capobianco, Michael F., tr. see Nervo, Amado.

Capobianco, R. J., jt. auth. see Dunn, L.

Capocaccia, L., et al, eds. The Epidemiology & Prevention of Gallstone Disease. 1984. text 147.50 (*0-85200-850-3*) Kluwer Academic.

— Recent Advances in the Epidemiology & Prevention of Gallstone Disease: Proceedings of the Second International Workshop on Epidemiology & Prevention of Gallstone Disease. (Developments in Gastroenterology Ser.). 192p. 1991. text 126.50 (*0-7923-0994-4*) Kluwer Academic.

Capocaccia, Livio. Advances in Hepatic Encephalopathy & Metabolic Nitrogen Exchange. 672p. 1994. lib. bdg. 229.00 (*0-8493-8964-X*) CRC Pr.

Capocelli, Renato M., ed. Sequences. (Illus.). xii, 549p. 1989. 102.95 (*0-387-97186-6*) Spr-Verlag.

Capocelli, Renato M., et al, eds. Sequences II: Methods in Communication, Security & Computer Science. LC 92-32461. 488p. 1992. 144.95 (*0-387-97940-9*) Spr-Verlag.

***Capodagli, Bill.** Disney Way Fieldbook: How to Implement Walt Disney's Vision of Dream, Believe, Dare, Do in Your Own Company. 304p. 2000. pap. text 24.95 (*0-07-136106-5*) McGraw.

***Capodilupo, Lucia.** Thin Through the Power of the Spirit: Creating Paradise in Your Weight & World. 224p. 1999. pap. 11.95 (*0-87516-726-8*) DeVorss.

Capoeira, Nestor. The Little Capoeira Book. Ladd, Alex, tr. from POR. LC 95-2216. (Illus.). 150p. (Orig.). (C). 1995. pap. 11.95 (*1-55643-199-6*) North Atlantic.

Capoeman, Pauline, ed. see Storm, Jacqueline, et al.

Capogna, Vera Vullo. About Things You Find in the Woods? LC 99-32140. (Did You Ever Wonder? Ser.) (gr. k-3). 2000. 22.79 (*0-7614-0852-5*, Benchmark NY) Marshall Cavendish.

— Did You Ever Wonder?, 4 vols. 2000. boxed set 91.14 (*0-7614-0854-1*, Benchmark NY) Marshall Cavendish.

Capole, Dorinda, jt. auth. see Williams, Julie Pierce.

Capon. Architectural Theory, 2 vols. LC 98-30281. 738p. 1999. 210.00 (*0-471-97946-5*) Wiley.

Capon, B. & Rees, C. W., eds. Organic Reaction Mechanisms, 1969: An Annual Survey Covering the Literature Dated December 1968 Through November 1969. LC 66-23143. 720p. reprint ed. pap. 200.00 (*0-608-13714-6*, 205161800069) Bks Demand.

Capon, Brian. Botany for Gardeners: An Introduction & Guide. LC 89-20340. (Illus.). 220p. 1990. 23.95 (*0-88192-163-7*) Timber.

— Botany for Gardeners: An Introduction & Guide. LC 89-20340. (Illus.). 220p. 1992. pap. 17.95 (*0-88192-258-7*) Timber.

— Plant Survival: Adapting to a Hostile World. LC 93-43342. (Illus.). 144p. (J). 1994. 24.95 (*0-88192-283-8*); pap. 15.95 (*0-88192-287-0*) Timber.

***Capon, Claire.** Understanding Organisational Context. 352p. (Orig.). 1999. pap. 51.50 (*0-273-63162-4*, Pub. by F T P-H) Trans-Atl Phila.

***Capon, David S.** Le Corbusier's Legacy: Principles of Twentieth Century Architectural Theory. LC 98-30281. (Architectural Theory Ser.). 456p. (C). 1999. 124.50 (*0-471-98589-9*) Wiley.

Capon, David S. The Vitruvian Fallacy: A History of the Categories in Architecture & Philosophies. LC 98-30281. (Architectural Theory Ser.: 1). 282p. (C). 1999. 124.50 (*0-471-98588-0*) Wiley.

Capon, Jack. Balance Activities. Alexander, Frank, ed. (Perceptual-Motor Development Ser.: Bk. 3). (Illus.). 34p. 1994. reprint ed. pap., teacher ed. 9.00 (*0-915256-38-X*, 123) Front Row.

— Ball, Rope, Hoop Activities. rev. ed. Alexander, Frank, ed. (Perceptual-Motor Development Ser.: Bk. 2). (Illus.). 54p. 1994. reprint ed. pap., teacher ed. 9.00 (*0-915256-37-1*, 122) Front Row.

— Basic Movement Activities. rev. ed. Alexander, Frank, ed. (Perceptual-Motor Development Ser.: Bk. 1). (Illus.). 27p. 1994. reprint ed. pap., teacher ed. 9.00 (*0-915256-36-3*, 121) Front Row.

— Bean Bag, Rhythm Stick Activities. rev. ed. Alexander, Frank, ed. (Perceptual-Motor Development Ser.: Bk. 4). (Illus.). 28p. 1994. reprint ed. pap., teacher ed. 9.00 (*0-915256-39-8*, 124) Front Row.

— Perceptual Motor Development Series, 5 bks. Incl. Balance Activities. (J). (gr. k-6). 1975. pap. 6.95 (*0-8224-5302-9*); Ball, Rope, Hoop Activities. (J). (gr. k-6). 1975. pap. 6.95 (*0-8224-5301-0*); Basic Movement Activities. (J). (gr. k-6). 1975. pap. 6.95 (*0-8224-5300-2*); Beanbag, Rhythm-Stick Activities. (J). (gr. k-6). 1975. pap. 6.95 (*0-8224-5303-7*); Tire, Parachute Activities. (J). (gr. k-6). 1975. pap. 6.95 (*0-8224-5304-5*); (J). (gr. k-6). 1975. pap. write for info. (*0-318-55298-1*) Fearon Teacher Aids.

— Perceptual-Motor Lesson Plans Level 2: Basic & "Practical" Lesson Plans for Perceptual-Motor Programs in Preschool & Elementary Grades, Level 2. 4th ed. Alexander, Frank, ed. (Illus.). 236p. 1999. teacher ed., spiral bd. 23.00 (*0-915256-04-5*) Front Row.

***Capon, Jack.** Perceptual-Motor Lesson Plans - Level 1: Basic & "Practical" Lesson Plans for Perceptual-Motor Programs in Preschool & Elementary Grades. 8th ed. Alexander, Frank, ed. LC 98-177428. (Illus.). 216p. 1998. pap., teacher ed. 19.00 (*0-915256-03-7*) Front Row.

Capon, Jack. Successful Movement Challenges: Movement Activities for the Developing Child. Alexander, Frank & Alexander, Diane, eds. (Illus.). 129p. (Orig.). 1981. pap. 14.00 (*0-915256-07-X*) Front Row.

— Tire, Parachute Activities. rev. ed. Alexander, Frank, ed. (Perceptual-Motor Development Ser.: Bk. 5). (Illus.). 31p. 1994. reprint ed. pap., teacher ed. 9.00 (*0-915256-40-1*, 125) Front Row.

Capon, Noel. Planning the Development of Builders, Leaders, & Managers for 21st-Century Business: Curriculum Review at Columbia Business School. 544p. (C). 1996. lib. bdg. 109.00 (*0-7923-9728-2*) Kluwer Academic.

— Toward an Integrative Explanation of Corporate Financial Performance. LC 96-46306. 424p. (C). 1996. lib. bdg. 151.50 (*0-7923-9831-9*) Kluwer Academic.

***Capon, Noel & Vanhonacker, Wilfried R.** The Asian Marketing Casebook. LC 98-474003. (Illus.). 1999. write for info. (*0-13-795550-2*) P-H.

Capon, Noel, et al. Corporate Strategic Planning. (Columbia Studies in Business, Government & Society). 592p. 1988. text 80.50 (*0-231-06380-6*) Col U Pr.

Capon, Paul, tr. see Duplessis, Yves.

Capon, Robert. Foolishness of Preaching. LC 97-39592. 164p. 1997. pap. text 18.00 (*0-8028-4315-8*) Eerdmans.

Capon, Robert F. The Astonished Heart: Reclaiming the Good News from the Lost-&-Found of Church History. 132p. (Orig.). 1996. pap. 12.00 (*0-8028-0791-7*) Eerdmans.

— Between Noon & Three: Romance, Law & the Outrage of Grace. LC 96-35871. 240p. (Orig.). 1997. pap. 18.00 (*0-8028-4222-4*) Eerdmans.

— The Man Who Met God in a Bar: The Gospel According to Marvin: A Novel. LC 89-78168. 143p. 1990. 15.95 (*0-911519-22-X*) Richelieu Court.

— The Mystery of Christ: And Why We Don't Get It. LC 93-26653. 202p. (Orig.). 1993. pap. 14.00 (*0-8028-0121-8*) Eerdmans.

— The Parables of Grace. 1991. pap. 14.00 (*0-8028-0304-0*) Eerdmans.

— The Parables of Judgement. 1993. pap. 14.00 (*0-8028-0491-8*) Eerdmans.

— The Parables of the Kingdom. 176p. 1991. reprint ed. pap. 14.00 (*0-8028-0605-8*) Eerdmans.

— The Supper of the Lamb: A Culinary Reflection. LC 78-14937. 271p. 1979. pap. 7.95 (*0-15-686893-8*, Harvest Bks) Harcourt.

***Capon, Robert Farrar.** The Fingerprints of God: Tracking the Divine Suspect Through a History of Images. 184p. 2000. pap. 15.00 (*0-8028-4768-4*) Eerdmans.

Capon, Robin. Drawing Techniques. (Crowood Art Class Ser.). (Illus.). 80p. 1996. pap. 19.95 (*1-85223-865-8*, Pub. by Crolwood) Trafalgar.

— Teach Yourself Drawing. (Illus.). 60p. 1995. pap. 11.95 (*0-8442-3641-1*, Teach Yrslf) NTC Contemp Pub Co.

— Watercolor Painting. (Teach Yourself Ser.). (Illus.). 192p. 1998. pap. 12.95 (*0-8442-0280-0*, 02800, Teach Yrslf) NTC Contemp Pub Co.

C

An Asterisk (*) at the beginning of an entry indicates that the title is appearing for the first time.

Capon, Stephen M. & Chambers, Linda A., eds. New Directions in Pediatric Hemotherapy. (Illus.). 144p. 1996. pap. text 65.00 (*1-56395-064-2*, PC97-960014) Am Assn Blood.

Capone, Charles A., Jr., et al. Providing Alternatives to Mortgage Disclosure: A Report to Congress. (Illus.). 176p. (Orig.). (C). 1996. pap. text 35.00 (*0-7881-2822-1*) DIANE Pub.

Capone, Donald, jt. auth. see Cheyney, Arnold B.

Capone, Douglas G., jt. ed. see Carpenter, Edward J.

Capone, Lisa. The Conservationworks Book: Practical Conservation Tips for the Home & Outdoors. LC 92-6836. (Illus.). 96p. 1992. pap. 7.95 (*1-878239-11-2*) AMC Books.

Capone, Robert J., jt. auth. see Boden, William E.

Caponegro, Mary. 5 Doubts. 152p. 1998. 19.95 (*1-56886-059-5*) Marsilio Pubs.

— The Star Cafe. 192p. 1991. pap. 8.95 (*0-393-30791-3*) Norton.

Caponera, Dante A. Principles of Water Law & Administration: National & International. (Illus.). 280p. (C). 1992. text 128.00 (*90-5410-108-3*, Pub. by A A Balkema) Ashgate Pub Co.

Caponetto, Salvatore. The Protestant Reformation in Sixteenth-Century Italy. Tedeschi, John & Tedeschi, Anne C., trs. from ITA. LC 98-3776. (Sixteenth Century Essays & Studies: No. 43). Orig. Title: La Riforma Protestante Nell'Italia del Cinquecento. (Illus.). 416p. 1999. 45.00 (*0-943549-67-1*) Truman St Univ.

Caponetto, Salvatore, ed. Benedetto Da Mantova: Il Beneficio Di Cristo. LC 72-3471. (Corpus Reformatorum Italicorum & Biblioteca Ser.). (ITA & LAT., Illus.). 558p. 1972. 45.00 (*0-87580-035-1*) N Ill U Pr.

Caponi. Paul Bowles. LC 98-34789. 1998. 32.00 (*0-8057-4560-2*, Twyne) Mac Lib Ref.

Caponi, Gena D. Paul Bowles: Romantic Savage. LC 93-35581. (Illus.). xx, 304p. (C). 1994. 36.95 (*0-8093-1923-3*) S Ill U Pr.

Caponi, Gena D., ed. Conversations with Paul Bowles. LC 93-25038. (Literary Conversations Ser.). 175p. 1993. pap. 15.95 (*0-87805-650-5*); text 39.50 (*0-87805-649-1*) U Pr of Miss.

— Signifyin(g), Sanctifyin' & Slam Dunking: A Reader in African American Expressive Culture. LC 99-18345. 480p. 1999. 60.00 (*1-55849-182-1*); pap. 22.95 (*1-55849-183-X*) U of Mass Pr.

Caponi, Laura & Migliorini, Paola. Antibody Usage in the Lab. LC 99-11672. (Springer Lab Manual Ser.). 160p. 1999. 62.00 (*3-540-65148-9*) Spr-Verlag.

Caponigri, A. Robert, tr. see Pico Della Mirandola, Giovanni.

Caponigri, Aloysius R. Modern Catholic Thinkers: An Anthology. (Essay Index Reprint Ser.). 650p. reprint ed. lib. bdg. 40.50 (*0-8290-0784-9*) Irvington.

Caponigri, Aloysius R., ed. Modern Catholic Thinkers. LC 78-117775. (Essay Index Reprint Ser.). 1977. 42.95 (*0-8369-1787-1*) Ayer.

***Caponigro, Jeffrey R.** The Crisis Counselor: A Step-By-Step Guide to Managing a Business Crisis. LC 99-16463. 320p. 2000. pap. 16.95 (*0-8092-2490-9*, 249090, Contemporary Bks) NTC Contemp Pub Co.

Caponigro, Jeffrey R. The Crisis Counselor: The Executive's Guide to Avoiding, Managing & Thriving on Crisis That Occur in All Businesses. LC 97-77202. 282p. 1997. 24.95 (*0-9659606-0-9*) Barker Business Bks.

Caponigro, John Paul. Adobe Photoshop Master Class: John Paul Caponigro. 200p. (C). 1999. pap. 50.00 (*0-201-35499-3*, Pub. by Adobe Pr) Peachpit Pr.

Caponigro, Paul. Megaliths. 1986. 75.00 (*0-685-17622-3*) Little.

Caponnetto, Antonio. The Black Legends & Catholic Hispanic Culture: Liberation Theology & the History of the New World. Lopez-Gaston, Jose R. & Lopez-Gaston, Rosa M., trs. from SPA. (Orig.). 1991. pap. 10.00 (*0-9626257-3-6*) CBCCU Amer.

Capoore, jt. auth. see Sidwell.

Caporale, Lynn H., ed. Molecular Strategies in Biological Evolution. LC 99-28213. 350p. 1999. text 120.00 (*1-57331-192-8*) NY Acad Sci.

Caporale, Lynne H. Molecular Strategies in Biological Evolution LC 99-28213. (Annals of the New York Academy of Science Ser.). 1999. write for info. (*1-57331-193-6*) NY Acad Sci.

Caporale, Rocco, ed. The Italian Americans Through the Generations. 1982. 9.95 (*0-934675-15-5*); 19.95 (*0-685-17670-3*) Am Italian.

Caporale, Rocco, ed. see Symposium on the Culture of Unbelief Staff.

***Caporaso, J.** Challenges & Dilemmas of European. 160p. 2000. text 55.00 (*0-8133-2582-X*) Westview.

— The European Union: Dilemmas of Regional Integration. LC 00-23372. 160p. 2000. pap. text 17.00 (*0-8133-2583-8*) Westview.

Caporaso, James A., ed. The Elusive State: International & Comparative Perspective. 288p. (C). 1989. text 49.95 (*0-8039-3381-9*); pap. text 24.00 (*0-8039-3382-7*) Sage.

— The Elusive State: International & Comparative Perspectives. LC 89-34763. 285p. 1989. reprint ed. pap. 88.40 (*0-608-03002-3*, 206345200006) Bks Demand.

Caporaso, James A. & Levine, David P. Theories of Political Economy. (Illus.). 253p. (C). 1992. text 59.95 (*0-521-41561-6*) Cambridge U Pr.

— Theories of Political Economy. (Illus.). 253p. (C). 1992. pap. text 18.95 (*0-521-42578-6*) Cambridge U Pr.

Caporaso, James A. & Roos, Leslie L., Jr., eds. Quasi-Experimental Approaches: Testing Theory & Evaluating Policy. LC 72-96703. 388p. (C). reprint ed. 120.30 (*0-8357-9467-9*, 201146800078) Bks Demand.

Caporello-Szykman, Corradina. The Boccaccian Novella: The Creation & Waning of a Genre. Scaglione, Aldo, ed. (Studies in Italian Culture: Literature in History: Vol. 2). 167p. 1990. 49.95 (*0-8204-1134-5*) P Lang Pubng.

Capossela. Guide to Peer Tutoring. LC 99-166550. (C). 1998. pap. text 14.00 (*0-15-508159-4*, Pub. by Harcourt Coll Pubs) Harcourt.

— Language Matters. (C). 1995. pap. text 35.00 (*0-15-502004-8*); pap. text, teacher ed. 30.00 (*0-15-502159-1*) Harcourt Coll Pubs.

Capossela, Cappy & Warnock, Sheila. Share the Care: How to Organize a Group to Care For Someone Who is Seriously Ill. 320p. 1995. pap. 13.00 (*0-684-81136-7*, Fireside) S&S Trade Pap.

Capossela, Jim. Ice Fishing: A Complete Guide... Basic to Advanced. LC 91-45934. (Illus.). 256p. (Orig.). 1992. pap. 16.00 (*0-88150-234-0*, Pub. by Countryman) Norton.

Capossela, Jim, et al. Good Fishing in the Catskills: From the Waters of the Capital District to the Delaware River. 2nd rev. ed. LC 92-11469. (Good Fishing Ser.). (Illus.). 280p. 1992. pap. 16.00 (*0-88150-237-5*, Pub. by Countryman) Norton.

Capossela, Toni-Lee, ed. Critical Writing Workshop: Designing Writing Assignments to Foster Critical Thinking. LC 93-9449. 225p. (C). 1993. pap. text 25.00 (*0-86709-319-6*, 0319, Pub. by Boynton Cook Pubs) Heinemann.

Capote, Lea R., jt. ed. see O'Leary, J. Patrick.

Capote, Lea R., ed. see O'Leary, Patrick J.

Capote, Maria. Agustin Acosta: El Modernista y Su Isla. LC 89-81546. (SPA., Illus.). 260p. (Orig.). 1990. pap. 19.00 (*0-89729-550-1*) Ediciones.

Capote, Truman. Answered Prayers: The Unfinished Novel. LC 93-43496. 1994. pap. 12.00 (*0-679-75182-3*) Vin Bks.

— Un Arbre De Nuit. (FRE.). 224p. 1981. pap. 10.95 (*0-7859-1944-9*, 2070373398) Fr & Eur.

— Breakfast at Tiffany's: A Short Novel & Three Stories. 196p. 1994. 14.95 (*0-679-60085-X*) Random.

— Breakfast at Tiffany's: And & Three Stories. LC 93-10163. 1993. pap. 11.00 (*0-679-74565-3*) Vin Bks.

— Breakfast at Tiffany's & Other Stories. 1976. 17.95 (*0-8488-0446-5*) Amereon Ltd.

— A Capote Reader. 1998. pap. 18.00 (*0-375-75149-1*) Modern Lib NY.

— A Christmas Memory. LC 88-36452. (Illus.). 40p. (J). (gr. 2 up). 1989. 19.00 (*0-679-80040-9*, Pub. by Knopf Bks Yng Read) Random.

— A Christmas Memory, One Christmas, & the Thanksgiving Visitor. (J). 1996. 13.50 (*0-679-60237-2*) Modern Lib NY.

— De Sang-Froid. (FRE.). 1972. pap. 11.95 (*0-7859-1690-3*, 2070360598) Fr & Eur.

— The Grass Harp. 1954. pap. 5.25 (*0-8222-0476-2*) Dramatists Play.

— The Grass Harp: Including a Tree of the Night & Other Stories. LC 93-19633. 1993. pap. 11.00 (*0-679-74557-2*) Vin Bks.

— Grass Harp Movie Tie-In. 112p. 1996. pap. 9.00 (*0-679-76670-7*) Vin Bks.

— The Grassharp & a Tree of Night. 216p. Date not set. 20.95 (*0-8488-2228-5*) Amereon Ltd.

— In Cold Blood. 1966. 24.95 (*0-394-43023-9*) Random.

***Capote, Truman.** In Cold Blood. LC 99-51693. 440p. 2000. 32.95 (*1-56000-451-7*) Transaction Pubs.

Capote, Truman. In Cold Blood. 1993. reprint ed. lib. bdg. 27.95 (*1-56849-152-2*) Buccaneer Bks.

— In Cold Blood: A True Account of a Multiple Murder & Its Consequences. LC 92-50211. 434p. 1992. 15.95 (*0-679-60023-X*) Modern Lib NY.

— In Cold Blood: A True Account of a Multiple Murder & Its Consequences. 343p. 1994. pap. 12.00 (*0-679-74558-0*) Vin Bks.

— Music for Chameleons. LC 93-42198. 1994. pap. 12.00 (*0-679-74566-1*) Vin Bks.

— Music for Chamelons. 283p. Date not set. 23.95 (*0-8488-2227-7*) Amereon Ltd.

— Musique pour Cameleon. (FRE.). 308p. 1991. pap. 11.95 (*0-7859-2144-3*, 2070382672) Fr & Eur.

— Un Noel-l'Invite d'un Jour. (ENG & FRE.). 145p. 1991. pap. 14.95 (*0-7859-2180-X*, 2070384373) Fr & Eur.

— Other Voices, Other Rooms. 1994. lib. bdg. 24.95 (*1-56849-388-6*) Buccaneer Bks.

— Other Voices, Other Rooms. LC 98-48265. 245 p. 1999. write for info. (*0-7540-3681-2*) Chivers N Amer.

***Capote, Truman.** Other Voices, Other Rooms. LC 98-48265. 1999. 25.95 (*0-7838-8491-5*) Macmillan Gen Ref.

Capote, Truman. Other Voices, Other Rooms. 1994. pap. 12.00 (*0-679-74564-5*) Vin Bks.

— Petit Dejeuner Chez Tiffany. (FRE.). 192p. 1973. pap. 10.95 (*0-7859-1741-1*, 2070363643) Fr & Eur.

— The Thanksgiving Visitor. LC 95-1503. (Illus.). 40p. (J). 1996. 19.00 (*0-679-83898-8*) Knopf.

Capotorti, Francesco, et al. The European Union Treaty: Commentary on the Draft Adopted by the European Parliament on 14 February 1984. 250p. 1987. 85.00 (*0-19-825548-9*) OUP.

Capotosto, Rosario. Two Hundred Original Shop Aids & Jigs for Woodworking. LC 87-10144. (Illus.). 366p. 1987. pap. 17.95 (*0-8069-6582-7*) Sterling.

Capouya, Emile, ed. Classic American Love Poems. (Illus.). 130p. 1999. 17.50 (*0-7818-0645-3*) Hippocrene Bks.

Capouya, Emile & Capouya, Keitha, eds. Classic English Love Poems. LC 97-24432. (Illus.). 130p. 1998. 17.50 (*0-7818-0572-4*) Hippocrene Bks.

Capouya, Emile & Tompkins, Keitha, eds. The Essential Kropotkin. 296p. (C). 1975. pap. 7.20 (*0-87140-400-1*) Liveright.

Capouya, Keitha, jt. ed. see Capouya, Emile.

Capova, M. & Kolbaska, V. Nebojte Sa Pisomnych Prac Z Matematiky (Don't Be Afraid of Mathematical Tests) (SLO.). 216p. 1997. pap. write for info. (*80-08-02433-X*, Pub. by Slov Pegagog Naklad) IBD Ltd.

Capowski, J. J. Computer Techniques in Neuroanatomy. (Illus.). 502p. (C). 1989. text 115.00 (*0-306-43263-3*, Kluwer Plenum) Kluwer Academic.

Capozzi, James D. Beside Quiet Waters: Reflections on the Psalms in Our Everyday Lives. LC 98-55720. 208p. 1999. pap. 16.95 (*0-8264-1145-2*) Continuum.

***Capozzi, John M.** Get a Grip! (Illus.). 160p. 2000. 19.95 (*0-9656410-5-8*) JMC Industries.

Capozzi, John M. A Spirit of Greatness: Stories from the Employees of American Airlines. 244p. 1998. 24.95 (*0-9656410-3-1*) JMC Industries.

Capozzi, Rocco, ed. Reading Eco: An Anthology. LC 96-48021. (Advances in Semiotics Ser.). 1997. 39.95 (*0-253-33275-3*); pap. 18.95 (*0-253-21116-6*) Ind U Pr.

Capozziello, Vincent, Jr. Planning My Career. (YA). (gr. 7 up). 1998. student ed. 5.50 (*0-912486-82-1*) Finney Co.

Capozzoli, Cathy. Julie's Mustard Seed. (Illus.). 48p. (J). 1998. pap. text 12.99 (*0-8054-1717-6*) Broadman.

***Capozzoli, Thomas K. & McVey, R. Steve.** Killer Kids & Gangs: Managing Violence in Schools. LC 99-52301. (Illus.). 156p. 1999. per. 24.95 (*1-57444-283-X*) St Lucie Pr.

Capozzoli, Thomas K. & McVey, R. Steve. Managing Violence in the Workplace. 152p. 1996. boxed set 49.95 (*1-57444-033-0*) St Lucie Pr.

Capp, A. Li'l Abner Dailies. (Li'l Abner Dailies Ser.: Vol. XXI). 1995. pap. 18.95 (*0-87816-262-3*) Kitchen Sink.

— Li'l Abner Dailies. (Li'l Abner Dailies Ser.: Vol. XXII). 1995. pap. 20.95 (*0-87816-271-2*) Kitchen Sink.

Capp, Al. Fearless Fosdick. Schreiner, Dave & Collins, Max Allan, eds. LC 90-43616. (Illus.). 112p. (Orig.). 1991. reprint ed. pap. 11.95 (*0-87816-108-2*) Kitchen Sink.

— Fearless Fosdick: The Hole Story! Schreiner, Dave, ed. LC 92-8056. (Illus.). 128p. (Orig.). 1992. pap. 11.95 (*0-87816-164-3*) Kitchen Sink.

— Lil Abner, No. 24. Couch, N. C. Christopher, ed. (Illus.). 176p. 1997. pap. 18.95 (*0-87816-316-6*) Kitchen Sink.

— Lil Abner, No. 24. 2nd ed. Couch, N. C. Christopher, ed. (Illus.). 176p. 1997. 34.95 (*0-87816-317-4*) Kitchen Sink.

— Li'l Abner, No. 26. 184p. 1998. pap. 22.95 (*0-87816-290-9*) Kitchen Sink.

— Li'l Abner, No. 27. 176p. 1998. pap. 22.95 (*0-87816-295-X*) Kitchen Sink.

— Li'l Abner, No. 27. 1999. write for info. (*0-87816-296-8*) Kitchen Sink.

— Li'l Abner, Vol. 17. Vance, James, ed. (Illus.). 160p. 1993. 34.95 (*0-87816-209-7*) Kitchen Sink.

— Li'l Abner, Vol. 19. 2nd ed. Vance, James, ed. (Illus.). 160p. 1994. 34.95 (*0-87816-249-6*) Kitchen Sink.

— Li'l Abner, Vol. 21. 2nd ed. (Illus.). 176p. 1995. 34.95 (*0-87816-263-1*) Kitchen Sink.

— Li'l Abner, Vol. 22. (Illus.). 192p. 1995. 40.00 (*0-87816-272-0*) Kitchen Sink.

— Li'l Abner, Vol. 23. (Illus.). 176p. 1995. 34.95 (*0-87816-305-0*) Kitchen Sink.

— Li'l Abner: Li'l Abner Meets the Shmoo, No. 27. (Li'l Abner Dailies Ser.). (Illus.). 180p. 1998. reprint ed. pap. 22.95 (*0-87816-116-3*) Kitchen Sink.

— Li'l Abner Dailies, Vol. 23. (Illus.). 176p. 1996. pap. text 18.95 (*0-87816-304-2*) Kitchen Sink.

— Li'l Abner Dailies, 1959. (Li'l Abner Dailies Ser.: Vol. 25). (Illus.). 184p. 1996. 34.95 (*0-87816-279-8*); pap. 18.95 (*0-87816-278-X*) Kitchen Sink.

Capp, Al. Li'l Abner Dailies 1940, Vol.VI. Schreiner, Dave, ed. LC 88-12831. (Li'l Abner Dailies Ser.). (Illus.). 174p. 1989. pap. 16.95 (*0-87816-059-0*) Kitchen Sink.

— Li'l Abner Dailies 1945, Vol. 11. Schreiner, Dave & Gardner, Madeline, eds. (Al Capp's Li'l Abner Ser.). (Illus.). 158p. 1991. reprint ed. pap. 18.95 (*0-87816-083-3*) Kitchen Sink.

— Li'l Abner Dailies 1944, Vol. 10. Schreiner, Dave, ed. LC 88-12831. (Li'l Abner Dailies Ser.: Vol. X). (Illus.). 168p. 1990. pap. 18.95 (*0-87816-079-5*) Kitchen Sink.

— Li'l Abner Dailies 1949 Vol. 15: Kick in the Kigmies! limited ed. Schreiner, Dave, ed. (Illus.). 176p. 1993. 34.95 (*0-87816-126-0*) Kitchen Sink.

— Li'l Abner Dailies 1941, Vol. VII. Schreiner, Dave, ed. LC 88-12831. (Li'l Abner Dailies Ser.). (Illus.). 1990. 27.95 (*0-87816-064-7*) Kitchen Sink.

— Li'l Abner Dailies 1946, Vol. 12. LC 88-12831. (Illus.). 168p. 1991. pap. 18.95 (*0-87816-092-2*) Kitchen Sink.

— Li'l Abner Dailies 1943, Vol. IX. Schreiner, Dave, ed. LC 88-12831. (Illus.). 1990. 29.95 (*0-87816-073-6*) Kitchen Sink.

— Li'l Abner Dailies 1939, Vol. 5. Schreiner, Dave & Cairol, Julie C., eds. LC 88-12831. (Illus.). 176p. 1989. 27.95 (*0-87816-056-6*) Kitchen Sink.

Capp, Al. Li'l Abner Dailies, 1938: Abner in the Orphanage, Strange Gal in the Swamp. Schreiner, Dave, ed. LC 88-12831. (Li'l Abner Dailies Ser.: Vol. IV). (Illus.). 168p. 1989. 27.95 (*0-87816-051-5*); pap. 16.95 (*0-87816-052-3*) Kitchen Sink.

— Li'l Abner Dailies, 1950: In Search of the Perfect Woman. limited ed. Schreiner, Dave, ed. (Li'l Abner Dailies Ser.: Vol. 16). (Illus.). 184p. 1993. 34.95 (*0-87816-143-0*) Kitchen Sink.

— Li'l Abner Daily Strips, 1951. Schreiner, Dave, ed. (Li'l Abner Dailies Ser.: Vol. 17). (Illus.). 180p. 1993. pap. 18.95 (*0-87816-210-0*) Kitchen Sink.

— Li'l Abner, 1952, Vol. 18. Schriener, Dave, ed. (Illus.). 176p. (YA). (gr. 6 up). 1994. reprint ed. 34.95 (*0-87816-242-9*) Kitchen Sink.

— My Well-Balanced Life on a Wooden Leg. LC 91-6728. (Illus.). 128p. 1991. 15.95 (*0-936784-93-8*) J Daniel.

Capp, Al & Van Buren, Raeburn. Abbie an' Slats, Vol. 1. Galewitz, Herb, ed. (U. S. Classics Ser.). (Illus.). 80p. (Orig.). 1983. pap. 5.95 (*0-912277-14-9*) K Pierce Bks.

Capp, Al, et al. Abbie an' Slats, Vol. 2. Galewitz, Herb, ed. (U. S. Classics Ser.). (Illus.). 80p. (Orig.). 1984. pap. 5.95 (*0-912277-24-6*) K Pierce Bks.

Capp, Bernard. Cromwell's Navy: The Fleet & the English Revolution, 1648-1660. 432p. 1992. reprint ed. pap. text 32.00 (*0-19-820393-4*) OUP.

Capp, Carolyn, jt. auth. see Silvious, Jan.

***Capp, Charles.** La Esperanza, Companera De La Fe. (SPA.). 48p. 1999. pap. write for info. (*1-58633-003-9*) Libros Intern.

— El Poder Creativo de Dios: Obrara para Usted. (SPA.). 32p. 1999. pap. write for info. (*1-58633-005-5*) Libros Intern.

— El Poder Creativo de Dios para Sanar. (SPA.). 64p. 1999. pap. write for info. (*1-58633-004-7*) Libros Intern.

— Siembra y Cosecha. (SPA.). 48p. 1999. pap. write for info. (*1-58633-002-0*) Libros Intern.

Capp, Fiona. Night Surfing. 213p. (Orig.). 1997. pap. 12.95 (*1-86373-913-0*, Pub. by Allen & Unwin Pty) IPG Chicago.

Capp, Glenn Richard, et al. Basic Oral Communication. 5th ed. 360p. (C). 1989. pap. text 39.00 (*0-13-065996-7*) P-H.

***Capp, Kristin, photos by.** Americana. (Illus.). 2000. 65.00 (*3-908163-25-0*, Pub. by Edit Stemmle) Abbeville Pr.

Capp, Kristin, photos by. Hutterite: A World of Grace. (Illus.). 145p. 1998. 75.00 (*3-908161-29-0*) Abbeville Pr.

Capp, Richard. Crown of Thorns. Young, Billie, ed. LC 77-78802. 1979. 22.95 (*0-87949-096-9*) Ashley Bks.

Capp, Robert A. & Bush, Robert G. Glass Etching: Fifty-Two Patterns with Complete Instructions. (Crafts Ser.). (Illus.). 64p. (Orig.). 1984. pap. 5.95 (*0-486-24578-0*) Dover.

Cappa, Stefano F. Cognitive Neurology. 1998. 38.00 (*1-86094-128-1*) World Scientific Pub.

Cappadelta, Luigi, tr. see Von Funk, Franz X.

Cappaert, David, jt. auth. see Monroe, Martha C.

Cappaert, David, ed. see Braus, Judy A. & Monroe, Martha C.

Cappaert, David, ed. see Disinger, John F. & Monroe, Martha C.

Cappaert, David, ed. see Pennock, Margaret T. & Bardwell, Lisa V.

Cappalli, Richard B. The American Common Law Method. LC 96-41156. 300p. 1997. lib. bdg. 95.00 (*1-57105-041-8*) Transnatl Pubs.

— Rights & Remedies under Federal Grants. LC 79-12004. 414p. reprint ed. pap. 128.40 (*0-608-16706-1*, 202679500052) Bks Demand.

Cappannelli, George. Sensational Ladies: A Handbook for Women Who Want More. 90p. 1989. 14.95 (*0-685-29401-3*) Onlife Pub.

Capparell, Stephanie, jt. auth. see Morrell, Margot.

Cappas, Alberto O. Disintegration of the Puertoricans: Puertoricans Con Games & Other Poems. 55p. 1997. pap. 20.00 (*0-9656807-0-3*, CPAOC41546) D Pedro.

Cappel, Constance. Utopian Colleges, Vol. 38. LC 98-8577. (American University Studies: Vol. XIV). XI, 148p. (C). 1999. pap. text 32.95 (*0-8204-2056-5*) P Lang Pubng.

Cappel, Jerry & Smith, Lawanda. Transitions. (Extensions Adult Elective Bible Study Ser.). 56p. pap. 9.00 (*1-57312-113-4*); pap. 3.00 (*1-880837-62-5*) Smyth & Helwys.

Cappel, Michelle E. Anthology of the Soul: From Crisis to Recovery. 89p. (Orig.). 1996. pap. 12.50 (*0-9653666-0-X*) M E Cappel.

— The Survival Guide: Tips for Coping for Patients of Spiritual Healing. (Illus.). 50p. (Orig.). 1997. pap. 10.95 (*0-9653666-1-8*) M E Cappel.

Cappel, Robert P. S. W. A. T. Team Manual. (Illus.). 150p. 1979. pap. 25.00 (*0-87364-169-8*) Paladin Pr.

Cappeliez, Philippe & Flynn, Robert J., eds. Depression & the Social Environment: Research & Intervention with Neglected Populations. 448p. 1993. 65.00 (*0-7735-0960-7*, Pub. by McG-Queens Univ Pr) CUP Services.

Cappell & Howard. New York in American History. 64p. 1987. student ed. 4.50 (*0-910307-14-8*) Comp Pr.

Cappell, Howard D., et al, eds. Research Advances in Alcohol & Drug Problems, Vol. 9. 315p. 1986. 79.50 (*0-306-42426-6*, Plenum Trade) Perseus Pubng.

***Cappell, Ian.** Awakening. 2000. pap. 11.95 (*1-902644-30-1*) Prowler Pr.

Cappell, James J., jt. ed. see Deakin, Edward B.

Cappell, Ralph & Howard, Ethel M. Reading & Writing about Health Careers. (Career Ser.). 79p. 1984. student ed. 4.25 (*0-910307-02-4*) Comp Pr.

— Reading & Writing about Office Careers. (Career Ser.). 79p. 1986. student ed. 4.50 (*0-910307-06-7*) Comp Pr.

Cappell, Ralph, jt. auth. see Howard, Ethel M.

***Cappell, S.** Three-manifold Invariants Using Symplectic Geometry of Representation Varieties. 1999. 28.00 (*981-02-4019-8*) WSC Inst MA Studies.

***Cappell, Sylvain.** Papers Dedicated to C.T.C. Wall, 145. (Annals of Mathematics Studies). 2000. pap. text 35.00 (*0-691-04938-6*, Pub. by Princeton U Pr) Cal Prin Full Svc.

— Surveys on Surgery Theory Vol. 1: Papers Dedicated to C. T. C. Wall. (Annals of Mathematics Studies: Vol. 145). 440p. 2000. 89.50 (*0-691-04937-8*, Pub. by Princeton U Pr) Cal Prin Full Svc.

Cappella, Joseph N., jt. auth. see Jamieson, Kathleen H.

Cappellari, Bartolomeo Alberto, see Gregory XVI, pseud.

Cappellazzo, Amy. In Company: Robert Creeley's Collaborations. (Illus.). 120p. 1999. pap. 24.95 (*0-8078-4833-6*) U of NC Pr.

***Cappellazzo, Amy.** Making Time: Considering Time as a Material in Contemporary Video & Film. 2000. pap. 25.00 (*0-9676480-0-9*) Palm Bch Inst.

Cappellazzo, Amy. Suzanne McClelland: Recent Works on Paper. LC 98-61360. (Illus.). 18p. 1998. pap. 8.00 (*1-890949-02-7*) UNC Greensboro.

— Wildlife or the Impossibility of Mistaking Nature. LC 98-60509. (Illus.). 23p. 1998. pap. 5.00 (*1-890949-01-9*) UNC Greensboro.

Cappellazzo, Amy, et al. Desert Cliche: Israel Now - Local Images. Kassovsky, Daria, tr. LC 96-78969. (ENG & HEB., Illus.). (Orig.). 1996. pap. 18.00 (*1-880511-07-X*) Bass Museum.

Cappelletti, M., jt. auth. see Seccombe, M.

Cappelletti, Paulo. Flash Memories. LC 99-25278. 1999. write for info. (*0-7923-8487-3*) Kluwer Academic.

Cappelli. The New Deal at Work: Managing the market-Driven Workforce. LC 98-42221. 320p. 1999. 29.95 (*0-87584-668-8*, HBS Pr) Harvard Busn.

Cappelli, Adriano, ed. Dizionario di Abbreviature Latine Ed Italiane. (ITA & LAT., Illus.). 531p. 1990. 45.00 (*0-913298-95-6*) S F Vanni.

Cappelli, Peter. Airline Labor Relations in the Global Era: The New Frontier. LC 94-48393. 250p. 1995. 45.00 (*0-87546-343-6*, ILR Press) Cornell U Pr.

Cappelli, Peter, ed. Airline Labor Relations in the Global Era: The New Frontier. 304p. 1995. pap. 19.95 (*0-87546-344-4*, ILR Press) Cornell U Pr.

***Cappelli, Peter, ed.** Employment Practices & Corporate Strategy. LC 98-48334. (Illus.). 240p. 1999. 29.95 (*0-19-512859-1*) OUP.

Cappelli, Peter, ed. Training & Development. LC 93-37289. (International Library of Management). 512p. 1994. 224.95 (*1-85521-353-2*, Pub. by Dartmth Pub) Ashgate Pub Co.

Cappelli, Peter & National Policy Association (U.S.). Committee on New American Realities. Change at Work: Trends That Are Transforming the Business of Business. LC 97-65394. 1997. write for info. (*0-89068-137-6*) Natl Planning.

Cappelli, Peter, et al. Change at Work. LC 96-23911. (Illus.). 288p. 1997. 32.00 (*0-19-510327-0*) OUP.

Cappelli, William S., ed. see Gartner Group, Inc. Staff.

Cappellin, Riccardo & Nujkamp, Peter. Spatial Context of Technological Development. (Illus.). 513p. 1990. text 109.95 (*0-566-07149-5*, Pub. by Avebry) Ashgate Pub Co.

Cappellin, Riccardo, jt. auth. see Molle, Willem.

Cappellini, V., ed. Time-Varying IMage Processing & Moving Object Recognition, No. 4. 1997. write for info. (*0-614-17887-8*) Elsevier.

— Time-Varying Image Processing & Moving Object Recognition: Proceedings of the 4th International Workshop, Florence, Italy, June 1993, No. 3. (Illus.). 444p. 1994. 194.50 (*0-444-81467-1*) Elsevier.

Cappellini, Vito, ed. Data Compression & Error Control Techniques with Applications. 1985. text 97.00 (*0-12-159260-X*) Acad Pr.

— Time-Varying Image Processing & Moving Object Recognition: Proceedings of the 5th International Workshop, Florence, Italy, September 5-6, 1996. LC 97-23533. 346p. 1997. 184.50 (*0-444-82307-7*) Elsevier.

Cappellitti, Mauro, et al, eds. Integration Through Law - Europe & the American Federal Experience: The Legal Integration of Energy Markets, Vol. 5. (European University Institute, Series A (Law): Vol. 2-5). xxvii, 176p. 1987. lib. bdg. 64.65 (*3-11-010743-0*) De Gruyter.

Cappello & Komoroske, Frances E. Lender Liability. 2nd ed. 1996. ring bd. 115.00 (*0-327-03900-0*, 81389-10, MICHIE) LEXIS Pub.

Cappello, A. Barry & Komoroske, Frances E. Lender Liability. 1987. ring bd. 80.00 (*1-55943-164-4*, MICHIE) LEXIS Pub.

— Lender Liability. 2nd ed. 800p. 1993. spiral bd. 130.00 (*0-250-40702-7*, MICHIE) LEXIS Pub.

***Cappello, A. Barry & Komoroske, Frances E.** Lender Liability. 3rd ed. 800p. 1999. ring bd. write for info. (*0-327-04967-7*, 8138911) LEXIS Pub.

Cappello, A. Barry & Komoroske, Frances E. Lender Liability, No. 1. 1987. suppl. ed. 34.00 (*0-685-66651-4*, MICHIE) LEXIS Pub.

— Lender Liability, No. 2. 1987. suppl. ed. 32.50 (*1-55943-064-8*, MICHIE) LEXIS Pub.

— Lender Liability, No. 3. 1987. suppl. ed. 28.00 (*1-55943-864-9*, MICHIE) LEXIS Pub.

— Lender Liability, No. 4. 1987. suppl. ed. 34.00 (*1-55943-765-0*, MICHIE) LEXIS Pub.

Cappello, Carl, jt. ed. see Kline, Linda J.

***Cappello, Dominic.** Ten Talks Parents Must Have with Their Children about Violence. 288p. 2000. pap. 12.95 (*0-7868-8549-1*, Pub. by Hyperion) Time Warner.

Cappello, Dominic, jt. auth. see Stein, Nan.

Cappello, Eve. Act, Don't React: Programming Yourself for Success SD 8 & Workbook. 3rd ed. 192p. (C). 1988. pap., wbk. ed. 15.95 (*0-8403-4848-7*) Eve Cappello.

***Cappello, Eve.** Great Sex after 50: Reinventing Yourself & Reaching New Sexual Heights at Any Age. 100p. 2000. pap. text 10.95 (*0-9639037-1-3*, Dr Eve Pub) Eve Cappello.

Cappello, Eve. The "New" Professional Touch. 2nd ed. 128p. 1988. pap. 10.00 (*0-8403-4910-6*) Eve Cappello.

— The Perfectionist Syndrome: How to Stop Driving Yourself & Everyone Else Crazy. 169p. 1990. pap. text 14.95 (*0-8403-5744-3*) Eve Cappello.

***Cappello, Eve.** The Professional Touch: How to Think, Act, Write & Look Your Professional Best. rev. ed. 108p. 2000. pap. text 10.95 (*0-9639037-2-1*, Dr Eve Pub) Eve Cappello.

Cappello, Eve. Why Aren't More Women Running the Show? How Women Can Stop Being Their Own Worst Enemies, Handle Men, Power & Sexual Harassment. 84p. (Orig.). 1994. pap. text 10.00 (*0-9639037-0-5*) Eve Cappello.

Cappello, Mary. Night Bloom. LC 98-19582. 280p. 1998. 24.00 (*0-8070-7216-8*) Beacon Pr.

— Night Bloom: An Italian-American Life. LC 98-19582. 280p. 1999. pap. 16.00 (*0-8070-7217-6*) Beacon Pr.

Cappello, Sharyn, jt. auth. see Jaffe, Merle.

Cappelloni, Nancy. Ethnic Cooking the Microwave Way. LC 93-29543. (Easy Menu Ethnic Cookbooks Ser.). (Illus.). 48p. (J). (gr. 5 up). 1994. pap. 5.95 (*0-8225-9660-1*, First Ave Edns) Lerner Pub.

— Ethnic Cooking the Microwave Way. LC 93-29543. (Easy Menu Ethnic Cookbooks Ser.). (Illus.). 48p. (YA). (gr. 5 up). 1994. lib. bdg. 19.93 (*0-8225-0929-6*, Lerner Publctns) Lerner Pub.

Cappelorn, Niels J. & Deuser, Hermann, eds. Kierkegaard Studies - Yearbook 1997. 500p. 1997. 143.00 (*3-11-015906-6*) De Gruyter.

— Kierkegaard Studies Yearbook, 1996. (ENG & GER.). viii, 575p. (C). 1996. lib. bdg. 131.85 (*3-11-015188-X*) De Gruyter.

Cappelorn, Niels J. & Stewart, Jon, eds. Kierkegaard Revisited: Proceedings from the Conference "Kierkegaard & the Meaning It" Copenhagen, may 5-9, 1996. LC 97-28986. 508p. 1997. text 145.35 (*3-11-015718-7*) De Gruyter.

***Cappels, Thomas M.** Financially Focused Quality LC 99-28173. 312p. 1999. boxed set 39.95 (*1-57444-248-1*) St Lucie Pr.

Cappenberg, T. E. & Steenbergen, C. L., eds. Measurement of Microbial Activities in the Carbon Cycle in Aquatic Ecosystems: Proceedings of the Third International Workshop, 18-21 Aug., 1986. (Advances in Limnology Ser.: Vol. 31). (GER., Illus.). xii, 390p. 1988. pap. text 103.00 (*3-510-47029-X*, Pub. by E Schweizerbartsche) Balogh.

Capper, Charles. Margaret Fuller: An American Romantic Life: The Private Years. (Illus.). 456p. 1992. text 65.00 (*0-19-504579-3*) OUP.

— Margaret Fuller: The Public Years. (Illus.). 320p. Date not set. 29.95 (*0-19-506313-9*) OUP.

— Margaret Fuller an American Romantic Life: The Private Years, Vol. 1. (Illus.). 456p. 1994. reprint ed. pap. 18.95 (*0-19-509267-8*) OUP.

Capper, Charles & Wright, Conrad E., eds. Transient & Permanent: The Transcendentalist Movement & Its Contexts. LC 99-35220. (Studies in American History & Culture Ser.: Vol. 5). (Illus.). 650p. 1999. 75.00 (*0-934909-76-8*, Pub. by Mass Hist Soc) NE U Pr.

Capper, Charles, jt. auth. see Hollinger, David A.

Capper, Colleen A., ed. Educational Administration in a Pluralistic Society. LC 92-8122. (SUNY Series, the Social Context of Education). 323p. (C). 1993. text 64.50 (*0-7914-1373-X*); pap. text 21.95 (*0-7914-1374-8*) State U NY Pr.

***Capper, Colleen A., et al.** Meeting the Needs of Students of All Abilities: How Leaders Go Beyond Inclusion. (Illus.). 168p. 2000. pap., wbk. ed. 32.95 (*0-7619-7501-2*); lib. bdg., wbk. ed. 69.95 (*0-7619-7500-4*) Corwin Pr.

Capper, D. M. The C++ Programming Language for Scientists, Engineers, & Mathematicians. LC 93-47975. 502p. 1994. 42.95 (*0-387-19847-4*) Spr-Verlag.

— The C++ Programming Language for Scientists, Mathematicians & Engineers. 1996. pap. 42.95 (*3-540-19847-4*) Spr-Verlag.

Capper, Joanne. Testing to Learn--Learning to Test. LC 96-32876. 1996. pap. 28.95 (*0-87207-145-6*) Intl Reading.

Capper, Lizanne. That's My Child: Strategies for Parents of Children with Disabilities. 200p. 1996. pap. text 10.95 (*0-87868-595-2*, Child-Family Pr) Child Welfare.

Capper, Peter, ed. Properties of Narrow-Gap Cadmium-Based Compounds. (EMIS Datareviews Ser.: No. 10). 650p. 1994. boxed set 295.00 (*0-85296-880-9*) INSPEC Inc.

Capper, Phillip. Latent Damage Act, 1986: Impact on the Professions & the Construction Industry. (C). 1987. 285.00 (*0-7855-4107-1*, Pub. by Witherby & Co) St Mut.

Capper, Phillip, et al, eds. Emden's Construction Law. ring bd. write for info. (*0-406-99811-6*, ECL8ASET, MICHIE) LEXIS Pub.

Capper, Phillip & Susskind, Richard. Latent Damage Law: The Expert System. 120p. 1988. boxed set 60.00 (*0-406-02362-X*, UK, MICHIE) LEXIS Pub.

Capper, Richard. A Project-by-Project Approach to Quality: A Practical Handbook for Individuals, Teams, & Organizations. LC 97-20129. 277p. 1998. 96.95 (*0-566-07925-9*, Pub. by Gower) Ashgate Pub Co.

Capper, W. M. & Johnson, D., eds. The Faith of a Surgeon: Belief & Experience in the Life of Arthur Rendle Short. 160p. 1976. pap. 8.95 (*0-85364-198-6*) Attic Pr.

Cappetta, Cynthia. Chairs, Chairs, Chairs! (Rookie Readers Ser.). (Illus.). 32p. (gr. k-3). 1999. lib. bdg. 4.95 (*0-516-26474-5*) Childrens.

— Chairs, Chairs, Chairs! LC 98-9916. (Rookie Readers Ser.). (Illus.). 32p. (J). (gr. 1-2). 1999. 17.50 (*0-516-21542-6*) Childrens.

Cappetta, Henri. Chondrichthyes II: Mesozoic & Genozoic Elasmobranhii. (Handbook of Paleoichthyology: Vol. 3B). (Illus.). 193p. 1987. text 225.00 (*3-437-30393-7*) Lubrecht & Cramer.

Cappetti, Carla. Writing Chicago: Modernism, Ethnography, & the Novel. Arac, Jonathan, ed. LC 92-41092. (Social Foundations of Aesthetic Forms Ser.). 320p. (C). 1993. pap. 21.00 (*0-231-08129-4*); text 57.50 (*0-231-08128-6*) Col U Pr.

Cappi, Hughes De, see Fulvio, Andrea.

Cappi, Paul & Collins, Mary. A Level Paper. (Lecture Notes Ser.). 328p. 1995. pap. 28.00 (*1-87424.-74-0*, Pub. by Cavendish Pubng) Gaunt.

Cappi, Paul, ed. see Booth, Penny, et al.

Cappiello. Case Studies for Family Nurse Practitioners. LC 98-11267. (Illus.). 360p. (C). (gr. 13). 1998. pap. text 39.95 (*0-8151-1559-8*, 31762) Mosby Inc.

Cappiello, Frank A., Jr. Finding the Next Super Stock. 64p. 1983. pap. 8.95 (*0-89709-100-0*, 30031) McGraw-Hill Prof.

— Frank Cappiellos New Guide to Finding. 1990. pap. 12.95 (*0-8306-9041-7*) McGraw-Hill Prof.

Cappiello, Rose. Oh Lucky Country. Rando, Gaetano, tr. from ITA.Tr. of Paese Fortunato. 236p. 1985. pap. 16.95 (*0-7022-1935-5*, Pub. by Univ Queensland Pr) Intl Spec Bk.

Cappleman, Helen C. Jumpstart to Language Power: A Literacy Program for At-Risk Students, Incl. blackline masters. LC 90-61866. (Illus.). 292p. (C). 1990. teacher ed., spiral bd. 20.00 (*1-886131-24-4*, JS) Math Lrning.

Cappleman, Helen G. Success in Reading & Writing: Grade 2. 2nd ed. (Illus.). 288p. 1991. 27.95 (*0-673-36002-4*, GoodYrBooks) Addson-Wesley Educ.

Cappleman, Henel G. Success in Reading & Writing: Grade 1. 2nd ed. (Illus.). 288p. 1991. 27.95 (*0-673-36001-6*, GoodYrBooks) Addson-Wesley Educ.

Cappon, Daniel. Eating, Loving & Dying: A Psychology of Appetites. LC 72-97151. 130p. reprint ed. pap. 40.30 (*0-608-30215-5*, 201916500010) Bks Demand.

— Intuition: Harnessing the Hidden Power of the Mind. 211p. 1998. text 22.00 (*0-7881-5541-5*) DIANE Pub.

— Intuition & Management: Research & Application. LC 94-2993. 224p. 1994. 57.95 (*0-89930-850-3*, Quorum Bks) Greenwood.

Cappon, Lester, ed. Atlas of Early American History: The Revolutionary Era, 1760-1790. 1976. 250.00 (*0-911028-00-5*) Princeton U Pr.

Cappon, Lester J., ed. The Adams-Jefferson Letters: The Complete Correspondence Between Thomas Jefferson & Abigail & John Adams. LC 88-14258. (Institute of Early American History & Culture Ser.). lii, 638p. (C). 1988. reprint ed. 55.00 (*0-8078-1807-0*); reprint ed. pap. 19.95 (*0-8078-4230-3*) U of NC Pr.

Cappon, Rene J. Associated Press Guide to News Writing. 176p. 1991. per. 11.95 (*0-13-053679-2*, Arc) IDG Bks.

Capps, jt. auth. see Penson.

Capps, ed. see Brown, Lowell.

Capps, Anita A. See Rock City Barns Vol. 1: A Tennessee Tradition. LC 96-70305. (Illus.). 112p. 1997. 26.95 (*0-9654815-0-6*) See Rock City.

Capps, Annette. Reverse the Curse in Your Body & Emotions. 106p. (Orig.). 1987. pap. 4.95 (*0-9618975-0-3*) Annette Capps.

— Understanding Persecution. 32p. 1982. pap. 1.00 (*0-89274-214-3*, HH-214) Harrison Hse.

Capps, Annette, jt. auth. see Capps, Charles.

Capps, Benjamin. The Brothers of Uterica. LC 87-23387. (Southwest Life & Letters Ser.). 320p. 1988. reprint ed. pap. 10.95 (*0-87074-258-2*) SMU Press.

— The Brothers of Uterica: A Novel. LC 87-23387. (Southwest Life & Letters Ser.). 320p. 1988. reprint ed. 22.50 (*0-87074-257-4*) SMU Press.

— The Heirs of Franklin Woodstock. LC 88-39269. 196p. 1989. 17.95 (*0-87565-036-8*) Tex Christian.

— Sam Chance. LC 87-9757. (Southwest Life & Letters Ser.). 282p. 1987. reprint ed. pap. 10.95 (*0-87074-251-5*) SMU Press.

— Sam Chance: A Novel. LC 87-9757. (Southwest Life & Letters Ser.). 282p. 1987. reprint ed. 22.50 (*0-87074-250-7*) SMU Press.

— The Trail to Ogallala. LC 85-4721. (Texas Tradition Ser.: No. 3). 286p. 1985. reprint ed. 16.95 (*0-87565-012-0*); reprint ed. pap. 9.95 (*0-87565-013-9*) Tex Christian.

— The Warren Wagontrain Raid: The First Complete Account of an Historic Indian Attack & Its Aftermath. LC 89-42897. (Southwest Life & Letters Ser.). (Illus.). 328p. 1989. reprint ed. pap. 12.95 (*0-87074-295-7*) SMU Press.

— The White Man's Road. LC 88-42633. (Southwest Life & Letters Ser.). 328p. 1988. reprint ed. pap. 10.95 (*0-87074-272-8*) SMU Press.

— The White Man's Road: A Novel. LC 88-42633. (Southwest Life & Letters Ser.). 328p. 1988. reprint ed. 22.50 (*0-87074-281-7*) SMU Press.

— Woman of the People. LC 98-47729. Vol. 26. 248p. 1999. pap. 15.95 (*0-87565-195-X*) Tex Christian.

Capps, Charles. Authority in Three Worlds. 266p. (Orig.). 1980. mass mkt. 5.99 (*0-89274-281-X*, HH-281) Harrison Hse.

— Can Your Faith Fail? 53p. 1978. mass mkt. 4.99 (*0-89274-105-8*, HH-105) Harrison Hse.

— Changing the Seen & Shaping the Unseen. 57p. 1981. mass mkt. 4.99 (*0-89274-220-8*, HH-220) Harrison Hse.

— End Time Events. LC 97-191753. 256p. 1999. 19.99 (*0-89274-946-6*, HH-946) Dake Pub.

— Faith & Confession. 320p. 1992. pap. 12.99 (*0-89274-914-8*, HH-914) Harrison Hse.

— Faith & Confessions. 1992. pap. 12.99 (*1-57794-132-2*) Harrison Hse.

— God's Creative Power for Healing: Minibook. 48p. 1991. pap. 1.25 (*0-89274-815-X*, HH-815) Harrison Hse.

— God's Creative Power Will Work for You. 32p. 1976. pap. 1.00 (*0-89274-024-8*) Harrison Hse.

— God's Image of You. 77p. 1985. mass mkt. 4.99 (*0-89274-376-X*) Harrison Hse.

— Hope: A Partner to Faith. 38p. (Orig.). 1986. pap. 1.50 (*0-89274-396-4*, HH-396) Harrison Hse.

— How to Have Faith in Your Faith. 112p. 1988. mass mkt. 4.99 (*0-89274-415-4*, HH-415) Harrison Hse.

— How You Can Avoid Tragedy. pap. 6.99 (*0-89274-847-8*, HH-847) Harrison Hse.

— How You Can Avoid Tragedy. 192p. 1981. mass mkt. 6.99 (*0-89274-467-7*, HH-467) Harrison Hse.

— Jesus, Our Intercessor. LC 94-237584. 144p. 1999. pap. 7.99 (*0-89274-853-2*, HH-853) Dake Pub.

— Kicking over Sacred Cows. 208p. 1987. mass mkt. 5.99 (*0-89274-409-X*, HH-409) Harrison Hse.

— The Light of Life in the Spirit of Man. (Orig.). 1987. pap. 4.99 (*0-89274-470-7*, HH-470) Harrison Hse.

— The Messenger of Satan. 64p. 1993. pap. 5.99 (*0-89274-633-5*, HH-633) Harrison Hse.

— El Poder Creador de Dios. (Mini-Bks.).Tr. of God's Creative Power Will Work for You. (SPA.). 32p. 1980. pap. 0.99 (*0-89274-335-2*, HH-335) Harrison Hse.

— El Poder Creador de Dios para Sanar.Tr. of God's Creative Power for Healing. (SPA.). 64p. (Orig.). 1995. mass mkt. 1.00 (*0-89274-825-7*, HH-825) Harrison Hse.

— Seedtime & Harvest: Minibook. 39p. (Orig.). 1986. pap. 1.00 (*0-89274-397-2*) Harrison Hse.

— The Substance of Things. 64p. (Orig.). 1989. pap. 4.99 (*0-89274-599-1*, HH599) Harrison Hse.

— Success Motivation Through the Word. 272p. 1982. mass mkt. 5.99 (*0-89274-183-X*, HH-183) Harrison Hse.

— Tongue: A Creative Force. 159p. (Orig.). 1976. mass mkt. 5.99 (*0-89274-061-2*) Harrison Hse.

— The Tongue: A Creative Force. 1999. pap. 6.99 (*0-89274-006-X*) Dake Pub.

Capps, Charles & Capps, Annette. Angels. 144p. (Orig.). 1995. pap. 5.99 (*0-89274-743-9*, HH-743) Harrison Hse.

Capps, Claudius M., ed. Blue & the Gray. LC 70-75710. (Granger Index Reprint Ser.). 1977. 19.95 (*0-8369-6005-X*) Ayer.

Capps, Clive, jt. auth. see Bolton, Tim.

Capps, Donald. Agents of Hope: A Pastoral Psychology. LC 94-31466. 176p. 1995. 17.00 (*0-8006-2578-1*, 1-2578, Fortress Pr) Augsburg Fortress.

— The Child's Song: The Religious Abuse of Children. LC 94-27462. 208p. (Orig.). 1995. pap. 19.95 (*0-664-25554-X*) Westminster John Knox.

***Capps, Donald.** Deadly Sins & Saving Virtues. 162p. 2000. pap. 18.00 (*1-57910-247-6*) Wipf & Stock.

Capps, Donald. The Depleted Self: Sin in a Narcissistic Age. LC 92-7931. 192p. (Orig.). 1993. pap. 18.00 (*0-8006-2587-0*, 1-2587, Fortress Pr) Augsburg Fortress.

***Capps, Donald.** Jesus: A Psychological Biography. 2000. 29.99 (*0-8272-1713-7*) Chalice Pr.

Capps, Donald. Living Stories: Pastoral Counseling in Congregational Context. LC 98-9235. 1998. pap. text 16.00 (*0-8006-3073-4*, 1-3073, Fortress Pr) Augsburg Fortress.

— Men, Religion & Melancholia: James, Otto, Jung & Erikson. LC 96-36548. 240p. 1997. 32.00 (*0-300-06971-5*) Yale U Pr.

— The Poet's Gift: Toward the Renewal of Pastoral Care. 176p. (Orig.). 1993. pap. 19.95 (*0-664-25403-9*) Westminster John Knox.

— Reframing: A New Method in Pastoral Care. LC 89-37499. 192p. (Orig.). 1990. pap. 18.00 (*0-8006-2413-0*, 1-2413) Augsburg Fortress.

— Religion, Society & Psychoanalysis: Readings in Contemporary Theory. Jacobs, Janet L., ed. LC 97-573. 288p. (C). 1997. pap. text 27.00 (*0-8133-2648-6*, Pub. by Westview) HarpC.

— Social Phobia: Alleviating Anxiety in an Age of Self-Promotion. LC 99-29806. 1999. pap. 21.99 (*0-8272-3440-6*) Chalice Pr.

Capps, Donald & Dittes, James E. The Hunger of the Heart: Reflections on the Confessions of Augustine. Gaede, S. D., ed. (Monographs). 352p. (Orig.). (C). 1990. pap. 12.00 (*0-932566-07-3*) Soc Sci Stud Rel.

Capps, Donald & Fenn, Richard K., eds. Individualism Reconsidered: Readings Bearing on the Endangered Self in Modern Society. (Center for Religion, Self & Society Monograph: No. 1). 400p. (C). 1992. pap. text 20.00 (*1-882380-00-2*) Princeton Theol Sem.

Capps, Donald & Jacobs, Janet L., eds. The Struggle for Life No. 9: A Companion to William James's the Varieties of Religious Experience. LC 95-71180. 320p. 1995. 18.00 (*1-882380-02-9*) Soc Sci Stud Rel.

Capps, Donald, jt. ed. see Fenn, Richard K.

Capps, Donald, jt. ed. see Reynolds, Frank E.

Capps, Edward. From Homer to Theocritus: A Manual of Greek Literature. 1977. text 24.95 (*0-8369-8184-7*, 8322) Ayer.

Capps, Edward, ed. & intro. see Menander.

Capps, Emerson, jt. auth. see Camerer, M. C.

Capps, Ferald B., jt. auth. see Weber, David B.

Capps, Finis H. From Isolation to Involvement: The Swedish Immigrant Press in America, 1914-1945. 238p. 1966. 3.00 (*0-318-16616-X*, SP13) Swedish-Am.

Capps, Gavin, jt. auth. see Panayiotopoulos, Prodromos.

Capps, Jack L. Emily Dickinson's Reading, 1836-1886. LC 66-14439. 242p. reprint ed. pap. 75.10 (*0-8357-3402-1*, 203965900013) Bks Demand.

Capps, James. Webster's New World Easy Crossword Key. LC 97-774. 548p. 1997. 10.95 (*0-02-861837-8*) Macmillan.

Capps, Lisa. Constructing Panic: The Discourse of Agoraphobia. 256p. 1997. pap. text 16.50 (*0-674-16549-7*) HUP.

Capps, Lisa & Ochs, Elinor. Constructing Panic: The Discourse of Agoraphobia. LC 95-22566. 224p. (C). 1995. text 33.95 (*0-674-16548-9*) HUP.

Capps, Lisa, jt. auth. see Sigman, Marian.

Capps, Marcia M. The Waiting Land: And Other Poems. LC 89-35147. 64p. (Orig.). 1989. pap. 7.50 (*0-931832-35-7*) Fithian Pr.

Capps, Michael H., jt. auth. see Miner, John B.

Capps, Randall & O'Connor, J. Regis. Fundamentals of Effective Speech Communication. 272p. (C). 1984. reprint ed. pap. text 23.00 (*0-8191-3534-8*) U Pr of Amer.

Capps, Robert S. Hannibal's Lieutenant: A Unique Biography of Hannibal (247-183 B.C.) LC 94-75074. (Illus.). 349p. 1994. 16.75 (*0-9640665-0-5*) Manor Hse VA.

Capps, Steve. The Programmer's Online Companion Inside Macintosh. LC 70-991. 1970. 2995.00 (*0-201-12214-6*) Addison-Wesley.

Capps, Walter, intro. Thomas Merton: Preview of the Asian Journey. 120p. 1991. reprint ed. pap. 8.95 (*0-8245-1124-7*) Crossroad NY.

Capps, Walter H. The New Religious Right: Piety, Patriotism & Politics. LC 90-39818. 253p. 1990. pap. 15.95 (*0-87249-741-0*) U of SC Pr.

— Religious Studies: The Making of a Discipline. LC 95-6956. 400p. 1995. pap. 30.00 (*0-8006-2535-8*, 1-2535, Fortress Pr) Augsburg Fortress.

— The Unfinished War: Vietnam & the American Conscience. 2nd ed. LC 81-66193. 224p. 1983. pap. 15.50 (*0-8070-0411-1*) Beacon Pr.

Capps, Walter H., ed. Seeing with a Native Eye: Contributions to the Study of Native American Religion. LC 76-9980. 1976. pap. 6.95 (*0-06-061312-2*, RD-177) Harper SF.

— The Vietnam Reader. (Illus.). 288p. 1991. 45.00 (*0-415-90126-X*, A3261) Routledge.

— The Vietnam Reader. (Illus.). 320p. (C). (gr. 13). 1991. pap. 22.99 (*0-415-90127-8*, A3265) Routledge.

Cappuccinelli, Piero & Morris, N. Ronald, eds. Microtubules in Microorganisms. LC 82-13003. (Microbiology Ser.: No. 8). (Illus.). 428p. reprint ed. pap. 132.70 (*0-7837-0636-7*, 204098000019) Bks Demand.

Cappuccino, James G. Microiology Lab Manual. 5th ed. LC 98-18844. 477p. (C). 1998. pap. text, lab manual ed. 42.00 (*0-8053-7646-1*) Benjamin-Cummings.

Cappuccino, James G. & Sherman, Natalie. Microbiology: A Laboratory Manual. 2nd ed. (Biology Ser.). (Illus.). 466p. (C). 1987. pap. text 20.76 (*0-201-11636-7*) Addison-Wesley.

Cappuccino, Naomi & Price, Peter W., eds. Population Dynamics: New Approaches & Synthesis. (Illus.). 429p. 1995. text 79.00 (*0-12-159270-7*) Acad Pr.

Capra. Pristine Lessons for the E-Trader. 1999. 24.95 (*0-07-134651-1*) McGraw.

C

***Capra, Daniel J. & Saltzburg, Stephan A.** Evidence: The Objection Method, 1999 Supplement. 135p. 1999. pap. write for info. (*0-327-01312-5*, 1135910) LEXIS Pub.

Capra, Daniel J. & Saltzburg, Stephen A. American Criminal Procedure: Cases & Commentary (American Casebook Series) 5th ed. (Paralegal). 1508p. (C). 1996. text 55.00 (*0-314-07214-4*) West Pub.

— American Criminal Procedure, Cases & Commentary: 1995 Supplement. 4th ed. (American Casebook Ser.). 350p. 1995. pap. text 15.50 (*0-314-06874-0*) West Pub.

***Capra, Daniel J., et al.** The Federal Rules of Evidence Manual, August 1999 Cumulative Supplement: Pocketpart. 7th ed. 1999. write for info. (*0-327-01524-1*, 6654323) LEXIS Pub.

— The Federal Rules of Evidence Manual, August 1999 Cumulative Supplement Vol. 1: Pocketpart. 7th ed. 1999. write for info. (*0-327-01522-5*, 6654123) LEXIS Pub.

— The Federal Rules of Evidence Manual, August 1999 Cumulative Supplement Vol. 2: Pocketpart. 7th ed. 1999. write for info. (*0-327-01523-3*, 6654223) LEXIS Pub.

Capra, Daniel J., jt. auth. see Saltzburg, Stephen A.

Capra, Daniel J., ed. see Saltzburg, Stephen A.

Capra, Dominick L. History & Memory after Auschwitz. LC 97-41845. (Illus.). 232p. 1998. pap. 15.95 (*0-8014-8496-0*); text 39.95 (*0-8014-3496-3*) Cornell U Pr.

Capra, Donald J., jt. auth. see Zanetti, Maurizio.

Capra, Doug. A Handful of Pebbles: Stories from Seward History. (Illus.). 66p. (Orig.). 1995. pap. 8.00 (*0-9646517-0-X*) Yankee-Sourdough Pubns.

— Something to Be Remembered: Stories from Seward History. (Illus.). 80p. 1996. pap. 9.00 (*0-9646517-1-8*) Yankee-Sourdough Pubns.

Capra, Frank, Jr. The Name above the Title: An Autobiography. 1985. pap. 11.95 (*0-394-71205-6*) Vin Bks.

— The Name above the Title: An Autobiography. LC 96-47921. (Illus.). 534p. 1997. reprint ed. pap. 18.95 (*0-306-80771-8*) Da Capo.

Capra, Fritjof. The Tao of Physics: An Exploration of the Parallels Between Modern Physics & Eastern Mysticism. 3rd rev. ed. LC 91-52520. (Illus.). 368p. 1991. pap. 14.00 (*0-87773-594-8*, Pub. by Shambhala Pubns) Random.

— The Turning Point. 468p. 1983. pap. 17.95 (*0-553-34572-9*, New Age Bks) Bantam.

— The Web of Life: A New Understanding of Living Systems. (Illus.). 368p. 1997. pap. 14.95 (*0-385-47676-0*, Anchor NY) Doubleday.

Capra, Fritjof, told to. The Tao of Physics: An Exploration of the Parallels Between Modern Physics & Easter Mysticism. 25th ed. LC 99-35683. 368p. 2000. pap. 15.95 (*1-57062-519-0*, Pub. by Shambhala Pubns) Random.

Capra, Fritjof, et al. Belonging to the Universe: Explorations on the Frontiers of Science & Spirituality. LC 90-56454. 240p. 1992. reprint ed. pap. 14.00 (*0-06-250195-X*, Pub. by Harper SF) HarpC.

Capra, Fritjof, jt. auth. see Berendt, Joachim-Ernst.

Capra, J. D., ed. Antibody Engineering. LC 96-34316. (Chemical Immunology Ser.: Vol. 65, 1996). (Illus.). xii, 212p. 1996. 195.75 (*3-8055-6356-6*) S Karger.

Capra, J. Donald, jt. auth. see Kindt, Thomas J.

Capra, J. Donald, jt. auth. see Zanetti, Maurizio.

Capra, J. Donald, jt. ed. see Zanetti, Maurizio.

***Caprara, Collette, ed.** Violence - Free Zone Initiatives: Models of Successful Grassroots Youth Intervention. (Illus.). 163p. 1999. pap. write for info. (*0-9673945-1-1*) Natl Ctr Neighbor.

— Violence - Free Zone Initiatives Tool Kit. 100p. 1999. pap. text. write for info. (*0-9673945-0-3*) Natl Ctr Neighbor.

***Caprara, Gian Vittorio & Cervone, Daniel.** Personality: Determinants, Dynamics, & Potentials. (Illus.). 480p. 2000. write for info. (*0-521-58310-1*); pap. write for info. (*0-521-58748-4*) Cambridge U Pr.

***Caprara, Giovanni.** Living in Space: From Science Fiction to the International Space Station. (Illus.). 216p. 2000. pap. 29.95 (*1-55209-549-5*) Firefly Bks Ltd.

Capretz, Luiz F. & Capretz, Miriam A. Object-Oriented Software: Design & Maintenance. LC 96-21637. (Series on Software Engineering & Knowledge). 288p. 1996. write for info. (*981-02-2731-0*) World Scientific Pub.

Capretz, Miriam A., jt. auth. see Capretz, Luiz F.

Capretz, Pierre J. French in Action: A Beginning Course in Language & Culture. 100.00 (*0-300-05339-8*) Yale U Pr.

— French in Action: A Beginning Course in Language & Culture, Pt. I & II. Vol. II. 1987. audio 65.00 (*0-300-04138-1*) Yale U Pr.

— French in Action: A Beginning Course in Language & Culture, Se, Pts. I & II. 476p. 1987. teacher ed. 20.00 (*0-300-04163-2*) Yale U Pr.

— French in Action: A Beginning Course in Language & Culture, Set, Pts. I & II. 553p. 1987. student ed. 28.00 (*0-300-03656-6*) Yale U Pr.

— French in Action: A Beginning Course in Language & Culture: Part I. 1987. student ed. 14.00 (*0-318-72974-1*) Yale U Pr.

— French in Action: A Beginning Course in Language & Culture: Part I, Pt. II. Vol. II. 235p. 1987. teacher ed. 12.50 (*0-300-04161-6*) Yale U Pr.

— French in Action Textbook. LC 86-51339. 323p. 1987. 40.00 (*0-300-03655-8*) Yale U Pr.

Capretz, Pierre J., et al. French in Action, Pt. 1. 2nd ed. LC 93-28562. (FRE., Illus.). 400p. audio 100.00 (*0-300-05829-2*) Yale U Pr.

— French in Action, Pt. 2. 2nd ed. LC 93-28562. (FRE., Illus.). 400p. audio 100.00 (*0-300-05830-6*) Yale U Pr.

— French in Action: A Beginning Course in Language & Culture. 2nd ed. LC 93-28562. (Illus.). 400p. 1994. 50.00 (*0-300-05821-7*); teacher ed. 25.00 (*0-300-05824-1*) Yale U Pr.

— French in Action: A Beginning Course in Language & Culture, Pt. 1. 2nd ed. LC 93-28562. (Illus.). 400p. 1994. student ed. 16.00 (*0-300-05827-6*) Yale U Pr.

— French in Action: A Beginning Course in Language & Culture, Pt. 1. 2nd ed. LC 93-28562. Vol. 1. (Illus.). 400p. 1994. student ed. 21.50 (*0-300-05822-5*) Yale U Pr.

— French in Action: A Beginning Course in Language & Culture, Pt. 2. 2nd ed. LC 93-28562. (Illus.). 400p. 1994. student ed. 16.00 (*0-300-05828-4*) Yale U Pr.

— French in Action: A Beginning Course in Language & Culture, Pt. 2. 2nd ed. LC 93-28562. Vol. 2. (Illus.). 400p. 1994. student ed. 21.50 (*0-300-05823-3*) Yale U Pr.

— French in Action: A Beginning Course in Language & Culture: Part I. 1987. student ed. 12.00 (*0-300-03940-9*); student ed. 18.00 (*0-300-03937-9*); student ed. 18.00 (*0-300-03938-7*) Yale U Pr.

— French in Action: A Beginning Course in Language & Culture: Part I, Pt. I. 1987. 65.00 (*0-300-04137-3*) Yale U Pr.

— French in Action: A Beginning Course in Language & Culture: Part I, Pt. I. Vol. I. 241p. 1987. teacher ed. 12.50 (*0-300-03657-4*) Yale U Pr.

— French in Action: A Beginning Course in Language & Culture, the Capretz Method, Vol. 1. 2nd ed. Vol. 1. 1997. 35.00 (*0-300-07265-1*) Yale U Pr.

— French in Action: A Beginning Course in Language & Culture, the Capretz Method, Vol. 2. 2nd ed. Vol. 2. 1997. 35.00 (*0-300-07267-8*) Yale U Pr.

Capri, Anton Z. Non-Relativistic Quantum Mechanics. 2nd ed. LC 85-14933. (Lecture Notes & Supplements in Physics Ser.: No. 19). (Illus.). 653p. (C). 1985. 61.00 (*0-8053-1505-5*) Addison-Wesley.

Capri, Antonio. Il Settecento Musicale in Europa. LC 77-5523. (Music Reprint Ser.). 1977. reprint ed. lib. bdg. 49.50 (*0-306-77413-5*) Da Capo.

Capri-Karka, C. Love & the Symbolic Journey in the Poetry of Cavafy, Eliot & Seferis. LC 82-81629. 374p. 1982. pap. text 12.00 (*0-918618-21-5*) Pella Pub.

Capri-Karka, Carmen. War in the Poetry of George Seferis. LC 85-62597. 240p. 1986. 25.00 (*0-918618-28-2*); pap. 11.00 (*0-918618-27-4*) Pella Pub.

Capri-Karka, Carmen, ed. 600 Modern Greek Verbs. (GRE.). 500p. 1997. pap. 35.00 (*0-918618-68-1*) Pella Pub.

Capria, Michael. Promise of the Fountain: Health Secrets for Life, Longevity & Freedom from Fear of Disease. (Illus.). 264p. (Orig.). 1993. pap. text 15.95 (*0-9638492-0-4*) Plumosa Pr.

***Caprice-Konstantine, R.** Mathematics Competency, 2000: Algebra & Geometry Refresher Course. (C). 2000. pap. 8.50 (*0-7442-0105-5*) Montezuma.

Capricornus, Samuel. Samuel Capricornus Vol. III: Geistliche Harmonien. Walker, Paul, ed. (Collegium Musicum: Yale University Ser.: Series II, Vol. 13). (Illus.). xviii, 258p. 1997. pap. 90.00 (*0-89579-380-6*) A-R Eds.

Caprio. Sexually Adequate Female. 1979. pap. 3.00 (*0-87980-146-8*) Wilshire.

— Sexually Adequate Male. 1979. pap. 3.00 (*0-87980-147-6*) Wilshire.

Caprio & Berger. Healing Yourself with Self-Hypnosis. LC 97-53295. 320p. 1998. pap. 12.95 (*0-7352-0004-1*) PH Pr.

Caprio, Anthony, jt. auth. see Carton, Dana.

Caprio, Betsy & Hedberg, Thomas M. Coming Home: A Handbook for Exploring the Sanctuary Within. LC 85-61739. (Illus.). 288p. (Orig.). 1986. pap. 14.95 (*0-8091-2739-3*); pap., teacher ed. 9.95 (*0-8091-2787-3*) Paulist Pr.

Caprio, Frank & Berger, Joseph R. Healing Yourself with Self-Hypnosis. 2nd rev. expanded ed. 320p. (C). 1998. pap. text 12.95 (*0-13-906611-X*) P-H.

Caprio, Frank S. & Berger, Joseph R. Helping Yourself with Self Hypnosis: A Modern Guide to Self-Improvement & Successful Living. 2nd ed. 228p. (C). 1988. pap. text 9.95 (*0-13-386764-1*) P-H.

Caprio, Frank S., et al. Healing Yourself with Self-Hypnosis. 2nd rev. expanded ed. LC 97-53295. 288p. (C). 1998. 30.00 (*0-13-906678-0*) P-H.

Caprio, Gerard, et al, eds. Building Sound Finance in Emerging Market Economies: Proceedings of a Conference Held in Washington, D.C., June 10-11,1993. LC 94-7903. 1994. 27.50 (*1-55775-380-6*) Intl Monetary.

Caprio, Gerard, Jr., et al, eds. Financial Reform: Theory & Experience. (Illus.). 492p. 1996. pap. text 24.95 (*0-521-57424-2*) Cambridge U Pr.

Caprio, Gerard, et al, eds. Preventing Bank Crises: Lessons from Recent Global Bank Failures. (EDI Development Studies). 392p. 1998. pap. 40.00 (*0-8213-4202-9*, 14202) World Bank.

Caprio, Gerard, Jr. & Honohan, Patrick, eds. Monetary Policy Instruments for Developing Countries. 148p. 1991. pap. 22.00 (*0-8213-1969-8*, 11969) World Bank.

Caprio, Gerard, Jr. & Vittas, Dimitri, eds. Reforming Financial Systems: Historical Implications for Policy. (Illus.). 232p. (C). 1997. text 52.95 (*0-521-58115-X*) Cambridge U Pr.

Caprio, M. Compulsion. mass mkt. 6.95 (*0-7472-4306-9*, Pub. by Headline Bk Pub) Trafalgar.

— Taboo. mass mkt. 6.95 (*0-7472-4552-5*, Pub. by Headline Bk Pub) Trafalgar.

— Two Weeks in May. mass mkt. 6.95 (*0-7472-4229-1*, Pub. by Headline Bk Pub) Trafalgar.

Caprio-Prevette, May D., jt. auth. see Fry, Prem S.

***Caprioglio, Filippo.** Giovanni Caprioglio: The Light of the Modernity. 2000. pap. 25.00 (*88-7838-081-4*) L'Arca IT.

Capriola, Arlene & Swensen, Rigmor. Once upon a Time, 10 vols. Mastry, Cherisse, ed. (Illus.). 320p. (J). (gr. k-2). 1998. pap., wbk. ed. 69.50 (*1-57022-144-8*, ECS1448) ECS Lrn Systs.

— Once upon a Time: Chicken Licken. Mastry, Cherisse, ed. (Illus.). 32p. (J). (gr. k-2). 1998. pap., wbk. ed. 6.95 (*1-57022-139-1*, ECS1391) ECS Lrn Systs.

— Once upon a Time: Jack & the Beanstalk. Mastry, Cherisse, ed. (Illus.). 32p. (J). (gr. k-2). 1998. pap., wbk. ed. 6.95 (*1-57022-142-1*, ECS1421) ECS Lrn Systs.

— Once upon a Time: Little Red Riding Hood. Mastry, Cherisse, ed. (Illus.). 32p. (J). (gr. k-2). 1998. pap., wbk. ed. 6.95 (*1-57022-136-7*, ECS1367) ECS Lrn Systs.

— Once upon a Time: The Billy Goats Gruff. Mastry, Cherisse, ed. (Illus.). 32p. (J). (gr. k-2). 1998. pap., wbk. ed. 6.95 (*1-57022-135-9*, ECS1359) ECS Lrn Systs.

— Once upon a Time: The Boy Who Cried Wolf. Mastry, Cherisse, ed. (Illus.). 32p. (J). (gr. k-2). 1998. pap., wbk. ed. 6.95 (*1-57022-143-X*, ECS143X) ECS Lrn Systs.

— Once upon a Time: The Elves & the Shoemaker. Mastry, Cherisse, ed. (Illus.). 32p. (J). (gr. k-2). 1998. pap., wbk. ed. 6.95 (*1-57022-141-3*, ECS1413) ECS Lrn Systs.

— Once upon a Time: The Gingerbread Man. Mastry, Cherisse, ed. (Illus.). 32p. (J). (gr. k-2). 1998. pap., wbk. ed. 6.95 (*1-57022-138-3*, ECS1383) ECS Lrn Systs.

— Once upon a Time: The Little Red Hen. Mastry, Cherisse, ed. (Illus.). 32p. (J). (gr. k-2). 1998. pap., wbk. ed. 6.95 (*1-57022-140-5*, ECS1405) ECS Lrn Systs.

— Once upon a Time: The Three Bears. Mastry, Cherisse, ed. (Illus.). 32p. (J). (gr. k-2). 1998. pap., wbk. ed. 6.95 (*1-57022-134-0*, ECS1340) ECS Lrn Systs.

— Once upon a Time: The Three Little Pigs. Mastry, Cherisse, ed. (Illus.). 32p. (J). (gr. k-2). 1998. pap., wbk. ed. 6.95 (*1-57022-137-5*, ECS1375) ECS Lrn Systs.

***Capriola, Arlene & Swenson, Rigmor.** The Boy Who Cried Wolf. Mastry, Cherisse, ed. (Once upon a Time Ser.). (Illus.). (J). (gr. k-2). 1998. pap., wbk. ed. Price not set. incl. audio (*1-57022-170-7*) ECS Lrn Systs.

— Chicken Licken. Mastry, Cherisse, ed. (Once upon a Time Ser.). (Illus.). (J). (gr. k-2). 1998. pap., wbk. ed. Price not set. incl. audio (*1-57022-171-5*) ECS Lrn Systs.

— The Elves & the Shoemaker. Mastry, Cherisse, ed. (Once Upon a Time Ser.). (Illus.). (J). (gr. k-2). 1998. pap., wbk. ed. Price not set. incl. audio (*1-57022-172-3*) ECS Lrn Systs.

— The Gingerbread Man. Mastry, Cherisse, ed. (Once upon a Time Ser.). (Illus.). (J). (gr. k-2). 1998. pap., wbk. ed. Price not set. incl. audio (*1-57022-173-1*) ECS Lrn Systs.

— Jack & the Beanstalk. Mastry, Cherisse, ed. (Once upon a Time Ser.). (Illus.). (J). (gr. k-2). 1998. pap., wbk. ed. Price not set. incl. audio (*1-57022-174-X*) ECS Lrn Systs.

— The Little Red Hen. Mastry, Cherisse, ed. (Once upon a Time Ser.). (Illus.). (J). (gr. k-2). 1998. pap., wbk. ed. Price not set. incl. audio (*1-57022-175-8*) ECS Lrn Systs.

— Little Red Riding Hood. Mastry, Cherisse, ed. (Once upon a Time Ser.). (Illus.). (J). (gr. k-2). 1998. pap., wbk. ed. Price not set. incl. audio (*1-57022-176-6*) ECS Lrn Systs.

— The Three Bears. Mastry, Cherisse, ed. (Once upon a Time Ser.). (Illus.). (J). (gr. k-2). 1998. pap., wbk. ed. Price not set. incl. audio (*1-57022-177-4*) ECS Lrn Systs.

— The Three Billy Goats Gruff. Mastry, Cherisse, ed. (Once upon a Time Ser.). (Illus.). (J). (gr. k-2). 1998. pap., wbk. ed. Price not set. incl. audio (*1-57022-169-3*) ECS Lrn Systs.

Capriola, Arlene & Swenson, Rigmor. The Three Little Pigs. Mastry, Cherisse, ed. (Once upon a Time Ser.). (Illus.). 32p. (J). (gr. k-2). 1998. pap., wbk. ed. Price not set. incl. audio (*1-57022-178-2*, ECS1782) ECS Lrn Systs.

Caprioli, Joseph, jt. auth. see Weber, Jorg.

Caprioli, R. M., ed. Continuous-Flow Fast Atom Bombardment Mass Spectrometry. LC 90-12683. (Illus.). 201p. 1990. reprint ed. pap. 62.40 (*0-608-06834-9*, 206703100009) Bks Demand.

Caprioli, Richard M., III, et al, eds. Mass Spectrometry in Biomolecular Sciences: Proceedings of the NATO Advanced Study Institute, Lacco Ameno, Ischia, Italy, June 23 - July 5, 1993. (NATO Advanced Science Institute Ser.: Pt. C). 548p. (C). 1996. text 276.00 (*0-7923-3946-0*) Kluwer Academic.

Caprioli, Richard M., et al, eds. Selected Topics in Mass Spectrometry in Biomolecular Sciences: Proceedings of the NATO Advanced Study Institute on Mass Spectrometry in the Biomolecular Sciences, Altavilla-Milicia (PA), Italy, 7-18 July 1996. LC 97-32177. (NATO Advanced Science Institute Ser.: No. 504). 612p. 1997. text 307.50 (*0-7923-4849-4*) Kluwer Academic.

***Capriolo, Paola.** A Man of Character. 192p. 2000. pap. 15.00 (*1-85242-605-5*) Serpents Tail.

Capriolo, Paola & Heron, Liz. Woman Watching. 214p. 1998. pap. 13.99 (*1-85242-520-2*) Serpents Tail.

Caprione, Carol. Opportunities in Food Services. (Illus.). 160p. 1986. 13.95 (*0-8442-6252-8*, VGM Career) NTC Contemp Pub Co.

— Opportunities in Food Services. (Illus.). 160p. 1988. pap. 10.95 (*0-8442-6253-6*, VGM Career) NTC Contemp Pub Co.

Capriotti, Emile. The Grounds & Limits of Political Obligation. LC 91-4068. (American University Studies: Philosophy: Ser. V, Vol. 125). VI, 203p. 1993. 40.95 (*0-8204-1605-3*) P Lang Pubng.

Capriulo, Gerard M. Ecology of Marine Protozoa. (Illus.). 384p. 1990. text 125.00 (*0-19-504316-2*) OUP.

Capriz, G. Continua with Microstructure. (Tracts in Natural Philosophy Ser.: Vol. 35). 105p. 1989. 79.95 (*0-387-96886-5*) Spr-Verlag.

Caprock Girl Scout Council Staff. Gatherings. LC 92-28196. (Illus.). 1992. 12.95 (*0-87197-349-9*) Favorite Recipes.

Capron. Computers: Tools For An Information Age. (C). 1997. pap. text 86.00 (*0-201-30745-6*) Addison-Wesley.

***Capron.** Computers: Tools for an Information Age. 6th ed. 1999. pap. 59.00 (*0-201-61211-9*) P-H.

— Computers: Tools for the Information Age. 6th ed. 1999. pap. 46.00 (*0-201-61212-7*) P-H.

Capron. Essential Computing with DOS & Windows. 2nd ed. (C). 1996. text 62.81 (*0-8053-3460-2*) Longman.

Capron. Essential Computing Word 6 Window Microsoft Excel 5 Window. 1996. 54.00 (*0-8053-3440-8*) Benjamin-Cummings.

— Essentials Computing Word 6 Windows. 1995. 67.00 (*0-8053-3458-0*) Benjamin-Cummings.

Capron. Tool Info Age Struct Bas. 4th ed. (C). 1996. text 52.00 (*0-8053-3446-7*) Benjamin-Cummings.

Capron & Fenton, Erfert. Computers: Tools for an Information Age, Q-Basic & Netscape 4.0. (C). 1998. pap. text 80.00 (*0-201-43467-9*) Addison-Wesley.

Capron, A., et al, eds. Current Topics in Microbiology & Immunology. (Molecular & Cellular Mechanisms: Vol. 189). 210p. 1994. 153.95 (*0-387-57259-7*) Spr-Verlag.

Capron, A., ed. see Dangl, J. L.

Capron, Alexander M., et al, eds. Genetic Counseling: Fact, Values & Norms. LC 79-1736. (Alan R. Liss Ser.: Vol. 15, No. 2). 1979. 41.00 (*0-685-03289-2*) March of Dimes.

Capron, Alexander M., jt. auth. see Katz, Jay.

Capron, Alexander M., ed. see Birnbaum, Irwin M.

Capron, Alexander M., ed. see Institute of Medicine Staff.

Capron, E. W. Modern Spiritualism: Its Facts & Fanaticisms. LC 75-36833. (Occult Ser.). 1976. reprint ed. 35.95 (*0-405-07945-1*) Ayer.

Capron, H. L. Capron Essentials Including DOS 5.0/Windows 3.1, Lotus 123 Release 2.2, Wordperfect 5.1 & Qbasic. (C). 1993. pap. text 0.00 (*0-8053-1504-7*) Addison-Wesley.

— Capron Tools D6 Qw for Bundle or Canada. 1994. pap. text. write for info. (*0-8053-8858-3*) Addison-Wesley.

— Capron's Pocket Internet: 2001 Sites. LC 98-168856. 224p. (C). 1997. pap. text 17.00 (*0-201-31112-7*) Addison-Wesley.

— Computers: Tools For An Information Age. (C). 1995. 44.66 (*0-8053-0718-4*) Addison-Wesley.

— Computers: Tools For An Information Age. LC 97-26773. 27p. (C). 1997. pap. text 46.00 (*0-201-30559-3*) Addison-Wesley.

— Computers: Tools for an Information Age, Brief Edition (Chapters 1-8) 320p. (C). 1997. pap. text 47.00 incl. audio compact disk (*0-201-35205-2*, Prentice Hall) P-H.

— Computers: Tools for an Information Age (Chapters 1-16) 5th ed. 540p. (C). 1997. pap. text 59.00 (*0-201-35202-8*, Prentice Hall) P-H.

— DOS. (C). 1993. pap. text 52.66 (*0-8053-1449-0*) Addison-Wesley.

— ESS MS WORK3.0 PCS CB. 1995. pap. text 59.33 (*0-8053-2961-7*) Addison-Wesley.

— Essential Computing. (C). 1992. pap. text 36.33 (*0-8053-0849-0*) Addison-Wesley.

— ESSN B DOS5.0 WRD5.1 PK. (C). 1993. pap. text 36.33 (*0-8053-1439-3*) Addison-Wesley.

— ESSN DOS3.3&WIN3.0 DB3PK. (C). 1993. pap. text 40.33 (*0-8053-1484-9*) Addison-Wesley.
— ESSN DOS3.3&WIN3.0QBA PK. (C). 1993. pap. text 36.33 (*0-8053-1463-6*) Addison-Wesley.
— ESSN DOS5.0&WIN3.1 DB4PK. (C). 1995. pap. text 36.33 (*0-8053-1489-X*) Addison-Wesley.
— ESSN DOS5.0&WIN3.1 D3 PK. (C). 1993. pap. text 36.33 (*0-8053-1493-8*) Addison-Wesley.
— ESSN DOS5.0&WIN3.1 QB PK. (C). 1993. pap. text 40.33 (*0-8053-1469-5*); pap. text 36.33 (*0-8053-1518-7*); pap. text 40.33 (*0-8053-1535-7*) Addison-Wesley.
— ESSN DOS5.0&WIN3.1 WP PK. (C). 1995. pap. text 32.00 (*0-8053-1507-1*) Addison-Wesley.
— ESSN DOS5.0&WIN3.1DB3 PK. (C). 1993. pap. text 36.33 (*0-8053-1491-1*) Addison-Wesley.
— ESSN DOS5.0&WIN3.1DB4 PK. (C). 1993. pap. text 36.33 (*0-8053-1506-3*) Addison-Wesley.
— ESSN DOS5.0&WIN3.1WRD PK. (C). 1993. pap. text 36.33 (*0-8053-1516-0*) Addison-Wesley.
— ESSN LOTUS R2.2DB3+QB PK. (C). 1997. pap. text 36.33 (*0-8053-1495-4*) Addison-Wesley.
— ESSN&DOS 5.0&WIN3.1 PKG. (C). 1995. pap. text 36.33 (*0-8053-1443-1*) Addison-Wesley.
— ESSN&DOS5.0&WIN&3.1DB4PK. (C). 1993. pap. text 40.33 (*0-8053-1461-X*) Addison-Wesley.
— ESSN&LOTUS REL2.2&.4 PKG. (C). 1993. pap. text 28.66 (*0-8053-1446-6*) Addison-Wesley.
— Qbasic. (C). 1995. pap. text 50.66 (*0-8053-1428-8*) Addison-Wesley.
— Select Custom Book for Bundle or Canada. (C). 1993. pap. text 0.00 (*0-8053-8838-9*) Addison-Wesley.
— SELECT LOTUS123 REL4 WIN. 224p. (C). 1995. pap. text 26.00 (*0-8053-2933-1*) Addison-Wesley.
— Select Visual Basic 3.O for Windows. 192p. (C). 1995. pap. text 29.00 (*0-8053-3874-8*) Addison-Wesley.
— TOOL CUS&DOS3.3&WIN3.0. (C). 1997. pap. text 73.66 (*0-8053-1511-X*) Addison-Wesley.
— TOOL CUS&DOS3.3&WIN3.0LO. (C). 1995. pap. text 73.66 (*0-8053-1477-6*) Addison-Wesley.
— TOOL CUS&DOS3.3&WIN3.0WR. (C). 1993. pap. text 66.66 (*0-8053-1479-2*) Addison-Wesley.
— TOOL CUS&DOS5.0&WIN3.1. (C). 1993. pap. text 66.66 (*0-8053-1503-9*); pap. text 66.66 (*0-8053-1510-1*) Addison-Wesley.
— TOOL CUS&DOS5.0&WIN3.1. (C). 1995. pap. text 66.66 (*0-8053-1515-2*) Addison-Wesley.
— TOOL CUS&DOS5.0&WIN3.1. (C). 1997. pap. text 73.66 (*0-8053-1508-X*) Addison-Wesley.
— TOOL CUS&DOS5.0&WIN3.1WD. (C). 1997. pap. text 59.66 (*0-8053-1525-X*) Addison-Wesley.
— TOOL CUS&LOTUS&R2.3&2.4W. (C). 1993. pap. text 73.66 (*0-8053-1480-6*) Addison-Wesley.
— TOOL CUS&LOTUS123 R2.2BA. (C). 1993. pap. text 59.66 (*0-8053-1475-X*) Addison-Wesley.
— TOOL CUS&LOT123 R2.2DBAS. (C). 1995. pap. text 59.66 (*0-8053-1526-8*) Addison-Wesley.
— TOOL CUS&QBAS WRK2.0 PCS. (C). 1993. pap. text 73.66 (*0-8053-1473-3*) Addison-Wesley.
— TOOL CUS&QUAT4.0&5.0DBAS. (C). 1993. pap. text 66.66 (*0-8053-1530-6*) Addison-Wesley.
— TOOL CUS&WRD5.1 DBAS5MOD. (C). 1995. pap. text 59.66 (*0-8053-1492-X*) Addison-Wesley.
— TOOL CUST&DOS5.0&WIN3.1. (C). 1993. pap. text 73.66 (*0-8053-1512-8*) Addison-Wesley.
— TOOL DOS3.3&WIN3.0MOD PK. (C). 1995. pap. text 70.66 (*0-8053-1486-5*) Addison-Wesley.
— TOOL DOS5.0&WIN3.1DB3 PK. (C). 1995. pap. text 57.33 (*0-8053-1538-1*) Addison-Wesley.
— TOOL DOS5.0WN3.1 DB4 PKG. (C). 1995. pap. text 70.66 (*0-8053-1460-1*) Addison-Wesley.
— TOOL LOTUS R2.3&2.4WD PK. (C). 1993. pap. text 57.33 (*0-8053-1482-2*) Addison-Wesley.
— TOOL LOTUS 2.2 WD DB3 PK. (C). 1993. pap. text 70.66 (*0-8053-1481-4*) Addison-Wesley.
— TOOL&DOS5.0 WRD5.1 PX PK. (C). 1993. pap. text 70.66 (*0-8053-1426-1*) Addison-Wesley.
— TOOL&DOS5.0&WIN3.1 DB PK. (C). 1993. pap. text 57.33 (*0-8053-1440-7*) Addison-Wesley.
— TOOL&DOS5.0&WIN3.1WRD5.1. (C). 1993. pap. text 73.66 (*0-8053-1534-9*) Addison-Wesley.
— TOOL&LOTUS123 R2.2 DBAS4. (C). 1993. pap. text 66.66 (*0-8053-1527-6*) Addison-Wesley.
— TOOL&WRD5.1 BASIC MOD PK. (C). 1993. pap. text 57.33 (*0-8053-1442-3*) Addison-Wesley.
— TOOLS CUS BOUND&EXCEL3.0. (C). 1995. pap. text 52.66 (*0-8053-1457-1*) Addison-Wesley.
— Tools for an Information Age. (C). 1993. pap. text 80.66 (*0-8053-1459-8*) Addison-Wesley.
— Tools for an Information Age Custom Book Block. 4th ed. 1996. pap. text 38.66 (*0-8053-0663-3*) Addison-Wesley.
— Tools Plus Basic. (C). 1995. pap. text 50.66 (*0-8053-6120-0*) Addison-Wesley.
— TOOLS&DOS3.3&WIN3.0 PKG. (C). 1995. pap. text 70.66 (*0-8053-1441-5*) Addison-Wesley.
— TOOLS&DOS5.0 WIN LOTS PK. (C). 1995. pap. text 70.66 (*0-8053-1429-6*) Addison-Wesley.
— TOOLS&DOS5.0 WIN3.0 PK. (C). 1995. pap. text 50.66 (*0-8053-1436-9*) Addison-Wesley.
— TOOLS&DOS5.0 WIN3.1DB PK. (C). 1993. pap. text 70.66 (*0-8053-1434-2*) Addison-Wesley.
— TOOLS&LOT2.2 WRD5.1 PKG. (C). 1993. pap. text 57.33 (*0-8053-1427-X*) Addison-Wesley.
— TOOLS&MS WRK2.0PC MOD PK. (C). 1995. pap. text 64.00 (*0-8053-1438-5*) Addison-Wesley.

Capron, H. L. Understood Betsy. 1994. text 36.33 (*0-8053-1520-9*) Addison-Wesley.

***Capron, Harriet.** Capron's Pocket Internet Guide: 4001 Sites. 2nd ed. 384p. (C). 1999. pap. 16.00 (*0-201-61195-3*, Prentice Hall) P-H.

Capron, Harriet. Computers: Tools for an Information Age. 320p. (C). 1997. pap. text. write for info. (*0-201-33614-6*) Addison-Wesley.
— Computers Brief: Tools for an Information Age, Brief Edition. 2nd ed. LC 99-23733. 304p. (C). 1999. pap. text 46.67 incl. audio compact disk (*0-201-47660-6*, Prentice Hall) P-H.
— Computers Standard: Tools for an Information Age, Standard Edition. 6th ed. LC 99-23915. 530p. (C). 1999. pap. text 60.00 incl. audio compact disk (*0-201-47659-2*, Prentice Hall) P-H.

Capron, Harriet L. Capron Tools: DOS 6.0 for Windows 3.1, Word 6 for Windows, Excel 5 foe Windows. 1996. pap. text 84.33 (*0-8053-5786-6*) Addison-Wesley.
— Capron Tools: DOS 6.0 for Windows 3.1, Wordperfect 5.1, Excel 4.0 for Windows Qbasic for Beginners. 1996. pap. text 94.00 (*0-8053-5782-3*) Addison-Wesley.
— CIS&LOTUSWRKS3.0&STU 3.5. (C). 1993. student ed. 85.33 (*0-8053-9713-2*) Addison-Wesley.
— ESS COMPT WRDPRFT 6.0WIN. 2nd ed. (C). 1995. pap. text 58.00 (*0-8053-3767-9*) Addison-Wesley.
— ESS COMPTG CHPTR12 14 MS. 2nd ed. (C). 1995. pap. text 64.66 (*0-8053-3763-6*) Addison-Wesley.
— ESS COMPTG DOS5.0&WIN3.1. 2nd ed. (C). 1995. pap. text 58.00 (*0-8053-3762-8*) Benjamin-Cummings.
— ESS COMPTG LOTUS 1 2 3. 2nd ed. (C). 1995. text 47.80 (*0-201-61149-X*) Addison-Wesley.
— ESSEN CMPUT DOS5.&WIN3.1. 2nd ed. (C). 1995. text 40.31 (*0-8053-3477-7*) Benjamin-Cummings.
— ESSEN CMPUT DOS6&WRD&EX5. 2nd ed. (C). 1996. text 59.00 (*0-8053-3479-3*) Benjamin-Cummings.
— ESSEN COMPT DOS6.0&STRUC. 2nd ed. (C). 1996. text 67.00 (*0-8053-5870-6*) Benjamin-Cummings.
— ESSEN COMPUT A DOS6.0&PK. 2nd ed. (C). 1996. text 69.38 (*0-8053-3442-4*) Benjamin-Cummings.
— ESSEN COMPUT A LOT123 R4. 2nd ed. (C). 1996. text 61.88 (*0-8053-5291-0*) Benjamin-Cummings.
— ESSEN COMPUT A WRD6.0WIN. 2nd ed. (C). 1996. text 69.00 (*0-8053-5860-9*) Benjamin-Cummings.
— ESSEN COMPUT DOS3LOT PK. 2nd ed. (C). 1997. text 67.00 (*0-8053-3473-4*) Benjamin-Cummings.
— ESSEN COMPUT DOS6.0&WIN3. 2nd ed. (C). 1996. text 67.00 (*0-8053-5879-X*) Benjamin-Cummings.
— ESSEN COMPUT LOTUS DBAS3. 2nd ed. (C). 1996. text 59.00 (*0-8053-5863-3*) Benjamin-Cummings.
— ESSEN COMPUT LOTUS123 R5. 2nd ed. (C). 1997. text 45.00 (*0-8053-5293-7*) Benjamin-Cummings.
— ESSEN COMPUT LOT123 DBS4. 2nd ed. (C). 1996. text 59.00 (*0-8053-5861-7*) Benjamin-Cummings.
— ESSEN COMPUT LOT123 PARA. 2nd ed. (C). 1997. text 51.56 (*0-8053-5294-5*) Benjamin-Cummings.
— ESSEN COMPUT WRD6 WIN AC. 2nd ed. (C). 1996. text 62.81 (*0-8053-5274-0*) Benjamin-Cummings.
— ESSEN COMPUT WRD6&ACC PK. 2nd ed. (C). 1995. text 55.31 (*0-8053-3466-1*) Benjamin-Cummings.
— ESSEN COMPUTG A WRD6 WIN. 2nd ed. (C). 1997. text 51.56 (*0-8053-5285-6*) Benjamin-Cummings.
— ESSEN COMPUTG DOS5.0&WIN. 2nd ed. (C). 1996. text 55.31 (*0-8053-5313-5*) Benjamin-Cummings.
— ESSEN COMPUTG DOS6.0&WIN. 2nd ed. (C). 1997. text 59.06 (*0-8053-5286-4*) Benjamin-Cummings.
— ESSEN COMPUTING WORK WINDOWS PK. 2nd ed. (C). 1995. text 54.38 (*0-8053-3461-0*) Benjamin-Cummings.
— ESSEN COMUT LOTUS R2.3&2. 2nd ed. (C). 1996. text 66.00 (*0-8053-3444-0*) Benjamin-Cummings.
— ESSEN DOS 6.0&WIN LOT R4. 2nd ed. (C). 1996. text 55.31 (*0-8053-5847-1*) Benjamin-Cummings.
— ESSEN WRD6 WIN EXCL POW4. 2nd ed. (C). 1996. text 59.00 (*0-8053-3487-4*) Benjamin-Cummings.
— ESSENT COMPUT A WRK3 PCS. 2nd ed. (C). 1996. text 65.00 (*0-8053-3485-8*) Benjamin-Cummings.
— Essential Computer: Basic Structure. 2nd ed. (C). 1996. text 69.00 (*0-8053-3486-6*) Benjamin-Cummings.
— Essential Computing. (C). 1992. pap. text 36.33 (*0-8053-0819-9*) Addison-Wesley.
— Essential Computing. 2nd ed. (C). 1995. pap. text 63.00 (*0-8053-3761-X*) Benjamin-Cummings.
— Essential Computing: Structure Basic of Microsoft. 2nd ed. (C). 1995. pap. text 65.33 (*0-8053-3764-4*) Addison-Wesley.
— Essential Computing Dos 6.0&Win3.1 Lotus Pk. (C). 1995. text 55.31 (*0-8053-3465-3*) Longman.
— Essential Computing with DOS 5.0. 2nd ed. (C). 1996. text 67.00 (*0-8053-3463-7*) Benjamin-Cummings.
— Essential Computing with Excel 5.0. 2nd ed. (C). 1996. text 50.00 (*0-8053-5878-1*) Benjamin-Cummings.
— Essentials of Computing. 2nd ed. 412p. 1993. pap. text, teacher ed. 39.00 (*0-8053-1381-8*) Benjamin-Cummings.
— Essentials of Computing. 2nd ed. (C). 1996. pap. text 45.94 (*0-8053-1604-3*) Benjamin-Cummings.
— ESSN COMPUTING D6 PW CB. 2nd ed. (C). 1995. pap. text 48.66 (*0-8053-3711-3*) Addison-Wesley.
— Pascal. 1995. 56.00 (*0-8053-1146-7*) Addison-Wesley.
— Printed Tstbnk Essen Cmp. 2nd ed. 412p. 1993. pap. text 18.00 (*0-8053-1382-6*) Benjamin-Cummings.
— Select Essentials of Computing 2Nd Version (B) with Planet Internet. 2nd ed. (C). 1996. pap. text 29.33 (*0-8053-1611-6*) Addison-Wesley.
— Select Modules: Word 6.0 & Excel 5 for Windows, Powerpoint 4 DOS. (C). 1995. pap. text 44.33 (*0-8053-3880-2*) Benjamin-Cummings.
— TOOL INFO AGE A DOS POW4. 4th ed. (C). 1996. text 67.50 (*0-8053-5176-0*) Benjamin-Cummings.
— TOOL INFO AGE A DOS6.1&W. 4th ed. (C). 1997. text 69.38 (*0-8053-5282-1*) Benjamin-Cummings.
— TOOL INFO AGE A LOTUS123. 4th ed. (C). 1996. text 75.00 (*0-8053-9734-5*) Benjamin-Cummings.
— TOOL INFO AGE A WRK3 WIN. 4th ed. (C). 1996. text 80.00 (*0-8053-5894-3*) Benjamin-Cummings.
— TOOL INFO AGE DOS6&ACC2. 4th ed. (C). 1996. text 77.00 (*0-8053-5891-9*) Benjamin-Cummings.
— TOOL INFO AGE DOS6&QUBAS. 4th ed. (C). 1996. text 64.69 (*0-8053-5316-X*) Benjamin-Cummings.
— TOOL INFO AGE DOS6&WIN3. 4th ed. (C). 1996. text 72.19 (*0-8053-5853-6*) Benjamin-Cummings.
— TOOL INFO AGE LOT WRD5.1. 4th ed. (C). 1996. text 61.00 (*0-8053-5896-X*) Benjamin-Cummings.
— TOOL INFO AGE QUATT6 WIN. 4th ed. (C). 1996. text 71.25 (*0-8053-5307-0*) Benjamin-Cummings.
— TOOL LOT123 R4 WIN PARAD. 4th ed. (C). 1996. text 64.69 (*0-8053-5846-3*) Benjamin-Cummings.
— Tools for An Information Age: Excel 5 Net. 4th ed. (C). 1997. text 53.44 (*0-8053-5302-X*) Benjamin-Cummings.
— Tools IM. 5th ed. (C). 1998. pap. text, teacher ed. 14.95 (*0-201-31563-7*) Addison-Wesley.
— Tools Info Age a Structr. 4th ed. (C). 1996. text 67.00 (*0-8053-5895-1*) Benjamin-Cummings.
— TOOLS INFO AGE DOS6 ACC2. 4th ed. (C). 1997. text 67.50 (*0-8053-9722-1*) Benjamin-Cummings.
— TOOLS INFO AGE DOS6 QBAS. (C). 1996. text 64.69 (*0-8053-9732-9*) Benjamin-Cummings.
— TOOLS INFO AGE DOS6&EXCL. 4th ed. (C). 1997. text 60.94 (*0-8053-9721-3*) Benjamin-Cummings.

Capron, Margie L., jt. auth. see Cobaugh, Barbara A.

Caproni, Gianni. Gli Aeroplani C: Studi-Progetti-Realizzazioni dal 1908 al 1935. Gilbert, James B., ed. LC 79-7234. (Flight: Its First Seventy-Five Years Ser.).Tr. of Caproni Airplanes: Studies, Plans, Fulfillments from 1908 to 1935. (ITA., Illus.). 1980. reprint ed. lib. bdg. 68.95 (*0-405-12150-4*) Ayer.

Caproni, Giorgio. The Wall of the Earth. 110p. 1992. pap. 10.00 (*0-920717-53-5*) Guernica Editions.

Caproni, Nathan. Washington's Best Lake Fly Fishing. 180p. 1995. pap. 21.95 (*1-57188-027-5*) F Amato Pubns.

***Capros, P., et al.** Climate Technology Strategies: Controlling Greenhouse Gases, Policy & Technology Options. LC 99-51995. (ZEW Economic Studies: Vol. 3). xviii, 365p. 1999. pap. 73.00 (*3-7908-1229-3*) Spr-Verlag.
— Climate Technology Strategies Vol. 2: The Macro-Economic Cost & Benefit or Reducing Greenhouse Gas Emissions in the European Union. (ZEW Economic Studies: Vol. 4). xiv, 224p. 1999. pap. 63.00 (*3-7908-1230-7*) Spr-Verlag.

Capros, Pantelis & Meulders, Daniele, eds. Budgetary Policy Modelling: Public Expenditures. (Routledge New International Studies in Economic Modelling). 288p. (C). 1996. 100.00 (*0-415-14235-0*) Routledge.

Capsanis, George. The Eros of Repentance. Amis, Robin, ed. Golitzyn, Alexander, tr. from GRE. 96p. (Orig.). (C). 1992. pap. text 7.95 (*0-685-57526-8*) Praxis Inst.
— The Eros of Repentance. Golitzin, Alexander, tr. 104p. (Orig.). 1992. pap. 11.95 (*1-872292-04-6*) Praxis Inst.

Capshew, James H. Psychologists on the March: Science, Practice, & Professional Identity in America, 1929-1969. LC 97-47526. (Studies in the History of Psychology). 304p. (C). 1998. 59.95 (*0-521-56267-8*); pap. 19.95 (*0-521-56585-5*) Cambridge U Pr.

Capstick, P. A Man Called Lion. (Illus.). 275p. 1994. 24.95 (*1-57157-011-X*) Safari Pr.

Capstick, Peter H. The African Adventurers: A Return to the Silent Places. 288p. 1992. text 22.95 (*0-312-07622-3*) St Martin.
— Death in a Lonely Land: More Tales of Hunting, Fishing & Shooting. (Illus.). 304p. 1990. text 23.95 (*0-312-03810-0*) St Martin.
— Death in the Dark Continent. 8th ed. (Illus.). 320p. 1983. text 22.95 (*0-312-18615-0*) St Martin.
— Death in the Long Grass. LC 77-9224. (Illus.). 1978. text 23.95 (*0-312-18613-4*) St Martin.
— Death in the Silent Places. 8th ed. 320p. 1981. text 23.95 (*0-312-18618-5*) St Martin.
— Last Horizons: Hunting, Fishing & Shooting on Five Continents. (Illus.). 288p. 1988. text 23.95 (*0-312-02535-1*) St Martin.
— The Last Ivory Hunter. (Illus.). 288p. 1988. text 21.95 (*0-312-00048-0*) St Martin.
— Maneaters. (Illus.). 200p. 1981. 17.95 (*0-8227-3023-5*) Petersen Pub.
— Maneaters. (Illus.). 178p. 1993. 24.95 (*1-57157-117-5*) Safari Pr.
— Peter Capstick's Africa: Return to the Long Grass. 320p. 1987. text 35.00 (*0-312-00670-5*) St Martin.
— Safari - The Last Adventure: How You Can Share in It. (Illus.). 352p. 1984. text 23.95 (*0-312-69657-4*) St Martin.
— Sands of Silence: On Safari in Namibia. (Illus.). 288p. 1991. text 35.00 (*0-312-06459-4*) St Martin.
— Warrior: The Legend of Colonel Richard Meinertzhagan. 3rd ed. LC 97-31884. (Illus.). 320p. 1998. text 23.95 (*0-312-18271-6*) St Martin.

Capstoen Press Geography Department. One Nation. 1999. 152.00 (*1-56065-813-4*) Capstone Pr.

Capstone Press, jt. auth. see Kummer, Patricia K.

Capstone Press Editors. Delaware. LC 98-43356. (One Nation Ser.). (J). 1999. 19.00 (*0-7368-0116-2*, Cpstone High Low) Capstone Pr.
— Oklahoma. LC 98-31227. (One Nation Ser.). (J). 1999. 19.00 (*0-7368-0117-0*, Cpstone High Low) Capstone Pr.
— Puerto Rico. LC 98-44035. (One Nation Ser.). (Illus.). 48p. (J). (gr. 3-7). 1999. 19.00 (*0-7368-0118-9*, Cpstone High Low) Capstone Pr.
— Rhode Island. LC 98-37333. (One Nation Ser.). (J). 1999. 19.00 (*0-7368-0119-7*, Cpstone High Low) Capstone Pr.
— South Dakota. LC 98-43043. (One Nation Ser.). (J). 1999. 19.00 (*0-7368-0120-0*, Cpstone High Low) Capstone Pr.
— Vermont. LC 98-31223. (One Nation Ser.). (J). 1999. 19.00 (*0-7368-0121-9*, Cpstone High Low) Capstone Pr.

Capstone Press Editors, jt. auth. see Kummer, Patricia K.

Capstone Press Geogra Staff. Arkansas, 4. (One Nation Ser.). (J). 1998. 19.00 (*0-516-21472-1*) Childrens.
— Idaho, 11. (One Nation Ser.). (J). 1998. 19.00 (*0-516-21473-X*) Childrens.
— Iowa, 14. (One Nation Ser.). (J). 1998. 19.00 (*0-516-21474-8*) Childrens.
— Kansas, 15. (One Nation Ser.). (J). 1998. 19.00 (*0-516-21475-6*) Childrens.
— Kentucky, 16. (One Nation Ser.). (J). 1998. 19.00 (*0-516-21476-4*) Childrens.
— Maryland, 19. Vol. 19. (Illus.). 48p. (J). (gr. 3-7). 1998. 19.00 (*0-516-21303-2*) Childrens.
— Nevada, 27. (One Nation Ser.). (J). 1998. 19.00 (*0-516-21478-0*) Childrens.
— New Hampshire, 28. (J). 1998. 19.00 (*0-516-21304-0*) Childrens.
— North Dakota, 33. (One Nation Ser.). (J). 1998. 19.00 (*0-516-21479-9*) Childrens.
— Utah, 40. (J). 1998. 19.00 (*0-516-21306-7*) Childrens.
— Washington, D.C., 43. (J). 1998. 19.00 (*0-516-21307-5*) Childrens.
— West Virginia, 44. (One Nation Ser.). (J). 1998. 19.00 (*0-516-21308-3*) Childrens.
— Wyoming, 46. (One Nation Ser.). (J). 1998. 19.00 (*0-516-21309-1*) Childrens.

Capstone Press Geograhpy Department. One Nation: An American Government Text with Readings. 1999. 152.00 (*1-56065-812-6*) Capstone Pr.

Capstone Press Geograhy Staff. One Nation. 1999. 152.00 (*1-56065-658-1*) Capstone Pr.

Capstone Press, Geography Department Staff. Alabama. (One Nation Ser.). (Illus.). 48p. (J). (gr. 3-7). 1997. lib. bdg. 19.00 (*0-516-20925-6*) Childrens.
— Alaska. LC 97-40817. (One Nation Ser.). (Illus.). 48p. (J). (gr. 3-7). 1998. lib. bdg. 19.00 (*1-56065-679-4*) Capstone Pr.

Capstone Press Geography Department Staff. Arizona. (One Nation Ser.). (Illus.). 48p. (J). (gr. 3-7). 1996. lib. bdg. 19.00 (*0-516-20267-7*) Childrens.

***Capstone Press, Geography Department Staff.** Celebrate!, 4 vols. 1999. 76.00 (*0-516-29999-9*, Bridgestone Bks) Capstone Pr.

Capstone Press Geography Department Staff. Colorado. (One Nation Ser.). (Illus.). 48p. (J). (gr. 3-7). 1996. 19.00 (*0-516-20112-3*) Childrens.
— Florida. (One Nation Ser.). (Illus.). 48p. (J). (gr. 3-7). 1996. lib. bdg. 19.00 (*0-516-20111-5*) Childrens.

Capstone Press, Geography Department Staff. Hawaii. (One Nation Ser.). (Illus.). 48p. (J). (gr. 3-7). 1997. lib. bdg. 19.00 (*0-516-20926-4*) Childrens.

Capstone Press Geography Department Staff. Illinois. (One Nation Ser.). (Illus.). 48p. (J). (gr. 3-7). 1996. 19.00 (*0-516-20108-5*) Childrens.
— Louisiana. (One Nation Ser.). (Illus.). 48p. (J). (gr. 3-7). 1996. 19.00 (*0-516-20269-3*) Childrens.

Capstone Press, Geography Department Staff. Maine. (One Nation Ser.). (Illus.). 48p. (J). (gr. 3-7). 1997. lib. bdg. 19.00 (*0-516-20927-2*) Childrens.

Capstone Press Geography Department Staff. Massachusetts. (One Nation Ser.). (Illus.). 48p. (J). (gr. 3-7). 1996. 19.00 (*0-516-20264-2*) Childrens.
— Michigan. (One Nation Ser.). (Illus.). 48p. (J). (gr. 3-7). 1996. 19.00 (*0-516-20263-4*) Childrens.
— Minnesota. (One Nation Ser.). 1997. 19.00 (*0-516-20530-7*) Childrens.

Capstone Press, Geography Department Staff. Missouri. (One Nation Ser.). (Illus.). 48p. (J). (gr. 3-7). 1997. lib. bdg. 19.00 (*0-516-20928-0*) Childrens.
— Montana. (One Nation Ser.). (Illus.). 48p. (J). (gr. 3-7). 1997. lib. bdg. 19.00 (*0-516-20929-9*) Childrens.

Capstone Press Geography Department Staff. Nebraska. (One Nation Ser.). (Illus.). 48p. (J). (gr. 3-7). 1996. lib. bdg. 19.00 (*0-516-20270-7*) Childrens.

Capstone Press, Geography Department Staff. New Jersey. (One Nation Ser.). (Illus.). 48p. (J). (gr. 3-7). 1997. lib. bdg. 19.00 (*0-516-20930-2*) Childrens.
— New Mexico. (One Nation Ser.). (Illus.). 48p. (J). (gr. 3-7). 1997. lib. bdg. 19.00 (*0-516-20931-0*) Childrens.

Capstone Press Geography Department Staff. New York. (One Nation Ser.). (Illus.). 48p. (J). (gr. 3-7). 1996. lib. bdg. 19.00 (*0-516-20107-7*) Childrens.

Capstone Press, Geography Department Staff. North Carolina. (One Nation Ser.). (Illus.). 48p. (J). (gr. 3-7). 1997. lib. bdg. 19.00 (*0-516-20932-9*) Childrens.

Capstone Press Geography Department Staff. Ohio. (One Nation Ser.). (Illus.). 48p. (J). (gr. 3-7). 1996. lib. bdg. 19.00 (*0-516-20266-9*) Childrens.

***Capstone Press Geography Department Staff.** Oklahoma. 1999. 19.93 (*0-516-21795-X*) Capstone Pr.

Capstone Press Geography Department Staff. One Nation. 1999. 152.00 (*0-7368-0122-7*); 114.00 (*0-7368-0150-2*, Cpstone High Low) Capstone Pr.
— Pennsylvania. (One Nation Ser.). (Illus.). 48p. (J). (gr. 3-7). 1996. 19.00 (*0-516-20265-0*) Childrens.

***Capstone Press Geography Department Staff.** Puerto Rico, 36. 1999. 19.93 (*0-516-21796-8*) Capstone Pr.
— Rhode Island. 1999. 19.93 (*0-516-21797-6*) Capstone Pr.
— South Dakota. 1999. 19.93 (*0-516-21798-4*) Capstone Pr.

Capstone Press Geography Department Staff. Tennesee. (Illus.). 48p. (gr. 3-7). 1998. lib. bdg. 19.00 (*1-56065-682-4*) Capstone Pr.
— Texas. (One Nation Ser.). (Illus.). 48p. (J). (gr. 3-7). 1996. 19.00 (*0-516-20110-7*) Childrens.

***Capstone Press Geography Department Staff.** Vermont. 1999. 19.93 (*0-516-21799-2*) Capstone Pr.

Capstone Press Geography Department Staff. Washington. (One Nation Ser.). (Illus.). 48p. (J). (gr. 3-7). 1996. 19.00 (*0-516-20268-5*) Childrens.

Capstone Press Geography Departure Staff. One Nation?, 6 Vols. 1999. 114.00 (*1-56065-656-5*) Capstone Pr.

C

Capstone Press Geography Staff. Mississippi, 23. (One Nation Ser.). 1999. 19.00 (*0-516-21477-2*) Childrens.

— One Nation. 1999. 152.00 (*1-56065-657-3*) Capstone Pr.

Capstone Press Staff. Abraham Lincoln. (J). 1998. 14.00 (*0-516-21376-8*) Childrens.

— African-American Astronauts. (Capstone Short Biographies Ser.). (J). 1998. 19.00 (*0-516-21334-2*) Childrens.

— African-American Aviators. (Capstone Short Biographies Ser.). (J). 1998. 19.00 (*0-516-21335-0*) Childrens.

— African-American Inventors, II, 1 vol. (Capstone Short Biographies Ser.). (J). 1998. 19.00 (*0-516-21336-9*) Childrens.

— African-American Inventors, III. (Capstone Short Biographies Ser.). (J). 1998. 19.00 (*0-516-21337-7*) Childrens.

— African Civilizations. (First Bks.). 1998. 132.00 (*0-531-19493-0*) Watts.

***Capstone Press Staff.** Alimentos, 2 vols. 1998. 28.00 (*0-516-29816-X*) Childrens.

Capstone Press Staff. Animales de La Granja, 4 vols. 1998. 56.00 (*0-516-29814-3*) Childrens.

— Autobuses Escolares. (J). 1998. 14.00 (*0-516-21385-7*) Childrens.

— Bibliotecarlos y Bibliotecarias. (J). 1998. 14.00 (*0-516-21362-8*) Childrens.

***Capstone Press Staff.** Biografias, 4 vols. 1998. 56.00 (*0-516-29815-1*) Childrens.

Capstone Press Staff. Bomberos y Bomberas. (J). 1998. 14.00 (*0-516-21363-6*) Childrens.

— Bridgestone Animals. (J). 1998. 252.00 (*0-516-29798-8*) Childrens.

— Calabazas. (J). 1998. 14.00 (*0-516-21380-6*) Childrens.

— Camiones Do Bomberos. (J). 1998. 14.00 (*0-516-21384-9*) Childrens.

— Capstone Short Biographies. (J). 1998. 152.00 (*0-516-29743-0*) Childrens.

— Cerdos. (J). 1998. 14.00 (*0-516-21372-5*) Childrens.

— Cesar Chavez. (J). 1998. 14.00 (*0-516-21377-6*) Childrens.

— Choferes de Autobuses Excolares. (J). 1998. 14.00 (*0-516-21365-2*) Childrens.

Capstone Press Staff. Christmas Around the World. (Illus.). 24p. 95.60 (*0-7368-0456-0*, Bridgestone Bks) Capstone Pr.

C

Capstone Press Staff. Connecticut. (One Nation Ser.). (Illus.). (J). 1997. lib. bdg. 19.00 (*0-516-20527-7*) Childrens.

***Capstone Press Staff.** Delaware. 1999. 19.93 (*0-516-21794-1*) Capstone Pr.

Capstone Press Staff. Dentistas. (J). 1998. 14.00 (*0-516-21366-0*) Childrens.

— Doctores y Doctoras. (J). 1998. 14.00 (*0-516-21367-9*) Childrens.

— Enfermeras y Enfermeros. (J). 1998. 14.00 (*0-516-21368-7*) Childrens.

***Capstone Press Staff.** Field Trips, 4 Vols. 1999. 53.00 (*0-516-29738-4*) Capstone Pr.

Capstone Press Staff. First Books--America at War. (gr. 4-7). 1998. 176.00 (*0-531-19226-1*) Watts.

— George Washington. (J). 1998. 14.00 (*0-516-21378-4*) Childrens.

— Georgia. (One Nation Ser.). (Illus.). (J). 1997. 19.00 (*0-516-20528-5*) Childrens.

— Greek & Roman Mythology. 1998. 76.00 (*0-531-19245-8*) Childrens.

— In Their Own Voices. 1998. 44.00 (*0-531-19408-6*) Watts.

— Indiana. (One Nation Ser.). (Illus.). (J). 1997. lib. bdg. 19.00 (*0-516-20529-3*) Childrens.

— John F. Kennedy. (Illus.). 24p. (J). (gr. k-3). 1998. 14.00 (*0-516-21379-2*) Childrens.

— Lives in Science. 1998. 48.00 (*0-531-19407-8*) Watts.

— Manzanas. (J). 1998. 14.00 (*0-516-21381-4*) Childrens.

— Maquinas Simples, 2 vols. 1998. 28.00 (*0-516-29817-8*) Childrens.

***Capstone Press Staff.** On the Road. 1999. 80.00 (*0-531-19418-3*) Capstone Pr.

Capstone Press Staff. Ovejas. (J). 1998. 14.00 (*0-516-21373-3*) Childrens.

Capstone Press Staff. Palancas. Price not set. (*1-56065-793-6*) Capstone Pr.

Capstone Press Staff. Palancas. (J). 1998. 14.00 (*0-516-21382-2*) Childrens.

Capstone Press Staff. Poleas. Price not set. (*1-56065-794-4*) Capstone Pr.

Capstone Press Staff. Poleas. (J). 1998. 14.00 (*0-516-21383-0*) Childrens.

— Policias. (J). 1998. 14.00 (*0-516-21370-9*) Childrens.

***Capstone Press Staff.** Servidores Comunitarios, 10 vols. 1998. 140.00 (*0-516-29813-5*) Childrens.

Capstone Press Staff. Tennessee, 38. Vol. 38. (Illus.). 48p. (J). (gr. 3-7). 1998. 19.00 (*0-516-21305-9*) Childrens.

Capstone Press Staff. Transportes. 23.90 (*0-7368-0148-0*, Bridgestone Bks) Capstone Pr.

— Transportes, 2 vols. 1998. 28.00 (*0-516-29818-6*) Childrens.

Capstone Press Staff. U.S. Air Force Special Forces: Combat Controllers. 1999. 20.00 (*0-531-12012-0*) Watts.

— U.S. Air Force Special Forces: Pararescue. 1999. 20.00 (*0-531-12013-9*) Watts.

— U.S. Air Force Special Forces: Special Operations Wings. (Warfare & Weapons Ser.). 1999. 20.00 (*0-531-12008-2*) Watts.

— U.S. Army Special Operations Command: Night Stalkers-Special Operations Aviation. (Warfare & Weapons Ser.). 1999. 20.00 (*0-531-12009-0*) Watts.

— U.S. Marine Corps Special Forces: Recon Marines. (Warfare & Weapons Ser.). 1999. 20.00 (*0-531-12010-4*) Watts.

— U.S. Navy Special Forces: SEAL Teams. (Warfare & Weapons Ser.). 1999. 20.00 (*0-531-12011-2*) Watts.

— Vacas. (J). 1998. 14.00 (*0-516-21375-X*) Childrens.

— Veterinarios y Veterinarias. (J). 1998. 14.00 (*0-516-21371-7*) Childrens.

— Women in Earth Science Careers. (Capstone Short Biographies Ser.). (J). 1998. 19.00 (*0-516-21390-3*) Childrens.

— Women in Engineering Careers. (Capstone Short Biographies Ser.). (J). 1998. 19.00 (*0-516-21391-1*) Childrens.

Capstone Press Staff, ed. Women in Physical Science Careers. (Capstone Short Biographies Ser.). (J). 1998. 19.00 (*0-516-21393-8*) Childrens.

Capstone Press Staff & Ready, Dee. Autobuses Escolares. Schon, Isabel, ed. Ferrer, Martin Luis Guzman, tr. 15.93 (*1-56065-792-8*, Bridgestone Bks) Capstone Pr.

Capstone Press Staff, jt. auth. see Kummer, Patricia K.

***Capstone Publishers Staff, tr.** Chinese International Inductive Study Bible New Testament. (Illus.). 2000. 42.99 (*1-888655-66-6*) Precept Ministries.

Capstone Publishers Staff, tr. see Arthur, Kay.

***Capstone Publishing Staff.** Harnessing The Power of If. 1999. pap. text 15.95 (*1-84112-068-5*) Capstone Pub.

***Capsuto, Steven.** Alternate Channels: The Uncensored Story of Gay & Lesbian Images on Radio & Television. 432p. 2000. pap. 18.00 (*0-345-41243-5*) Ballantine Pub Grp.

Capt, E. Raymond. The Glory of the Stars. LC 79-116390. (Illus.). 144p. (Orig.). 1976. pap. 7.00 (*0-934666-02-4*) Artisan Pubs.

— The Great Pyramid Decoded. rev. ed. LC 78-101677. (Illus.). 96p. 1978. pap. 6.00 (*0-934666-01-6*) Artisan Pubs.

— Jacob's Pillar. LC 79-116385. (Illus.). 96p. 1977. pap. 5.00 (*0-934666-03-2*) Artisan Pubs.

— King Solomon's Temple. LC 79-54774. (Illus.). 96p. 1979. pap. 5.00 (*0-934666-05-9*) Artisan Pubs.

— Lost Chapter of Acts of the Apostles. 32p. 1982. pap. 4.00 (*0-934666-09-1*) Artisan Pubs.

— Missing Links Discovered in Assyrian Tablets. LC 84-72709. (Illus.). 256p. (C). 1985. 16.00 (*0-934666-17-2*); pap. 11.00 (*0-934666-15-6*) Artisan Pubs.

— Our Great Seal - Symbols of Our Heritage & Our Destiny. LC 79-53862. 96p. (Orig.). 1979. pap. 5.00 (*0-934666-00-8*) Artisan Pubs.

— Petra. LC 87-70766. (Illus.). 128p. 1987. pap. 6.00 (*0-934666-23-7*) Artisan Pubs.

— The Resurrection Tomb. LC 88-71638. (Illus.). 80p. 1988. pap. 4.00 (*0-934666-24-5*) Artisan Pubs.

— Scottish Declaration of Independence. enl. rev. ed. (Illus.). 64p. 1996. pap. 4.50 (*0-934666-11-3*) Artisan Pubs.

— Stonehenge & Druidism. rev. ed. LC 79-54773. (Illus.). 96p. 1979. pap. 5.00 (*0-934666-04-0*) Artisan Pubs.

— Study in Pyramidology. LC 86-70103. (Illus.). 264p. (Orig.). 1986. 16.00 (*0-934666-20-2*); pap. 11.00 (*0-934666-21-0*) Artisan Pubs.

— The Traditions of Glastonbury. LC 82-72525. (Illus.). 128p. (Orig.). 1983. pap. 7.00 (*0-934666-10-5*) Artisan Pubs.

Captain Abb. Flying Safe in America: My Version. 2nd ed. LC 95-171025. (Illus.). 256p. 1994. pap. 25.00 (*0-8059-3601-7*) Dorrance.

Captain Comal's Staff. Cartridge Graphics & Sound. (Amazing Adventures of Captain COMAL Ser.). (Illus.). 64p. (Orig.). (J). (gr. 6 up). 1984. pap. 6.95 (*0-928411-02-8*) COMAL Users.

Captain-Hidalgo, Yvonne. The Culture of Fiction in the Works of Manuel Zapata Olivella. 200p. (C). 1993. text 34.95 (*0-8262-0891-6*) U of Mo Pr.

Captain Jester. Aesops' Airline Tales. 128p. 1998. pap. 6.99 (*0-9663644-5-7*) Home Made Bks.

***Captain, Myrtle L.** The Warden & His Brother: From Their Mother's Point of View. LC 98-91090. 2000. pap. 12.95 (*0-533-13046-8*) Vantage.

Captain, Rod, jt. auth. see Stebbins, Susie.

Captain Visual. Captain Visual's Big Book of Balloon Art! A Complete Book of Balloonology for Beginners & Advanced Twisters. (Illus.). 144p. 1995. pap. 9.95 (*0-8065-1641-0*, Citadel Pr) Carol Pub Group.

Captaini Visual. Captain Visual's Big Book of Holiday Balloon Artsculptures for Every Celebration of the Year. LC 97-20751. (Illus.). 144p. 1997. pap. text 15.95 (*0-8065-1920-7*, Citadel Pr) Carol Pub Group.

CAPTECH '98 Staff, et al. Modelling & Motion Capture Techniques for Virtual Environments: International Workshop, Captech'98, Geneva, Switzerland, November 1998: Proceedings: International Workshop, Captech '98, Geneva, Switzerland, November 26-27, 1998: Proceedings, 153. LC 98-49869. (Lecture Notes in Computer Science Ser.). 271 p. 1998. pap. 49.00 (*3-540-65353-8*) Spr-Verlag.

Captive Care Working Party, Primate Society of Gre & UFAW Staff. The Welfare of Pet Marmosets. (C). 1996. pap. 23.00 (*0-900767-42-1*, Pub. by Univs Fed Animal Welfare) St Mut.

Captor, Renee S. Library Research for the Analysis of Public Policy. (Learning Packages in the Policy Sciences Ser.: No. 19). 36p. (Orig.). 1979. pap. text 8.50 (*0-936826-08-8*) PS Assocs Croton.

Capture, George P. Powwow. LC 90-80178. (Illus.). 64p. 1989. pap. 7.50 (*0-931618-29-0*) Buffalo Bill Hist Ctr.

Capua, A. G. De, see De Capua, A. G.

Capuano, Thomas M., ed. Texto y Concordancia del Compendio de los Boticarios, Saladino de Ascoli, Valladolid, 1515. (Medieval Spanish Medical Texts Ser.: No. 30). (SPA.). 36p. 1990. 10.00 incl. fiche (*0-940639-60-2*) Hispanic Seminary.

— Textos y Concordancias del Libro de Medecina Llamado Macer: Andres de Burgos, Granada 1518 y 1519. (Medieval Spanish Medical Texts Ser.: No. 32). (SPA.). 20p. 1991. 10.00 incl. fiche (*0-940639-66-1*) Hispanic Seminary.

Capuano, Thomas M., ed. see Aemilianus, Palladius R.

Capuchin, Edward R. Foundations of Christian Music: The Music of Pre-Constantinian Christianity. LC 95-20948. (American Essays in Liturgy Ser.). 128p. (Orig.). 1996. pap. 10.95 (*0-8146-2396-4*) Liturgical Pr.

Capuchin, Peter M. Collected Teachings on Christian Healing. vi, 151p. 1998. pap. 10.00 (*0-936269-02-2*) Hse of Peace.

***Capucilli, Alyssa.** Bear Hugs. (Road to Reading Mile 1 Ser.). (Illus.). (J). 2000. 10.99 (*0-307-46113-0*); pap. 3.99 (*0-307-26113-1*, Goldn Books) Gldn Bks Pub Co.

***Capucilli, Alyssa & Arnold, Tedd.** Inside a Zoo in the City. LC 99-46235. (J). 2000. 11.95 (*0-590-99715-7*) Scholastic Inc.

Capucilli, Alyssa S. Good Morning, Pond. LC 93-29311. (Illus.). 32p. (J). (ps-2). 1994. 13.95 (*1-56282-674-3*, Pub. by Hyprn Child); lib. bdg. 13.89 (*1-56282-675-1*, Pub. by Hyprn Child) Little.

— Inside a Barn in the Country. LC 92-30491. (Illus.). 32p. (J). (ps-1). 1995. 10.95 (*0-590-46999-1*, Cartwheel) Scholastic Inc.

— Peekaboo Bunny. LC 92-62493. (Illus.). 24p. (J). (ps-k). 1994. 6.95 (*0-590-46754-9*, Cartwheel) Scholastic Inc.

Capucilli, Alyssa Satin. Babysits. (ps-1). pap. 6.95 (*0-694-01517-2*) HarpC.

Capucilli, Alyssa Satin. Bathtime for Biscuit. LC PZ7.C179Bat 1998. (My First I Can Read Bks.). (Illus.). 32p. (J). (ps-k). 1998. lib. bdg. 12.89 (*0-06-027938-9*) HarpC.

— Bathtime for Biscuit. LC PZ7.C179Bat 1998. (My First I Can Read Bks.). (Illus.). 32p. (J). (ps-k). 1998. 12.95 (*0-06-027937-0*) HarpC Child Bks.

— Bathtime for Biscuit. LC 97-49663. (My First I Can Read Bks.). (Illus.). 32p. (J). (ps-k). 1999. pap. 3.95 (*0-06-444264-0*) HarpC Child Bks.

Capucilli, Alyssa Satin. Bedtime for Biscuit. (Biscuit Ser.). (Illus.). (J). (ps-1). bds. 4.95 (*0-694-01524-5*) HarperAudio.

— Best Friends. (ps-1). pap. 6.95 (*0-694-01518-0*) HarpC.

Capucilli, Alyssa Satin. Biscuit. LC 95-9716. (My First I Can Read Bks.). (Illus.). 32p. (J). (ps-k). 1996. 12.95 (*0-06-026197-8*) HarpC Child Bks.

— Biscuit. LC 95-9716. (My First I Can Read Bks.). (Illus.). 32p. (J). (ps-2). 1996. lib. bdg. 14.89 (*0-06-026198-6*) HarpC Child Bks.

— Biscuit. (My First I Can Read Bks.). (Illus.). (J). (ps-k). 1999. pap. 8.95 incl. reel tape (*0-694-70101-7*, HarpFestival) HarpC Child Bks.

— Biscuit. (My First I Can Read Bks.). (Illus.). (J). (ps-k). 1997. 8.95 (*0-606-11135-2*, Pub. by Turtleback) Demco.

— Biscuit. (My First I Can Read Bks.). (Illus.). 32p. (J). (ps-k). 1997. reprint ed. pap. 3.95 (*0-06-444212-8*, HarpTrophy) HarpC Child Bks.

Capucilli, Alyssa Satin. Biscuit & Daisy. (Biscuit Ser.). (Illus.). (J). (ps-1). bds. 4.95 (*0-694-01520-2*, HarpFestival) HarpC Child Bks.

— Biscuit & Puddles. (Biscuit Ser.). (Illus.). (J). (ps-1). bds. 4.95 (*0-694-01523-7*) HarperAudio.

— Biscuit at the Beach. (Biscuit Ser.). (J). (ps-1). bds. 4.95 (*0-694-01521-0*, HarpFestival) HarpC Child Bks.

Capucilli, Alyssa Satin. Biscuit Finds a Friend. LC 96-18368. (My First I Can Read Bks.). (Illus.). 32p. (J). (ps-k). 1997. 12.95 (*0-06-027412-3*); lib. bdg. 14.89 (*0-06-027413-1*) HarpC Child Bks.

— Biscuit Finds a Friend. LC 96-18368. (My First I Can Read Bks.). (Illus.). 32p. (J). (ps-k). 1998. pap. 3.95 (*0-06-444243-8*) HarpC Child Bks.

— Biscuit Finds a Friend. (My First I Can Read Bks.). (Illus.). (J). (ps-k). 1998. 8.95 (*0-606-13203-1*, Pub. by Turtleback) Demco.

— Biscuit Goes to School. (Biscuit Ser.). (Illus.). 24p. (J). (ps-1). 12.95 (*0-06-028682-2*); write for info. (*0-06-443616-0*) HarpC.

***Capucilli, Alyssa Satin.** Biscuit Goes to School. (Biscuit Ser.). (Illus.). 24p. (J). (ps-1). 2001. lib. bdg. 12.89 (*0-06-028683-0*) HarpC Child Bks.

— Biscuit Mini Book & Puppy. (Biscuit Ser.). (Illus.). (J). (ps-1). 1999. 14.95 (*0-694-01444-3*) HarpC Child Bks.

— Biscuit Treasury (Omnibus) (Biscuit Ser.). (Illus.). (J). (ps-1). 2000. write for info. (*0-06-029128-1*) HarpC Child Bks.

— Biscuit Wants to Play. (Illus.). (J). 2001. lib. bdg. write for info. (*0-06-028070-0*) HarpC Child Bks.

— Biscuit Wants to Play. (Biscuit Ser.). (Illus.). (J). (ps-1). 2001. write for info. (*0-06-028069-7*) HarpC Child Bks.

— Biscuit's Christmas. LC 99-69747. (Biscuit Ser.). (Illus.). 16p. (J). (ps-1). 2000. 6.95 (*0-694-01516-4*, HarpFestival) HarpC Child Bks.

Capucilli, Alyssa Satin. Biscuit's New Trick. LC 99-23004. (My First I Can Read Bks.). (Illus.). 32p. (J). (ps-k). 2000. 12.95 (*0-06-028067-0*); lib. bdg. 12.89 (*0-06-028068-9*) HarpC Child Bks.

— Biscuit's Picnic. LC 98-72312. (Biscuit Ser.). (Illus.). 24p. (J). (ps-1). 1998. 12.95 (*0-06-028072-7*) HarpC Child Bks.

— Biscuit's Vacation. (Biscuit Ser.). (Illus.). 24p. (J). (ps-1). 12.95 (*0-06-028680-6*); write for info. (*0-06-443618-7*) HarpC.

***Capucilli, Alyssa Satin.** Biscuit's Vacation. (Biscuit Ser.). (Illus.). 24p. (J). (ps-1). 2002. lib. bdg. 12.89 (*0-06-028681-4*) HarpC Child Bks.

— Biscuit's Valentine's Day. LC 99-71632. (Biscuit Ser.). (Illus.). 20p. (J). (ps-1). 2000. 6.95 (*0-694-01222-X*, HarpFestival) HarpC Child Bks.

— Camps Out. 8p. pap. 6.95 (*0-694-01525-3*) HarpC.

Capucilli, Alyssa Satin. Happy Birthday, Biscuit! (Biscuit Ser.). (Illus.). (J). (ps-1). Date not set. pap. write for info. (*0-06-443565-2*) HarpC Child Bks.

— Happy Birthday, Biscuit! LC 98-41514. (Biscuit Ser.). (Illus.). 24p. (J). (ps-1). 1999. 12.95 (*0-06-028355-6*) HarpC Child Bks.

— Happy Birthday, Biscuit! LC 98-41514. (Biscuit Ser.). (Illus.). 24p. (J). (ps-1). 1999. lib. bdg. 13.89 (*0-06-028361-0*) HarpC Child Bks.

— Happy Halloween, Biscuit! LC 98-75747. (Biscuit Ser.). (Illus.). 20p. (J). (ps-1). 1999. 6.95 (*0-694-01220-3*, HarpFestival) HarpC Child Bks.

— Happy Thanksgiving, Biscuit! LC 98-75748. (Biscuit Ser.). (Illus.). 20p. (J). (ps-1). 1999. 6.95 (*0-694-01221-1*) HarpC Child Bks.

— Hello, Biscuit! LC 98-70489. (Biscuit Ser.). (Illus.). 24p. (J). (ps-1). 1998. 12.95 (*0-06-028071-9*) HarpC Child Bks.

— Inside a House That Is Haunted: A Rebus Read-Along Story. LC 97-38398. (Illus.). 32p. (J). (ps-1). 1998. 11.95 (*0-590-99716-5*, Pub. by Scholastic Inc) Penguin Putnam.

Capucilli, Alyssa Satin. Lost & Found. 8p. (ps-1). pap. 6.95 (*0-694-01526-1*) HarpC.

— My First Biscuit Library, 3 bks. (Illus.). (J). (ps up). 2000. pap. 9.95 (*0-694-01457-5*) HarpC Child Bks.

— Paw Print. (ps-1). pap. 6.95 (*0-694-01519-9*) HarpC.

— Potty Book - For Boys. (Illus.). 32p. (J). 2000. 5.95 (*0-7641-5232-7*) Barron.

— Potty Book - For Girls. (Illus.). 32p. (J). 2000. 5.95 (*0-7641-5231-9*) Barron.

— Trip to the Farm. (ps-1). pap. 9.95 (*0-694-01522-9*) HarpC.

Capucilli, Alyssa Satin & Schories, Pat. Happy Easter, Biscuit! LC 99-71631. (Biscuit Ser.). (Illus.). 20p. (J). (ps-1). 2000. 6.95 (*0-694-01223-8*) HarpC Child Bks.

Capul, Jean-Yves. Dictionnaire d'Economie et de Sciences Sociales. (FRE.). 475p. 1993. pap. 29.95 (*0-7859-5616-6*, 2218059363) Fr & Eur.

Capula, Massimo. Simon & Schuster's Guide to Reptiles & Amphibians of the World. 256p. 1990. per. 14.00 (*0-671-69098-1*, Fireside) S&S Trade Pap.

Capulet, Nancy & Blachman, Nancy. Putting Your Heart Online. (Illus.). xvi, 244p. 1998. pap. 14.95 (*0-9663774-0-0*) Variable Symbols.

— Putting Your Heart Online: Matchmaker Edition. (Illus.). xvi, 237p. 1998. pap. 14.95 (*0-9663774-1-9*) Variable Symbols.

***Capullo, Greg.** Creech: Rage Against Death, 1. 1999. pap. text 9.95 (*1-58240-100-4*) Image Comics.

Capulong-Hallenberg, Virginia S. Philippine Foreign Policy Toward the U. S., 1972-1980: Reorientation? (Stockholm Studies in Politics: No. 33). 292p. (Orig.). 1987. pap. 83.00 (*91-7146-478-6*, Pub. by Stockholms Universitet) Coronet Bks.

Capurro, Juan R. Las Cinco Dimensiones de la Prosperidad.Tr. of Five Dimensions of Prosperity. (SPA.). 1997. 9.99 (*0-88113-408-2*, B079-4082) Caribe Betania.

Capurro, Luis R. & Reid, Joseph L., eds. Contributions on the Physical Oceanography of the Gulf of Mexico. LC 72-170030. (Texas A & M University Oceanographic Studies: No. 2). (Illus.). 308p. reprint ed. pap. 95.50 (*0-608-18173-0*, 203288900081) Bks Demand.

***Capurro, Scott.** Fowl Play. 279p. 2000. pap. 17.95 (*0-7472-7571-8*, Pub. by Headline Bk Pub) Trafalgar.

Capus, Joseph M. Metal Powders: A Global Survey of Production, Applications & Markets. 200p. 1993. pap. 994.00 (*1-85617-174-4*) Elsevier.

— Metal Powders Global Survey. LC 96-204723. 1996. pap. text 1253.00 (*1-85617-287-2*) Elsevier.

Capus, Joseph M. & German, Randall M., eds. Advances in Powder Metallurgy & Particulate Materials - 1992, 9 vols., Set. LC 92-81743. Orig. Title: Compiled by. (Illus.). 4576p. 1992. text 300.00 (*1-878954-19-9*) Metal Powder.

Capute, Arnold J., et al, eds. Learning Disabilities Spectrum: ADD, ADHD, & LD. LC 93-39701. 265p. 1994. pap. text 32.50 (*0-912752-33-5*) York Pr.

Capute, Arnold J. & Accardo, Pasquale J. Developmental Disabilities in Infancy & Childhood Vol. I: Neurodevelopmental Diagnosis & Treatment, vol. 1. 2nd ed. LC 94-34249. 736p. 1996. boxed set 120.00 (*1-55766-178-2*) P H Brookes.

— Developmental Disabilities in Infancy & Childhood Vol. II: The Spectrum of Developmental Disabilities. 2nd ed. LC 94-34249. 624p. 1996. boxed set 110.00 (*1-55766-194-4*) P H Brookes.

Caputi, Anthony. Pirandello & the Crisis of Modern Consciousness. LC 87-10801. 184p. 1988. text 24.95 (*0-252-01468-5*) U of Ill Pr.

Caputi, Anthony F. Buffo: The Genius of Vulgar Comedy. LC 78-15992. (Illus.). 263p. reprint ed. pap. 81.60 (*0-8357-8820-2*, 205674500085) Bks Demand.

— Pirandello & the Crisis of Modern Consciousness. fac. ed. LC 87-10801. 183p. 1988. pap. 56.80 (*0-7837-7610-1*, 204736200007) Bks Demand.

Caputi, Anthony F., ed. Eight Modern Plays. 2nd ed. (Critical Editions Ser.). 512p. (Orig.). (C). 1991. pap. text 20.25 (*0-393-96015-3*) Norton.

Caputi, Gary. Fishing for Striped Bass. Barrett, Linda, ed. (Illus.). 232p. (Orig.). 1993. pap. 18.95 (*0-923155-19-8*) Fisherman Lib.

Caputi, Jane. The Age of Sex Crime. LC 87-70344. (Illus.). 246p. 1987. 24.95 (*0-87972-385-8*) Bowling Green Univ Popular Press.

— Gossips, Gorgons & Crones: The Fates of the Earth. LC 93-18885. (Illus.). 400p. (Orig.). 1993. pap. text 14.95 (*1-879181-05-3*) Bear & Co.

Caputi, Jane, jt. auth. see Daly, Mary.

An Asterisk (*) at the beginning of an entry indicates that the title is appearing for the first time.

Caputi, Mary. Voluptuous Yearnings: A Feminist Theory of the Obscene. (New Feminist Perspectives Ser.). 144p. (Orig.). (C). 1994. pap. text 19.95 (*0-8476-7886-5*); lib. bdg. 49.50 (*0-8476-7885-7*) Rowman.

Caputi, Natalino. Guide to the Unconscious. LC 83-24620. 172p. (Orig.). 1984. pap. 19.95 (*0-89135-042-X*) Religious Educ.

— Unconscious: A Guide to the Sources. LC 85-1979. (American Theological Library Association Monograph: No. 16). 161p. 1985. 24.00 (*0-8108-1798-5*) Scarecrow.

***Caputi, Robert J.** Neville Chamberlain & Appeasement. LC 99-23975. 272p. 2000. 45.00 (*1-57591-027-6*) Susquehanna U Pr.

Caputo, jt. auth. see Hazel.

Caputo, A., ed. Biological Basis of Clinical Effect of Bleomycin. (Progress in Biochemical Pharmacology Ser.: Vol. 11). (Illus.). 200p. 1976. 110.50 (*3-8055-2338-6*) S Karger.

Caputo, A., jt. ed. see Silvestrini, B.

Caputo, A. G. The Afterlife Connection, Heavenly Reflection. (Illus.). 144p. 1988. 12.95 (*0-929484-00-2*) Crystal Pl Inc.

Caputo, Algelo A. & Standlee, Jon P. Biomechanics in Clinical Dentistry. (Illus.). 224p. 1987. text 82.00 (*0-86715-178-1*) Quint Pub Co.

Caputo, C. & Jannini, P. A. Italian-French - French-Italian Commercial Dictionary: Vocabolario Commerciale Italiano-Francese-Italiano. (FRE & ITA.). 257p. 1982. reprint ed. 59.95 (*0-8288-0110-X*, M14304) Fr & Eur.

Caputo, Don D. Against Ethics: Contributions to a Poetics of Obligation with Constant Reference to Deconstruction. LC 92-41567. (Studies in Continental Thought). 304p. 1993. 39.95 (*0-253-31313-9*) Ind U Pr.

— Against Ethics: Contributions to a Poetics of Obligation with Constant Reference to Deconstruction. LC 92-41567. (Studies in Continental Thought). 304p. 1993. pap. text 18.95 (*0-253-20816-5*) Ind U Pr.

Caputo, F., jt. ed. see Heck, A.

Caputo, Gregory M., ed. see Kammerer, William S.

Caputo, Janette S. Stress & Burnout in Library Service. LC 90-41637. 184p. 1991. pap. 24.95 (*0-89774-602-3*) Oryx Pr.

Caputo, John & Yount, Mark, eds. Foucault & the Critique of Institutions. LC 92-33881. (Studies of the Greater Philadelphia Philosophy Consortium). 240p. (C). 1993. 50.00 (*0-271-00881-4*); pap. 18.95 (*0-271-00938-1*) Pa St U Pr.

Caputo, John, et al. Interpersonal Communication: Competence Through Critical Thinking. 2nd ed. LC 96-26384. 394p. (C). 1996. pap., per. 34.95 (*0-7872-2224-0*) Kendall-Hunt.

Caputo, John, jt. auth. see Hazel, Harry C.

Caputo, John, ed. see Wynyard, Robin.

Caputo, John D. Demythologizing Heidegger. LC 93-461. (Indiana Series In Philosophy of Religion). 246p. 1993. pap. 16.95 (*0-253-20838-6*) Ind U Pr.

Caputo, John D. Demythologizing Heidegger. LC 93-461. (Indiana Series In Philosophy of Religion). 246p. 1993. 16.95 (*0-253-31306-6*) Ind U Pr.

— God, the Gift & Postmodernism. LC 99-32397. (Series in the Philosophy of Religion). 368p. 1999. pap. 49.95 (*0-253-33572-8*) Ind U Pr.

Caputo, John D. Heidegger & Aquinas: An Essay on Overcoming Metaphysics. LC 82-71398. 308p. 1982. 35.00 (*0-8232-1097-9*); pap. 17.50 (*0-8232-1098-7*) Fordham.

***Caputo, John D.** More Radical Hermeneutics: On Not Knowing Who We Are. LC 99-88428. (Studies in Continental Thought). 336p. 2000. pap. 19.95 (*0-253-21387-8*); lib. bdg. 44.95 (*0-253-33747-X*) Ind U Pr.

Caputo, John D. The Mystical Element in Heidegger's Thought. rev. ed. LC 77-92257. xxvi, 292p. 1986. pap. 17.50 (*0-8232-1153-3*) Fordham.

— The Prayers & Tears of Jacques Derrida: Religion Without Religion. LC 96-47839. (Indiana Series in the Philosophy of Religion). 1997. 39.95 (*0-253-33268-0*); pap. 19.95 (*0-253-21112-3*) Ind U Pr.

— Radical Hermeneutics: Repetition, Deconstruction & the Hermeneutic Project. LC 86-46143. (Studies in Phenomenology & Existential Philosophy). 332p. 1988. 39.95 (*0-253-34785-8*); pap. 18.95 (*0-253-20442-9*, MB-442) Ind U Pr.

Caputo, John D., ed. Deconstruction in a Nutshell: A Conversation with Jacques Derrida. LC 96-45189. (Perspectives in Continental Philosophy Ser.: Vol. 1). xv, 215p. 1996. pap. 17.95 (*0-8232-1755-8*); text 25.00 (*0-8232-1754-X*) Fordham.

***Caputo, John D. & Scanlon, Michael J.** God, the Gift, & Postmodernism LC 99-32397. (Indiana Series in the Philosophy of Religion). 1999. pap. 19.95 (*0-253-21328-2*) Ind U Pr.

Caputo, Kathryn. How to Produce a Successful Crafts Show. LC 96-28941. (Illus.). 160p. 1997. pap. 14.95 (*0-8117-2797-1*) Stackpole.

— How to Show & Sell Your Crafts. LC 97-23813. (Illus.). 160p. 1997. pap. 18.99 (*1-55870-447-7*, Betrwy Bks) F & W Pubns Inc.

— How to Start Making Money with Your Crafts. (Illus.). 160p. 1995. pap. 18.99 (*1-55870-400-0*, Betrwy Bks) F & W Pubns Inc.

— How to Start Making Money with Your Crafts. rev. ed. LC 98-54848. (Illus.). 192p. 1999. pap. 18.99 (*1-55870-518-X*, 70437, Betrwy Bks) F & W Pubns Inc.

Caputo, Kim. CMM Implementation Guide: Choreographing Software Process Improvement. LC 97-51575. 336p. (C). 1998. pap. text 49.95 (*0-201-37938-4*) Addison-Wesley.

Caputo, Larry. Sno-Jobs of America: America's Handbook of Snowjobs. Blanchard, Clay, ed. 314p. (Orig.). 1995. pap. text 8.00 (*0-9646991-0-9*) Brookdale Pub.

Caputo, Luciano V. Questioned Document Case Studies. LC 82-3563. (Illus.). 100p. 1982. text 55.95 (*0-88229-259-5*) Burnham Inc.

Caputo-Mayr, Maria L. & Herz, Julius M., eds. Franz Kafka: Eine Kommentierte Bibliographie der Sekundarliteratur. 2nd enl. rev. ed. 850p. 1997. write for info. (*3-907820-65-7*) K G Saur Verlag.

— Franz Kafkas Werke: Eine Bibliographie der Primarliteratur. 2nd enl. rev. ed. 1997. write for info. (*3-907820-64-9*) K G Saur Verlag.

***Caputo, Michael.** God: Seen Through the Eyes of the Greatest Minds. (Illus.). 250p. 2000. 16.99 (*1-58229-132-2*) Howard Pub LA.

Caputo, Philip. Delcorso's Gallery: A Novel. LC 90-56437. 368p. 1991. reprint ed. pap. 11.00 (*0-06-098606-9*, Perennial) HarperTrade.

— Exiles. 368p. 1998. pap. 13.00 (*0-679-76838-6*) Vin Bks.

— Exiles: Three Short Novels. LC 96-44459. 1997. 25.00 (*0-679-45038-6*) Knopf.

— A Rumor of War. LC 96-19314. 1996. 0.85 (*0-8050-4965-7*) H Holt & Co.

— A Rumor of War. 356p. 1996. pap. 11.95 (*0-8050-4695-X*) H Holt & Co.

— A Rumor of War. large type ed. (Niagara Large Print Ser.). 512p. 1997. 29.50 (*0-7089-5864-8*) Ulverscroft.

***Caputo, Philip.** The Voyage. LC 99-23568. (Illus.). 416p. 1999. 26.00 (*0-679-45039-4*) Knopf.

— The Voyage. 2000. reprint ed. pap. 14.00 (*0-679-76839-4*) Knopf.

***Caputo, Raffaele & Burton, Geoff.** Second Take: Australian Film-Makers Talk. (Illus.). 352p. 2000. pap. 19.95 (*1-86448-765-8*, Pub. by Allen & Unwin Pty) IPG Chicago.

***Caputo, Richard K.** Advantage White & Male, Disadvantage Black & Female. 208p. 1999. 20.95 (*1-58244-030-1*) Rutledge Bks.

Caputo, Richard K. Management Information Systems in Human Services: Implications for the Distribution of Authority & Decision Making. 166p. 1987. 49.95 (*0-86656-663-5*) Haworth Pr.

— Management Information Systems in Human Services: Implications for the Distribution of Authority & Decision Making. 166p. 1988. pap. 14.95 (*0-86656-822-0*) Haworth Pr.

— Welfare & Freedom American Style II: The Role of the Federal Government, 1941-1980. LC 93-43063. (Federal Responses to People in Need Ser.: Vol. 2). 694p. (C). 1994. lib. bdg. 64.50 (*0-8191-9398-4*) U Pr of Amer.

***Caputo, Robert.** Cisco Packetized Voice & Data Integration. LC 99-40271. (Cisco Technical Expert Ser.). 352p. 1999. pap. 55.00 (*0-07-134777-1*) McGraw.

Caputo, Robert, jt. auth. see Burian, Peter.

Caputo, Rudolph R., jt. auth. see Aubry, Arthur S., Jr.

Caputo, Ruggero, et al. Pediatric Dermatology & Dermatopathology, Vol. 3. (Illus.). 516p. 1995. 165.00 (*0-683-01437-4*) Lppncott W & W.

— Pediatric Dermatology & Dermatopathology, Vol. IV. (Illus.). 476p. 1995. 165.00 (*0-683-01438-2*) Lppncott W & W.

— Pediatric Dermatology & Dermatopathology: A Text & Atlas. LC 88-36885. (Illus.). 391p. write for info. (*0-8121-1166-4*); write for info. (*0-8121-1314-4*); text 150.00 (*0-318-67251-0*) Lppncott W & W.

— Pediatric Dermatology & Dermatopathology: A Text & Atlas, IV. LC 88-36885. (Illus.). 391p. write for info. (*0-8121-1316-0*) Lppncott W & W.

***Caputo, Ruggero, et al.** Text Atlas of Pathology of the Foot. (Illus.). 216p. 2000. 89.95 (*1-85317-787-3*, Pub. by Martin Dunitz) Blackwell Sci.

Caputo, Sal, ed. see Bouchard, P. J. & Pellet, Lizz.

Caputo, Sal, ed. see Domoradzki, Stan.

Caputo, Sal, ed. see Radke, Linda F.

***Caputo, Salvatore, et al, eds.** Letters of Love: Stories from the Heart. LC 99-89590. 2000. pap. 12.95 (*1-877749-35-4*) Five Star AZ.

Caputo, Salvatore, jt. auth. see Ross, Debbie.

Caputo, Salvatoro, ed. see Pagano, Ricki S.

Caputo, Silvio J., Jr. The Death of Spring. LC 81-14952. 1985. pap. 13.95 (*0-87949-201-5*, 81-14952) Ashley Bks.

Caputo, Susan, jt. auth. see Ziol, Elaine.

Caputo, Tony. How to Self-Publish Your Own Comic Book. LC 96-37271. (Illus.). 176p. 1996. 19.95 (*0-8230-2455-5*) Watsn-Guptill.

Caputto, R. & Marsan, Cosimo A., eds. Neural Transmission, Learning, & Memory. LC 83-2969. (International Brain Research Organization Monograph Ser.: No. 10). (Illus.). 301p. 1983. reprint ed. pap. 93.40 (*0-608-00645-9*, 206123300007) Bks Demand.

Capuzzi, Dare & Gross, Douglas R. Introduction to Counseling Profession. 2nd ed. LC 96-46277. 528p. 1997. 79.00 (*0-205-26535-9*) Allyn.

Capuzzi, Dave. Suicide Prevention in the Schools: Guidelines for Middle & High School Settings. LC 93-33197. 128p. 1994. pap. text 29.95 (*1-55620-127-3*, 72581) Am Coun Assn.

Capuzzi, Dave & Gross, Doug. Introduction to Group Counseling. 2nd ed. 528p. (C). 1998. text 59.00 (*0-89108-259-X*, 9802) Love Pub Co.

Capuzzi, Dave & Gross, Douglas. Counseling & Psychotherapy. 2nd ed. LC 98-8649. 501p. (C). 1998. 67.00 (*0-13-569955-X*) P-H.

Capuzzi, David. Counseling & Psychotherapy: Theories & Interventions. 1994. teacher ed. 6.00 (*0-02-319212-7*, Macmillan Coll) P-H.

Capuzzi, David & Gross, Doug. An Introduction to the Counseling Profession. 2nd ed. (C). 1996. teacher ed. write for info. (*0-205-26589-8*, T6589-0) Allyn.

Capuzzi, David & Gross, Douglas. Student Handbook for Introduction to Group Counseling. 200p. 1998. pap. text 19.95 (*0-89108-261-1*, 9804) Love Pub Co.

Capuzzi, David & Gross, Douglas R. Counseling & Psychotherapy: Theories & Interventions. (Illus.). 544p. (C). 1994. teacher ed. write for info. (*0-318-72454-5*) Macmillan.

***Capuzzi, David & Gross, Douglas R.** Introduction to the Counseling Profession. 3rd ed. 512p. 2000. 73.00 (*0-205-32196-8*) Allyn.

***Capuzzi, David & Gross, Douglas R., eds.** Youth at Risk: A Prevention Resource for Counselors, Teachers & Parents. 3rd ed. LC 99-41560. 526p. 1999. pap. text 39.95 (*1-55620-219-9*, 72665) Am Coun Assn.

Capuzzo-Dolcetta, Roberto, et al, eds. Physical Processes in Fragmentation & Star Formation. (C). 1990. text 236.50 (*0-7923-0769-0*) Kluwer Academic.

Capuzzo, Judith M. & Kester, Dana R. Biological Processes & Wastes in the Ocean. Duedall, Iver. W. et al, eds. LC 84-29733. (Oceanic Processes in Marine Pollution Ser.: Vol. 1). 280p. (C). 1986. lib. bdg. 59.50 (*0-89874-810-0*) Krieger.

Capuzzo, Michael & Banik Capuzzo, Teresa. Cat Caught My Heart: Purrfect Tales of Wisdom, Hope & Love. 288p. 1999. mass mkt. 6.50 (*0-553-58101-5*) Bantam.

— Our Best Friends: Wagging Tales to Warm the Heart. 304p. 1999. mass mkt. 6.50 (*0-553-58104-X*) Bantam.

Capwell, Charles. The Music of the Bauls of Bengal. LC 84-27824. (Illus.). 254p. 1986. reprint ed. pap. 78.80 (*0-608-07347-4*, 206757500009) Bks Demand.

Capwell, Gerald & Resnick, Barry. SABRE Reservations: Basic & Advanced Training. 304p. 1993. pap., teacher ed. write for info. (*0-538-70620-1*) S-W Pub.

Capwell, Gerald K. & Resnick, Barry P. SABRE Reservations: Basic & Advanced Training. 2nd ed. LC 92-17416. 1993. pap. 38.95 (*0-538-70619-8*) S-W Pub.

Capy, Pierre, ed. Evolution & Impact of Transposable Elements. LC 97-23957. (Contemporary Issues in Genetics & Evolution Ser.). 307p. 1998. lib. bdg. 199.00 (*0-7923-4690-4*) Kluwer Academic.

Caquot, A., et al, eds. Melanges Bibliques et Orientaux en l'Honneur de M. Mathias Delcor. (Alter Orient und Altes Testament Ser.: Vol. 215). (FRE, SPA & GER.). x, 448p. 1985. text 107.50 (*3-7887-0799-2*, Pub. by NeukirchenerV) Eisenbrauns.

Car & Parts Staff. Resurrection of Vicky. (Illus.). 218p. 1995. pap. text 12.95 (*1-880524-12-0*) Cars & Parts.

Cara. Night, Night Baby Mouseling. (Tiny Touch Bks.). (Illus.). 1994. 7.50 (*0-8378-7623-0*) Gibson.

Cara, M., jt. auth. see Babuska, V.

Caraballo, Daisy. La Prosa de Luis Lloren Torres: Estudio y Antologia. LC 83-27416. xiv, 286p. 1986. pap. 10.50 (*0-8477-3802-7*) U of PR Pr.

Carabasi, R. Anthony, III, jt. auth. see Jarrell, Bruce E.

Carabasi, R. Anthony, III, jt. ed. see Jarrell, Bruce E.

Carabella, Monica, jt. auth. see Massa, Renato.

Carabelli, Giancarlo, tr. from ITA. On Hume & Eighteenth-Century Aesthetics: The Philosopher on a Swing. LC 94-27991. Vol. 22.Tr. of Intorno a Hume. (Illus.). XI, 222p. (C). 1995. text 48.95 (*0-8204-2528-1*) P Lang Pubng.

Carabelli, Umberto & Sciarra, Silvana. New Patterns of Collective Labour Law in Central Europe: Czech & Slovak Republics, Hungary, Poland (Nuovi Modelli di Diritto Sindacale Nell'Europa Centrale: Repubbliche Ceca e Slovacca, Ungheria, Polonia) LC 99-215182. xiii, 495 p. 1996. write for info. (*88-14-05075-9*, Pub. by Giuffre) IBD Ltd.

Carabello, Blase, ed. Cardiology Pearls. (Illus.). 256p. (Orig.). 1993. pap. text 46.95 (*0-932883-96-6*) Hanley & Belfus.

Carabello, Blase A., jt. ed. see Vetrovec, George W.

***Carabetta, Natalie.** Carmen from Spain. (Little Activity Bks.). (Illus.). (J). 1999. pap. 1.00 (*0-486-40755-1*) Dover.

Carabetta, Natalie. Frances Hodgson Burnett's the Secret Garden. LC 94-26078. (All Aboard Reading Ser.: Level 3). 48p. (J). (gr. 2-3). 1995. pap. 3.95 (*0-448-40736-1*, G & D) Peng Put Young Read.

— A Little Princess. LC 96-22426. (All Aboard Reading Ser.: Level 3). 48p. (J). (gr. 2-3). 1996. pap. 3.95 (*0-448-41327-2*, G & D); lib. bdg. 13.99 (*0-448-41329-9*, G & D) Peng Put Young Read.

Carabillo, Toni & Meuli, Judith. The Feminization of Power. (Illus.). 166p. (Orig.). (YA). (gr. 8-12). 1988. pap. 8.95 (*0-929037-02-2*) Fund Feminist Majority.

Carabillo, Toni, et al. Feminist Chronicles, 1953-1993. LC 93-12500. (Illus.). 320p. (C). 1993. pap. 24.95 (*0-9634912-0-2*) Womens Graphics.

Carabine, Deirdre. The Unknown God: Negative Theology in the Platonic Tradition: Plato to Eriugena. (Louvain Theological & Pastoral Monographs: Vol. 19). 358p. 1995. pap. 25.00 (*0-8028-0558-2*) Eerdmans.

***Carabine, Dierdre.** John Scottus Eriugena. LC 99-29192. (Great Medieval Thinkers Ser.). 144p. 2000. pap. 16.95 (*0-19-511362-4*); text 35.00 (*0-19-511361-6*) OUP.

Carabine, Keith, ed. Joseph Conrad: Critical Assessments, 4 vols., Set. (Writers in English Ser.). (Illus.). 2912p. (C). (gr. 13). 1992. text, boxed set 535.00 (*1-873403-04-6*, A9683) Routledge.

Carabine, Keith, et al, eds. Joseph Conrad Vol. II: Eastern & Western Perspectives. (East European Monographs: No. 370). 285p. 1993. 50.00 (*0-88033-267-0*, 370, Pub. by East Eur Monographs) Col U Pr.

— Joseph Conrad, Eastern & Western Perspectives Vol. 1: Conrad's Literary Career. 450p. (C). 1993. text 69.50 (*0-88033-250-6*, 353, Pub. by East Eur Monographs) Col U Pr.

***Carabine, Keith & Knowles, Owen.** James, Conrad, & Other Relations. 360p. 1998. text 50.00 (*0-88033-974-8*, Pub. by East Eur Monographs) Col U Pr.

Carabine, Keith, ed. see Conrad, Joseph.

Carabine, Sue. A Cat's Night Before Christmas. LC 97-126675. (Illus.). 60p. 1996. 5.95 (*0-87905-761-0*) Gibbs Smith Pub.

— Dad's Night Before Christmas. (Little Night Before Christmas Bks.: Vol. 13). (Illus.). 60p. 1999. 5.95 (*0-87905-926-5*) Gibbs Smith Pub.

— A Dog's Night Before Christmas. LC 97-176721. (Little Night Before Christmas Ser.). (Illus.). 60p. 1996. 5.95 (*0-87905-762-9*) Gibbs Smith Pub.

— Grandma's Night Before Christmas. (Night Before Christmas Ser.: Vol. 13). (Illus.). 60p. 1998. 5.95 (*0-87905-820-X*) Gibbs Smith Pub.

— Grandpa's Night Before Christmas. (Little Night Before Christmas Bks.: Vol. 14). (Illus.). 60p. 1999. 5.95 (*0-87905-927-3*) Gibbs Smith Pub.

***Carabine, Sue.** The Night Before Christmas in Colorado. (Little Night Before Christmas Ser.: Vol. 18). (Illus.). 60p. 2000. 5.95 (*0-87905-997-4*) Gibbs Smith Pub.

Carabine, Sue. The Night Before Christmas in Florida. (Little Night Before Christmas Bks.: Vol. 15). (Illus.). 60p. 1999. 5.95 (*0-87905-928-1*) Gibbs Smith Pub.

***Carabine, Sue.** The Night Before Christmas in Seattle. (Little Night Before Christmas Bks.: Vol. 16). (Illus.). 60p. 1999. 5.95 (*0-87905-929-X*) Gibbs Smith Pub.

— The Night Before Christmas in Utah. (Little Night Before Christmas Ser.: Vol. 17). (Illus.). 60p. 2000. 5.95 (*0-87905-981-8*) Gibbs Smith Pub.

Carabine, Sue. A Teacher's Night Before Christmas. LC 97-126679. (Little Night Before Christmas Ser.). (Illus.). 60p. 1996. 8.95 (*0-87905-764-5*) Gibbs Smith Pub.

Carabini, Louis E., ed. see Steed, Robin.

Carabis, Anne. The Magic Rocking Chair. (Illus.). 28p. (Orig.). (J). (ps-3). 1980. pap. 3.50 (*0-9605802-0-4*) Carabis.

Carabott, Philip, ed. Greek Society in the Making, 1863-1913: Realities, Symbols & Visions. LC 97-17845. (Publications of the Centre for Hellenic Studies, King's College London: Vol. 3). 300p. 1997. text 83.95 (*0-86078-612-9*, DF825.G74, Pub. by Variorum) Ashgate Pub Co.

Caracas Report on Alternative Indicators Staff. Redefining Wealth & Progress: New Ways to Measure Economic, Social & Environmental Change. LC 90-892. 112p. (Orig.). 1990. pap. 9.95 (*0-942850-24-6*) Bootstrap Pr.

Caracci, Julie M. The Red Colt. (Illus.). 70p. (Orig.). (YA). (gr. 5-6). 1996. pap. 4.50 (*1-57502-265-6*, PO949) Morris Pubng.

Caraccilo, Dominic J. The Ready Brigade of the 82nd Airborne in Desert Storm: A Combat Memoir by a Headquarters Company Commander. LC 92-50945. (Illus.). 223p. (YA). (gr. 8-12). 1993. pap. 19.95 (*0-89950-829-4*) McFarland & Co.

— Surviving Bataan & Beyond: Colonel Irvin Alexander's Odyssey As a Japanese Prisoner of War. LC 98-47675. (Illus.). 224p. 1999. 24.95 (*0-8117-1596-5*) Stackpole.

Caracciolla, Mariella. Houses & Palaces of Majorca. LC 96-61061. (Illus.). 288p. 1996. text 60.00 (*1-86064-141-5*) St Martin.

Caracciolo, Ana, tr. Spanish Scripts. (SPA.). 30p. 1985. pap. 10.00 (*1-58302-087-X*, BSP-02) One Way St.

***Caracciolo, Lucio, et al.** The Italian Commonwealth. LC 99-30824. (Significant Issues Ser.). 92p. (C). 1999. pap. text 15.95 (*0-89206-354-8*) CSIS.

Caracciolo, Lucio, et al. What Italy Stands For. LC 97-27648. (Significant Issues Ser.). xxii, 82 p. 1997. pap. 15.95 (*0-89206-325-4*) CSIS.

Caracciolo, Nicola. Uncertain Refuge: Italy & the Jews During the Holocaust. Koffler, Florette R. & Koffler, Richard, eds. & trs. by. LC 94-16156. (Illus.). 224p. 1995. 16.95 (*0-252-06424-0*); text 39.50 (*0-252-01923-7*) U of Ill Pr.

Caracciolo, Shirley D., tr. see Banti, Anna.

Caraceni, T., et al, eds. New Vistas in Parkinson's Disease. (Journal of Neural Transmission: Suppl. 22). (Illus.). 280p. 1986. pap. 68.00 (*0-387-81929-0*) Spr-Verlag.

Carachei, Maria E., tr. see Buckingham, Betty Jo, ed.

Caraco, Edward P. Profile of a Collector: The Collection of Muriel Bultman Francis. LC 85-43432. (Illus.). 132p. 1985. pap. 18.95 (*0-89494-024-4*) New Orleans Mus Art.

Caracostas, Paraskevas, et al. Society, the Endless Frontier: A European Vision of Research & Innovation Policies for the 21st Century. LC 99-196219. (EUR Ser.). 202 p. 1998. write for info. (*92-828-1186-7*, Pub. by Comm Europ Commun) Intl Pubns Serv.

Caradec, F. Dictionary Francais Argotique, Populaire. (FRE.). 1998. 59.95 (*0-320-00254-3*) Fr & Eur.

Caradec, Francois. Dictionnaire du Francais Argotique et Populaire.Tr. of Dictionary of Slang & Polpular French. (FRE.). 255p. 1977. pap. 17.95 (*0-8288-5385-1*, M4968) Fr & Eur.

Caradente, Giovanni, text. Caro at the Trajan Markets, Rome. LC 93-24436. (Illus.). 128p. 1994. 60.00 (*0-87951-525-2*, Pub. by Overlook Pr) Penguin Putnam.

Caradine, Richard W. Federal Advisory Committee Act: Views of Committee Members & Agencies on Federal Advisory Committee Issues. (Illus.). 63p. (C). 1999. pap. text 20.00 (*0-7881-7787-7*) DIANE Pub.

***Caradine, Richard W.** Federal Lobbying: Differences in Lobbying Definitions & Their Impact. (Illus.). 52p. (C). 2000. pap. text 20.00 (*0-7881-8494-6*) DIANE Pub.

Caradja, Catherine. Princess Catherine. 2nd ed. Britt, Dorothy, ed. (Illus.). 212p. 1991. pap. 15.00 (*1-881809-26-9*) Gabriel TX.

Caradoc Of Llancarfan. The Historie of Cambria, Now Called Wales. Lhoyd, H., tr. LC 70-26025. (English Experience Ser.: No. 163). 402p. 1969. reprint ed. 65.00 (*90-221-0163-0*) Walter J Johnson.

Caradon, et al. Greece & Cyprus in History: Essays by Lord Caradon, et al. Koumoulides, John T., ed. (Illus.). 235p. 1985. lib. bdg. 38.50 (*90-256-0905-8*, Pub. by AM Hakkert) Coronet Bks.

C

Caradus, S. R. Calkin Algebras & Algebras of Operators on Banach Spaces. (Lecture Notes in Pure & Applied Mathematics Ser.: Vol. 9). (Illus.). 160p. 1974. pap. text 125.00 (*0-8247-6246-0*) Dekker.

Carafa, Michelle. Le Nozze di Lammermoor, Vol. 2. (Italian Opera 1810-1840 Ser.). 378p. 1986. text 30.00 (*0-8240-6551-4*) Garland.

***Carafano, James Jay.** After D-Day: Operation Cobra & the Normandy Breakout. LC 99-34324. (Art of War Ser.). 295p. 2000. lib. bdg. 55.00 (*1-55587-885-7*) L Rienner.

Caraffa, Sharon. Kitten: Growin' up the Hard Way. LC 93-79923. 304p. 1994. pap. 14.95 (*1-884164-97-8*) Hogan-Ross.

Carafiol, Peter C. Transcendent Reason: James Marsh & the Forms of Romantic Thought. LC 82-13617. xviii, 222p. 1982. 49.95 (*0-8130-0732-1*) U Press Fla.

Carafoli, E. Wing Theory in Supersonic Flow. 1969. 271.00 (*0-08-012330-9*, Pub. by Pergamon Repr) Franklin.

Carafoli, Ernesto. Calcium as Cellular Regulator. LC 97-48843. (Illus.). 656p. 1999. text 150.00 (*0-19-509421-2*) OUP.

***Carafoli, Ernesto & Krebs, J. R., eds.** Calcium Homeostasis. LC 00-39467. (Topics in Biological Inorganic Chemistry Ser.: Vol. 3). (Illus.). x, 198p. 2000. 110.00 (*3-540-67175-7*) Spr-Verlag.

Carafoli, John. Food Photography & Styling: How to Prepare, Light & Photograph Delectable Food & Drinks. LC 92-16258. (Illus.). 144p. 1992. pap. 22.50 (*0-8174-3899-8*, Amphoto) Watsn-Guptill.

Caragata, Patrick J. The Economic & Compliance Consequences of Taxation: A Report on the Health of the Tax System in New Zealand. LC 98-22976. 1998. 120.00 (*0-7923-8185-8*) Kluwer Academic.

Caragata, Warren. Alberta Labour: A Heritage Untold. 162p. 1979. 24.95 (*0-88862-264-3*, Pub. by J Lorimer) Formac Dist Ltd.

Carageorgos, Panayotis. Meditation: On the Iron Testament. LC 99-187126. 60p. 1998. pap. 9.95 (*1-85756-385-9*, Pub. by Janus Pubng) Paul & Co Pubs.

Caragonne, Alexander. The Texas Rangers: Notes from the Architectural Underground. LC 94-27395. (Illus.). 462p. 1995. 52.50 (*0-262-03218-X*) MIT Pr.

Caragonne, Alexander, ed. see Rowe, Colin.

Caragonne, George, jt. auth. see Morrow, Gray.

Caragounis, Chrys. Peter & the Rock. (Beiheft zur Zeitschrift fuer die Alttestamentliche Wissenschaft Ser.: Vol. 58). ix, 157p. 1990. lib. bdg. 49.25 (*3-11-012396-7*) De Gruyter.

Caragounis, Chrys C. The Son of Man: Vision & Interpretation. ix, 310p. 1986. lib. bdg. 87.50 (*3-16-144963-0*, Pub. by JCB Mohr) Coronet Bks.

Caragounis, Chrys C., ed. see Fridrichsen, Anton.

Caraher, Brian G. Wordsworth's "Slumber" & the Problematics of Reading. 288p. 1991. 40.00 (*0-271-00720-6*) Pa St U Pr.

Caraher, Kim. There's a Bat on the Balcony. LC 92-34260. (Voyages Ser.). (Illus.). (J). 1993. 4.25 (*0-383-03660-7*) SRA McGraw.

Caraher, Meg. Second Story Sally. LC 98-223863. 63 p. 1999. write for info. (*0-7608-1931-9*) Sundance Pub.

Caraion, Ion. The Error of Being: Poems. Dorian, M. & Urdang, E. B., trs. from RUM. LC 93-71946. 142p. 1994. pap. 16.95 (*1-85610-030-8*, Pub. by Forest Bks) Dufour.

Caraker, Mary. Elina, Mistress of Laukko: A Novel. LC 97-4377. 160p. 1997. pap. 12.95 (*0-87839-120-7*) North Star.

— Women of the Kalevala: Stories Based on the Great Finnish Epic. LC 96-26021. viii, 120p. 1996. pap. 12.95 (*0-87839-106-1*) North Star.

Caraley, Demetrios. Doing More with Less: Cutback Management in New York City. 160p. (Orig.). pap. 7.00 (*0-910955-01-8*) Columbia U GPPPA.

— The New American Interventionism. LC 99-14696. 320p. 1999. pap. 22.50 (*0-231-11849-X*) Col U Pr.

Caraley, Demetrios, ed. Critical Issues for Clinton's Domestic Agenda. LC 93-74869. 224p. 1994. reprint ed. pap. 19.95 (*1-884853-00-5*) Acad Poli Sci.

Caram, Betsy, ed. see Bailey, Brian J.

Caram, Eva L., ed. see Escandon, Maria, et al.

Caram, Eve. Wintershine: A Book of Maps, Pictures, Laments, Celebrations, Praise. 100p. 1994. pap. 11.95 (*0-911051-74-0*) Plain View.

Caram, Eve L. Dear Corpus Christi. 146p. 1992. pap. 12.95 (*0-911051-59-7*) Plain View.

Caram, Paul, ed. see Bailey, Brian J.

Caram, Paul G., ed. see Bailey, Brian J.

Caramagno, Thomas C. The Flight of the Mind: Virginia Woolf's Art & Manic-Depressive Illness. 1992. 48.00 (*0-520-07280-4*, Pub. by U CA Pr) Cal Prin Full Svc.

— The Flight of the Mind: Virginia Woolf's Art & Manic-Depressive Illness. LC 91-38836. (Illus.). 362p. (C). 1996. pap. 16.95 (*0-520-20504-9*, Pub. by U CA Pr) Cal Prin Full Svc.

Caraman, P. N-Dimensional Quasiconformal Mappings. 554p. 1974. text 146.00 (*0-85626-005-3*) Gordon & Breach.

— Victoria Sobre la Vida Egocentrica.Tr. of Victory over the Self-Centered Life. (SPA.). 94p. pap. 8.99 (*0-7899-0240-0*, 550110) Editorial Unilit.

Caraman, Philip. A Study in Friendship: St. Robert Southwell & Henry Garnet. LC 95-80587. (Studies on Jesuit Topics IV: Series IV, Vol. 16). xii, 124p. (Orig.). 1995. pap. 14.95 (*1-880810-15-8*) Inst Jesuit.

— Tibet: The Jesuit Century. LC 97-72349. (Series IV: Vol. 20). viii, 154p. 1997. pap. 14.95 (*1-880810-29-8*) Inst Jesuit.

Caraman, Philip, tr. see Gerard, John.

***Caramani, Daniele & Mannheim Centre Staff.** Elections in Europe, 1815-1995. (Societies of Europe Ser.). 1120p. 2000. 325.00 incl. cd-rom (*1-56159-243-9*) Groves Dictionaries.

Caramazza, Alfonso. Issues in Reading, Writing & Speaking: A Neuropsychological Perspective. (Neuropsychology & Cognition Ser.). 464p. 1990. text 155.00 (*0-7923-0996-0*) Kluwer Academic.

Caramazza, Alfonso, ed. Cognitive Neuropsychology & Neurolinguistics: Advances in Models of Cognitive Function & Impairment. 312p. 1990. 89.95 (*0-89859-892-3*) L Erlbaum Assocs.

Caramazza, Alfonso & Zurif, Edgar B., eds. Language Acquisition & Language Breakdown: Parallels & Divergencies. LC 77-4789. 351p. reprint ed. pap. 108.90 (*0-7837-2184-6*, 204252200004) Bks Demand.

Caramel, Luciano. Medardo Rosso: Impressions in Wax & Bronze: 1882-1906. Wasilik, Jeanne M. et al, trs. (Illus.). 112p. 1988. 30.00 (*1-878607-03-0*); pap. 25.00 (*1-878607-02-2*) Kent Gallery.

— Towards the Seventies: Art in Italy in the 1970s. 1997. pap. 35.00 (*88-8158-101-9*, Pub. by Charta) Dist Art Pubs.

Caramella, D. Radiologist & the Internet. LC 98-41691. 1998. pap. text 59.00 (*3-540-63151-8*) Spr-Verlag.

Caramello, Charles. Henry James, Gertrude Stein, & the Biographical Act. LC 95-34701. (Illus.). 416p. (C). 1996. text 45.00 (*0-8078-2267-1*) U of NC Pr.

— Silverless Mirrors: Book, Self, & Postmodern American Fiction. LC 83-14841. 1983. pap. 27.95 (*0-8130-0722-4*) U Press Fla.

— Silverless Mirrors: Book, Self & Postmodern American Fiction. LC 83-14841. xi, 250p. 1983. 25.00 (*0-8130-0772-0*) U Press Fla.

Caramia. A Guide for Jazz Piano Harmonization. 24p. 1983. 3.95 (*0-8497-5206-X*, WP95) Kjos.

Caramia, Tony. Folksongs Revisited. (Frances Clark Library for Piano Students). 16p. 1983. pap. text 3.50 (*0-913277-03-7*) Summy-Birchard.

— Six Sketches. Clark, Frances & Goss, Louise, eds. (Frances Clark Presents Ser.). 12p. 1985. pap. text 2.95 (*0-913277-17-7*) Summy-Birchard.

— Sounds of Jazz, Bk. 1. 16p. 1983. pap. text 3.50 (*0-913277-01-0*) Summy-Birchard.

— Sounds of Jazz, Bk. 2. 16p. 1983. pap. text 3.50 (*0-913277-02-9*) Summy-Birchard.

Caramitti, Mario. How to Eat Out in Russia. (Illus.). Date not set. pap. 6.95 (*88-7301-103-9*, Pub. by Gremese Intl) Natl Bk Netwk.

Caran, S. Christopher, jt. auth. see Kutac, Edward A.

Carande, Robert J. Automation in Library Reference Services: A Handbook. LC 92-19417. (Library Management Collection). 208p. 1992. lib. bdg. 59.95 (*0-313-27837-7*, CHU, Greenwood Pr) Greenwood.

— Information Sources for Virtual Reality: A Research Guide. LC 92-45083. 184p. 1993. lib. bdg. 55.00 (*0-313-28804-6*, GR8804, Greenwood Pr) Greenwood.

Carandente, Gionvanni, contrib. by. Marino Marini: Catalogue Raisonne, Sculpture. (Illus.). 384p. 1999. boxed set 90.00 (*88-8118-390-0*, Pub. by Skira IT) Abbeville Pr.

Carandente, Giouanni. Alexander Calder's Teodelapio at Spoleto. 1996. pap. 29.95 (*88-8158-075-6*, Pub. by Charta) Dist Art Pubs.

— Mark Di Suvero in Venice. (Illus.). 52p. 1996. pap. text 29.95 (*88-8158-035-7*, Pub. by Charta) Dist Art Pubs.

Carandente, Giovanni & Dupin, Jacques. Calder: With Eight Original Lithographs. (Illus.). 24p. 1968. pap. 300.00 (*1-55660-138-7*) A Wofsy Fine Arts.

Caranfa, Angelo. Camille Claudel: A Sculpture of Interior Solitude. LC 98-28188. (Illus.). 214p. 1999. 39.50 (*0-8387-5391-4*) Bucknell U Pr.

— Claudel: Beauty & Grace. LC 87-47982. (Illus.). 192p. 1989. 29.50 (*0-8387-5134-2*) Bucknell U Pr.

— Proust: The Creative Silence. LC 88-43408. (Illus.). 208p. 1990. 36.50 (*0-8387-5165-2*) Bucknell U Pr.

Caranfa, Angelo, jt. ed. see Gendreau, Francis R.

Carangelo, Bob. Common Sense vs. Common Thinking: Two Men from Nowhere. Carangelo, Richard M., ed. (Illus.). 60p. (Orig.). 1995. pap. 5.95 (*0-9650601-0-1*) Deerwood Pr.

— Ignorance Can Be Cured But Stupid Is Forever: More on Common Sense. Date not set. pap. 25.00 (*0-9650601-4-4*) Deerwood Pr.

Carangelo, Lori. Adopt-a-Quote: Bridging the Adoption Experience. 50p. 2000. pap. 9.95 (*0-942605-04-7*) Access Pr CA.

***Carangelo, Lori.** Angels A to Z... The Heavenly & Earthly Kind. (Illus.). 144p. 1999. pap. 12.95 (*0-942605-06-3*) Access Pr CA.

— Better Than Sex Italian Take-Out Cookbook: Eat in Or Out-- Italian Restaurants, Worldwide, Share Their Recipe Secrets. (Illus.). 300p. 2000. pap. 24.95 (*0-942605-15-2*) Access Pr CA.

Carangelo, Lori. Born Losers: Billion Dollar Babies in America's Foster Care, Adoption & Prison Systems. rev. ed. (Illus.). 250p. 1999. pap. 19.95 (*0-942605-07-1*) Access Pr CA.

***Carangelo, Lori.** Chosen Children: Adoptees & Others in Prison Tell Their Stories. 200p. 2000. pap. 16.95 (*0-942605-11-X*) Access Pr CA.

— 8 Ball Cafe: True Tale of Two Adoptions, Addictions, Incarcerations & Resurrections. (Illus.). 150p. 2000. pap. 12.95 (*0-942605-10-1*) Access Pr CA.

Carangelo, Lori. Homestyle Italian Cooking. LC 97-11511. (Homestyle Cooking Ser.). (Illus.). 192p. 1997. pap. 16.95 (*0-89594-867-2*) Crossing Pr.

***Carangelo, Lori.** No Remorse: The Untold Story of a Parent Killer. 150p. 2000. pap. 12.95 (*0-942605-13-6*) Access Pr CA.

Carangelo, Lori. The Ultimate Search Book: Worldwide Adoption & Vital Records (1999 Edition) 3rd rev. ed. LC 96-86225. Orig. Title: Ultimate Search Book: What Government & Search Books Don't Want You to Know. 291p. 1998. pap. 29.95 (*1-877677-85-X*, A0075, Precision Index) Herit Quest.

***Carangelo, Lori.** The Ultimate Search Book 2000 Edition: Worldwide Adoption, Genealogy & Other Search Secrets. rev. ed. LC 98-86225. (Illus.). 300p. 2000. pap. 29.95 (*0-942605-12-8*) Access Pr CA.

***Carangelo, Lori, ed.** Statistics of Adoption 2000 Edition. 50p. 2000. pap. 9.95 (*0-942605-05-5*) Access Pr CA.

Carangelo, Lori, ed. see Reyburn, Stanley S.

Carangelo, Lori, ed. see Turkington, Cleil.

Carangelo, Richard M., ed. see Carangelo, Bob.

Carapetis, Steve, et al. The Road Maintenance Initiative: Building Capacity for Policy Reform: Report on the Policy Seminars. (EDI Seminar Ser.: Vol. 1). 106p. 1991. pap. 22.00 (*0-8213-1859-4*, 11859) World Bank.

***Carapezza, Edward M., et al, eds.** Unattended Ground Sensor Technologies & Applications. 280p. 1999. pap. text 72.00 (*0-8194-3187-7*) SPIE.

***Carapezza, Edward M. & Law, David B., eds.** Sensors, C3I, Information & Training Technologies for Law Enforcement. LC 99-229020. 394p. 1999. pap. text 89.00 (*0-8194-3043-9*) SPIE.

Carapezza, Edward M., jt. ed. see Spector, Donald.

Carapico, Sheila. Civil Society in Yemen: The Political Economy of Activism in Modern Arabia. LC 97-23259. (Middle East Studies: No. 9). 256p. (C). 1998. text 59.95 (*0-521-59098-1*) Cambridge U Pr.

Caras. The Trashing of America. 1992. write for info. (*0-201-52367-1*) Addison-Wesley.

Caras, Paul. Buddhism & Its Christian Critics. 316p. (C). 1987. 29.00 (*81-85132-01-1*) S Asia.

Caras, Roger. New Treasury of Cat Stories. 512p. 1997. 27.00 (*0-88486-172-4*, Bristol Park Bks) Arrowood Pr.

— A Perfect Harmony: The Intertwining Lives of Animals & Humans Throughout History. 272p. 1997. per. 12.00 (*0-684-83531-2*, Fireside) S&S Trade Pap.

— The Roger Caras Dog Book. 3rd ed. (Illus.). 320p. 1996. 21.95 (*0-87131-814-8*); pap. 14.95 (*0-87131-799-0*) M Evans.

— Roger Caras' Treasury of Great Cat Stories. 512p. 1990. 9.98 (*0-88365-763-5*) Galahad Bks.

— Roger Caras' Treasury of Great Dog Stories. 512p. 1990. 9.98 (*0-88365-764-3*) Galahad Bks.

— Roger Caras Treasury of Great Fishing Stories. 544p. 1996. 27.00 (*0-88486-142-2*, Bristol Park Bks) Arrowood Pr.

Caras, Roger. Roger Caras' Treasury of Great Horse Stories. 512p. 1993. 9.98 (*0-88365-840-2*) Galahad Bks.

Caras, Roger, ed. Roger Caras' Treasury of Classic Nature Tales. 528p. 1997. 10.99 (*1-57866-009-2*) Galahad Bks.

— Roger Caras' Treasury of Great Horse Stories. 512p. 1994. pap. 15.95 (*0-452-27307-2*, Truman Talley) St Martin.

Caras, Roger & Kirk, Robert W. Harper Illustrated Handbook Of Dogs. LC 85-1330. (Illus.). 319p. 1992. pap. 23.00 (*0-06-273164-5*) HarpC.

— Harper's Illustrated Handbook of Cats. (Illus.). 191p. 1992. pap. 16.00 (*0-06-273165-3*) HarpC.

Caras, Roger A. The Bond: People & Their Animals. LC 97-17616. (Illus.). 144p. 1997. 29.50 (*0-684-83082-5*) Simon & Schuster.

— Cat Is Watching: A Look at the Way Cats See Us. 240p. 1997. 7.99 (*0-88365-965-6*) Galahad Bks.

— The Cats of Thistle Hill: A Mostly Peaceable Kingdom. LC 93-42775. 240p. 1994. 22.00 (*0-671-75462-9*) S&S Trade.

— A Dog Is Listening: The Way Some of Our Closest Friends View Us. 240p. 1998. 7.99 (*1-57866-017-3*) Galahad Bks.

— A Dog Is Listening: The Way Some of Our Closest Friends View Us. (Illus.). 240p. 1993. pap. 12.00 (*0-671-79726-3*, Fireside) S&S Trade Pap.

— A Most Dangerous Journal. 1999. pap. 4.99 (*0-14-038227-5*) Viking Penguin.

***Caras, Roger A.** New Roger Caras Treasury of Great Cat Stories. 512p. 2000. 11.99 (*1-57866-098-X*) Galahad Bks.

Caras, Roger A. A Perfect Harmony. 256p. 1996. 22.50 (*0-684-81100-6*) S&S Trade.

***Caras, Roger A.** The Road to Westminister. 256p. 2001. 25.95 (*0-446-52644-4*) Warner Bks.

Caras, Roger A. Roger Caras' Treasury of Great Fishing Stories. 1998. pap. 13.95 (*0-88486-190-2*, Bristol Park Bks) Arrowood Pr.

***Caras, Roger A.** Roger Caras Treasury of Great Fishing Stories. 544p. 1999. 10.99 (*1-57866-052-1*) Galahad Bks.

Caras, Roger A., ed. Harper's Illustrated Handbook of Dogs. (Illus.). (Orig.). 1988. write for info. (*0-318-63753-7*) Chanticleer.

Caras, Roger A., intro. Roger Caras' Treasury of Great Dog Stories. 512p. 1988. pap. 12.50 (*0-525-48428-0*, 01212-360, Truman Talley) St Martin.

Carasa Collective Staff. Women under Attack: Victories, Backlash & the Fight for Reproductive Freedom. Davis, Susan E., ed. LC 88-26350. 80p. 1988. pap. 5.00 (*0-89608-356-X*) South End Pr.

Carasik, Anne. Linux System Administration. LC QA76.76.O63C3729. 480p. 1998. pap. text 39.99 (*0-7645-7008-0*, M&T Bks) IDG Bks.

— UNIX Secure Shell. 1999. pap., student ed. 39.99 (*0-07-134933-2*) McGraw.

Carasik, Anne. Unix Secure Shell Tools. 29.99 (*0-07-212273-0*) McGraw.

Carasso, C., et al, eds. Nonlinear Hyperbolic Problems. (Lecture Notes in Mathematics Ser.: Vol. 1270). 341p. 1987. pap. 47.90 (*0-387-18200-4*) Spr-Verlag.

— Nonlinear Hyperbolic Problems. (Lecture Notes in Mathematics Ser.: Vol. 1402). 255p. 1989. 37.30 (*0-387-51746-4*) Spr-Verlag.

Carasso, M. & Becker, Martin, eds. Solar Thermal Central Receiver Systems Vol. 3: Performance Evaluation Standards for Solar Central Receivers. 150p. 1991. 47.95 (*0-387-53270-6*) Spr-Verlag.

Carath Eodory, Constantin. Conformal Representation. LC 97-47129. 1998. pap. 6.95 (*0-486-40028-X*) Dover.

Carathanassis, Mani. Expert MVS-ESA JCL: Guide to Advanced Techniques. 1991. 60.00 (*0-07-009820-4*) McGraw.

Caratheodory, Constantin. Algebraic Theory of Measure & Integration. 2nd ed. Finsler, P. et al, eds. Linton, Fred E., tr. from GER. LC 63-13094. 378p. (C). 1986. 27.50 (*0-8284-0161-6*) Chelsea Pub.

— Calculus of Variations & Partial Differential Equations of the First Order. 2nd ed. LC 81-71519. (Illus.). 421p. 1982. text 29.50 (*0-8284-0318-X*) Chelsea Pub.

— Theory of Functions, 1. 2nd ed. LC 60-16838. 22.95 (*0-8284-0097-0*) Chelsea Pub.

— Theory of Functions, 2. 2nd ed. LC 60-16838. 24.95 (*0-8284-0106-3*) Chelsea Pub.

— Vorlesungen Ueber Reelle Funktionen. 3rd ed. LC 63-11321. 1968. 29.50 (*0-8284-0038-5*) Chelsea Pub.

Caratini, Roger. Dictionnaire des Decouvertes. (FRE.). 486p. 1990. 115.00 (*0-7859-8136-5*, 2863913522) Fr & Eur.

— Dictionnaire des Personnages de la Revolution. (FRE.). 575p. 1988. 79.95 (*0-7859-7943-3*, 2714422322) Fr & Eur.

— Larousse Dictionnaire des Nationalites et des Minorites de L'Ex-URSS. (FRE.). 255p. 1992. pap. 29.95 (*0-7859-7687-6*, 2037202636) Fr & Eur.

Caratini, Roger, ed. Sciences Sociales 1. (FRE.). 160p. 1971. 49.95 (*0-8288-6478-0*, M-6510) Fr & Eur.

— Sciences Sociales 2: Linguistique. (FRE.). 160p. 1971. 49.95 (*0-8288-6479-9*, M-6511) Fr & Eur.

Caratozzolo, Marie & Abrams, Joanne, eds. The No-Time-to-Cook Cookbook: Fabulous Dishes for Today's Fast-Paced Lifestyle. LC 98-36064. (Illus.). 240p. Date not set. 19.95 (*0-89529-859-7*, Avery) Penguin Putnam.

Caratti, G., jt. auth. see Rasmussen, B.

Caratti, G., jt. auth. see Van Overstraeten, R. J.

Caratzas, Stam C. Les Tzacones. (Supplementa Byzantina Ser.: Vol. 4). (C). 1976. 392.35 (*3-11-004799-3*) De Gruyter.

Caraulia, Algene & Steiger, Linda. Nonviolent Crisis Intervention: Learning to Defuse Explosive Behavior. Wyka, Eugene T. & Christensen, Sandra, eds. LC 97-156982. 139p. 1997. text 59.00 (*0-9651733-2-1*) Crisis Prevent.

Caravaggio, Jean. Cervantes. (SPA., Illus.). 431p. 1998. 24.95 (*84-239-9915-7*, Pub. by Espasa Calpe) Continental Bk.

Caravale, G. A., ed. Marx & Modern Economic Analysis, 2 vols., Set. (Illus.). 538p. 1991. text 215.00 (*1-85278-435-0*) E Elgar.

Caravale, Giovanni. Equilibrium & Economic Theory. LC 96-33541. 216p. (C). 1997. 80.00 (*0-415-14299-7*) Routledge.

Caravale, Giovanni A. & Tosato, Domenico A. Ricardo & the Theory of Value Distribution & Growth. (Modern Revivals in Economics Ser.). (C). 1993. text 61.95 (*0-7512-0257-6*, Pub. by Gregg Revivals) Ashgate Pub Co.

Caravan, Jill. American Barns: A Pictorial History. LC 93-87595. (Illus.). 80p. 1995. 12.98 (*1-56138-471-2*, Courage) Running Pr.

— American Country Churches: A Pictorial History. LC 96-69268. (Illus.). 80p. 1996. 12.98 (*1-56138-789-4*, Courage) Running Pr.

— American Covered Bridges: A Pictorial History. (Illus.). 80p. 1995. 12.98 (*1-56138-472-0*, Courage) Running Pr.

— American Lighthouses: A Pictorial History. LC 96-68393. (Illus.). 80p. 1996. 12.98 (*1-56138-788-6*, Courage) Running Pr.

— Identification Guide to Cat Breeds. (Illus.). 96p. 1996. write for info. (*1-57215-149-8*) World Pubns.

— You're OK, Your Cat's OK. 1992. 12.98 (*1-55521-816-4*) Bk Sales Inc.

— You're OK, Your Dog's OK. 1992. 12.98 (*1-55521-817-2*) Bk Sales Inc.

Caravatta, Michael. Let's Work Smarter, Not Harder: How to Engage Your Entire Organization in the Execution of Change. LC 97-3241. 283p. 1997. pap. 32.00 (*0-87389-386-7*, H0975) ASQ Qual Pr.

Caravelis, Georges. European Monetary Union: An Application of the Fundamental Principles of Monetary Theory. LC 94-8707. 320p. 1994. 77.95 (*1-85628-885-4*, Pub. by Avebry) Ashgate Pub Co.

***Caravella, Frank J.** The Execution of Lieutenant Edy Haller. LC 99-91118. 1999. 25.00 (*0-7388-0622-6*); pap. 18.00 (*0-7388-0623-4*) Xlibris Corp.

Caravella, Jack, ed. see Abrams, Sandy, et al.

Caravella, Jack, ed. see Virtue, Doreen L.

Caravella, Lorenzo. Mouth of God. 1999. pap. text 21.95 (*1-887472-07-X*) Sunstar Pubng.

Caraw, Peggy & Deming, Vasudha K. The Big Book of Customer Service Training Games: Quick, Fun Activities for Training Customer Service Reps, & Anyone Else Who Deals with Customers. (Illus.). 224p. 1998. pap. 17.95 (*0-07-077974-0*) McGraw.

Carawan, Candie, jt. auth. see Carawan, Guy.

Carawan, Candie, jt. ed. see Carawan, Guy.

Carawan, Edwin. Rhetoric & the Law of Draco. 428p. 1998. text 95.00 (*0-19-815086-5*) OUP.

Carawan, Guy & Carawan, Candie. Voices from the Mountains. LC 96-19867. 1996. pap. 24.95 (*0-8203-1882-5*) U of Ga Pr.

Carawan, Guy & Carawan, Candie, eds. Ain't You Got a Right to the Tree of Life? The People of Johns Island, South Carolina - Their Faces, Their Words & Their Songs. enl. rev. ed. LC 89-4846. (Brown Thrasher Bks.). (Illus.). 256p. 1994. reprint ed. pap. 22.50 (*0-8203-1643-1*) U of Ga Pr.

— Sing for Freedom: The Story of the Civil Rights Movement Through Its Songs. (Illus.). 312p. 1990. reprint ed. pap. 14.95 (*0-9626704-4-8*); reprint ed. lib. bdg. 39.95 (*0-9626704-5-6*) Sing Out.

Caraway, Caren. African Designs from the Congo, Nigeria, the Cameroons & the Guinea Coast. (International Design Library). (Illus.). 144p. (Orig.). 1987. pap. 15.95 (*0-88045-093-2*) Stemmer Hse.

— African Designs of Nigeria & the Cameroons. (International Design Library). (Illus.). 48p. (Orig.). 1984. pap. 5.95 (*0-88045-060-6*) Stemmer Hse.

— African Designs of the Congo. (International Design Library). (Illus.). 48p. (Orig.). 1986. pap. 5.95 (*0-88045-083-5*) Stemmer Hse.

— African Designs of the Guinea Coast. (International Design Library). (Illus.). 48p. (Orig.). 1985. pap. 5.95 (*0-88045-064-9*) Stemmer Hse.

— Applique Quilts. (International Design Library). (Illus.). 56p. (Orig.). 1981. pap. 5.95 (*0-916144-78-X*) Stemmer Hse.

— Aztec & Other Mexican Indian Designs. 4th ed. LC 90-101016. (International Design Library). (Illus.). 48p. 1984. pap. 6.95 (*0-88045-051-7*, Intl Design) Stemmer Hse.

— Designs of the South Pacific. (International Design Library). (Illus.). 48p. (Orig.). 1983. pap. 5.95 (*0-88045-036-3*) Stemmer Hse.

— Eastern Woodland Indian Designs. (International Design Library). (Illus.). 48p. (Orig.). 1984. pap. 5.95 (*0-88045-057-6*) Stemmer Hse.

— Hawaiian & Easter Island Designs. (International Design Library). (Illus.). 48p. (Orig.). 1985. pap. 5.95 (*0-88045-071-1*) Stemmer Hse.

— The Mayan Design Book. (International Design Library). (Illus.). 56p. 1981. pap. 6.95 (*0-916144-80-1*) Stemmer Hse.

— The Mola Design Book. 5th ed. (International Design Library). (Illus.). 48p. 1981. pap. 6.95 (*0-916144-71-2*, Naturencyclop) Stemmer Hse.

— Native American Designs: Collected Edition. (International Design Library). (Illus.). 240p. (Orig.). 1993. pap. 27.95 (*0-88045-125-4*) Stemmer Hse.

— Northwest Indian Designs. 5th ed. (International Design Library). (Illus.). 48p. 1982. pap. 6.95 (*0-916144-98-4*, Naturencyclop) Stemmer Hse.

— Peruvian Textile Designs. (International Design Library). (Illus.). 48p. 1983. pap. 5.95 (*0-88045-026-6*) Stemmer Hse.

— Pieced Quilts. (International Design Library). (Illus.). 48p. (Orig.). 1981. pap. 5.95 (*0-916144-79-8*) Stemmer Hse.

— Plains Indian Designs. (International Design Library). (Illus.). 48p. (Orig.). 1984. pap. 5.95 (*0-88045-050-9*) Stemmer Hse.

— Southeast Asian Textile Designs. (International Design Library). (Illus.). 48p. (Orig.). 1983. pap. 5.95 (*0-88045-034-7*) Stemmer Hse.

— Southeastern Woodland Indian Designs. (International Design Library). (Illus.). 48p. (Orig.). 1985. pap. 5.95 (*0-88045-072-X*) Stemmer Hse.

— Southwest American Indian Designs. 4th ed. (International Design Library). (Illus.). 48p. 1983. pap. 5.95 (*0-88045-035-5*, Intl Design) Stemmer Hse.

Caraway, Hattie W. Silent Hattie Speaks: The Personal Journal of Senator Hattie Caraway, 9. Kincaid, Diane D., ed. LC 78-22136. (Contributions in Women's Studies: No. 9). (Illus.). 151p. 1979. 49.95 (*0-313-20820-4*, KSI/, Greenwood Pr) Greenwood.

Caraway, James E. Whitehead's Philosophical Theology. 284p. 1997. pap. 17.00 (*1-883058-63-5*, Inst of Global) Global Pubns.

Caraway, James E., ed. Mediterranean Perspectives: Literature, Social Studies & Philosophy. (Mediterranean Perspectives Ser.). 176p. 1996. pap. 17.00 (*1-883058-20-1*, Dowling College) Global Pubns.

— Mediterranean Perspectives: Philosophy, Literature, History, & Art. (Mediterranean Perspectives Ser.). 217p. 1997. pap. 17.00 (*1-883058-38-4*, Dowling College) Global Pubns.

Caraway, Jane. One Windy Day. (Ready-Set-Read Ser.). (Illus.). 32p. (J). (ps-3). 1990. lib. bdg. 21.40 (*0-8172-3579-5*) Raintree Steck-V.

— One Windy Day. 28p. (J). (ps-3). 1995. pap. text 4.95 (*0-8114-6744-9*) Raintree Steck-V.

Caraway, Nancie. Segregated Sisterhood: Racism & the Politics of American Feminism. LC 91-2528. 296p. (C). 1991. 42.50 (*0-87049-719-7*); pap. text 19.95 (*0-87049-720-0*) U of Tenn Pr.

Caray, Skip, jt. auth. see Farmer, Don.

Carayon, Pascale, ed. A Special Issue of The International Journal of Human-Computer Interaction. 147p. 1998. pap. write for info. (*0-8058-9847-6*) L Erlbaum Assocs.

***Carbado, Devon, ed.** Black Men on Race, Gender, & Sexuality: A Critical Reader. LC 98-31404. (Critical America Ser.). 400p. 1999. text 65.00 (*0-8147-1552-4*) NYU Pr.

Carbado, Devon, ed. Black Men on Race, Gender & Sexuality: A Critical Reader. LC 98-31404. (Critical America Ser.). 400p. 1999. pap. 24.95 (*0-8147-1553-2*) NYU Pr.

Carbajal, Arias. Plantas Medicinales.Tr. of Healing Plants. 215p. (Orig.). 1997. pap. text 6.98 (*968-15-0735-5*) Ed Mex.

***Carbajal, Brent J.** The Veracity of Disguise in Selected Works of Jose Donoso: Illusory Deception. LC 00-24541. (Hispanic Literature Ser.: 55). 128p. 2000. 59.95 (*0-7734-7752-7*) E Mellen.

Carbajal, Greg, jt. ed. see Haberman, Lawrence.

Carbajal, Greg, jt. illus. see Haberman, Lawrence.

Carbajal, Xavier J. The Jesus Machine. unabridged ed. Jodway, Sherry, ed. 296p. (Orig.). 1997. pap. 5.99 (*0-9654507-1-6*, 7154) New Future Pub.

— Lady President. unabridged ed. Jodway, Sherry L., ed. LC 97-92604. 340p. 1997. 24.95 (*0-9654507-0-8*) New Future Pub.

Carbajal, Xavier J. & Jodway, Sherry L., eds. Captain Nemo, Vol. 13. unabridged ed. LC TXU 612 429. xv, 413p. 1996. pap. 4.99 (*0-9654507-5-9*, 13048) New Future Pub.

— Captain Nemo, Vol. 16. unabridged ed. LC TXU 612 429. xv, 413p. 1996. 24.95 (*0-9654507-4-0*, 13048) New Future Pub.

Carbajal, Xavier J. & Malia, Joe H. Horizontal Rain, Vol. 1. unabridged ed. Jodway, Sherry L., ed. 340p. 1998. 24.95 (*0-9654507-9-1*, 13057) New Future Pub.

Carbajo, Antonio. Expresiones Idiomaticas. (SPA.). 1997. pap. 8.98 (*968-13-2053-0*, Pub. by Edit Diana) Libros Fronteras.

Carball. Apocalipsis.Tr. of Revelation. (SPA.). 496p. 1998. pap. 15.99 (*0-8254-1107-6*) Kregel.

Carballido, Emilio. La Caja Vacia (The Empty Box) (SPA.). 151p. 1974. pap. 6.99 (*968-16-1085-7*, Pub. by Fondo) Continental Bk.

— Un Enorme Animal Nube (The Enormous Animal Cloud) (SPA.). (J). (gr. 1-3). 1994. 12.99 (*968-16-4231-7*, Pub. by Fondo) Continental Bk.

***Carballido, Emilio.** Felicidad. Gann, Myra S., ed. & intro. by. (SPA.). 110p. (C). 1999. pap. text 15.00 (*0-9643288-2-8*) Danzon Pr.

Carballido, Emilio. La Historia de Sputnik y David (The Story of Sputnik & David) (SPA., Illus.). 48p. (J). (gr. 3-4). 1992. reprint ed. pap. 5.99 (*968-16-3678-3*, Pub. by Fondo) Continental Bk.

— Loros en Emergencias (Parrots in Danger) (SPA., Illus.). 46p. (J). (gr. 5-6). 1993. pap. 5.99 (*968-16-4230-9*, Pub. by Fondo) Continental Bk.

— The Norther. LC 68-54901. (Texas Pan-American Ser.). Orig. Title: El Norte. (Illus.). 101p. reprint ed. pap. 31.40 (*0-8357-7753-7*, 203611100002) Bks Demand.

— Orinoco, Rosa de Dos Aromas y Otras Piezas Dramaticas (Orinoco, Rose of Two Fragrances & Other Dramatic Pieces) (SPA.). 270p. 1994. pap. 8.99 (*968-16-4161-2*, Pub. by Fondo) Continental Bk.

— Rosalba y los Llaveros, y Otras Obras de Teatro (Rosalba & the Jailers, & Other Plays) (SPA.). 208p. 1984. pap. 7.99 (*968-16-1615-4*, Pub. by Fondo) Continental Bk.

— Teatro de Carballido (The Theater of Carballido) (SPA.). 273p. 1976. pap. 8.99 (*968-16-0963-8*, Pub. by Fondo) Continental Bk.

— El Tren Que Corria (The Train That Ran) (SPA., Illus.). 144p. 1984. pap. 5.99 (*968-16-1652-9*, Pub. by Fondo) Continental Bk.

***Carballo, Arles.** In the Shadow of Gleam. large type ed. Koenigsberg, Linda, ed. 165p. 1999. 23.95 (*0-9672603-0-2*) Carbapress.

***Carballo, Arles, et al.** In the Shadow of Gleam. 2nd ed. 218p. 2000. 23.95 (*0-9672603-1-0*) Carbapress.

Carballo, Carl D. Eskomos - Their Health, Activities & Behavior: Index of New Information. 150p. 1998. 47.50 (*0-7883-2030-0*); pap. 44.50 (*0-7883-2031-9*) ABBE Pubs Assn.

Carballo, M., jt. ed. see Bankowski, Z.

Carballo, Manuel & Bane, Mary J., eds. The State & the Poor in the Nineteen Eighties. 328p. (C). 1984. 49.95 (*0-86569-064-2*, T064, Auburn Hse) Greenwood.

Carballosa, Cosette A. Mi Infancia en Cuba: (Lo Visto y Lo Vivido Por una Nina de Doce Anos) LC 96-83524. (Coleccion Cuba y Sus Jueces). (SPA.). 122p. (Orig.). 1996. pap. 13.00 (*0-89729-796-2*) Ediciones.

Carballosa, Evis L. Colosenses. (SPA.). 176p. 1996. pap. 8.99 (*0-8254-1106-8*, Edit Portavoz) Kregel.

— Daniel y el Reino Mesianico. 288p. 1979. pap. 9.99 (*0-8254-1101-7*, Edit Portavoz) Kregel.

— La Deidad de Cristo. (SPA.). 176p. 1982. mass mkt. 5.25 (*0-8254-1102-5*, Edit Portavoz) Kregel.

— El Dictador del Futuro. (SPA.). 96p. 1978. mass mkt. 3.99 (*0-8254-1103-3*, Edit Portavoz) Kregel.

— Filipenses: Un Comentario Exegetico y Practico. Orig. Title: Phillippians: Commentary. (SPA.). 128p. 1991. pap. 6.99 (*0-8254-1104-1*, Edit Portavoz) Kregel.

— Romanos. (SPA.). 352p. 1994. pap. 11.99 (*0-8254-1105-X*, Edit Portavoz) Kregel.

— Santiago: Una Fe en Accion. (SPA.). 352p. (Orig.). 1986. pap. 11.99 (*0-8254-1112-2*, Edit Portavoz) Kregel.

Carbarga, Leslie. Trademark Designs of the '20s. 112p. 1991. pap. 7.95 (*0-486-26858-6*) Dover.

Carbarga, Leslie, compiled by. Borders, Vol. 4. LC 91-70262. 64p. 1991. pap. text 7.95 (*0-88108-086-1*) Art Dir.

Carbato, Charles E. Bouger Gravity Anomalies of the San Fernando Valley, California. LC 65-63511. (University of California Publications in Social Welfare: Vol. 46, No. 1). 49p. reprint ed. pap. 30.00 (*0-8357-7363-9*, 201179200080) Bks Demand.

Carbaugh. Contemporary Economics: An Application. LC 99-57845. 2000. pap. 41.00 (*0-324-00216-5*) Sth-Wstrn College.

***Carbaugh.** Contemporary Economics: An Applicatons Approach. 2000. pap. 17.50 (*0-324-02439-8*) Sth-Wstrn College.

— International Economics. 7th ed. LC 98-51511. 30p. 1999. pap. 91.95 (*0-324-00108-8*) Thomson Learn.

— International Economics. 8th ed. (SWC-Economics Ser.). 2001. pap. 25.95 (*0-324-05590-0*) Sth-Wstrn College.

— International Economics. 8th ed. (SWC-Economics Ser.). (C). 2001. text 63.50 (*0-324-05589-7*) Sth-Wstrn College.

Carbaugh, Donal. Situating Selves: The Communication of Social Identities in American Scenes. LC 95-16183. (SUNY Series, Human Communication Processes). 238p. (C). 1996. text 59.50 (*0-7914-2827-3*); pap. text 19.95 (*0-7914-2828-1*) State U NY Pr.

— Talking American: Cultural Discourses on Donahue. Dervin, Brenda, ed. LC 88-10455. (Communication & Information Science Ser.). 272p. 1988. pap. 39.50 (*0-89391-477-0*); text 73.25 (*0-89391-492-4*) Ablx Pub.

Carbaugh, Donal, ed. Cultural Communication & Intercultural Contact. 456p. (C). 1990. pap. 45.00 (*0-8058-0727-6*); text 125.00 (*0-8058-0167-7*) L Erlbaum Assocs.

Carbaugh, Ella M. Come into My Garden. 69p. 1994. pap. 6.95 (*0-9642705-0-1*) E M Carbaugh.

Carbaugh, Gary & Spurr, Dick. Colorado Reel & Old Fishing Tackle: A Collector's Guide. 128p. 1994. pap. 16.00 (*1-882418-14-X*) Centenn Pubns.

***Carbaugh, Marsha Wilson.** The Barbour Collection of Connecticut Town Vital Records Vol. 21: Killingworth 1667-1850, Ledyard 1836-1855, Lisbon 1786-1850. White, Lorraine C., ed. 244p. 1999. pap. 25.00 (*0-8063-1598-9*) Genealog Pub.

Carbaugh, Robert. International Economics. 5th ed. (HB - Economics Ser.). 1994. text, suppl. ed. 36.95 (*0-538-84444-2*) S-W Pub.

— International Economics. 5th ed. (HB - Economics Ser.). 1994. mass mkt., student ed. 22.95 (*0-538-84443-4*) S-W Pub.

— International Economics. 6th ed. LC 97-5123. (Hv - International Economics Ser.). 1997. mass mkt. 64.95 (*0-538-86641-1*); mass mkt., student ed. 19.95 (*0-538-86642-X*) S-W Pub.

Carbaugh, Robert J. International Economics. 2nd ed. (SWC-Economics). 349p. (C). 1984. mass mkt. 36.00 (*0-534-03831-X*) S-W Pub.

— International Economics. 3rd ed. (SWC-Economics). 340p. (C). 1988. mass mkt. 44.50 (*0-534-09414-7*) S-W Pub.

— International Economics. 5th ed. LC 94-13411. (C). 1994. pap. 74.69 (*0-538-84427-2*) S-W Pub.

Carbaugh, Robert J. & Fan, Liang-Shing. The International Monetary System: History, Institutions, Analyses. LC 75-38829. vii, 168p. 1976. 19.95 (*0-7006-0141-4*) U Pr of KS.

***Carbbo, Rambon.** Molecular Quantum Similarity in QSAR & Drug Design. LC 00-41287. (Lecture Notes in Chemistry Ser.). (Illus.). 2000. pap. write for info. (*3-540-67581-7*) Spr-Verlag.

***Carbeck, Hank.** MCSE Guide to Frontpage 2000. (Networking Ser.). (C). 2000. text 45.00 (*0-619-01568-3*) Course Tech.

Carbeck, Hank. Thompson's Introduction to Maternity & Pediatric Nursing. 3rd ed. Wood, Terri, ed. LC 98-38331. (Illus.). 1008p. (C). 1998. text 44.95 (*0-7216-7557-3*, W B Saunders Co) Harcrt Hlth Sci Grp.

Carberry, Ed, ed. Communicating Stock Options: Practical Tips & Techniques for Communicating Stock Options to Employees. 184p. (Orig.). 1999. pap. write for info. (*0-926902-52-0*) NCEO.

Carberry, Ann. Alice & the Gunfighter. 368p. (Orig.). 1996. mass mkt. 5.50 (*0-380-77882-3*, Avon Bks) Morrow Avon.

— Frannie & the Charmer. (Four Roses Ser.: No. 2). 384p. (Orig.). 1996. mass mkt. 4.99 (*0-380-77881-5*, Avon Bks) Morrow Avon.

***Carberry, Ann.** Frontier Bride. large type ed. 368p. 1999. 31.99 (*0-7089-4095-1*, Linford) Ulverscroft.

Carberry, Ann. Maggie & the Gambler. 384p. (Orig.). 1995. mass mkt. 4.99 (*0-380-77880-7*, Avon Bks) Morrow Avon.

***Carberry, Ann.** Nevada Heat. large type ed. 416p. 1999. 31.99 (*0-7089-4130-3*) Ulverscroft.

Carberry, Ann. The Scoundrel. 352p. (Orig.). 1995. mass mkt. 5.50 (*0-515-11705-6*, Jove) Berkley Pub.

Carberry, Charles M., et al. Money Laundering: Reporting & Regulatory Requirements. 1993. ring bd. 35.00 (*0-317-05404-X*, 00621) NY Law Pub.

Carberry, Edward. Glassblowing: An Introduction to Artistic & Scientific Flameworking. rev. ed. LC 88-62399. (Illus.). 230p. (C). 1994. spiral bd. 48.95 (*0-9601682-6-5*) MGLS Inc.

— Glassblowing: An Introduction to Artistic & Scientific Flameworking. 2nd rev. ed. LC 88-62399. (Illus.). 230p. (C). 1994. 68.95 (*0-9601682-7-3*) MGLS Inc.

Carberry, Edward & Eliason, Robert. Everyday Chemicals. 2nd ed. LC 89-85613. (Illus.). iv, 114p. (C). 1989. pap. text 14.95 (*0-685-29170-7*) Bluestem Chemicals.

— Food for Thought. 2nd ed. LC 89-85614. (Illus.). iv, 144p. (C). 1989. pap. text 16.95 (*0-685-29169-3*) Bluestem Chemicals.

Carberry, Edward J. Corporate Governance in Employee - Ownership Companies, 31p. (Orig.). 1996. pap. 15.00 (*0-926902-30-X*) NCEO.

Carberry, H. D. It Takes a Mighty Fire. Baugh, Edward, ed. LC 97-198283. 70p. 1997. pap. 15.00 (*976-8100-80-X*, Pub. by Ian Randle) Paul & Co Pubs.

Carberry, J. C. Cobol. (Computers & Their Applications Ser.). 1986. text 36.95 (*0-470-20755-8*) P-H.

***Carberry, J. W. & Tyrer, N.** Child of the Happy Valley. 1999. 24.95 (*0-434-00729-3*, Pub. by Random) Trafalgar.

Carberry, James J. Chemical Reaction & Reactor Engineering. Varma, Arvind, ed. (Chemical Industries Ser.: Vol. 26). (Illus.). 1088p. 1986. text 295.00 (*0-8247-7543-0*) Dekker.

— Chemistry & Catalytic Reaction Engineering. (Chemical Engineering Ser.). (Illus.). 704p. (C). 1976. 107.19 (*0-07-009790-9*) McGraw.

Carberry, John. The Book of the Rosary. LC 83-62424. 120p. (Orig.). 1983. pap. 4.50 (*0-87973-610-0*, 610) Our Sunday Visitor.

— Reflections & Prayers for Visits with Our Eucharistic King. 56p. 1992. pap. 2.50 (*0-8198-6436-6*) Pauline Bks.

Carberry, Sandra. Plan Recognition in Natural Language Dialogue. (Bradford - ACL-MIT Press Series in Natural Language Processing). 240p. 1990. 44.00 (*0-262-03167-1*, Bradford Bks) MIT Pr.

Carbert, Louise I. Agrarian Feminism: The Politics of Ontario Farm Women. (Illus.). 255p. 1995. text 50.00 (*0-8020-2931-0*); pap. text 19.95 (*0-8020-7756-0*) U of Toronto Pr.

Carbery, Mary. Mary Carbery's West Cork Journals, 1898-1901. Sandford, Jeremy, ed. LC 96-130570. (Illus.). 320p. 1998. pap. 29.95 (*1-874675-36-8*, Pub. by Lilliput Pr) Irish Bks Media.

Carbery, Thomas F. Consumers in Politics: A History & General Review of the Co-operative Party. LC 68-56547. vii, 276p. 1969. 39.50 (*0-678-06754-6*) Kelley.

***Carbin, Eddie.** Arty the Part-Time Astronaut. 36p. (J). (gr. 1-7). 2000. pap. 19.95 (*0-9675299-0-5*) Three Pounds Pr.

Carbine, Jason A., jt. ed. see Reynolds, Frank E.

Carbine, Michael E. Health Care & the Law, Vol. I. (Papers of the Roscoe Pound Foundation Ser.). 50p. 1988. pap. 20.00 (*0-933067-07-0*) Roscoe Pound Inst.

— Health Care & the Law: Reports on Three Roundtable Discussions, Vol. III. 68p. 1990. pap. 20.00 (*0-933067-10-0*) Roscoe Pound Inst.

— Medical Quality & the Law: Final Report of the 1989 Chief Justice Earl Warren Conference on Advocacy in the United States. 116p. (Orig.). 1989. pap. 25.00 (*0-941916-60-X*) Roscoe Pound Inst.

Carbo-Dorca, R. & Mezey, Paul G. Advances in Molecular Similarity, Vol. 2. Date not set. 112.50 (*0-7623-0258-5*) Jai Pr.

Carbo-Dorca, Ramon & Mezey, P. G., eds. Advances in Molecular Similarity, Vol. 1. 287p. 1996. 112.50 (*0-7623-0131-7*) Jai Pr.

Carbo, Ilka. Guia Deportiva. (ENG & SPA.). 54p. 1994. pap. write for info. (*0-929441-65-6*) Pubns Puertorriquenas.

Carbo, Marie. How to Record Books for Maximum Reading Gains. 3rd ed. LC 89-29528. (Illus.). 118p. (Orig.). 1997. reprint ed. pap. 19.95 (*0-929192-15-X*) Natl Read Styles Inst.

Carbo, Marie & Cole, Richard W. What Every Principal Should Know about Teaching Reading: How to Raise Test Scores & Nurture a Love of Reading. 2nd ed. (Illus.). 192p. (Orig.). 1997. reprint ed. pap. 19.95 (*1-883186-00-5*) Natl Read Styles Inst.

Carbo, Marie, et al. Teaching Students to Read Through Their Individual Learning Styles. rev. ed. (Illus.). 320p. (C). 1986. 42.00 (*0-8359-7517-7*) P-H.

Carbo, Nick. El Grupo McDonald's. (SPA.). 80p. (Orig.). 1995. pap. 10.95 (*1-882688-08-2*) Tia Chucha Pr.

***Carbo, Nick.** Secret Asian Man. LC 00-130213. 60p. 2000. pap. 10.95 (*1-882688-24-4*, Pub. by Tia Chucha Pr) Northwestern U Pr.

Carbo, Nick, ed. Returning a Borrowed Tongue: An Anthology of Philipino & Filipino American Poetry. 320p. (Orig.). (YA). (gr. 11-12). 1996. pap. 14.95 (*1-56689-043-8*) Coffee Hse.

***Carbo, Nick & Tabios, Eileen, eds.** Babaylan: An Anthology of Filipina & Filipina American Writers. LC 00-35525. 240p. 2000. pap. 16.95 (*1-879960-59-1*) Aunt Lute Bks.

Carbon, C., jt. ed. see Kayser, F. H.

Carbon, Max W. Nuclear Power: Villain or Victim? Our Most Misunderstood Source of Electricity. LC 97-91918. (Illus.). xii, 100p. 1997. pap. 13.95 (*0-9658096-0-9*) Pebble Beach.

Carbon, Ramon, ed. Molecular Similarity & Reactivity. LC 94-46540. (Understanding Chemical Reactivity Ser.: Vol. 14). 1995. text 166.00 (*0-7923-3309-8*) Kluwer Academic.

Carbonara, Nancy T. Techniques for Observing Normal Child Behavior. LC 61-9991. 32p. 1961. pap. 3.95 (*0-8229-5043-X*) U of Pittsburgh Pr.

Carbonara, R. S., ed. see Symposium on Surface Analysis Techniques for Metal.

***Carbonari, Polly, photos by.** Basic Equine Energy Balancing: A Horseman's Horse Therapy. 2nd ed. (Illus.). 120p. 1998. 24.95 (*1-892413-00-0*) Lazy P Inc.

— The Horse Show. (Illus.). 40p. (J). (ps-5). 1997. 6.95 (*0-9645477-6-7*) Lazy P Inc.

— The Riding Lesson. 2nd ed. (Illus.). 40p. (J). (ps-5). 1996. 6.95 (*0-9645477-7-5*) Lazy P Inc.

— The Trail Ride. (Illus.). 40p. (J). (ps-5). 1998. 6.95 (*1-892413-01-9*) Lazy P Inc.

***Carbone, Alessandra & Semmes, Stephen.** A Graphic Apology for Symmetry & Implicitness. (Oxford Mathematical Monographs). (Illus.). 592p. 2000. text 120.00 (*0-19-850729-1*) OUP.

Carbone, Claudia. Antipasti! The Art of Italian Appetizers. LC 97-26248. (Pane & Vino Ser.). (Illus.). 128p. (gr. 11). 1999. 17.95 (*0-7835-5269-6*) Time-Life.

— Women Ski. 2nd ed. 1996. pap. 14.95 (*0-915009-55-2*) World Leis Corp.

Carbone, David P., jt. auth. see Gazdar, Adi F.

Carbone, E., jt. ed. see Strata, P.

***Carbone, Elisa.** Sarah & the Naked Truth. LC 99-33714. 112p. (J). 2000. lib. bdg. 17.99 (*0-375-90264-3*) Knopf.

Carbone, Elisa. Sarah & the Naked Truth. LC 99-33714. 144p. (J). (gr. 5-8). 2000. 15.95 (*0-375-80264-9*) Knopf.

— Starting School with an Enemy. LC 97-33366. 112p. (J). (gr. 5 up). 1998. 16.00 (*0-679-88639-7*, Pub. by Knopf Bks Yng Read) Random.

An Asterisk (*) at the beginning of an entry indicates that the title is appearing for the first time.

— Starting School with an Enemy. (J). 1999. pap. 4.99 (*0-679-88640-0*, Pub. by Knopf Bks Yng Read) Random.

— Starting School with an Enemy. LC 97-33366. 112p. (J). (gr. 5 up). 1998. lib. bdg. 17.99 (*0-679-98639-1*, Pub. by Random Bks Yng Read) Random.

*__Carbone, Elisa.__ Stealing Freedom. (YA). 2001. pap. 5.50 (*0-440-41707-4*) BDD Bks Young Read.

Carbone, Elisa. Stealing Freedom. 272p. (J). (gr. 5 up). 1998. 17.00 (*0-679-89307-5*, Pub. by Random Bks Yng Read) Random.

— Stealing Freedom. 160p. (YA). (gr. 5-9). 1999. lib. bdg. 18.99 (*0-679-99307-X*, Pub. by Random Bks Yng Read) Random.

*__Carbone, Elisa.__ The Surfmen of Pea Island. (YA). 2001. 18.99 (*0-375-90664-9*) Random.

— The Surfmen of Pea Island. (YA). 2001. mass mkt. 16.95 (*0-375-80664-4*, Pub. by Random Bks Yng Read) Random.

Carbone, Elisa L. Corey's Story. LC 96-43564. (J). 1997. pap. 9.95 (*0-914525-30-1*) Waterfront Bks.

— My Dad's Definitely Not a Drunk! Weber, Susan B., ed. LC 92-53883. (Illus.). 116p. (Orig.). (J). (gr. 4-9). 1992. pap. text 7.95 (*0-914525-22-0*) Waterfront Bks.

— Teaching Large Classes: Tools & Strategies. LC 98-19671. (Survival Skills for Scholars Ser.). 96p. 1998. 38.50 (*0-7619-0974-5*); pap. 17.50 (*0-7619-0975-3*) Sage.

Carbone, George A., ed. see Toscano, Mario.

Carbone, Joyce. Apologies to Thelonious. 50p. (Orig.). 1996. pap. 5.95 (*1-878116-56-8*) JVC Bks.

— Chela's Song: The Beginning of This Journey. LC 91-93084. (Illus.). 124p. (Orig.). 1991. pap. 8.95 (*1-878116-10-X*) JVC Bks.

— Cosmic Interlude. LC 90-91792. (Illus.). 94p. (Orig.). 1990. lib. bdg. 7.95 (*1-878116-00-2*) JVC Bks.

— Dream Sequence, No. 1. (Illus.). 44p. 1994. 5.95 (*1-878116-31-2*) JVC Bks.

— Dream Sequence, No. 2. (Illus.). 56p. 1994. pap. 5.95 (*1-878116-32-0*) JVC Bks.

— Ragged Prison Blues. 50p. (Orig.). 1996. pap. 5.95 (*1-878116-58-4*) JVC Bks.

— Two Plays, One Day & a Third. limited ed. (Illus.). 100p. (Orig.). 1997. pap. 9.95 (*1-878116-68-1*) JVC Bks.

Carbone, Joyce, intro. In Retrospect. 42p. (Orig.). 1994. 5.95 (*1-878116-30-4*) JVC Bks.

Carbone, Joyce & Pine, Ana. New Age Women. LC 90-92049. (Illus.). 79p. (Orig.). 1990. pap. 7.95 (*1-878116-02-9*) JVC Bks.

Carbone, Joyce, jt. auth. see Cauchi, Patrick.

Carbone, Joyce, jt. auth. see Metzger, Wendell.

Carbone, Joyce, jt. auth. see Weinman, Paul.

Carbone, Joyce, ed. see Allen, Blair H.

Carbone, Joyce, ed. see Duplij, Steven.

Carbone, Joyce, ed. see Galioto, Salvatore.

Carbone, Joyce, ed. see Lifshin, Lyn.

Carbone, Joyce, ed. see Metzger, Wendell.

Carbone, Joyce, ed. see Niditch, B. Z.

Carbone, Joyce, ed. see Tribune, George.

Carbone, Joyce, ed. see Verrilli, Joseph.

*__Carbone, June.__ From Partners to Parents: The Second Revolution in Family Law. 2000. pap. text 18.50 (*0-231-11117-7*) Col U Pr.

— From Partners to Parents: The Second Revolution of Family Law. 2000. 49.50 (*0-231-11116-9*) Col U Pr.

*__Carbone, Ken.__ The Virtuoso: Face to Face with 40 Extraordinary Talents. LC 98-46260. (Illus.). 122p. 1999. text 30.00 (*1-55670-908-0*) Stewart Tabori & Chang.

Carbone, Linda. Marvelous Math Masters. (J). (gr. 6-8). 1995. spiral bd. 17.95 (*1-881641-02-3*) Pencil Point.

Carbone, Linda & Decker, Ed. A Little Pregnant: Our Memoir of Fertility, Infertility & a Marriage. LC 99-19217. 240p. 1999. 23.00 (*0-87113-751-8*, Pub. by Grove-Atltic) Publishers Group.

Carbone, Nick, jt. auth. see Crump, Eric.

Carbone, Paul, ed. see Yancik, Rosemary.

Carbone, Peter F. The Social & Educational Thought of Harold Rugg. LC 75-36176. 238p. reprint ed. pap. 73.80 (*0-608-11947-4*, 202337400032) Bks Demand.

Carbone, Peter F., Jr. Value Theory & Education. LC 86-27822. 288p. 1987. lib. bdg. 29.50 (*0-89874-976-X*) Krieger.

Carbone, Sonny. Three Shots in the Night. Literacy Volunteers of New York City Staff, ed. (New Writers' Voices Ser.). (Illus.). 64p. (Orig.). 1992. pap. text 3.50 (*0-929631-63-3*, Signal Hill) New Readers.

Carbone, Teresa A. Masterpieces of American Painting from the Brooklyn Museum. LC 96-78480. (Illus.). 103p. 1996. 25.00 (*0-614-29364-2*) V Jordan Fine Art.

*__Carbone, Teresa A. & Hills, Patricia.__ Eastman Johnson: Painting America. LC 99-14456. (Illus.). 272p. 1999. 65.00 (*0-8478-2214-1*, Pub. by Rizzoli Intl) St Martin.

Carbone, Teresa A., et al. Eastman Johnson: Painting America. LC 99-14456. 1999. write for info. (*0-87273-138-3*) Bklyn Mus.

Carbonel, Daniele. Oro Plata. Date not set. 100.00 (*2-908228-14-9*, Pub. by Assouline) Rizzoli Intl.

Carbonell, J. G., ed. see Calmet, Jacques & Plaza, Jan.

Carbonell, J. G., ed. see Kompe, Ralf.

Carbonell, J. G., ed. see Lenzerini, Maurizio.

Carbonell, J. G., ed. see Nienhuys-Cheng, S. H. & De Wolf, R.

Carbonell, J. G., ed. see Ossowski, Sascha.

Carbonell, J. G., ed. see Reinartz, Thomas.

Carbonell, J. G., ed. see Schaub, Torsten.

Carbonell, J. G., ed. see Zhong, N. & Zhou, L.

Carbonell, Joyce L. Psychology of Violent Women. 200p. 1996. lib. bdg. 39.95 (*1-57444-051-9*, SL0519) St Lucie Pr.

Carbonell, Joyce L. & Figley, Charles R., eds. The Active Ingredient in Psychological Treatments for Anxiety. 280p. 1994. lib. bdg. 39.95 (*1-57444-049-7*, SL0497) St Lucie Pr.

Carbonell, Maria G. Volver. (Coleccion Espejo de Paciencia). (SPA., Illus.). 122p. (Orig.). 1980. pap. 5.95 (*0-89729-290-1*) Ediciones.

Carbonell, Montserrat, jt. auth. see Johnsgard, Paul A.

Carbonell, S. Complete Italian & Spanish Phraseological Dictionary: Dizionario Fraseologico Completo Italiano-Spagnole e Spagnole-Italiano, Vol. 1. (ITA & SPA.). 840p. 1987. lib. bdg. 4200.00 (*0-8288-3361-3*) Fr & Eur.

— Complete Phraseological Dictionary, Spanish-Italian: Dizionario Fraseologico Completo, Vol. 2. (ITA & SPA.). 1524p. 1987. lib. bdg. 5200.00 (*0-8288-3362-1*) Fr & Eur.

Carbonell Vaya, Enrique J., jt. ed. see Rothengatter, Talib.

Carbonetti, Jeanne. The Tao of Watercolor: A Revolutionary Approach to the Practice of Painting. LC 97-47316. (Zen of Creativity Ser.). (Illus.). 112p. 1998. pap. 19.95 (*0-8230-5057-2*) Watsn-Guptill.

*__Carbonetti, Jeanne.__ The Yoga of Drawing: Uniting Body, Mind & Spirit in the Art of Drawing. LC 99-18113. 112p. 1999. pap. text 19.95 (*0-8230-5972-3*) Watsn-Guptill.

Carbonetti, Jeanne. The Zen of Creative Painting: An Elegant Design for Revealing Your Muse. LC 98-35575. 112p. 1998. pap. 19.95 (*0-8230-5973-1*) Watsn-Guptill.

Carbonetto, S., ed. The Extracellular Matrix in Neural Development & Regeneration: Journal: Developmental Neuroscience, Vol. 11, No. 4-5, 1989. (Illus.). 156p. 1989. pap. 94.00 (*3-8055-5056-1*) S Karger.

Carboni, David K. Geriatric Medicine in the United States & Great Britain, 1. LC 82-9245. (Contributions to the Study of Aging Ser.: No. 1). (Illus.). 159p. 1982. 49.95 (*0-313-23437-X*, CAO/, Greenwood Pr) Greenwood.

Carboni, Polly & Crowther, Jean D. Country Life: Counted Cross-Stitch. (Illus.). 8p. (Orig.). 1987. pap. 5.98 (*0-88290-294-6*) Horizon Utah.

— Country Wisdom: Counted Cross-Stitch. (Illus.). 8p. (Orig.). 1987. pap. 5.98 (*0-88290-295-4*) Horizon Utah.

Carboni, Rudolph A. Planning & Managing Industry-University Research Collaborations. LC 92-14724. 240p. 1992. 59.95 (*0-89930-769-8*, CHZ, Quorum Bks) Greenwood.

Carboni, Stefano, jt. auth. see Swietochowski, Marie L.

Carbonneau, Thomas E. Alternative Dispute Resolution: Melting the Lances & Dismounting the Steeds. LC 89-4703. 352p. 1989. text 34.95 (*0-252-01640-8*) U of Ill Pr.

— Cases & Materials on Commercial Arbitration. LC 97-5168. (Adams & Reese Legal Ser.). 658p. 1997. 55.00 (*1-57823-018-7*) Juris Pubng.

*__Carbonneau, Thomas E.__ Cases & Materials on the Law & Practice of Arbitration. 2nd ed. LC 99-54007. 1999. 75.00 (*1-57823-037-3*) Juris Pubng.

Carbonneau, Thomas E. Lex Mercatoria & Arbitration: A Discussion of the New Law Merchant. LC 97-46193. 1997. 85.00 (*1-57823-023-3*) Juris Pubng.

— Lex Mercatoria & Arbitration: A Discussion of the New Law Merchant. LC 98-17861. 1998. 100.00 (*90-411-0586-7*) Kluwer Law Intl.

Carbonneau, Thomas E., ed. Lex Mercatoria & Arbitration. 250p. 1990. 85.00 (*0-929179-35-8*) Juris Pubng.

Carbotte, J. P., et al, eds. Electron-Phonon Interaction in Oxide Superconductors: Proceedings of the First CINVESTAV - Superconductivity Symposium, Oaxtepec, Mexico, 11-14 December 1990. 400p. (C). 1991. text 104.00 (*981-02-0725-5*) World Scientific Pub.

Carbotti, Richard. Newport Houses. (Birds Pack Ser.). 8p. (J). (gr. k-2). 1993. pap. write for info. (*1-882563-01-8*) Lamont Bks.

— Summer Festivals. (Geronomo Pack Ser.). 8p. (J). (gr. k-2). 1993. pap. write for info. (*1-882563-09-3*) Lamont Bks.

Carby, Hazel V. Culture in Babylon: Black Britain & African America. 280p. 1999. 60.00 (*1-85984-884-2*, Pub. by Verso) Norton.

— Cultures in Babylon: Black Britain & African America. (Haymarket Ser.). 282p. 1999. pap. 18.00 (*1-85984-281-X*, Pub. by Verso) Norton.

*__Carby, Hazel V.__ Race Men. 240p. 2000. pap. 15.95 (*0-674-00404-3*) HUP.

— Race Men: The W. E. B. Du Bois Lectures. LC 98-14077. (W. E. B. Du Bois Lectures). 192p. 1998. 24.00 (*0-674-74558-2*) HUP.

Carby, Hazel V. Reconstructing Womanhood: The Emergence of the Afro-American Woman Novelist. 240p. 1989. pap. text 19.95 (*0-19-506071-7*) OUP.

Carby, Keith & Thakur, Manab. Transactional Analysis at Work. 98p. (C). 1976. 80.00 (*0-85292-133-0*) St Mut.

Carby-Samuels, Horace. Work, the Economy & Human Development. Date not set. write for info. (*0-9681906-1-8*) Agora Publ.

*__Carcach, Carlos & Leverett, Simon.__ Recidivism among Juvenile Offenders: An Analysis of Times to Reappearance in Court. (Research & Public Policy Series: Vol. 17). 25p. 1999. pap. 75.00 (*0-642-24113-9*, Pub. by Aust Inst Criminology) St Mut.

*__Carcach, Carlos & Muscat, Glenn.__ Juveniles in Australian Corrective Instititions 1981-1998, with a Statistical Review of the Year 1998. 61p. 1999. pap. 76.00 (*0-642-24118-X*, Pub. by Aust Inst Criminology) St Mut.

Carcach, Carlos, jt. auth. see Mukherjee, Satyanshu Kumar.

Carcach, Carols, jt. auth. see James, Marianne.

Carcaci, Diana Di, see Cardella, Lara.

Carcamo, Luis. Diccionario para Ingenieros y Tecnicos Frances-Espanol-Frances. (FRE & SPA.). 1106p. 195.00 (*0-8288-0671-3*, S2560) Fr & Eur.

— Dictionary for Engineers & Technicians: Dictionnaire pour Ingenieurs et Techniciens: Francais-Espagnol-Francais. 4th ed. (ENG & FRE.). 1988. write for info. (*0-8288-2103-8*, F12480) Fr & Eur.

Carcamo, Otila & Calderon, Wilfredo. La Mujer Integral. (SPA.). 88p. 1984. pap. 1.95 (*0-938127-03-9*) Publ Senda de Vida.

Carcano, Minerva G. 365 More Meditations for Women. LC 91-33363. 352p. 1992. pap. 12.00 (*0-687-41888-7*) Dimen for Liv.

*__Carcano, Robert.__ Purposes & Procedures of the NAIC Securities Valuation Office. 160p. 2000. pap. 65.00 (*0-89382-664-2*) Nat Assn Insurance.

— Purposes & Procedures of the NAIC Securities Valuation Office. rev. ed. 160p. 1998. pap. 65.00 (*0-89382-567-0*) Nat Assn Insurance.

Carcano, Robert, ed. Purposes & Procedures of the NAIC Securities Valuation Office. rev. ed. 160p. 1998. ring bd. 65.00i (*0-89382-519-0*, SVO-PP97-2) Nat Assn Insurance.

Carcassi, M. Carcassi 25 Progressive Studies. 48p. 1993. pap. 14.95 (*0-7935-1868-7*, 00696505); pap. 17.95 (*0-7935-1867-9*, 00696506) H Leonard.

Carcassi, M. Classical Guitar Method. rev. ed. 128p. 1962. pap. 11.95 (*0-8258-0049-8*, 0762) Fischer Inc NY.

Carcassi, Matteo. Melodic & Progressive Etudes. Stang, Aaron, ed. 36p. (Orig.). (C). 1985. pap. text 8.00 (*0-7692-1304-9*, K04253) Wrner Bros.

Carcasson, R. H. The Swallowtail Butterflies of East Africa. 1984. 30.00 (*0-7855-0675-6*) St Mut.

Carcaterra, Lorenzo. Apaches. 1998. mass mkt. 6.99 (*0-345-42537-5*) Ballantine Pub Grp.

— Apaches. 1998. mass mkt. 6.99 (*0-345-42251-1*) Ballantine Pub Grp.

— A Safe Place: The Story of a Father, a Son, a Murder. 1994. mass mkt. 6.99 (*0-345-38348-6*) Ballantine Pub Grp.

— Shadows. 1998. 18.00 (*0-375-40332-9*) Knopf.

— Sleepers. 1996. mass mkt. 6.99 (*0-345-40411-4*) Ballantine Pub Grp.

— Sleepers. 1996. pap. 6.99 (*0-345-90999-2*) Ballantine Pub Grp.

— Sleepers. 1998. pap. 6.99 (*0-345-91465-1*) Ballantine Pub Grp.

Carceles, Michael & Torra, Elizabeth. Yes! Life of a Blessed Josemaria for Young Readers. 110p. 1994. pap. 11.95 (*0-933932-68-5*) Scepter Pubs.

Carcell, Roland A. Hitting the Wall: How to Rescue Your Relationship with a Single Conversation. 36p. (Orig.). Date not set. pap. 5.95 (*0-9648800-0-8*) Granite-Collen.

Carcello, Joseph V., jt. auth. see Williams, Jan R.

Carchedi, Guglielmo. Frontiers of Political Economy. LC 91-30577. 320p. (C). 1992. pap. 20.00 (*0-86091-566-2*, A6406, Pub. by Verso) Norton.

Carchedi, Guglielmo, jt. ed. see Freeman, Alan.

Carcilaso de la Vega, Inca. Comentarios Reales de Los Incas (Royal Commentaries of The Incas), Vols. I & II. (SPA.). 441p. 1991. pap. 18.99 (*968-16-4892-7*, Pub. by Fondo) Continental Bk.

Carcio, Helen A. Management of the Infertile Woman. LC 97-42828. 320p. 1998. pap. text 39.95 (*0-7817-1044-8*) Lppncott W & W.

Carcio, Helen N. Advanced Health Assessment of Women: Clinical Skills & Procedures. LC 98-44544. 1999. write for info. (*0-7817-1826-0*) Lppncott W & W.

Carcioppolo, James L. The Lost Sonnets of Cyrano de Bergerac: A Poetic Fiction. LC 97-92863. (Illus.). xiii, 115p. 1998. pap. 12.00 (*0-9662204-0-4*) Lost Sonnet Pubg.

Carco, Diane M., jt. auth. see Petersen, Brad L.

Carcopino, Jerome. Daily Life in Ancient Rome: The People & the City at the Height of the Empire. Rowell, Henry T., ed. Lorimer, E. O., tr. (FRE., Illus.). 1960. pap. 18.00 (*0-300-00031-6*, Y28) Yale U Pr.

— Le Vatican. large type ed. (FRE., Illus.). 225p. 1958. lib. bdg. 150.00 (*0-8288-3947-6*) Fr & Eur.

Card. Linux Kernel Book pap. text. write for info. (*0-471-49178-0*) Wiley.

Card, jt. auth. see Smith.

Card, Brigham Y., et al, eds. The Mormon Presence in Canada. LC 90-34484. (Illus.). 408p. reprint ed. pap. 126.50 (*0-608-08566-9*, 206908900002) Bks Demand.

*__Card, C. J.__ My Loving Familiar. (Magical Love Ser.). 2000. mass mkt. 5.99 (*0-515-12728-0*, Jove) Berkley Pub.

Card, C. J. One Wish. (Magical Love Ser.: Vol. 4). 308p. 1998. mass mkt. 5.99 (*0-515-12354-4*, Jove) Berkley Pub.

Card, Cheryl N. Discover the Power of Introversion: What Most Introverts Are Never Told & Extraverts Learn the Hard Way. 1993. pap. 9.95 (*1-878287-42-7*) Type & Temperament.

Card, Claudia. Lesbian Choices. LC 94-12527. (Between Men - Between Women Ser.). 320p. 1994. 41.00 (*0-231-08008-5*) Col U Pr.

— Lesbian Choices. 1995. pap. 19.00 (*0-231-08009-3*) Col U Pr.

— On Feminist Ethics & Politics. LC 99-11259. (Feminist Ethics Ser.). 368p. 1999. pap. 19.95 (*0-7006-0968-7*) U Pr of KS.

— The Unnatural Lottery: Character & Moral Luck. LC 96-1316. 232p. 1996. 59.95 (*1-56639-452-X*); pap. 24.95 (*1-56639-453-8*) Temple U Pr.

Card, Claudia, ed. Adventures in Lesbian Philosophy. LC 94-3921. (Hypatia Bks.). 320p. 1994. 39.95 (*0-253-31308-2*) Ind U Pr.

— Adventures in Lesbian Philosophy. LC 94-3921. (Hypatia Bks.). 320p. 1994. pap. 16.95 (*0-253-20899-8*) Ind U Pr.

— Feminist Ethics. LC 91-6753. viii, 304p. 1991. pap. 16.95 (*0-7006-0483-9*) U Pr of KS.

*__Card, Claudia, ed.__ On Feminist Ethics & Politics. LC 99-11259. (Feminist Ethics Ser.). 368p. 1999. 45.00 (*0-7006-0967-9*) U Pr of KS.

Card, D., jt. auth. see Ashenfelter, O.

Card, Dave, jt. auth. see Rutter, Michael.

Card, David. Myth & Measurement: The New Economics of the Minimum Wage. 432p. 1995. pap. text 16.95 (*0-691-04823-1*, Pub. by Princeton U Pr) Cal Prin Full Svc.

Card, David & Freeman, Richard B., eds. Small Differences That Matter: Labor Markets & Income Maintenance in Canada & the United States. LC 93-10513. (National Bureau of Economic Research Comparative Labor Markets Ser.: Vol. 1). (Illus.). 288p. 1993. 29.95 (*0-226-09283-6*) U Ch Pr.

Card, David & Krueger, Alan. Myth & Measurement: The New Economics of the Minimum Wage. 384p. 1995. text 55.00 (*0-691-04390-6*, Pub. by Princeton U Pr) Cal Prin Full Svc.

Card, David, jt. auth. see Rutter, Michael.

Card, David, jt. ed. see Blank, Rebecca M.

Card, Emily. Global Investing. 1998. write for info. (*0-8129-2846-6*, Times Bks) Crown Pub Group.

Card, Emily & Miller, Adam. Business Capital for Women: An Essential Handbook for Entrepreneurs. 291p. 1996. pap. 16.95 (*0-02-860854-2*) Macmillan.

— Managing Your Inheritance: Getting It, Keeping It, Growing It; Making the Most of an Inheritance. LC 95-13765. 288p. 1997. pap. 15.00 (*0-8129-2600-5*, Times Bks) Crown Pub Group.

Card, Emily W. The Single Parent's Money Guide: Thriving On. 208p. 1996. 14.95 (*0-02-861119-5*) Macmillan.

Card, Emily W. & Kelly, Christie W. New Families, New Finances Money Skills for Today's Nontraditional Families. LC 97-37906. (Wiley Personal Finance Solutions Your Family Matters Ser.). 285p. 1998. pap. 14.95 (*0-471-19612-6*) Wiley.

Card, Hermon R. The Poetry of Teaching. 65p. 1998. pap. 10.00 (*0-9664103-2-7*) Thornetree Hill.

Card, Howard C. Artificial Neural Networks: Hardware or Software? (Progress in Neural Processing Ser.). 1999. 46.00 (*981-02-3733-2*) World Scientific Pub.

Card, James. Seductive Cinema: The Art of Silent Film. LC 99-12431. 1999. reprint ed. pap. 19.95 (*0-8166-3390-8*) U of Minn Pr.

Card, James Van Dyck. An Anatomy of Penelope. LC 82-49195. 168p. 1985. 31.50 (*0-8386-3158-4*) Fairleigh Dickinson.

Card, Josefina J., ed. The American Family: A Compendium of Data & Sources. LC 93-24328. (Reference Library of Social Science). 560p. 1994. text 25.00 (*0-8153-1492-2*, SS925) Garland.

— Handbook of Adolescent Sexuality & Pregnancy: Research & Evaluation Equipment. LC 93-2673. (Illus.). 294p. (C). 1993. text 69.95 (*0-8039-4595-7*) Sage.

Card, Josephina T., ed. see Park, Jane & Muller, Kathryn.

Card, Lester. Norwalk Cemeteries. 152p. 1997. reprint ed. pap. 21.00 (*0-8328-5676-2*) Higginson Bk Co.

Card, Linda, jt. auth. see Card, Ron.

Card, M. Dictionary of Computer Terms of Printing & Publishing: English & French. (ENG & FRE.). 136p. 1992. 85.00 (*0-7859-0500-6*, 2852066823) Fr & Eur.

— Dictionnaire des Termes Typographiques et de Design. (ENG & FRE.). 192p. 1992. 175.00 (*0-7859-9272-3*) Fr & Eur.

Card, Margaret. Angelina Trueheart & the Fox. LC 93-26224. (Illus.). (J). 1994. 4.25 (*0-383-03732-8*) SRA McGraw.

Card, Michael. Come to the Cradle. LC 93-10325. 1993. 12.95 (*0-917143-24-8*) Sparrow TN.

— The Parable of Joy. (Illus.). 288p. 1995. 19.99 (*0-7852-8229-7*, J Thoma Bks) Nelson.

— The Promise: The Celebration of the Birth of Christ. Hazard, David, ed. (Illus.). 48p. 1991. 10.95 (*0-917143-07-8*) Sparrow TN.

— Sleep Sound in Jesus. (Illus.). 32p. 1990. 16.99 (*0-89081-792-8*) Harvest Hse.

— Tell Me Why: Eternal Answers to Children's Timeless Questions. LC 99-21448. (Tell Me Ser.). (Illus.). 48p. (J). (ps-3). 1999. 16.99 (*1-58134-031-1*) Crossway Bks.

*__Card, Michael.__ A Violent Grace. LC 99-50836. 182p. 2000. 12.99 (*1-57673-688-1*, Pub. by Multnomah Pubs) GL Services.

Card, Michael, jt. auth. see Card, Susan.

Card, Michael, jt. auth. see Smith, Scotty.

Card, Orson Scott. Alvin Journeyman. (Tales of Alvin Maker Ser.: Vol. IV). 384p. 1995. 23.95 (*0-312-85053-0*) Tor Bks.

— Alvin Journeyman. (Tales of Alvin Maker Ser.). 1996. 12.09 (*0-606-11033-X*, Pub. by Turtleback) Demco.

— Alvin Journeyman, Vol. 1. (The Tales of Alvin Maker Ser.). 1996. mass mkt. 6.99 (*0-8125-0923-4*, Pub. by Tor Bks) St Martin.

— The Call of Earth. (Homecoming Saga Ser.: No. 2). 352p. 1994. mass mkt. 5.99 (*0-8125-3261-9*, Pub. by Tor Bks) St Martin.

— The Call of Earth. LC 92-36971. (Homecoming Ser.: No. 2). 1994. 12.09 (*0-606-11472-6*, Pub. by Turtleback) Demco.

— The Call of Earth. deluxe limited ed. LC 92-36971. (Homecoming Saga Ser.: No. 2). 304p. 1993. 200.00 (*0-312-85477-3*, Pub. by Tor Bks) St Martin.

— The Changed Man, Vol. 1. 1992. mass mkt. 4.99 (*0-8125-3365-8*, Pub. by Tor Bks) St Martin.

— Characters & Viewpoint. (Elements of Fiction Writing Ser.). 182p. 1999. pap. 12.00 (*0-89879-927-9*, Wrtrs Digest Bks) F & W Pubns Inc.

— Children of the Mind. (Ender Wiggins Saga Ser.). 370p. 1997. mass mkt. 6.99 (*0-8125-2239-7*, Pub. by Tor Bks) St Martin.

An Asterisk (*) at the beginning of an entry indicates that the title is appearing for the first time.

— Children of the Mind. (Ender Ser.: Vol. 4). 1997. mass mkt. 6.99 (*0-614-27801-5*) Tor Bks.

— Children of the Mind. limited ed. 1996. 200.00 (*0-312-86191-5*) St Martin.

— Cruel Miracles, Vol. 3. (Maps in a Mirror Ser.: No. 3). 256p. 1992. reprint ed. mass mkt. 4.99 (*0-8125-2304-0*, Pub. by Tor Bks) St Martin.

— Dragons of Darkness. LC 81-215874. (Ace Science Fiction Ser.). xii, 351 p. 1981. 6.95 (*0-441-16662-8*) Ace Bks.

— Dragons of Light. LC 81-129331. (Ace Science Fiction Special Ser.). 317 p. 1980. 7.95 (*0-441-16660-1*) Ace Bks.

— Earthborn. limited ed. (Homecoming Saga Ser.: No. 5). 384p. 1995. 200.00 (*0-312-85928-7*, Pub. by Tor Bks) St Martin.

— Earthborn. limited ed. (Homecoming Saga Ser.: No. 5). 1996. mass mkt. 6.99 (*0-8125-3298-8*, Pub. by Tor Bks) St Martin.

— Earthborn, 5. (Homecoming Ser.: No. 5). 1996. 12.09 (*0-606-11475-0*, Pub. by Turtleback) Demco.

— Earthfall. (Homecoming Saga Ser.: No. 4). 352p. 1996. pap. write for info. (*0-614-05511-3*); mass mkt. 5.99 (*0-8125-3296-1*, Pub. by Tor Bks) St Martin.

— Earthfall. (Homecoming Ser.: No. 4). 1996. 12.09 (*0-606-11474-2*, Pub. by Turtleback) Demco.

— Enchantment. LC PS3553.A655E495 1999. 390p. 1999. 25.00 (*0-345-41687-2*, Del Rey) Ballantine Pub Grp.

***Card, Orson Scott.** Enchantment. 2000. mass mkt. 6.99 (*0-345-41688-0*, Del Rey) Ballantine Pub Grp.

— Enchantment. (Illus.). (J). 2000. 12.34 (*0-606-18096-6*) Turtleback.

Card, Orson Scott. Ender's Game. (Ender Ser.). 256p. 1992. pap. 12.95 (*0-312-85323-8*, Pub. by Tor Bks) St Martin.

— Ender's Game. (Ender Ser.: No. 1). 1994. pap. 6.99 (*0-8125-5070-6*, Pub. by Tor Bks) St Martin.

— Ender's Game. (Ender Ser.: No. 1). 384p. 1994. mass mkt. 5.99 (*0-8125-2358-X*) Tor Bks.

— Ender's Game. (Ender Wiggins Saga Ser.). (J). 1985. 11.09 (*0-606-04043-9*, Pub. by Turtleback) Demco.

— Ender's Game. limited ed. (Ender Ser.). 256p. 1992. 200.00 (*0-312-85402-1*, Pub. by Tor Bks) St Martin.

— Ender's Game. 4th ed. (Ender Ser.). 368p. 1985. 23.95 (*0-312-93208-1*, Pub. by Tor Bks) St Martin.

***Card, Orson Scott.** Ender's Shadow. 2000. 24.95 (*0-312-85758-6*) St Martin.

— Ender's Shadow. 2000. mass mkt. 6.99 (*0-8125-7571-7*) Tor Bks.

— Ender's Shadow. deluxe ed. 384p. 1999. lthr. 200.00 (*0-312-87297-6*, Pub. by Tor Bks) St Martin.

— Ender's Shadow. 5th ed. LC 99-35824. (Ender Wiggins Saga Ser.). 379p. 1999. 24.95 (*0-312-86860-X*, Pub. by Tor Bks) St Martin.

Card, Orson Scott. Flux. (Map in a Mirror Ser.: Vol. 2). 288p. 1992. mass mkt. 4.99 (*0-8125-1685-0*, Pub. by Tor Bks) St Martin.

— The Folk of the Fringe. 1989. 22.00 (*0-932096-49-2*) Phantasia Pr.

— The Folk of the Fringe. 320p. 1990. mass mkt. 4.95 (*0-8125-0086-5*, Pub. by Tor Bks) St Martin.

— Future On Fire. 1991. mass mkt. 4.95 (*0-8125-1183-2*, Pub. by Tor Bks) St Martin.

***Card, Orson Scott.** Future On Ice. 1998. mass mkt. 4.99 (*0-8125-1190-5*) Tor Bks.

— Future On Ice. 432p. 2000. 15.95 (*0-312-87296-8*, Pub. by Tor Bks) St Martin.

Card, Orson Scott. Hart's Hope. 1992. mass mkt. 4.99 (*0-8125-2135-8*, Pub. by Tor Bks) St Martin.

— Heartfire. LC 98-3041. 304p. 1998. 24.95 (*0-312-85054-9*) St Martin.

— Heartfire. (Tales of Alvin Maker Ser.). 336p. 1999. mass mkt. 6.99 (*0-8125-0924-2*, Pub. by Tor Bks) St Martin.

— Heartfire. limited ed. LC 98-3041. 1999. 200.00 (*0-312-86728-X*) St Martin.

— Homebody: A Novel. LC 97-37627. 304p. (YA). 1998. 24.00 (*0-06-017655-5*) HarpC.

— Homebody: A Novel. 448p. 1999. mass mkt. 6.99 (*0-06-109399-8*, Harp PBks) HarpC.

— How to Write Science Fiction & Fantasy. (Genre Writing Ser.). 176p. 1990. 14.99 (*0-89879-416-1*, Wrtrs Digest Bks) F & W Pubns Inc.

— Lost Boys: A Novel. 544p. 1993. mass mkt. 6.99 (*0-06-109131-6*, Harp PBks) HarpC.

— Magic Mirror. LC 99-27497. (Illus.). 32p. 1999. 15.95 (*0-87905-876-5*) Gibbs Smith Pub.

— Maps in a Mirror: The short fiction of Orson Scott Card. 544p. 1990. 24.95 (*0-312-85047-6*, Pub. by Tor Bks) St Martin.

— The Memory of Earth. (Homecoming Saga Ser.: No. 1). 336p. 1993. mass mkt. 5.99 (*0-8125-3259-7*, Pub. by Tor Bks) St Martin.

— The Memory of Earth. (Homecoming Ser.: No. 1). 1993. 11.09 (*0-606-11471-8*, Pub. by Turtleback) Demco.

— The Memory of Earth. deluxe limited ed. (Homecoming Saga Ser.: No. 1). 336p. 1992. 200.00 (*0-312-85348-3*, Pub. by Tor Bks) St Martin.

— Monkey Sonatas. (Maps in a Mirror Ser.: No. 4). 320p. 1993. mass mkt. 4.99 (*0-8125-2367-9*, Pub. by Tor Bks) St Martin.

— Pastwatch. limited ed. 1996. 200.00 (*0-312-86122-2*, Pub. by Tor Bks) St Martin.

— Pastwatch: The Flood. 1998. write for info. (*0-312-85845-0*) Tor Bks.

— Pastwatch: The Redemption of Christopher Columbus. 352p. 1996. 23.95 (*0-312-85058-1*) Tor Bks.

— Pastwatch: The Redemption of Christopher Columbus. 1997. mass mkt. 6.99 (*0-8125-0864-5*, Pub. by Tor Bks) St Martin.

Card, Orson Scott. Pastwatch, the Redemption of Christopher Columbus. LC 95-44927. 1997. 12.09 (*0-606-11724-5*, Pub. by Turtleback) Demco.

Card, Orson Scott. Prentice Alvin, 3. (Tales of Alvin Maker Ser.). 1989. 11.09 (*0-606-11761-X*, Pub. by Turtleback) Demco.

— Prentice Alvin, Vol. 3. (Tales of Alvin Maker Ser.: Bk. III). 1989. mass mkt. 4.95 (*0-8125-0212-4*, Pub. by Tor Bks) St Martin.

— Red Prophet. (Tales of Alvin Maker Ser.: Bk. II). 320p. 1992. mass mkt. 4.99 (*0-8125-2426-8*, Pub. by Tor Bks) St Martin.

— Red Prophet, 2. (Tales of Alvin Maker Ser.). 1988. 12.09 (*0-606-11784-9*, Pub. by Turtleback) Demco.

— Saints. 720p. 1993. mass mkt. 5.99 (*0-8125-3521-9*, Pub. by Tor Bks) St Martin.

— Seventh Son. LC 86-51490. (Tales of Alvin Maker Ser.: No. 1). 256p. 1993. mass mkt. 4.99 (*0-8125-3305-4*, Pub. by Tor Bks) St Martin.

— Seventh Son. (Tales of Alvin Maker Ser.). 1987. 11.09 (*0-606-04134-6*, Pub. by Turtleback) Demco.

***Card, Orson Scott.** Shadow of the Hegemon. 2000. 25.95 (*0-312-87651-3*) Tor Bks.

Card, Orson Scott. The Ships of Earth. (Homecoming Saga Ser.: No. 3). 384p. 1995. mass mkt. 5.99 (*0-8125-3263-5*, Pub. by Tor Bks) St Martin.

— The Ships of Earth. LC 93-42549. (Homecoming Ser.: No. 3). 1995. 12.09 (*0-606-11473-4*, Pub. by Turtleback) Demco.

— The Ships of Earth. deluxe limited ed. (Homecoming Saga Ser.: No. 3). 384p. 1994. 200.00 (*0-312-85660-1*, Pub. by Tor Bks) St Martin.

— Songmaster. 1992. mass mkt. 4.99 (*0-8125-3322-4*) Tor Bks.

— Songmaster. 1993. mass mkt. 6.99 (*0-8125-2486-1*, Pub. by Tor Bks) St Martin.

— Songmaster. 1992. reprint ed. lib. bdg. 22.00 (*0-7278-4654-X*) Severn Hse.

— Speaker for the Dead. (Ender Ser.: No. 1). 304p. 1992. pap. 12.95 (*0-312-85325-4*, Pub. by Tor Bks) St Martin.

Card, Orson Scott. Speaker for the Dead. (Ender Wiggins Saga Ser.: No. 2). 382p. 1994. pap. 5.99 (*0-8125-5075-7*, Pub. by Tor Bks) St Martin.

Card, Orson Scott. Speaker for the Dead. (Ender Wiggins Saga Ser.). 1994. 12.09 (*0-606-11866-7*, Pub. by Turtleback) Demco.

— Speaker for the Dead. 2nd ed. 432p. 1986. 21.95 (*0-312-93738-5*, Pub. by Tor Bks) St Martin.

***Card, Orson Scott.** Stone Tables. 2000. pap. 17.95 (*1-57345-663-2*) Deseret Bk.

Card, Orson Scott. Stone Tables: A Novel. LC 97-35881. 432p. 1998. 19.95 (*1-57345-115-0*) Deseret Bk.

— The Tales of Alvin Maker. 1995. boxed set 14.93 (*0-8125-3662-2*) Tor Bks.

— The Treasure Box. 384p. 1997. mass mkt. 6.99 (*0-06-109398-X*, Harp PBks) HarpC.

— Treasure Box: A Novel. large type ed. LC 96-34828. (Cloak & Dagger Ser.). 485p. 1996. 23.95 (*0-7862-0887-2*) Thorndike Pr.

— The Worthing Saga. 480p. 1992. mass mkt. 5.99 (*0-8125-3331-3*, Pub. by Tor Bks) St Martin.

— Wyrms. 1992. mass mkt. 4.99 (*0-8125-2136-6*, Pub. by Tor Bks) St Martin.

— Xenocide. (Ender Wiggins Saga Ser.). 592p. 1992. mass mkt. 6.99 (*0-8125-0925-0*, Pub. by Tor Bks) St Martin.

— Xenocide. (Ender Wiggins Saga Ser.). 1992. 12.09 (*0-606-12119-6*, Pub. by Turtleback) Demco.

— Xenocide. 2nd ed. 416p. 1996. pap. 13.95 (*0-312-86187-7*) St Martin.

Card, Orson Scott, ed. Future on Ice. LC 98-23524. 432p. (YA). (gr. 10 up). 1998. 24.95 (*0-312-86694-1*, Pub. by Tor Bks) St Martin.

Card, Orson Scott & Dollahite, David, eds. Turning Hearts: Short stories on family life. LC 94-79640. 1994. pap. 10.95 (*0-88494-948-6*) Bookcraft Inc.

Card, Orson Scott & Ferrell, Keith, eds. Black Mist: And Other Japanese Futurers. 320p. 1997. pap. 5.99 (*0-88677-767-4*, Pub. by DAW Bks) Penguin Putnam.

Card, Orson Scott & Kidd, Kathryn H. Lovelock. 320p. 1995. 5.99 (*0-8125-1805-5*, Pub. by Tor Bks) St Martin.

Card, Orson Scott, ed. see Williams, Walter Jon & Watson, Ian.

Card, Peter W. Early Vehicle Lighting. 1989. pap. 25.00 (*0-85263-843-4*, Pub. by Shire Pubns) St Mut.

— Motor Car Mascots & Badges. 1989. pap. 30.00 (*0-7478-0117-7*, Pub. by Shire Pubns) St Mut.

Card, Remy & Dumas, Eric. The Linux Kernel Book. LC 98-18121. 548p. 1998. pap. text 49.00 incl. cd-rom (*0-471-98141-9*) Wiley.

Card, Richard. Crime & Disorder Act 1998: A Practitioner's Guide. LC 98-196548. 376p. 1998. write for info. (*0-85308-490-4*) Jordan Pubng.

— Public Order - the New Law. 170p. 1987. reprint ed. pap. 30.00 (*0-406-50440-7*, U.K., MICHIE) LEXIS Pub.

Card, Richard & James, Jennifer. Law for Accountancy Students. 655p. 1994. pap. 38.00 (*0-406-02001-9*, UK, MICHIE) LEXIS Pub.

Card, Richard, et al. Card, Murdoch & Schofield: Law for Estate Management Students. 4th ed. LC 95-132534. 1994. pap. write for info. (*0-406-02879-6*, CMSE4, MICHIE) LEXIS Pub.

— Law for Estate Management Students. 3rd ed. 745p. 1990. pap. 44.00 (*0-406-51173-X*, UK, MICHIE) LEXIS Pub.

Card, Richard, jt. auth. see English, Jack.

Card, Ron & Card, Linda. Virginia: A Pictorial Guide to the Old Dominion. 52p. 1992. pap. write for info. (*0-9620127-0-X*) Cards Unltd.

Card, Stuart, et al. Readings in Information Visualization: Using Vision to Think. LC 98-53660. 576p. (C). 1999. pap. 69.95 (*1-55860-533-9*) Morgan Kaufmann.

Card, Stuart K., et al. The Psychology of Human-Computer Interaction. 488p. (C). 1983. pap. 55.00 (*0-89859-859-1*) L Erlbaum Assocs.

Card, Susan. A Season of Joy: Celebrating the True Meaning of Christmas. LC 99-21704. (Illus.). 80p. 1999. 16.99 (*0-7369-0110-8*) Harvest Hse.

Card, Susan & Card, Michael. The Homeschool Journey: Our Family's Adventure in Learning Together. LC 97-7435. 250p. (Orig.). 1997. pap. 9.99 (*1-56507-568-4*) Harvest Hse.

Cardale, J. C. Zoological Catalogue of Australia Vol. 10: Hymenoptera: Apoidea. 406p. 1993. 59.95 (*0-644-29080-3*, Pub. by CSIRO) Accents Pubns.

Cardamme, Tom. Studio Smarts: How to Adapt to the Business of Desktop Publishing. LC 97-73444. 104p. 1997. pap. 12.95 (*0-88108-203-1*) Art Dir.

Cardamone, Donna G., ed. see Willaert, Adrian, et al.

Cardamone, Jeanette M. & Baker, Mary T., eds. Historic Textiles, Papers & Polymers in Museums. (ACS Symposium Ser.). 125.00 (*0-8412-3652-6*, Pub. by Am Chemical) OUP.

Cardamone, Stevie & Butler, Kathleen A. The Constitution in Style. 60p. 1987. pap. 9.95 (*0-945852-02-9*) Learners Dimension.

Cardamone, Tom. How to Plot & Construct Charts & Graphs. (Illus.). 1987. 17.95 (*0-88108-043-8*); pap. 13.95 (*0-88108-044-6*) Art Dir.

Cardamone, Tom, ed. How to Spec & Buy Type. LC 88-70437. 104p. 1988. pap. 14.50 (*0-88108-050-0*); text 17.50 (*0-88108-049-7*) Art Dir.

Cardan, Joseph. The Astrological Aphorisms of Cardan. Lilly, William, ed. 1990. reprint ed. pap. 3.95 (*1-55818-101-6*, Sure Fire) Holmes Pub.

Cardana, Claudia. Taste of Malta: A Hippocrene Original Cookbook. LC 97-41257. (Original Cookbook Ser.). 305p. 1998. 24.95 (*0-7818-0524-4*) Hippocrene Bks.

Cardanha, Judith. Career Math Skills. 256p. (C). 1993. text 12.40 (*0-256-13838-9*, Irwn McGrw-H) McGrw-H Hghr Educ.

— Career Reading Skills. 320p. (C). 1993. text 16.40 (*0-256-13836-2*, Irwn McGrw-H) McGrw-H Hghr Educ.

— Career Writing Skills. 192p. (C). 1993. text 14.00 (*0-256-13835-4*, Irwn McGrw-H) McGrw-H Hghr Educ.

Cardanha, Judith M. Career Math Skills. 1993. teacher ed. 16.78 (*0-256-13842-7*, Irwn McGrw-H) McGrw-H Hghr Educ.

— Career Reading Skills. 1993. teacher ed. 11.99 (*0-256-13837-0*, Irwn McGrw-H) McGrw-H Hghr Educ.

— Career Writing Skills. 1993. teacher ed. 16.78 (*0-256-13841-9*, Irwn McGrw-H) McGrw-H Hghr Educ.

Cardano, Girolamo. Ars Magna: or The Rules of Algebra. (Illus.). xxiv, 267p. 1993. reprint ed. pap. text 8.95 (*0-486-67811-3*) Dover.

— Cardanus Comforte. Bedingfield, T., ed. LC 77-6565. (English Experience Ser.: No. 82). 204p. 1969. reprint ed. 25.00 (*90-221-0082-0*) Walter J Johnson.

Cardarelle-Hermans, Jeff, jt. auth. see Cardarelle-Hermans, Mary J.

Cardarelle-Hermans, Mary J. & Cardarelle-Hermans, Jeff. Eating Economically - Just Plain Smart: How We Feed Our Family of 7 for Less Than $50 Per Week. (Illus.). 128p. 1998. pap. 14.99 (*0-9661400-0-1*) M J & J C-H.

***Cardarelli, Francois.** Scientific Unit Conversion: A Practical Guide to Metrication. 2nd ed. LC 98-20455. xiv, 488p. 1999. pap. 49.95 (*1-85233-043-0*, Pub. by Spr-Verlag) Spr-Verlag.

Cardarelli, Francois. Scientific Unit Conversion: Practical Guide to Metrication, Vol. XVI. (Illus.). 472p. 1997. pap. 39.95 (*3-540-76022-9*) Spr-Verlag.

***Cardarelli, Franpcois.** Materials Handbook: A Concise Desktop Reference. LC 99-20194. 510p. 2000. 116.00 (*1-85233-168-2*, Pub. by Spr-Verlag) Spr-Verlag.

Cardarelli, Nate F. Controlled Release Pesticides Formulations. (Uniscience Ser.). 224p. 1976. 124.95 (*0-8493-5114-6*, SB951) CRC Pr.

Cardarelli, Nate F., ed. Role of the Thymus in Health & Senescence, Vol. 1: Thymus & Immunity. LC 88-39539. 368p. 1989. 172.00 (*0-8493-6909-6*, QP188, CRC Reprint) Franklin.

— Role of the Thymus in Health & Senescence, Vol. 1: Thymus & Immunity, II. LC 88-39539. 368p. 1989. 197.00 (*0-8493-6910-X*, QP188, CRC Reprint) Franklin.

— Tin As a Vital Nutrient: Implications in Cancer Prophylaxis & Other Physiological Processes. 336p. 1986. 138.00 (*0-8493-6579-1*, RC271, CRC Reprint) Franklin.

Cardell, Kerry. On Reading Paradise Lost. 91p. (C). 1980. 25.00 (*0-86828-050-X*, Pub. by Deakin Univ) St Mut.

Cardella, Lara. Good Girls Don't Wear Trousers. Di Carcaci, Diana, tr. from ITA. 128p. 1994. 16.45 (*1-55970-263-X*, Pub. by Arcade Pub Inc) Time Warner.

— Volevo i Pantaloni: B Level. text 8.95 (*0-8219-1056-6*) EMC-Paradigm.

Cardelle, Frank. Journey to Brotherhood: Awakening, Healing & Connecting Men's Hearts. 308p. 1991. 21.95 (*0-89876-153-0*) Gardner Pr.

Cardelle, Robert. Youth & Adult: The Shared Journey Toward Wholeness. LC 88-11699. 1989. pap. 19.95 (*0-89876-155-7*) Gardner Pr.

Cardelli, Luca, jt. auth. see Abadi, Martin.

Carden. Song of the Thunderbird. 1996. pap. text 29.95 (*0-7935-6322-4*) H Leonard.

Carden, contrib. by. Fugue in G Minor. 1996. pap. text 24.95 (*0-7935-6387-9*) H Leonard.

Carden & Cherry Advertising Agency, Inc. Staff, ed. see Worrell, Ernest P.

Carden, A. E., ed. see American Society for Testing & Materials Staff, et al.

Carden, Allen D. The Missouri Harmony: or A Collection of Psalm & Hymn Tunes, & Anthems. LC 93-41235. xx, 240p. 1994. pap. 12.00 (*0-8032-6114-4*, Bison Books) U of Nebr Pr.

Carden, Barbara. When I First Saw the Moon: A Journey of Triumph & Celebration. LaRusso, Carol, ed. LC 97-68599. 304p. 1997. pap. 19.95 (*0-9658179-4-6*) Divine Grace.

Carden, Connie & Ballard, Patti. San Jacinto Battleground State Historical Park: A Teacher's Curriculum Guide. Spasic, Larry et al, eds. (Illus.). 147p. ring bd. 10.75 (*0-940803-01-1*) SJ Mus Hist Assn.

Carden, Frank. Telemetry Systems Design. LC 95-19077. (Illus.). 256p. 1995. 93.00 (*0-89006-800-3*) Artech Hse.

Carden, Gary & Anderson, Nina. Belled Buzzards, Hucksters & Grieving Spectres: Appalachian Tales, Strange, True & Legendary. Bledsoe, Jerry, ed. LC 94-70669. (Illus.). 208p. 1994. pap. 13.95 (*1-878086-28-6*, Pub. by Down Home NC) Blair.

Carden, Gary, jt. auth. see Davenport, Tom.

Carden, Gary, jt. auth. see Paxton, Collin Wilcox.

***Carden, Gary N.** Mason Jars in the Flood: And Other Stories. LC 99-58227. 1999. 16.95 (*1-887905-22-7*) Pkway Pubs.

Carden, John. A Procession of Prayers: Meditations & Prayers from Around the World. 320p. 1997. pap. 25.00 (*0-304-70139-4*) Continuum.

— A Procession of Prayers: Meditations & Prayers from Around the World. LC 97-46455. 352p. 1998. pap. 16.95 (*0-8192-1752-2*) Morehouse Pub.

Carden, Joy C. Music in Lexington Before 1840. LC 80-83683. 148p. 1980. pap. 9.95 (*0-912839-05-8*) Lexington-Fayette.

***Carden, Judith, et al.** God Things Come in Small Packages: Celebrating the Little Things in Life. (God Things Come in Small Packages Ser.). (Illus.). 128p. 2000. 12.95 (*1-892016-28-1*, Pub. by Starburst) Natl Bk Netwk.

— God Things Come in Small Packages for Moms: Rejoicing in the Simple Pleasures of Motherhood. (God Things Come in Small Packages Ser.). (Illus.). 128p. 2000. 12.95 (*1-892016-29-X*, Pub. by Starburst) Natl Bk Netwk.

Carden, Maren L. The New Feminist Movement. LC 73-83889. 226p. 1974. 35.00 (*0-87154-196-3*) Russell Sage.

— Oneida: Utopian Community to Modern Corporation. LC 98-6533. 1998. pap. text 17.95 (*0-8156-0523-4*) Syracuse U Pr.

Carden, Richard, jt. auth. see Sophocles.

Carden, Ron M. German Policy Toward Neutral Spain, 1914-1918. (Modern European History Ser.). 320p. 1987. text 15.00 (*0-8240-8047-5*) Garland.

***Cardena, Etzel, et al.** Varieties of Anomalous Experience: Examining the Scientific Evidence. LC 99-45473. 488p. 2000. text 39.95 (*1-55798-625-8*, 431-629A) Am Psychol.

Cardenal, Ernesto. Abide in Love. Livingstone, Dinah, tr. from SPA. LC 95-18293. (Illus.). 160p. (Orig.). 1995. pap. 13.00 (*1-57075-011-4*) Orbis Bks.

— Apocalypse & Other Poems. Pring-Mill, Robert & Walsh, Donald D., eds. LC 77-7280. 1977. pap. 7.95 (*0-8112-0662-9*, NDP441, Pub. by New Directions) Norton.

— Cosmic Canticle. Lyons, John, tr. from SPA. LC 93-24154. 490p. 1993. 24.95 (*1-880684-07-1*) Curbstone.

— The Doubtful Strait. Lyons, John & Williams, Tamara R., trs. from SPA. LC 94-633.Tr. of Estrecho Dudoso. 224p. 1995. pap. 14.95 (*0-253-20903-X*) Ind U Pr.

— Flights of Victory. Zimmerman, Marc, tr. LC 84-5278. 123p. 1988. pap. 12.95 (*0-915306-74-3*) Curbstone.

— Flights of Victory (Vuelos de Victoria) Zimmerman, Marc, ed. & tr. by. LC 84-5278. 160p. reprint ed. pap. 49.60 (*0-8357-4058-7*, 203674800005) Bks Demand.

— Golden UFOs: The Indian Poems Los Ovnis de Oro: Poemas Indios. LC 91-33638. (Illus.). 480p. 1992. text 52.50 (*0-253-31302-3*); pap. text 10.95 (*0-253-20677-4*, MB-677) Ind U Pr.

— The Gospel in Solentiname, Vol. 1. Walsh, Donald D., tr. LC 76-2681. Orig. Title: El Evangelio en Solentiname. 288p. (Orig.). 1976. reprint ed. pap. 89.30 (*0-7837-9861-X*, 206059000001) Bks Demand.

— The Gospel in Solentiname, Vol. 2. Walsh, Donald D., tr. LC 76-2681. Orig. Title: El Evangelio en Solentiname. 272p. (Orig.). 1976. reprint ed. pap. 84.40 (*0-7837-9862-8*, 206059000002) Bks Demand.

— The Gospel in Solentiname, Vol. 4. Walsh, Donald D., tr. LC 76-2681. Orig. Title: El Evangelio en Solentiname. 288p. (Orig.). 1976. reprint ed. pap. 89.30 (*0-7837-9864-4*, 206059000004) Bks Demand.

— Homage to the American Indians. Altschul, Carlos & Altschul, Monique, trs. LC 73-8111. (Illus.). 123p. reprint ed. pap. 38.20 (*0-608-10720-4*, 202049700018) Bks Demand.

— In Cuba. Walsh, Donald D., tr. from SPA. & pref. by. LC 74-8493. 352p. 1974. pap. 9.95 (*0-8112-0538-X*, NDP377, Pub. by New Directions) Norton.

— Love. 142p. 1994. pap. 21.00 (*0-85532-344-2*, Pub. by Srch Pr) St Mut.

— Marilyn Monroe & Other Poems. 136p. 1994. pap. 21.00 (*0-85532-358-2*, Pub. by Srch Pr) St Mut.

— Quetzalcoatl. Ross, Clifton, tr. from SPA. & intro. by. (Illus.). 59p. 1992. pap. 9.95 (*0-915117-38-X*) Freedom Voices Pubns.

***Cardenal, Ernesto.** Vida Perdida. 1999. pap. 24.95 (*84-322-0832-9*) Planeta.

Cardenal, Ernesto, tr. The Gospel in Solentiname, Vol. 3. LC 76-2681. Orig. Title: El Evangelio en Solentiname. 320p. (Orig.). 1976. reprint ed. pap. 99.20 (*0-7837-9863-6*, 206059000003) Bks Demand.

Cardenal, Ernesto, et al. Ergo! The Bumbershoot Literary Magazine, Vol. 6, No. 1. 96p. (Orig.). 1991. pap. 6.00 (*0-929696-03-4*) Bumbershoot.

Cardenal, Jaime C. La Prensa: The Republic of Paper. LC 88-24295. (Focus on Issues Ser.: No. 5). (Illus.). 206p. (Orig.). (C). 1989. 22.95 (*0-932088-24-4*); pap. text 9.95 (*0-932088-25-2*) Freedom Hse.

Cardenas. Research Foundations Object Oriented. (C). 1995. pap. text 42.00 (*0-13-456476-6*) P-H.

Cardenas, Alfonso F., et al. Computer Science. LC 71-169162. 534p. reprint ed. pap. 165.60 (*0-8357-9861-5*, 205517200011) Bks Demand.

Cardenas, Anthony J. The Text & Concordance of Biblioteca Nacional Manuscript Res. 270-217: Libro Que Es Hecho de las Animalias Que Cazan: The Book of Moamin. (Spanish Ser.: No. 38). 24p. 1987. 10.00 incl. fiche (*0-942260-99-6*) Hispanic Seminary.

Cardenas-Arroyo, Felipe & Guhl-Nannetti, Felipe. Bioantropologia, Vol. 2, No. 2. (SPA., Illus.). 42p. 1992. pap. 6.00 (*1-877812-63-3*, UA006) UPLAAP.

Cardenas-Arroyo, Felipe, jt. ed. see Langebaek, Carl H.

Cardenas, Blandina, jt. auth. see Cardenas, Jose A.

Cardenas, Elaine, jt. auth. see Wheeler, Joseph.

***Cardenas, Enrique, et al.** An Economic History of 20th Century Latin America. 3 vols. LC 00-40449. 2000. write for info. (*0-333-63342-3*) St Martin.

Cardenas, Gilberto, jt. auth. see Chapa, Jorge.

Cardenas, Gilberto, jt. ed. see Ugalde, Antonio.

Cardenas, Hugo, et al. Artesania Textil Andina. 236p. 1988. pap. 17.50 (*1-85339-369-X*, Pub. by Intermed Tech) Stylus Pub VA.

Cardenas, Jeffrey. Marquesa: A Place & Time with Fish. (Illus.). 125p. 1995. 50.00 (*0-9620609-9-2*) Meadow Run Pr.

Cardenas, Jose A. All Pianos Have Keys & Other Stories. 134p. (Orig.). 1994. pap. 12.70 (*1-878550-53-5*) Inter Dev Res Assn.

— My Spanish Speaking Left Foot. 135p. (Orig.). 1997. pap. 9.00 (*1-878550-59-4*) Inter Dev Res Assn.

— Texas School Finance Reform: An IDRA Perspective. LC 97-183194. 387p. 1997. 30.00 (*1-878550-63-2*) Inter Dev Res Assn.

Cardenas, Jose A. & Cardenas, Blandina. The Theory of Incompatibilities: A Conceptual Framework for Responding to the Educational Needs of Hispanic Americans. 23p. (Orig.). 1977. pap. text 2.50 (*1-878550-06-3*) Inter Dev Res Assn.

Cardenas, Jose A. & Ramirez, Blandina C. La Teoria de las Incompatibilidades. Vergara, Fausto, tr. from ENG. (SPA.). 19p. 1981. pap. text 4.00 (*1-878550-39-X*) Inter Dev Res Assn.

Cardenas, Juan, ed. see Robles, Mireya.

Cardenas, Lupe, jt. auth. see Alarcon, Justo S.

Cardenas, M. L., jt. auth. see Cornish-Bowden, A.

Cardenas, Magolo. Con Mis Ojos a los Muertos (With My Eyes on the Dead) (SPA.). 160p. 1993. pap. 6.99 (*968-16-4164-7*, Pub. by Fondo) Continental Bk.

— Maria Contra Viento y Marea. (SPA., Illus.). 191p. 1994. pap. 6.99 (*968-16-4229-5*, Pub. by Fondo) Continental Bk.

Cardenas, Margarita, tr. see Burke, Ray & Herron, Ron.

Cardenas, Raul de. Las Sombras No Se Olvidan. rev. ed. (SPA.). 57p. 1993. pap. text 3.95 (*1-885901-01-1*) Presbyters Peartree.

Cardenas-Ruiz, Manuel, ed. from FRE. Cronicas Francesas de los Indios Caribes. LC 79-11655. (SPA., Illus.). xii, 624p. (Orig.). 1981. pap. 15.00 (*0-8477-0852-7*) U of PR Pr.

Cardenas-Ruiz, Manuel, ed. see Labat, Jean B.

Cardenas, Tony. Back in Balance - Back in Action: The Complete Guide to the Self-Treatment & Prevention of Back Pain. (Illus.). 150p. (Orig.). 1994. 19.95 (*0-9641656-0-0*); pap. 14.95 (*0-685-75262-3*) T H I N K Pr.

Cardenosa, Gilda. Breast Imaging: A Teaching File. (Teaching File Ser.). (Illus.). 425p. 1998. write for info. (*0-683-30218-3*) Lppncott W & W.

— Breast Imaging Companion. LC 96-29273. 456p. 1996. text 63.00 (*0-397-51778-5*) Lppncott W & W.

Carder, C. H. The Shamblin Family History of West Virginia. LC 97-66114. 196p. 1997. pap. 12.00 (0-87012-575-3) McClain.

THE SHAMBLIN FAMILY OF WEST VIRGINIA traces the Shamblin descendants of the earliest pioneers of that name in West Virginia to well into this century. Most members of the family living in West Virginia should be able to find their grandparents in this book & trace their ancestry back to the pioneer settlers. *Publisher Paid Annotation.*

Carder, Charles E. Falling Blocks & Other Single Shots from Hopkins & Allen. 71p. 1996. pap. text 17.95 (*0-9635451-2-4*) Aero Print.

— Side by Sides of the World. 1997. pap. write for info. (*0-7880-0930-3*, Fairway Pr) CSS OH.

— Tip up Shotguns from Hopkins & Allen Arms Company. 60p. 1994. pap. text 13.95 (*0-9635451-1-6*) Aero Print.

Carder, Clarence A., ed. Lees-McRae College Recipe Book. (Illus.). 1984. 5.50 (*0-317-00834-X*) Puddingstone.

Carder, Dave. Secrets of Your Family Tree: Healing for Adult Children of Dysfunctional Families. pap. 14.99 (*0-8024-7749-6*, 281) Moody.

Carder, Dave, et al. Torn Asunder: Recovering from Extramarital Affairs. expanded rev. ed. pap. 14.99 (*0-8024-7748-8*, 301) Moody.

Carder, David. Promises from Proverbs. 1984. pap. 11.70 (*0-310-36782-4*, 12732P) Zondervan.

Carder, Jennifer, ed. see Deaton, James.

Carder, Kenneth. Sermons on United Methodist Beliefs. (Orig.). 1991. pap. 8.95 (*0-687-38002-2*) Abingdon.

Carder, Kenneth L. A Bishop's Reflections. LC 96-69127. 144p. 1996. pap. 11.95 (*1-881576-99-X*) Providence Hse.

— Living Our Beliefs: The United Methodist Way. LC 96-84123. 144p. 1996. pap. 15.95 (*0-88177-169-4*, DR169) Discipleship Res.

Carder, Paul, ed. see Oakland, Roger.

Carder, Polly, ed. Eclectic Curriculum in American Music Education. rev. ed. (Illus.). 176p. 1990. reprint ed. pap. 21.00 (*0-940796-77-5*, 1503) MENC.

Carder, Shirl. Nut Lover's Cookbook. LC 84-70857. 160p. 1984. pap. 6.95 (*0-89087-405-0*) Celestial Arts.

Carder, Susie F. Passion: A Salon Professional's Handbook for Building a Successful Business. (Illus.). 200p. (Orig.). 1996. pap. 19.95 (*0-9650777-8-0*) Carder Creative.

Carder, Thomas. Handling of Radiation Accident Patients by Para-Hospital Personnel. 2nd ed. 240p. 1993. boxed set 79.95 (*0-8493-8696-9*, RC93) CRC Pr.

Cardew, A. G., jt. auth. see Natesa, Sastri S.

Cardew, Cornelius, tr. see Eimert, Herbert & Stockhausen, Karlheinz, eds.

Cardew, Cornelius, tr. see Webern, Anton.

Cardew, F. G. The Services of the Bengal Native Army. 576p. 1990. 105.00 (*0-948251-69-7*, Pub. by Picton) St Mut.

Cardew, G. F. Bengal Native Army to Year Eighteen Ninety-Five: A Sketch of the Services. (Illus.). 576p. 1971. reprint ed. 10.00 (*0-88065-025-7*) Scholarly Pubns.

Cardew, Gail, jt. auth. see Chadwick, Derek.

Cardew, Gail, jt. auth. see Chadwick, Derek J.

Cardew, Gail, jt. ed. see Bock, Gregory R.

Cardew, P. T. & Level, M. S., eds. Membrane Processes: A Technology Guide. (Special Publication Ser.: Vol. 238). viii, 326p. 1999. pap. 100.00 (*0-85404-454-X*) Spr-Verlag.

***Cardew, Philip.** A Translation of Porskifiroinga (Gull Poris) Saga. LC 00-24198. (Scandinavian Studies: 5). 200p. 2000. 79.95 (*0-7734-7795-0*) E Mellen.

Cardiel, Patrice, jt. auth. see Trisler, Alana.

Cardiel, Patrice H., jt. auth. see Trisler, Alana.

Cardiff, David, jt. auth. see Scannell, Paddy.

Cardiff, Gladys. A Bare Unpainted Table. LC 98-66494. 64p. 1999. 22.00 (*0-932826-69-5*) New Issues MI.

— A Bare Unpainted Table. LC 98-66494. (Poetry Ser.). 64p. 1999. pap. 12.00 (*0-932826-67-9*) WMU Poetry & Prose.

Cardiff, Ira D. What Great Men Think of Religion. LC 71-161322. (Atheist Viewpoint Ser.). 504p. 1976. reprint ed. 31.95 (*0-405-03625-6*) Ayer.

***Cardiff, Janet.** Janet Cardiff: The Missing Voice (Case Study B) (Illus.). 72p. 2000. pap. 40.00 (*1-902201-07-8*) Dist Art Pubs.

Cardiff Law School, Centre for Legal Aspects of Me, ed. Butterworths Medico-Legal Reports. 160p. 1992. boxed set 58.00 (*0-406-44001-8*, UK, MICHIE) LEXIS Pub.

Cardiff, Pam. Blast from the Past. LC 95-221827. 80p. (J). (gr. 5-9). 1996. pap. text 2.95 (*0-8114-9327-X*) Raintree Steck-V.

Cardigan, Jim. Ronald Reagan: A Remarkable Life. (Illus.). 128p. 1995. pap. 12.95 (*0-8362-0449-2*) Andrews & McMeel.

Cardillo, Alberto. Altra Meta del Cielo: Italian Poetry. 31p. 1987. pap. 5.00 (*0-89304-577-2*) Cross-Cultrl NY.

Cardillo, Brent, jt. auth. see Brannon, Tom.

Cardillo, G., jt. auth. see Cainelli, G.

Cardillo, Joe. No Surrender. LC 93-85853. (Orig.). (YA). 1993. pap. 11.95 (*0-9624082-1-2*) Stone Buzzard.

— Pulse. 1999. pap. 4.99 (*0-14-038177-5*) Viking Penguin.

— The Rock n' Roll Journals: Poems by Joe Cardillo. (Illus.). 1989. pap. 6.95 (*0-9624082-0-4*) Stone Buzzard.

— Turning Toward Morning. 64p. 1986. reprint ed. 19.95 (*0-89002-237-2*); reprint ed. pap. 6.95 (*0-89002-236-4*) Northwoods Pr.

Cardillo, Rod. Totally Orchids. (Totally Flowers Ser.). (Illus.). 96p. 1996. pap. 5.95 (*0-89087-782-3*) Celestial Arts.

Cardin, Carlton. Understanding Computer Telephony. 1997. 34.95 (*0-936648-83-X*) Telecom Bks.

Cardin, Clifton D. Bossier Parish Headstones: A Complete Inventory. LC 97-92383. 528p. (Orig.). 1997. pap. 39.95 (*0-9637507-2-0*) C D Cardin.

— Bossier Parish History, 1843-1993: The First 150 Years. 253p. 1993. 29.95 (*0-9637507-1-2*); pap. 19.95 (*0-9637507-0-4*) C D Cardin.

***Cardin, Clifton D.** Bossier Parish, LA. (Images of America Ser.). (Illus.). 128p. 1999. pap. 18.99 (*0-7385-0172-7*) Arcadia Publng.

Cardin, D. J., et al. Chemistry of Organo-Zirconium & Hafnium Compounds. LC 85-14059. 451p. 1986. text 139.00 (*0-470-20204-1*) P-H.

Cardin, Nina B., ed. Out of the Depths I Call to You: A Book of Prayers for the Married Jewish Woman. LC 91-15950. 148p. 1995. reprint ed. pap. text 25.00 (*1-56821-411-1*) Aronson.

***Cardin, Nina Beth.** The Tapestry of Jewish Time: A Spiritual Guide to Holiday & Life-Cycle Events. LC 99-88876. (Illus.). 320p. 2000. pap. 24.95 (*0-87441-645-0*) Behrman.

Cardin, Nina Beth. Tears of Sorrow, Seeds of Hope: A Jewish Spiritual Companion for Infertility & Pregnancy Loss. 160p. 1999. 19.95 (*1-58023-017-2*) Jewish Lights.

Cardin, Pierre. Pierre Cardin. 1997. 50.00 (*2-08-013642-9*, Pub. by Flammarion) Abbeville Pr.

Cardinal, Agnes, et al, eds. Women's Writing on the First World War. LC 99-15282. 392p. 2000. 35.00 (*0-19-812280-2*) OUP.

Cardinal, Andre. Etude Sur les Ectocarpacees de la Manche. (Illus.). 1965. pap. 48.00 (*3-7682-5415-1*) Lubrecht & Cramer.

Cardinal, Bradley. Physical Fitness: The Hub of the Wellness Wheel. 2nd ed. 256p. (C). 1994. spiral bd. 21.95 (*0-8403-9360-1*) Kendall-Hunt.

***Cardinal, Catherine.** The Ten Commandments of Relationships. LC 00-35533. 2000. write for info. (*0-7407-0993-3*) Andrews & McMeel.

Cardinal, Catherine. The Ten Commandments of Self-Esteem. LC 97-41455. 1998. write for info. (*0-8362-5196-2*) Andrews & McMeel.

Cardinal, Catherine S. The Button Box. (Illus.). 40p. (Orig.). (J). (gr. 3 up). 1992. write for info. (*0-9630655-1-3*) Garden Gate.

— Charlotte Pug: (The Walnut War) (Illus.). 16p. (J). (gr. k-5). 1994. pap. 3.40 (*0-9630655-2-1*) Garden Gate.

— Mud Grape Pie. 29p. (J). (gr. k-6). 1991. pap. 6.00 (*0-9630655-0-5*) Garden Gate.

Cardinal, Don, ed. see Biklin, Doug.

Cardinal, Douglas J. & Armstrong, Jeannette C. The Native Creative Process: A Collaborative Discourse. (Illus.). 128p. 1991. pap. 21.95 (*0-919441-26-2*, Pub. by Theytus Bks) Orca Bk Pubs.

Cardinal, Etienne, jt. ed. see Chhem, Rethy.

Cardinal Gibbons. Faith of Our Fathers. LC 80-51331. 352p. 1980. reprint ed. pap. 16.50 (*0-89555-158-6*) TAN Bks Pubs.

Cardinal, Ginger. The Rats: An Owner's Guide to a Happy, Healthy Pet. LC 97-25735. 126p. 1997. 12.95 (*0-87605-428-9*) Howell Bks.

***Cardinal, Harold.** The Unjust Society. 166p. 2000. pap. 19.95 (*0-295-97909-7*) U of Wash Pr.

Cardinal Henry E. Manning. The Fourfold Sovereignty of God. LC 86-51264. 185p. 1986. reprint ed. pap. 5.00 (*0-89555-308-2*) TAN Bks Pubs.

— Sin & Its Consequences. rev. ed. LC 86-50420. 200p. 1991. reprint ed. pap. 6.00 (*0-89555-299-X*) TAN Bks Pubs.

Cardinal, Marie. Au Pays de Mes Racines. (FRE.). 1982. pap. 10.95 (*0-7859-3107-4*) Fr & Eur.

— Autrement Dit. (FRE.). 1988. pap. 10.95 (*0-7859-3097-3*) Fr & Eur.

— Cet Ete La. (FRE.). 1980. pap. 10.95 (*0-7859-3103-1*) Fr & Eur.

— La Cle sur la Porte. (FRE.). 1975. pap. 10.95 (*0-7859-3075-2*) Fr & Eur.

— Comme Si de Rien n'Etait. (FRE.). 1992. pap. 10.95 (*0-7859-3168-6*, 2253059188) Fr & Eur.

— Ecoutez la Mer. (FRE.). 1978. pap. 10.95 (*0-7859-3209-7*, 2266006525) Fr & Eur.

— Les Grands Desordres. (FRE.). 1989. pap. 12.95 (*0-7859-3152-X*, 2253051195) Fr & Eur.

— In Other Words. Cooper, Amy, tr. from FRE. LC 95-8257.Tr. of Autrement Dit. 216p. 1995. 24.95 (*0-253-32929-9*); pap. 12.95 (*0-253-20992-7*) Ind U Pr.

— Les Mots pour le Dire. (FRE.). 1977. pap. 10.95 (*0-7859-3093-0*) Fr & Eur.

— Le Mule de Corbillard. (FRE.). 1979. pap. 10.95 (*0-7859-3210-0*, 2266006614) Fr & Eur.

— Le Passe Empiete. (FRE.). 1984. pap. 12.95 (*0-7859-3123-6*) Fr & Eur.

— La Sourciere. (FRE.). 1978. pap. 10.95 (*0-7859-3208-9*, 2266006495) Fr & Eur.

— Une Vie pour Deux. (FRE.). 1980. pap. 12.95 (*0-7859-3102-3*) Fr & Eur.

— Words to Say It. 9th ed. Goodheart, Pat, ed. & tr. by. from FRE.Tr. of Les/Mots Pour le Dire. (ENG.). 308p. (Orig.). (C). 1994. pap. 22.95 (*0-941324-09-5*) Van Vactor & Goodheart.

***Cardinal, Ratzinger.** Many Religions, One Covenant. 1999. pap. 11.95 (*0-89870-753-6*) Ignatius Pr.

Cardinal, Roger, et al. Visions from the Left Coast: California Self-Taught Artists. LC 95-74807. (Illus.). 66p. (Orig.). 1995. pap. 19.95 (*1-880658-08-9*) San Barb CAF.

Cardinal, Roger, jt. auth. see Bowman, Russell.

Cardinal, Roger, jt. ed. see Elsner, John.

Cardinale, Diane, ed. see Edmund, Norman W.

Cardinale, Gary, jt. auth. see Rulien, Diane E.

Cardinale, Susan, compiled by. Anthologies by & about Women: An Analytical Index. LC 81-13423. 822p. 1982. lib. bdg. 105.00 (*0-313-22180-4*, CAB/, Greenwood Pr) Greenwood.

Cardinale, Susan, jt. compiled by see Smith, Hilda.

Cardinaletti, Anna & Guasti, Maria T., eds. Syntax & Semantics Vol. 28: Small Clauses. (Illus.). 333p. 1995. text 84.95 (*0-12-613528-2*) Acad Pr.

Cardinali, D. P. Manual de Neurofisiologia. (SPA.). 339p. 1992. pap. 28.50 (*84-7978-005-3*, Pub. by Ediciones Diaz) IBD Ltd.

Cardinali, D. P. & Fraschini, F., eds. Psycho-Immune-Neuroendocrine Integrative Mechanisms. (Biological Signals & Receptors Ser.: Vol. 7, No. 1, 1998). (Illus.). 74p. 1998. pap. 33.25 (*3-8055-6685-9*) S Karger.

Cardinali, Luca. Origo Gentis Romanae: De Viris Illustribus, Concordantiae et Indices. (Alpha-Omega, Reihe A Ser.: Bd. CLXXXVI). (GER.). 549p. 1997. write for info. (*3-487-10494-6*) G Olms Pubs.

Cardinali, Rick. Instant Guitar Chords. (Illus.). 48p. 1991. pap. 15.95 (*0-7119-1815-5*, AM74709) Music Sales.

Cardini, Leo. Mineshaft Nights. Douglas, Jerry, ed. (Illus.). 183p. (Orig.). 1990. pap. 10.95 (*0-943383-01-3*) FirstHand Ltd.

Cardiovascular Disease Conference Staff. Clinical Application of Current Techniques & Treatment in Cardiology: Proceedings of the Cardiovascular Disease Conference, 6th, Snowmass at Aspen, Colorado, 1975. Vogel, H. K., ed. (Advances in Cardiology Ser.: Vol. 17). 1976. 109.75 (*3-8055-2267-3*) S Karger.

— Future Directions in the Management of Cardiac Disease: Proceedings of the Cardiovascular Disease Conference, 7th, Snowmass at Aspen, Colorado, 1976. Vogel, H. K., ed. (Advances in Cardiology Ser.: Vol. 20). 1977. 65.25 (*3-8055-2412-9*) S Karger.

— Hypoxia, High Altitude & the Heart: Proceedings of the Cardiovascular Disease Conference, 1st, Snowmass at Aspen, Colorado, 1970. Vogel, J. H., ed. (Advances in Cardiology Ser.: Vol. 5). 1970. 61.75 (*3-8055-0728-3*) S Karger.

— Integrated Medical-Surgical Care in Acute Coronary Artery Disease: Proceedings of the Cardiovascular Disease Conference, 5th, Snowmass at Aspen, Colorado, Jan. 1974. Vogel, J. H., ed. (Advances in Cardiology Ser.: Vol. 15). x, 199p. 1975. 94.00 (*3-8055-2098-0*) S Karger.

— Myocardial Infarction: Proceedings of the Cardiovascular Disease Conference, 3rd, Snowmass at Aspen, CO, Jan. 1972. Vogel, J. H., ed. (Advances in Cardiology Ser.: Vol. 9). 1973. 85.25 (*3-8055-1373-9*) S Karger.

— A Perspective on New Techniques in Congenital & Acquired Heart Disease: Proceedings of the Cardiovascular Disease Conference, 4th, Snowmass at Aspen, Colorado, Jan. 1973. Vogel, J., ed. (Advances in Cardiology Ser.: Vol. 11). 1974. 95.00 (*3-8055-1654-1*) S Karger.

— Results & Evaluation of New Methodology in Cardiology: Proceedings of the Cardiovascular Disease Conference, 8th, Snowmass at Aspen, Colorado, Jan. 10-14, 1977. Vogel, J. H., ed. (Advances in Cardiology Ser.: Vol. 22). 1977. 117.50 (*3-8055-2748-9*) S Karger.

Cardiovascular Medicine Staff & Kressel, Herbert Y. Cardiovascular Medicine, Vol. 1. fac. ed. LC 81-48504. 388p. pap. 120.30 (*0-7837-7224-6*, 204707400001) Bks Demand.

***Cardis, A. B. & Webster, M. N.** Gear Oil Micropitting Evaluation. (Technical Papers: Vol. 99FTM4). 16p. 1999. pap. 30.00 (*1-55589-742-8*) AGMA.

Cardis, E. & Gilbert, E. Combined Analyses of Cancer Mortality among Nuclear Industry Workers in Canada, the United Kingdom & the United States of America. (IARC Technical Report Ser.: No. 25). 147p. 1995. text 30.00 (*92-832-1440-4*) World Health.

Cardis, Julia, jt. auth. see Smith, Kendall.

Cardo, Francesco, jt. auth. see Proudfoot, Anna.

Cardo, Horacio. The Story of Chess. LC 99-194894. (Illus.). 48p. (J). (gr. 3 up). 1998. 16.95 (*0-7892-0250-6*, Abbeville Kids) Abbeville Pr.

Cardo, Ras. Let the Dead Bury Their Dead: Bad Company. (Ras Cardo Speaks Ser.). 110p. 1995. pap. 30.95 (*1-883427-93-2*, RAS9949-C) Crnerstone GA.

***Cardo, Ras.** Vexations to the Spirit - Ras Cardo Prophesy: Issues Affecting Reggae Music, Its Mission, Its Prophets. (Illus.). 99p. 1999. pap. write for info. (*1-58470-049-1*, RAS1949) Crnerstone GA.

Cardo, Ras & Dennis, Gartie. This Is Jamaica - Reggae - & Rastafari: The Book of Truths - Eye on Jamaica. (Reggae Family Ser.). (Illus.). 200p. (Orig.). 1995. pap. 9.95 (*1-883427-92-4*, RAS9949-A) Crnerstone GA.

Cardon, A. & Fransen, L. Dynamic Semiconductor RAM Structures. (European Patent Office Ser.: Vol. 1). (Illus.). 488p. 1984. 208.00 (*0-08-030578-4*, Pub. by Pergamon Repr) Franklin.

Cardon, A. H., et al, eds. Progress in Durability Analysis of Composite Systems: Proceedings of the International Conference on the Subject, DURACOSYS 95, Brussels, 16-21 July 1995. (Illus.). 336p. (C). 1996. text 136.00 (*90-5410-809-6*, Pub. by A A Balkema) Ashgate Pub Co.

Cardon, A. H. & Verchery, G., eds. Mechanical Characterisation of Load Bearing Fibre Composite Laminates: Proceedings of the European Mechanics Colloquium 182, Mechanical Characterisation of Load Bearing Fibre Composite Laminates Brussels, Belgium, August 29-31, 1984. 264p. 1985. 66.75 (*0-85334-379-9*) Elsevier.

Cardon, Albert H., ed. Durability Analysis of Structural Composite Systems: Reliability, Risk Analysis & Prediction of Safe Residual Structural Integrity. LC 99-227041. (Illus.). 204p. (C). 1996. text 104.00 (*90-5410-640-9*, Pub. by A A Balkema) Ashgate Pub Co.

Cardon, Charlotte M., jt. auth. see Cabat, Erni.

Cardon, Charlotte M., tr. see Cabat, Erni.

***Cardon, H., et al, eds.** Recent Developments in Durability Analysis of Composite Systems: Proceedings of the Fourth International Conference, Brussels, Belgium, 11-14 July 1999. 500p. (C). 2000. text 99.00 (*90-5809-103-1*, Pub. by A A Balkema) Ashgate Pub Co.

Cardona, Dwardu, ed. see Greenberg, Lewis M.

Cardona, Dwardu, ed. see Wescott, Roger W.

Cardona, Francisco J. & Cardona, Maria E. Handbook of Latin American Studies, Author Index to Numbers 1-28. LC 36-32633. 1968. 52.95 (*0-8130-0265-6*) U Press Fla.

Cardona, George. Panini: A Survey of Research. (Trends in Linguistics, State-of-the-Art Reports: No. 6). 1976. pap. 80.80 (*90-279-3435-5*) Mouton.

— Panini - History Work & Its Tradition Vol. 1: Background & Introduction. LC 98-909891. (C). 1997. 60.00 (*81-208-0419-8*, Pub. by Motilal Bnarsidass) S Asia.

***Cardona, George.** Recent Research in Peaminian Studies. LC 99-933528. xi, 327p. 1999. pap. 200.00 (*81-208-1637-4*, Pub. by Motilal Bnarsidass) St Mut.

Cardona-Hine, Alvaro. A History of Light: A Memoir. LC 97-27176. 128p. 1997. pap. 11.95 (*1-890932-00-0*) Sherman Asher Pub.

— Thirteen Tangos for Stravinsky. 144p. 1999. 21.00 (*1-890932-11-6*); pap. 15.00 (*1-890932-07-8*) Sherman Asher Pub.

— Words on Paper. 1974. pap. 2.50 (*0-88031-013-8*) Invisible-Red Hill.

Cardona-Hine, Alvaro, jt. auth. see Patten, Christine T.

Cardona-Hine, Alvaro, jt. auth. see Pena, Alfredo C.

Cardona-Hine, Alvaro, tr. see Vallejo, Cesar.

An Asterisk (*) at the beginning of an entry indicates that the title is appearing for the first time.

Cardona, Jose. Disney Pop-up Book of Actions. LC 92-70935. (Pop-up Bks.). 12p. (J). (ps-k). 1993. 7.95 (*1-56282-506-2*, Pub. by Disney Pr) Little.
— Disney's Pop-up Book of Things That Go. LC 92-56160. (Pop-up Bks.). 12p. (J). (ps-k). 1993. 7.95 (*1-56282-509-7*, Pub. by Disney Pr) Little.
Cardona, Jose & Dubowski, Cathy. The Aristocats. LC 94-74640. (Illus.). 32p. (J). 1996. 12.45 (*0-7868-3081-6*, Pub. by Disney Pr) Little.
Cardona, Jose M., jt. auth. see David, Luke.
Cardona, Luis A. An Annotated Bibliography on Puerto Rican Materials & Other Sundry Matters. LC 83-50536. (Illus.). 154p. (Orig.). (C). 1983. text 36.95 (*0-914199-00-5*) Carreta Pr.
— Contributions of the Hispanics to the United States of America, Vol. 1. LC 91-71254. 75p. (Orig.). 1991. pap. 13.95 (*0-914199-08-0*) Carreta Pr.
— A Directory of Doctoral Research on Puerto Ricans in the United States of America. LC 89-83369. 136p. (Orig.). 1990. pap. text 33.95 (*0-914199-07-2*) Carreta Pr.

— History of Puerto Ricans in the United States of America, Vol. I. 2nd rev. ed. Luis A. Cardona. LC 95-69044. (Illus.). 525p. (Orig.). (C). 1995. pap. 38.95 (0-914199-09-9) Carreta Pr.
The focus of these books is a historical account of Puerto Ricans in the U.S. to the present. Volume I begins with the Tainos Indians, the African slaves & the American military invasion. We see the megalopolis that little old New York became, its ethnic enclaves & the Puerto Rican search for the good life. American ships anchored in Puerto Rican ports. These vessels, after discharging goods & business persons, returned to American ports empty. It was good economics for ships to carry passengers both ways. A HISTORY OF THE PUERTO RICANS IN THE U.S.A. Luis A. Cardona. 1998. 42 photos, p. 500. Vol. II $38.95 1970-present. ISBN 0-914199-10-2. LCCN 98-071230. In Volume II Puerto Ricans continue in a complex industrial society. They sought support from each other in a strange land. With time, they became acquainted with their extended homeland & explored other areas. The crucial issues throughout Volume II are education, employment, health & housing. The political status & languages Spanish vs. English, their identity & their place in the world became all time consuming matters. We witness Puerto Ricans developing organizational skills & becoming a political force. To order contact: Carreta Press, 365 Singletree Trace, Alpharetta, GA 30004. (770) 770-5680. ***Publisher Paid Annotation.***

— A History of Puerto Ricans in the United States of America, Vol. I. 2nd rev. ed. LC 95-69044. (Illus.). 525p. (Orig.). (C). 1995. pap. 38.95 (*0-914199-09-9*) Carreta Pr.
— A History of the Puerto Ricans in the United States of America, Vol. II. LC 98-71230. (Illus.). 500p. 1998. pap. 38.95 (*0-914199-10-2*) Carreta Pr.
— Looking for Employment in the United States. 1997. 11.95 (*0-914199-05-6*) Carreta Pr.
Cardona, Luis A., ed. A Selected Directory of Audio Visual Materials on Puerto Rico & the Puerto Ricans. 70p. (Orig.). 1984. pap. text 8.95 (*0-914199-02-1*) Carreta Pr.
Cardona, Luis Antonio. A Short History of Puerto Ricans in the U. S. 380p. (Orig.). 1999. pap. 28.95 (*0-914199-11-0*) Carreta Pr.
Cardona, M., ed. Light Scattering in Solids I. 2nd ed. (Topics in Applied Physics Ser.: Vol. 8). (Illus.). 363p. 1982. 69.95 (*0-387-11913-2*) Spr-Verlag.
— Thin Films & Small Particles: 5th Latin American Symposium on Surface Physics. 450p. (C). 1989. text 93.00 (*9971-5-0720-X*) World Scientific Pub.
Cardona, M., et al, eds. Self-Trapped Excitons. 2nd rev. ed. LC 96-29440. (Illus.). 424p. 1996. pap. 69.00 (*3-540-60446-4*) Spr-Verlag.
***Cardona, M. & Guentherodt, G., eds.** Light Scattering in Solids VIII: Fullerenes, Semiconductor Surfaces, Coherent Phonons. (Topics in Applied Physics Ser.: Vol. 76). (Illus.). 250p. 1999. 89.95 (*3-540-66085-2*) Spr-Verlag.
— Light Scattering in Solids VII: Crystal-Field & Magnetic Excitations. (Topics in Applied Physics Ser.: Vol. 75). (Illus.). 250p. 1999. 99.00 (*3-540-66075-5*) Spr-Verlag.
Cardona, M. & Guentherodt, G., eds. Light Scattering in Solids III: Recent Results. (Topics in Applied Physics Ser.: Vol. 51). (Illus.). 305p. 1982. 91.95 (*0-387-11513-7*) Spr-Verlag.
— Light Scattering in Solids II: Basic Concept & Instrumentation. (Topics in Applied Physics Ser.: Vol. 50). (Illus.). 251p. 1982. 91.95 (*0-387-11380-0*) Spr-Verlag.
Cardona, M. & Guntherodt, G., eds. Light Scattering in Solids, No. V. (Topics in Applied Physics Ser.: Vol. 66). (Illus.). 345p. 1989. 102.95 (*0-387-50400-1*) Spr-Verlag.
— Light Scattering in Solids IV: Electronic Scattering, Spin Effects, SERS & Morphic Effects. LC 83-13095. (Topics in Applied Physics Ser.: Vol. 54). (Illus.). 560p. 1984. 97.95 (*0-387-11942-6*) Spr-Verlag.
— Light Scattering in Solids VI: Recent Results Including High-TC Superconductivity. (Topics in Applied Physics Ser.: Vol. 68). (Illus.). xiv, 526p. 1991. 135.95 (*0-387-53614-0*) Spr-Verlag.
Cardona, M., jt. ed. see Castro, G. R.
Cardona, M., ed. see Fick, E. & Sauermann, G.
Cardona, M., ed. see Fulde, P.
Cardona, M., ed. see Inui, Tomoyuki, et al.
Cardona, M., ed. see Isihara, A.
Cardona, M., ed. see Isihara, Akira.
Cardona, M., ed. see Kalt, H.
Cardona, M., ed. see Kubo, R., et al.
Cardona, M., jt. ed. see Ley, L.
Cardona, M., jt. ed. see Ponce, F. A.
Cardona, M., ed. see Shah, Jagdeep.
Cardona, M., ed. see Spaeth, Johann-Martin, et al.
Cardona, M., ed. see Toda, Morikazu, et al.
Cardona, Manuel, jt. auth. see Yu, Peter Y.
Cardona, Maria E., jt. auth. see Cardona, Francisco J.
Cardona, Miguel P. Diccionari de Quimica. (CAT.). 110p. 1984. pap. 11.95 (*0-7859-6473-8*) Fr & Eur.
Cardona, Richard. Teach Yourself Java for Macintosh in 21 Days. LC 96-212612. 600p. 1996. pap. text 40.00 incl. cd-rom (*1-56830-280-0*) Hayden.
***Cardona, Rodolfo & Cockcroft, James, eds.** Hispanics of Achievement. (Illus.). 112-128p. (J). 1999. 99.50 (*0-7910-3762-2*) Chelsea Hse.
Cardona, Rodolfo & Cockcroft, James, eds. Juan Ponce de Leon: Spanish Explorer. (Hispanics of Achievement Ser.). (Illus.). 120p. (YA). (gr. 5 up). 1995. lib. bdg. 19.95 (*0-7910-2023-1*) Chelsea Hse.
Cardona, Rudolph, ed. see Perez Galdos, Benito.
Cardona, Virginia D., et al. Trauma Nursing: From Resuscitation Through Rehabilitation. 2nd ed. LC 92-49094. (Illus.). 944p. 1993. text 104.00 (*0-7216-4333-7*, W B Saunders Co) Harcrt Hlth Sci Grp.
Cardone, Bonnie J. Fireside Diver. LC 95-32810. (Illus.). 326p. 1995. reprint ed. pap. 14.95 (*1-881652-09-2*) Aqua Quest.
***Cardone, Christine & Puntillo, Timothy.** The Birthday Book. 120p. 2000. 22.95 (*0-9700192-2-X*) Ink.
Cardone, Christine, jt. auth. see Puntillo, Timothy.
Cardone, David A., jt. auth. see Newbrough, John B.
Cardone, Frances. This Is My Story - This Is My Song. LC 94-75410. 192p. 1994. lib. bdg. 14.95 (*1-883928-05-2*) Longwood.
Cardone, Laurel. Fodor's How to Pack: Experts Share Tips & Techniques to Make Packing a Breeze. LC 98-108727. 160p. 1997. pap. 9.00 (*0-679-03517-6*) Fodors Travel.
Cardoni, Agnes T. Women's Ethical Coming-of-Age: Adolescent Female Characters in the Prose Fiction of Tillie Olsen. LC 97-37712. 136p. (C). 1997. 34.50 (*0-7618-0923-6*) U Pr of Amer.
Cardoni, Edmund, ed. Blatant Artifice: An Annual Anthology of Short Fiction by Visiting Writers, 1984-85. 142p. 1987. pap. 5.95 (*0-936739-03-7*) Hallwalls Inc.
Cardonick, Isabell, jt. auth. see Feldgus, Eileen.
Cardonnoy, Eric L. Les Reflexions d'Elias Canetti: Une Esthetique de la Discontinuite. (Contacts Ser.: Series III, Vol. 38). (FRE.). 338p. 1997. 47.95 (*3-906754-81-2*, Pub. by P Lang) P Lang Pubng.
Cardonsky, Sam. Mary Dugan's Dependable Home. 1988. 21.95 (*0-689-11937-2*) Atheneum Yung Read.
Cardos, Amalia, ed. La Epoca Clasica: Nuevos Hallazgos, Nuevas Ideas. (SPA.). 520p. 1990. pap. 18.00 (*1-877812-39-0*, IN012) UPLAAP.
Cardos de Mendez, Amalia. La Epoca Clasica: Nuevos Hallazgos, Nuevas Ideas. (SPA.). 520p. 1990. pap. 18.00 (*1-877812-65-X*, IN012) UPLAAP.
Cardoso, Ana I., ed. Stochastic Analysis & Applications in Physics: Proceedings of the NATO Advanced Study Institute, Funchal, Madeira, Portugal, August 6-19, 1993. (NATO Advanced Science Institutes: Series C). 472p. (C). 1994. text 264.50 (*0-7923-3197-4*) Kluwer Academic.
Cardoso, Eliana & Helwege, Ann. Cuba after Communism. (Illus.). 160p. 1992. 24.50 (*0-262-03197-3*) MIT Pr.
— Latin America's Economy: Diversity, Trends & Conflicts. 354p. 1995. pap. text 22.00 (*0-262-53125-9*) MIT Pr.
Cardoso, Ersillo, jt. auth. see Rouse.
Cardoso, F. A., et al, eds. Partial Differential Operators. (Lecture Notes in Mathematics Ser.: Vol. 1324). viii, 433p. 1988. 57.95 (*0-387-50111-8*) Spr-Verlag.
Cardoso, Fernando E. & Faletto, Enzo. Dependency & Development in Latin America. Urquidi, Marjory M., tr. LC 75-46033. 1979. pap. 16.95 (*0-520-03527-5*, Pub. by U CA Pr) Cal Prin Full Svc.
Cardoso, Homem, jt. auth. see Carita, Helder.
***Cardoso, J.** Fuzziness in Petri Nets. LC 98-44475. (Illus.). 318p. 1999. 90.00 (*3-7908-1158-0*) Spr-Verlag.
Cardoso, Joel A. Metabolism with Inborn Errors: Medical Subject Analysis with Bibliography. LC 87-47681. 150p. 1987. 47.50 (*0-88164-635-0*); pap. 44.50 (*0-88164-636-9*) ABBE Pubs Assn.
Cardoso, Lawrence A. Mexican Emigration to the United States, 1897-1931: Socio-Economic Patterns. LC 79-20029. 215p. reprint ed. pap. 66.70 (*0-7837-1904-3*, 204210800001) Bks Demand.
Cardoso, Luis, jt. auth. see Almodovar, Antonio.
Cardoso, O., jt. auth. see Tabeling, P.
Cardoso Ramon, Manuel. Pulmonary Radiology. LC 98-52914. 400p. 1998. text 80.00 (*0-7817-1449-4*) Lppncott W & W.
Cardot, Joe J. AIDS: It May Not Be Too Late. 56p. (Orig.). 1989. pap. 4.99 (*0-685-28032-2*) Srch Fndtn.
Cardoulis, John N. A Friendly Invasion II: A Personal Touch. 224p. 1993. 15.95 (*1-895387-27-2*) Creative Bk Pub.
Cardoza, Anne. Opportunities in Homecare Services Careers. LC 92-37879. (Opportunities In . . . Ser.). (Illus.). 160p. pap. 12.95 (*0-8442-4062-1*, 297OIHS, VGM Career) NTC Contemp Pub Co.
— Opportunities in Homecare Services Careers. LC 92-37879. (Opportunities in...Ser.). (Illus.). 160p. 1994. 14.95 (*0-8442-4061-3*, 40613, VGM Career) NTC Contemp Pub Co.
Cardoza, Anthony L. Agrarian Elites & Italian Fascism: The Province of Bologna, 1901-1926. LC 82-47585. 495p. reprint ed. pap. 153.50 (*0-8357-7892-4*, 203631100002) Bks Demand.
— Aristocrats in Bourgeois Italy: The Piedmontese Nobility, 1861-1930. LC 97-1848. (Studies in Italian History & Culture). (Illus.). 264p. (C). 1998. text 59.95 (*0-521-59303-4*) Cambridge U Pr.
Cardoza, Avery. Avery Cardoza's Let it Ride: Caribbean Stud Poker. LC 97-94717. (Illus.). 168p. 1998. pap. 12.95 (*0-940685-12-4*) Cardoza Pub.
— The Basics of Winning Baccarat. LC 92-81295. (Illus.). 64p. 1992. mass mkt. 4.95 (*0-940685-30-2*, Gambling Res) Cardoza Pub.
— Basics of Winning Bingo. rev. ed. LC 97-94818. 64p. 1998. mass mkt. 4.95 (*0-940685-31-0*) Cardoza Pub.
— Basics of Winning Sports Betting. LC 97-94820. 64p. 1998. mass mkt. 4.95 (*0-940685-98-1*) Cardoza Pub.
— Casino Craps for the Winner. 4th ed. LC 97-68731. (Illus.). 128p. 1998. pap. 9.95 (*0-940685-87-6*) Cardoza Pub.
— Complete Guide to Successful Publishing: How to Create, Print, Distribute & Make Money Publishing. LC 97-94721. 432p. 1998. pap. text 19.95 (*0-940685-94-9*) Cardoza Pub.
— How to Play Winning Poker. 3rd rev. ed. LC 96-71758. 160p. 1997. pap. 12.95 (*0-940685-75-2*) Cardoza Pub.
— How to Win at Gambling. 3rd ed. LC 97-65217. 384p. 1997. pap. 14.95 (*0-940685-61-2*) Cardoza Pub.
— Secrets of Winning Slots. LC 97-94709. (Illus.). 176p. 1998. pap. 12.95 (*0-940685-96-5*) Cardoza Pub.
***Cardoza, Avery.** Secrets of Winning Video Poker. 2000. pap. 14.95 (*1-58042-023-0*, Pub. by Cardoza Pub) LPC Group.
Cardoza, Avery. Secrets of Winning Video Poker. LC 98-74284. (Illus.). 168p. 2000. pap. 14.95 (*1-58042-013-3*, Pub. by Cardoza Pub) LPC Group.
— Winners Playbook. 2nd ed. LC 94-68041. (Illus.). 128p. 1995. pap. 5.95 (*0-940685-53-1*) Cardoza Pub.
— Winning Casino Blackjack for the Non-Counter. rev. ed. LC 98-74286. 144p. 1999. pap. 12.95 (*1-58042-011-7*) Cardoza Pub.
— Winning Casino Play. rev. ed. LC 98-74285. 320p. 1999. pap. 7.95 (*1-58042-012-5*) Cardoza Pub.
Cardoza, Jim D. & Herfkens, Robert J. MRI Survival Guide. LC 93-41765. 240p. 1994. text 63.00 (*0-7817-0180-5*) Lppncott W & W.
Cardoza, Luis. Andre Breton - Malevich. (SPA.). pap. 10.99 (*968-16-3789-5*, Pub. by Fondo) Continental Bk.
***Cardoza, Monica McCabe.** You Can Write a Column. (You Can Write It! Ser.). 128p. 2000. pap. 12.99 (*0-89879-924-4*, Wrtrs Digest Bks) F & W Pubns Inc.
***Cardoza-Orlandi, Carlos F.** Mission: An Essential Guide. 1999. 15.00 (*0-687-05472-9*) Abingdon.
Cardoza y Aragon. El Rio: Novelas de Caballeria. (SPA.). 29.99 (*968-16-5037-9*, Pub. by Fondo) Continental Bk.
Cardoza y Aragon, Luis. Guatemala: Las Lineas de Su Mano (The Lines on Her Hand) 3rd ed. (SPA.). 455p. 1986. reprint ed. pap. 10.99 (*968-16-2309-6*, Pub. by Fondo) Continental Bk.
Cardozier, V. R. American Higher Education: An International Perspective. 209p. 1987. 91.95 (*0-566-05428-0*, Pub. by Avebry) Ashgate Pub Co.
— Colleges & Universities in World War II. LC 92-18877. 264p. 1993. 55.00 (*0-275-94432-8*, C4432, Praeger Pubs) Greenwood.
— The Mobilization of the U. S. in World War II: How the Government, Military & Industry Prepared for War. LC 94-48001. 277p. 1995. lib. bdg. 42.50 (*0-7864-0076-5*) McFarland & Co.
— University of Texas of the Permian Basin: A History. LC 98-28988. (Illus.). 288p. (Orig.). 1998. pap. 19.95 (*1-57168-269-4*, Eakin Pr) Sunbelt Media.
Cardozier, V. Ray, ed. Important Lessons from Innovative Colleges & Universities. LC 85-644752. (New Directions for Higher Education Ser.: No. HE 82). 112p. (Orig.). 1993. pap. 22.00 (*1-55542-690-5*) Jossey-Bass.
Cardozo. Urogynecology. 1997. text 110.00 (*0-443-05058-9*, C0827) Church.
Cardozo, Arlene R. Jewish Family Celebrations. (Illus.). 288p. 1985. pap. 11.95 (*0-312-44232-7*) St Martin.
— Sequencing. 2nd ed. 355p. 1996. reprint ed. pap. 13.95 (*0-9651238-0-4*) Brownstne Bks.
Cardozo, Benjamin N. The Growth of the Law. LC 73-8154. 145p. 1973. reprint ed. lib. bdg. 65.00 (*0-8371-6953-4*, CAGL, Greenwood Pr) Greenwood.
— Law & Literature & Other Essays & Addresses. 190p. 1986. reprint ed. 35.00 (*0-8377-2009-5*, Rothman) W S Hein.
— Law Is Justice: Notable Opinions of Mr. Justice Cardozo, 1938. Sainer, A. L., ed. LC 99-34154. 1999. reprint ed. 75.00 (*1-58477-010-4*) Lawbk Exchange.
— Nature of the Judicial Process. (Storrs Lectures). (C). 1960. pap. 14.00 (*0-300-00033-2*, Y21) Yale U Pr.
— Nature of the Judicial Process. 180p. 1997. reprint ed. 55.00 (*1-57588-214-0*, 311210) W S Hein.
— The Nature of the Judicial Process. 8th ed. (Storrs Lectures). 180p. 1998. reprint ed. 55.00 (*1-56169-420-7*) Gaunt.
***Cardozo, Benjamin N.** The Paradoxes of Legal Science. LC 00-24469. 2000. write for info. (*1-58477-097-X*) Lawbk Exchange.
Cardozo, Benjamin N. The Paradoxes of Legal Science. LC 76-104241. 142p. 1970. reprint ed. lib. bdg. 58.50 (*0-8371-3263-0*, CALS, Greenwood Pr) Greenwood.
Cardozo, Christopher. Native Nations: First Americans As Seen by Edward S. Curtis. White, Antoinette, ed. (Illus.). 160p. 1993. 75.00 (*0-8212-2052-7*, Pub. by Bulfinch Pr) Little.
***Cardozo, Dick & Rao, Dileep.** NYT Business Financing: 25 Keys to Raising Money. LC 99-27690. 104p. 1999. pap. 12.95 (*0-86730-770-6*) Lebhar Friedman.
Cardozo-Freeman, Inez. Chief: The Life History of Eugene Delorme, Imprisoned Santee Sioux. LC 94-7336. (American Indian Lives Ser.). (Illus.). xxxvi, 219p. 1994. text 35.00 (*0-8032-1469-3*) U of Nebr Pr.
Cardozo, Jacob N. Notes on Political Economy. LC 72-187225. (Reprints of Economic Classics Ser.). xiv, 273p. 1972. reprint ed. 45.00 (*0-678-00860-4*) Kelley.
***Cardozo, L.** HRT & Urogenital Aging. 2001. write for info. (*1-84214-029-9*) Prthnon Pub.
Cardozo, Lida L., jt. auth. see Kindersley, David.
Cardozo, Linda, et al. Basic Urogynaecology. LC 92-48233. 176p. 1993. 55.00 (*0-19-262360-5*) OUP.
— Basic Urogynecology. LC 92-48233. 176p. 1993. pap. 27.50 (*0-19-262359-1*) OUP.
Cardozo, Nancy. Creature to Creature. (Illus.). 82p. (Orig.). 1987. pap. 7.00 (*0-913057-37-1*) Confront Mag Pr.
— Creature to Creature. deluxe limited ed. (Illus.). 82p. (Orig.). 1987. 20.00 (*0-913057-38-X*) Confront Mag Pr.
— Maud Gonne. Orig. Title: Lucky Eyes & a High Heart. (Illus.). 468p. (C). 1990. reprint ed. pap. 16.95 (*0-941533-95-6*, NAB) I R Dee.
— Using the Natural Light: Selected Poems. LC 91-61718. (Orig.). 1991. pap. 7.95 (*0-9621570-3-1*) North Lights.
Cardozo, Richard N. Product Policy: Cases & Concepts. LC 78-67939. 1979. text. write for info. (*0-201-00888-2*) Addison-Wesley.
Cardozo, Sidney B. & Hirano, Masaaki. Uncommon Clay: The Life & Pottery of Rosanjin. 1998. pap. 28.00 (*4-7700-2381-2*, Pub. by Kodansha Intl) Kodansha.
CARDRI Staff, ed. Saddam's Iraq: Revolution or Reaction? 2nd ed. LC 88-20588. 288p. (C). 1988. pap. 22.50 (*0-86232-821-7*, Pub. by St Martin) St Martin.
Cardu, Petru. Trapped Strawberry: Poems. Walker, B. & Marinkov, D., trs. from CRO. 96p. (Orig.). 1990. pap. 16.95 (*0-948259-83-3*, Pub. by Forest Bks) Dufour.
Carducci, Bernardo. The Shy Life: Understanding, Hope & Healing. LC 98-18482. 400p. 1999. 25.00 (*0-06-018247-4*) HarpC.
***Carducci, Bernardo J.** The Pocket Guide to Making Successful Small Talk: How to Talk to Anyone Anytime Anywhere about Anything. unabridged ed. 90p. 1999. pap. 9.95 (*0-9677517-0-5*, PGP001) Pocket Guide IN.
Carducci, Bernardo J. The Psychology of Personality. LC 97-25802. 1997. pap. 76.95 (*0-534-35019-4*) Brooks-Cole.
Carducci, Bernice. Shyness: A Bold New Approach. 400p. 2000. pap. 15.00 (*0-06-093068-3*, Perennial) HarperTrade.
Carducci, Joe. Rock & the Pop Narcotic. 2nd rev. ed. (Illus.). 532p. 1995. pap. 18.00 (*1-880985-11-X*) Two Thirteen Sixty-one.
***Carduck, Christian.** International Procurement Offices: Internal Service Providers in Procurement Organizations of Multinational Corporations. (European University Studies: Vol. 2595). xx, 294p. 2000. pap. 52.95 (*0-8204-4749-8*) P Lang Pubng.
Cardulle, Bert. Practical Film Criticism - An Enlightened Approach to Moviegoing. LC 99-15808. (Studies in History & Criticism of Film: Vol. 1). 324p. 1999. text 99.95 (*0-7734-7967-8*) E Mellen.
Cardullo. Perspectives on the Godfather, Set, Pts. 1 & 2. 1996. 50.00 (*0-8161-1612-1*, Hall Reference) Macmillan.
Cardullo, Bert. Dramatic Considerations: Essays in Criticism, 1977-1987. LC 91-10926. (American University Studies: Theatre Arts: Ser. XXVI, Vol. 11). 172p. (C). 1992. text 36.95 (*0-8204-1586-3*) P Lang Pubng.
— Film Chronicle: Critical Dispatches from a Forward Observer, 1987-1992. LC 93-832. (American Univ. Studies, XXVI, Theatre Arts: Vol. 22). (Illus.). XVIII, 294p. (C). 1994. text 59.95 (*0-8204-2206-1*) P Lang Pubng.
— Indelible Images: New Perspectives on Classic Films. LC 86-34014. (Illus.). 322p. (C). 1987. pap. text 27.00 (*0-8191-6150-0*); lib. bdg. 50.50 (*0-8191-6149-7*) U Pr of Amer.
— Theatrical Reflections: Notes on the Form & Practice of Drama. LC 92-22552. (American University Studies: Theatre Arts: Ser. XXVI, Vol. 15). VII, 276p. (C). 1993. text 49.95 (*0-8204-1935-4*) P Lang Pubng.
— What Is Neorealism? A Critical English-Language Bibliography of Italian Cinematic Neorealism. 158p. (C). 1991. lib. bdg. 36.50 (*0-8191-7756-3*) U Pr of Amer.
Cardullo, Bert, ed. Before His Eyes: Essays in Honor of Stanley Kauffmann. (Illus.). 198p. (Orig.). (C). 1987. pap. text 22.50 (*0-8191-5637-X*); lib. bdg. 44.00 (*0-8191-5636-1*) U Pr of Amer.
— The Film Criticism of Vernon Young. 462p. (Orig.). (C). 1990. lib. bdg. 56.50 (*0-8191-7846-2*) U Pr of Amer.
— The Theater of Fernand Crommelynck: Eight Plays. Piette, Alain, tr. from FRE. LC 97-47160. (Lancaster Pamphlets Ser.). 424p. 1998. 57.50 (*1-57591-002-0*) Susquehanna U Pr.
— What Is Dramaturgy? LC 93-2357. (American University Studies: Vol. 20). VIII, 258p. (C). 1995. pap. text 29.95 (*0-8204-2177-4*) P Lang Pubng.
Cardullo, Bert, et al, eds. Playing to the Camera: Film Actors Discuss Their Craft. LC 97-1644. (Illus.). 384p. 1997. pap. 16.95 (*0-300-07051-9*) Yale U Pr.
— Playing to the Camera: Film Actors Discuss Their Craft. LC 97-1644. (Illus.). 384p. 1998. 35.00 (*0-300-06983-9*) Yale U Pr.

C

An Asterisk (*) at the beginning of an entry indicates that the title is appearing for the first time.

Cardullo, Bert, tr. German-Language Comedy: A Critical Anthology. LC 91-50195. 304p. 1992. 50.00 (*0-945636-24-5*) Susquehanna U Pr.

Cardullo, Bert, jt. auth. see Piette, Alain.

Cardullo, Bert, ed. & tr. see Bazin, Andre.

Cardullo, M. W. Introduction to Managing Technology. LC 96-31564. (Engineering Management Ser.). 282p. 1996. 54.95 (*0-86380-204-4*) Wiley.

Carduner, Jean, ed. Pratiques Culturelles. LC 81-50963. (Michigan Romance Studies: Vol. 3). 188p. 1983. pap. 15.00 (*0-939730-02-2*) Mich Romance.

Carduner, Sylvia & Hagiwara, Michio P. D'Accord: La Prononciation Du Francais International: Acquisition et Perfectionnement. Ep. (C). 1982. cd-rom 108.95 (*0-471-86757-8*) Wiley.

— D'Accord : LA Prononciation Du Francais Internationale: Acquisitio Et Perfectio, Net. LC 82-13123. (FRE.). 320p. (C). 1982. text 58.95 (*0-471-09729-2*) Wiley.

Cardus, David, jt. ed. see Blocker, William, Jr.

Cardus, Neville. Autobiography. LC 75-37825. (Illus.). 288p. 1976. reprint ed. lib. bdg. 65.00 (*0-8371-8577-7*, CAAU, Greenwood Pr) Greenwood.

— Composers Eleven. (Essay Index Reprint Ser.). (Illus.). 1958. 23.95 (*0-8369-1554-2*) Ayer.

— English Cricket. (Illus.). 96p. 1997. 11.95 (*1-85375-252-5*) Prion.

Cardwell. Turning Points in Western Technology. 256p. 1972. pap. text 8.95 (*0-614-18188-7*, Sci Hist) Watson Pub Intl.

***Cardwell, Andrew.** Relative Strength Index Advantage: Combining RSI & Other Analysis Techniques into a Winning Merger. (Irwin Trader's Edge Ser.). (Illus.). 320p. 2000. 59.95 (*0-07-136209-6*) McGraw.

Cardwell, Ann. Crazy to Kill. large type ed. 1990. pap. 16.99 (*0-7089-6905-4*) Ulverscroft.

Cardwell, Cardwell, ed. From the Heart of a Poet, 2 vols., 1. (Illus.). 225p. (Orig.). 1984. pap. 8.45 (*0-916395-12-X*) Hieroglyphics.

— From the Heart of a Poet, 2 vols., 2. (Illus.). 225p. (Orig.). 1984. write for info. (*0-916395-15-4*) Hieroglyphics.

— From the Heart of a Poet, 2 vols., Set. (Illus.). 225p. (Orig.). 1984. write for info. (*0-916395-18-9*) Hieroglyphics.

Cardwell, Carolyn E. Kids, Cats & Puppydogs, Vol. 1. (Illus.). 250p. (Orig.). 1987. pap. 10.95 (*0-916395-14-6*, KC-1) Hieroglyphics.

— Sands of Time, Vol. 1. (Illus.). 225p. (Orig.). 1986. pap. 10.95 (*0-916395-21-9*, ST-1) Hieroglyphics.

— Sands of Time, Vol. 2. (Illus.). 225p. (Orig.). 1986. pap. 10.95 (*0-916395-23-5*, ST-2) Hieroglyphics.

— Tidings to a Tick, Vol. 1. (Illus.). 225p. (Orig.). 1988. pap. 10.95 (*0-916395-17-0*, TT-1) Hieroglyphics.

Cardwell, Carolyn E., ed. Dreams & Wishes, 2 Vols., 1, (Illus.). 225p. (Orig.). 1986. pap. 8.45 (*0-916395-20-0*, DW-1) Hieroglyphics.

— Dreams & Wishes, 2 Vols., 2, (Illus.). 225p. (Orig.). 1986. pap. 10.95 (*0-916395-22-7*) Hieroglyphics.

— My Heart Speaks to Thee, Vol. 1. (Illus.). 250p. 1985. pap. 10.95 (*0-916395-02-2*, MH-1) Hieroglyphics.

— My Heart Speaks to Thee, Vol. 2. (Illus.). 250p. 1985. pap. 10.95 (*0-916395-05-7*, MH-2) Hieroglyphics.

— Odes to a Cockroach, Vol. 2. (Illus.). 250p. (Orig.). 1985. pap. 10.95 (*0-916395-03-0*, OC-2) Hieroglyphics.

— Teardrops & Laughter, 3 vols. (Illus.). 250p. (Orig.). 1984. pap. write for info. (*0-916395-10-3*) Hieroglyphics.

— Teardrops & Laughter, 3 vols., 1. (Illus.). 250p. (Orig.). 1984. pap. 10.95 (*0-916395-01-4*, TD-1) Hieroglyphics.

— Teardrops & Laughter, 3 vols., 2. (Illus.). 250p. (Orig.). 1984. pap. 8.45 (*0-916395-04-9*, TD-2) Hieroglyphics.

— Teardrops & Laughter, 3 vols., Vol. 3. (Illus.). 250p. (Orig.). 1985. pap. 8.45 (*0-916395-07-3*, TD-3) Hieroglyphics.

Cardwell, Carolyn E., pref. Odes to a Cockroach, Vol. 1. (Illus.). 250p. (Orig.). 1984. pap. 10.95 (*0-916395-00-6*, 0C-1) Hieroglyphics.

Cardwell, Donald. Technology. 1995. pap. 19.95 (*0-393-31192-9*) Norton.

Cardwell, Guy, ed. see Twain, Mark, pseud.

***Cardwell, Harold D., Sr. & Cardwell, Priscilla D.** Port Orange. (Images of America Ser.). (Illus.). 128p. 2000. pap. 18.99 (*0-7385-0618-4*) Arcadia Publng.

***Cardwell, James Moss.** Mrs. Hudson? Mrs. Hudson!! A Conceptual Narrative Treatment of an Original Musical. (Illus.). 2000. 30.00 (*1-55246-207-2*) Battered Silicon.

Cardwell, Jerry. Sailing Big on a Small Sailboat. 2nd ed. LC 97-41470. (Illus.). 208p. 1997. pap. 17.50 (*1-57409-007-0*) Sheridan.

Cardwell, Kenneth H. Bernard Maybeck: Artisan, Architect, Artist. 5th ed. (California Architecture & Architects Ser.: Vol. 8). (Illus.). 255p. 1995. reprint ed. pap., per. 29.95 (*0-912158-99-9*) Hennessey.

Cardwell, Margaret, ed. see Dickens, Charles.

Cardwell, Margaret, ed. & intro. see Dickens, Charles.

Cardwell, Margaret, ed. & notes see Dickens, Charles.

Cardwell, Michael. Milk Quotas: European Community & United Kingdom Law. 258p. 1996. text 65.00 (*0-19-825940-9*) OUP.

Cardwell, Priscilla D., jt. auth. see Cardwell, Harold D., Sr.

Cardwell, R. A., ed. see De Espronceda, Jose.

Cardwell, Richard, ed. Lord Byron the European: Essays from the International Byron Society. LC 97-24022. (Studies in British Literature: No. 31). 240p. 1997. text 89.95 (*0-7734-8593-7*) E Mellen.

Cardwell, Richard A. & Landeira, Ricardo. Jose de Zorilla: Centennial Readings, 1893-1993. 170p. 1993. pap. 30.00 (*0-900572-82-5*) Society Sp & Sp-Am.

Cardwell, Richard A. & McGuirk, Bernard, eds. Que Es el Modernismo? Nueva Encuesta, Neuvas Lecturas. LC 92-64364. (SPA.). 456p. 1993. pap. 60.00 (*0-89295-067-6*) Society Sp & Sp-Am.

Cardwell, Richard A., ed. see Jimenez, Juan Ramon.

Cardwell, Rick D., et al, eds. Aquatic Toxicology & Hazard Assessment: Seventh Symposium- STP 854. LC 84-70338. (Illus.). 590p. 1985. text 60.00 (*0-8031-0410-3*, STP854) ASTM.

Cardwell, Tammy. Front Porch History: Researching & Telling Your Family's Stories. 80p. (Orig.). (J). (gr. 5-12). 1997. pap. 9.95 (*1-882514-51-3*) Greenleaf TN.

Cardy, Chris. Personal Safety: A Training Resource Manual. 218p. 1992. ring bd. 212.95 (*1-85904-045-4*, Pub. by Gower) Ashgate Pub Co.

— Training for Personal Safety at Work. 224p. 1995. pap. 131.95 (*0-566-07680-2*) Ashgate Pub Co.

Cardy, J., ed. Finite-Size Scaling. (Current Physics Sources & Comments Ser.: Vol. 2). x, 374p. 1988. pap. 68.00 (*0-444-87110-1*) Elsevier.

Cardy, John. Scaling & Renormalization in Statistical Physics. (Cambridge Lecture Notes in Physics Ser.: No. 5). 256p. 1996. pap. text 34.95 (*0-521-49959-3*) Cambridge U Pr.

Cardy, Michael, et al, eds. Narrative Voices in Modern French Fiction. LC 97-187106. 258p. 1997. 55.00 (*0-7083-1394-9*, Pub. by Univ Wales Pr) Paul & Co Pubs.

***Cardy, Michael & Connon, Derek, eds.** Aspects of Twentieth-Century Theatre in French. 243p. 2000. pap. 40.95 (*0-8204-4635-1*) P Lang Pubng.

Cardy, Michael, tr. see Pouchot, Pierre.

***Cardy, Nick, photos by.** The Art of Nick Cardy. (Illus.). 176p. (C). 1999. pap. 24.95 (*0-9673848-0-X*) Coates Pubg Inc.

***Cardy, Peter, et al.** Keeping Patients in the Dark: Should Prescription Medicines Be Advertised Direct to Consumers. (Choice in Welfare Ser.: No. 51). 45p. 1999. pap. 12.95 (*0-255-36454-7*, Pub. by Inst Economic Affairs) Coronet Bks.

Cardy, Robert L., et al, eds. Advances in Managerial Cognition & Organizational Information Processing, Vol. 4. 275p. 1991. 73.25 (*1-55938-012-8*) Jai Pr.

Cardy, Robert L. & Dobbins, Gregory H. Performance Appraisal: Alternative Perspectives. LC 93-19694. (Human Resource Management Ser.). (C). 1993. mass mkt. 37.95 (*0-538-81383-0*, GJ65AA) S-W Pub.

Care, Henry. English Liberties, or The Free-Born Subject's Inheritance. 6th ed. LC 75-31087. reprint ed. 37.50 (*0-404-13505-6*) AMS Pr.

***Care, Jennifer Corrin, et al.** Introduction to South Pacific Law. 402p. 1999. pap. 36.00 (*1-85941-431-1*, 18125) Cavendish Pubng.

***Care, Norman S.** Decent People. LC 00-38737. 2000. pap. write for info. (*0-7425-0709-2*) Rowman.

Care, Norman S. Living with One's Past: Personal Fates & Moral Pain. 248p. 1996. pap. text 24.95 (*0-8476-8237-4*); lib. bdg. 60.50 (*0-8476-8236-6*) Rowman.

Care, Norman S. & Landesman, Charles, eds. Readings in the Theory of Action. LC 68-27339. 446p. reprint ed. pap. 138.30 (*0-608-30637-1*, 205005000059) Bks Demand.

Care, Norman S., ed. see Oberlin Colloquium in Philosophy Staff.

Careaga, Andrew. A Divine Appointment in Washington, D.C. Sharing the Gospel in Cyberspace. LC 98-75141. 172p. 1998. pap. 9.99 (*1-56384-160-6*) Huntington Hse.

Careathers, Christie S. Order My Steps in Thy Word: Contentment in Psalm over 600 Scriptures. LC 95-69872. 80p. 1995. pap. write for info. (*1-57502-022-X*, P00411) Morris Pubng.

Careau, Rachel. Itineraries. 32p. 1991. pap. 4.00 (*0-685-56975-6*) St Lazaire.

***Caredo, Keith, et al, eds.** Independent Women's Specialty Stores, 2000. 640p. 1999. pap. 189.95 (*0-87228-129-9*) Douglas Pubns.

— Metro Women's & Children's & Fashion Accessories Buyers. 184p. 1999. write for info. (*0-87228-134-5*) Douglas Pubns.

Career Development Center Staff. Choices & Challenges: Foundations for Career Planning. 135p. (Orig.). 1996. pap. text 14.95 (*1-889688-00-2*) IU Custom Pub.

— Choices & Challenges Job Search Strategies for Liberal Arts Students. 182p. (C). 1997. pap. text 14.95 (*1-889688-01-0*) IU Custom Pub.

Career Directions Staff. Achieve It: Multi User. 22p. 1999. pap. text 499.00 (*0-7872-5609-9*, 41560901) Kendall-Hunt.

— Achieve It: Single User. 22p. 1999. pap. text 59.95 (*0-7872-5608-0*, 41560801) Kendall-Hunt.

***Career Directions Staff.** Achieve It! Workbook. 208p. 1999. ring bd. 37.95 (*0-7872-6152-1*) Kendall-Hunt.

***Career Guide Staff.** Finance 2000. (Career Guide Finance Ser.). (Illus.). 1999. pap. 24.95 (*1-57851-190-9*, HBS Pr) Harvard Busn.

Career Press. Commitment to Excellence: Quotations That Lift the Spirit Toward Excellence. LC 98-8600. 128p. 1998. pap. 7.99 (*1-56414-387-2*) Career Pr Inc.

— The Essence of Attitude: Quotations for Igniting Positive Attitudes. LC 98-28301. 128p. 1998. pap. 7.99 (*1-56414-383-X*) Career Pr Inc.

— The Magic of Motivation: Quotations to Empower Dreams for the Road to Success. LC 98-28303. 128p. 1998. pap. 7.99 (*1-56414-385-6*) Career Pr Inc.

— The Power of Goals: Quotations to Strengthen Your Climb to New Heights. LC 98-28304. 128p. 1998. pap. 7.99 (*1-56414-384-8*) Career Pr Inc.

Career Press Editors. 101 Great Resumes: Unique Resumes, Creative Resumes, but Most Important, Resumes that Work! LC 95-50099. 210p. 1996. pap. 9.99 (*1-56414-201-9*) Career Pr Inc.

Career Press Editors & Mohler, Lisa. Resumes! Resumes! Resumes! Top Career Experts Show You the Job-Training Resumes That Sold Them. 3rd ed. LC 97-17756. 192p. 1997. pap. 10.99 (*1-56414-309-0*) Career Pr Inc.

Career Press, Inc. Staff. Business Finance for the Numerically Challenged. LC 97-37337. 160p. 1997. pap. 11.99 (*1-56414-314-7*) Career Pr Inc.

— Business Math for the Numerically Challenged. LC 97-36693. 160p. 1997. pap. 11.99 (*1-56414-316-3*) Career Pr Inc.

Career Press Staff. The Best of Success: Quotations to Illuminate the Journey of Success. LC 98-29821. 128p. 1998. pap. 7.99 (*1-56414-386-4*) Career Pr Inc.

— Dictionary of Occupational Titles, Vol. 1. 1995. pap. 21.95 (*0-8442-4143-1*) NTC Contemp Pub Co.

— Dictionary of Occupational Titles, Vol. 2. 1994. pap. 21.95 (*0-8442-4145-8*) NTC Contemp Pub Co.

***Career Press Staff.** 2,001 Things That Won't Make It into the 21st Century. LC 99-41526. 176p. 1999. pap. 8.99 (*1-56414-439-9*) Career Pr Inc.

Career Press Staff, ed. Motivation & Goal Setting: A Quick & Hardy Guide for Any Manager or Business Owner. 2nd ed. (Business Desk Reference Ser.). 128p. 1993. pap. 8.95 (*1-56414-111-X*) Career Pr Inc.

— Powerful Presentation Skills: A Quick & Handy Guide for Any Manager or Business Owner. LC 93-22387. (Business Desk Reference Ser.). 128p. (Orig.). 1993. pap. 8.95 (*1-56414-109-8*) Career Pr Inc.

— Powerful Telephone Skills: A Quick & Handy Guide for Any Manager or Business Owner. (Business Desk Reference Ser.). 128p. 1993. pap. 8.95 (*1-56414-107-1*) Career Pr Inc.

— The Supervisor's Handbook: A Quick & Handy Guide for Any Manager or Business Owner. 2nd ed. (Business Desk Reference Ser.). 128p. 1993. pap. 8.95 (*1-56414-106-3*) Career Pr Inc.

— Understanding the Bottom Line: Finance for Nonfictional Managers & Business Owners. 2nd ed. LC 93-17887. (Business Desk Reference Ser.). 128p. 1993. pap. 8.95 (*1-56414-108-X*) Career Pr Inc.

— Winning with Teamwork: Quotations to Inspire the Power of Teamwork. LC 98-28302. 128p. 1998. pap. 7.99 (*1-56414-388-0*) Career Pr Inc.

Career Press Staff, ed. see Barnes, Ginny Pearson.

Career Press Staff, ed. see Capezio, Peter.

Career Press Staff, ed. see McKenna, Colleen.

Career Resources Staff. The North Carolina Employment Guide, 1995. 170p. 1994. pap. 34.95 (*1-881803-04-X*) Career Res.

CareerSource Staff. Who's Hiring in Atlanta? 2nd ed. Hines, Steve, ed. (Fast Track Job Search Ser.). 320p. (C). 1999. pap. 14.95 (*0-929255-23-2*) CareerSource.

Carefoot, George M., jt. auth. see Browne, Laynie.

Carefree & Cave Creek Residents Staff. Carefree - Cave Creek Foothills: Life in the Sonoran Sun. LC 90-82286. (Illus.). 264p. 1990. pap. text 17.95 (*0-9626269-1-0*) Foothills Comm Fndtn.

Careless, Anthony. Initiative & Response: The Adaptation of Canadian Federalism to Regional Economic Development. (Canadian Public Administration Ser.). 1977. 44.95 (*0-7735-0280-7*, Pub. by McG-Queens Univ Pr) CUP Services.

Careless, Anthony G. Initiative & Response: The Adaptation of Canadian Federalism to Regional Economic Development. LC 77-368201. (Canadian Public Administration Ser.). 254p. reprint ed. pap. 78.80 (*0-7837-2627-9*, 204297700006) Bks Demand.

***Careless, Dolores A.** An Unfortunate Likeness. Mitchell, Frances G. & Paon, Michelle, eds. (Illus.). 144p. 1998. pap. 9.95 (*1-895814-05-7*) NewWorld Pub.

Careless, J. M. Canada: A Story of Challenge. (Illus.). 449p. 1991. pap. 7.95 (*0-7736-7354-7*) Genl Dist Srvs.

Careless, J. M., ed. The Pre-Confederation Premiers: Ontario Government Leaders 1841 to 1867. (Ontario Historical Studies). 368p. 1985. pap. 16.95 (*0-8020-6590-2*) U of Toronto Pr.

Careless, James M., ed. The Pre-Confederation Premiers: Ontario Government Leaders, 1841-1867. LC 80-501684. (Ontario Historical Studies). 358p. reprint ed. pap. 111.00 (*0-608-16708-8*, 205611900050) Bks Demand.

Careless, Ric. To Save the Wild Earth: Field Notes from the Environmental Frontline. LC 98-130258. (Illus.). 256p. 1998. pap. 15.95 (*0-89886-567-0*) Mountaineers.

Carell, Paul. Foxes of the Desert: The Story of the Afrikakorps. LC 94-65576. (Luftwaffe Profile Ser.). (Illus.). 370p. (YA). (gr. 10-13). 1996. 29.95 (*0-88740-659-9*) Schiffer.

— Invasion! They're Coming! The German Account of the D-Day Landings & the 80 Days' Battle for France. Johnston, David, tr. from GER. LC 94-68032. (Illus.). 292p. 1995. 29.95 (*0-88740-716-1*) Schiffer.

— Operation Barbarossa in Photographs: The War in Russia As Photographed by the Soldiers, with a New Preface by the Author. LC 90-62986. (Illus.). 460p. 1991. 49.95 (*0-88740-280-1*) Schiffer.

— Scorched Earth: The Russian-German War, 1943-1944. LC 93-87471. (Illus.). 556p. 1994. 39.95 (*0-88740-598-3*) Schiffer.

— Stalingrad: The Defeat of the German 6th Army. LC 92-62188. (Illus.). 352p. 1992. 29.95 (*0-88740-469-3*) Schiffer.

Carella, Angelo, ed. Autologous Stem Cell Transplantation: Biological & Clinical Results in Malignancies. (Advances in Blood Disorders Ser.: Vol. 2). 600p. 1997. text 150.00 (*3-7186-5933-6*, Harwood Acad Pubs) Gordon & Breach.

Carella, C. J. GURPS Martial Arts: Exotic Combat from All Cultures. 2nd ed. Punch, Sean & Butler, Lillian, eds. (Illus.). 160p. 1996. pap., suppl. ed. 22.95 (*1-55634-314-0*, 6036, Pub. by S Jackson Games) BookWorld.

— GURPs Voodoo: The Shadow War. Pinsonneault, Susan, ed. (Illus.). 128p. 1995. pap., suppl. ed. 19.95 (*1-55634-300-0*, 6071) S Jackson Games.

— Rifts Psyscape. Siembieda, Kevin & Marcinszyn, Alex, eds. (Rifts Worldbook Ser.: Vol. 12). (Illus.). 160p. (Orig.). 1997. pap. 16.95 (*0-916211-94-0*) Palladium Bks.

Carella, C. J. & Siembieda, Kevin. Between the Shadows. (Nightbane Ser.: Vol. 1). (Illus.). 160p. (Orig.). (YA). (gr. 8 up). 1996. pap. 16.95 (*0-916211-90-8*, 731) Palladium Bks.

— Jucier Uprising. Kirsten, Kevin, ed. (Rifts Worldbook Ser.: Vol. 10). (Illus.). 160p. (Orig.). (YA). (gr. 8 up). 1996. pap. 16.95 (*0-916211-92-4*, 820) Palladium Bks.

— Nightlands. Marciniszyn, Alex et al, eds. (Nightbane Worldbook Ser.: Vol. 2). (Illus.). 144p. (Orig.). (YA). (gr. 8 up). 1996. pap. 16.95 (*0-916211-97-5*, 732) Palladium Bks.

Carella, C. J., et al. Pantheons of the Megaverse. Marciniszyn, Alex et al, eds. (Rifts Conversion Bks.: No. 2). (Illus.). 208p. (Orig.). (YA). (gr. 8 up). 1994. pap. 20.95 (*0-916211-68-1*, 811) Palladium Bks.

Carella, C. J., jt. auth. see Siembieda, Kevin.

Carella, Michael J. Matter, Morals & Medicine: The Ancient Greek Origins of Science, Ethics & the Medical Profession. (American University Studies: Philosophy: Ser. V, Vol. 110). (Illus.). XIV, 361p. 1991. 43.95 (*0-8204-1432-8*) P Lang Pubng.

Carelli-Gilbert, Marti. Half Time. 1990. pap. 9.95 (*0-9626967-0-6*) R J Prodns.

Carello, Adrian N. The Northern Question: Italy's Participation in the European Economic Community & the Mezzogiorno's Underdevelopment. LC 87-40642. (Illus.). 216p. 1989. 38.50 (*0-87413-342-4*) U Delaware Pr.

Caren, Eric. The Civil War Extra: From the Pages of the Charleston Mercury & the New York Times, Vol. 1. 1999. 24.99 (*0-7858-1137-0*) Bk Sales Inc.

— The Civil War Extra: From the Pages of the Charleston Mercury & the New York Times, Vol. 2. 1999. 24.99 (*0-7858-1150-8*) Bk Sales Inc.

— Extra-Titanic. 1998. 19.99 (*0-7858-1030-7*) Bk Sales Inc.

— New York Extra, 1693-1939, Vol. 1. 1999. 24.99 (*0-7858-1138-9*) Bk Sales Inc.

— Texas Extra: A Newspaper History of the Lone Star State. 1999. 24.99 (*0-7858-1082-X*, Castle Bks Inc) Bk Sales Inc.

— World War II Extra, Vol. 1. 1999. 24.99 (*0-7858-1136-2*) Bk Sales Inc.

Carenas, F. & Ferrando, Jose. La Sociedad Espanola en la Novela de la Postguerra. 1971. 10.95 (*0-88303-997-4*) E Torres & Sons.

Carenen, John. Son-Up, Son-Down. (Trilogy Ser.: Bk. 3). 1990. pap. 7.50 (*0-87868-347-X*, 3470) Child Welfare.

Carens, ed. Critical Essays on Joyce's Portrait of the Artist As a Young Man. LC 98-18912. 326p. 1998. 49.00 (*0-7838-0035-5*, G K Hall & Co) Mac Lib Ref.

Carens, James F., jt. ed. see Bowen, Zack R.

Carens, James F., ed. see Buttel, Robert.

Carens, James F., ed. see Kenney, Edwin J.

Carens, James F., ed. see Skelton, Robin.

Carens, James F., ed. see Sullivan, Eileen.

***Carens, Joseph H.** Culture, Citizenship, & Community: A Contextual Exploration of Justice As Evenhandedness. LC 99-48977. 156p. 2000. text 65.00 (*0-19-829751-3*); pap. text 29.95 (*0-19-829768-8*) OUP.

Carens, Joseph H. Equality, Moral Incentives, & the Market. LC 80-36774. (Illus.). 264p. 1994. pap. text 19.00 (*0-226-09269-0*) U Ch Pr.

— Equality, Moral Incentives & the Market: An Essay in Utopian Politico-Economic Theory. LC 80-36774. 264p. reprint ed. pap. 81.90 (*0-608-09279-7*, 205415300004) Bks Demand.

Carens, Joseph H., ed. Democracy & Possessive Individualism: The Intellectual Legacy of C. B. Macpherson. LC 92-17915. (SUNY Series in Political Theory: Contemporary Issues). 298p. (C). 1993. text 64.50 (*0-7914-1457-4*); pap. text 21.95 (*0-7914-1458-2*) State U NY Pr.

— Is Quebec Nationalism Just? Perspectives from Anglophone Canada. (Illus.). 240p. 1995. text 60.00 (*0-7735-1341-8*) McG-Queens Univ Pr.

— Is Quebec Nationalism Just? Perspectives from Anglophone Canada. (Illus.). 240p. (C). 1995. pap. 22.95 (*0-7735-1342-6*, Pub. by McG-Queens Univ Pr) CUP Services.

Careri, Enrico. Francesco Geminiani, 2 vols., Vol. 1: Life & Works. LC 92-41355. (Illus.). 314p. 1993. text 62.00 (*0-19-816300-2*, Clarendon Pr) OUP.

— Francesco Geminiani, 2 vols., Vol. 2: Thematic Catalogue. LC 92-41355. 1993. write for info. (*0-19-816301-0*, Clarendon Pr) OUP.

Careri, Giorgio. Order & Disorder in Matter. 162p. (C). 1984. write for info. (*0-8053-1700-7*); pap. 25.95 (*0-8053-1725-2*) Addison-Wesley.

Careri, Giovanni. Bernini: Flights of Love, the Art of Devotion. Lappin, Linda, tr. (Illus.). 168p. 1995. pap. text 16.95 (*0-226-09273-9*) U Ch Pr.

— Bernini: Flights of Love, the Art of Devotion. Lappin, Linda, tr. (Illus.). 168p. 1996. lib. bdg. 39.95 (*0-226-09272-0*) U Ch Pr.

Carerra, Kathleen. Nantahla Love Feast. LC 87-71620. (Gazebo Romance Ser.). 200p. 1987. 15.95 (*0-89227-075-6*) Commonwealth Pr.

Cares. But Not Always. 1999. pap. 13.00 (*0-525-44760-1*) NAL.

C

An Asterisk (*) at the beginning of an entry indicates that the title is appearing for the first time.

Caress, Jay, jt. auth. see Hybels, Bill.

Caret. Better Think Chemistry. 1993. 42.00 (*0-697-22801-0*) McGraw.

— Found. Inorg. Chem. & SG Student Manual. 1997. 61.50 (*0-07-561238-0*) McGraw.

— General Organic & Biochemistry. 1993. lab manual ed. 13.25 (*0-697-22746-4*) McGraw.

— General Organic & Biochemistry (Cooke) 1993. 14.50 (*0-697-22614-X*) McGraw.

— General Organic Biochemistry. 1993. lab manual ed. 12.25 (*0-697-22597-6*) McGraw.

— Princ. Organic Biol. & SSG Student Manual. 2nd ed. 1997. 57.74 (*0-07-561226-7*) McGraw.

— Principles & Applications of Inorganic Organizations. 1992. pap. 11.25 (*0-697-17024-1*) McGraw.

— Trans Foundations Inorganic. 1995. 155.00 (*0-697-21247-5*) McGraw.

Caret, et al. Found of Inorganic/Organic. 2nd ed. 2001. 55.25 (*0-697-34850-4*, WCB McGr Hill) McGrw-H Hghr Educ.

— Foundations Inorganic, Organic & Biological. 1995. teacher ed. 18.75 (*0-697-21243-2*, WCB McGr Hill) McGrw-H Hghr Educ.

— Foundations of Inorganic & Organic Chemistry: Student Study Art Notebook. 1995. pap. (*0-697-34313-8*, WCB McGr Hill) McGrw-H Hghr Educ.

— Solman - Principles & Applications in Inorganic... 2nd ed. 1996. pap. 28.75 (*0-697-25005-9*) McGraw.

Caret, Robert L. & Topping, Joseph J. Principles & Applications of Organic & Biological Chemistry. 2nd ed. 528p. (C). 1997. per. write for info. (*0-07-114294-0*, WCB McGr Hill) McGrw-H Hghr Educ.

Caret, Robert L., et al. Foundations of Inorganic, Organic & Biological Chemistry: A Medical Perspective. 94p. (C). 1994. text, student ed. write for info. (*0-697-26037-2*, WCB McGr Hill) McGrw-H Hghr Educ.

— Principles & Applications of Inorganic, Organic, & Biological Chemistry. 2nd ed. LC 96-83936. 736p. (C). 1996. text 83.68 (*0-697-25003-2*, WCB McGr Hill) McGrw-H Hghr Educ.

— Principles & Applications of Organic & Biological Chemistry. 576p. (C). 1993. text, student ed. 23.12 (*0-697-14871-8*, WCB McGr Hill) McGrw-H Hghr Educ.

— Principles & Applications of Organic & Biological Chemistry. (C). 1995. text, student ed. write for info. (*0-697-29619-9*, WCB McGr Hill) McGrw-H Hghr Educ.

— Principles & Applications of Organic & Biological Chemistry. 2nd ed. LC 96-83906. 560p. (C). 1996. text 46.50 (*0-697-25002-4*, WCB McGr Hill) McGrw-H Hghr Educ.

— Principles & Applications of Organic & Biological Chemistry: (With Solutions Manual) 2nd ed. 240p. (C). 1996. text, student ed. 24.37 (*0-697-37661-3*, WCB McGr Hill) McGrw-H Hghr Educ.

Caret, Robert L., jt. auth. see Plante, Patricia R.

Caretta, Fernando. Insatiable. (Illus.). 96p. 1998. pap. 12.95 (*1-56097-346-3*, Pub. by Fantagraph Bks) Seven Hills Bk.

Carev, Bonnie. Baba Yaga's Geese & Other Russian Stories. LC 73-77852. (Illus.). 128p. reprint ed. pap. 39.70 (*0-8357-5936-9*, 205622500056) Bks Demand.

Carew. Piano & Its Music 1770-1850. 76.95 (*0-85967-969-1*) Ashgate Pub Co.

Carew & Mylroie. Earth History. 1999. text 36.80 (*0-697-11447-3*) McGraw.

Carew, Anthony. Labour under the Marshall Plan: The Politics of Productivity & the Marketing of Management Science. LC 87-211445. 303p. reprint ed. pap. 94.00 (*0-608-10581-3*, 207120200009) Bks Demand.

***Carew, Anthony, et al.** The International Confederation of Free Trade Unions: Edited by Marcel van der Linden. Van der Linden, Marcel, ed. (International & Comparative Social History Ser.: Vol. 3). 616p. (C). 2000. text 77.95 (*0-8204-4643-2*) P Lang Pubng.

Carew, Crystal S. Action Advertiser Marketplace Recipes, 1981-87, Vol. 1: A Collection from Our Readers. 300p. (Orig.). 1988. pap. text 7.95 (*0-9620986-0-4*) Action Advertising Inc.

***Carew, Edna.** Fast Money 4: The Bestselling Guide to Australia's Financial Markets. (Illus.). 352p. 1999. pap. 34.95 (*1-86448-994-4*, Pub. by Allen & Unwin Pty) Paul & Co Pubs.

Carew, Edna. The Language of Money. 3rd ed. 368p. 1996. pap. 34.95 (*1-86373-966-1*, Pub. by Allen & Unwin Pty) Paul & Co Pubs.

Carew, Edna, jt. auth. see Slatyer, Will.

Carew, Henry. The Vampires of the Andes. Reginald, R. & Menville, Douglas A., eds. LC 77-84206. (Lost Race & Adult Fantasy Ser.). 1978. reprint ed. lib. bdg. 29.95 (*0-405-10962-8*) Ayer.

Carew, Jack. The Mentor: 15 Keys to Achieving Success in Sales, Business & Life. 224p. 1999. pap. 13.95 (*0-452-28021-4*, Plume) Dutton Plume.

— The Mentor: 15 Keys to Success in Sales, Business, & Life. LC 97-49231. 160p. 1998. 19.95 (*1-55611-541-5*, Pub. by D I Fine) Penguin Putnam.

— You'll Never Get No for an Answer. 224p. 1990. per. 14.00 (*0-671-73649-3*) PB.

Carew, James L., ed. Proceedings of the 8th Symposium on the Geology of the Bahamas & Other Carbonate Regions. (Illus.). 213p. (C). 1997. pap. text 25.00 (*0-935909-63-X*) Bahamian.

Carew, James L. & Mylroie, John E. Geology & Karst of San Salvador Island, Bahamas: A Field Trip Guidebook. (Illus.). 32p. (Orig.). (C). 1994. pap. text 7.00 (*0-935909-50-8*) Bahamian.

***Carew, James L., et al.** The Geology of South Andros Island Bahamas: A Reconnaissance Report for the 9th Symposium on the Geology of the Bahamas Field Trip. (Illus.). 30p. (C). 1998. pap. text 8.00 (*0-935909-65-6*) Bahamian.

Carew, James L., jt. auth. see Mylroie, John E.

Carew, Jan. Fulcrums of Change: Origins of Racism in the Americas & Other Essays. LC 86-71492. 240p. 1988. 29.95 (*0-86543-032-2*); pap. 9.95 (*0-86543-033-0*) Africa World.

— Rape of Paradise: Columbus & the Origin of Western Racism. LC 94-16194. 232p. 1994. pap. text 14.95 (*1-881316-79-3*) A&B Bks.

Carew, Jean. Look Back, My Love. large type ed. (Linford Romance Large Print Ser.). 288p. 1995. pap. 16.99 (*0-7089-7679-4*, Linford) Ulverscroft.

— Nurse's Masquerade. large type ed. (Linford Romance Library). 256p. 1994. pap. 16.99 (*0-7089-7518-6*, Linford) Ulverscroft.

— Run, Nurse, Run. large type ed. (Linford Mystery Library). 272p. 1996. pap. 16.99 (*0-7089-7852-5*, Linford) Ulverscroft.

Carew, Jean V. & Lightfoot, Sara L. Beyond Bias: Perspectives on Classrooms. LC 78-20997. (Illus.). 291p. 1979. 32.00 (*0-674-06882-3*) HUP.

Carew, Lawrence F. Healer of Hearts, Healer of Minds. LC 88-70965. 336p. (Orig.). 1988. pap. 9.95 (*0-943773-00-8*) Community Cross.

Carew, M. Jane. Making Disciples: A Comprehensive Catechesis for the RCIA Catechumenate. 1997. spiral bd. 32.95 (*0-87973-363-2*) Our Sunday Visitor.

Carew, Thomas. Poems of Thomas Carew. Vincent, Arthur, ed. LC 76-38343. (Select Bibliographies Reprint Ser.). 1977. 19.95 (*0-8369-6760-7*) Ayer.

Carew, Thomas J. Behavioral Neurobiology: The Cellular Organization of Natural Behavior. (Illus.). (C). 2000. text. write for info. (*0-87893-084-1*) Sinauer Assocs.

Carew, Thomas J. & Kelley, Darcy B., eds. Perspectives in Neural Systems & Behavior. (MBL Lectures in Biology: Vol. 10). 276p. 1989. pap. 145.00 (*0-471-56218-1*) Wiley.

Carew, Thomas J., et al. Mechanistic Relationships Between Development & Learning: Report of the Dahlem Workshop on Mechanistic Relationships Between Development & Learning, Berlin, January 19-25, 1997. LC 98-17869. (Dahlem Workshop Reports). 336p. 1998. 165.00 (*0-471-97702-0*) Wiley.

***Carew, Wally.** Men of Spirit, Men of Sports. LC 99-67279. 212p. 2000. pap. 14.95 (*1-929039-00-X*) Ambasdr Bks.

***Carey.** Creating Web Pages with HTML: Brief Enhanced. (New Perspectives Ser.). (C). 1998. text 15.95 (*0-7600-5794-X*) Course Tech.

— Creating Websites with HTML. 2nd ed. (New Perspectives Ser.). (C). 2000. text 21.95 (*0-619-01966-2*) Course Tech.

— Creating Websites with HTML: Comprehensive. 2nd ed. (New Perspectives Ser.). (C). 2000. text 44.95 (*0-619-01968-9*) Course Tech.

— Creating Websites with Html: Introductory. 2nd ed. (C). 2000. 31.95 (*0-619-01967-0*) Course Tech.

— Creating Websites with HTML & DHTML. (New Perspectives Ser.). (C). 2000. text 49.95 (*0-619-01969-7*) Course Tech.

— Creatng Web Pages with HTML: An Introduction. (New Perspectives Ser.). (C). 1997. text 31.95 (*0-7600-5532-7*) Course Tech.

Carey. Data Analysis with MS Excel 5 for Windows. 1994. text 21.25 (*1-56527-525-X*) Course Tech.

***Carey.** Dirty Jokes & Beers: Stories of the Unrefined. 256p. 2000. pap. 12.95 (*0-7868-8559-9*, Pub. by Hyperion) Time Warner.

Carey. King of Mysteries. 22.00 (*0-06-061248-7*) HarpC.

Carey. NP Inet Using Netscape Communicator Software. (New Perspectives Ser.). (C). 1997. pap. 21.95 (*0-7600-5764-8*) Course Tech.

— NP on Dynamic HTML. (New Perspectives Ser.). (C). 2000. pap. 33.95 (*0-619-01918-2*) Course Tech.

Carey. Organic Chem. 3rd ed. 1996. 89.74 (*0-07-844757-7*) McGraw.

— Organic Chemistry. 3rd ed. 1995. pap., student ed. 50.94 (*0-07-011223-1*) McGraw.

— Organic Chemistry. 4th ed. LC 99-45791. 2000. 84.00 (*0-07-290501-8*) McGraw.

— Organic Chemistry & SG Student Manual. 3rd ed. 1997. 65.50 (*0-07-561227-5*) McGraw.

***Carey.** Politics & Society in Post-communist. 2000. 70.00 (*0-8133-3743-7*, Pub. by Westview) HarpC.

Carey. Sting Ship Line. 1999. pap. 9.98 (*0-671-04412-5*) PB.

***Carey.** Wave Craze. 24p. 2000. pap. 3.99 (*0-307-13261-7*) Gldn Bks Pub Co.

Carey. Webquester: Socialology. 2nd ed. 150p. 1999. spiral bd. 13.13 (*0-07-235616-2*) McGraw.

— Webquester: Sociology. 1998. 10.00 (*0-697-39953-2*) McGraw.

— Wuthering Heights (Bronte) (Barron's Book Notes Ser.). (C). 1984. pap. 3.95 (*0-8120-3448-1*) Barron.

Carey, ed. Greek Orators No. VI: Apollodorus, Against Neaira. 1992. 59.99 (*0-85668-525-9*, Pub. by Aris & Phillips) David Brown.

— Greek Orators VI: Apollodorus, Against Neaira. 1992. pap. 22.00 (*0-85668-526-7*, Pub. by Aris & Phillips) David Brown.

***Carey & Oja.** New Perspectives on MS Win 98. (New Perspectives Ser.). (C). 1999. ring bd. 16.50 (*0-7600-6547-0*) Course Tech.

Carey & Parsons. New Perspectives on Window 98 for Power Users. 10th ed. (New Perspectives Ser.). (C). 1998. pap. 42.95 (*0-7600-7272-8*) Course Tech.

Carey & Salkind. Microsoft Windows 98 Plus. (Illus.). (C). 1998. pap. 38.95 (*0-7600-5485-1*) Course Tech.

Carey & Stone. The Pentecostal Minister's Sermon Resource Manual, Vol. I. LC 87-72041. Vol. 1. (Illus.). 1987. 15.99 (*0-87148-721-7*) Pathway Pr.

— The Pentecostal Minister's Sermon Resource Manual, Vol. 2. Vol. 2. (Illus.). 1988. 15.99 (*0-87148-950-3*) Pathway Pr.

— Pentecostal Resource Manual, Vol. 3. Vol. 3. (Illus.). 1990. 15.99 (*0-87148-951-1*) Pathway Pr.

Carey, jt. auth. see Johnson.

Carey, jt. auth. see Mayo.

Carey, ed. see Roxburgh, William.

Carey, A. L., et al, eds. Confronting the Infinite: Proceedings of a Conference in Honour of H. S. Green & C. A. Hurst, University of Adelaide, Adelaide, South Australia 14-17 February, 1994. viii, 321p. 1995. text 78.00 (*981-02-2413-3*, Pmton-P2891) World Scientific Pub.

Carey, Alan & Carey, Sandy. Buffalo. (Illus.). 80p. Date not set. 10.98 (*0-7858-0830-2*) Bk Sales Inc.

— Eagle. (Creatures of the Wild Ser.). (Illus.). 80p. 1998. 10.98 (*0-7858-0826-4*) Bk Sales Inc.

— Moose. (Illus.). 80p. Date not set. 10.98 (*0-7858-0827-2*) Bk Sales Inc.

— Wolf. (Illus.). 80p. Date not set. 10.98 (*0-7858-0828-0*) Bk Sales Inc.

Carey, Alan C. The Reluctant Raiders: The Story of United States Navy Bombing Squadron VB/VPB-109 in WW II. LC 98-89153. (Illus.). 240p. 1999. 29.95 (*0-7643-0757-6*) Schiffer.

***Carey, Alan C.** We Flew Alone, US Navy B-24 Squadrons in the Pacific: February Forty Three to September Forty Four. (Illus.). 120p. 2000. pap. 19.95 (*0-7643-1170-0*) Schiffer.

Carey, Alan L. & Murray, Michael K., eds. Geometric Analysis & Lie Theory in Mathematics & Physics. (Australian Mathematical Society Lecture Ser.: Vol. 11). 304p. (C). 1997. pap. text 42.95 (*0-521-62490-8*) Cambridge U Pr.

Carey, Alex & Lohrey, Andrew. Taking the Risk Out of Democracy: Corporate Propaganda Versus Freedom & Liberty. LC 96-20817. (History of Communication Ser.). 240p. 1997. pap. text 15.95 (*0-252-06616-2*) U of Ill Pr.

Carey, Alice. Family Camping. (Trailside Series Guide). Date not set. pap. write for info. (*0-393-31477-4*, Norton Paperbks) Norton.

Carey, Andrew B., jt. ed. see Gutierrez, Ralph J.

Carey, Ann. The Dachshund: An Owner's Guide to a Happy, Healthy Pet. LC 95-15662. (Owner's Guide to a Happy, Healthy Pet Ser.). (Illus.). 160p. 1995. 12.95 (*0-87605-386-X*) Howell Bks.

— Sisters in Crisis: The Tragic Unravelling of Women's Religious Communities. LC 96-70435. 368p. 1997. 19.95 (*0-87973-655-0*) Our Sunday Visitor.

Carey, Anthony G. Parties, Slavery, & the Union in Antebellum Georgia. LC 96-30786. 1997. 60.00 (*0-8203-1898-1*) U of Ga Pr.

Carey, Barbara. The Ground of Events. LC 94-182370. 80p. pap. 9.95 (*1-55128-009-4*, Pub. by Mercury Bk) LPC InBook.

— Undressing the Dark. 80p. 1986. pap. 12.95 (*0-919627-01-3*, Pub. by Quarry Pr) LPC InBook.

— The Year in Pictures. 80p. 1989. pap. 12.95 (*0-919627-53-6*, Pub. by Quarry Pr) LPC InBook.

Carey, Belva. Maranatha Vol. 2: My Many Phases. (Illus.). 117p. (Orig.). 1997. pap. 8.00 (*0-614-28589-5*) Careys Pub Co.

— Poetry of Love: Baby Boomers. (Poetry...Mostly Faith Ser.). (Illus.). 72p. (Orig.). (J). (gr. 6 up). 1987. pap. 5.95 (*0-9617859-0-X*) Careys Pub Co.

Carey, Bill, et al. How to Sell Your Home Without a Broker. 2nd ed. LC 96-22882. 238p. 1996. 29.95 (*0-471-15286-2*); pap. 18.95 (*0-471-15285-4*) Wiley.

***Carey, Bill, et al.** How to Sell Your Home Without a Broker. 3rd ed. 288p. 2000. pap. 19.95 (*0-471-38881-5*) Wiley.

Carey, Bill, jt. auth. see Carey, Chantal Howell.

Carey, Carol W. Fayette County, Ohio: A Pictorial History. LC 93-24069. 1993. write for info. (*0-89865-874-8*) Donning Co.

***Carey, Chantal Howell & Carey, Bill.** Going Going Gone! Auctioning Your Home for Top Dollar. LC 99-52513. 256p. 2000. pap. 16.95 (*0-471-37757-0*) Wiley.

Carey, Charles F., jt. auth. see Washington University School of Medicine Departmen.

Carey, Charles H. General History of Oregon. 3rd ed. LC 70-140122. (Illus.). 968p. 1971. 35.00 (*0-8323-0221-X*) Binford Mort.

Carey, Charles Henry, ed. The Oregon Constitution & Proceedings & Debates of the Constitutional Convention of 1857. 543p. 1926. 14.95 (*0-87595-092-2*) Oregon Hist.

***Carey, Charles W., Jr.** The Emancipation Proclamation. LC 99-19260. (Journey to Freedom Ser.). (Illus.). 32p. (YA). (gr. 4 up). 1999. lib. bdg. 24.21 (*1-56766-620-5*) Childs World.

Carey, Charles W. George Washington Carver. LC 98-47048. (Journey to Freedom Ser.). (Illus.). 32p. (J). (gr. 2-6). 1998. lib. bdg. 24.21 (*1-56766-569-1*) Childs World.

Carey, Chipper, jt. auth. see Carey, Skip.

Carey, Chris. The American Darts Organization Book of Darts. (Illus.). 112p. 1994. pap. 9.95 (*1-55821-247-7*) Lyons Pr.

— U. S. Chemical & Biological Defense Respirators: An Illustrated History. LC 97-67596. 224p. 1998. 45.00 (*0-7643-0387-2*) Schiffer.

***Carey, Chris, tr.** Aeschines. (Oratory of Classical Ser.). 270p. 2000. 45.00 (*0-292-71222-7*); pap. 19.95 (*0-292-71223-5*) U of Tex Pr.

Carey, Chris, ed. see Rohm, Robert A.

Carey, Christopher. A Commentary of Five Odes of Pindar. rev. ed. Connor, W. R., ed. LC 80-2644. (Monographs in Classical Studies). 1981. lib. bdg. 26.00 (*0-405-14032-0*) Ayer.

— A Commentary on Five Odes of Pindar. 1981. 30.95 (*0-88143-028-5*) Ayer.

— Trials from Classical Athens. LC 96-47561. 256p. (C). 1997. 80.00 (*0-415-10760-1*); pap. 25.99 (*0-415-10761-X*) Routledge.

Carey, Christopher, ed. see Demosthenes.

Carey, Christopher, ed. see Lysias.

***Carey, Craig R.** Below Zero. (Illus.). (J). 2000. pap. 3.99 (*0-307-20127-9*) Gldn Bks Pub Co.

— Hit the Dirt. (Extreme Sports Ser.). (Illus.). (J). 2000. pap. 3.99 (*0-307-20126-0*) Gldn Bks Pub Co.

Carey, Cynthia, ed. Avian Energetics & Nutritional Ecology. LC 95-15905. 464p. (gr. 13). 1996. write for info. (*0-412-03701-7*) Kluwer Academic.

Carey, D. P., et al, eds. Recent Advances in Canine & Feline Nutritional Research: Proceedings of the 1996 IAMS International Nutrition Symposium. 284p. 1997. text 7.00 (*1-882203-09-7*) Orange Frazer.

Carey, Daniel P., jt. ed. see Reinhart, Gregory A.

Carey, Dave. The Ways We Choose: Lessons for Life from a POW's Experience. LC 99-47019. 224p. 2000. pap. 15.95 (*1-58151-042-X*, Pub. by BookPartners) Midpt Trade.

Carey, David C. The Optics of Charged Particle Beams. (Accelerators & Storage Rings Ser.: Vol. 6). xviii, 298p. 1987. text 209.00 (*3-7186-0350-0*) Gordon & Breach.

Carey, Dean. The Actor's Audition Manual, Vol. 1. (Orig.). pap. 19.95 (*0-86819-516-2*, Pub. by Currency Pr) Accents Pubns.

— Masterclass: The Actor's Manuals for Men. (Nick Hern Bks.). (Illus.). 2000. pap. 27.95 (*1-85459-233-5*) Theatre Comm.

— Masterclass: The Actor's Manuals for Women. (Nick Hern Bks.). 2000. pap. 27.95 (*1-85459-238-6*) Theatre Comm.

Carey, Dean, ed. Masterclass: The Actor's Audition Manual for Men. 246p. 1995. pap. 10.95 (*0-435-08678-2*, 08678) Heinemann.

— Masterclass: The Actor's Audition Manual for Women. 246p. 1995. pap. 10.95 (*0-435-08679-0*, 08679) Heinemann.

Carey, Debi. Private Medical Practice: Getting Started & Making It Work. LC 97-10674. 320p. 1997. 175.00 (*0-7863-1118-5*, Irwn Prfssnl) McGraw-Hill Prof.

Carey, Denis. Medical Negligence Litigation. 176p. 1998. pap. 40.00 (*1-85811-162-5*, Pub. by CLT Prof) Gaunt.

***Carey, Denis.** Pension Loss in Personal Injuries. 60p. 1999. 30.00 (*1-85811-126-9*, Pub. by CLT Prof) Gaunt.

Carey, Denis. Personal Injury Litigation: Legal Practice Course Guides. 251p. 1995. pap. 34.00 (*1-85431-463-7*, Pub. by Blackstone Pr) Gaunt.

— Personal Injury Litigation: Legal Practice Course Guides. rev. ed. 200p. Date not set. pap. 34.00 (*1-85431-514-5*, Pub. by Blackstone Pr) Gaunt.

— Tripping & Slipping. 100p. 1997. pap. 33.00 (*1-85811-139-0*, Pub. by CLT Prof) Gaunt.

***Carey, Dennis C. & Ogden, Dayton.** CEO Succession. (Illus.). 224p. 2000. 25.00 (*0-19-512713-7*) OUP.

***Carey, Dian.** Star Trek Voyager: Season Six Novelization. (J). 1999. per. 6.50 (*0-671-04295-5*) Aladdin.

Carey, Diana & Large, Judy. Festivals Family & Food: A Guide to Multi-Cultural Celebration. (Lifeways Ser.). (Illus.). 216p. (Orig.). 1982. pap. text 18.95 (*0-9507062-3-X*, 654, Pub. by Hawthorn Press) Anthroposophic.

— Festivals Together: A Guide to Multi-Cultural Celebration. (Lifeways Ser.). (Illus.). 223p. (Orig.). 1993. pap. text 19.95 (*1-869890-46-9*, Pub. by Hawthorn Press) Anthroposophic.

Carey, Diana L. Best Destiny. 1997. per. 12.99 (*0-671-01945-7*) PB.

Carey, Diane. Battlestation! Star Trek, No. 31. (Star Trek Ser.: No. 13). 1991. mass mkt. 4.99 (*0-671-74025-3*) PB.

— Battlestations. 1999. mass mkt. 3.99 (*0-671-03858-3*) PB.

— Best Destiny. Ripin, Kevin, ed. (Star Trek Ser.). 416p. 1993. reprint ed. mass mkt. 5.99 (*0-671-79588-0*, Star Trek) PB.

***Carey, Diane.** Challenger. (Star Trek Ser.: Vol. 6). 304p. 2000. mass mkt. 6.50 (*0-671-04298-X*, Star Trek) PB.

Carey, Diane. Descent. (Star Trek: The Next Generation Ser.). 1993. per. 5.99 (*0-671-88267-8*) PB.

— Dominion War No. 2: Call to Arms. (Star Trek Ser.). 1998. per. 6.50 (*0-671-02497-3*, Star Trek) PB.

— Dominion War No. 4: Sacrifice of Angels. (Star Trek Ser.). 1998. mass mkt. 6.50 (*0-671-02498-1*, Star Trek) PB.

— Dreadnought. 1999. mass mkt. 3.99 (*0-671-03852-4*) PB.

— End of Season Cliffhanger. (Star Trek: Deep Space Nine Ser.). 1994. mass mkt. 5.50 (*0-671-50604-8*) PB.

— Final Frontier. (Giant Star Trek). (Orig.). 1989. 5.99 (*0-671-69655-6*, Star Trek) PB.

— Flashback. (Star Trek). 1996. per. 5.99 (*0-671-00383-6*, Star Trek) PB.

— Ghost Ship, No. 1. (Star Trek: The Next Generation Ser.). 1991. mass mkt. 5.50 (*0-671-74608-1*) PB.

— The Great Starship Race. (Star Trek Ser.: No. 67). 288p. 1993. mass mkt. 5.99 (*0-671-87250-8*) PB.

— Invasion! No. 1: First Strike. (Star Trek: Deep Space Nine Ser.: No. 79). 1996. mass mkt. 6.50 (*0-671-54002-5*, Star Trek) PB.

— Red Sector: Double Helix, No. 3. (Star Trek Next Generation Ser.: Vol. 3). 293p. 1999. per. 6.50 (*0-671-03257-7*, Star Trek) PB.

— Ship of the Line. (Star Trek Ser.). 320p. 1984. 1.50 (*0-671-00924-9*, Star Trek) PB.

***Carey, Diane.** Ship of the Line. (Star Trek Ser.). 320p. 1999. reprint ed. mass mkt. 6.50 (*0-671-00925-7*, Star Trek) PB.

C

— Star Trek Best Destiny. 1999. pap. 9.98 (*0-671-04410-9*) PB.

— Star Trek Deep Space Nine Final Episode, 1. (Star Trek Deep Space Nine (Unnumbered) Ser.). 1999. per. 6.50 (*0-671-03476-6*) PB.

Carey, Diane. Starfleet Academy. (Star Trek Ser.). 1997. per. 5.99 (*0-671-01550-8*, Star Trek) PB.

— Station Rage. (Star Trek: Deep Space Nine Ser.: No. 13). 1995. mass mkt. 5.99 (*0-671-88561-8*) PB.

— Trial & Tribulations. (Star Trek Ser.). 1984. mass mkt. 1.50 (*0-671-00902-8*) PB.

***Carey, Diane.** Wagon Train to the Stars. (Star Trek Ser.: Bk. 1). 400p. 2000. per. 6.50 (*0-671-04296-3*) PB.

Carey, Diane. The Way of the Warrior. (Star Trek: Deep Space Nine Ser.: 01). 1995. mass mkt. 5.99 (*0-671-56813-2*) PB.

***Carey, Diane & Smith, Dean Wesley.** Belle Terre. (Star Trek Ser.: Vol. 90). 288p. 2000. per. 6.50 (*0-671-04297-1*) PB.

Carey, Diane, et al. Star Trek: Day of Honor Omnibus. 1200p. 1999. pap. 16.00 (*0-671-02813-8*, Star Trek) PB.

Carey, Diane L. Ancient Blood: The/Day of Honor. (Star Trek Ser.). 1997. per. 7.99 (*0-671-00238-4*) PB.

— Buried Alive. (Distress Call 911 Ser.: No. 2). 192p. (YA). (gr. 7 up). 1996. per. 3.99 (*0-671-55307-0*) PB.

— Cadet Kirk. (Starfleet Academy Ser.: No. 3). (J). (gr. 3-6). 1996. per. 3.99 (*0-671-00077-2*) PB.

— Cadet Kirk. LC 49-244350. (Starfleet Academy Ser.). 1996. 9.09 (*0-606-10944-7*, Pub. by Turtleback) Demco.

— Danger Zone. (Distress Call 911 Ser.: No. 3). 192p. (YA). (gr. 7 up). 1996. per. 3.99 (*0-671-55309-7*) PB.

— Invasion Omnibus. (Star Trek Ser.). 960p. 1998. mass mkt. 14.00 (*0-671-02185-0*) PB.

— Million Dollar Mistake: Distress Call 911. 5th ed. (Distress Call 911 Ser.: No. 5). 192p. (YA). (gr. 7 up). 1996. per. 3.99 (*0-671-00095-0*) PB.

— Promise Me You'll Stop Me: Distress Call 911. 7th ed. (Distress Call 911 Ser.: No. 7). (YA). 1997. per. 3.99 (*0-671-00097-7*) PB.

— Roughing It: Distress Call 911. 7th ed. (Distress Call 911 Ser.: No. 6). (YA). (gr. 7 up). 1996. mass mkt. 3.99 (*0-671-00096-9*) PB.

— Twist of Fate. (Distress Call 911 Ser.: No. 1). 192p. (J). (gr. k-7). 1996. mass mkt. 3.99 (*0-671-55306-2*) PB.

— Voyager Season Premier: Star Trek. 1995. per. 5.99 (*0-671-55193-0*) PB.

— Worth Dying For. (Distress Call 911 Ser.: No. 4). (YA). (gr. 7 up). 1996. per. 3.99 (*0-671-55308-9*) PB.

Carey, Diane L. & Janeway, Kathryn. The Fire Ship No. 4: The Captain's Table. (Star Trek Ser.). 274p. 1998. mass mkt. 6.50 (*0-671-01467-6*) PB.

Carey, Diane L. & Kirkland, James C. First Frontier. (Star Trek Ser.: No. 75). 400p. 1995. mass mkt. 5.99 (*0-671-52045-8*, Pocket Books) PB.

Carey, Diane L., jt. auth. see Case, Linda P.

Carey, D.L. Buried Alive. (Distress Call 911 Ser.). 1996. 9.09 (*0-606-10783-5*, Pub. by Turtleback) Demco.

— Danger Zone. (Distress Call 911 Ser.). 1996. 9.09 (*0-606-10784-3*, Pub. by Turtleback) Demco.

— Million Dollar Mistake. (Distress Call 911 Ser.). 1996. 9.09 (*0-606-10786-X*, Pub. by Turtleback) Demco.

— Promise You'll Stop Me. (Distress Call 911 Ser.). (J). 1997. 9.09 (*0-606-11263-4*, Pub. by Turtleback) Demco.

Carey, D.L. Roughing It. (Distress Call 911 Ser.). 1996. 9.09 (*0-606-11262-6*, Pub. by Turtleback) Demco.

Carey, D.L. Twist of Fate. (Distress Call 911 Ser.). 1996. 9.09 (*0-606-10172-1*, Pub. by Turtleback) Demco.

Carey, D.L. Worth Dying For. (Distress Call 911 Ser.). 1996. 9.09 (*0-606-10785-1*, Pub. by Turtleback) Demco.

Carey, Donald E. & Carey, Neil G. Fighting the Bolsheviks: The Russian War Memoir of Private First Class Donald E. Carey, U. S. Army 1918-1919. LC 97-16772. (Illus.). 240p. 1997. 24.95 (*0-89141-631-5*) Presidio Pr.

Carey, Doris E. Echoes of a Soul in Anguish. (Orig.). 1997. pap. 8.95 (*0-533-12339-9*) Vantage.

Carey, Drew. Dirty Jokes & Beer: Stories of the Unrefined. LC 97-194470. (Illus.). 224p. 1997. 22.45 (*0-7868-6351-X*, Pub. by Hyperion) Time Warner.

— Dirty Jokes & Beer: Stories of the Unrefined. LC PN2287.C27A3 . 272p. 1998. mass mkt. 6.99 (*0-7868-8939-X*, Pub. by Hyperion) Time Warner.

Carey, E. Chris, ed. see Rohm, Robert A.

***Carey, Edward.** Observatory Mansions. 2001. 23.00 (*0-609-60680-8*) Crown Pub Group.

Carey, Eileen Andrew. The Bishop & I. 1998. pap. 10.99 (*0-340-65652-2*, Pub. by Hodder & Stought Ltd) Trafalgar.

Carey, Elizabeth. The Tragedy of Mariam (1613) Dunstan, A. C. & Greg, W. W., eds. (Malone Society reprints Ser.: No. 42). (Illus.). 92p. 1992. text 52.00 (*0-19-729017-5*) OUP.

Carey, Elizabeth L. The Commands of Jesus. 167p. 1997. pap. text 16.95 (*1-891331-01-9*, 1002) Nebbadoon Pr.

— Jesus' Healings: A Closer Look. 153p. 1995. pap. text 16.95 (*1-891331-00-0*, 1001) Nebbadoon Pr.

Carey, Ernestine G., jt. auth. see Gilbreth, Frank B., Sr.

Carey, Ernestine Gilbreth, jt. auth. see Gilbreth, Frank B., Jr.

Carey, Floyd & Stone, Hoyt, compiled by. The Pentecostal Minister Sermon Resource Manual, Vol. 5. Vol. 5. (Illus.). 328p. 1996. 16.99 (*0-87148-968-6*) Pathway Pr.

Carey, Floyd D. Sermon Resource Manual. 1997. 59.99 (*5-559-30297-X*) Pathway Pr.

***Carey, Frances.** The Apocalypse & the Shape of Things to Come. 2000. pap. text 39.95 (*0-8020-8325-0*) U of Toronto Pr.

Carey, Francis A. Advanced Organic Chemistry, Pt. A - Structure & Mechanisms. LC 76-54956. 609p. reprint ed. pap. 188.80 (*0-8357-5129-5*, 202472000001) Bks Demand.

— Advanced Organic Chemistry, Pt. B - Reactions & Synthesis. abr. ed. LC 76-54956. 547p. pap. 169.60 (*0-8357-5130-9*, 202472000002) Bks Demand.

— Organic Chemistry. 2nd ed. (C). 1991. text 78.50 (*0-07-009934-0*); pap. text, student ed. 45.00 (*0-07-009935-9*) McGraw.

— Organic Chemistry. 3rd ed. LC 95-25237. 1151p. (C). 1995. 102.81 (*0-07-011212-6*) McGraw.

***Carey, Francis A.** Organic Chemistry. 4th ed. LC 99-45791. 2000. write for info. (*0-07-117499-0*) McGraw.

***Carey, Francis A. & Atkins, Robert C.** Study Guide & Solutions Manual to Accompany Organic Chemistry, Fourth Edition. LC 99-47983. 2000. write for info. (*0-07-290510-7*) McGrw-H Hghr Educ.

***Carey, Francis A. & Sundberg, Richard J.** Advanced Organic Chemistry. 4th ed. LC 00-27456. 2000. pap. write for info. (*0-306-46243-5*, Kluwer Plenum) Kluwer Academic.

Carey, Frank & Naas, Jayni. Kansas Cookbook: Recipes from the Heartland. LC 89-51768. (Illus.). x, 478p. (Orig.). 1989. pap. 16.95 (*0-7006-0418-9*) U Pr of KS.

Carey, Frank, jt. auth. see Sheffler, William L.

Carey, Frank A. & Sundberg, R. J. Advanced Organic Chemistry: Reactions & Synthesis, Pt. B. 3rd ed. LC 90-6851. (Illus.). 830p. (C). 1990. pap. text 37.50 (*0-306-43457-1*, Kluwer Plenum) Kluwer Academic.

— Advanced Organic Chemistry: Structure & Mechanisms, Pt. A. 3rd ed. LC 90-6851. (Illus.). 832p. (C). 1990. pap. text 37.50 (*0-306-43447-4*, Kluwer Plenum) Kluwer Academic.

— Advanced Organic Chemistry Pt. A: Structure & Mechanisms. 3rd ed. LC 90-6851. (Illus.). 832p. (C). 1990. 90.00 (*0-306-43440-7*, Kluwer Plenum) Kluwer Academic.

— Advanced Organic Chemistry Pt. B: Reactions & Synthesis. 3rd ed. LC 90-6851. (Illus.). 830p. (C). 1990. 90.00 (*0-306-43456-3*, Kluwer Plenum) Kluwer Academic.

Carey, Frank A., jt. auth. see Atkins, Robert C.

Carey, G. F., et al. Circuit, Device, & Process Simultaion: Mathematical & Numerical Aspects. LC 95-49408. 440p. 1996. 195.00 (*0-471-96019-5*) Wiley.

Carey, G. V. Mind the Stop: A Brief Guide to Punctuation. (Illus.). (J). pap. 11.95 (*0-14-051072-9*, Pub. by Pnguin Bks Ltd) Trafalgar.

Carey, G. W. The Chemistry of the Cosmos: Armageddon, Astrology, Wonders & Possibilities of the Human Body, Paradoxes of Civilization & the Coming Man. 1991. lib. bdg. 79.95 (*0-8490-4249-6*) Gordon Pr.

— The Chemistry Wonders of the Human Body. 1991. lib. bdg. 74.50 (*0-8490-4133-3*) Gordon Pr.

— Relation of the Mineral Salts of the Body to the Signs of the Zodiac. 1991. lib. bdg. 69.00 (*0-8490-4248-8*) Gordon Pr.

Carey, Gary. Anita Loos: A Biography. LC 89-204802. xiii, 331 p. 1988. write for info. (*0-7475-0294-3*) Blmsbury Pub.

— Babbitt Notes. (Cliffs Notes Ser.). 72p. 1964. pap. 4.95 (*0-8220-0219-1*, Cliff) IDG Bks.

— Brothers Karamazov Notes. (Cliffs Notes Ser.). 96p. 1964. pap. 4.95 (*0-8220-0265-5*, Cliff) IDG Bks.

— Great Expectations Notes. (Cliffs Notes Ser.). 64p. 1982. pap. 4.95 (*0-8220-0551-4*, Cliff) IDG Bks.

— Idiot Notes. (Cliffs Notes Ser.). 112p. (Orig.). 1968. pap. 4.50 (*0-8220-0627-8*, Cliff) IDG Bks.

— Mrs. Dalloway Notes. (Cliffs Notes Ser.). 64p. 1970. pap. 4.95 (*0-8220-0855-6*, Cliff) IDG Bks.

— Plague Notes. (Cliffs Notes Ser.). 80p. 1967. pap. 4.95 (*0-8220-1039-9*, Cliff) IDG Bks.

— Romeo & Juliet Notes. (Cliffs Notes Ser.). 72p. 1960. pap. 4.95 (*0-8220-0074-1*, Cliff) IDG Bks.

— Stranger Notes. (Cliffs Notes Ser.). 72p. (Orig.). 1965. pap. 4.95 (*0-8220-1229-4*, Cliff) IDG Bks.

Carey, Gary. The Sun Also Rises: Notes. (Cliffs Notes Ser.). 80p. 1964. pap. 4.95 (*0-8220-1237-5*, Cliff) IDG Bks.

Carey, Gary, ed. Shakespeare's Minor Plays Notes. (Cliffs Notes Ser.). 1991. pap. 7.95 (*0-8220-0059-8*, Cliff) IDG Bks.

Carey, Gary & Jorgenson, Paul A. Othello Notes. (Cliffs Notes Ser.). 88p. 1959. pap. 4.95 (*0-8220-0063-6*, Cliff) IDG Bks.

Carey, Gary & Snodgrass, Mary E. A Multicultural Dictionary of Literary Terms. LC 98-35221. (Illus.). 192p. 1998. pap. 29.50 (*0-7864-0552-X*) McFarland & Co.

Carey, Gary K. The Old Man & the Sea Notes. (Cliffs Notes Ser.). 64p. (Orig.). (C). 1973. pap. 4.95 (*0-8220-0935-8*, Cliff) IDG Bks.

— The Red Pony, Chrysanthemums & Flight Notes. (Cliffs Notes Ser.). 56p. (Orig.). 1978. pap. text 4.95 (*0-8220-1135-2*, Cliff) IDG Bks.

Carey, George. Canterbury Letters to the Future. LC 98-32000. 240p. 1999. pap. 12.95 (*0-8192-1753-0*) Morehouse Pub.

— A Charter for the Church: Sharing a Vision for the 21st Century. LC 93-26327. 236p. 1993. pap. 14.95 (*0-8192-1612-7*) Morehouse Pub.

— The Church in the Market Place: An Inspiring Story of Witness & Renewal. LC 90-25405. 160p. 1991. pap., student ed. 9.95 (*0-8192-1562-7*) Morehouse Pub.

— A Faraway Time & Place: Lore of the Eastern Shore. Dorson, Richard M., ed. LC 77-70586. (International Folklore Ser.). (Illus.). 1977. reprint ed. lib. bdg. 24.95 (*0-405-10086-8*) Ayer.

— I Believe. LC 91-17587. 208p. (Orig.). 1991. pap. 12.95 (*0-8192-1579-1*) Morehouse Pub.

— Spiritual Journey. LC 93-45516. 160p. (Orig.). 1994. pap. 10.95 (*0-8192-1595-3*) Morehouse Pub.

— Why I Believe in a Personal God: The Credibility of Faith in a Doubting Culture. 152p. 1991. per. 8.99 (*0-87788-947-3*, H Shaw Pubs) Waterbrook Pr.

Carey, George, ed. The Bible for Everyday Life. 398p. 1996. pap. 20.00 (*0-8028-4157-0*) Eerdmans.

Carey, George & Frohnen, Bruce, eds. Order & Freedom: The Conservative Vision of Community. LC 98-23398. 216p. (Orig.). 1998. 53.00 (*0-8476-8660-4*); pap. 22.95 (*0-8476-8661-2*) Rowman.

Carey, George, jt. auth. see Kendall, Willmoore.

Carey, George G. Maryland Folklore. LC 89-40302. (Illus.). 175p. 1989. pap. 12.95 (*0-87033-396-8*, Tidewtr Pubs) Cornell Maritime.

Carey, George G., ed. A Sailor's Songbag: An American Rebel in an English Prison, 1777-1779. LC 75-32483. (Illus.). 176p. 1976. reprint ed. pap. 54.60 (*0-608-01707-8*, 206236200002) Bks Demand.

Carey, George W. The Biochemic System of Medicine. 26th ed. 535p. 1996. spiral bd. 38.50 (*0-7873-0144-2*) Hlth Research.

— The Chemistry & Wonders of the Human Body. 156p. 1996. reprint ed. spiral bd. 12.00 (*0-7873-0142-6*) Hlth Research.

— The Chemistry of Human Life. 78p. 1996. reprint ed. spiral bd. 11.00 (*0-7873-0141-8*) Hlth Research.

— Chemistry of the Cosmos. 144p. 1996. reprint ed. spiral bd. 10.50 (*0-7873-0140-X*) Hlth Research.

— Course of Instructions in the Biochemic Pathology of Disease: Includes Twelve Cell Salts of the Zodiac. 31p. 1996. reprint ed. spiral bd. 11.50 (*0-7873-0145-0*) Hlth Research.

— The Federalist: Design for a Constitutional Republic. 216p. (C). 1995. pap. text 12.95 (*0-252-06449-6*) U of Ill Pr.

— In Defense of the Constitution. expanded rev. ed. LC 94-38245. xii, 202p. 1995. 14.00 (*0-86597-137-4*); pap. 7.50 (*0-86597-138-2*) Liberty Fund.

— Relation of the Mineral Salts of the Body to the Signs of the Zodiac. 50p. 1992. pap. 5.00 (*0-89540-208-4*, SB-208, Sun Bks) Sun Pub.

— The Tree of Life. 60p. 1985. reprint ed. spiral bd. 16.00 (*0-7873-1225-8*) Hlth Research.

— Twelve Cell Salts of the Zodiac. 31p. 1994. reprint ed. spiral bd. write for info. (*0-7873-1224-X*) Hlth Research.

Carey, George W., ed. Order, Freedom, & the Polity: Critical Essays on the Open Society. 196p. (Orig.). 1986. pap. text 20.00 (*0-8191-5156-4*); lib. bdg. 45.00 (*0-8191-5155-6*) U Pr of Amer.

Carey, George W. & Perry, Inez E. God-Man: The Word Made Flesh (1920) 176p. 1996. reprint ed. pap. 11.95 (*1-56459-942-6*) Kessinger Pub.

— God-Man, the Word Made Flesh. 176p. 1920. reprint ed. spiral bd. 15.50 (*0-7873-0143-4*) Hlth Research.

— The Zodiac & the Salts of Salvation. LC 77-166412. 352p. 1989. pap. 16.95 (*0-87728-708-2*) Weiser.

Carey, George W. & Schall, James V., eds. Essays on Christianity & Political Philosophy. (ISI Roots of Western Culture Ser.). 144p. (Orig.). (C). 1985. pap. text 18.00 (*0-8191-4276-X*) U Pr of Amer.

Carey, George W., et al. Relation of the Mineral Salts of the Body to the Signs of the Zodiac. 50p. 1996. reprint ed. spiral bd. 11.00 (*0-7873-0146-9*) Hlth Research.

Carey, George W., jt. auth. see Kendall, Willmoore.

Carey, George W., jt. auth. see Perry, Inez E.

Carey, George W., jt. ed. see Hyneman, Charles S.

Carey, George W., ed. see Kirk, Russell, et al.

Carey, Ginger. Research Made Easy. 88p. 1996. teacher ed. 10.00 (*1-56417-846-3*, GA1553) Good Apple.

Carey, Graham F. Computational Grids: Generations, Adaptation & Solution Strategies. LC 96-29510. 472p. 1997. 80.00 (*1-56032-635-2*) Hemisp Pub.

Carey, Graham F., ed. Finite Element Modeling of Environmental Problems: Surface & Subsurface Flow & Transport. LC 95-7311. 392p. 1995. 175.00 (*0-471-95662-7*) Wiley.

Carey, Greg. Elusive Apocalypse. LC 99-28149. (Studies in American Biblical Hermeneutics: Vol. 15). 192p. 1999. pap. 18.95 (*0-86554-632-0*) Mercer Univ Pr.

Carey, Greg, jt. ed. see Bloomquist, L. Gregory.

Carey, Harry, Jr. Company of Heroes: My Life As an Actor in the John Ford Stock Company. 218p. 1996. pap. 14.95 (*1-56833-068-5*) Madison Bks UPA.

— Company of Heroes: My Life As an Actor in the John Ford Stock Company. LC 94-8074. (Filmmakers Ser.: No. 42). (Illus.). 278p. 1994. 31.00 (*0-8108-2865-0*) Scarecrow.

Carey, Helen. On a Wing & a Prayer. 416p. 1998. 27.00 (*1-85797-642-8*, Pub. by Orion Pubng Grp) Trafalgar.

— Some Sunny Day. 380p. 1996. pap. 17.95 (*1-85797-617-7*, Pub. by Orion Pubng Grp) Trafalgar.

Carey, Helen, jt. auth. see Greenberg, Judith.

Carey, Henry. The Dramatic Works. (Anglistica & Americana Ser.: No. 101). 256p. 1982. reprint ed. 95.00 (*3-487-07183-5*) G Olms Pubs.

Carey, Henry. Musical Century. fac. ed. (Monuments of Music & Music Literature in Facsimile, I Ser.: Vol. 22). 9p. 1976. lib. bdg. 65.00 (*0-8450-2022-6*) Broude.

Carey, Henry. Poems. (BCL1-PR English Literature Ser.). 261p. 1992. reprint ed. lib. bdg. 79.00 (*0-7812-7329-3*) Rprt Serv.

Carey, Henry C. Collected Works, 6 vols. 1972. 600.00 (*0-87968-885-8*) Gordon Pr.

— Essay on the Rate of Wages. LC 77-119647. reprint ed. 24.50 (*0-404-01392-9*) AMS Pr.

— Essay on the Rate of Wages. LC 64-66155. (Reprints of Economic Classics Ser.). 255p. 1965. reprint ed. 22.50 (*0-678-00081-6*) Kelley.

— The Harmony of Interests: Agricultural, Manufacturing & Commercial. LC 68-18572. (Reprints of Economic Classics Ser.). 235p. 1967. reprint ed. 39.50 (*0-678-00246-0*) Kelley.

— The Past, the Present, & the Future. LC 67-18573. (Reprints of Economic Classics Ser.). 474p. 1967. reprint ed. 49.50 (*0-678-00245-2*) Kelley.

— Principles of Political Economy, 3 Vols, Set. LC 65-16983. (Reprints of Economic Classics Ser.). 1965. reprint ed. 125.00 (*0-678-00071-9*) Kelley.

— Principles of Social Science, 3 Vols, Set. LC 63-22257. (Reprints of Economic Classics Ser.). 1963. reprint ed. 150.00 (*0-678-00013-1*) Kelley.

— The Unity of Law: As Exhibited in the Relation of Physical, Social, Mental & Moral Science. LC 67-18575. (Reprints of Economic Classics Ser.). (Illus.). xxiii, 433p. 1967. reprint ed. 49.50 (*0-678-00247-9*) Kelley.

Carey, Hilary. Believing in Australia: A Cultural History of Religions. (Illus.). 288p. 1997. pap. 27.95 (*1-86373-950-5*, Pub. by Allen & Unwin Pty) Paul & Co Pubs.

Carey, Hilary M. Courting Disaster: Astrology at the English Court & University in the Later Middle Ages. LC 91-17383. 296p. 1992. text 55.00 (*0-312-06723-2*) St Martin.

Carey, Howard R. Journey into Light & Joy. LC 79-53905. (Illus.). 180p. 1979. pap. 4.50 (*0-87516-380-7*) DeVorss.

Carey, Hugh. Duet for Two Voices: An Informal Biography of Edward Dent Compiled from His Letters to Clive Carey. LC 78-62115. (Illus.). 224p. reprint ed. pap. 63.90 (*0-608-17575-7*, 2030583) Bks Demand.

***Carey, J. C.** Carey's Index: State of California California Code of Regulations Title Is Crime Prevention & Correction. 240p. (C). 2000. pap. 18.95 (*0-9678785-0-0*) A F E R Pubng.

Carey, J. Christopher, jt. auth. see Rayburn, William F.

Carey, Jacqueline. Angels: Celestial Spirits in Legend & Art. LC 97-37024. (Illus.). 128p. 1997. 16.98 (*1-56799-603-5*, MetroBooks) M Friedman Pub Grp Inc.

***Carey, Jacqueline.** Kushiel's Dart. 2001. text 24.95 (*0-312-87238-0*) St Martin.

Carey, Jacqui. Beginners Guide to Braiding: The Craft of Kumihimi. (Illus.). 64p. (Orig.). 1997. pap. 15.95 (*0-85532-828-2*, 8282, Pub. by Srch Pr) A Schwartz & Co.

Carey, James. About Pay. Racine, Robert, ed. LC 93-73209. (Fifty-Minute Ser.). (Illus.). 80p. (Orig.). 1994. pap. 10.95 (*1-56052-267-4*) Crisp Pubns.

***Carey, James.** San Francisco Design Patterns: Blueprints for Business Software. LC 99-89298. (Illus.). 320p. 2000. pap. text 44.95 (*0-201-61644-0*) Addison-Wesley.

Carey, James, jt. auth. see Carey, Morris.

Carey, James E., et al, eds. Manual of Nuclear Medicine Procedures. 4th ed. 248p. 1983. 139.00 (*0-8493-0708-2*, R78, CRC Reprint) Franklin.

***Carey, James P. & Bocchino, Anthony J.** Illinois Evidence with Objections. 2000. 25.95 (*1-55681-656-1*) Natl Inst Trial Ad.

Carey, James R. Applied Demography for Biologists: With Special Emphasis on Insects. (Illus.). 224p. 1993. text 55.00 (*0-19-506687-1*) OUP.

Carey, James W. Communication As Culture: Essays on Media & Society. (Media & Popular Culture Ser.: No. 1). 1988. pap. 16.95 (*0-04-445064-8*) Routledge.

— Communication As Culture: Essays on Media & Society. (Media & Popular Culture Ser.). 256p. (C). 1988. pap. 18.99 (*0-415-90725-X*) Routledge.

Carey, James W., ed. Media Myths & Narratives: Television & the Press. (Sage Annual Reviews of Communication Research Ser.: Vol. 15). 270p. (C). 1987. text 58.00 (*0-8039-3048-8*); pap. text 26.00 (*0-8039-3049-6*) Sage.

— Media, Myths, & Narratives: Television & the Press. LC 87-36962. (Sage Annual Reviews of Communication Research Ser.: No. 15). 264p. 1988. reprint ed. pap. 81.90 (*0-608-01532-6*, 205957600002) Bks Demand.

Carey, Jane. Exploring the Piedmont of North Carolina. (Illus.). 1985. pap. 9.95 (*0-936179-01-5*) Provincial NC.

***Carey, Janet Lee.** Molly's Fire. LC 99-47058. (Illus.). (YA). (gr. 5-9). 2000. 16.00 (*0-689-82612-5*) Atheneum Yung Read.

Carey, Jennifer, ed. see James, Will.

Carey, Jennifer, ed. see Kelly, Robert E.

Carey, Jennifer, ed. see Norton, O. Richard.

Carey, Jennifer L. Cocker Spaniels. (Owner's Companion Ser.). (Illus.). 272p. 1993. 39.95 (*1-85223-488-1*, Pub. by Crolwood) Trafalgar.

Carey, Joan & Johnson, Steven M. Microsoft Windows 98 - Illustrated Advanced. (Illus.). 216p. spiral bd. 20.95 (*0-7600-6084-3*, Pub. by Course Tech) Thomson Learn.

Carey, Joan & Poindexter, Sandra. New Perspectives on Microsoft Internet Explorer 4.0: Introductory. 10th ed. (New Perspectives Ser.). 200p. (C). 1998. pap. 21.95 (*0-7600-5785-0*) Course Tech.

Carey, Joan & Poindexter, Sandra E. New Perspectives on Microsoft Internet Explorer 5 - Brief. 176p. per. 18.95 (*0-7600-7121-7*, Pub. by Course Tech) Thomson Learn.

— New Perspectives on Microsoft Internet Explorer 5 - Introductory. 272p. per. 21.95 (*0-7600-7122-5*, Pub. by Course Tech) Thomson Learn.

— New Perspectives on Netscape Communicator 6.0 - Brief. 160p. per. 18.95 (*0-7600-7133-0*, Pub. by Course Tech) Thomson Learn.

— New Perspectives on Netscape Communicator 6.0 - Introductory. 256p. per. 21.95 (*0-7600-7134-9*, Pub. by Course Tech) Thomson Learn.

Carey, Joel. California Peace Officers Legal Sourcebook 1997 Field Guide. 3rd ed. 300p. 1996. 7.75 (*1-889110-01-9*) CA District Attys.

Carey, John. English Renaissance Studies: Presented to Dame Helen Gardner in Honour of Her Seventieth Birthday. (Illus.). 312p. 1980. text 59.00 (*0-19-812093-1*) OUP.

An Asterisk (*) at the beginning of an entry indicates that the title is appearing for the first time.

— John Milton: Complete Shorter Poems. 2nd ed. (Laep Ser.). 560p. (C). 1997. pap. 36.93 (*0-582-01985-0*) Addison-Wesley.

***Carey, John.** King of Mysteries: Early Irish Religious Writings. 320p. 2000. pap. 29.95 (*1-85182-572-X*, Pub. by Four Cts Pr) Intl Spec Bk.

Carey, John. King of Mysteries: Irish Religious Writing, A. D. 600-1200. LC 98-167589. 304p. 1998. boxed set 55.00 (*1-85182-340-9*, Pub. by Four Cts Pr) Intl Spec Bk.

— Milton: Complete Short Poems. 2nd ed. (Laep Ser.). 531p. (C). 1997. pap. 88.00 (*0-582-01984-2*) Addison-Wesley.

***Carey, John.** A Single Ray of the Sun: Religious Speculation in Early Ireland. (Celtic Studies Publications: Vol. 3). 136p. 1999. pap. 14.50 (*1-891271-03-2*) Celtic Studies.

Carey, John. U. N. Protection of Civil & Political Rights, Vol. 1. LC 71-104674. (Procedural Aspects of International Law Ser.). xiii, 205p. 1970. 45.00 (*0-8156-2146-9*, 306480) W S Hein.

Carey, John, ed. Eyewitness to History. LC 88-1699. 752p. 1988. text 29.95 (*0-674-28750-9*) HUP.

— Eyewitness to History. 752p. 1990. pap. 13.00 (*0-380-70895-7*, Avon Bks) Morrow Avon.

— Eyewitness to History. 752p. 1997. reprint ed. pap. 15.00 (*0-380-72968-7*, Avon Bks) Morrow Avon.

— Eyewitness to Science. LC 97-8132. 560p. 1997. pap. 16.95 (*0-674-28755-X*) HUP.

— John Milton: Complete Shorter Poems. (Longman Annotated English Poets Ser.). (Illus.). 531p. (C). 1989. pap. text 39.00 (*0-582-48456-1*, 73262) Longman.

— Short Stories & the Unbearable Bassington. LC 93-45276. (World's Classics WC Ser.). 342p. (Orig.). 1994. pap. 10.95 (*0-19-283169-0*) OUP.

— United Nations Law Reports Vol. 32: September 1997-August 1998. 1997. ring bd. 150.00 (*0-8027-2965-7*) Walker & Co.

Carey, John, et al, eds. Ecotoxicological Risk Assessment of the Chlorinated Organic Chemicals. LC 98-4840. (Illus.). 1998. 98.00 (*1-880611-07-4*) SETAC.

***Carey, John, et al, eds.** Studies in Irish Hagiography. 288p. 1999. 65.00 (*1-85182-486-3*, Pub. by Four Cts Pr) Intl Spec Bk.

***Carey, John, et al.** Ild'anach Ild'irech: A Festschrift for Proinsias Mac Cana. (Celtic Studies Publications: Vol. IV).Tr. of Many Gifts for the Multi-Talented Man. xviii, 312p. 1999. text 45.00 (*1-891271-01-6*) Celtic Studies.

Carey, John, jt. auth. see Koch, John T.

Carey, John, ed. see Donne, John.

Carey, John, ed. see Hogg, James.

Carey, John, tr. see Koch, John T., ed.

Carey, John A. Judicial Reform in France Before the Revolution of 1789. LC 81-6463. (Historical Studies: No. 99). (Illus.). 176p. 1982. 25.00 (*0-674-48878-4*) HUP.

Carey, John J. Carlyle Marney: A Pilgrim's Progress. LC 80-82573. xii, 156p. 1980. pap. text 5.95 (*0-86554-001-2*, H002) Mercer Univ Pr.

— Kairos & Logos: Studies in the Roots & Implications of Tillich Society. LC 84-6738. xxii, 284p. 1984. reprint ed. 15.95 (*0-86554-106-X*, MUP/H100) Mercer Univ Pr.

***Carey, John J.** A Marine from Boston: A First Person Story of a U. S. Marine in World War II: Boot Camp, New River, Samoa, Guadalcanal, Bougainville. LC 00-34109. 2000. write for info. (*1-880774-26-7*) Ferguson.

— Paulus, Then & Now: A Study of Paul Tillich's Theological World & the Continuing Relevance of His Work. 2000. 29.95 (*0-86554-681-9*, H531) Mercer Univ Pr.

Carey, John J. The Sexuality Debate in North American Churches, 1988-1993: Controversies, Unresolved Issues, Future Prospects. LC 94-38866. 324p. 1995. text 99.95 (*0-7734-9111-2*) E Mellen.

Carey, John J., intro. The Christian Argument for Gays & Lesbians in the Military: Essays by Mainline Church Leaders. LC 93-21573. 58p. 1993. text 39.95 (*0-7734-9315-8*) E Mellen.

Carey, John L. Professional Ethics of Public Accounting. Brief, Richard P., ed. LC 80-1476. (Dimensions of Accounting Theory & Practice Ser.). 1980. reprint ed. lib. bdg. 17.95 (*0-405-13506-8*) Ayer.

— The Rise of the Accounting Profession, 2 vols., 1. LC 75-7181. 405p. reprint ed. 125.60 (*0-608-16955-2*, 202759100001) Bks Demand.

— The Rise of the Accounting Profession, 2 vols., 2. LC 75-7181. 561p. reprint ed. 174.00 (*0-608-16956-0*, 202759200002) Bks Demand.

Carey, John M. Term Limits & Legislative Representation. (Illus.). 229p. (C). 1996. text 59.95 (*0-521-55233-8*) Cambridge U Pr.

— Term Limits & Legislative Representation. LC 99-162520. (Illus.). xiii, 216p. (C). 1998. pap. 17.95 (*0-521-64601-4*) Cambridge U Pr.

***Carey, John M.** Term Limits in State Legislatures. 192p. (C). 2000. text 49.50 (*0-472-09699-0*, 09699) U of Mich Pr.

Carey, John M. & Shugart, Matthew S., eds. Executive Decree Authority. LC 97-50077. (Illus.). 346p. (C). 1998. text 64.95 (*0-521-59255-0*); pap. text 24.95 (*0-521-59722-6*) Cambridge U Pr.

***Carey, John M., et al.** Term Limits in State Legislatures. LC 00-23333. 192p. (C). 2000. pap. text 18.95 (*0-472-06699-4*, 06699) U of Mich Pr.

Carey, John M., jt. auth. see Shugart, Matthew S.

Carey, Jonathan S., jt. auth. see Ahlstrom, Sydney E.

Carey Jones. Pattern of a Dependent Economy. LC 77-157955. (Illus.). 162p. 1972. reprint ed. lib. bdg. 65.00 (*0-8371-6178-9*, CADE, Greenwood Pr) Greenwood.

***Carey, Juanita S.** E. W. Bullinger: A Biography. rev. ed. 2000. pap. 13.99 (*0-8254-2372-4*) Kregel.

Carey, Karla. Julie & Jackie & the Calendar: A Children's Book. LC 88-12894. (Julie & Jackie Ser.). (Illus.). 61p. (J). 1990. reprint ed. pap. 8.00 incl. audio (*1-55768-025-6*) LC Pub.

— Julie & Jackie & the Calendar: The Music Book. LC 88-12894. (Julie & Jackie Ser.). (Illus.). 61p. (J). 1990. reprint ed. pap. 6.00 incl. audio (*1-55768-175-9*) LC Pub.

— Julie & Jackie & the Calendar: The Music Book (with Song Lyrics, Complete Narration & Cassette) LC 88-12894. (Julie & Jackie Ser.). (Illus.). 61p. (J). 1990. reprint ed. pap. 9.95 (*1-55768-200-3*); reprint ed. pap. 9.95 (*1-55768-000-0*) LC Pub.

— Julie & Jackie & the Calendar: The Musical Play. LC 88-12894. (Julie & Jackie Ser.). (Illus.). 61p. (J). 1990. reprint ed. pap. 35.00 incl. audio (*1-55768-150-3*) LC Pub.

— Julie & Jackie at Christmas-Time: The Music Book. (Julie & Jackie Ser.). (Illus.). 69p. (YA). 1990. 14.00 incl. audio (*1-55768-201-1*) LC Pub.

— Julie & Jackie at Christmas-Time: The Musical Play. LC 88-12909. (Julie & Jackie Ser.). (Illus.). 39p. (J). 1990. reprint ed. pap. 35.00 incl. audio (*1-55768-151-1*) LC Pub.

— Julie & Jackie at the Circus: The Musical Play. LC 88-12910. (Julie & Jackie Ser.). (Illus.). 44p. (J). 1990. pap. 35.00 incl. audio (*1-55768-152-X*) LC Pub.

— Julie & Jackie at the Circus: The Narration & Music Book. (Julie & Jackie Ser.). (Illus.). 57p. (YA). 1990. pap. 18.95 (*1-55768-002-7*); pap. 9.95 (*1-55768-202-X*) LC Pub.

— Julie & Jackie Go A'Journeying: A Children's Book. LC 88-9171. (Julie & Jackie Ser.). (Illus.). 73p. (J). 1990. pap. 8.00 incl. audio (*1-55768-028-0*) LC Pub.

— Julie & Jackie Go A'Journeying: The Musical Play. LC 88-9171. (Julie & Jackie Ser.). (Illus.). 73p. (J). 1990. pap. 35.00 incl. audio (*1-55768-153-8*) LC Pub.

— Julie & Jackie Go a'Journeying: The Narration & Music Book. (Julie & Jackie Ser.). (Illus.). 76p. (YA). 1990. pap. 9.95 (*1-55768-203-8*) LC Pub.

— Julie & Jackie Go a'Journeying: The Play & Musical Play (with Music Book, Story-&-Song Cassette & Piano Cassette) LC 88-9171. (Julie & Jackie Ser.). (Illus.). 73p. (J). 1990. audio 8.00 (*1-55768-003-5*) LC Pub.

— Julie & Jackie on the Ranch: The Musical Play. LC 88-12911. (Julie & Jackie Ser.). (Illus.). 46p. (J). 1990. reprint ed. pap. 35.00 incl. audio (*1-55768-154-6*) LC Pub.

— Julie & Jackie on the Ranch: The Narration & Music Book. (Julie & Jackie Ser.). (Illus.). 91p. (YA). 1990. pap. 9.95 (*1-55768-204-6*) LC Pub.

— Julie & Jackie on the Ranch: The Play & Musical Play (with Music Book, Story-&-Song Cassette & Piano Cassette) LC 88-12911. (Julie & Jackie Ser.). (Illus.). 46p. (J). 1990. reprint ed. audio 8.00 (*1-55768-004-3*) LC Pub.

— Poems for Piano: Poems (with Descriptive Music) (Reflections in Thought, from Dawn to Dusk Ser.). 50p. 1988. pap. 10.00 (*1-55768-518-5*); audio 8.00 (*1-55768-538-X*) LC Pub.

Carey, Kathleen, jt. auth. see Mary Ann.

Carey, Kay. The Awakening Notes. (Cliffs Notes Ser.). 80p. (Orig.). (C). 1980. pap. text 4.95 (*0-8220-0218-3*, Cliff) IDG Bks.

Carey, Ken. Flat Rock Journal: A Day in the Ozark Mountains. large type ed. LC 94-7688. 276p. 1994. reprint ed. lib. bdg. 21.95 (*0-8161-7433-4*, G K Hall Lrg Type) Mac Lib Ref.

— Return of the Bird Tribes. LC 90-56460. 240p. 1991. reprint ed. pap. 15.00 (*0-06-250188-7*, Pub. by Harper SF) HarpC.

— The Starseed Transmissions. LC 90-56461. 112p. 1991. reprint ed. pap. 12.00 (*0-06-250189-5*, Pub. by Harper SF) HarpC.

— The Third Millennium: Living in the Posthistoric World. LC 94-39494. 224p. 1996. pap. 13.00 (*0-06-251408-3*, Pub. by Harper SF) HarpC.

— Vision: A Personal Call to Create a New World. LC 91-58901. 112p. 1992. pap. 12.00 (*0-06-250179-8*, Pub. by Harper SF) HarpC.

Carey, Kimball, jt. auth. see Baker, Robert.

Carey, Larry & Tompkins, Sylvia. 1005 Salt & Pepper Shakers. LC 99-61080. (Illus.). 160p. 1999. pap. 29.95 (*0-7643-0880-7*) Schiffer.

— 1004 Salt & Pepper Shakers. LC 97-81443. 160p. 1998. pap. 29.95 (*0-7643-0553-0*) Schiffer.

***Carey, Larry & Tompkins, Sylvia.** One Thousand Six Salt & Pepper Shakers: Advertising. (Illus.). 176p. 2000. pap. 29.95 (*0-7643-1185-9*) Schiffer.

Carey, Larry & Tompkins, Sylvia. 1003 Salt & Pepper Shakers. LC 96-29169. 176p. (gr. 10). 1997. pap. 29.95 (*0-7643-0112-8*) Schiffer.

— 1002 Salt & Pepper Shakers: Nodders, Fitz & Floyd, Parkcraft with Prices. abr. ed. LC 95-6996. (Illus.). 112p. (Orig.). 1995. pap. 19.95 (*0-88740-789-7*) Schiffer.

— Salt & Pepper Shakers. LC 94-65428. (Illus.). 112p. (Orig.). 1994. pap. 19.95 (*0-88740-607-6*) Schiffer.

Carey, Larry, ed. see Bandyk.

Carey, Larry, ed. see Marcet, Jorge E.

Carey, Larry, ed. see Norman, James.

Carey, Larry C., ed. see Marcet, Jorge.

Carey, Larry C., ed. see Marcet, Jorge E.

Carey, Larry L. Colonial & Revolutionary American Literature: Recent Scholarship, since Nineteen Seventy-Five. (C). 1989. text 22.95 (*0-8290-0742-3*) Irvington.

Carey, Linda, et al. Topic Talk: An Interactive Communication Program for Adults. Drolet, Cindy & Gilles-Brown, C., eds. (Illus.). 239p. 1991. spiral bd. 89.00 (*0-9609464-5-4*, 8505) Imaginart Intl.

***Carey, Lisa.** In the Country of the Young. 320p. 2000. 24.00 (*0-380-97675-7*, Wm Morrow) Morrow Avon.

— In the Country of the Young. Hershey, J. H., ed. 2001. mass mkt. write for info. (*0-380-79967-7*, Avon Bks) Morrow Avon.

***Carey, Lisa A.** The Mermaids Singing. LC 97-36438. 257p. 1998. mass mkt. 22.00 (*0-380-97674-9*, Avon Bks) Morrow Avon.

Carey, Lisa A. The Mermaids Singing. LC 97-36438. 352p. (gr. 8 up). 1999. mass mkt. 6.99 (*0-380-79960-X*, Avon Bks) Morrow Avon.

Carey, Lois J. Sandplay Therapy with Children & Families. LC 97-50266. xxix, 205 p. 1998. 40.00 (*0-7657-0161-8*) Aronson.

Carey, Lois J., jt. ed. see Schaefer, Charles E.

Carey, Lou M. Measuring & Evaluating School Learning. 2nd ed. LC 93-35571. 480p. 1993. 76.00 (*0-205-12865-3*) Allyn.

— Measuring & Evaluating School Learning. 2nd ed. 480p. 1994. pap. text, student ed. 23.00 (*0-205-16094-8*, H6094-0) Allyn.

***Carey, Lou M.** Measuring & Evaluating School Learning. 3rd ed. 560p. 2000. 44.25 (*0-205-32388-X*) Allyn.

Carey, Lou M. Measuring & Evaluating School Learning 1987. 2nd ed. 1994. pap., teacher ed. write for info. (*0-205-12866-1*, H2866-5) Allyn.

Carey, Lou M., jt. auth. see Dick, Walter.

Carey, Louis F. The Bible Is True, but It's Not the Truth! v, 131p. 1996. pap. write for info. (*0-9651471-0-X*) LFC Bible.

Carey, M. F. Freemasonry in All Ages Being a Sketch of Its History, Philosophy, & Ethical Teaching. 384p. 1998. reprint ed. pap. 27.95 (*0-7661-0448-6*) Kessinger Pub.

Carey, MacDonald. Out of Heart. Adler, Andrew & Adler, Roger, eds. 1979. 5.95 (*0-916844-04-8*) Turtle Pr.

— That Further Hill. 1987. pap. 8.95 (*0-941017-12-5*) Bombshelter Pr.

Carey, Margaret. Beads & Beadwork of West & Central Africa. (Ethnography Ser.: No. 21). (Illus.). 56p. 1989. pap. 10.50 (*0-7478-0100-2*, Pub. by Shire Pubns) Parkwest Pubns.

Carey, Margaret S. & Hainline, Patricia H. Sweet Home in the Oregon Cascades. (Illus.). 140p. 1979. pap. 7.95 (*0-934784-04-3*) Calapooia Pubns.

Carey, Marian. Recipe Finder. (Illus.). 103p. (Orig.). pap. 14.95 (*0-9620559-0-5*) M J Carey.

Carey, Martha I. Lifestyle Workshops. LC 88-9142. 455p. 1989. reprint ed. pap. 141.10 (*0-608-04293-5* 206507200012) Bks Demand.

Carey, Mary. My 3 Lives in Headlines. LC 96-29630. (Illus.). 360p. 1997. 27.95 (*1-57168-125-6*, 125-6, Eakin Pr) Sunbelt Media.

***Carey, Mary.** Two for Texas: The Extraordinary Story of Kian & Jane Long. LC 99-36608. (J). 1999. 14.95 (*1-57168-292-9*, Eakin Pr) Sunbelt Media.

Carey, Mary, ed. see Massachusetts General Hospital Department of Nursing Staff.

Carey, Mathew. Autobiographical Sketches. LC 70-125683. (American Journalists Ser.). 1977. reprint ed. 23.95 (*0-405-01660-3*) Ayer.

— Autobiographical Sketches. (American Biography Ser.). 156p. 1991. reprint ed. lib. bdg. 69.00 (*0-7812-8060-5*) Rprt Serv.

— Olive Branch: Or, Faults on Both Sides, Federal & Democratic. LC 69-16848. (Select Bibliographies Reprint Ser.). 1977. 29.95 (*0-8369-5002-X*) Ayer.

— Short Account of the Malignant Fever, Lately Prevalent in Philadelphia. LC 73-112531. (Rise of Urban America Ser.). 1970. reprint ed. 15.95 (*0-405-02441-X*) Ayer.

***Carey, Max.** The Superman Complex: Achieving the Balance That Leads to True Success. LC 99-61752. 240p. 1999. 22.00 (*1-56352-516-X*) Longstreet.

Carey, Michael. Carpenter of Song: Poems from Trees. (Illus.). 80p. 1998. pap. 14.00 (*0-931209-77-3*, Loess Hills Bks) Mid-Prairie Bks.

***Carey, Michael.** Heraclitean Fire: Journeying on the Path of Leadership. 144p. (C). 1999. per. 26.95 (*0-7872-6286-2*) Kendall-Hunt.

Carey, Michael. Honest Effort. 1991. pap. 7.95 (*0-930100-39-5*) Holy Cow.

— Honest Effort: Poems. 1991. 14.95 (*0-930100-38-7*) Holy Cow.

— Honest Effort: Poems by Michael Carey. 91p. 1995. pap. 9.95 (*0-931209-56-0*) Mid-Prairie Bks.

— Nishnabotna: Poems, Prose & Dramatic Scenes from the Natural & Oral History of Southwest Iowa. (Illus.). 124p. 1995. pap. 12.95 (*0-931209-62-5*) Mid-Prairie Bks.

— The Noise the Earth Makes. (Iowa Poets Ser.: No. 1). (Illus.). 56p. (Orig.). 1985. 25.00 (*0-931757-19-3*); pap. 15.00 (*0-931757-20-7*) Pterodactyl Pr.

— Poetry: Starting from Scratch, a Two Week Lesson Plan for Teaching Poetry Writing. LC 88-82550. 120p. 1989. pap. 5.95 (*0-934988-17-X*) Foun Bks.

Carey, Michael, ed. Voices on the Landscape: Contemporary Iowa Poets. 193p. 1996. 25.00 (*0-931209-64-1*, Loess Hills Bks); pap. 14.00 (*0-931209-65-X*, Loess Hills Bks) Mid-Prairie Bks.

***Carey, Michael & Smale, Stephen T.** Transcriptional Regulation in Eukaryotes: Concepts, Strategies, & Techniques. LC 99-49636. 640p. (C). 1999. text 150.00 (*0-87969-537-4*) Cold Spring Harbor.

Carey, Michael J., jt. ed. see Balaam, David N.

Carey, Michael P., jt. auth. see Wincze, John P.

***Carey-Miller, David.** Land Title in South Africa. 2000. pap. 91.50 (*0-7021-5120-3*, Pub. by Juta & Co) Gaunt.

Carey, Miriam. 52 Romantic Outings in Greater Cleveland: A Couple's Guide to Fun & Romance in Greater Cleveland. (Illus.). 208p. 2000. pap. 13.95 (*1-886228-21-3*) Gray & Co Pubs.

***Carey, Morris & Carey, James.** Home Maintenance for Dummies. (Illus.). 384p. 2000. pap. 19.99 (*0-7645-5215-5*) IDG Bks.

Carey, Morris & Carey, James. Home Remodeling for Dummies. LC 98-86811. (For Dummies Ser.). (Illus.). 432p. 1998. pap. 19.99 (*0-7645-5088-8*) IDG Bks.

***Carey, Nancy.** Parent Involvement in Children's Education: Efforts by Public Elementary Schools. LC 98-115864. 59p. 1998. pap. 5.00 (*0-16-049388-9*) USGPO.

Carey, Neil. Guide to the Queen Charlotte Islands. 12th ed. 160p. 1998. pap. text 9.95 (*1-55192-144-8*) Raincoast Bk.

Carey, Neil, ed. see Twining, Merrill B.

Carey, Neil G. Puffin Cove: A Queen Charlotte Islands Odyssey. 178p. 1984. pap. 11.95 (*0-88839-216-8*) Hancock House.

Carey, Neil G., jt. auth. see Carey, Donald E.

Carey, Nora. Perfect Preserves: Provisions from the Kitchen Garden. (Illus.). 256p. 1995. pap. 24.95 (*1-55670-401-1*) Stewart Tabori & Chang.

Carey, Omer & Olson, Dean. Opportunity Management: Strategic Planning for Small Business. write for info. (*0-318-58210-4*) P-H.

Carey, Omer L., ed. The Military-Industrial Complex & United States Foreign Policy. LC 71-8835. 74p. reprint ed. pap. 30.00 (*0-608-18354-7*, 203303500083) Bks Demand.

Carey, P. Bradley. The Darkness in the Light: The Book on Cult Recognition. LC 99-94604. 106p. 1999. pap. 19.95 (*0-7392-0084-4*, No. PO2951) Morris Pubng.

Carey, Patrick. An Immigrant Bishop: John England's Adaptation of Irish Catholicism to American Republicanism. LC 79-63860. (Monographs: Vol. 36). (Illus.). ix, 236p. 1982. 14.95 (*0-930060-16-4*) US Cath Hist.

— Internet Student Survival Guide with Netscape Navigator Software. (Illus.). 48p. 1996. text, mass mkt. write for info. incl. 3.5 ld (*0-7600-4173-3*) Course Tech.

— New Perspectives on Creating Web Pages with HTML: Brief. (New Perspectives Ser.). 64p. 1996. pap. 8.00 (*0-7600-4585-2*) Course Tech.

Carey, Patrick. New Perspectives on Creating Web Pages with HTML -- Comprehensive. 512p. per. 44.95 (*0-7600-6484-9*, Pub. by Course Tech) Thomson Learn.

Carey, Patrick. New Perspectives on Microsoft FrontPage 97. 336p. (C). 1998. pap. 31.95 (*0-7600-5417-7*) Course Tech.

***Carey, Patrick.** Rediscovering the Old Tokaido: In the Footsteps of Hiroshige. 176p. 2000. boxed set 29.95 (*1-901903-10-9*, Pub. by Global Oriental) Midpt Trade.

Carey, Patrick. Street Level. 1989. boxed set 10.00 (*0-685-29147-2*) Cottage Wordsmiths.

Carey, Patrick, ed. American Catholic Religious Thought. 272p. 1987. pap. 19.95 (*0-8091-2884-5*) Paulist Pr.

— Orestes A. Brownson: Selected Writings. (Sources of American Spirituality Ser.). 1991. 24.95 (*0-8091-0433-4*) Paulist Pr.

— Pastoral Letters & Statements of the U. S. Catholic Bishops, 1989 to 1997, Vol. 6. 916p. (C). 1998. 39.95 (*1-57455-174-4*) US Catholic.

Carey, Patrick & Ambrosia, Angela. The Internet - Illustrated, Incl. instr. resource kit, test bank, transparency. (Illustrated Ser.). 160p. (C). 1995. pap. 20.95 (*1-56527-528-4*) Course Tech.

Carey, Patrick & Berk, Kenneth. Data Analysis with Microsoft Excel: Windows '95 Edition. LC 97-14883. (Business Statistics Ser.). 512p. (C). 1997. pap. 37.95 (*0-534-52929-1*) Wadsworth Pub.

Carey, Patrick, et al. Microsoft Windows 98 - Illustrated Basic. (Illus.). 184p. spiral bd. 20.95 (*0-7600-6083-5*, Pub. by Course Tech) Thomson Learn.

Carey, Patrick, et al. Microsoft Windows 95: Illustrated PLUS Edition. 296p. 1996. teacher ed. 18.50 (*0-7600-4056-7*) Course Tech.

Carey, Patrick, ed. see Ignatow, David.

Carey, Patrick W. The Roman Catholics, 6. LC 93-20125. (Denominations in America Ser.: No. 6). 400p. 1993. lib. bdg. 65.00 (*0-313-25439-7*, CRT/, Greenwood Pr) Greenwood.

— The Roman Catholics in America. LC 93-20125. 208p. 1996. pap. 18.95 (*0-275-95802-7*, Praeger Pubs) Greenwood.

Carey, Patrick W., anno. Orestes A. Brownson: A Bibliography, 1826-1876. annot. ed. LC 96-45810. (Orestes A. Brownson's Collected Works: No. 10). 212p. (Orig.). 1996. pap. 25.00 (*0-87462-634-X*) Marquette.

Carey, Patrick W. & Lienhard, Joseph T. Biographical Dictionary of Christian Theologians. LC 99-22143. 608p. 2000. lib. bdg. 125.00 (*0-313-29649-9*, Greenwood Pr) Greenwood.

Carey, Patrick W. & Muller, Earl C., eds. Theological Education in the Catholic Tradition: Contemporary Challenges. LC 96-51970. 396p. (Orig.). 1997. pap. 29.95 (*0-8245-1672-9*, Herdr & Herdr) Crossroad NY.

Carey, Patrick W., jt. auth. see Brownson, Orestes A.

Carey, Patsy. Activities for Any Literature Unit. 1997. pap. text 9.95 (*1-57690-004-5*) Tchr Create Mat.

Carey, Patsy & Kilpatrick, Susan. Charlotte's Web: A Literature Unit. (Literature Units Ser.). (Illus.). 48p. (Orig.). 1993. pap. 7.95 (*1-55734-435-3*) Tchr Create Mat.

— Strega Nona: A Literature Unit. (Literature Units Ser.). (Illus.). 48p. (Orig.). (J). (gr. k-3). 1993. pap., student ed. 7.95 (*1-55734-436-1*) Tchr Create Mat.

Carey, Paul, ed. Protein Engineering & Design. LC 96-2000. (Illus.). 361p. 1996. text 79.95 (*0-12-159640-0*) Acad Pr.

Carey, Peter. The Archive of Yogyakarta: Documents Relating to Politics & Internal Court Affairs, Vol.1. (Oriental Documents Ser.: Vol. III). (Illus.). 1981. 84.00 (*0-19-725997-9*) OUP.

C

— The Big Bazoohley. LC 95-15282. (Illus.). 96p. (J). (gr. 3-7). 1995. 14.95 (*0-8050-3855-8*, J Macrae Bks) H Holt & Co.

— The Big Bazoohley. LC 95-15282. (Illus.). 144p. (J). (gr. 4-7). 1996. pap. 4.99 (*0-698-11420-5*, PapStar) Peng Put Young Read.

— The Big Bazoohley. 1996. 9.05 (*0-606-11120-4*, Pub. by Turtleback) Demco.

— The Big Bazoohley. (Storybridge Ser.). 96p. (J). (gr. 3-7). 1995. pap. 9.95 (*0-7022-2832-X*, Pub. by Univ Queensland Pr) Intl Spec Bk.

— Blackstone's Guide to the Data Protection Act, 1998. 176p. 1998. pap. 44.00 (*1-85431-866-7*) Gaunt.

— Bliss. LC 95-35375. 304p. 1996. pap. 13.00 (*0-679-76719-3*) Random.

Carey, Peter. The British in Java, 1811-1816: A Javanese Account. (Oriental Documents Ser.: No.10). (Illus.). 634p. 1992. text 95.00 (*0-19-726062-4*) OUP.

Carey, Peter. The Fat Man in History. LC 92-56374. 1993. pap. 12.00 (*0-679-74332-4*, Vin) Random.

— The Fat Man in History. 1994. pap. 14.95 (*0-7022-2799-4*, Pub. by Univ Queensland Pr) Intl Spec Bk.

— The Fat Man in History: 50th Anniversary Edition. 1998. reprint ed. pap. 19.95 (*0-7022-3020-0*, Pub. by Univ Queensland Pr) Intl Spec Bk.

— Illywhacker. LC 95-43450. 1996. pap. 16.00 (*0-679-76790-8*) Knopf.

***Carey, Peter.** Jack Maggs. LC 97-36893. 309p. 1998. 24.00 (*0-679-44008-9*) Knopf.

— Jack Maggs. LC 97-36893. 357p. 1999. pap. 13.00 (*0-679-76037-7*) Vin Bks.

Carey, Peter. Jack Maggs. large type ed. LC 98-22305. 530p. 1998. 26.95 (*0-7838-0285-4*, G K Hall Lrg Type) Mac Lib Ref.

— A Letter to Our Son. LC 95-119184. 1994. 19.95 (*0-7022-2764-1*, Pub. by Univ Queensland Pr) Intl Spec Bk.

— Oscar & Lucinda. large type ed. 818p. 1989. reprint ed. 20.95 (*1-85089-318-7*, Pub. by ISIS Lrg Prnt) Transaction Pubs.

— Oscar & Lucinda: Movie Tie-in. LC 97-6669. 1997. pap. 13.00 (*0-679-77750-4*) Vin Bks.

— The Tax Inspector. LC 92-56375. 1993. pap. 13.00 (*0-679-73598-4*) Vin Bks.

***Carey, Peter.** The True History of the Kelly Gang. 2001. 26.00 (*0-375-41084-8*) Knopf.

Carey, Peter. The Unusual Life of Tristan Smith. 432p. 1996. pap. 15.00 (*0-679-76036-9*) Random.

— The Unusual Life of Tristan Smith: A Novel. 1995. 24.00 (*0-679-43888-2*) Knopf.

Carey, Peter, jt. auth. see Cox, Steve.

Carey, Peter, jt. auth. see Mayo, Sandra M.

Carey, Peter, jt. ed. see Hoadley, Mason C.

Carey, Peter B. & Bentley, G. Carter, eds. East Timor at the Crossroads: The Forging of a Nation. LC 95-4940. 256p. 1995. text 30.00 (*0-8248-1787-7*); pap. text 15.75 (*0-8248-1788-5*) UH Pr.

Carey, Phyllis, ed. Wagering on Transcendence: The Search for Meaning in Literature. LC 97-14762. 320p. 1997. pap. 24.95 (*1-55612-982-3*, LL1982) Sheed & Ward WI.

Carey, Phyllis & Jewinski, Ed, eds. Re: Joyce 'n Beckett. LC 91-31853. xviii, 199p. 1992. 30.00 (*0-8232-1340-4*); pap. 19.95 (*0-8232-1341-2*) Fordham.

Carey, Phyllis, jt. ed. see Goetz-Stankiewicz, Marketa.

Carey, Phyllis, jt. ed. see Malloy, Catharine.

Carey, R. Neill, jt. auth. see Cembrowski, George S.

Carey, Raymond G. & Lloyd, Robert C. Measuring Quality Improvement in Healthcare: A Guide to Statistical Process Control Applications. LC 95-5101. 208p. 1995. pap. 26.95 (*0-527-76293-8*) Productivity Inc.

Carey, Raymond G., jt. auth. see Posavac, Emil.

***Carey, Richard & McKee, Linda Jones.** Pennsylvania Wineries. LC 99-43759. 2000. 19.95 (*0-8117-2877-3*) Stackpole.

Carey, Richard A. Against the Tide: The Fate of the New England Fisherman. LC 99-18146. 381p. 1999. 23.00 (*0-395-76530-7*) HM.

***Carey, Richard A.** Against the Tide: The Fate of the New England Fisherman. 384p. 2000. pap. 13.00 (*0-618-05698-X*) HM.

Carey, Rikk & Bell, Gavin. The Annotated VRML 2.0 Reference Manual. 1997. pap. 39.95 (*0-614-28441-4*) Addison-Wesley.

— VRML Annotated Reference. LC 97-6495. 528p. (C). 1997. pap. text 39.95 (*0-201-41974-2*) Addison-Wesley.

Carey, Robert. Career Transition: A Guide for Federal Employees in a Time of Turmoil. (Illus.). 105p. 1996. pap. text 14.95 (*0-936295-63-5*) FPMI Comns.

Carey, Robert D. & Furbay, John H. Freedom Ships. (Illus.). 358p. 1999. pap. 14.95 (*0-9669613-0-7*, 101) Af-Am Links Pr.

Carey, Robert F., jt. auth. see Farr, Roger C.

Carey, Robert F., jt. auth. see Siegel, Majorie.

Carey, Robert L. Daniel Webster As an Economist. LC 29-15020. (Columbia University. Studies in the Social Sciences: No. 313). reprint ed. 20.00 (*0-404-51313-1*) AMS Pr.

Carey, Robin. Baja Journey: Reveries of a Sea-Kayaker. LC 88-18665. 184p. 1989. 29.95 (*0-89096-347-9*); pap. 15.95 (*0-89096-392-4*) Tex A&M Univ Pr.

— North Bank: Claiming a Place on the Rogue. LC 98-25222. 128p. 1998. 19.95 (*0-87071-448-1*) Oreg St U Pr.

Carey, Ron. Rebel with A Cause. Date not set. 22.00 (*1-56584-419-X*) Norton.

***Carey, Rosalie.** A Theatre in the House: The Carey's Globe. 168p. 1999. pap. 34.95 (*1-877133-66-3*, Pub. by Univ Otago Pr) Intl Spec Bk.

Carey, S. Warren. Theories of the Earth & Universe: A History of Dogma in the Earth Sciences. LC 87-6433. (Illus.). 432p. 1988. 59.50 (*0-8047-1364-2*) Stanford U Pr.

Carey Sabbah, Ann. Kurds. LC 98-36150. (Endangered Cultures Ser.). (Illus.). 32p. (YA). (gr. 4 up). 1999. lib. bdg. 21.30 (*1-887068-92-9*) Smart Apple.

— Tuaregs. LC 98-46705. (Endangered Cultures Ser.). (Illus.). 32p. (YA). (gr. 4 up). 1999. lib. bdg. 21.30 (*1-887068-93-7*) Smart Apple.

Carey, Sandra H. Sexual Harassment: A Management Issue. write for info. (*0-8290-1055-6*) Irvington.

Carey, Sandy, jt. auth. see Carey, Alan.

Carey, Selena, jt. auth. see Trina.

Carey, Shelley J. Science for All Cultures. (Illus.). 72p. 1993. pap. text 16.50 (*0-87355-122-2*) Natl Sci Tchrs.

***Carey, Skip & Carey, Chipper.** Jungle Paradise, Almost. LC 99-93809. 299p. 2000. pap. 14.95 (*0-533-13166-9*) Vantage.

Carey, Stephen C. Marketing & Selling to Associations & Nonprofits in the New Millennium: A Service Providers Guide to Understanding a Changing Association Marketplace. 75p. 1999. pap. text 38.50 (*0-9666966-0-3*) Assn Mktg Mgmt Res.

Carey, Stephen S. A Beginner's Guide to Scientific Method. 124p. 1993. pap. 18.95 (*0-534-21126-7*) Wadsworth Pub.

— A Beginner's Guide to Scientific Method. 2nd ed. LC 97-22064. 200p. (C). 1997. 25.95 (*0-534-52843-0*) Wadsworth Pub.

— Introduction to Argument Analysis: A Critical Thinking Hand Book. 2nd ed. 144p. (C). 1992. per. 23.95 (*0-8403-8197-2*) Kendall-Hunt.

***Carey, Stephen S.** The Uses & Abuses of Argument: Critical Thinking & Fallacious Reasoning. LC 99-23923. xii, 292p. 1999. pap. text 29.99 (*0-7674-0517-X*) Mayfield Pub.

Carey, Susan & Gelman, Rochel, eds. The Epigenesis of Mind: Essays on Biology & Cognition. 360p. 1991. text 69.95 (*0-8058-0438-2*) L Erlbaum Assocs.

Carey, Susan, jt. auth. see Brown, Roberta S.

Carey, Suzanne. Baby Swap. (Romance Ser.: No. 880). 1992. per. 2.69 (*0-373-08880-9*) Silhouette.

— The Bride Price. 1997. per. 3.25 (*0-373-19247-9*, 1-19247-5) Silhouette.

— Dad Galahad. (Romance Ser.). 1993. per. 2.69 (*0-373-08928-7*, 5-08928-9) Silhouette.

— The Daddy Project: (Bundles of Joy) (Romance Ser.). 1995. per. 2.99 (*0-373-19072-7*, 1-19072-7) Silhouette.

— Eleanora's Ghost. (Intimate Moments Ser.). 1993. per. 3.50 (*0-373-07518-9*, 5-07518-9) Silhouette.

— Father by Marriage. 1995. per. 2.99 (*0-373-19120-0*, 1-19120-4) Silhouette.

— The Greek Tycoon: The World's Most Eligible Bachelor. Vol. 8. 1999. per. 4.50 (*0-373-65025-6*, 1-65025-8, Harlequin) Harlequin Bks.

— Home for Thanksgiving. (Romance Ser.: No. 825). 1991. per. 2.59 (*0-373-08825-6*) Silhouette.

— The Male Animal. (Silhouette Romance Ser.). 1994. per. 2.75 (*0-373-19025-5*, 1-19025-5) Harlequin Bks.

— Marry Me Again. (Silhouette Romance Ser.). 1994. per. 2.75 (*0-373-19001-8*, 5-19001-2) Harlequin Bks.

— Marry Me Again. (Romance Ser.). 1997. per. 95.76 (*0-373-91001-0*, 5-91001-3) Silhouette.

— Mystery Heiress. (Fortune's Children Ser.). 256p. 1997. per. 4.50 (*0-373-50185-4*, 1-501857) Harlequin Bks.

— Navajo Wedding. (Romance Ser.: No. 855). 1992. per. 2.69 (*0-373-08855-8*, 5-08855-4) Silhouette.

— Never Say Goodbye. (Intimate Moments Ser.: No. 330). 1990. per. 2.95 (*0-373-07330-5*) Silhouette.

— Strangers When We Meet. (Intimate Moments Ser.: No. 392). 1991. per. 3.25 (*0-373-07392-5*) Silhouette.

— Sweet Bride of Revenge. 1998. per. 3.50 (*0-373-19300-9*, 1-19300-2) Silhouette.

— True to the Fire. (Intimate Moments Ser.: No. 435). 1992. mass mkt. 3.39 (*0-373-07435-2*, 5-07435-6) Harlequin Bks.

— Villa Voglia. (Horizon Ser.). (FRE.). 1994. pap. 3.50 (*0-373-39290-7*, 1-39290-1) Harlequin Bks.

***Carey, Suzanne.** When Love Walks In. (Special Edition Ser.). 2000. mass mkt. 4.50 (*0-373-24341-3*, 1-24341-9) Silhouette.

Carey, Suzanne. Whose Baby? (Intimate Moments Ser.). 1996. per. 3.99 (*0-373-07715-7*, 1-07715-5) Silhouette.

Carey, Terence. Therese of Lisieux - A Discovery of Love: Selected Spiritual Writings. 3rd ed. 144p. 1992. pap. 9.95 (*1-56548-072-4*) New City.

Carey, Thomas E., jt. ed. see Wolf, Gregory T.

***Carey, Timothy.** Mountjoy: The Story of a Prison. 2000. pap. 22.95 (*1-898256-89-6*, Pub. by Collins Press) Dufour.

Carey, Tom. Baby's Fortieth Birthday Book. (Illus.). 80p. (Orig.). 1994. pap. 10.95 (*1-877590-97-5*) DE Pr IL.

— The Club Thrower's Handbook. (Illus.). 112p. (Orig.). 1995. pap. 9.95 (*1-877590-91-6*) DE Pr IL.

— Desire: Poems, 1986-1996. LC 97-23600. 1997. pap. 10.00 (*0-9651558-4-6*) Painted Leaf.

— The Marriage Dictionary. (Illus.). 128p. (Orig.). 1993. pap. 6.95 (*1-877590-99-1*) DE Pr IL.

— The Modern Guide to Sex Etiquette, Too! (Illus.). 112p. (Orig.). 1995. pap. 7.95 (*1-877590-90-8*) DE Pr IL.

— Teed Off! The Modern Guide to Golf. (Illus.). 112p. (Orig.). 1995. pap. 7.95 (*1-877590-92-4*) DE Pr IL.

— The Ugly Truth about Men: A Guide to the Weaker Sex. Carle, Cliff, ed. 128p. (Orig.). 1993. pap. 5.95 (*0-918259-46-0*) CCC Pubns.

— Your Baby: An Owner's Manual. 1996. pap. text 7.95 (*1-877590-83-5*) DE Pr IL.

Carey, Tom & Schnem, Greg. Til What Do We Part? A Wedding Planner to the Etiquette Impaired. (Illus.). 128p. (Orig.). 1996. pap. 7.95 (*1-877590-84-3*) DE Pr IL.

Carey, Tony. Crisis or Conference! A Planner's Pocket Guide for Organizing Conferences. 104p. 1997. pap. 13.95 (*1-85835-463-3*, Indust Soc) Stylus Pub VA.

Carey, Valerie S. The Devil & Mother Crump. LC 87-64. (Illus.). 40p. (J). (gr. k-3). 1987. 11.95 (*0-06-020982-8*) HarpC Child Bks.

— The Devil & Mother Crump. LC 87-64. (Trophy Picture Bk.). (Illus.). 40p. (J). (gr. 2-5). 1992. pap. 4.95 (*0-06-443278-5*, HarpTrophy) HarpC Child Bks.

— Tsugele's Broom. LC 92-9873. (Laura Geringer Bks.). (Illus.). 48p. (J). (gr. k-3). 1993. lib. bdg. 14.89 (*0-06-020987-9*) HarpC Child Bks.

Carey, Van P. Liquid-Vapor Phase-Change Phenomena: An Introduction to the Thermophysics of Vaporization & Condensation in Heat Transfer Equipment. 700p. 1992. pap. text 66.95 (*1-56032-074-5*) Hemisp Pub.

— Statistical Thermodynamics & Microscale Thermophysics. LC 98-45449. (Illus.). 432p. 1999. 110.00 (*0-521-65277-4*); pap. 49.95 (*0-521-65420-3*) Cambridge U Pr.

Carey, Vincent, jt. ed. see Carroll, Clare.

Carey, W. Dictionary of the Bengali Language, 2 Vols. (BEN & ENG.). 2160p. 1981. 195.00 (*0-8288-1120-2*, M14468) Fr & Eur.

Carey, W. B. & McDevitt, S. C., eds. Clinical & Educational Applications of Temperament Research. 208p. 1989. 38.75 (*90-265-0971-5*) Swets.

Carey, W. W. History of Spencerville. (Illus.). 125p. 1996. reprint ed. pap. 17.00 (*0-8328-5016-0*) Higginson Bk Co.

Carey, Wayne J. & Habbart, Ellisa O. Delaware Limited Liability Company Forms & Practice Manual. LC 94-36232. 626p. 1995. ring bd. 219.90 (*0-9637468-4-7*) Data Trace Pubng.

Carey-Webb, Allen. Maring Subject(s) Literature & the Emergence of the National Identity. Hart, Jonathan, ed. LC 97-32709. (Comparative Literature & Cultural Studies Ser.: Vol. 4). (Illus.). 256p. 1998. text 55.00 (*0-8153-2896-6*, H2072) Garland.

Carey-Webb, Allen & Benz, Stephen, eds. Teaching & Testimony: Rigoberta Menchu & the North American Classroom. LC 96-592. (SUNY Series, Interruptions). 391p. (C). 1996. text 71.50 (*0-7914-3013-8*); pap. text 24.95 (*0-7914-3014-6*) State U NY Pr.

Carey, William. An Enquiry: An Enquiry into the Obligations of Christians to Use Means for the Conversion of the Heathens. Pretlove, John, ed. 65p. (C). 1988. reprint ed. pap. text 5.95 (*0-317-93396-5*) Criswell Pubns.

Carey, William B. & Jablow, Martha M. Understanding Your Child's Temperament. 1997. 23.95 (*0-614-28004-4*) Macmillan USA.

— Understanding Your Child's Temperament: A Revolutionary Approach to Parenting. 228p. 1999. reprint ed. text 24.00 (*0-7881-6485-6*) DIANE Pub.

Carey, William B. & McDevitt, Sean C. Coping with Children's Temperament: A Guide for Professionals. LC 95-8624. 256p. 1995. 42.00 (*0-465-01432-1*, Pub. by Basic) HarpC.

Carey, William B. & McDevitt, Sean C., eds. Prevention & Early Intervention: Individual Differences As Risk Factors for the Mental Health of Children - A Festschrift for Stella Chess & Alexander Thomas. LC 93-25940. 328p. 1994. text 47.95 (*0-87630-723-3*) Brunner-Mazel.

Carey, William D. & Fise, Thomas F., eds. Gastroenterology Practice Management. LC 93-14755. 280p. 1993. 70.00 (*0-89640-237-1*) Igaku-Shoin.

Carey, William T. Law Students: How to Get a Job When There Aren't Any. 102p. (Orig.). (C). 1986. lib. bdg. 9.75 (*0-89089-325-X*) Carolina Acad Pr.

Carezani, Ricardo L. Autodynamics: Fundamental Basis for a New Relativistic Mechanics. SAA Staff, ed. LC 98-86262. 250p. (C). 1998. pap. text 25.00 (*0-9665533-0-6*) SAA.

Carfagna, C., ed. Liquid Crystalline Polymers: Proceedings of the International Workshop, WLCP 93, Capri, Italy, June 1-4, 1993. LC 93-43406. 272p. 1994. text 145.25 (*0-08-042149-0*, Pergamon Pr) Elsevier.

Carfagna, Rosemarie. Divine Designs: Exercises for Spiritual Growth. 192p. (Orig.). 1996. pap. 14.95 (*1-55612-862-2*, LL1862) Sheed & Ward WI.

— Educating Women at Ursuline College: Curriculum, Collaboration, & Growth. LC 97-52367. (Women's Studies Ser.: Vol. 18). 280p. 1998. 89.95 (*0-7734-8479-5*) E Mellen.

Carfagno, Vincent R., tr. see Reich, Wilhelm.

Carfax, Catherine. To Die a Little. large type ed. 432p. 1986. 27.99 (*0-7089-1499-3*) Ulverscroft.

Carfi, John & Carle, Cliff. Getting Even with the Answering Machine & Voice Mail: What to Say When You Reach a Machine. 128p. 1996. pap. 5.95 (*0-918259-99-1*) CCC Pubns.

Carfi, John & Carle, Cliff. The Greatest Answering Machine Messages of All Time. 128p. 1994. pap. 4.95 (*0-918259-54-1*) CCC Pubns.

Carfi, John & Carle, Cliff. Never a Dull Card. (Illus.). 160p. (Orig.). 1992. pap. 5.95 (*0-918259-40-1*) CCC Pubns.

— No Hang-Ups: Funny Answering Machine Messages. (Illus.). 132p. (Orig.). 1984. pap. 3.95 (*0-918259-00-2*) CCC Pubns.

— No Hang-Ups III: Funny Answering Machine Messages. (Illus.). 96p. (Orig.). (YA). 1988. pap. 3.95 (*0-918259-12-6*) CCC Pubns.

Carfora, M., et al. Integrable Systems & Quantum Groups. 200p. 1992. text 67.00 (*981-02-1007-8*) World Scientific Pub.

***Carfrae, Nancy, ed.** Who's Who in International Organizations: A Biographical Encyclopedia of More Than 13,000 Leading Personalities, 3 vols. 3rd ed. 1300p. 1999. 480.00 (*3-598-11398-6*, Pub. by K G Saur Verlag) Bowker.

***Cargal, James M.** Discrete Mathematics for Beginners. (Illus.). 2000. 39.95 (*0-8176-4172-6*) Birkhauser.

Cargal, Michael. The Captain's Guide to Liferaft Survival. (Illus.). 200p. 1990. 24.95 (*0-924486-00-7*) Sheridan.

Cargan. Sociological Footprints. 2nd ed. (Sociology - Introductory Level Ser.). 1982. pap. write for info. (*0-534-02253-7*) Wadsworth Pub.

— Sociological Footprints. 5th ed. (Sociology Ser.). 1990. pap. text 16.50 (*0-534-14654-6*); mass mkt., teacher ed. write for info. (*0-534-14653-8*) Wadsworth Pub.

— Sociological Footprints. 6th ed. (Sociology - Introductory Level Ser.). 1993. teacher ed. 24.00 (*0-534-20803-7*) Wadsworth Pub.

Cargan & Ballantine, Jeanne H. Sociological Footprints. 8th ed. LC 99-19047. (Sociology - Intro Level Ser.). 1999. pap. 35.95 (*0-534-56502-6*) Wadsworth Pub.

Cargan, Jonathan, et al. USMLE Step 1: United States Medical Licensing Examination. LC 97-67179. 1200p. 1998. pap. 39.95 (*0-87891-074-3*) Res & Educ.

Cargan, Leonard. Sociological Footprints. 7th ed. LC 96-26098. (Sociology Ser.). 1996. pap. 23.50 (*0-534-50488-4*) Wadsworth Pub.

Cargan, Leonard & Ballantine, Jeanne H. Sociological Footprints: Introductory Readings in Sociology. 3rd ed. LC 78-69541. (C). 1984. mass mkt. 13.00 (*0-534-03669-4*) Wadsworth Pub.

— Sociological Footprints: Introductory Readings in Sociology. 6th ed. 555p. 1993. mass mkt. 21.50 (*0-534-20802-9*) Wadsworth Pub.

Cargan, Leonard & Ballantine, Jeanne H., eds. Sociological Footprints: Introductory Readings in Sociology. 4th ed. 482p. (C). 1987. mass mkt. 16.00 (*0-534-08538-5*) Wadsworth Pub.

— Sociological Footprints: Introductory Readings in Sociology. 5th ed. 456p. (C). 1990. mass mkt. 16.50 (*0-534-14652-X*) Wadsworth Pub.

Cargan, Leonard & Melko, Matthew. Singles: Myths & Realities. LC 81-23343. (New Perspectives on Family Ser.). (Illus.). 287p. reprint ed. pap. 89.00 (*0-8357-8482-7*, 203474900091) Bks Demand.

Cargas, Harry J. Daniel Berrigan & Contemporary Protest Poetry. 1972. pap. 13.95 (*0-8084-0352-4*) NCUP.

— Face to Face: A Book about the Holocaust for the Christian Reader. 1988. 19.95 (*0-940461-07-2*) Seth Pr.

— Reflections of a Post-Auschwitz Christian. LC 88-26798. 160p. (C). 1989. pap. 17.95 (*0-8143-2096-1*) Wayne St U Pr.

— Reflections of a Post-Auschwitz Christian. LC 88-26798. (Illus.). 159p. reprint ed. pap. 49.30 (*0-608-10604-6*, 2071226) Bks Demand.

— The Unnecessary Problem of Edith Stein. 135p. (C). 1994. lib. bdg. 37.50 (*0-8191-8781-X*) U Pr of Amer.

— Voices from the Holocaust. LC 92-20178. 184p. 1993. pap. 16.50 (*0-8131-0825-X*) U Pr of Ky.

Cargas, Harry J., ed. Holocaust Scholars Write to the Vatican. 58. LC 98-14233. (Contributions to the Study of Religion Ser.: 58). 176p. 1998. 49.95 (*0-313-30487-4*, Greenwood Pr) Greenwood.

— Problems Unique to the Holocaust. LC 98-41612. 194p. 1999. 22.50 (*0-8131-2101-9*) U Pr of Ky.

Cargas, Harry J., ed. see Panikkar, Raimon.

Cargas, Harry J., ed. see Wiesel, Elie.

Cargas, Nonnie. Gingerbread Houses: Baking & Building Memories. LC 99-61262. 192p. 1999. pap. 23.95 (*0-87341-711-9*) Krause Pubns.

Carger, Chris L. Of Borders & Dreams: A Mexican-American Experience of Urban Education. 176p. 1996. 40.00 (*0-8077-3523-X*); pap. 17.95 (*0-8077-3522-1*) Tchrs Coll.

Cargile, Michael E. Spike's Grand Adventure. (Illus.). 32p. (J). (ps-6). 1998. pap. 9.95 (*0-9665995-0-0*) Spike Enters.

Cargile, Phillip. Old Friends & Married People. LC 96-94730. 184p. 1998. pap. 13.95 (*0-9653711-0-7*, Pub. by IP Books) Barnes & Noble Inc.

Cargile, William A. Why Adam, Lord? And Why the Israelites? LC 98-218025. vii, 191p. 1998. write for info. (*1-884707-86-6*) Lifestyles.

Cargill. Essential C++ Programming for Non-C Programmers. 1995. write for info. (*0-201-41868-1*) Addison-Wesley.

Cargill, B. F., et al. Potato Storage Technology & Practice: Proceedings of an International Symposium. LC 88-83722. 340p. (Orig.). 1989. pap. 44.00 (*0-916150-99-2*, C0189) Am Soc Ag Eng.

Cargill, Carol, ed. A TESOL Professional Anthology: Culture. 120p. 1987. pap. 22.54 (*0-8325-0347-9*) NTC Contemp Pub Co.

— A TESOL Professional Anthology: Grammar & Composition. 120p. 1987. pap. 22.54 (*0-8325-0345-2*) NTC Contemp Pub Co.

— A TESOL Professional Anthology: Listening, Speaking, & Reading. 120p. 1987. pap. 22.54 (*0-8325-0346-0*) NTC Contemp Pub Co.

— A TESOL Professional Anthology: The Primary & Elementary Classroom. 120p. 1987. pap. 22.54 (*0-8325-0348-7*) NTC Contemp Pub Co.

Cargill, G. S., III, et al, eds. Phase Transitions in Condensed Systems - Experiments & Theory, Vol. 57. (Materials Research Society Symposium Proceedings Ser.). 1987. text 17.50 (*0-931837-22-7*) Materials Res.

Cargill, Jack. Athenian Settlements of the Fourth Century B. C. LC 95-7098. (Mnemosyne, Bibliotheca Classica Batava Ser.: Supplementum Ser.: Vol. 145). xxvii, 487p. 1995. 187.50 (*90-04-09991-3*) Brill Academic Pubs.

***Cargill, Jack.** Handbook for Ancient History Classes. 86p. 1999. 10.50 (*0-941690-93-8*) Regina Bks.

An Asterisk (*) at the beginning of an entry indicates that the title is appearing for the first time.

Cargill, Jennifer, ed. Library Management & Technical Services: The Changing Role of Technical Services in Library Organizations. LC 88-6824. (Journal of Library Administration: Vol. 9, No. 1). (Illus.). 154p. 1988. text 4.95 (*0-86656-779-8*) Haworth Pr.

Cargill, Jennifer, jt. ed. see Von Dran, Gisela M.

Cargill, Kathleen M. Waiting for the Big One. unabridged ed. Goessling, Maura, ed. (Illus.). x, 188p. (Orig.). 1996. pap. 16.95 (*0-9655503-0-3*) Beekeepers Pr.

Cargill, Katrin. Bed Linens. 1998. 23.00 (*0-609-60126-1*) C Potter.

— Easy Country: A New Approach to Country Style. LC 98-70702. (Illus.). 160p. (gr. 8). 1998. 27.50 (*0-8212-2469-7*) Little.

— Fabrications: Over One Thousand Ways to Decorate Your Home with Fabric. LC 93-28744. (Illus.). 192p. 1994. 45.00 (*0-8212-2083-7*, Pub. by Bulfinch Pr) Little.

***Cargill, Katrin.** Fabrications: Over 1000 Ways to Decorate Your Home with Fabric. (Illus.). 192p. 1999. pap. 26.95 (*0-8212-2590-1*, Pub. by Bulfinch Pr) Little.

Cargill, Katrin. Home Living Workbooks: Lampshades. LC 96-218917. 112p. 1996. 23.00 (*0-517-70671-7*) C Potter.

— Painted Furniture: Making Ordinary Furniture Extrordinary with Paint, Pattern & Color. LC 98-75319. 128p. (gr. 8). 1999. 27.50 (*0-8212-2541-3*) Little.

— Simple Beds LC 98-234376. (Soft Furnishing Workbooks Ser.). 112p. 1998. write for info. (*1-900518-35-X*) Ryland Peters & Small.

— Simple Curtains. 1998. 23.00 (*0-609-60125-3*) C Potter.

— Simple Curtains. LC 98-234380. (Soft Furnishing Workbooks Ser.). 112p. 1998. write for info. (*1-900518-34-1*) Ryland Peters & Small.

Cargill, Kristi. Nana's New Home: A Comforting Story Explaining Alzheimer's Disease to Children. Smith, Gwen C., ed. (Illus.). 32p. (J). (ps-6). 1997. pap. text 11.99 (*0-9660566-0-4*) KrisPer.

Cargill, Linda. Dreadful Sorry. (YA). (gr. 7 up). Date not set. 4.99 (*0-614-19203-X*, Point) Scholastic Inc.

— Pool Party. 211p. (YA). (gr. 7 up). 1996. mass mkt. 3.99 (*0-590-58111-2*) Scholastic Inc.

— Pool Party. (YA). 1996. 9.09 (*0-606-09762-7*, Pub. by Turtleback) Demco.

— The Surfer. 176p. (J). (gr. 7-9). 1995. mass mkt. 3.99 (*0-590-22215-5*) Scholastic Inc.

— To Follow the Goddess. LC 90-83559. 288p. (Orig.). 1991. pap. 9.95 (*0-9627258-7-0*) Cheops Bks.

Cargill, Marie. Acupuncture: A Viable Medical Alternative. LC 94-12069. 200p. 1994. pap. 12.95 (*0-275-94881-1*, Praeger Pubs) Greenwood.

Cargill, Marie E. Well Women: Healing the Female Body Through Traditional Chinese Medicine. LC 97-16135. 144p. 1998. pap. 12.95 (*0-89789-543-6*, Bergin & Garvey) Greenwood.

***Cargill, Mary Terrell & Huynh, Jade Quang, eds.** Voices of Vietnamese Boat People: 19 Narratives of Escape & Survival. (Illus.). 200p. 2000. per. 32.50 (*0-7864-0785-9*) McFarland & Co.

Cargill, Morris. Jamaica Farewell. LC 94-45638. 240p. 1995. pap. 7.95 (*1-56980-031-6*) Barricade Bks.

Cargill, Oscar. Drama & Liturgy. (BCL1-PR English Literature Ser.). 151p. 1992. reprint ed. lib. bdg. 69.00 (*0-7812-7256-4*) Rprt Serv.

Cargill, R. W., ed. Carbon Monoxide, No. 43. (Illus.). 330p. 1990. 118.50 (*0-08-030733-7*, 1901; 1906; 230, Pergamon Pr) Elsevier.

Cargill, S. T. The Philosophy of Analogy & Symbolism. 264p. 1996. reprint ed. pap. 19.95 (*1-56459-586-2*) Kessinger Pub.

Cargill, Thomas F. & Garcia, Gillian. Financial Deregulation & Monetary Control: Historical Perspective & Impact of the 1980 Act. (Publication Ser.: No. 259). 154p. (C). 1982. pap. 3.58 (*0-8179-7592-6*) Hoover Inst Pr.

Cargill, Thomas F. & Royama, Shoichi. The Transition of Finance in Japan & the United States: A Comparative Perspective. (Publication Ser.: No. 372). 242p. (C). 1988. text 25.95 (*0-8179-8721-5*); pap. text 18.95 (*0-8179-8722-3*) Hoover Inst Pr.

***Cargill, Thomas F., et al.** Financial Policy & Central Banking in Japan. (Illus.). 273p. (C). 2000. 27.95 (*0-262-03285-6*) MIT Pr.

Cargill, Thomas F., et al. The Political Economy of Japanese Monetary Policy. LC 97-3717. 248p. 1997. 35.50 (*0-262-03247-3*) MIT Pr.

Cargill, Tom. Elements of C Plus Plus Programming Style. (Illus.). 248p. (C). 1992. pap. text 35.95 (*0-201-56365-7*) Addison-Wesley.

— TEC Course - C++ Workshop for Non-C Programmers. 1991. ring bd. write for info. (*0-201-41898-3*) Addison-Wesley.

Cargo, David N. & Mallory, Bob F. Man & His Geologic Environment. 2nd ed. LC 76-7655. (C). 1977. text. write for info. (*0-201-00894-7*) Addison-Wesley.

Cargo, Douglas B. Solid Wastes: Factors Influencing Generation Rates. LC 78-16823. (University of Chicago, Department of Geography, Research Paper Ser.: No. 174). 112p. 1978. reprint ed. pap. 34.80 (*0-608-02237-3*, 206279700004) Bks Demand.

Cargo, Robert T. A Concordance to Baudelaire's "Les Fleurs du Mal" LC 73-15399. 417p. 1975. reprint ed. lib. bdg. 65.00 (*0-8371-7197-0*, CACB, Greenwood Pr) Greenwood.

Cargo Systems International Staff, ed. Bulktrans Eighty-Nine. (C). 1989. 150.00 (*0-907499-64-3*, Pub. by Cargo Systs) St Mut.

— Bulktrans Eighty-One. (C). 1981. 150.00 (*0-907499-15-5*, Pub. by Cargo Systs) St Mut.

— Bulktrans Eighty-Three. (C). 1983. 155.00 (*0-7855-6732-1*, Pub. by Cargo Systs) St Mut.

— Bulktrans Ninety-One. (C). 1991. 450.00 (*0-907499-73-2*, Pub. by Cargo Systs) St Mut.

— Container Handling & Transport. 244p. (C). 1990. 160.00 (*0-907499-32-5*, Pub. by Cargo Systs) St Mut.

— Container Repair & Depot Conference, 4th. (C). 1988. 200.00 (*0-7855-6733-X*, Pub. by Cargo Systs) St Mut.

— Container Technology Conference, 7th. (C). 1988. 150.00 (*0-907499-61-9*, Pub. by Cargo Systs) St Mut.

— East-West Interfreight Ninety-One. (C). 1991. 150.00 (*0-907499-72-4*, Pub. by Cargo Systs) St Mut.

— Fifth Container Technology Conference. (C). 1984. text 125.00 (*0-907499-44-9*, Pub. by Cargo Systs) St Mut.

— Guide to Food Transport: Fruit & Vegetables. 250p. (C). 1990. 200.00 (*87-89010-98-1*, Pub. by Cargo Systs) St Mut.

— Guide to Food Transport: Meat, Fish & Dairy. (C). 1990. 200.00 (*87-89010-97-3*, Pub. by Cargo Systs) St Mut.

— Intermodal - The Boom Years. (C). 1990. 175.00 (*0-907499-65-1*, Pub. by Cargo Systs) St Mut.

— Intermodal, 88. (C). 1988. 175.00 (*0-907499-62-7*, Pub. by Cargo Systs) St Mut.

— Intermodal, 89. (C). 1989. 175.00 (*0-907499-67-8*, Pub. by Cargo Systs) St Mut.

— Reefer Trans 89. (C). 1989. 150.00 (*0-907499-68-6*, Pub. by Cargo Systs) St Mut.

— Terminal Operations Conference, 5th. (C). 1988. 200.00 (*0-907499-59-7*, Pub. by Cargo Systs) St Mut.

— Terminal Operations Conference, 6th. (C). 1990. 200.00 (*0-907499-69-4*, Pub. by Cargo Systs) St Mut.

Cargo Systems Staff. Bulk Handling & Transport Conference, Vol. V. 1985. 195.00 (*0-907499-48-1*, Pub. by Cargo Systs) St Mut.

— The Changing Maritime Environment. 1981. 200.00 (*0-907499-14-7*, Pub. by Cargo Systs) St Mut.

— Container Efficiency & Shipping. 1985. 195.00 (*0-907499-51-1*, Pub. by Cargo Systs) St Mut.

— Container Handling & Transport. 1983. 250.00 (*0-907499-31-7*, Pub. by Cargo Systs) St Mut.

— Container Repair, Vol. III. 1985. 210.00 (*0-907499-50-3*, Pub. by Cargo Systs) St Mut.

— Container Technology, Vol. V. 1985. 195.00 (*0-7855-2042-2*, Pub. by Cargo Systs) St Mut.

— Terminal Operations, Vol. II. 1980. 195.00 (*0-907499-12-0*, Pub. by Cargo Systs) St Mut.

Cargo Systems Staff, ed. Bulk Handling & Transport Conference, Vol. III. 1981. 195.00 (*0-907499-13-9*, Pub. by Cargo Systs) St Mut.

— Bulk Handling & Transport Conference, Vol. IV. 1983. 195.00 (*0-907499-36-8*, Pub. by Cargo Systs) St Mut.

— Coal Trans, '84. 1984. 210.00 (*0-907499-43-0*, Pub. by Cargo Systs) St Mut.

— CoalPower, '87. 1987. 195.00 (*0-907400-59-0*, Pub. by Cargo Systs) St Mut.

— CoalTrans, 1981. 1981. 195.00 (*0-907499-19-8*, Pub. by Cargo Systs) St Mut.

— CoalTrans, 1982. 1982. 195.00 (*0-907499-29-5*, Pub. by Cargo Systs) St Mut.

— Computers in Transportation. 1987. 195.00 (*0-7855-2043-0*, Pub. by Cargo Systs) St Mut.

— Container Repair, Vol. II. 1983. 395.00 (*0-907499-38-4*, Pub. by Cargo Systs) St Mut.

— Container Shipping, Vol. II. 1981. 195.00 (*0-907499-20-1*, Pub. by Cargo Systs) St Mut.

— Container Technology, Vol. IV. 1982. 300.00 (*0-907499-30-9*, Pub. by Cargo Systs) St Mut.

— Container Technology, Vol. VI. 1986. 225.00 (*0-907499-55-4*, Pub. by Cargo Systs) St Mut.

— Containerisation Asia. 1990. 395.00 (*0-907499-40-6*, Pub. by Cargo Systs) St Mut.

— Port Engineering Seminar. 1986. 220.00 (*0-907499-54-6*, Pub. by Cargo Systs) St Mut.

— Safe Ship - Safe Cargo, Vol. II. 1987. 210.00 (*0-907499-56-2*, Pub. by Cargo Systs) St Mut.

— Ship Choice in the Container Age. 1980. 200.00 (*0-905394-07-0*, Pub. by Cargo Systs) St Mut.

— Terminal Operations, Vol. III. 1983. 195.00 (*0-907499-39-2*, Pub. by Cargo Systs) St Mut.

Cargonne, Alexander, ed. see Rowe, Colin.

Carhart, Alfreda. Masoud the Bedouin. LC 76-150541. (Short Story Index Reprint Ser.). (Illus.). 1977. reprint ed. 20.95 (*0-8369-3838-0*) Ayer.

Carhart, Clare, jt. auth. see Strohmer, Joanne C.

Carhart, Jane M., jt. ed. see Kline, Linda J.

Carhart, Ross. Raven. 100p. 1998. pap. 8.95 (*1-57502-877-8*, PO2387) Morris Pubng.

Carhart, Tom. Iron Soldiers. Tobias, Eric, ed. LC 94-172439. viii, 320p. (Orig.). 1994. mass mkt. 5.99 (*0-671-79165-6*) PB.

***Caria, Mario.** Measurement Analysis: An Introduction to the Statistical Analysis of Laboratory Data In Physics, Chemistry & the Life Sciences. 280p. 2000. 48.00 (*1-86094-231-8*, Pub. by Imperial College) World Scientific Pub.

Cariaga-Barden, Regina & Onorato, Michael P., eds. Saturnino Q. Cariaga: His American Dream. 1988. 14.00 (*0-930046-11-0*) CSUF Oral Hist.

***Cariaga, Catalina.** Cultural Evidence. Spahr, Juliana, ed. (Illus.). 87p. 1999. pap. 12.00 (*0-9666303-5-1*, Pub. by A A Arts) SPD-Small Pr Dist.

Carias, Guillo, ed. see De Carias, Maria R.

Caribbean Central American Action Staff. Caribbean Basin Profile: 1988. rev. ed. Koukal, Lisa, ed. (Illus.). 383p. (C). 1998. pap. text 20.00 (*0-944804-00-4*) CLAA.

Caribbean Community Staff. Caricom's Trade: A Quick Reference to Some Summary Data, 1985-1992 LC 98-832934. xiii, 118 p. 1994. write for info. (*976-600-102-2*) Carib Comm Sec.

— Regional Cultural Policy of the Caribbean Community. LC 98-832933. 70 p. 1997. write for info. (*976-600-108-1*) Carib Comm Sec.

Caribbean Geological Conference Staff. Caribbean Geophysical, Tectonic & Petrologic Studies: Proceedings of the Caribbean Geological Conference, 5th, St. Thomas, Virgin Islands, 1968. Donnelly, Thomas W., ed. LC 74-165441. (Geological Society of America, Memoir Ser.: No. 130). 274p. reprint ed. pap. 85.00 (*0-608-13956-4*, 202502500041) Bks Demand.

Caribe Editorial Staff. Historias Biblicas. (SPA.). (J). (ps-3). 1992. pap. 9.99 (*0-88113-206-3*) Caribe Betania.

***Caribe Editorial Staff.** El Regalo de Dios para las Madres. (SPA.). 2000. pap. 6.99 (*0-88113-573-9*) Caribe Betania.

Caric, Marijana. Concentrated & Dried Dairy Products. LC 93-37115. 249p. 1993. 110.00 (*1-56081-531-0*, Wiley-VCH) Wiley.

Caricature Carvers of America Staff. Carving the CCA Circus: Cartooning in Wood by America's Top Carvers. (Illus.). 123p. 1997. pap. 19.95 (*1-56523-094-9*) Fox Chapel Pub.

— Carving the Full Moon Saloon: The Art of Caricature in Wood. LC 96-197711. 116p. 1995. 29.95 (*1-56523-067-1*) Fox Chapel Pub.

Caricatures Carvers of America, jt. auth. see Wolfe, Tom James.

Carich, Mark S. & Adkerson, Donya L. Adult Sexual Offender Assessment Packet. Bear, Euan, ed. 96p. (Orig.). 1995. pap. text 8.00 (*1-884444-19-9*) Safer Soc.

Carick, Valery. Picture Folk-Tales. Orig. Title: Valery Carick's Picture Folk-Tales. (Illus.). vi, 90p. (J). 1992. reprint ed. pap. 1.00 (*0-486-27083-1*) Dover.

Caridono, Ron. The Complete Ford Flathead V8 Engine Manual. (Illus.). 200p. 1995. pap. 22.95 (*1-884089-11-9*) CarTech.

Carifio, Benjamin V., jt. ed. see Fawcett, James T.

Carigan, William. Ad Lib: Flying the B-24 Liberator in World War II. 100p. 1993. reprint ed. pap. 17.00 (*0-89745-099-X*) Sunflower U Pr.

— Flying Game. LC 74-13775. 1974. 7.95 (*0-9605986-1-8*) Juniper Pubs.

— Staves for Louisville. LC 81-81067. 1981. 10.95 (*0-9605986-0-X*) Juniper Pubs.

Carignan, Michael J. The First Witness. (Illus.). (J). (ps-6). 1998. mass mkt. 4.95 (*1-892589-00-1*) Madjec Jet.

Carija Brandt, Janet. Folk Art Animals: 25 Fanciful Applique' Designs. LC 98-4509. (Illus.). 88p. 1998. pap. 19.95 (*1-56477-222-5*, B342) Martingale & Co.

***Carillet, Jean-Bernard & Wheeler, Tony.** Diving & Snorkeling Tahiti & French Polynesia. (Illus.). 144p. 2000. pap. 16.95 (*1-86450-071-9*) Lonely Planet.

***Carilli, C. L., et al, eds.** Highly Redshifted Radio Lines. LC QB479.5.H54 1999. (Conference Series Proceedings). 284p. 1999. text 52.00 (*1-886733-76-7*) Astron Soc Pacific.

Carilli, Christopher L. & Harris, Daniel L., eds. Cygnus A--Study of a Radio Galaxy. (Illus.). 281p. (C). 1996. text 69.95 (*0-521-55343-1*) Cambridge U Pr.

Carilli, Theresa. Women as Lovers: Two Plays: Dolores Street & Country Wine. LC 93-81345. (Drama Ser.: No. 11). 265p. 1996. pap. 15.00 (*1-55071-007-9*) Guernica Editions.

Carilli, Theresa, jt. ed. see Kamalipour, Yahya R.

Carillo, Charles. My Ride with Gus. 256p. 1996. 22.00 (*0-671-53568-4*, PB Hardcover) PB.

— My Ride with Gus. 1997. per. 5.99 (*0-671-53569-2*) PB.

Carillo, Jo, ed. Readings in American Indian Law: Recalling the Rhythm of Survival. LC 97-23754. 304p. 1998. text 69.95 (*1-56639-581-X*); pap. text 29.95 (*1-56639-582-8*) Temple U Pr.

Carillo, M. Elena, jt. ed. see Wright, Michael.

Carillo, S., et al, eds. Nonlinear Evolution Equations & Dynamical Systems. (Research Reports in Physics). (Illus.). 200p. 1990. pap. 51.00 (*0-387-51983-1*) Spr-Verlag.

Carillon, Bill. Contractor's Profit Manual: Putting the Pieces Together to Maximize Profits. LC 98-89874. 365p. 1999. 25.00 (*0-7388-0305-7*); pap. 15.00 (*0-7388-0306-5*) Xlibris Corp.

CARIMAR Staff, tr. see Baralt, Guillermo A.

Carimati, R. Diccionario Enciclopedico De Geologia. (SPA.). 271p. 1989. 39.95 (*0-7859-6408-8*, 8486761174) Fr & Eur.

Carin, Arthur A. Guided Discovery Activities. 4th ed. LC 96-28519. 258p. (C). 1996. pap. text 38.00 (*0-13-506940-8*) P-H.

— Teaching Modern Science. 7th ed. LC 96-26853. 379p. (C). 1996. pap. text 57.00 (*0-13-457060-X*) P-H.

— Teaching Science Through Discovery. 8th ed. LC 96-27830. 1996. text 71.00 (*0-13-234089-5*, Merrill Pub Co) Macmillan.

***Carin, Arthur A. & Bass, Joel E.** Activities for Teaching Science as Inquiry. 5th ed. LC 00-41883. (Illus.). 2000. write for info. (*0-13-021281-4*) P-H.

— Methods for Teaching Science as Inquiry. 8th ed. LC 00-41879. (Illus.). 2000. pap. write for info. (*0-13-021283-0*) P-H.

Carin, L. & Felsen, L. B. Ultra-Wideband, Short-Pulse Electromagnetics No. 2: Proceedings of the Second International Conference Held at Weber Research Institute, Polytechnic University, Brooklyn, New York, April 7-9, 1994, Vol. 2. LC 95-17339. (Illus.). 620p. (C). 1995. text 167.00 (*0-306-45002-X*, Kluwer Plenum) Kluwer Academic.

Carin, Martha & Rosenthal, Joel Thomas. Food & Eating in Medieval Europe. LC 98-16277. 200p. 1998. 45.00 (*1-85285-148-1*) Hambledon Press.

Carin, V. S., et al. Nine Papers on Foundations, Algebra, Topology, Functions of a Complex Variable. (Translations Ser.: Series 2, Vol. 15). 349p. 1960. 41.00 (*0-8218-1715-9*, TRANS2/15) Am Math.

Caringer, Denise L., ed. Cottage Style: Furniture, Fabrics, Colors. LC 97-75847. (Illus.). 216p. 1997. 29.95 (*0-696-20777-X*, Better Homes) Meredith Bks.

— Step-by-Step Kitchen & Bath Projects. (Illus.). 112p. 1998. pap. 12.95 (*0-696-20778-8*, Better Homes) Meredith Bks.

Carington, Edward, ed. see Covan, Penney.

Carington, Whately. Matter, Mind & Meaning. LC 78-111818. (Essay Index Reprint Ser.). 1977. 23.95 (*0-8369-1596-8*) Ayer.

Carini, E. Take Another Look. (J). (ps-3). 1969. pap. 1.50 (*0-685-03910-2*) P-H.

Carini, Louis. Three Axioms for a Theory of Conduct: Philosophy, & the Humanistic Science of Psychology. 108p. (Orig.). (C). 1984. pap. text 13.50 (*0-8191-3971-8*) U Pr of Amer.

Carini, Mario A. Milwaukee's Italians: The Early Years. Goodrich, Austin, ed. (Illus.). 180p. 1999. pap. 12.95 (*0-9670696-0-2*) Italian Comm Ctr Milwaukee.

Carini, Patricia F. On Value in Education. (Occasional Papers). 33p. (C). 1987. pap. 5.00 (*0-918374-23-5*) City Coll Wk.

Carino, Gina, tr. see Fernandez-Galiano, Luis.

Carino, Maria Ledvina. In the Garden of the Three Islands: Poems. 120p. 1994. pap. 11.95 (*1-55921-117-2*, Asphodel Pr) Moyer Bell.

Carino, Nicholas J., jt. auth. see Malhotra, V. M.

Carino, Peter A. Basic Writing: Process & Purpose. 2nd ed. 464p. (C). 1997. pap. text 53.00 (*0-673-99294-2*) Addison-Wesley Educ.

Carino, Theresa C. China & the Overseas Chinese in Southeast Asia. vii, 115p. (Orig.). (C). 1986. pap. 12.50 (*971-10-0231-0*, Pub. by New Day Pub) Cellar.

— Chinese Big Business in the Philippines: Political Leadership & Change. LC 98-837329. 167p. 1998. 35.00 (*981-210-125-X*) Intl Spec Bk.

Carion, Marion C. Let Night Touch You. unabridged ed. (Message from Yin Ser.: Vol. 2). 32p. 1999. pap. 6.00 (*1-890185-02-7*) Half-Moon.

— Listen to the Moon Pt. 1: Message from Yin. 32p. (Orig.). 1997. pap. 6.00 (*1-890185-01-9*) Half-Moon.

Cariou, Gail, jt. auth. see Shep, R. L.

Cariou, Mavis, et al, eds. Canadian Selection: Books & Periodicals for Libraries. 2nd ed. 517p. 1986. text 85.00 (*0-8020-4630-4*) U of Toronto Pr.

***Cariou, Patrick, photos by.** Yes Rasta. (Illus.). 2000. 60.00 (*1-57687-073-1*, pwerHse Bks) pwerHse Cultrl.

Cariou, Warren. The Exalted Company of Roadside Martyrs. 270p. 1999. pap. 12.95 (*1-55050-145-3*) Coteau.

Caris, John. Foundation for a New Consciousness. LC 86-20201. (Illus.). 136p. (Orig.). 1987. pap. 8.95 (*0-9607320-1-2*) Westgate Hse.

— Reality Inspector. (Illus.). 1982. pap. 7.95 (*0-9607320-0-4*) Westgate Hse.

Caris, Susan L. Community Attitudes Toward Pollution. LC 78-13164. (University of Chicago, Department of Geography, Research Paper Ser.: No. 188). 227p. 1978. reprint ed. pap. 70.40 (*0-608-02238-1*, 206279800001) Bks Demand.

Caris, Timothy N. Essential Hypertension: A Strategy for Individualized Treatment. LC 89-64149. 130p. (Orig.). 1990. pap. 11.95 (*0-945892-01-2*) JBK Pub.

Carisano, Rita. Deposit Insurance: Theory, Policy & Evidence. (Luiss Ser.). 203p. 1992. 67.95 (*1-85521-174-2*, Pub. by Dartmth Pub) Ashgate Pub Co.

Carisella, P. J. The Dance of the Twelve Apostles. Caso, A., ed. (Illus.). 274p. 1991. text 17.95 (*0-8283-1935-9*) Branden Bks.

Carisella, P. J., jt. auth. see Schofield, William.

Carish, Sharon, ed. see Headley, Barbara J.

Carisse, Colette. Planification des Naissances en Milieu Canadien-Francais. LC 66-56044. (FRE.). 228p. reprint ed. pap. 70.70 (*0-7837-6944-X*, 204677300003) Bks Demand.

Caristi, Anthony J., ed. IEEE-488 General Purpose Instrumentation Bus Manual. 253p. 1989. text 84.00 (*0-12-159820-9*) Acad Pr.

Caristi, Dom. Expanding Free Expression in the Marketplace: Broadcasting & the Public Forum. LC 91-40950. 192p. 1992. 52.95 (*0-89930-720-5*, CTK, Quorum Bks) Greenwood.

Caristi, Gabriella & Mitidieri, Enzo. Reaction Diffusion Systems. LC 97-35931. (Lecture Notes in Pure & Applied Mathematics). (Illus.). 432p. 1997. pap. text 175.00 (*0-8247-0125-9*) Dekker.

Caristi, Vincent, et al. Tracers. 71p. 1987. pap. 5.25 (*0-8222-1164-5*) Dramatists Play.

Cariston, Nina. Summer Clouds. large type ed. 352p. 1996. 27.99 (*0-7089-3479-X*) Ulverscroft.

***Carita, Helder.** Palaces of Goa: Models & Types of Indo-Portuguese Architecture. 224p. 1999. 60.00 (*1-900826-10-0*, Pub. by M T Train) Antique Collect.

Carita, Helder & Cardoso, Homem. Portuguese Gardens. (Illus.). 320p. 1991. 79.50 (*1-85149-101-5*) Antique Collect.

Caritat, Patrice De, see Reimann, Clemens & De Caritat, Patrice.

Caritat, Patrice De, see Saether, Ola M.

Caritat, Patrice De, see Saether, Ola M. & De Caritat, Patrice.

Caritat, Patrice De, see Saether, Ola M.

Caritat, Patrice De, see Saether, Ola M. & De Caritat, Patrice.

Carithers, Jeanine A., jt. auth. see Dellmann, H. Dieter.

Caritt, E. F., tr. see Croce, Benedetto.

***Carius, Alexander & Lietzmann, Kurt M., eds.** Environmental Change & Security: A European Perspective. LC 99-51550. (Illus.). xxvi, 322p. 2000. 79.95 (*3-540-66179-4*) Spr-Verlag.

Carkeet, David. Double Negative. Rosenman, Jane, ed. 252p. 1991. reprint ed. pap. 7.95 (*0-671-73690-6*, WSP) PB.

— The Error of Our Ways: A Novel. 320p. 1997. 25.00 (0-8050-4502-3) H Holt & Co.

— The Error of Our Ways: A Novel. 256p. 1998. pap. text 13.00 (0-8050-5604-1) H Holt & Co.

— The Error of Our Ways: A Novel. large type ed. (Niagara Large Print Ser.). 352p. 1997. 29.50 (0-7089-5865-6) Ulverscroft.

— The Full Catastrophe. Rosenman, Jane, ed. 324p. 1991. reprint ed. pap. 12.00 (0-671-73245-5, WSP) PB.

— Quiver River. LC 90-24095. (Laura Geringer Bks.). 224p. (YA). (gr. 7 up). 1991. 14.95 (0-06-022453-3) HarpC Child Bks.

— The Silent Treatment. LC 87-45567. (Charlotte Zolotow Bk.). 288p. (YA). (gr. 7 up). 1990. pap. 3.25 (0-06-447014-8, HarpTrophy) HarpC Child Bks.

Carkesse, James. Lucida Intervalla: Containing Divers Miscellaneous Poems, Written at Finsbury & Bethlem by the Doctors Patient Extraordinary. LC 92-25461. (Augustan Reprints Ser.: Nos. 195-196). 1979. reprint ed. 21.50 (0-404-70195-7, PR339) AMS Pr.

Carkhuff, Robert R. Art of Helping, Vol. VII. 140p. 1993. teacher ed. 12.95 (0-87425-232-6); student ed. 12.95 (0-87425-233-4); pap. text 24.95 (0-87425-231-8) HRD Press.

***Carkhuff, Robert R.** Art of Helping, Vol. 8. 8th ed. 2000. pap. 34.95 (0-87425-530-9) HRD Press.

Carkner, Gordon, jt. auth. see Green, Michael.

Carko Glu Ali, et al. The Political Economy of Regional Cooperation in the Middle East. LC 98-17666. 272p. (C). 1998. 100.00 (0-415-19445-8) Routledge.

***Carl.** The Dungeon of Death. 32p. 2000. pap. 9.95 (0-7869-1622-2) TSR Inc.

***Carl, Andreas.** Medical Boards - Step 1 Made Ridiculously Simple. 2nd ed. (Illus.). 367p. (Orig.). (C). 1999. pap. text 24.95 (0-940780-39-9) MedMaster.

Carl, Andreas. Medical Boards - Step 2 Made Ridiculously Simple. LC 97-122209. 356p. 1999. pap. text 24.95 (0-940780-28-3) MedMaster.

— Medical Boards Step 3 Made Ridiculously Simple. (Illus.). 285p. 1999. pap. text 22.95 (0-940780-37-2) MedMaster.

***Carl, Andreas.** NCLEX-RN Made Ridiculously Simple. (Illus.). 379p. 2000. pap. text 24.95 (0-940780-35-6) MedMaster.

Carl, Angela. Child Abuse: What You Can Do about It. 128p. 1993. reprint ed. pap., teacher ed. 6.99 (0-89900-462-8) College Pr Pub.

— Good Hugs & Bad Hugs: How Can You Tell? 32p. 1993. reprint ed. pap., student ed. 3.99 (0-89900-463-6) College Pr Pub.

***Carl, Ann B.** A Wasp among Eagles: A Woman Military Test Pilot in World War II. LC 98-39772. (Illus.). 142p. 1999. 21.95 (1-56098-842-8) Smithsonian.

Carl, Beverly M. Economic Integration among Developing Nations: Law & Policy. LC 85-30777. 304p. 1986. 69.50 (0-275-92060-7, C2060, Praeger Pubs) Greenwood.

***Carl, Beverly M.** Trade & the Developing World in the 21st Century. 800p. 2000. 165.00 (1-57105-070-1) Transnatl Pubs.

Carl, Craig, ed. New Jersey Style. (Illus.). 72p. 1991. 29.95 (0-934590-35-4) Visual Refer.

Carl, Douglas. Counseling Same-Sex Couples. 160p. (C). 1990. 19.95 (0-393-70107-7) Norton.

Carl, Elsie. Neryugngaunga Naunerrlugnek (I Can Eat Plants) (ESK., Illus.). 16p. (J). (gr. k-3). 1998. pap. text 6.00 (1-58084-034-5) Lower Kuskokwim.

Carl, Elsie & Mann, Mary J. Eren'am Erenra. large type ed. (ESK., Illus.). 12p. (J). (gr. k-3). 1998. pap. text 6.00 (1-58084-021-3) Lower Kuskokwim.

— Inaqam Ikamrcuallra. large type ed. (ESK., Illus.). 12p. (J). (gr. k-3). 1997. pap. text 6.00 (1-58084-005-1) Lower Kuskokwim.

Carl, Frank. Courting the King of Terrors. LC 89-90873. 176p. 1990. pap. 7.95 (0-914984-18-7) Starburst.

Carl H. Pforzheimer Library Staff. The Carl H. Pforzheimer Library, English Literature, 1475-1700, 3 vols. Jackson, William A. & Unger, Emma V., eds. LC 97-7541. (Illus.). 1350p. 1997. reprint ed. 350.00 (1-884718-33-7) Oak Knoll.

Carl, Hans. Bubble, Bubble, Toil & Trouble. 254p. (C). 1991. 45.00 (0-7223-2498-7, Pub. by A H S Ltd) St Mut.

Carl, Iris M., ed. Seventy-Five Years of Progress: Prospects for School Mathematics. LC 95-10255. (Illus.). 340p. 1995. 25.95 (0-87353-418-2) NCTM.

***Carl, Jason.** Apocalypse Stone. (AD & D Accessory Ser.). (Illus.). 96p. 2000. pap. 16.95 (0-7869-1614-1) TSR Inc.

— Camarilla Guide. (Mind's Eye Theatre Ser.). 2000. pap. 14.95 (1-56504-731-1) White Wolf.

Carl, Jason & DeFreest, Shane. Secrets of Elysium. (Mind's Eye Theatre Ser.). (Illus.). 1998. pap. 15.00 (1-56504-536-X, 5012) White Wolf.

***Carl, Jason, et al.** Laws of the Night. limited rev. ed. (Mind's Eye Theatre Ser.). (Illus.). 256p. 1999. 33.95 (1-56504-699-4, 5015) White Wolf.

Carl, Jason, et al. Laws of the Night. rev. ed. (Mind's Eye Theatre Ser.). (Illus.). 256p. 1999. pap. 19.95 (1-56504-589-0, 5013) White Wolf.

Carl, Kathy, jt. auth. see Cook, Shirley.

***Carl, Lindahl & Alan, Jabbour.** Treasury of American Folktales: From the Collections of the Library of Congress. 2001. lib. bdg. 65.00 (1-57607-156-1) ABC-CLIO.

Carl-Mitchell, Smoot & Quarterman, John S. Practical Internetworking with TCP - IP & Unix. LC 92-41015. (Illus.). 496p. (C). 1993. 54.95 (0-201-58629-0) Addison-Wesley.

— UniForum Technology Guide: Electronic Mail De-Mystified. 34p. pap. text 10.00 (0-936593-15-6) UniForum.

***Carl, Nina.** You Know That You're a Woman over Forty When... 16p. 2000. pap. 8.95 (0-8059-4807-4) Dorrance.

Carl, Peter, jt. auth. see Allison, Stacy.

Carl, Robert A. Men of the Sea. (Illus.). 325p. (Orig.). 1993. pap. 10.95 (0-9637332-0-6) R Carl.

***Carl, S. & Heikkilha, Seppo.** Nonlinear Differential Equations in Ordered Spaces, Vol. 111. LC 00-30835. (Monographs & Surveys in Pure & Applied Mathematics). 336p. 2000. boxed set 74.95 (1-58488-068-6, Chap & Hall CRC) CRC Pr.

Carl Vinson Institute of Government Staff, jt. auth. see Jackson, Edwin L.

Carl, Wilhelm H. Data Communication Pocket Dictionary: Taschenwoerterbuch der Datenkommunikation. (ENG, FRE & GER.). 290p. 1982. 85.00 (0-8288-0269-6, M14466) Fr & Eur.

Carl, Wilhelm H. & Amkreutz, Johann J. English, German & French Dictionary of Data Processing: Woerterbuch der Datenverarbeitung, 2 vols. 3rd ed. 1944p. 1986. 225.00 (0-8288-0268-8, M8060) Fr & Eur.

Carl, William J., III. Church People Beware! 1992. pap. 6.75 (1-55673-426-3, 9229) CSS OH.

Carl, William J., Jr., ed. Graying Gracefully: Preaching to Older Adults. LC 96-43254. 176p. (Orig.). 1997. pap. 16.95 (0-664-25722-4) Westminster John Knox.

Carl, Wolfgang. Frege's Theory of Sense & Reference: Its Origins & Scope. LC 93-48145. (Modern European Philosophy Ser.). 230p. (C). 1994. text 64.95 (0-521-39135-0); pap. text 21.95 (0-521-39816-9) Cambridge U Pr.

Carlan, Audrey. Everyday Math for the Numerically Challenged. LC 98-10725. (Numerically Challenged Ser.). 160p. 1998. pap. 11.99 (1-56414-355-4) Career Pr Inc.

Carlan, Betty, et al, eds. The Heritage of Talladega County, Alabama. (Heritage of Alabama Ser.: No. 61). (Illus.). 280p. 1998. 55.00 (1-891647-23-7) Herit Pub Consult.

Carland. Small Business Management: Tools for Success. 2nd ed. LC 97-94633. 1998. 68.95 (0-87393-719-8) Dame Pubns.

Carland, Jim & Carland, JoAnn. Small Business Management: Tools for Success. 696p. (C). 1990. text 50.50 (0-534-92036-5) S-W Pub.

Carland, JoAnn, jt. auth. see Carland, Jim.

Carland, John M. The Colonial Office & Nigeria, 1898-1914. (Publication Ser.: No. 314). 258p. 1985. lib. bdg. 10.78 (0-8179-8141-1) Hoover Inst Pr.

Carland, Maria Pinto, ed. see School of Foreign Service, Georgetown University S.

Carlander, Kenneth D. Handbook of Freshwater Fishery Biology. 384p. (Orig.). 1997. pap. text 52.95 (0-8138-2999-2) Iowa St U Pr.

Carlano, Marianne. French Textiles, from the Middle Ages through the Second Empire. LC 84-51324. (Illus.). 202p. 1985. pap. 30.00 (0-918333-02-4) Wadsworth Atheneum.

***Carlassare, Elizabeth.** DotCom Divas: 20 Profiles of Successful Web Companies & the Women Who Founded Them. (Illus.). 2001. 21.95 (0-07-136242-8) McGraw.

***Carlat, Daniel J.** Psychiatric Interview: A Practical Guide. LC 98-44274. 1999. 29.95 (0-683-30735-5) Lppncott W & W.

Carlaw, Alan, ed. Eagles in the Sky: The RAF ay 75 - a Celebration. (Illus.). 160p. 1994. 35.00 (1-85158-518-4, Pub. by Mainstream Pubng) Trafalgar.

Carlaw, Florence B. I Remember Ray: A Celebration. 128p. (Orig.). 1995. pap. 9.95 (0-89914-047-5) Third Party Pub.

***Carlaw, Peggy & Deming, Vasudha Kathleen.** The Big Book of Selling Games: Quick, Fun Activities for Improving Selling Skills or Livening Up a Sales Meeting. (Big Book of Business Games Ser.). (Illus.). 214p. 1999. pap. 17.95 (0-07-134336-9) McGraw.

Carlaw, Raymond W., ed. Perspectives on Community Health Education: A Series of Case Studies. LC 80-54741. 224p. (C). 1982. pap. text 9.95 (0-89914-007-6) Third Party Pub.

Carlaw, Raymond W. & Ward, William B., eds. Primary Health Care: The African Experience. LC 80-54741. (Case Studies in Community Health Education: Vol. 2). 472p. 1988. pap. 19.95 (0-89914-025-4) Third Party Pub.

Carlberg, Conrad. Using MS Excel 97. LC 97-69800. 359p. 1997. 19.99 (0-7897-1440-X) Que.

Carlberg, Conrad, jt. auth. see Ivens, Kathy.

Carlberg, David. Cleanroom Microbiology for the Non-Microbiologist. 154p. 1995. 119.00 (0-935184-73-2) Interpharm.

Carlberg, Jan. The Hungry Heart: Daily Devotions from the Old Testament. 220p. 1997. reprint ed. 16.95 (1-56563-294-X) Hendrickson MA.

— The Welcome Song: And Other Stories from a Place Called Home. LC 98-48394. 176p. 1999. 12.99 (0-8007-1761-9) Revell.

Carlberg, M. European Monetary Union: Theory, Evidence, & Policy. LC 99-14659. (Contributions to Economics Ser.). (Illus.). xiv, 255p. 1999. pap. 56.00 (3-7908-1191-2) Spr-Verlag.

— International Economic Growth, Vol. X. (Contributions to Economics Ser.). (Illus.). 216p. 1997. pap. 67.00 (3-7908-0995-0) Spr-Verlag.

— Intertemporal Macroeconomics: Deficits, Unemployment, & Growth. (Contributions to Economics Ser.). (Illus.). x, 240p. 1998. pap. 59.00 (3-7908-1096-7) Spr-Verlag.

— Monetary & Fiscal Dynamics. Bos, Dieter et al, eds. (Studies in Contemporary Economics). (Illus.). viii, 194p. 1992. 59.95 (0-387-91423-4) Spr-Verlag.

— Open Economy Dynamics. (Contributions to Economics Ser.). (Illus.). x, 203p. 1993. 61.95 (0-387-91456-0) Spr-Verlag.

— Sustainability & Optimality of Public Debt. (Illus.). x, 217p. 1995. 61.00 (3-7908-0834-2) Spr-Verlag.

***Carlberg, Michael.** Economic Policy in a Monetary Union. LC 00-44066. 2000. write for info. (3-540-67558-2) Spr-Verlag.

Carlberg, Nancy E. Becoming a Professional Genealogist. 250p. (Orig.). 1991. pap. 20.00 (0-944878-13-X) Carlberg Pr.

— Beginning Census Research. 160p. (Orig.). 1991. pap. 15.00 (0-944878-14-8) Carlberg Pr.

— Beginning English Research. 175p. 1993. pap. 15.00 (0-944878-26-1) Carlberg Pr.

— Beginning Norwegian Research. 160p. (Orig.). 1991. pap. 15.00 (0-944878-12-1) Carlberg Pr.

— Beginning Swedish Research. LC 89-156347. 150p. (Orig.). 1989. pap. 15.00 (0-944878-05-9) Carlberg Pr.

— Climbing the Family Tree with Nancy. LC 87-400889. 142p. (Orig.). 1986. pap. 15.00 (0-944878-00-8) Carlberg Pr.

— Ecological Living on a Shoestring. 180p. (Orig.). 1991. pap. 15.00 (0-944878-15-6) Carlberg Pr.

— Gentle Living in England. 160p. (Orig.). 1992. pap. 15.00 (0-944878-20-2) Carlberg Pr.

— Gentle Living on a Shoestring: How to Live Rich When You're Not. 175p. (Orig.). 1991. pap. 15.00 (0-944878-19-9) Carlberg Pr.

— Getting a Quick Start up Your Family Tree. 155p. (Orig.). 1993. pap. 10.00 (0-944878-27-X) Carlberg Pr.

— How to Survive the Genealogy Bug Without Going Broke. 50p. (Orig.). 1993. pap. 5.00 (0-944878-22-9) Carlberg Pr.

— Midwest Research. (Illus.). 110p. (Orig.). 1991. pap. 5.00 (0-944878-11-3) Carlberg Pr.

— Nancy's Easy Filing System. 50p. (Orig.). 1987. pap. 5.00 (0-944878-01-6) Carlberg Pr.

— Overcoming Dead Ends. 320p. (Orig.). 1991. pap. 20.00 (0-944878-10-5) Carlberg Pr.

— Preserving Your Family Heritage. LC 87-162874. 100p. (Orig.). 1987. pap. 5.00 (0-944878-04-0) Carlberg Pr.

— Researching in Salt Lake City. rev. ed. 260p. (Orig.). 1993. pap. 20.00 (0-944878-24-5) Carlberg Pr.

— Teaching Genealogy. (Illus.). 340p. (Orig.). 1988. pap. 25.00 (0-944878-07-5) Carlberg Pr.

— Toy Making on a Budget. 40p. 1993. pap. 5.00 (0-944878-28-8) Carlberg Pr.

— Travelling to England to Find Your Roots (Cheap) 200p. (Orig.). 1989. pap. 15.00 (0-944878-06-7) Carlberg Pr.

— Using the Family History Library Computer System: Including the Library Catalog, Ancestral File, International Genealogical Index. 90p. (Orig.). 1991. pap. 15.00 (0-944878-08-3) Carlberg Pr.

— Using the Los Angeles Family History Center. rev. ed. 160p. 1991. reprint ed. pap. 15.00 (0-944878-03-2) Carlberg Pr.

— Using the 1992 IGI on Microfiche. 55p. 1993. pap. 3.00 (0-944878-29-6) Carlberg Pr.

— Using the Orange Family History Center. 160p. 1992. pap. 10.00 (0-944878-23-7) Carlberg Pr.

— Using the Personal Ancestral File. 120p. (Orig.). 1991. pap. 15.00 (0-944878-09-1) Carlberg Pr.

— Writing a Family History. 150p. (Orig.). 1991. pap. 15.00 (0-944878-16-4) Carlberg Pr.

— Writing a Non-Fiction Book the Easy Way. 150p. (Orig.). 1991. pap. 15.00 (0-944878-17-2) Carlberg Pr.

Carlberg, Nancy E. & Jenkins, Pamela T. Thrift Shopping in England. 175p. (Orig.). 1992. pap. 15.00 (0-944878-21-0) Carlberg Pr.

Carlberg, Nancy E. & Keating, Norma S. Beginning Danish Research. 160p. (Orig.). 1991. pap. 20.00 (0-944878-18-0) Carlberg Pr.

Carlberg, Scott. Corporate Video Survival. (Illus.). 192p. 1991. 45.95 (0-86729-280-6, Focal) Buttrwrth-Heinemann.

Carlbom, Ingrid. High-Performance Graphics System Architecture: A Methodology for Design & Evaluation. LC 84-2673. (Computer Science: Systems Programming Ser.: No. 21). (Illus.). 182p. reprint ed. pap. 56.50 (0-8357-1595-7, 207036600088) Bks Demand.

Carlborg, Kenneth, jt. auth. see Warwick, Robert T.

Carle. Don't Bet on Prince. 264p. 1999. pap. 12.95 (1-58238-024-4, Whitman Coin) St Martin.

Carle. Mixed-Up Chameleon Coloring Book. 32p. (J). Date not set. 3.95 (0-694-00713-7, HarpFestival) HarpC Child Bks.

Carle. Women, Housewives, Whores. 1994. pap. 12.95 (0-9642208-0-6) Buckhorn Bks.

Carle, Cliff. No Hang-Ups II. (Illus.). 96p. (Orig.). 1986. pap. 3.95 (0-918259-05-3) CCC Pubns.

Carle, Cliff, jt. auth. see Ben-Meir, Ron.

Carle, Cliff, jt. auth. see Carfi, John.

Carle, Cliff, ed. see Arnold, R. Steven.

Carle, Cliff, ed. see Baynham, John.

Carle, Cliff, ed. see Bean, R. S.

Carle, Cliff, ed. see Boulanger, Ari A.

Carle, Cliff, ed. see Boulevard, Roscoe.

Carle, Cliff, ed. see Carey, Tom.

Carle, Cliff, ed. see Chamberlain, Cathi.

Carle, Cliff, ed. see Choate, Scott.

Carle, Cliff, ed. see Deboer, Cy.

Carle, Cliff, ed. see Della Valle, Paula & Peterson, Lennie.

Carle, Cliff, ed. see Dutter, Barry & Kurth, Steve.

Carle, Cliff, ed. see Feinsinger, Paul R.

Carle, Cliff, ed. see Francis, Chuck.

Carle, Cliff, ed. see Glasbergen, Randy.

Carle, Cliff, ed. see Glickman, Bob.

Carle, Cliff, ed. see Goffe, Toni.

Carle, Cliff, ed. see Goll, Charles.

Carle, Cliff, ed. see Hellweg, Paul, et al.

Carle, Cliff, ed. see Hunt, Patrick.

Carle, Cliff, ed. see Hutchings, Anthony.

Carle, Cliff, ed. see Karol, Jim & CCC Staff.

Carle, Cliff, ed. see Karpinski, Peter.

Carle, Cliff, ed. see Kelley, David W.

Carle, Cliff, ed. see King, Jan B.

Carle, Cliff, ed. see King, Jan & King, Jerry.

Carle, Cliff, ed. see King, Jerry.

Carle, Cliff, ed. see Kohl, Joel.

Carle, Cliff, ed. see Kolness, John.

Carle, Cliff, ed. see Kramer, Jill.

Carle, Cliff, ed. see Lawn, Robert.

Carle, Cliff, ed. see Lindway, Russ.

Carle, Cliff, ed. see Lucques.

Carle, Cliff, ed. see Michaels, Jon.

Carle, Cliff, ed. see Mullan, Desmond.

Carle, Cliff, ed. see Nordstrom, David.

Carle, Cliff, ed. see O'Brien, Tim.

Carle, Cliff, ed. see Pascoe, Jed.

Carle, Cliff, ed. see Peterson, Lennie.

Carle, Cliff, ed. see Phillips, Steve.

Carle, Cliff, ed. see Porteus, Richard.

Carle, Cliff, ed. see Reynolds, Dan.

Carle, Cliff, ed. see Rubino, Anthony.

Carle, Cliff, ed. see Rumsey, Dusty.

Carle, Cliff, ed. see Sahner, Fred.

Carle, Cliff, ed. see Scarborough, Steve.

Carle, Cliff, ed. see Schuman, Eric.

Carle, Cliff, ed. see Shank, Mary B. & Tumy, Suzanne.

Carle, Cliff, ed. see Shape, Laraine.

Carle, Cliff, ed. see Smith, Bruce T. & Burns, Laura G.

Carle, Cliff, ed. see Smith, Bruce T., et al.

Carle, Cliff, ed. see Smith, Don.

Carle, Cliff, ed. see Sorg, Leslie.

Carle, Cliff, ed. see Stein, Eric.

Carle, Cliff, ed. see Strand, Ed.

Carle, Cliff, ed. see Strnad, Ed.

Carle, Cliff, ed. see Sullivan, Kenyata.

Carle, Cliff, ed. see Twain, M. N. & Smith, Don.

Carle, Cliff, ed. see White, I. B.

Carle, Cliff, ed. see Williams, Marsha P. & Price, Mike.

Carle, Cliff, ed. see Williams, Steve D.

Carle, Cliff, ed. see Wilson, Scott.

Carle, Cliff, ed. see Zahn, Bob.

Carle, Cliff, ed. see Zobel, Allia.

Carle, Cliff, ed. see Zurluini, Paul.

***Carle, David.** Drowning the Dream: California's Water Choices at the Millennium. LC 99-54444. 256p. 2000. 45.00 (0-275-96719-0, Praeger Pubs) Greenwood.

Carle, David. Mono Lake Viewpoint. (Illus.). 136p. (Orig.). 1993. pap. 5.00 (0-932347-06-1) Artemisia Pr.

***Carle, Eric.** Animals Animals. LC 88-31646. (Illus.). 96p. (J). (ps-3). 1999. 7.99 (0-698-11855-3, PapStar) Peng Put Young Read.

Carle, Eric. The Art of Eric Carle. LC 95-24940. (Illus.). 128p. (J). (gr. 3 up). 1996. 35.00 (0-399-22937-X, Philomel) Peng Put Young Read.

Carle, Eric. The Art of Eric Carle. LC 91-646. (Illus.). 124p. (J). (gr. k up). 1993. pap. 29.95 (0-88708-176-2, Picture Book Studio) S&S Childrens.

Carle, Eric. The Carle Slipcase Set: The Very Hungry Caterpillar; The Very Busy Spider; The Very Quiet Cricket. (Illus.). 32p. (J). (ps-3). Date not set. 52.85 (0-399-22623-0) Putnam Pub Group.

— Catch the Ball! (Play-&-Read Book Ser.). (Illus.). 12p. (J). (ps). 1998. bds. 6.95 (0-590-32845-X, Cartwheel) Scholastic Inc.

— Do You Want to Be My Friend? LC 88-4169. (Illus.). 32p. (J). (ps-k). 1988. 5.95 (0-399-21598-0, Philomel) Peng Put Young Read.

— Do You Want to Be My Friend. LC 70-140643. (Illus.). 40p. (J). (ps-2). 1971. 15.95 (0-690-24276-X) HarpC Child Bks.

— Do You Want to Be My Friend. LC 70-140643. (Illus.). 40p. (J). (ps-3). 1971. lib. bdg. 15.89 (0-690-01137-7) HarpC Child Bks.

— Do You Want to Be My Friend. (Illus.). 15p. (J). (ps-1). 1995. 7.95 (0-694-00709-9, HarpFestival) HarpC Child Bks.

— Do You Want to Be My Friend. LC 70-140643. (Trophy Picture Bk.). (Illus.). 40p. (J). (ps-2). 1987. reprint ed. pap. 6.95 (0-06-443127-4, HarpTrophy) HarpC Child Bks.

***Carle, Eric.** Does a Kangaroo Have a Mother, Too? (J). 2002. 7.95 (0-694-01456-7, HarpFestival) HarpC Child Bks.

— Does a Kangaroo Have a Mother, Too? LC 99-36147. 32p. (J). (ps-1). 2002. pap. 6.95 (0-06-443642-X) HarpC Child Bks.

— Does a Kangaroo Have a Mother, Too. LC 99-36147. (Illus.). 32p. (J). (ps-1). 2000. 16.95 (0-06-028768-3); lib. bdg. 16.89 (0-06-028767-5) HarpC Child Bks.

Carle, Eric. Draw Me a Star. LC 91-29055. (Illus.). 40p. (J). (ps up). 1992. 16.95 (0-399-21877-7, Philomel) Peng Put Young Read.

— Draw Me a Star. (Illus.). 40p. (J). 1998. pap. 6.99 (0-698-11632-1, PapStar) Peng Put Young Read.

— Draw Me a Star. (J). 1998. 12.19 (0-606-12924-3, Pub. by Turtleback) Demco.

***Carle, Eric.** Dream Snow. LC 99-59200. (Illus.). 32p. (J). (ps-1). 2000. 21.99 (0-399-23579-5) Peng Put Young Read.

— Eric Carle Activity Kit. (J). 2000. write for info. (0-06-028837-X) HarpC Child Bks.

Carle, Eric. Eric Carle's Dragons, Dragons: And Other Creatuers That Never Were. Whipple, Laura, ed. LC 91-11986. (Illus.). 72p. (J). (ps up). 1991. 18.95 (0-399-22105-0, Philomel) Peng Put Young Read.

— Eric Carle's Dragons, Dragons & Other Creatures That Never Were. LC 91-11986. 1991. 13.15 (0-606-09242-0, Pub. by Turtleback) Demco.

An Asterisk (*) at the beginning of an entry indicates that the title is appearing for the first time.

— Eric Carle's Treasury of Classic Stories for Children. LC 87-22072. 160p. (J). (gr. k-3). 1995. pap. 9.95 (*0-590-50213-1*, Cartwheel) Scholastic Inc.

— Eric Carle's Treasury of Classic Stories for Children By Aesop, Hans Christian Andersen. 1988. 15.15 (*0-606-07485-6*, Pub. by Turtleback) Demco.

— Flora & Tiger: 19 Very Short Stories from My Life. LC 97-1430. (Illus.). 64p. (J). (gr. 3-7). 1997. 17.95 (*0-399-23203-6*, Philomel) Peng Put Young Read.

— From Head to Toe. LC 95-53141. (Illus.). 32p. (J). (gr. k-3). 1997. lib. bdg. 16.89 (*0-06-023516-0*) HarpC Child Bks.

— From Head to Toe. LC 95-53141. (Illus.). 32p. (J). (ps-3). 1997. 16.95 (*0-06-023515-2*) HarpC Child Bks.

— From Head to Toe. (Illus.). 26p. (J). (ps-k). 1999. 7.95 (*0-694-01301-3*, HarpFestival) HarpC Child Bks.

— From Head to Toe. LC 95-53141. (Illus.). 32p. (J). (ps-3). 1999. pap. 6.95 (*0-06-443596-2*, HarpTrophy) HarpC Child Bks.

— The Grouchy Ladybug. LC 95-26581. (Illus.). 48p. (J). (ps-1). 1996. lib. bdg. 16.89 (*0-06-027088-8*) HarpC Child Bks.

— The Grouchy Ladybug. LC 95-26581. (Illus.). 48p. (J). (ps-3). 1996. 16.95 (*0-06-027087-X*); pap. 6.95 (*0-06-443450-8*, HarpTrophy) HarpC Child Bks.

— The Grouchy Ladybug. LC 95-26581. 1996. 12.15 (*0-606-09371-0*, Pub. by Turtleback) Demco.

— Grouchy Ladybug. LC 77-3170. (Illus.). 48p. (J). (ps-1). 1977. 15.00 (*0-690-01391-4*) HarpC Child Bks.

— Grouchy Ladybug. LC 77-3170. (Trophy Picture Bk.). (Illus.). 48p. (J). (ps-2). 1986. reprint ed. pap. 5.95 (*0-06-443116-9*, HarpTrophy) HarpC Child Bks.

— The Grouchy Ladybug Board Book. (Illus.). 44p. (J). (ps-k). 1999. 7.95 (*0-694-01320-X*) HarpC Child Bks.

— Grouchy Ladybug Doll. (Illus.). (J). (ps-3). 1996. 10.95 (*0-694-00716-1*, HarpFestival) HarpC Child Bks.

— Grouchy Ladybug, The (Spanish edition) La mariquita malhumorada. L'Hoeste, Simon S., tr. from SPA. LC 95-35719. (SPA., Illus.). 48p. (J). (gr. k-2). 1996. 16.95 (*0-06-027089-6*, HpArco Iris) HarpC Child Bks.

— Grouchy Ladybug, The (Spanish edition) La mariquita malhumorada. L'Hoeste, Simon S., tr. from SPA. LC 95-35719. (Trophy Picture Bk.). (SPA., Illus.). 48p. (J). (ps-1). 1996. pap. 7.95 (*0-06-443449-4*, HpArco Iris) HarpC Child Bks.

— Have You Seen My Cat? (Illus.). 24p. (J). (ps-k). 1996. bds. 6.99 (*0-689-80378-8*) Litle Simon.

— Have You Seen My Cat? LC 88-4170. (Illus.). 32p. (J). (ps). 1988. 5.95 (*0-399-21597-2*, Philomel) Peng Put Young Read.

— Have You Seen My Cat? LC 87-15262. (Illus.). 28p. (J). (ps up). 1991. 16.00 (*0-88708-054-5*, Picture Book Studio) S&S Childrens.

— Have You Seen My Cat? (Illus.). 32p. (J). (ps-3). 1991. 4.99 (*0-590-44461-1*, Blue Ribbon Bks) Scholastic Inc.

— Have You Seen My Cat? (J). 1997. 11.19 (*0-606-12962-6*, Pub. by Turtleback) Demco.

— Have You Seen My Cat? 97th ed. (Illus.). 32p. (J). (ps-2). 1997. per. 5.99 (*0-689-81731-2*) S&S Childrens.

***Carle, Eric.** Hello, Red Fox. (J). 1998. per. write for info. (*0-689-00581-4*) S&S Childrens.

Carle, Eric. Hello, Red Fox. LC 97-15473. 32p. (J). (ps-4). 1998. per. 15.99 (*0-689-81775-4*) S&S Trade.

— The Honeybee & the Robber: A Pop-Up Book. LC 80-23936. (Illus.). 16p. (J). (ps-3). 1995. 18.95 (*0-399-20767-8*, Philomel) Peng Put Young Read.

— A House for Hermit Crab. LC 87-29261. (Illus.). 32p. (J). (ps up). 1991. 16.00 (*0-88708-056-1*, Picture Book Studio) S&S Childrens.

— A House for Hermit Crab. LC 90-25388. (Pixies Ser.). (Illus.). 32p. (J). (gr. k up). 1991. reprint ed. 4.95 (*0-88708-168-1*, Picture Book Studio) S&S Childrens.

— I See a Song. LC 72-9249. 32p. (J). (ps-3). 1996. pap. text 4.95 (*0-590-25213-5*) Scholastic Inc.

— I See a Song. LC 72-9249. 1996. 10.15 (*0-606-09449-0*, Pub. by Turtleback) Demco.

— Let's Paint a Rainbow. (Play-&-Read Book Ser.). (Illus.). 12p. (YA). (ps). 1998. bds. 6.95 (*0-590-32844-1*, Cartwheel) Scholastic Inc.

— Little Cloud. LC 95-38119. (Illus.). 32p. (J). (gr. k-2). 1996. 15.95 (*0-399-23034-3*, Philomel) Peng Put Young Read.

— Little Cloud. LC 98-189863. (Illus.). 28p. (J). (ps-1). 1998. bds. 6.99 (*0-399-23191-9*, Philomel) Peng Put Young Read.

Carle, Eric. Mixed-Up Chameleon. (J). 1984. 12.15 (*0-606-03618-0*, Pub. by Turtleback) Demco.

Carle, Eric. The Mixed-Up Chameleon. rev. ed. LC 83-45950. (Trophy Picture Bk.). (Illus.). 32p. (J). (ps-3). 1988. reprint ed. pap. 6.95 (*0-06-443162-2*, HarpTrophy) HarpC Child Bks.

— The Mixed-Up Chameleon Board Book. 32p. (J). (ps up). 1998. 7.95 (*0-694-01147-9*) HarpC Child Bks.

— The Mixed-Up Chameleon Revised. 2nd ed. LC 83-45950. (Illus.). 32p. (J). (ps-3). 1984. 15.95 (*0-690-04396-1*); lib. bdg. 15.89 (*0-690-04397-X*) HarpC Child Bks.

— The Mixed-Up Chameleon Sticker Book. LC 75-5505. (Illus.). 32p. (J). (ps-2). 1993. 7.95 (*0-694-00448-0*, HarpFestival) HarpC Child Bks.

— My Apron. (Illus.). 32p. (J). (gr. k). 1994. 22.95 (*0-399-22824-1*, Philomel) Peng Put Young Read.

— My Apron. LC 93-36342. (Illus.). 40p. (J). (gr. 1 up). 1995. 13.95 (*0-399-22685-0*, Philomel) Peng Put Young Read.

Carle, Eric. MY VERY 1ST BK COLORS. LC 72-83776. (My Very First Library). (Illus.). 10p. (J). (ps-1). 1985. 4.95 (*0-694-00011-6*) HarpC Child Bks.

— MY VERY 1ST BK NUMBERS. LC 72-83777. (My Very First Library). (Illus.). 10p. (J). (ps-1). 1985. 4.95 (*0-694-00012-4*) HarpC Child Bks.

Carle, Eric. My Very First Book of Colors. LC 72-83776. (My Very First Library). (Illus.). 10p. (J). (ps). 1985. 2.95 (*0-690-57365-0*) HarpC Child Bks.

Carle, Eric. MY VERY 1ST BK FOOD. LC 85-45259. (My Very First Library). (Illus.). 10p. (J). (ps). 1986. 2.95 (*0-694-00130-9*) HarpC Child Bks.

— MY VERY 1ST BK HEADS. LC 85-45260. (My Very First Library). (Illus.). 10p. (J). (ps). 1986. 2.95 (*0-694-00128-7*) HarpC Child Bks.

Carle, Eric. My Very First Book of Numbers. LC 72-8377. (My Very First Library). (Illus.). 10p. (J). (ps). 1985. 2.95 (*0-690-57366-9*) HarpC Child Bks.

— My Very First Book of Shapes. LC 72-83778. (My Very First Library). (Illus.). 10p. (J). (ps). 1985. 2.95 (*0-690-57367-7*) HarpC Child Bks.

Carle, Eric. MY VERY 1ST BK OF SHAPES. LC 72-83778. (My Very First Library). (Illus.). 10p. (J). (ps-1). 1985. 4.95 (*0-694-00013-2*) HarpC Child Bks.

— MY VERY 1ST BK TOOLS. LC 85-45258. (My Very First Library). (Illus.). 10p. (J). (ps). 1986. 2.95 (*0-694-00129-5*) HarpC Child Bks.

— MY VERY 1ST BK TOUCH. LC 84-47894. (My Very First Library). (Illus.). 10p. (J). (ps). 1986. 2.95 (*0-694-00095-7*) HarpC Child Bks.

Carle, Eric. My Very First Book of Words. LC 72-83779. (My Very First Library). (Illus.). 10p. (J). (ps-1). 1985. 2.95 (*0-690-57368-5*) HarpC Child Bks.

Carle, Eric. MY VERY 1ST BK WORDS. LC 72-83779. (My Very First Library). (Illus.). 10p. (J). (ps-1). 1985. 4.95 (*0-694-00014-0*) HarpC Child Bks.

Carle, Eric. One, Two, Three to the Zoo. LC 81-8609. (Illus.). 32p. (J). (ps-1). 1982. 15.95 (*0-399-61172-X*, Philomel) Peng Put Young Read.

— One, Two, Three to the Zoo. (Illus.). 34p. (J). (ps-2). 1990. pap. 7.95 (*0-399-21970-6*, Sandcastle Bks) Putnam Pub Group.

— 1, 2, 3 to the Zoo: A Counting Book. (J). 1968. 13.15 (*0-606-04498-1*, Pub. by Turtleback) Demco.

— La Oruga Muy Hambrienta (The Very Hungry Caterpillar) LC 79-13202. (SPA., Illus.). 32p. (J). (ps-2). 1994. 18.95 (*0-399-22780-6*, Philomel) Peng Put Young Read.

— Pancakes, Pancakes! LC 88-32438. (Illus.). 32p. (J). (ps-3). 1998. per. 5.99 (*0-689-82246-4*) Aladdin.

— Pancakes, Pancakes! 40p. (J). (ps-3). 1992. 5.95 (*0-590-44453-0*, Blue Ribbon Bks) Scholastic Inc.

Carle, Eric. Pancakes, Pancakes! (Blue Ribbon Bks.). (J). 1990. 11.19 (*0-606-02825-0*, Pub. by Turtleback) Demco.

Carle, Eric. Pancakes, Pancakes! LC 88-32438. (Illus.). 32p. (J). (ps up). 1991. reprint ed. 16.00 (*0-88708-120-7*, Picture Book Studio) S&S Childrens.

— Pancakes, Pancakes! Mini Book. LC 88-32438. (Illus.). 28p. (J). 1992. 4.95 (*0-88708-275-0*, Picture Book Studio) S&S Childrens.

— Papa, Please Get the Moon for Me. LC 91-14561. (Pixies Ser.). (Illus.). 28p. (J). (gr. k up). 1991. 5.95 (*0-88708-177-0*) S&S Childrens.

— Papa, Please Get the Moon for Me. LC 85-29785. (Illus.). 40p. (J). (ps up). 1991. 19.00 (*0-88708-026-X*, Picture Book Studio) S&S Childrens.

***Carle, Eric.** Papa Please Get the Moon for Me. (Illus.). 32p. (J). (gr. k-3). 1999. pap. 9.99 (*0-689-82959-0*) Litle Simon.

Carle, Eric. Rooster's Off to See the World. LC 86-25509. (Illus.). 28p. (J). (ps up). 1991. 16.00 (*0-88708-042-1*, Picture Book Studio) S&S Childrens.

— Rooster's Off to See the World. (Illus.). 32p. (J). (ps-3). 1997. pap. 12.95 (*0-689-81772-X*) S&S Childrens.

— Rooster's Off to See the World. LC 86-25509. (Illus.). 32p. (ps-3). 1999. per. 5.99 (*0-689-82684-2*, 076714005990) S&S Childrens.

— Rooster's Off to See the World. LC 91-15246. (Pixies Ser.). (Illus.). 28p. (J). (gr. k up). 1992. reprint ed. 4.95 (*0-88708-178-9*, Picture Book Studio) S&S Childrens.

— Roosters off to See the World. rev. ed. (Illus.). 32p. (J). (ps-3). 1998. pap. 12.95 (*0-689-82158-1*) S&S Childrens.

— The Secret Birthday Message. LC 75-168726. (Illus.). 32p. (J). (ps-3). 1972. 15.95 (*0-690-72347-4*); lib. bdg. 15.89 (*0-690-72348-2*) HarpC Child Bks.

— The Secret Birthday Message. LC 85-45403. (Trophy Picture Bk.). (Illus.). 32p. (J). (ps-3). 1986. pap. 6.95 (*0-06-443099-5*, HarpTrophy) HarpC Child Bks.

— Secret Birthday Message. 1986. 11.15 (*0-606-00976-0*, Pub. by Turtleback) Demco.

— The Secret Birthday Message: Miniature Edition. LC 91-8306. (Illus.). 26p. (J). (ps-3). 1991. 4.95 (*0-06-020102-9*) HarpC Child Bks.

— The Secret Birthday Message Board Book. (Illus.). 22p. (J). (ps up). 1998. 7.95 (*0-694-01148-7*) HarpC Child Bks.

— Stories for All Seasons: A House for Hermit Crab; The Tiny Seed; Rooster's off to See the World. LC 98-85110. (Illus.). 96p. (J). (ps up). 1998. 19.95 (*0-689-82225-1*) S&S Bks Yung.

— The Tiny Seed. LC 86-2534. (Illus.). 36p. (J). (ps up). 1991. 16.00 (*0-88708-015-4*, Picture Book Studio) S&S Childrens.

— The Tiny Seed. 2nd ed. LC 86-2534. (Pixies Ser.). (Illus.). 36p. (J). (gr. k up). 1991. reprint ed. 4.95 (*0-88708-155-X*, Picture Book Studio) S&S Childrens.

— The Tiny Seed Mini-Book & Seed Set. (Illus.). 40p. (J). (ps-3). 1998. per. 12.95 (*0-689-81966-8*) Litle Simon.

— Today Is Monday. LC 91-45866. (Illus.). 32p. (J). (ps-1). 1993. 15.95 (*0-399-21966-8*, Philomel) Peng Put Young Read.

— Today Is Monday. (Illus.). 32p. (J). (ps-1). 1997. pap. 6.99 (*0-698-11563-5*, PapStar) Peng Put Young Read.

Carle, Eric. Today Is Monday. (J). 1997. 12.15 (*0-606-11994-9*, Pub. by Turtleback) Demco.

Carle, Eric. The Very Busy Spider. LC 84-5907. (Illus.). 22p. (J). (ps-3). 1985. 19.95 (*0-399-21166-7*, Philomel) Peng Put Young Read.

— The Very Busy Spider. LC 84-5907. (Illus.). 24p. (J). (ps-2). 1989. 6.95 (*0-399-21592-1*, Philomel) Peng Put Young Read.

— The Very Busy Spider. LC 84-5907. (Illus.). 24p. (J). (ps up). 1995. bds. 9.95 (*0-399-22919-1*, Philomel) Peng Put Young Read.

***Carle, Eric.** The Very Busy Spider. (Illus.). 32p. (J). 2000. 15.99 (*0-399-23566-3*) Peng Put Young Read.

Carle, Eric. The Very Clumsy Click Beetle. LC 97-33417. (Illus.). 32p. (J). 1999. 22.99 (*0-399-23201-X*, Philomel) Peng Put Young Read.

— The Very Clumsy Click Beetle. 1998. 275.88 (*0-399-23264-8*) Putnam Pub Group.

— The Very Hungry Caterpillar. LC 79-13202. (Illus.). 26p. (J). (ps-2). 1969. 19.99 (*0-399-20853-4*, Philomel) Peng Put Young Read.

— The Very Hungry Caterpillar. LC 79-13202. (Illus.). 23p. (J). (ps-3). 1986. 15.95 (*0-399-21301-5*, Philomel) Peng Put Young Read.

— The Very Hungry Caterpillar. LC 79-13202. (Illus.). 26p. (J). (ps up). 1994. bds. 9.99 (*0-399-22690-7*, Philomel) Peng Put Young Read.

— The Very Hungry Caterpillar. (CHI & ENG., Illus.). 28p. (J). (ps-2). pap. 6.95 (*1-85269-126-3*); pap. 6.95 (*1-85269-130-1*) Writers & Readers.

— The Very Hungry Caterpillar. (ARA & ENG., Illus.). 28p. (J). (ps-5). pap. 6.95 (*1-85269-124-7*) Writers & Readers.

— The Very Hungry Caterpillar: Mini Book & Plush Package. (Illus.). 26p. (J). (ps-3). 1991. 15.95 (*0-399-22049-6*, Philomel) Peng Put Young Read.

Carle, Eric. The Very Hungry Caterpillar Plush Caterpillar. 4.00 (*0-399-21659-6*) Peng Put Young Read.

Carle, Eric. The Very Lonely Firefly. LC 94-27827. (Illus.). 27p. (J). (ps-3). 1995. 19.95 (*0-399-22774-1*, Philomel) Peng Put Young Read.

— The Very Lonely Firefly. (Illus.). 32p. (J). (ps). 1999. bds. 10.99 (*0-399-23427-6*, Philomel) Peng Put Young Read.

— The Very Quiet Cricket. LC 89-78317. (Illus.). 26p. (J). (ps-k). 1997. bds. 10.99 (*0-399-22684-2*, Philomel) Peng Put Young Read.

— The Very Quiet Cricket: A Multi-Sensory Book. LC 89-78317. (Illus.). 28p. (J). (ps-3). 1990. 19.99 (*0-399-21885-8*, Philomel) Peng Put Young Read.

— Walter the Baker. 40p. (J). 1998. mass mkt. 5.99 (*0-689-82088-7*) Aladdin.

— Walter the Baker. LC 94-32364. (Illus.). 40p. (J). (ps-3). 1995. mass mkt. 16.00 (*0-689-80078-9*) S&S Bks Yung.

— Walter the Baker. LC 93-20124. (J). (gr. 1-8). 1993. 15.95 (*0-88708-331-5*, Picture Book Studio) S&S Childrens.

***Carle, Eric.** Walter the Baker. (J). 1998. 11.19 (*0-606-13888-9*, Pub. by Turtleback) Demco.

Carle, Eric. What's for Lunch? (Play-&-Read Book Ser.). (Illus.). 12p. (J). (ps). 1998. bds. 6.95 (*0-590-32842-5*) Scholastic Inc.

— You Can Make a Collage: A Very Simple How-To Book. LC 98-235168. (Illus.). 72p. (J). (gr. k up). 1998. student ed., spiral bd. 19.95 (*1-57054-207-4*) Klutz.

Carle, Eric. The Hole in the Dike. 32p. (J). (ps-2). 1993. pap. 4.95 (*0-590-46146-X*) Scholastic Inc.

Carle, Eric, et al. Eric Carle's Treasury of Classic Stories for Children. LC 87-22072. (Illus.). 160p. (J). (ps-4). 1988. 24.95 (*0-531-05742-9*) Orchard Bks Watts.

***Carle, Gilda.** He's Not All That! How to Attract the Good Guys. LC 00-43062. 2001. write for info. (*0-06-019924-5*, Cliff Street) HarperTrade.

Carle, James, tr. see Dabrowski, Hans-Peter.

Carle, James, tr. see Nowarra, Heinz J.

Carle, Jan. How to Begin & End a Conversation in Unforgettable Style. 1997. 8.95 (*0-533-12022-5*) Vantage.

Carle, John, ed. Silhouettes in the Electric Sky: The Best Poetry from Two Years of Gravity. LC 98-96655. (Illus.). 128p. 1998. pap. 12.00 (*0-9667228-0-9*) Newtons Baby.

Carle, M., jt. auth. see Pastor, Reyna.

Carle, Robert D. & DeCaro, Louis A., Jr., eds. Signs of Hope in the City: Ministries of Community Renewal. rev. ed. LC 99-29086. 280p. 1999. pap. 18.00 (*0-8170-1324-5*) Judson.

Carle, S., jt. auth. see Aiken, Conrad.

Carle, Teet, jt. auth. see Webb, Richard.

Carlebach, Diane. Peace Scholars: Learning Through Literature, Grade 3. Burke, James A., II et al, eds. (Illus.). 206p. (J). (gr. 3). 1996. pap. text, teacher ed. 29.95 (*1-878227-44-0*) Peace Educ.

— Peace Scholars: Learning Through Literature, Student Activity Book. Burke, James A., II et al, eds. (Illus.). 72p. (J). (gr. 3). 1996. pap. text 3.39 (*1-878227-45-9*) Peace Educ.

Carlebach, Diane & Dickmann, Catherine H. Peace Scholars: Learning Through Literature, Grade 4. Burke, James A., II, ed. (Peace Scholars: Learning Through Literature Ser.). (Illus.). (J). 1999. pap., teacher ed. 29.95 (*1-878227-55-6*) Peace Educ.

Carlebach, Elisheva. In Pursuit of Hersey: Rabbi Moses Hagiz & the Sabbatian Controversy. 364p. 1994. pap. 25.50 (*0-231-07191-4*) Col U Pr.

Carlebach, Elisheva, ed. see Yerushalmi, Yosef H.

Carlebach, Joseph. Ausgewahlte Schriften, 2 vols. Gillis-Carlebach, Miriam, ed. (GER.). xviii, 1351p. 1982. write for info. (*3-487-07140-1*) G Olms Pubs.

Carlebach, Michael, Jr., jt. auth. see Provenzo, Eugene F.

Carlebach, Michael L. American Photo Journalism Comes of Age. LC 97-17446. (Illus.). 224p. (Orig.). 1997. pap. 29.95 (*1-56098-786-3*) Smithsonian.

— The Origins of Photojournalism in America. LC 91-40145. (Illus.). 208p. (Orig.). 1992. pap. 29.95 (*1-56098-159-8*) Smithsonian.

Carlebach, Shlomo & Mesinai, Susan Y. Shlomo's Stories: Selected Tales. LC 94-7560. 296p. 1995. 30.00 (*1-56821-215-1*) Aronson.

Carlee, Roberta. The Last Gladiator. LC 79-91303. (Illus.). 291p. 1979. 12.50 (*0-935680-00-4*) Kentucke Imprints.

Carleen, Sally. A Bride in Waiting: On the Way to a Wedding. (Romance Ser.: No. 1376). 1999. per. 3.50 (*0-373-19376-9*, 1-19376-2) Silhouette.

— Cody's Christmas Wish. 1995. per. 2.99 (*0-373-19124-3*, 1-19124-6) Silhouette.

— L' Enfant Retrouve. (FRE.). 1998. mass mkt. 3.50 (*0-373-39478-0*, 1-39478-2) Harlequin Bks.

— A Gift for the Groom: On the Way to a Wedding... (Romance Ser.: Bk. 1382). 1999. per. 3.50 (*0-373-19382-3*, 1-19382-0) Silhouette.

— An Improbable Wife. (Romance Ser.). 1995. per. 2.99 (*0-373-19101-4*, 1-19101-4) Silhouette.

— My Favorite Husband. (Romance Ser.). 1996. per. 3.25 (*0-373-19183-9*, 1-19183-2) Silhouette.

— Un Papa pour Noel. (Horizon Ser.: Bk. 492). 1999. mass mkt. 3.50 (*0-373-39492-6*, 1-39492-3) Harlequin Bks.

— Porcupine Ranch. 1997. per. 3.25 (*0-373-19221-5*, 1-19221-0) Silhouette.

— The Prince's Heir. (Romance Ser.: No. 1397). 1999. per. 3.50 (*0-373-19397-1*, 1-19397-8) Silhouette.

— With This Child . . . (Romance Ser.: No. 1281). 1998. per. 3.50 (*0-373-19281-9*, 1-19281-4) Silhouette.

Carlen, Claudia, ed. The Papal Encyclicals, 1740-1981, 5 vols., Set. LC 81-84885. 1990. 495.00 (*0-87650-259-1*) Pierian.

— Papal Pronouncements, a Guide, 1740-1978, 2 vols., Set. 1991. 195.00 (*0-87650-266-4*) Pierian.

Carlen, Daniel D. How to Get Out of the Woods. . . When You find Yourself Hunkered down in Your Favorite Hiding Place. Bayuk, Shelah S., ed. 15p. 1998. pap. 2.50 (*1-892172-04-6*) Writing Matters.

Carlen, Eric, et al, eds. Advances in Differential Equations & Mathematical Physics: 1997 Georgia Tech-UAB International Conference on Differential Equations & Mathematical Physics, March 23-29, 1997, Georgia Institute of Technology. LC 97-48877. (Contemporary Mathematics Ser.: Vol. 217). 221p. 1998. pap. 44.00 (*0-8218-0861-3*, CONM/217) Am Math.

Carlen, Henry. Live Healthier, Live Longer. large type ed. 195p. 1997. pap. 12.95 (*0-9654810-0-X*) Nutri-fit Pubns.

Carlen, Louis & Faussner, Hans C. Nikolaus Grass: Alm und Wein. (GER.). x, 436p. 1990. 128.00 (*3-615-00036-6*, Pub. by Weidmann) Lubrecht & Cramer.

— Nikolaus Grass: Ausgewahlte Aufsatze zum 80. Geburtstag. (GER.). xix, 545p. 1993. 148.00 (*3-615-00095-1*, Pub. by Weidmann) Lubrecht & Cramer.

Carlen, Pat. Jigsaw: A Political Criminology of Youth Homelessness. 192p. (C). 1996. 112.95 (*0-335-19681-0*); pap. 31.95 (*0-335-19680-2*) OpUniv Pr.

Carlen, Pat, et al, eds. Criminal Women: Some Autobiographical Accounts. 252p. 1993. pap. 24.95 (*0-7456-0088-3*) Blackwell Pubs.

Carlen, Pat & Collison, Mike, eds. Radical Issues in Criminology. 212p. 1980. 44.00 (*0-389-20083-2*, 06856) B&N Imports.

Carlen, Pat & Cook, Dee. Paying for Crime. 176p. 1989. 113.00 (*0-335-09938-6*); pap. 34.95 (*0-335-09937-8*) OpUniv Pr.

Carlen, Pat & Worrall, Anne, eds. Gender, Crime & Justice. 224p. 1987. pap. 34.95 (*0-335-15504-9*) OpUniv Pr.

Carlen, Pat, et al. Truancy: The Politics of Compulsory Schooling. 176p. 1992. 123.00 (*0-335-09615-8*); pap. 34.95 (*0-335-09614-X*) OpUniv Pr.

Carleo. ATC Modules Part 2: Automotive Parts. 1997. 38.95 (*0-8273-8509-9*) Delmar.

Carleone, J., ed. Tactical Missile Warheads. (PAAS Ser.: Vol. 155). 745p. 1993. 109.95 (*1-56347-067-5*, V-155) AIAA.

Carles, Emilie. A Life of Her Own: The Transformation of a Countrywoman in 20th-Century France. Goldberger, Avriel H., tr. (Illus.). 304p. 1992. pap. 14.95 (*0-14-016965-2*, Penguin Bks) Viking Penguin.

Carles, M., ed. see Pidal, Ramon M.

Carles, Philippe. Dictionnaire du Jazz. (FRE.). 1160p. 1988. pap. 55.00 (*0-7859-7798-8*, 2221045165) Fr & Eur.

Carlesi, M., jt. auth. see Bjarnson, B. A.

Carlesimo, Thomas F., tr. see Brown, Mary E., ed.

Carleson, David, jt. auth. see Dickson, Bruce.

Carleson, L. & Gamelin, T. Complex Dynamics. LC 92-32457. (Universitext Ser.). (Illus.). 175p. 1996. 34.95 (*0-387-97942-5*) Spr-Verlag.

Carleson, Lennart, jt. auth. see Salem, Raphael.

Carleson, Thomas E., et al, eds. Separation Techniques in Nuclear Waste Management. 334p. 1995. boxed set 249.00 (*0-8493-4876-5*, 4876) CRC Pr.

Carless, Jacqueline, jt. auth. see Simpson, Struan.

Carless, Jennifer. Renewable Energy: A Concise Guide to Green Alternatives. LC 92-35137. 224p. (YA). 1993. 19.95 (*0-8027-8214-0*) Walker & Co.

— Taking Out the Trash: A No-Nonsense Guide to Recycling. LC 91-43855. 249p. 1992. pap. 19.95 (*1-55963-170-8*) Island Pr.

Carleton, A. Cold Air Mesocyclones in the Arctic & Antarctic. 396p. 1996. pap. text 42.00 (*90-5699-061-6*) Gordon & Breach.

Carleton, Andrew M. Satellite Remote Sensing in Climatology. 1991. 99.95 (*0-8493-7720-X*) CRC Pr.

Carleton College Faculty Staff. Plain Songs: Stories & Poems by Carleton Writers. (Orig.). 1990. pap. 11.95 (*0-9613911-5-4*) Carleton Coll.

Carleton, Don E. Breed So Rare: The Life of J. R. Parten, Liberal Texas Oilman, 1896-1992. LC 98-14630. (Illus.). 50p. 1998. 39.95 (*0-87611-166-5*) Tex St Hist Assn.

Carleton, F. J. & Agalloco, J. P. Validation of Pharmaceutical Processes. 2nd expanded rev. ed. LC 98-44757. (Illus.). 856p. 1998. text 195.00 (*0-8247-9384-6*, 9384-6) Dekker.

***Carleton, Geoffrey.** Birds of Essex County, New York. 3rd rev. ed. Peterson, John M., ed. & photos by by. Greene, Warren et al, photos by. LC 99-72086. (Illus.). viii, 56p. 1999. pap. 8.95 (*0-9668819-1-5*) High Peaks.

Carleton, George W., ed. Suppressed Book about Slavery. LC 68-28987. (American Negro: His History & Literature. Series 1). (Illus.). 1978. reprint ed. 21.95 (*0-405-01806-1*) Ayer.

Carleton, Gregory. The Politics of Reception: Critical Constructions of Mikhail Zoshenko. LC 98-29222. (Studies in Russian Literature & Theory). 248p. 1998. text 54.95 (*0-8101-1609-X*) Northwestern U Pr.

***Carleton, Hiram.** Genealogical & Family History of the State of Vermont: A Record of the Achievements of Her People in the Making of a Commonwealth & the Founding of a Nation, 2 vols. (Illus.). 1474p. 2000. reprint ed. pap. 145.00 (*0-8063-4794-5*, Pub. by Clearfield Co) ACCESS Pubs Network.

Carleton, James H. The Prairie Logbooks: Dragoon Campaigns to the Pawnee Villages in 1844, & to the Rocky Mountains in 1845. Pelzer, Louis, ed. & intro. by. LC 82-24755. 311p. 1983. reprint ed. pap. 96.50 (*0-608-03489-4*, 206420400008) Bks Demand.

Carleton, Jerry, jt. auth. see Stock, Edwin.

Carleton, Jetta. The Moonflower Vine. (J). 1995. reprint ed. lib. bdg. 24.95 (*1-56849-617-6*) Buccaneer Bks.

Carleton, Mark T. River Capital: An Illustrated History of Baton Rouge. LC 96-78831. (Illus.). 274p. 1996. 39.95 (*0-9654754-0-9*) Am Historical Pr.

Carleton, Nancy, ed. see Barnes, Robert.

Carleton, Nancy, ed. see Heart, Kimberley.

Carleton, Nancy, ed. see Huffines, LaUna.

Carleton, Nancy, ed. see Loomans, Diane.

Carleton, Nancy, ed. see Loomans, Diane & Loomans, Julia.

Carleton, Nancy, ed. see Miller, Carolyn G.

Carleton, Nancy, ed. see Millman, Dan.

Carleton, Nancy, ed. see Parker, Alice A.

Carleton, Nancy, ed. see Roads, Michael J.

Carleton, Nancy, ed. see Taylor, Terry L.

Carleton, R. Milton. Vegetables for Today's Gardens. 1979. pap. 2.00 (*0-87980-226-X*) Wilshire.

Carleton, R. O., jt. auth. see Jaffe, A.

Carleton University History Collaborative Staff. Urban & Community Development in Atlantic Canada, 1867-1991: Enterprise in a Maritime Setting, 1787-1920. (Mercury Ser.: History No. 44). (Illus.). 146p. 1994. pap. 19.95 (*0-660-14017-9*, Pub. by CN Mus Civilization) U of Wash Pr.

Carleton, William. The Black Prophet, 1847. LC 96-2990. (Hibernia Ser.). (Illus.). 1996. 105.00 (*1-85477-216-3*) Continuum.

— Fardorougha the Miser: or The Convicts of Lisnamona. LC 79-8245. reprint ed. 44.50 (*0-404-61805-7*) AMS Pr.

— The Tithe Proctor: Being a Tale of the Tithe Rebellion in Ireland. LC 79-8246. reprint ed. 44.50 (*0-404-61806-5*) AMS Pr.

— Traits & Stories of the Irish Peasantry, I. (Illus.). (C). 1990. text 72.00 (*0-389-20908-2*) B&N Imports.

— Traits & Stories of the Irish Peasantry, II. (Illus.). (C). 1990. text 72.00 (*0-389-20909-0*); pap. text 22.00 (*0-389-20942-2*) B&N Imports.

— Traits & Stories of the Irish Peasantry: With Illustrations by Phiz, Wrightson Lee & Others, 4 Vols. LC 79-163022. (Short Story Index Reprint Ser.). (Illus.). 1977. reprint ed. 88.95 (*0-8369-3936-0*) Ayer.

— Valentine M'Clutchy; The Irish Agent: The Chronicles of Castle Cumber Property, with the Pious Aspirations of Solomon M'Slime, 3 vols., 2 bks., Set. LC 79-8247. reprint ed. 84.50 (*0-404-61807-3*) AMS Pr.

— Works of William Carleton, 2 Vols, Set. LC 77-106257. (Short Story Index Reprint Ser.). 1977. 96.95 (*0-8369-3294-3*) Ayer.

Carletti, Alessandro, jt. auth. see Ghisotti, Andrea.

Carletti, Silvana, et al. The Library-Classroom Connection. 136p. (C). 1991. pap. text 18.00 (*0-435-08711-8*, 08711) Heinemann.

Carletti, Silvana, et al. The Library Classroom Connection. 136p. (J). 1994. pap. 24.25 (*0-921217-66-8*) Pembroke Pubs.

Carlevale, John M. Observing, Recording, Interpreting Child Behavior: Guide & Workbook. 2nd rev. ed. 120p. 1990. pap. text 15.95 (*0-940139-15-4*) Consortium RI.

Carlevale, John M., Sr. Observing, Recording, Interpreting Child Behavior: Guide & Workbook. 3rd rev. ed. 124p. 1997. pap. text 14.95 (*0-940139-44-8*) Consortium RI.

Carlevale, John M. Parent & Child Relations. 256p. (C). 1991. pap. text 16.95 (*0-940139-23-5*) Consortium RI.

— Parent & Child Relations. 2nd ed. (Illus.). 292p. 1999. text 22.95 (*0-940139-49-9*) Consortium RI.

— Student Teaching Manual. 3rd ed. 230p. 1997. pap. text 19.95 (*0-940139-36-7*) Consortium RI.

Carley. Introduction to Electrical & Computer Engineering. 1999. lab manual ed. 15.74 (*0-07-012008-0*) McGraw.

— Introduction to Electrical & Computer Engineering. 2000. 60.50 (*0-07-012007-2*) McGraw.

— Sharing the World: Sustainable Living & Global Equity in the Twenty-First Century. LC 98-191036. 227p. 1998. text 59.95 (*0-312-21367-0*) St Martin.

— Technical Guide to Automotive Emission Systems: Education Version. (Automotive Technology Ser.). 1994. pap. 34.95 (*0-8273-7135-7*, VNR) Wiley.

Carley, A. F. & Morgan, P. H. Computational Methods in the Chemical Sciences. (Ellis Horwood Series in Inorganic Chemistry). 1989. text 115.00 (*0-470-21490-2*) P-H.

Carley, Dave. Taking Liberties & Into: Taking Liberties. LC 93-228796. 96p. (Orig.). 1997. pap. 10.95 (*0-88754-512-2*) Theatre Comm.

— A View from the Roof. LC 98-135039. 96p. (Orig.). 1998. pap. 12.95 (*0-88754-525-4*) Theatre Comm.

Carley, Edward, III, photos by. If Only Words Could Say. (Illus.). 64p. (Orig.). 1997. pap. 10.00 (*1-890138-00-2*) Poet Journals.

— Words Just Keep on Coming: Rap Is Poetry but Poetry Ain't All Rap. (Illus.). 64p. (Orig.). 1997. pap. 10.00 (*1-890138-02-9*) Poet Journals.

Carley, Isabel M. Simple Settings of American Folk Songs & Rhymes for Orff Ensemble, Bk. 1: CDEGA Pentatonic. 1974. pap. 2.00 (*0-918812-06-2*, SE 0122) MMB Music.

— Simple Settings of American Folk Songs & Rhymes for Orff Ensemble, Bk. 2: CDEGA Pentatonic. 2nd rev. ed. 1974. reprint ed. pap. 2.00 (*0-918812-07-0*, SE 0123) MMB Music.

Carley, James, intro. Arthurian Poets: Algernon Charles Swinburne. 256p. (Orig.). 1996. pap. 29.95 (*0-85115-546-4*) Boydell & Brewer.

Carley, James F., ed. Whittington's Dictionary of Plastics. 3rd expanded rev. ed. LC 93-60943. 575p. (Orig.). (C). 1993. 99.95 (*1-56676-090-9*) Technomic.

***Carley, James P., ed.** Glastonbury Abbey & the Arthurian Tradition. (Arthurian Studies: Vol. 0261-9814). 384p. 2000. 75.00 (*0-85991-572-7*) Boydell & Brewer.

Carley, James P., intro. Arthurian Poets: Matthew Arnold & William Morris. 90p. 1995. reprint ed. pap. 17.95 (*0-85115-544-8*) Boydell & Brewer.

Carley, James P. & Riddy, Felicity, eds. Arthurian Literature, No. XII. (Illus.). 208p. (C). 1993. 75.00 (*0-85991-397-X*, DS Brewer) Boydell & Brewer.

— Arthurian Literature, Vol. XIII. (Illus.). 199p. (C). 1995. 75.00 (*0-85991-449-6*, DS Brewer) Boydell & Brewer.

— Arthurian Literature, Vol. XV. (Illus.). 228p. 1997. 75.00 (*0-85991-518-2*) Boydell & Brewer.

— Arthurian Literature, Vol. 16. 226p. 1998. 75.00 (*0-85991-531-X*) Boydell & Brewer.

— Arthurian Literature XIV, Vol. 14. (Arthurian Literature Ser.). (Illus.). 180p. 1996. 75.00 (*0-85991-482-8*) Boydell & Brewer.

Carley, James P., jt. ed. see Abrams, Lesley.

Carley, James P., jt. ed. see Shichtman, Martin B.

***Carley, Jeanne.** Flower Child. 1999. 10.95 (*0-7407-0131-2*) Andrews & McMeel.

— Grin & Ferret: A Warm & Fuzzy Guide to Life. 1999. 4.95 (*0-7407-0132-0*) Andrews & McMeel.

— Warm & Fuzzy Friends: A Ferret Guide to Friendship. 2000. pap. 4.95 (*0-7407-1210-1*) Andrews & McMeel.

Carley, Joyce. Spirit Verse: The Ten Commandments & Other Twentieth Century Perspectives. 130p. 1999. pap. 12.00 (*1-890138-03-7*) Poet Journals.

Carley, Kathleen M. & Prietula, Michael J., eds. Computational Organization Theory. 336p. 1994. text 69.95 (*0-8058-1406-X*) L Erlbaum Assocs.

Carley, Kathleen M., jt. auth. see Kaufer, David S.

Carley, Ken. Gems & Stones: Scientific Properties & Aspects of Twenty Two-A Comparative Study Based upon the Edgar Cayce Psychic Readings. rev. ed. 73p. 1979. pap. 6.95 (*0-87604-110-1*, 214) ARE Pr.

***Carley, Kenneth.** Minnesota in the Civil War: An Illustrated History. LC 00-40180. (Illus.). 2000. write for info. (*0-87351-387-8*) Minnesota Historical Society.

Carley, Kenneth. The Sioux Uprising of 1862. rev. ed. LC 76-16499. (Illus.). v, 102p. 1976. pap. 8.50 (*0-87351-103-4*) Minn Hist.

Carley, L. Richard. Experimental Context for Introduction to Electrical & Computer Engineering. 2nd ed. (C). 1997. pap. 37.81 (*0-07-290362-7*) McGrw-H Hghr Educ.

Carley, L. Richard & Gyurcsik, Ronald S., eds. Computer-Aided Design of Analog Circuits & Systems. LC 93-17165. (International Series in Engineering & Computer Science, VLSI, Computer Architecture, & Digital Screen Processing). 120p. (C). 1993. text 127.00 (*0-7923-9351-1*) Kluwer Academic.

Carley, L. Richard, jt. auth. see Moon, Jaekyun.

Carley, Larry. LP-Gas Training Guidebooks, 5 vols., Set. Fox, John B., ed. 1984. pap. 100.00 (*0-88466-004-4*) NPGA.

— A Technician's Guide to Auto Emission Systems. LC 94-22901. 352p. 1994. pap., student ed. 37.50 (*0-8273-7048-2*) Delmar.

Carley, Larry W. Do-It-Yourself Car Care. (Illus.). 224p. (Orig.). 1987. 12.95 (*0-8306-0843-5*, 2143) McGraw-Hill Prof.

— Ford Escort Mercury Lynx Cars, (Nineteen Eighty-Oneto Nineteen Eighty-Four) Do-it-Yourself Car Care. (Illus.). 352p. (Orig.). 1984. pap. 13.95 (*0-8306-2133-4*, 2133) McGraw-Hill Prof.

***Carley, Leila.** From Sea to Shining Sea: A Bike Trip to 48 State Capitals & the District of Columbia. (Illus.). 116p. 1999. pap. write for info. (*1-882194-57-8*) TN Valley Pub.

Carley, Lionel. Delius: A Life in Letters, Nineteen Hundred Nine to Nineteen Thirty-Four, Vol. 2. 500p. 1988. text 104.95 (*0-85967-717-6*, Pub. by Scolar Pr) Ashgate Pub Co.

Carley, Lionel. Delius: A Life in Letters 1862-1908, Vol.1. 494p. 1983. 121.95 (*0-85967-656-0*) Ashgate Pub Co.

Carley, Lionel. Frederick Delius: Music, Art & Literature. LC 97-3005. (Illus.). 350p. 1997. text 96.95 (*1-85928-222-9*, Pub. by Ashgate Pub) Ashgate Pub Co.

Carley, Lionel, ed. Delius: A Life in Letters, 1862-1908. (Illus.). 500p. 1984. 48.00 (*0-674-19570-1*) HUP.

Carley, Lionel & Threlfall, Robert. Delius: A Life in Pictures. (Illus.). 1978. 34.50 (*0-19-315437-4*) OUP.

Carley-Macauly, K. W., ed. Radioactive Waste: Advanced Management Methods for Medium-Active Liquid Waste, Vol. 1. (Radioactive Waste Management Ser.). viii, 328p. 1981. text 372.00 (*3-7186-0060-9*) Gordon & Breach.

Carley, Maurine, jt. auth. see Trenholm, Virginia C.

Carley, Michael. Rational Techniques in Policy Analysis. 1980. pap. text 38.95 (*0-566-05491-4*, Pub. by Dartmth Pub) Ashgate Pub Co.

Carley, Michael & Christie, Ian. Managing Sustainable Development. LC 92-35224. 1993. pap. 19.95 (*0-8166-2339-2*) U of Minn Pr.

Carley, Michael & Spapens, Philippe. Sharing the World: Sustainable Living & Global Equity in the 21st Century. (Illus.). 192p. 1997. pap. 28.00 (*1-85383-463-7*, Pub. by Escan Pubns) Island Pr.

Carley, Michael J. 1939: The Alliance That Never Was & the Coming of World War II. LC 99-24873. (Illus.). 352p. 1999. 28.95 (*1-56663-252-8*, Pub. by I R Dee) Natl Bk Netwk.

Carley, Michelle. Big E-Z Bookkeeping, No. 1: Business System Without Payroll. (Illus.). 1991. spiral bd. 45.00 (*0-9634040-0-8*, TX 3 196393) Big E-Z Bkkeeping.

— Big E-Z Bookkeeping, No. 2: Business System with Payroll. (Illus.). 79p. 1991. spiral bd. 45.00 (*0-9634040-1-6*, TX 3 196393) Big E-Z Bkkeeping.

Carley, Nancy C. From Tears to Triumph. 142p. 1992. per. 7.95 (*0-945383-35-5*, 945-5827) Teach Servs.

Carley, Rachel. Cabin Fever: Rustic Style Comes Home. LC 98-21134. (Illus.). 208p. 1998. 34.50 (*0-684-84422-2*) S&S Trade.

— Cuba: 400 Years of Architectural Heritage. LC 97-9188. (Illus.). 224p. 1997. 49.95 (*0-8230-1129-1*) Watsn-Guptill.

***Carley, Rachel.** Cuba: 400 Years of Architectural Heritage. (Illus.). 224p. 2000. pap. 29.95 (*0-8230-1128-3*) Watsn-Guptill.

Carley, Rachel. A Guide to Biltmore Estate. LC 94-11621. 1994. write for info. (*1-885378-00-9*); pap. write for info. (*1-885378-01-7*) Biltmore.

— The Visual Dictionary of American Domestic Architecture. LC 94-20071. (Illus.). 89p. 1995. 40.00 (*0-8050-2646-0*); pap. 19.95 (*0-8050-4563-5*, Owl) H Holt & Co.

— The Visual Dictionary of American Domestic Architecture. (Illus.). 1997. pap. 18.95 (*0-614-28153-9*, Owl) H Holt & Co.

Carley, Robert. Final Performance. 122p. (C). 1989. 60.00 (*0-7223-2233-X*, Pub. by A H S Ltd) St Mut.

— Some That Smile. 113p. (C). 1989. 40.00 (*0-7223-2298-4*, Pub. by A H S Ltd) St Mut.

Carley, Royal V., ed. Twenty-Third Psalm for Today. LC 73-101450. (Illus.). (J). (gr. 3 up). 1971. 6.95 (*0-8378-2001-4*) Gibson.

Carley, V. A. Student Aid in the Secondary Schools of the United States. LC 77-176626. (Columbia University. Teachers College. Contributions to Education Ser.: No. 594). reprint ed. 37.50 (*0-404-55594-2*) AMS Pr.

Carlgren, Ingrid, et al, eds. Research on Teachers' Thinking & Practice. LC 94-38648. 224p. 1995. pap. 29.95 (*0-7507-0431-4*, Falmer Pr); text 85.00 (*0-7507-0430-6*, Falmer Pr) Taylor & Francis.

Carlhian, Jean Paul, jt. auth. see Park, Edwards.

Carli, Alarico & Favaro, Antonio. Bibliografia Galileana, 1568-1895. 403p. 1998. reprint ed. 65.00 (*1-57898-111-5*) Martino Pubng.

***Carli, Audrey.** Valiant Victory. 170p. 2000. pap. write for info. (*0-7880-1613-X*, Fairway Pr) CSS OH.

Carli, Audrey. When Jesus Holds Our Hand. 72p. (Orig.). 1987. pap. 3.95 (*0-9618664-0-3*) AMC Pub.

Carli, Camillo. Fabio. 1989. pap. write for info. (*2-89135-020-0*) Guernica Editions.

Carli, E. De, see Conca, F.

Carli, G. & Zimmermann, M. Towards the Neurobiology of Chronic Pain. LC 96-40280. (Progress in Brain Research Ser.: 110). 290p. 1996. 201.00 (*0-444-82149-X*) Elsevier.

***Carli, Patti.** Official Annual Statement Blanks of the NAIC: Hospital, Medical, Dental & Indemnity Corporations. rev. ed. 106p. 1999. ring bd. write for info. (*0-89382-529-8*, ASB-MU99) Nat Assn Insurance.

Carli, Patti, ed. Annual Statement Instructions: Property & Casualty. 14th rev. ed. 380p. (C). 1997. ring bd. 175.00 (*0-89382-427-5*, ASI-PM) Nat Assn Insurance.

— NAIC Report on Receiverships. rev. ed. Orig. Title: Contact Person Report. 672p. (C). 1995. ring bd. 75.00 (*0-89382-360-0*, CPR-ZB) Nat Assn Insurance.

— 1997 Annual Statement Instructions - Title. 6th rev. ed. 316p. (C). 1997. ring bd. 125.00 (*0-89382-472-0*, ASI-TM) Nat Assn Insurance.

— 1997 Annual Statement Instructions - Limited Health Services Organizations (LHSO) 6th rev. ed. 108p. (C). 1997. ring bd. 75.00 (*0-89382-471-2*, ASI-SM) Nat Assn Insurance.

— 1997 Annual Statement Instructions - Hospital, Medical, Dental Service & Indemnity Corporation (HMDI) 6th rev. ed. 252p. (C). 1997. ring bd. 75.00 (*0-89382-469-0*, ASI-MM) Nat Assn Insurance.

— 1997 Annual Statement Instructions - Health Maintenance Organization. 7th rev. ed. 137p. (C). 1997. ring bd. 175.00 (*0-89382-468-2*, ASI-HM) Nat Assn Insurance.

— 1997 Annual Statement Instructions - Fraternal. 11th rev. ed. 418p. (C). 1997. ring bd. 175.00 (*0-89382-473-9*, ASI-FM) Nat Assn Insurance.

— 1997 Annual Statement Instructions - Life. 13th rev. ed. 488p. (C). 1997. ring bd. 175.00 (*0-89382-474-7*, ASI-LM) Nat Assn Insurance.

***Carli, Patti, ed.** Offical Annual Statement Blanks of the NAIC: Hospital, Medical, Dental & Indemnity Corporations. rev. ed. 106p. 1999. ring bd. 100.00 (*0-89382-616-2*) Nat Assn Insurance.

— Offical Annual Statement Blanks of the NIAC: Health Maintenance Organizations. rev. ed. 100p. 1999. ring bd. 125.00 (*0-89382-609-X*, ASB-H499) Nat Assn Insurance.

— Offical Annual Statement Blanks of the NIAC: Limited Health Services Organizations. rev. ed. 100p. 1999. ring bd. 100.00 (*0-89382-610-3*, ASB-S499) Nat Assn Insurance.

— Offical Annual Statement Blanks of the NIAC: Separate Accounts. rev. ed. 75p. 1999. pap. 25.00 (*0-89382-617-0*) Nat Assn Insurance.

— Offical Annual Statement Blanks of the NIAC: Title. rev. ed. 130p. 1999. ring bd. 100.00 (*0-89382-615-4*, ASB-T499) Nat Assn Insurance.

— Official Annual Statement Blanks of the NAIC: Franternal for 2001. 130p. 2000. ring bd. 175.00 (*0-89382-996-X*, ASB-FU00) Nat Assn Insurance.

— Official Annual Statement Blanks of the NAIC: Fraternal. rev. ed. 158p. 1998. ring bd. 175.00 (*0-89382-527-1*, ASB-FU98) Nat Assn Insurance.

— Official Annual Statement Blanks of the NAIC: Fraternal. rev. ed. 160p. 1999. ring bd. 175.00 (*0-89382-613-8*, ASB-FU99) Nat Assn Insurance.

— Official Annual Statement Blanks of the NAIC: Health Maintenance Organizations. 99p. 1998. ring bd. write for info. (*0-89382-523-9*, ASB-HU98) Nat Assn Insurance.

— Official Annual Statement Blanks of the NAIC: Life. rev. ed. 182p. 1998. ring bd. 175.00 (*0-89382-525-5*, ASB-LU98) Nat Assn Insurance.

— Official Annual Statement Blanks of the NAIC: Life. rev. ed. 184p. 1999. ring bd. 175.00 (*0-89382-612-X*, ASB-LU99) Nat Assn Insurance.

— Official Annual Statement Blanks of the NAIC: Life for 2001. 130p. 2000. ring bd. 175.00 (*0-89382-995-1*, ASB-LU00) Nat Assn Insurance.

— Official Annual Statement Blanks of the NAIC: Property & Casualty. rev. ed. 240p. 1998. ring bd. 175.00 (*0-89382-526-3*, ASB-PU98) Nat Assn Insurance.

— Official Annual Statement Blanks of the NAIC: Property & Casualty. rev. ed. 242p. 1999. ring bd. 175.00 (*0-89382-611-1*, ASB-PU99) Nat Assn Insurance.

— Official Annual Statement Blanks of the NAIC: Property & Casualty for 2001. 290p. 2000. ring bd. 175.00 (*0-89382-994-3*, ASB-PU00) Nat Assn Insurance.

— Official Annual Statement Blanks of the NAIC: Separate Accounts. rev. ed. 51p. 1998. ring bd. 50.00 (*0-89382-524-7*, ASB-AS98) Nat Assn Insurance.

— Official Annual Statement Blanks of the NAIC: Title. rev. ed. 128p. 1998. ring bd. 150.00 (*0-89382-528-X*, ASB-TU98) Nat Assn Insurance.

Carli, Patti, ed. Official NAIC Annual Statement Blanks: Fraternal. 3rd rev. ed. 160p. 1996. ring bd. 100.00 (*0-89382-392-9*) Nat Assn Insurance.

— Official NAIC Annual Statement Blanks: Fraternal. 4th rev. ed. 162p. (C). 1997. ring bd. 100.00 (*0-89382-450-X*, ASB-FM) Nat Assn Insurance.

— Official NAIC Annual Statement Blanks: Health Maintenance Organization. rev. ed. 68p. (C). 1997. ring bd. 75.00 (*0-89382-452-6*, ASB-HM) Nat Assn Insurance.

— Official NAIC Annual Statement Blanks: Health Maintenance Organizations. 3rd rev. ed. 52p. 1996. ring bd. 75.00 (*0-89382-393-7*) Nat Assn Insurance.

— Official NAIC Annual Statement Blanks: Hospital, Medical, & Dental Service or Indemnity Corporation. 3rd rev. ed. 114p. 1996. ring bd. 75.00 (*0-89382-394-5*) Nat Assn Insurance.

— Official NAIC Annual Statement Blanks: Hospital, Medical, Dental or Indemnity. 6th rev. ed. 104p. (C). 1997. ring bd. 75.00 (*0-89382-453-4*, ASB-MM) Nat Assn Insurance.

— Official NAIC Annual Statement Blanks: Life, Accident, & Health. 3rd rev. ed. 192p. 1996. ring bd. 100.00 (*0-89382-390-2*) Nat Assn Insurance.

— Official NAIC Annual Statement Blanks: Life, Accident, & Health. 4th rev. ed. 190p. (C). 1997. ring bd. 100.00 (*0-89382-449-6*, ASB-LM) Nat Assn Insurance.

— Official NAIC Annual Statement Blanks: Limited Health Service Organization. 46p. 1996. ring bd. 75.00 (*0-89382-395-3*) Nat Assn Insurance.

— Official NAIC Annual Statement Blanks: Limited Health Service Organization. 6th rev. ed. 51p. (C). 1997. ring bd. 75.00 (*0-89382-451-8*, ASB-SM) Nat Assn Insurance.

— Official NAIC Annual Statement Blanks: Property & Casualty. 3rd rev. ed. 100.00p. 1996. ring bd. 100.00 (*0-89382-389-9*) Nat Assn Insurance.

— Official NAIC Annual Statement Blanks: Property & Casualty. 4th rev. ed. 240p. (C). 1997. ring bd. 100.00 (*0-89382-448-8*, ASB-PM) Nat Assn Insurance.

— Official NAIC Annual Statement Blanks: Separate Accounts. 2nd rev. ed. 57p. (C). 1997. ring bd. 25.00 (*0-89382-456-9*) Nat Assn Insurance.

— Official NAIC Annual Statement Blanks: Separate Accounts. 3rd rev. ed. 52p. 1996. ring bd. 100.00 (*0-89382-391-0*) Nat Assn Insurance.

— Official NAIC Annual Statement Blanks: Title. rev. ed. 132p. (C). 1997. ring bd. 75.00 (*0-89382-454-2*, ASB-TM) Nat Assn Insurance.

— Official NAIC Annual Statement Blanks: Title Insurance Companies. 3rd rev. ed. 114p. 1996. ring bd. 75.00 (*0-89382-396-1*) Nat Assn Insurance.

— Report on Receiverships. rev. ed. 756p. (C). 1997. ring bd. 125.00i (*0-89382-504-2*, CPR-ZS97) Nat Assn Insurance.

— Report on Receiverships for 1996. 10th rev. ed. 740p. (C). 1996. ring bd. 125.00 (*0-89382-433-X*, CPR-ZS) Nat Assn Insurance.

C

An Asterisk (*) at the beginning of an entry indicates that the title is appearing for the first time.

Carlie, Michael K. & Minor, Kevin I. Prisons Around the World: Studies in International Penology. 336p. (C). 1992. text. write for info. (*0-697-14310-4*) Brown & Benchmark.

Carlier, Alexandra. Ten Late Breakfasts. LC 88-21935. (Ten Menus Ser.). (Illus.). 128p. 1989. 19.95 (*0-940793-24-5*) Interlink Pub.

Carlier, Auguste. Marriage in the United States. LC 70-169376. (Family in America Ser.). 200p. 1977. reprint ed. 23.95 (*0-405-03853-4*) Ayer.

Carlier, R. Dictionnaire des Citations Francaises. (FRE.). 1998. 59.95 (*0-320-00248-9*) Fr & Eur.

Carlile, Clark Stites & Hensley, Dana. 38 Basic Speech Experiences. 10th rev. ed. LC 98-198218. xxxiv, 350p. 1999. 30.00 (*0-931054-53-2*) Clark Pub.

Carlile, Candy. Book Report Big Top. (Learning Works Reading Ser.). (Illus.). 48p. (J). (gr. 1-4). 1980. pap. 6.95 (*0-88160-009-1*, LW111) Learning Wks.

— Crafts with Rhymes - Discovering God's Love: Age 5-10. (Crafts with Rhymes Ser.). (Illus.). 64p. pap. 9.95 (*0-937282-59-6*) Rainbow CA.

***Carlile, Clancy.** The Paris Pilgrims. 464p. 2000. pap. 14.00 (*0-7867-0753-4*, Pub. by Carroll & Graf) Publishers Group.

***Carlile, Clark.** Thirty-Eight Basic Speech Experiences. 1999. pap., teacher ed. 8.00 (*0-931054-55-9*) Clark Pub.

***Carlile, Clark & Hensley, Dana.** Thirty-Eight Basic Speech Experiences. 1999. pap. 20.00 (*0-931054-54-0*) Clark Pub.

Carlile, Cynthia & McKee, Sharon, trs. from RUS. Anton Chekhov & His Times. LC 95-5839. 368p. 1995. 24.00 (*1-55728-391-5*) U of Ark Pr.

Carlile, Glenda. Buckskin, Calico & Lace: Oklahoma's Territorial Women. Warren, Clifton, ed. 116p. (Orig.). 1990. pap. text 10.95 (*0-9628214-0-3*) Sthrn Hills Pub.

— Petticoats, Politics, & Pirouettes: Oklahoma Women from 1900 to 1950. Welsh, Carol, ed. LC 95-92460. (Illus.). 120p. 1995. pap. 12.95 (*0-9628214-4-6*) Sthrn Hills Pub.

Carlile, Henry. Rain. LC 93-73476. (Poetry Ser.). 88p. (Orig.). 1994. pap. 11.95 (*0-88748-167-1*) Carnegie-Mellon.

— Running Lights. LC 80-67971. 66p. (C). 1981. 9.00 (*0-937872-00-8*); pap. 5.00 (*0-937872-01-6*) Dragon Gate.

Carlile, Janice B., jt. auth. see Bannister, Barbara J.

Carlile, Lonny E. & Tilton, Mark, eds. Is Japan Really Changing Its Ways? Regulatory Reform & the Japanese Economy. LC 98-25374. 180p. 1998. 39.95 (*0-8157-1292-8*); pap. 16.95 (*0-8157-1291-X*) Brookings.

Carlile, Lonny E., tr. see Masumi, Junnosuke.

Carlile, M. J., et al. Molecular & Cellular Aspects of Microbial Evolution. LC 80-42172. (Society for General Microbiology Symposium Ser.: No. 32). (Illus.). 378p. 1981. text 110.00 (*0-521-24108-1*) Cambridge U Pr.

Carlile, Michael J. & Watkinson, Sarah. The Fungi. 320p. 1994. text 83.00 (*0-12-159959-0*) Acad Pr.

— The Fungi. 496p. (C). 1995. reprint ed. pap. text 42.00 (*0-12-159960-4*) Acad Pr.

Carlile, Richard. Manual of Freemasonry: The First Three Degrees; the Royal Arch & Knights Templar Druids. 311p. 1992. reprint ed. pap. 30.00 (*1-56459-197-2*) Kessinger Pub.

— What Is Love? LC 98-30215. 1998. 15.00 (*1-85984-851-6*, Pub. by Verso) Norton.

Carlile, Simon. The Generation & Applications of Virtual Auditory Space. LC 96-14117. (Neuroscience Intelligence Unit Ser.). 1996. 99.00 (*1-57059-341-8*) Landes Bioscience.

Carlile, Thelma. Mealtimes & Memories: Fond Reflections of Family, Friends & Food. 430p. 1995. pap. 16.95 (*0-9644579-0-3*) Sunline.

Carlile, Vowery D. Monsters, Magic & Make-Believe. (J). Date not set. teacher ed. 12.95 (*1-56644-956-1*, 956-1AP) Educ Impress.

— Multicultural Legends & Tales. (J). (gr. 1-4). Date not set. teacher ed. 12.95 (*1-56644-974-X*) Educ Impress.

— A Pot Full of Tales. (J). Date not set. teacher ed. 12.95 (*1-56644-972-3*, 011-4AP) Educ Impress.

Carlile, W. R. Control of Crop Diseases. 2nd ed. (Illus.). 161p. (Orig.). (C). 1995. pap. text 20.95 (*0-521-48345-X*) Cambridge U Pr.

Carlile, William W. The Evolution of Modern Money. LC 69-17029. (Reprints of Economic Classics Ser.). xxiii, 373p. 1969. reprint ed. 49.50 (*0-678-00467-6*) Kelley.

Carlin. Pierre Corneille Revisited. LC 98-34788. 1998. 32.00 (*0-8057-4561-0*, Twyne) Mac Lib Ref.

Carlin, jt. auth. see Earle.

Carlin, Alan. Environmental Investments: The Cost of a Clean Environment. (Illus.). 511p. (Orig.). (C). 1994. pap. text 60.00 (*0-7881-0656-2*) DIANE Pub.

Carlin, Albert S., jt. ed. see Doerr, Hans O.

Carlin, Angela G., ed. Baldwin's Ohio Practice, Merrick-Rippner Probate Law, 4 vols. 5th ed. LC 97-149204. 3898p. 1997. 330.00 (*0-8322-0697-0*) Banks-Baldwin.

Carlin, Bob, jt. auth. see Carlin, Richard.

Carlin, Bradley P. Bayes & Empirical Bayes Methods for Data Analysis. (Monographs on Statistics & Applied Probability). 416p. (gr. 13). 1996. boxed set 54.95 (*0-412-05611-9*, Chap & Hall CRC) CRC Pr.

***Carlin, Bradley P. & Louis, Thomas A.** Bayes & Empirical Bayes Methods for Data Analysis. 2nd ed. LC 00-38242. (Texts in Statistical Science Ser.). 2000. pap. write for info. (*1-58488-170-4*) St Lucie Pr.

Carlin, Chip, ed. Do You Understand? Handbook. 119p. 1989. teacher ed. 4.00 (*0-930713-61-3*); pap. text 10.00 (*0-318-41708-1*) Lit Vol Am.

Carlin, Chip, ed. see Broadway, Beth A.

Carlin, Chip, ed. see Literacy Volunteers Computer Task Force Staff.

Carlin, Chip, ed. see Price, Margaret.

Carlin, Christopher J. Protecting Niagara: A History of the Niagara County Sheriff's Office. Colangelo, Paul G., ed. (Illus.). 242p. (Orig.). 1995. 17.00 (*0-9645195-1-8*); pap. 10.00 (*0-9645195-4-2*); lib. bdg. 17.00 (*0-9645195-2-6*) AEGIS Pr.

***Carlin, Claire L.** Women Reading Corneille: Feminist Psychocriticisms of "Le Cid" LC 99-21632. (Contemporary Critical Concepts & Pre-Enlightenment Literature Ser.: Vol. 4). 184p. (C). 2000. 44.95 (*0-8204-4494-4*) P Lang Pubng.

Carlin, Crystal, jt. ed. see Tillman, Jamie.

Carlin, Daniel. Browning's Hatreds. LC 93-2907. 288p. (C). 1993. 48.00 (*0-19-811229-7*, Clarendon Pr) OUP.

Carlin, Deborah. Cather, Canon, & the Politics of Reading. LC 92-12670. 208p. 1992. 30.00 (*0-87023-822-1*) U of Mass Pr.

Carlin, Diana, jt. auth. see Hensley, Dana.

Carlin, Diana B. & McKinney, Mitchell S. The 1992 Presidential Debates in Focus. LC 94-12350. (Political Communication Ser.). 296p. 1994. 65.00 (*0-275-94846-3*, Praeger Pubs) Greenwood.

Carlin, Diana B. & Payne, James. Public Speaking Today. 3rd ed. LC 98-14372. 1998. 49.94 (*0-8442-0369-6*) NTC Contemp Pub Co.

Carlin, Diana P. & Moore, Meredith A., eds. The Landon Lecture Series on Public Issues: The First Twenty Years, 1966-1986. 888p. (C). 1990. lib. bdg. 92.00 (*0-8191-7403-3*) U Pr of Amer.

Carlin, George. Brain Droppings. LC 96-52373. 272p. (J). 1997. 19.45 (*0-7868-6313-7*, Pub. by Hyperion) Time Warner.

— Brain Droppings. 272p. (J). 1998. reprint ed. pap. 10.45 (*0-7868-8321-9*, Pub. by Hyperion) Time Warner.

***Carlin, George.** Napalm & Silly Putty: George Carlin. 272p. 2001. 21.00 (*0-7868-6413-3*, Pub. by Hyperion) Time Warner.

— Untitled Autobiography. (Illus.). 224p. 2001. 18.95 (*0-7868-6088-X*, Pub. by Hyperion) Little.

Carlin, Herbert J. & Civalleri, Paolo. Wideband Circuit Design. LC 97-26966. (Electronic Engineering Systems Ser.). 544p. 1997. boxed set 104.95 (*0-8493-7897-4*) CRC Pr.

***Carlin, Jane D. & Teigland, Lauren A., contrib. by.** Current Developments in the European Capital Markets: The Impact of a Single Currency. LC 99-161986. (Corporate Law & Practice Course Handbook Ser.). 840 p. 1998. 129.00 (*0-87224-548-9*) PLI.

Carlin, John. How to Invest in Your First Works of Art: A Guide for the New Collector. LC 89-29020. (Illus.). 104p. (Orig.). 1990. pap. 11.95 (*1-878274-03-1*) Yarrow Pr.

Carlin, Joi. La Cama de Mama: Mommy's Bed Is Best. (SPA., Illus.). 24p. (J). pap. 6.95 (*980-257-167-9*) Volcano Pr.

Carlin, Katherine E., jt. auth. see Brandes, Ray.

Carlin, Martha. Medieval Southwark. LC 95-47679. 351p. 1996. 60.00 (*1-85285-116-3*) Hambledon Press.

Carlin, Matthew. Hide & Seek: A Comedy. (Illus.). 32p. 1985. pap. 3.50 (*0-88680-243-1*) I E Clark.

Carlin, Matthew, jt. auth. see Tissot, John.

Carlin, Michael J. Trial: Ordeal of the U. S. S. Enterprise, 14 January 1969. (Illus.). 256p. 1993. 24.95 (*0-9647533-0-8*) Tuscarora Pr.

***Carlin, Michael Joe.** Trial: Ordeal of the USS Enterprise, 14 January 1969. ed. 259p. 2000. pap. 19.95 (*0-9647533-1-6*) Tuscarora Pr.

Carlin, Mike, ed. Superman: Panic in the Sky. (Illus.). 192p. (J). 1993. mass mkt. 9.95 (*1-56389-094-1*, Pub. by DC Comics) Time Warner.

Carlin, Mike, et al. Star Trek: The Next Generation-Beginnings. LC 96-228592. (Illus.). 160p. 1995. mass mkt. 19.95 (*1-56389-200-6*) DC Comics.

Carlin, Mike, ed. see Ordway, Jerry.

Carlin, Norah. The Causes of the English Civil War. LC 98-39044. (Historical Association Studies). 224p. 1998. 49.95 (*0-631-20450-4*); pap. 19.95 (*0-631-20451-2*) Blackwell Pubs.

Carlin, Patricia L. Shakespeare's Mortal Men: Overcoming Death in History, Comedy, & Tragedy. LC 92-8722. (Studies in Shakespeare: Vol. 1). VIII, 250p. (C). 1993. text 49.95 (*0-8204-1563-4*) P Lang Pubng.

Carlin, Paul W., Sr. Behind Enemy Lines. (Illus.). 137p. (Orig.). 1989. pap. text 12.00 (*0-317-93531-3*) Kerusso Co.

— Treasures of Darkness. (Illus.). 158p. (Orig.). 1989. pap. text 7.95 (*0-317-93532-1*) Kerusso Co.

Carlin, Peter. Brave New Bride. (Illus.). 80p. (Orig.). 1992. mass mkt. 8.99 (*0-446-39330-4*, Pub. by Warner Bks) Little.

Carlin, Peter, jt. auth. see Allison, Stacy.

Carlin, R. L. Magnetochemistry. (Illus.). 350p. 1985. 130.95 (*0-387-15816-2*) Spr-Verlag.

Carlin, R. T., et al, eds. Molten Salts: 10th International Symposium. (Proceedings Ser.: Vol. 96-7). (Illus.). 568p. 1996. 92.00 (*1-56677-159-5*) Electrochem Soc.

Carlin, Richard. Animal Songs for Children. (Illus.). 64p. 1985. pap. 10.95 (*0-8256-2441-X*, AM60062) Music Sales.

— The English Concertina. (Illus.). 64p. pap. 12.95 (*0-8256-0189-4*, OK63297, Oak) Music Sales.

— How to Play the Autoharp. (Illus.). 48p. 1985. pap. 5.95 (*0-8256-2338-3*, AM37235) Music Sales.

— Jazz. (World of Music Ser.). (Illus.). 160p. (J). (gr. 5-9). 1991. 19.95 (*0-8160-2229-1*) Facts on File.

— The Lullaby Book. (Illus.). 64p. 1997. pap. 9.95 (*0-8256-2337-5*, AM37029) Music Sales.

***Carlin, Richard.** Rock & Roll: 1955-1970. (Illus.). 126p. 1999. 22.95 (*0-7351-0211-2*) Replica Bks.

Carlin, Richard, compiled by. The Gow Collection of Scottish Dance Music. (Illus.). 256p. 1986. pap. 21.95 (*0-8256-0307-2*, OK64881, Oak) Music Sales.

***Carlin, Richard & Carlin, Bob.** Southern Exposure: The Story of Southern Music in Pictures & Words. (Illus.). 160p. 2000. pap. write for info. (*0-8230-8426-4*) Watsn-Guptill.

Carlin, Richard L., ed. Transition Metal Chemistry, 1. LC 65-27431. 319p. 1965. pap. 98.90 (*0-8357-8000-7*, 202712700001) Bks Demand.

— Transition Metal Chemistry, 2. LC 65-27431. 360p. 1966. pap. 111.60 (*0-8357-8001-5*, 202712700002) Bks Demand.

— Transition Metal Chemistry, 3. LC 65-27431. 371p. 1967. pap. 115.10 (*0-8357-8002-3*, 201769600003) Bks Demand.

— Transition Metal Chemistry, 4. LC 65-27431. 365p. 1968. pap. 113.20 (*0-8357-8003-1*, 202712700004) Bks Demand.

— Transition Metal Chemistry, 5. LC 65-27431. 317p. 1969. pap. 98.30 (*0-8357-8004-X*, 202712700005) Bks Demand.

— Transition Metal Chemistry, 7. LC 65-27431. 378p. 1972. pap. 117.20 (*0-8357-8005-8*, 202712700007) Bks Demand.

— Transition Metal Chemistry, Vol. 6. LC 65-27431. 340p. 1970. reprint ed. pap. 105.40 (*0-7837-0018-0*, 202712700006) Bks Demand.

***Carlin, Stephanie & Womack, Alexandria.** Creating a Knowledge-Sharing Culture. Elliot, Susan, ed. (Illus.). 92p. 1999. ring bd. 395.00 (*1-928593-17-8*) Am Prodtv Qual.

Carlin, Stephanie, et al. Expanding Knowledge Management Externally: Putting Your Knowledge to Work for Customers. Elliott, Susan, ed. (Illus.). 111p. 1998. spiral bd. 495.00 (*1-928593-03-8*) Am Prodtv Qual.

Carlin, Tom & McMeen, Albert. Analyzing Financial Statements. 4th ed. (Illus.). 360p. 1993. pap. text 46.00 (*0-89982-315-7*) Am Bankers.

Carlin, Vivian F. & Greenberg, Vivian E. Should Mom Live with Us? And Is Happiness Possible If She Does? 193p. 1999. text 19.00 (*0-7881-6148-2*) DIANE Pub.

Carlin, Vivian F. & Mansberg, Ruth. If I Live to Be One Hundred: Congregate Housing for Later Life. 216p. 1984. 17.95 (*0-13-450387-2*, Parker Publishing Co); pap. 8.95 (*0-13-450379-1*, Parker Publishing Co) P-H.

Carlin, Vuyelwa. How We Dream of the Dead. 70p. 1996. pap. 15.95 (*1-85411-139-6*, Pub. by Seren Bks) Dufour.

— Midas's Daughter. 80p. (Orig.). 1991. pap. 15.95 (*1-85411-054-3*, Pub. by Seren Bks) Dufour.

Carlin, Wendy & Soskice, David W. Macroeconomics & the Wage Bargain: A Modern Approach to Employment, Inflation, & the Exchange Rate. (Illus.). 496p. 1990. 78.00 (*0-19-877245-9*); pap. text 38.00 (*0-19-877244-0*) OUP.

Carlin, William P. The Memoirs of Brigadier General William Passmore Carlin, U.S.A. Girardi, Robert I. & Hughes, Nathaniel C., eds. LC 99-12594. (Illus.). 352p. (Orig.). 1999. text 50.00 (*0-8032-1494-4*) U of Nebr Pr.

Carline, Jan D., et al. Mountaineering First Aid: A Guide to Accident Response & First Aid Care. 4th ed. LC 96-15825. (Illus.). 144p. 1996. pap. 10.95 (*0-89886-478-X*) Mountaineers.

Carline, Richard. Pictures in the Post: The Story of the Picture Postcard. LC 70-190038. 128p. 1971. pap. 7.95 (*0-913782-04-1*); pap. 7.95 (*0-685-08357-8*) Deltiologists Am.

Carliner, David, et al. The Rights of Aliens & Refugees: The Basic ACLU Guide to Alien & Refugee Rights. 2nd rev. ed. LC 89-11570. 240p. (C). 1990. pap. 9.95 (*0-8093-1598-X*) S Ill U Pr.

Carliner, Geoffrey, jt. ed. see Alesina, Alberto.

Carliner, Michael, jt. auth. see Ahluwalia, Gopal.

Carliner, Saul, jt. auth. see Barnum, Carol M.

Carling, Alan. Social Division. 360p. 1991. pap. 18.95 (*0-86091-553-0*, A4518) Verso.

Carling, Chris. How to Run a Voluntary Group: A Guide to Successful Organisation & Management. 160p. 1995. pap. 19.95 (*1-85703-135-0*, Pub. by How To Bks) Trans-Atl Phila.

Carling, E. B. & Kopal, Zdenek, eds. Photometric & Spectroscopic Binary Systems. xii, 546p. 1981. text 247.50 (*90-277-1281-6*) Kluwer Academic.

Carling, E. B., jt. ed. see Dyson, J. E.

Carling, Finn. Commission. Muinzer, Louis A., tr. from NOR. 176p. 1993. 30.00 (*0-7206-0896-1*, Pub. by P Owen Ltd) Dufour.

— Diary for a Dead Husband. LC 99-200318. 176p. 1998. 29.95 (*0-7206-1037-0*, Pub. by P Owen Ltd) Dufour.

— Under the Evening Sky. Muinzer, L. A., tr. from NOR. 120p. 1993. 30.00 (*0-7206-0783-3*, Pub. by P Owen Ltd) Dufour.

Carling, Finn & Haecker, Theodor. And Yet We Are Human & Kierkegaard: The Cripple, 2 vols. Phillips, William R. & Rosenberg, Janet, eds. Bruyn, C. V., tr. from NOR. LC 79-6897. (Physically Handicapped in Society Ser.). (Illus.). 1980. reprint ed. lib. bdg. 25.95 (*0-405-13108-9*) Ayer.

Carling, P. A. & Dawson, M., eds. Advances in Fluvial Dynamics & Stratigraphy. LC 95-49524. 546p. 1996. 225.00 (*0-471-95330-X*) Wiley.

Carling, Paul A. & Petts, G. E. Lowland Floodplain Rivers: Geomorphological Perspectives. LC 91-21774. (British Geomorphological Research Group Symposia Ser.). 318p. 1992. 315.00 (*0-471-93119-5*) Wiley.

Carling, Paul J. Return to Community: Building Support Systems for People with Psychiatric Disabilities. 348p. 1994. pap. text 23.00 (*0-89862-323-5*) Guilford Pubns.

***Carling, W.** My Autobiography, Bill Carling. 1998. text 35.00 (*0-340-69658-3*, Pub. by Hodder & Stought Ltd) Trafalgar.

Carlini, John, tr. see Grisman, David & Rice, Tony.

Carlini, John, tr. see O'Connor, Mark.

Carlino, Andrea. Construction of the Body. Tedeschi, John, tr. 1997. pap. text 16.95 (*0-226-09288-7*) U Ch Pr.

— Construction of the Body. Tedeschi, John & Tedeschi, Anne C., trs. LC 99-25338. 266p. 2000. 29.00 (*0-226-09287-9*) U Ch Pr.

Carlino, Cristina. The Rainbow Connection: Seven Steps for Making Miracles Happen. LC 98-42349. 368p. 1999. 22.95 (*0-385-49387-8*) Doubleday.

Carlino, Lewis J. The Brick & the Rose. 1959. pap. 3.25 (*0-8222-0150-X*) Dramatists Play.

— Cages: Snowangel & Epiphany. 1964. pap. 5.25 (*0-8222-0174-7*) Dramatists Play.

— The Dirty Old Man. 1964. pap. 3.25 (*0-8222-0312-X*) Dramatists Play.

— The Exercise. 1968. pap. 5.25 (*0-8222-0373-1*) Dramatists Play.

— High Sign, & Sarah & the Sax: Two Short Plays. 1963. pap. 5.25 (*0-8222-0519-X*) Dramatists Play.

— Junk Yard. 1959. pap. 5.25 (*0-8222-0605-6*) Dramatists Play.

— Telemachus Clay. 114p. 1964. 16.95 (*0-910278-12-1*) Boulevard.

— Telemachus Clay. LC 64-17945. 1963. pap. 5.25 (*0-8222-1116-5*) Dramatists Play.

— Two Short Plays by Lewis John Carlino: Mr. Flannery's Ocean & Objective Case. 1962. pap. 5.25 (*0-8222-0781-8*) Dramatists Play.

— Used Car for Sale. 1959. pap. 3.25 (*0-8222-1197-1*) Dramatists Play.

Carlinsky, Dan. The Complete Bible Quiz Book. 160p. 1988. 4.99 (*0-517-23278-2*) Random Hse Value.

Carlinsky, Dan & Goodgold, Ed. The Armchair Conductor. 96p. 1991. pap. 11.95 (*0-440-50415-5*, Dell Trade Pbks) Dell.

Carlip, Hillary. Girl Power: Young Women Speak Out. (Illus.). 368p. (Orig.). 1995. mass mkt. 13.99 (*0-446-67021-9*, Pub. by Warner Bks) Little.

Carlisi, jt. auth. see Steer.

Carlisi, Karen. Authentic & Aware. (College ESL Ser.). (J). 1994. mass mkt., teacher ed. 7.95 (*0-8384-4255-2*); student ed., suppl. ed. 29.95 incl. audio (*0-8384-4254-4*) Heinle & Heinle.

— Authentic & Aware: Advanced Conversation Strategies. (College ESL Ser.). 112p. (J). 1994. mass mkt. 26.95 (*0-8384-3957-8*) Heinle & Heinle.

Carlisi, Karen & Christie, Susana. Tapestry: Listening & Speaking, Level 3. LC 99-54093. (C). 2000. pap. text, student ed. 25.95 (*0-8384-0023-X*) Heinle & Heinle.

Carlisi, Karen & Stevens, Robin. Looking at Our Lives: Picture Dictionary. (Illus.). 72p. (J). (gr. k-9). 1996. pap. 12.95 incl. audio (*0-9649379-0-5*) EECI.

— Looking at Our Lives Picture Dictionary. (Illus.). (Orig.). (J). (gr. 4-6). 1997. pap. text, teacher ed. 19.95 (*0-9649379-2-1*); pap. text, wbk. ed. 9.95 (*0-9649379-1-3*); audio 16.95 (*0-614-24873-6*) EECI.

Carlisky, Nestor J., et al. Living Without a Project: Psychoanalysis & the Postmodern Society. Pozzi, Dora C., tr. LC 97-23742. 112p. 1997. 38.50 (*0-7618-0830-2*); pap. 19.50 (*0-7618-0831-0*) U Pr of Amer.

Carlisle, A. L. Washington, D. C. (Illus.). 1986. reprint ed. pap. 6.95 (*1-879295-20-2*) L B Prince.

Carlisle, Andrea. The Riverhouse Stories: How Pubah S. Queen & Lazy LaRue Save the World. LC 86-20783. (Illus.). 125p. (Orig.). 1993. reprint ed. pap. 8.95 (*0-933377-24-X*, Pub. by Eighth Mount Pr) Consort Bk Sales.

Carlisle, Anthony. An Essay on the Disorders of Old Age, & on the Means for Prolonging Human Life. Kastenbaum, Robert J., ed. LC 78-22183. (Aging & Old Age Ser.). 1979. reprint ed. lib. bdg. 15.95 (*0-405-11802-3*) Ayer.

Carlisle, Barbara. The Crane Wife. LC 98-224909. (J). (gr. 1-7). 1997. pap. 6.00 (*0-87602-358-8*) Anchorage.

Carlisle, Barbara & Drapeau, Don. Hi-Concept-Lo Tech: Theatre for Everyone in Any Place. LC 95-51736. 275p. (Orig.). 1996. pap. 19.95 (*0-435-07001-0*, 07001) Heinemann.

Carlisle, Barbara, ed. see McDaniel, Nello & Thorn, George.

***Carlisle, Betsy A., et al.** 101 Medication Tips for People with Diabetes. LC 99-23163. (Illus.). 128p. 1999. pap. 14.95 (*1-58040-032-9*, 00329Q, Pub. by Am Diabetes) NTC Contemp Pub Co.

Carlisle, Bob. Butterfly Kisses: A Narrative Poem Celebrating the Love Between Fathers & Daughters. (Little Golden Storybks.). 24p. (J). (ps-k). 1997. 3.99 (*0-307-16190-0*, 16190, Goldn Books) Gldn Bks Pub Co.

Carlisle, Bob. Butterfly Kisses: Tender Thoughts Shared Between Fathers & Daughters. LC 97-74418. (Illus.). 48p. 1997. 9.99 (*0-8499-5353-7*) Word Pub.

Carlisle, Bob. Butterfly Kisses & Bittersweet Tears. LC 97-46460. 1998. 15.99 (*0-8499-1339-X*) Word Pub.

— Father's Love, 1. 1998. 9.99 (*0-8499-5475-4*) Word Pub.

— Journal of Butterfly Kisses: A Journal of Reflections. (Illus.). 112p. 12.99 (*0-8499-5354-5*) Word Pub.

— Sons: A Father's Legacy: Heart-Lifting Stories of Dads & Their Boys, 1. LC 99-14396. 1999. 16.99 (*0-8499-1611-9*) Word Pub.

Carlisle, Bob & Carlisle, Brooke. Butterfly Kisses: A Narrative Poem Celebrating the Love Between Fathers & Daughters. (Little Golden Bks.). (J). 1997. 6.99 incl. audio (*0-307-14462-3*, 14462, Goldn Books) Gldn Bks Pub Co.

— Butterfly Kisses: A Narrative Poem Celebrating the Love Between Fathers & Daughters. (Little Golden Bks.). 24p. (J). (ps-k). 1997. 2.29 (*0-307-98872-4*, 98872, Goldn Books) Gldn Bks Pub Co.

Carlisle, Brooke, jt. auth. see Carlisle, Bob.

C

Carlisle, Chris, ed. World Affairs Organizations in Northern California: A Guide to the Field. 230p. 1995. pap. 11.00 (*0-912018-25-9*) World Without War.

Carlisle Civic Club Staff. Carlisle Old & New. (Illus.). 173p. 1997. reprint ed. lib. bdg. 26.00 (*0-8328-6399-8*) Higginson Bk Co.

Carlisle, Clancy. The Paris Pilgrims. 496p. 1999. 25.00 (*0-7867-0615-5*) Carroll & Graf.

Carlisle, Cynthia, jt. auth. see Gallahue, David L.

Carlisle, D. M. The Harvest Is Sure. large type ed. 1990. pap. 16.99 (*0-7089-6908-9*) Ulverscroft.

— The Secret of the Chateau. large type ed. (Linford Romance Library). 304p. 1987. pap. 8.95 (*0-7089-6434-6*, Linford) Ulverscroft.

Carlisle, Dan & Adams, Dolph. Taking More Birds: A Practical Handbook for Success at Sporting Clays & Wing Shooting. (Illus.). 160p. 1995. pap. 15.95 (*1-55821-473-9*, 24739) Lyons Pr.

***Carlisle, David.** What Makes the Trumpet Play. LC 99-65453. (Illus.). 60p. (C). 1999. pap. text 6.99 (*1-893181-26-X*, Simon & Northrop) Le Gesse Stevens.

Carlisle, David B. Dinosaurs, Diamonds, & Things from Outer Space: The Great Extinction. LC 94-32694. xx, 241p. 1995. 45.00 (*0-8047-2392-3*) Stanford U Pr.

— Dinosaurs, Diamonds & Things from Outer Space: The Great Extinction. LC 94-32694. xx, 241p. 1995. pap. 17.95 (*0-8047-2494-6*) Stanford U Pr.

— Human Sex Change & Sex Reversal: Transvestism & Transsexualism. LC 97-51520. (Symposium Ser.: Vol. 45). 456p. 1998. text 109.95 (*0-7734-8496-5*) E Mellen.

Carlisle, Don & Adams, Dolph. Taking More Birds. (Illus.). 160p. 1993. 19.95 (*1-55821-231-0*) Lyons Pr.

Carlisle, Donna. Cast Adrift. (Desire Ser.: No. 700). 1992. per. 2.89 (*0-373-05700-8*, 5-05700-5) Harlequin Bks.

— Stealing Savannah. (Desire Ser.). 1994. per. 2.99 (*0-373-05852-7*, 5-05852-4) Silhouette.

Carlisle, Edward E. & Carlisle, Josephine. Historical Sketches of the Ancient Negro. (African Studies). reprint ed. 20.00 (*0-938818-39-2*) ECA Assoc.

Carlisle, Edward E. & Carlisle, Josephine E. Historical Sketches of the Ancient Negro: A Compilation. (Illus.). 97p. 1998. reprint ed. pap. 15.95 (*1-58073-017-5*) BCP Bks.

Carlisle, Ellen. Smooth Moves: The Relocation Guide for Families on the Move. LC 98-88433. x, 107p. 1999. per. 12.95 (*0-9667827-0-4*) Teacup Press.

Carlisle, Eric. West Coast River Angling. (Illus.). 192p. 1990. pap. 12.95 (*0-88839-212-5*) Hancock House.

Carlisle, Erica & Carlisle, Vanessa. I Was My Mother's Bridesmaid: Young Adults from Blended Families Tell It Like It Is. LC 99-31412. 256p. 1999. pap. 13.95 (*1-885171-34-X*) Wldcat Canyon.

Carlisle, Frederick. Wayne County Historical & Pioneer Society Chronography of Notable Events in the History of the Northwest Territory & Wayne County, 1651-1890: Together with Biographical Sketches of the Early Explorers & Pioneers. (Illus.). 484p. 1997. reprint ed. lib. bdg. 52.50 (*0-8328-6793-4*) Higginson Bk Co.

Carlisle, H. A. The History of Lowndesville, South Carolina. LC 95-40946. 1999. 32.50 (*0-87152-495-3*) Reprint.

Carlisle, Helen T. Song for Tomorrow: A Collection of Poetry. 80p. (Orig.). 1998. pap. 9.95 (*1-892038-01-3*) Ravenwood Pub.

***Carlisle, Henry.** Jonah Man. 272p. 2000. pap. 13.95 (*0-312-24207-7*) St Martin.

Carlisle, Henry & Carlisle, Olga A. The Idealists. LC 98-44018. 288p. 1999. text 23.95 (*0-312-20054-4*, Thomas Dunne) St Martin.

***Carlisle, Henry Olga.** Idealists: A Novel of Revolutionary Russia. 256p. 2000. text 14.95 (*0-312-25394-X*) St Martin.

Carlisle, Howard M. Colonist Fathers, Corporate Sons: A Selective History of the Call Family. (Illus.). xiv, 267p. 1996. 19.95 (*0-9651936-0-8*) Calls Trust.

Carlisle, Isabel, jt. auth. see Gooding, Mel.

Carlisle, Janice, ed. see Dickens, Charles.

Carlisle, Jody, jt. auth. see Cook, Carole.

***Carlisle, John & Maguire, Joseph.** Mastering Data Modeling Using Logical Data Structures. 2000. 44.95 incl. cd-rom (*0-201-70045-X*) Addison-Wesley.

Carlisle, John A. & Parker, Robert C. Beyond Negotiation: Redeeming Customer-Supplier Relationships. LC 88-20733. 200p. 1989. 118.00 (*0-471-92203-X*) Wiley.

Carlisle, John C. A Simple & Vital Design: The Story of the Indiana Post Office Murals. (Illus.). viii, 104p. 1995. pap. 19.95 (*0-87195-110-X*) Ind Hist Soc.

Carlisle, John M. Red Arrow Men: Stories about the 32nd Division on the Villa Verde. (Combat Arms Ser.: No. 22). 215p. 1990. reprint ed. 29.95 (*0-89839-149-0*) Battery Pr.

Carlisle, Josephine, jt. auth. see Carlisle, Edward E.

Carlisle, Josephine E., jt. auth. see Carlisle, Edward E.

Carlisle, Kenneth E. Analyzing Jobs & Tasks. LC 85-20661. (Techniques in Training & Performance Development Ser.). (Illus.). 230p. 1986. 39.95 (*0-87778-194-X*) Educ Tech Pubns.

Carlisle, Kim. The Special Raccoon: Helping Children Learn about Handicaps & Love. LC 94-66764. 1994. pap. 9.95 (*0-88282-096-6*) New Horizon NJ.

Carlisle, Lenore, jt. ed. see Benedict, Susan.

Carlisle, Madelyn. Let's Investigate Beautiful, Bouncy Balloons. (Illus.). 32p. (J). (gr. 4-7). 1992. pap. 4.95 (*0-8120-4734-6*) Barron.

— Let's Investigate Magical, Mysterious Meteorites. LC 92-12776. (Illus.). 32p. (J). (gr. 4-7). 1992. pap. 4.95 (*0-8120-4733-8*) Barron.

— Let's Investigate Sparkling, Silent Snow. (Illus.). 32p. (J). (gr. 4-7). 1992. pap. 4.95 (*0-8120-4736-2*) Barron.

Carlisle, Madelyn W. Beautiful, Bouncy Balloons. LC 92-1177. (Let's Investigate Ser.). (Illus.). 32p. (J). (gr. 2-6). 1996. lib. bdg. 14.45 (*1-56674-131-9*) Forest Hse.

— Let's Investigate Series, 6 vols., Set. (Illus.). 192p. (J). (gr. 2-6). 1997. lib. bdg. 86.70 (*1-56674-929-8*) Forest Hse.

— Magical, Mysterious Meteorites. LC 92-12776. (Let's Investigate Ser.). (Illus.). 32p. (J). (gr. 2-6). 1996. lib. bdg. 14.45 (*1-56674-132-7*) Forest Hse.

— Marvelously Meaningful Maps. LC 92-19788. (Let's Investigate Ser.). (Illus.). 32p. (J). (gr. 2-6). 1996. lib. bdg. 14.45 (*1-56674-133-5*) Forest Hse.

— Slippery, Splendid Sea Creatures. LC 92-45206. (Let's Investigate Ser.). (Illus.). 32p. (J). (gr. 2-6). 1996. lib. bdg. 14.45 (*1-56674-134-3*) Forest Hse.

— Soft, Shimmering Sand. LC 92-44756. (Let's Investigate Ser.). (Illus.). 32p. (J). (gr. 2-6). 1996. lib. bdg. 14.45 (*1-56674-148-3*) Forest Hse.

— Sparkling, Silent Snow. LC 92-16832. (Let's Investigate Ser.). (Illus.). 32p. (J). (gr. 2-6). 1996. lib. bdg. 14.45 (*1-56674-149-1*) Forest Hse.

Carlisle, Madelyn Wood. The Magical, Mysterious Meteorites. (Let's Investigate Ser.). 1992. 10.15 (*0-606-01638-4*, Pub. by Turtleback) Demco.

— Marvelously Meaningful Maps. (Let's Investigate Ser.). 1992. 10.15 (*0-606-01639-2*, Pub. by Turtleback) Demco.

Carlisle, Marcia, ed. Madeleine: An Autobiography. 364p. 1986. reprint ed. 9.95 (*0-89255-108-9*) Persea Bks.

Carlisle, Miriam & Levaniouk, Olga, eds. Nine Essays on Homer. LC 99-11159. (Greek Studies). 272p. 1999. pap. 21.95 (*0-8476-9424-0*) Rowman.

***Carlisle, Miriam & Levaniouk, Olga, eds.** Nine Essays on Homer. LC 99-11159. (Greek Studies). 10p. 1999. 57.50 (*0-8476-9423-2*) Rowman.

Carlisle, Norman. Treasure Hunting in the U. S. A. 24.95 (*0-89190-324-0*) Amereon Ltd.

Carlisle, Olga A. Under a New Sky: A Reunion with Russia. 1993. 21.95 (*0-685-63199-0*) HM.

Carlisle, Olga A., jt. auth. see Carlisle, Henry.

***Carlisle, Olga Andreyev.** Far from Russia: A Memoir. 192p. 2000. text 22.95 (*0-312-25245-5*, Thomas Dunne) St Martin.

Carlisle, Patti, ed. see Leary, Brian.

Carlisle, Patti, ed. see Leary, Brian & MacDorman, John.

***Carlisle, Paul B. & Porowski, James P.** Strength for the Journey: A Biblical Perspective on Discouragement & Depression. 192p. 1999. pap. text 12.95 (*0-7673-9105-5*, LifeWy Press) LifeWay Christian.

Carlisle, Richard G., jt. auth. see Freilich, Robert H.

***Carlisle, Robert.** Exercises in English Phonology & Morphology. 98p. (C). 1999. per. 18.95 (*0-7872-6442-3*) Kendall-Hunt.

— Exercises in English Syntax. 90p. (C). 1999. per. 20.95 (*0-7872-6594-2*) Kendall-Hunt.

— Lectures in the Structure of English. 210p. (C). 1999. per. 26.95 (*0-7872-6443-1*, 41644301) Kendall-Hunt.

Carlisle, Robert B. The Proffered Crown: Saint-Simonianism & the Doctrine of Hope. LC 87-45481. (Johns Hopkins University Studies in Historical & Political Science: Series 105, No. 3). 286p. 1987. reprint ed. pap. 88.70 (*0-608-06706-7*, 206690300009) Bks Demand.

Carlisle, Robert D. Eye of the Glider: Shadow on Cape Cod. unabridged ed. (Illus.). 180p. (Orig.). 1996. pap. 14.95 (*1-888999-00-4*) Stage Neck.

Carlisle, Robert L. Cats over the Atlantic: VPB-73 in World War II. (Illus.). 192p. (Orig.). 1995. pap. 9.95 (*1-56474-124-9*) Fithian Pr.

— P-Boat Pilot: With a Patrol Squadron in the Battle of the Atlantic. LC 92-33211. (Illus.). 158p. (Orig.). 1993. pap. 9.95 (*1-56474-046-3*) Fithian Pr.

— Tower, This Is Andy & Other Flying Stories from Northeast Nebraska. LC 91-18416. (Illus.). 178p. (Orig.). (YA). 1991. pap. 8.95 (*0-934988-24-2*, CIP) Foun Bks.

Carlisle, Rodney P. Management of the United States Navy Research & Development Centers During the Cold War Era: Survey Guide to Reports. 137p. 1997. per. 10.00 (*0-16-061335-3*) USGPO.

Carlisle, Rodney P. Navy RDT&E Planning in an Age of Transition: A Survey Guide to Contemporary Literature. LC 97-39907. 1997. write for info. (*0-945274-37-8*) Naval Hist Ctr.

***Carlisle, Rodney P.** Relationship of Science & Technology: Bibliographic Guide. 96p. 1998. per. 5.50 (*0-16-061338-8*) USGPO.

Carlisle, Rodney P. Where the Fleet Begins: A History of the David Taylor Research Center, 1898-1998. LC 98-24955. (Illus.). 689p. 1998. 48.00 (*0-16-049442-7*) USGPO.

***Carlisle, Rodney P. & Monetta, Dominic J.** Brandy, Our Man in Acapulco: The Life & Times of Colonel Frank M. Brandstetter. LC 99-22172. (Illus.). 377p. 1999. 29.95 (*1-57441-069-5*, Pub. by UNTX Pr) Tex A&M Univ Pr.

Carlisle, Rodney P. & Naval Historical Center (U. S.) Staff. The Relationship of Science & Technology: A Bibliographic Guide. LC 97-39894. 1997. write for info. (*0-945274-38-6*) Naval Hist Ctr.

Carlisle, Rodney P. & Zenzen, Joan M. Supplying the Nuclear Arsenal: American Production Reactors, 1942-1992. LC 95-44410. (Illus.). 296p. (C). 1996. text 48.00 (*0-8018-5207-2*) Johns Hopkins.

Carlisle, Ronald C. The Story of "Woodville" The History, Architecture & Archaeology of a Western Pennsylvania Farm. LC 98-68137. (Illus.). 184p. 1998. pap. text 18.95 (*0-916670-19-8*) Pitt Hist & Landmks Found.

Carlisle, Ronald C., ed. & intro. see Anfinson, Scott F., et al.

Carlisle, Sheila. Pattern Words: 3 Letters to Eight Letters in Length. 140p. (Orig.). 1986. pap. 20.80 (*0-89412-135-9*) Aegean Park Pr.

— Pattern Words: 9-Letters in Length. 167p. (Orig.). 1986. pap. 20.80 (*0-89412-146-4*) Aegean Park Pr.

Carlisle, Sheila, ed. U. S. Naval Cryptographic Activities in the Philippines Prior to World War II. 108p. 1994. pap. 20.80 (*0-89412-222-3*) Aegean Park Pr.

Carlisle, Sidney B. Cooking 101. 142p. 1994. pap. 10.95 (*0-9643380-0-9*) Riviera Publng.

— One Hundred Years of Bread: Classic Breads from Your Bread Machine. LC 96-207995. 128p. 1995. pap. 11.95 (*0-9643380-1-7*) Riviera Publng.

Carlisle, Thomas. Bonstonofavitch! LC 74-78089. (Illus.). 176p. (Orig.). 1974. pap. 7.95 (*0-914580-00-0*) Angst World.

— A Ride on the Wave of the Future: An Essay on Human Potential. LC 78-55736. (Illus.). 1978. 4.00 (*0-914580-08-6*) Angst World.

Carlisle, Thomas J. Beginning with Mary: Women of the Gospels in Portrait. fac. ed. LC 86-11570. 118p. (Orig.). 1986. reprint ed. pap. 36.60 (*0-7837-7947-X*, 204770300008) Bks Demand.

— Eve & After: Old Testament Women in Portrait. fac. ed. LC 84-1551. 155p. 1984. reprint ed. pap. 48.10 (*0-7837-7948-8*, 204770400008) Bks Demand.

— Journey with Job: Poems. LC 75-34230. 94p. reprint ed. pap. 30.00 (*0-8357-9129-7*, 201283000083) Bks Demand.

— You! Jonah! LC 68-20587. (Illus.). 64p. reprint ed. pap. 30.00 (*0-8357-9134-3*, 201275000083) Bks Demand.

Carlisle, Vanessa, jt. auth. see Carlisle, Erica.

Carlisle, William. Bill Carlisle, Lone Bandit. (American Autobiography Ser.). 220p. 1995. reprint ed. lib. bdg. 79.00 (*0-7812-8473-2*) Rprt Serv.

Carlizza, A., jt. ed. see Allegra, C.

Carll, Elizabeth K. Violence in Our Lives: Impact on Workplace, Home & Community. 240p. 1998. pap. 29.99 (*0-205-17085-4*) Allyn.

Carll, George K., ed. see Schwartz, Adolph A., pseud.

Carll, Steve. Trace a Moment's Closure for Clues. 40p. (Orig.). 1996. pap. write for info. (*0-9651401-1-3*) Logodaedalus.

Carlo. Merchandising Mathematics. 2nd ed. (Trade/Tech Math Ser.). 1981. pap., teacher ed. 10.00 (*0-8273-1417-5*) Delmar.

Carlo, jt. ed. see Kobmaly.

Carlo, Andrea De, see De Carlo, Andrea.

Carlo, Ciovanni D. Cartas de Amor a Una Mujor Casada. (SPA.). 64p. 1999. pap. 10.00 (*0-7392-0188-3*, PO3084) Morris Pubng.

Carlo, Donald T. De, see De Carlo, Donald T.

Carlo, George L. Wireless Phones & Health: Scientific Progress. LC 98-46064. viii, 413p. 1998. write for info. (*0-7923-8347-8*) Kluwer Academic.

Carlo, James, et al. Practical Networking with Token Ring: Improving Network Operations with Dedicated & Base Token Ring. (ITCP-US Computer Science Ser.). 350p. 1997. pap. 39.99 (*1-85032-884-6*) ITCP.

Carlo, James T. Understanding Token Ring Protocols & Standards: Newwork Engineering & Management. LC 98-30074. 1998. 93.00 (*0-89006-458-X*) Artech Hse.

Carlo, Jean F. & Fosdick, Rose A. A Treasured Heritage. Dickey, Terry P. & Krumhardt, Andrea P., eds. (Illus.). 61p. (Orig.). 1988. pap. 12.50 (*0-931163-04-8*) U Alaska Museum.

Carlo, Mark De, see De Carlo, Mark.

Carlo, Philip. The Intruder. 1996. text 21.95 (*0-8217-5123-9*) NAL.

— The Night Stalker. LC 97-208386. 576p. 1997. mass mkt. 5.99 (*0-7860-0379-0*, Pinncle Kensgtn) Kensgtn Pub Corp.

***Carlo, Philip.** Night Stalker. 2000. mass mkt. 6.50 (*0-7860-1362-1*, Pinncle Kensgtn) Kensgtn Pub Corp.

— The Night Stalker: The Life & Crimes of Richard Ramirez. 1996. 16.95 incl. audio (*1-882071-83-2*, 634043) B&B Audio.

Carlo, Phillip. The Night Stalker: The True Story of America's Most Feared Serial Killer. LC 96-75279. 432p. 1996. pap. 22.95 (*1-57566-030-X*) Kensgtn Pub Corp.

Carlo-Stella, jt. auth. see Boullart.

Carlock, C. Jesse & Hagerty, Patricia. Bridges to Intimacy: A Workbook for Couples From Dysfunctional Families. 1991. pap. 14.95 (*1-55691-037-1*, 371) Learning Pubns.

Carlock, Chuck. Firebirds. (Illus.). 320p. 1997. reprint ed. mass mkt. 6.50 (*0-553-57705-0*, Spectra) Bantam.

Carlock, Jesse C. & Frey, Diane. Enhancing Self-Esteem. 3rd ed. LC 98-26790. 1998. pap. 31.95 (*1-56032-396-5*) Hemisp Pub.

Carlock, L. L. The Electronic Office & You: Managing Your Productivity. 192p. 1985. text 10.56 (*0-07-027978-0*) McGraw.

Carlock, M. P. Tschudy: History & Genealogy of the Judy-Judah-Tschudy-Tschudin Family Who Have Lived in America, Switzerland & Other Countries of the World, Including Connected Families. (Illus.). 576p. 1992. reprint ed. pap. 86.00 (*0-8328-2511-5*); reprint ed. lib. bdg. 96.00 (*0-8328-2510-7*) Higginson Bk Co.

Carlock, Marion P. Carlock: History of the Carlock Family & Adventures of Pioneer Americans, Including the Kimbrough, Goodpasture, Hoyl, Fite, Fancher, Lee, Wells & Other Connecting Families. (Illus.). 654p. 1997. reprint ed. pap. 97.50 (*0-8328-7851-0*); reprint ed. lib. bdg. 107.50 (*0-8328-7850-2*) Higginson Bk Co.

Carlock, Marty. A Guide to Public Art in Greater Boston: From Newburyport to Plymouth. rev. ed. Rosenberg, Dan, ed. LC 93-34413. (Illus.). 256p. (Orig.). 1993. pap. 12.95 (*1-55832-062-8*) Harvard Common Pr.

Carlock, Michaela. Planet Dreams. LC 97-75467. 336p. (Orig.). 1998. pap. 13.95 (*0-9653024-2-3*) Keswick Hse.

Carlock, Randel S. The Need for Organizational Development in Successful Entrepreneurial Firms. rev. ed. LC 94-30161. (Garland Studies in Entrepreneurship). (Illus.). 280p. 1994. text 58.00 (*0-8153-1731-X*) Garland.

Carlock, Robert H. The Hashknife: The early Days of the Aztec Land & Cattle Co., Ltd. (Great West & Indian Ser.: Vol. 60). (Illus.). 1994. 49.95 (*0-87026-087-1*) Westernlore.

Carloftis, Lucille B. Favorite Recipes from a Treasury of Country Inns. 1998. pap. text 19.95 (*1-57072-076-2*) Overmountain Pr.

Carlomagno, G. M., et al, eds. Computational Methods & Experimental Measurements VIII. LC 97-66709. 712p. 1997. 317.00 (*1-85312-463-X*, 463X) Computational Mech MA.

Carlomagno, G. M. & Brebbia, C. A., eds. Computational Methods & Experimental Measurements VII. 264p. 1995. 319.00 (*1-85312-313-7*) Computational Mech MA.

Carlomagno, G. M. & Brebbia, Carlos A., eds. Computational Methods & Experimental Measurements IX. (Computational Engineering Ser.: Vol. 2). 648p. 1999. 369.00 (*1-85312-683-7*, 6837) Computational Mech MA.

— Computational Methods & Experimental Measurements VII, Vol. VII. LC 95-67481. (CMEM Ser.: Vol. 7). 784p. 1995. 319.00 (*1-56252-237-X*, 3137) Computational Mech MA.

— Computational Methods & Experimental Measures, 2 vols., Vol. 1: Computers & Experiments in Fluid Flow. LC 89-60541. (CMEM Ser.: Vol. 4). 483p. 1989. 101.50 (*0-945824-17-3*) Computational Mech MA.

— Computational Methods & Experimental Measures, 2 vols., Vol. 2: Computers & Experiments in Stress Analysis. LC 89-60541. (CMEM Ser.: Vol. 4). 481p. 1989. 101.50 (*0-945824-18-1*) Computational Mech MA.

Carlomagno, G. M., jt. ed. see Brebbia, Carlos A.

Carlomagno, Sergio. Pragmatic Approaches to Aphasia Therapy. (Illus.). 170p. (Orig.). (C). 1994. pap. text 42.50 (*1-56593-244-7*, 0568) Singular Publishing.

Carlon, Patricia. Crime of Silence. LC 99-18840. 1999. 25.95 (*0-7862-1905-X*) Mac Lib Ref.

— Crime of Silence. LC 98-15803. (Soho Crime Ser.). 196p. 1998. 21.00 (*1-56947-131-2*) Soho Press.

— Crime of Silence. (Soho Crime Ser.). 208p. 1999. pap. 12.00 (*1-56947-172-X*) Soho Press.

***Carlon, Patricia.** Hush It's a Game. 2001. 22.00 (*1-56947-214-9*) Soho Press.

Carlon, Patricia. The Price of an Orphan. LC 99-30787. 208p. 1999. 22.00 (*1-56947-173-8*) Soho Press.

***Carlon, Patricia.** The Price of an Orphan. 272p. 2000. pap. 12.00 (*1-56947-195-9*) Soho Press.

Carlon, Patricia. The Running Woman. LC 97-16842. 196p. 1998. 21.00 (*1-56947-110-X*) Soho Press.

— The Running Woman. LC 97-16842. (Soho Crime Ser.). 189p. 1998. pap. 12.00 (*1-56947-132-0*) Soho Press.

— The Running Woman. large type ed. LC 98-42625. 1999. 30.00 (*0-7862-1671-9*) Thorndike Pr.

— The Souvenir. LC 95-18477. 183p. 1996. 20.00 (*1-56947-048-0*) Soho Press.

— The Souvenir. LC 95-18477. (Soho Crime Ser.). 183p. 1996. pap. 12.00 (*1-56947-065-0*) Soho Press.

***Carlon, Patricia.** The Unquiet Night. LC 99-48518. (Soho Crime Ser.). 192p. 2000. 22.00 (*1-56947-194-0*) Soho Press.

— The Unquiet Night. 2001. pap. 12.00 (*1-56947-213-0*) Soho Press.

Carlon, Patricia. The Whispering Wall. LC 96-20040. 212p. 1996. 20.00 (*1-56947-066-9*) Soho Press.

— The Whispering Wall. LC 96-20040. 208p. 1998. pap. 12.00 (*1-56947-111-8*) Soho Press.

Carlone, Judith, jt. auth. see Burchard, Elizabeth.

***Carlos, et al.** Empowerment Takes More Than a Minute. 144p. 2000. 5.98 (*1-56731-368-X*, MJF Bks) Fine Comms.

Carlos, ed. see Charles.

Carlos, Alberto, ed. see Hernandez, Jose.

Carlos, Alberto, ed. see Hernandez, Jose, et al.

Carlos, Manuel L. State Policies, State Penetration & Ecology: Comparative Analysis of Uneven Development & Underdevelopment in Mexico's Micro Agrarian Regions. (Research Reports: No. 19). 39p. (Orig.). (C). 1981. pap. 5.00 (*0-935391-18-5*, RR-19) UCSD Ctr US-Mex.

Carlos, Peter. Praise the High Grass. 1977. 1.50 (*0-918476-01-1*) Cornerstone Pr.

Carlotto, Mark. Martian Enigmas: The Face, Pyramids & Other Unusual Objects on Mars. LC 91-32489. (Illus.). 123p. 1991. 29.95 (*1-55643-092-2*) North Atlantic.

Carlotto, Mark J. The Martian Enigmas - A Closer Look: The Face, Pyramids & Other Unusual Objects on Mars. 2nd ed. LC 96-49796. (Illus.). 160p. 1997. pap. 18.95 (*1-55643-242-9*) North Atlantic.

***Carlough, Curt, et al, eds.** The Next Station Will Be... An Album of Photographs of Railroad Depots in 1910. 2nd rev. ed. LC 99-67001. (Illus.). 64p. 1999. pap. 17.95 (*0-941652-15-7*) NJ Midland Railroad.

Carlow, Joyce. Darling Mama. 352p. 1999. mass mkt. 5.50 (*0-8217-6202-8*) Kensgtn Pub Corp.

— Defiant Captive. 352p. 1998. mass mkt. 4.99 (*0-8217-5899-3*, Zebra Kensgtn) Kensgtn Pub Corp.

— Highland Desire. 384p. 1998. mass mkt. 4.99 (*0-8217-6058-0*, Zebra Kensgtn) Kensgtn Pub Corp.

***Carlow, Joyce.** Highland Fire. (Zebra Splendor Historical Romances Ser.). 320p. 1999. mass mkt. 4.99 (*0-8217-6225-7*) Kensgtn Pub Corp.

— Highland Flame. (Zebra Splendor Historical Romances Ser.). 384p. 1999. mass mkt. 4.99 (*0-8217-6414-4*, Zebra Kensgtn) Kensgtn Pub Corp.

Carlow, Joyce. Sinfully Delicious, 1. 352p. 1999. mass mkt. 5.99 (*0-8217-6257-5*) Kensgtn Pub Corp.

— So Speaks the Heart. 304p. 1997. mass mkt. 4.99 (*0-8217-5785-7*, Zebra Kensgtn) Kensgtn Pub Corp.

An Asterisk (*) at the beginning of an entry indicates that the title is appearing for the first time.

— Timeswept Passion. 320p. 1997. mass mkt. 4.99 (*0-8217-5567-6*, Zebra Kensgtn) Kensgtn Pub Corp.

Carlow, Joyce, et al. Snow Kisses. 288p. 1998. mass mkt. 4.99 (*0-8217-6056-4*, Zebra Kensgtn) Kensgtn Pub Corp.

— Timeswept Summer. 496p. 1998. pap. 5.99 (*0-8217-5949-3*, Zebra Kensgtn) Kensgtn Pub Corp.

***Carlowicz, Michael J. & Lopez, Ramon E.** Storms from the Sun. 224p. 2000. 24.95 (*0-07-135685-1*) McGraw.

***Carlozzi, Annette D.** Negotiating Small Truths. (Illus.). 1999. pap. write for info. (*0-935213-24-4*) J S Blanton Mus.

Carlozzi, Annette D., ed. 60th Annual Art Faculty Exhibition. (Illus.). 112p. 1998. pap. 13.95 (*0-935213-13-9*) J S Blanton Mus.

Carlozzi, Annette M., jt. auth. see Fenton, Julia A.

Carlozzi, Carl G. The Biblical Message of Healing. 116p. 1992. pap. 8.95 (*0-89869-230-X*) Church Pub Inc.

— New Episcopal Way: Masters Book. 128p. (J). (gr. 6). 1989. pap. 8.95 (*0-8192-4102-4*) Morehouse Pub.

— New Episcopal Way: Students Book. 128p. (J). (gr. 6). 1989. pap. 7.95 (*0-8192-4101-6*) Morehouse Pub.

— Through Life's Window. 96p. 1989. 13.95 (*0-89869-207-5*) Church Pub Inc.

Carlozzi, Carl G., ed. Prayers for Pastor & People. 310p. 1984. 19.95 (*0-89869-108-7*) Church Pub Inc.

Carlquist, S. Comparative Wood Anatomy. (Wood Science Ser.). (Illus.). 450p. 1988. 358.95 (*0-387-18827-4*) Spr-Verlag.

Carlquist, Sherwin. Hawaii: A Natural History. 2nd ed. LC 80-81407. (Illus.). 484p. (C). 1993. pap. text 35.00 (*0-915809-19-2*) Natl Trop Bot.

— Man Naturally: Photos by Sherwin Carlquist. LC 96-228854. (Illus.). 224p. 1996. 39.00 (*0-9648861-0-3*) Pinecone Press.

— Natural Man: Photographs by Sherwin Carlquist. (Illus.). 256p. 1991. 35.00 (*0-9648861-2-X*) Pinecone Press.

— Outsiders: Fifteen Funny Gay Stories. 224p. 1996. 12.00 (*0-9648861-1-1*) Pinecone Press.

Carlquist, Sherwin, photos by. Natural Male: Photographs by Sherwin Carlquist. (Illus.). 220p. 1999. 42.00 (*0-9648861-3-8*) Pinecone Press.

Carls, Kenneth, jt. auth. see Schmiechen, James.

Carls, Stephen D. Louis Loucheur & the Shaping of Modern France, 1916-1931. LC 92-40840. (Illus.). 416p. 1993. text 60.00 (*0-8071-1787-0*) La State U Pr.

Carls, Uwe & Lucko, Peter, eds. Form, Function & Variation in English: Studies in Honour of Klaus Hansen. LC 99-19702. (Illus.). IV, 372p. (C). 1999. pap. text 56.95 (*0-8204-3567-8*) P Lang Pubng.

Carlsen, Clarence J., tr. see Hallesby, O.

Carlsen, D. & Tryon, V. Communication: Graphic Arts. 1976. pap. 10.16 (*0-13-153189-1*) P-H.

***Carlsen, Frances L., ed.** Harris Manufacturers Directory: National Edition, 1999, 2 vols., Set. 3512p. 1999. 549.00 (*1-55600-683-7*) Harris InfoSource.

— Harris New England Manufacturers Directory, 1999. 1248p. 1999. 199.00 (*1-55600-684-5*) Harris InfoSource.

— Nevada Manufacturers Register 2000. 374p. 2000. pap. 61.00 (*1-55600-691-8*) Database Pub Co.

Carlsen, Frances L., ed. Wyoming Manufacturers Register 2000. 243p. 1999. pap. 57.00 (*1-55600-689-6*) Harris InfoSource.

Carlsen, Frances L., ed. see Harris InfoSource Staff.

Carlsen, G. Robert. English Literature: A Chronological Approach. 976p. 1985. text 32.80 (*0-07-009845-X*) McGraw.

— Focus. 4th ed. (Themes & Writers Ser.). (Illus.). 640p. (gr. 7). 1985. text 27.60 (*0-07-009801-8*) McGraw.

— Insights. 4th ed. (Themes & Writers Ser.). (Illus.). 800p. (gr. 9). 1985. text 29.08 (*0-07-009809-3*) McGraw.

— Perception. 4th ed. (Themes & Writers Ser.). (Illus.). 640p. (gr. 8). 1985. text 27.60 (*0-07-009805-0*) McGraw.

Carlsen, G. Robert & Gilbert, Miriam. British & Western Literature. 3rd ed. (Themes & Writers Ser.). (Illus.). 1979. text 33.36 (*0-07-009871-9*) McGraw.

Carlsen, G. Robert & Tovatt, Anthony. Insights: Themes in Literature. 2nd ed. LC 72-641. (Themes & Writers Ser.). 758 p. 1973. write for info. (*0-07-009903-0*) McGraw.

Carlsen, G. Robert, et al. American Literature: A Chronological Approach. 896p. 1985. text 44.70 (*0-07-009844-1*) McGraw.

— American Literature: A Thematic Approach. 4th ed. 1985. text 31.20 (*0-07-009817-4*) McGraw.

— American Literature: Themes & Writers. 3rd ed. (Illus.). (gr. 11). 1979. text 32.48 (*0-07-009867-0*) McGraw.

— British & Western Literature: A Thematic Approach. 4th ed. 800p. 1985. text 44.70 (*0-07-009821-2*) McGraw.

— Encounters. 832p. 1985. text 29.08 (*0-07-009813-1*) McGraw.

***Carlsen, Gary.** The Candida Yeast Answer. 323p. 1999. pap. text 19.95 (*1-57636-079-2*, Pub. by SunRise Pbl) Granite UT.

Carlsen, Hanne. A Bibliography to the Classical Tradition in English Literature. 164p. (Orig.). 1985. pap. text 42.50 (*87-88648-06-0*) Coronet Bks.

Carlsen, Ivana, tr. see Torga, Miguel.

Carlsen, James C. Melodic Perception: A Program for Self-Instruction. 1965. text 23.95 (*0-07-009975-8*) McGraw.

Carlsen, John. Economic & Social Transformation in Rural Kenya. (Centre for Development Research Publications: No. 4). 230p. 1980. 18.95 (*91-7106-170-3*, Pub. by Nordic Africa) Transaction Pubs.

Carlsen, Jorn, ed. O Canada: Essays on Canadian Literature & Culture. (The Dolphin Ser.: No. 25). (Illus.). 256p. (C). 1995. pap. 19.95 (*87-7288-376-6*, Pub. by Aarhus Univ Pr) David Brown.

Carlsen, L. R-oneR-twoCSO-x Structures in the Conversion of Thiocarbonyl Compounds into the Corresponding Oxo Derivatives, Vol. 3. 44p. 1983. pap. text 85.00 (*3-7186-0184-2*) Gordon & Breach.

Carlsen, Mary B. Creative Aging. 256p. 1996. pap. 17.00 (*0-393-70226-X*) Norton.

— Meaning-Making: Therapeutic Processes in Adult Development. (Professional Bks.). 1988. 25.95 (*0-393-70049-6*) Norton.

Carlsen, Philip. The Player-Piano Music of Conlon Nancarrow: An Analysis of Selected Studies. LC 87-832360. (I.S.A.M. Monographs: No. 26). 86p. (Orig.). 1988. pap. 12.00 (*0-914678-29-9*) Inst Am Music.

Carlsen, Robert D. Encyclopedia of Business Charts. 1977. text 55.00 (*0-13-275321-9*) P-H.

Carlsen, Robert S. The War for Heart & Soul of a Highland Maya Town. LC 96-35613. (Illus.). 224p. 1997. 35.00 (*0-292-71193-X*); pap. 14.95 (*0-292-71194-8*) U of Tex Pr.

***Carlser, Frances L., ed.** Harris Manufacturers Directory, 1998: National Edition, 2 vols. 1998. 520.00 (*1-55600-616-0*) Harris InfoSource.

Carlshausen, John. Thoughts of a Money Lender. LC 97-90979. ix, 229p. 1998. pap. 12.95 (*0-533-12524-3*) Vantage.

Carlsnaes, Walter. The Concept of Ideology & Political Analysis: A Critical Examination of Its Usage by Marx, Lenin, & Mannheim, 17. LC 80-1202. (Contributions in Philosophy Ser.: No. 17). 274p. 1981. 55.00 (*0-313-22267-3*, CCI/) Greenwood.

— Energy Vulnerability & National Security: The Energy Crises, Domestic Policy Responses, & Logic of Swedish Neutrality. 224p. 1992. 54.00 (*0-86187-988-0*) St Martin.

Carlsnaes, Walter & Smith, Steve, eds. European Foreign Policy: The EC & Changing Perspectives in Europe. (Modern Politics Ser.: Vol. 24). 320p. 1994. 75.00 (*0-8039-8816-8*); pap. 28.50 (*0-8039-8817-6*) Sage.

Carlson. Barrio Street Carnival Dreams. (J). 1996. pap. 15.95 (*0-8050-4584-8*) St Martin.

— Behavioral Therapy with Dr. Richard Stuart. 1998. VHS 95.00 (*0-205-28358-6*) Allyn.

— Carlson's Guide to Landscape Painting. (Illus.). 144p. reprint ed. pap. 8.95 (*0-486-22927-0*) Dover.

— Cases in Managerial Data Analysis. (Business Statistics Ser.). 1997. pap., student ed. 21.25 (*0-534-51722-6*) Wadsworth Pub.

***Carlson.** Communication in World Business & Industry. 546p. 1999. pap. text 40.00 (*0-536-02834-6*) S&S Trade.

Carlson. Communication Systems. 3rd ed. 1983. 27.50 (*0-07-009961-8*) McGraw.

— Communication Systems. 4th ed. 2001. 59.50 (*0-07-011127-8*) McGraw.

— Corrections. LC 98-4016. 1998. pap. 68.95 (*0-534-53496-1*) Brooks-Cole.

— Dialogue Games. (Studies in Linguistics & Philosophy). 1985. pap. text 54.00 (*90-277-1951-9*) Kluwer Academic.

— Discovering the Universe. 5th ed. 1999. teacher ed. write for info. (*0-7167-3575-X*) W H Freeman.

— Experiential Therapy with Dr. Gus Napier. 1998. VHS 95.00 (*0-205-28364-0*) Allyn.

— Family Therapy. (C). 1999. pap. text 56.00 (*0-205-27403-X*, Macmillan Coll) P-H.

***Carlson.** Fire in the Valley. 463p. 1999. 34.95 (*0-07-135895-1*) McGraw.

Carlson. Foundations of Physiological Psychology. 4th ed. LC 98-38532. 544p. 1998. text 80.00 (*0-205-28311-X*) Allyn.

— Indiscretion Finitude. LC 98-19277. 1999. lib. bdg. 45.00 (*0-226-09293-3*) U Ch Pr.

***Carlson.** Individual Investor's Revolution. 366p. 2000. pap. 15.95 (*0-07-135785-8*) McGraw.

Carlson. Object Relations Therapy with Dotors Jill & David Scharff. 1998. VHS 95.00 (*0-205-28354-3*) Allyn.

— Out of Inferno: Strindberg's Reawakening As an Artist. LC 95-35409. (McLellan Bks.). (Illus.). 412p. (C). 1996. pap. 24.95 (*0-295-97564-4*) U of Wash Pr.

— Physiology of Behavior. 6th ed. 1998. pap. text, student ed. 21.00 (*0-205-27435-8*) P-H.

— Primary Care Women No. 2. 2nd ed. 2001. pap. text. write for info. (*0-323-01065-2*) Mosby Inc.

— Springs: Troubleshooting & Failure Analysis. (Engineering Troubleshooting Ser.: Vol. 1). (Illus.). 192p. 1980. text 125.00 (*0-8247-1003-7*) Dekker.

— Statistical Methods. (C). 1995. pap. text 17.00 (*0-03-098110-7*) Harcourt Coll Pubs.

— Strategic Therapy with Dr. James Coyne. 1998. VHS 95.00 (*0-205-28341-1*) Allyn.

***Carlson.** Sweden. LC 98-31485. (Illus.). 1999. 24.26 (*0-8172-5407-2*) Raintree Steck-V.

Carlson. Through the Looking Glass. 2nd ed. LC 99-35391. 256p. 1999. pap. 19.38 (*0-07-228605-9*) McGraw.

Carlson. Topology of Surfaces. 300p. text. write for info. (*0-471-35544-5*) Wiley.

Carlson & Bright. Maine Objections at Trial. 190p. 1991. pap. text 39.50 (*0-327-03911-6*, 81660-10, MICHIE) LEXIS Pub.

— Missouri Objection at Trial. 200p. 1993. pap. text 39.50 (*0-327-03968-X*, 81943-10, MICHIE) LEXIS Pub.

Carlson & Heintz. College Accounting Pts. 1 & 2. 12th ed. (Swc-Accounting Ser.). 1986. mass mkt. 30.75 (*0-538-01843-7*) S-W Pub.

Carlson & Kjos. Bowenian Therapy Guerin. 1998. VHS 95.00 (*0-205-28360-8*) Allyn.

— Family Therapy. 1999. pap. text, wbk. ed. 20.00 (*0-205-27404-8*) Allyn.

— Feminist Therapy Rampage with Dr. Cheryl Rampage. 1998. VHS 95.00 (*0-205-28348-9*) Allyn.

Carlson & Lyle. Geology. 136p. (C). 1998. pap. text 12.50 (*0-536-01197-4*) S&S Trade.

Carlson, et al. Evidence in the 90s: Appendix. 3rd ed. 1991. text. write for info. (*0-87473-740-0*, 10680-10, MICHIE) LEXIS Pub.

— Evidence in the 90's: 1993 Supplement. 1993. 5.50 (*1-55834-105-6*, 10682-10, MICHIE) LEXIS Pub.

— Federal Rules of Evidence: 1997 Appendix. 28p. 1997. pap. write for info. (*1-55834-580-9*, 10681-11, MICHIE) LEXIS Pub.

Carlson, et al. Minnesota Objections at Trial. 200p. 1992. pap. text 39.50 (*0-327-03912-4*, 81875-10, MICHIE) LEXIS Pub.

Carlson, jt. auth. see Gac.

Carlson, Anita L. Adventures in Yooperland Vol. 1: The Good Old Times. (Illus.). 20p. (J). (ps-6). 1996. spiral bd. 10.00 (*0-9662539-1-4*) Bks By Anita.

— Adventures in Yooperland Vol. 3: A Tale of Charlie & Clara Chipmunk. (Illus.). 16p. (J). (ps-1). 1997. spiral bd. 8.00 (*0-9662539-2-2*) Bks By Anita.

Carlson, William A., ed. see California Redevelopment Association Staff.

Carlson, A., jt. auth. see Youtz, H.

Carlson, A. B. Communications Systems. 3rd ed. (Electrical Engineering Ser.). 704p. (C). 1986. 102.81 (*0-07-009960-X*) McGraw.

Carlson, A. Bruce & Gisser, David G. Electrical Engineering: A Solution Manual. LC 80-21519. (Electrical Engineering Ser.). 640p. (C). 1981. teacher ed. 3.25 (*0-201-03941-9*) Addison-Wesley.

— Electrical Engineering: Concepts & Applications. LC 80-21519. (Electrical Engineering Ser.). 640p. (C). 1981. text. write for info. (*0-201-03940-0*) Addison-Wesley.

Carlson, Albert D., jt. auth. see Soucek, Branko.

Carlson, Allan. Family Questions: Reflections on the American Social Crisis. 335p. 1988. 44.95 (*0-88738-206-1*) Transaction Pubs.

— Family Questions: Reflections on the American Social Crisis. 335p. (C). 1988. pap. 24.95 (*1-56000-555-6*) Transaction Pubs.

***Carlson, Allan.** The New Agrarian Mind: The Movement Toward Decentralist Thought in 20th Century America. LC 99-56518. 197p. 1999. 29.95 (*1-56000-42!-5*) Transaction Pubs.

Carlson, Allan. The Swedish Experiment in Family Politics: The Myrdals & the Interwar Population Crisis. 314p. 1989. 44.95 (*0-88738-299-1*) Transaction Pubs.

Carlson, Allan & Check, Christopher. Culture & Crime. (Independent Policy Reports). 58p. 1996. pap. 6.95 (*0-945999-47-X*) Independent Inst.

***Carlson, Allen.** Aesthetics & the Environment: Appreciation of Nature Art & Architecture. LC 99-28959. 1999. text. write for info. (*0-415-20683-9*) Routledge.

Carlson, Althea. Riding a White Horse: Ted Turner's Goodwill Games & Other Crusades. LC 98-70400. 272p. 1998. pap. 19.95 (*0-9663743-0-4*, 9663743) Episcopal Pr.

Carlson, Alvar W. Spanish-American Homeland: Four Centuries in New Mexico's Rio Arriba. LC 90-4345. (Creating the North American Landscape Ser.). (Illus.). 312p. 1991. text 42.50 (*0-8018-3990-4*) Johns Hopkins.

Carlson, Amy Greimann & Habegger, Larry, eds. The Gift of Birds: True Encounters with Avian Spirits. LC 99-36686. (Travelers' Tales Ser.). 300p. 1999. pap. 17.95 (*1-885211-41-4*, 41-4, Pub. by Trvlers Tale) OReilly & Assocs.

Carlson, Amy Greimann, jt. ed. see George, Donald W.

Carlson, Amy Greimann, jt. ed. see Habegger, Larry.

Carlson, Andrea. Creating a Climate of Hope: Ten Neighborhoods Tackle the Drug Crisis. O'Neil, Jean, ed. 84p. 1992. pap. 14.95 (*0-934513-19-8*, M23A) Natl Crime DC.

— Teens, Crime, & the Community in Boys & Girls Clubs. O'Neil, Jean, ed. 23p. (Orig.). 1995. pap. 9.95 (*0-934513-72-4*, TCCB&G) Natl Crime DC.

***Carlson, Andrea & Kelly, Theresa.** Standing in the Gap. Kirby, Judy, ed. 59p. 1999. pap. 12.95 (*0-934513-88-0*) Natl Crime DC.

***Carlson, Anita.** Adventures in Yooperland Vol. 4: Golden School Days in War Years. Fudala, Linda, ed. (Illus.). 125p. (YA). (gr. 7-12). 2000. pap. 16.00 (*0-9662539-4-9*) Bks By Anita.

Carlson, Ann D. Flannelboard Stories for Infants & Toddlers. LC 98-54724. 196p. (J). 1999. 25.00 (*0-8389-0759-8*) ALA.

— The Preschooler & the Library. LC 91-18073. (Illus.). 172p. 1991. 28.00 (*0-8108-2457-4*) Scarecrow.

Carlson, Ann L., jt. auth. see Kovacs, Diane K.

Carlson, Anna L. The Candy Cruncher. 2nd ed. LC 80-83738. (Illus.). 24p. (J). (gr. k-4). 1981. pap. 1.95 (*0-939938-03-0*) Karwyn Ent.

— The Cookie Looker. 2nd ed. LC 80-82182. (Illus.). (J). (gr. k-4). 1980. pap. 1.95 (*0-939938-01-4*) Karwyn Ent.

— Homer Bear's Secret. (Illus.). 24p. (Orig.). (J). (gr. k-4). 1983. pap. 1.95 (*0-939938-05-7*) Karwyn Ent.

— The Mouse Family's Christmas. (Illus.). 24p. (Orig.). (J). (gr. k-4). 1983. pap. 1.95 (*0-939938-04-9*) Karwyn Ent.

— Stories to Treasure. (Illus.). 24p. (Orig.). (J). (ps-5). 1984. pap. 62.40 (*0-939938-06-5*) Karwyn Ent.

— Toady Tales. 2nd ed. LC 80-83018. 24p. (J). (gr. k-4). 1980. pap. 1.95 (*0-939938-02-2*) Karwyn Ent.

Carlson, Anna L. & Wynne, Diana. My Brother & I Like Cookies. 2nd ed. LC 80-81624. (Illus.). 96p. (Orig.). (J). (gr. 1-7). 1980. pap. 4.95 (*0-939938-00-6*) Karwyn Ent.

Carlson, Anne. The Meatless Galley Cookbook. LC 95-30807. (Illus.). 192p. 1995. pap. 16.95 (*0-9639566-2-0*) Seaworthy WI.

Carlson, Anton J., et al. The Machinery of the Body. enl. rev. ed. LC 61-14536. 1993. lib. bdg. 30.00 (*0-226-09279-8*) U Ch Pr.

— The Machinery of the Body. 5th enl. rev. ed. LC 61-14536. (Illus.). 752p. reprint ed. pap. 200.00 (*0-608-09280-0*, 205415400004) Bks Demand.

Carlson, Arvid C. & Sundaram, Sam L. Ssri Reductn JFET Parmtr. LC 92-25875. (Six Sigma Research Institute Ser.). 1993. pap. text 10.95 (*0-201-63429-5*) Addison-Wesley.

Carlson, Avis D. Small World...Long Gone LC 78-22046. 1979. write for info. (*0-89340-188-9*) Chivers N Amer.

Carlson, B. Airplane Kill Cookbook: A Collection of Spurious Recipes Using Ventre Montant (French for Belly-Up) (Illus.). 110p. 1996. pap. 7.95 (*1-57166-056-9*) Quixote Pr IA.

— Aphrodisiac Cooking. (Illus.). 242p. 1993. spiral bd. 11.95 (*1-878488-83-X*) Hearts N Tummies.

— Aphrodisiac Cooking. (Illus.). 160p. 1994. spiral bd. 5.95 (*1-57166-007-0*) Hearts N Tummies.

— Apples Apples Apples. (Illus.). 176p. 1997. spiral bd. 5.95 (*1-57166-084-4*) Hearts N Tummies.

— Arkansas Cookin' (Illus.). 160p. 1994. spiral bd. 5.95 (*1-57166-002-X*) Hearts N Tummies.

— The Best of the Mississippi River Ghosts. (Illus.). 182p. 1997. pap. 9.95 (*1-57166-081-X*) Quixote Pr IA.

— Cooking with Things That Go "Cluck" (Illus.). 176p. (J). 1998. spiral bd. 5.95 (*1-57166-113-1*) Hearts N Tummies.

— Cooking with Things That Go Moo. (Illus.). 160p. 1994. spiral bd. 5.95 (*1-57166-016-X*) Hearts N Tummies.

— Cooking with Things That Go "Oink" (Illus.). 176p. (J). 1998. spiral bd. 5.95 (*1-57166-114-X*) Hearts N Tummies.

— Dakota Cookin' (Illus.). 160p. 1994. spiral bd. 5.95 (*1-878488-97-X*) Hearts N Tummies.

— Dear Tabby. (Illus.). 83p. 1993. pap. 5.95 (*1-878488-78-3*) Quixote Pr IA.

— Depression Times Cookbook. (Illus.). 226p. 1993. spiral bd. 11.95 (*1-878488-84-8*) Hearts N Tummies.

— Dial-a-Dream Cookbook. (Illus.). 236p. 1996. spiral bd. 11.95 (*1-57166-019-4*) Hearts N Tummies.

— Good Cookin' from the Plain People. (Illus.). 160p. 1994. spiral bd. 5.95 (*1-57166-009-7*) Hearts N Tummies.

— Hill Country Cookin' (Illus.). 160p. 1994. spiral bd. 5.95 (*1-57166-005-4*) Hearts N Tummies.

— Hormone Helper Cookbook. (Illus.). 238p. 1996. spiral bd. 11.95 (*1-57166-020-8*) Hearts N Tummies.

— Idaho Cooking. (Illus.). 176p. 1998. spiral bd. 5.95 (*1-57166-110-7*) Hearts N Tummies.

— Illinois Cookin' (Illus.). 160p. 1994. spiral bd. 5.95 (*1-57166-003-8*) Hearts N Tummies.

— Indiana Cookin' (Illus.). 160p. 1996. spiral bd. 5.95 (*1-57166-049-6*) Hearts N Tummies.

— Iowa Cookin' (Illus.). 160p. 1994. spiral bd. 5.95 (*1-878488-98-8*) Hearts N Tummies.

— Kansas Cookin' (Illus.). 160p. 1996. spiral bd. 5.95 (*1-57166-076-3*) Hearts N Tummies.

— Michigan Cookin' (Illus.). 160p. 1994. spiral bd. 5.95 (*1-878488-99-6*) Hearts N Tummies.

— Michigan's Roadkill Cookbook. (Illus.). 112p. 1994. pap. 7.95 (*1-878488-75-9*) Quixote Pr IA.

— Michigan's Vanishing Outhouse. (Illus.). 183p. 1994. pap. 9.95 (*1-878488-77-5*) Quixote Pr IA.

— Midwest Small Town Cookin' (Illus.). 160p. 1994. spiral bd. 5.95 (*1-57166-006-2*) Hearts N Tummies.

— Minnesota Cooking. (Illus.). 160p. 1994. spiral bd. 5.95 (*1-57166-000-3*) Hearts N Tummies.

— Missouri Cooking. (Illus.). 160p. 1994. spiral bd. 5.95 (*1-57166-001-1*) Hearts N Tummies.

— New Jersey Cooking. (Illus.). 160p. 1997. spiral bd. 5.95 (*1-57166-090-9*) Hearts N Tummies.

— New York Cooking. (Illus.). 160p. 1997. spiral bd. 5.95 (*1-57166-079-8*) Hearts N Tummies.

— Ohio Cookin' (Illus.). 160p. 1997. spiral bd. 5.95 (*1-57166-077-1*) Hearts N Tummies.

— The Orchards, Berry Patches & Garden Cookbook. (Illus.). 230p. 1997. spiral bd. 11.95 (*1-57166-082-8*) Hearts N Tummies.

— Oregon Cooking. (Illus.). 176p. 1998. spiral bd. 5.95 (*1-57166-112-3*) Hearts N Tummies.

— Out Behind the Barn. (Illus.). 137p. 1996. pap. 9.95 (*1-57166-054-2*) Quixote Pr IA.

— Out Behind the Barn: A Celebration of Iowa's Sesquicentennial 1996. (Illus.). 137p. 1996. pap. 9.95 (*1-57166-055-0*) Quixote Pr IA.

— Pennsylvania Cooking. (Illus.). 160p. 1997. spiral bd. 5.95 (*1-57166-078-X*) Hearts N Tummies.

— Pregnant Lady Cooking. (Illus.). 160p. 1994. spiral bd. 5.95 (*1-57166-008-9*) Hearts N Tummies.

— Revenge of Roadkill. (Illus.). 117p. 1993. pap. 7.95 (*1-878488-42-2*) Quixote Pr IA.

— Some Awfully Tame but Kinda Funny Stories about Early Dakota Ladies of the Evening. (Illus.). 172p. 1992. pap. 9.95 (*1-878488-46-5*) Quixote Pr IA.

— Washington Cooking. (Illus.). 176p. 1998. spiral bd. 5.95 (*1-57166-111-5*) Hearts N Tummies.

— Wisconsin Cookin' (Illus.). 160p. 1994. spiral bd. 5.95 (*1-57166-004-6*) Hearts N Tummies.

— Working Girl Cooking. (Illus.). 160p. 1994. spiral bd. 5.95 (*1-57166-010-0*) Hearts N Tummies.

Carlson, Barbara. Food Festivals: Eating Your Way from Coast to Coast. LC 97-971. (Illus.). 428p. 1997. 14.95 (*1-57859-003-5*, 00156898) Visible Ink Pr.

— This Broad's Life: Raucous Riveting Autobiography of the Most Outrageous Radio Talk-Show Host. (Illus.). 288p. 1997. per. 14.00 (*0-671-52304-X*, PB Trade Paper) PB.

Carlson, Barbara, et al. Taking Care of Me: (So I Can Take Care of My Children) LC 94-23012. (Tools for Everyday Parenting Ser.). (Illus.). 112p. (Orig.). 1998. lib. bdg. 18.95 (*1-884734-03-0*) Parenting Pr.

Carlson, Barbara S. Between This World. 34p. (Orig.). 1996. pap. 5.50 (*0-9647127-5-X*) Coreopsis Bks.

C

An Asterisk (*) at the beginning of an entry indicates that the title is appearing for the first time.

Carlson, Betty & Smith, Jane S. Great Christian Hymn Writers. rev. ed. LC 97-15861. 224p. 1997. pap. 11.99 (*0-89107-944-0*) Crossway Bks.

Carlson, Betty, jt. auth. see Smith, Jane S.

*__Carlson, Beverly C.__ When We Came Here to Dwell. LC 00-190865. 291p. 2000. 25.00 (*0-7388-2050-4*); pap. 18.00 (*0-7388-2051-2*) Xlibris Corp.

Carlson, Bob. Walking for Health Fitness & Sport. 320p. (Orig.). 1996. pap. 15.95 (*1-55591-236-2*) Fulcrum Pub.

Carlson, Bonnie E. & Cervera, Neil. Inmates & Their Wives: Incarceration & Family Life, 14. LC 92-19428. (Studies in Social Welfare Policies & Programs: No. 14). 176p. 1992. 47.95 (*0-313-27481-9*, CIJ, Greenwood Pr) Greenwood.

Carlson, Brian M. Itasca County: It's Fair, Agricultural Association, & Agriculture. 256p. 1993. pap. 16.95 (*0-9636002-0-6*) Itasca Cnty.

Carlson, Bruce. Arkansas Roadkill Cookbook. (Illus.). 112p. 1992. pap. 7.95 (*1-878488-73-2*) Quixote Pr IA.

— A Cookbook for Them What Ain't Done a Whole Lot of Cookin' (Illus.). 252p. 1993. spiral bd. 11.95 (*1-878488-85-6*) Hearts N Tummies.

— Cookin' a la Nude. (Illus.). 152p. 1995. spiral bd. 9.95 (*1-57166-024-0*) Black Iron.

— Cooking with Spirits. (Illus.). 160p. 1995. spiral bd. 5.95 (*1-57166-017-8*) Black Iron.

— Cooking with Things That Go Splash. (Illus.). 160p. 1995. spiral bd. 5.95 (*1-57166-015-1*) Black Iron.

— Covered Bridges Cookbook. (Illus.). 224p. 1995. spiral bd. 11.95 (*1-57166-029-1*) Hearts N Tummies.

— The Dakotas' Vanishing Outhouse: A Collection of Illustrations & Stories about a Rapidly Vanishing Institution in the Dakotas, the Little Outhouse Out Back. (Illus.). 175p. (Orig.). 1990. pap. 9.95 (*1-878488-23-6*) Quixote Pr IA.

— Electric Circuits. (C). 1996. text. write for info. (*0-201-52226-8*) Addison-Wesley.

— A Field Guide to Illinois Critters. (Illus.). 109p. (Orig.). 1991. pap. 7.95 (*1-878488-49-X*) Quixote Pr IA.

— A Field Guide to Iowa's Critters. (Illus.). 105p. (Orig.). 1991. pap. 7.95 (*1-878488-34-1*) Quixote Pr IA.

— A Field Guide to Missouri's Critters. (Illus.). 109p. (Orig.). 1991. pap. 7.95 (*1-878488-45-7*) Quixote Pr IA.

— Flat-Out Dirt Cheap Cookin. (Illus.). 258p. 1993. spiral bd. 11.95 (*1-878488-87-2*) Black Iron.

— Ghosts of the Iowa Great Lakes. (Illus.). 174p. (Orig.). 1989. pap. 9.95 (*1-878488-11-2*) Quixote Pr IA.

— The Great Midwest American Wild Critter Cookbook. (Illus.). 214p. 1992. spiral bd. 11.95 (*1-878488-71-6*) Black Iron.

— Hunting-in-the-Nude Cookbook. LC 96-144827. (Illus.). 150p. 1994. spiral bd. 9.95 (*1-878488-93-7*) Black Iron.

— Illinois Vanishing Outhouse: A Collection of Photographs, Illustrations, & Stories about a Rapidly Vanishing Institution in Illinois, the Little Outhouse Out Back. (Illus.). 172p. (Orig.). 1989. pap. 9.95 (*1-878488-22-8*) Quixote Pr IA.

— Indian Cooking Cookbook. LC 96-144839. (Illus.). 150p. 1992. spiral bd. 9.95 (*1-57166-018-6*) Black Iron.

— Iowa: "The Land Between the Vowels" (Illus.). 146p. (Orig.). 1989. pap. 9.95 (*1-878488-15-5*) Quixote Pr IA.

— Iowa's Road Kill Cookbook: A Collection of Spurious Recipes Using Ventre Montant (French for Belly-Up) Animals One Finds on Iowa Highways. (Illus.). 102p. (Orig.). 1989. pap. 7.95 (*1-878488-13-9*) Quixote Pr IA.

— Kansas Roadkill Cookbook. (Illus.). 120p. 1995. pap. 7.95 (*1-57166-027-5*) Quixote Pr IA.

— Lake Country Cooking Book. (Illus.). 238p. 1993. spiral bd. 11.95 (*1-878488-88-0*) Black Iron.

— Minnesota's Roadkill Cookbook. (Illus.). 112p. 1992. pap. 7.95 (*1-878488-74-0*) Quixote Pr IA.

— Minnesota's Vanishing Outhouse: A Collection of Illustrations & Stories about a Rapidly Vanishing Institution in Minnesota, the Little Outhouse Out Back. (Illus.). 168p. (Orig.). 1991. pap. 9.95 (*1-878488-26-0*) Quixote Pr IA.

— Mississippi River Cookin' Book. (Illus.). 214p. (Orig.). 1989. spiral bd. 11.95 (*1-878488-09-0*) Hearts N Tummies.

— Missouri's Roadkill Cookbook. (Illus.). 110p. (Orig.). 1991. pap. 7.95 (*1-878488-44-9*) Quixote Pr IA.

— Old Iowa Houses: New Loves. (Illus.). 173p. (Orig.). 1991. pap. 9.95 (*1-878488-37-6*) Quixote Pr IA.

— One Hundred One Ways to Use a Dead Riverfly. (Illus.). 106p. (Orig.). 1991. pap. 7.95 (*1-878488-60-0*) Quixote Pr IA.

— Roaring Twenties Cookbook. (Illus.). 224p. 1993. spiral bd. 11.95 (*1-878488-86-4*) Hearts N Tummies.

— Some Awfully Tame, but Kinda Funny Stories about Early Illinois Ladies-of-the-Evening. (Illus.). 152p. (Orig.). 1990. pap. 9.95 (*1-878488-25-2*) Quixote Pr IA.

— Some Awfully Tame, but Kinda Funny Stories about Early Iowa Ladies of the Evening. (Illus.). 172p. (Orig.). 1989. pap. 9.95 (*1-878488-18-X*) Quixote Pr IA.

— Some Awfully Tame, but Kinda Funny Stories about Early Missouri Ladies-of-the-Evening. (Illus.). 169p. (Orig.). 1990. pap. 9.95 (*1-878488-24-4*) Quixote Pr IA.

— South Dakota's Roadkill Cookbook: A Collection of Spurious Recipes Using Ventre Montant (French for Belly-Up) Animals One Finds on South Dakota Highways. (Illus.). 104p. (Orig.). 1990. pap. 7.95 (*1-878488-19-8*) Quixote Pr IA.

— Underground Missouri. (Illus.). 172p. (Orig.). 1991. pap. 9.95 (*1-878488-47-3*) Quixote Pr IA.

— Wisconsin's Roadkill Cookbook. (Illus.). 106p. (Orig.). 1991. pap. 7.95 (*1-878488-40-6*) Quixote Pr IA.

— Wisconsin's Vanishing Outhouse: A Collection of Illustrations & Stories about a Rapidly Vanishing Insitution in Wisconsin, the Little Outhouse Out Back. (Illus.). 168p. (Orig.). 1990. pap. 9.95 (*1-878488-27-9*) Quixote Pr IA.

Carlson, Bruce, ed. The Schubert Club Museum. (Illus.). 64p. (Orig.). 1990. pap. 10.00 (*0-912373-05-9*) Schubert.

Carlson, Bruce, intro. Song of India. (Illus.). 40p. (Orig.). 1992. pap. 5.00 (*0-912373-06-7*) Schubert.

Carlson, Bruce, ed. see Bell, Netha & Scholl, Gary.

Carlson, Bruce, ed. see Erickson, Lori.

Carlson, Bruce, ed. see Welch, Tom.

Carlson, Bruce, ed. & illus. see Thomas, Robert.

Carlson, Bruce, ed. & illus. see Wallace, Pat.

Carlson, Bruce A. Circuits: Engineering Cncpts & Analysis Linear Elec Circuits. LC 99-41780. 840p. 2000. 96.95 (*0-534-37097-7*) Thomson Learn.

Carlson, Bruce A. Circuits: Engineering Concepts & Analysis of Linear Electric Circuits. LC 96-18043. 860p. 1996. pap. 61.95 (*0-471-15667-1*) Wiley.

Carlson, Bruce M. Patten's Foundations of Embryology. 6th ed. LC 96-75396. 752p. (C). 1996. 85.63 (*0-07-009940-5*) McGraw.

— Pattern's Foundations of Embryology. 5th ed. (C). 1988. text 77.25 (*0-07-009902-2*) McGraw.

Carlson, Bruce M., tr. see Polezhaev, L. V.

Carlson, Bryce. Blackjack for Blood: The Card-Counters Bible, & Complete Winning Guide. 1992. pap. 19.95 (*0-9633684-0-0*) CompuStar Pr.

Carlson, C., et al. Exclusive Reactions of High Momentum Transfers. 308p. 1994. text 99.00 (*981-02-1768-4*) World Scientific Pub.

Carlson, C. C. Escape the Coming Night. write for info. (*0-8499-0726-8*) J Countryman.

Carlson, C. C., jt. auth. see Jeremiah, David.

Carlson, C. C., jt. auth. see Lindsey, Hal.

Carlson, C. P., Jr. Justification in Earlier Medieval Theology. 157p. 1975. pap. text 65.00 (*90-247-1709-4*, Pub. by M Nijhoff) Kluwer Academic.

Carlson, Cari, jt. auth. see Hellstrom, Lawrence.

Carlson, Carl W. & Hodder, Michael, eds. The American Numismatic Association Anthology. (Illus.). 372p. 1991. text 65.00 (*0-943161-32-0*) Bowers & Merena.

*__Carlson, Carol.__ Sandcastles in The Rain. 1999. pap. text 12.99 (*1-888848-27-8*) Western Front.

Carlson, Carole C., jt. auth. see Corcoran, John.

Carlson, Carole C., jt. auth. see Lindsey, Hal.

Carlson, Carole C., jt. auth. see Rogers, Dale Evans.

Carlson, C.C., jt. auth. see Jeremiah, David.

Carlson, Charles & Evers, Yvonne. CUES Job Write: Credit Union Position Description Manual. 122p. (Orig.). 1991. pap. 89.00 (*1-889394-15-7*) Credit Union Execs.

Carlson, Charles B. Buying Stocks Without a Broker: Commission-Free Investing Through Company Dividend Reinvestment Plans. 2nd ed. (Illus.). 448p. 1995. pap. 17.95 (*0-07-011501-X*) McGraw.

— Buying Stocks Without a Broker: Commission-Free Investing Through Company Dividend Reinvestment Plans. 2nd ed. 1996. text 29.95 (*0-07-011500-1*) McGraw.

— Chuck Carlson's 60 Second Investor: 201 Tips, Tools & Tactics for the Time-Strapped Investor. LC 97-23170. 304p. 1997. pap. 12.95 (*0-07-011892-2*) McGraw.

*__Carlson, Charles B.__ Eight Steps to Seven Figures: The Strategies Today's "Mainstream" Inventors Have Used to Become Millionaires. 336p. 2000. 24.95 (*0-385-49731-8*) Doubleday.

Carlson, Charles B. Free Lunch on Wall Street: Perks, Freebies, & Giveaways for Investors. 234p. 1993. pap. 14.95 (*0-07-009979-0*) McGraw.

— No-Load Stocks: How to Buy Your First Share & Every Share Directly from the Company-With No Broker's Fee. expanded rev. ed. LC 96-36839. (Illus.). 275p. 1996. pap. 16.95 (*0-07-011880-9*) McGraw.

*__Carlson, Charles E. & Tenuta, Rosemary.__ CUES 1999 Compensation Manuel. 170p. 1999. pap. 289.00 (*1-889394-45-9*) Credit Union Execs.

*__Carlson, Charlie.__ The First Florida Cavalry Regiment C. S. A. LC 99-21317. 1999. 12.95 (*1-877633-43-7*) Luthers.

Carlson, Charlie. Strange Florida: The Unexplained & Unusual. LC 97-39306. (Illus.). 112p. 1997. pap. 9.95 (*1-877633-39-9*) Luthers.

Carlson, Chip. Tom Horn: Killing Men Is My Specialty...: The Definitive History of the Notorious Wyoming Stock Detective. (Illus.). 261p. (Orig.). 1991. pap. 16.95 (*0-9630248-0-9*) Beartooth.

Carlson, Chuck. Green Bay Packer's Pocket Primer. Kidson, Darcie, ed. LC 97-22758. (Illus.). 96p. (Orig.). 1997. pap. 8.95 (*1-886110-16-6*, Pub. by Addax Pubng) Midpt Trade.

— The Individual Investor Revolution: Unlock the Secrets of Wall Street & Invest Like a Pro. (Illus.). 366p. 1998. 21.95 (*0-07-012049-8*) McGraw.

— Mulligans 4 All: 101 Excuses, Alibis & Observations on the Game of Golf. LC 98-24658. (Illus.). 144p. 1998. 9.95 (*1-886110-58-1*) Addax Pubng.

— Puck! Kirby Puckett: Baseball's Last Warrior. Cameron, Steve, ed. LC 97-13818. 224p. 1997. 22.95 (*1-886110-14-X*, Pub. by Addax Pubng) Midpt Trade.

— Titletown Again: The Super Bowl Season of the 1996 Green Bay Packers. Cameron, Steve, ed. LC 97-70764. Orig. Title: Official Story of the 1996 Green Bay Packers. (Illus.). 144p. 1997. 26.95 (*1-886110-21-2*); pap. 16.95 (*1-886110-22-0*) Addax Pubng.

*__Carlson, Cindy & Weisl, Angela J.__ Constructions of Widowhood & Virginity In the Middle Ages. LC 99-27418. (New in the Middle Ages Ser.). 350p. 1999. text 49.95 (*0-312-21136-8*) St Martin.

Carlson, Cindy L., jt. auth. see Grotevant, Harold D.

Carlson, Cody. Out of the Darkness: The Mystery & Majesty of God's Creation. (Illus.). 216p. 1998. 50.00 (*1-888237-13-9*) Baxter Pr.

Carlson, Constance. Garage Sales 101. (Illus.). 70p. 1998. 9.95 (*0-9665203-0-0*) Mouths in Motion.

Carlson, D. Proceedings of the Symposium on Chemical Aspects of High-Tc Superconductors. vii, 412p. 1990. text 1229.00 (*2-88124-450-5*) Gordon & Breach.

Carlson, D. & Shield, R., eds. Finite Elasticity. 1982. lib. bdg. 222.50 (*90-247-2629-8*) Kluwer Academic.

Carlson, D. A. & Haurie, A. B. Infinite Horizon Optimal Control. (Lecture Notes in Economics & Mathematical Systems Ser.: Vol. 290). xi, 254p. 1987. pap. 33.70 (*0-387-17824-4*) Spr-Verlag.

Carlson, D. A., et al. Infinite Horizon Optimal Control: Deterministic & Stochastic Systems. 2nd enl. rev. ed. xvi, 332p. 1991. 110.00 (*0-387-54249-3*) Spr-Verlag.

Carlson, D. S., ed. Craniofacial Biology. (Craniofacial Growth Ser.: Vol. 10). (Illus.). 269p. 1981. 43.00 (*0-929921-07-0*) UM CHGD.

Carlson, D. S. & McNamara, J. A., eds. Muscle Adaptation in the Craniofacial Region. (Craniofacial Growth Ser.: Vol. 8). (Illus.). 252p. 1978. 45.00 (*0-929921-05-4*) UM CHGD.

Carlson, D. S., jt. ed. see Ribbens, Katherine A.

Carlson, Dale. Confessions of a Brain-Impaired Writer. LC 98-7369. 220p. 1999. pap. 14.95 (*1-884158-24-2*, Pub. by Bick Pub Hse) BookWorld.
Autobiography, woman author, publisher, writer of children's books, psychology books, learning disabled. Memoir of an ALA Notable Book author, her life as writer, publisher, teacher, wildlife rehabilitator, lover, wife, mother - complicated with high IQ, social learning disabilities, right-brain impairment that create success in her career & havoc in her personal life. Carlson writes "with intelligence, spunk & wit."--The New York Times Book Review. "Carlson captures with ferocity the dilemmas experienced by people with right-hemisphere learning disabilities."--Dr. Kathleen Laundy, Yale School of Medicine. Available at BookWorld Services, Ingram, Baker & Taylor. Or order, Bick Pub. House, 307 Neck Rd., Madison, CT, 06443. Distributed by BookWorld Services. *Publisher Paid Annotation.*

-Stop the Pain: Adult Meditations. LC 99-40026. (Illus.). 224p. 2000. pap. 14.95 (*1-884158-21-8*) Bick Pub Hse.
What is meditation? There are many ways into meditation. Learn to quiet the brain's noise so you can hear, watch & understand the ways of yourself in daily life. Medication techniques to end the psychological sufferings of depression, anger, hurt, anxiety, loneliness, marital & sexual stress, tension over family, work, money. Publishers Weekly says Carlson's work is "a practical focus on psychological survival skills." Times says she writes "with intelligence, spark & wit." Available at BookWorld Services, Ingram, Baker & Taylor or Book Co. To order: Bick Publishing House, 307 Neck Road, Madison, Ct. 06403, (203) 245-0073. Distributed by BookWorld Services, Inc. *Publisher Paid Annotation.*

-Stop the Pain: Teen Meditations. LC 98-28757. (Psychology for Teenagers Ser.: No. 3). (Illus.). 189p. (Orig.). (YA). (gr. 5-9). 1999. pap. 14.95 (*1-884158-23-4*) Bick Pub Hse.
What is meditation? Many ways into meditation. Learn to quiet the brain's noise so you can hear, watch, understand the ways of yourself in daily life. Meditation techniques to end the psychololgical suffering of depression, anger, hurt, anxiety, loneliness, martial & sexual stress, tension over family, work, money. Publishers Weekly says Carlson's work" is a practical focus on psychological survival skills." NY Times says she writes "with intelligence, spunk & wit." Available at BookWorld Services, Ingram, Baker & Taylor. To order: Bick Publishing House, 3207 Neck Road, Madision, CT 06443. (203) 245-0073. Distributed by BookWorld Services. *Publisher Paid Annotation.*

Carlson, Dale & Ruth, Irene. Wildlife Care for Birds & Mammals: Basic Manuals Wildlife Rehabilitation, 7 vols. in 1. 3rd ed. LC 96-79851. (Illus.). 288p. (Orig.). 1997. pap. 59.70 (*1-884158-16-1*, Pub. by Bick Pub Hse) BookWorld.
Seven wildlife rehabilitation handbooks, under the direction of Wind Over Wings Rehabilitation Center, provide beginners with SAFE, step-by-step, text & picture guidance for independent rehabilitators, rehabilitation centers, parents, teachers, librarians & all who care about injured & orphaned small wildlife. The series is endorsed by wildlife rehabilitation centers, national wildlife magazines & veterinarians. Richard A. Alter, DVM says: "These compact handbooks present safe, responsible wildlife care, first aid treatment, with appropriate initial care, habitat design, captive diets & basic rehabilitation & release techniques." Included are instructions on who to call for help & advice, how to get licensed, & to bring to those who want to learn & teach basic rehabilitation, the professional information of rehabilitators in an easy-to-use, uncomplicated style. The illustrated series includes: I Found A Baby Bird, What Do I Do? 64 p. $9.95 (1-884158-00-5); I Found A Baby Duck, What Do I Do? 64 p. $9.95 (1-884158-02-1), I Found A Baby Opossum, What Do I Do? 64 p. $9.95 (1-884158-06-4); I Found A Baby Rabbit, What Do I Do? 64 p. $9.95 (1-884158-03-X), I Found A Baby Raccoon, What Do I Do? 64 p. $9.95 (1-884158-05-6), I Found A Baby Squirrel, What Do I Do? 64p. $9.95 (1-884158-01-3), FIRST AID FOR WILDLIFE, 64p. $9.95 (1-884158-14-5). Sep. vol. set of 7 (1-884158-04-8). Available at: BookWorld Services, Ingram, Baker & Taylor Book Company. To order: Bick Publishing House, 307 Neck Road, Madison, CT 06443. 203-245-0073. Distributed by: BookWorld Services, Inc. 800-444-2524. *Publisher Paid Annotation.*

Carlson, Dale, jt. auth. see Carlson, Hannah.

Carlson, Dale B. & Carlson, Hannah. Girls Are Equal Too: Teenage Girls How-to-Survive Book. 2nd rev. ed. LC 97-31718. (Psychology for Teenagers Ser.: Vol. 1). (Illus.). 250p. (YA). (gr. 6-12). 1998. pap. 14.95 (*1-884158-18-8*, Pub. by Bick Pub Hse) BookWorld.

-Where's Your Head? Teenage Psychology. 2nd rev. ed. LC 97-31717. (Psychology for Teenagers Ser.: Vol. 2). (Illus.). 320p. (YA). (gr. 6-12). 1998. pap. 14.95 (*1-884158-19-6*) Bick Pub Hse.
How to understand yourself, your teens, your parents, peers, your past, present & future: mental illness, learning disabilities, addictions, teenage problems. Christopher Award. "Readable, humorous, introduction to psychology for junior & senior high school."--SCHOOL LIBRARY JOURNAL. "Discusses entire range of human psychological development while focusing on the mind, feelings & behaviors of teenagers so they can understand their personality formation."--LIBRARY OF CONGRESS. Available at BookWorld Services, Ingram, Baker & Taylor. Or order: Bick Pub. House, 307 Neck Rd., Madison, CT 06443, 203-245-0073. Distributed by BookWorld Services. *Publisher Paid Annotation.*

Carlson, Dan. The Ins & Outs of Mormonism. LC 99-94670. 442p. 1998. pap. 14.95 (*0-9669025-0-5*) Carlsons Pubg.

Carlson, Daniel, et al. At Road's End: Transportation & Land Use Choices for Communities. 288p. (C). 1995. pap. text 40.00 (*1-55963-338-7*) Island Pr.

Carlson, Daniel F. Wordfinding: A Language Rehabilitation Manual for Aphasic Adults. rev. ed. Drolet, Cindy, ed. LC 87-82069. 155p. 1990. spiral bd. 59.00 (*0-9609464-4-6*, 8500) Imaginart Intl.

Carlson, Daniel J. A la Recherche des Mots: French Edition of the Word-Finding Program. Desmarais, Chantal, ed. Archambault, Lise, tr. (FRE.). 155p. 1993. spiral bd. 68.00 (*0-9609464-9-7*, 8510) Imaginart Intl.

— Auditory & Reading Comprehension: Intriguing Exercises for Language Rehabilitation. Drolet, Cindy & Gilles-Brown, C., eds. 327p. 1993. spiral bd. 54.00 (*1-883315-04-2*, 8455) Imaginart Intl.

— Encontrando Palabras: Spanish Edition of the Word-Finding Program. rev. ed. Montalbetti, Rocio, ed. Natividad, Oscar, tr. (SPA.). 155p. 1993. spiral bd. 68.00 (*1-883315-01-8*, 8511) Imaginart Intl.

Carlson, Dave. The Hike of Life. (Illus.). 250p. (Orig.). 1997. pap. 12.95 (*0-9649775-1-6*) Planet Books.

— Moose Don't Fly! Essays by Dave Carlson. (Illus.). 220p. 1995. pap. 12.95 (*0-9649775-0-8*) Planet Books.

— Pressure Points: Stress. (Inter Acta Ser.). (Illus.). 6p. (C). 1994. teacher ed., ring bd. 1.25 (*1-885702-95-7*, 741-060t, Inter Acta); student ed., ring bd. 3.25 (*1-885702-94-9*, 741-060s, Inter Acta) WSN Pr.

— The Way the Stick Floats: Wandering Outdoor Trails with Dave Carlson. Kinderman, Wendy, ed. (Illus.). 150p. 1997. pap. 12.95 (*0-9649775-4-0*) Planet Books.

Carlson, David. Counseling & Self-Esteem. (Resources for Christian Counseling Ser.). pap. 10.99 (*0-8499-3614-4*) Word Pub.

— Counseling & Self-Esteem. (Resources for Christian Counseling Ser.: Vol. 13). 268p. 18.99 (*0-8499-0479-X*) Word Pub.

— Linear Algebra. Bennett, Heather, ed. (Electronic Companion Ser.). (Illus.). 300p. (Orig.). (C). 1998. pap. text, wbk. ed. write for info. (*1-888902-54-X*); pap. text, wbk. ed. write for info. incl. cd-rom (*1-888902-76-0*) Cogito Lrning.

— Ready-to-Use Outdoor Recreations Spot Illustrations. (Clip Art Ser.). 64p. 1985. pap. 5.95 (*0-486-24784-8*) Dover.

— Ready-to-Use Sports Illustrations (Clip Art) 81st ed. (Pictorial Archive Ser.). (Illus.). 64p. (Orig.). 1982. pap. 5.95 (*0-486-24344-3*) Dover.

An Asterisk (*) at the beginning of an entry indicates that the title is appearing for the first time.

Carlson, David, et al, eds. Resources for Teaching Linear Algebra. LC 97-70503. (Notes Ser.: No. 42). 306p. (Orig.). (C). 1997. pap. text 35.95 (*0-88385-150-4*, NTE-42) Math Assn.

Carlson, David, jt. auth. see Gilmore, Grant.

Carlson, David, ed. see Instrument Society of America Staff.

Carlson, David A., ed. Corrugating Defect Terminology: Fabrication Manual for Corrugated Box Plants. 5th rev. ed. (Illus.). 234p. 1988. 60.00 (*0-89852-453-9*, 0101R153) TAPPI.

Carlson, David F. & Goodrich, Peter, eds. Law & the Postmodern Mind: Essays on Psychoanalysis & Jurisprudence. LC 97-33739. 328p. (C). 1998. text 49.50 (*0-472-10841-7*, 10841) U of Mich Pr.

Carlson, David L. & Bryant, Vaughn M. Through the Looking Glass: Readings in Anthropology. (C). 1996. pap. text 18.74 (*0-07-011884-1*) McGraw.

Carlson, David R. English Humanist Books: Writers & Patrons, Manuscripts & Print, 1475-1525. LC 93-93049. (Illus.). 275p. 1993. text 50.00 (*0-8020-2911-6*) U of Toronto Pr.

Carlson, David S., ed. see Achenbaum, W. Andrew, et al.

Carlson, David S., ed. see Enlow, Donald H., et al.

Carlson, David S., jt. ed. see Goldstein, Steven A.

Carlson, David S., jt. ed. see Hunter, W. Stuart.

Carlson, David S., ed. see Sessle, et al.

Carlson, Dean. So This Is Farming: A Journal. (Illus.). 184p. (Orig.). 1988. 14.95 (*0-934860-51-3*); pap. 8.95 (*0-934860-50-5*) Adventure Pubns.

Carlson, Deanna, ed. see Sherman, Amy.

***Carlson, Deanna L.** The Welfare of My Neighbor: Living Out Christ's Love for the Poor. LC 99-74542. (Illus.). 138p. 1999. pap. 10.00 (*1-55872-002-2*) Fam Res Council.

***Carlson, Deborah Marks & Foster, Betty.** Reaching Communities with Alzheimer's Education, Advanced Train-the-Trainer Manual. 2nd rev. ed. xxxviii, 552p. (C). 2000. ring bd. 189.95 (*0-9678744-0-8*) Eymann.

Carlson, Delbert G. & Giffin, James M. Dog Owner's Home Veterinary Handbook. 2nd rev. ed. (Illus.). 448p. 1992. 25.00 (*0-87605-537-4*) Howell Bks.

Carlson, Delbert G., et al. The Cat Owner's Home Veterinary Handbook. rev. expanded ed. LC 95-6632. (Illus.). 448p. 1995. 24.95 (*0-87605-796-2*) Howell Bks.

Carlson, Dennis. Making Progress: Education & Culture in New Times. 168p. (C). 1996. 45.00 (*0-8077-3577-9*); pap. text 19.95 (*0-8077-3576-0*) Tchrs Coll.

— Teachers & Crisis: Urban School Reform & Teachers' Work Culture. 320p. (Orig.). 1992. pap. 15.95 (*0-685-50333-X*, A4269) Routledge.

— Teachers & Crisis: Urban School Reform & Teachers' Work Culture. (Critical Social Thought Ser.). 320p. (Orig.). (C). 1992. pap. 18.99 (*0-415-90270-3*) Routledge.

Carlson, Dennis & Apple, Michael W., eds. Power/Knowledge/Pedagogy: The Meaning of Democratic Education in Unsettling Times. (Edge Ser.). 368p. 1999. pap. 28.00 (*0-8133-9138-5*, Pub. by Westview) HarpC.

Carlson, Dennis G. African Fever: A Study of British Science, Technology, & Politics in West Africa, 1787-1864. LC 81-5621. 1984. 15.95 (*0-88202-196-6*) Watson Pub Intl.

Carlson, Dolley. Christmas Gifts from the Heart: Wrapped in Joyous Celebration & Tied with a Ribbon of Love. LC 99-29792. 1999. 12.99 (*0-7814-3319-3*) Chariot Victor.

— Gifts from the Heart: Thoughtful Ways to Bless Those You Love. 64p. 1998. 10.99 (*1-56476-723-X*, Victor Bks) Chariot Victor.

***Carlson, Dolley.** Mr. & Mrs. Gifts from the Heart. LC 99-39105. (Illus.). 64p. 2000. 12.99 (*0-7814-3381-9*) Chariot Victor.

***Carlson, Dolley & Lazor-Bahr, Beverly.** Friendship Gifts from the Heart. LC 00-42187. (Illus.). 2001. write for info. (*0-7814-3477-7*) Cook.

Carlson, Donn & Carlson, Roger. Earth Science College Edition: Invitation to Inquiry a Comprehensive Program of Inquiry Activities in Earth Science. (Illus.). 256p. (C). 1995. ring bd. 33.00 (*1-878276-53-0*) Educ Systs Assocs Inc.

— Physical Science Electricity/Electronics Instructor's Manual. (Invitation to Inquiry a Comprehensive Program of Inquiry Activities in Physical Science Ser.). (Illus.). 98p. (YA). (gr. 6-12). 1990. 20.00 (*1-878276-16-6*) Educ Systs Assocs Inc.

— Physical Science Electricity/Electronics Student Activity Packet. (Invitation to Inquiry a Comprehensive Program of Inquiry Activities in Physical Science Ser.). (Illus.). 85p. (YA). (gr. 6-12). 1990. ring bd. 8.00 (*1-878276-09-3*) Educ Systs Assocs Inc.

— Physical Science Light/Computer Instructor's Manual. (Invitation to Inquiry a Comprehensive Program of Inquiry Activities in Physical Science Ser.). (Illus.). 124p. (YA). (gr. 6-12). 1990. 20.00 (*1-878276-18-2*) Educ Systs Assocs Inc.

— Physical Science Light/Computer Labs Student Activity Packet. (Invitation to Inquiry a Comprehensive Program of Inquiry Activities in Physical Science Ser.). (Illus.). 102p. (YA). (gr. 6-12). 1990. ring bd. 8.00 (*1-878276-11-5*) Educ Systs Assocs Inc.

— Physical Science Magnetism Instructor's Manual. (Invitation to Inquiry a Comprehensive Program of Inquiry Activities in Physical Science Ser.). (Illus.). 80p. (YA). (gr. 6-12). 1990. 15.00 (*1-878276-17-4*) Educ Systs Assocs Inc.

— Physical Science Magnetism Student Activity Packet. (Invitation to Inquiry a Comprehensive Program of Inquiry Activities in Physical Science Ser.). (Illus.). 66p. (YA). (gr. 6-12). 1990. ring bd. 6.00 (*1-878276-10-7*) Educ Systs Assocs Inc.

— Physical Science Measurement Instructor's Manual. (Invitation to Inquiry a Comprehensive Program of Inquiry Activities in Physical Science Ser.). (Illus.). 77p. (YA). (gr. 6-12). 1990. 15.00 (*1-878276-13-1*) Educ Systs Assocs Inc.

— Physical Science Measurement Student Activity Packet. (Invitation to Inquiry a Comprehensive Program of Inquiry Activities in Physical Science Ser.). (Illus.). 77p. (YA). (gr. 6-12). 1990. ring bd. 6.00 (*1-878276-12-3*) Educ Systs Assocs Inc.

— Physical Science Mechanics/Computer Labs Instructor's Manual. (Invitation to Inquiry a Comprehensive Program of Inquiry Activities in Physical Science Ser.). (Illus.). 114p. (YA). (gr. 6-12). 1990. 20.00 (*1-878276-15-8*) Educ Systs Assocs Inc.

— Physical Science Mechanics/Computer Labs Student Activity Packet. (Invitation to Inquiry a Comprehensive Program of Inquiry Activities in Physical Science Ser.). (Illus.). 102p. (YA). (gr. 6-12). 1990. ring bd. 8.00 (*1-878276-08-5*) Educ Systs Assocs Inc.

— Physical Science Microchemistry Student Activity Packet. (Invitation to Inquiry a Comprehensive Program of Inquiry Activities in Physical Science Ser.). (Illus.). 136p. (YA). (gr. 6-12). 1990. ring bd. 10.00 (*1-878276-06-9*) Educ Systs Assocs Inc.

— Physical Science Middle School Student Activity Packet. (Invitation to Inquiry a Comprehensive Program of Inquiry Activities in Physical Science Ser.). (Illus.). 290p. (YA). (gr. 6-12). 1990. ring bd. 16.00 (*1-878276-21-2*) Educ Systs Assocs Inc.

— Physical Science Variables Instructor's Manual. (Invitation to Inquiry a Comprehensive Program of Inquiry Activities in Physical Science Ser.). (Illus.). 38p. (YA). (gr. 6-12). 1990. 8.00 (*1-878276-14-X*) Educ Systs Assocs Inc.

— Physical Science Variables Student Activity Packet. (Invitation to Inquiry a Comprehensive Program of Inquiry Activities in Physical Science Ser.). (Illus.). 36p. (YA). (gr. 6-12). 1990. ring bd. 4.00 (*1-878276-07-7*) Educ Systs Assocs Inc.

Carlson, Donn, et al. Earth Science Astronomy Instructor's Manual. (Invitation to Inquiry a Comprehensive Program of Inquiry Activities in Physical Science Ser.). (Illus.). 106p. (YA). (gr. 6-12). 1995. 25.00 (*1-878276-54-9*) Educ Systs Assocs Inc.

— Earth Science Astronomy Student Activity Packet. (Invitation to Inquiry a Comprehensive Program of Inquiry Activities in Physical Science Ser.). (Illus.). 82p. (YA). (gr. 6-12). 1995. ring bd. 10.00 (*1-878276-55-7*) Educ Systs Assocs Inc.

— Earth Science Geology Instructor's Manual. (Invitation to Inquiry a Comprehensive Program of Inquiry Activities in Physical Science Ser.). (Illus.). 105p. (YA). (gr. 6-12). 1994. 25.00 (*1-878276-32-8*) Educ Systs Assocs Inc.

— Earth Science Geology Student Activity Packet. (Invitation to Inquiry a Comprehensive Program of Inquiry Activities in Physical Science Ser.). (Illus.). 74p. (YA). (gr. 6-12). 1994. ring bd. 10.00 (*1-878276-49-2*) Educ Systs Assocs Inc.

— Earth Science Meteorology Instructor's Manual. (Invitation to Inquiry a Comprehensive Program of Inquiry Activities in Physical Science Ser.). (Illus.). 96p. (YA). (gr. 6-12). 1995. 25.00 (*1-878276-56-5*) Educ Systs Assocs Inc.

— Earth Science Meterology Student Activity Packet. (Invitation to Inquiry a Comprehensive Program of Inquiry Activities in Physical Science Ser.). (Illus.). 66p. (YA). (gr. 6-12). 1995. ring bd. 10.00 (*1-878276-57-3*) Educ Systs Assocs Inc.

— Physical Science College Edition. (Invitation to Inquiry a Comprehensive Program of Inquiry Activities in Physical Science Ser.). (Illus.). 156p. (C). 1995. ring bd. 33.00 (*1-878276-22-0*) Educ Systs Assocs Inc.

Carlson, Donn A. & Carlson, Roger L. Physical Science Microchemistry Instructor's Manual: A New Concept in Teaching Chemistry. (Invitation to Inquiry a Comprehensive Program of Inquiry Activities in Physical Science for Middle Through Secondary Schools Ser.). (Illus.). 167p. (Orig.). 1990. 25.00 (*1-878276-19-0*) Educ Systs Assocs Inc.

— Physical Science Middle School Instructor's Manual. (Science: Invitation to Inquiry Ser.). (Illus.). 279p. 1990. teacher ed. 40.00 (*1-878276-20-4*) Educ Systs Assocs Inc.

— Physical Science Resource Manual: A Comprehensive Program of Inquiry Activities in Physical Science for Middle Through Secondary School. (Science: Invitation to Inquiry a Comprehensive Program of Inquiry Acticities in Physical Science for Middle Through Secondary Schools Ser.). (Illus.). 712p. (Orig.). 1990. teacher ed. 75.00 (*1-878276-05-0*) Educ Systs Assocs Inc.

Carlson, Donna, ed. see Melville, Herman.

Carlson, Dosia. Engaging in Ministry with Older Adults. LC 97-73983. 182p. 1997. pap. 16.75 (*1-56699-186-2*, AL185) Alban Inst.

— Rituals of the Celebration of Later Life. (Older Adult Issues Ser.). 50p. 1999. pap. 4.50 (*0-664-50087-0*) Geneva Press.

Carlson, Douglas. At the Edge. 98p. (Orig.). 1989. pap. 9.00 (*0-934834-29-6*) White Pine.

Carlson, Douglas W., et al. Guide to the Papers in the John Hunter Walker Collection, 1911-1953. LC 80-16678. (Robert B. Downs Publication Fund: No. 6). 114p. 1980. 10.00 (*0-87845-056-4*) U of Ill Grad Sch.

***Carlson, Dwight.** Overcoming Hurts & Anger: Freedom from Negative Emotions. rev. expanded ed. LC 99-57244. 200p. 2000. pap. 8.99 (*0-7369-0196-5*) Harvest Hse.

Carlson, Dwight L. Overcoming Hurts & Anger. LC 80-83852. 1981. pap. 7.99 (*0-89081-277-2*) Harvest Hse.

— Run & Not Be Weary - Chinese Edition. Liu, J. Y., tr. (CHI.). 231p. 1998. pap. 8.00 (*1-56582-041-X*) Christ Renew Min.

— Why Do Christians Shoot Their Wounded? Helping (Not Hurting) Those with Serious Emotional Difficulties. LC 93-43019. 180p. (Orig.). 1994. pap. 10.99 (*0-8308-1666-6*, 1666) InterVarsity.

Carlson, Edgar M. The Church & the Public Conscience. LC 79-8710. 104p. 1981. reprint ed. lib. bdg. 49.50 (*0-313-22195-2*, CACH, Greenwood Pr) Greenwood.

— The Classic Christian Faith: Chapel Meditations Based on Luther's Small Catechism. LC 59-9093. 171p. reprint ed. pap. 53.10 (*0-608-16667-7*, 202691200053) Bks Demand.

Carlson, Edith. Phantoms of Divinity: The Collapse of Traditional Faith. LC 92-6724. 150p. (C). 1992. 24.95 (*0-87975-718-3*) Prometheus Bks.

Carlson, Edward H. Kids & the Franklin. (Illus.). 200p. 1984. 19.95 (*0-8359-3664-3*) P-H.

Carlson, Effie B. A Bio-Bibliographical Dictionary of Twelve-Tone & Serial Composers. LC 79-8959. 233p. reprint ed. pap. 72.30 (*0-8357-7213-6*, 201234700081) Bks Demand.

Carlson, Elizabeth. Best of All. 320p. 1993. mass mkt. 3.99 (*0-8217-4055-5*, Zebra Kensgtn) Kensgtn Pub Corp.

Carlson, Elizabeth, et al. Task Force on Education for Children with Disabilities--Year II (Minnesota) Final Report. (Illus.). 91p. 1998. reprint ed. pap. text 25.00 (*0-7881-4245-3*) DIANE Pub.

Carlson, Elizabeth H. Small Wonders: Tiny Treasures in Patchwork & Applique. LC 98-43430. (Illus.). 96p. 1999. pap. 24.95 (*1-56477-250-0*, B361, That Patchwrk Pl) Martingale & Co.

Carlson, Ellsworth C. The Foochow Missionaries, 1847-1880. LC 72-97832. (East Asian Monographs: No. 51). 267p. 1973. pap. 30.00 (*0-674-30735-6*) HUP.

— Kaiping Mines, 1877 to 1912. 2nd rev. ed. LC 71-148943. (East Asian Monographs: No. 3). 243p. 1971. pap. 20.00 (*0-674-49700-7*) HUP.

Carlson, Elof A. The Gene: A Critical History. LC 89-24427. (History of Science & Technology Reprint Ser.). (Illus.). 313p. 1989. reprint ed. pap. 97.10 (*0-608-00043-4*, 206080900006) Bks Demand.

— Genes, Radiation & Society: The Life & Work of H. J. Muller. LC 81-5486. (Illus.). 472p. reprint ed. pap. 146.40 (*0-8357-5534-7*, 203514700093) Bks Demand.

— Human Genetics. 432p. (C). 1983. text 51.56 (*0-669-05559-X*); teacher ed. 2.66 (*0-669-06724-5*) HM Trade Div.

Carlson, Elof A., jt. ed. see Muller, Hermann Joseph.

Carlson, Elof Axel. Human Genetics. 2nd ed. Date not set. pap. text 30.00 (*0-697-11657-3*) McGraw.

Carlson, Elwood & Carlson, Ruth. Navy Marriages & Deployment. 114p. (Orig.). 1984. pap. text 18.00 (*0-8191-4159-3*); lib. bdg. 40.00 (*0-8191-4158-5*) U Pr of Amer.

Carlson, Eric. The Holiday Wreath Book: Eighty Wreaths to Celebrate Birthdays, Anniversaries & Holidays Throughout the Year. LC 92-47698. (Illus.). 112p. 1992. 27.95 (*0-8069-8696-4*) Sterling.

Carlson, Eric J. Marriage & the English Reformation. (Family, Sexuality & Social Relations in Past Times Ser.). 352p. (C). 1994. 66.95 (*0-631-16864-8*) Blackwell Pubs.

Carlson, Eric J., ed. Religion & the English People, 1500-1640: New Voices/New Perspectives. LC 98-3778. (Sixteenth Century Essays & Studies: No. 45). (Illus.). 312p. 1998. 40.00 (*0-943549-62-0*) Truman St Univ.

Carlson, Eric J., jt. auth. see Parker, Kenneth L.

***Carlson, Eric M.** Long-Term Care Advocacy. LC 99-43080. 1050p. 1999. 135.00 (*0-8205-4153-2*) Bender.

Carlson, Eric S. I Remember Julia: Voices of the Disappeared. LC 96-5021. 169p. (C). 1996. pap. 19.95 (*1-56639-437-6*) Temple U Pr.

— I Remember Julia: Voices of the Disappeared. LC 96-5021. 169p. (C). 1996. lib. bdg. 69.95 (*1-56639-430-9*) Temple U Pr.

Carlson, Eric T., ed. Classics in Psychiatry Ser., 46 vols. 1976. 1985.50 (*0-405-07410-7*) Ayer.

Carlson, Eric T., ed. see Rush, Benjamin.

Carlson, Eric W., ed. A Companion to Poe Studies. LC 95-40034. 624p. 1996. lib. bdg. 105.00 (*0-313-26506-2*, Greenwood Pr) Greenwood.

— Critical Essays on Edgar Allan Poe. (Critical Essays Ser.). 200p. 1987. 49.00 (*0-8161-8878-5*, Hall Reference) Macmillan.

Carlson, Eric W., jt. auth. see Poe, Edgar Allan.

Carlson, Eric W., ed. & intro. see Emerson, Ralph Waldo.

Carlson, Eric W., intro. see Poe, Edgar Allan.

Carlson, Erik. Consequentialism Reconsidered. (Theory & Decision Library: Series A). 170p. (C). 1995. lib. bdg. 107.00 (*0-7923-3547-3*, Pub. by Kluwer Academic) Kluwer Academic.

Carlson, Eve B. Trauma Assessments: A Clinician's Guide. LC 97-17254. 307p. 1997. lib. bdg. 30.00 (*1-57230-251-8*, 0231) Guilford Pubns.

Carlson, Eve B., ed. Trauma Research Methodology. LC 95-26829. viii, 291p. (Orig.). 1996. pap. text 18.95 (*0-9629164-8-X*, CATR) Sidran Pr.

Carlson, Evelyn, et al. Vintage. Traxler, Patricia, ed. (Illus.). 104p. (Orig.). 1984. pap. 5.00 (*0-932199-00-3*) Smoky Hill.

Carlson, Faith. Creating Communication Displays. (Illus.). 153p. 1997. ring bd. 40.00 (*1-886498-05-9*, 8-0014) Poppin & Co.

— PICSYMS Categorical Dictionary. 186p. 1995. reprint ed. pap. 35.00 (*1-886498-02-4*, 8-0006) Poppin & Co.

— Poppin's Cut & Paste with 1000 Plus DynaSyms. (Illus.). 74p. 1994. pap. 15.00 (*1-886498-00-8*, 8-0002) Poppin & Co.

— Poppin's DynaSyms 1700+ 47p. 1995. pap. 20.00 (*1-886498-01-6*, 8-0005) Poppin & Co.

— Poppin's Mini DynaSyms 1700+ (Illus.). 27p. (Orig.). 1996. pap. 17.00 (*1-886498-03-2*, 8-0012) Poppin & Co.

Carlson, Faith & Harlan, Nancy T. Poppin's DynaSyms Test-Probe. (Illus.). 1332p. 1997. ring bd. 50.00 (*1-886498-06-7*, 8-0015) Poppin & Co.

Carlson-Finnerty, Lavonne, jt. auth. see Robinson, Lynn A.

Carlson, Fran. Growing Your Family Medical Tree. large type ed. LC 97-94338. 60p. 1997. boxed set 14.95 (*0-9660319-0-3*, 001) KISS.

Carlson, Frances C. Cave Creek & Carefree, Arizona: A History of the Desert Foothills. 3rd ed. LC 88-82253. (Illus.). 200p. 1996. reprint ed. 22.95 (*0-9621136-0-3*) Encanto Pr.

Carlson, Frances C., ed. Montana Manufacturers Register 1999. 373p. 1999. 61.00 (*1-55600-686-1*) Harris InfoSource.

Carlson, Fred. The Cow Punchers' Cookbook. (Illus.). 150p. 1995. spiral bd. 9.95 (*1-57166-028-3*) Black Iron.

Carlson, Frederick L., frwd. Thoughts in Time. limited ed. (Illus.). 61p. 1984. 20.00 (*0-89904-006-3*) Crumb Elbow Pub.

Carlson, G. Our Faith & Fellowship. LC 77-75023. (Radiant Life Ser.). 128p. 1977. pap. 4.99 (*0-88243-908-1*, 02-0908) Gospel Pub.

Carlson, G. Raymond. How to Study the Bible. (Spiritual Discovery Ser.). 112p. 1995. pap., teacher ed. 9.95 (*0-88243-208-7*); pap., student ed. 4.95 (*0-88243-108-0*) Gospel Pub.

— The Life Worth Living. LC 75-22607. (Radiant Life Ser.). 128p. 1975. pap. 3.95 (*0-88243-876-X*, 02-0876); pap., teacher ed. 5.50 (*0-88243-160-9*, 32-0160) Gospel Pub.

— Our Faith & Fellowship. LC 77-75023. (Radiant Life Ser.). 128p. 1977. pap., teacher ed. 5.50 (*0-88243-178-1*, 32-0178) Gospel Pub.

— Prayer & the Christian's Devotional Life. LC 80-83522. (Radiant Life Ser.). 124p. 1981. pap. 3.95 (*0-88243-878-6*, 02-0878); pap., teacher ed. 5.50 (*0-88243-190-0*, 32-0190) Gospel Pub.

— Romans: Finding Freedom in Chirst. (Spiritual Discovery Ser.). 126p. 1997. pap., teacher ed. 9.95 (*0-88243-219-2*, 02-0219) Gospel Pub.

— Romans: Finding Freedom in Christ. 110p. 1997. pap., student ed. 4.95 (*0-88243-119-6*) Gospel Pub.

Carlson, Gary. Land Value Taxation: Impact Analysis on Omaha-Douglas County, Nebraska. 72p. (Orig.). 1976. pap. 6.00 (*1-55719-043-7*) U NE CPAR.

— Teenage Mutant Ninja Turtles: A New Beginning. (Illus.). 112p. 1997. pap. 9.95 (*1-887279-56-3*) Image Comics.

Carlson, Gary & Ecker, Chris, eds. Your Big Book of Big Bang Comics. (Big Bang Comics Ser.). (Illus.). 80p. 1998. pap. 11.00 (*1-887279-88-1*) Image Comics.

Carlson, Gayle F. & Steinacher, Terry L. Nebraska Highway Archaeological & Historical Investigations, 1969-1975. (Publications in Archaeology: No. 10). 191p. 1984. 2.00 (*0-933307-09-8*) Nebraska Hist.

Carlson, Gene P., intro. Leadership Curriculum. (Illus.). 108p. 1987. ring bd. 150.00 (*0-685-59453-X*) IFSTA.

Carlson, Gene P. & Vandevort, William J., eds. Practicas y Teorias para Bomberos. 6th ed. Ventura, Mitch, tr. & intro. by. LC 91-72468. (SPA., Illus.). 347p. 1991. pap. text 23.00 (*0-87939-095-6*) IFSTA.

Carlson, Gene P., ed. see Fleischner, Robert.

Carlson, Gene P., jt. ed. see FPP Staff.

Carlson, Gene P., ed. see IFSTA Committee.

Carlson, Gene P., ed. see IFSTA Committee & FPP Staff.

Carlson, Gene P., ed. see IFSTA Committee, et al.

Carlson, Gene P., ed. see ISFTA Committee.

Carlson, Gene P., ed. see Walker, Susan S.

Carlson, Gene P., ed. & intro. see IFSTA Committee.

Carlson, Gene P., ed. & intro. see Wiley-Jones, Rhonda.

Carlson, George, jt. auth. see Nottage, James.

Carlson, George A. George Carlson: The Spirit of the Tarahumara. Maxon, Gayle & Hopkins, Quincie, eds. LC 85-92063. (Illus.). 52p. 1985. 18.00 (*0-935037-00-4*) G Peters Gallery.

Carlson, George G. Real Estate Accounting & Reporting Manual. LC 98-196196. 1998. write for info. (*0-7913-2912-7*) Warren Gorham & Lamont.

Carlson, Gerald. Hometown Folks: A Finnish-American Saga. LC 97-15065. 1997. pap. 12.95 (*0-87839-115-0*) North Star.

Carlson, Gerald A., et al, eds. Agricultural & Environmental Resource Economics. LC 92-21524. (Oxford Biological Resource Management Ser.). (Illus.). 544p. 1993. text 57.00 (*0-19-507651-6*) OUP.

Carlson, Gerald P. & Blackwell, Harold E. Bowling Basics: A Step by Step Approach. 4th ed. LC 97-169560. 128p. (C). 1997. per. 11.95 (*0-7872-3610-1*) Kendall-Hunt.

Carlson, Glenn E. Airplane Talk: Complete Book of VFR & IFR Communications. 2nd ed. (Illus.). 276p. (C). 1993. pap. 17.95 (*0-9611954-0-1*) Aviation.

— Angie the Aviator. 68p. 11.95 (*0-317-56126-X*) Watosh Pub.

***Carlson, Glenn E.** Angie the Aviator. large type ed. Robinson, Helen, ed. (Illus.). 56p. (J). (gr. 2-9). 1999. 21.95 (*0-9611954-4-4*) Watosh Pub.

Carlson, Glenn E., et al. Granny Karate's Kitchen: Romance Through Cooking Non-Beef Gourmet Recipes Jerk-Proof. Barbagallo, Cathy, ed. (For the Bachelor Out to Impress Ser.). (Illus.). 224p. (Orig.). 1989. spiral bd. 19.95 (*0-9611954-3-6*) Watosh Pub.

Carlson, Glenn R., jt. auth. see Brandes, Charles H.

Carlson, Gordon E. Signal & Linear System Analysis. 768p. 1994. text 90.95 (*0-471-12499-0*) Wiley.

— Signal & Linear System Analysis. 2nd ed. LC 97-33237. 768p. 1998. text 103.95 (*0-471-12465-6*) Wiley.

C

An Asterisk (*) at the beginning of an entry indicates that the title is appearing for the first time.

Carlson, Greg N. & Pelletier, Francis Jeffry, eds. The Generic Book. LC 94-32400. 474p. 1995. lib. bdg. 105.00 (*0-226-09291-7*) U Ch Pr.

— The Generic Book. LC 94-32400. 474p. 1995. pap. text 37.95 (*0-226-09292-5*) U Ch Pr.

Carlson, Greg N. & Tanenhaus, Michael K., eds. Linguistic Structure in Language Processing. (C). 1988. lib. bdg. 167.00 (*1-55608-074-3*) Kluwer Academic.

Carlson, Gregory C. Understanding Teaching: Effective Bible Teaching for the 21st Century. 96p. 1998. pap. 9.95 (*0-910566-73-9*); teacher ed., ring bd. 24.95 (*0-910566-74-7*) Evang Trg Assn.

***Carlson, Gustav.** Total Exposure: Controlling Your Company's Image in the Glare of the Business Media Explosion. LC 99-40039. 304p. 1999. 27.95 (*0-8144-0484-7*) AMACOM.

Carlson, H. G. Mysteries of the Unexplained. LC 95-100126. (Illus.). 192p. 1994. pap. 15.95 (*0-8092-3497-1*, 349710, Contemporary Bks) NTC Contemp Pub Co.

***Carlson, Hannah. The Courage to Lead: Start Your Own Mutual Support Group, 1. (Illus.). 224p. 2000. pap. 14.95 (*1-884158-25-0*) Bick Pub Hse.**

Start your own mutual support group for mental illness, whether manic-depression, schizophrenia, obsessive-compulsive disorder, alcoholism & drug-addiction, eating & other addictive disorders, phobia. We cannot live in our doctors' offices or only on medication. We need each other to learn freedom from mental illness. This book has information & resources, life stories, diagnoses, treatments, bibliography. "A practical guide for general audiences." --Dr. Kathleen C., Laundy, Psy.D. Yale School of Medicine. Available at BookWorld Services, Ingram, Baker & Taylor. To order: Bick Publishing House, 307 Neck Road, Madison, CT. 06443. 203/245-0073. Distributed by BookWorld Services. ***Publisher Paid Annotation.***

Carlson, Hannah & Carlson, Dale. Basic Manuals for Friends of the Disabled Series, 6 vols. Incl. I Have a Friend in a Wheelchair: Basic Manuals for Friends of the Disabled. Douglas, Hope M. LC 95-79843. 64p. (Orig.). 1995. pap. 9.95 (*1-884158-09-9*, Pub. by Bick Pub Hse); I Have a Friend Who Is Blind: Basic Manuals for Friends of the Disabled. Douglas, Hope M. LC 95-79842. 64p. (Orig.). 1995. pap. 9.95 (*1-884158-07-2*, Pub. by Bick Pub Hse); I Have a Friend Who Is Deaf: Basic Manuals for Friends of the Disabled. Douglas, Hope M. LC 95-79840. 64p. (Orig.). 1995. pap. 9.95 (*1-884158-08-0*, Pub. by Bick Pub Hse); I Have a Friend with Learning Disabilities: Basic Manuals for Friends of the Disabled. Kinrade, Richard A. LC 96-84059. 64p. 1996. pap. 9.95 (*1-884158-12-9*, Pub. by Bick Pub Hse); I Have a Friend with Mental Illness: Basic Manuals for Friends of the Disabled. Kinrade, Richard A. LC 96-84060. 64p. (Orig.). 1996. pap. 9.95 (*1-884158-13-7*, Pub. by Bick Pub Hse); I Have a Friend With Mental Retardation: Basic Manuals for Friends of the Disabled. Douglas, Hope M. LC 95-79840. 64p. (Orig.). 1995. pap. 9.95 (*1-884158-10-2*, Pub. by Bick Pub Hse); LC 96-84060. 1996. Set pap. 59.70 (*1-884158-11-0*, Pub. by Bick Pub Hse) BookWorld.

Carlson, Hannah & Carlson, Dale. Living with Disabilities: Basic Manuals for Friends of the Disabled, 6 vols. in 1. 2nd ed. LC 96-79850. (Illus.). 352p. (Orig.). 1997. pap. 59.70 (*1-884158-15-3*, Pub. by Bick Pub Hse) BookWorld.

Six introductory handbooks about disabilities & special needs, under the direction of Hannah Carlson, M.Ed., CRC, provide basic information for friends, families, teachers, employers & anyone concerned about people with disabilities. Covered are: medical conditions & causes; behaviors, feelings, rehabilitation, resources, ADA rights, funds, adaptive technology, life stories of child & adult models in all fields. "Excellent introductory handbooks offer professional information in an easy-to-use style for the general audience."--Kathleen Laundy, Psy.D., M.S.W., Yale School of Medicine. The series is endorsed by rehabilitation facilities, doctors, therapists. Included are appendices of national & local organizations that serve each disability, technological resources, adaptive devices information, lists of national & regional support centers, who to call for referrals, help & advice. The illustrated series includes: I HAVE A FRIEND WHO IS BLIND, 64 p. $9.95. (1-884158-07-2); I HAVE A FRIEND WHO IS DEAF, 64 p. $9.95 (1-884158-08-0); I HAVE A FRIEND WITH LEARNING DISABILITIES, 64 p. $9.95 (1-884158-12-9); I HAVE A FRIEND WITH MENTAL ILLNESS, 64 p. $9.95 (1-884158-13-7); I HAVE A FRIEND WITH MENTAL RETARDATION, 64 p. $9.95 (1-884158-10-2); I HAVE A FRIEND IN A WHEELCHAIR, 64 p. $9.95 (1-884158-09-9). Sep. vol. set of 6 (1-884158-11-0). Available at: BookWorld Services, Ingram, Baker & Taylor Book Company. To order: Bick Publishing House, 307 Neck Road, Madison, CT 06443. 203-245-0073. Distributed by: BookWorld Services, Inc. ***Publisher Paid Annotation.***

Carlson, Hannah, jt. auth. see Carlson, Dale B.

Carlson, Harold. Spring Manufacturing Handbook. LC 82-12750. (Mechanical Engineering Ser.: No. 15). (Illus.). 384p. reprint ed. pap. 119.10 (*0-7837-0939-0*, 204124400019) Bks Demand.

Carlson, Harry G., ed. see Lamm, Martin.

Carlson, Harry G., tr. see Friis, Erik J., et al, eds.

Carlson, Harry G., tr. see Strindberg, August.

Carlson, Helen & Falk, Dennis R. Multimedia in Higher Education: A Practical Guide to New Tools for Interactive Teaching & Learning. 176p. 1995. 42.50 (*1-57387-002-1*) Info Today Inc.

Carlson, Helen S. Nevada Place Names: A Geographical Dictionary. LC 74-13877. 296p. 1974. reprint ed. pap. 84.40 (*0-608-01266-1*, 2062015) Bks Demand.

— Nevada Place Names: A Geographical Dictionary. LC 74-13877. (Illus.). 296p. 1974. reprint ed. pap. 21.95 (*0-87417-094-X*) U of Nev Pr.

Carlson, J. D., et al, eds. Electrorheological Fluids: Proceedings of the 2nd International Conference on ER Fluids. LC 90-70350. 550p. 1990. pap. 69.95 (*0-87762-739-8*) Technomic.

Carlson, J. E. & Budd, T. H., eds. Proceedings of the 1997 Rapid Excavation Tunneling Conference. LC 96-72547. (Illus.). 874p. 1997. 83.00 (*0-87335-148-7*, 148-7) SMM&E Inc.

Carlson, J. G., et al, eds. Clinical Applied Psychophysiology. (Behavioral Psychophysiology Ser.). (Illus.). 292p. (C). 1994. 49.50 (*0-306-44555-7*, Plenum Trade) Perseus Pubng.

Carlson, J. G. & Seifert, A. R. International Perspectives on Self-Regulation & Health. (Behavioral Psychophysiology & Medicine Ser.). (Illus.). 310p. (C). 1991. text 60.00 (*0-306-43557-8*, Kluwer Plenum) Kluwer Academic.

Carlson, J. Lon, jt. auth. see Skaggs, Neil T.

Carlson, Jack C. & Stewart, Elizabeth J. Hiker's Guide to the Superstition Wilderness: With History & Legends of Arizona's Lost Dutchman Gold Mine. LC 94-94270. (Illus.). 320p. (Orig.). 1999. pap. 14.95 (*1-884224-05-9*) CC Pub.

Carlson, James. PPP Debugging. LC 97-41553. 240p. (C). 1997. pap. text 29.95 (*0-201-18539-3*) Addison-Wesley.

Carlson, James A., et al. Complex Geometry & Lie Theory. LC 91-25148. (PSPUM Ser.: No. 53). 348p. 1992. text 73.00 (*0-8218-1492-3*, PSPUM/53) Am Math.

Carlson, James B. Raising Healthy Beef Cattle. 2nd rev. ed. (Raising Healthy Animals under Primitive Conditions Ser.). (Illus.). 125p. 1990. pap. 9.00 (*1-886532-06-0*) Christian Vet.

Carlson, James M. Prime Time Law Enforcement: Crime Show Viewing & Attitudes Toward the Criminal Justice System. LC 85-9420. 238p. 1985. 38.95 (*0-275-90070-3*, C0070, Praeger Pubs) Greenwood.

***Carlson, Jeff.** Palm Organizers. 2nd ed. (Visual QuickStart Guides Ser.). (Illus.). 304p. 2000. pap. text 16.99 (*0-201-70063-8*) Addison-Wesley.

Carlson, Jeff. Palm III & PalmPilot: Visual QuickStart Guide. LC 99-190536. (Visual QuickStart Guides Ser.). 264p. (C). 1998. pap. text 15.99 (*0-201-35390-3*, Pub. by Peachpit Pr) Addison-Wesley.

***Carlson, Jeff & Fleishman, Glenn.** Real World Adobe GoLive 4. (Real World Ser.). 760p. 1999. pap. 44.99 (*0-201-35474-8*) Peachpit Pr.

— Real World Adobe Golive 5. 776p. 2000. pap. text 44.99 (*0-201-70406-4*) Peachpit Pr.

Carlson, Jefferey J. California Tort Guide: May 1994 Update. 2nd ed. Peyrat, Paul I., ed. LC 78-633174. 356p. 1994. pap. text 38.00 (*0-88124-741-3*, TO-32281) Cont Ed Bar-CA.

Carlson, Jeffrey, et al. Web Site Graphics: Color. (Website Graphics Ser.). (Illus.). 96p. 1999. pap. 15.99 (*1-56496-516-3*) Rockport Pubs.

— Web Site Graphics: Navigation. (Website Graphics Ser.). (Illus.). 96p. 1999. pap. 15.99 (*1-56496-518-X*) Rockport Pubs.

— Web Site Graphics: Typography. (Website Graphics Ser.). (Illus.). 96p. 1999. pap. 15.99 (*1-56496-517-1*) Rockport Pubs.

Carlson, Jeffrey D. A Historical Album of Minnesota. LC 92-41136. (Historical Albums Ser.). (Illus.). 64p. (J). (gr. 4-8). 1994. pap. 6.95 (*1-56294-757-5*); lib. bdg. 23.40 (*1-56294-006-6*) Millbrook Pr.

Carlson, Jerry. Details for Locating & Catching Fish. LC 98-175620. (Illus.). 136p. 1998. pap. 10.95 (*0-9661906-0-2*) Back Bay MN.

Carlson, Jerry, ed. Advances in Cognition & Educational Practice, Vol. 3. 256p. 1995. 78.50 (*1-55938-766-1*) Jai Pr.

Carlson, Jerry, et al, eds. Advances in Cognition & Educational Practice, 2 pts., Vol. 4. 304p. 1997. 78.50 (*0-7623-0105-8*) Jai Pr.

— Advances in Cognition & Educational Practice Vol. 5: Conceptual Issues in Research in Intelligence. 1998. 78.50 (*0-7623-0423-5*) Jai Pr.

— Advances in Cognition & Educational Practice Vol. 6, Pt. B: Conceptual Issues in Research in Intelligence. LC 97-18549. Date not set. 78.50 (*0-7623-0424-3*) Jai Pr.

Carlson, Jerry & Butterfield, E. C., eds. Advances in Cognition & Educational Practice: Applications: Remediation, Vol. 1, Pt. B. 240p. 1992. 78.50 (*1-55938-485-9*) Jai Pr.

— Advances in Cognition & Educational Practice: Children's Writing: Towards a Process Theory of the Development of Skilled Writing, Vol. 2: Childrens Writing. 224p. 1994. 78.50 (*1-55938-108-6*) Jai Pr.

— Advances in Cognition & Educational Practice: Cognition & Educational Practice, 2 vols., Set, Vol. 1. 1992. 157.00 (*1-55938-484-0*) Jai Pr.

— Advances in Cognition & Educational Practice: Theoretical Issues Intelligence, Vol. 1, Pt. A. 264p. 1992. 78.50 (*1-55938-483-2*) Jai Pr.

Carlson, Jerry S., et al. Study Abroad: The Experience of American Undergraduates, 37. LC 89-49243. (Contributions to the Study of Education Ser.: No. 37). (Illus.). 264p. 1990. 62.95 (*0-313-27385-5*, CSH/, Greenwood Pr) Greenwood.

Carlson, Jodi L., jt. ed. see Taira, Ellen D.

Carlson, Jody. George C. Wallace & the Politics of Powerlessness. LC 79-65225. 332p. 1981. 44.95 (*0-87855-344-4*) Transaction Pubs.

Carlson, Joel. No Neutral Ground. 4.95 (*0-7043-3158-6*, Pub. by Quartet) Charles River Bks.

Carlson, John, jt. ed. see Fabozzi, Frank J.

Carlson, John A. Gambler's Ruin in Foreign Exchange Markets. (Illus.). 25p. (Orig.). (C). 1993. pap. text 30.00 (*1-56806-916-2*) DIANE Pub.

Carlson, John E. & Lassey, William R. Rural Society & Environment in America. (Agricultural Sciences Ser.). (Illus.). 448p. (C). 1981. text 59.50 (*0-07-009959-6*) McGraw.

Carlson, John F. Carlson's Guide to Landscape Painting. 1984. 24.25 (*0-8446-6102-3*) Peter Smith.

Carlson, John G. & Hatfield, Elaine. Psychology of Emotion. (Illus.). 519p. (C). 1992. text 74.00 (*0-03-055419-5*, Pub. by Harcourt Coll Pubs) Harcourt.

Carlson, John G. & Yao, Andrew C. MROM: Micro Routines for Operations Management. 1991. pap. 40.00 (*0-685-51816-7*) Pearson Custom.

Carlson, John G. & Yao, Andrew C. MROM: Micro Routines for Operations Management. 2nd ed. 266p. (C). 1994. text 68.00 (*0-536-58621-7*) Pearson Custom.

Carlson, John G., jt. auth. see Barge, Bruce N.

Carlson, John G., jt. auth. see Hall, P. Owen.

Carlson Johnson, Linda. Rain Forests: A Pro/Con Issue. LC 98-34060. (Hot Pro/Con Issues Ser.). (Illus.). 64p. (YA). (gr. 6 up). 1999. lib. bdg. 19.95 (*0-7660-1202-6*) Enslow Pubs.

Carlson, Jon & Lewis, Judith. Counseling the Adolescent: Individual, Family, & School Interventions. 3rd ed. 472p. (C). 1998. text 49.00 (*0-89108-257-3*, 9708) Love Pub Co.

Carlson, Jon & Lewis, Judith A., eds. Family Counseling: Strategies & Issues. 1991. pap. 27.00 (*0-89108-219-0*, 9102) Love Pub Co.

Carlson, Jon & Slavik, Steven. Techniques in Adlerian Psychology. LC 97-8530. 1997. pap. write for info. (*1-56032-555-0*) Hemisp Pub.

***Carlson, Jon & Sperry, Len.** Brief Therapy with Individuals & Couples. LC 00-28969. 571p. 2000. 59.95 (*1-891944-43-6*) Zeig Tucker.

Carlson, Jon & Sperry, Len. The Intimate Couple. LC 98-29774. 1998. 44.95 (*0-87630-880-9*) Brunner-Mazel.

Carlson, Jon & Sperry, Len, eds. The Disordered Couple. LC 97-24085. xxiii, 342p. 1997. 45.95 (*0-87630-815-9*) Brunner-Mazel.

Carlson, Jon, et al. Family Therapy: Insuring Treatment Efficacy. LC 96-32435. (Counseling Ser.). 290p. (C). 1996. mass mkt. 65.95 (*0-534-16698-9*) Brooks-Cole.

— Study Guide to Accompany Psychopathology & Psychotherapy: Diagnosis & Treatment. LC 97-43842. 1998. 9.95 (*1-56032-554-2*) Hemisp Pub.

Carlson, Jon, jt. auth. see Dinkmeyer, Don C.

Carlson, Jon, jt. auth. see Sperry, Len.

Carlson, Jon, jt. auth. see Watts, Richard E.

Carlson, Jon F. Modules & Group Algebras. (Lectures in Mathematics). 1996. 26.50 (*0-8176-5389-9*); 26.50 (*3-7643-5389-9*) Birkhauser.

Carlson, Jonathan C. Basic Law Text: Criminal Law. (Winning in Law School Ser.). 175p. (Orig.). (C). 1992. pap. text 12.95 (*0-915667-20-7*) Spectra Pub Co.

Carlson, Jude, ed. see Bishop, Dorothy.

Carlson, Judy. Harriet Tubman: Call to Freedom. LC 89-90818. (Great Lives Biography Ser.). (Illus.). 118p. (J). (gr. 5-9). 1989. pap. 4.99 (*0-449-90376-1*, Columbine) Fawcett.

Carlson, Judy. Harriet Tubman: Call to Freedom. (Great Lives Ser.). 1989. 10.09 (*0-606-01349-0*, Pub. by Turtleback) Demco.

Carlson, Judy. Here Comes Kate! (Real Readers Ser.: Level Blue). (Illus.). 32p. (J). (gr. 1-4). 1989. pap. 4.95 (*0-8114-6713-9*) Raintree Steck-V.

— Here Comes Kate! (Real Readers Ser.: Level Blue). (Illus.). 32p. (J). (ps-3). 1995. lib. bdg. 21.40 (*0-8172-3515-9*) Raintree Steck-V.

— Nothing Is Impossible, Said Nelly Bly. (Real Readers Ser.: Level Blue). (Illus.). 32p. (J). (gr. 1-4). 1989. pap. 4.95 (*0-8114-6721-X*) Raintree Steck-V.

Carlson, Julia. Snowboarding: A Woman's Guide. (Illus.). 144p. 1998. pap. text 14.95 (*0-07-012038-2*, Ragged Mntain) McGraw-Hill Prof.

Carlson, Julie, jt. auth. see Johnson, Sue.

Carlson, K. C., ed. see Gaiman, Neil.

Carlson, K. C., ed. see Wolfman, Marv.

Carlson, Karen J. & Eisenstat, Stephanie A. Primary Care of Women. (Illus.). 608p. (C). (gr. 13). 1995. text 79.95 (*0-8016-7677-0*, 07677) Mosby Inc.

Carlson, Karen J., et al. The Harvard Guide to Women's Health. (Illus.). 704p. 1996. 39.95 (*0-674-36768-5*) HUP.

— The Harvard Guide to Women's Health. (Illus.). 704p. 1996. pap. 24.95 (*0-674-36769-3*); pap. 39.95 incl. cd-rom (*0-674-36771-5*) HUP.

— The Women's Concise Guide to a Healthier Heart. LC 97-17310. (Illus.). 144p. 1997. 24.95 (*0-674-95483-1*); pap. 12.95 (*0-674-95484-X*) HUP.

— The Women's Concise Guide to Emotional Well-Being. LC 97-21277. 256p. 1997. 31.00 (*0-674-95490-4*); pap. 14.95 (*0-674-95491-2*) HUP.

Carlson, Karyl & Gjovaag, Eric. Queen Ann in Oz. (Illus.). 128p. (J). (gr. 2 up). 1993. 44.95 (*0-929605-26-8*); pap. 9.95 (*0-929605-25-X*) Books of Wonder.

Carlson, Katherine. Casualties. LC 82-61652. (Minnesota Voices Project Ser.: No. 9). (Illus.). 124p. 1982. pap. 5.00 (*0-89823-041-1*) New Rivers Pr.

Carlson, Kathie. In Her Image: The Unhealed Daughter's Search for Her Mother. LC 89-42623. (Illus.). 168p. 1990. pap. 16.00 (*0-87773-584-0*, Pub. by Shambhala Pubns) Random.

— Life's Daughter - Death's Bride: Inner Transformations Through the Goddess Demeter-Persephone. LC 97-9007. 1997. 27.50 (*0-87773-903-X*, Pub. by Shambhala Pubns) Random.

Carlson, Kathy, ed. see American Society of Post Anesthesia Nurses Staff.

Carlson, KC, ed. see Moore, Alan.

Carlson, KC, ed. see Motter, D. & Askwith, M.

Carlson, Keith T. The Twisted Road to Freedom: America's Granting of Independence to the Philippines. LC 95-947380. 176p. (C). 1996. pap. text 16.00 (*971-542-051-6*, Pub. by U of Philippines Pr) UH Pr.

Carlson, Ken. Star Mana: The Healing Energies of Hawaii. (Illus.). 148p. 1998. pap. 14.00 (*0-9659716-0-0*) Starmen Pr.

Carlson, Kenneth E., jt. auth. see McDonald, Douglas C.

Carlson, Kenneth N. California Football Scorebook. (Illus.). 294p. (Orig.). 1991. pap. 8.25 (*0-938428-11-X*) Rain Belt.

— College Basketball Scorebook. LC 91-152490. (Illus.). 984p. (Orig.). 1990. pap. 22.50 (*0-938428-10-1*) Rain Belt.

— Football Scores & Schedules - The Book. (Illus.). 493p. 1998. pap. 15.50 (*0-938428-17-9*) Rain Belt.

— Manual for Travel Counsellors. 15th rev. ed. LC 89-114573. (Illus.). 304p. 1996. pap. text 27.50 (*0-938428-08-X*) Rain Belt.

— Pro Football Scorebook. 3rd ed. LC 94-105968. 610p. 1993. pap. 14.50 (*0-938428-12-8*) Rain Belt.

— Secret Code Book. 112p. (Orig.). 1994. pap. 9.95 (*0-938428-13-6*) Rain Belt.

— Small College & Rugby Football Scorebook. (Illus.). 816p. (Orig.). 1995. pap. 19.75 (*0-938428-14-4*) Rain Belt.

Carlson, Kim, ed. Portland Best Places: Restaurants, Lodgings, Shopping, Nightlife, Arts, Sights, Outings. 4th rev. ed. (Best Places Ser.). 368p. 1998. pap. 16.95 (*1-57061-123-8*) Sasquatch Bks.

Carlson, Kimberly S., jt. auth. see McCutcheon, Gregory K.

Carlson, Kit. Bringing up Baby: Wild Animal Families. (Animal Planet Ser.). 1998. 15.19 (*0-606-13227-9*, Pub. by Turtleback) Demco.

Carlson, Kit, jt. auth. see Needles, Colleen.

Carlson, Kristine, jt. auth. see Carlson, Richard.

Carlson, Kurt. The FamilyPC Software Buyer's Guide. LC 96-208019. (Illus.). 320p. (J). 1996. pap. 24.45 (*0-7868-8205-0*, Pub. by Hyperion) Time Warner.

Carlson, Kyogen. Zen in the American Grain: Discovering the Teachings at Home. 1994. pap. 9.95 (*0-88268-158-3*) Station Hill Pr.

***Carlson, L. A., et al, eds.** Delirium in the Elderly: Epidemiological, Pathogenetic, Diagnostic & Treatment Aspects, 3rd Symposium on Aging & Aging Disorders, Stockholm, September, 1998. (Dementia & Geriatric Cognitive Disorders Ser.: Vol. 10, No. 5). (Illus.). 126p. 1999. pap. 39.25 (*3-8055-6967-X*) S Karger.

Carlson, L. A., et al, eds. Vascular Dementia: Etiological, Pathogenetic, Clinical & Treatment Aspects. (Journal: Dementia: Vol. 5, Nos. 3-4, 1994). (Illus.). iv, 86p. 1994. pap. 97.50 (*3-8055-5984-4*) S Karger.

Carlson, Lage, ed. Boxes for the Protection of Books: Their Design & Construction. rev. ed. (Illus.). 220p. (C). 1998. pap. text 30.00 (*0-7881-7091-0*) DIANE Pub.

Carlson, Larry G. Molecular Ramjet: And Other Bedtime Stories . . . (Illus.). 212p. (YA). (gr. 7-9). 1989. pap. 4.95 (*0-929301-01-3*) TadAlex Bks.

Carlson, Lars A. & Olsson, Anders G., eds. Treatment of Hyperlipoproteinemia. LC 83-42855. 304p. 1984. reprint ed. pap. 94.30 (*0-608-00360-3*, 206107700007) Bks Demand.

Carlson, Lars A. & Pernow, Bengt, eds. Metabolic Risk Factors in Ischemic Cardiovascular Disease. LC 80-5835. 263p. 1982. reprint ed. pap. 81.60 (*0-608-00308-5*, 206102500007) Bks Demand.

Carlson, Lars A., ed. see International Conference on Atherosclerosis Staff.

Carlson, Laura, et al, eds. Literary Laurels: A Reader's Guide to Award-Winning Fiction. 80p. (Orig.). 1995. pap. 9.95 (*0-9647361-0-1*) Hillyard.

— Literary Laurels - Kid's Edition: A Guide to Award-Winning Children's Books. LC 96-180880. 138p. (Orig.). 1996. pap. 11.95 (*0-9647361-1-X*) Hillyard.

Carlson, Lauri. Well in Dialogue Games: A Discourse Analysis of the Interjection "Well" in Idealized Conversation. LC 85-4029. (Pragmatics & Beyond Ser.: Vol. V-5). ix, 104p. (Orig.). 1985. pap. 38.00 (*0-915027-27-5*) J Benjamins Pubng Co.

Carlson, Laurie. Boss of the Plains: The Hat That Won the West. LC 97-30995. (Illus.). (J). (gr. 2-4). 1998. 16.95 (*0-7894-2479-7*) DK Pub Inc.

— Classical Kids: An Activity Guide to Life in Ancient Greece & Rome. LC 97-52676. (Illus.). 184p. (J). (gr. 4-6). 1998. pap. 14.95 (*1-55652-290-8*) Chicago Review.

— EcoArt! Earth-Friendly Art & Craft Experiences for 3- to 9-Year-Olds. LC 92-21347. (Kids Can! Ser.: No. 8). (Illus.). 160p. (Orig.). (J). (ps-4). 1993. pap. 12.95 (*0-913589-68-3*) Williamson Pub Co.

— Green Thumbs: A Kid's Activity Guide to Indoor & Outdoor Gardening. LC 94-41895. (Illus.). 144p. (Orig.). (J). (ps-4). 1995. pap. 12.95 (*1-55652-238-X*) Chicago Review.

— Kids Create! Art & Craft Experiences for 3 to 9 Year Olds. Williamson, Susan, ed. LC 90-33677. (Kids Can! Ser.). (Illus.). 160p. (Orig.). (J). (ps-4). 1990. pap. 12.95 (*0-913589-51-9*) Williamson Pub Co.

Carlson, Laurie. More Than Moccasins: A Kid's Activity Guide to Traditional North American Indian Life. LC 93-39922. (Illus.). 200p. (J). (gr. k-6). 1994. pap. 12.95 (*1-55652-213-4*) Chicago Review.

Carlson, Laurie & Dammel, Judith. Kids Camp! Activities for the Backyard or Wilderness. LC 94-41030. (Illus.). 176p. (Orig.). (J). (ps-7). 1995. pap. 12.95 (*1-55652-237-1*) Chicago Review.

Carlson, Laurie, jt. auth. see Carlson, Russ.

Carlson, Laurie, jt. auth. see DK Publishing Staff.

Carlson, Laurie M. Colonial Kids: An Activity Guide to Life in the New World. LC 97-13105. (Illus.). 160p. (J). (gr. k-7). 1997. pap. 12.95 (*1-55652-322-X*) Chicago Review.

— Days of Knights & Damsels: An Activity Guide. LC 97-36359. 174p. (J). 1998. pap. 14.95 (*1-55652-291-6*) Chicago Review.

— Kids Create!, Art & Craft Experiences for 3- To 9-Year-Olds. LC 90-33677. 1990. 18.05 (*0-606-10238-8*, Pub. by Turtleback) Demco.

— Westward Ho! An Activity Guide to the Wild West. LC 96-10841. (Illus.). 184p. (Orig.). (J). (gr. k-7). 1996. pap. 12.95 (*1-55652-271-1*) Chicago Review.

Carlson, Laurie W. A Fever in Salem: A New Interpretation of the New England Witch Trials. LC 99-27520. (Illus.). 224p. 1999. 24.95 (*1-56663-253-6*, Pub. by I R Dee) Natl Bk Netwk.

— On Sidesaddles to Heaven: The Women of the Rocky Mountain Mission. Cornell, Wayne, ed. LC 98-10199. (Illus.). 256p. 1998. 19.95 (*0-87004-384-6*) Caxton.

***Carlson, Laurie Winn.** A Fever in Salem: A New Interpretation of the New England Witch Trials. (Illus.). 224p. 2000. reprint ed. pap. 14.95 (*1-56663-309-5*, Pub. by I R Dee) Natl Bk Netwk.

Carlson, Leland H. Martin Marprelate, Gentleman: Master Job Throkmorton Laid Open in His Colors. LC 80-26442. (Illus.). 467p. 1981. reprint ed. pap. 144.80 (*0-608-03170-4*, 206362300007) Bks Demand.

***Carlson, Lenny.** John Jackson - Don't Let Your Deal Go Down. 88p. 1998. pap. 14.95 (*0-7866-3549-5*, 96795) Mel Bay.

Carlson, Lenny, tr. see Spence, Joseph.

Carlson, Leonard A. Indians, Bureaucrats, & Land: The Dawes Act & the Decline of Indian Farming, 36. LC 80-1709. (Contributions in Economics & Economic History Ser.: No. 36). 219p. 1981. 55.00 (*0-313-22533-8*, CDA/, Greenwood Pr) Greenwood.

Carlson, Les, jt. auth. see Macklin, M. Carolin.

Carlson, Lewis & Ferreira, James M. Beyond the Red, White, & Blue: A Student's Introduction to American Studies. 480p. (C). 1993. pap. text, per. 48.95 (*0-8403-8816-0*) Kendall-Hunt.

Carlson, Lewis H. We Were Each Other's Prisoners: An Oral History of World War II American & German Prisoners of War. 288p. 1998. pap. 15.00 (*0-465-09123-7*, Pub. by Basic) HarpC.

Carlson-Lichlyter, Lynette, et al. Green Horses: Stories & Poems to Share. LC 96-72044. (Illus.). 170p. (Orig.). 1996. pap. 7.95 (*0-9655485-0-3*) Soc of Literary.

Carlson, Linda. Executive Search Firms & Employment Agencies in Seattle: Job-Search Resources for the Executive, Manager & Professional. LC 97-94833. 200p. 1998. pap. 21.95 (*0-9627122-7-2*) Barrett St Prodns.

— Four Blocks Continued. LC 97-25847. (Illus.). 128p. 1997. pap. 16.95 (*0-89145-795-X*, 4900, Am Quilters Soc) Collector Bks.

— How to Find a Good Job in Seattle: Your Best Guide to Thousands of Puget Sound Employers. 7th ed. LC 98-92706. 504p. 1998. pap. 21.95 (*0-9627122-8-0*) Barrett St Prodns.

— Instructor's Manual to Accompany the Strengths Model: Case Management with People Suffering from Severe & Persistent Mental Illness. 54p. 1997. pap. text. write for info. (*0-19-512141-4*) OUP.

Carlson, Linda, ed. see Archer, Jeff.

Carlson, Linda, ed. see Diamond, Dickson.

Carlson, Linda, ed. see Fay, Jim, et al.

***Carlson, Linda F.** Plump: Survival of the Fattest. Boucke, Laurie, ed. LC 99-43574. (Illus.). 1999. pap. 12.50 (*1-888580-12-7*) White-Boucke.

Carlson, Linda G. Roots, Feathers & Blooms: 4-Block Quilts Their History & Patterns, Bk. 1. 128p. 1995. pap. 16.95 (*0-89145-825-5*, 3789, Am Quilters Soc) Collector Bks.

***Carlson, Linda Sonnett.** Pathways Through Pain: A Spiritual Journey. LC 99-44303. 2000. pap. write for info. (*1-880090-96-1*) Galde Pr.

Carlson, Lisa. Caring for the Dead: Your Final Act of Love. LC 98-27893. 640p. 1998. pap. 29.95 (*0-942679-21-0*) Upper Access.

Carlson, Lisa, ed. see Carse, Mary.

Carlson, Liz. Fun with Paint & Stitch. 20p. 1993. pap. 6.95 (*1-883504-04-X*) Sew-Art Int.

Carlson, Loren M. Bibliography of South Dakota Government. 1951. 5.00 (*1-55614-024-X*) U of SD Gov Res Bur.

— Dakota Preposition: Panacea or Nightmare for South Dakota? 1980. 1.00 (*1-55614-032-0*) U of SD Gov Res Bur.

— South Dakota Budgetary Developments: Process & Trends, 1967-1983. 1984. 1.00 (*1-55614-116-5*) U of SD Gov Res Bur.

— State Budgeting in South Dakota. 1967. 1.00 (*1-55614-006-1*) U of SD Gov Res Bur.

Carlson, Lori. Sol a Sol. LC 97-18574. (Illus.). 32p. (J). 1995. 15.95 (*0-8050-4373-X*) H Holt & Co.

— The Truth about You: Self-Image. (Inter Acta Ser.). (Illus.). 4p. (C). 1994. teacher ed., ring bd. 1.25 (*1-885702-81-7*, 741-059t, Inter Acta); student ed., ring bd. 3.25 (*1-885702-80-9*, 741-059s, Inter Acta) WSN Pr.

Carlson, Lori, ed. Cool Salsa: Bilingual Poems on Growing up Latino in the United States. LC 93-45798. (ENG & SPA.). 160p. (YA). (gr. 7 up). 1995. mass mkt. 4.50 (*0-449-70436-X*, Juniper) Fawcett.

— Cool Salsa: Bilingual Poems on Growing up Latino in the United States. (YA). (gr. 8 up). 1995. 14.95 (*0-8050-3135-9*, Bks Young Read) H Holt & Co.

Carlson, Lori, jt. ed. see MacShane, Frank.

Carlson, Lori M. American Eyes: New Asian-American Short Stories for Young Adults. (J). (gr. 7). 1996. mass mkt. 4.50 (*0-449-70448-3*) Fawcett.

— Bilingual Plays Anthology. (J). 1999. lib. bdg. write for info. (*0-688-16238-X*, Wm Morrow) Morrow Avon.

— Hurray for Three Kings' Day! LC 97-20937. 32p. (J). 1999. 16.00 (*0-688-16239-8*, Wm Morrow) Morrow Avon.

***Carlson, Lori M.** Hurray for Three Kings' Day! LC 97-20937. 32p. (J). 1999. 15.93 (*0-688-16240-1*, Wm Morrow) Morrow Avon.

Carlson, Lori M. Where Angels Glide at Dawn: New Stories from Latin America. 1993. 9.05 (*0-606-02982-6*, Pub. by Turtleback) Demco.

— You're On! Seven Plays in English & Spanish. LC 99-17222. (SPA., Illus.). 144p. (J). (gr. 3-7). 1999. 17.00 (*0-688-16237-1*, Wm Morrow) Morrow Avon.

Carlson, Lori M., ed. American Eyes: New Asian-American Short Stories for Young Adults. 160p. (J). (gr. 7 up). 1995. 14.95 (*0-8050-3544-3*) H Holt & Co.

— Barrio Streets, Carnival Dreams: Three Generations of Latino Artistry. (Illus.). 127p. (YA). (gr. 7-12). 1998. 16.00 (*0-7881-5782-5*) DIANE Pub.

— Barrio Streets, Carnival Dreams: Three Generations of Latino Artistry. LC 95-41317. 96p. (YA). (gr. 6 up). 1995. 15.95 (*0-8050-4120-6*, Edge Books) H Holt & Co.

Carlson, Lori M. & Ventura, Cynthia L. Where Angels Glide at Dawn: New Stories from Latin America. LC 90-6697. (Trophy Bk.). 128p. (J). (gr. 5 up). 1993. pap. 4.50 (*0-06-440464-1*, HarpTrophy) HarpC Child Bks.

Carlson, Lori M. & Ventura, Cynthia L., eds. Where Angels Glide at Dawn: New Stories from Latin America. LC 90-6697. (Illus.). 128p. (J). (gr. 5 up). 1990. lib. bdg. 13.89 (*0-397-32425-1*) HarpC Child Bks.

— Where Angels Glide at Dawn: New Stories from Latin America. LC 90-6697. (Illus.). 128p. (YA). (gr. 5 up). 1990. 14.00 (*0-397-32424-3*) HarpC Child Bks.

***Carlson, Lori Marie.** The Sunday Tertulia. 224p. 2000. 22.00 (*0-06-019536-3*) HarpC.

Carlson, Luis A. Language-Structured Auditory Retention Span Test (LARS) rev. ed. 1989. write for info. (*0-87879-881-1*); 9.00 (*0-87879-882-X*); lp 18.00 (*0-87879-880-3*) Acad Therapy.

***Carlson, Margaret.** The Canning Season. LC 98-14061. (First Person Ser.). 32p. (gr. 2-4). 1999. pap. 7.95 (*1-57505-283-0*, Carolrhoda) Lerner Pub.

Carlson, Margaret. The Canning Season. LC 98-14061. (First Person Book Ser.). (Illus.). 40p. (J). (gr. 2-4). 1999. 19.93 (*1-57505-260-1*) Lerner Pub.

Carlson, Margery V. Message from the Blueberries & Other Poems. (Illus.). 144p. 1999. pap. write for info. (*0-9670922-0-5*) GA Poetry Socy.

— Vala Fastel & Other Essays. (Illus.). 184p. 1999. pap. write for info. (*0-9650673-9-4*) Dolphs & Orchs.

Carlson, Maria. No Religion Higher Than Truth: A History of the Theosophical Movement in Russia, 1875-1922. LC 92-19451. (Illus.). 304p. (C). 1993. text 49.50 (*0-691-05682-X*, Pub. by Princeton U Pr) Cal Prin Full Svc.

Carlson, Maria, tr. see Prokofiev, Sergei.

Carlson, Marifran. Feminismo! The Woman's Movement in Argentina from Its Beginnings to Eva Peron. (Illus.). 225p. 1988. 25.00 (*0-89733-152-4*); pap. 12.00 (*0-89733-168-0*) Academy Chi Pubs.

Carlson, Marvin. Deathtraps: The Postmodern Comedy Thriller. LC 92-45237. 224p. 1993. 35.00 (*0-253-31305-8*); 14.95 (*0-253-20826-2*) Ind U Pr.

— The Italian Shakespearians: Performances by Ristori, Salvini, & Rossi in England & America. LC 84-48131. (Illus.). 224p. 1986. 35.00 (*0-918016-76-2*) Folger Bks.

— Performance: A Critical Introduction. LC 95-41701. 256p. (C). 1996. 85.00 (*0-415-13702-0*); pap. 20.99 (*0-415-13703-9*) Routledge.

— Places of Performance: The Semiotics of Theatre Architecture. LC 88-47936. (Illus.). 224p. 1989. text 49.95 (*0-8014-2254-X*) Cornell U Pr.

— Places of Performance: The Semiotics of Theatre Architecture. LC 88-47936. (Illus.). 224p. 1993. pap. text 21.95 (*0-8014-8094-9*) Cornell U Pr.

— Theatre Semiotics: Signs of Life. LC 89-45193. (Advances in Semiotics Ser.). 144p. 1990. 25.95 (*0-253-31315-5*) Ind U Pr.

— Theories of the Theatre: A Historical & Critical Survey from the Greeks to the Present. 560p. 1993. pap. text 19.95 (*0-8014-8154-6*) Cornell U Pr.

Carlson, Marvin, tr. see Antoine, Andre.

Carlson, Marvin A. Voltaire & the Theatre of the Eighteenth Century, 84. LC 98-17533. (Contributions in Drama & Theatre Studies: Vol. 84). 208p. 1998. 59.95 (*0-313-30302-9*, Greenwood Pr) Greenwood.

Carlson, Mary. Beanie the Brownie & the Great Christmas Caper. (Illus.). 32p. (Orig.). (J). 1996. write for info. (*0-614-26216-X*) Jrnl Sentinel.

***Carlson, Mary.** Journey from Cornwall. 244p. 2000. pap. 12.95 (*1-878569-69-4*, Waubesa Pr) Badger Bks Inc.

Carlson, Mary. The Vermont State Office of Economic Opportunity: A Case Study in Organizational Relationships. (Occasional Papers: No. 16). (Illus.). 68p. 1993. pap. text 7.50 (*0-944277-25-X*) U VT Ctr Rsch VT.

Carlson, Mary, jt. auth. see Carlson, Stuart.

Carlson, Mary, jt. auth. see Riley, Jane.

***Carlson, Maureen.** Family & Friends in Polymer Clay: Techniques for Making Character Dolls & Whimsical Figures. LC 99-43672. (Illus.). 128p. 2000. pap. 22.99 (*0-89134-927-8*, North Lght Bks) F & W Pubns Inc.

Carlson, Maureen. How to Make Clay Characters. LC 96-38418. (Illus.). 128p. 1997. pap. 22.99 (*0-89134-721-6*, North Lght Bks) F & W Pubns Inc.

Carlson, Melanie, jt. auth. see LeNoir, Anna.

Carlson, Melinda, ed. see Hanson, John B.

Carlson, Melody. The Ark That Noah Built. LC 97-3377. (Illus.). 40p. (J). 1997. 9.99 (*1-57673-058-1*, Gold n Honey) Zondervan.

— Autumn Secrets. LC 98-220292. (Allison Chronicles Ser.). 192p. 1998. pap. 5.99 (*1-55661-959-6*) Bethany Hse.

— Awakening Heart. LC 97-45445. (Portraits Ser.). 288p. 1998. pap. 8.99 (*1-55661-998-7*) Bethany Hse.

— Benjamin's Box: A Resurrection Story. LC 96-43715. (Illus.). 40p. (J). 1997. 10.99 (*1-57673-139-1*, Gold n Honey) Zondervan.

Carlson, Melody. Benjamin's Box: An Easter Story. (Illus.). (J). (gr. k-5). 1997. 7.97 (*0-310-70044-2*) Zondervan.

Carlson, Melody. Cherished Wish. LC 97-33853. (Allison Chronicles Ser.). 16p. (J). 1998. pap. 5.99 (*1-55661-958-8*) Bethany Hse.

— Daniel & the Lions Den. (Story Pockets Ser.). 1997. 4.99 (*1-57673-166-9*, Gold n Honey) Zondervan.

***Carlson, Melody.** The Day the Circus Came to Town. LC 99-86595. (Illus.). 32p. (J). (ps-3). 2000. 14.99 (*1-58134-158-X*) Crossway Bks.

— Diary of a Teenage Girl. (Illus.). (YA). 2000. pap. 12.99 (*1-57673-735-7*) Multnomah Pubs.

Carlson, Melody. Dreams of Promise. (Allison Chronicles Ser.). 176p. 1999. pap. 5.99 (*1-55661-960-X*) Bethany Hse.

***Carlson, Melody.** Everything I Long For. LC 99-41914. (Whispering Pines Ser.: Bk. 2). 250p. 2000. pap. 9.99 (*0-7369-0062-4*) Harvest Hse.

— Farmer Brown's Field Trip. LC 99-53086. (Illus.). 40p. (J). (gr. 2-6). 2000. 9.99 (*1-58134-142-3*) Crossway Bks.

Carlson, Melody. Fruit Troop - Anna Apple. LC 99-158695. (Fruit Troop Action Ser.). (Illus.). 8p. (J). (ps) 1997. bds. 6.99 (*1-57673-195-2*, Gold n Honey) Zondervan.

— Fruit Troop - Blackberry Bart. (Fruit Troop Action Ser.). (Illus.). 8p. (J). (ps). 1997. bds. 6.99 (*1-57673-199-5*, Gold n Honey) Zondervan.

— Fruit Troop - Gladys Grape. (Fruit Troop Action Ser.). (Illus.). 8p. (J). (ps). 1997. bds. 6.99 (*1-57673-193-6*, Gold n Honey) Zondervan.

— Fruit Troop - Lyle Lemon. (Fruit Troop Action Ser.). (Illus.). 8p. (J). (ps). 1997. bds. 6.99 (*1-57673-196-0*, Gold n Honey) Zondervan.

— Fruit Troop - Peachy Pete. (Fruit Troop Action Ser.). (Illus.). 8p. (J). (ps). 1997. bds. 6.99 (*1-57673-194-4*, Gold n Honey) Zondervan.

— Fruit Troop - Penny Pear. (Fruit Troop Action Ser.). (Illus.). 8p. (J). (ps). 1997. bds. 6.99 (*1-57673-192-8*, Gold n Honey) Zondervan.

— Fruit Troop - Pineapple Paul. (Fruit Troop Action Ser.). (Illus.). 8p. (J). (ps). 1997. bds. 6.99 (*1-57673-197-9*, Gold n Honey) Zondervan.

— Fruit Troop - Strawberry Sam. (Fruit Troop Action Ser.). (Illus.). 8p. (J). (ps). 1997. bds. 6.99 (*1-57673-191-X*, Gold n Honey) Zondervan.

— Fruit Troop - Tammy Tangerine. (Fruit Troop Action Ser.). (Illus.). 8p. (J). (ps). 1997. bds. 6.99 (*1-57673-198-7*, Gold n Honey) Zondervan.

***Carlson, Melody.** God Goes with Me. (Illus.). 20p. (J). (ps-k). 2000. bds. 7.99 (*1-58134-160-1*) Crossway Bks.

Carlson, Melody. God Lives in My House. (Illus.). 20p. (J). (ps-3). 1999. bds. 7.99 (*1-58134-070-2*) Crossway Bks.

***Carlson, Melody.** God Made Them All. (Illus.). 20p. (J). (ps-1). 2000. bds. 7.99 (*1-58134-159-8*) Crossway Bks.

Carlson, Melody. Gold & Honey Bible. LC 97-17256. (Illus.). (J). 1997. 17.99 (*1-57673-179-0*, Gold n Honey) Zondervan.

— The Greatest Gift. LC 97-19582. (Illus.). 48p. (J). 1997. 14.99 (*1-57673-190-1*, Gold n Honey) Zondervan.

— Heartland Skies, No. 1. LC 97-36406. (Cowboy Ser.). 1998. pap. 9.99 (*1-57673-264-9*, Palisades OR) Multnomah Pubs.

***Carlson, Melody.** Hi, I'm Blackbeary: The Fruit of the Spirit is Peace. (Illus.). 16p. (J). (ps-k). 2000. 6.99 (*1-58134-182-2*) Crossway Bks.

— Hi, I'm Hucklebeary: The Fruit of the Spirit is Love. (Beary Patch Bears Ser.). (Illus.). 16p. (J). (ps-k). 2000. 6.99 (*1-58134-180-6*) Crossway Bks.

— Hi, I'm Razzbeary: The Fruit of the Spirit is Joy. (Beary Patch Bears Ser.). (Illus.). 16p. (J). (ps-k). 2000. 6.99 (*1-58134-181-4*) Crossway Bks.

Carlson, Melody. Homeward. LC 97-11833. 348p. 1998. pap. 10.99 (*1-57673-029-8*, Multnomah Bks) Multnomah Pubs.

— I Can Count on God. (Illus.). 20p. (J). (ps-3). 1999. bds. 7.99 (*1-58134-071-0*) Crossway Bks.

***Carlson, Melody.** It's Not Funny, I've Lost My Money. LC 00-8836. (Illus.). 40p. (J). (ps-3). 2000. 9.99 (*1-58134-183-0*) Crossway Bks.

Carlson, Melody. Jammin' with the Fruit Troop Color Book. (Stories, Songs, & Riddles Ser.). 64p. (J). 1998. pap. 9.99 incl. audio (*1-57673-305-X*, Gold n Honey) Zondervan.

— Jonah & the Big Fish. (Story Pockets Ser.). 1997. 4.99 (*1-57673-169-3*, Gold n Honey) Zondervan.

— King of the Stable. LC 98-19486. (Illus.). 32p. (J). (ps-5). 1998. 14.99 (*1-58134-032-X*) Crossway Bks.

***Carlson, Melody.** Looking for You All My Life. (Whispering Pines Ser.). 300p. 2000. pap. 9.99 (*0-7369-0063-2*) Harvest Hse.

Carlson, Melody. The Lost Lamb. LC 99-13300. (Illus.). 40p. (J). (ps-3). 1999. 9.99 (*1-58134-072-9*) Crossway Bks.

***Carlson, Melody.** Lullaby Bible. LC 97-43520. (Illus.). 48p. (J). (ps). 1998. 10.99 (*1-57673-252-5*, Gold n Honey) Zondervan.

Carlson, Melody. Moses in the Bulrushes. (Story Pockets Ser.). 1997. 4.99 (*1-57673-168-5*, Gold n Honey) Zondervan.

— Noah & the Ark. (Story Pockets Ser.). 1997. 4.99 (*1-57673-167-7*, Gold n Honey) Zondervan.

***Carlson, Melody.** O Come Let Us Adore Him. (Illus.). 96p. 2000. 12.99 (*1-58134-200-4*) Crossway Bks.

Carlson, Melody. On Hope's Wings. LC 97-33854. (Allison Chronicles Ser.). 192p. (J). 1998. pap. 5.99 (*1-55661-957-X*) Bethany Hse.

— The Other Brother. LC 99-16674. (Illus.). 40p. (J). (gr. 3-6). 1999. 9.99 (*1-58134-122-9*) Crossway Bks.

***Carlson, Melody.** A Place to Come Home to. LC 99-14245. (Whispering Pine Ser.). 300p. 1999. pap. 9.99 (*0-7369-0053-5*) Harvest Hse.

Carlson, Melody. Sea Hag's Treasure. LC 96-37886. (Illus.). 48p. (J). (ps-3). 1997. 12.99 (*1-57673-055-7*, Gold n Honey) Zondervan.

— Shades of Light. LC 98-12014. 232p. 1998. pap. 9.99 (*1-57673-283-5*, Palisades OR) Multnomah Pubs.

***Carlson, Melody.** Take Time: A Moment for the Heart. LC 99-87149. 2000. 14.99 (*0-8054-2359-1*) Broadman.

Carlson, Melody. A Tale of Two Houses. LC 97-45004. (Illus.). 40p. (J). (ps up). 1998. 9.99 (*1-57673-314-9*, Gold n Honey) Zondervan.

— Tupsu: The Squirrel Who Was Afraid. LC 96-49451. (Illus.). 48p. (J). (ps-3). 1997. 12.99 (*1-57673-052-2*, Gold n Honey) Zondervan.

— The War of the Weeds. LC 97-45005. (Fruit Troop Adventure Ser.). (Illus.). 32p. (J). (ps). 1998. 9.99 (*1-57673-308-4*, Gold n Honey) Zondervan.

— What Nick & Holly Found in Grandpa's Attic. LC 98-14993. (Illus.). 40p. (J). 1998. 10.99 (*1-57673-372-6*) Zondervan.

— The Wise Man's House. LC 96-50929. 286p. 1997. pap. 9.99 (*1-57673-070-0*) Multnomah Pubs.

— The Wonder of Christmas: A Family Advent Journey. LC 99-32348. (Illus.). 144p. (J). (gr. 2-6). 1999. 14.99 (*1-58134-105-9*) Crossway Bks.

— The Wonder of Christmas: A Family Advent Journey. (Illus.). 48p. (J). (ps-3). 1999. pap. 3.99 (*1-58134-130-X*) Crossway Bks.

***Carlson, Melody, compiled by.** The Storyteller's Collection: Tales of Far off Places. (Illus.). 320p. 2000. pap. 16.99 (*1-57673-738-1*) Multnomah Pubs.

Carlson, Melody, jt. auth. see Tada, Joni Eareckson.

Carlson, Merry, jt. auth. see Anderson, Ken.

Carlson, Mim. Team-Based Fundraising Step-by-Step: A Total Organization Model. LC 99-59677. 1999. 26.95 (*0-7879-4367-3*) Jossey-Bass.

Carlson, Mim & Support Centers of America Staff. Winning Grants Step by Step: Support Centers of America's Complete Workbook for Planning, Developing, & Writing Successful Proposals. LC 95-16793. (Nonprofit Sector Ser.). 128p. 1995. pap. text 25.95 (*0-7879-0118-0*) Jossey-Bass.

Carlson-Mineau, Anita. Poems & Things for Pondering. 20p. 1995. pap. 5.00 (*0-9662539-3-0*) Bks By Anita.

***Carlson, Moira.** Herbs for the Pacific Northwest. (Illus.). 232p. 2000. pap. 24.95 (*1-894143-05-1*, Pub. by S Pr Ltd) SCB Distributors.

Carlson, N. Kay. Mission: Faithful: A Christian Adventure Novel. 225p. 1999. pap. 7.95 (*0-9665487-2-8*) T Carlson.

Carlson, N. Kay, ed. see Carlson, Thomas E.

Carlson, Nancy. ABC I Like Me! LC 96-45118. 32p. (J). 1997. 14.99 (*0-670-87458-2*) Viking Penguin.

— ABC, I Like Me. 32p. (ps-k). 1999. pap. 5.99 (*0-14-056485-3*, PuffinBks) Peng Put Young Read.

— Bunnies & Their Hobbies. LC 83-23161. (Illus.). 32p. (J). (ps-3). 1984. lib. bdg. 17.27 (*0-87614-257-9*, Carolrhoda) Lerner Pub.

— Bunnies & Thier Hobbies. (Nancy Carlson's Neighborhood Ser.). (Illus.). 32p. (J). 1997. pap. text 4.95 (*1-57505-066-8*, Carolrhoda) Lerner Pub.

— Harriet & the Garden. LC 81-18136. (Illus.). 32p. (J). (ps-3). 1982. lib. bdg. 17.27 (*0-87614-184-X*, Carolrhoda) Lerner Pub.

— Harriet & the Garden. (Nancy Carlson's Neighborhood Ser.). (Illus.). 32p. (J). (ps-3). 1997. pap. text 4.95 (*1-57505-065-X*, Carolrhoda) Lerner Pub.

— Harriet & the Roller Coaster. (Nancy Carlson's Neighborhood Ser.). (Illus.). 32p. (J). (ps-3). 1994. pap. 4.95 (*0-87614-850-X*, First Ave Edns); lib. bdg. 17.27 (*0-87614-183-1*, First Ave Edns) Lerner Pub.

— Harriet & the Roller Coaster. unabridged ed. (Illus.). (J). (gr. k-3). 24.95 incl. audio (*0-941078-56-6*); pap. 15.95 incl. audio (*0-941078-54-X*) Live Oak Media.

— Harriet & the Roller Coaster, 4 bks., Set. unabridged ed. (Illus.). (J). (gr. k-3). pap. 31.95 incl. audio (*0-941078-55-8*) Live Oak Media.

— Harriet & Walt. (Nancy Carlson's Neighborhood Ser.). (Illus.). 32p. (J). (ps-3). 1994. pap. 4.95 (*0-87614-851-8*, First Ave Edns); lib. bdg. 17.27 (*0-87614-185-8*, First Ave Edns) Lerner Pub.

— Harriet & Walt. unabridged ed. (Illus.). (J). (gr. k-3). 24.95 incl. audio (*0-941078-59-0*); pap. 15.95 incl. audio (*0-941078-57-4*) Live Oak Media.

— Harriet & Walt, Set. unabridged ed. (Illus.). (J). (gr. k-3). pap. 31.95 incl. audio (*0-941078-58-2*) Live Oak Media.

An Asterisk (*) at the beginning of an entry indicates that the title is appearing for the first time.

— Harriet's Halloween Candy. (Nancy Carlson's Neighborhood Ser.). (Illus.). 32p. (J). (ps-3). 1994. pap. 4.95 (*0-87614-850-X*, First Ave Edns); lib. bdg. 17.27 (*0-87614-182-3*, First Ave Edns) Lerner Pub.

— Harriet's Halloween Candy. unabridged ed. (Illus.). (J). (gr. k-3). 24.95 incl. audio (*0-941078-53-1*); pap. 15.95 incl. audio (*0-941078-51-5*) Live Oak Media.

— Harriet's Halloween Candy, 4 bks., Set. unabridged ed. (Illus.). (J). (gr. k-3). pap. 31.95 incl. audio (*0-941078-52-3*) Live Oak Media.

— Harriet's Recital. (Nancy Carlson's Neighborhood Ser.). (Illus.). 32p. (J). (ps-3). 1994. pap. 4.95 (*0-87614-853-4*, First Ave Edns); lib. bdg. 17.27 (*0-87614-181-5*, First Ave Edns) Lerner Pub.

— Harriet's Recital. unabridged ed. (Illus.). (J). (gr. k-3). 1985. 24.95 incl. audio (*0-941078-69-8*); pap. 15.95 incl. audio (*0-941078-67-1*) Live Oak Media.

— Harriet's Recital, 4 bks., Set. unabridged ed. (Illus.). (J). (gr. k-3). 1985. pap. 31.95 incl. audio (*0-941078-68-X*) Live Oak Media.

***Carlson, Nancy.** Hooray for Grandpartent's Day. (Illus.). (J). 2000. 15.99 (*0-670-88876-1*, Viking Child) Peng Put Young Read.

Carlson, Nancy. How to Lose All of Your Friends. LC 92-28368. 32p. (J). (ps-3). 1994. 14.99 (*0-670-84906-5*, Viking Child) Peng Put Young Read.

— How to Lose All Your Friends. (J). 1997. pap. 5.99 (*0-14-055862-4*) Viking Penguin.

— I Like Me! (Story Tapes Ser.). (Illus.). 32p. (J). (ps-3). 1996. pap. 7.99 incl. audio (*0-14-095402-3*, PuffinBks) Peng Put Young Read.

— Kings Highway. (Poetry Ser.). (Orig.). 1997. pap. 10.00 (*0-614-27188-6*) Wash Writers Pub.

— Life Is Fun! (Illus.). 32p. (J). (ps-3). 1996. pap. 5.99 (*0-14-054445-3*, PuffinBks) Peng Put Young Read.

— Louanne Pig in Making the Team. unabridged ed. (Illus.). (J). (gr. k-3). 1987. pap. 15.95 incl. audio (*0-87499-038-6*) Live Oak Media.

— Louanne Pig in Making the Team, Set. unabridged ed. (Illus.). (J). (gr. k-3). 1987. 24.95 incl. audio (*0-87499-040-8*); pap., teacher ed. 31.95 incl. audio (*0-87499-039-4*) Live Oak Media.

— Louanne Pig in the Mysterious Valentine. (Illus.). 32p. 1996. pap. text 4.95 (*1-57505-032-3*, Carolrhoda) Lerner Pub.

— Louanne Pig in The Mysterious Valentine. unabridged ed. (Illus.). (J). (gr. 1-3). 1988. pap. 15.95 incl. audio (*0-87499-086-6*) Live Oak Media.

— Louanne Pig in The Mysterious Valentine, Set. (Illus.). (J). (gr. 1-3). 1988. 24.95 incl. audio (*0-87499-087-4*) Live Oak Media.

— Louanne Pig in The Mysterious Valentine, 4 bks., Set. unabridged ed. (Illus.). (J). (gr. 1-3). 1988. pap., teacher ed. 31.95 incl. audio (*0-87499-088-2*) Live Oak Media.

— Louanne Pig in the Perfect Family. unabridged ed. (Illus.). (J). (gr. k-3). 1987. 24.95 incl. audio (*0-87499-037-8*); pap. 15.95 incl. audio (*0-87499-035-1*) Live Oak Media.

— Louanne Pig in the Perfect Family, 4 bks., Set. (Illus.). (J). (gr. k-3). 1987. pap., teacher ed. 31.95 incl. audio (*0-87499-036-X*) Live Oak Media.

— Louanne Pig in Witch Lady. (Nancy Carlson's Neighborhood Ser.). (Illus.). 32p. (J). (ps-2). 1997. pap. text 4.95 (*1-57505-234-2*, Carolrhoda) Lerner Pub.

— Loudmouth George & the Big Race. LC 83-5191. (Illus.). 32p. (J). (ps-3). 1983. lib. bdg. 17.27 (*0-87614-215-3*, Carolrhoda) Lerner Pub.

— Loudmouth George & the Bir Race. (Illus.). 32p. 1996. pap. text 4.95 (*1-57505-033-1*, Carolrhoda) Lerner Pub.

— Loudmouth George & the Cornet. LC 82-22171. (Illus.). 32p. (J). (ps-3). 1983. lib. bdg. 17.27 (*0-87614-214-5*, Carolrhoda) Lerner Pub.

— Loudmouth George & the Cornet. (Nancy Carlson's Neighborhood Ser.). (Illus.). 32p. (J). (ps-2). 1997. pap. text 4.95 (*1-57505-235-0*, Carolrhoda) Lerner Pub.

— Loudmouth George & the Fishing Trip. LC 82-22159. (Illus.). 32p. (J). (ps-3). 1983. lib. bdg. 17.27 (*0-87614-213-7*, Carolrhoda) Lerner Pub.

— Loudmouth George & the Fishing Trip. (Illus.). 32p. (J). (ps-3). 1994. pap. 4.95 (*0-87614-623-X*, Carolrhoda) Lerner Pub.

— Loudmouth George & the Fishing Trip. unabridged ed. (Illus.). (J). (gr. k-3). 1986. 24.95 incl. audio (*0-87499-019-X*); pap. 15.95 incl. audio (*0-87499-017-3*) Live Oak Media.

— Loudmouth George & the Fishing Trip, 4 vols., Set. (Illus.). (J). (gr. k-3). 1986. pap., teacher ed. 31.95 incl. audio (*0-87499-018-1*) Live Oak Media.

— Loudmouth George & the New Neighbors. LC 83-7298. (Illus.). 32p. (J). (ps-3). 1983. lib. bdg. 17.27 (*0-87614-216-1*, Carolrhoda) Lerner Pub.

— Loudmouth George & the New Neighbors. (Nancy Carlson's Neighborhood Ser.). (Illus.). 32p. (J). (ps-2). 1997. pap. text 4.95 (*0-87614-622-1*) Lerner Pub.

— Loudmouth George & the Sixth Grade Bully. (Nancy Carlson's Neighborhood Ser.). (Illus.). 32p. (J). (ps-3). 1994. pap. 4.95 (*0-87614-624-8*, First Ave Edns); lib. bdg. 17.27 (*0-87614-217-X*, First Ave Edns) Lerner Pub.

— Loudmouth George & the Sixth Grade Bully. unabridged ed. (Illus.). (J). (gr. k-3). 1986. 24.95 incl. audio (*0-87499-016-5*); pap. 15.95 incl. audio (*0-87499-014-9*) Live Oak Media.

— Loudmouth George & the Sixth Grade Bully, 4 bks., Set. (Illus.). (J). (gr. k-3). 1986. pap., teacher ed. 31.95 incl. audio (*0-87499-015-7*) Live Oak Media.

— Making the Team. (Nancy Carlson's Neighborhood Ser.). (Illus.). 32p. (J). (ps-3). 1994. pap. 4.95 (*0-87614-855-0*, First Ave Edns); lib. bdg. 17.27 (*0-87614-281-1*, First Ave Edns) Lerner Pub.

— Me Gusto Como Soy. LC 96-39622.Tr. of I Like Me!. (SPA.). 32p. (J). (ps-2). 1997. 14.99 (*0-670-86960-0*) Penguin Putnam.

— The Perfect Family. (Illus.). 32p. (J). (ps-3). 1985. pap. 4.95 (*0-87614-854-2*, Carolrhoda) Lerner Pub.

— The Perfect Family. LC 85-4123. (Illus.). 32p. (J). (ps-3). 1985. lib. bdg. 17.50 (*0-87614-280-3*, Carolrhoda) Lerner Pub.

— Sit Still. 1998. 11.19 (*0-606-13776-9*, Pub. by Turtleback) Demco.

— Sit Still. 32p. (J). (ps-2). 1998. pap. 5.99 (*0-14-056202-8*) Viking Penguin.

***Carlson, Nancy.** Snowden. (Illus.). 32p. (J). (ps-3). 2000. pap. 5.99 (*0-14-056769-0*, PuffinBks) Peng Put Young Read.

Carlson, Nancy. The Talent Show. LC 85-4122. (Nancy Carlson's Neighborhood Ser.). (Illus.). 32p. (J). (ps-3). 1985. pap. 4.95 (*1-57505-064-1*, Carolrhoda); lib. bdg. 12.95 (*0-87614-284-6*, Carolrhoda) Lerner Pub.

— Witch Lady. LC 85-3756. (Illus.). 32p. (J). (ps-1). 1985. lib. bdg. 12.95 (*0-87614-283-8*, Carolrhoda) Lerner Pub.

Carlson, Nancy, jt. auth. see Quina, Kathryn.

Carlson, Nancy, ed. see Pederson, Rolf A.

Carlson, Nancy B., et al. Clinical Procedures for Ocular Examination. 2nd ed. LC 95-49332. 493p. (C). 1996. pap. 44.95 (*0-8385-1319-0*, A1319-1, Apple Lange Med) McGraw.

Carlson, Nancy L. Arnie & the New Kid. (Picture Puffin Ser.). (Illus.). 32p. (J). (ps-3). 1992. pap. 5.99 (*0-14-050945-3*, PuffinBks) Peng Put Young Read.

— Arnie & the New Kid. (Picture Puffin Ser.). (Illus.). (J). 1992. 10.19 (*0-606-01678-3*, Pub. by Turtleback) Demco.

— Arnie & the Skateboard Gang. (Picture Puffin Ser.). 1997. 10.19 (*0-606-11057-7*, Pub. by Turtleback) Demco.

— Arnie & the Stolen Markers. (Picture Puffin Ser.). (Illus.). (J). 1989. 10.19 (*0-606-01679-1*, Pub. by Turtleback) Demco.

— I Like Me! (Picture Puffin Ser.). (Illus.). 32p. (J). (ps-3). 1990. pap. 5.99 (*0-14-050819-8*, PuffinBks) Peng Put Young Read.

— I Like Me! LC 92-25330. (J). 1993. pap. 19.99 (*0-14-054846-7*, PuffinBks) Peng Put Young Read.

Carlson, Nancy L. I Like Me! (Picture Puffin Ser.). (Illus.). (J). 1988. 9.19 (*0-606-03965-1*, Pub. by Turtleback) Demco.

Carlson, Nancy L. I Like Me. (Illus.). 32p. (J). (ps-1). 1988. 15.99 (*0-670-82062-8*, Viking Child) Peng Put Young Read.

***Carlson, Nancy L.** It's Going to Be Perfect. (Picture Puffin Ser.). (Illus.). 40p. (J). (ps-3). 2000. pap. 5.99 (*0-14-056723-2*, PuffinBks) Peng Put Young Read.

Carlson, Nancy L. It's Going to Be Perfect. LC 97-27689. (Illus.). 32p. (J). (gr. k-3). 1998. 15.99 (*0-670-87802-2*) Viking Penguin.

— Life is Fun. LC 93-14666. 1996. 10.19 (*0-606-09554-3*, Pub. by Turtleback) Demco.

— Look Out Kindergarten, Here I Come! LC 98-47039. (Illus.). 32p. (J). (ps-1). 1999. 15.99 (*0-670-88378-6*) Viking Penguin.

— Snowden. LC 98-13099. (Illus.). 32p. (J). (ps-3). 1998. 15.99 (*0-670-88078-7*, Viking) Viking Penguin.

Carlson, Nancy L. Visit to Grandma's. 1993. 10.19 (*0-606-06077-4*, Pub. by Turtleback) Demco.

Carlson, Nancy N. Kings Highway. LC 97-8504. 1997. write for info. (*0-931846-50-1*) Wash Writers Pub.

Carlson, Natalie S. Family under the Bridge. (J). 1989. 10.05 (*0-606-04031-5*, Pub. by Turtleback) Demco.

— The Family Under the Bridge. LC 58-5292. (Illus.). 112p. (J). (ps-3). 1958. lib. bdg. 15.89 (*0-06-020991-7*) HarpC Child Bks.

— The Family Under the Bridge. LC 58-5292. (Trophy Bk.). (Illus.). 112p. (J). (gr. 2-6). 1989. pap. 5.95 (*0-06-440250-9*, HarpTrophy) HarpC Child Bks.

Carlson, Neal. Aircraft Fabric Covering. IAP, Inc. Staff, ed. LC 93-20622. (Aviation Maintenance Training Course Ser.). (Illus.). 54p. (C). 1978. pap. 11.40 (*0-89100-077-1*, JS312636) Jeppesen Sanderson.

Carlson, Neal & IAP, Inc. Staff. Aircraft Painting & Finishing. 2nd ed. LC 93-24822. (Aviation Maintenance Training Course Ser.). (Illus.). 67p. (C). 1985. pap. 13.45 (*0-89100-152-2*, JS312638) Jeppesen Sanderson.

Carlson, Neil H. & Buskist, William. Psychology: The Science of Behavior. 5th ed. LC 96-3411. 683p. 1996. 84.00 (*0-205-19345-5*) Allyn.

Carlson, Neil R. Foundation of Physiological Psychology. 620p. (C). 1988. text 50.00 (*0-205-11261-7*, H12610) Allyn.

— Physiology of Behavior. 6th ed. 144p. (C). 1997. text, teacher ed. write for info. (*0-205-27432-3*, T7432-2) Allyn.

— Physiology of Behavior. 6th ed. LC 97-41384. 736p. 1997. 83.00 (*0-205-27340-8*) P-H.

***Carlson, Neil R.** Physiology of Behavior. 7th ed. LC 00-38093. 720p. 2000. pap. 80.00 (*0-205-30840-6*) Allyn.

Carlson, Neil R. Psychology: The Science of Behavior. 3rd ed. 800p. 1989. text 48.00 (*0-205-12166-7*, H21660); trans. 100.00 (*0-685-29842-6*, H21694) Allyn.

Carlson, Neil R. & Buskist, William. Annotated Instructor's Edition: The Science of Behavior. 5th annot. ed. (C). 1996. teacher ed. write for info. (*0-205-26194-9*, T6194-9) Allyn.

— Psychology: The Science of Behavior, Test Bank. 5th ed. (C). 1997. write for info. (*0-205-26196-5*, T6196-4) Allyn.

Carlson, Nils W. Monolithic Diode-Laser Arrays. LC 94-11598. (Electronics & Photonics Ser.: Vol. 33). 1994. 75.95 (*0-387-57910-9*) Spr-Verlag.

Carlson, Noan. The Lopsided Angel. LC 96-79034. (Illus.). 176p. (Orig.). 1996. pap. 9.95 (*1-882420-29-2*) Hearth KS.

Carlson, Nolan. Lewis & Clark & Davey Hutchins. LC 93-80993. (Illus.). 158p. (Orig.). (J). (gr. 4-8). 1994. pap. 6.95 (*1-882420-08-X*, 1-882420-08-X) Hearth KS.

— Shiner's Return. LC 95-78134. (Illus.). 146p. (YA). (gr. 4-8). 1995. pap. 6.95 (*1-882420-25-X*) Hearth KS.

— Summer & Shiner. LC 92-71256. (Illus.). 158p. (YA). (gr. 4-8). 1992. pap. 6.95 (*0-9627947-4-0*) Hearth KS.

Carlson, Norman, ed. Chicago South Shore & South Bend Railroad: How the Medal Was Won. LC 85-72308. 160p. 1985. 20.00 (*0-915348-24-1*, B-124) Central Electric.

— Thirty Years Later: The Shore Line. LC 85-72307. (NS-300 Ser.). (Illus.). 32p. (Orig.). 1985. pap. 6.00 (*0-915348-00-4*, NS-300) Central Electric.

Carlson, Norman, jt. ed. see Krambles, George.

Carlson, Norman, ed. see Middleton, William D.

Carlson, Oliver. Brisbane: A Candid Biography. LC 75-98829. 1970. reprint ed. lib. bdg. 75.00 (*0-8371-2980-X*, CABR, Greenwood Pr) Greenwood.

Carlson, Oliver & Bates, Ernest S. Hearst, Lord of San Simeon. LC 70-98830. 332p. 1970. reprint ed. lib. bdg. 59.75 (*0-8371-2847-1*, CAHE, Greenwood Pr) Greenwood.

Carlson, P. Collecting Toy Trains. 1994. pap. 19.95 (*1-872727-56-5*, Perigee Bks) Berkley Pub.

Carlson, P., et al. First Biennial Conference on Low Energy Antiproton Physics. 560p. 1991. text 137.00 (*981-02-0444-2*) World Scientific Pub.

Carlson, P. M. Bloodstream. 1996. pap. 5.99 (*0-671-76978-2*) S&S Trade.

— Gravestone. Chelius, Jane, ed. 352p. 1994. reprint ed. mass mkt. 5.50 (*0-671-76975-8*) PB.

— Renowned Be Thy Grave: or The Murderous Miss Mooney. LC 98-181217. 232p. 1998. pap. 16.00 (*1-885941-23-4*) Crippen & Landru.

— Renowned Be Thy Grave: or The Murderous Miss Mooney. deluxe limited ed. LC 98-181217. 252p. 1998. 30.00 (*1-885941-22-6*) Crippen & Landru.

***Carlson, Pat M.** Murder Unrenovated. LC 99-35100. (Mystery Ser.). 248p. 1999. pap. 19.95 (*0-7862-2077-5*, Five Star MI) Mac Lib Ref.

Carlson, Patricia H. Sacred Echoes. (Illus.). 140p. (Orig.). 1995. pap. 11.50 (*0-9645393-4-9*) P H S Carlson.

Carlson, Patricia M., jt. auth. see Darlington, Richard B.

Carlson, Paul, jt. auth. see Rossiter, Sean.

Carlson, Paul, ed. see Williams, J. W.

***Carlson, Paul H.** Cowboy Way: An Exploration of History & Culture. LC 99-40584. 1999. 29.95 (*0-89672-425-5*) Tex Tech Univ Pr.

— Empire Builder in the Texas Panhandle: William Henry Bush. LC 96-10628. (Illus.). 256p. 1996. 29.95 (*0-89096-712-1*) Tex A&M Univ Pr.

Carlson, Paul H. Pecos Bill: A Military Biography of William R. Shafter. LC 88-36465. (Illus.). 240p. 1989. 39.95 (*0-89096-348-7*) Tex A&M Univ Pr.

— The Plains Indians. LC 98-13697. (Elma Dill Russell Spencer Series in the West & Southwest: Vol. 19). (Illus.). 256p. 1998. 29.95 (*0-89096-828-4*); pap. 16.95 (*0-89096-817-9*) Tex A&M Univ Pr.

— Texas Woollybacks: The Range Sheep & Goat Industry. LC 82-40311. (Illus.). 256p. 1982. 29.95 (*0-89096-133-6*) Tex A&M Univ Pr.

***Carlson, Paul R.** Christianity after Auschwitz. LC 00-190164. 456p. 2000. pap. 18.00 (*0-7388-1584-5*) Xlibris Corp.

— Christianity after Auschwitz: Evangelicals Encounter Judaism in the New Millennium. LC 00-190164. 456p. 2000. 25.00 (*0-7388-1583-7*) Xlibris Corp.

Carlson, Paul V., jt. auth. see Hunter, Madeline C.

Carlson, Paula J. & Hawkins, Peter S., eds. Listening for God Vol. 1: Contemporary Literature & the Life of Faith. 1994. pap., teacher ed. 3.99 (*0-8066-2716-6*, 10-27166, Augsburg) Augsburg Fortress.

— Listening for God Leader's Guide Vol. 2: Contemporary Literature & the Life of Faith. 1996. pap., teacher ed. 3.99 (*0-8066-2845-6*, 10-28456) Augsburg Fortress.

— Listening for God Reader Vol. 1: Contemporary Literature & the Life of Faith. LC 93-50662. 1994. pap. 12.99 (*0-8066-2715-8*, 10-27158) Augsburg Fortress.

— Listening for God Reader Vol. 2: Contemporary Literature & the Life of Faith. 144p. 1996. pap. 12.99 (*0-8066-2844-8*, 10-28448) Augsburg Fortress.

Carlson, Peggie. The Girls Are Coming. LC 99-20893. 208p. 1999. 24.95 (*0-87351-375-4*, Borealis Book); pap. 15.95 (*0-87351-376-2*, Borealis Book) Minn Hist.

Carlson, Peter M. & Garrett, Judith S. Handbook of Prison & Jail Administration: Organization, Principles & Practice. 750p. 1998. 95.00 (*0-8342-0867-9*, 08679) Aspen Pub.

Carlson, Pierce. Collecting Toy Trains. 144p. 1993. pap. 19.95 (*1-883685-01-X*) Pincushion Pr.

Carlson, R. Design & Optimization in Organic Synthesis. (Data Handling in Science & Technology Ser.: Vol. 8). xvi,536p. 1992. 249.50 (*0-444-89201-X*) Elsevier.

Carlson, R. F., et al. North American Apples: Varieties, Rootstocks, Outlook. (Illus.). 197p. 1970. text 15.00 (*0-87013-157-5*) Mich St U Pr.

Carlson, R. M., jt. ed. see Croasmun, W. R.

Carlson, R. W., ed. Packages for Transportation & Storage of Radioactive Materials. (PVP Ser.: Vol. 254). 116p. 1993. 40.00 (*0-7918-0981-1*, H00813) ASME.

— Transport & Storage of Radioactive Materials. 83p. 1996. pap. text 70.00 (*0-7918-1781-4*, TS283) ASME Pr.

— Transport & Storage of Radioactive Materials: Proceedings of the Pressure Vessel & Piping Conference, Minneapolis, MN, 1994. LC 94-71747. (PVP Ser.: Vol. 284). 53p. 1994. pap. 25.00 (*0-7918-1357-6*) ASME.

Carlson, R. W., et al, eds. Transport & Storage of Radioactive Materials, 1995. LC 94-71747. (Proceedings of the 1995 ASME/JSME Pressure Vessels & Piping Conference Ser.: PVP-Vol. 307). 192p. 1995. 100.00 (*0-7918-1338-X*, H00970) ASME.

Carlson, Randy, jt. auth. see Leman, Kevin.

Carlson, Reinhold A. & Di Giandomenico, Robert. Understanding Building Automation Systems: Direct Digital Control Energy Management Life Safety. 225p. 1991. 79.95 (*0-87629-211-2*, 67284) R S Means.

Carlson, Reynold E. British Block Grants & Central-Local Finance. LC 78-64203. (Johns Hopkins University. Studies in the Social Sciences. Thirtieth Ser. 1912: 1). 224p. 1980. reprint ed. 37.50 (*0-404-61309-8*) AMS Pr.

***Carlson, Rhonda.** How to Attain Your HRMS Vision. 115p. 1999. pap. 49.00 (*0-8080-0374-7*) CCH INC.

Carlson, Rhonda. Introduction to Paralegalism. 91st ed. 112p. (C). 1996. text, student ed. 14.37 (*0-256-24050-7*, Irwn McGrw-H) McGrw-H Hghr Educ.

— Irwin's Introduction to Paralegal Studies. LC 96-21355. 480p. (C). 1996. text 49.95 (*0-256-18592-1*, Irwn McGrw-H) McGrw-H Hghr Educ.

Carlson, Rhonda, jt. auth. see Wildman, Iris J.

Carlson, Richard. The Business of Bodywork. 54p. (Orig.). 1987. pap. text 9.95 (*0-916147-08-8*) Regent Pr.

— Don't Sweat, 4 vols., Vols. 1-4. (Don't Sweat the Small Stuff Ser.). 1998. 327.00 (*0-7868-9847-X*, Pub. by Hyperion) Little.

— Don't Sweat the Small Stuff, 3 vols. 816p. 1999. boxed set 29.95 (*0-7868-8517-3*, Pub. by Hyperion) Little.

— Don't Sweat the Small Stuff. 256p. 2001. pap. 11.95 (*0-7868-8420-7*, Pub. by Hypm Ppbks) Little.

***Carlson, Richard.** Don't Sweat the Small Stuff . . . And It's All Small Stuff: Simple Ways to Keep the Little Things from Taking over Your Life. 144p. 1999. pap. 13.95 (*0-7868-8430-4*, Pub. by Hyperion) Little.

Carlson, Richard. Don't Sweat the Small Stuff . . . And It's All Small Stuff: Simple Ways to Keep the Little Things from Taking over Your Life. deluxe gif. ed. (J). 1997. 19.95 (*0-7868-6410-9*, Pub. by Hyperion) Time Warner.

Carlson, Richard. Don't Sweat the Small Stuff . . . And It's All Small Stuff: Simple Ways to Keep the Little Things from Taking over Your Life, BF637.B4C35. LC 96-13822. 272p. (J). 1997. pap. 10.45 (*0-7868-8185-2*, Pub. by Hyperion) Time Warner.

Carlson, Richard. Don't Sweat the Small Stuff at Work. large type ed. LC 98-13597. 1998. 27.95 (*0-7838-0141-6*, G K Hall Lrg Type) Mac Lib Ref.

***Carlson, Richard.** Dont Sweat the Small Stuff for Teens: Simple Ways to Keep Your Cool in Stressful Times. 2000. pap. 11.95 (*0-7868-8597-1*, Pub. by Hyperion) Time Warner.

Carlson, Richard. A Don't Sweat the Small Stuff Treasury. LC 99-60269. (Don't Sweat the Small Stuff Ser.). 98p. 1999. 5.95 (*0-7868-6576-8*, Pub. by Hyperion) Little.

***Carlson, Richard.** Don't Sweat the Small Stuff Treasury: A Special Collection for Friends. 112p. 2000. 5.95 (*0-7868-6625-X*, Pub. by Hyperion) Time Warner.

— Don't Sweat the Small Stuff Treasury: A Special Collection for New Parents. LC 99-37512. 112p. (YA). 2000. 5.95 (*0-7868-6626-8*, Pub. by Disney Pr) Time Warner.

— Don't Sweat the Small Stuff Treasury: A Special Collection for Newlyweds. 112p. 2000. 5.95 (*0-7868-6623-3*, Pub. by Hyperion) Time Warner.

— Don't Sweat the Small Stuff Treasury: A Special Collection for the Office. LC 99-37514. 112p. (YA). 2000. 5.95 (*0-7868-6624-1*, Pub. by Disney Pr) Time Warner.

Carlson, Richard. A Don't Sweat the Small Stuff Treasury: A Special Selection for Fathers. LC 99-60271. (Don't Sweat the Small Stuff Ser.). 99p. 1999. 5.95 (*0-7868-6574-1*, Pub. by Hyperion) Little.

***Carlson, Richard.** Don't Sweat the Small Stuff Treasury: A Special Selection for Graduates. LC 99-60270. (Don't Sweat the Small Stuff Ser.). 98p. 1999. 5.95 (*0-7868-6575-X*, Pub. by Hyperion) Little.

Carlson, Richard. Don't Sweat the Small Stuff Treasury: A Special Selection for Mothers. LC 99-60272. 100p. 1999. pap. text 5.95 (*0-7868-6573-3*, Pub. by Hyperion) Little.

— Don't Sweat the Small Stuff with Your Family: Simple Ways to Keep Loved Ones & Household Chaos from Taking over Your Life. LC 98-11149. 176p. (J). 1998. pap. 11.45 (*0-7868-8337-5*, Pub. by Hyperion) Time Warner.

— The Don't Sweat the Small Stuff Workbook: Exercises, Questions, & Self-Tests to Help You Keep the Little Things from Taking over Your Life. LC 98-231268. 240p. 1998. pap., wbk. ed. 12.95 (*0-7868-8351-0*, Pub. by Hyperion) Time Warner.

— Don't Worry, Make Money: Spiritual & Practical Ways to Create Abundance & More Fun in Your Life. LC 97-14459. 240p. (J). 1997. 15.95 (*0-7868-6321-8*, Pub. by Hyperion) Time Warner.

***Carlson, Richard.** Don't Worry, Make Money: Spiritual & Practical Ways to Create Abundance & More Fun in Your Life. 240p. (J). 1998. pap. 11.45 (*0-7868-8360-X*, Pub. by Hyperion) Time Warner.

Carlson, Richard. Form or Formula Drawing & Drawings. (Illus.). 56p. (Orig.). 1986. pap. 2.50 (*0-943651-14-X*) Hudson Riv.

— Handbook for the Heart, Vol. 1. 240p. 1998. pap. 12.95 (*0-316-12004-9*) Little.

Carlson, Richard. Handbook for the Soul. large type ed. 240p. 1996. pap. 12.95 (*0-316-12822-8*, Back Bay) Little.

— Mes Despacio. 1998. pap. text 19.95 (*84-253-3152-8*) Distribks Inc.

— No Te Ahogues En Un Vaso De Agua. 1998. pap. 22.95 (*84-253-3199-4*) Distribks Inc.

An Asterisk (*) at the beginning of an entry indicates that the title is appearing for the first time.

— No Te Preocupes, Gana Dinero: Los Metodos Mas Practicos de Crear Abundancia y Alegria en su Vida. (SPA.). 1998. pap. 22.95 (*84-253-3247-8*) Distribks Inc.
Carlson, Richard. Shortcut Through Therapy: Ten Principles of Growth-Oriented, Contented Living. 224p. (Orig.). 1995. pap. 11.95 (*0-452-27383-8*, Plume) Dutton Plume.
— Slowing Down to the Speed of Life. LC 97-5358. 1997. 20.00 (*0-06-251453-9*, Pub. by Harper SF) HarpC.
***Carlson, Richard.** Untitled Carlson Non Fiction #2 2000. 15.95 (*0-7868-6379-X*, Pub. by Disney Pr) Time Warner.
Carlson, Richard. Usted Si Puede Ser Feliz Pase Lo Que Pase: Cinco Principios para Mantener en Perspectiva Su Vida. LC 98-35596. (SPA.). 184p. 1998. pap. 12.95 (*1-57731-049-7*) New Wrld Lib.
— Vous Pouvez Etre Heureux de Toute Facon. (FRE.). 1998. 14.95 (*2-89466-017-0*) Edns Roseau.
***Carlson, Richard.** You Can Be Happy No Matter What: Five Principles for Keeping Life in Perspective. 2nd gif. ed. LC 97-15902. 192p. 1999. 18.00 (*1-57731-110-8*, Pub. by New Wrld Lib) Publishers Group.
Carlson, Richard. You Can Be Happy No Matter What: Five Principles for Keeping Life in Perspective. 2nd rev. ed. LC 97-15902. 176p. 1997. pap. 10.95 (*1-57731-064-0*) New Wrld Lib.
— You Can Feel Good Again: Common-Sense Strategies for Releasing Unhappiness & Changing Your Life. 180p. 1994. pap. 11.95 (*0-452-27242-4*, Plume) Dutton Plume.
Carlson, Richard, ed. Illinois Communications Guide. 492p. 1993. pap. 29.95 (*0-939430-21-5*) Scanner Master.
Carlson, Richard. Don't Sweat the Small Stuff at Work. 272p. 1999. pap. 11.95 (*0-7868-8336-7*, Pub. by Hyperion) Time Warner.
Carlson, Richard & Bailey, Joseph. Slowing Down to the Speed of Life: How to Create a More Peaceful, Simpler Life from the Inside Out. LC 97-5358. (Illus.). 240p. 1998. pap. 12.00 (*0-06-251454-7*) HarpC.
Carlson, Richard & Carlson, Kristine. Don't Sweat the Small Stuff in Love: Simple Ways to Nurture & Strengthen Your Relationships While Avoiding the Habits That Break down Your Loving Connections. LC 99-27271. 272p. 1999. 15.95 (*0-7868-6509-1*, Pub. by Hyperion) Time Warner.
Carlson, Richard & Goldman, Bruce. Fast Forward: Where Technology, Demographics & History Will Take America & the World in the Next Thirty Years. LC 93-39546. 384p. 1994. 25.00 (*0-88730-597-0*, HarpBusn) HarpInfo.
— Twenty Twenty Visions: Long View of a Changing World. (Portable Stanford Bks.). 246p. (Orig.). 1991. pap. 12.95 (*0-916318-44-3*) Stanford Alumni Assn.
Carlson, Richard & Moran, Ted. Scanner Master Chicagoland Guide. (Illus.). 168p. 1995. pap. 13.95 (*0-939430-32-0*) Scanner Master.
Carlson, Richard & Shield, Benjamin, eds. For the Love of God: Handbook for the Spirit. 2nd rev. ed. LC 97-28695. 224p. 1997. 20.00 (*1-57731-061-6*) New Wrld Lib.
— Handbook for the Soul. large type ed. 1996. 22.95 (*0-7838-1855-6*, G K Hall Lrg Type) Mac Lib Ref.
— Healers on Healing. 224p. (Orig.). 1989. pap. 14.95 (*0-87477-494-2*, Tarcher Putnam) Putnam Pub Group.
Carlson, Richard, jt. ed. see Shield, Benjamin.
Carlson, Richard A. Experienced Cognition. LC 97-17199. 500p. 1997. pap. 45.00 (*0-8058-1733-6*) L Erlbaum Assocs.
— Experienced Cognition. LC 97-17199. 500p. 1997. write for info. (*0-8058-1732-8*) L Erlbaum Assocs.
***Carlson, Richard F.** Science & Christianity: Four Views. 240p. 2000. pap. 15.99 (*0-8308-2262-3*) InterVarsity.
Carlson, Richard P., jt. auth. see Hedahl, Susan K.
Carlson, Richard R. Carlson's Federal Employment Laws. annot. ed. LC 96-76324. 1500p. 1996. pap. text. write for info. (*0-7620-0067-8*) West Group.
— Texas Employment Law, Pt. I. Neighbors, Charles, ed. 640p. (Orig.). 55.00 (*0-945701-05-5*) Sterling TX.
— Texas Employment Law, Pt. II. Neighbors, Charles, ed. 640p. (Orig.). 55.00 (*0-685-35545-4*) Sterling TX.
Carlson, Richard W. & Geheb, Michael A., eds. Principles & Practice of Medical Intensive Care. (Illus.). 1824p. 1993. text 220.00 (*0-7216-3396-X*, W B Saunders Co) Harcrt Hlth Sci Grp.
Carlson, Rick J. The End of Medicine. LC 75-6856. (Health, Medicine & Society Ser.). 303p. reprint ed. pap. 94.00 (*0-608-13375-2*, 205572900034) Bks Demand.
Carlson, Rick J., et al. The Future of Work & Health. LC 85-18627. (Illus.). 215p. (Orig.). 1985. 49.95 (*0-86569-088-X*, Auburn Hse) Greenwood.
Carlson, Rob. Mount St. Helens: The Eruption & Recovery of a Volcano. LC 90-31009. (Illus.). 160p. 1990. pap. 19.95 (*0-912365-32-3*) Sasquatch Bks.
Carlson, Robert. A Grammar of Supyire. LC 94-5259. (Grammar Library: No. 14). 787p. (C). 1994. lib. bdg. 267.70 (*3-11-014057-8*) Mouton.
— Reframing & Reform: Perspectives on Organization, Leadership, & School Change. LC 95-11579. 343p. (Orig.). (C). 1995. pap. text 52.00 (*0-8013-1106-3*) Longman.
Carlson, Robert, jt. auth. see Coddington, Earl A.
Carlson, Robert, ed. see Ford, Judy & Ross, William A.
Carlson, Robert, ed. see Ross, William A.
Carlson, Robert, ed. see Ross, William A. & Ford, Judy.
Carlson, Robert, ed. see United States Gypsum Co., Marketing Communications.
Carlson, Robert A. Conceptual Learning: From Mollusks to Adult Education. LC 73-72. (Occasional Papers: No. 35). 1973. pap. 2.00 (*0-87060-058-3*, OCP 35) Syracuse U Cont Ed.
Carlson, Robert C. How to Handle & Win a Federal Tax Appeal: A Complete Guide for the Tax Professional. (Illus.). 516p. (C). 1988. text 40.00 (*0-685-43921-6*) P-H.
Carlson, Robert F. & Technical Council on Cold Regions Engineering Staf. Cold Regions Engineering: The Cold Regions Infrastructure--An International Imperative for the 21st Century: Proceedings of the Eighth International Conference on Cold Regions Engineering, University of Alaska Fairbanks, Fairbanks, Alaska, August 12-16, 1996. LC 96-31480. 968p. 1996. 87.00 (*0-7844-0190-X*) Am Soc Civil Eng.
Carlson, Robert K. Truth in Trial: Liberal Education Be Hanged. (Illus.). 213p. (Orig.). 1995. pap. 13.95 (*1-883357-91-8*, Crisis Bks) Dumb Ox Bks.
— Truth on Trial: Liberal Education Be Hanged. (Illus.). 213p. 1995. 22.00 (*1-883357-90-X*, Crisis Bks) Dumb Ox Bks.
Carlson, Robert S., et al. International Finance: Cases & Simulation. LC 80-81213. 400p. 1980. pap. text. write for info. (*0-201-00903-X*) Addison-Wesley.
Carlson, Robert V. & Ducharme, Edward R., eds. School Improvement: Theory & Practice, a Book of Readings. (Illus.). 1228p. (Orig.). (C). 1987. lib. bdg. 99.00 (*0-8191-5815-1*) U Pr of Amer.
Carlson, Robert W. The Palatine Ship: Ghost Ship of Block Island. 60p. 1994. pap. 7.95 (*1-886066-00-0*) Ctr Archaeoastronomy.
Carlson, Rodger D. The Economics of Geothermal Power in California. Bruchey, Stuart, ed. LC 78-22666. (Energy in the American Economy Ser.). (Illus.). 1979. lib. bdg. 18.95 (*0-405-11970-4*) Ayer.
Carlson, Roger, jt. auth. see Carlson, Donn.
Carlson, Roger L., jt. auth. see Carlson, Donn A.
Carlson, Ron. Betrayed by F. Scott Fitzgerald. 224p. 1984. reprint ed. pap. 6.95 (*0-393-30168-0*) Norton.
— The Hotel Eden: Stories. 224p. 1998. pap. 12.95 (*0-14-027389-1*) Viking Penguin.
Carlson, Ron, jt. auth. see Decker, Ed.
Carlson, Ron, jt. auth. see Winter, MaryJean.
Carlson, Ronald. Pocket Proof of Facts: Proof of Facts & How to Deal with the Difficult Judge. 1993. 29.95 (*0-614-06017-6*, 4324); audio 95.00 (*0-614-06018-4*) Natl Prac Inst.
— Successful Techniques for Civil Trials. 1992. 105.00 (*0-614-06021-4*, 4007) Natl Prac Inst.
Carlson, Ronald & Imwinkelreid, Edward J. Dynamic Trial Practice. 1995. 39.95 (*0-614-06012-5*, 3327) Natl Prac Inst.
Carlson, Ronald & Winter, Mary J. Transforming Functions. (Illus.). 140p. (YA). (gr. 8-12). 1997. pap. text 18.95 (*1-55953-302-1*) Key Curr Pr.
Carlson, Ronald L. Adjudication of Criminal Justice: Problems & References. (American Casebook Ser.). 130p. (C). 1986. pap. 20.50 (*0-314-25371-8*) West Pub.
— Criminal Justice Procedure. 5th ed. LC 94-73268. 344p. (C). 1995. pap. text 33.95 (*0-87084-136-X*) Anderson Pub Co.
— Criminal Justice Procedure. 6th ed. LC 98-45363. 396p. 1998. pap. 37.95 (*0-87084-211-0*, KF9619) Anderson Pub Co.
— Maine Objections at Trial. 190p. 1991. pap. 39.50 (*0-614-05889-9*, MICHIE) LEXIS Pub.
— Successful Techniques for Civil Trials. 2nd ed. LC 92-72360. 1993. 97.50 (*0-318-00076-8*) West Group.
Carlson, Ronald L. & Bright, Myron H. Maine Objections at Trial. 200p. 1991. pap. 39.50 (*0-88063-321-2*, MICHIE) LEXIS Pub.
— New Hampshire Objections at Trial. 200p. 1992. pap. 39.50 (*0-88063-822-2*, MICHIE) LEXIS Pub.
— Objections at Trial. 2nd ed. LC 93-25116. 280p. 1993. pap. 29.95 (*1-56257-349-7*, MICHIE) LEXIS Pub.
— Oregon Objections at Trial. LC 92-13850. 190p. 1992. pap. 39.50 (*1-56257-163-X*, MICHIE) LEXIS Pub.
Carlson, Ronald L. & Iminkelried, Edward J. Dynamics to Trial Practice, Problems & Materials, 1990 Supplement. (American Casebook Ser.). 44p. 1990. pap. text 3.95 (*0-685-49444-6*) West Pub.
Carlson, Ronald L. & Imwinkelried, Edward A. Dynamics of Trial Practice: Problems & Materials. 2nd ed. (American Casebook Ser.). 571p. (C). 1995. pap. 36.50 (*0-314-04314-4*) West Pub.
— Dynamics of Trial Practice Problems & Materials: Fall 1997 Supplement. annuals 2nd ed. (American Casebook Ser.). 45p. 1997. pap. text, suppl. ed. write for info. (*0-314-22744-X*) West Pub.
— Dynamics of Trial Practice, Problems & Materials, Teacher's Manual to Accompany. 2nd ed. (American Casebook Ser.). 100p. (C). 1994. pap. text. write for info. (*0-314-05986-5*) West Pub.
Carlson, Ronald L., et al. Evidence: Teaching Material Science & Statutes, 1997. 4th ed. LC 97-73314. 942p. 1997. text 55.00 (*1-55834-540-X*, 10680-11, MICHIE) LEXIS Pub.
— Minnesota Objections at Trial. 200p. 1992. pap. 39.50 (*0-88063-824-9*, 81875, MICHIE) LEXIS Pub.
— Missouri Objections at Trial. LC 93-11002. 200p. 1993. pap. 39.50 (*0-250-42765-6*, MICHIE) LEXIS Pub.
— Virginia Objections at Trial. LC 93-28249. 280p. 1993. pap. 39.50 (*0-250-42767-2*, MICHIE) LEXIS Pub.
Carlson, Roseann J., jt. auth. see Poort, Jon M.
Carlson, Roy, ed. Contemporary Northwest Writing: A Collection of Poetry & Fiction. 208p. 1979. text 24.95 (*0-87071-324-8*); pap. text 15.95 (*0-87071-323-X*) Oreg St U Pr.
Carlson, Roy & Dalla Bona, Luke, eds. Early Human Occupation in British Columbia. LC 96-127667. (Illus.). 261p. 1995. pap. 35.95 (*0-7748-0535-8*, E78) U of Wash Pr.
Carlson, Russ & Carlson, Laurie. Companions Through Crisis: A Family Struggles with Chronic Illness, Life Threatening Surgery, & God's Providence. 119p. 1995. pap. 7.95 (*0-910452-79-2*) Covenant.
Carlson, Ruth, jt. auth. see Carlson, Elwood.
Carlson, Ruth K. Sparkling Words. 1979. 29.35 (*0-88252-009-1*) Paladin Hse.
— Speaking Aids Through the Grades. LC 74-14719. 93p. reprint ed. pap. 30.00 (*0-8357-3459-5*, 203972100013) Bks Demand.
Carlson, Sally, jt. auth. see Anderson, Bob.
Carlson, Shawn, jt. auth. see Scientific American Staff.
Carlson, Signe M., ed. see Wikstrom, Karl S.
Carlson, Stephen, ed. see White, Mary B.
Carlson, Stephen P. From Boston to the Berkshires: A Pictorial Review of Electric Transportation in Massachusetts. LC 87-5124. (Bulletin Ser.: No. 21). (Illus.). 160p. (Orig.). 1990. pap. 24.95 (*0-938315-03-X*) Boston St Rwy.
Carlson, Steve. The Best Home for Less. 320p. 1992. pap. 12.50 (*0-380-76540-3*, Avon Bks) Morrow Avon.
— Hitting Your Mark: What Every Actor Really Needs to Know on a Hollywood Set. LC 97-52160. xvi, 197 p. 1999. 16.95 (*0-941188-69-8*) M Wiese.
— Introduction to HDL-Based Design Using VHDL. (Illus.). 176p. (Orig.). 1990. pap. text 49.95 (*0-9625929-0-0*) Synopsys.
— Your Low-Tax Dream House: A New Approach to Slashing the Costs of Home Ownership. (Illus.). 304p. (Orig.). 1989. pap. 12.95 (*0-942679-07-5*) Upper Access.
Carlson, Stuart & Carlson, Mary. Beanie the Brownie & the Great Christmas Caper. (Illus.). 32p. (Orig.). (J). 1996. pap. 3.99 (*0-9655586-0-6*) Jrnl Sentinel.
Carlson, Sune. Executive Behaviour. 157p. 1991. reprint ed. pap. 43.00 (*91-554-2485-6*) Coronet Bks.
Carlson, Sune, Jr. Executive Behaviour: A Study of the Workload & the Working Methods of Managing Directors. Chandler, Alfred D., ed. LC 79-7535. (History of Management Thought & Practice Ser.). 1980. reprint ed. lib. bdg. 18.95 (*0-405-12317-5*) Ayer.
Carlson, Sune. A Study on the Pure Theory of Production. LC 65-18333. (Reprints of Economic Classics Ser.). vii, 128p. 1965. reprint ed. 27.50 (*0-678-00009-3*) Kelley.
Carlson, Susan. Women & Comedy: Rewriting the British Theatrical Tradition. 400p. 1991. text 44.50 (*0-472-10187-0*, 10187) U of Mich Pr.
— Women of Grace: James's Plays & the Comedy of Manners. LC 84-23932. (Studies in Modern Literature: No. 48). 199p. reprint ed. pap. 61.70 (*0-8357-1617-1*, 207053600001) Bks Demand.
Carlson, Susan C. Wyoming Historical Markers at 55 MPH: A Guide to Historical Markers & Monuments on Wyoming Highways. Jost, Loren, ed. LC 94-225029. (Illus.). 104p. (Orig.). (C). 1994. pap. 12.00 (*0-9630248-2-5*) Beartooth.
***Carlson, Susan E.** Free-Style Quilts: A "No Rules" Approach. Rymer, Cyndy & Koolish, Lynn, eds. LC 99-50975. (Illus.). 96p. 2000. pap. 23.95 (*1-57120-102-5*, Pub. by C & T Pub) Watsn-Guptill.
Carlson, Sven H. Trade & Dependency: Studies in the Expansion of Europe. 188p. (Orig.). 1984. pap. text 33.50 (*91-554-1628-4*) Coronet Bks.
Carlson, Sylvia E. & Carlson, Verne. The Professional Cameraman's Handbook. 4th rev. ed. (Illus.). 578p. 1994. 52.95 (*0-240-80080-X*, Focal) Buttrwrth-Heinemann.
Carlson, Sylvia E., jt. auth. see Carlson, Verne.
Carlson, T., et al, eds. X-Ray & Inner-Shell Processes. (AIP Conference Proceedings Ser.: No. 215). 900p. 1991. 99.00 (*0-88318-790-6*) Am Inst Physics.
Carlson, Teresa B., jt. auth. see Hanrahan, Stephanie J.
***Carlson, Theodore J.** Democracy, from Whence? LC 99-97497. 2000. pap. 8.95 (*0-533-13397-1*) Vantage.
Carlson, Theodore L. The Illinois Military Tract. Bruchey, Stuart, ed. LC 78-56707. (Management of Public Lands in the U. S. Ser.). (Illus.). 1979. reprint ed. lib. bdg. 18.95 (*0-405-11322-6*) Ayer.
Carlson, Thomas. Muskegon - At the Peak of the Lumber Area: A Pictorial Companion to the Novel "Sawdust Fires" (Illus.). 30p. 1998. pap. 8.50 (*0-9665487-1-X*) T Carlson.
Carlson, Thomas A. Indiscretion: Finitude & the Naming of God. LC 98-19277. 1999. pap. text 18.00 (*0-226-09294-1*) U Ch Pr.
Carlson, Thomas A., tr. see Marion, Jean-Luc.
Carlson, Thomas E. Sawdust Fires: The Tumultuous End of Muskegon's Lumber Era - A Novel. Carlson, N. Kay, ed. (Illus.). vi, 186p. 1998. pap. 8.50 (*0-9665487-0-1*) T Carlson.
Carlson, Thorsten R. HBJ Spelling Signature Edition Blue Consumable Version 1. 88th ed. (J). 1988. pap. text 12.90 (*0-15-327070-5*) Harcourt.
Carlson, Thorsten R., ed. HBJ Spelling Signature Edition Red Level 2. 88th ed. (J). 1988. text 28.90 (*0-15-327078-0*) Harcourt.
Carlson, Ticien, ed. see Block, Janice & Rankine, David.
Carlson, Toby. Mid-Latitude Weather Systems. (Illus.). 512p. (C). 1991. pap. text 39.95 (*0-04-551116-0*, A8240) Routledge.
Carlson, Toby N. Mid-Latitude Weather Systems. LC 98-73847. (Illus.). 507p. 1998. pap. 42.00 (*1-878220-30-6*) Am Meteorological.
Carlson, Trudy. Ben's Story: The Symptoms of Depression, ADHD, & Anxiety That Caused His Suicide. LC 96-83889. (Illus.). 144p. (Orig.). 1998. pap. 9.95 (*0-9642443-6-5*) Benline Pr.
— Depression in the Young: What We Can Do to Help Them. LC 96-83676. 176p. (Orig.). 1998. pap. 9.95 (*0-9642443-5-7*) Benline Pr.
— Learning Disabilities: How to Recognize & Manage Learning & Behavioral Problems in Children. LC 95-94110. 144p. (Orig.). 1997. pap. 14.95 (*0-9642443-2-2*) Benline Pr.
— The Life of a Bipolar Child: What Every Parent & Professional Needs to Know. 288p. 2000. pap. 18.95 (*0-9642443-7-3*) Benline Pr.
— The Suicide of My Son: A Story of Childhood Depression. LC 94-96796. 272p. (Orig.). 1995. pap., per. 16.95 (*0-9642443-1-4*) Benline Pr.
— Suicide Survivor's Handbook: A Guide for the Bereaved & Those Who Wish to Help Them. LC 94-96837. 160p. (Orig.). 1995. pap., per. 14.95 (*0-9642443-0-6*) Benline Pr.
— Tragedy: Finding a Hidden Meaning: How to Transform the Tragedies in Your Life into Personal Growth. LC 95-94111. 144p. (Orig.). 1997. pap. 14.95 (*0-9642443-3-0*) Benline Pr.
Carlson, Vada. Broken Pattern: Sunlight & Shadows of Hopi History. LC 85-18797. (Illus.). 208p. 1985. pap. 8.95 (*0-87961-149-9*) Naturegraph.
Carlson, Verne. International Electrical Power & Television Systems. (International Film - Video Image Method Ser.: No. 1). (Illus.). 148p. (Orig.). 1992. pap. 9.95 (*0-937844-02-0*) Caverne Pub.
— Translation of Film/Video Terms into French. LC 84-203565. (Video Terms into Ser.: Vol. 1). (ENG & FRE.). 180p. (Orig.). 1984. pap. 17.95 (*0-943288-00-2*, Double C Pub) Caverne Pub.
— Translation of Film/Video Terms into German. LC 84-203565. (Video Terms into Ser.: Vol. 2). (ENG & GER.). 180p. (Orig.). 1984. pap. 17.95 (*0-943288-01-0*, Double C Pub) Caverne Pub.
— Translation of Film/Video Terms into Italian. LC 84-203565. (Video Terms into Ser.: Vol. 3). (ENG & ITA.). 180p. (Orig.). 1984. pap. 17.95 (*0-943288-02-9*, Double C Pub) Caverne Pub.
— Translation of Film/Video Terms into Japanese. LC 84-203565. (Video Terms into Ser.: Vol. 5). (ENG & JPN.). 180p. (Orig.). 1984. pap. 17.95 (*0-943288-04-5*, Double C Pub) Caverne Pub.
— Translation of Film/Video Terms into Series (French, German, Italian, Spanish, Japanese), 5 vols. LC 84-203565. (Translation of Film/Video Terms into Ser.). (ENG, FRE, GER, ITA & JPN.). 1984. pap. 89.75 (*0-943288-05-3*, Double C Pub) Caverne Pub.
— Translation of Film/Video Terms into Spanish. LC 84-203565. (Video Terms into Ser.: Vol. 4). (ENG & SPA.). 180p. (Orig.). 1984. pap. 17.95 (*0-943288-03-7*, Double C Pub) Caverne Pub.
Carlson, Verne & Carlson, Sylvia E. Professional Lighting Handbook. 2nd ed. (Illus.). 256p. 1991. 52.95 (*0-240-80020-6*, Focal) Buttrwrth-Heinemann.
Carlson, Verne, jt. auth. see Carlson, Sylvia E.
Carlson, Vicki K., jt. ed. see Cicchetti, Dante.
Carlson, Victor & Ittmann, John. French Printmaking, 1715-1814: Regency to Empire. (Illus.). 371p. 1984. pap. 65.00 (*0-912964-23-5*) A Wofsy Fine Arts.
Carlson, Victor, jt. auth. see Campbell, Richard J.
Carlson, Victor I. Picasso Drawings & Watercolors, 1899-1907 in the Collection of the Baltimore Museum of Art. LC 76-41022. 1977. 25.00 (*0-912298-43-X*); pap. 17.50 (*0-912298-42-1*) Baltimore Mus.
Carlson, Virginia L. The Availability of Women Workers: Effects on Company Location. LC 97-35311. (Studies in the History of American Labor). (Illus.). 143p. 1997. text 44.00 (*0-8153-3009-X*) Garland.
Carlson, W. Bernard. Innovation as a Social Process: Elihu Thomson & the Rise of General Electric. (Studies in Economic History & Policy: The United States in the Twentieth Century). (Illus.). 399p. (C). 1991. text 57.95 (*0-521-39317-5*) Cambridge U Pr.
***Carlson, William & Vance, Daniel J.** William "Bill" Carlson, an Autobiography: The Founder of Carlson Craft. (Illus.). 80p. 1999. pap. 7.99 (*0-9672014-0-3*) Advance Creat.
Carlson, William, et al. Thrinaxodon: Digital Atlas of the Skull. (Illus.). 1995. 35.00 (*0-292-77072-3*) U of Tex Pr.
Carlson, William L. Cases in Managerial Data Analysis. LC 96-5521. (C). 1996. pap. 29.95 (*0-534-51721-8*) Wadsworth Pub.
Carlson, William L. & Thorne, Betty. Applied Statistical Methods: For Business, Economics & the Social Sciences. LC 96-20962. 902p. (C). 1996. 101.33 (*0-13-570847-8*) P-H.
Carlsson. Ownership: Strategic Corporate Governance in the New Economy. text 37.00 (*0-471-63219-8*) Wiley.
Carlsson, A., et al, eds. Psychiatry, Psychoimmunology & Viruses. (Key Topics in Brain Research Ser.). 180p. 1999. pap. 84.00 (*3-211-83249-1*) Spr-Verlag.
Carlsson, A. J., jt. auth. see Wu, Xue-Ren.
Carlsson, B., et al. The Importance of Technology & the Permanence of Structure in Industrial Growth. 238p. (Orig.). 1978. pap. text 42.50 (*91-7204-084-X*) Coronet Bks.
Carlsson, Bo. Industrial Dynamics: Technological, Organizational, & Structural Changes in Industries & Firms. 336p. (C). 1989. lib. bdg. 147.50 (*0-7923-9044-X*) Kluwer Academic.
— Technological Systems. LC 97-16536. 1997. lib. bdg. 120.00 (*0-7923-9940-4*) Kluwer Academic.
Carlsson, Bo, ed. Technological Systems. (Economics of Science, Technology & Innovation Ser.: No. 10). 344p. 1997. pap. 44.00 (*0-7923-9972-2*) Kluwer Academic.
— Technological Systems & Economic Performance: The Case of Factory Automation. LC 95-14924. (Economics of Science, Technology & Innovation Ser.: Vol. 5). 512p. (C). 1995. lib. bdg. 125.00 (*0-7923-3512-0*) Kluwer Academic.
Carlsson, Bo & Henriksson, Rolf G. Development Blocks & Industrial Transformation: The Dahmenian Approach to Economic Development. (Industrial Institute for Economic & Social Research Report Ser.). 154p. 1991. 61.50 (*91-7204-372-5*) Coronet Bks.
Carlsson, Bo K. Sweden. (Modern Industrial World Ser.). (Illus.). 48p. (J). (gr. 6-8). 1995. lib. bdg. 24.26 (*1-56847-436-9*) Raintree Steck-V.

C

An Asterisk (*) at the beginning of an entry indicates that the title is appearing for the first time.

Carlsson, C. Decision Support Systems: Myth or Reality. 400p. 2000. 75.00 (*0-08-040258-5*, Pergamon Pr) Elsevier.

Carlsson, Chris, ed. Bad Attitude: The Processed World Anthology. 272p. (gr. 13). 1990. pap. 20.00 (*0-86091-946-3*, Pub. by Verso) Norton.

Carlsson, Claes-Goran, jt. auth. see Murkes, Jakob.

Carlsson, G., et al, eds. Algebraic Topology. (Lecture Notes in Mathematics Ser.: Vol. 1370). ix, 456p. 1989. 66.95 (*0-387-51118-0*) Spr-Verlag.

Carlsson, Gosta. Mass Response & Individual Choice: The Sociology of Behavioral Trends. 154p. (Orig.). 1987. pap. 52.00 (*91-22-01172-2*) Coronet Bks.

***Carlsson, Gunnar E. & Magnusson, Tomas.** Management of Temporomandibular Disorders in the General Dental Practice. LC 99-16117. 1999. write for info. (*0-86715-367-9*) Quint Pub Co.

Carlsson, Ingegard M., jt. auth. see Smith, Gudmund J.

Carlsson, J., ed. Mechanical Behaviour of Materials: Proceedings of the 4th International Conference on Mechanical Behaviour of Materials, Stockholm, Sweden August 15-19, 1983, 2 vols., No. IV. (International Series of Monographs on the Strength & Fracture of Materials & Structures). (Illus.). 1175p. 1984. 559.00 (*0-08-029340-9*, Pub. by Pergamon Repr) Franklin.

Carlsson, Jerker. The Limits to Structural Change: A Comparative Study of Foreign Direct Investments in Liberia & Ghana, 1950-71. 299p. 1981. write for info. (*91-7106-190-8*, Pub. by Nordic Africa) Transaction Pubs.

— Transnational Companies in Liberia. (Research Report Ser.: No. 37). 51p. 1977. write for info. (*91-7106-107-X*, Pub. by Nordic Africa) Transaction Pubs.

Carlsson, Jerker, ed. Recession in Africa. (Seminar Proceedings Ser.: No. 15). 204p. 1983. write for info. (*91-7106-218-1*, Pub. by Nordic Africa) Transaction Pubs.

— South-South Relations in a Changing World Order. (Seminar Proceedings Ser.: No. 14). 168p. 1982. write for info. (*91-7106-206-8*, Pub. by Nordic Africa) Transaction Pubs.

Carlsson, Jerker, et al, eds. Foreign Aid in Africa: Learning from Country Experiences. LC 98-132759. 224p. 1998. pap. 26.95 (*91-7106-414-1*, Pub. by Almqvist Wiksell) Transaction Pubs.

Carlsson, Jerker, jt. auth. see Saasa, Oliver.

Carlsson, Jerker, jt. ed. see Wohlgemuth, Lennart.

Carlsson, L. A., ed. Thermoplastic Composite Materials. (Composite Materials Ser.: No. 7). xii,390p. 1991. 198.50 (*0-444-88118-2*) Elsevier.

Carlsson, Leif A. & Pipes, R. Byron. Experimental Characterization of Advanced Composite Materials. LC 96-61023. 195p. 1996. text 159.95 (*1-56676-433-5*) Technomic.

Carlsson, Leif A., ed. see Center for Composite Materials Staff.

Carlsson, Olle & Lundgren, Stefan. Svalbard: Land Beyond the North Cape. 64p. 1994. 15.95 (*0-9641652-0-1*) Spec Expedit.

Carlsson-Paige, Nancy. Best Day of the Week. LC 98-14401. (Illus.). 32p. (J). (ps-1). 1998. pap. 10.95 (*1-884834-52-3*, 7070) Redleaf Pr.

Carlsson-Paige, Nancy & Levin, Diane. The War Play Dilemma: Balancing Needs & Values in the Early Childhood Classroom. LC 87-7086. (Early Childhood Education Ser.). 120p. (C). 1987. pap. text 13.95 (*0-8077-2875-6*) Tchrs Coll.

Carlsson-Paige, Nancy & Levin, Diane E. Before Push Comes to Shove: Building Conflict & Resolution Skills with Children. LC 98-14644. (Illus.). 100p. 1998. pap. 14.95 (*1-884834-53-1*, 1557) Redleaf Pr.

— Helping Young Children Understand Peace, War, & the Nuclear Threat. LC 84-63040. (Illus.). pap. 3.00 (*0-935989-16-1*, NAEYC #321) Natl Assn Child Ed.

— Who's Calling the Shots: How to Respond Effectively to Children's Fascination with War Play, War Toys & Violent TV. (Illus.). 204p. 1990. pap. 14.95 (*0-86571-165-8*) New Soc Pubs.

Carlsson, Stig G. The Distinctive Rhodesian Ridgeback. LC 98-34966. 1999. text 29.95 (*1-58245-039-0*) Howell Bks.

Carlsson, Susanne C. Charles & Elsa Chauvel - Movie Pioneers: Thirty Years of Australian Film Making. 1989. pap. 29.95 (*0-7022-2251-8*) Intl Spec Bk.

— Charles & Elsa Chauvel - Movie Pioneers: Thirty Years of Australian Film Making. 1989. 49.95 (*0-7022-2213-5*, Pub. by Univ Queensland Pr) Intl Spec Bk.

Carlstedt-Duke, J., et al. The Steroid-Thyroid Hormone Receptor Family & Gene Regulation. (Congress Reports: No. 4). 400p. 1989. 87.50 (*0-8176-2275-6*) Birkhauser.

Carlstein, Edward, et al, eds. Change-Point Problems. LC 94-79176. (Lecture Notes-Monographs: Vol. 23). vii, 385p. 1994. 45.00 (*0-940600-34-X*) Inst Math.

Carlston, D. E., jt. auth. see Wyer, Robert S.

Carlston, Eloise, jt. auth. see Wolfersperger, Shirley K.

Carlston, Erin G. Thinking Fascism: Sapphic Modernism & Fascist Modernity. LC 97-28947. 1998. write for info. (*0-8047-3088-1*) Stanford U Pr.

Carlston, Kenneth S. Law & Structures of Social Action. LC 80-19159. (Library of World Affairs: No. 30). 288p. 1980. reprint ed. lib. bdg. 59.75 (*0-313-20837-9*, CALW, Greenwood Pr) Greenwood.

— The Process of International Arbitration. LC 74-152591. 318p. 1972. reprint ed. lib. bdg. 65.00 (*0-8371-6024-3*, CAIA, Greenwood Pr) Greenwood.

Carlstone, Ed. Bubba's Big Banana Cream Crime: Resisting Temptation. (Quigley's Village Ser.: Vol. 8). (J). (ps-2). 12.99 incl. VHS (*0-310-58319-5*) Zondervan.

— The Great Treehouse Disaster: Cooperation. (Quigley's Village Ser.: Vol. 3). (J). (ps-2). 12.99 incl. VHS (*0-310-58259-8*, V5560) Zondervan.

— Shakeups & Showdowns, Vol. 12. (Quigley's Village Ser.). (J). 1993. 12.99 incl. VHS (*0-310-58329-2*) Zondervan.

— The Super Shoot for the Stars Space Station: Responsibility. (Quigley's Village Ser.: Vol. 1). (J). (ps-2). 12.99 incl. VHS (*0-310-58279-2*, V6790) Zondervan.

Carlstrom. Out & about with Jesse Bear. 1996. 14.95 (*0-02-717274-0*) Macmillan.

Carlstrom, Anders. Policy Capturing in Target Selection: U. S. & Swedish Army Aviators & Social Judgment Theory. LC 97-170685. (Studia Psychologica Upsaliensia: No. 15). (Illus.). 74p. (Orig.). 1996. pap. 33.50 (*91-554-3810-5*, Pub. by Uppsala Univ Acta Univ Uppsaliensis) Coronet Bks.

Carlstrom, Elis, et al. Language & Liberation for RC Translators. 1997. pap. 3.00 (*1-885357-55-9*) Rational Isl.

Carlstrom, Nancy. Guess Who's Coming, Jesse Bear. LC 96-12115. 32p. (J). (ps-k). 1998. 15.00 (*0-689-80702-3*) S&S Childrens.

Carlstrom, Nancy. I'm Not Moving, Mama! (Illus.). (J). 1990. 11.44 (*0-606-17924-0*) Turtleback.

Carlstrom, Nancy. Jesse Its About Time. 32p. (J). (ps-k). 1998. per. 5.99 (*0-689-81849-1*) S&S Childrens.

— Merry Christmas Jesse Bear. LC 99-22599. (J). 2000. per. 15.00 (*0-689-81962-5*) S&S Bks Yung.

— What a Scare, Jesse Bear. LC 98-22087. (Illus.). 32p. (J). (gr. k-3). 1999. per. 15.00 (*0-689-81961-7*) S&S Bks Yung.

— You're the Best, Jesse Bear. (J). 2001. 16.00 (*0-689-80701-5*) S&S Childrens.

Carlstrom, Nancy W. Bizz Buzz Chug-a-Chug. (Jesse Bear Ser.). (Illus.). 14p. (J). (ps-k). 1997. 4.99 (*0-689-80730-9*) S&S Childrens.

— Blow Me a Kiss, Miss Lilly. LC 89-34505. (Illus.). 32p. (J). (ps-3). 1990. 13.00 (*0-06-021012-5*); lib. bdg. 15.89 (*0-06-021013-3*) HarpC Child Bks.

— Does God Know How to Tie Shoes? (Illus.). 32p. (J). (ps-3). 1993. pap. 7.50 (*0-8028-5125-8*, Eerdmans Bks) Eerdmans.

— Does God Know How to Tie Shoes? (Illus.). 32p. (J). (ps-3). 1993. 15.00 (*0-8028-5074-X*, Eerdmans Bks) Eerdmans.

— Glory. LC 97-7882. (Illus.). (J). 2000. write for info. (*0-8028-5143-6*) Eerdmans.

— Happy Birthday, Jesse Bear! LC 93-25180. (Illus.). 32p. (J). (ps-1). 1994. text. write for info. (*0-02-717277-5*, Mac Bks Young Read) S&S Childrens.

— Hooray for Me, Hooray for You, Hooray for Blue. (Jesse Bear Ser.). (Illus.). 14p. (J). (ps-k). 1997. 4.99 (*0-689-80727-9*) S&S Childrens.

— How Do You Say It Today, Jesse Bear? LC 91-21939. (Illus.). 32p. (Orig.). (J). (ps-1). 1992. text 15.00 (*0-02-717276-7*, Mac Bks Young Read) S&S Childrens.

— How Do You Say It Today, Jesse Bear? (Illus.). 32p. (Orig.). 1999. pap. 5.99 (*0-689-82424-6*) S&S Childrens.

— I Love You Mama, Any Time of the Year. (Illus.). 14p. (J). (ps-k). 1997. 4.99 (*0-689-80729-5*) S&S Childrens.

— I Love You, Mama, Any Time of the Year. (Illus.). (J). (ps-k). 1997. bds. 4.99 (*0-614-29098-8*) Litle Simon.

— I Love You Papa, in All Kinds of Weather. (Illus.). (J). (ps-k). 1997. bds. 4.99 (*0-614-29099-6*) Litle Simon.

— I Love You Papa, in All Kinds of Weather. (Illus.). 14p. (J). (ps-k). 1997. 4.99 (*0-689-80728-7*) S&S Childrens.

***Carlstrom, Nancy W.** I'm Not Moving, Mama! 32p. (J). (gr. k-3). 1999. pap. 5.99 (*0-689-82881-0*) Aladdin.

Carlstrom, Nancy W. I'm Not Moving, Mama! LC 89-38151. (Illus.). 32p. (J). (ps-1). 1990. lib. bdg. 13.95 (*0-02-717286-4*, Mac Bks Young Read) S&S Childrens.

— Jesse Bear, What Will You Wear? LC 94-482. (Illus.). 32p. (J). (gr. 2-6). 1994. 19.95 (*0-689-71878-0*) Aladdin.

— Jesse Bear, What Will You Wear? LC 85-10610. (Illus.). 32p. (J). (ps-k). 1996. per. 5.99 (*0-689-80623-X*) Aladdin.

— Jesse Bear, What Will You Wear? LC 85-10610. (Illus.). 32p. (J). (ps-k). 1986. lib. bdg. 15.00 (*0-02-717350-X*, Mac Bks Young Read) S&S Childrens.

— Jesse Bear, What Will You Wear? Chunky Board Book. (Illus.). 16p. (J). (ps-k). 1996. per. 6.99 (*0-689-80930-1*) S&S Bks Yung.

— Jesse Bear's Tum Tum Tickle. (Illus.). 10p. (J). (ps up). 1994. mass mkt. 5.95 (*0-689-71716-4*) Aladdin.

— Let's Count It Out, Jesse Bear. (Illus.). 32p. (J). (ps-1). 1996. per. 15.00 (*0-689-80478-4*) S&S Childrens.

— Moose in the Garden. LC 89-29407. (Illus.). 32p. (J). (ps-2). 1990. 13.95 (*0-06-021015-X*) HarpC Child Bks.

— Raven & River. LC 95-14773. (Illus.). 32p. (J). (gr. k-3). 1997. 15.95 (*0-316-12894-5*) Little.

— Rise & Shine. LC 92-21696. (Illus.). 32p. (J). (ps-2). 1993. 15.00 (*0-06-021451-1*) HarpC Child Bks.

— The Snow Speaks. (Illus.). (J). (ps-3). 1992. 15.95 (*0-316-12861-9*) Little.

— The Snow Speaks. (Illus.). 32p. (J). (gr. k-3). 1995. pap. 4.95 (*0-316-12830-9*) Little.

— Swim the Silver Sea, Joshie Otter. LC 91-26168. (Illus.). 32p. (J). (ps). 1997. pap. 6.99 (*0-698-11447-7*, PapStar) Peng Put Young Read.

— Thanksgiving Day at Our House. LC 98-49254. (Illus.). 32p. (J). (gr. k-3). 1999. per. 14.00 (*0-689-80360-5*) S&S Bks Yung.

— Where Does the Night Hide? LC 89-32910. (Illus.). 32p. (J). (ps-1). 1990. lib. bdg. 13.95 (*0-02-717390-9*, Mac Bks Young Read) S&S Childrens.

***Carlstrom, Nancy W.** Who Said Boo? Halloween Poems for the Very Young. (Illus.). 32p. (J). 1999. per. 5.99 (*0-689-83151-X*) Aladdin.

Carlstrom, Nancy W. Who Said Boo? Halloween Poems for the Very Young. (Illus.). 32p. (J). 1995. 14.00 (*0-689-80308-7*) S&S Bks Yung.

— Wild Wild Sunflower Child Anna. LC 86-18226. (Illus.). 32p. (J). (ps-1). 1987. lib. bdg. 14.95 (*0-02-717360-7*, Mac Bks Young Read) S&S Childrens.

Carlstrom, Nancy White. Better Not Get Wet, Jesse Bear. LC 87-10810. (Illus.). 32p. (J). (ps-k). 1988. lib. bdg. 15.00 (*0-02-717280-5*, Mac Bks Young Read) S&S Childrens.

— Better Not Get Wet, Jesse Bear. (Illus.). 32p. (J). (ps-k). 1997. per. 5.99 (*0-689-81055-5*) S&S Childrens.

— Better Not Get Wet, Jesse Bear. (Aladdin Picture Bks.). 1997. 11.19 (*0-606-11117-4*, Pub. by Turtleback) Demco.

— Deer Eyes. (J). 1994. write for info. (*0-316-17720-2*) Little.

***Carlstrom, Nancy White.** Happy Birthday, Jesse Bear! 32p. (J). (ps-1). 2000. pap. 5.99 (*0-689-83311-3*) Aladdin.

— Happy Birthday Jesse Bear. (Illus.). (J). 2000. 11.44 (*0-606-17922-4*) Turtleback.

— It's about Time Jesse Bear. (Illus.). (J). 1999. pap. 13.40 (*0-613-08100-5*) Econo-Clad Bks.

— It's about Time, Jesse Bear: And Other Rhymes. (J). 1998. 11.19 (*0-606-13529-4*, Pub. by Turtleback) Demco.

Carlstrom, Nancy White. Jesse Bear, What Will You Wear? (J). 1996. 10.85 (*0-606-09490-3*, Pub. by Turtleback) Demco.

— Snow Speaks. (J). 1992. 10.40 (*0-606-08177-1*) Turtleback.

***Carlstrom, Nancy White.** The Way to Wyatt's House. (Illus.). 32p. (J). (gr. k-3). 2000. write for info. (*0-8027-8740-1*); lib. bdg. write for info. (*0-8027-8742-8*) Walker & Co.

Carlstrom, Nancy White. Who Gets the Sun Out of Bed? LC 91-32313. 1992. 10.15 (*0-606-10066-0*, Pub. by Turtleback) Demco.

— Wild Wild Sunflower Child Anna. 1991. 11.19 (*0-606-04847-2*, Pub. by Turtleback) Demco.

Carlton. NBA Jam Tournament Edition Official Game Secrets. 1995. pap. text 12.95 (*0-7615-0189-4*) Prima Pub.

Carlton. Paranormal. 240p. 78.95 (*0-7546-0170-6*) Ashgate Pub Co.

Carlton. Principles of Radiographic Imaging. 2nd ed. (Radiographic Technology Ser.). 96p. 1996. teacher ed. 18.00 (*0-8273-6865-8*) Delmar.

— Principles of Radiographic Imaging. 2nd ed. (Radiographic Technology Ser.). (C). 1996. lab manual ed. 23.00 (*0-8273-6866-6*) Delmar.

— Principles of Radiographic Positioning & Procedures Pocket Guide. 2nd ed. LC 98-43726. 448p. (C). 1999. pap. 21.95 (*0-8273-6372-9*) Delmar.

— State Sovereigns, & Society: Essays in Early Modern English History in Honour of A. J. Slavin. LC 97-26828. 288p. 1997. text 55.00 (*0-312-21045-0*) St Martin.

Carlton, ed. Modern Industrial Organization. 3rd ed. LC 99-25713. 780p. (C). 1999. 98.00 (*0-321-01145-7*) Addson-Wesley Educ.

Carlton-Alexander, Sandra. Black Butterflies: Stories of the South in Transition. 131p. 1994. pap. 14.95 (*1-879934-18-3*) St Andrews NC.

Carlton, Bea. In the Foxes' Lair, Vol. 3. rev. ed. (Randolph Mystery Ser.). 184p. 1999. pap. 8.99 (*0-9658103-7-2*) SonLife Pub.

— In the House of the Enemy. rev. ed. (Randolph Mystery Ser.). 189p. (Orig.). 1999. reprint ed. pap. 8.99 (*0-9658103-8-0*) SonLife Pub.

Carlton, Bea. Mystery at Natural Bridge. (Orig.). (J). (gr. 4-7). Date not set. pap. 5.95 (*0-9658103-2-1*) SonLife Pub.

Carlton, Bea. Voices from the Mist, Vol. 2. (SonLight Mysteries Ser.: Vol. 3). 207p. (Orig.). 1998. pap. 8.99 (*0-9658103-9-9*) SonLife Pub.

Carlton, Bea & Kircher, Anne. You Can Do Christian Puppets: A Beginner's Book of Puppet Craft & Playscripts. Zapel, Arthur L., ed. LC 89-3210. (Illus.). 176p. 1989. pap. 12.95 (*0-916260-58-5*, B196) Meriwether Pub.

***Carlton, Bea, et al.** Where's Jessie? unabridged ed. (Son Life Mysteries Ser.). 2000. pap. 8.99 (*0-9658103-6-4*, SLN-10) SonLife Pub.

***Carlton, Bob.** Laughter of Stones. 10p. 1999. pap. 2.00 (*0-9674487-4-3*) Good SAMAR.

***Carlton Books Staff.** The Derrieres. (Objects of Desire Ser.). (Illus.). 128p. 2000. 14.95 (*1-85868-871-X*, Pub. by Carlton Bks Ltd) Natl Bk Netwk.

— Legs. (Objects of Desire Ser.). (Illus.). 128p. 2000. 14.95 (*1-85868-870-1*, Pub. by Carlton Bks Ltd) Natl Bk Netwk.

Carlton Books Staff. Millennium Time Capsule. 1999. pap. 24.95 (*1-85868-647-4*, Pub. by Carlton Bks Ltd) Natl Bk Netwk.

— Romantic Photograph Album. (Illus.). 1999. 20.00 (*1-85868-323-8*, Pub. by Carlton Bks Ltd) Natl Bk Netwk.

— Super NES Games Unauthorized Power Tips Book, Vol. 2. 1994. pap. 14.95 (*1-55958-686-9*) Prima Pub.

— Urban Strike Official Power Play Guide with Desert & Jungle Strike. LC 94-236664. 96p. 1994. pap. 12.95 (*1-55958-687-7*) Prima Pub.

Carlton, Bronwyn. Auberon's Tale: The Books of Faerie. 128p. 1999. pap. text 14.95 (*1-56389-502-1*, Pub. by DC Comics) Time Warner.

— The Big Book of Death. (Factoid Books Big Book Ser.: Vol. 3). (Illus.). 1995. pap. 12.95 (*1-56389-166-2*, Pub. by DC Comics) Time Warner.

Carlton, Bronwyn & Reiber, John Ney. Books of Faerie. LC 98-222988. (Illus.). 144p. 1998. pap. text 14.95 (*1-56389-401-7*, Pub. by DC Comics) Time Warner.

Carlton-Carew, Miranda A., jt. ed. see Snider, Don M.

Carlton, Charles. Archbishop William Laud. 320p. 1987. lib. bdg. 65.00 (*0-7102-0463-9*, Routledge Thoemms) Routledge.

— Charles I: The Personal Monarch. 2nd ed. (Illus.). 434p. (C). 1995. pap. 25.99 (*0-415-12565-0*) Routledge.

— Charles I: The Personal Monarch. 2nd ed. LC 95-6998. (Illus.). 424p. (C). (gr. 13). 1995. 75.00 (*0-415-12141-8*, C0212) Routledge.

— Descriptive Syntax of the Old English Charters. LC 73-102955. (Janua Linguarum, Series Practica: No. 111). (Illus.). (Orig.). 1970. pap. text 49.25 (*90-279-0744-7*) Mouton.

— Going to the Wars: The Experience of the British Civil Wars, 1638-1651. (Illus.). 440p. (C). 1994. pap. 29.99 (*0-415-10391-6*) Routledge.

— Royal Childhoods. (Illus.). 192p. (C). 1986. 29.95 (*0-7102-0185-0*, Routledge Thoemms) Routledge.

Carlton, Charles, et al. Romanian Poetry in English Translation. LC 98-128784. 160p. 1997. 40.00 (*973-98091-6-2*, Pub. by Ctr Romanian Studies) Intl Spec Bk.

Carlton, Charles M., tr. see Marino, Adrian.

Carlton, Clark. The Faith - an Orthodox Catechism: Understanding Orthodox Christianity. LC 97-174073. 288p. 1997. pap. 22.95 (*0-9649141-1-5*) Regina Orthodox.

***Carlton, Clark.** The Homeland of Your Heart's Desire: The Orthodox Teaching on How to Be Saved. 57p. 2000. pap. 9.95 (*1-928653-00-6*) Regina Orthodox.

Carlton, Clark. The Truth: What Every Roman Catholic Should Know about the Orthodox Church. 272p. 1999. pap. 22.95 (*0-9649141-8-2*) Regina Orthodox.

— The Way: What Every Protestant Should Know about the Orthodox Church. LC 98-106897. 200p. 1995. pap. 22.95 (*0-9649141-2-3*) Regina Orthodox.

***Carlton, David.** Churchill & the Soviet Union. LC 99-42908. 256p. 2000. pap. 27.95 (*0-7190-4107-4*, Pub. by Manchester Univ Pr) St Martin.

— Churchill & the Soviet Union. LC 99-42908. 256p. 2000. text 69.95 (*0-7190-4106-6*, Pub. by Manchester Univ Pr) St Martin.

Carlton, David. Dallas Doc! From Barnyard Pigs to Skyscraper Cats - All the Amazing Critters in the Life of a Texas-Style Vet. LC 99-49619. 224p. (Orig.). 1999. pap. 14.00 (*1-888843-53-5*) Bridgeline Pr.

— Great Britain & NATO: A Parting of the Ways? (C). 1990. 35.00 (*0-907967-01-9*, Pub. by Inst Euro Def & Strat) St Mut.

Carlton, David, et al, eds. Rising Tension in Eastern Europe & the Former Soviet Union. LC 95-47704. (Illus.). 216p. 1996. 77.95 (*1-85521-666-3*, Pub. by Dartmth Pub) Ashgate Pub Co.

Carlton, David & Ingram, Paul, eds. The Search for Stability in Russian & the Former Soviet Bloc. LC 97-2266. (Studies in Disarmament & Conflicts). 228p. 1997. 72.95 (*1-85521-897-6*, Pub. by Ashgate Pub) Ashgate Pub Co.

Carlton, David L. Mill & Town in South Carolina, 1880-1920. LC 82-7753. xii, 313p. (C). 1982. pap. text 19.95 (*0-8071-1059-0*) La State U Pr.

Carlton, Dennis & Perloff, Joseph K. Modern Industrial Organization. 2nd ed. (C). 1994. pap. text 83.44 (*0-673-46902-6*) Addson-Wesley Educ.

Carlton, Donald M. Riding a Good Horse: Tales & Tips from an Old Horseman. Kelly, Patricia P., ed. (Illus.). 240p. 1999. pap. 14.95 (*0-9667682-0-5*) Sweetgrass Pr.

Carlton, Donna. Looking for Little Egypt. LC 94-79660. (Illus.). 120p. (Orig.). 1995. pap. 14.95 (*0-9623998-1-7*) Intl Dance Discovery.

***Carlton, E. B. & Weikart, P. S.** Guide to Rhythmically Moving, Vol. 4. 72p. 1999. pap. 9.95 (*1-57379-049-4*) High-Scope.

Carlton, E. B. & Weikart, Phyllis S. Guide to Rhythmically Moving 1. LC 98-114570. 60p. 1996. 9.95 (*1-57379-004-4*, M1009) High-Scope.

— Guide to Rhythmically Moving 2. LC 98-114570. 72p. 1996. 9.95 (*1-57379-015-X*, M1011) High-Scope.

Carlton, Elizabeth & Weikart, Phyllis S. Foundations in Elementary Education: Music. LC 94-26875. (K-Three Curriculum Ser.). (Illus.). 375p. 1993. 39.95 (*0-929816-60-9*, E3005) High-Scope.

Carlton, Elizabeth B., jt. auth. see Weikart, Phyllis S.

Carlton, Eric. Faces of Despotism. LC 94-31293. 272p. 1995. 69.95 (*1-85928-045-5*, Pub. by Scolar Pr) Ashgate Pub Co.

— The Few & the Many: A Typology of Elites. 232p. 1996. 78.95 (*1-85928-194-X*, Pub. by Scolar Pr) Ashgate Pub Co.

— Massacre: An Historical Perspective. LC 93-12373. 240p. (C). 1993. write for info. (*0-7185-1469-6*) St Martin.

— Massacres: A Historical Perspective. 207p. 1994. 67.95 (*1-85928-017-X*, Pub. by Scolar Pr) Ashgate Pub Co.

— Occupation: The Policies & Practices of Military Conquerors. 200p. (C). 1992. text 58.50 (*0-389-20981-3*) B&N Imports.

— Patterns of Belief Vol. 1: Peoples & Religion. 130p. 1973. pap. 6.95 (*0-04-377004-5*) Attic Pr.

— Patterns of Belief Vol. 2: Religions in Society. 140p. 1973. pap. 6.95 (*0-04-377005-3*) Attic Pr.

— The State Against the State: The Theory & Practice of the Coup d'Etat. LC 96-43351. 256p. 1997. text 78.95 (*1-85928-231-8*, Pub. by Scolar Pr) Ashgate Pub Co.

— Treason: Meaning & Motives. LC 98-18991. 208p. 1998. text 78.95 (*1-85928-371-3*, K5252.C37, Pub. by Scolar Pr) Ashgate Pub Co.

— War & Ideology. 216p. (C). 1990. pap. text 66.50 (*0-389-20945-7*) B&N Imports.

Carlton, Fields, Ward, Emmanuel, Smith & Cutler Staff. Florida Environmental Law Handbook. 383p. 1992. pap. text 89.00 (*0-86587-291-0*) Gov Insts.

Carlton-Ford, Steven. The Effects of Ritual & Charisma: The Creation of Collective Effervescence & the Support of Psychic Strength. LC 93-7105. (Cults & Nonconventional Religious Groups Ser.). 256p. 1993. text 30.00 (*0-8153-1251-2*) Garland.

Carlton, Frank E. Marine Recreational Fisheries, No. 6. Clepper, Henry, ed. 1981. 15.00 (*0-685-10270-X*) Sport Fishing.

— Marine Recreational Fisheries, No. 7. Clepper, Henry, ed. 1982. 15.00 (*0-685-10271-8*) Sport Fishing.

— Marine Recreational Fisheries, Vol. 3. Clepper, Henry, ed. LC 76-22389. 1978. 15.00 (*0-686-65030-1*) Sport Fishing.

— Marine Recreational Fisheries, Vol. 4. Clepper, Henry, ed. LC 76-22389. 1979. 15.00 (*0-686-65031-X*) Sport Fishing.

— Marine Recreational Fisheries, Vol. 5. Clepper, Henry, ed. LC 76-22389. 1980. 15.00 (*0-686-70340-5*) Sport Fishing.

— Marine Recreational Fisheries, Vol. 8. Clepper, Henry, ed. 1983. 15.00 (*0-317-45803-5*) Sport Fishing.

— Marine Recreational Fisheries, Vol. 9. Clepper, Henry, ed. 1984. 15.00 (*0-317-30084-9*) Sport Fishing.

— Marine Recreational Fisheries, Vol. 10. Clepper, Henry, ed. 1986. write for info. (*0-318-60770-0*) Sport Fishing.

— Marine Recreational Fisheries, Vol. 14. Clepper, Henry, ed. 199p. write for info. (*0-318-69747-5*) Sport Fishing.

Carlton, Geoff, jt. auth. see Moore, Jeff.

Carlton, James T. Molluscan Introductions & Transfers: Risks Considerations & Implications. (Illus.). 1994. pap. text 3.00 (*0-943676-58-4*) MD Sea Grant Col.

Carlton, James T., jt. ed. see Smith, Ralph.

Carlton, Jane, jt. auth. see Roguemore, Patt.

Carlton, Jane C. The Everyday & the Eternal. 1998. pap. 8.95 (*0-533-12716-5*) Vantage.

Carlton, Jean. Panic No More: Your Guide to Overcome Panic Attacks. 288p. (Orig.). 1994. pap. 12.95 (*0-9639632-9-5*) Stonehorse.

***Carlton, Jean.** Posh, Vol. 1. 2000. pap. 15.95 (*0-9639632-6-0*) Stonehorse.

Carlton, Jean. Victim No More: Your Guide to Overcome Revictimization. 288p. 1995. pap. 13.95 (*0-9639632-7-9*) Stonehorse.

Carlton, Jenean. Frames & Lenses. (Basic Bookshelf for Eyecare Professionals Ser.). (Illus.). 170p. 1999. pap. text 30.00 (*1-55642-364-0*, 63640) SLACK Inc.

Carlton, Jerry W., jt. auth. see Blumer, Evalyn A.

***Carlton, Jim.** Apple: The Inside Story of Intrigue, Egomania & Business Blunders. 463p. 2000. reprint ed. text 27.00 (*0-7881-9068-7*) DIANE Pub.

Carlton, Jim. Apple: The Inside Story of Intrigue, Egomania & Business Blunders. rev. ed. LC 98-39061. 480p. 1998. pap. 16.00 (*0-88730-965-8*) HarpC.

Carlton, Joseph R. Carlton's Complete Reference Book of Music. LC 44-181. (Illus.). 729p. (C). 1980. lib. bdg. 40.00 (*0-937348-00-7*) Carlton Pubns CA.

***Carlton, Josephine.** Life Messages: Inspiration for the Woman's Soul. 224p. 2000. 14.95 (*0-7407-0023-5*) Andrews & McMeel.

Carlton, J.S. Marine Propellers & Propulsion. LC 94-222746. 432p. 1994. 215.00 (*0-7506-1143-X*) Buttrwrth-Heinemann.

***Carlton, Katharine Tasheff.** Webworks: E-Commerce. 2001. 40.00 (*1-56496-661-5*) Rockport Pubs.

Carlton, Ken. The Dating Game. LC 96-96452. 224p. 1996. mass mkt. 5.99 (*0-380-78799-7*, Avon Bks) Morrow Avon.

— What Men Want from the Women They Love. 240p. (Orig.). 1996. mass mkt. 4.99 (*0-380-77497-6*, Avon Bks) Morrow Avon.

Carlton, Kevin & Parkinson, Eric. Physical Sciences: A Primary Teacher's Guide. (Illus.). 192p. 1994. pap. 35.95 (*0-304-32766-2*) Continuum.

Carlton-LaNey, Iris & Burwell, N. Yolanda, eds. African American Community Practice Models: Historical & Contemporary Responses. LC 96-12676. 114p. (C). 1996. 39.95 (*1-56024-791-6*) Haworth Pr.

***Carlton-LaNey, Iris B., et al.** Preserving & Strengthening Small Towns & Rural Communities. LC 99-33081. 401p. 1999. 36.95 (*0-87101-310-X*, NASW Pr) Natl Assn Soc Wkrs.

Carlton, Les G., jt. auth. see Carlton, Mary J.

Carlton, Lowis. Famous Florida Recipes. LC 72-170802. (Illus.). 80p. 1972. pap. 4.95 (*0-8200-0804-4*) Great Outdoors.

— Florida Seafood Cookery. LC 91-70788. (Illus.). 144p. (Orig.). 1991. pap. 9.95 (*0-8200-0809-5*) Great Outdoors.

Carlton, Lucille. Sex, Love & Chronic Illness LC 94-66888. 141p. 1994. write for info. (*0-9641712-0-1*) Natl Parkinson.

Carlton, Mary J. & Carlton, Les G. Teaching Sport Skills Study Guide. LC 87-19687. (Illus.). 224p. 1988. ring bd. 32.00 (*0-87322-021-8*, ACEP0205) Human Kinetics.

Carlton, Mike. Great Smoky Mountains National Park: A Wildlife Watcher's Guide. LC 95-24502. (Wildlife Watcher's Guide Ser.). (Illus.). 144p. 1996. pap. 11.95 (*1-55971-544-8*, NorthWord Pr) Creat Pub Intl.

— Tennessee Wonders: A Pictorial Guide to the Parks. LC 94-5228. (Illus.). 1994. pap. 18.95 (*1-55853-289-7*) Rutledge Hill Pr.

Carlton, Pamela J., et al. Human Diseases: A Systemic Approach: Teachers Manual & Testbank. 4th ed. (Illus.). 474p. 1995. teacher ed. write for info. (*0-8385-3929-7*, A3929-5) Appleton & Lange.

Carlton, Peter L. A Primer of Behavioral Pharmacology. LC 83-9083. (Illus.). 301p. (C). 1983. pap. text 17.60 (*0-7167-1451-5*) W H Freeman.

Carlton Press Staff, ed. see Blair, Jayne.

Carlton, R. Scott. International Encyclopaedic Dictionary of Philately. 3rd ed. LC 96-76695. 500p. 1997. 39.95 (*0-87341-448-9*) Krause Pubns.

— International Encyclopedic Dictionary of Numismatics. LC 95-82430. (Illus.). 500p. 1996. 39.95 (*0-87341-443-8*, NND) Krause Pubns.

***Carlton, Richard R.** Principles of Radiographic Imaging: An Art & a Science. (Illus.). 2000. 64.95 (*0-7668-1300-2*) Delmar.

Carlton, Richard R. Principles of Radiographic Imaging: An Art & a Science. 2nd ed. (Radiographic Technology Ser.). (Illus.). 736p. (C). 1996. mass mkt. 77.95 (*0-8273-6864-X*) Delmar.

Carlton, Richard R. & Adler, Arlene M. Principles of Radiographic Imaging. 1990. text 53.50 (*0-8273-3605-5*) Delmar.

— Principles of Radiographic Imaging: Instructor's Guide. 1991. pap., teacher ed. 18.00 (*0-8273-3606-3*) Delmar.

Carlton, Richard R., et al. Principles of Radiographic Imaging: Lab Manual. 1992. pap., wbk. ed., lab manual ed. 21.95 (*0-8273-3607-1*) Delmar.

Carlton, Richard R., jt. auth. see Adler, Arlene M.

Carlton, Rick, jt. ed. see Adler, Arlene.

Carlton, Robert W., jt. auth. see Bothwell, Thomas H.

Carlton, Stuart, tr. see Ruggieri, Claude-Fortune.

Carlton, Susan & Myers, Coco. The Nanny Book: The Smart Parent's Guide to Hiring, Firing, & Every Sticky Situation in Between. LC 98-50583. 1999. pap. 14.95 (*0-312-19933-3*) St Martin.

Carlton, Susan R., jt. auth. see Slattery, Patrick J.

Carlton, Suzanne & Brockington, Crystal W., eds. Promoting the Profession: A Resource Guide for Marketing & Publicizing Occupational Therapy. 129p. (Orig.). 1993. pap. text 16.00 (*1-56900-002-6*) Am Occup Therapy.

Carlton, Terence R. Introduction to the Phonological History of the Slavic Languages. 462p. (Orig.). 1991. pap. text 24.95 (*0-89357-223-3*) Slavica.

Carlton, W. The Christian Response to the Industrial Capitalism. 1990. pap. 38.00 (*0-7220-1975-0*) St Mut.

Carlton, W. E. Jack. It Took Their Kind: An Account of the Development of North Central Texas. 1994. 19.95 (*0-614-06086-9*) Texian.

Carlton, Wendy, ed. see Ford, Debbie.

Carlton, William W. Thomson's Special Veterinary Pathology. 3rd ed. 700p. Date not set. text. write for info. (*0-323-00560-8*, Pub. by Mosby) Saunders.

Carlton, William W. & McGavin, M. Donald. Thomson's Special Veterinary Pathology, Vol. 2. 2nd ed. (Illus.). 672p. (C). (gr. 13). 1995. text 102.00 (*0-8016-7968-0*, 07968) Mosby Inc.

Carluccio, Ann. Passion for Pasta. rev. ed. LC 94-28410. (Illus.). 192p. 1994. 17.95 (*1-56426-065-8*) Cole Group.

Carluccio, Antonio. Antonio Carluccio's Italian Feast. LC 98-46004. 1999. pap. 22.95 (*1-884656-09-9*) W One Hund Seventy Five.

— Antonio Carluccio's Southern Italian Feast. 1999. pap. text 22.95 (*1-884656-11-0*) W One Hund Seventy Five.

— Music & Menus from Italy: A Cookbook with Compact Disc. (Illus.). 96p. 1996. 24.95 incl. audio compact disk (*1-85793-529-2*, Pub. by Pavilion Bks Ltd) Trafalgar.

— A Taste of Italy. 1986. 24.95 (*0-316-12858-9*) Little.

Carluccio, Antonio & Carluccio, Priscilla. Carluccio's Complete Italian Food. LC 97-67797. (Illus.). 320p. 1997. 35.00 (*0-8478-2037-8*, Pub. by Rizzoli Intl) St Martin.

Carluccio, Antonio, et al. Great Food: Over 175 Recipes from Six of the World's Greatest Chefs. LC 98-17732. (Illus.). 280p. 1998. 26.95 (*1-884656-05-6*) W One Hund Seventy Five.

Carluccio, Michael J. The Fun of Transforming Pt. 2: The Holy Trio. (Teaching Sanity in an Insane World Ser.). (Illus.). 65p. (Orig.). (C). 1991. pap. text 4.00 (*1-878032-06-2*) Clear Thinking.

— Holy Trio. (Teaching Sanity in an Insane World Ser.). (Illus.). 64p. (C). 1991. pap. text 4.00 (*1-878032-05-4*) Clear Thinking.

— Teaching Sanity in an Insane World: The Unholy Trio, 3 pts. (Illus.). 255p. 1990. pap. 10.00 (*1-878032-01-1*) Clear Thinking.

— Teaching Sanity in an Insane World: The Unholy Trio, Pt. 1. (Illus.). 81p. 1989. pap. 4.00 (*0-685-36279-5*) Clear Thinking.

— Teaching Sanity in an Insane World: The Unholy Trio, Pt. 2. (Illus.). 80p. 1989. pap. 4.00 (*1-878032-03-8*) Clear Thinking.

Carluccio, Priscilla, jt. auth. see Carluccio, Antonio.

Carlup, Steven. Quantum Gravity in 2 + 1 Dimensions. LC 97-42893. (Monographs on Mathematical Physics). (Illus.). 287p. (C). 1998. 80.00 (*0-521-56408-5*) Cambridge U Pr.

Carlus, Charlotte, tr. see Gaddie, Mary, et al.

Carlut. French Oral & Written Review. 5th ed. (C). 1993. pap. text, wbk. ed., lab manual ed. 36.00 (*0-03-075901-3*) Harcourt Coll Pubs.

Carlut, Charles & Meiden, Walter. French for Oral & Written Review. 5th ed. 448p. (C). 1993. pap. text 50.00 (*0-03-075899-8*) Harcourt Coll Pubs.

Carlyle, A. J., ed. see Crabbe, George.

Carlyle, Alexander. An Argument to Prove That the Tragedy of Douglas Ought to Be Publickly Burned by the Hands of the Hangman. LC 78-67650. reprint ed. 24.50 (*0-404-17185-0*) AMS Pr.

Carlyle, Alexander, ed. see Carlyle, Jane B.

Carlyle, Alexander, ed. see Carlyle, Thomas.

Carlyle, Alexander J. Political Liberty. 220p. 1963. 26.00 (*0-7146-1551-X*, Pub. by F Cass Pubs) Intl Spec Bk.

— Political Liberty: A History of the Conception in the Middle Ages & Modern Times. LC 80-18967. 220p. 1980. reprint ed. lib. bdg. 59.50 (*0-313-21482-4*, CAPL, Greenwood Pr) Greenwood.

Carlyle, Carolyn. Mercy Hospital: Crisis! 128p. (Orig.). (J). (gr. 5). 1993. pap. 3.50 (*0-380-76846-1*, Avon Bks) Morrow Avon.

— Mercy Hospital: Don't Tell Mrs. Harris. 128p. (Orig.). (YA). 1993. pap. 3.50 (*0-380-76848-8*, Avon Bks) Morrow Avon.

— Mercy Hospital: Dr. Cute. 128p. (Orig.). (YA). 1993. pap. 3.50 (*0-380-76849-6*, Avon Bks) Morrow Avon.

— Mercy Hospital: The Best Medicine. 128p. (Orig.). (J). 1993. pap. 3.50 (*0-380-76847-X*, Avon Bks) Morrow Avon.

Carlyle, E. I. William Cobbett. 1972. 59.95 (*0-8490-1301-1*) Gordon Pr.

Carlyle, Ivor. Scroll Saw Toy Projects. LC 99-216418. 1999. pap. text 19.95 (*1-86108-094-8*) Guild Master.

***Carlyle, Ivor.** Scrollsaw Toys for All Ages. (Illus.). 2000. pap. 19.95 (*1-86108-146-4*) Guild Master.

Carlyle, Jane B. Jane Welsh Carlyle: Letters to Her Family. (BCL1-PR English Literature Ser.). 390p. 1992. reprint ed. lib. bdg. 89.00 (*0-7812-7483-4*) Rprt Serv.

— Letters & Memorials of Jane Welsh Carlyle, 3 vols., Set. LC 79-37683. 1168p. 1983. reprint ed. 230.00 (*0-404-56709-6*) AMS Pr.

— New Letters & Memorials of Jane Welsh Caryle, 2 vols., Set. Carlyle, Alexander, ed. LC 78-37672. (Illus.). 1983. reprint ed. 150.00 (*0-404-56724-X*) AMS Pr.

Carlyle, Jane W. I Too Am Here: Selections from the Letters of Jane Welsh Carlyle. LC 76-11093. 327p. reprint ed. pap. 93.20 (*0-608-13406-6*, 2022471) Bks Demand.

Carlyle, Jane W., jt. auth. see Carlyle, Thomas.

Carlyle, L. Dark Deception. mass mkt. 6.95 (*0-7472-5273-4*, Pub. by Headline Bk Pub) Trafalgar.

— Liaison Curtain Calls. 1997. mass mkt. 6.95 (*0-7472-5579-2*, Pub. by Headline Bk Pub) Trafalgar.

— Liaison Velvet Vices. 1997. mass mkt. 6.95 (*0-7472-5767-1*, Pub. by Headline Bk Pub) Trafalgar.

— Sensual Storm. mass mkt. 6.95 (*0-7472-5274-2*, Pub. by Headline Bk Pub) Trafalgar.

— Voluptuous Voyage. pap. 6.95 (*0-7472-5145-2*, Pub. by Headline Bk Pub) Trafalgar.

— Willful Ways. mass mkt. 6.95 (*0-7472-5465-6*, Pub. by Headline Bk Pub) Trafalgar.

Carlyle, Linda P. God & Joseph & Me. (Child's Steps to Jesus Ser.: No. 1). 32p. (J). 1992. 7.99 (*0-8163-1092-0*) Pacific Pr Pub Assn.

— Grandma Stepped on Fred. (Child's Steps to Jesus Ser.: No. 3). 32p. (J). 1992. 7.99 (*0-8163-1094-7*) Pacific Pr Pub Assn.

— Rescued from the River. (Child's Steps to Jesus Ser.: No. 2). 25p. (J). 1992. 7.99 (*0-8163-1093-9*) Pacific Pr Pub Assn.

***Carlyle, Linda Porter.** Child's Steps to Jesus. (Illus.). (J). 2000. 25.95 (*0-8163-1185-4*) Pacific Pr Pub Assn.

Carlyle, Linda Porter. Cookies in the Mailbox Vol. 5: A Book about the Bible. Sox, Aileen, ed. (Child's Steps to Jesus Ser.). (Illus.). 24p. (J). (ps-2). 1993. 7.99 (*0-8163-1122-6*) Pacific Pr Pub Assn.

— Max Moves In Vol. 4: A Book about Obeying. Sox, Aileen, ed. (Child's Steps to Jesus Ser.). (Illus.). 24p. (J). 1992. 7.99 (*0-8163-1095-5*, 0-8163-1095-5) Pacific Pr Pub Assn.

Carlyle, Liz. My False Heart. 1999. per. 6.50 (*0-671-04054-5*) S&S Trade.

***Carlyle, Liz.** A Woman Scorned. 448p. 2000. per. 6.50 (*0-671-03826-5*, Sonnet Bks) PB.

***Carlyle, Lizanne.** Beauty Like the Night. 2000. 6.50 (*0-7434-1054-8*) PB.

Carlyle, Lizanne. The Rose Window. large type ed. 256p. 1992. pap. 16.99 (*0-7089-7140-7*) Ulverscroft.

Carlyle, Margaret. The Awakening of Southern Italy. LC 85-14821. (Illus.). 147p. 1985. reprint ed. lib. bdg. 59.50 (*0-313-25044-8*, CAAW, Greenwood Pr) Greenwood.

Carlyle, Richard. An Answer to Prayer. (Illus.). 130p. 1997. pap. text 9.95 (*0-9658767-0-5*) Rocky Point.

Carlyle, Sue. Move to Learn: Physical Activities for Young Children. (Illus.). 1986. reprint ed. pap. text 8.95 (*0-941376-02-8*) Bleecker St Pub.

***Carlyle, Thomas.** A Carlyle Reader: Selections from the Writings of Thomas Carlyle. Tennyson, G. B., ed. LC 99-74754. (C). 2000. pap. text 15.95 (*1-58390-008-X*, Copley Editions) Copley Pub.

— Early Letters, 1814-1826, 2 vols. in 1. Norton, Charles E., ed. (Anglistica & Americana Ser.: No. 165). (Illus.). xxii, 775p. 1976. reprint ed. 160.00 (*3-487-05937-1*) G Olms Pubs.

Carlyle, Thomas. History of Friedrich II of Prussia, Called Frederick the Great. Clive, John, ed. LC 79-82375. (Classic European Historians Ser.). 519p. reprint ed. pap. 160.90 (*0-608-13456-2*, 202004200016) Bks Demand.

— How Smart Are You? Test Your History IQ. 64p. pap. 2.95 (*0-9637056-6-0*) Blck Dog & Leventhal.

— Letters: 1826-1836 : vol. 1/2 : 1826-1832 : 1832-1836 : 2 vol. in 1, 2 vols. in 1. Norton, Charles E., ed. (Anglistica & Americana Ser.: No. 171). (Illus.). viii, 841p. 1977. reprint ed. 160.00 (*3-487-06285-2*) G Olms Pubs.

— The Letters of Thomas Carlyle. 1971. reprint ed. 39.00 (*0-403-00897-2*) Scholarly.

— The Letters of Thomas Carlyle, 1826-1836, 2 vols, Set. Norton, Charles E., ed. LC 70-39194. (Select Bibliographies Reprint Ser.). 1977. 53.95 (*0-8369-6796-8*) Ayer.

— The Letters of Thomas Carlyle to His Brother Alexander: With Related Family Letters. Marrs, Edwin W., Jr., ed. LC 68-21978. 848p. reprint ed. pap. 200.00 (*0-7837-2058-0*, 204233300004) Bks Demand.

— The Letters of Thomas Carlyle to John Stuart Mill, John Sterling & Robert Browning. Carlyle, Alexander, ed. LC 77-95420. (English Biography Ser.: No. 31). 1969. reprint ed. lib. bdg. 75.00 (*0-8383-0964-X*) M S G Haskell Hse.

— The Letters of Thomas Carlyle to John Stuart Mill, John Sterling & Robert Browning. (BCL1-PR English Literature Ser.). 311p. 1992. reprint ed. lib. bdg. 89.00 (*0-7812-7486-9*) Rprt Serv.

— Letters to His Youngest Sister. Copeland, C. T., ed. (Anglistica & Americana Ser.: No. 30). 284p. 1968. reprint ed. 80.00 (*0-685-25148-9*, 05102208) G Olms Pubs.

— Life of Fredrich Schiller. 200p. 1994. pap. 25.00 (*0-87556-790-8*) Saifer.

— The Love Letters of Thomas Carlyle & Jane Welsh, 2 vols. Carlyle, Alexander, ed. LC 75-30016. (Illus.). reprint ed. 135.00 (*0-404-14050-5*) AMS Pr.

— Montaigne: And Other Essays, Chiefly Biographical. LC 72-13208. (Essay Index Reprint Ser.). 1977. reprint ed. 25.95 (*0-8369-8149-9*) Ayer.

— New Letters, 2 vols., Set. (BCL1-PR English Literature Ser.). 1992. reprint ed. lib. bdg. 150.00 (*0-7812-7487-7*) Rprt Serv.

— New Letters, 2 vols., Set. (Anglistica & Americana Ser.: No. 42). (Illus.). 1969. reprint ed. 150.00 (*0-685-66442-2*, 05102525) G Olms Pubs.

— New Letters of Thomas Carlyle, 2 vols., Set. Carlyle, Alexander, ed. LC 75-108465. (Illus.). 1970. reprint ed. 49.00 (*0-403-00204-4*) Scholarly.

— On Heroes, Hero-Worship & the Heroic in History. LC 91-33937. (Charlotte & Norman Strouse Edition of the Writings of Thomas Carlyle: Vol. 1). 622p. (C). 1992. 55.00 (*0-520-07515-3*, Pub. by U CA Pr) Cal Prin Full Svc.

— On Heroes, Hero-Worship & the Heroic in History. Niemeyer, Carl, ed. & intro. by. LC 66-12130. (Illus.). xxv, 257p. 1966. pap. text 12.00 (*0-8032-5030-4*, Bison Books) U of Nebr Pr.

— Past & Present. Altick, Richard D., ed. LC 77-70381. (Gotham Library). 294p. (C). 1977. pap. text 18.50 (*0-8147-0562-6*) NYU Pr.

— Past & Present (1909) 348p. 1998. reprint ed. pap. 19.95 (*0-7661-0713-2*) Kessinger Pub.

— Reminiscences. Fielding, K. J. & Campbell, Ian, eds. LC 97-7081. (The World's Classics Ser.). 512p. 1997. pap. 15.95 (*0-19-281748-5*) OUP.

— Reminiscences, 2 vols. Froude, James A., ed. LC 71-144936. (Literature Ser.). 1972. reprint ed. 29.00 (*0-403-00898-0*) Scholarly.

***Carlyle, Thomas.** Reminiscences: Nineteenth-Century British Literature. (World Classics Ser.). 512p. 1999. pap. 15.95 (*0-19-283889-X*) OUP.

— Sartor Resartus. McSweeney, Kerry & Sabor, Peter, eds. (Oxford World's Classics Ser.). 320p. 1999. pap. 11.95 (*0-19-283673-0*) OUP.

Carlyle, Thomas. Scottish & Other Miscellanies. (BCL1-PR English Literature Ser.). 339p. 1992. reprint ed. lib. bdg. 89.00 (*0-7812-7485-0*) Rprt Serv.

— Selected Writings. Shelston, Alan, ed. (English Library). 400p. 1980. pap. 14.95 (*0-14-043065-2*, Penguin Classics) Viking Penguin.

— Thomas Carlyle's Life of Friedrich Schiller. (GERM Ser.). xv, 92p. 1992. 55.00 (*1-879751-10-0*) Camden Hse.

— The Works of Thomas Carlyle, 30 vols. Traill, H. D., ed. LC 79-22238. (BCL Ser. II). reprint ed. 2535.00 (*0-404-09800-2*) AMS Pr.

— The Works of Thomas Carlyle, 30 vols., Set. (BCL1-PR English Literature Ser.). 1992. reprint ed. lib. bdg. 2700.00 (*0-7812-7484-2*) Rprt Serv.

Carlyle, Thomas, ed. Latter-Day Pamphlets. LC 72-37771. (Essay Index Reprint Ser.). 1977. reprint ed. 23.95 (*0-8369-2584-X*) Ayer.

Carlyle, Thomas, et al, trs. Novellas of Ludwig Tieck & E. T. A. Hoffmann. (GERM Ser.: Vol. 58). xiv, 3178p. 1992. reprint ed. 55.00 (*0-938100-90-4*) Camden Hse.

Carlyle, Thomas & Carlyle, Jane W. The Collected Letters of Thomas & Jane Welsh Carlyle, Vol. 10. LC 71-101132. 1985. text 49.95 (*0-8223-0611-5*) Duke.

Carlyle, Thomas, et al. Sartor Resartus: The Life & Opinions of Herr Teufelsdr Ockh in Three Books. LC 97-3100. (Norman & Charlotte Strouse Edition of the Writings of Thomas Carlyle: Vol. 2). 646p. 2000. 60.00 (*0-520-20928-1*, Pub. by U CA Pr) Cal Prin Full Svc.

Carlyle, Thomas, jt. auth. see Emerson, Ralph Waldo.

Carlyle, Thomas, tr. see Burton, Michael & Goethe, Johann Wolfgang Von.

Carlyle, Thomas, tr. see Goethe, Johann Wolfgang Von.

Carlyle, Thomas, tr. see Musaus, Johann Karl August, et al.

Carlyle, Thomas, tr. see Richter, Johann P.

Carlyle, Viveca. Sweet Lies. 352p. 1997. mass mkt. 4.99 (*0-7860-0425-8*, Pinncle Kensgtn) Kensgtn Pub Corp.

Carlyle, Womble, Sandridge & Rice Staff, et al. North Carolina Environmental Law Handbook. 388p. 1994. pap. text 89.00 (*0-86587-306-2*) Gov Insts.

Carlyon, R. P., et al, eds. Processing of Complex Sounds by the Auditory System: Proceedings of a Royal Society Discussion Meeting Held on 4-5 December 1991. LC 92-28567. (Illus.). 146p. (C). 1993. text 55.00 (*0-19-852272-X*, Clarendon Pr) OUP.

Carlysle, Viveca. All That Glitters. 256p. 1999. mass mkt. 4.99 (*0-7860-0609-9*) Kensgtn Pub Corp.

— Return to Love. 1999. mass mkt. 4.99 (*1-58314-035-2*) BET Bks.

Carlzon, Jan. Moments of Truth. LC 87-1070. 160p. 1987. 22.50 (*0-88730-200-9*, HarpBusn) HarpInfo.

— Moments of Truth. LC 88-45644. 160p. 1989. reprint ed. pap. 13.00 (*0-06-091580-3*, PL 1580, Perennial) HarperTrade.

Carm, T. O., jt. auth. see Schmidt, Herbert.

Carmack, Daniel F. Ohio Probate. LC 79-91159. (Practice Systems Library Manual). 120.00 (*0-317-00549-9*) West Group.

C

— Ohio Probate. LC 79-91159. (Practice Systems Library Manual). 1991. suppl. ed. 50.00 (*0-317-03201-1*) West Group.

Carmack, Derin. Seven Steps to Freedom. 31p. 1986. pap. 3.00 (*0-937093-25-4*) Jewel Pr.

Carmack, Doris. New Horizons in Quilting. 47p. 1992. pap. 14.95 (*1-883504-03-1*) Sew-Art Int.

Carmack, Joyce, jt. contrib. by see O'Kain, David.

Carmack, Lisa. Philippe in Monet's Garden. (J). (ps-1). 1998. 10.95 (*0-87846-456-5*) Mus Fine Arts Boston.

Carmack, Melanie Z. P Is for Pioneers: An Alphabet Book for LDS Children. LC 97-92940. (Illus.). 32p. (J). 1997. 14.95 (*0-9656612-0-2*) Buffalo Bks.

***Carmack, Noel A. & Davidson, Karen Lynn, eds.** Out of the Black Patch: The Autobiography of Effie Marquess Carmack, Folk Musician, Artist, & Writer. LC 99-6901. (Life Writings of Frontier Women Ser.: Vol. 4). (Illus.). 380p. 1999. 29.95 (*0-87421-279-0*) Utah St U Pr.

Carmack, Rita J. Image to Image, Vol. 1. 146p. 1985. pap. 5.00 (*0-88144-047-7*) Jewel Pr.

— Image to Image, Vol. II. 155p. 1986. pap. 5.00 (*0-937093-00-9*) Jewel Pr.

— Life Is More Important Than Food. 39p. 1987. pap. 5.00 (*0-937093-05-X*) Jewel Pr.

— Set My Heart Free. 144p. 1984. pap. 5.00 (*0-88144-031-0*) Jewel Pr.

Carmack, Robert M. Harvest of Violence: The Maya Indians & the Guatemalan Crisis. LC 87-40550. (Illus.). 352p. 1992. pap. 13.95 (*0-8061-2459-8*) U of Okla Pr.

— Rebels of Highland Guatemala: The Quiche-Mayas of Momostenango. LC 95-18047. (Civilization of the American Indian Ser.: Vol. 215). (Illus.). 560p. 1996. 39.95 (*0-8061-2760-0*) U of Okla Pr.

Carmack, Robert M., et al, eds. The Legacy of Mesoamerica: History & Culture of a Native American Civilization. LC 94-31722. (Exploring Cultures Ser.). 494p. 1995. pap. text 42.00 (*0-13-337445-9*) P-H.

Carmack, Robert M., jt. auth. see Wallace, Dwight T.

Carmack, Sharon D. Genealogist's Guide to Discovering Your Female Ancestors. LC 97-48297. (Genealogiset's Guide to Discovering Your Ancestors Ser.). 144p. 1998. pap. 17.99 (*1-55870-472-8*, Betrwy Bks) F & W Pubns Inc.

— The Genealogy Sourcebook. LC 97-35878. 266p. 1998. reprint ed. 26.00 (*1-56565-794-2*, Extension Pr) Lowell Hse.

— The Genealogy Sourcebook. 288p. 1998. reprint ed. pap. 17.95 (*0-7373-0007-8*, 00078W) NTC Contemp Pub Co.

***Carmack, Sharon DeBartolo.** A Genealogist's Guide to Discovering Your Immigrant & Ethnic Ancestors. 192p. 2000. pap. 18.99 (*1-55870-524-4*) F & W Pubns Inc.

Carmack, Sharon DeBartolo. Italian-American Family History: A Guide to Researching & Writing about Your Heritage. LC 96-79437. 139p. 1997. pap. 12.95 (*0-8063-1527-X*) Genealog Pub.

— Organizing Your Family History Search: Efficient & Effective Ways to Gather & Protect Your Genealogical Research. LC 99-21643. (Illus.). 176p. 1999. pap. 16.99 (*1-55870-511-2*, 70425, Betrwy Bks) F & W Pubns Inc.

Carmack, William, et al. Native American Research Information Service. LC 83-70626. (American Indian Handbook & Manual Ser.). 275p. 1983. pap. 15.00 (*0-935626-11-5*) U Cal AISC.

Carmagnani, Marcello. Estado y Mercado. (SPA.). pap. 15.99 (*968-16-4391-7*, Pub. by Fondo) Continental Bk.

Carmagnani, Marcelo. Federalismos Lationamericanos. (SPA.). pap. 15.99 (*968-16-4216-3*, Pub. by Fondo) Continental Bk.

Carman. Mission 3:16 Devotional. 144p. 1998. pap. 9.99 (*1-57778-098-1*, Pub. by Albury Pub) Appalach Bk Dist.

— Radically Saved. 1993. pap. text 15.99 (*0-89274-638-6*) Harrison Hse.

— Riot Manual. Date not set. pap. text 4.99 (*0-917143-46-9*) Sparrow TN.

Carman, Bliss. Songs from Vagabondia. (BCL1-PR English Literature Ser.). 54p. 1992. reprint ed. lib. bdg. 59.00 (*0-7812-7495-8*) Rprt Serv.

Carman, Bliss, ed. The World's Best Poetry, 10 vols, Set. 1975. lib. bdg. 1200.00 (*0-87968-323-6*) Gordon Pr.

— The World's Best Poetry: Foundation Volumes I-X. LC 81-83524. 4944p. 1982. reprint ed. lib. bdg. 599.99 (*0-89609-300-X*) Roth Pub Inc.

Carman, Bliss & Hovey, Richard. Songs from Vagabondia. LC 68-57593. 1970. reprint ed. lib. bdg. 69.50 (*0-8371-1800-X*, CASO, Greenwood Pr) Greenwood.

Carman, Carol J. Sweatlodge Participation among Nez Perce Women. 121p. (C). 1989. pap. text 13.75 (*1-55567-069-5*) Coyote Press.

***Carman, Charles H.** Images of Humanists Ideals in Italian Renaissance Art. LC 99-86703. (Studies in Art History: Vol. 2). 208p. 2000. text 89.95 (*0-7734-7804-3*) E Mellen.

Carman, Elizabeth, jt. auth. see Carman, Neil.

Carman, G. P., et al, eds. Adaptive Material Systems Vol. 206-58: Adaptive Material Systems. LC 95-77293. (1995 Joint ASME Applied Mechanics & Materials Summer Meeting Ser.: Vol. 206). 160p. 1995. 96.00 (*0-7918-1321-5*, H00953) ASME.

Carman, G. P. & Garcia, E., eds. Adaptive Structures & Material Systems. LC 93-73594. (AD Ser.: Vol. 35). 463p. 1994. pap. 85.00 (*0-7918-1041-0*) ASME.

Carman, Gary D., jt. ed. see Small, Richard W.

Carman, Gary O. & Farragher, Brian J. Quality Indicators for Residential Programs: A Survey Instrument. 1994. pap. 16.95 (*0-87868-590-1*) Child Welfare.

Carman, Gary O. & Sage, Daniel D. Evaluation Criteria for Special Education in Residential Schools. 30p. 1991. pap. 16.95 (*0-87868-455-7*) Child Welfare.

Carman, Harry J. Street Surface Railway Franchises of New York City. LC 76-77998. (Columbia University. Studies in the Social Sciences: No. 200). reprint ed. 37.50 (*0-404-51200-3*) AMS Pr.

Carman, Harry J., ed. Jesse Buel, Agricultural Reformer: Selections from His Writings. LC 72-2835. (Use & Abuse of America's Natural Resources Ser.). 650p. 1972. reprint ed. 41.95 (*0-405-04503-4*) Ayer.

Carman, Harry J. & Thompson, Arthur W. A Guide to the Principal Sources for American Civilization, 1800-1900, in the City of New York: Manuscripts. LC 60-6935. 501p. reprint ed. pap. 155.40 (*0-608-11281-X*, 201320900083) Bks Demand.

Carman, Harry J., ed. see Eliot, Jared.

Carman, Hoy F. U. S. Agricultural Response to Income Taxation. LC 97-10763. 224p. 1997. 52.95 (*0-8138-2175-4*) Iowa St U Pr.

Carman, Jana, jt. auth. see Souder, Patricia.

Carman, John. Ancient Warfare. (Illus.). 256p. 2000. 44.95 (*0-7509-1795-4*) Bks Intl VA.

Carman, John & Hall, Clare. Valuing Ancient Things: Archaeology & Law. LC 95-24873. 288p. 1996. 120.00 (*0-7185-0012-1*) Bks Intl VA.

Carman, John & Narayanan, Vasudha. The Tamil Veda: Pillan's Interpretation of the Tiruvaymoli. 342p. 1989. pap. text 24.00 (*0-226-09306-9*); lib. bdg. 60.00 (*0-226-09305-0*) U Ch Pr.

Carman, John B. & Hopkins, Steven P. Tracing Common Themes: Comparative Courses in the Study of Religion. 318p. 1991. 44.95 (*1-55540-563-0*, 00 01 16); pap. 34.95 (*1-55540-564-9*, 00 01 16) Duke.

Carman, John B. & Streng, Frederick. Spoken & Unspoken Thanks: Some Comparative Soundings. (Studies in World Religions). 170p. (C). 1989. pap. 20.95 (*1-55540-282-8*) Harvard U Wrld Relig.

Carman, John B., jt. ed. see Dawe, Donald G.

Carman, John B., tr. see Vesalius, Andreas.

Carman, Judy McCoy. Born to Be Blessed: Seven Keys to Joyful Living. 1999. pap. 14.95 (*1-58501-005-7*) CeShore Pubg.

Carman, Laura J. Louisiana Successions. 2nd ed. LC 98-89051. 800p. 1998. 150.00 (*0-327-00707-9*, 6879011) LEXIS Pub.

***Carman, Laura J.** Louisiana Successions, 1999 Supplement: Pocketpart. 100p. 1999. suppl. ed. write for info. (*0-327-01690-6*, 6879413) LEXIS Pub.

Carman, Laura Junge. Louisiana Successions. 2nd ed. 914p. 115.00 (*0-327-10171-7*) LEXIS Pub.

Carman, M. G. & Flack, J. G. Gordon - Macy: Allied Fammlies: Gordon-Macy & Hiddleston-Curtis Et Al. (Illus.). 293p. 1991. reprint ed. pap. 45.00 (*0-8328-1891-7*); reprint ed. lib. bdg. 55.00 (*0-8328-1890-9*) Higginson Bk Co.

Carman, Marilyn J., jt. auth. see Carman, Robert A.

Carman Ministries Staff. No Monsters: A Storybook for Kids. LC 97-163194. 32p. (J). (ps-3). 1996. 7.99 (*1-880089-35-1*, Pub. by Albury Pub) Appalach Bk Dist.

— R. I. O. T. Devotional: Righteous Truths That Will Invade Your Life, Vol. 1. LC 97-159968. 128p. (YA). 1996. pap. 4.99 (*1-880089-38-6*, Pub. by Albury Pub) Appalach Bk Dist.

— R. I. O. T. Devotional: Righteous Truths That Will Invade Your Life, Vol. 2. 128p. (YA). 1996. pap. 4.99 (*1-880089-39-4*, Pub. by Albury Pub) Appalach Bk Dist.

— Radically Saved. 64p. 1996. pap. 1.50 (*1-880089-91-2*, Pub. by Albury Pub) Appalach Bk Dist.

— Satan, Bite the Dust! A Storybook for Kids. 32p. (J). (ps-3). 1996. 7.99 (*1-880089-34-3*, Pub. by Albury Pub) Appalach Bk Dist.

***Carman, Neil & Carman, Elizabeth.** Cosmic Cradle: Souls Waiting in the Wings for Birth. (Illus.). 750p. 2000. pap. 21.95 (*1-887472-71-1*) Sunstar Pubng.

Carman, Oneal. The Final Triumph: The Book of Revelation Revealed. 235p. (Orig.). (C). Date not set. pap. 12.95 (*0-9649675-0-2*) Gospel Gold.

— Golden Age, 2000: Coming of the Prince. rev. ed. Eldredge, A., ed. 230p. 1994. pap. 10.00 (*1-885857-09-8*) Four Wnds Pubng.

— The Handshake That Shook the World. 48p. (Orig.). (C). 1994. pap. 3.95 (*0-9649675-1-0*) Gospel Gold.

Carman, Paul & Tigwell, Paul. CATIA Reference Guide. LC 98-9653. 608p. (C). 1998. pap. 52.95 (*1-56690-155-3*) Thomson Learn.

— Inside CATIA. 2nd ed. LC 97-47325. 424p. (C). 1998. pap. 95.95 (*1-56690-153-7*, 2017) Thomson Learn.

Carman, Peter. Quantitative Investment for the Global Markets: Strategies, Tactics, & Advanced Analytical Techniques. (Glenlake Business Monographs). 400p. 1998. 65.00 (*1-884964-71-0*) Fitzroy Dearborn.

Carman, Peter, ed. Quantitative Investing for the Global Markets: Strategies, Tactics & Advanced Analytical Techniques. 400p. 1997. 65.00 (*1-888998-03-2*) Glenlake Pub.

Carman, Rebecca W., jt. ed. see Bassuk, Ellen L.

Carman, Robert A. & Adams, Royce W., Jr. Study Skills: A Student's Guide for Survival. 2nd ed. LC 83-5925. (Self-Teaching Guides Ser.: No. 1-581). 272p. (C). 1984. pap. 16.95 (*0-471-88911-3*) Wiley.

Carman, Robert A. & Carman, Marilyn J. Quick Arithmetic: A Self-Teaching Guide. 2nd ed. LC 83-3531. 304p. 1984. pap. 17.95 (*0-471-88966-0*, 1-581) Wiley.

Carman, Robert A. & Saunders, Hal M. Mathematics for the Trades: A Guided Approach. 5th ed. LC 98-18951. 617p. (C). 1998. pap. text 71.00 (*0-13-907783-9*) P-H.

Carman, Robert A., jt. auth. see Cain, Jack.

Carman, Rochelle A. Fifty Great Ideas to Celebrate Casimir Pulaski Day: A Teacher's Guide. 20p. 1995. pap. text 6.95 (*1-886325-14-6*) DanNiall Pubng.

— Stanley the Sleuth Uncovers the Story of Casimir Pulaski. LC 94-93853. (Illus.). 40p. (J). (gr. k-4). 1995. 14.95 (*1-886325-18-9*) DanNiall Pubng.

***Carman, Wayne.** Elvis's Karate Legacy: The Untold Story of Elvis Presley's Faith, Spirit & Discipline. (Illus.). 268p. 1998. 39.95 (*0-9665537-0-5*) Legacy Ent.

Carmandi, Olivia R. MVS-JCL (OS-390) Quick Reference Guide. 2nd rev. ed. (Mainframe Ser.). 80p. 1998. pap. text 22.00 (*1-892559-00-5*) M V S Train.

— MVS-TSO (OS-390) Quick Reference Guide. 2nd rev. ed. (Mainframe Ser.). 113p. 1998. pap. text 22.00 (*1-892559-01-3*) M V S Train.

Carmandi, Olivia R., ed. see Gargiulo, Gabriel F.

***Carmann, Martin.** Mensch: Moral--Religion: Kant-lekturen Aus der Polykontexturalen Gesellschaft. (Beitrage zur Rationalen Theologie Ser.). 373p. 1999. 56.95 (*3-631-34738-3*) P Lang Pubng.

Carmean, E. A., Jr. Helen Frankenthaler: A Paintings Retrospective. Whelchel, Harriet, ed. LC 88-39301. (Illus.). 120p. (Orig.). 1989. pap. write for info. (*0-929865-01-4*) Mod Art Mus Ft Worth.

Carmean, E. A., Jr., frwd. Dubuffet Prints from the Museum of Modern Art. LC 88-36830. (Illus.). 107p. (Orig.). 1989. pap. 19.95 (*0-929865-02-2*) Mod Art Mus Ft Worth.

Carmean, E. A., Jr. & Morgan, Robert C. Nancy Graves: Recent Works. 40p. 1993. pap. 15.00 (*0-9624565-3-5*) Univ MD Fine Arts.

Carmean, Karen. Ernest J. Gaines: A Critical Companion. LC 97-48578. (Critical Companions to Popular Contemporary Writers Ser.). 184p. 1998. 29.95 (*0-313-30286-3*, Greenwood Pr) Greenwood.

Carmean, Karen. Toni Morrison's World of Fiction. vi, 127p. 1993. 28.50 (*0-87875-432-6*) Whitston Pub.

Carmean, Karen & Gaston, George M. Robert Shaw: More Than a Life. LC 93-25434. (Illus.). 350p. 1994. 22.95 (*1-56833-021-9*) Madison Bks UPA.

Carmel. Global Software Teams. LC 98-53011. 208p. 1998. pap. 39.00 (*0-13-924218-X*) P-H.

Carmel, Abraham. So Strange My Path: A Spiritual Pilgrimage. rev. ed. LC 93-1282. 296p. 1993. pap. 9.95 (*0-8197-0040-1*) Bloch.

Carmel, Amos. Israel: Vision & Reality. (Illus.). 224p. 1992. 38.00 (*965-05-0629-2*, Pub. by Israel Ministry Def) Gefen Bks.

Carmel, Aryeh, tr. see Dessler, Rabbi E.

Carmel, Hesi. Intelligence for Peace: The Role of Intelligence in Times of Peace. LC 99-21115. (Peacekeeping Ser.). 288p. 1999. 59.50 (*0-7146-4950-3*, Pub. by F Cass Pubs) Intl Spec Bk.

***Carmel, Hesi.** Intelligence for Peace: The Role of Intelligence in Times of Peace. LC 99-21115. (Peacekeeping Ser.). 288p. 1999. pap. 27.50 (*0-7146-8009-5*, Pub. by F Cass Pubs) Intl Spec Bk.

Carmel, Paula, jt. auth. see Toomey, Marilyn M.

Carmel, Shlomo, tr. see Rubinowitz, Chaim D.

Carmel, Shlomo, tr. see Yerushalmi, Shmuel.

Carmeli, M., et al. Gauge Fields: Classification & Equations of Motion. 148p. (C). 1989. text 30.00 (*9971-5-0745-5*) World Scientific Pub.

— Gravitation: SL (2, C) Gauge Theory & Conservation Laws. 116p. (C). 1990. text 30.00 (*981-02-0160-5*) World Scientific Pub.

Carmeli, Moshe. Classical Fields: General Relativity & Gauge Theory. LC 82-2704. (Wiley-Interscience Publications). 670p. reprint ed. pap. 200.00 (*0-7837-2390-3*, 204007500006) Bks Demand.

***Carmeli, Moshe.** Group Theory & General Relativity: Representations of the Lorentz Group & Their Applications to the Gravitational Field. 400p. 2000. 58.00 (*1-86094-234-2*, Pub. by Imperial College) World Scientific Pub.

Carmeli, Moshe & Malin, S. Representations of the Rotation & Lorentz Groups: An Introduction. LC 76-3337. (Lecture Notes in Pure & Applied Mathematics Ser.: No. 16). 133p. reprint ed. pap. 41.30 (*0-7837-4228-2*, 204391500012) Bks Demand.

***Carmeli, Moshe & Malin, Shimon.** The Theory of Spinors: An Introduction. LC 00-26040. 230p. 2000. 36.00 (*981-02-4261-1*) World Scientific Pub.

Carmeliet, P. Production, Release & Paracrine Action of Acetylcholine in the Anterior Pituitary of the Rat. No. 10. 123p. (Orig.). 1989. pap. 32.50 (*90-6186-316-3*, Pub. by Leuven Univ) Coronet Bks.

Carmelinc, Vizcarrondo. Campanerito Azul: Poemas para Ninos. LC 84-28124. (Ninos y Letras Ser.). (Illus.). 72p. (C). 1985. pap. 5.00 (*0-8477-3528-1*) U of PR Pr.

***Carmelita, C.** Lost Souls & Fallen Spirits, 1. (Tien-Tu Ser.). 305p. 1999. pap. 15.00 (*0-9668012-6-1*) Enlighten Noah.

Carmelite Sisters of Indianapolis Staff. The Woman's Prayer Companion. 218p. 1993. pap. 13.95 (*1-886873-04-6*) Carmelites IN.

Carmelite Sisters of the Eucharist of Colchester,, tr. see Piat, Stephane-Joseph.

Carmelites of Indianapolis Staff. Companion to the Brevairy: A Four-Week Psalter with Intercessions. rev. ed. 184p. 1999. pap. 9.95 (*1-886873-14-3*) Carmelites IN.

— Hidden Friends: Growing in Prayer. LC 96-145866. (Illus.). 100p. (Orig.). 1995. pap. 9.95 (*1-55612-824-X*) Sheed & Ward WI.

— People's Companion to the Breviary: Revised & Expanded Edition of the New Companion to the Breviary with Seasonal Supplement, 2 vols. Incl. Vol. 1. LC 96-228014. 576p. 1997. pap. (*1-886873-09-7*); Vol. 2. LC 96-228014. 560p. 1997. pap. (*1-886873-11-9*); LC 96-228014. 1997. Set pap. 29.95 (*1-886873-12-7*) Carmelites IN.

Carmelites of Indianapolis Staff, rev. Scripture Readings: Advent to Pentecost. 420p. 1989. pap. 12.00 (*1-886873-00-3*) Carmelites IN.

— Scripture Readings: Ordinary Time Weeks 10-34. 356p. 1990. pap. 12.00 (*1-886873-01-1*) Carmelites IN.

Carmell, Aryeh. Aiding Talmud Study. 5th ed. (Illus.). 88p. 1987. pap. 9.95 (*0-87306-428-3*) Feldheim.

— Masterplan, Judaism: Its Program, Meanings, & Goals. 1991. pap. 17.95 (*0-87306-581-6*) Feldheim.

***Carmell, Aryeh.** Masterplan, Judaism: Its Program, Meanings, & Goals. 1999. 11.95 (*1-58330-369-3*) Feldheim.

— Strive for Truth, 3 vols. 34.95 (*1-58330-352-9*) Feldheim.

— Strive for Truth, 6 vols. 1999. 109.95 (*1-58330-350-2*) Feldheim.

— Strive for Truth, Vols. 5 & 6. 1999. 39.95 (*1-58330-354-5*) Feldheim.

— Strive for Truth: Sanctuaries in Time, Vol. 4. 18.95 (*0-87306-692-8*) Feldheim.

Carmell, Aryeh & Domb, Cyril, eds. Challenge. 1978. 23.95 (*0-87306-174-8*) Feldheim.

Carmell, Aryeh, tr. see Dessler, E. E.

Carmell, Pamella, tr. & intro. see Male, Belkis C.

Carmelle, Susan A. Children of Impaired Parents: Index of New Information for Reference & Research. 160p. 1997. 47.50 (*0-7883-1752-0*); pap. 44.50 (*0-7883-1753-9*) ABBE Pubs Assn.

Carmello, Charles. La Mattanza: The Sicilian Madness. LC 86-22965. 407p. 1986. 17.95 (*0-88191-040-6*) Freundlich.

Carmelly, Felicia S. Shattered! 50 Years of Silence: History & Voices from the Tragedy in Romania & Transnistria. LC 96-931348. (Illus.). xxvi, 506p. 1997. write for info. (*0-9699521-0-4*) Transnistria.

Carmen Baerga, Maria Del, see Del Carmen Baerga, Maria.

Carmen, Christopher U. How to Search & Negotiate for Office Space. 72p. 1999. pap. 49.95 (*1-928742-02-5*) Vision Pubns IN.

Carmen, Christopher U., jt. auth. see Chessler, Karen E.

Carmen, Concepcion M. Del, see Silva, Carlos & Del Carmen, Concepcion M.

Carmen De La Cal, Maria, ed. Recetas: Biblioteca Universitaria, Salamanca MS.2262. (Medieval Spanish Medical Texts Ser.: No. 20). (SPA.). 6p. 1987. 10.00 incl. fiche (*0-940639-16-5*) Hispanic Seminary.

Carmen, Edna Creekmore. A Day of Rest. (Illus.). 184p. (YA). (gr. 4-9). 1994. pap. 9.75 (*0-935680-57-8*) Kentucke Imprints.

Carmen, Elaine H. The Rape Victim: A Project of the Committee on Women of the American Psychiatric Association. LC 76-5627. 110p. reprint ed. pap. 34.10 (*0-8357-7799-5*, 203616400002) Bks Demand.

Carmen, Elaine H., jt. ed. see Rieker, Patricia P.

Carmen, G. E., et al. Residue Reviews, Vol. 62. LC 62-18595. (Illus.). 176p. 1976. 101.00 (*0-387-90158-2*) Spr-Verlag.

Carmen, John, et al, eds. Managing Archaeology. LC 94-47092. (TAG Ser.). (Illus.). 280p. (C). (gr. 13). 1995. 75.00 (*0-415-10674-5*, C0033) Routledge.

Carmen, John & Juergensmeyer, Mark, eds. Bibliography of Comparative Religious Ethics. 817p. (C). 1991. text 130.00 (*0-521-34448-4*) Cambridge U Pr.

Carmen, Oneal. Golden Age, 2000: Coming of the Prince. 2nd rev. ed. 230p. 1994. pap. write for info. (*0-614-10116-6*) Gospel Gold.

Carmen, Richard, ed. The Consumer Handbook on Hearing Loss & Hearing Aids: A Bridge to Healing. (Illus.). 262p. 1998. pap. 18.95 (*0-9661826-0-X*) Auricle Ink.

Carment, Bill, jt. auth. see Alcock, Jim.

***Carment, David & Harvey, Frank.** Preventing, Managing & Resolving Intrastate Ethnic Conflict: An Evaluation of Theory & Evidence. LC 99-86108. (Praeger Studies on Ethnic & National Identities in Politics). 224p. 2000. 49.00 (*0-275-96979-7*, C6979, Praeger Pubs) Greenwood.

Carment, David & James, Patrick, eds. Wars in the Midst of Peace: The International Politics of Ethnic Conflict. LC 96-51262. (Policy & Institutional Studies). 302p. 1997. pap. 19.95 (*0-8229-5626-8*); text 45.00 (*0-8229-3975-4*) U of Pittsburgh Pr.

Carment, David, ed. see Stack, John.

Carmer, Carl. The Hudson. 434p. 1993. reprint ed. lib. bdg. 99.00 (*0-7812-5118-4*) Rprt Serv.

— The Hudson. 50th rev. ed. LC 39-27579. (Illus.). xii, 338p. (C). 1989. pap. 20.00 (*0-8232-1226-2*) Fordham.

— Listen for a Lonesome Drum. 381p. 1993. reprint ed. lib. bdg. 89.00 (*0-7812-5119-2*) Rprt Serv.

— Listen for a Lonesome Drum: A York State Chronicle. LC 94-42361. 450p. 1995. pap. 17.95 (*0-8156-0261-8*) Syracuse U Pr.

— My Kind of Country: Favorite Writings about New York. LC 94-42338. 292p. 1995. pap. 15.95 (*0-8156-0310-X*) Syracuse U Pr.

***Carmer, Carl.** Stars Fell on Alabama. (Orig.). 2000. pap. 19.95 (*0-8173-1072-X*) U of Ala Pr.

Carmer, Carl. Stars Fell on Alabama. LC 85-8107. (Library of Alabama Classics). 320p. (Orig.). 1985. reprint ed. pap. 19.95 (*0-8173-0235-2*) U of Ala Pr.

Carmer, Carl, ed. Tavern Lamps Are Burning: Literary Journeys Through Six Regions & Four Centuries of New York. rev. ed. LC 96-28634. (Illus.). xix, 567p. 1996. reprint ed. 35.00 (*0-8232-1697-7*); reprint ed. pap. 19.95 (*0-8232-1698-5*) Fordham.

Carmer, Carl L. For the Rights of Men. LC 75-86740. (Essay Index Reprint Ser.). 1977. 18.95 (*0-8369-1175-X*) Ayer.

Carmi, A. & Schneider, Stephen H., eds. Hospital Law. (Medicolegal Library: Vol. 7). 225p. 1988. 118.00 (*0-387-18642-5*) Spr-Verlag.

Carmi, Amnon. Forensic Psychiatry. Levy, Amihay et al, eds. (Psychiatry, Law & Ethics Ser.). iii, 377p. 1999. pap. 55.00 (*965-7077-05-2*, 324090) W S Hein.

Carmi, Amnon, jt. ed. see Beran, Roy G.

An Asterisk (*) at the beginning of an entry indicates that the title is appearing for the first time.

***Carmi, Daniella.** Samir & Yonatan. LC 99-30705. (Illus.). 160p. (J). (gr. 3-7). 2000. 15.95 (0-439-13504-4, A A Levine) Scholastic Inc.

Carmi, Giora. The Greatest of All: A Japanese Folktale. LC 90-23658. 32p. (J). (gr. k-3). 1991. lib. bdg. 16.95 (0-8234-0885-X) Holiday.

— The Old Woman & Her Pig. 32p. (J). (ps-3). 1992. pap. 6.95 (0-8234-1234-2) Holiday.

— The Old Woman & Her Pig. LC 91-44185. 32p. (J). (gr. k-3). 1992. lib. bdg. 16.95 (0-8234-0970-8) Holiday.

Carmi, S., ed. see AIAA-ASME Joint Fluids, Plasma Thermophysics, & Heat Transfer Staff.

Carmi, Shlomo & Aung, Win, eds. Engineering Education: Curriculum Innovation & Integration. 460p. 1992. pap. text 40.00 (0-939204-50-9) Eng Found.

Carmi, T. At the Stone of Losses. Schulman, Grace, tr. from HEB. (Illus.). 192p. (Orig.). (C). 1983. pap. 15.95 (0-520-05107-6, Pub. by U CA Pr) Cal Prin Full Svc.

Carmi, T., ed. The Penguin Book of Hebrew Verse. (ENG & HEB.). 448p. (Orig.). 1981. pap. 18.95 (0-14-042197-1, Penguin Bks) Viking Penguin.

Carmical, Frank D. The Omega Reunion. 110p. (Orig.). 1986. pap. 3.95 (0-9607576-5-1) Redencion Viva.

Carmical, Phil, ed. see Warren, Bill.

Carmical, Phillip, ed. see Barrett, Anna P.

Carmical, Phillip, ed. see Kelsaw, James W., Sr.

Carmical, Phillip, ed. see Night, Joseph.

Carmical, Phillip, ed. see Roy, Ann S.

Carmical, Phillip D., ed. see Hayes, Warren S.

Carmical, Phillip D., ed. see Young, Ron.

Carmichael. Color Atlas of Osteochondrosis in the Dog. (Illus.). 1993. write for info. (0-8151-1438-9) Mosby Inc.

Carmichael, Alexander. Celtic Prayers. 128p. 1996. pap. 6.00 (0-385-48241-8, Image Bks) Doubleday.

— Thou Harp of My Music: Love Songs from the Gaelic. 128p. 1999. pap. 9.95 (0-86315-293-7) Anthroposophic.

Carmichael, Alexander, ed. Carmina Gadelica: Hymns & Incantations from the Gaelic. (Illus.). 512p. (Orig.). 1992. pap. 19.95 (0-940262-50-9, Lindisfarne) Anthroposophic.

Carmichael, Alexander, tr. from GAE. New Moon of the Seasons: Prayers from the Highlands & Islands. 160p. 1992. reprint ed. pap. 8.95 (0-940262-51-7, Lindisfarne) Anthroposophic.

— The Sun Dances: Prayers & Blessings from the Gaelic. 144p. 1990. pap. 9.95 (0-86315-503-0, 448, Pub. by Floris Bks) Anthroposophic.

Carmichael, Alexander D. Ocean Engineering Power Systems. LC 74-4343. (Massachusetts Institute of Technology, Sea Grant Program Ser.: Report No. MITSG 74-15). (Illus.). 206p. 1974. reprint ed. pap. 63.90 (0-7837-9068-6, 204981700003) Bks Demand.

Carmichael, Amy. Candles in the Dark. 1982. pap. text 5.99 (0-87508-085-5) Chr Lit.

— Edges of His Ways. 1992. pap. 11.99 (0-87508-062-6) Chr Lit.

— Figures of the True. 1991. pap. 1.95 (0-87508-065-0) Chr Lit.

— God's Missionary. 1992. pap. 3.50 (0-87508-323-4) Chr Lit.

— Gold by Moonlight. 232p. 1992. pap. 11.99 (0-87508-087-1) Chr Lit.

— Gold Cord. 1992. pap. 12.99 (0-87508-068-5) Chr Lit.

— His Thoughts Said... His Father Said. 1993. pap. 4.99 (0-87508-069-3) Chr Lit.

— If. 1988. mass mkt. 3.75 (0-87508-429-X) Chr Lit.

— If. 1992. pap. 4.99 (0-87508-071-5) Chr Lit.

— Mimosa. 1992. mass mkt. 5.99 (0-87508-074-X) Chr Lit.

— Mountain Breezes: The Collected Poems of Amy Carmichael. 470p. 1999. 29.95 (0-87508-790-6, 790) Chr Lit.

— Mountain Breezes: The Collected Poems of Amy Carmichael. 470p. 1999. pap. 15.95 (0-87508-789-2, 789) Chr Lit.

— Rose from Brier. 1992. mass mkt. 6.99 (0-87508-077-4) Chr Lit.

— Thou Givest... They Gather. 1991. pap. 6.99 (0-87508-083-9) Chr Lit.

— Toward Jerusalem. 1989. pap. 5.99 (0-87508-080-4) Chr Lit.

— A Very Present Help: Life Messages of Great Christians. LC 96-26543. (Life Messages of Great Christians Ser.: Vol. 1). 180p. (Orig.). 1996. pap. 10.99 (0-89283-978-3, Vine Bks) Servant.

— Whispers of His Power. 288p. 1993. pap. 11.99 (0-87508-317-X) Chr Lit.

— You Are My Hiding Place. rev. ed. Hazard, David, ed. (Rekindling the Inner Fire Ser.: Vol. 2). 128p. 1991. pap. 8.99 (1-55661-205-2) Bethany Hse.

Carmichael, Amy, et al. Learning of God. 1986. pap. 8.99 (0-87508-086-3) Chr Lit.

Carmichael, Amy W. If. (Illus.). 64p. 1980. 5.70 (0-310-42202-7, 6885P) Zondervan.

Carmichael, Andy, ed. Developing Business Objects. LC 97-17361. (Managing Object Technology Ser.: No. 11). 336p. 1998. pap. text 39.95 (0-521-64825-4) Cambridge U Pr.

— Object Development Methods. LC 93-87695. (Advances in Object Technology Ser.: No. 3). 374p. 1994. pap. 39.95 (0-13-131591-9) Cambridge U Pr.

Carmichael, Ann, jt. auth. see Sparkman, Brandon B.

Carmichael, Ann Carlisle, ed. see Fitzhugh, Robert H.

***Carmichael, C. J.** A Daughter's Place. (Superromance Ser.). 2000. mass mkt. 4.50 (0-373-70956-0, 1709567) Harlequin Bks.

— Fourth Child, Vol. 917. (Harlequin Super Romance Ser.). 2000. mass mkt. 4.50 (0-373-70917-X) Harlequin Bks.

— Her Best Friend's Baby: (9 Months Later) (Superromance Ser.: No. 891). 2000. mass mkt. 4.25 (0-373-70891-2, 1-70891-6, Harlequin) Harlequin Bks.

Carmichael, C. J. Jessie's Father: Family Man. (Superromance Ser.: Bk. 851). 1999. per. 4.25 (0-373-70851-3, 1-70851-0) Harlequin Bks.

***Carmichael, C. J.** Safe at Home. (Superromance Ser.: No. 892). 2000. mass mkt. 4.25 (0-373-70892-0, 1-70892-4, Harlequin) Harlequin Bks.

Carmichael, C. J. Same Place, Same Time. (Intrigue Ser.: Bk. 548). 2000. per. 3.99 (0-373-22548-2, 1-22548-1) Harlequin Bks.

Carmichael, Calum & Daube, David. Law, Morality & Religion: Global Perspectives. Watson, Alan, ed. LC 96-27777. (Studies in Comparative Legal History). 226p. 1996. 40.00 (1-882239-08-3) Robbins Collection.

Carmichael, Calum, et al. Essays on Law & Religion: The Berkeley & Oxford Symposia in Honour of David Daube. LC 93-32732. (Studies in Comparative Legal History). 107p. (C). 1993. 30.00 (1-882239-02-4) Robbins Collection.

Carmichael, Calum C. The Story of Creation: Its Origin & Its Interpretation in Philosophy & the Fourth Gospel. LC 96-6131. 144p. 1996. text 27.50 (0-8014-3261-8) Cornell U Pr.

Carmichael, Calum M. Law & Narrative in the Bible: The Evidence of the Deuteronomic Laws & the Decalogue. LC 85-4214. 356p. (C). 1985. 47.50 (0-8014-1792-9) Cornell U Pr.

— Law, Legend, & Incest in the Bible: Leviticus 18-20. LC 96-52609. 224p. 1996. text 35.00 (0-8014-3388-6) Cornell U Pr.

— The Origins of Biblical Law: The Decalogues & the Book of the Covenant. LC 92-6908. 272p. 1992. text 37.50 (0-8014-2712-6) Cornell U Pr.

— The Spirit of Biblical Law. LC 96-21568. (Spirit of the Laws Ser.). 1996. text 35.00 (0-8203-1845-0) U of Ga Pr.

Carmichael, Calum M., ed. see Daube, David.

Carmichael, Calum M., ed. & tr. see Daube, David.

Carmichael, Carrie, jt. auth. see Storch, Marcia L.

***Carmichael, Cathie, compiled by.** Croatia. (World Bibliographical Ser.: Vol. 216). 300p. 1999. lib. bdg. 64.00 (1-85109-285-4) ABC-CLIO.

Carmichael, Cathie, compiled by. Slovenia. LC 96-191948. (World Bibliographical Ser.: Vol. 186). 194p. 1996. lib. bdg. 66.00 (1-85109-239-0, DR1375) ABC-CLIO.

Carmichael, Cathie, jt. auth. see Gow, James.

Carmichael, Cathie, jt. ed. see Barbour, Stephen.

Carmichael, Chris & Burke, Edmund R. Fitness Cycling. LC 93-42156. (Fitness Spectrum Ser.). (Illus.). 176p. 1994. pap. 14.95 (0-87322-460-4, PCAR0460) Human Kinetics.

Carmichael, Clay. Bear at the Beach. LC 95-46289. (Illus.). 48p. (J). (gr. 1-3). 1996. 13.95 (1-55858-569-9, Pub. by North-South Bks NYC); lib. bdg. 13.88 (1-55858-570-2, Pub. by North-South Bks NYC) Chronicle Bks.

— Bear at the Beach. LC 95-46289. (Illus.). 48p. (J). (gr. 1-3). 1998. pap. 5.95 (1-55858-903-1, Pub. by North-South Bks NYC) Chronicle Bks.

***Carmichael, Clay.** Bear at the Beach. (Illus.). (J). 1998. 11.40 (0-606-18315-9) Turtleback.

— El Osito Usado. Moro, Elena, tr.Tr. of Used-Up Bear. (SPA., Illus.). 48p. (J). (gr. 1-3). 2000. pap. 5.95 (0-7358-1306-X, Pub. by North-South Bks NYC) Chronicle Bks.

— El Osito Usado.Tr. of Used-Up Bear. (SPA., Illus.). (J). 2000. 11.40 (0-606-18319-1) Turtleback.

— Used-Up Bear. LC 97-32225. (Illus.). 48p. (J). (gr. 1-3). 1998. lib. bdg. 13.88 (1-55858-902-3, Pub. by North-South Bks NYC) Chronicle Bks.

***Carmichael, Clay.** Used-Up Bear. LC 97-32225. (Illus.). 48p. (J). (gr. 1-3). 1998. 13.95 (1-55858-901-5, Pub. by North-South Bks NYC) Chronicle Bks.

— Used-Up Bear. (Illus.). 48p. (J). (gr. k-3). 2000. pap. 5.95 (0-7358-1305-1, Pub. by North-South Bks NYC) Chronicle Bks.

Carmichael, Cynthia G. AIDS & HIV Essentials. 83p. 1999. pap. text 22.00 (1-879772-13-2) Health Studies.

— HIV/AIDS Primary Care Handbook. 228p. (C). 1995. pap. text 19.95 (0-8385-3557-7, A3557-4, Apple Lange Med) McGraw.

Carmichael, D. G. Engineering Queues in Construction & Mining. (Engineering Science Ser.). 378p. 1987. text 69.95 (0-470-20831-7) P-H.

Carmichael, D. G., jt. ed. see Wakefield, R. R.

***Carmichael, D. R.** Wiley Practitioner's Guide to GAAS: Student Guide. 528p. 1998. pap. 37.95 (0-471-29853-0) Wiley.

***Carmichael, D. R., et al.** Accountant's Handbook, 2 vols. Set. 9th ed. Incl. Vol. 1. Accountant's Handbook. 9th ed. LC 98-39840. 1056p. 1999. pap. 80.00 (0-471-29594-9); Vol. 2. Accountant's Handbook. 9th ed. LC 98-39840. 768p. 1999. pap. 80.00 (0-471-29595-7); LC 98-39840. 1808p. 1999. Set pap. 135.00 (0-471-29122-6) Wiley.

Carmichael, D. R., jt. auth. see Guy, Dan M.

Carmichael, David. Construction Engineering Networks: Techniques, Planning & Management. 1989. text 76.95 (0-470-21491-0) P-H.

Carmichael, David L. & Hubert, Jane, eds. Sacred Sites Sacred Places. (One World Archaeology Ser.: 23). (Illus.). 328p. (C). 1997. pap. 32.99 (0-415-15226-7) Routledge.

Carmichael, Douglas R. & Willingham, John J. Auditing Concepts & Methods: A Guide to Current Theory & Practice. 6th ed. LC 95-33427. 621p. (C). 1995. 89.06 (0-07-011058-1) McGraw.

Carmichael, Douglas R., et al. Accounting & Auditing Update Handbook 1989. LC 89-643780. 461p. reprint ed. pap. 143.00 (0-8357-4114-1, 203689400005) Bks Demand.

— Accounting & Auditing Update Handbook, 1991. fac. ed. LC 89-643780. 488p. 1990. pap. 151.30 (0-7837-8238-1, 204900200009) Bks Demand.

Carmichael, Douglas R., et al. Guide to Audits of Employee Benefit Plans, 3 vols. Incl. Vol. 1. 1997. ring bd. 172.00 (0-7646-0320-5); Vol. 2. 1997. ring bd. 172.00 (0-7646-0321-3); Vol. 3. 1997. ring bd. 172.00 (0-7646-0322-1); 172.00 (0-7646-0319-1) Prctnrs Pub Co.

— Guide to Audits of Employee Benefit Plans, 3 vols. 1999. ring bd. 180.00 (0-7646-0940-8) Prctnrs Pub Co.

Carmichael, Douglas R., et al. Guide to Audits of Employee Benefit Plans, Vol. 1. 1998. ring bd. write for info. (0-7646-0634-4) Prctnrs Pub Co.

***Carmichael, Douglas R., et al.** Guide to Audits of Employee Benefit Plans, Vol. 1. 1999. ring bd. write for info. (0-7646-0941-6) Prctnrs Pub Co.

Carmichael, Douglas R., et al. Guide to Audits of Employee Benefit Plans, Vol. 2. 1998. ring bd. write for info. (0-7646-0635-2) Prctnrs Pub Co.

***Carmichael, Douglas R., et al.** Guide to Audits of Employee Benefit Plans, Vol. 2. 1999. ring bd. write for info. (0-7646-0942-4) Prctnrs Pub Co.

Carmichael, Douglas R., et al. Guide to Audits of Employee Benefit Plans, Vol. 3. 1998. ring bd. write for info. (0-7646-0636-0) Prctnrs Pub Co.

***Carmichael, Douglas R., et al.** Guide to Audits of Employee Benefit Plans, Vol. 3. 1999. ring bd. write for info. (0-7646-0943-2) Prctnrs Pub Co.

Carmichael, Douglas R., et al. Guide to Audits of Employee Benefit Plans, Vols. 1-3. 1998. ring bd. 180.00 (0-7646-0633-6) Prctnrs Pub Co.

— Guide to Audits of Financial Institutions, 4 vols. Incl. Vol. 1. Guide to Audits of Financial Institutions. Ecklund, Kathy J. & Brauer, David C. 1998. ring bd. 278.00 (0-7646-0506-2); Vol. 2. Guide to Audits of Financial Institutions. Ecklund, Kathy J. & Brauer, David C. 1998. ring bd. (0-7646-0507-0); Vol. 3. Guide to Audits of Financial Institutions. Ecklund, Kathy J. & Brauer, David C. 1998. ring bd. 278.00 (0-7646-0508-9); Vol. 4. Guide to Audits of Financial Institutions. Ecklund, Kathy J. & Brauer, David C. 1998. ring bd. 278.00 (0-7646-0509-7); Vol. 1. Ecklund, Kathy J. 1997. ring bd. (1-56433-998-X); Vol. 2. Ecklund, Kathy J. 1997. ring bd. (1-56433-999-8); Vol. 3. Eklund, Kathy J. 1997. ring bd. (0-7646-0000-1); Vol. 4. Ecklund, Kathy J. 1997. ring bd. (0-7646-0001-X); 265.00 (1-56433-997-1); 278.00 (0-7646-0505-4) Prctnrs Pub Co.

— A Guide to Audits of Local Governments, 4 vols. Incl. Vol. 1. 1997. ring bd. (0-7646-0081-8); Vol. 2. 1997. ring bd. (0-7646-0082-6); Vol. 3. 1997. ring bd. (0-7646-0083-4); Vol. 4. 1997. ring bd. (0-7646-0084-2); 165.00 (0-7646-0080-X) Prctnrs Pub Co.

— Guide to Audits of Nonprofit Organizations, 3 vols. Incl. Vol. 1. Guide to Audits of Nonprofit Organizations. Holland, Stephen F. 1998. ring bd. 184.00 (0-7646-0438-4); Vol. 2. Guide to Audits of Nonprofit Organizations. Holland, Stephen E. 1998. ring bd. 184.00 (0-7646-0439-2); Vol. 3. Guide to Audits of Nonprofit Organizations. Holland, Stephen E. 1998. ring bd. 184.00 (0-7646-0440-6); Vol. 1. Holland, Stephen E. 1997. ring bd. (0-7646-0172-5); Vol. 2. Holland, Stephen E. 1997. ring bd. (0-7646-0173-3); Vol. 3. Holland, Stephen E. 1997. ring bd. (0-7646-0174-1); 184.00 (0-7646-0437-6) Prctnrs Pub Co.

Carmichael, Douglas R., et al. Guide to Audits of Nonprofit Organizations, 3 vols. Incl. Vol. 1. Guide to Audits of Nonprofit Organizations. Holland, Stephen F. 1998. ring bd. 184.00 (0-7646-0438-4); Vol. 2. Guide to Audits of Nonprofit Organizations. Holland, Stephen E. 1998. ring bd. 184.00 (0-7646-0439-2); Vol. 3. Guide to Audits of Nonprofit Organizations. Holland, Stephen E. 1998. ring bd. 184.00 (0-7646-0440-6); Vol. 1. Holland, Stephen E. 1997. ring bd. (0-7646-0172-5); Vol. 2. Holland, Stephen E. 1997. ring bd. (0-7646-0173-3); Vol. 3. Holland, Stephen E. 1997. ring bd. (0-7646-0174-1); 177.00 (0-7646-0171-7) Prctnrs Pub Co.

Carmichael, Douglas R., et al. Guide to Construction Contractors, 3 vols. Incl. Vol. 1. 1997. ring bd. 172.00 (0-7646-0258-6); Vol. 2. 1997. ring bd. 172.00 (0-7646-0259-4); Vol. 3. 1997. ring bd. 172.00 (0-7646-0260-8); 172.00 (0-7646-0257-8) Prctnrs Pub Co.

***Carmichael, Douglas R., et al.** Guide to Construction Contractors, 3 vols. 1999. ring bd. 180.00 (0-7646-0798-7) Prctnrs Pub Co.

Carmichael, Douglas R., et al. Guide to Construction Contractors, Vol. 1. 1998. ring bd. write for info. (0-7646-0548-8) Prctnrs Pub Co.

***Carmichael, Douglas R., et al.** Guide to Construction Contractors, Vol. 1. 1999. ring bd. write for info. (0-7646-0799-5) Prctnrs Pub Co.

Carmichael, Douglas R., et al. Guide to Construction Contractors, Vol. 2. 1998. ring bd. write for info. (0-7646-0549-6) Prctnrs Pub Co.

***Carmichael, Douglas R., et al.** Guide to Construction Contractors, Vol. 2. 1999. ring bd. write for info. (0-7646-0800-2) Prctnrs Pub Co.

Carmichael, Douglas R., et al. Guide to Construction Contractors, Vol. 3. 1998. ring bd. write for info. (0-7646-0550-X) Prctnrs Pub Co.

***Carmichael, Douglas R., et al.** Guide to Construction Contractors, Vol. 3. 1999. ring bd. write for info. (0-7646-0801-0) Prctnrs Pub Co.

Carmichael, Douglas R., et al. Guide to Construction Contractors, Vols. 1-3. 1998. ring bd. 180.00 (0-7646-0547-X) Prctnrs Pub Co.

— Guide to Small Business Consulting Engagements. 1997. ring bd. write for info. (0-7646-0151-2) Prctnrs Pub Co.

— A Guide to Small Business Consulting Engagements, 3 vols. Incl. Vol. 1. Guide to Small Business Consulting Engagements. 1997. ring bd. (0-7646-0149-0); 156.00 (0-7646-0148-2) Prctnrs Pub Co.

— Guide To Small Business Consulting Engagements, 3 vols. Incl. Vol. 1. 1998. ring bd. 164.00 (0-7646-0415-5); Vol. 2. 1998. ring bd. 164.00 (0-7646-0416-3); Vol. 3. 1998. ring bd. 164.00 (0-7646-0417-1); 164.00 (0-7646-0414-7) Prctnrs Pub Co.

— Guide to Small Business Consulting Engagements, Vol. 2. 1997. ring bd. write for info. (0-7646-0150-4) Prctnrs Pub Co.

— PPC's Guide To Audits of Small Businesses, 4 vols. Incl. Vol. 1. 1998. ring bd. 164.00 (0-7646-0427-9); Vol. 2. 1998. ring bd. 164.00 (0-7646-0428-7); Vol. 3. 1998. ring bd. 164.00 (0-7646-0429-5); Vol. 4. 1998. ring bd. 164.00 (0-7646-0430-9); 164.00 (0-7646-0426-0) Prctnrs Pub Co.

— PPC's Guide to Audits of Small Businesses, 4 vols. Incl. Vol. 1. 1997. ring bd. (0-7646-0180-6); Vol. 2. 1997. ring bd. (0-7646-0181-4); Vol. 3. 1997. ring bd. (0-7646-0182-2); Vol. 4. 1997. ring bd. (0-7646-0183-0); 150.00 (1-56433-947-5); 156.00 (0-7646-0179-2) Prctnrs Pub Co.

Carmichael, E., et al. Preparing for Global Change Vol. 9: A Midwestern Perspective. (Illus.). 302p. 1994. 100.00 (90-5103-102-5, Pub. by SPB Acad Pub) Balogh.

Carmichael, E. M. Timber Engineering: Practical Design Studies. 280p. (C). (gr. 13). 1984. pap. 39.99 (0-419-12700-3) Chapman & Bkman.

Carmichael, E. S. & Eugster, H. P., eds. Thermodynamic Modelling of Geological Materials: Minerals, Fluids, Melts. (Reviews in Mineralogy Ser.: Vol. 17). 499p. 1987. per. 28.00 (0-939950-21-9) Mineralogical Soc.

Carmichael, Elizabeth & Sayer, Chloe. The Skeleton at the Feast: The Day of the Dead in Mexico. LC 91-66304. (Illus.). 192p. (Orig.). 1991. pap. 29.95 (0-292-77658-6) U of Tex Pr.

Carmichael, Emily. Autumnfire. 1987. mass mkt. 3.95 (0-446-34717-5, Pub. by Warner Bks) Little.

— Finding Mr. Right: Sometimes Love Is Heaven-Sent. 368p. 1999. mass mkt. 5.50 (0-553-57874-X) Bantam.

— A Ghost for Maggie. 384p. 1999. mass mkt. 5.50 (0-553-57875-8) Bantam.

— Gold Dust. 352p. 1996. mass mkt. 5.99 (0-446-60297-3, Pub. by Warner Bks) Little.

— Lawless. 384p. (Orig.). 1993. mass mkt. 4.99 (0-446-36409-6, Pub. by Warner Bks) Little.

— Outcast. 368p. (Orig.). 1995. mass mkt. 5.99 (0-446-36411-8, Pub. by Warner Bks) Little.

— Surrender. 432p. 1988. mass mkt. 3.95 (0-446-35200-4, Pub. by Warner Bks) Little.

— Touch of Fire. 352p. 1989. mass mkt. 3.95 (0-446-35548-8, Pub. by Warner Bks) Little.

— Visions of the Heart. 1990. mass mkt. 4.95 (0-446-35748-0, Pub. by Warner Bks) Little.

— Windfall. 416p. 1997. mass mkt. 5.99 (0-446-60298-1, Pub. by Warner Bks) Little.

Carmichael, Fitzhugh L. & Nassimbene, Raymond. Changing Aspects of Urban Relief. LC 72-173446. (FDR & the Era of the New Deal Ser.). 94p. 1971. reprint ed. lib. bdg. 19.50 (0-306-70370-X) Da Capo.

Carmichael, Fred. Meet My Husbands: A Comedy in Two Acts. LC 98-232326. 94 p. 1997. write for info. (0-573-60230-1) French.

Carmichael, G., et al, eds. Sea Fare Cookbook. 184p. 1992. pap. 18.00 (0-913235-82-2, 530.15P) Am Fisheries Soc.

Carmichael, Harry. Deadly Nightcap. large type ed. (Linford Mystery Library). 432p. 1997. pap. 16.99 (0-7089-5095-7) Ulverscroft.

— A Grave for Two. large type ed. (Linford Mystery Library). 368p. 1997. pap. 16.99 (0-7089-5108-2, Linford) Ulverscroft.

— The Motive. large type ed. 320p. 1983. 27.99 (0-7089-0954-X) Ulverscroft.

— Post-Mortem. large type ed. 1978. 27.99 (0-7089-0142-5) Ulverscroft.

— A Slightly Bitter Taste. large type ed. (Linford Mystery Library). 480p. 1997. pap. 16.99 (0-7089-5160-0) Ulverscroft.

***Carmichael, Hoagy.** The Hoagy Carmichael Centennial Collection. (Illus.). 248p. 1999. otabind 19.95 (0-7935-8660-7) H Leonard.

Carmichael, Hoagy. Raffles & Other Singing Stories. Stearns, Helen M., ed. (Illus.). 44p. (J). (ps up). 1989. 14.95 (0-9614281-5-5, 1477, Cricketfld Pr) Picton Pr.

— Stardust Road. (American Autobiography Ser.). 156p. 1995. reprint ed. lib. bdg. 69.00 (0-7812-8474-0) Rprt Serv.

— The Stardust Road: Music Book Index. 1993. reprint ed. lib. bdg. 69.00 (0-7812-9575-0) Rprt Serv.

Carmichael, Hoagy, et al. The Stardust Road & Sometimes I Wonder: The Autobiography of Hoagy Carmichael. LC 98-46948. 512p. 1999. mass mkt. 17.95 (0-306-80899-4, Pub. by Da Capo) HarpC.

Carmichael, Hoagy B., jt. auth. see Garrison, Everett.

Carmichael, Howard. An Open Systems Approach to Quantum Optics: Lectures Presented at the Universite Libre de Bruxelles, October 28 to November 4, 1991. LC 93-19394. (Lecture Notes in Physics, New Series, Monographs: Vol. M18). x, 179p. 1993. 51.95 (0-387-56634-1) Spr-Verlag.

***Carmichael, Howard.** Quantum Statistical Methods in Quantum Optics. LC 98-40873. (Texts & Monographs in Physics Ser.). 1999. 64.95 (3-540-54882-3) Spr-Verlag.

Carmichael, J. & Strzepek, K. Industrial Water Use & Treatment Practices. 140p. 1987. text 90.00 (1-85148-019-6, Tycooly Pub) Weidner & Sons.

Carmichael, J. W., et al. Project SOAR: Stress on Analytical Reasoning. 186p. (C). 1989. pap. text 11.80 (0-87563-354-4) Stipes.

Carmichael, Jack B. Black Knight. (Trilogy of the Cousin Ser.). 89p. (Orig.). (YA). (gr. 12). 1991. pap. 9.95 (*0-9626948-1-9*) Dynamics MI.

***Carmichael, Jack B.** Hear Me, America! & Other Verse & Prose. 100p. 1999. lib. bdg. 21.95 incl. audio compact disk (*0-9626948-5-1*) Dynamics MI.

Carmichael, Jack B. The Humpty Boys in Michigan. 38p. (Orig.). 1996. pap. 9.95 (*0-9626948-4-3*) Dynamics MI.

— Memoirs of the Great Gorgeous. 50p. (Orig.). 1992. pap. 7.95 (*0-9626948-3-5*) Dynamics MI.

— Tales of the Cousin. (Trilogy of the Cousin Ser.). 80p. (Orig.). (YA). (gr. 12). 1992. pap. 9.95 (*0-9626948-2-7*) Dynamics MI.

Carmichael, Jacqueline M. Trumpeting a Fiery Sound: History & Folklore in Margaret Walker's Jubilee. LC 98-3672. 208p. 1998. text 35.00 (*0-8203-2010-2*) U of Ga Pr.

Carmichael, Jae, intro. Women Painters East-West. (Illus.). 100p. 1974. pap. 3.00 (*1-877921-21-1*) Pacific Asia.

Carmichael, James V., Jr., ed. Daring to Find Our Names: The Search for Lesbigay Library History, 5. LC 97-48579. (Beta Phi Mu Monograph). 272p. 1998. 59.95 (*0-313-29963-3*, Greenwood Pr) Greenwood.

Carmichael, Jean. Software Directory for Home Builders & Remodelers, 1996. 5th rev. ed. 112p. 1995. pap. 24.75 (*0-86718-413-2*) Home Builder.

— Software Product Directory for Builders & Remodelers: Updated for 1997. 6th rev. ed. 84p. 1997. pap. 24.75 (*0-86718-422-1*) Home Builder.

Carmichael, Jean, et al. CAD Reference Guide for Residential Construction. 112p. (Orig.). 1995. pap. 27.50 (*0-86718-415-9*) Home Builder.

Carmichael, Jeanne. A Match Made in Heaven. (Regency Romance Ser.). 1993. per. 2.99 (*0-373-31199-0*, 1-31199-2) Harlequin Bks.

— A Match Made in Heaven. 1999. per. 3.75 (*0-373-31222-9*) Harlequin Bks.

— Quest for Vengeance. rev. ed. (Regency Romance Ser.: No. 167). 1992. mass mkt. 2.99 (*0-373-31167-2*, 1-31167-9) Harlequin Bks.

Carmichael, Jim. Guns & Shooting Yearbook, 1988. 1988. 19.95 (*1-55654-025-6*) Times Mir Mag Bk Div.

***Carmichael, Joel.** Russia: An Illustrated History. (Illus.). 164p. 1998. 14.95 (*0-7818-0689-5*) Hippocrene Bks.

Carmichael, Joel. Satanizing of the Jews: Origin & Development of Mystical Anti-Semitism. 210p. 1995. pap. 10.95 (*0-88064-152-5*) Fromm Intl Pub.

— Satanizing of the Jews: Origin & History of Mystical Anti-Semitism. 210p. 1992. 18.95 (*0-88064-132-0*) Fromm Intl Pub.

— The Unriddling of Christian Origins: A Secular Account. LC 95-16635. 425p. 1995. 35.95 (*0-87975-952-6*) Prometheus Bks.

Carmichael, Joel, tr. see Aldanov, Mark.

Carmichael, Joel, tr. see Brockelmann, Carl.

Carmichael, Joel, tr. see Tolstoy, Leo.

Carmichael, John, Jr. & Bulmer, Charles. Labor & Employment Policy. (Orig.). (C). 1979. pap. 15.00 (*0-918592-35-6*) Pol Studies.

Carmichael, John P. My Greatest Day in Baseball. LC 95-40142. xii, 245p. 1996. pap. 12.95 (*0-8032-6368-6*, Bison Books) U of Nebr Pr.

Carmichael, Judy. You Can Play Stride Piano. pap. 19.95 incl. audio compact disk (*0-943748-79-8*) Ekay Music.

Carmichael, K. S. Corporation Tax Manual. pap. write for info. (*0-406-50261-7*, MICHIE) LEXIS Pub.

— Ranking, Spicer & Pegler: Executorship Law & Accounts. 23rd ed. 1988. 120.00 (*0-406-67901-0*, U.K., MICHIE) LEXIS Pub.

— Spicer & Pegler's Executorship Law & Accounts. 24th ed. boxed set. write for info. (*0-406-03598-9*, U.K., MICHIE) LEXIS Pub.

Carmichael, K. S. & Wolstenholme, P. H. Taxation of Lloyd's Underwriters. 4th ed. 1994. write for info. (*0-406-01138-9*, UK, MICHIE) LEXIS Pub.

Carmichael, Kay. For Crying Out Loud! 256p. (C). 1993. pap. write for info. (*1-874640-30-0*, Pub. by Argyll Pubng) St Mut.

Carmichael, Nancie. The Deeper Life. LC 99-34603. 1999. pap. text 9.99 (*0-8423-8586-X*) Tyndale Hse.

— Desperate for God: How He Meets Us When We Pray. LC 99-23343. 208p. 1999. 15.99 (*1-58134-089-3*) Crossway Bks.

— Your Life, God's Home: Knowing the Joy of His Presence. LC 98-19635. 208p. 1998. 15.99 (*1-58134-017-6*) Crossway Bks.

Carmichael, Nancie, jt. auth. see Carmichael, William.

Carmichael, Oliver C. Graduate Education: A Critique & a Program. LC 77-4229. 213p. 1977. reprint ed. lib. bdg. 59.50 (*0-8371-9585-3*, CAGE, Greenwood Pr) Greenwood.

— Universities: Commonwealth & American; a Comparative Study. LC 70-167323. (Essay Index Reprint Ser.). 1977. reprint ed. 22.95 (*0-8369-2760-5*) Ayer.

Carmichael, Paul. Central Local Government Relations in the 1980's. 368p. 1995. 82.95 (*1-85972-033-1*, Pub. by Avebury) Ashgate Pub Co.

Carmichael, Paul, jt. ed. see Dickson, Brice.

Carmichael, Pele & Hill, Leonard. The World's Most Beautiful Seashells. Ohr, Tim, ed. (World Nature Ser.). 240p. 1995. pap. 22.95 (*1-884942-00-8*) Wrld Tampa.

— The World's Most Beautiful Seashells. Ohr, Tim, ed. (World's Most Ser.). 240p. 1995. 34.95 (*1-884942-03-2*) Wrld Tampa.

Carmichael, Pete. Florida's Fabulous Reptiles & Amphibians. 128p. 1991. pap. 15.95 (*0-911977-11-2*) Wrld Tampa.

Carmichael, Pete, jt. auth. see Williams, Winston.

Carmichael, Peter. Nomads. (Illus.). 160p. 1993. 45.00 (*1-85585-061-3*) Trafalgar.

Carmichael, Peter L. The Purcell, Crenshaw & Letcher Artillery. (Virginia Regimental Histories Ser.). (Illus.). 234p. 1990. 19.95 (*0-930919-93-9*) H E Howard.

Carmichael, Peter S. Lee's Young Artillerist: William R. J. Pegram. (Nation Divided Ser.). 222p. 1998. reprint ed. pap. 15.95 (*0-8139-1828-6*) U Pr of Va.

Carmichael, Rachel, jt. auth. see Loney, Kevin.

Carmichael, Richard D. The Logic of Discovery. LC 74-26255. (History, Philosophy & Sociology of Science Ser.). 1975. reprint ed. 24.95 (*0-405-06583-3*) Ayer.

Carmichael, Richard E. Politics & Economics in America: The Way We Came to Be. LC 97-20172. 384p. 1997. 29.50 (*1-57524-056-4*) Krieger.

Carmichael, Robert D. & Smith, Edwin R. Mathematical Tables & Formulas. 269p. (C). 1962. pap. 6.95 (*0-486-60111-0*) Dover.

Carmichael, Robert S. Handbook of Physical Properties of Rocks: Seismic Velocities, Vol. I. 416p. 1982. 231.00 (*0-8493-0226-9*, QE431, CRC Reprint) Franklin.

— Handbook of Physical Properties of Rocks: Seismic Velocities, Vol. II. 360p. 1982. 199.00 (*0-8493-0227-7*, CRC Reprint) Franklin.

— Handbook of Physical Properties of Rocks: Seismic Velocities, Vol. III. 360p. 1984. lib. bdg. 128.00 (*0-8493-0228-5*, CRC Reprint) Franklin.

— Practical Handbook of Physical Properties of Rocks & Minerals. 744p. 1988. lib. bdg. 89.95 (*0-8493-3703-8*, QE431) CRC Pr.

***Carmichael, Stephen & Stoddard, Susan.** Climbing Mount Kilimanjaro. (Illus.). 112p. 1999. pap. 11.95 (*0-936741-12-0*) Medi-Ed Pr.

Carmichael, Stephen W. The Adrenal Medulla, 1989-1991. 672p. 1992. lib. bdg. 110.00 (*0-8493-4449-2*) CRC Pr.

Carmichael, Stephen W. & Stoddard, Susan L. The Adrenal Medulla. 646p. 1989. lib. bdg. 88.00 (*0-936923-28-8*) Telford Pr.

Carmichael, Stokely S. & Hamilton, Charles V. Black Power: The Politics of Liberation in America. LC 92-60284. 1992. pap. 12.00 (*0-679-74313-8*) Vin Bks.

Carmichael, Thomas & Lee, Alison, eds. Postmodern Times: A Critical Guide to the Contemporary. LC 99-28171. 250p. 1999. 36.00 (*0-87580-251-6*) N Ill U Pr.

Carmichael, Thomas, jt. auth. see Willis, Ron L.

Carmichael, Thomas, jt. ed. see Kreiswirth, Martin.

Carmichael, Virginia. Framing History: The Rosenberg Story & the Cold War. LC 92-14752. (American Culture Ser.: Vol. 6). 288p. (C). 1992. pap. 19.95 (*0-8166-2042-3*); text 49.95 (*0-8166-2041-5*) U of Minn Pr.

Carmichael, William. Habits of a Healthy Home: Preparing the Ground in Which Your Children Can Grow. LC 97-21403. 1997. 11.99 (*0-8423-1490-3*) Tyndale Hse.

Carmichael, William & Carmichael, Nancie. The Best Things Ever Said about Parenting. (Healthy Home Bks.). 256p. 1996. 9.99 (*0-8423-0151-8*) Tyndale Hse.

— Lord, Bless My Child. LC 95-12643. 256p. 1995. 19.99 (*0-8423-2047-4*) Tyndale Hse.

— Lord, Bless This Marriage. LC 98-31854. 226p. 1999. 19.99 (*0-8423-3855-1*) Tyndale Hse.

— 601 Quotes about Marriage & Family. LC 98-17264. 1998. 10.95 (*0-8423-7894-4*) Tyndale Hse.

Carmicheal, David W. & Maull, Diana. Guide to the Collections of the Westchester County Archives. 1993. pap. 10.00 (*0-9626844-1-4*) West Cnty Archives.

Carmichel, Jim. The Complete Just Jim. 2nd ed. Wolfe, Dave, ed. (Illus.). 128p. (C). 1981. text 13.50 (*0-935632-09-3*) Wolfe Pub Co.

Carmichel, V., ed. see Stockner, M. F.

Carmien, Edward. Daggerfall: Unauthorized Strategy Guide. LC 96-68917. 176p. 1996. pap., per. 19.99 (*0-7615-0715-9*) Prima Pub.

— Lands of Lore: Guardians of Destiny Unauthorized Game Secrets. LC 96-70477. 192p. 1997. pap., per. 14.99 (*0-7615-0928-3*) Prima Pub.

Carmignac, Jean. The Birth of the Synoptic Gospels. Wrenn, Michael J., tr. from FRE. 109p. 1986. pap. 5.95 (*0-8199-0887-8*, Frncscn Herld) Franciscan Pr.

Carmignani, C., jt. ed. see Maino, Giuseppe.

Carmilly-Weinberger, Moshe. The Road to Life: The Rescue Operation of Jewish Refugees on the Hungarian-Romanian Border in Transylvania, 1936-1944. (Illus.). 189p. 1994. 17.95 (*0-88400-175-X*, Pub. by Schreiber Pub) Natl Bk Netwk.

Carmin, Marilyn. Scroll Saw Relief: 70+ Patterns Included. 120p. 1999. pap. 14.95 (*1-56523-107-4*) Fox Chapel Pub.

Carminati, J. Dictionnaire Imaginaire Stations Metro. (FRE.). 1998. 35.00 (*0-320-00180-6*) Fr & Eur.

Carmine, D., jt. auth. see Engelman, S.

Carmine, Mary & Baynton, Martin. Daniel Et Ses Dinosaures.Tr. of Daniel et Ses Dinosaures. (FRE., Illus.). (J). pap. 13.99 incl. audio (*0-590-74149-7*) Scholastic Inc.

— Daniel Et Ses Dinosaures, Big Bk. large type ed.Tr. of Daniel et Ses Dinosaures. (FRE., Illus.). (J). pap. 29.99 (*0-590-74124-1*) Scholastic Inc.

— Daniel's Dinosaur.Tr. of Daniel et Ses Dinosaures. (FRE., Illus.). (J). pap. 6.99 (*0-590-74121-7*) Scholastic Inc.

***Carmine, Rudy Ilario.** Divorce Not Granted. LC 99-94960. 1999. pap. 7.95 (*0-533-13237-1*) Vantage.

Carmines, Edward G. & Stimson, James A. Issue Evolution: Race & the Transformation of American Politics. 234p. 1989. pap. text 17.95 (*0-691-02331-X*, Pub. by Princeton U Pr) Cal Prin Full Svc.

Carmines, Edward G. & Zeller, Richard A. Reliability & Validity Assessment. LC 79-67629. (Quantitative Applications in the Social Sciences Ser.: No. 17). (Illus.). 70p. 1979. pap. 10.95 (*0-8039-1371-0*) Sage.

Carmines, Edward G., jt. auth. see McIver, John P.

Carmines, Edward G., jt. auth. see Sniderman, Paul M.

Carmo Bogo, Maria Do, see Do Carmo Bogo, Maria.

Carmo, Jose, jt. ed. see Brown, Mark A.

Carmo, M. Do, ed. Geometry & Topology. (Lecture Notes in Mathematics Ser.: Vol. 597). 1977. 52.95 (*0-387-08345-6*) Spr-Verlag.

Carmo, R. J. Do, see Do Carmo, R. J., ed.

Carmody, Brendan P. Conversion & Jesuit Schooling in Zambia. LC 91-27038. (Studies in Christian Mission: Vol. 4). (Illus.). xxix, 179p. 1992. 82.00 (*90-04-09428-8*) Brill Academic Pubs.

Carmody, Brian. Fruit Cocktail Diaries. 1994. 15.95 (*0-312-11796-5*) St Martin.

Carmody, D. S. Instrument Pilot Test Guide 1996-1998: FAA Practical & Computer-Based Airman Knowledge. LC 97-136580. (Illus.). 288p. 1996. pap., student ed. 44.95 (*0-07-011661-X*) McGraw.

— Private Pilot Test Guide, 1996-1998: FAA Practical & Computer-Based Airman Knowledge with Disk. LC 95-50764. 257p. 1996. pap. 34.95 (*0-07-912308-2*) McGraw.

***Carmody, Denise.** Los Grandes Maestros de la Humanidad. 1999. pap. 9.95 (*84-08-02832-4*) Planeta Edit.

Carmody, Denise L. Christian Ethics: An Introduction Through History & Current Issues. LC 92-18411. 240p. (C). 1992. pap. text 42.00 (*0-13-131533-1*) P-H.

— Christian Feminist Theology: A Constructive Interpretation. 304p. (C). 1995. pap. 28.95 (*1-55786-587-6*) Blackwell Pubs.

— Christian Feminist Theology: A Constructive Interpretation. 304p. (C). 1995. 66.95 (*1-55786-586-8*) Blackwell Pubs.

— Feminism & Christianity: A Two-Way Reflection. 188p. (Orig.). (C). 1990. reprint ed. pap. text 19.00 (*0-8191-7855-1*) U Pr of Amer.

— The Good Alliance: Feminism, Religion & Education. 132p. (Orig.). (C). 1991. pap. text 20.00 (*0-8191-8045-9*); lib. bdg. 39.50 (*0-8191-8044-0*) U Pr of Amer.

— An Ideal Church: A Meditation. LC 98-55906. 104p. 1999. pap. 6.95 (*0-8091-3885-9*) Paulist Pr.

— Religious Woman: Contemporary Reflections on Eastern Texts. 143p. (Orig.). (C). 1998. pap. text 10.00 (*0-7881-5238-6*) DIANE Pub.

— Responses to One Hundred One Questions about Feminism. (Responses to 101 Questions Ser.). 144p. (Orig.). 1994. pap. 8.95 (*0-8091-3438-1*) Paulist Pr.

— Virtuous Woman: Reflections on Christian Feminist Ethics. LC 92-17952. 180p. (Orig.). 1992. pap. 17.50 (*0-88344-817-3*) Orbis Bks.

— Women & World Religions. 2nd ed. 256p. (C). 1988. pap. text 26.80 (*0-13-962424-4*) P-H.

Carmody, Denise L. & Carmody, John T. Bonded in Christ's Love: Being a Member of the Church. 240p. (Orig.). (C). 1986. pap. 9.95 (*0-8091-2791-1*) Paulist Pr.

— Christianity: An Introduction. 273p. (C). 1982. pap. write for info. (*0-534-01181-0*) Wadsworth Pub.

— Christianity: An Introduction. 2nd ed. 252p. (C). 1988. pap. 20.25 (*0-534-09474-0*) Wadsworth Pub.

— Christianity: An Introduction. 3rd ed. LC 94-25007. 260p. 1994. 42.95 (*0-534-21360-X*) Wadsworth Pub.

— Corn & Ivy: Spiritual Reading in Ruth & Jonah. LC 95-34898. 192p. (Orig.). (C). 1995. pap. 16.00 (*1-56338-134-6*) TPI PA.

— Eastern Ways to the Center: An Introduction to Asian Religions. 238p. (C). 1983. pap. write for info. (*0-534-01342-2*) Wadsworth Pub.

— Exploring American Religion. LC 89-34098. xii, 376p. (C). 1990. text 53.95 (*0-87484-750-8*, 750) Mayfield Pub.

— In the Path of the Masters: Understanding the Spirituality of Buddha, Confucius, Jesus, & Muhammad. LC 96-11387. 234p. (C). 1996. pap. 20.95 (*1-56324-863-8*) M E Sharpe.

— In the Path of the Masters: Understanding the Spirituality of Buddha, Confucius, Jesus, & Muhammad. 256p. 1995. 17.95 (*1-55778-409-4*) Paragon Hse.

— Mysticism: Holiness East & West. 336p. 1996. pap. text 24.95 (*0-19-508819-0*) OUP.

— Native American Religions: An Introduction. LC 93-15547. 288p. 1993. pap. 14.95 (*0-8091-3404-7*) Paulist Pr.

— Original Visions: The Religions of Oral Peoples. (Illus.). 176p. (Orig.). (C). 1992. pap. text 19.40 (*0-02-319395-6*, Macmillan Coll) P-H.

— Prayer in World Religions. LC 89-48198. 176p. reprint ed. pap. 54.60 (*0-608-20188-X*, 207144700012) Bks Demand.

— The Range of Religion: An Introductory Reader. (Illus.). 450p. (Orig.). (C). 1991. pap. text 54.00 (*0-02-319391-3*, Macmillan Coll) P-H.

— The Republic of Many Mansions: Foundations of American Religious Thought. 288p. (C). 1990. pap. 16.95 (*1-55778-392-6*) Paragon Hse.

— Serene Compassion: A Christian Appreciation of Buddhist Holiness. 144p. 1996. 30.00 (*0-19-509969-9*) OUP.

— Stories of Eastern Religions. LC 91-18925. 242p. (C). 1992. pap. text 35.95 (*1-55934-054-1*, 1054) Mayfield Pub.

— Ways to the Center: An Introduction to World Religions. 432p. (C). 1981. pap. write for info. (*0-534-00890-9*) Wadsworth Pub.

— Ways to the Center: An Introduction to World Religions. 2nd ed. 416p. (C). 1984. pap. write for info. (*0-534-03121-8*) Wadsworth Pub.

— Ways to the Center: An Introduction to World Religions. 3rd ed. 470p. (C). 1989. pap. write for info. (*0-534-09954-8*) Wadsworth Pub.

— Ways to the Center: An Introduction to World Religions. 4th ed. 489p. (C). 1992. 38.00 (*0-534-19182-7*) Wadsworth Pub.

— Western Ways to the Center: An Introduction to Western Religions. 252p. (C). 1983. pap. write for info. (*0-534-01328-7*) Wadsworth Pub.

Carmody, Denise L. & Carmody, John T., eds. The Future of Prophetic Christianity: Essays in Honor of Robert McAfee Brown. LC 93-117628. (Illus.). 185p. reprint ed. pap. 57.40 (*0-608-20260-6*, 207151900012) Bks Demand.

Carmody, Denise L., jt. auth. see Carmody, John T.

Carmody, Denise Lardner & Carmody, John. The Story of World Religions. LC 87-24857. 503p. (C). 1988. text 53.95 (*0-87484-756-7*, 756) Mayfield Pub.

— The Story of World Religions: Instructor's Manual. (C). 1988. pap. text, teacher ed. write for info. (*0-87484-874-1*, 874) Mayfield Pub.

Carmody, Donald, jt. auth. see Klein, Carol.

Carmody, Douglas S. Basic Airplane Maintenance & Repair: A Manual for Owners, Builders, Mechanics, & Pilots. LC 97-28746. (Illus.). 346p. 1998. pap. 34.95 (*0-07-011937-6*) McGraw.

— Northeast & Eastern Canada. LC 99-18950. (Pilot's Travel & Recreation Guides). 1999. pap. 24.95 (*0-07-001743-3*) McGraw.

— Opportunities in Aircraft Maintenance Careers. (Opportunities in... Ser.). 160p. 1999. pap. 11.95 (*0-8442-3581-4*) NTC Contemp Pub Co.

— The Pilot's Travel & Recreation Guide: Northwest & Western Canada. 1999. pap. 24.95 (*0-07-001744-1*) Osborne-McGraw.

— The Pilot's Travel & Recreation Guide: Southeast & the Caribbean. LC 98-34944. (Illus.). 330p. 1998. pap. 24.95 (*0-07-001648-8*) McGraw.

— The Pilot's Travel & Recreation Guide: Southwest & Baja. LC 98-34945. (Illus.). 234p. 1998. pap. 24.95 (*0-07-001647-X*) McGraw.

***Carmody, Isobelle.** The Farseekers, Vol. 2. (Obernewtyn Chronicles Ser.). 304p. 2000. 23.95 (*0-312-86957-6*, Pub. by Tor Bks) St Martin.

Carmody, Isobelle. The Gathering. LC 93-31844. (J). 1996. 10.09 (*0-606-10191-8*, Pub. by Turtleback) Demco.

— The Gathering. 288p. (J). (gr. 7). 1996. pap. 4.99 (*0-14-036059-X*) Viking Penguin.

***Carmody, Isobelle.** Obernewtyn. LC 99-38130. 256p. 1999. 22.95 (*0-312-86958-4*, Pub. by Tor Bks) St Martin.

— Obernewtyn. 2000. mass mkt. 6.99 (*0-8125-8422-8*) Tor Bks.

Carmody, James K., ed. The Chick & Ruth Delly Joke Book. (Illus.). 125p. (Orig.). 1988. pap. 8.55 (*0-317-91231-3*) Levitt Charitable.

Carmody, Jan B., ed. Crimes of Violence: Australian Responses to Rape & Child Sexual Assault. 256p. 1993. pap. 19.95 (*1-86373-202-0*, Pub. by Allen & Unwin Pty) Paul & Co Pubs.

Carmody, Jennifer, jt. auth. see Strang, Gilbert.

Carmody, Jim. Rereading Moliere: Mise en Scene from Antione to Vitez. (Theater: Theory - Text - Performance Ser.). 200p. (C). 1993. text 44.50 (*0-472-10466-7*, 10466) U of Mich Pr.

Carmody, John. Cancer & Faith: Reflections on Living with a Terminal Illness. LC 94-60080. 160p. (Orig.). 1994. pap. 9.95 (*0-89622-594-1*) Twenty-Third.

— How to Handle Trouble. large type ed. LC 93-36842. 1994. lib. bdg. 20.95 (*0-8161-5912-2*, G K Hall Lrg Type) Mac Lib Ref.

— How to Handle Trouble: A Guide to Peace of Mind. 1994. mass mkt. 4.99 (*0-8041-1265-7*) Ivy Books.

— Living with God: In Good Times & Bad. LC 95-43605. 168p. (Orig.). 1996. pap. 13.95 (*0-8245-1541-2*) Crossroad NY.

— Psalms for Times of Trouble. LC 94-60847. 176p. (Orig.). 1995. pap. 9.95 (*0-89622-614-X*) Twenty-Third.

— Reexamining Conscience. 144p. (Orig.). 1984. 8.95 (*0-8164-2405-5*) Harper SF.

Carmody, John & Lstiburek, Joseph. Moisture Control Handbook: Principles & Practices for Residential & Small Commercial Buildings. LC 93-11064. (Illus.). xiv, 214 p. 1993. text 52.95 (*0-442-01432-5*, VNR) Wiley.

Carmody, John & Sterling, Ray. Underground Space Design: A Guide to Subsurface Utilization & Design for People in Underground Spaces. LC 92-33460. 1993. text 72.95 (*0-442-01383-3*, VNR) Wiley.

Carmody, John & Sterling, Raymond L. Underground Space Design: A Guide to Subsurface Utilization & Design for People. 328p. 1993. 90.00 (*0-471-28548-X*, VNR) Wiley.

Carmody, John, et al. Residential Windows: A Guide to New Technology & Energy Performance. LC 96-28781. (Illus.). 192p. 1996. pap. 22.00 (*0-393-73004-2*, Norton Paperbks) Norton.

***Carmody, John, et al.** Residential Windows Pennsylvania. 2nd ed. (Illus.). 224p. 2000. pap. 26.95 (*0-393-73053-0*) Norton.

Carmody, John, jt. auth. see Carmody, Denise Lardner.

Carmody, John, jt. auth. see Herzog, Peter.

Carmody, John, jt. auth. see Lstiburek, Joseph.

Carmody, John T. God Is No Illusion: Meditations on the End of Life. LC 96-42947. 128p. (Orig.). 1997. pap. 14.00 (*1-56338-188-5*) TPI PA.

— Toward a Male Spirituality. LC 89-50905. x, 128p. 1989. pap. 7.95 (*0-89622-410-4*) Twenty-Third.

Carmody, John T. & Carmody, Denise L. Christian Uniqueness & Catholic Spirituality. LC 90-42842. 1990. pap. 12.95 (*0-8091-3197-8*) Paulist Pr.

Carmody, John T., jt. auth. see Carmody, Denise L.

Carmody, John T., jt. ed. see Carmody, Denise L.

Carmody, Maurice. The Leonine Union of the Order of Friars Minor, 1897. (History Ser.). 234p. 1994. pap. 20.00 (*1-57659-084-4*) Franciscan Inst.

Carmody, Michael. Filled with the Fullness of God. LC 96-6891. 32p. (Orig.). 1997. pap. 5.95 (*0-910487-39-1*) Royalty Pub.

C

An Asterisk (*) at the beginning of an entry indicates that the title is appearing for the first time.

Carmody, Michael A. Triumph in the Wilderness. LC 95-68742. 52p. (Orig.). 1995. pap. 5.00 (0-910487-33-2) Royalty Pub.

Carmon. Immigration & Integration in Industrial Societies. LC 96-7686. 280p. 1996. text 65.00 (0-312-15962-5) St Martin.

Carmon, Mike. Create Senergy: Conscious Living & Healing into the Millenium, 1999. 239p. 1998. pap. 19.95 (1-893150-00-3) Caritt Pubng.

Carmon, Naomi, ed. Neighborhood Policy & Practice. (Orig.). 1987. pap. 15.00 (0-944285-00-7) Pol Studies.

Carmona. Public Places Urban Spaces. 129p. 1999. pap. text 49.95 (0-7506-3632-7) Buttrwrth-Heinemann.

Carmona-Agosto, Vivian, ed. The Bit. Albornoz, Fernando, tr. (Rotary Drilling Ser.: Unit I, Lesson 2). (SPA., Illus.). 55p. (Orig.). 1981. pap. text 14.00 (0-88698-030-5, 2.10232) PETEX.

— Safety on the Rig. 2nd ed. Albornoz, Fernando, tr. (Rotary Drilling Ser.: Unit I, Lesson 10). (SPA., Illus.). 77p. 1981. pap. text 14.00 (0-88698-038-0, 2.11032) PETEX.

— Wind, Waves & Weather. Rossman, Marcela, tr. (Rotary Drilling Ser.: Unit V, Lesson 1). (SPA., Illus.). 49p. (Orig.). 1982. pap. text 14.00 (0-88698-046-1, 2.50112) PETEX.

Carmona-Agosto, Vivian, tr. see Albornoz, Fernando, ed.

Carmona, Gerardo, et al. Michael Faraday: Un Genio de la Fisica. (Ciencia para Todos Ser.). (SPA.). pap. 6.99 (968-16-4439-5, Pub. by Fondo) Continental Bk.

Carmona, J., et al, eds. Non-Commutative Harmonic Analysis & Lie Groups. (Lecture Notes in Mathematics Ser.: Vol. 1243). v, 309p. 1987. 47.95 (0-387-17701-9) Spr-Verlag.

Carmona, J. & Vergne, M., eds. Non-Commutative Harmonic Analysis & Lie Groups. (Lecture Notes in Mathematics Ser.: Vol. 1020). 187p. 1983. 32.95 (0-387-12717-8) Spr-Verlag.

Carmona, Jose. Adolescent Blues. 60p. 1994. 12.95 (0-8403-7881-5) Kendall-Hunt.

Carmona, Jose, jt. auth. see Gorokhova, Elena.

Carmona, Maria & Stewart, Kathryn. A Review of Alternative Activities & Alternatives Programs in Youth-Oriented Prevention. 44p. (C). 1998. pap. text 15.00 (0-7881-4778-1) DIANE Pub.

***Carmona, Maria G.** A Guide for Evaluating Prevention Effectiveness. (Illus.). 58p. (C). 2000. reprint ed. pap. text 20.00 (0-7881-8410-5) DIANE Pub.

Carmona, Matthew, jt. auth. see Punter, John.

Carmona, P., et al, eds. Spectroscopy of Biological Molecules: Modern Trends. LC 97-23871. 676p. 1997. text 249.00 (0-7923-4685-8) Kluwer Academic.

Carmona, R., et al. Ecole d'Ete de Probabilites de Saint Flour XIV - 1984. (Lecture Notes in Mathematics Ser.: Vol. 1180). x, 439p. 1986. pap. 43.40 (0-387-16441-3) Spr-Verlag.

— Practical Time-Frequency Analysis: Gabor & Wavelet Transforms with an Implementation in Wavelet Analysis & Its Applications, Vol. 9. LC 98-22862. (Wavelet Analysis And Its Applications ;). (Illus.). 490p. (C). 1998. text 65.00 (0-12-160170-6) Acad Pr.

Carmona, R. A. & Nualart, D. Nonlinear Stochastic Integrators, Equations & Flows, Vol. 6. x, 160p. 1990. text 134.00 (2-88124-733-4) Gordon & Breach.

Carmona, Rafael F. The Iron Stallion: Harley-Davidson, an American Love Story. LC 90-71078. 144p. 1990. 39.95 (0-9626928-7-5, 213-473-7223) Hirshberg.

Carmona, Rene & LaCroix, Jean. Spectral Theory of Random Schrodinger Operators. (Probability & Its Applications Ser.). 587p. 1990. 72.50 (0-8176-3486-X) Birkhauser.

Carmona, Rene A. & Molchanov, S. A. Parabolic Anderson Problem & Intermittency. LC 93-48271. (Memoirs of the American Mathematical Society Ser.: No. 518). 125p. 1994. pap. 34.00 (0-8218-2577-1, MEMO/108/518) Am Math.

Carmona, Rene A. & Rozovskii, Boris, eds. Stochastic Partial Differential Equations: Six Perspectives. LC 98-38392. (Mathematical Surveys & Monographs). 337p. 1998. 49.00 (0-8218-0806-0) Am Math.

Carmona, Soledad San Miguel, see Balster, Brigitte.

Carmony. Fundamentals in Data Structure. (C). 1991. text, teacher ed. write for info. (0-7167-8241-3) W H Freeman.

— Turbo Pascal. (C). 1991. text, teacher ed. 24.00 (0-7167-8231-6) W H Freeman.

Carmony & Blais. Physics Engineers & Scientists. Date not set. text 45.00 (0-697-11137-7) McGraw.

— Physics Engineers & Scientists. 1999. pap. text, student ed. 15.00 (0-697-11139-3) McGraw.

Carmony, Donald F. Indiana, 1816 to 1850: The Pioneer Period. LC 97-36392. (History of Indiana Ser.: Vol. 2). xiv, 924p. 1998. 39.95 (0-87195-124-X); pap. 29.95 (0-87195-125-8) Ind Hist Soc.

Carmony, Donald F. & Elliott, Josephine M. New Harmony, Indiana: Robert Owen's Seedbed for Utopia. (Illus.). 102p. 1999. pap. 5.99 (0-9640288-7-5) Univ So IN.

Carmony, Lowell A. & Holliday, Robert L. A First Course in Modula-2. (C). 1990. pap. text 32.80 (0-7167-8229-4, Computer Sci Pr) W H Freeman.

Carmony, Lowell A., et al. Problem Solving in Apple PASCAL. (Computers & Math Ser.). 213p. (YA). (gr. 10-12). 1984. disk 16.80 (0-7167-8170-0, Computer Sci Pr) W H Freeman.

Carmony, Marvin, jt. auth. see Baker, Ronald L.

Carmony, Neil B. Onza! The Hunt for a Legendary Cat. LC 95-75822. (Illus.). 208p. 1995. 20.00 (0-944383-29-7); pap. 12.95 (0-944383-28-9) High-Lonesome.

Carmony, Neil B. & Brown, David E., eds. Tales from Tiburon: An Anthology of Adventures in Seriland. LC 82-51171. (Illus.). 146p. (Orig.). 1983. 15.95 (0-9610126-1-7); pap. 9.95 (0-9610126-0-9) SW Nat Hist Assn.

— Tough Times in Rough Places: Personal Narratives of Adventure, Death & Survival on the Western Frontier. LC 92-71023. (Illus.). 296p. 1995. reprint ed. pap. 14.95 (0-944383-26-2) High-Lonesome.

Carmony, Neil B., jt. auth. see Brown, David E.

Carmony, Neil B., jt. ed. see Brown, David.

Carmony, Neil B., ed. see Gatto, Steve.

Carmony, Neil B., ed. see Gray, John Plesent.

Carmony, Neil B., ed. see Hand, George.

Carmony, Neil B., ed. see Lilly, Ben.

Carmouche, R. & Kelly, N. Behavioural Studies in Hospitality Management. 232p. 1994. mass mkt. 29.95 (0-412-60850-2) Chapman & Hall.

Carmy, Shalom. Jewish Perspectives on the Experience of Suffering. LC 98-36383. 1999. 40.00 (0-7657-6050-9) Aronson.

Carn, John B. Vietnam Blues. 272p. (Orig.). (J). 1988. mass mkt. 3.25 (0-87067-730-6) Holloway.

Carn, Neil G., et al. Real Estate Market Analysis: Techniques & Applications. (Illus.). 368p. (C). 1988. text 51.00 (0-13-763368-8) P-H.

Carnaby, Ann J. A Guidebook for Creating Three Dimensional Theatre Art. LC 96-43402. 256p. 1997. pap. 26.95 (0-435-07000-2) Heinemann.

***Carnaby, Steven.** Designs for Living: A Comparative Approach to Normalisation for the New Millennium. 246p. 1999. text 69.95 (1-84014-831-4, Pub. by Ashgate Pub) Ashgate Pub Co.

Carnaghan, Robert & Bracewell-Milnes, Barry. Testing the Market: Competitive Tendering for Government Services in Britain & Abroad. (Research Monographs: No. 49). 164p. 1993. pap. 39.50 (0-255-36317-6, Pub. by Inst Economic Affairs) Coronet Bks.

Carnagie, Julie. Holocaust Reference Library: Cumulative Index. LC 99-160741. 32 p. 1999. write for info. (0-7876-1924-8) Gale.

Carnagie, Julie, jt. auth. see Saari, Peggy.

Carnagie, Julie L., ed. see Saari, Peggy.

Carnagie, Julie L., ed. see Weigel, Marlene.

Carnahan, Brice, ed. Computers in Chemical Engineering Education. 288p. 1996. 15.00 (0-9655891-0-2) CACHE Corp.

— Foundations of Computer-Aided Process Operations. LC 98-52902. (Symposium Ser.: Vol. 94). 1999. 90.00 (0-8169-0776-5, S-320) Am Inst Chem Eng.

Carnahan, Brice, et al. Applied Numerical Methods. 624p. (C). 1990. reprint ed. 79.50 (0-89464-486-6) Krieger.

Carnahan, Cathy. Miramichi Seasons. LC 98-95022. (Illus.). 128p. 1998. write for info. (0-88780-468-3) FMC.

Carnahan, Cathy, photos by. Miramichi Magic. LC 96-950144. (Illus.). 112p. 1996. bds. 29.95 (0-88780-380-6, Pub. by Formac Publ Co) Formac Dist Ltd.

Carnahan, Charles W. Conflict of Law & Life Insurance Contracts. 2nd ed. LC 58-11622. xviii, 768p. 1958. lib. bdg. 37.50 (0-89941-361-7, 500270) W S Hein.

Carnahan Conference on Security Technology Staff. Proceedings of the Carnahan Conference on Security Technology, 1987. De Vore, R. William & Jackson, John S., eds. LC 82-646157. (Illus.). 147p. 1987. pap. 10.00 (0-89779-068-5, UKY BU143) OES Pubns.

Carnahan, David H. Prologue in the Old French & Provencal Mystery. LC 68-55160. (Studies in French Literature: No. 45). 1969. reprint ed. lib. bdg. 75.00 (0-8383-0519-9) M S G Haskell Hse.

Carnahan, Douglas G. A Business Guide to a California Small Claims Court. 1992. pap. 44.00 (1-55943-162-8, MICHIE) LEXIS Pub.

Carnahan, James R. Secret Ritual of the Pythian Knighthood. 101p. 1993. reprint ed. pap. 16.95 (1-56459-383-5) Kessinger Pub.

***Carnahan, Jean.** If Walls Could Talk: The Story of Missouri's First Families LC 99-179471. xviii, 430 p. 1998. write for info. (0-9668992-0-2) MMPI.

Carnahan, John, et al. Pagan Shore: Ireland in the Age of King Arthur. Shirley, Sam, ed. (Pendragon Roleplaying Ser.). (Illus.). 125p. 1994. pap. 18.95 (1-56882-016-X, 2713) Chaosium.

Carnahan, Martha, ed. see Bohnet, Jeanne.

Carnahan, Melody Sumner, ed. see Cage, John, et al.

Carnahan, Paul, compiled by. A Guide to Vermontiana Collections at Academic, Special & Selected Public Libraries. 62p. 1995. pap. text 7.50 (0-944277-26-8) U VT Ctr Rsch VT.

Carnahan, Peter. Schooner Master: A Portrait of David Stevens. LC 89-32336. 207p. 1989. reprint ed. pap. 64.20 (0-608-00549-5, 206142800008) Bks Demand.

***Carnahan, Sumner.** The Form, 1970-1979. rev. ed. (Illus.). 108p. 2000. pap. 20.00 (0-936050-02-0, Pub. by Burning Bks) SPD-Small Pr Dist.

Carnahan, Sumner. Thirteen Stories: Sumner Carnahan. limited ed. (Illus.). 160p. 1995. pap. 13.00 (0-936050-13-6) Burning Bks.

— The Time Is Now. 3rd rev. ed. (Illus.). 80p. 1998. pap. 20.00 incl. audio compact disk (0-936050-15-2) Burning Bks.

***Carnahan, Sumner & Rinpoche, Lama Kunga.** In the Presence of My Enemies: Memoir of a Tibetan Nobleman. LC 94-43886. (Illus.). 256p. 2000. reprint ed. 24.95 (1-57416-044-3); reprint ed. pap. 14.95 (1-57416-045-1) Clear Light.

Carnahan, Sumner, jt. auth. see Brandauer, Aline Chipman.

Carnahan, Sumner, jt. auth. see Golden, Barbara.

Carnahan, William E., ed. see Post, Ruth N.

***Carnal, Barbara J.** Your Mistress: Emerging from a Codependent Relationship. unabridged ed. 92p. 1999. pap. 18.00 (0-9674072-0-6, 10799) Patchwork Fmly.

Carnall, Colin. Managing Change. (Self-Development for Managers Ser.). 128p. (C). 1990. pap. 17.95 (0-415-04463-4, A6268) Thomson Learn.

— Strategic Change. LC 97-180573. (Management Reader Ser.). 288p. 1997. pap. text 39.95 (0-7506-1932-5) Buttrwrth-Heinemann.

Carnall, Geoffrey, ed. see Butt, John.

Carnall, Geoffrey, ed. see Sykes, Marjorie.

Carnall, William T. & Choppin, Gregory R., eds. Plutonium Chemistry. LC 83-6057. (Symposium Ser.: No. 216). 484p. 1983. lib. bdg. 60.95 (0-8412-0772-0) Am Chemical.

— Plutonium Chemistry. LC 83-6057. (ACS Symposium Ser.: No. 216). (Illus.). 496p. 1983. reprint ed. pap. 153.80 (0-608-03200-X, 206371900007) Bks Demand.

Carnap, Rudolf. Foundations of Logic & Mathematics. (Foundations of the Unity of Science Ser.: Vol. 1, No. 3). 1937. pap. text 4.50 (0-226-57578-0, P402) U Ch Pr.

— Foundations of Logic & Mathematics: The Theory of Paronymy. LC 40-3146. 79p. reprint ed. pap. 30.00 (0-608-09436-6, 205423600004) Bks Demand.

— An Introduction of the Philosophy of Science. unabridged ed. (Illus.). 320p. 1995. pap. text 8.95 (0-486-28318-6) Dover.

— Introduction to Semantics & Formalization of Logic. LC 58-13846. (His Studies in Semantics: Nos. 1-2). 445p. reprint ed. pap. 138.00 (0-7837-2987-1, 205746400006) Bks Demand.

— Introduction to Symbolic Logic & Its Applications. 241p. (C). 1958. pap. 7.95 (0-486-60453-5) Dover.

— Meaning & Necessity: A Study in Semantics & Modal Logic. 2nd ed. 272p. 1988. pap. text 22.00 (0-226-09347-6, Midway Reprint) U Ch Pr.

— Philosophy & Logical Syntax. (Key Texts Ser.). 99p. 1996. pap. 14.95 (1-85506-428-6) Bks Intl VA.

— Philosophy & Logical Syntax. LC 75-41050. (BCL Ser. II). reprint ed. 21.50 (0-404-14518-3) AMS Pr.

— The Unity of Science, 1934 Edition. Black, M., tr. & intro. by. (Key Texts Ser.). 101p. 1996. reprint ed. pap. 13.00 (1-85506-391-3) Bks Intl VA.

Carnap, Rudolf, jt. auth. see Quine, Willard V.

***Carnavali, M. D. Candia & Bonasoro, F., eds.** Echinoderm Research, 1998: Proceedings of the 5th European Conference on Echinoderms, Milan, Italy, 7-12 September, 1998. (Illus.). 580p. 1999. text 165.00 (90-5809-102-3) A A Balkema.

Carnazza, Joseph. Succession - Replacement Planning: Programs & Practices. 1982. pap. 12.00 (0-317-11511-1) CU Ctr Career Res.

Carncross Chandler, Janet. Flight of the Wild Goose. LC 89-16270. (Illus.). 96p. (Orig.). 1989. pap. 8.00 (0-918949-07-6) Martz.

Carnduff, John. An Introduction to Organic Chemistry. LC 78-16664. 208p. reprint ed. pap. 64.50 (0-608-16330-9, 202667800051) Bks Demand.

Carne. Shape & Shape Theory. LC 99-12433. 318p. (C). 1999. 120.00 (0-471-96823-4) Wiley.

— Telecommunications Topics: Applications of Functions & Probabilities in Electronic Communications. LC 98-4540. 416p. (C). 1998. 75.00 (0-13-645565-4, Prentice Hall) P-H.

Carne, D., et al, eds. Vibration, Shock, Damage, & Identification of Mechanical Systems. LC 93-72640. (DE Ser.: Vol. 64). 124p. 1993. 37.50 (0-7918-1180-8, G00825) ASME.

Carne, E. B. Modern Telecommunications. LC 84-16103. (Applications of Communications Theory Ser.). (Illus.). 306p. (C). 1984. 69.50 (0-306-41841-X, Plenum Trade) Perseus Pubng.

Carne, E. Bryan. Telecommunications Primer: Signals, Building Blocks & Networks. 2nd ed. LC 99-20391. (Feher/Prentice Hall Digital & Wireless Communciation Ser.). 832p. 1999. 65.00 (0-13-022155-4) P-H.

Carne, F. Erick. Shorelines of the Great Lakes. (Illus.). 127p. 1996. pap. 24.95 (1-882376-25-0) Thunder Bay Pr.

Carne, Marcel, jt. auth. see Prevert, Jacques.

Carne, Paul, et al. Cambridge Practice Tests for First Certificate 1. 1996. teacher ed. 13.95 (0-521-49897-X); student ed. 11.95 (0-521-49896-1) Cambridge U Pr.

— Cambridge Practice Tests for First Certificate 2. 1997. teacher ed. 13.95 (0-521-49901-1); student ed. 11.95 (0-521-49900-3) Cambridge U Pr.

Carne-Ross, D. S., ed. see Horace.

Carne, William F., jt. auth. see Wolber, Greg J.

***Carneal, Garry.** Case Management State Laws: A 50 State Survey of Health & Insurance Statutory Codes. 118p. 1999. 25.00 (1-930104-02-2) U R A C.

***Carneal, Garry, et al, eds.** The Credentialing Guide. 252p. 2000. 195.00 (1-930104-05-7) U R A C.

***Carneal, Garry & Makwana, Kashmira, eds.** URAC Directory of Accredited Organizations: 1999-2000 Edition. 362p. 1999. 39.00 (1-930104-04-9) U R A C.

Carneal, Garry, ed. see Goddard, Thomas G.

Carneal, Herb & Thornley, Stew. Hi Everybody! 232p. 1995. 21.95 (0-931714-69-9, Pub. by Nodin Pr) Bookmen Inc.

Carnegie. The People Who Came, Bk. 2. Date not set. pap. text. write for info. (0-582-76658-3, Pub. by Addison-Wesley) Longman.

Carnegie, jt. auth. see Coughlan.

Carnegie, Andrew. The Autobiography of Andrew Carnegie. 396p. 1986. reprint ed. pap. text 18.95 (1-55553-001-X) NE U Pr.

— Autobiography of Andrew Carnegie. 1993. reprint ed. lib. bdg. 89.00 (0-7812-5441-8) Rprt Serv.

— Empire of Business. LC 68-23280. 307p. 1968. reprint ed. lib. bdg. 55.00 (0-8371-0037-2, CAEB, Greenwood Pr) Greenwood.

— The Gospel of Wealth. LC 98-11060. 32p. 1998. reprint ed. 9.95 (1-55709-471-3) Applewood.

— A Look Ahead. 1996. lib. bdg. 251.75 (0-8490-5940-2) Gordon Pr.

— Miscellaneous Writings. Hendrick, Burton J., ed. LC 68-58777. (Essay Index Reprint Ser.). 1977. 44.95 (0-8369-0105-3) Ayer.

Carnegie Commission on Preventing Deadly Conflict. Preventing Deadly Conflict: Final Report. LC 98-29056. 257p. 1998. pap. write for info. (1-885039-01-8) Carnegie Corp.

Carnegie Commission on Science, Technology, & Gove. Science & Technology in U. S. International Affairs. (Illus.). 125p. (Orig.). 1992. pap. write for info. (1-881054-00-4) Carnegie Comm Sci.

Carnegie Commission on Science, Technology, & Gove & Branscomb, Lewis M. In the Natural Interest: The Federal Government in the Reform of K-12 Math & Science Education. (Illus.). 76p. 1993. reprint ed. pap. write for info. (1-881054-14-4) Carnegie Comm Sci.

Carnegie Commission on Science, Technology, & Gove & Inman, B. R. Technology & Economic Performance: Organizing the Executive Branch for a Stronger National Technology Base. 58p. 1993. reprint ed. pap. write for info. (1-881054-15-2) Carnegie Comm Sci.

Carnegie Commission on Science, Technology, & Gove & Kaplan, Helene L. Science & Technology in Judicial Decision Making: Creating Opportunities & Meeting Challenges. 92p. (Orig.). 1993. pap. write for info. (1-881054-08-X) Carnegie Comm Sci.

Carnegie Commission on Science, Technology, & Gove & Perry, William J. New Thinking & American Defense Technology. 2nd ed. 48p. 1993. pap. write for info. (1-881054-12-8) Carnegie Comm Sci.

Carnegie Council on Adolescent Development Staff. Great Transitions: Preparing Adolescents for a New Century. Community Scribes Staff, ed. LC 95-37472. (Illus.). (Orig.). 1995. pap. text 6.00 (0-9623154-4-3) CCAD DC.

— A Matter of Time: Risk & Opportunity in the Nonschool Hours. Quinn, Jane & Takanishi, Ruby, eds. LC 92-37832. (Illus.). (Orig.). 1992. pap. text 9.00 (0-9623154-3-5) CCAD DC.

Carnegie Council on Adolescent Development's Task. Turning Points: Preparing American Youth for the 21st Century. 2nd ed. (Illus.). 108p. 1989. reprint ed. pap. 6.00 (0-9623154-1-9) CCAD DC.

Carnegie Council on Ethics & International Affairs Staff. Ethics & International Affairs: A Reader. 2nd rev. ed. Rosenthal, Joel H., ed. & pref. by. LC 98-45147. 484p. 1999. pap. 23.95 (0-87840-725-1) Georgetown U Pr.

Carnegie Council on Policy Studies in Higher Educa. The Carnegie Council on Policy Studies in Higher Education: A Summary of Reports & Recommendations. LC 80-7999. 503p. reprint ed. pap. 156.00 (0-8357-4871-5, 203780300009) Bks Demand.

— Fair Practices in Higher Education: Rights & Responsibilities of Students & Their Colleges in a Period of Intensified Competition for Enrollment: A Report of the Carnegie Council. LC 79-84232. (Carnegie Council Ser.). 117p. reprint ed. pap. 36.30 (0-608-14909-8, 202567100045) Bks Demand.

— The Federal Role in Postsecondary Education: Unfinished Business, 1975-1980: A Report. LC 75-4482. (Carnegie Council Ser.). 111p. reprint ed. pap. 34.50 (0-608-12984-4, 202387200034) Bks Demand.

— Giving Youth a Better Chance: Options for Education, Work & Service: A Report, with Recommendations of the Carnegie Council on Policy Studies in Higher Education. LC 79-90851. (Carnegie Council Ser.). 365p. reprint ed. pap. 113.20 (0-8357-4934-7, 203786400009) Bks Demand.

— Low or No Tuition: The Feasibility of a National Policy for the First Two Years of College: An Analytical Report. LC 75-4276. 96p. reprint ed. pap. 30.00 (0-608-12985-2, 202387300034) Bks Demand.

— Making Affirmative Action Work in Higher Education: Analysis of Institutional & Federal Policies with Recommendations: A Report of the Carnegie Council. LC 75-27205. (Carnegie Council Ser.). 298p. reprint ed. pap. 92.40 (0-608-14787-7, 202565100045) Bks Demand.

— Progress & Problems in Medical & Dental Education: Federal Support Versus Federal Control. LC 76-11964. (Carnegie Council Ser.). 192p. reprint ed. pap. 59.60 (0-608-12272-6, 202378000034) Bks Demand.

— Selective Admissions in Higher Education: Public Policy & Academic Policy, the Pursuit of Fairness in Admissions to Higher Education, the Status of Selective Admissions. LC 77-88501. 272p. reprint ed. pap. 84.40 (0-608-12986-0, 202387400034) Bks Demand.

— The States & Private Higher Education: Problems & Policies in a New Era. LC 77-90808. (Carnegie Council Ser.). 222p. 1977. reprint ed. pap. 68.90 (0-608-10336-5, 202378100034) Bks Demand.

— Three Thousand Futures: The Next Twenty Years for Higher Education: Final Report. LC 79-9675. (Carnegie Council Ser.). (Illus.). 461p. reprint ed. pap. 143.00 (0-8357-4873-1, 203780500009) Bks Demand.

Carnegie, Dale. Como Disfrutar de la Vida y del Trabajo. 1997. pap. text 10.98 (968-446-080-5) Hermes Edit.

— Como Ganar Amigos E Influir Sobre Las Personas. 1997. pap. text 14.50 (968-446-052-X) Hermes Edit.

— Como Hablar Bien en Publico. 1997. pap. text 17.50 (968-446-116-X) Hermes Edit.

Carnegie, Dale. Como Suprimir Las Preocupaciones y Disfrutar De la Vida. 1997. pap. text 16.50 (968-446-064-3) Hermes Edit.

— Dale Carnegie's Biographical Roundup. LC 77-117764. (Essay Index Reprint Ser.). 1977. 24.95 (0-8369-1788-X) Ayer.

— Dale Carnegie's Lifetime Plan for Success: Three Bestselling Works in One Volume, 1. 816p. 1998. 12.99 (1-57866-039-4) Galahad Bks.

— How to Develop Self Confidence. 1991. per. 6.99 (0-671-74607-3) PB.

C

An Asterisk (*) at the beginning of an entry indicates that the title is appearing for the first time.

— How to Enjoy Your Life & Job. 1990. per. 6.99 (*0-671-70826-0*) PB.
— How to Stop Worrying & Start Living. rev. ed. 358p. 1990. per. 7.50 (*0-671-73335-4*) PB.
— How to Stop Worrying & Start Living. rev. ed. 1984. 15.50 (*0-671-50619-6*) S&S Trade.
— How to Win Friends & Influence People. 260p. 1998. per. 12.00 (*0-671-02703-4*) S&S Trade.
— How to Win Friends & Influence People. 1936. 12.09 (*0-606-03008-5*, Pub. by Turtleback) Demco.
— How to Win Friends & Influence People. rev. ed. LC 94-176452. 276p. 1990. per. 7.50 (*0-671-72365-0*) PB.
— The Leader in You. (Illus.). 256p. 1995. per. 7.50 (*0-671-51998-0*) PB.
— Leader in You. 240p. 1993. 21.50 (*0-671-79809-X*) S&S Trade.
— The Leader in You: How to Stop Worrying & Start Living/How to Win Friends & Influence People. 1996. mass mkt. 20.97 (*0-671-85152-7*) PB.
— Lincoln the Unknown. 256p. 1993. reprint ed. lib. bdg. 29.95 (*0-89968-320-7*, Lghtyr Pr) Buccaneer Bks.
— Quick & Easy Way to Effective Speaking. 1990. per. 7.50 (*0-671-72400-2*) PB.

Carnegie, Dale & Carnegie, Dorothy. How to Win Friends & Influence People. rev. ed. 1981. 17.45 (*0-671-42517-X*) S&S Trade.

Carnegie, David W. Letters from Nigeria, 1899-1900. O'Hear, Ann, ed. LC 92-41951. (C). 1992. 30.00 (*0-942615-16-6*) U Wis African Stud.

Carnegie, Dorothy, jt. auth. see Carnegie, Dale.

Carnegie Endowment for International Peace Staff. American Labor in a Changing World Economy. Morehouse, Ward, ed. LC 78-15545. (Praeger Special Studies). 340p. 1980. 75.00 (*0-275-90460-1*, C0460, Praeger Pubs) Greenwood.

***Carnegie Endowment for International Peace Staff.** Arbitrations & Diplomatic Settlements of the United States. LC 99-56486. 2000. write for info. (*1-57588-537-9*) W S Hein.
— The Consortium: The Official Text of the Four-Power Agreement for a Loan to China & Relevant Documents. LC 99-47538. 1999. write for info. (*1-57588-593-X*) W S Hein.
— Documents Relating to the Controversy over Neutral Rights Between the United States & France, 1797-1800. LC 99-47419. 1999. write for info. (*1-57588-584-0*) W S Hein.
— Documents Respecting the Limitation of Armaments. LC 99-48401. 1999. write for info. (*1-57588-582-4*) W S Hein.
— Extracts from American & Foreign Works on International Law Concerning the Armed Neutrality of 1780 & 1800. LC 99-47545. 2000. write for info. (*1-57588-603-0*) W S Hein.
— The Final Acts of the 1st & 2nd Hague Peace Conferences, Together with the Draft Convention on a Judicial Arbitration Court. LC 99-56478. 2000. write for info. (*1-57588-546-8*) W S Hein.
— The Geneva Convention of 1906 for the Amelioration of the Condition of the Wounded in Armies in the Field. LC 99-48404. 1999. write for info. (*1-57588-581-6*) W S Hein.
— The Hague Convention (VIII) of 1907 Relative to the Laying of Automatic Submarine Contact Mines. LC 99-48421. 2000. write for info. (*1-57588-552-2*) W S Hein.
— The Hague Convention (XI) of 1907 Relative to Certain Restrictions with Regard to the Exercise of the Right of Capture in Naval War. LC 99-48406. 1999. write for info. (*1-57588-554-9*) W S Hein.
— The Hague Convention (V) of 1907 Respecting the Rights & Duties of Neutral Powers & Persons in Case of War on Land. LC 99-52088. 1999. write for info. (*1-57588-549-2*) W S Hein.
— The Hague Convention (IX) of 1907 Concerning Bombardment by Naval Forces in Time of War. LC 99-48407. 1999. write for info. (*1-57588-553-0*) W S Hein.
— The Hague Convention (II) of 1907 Respecting the Limitation of the Employment of Force for the Recovery of Contract Debts. LC 99-56477. 2000. write for info. (*1-57588-547-6*) W S Hein.
— The Hague Convention (XIII) of 1907 Concerning the Rights & Duties of Neutral Powers in Naval War. LC 99-48405. 2000. write for info. (*1-57588-556-5*) W S Hein.
— The Hague Convention (III) of 1907 Relative to the Opening of Hostilities. LC 99-56476. 2000. write for info. (*1-57588-548-4*) W S Hein.
— The Hague Convention XIII of 1907 Relative to the Creation of an International Prize Court. LC 99-48408. 1999. write for info. (*1-57588-555-7*) W S Hein.
— The Hague Conventions of 1899 (III) & 1907 (IV) Respecting the Laws & Customs of War on Land. LC 99-56482. 2000. write for info. (*1-57588-541-7*) W S Hein.
— The Hague Conventions of 1899 (I) & 1907 (I) for the Pacific Settlement of International Disputes. LC 99-56483. 2000. write for info. (*1-57588-540-9*) W S Hein.
— The Hague Conventions of 1899 (III) & 1907 (X) for Adaptations to Maritime Warfare of the Principles of the Geneva Convention. LC 99-56480. 2000. write for info. (*1-57588-542-5*) W S Hein.
— The Hague Declaration (IV, 3) of 1899 Concerning Expanding Bullets. LC 99-56475. 2000. write for info. (*1-57588-545-X*) W S Hein.
— The Hague Declaration (IV, 2) of 1899 Concerning Asphyxiating Gases. LC 99-56479. 2000. write for info. (*1-57588-544-1*) W S Hein.
— The Hague Declarations of 1899 (IV, I) & 1907 (XIV) Prohibiting the Discharge of Projectiles & Explosives from Balloons. LC 99-56481. 2000. write for info. (*1-57588-543-3*) W S Hein.
— Official Communications & Speeches Relating to Peace Proposals, 1916-1917. LC 99-48403. 1999. write for info. (*1-57588-583-2*) W S Hein.
— Opinions of the Attorneys General & Judgments of the Supreme Court & the Court of Claims of the United States Relating to the Controversy over Neutral Rights Between the United States & France, 1797-1800. LC 99-48343. 2000. write for info. (*1-57588-597-2*) W S Hein.
— Signatures, Ratifications, Adhesions & Reservations to the Conventions & Declarations of the First & Second Hague Peace Conferences. LC 99-56484. 2000. write for info. (*1-57588-539-5*) W S Hein.
— The Sino-Japanese Negotiations of 1915: Japanese & Chinese Documents & Chinese Official Statement. LC 99-46133. 2000. write for info. (*1-57588-585-9*) W S Hein.

Carnegie Endowment for International Peace Staff. The Sino-Japanese Negotiations of 1915: Japanese & Chinese Documents & Chinese Official Statement. LC 75-36222. reprint ed. 27.50 (*0-404-14473-X*) AMS Pr.

***Carnegie Endowment for International Peace Staff.** Treaties & Agreements with & Concerning China, 1919-1929. LC 99-46132. 1999. write for info. (*1-57588-586-7*) W S Hein.

Carnegie Endowment for International Peace Staff. United Nations Studies, 11 vols. 1980. lib. bdg. 495.00 (*0-313-20320-2*, UNSS, Greenwood Pr) Greenwood.

Carnegie Endowment for International Peace Staff, ed. International Conciliation, 39 vols. 1997. reprint ed. 3995.00 (*1-57588-195-0*, 310840) W S Hein.

***Carnegie Endowment for International Peace Staff & Council on Foreign & Defense Policy Staff, eds.** U. S.-Russian Relations at the Turn of the Century: Reports of the Working Groups Organized by the Carnegie Endowment for International Peace, Washington & the Council on Foreign & Defense Policy, Moscow. LC 00-8416. 2000. write for info. (*0-87003-177-5*) Carnegie Endow.

Carnegie Endowment for International Peace Staff & Leiken, Robert S. Central America: Anatomy of Conflict. LC 83-27440. 1984. 40.00 (*0-08-030950-X*, Pergamon Pr) Elsevier.

Carnegie Endowment for International Peace Staff, jt. auth. see Alvarez, Alejandro G.

Carnegie Endowment for International Peace Staff, jt. auth. see Atwater, Elton.

Carnegie Endowment for International Peace Staff, jt. auth. see Feilchenfeld, Ernst H.

Carnegie Endowment for International Peace Staff, jt. auth. see Foster, John Watson.

Carnegie Endowment for International Peace Staff, jt. auth. see International Peace Conference Staff.

Carnegie Endowment for International Peace Staff, jt. auth. see Lansing, Robert.

Carnegie Endowment for International Peace Staff, jt. auth. see Permanent Court of Arbitration Staff.

Carnegie Endowment for International Peace Staff, jt. auth. see Riesenfeld, Stefan A.

Carnegie Endowment for International Peace Staff, jt. auth. see Ritchie, Hugh.

Carnegie Endowment for International Peace Staff, jt. auth. see Root, Elihu.

Carnegie Endowment for International Peace Staff, jt. auth. see Scott, James Brown.

Carnegie Endowment National Commission on America. Changing Our Ways: America & the New World. LC 92-27961. 1992. 9.95 (*0-87003-034-5*) Carnegie Endow.

Carnegie Endowment Study Group on International Tr, jt. auth. see Serra, Jaime.

Carnegie Endowment Study Group Staff. Limited Partnership: Russia-China Relations in a Changing Asia: Report of the Carnegie Endowment Study Group on Russia-China Relations. 48p. 1998. pap. 6.95 (*0-87003-133-3*) Carnegie Endow.

Carnegie Foundation for the Advancement of Teachin. A Classification of Institutions of Higher Education, 1987. LC 85-28030. (Carnegie Foundation Technical Report Ser.). 154p. reprint ed. pap. 47.80 (*0-7837-6303-4*, 204601800010) Bks Demand.
— The Financial Status of the Professor in America & in Germany, Vol. 2. Metzger, Walter P., ed. LC 76-55175. (Academic Profession Ser.). (Illus.). 1977. reprint ed. lib. bdg. 17.95 (*0-405-10003-5*) Ayer.
— The International Academic Profession: Portraits of Fourteen Countries. Altbach, Philip G., ed. LC 96-42993. (Special Reports). 700p. (C). 1997. pap. text 20.00 (*0-931050-53-7*) Carnegie Fnd Advan Teach.
— Missions of the College Curriculum: A Contemporary Review with Suggestions: A Commentary. LC 77-84320. (Carnegie Council Ser.). (Illus.). 344p. reprint ed. pap. 106.70 (*0-8357-4872-3*, 203780400009) Bks Demand.
— More Than Survival: Prospects for Higher Education in a Period of Uncertainty: A Commentary with Recommendations. LC 75-4481. (Carnegie Council Ser.). 182p. reprint ed. pap. 56.50 (*0-608-17069-0*, 202774800056) Bks Demand.
— The States & Higher Education: A Proud Past & a Vital Future: A Commentary of the Carnegie Foundation for the Advancement of Teaching Staff. LC 76-11958. (Carnegie Council Ser.). 112p. reprint ed. pap. 34.80 (*0-608-12572-5*, 202398200035) Bks Demand.

Carnegie Foundation for the Advancement of Teachin, jt. auth. see Boyer, Ernest L.

Carnegie, Garry. Pastoral Accounting in Colonial Australia: A Case Study of Unregulated Accounting. LC 97-33178. (New Works in Accounting History). (Illus.). 308p. 1997. text 67.00 (*0-8153-3037-5*) Garland.

***Carnegie, Garry D. & Parker, Robert H., eds.** Professional Accounting & Audit in Australia, 1880-1900. LC 99-33042. (New Works in Accounting History). 288p. 1999. reprint ed. 71.00 (*0-8153-3446-X*) Garland.

Carnegie, Garry D. & Wolnizer, Peter W., eds. Accounting History Newsletter, 1980-1989 & Accounting History, 1989-1994: A Tribute to Robert William Gibson. LC 95-51443. (New Works in Accounting History). (Illus.). 416p. 1996. reprint ed. text 88.00 (*0-8153-2268-2*) Garland.

Carnegie, Herb. A Fly in a Pail of Milk: The Herb Carnegie Story. LC 97-208347. (Illus.). 201p. 1996. pap. 16.00 (*0-88962-604-9*, Pub. by Mosaic) Midpt Trade.

Carnegie Institute of Technology, Department of En. Six Satirists. LC 72-1315. (Essay Index Reprint Ser.). 1977. reprint ed. 15.95 (*0-8369-2838-5*) Ayer.

Carnegie Institute of Technology, Department of En, ed. Lovers Meeting: Discussions of Five Plays by Shakespeare. LC 72-1335. (Essay Index Reprint Ser.). 1977. reprint ed. 15.95 (*0-8369-2836-9*) Ayer.
— Six Novelists: Stendhal, Dostoevski, Tolstoy, Hardy, Dreiser & Proust. LC 72-1311. (Essay Index Reprint Ser.). 1977. reprint ed. 18.95 (*0-8369-2837-7*) Ayer.

Carnegie Institute of Technology, Department of En, et al. Studies in Faulkner. LC 72-1325. (Essay Index Reprint Ser.). 1977. reprint ed. 17.95 (*0-8369-2839-3*) Ayer.

Carnegie Institute of Technology, Department of En, ed. see Broes, Arthur T.

Carnegie Institute of Washington Staff. Notes on Middle American Archaeology & Ethnology, 5 vols. Nos. 1-131, Set. reprint ed. 362.50 (*0-685-78166-6*) AMS Pr.

Carnegie Institute Staff. American Painting: Sixteen Seventy to Nineteen Forty. (Illus.). 306p. 1940. pap. 50.00 (*0-915346-77-X*) A Wofsy Fine Arts.
— American Painting in the Nineteen Forties, 8 vols., Set. (Illus.). 1945. pap. 150.00 (*0-915346-80-X*) A Wofsy Fine Arts.

Carnegie Institution of Washington Staff. Albany Catalogue of 20,811 Stars for the Epoch 1910: Prepared at the Dudley Observatory , Albany, New York. LC 32-5590. (Carnegie Institution of Washington Publication Ser.: No. 419). 484p. pap. 150.10 (*0-8357-5295-X*, 200608400060) Bks Demand.
— Contributions to Embryology, Vol. 38, Nos. 259-263. LC 66-24191. (Carnegie Institution of Washington Publication Ser.: Vol. 625). (Illus.). 215p. reprint ed. pap. 66.70 (*0-608-06225-1*, 206655400038) Bks Demand.
— Year Book, No. 77, 1977-1978. LC 03-16716. (Airplane, Missile, & Spacecraft Structures Ser.: Vol. 2). 1006p. reprint ed. pap. 200.00 (*0-608-10646-1*, 207126700077) Bks Demand.
— Year Book, No. 87, 1987-1988. LC 03-16716. (Papers in International Studies: Southeast Asia Ser.: No. 2). 235p. reprint ed. pap. 72.90 (*0-608-10655-0*, 207126700087) Bks Demand.
— Year Book, No. 89, 1989-1990. LC 03-16716. (Holden-Day Series in Physical Techniques in Chemistry). 205p. reprint ed. pap. 63.60 (*0-608-10657-7*, 207126700089) Bks Demand.
— Year Book, No. 90, 1990-1991. LC 03-16716. 183p. reprint ed. pap. 56.80 (*0-608-10658-5*, 207126700090) Bks Demand.
— Year Book, No. 91, 1991-1992. LC 03-16716. (Illus.). 200p. reprint ed. pap. 62.00 (*0-608-10659-3*, 207126700091) Bks Demand.
— Year Book: A Marxist Critique & Alternative, No. 93, 1993-1994. LC 03-16716. 200p. reprint ed. pap. 62.00 (*0-608-10661-5*, 207126700093) Bks Demand.
— Year Book: A Political Study of Two Sardinian Communities, No. 92, 1992-1993. LC 03-16716. 208p. reprint ed. pap. 64.50 (*0-608-10660-7*, 207126700092) Bks Demand.
— Year Book: A Prison Camp Society, No. 94, 1994-1995. LC 03-16716. (Illus.). 200p. reprint ed. pap. 62.00 (*0-608-10662-3*, 207126700094) Bks Demand.
— Year Book: Privacy at the Workplace, No. 88, 1988-1989. LC 03-16716. (AMA Management Briefing Ser.). 207p. reprint ed. pap. 64.20 (*0-608-10656-9*, 207126700088) Bks Demand.
— Year Book 1985-1986, No. 85. LC AS0032.A3. 198p. reprint ed. pap. 61.40 (*0-608-10653-4*, 207126700085) Bks Demand.
— Year Book 1984-1985, No. 84. LC AS0032.A3. (Illus.). 206p. reprint ed. pap. 63.90 (*0-608-10652-6*, 207126700084) Bks Demand.
— Year Book 1981-1982, No. 81. LC AS0032.A3. 756p. reprint ed. pap. 200.00 (*0-608-10650-X*, 207126700081) Bks Demand.
— Year Book1986-1987, No. 86. LC AS0032.A3. 205p. reprint ed. pap. 63.60 (*0-608-10654-2*, 207126700086) Bks Demand.
— Year Book 1980-1981, No. 80. LC AS0032.A3. (Illus.). 730p. reprint ed. pap. 200.00 (*0-608-10649-6*, 207126700080) Bks Demand.
— Year Book 1978-1979, No. 78. LC AS0032.A3. 854p. reprint ed. pap. 200.00 (*0-608-10647-X*, 207126700078) Bks Demand.
— Year Book1979-1980, No. 79. LC AS0032.A3. 705p. reprint ed. pap. 200.00 (*0-608-10648-8*, 207126700079) Bks Demand.
— Year Book 1976-1977, No. 76. LC AS0032.A3. 955p. reprint ed. pap. 200.00 (*0-608-10645-3*, 207126700072) Bks Demand.

Carnegie Institution of Washington Staff, et al. Genetic Studies with Bacteria. LC 57-1751. (Carnegie Institution of Washington Publication Ser.: Vol. 612). (Illus.). 142p. reprint ed. pap. 44.10 (*0-608-06223-5*, 206655200008) Bks Demand.
— Studies of Cenozoic Vertebrates of Western North America & of Fossil Primates. LC 43-2808. (Carnegie Institution of Washington Publication Ser.: Vol. 530). (Illus.). 259p. reprint ed. pap. 80.30 (*0-608-06221-9*, 206655000008) Bks Demand.
— Year Book 1982, No. 81. LC AS0032.A3. 744p. reprint ed. pap. 200.00 (*0-608-10651-8*, 207126700082) Bks Demand.

Carnegie, James. Jonas Fisher: A Poem in Brown & White. Fredeman et al, eds. 264p. 1986. lib. bdg. 15.00 (*0-8240-8621-X*) Garland.
— Suomiria: A Fantasy. Reginald, R. & Menville, Douglas A., eds. LC 75-46307. (Supernatural & Occult Fiction Ser.). 1976. reprint ed. lib. bdg. 26.95 (*0-405-08170-7*) Ayer.

Carnegie, L. & Carnegie Library of Pittsburgh, Science & Technolo. Index to Handicraft Books 1974-1984. LC 85-40857. (Illus.). 424p. 1986. text 49.95 (*0-8229-3532-5*) U of Pittsburgh Pr.

Carnegie Library of Pittsburgh, Science & Technolo, jt. auth. see Carnegie, L.

Carnegie Library of Pittsburgh Staff. Science & Technology Desk Reference. 2nd ed. LC 96-26601. 795p. 1996. 60.00 (*0-8103-9176-7*) Gale.

Carnegie, Liz, et al. The People's Palace Book of Glasgow. LC 99-219339. 128p. 1998. pap. 19.95 (*1-84018-068-4*, Pub. by Mainstream Pubng) Trafalgar.

Carnegie, Mary E. The Path We Tread: Blacks in Nursing Worldwide, 1854-1994. 3rd ed. LC 94-49183. 1995. 30.95 (*0-88737-640-1*) Natl League Nurse.

Carnegie-Mellon University Staff & DeGroot, Morris H. Probability & Statistics. 2nd ed. LC 84-6269. 678p. (C). 1986. 110.00 (*0-201-11366-X*); pap. text, teacher ed. 7.25 (*0-201-11367-8*) Addison-Wesley.

Carnegie Mellon University Staff & Software Engineering Institute Staff. The Capability Maturity Model: Guidelines for Improving the Software Process. (SEI Series Software Engineering). (Illus.). 464p. (C). 1995. 59.95 (*0-201-54664-7*) Addison-Wesley.

Carnegie Museum of Natural History, Division of Ed. Dippy Diplodocus: Story & Gameboard. (Illus.). 16p. (Orig.). (J). (ps-2). 1988. pap. 4.95 (*0-911239-23-5*) Carnegie Mus.
— Dippy Diplodocus: Story Only. (Illus.). 16p. (Orig.). (J). (ps-2). 1988. pap. 1.50 (*0-911239-40-5*) Carnegie Mus.

Carnegie Museum of Natural History Staff. Discover Dinosaurs Activity Book: A Comprehensive Teacher's Guide for Elementary & Middle Schools. (Discover Ser.). (Illus.). 40p. (Orig.). (J). (gr. 2-7). 1995. pap. 6.95 (*0-911239-47-2*) Carnegie Mus.

Carnegie Museum of Natural History Staff, jt. ed. see Bol, Marsha C.

Carnegie, R. H. Outlook for Mineral Commodities. (Report Ser.). 39p. 1986. pap. 10.00 (*1-56708-068-5*) Grp of Thirty.

Carnegie Task Force Staff. Starting Points: Meeting the Needs of Our Youngest Children. LC 94-8825. 1994. write for info. (*1-885039-00-X*) Carnegie Corp.

Carnegie, Winnie. Ugie Pearls & Other Stories. 96p. 1997. pap. 21.00 (*1-84017-004-2*) St Mut.

Carnegy, Daphne. Tin Glazed Earthenware. (Illus.). 176p. 1993. reprint ed. 34.95 (*0-9650786-8-X*) Gentle Br.
— Tin-Glazed Earthenware: From Maiolica, Faience & Delftware to the Contemporary. (Illus.). 144p. 1997. text. write for info. (*976-8097-73-6*) Gordon & Breach.

Carnegy, Vicky. Fashions of a Decade: The 1980s. Cumming, Valerie & Feldman, Elane, eds. (Illus.). 64p. (J). (gr. 4-9). 1990. 19.95 (*0-8160-2471-5*) Facts on File.

***Carnehl, Jeff.** Creative Clips: Clip Art & Awards for Christian Classrooms. 1999. pap. 12.99 (*0-570-05383-8*) Concordia.

***Carneiro.** Anthropology & Cultural Evolutionism. 2000. 45.00 (*0-8133-3765-8*, Pub. by Westview); pap. 15.00 (*0-8133-3766-6*, Pub. by Westview) HarpC.

Carneiro, F. L., et al, eds. Offshore Engineering. LC 97-80093. 520p. 1997. 225.00 (*1-85312-537-7*, 5377) Computational Mech MA.

Carneiro, F. L., ed. see International Conference on Offshore Structures En.

***Carneiro, Robert L.** The Muse of History & the Science of Culture. LC 00-25106. (Illus.). 300p. 2000. pap. 37.50 (*0-306-46273-7*) Kluwer Academic.

Carneiro, Robert L., ed. see Spencer, Herbert.

Carnejo-Polar, Antonio, ed. see De Turner, Clorinda M.

Carnelia, Craig, jt. auth. see Lucas, Craig.

***Carnell.** Starwarped. 176p. 1998. 19.95 (*0-671-01194-4*, Pocket Books) PB.

Carnell, Corbin S. Bright Shadow of Reality: Spiritual Longing in C. S. Lewis. LC 99-234498. 180p. 1999. reprint ed. pap. 16.00 (*0-8028-4627-0*) Eerdmans.

Carnell, Edward J. An Introduction to Christian Apologetics. 6th rev. ed. LC 97-74705. 352p. 1996. pap. 19.99 (*0-938462-19-9*) Green Leaf CA.

Carnell, Eileen, jt. auth. see Askew, Susan.

Carnell, Paul. Alternatives to Factory Farming: An Economic Appraisal. 1983. 45.00 (*0-7855-1118-0*) St Mut.

Carnell, Suzanne. A Treasury of Pet Stories. LC 96-34092. (Illus.). 160p. (J). 1997. 6.95 (*0-7534-5074-7*) LKC.

Carner. Jazz since 1900. 1997. 75.00 (*0-02-864555-3*, Hall Reference) Macmillan.

Carner, Charles. Venicewalks. 1995. pap. 12.95 (*0-8050-1139-0*, Owl) H Holt & Co.

Carner, Gary, compiled by. Jazz Performers: An Annotated Bibliography of Biographical Materials, 26. LC 90-31765. (Music Reference Collection: No. 26). 384p. 1990. lib. bdg. 55.00 (*0-313-26250-0*, CJZ, Greenwood Pr) Greenwood.

Carner, Mosco. Alban Berg. 2nd rev. ed. LC 82-21279. (Illus.). 314p. 1983. pap. 24.50 (*0-8419-1256-4*); text 49.95 (*0-8419-0841-9*) Holmes & Meier.
— Puccini: A Critical Biography. 3rd rev. ed. (Illus.). 566p. 1992. 59.95 (*0-8419-1326-9*) Holmes & Meier.

An Asterisk (*) at the beginning of an entry indicates that the title is appearing for the first time.

Carner, Mosco, jt. auth. see Lenormand, Rene.

Carner-Ribalta, J. Gaspar de Portola: Explorer of California. 2nd rev. ed. LC 90-70278. (Illus.). 200p. 1990. reprint ed. pap. 12.95 (*0-938711-07-5*) Tecolote Pubns.

Carner-Ribalta, Josep. The Catalan Nation & Its People. (Illus.). 223p. (Orig.). 1995. pap. write for info. (*0-9648109-0-5*) Am Inst Catalan Stud.

Carnes, Barbara, jt. auth. see Johnson, Dora B.

Carnes, Bruce A., jt. auth. see Olshansky, S. Jay.

Carnes, Del. How to Make Money in Cake Decorating: Owning & Operating a Successful Business in Your Home. rev. ed. (How to Profit Ser.: Vol. 1). (Illus.). 192p. 1987. pap. 10.99 (*0-685-01386-3*) Deco-Pr Pub.

Carnes, Del, ed. see Murphy, Esther.

Carnes, Elizabeth A., ed. see De Kunffy, Charles.

Carnes, Jim. Us & Them: A History of Intolerance in America. (Illus.). 136p. (J). 1996. text 25.00 (*0-19-510378-5*) OUP.

— Us & Them: A History of Intolerance in America. (Illus.). 136p. 1999. pap. 12.95 (*0-19-513125-8*) OUP.

Carnes, Mark. American Life in Modern Times. 128p. (C). 2001. 17.00 (*0-02-319397-2*, Macmillan Coll) P-H.

Carnes, Mark C. Anglo-American Negotiations on Sharing Atomic Secrets, December 1942-July 1943. (Pew Case Studies in International Affairs). 50p. (C). 1993. pap. text 3.50 (*1-56927-335-9*) Geo U Inst Dplmcy.

— Mapping America's Past: A Historical Atlas. (Illus.). 288p. 1996. 50.00 (*0-8050-4927-4*) H Holt & Co.

— Past Imperfect: History According to the Movies. (Illus.). 320p. 1995. pap. 17.95 (*0-8050-3760-8*) H Holt & Co.

— Secret Ritual & Manhood in Victorian America. 240p. (C). 1989. 37.50 (*0-300-04424-0*) Yale U Pr.

— Secret Ritual & Manhood in Victorian America. 296p. (C). 1991. reprint ed. pap. 19.00 (*0-300-05146-8*) Yale U Pr.

Carnes, Mark C., ed. Past Imperfect: History According to the Movies. LC 95-354. (Reference Bks.). (Illus.). 88p. 1995. 30.00 (*0-8050-3759-4*) H Holt & Co.

Carnes, Mark C. & Griffen, Clyde, eds. Meanings for Manhood: Constructions of Masculinity in Victorian America. LC 90-32943. 288p. 1990. pap. text 17.95 (*0-226-09365-4*) U Ch Pr.

— Meanings for Manhood: Constructions of Masculinity in Victorian America. LC 90-32943. 288p. 1990. lib. bdg. 48.00 (*0-226-09364-6*) U Ch Pr.

Carnes, Mark C., jt. auth. see Garraty, John A.

Carnes, Mark C., ed. see American Council of Learned Societies.

Carnes, Mark C., jt. ed. see Garraty, John A.

Carnes, Molly, jt. auth. see Kindig, Mary N.

Carnes, Pack. Fable Scholarship: An Annotated Bibliography. LC 82-48494. 480p. 1985. text 10.00 (*0-8240-9229-5*) Garland.

Carnes, Patrick. The Betrayal Bond: Breaking Free of Exploitive Relationships. LC 97-35071. 250p. 1997. pap. 11.95 (*1-55874-526-2*) Health Comm.

— Contrary to Love: Helping the Sexual Addict. 280p. pap. 12.95 (*1-56838-059-3*) Hazelden.

— Don't Call It Love. 448p. 1992. pap. 15.95 (*0-553-35138-9*) Bantam.

— Out of Betrayal: Breaking Free of Exploitive Relationships. 250p. 1996. pap. 11.95 (*1-55874-393-6*, 3936) Health Comm.

— Out of the Shadows: Understanding Sexual Addiction. 2nd ed. Orig. Title: Sexual Addiction. 182p. 1992. pap. 14.95 (*1-56838-055-0*) Hazelden.

— Sexual Anorexia: Overcoming Sexual Self-Hatred. LC 97-12610. 250p. pap. 14.95 (*1-56838-144-1*, 1316 A) Hazelden.

Carnes, Patrick, et al. Open Hearts: Renewing Relationships with Recovery, Romance & Reality. 236p. pap. 19.95 (*1-929866-00-3*, Pub. by Gentle Path Pr) Hazelden.

Carnes, Patrick J. A Gentle Path Through the Twelve Steps: The Classic Guide for All People in the Process of Recovery. rev. ed. (Illus.). 310p. 1994. pap. 16.00 (*1-56838-058-5*) Hazelden.

Carnes, Roberta. Global Learning (Aprendizaje Mundial) (Illus.). 32p. (Orig.). pap. 8.00 (*0-9644298-0-2*) Sunshine Corner.

Carnes, Robin & Craig, Sally. Sacred Circles: A Guide to Creating Your Own Women's Spirituality Group. LC 97-13381. 240p. 1998. pap. 17.00 (*0-06-251522-5*, Pub. by Harper SF) HarpC.

***Carnes, Ruth J.** Ben Milam. LC 00-26507. 2000. write for info. (*1-57168-398-4*, Eakin Pr) Sunbelt Media.

Carnes, Ruth J. David G. Burnet: From New Jersey to Texas. 64p. (J). 1997. pap. 6.95 (*1-57168-139-6*, Eakin Pr) Sunbelt Media.

***Carnes, Shawn.** Pool of Radiance: Attack on Myth Drannor. (Forgotten Realms Ser.). 2000. pap. text 17.95 (*0-7869-1710-5*) Wizards Coast.

Carnes, Stan, jt. auth. see Slifer, Stephen.

Carnes, Susan, ed. see Adams, Pamela W. & Baskett, Kathryn.

Carnes, Susan D., ed. see Adams, Pamela W.

Carnes, Susan D., ed. see Adams, Pamela W. & Baskett, Kathryn K.

***Carnes, Tony & Karpathakis, Anna, eds.** New York Glory: Religions in the City. 2000. text 60.00 (*0-8147-1600-8*); pap. text 19.50 (*0-8147-1601-6*) NYU Pr.

Carnes, W. Stansbury & Slifer, Stephen D. The Atlas of Economic Indicators: A Visual Guide to Market Forces. LC 91-58515. 192p. 1991. 24.95 (*0-88730-500-8*, HarpBusn) HarpInfo.

— The Atlas of Economic Indicators: A Visual Guide to Market Forces & the Federal Reserve. LC 91-58515. (Illus.). 240p. 1992. reprint ed. pap. 15.00 (*0-88730-537-7*, HarpBusn) HarpInfo.

Carnesale, Albert & Haass, Richard N., eds. Superpower Arms Control: Setting the Record Straight. LC 87-1372. 392p. 1987. pap. 34.95 (*0-88730-228-9*, HarpBusn); pap. 18.95 (*0-88730-229-7*, HarpBusn) HarpInfo.

Carness, Fern, et al. The Healthy Workplace: Health Fairs for Your Wealthfare. 70p. (Orig.). 1995. pap. text 30.00 (*0-9628334-4-4*) WELCOA.

Carnevale, Anthony, et al. Training in America: The Organization & Strategic Role of Training. LC 89-28662. (Management Ser.). 450p. 1990. text 36.95 (*1-55542-203-9*) Jossey-Bass.

Carnevale, Anthony P. America & the New Economy: How New Competitive Standards Are Radically Changing American Workplaces. LC 91-19307. (Management Ser.). 291p. 1991. text 35.95 (*1-55542-371-X*) Jossey-Bass.

— A Society Based on Work. 102p. 1984. 8.75 (*0-318-22200-0*, IN270) Ctr Educ Trng Employ.

— Tools & Activities for a Diverse Work Force. 464p. 1995. 149.95 (*0-07-011375-0*) McGraw.

Carnevale, Anthony P. & Gainer, Andleila J. The Learning Enterprise. (Illus.). 54p. (Orig.). (C). 1993. pap. text 30.00 (*1-56806-382-2*) DIANE Pub.

Carnevale, Anthony P., et al. Training the Technical Work Force. LC 89-48806. (Management Ser.). 220p. 1990. text 36.95 (*1-55542-201-2*) Jossey-Bass.

— Workplace Basics Training Manual. LC 89-48805. (Management Ser.). 304p. 1990. text 45.95 (*1-55542-204-7*) Jossey-Bass.

Carnevale, David G. Trustworthy Government: Leadership & Management Strategies for Building Trust & High Performance. LC 94-38540. (Public Administration Ser.). 255p. 1995. 29.95 (*0-7879-0062-1*) Jossey-Bass.

Carnevale, Ellen S., jt. ed. see Galagan, Patricia A.

Carnevale, Peter J., jt. auth. see Pruitt, Dean G.

Carnevali de Hawthorn, Gloria, tr. see Hawthorn, Geoffrey.

Carnevali, Doris L. Diagnostic Reasoning & Treatment Decision Making. 288p. 1993. pap. text 36.95 (*0-397-54921-0*) Lppncott W & W.

— Nursing Management for the Elderly. 3rd ed. Patrick, Maxine, ed. LC 92-20793. (Illus.). 688p. 1993. text 53.00 (*0-397-54898-2*) Lppncott W & W.

Carney. Career Planning: Skills to Build. 2nd ed. (Counseling Ser.). 1987. pap. write for info. (*0-534-07177-5*) Brooks-Cole.

— Career Planning: Skills to Build a Future. (Counseling Ser.). 1981. pap. 15.75 (*0-534-23350-3*) Brooks-Cole.

— Career Planning Skills to Build a Future. (Counseling Ser.). 1981. pap. 2.00 (*0-534-25860-3*) Brooks-Cole.

— An Introduction to QBasic. (C). 1996. pap. text. write for info. (*0-03-007593-9*) Harcourt Coll Pubs.

— Other Mississippi. 1994. pap. 14.95 (*0-938252-01-1*) Coffeetable.

Carney. Using the Newspaper in the Writing Process. (Illus.). (J). (gr. 3-5). 1996. pap., wbk. ed. 9.95 (*1-55734-479-5*) Tchr Create Mat.

— Using the Newspapers to Teach Reading Skills. (Illus.). (J). (gr. 3-5). 1996. pap., wbk. ed. 9.95 (*1-55734-466-3*) Tchr Create Mat.

Carney & Wells. Working Well, Living Well: Discover the Career Within You. 5th ed. LC 98-26828. (Counseling Ser.). 1998. pap. 37.95 (*0-534-35767-9*) Brooks-Cole.

Carney, Andrew L. & Anderson, Evelyn M., eds. Diagnosis & Treatment of Brain Ischemia: CT Brain Blood Flow, Brain Hemodynamics, & Carotid & Vertebral Artery Surgery. LC 80-5669. (Advances in Neurology Ser.: Vol. 30). 423p. 1981. reprint ed. pap. 131.20 (*0-608-00316-6*, 206103300007) Bks Demand.

Carney, Betty & Adams, Keith. Let's Make a Scene. LC 89-60299. 52p. (Orig.). 1989. pap. 8.95 (*0-916809-28-5*) Scott Pubns MI.

***Carney, Bruce & Ellis & Associates Staff.** Aquatic Inservice Manual. (Illus.). 64p. (C). 1999. pap. text 38.75 (*0-7637-1193-4*) JB Pubns.

Carney, Cary M. Native American Higher Education in the United States. LC 99-14822. 226p. 1999. 32.95 (*1-56000-417-7*) Transaction Pubs.

Carney, Cathey. The Old Huntsville Book of Recipes & Timeless Tips. 1995. 15.95 (*0-9650939-0-5*) Old Huntsville.

Carney, Charles & Misiroglu, Gina. Space Jam: Michael & Bugs Hit the Big Screen. (Illus.). 175p. 1998. text 20.00 (*0-7881-5851-1*) DIANE Pub.

Carney, Cindy, jt. auth. see Boardman, Mark.

Carney, Clandion. Urbanization. Hayner, Stephen & Aeschliman, Gordon, eds. (Global Issues Bible Study Ser.). 48p. (Orig.). 1990. pap., wbk. ed. 4.99 (*0-8308-4904-1*, 4904) InterVarsity.

Carney, Clarke G. & Wells, Cinda F. Career Planning: Skills to Build Your Future. 2nd ed. LC 86-21625. 272p. (C). 1986. pap. 17.75 (*0-534-07176-7*) Brooks-Cole.

— Discover the Career Within You. 3rd ed. 312p. (C). 1990. pap. 21.95 (*0-534-14952-9*) Brooks-Cole.

— Discover the Career Within You. 4th rev. ed. LC 94-21844. 336p. 1994. pap. 22.50 (*0-534-25638-4*) Brooks-Cole.

Carney, Cynthia J., jt. auth. see Grundfast, Kenneth.

Carney, David. All about Myth: An Introduction to Mythanalysis. LC 90-85386. 147p. (Orig.). 1990. pap. 10.00 (*1-879320-00-2*) Adastra.

— Soul of Darkness: Introduction to African Metaphysics, Philosophy & Religion. LC 91-72774. (Illus.). 146p. (Orig.). 1991. pap. 10.00 (*1-879320-01-0*) Adastra.

***Carney, David E., ed.** To Promote the General Welfare: A Communitarian Legal Reader. LC 99-29371. 320p. 1999. 65.00 (*0-7391-0032-7*) Lxngtn Bks.

Carney, David E., jt. ed. see Etzioini, Amitai.

Carney, Debra. Using the Newspapers to Teach Reading Skills. 1997. pap. text 11.95 (*1-55734-467-1*) Tchr Create Mat.

Carney, Desmond N., ed. Lung Cancer. (An Arnold Publication). 280p. 1995. text 95.00 (*0-340-56759-7*, Pub. by E A) OUP.

Carney, Diana & Farrington, John. Natural Resource Management & Institutional Change. LC 97-44290. 136p. (C). 1998. 60.00 (*0-415-18604-8*) Routledge.

Carney, Edward. English Spelling. LC 96-47573. (Language Workbooks Ser.). 112p. (C). 1997. pap. 14.99 (*0-415-16109-6*) Routledge.

Carney, Edward M. A Survey of English Spelling. LC 93-3378. 544p. (C). (gr. 13). 1993. 100.00 (*0-415-09270-1*, B0010) Routledge.

Carney, Edward M., Jr., et al. The American Business Manual, 3 vols., Set. Chandler, Alfred D., ed. LC 79-7536. (History of Management Thought & Practice Ser.). 1980. reprint ed. lib. bdg. 113.95 (*0-405-12318-3*) Ayer.

— The American Business Manual, 3 vols., Vol. 1. Chandler, Alfred D., ed. LC 79-7536. (History of Management Thought & Practice Ser.). 1980. reprint ed. lib. bdg. 37.95 (*0-405-12319-1*) Ayer.

— The American Business Manual, 3 vols., Vol. 2. Chandler, Alfred D., ed. LC 79-7536. (History of Management Thought & Practice Ser.). 1980. reprint ed. lib. bdg. 37.95 (*0-405-12320-5*) Ayer.

— The American Business Manual, 3 vols., Vol. 3. Chandler, Alfred D., ed. LC 79-7536. (History of Management Thought & Practice Ser.). 1980. reprint ed. lib. bdg. 37.95 (*0-405-12321-3*) Ayer.

***Carney, Elizabeth D.** Women & Monarchy in Macedonia. LC 99-37790. 384p. 2000. 42.95 (*0-8061-3212-4*) U of Okla Pr.

Carney, Ellen. Historic Soda Springs: An Oasis on the Oregon Trail. (Illus.). 402p. 1998. pap. 22.50 (*0-9636479-3-8*) Traildust Pub.

— The Oregon Trail: Ruts, Rogues & Reminiscences. (Illus.). 322p. (Orig.). 1993. pap. 17.50 (*0-9636479-0-3*) Traildust Pub.

— River of Beaver, Stream of Gold. (Illus.). 156p. (Orig.). 1994. pap. 12.50 (*0-9636479-1-1*) Traildust Pub.

Carney, Ellen & Johnson, Elaine S. The Mountain Carriboo: And Other Gold Camps in Idaho. 2nd ed. (Illus.). 238p. 1994. pap. write for info. (*0-9636479-2-X*) Traildust Pub.

Carney, Eunice, jt. auth. see Duncan, Kate.

Carney, Faye. Larousse Grande Dictionnaire Francais-Anglais, Anglais-Francais, Vol. 1. (ENG & FRE.). 978p. 1993. 65.00 (*0-614-00398-9*, 2034013018) Fr & Eur.

— Larousse Grande Dictionnaire Francais-Anglais, Anglais-Francais, 2 vols., Vol. 2. (ENG & FRE.). 125.00 (*0-7859-7564-0*, 203401300X) Fr & Eur.

Carney, Francis L. Criminality & Its Treatment: Paxtuxent Experience. LC 88-8444. 168p. (C). 1989. lib. bdg. 21.50 (*0-89464-348-7*) Krieger.

Carney, Frederick S., tr. & abr. see Althusius, Johannes.

Carney, Gene. Romancing the Horsehide: Baseball Poems on Players & the Game. LC 92-42356. (Illus.). 127p. 1993. lib. bdg. 18.95 (*0-89950-838-3*) McFarland & Co.

Carney, George. Physics: Electricity. 3rd ed. 228p. (C). 1995. pap. text, ring bd. 32.95 (*0-7872-0947-3*) Kendall-Hunt.

Carney, George O., ed. Baseball, Barns, & Bluegrass: A Geography of American Folklife. LC 97-42879. (Illus.). 320p. 1998. 64.00 (*0-8476-8600-0*) Rowman.

— Baseball, Barns & Bluegrass: A Geography of American Folklife. LC 97-42879. (Illus.). 320p. 1998. pap. 23.95 (*0-8476-8601-9*) Rowman.

— Fast Food, Stock Cars & Rock-n-Roll: Place in American Popular Culture. 328p. (C). 1995. pap. text 27.95 (*0-8476-8080-0*); lib. bdg. 72.00 (*0-8476-8079-7*) Rowman.

— The Sounds of People & Places: Readings in the Geography of American Folk & Popular Music. LC 87-10481. (Illus.). 362p. (Orig.). (C). 1987. pap. text 26.00 (*0-8191-6414-3*) U Pr of Amer.

— The Sounds of People & Places: Readings in the Geography of American Folk & Popular Music. 2nd ed. 320p. (Orig.). (C). 1993. lib. bdg. 62.50 (*0-8476-7787-7*) Rowman.

— The Sounds of People & Places: Readings in the Geography of American Folk & Popular Music. 2nd ed. 356p. (Orig.). (C). 1994. pap. text 27.95 (*0-8476-7788-5*) Rowman.

Carney, Glandion & Long, Bill. Longing for God: Prayer & the Rhythms of Life. LC 93-41899. Orig. Title: The Rhythm of Live & the Psalms. 228p. 1993. pap. 10.99 (*0-8308-1665-8*, 1665) InterVarsity.

Carney, Glandion & Long, William. Trusting God Again: Regaining Hope after Disappointment or Loss. LC 95-7840. 237p. (Orig.). 1995. pap. 10.99 (*0-8308-1609-7*, 1609) InterVarsity.

Carney, Glandion & Moore, Coleman. A Beginner's Guide to Spiritual Formation. 48p. 1998. spiral bd. 6.25 (*1-56212-340-8*, 1360-0100) CRC Pubns.

***Carney, Ian.** Sugar Buzz: Live at Budokan! 2000. pap. 12.50 (*1-899866-33-7*) Slab-O-Concrete Pubns.

Carney, J. W. Massachusetts Criminal Practice Forms. 1994. write for info. (*1-56257-219-9*, MICHIE) LEXIS Pub.

Carney, James. Medieval Irish Lyrics with the Irish Bardic Poet. 176p. 1985. pap. 13.95 (*0-85105-360-2*, Pub. by Smyth) Dufour.

— The Playboy & the Yellow Lady. 240p. 1986. pap. 10.95 (*0-905169-82-4*, Pub. by Poolbeg Pr) Dufour.

***Carney, James L.** Mystery Stories: A Journey Through the Rosary. unabridged ed. LC 99-64130. (Illus.). xviii, 404p. 2000. pap. 24.95 (*0-9673328-0-X*) Crown of Mary Pubg Co.

Carney, James L. The Seton Miracles, Weeping Statues & Other Wonders. 3rd rev. ed. LC 98-67910. (Illus.). xvi, 122p. 1998. pap. 14.95 (*0-9666234-0-1*) Marian Found.

Carney, Jennifer, jt. auth. see Podjasek, Jill H.

Carney, Jerome P. Fire Protection During Construction: A Critical Time. 1984. 4.65 (*0-318-03824-2*, TR84-7) Society Fire Protect.

Carney, Jessica. Who's There? The Life & Career of William Hartnell. LC 97-105635. (Illus.). 224p. 1996. text 22.95 (*1-85227-514-6*, Pub. by Virgin Bks) London Brdge.

***Carney, Jo Eldridge, ed.** Renaissance & Reformation, 1500-1620: A Biographical Dictionary. LC 99-462063. (The Great Cultural Eras of the Western World). 2000. lib. bdg. write for info. (*0-313-30574-9*) Greenwood.

Carney, Joan M., jt. auth. see Gerring, Joan P.

Carney, John & Alcerro, Angela. La Migracion de Inmigrantes Indocumentados Mexicanos: Y la Politica para Gestionarla. (ENG & SPA., Illus.). 84p. (Orig.). 1995. pap. 6.00 (*1-879861-13-5*) Consensus Pubs.

Carney, John F., III, ed. Effectiveness of Highway Safety Improvements. (Conference Proceedings Ser.). 295p. 1986. 5.00 (*0-87262-520-6*) Am Soc Civil Eng.

Carney, John P. Governing a Changing United States. 4th ed. 250p. (C). 1999. pap. 15.00 (*1-879861-17-8*) Consensus Pubs.

— Irish Race in America & in Hibernia: Added Reference to Spanish, Asian, & Aboriginal Antecedents. 100p. (C). 1996. pap. 6.50 (*1-879861-11-9*) Consensus Pubs.

Carney, John P. & Alcerro, Angela. Governing a Changing California. 6th ed. 116p. (C). 1999. pap. 6.00 (*1-879861-15-1*) Consensus Pubs.

Carney, Louis P. Corrections: Treatment & Philosophy. (Criminal Justice Ser.). (Illus.). 1980. text 25.95 (*0-685-03806-8*) P-H.

Carney, Margaret. At Grandpa's Sugar Bush. LC 96-931694. (Illus.). 32p. (J). (ps-1). 1998. 16.95 (*1-55074-341-4*, Pub. by Kids Can Pr) Genl Dist Srvs.

— The First Franciscan Woman: Clare of Assisi & Her Form of Life. LC 93-7917. 261p. 1993. pap. 12.95 (*0-8199-0962-9*) Franciscan Pr.

Carney, Margaret, et al. Charles Fergus Binns: The Father of American Studio Ceramics, Including a Catalogue Raisonne. LC 97-46898. (Illus.). 256p. 1998. 50.00 (*1-55595-144-9*, Pub. by Hudson Hills) Natl Bk Netwk.

Carney, Marie T. Come Walk with Me, Against All Odds. LC 98-90027. 1998. pap. 9.95 (*0-533-12686-X*) Vantage.

Carney, Mary L. Bubble Gum & Chalk Dust. LC 82-4041. 96p. 1982. pap. 7.95 (*0-687-03987-8*) Abingdon.

— Too Tough to Hurt. 128p. (J). 1991. pap. 6.99 (*0-310-28621-2*) Zondervan.

***Carney, Miriam.** Spiritual Treasures: A Collection of Short Stories, Poems, Essays & Insights, 3 vols. large type ed. (Illus.). 71p. 2000. ring bd. 10.00 (*0-9702530-0-1*) Angels Amngst Us.

Carney, Ray. American Vision: The Films of Frank Capra. LC 95-49517. (Illus.). 534p. 1996. reprint ed. pap. 24.95 (*0-8195-6301-3*, Wesleyan Univ Pr) U Pr of New Eng.

— The Films of John Cassavetes: Pragmatism, Modernism, & the Movies. (Cambridge Film Classics Ser.). (Illus.). 334p. (C). 1994. pap. text 17.95 (*0-521-38815-5*) Cambridge U Pr.

***Carney, Ray & Quart, Leonard.** The Films of Mike Leigh: Embracing the World. LC 99-30993. (Film Classics Ser.). (Illus.). 224p. (C). 2000. 49.95 (*0-521-48043-4*); pap. 18.95 (*0-521-48518-5*) Cambridge U Pr.

Carney, Ray, jt. auth. see Cassavetes, John.

Carney, S. H., Jr. Genealogy of the Carney Family, Descendants of Mark Carney & Suzann Gow, His Wife, of Pownalboro, Maine, 1751-1903. (Illus.). 227p. 1989. reprint ed. pap. 34.00 (*0-8328-1313-3*); reprint ed. lib. bdg. 42.00 (*0-8328-1312-5*) Higginson Bk Co.

Carney, Seamus. The Appin Murder: The Killing of the Red Fox. (Illus.). 206p. pap. 13.95 (*1-874744-21-1*, Pub. by Birlinn Ltd) Dufour.

Carney, Sheila, jt. auth. see Burns, Helen Marie.

Carney, T. F. The Shape of the Past: Models & Antiquity. (Illus.). 1975. 30.00 (*0-685-01230-1*) Coronado Pr.

Carney, T. F., ed. John the Lydian, de Magistratibus: On the Magistracies of the Roman Constitution. 127p. 1971. pap. 7.50 (*0-87291-031-8*) Coronado Pr.

Carney, Teddy & Hawkins, David R. Power vs. Force: Synopsis & Study Guide. 70p. (Orig.). 1998. pap., wbk. ed. 10.95 (*0-9643261-6-7*) Veritas AZ.

Carney, Terry. Law at the Margins: Toward Social Participation? 214p. 1991. text 59.00 (*0-19-553219-8*) OUP.

Carney, Terry & Hanks, Peter. Social Security in Australia. 376p. 1994. pap. text 45.00 (*0-19-553562-6*) OUP.

Carney, Terry & Tait, David. Adult Guardianship Experiment: Tribunals & Popular Justice. 229p. 1997. pap. 39.00 (*1-86287-264-3*, Pub. by Federation Pr) Gaunt.

Carney, Timothy M., ed. Communist Party Power in Kampuchea (Cambodia) Documents & Discussion. LC 76-152199. (Southeast Asia Program, Cornell University, Data Paper Ser.: No. 106). 86p. reprint ed. pap. 30.00 (*0-8357-2558-8*, 204024900015) Bks Demand.

Carney, Tom. Bird Dogs & Betty Cakes: More Notes from the Outdoors. LC 98-140273. (Illus.). 160p. 1998. pap. 12.95 (*0-9637085-3-8*) Partrdge Pointe.

— Natural Wonders of Michigan: A Guide to Parks, Preserves & Wild Places. (Natural Wonders Ser.). (Illus.). 180p. (Orig.). 1995. pap. 9.95 (*1-56626-078-7*, Cntry Rds Pr) NTC Contemp Pub Co.

***Carney, Tom.** Natural Wonders of Michigan: Exploring Wild & Scenic Places. 2nd ed. LC 98-50001. (Natural Wonders of... Ser.). 192p. 1999. pap. 14.95 (*0-658-00176-0*, 001760, Cntry Rds Pr) NTC Contemp Pub Co.

Carney, Tom. Sun-Drenched Days, Two-Blanket Nights: A Sportsman Takes Note. (Illus.). (Orig.). 1995. pap. 10.95 (*0-9637085-6-2*) Partrdge Pointe.

Carney, Tom, ed. Publishing by Microcomputer: Its Potential & Its Problems. 184p. 1990. 75.00 (*1-870167-04-X*, Pub. by P Francis) St Mut.

Carney, Vaughn A. Swiss Movement. unabridged ed. 1998. pap. 18.95 (*1-892896-05-2*) Buy Books.

Carney, William. Cities. 80p. (Orig.). 1985. pap. 5.95 (*0-938190-58-X*) North Atlantic.

— The Real Thing. 1995. pap. 10.95 (*1-56333-280-9*, R Kasak Bks) Masquerade.

Carnicelli, D. D., ed. see Petrarca, Francesco.

Carnicelli, Thomas A., ed. see Augustine, Saint.

***Carnicelli, Tom.** Word Study: A Way into Reading, Writing, & Thinking. 2001. pap. text. write for info. (*0-86709-565-2*, Pub. by Boynton Cook Pubs) Heinemann.

Carnick, Cliff, ed. see Fisher, Carmen J. & Jefford, Jack.

Carnicke, Sharon. Stanislavsky in Focus. (Illus.). 252p. 1998. text 25.00 (*90-5755-069-5*) Gordon & Breach.

***Carnicke, Sharon M.** Stanislavsky in Focus. (Illus.). 252p. 1998. pap. text 23.00 (*90-5755-070-9*, Harwood Acad Pubs) Gordon & Breach.

Carnicke, Sharon M. The Theatrical Instinct: Nikolai Evreinov & the Russian Theatre of the Early Twentieth Century. LC 88-31364. (American University Studies: Theatre Arts: Ser. XXVI, Vol. 2). XII, 247p. (C). 1989. text 45.50 (*0-8204-1073-X*) P Lang Pubng.

***Carnie, Andrew & Guilfoyle, Eithne, eds.** The Syntax of the Verb Initial Languages. LC 99-40359. (Oxford Studies in Comparative Syntax Ser.). 272p. 2000. text 49.95 (*0-19-513222-X*); pap. text 24.95 (*0-19-513223-8*) OUP.

Carnie, Fiona, et al, eds. Freeing Education: Steps Towards Real Choice & Diversity in Schools. LC 96-205980. (Educational Ser.). 192p. 1996. pap. text 16.95 (*1-869890-82-5*, Pub. by Hawthorn Press) Anthroposophic.

Carnie, L. V. Chi Gung: Chinese Healing, Energy, & Natural Magick. LC 97-32002. (Illus.). 288p. (Orig.). 1999. pap. 17.95 (*1-56718-113-9*) Llewellyn Pubns.

Carnielli, et al. Methods & Applications of Mathematical Logic: (Proceedings of the Latin American Symposium on Mathematical Logic, 7th) LC 87-33651. (Contemporary Mathematics Ser.: No. 69). 250p. 1988. pap. 36.00 (*0-8218-5076-8*, CONM/69) Am Math.

Carnielli, Walter A., jt. auth. see Epstein, Richard L.

Carniglia, Stephen C. & Barna, Gordon L. Handbook of Industrial Refractories Technology: Principles, Types, Properties & Applications. LC 92-4458. (Illus.). 627p. 1992. 159.00 (*0-8155-1304-6*) Noyes.

Carnignan, Ann M., et al, eds. Gerontologic Nursing. LC 94-31990. (NSNA Review Ser.). 224p. (C). 1995. pap. 31.95 (*0-8273-6484-9*) Delmar.

Carnine, Douglas, et al. Direct Instruction Reading. 3rd ed. LC 96-38830. 420p. (C). 1996. 76.33 (*0-13-602566-8*) P-H.

Carnine, Douglas, jt. auth. see Kameenui, Edward J.

***Carnine, Jay.** California Hot Rodder. (Illus.). 200p. 2000. pap. 24.95 (*0-949398-10-1*, 130729AE, Pub. by Graffiti) Motorbooks Intl.

***Carniol, Paul.** Facial Rejuvenation. 464p. 2000. 149.00 (*0-471-31846-9*) Wiley.

Carniol, Paul J. Laser Skin Rejuvenation. LC 98-21400. 256p. 1998. text 95.00 (*0-7817-1561-X*) Lppncott W & W.

Carnley, Peter. The Structure of Resurrection Belief. (Illus.). 408p. 1987. 95.00 (*0-19-826679-0*) OUP.

Carno, Deni, ed. see Clayton, Brad.

Carnochan, Brigitte, photos by. Colors of the Imagination: Painted Flowers & Nudes. LC 98-127575. (Illus.). 32p. 1997. 12.00 (*0-9659635-0-0*) B Carnochan.

***Carnochan, Peter.** Looking for Ground: Countertransference, Epistemology & the Problem of Value. LC 00-26372. 2000. write for info. (*0-88163-324-0*) Analytic Pr.

Carnochan, W. B. The Battleground of the Curriculum: Liberal Education & American Experience. LC 92-40401. 186p. 1993. 35.00 (*0-8047-2147-5*) Stanford U Pr.

— Battleground of the Curriculum: Liberal Education & American Experience. xiv, 174p. 1994. pap. 13.95 (*0-8047-2364-8*) Stanford U Pr.

— Gibbon's Solitude: The Inward World of the Historian. LC 86-30200. 248p. 1987. 37.50 (*0-8047-1363-4*) Stanford U Pr.

Carnochan, W. B., ed. see Etherege, George.

Carnois, Bernard & Booth, David. The Coherence of Kant's Doctrine of Freedom. LC 86-15935. xvi, 192p. (C). 1987. 28.95 (*0-226-09394-8*) U Ch Pr.

Carnot, Sadi. Reflections on the Motive Power of Fire. (Illus.). 1990. 16.50 (*0-8446-1809-8*) Peter Smith.

Carnov, Martin. Industrialization in a Latin American Common Market. LC 73-161596. 293p. reprint ed. pap. 90.90 (*0-608-12156-8*, 202536800043) Bks Demand.

Carnovale, Marco, ed. European Security & International Institutions after the Cold War. LC 94-34879. 300p. 1995. text 75.00 (*0-312-12488-0*) St Martin.

***Carnovale, Norbert.** George Gershwin: A Bio-bibliography, 76. LC 99-46018. (Bio-bibliographies in Music Ser.). 632p. 2000. lib. bdg. write for info. (*0-313-26003-6*) Greenwood.

Carnovale, Norbert. Gunther Schuller: A Bio-Bibliography, 6. LC 87-7507. (Bio-Bibliographies in Music Ser.: No. 6). 350p. 1987. lib. bdg. 65.00 (*0-313-25084-7*, CGS, Greenwood Pr) Greenwood.

Carnovale, Richard L., jt. auth. see Pierce, Mark F.

Carnovsky, Morris & Sander, Peter. The Actor's Eye: Seeing & Being Seen. 1983. pap. 8.95 (*0-933826-62-1*) PAJ Pubns.

Carnoy, Albert J. Le Latin d'Espagne d'Apres les Inscriptions. 293p. 1983. reprint ed. 65.00 (*3-487-03384-4*) G Olms Pubs.

Carnoy, David, jt. auth. see Carnoy, Martin.

Carnoy, Emile. Dictionnaire Biographique International Des Ecrivains. (FRE.). 946p. 1987. reprint ed. 240.00 (*3-487-06703-X*) G Olms Pubs.

Carnoy, Martin. Faded Dreams: Politics & Economics of Race in America. rev. ed. (Illus.). 296p. 1996. pap. 18.95 (*0-521-57639-3*) Cambridge U Pr.

— Faded Dreams: The Politics & Economics of Race in America. (Illus.). 296p. (C). 1994. text 49.95 (*0-521-47062-5*) Cambridge U Pr.

***Carnoy, Martin.** Sustaining the New Economy: Work, Family & Community in the Information Age. LC 00-27030. 240p. 2000. 39.95 (*0-674-00373-X*) HUP.

Carnoy, Martin, ed. International Encyclopedia of Economics of Education. 2nd ed. (Resources in Education Ser.: Vol. 2). 458p. 1995. 181.50 (*0-08-042303-5*) Elsevier.

Carnoy, Martin & Carnoy, David. Fathers of a Certain Age: The Joys & Problems of Middle-Aged Fatherhood. LC 97-612. 192p. 1997. pap. text 12.95 (*1-57749-031-2*) Fairview Press.

Carnoy, Martin & Levin, Henry M. Schooling & Work in the Democratic State. LC 83-40697. 320p. 1985. 45.00 (*0-8047-1242-5*); pap. 17.95 (*0-8047-1289-1*) Stanford U Pr.

Carnoy, Martin & Samoff, Joel. Education & Social Transition in the Third World. (Illus.). 350p. (Orig.). 1990. pap. text 22.95 (*0-691-02311-5*, Pub. by Princeton U Pr) Cal Prin Full Svc.

Carnoy, Martin, et al. The New Global Economy in the Information Age: Reflections on Our Changing World. LC 92-33652. 170p. (C). 1993. pap. 15.95 (*0-271-00910-1*) Pa St U Pr.

Carns. The Struggle for Democracy. 2nd ed. (C). 1995. teacher ed. write for info. (*0-673-55667-0*) Addson-Wesley Educ.

Carns, Michael P., comment. Spacecast 2020: Surveillance & Reconnaissance...The U. S. Air Force's Future in Space. 64p. (Orig.). (C). 1995. pap. text 30.00 (*0-7881-2539-7*) DIANE Pub.

Carns, Pauli, ed. see Haas, Chris.

Carnuche, William. A Journey of a Lifetime. 224p. 1995. 19.95 (*0-9646225-0-5*) Pitt Pub & Co.

Carnus, Jean. L' Hotel Hurluberlu et Autres Histoires: Harebrain Hotel & Other Stories. No. 1.Tr. of Harebrain Hotel & Other Stories. (ENG & FRE., Illus.). 120p. 1985. pap. 4.25 (*0-940038-03-X*) Andante Pub.

Carnwath, Drew. Johnnyville/Total Body Washout: "Johnnyville: An Official Secrets Act" & "Total Body Washout" LC 98-183642. 96p. (Orig.). 1998. pap. 13.95 (*0-88754-555-6*) Theatre Comm.

Carnwath, Squeak. Squeak Carnwath: Lists, Observations & Counting. LC 95-23315. 108p. 1996. 29.95 (*0-8118-1220-0*); pap. 18.95 (*0-8118-1171-9*) Chronicle Bks.

Caro, Adrian Del, see Del Caro, Adrian.

Caro, Adrian Del, see Szyszkowitz, Gerald.

Caro, Adrian Del, see Del Caro, Adrian, ed.

Caro, Adrian Del, see Szyszkowitz, Gerald.

Caro, Adrian Del, see Callaway, H. G. & Del Caro, Adrian, frwds.

Caro Baroja, Julio. The World of the Witches. Glendinning, O. N., tr. LC 64-15829. (The Nature of Human Society Ser.). (Illus.). 339p. reprint ed. pap. 105.10 (*0-608-09379-3*, 205412400004) Bks Demand.

Caro, Colin G., jt. ed. see Jaffrin, Michel Y.

Caro, Francis A. De, see De Caro, Francis A., compiled by.

Caro, Francis G., ed. Readings in Evaluation Research. 2nd ed. LC 76-12706. 436p. 1977. 50.00 (*0-87154-201-3*) Russell Sage.

Caro, Francis G. & Blank, Arthur E. Caring for the Elderly at Home: A Policy Perspective on Consumer Experiences with Publicly-Funded Home Care Programs in New York City. LC 89-105204. 143p. 1987. pap. text 12.00 (*0-88156-052-9*) Comm Serv Soc NY.

Caro, Francis G. & Blank, Arthur E., eds. Quality Impact of Home Care for the Elderly. LC 88-11292. (Home Health Care Services Quarterly Ser.: Vol. 9, Nos. 2 & 3). (Illus.). 204p. 1989. text 39.95 (*0-86656-820-4*) Haworth Pr.

Caro, Francis G. & Simpson, Patricia. Definitions & Realities of Poverty. LC 90-198046. 68p. 1988. 6.50 (*0-88156-097-9*) Comm Serv Soc NY.

Caro, Francis G., et al. Barriers to Prenatal Care: An Examination of Use of Prenatal Care among Low-Income Women in New York City. LC 89-170885. 122p. 1988. pap. 11.00 (*0-88156-069-3*) Comm Serv Soc NY.

Caro, Frank De, see De Caro, Frank.

Caro, G. De, see De Caro, G.

Caro, Ina. The Road from the Past. 352p. 1996. pap. 16.00 (*0-15-600363-5*) Harcourt.

Caro, Janice E., jt. auth. see Oster, Gerald D.

Caro, Joseph J. Hopalong Cassidy Collectibles. (Illus.). 290p. 1997. pap. 42.50 (*0-9628078-1-8*) Cowboy Collector.

Caro, Michael A. Carmina Latina et Latinae Interpretationes. rev. ed. (LAT.). 273p. 1993. pap. 19.95 (*0-9637760-0-2*) A Becerra.

Caro, Mike. Caro's Fundamental Secrets of Poker. (Illus.). (Orig.). 1991. pap. 12.95 (*1-880069-00-8*) M Caro Univ Pr.

— Caro's Fundamental Secrets of Winning Poker. 3rd ed. LC 95-68284. (Illus.). 160p. 1996. pap. 9.95 (*0-940685-57-4*) Cardoza Pub.

— Gambling Times Quiz Book. (Illus.). 270p. 1984. pap. 5.95 (*0-89746-031-6*) Gambling Times.

— New Poker Games. 156p. 1984. pap. 6.95 (*0-89746-040-5*) Gambling Times.

Caro, N. Raten Sie Mal. (GER.). 118p. (C). 1984. pap. text 24.75 (*3-12-550800-2*, Pub. by Klett Edition) Intl Bk Import.

Caro, Paul. Water. 155p. 1993. pap. 11.95 (*0-07-009990-1*) McGraw.

Caro, Robert A. Means of Ascent: The Years of Lyndon Johnson. 1990. 30.00 (*0-394-52835-2*) Knopf.

— Means of Ascent: The Years of Lyndon Johnson. LC 90-50483. Vol. 2. 592p. 1991. pap. 18.00 (*0-679-73371-X*) Vin Bks.

— Path to Power. LC 89-40608. 1990. pap. 19.00 (*0-679-72945-3*) Vin Bks.

— The Path to Power: The Years of Lyndon Johnson, Vol. 1. LC 82-47811. 1982. 29.95 (*0-394-49973-5*) Knopf.

— The Power Broker: Robert Moses & the Fall of New York. LC 73-20751. (Illus.). 1296p. 1974. 50.00 (*0-394-48076-7*) Knopf.

— The Power Broker: Robert Moses & the Fall of New York. 1975. pap. 24.00 (*0-394-72024-5*) Vin Bks.

Caro, T. M. Cheetahs of the Serengeti Plains: Groups Living in an Asocial Species. LC 93-35466. (Wildlife Behavior & Ecology Ser.). 500p. (C). 1994. pap. text 26.95 (*0-226-09434-0*); lib. bdg. 70.00 (*0-226-09433-2*) U Ch Pr.

Caro, Tim, ed. Behavioral Ecology & Conservation Biology. (Illus.). 608p. 1998. text 95.00 (*0-19-510489-7*); pap. text 55.00 (*0-19-510490-0*) OUP.

Carocci, Giampiero. The Officers' Camp. Hochfield, George, tr. from ITA. LC 97-10067. 1997. 49.95 (*0-8101-6025-0*, Marlboro); pap. text 15.95 (*0-8101-6026-9*) Northwestern U Pr.

***Carodine, Ken.** All the Tea. 250p. 2000. pap. 14.95 (*1-58752-000-1*) Timberwolf Pr.

***Caroe, Olaf.** The Panthans. 544p. 2000. text 110.00 (*0-7103-0682-2*) Col U Pr.

Caroe, Olaf. The Pathans: 500 B.C.-A.D., 1957. With a New Epilogue. (Illus.). 544p. 1984. text 39.95 (*0-19-577221-0*) OUP.

— Wells of Power: The Oil Fields of South-Western Asia. (Middle East in the 20th Century Ser.). 1976. reprint ed. lib. bdg. 29.50 (*0-306-70825-6*) Da Capo.

Caroff, Joe. Converging Lines. LC 98-90115. 1998. pap. 10.95 (*0-533-12720-3*) Vantage.

Caroff, Phyllis & Gottesfeld, Mary, eds. Psychosocial Studies. LC 86-22806. 185p. 1987. text 32.50 (*0-89876-100-X*) Gardner Pr.

Caroff, Phyllis, jt. ed. see Mailick, Mildred D.

Carol. On Fundamental Rights. (C). Date not set. write for info. (*0-8147-7994-8*) NYU Pr.

Carol & Grant, Lucinda. Jump Now, Look Later: New Ways to Beat Your Fears. (Illus.). v, 111p. 1998. pap. 10.00 (*0-9662717-0-X*, 1001) Success NOW LA.

Carol, jt. auth. see Green.

Carol A. Keene, ed. & intro. see Bradley, F. H.

***Carol, Angela.** St. Raphael: Angel of Marriage, of Healing, of Happy Meetings, of Joy & of Travel. LC 99-70785. 39p. 1999. pap. 2.00 (*0-89555-650-2*, 1595) TAN Bks Pubs.

Carol, Anne. Dictionnaire d'Histoire du XXe Siecle. (FRE.). 499p. 1993. pap. 24.95 (*0-7859-7792-9*, 2218071924) Fr & Eur.

Carol, Avedon. Nudes, Prudes & Attitudes: Pornography & Censorship. LC 95-137372. 208p. pap. 18.95 (*1-873797-13-3*, Pub. by New Clarion) Paul & Co Pubs.

— Nudes, Prudes & Attitudes: Pornography & Censorship. LC 95-137372. 208p. 1994. 45.00 (*1-873797-14-1*, Pub. by New Clarion) Paul & Co Pubs.

Carol, Avedon, jt. auth. see Assiter, Alison.

Carol, Bonnie. Dust off That Dulcimer & Dance. 1983. pap. 9.95 (*0-88284-256-0*, 2071) Alfred Pub.

Carol, Brennan. Headhunt. 224p. 1994. reprint ed. pap. 4.50 (*0-425-14125-X*, Prime Crime) Berkley Pub.

Carol Chambers-Benjamin Employee for Licensing by Loren Inc., Staff, ed. see Johnson, Loren, et al.

Carol, Daniel S., jt. ed. see Brower, David J.

Carol, Ignacio, jt. ed. see Bazant, Zdenek.

Carol, Jacqueline. How to Meet a Superstar. (Full House Michelle & Friends Ser.). 96p. (J). (gr. 2-4). 2000. per. 3.99 (*0-671-04195-9*, Minstrel Bks) PB.

Carol, Juniper. A History of the Controversy Over the "Debitum Peccati" (Theology Ser.). xiv, 260p. 1978. pap. 7.00 (*1-57659-026-7*) Franciscan Inst.

Carol, Juniper B., tr. see Pancheri, Francesco S.

***Carol-Libman, David.** The Essential Drumset Method. 64p. 1999. pap. 19.95 (*0-7866-3395-6*, 97058BCD) Mel Bay.

Carol, Nina. Waif. LC 97-68824. 109p. 1997. pap. 13.95 (*0-9659915-0-4*) Still Water.

Carol, Ruth, ed. Alternatives for Women with Endometriosis: A Guide by Women for Women. LC 94-10122. 176p. (Orig.). 1994. pap. 12.95 (*1-879427-12-5*) Third Side Pr.

Carola. Human Anatomy. 1992. teacher ed. 30.62 (*0-07-011119-7*) McGraw.

— Human Anatomy Visiquizzes. 1992. 28.12 (*0-07-026488-0*) McGraw.

— Users Guide to Human Anatomy & Physiology. 1990. 63.00 (*0-07-010502-2*) McGraw.

***Carola, Dorothy Kosinski.** Learning about Liturgy: Catechesis for Children & Their Families. 192p. 2000. pap. 37.95 (*0-89390-497-X*) Resource Pubns.

— Learning about the Liturgical Seasons: Catechesis fo Children & Their Families. 80p. 1999. pap. 24.95 (*0-89390-495-3*) Resource Pubns.

Carola, Leslie C. The Irish: A Treasury of Art & Literature. (Illus.). 384p. 1995. 24.95 (*0-88363-701-4*) H L Levin.

Carola, Robert, et al. Human Anatomy. (C). 1991. text 75.25 (*0-07-010527-8*); pap. text, student ed. 25.00 (*0-07-010547-2*) McGraw.

— Human Anatomy. (C). 1992. pap. text, lab manual ed. 28.50 (*0-07-011118-9*) McGraw.

— Human Anatomy & Physiology. (C). 1992. pap. text, student ed. 27.25 (*0-07-010972-9*) McGraw.

— Human Anatomy & Physiology. 2nd ed. (C). 1992. pap. text, student ed. 25.50 (*0-07-010971-0*) McGraw.

— Human Anatomy & Physiology. 2nd ed. (C). 1992. text 273.12 (*0-07-010978-8*) McGraw.

Carola, Robert, jt. auth. see Rechtschaffen, Joseph S.

Carola, Robert, jt. auth. see Ritchie, Donald D.

Carola, Rovert, et al. Human Anatomy & Physiology. 3rd ed. 1120p. (C). 1994. 95.94 (*0-07-011171-5*) McGraw.

Carolan, Christopher L. The Spiral Calendar & Its Effect on Financial Markets & Human Events. (Illus.). 159p. 1992. 49.00 (*0-932750-21-4*) New Classics Lib.

Carolan, Nicholas. A Harvest Saved: Francis O'Neill & Irish Music in Chicago. LC 97-201030. (Illus.). 84p. 1997. pap. 18.95 (*1-900428-11-3*, Pub. by Ossian) Music Sales.

Carolan, Nicholas & Munnelly, Tom, eds. Breandan Breathnach. 320p. 1996. 39.50 (*1-85182-231-3*, Pub. by Four Cts Pr) Intl Spec Bk.

Carolan, Trevor, tr. see Ching-Yuen, Loy.

Carolane, J., jt. auth. see Hackett, C.

Caroli, Betty. Roosevelt Women. LC 98-37072. 528p. 1998. 30.00 (*0-465-07133-3*, Pub. by Basic) HarpC.

— The Roosevelt Women. Date not set. pap. 18.00 (*0-465-07134-1*, Pub. by Basic) HarpC.

Caroli, Betty B. First Ladies. expanded ed. (Illus.). 496p. 1995. 35.00 (*0-19-509944-3*); pap. 16.95 (*0-19-509228-7*) OUP.

— Inside the White House: Celebrating the First 200 Years of America's Most Famous Home. rev. ed. (Illus.). 224p. 1994. 29.95 (*1-55859-818-9*) Abbeville Pr.

Caroli, Betty B., et al, eds. The Italian Immigrant Woman in North America. 1977. 9.95 (*0-934675-10-4*) Am Italian.

Caroli, Betty B., jt. auth. see Kessner, Thomas.

***Caroli, Betty Boyd.** Inside the White House: America's Most Famous Home. 224p. 1999. 29.95 (*0-7621-0143-1*, Pub. by RD Assn) Penguin Putnam.

Caroli, Betty L. Immigrants Who Returned Home. (Peoples of North America Ser.). (Illus.). 20p. (YA). (gr. 5 up). 1990. lib. bdg. 19.95 (*0-87754-864-1*) Chelsea Hse.

Caroli, S., jt. ed. see Minoia, C.

Caroli, Sergio, ed. Element Speciation in Bioinorganic Chemistry. LC 95-11167. (Chemical Analysis Ser.: Vol. 135). (Illus.). 474p. 1996. 115.00 (*0-471-57641-7*, Wiley-Interscience) Wiley.

— Improved Hollow Cathode Lamps for Atomic Spectroscopy. LC 85-900. (Analytical Chemistry Ser.). 232p. 1985. text 97.00 (*0-470-20209-2*) P-H.

Caroli, Sergio, jt. auth. see Milazzo, Guilio.

Carolie, Koster. Art of Cooking: More Than 1001 Choice Recipes. 1999. 100.00 (*0-627-02102-6*) J L Van Schaik.

Carolin, Birgit, jt. auth. see Milner, Pat.

Carolina Biological Supply Company Staff. Biology: The Dynamics of Life: 1997 Laboratory Activities Materials List. 52p. 1997. pap., teacher ed. write for info. (*0-89278-003-7*) Carolina Biological.

— Carolina Science & Math Catalog 70. rev. ed. (Illus.). 1225p. 1999. pap. text, teacher ed. 17.95 (*0-89278-002-9*) Carolina Biological.

Carolina Hospital Staff & Cantera, Jorge, eds. A Century of Cuban Writers in Florida: Selected Prose & Poetry. LC 96-20647. 256p. (Orig.). 1996. pap. 14.95 (*1-56164-104-9*) Pineapple Pr.

Caroline H.-ational Research Council Staff. Critical Perspectives on Schooling & Fertility in the Developing World. Bledsoe, Caroline H. et al, eds. LC 98-40216. 336p. 1999. pap. text 47.00 (*0-309-06191-1*) Natl Acad Pr.

Caroline, Nancy L. Ambulance Calls: Review Problems in Emergency Care. 2nd ed. 1987. pap. text 22.00 (*0-316-12871-6*, Little Brwn Med Div) Lppncott W & W.

— Emergency Care in the Streets. 3rd ed. 1987. 25.50 (*0-316-12879-1*, Little Brwn Med Div) Lppncott W & W.

— Emergency Care in the Streets. 3rd ed. 610p. (C). 1987. pap. 19.00 (*0-685-17577-4*, Little Brwn Med Div) Lppncott W & W.

— Emergency Care in the Streets. 5th ed. LC 94-30822. (Illus.). 1087p. 1995. pap. text 51.95 (*0-316-12891-0*) Lppncott W & W.

— Emergency Medical Technician Instructor's Manual. 2nd ed. 1987. teacher ed. 18.50 (*0-316-12881-3*, Little Brwn Med Div) Lppncott W & W.

— Emergency Medical Technician Workbook. 3rd ed. 392p. 1991. pap. text, wbk. ed. 17.00 (*0-316-12887-2*) Lppncott W & W.

— Emergency Medical Treatment. 3rd ed. 644p. 1991. pap. text 37.00 (*0-316-12886-4*) Lppncott W & W.

— Emergency Medical Treatment: A Text for EMT-As & EMT-Intermediates. 2nd ed. 1987. 24.00 (*0-316-12878-3*, Little Brwn Med Div); teacher ed. 7.95 (*0-316-12880-5*, Little Brwn Med Div); student ed. 15.50 (*0-316-12882-1*, Little Brwn Med Div) Lppncott W & W.

— Handbook of Prehospital Medications. LC 94-32684. 144p. 1995. pap. text 17.00 (*0-316-55447-2*) Lppncott W & W.

— Study Guide for Emergency Care in the Streets. 5th ed. (Illus.). 569p. 1995. pap. text, student ed. 26.00 (*0-316-12893-7*) Lppncott W & W.

Caroline, Nancy L., jt. auth. see McClintock, James C.

Caroline, Nancy L., jt. auth. see Waller, Alexander.

Carolissen, Ron, jt. auth. see Hall, Dorothea.

Caroll, David. French Literary Fascism: Nationalism, Anti-Semitism & the Ideology of Culture. LC 94-20035. 320p. 1995. text 39.50 (*0-691-03723-X*, Pub. by Princeton U Pr) Cal Prin Full Svc.

C

An Asterisk (*) at the beginning of an entry indicates that the title is appearing for the first time.

Caroll, Frieda. Recession Proofing Possibilities Workshop. 80p. 1999. pap., wbk. ed. 39.95 (*1-890928-44-5*) Frieda Carroll.

Caroll, John. 4X4 Vehicles. (Illus.). 80p. (Orig.). 1996. pap. 14.95 (*0-88317-195-3*) Stoeger Pub Co.

Carolle, Lisa. The Secrets of Yashir. 190p. mass mkt. 4.99 (*1-896329-22-5*) Picasso Publ.

***Carollo, C. Marcella, et al, eds.** The Formation of Galactic Bulges. LC 99-43050. (Cambridge Contemporary Astrophysics Ser.). (Illus.). 224p. (C). 2000. 69.95 (*0-521-66334-2*) Cambridge U Pr.

Carollo, John, jt. auth. see Holder, Bill.

Carolus, Roger & Nelson, Donald. Business-Focused QAR Manual. 3rd rev. ed. Campbell, Lee A., ed. 160p. 1996. pap. 150.00 (*0-89413-365-9*, A585) Inst Inter Aud.

Caron, Aimery P. & Highfield, Arnold R. St. Croix under French Dominion, 1650-1733. (Illus.). 200p. (Orig.). 1984. pap. text 10.00 (*0-916611-00-0*) Antilles Pr.

Caron, Ann F. Don't Stop Loving Me: A Reassuring Guide for Mothers of Adolescent Daughters. LC 91-50510. 240p. 1992. reprint ed. pap. 13.00 (*0-06-097402-8*, Perennial) HarperTrade.

— Mothers & Daughters: Searching for New Connections. LC 97-52977. 288p. 1998. 25.00 (*0-8050-5149-X*) H Holt & Co.

— Mothers to Daughters: Searching for New Connections. 288p. 1999. pap. 13.00 (*0-8050-5150-3*) St Martin.

— Strong Mothers, Strong Sons: Raising Adolescent Boys in the 90's. 256p. 1995. 22.50 (*0-8050-2499-9*) H Holt & Co.

— Strong Mothers, Strong Sons: Raising the Next Generation of Men. LC 94-40537. 336p. 1995. pap. 14.00 (*0-06-097648-9*, Perennial) HarperTrade.

Caron, Barbara. Navigating Compass Designs. LC 98-27957. 1998. pap. text 19.95 (*0-89145-896-4*, 4889, Am Quilters Soc) Collector Bks.

Caron, Barbara, ed. see Genereux, Diane & Huntsberger, Briana.

Caron, D. Phillip. Bamboo. McGuirt, Curtis R., ed. & intro. by. (Illus.). 16p. 1994. pap. 4.00 (*1-885799-00-4*) October Release.

— Eagles & Other Prey: A Vietnam Experience in Prose & Poetry. Burton, Margaret E., ed. LC 88-29177. (Illus.). 80p. (Orig.). 1989. pap. 8.95 (*0-938310-09-7*) Volunteer Pubns.

— How Hawkhouse Went. Fleming, Harold, ed. (Illus.). 24p. 1994. 4.00 (*0-910047-02-2*) Black Willow.

— Wellspring. McGuirt, Curtis R., ed. (Illus.). 28p. (Orig.). 1994. pap. 4.00 (*1-885799-01-2*) October Release.

Caron, David D. Resolution of Private International Disputes. (C). 2000. text. write for info. (*0-87084-779-1*) Anderson Pub Co.

— Resolution of Private International Disputes: Documentary Supplement. 2000. pap. write for info. (*0-87084-781-3*) Anderson Pub Co.

Caron, David D. & Buderi, Charles L. Perspectives on U. S. Policy Toward the Law of the Sea: Prelude to the Final Session of the Third U. N. Conference of the Sea, Occasional Paper No. 35. 98p. 1985. 5.00 (*0-911189-12-2*) Law Sea Inst.

***Caron, David D. & Crook, John R., eds.** The Iran-United States Claims Tribunal & the Process of International Claims Resolution. 450p. 2000. 125.00 (*1-57105-113-9*) Transnatl Pubs.

Caron, Denis R. Connecticut Foreclosure - Supplement. 1991. 55.00 (*0-910051-27-5*) CT Law Trib.

— Connecticut Foreclosures: An Attorney's Manual of Practice & Procedure. 2nd ed. 350p. 1989. 135.00 (*0-910051-26-7*) CT Law Trib.

Caron, Francois. An Economic History of Modern France. Bray, Barbara, tr. from FRE. (Columbia Economic History of the Modern World Ser.). 360p. 1979. text 69.00 (*0-231-03860-7*) Col U Pr.

Caron, Francois, et al, eds. Innovations in the European Economy Between the Wars. LC 95-1423. 340p. 1995. lib. bdg. 125.50 (*3-11-013582-5*) De Gruyter.

Caron, George R. & Meares, Charlotte E. Fire of a Thousand Suns: The George R. "Bob" Caron Story, Tail Gunner of the Enola Gay. (Illus.). 272p. 1995. pap. 14.95 (*0-9639014-9-4*) WEB Pubng.

***Caron, Gerald, et al.** Women Also Journeyed with Him: Feminist Perspectives on the Bible. 232p. 2000. pap. 24.95 (*0-8146-5892-X*, M Glazier) Liturgical Pr.

Caron, Jacques, ed. Kierkegaard Aujourd'hui: Recherches Kierkegaardiennes au Danemark et en France. 179p. pap. 24.75 (*87-7838-335-8*) Odense Univ.

Caron, James E. & Inge, M. Thomas, eds. Sut Lovingood's Nat'ral Born Yarnspinner: Essays on George Washington Harris. (Illus.). 344p. 1996. text 44.95 (*0-8173-0821-0*) U of Ala Pr.

Caron, Jean. An Introduction to Psycholinguistics. Pownall, Tim, tr. 1992. text 40.00 (*0-8020-5026-3*) U of Toronto Pr.

— An Introduction to Psycholinguistics. Pownall, Tim, tr. 1992. pap. text 20.95 (*0-8020-7743-9*) U of Toronto Pr.

Caron, Jonathan F. American Souvenir Teaspoon Handbook. LC 90-92280. (Illus.). 247p. (Orig.). 1991. pap. 19.95 (*0-9628713-0-3*) J F Caron.

Caron, Kathy. Inside City Hall: A Guide to City Government in Portland, Maine. LC 88-80587. (Illus.). 75p. (Orig.). 1988. pap. 12.95 (*0-9620895-0-8*) Ledgewood Consult.

Caron, L. G., jt. ed. see Jerome, D.

Caron, Louis. The Draft Dodger. Homel, David T., tr. (ENG & FRE.). 160p. (Orig.). 1980. pap. 9.95 (*0-88784-085-X*, Pub. by Hse of Anansi Pr) Genl Dist Srvs.

***Caron, Lucille & St. Jacques, Phil.** Addition & Subtraction. LC 99-39205. (Math Success Ser.). 2000. 17.95 (*0-7660-1432-0*) Enslow Pubs.

— Fractions & Decimals. (Math Success Ser.). (Illus.). 64p. (YA). (gr. 4-10). 2000. lib. bdg. 17.95 (*0-7660-1430-4*) Enslow Pubs.

— Percents & Ratios. (Math Success Ser.). (Illus.). 64p. (YA). (gr. 4-10). 2000. lib. bdg. 17.95 (*0-7660-1435-5*) Enslow Pubs.

— Pre-Algebra & Algebra. (Math Success Ser.). (Illus.). 64p. (YA). (gr. 4-10). 2000. lib. bdg. 17.95 (*0-7660-1434-7*) Enslow Pubs.

Caron, Martine M., jt. auth. see Bond, Mary E.

Caron, Melissa. The Last (Lose & Stay Trim) Program: A Holistic Approach to Weight Loss. 87p. 1997. ring bd. 29.00 (*0-9657924-0-4*, 1001) Write Prodns.

***Caron, Michel & Seve, Annie-Pierre, eds.** Lectins & Pathology. 216p. 2000. text 95.00 (*90-5702-491-8*, Harwood Acad Pubs) Gordon & Breach.

Caron, Mona, jt. auth. see Shah, Idries.

Caron, Paul L., et al, eds. Federal Income Tax Anthology. 680p. 1997. pap. 29.95 (*0-87084-283-8*) Anderson Pub Co.

— Federal Wealth Transfer Tax Anthology. 500p. 1998. pap. 29.95 (*0-87084-280-3*) Anderson Pub Co.

Caron, Sandra. Human Sexuality: Cross Cultural Perspectives 238p. (C). 1997. text 31.80 (*0-536-59993-9*) Pearson Custom.

Caron, Sandra L. Cross Cultural Human Sexuality. LC 98-125180. 201p. 1997. pap. text 29.00 (*0-205-27416-1*) P-H.

***Caron, Timothy P.** Struggles over the Word: Race & Religion in O'Connor, Faulkner, Hurston & Wright. 160p. 2000. 26.95 (*0-86554-669-X*) Mercer Univ Pr.

Caron, Vicki. Between France & Germany: The Jews of Alsace-Lorraine, 1871-1918. LC 88-2131. 296p. 1988. 39.50 (*0-8047-1443-6*) Stanford U Pr.

— Uneasy Asylum: France & the Jewish Refugee Crisis, 1933-1942. LC 98-36350. (Studies in Jewish History & Culture). 730p. 1998. 65.00 (*0-8047-3312-0*) Stanford U Pr.

Carona, Mike, jt. auth. see Wills, Maralys.

Carona, Philip. Power Skills in Science. 1979. pap. text 4.95 (*0-07-010134-5*) McGraw.

Carona, Philip B. The Microscope & How to Use It. LC 73-131927. (Instruments of Science Ser.). (Illus.). 63p. reprint ed. pap. 30.00 (*0-608-15597-7*, 202967000062) Bks Demand.

Carone, Pasquale A., et al, eds. History of Mental Health & Industry. (Problems of Industrial Psychiatric Medicine Ser.: Vol. 10). 128p. 1985. 30.95 (*0-89885-207-2*, Kluwer Acad Hman Sci) Kluwer Academic.

Carone, Pasquale A., ed. see Yolles, Stanley F.

Carone, Sadia. Circle Words. 2nd ed. 89p. 1995. 11.00 (*0-9673055-0-0*) Alternate Society Pr.

Caronna. Acute & Recurrent Unconsciousness. Date not set. text 15.99 (*0-7506-9542-0*) Buttrwrth-Heinemann.

Caronni, Ernesto P. Craniofacial Surgery. 620p. 1985. 89.50 (*0-316-12877-5*, Little Brwn Med Div) Lppncott W & W.

Caroons, Steven, jt. auth. see Harris, Elaine K.

Caropreso, Frank & Conference Board Staff. Communications Strategies for Changing Times. LC 93-218711. (Conference Board Report Ser.). 47 p. 1991. write for info. (*0-8237-0412-2*) Conference Bd.

***Carosa, Christopher.** Due Diligence: The Individual Trustee's Guide to Selecting & Monitoring A Professional Investm. (Illus.). 160p. 1999. pap. 19.95 (*0-9669745-0-6*) Ardman Regional Ltd.

Caroscio, James T. Caring for ALS Patients: A Guide for Patient Care. (Illus.). 224p. 1986. 37.00 (*0-86577-246-0*) Thieme Med Pubs.

Caroselli, Marlena. The Language of Leadership. 3rd ed. 253p. 1990. reprint ed. 24.95 (*0-922411-05-0*) CPD NY.

Caroselli, Marlene. Breakthrough Creativity! Developing Ideas That Make a Difference. LC 94-14081. 92p. 1994. pap. 14.95 (*0-527-76244-X*) Productivity Inc.

— Communicate with Quality: Tips & Techniques for Continuous Improvement of the Communications Process. 104p. (Orig.). 1991. pap. 9.95 (*0-922411-01-8*) CPD NY.

— Continuous Learning in Organizations: Fifty Principles & One Hundred Fifty Activities. 300p. 1994. ring bd. 99.95 (*0-87425-978-9*) HRD Press.

— Defeating Procrastination: 52 Fail Safe Tips for Keeping Time on Your Side. Scanlon, Kelly & Cole, Mason, eds. LC 96-69847. (Self-Study Sourcebook Ser.). (Illus.). 189p. 1997. pap. 15.95 (*1-57294-078-6*, 13-0017) SkillPath Pubns.

— Empower Yourself! A Take-Charge Assistant Book. LC 97-18762. (Take-Charge Assistant Book Ser.: No. 1). 128p. 1997. pap. 12.95 (*0-8144-7951-0*) AMACOM.

— Empowerment Works: A Guide for Supervisors & Employees. Miller, Karen M., ed. LC 98-74672. (How-to Book Ser.). 88p. 1999. pap. 12.95 (*1-884926-97-5*, EMPMT) Amer Media.

— Great Session Openers, Closers, & Energizers: Quick Activities for Warming up Your Audience & Ending on a High Note. LC 97-48489. 300p. 1998. 79.95 (*0-07-012009-9*); pap. 34.95 (*0-07-012010-2*) McGraw-Hill Prof.

— Hiring & Firing: What Every Manager Needs to Know. rev. ed. (Illus.). 119p. 1991. 12.95 (*1-878542-35-4*, 12-0008) SkillPath Pubns.

— Info-Flood: How to Swim in a Sea of Information Without Going Under. Scanlon, Kelly, ed. LC 96-70931. (Self-Study Sourcebook Ser.). (Illus.). 172p. 1997. pap. 15.95 (*1-57294-041-7*, 13-0013) SkillPath Pubns.

— The Innovative Secretary. Scanlon, Kelly, ed. LC 95-69804. (Self-Study Sourcebook Ser.). (Illus.). 178p. 1996. pap. 15.95 (*1-57294-013-1*, 13-0011) SkillPath Pubns.

***Caroselli, Marlene.** Leadership Skills for Managers. (Briefcase Bks.). 2000. pap. 14.95 (*0-07-136430-7*) McGraw.

Caroselli, Marlene. Meetings That Work. rev. ed. 123p. 1995. 12.95 (*1-878542-24-9*, 12-0006) SkillPath Pubns.

***Caroselli, Marlene.** Memory Tips for the Forgetful. LC 98-70097. (Illus.). 126p. 1999. pap. write for info. (*1-883553-80-6*) R Chang Assocs.

Caroselli, Marlene. P. E. R. S. U. A. D. E. Communication Strategies That Move People to Action. Scanlon, Kelly, ed. LC 96-67386. 177p. (Orig.). 1996. pap. 15.95 (*1-57294-053-0*, 13-0019) SkillPath Pubns.

— PowerWriting. LC 88-92374. 74p. (Orig.). (C). 1988. pap. 9.95 (*0-922411-00-X*) CPD NY.

— Promoting Yourself: 50 Ways to Increase Your Prestige, Power, & Paycheck. Scanlon, Kelly, ed. LC 95-68998. (Illus.). 139p. (Orig.). 1995. 15.95 (*1-878542-89-3*) SkillPath Pubns.

— Quality Care: Prescription for Injecting Quality into Health Care Systems. LC 97-163014. (Illus.). 304p. 1997. boxed set 69.95 (*1-57444-043-8*) St Lucie Pr.

— Quality-Driven Designs: Thirty-Six Activities to Reinforce TQM Concepts. LC 92-60880. 120p. 1992. ring bd. 89.95 (*0-88390-061-0*, Pfffr & Co) Jossey-Bass.

— Quality Games for Trainers: 101 Playful Lessons in Quality & Continuous Improvements. LC 95-40601. (Illus.). 304p. 1995. 79.95 (*0-07-011502-8*); pap. 34.95 (*0-07-011503-6*) McGraw.

— The Quality Secretary: Success Secrets from TQM Support Staff. 150p. (Orig.). 1992. pap. 9.95 (*0-922411-02-6*) CPD NY.

— That's No Problem: A Problem-Free Approach to Problem Solving. Jensen, Jill, ed. LC 97-70155. (How-To Book Ser.). 123p. 1997. pap. 12.95 (*1-884926-74-6*, PROBL) Amer Media.

— Thinking on Your Feet: Tools to Communicate Clearly & Convincingly. Pohl, Nina, ed. LC 91-76252. (Fifty-Minute Ser.). (Illus.). 86p. (Orig.). 1992. pap. 10.95 (*1-56052-117-1*) Crisp Pubns.

Caroselli, Marlene & Edison, Linda. Quality Care: Prescription for Injecting Quality into Healthcare Systems. 1998. lib. bdg., teacher ed. 39.95 (*1-57444-138-8*, SL1388) St Lucie Pr.

Caroselli, Marlene & Harris, David. Risk-Taking: Fifty Ways to Turn Risks into Rewards. (Self-Study Sourcebook Ser.). xii, 148p. (Orig.). 1993. pap. 15.95 (*1-878542-32-X*, 13-0003) SkillPath Pubns.

Caroselli, Susan L. Italian Panel Paint Early Renaissance. LC 94-79755. (Illus.). 136p. 1995. 40.00 (*0-295-97434-6*) U of Wash Pr.

— The Painted Enamels of Limoges. LC 92-85528. (Illus.). 208p. 1993. 50.00 (*0-500-97406-3*, Pub. by Thames Hudson) Norton.

Caroso, Fabritio. Courtly Dance of the Renaissance: A New Translation & Edition of the Nobilta di Dame (1600) (Illus.). 423p. 1995. pap. text 14.95 (*0-486-28619-3*) Dover.

Caroso, Fabrizio. Il Ballarino. fac. ed. (Monuments of Music & Music Literature in Facsimile Ser., Series I: Vol. 46). (Illus.). 1967. lib. bdg. 75.00 (*0-8450-2246-6*) Broude.

Carosso, Rebecca B. Technical Communication. 522p. (C). 1986. pap. write for info. (*0-534-06180-X*) Wadsworth Pub.

Carosso, Vincent P. The Morgans: Private International Bankers, 1854-1913. LC 86-14829. (Harvard Studies in Business History: No. 38). (Illus.). 904p. 1987. 69.95 (*0-674-58729-4*) HUP.

Carosso, Vincent P., ed. The Boston Stock Exchange: An Original Anthology. LC 75-2622. (Wall Street & the Security Market Ser.). 1975. 35.95 (*0-405-06949-9*) Ayer.

— The Chicago Securities Market: An Original Arno Press Anthology. LC 75-2627. (Wall Street & the Security Market Ser.). 1975. 18.95 (*0-405-06953-7*) Ayer.

— Finance & Industry: The New York Stock Exchange: Banks, Bankers, Business Houses, & Moneyed Institutions of the Great Metropolis of the United States. LC 75-2620. (Wall Street & the Security Market Ser.). 1975. reprint ed. 25.95 (*0-405-06947-2*) Ayer.

— The New York Stock Market: An Original Anthology. LC 75-2656. (Wall Street & the Security Market Ser.). 1975. 52.95 (*0-405-06981-2*) Ayer.

— Regulation of the Security Markets: An Original Anthology. LC 75-2662. (Wall Street & the Security Market Ser.). 1975. 35.95 (*0-405-06986-3*) Ayer.

— Two Private Banking Partnerships: An Original Anthology. LC 75-2676. (Wall Street & the Security Market Ser.). (Illus.). 1975. 50.95 (*0-405-07238-4*) Ayer.

— Wall Street & the Security Markets, 58 vols., Vol. 30. 1975. reprint ed. 770.00 (*0-405-19007-7*) Ayer.

— Wall Street & the Security Markets, 58 vols., Vols. 1[00ad]29. 1975. reprint ed. 2103.00 (*0-405-12493-7*) Ayer.

Carosso, Vincent P. & Bruchey, Stuart, eds. The Survival of Small Business. LC 78-18155. (Small Business Enterprise in America Ser.). 1979. lib. bdg. 28.95 (*0-405-11512-1*) Ayer.

Carosso, Vincent P., jt. ed. see Bruchey, Stuart.

Carosso, Vincent P., ed. see Bruchey, Stuart.

Carosso, Vincent P., jt. ed. see Bruchey, Stuart.

Carosso, Vincent P., ed. see Bunn, Verne A.

Carosso, Vincent P., ed. see Bunzel, John A.

Carosso, Vincent P., ed. see Carpenter, Walter H., Jr. & Handler, Edward.

Carosso, Vincent P., ed. see Christensen, Roland C.

Carosso, Vincent P., ed. see Commerce Clearing House, Inc.

Carosso, Vincent P., ed. see Daughters, Charles G.

Carosso, Vincent P., ed. see Flink, Salomon J.

Carosso, Vincent P., ed. see Glover, John D.

Carosso, Vincent P., ed. see Haas, Harold M.

Carosso, Vincent P., ed. see Hollander, Edward, et al.

Carosso, Vincent P., ed. see Howard, Marshall C.

Carosso, Vincent P., ed. see Kaplan, Abraham D.

Carosso, Vincent P., ed. see Konopa, Leonard J.

Carosso, Vincent P., ed. see Lumer, Wilfred.

Carosso, Vincent P., ed. see McGee, John S.

Carosso, Vincent P., ed. see Merwin, Charles L.

Carosso, Vincent P., ed. see Morris, Bruce R.

Carosso, Vincent P., ed. see Neifeld, Morris R.

Carosso, Vincent P., ed. see Pepper, Roger S.

Carosso, Vincent P., ed. see Proxmire, William.

Carosso, Vincent P., ed. see Richards, Max D.

Carosso, Vincent P., ed. see Schor, Stanley S.

Carosso, Vincent P., ed. see Still, Jack W.

Carosso, Vincent P., ed. see Tosiello, Rosario J.

Carosso, Vincent P., ed. see U. S. House of Representative Subcommittee No. 2 o.

Carosso, Vincent P., ed. see U. S. House of Representatives Select Committee on.

Carosso, Vincent P., ed. see U. S. Senate Committee on Banking & Currency.

Carosso, Vincent P., ed. see U. S. Senate Select Committee on Small Business, S.

Carosso, Vincent P., ed. see Vatter, Harold G.

Carosso, Vincent P., ed. see Vatter, Paul A.

Carosso, Vincent P., ed. see Weissman, Rudolph L.

Carosso, Vincent P., ed. see Zeigler, Harmon.

Carotenuto, Aldo. The Call of the Daimon: Love & Truth in the Writings of Franz Kafka: the Trial & the Castle. Nobar, Charles, tr. LC 93-29052. (ITA.). 376p. (Orig.). 1994. pap. 19.95 (*0-933029-83-7*) Chiron Pubns.

— The Difficult Art: A Critical Discourse on Psychotherapy. Tambureno, Joan, tr. from ITA. LC 92-7870. 312p. (Orig.). 1992. pap. 5.95 (*0-933029-64-0*) Chiron Pubns.

— Eros & Pathos. 144p. 1989. pap. 16.00 (*0-919123-39-2*, Pub. by Inner City Bks) BookWorld.

— Kant's Dove: The History of Transference in Psychoanalysis. Tambureno, Joan, tr. from ITA. 184p. (Orig.). 1990. pap. 8.95 (*0-933029-50-0*) Chiron Pubns.

— The Spiral Way. 144p. 1995. pap. 16.00 (*0-919123-24-4*, Pub. by Inner City Bks) BookWorld.

— To Love, to Betray: Life As Betrayal. LC 95-51849.Tr. of Amare Tradire. 200p. (Orig.). 1996. pap. 14.95 (*0-933029-97-7*, 977) Chiron Pubns.

— The Vertical Labyrinth. 144p. 1985. pap. 16.00 (*0-919123-19-8*, Pub. by Inner City Bks) BookWorld.

Carothers, Diane F. Self-Instruction Manual for Filing Catalog Cards. LC 81-3606. 127p. reprint ed. pap. 39.40 (*0-7837-5916-9*, 204571500007) Bks Demand.

Carothers, Doris. Chronology of the Federal Emergency Relief Administration: May 12, 1933 to December 31, 1935. LC 70-165681. (Research Monographs: Vol. 6). 1971. reprint ed. lib. bdg. 19.50 (*0-306-70338-6*) Da Capo.

Carothers, J. Edward. Caring for the World: A Christian Religious Experience. fac. ed. LC 82-195056. (Illus.). 146p. pap. 45.30 (*0-7837-7709-4*, 204746800007) Bks Demand.

— Living with the Parables: Jesus & the Reign of God. LC BT0738.. 145p. (Orig.). 1984. reprint ed. pap. 45.00 (*0-608-00244-5*, 206074600006) Bks Demand.

Carothers, James B. & Faulkner, William. William Faulkner's Short Stories. LC 85-8523. (Studies in Modern Literature: No. 34). 183p. reprint ed. pap. 52.20 (*0-8357-1500-0*, 2070630) Bks Demand.

Carothers, James E. & Gasten, Ruth S. Helping Children to Like Themselves: Activities for Building Self-Esteem. 1978. pap. 4.95 (*0-9602090-1-8*) RJ Assocs.

Carothers, John C. African Mind in Health & Diseases: A Study in Ethnopsychiatry, No. 17--17. LC 73-100260. 177p. 1970. reprint ed. lib. bdg. 35.00 (*0-8371-2864-1*, CMI&) Greenwood.

Carothers, Katie. Croutons. 1993. pap. 10.95 (*0-9639528-2-X*, Blue Beg Pub) Valentine CA.

— White Trash. 200p. (C). 1994. pap. 10.95 (*0-9639528-0-3*, Blue Beg Pub) Valentine CA.

Carothers, Merlin R. Answers to Praise. 169p. (Orig.). 1972. pap. 6.95 (*0-943026-07-5*) Carothers.

— The Bible on Praise. 32p. (Orig.). 1981. pap. 3.25 (*0-943026-03-2*) Carothers.

— Bringing Heaven into Hell. 120p. (Orig.). 1976. pap. 6.95 (*0-943026-10-5*) Carothers.

— De la Prision a la Alabanza.Tr. of Prison to Praise. (SPA.). 128p. 1975. pap. 5.99 (*0-8297-0447-7*) Vida Pubs.

Carothers, Merlin R. Del Temor a la Fe.Tr. of From Fear to Faith. 1997. pap. text 8.99 (*0-88113-484-8*) Caribe Betania.

Carothers, Merlin R. From Fear to Faith. LC 96-36579. 1997. pap. 11.99 (*0-7852-7358-1*) Nelson.

— Let Me Entertain You. 1992. 6.95 (*0-943026-21-0*) Carothers.

— More Power to You. 143p. (Orig.). 1982. pap. 6.95 (*0-943026-00-8*) Carothers.

— El Poder de la Alabanza. (SPA.). 224p. 1996. pap. 6.99 (*0-8297-0444-2*) Vida Pubs.

— Power in Praise. 143p. 1972. pap. 6.95 (*0-943026-01-6*) Carothers.

— Power in Praise: Giant Print. 1992. 7.95 (*0-943026-23-7*) Carothers.

— Praise Works. 161p. (Orig.). 1973. pap. 6.95 (*0-943026-06-7*) Carothers.

— Prison to Praise. 106p. 1970. pap. 3.95 (*0-943026-02-4*) Carothers.

— Prison to Praise: Giant Print. 106p. (Orig.). 1970. pap. 5.95 (*0-943026-08-3*) Carothers.

— Respuestas a la Alabanza Revisada.Tr. of Answers to Praise. (SPA.). 144p. 1995. pap. 7.99 (*0-8297-2035-9*) Vida Pubs.

C

— Victory on Praise Mountain. 175p. 1979. pap. 6.95 (0-943026-04-0) Carothers.
— Walking & Leaping. 129p. (Orig.). 1974. pap. 6.95 (0-943026-05-9) Carothers.
— What's on Your Mind? 1984. pap. 6.95 (0-943026-13-X) Carothers.
Carothers, N. L. Real Analysis. LC 98-31982. (Illus.). 420p. (C). 1999. text. write for info. (0-521-49749-3); pap. text 29.95 (0-521-49756-6) Cambridge U Pr.
Carothers, Neil. Fractional Money: A History of Small Coins & Fractional Paper Currency of the United States. (Illus.). 392p. 1988. reprint ed. pap. 19.95 (0-943161-12-6) Bowers & Merena.
— Fractional Money: A History of the Small Coins & Fractional Paper Currency of the United States. LC 65-26361. (Reprints of Economic Classics Ser.). xiii, 372p. 1967. reprint ed. 49.50 (0-678-00253-3) Kelley.
Carothers, Robert L. Freedom & Other Times. 48p. 1972. write for info. (0-318-64116-X) Poets Pr.
Carothers, Roberta, jt. auth. see McKeon, James.
Carothers, Steven W. Wildlife of the Colorado Plateau. (Illus.). 50p. 1993. pap. 5.95 (0-89734-063-9) Mus Northern Ariz.
Carothers, Steven W. & House, Dorothy A. Birds of Prey. (Plateau Ser.). (Illus.). 50p. 1993. pap. 6.95 (0-89734-110-4) Mus Northern Ariz.
***Carothers, Thomas.** Aiding Democracy Abroad: The Learning Curve. LC 99-45358. 1999. pap. write for info. (0-87003-169-4) Carnegie Endow.
Carothers, Thomas. Assessing Democracy Assistance: The Case of Romania. 144p. 1996. 12.95 (0-87003-102-3) Carnegie Endow.
— In the Name of Democracy: U. S. Policy Toward Latin America in the Regan Years. 1993. pap. 16.95 (0-520-08260-5, Pub. by U CA Pr) Cal Prin Full Svc.
Carotta, Michael. Being Catholic. Zanzig, Thomas, ed. (Discovering Program Ser.). (Illus.). 50p. 1989. teacher ed. 6.00 (0-88489-189-5); text 3.00 (0-88489-188-7) St Marys.
— Director's Manual: Discovering: A Junior High Religion Program. Zanzig, Thomas, ed. (Discovering Program Ser.). 134p. 1989. teacher ed., ring bd. 56.00 (0-88489-212-3) St Marys.
— Learning to Communicate. Zanzig, Thomas, ed. (Discovering Program Ser.). (Illus.). 46p. 1989. teacher ed. 6.00 (0-88489-199-2); pap. 3.00 (0-88489-198-4) St Marys.
Carotta, Michael & Dillon, Valerie V. Growing up Sexually. Zanzig, Thomas, ed. (Discovering Program Ser.). (Illus.). 51p. 1989. teacher ed. 6.00 (0-88489-193-3); text 3.00 (0-88489-192-5) St Marys.
Carousel Staff. Scott Joplin Melody Dicer. (Orig.). 1983. pap. text 8.95 (0-935474-16-1) Carousel Pubns Ltd.
Carousso, Dorothee H. How to Search for Your Revolutionary Patriot in Pennsylvania. (Special Publications: No. 2). 12p. 1994. reprint ed. pap. 2.00 (1-887099-01-8) Geneal Soc Pa.
Carovillano, R. L. & Forbes, J. M., eds. Solar-Terrestial Physics: Principles & Theoretical Foundations. 1983. text 376.50 (90-277-1632-3) Kluwer Academic.
Carovillano, R. L., ed. see Conference on Physics of the Magnetosphere, Boston.
***Carovillano, Robert L., et al, eds.** Sun-Earth Plasma Connections. LC 99-28915. (Geophysical Monograph Ser.: Vol. 109). 11p. 1999. 67.00 (0-87590-092-5) Am Geophysical.
Carow, Robert. Compensation of Civil Service Employees: A Study of United States & United Kingdom Policy, 1625-1995. rev. ed. LC 96-41527. (Studies in the History of American Labor). (Illus.). 234p. 1996. text 68.00 (0-8153-2542-8) Garland.
Carozza, Carl, jt. auth. see Silver, Abigail.
Carozzi, Albert V., tr. see Gohau, Gabriel.
Carozzi, Albert V., tr. see Trompette, Ronald.
Carozzi, Marguerite, ed. see Ellenberger, Francois.
Carozzi, Marguerite, ed. & tr. see Gohau, Gabriel.
Carozzi, Marguerite, tr. see Gohau, Gabriel.
Carp, E. Wayne. Family Matters: Secrecy & Disclosure in the History of Adoption. LC 97-40023. 288p. 1999. text 29.00 (0-674-79668-3) HUP.
***Carp, E. Wayne.** Family Matters: Secrecy & Disclosure in the History of Adoption. 2000. pap. 16.95 (0-674-00186-9) HUP.
Carp, E. Wayne. To Starve the Army at Pleasure: Continental Army Administration & American Political Culture, 1775-1783. LC 83-19697. (Illus.). xv, 305p. 1984. pap. 16.95 (0-8078-4269-9) U of NC Pr.
Carp, Frances M. Elder Abuse & Neglect at Home: A Research Perspective. LC 99-35045. (Illus.). 224p. 1999. text 36.95 (0-8261-1291-9) Springer Pub.
***Carp, Matatias.** Holocaust in Romania. 300p. 2000. 39.95 (0-9665734-7-1) Simon Publns.
Carp, Robert A. & Rowland, C. K. Policymaking & Politics in the Federal District Courts. LC 82-13462. 220p. 1983. text 30.00 (0-87049-369-8) U of Tenn Pr.
Carp, Robert A. & Stidham, Ronald. Federal Courts. 2nd ed. 253p. 1990. 21.95 (0-87187-580-2) Congr Quarterly.
— The Federal Courts. 3rd ed. LC 98-9246. 236p. 1998. 23.95 (0-87187-820-8) CQ Products.
— Judicial Process in America. 3rd ed. LC 95-16858. 420p. (YA). (gr. 11). 1995. pap. text 34.95 (0-87187-833-X) Congr Quarterly.
— Judicial Process in America. 4th ed. LC 98-5039. 408p. 1998. 42.95 (1-56802-394-4) Congr Quarterly.
Carp, Robert A., jt. auth. see Rowland, C. K.
***Carp, Roger.** Classic Lionel Display Layouts You Can Build. (Illus.). 2000. pap. 16.95 (0-89778-509-6) Kalmbach.
Carp, Roger. Lionel's Model Builder: The Magazine That Shaped the Toy Train Hobby. Thompson, Terry, ed. (Illus.). 96p. 1998. pap. 15.95 (0-89778-446-4, 10-8235, Kalmbach Books) Kalmbach.
— The World's Greatest Toy Train Maker: Insiders Remember Lionel. LC 97-223678. (Illus.). 112p. 1997. 24.95 (0-89778-439-1, 10-8225, Kalmbach Books) Kalmbach.
Carp, Roger, ed. Greenberg's Repair & Operating Manual for Lionel Trains, 1945-69. 7th ed. LC 98-136867. (Illus.). 752p. 1998. pap. 21.95 (0-89778-455-3, 10-8160, Kalmbach Books) Kalmbach.
Carp, Roger, ed. see Ambrose, Paul V.
Carpanetto, Dino, jt. auth. see Ricuperati, Guisseppe.
Carpelan, Bo. Axel. McDuff, David, tr. 376p. 1998. 26.95 (0-8101-1617-0, Hydra Bks) Northwestern U Pr.
— Room Without Walls: Selected Poems. Born, Anne, tr. & intro. by. 143p. 1987. pap. 14.95 (0-318-39997-0) Dufour.
— Room Without Walls: Selected Poems. 143p. 1987. pap. 16.95 (0-948259-08-6) Dufour.
— Urwind. McDuff, David, tr. from FIN. LC 97-189508. 220p. 1997. pap. 24.95 (1-85754-250-9, Pub. by Carcanet Pr) Paul & Co Pubs.
— Urwind. McDuff, David, tr. from SWE. 200p. 1998. 24.95 (0-8101-1618-9, Hydra Bks) Northwestern U Pr.
Carpender, Rhys. The Sculpture of the Nike Temple Parapet. Date not set. write for info. (0-8434-0126-5, Pub. by McGrath NH) Ayer.
***Carpenito, Lynda J.** Nursing Care Plans & Documentation: Nursing Diagnoses & Collaborative Problems. 3rd ed. LC 98-46595. 825p. 1998. pap. write for info. (0-7817-1742-6) Lppncott W & W.
Carpenito, Lynda Juall. Handbook of Nursing Diagnosis. 8th ed. LC 99-10471. 17p. 1999. write for info. (0-7817-1971-2) Lppncott W & W.
***Carpenito, Lynda Juall.** Nursing Diagnosis: Application to Clinical Practice. 8th ed. LC 99-36287. 1,232p. 2000. pap. text 36.95 (0-7817-1970-4) Lppncott W & W.
Carpenter. Acts of Fiction: Resistance & Resolution from Sade to Baudelaire. (C). 1995. pap. text 18.95 (0-271-01449-0) Pa St U Pr.
— Power of Public Speaking: Eloquence That Works. LC 99-182785. 180p. (C). 1998. pap. text 14.95 (0-205-27124-3) P-H.
— Quality Multimedia Systems. (Multimedia Ser.). 1997. mass mkt. 43.95 (0-534-23364-3) Wadsworth Pub.
— Social Cognition Joint. 1998. pap. text 14.00 (0-226-09461-8) U Ch Pr.
— Working for Health: The History of COHSE. (C). 1988. pap. 25.00 (0-85315-682-4, Pub. by Lawrence & Wishart) NYU Pr.
Carpenter, ed. Market-Driving Strategies. (C). 1998. text. write for info. (0-321-01414-6) Addson-Wesley Educ.
— Market Driving Strategies. (C). 1996. text. write for info. (0-321-40453-X) Addson-Wesley Educ.
— Market-Driving Strategies: A Reader. LC 97-195665. 540p. (C). 1997. pap. text 49.00 (0-321-01413-8) Addson-Wesley Educ.
Carpenter, et al. Markt Drivng Strat Rdr. (C). 1995. text 25.00 (0-673-99601-8) Addson-Wesley Educ.
Carpenter, A. A Genealogical History of the Rehoboth Branch of the Carpenter Family in America, Brought down from Their English Ancestor, John Carpenter, 1303. (Illus.). 921p. 1989. reprint ed. pap. 112.00 (0-8328-0365-0); reprint ed. lib. bdg. 122.00 (0-8328-0364-2) Higginson Bk Co.
— Sea Drift: Full Score for Orchestra. 40p. 1989. pap. 15.00 (0-7935-3610-3, 50488512) H Leonard.
Carpenter, Alejo. El Siglo de las Luces. 1999. 24.95 (84-322-0757-8) E Seix Barral.
Carpenter, Alice B. & Carpenter, Buddy. Questions & Answers in Quartz Watch Repairing. 1989. 12.95 (0-918845-13-0) Am Watchmakers.
Carpenter, Allan. Benin (Dahomey) Owen, Wilfred, ed. LC 77-20877. (Enchantment of Africa Ser.). 96p. (YA). (gr. 6-12). reprint ed. pap. 30.00 (0-8357-3475-7, 203976200013) Bks Demand.
— The Encyclopedia of the Central West. fac. ed. LC 89-25849. (Illus.). 544p. 1990. reprint ed. pap. 168.70 (0-7837-8151-2, 204785600008) Bks Demand.
Carpenter, Allan & Balow, Tom. Algeria. LC 77-20876. (Enchantment of Africa Ser.). 96p. (YA). (gr. 6-12). reprint ed. pap. 30.00 (0-8357-3474-9, 203976100013) Bks Demand.
— Botswana. Cohen, Ronald, ed. LC 72-10379. (Enchantment of Africa Ser.). 94p. (YA). (gr. 6-12). reprint ed. pap. 30.00 (0-8357-3476-5, 203976300013) Bks Demand.
Carpenter, Allan & Maginnis, Matthew. Burundi. Rowe, John, ed. LC 73-4971. (Enchantment of Africa Ser.). 93p. (YA). (gr. 6-12). reprint ed. pap. 30.00 (0-8357-2700-9, 203976400013) Bks Demand.
Carpenter, Allan & Provorse, Carl. Facts about the Cities. 2nd ed. (Illus.). 632p. 1996. 65.00 (0-8242-0897-8) Wilson.
— The World Almanac of the U. S. A. World Almanac Editors, ed. 1996. pap. 9.95 (0-88687-791-1); pap. 19.95 (0-88687-792-X) Wrld Almnc.
— The World Almanac of the U. S. A. (Illus.). 416p. 1998. pap. 10.95 (0-88687-831-4) Wrld Almnc.
Carpenter, Allan, et al. Between Two Rivers: Iowa Year by Year, 1846-1996. LC 97-38304. (Illus.). 377p. 1997. pap. 16.95 (0-8138-2735-3) Iowa St U Pr.
Carpenter, Amanda. Cry Wolf. (Presents Ser.). 1993. mass mkt. 2.99 (0-373-11596-2, 1-11596-3) Harlequin Bks.
— Perfect Chance. (Harlequin Presents Ser.: No. 1826). 1996. per. 3.50 (0-373-11826-0, 1-11826-4) Harlequin Bks.
— Piege Dore por une Actrice. (Azur Ser.: Bk. 736). 1999. mass mkt. 3.50 (0-373-34736-7, 1-34736-8) Harlequin Bks.
— A Solitary Heart. (Presents Ser.). 1994. per. 2.99 (0-373-11635-7, 1-11635-9) Harlequin Bks.
Carpenter, Andrew, ed. Verse in English from Eighteenth-Century Ireland. LC 98-162129. 623p. 1998. 60.00 (1-85918-103-1, Pub. by Cork Univ); pap. 29.95 (1-85918-104-X, Pub. by Cork Univ) Intl Spec Bk.
Carpenter, Angelica S. & Shirley, Jean. Frances Hodgson Burnett: Beyond the Secret Garden. (Biographies Ser.). (Illus.). 128p. (J). (gr. 5 up). 1990. lib. bdg. 23.93 (0-8225-4905-0, Lerner Publctns) Lerner Pub.
Carpenter, Angelica S. & Shirley, Jean. Frances Hodgson Burnett: Beyond the Secret Garden. (Biographies Ser.). (YA). (gr. 5 up). 1992. pap. 2.98 (0-8225-9610-5, First Ave Edns) Lerner Pub.
— Robert Louis Stevenson: Finding Treasure Island. LC 96-48274. (J). 1997. lib. bdg. 23.93 (0-8225-4955-7, Lerner Publctns) Lerner Pub.
Carpenter, Anita, jt. auth. see Gabrielson, Christine.
Carpenter, Anne N. Ma's Ram & Other Poems. LC 85-1893. (Eileen W. Barnes Award Ser.). (Illus.). 80p. (Orig.). 1985. pap. 6.50 (0-938158-06-6) Saturday Pr.
***Carpenter, Art.** Annotate: Simply the Basics. 110p. (C). 1999. pap. 14.95 (1-58025-578-7) SAS Publ.
Carpenter, Art. Carpenter's Complete Guide to the SAS(R) Macro Language. LC 98-226399. 244p. (C). 1998. pap. 29.95 (1-58025-137-4, BR56100) SAS Publ.
Carpenter, Arthur L. & Shipp, Charles E. Quick Results with SAS/GRAPH Software. 272p. (C). 1995. pap. 32.95 (1-55544-683-3, BR55127) SAS Publ.
Carpenter, B. E. & Doran, R. W., eds. A. M. Turing's: ACE Report of 1946. (Charles Babbage Institute Reprint Series for the History of Computing). 125p. 1986. 30.00 (0-262-03114-0) MIT Pr.
Carpenter, B. Stephen, et al, eds. Computers in Activation Analysis & Gamma-Ray Spectroscopy: Proceedings. LC 79-19600. (DOE Symposium Ser.). 905p. 1979. pap. 30.50 (0-87079-117-6, CONF-780421); fiche 9.00 (0-87079-169-9, CONF-780421) DOE.
Carpenter, Barbara. Blue Riband of the Heather. 2nd ed. (Illus.). 160p. 1996. text 34.95 (0-85236-318-4, Pub. by Farming Pr) Diamond Farm Bk.
— National Sheepdog Champions of Britain & Ireland. (Illus.). 338p. 1994. text 49.95 (0-85236-282-X, Pub. by Farming Pr) Diamond Farm Bk.
Carpenter, Barbara, ed. Ethnic Heritage in Mississippi. LC 92-5655. (Illus.). 192p. 1992. pap. text 17.95 (0-87805-578-9) U Pr of Miss.
Carpenter, Barbara, jt. illus. see Carpenter, Don.
Carpenter, Barry, ed. Families in Context: Emerging Trends in Family Support & Early Intervention. LC 98-102233. 176p. 1997. pap. 24.95 (1-85346-489-9, Pub. by David Fulton) Taylor & Francis.
Carpenter, Barry, et al, eds. Enabling Access: Effective Teaching & Learning for Pupils with Learning Difficulties. LC 97-121417. 384p. 1996. pap. 27.95 (1-85346-420-1, Pub. by David Fulton) Taylor & Francis.
Carpenter, Barry K. Determination of Organic Reaction Mechanisms. 272p. 1984. 99.95 (0-471-89369-2) Wiley.
***Carpenter, Belinda J.** Re-thinking Prostitution: Feminism, Sex, & the Self. LC 98-44636. (Eruptions Ser.: No. 6). 168p. (C). 2000. pap. text 24.95 (0-8204-4417-0) P Lang Pubng.
Carpenter, Beth. Strength of the Spirit: One Woman's Journey Towards Health & Enlightenment Through a 10 Year Battle with Cancer. 192p. 1999. pap. 12.95 (0-9670836-0-5) Violet Crwn.
Carpenter, Betty O. The Brosh. LC 98-87506. 325p. 1998. pap. 15.00 (0-7388-0094-5) Xlibris Corp.
— The Brosh: Brosh - Bionic Replacement of Species Humanoid. LC 98-87506. 325p. 1998. 25.00 (0-7388-0093-7) Xlibris Corp.
— Lady of the Lake. LC 98-89881. 365p. 1999. 25.00 (0-7388-0315-4); pap. 15.00 (0-7388-0316-2) Xlibris Corp.
— Tutoring for Pay: Earn While You Help Others Learn. 214p. 1991. pap. 31.95 (0-398-06041-X) C C Thomas.
— Tutoring for Pay: Earn While You Help Others Learn. 214p. (C). 1991. text 48.95 (0-398-05714-1) C C Thomas.
***Carpenter, Betty P.** How to Prevent Falls: A Comprehensive Guide to Better Balance. 4th rev. ed. (Illus.). 105p. 1999. pap. 11.95 (0-9621031-5-2) Sr Fitness Prodns.
Carpenter, Bettye H., ed. Main Course: Heritage & Hope Cookbook. (Illus.). 304p. 1988. pap. 12.95 (0-317-91270-4) S Main Baptist Ch.
Carpenter, Bob. Type-Logical Semantics. LC 97-863. (Language, Speech & Communication Ser.). (Illus.). 550p. 1997. 60.00 (0-262-03248-1, Bradford Bks) MIT Pr.
— Type-Logical Semantics. LC 97-863. (Language, Speech & Communication Ser.). (Illus.). 550p. 1998. pap. text 35.00 (0-262-53149-6, Bradford Bks) MIT Pr.
Carpenter, Bogdana. Monumenta Polonica. (Michigan Slavic Materials Ser.: No. 31). 1990. 27.50 (0-930042-68-9) Mich Slavic Pubns.
— The Poetic Avant-Garde in Poland, 1918-1939. LC 83-1126. (Publications on Russia & Eastern Europe of the School of International Studies: No. 11). (Illus.). 254p. 1983. 25.00 (0-295-95996-7) U of Wash Pr.
Carpenter, Bogdana, tr. see Herbert, Zbigniew.
Carpenter, Bonnie L., jt. auth. see Hunt, Jan.
Carpenter, Brown H., jt. ed. see Thomas, Erwin K.
Carpenter, Bruce N., ed. Personal Coping: Theory, Research, & Application. LC 92-8378. 276p. 1992. 65.00 (0-275-93012-2, C3012, Praeger Pubs) Greenwood.
Carpenter, Bruce N., jt. auth. see Hansson, Robert O.
Carpenter, Bruce W. W. O. J. Nieuwenkamp: First Artist in Bali. 208p. 1998. 45.00 (962-593-318-2) Tuttle Pubng.
Carpenter, Bryant. The Classic Experience: The Hampton Classic, Bridgehampton, NY. limited ed. (Illus.). 200p. 1994. 55.00 (0-9645332-0-0) C Miller.
Carpenter, Buddy, jt. auth. see Carpenter, Alice B.
Carpenter, C. Dale, jt. auth. see Schulz, Jane B.
Carpenter, C. P., 2nd & Mayfield, M. J., eds. Proceedings of the Fuel Cells '94 Contractors Review Meeting (Aug. 1994) (Fuel Cell Information Ser.: Vol. IV). (Illus.). 100p. 1996. lib. bdg. 135.00 (0-89934-304-X, BT959) Bus Tech Bks.
Carpenter, C. R., ed. Behavioral Regulators of Behavior in Primates. LC 72-3602. (Illus.). 303p. 1974. 40.00 (0-8387-1099-9) Bucknell U Pr.
Carpenter, C. Tyler & Yeatts, Edward H. Stars Without Garters! The Memoirs of Two Gay GIs in WWII. LC 96-13649. (Illus.). 160p. 1996. 20.00 (1-886360-03-0); pap. 12.00 (1-886360-04-9) Alamo Sq Pr.
Carpenter, Carol, jt. auth. see Carpenter, Phil.
Carpenter, Carol B., jt. auth. see Rakow, Sue F.
Carpenter, Cathy, ed. see Fringe Festival-Los Angeles Staff & Community Arts Resources, Inc. Staff.
Carpenter, Catrine. Teach Yourself Beginner's French. (ENG & FRE., Illus.). 240p. 1995. pap. 8.95 (0-8442-3767-1, Teach Yrslf) NTC Contemp Pub Co.
— Teach Yourself Beginner's French, 2 cass., Set. (Teach Yourself Ser.). (FRE.). 240p. 1996. pap. 17.95 incl. audio (0-8442-3879-1, Teach Yrslf) NTC Contemp Pub Co.
— Teach Yourself French, Beginner's. (Teach Yourself Ser.). 1992. 13.95 (0-8288-8322-X); 33.95 incl. audio (0-8288-8323-8) Fr & Eur.
Carpenter, Catrine & Broady, Elspeth. Savoir-Faire: An Advanced French Course. LC 98-36168. (FRE.). 1999. write for info. (0-415-15311-5); pap. 24.99 (0-415-13090-5) Routledge.
Carpenter, Cecelia S. Fort Nisqually: A Documented History of Indian & British Interaction. LC 86-71238. (Illus.). 216p. (Orig.). 1986. pap. 13.95 (0-9616969-0-7) Tahoma Pubns.
— How to Research American Indian Blood Lines. (Illus.). 110p. 1987. pap. 9.00 (0-318-50024-8) Herit Quest.
Carpenter, Cecelia S. How to Research American Indian Blood Lines: Manual on American Indian Genealogy Research. 108p. pap. 8.95 (0-945433-00-X) Herit Quest.
Carpenter, Cecelia S. Leschi, Last Chief of the Nisquallies. (Illus.). 56p. 1986. reprint ed. pap. 5.00 (0-945433-11-5) Herit Quest.
— Tears of Internment: The Indian History of Fox Island & the Puget Sound Indian War. LC 96-96300. (Illus.). 102p. (Orig.). 1996. pap. 11.00 (0-9616969-2-3) Tahoma Pubns.
— They Walked Before: The Indians of Washington State. rev. ed. LC 89-91967. (Illus.). 75p. 1989. reprint ed. pap. 10.00 (0-9616969-1-5) Tahoma Pubns.
— Where the Waters Begin: The Traditional Nisqually Indian History of Mount Rainier. (Illus.). 108p. (Orig.). 1994. pap. text 10.95 (0-914019-33-3, 5339) NW Interpretive.
Carpenter, Chad. Tundra: Cartoons from the Last Frontier. (Illus.). 118p. (Orig.). 1993. pap. 10.00 (1-878100-54-8) Todd Commns.
— Tundra III: Even More Cartoons of a Northerly Nature. (Illus.). 128p. (Orig.). 1995. pap. 10.00 (1-878100-67-X) Todd Commns.
— Tundra Trilogy. 1995. pap. 25.00 (1-878100-33-5) Todd Commns.
— Tundra II: More Cartoons from the Last Frontier. (Illus.). 64p. (Orig.). 1994. pap. 10.00 (1-878100-55-6) Todd Commns.
Carpenter, Charles, Jr. Gorham Silver, 1831-1981. rev. ed. (Illus.). 296p. 1997. 95.00 (1-55660-244-8) A Wofsy Fine Arts.
Carpenter, Charles. Theology as the Road to Holiness in St. Bonaventure. LC 99-201768. (Theological Inquirers Ser.). 240p. 1999. pap. 23.95 (0-8091-3861-1) Paulist Pr.
Carpenter, Charles, Jr. Tiffany Silver. rev. ed. (Illus.). 288p. 1997. 95.00 (1-55660-243-X) A Wofsy Fine Arts.
***Carpenter, Charles A.** Dramas of the Nuclear Age--A Descriptive List of English-Language Plays. LC 99-47309. (Studies in Comparative Literature: Vol. 29). 104p. 2000. text 59.95 (0-7734-7891-4) E Mellen.
Carpenter, Charles A. Dramatists & the Bomb: American & British Playwrights Confront the Nuclear Age, 1945-1964, 91. LC 98-37715. (Contributions in Drama & Theatre Studies: Vol. 91). 208p. 1999. 57.95 (0-313-30713-X) Greenwood.
— Modern British Drama. LC 76-4654. (Goldentree Bibliographies Series in Language & Literature). (C). 1979. pap. text 14.95 (0-88295-559-4) Harlan Davidson.
— Modern Drama Scholarship & Criticism, 1981-1990: An International Bibliography. LC 97-206771. 625p. 1996. text 85.00 (0-8020-0914-X) U of Toronto Pr.
Carpenter, Charles A., ed. Modern Drama Scholarship & Criticism, 1966-1980: An International Bibliography. 624p. 1986. text 80.00 (0-8020-2549-8) U of Toronto Pr.
Carpenter, Charles C. & Krupa, James J. Oklahoma Herpetology: An Annotated Bibliography. LC 88-38318. (Oklahoma Museum of Natural History Publication Ser.). 272p. 1989. 26.95 (0-8061-2210-2) U of Okla Pr.
Carpenter, Charles C., jt. auth. see Barondess, Jeremiah A.
Carpenter, Charles F. The Purchasing Role: A View from the Top. LC 77-6349. (AMA Management Briefing Ser.). 31p. reprint ed. pap. 30.00 (0-608-14414-2, 205169800002) Bks Demand.
Carpenter, Charles H. Portraits of Native Americans: Photographs from the 1904 Louisiana Purchase Exposition. (Illus.). 48p. 1994. pap. 9.95 (1-56584-160-3, Pub. by New Press NY) Norton.

C

Carpenter, Charles H., et al. The Odyssey of a Collector. Freshman, Phil, ed. (Illus.). 160p. (Orig.). 1996. pap. 29.95 (*0-88039-032-8*) Mus Art Carnegie.

Carpenter, Christina, ed. see Swaim, Jessica.

Carpenter, Christina D., ed. see Bauld, Jane S.

Carpenter, Christina D., ed. see Maguire, Arlene.

Carpenter, Christina D., ed. see Raya-Norman, Faye.

Carpenter, Christine. Locality & Polity: A Study of Warwickshire Landed Society, 1401-1499. 811p. (C). 1992. text 135.00 (*0-521-37016-7*) Cambridge U Pr.

— The Wars of the Roses: Politics & the Constitution in England, C. 1437-1509. LC 97-7038. (Medieval Textbooks Ser.). 312p. (C). 1997. text 59.95 (*0-521-26800-1*) Cambridge U Pr.

— The Wars of the Roses: Politics & the Constitution in England, c. 1437-1509. (Medieval Textbooks Ser.). 312p. (C). 1997. pap. text 19.95 (*0-521-31874-2*) Cambridge U Pr.

Carpenter, Christine, ed. The Armburgh Papers: The Brokholes Inheritance in Warwickshire, Hertfordshire & Essex, 1417-1453. LC 98-7954. 222p. 1998. 63.00 (*0-85115-624-X*) Boydell & Brewer.

— Kingsford's Stonor Letters & Papers, 1290-1483. LC 95-21109. (Camden Classic Reprints Ser.: No. 1). (Illus.). 531p. (C). 1996. text 64.95 (*0-521-55467-5*); pap. text 24.95 (*0-521-55586-8*) Cambridge U Pr.

Carpenter, Christine M. All Bible Women of Great Faith. (All the Women in the Bible Ser.: Vol. 5). (Illus.). 208p. 1997. pap. 16.95 (*1-887999-03-5*) CMC Pr OR.

— All Influential Bible Women. (All the Women in the Bible Ser.: Vol. 6). (Illus.). 200p. 1997. pap. 16.95 (*1-887999-11-6*) CMC Pr OR.

— All the Women in the Bible, 6 vols., Set. (Illus.). (Orig.). 1997. pap. write for info. (*1-887999-56-6*) CMC Pr OR.

— All the Women in the Bible: Mothers & Daughters. LC 96-84500. (All the Women in the Bible Ser.: Vol. 2). (Illus.). 304p. (Orig.). 1998. pap. 16.95 (*1-887999-58-2*) CMC Pr OR.

— All the Women in the Bible Vol. 1: The Women Around Jesus. LC 96-86622. (Illus.). 272p. (Orig.). 1996. pap. 16.95 (*1-887999-53-1*) CMC Pr OR.

— All Wives, Widows & Concubines. (All the Women in the Bible Ser.: Vol. 4). (Illus.). 216p. 1998. pap. 16.95 (*1-887999-60-4*) CMC Pr OR.

— Virtues Spiritual Growth Guide. LC 96-84478. (Illus.). 200p. (Orig.). 1997. pap. 16.95 (*1-887999-50-7*) CMC Pr OR.

Carpenter, Clarence R. A Field Study in Siam of the Behavior & Social Relations of the Gibbon. LC 84-16897. (Comparative Psychology Monographs: Vol. 16, No. 5, Serial No. 84). (Illus.). 224p. reprint ed. 42.50 (*0-404-15855-2*) AMS Pr.

— A Field Study of the Behavior & Social Relations of Howling Monkeys. LC 76-44703. 1985. reprint ed. 40.00 (*0-404-15854-4*) AMS Pr.

***Carpenter, Clive.** The Changing World of Weather. (Illus.). 194p. 1999. 28.95 (*0-7351-0202-3*) Replica Bks.

Carpenter, Connie, jt. auth. see Phinney, Davis.

Carpenter, D. A. The Reign of Henry III. LC 96-5798. 480p. 1996. 65.00 (*1-85285-137-6*) Hambledon Press.

Carpenter, D. H. Hoagland: History & Genealogy of the Hoagland Family. (Illus.). 276p. 1990. reprint ed. pap. 42.00 (*0-8328-1603-5*); reprint ed. lib. bdg. 52.00 (*0-8328-1602-7*) Higginson Bk Co.

Carpenter, Dale. Hitchhiking in America: Using the Golden Thumb. (Illus.). 142p. (Orig.). 1992. pap. 6.00 (*0-9631910-0-4*) Lies Told Pr.

Carpenter, Dan. Hard Pieces: Dan Carpenter's Indiana. Hoppe, David, ed. LC 93-9960. 232p. 1993. 27.50 (*0-253-31316-3*); pap. 14.95 (*0-253-31317-1*) Ind U Pr.

***Carpenter, Dana & Winfree, Woody, eds.** I Am Beautiful Vol. 2: A Celebration of Women. 2nd rev. ed. (Illus.). 192p. 1999. reprint ed. 24.95 (*0-9675113-0-5*, Pub. by Sole Sisters) Allnce Hse.

Carpenter, Daniel H. History & Genealogy of the Carpenter Family in America from the Settlement at Providence, Rhode Island, 1637-1901. (Illus.). 375p. 1989. reprint ed. pap. 55.25 (*0-8328-0367-7*); reprint ed. lib. bdg. 63.25 (*0-8328-0366-9*) Higginson Bk Co.

Carpenter, Darin. Tundra Presents: And Now, a Break from Sanity. LC 96-60912. (Illus.). 136p. 1996. pap. 10.00 (*1-878100-35-1*) Todd Commns.

Carpenter, Darlene. Spiritual Nurturing: How to Help Your Child Grow Spiritually. LC 99-90357. 96p. 1999. pap. 7.99 (*0-9671274-0-8*) Carpenter Shop.

Carpenter, Dave, jt. auth. see Lambert, Larry.

Carpenter, David. Banjo Lessons. LC 97-160413. 288p. 1997. pap. 17.95 (*1-55050-108-9*, Pub. by Coteau) Genl Dist Srvs.

— Courting Saskatchewan: A Celebration of Winter Feasts, Summer Loves & Rising Brookies. 196p. 1998. pap. 14.95 (*1-55054-617-1*, Pub. by DGL) Orca Bk Pubs.

Carpenter, David A. Revelation, History, & the Dialogue of Religions: A Study of Bhartrhari & Bonaventure. LC 95-21567. (Faith Meets Faith Ser.). 250p. (Orig.). 1995. pap. 23.00 (*1-57075-039-4*) Orbis Bks.

— William Stafford. LC 86-70651. (Western Writers Ser.: No. 72). 51p. (Orig.). 1986. pap. 4.95 (*0-88430-046-3*) Boise St U W Writ Ser.

Carpenter, David M. Flame Powerer: The Story of America's First Jet Plane - the Bell Aerocomet P-59A. (Illus.). 78p. (Orig.). 1992. pap. 9.95 (*0-9633387-0-6*) Jet Pioneers Am.

Carpenter, David O., ed. Cellular Pacemakers, 2 vols., Vol. 1: Mechanisms of Pacemaker Generation. LC 81-11711. (Illus.). 344p. 1982. reprint ed. pap. 106.70 (*0-7837-3536-7*, 205775600001) Bks Demand.

— Cellular Pacemakers, 2 vols., Vol. 2. LC 81-11711. (Illus.). 383p. 1982. reprint ed. pap. 118.80 (*0-7837-3537-5*, 205775600002) Bks Demand.

Carpenter, David O. & Ayrapetyan, Sinerik, eds. Biological Effects of Electric & Magnetic Fields Vol. 1: Sources & Mechanisms. LC 93-44938. (Illus.). 369p. 1994. text 104.00 (*0-12-160261-3*) Acad Pr.

— Biological Effects of Electric & Magnetic Fields Vol. 2: Clinical Applications & Therapeutic Effects. LC 93-44938. (Illus.). 357p. 1994. text 104.00 (*0-12-160262-1*) Acad Pr.

Carpenter, David R. Electrician's Technical Reference for Motors. LC 98-17357. 288p. 1998. 36.95 (*0-8273-8513-7*) Delmar.

***Carpenter, David R.** Motor Controls. LC 99-32122. (Electricians Technical Reference Ser.). 352p. 1999. 39.95 (*0-8273-8514-5*) Delmar.

***Carpenter, Dean E., et al.** Regional Ecosystem Assessment Decision Support for Ecosystem Management. (Environmental Sciences Library). (Illus.). 2000. 65.00 (*0-632-04311-3*) Blackwell Sci.

Carpenter, Deb. Nature's Beauty Kit: Cosmetic Recipes You Can Make at Home. (Illus.). 148p. (Orig.). (YA). 1995. pap. 9.95 (*1-55591-221-4*) Fulcrum Pub.

Carpenter, Deb, jt. auth. see DeNayer, Lyn.

Carpenter, Delburn. The Radical Pietists. LC 72-13586. (Illus.). 42.50 (*0-404-11008-8*) AMS Pr.

Carpenter, Delores B. The Early Days of Cape Cod Community College. (Illus.). 200p. (Orig.). 1989. text 25.00 (*0-9624103-0-6*) Cape Cod Cmnt Col.

— Early Encounters: Native Americans & Europeans in New England - Selected Papers of W. Sears. (Illus.). 258p. 1995. pap. 19.95 (*0-87013-411-6*) Mich St U Pr.

— The Selected Letters of Lidian Jackson Emerson. LC 86-16102. (Illus.). 384p. 1987. text 42.00 (*0-8262-0610-7*, 83-36240) U of Mo Pr.

Carpenter, Delores B., jt. auth. see Nickerson, Warren S.

***Carpenter, Diana Lynn.** Don't You Know... Queens Don't Stand on the Corner? Amundson, Patricia A., ed. (Illus.). 1999. pap. 19.95 (*0-9671300-0-X*) Lady Diana Min.

— Don't You Know... Queens Don't Stand on the Corner? 2nd rev. ed. Hager, Penny Marie, ed. (Illus.). 276p. 1999. pap. 19.99 (*0-9671300-1-8*) Lady Diana Min.

Carpenter, Don & Carpenter, Barbara. The Untold Stories of the World Cup Soccer Championships: Nothing Like It Before. LC 98-2765. 180p. 1998. pap. 12.50 (*978-2765-01-5*) Royal Prod.

Carpenter, Dona R. & Hudacek, Sharon. On Doctoral Education in Nursing: The Voice of the Student. 1996. 27.95 (*0-88737-670-3*) Natl League Nurse.

Carpenter, Dona R., jt. auth. see Streubert, Helen J.

Carpenter, Donald, jt. auth. see Sullivan, Darryl M.

Carpenter, Donald H. Dueling Voices. 427p. 1993. 24.95 (*0-914339-42-7*, Pub. by P E Randall Pub) U Pr of New Eng.

Carpenter, Donna. Business Masters 3, Vol. 3. Date not set. 14.00 (*0-88730-987-9*, HarpBusn) HarpInfo.

***Carpenter, Donna.** Business Masters 3, Vol. 3. 224p. 2000. 19.00 (*0-88730-773-6*, HarpBusn) HarpInfo.

Carpenter, Donna. Business Masters 4, Vol. 4. Date not set. 14.00 (*0-88730-988-7*, HarpBusn) HarpInfo.

***Carpenter, Donna.** Business Masters 4, Vol. 4. 224p. 1998. 19.00 (*0-88730-774-4*, HarpBusn) HarpInfo.

Carpenter, Donna. Country Inns: Ontario's Best Getaways. LC 98-229776. 1997. pap. text 11.95 (*1-55046-236-9*, Pub. by Boston Mills) Genl Dist Srvs.

— St. Jacobs: A Day in the Country Guidebook. 1997. pap. 5.00 (*1-55046-252-0*, Pub. by Boston Mills) Genl Dist Srvs.

— Daytripper Vol. 4: 50 Trips in Cottage Country. LC 99-179995. Vol. 4. (Illus.). 176p. (Orig.). 1996. pap. 12.95 (*1-55046-161-3*, Pub. by Boston Mills) Genl Dist Srvs.

Carpenter, Donna. Daytripper, No. 2: Fifty Trips in & Around Toronto. Hudson, Noel, ed. LC 97-188792. (Illus.). 120p. (Orig.). 1992. pap. 14.50 (*1-55046-033-1*, Pub. by Boston Mills) Genl Dist Srvs.

Carpenter, Donna & Wiersema, Fred. Customer Service: Extraordinary Results at Southwest Airlines, Charles Schwab, Land's End, American Express, Staples & USAA, Vol. 2. LC 98-24870. (Business Masters). 224p. 1998. 24.00 (*0-88730-772-8*, HarpBusn) HarpInfo.

Carpenter, Donna G. Daytripper 1: 50 Trips in Southwestern Ontario. rev. ed. LC 97-118866. (Illus.). 176p. 1996. pap. 12.95 (*1-55046-179-6*, Pub. by Boston Mills) Genl Dist Srvs.

— Daytripper 3: 50 Trips in & Around Eastern Ontario. LC 97-188796. Vol. 3. (Illus.). 120p. 1994. pap. 15.95 (*1-55046-094-3*, Pub. by Boston Mills) Genl Dist Srvs.

***Carpenter, Donna M. G.** Camper's Guide to Ontario's Best Parks. (Illus.). 168p. 2000. pap. 13.95 (*1-55046-315-2*) Boston Mills.

Carpenter, Donna S. The Mutual Fund Tax Guide, 1990. 4th ed. (Illus.). 129p. 1990. pap. 7.95 (*0-317-92282-3*) Fidelity MA.

Carpenter, Dora, jt. auth. see Janes, Michael.

Carpenter, Dora, jt. auth. see Janes, Michael.

Carpenter, Doug & Pryor, Carolyn. Western Pleasure: Training & Showing to Win. Feinberg, Robert, ed. & illus. by. (Masters Ser.). 190p. 1995. 29.95 (*0-9625898-3-7*) EquiMedia.

Carpenter, Dwayne E. Alfonso X & the Jews: An Edition of & Commentary on Siete Partidas 7.24 "De los Judios" fac. ed. LC 86-11425. (University of California Publications in Entomology: No. 115). 173p. 1986. reprint ed. pap. 53.70 (*0-7837-8130-X*, 204793700008) Bks Demand.

Carpenter, E. J., et al, eds. Marine Pelagic Cyanobacteria: Trichodesmium & Other Diazotrophs. (C). 1992. text 185.00 (*0-7923-1614-2*) Kluwer Academic.

***Carpenter, E. M., ed.** Pattern Formation in the Developing Nervous System. (Developing Neuroscience Ser.: Vol. 22). (Illus.). 74p. 2000. pap. 25.25 (*3-8055-7086-4*) S Karger.

Carpenter, Edmund, jt. auth. see Schuster, Carl.

Carpenter, Edmund J. The Mayflower Pilgrims. (Illus.). 256p. (YA). (gr. 7-12). 1993. pap. text 3.95 (*1-930092-17-2*, CLP29995) Christian Liberty.

Carpenter, Edmund J. Roger Williams. LC 72-13. (Select Bibliographies Reprint Ser.). 1977. reprint ed. 19.95 (*0-8369-9955-X*) Ayer.

Carpenter, Edward. A Bibliography of Edward Carpenter. 1972. 59.95 (*0-87968-737-1*) Gordon Pr.

— Days with Walt Whitman: With Some Notes on His Life & Work. LC 78-22293. (Gay Experience Ser.). reprint ed. 41.50 (*0-404-61522-8*) AMS Pr.

— Days with Walt Whitman with Some Notes on His Life & Work. 200p. 1998. reprint ed. pap. 14.95 (*0-7661-0120-7*) Kessinger Pub.

— The Drama of Love & Death: A Study of Human Evolution & Transfiguration. 303p. 1996. reprint ed. pap. 24.95 (*1-56459-616-8*) Kessinger Pub.

— From Adam's Peak to Elephanta: Sketches of Ceylon & India LC 99-932497. xx, 370p. 1999. write for info. (*81-206-1233-7*, Pub. by Asian Educ Servs) S Asia.

— The Intermediate Sex: A Study of Some Transitional Types of Men & Women. 2nd ed. LC 78-22294. (Gay Experience Ser.). reprint ed. 39.50 (*0-404-61524-4*) AMS Pr.

— Intermediate Sex (1912) 178p. 1999. reprint ed. pap. 16.95 (*0-7661-0745-0*) Kessinger Pub.

— Intermediate Types among Primitive Folk. LC 75-12308. (Homosexuality Ser.). 1975. reprint ed. 19.95 (*0-405-07352-6*) Ayer.

— Love's Coming-of-Age: A Series of Papers on the Relations of the Sexes (1912) 164p. 1999. reprint ed. pap. 16.95 (*0-7661-0737-X*) Kessinger Pub.

— Pagan & Christian Creeds. 1972. 59.95 (*0-8490-0794-1*) Gordon Pr.

— Pagan & Christian Creeds: Their Origin & Meaning. 319p. 1996. reprint ed. spiral bd. 18.50 (*0-7873-0147-7*) Hlth Research.

— Pagan & Christian Creeds: Their Origin & Meaning. 318p. 1992. reprint ed. pap. 24.95 (*1-56459-211-1*) Kessinger Pub.

***Carpenter, Edward.** Towards Democracy (1912) 528p. 1999. reprint ed. pap. 29.95 (*0-7661-0775-2*) Kessinger Pub.

Carpenter, Edward. Visit to a Gnani. 65p. 1971. reprint ed. 11.00 (*0-911662-44-8*) Yoga.

Carpenter, Edward & Barnefield, George. Psychology of the Poet Shelley. LC 72-1334. (English Literature Ser.: No. 33). 1972. reprint ed. lib. bdg. 75.00 (*0-8383-1431-7*) M S G Haskell Hse.

Carpenter, Edward & Carpenter, Louis. Samuel Carpenter & His Descendants. (Illus.). 320p. 1989. reprint ed. pap. 48.00 (*0-8328-0369-3*); reprint ed. lib. bdg. 56.00 (*0-8328-0368-5*) Higginson Bk Co.

Carpenter, Edward, jt. auth. see Cunningham Graham, R. B.

Carpenter, Edward J. & Capone, Douglas G., eds. Nitrogen in the Marine Environment. LC 83-2829. 1983. text 142.00 (*0-12-160280-X*) Acad Pr.

Carpenter, Edward K. Urban Design Case Studies: A Service of Urban Design Newsletter: 3rd Awards Program LC 79-84894. 111p. 1979. write for info. (*0-915734-25-7*) RC Pubns.

Carpenter, Elizabeth. Microsoft Access 97 Intermediate. 1999. pap. text 28.95 (*1-58163-086-7*) CPI Train.

Carpenter, Elizabeth & Freund, Sam. Kids Eat New York. (Orig.). 1997. pap. 11.95 (*0-614-29505-X*) Little Bkrm.

Carpenter, Elizabeth & Martin, Rick. FrontPage 98 Basics. Adams, Pamela W. & Davis, Jenell, eds. (Internet Ser.). 1999. pap. text 28.95 (*1-58163-084-0*) CPI Train.

— Getting Started with HTML Basics. Adams, Pamela W. & Davis, Jenell, eds. (Internet Ser.). (Illus.). 58p. 1998. pap. text 28.95 (*1-58163-063-8*) CPI Train.

Carpenter, Elizabeth, jt. auth. see Adams, Pamela W.

Carpenter, Elizabeth, jt. auth. see Freund, Sam.

Carpenter, Elizabeth, ed. see Adams, Pamela W.

Carpenter, Eric. Young Christopher Columbus: Discoverer of New Worlds. (Troll First-Start Biography Ser.). (J). 1992. 8.70 (*0-606-02364-X*, Pub. by Turtleback) Demco.

— Young Christopher Columbus: Discoverer of the New Worlds. LC 91-24975. (Illus.). 32p. (J). (gr. k-2). 1996. pap. 3.50 (*0-8167-2527-6*) Troll Communs.

— Young Davy Crockett: Frontier Pioneer. LC 95-7598. (First-Start Biography Ser.). (Illus.). 32p. (J). (gr. k-2). 1995. pap. text 3.50 (*0-8167-3759-2*) Troll Communs.

— Young Davy Crockett: Frontier Pioneer. LC 95-7598. (First-Start Biography Ser.). (Illus.). 32p. (J). (gr. k-2). 1997. lib. bdg. 17.25 (*0-8167-3758-4*) Troll Communs.

— Young Thurgood Marshall: Fighter for Equality. LC 95-10023. (First-Start Biography Ser.). (Illus.). 32p. (J). (gr. 1-4). 1997. pap. 3.50 (*0-8167-3771-1*) Troll Communs.

— Young Thurgood Marshall: Fighter for Equality. LC 95-10023. (First-Start Biography Ser.). (Illus.). 332p. (J). (gr. k-2). 1997. lib. bdg. 17.25 (*0-8167-3770-3*) Troll Communs.

— Young Thurgood Marshall: Fighter for Equality. LC 95-10023. (Troll First-Start Biography Ser.). 1996. 8.70 (*0-606-10103-9*, Pub. by Turtleback) Demco.

Carpenter, Esther B. & Hazard, Caroline. South County Studies: Of Some Eighteenth Century Persons, Places & Conditions. in That Portion of Rhode Island Called Narragansett. LC 75-160961. (Select Bibliographies Reprint Ser.). 1977. reprint ed. 23.95 (*0-8369-5829-2*) Ayer.

Carpenter, Eugene E. A Biblical Itinerary: In Search of Method, Form & Content, Essays in Honor of George W. Coats. LC 97-201138. (JSOTS Ser.: Vol. 240). 194p. 1997. 57.50 (*1-85075-653-8*, Pub. by Sheffield Acad) CUP Services.

***Carpenter, Eugene E.** Holman Treasury of Key Bible Words: 200 Greek & 200 Hebrew Words Explained & Defined. 2000. pap. 14.99 (*0-8054-9352-2*) Broadman.

Carpenter, F. B. The Inner Life of Abraham Lincoln: Six Months at the White House. LC 95-20127. xxi, 352p. 1995. pap. 14.00 (*0-8032-6365-1*, Bison Books) U of Nebr Pr.

Carpenter, F. I. A Reference Guide to Edmund Spenser. 1980. 16.50 (*0-8446-1102-6*) Peter Smith.

Carpenter, F. M., et al. Coal Age Fossils from Mazon Creek. (Scientific Papers: Vol. III, Nos. 1-4). (Illus.). 147p. 1979. pap. 4.00 (*0-89792-082-1*) Ill St Museum.

Carpenter, Farrington R. Confessions of a Maverick: An Autobiography of Farrington R. Carpenter. LC 84-50023. (Illus.). x, 222p. (Orig.). 1984. pap. text 9.95 (*0-942576-27-6*) CO Hist Soc.

Carpenter, Frances. Tales of a Basque Grandmother. 1976. 23.95 (*0-8488-0941-6*) Amereon Ltd.

— Tales of a Chinese Grandmother. 293p. (J). (gr. 5-6). reprint ed. lib. bdg. 24.95 (*0-89190-481-6*, Rivercity Pr) Amereon Ltd.

— Tales of a Chinese Grandmother. 1993. reprint ed. lib. bdg. 21.95 (*1-56849-155-7*) Buccaneer Bks.

— Tales of a Chinese Grandmother. LC 72-77514. (Illus.). 302p. (J). (gr. 3-8). 1972. reprint ed. pap. 8.95 (*0-8048-1042-7*) Tuttle Pubng.

— Tales of a Korean Grandmother. 1976. 24.95 (*0-8488-0944-0*) Amereon Ltd.

— Tales of a Korean Grandmother. (Tut Bks.). (J). 1973. 14.05 (*0-606-04140-0*, Pub. by Turtleback) Demco.

— Tales of a Korean Grandmother. LC 72-77515. (Illus.). 320p. (J). (gr. 3-8). 1972. pap. 8.95 (*0-8048-1043-5*) Tuttle Pubng.

— Tales of a Russian Grandmother. 1976. 22.95 (*0-8488-0942-4*) Amereon Ltd.

— Tales of a Swiss Grandmother. 1976. 22.95 (*0-8488-0943-2*) Amereon Ltd.

— Wonder Tales of Dogs & Cats. 1976. 21.95 (*0-8488-0945-9*) Amereon Ltd.

— Wonder Tales of Seas & Ships. 1976. 25.95 (*0-8488-0946-7*) Amereon Ltd.

Carpenter, Frances H., et al. Popular Reporting: Local Government Financial Reports to the Citizenry. LC 92-70489. (Research Report Ser.). ix, 69p. 1992. write for info. (*0-910065-47-0*) Finan Acct Found.

Carpenter, Frank. Bouquet of Memories for Mother. 1990. pap. 5.95 (*0-937769-14-2*) Mark Inc CA.

Carpenter, Frank G. How the World Is Fed. 1977. lib. bdg. 59.95 (*0-8490-2021-2*) Gordon Pr.

Carpenter, Frederic I., ed. see Cox, Leonard.

Carpenter, Frederick I. American Literature & the Dream. LC 68-57310. (Essay Index Reprint Ser.). 1979. 20.95 (*0-8369-0276-9*) Ayer.

— Emerson & Asia. LC 67-30810. (Studies in Comparative Literature: No. 35). 1969. reprint ed. lib. bdg. 75.00 (*0-8383-0710-8*) M S G Haskell Hse.

— English Lyric Poetry, Fifteen Hundred to Seventeen Hundred. LC 77-76942. (Granger Index Reprint Ser.). 1977. 20.95 (*0-8369-6006-8*) Ayer.

— Metaphor & Simile in Minor Elizabethan Drama. LC 77-136372. (Chicago. University. English Studies: No. 4). reprint ed. 37.50 (*0-404-50264-4*) AMS Pr.

Carpenter, Freeman. 60 Years an Alcoholic - 50 Years Without a Drink. LC 96-90221. 416p. (Orig.). 1996. pap. 17.95 (*0-9651618-4-6*) Unique Educ.

Carpenter, G. Introduction to South African Constitutional Law. 479p. 1987. pap. 108.00 (*0-409-01785-X*, SA, MICHIE) LEXIS Pub.

— Some Mathematical Questions in Biology, Circadian Rhythms. LC 86-72815. (Lectures in Mathematics in the Life Sciences: Vol. 19). 54p. 1987. pap. 22.00 (*0-8218-1169-X*, LLSCI/19) Am Math.

Carpenter, G., jt. auth. see Bekker, J. C.

Carpenter, G. H. Insect Transformation. 282p. 1985. pap. 175.00 (*0-7855-0369-2*, Pub. by Intl Bks & Periodicals) St Mut.

Carpenter, Gail A. & Grossberg, Stephen, eds. Neural Networks for Vision & Image Processing. (Illus.). 504p. 1992. pap. text 59.50 (*0-262-53108-9*, Bradford Bks) MIT Pr.

— Pattern Recognition by Self-Organizing Neural Networks. 650p. 1991. 65.00 (*0-262-03176-0*, Bradford Bks) MIT Pr.

Carpenter, Gary. What the Bible Says about the Heart. 308p. (C). 1991. text 13.99 (*0-89900-267-6*) College Pr Pub.

Carpenter, Gene C. Business Broker's Manual. rev. ed. LC 86-50900. (Illus.). 250p. (Orig.). 1995. pap. text 39.95 (*0-940867-00-1*) Trend Pubns.

— How to Sell Your Own Business. LC 95-60162. (Illus.). 240p. (Orig.). 1995. pap. text 29.95 (*0-940867-04-4*) Trend Pubns.

Carpenter, Geoffrey. A Secondary Annotated Bibliography of John Winthrop, 1588-1649. LC 91-11030. (Studies in the Seventeenth Century: No. 5). 193p. 1991. 49.50 (*0-404-61725-5*) AMS Pr.

Carpenter, Gilbert C., Sr. & Carpenter, Gilbert C., Jr. Mary Baker Eddy: Her Spiritual Footsteps. 281p. 1987. 10.95 (*1-878641-02-6*) Aequus Inst Pubns.

Carpenter, Gilbert C., Jr., jt. auth. see Carpenter, Gilbert C., Sr.

Carpenter, Gordon L., jt. auth. see Roden, Martin S.

Carpenter, Gretchen, tr. see Wiechers, M.

Carpenter, Harry W., jt. auth. see Leedom, Tim C.

***Carpenter, Hugh.** The Great Ribs Book. LC 99-227427. (Hot Ser.). (Illus.). 160p. 1999. pap. 14.95 (*1-58008-071-5*) Ten Speed Pr.

Carpenter, Hugh. Pacific Flavors: Oriental Recipes for a Contemporary Kitchen. LC 87-26775. (Illus.). 272p. 1988. 40.00 (*1-55670-020-2*) Stewart Tabori & Chang.

C

— Pacific Flavors: Oriental Recipes for a Contemporary Kitchen. LC 87-26775. (Illus.). 272p. 1993. pap. 23.50 (*1-55670-333-3*) Stewart Tabori & Chang.

Carpenter, Hugh & Sandison, Teri. Chopstix: Quick Cooking with Pacific Flavors. LC 89-28334. (Illus.). 208p. 1990. 32.50 (*1-55670-133-0*) Stewart Tabori & Chang.

— Fast Appetizers. LC 99-20151. (Illus.). 112p. 1999. pap. text 17.95 (*1-58008-049-9*) Ten Speed Pr.

— Fusion Food Cookbook. LC 94-19146. (Illus.). 232p. 1994. 40.00 (*1-885183-00-3*) Artisan.

— Hot Barbecue. LC 96-36818. (Illus.). 112p. (Orig.). 1997. pap. 17.95 (*0-89815-900-8*) Ten Speed Pr.

— Hot Chicken. LC 95-16344. (Illus.). 104p. 1995. pap. 17.95 (*0-89815-771-4*) Ten Speed Pr.

— Hot Pasta. LC 96-16605. (Illus.). 112p. 1996. pap. 17.95 (*0-89815-857-5*) Ten Speed Pr.

— Hot Vegetables. LC 98-17031. (Illus.). 112p. 1998. pap. 17.95 (*0-89815-975-X*) Ten Speed Pr.

— Hot Wok. (Illus.). 112p. (Orig.). 1995. pap. 17.95 (*0-89815-678-5*) Ten Speed Pr.

— Quick Cooking with Pacific Flavors. LC 97-9785. (Illus.). 208p. 1997. 35.00 (*1-55670-645-6*) Stewart Tabori & Chang.

Carpenter, Humphrey. The Captain Hook Affair. (J). write for info. (*0-318-59418-8*) HM.

***Carpenter, Humphrey.** Dennis Potter: A Biography. 2nd ed. (Illus.). 704p. 1999. text 40.00 (*0-312-22126-6*) St Martin.

— Dennis Potter: The Authorized Biography. LC 99-202383. 1998. text. write for info. (*0-571-17685-2*) Faber & Faber.

Carpenter, Humphrey. Elephants Don't Bounce. (J). write for info. (*0-318-59417-X*) HM.

— The Inklings: C. S. Lewis, J. R. R. Tolkien, Charles Williams, & Their Friends. LC 78-40524. 287 p. 1978. write for info. (*0-04-809011-5*, Pub. by Allen & Unwin Pty) Paul & Co Pubs.

***Carpenter, Humphrey.** J. R. R. Tolkien: A Biography. (Illus.). 288p. 2000. pap. 14.00 (*0-618-05702-1*) HM.

Carpenter, Humphrey. Jesus. (Past Masters Ser.). 110p. 1983. pap. text 9.95 (*0-19-283016-3*) OUP.

— The Joshers: or London to Birmingham with Albert & Victoria. (J). write for info. (*0-318-59419-6*) HM.

***Carpenter, Humphrey.** Letters of J. R. R. Tolkien. LC 00-36939. (Illus.). 480p. 2000. pap. 15.00 (*0-618-05699-8*) HM.

— Mr. Majeika. 96p. (J). (gr. 3-6). 1985. pap. 7.95 (*0-14-031677-9*, Pub. by Pnguin Bks Ltd) Trafalgar.

— Mr. Majeika & the Dinner Lady. (J). 1993. pap. 7.95 (*0-14-032762-2*, Pub. by Pnguin Bks Ltd) Trafalgar.

— Mr. Majeika & the Ghost Train. (Illus.). (J). 1998. pap. 7.95 (*0-14-036641-5*, Pub. by Pnguin Bks Ltd) Trafalgar.

— Mr. Majeika & the School Book. (Illus.). (J). 1993. pap. 7.95 (*0-14-034834-4*, Pub. by Pnguin Bks Ltd) Trafalgar.

— Mr. Majeika & the School Caretaker. 96p. (J). 1998. pap. 7.95 (*0-14-037123-0*, Pub. by Pnguin Bks Ltd) Trafalgar.

— Mr. Majeika & the School Inspector. (Illus.). 96p. (J). (gr. 3-6). 1993. pap. 7.95 (*0-14-036288-6*, Pub. by Pnguin Bks Ltd) Trafalgar.

— Mr. Majeika & the School Play. (Illus.). 96p. (J). (gr. 3-6). 1993. pap. 7.95 (*0-14-034358-X*, Pub. by Pnguin Bks Ltd) Trafalgar.

— Mr. Majeika Vanishes. (Illus.). 96p. (J). 1998. pap. 7.95 (*0-14-037840-5*, Pub. by Pnguin Bks Ltd) Trafalgar.

— Mr. Majeika's Postbag. (Illus.). pap. 7.95 (*0-14-036648-2*, Pub. by Pnguin Bks Ltd) Trafalgar.

— Mr. Majeika & the Haunted Hot. (Illus.). 1989. pap. 7.95 (*0-14-032360-0*, Pub. by Pnguin Bks Ltd) Trafalgar.

— Mr. Majeika & the Music Teacher. (J). 1988. pap. 7.95 (*0-14-032141-1*, Pub. by Pnguin Bks Ltd) Trafalgar.

— Robert Runcie. 288p. 1996. text 40.00 (*0-340-57107-1*, Pub. by Hodder & Stought Ltd) Trafalgar.

Carpenter, Humphrey. Robert Runcie: The Reluctant Archbishop. (Illus.). 404p. 1997. pap. 13.95 (*0-340-66004-X*, Pub. by Hodder & Stought Ltd) Trafalgar.

— The Solitary Volcano. (J). write for info. (*0-318-59414-5*) HM.

Carpenter, Humphrey. Tolkien. 1978. mass mkt. 2.50 (*0-345-27256-0*) Ballantine Pub Grp.

Carpenter, Humphrey. The Wind in the Willows. (J). write for info. (*0-318-59416-1*) HM.

Carpenter, Humphrey & Prichard, Mari. The Oxford Companion to Children's Literature. (J). write for info. (*0-318-59415-3*) HM.

— The Oxford Companion to Children's Literature. (Illus.). 600p. 1999. pap. 24.95 (*0-19-860228-6*) OUP.

Carpenter, Humphrey, ed. see Tolkien, J. R. R.

Carpenter, Inta G. A Latvian Storyteller: The Repertoire of Janis Plavnieks. Dorson, Richard M., ed. LC 80-725. (Folklore of the World Ser.). 1981. lib. bdg. 28.95 (*0-405-13306-5*) Ayer.

Carpenter, Inta G. & Dorson, Richard M., eds. Folklore in the Calumet Region: Special Issue, Indiana Folklore, Vol. 10. LC 80-7779. (Folklore of the World Ser.). (Illus.). 1981. reprint ed. lib. bdg. 18.95 (*0-405-13341-3*) Ayer.

Carpenter, J. A., ed. Drug Interactions: The Effects of Alcohol & Meprobamate Applied Singly & Jointly in Human Subjects. (Journal of Studies on Alcohol: Suppl. No. 7). 1975. 10.00 (*0-911290-02-8*) Rutgers Ctr Alcohol.

Carpenter, J. D. Swimming at Twelve Mile. 70p. 1979. 3.95 (*0-920806-01-5*) U of Toronto Pr.

Carpenter, J. Estlin. The Life & Work of Mary Carpenter. 2nd ed. LC 77-172564. (Criminology, Law Enforcement, & Social Problems Ser.: No. 145). (Illus.). 420p. 1974. reprint ed. lib. bdg. 28.00 (*0-87585-145-2*) Patterson Smith.

— Theism in Medieval India. 564p. reprint ed. text 37.50 (*0-685-13399-0*) Coronet Bks.

Carpenter, Jack. Street Wise: A Colorful Look at the Avenues in Syracuse. rev. ed. (Illus.). 70p. 1996. pap. 7.95 (*0-9648622-1-2*) Pine Grve Pr.

Carpenter, Jack, jt. auth. see Shaughnessy, Diane.

Carpenter, Jack, jt. auth. see Waterman, Waldo D.

Carpenter, Jake, ed. see Beylin, Simon.

Carpenter, James, et al. Exotic Animal Formulary. 2nd ed. 384p. (C). 1999. pap. text. write for info. (*0-7216-8312-6*, W B Saunders Co) Harcrt Hlth Sci Grp.

Carpenter, Jane, jt. auth. see Hatchfield, Pamela.

Carpenter, Jason D., jt. auth. see Carter, Benjamin F.

Carpenter, Jean. Nutrition Model. Fusaro, Diane, ed. 64p. (J). (gr. 5-8). 1998. pap. text. write for info. (*0-614-22244-3*) Hubbard Sci.

Carpenter, Jeanne. Naked As We Stand. LC 96-79571. 165p. 1997. 12.95 (*0-9655354-1-X*) About Time Pub.

***Carpenter, Jeff.** P.E. Teacher's Complete Fitness & Skills Development Activities Program. LC 99-37792. 2000. write for info. (*0-13-022817-6*) P-H.

Carpenter, Jeff & Tunnell, Diane. Elementary P.E. Teacher's Survival Guide. LC 94-2806. 368p. (C). 1994. spiral bd. 28.95 (*0-13-302993-X*, Parker Publishing Co) P-H.

Carpenter, Jennifer & MacLean, Sally-Beth, eds. Power of the Weak: Studies on Medieval Women. LC 94-45063. (Illus.). 240p. (C). 1995. text 39.95 (*0-252-02169-X*); pap. text 14.95 (*0-252-06504-2*) U of Ill Pr.

***Carpenter, Jennifer M., et al.** Executive Compensation & Shareholder Value: Theory & Evidence. LC 98-23576. (New York University Salomon Center Series on Financial Markets & Institutions). 29p. 1998. write for info. (*0-7923-8179-3*) Kluwer Academic.

Carpenter, Jesse T. The South As a Conscious Minority, 1789-1861: A Study in Political Thought. (BCL1 - United States Local History Ser.). 315p. 1991. reprint ed. text 89.00 (*0-7812-6286-0*) Rprt Serv.

Carpenter, Jill, ed. Of Frogs & Toads: Poems & Short Prose Featuring Amphibians. LC 98-93863. (Illus.). 131p. 1998. pap. 10.95 (*0-9666674-0-9*) Ione Pr.

Carpenter, Jill, jt. ed. see Priestley, Mary P.

Carpenter, Joel. In the Dark: Secret Weapons, UFOs, & the USAF. 1994. 22.95 (*0-8306-4360-5*) McGraw-Hill Prof.

Carpenter, Joel A. Revive Us Again: The Reawakening of American Fundamentalism. LC 97-13227. (Illus.). 368p. 1997. 30.00 (*0-19-505790-2*) OUP.

— Revive Us Again: The Reawakening of American Fundamentalism. (Illus.). 368p. 1999. pap. 16.95 (*0-19-512907-5*) OUP.

Carpenter, Joel A. & Shenk, Wilbert R., eds. Earthen Vessels: American Evangelicals & Foreign Missions, 1880-1980. LC 90-32559. 368p. reprint ed. pap. 114.10 (*0-7837-5553-8*, 204532800005) Bks Demand.

Carpenter, John. A Most Excellent Instruction for Keeping Merchants Bookes of Accounts. LC 76-57368. (English Experience Ser.: No. 786). 1977. reprint ed. lib. bdg. 30.00 (*90-221-0786-8*) Walter J Johnson.

Carpenter, John, et al, eds. Prehistory of the Borderlands: Recent Research in the Archaeology of Northern Mexico & the Southern Southwest. LC 97-70874. (Archaeological Ser.: No. 186). 175p. 1997. pap. 14.95 (*1-889747-51-3*) Ariz St Mus.

Carpenter, John, jt. auth. see Astwood, Philip.

Carpenter, John, jt. auth. see Laurence, Desmond R.

Carpenter, John, tr. see Herbert, Zbigniew.

Carpenter, John A. The Star Spangled Banner. ed. 1.99 (*1-58627-200-4*) Electric Umb OR.

— Sword & Olive Branch: Oliver Otis Howard. LC 99-33067. (North's Civil War Ser.: Vol. 10). 379p. 1999. pap. 19.95 (*0-8232-1988-7*, Pub. by Fordham) BookMasters.

***Carpenter, John A.** Sword & Olive Branch: Oliver Otis Howard. LC 99-33067. (North's Civil War Ser.: Vol. 10). 379p. 1999. 35.00 (*0-8232-1987-9*, Pub. by Fordham) BookMasters.

Carpenter, John T., jt. auth. see Mirviss, Joan B.

Carpenter, John W. John W. Carpenter's Kentucky Courthouses. (Illus.). 288p. 1988. text 36.00 (*0-9621337-0-1*) J W Carpenter Pub.

Carpenter, Johonet H. The Well of Understanding. LC 82-61176. (Illus.). 136p. 1982. 15.95 (*0-9609378-0-3*) Sophia Pr.

Carpenter, Joseph E. Theism in Medieval India. LC 77-27152. (Hibbert Lectures: 1919). reprint ed. 62.50 (*0-404-60419-6*) AMS Pr.

Carpenter, Judith A. Human Anatomy - Biology 161. Mayer, Laurence P., ed. (Illus.). 270p. 1997. pap. text, lab manual ed. 15.82 (*1-889766-05-4*) Columbus State Bks.

Carpenter, Juliet W., jt. auth. see Shiba, Ryotar O.

Carpenter, Juliet W., tr. see Kimura, Fumi.

Carpenter, Juliet W., tr. see Miyamoto, Masao.

Carpenter, Juliet W., tr. see Oka, Isaburo.

Carpenter, Juliet Winters, tr. see Abe, Kobo.

Carpenter, Juliet Winters, tr. see Shimamoto, Kazunori.

Carpenter, Karen & Howard, Susie. Something Happened in My House: A Journey of Children's Grief. (Illus.). 36p. (Orig.). (J). (gr. 3-8). 1993. pap. 9.95 (*1-883613-01-9*) Byte Size.

Carpenter, Kathryn H., ed. Sourcebook on Parenting & Child Care. LC 94-39012. 288p. 1994. spiral bd. 35.00 (*1-57356-158-4*) Oryx Pr.

***Carpenter, Kenneth.** Eggs, Nests & Baby Dinosaurs. LC 99-42739. (Illus.). 336p. 1999. 35.00 (*0-253-33497-7*) Ind U Pr.

Carpenter, Kenneth. The First Three-Hundred-Fifty Years of the Harvard University Library. 216p. 1986. 22.00 (*0-317-59524-5*) Gutman Lib.

— Pacific Islands. LC 95-22632. (OIES Country Guide Ser.). 1996. 20.00 (*0-929851-56-0*) Am Assn Coll Registrars.

Carpenter, Kenneth, et al, eds. Dinosaur Eggs & Babies. (Illus.). 388p. (C). 1994. text 85.00 (*0-521-44342-3*) Cambridge U Pr.

— Dinosaur Eggs & Babies. (Illus.). 388p. 1996. pap. text 31.95 (*0-521-56723-8*) Cambridge U Pr.

Carpenter, Kenneth & Currie, Philip J., eds. Dinosaur Systematics: Approaches & Perspectives. (Illus.). 375p. (C). 1990. 69.95 (*0-521-36672-0*) Cambridge U Pr.

— Dinosaur Systematics: Approaches & Perspectives. (Illus.). 334p. (C). 1992. pap. text 36.95 (*0-521-43810-1*) Cambridge U Pr.

Carpenter, Kenneth E. The First Three Hundred Fifty Years of the Harvard University Library. 216p. (C). 1986. write for info. (*1-882477-01-4*) Harv U Lib.

— Speculation in Gold & Silver, Vol. 14. LC 74-367. 1974. 16.95 (*0-405-05928-0*) Ayer.

Carpenter, Kenneth E., ed. British Labour Struggles: Contemporary Pamphlets, 1727-1850, 32 bks., Set. 1972. 693.00 (*0-405-04410-0*) Ayer.

— Gold & Silver in the Presidential Campaign of 1896, Vol. 5. LC 74-366. 1974. 25.95 (*0-405-05927-2*) Ayer.

— Gold Mining Company Prospect Uses: California, Alaska, Arizona, Colorado, Idaho, Utah, 2 pts., Vol. 6. LC 74-365. (Illus.). 1974. 35.95 (*0-405-05926-4*) Ayer.

Carpenter, Kenneth E., et al. The Legacy of James Bowdoin, III. LC 93-79512. (Illus.). 268p. 1994. 39.95 (*0-916606-27-9*) Bowdoin Coll.

Carpenter, Kenneth E., ed. see Coughlin.

***Carpenter, Kenneth J.** Beriberi, White Rice & Vitamin B: A Disease, a Cause & a Cure. LC 99-53339. 328p. 2000. 40.00 (*0-520-22053-6*, Pub. by U CA Pr) Cal Prin Full Svc.

Carpenter, Kenneth J. Protein & Energy: A Study of Changing Ideas in Nutrition. LC 93-32130. (Illus.). 296p. (C). 1994. text 42.95 (*0-521-45209-0*) Cambridge U Pr.

***Carpenter, Kevin.** The Robin Hood Encyclopedia. 2001. lib. bdg. 45.00 (*1-57607-187-1*) ABC-CLIO.

***Carpenter, Kim, et al.** The Vow: The Kim & Krickitt Carpenter Story. (Illus.). 240p. 2000. 19.99 (*0-8054-2130-0*) Broadman.

Carpenter, Kristy & Mansel, Philip. The French Bemigres in Europe & the Struggle Against Revolution, 1789-1814. LC 99-20923. 236p. 1999. text 65.00 (*0-312-22381-1*) St Martin.

Carpenter, L. CaseFiles: Interactive Studies in Language Assessment. 250p. (C). 1996. pap. text 45.00 incl. disk (*0-930599-38-1*) Thinking Pubns.

Carpenter, L. G. Vacuum Technology: An Introduction. 2nd fac. ed. LC 83-153551. (Illus.). 128p. 1983. reprint ed. pap. 39.70 (*0-7837-7987-9*, 204774300008) Bks Demand.

Carpenter, Larry. Conan Lord of the Black River. 1996. mass mkt. 5.99 (*0-8125-5266-0*, Pub. by Tor Bks) St Martin.

— Conan the Outcast. 1991. pap. 3.95 (*0-8125-0928-5*, Pub. by Tor Bks) St Martin.

Carpenter, Leo. The Altonberrys of Sandwich Bay. Helms, Michael, ed. LC 97-70438. (Illus.). 128p. (Orig.). 1997. pap. 14.95 (*0-9653966-6-5*) Karmichael Pr.

Carpenter, Leona, et al, eds. Towards the Digital Library: The British Library's Initiatives for Access Programme. LC 98-183175. (Illus.). 208p. (Orig.). 1997. pap. 45.00 (*0-7123-4540-X*) British Lib Document.

Carpenter, Leonard. Conan, Scourge of the Bloody Coast. 256p. (Orig.). 1994. mass mkt. 4.99 (*0-8125-2488-8*, Pub. by Tor Bks) St Martin.

— Conan the Gladiator. 288p. 1995. mass mkt. 4.99 (*0-8125-2492-6*, Pub. by Tor Bks) St Martin.

— Conan the Great. 288p. 1990. pap. 3.95 (*0-8125-0714-2*, Pub. by Tor Bks) St Martin.

— Conan the Savage. 288p. 1992. pap. 7.99 (*0-8125-2238-9*) Tor Bks.

— Conan the Savage. 288p. 1993. mass mkt. 4.50 (*0-8125-1412-2*, Pub. by Tor Bks) St Martin.

— Conan the Warlord. 288p. 1988. reprint ed. pap. 3.50 (*0-8125-4268-1*, Pub. by Tor Bks) St Martin.

Carpenter, Linda J. Legal Concepts in Sport: A Primer. 124p. (Orig.). 1995. pap. 25.00 (*0-88314-567-7*, 302-10006) AAHPERD.

Carpenter, Linda J. & Acosta, Vivian. Parent & Educators Title IX Team Project Workshop Kit: P. E. T. T. Project. 63p. 1995. ring bd., wbk. ed. 15.00 (*0-88314-803-X*, 303-10036) AAHPERD.

Carpenter, Linda J. & Acosta, Vivian, eds. NAGWS Title IX Toolbox. 217p. (Orig.). 1992. pap. text 16.00 (*0-88314-536-7*, 303-10021) AAHPERD.

Carpenter, Lloyd S. Ocean Floor Mysteries Vol. 1: The Amazing Mystery of the Great Face on the Pacific Ocean Floor. unabridged ed. LC 97-92205. (Illus.). x, 244p. 1997. pap. write for info. (*0-9659627-0-9*) Spiral Ent Publ.

Carpenter, Louis, jt. auth. see Carpenter, Edward.

Carpenter, Lucas, ed. The Autobiography of John Gould Fletcher. LC 87-34660. Orig. Title: Life Is My Song. 432p. 1989. reprint ed. text 32.00 (*1-55728-031-2*) U of Ark Pr.

Carpenter, Lucas, ed. see Fletcher, John G.

Carpenter, Lucas, ed. see Page, Thomas N.

Carpenter, Lynette & Kolmar, Wendy K. Ghost Stories by British & American Women: A Selected, Annotated Bibliography. LC 97-52758. 232p. 1998. 50.00 (*0-8240-5540-3*, H1204) Garland.

Carpenter, Lynette & Kolmar, Wendy K., eds. Haunting the House of Fiction: Feminist Perspectives on Ghost Stories by American Women. LC 90-12910. (Illus.). 280p. 1991. 30.00 (*0-87049-688-3*) U of Tenn Pr.

Carpenter, Lynne & Greenberg, Joel. A Birder's Guide to the Chicago Region. LC 99-35856. 210p. 2000. pap. 30.00 (*0-87580-582-5*, 582-5) N Ill U Pr.

Carpenter, M. B. & Jayaraman, A., eds. The Basal Ganglia Vol. 2: Structure & Function: Current Concepts. LC 87-15300. (Advances in Behavioral Biology Ser.: Vol. 32). (Illus.). 560p. 1987. 125.00 (*0-306-42616-1*, Plenum Trade) Perseus Pubng.

Carpenter, M. S., tr. see Boyer, S. & Mari, J. L.

Carpenter, Malcolm B. Core Text of Neuroanatomy. 4th ed. (Illus.). 496p. 1991. pap. 39.00 (*0-683-01457-9*) Lppncott W & W.

Carpenter, Margaret. Season's of Change. 56p. 1983. 22.00 (*0-942494-60-1*) Coleman Pub.

***Carpenter, Marian K.** Arabian Legends: Outstanding Arabian Stallions & Mares. (Illus.). 280p. 1999. 21.95 (*0-911647-48-1*, Pub. by Western Horseman) Mountain Pr.

Carpenter, Marilyn D. A Feather for My Wing: A Life Lost, a Life Regained. (Illus.). 95p. 1999. 13.95 (*0-942407-40-7*) Father & Son.

Carpenter, Marj. And a Little Bit Farther: More Stories of Missions "To the Ends of the Earth" LC 98-13596. 112p. 1998. pap. 10.95 (*0-664-50032-3*) Geneva Press.

— To the Ends of the Earth. LC 98-20785. 1998. pap. 9.95 (*1-57153-942-5*) Westminster John Knox.

Carpenter, Mark. Basic Stage Lighting. 113p. 1996. pap. 17.95 (*0-86840-360-1*) Intl Spec Bk.

— Brazil: An Awakening Giant. LC 87-13417. (Discovering Our Heritage Ser.). (Illus.). 128p. (YA). (gr. 5 up). 1988. text, lib. bdg. 14.95 (*0-87518-366-2*, Dillon Silver Burdett) Silver Burdett Pr.

— Brazil: An Awakening Giant. 2nd ed. LC 96-25522. (Discovering Our Heritage Ser.). (J). 1997. lib. bdg. 14.95 (*0-382-39310-4*, Dillon Silver Burdett) Silver Burdett Pr.

Carpenter, Marlene. The Link Between Language & Consciousness: A Practical Philosophy. 120p. (Orig.). (C). 1991. pap. text 19.00 (*0-8191-8090-4*); lib. bdg. 39.50 (*0-8191-8089-0*) U Pr of Amer.

Carpenter, Mary. Juvenile Delinquents, Their Condition & Treatment. LC 76-108224. (Criminology, Law Enforcement, & Social Problems Ser.: No. 107). 1970. reprint ed. lib. bdg. 15.00 (*0-87585-107-X*) Patterson Smith.

— Our Convicts, 2 vols. in 1. LC 69-16229. (Criminology, Law Enforcement, & Social Problems Ser.: No. 88). 1969. reprint ed. 30.00 (*0-87585-080-4*) Patterson Smith.

— Reformatory Prison Discipline As Developed by the Rt. Hon. Sir Walter Crofton in the Irish Convict Prisons. LC 67-26667. (Criminology, Law Enforcement, & Social Problems Ser.: No. 2). 1967. reprint ed. 13.00 (*0-87585-002-2*) Patterson Smith.

— Reformatory Schools for the Children of the Perishing & Dangerous Classes & for Juvenile Offenders: With Index Added. LC 72-108223. (Criminology, Law Enforcement, & Social Problems Ser.: No. 106). 1970. reprint ed. lib. bdg. 15.00 (*0-87585-106-1*) Patterson Smith.

Carpenter, Mary B. Who Am I? (Illus.). 219p. 1986. pap. 11.95 (0-9617470-0-5) McClain.

A genealogical study of the Bower, Taylor & related families. *Publisher Paid Annotation.*

Carpenter, Mary C. The Songs of Mary Chapin Carpenter. 112p. 1991. per. 14.95 (*0-7935-0341-8*, 00490542) H Leonard.

Carpenter, Mary E. A Summer on Choctaw Mountain. LC 97-23279. (Illus.). 36p. (J). (gr. 2-6). 1997. lib. bdg. 19.95 (*1-55618-162-0*) Brunswick Pub.

Carpenter, Mary W. George Eliot & the Landscape of Time: Narrative Form & Protestant Apocalyptic History. LC 85-31831. (Studies in Religion). 260p. reprint ed. pap. 80.60 (*0-7837-0313-9*, 204063500018) Bks Demand.

Carpenter, Max H. & Waldo, Wayne M. Real Time Method of Radar Plotting. LC 89-156916. (Illus.). 48p. 1975. reprint ed. pap. text 20.00 (*0-87033-204-X*) Cornell Maritime.

Carpenter, Mecca B., ed. see St. Joseph Hospital Staff, et al.

***Carpenter, Mecca Reitman.** No Regrets: Dr. Ben Reitman & the Women Who Loved Him. LC 97-91152. (Illus.). 212p. 1999. pap. 19.95 (*0-9650584-0-9*) Southside Pr.

Carpenter, Michael, ed. National & International Bibliographic Databases: Trends & Prospects. LC 88-15285. (Cataloging & Classification Quarterly Ser.: Vol. 8, Nos. 3 & 4). (Illus.). 277p. 1988. text 49.95 (*0-86656-749-6*) Haworth Pr.

Carpenter, Michael, jt. auth. see Jefferys, Steve.

Carpenter, Michael A. Corporate Authorship: Its Role in Library Cataloging, 34. LC 80-1026. (Contributions in Librarianship & Information Science Ser.: No. 34). 200p. 1981. 49.95 (*0-313-22065-4*, CAU/, Greenwood Pr) Greenwood.

Carpenter, Michael J. Green Mountain Troopers: Vermont & Its State Police. LC 97-91600. (Illus.). 310p. 1997. 29.95 (*1-889373-04-4*, PTR9) Prof Trning.

Carpenter, Mick. Normality Is Hard Work: Trade Unions & the Politics of Community Care. LC 97-191455. 168p. (C). 1994. pap. 29.50 (*0-85315-803-7*, Pub. by Lawrence & Wishart) NYU Pr.

Carpenter, Mimi G. Mermaid in a Tidal Pool. (Illus.). 32p. (Orig.). (J). (ps-6). 1985. pap. 8.95 (*0-9614628-0-9*) Beachcomber Pr.

— Of Lucky Pebbles & Mermaids Tears. (Illus.). 32p. (J). (ps-5). 1994. pap. 9.95 (*0-9614628-2-5*) Beachcomber Pr.

An Asterisk (*) at the beginning of an entry indicates that the title is appearing for the first time.

— What the Sea Left Behind. LC 81-66251. (Illus.). 32p. (J). (gr. k-2). 1981. pap. 9.95 (*0-89272-123-5*) Down East.

Carpenter, Minnie L. William Booth. 1986. pap. 7.99 (*0-88019-185-6*) Schmul Pub Co.

Carpenter, Morgan, et al. The Employment of People with Disabilities in Small & Medium-Sized Enterprises. LC 98-196275. 149 p. 1998. 25.00 (*92-828-2949-9*, Pub. by Comm Europ Commun) Bernan Associates.

Carpenter, Nan. A Quiver of Quizzes for Quidnuncs. 1984. pap. 6.95 (*0-8158-0420-2*) Chris Mass.

Carpenter, Nan Cooke. Music in the Medieval & Renaissance Universities. LC 70-171380. (Music Ser.). (Illus.). 394p. 1972. reprint ed. lib. bdg. 45.00 (*0-685-01357-X*) Da Capo.

Carpenter, Nancy. The Velveteen Rabbit. abr. ed. LC 92-6036. (Chunky Shape Bks.). 22p. (J). (ps). 1993. 3.99 (*0-679-83617-9*, Pub. by Random Bks Yng Read) Random.

Carpenter, Nancy, jt. auth. see Belton, Sandra.

Carpenter, Nancy, jt. illus. see Bowdish, Lynea.

Carpenter, Nancy Sippel. Land of Unicorns, 1 vol. (Nature Sticker Stories Ser.). (ps-1). 1999. pap. text 4.99 (*0-448-41984-X*) Putnam Pub Group.

Carpenter, Nathanael. Achitophel, or the Picture of a Wicked Politician. LC 79-84094. (English Experience Ser.: No. 914). 76p. 1979. reprint ed. lib. bdg. 20.00 (*90-221-0914-3*) Walter J Johnson.

— Geography Delineated Forth in Two Books, Set. LC 76-57369. (English Experience Ser.: No. 787). 1977. reprint ed. lib. bdg. 75.00 (*90-221-0787-6*) Walter J Johnson.

Carpenter, Niles. Immigrants & Their Children, 1920. Ozer, Jerome S., ed. LC 70-78038. (American Immigration Collection. Series 1). 1969. reprint ed. 20.95 (*0-405-00504-0*) Ayer.

Carpenter, Norman T., jt. auth. see Kreitzberg, Charles B.

Carpenter, Novella, jt. auth. see Vogel, Traci.

Carpenter, P. A., jt. ed. see Just, M. A.

Carpenter, P. W., jt. auth. see Houghton, E. L.

Carpenter, Patricia. Away for the Holiday. Anderson, Marvel & Hammel, Bette, eds. LC 87-7332. 160p. 1987. pap. 9.95 (*0-944283-00-4*) PCA Pub.

— Away for the Holiday. 2nd ed. Anderson, Marvel & Hammel, Bette, eds. LC 87-7332. 350p. 1988. pap. 12.95 (*0-944283-01-2*) PCA Pub.

Carpenter, Patricia, ed. & tr. see Schoenberg, Arnold.

Carpenter, Pearl E. The Duck Book: Basics for Painting Wood-Carved Ducks & Birds. (Illus.). (Orig.). 1984. student ed., spiral bd. 13.95 (*0-9614021-0-5*) Shades Mother Nat.

— Painting Textured Carvings. (Illus.). 42p. (Orig.). 1991. student ed., spiral bd. 13.95 (*0-9614021-1-3*) Shades Mother Nat.

Carpenter, Peter & Western, John. Starting a Career. (C). 1989. pap. 60.00 (*0-86431-052-8*, Pub. by Aust Council Educ Res) St Mut.

***Carpenter, Phil.** Ebrands: Building an Internet Business at Breakneck Speed. LC 99-89360. 2000. 25.95 (*0-87584-929-6*, HBS Pr) Harvard Busn.

Carpenter, Phil & Carpenter, Carol. Marketing Yourself to the Top Business Schools. 224p. 1995. pap. 15.95 (*0-471-11817-6*) Wiley.

Carpenter, Philip L. & Walker, Theodore D. Plants in the Landscapes. 2nd ed. (Illus.). 401p. (C). 1998. reprint ed. text 45.95 (*1-57766-018-8*) Waveland Pr.

Carpenter, Philip P. Catalogue of the Reigen Collection of Mazatlan Shells in the British Museum No. 8: Special Publication. (Illus.). 576p. 1967. reprint ed. 9.00 (*0-87710-371-2*) Paleo Res.

***Carpenter, Phyllis & Ford, Marti.** Sparky's Excellent Misadventures: My A. D. D. Journal by Me (Sparky) LC 99-39111. (Illus.). 32p. (J). (gr. k-6). 1999. pap. 14.95 (*1-55798-606-1*, 441-6061, Magination Press) Am Psychol.

Carpenter, Rachel L. A Practical Guide to Prepare for & Survive Widowhood. 1990. pap. 5.95 (*0-9628080-0-8*) Carpenter Ventures.

Carpenter, Rebecca. Canadian Business: Guide to Business Schools. 384p. (C). 1999. pap., student ed. 19.95 (*0-471-64324-6*) Wiley.

Carpenter, Rhys. Greek Sculpture. LC 60-14233. (Illus.). 1971. reprint ed. pap. text 12.95 (*0-226-09475-8*, P436) U Ch Pr.

— Greek Sculpture, a Critical Review. LC 60-14233. (Illus.). 336p. reprint ed. pap. 104.20 (*0-608-09281-9*, 205415500004) Bks Demand.

— Greeks in Spain. LC 74-161505. reprint ed. 20.00 (*0-404-01394-5*) AMS Pr.

Carpenter, Richard A. Assessing Tropical Forest Lands: Suitability for Sustainable Uses. 352p. 1982. text 105.00 (*0-907567-02-9*, Tycooly Pub); pap. text 65.00 (*0-907567-07-X*, Tycooly Pub) Weidner & Sons.

Carpenter, Richard C. Thomas Hardy. (English Authors Ser.). 224p. 1964. 32.00 (*0-8057-1244-5*) Macmillan.

Carpenter, Richard V., ed. History of Boone County: With Biographical Sketches. (Reprinted Without Historical Encylopedia of Illinois, Available Separately) (Illus.). 282p. 1997. reprint ed. lib. bdg. 36.00 (*0-8328-5714-9*) Higginson Bk Co.

Carpenter, Robert. Glycine from the People's Republic of China: An International Trade Investigation. (Illus.). 57p. (Orig.). (C). 1994. pap. text 30.00 (*0-7881-1609-6*) DIANE Pub.

Carpenter, Robert A. Technology in the Music Classroom. 76p. (Orig.). 1991. pap. 8.95 (*0-88284-493-8*, 4700) Alfred Pub.

Carpenter, Robert L. The Logic of Typed Feature Structures: With Applications to Unification Grammars, Logic Programs & Constraint Resolution. (Cambridge Tracts in Theoretical Computer Science Ser.: No. 32). (Illus.). 280p. (C). 1992. text 39.95 (*0-521-41932-8*) Cambridge U Pr.

Carpenter, Rod. QS-9000 Essentials. LC 97-37955. 1997. 49.95 (*1-56990-240-2*) Hanser-Gardner.

Carpenter, Roger. Neurophysiology. 3rd ed. (Illus.). 322p. 1996. pap. text 43.95 (*0-340-60880-3*, Pub. by E A) OUP.

Carpenter, Roger & Robson, John, eds. Vision Research: A Practical Guide to Laboratory Methods. LC 98-19461. (Illus.). 352p. 1999. text, lab manual ed. 55.00 (*0-19-852319-X*) OUP.

Carpenter, Ronald H. The Eloquence of Frederick Jackson Turner. LC 83-8370. 244p. reprint ed. pap. 75.70 (*0-7837-6677-7*, 204629300011) Bks Demand.

— Father Charles E. Coughlin: Surrogate Spokesman for the Disaffected, 28. LC 97-52296. (Great American Orators Ser.: Vol. 28). 224p. 1998. lib. bdg. 69.50 (*0-313-29040-7*, Greenwood Pr) Greenwood.

Carpenter, Ronald H., jt. auth. see Duffy, Bernard K.

Carpenter, S. R., ed. Complex Interactions in Lake Communities. (Illus.). 320p. 1990. 124.00 (*0-387-96684-6*) Spr-Verlag.

Carpenter, Scott. Acts of Fiction: Resistance & Resolution from Sade to Baudelaire. LC 94-42527. (Illus.). 192p. 1995. 35.00 (*0-271-01450-4*) Pa St U Pr.

— Deep Flight. LC 96-162930. 1994. mass mkt. write for info. (*0-671-75903-5*) PB.

***Carpenter, Scott.** Reading Lessons: An Introduction to Theory. LC 99-31353. 174p. 1999. pap. text 25.00 (*0-13-021100-1*) P-H.

Carpenter, Scott. The Steel Albatross. Chelius, Jane, ed. 384p. 1992. reprint ed. mass mkt. 5.99 (*0-671-67314-9*) PB.

Carpenter, Scott & Denis, Francois. Vagabondages Litteraires: Initiation a la litterature d'expression francaise. 256p. (C). 1995. pap. 31.25 (*0-07-011444-7*) McGraw.

Carpenter, Scott, jt. auth. see McClung, Paul J.

Carpenter, Scott, tr. see Maravelas, Paul, ed.

Carpenter, Sharon. Scissor Sorcery: Cutting Activities for Early Childhood. LC 83-83236. (Illus.). 241p. (J). (ps-2). 1985. lib. bdg. 29.95 (*0-89334-170-3*, 170-3) Humanics Ltd.

— Scissor Sorcery: Cutting Activities for Early Childhood Programs. LC 83-83236. 241p. (Orig.). (J). (ps-2). 1985. pap. 19.95 (*0-89334-076-6*) Humanics Ltd.

Carpenter, Sharon M. & Carpenter, Toni G. The Hurricane Handbook: A Practical Guide for Residents of the Hurricane Belt. 2nd ed. (Illus.). 128p. (Orig.). 1999. pap. 14.95 (*1-892629-03-8*) Tail Tours.

Carpenter, Stanley B., jt. ed. see De Vore, R. William.

Carpenter, Stephanie L., jt. auth. see King-Sears, Margaret E.

Carpenter, Stephen. Dreidel, Dreidel, Dreidel Board Book. LC 98-231800. (Illus.). 12p. (J). (ps up). 1998. 6.95 (*0-694-01217-3*) HarpC.

— Farmers' Guide to Getting a Guaranteed Loan. 62p. 1998. pap. 15.00 (*1-890508-01-2*) Farmers Leg Act.

— Farmers' Guide to Guaranteed Loan Servicing. 61p. 1998. pap. 15.00 (*1-890508-02-0*) Farmers Leg Act.

— Farmers' Guide to Guaranteed Loans. 123p. 1998. pap. 25.00 (*1-890508-03-9*) Farmers Leg Act.

Carpenter, Stephen. The New Adventures of Mother Goose: Gentle Rhymes for Happy Times. LC 93-11129. 32p. (J). 1993. 15.00 (*0-88166-201-1*) Meadowbrook.

Carpenter, Stephen, et al. Farmers' Guide to Disaster Assistance. 2nd ed. 232p. 1997. pap. 40.00 (*1-890508-00-4*) Farmers Leg Act.

Carpenter, Stephen R. & Kitchell, James F., eds. The Trophic Cascade in Lakes. (Studies in Ecology). (Illus.). 399p. 1996. pap. text 32.95 (*0-521-56684-3*) Cambridge U Pr.

Carpenter, Steven E. Monograph of Crocicreas: Ascomycetes, Helotiales, Helotiaceae. LC 81-4025. (Memoirs Ser.: Vol. 33). (Illus.). 290p. 1981. pap. 26.50 (*0-89327-230-2*) NY Botanical.

Carpenter, Stirling & Karpati, George. Pathology of Skeletal Muscle. LC 84-1849. (Illus.). 798p. reprint ed. pap. 200.00 (*0-8357-4662-3*, 203759200008) Bks Demand.

***Carpenter, Stirling & Karpati, George.** Pathology of Skeletal Muscle. 2nd ed. (Illus.). 584p. 2000. text 195.00 (*0-19-506364-3*) OUP.

Carpenter, Sue. Past Lives: True Stories of Reincarnation. 1995. mass mkt. 5.95 (*0-86369-906-5*, Pub. by Virgin Bks) London Brdge.

— Patterns & Patchwork: Mountain Dulcimer Fingerpicking Made Easy. LC 91-91870. (Illus.). 152p. (Orig.). 1991. pap. 20.00 (*0-9629028-0-2*) S Carpenter.

Carpenter, Sue E. & Rock, John A., eds. Pediatric & Adolescent Gynecology. 496p. 1991. text 80.00 (*0-88167-839-2*) Lppncott W & W.

Carpenter, Sue Ellen Koehler & Rock, John A. Pediatric & Adolescent Gynecology. 2nd ed. 576p. text 89.00 (*0-7817-1781-7*) Lppncott W & W.

Carpenter, Susan L. & Kennedy, W. J. Managing Public Disputes: A Practical Guide to Handling Conflict & Reaching Agreements. LC 87-46342. (Management Ser.). 311p. 1988. text 37.45 (*1-55542-080-X*) Jossey-Bass.

Carpenter, Susan M. & Kendall, Florence P. Golfers, Take Care of Your Back. LC 94-90020. (Illus.). 118p. (Orig.). 1995. pap. 16.50 (*0-9637535-0-9*) Thistle Ridge.

Carpenter, Sylvia. How to Get a Job in the Airlines. 97p. 1986. 25.00 (*0-934748-23-3*) Broughton Hall.

Carpenter, Sylvia, jt. auth. see Hancock, Robert.

Carpenter, T. G. The Environmental Impact of Railways. LC 93-46722. 394p. 1994. 165.00 (*0-471-94828-4*) Wiley.

Carpenter, Ted G. Beyond NATO: Staying Out of Europe's Wars. LC 94-23704. 180p. 1994. 18.95 (*1-882577-16-7*); pap. 9.95 (*1-882577-17-5*) Cato Inst.

— Captive Press: Foreign Policy Crises & the First Amendment. 315p. 1995. pap. text 14.95 (*1-882577-23-X*) Cato Inst.

— Delusions of Grandeur: The United Nations & Global Intervention. LC 97-16247. 184p. 1997. 19.95 (*1-882577-49-3*); pap. text 10.95 (*1-882577-50-7*) Cato Inst.

— Search for Enemies: America's Alliances after the Cold War. 228p. 1992. 15.95 (*0-932790-96-8*); pap. 12.95 (*0-932790-95-X*) Cato Inst.

Carpenter, Ted G., ed. America Entangled: The Persian Gulf Crisis & Its Consequences. 116p. 1991. pap. 3.00 (*0-932790-85-2*) Cato Inst.

— The Future of NATO. LC 95-193722. 319p. 1995. 37.50 (*0-7146-4647-4*, Pub. by F Cass Pubs); pap. 19.50 (*0-7146-4171-5*, Pub. by F Cass Pubs) Intl Spec Bk.

***Carpenter, Ted G., ed.** NATO's Empty Victory: A Postmortem on the Balkan War. 152p. 2000. pap. 9.95 (*1-882577-86-8*, Pub. by Cato Inst) Natl Bk Netwk.

Carpenter, Ted G. & Conry, Barbara, eds. NATO Enlargement: Illusions & Reality. 284p. 1998. 21.95 (*1-882577-58-2*); pap. 11.95 (*1-882577-59-0*) Cato Inst.

Carpenter, Ted G., jt. ed. see Bandow, Doug.

Carpenter, Ted Galen. Captive Press: Foreign Policy Crises & the First Amendment. 315p. 1995. 24.95 (*1-882577-22-1*) Cato Inst.

***Carpenter, Ted Galen & Dorn, James A., eds.** China's Future: Constructive Partner or Emerging Threat? 220p. 2000. 19.95 (*1-882577-87-6*, Pub. by Cato Inst); pap. 10.95 (*1-882577-88-4*, Pub. by Cato Inst) Natl Bk Netwk.

Carpenter, Teresa. The Baby Due Date. (Special Edition Ser.: Bk. 1260). 1999. per. 4.25 (*0-373-24260-3*, 1-24260-1) Silhouette.

— Missing Beauty. 1989. mass mkt. 5.99 (*0-7860-0449-5*, Pinncle Kensgtn) Kensgtn Pub Corp.

Carpenter, Teresa, jt. auth. see Clark, Marcia.

Carpenter, Terry, ed. see Smith, Paula.

Carpenter, Thomas. Summer Furniture: Practical Designs for the Backyard. (Illus.). 128p. 1994. pap. 18.95 (*0-921820-89-5*) Firefly Bks Ltd.

Carpenter, Thomas A. & Edwards, Frank B. Kids, Computers & You: What Parents Can Do Now to Prepare Their Children for the Future. (Illus.). 180p. 1996. write for info. (*0-921285-39-6*); pap. write for info. (*0-921285-38-8*) Bungalo Books.

Carpenter, Thomas H. Art & Myth in Ancient Greece. LC 88-51326. (World of Art Ser.). (Illus.). 1991. pap. 14.95 (*0-500-20236-2*, Pub. by Thames Hudson) Norton.

— Dionysian Imagery in Archaic Greek Art: Its Development in Black-Figure Vase Painting. (Oxford Monographs on Classical Archaeology). 192p. 1986. 95.00 (*0-19-813222-0*) OUP.

— Dionysian Imagery in Fifth Century Athens. LC 97-162434. (Oxford Monographs on Classical Archaeology). (Illus.). 170p. 1997. text 85.00 (*0-19-815038-5*) OUP.

Carpenter, Thomas H., ed. Beazley Addenda: Additional References to ABV, ARV2 & Paralipomena. 2nd ed. (British Academy Ser.). 536p. 1989. text 95.00 (*0-19-726069-1*) OUP.

Carpenter, Thomas H. & Faraone, Christopher A. Masks of Dionysus. LC 92-54965. (Myth & Poetics Ser.). (Illus.). 360p. 1993. text 52.50 (*0-8014-2779-7*); pap. text 19.95 (*0-8014-8062-0*) Cornell U Pr.

Carpenter, Thomas H. & Gula, Robert J. Mythology: Greek & Roman. (Illus.). (gr. 10). 1977. pap. text 9.25 (*0-88334-089-5*) Longman.

***Carpenter, Thomas J.** Silt Fence That Works. (Illus.). 56p. 1999. text 34.95 (*0-9672733-0-7*) carpenter erosion.

Carpenter, Thomas P. Children's Mathematics: Cognitively Guided Instruction. LC 98-49595. 1999. 23.00 (*0-325-00137-5*) Heinemann.

Carpenter, Thomas P., et al, eds. Rational Numbers: An Interaction of Research. (Studies in Mathematical Thinking & Learning). 392p. 1993. text 79.95 (*0-8058-1135-4*) L Erlbaum Assocs.

Carpenter, Thorne M., jt. auth. see Benedict, Francis G.

Carpenter, Tom. Dialogue on Awakening: Communion with Jesus. 288p. (Orig.). 1992. pap. 14.95 (*0-9633051-0-7*) Carpenters HI.

Carpenter, Tom & Taylor, Jeff. The Basement Book: Upstairs Downstairs: Reclaiming the Wasted Space in Your Basement. Estabrook, Barry, ed. (Illus.). 128p. (Orig.). 1996. pap. 18.95 (*1-881527-99-9*, Chapters Bks) HM.

Carpenter, Tom J. & Van Norman, Jim. Mule Deer: Hunting Today's Trophies. LC 98-84096. (Illus.). 256p. 1998. pap. 19.95 (*0-87341-563-9*, HTMD) Krause Pubns.

Carpenter, Toni G., jt. auth. see Carpenter, Sharon M.

Carpenter, Victor. Stations of the Spirit. LC 89-52162. 148p. (Orig.). 1990. pap. 10.00 (*0-931104-28-9*) SunInk Pubn.

Carpenter, Victor, tr. see Lehrmann, Charles C.

Carpenter, Virginia. Dragonflies & Damselflies of Cape Cod. 2nd ed. (Natural History Ser.: No. 4). (Illus.). 96p. 1997. pap. 10.95 (*0-916275-06-X*) Cape Cod Mus Nat His.

Carpenter, Virginia L. A Child's History of Placentia. rev. ed. LC 84-81997. (Illus.). 80p. 1984. 6.50 (*0-943480-57-4*) Friis-Pioneer Pr.

— Placentia, a Pleasant Place. 2nd enl. ed. LC 88-51559. (Illus.). 294p. 1988. 15.95 (*0-943480-67-1*) Friis-Pioneer Pr.

Carpenter, Vivian, ed. Don't Take Candy from a Stranger. (Illus.). 79p. 1985. write for info. (*0-915741-01-6*) C D Stampley Ent.

Carpenter, W. B. Popular Encyclopedia of Natural Sciences. 584p. 1991. 300.00 (*81-7041-245-5*, Pub. by Scientific Pubs) St Mut.

Carpenter, W. B., et al. Introduction to the Study of the Foraminifera. 1965. reprint ed. 37.50 (*0-934454-52-3*) Lubrecht & Cramer.

Carpenter, W. Boyd. The Spiritual Message of Dante. 278p. 1997. reprint ed. pap. 19.95 (*0-7661-0038-3*) Kessinger Pub.

Carpenter, W. Scott, jt. auth. see McClung, Paul J.

Carpenter, Walter H., Jr. & Handler, Edward. Small Business & Pattern Bargaining. Bruchey, Stuart & Carosso, Vincent P., eds. LC 78-18953. (Small Business Enterprise in America Ser.). 1979. reprint ed. lib. bdg. 21.95 (*0-405-11461-3*) Ayer.

Carpenter, William. The Hours of Morning: Poems 1976-79. LC 81-7452. (Virginia Commonwealth University Series for Contemporary Poetry). 90p. reprint ed. pap. 30.00 (*0-7837-3567-7*, 204342500009) Bks Demand.

— A Keeper of Sheep. LC 94-7049. 340p. 1994. 21.95 (*1-57131-000-2*) Milkweed Ed.

— A Keeper of Sheep. 340p. 1996. reprint ed. pap. 13.95 (*1-57131-007-X*) Milkweed Ed.

— Learning by Building: Design & Construction in Architectural Education. LC 96-49073. (Architecture Ser.). (C). 1997. pap. 39.95 (*0-442-02350-2*, VNR) Wiley.

Carpenter, William A. The Exemplar: A Guide to a Mason's Actions. (Illus.). iii, 88p. 1985. lthr. 25.70 (*0-9617310-4-4*) Grnd Lodge F&AMOP.

— The Exemplar: A Guide to a Mason's Actions. (Illus.). iii, 88p. 1985. reprint ed. 17.50 (*0-9617310-5-2*) Grnd Lodge F&AMOP.

— The Exemplar: A Guide to a Mason's Actions. (Illus.). iii, 88p. 1995. reprint ed. pap. 12.95 (*0-9617310-6-0*) Grnd Lodge F&AMOP.

Carpenter, William B. Nature & Man: Essays Scientific & Philosophical. LC 78-72791. (Brainedness, Handedness, & Mental Abilities Ser.). reprint ed. 34.50 (*0-404-60855-8*) AMS Pr.

— On the Use & Abuse of Alcoholic Liquors, in Health & Disease. Grob, Gerald N., ed. LC 80-1216. (Addiction in America Ser.). 1981. reprint ed. lib. bdg. 18.95 (*0-405-13572-6*) Ayer.

Carpenter, William B. Principles of Mental Physiology. 763p. 160.00 (*1-85506-662-9*) Thoemmes Pr.

Carpenter, William B. The Spiritual Message of Dante. 1977. 21.95 (*0-8369-7103-5*, 7937) Ayer.

Carpenter, William J. Learning by Building: Design & Construction in Architectural Education. 180p. 1997. pap. 49.95 (*0-471-28793-8*, VNR) Wiley.

Carpenter, William M. & Wiencek, David G., eds. Asian Security Handbook: An Assessment of Political-Security Issues in the Asia-Pacific Region. LC 96-6319. 318p. (C). 1996. text 76.95 (*1-56324-813-1*, East Gate Bk) M E Sharpe.

— Asian Security Handbook: An Assessment of Political-Security Issues in the Asia-Pacific Region. LC 96-6319. 318p. (C). (gr. 13). 1996. pap. text 30.95 (*1-56324-814-X*, East Gate Bk) M E Sharpe.

Carpenter, William M., jt. auth. see Gibert, Stephen P.

Carpenter, William M., jt. ed. see Cline, Ray S.

Carpenter, William M., jt. ed. see Gibert, Stephen P.

Carpenter, William M., jt. ed. see Wiencek, David G.

Carpenter, William S. Foundations of Modern Jurisprudence. LC 58-5314. 1958. 26.50 (*0-8290-2368-2*) Irvington.

— Power Boating: The Great Ideas Book: How to Buy & Sell, Equipment, Trailer, Operate, Maintain, Store, & Insure Your Power Boat Successfully! Borer, Brooke M., ed. LC 94-78110. (Illus.). 261p. (Orig.). 1995. pap. 19.95 (*1-883818-09-5*) Gemini Marine.

— The Unfinished Business of Civil Service Reform. LC 79-16863. 128p. 1980. reprint ed. lib. bdg. 35.00 (*0-313-22051-4*, CACS, Greenwood Pr) Greenwood.

Carpenter, William S., et al. Trailer Boater's Basic Handbook. LC 93-91422. 150p. 1993. pap. 19.95 (*1-883818-02-8*) Gemini Marine.

Carpenter, William T., jt. auth. see Strauss, John S.

Carpenter, William W. Certain Phases of the Administration of High School Chemistry. LC 70-176627. (Columbia University. Teachers College. Contributions to Education Ser.: No. 191). reprint ed. 37.50 (*0-404-55191-2*) AMS Pr.

Carpenteri, Stephen D. Osprey: The Fish Hawk. LC 96-46821. (Wildlife Ser.). 144p. 1997. pap. 14.95 (*1-55971-590-1*, NorthWord Pr) Creat Pub Intl.

Carpenteri, Steve, photos by see Ricciuti, Edward R.

Carpentier, A. El Reino de Este Mundo.Tr. of King of This World. (SPA.). 1997. pap. 7.95 (*84-322-3015-4*, Pub. by E Seix Barral) Continental Bk.

Carpentier, Alain, et al, eds. Cardiac Bioassist. LC 96-41246. (Bakken Research Center Ser.: Vol. 11). (Illus.). 656p. 1997. 125.00 (*0-87993-647-9*) Futura Pub.

Carpentier, Alejo. El Arpa y la Sombra (The Harp & the Shadow) (SPA.). 241p. 1994. 23.99 (*84-375-0376-0*, Pub. by Fondo) Continental Bk.

— Concert Baroque. (FRE.). 119p. 1978. pap. 10.95 (*0-7859-1871-X*, 2070370208) Fr & Eur.

— Concierto Barroco. (Caribbean Collection). 1994. pap. 9.50 (*0-8477-0183-2*) U of PR Pr.

— Cuentos Completos. (SPA.). 219p. 1980. 8.95 (*0-8288-7078-0*) Fr & Eur.

— Explosion in a Cathedral. Sturrock, John, tr. 351p. 1989. pap. 14.00 (*0-374-52198-0*) FS&G.

— Guerre Du Temps et Autres Nouvelles. 212p. 1989. pap. 11.95 (*0-7859-2238-5*, 207038120X) Fr & Eur.

C

— The Harp & the Shadow. Christensen, Thomas & Christensen, Carol, trs. from SPA. LC 89-13391. 176p. 1992. reprint ed. pap. 11.95 (*1-56279-024-2*) Mercury Hse Inc.

— La Harpe et l'Ombre. (FRE.). 204p. 1979. pap. 10.95 (*0-7859-2036-6*, 2070377423) Fr & Eur.

— The Kingdom of This World. De Onis, Harriet, tr. 190p. 1989. pap. 10.00 (*0-374-52197-2*) FS&G.

— The Lost Steps. De Onis, Harriet, tr. 280p. 1989. pap. 12.00 (*0-374-52199-9*) FS&G.

— La Partage des Eaux. (FRE.). 1976. pap. 11.95 (*0-7859-1827-2*, 2070367959) Fr & Eur.

— Pasos Perdidos. (SPA.). 175p. 1953. 11.00 (*0-8288-8563-X*); 11.00 (*0-8288-8589-3*) Fr & Eur.

— Pasos Perdidos. 1998. pap. 13.95 (*0-14-026193-1*) Viking Penguin.

— Los Pasos Perdidos. (SPA.). pap. 14.95 (*84-376-0502-4*, Pub. by Ediciones Catedra) Continental Bk.

— Reasons of State. Patridge, Frances, tr. from SPA.Tr. of El/Recurso Del Metodo. 320p. 1981. pap. 4.95 (*0-904613-52-6*) Writers & Readers.

— El Reino de Este Mundo. (SPA.). 7.50 (*0-8288-2557-2*, 5818) Fr & Eur.

— El Reino de Este Mundo. (Caribbean Collection). 1994. pap. 6.25 (*0-8477-0187-5*) U of PR Pr.

— Le Royaume De Ce Monde. (FRE.). 192p. 1980. pap. 10.95 (*0-7859-1927-9*, 2070372480) Fr & Eur.

— Le Siecle des Lumieres. (FRE.). 461p. 1977. pap. 11.95 (*0-7859-1862-0*, 2070369811) Fr & Eur.

— El Siglo de las Luces. (SPA.). pap. 13.50 (*84-322-3002-2*, Pub. by E Seix Barral) Continental Bk.

— Siglo de las Luces. 2nd ed. 420p. 1989. pap. 15.95 (*0-7859-5172-5*) Fr & Eur.

— Vision de America. 1999. pap. text 18.95 (*84-322-0765-9*, Pub. by E Seix Barral) Continental Bk.

Carpentier, Andre, jt. ed. see Cohen, Matt.

Carpentier, Bonnie A. & Sevenants, Michael R., eds. Supercritical Fluid Extraction & Chromatography: Techniques & Applications. LC 88-3466. (Symposium Ser.: No. 366). (Illus.). ix, 253p. 1988. 65.95 (*0-8412-1469-7*) Am Chemical.

Carpentier, Charlotte & Dietz, Kevin C., eds. Using Netscape Communicator: Module 1. (Illus.). 182p. 1997. pap. text 20.00 (*0-7423-0006-4*) ComputerPREP.

Carpentier, John. Price Guide to Packers Memorabilia. LC 97-80607. (Illus.). 304p. 1998. pap. 17.95 (*0-87341-572-8*, GBMEM) Krause Pubns.

Carpentier, M. H., jt. ed. see Smith, B. L.

Carpentier, Marcel. Your First Puppy. (Illus.). 32p. (Orig.). (J). (gr. 1-6). 1991. pap. 2.29 (*0-86622-064-X*, YF-119) TFH Pubns.

Carpentier, Martha C. Ritual, Myth & the Modernist Text: The Influence of Jane Ellen Harrison on Joyce, Eliot & Woolf. (Library of Anthropology: Vol. 12). 264p. 1998. text 33.00 (*90-5700-517-4*, ECU42, Harwood Acad Pubs) Gordon & Breach.

Carpentier, Michel H. Principles of Modern Radar Systems. LC 88-10563. (Artech House Radar Library). 320p. reprint ed. pap. 99.20 (*0-7837-0413-5*, 204073500018) Bks Demand.

Carpeatier, Michel-Henri, jt. ed. see Smith, Bradford L.

Carpentier, P. H., ed. European Conference on Microcirculation: 20th Conference, Paris, August/September 1998: Abstracts. (Journal of Vascular Research Ser.: Vol. 35, Suppl. 2 (1998)). 114p. 1998. pap. 29.75 (*3-8055-6747-2*) S Karger.

Carpentier, Posey. Posey Carpentier's Master Plan for Real Estate Selling Success. (Illus.). 186p. 1984. 19.95 (*0-13-687716-8*, Busn) P-H.

Carpentier, Tai & Beaumont, Clive. Kai Korero: A Cook Islands Maori Coursebook. 1996. audio 8.95 (*0-908597-15-0*) UH Pr.

— Kai Korero: A Cook Islands Maori Coursebook. (Illus.). 160p. 1996. pap. text 25.00 (*0-908597-14-2*); pap. text 32.00 incl. audio (*0-8248-1862-8*) UH Pr.

Carpentier, Y. A., jt. ed. see Wilmore, D. W.

Carpentieri, Anthony C. Frank & Joe Turn Blue. 3rd rev. ed. (Illus.). 248p. 1995. spiral bd. 24.95 (*0-9639949-9-9*) SynSine Pr.

Carpentieri, J. D., ed. see Purcell, Julia A.

Carpentieri, Tony & Mular, Paul. Hardy & Hardy Investigations. 3rd rev. ed. (Illus.). 600p. 1998. spiral bd. 56.95 (*1-891388-00-2*) SynSine Pr.

Carpentieri, Tony, ed. see DiCristo, Rose Marie, et al.

Carpentieri, Tony, ed. see Emburg, Kate.

Carpentieri, Tony, ed. see Knight, Melanie.

Carper. Business Law: Selected Court Cases. 1993. mass mkt. 23.25 (*0-314-02616-9*) West Pub.

— West Business Law. Date not set. text, teacher ed. 58.95 (*0-314-01952-9*) West Pub.

Carper, Donald L., et al. Understanding the Law. Perlee, Clyde, ed. 536p. (C). 1991. text 43.75 (*0-314-80723-3*) West Pub.

— Understanding The Law 2e. 2nd ed. LC 94-45062. (SWC-Business Law). 762p. (C). 1995. mass mkt. 48.75 (*0-314-04520-1*) West Pub.

— West's Business & Personal Law. LC 92-45780. 1994. mass mkt. 53.25 (*0-314-01391-1*) West Pub.

Carper, Helen. And Now the Magpie: A Selection of Winning Entries from 1983, 1984, 1985, 1986 - of the West Virginia Writers, Inc. Annual Awards Competition. 184p. 1987. pap. 7.95 (*0-941092-16-X*) Mtn St Pr.

Carper, Helen, ed. see McClure, Patricia & West Virginia Writers, Inc. Staff.

Carper, Helen, ed. see Weaver, Samuel R.

Carper, James. Using Building Systems: Modular, Panelized, Log, Dome. 118p. 1990. pap. 10.00 (*0-86718-314-4*) Home Builder.

Carper, James C., jt. auth. see Hunt, Thomas C.

Carper, James C., jt. auth. see Sears, James T.

Carper, James C., jt. ed. see Hunt, Thomas C.

Carper, Jean. The All-in-One Calorie Counter. 3rd rev. ed. 416p. (Orig.). 1993. mass mkt. 5.99 (*0-553-29843-7*) Bantam.

***Carper, Jean.** The Cancer Miracle. 2000. mass mkt. 5.99 (*0-06-101384-6*) HarpC.

Carper, Jean. Food--Your Miracle Medicine. 560p. 1998. mass mkt. 6.99 (*0-06-101330-7*) HarpC.

— Food--Your Miracle Medicine. LC 92-56208. 560p. 1994. pap. 15.00 (*0-06-098424-4*, Perennial) HarperTrade.

— The Food Pharmacy. 384p. 1989. pap. 15.95 (*0-553-34524-9*) Bantam.

— The Human Brain. 2000. pap. 14.00 (*0-06-098440-6*) HarpC.

— Miracle Cures: Dramatic New Scientific Discoveries Revealing the Healing Powers of Herbs, Vitamins, & Other Natural Remedies. 308p. 1998. text 25.00 (*0-7881-5907-0*) DIANE Pub.

— Miracle Cures: Dramatic New Scientific Discoveries Revealing the Healing Powers of Herbs, Vitamins, & Other Natural Remedies. LC 97-13747. 320p. 1998. pap. 14.00 (*0-06-098436-8*, Perennial) HarperTrade.

Carper, Jean. Miracle Cures: Dramatic New Scientific Discoveries Revealing the Healing Powers of Herbs, Vitamins, & Other Natural Remedies. abr. ed. 1997. audio 12.00 (*0-694-51848-4*, CPN 10112) HarperAudio.

Carper, Jean. Miracle Cures: Dramatic New Scientific Discoveries Revealing the Healing Powers of Herbs, Vitamins, & Other Natural Remedies. large type ed. LC 97-43877. (Large Print Bks.). 1998. 26.95 (*1-56895-516-2*) Wheeler Pub.

— The Miracle Heart: The Ultimate Guide to Preventing & Curing Heart Disease with Diet & Supplements. 336p. 2000. mass mkt. 5.99 (*0-06-101383-8*) HarpC.

— The National Medical Directory. (Orig.). 1985. pap. 11.95 (*0-671-49974-2*) PB.

Carper, Jean. Stop Aging Now! Carper,&Jean. abr. ed. 1995. audio 12.00 (*0-694-51581-7*, CPN 10061) HarperAudio.

Carper, Jean. Stop Aging Now! The Ultimate Plan for Staying Young & Reversing the Aging Process. large type ed. 435p. 1999. 26.95 (*0-7838-1546-8*, G K Hall Lrg Type) Mac Lib Ref.

— Stop Aging Now! The Ultimate Plan for Staying Young & Reversing the Aging Process. 894th ed. 384p. 1996. pap. 15.00 (*0-06-098500-3*) HarpC.

— Your Miracle Brain: Dramatic New Scientific Evidence Reveals How You Can Use Food & Supplements To. 400p. 2000. 26.00 (*0-06-018391-8*) HarpC.

***Carper, Jean.** Your Miracle Brain: Reader&tbd 1, large type ed. 496p. 2000. pap. 26.00 (*0-06-098510-0*) HarpC.

Carper, Joyce, jt. auth. see Carper, N. Gordon.

Carper, Kenneth L. Forensic Engineering. LC 97-51376. 384p. 1998. boxed set 74.95 (*0-8493-7483-9*) CRC Pr.

— Forensic Engineering. 353p. 1989. 50.00 (*0-444-01330-X*) P-H.

— Forensic Engineering. 2nd ed. (Civil Engineering - Advisors Ser.). 2000. 59.95 (*0-8493-7484-7*) CRC Pr.

Carper, Kenneth L. & Feld, Jacob. Construction Failure. 2nd ed. LC 96-33425. 528p. 1996. 99.00 (*0-471-57477-5*) Wiley.

Carper, N. Gordon & Carper, Joyce. The Meaning of History: A Dictionary of Quotations. LC 90-13977. 392p. 1990. lib. bdg. 65.00 (*0-313-26835-5*, CQH/, Greenwood Pr) Greenwood.

Carper, Richard. AIDS: The American Roads of Denial. Ewing, Joella, ed. (Illus.). 200p. (Orig.). 1990. pap. 11.50 (*0-930693-05-1*) Cross-Cultrl NY.

Carper, Richard L. Music, the Hidden Talent. (Illus.). 126p. (Orig.). (C). 1988. pap. 8.95 (*0-9620443-0-X*) Minimax Pub.

Carper, Steve. Milk is Not for Every Body: Living with Lactose Intolerance. LC 95-9950. 304p. 1995. 27.95 (*0-8160-3127-4*) Facts on File.

Carper, Steve, ed. The Defective Detectives: Mystery Parodies by the Great Humorists. LC 92-17734. 256p. 1992. pap. 9.95 (*0-8065-1367-5*, Citadel Pr) Carol Pub Group.

Carper, Steve & Dimoff, Timothy. How to Tell If Your Kids Are Using Drugs. 160p. 1992. 18.95 (*0-8160-2473-1*) Facts on File.

Carper, Steve, jt. auth. see Dimoff, Timothy.

Carper, Thomas. From Nature: Poems. LC 95-15478. (Poetry & Fiction Ser.). 80p. 1995. 16.95 (*0-8018-5208-0*) Johns Hopkins.

***Carpetto, George & Evanac, Diane M., eds.** Italian Americans of the 20th Century: From the Vine. 409p. 1999. 39.95 (*0-9673796-0-1*, Pub. by Grand Lodg FL) Wimmer Cos.

Carpi, Amilcare, ed. The Pharmacology of Cerebral Circulation. LC 70-182263. 370p. (C). 1972. 172.00 (*0-08-016209-6*, Pub. by Pergamon Repr) Franklin.

Carpin, Sarah. Seychelles. 4th ed. LC 98-32375. (Odyssey Passport Ser.). (Illus.). 232p. 1999. pap. 19.95 (*962-217-616-X*) Norton.

Carpineto, Jane. On the Vineyard: A Year in the Life of an Island. LC 98-5546. 272p. 1998. 24.95 (*0-312-15584-0*, Thomas Dunne) St Martin.

— On the Vineyard: A Year in the Life of an Island. 1999. pap. 13.95 (*0-312-20666-6*) St Martin.

Carpini, Giovanni Di Plan, see Di Plan Carpini, Giovanni.

Carpini, Joe D., jt. auth. see Cangelosi, Don.

Carpini, Joseph D., jt. auth. see Murko, Carole L.

Carpini, Michael X. What Americans Know about Politics & Why It Matters. 412p. 1997. pap. text 18.00 (*0-300-07275-9*) Yale U Pr.

***Carpiniello, Rick.** Messier: Hockey's Dragon Slayer. LC 99-36864. 1999. pap. text 17.95 (*0-9653846-9-1*) MCRHSI.

Carpinisan, Mariana, tr. see Stanescu, Nichita.

Carpino, Nancy. Christmas Rose. (Illus.). 23p. (J). 1996. 7.95 (*0-533-11428-4*) Vantage.

***Carpino, Nancy.** The Leprechaun & His Bag of Gold. LC 00-91172. (Illus.). 50p. (J). (gr. k-4). 2000. 8.95 (*1-928675-03-4*) N Carpino.

— The Tenor Mouse - Topo Tenori. LC 99-95701. (Illus.). 20p. (J). (gr. k-4). 1999. pap. 8.95 (*1-928675-01-8*) N Carpino.

— Veronica's Veil. (Illus.). 24p. 1999. pap. write for info. (*1-928675-02-6*) N Carpino.

Carpino, Nancy. What Makes a Snowflake Grow? (Illus.). 48p. (Orig.). (J). (gr. k-7). 1999. pap. 6.95 (*1-928675-00-X*) N Carpino.

Carpino, Pasquale. Recipes From Pasquale'S Kitchen. LC 84-10251. (Illus.). 212p. 1984. pap. 14.95 (*0-385-19307-6*) Doubleday.

***Carpino, Pasquale.** Today's Cooking with Chef Pasquale. (Illus.). 160p. 1999. pap. 19.95 (*1-894020-64-2*, Pub. by Warwick Publ) Firefly Bks Ltd.

Carpinteri, A. Minimum Reinforcement in Concrete Members. LC 99-18029. (International Series on Structural Integrity). 212p. 1999. 101.50 (*0-08-043022-8*, Pergamon Pr) Elsevier.

— Nonlinear Crack Models for Nonmetallic Materials LC 99-23128. 1999. write for info. (*0-7923-5750-7*) Kluwer Academic.

— Structural Engineering Fracture Mechanics. 1998. pap. 121.00 (*0-419-17950-X*) Thomson Learn.

Carpinteri, A., ed. Size-Scale Effects in the Failure Mechanisms of Materials & Structures. (Illus.). 608p. (C). 1995. 165.00 (*0-419-20520-9*, E & FN Spon) Routledge.

Carpinteri, A. & Aliabadi, M. H., eds. Computational Fracture Mechanics in Concrete Technology. LC 98-84459. (Advances in Fracture Mechanics Ser.: Vol. 3). 223p. 1999. 149.00 (*1-85312-507-5*, 5075) Computational Mech MA.

Carpinteri, A. & Brebbia, Carlos A., eds. Damage & Fracture Mechanics: Computer Aided Assessment & Control. LC 98-84575. (Structures & Materials Ser.: Vol. 9). 688p. 1998. 325.00 (*1-85312-583-0*, 5830) Computational Mech MA.

Carpinteri, A. & Mainardi, F., eds. Fractals & Fractional Calculus in Continuum Mechanics. (CISM International Centre for Mechanical Sciences Ser.: No. 378). viii, 348p. 1997. pap. 80.00 (*3-211-82913-X*) Spr-Verlag.

Carpinteri, A., jt. ed. see Shah, S.

Carpinteri, Alberto. Mechanical Damage & Crack Growth in Concrete. (Engineering Application of Fracture Mechanics Ser.). 1986. text 186.00 (*90-247-3233-6*) Kluwer Academic.

— Structural Mechanics A Unified Approach. LC 94-66939. (Illus.). 784p. (C). (gr. 13). 1997. 180.00 (*0-419-19160-7*, E & FN Spon) Routledge.

Carpinteri, Alberto, ed. Fracture Mechanics of Concrete: Material Characterization & Testing. 1984. text 168.50 (*90-247-2959-9*) Kluwer Academic.

Carpinteri, Andrea, ed. Handbook of Fatigue Crack Propagation in Metallic Structures. LC 94-41214. 1806p. 1994. 427.50 (*0-444-81645-3*) Elsevier.

***Carpio, Ralph.** The Constant Creator in You. LC 00-28601. 104p. 2000. 10.95 (*1-56825-075-4*, 075-4) Rainbow Books.

Carpman, Janet R. & Grant, Myron A. Design That Cares: Planning Health Facilities for Patients & Visitors. 2nd ed. LC 93-24698. 327p. (Orig.). 1993. 49.95 (*1-55648-106-3*, 043182) AHPI.

Carpou, Mary, ed. Greek Cookery: Marin. LC 75-41189. (Illus.). (Orig.). 1981. pap. text 12.00 (*0-9611164-0-4*) Ladies Philo.

Carpovich, E. A. Russian-English Science & Engineering Dictionary. (ENG & RUS.). 676p. 1988. 250.00 (*0-7859-7145-9*) Fr & Eur.

Carpovich, Eugene A. Russian-English Atomic Dictionary: Physics, Mathematics, Nucleonics. 2nd rev. ed. LC 57-8256. (ENG & RUS.). 1959. 20.00 (*0-911484-00-0*) Tech Dict.

— Russian-English Chemical Dictionary. 2nd ed. LC 61-11700. (ENG & RUS.). 1963. 30.00 (*0-911484-03-5*) Tech Dict.

— Russian-English Metals & Machines Dictionary. LC 60-12013. (ENG & RUS.). 1960. 20.00 (*0-911484-02-7*) Tech Dict.

Carpovich, Eugene A. & Carpovich, Vera V. Science & Engineering Dictionary: Russian-English. LC 87-50551. (ENG & RUS.). 1988. 90.00 (*0-911484-05-1*) Tech Dict.

Carpovich, Vera V. Solzhenitsyn's Peculiar Vocabulary: Russian - English Glossary. LC 76-3932. (ENG & RUS.). 1976. 20.00 (*0-911484-04-3*) Tech Dict.

Carpovich, Vera V., jt. auth. see Carpovich, Eugene A.

Carpozi, George, Jr. Nazi Gold: The Real Story of How America & Europe Ended up with Jewish Treasures. 400p. 1998. 25.95 (*0-88282-167-9*, Pub. by New Horizon NJ) Natl Bk Netwk.

Carpozi, George. Poison Pen. 368p. 1997. 20.00 (*1-56980-112-6*) Barricade Bks.

Carpozi, George, Jr., jt. auth. see Balsamo, William.

Carque, Otto. Key to Rational Dietetics. 38p. 1996. reprint ed. spiral bd. 13.00 (*0-7873-1151-0*) Hlth Research.

— Natural Foods: The Safe Way to Health. (Illus.). 350p. 1998. reprint ed. pap. text 35.00 (*0-87556-858-0*) Saifer.

— Natural Foods, the Safe Way to Health. 359p. 1996. reprint ed. spiral bd. 20.00 (*0-7873-0149-3*) Hlth Research.

— Rational Diet: An Advanced Treatise on the Food Question. 540p. 1996. reprint ed. spiral bd. 26.00 (*0-7873-0150-7*) Hlth Research.

— Vital Facts about Foods: A Guide to Health & Longevity. 208p. 1996. reprint ed. spiral bd. 16.50 (*0-7873-0148-5*) Hlth Research.

Carr. Antenna Toolkit. pap. 42.95 incl. cd-rom (*0-7506-3755-2*, Newnes) Buttrwrth-Heinemann.

— Antenna Toolkit. 2001. pap. 47.95 (*0-7506-4947-X*, Newnes) Buttrwrth-Heinemann.

Carr. Calculus for Engineers. (C). 1998. text. write for info. (*0-03-009363-5*) Harcourt Coll Pubs.

— Complex Numbers Made Simple. 128p. Date not set. pap. text 19.95 (*0-7506-2559-7*) Buttrwrth-Heinemann.

— Construction Cost Engineering. (C). 2001. text. write for info. (*0-06-361162-7*) Addson-Wesley Educ.

— Construction of Cost Engineering. (C). 2001. text. write for info. (*0-06-041191-0*) HarpC.

— Death & Dying. 474p. 1999. pap. text 61.00 (*0-536-02205-4*) S&S Trade.

— Delmar's Anatomy Coloring Book. (Allied Health Ser.). 1998. pap. 18.95 (*0-8273-5640-4*) Delmar.

— Differentiation Made Simple. 128p. Date not set. pap. text 19.95 (*0-7506-2560-0*) Buttrwrth-Heinemann.

***Carr.** Family Therapy. 2000. pap. write for info. (*0-471-49124-1*) Wiley.

— Human Behavior Organizations. 3rd ed. 1999. 40.00 (*0-07-239086-7*) McGraw.

Carr. Integration Made Simple. 128p. Date not set. pap. text 19.95 (*0-7506-2561-9*) Buttrwrth-Heinemann.

— Preliminary Calculus for Engineers. 94th ed. (C). 1994. pap. text 19.50 (*0-03-011647-3*) Harcourt.

— Prepare Year for New Advent. 1991. pap. 6.95 (*0-687-60010-3*); pap. 4.95 (*0-687-60011-1*) Abingdon.

— Rock N Roll Bible. 1980. pap. text 8.95 (*0-8129-0912-7*) Random.

***Carr, ed.** Is Shame the Central Affect of Disorders of the Self? (Psychoanalytic Inquiry Ser.: Vol. 19, No. 3). 1999. 20.00 (*0-88163-924-9*) Analytic Pr.

Carr & Blackwell. Reproductive Medicine. 2nd ed. 223p. (C). 1998. pap., student ed. 55.00 (*0-8385-8894-8*, Apple Lange Med) McGraw.

Carr & Meilgaard, Morten C. Sensory Evaluation Techniques. 1987. lib. bdg. 135.00 (*0-8493-5431-5*, TA418, CRC Reprint) Franklin.

Carr & Paquet. God, I've Got to Talk to You Again! LC 59-1315. (Arch Bks.). 24p. (Orig.). (J). (gr. k-4). 1985. pap. 1.99 (*0-570-06197-0*, 59-1315) Concordia.

Carr, et al. Speaking Out Women's Economic Empowerment in South Asia. 1996. pap. 54.00 (*0-7855-7492-1*, Pub. by Ratna Pustak Bhandar) St Mut.

Carr, jt. auth. see Benward, Bruce.

Carr, jt. auth. see Hafner.

Carr, jt. auth. see McCarthy.

Carr, jt. auth. see Straub.

Carr, A. Assessment Methodology in Orthopaedics. Pynsent, P. B. et al, eds. LC 96-37312. (Illus.). 273p. 1995. text 80.00 (*0-7506-2214-8*) Buttrwrth-Heinemann.

Carr, A., jt. ed. see Hails, J.

Carr, A. A. Eye Killers: A Novel. LC 94-36175. (American Indian Literature & Critical Studies: Vol. 13). 352p. 1995. 19.95 (*0-8061-2707-4*) U of Okla Pr.

— Eye Killers: A Novel. LC 94-36175. (American Indian Literature & Critical Studies Ser.: Vol. 13). 352p. (C). 1996. pap. 12.95 (*0-8061-2854-2*, 2854) U of Okla Pr.

Carr, A. Wesley, jt. auth. see Shapiro, Edward R.

Carr, Adrian. Organizational Psychology: Its Origins, Assumptions, & Implications for Educational Administration. 80p. (C). 1995. pap. 50.00 (*0-7300-0682-4*, Pub. by Deakin Univ) St Mut.

Carr, Adrienne, jt. auth. see Carr, John.

***Carr, Alan.** Clinical Psychology in Ireland: Empirical Studies of Professional Practice. LC 99-54657. (Studies in Health & Human Services: Vol. 36). 256p. 2000. 89.95 (*0-7734-7831-0*) E Mellen.

Carr, Alan. Family Therapy & Systemic Practice: Readings on Child Protection, Clinical Techniques & Empirical Foundations. 328p. (C). 1997. 62.00 (*0-7618-0912-0*); pap. 36.50 (*0-7618-0913-9*) U Pr of Amer.

— The Handbook of Child & Adolescent Clinical Psychology: A Contextual Approach. LC 98-25289. 1999. 150.00 (*0-415-19491-1*); pap. 50.00 (*0-415-19492-X*) Routledge.

— Positive Practice: A Step-by-Step Approach to Family Therapy. xiii, 264p. 1995. text 47.00 (*3-7186-5678-7*, Harwood Acad Pubs); pap. text 20.00 (*3-7186-5680-9*, Harwood Acad Pubs) Gordon & Breach.

***Carr, Alan.** What Works for Whom with Children & Adolescents? A Critical Review of Psychological Interventions with Children, Adolescents, & Their Families. LC 99-34148. 2000. write for info. (*0-415-22113-7*) Routledge.

Carr, Alan, jt. auth. see MacIntyre, Deirdre.

Carr, Alan B., jt. auth. see McGivney, Glen P.

Carr, Albert H. How to Attract Good Luck. 1979. pap. 10.00 (*0-87980-054-2*) Wilshire.

— Juggernaut: The Path of Dictatorship. LC 79-180393. reprint ed. 49.50 (*0-404-56109-8*) AMS Pr.

— Juggernaut, the Path of Dictatorship. LC 75-93325. (Essay Index Reprint Ser.). 1977. 30.95 (*0-8369-1280-2*) Ayer.

Carr, Alice. Dark Harvest. 336p. 1998. 27.00 (*0-7528-0076-0*) Trafalgar.

— The Last Summer. 324p. 1997. pap. 17.95 (*0-7528-0075-2*, Pub. by Orion Pubng Grp) Trafalgar.

***Carr, Alice.** Winter Roses. large type ed. 432p. 2000. 31.99 (*0-7505-1467-1*, Pub. by Mgna Lrg Print) Ulverscroft.

Carr, Amelia, tr. see Augustodunensis, Honorius.

Carr, Andrew & Harnden, Anthony. Orthopaedics in General Practice. LC 96-37668. (Illus.). 240p. 1997. pap. text 52.50 (*0-7506-2219-9*) Buttrwrth-Heinemann.

Carr, Angela. Toronto Architect Edmund Burke: Redefining Canadian Architecture. (Illus.). 248p. 1995. 49.95 (*0-7735-1217-9*, Pub. by McG-Queens Univ Pr) CUP Services.

Carr, Anne. The Theological Method of Karl Rahner. LC 76-51639. (American Academy of Religion, Dissertation Ser.: No. 19). 289p. reprint ed. pap. 89.60 (*0-608-30382-8*, 201755600007) Bks Demand.

An Asterisk (*) at the beginning of an entry indicates that the title is appearing for the first time.

Carr, Anne, ed. Academic Study of Religion: Proceedings. LC 74-14212. (American Academy of Religion. Section Papers). 162p. (C). reprint ed. 50.30 (*0-8357-9563-2*, 201755200007) Bks Demand.

Carr, Anne E. A Search for Wisdom & Spirit: Thomas Merton's Theology of the Self. LC 87-40352. 176p. (C). 1989. pap. text 11.50 (*0-268-01735-2*) U of Notre Dame Pr.

— Transforming Grace: Christian Tradition & Women's Experience. 288p. 1996. pap. 19.95 (*0-8264-0873-7*) Continuum.

Carr, Anne E. & Van Leeuwen, Mary S., eds. Religion, Feminism, & the Family. LC 96-8618. (Studies in the Family, Religion, & Culture). 400p. 1996. pap. 27.00 (*0-664-25512-4*) Westminster John Knox.

Carr, Annemarie W. Byzantine Illumination Eleven Fifty to Twelve Fifty: The Study of a Provincial Tradition. (Studies in Medieval Manuscript Illumination Chicago Visual Library: No. 47). (Illus.). 448p. 1987. lib. bdg. 95.00 (*0-226-68863-1*) U Ch Pr.

Carr, Archie. Handbook of Turtles: The Turtles of the United States, Canada, & Baja California. (Comstock Classic Handbooks Ser.). (Illus.). 560p. 1995. pap. text 39.95 (*0-8014-8254-2*) Cornell U Pr.

— High Jungles & Low. (Illus.). 272p. 1992. reprint ed. pap. 17.95 (*0-8130-1135-3*) U Press Fla.

— A Naturalist in Florida: A Celebration of Eden. Carr, Marjorie H., ed. LC 93-44919. (Illus.). 304p. (C). 1994. 37.00 (*0-300-05589-7*) Yale U Pr.

— A Naturalist in Florida: A Celebration of Eden. (Illus.). 304p. 1996. pap. 17.00 (*0-300-06854-9*) Yale U Pr.

— The Sea Turtle: So Excellent a Fishe. rev. ed. 292p. 1986. pap. 18.95 (*0-292-77595-4*) U of Tex Pr.

— Ulendo: Travels of a Naturalist in & Out of Africa. LC 92-34453. 344p. 1993. reprint ed. pap. 16.95 (*0-8130-1179-5*) U Press Fla.

— The Windward Road: Adventures of a Naturalist on Remote Caribbean Shores. LC 79-23624. (Illus.). xl, 266p. 1979. reprint ed. pap. 16.95 (*0-8130-0639-2*) U Press Fla.

Carr, Arthur A. Carr Book: Sketches of the Lives of Many of the Descendants of Robert & Caleb Carr, Whose Arrival on This Continent in 1635 Began the American Story of Our Family. (Illus.). 598p. 1997. reprint ed. pap. 89.50 (*0-8328-7855-3*); reprint ed. lib. bdg. 99.50 (*0-8328-7854-5*) Higginson Bk Co.

Carr, Arthur C., et al, eds. Grief: Selected Readings. LC 72-75176. 155p. 1974. pap. 7.50 (*0-930194-76-4*) Ctr Thanatology.

Carr, Arthur C., jt. auth. see Frazier, Shervert.

Carr, Arthur C., ed. see Tolstoy, Leo.

Carr, Arthur J. & Steinhoff, William R., eds. Points of Departure: Essays & Stories for College English. LC 74-167324. (Essay Index Reprint Ser.). (C). 1977. reprint ed. 39.95 (*0-8369-2449-5*) Ayer.

Carr, Audrey & Davis, Lou E. Housebreak Any Dog. LC 96-38852. 128p. 1997. pap. 11.95 (*0-8092-3074-7*, 307470, Contemporary Bks) NTC Contemp Pub Co.

Carr, B. History of England from the Close of the Saxon Heptarchy to the Declaration of Independence. 1954. 25.00 (*0-87556-047-4*) Saifer.

Carr, Banjamin. Benjamin Carr: Selected Secular & Sacred Songs. Meyer, Eve R., ed. (Recent Researches in American Music Ser.: No. RRAM15). (Illus.). 86, xxiiip. 1986. pap. 35.00 (*0-89579-204-4*) A-R Eds.

Carr, Barbara. The Planet of the Dinosaurs. LC 92-9287. (Illus.). 32p. (J). (gr. k-3). 1992. 16.95 (*0-89334-161-4*, 161-4) Humanics Ltd.

Carr, Barry. Mexican Communism, 1968-1983: Eurocommunism in the Americas? (Research Reports: No. 42). 36p. (Orig.). (C). 1985. pap. 5.00 (*0-935391-41-X*, RR-42) UCSD Ctr US-Mex.

Carr, Beau & Rychner, Lorenz M. Yamaha MTIX. Alexander, Peter L., ed. (Illus.). 72p. (C). 1987. pap. text 17.95 (*0-939067-74-9*) Alexander Pub.

Carr, Benjamin, et al. Anthology of Early American Key Board Music 1787-1830, Vol. 1. Clark, J. Bunker, ed. (Recent Researches in American Music Ser.: No. RRAM1). (Illus.). 1977. pap. 50.00 (*0-89579-098-X*) A-R Eds.

— Anthology of Early American Key Board Music 1787-1830, Vol. 2. Clark, J. Bunker, ed. (Recent Researches in American Music Ser.: No. RRAM2). (Illus.). 1977. pap. 45.00 (*0-89579-099-8*) A-R Eds.

Carr, Bernadette. A Woman's Touch. 320p. 1998. mass mkt. 4.99 (*0-505-52261-6*, Love Spell) Dorchester Pub Co.

Carr, Beth Ann, jt. auth. see Nelson, J. Ron.

Carr, Betty J. The Wisdom of His Word. Knox, Dahk & Pearson, Keith, eds. LC 96-213284. (Illus.). 170p. 1996. pap. text 14.95 (*1-881116-79-4*, Kinder Bks) Black Forest Pr.

Carr, Blair. A Case of Black or White. 240p. 1995. pap. 11.95 (*0-9647013-0-8*) Kudzu Pubns.

Carr Blood, William. Miracles! More Than Believing : Supernatural Events are Happening Today. LC 95-83204. xiii, 93 p. 1995. write for info. (*1-56043-573-9*) Destiny Image.

Carr, Brad, jt. auth. see Wright, J. B.

Carr, Brian, ed. Morals & Society in Asian Philosophy. (Curzon Studies in Asian Philosophy). 260p. (C). 1996. text 42.00 (*0-7007-0345-4*, Pub. by Curzon Pr Ltd) UH Pr.

***Carr, Brian & Mahalingam, Indira.** Companion Encyclopedia of Asian Philosophy. LC 00-32831. 2000. write for info. (*0-415-24038-7*) Routledge.

Carr, Brian & Mahalingam, Indira, eds. Companion Encyclopedia of Asian Philosophy. LC 96-29027. (Companion Encyclopedia Ser.). 1168p. (C). (gr. 13). 1997. 200.00 (*0-415-03535-X*, B3888) Routledge.

Carr-Brion, K. G., et al. Sampling Systems for Process Analysers. 2nd ed. LC 94-2204. (Illus.). 400p. 1996. 160.00 (*0-7506-1247-9*) Buttrwrth-Heinemann.

Carr, Bruce, ed. see International Beethoven Congress Staff.

Carr, Bruce R. & Blackwell, Richard E. Textbook of Reproductive Medicine. 645p. (C). 1993. pap. text 90.00 (*0-8385-8914-6*, A8914-2) Appleton & Lange.

— Textbook of Reproductive Medicine. 2nd ed. LC 97-37910. 790p. (C). 1999. 125.00 (*0-8385-8893-X*, Apple Lange Med) McGraw.

Carr, C. Caught in the Act: A Visual History of Contemporary Multimedia Performance. LC 96-83973. (Illus.). 128p. 1996. 60.00 (*0-89381-680-9*) Aperture.

— Klan & Tribe. 1999. 25.00 (*0-517-70506-0*) Random.

— On Edge: Performance at the End of the Twentieth Century. LC 93-8182. (Illus.). 357p. 1993. pap. 24.95 (*0-8195-6269-6*, Wesleyan Univ Pr) U Pr of New Eng.

Carr, C. & Neitzel, J. E. Style, Society, & Person: Archaeological & Ethnological Perspectives. LC 95-2530. (Interdisciplinary Contributions to Archaeology Ser.). (Illus.). 500p. (C). 1995. 72.50 (*0-306-44843-2*, Plenum Trade) Perseus Pubng.

Carr, C., et al. The Seven Pagodas on the Coromandal Coast. (Illus.). 244p. 1986. reprint ed. 37.50 (*0-8364-1726-7*, Pub. by Usha) S Asia.

Carr, C. T. The General Principles of the Law of Corporations: Being the Yorke Prize Essay for the Year 1902. xiii, 211p. 1984. reprint ed. lib. bdg. 42.00 (*0-8377-2006-0*, Rothman) W S Hein.

Carr, Caleb. The Alienist. LC 93-32766. 608p. 1995. mass mkt. 7.50 (*0-553-57299-7*) Bantam.

— The Alienist. LC 93-32766. 496p. 1994. 29.95 (*0-679-41779-6*) Random.

— The Angel of Darkness. 1998. mass mkt. 7.99 (*0-345-42763-7*) Ballantine Pub Grp.

— The Devil Soldier: The American Soldier of Fortune Who Became a God in China. 1995. pap. 15.00 (*0-679-76128-4*) Random.

***Carr, Caleb.** Killing Time. large type ed. 528p. 2000. 25.95 (*0-375-43076-8*) Random.

— Killing Time: A Novel. 336p. 2000. 25.95 (*0-679-46332-1*) Random.

Carr, Caleb, ed. see Bradley, Omar N.

Carr, Caleb, ed. see Grant, Ulysses S.

Carr, Caleb, ed. see Parkman, Francis.

Carr, Caleb, ed. see Roosevelt, Theodore.

Carr, Caleb, ed. see Von Clausewitz, Carl & Tzu, Sun.

Carr-Calthrop, C. W. Calthorpe: Notes on the Calthore & Calthrop in the Counties of Norfold & Lincolnshire & Elsewhere. 151p. 1994. reprint ed. pap. 24.00 (*0-8328-4137-4*); reprint ed. lib. bdg. 34.00 (*0-8328-4136-6*) Higginson Bk Co.

Carr, Camilla. Topsy Dingo Wild Dog. Richardson, Stewart, ed. 410p. 1989. 16.95 (*1-55972-013-1*, Birch Ln Pr) Carol Pub Group.

Carr, Caroline A., et al. Ophthalmic Anesthesia. 2nd ed. (Illus.). 288p. 1996. pap. text 65.00 (*0-340-56757-0*, Pub. by E A) OUP.

Carr, Carolyn, jt. ed. see Acomb, Craig.

Carr, Carolyn K. Hans Namuth Portraits. LC 98-50685. (Photography Ser.). (Illus.). 166p. 1999. 39.95 (*1-56098-809-6*) Smithsonian.

Carr, Carolyn K., et al. Revisiting the White City: American Art at the 1893 World's Fair. LC 92-37218. (Illus.). 408p. 1993. 60.00 (*0-937311-01-4*); pap. 35.00 (*0-937311-02-2*) Natl Mus Amer Art.

Carr, Cecil T. Concerning English Administrative Law. LC 70-38958. reprint ed. 20.00 (*0-404-01395-3*) AMS Pr.

Carr, Charles C. Alcoa, an American Enterprise. LC 72-5039. (Technology & Society Ser.). (Illus.). 292p. 1972. reprint ed. 26.95 (*0-405-04692-8*) Ayer.

Carr, Charles C., jt. auth. see Gause, Frank A.

***Carr, Charmian & Strauss, Jean A.** Forever Liesl: A Memoir of the Sound of Music. LC 99-38143. 245p. 2000. 23.95 (*0-670-88908-3*, Viking) Viking Penguin.

***Carr, Charmian & Strauss, Jean A. S.** Forever Liesl: A Memoir of the Sound of Music. large type ed. LC 00-28636. 488p. 2000. 26.95 (*0-7862-2558-0*) Thorndike Pr.

Carr, Chester C. Free Lance Adult Travel in Europe: Travel Without a Travel Agent or Tour. LC 88-92325. 112p. (Orig.). 1989. pap. 14.95 (*0-922958-02-5*) H W Parker.

Carr, Chester C., ed. Travel Photography Using Existing Light. LC 88-92326. (Orig.). 1989. pap. 12.95 (*0-922958-04-1*) H W Parker.

Carr, Chris, et al. Strategic Investment Decisions: A Comparative Study of Companies in the Motor Industry in the U. K. & West Germany. (Avebury Business Research Library). 407p. 1994. 91.95 (*1-85628-975-3*, Pub. by Avebry) Ashgate Pub Co.

Carr, Christopher. Handbook on Soil Resistivity Surveying. LC 82-4277. (Research Ser.: No. 2). (Illus.). 704p. (C). 1982. 20.00 (*0-942118-13-8*, CC79.S6C37) Ctr Amer Arche.

Carr, Christopher & Beaumont, John. SWOT Law of Evidence. 214p. (C). 1990. 90.00 (*1-85431-035-6*) St Mut.

— SWOT Law of Evidence. 4th ed. 210p. 1996. pap. 22.00 (*1-85431-486-6*, Pub. by Blackstone Pr) Gaunt.

Carr, Cindy L. Your Church Bulletin Board: 3-D Ideas for All Seasons. (Illus.). 64p. 1995. wbk. ed. 9.99 (*0-87227-185-4*, RBP5222) Reg Baptist.

Carr, Clare, ed. see Freelander, Iris.

Carr, Claudia J. Pastoralism in Crisis: The Dasanetch & Their Ethiopian Lands. LC 77-1252. (University of Chicago, Department of Geography, Research Paper Ser.: No. 180). 373p. 1977. reprint ed. pap. 115.70 (*0-608-02239-X*, 206279900004) Bks Demand.

Carr, Clay. Choice, Chance & Organizational Change: Practical Insights from Evolution for Business Leaders & Thinkers. 208p. 1996. 22.95 (*0-8144-0279-8*) AMACOM.

— The New Manager's Survival Manual. 2nd ed. LC 94-34049. 261p. 1995. 69.95 (*0-471-10986-X*); pap. 19.95 (*0-471-10987-8*) Wiley.

— 101 Most Common Mistakes. LC 97-199204. (C). 1997. pap. text 16.95 (*0-13-234170-0*) P-H.

— Team Leader's Problem Solver. LC 95-39795. 464p. 1995. text 39.95 (*0-13-409970-2*) P-H.

— Team Leader's Problem Solver. LC 95-39795. 350p. (C). 1995. pap. text 14.95 (*0-13-409962-1*) P-H.

Carr, Clay & Albright, Mary. The Manager's Troubleshooter: Pinpointing the Causes & Cures of 125 Tough Day-to-Day Problems. 2nd ed. 448p. (C). 1996. text 39.95 (*0-13-240318-8*) P-H.

Carr, Clay & Beer, Valorie. Personal Job Power: Discover Your Own Power Style for Work Satisfaction & Success. 224p. 1996. pap. 12.95 (*1-56079-599-9*) Petersons.

Carr, Clay & Fletcher, Mary A. The Manager's Troubleshooter: Pinpointing the Causes & Cures of 125 Tough Supervisory Problems. 496p. (C). 1990. text 39.95 (*0-13-552647-7*) P-H.

Carr, Craig L., ed. see Pufendorf, Samuel.

Carr, Cynthia, ed. Fever: The Art of David Wojnarowicz. LC 98-35322. (Illus.). 160p. 1999. 35.00 (*0-8478-2144-7*, Pub. by Rizzoli Intl) St Martin.

Carr, D. Explorations in Phenomenology. Casey, E. S., ed. (Selected Studies in Phenomenology & Existential Philosophy: Vol. 4). 448p. 1974. pap. text 112.50 (*90-247-1561-X*, Pub. by M Nijhoff) Kluwer Academic.

— Interpreting Husserl: Critical & Comparative Studies. (Phaenomenologica Ser.: No. 106). 308p. 1987. lib. bdg. 193.50 (*90-247-3505-X*, Pub. by M Nijhoff) Kluwer Academic.

***Carr, D. B.** An Atlas of Pain Management. (Encyclopedia of Visual Medicine Ser.). (Illus.). 120p. 2000. 85.00 (*1-85070-564-X*) Prthnon Pub.

Carr, D. S. & Ponikvar, A. L., eds. Proceedings - 3rd International Lead-Acid Battery Seminar. (Illus.). 410p. (Orig.). 1989. pap. 50.00 (*0-932893-03-1*) Intl Lead Zinc.

***Carr, Dalton.** Tales of a Bear Hunter. (Illus.). 140p. 2000. 24.95 (*1-57157-171-X*) Safari Pr.

Carr, Dan. The Ennead of Set-Heru. (Illus.). 20p. 1981. 25.00 (*0-939622-23-8*) Four Zoas Night Ltd.

— Our Savior Is Born. 24p. (J). (gr. 1 up). 1984. 8.99 (*0-570-04092-2*, 56-1460) Concordia.

Carr, Daniel B. & Jacox, Ada K. Acute Pain Management: Operative or Medical Procedures & Trauma Clinical Practice Guideline. (Illus.). 145p. (C). 1997. reprint ed. pap. text 30.00 (*0-7881-4611-4*) DIANE Pub.

Carr, Daniel M., ed. Washington County Men & Women of Nebraska: A Book of Portraits, Washington County Edition, Containing an Historical Review of Washington County, Compiled from Public & Private Records. (Illus.). 198p. 1995. reprint ed. lib. bdg. 29.50 (*0-8328-5054-3*) Higginson Bk Co.

Carr, David. Education, Knowledge, & Truth: Beyond the Post-Modern Impasse. LC 98-7427. (International Studies in the Philosophy of Education). 14p. 1999. write for info. (*0-415-16317-X*) Routledge.

— Flowering Shrubs: Step by Step to Growing Success. (Crowood Gardening Guides Ser.). 128p. 1992. pap. 16.95 (*1-85223-505-5*, Pub. by Crolwood) Trafalgar.

— Foreign Investment & Development in Egypt. LC 79-1230. 148p. 1979. 57.95 (*0-275-90338-9*, C0338, Praeger Pubs) Greenwood.

— Garden Trees: Step by Step to Growing Success. (Crowood Gardening Guides Ser.). (Illus.). 128p. 1991. pap. 16.95 (*1-85223-576-4*, Pub. by Crolwood) Trafalgar.

— The Paradox of Subjectivity: The Self in the Transcendental Tradition. LC 98-28135. 168p. 1999. text 35.00 (*0-19-512690-4*) OUP.

— Practical Container Gardening. (Illus.). 64p. 1992. pap. 8.95 (*1-85223-621-3*, Pub. by Crolwood) Trafalgar.

***Carr, David.** Professionalism & Ethics in Teaching. LC 99-23908. 304p. (C). 1999. text. write for info. (*0-415-18459-2*) Routledge.

Carr, David. Professionalism & Ethics in Teaching. LC 99-23908. (Professional Ethics Ser.). 304p. 2000. pap. 25.99 (*0-415-18460-6*) Routledge.

— Time, Narrative, & History. LC 85-45742. (Studies in Phenomenology & Existential Philosophy). 200p. 1991. pap. 13.95 (*0-253-20603-0*, MB 603) Ind U Pr.

— Topiary & Plant Sculpture: A Beginner's Step-by-Step Guide. (Illus.). 144p. 1995. pap. 22.95 (*1-85223-881-X*, Pub. by Crolwood) Trafalgar.

Carr, David & Steutel, J. W. Virtue Ethics & Moral Education. LC 98-47913. 1999. 75.00 (*0-415-17073-7*) Routledge.

Carr, David, tr. see Husserl, Edmund.

Carr, David K. & Hard, Kelvin J. Managing the Change Process: A Field Book for Change Agents, Team Leaders & Reengineering Managers. LC 95-36992. (Illus.). 272p. 1995. 34.95 (*0-07-012944-4*) McGraw.

Carr, David K. & Johansson, Henry J. Best Practices in Reengineering: What Works & What Doesn't in the Reengineering Process. 288p. 1995. 29.95 (*0-07-011224-X*) McGraw.

Carr, David K. & Littman, Ian D. Excellence in Government: Total Quality Management in the 1990s. 2nd ed. 1993. 39.95 (*0-944533-07-8*) Coopers Total Qlty.

Carr, David K., et al. Improvement Driven Government: Public Service for the 21st Century. (Excellence in Government Ser.). 592p. 1995. 39.95 (*0-944533-20-5*) Coopers Total Qlty.

Carr, David M. Reading the Fractures of Genesis: Historical & Literary Approaches. LC 95-46693. 424p. 1996. 44.95 (*0-664-22071-1*) Westminster John Knox.

Carr, David M., jt. ed. see Weis, Richard D.

***Carr, David W.** The Significance of Gorbachev's Economic Reforms. 102p. 1999. pap. 13.95 (*1-58244-031-X*) Rutledge Bks.

***Carr, Dawson.** The Cape Hatteras Lighthouse: Sentinel of the Shoals. LC 99-89872. (Illus.). 155p. 2000. pap. 10.95 (*0-8078-4876-X*) U of NC Pr.

Carr, Dawson. Gray Phantoms of the Cape Fear: Running the Civil War Blockade. LC 98-21315. (Illus.). 1998. pap. 14.95 (*0-89587-213-7*) Blair.

Carr, Dawson & Leonard, Mark. Looking at Paintings: A Guide to Technical Terms. LC 91-24329. (Looking at . . . Ser.). 84p. 1992. pap. 12.95 (*0-89236-213-8*) OUP.

Carr, Dawson W. Andrea Mantegna: The Adoration of the Magi. LC 97-17639. (Getty Museum Studies on Art). 106p. 1998. pap. 17.50 (*0-89236-287-1*, Pub. by J P Getty Trust) OUP.

Carr, Deborah, ed. see National Research Council Staff.

Carr, Denis H., ed. Contrast Media. (Illus.). 227p. 1988. text 132.00 (*0-443-03352-8*) Church.

Carr, Dodd S., ed. see Brown, Harvey E.

Carr, Donald A. Environmental Criminal Liability: Avoiding & Defending Enforcement. 500p. 1996. 155.00 (*0-87179-867-0*) BNA Books.

Carr, Donald D., pref. Industrial Minerals & Rocks. 6th ed. LC 93-84488. (Illus.). 1214p. (C). 1994. text 138.00 (*0-87335-103-7*) SMM&E Inc.

Carr, Donald D. & Herz, Norman, eds. Concise Encyclopedia of Mineral Resources. (Advances in Materials Science & Engineering Ser.: No. 2). (Illus.). 426p. 1989. 181.50 (*0-08-034734-7*, Pergamon Pr) Elsevier.

— Concise Encyclopedia of Mineral Resources. (Advances in Materials Science Ser.). 440p. 1989. 145.00 (*0-262-03155-8*) MIT Pr.

Carr, Donna S. Healthy Cuisine for Busy People: An Easy to Read Nutrition Guide with Quick Computerized Recipes & a Time Saving Menu Guide. (Illus.). 217p. 1989. pap. 11.95 (*0-9625338-0-7*) Braes Corp.

Carr, Dorothy, ed. see Dunn, Elsie M.

Carr, Duane. A Question of Class: The Redneck Stereotype in Southern Fiction. LC 96-38510. 188p. 1996. 45.95 (*0-87972-721-7*); pap. 19.95 (*0-87972-722-5*) Bowling Green Univ Popular Press.

***Carr, Duncan.** Thirty-One Days in the Kingdom of God. 64p. 2000. pap. 5.99 (*1-58158-002-9*, Fairmont Bks) McDougal Pubng.

C

Carr, E. H. The Romantic Exiles. 352p. 1998. pap. 22.95 (*1-897959-35-4*, Pub. by Serif) IPG Chicago.

Carr, Edson. Carr Family Records, Embracing the Records of the First Family Who Settled in America & Their Descendants, with Branches Who Came at a Later Date. (Illus.). 540p. 1989. reprint ed. pap. 68.00 (*0-8328-0371-5*); reprint ed. lib. bdg. 78.00 (*0-8328-0370-7*) Higginson Bk Co.

Carr, Edson I. History of Rockton, Winnebago Co., 1820 to 1898. (Illus.). 200p. 1997. reprint ed. lib. bdg. 27.50 (*0-8328-5793-9*) Higginson Bk Co.

Carr, Edward G. How to Teach Sign Language to Developmentally Disabled Children. (Teaching the Autistic Ser.). 54p. 1981. pap. 8.00 (*0-89079-063-9*, 1035) PRO-ED.

— Positive Behavior Support in People with Developmental Disabilities: A Research Synthesis. LC 99-22505. 108p. 1999. 31.95 (*0-940898-60-8*) Am Assn Mental.

Carr, Edward G., et al. Communication-Based Intervention for Problem Behavior: A User's Guide for Producing Positive Change. LC 94-11800. 288p. 1994. pap. 29.95 (*1-55766-159-6*, 1596) P H Brookes.

Carr, Edward H. The Bolshevik Revolution 1917-1923, 3 vols., 1. 1985. reprint ed. pap. 12.95 (*0-393-30195-8*) Norton.

— The Bolshevik Revolution 1917-1923, 3 vols., 2. 1985. reprint ed. pap. 13.95 (*0-393-30197-4*) Norton.

— The Bolshevik Revolution 1917-1923, 3 vols., 3. 1985. reprint ed. pap. 14.95 (*0-393-30199-0*) Norton.

— German-Soviet Relations Between the Two World Wars, 1919-1939. 1979. 18.95 (*0-405-10586-X*) Ayer.

— German-Soviet Relations Between the Two World Wars, 1919-1939. LC 83-12572. 146p. 1983. reprint ed. lib. bdg. 55.00 (*0-313-24117-1*, CAGS, Greenwood Pr) Greenwood.

— A History of Soviet Russia, 7 vols. Incl. 2. Bolshevik Revolution. 5. Socialism in One Country. 6. Socialism in One Country. 1960. Set. Socialism in One Country. 1964. 29.95 Vol. 1-3. Bolshevik Revolution. Vol. 1-3. Bolshevik Revolution. Vol. 1-3. Bolshevik Revolution. 1953. Vol. 4. Interregnum. 1954. Vol. 7. Socialism in One Country. 1964. Vol. 7. Socialism in One Country. 1964. Vols. 5-6. Socialism in One Country. write for info. (*0-318-54227-7*) Macmillan.

— Nueva Sociedad. 4th ed. (Ciencias Sociales Ser.: No. 39). (SPA.). 185p. 1984. pap. 3.00 (*0-8477-0039-9*) U of PR Pr.

— Twenty Year's Crisis. 450th ed. 256p. (gr. 8). 1964. pap. 15.00 (*0-06-131122-7*, TB1122, Torch) HarpC.

— What Is History? 1967. pap. 7.16 (*0-394-70391-X*, V391) Vin Bks.

Carr, Eileen, ed. see Bach, Penny B., et al.

Carr, Ellen & Killman, Judith A. Basics of Cancer Chemotherapy. 3rd rev. ed. (Illus.). 115p. (C). 1995. pap. 39.95 (*1-878025-71-6*) Western Schls.

Carr, Emily. Beloved Land: The World of Emily Carr. LC 96-4836. (Illus.). 112p. 1996. pap. 17.95 (*1-55054-474-8*) U of Wash Pr.

— The Complete Writings of Emily Carr. (Illus.). 893p. 1997. reprint ed. pap. 29.95 (*0-295-97626-8*) U of Wash Pr.

Carr, Ethan. Wilderness by Design: Landscape Architecture & the National Park Service. LC 97-22127. (Illus.). 378p. 1998. text 50.00 (*0-8032-1491-X*) U of Nebr Pr.

— Wilderness by Design: Landscape Architecture & the National Park Service. LC 97-22127. (Illus.). 378p. 1999. pap. 29.95 (*0-8032-6383-X*, Bison Books) U of Nebr Pr.

Carr, F. Rene Van De, see Van De Carr, F. Rene.

Carr, Fergus & Ifantis, Kostas. NATO in the New European Order. 270p. 1996. text 65.00 (*0-312-15815-7*) St Martin.

Carr, Fergus & Massey, Andrew. Public Policy in the New Europe: Eurogovernance in Theory & Practice. LC 99-30949. (New Horizons in Public Policy Ser.). 304p. 1999. 90.00 (*1-85898-982-5*) E Elgar.

Carr, Firpo. Wicked Words: Racism in the Dictionary. (Illus.). 144p. 1997. 24.95 (*0-9631293-5-X*) Prof Pr NC.

Carr, Frances A. Shaker Your Plate: Of Shaker Cooks & Cooking. LC 87-8242. (Illus.). 154p. (Orig.). 1985. pap. 14.95 (*0-87451-404-5*) U Pr of New Eng.

— Shaker Your Plate: Of Shaker Cooks & Cooking. LC 85-51982. (Illus.). 156p. (Orig.). 1985. pap. 12.95 (*0-915836-02-5*) United Soc Shakers.

Carr, Francis. Mozart & Constanze. 186p. 1985. mass mkt. 4.95 (*0-380-69884-6*, Avon Bks) Morrow Avon.

***Carr, Frank.** Partnering. LC 99-39379. 1999. write for info. (*1-57073-737-1*) Amer Bar Assn.

Carr, Frank. Sailing Barges. 464p. 1990. 83.00 (*0-86138-060-6*, Pub. by T Dalton) St Mut.

***Carr, Frank & Sutter, Pascal.** Confidential File 101. 324p. 2000. 24.95 (*0-9701583-0-0*) Angelhart.

Carr, Fred K. Patents Handbook: A Guide for Inventors & Researchers to Searching Patent Documents & Preparing & Making an Application. LC 95-7366. 237p. 1995. lib. bdg. 43.00 (*0-7864-0026-9*) McFarland & Co.

Carr, G. Masters of Fantasy. 1992. 9.98 (*0-88365-786-4*) Galahad Bks.

***Carr, G. Lawrence & Dumas, Paul, eds.** Accelerator-Based Sources of Infrared & Spectroscopic Applications. 1999. pap. text 62.00 (*0-8194-3261-X*) SPIE.

Carr, Gary. The Left Side of Paradise: The Screenwriting of John Howard Lawson. Kirkpatrick, Diane, ed. LC 84-2551. (Studies in Cinema: No. 26). 137p. reprint ed. 42.50 (*0-8357-1570-1*, 207046700095) Bks Demand.

Carr, Geoffrey. Tales from the Mines. 44p. 1987. 25.00 (*0-907496-45-8*, Pub. by JNM Pubns) St Mut.

Carr, Gerald A. Men's Gymnastic Handbook. (Illus.). 214p. 1981. pap., teacher ed. 14.95 (*0-88839-046-7*) Hancock House.

— Safety in Gymnastics. (Illus.). 248p. 1981. pap. 9.95 (*0-88839-054-8*) Hancock House.

Carr, Gerald F., et al, eds. Interdigitations: Essays for Irmengard Rauch. LC 98-11473. (Illus.). XXII, 762p. (C). 1999. text 89.00 (*0-8204-3802-2*) P Lang Pubng.

Carr, Gerald F., jt. ed. see Rauch, Irmengard.

Carr, Gerald L. Frederic Edwin Church: Catalogue Raisonne of Works of Art at Olana State Historical Site. (Illus.). 635p. (C). 1994. text 389.95 (*0-521-38540-7*) Cambridge U Pr.

***Carr, Gerry.** Fundamentals of Track & Field. 2nd rev. ed. LC 98-52218. (Illus.). 272p. 1999. pap. 19.95 (*0-7360-0008-9*, PCAR0008) Human Kinetics.

Carr, Gerry. Mechanics of Sport: A Practitioner's Guide. LC 95-52859. (Illus.). 224p. (Orig.). 1996. pap. text 24.00 (*0-87322-974-6*, PCAR0974) Human Kinetics.

***Carr, Glyn.** Death on Milestone Buttress. 187p. 2000. reprint ed. pap. 14.00 (*0-915230-29-1*) Rue Morgue.

***Carr, Glynis, ed.** New Essays in Ecofeminist Literary Criticism. 192p. 2000. 28.00 (*0-8387-5476-7*) Bucknell U Pr.

Carr, Glynis, ed. Turning the Century: Feminist Theory in the 1990s. LC 92-8980. (Review Ser.: Vol. 36, No. 2). 200p. (C). 1992. 22.00 (*0-8387-5241-1*) Bucknell U Pr.

Carr-Gomm, Philip. The Druid Way. (Earth Quest Ser.). (Illus.). 176p. 1993. pap. 15.95 (*1-85230-365-4*, Pub. by Element MA) Penguin Putnam.

— Elements of Druid Tradition. (Illus.). 144p. 1997. pap. 9.95 (*1-86204-031-1*, Pub. by Element MA) Penguin Putnam.

Carr-Gomm, Philip & Carr-Gomm, Stephanie. Druid Animal Oracle: Working with the Sacred Animals of the Druid Tradition. LC 94-25038. (Illus.). 184p. 1995. 24.95 (*0-671-50300-6*) S&S Trade.

Carr-Gomm, Sarah. Dictionary of Symbols in Western Art. LC 95-17577. (Illus.). 240p. 1995. 26.95 (*0-8160-3301-3*); pap. 14.95 (*0-8160-3326-9*) Facts on File.

Carr-Gomm, Stephanie, jt. auth. see Carr-Gomm, Philip.

Carr, Gregg. Residence & Social Status: The Development of 17th-Century London. LC 91-9481. (Harvard Studies in Sociology: Outstanding Dissertations & Monographs Twenty-Two Distinguished Works from the Past Fifty Years). 248p. 1991. text 20.00 (*0-8240-8423-3*) Garland.

Carr-Gregg, C. & Wetherell, D. F. Camilla: C. H. Wedgwood, 1901-1955 - A Life. (Modern History Ser.). 242p. 1990. pap. 27.95 (*0-86840-387-3*, Pub. by New South Wales Univ Pr) Intl Spec Bk.

***Carr, Griselda.** Pit Women: Coal Communities in Northern England in the Early Twentieth Century. 250p. 2000. pap. 65.00 (*0-85036-495-7*, Pub. by U Wales Pr) Paul & Co Pubs.

Carr, H. Arnold, jt. auth. see Fish, John P.

Carr, H. Wildon. Time & History in Contemporary Philosophy. 1970. reprint ed. pap. 39.95 (*0-8383-0120-7*) M S G Haskell Hse.

Carr, H. Wildon, tr. see Bergson, Henri.

Carr, Harold & Latham, Barbara. Technology in Clothing Manufacture. 2nd ed. LC 93-25907. (Illus.). 288p. 1994. pap. 34.95 (*0-632-03748-2*, Pub. by Blckwll Scitfc UK) Blackwell Sci.

Carr, Harold & Pomeroy, John. Fashion Design & Product Development. (Illus.). 224p. 1992. pap. 38.95 (*0-632-02893-9*) Blackwell Sci.

***Carr, Harold, et al.** Carr & Latham's Technology of Clothing Manufacture. 3rd ed. LC 00-35439. 2000. pap. write for info. (*0-632-05248-1*) Blackwell Sci.

Carr, Harry. Los Angeles, City of Dreams. 1992. reprint ed. lib. bdg. 75.00 (*0-7812-5010-2*) Rprt Serv.

Carr, Harvey. I Was on the Wrong Bear. 159p. 1992. pap. 9.95 (*0-912678-84-4*) Greenfld Rev Lit.

Carr, Heather. HTML: A Hands on Guide. (Illus.). 144p. 1997. spiral bd. 26.60 (*1-57426-045-6*) Computer Lit Pr.

Carr, Helen. Inventing the American Primitive: Politics, Gender & the Representation of Native American Literary Traditions, 1789-1936. LC 96-33848. 320p. (C). 1996. text 50.00 (*0-8147-1548-6*); pap. text 20.00 (*0-8147-1549-4*) NYU Pr.

— Jean Rhys. (Writers & Their Work Ser.). 95p. 1996. pap. text 17.00 (*0-7463-0717-9*, Pub. by Northcote House) U Pr of Miss.

Carr, Helen, ed. & photos by see Carr, John W.

Carr, Herbert W. The General Principle of Relativity in Its Philosophical & Historical Aspect. LC 75-3099. reprint ed. 27.50 (*0-404-59096-9*) AMS Pr.

— A Theory of Monads. LC 75-3101. reprint ed. 32.50 (*0-404-59098-5*) AMS Pr.

Carr, Hobart C. Early History of Iowa Railroads. Bruchey, Stuart, ed. LC 80-1277. (Railroads Ser.). 1981. lib. bdg. 18.95 (*0-405-13752-4*) Ayer.

***Carr, Houston.** Data Communications for Executives. 187p. 1999. 15.00 (*1-886855-30-7*) Tavenner Pub.

Carr, Houston. Management of End Use of Computing. (Illus.). 160p. 1999. pap. text 16.00 (*1-886855-28-5*) Tavenner Pub.

— Telecommunications Lab Manual. 196p. 1998. pap., lab manual ed. 12.00 (*1-886855-96-X*) Tavenner Pub.

Carr, Houston & Snyder, Charles. Management of Business Telecommunications. 560p. (C). 1996. text 55.35 (*0-256-21961-3*, Irwn McGrw-H) McGrw-H Hghr Educ.

Carr, Hugh. Encounter in the Wilderness. (Irish Play Ser.). 1980. pap. 2.95 (*0-912262-65-6*) Proscenium.

— Voices from a Far Country. 304p. 1996. pap. 18.95 (*0-85640-545-0*, Pub. by Blackstaff Pr) Dufour.

Carr-Hurtt, L. Denise, ed. see Carr, Monica M.

***Carr, I.** Love Child. 1999. text 35.00 (*0-340-68951-X*, Pub. by Hodder & Stought Ltd) Trafalgar.

— Lover's Meeting. mass mkt. 13.95 (*0-340-68950-1*, Pub. by Hodder & Stought Ltd) Trafalgar.

— Mary's Child. 1997. mass mkt. 13.95 (*0-340-65433-3*, Pub. by Hodder & Stought Ltd) Trafalgar.

Carr, Ian. Keith Jarrett: The Man & His Music. (Illus.). 264p. 1992. reprint ed. pap. 14.95 (*0-306-80478-6*) Da Capo.

***Carr, Ian.** Miles Davis: The Definitive Biography. LC 99-29423. (Illus.). 658p. 1999. pap. 18.95 (*1-56025-241-3*, Thunders Mouth) Avalon NY.

Carr, Ian, et al. The Rough Guide to Jazz: The Essential Companion to Artists & Albums. 912p. (Orig.). 1995. pap. 24.95 (*1-85828-137-7*, Penguin Bks) Viking Penguin.

Carr, Indira. Defamation on the Internet. 112p. 1998. pap. 33.00 (*1-85811-138-2*, Pub. by CLT Prof); pap. 42.00 (*1-85811-176-5*, Pub. by CLT Prof) Gaunt.

— International Trade Law. (Lecture Notes Ser.). 304p. 1996. pap. 28.00 (*1-874241-61-9*, Pub. by Cavendish Pubng) Gaunt.

***Carr, Indira.** Principles of International Trade Law. 519p. 1999. pap. 42.00 (*1-85941-383-8*, Pub. by Cavendish Pubng) Gaunt.

Carr, Indira & Kidner, Richard. Statutes & Conventions on International Trade. 2nd ed. 554p. 1995. pap. 25.00 (*1-85941-280-7*, Pub. by Cavendish Pubng) Gaunt.

Carr, Indira & Williams, Kate. Computers & Law. 288p. (Orig.). 1994. pap. text 29.95 (*1-871516-35-8*, Pub. by Intellect) Cromland.

Carr, Irene. Chrissie's Children. 320p. 1997. pap. 10.95 (*0-340-65435-X*, Pub. by Hodder & Stought Ltd) Trafalgar.

— Chrissie's Children. large type ed. (Ulverscroft Large Print Ser.). 496p. 1998. 29.99 (*0-7089-3924-4*) Ulverscroft.

***Carr, Irene.** Lovers Meeting. large type ed. 384p. 1999. 31.99 (*0-7089-4154-0*) Ulverscroft.

Carr, Irene. Mary's Child. large type ed. (Large Print Ser.). 656p. 1997. 27.99 (*0-7089-3698-9*) Ulverscroft.

Carr, J. Applications of Centre Manifold Theory. (Applied Mathematical Sciences Ser.: Vol. 35). 160p. 1997. pap. 41.00 (*0-387-90577-4*) Spr-Verlag.

Carr, J. & Isbell, P., eds. The U. K. Business Finance Directory, 1990. (C). 1991. lib. bdg. 289.50 (*1-85333-362-X*, Pub. by Graham & Trotman) Kluwer Academic.

Carr, J., jt. auth. see Steffens, J.

Carr, J., ed. see Bricault, G. C.

***Carr, J. L.** How Steeple Sinderby Wanderers Won the Fa Cup. (Prion Humor Classics Ser.). 1999. 15.95 (*1-85375-363-7*, Pub. by Prion) Trafalgar.

— A Month in the Country. (Classics). 152p. 2000. pap. 12.95 (*0-940322-47-1*, Pub. by NY Rev Bks) Midpt Trade.

Carr, Jacqueline B. Communicating & Relating. 3rd ed. 400p. (C). 1990. text. write for info. (*0-697-11516-X*) Brown & Benchmark.

— Communicating with Myself: A Journal. 2nd ed. 224p. (C). 1990. text. write for info. (*0-697-11518-6*) Brown & Benchmark.

Carr, Jacqueline H. & Rodak, Bernadette F. Clinical Hematology Atlas. Williams, Adrianne, ed. LC 98-5824. (Illus.). 224p. (C). 1998. pap. text 39.00 (*0-7216-4174-1*, W B Saunders Co) Harcrt Hlth Sci Grp.

Carr, Jacquelyn B. Crisis in Intimacy. LC 87-32560. 187p. (C). 1988. pap. 19.95 (*0-534-09006-0*) Brooks-Cole.

Carr, James A. American Foreign Policy During the French Revolution-Napoleonic Period, 1789-1815: A Bibliography. LC 94-2422. (Reference Library of Social Science). 192p. 1994. text 10.00 (*0-8240-5697-3*, SS593) Garland.

Carr, James E. & Wilder, David A. Functional Assessment & Intervention: An Introduction to the Assessment & Intervention of Problem Behavior. (High Tide Disability Ser.: Vol. 1). 46p. 1997. spiral bd. 10.95 (*0-9653744-5-9*) High Tide Pr.

Carr, James G. The Law of Electronic Surveillance. 2nd ed. LC 85-31406. (Criminal Law Ser.). 1986. ring bd. 145.00 (*0-87632-493-6*) West Group.

Carr, James G., jt. auth. see McCarthy, Francis B.

Carr, James H., ed. Crisis & Constraint in Municipal Finance: Local Fiscal Prospects in a Period of Uncertainty. LC 83-14280. 449p. 1984. pap. 1.00 (*0-88285-092-X*) Ctr Urban Pol Res.

Carr, James O. Carr Family of Duplin County, North Carolina. 65p. 1997. reprint ed. pap. 13.00 (*0-8328-7853-7*); reprint ed. lib. bdg. 23.00 (*0-8328-7852-9*) Higginson Bk Co.

Carr, James R. Numerical Analysis for the Geological Sciences. (Illus.). 592p. (C). 1994. 67.00 (*0-02-319511-8*, Macmillan Coll) P-H.

Carr, Jan. Ballet Party. LC 99-192204. (You're Invited to Mary-Kate & Ashley's Ser.). (Illus.). 48p. (J). (gr. 2-4). 1998. 12.95 (*0-590-29399-0*) Scholastic Inc.

***Carr, Jan.** Big Truck & Little Truck. LC 99-47323. (Illus.). 32p. (J). (ps-k). 2000. 15.95 (*0-439-07177-1*) Scholastic Inc.

Carr, Jan. Dark Day, Light Night. LC 93-45932. (Illus.). 32p. (ps-3). 1996. lib. bdg. 14.89 (*0-7868-2014-4*, Pub. by Hyprn Child) Little.

— Dark Day, Light Night. LC 93-45932. (Illus.). 32p. (J). (ps-3). 1996. 14.95 (*0-7868-0018-6*, Pub. by Hyprn Child) Time Warner.

— Dark Day, Light Night. 1997. 10.15 (*0-606-13314-3*, Pub. by Turtleback) Demco.

— Dark Day, Light Night. LC 93-45932. (Illus.). 32p. (J). (ps-3). 1997. reprint ed. pap. 4.95 (*0-7868-1201-X*, Pub. by Hyprn Ppbks) Little.

Carr, Jan. Disney's Hercules: The Hero. LC 97-77806. (Illus.). 24p. (J). 1997. 13.45 (*0-7868-3130-8*, Pub. by Disney Pr) Time Warner.

Carr, Jan. Doug's Secret Christmas. (Doug Picture Bks.). 32p. (J). (gr. k-4). 1999. pap. 4.99 (*0-7868-4351-9*, Pub. by Disney Pr) Time Warner.

***Carr, Jan.** Frozen Noses. LC 98-48540. (Illus.). 32p. (J). (gr. k-1). 1999. 15.95 (*0-8234-1462-0*) Holiday.

Carr, Jan. The Hunchback of Notre Dame: Upside Down & Topsy-Turvy. LC 95-74683. (Illus.). 24p. (J). (gr. k-3). 1996. 12.95 (*0-7868-3090-5*, Pub. by Disney Pr); 12.89 (*0-7868-5040-X*, Pub. by Disney Pr) Little.

— I Come in Peace. (J). 1996. pap. write for info. (*0-7868-4141-9*) Disney Pr.

— Swine Divine. LC 98-33500. (Illus.). 40p. (J). (ps-3). 1999. 15.95 (*0-8234-1434-5*) Holiday.

— Things to Do in Zoobilee Zoo. (Zoobilee Zoo Ser.). (Illus.). 32p. (J). (ps-3). 1988. pap. 1.95 (*0-590-42116-6*) Scholastic Inc.

— Toy Story: I Come in Peace. (Illus.). (J). 1996. pap. write for info. (*0-7868-5793-5*) Disney Pr.

Carr, Jan & Martin, Ann M. The Baby-Sitters Club: The Movie Keepsake. LC 95-211931. (Baby-Sitters Club Ser.). 48p. (J). (gr. 2-5). 1995. pap. 12.95 (*0-590-60405-8*) Scholastic Inc.

Carr, Jane M., et al. Sadlier Phonics: Level A. (Phonics Reading Ser.). (Illus.). 428p. 1997. pap. text, teacher ed. 45.45 (*0-8215-0811-3*) Sadlier.

— Sadlier Phonics: Level A. (Phonics Reading Ser.). (Illus.). 312p. (J). (gr. 1). 1997. pap. text 8.37 (*0-8215-0801-6*) Sadlier.

— Sadlier Phonics: Level B. (Phonics Reading Ser.). (Illus.). 350p. 1997. pap. text, teacher ed. 43.80 (*0-8215-0812-1*) Sadlier.

— Sadlier Phonics: Level B. (Phonics Reading Ser.). (Illus.). 224p. (J). (gr. 2). 1997. pap. text 8.19 (*0-8215-0802-4*) Sadlier.

— Sadlier Phonics: Level C. (Phonics Reading Ser.). (Illus.). 324p. 1997. pap. text, teacher ed. 43.80 (*0-8215-0813-X*) Sadlier.

— Sadlier Phonics: Level C. (Illus.). 208p. (J). (gr. 3). 1997. pap. text 8.19 (*0-8215-0803-2*) Sadlier.

— Sadlier Phonics: Level K. (Phonics Reading Ser.). (Illus.). 304p. 1997. pap. text, teacher ed. 42.00 (*0-8215-0810-5*) Sadlier.

— Sadlier Phonics: Level K. (Phonics Reading Ser.). (Illus.). 100p. (J). (ps-2). 1997. pap. text 6.69 (*0-8215-0800-8*) Sadlier.

Carr, Janet. Down's Syndrome: Children Growing Up: a Longitudinal Perspective. (Illus.). 216p. (C). 1995. pap. text 30.95 (*0-521-46933-3*) Cambridge U Pr.

Carr, Janet H. & Collins, Suzanne. Working Toward Independence: A Practical Guide to Teaching People with Learning Disabilities. 250p. 1992. pap. 27.50 (*1-85302-140-7*) Taylor & Francis.

***Carr, Janet H. & Shepherd.** Movement Science. 2nd ed. 2000. 55.00 (*0-8342-1747-3*) Aspen Pub.

Carr, Janet H. & Shepherd, Roberta B. A Motor Relearning Programme for Stroke. 2nd ed. 198p. (C). 1987. 54.00 (*0-87189-312-6*) Aspen Pub.

Carr, Janet H., jt. ed. see Yule, William.

Carr, Janet S. Scripture Scenes for Advent. 44p. 1995. pap. 7.95 (*1-877871-91-5*, 2580) Ed Ministries.

Carr, Janine C. A Child Went Forth: Reflective Teaching with Readers & Writers. LC 99-29498. 1999. pap. text 27.00 (*0-325-00171-5*) Heinemann.

Carr, Jean. Mowing the Rabbits. (Illus.). 48p. (Orig.). 1976. pap. 5.00 (*0-942908-03-1*) Pancake Pr.

Carr, Jean F., ed. see Emerson, Ralph Waldo.

Carr, Jeff O. Black Stuff: Poetry & Essays on the Afrikan-American Experience. 91p. 1998. pap. 9.95 (*0-9662118-0-4*) Third Eye TN.

Carr, Jerry E. National Water Summary, 1987, Hydrologic Events & Water Supply & Use. 565p. 1994. per. 49.00 (*0-16-061618-2*) USGPO.

Carr, Jess. Birth of a Book. LC 74-84706. 151p. 1974. 6.95 (*0-89227-010-1*) Commonwealth Pr.

— How a Book Is Born. LC 78-59112. 1978. 10.95 (*0-89227-041-1*) Commonwealth Pr.

— Intruder in the Wind. LC 87-71621. 248p. 1987. 15.95 (*0-89227-076-4*) Commonwealth Pr.

— The Midas Touch. LC 85-70064. 256p. 1986. 14.95 (*0-89227-112-4*) Commonwealth Pr.

— Ship Ride down the Spring Branch. LC 78-60480. 200p. 1978. 12.95 (*0-89227-048-9*) Commonwealth Pr.

Carr, Jim, jt. auth. see Hendel, John.

***Carr, Jim K.** Residential Foundations. LC 99-52183. (Illus.). 160p. 1999. pap. write for info. (*0-86718-509-0*) Home Builder.

Carr, Jo. Beyond Fact: Nonfiction for Children & Young People. LC 82-1601. 237p. reprint ed. pap. 73.50 (*0-8357-7156-3*, 202560900044) Bks Demand.

***Carr, Jody.** Lost & Found. 48p. 2000. mass mkt. write for info. (*0-06-101382-X*) HarpC.

Carr, Joe. Linear Integrated Circuits. LC 95-26394. (Illus.). 352p. 1996. pap. text 46.95 (*0-7506-2591-0*) Buttrwrth-Heinemann.

***Carr, Joe.** Rhythm Styles for Flatpicking Guitar. 32p. 1998. 17.95 (*0-7866-3496-0*, 96898BCD) Mel Bay.

— 25 Great Back-Up Licks for Flatpicking Guitar. 24p. 1998. 14.95 (*0-7866-3497-9*, 96899BCD) Mel Bay.

— Western Swing Guitar Style. 48p. 1997. pap. 17.95 incl. audio compact disk (*0-7866-0759-9*, 94906BCD) Mel Bay.

Carr, Joe & Munde, Alan. Prairie Nights to Neon Lights: The Story of Country Music in West Texas. (Illus.). 224p. 1995. text 35.00 (*0-89672-349-6*) Tex Tech Univ Pr.

— Prairie Nights to Neon Lights: The Story of Country Music in West Texas. LC 95-51753. (Illus.). 234p. 1997. pap. 18.95 (*0-89672-365-8*) Tex Tech Univ Pr.

Carr, Joe, jt. auth. see Bay, Mel.

Carr, Joe P., jt. auth. see Witynski, Karen.

Carr, John. Arizona Wildlife Viewing Guide. LC 92-53273. (Watchable Wildlife Ser.). (Illus.). 96p. (Orig.). 1992. pap. 8.95 (*1-56044-097-X*) Falcon Pub Inc.

— We Are an Easter People: The Triumph of God's Love in Our Lives: Participant's Workbook. 1990. pap. 4.95 (*0-687-61293-4*) Abingdon.

Carr, John & Carr, Adrienne. Power & Light Company: (Packet) 64p. 1994. pap. 13.95 (*0-8358-0698-7*) Upper Room Bks.

— Prepare Ye: For a New Advent of God's Love in Our World. 1991. pap., teacher ed. 7.00 (*0-8358-0628-6*) Upper Room Bks.

— Prepare Ye Participants Notebook: For a New Advent of God's Love in Our World. 1991. pap., student ed. 5.00 (*0-8358-0629-4*) Upper Room Bks.

— We Are an Easter People: The Triumph of God's Love in Our Lives Leaders Guide. 64p. 1990. pap., teacher ed. 9.00 (*0-8358-0602-2*) Upper Room Bks.

— We Are an Easter People: The Triumph of God's Love in Our Lives Participants Guide. 48p. 1990. pap., student ed. 6.00 (*0-8358-0603-0*) Upper Room Bks.

Carr, John C., jt. auth. see Grambs, Jean D.

Carr, John Dickson. The Bride of Newgate. 256p. (Orig.). 1994. pap. 4.95 (*0-7867-0102-1*) Carroll & Graf.

— The Burning Court. 224p. 1985. pap. 4.95 (*0-930330-27-7*) Intl Polygonics.

— Captain Cut-Throat. 306p. 1988. pap. 3.95 (*0-88184-437-3*) Carroll & Graf.

— Captain Cut-Throat. 240p. 1998. mass mkt. 4.95 (*0-7867-0547-7*) Carroll & Graf.

— Dark of the Moon. 256p. 1995. mass mkt. 4.95 (*0-7867-0222-2*) Carroll & Graf.

— Deadly Hall. 252p. 1989. pap. 3.95 (*0-88184-495-0*) Carroll & Graf.

— The Demoniacs. 197p. 1989. pap. 3.95 (*0-88184-543-4*) Carroll & Graf.

— The Devil in Velvet. 352p. 1994. mass mkt. 4.95 (*0-7867-0101-3*) Carroll & Graf.

— The Eight of Swords. 256p. 1986. mass mkt. 3.50 (*0-8217-1881-9*, Zebra Kensgtn) Kensgtn Pub Corp.

— The Emperor's Snuff Box. 304p. 1995. mass mkt. 4.95 (*0-7867-0223-0*) Carroll & Graf.

— Fell & Foul Play. Greene, Douglas G., ed. LC 90-55854. 368p. 1990. 19.95 (*1-55882-071-X*) Intl Polygonics.

— Fire, Burn! 268p. 1995. mass mkt. 4.50 (*0-7867-0175-7*) Carroll & Graf.

— The Ghosts' High Noon. 208p. 1990. mass mkt. 4.50 (*0-88184-673-2*) Carroll & Graf.

— Hag's Nook. 291p. 1976. lib. bdg. 25.95 (*0-89966-047-9*) Buccaneer Bks.

— Hag's Nook. 1985p. 1985. pap. 5.95 (*0-930330-28-5*) Intl Polygonics.

— He Who Whispers. 190p. 1986. pap. 5.95 (*0-930330-38-2*) Intl Polygonics.

— In Spite of Thunder. 224p. 1987. 3.50 (*0-88184-287-7*) Carroll & Graf.

— The Life of Sir Arthur Conan Doyle. 1976. 27.95 (*0-89109-973-5*) Amereon Ltd.

— The Life of Sir Arthur Conan Doyle. (Illus.). 310p. 1987. pap. 8.95 (*0-88184-372-5*) Carroll & Graf.

— The Lost Gallows. 344p. 1986. pap. 3.50 (*0-88184-202-8*) Carroll & Graf.

— Man Who Could Not Shudder. 1986. mass mkt. 3.50 (*0-8217-1703-0*, Zebra Kensgtn) Kensgtn Pub Corp.

— Most Secret. 235p. 1989. pap. 3.95 (*0-88184-542-6*) Carroll & Graf.

— The Murder of Sir Edmund Godfrey. 348p. 1989. reprint ed. pap. 12.95 (*1-55882-014-0*, Lib Crime Classics) Intl Polygonics.
— Nine Wrong Answers. 168p. 1995. mass mkt. 3.95 (*0-7867-0174-9*) Carroll & Graf.
— Panic in Box C. 272p. 1987. mass mkt. 3.50 (*0-88184-288-5*) Carroll & Graf.
— The Problem of the Wire Cage. 1986. mass mkt. 3.95 (*0-8217-3384-2*, Zebra Kensgtn) Kensgtn Pub Corp.
— Scandal at High Chimneys. 192p. 1988. mass mkt. 3.50 (*0-88184-394-6*) Carroll & Graf.
— The Sleeping Sphinx. (Dr. Fell Detective Ser.). 199p. 1985. pap. 4.95 (*0-930330-24-2*) Intl Polygonics.
— The Three Coffins. 1989. lib. bdg. 25.95 (*0-89966-048-7*) Buccaneer Bks.
— The Three Coffins. LC 79-690. 306p. 1979. reprint ed. 25.00 (*0-89366-259-3*) Ultramarine Pub.
— Till Death Do Us Part. 224p. 1989. reprint ed. pap. 5.95 (*1-55882-017-5*, Lib Crime Classics) Intl Polygonics.
— The Witch of the Low Tide. 186p. 1990. pap. 3.95 (*0-88184-672-4*) Carroll & Graf.

Carr, John Dickson & Stableford, Brian M. Papa La-Bas. 288p. 1998. mass mkt. 4.95 (*0-7867-0502-7*) Carroll & Graf.
Carr, John Dickson, see Dickson, Carter, pseud.
Carr, John Dickson, jt. auth. see Doyle, Adrian Conan.
Carr, John Dickson, jt. intro. see Doyle, Arthur Conan.
Carr, John F. & Pomeray, Sarah G. Assimilation of the Italian Immigrant: An Original Anthology. LC 74-17919. (Italian American Experience Ser.). (Illus.). 332p. 1975. reprint ed. 12.95 (*0-405-06392-X*) Ayer.
Carr, John L. Leigh Brackett: American Writer. (Booklet Ser.: No. 22). 67p. (Orig.). 1986. pap. 3.00 (*0-936055-23-5*) C Drumm Bks.
Carr, John L., jt. ed. see Nabhan, Gary P.
Carr, John L., jt. ed. see Parker, Theodore A., 3rd.
Carr, John R. The Paraflight Experience. LC 91-90953. (Illus.). 165p. 1997. reprint ed. pap. 16.95 (*0-9629429-6-0*) Waltz Pub.
Carr, John W. Factors Affecting Distribution of Trained Teachers Among Rural White Elementary Schools of North Carolina. LC 74-176628. (Columbia University. Teachers College. Contributions to Education Ser.: No. 269). reprint ed. 37.50 (*0-404-55269-2*) AMS Pr.
— The Physics of Electromagnetic Masses, Including the Derivation of E=mc2 from a Point Source. 3rd rev. ed. Carr, Helen, ed. & photos by by. (Illus.). 294p. 1998. pap. 35.00 (*0-9666831-5-3*) H Carr.
Carr, Jonathan. Mahler: A Biography. LC 97-9520. (Illus.). 272p. 1997. 29.95 (*0-87951-802-2*, Pub. by Overlook Pr) Penguin Putnam.
— Mahler: A Biography. 254p. 1999. pap. 16.95 (*0-87951-887-1*, Pub. by Overlook Pr) Penguin Putnam.
Carr, Joseph. Electronic Circuit Guidebook Vol. 1: Sensors. LC 97-65787. (Illus.). 339p. 1997. pap. 29.95 (*0-7906-1098-1*) Prompt Publns.
— Electronic Circuit Guidebook Vol. 2: IC Timers. LC 97-65787. (Illus.). 240p. 1997. pap. 29.95 (*0-7906-1106-6*) Prompt Publns.
— RadioScience Observing. (Illus.). 336p. 1998. pap. 34.95 (*0-7906-1127-9*) Prompt Publns.
***Carr, Joseph & Brown, John.** Introduction to Biomedical Equipment Technology. 4th ed. 720p. 2000. 98.00 (*0-13-010492-2*) Prntice Hall Bks.
Carr, Joseph, jt. auth. see Brindley, Keith.
Carr, Joseph, jt. auth. see Davies, John.
Carr, Joseph J. The Art of Science: A Practical Guide to Experiments, Observations, & Handling Data. LC 92-70471. (Illus.). 368p. 1992. pap. 19.95 (*1-878707-05-1*) LLH Tech Pub.
— Biomedical Equipment: Use, Maintenance & Management. 496p. (C). 1991. text 48.00 (*0-13-257577-9*, 740701) P-H.
— DC Power Supplies: A Technician's Guide. LC 96-25457. (Illus.). 326p. 1996. 39.95 (*0-07-011495-1*); pap. 24.95 (*0-07-011496-X*) McGraw.
— Designer's Handbook of Instrumentation & Control Circuits. 626p. 1991. text 161.00 (*0-12-160640-6*) Acad Pr.
— Digital Electronics Troubleshooting. 1980. pap. 14.95 (*0-8306-1250-5*, 1250P) McGraw-Hill Prof.
— Electronic Circuit Guidebook Vol. 3: Op Amps. LC 97-65787. (Electronic Circuit Guidebbook Ser.). (Illus.). 273p. 1997. pap. 29.95 (*0-7906-1131-7*, 61131) Prompt Publns.
— Electronic Circuit Guidebook Vol. 4: Electro-Optics. (Illus.). 416p. 1997. pap. 29.95 (*0-7906-1132-5*) Prompt Publns.
Carr, Joseph J. Electronic Circuit Guidebook Vol. 5: Digital Electronics. LC 97-65787. 234p. (Orig.). 1997. pap. text 29.95 (*0-7906-1129-5*) Prompt Publns.
— Electronic Circuit Guidebook Vol. 6: Oscillators. LC 97-65787. 240p. 1999. pap. 34.95 (*0-7906-1185-6*) Prompt Publns.
Carr, Joseph J. Electronic Devices. rev. ed. LC 92-34442. (Tech Ser.). Orig. Title: Mastering IC Electronics. 1992. pap. write for info. (*0-02-801302-6*) Glencoe.
— Elements of Electronic Instrumentation & Measurement. 3rd ed. LC 95-16744. 594p. (C). 1995. text 67.60 (*0-13-341686-0*) P-H.
— Elements of Microwave Technology. 416p. (C). 1989. teacher ed. write for info. (*0-15-522103-5*); write for info. (*0-318-65021-5*) SCP.
***Carr, Joseph J.** Exploring RF Circuits. LC 99-62441. 1999. pap. text 34.95 (*0-7906-1197-X*) Prompt Publns.
— Exploring Solid-State Amplifiers. LC 99-62439. 1999. pap. 19.95 (*0-7906-1192-9*) Prompt Publns.
Carr, Joseph J. Integrated Electronics: Operational Amplifiers & Linear ICs with Applications. (Illus.). 609p. (C). 1995. text 74.95 (*0-15-541360-0*) OUP.
***Carr, Joseph J.** Introduction to RF for Electronics & Communication Engineers. (Illus.). 320p. 2001. pap. 37.95 (*0-7506-4844-9*, Newnes) Buttrwrth-Heinemann.
— Joe Carr's Circuits Toolkit. LC 98-68670. 237p. 1998. 29.95 (*0-7906-1181-3*) Prompt Publns.
Carr, Joseph J. Linear IC Applications: A Designer's Handbook. LC 96-42135. (Illus.). 356p. 1996. pap. text 52.95 (*0-7506-3370-0*) Buttrwrth-Heinemann.
— Mastering IC Electronics. 448p. 1991. 32.95 (*0-8306-2185-7*, 3502); pap. 19.95 (*0-8306-2184-9*) McGraw-Hill Prof.
— Mastering Oscillator Circuits Through Projects & Experiments. LC 92-42360. 1993. text 27.95 (*0-8306-4067-3*); pap. text 17.95 (*0-8306-4066-5*) McGraw-Hill Prof.
— Mastering Solid-State Amplifiers. LC 92-10488. (Illus.). 304p. 1992. 29.95 (*0-8306-3082-1*, 3976); pap. 19.95 (*0-8306-3081-3*, 3976) McGraw-Hill Prof.
— Microwave & Wireless Communications Technology. 435p. 1996. pap. text 49.95 (*0-7506-9707-5*) Buttrwrth-Heinemann.
— Old-Time Radios: Restoration & Repair. (Illus.). 256p. 1990. pap. 16.95 (*0-8306-3342-1*) McGraw-Hill Prof.
— Old-Time Radios! Restoration & Repair. 264p. 1992. pap. 19.95 (*0-07-155735-0*) McGraw.
— Practical Antenna Handbook. (Illus.). 416p. 1989. 31.95 (*0-8306-9270-3*); pap. 21.95 (*0-8306-3270-0*) McGraw-Hill Prof.
— Practical Antenna Handbook. 2nd ed. LC 93-44428. 1994. 49.95 (*0-07-011104-9*); pap. 29.95 (*0-07-011105-7*) McGraw-Hill Prof.
— Practical Antenna Handbook. 3rd ed. LC 98-5964. 650p. 1998. pap. 49.95 incl. cd-rom (*0-07-012026-9*) McGraw.
— The Practical Antenna Handbook. 3rd ed. LC 98-5964. 574p. 1998. 54.95 incl. cd-rom (*0-07-012027-7*) McGraw.
***Carr, Joseph J.** Practical Radio Frequency Test & Measurement: A Technician's Handbook. LC 99-28220. 320p. 1999. pap. text 34.95 (*0-7506-7161-0*, Newnes) Buttrwrth-Heinemann.
Carr, Joseph J. The Radio Hobbyist's Handbook. (Illus.). 392p. 1982. 19.95 (*0-8306-1346-3*, 1346) McGraw-Hill Prof.
— RadioScience Observing, 2. (Radioscience Observing Ser.). 1999. pap. text 34.95 (*0-7906-1172-4*) Prompt Publns.
— Secrets of RF Circuit Design. (Illus.). 416p. 1991. 32.95 (*0-8306-8710-6*, 3710); pap. 19.95 (*0-8306-3710-9*) McGraw-Hill Prof.
— Secrets of RF Circuit Design. 2nd ed. 1996. text 49.95 (*0-07-912943-9*); pap. text 24.95 (*0-07-912944-7*) McGraw.
— Secrets of RF Circuit Design. 2nd ed. LC 96-30966. (Illus.). 464p. 1996. pap. 29.95 (*0-07-011673-3*); text 49.95 (*0-07-011672-5*) McGraw.
— Sensors & Circuits: Sensors, Transducers, & Supporting Circuits for Electronic Instrumentation, Measurement, & Control. LC 92-14958. 368p. (C). 1993. text 45.00 (*0-13-805631-5*) P-H.
***Carr, Joseph J.** The Technicians Radio Received Handbook. 304p. 2001. pap. 34.95 (*0-7506-7319-2*, Newnes) Buttrwrth-Heinemann.
Carr, Joseph J. & Brown, John M. Introduction to Biomedical Equipment Technology. LC 80-6218. (Electronic Technology Ser.). 430p. (C). 1981. pap. text 6.00 (*0-471-04144-0*) P-H.
— Introduction to Biomedical Equipment Technology. 3rd ed. LC 97-12570. (Illus.). 703p. 1997. teacher ed. 106.00 (*0-13-849431-2*) P-H.
Carr, Josephine. Monday's Child. 416p. (Orig.). 1999. mass mkt. 6.50 (*0-06-101381-1*) HarpC.
— My Beautiful Fat Friend. 1988. reprint ed. write for info. (*0-318-62360-9*) S&S Trade.
Carr, Judy, jt. auth. see Harris, Douglas E.
Carr, Judy F. & Harris, Douglas E. Getting It Together: A Process Workbook for Curriculum Development, Implementation, & Assessment. LC 92-37654. 318p. (C). 1993. pap. text 61.00 (*0-205-14173-0*, H41734, Longwood Div) Allyn.
Carr, Judy F., jt. auth. see Stevenson, S. Christopher.
***Carr, Julie B.** Countdown to a Miracle: The Making of Me. 296p. (YA). 1999. spiral bd. 12.95 (*0-9671428-0-6*) Motherly Way.
Carr, K. E. & Seed, T. M., eds. Ultrastructural Effects of Radiation on Tissues & Cells. (Illus.). 172p. (Orig.). 1983. pap. text 18.00 (*0-931288-29-0*) Scanning Microscopy.
Carr, K. E., et al. Physical, Chemical, Biochemical & Biological Techniques & Processes. Kraft, Guenther, ed. (Advances in Space Research Ser.: Vol. 18). 352p. 1995. pap. 194.50 (*0-08-042664-6*, Pergamon Pr) Elsevier.
Carr, Karen. Did Roman Government Matter? (Illus.). (C). text. write for info. (*0-472-10891-3*) U of Mich Pr.
Carr, Karen & England, Rupert, eds. Simulated & Virtual Realities: Elements of Perception. 250p. 1995. pap. 34.95 (*0-7484-0129-6*, Pub. by Tay Francis Ltd) Taylor & Francis.
— Simulated & Virtual Realities: Elements of Perception. 250p. 1995. 99.95 (*0-7484-0128-8*) Taylor & Francis.
Carr, Karen & Ivanhoe, Philip J. The Sense of Anti-Rationalism: Religious Thought of Zhuangzi & Kierkegaard. LC 99-44716. (Illus.). 208p. (C). 1999. pap. text 23.95 (*1-889119-10-5*) Seven Bridges.
Carr, Karen L. The Banalization of Nihilism: Twentieth-Century Responses to Meaninglessness. LC 90-27104. 196p. (C). 1992. text 21.50 (*0-7914-0833-7*) State U NY Pr.
Carr, Karyn. Journey Toward Tomorrow, No. 26. (Serenade Serenata Ser.). 1985. pap. 2.50 (*0-310-46912-0*, 15550P) Zondervan.
Carr, Katherine C. How to Develop a Policy & Procedure Manual for a Midwifery Service. 15p. (Orig.). 1988. pap. 3.95 (*0-937604-09-7*, Pennypr) Intl Childbirth.
Carr, Kathleen M., et al. Beyond Burlap: Idaho's Famous Potato Recipes. Jr. League of Boise, Inc. Staff & Hon, Romaine G., eds. LC 97-72093. (Illus.). 224p. 1997. 19.95 (*0-913743-97-6*) Jr League Boise.
Carr, Kathleen T. Polaroid Transfers: A Complete Visual Guide to Creating Image & Emulsion Transfers. LC 97-1132. (Illus.). 144p. 1997. pap. text 35.00 (*0-8174-5554-X*, Amphoto) Watsn-Guptill.
Carr, Kay J. Belleville, Ottawa, & Galesburg: Community & Democracy on the Illinois Frontier. LC 95-30743. (Illus.). 240p. 1996. 39.95 (*0-8093-2017-7*) S Ill U Pr.
Carr, Kay J., jt. ed. see Conzen, Michael P.
Carr-Lambert, Marsha. Everything in the World You Ever Wanted to Know about a Coral Reef. (Illus.). 72p. 1998. pap. text 10.00 (*0-9640940-5-3*) Teachers Little.
— Everything (in the World) You Ever Wanted to Know about Australia. 72p. write for info. (*0-9640940-1-0*) Teachers Little.
— Everything in the World You Ever Wanted to Know about Mysteries. (Illus.). 72p. (Orig.). 1997. pap. text 10.00 (*0-9640940-4-5*) Teachers Little.
— Everything (in the World) You Ever Wanted to Know about PIGS. 72p. write for info. (*0-9640940-6-2*) Teachers Little.
— Everything in the World You Ever Wanted to Know about Rain Forests. (Illus.). 72p. (Orig.). 1997. pap. text 10.00 (*0-9640940-2-9*) Teachers Little.
— Everything You Ever Wanted to Know about the Serengeti. (Illus.). 72p. (Orig.). 1997. pap. text 10.00 (*0-9640940-3-7*) Teachers Little.
Carr Lane Mfg. Co. Staff. Jig & Fixture Handbook. (Illus.). 430p. (C). 1995. 19.95 (*0-9622079-1-8*) Carr Ln.
— Modular Fixturing Handbook. (Illus.). 216p. (C). 1991. pap. text 12.00 (*0-9622079-0-X*) Carr Ln.
Carr, Leslie G. "Color-Blind" Racism. LC 97-4840. 240p. 1997. 45.00 (*0-7619-0443-3*); pap. 21.95 (*0-7619-0444-1*) Sage.
Carr, Lisa. Practical Boat Canvas Work. (Illus.). 1996. 25.95 (*1-85310-567-8*) Waterline.
Carr, Lois G., et al, eds. Colonial Chesapeake Society. LC 88-4719. (Institute of Early American History & Culture Ser.). (Illus.). xii, 512p. (C). 1988. 59.95 (*0-8078-1800-3*) U of NC Pr.
— Colonial Chesapeake Society. LC 88-4719. (Institute of Early American History & Culture Ser.). (Illus.). xii, 512p. 1991. pap. 24.95 (*0-8078-4343-1*) U of NC Pr.
Carr, Lois G., et al. Robert Cole's World: Agriculture & Society in Early Maryland. LC 90-26168. (Illus.). xxii, 384p. (C). 1991. 59.95 (*0-8078-1985-9*); pap 22.50 (*0-8078-4341-5*) U of NC Pr.
Carr, Lois Green. Declaration of Maryland. 1984. pap. text 5.00 (*0-942370-16-3*) MD St Archives.
Carr, Lois Green, intro. A Relation of the Successful Beginnings of the Lord Baltemore's Plantation in Mary-Land: Photographic Facsimile of 1634 Pamphlet. (Illus.). 64p. 1984. reprint ed. pap. 6.00 (*0-685-54617-9*) J C Brown.
Carr, Loretta. Covenant Land Covenant People. 1996. pap. 5.95 (*0-9648408-0-4*) Trumpet OR.
Carr, Lucien. Missouri, a Bone of Contention. LC 72-3761. (American Commonwealths Ser.: No. 11). reprint ed. 39.00 (*0-404-57211-1*) AMS Pr.
Carr, M. J. Ariel the Spy. LC 92-54512. (Little Mermaid Novels Ser.). (Illus.). 80p. (J). (gr. 1-4). 1993. pap. 2.95 (*1-56282-372-8*, Pub. by Disney Pr) Time Warner.
— Arista's New Boyfriend. LC 92-54511. (Little Mermaid Novels Ser.). (Illus.). 80p. (J). (gr. 1-4). 1993. pap. 2.95 (*1-56282-371-X*, Pub. by Disney Pr) Little.
— Be My Valentine. 32p. (J). (ps-3). 1992. pap. text 2.50 (*0-590-45131-6*) Scholastic Inc.
— Cabbage Patch Kids Visit the Doctor. (J). (ps-3). 1993. pap. 2.50 (*0-685-64929-6*) Scholastic Inc.
— The Cabbage Patch Kids Visit the Doctor. 32p. (J). (ps-3). 1993. pap. 2.50 (*0-590-46631-3*) Scholastic Inc.
— One Special Child. (Cabbage Patch Kids Ser.). (Illus.). 32p. (J). (ps-3). 1992. pap. 2.50 (*0-590-45460-9*) Scholastic Inc.
Carr, M. J. Wave Dancer is Missing: My Pretty Mermaid. LC 94-107424. 32p. (J). (ps-3). 1993. pap. 2.50 (*0-590-46604-6*) Scholastic Inc.
Carr, M. J., adapted by. A Little Princess. deluxe ed. LC 95-196150. 48p. (J). (gr. 4-7). 1995. pap. 12.95 (*0-590-48627-6*) Scholastic Inc.
Carr, M. J. & Baum, L. Frank. The Wizard of Oz: A Novelization. 96p. (J). (ps-3). 1993. pap. 3.25 (*0-590-46993-2*) Scholastic Inc.
Carr, M. L. Enough Is Enough. 158p. 1994. pap. 12.95 (*0-9642428-0-X*) M L Enter.
Carr, M. W. A Collection of Telugu Proverbs Translated, Illustrated & Explained Together with Some Sanskrit Proverbs Printed in the Devanagari & Telugu Characters. (C). 1988. reprint ed. 29.50 (*81-206-0261-7*, Pub. by Asian Educ Servs) S Asia.
— A Selection of Telegu Proverbs: Translated & Explained. 1986. 9.00 (*0-8364-1874-3*, Pub. by Usha) S Asia.
Carr, Marc. Last Sands in the Hourglass: Revelation Explored. Stanley, Majorie M., ed. 294p. (Orig.). 1989. pap. text 7.95 (*0-936369-14-0*) Son-Rise Pubns.
— Prosperity with Purpose. Biros, Florence K., ed. (Mini Teaching Ser.). 96p. (Orig.). 1987. pap. 3.95 (*0-936369-13-2*) Son-Rise Pubns.
Carr, Margaret A. Blindman's Bluff. large type ed. (Linford Mystery Library). 272p. 1987. pap. 16.99 (*0-7089-6360-9*, Linford) Ulverscroft.
— Blood Will Out. large type ed. (Linford Mystery Library). 295p. 1988. pap. 16.99 (*0-7089-6564-4*, Linford) Ulverscroft.
— Daggers Drawn. large type ed. (Linford Mystery Library). 256p. 1987. pap. 16.99 (*0-7089-6356-0*, Linford) Ulverscroft.
— Dare the Devil. large type ed. (Linford Mystery Library). 304p. 1989. pap. 16.99 (*0-7089-6728-0*, Linford) Ulverscroft.
— Dark Intruder. large type ed. (Linford Mystery Library). 1991. pap. 16.99 (*0-7089-7073-7*) Ulverscroft.
— An Innocent Abroad. large type ed. (Linford Mystery Library). 1989. pap. 16.99 (*0-7089-6745-0*) Ulverscroft.
— Lamb to the Slaughter. large type ed. (Linford Romance Library). 320p. 1992. pap. 16.99 (*0-7089-7239-X*) Ulverscroft.
— Love All Start. large type ed. (Linford Romance Library). 1991. pap. 16.99 (*0-7089-7043-5*) Ulverscroft.
— Out of the Past. large type ed. (Linford Mystery Library). 302p. 1989. pap. 16.99 (*0-7089-6640-3*, Linford) Ulverscroft.
— Sharendel. large type ed. (Linford Mystery Library). 368p. 1987. pap. 16.99 (*0-7089-6390-0*, Linford) Ulverscroft.
— Sitting Duck. large type ed. (Linford Mystery Library). 240p. 1988. pap. 16.99 (*0-7089-6617-9*, Linford) Ulverscroft.
— Spring into Love. large type ed. (Linford Romance Library). 1991. pap. 16.99 (*0-7089-7054-0*) Ulverscroft.
— Stolen Heart. large type ed. (Linford Romance Library). 1991. pap. 16.99 (*0-7089-7105-9*) Ulverscroft.
— A Time to Surrender. large type ed. (Linford Romance Library). 288p. 1993. pap. 16.99 (*0-7089-7317-5*, Linford) Ulverscroft.
— Too Close for Comfort. large type ed. (Linford Mystery Library). 276p. 1988. pap. 16.99 (*0-7089-6624-1*, Linford) Ulverscroft.
— Tread Warily at Midnight. large type ed. (Linford Mystery Library). 1988. pap. 16.99 (*0-7089-6508-3*) Ulverscroft.
— Twin Tragedy. large type ed. (Linford Mystery Library). 272p. 1987. pap. 16.99 (*0-7089-6453-2*, Linford) Ulverscroft.
— Wait for the Wake. large type ed. (Linford Mystery Library). 256p. 1989. pap. 16.99 (*0-7089-6736-1*, Linford) Ulverscroft.
— When Dreams Come True. large type ed. 320p. 1992. pap. 16.99 (*0-7089-7186-5*) Ulverscroft.
— Who's the Target? large type ed. (Linford Mystery Library). 256p. 1988. pap. 16.99 (*0-7089-6500-8*) Ulverscroft.
Carr, Marilyn. Blacksmith, Baker, Roofing Sheet Maker: Employment for Rural Women in Developing Countries. (Illus.). 158p. 1984. pap. 21.00 (*0-946688-15-X*, Pub. by Intermed Tech) Stylus Pub VA.
Carr, Marilyn, ed. Women & Food Security: The Experience of the SADCC Countries. (Orig.). 1991. pap. 21.00 (*1-85339-109-3*, Pub. by Intermed Tech); text 55.00 (*1-85339-118-2*, Pub. by Intermed Tech) Stylus Pub VA.
Carr, Marilyn, et al, eds. Speaking Out: Women's Economic Empowerment in South Asia. LC 97-128125. 252p. (Orig.). 1996. pap. 19.95 (*1-85339-382-7*, Pub. by Intermed Tech) Stylus Pub VA.
Carr, Marina. The Mai. LC 95-182206. 72p. 1997. pap. 14.95 (*1-85235-161-6*) Dufour.
— The Mai. LC 95-182206. 72p. 1997. 24.95 (*1-85235-162-4*, Pub. by Gallery Pr) Dufour.
***Carr, Marina.** Marina Carr: Plays 1: Low in the Dark; The Mai; Portia Coughlan; By the Bog of Cats... 368p. 2000. pap. 17.00 (*0-571-20011-7*) Faber & Faber.
Carr, Marion. A Proud Alliance. large type ed. (Magna Large Print Ser.). 408p. 1996. 27.99 (*0-7505-0966-X*, Pub. by Mgna Lrg Print) Ulverscroft.
Carr, Marjorie H., ed. see Carr, Archie.
Carr, Mark, ed. CPA Partner's Notebook. 62p. 1994. pap. text 24.50 (*0-9616858-5-X*) Strafford Pubns.
— Public Accounting Deskbook, 1994. 72p. (Orig.). 1994. pap. text 39.00 (*0-9616858-6-7*) Strafford Pubns.
Carr, Martha, ed. Motivation in Mathematics. LC 95-39941. 208p. (C). 1996. text 45.00 (*1-57273-026-9*); pap. text 20.95 (*1-57273-027-7*) Hampton Pr NJ.
Carr, Martha R. Wired: A Novel. 313p. 1993. pap. 14.95 (*0-9638639-0-8*) Nimrod Hse.
Carr, Martha R., ed. see August, Angel T.
Carr, Martha R., ed. see Doswell, J. William.
Carr, Marvin N. The Deliquescent Lights: Diamonds in the Desert. LC 96-90319. 384p. (Orig.). 1997. per. 19.95 (*0-9641226-6-9*) Trom Pubng.
— Men Are Cruel, but Women Are Dangerous: Mary & Sinclare. LC 95-90909. (Illus.). 400p. (Orig.). 1996. pap. 19.95 (*0-9641226-8-5*) Trom Pubng.
— Positively Negative: Reversing of the Magnetic Poles. LC 94-60567. 580p. (Orig.). 1994. per. 9.95 (*0-9641226-7-7*) Trom Pubng.
Carr, Mary, jt. auth. see Eversman, Sharon.
Carr, Mary C. The Dikler & His Circle. 128p. 1990. pap. 21.00 (*0-85131-341-8*, Pub. by J A Allen) St Mut.
Carr, Maureen A., jt. auth. see Benward, Bruce.
Carr, Melanie. French Lace. (Rainbow Romances Ser.). 160p. 1993. 14.95 (*0-7090-4898-X*) Parkwest Pubns.
Carr, Michael. The Complete Book of Weather: Forecasting, Tracking, & Understanding Weather & Weather Patterns. 2000. 24.95 (*0-07-134801-8*) McGraw.
— International Marine's Weather Predicting Simplified: How to Read Weather Charts & Satellite Images. LC 99-14304. (Illus.). 192p. 1999. 25.95 (*0-07-012031-5*, Ragged Mntain) McGraw-Hill Prof.
Carr, Michael & Darby. I Hate Brenda Book. (Illus.). 192p. 1993. mass mkt. 4.50 (*1-55817-797-3*, Pinncle Kensgtn) Kensgtn Pub Corp.
Carr, Michael H. Water on Mars. (Illus.). 248p. 1996. text 75.00 (*0-19-509938-9*) OUP.
Carr, Micheline H., jt. auth. see Crouch, James E.
Carr, Mike. Keeper of the Ancient King. 1983. 1.95 (*0-394-72317-1*) Random.

— Ruins of Ranghar. 1983. 1.95 (*0-394-72315-5*) Random.
***Carr, Monica M.** Buck O'Neil & I. Carr-Hurtt, L. Denise, ed. 75p. (YA). 2000. pap. 14.95 (*0-9700224-0-9*) Greene Pubns.
Carr, N. G., jt. auth. see Mann, N. H.
Carr, N. L. Viscosities of Natural Gas Components & Mixtures. (Research Bulletin Ser.: No. 23). iv, 59p. 1953. pap. 25.00 (*1-58222-054-9*) Inst Gas Tech.
Carr, Nicholas D., jt. ed. see Beynon, J.
Carr, Nick, jt. auth. see Stockbridge, Grant.
Carr, Pat. Night of the Luminarias. 120p. (Orig.). (C). 1986. write for info. (*0-941720-30-6*); pap. 5.95 (*0-941720-29-2*) Slough Pr TX.
— Sonahchi: A Collection of Myth Tales. LC 88-70067. 80p. (Orig.). 1988. pap. 8.95 (*0-938317-06-7*) Cinco Puntos.
— The Women in the Mirror. LC 77-24965. (Iowa Short Fiction Award Ser.). 152p. 1977. pap. 3.25 (*0-87745-082-X*) U of Iowa Pr.
Carr, Pat & Tracey, Steve. Mindstretchers, 4 vols., Level 2. Incl. Enchantments. 1983. pap. 5.95 (*0-8224-4508-5*); Great Explorations. 1983. pap. 5.95 (*0-8224-4507-7*); Star Gazing. 1983. pap. 5.95 (*0-8224-4505-0*); (J). (gr. 4-6). 1983. pap. write for info. (*0-318-57166-8*) Fearon Teacher Aids.
Carr, Patricia A., jt. auth. see Dignan, Mark.
***Carr, Patrick.** Sunshine States: Wild Times & Extraordinary Lives in the Land of Gators, Guns & Grapefruit. LC 99-29025. (Florida Sand Dollar Book Ser.). 237p. 1999. pap. 14.95 (*0-8130-1734-3*) U Press Fla.
Carr, Patrick, jt. auth. see Bowie, Angela.
Carr, Patrick, jt. auth. see Cash, Johnny.
***Carr, Peter.** Jimmy Archey: The Little Giant of the Trombone. (Jazzology Press Bks.: Vol. 7). (Illus.). 188p. 1999. pap. text 39.95 (*0-9638890-6-0*, Jazzology Pr) GHB Jazz Fnd.
Carr, Peter E. Censos, Padrones y Matriculas de la Poblacion de Cuba. LC 91-78402. (SPA.). 113p. (Orig.). 1993. pap. 25.95 (*0-9631209-3-X*) TCI Gene Res.
— Guide to Cuban Genealogical Research. LC 91-90691. 103p. 1991. pap. 19.95 (*0-9631209-0-5*) TCI Gene Res.
— Locating Your Ancestors in Cuban Cities: Methods & Resources. (Illus.). 65p. (Orig.). 1995. pap. 14.95 (*0-9631209-5-6*) TCI Gene Res.
— Records at the Archivo General de Indias in Seville, Spain: Their Usefulness for the Genealogist. 85p. (Orig.). 1995. pap. 18.95 (*0-9631209-9-9*) TCI Gene Res.
— San Francisco Passenger Departure Lists: January 3 to June 14, 1851, Vol. II. LC 92-90288. 160p. (Orig.). 1992. pap. 15.95 (*0-9631209-4-8*) TCI Gene Res.
— San Francisco Passenger Departure Lists: 15 January to 30 June 1852, Vol. IV. 175p. (Orig.). 1993. pap. 15.95 (*0-9631209-8-0*) TCI Gene Res.
— San Francisco Passenger Departure Lists: 15 July to 31 December 1851. (San Francisco Passenger Departure Lists Ser.: Vol. III). (Orig.). 1993. pap. 15.95 (*0-9631209-7-2*) TCI Gene Res.
— San Francisco Passenger Departure Lists Vol. I: September 30, 1850 to December 31, 1850, Vol. 1. LC 91-90704. 139p. 1991. pap. 15.95 (*0-9631209-2-1*) TCI Gene Res.
— San Francisco Passenger Departure Lists, 26 June 1852 to 31 December 1852, Vol. V. 38p. 1996. pap. 15.95 (*1-884579-03-5*) TCI Gene Res.
— Understanding Hispanic Surnaming Methods. (Illus.). 60p. (Orig.). 1995. pap. 17.95 (*0-9631209-6-4*) TCI Gene Res.
Carr, Philip. English Are Like That. LC 70-142613. (Essay Index Reprint Ser.). 1977. 23.95 (*0-8369-2041-4*) Ayer.
***Carr, Philip.** English Phonetics & Phonology: An Introduction. LC 99-19742. 232p. 1999. 54.95 (*0-631-19775-3*) Blackwell Pubs.
Carr, Philip. English Phonetics & Phonology: An Introduction. LC 99-19742. 232p. 1999. write for info. (*0-631-19776-1*) Blackwell Pubs.
Carr, Philip J., ed. The Organization of North American Prehistoric Chipped Stone Tool Technologies. LC 94-1508. (Archaeological Ser.: No. 7). (Illus.). vi, 136p. 1994. pap. 18.50 (*1-879621-14-2*); lib. bdg. 30.00 (*1-879621-15-0*) Intl Mono Prehstry.
Carr, Philippa, pseud. Daughters of England. large type ed. LC 95-13271. 482p. 1995. lib. bdg. 24.95 (*0-7838-1352-X*, G K Hall Lrg Type) Mac Lib Ref.
— The Lion Triumphant. 1976. 26.95 (*0-8488-0447-3*) Amereon Ltd.
— Saraband for Two Sisters. large type ed. 1981. 12.00 (*0-7089-0609-5*) Ulverscroft.
— The Song of the Siren. large type ed. 1981. 12.00 (*0-7089-0651-6*) Ulverscroft.
— We'll Meet Again. large type ed. LC 93-8425. 440p. 1993. lib. bdg. 22.95 (*1-56054-795-2*) Thorndike Pr.
Carr, Phyllis L., et al. The Medical Care of Women. LC 94-34774. (Illus.). 874p. 1995. text 105.00 (*0-7216-3779-5*, W B Saunders Co) Harcrt Hlth Sci Grp.
Carr, Rachel. Listen to Your Inner Self: A Ten-Week Program to Achieve the Healing Power Within You. 160p. 1993. pap. 16.95 (*0-8048-1827-4*) Tuttle Pubng.
— 24 Flower Arrangement Recipes. (Illus.). 65p. (Orig.). 1995. pap. 12.00 (*0-9634021-1-0*) Pennington CA.
Carr, Raymond. Modern Spain, 1875-1980. (Opus Ser.). (Illus.). 256p. 1981. pap. text 18.95 (*0-19-289090-5*) OUP.
— Spain: Eighteen Hundred Eight to Nineteen Seventy-Five. 2nd ed. (Oxford History of Modern Europe Ser.). 888p. 1982. pap. text 39.00 (*0-19-822128-2*) OUP.
***Carr, Raymond, ed.** Spain: A History. (Illus.). 300p. 2000. 40.00 (*0-19-820619-4*) OUP.
Carr, Raymond & Fusi, Juan P. Spain: Dictatorship to Democracy. 2nd ed. 304p. (C). 1981. pap. text 16.95 (*0-04-946014-5*) Routledge.
Carr, Raymond, jt. ed. see Lasky Schub, Joyce.
Carr, Rebecca. Hyde Park: A Bibliography, 1980. (Illus.). 25p. 1998. pap. text 8.00 (*0-913553-22-0*) Albert Hse Pub.
Carr, Richard & O'Con, Robert. Welding Practices & Procedures. (Illus.). 416p. 1983. pap. text 18.95 (*0-13-948059-5*) P-H.
Carr, Richard, jt. auth. see O'Con, Robert.
Carr, Richard H., jt. auth. see O'Con, Robert L.
***Carr, Richard J.** Wyndedanse: A Royal Chronicle of 17th Century Siam. LC 99-91762. 2000. 25.00 (*0-7388-1240-4*); pap. 18.00 (*0-7388-1241-2*) Xlibris Corp.
Carr, Richard W. Virtual Memory Management. LC 84-140. (Computer Science: Systems Programming Ser.: No. 20). (Illus.). 175p. reprint ed. pap. 54.30 (*0-8357-1533-7*, 207036700088) Bks Demand.
Carr, Robert, tr. see Rodriguez, Ileana.
Carr, Robert E. & Hayes, R. M. Wide Screen Movies: A History & Filmography of Wide Gauge Filmmaking. LC 86-43093. (Illus.). 516p. 1988. lib. bdg. 55.00 (*0-89950-242-3*) McFarland & Co.
Carr, Robert H., ed. see Conference of the Cryogenic Society of America, 5t.
Carr, Robert K. Supreme Court & Judicial Review. LC 74-98215. 304p. 1970. reprint ed. lib. bdg. 65.00 (*0-8371-3261-4*, CAJR, Greenwood Pr) Greenwood.
Carr, Robert K., jt. auth. see Kent, George C.
Carr, Roberta, ed. Directory of Art & Music Colleges. 3rd ed. 350p. (YA). (gr. 8-12). 1994. pap. 16.95 (*1-880468-09-3*) Col Connect.
— Directory of Unusual Majors. rev. ed. 100p. 1991. pap. text 25.00 (*1-880468-01-8*) Col Connect.
— Guide to Catholic Colleges & Universities. 2nd ed. 368p. (YA). (gr. 8-12). 1995. pap. 18.95 (*1-880468-10-7*) Col Connect.
— High School Student's Guide to Pre-College Programs. rev. ed. 480p. (YA). (gr. 8-12). 1994. pap. 16.95 (*1-880468-08-5*) Col Connect.
Carr, Roberta C. Couture: The Art of Fine Sewing. (Illus.). 208p. 1993. pap. 29.95 (*0-935278-28-1*) Palmer-Pletsch.
***Carr, Robyn.** Deep in the Valley. 2000. mass mkt. 5.99 (*1-55166-609-X*, 1-66609-8, Mira Bks) Harlequin Bks.
— The House on Olive Street. 408p. 1999. mass mkt. 5.99 (*1-55166-545-X*, Mira Bks) Harlequin Bks.
Carr, Ronnie, jt. ed. see Bancroft, Dennis.
***Carr, Rosamond Halsey & Halsey, Ann Howard.** Land of a Thousand Hills: My Life in Rwanda. (Illus.). 256p. 1999. 23.95 (*0-670-88780-3*, Viking) Viking Penguin.
— Land of a Thousand Hills: My Life in Rwanda. large type ed. LC 00-23135. 2000. 25.95 (*1-56895-858-7*, Compass) Wheeler Pub.
***Carr, Rosamund Halsey & Halsey, Ann Howard.** Land of a Thousand Hills: My Life in Rwanda. (Illus.). 2000. pap. 13.00 (*0-452-28202-0*) Penguin Books.
Carr, Rosanne. The Black Orchid Hotel. (Black Lace Ser.). 288p. (Orig.). 1996. mass mkt. 5.95 (*0-352-33060-0*, Pub. by Virgin Bks) London Brdge.
Carr, Roxanne. Avenging Angel. 256p. (Orig.). 1997. mass mkt. 5.95 (*0-352-33147-X*, Pub. by BLA4) London Brdge.
— Jewel of Xanadu. (Black Lace Ser.). 300p. 1996. mass mkt. 5.95 (*0-352-33037-6*, Pub. by Virgin Bks) London Brdge.
— Twin Temptations: Black Orchid/The Senses Bejewelled. (Black Lace Ser.). 1999. mass mkt. 6.95 (*0-352-33377-4*) Virgin Pubng.
Carr, Roy. A Century of Jazz: From Blues to Bop, Swing to Hip-Hop: A Hundred Years of Music, Musicians, Singers, & Styles. LC 97-204065. (Illus.). 256p. 1997. pap. 28.95 (*0-306-80778-5*) Da Capo.
Carr, Roy & Murray, Charles. David Bowie: An Illustrated Record. (Illus.). 120p. 1994. per. 14.95 (*0-906008-25-5*, Pub. by Plexus) Publishers Group.
Carr-Ruffino, Norma. Business Student's Guide to Course Assignments. 2nd ed. LC 90-80849. (Illus.). 425p. (C). 1991. pap. text 15.95 (*0-9625889-0-3*) Carlyle Pr.
***Carr-Ruffino, Norma.** Diversity Success Strategies. LC 98-48868. (Illus.). 368p. 1999. pap. text 19.95 (*0-7506-7102-5*) Buttrwrth-Heinemann.
Carr-Ruffino, Norma. Managing Diversity: People Skills For Multiculture. 2nd ed. LC 99-166750. 464p. 1998. pap. 40.00 (*0-536-00758-6*) Pearson Custom.
— The Promotable Woman: 10 Essential Skills for the New Millenium. 3rd ed. LC 97-23106. 312p. 1997. pap. 16.99 (*1-56414-323-6*) Career Pr Inc.
Carr, Ruth. The Fine Art of Loving. 304p. 1997. pap. 8.95 (*0-09-918462-1*, Pub. by Arrow Bks) Trafalgar.
Carr, Ruth, et al. Word of Mouth. 118p. 1997. pap. 13.95 (*0-85640-584-1*, Pub. by Blackstaff Pr) Dufour.
Carr, Sally. Dangereuse Lune de Miel. (Azur Ser.: No. 726). (FRE.). 1998. mass mkt. 3.50 (*0-373-34726-X*, 1-34726-9) Harlequin Bks.
— Juego de Mentiras. (Bianca Ser.). 1996. per. 3.50 (*0-373-33366-8*, 1-33366-5) Harlequin Bks.
— Une Mariee en Fuite. (Azur Ser.: Vol. 705). 1998. mass mkt. 3.50 (*0-373-34705-7*, 1-34705-3) Harlequin Bks.
Carr, Sally B., ed. see Fisher, Terry.
Carr, Sally B., ed. see Superior, Irving.
Carr, Sally G. & Hall, Bronwen. The Story of Beatrix Potter. (Classics for Children Ser.). 48p. (J). (gr. k-3). 1995. 15.00 (*1-888287-01-2*) Calvert Sch.
Carr, Sara L. I'd Rather Breathe! Stop Smoking Kit. LC 94-96720. 158p. (Orig.). 1994. pap. 7.95 (*1-886687-01-3*); vinyl bd. 24.95 incl. audio (*1-886687-00-5*) Grafik-FX.
Carr-Saunders, A. M. The Population Problem: A Study in Human Evolution. LC 73-14150. (Perspectives in Social Inquiry Ser.). 520p. 1974. reprint ed. 29.95 (*0-405-05496-3*) Ayer.
Carr-Saunders, Alexander M. New Universities Overseas. LC 77-7518. (Illus.). 1977. reprint ed. lib. bdg. 69.50 (*0-8371-9665-5*, CSNU, Greenwood Pr) Greenwood.
Carr, Sharon L. & Daugherty, Terry L. TMJ Pain Control: A Self-Help Program. (Illus.). 40p. 1989. 29.95 incl. audio (*0-924728-00-0*, TMJ Stress Ctr) MyoData.
Carr, Silvana E., et al, eds. The Critical Link: Interpreters in the Community, Papers from the First International Conference on Interpreting in Legal, Health & Social Service Settings, Geneva Park, Canada, 1-4 June 1995. LC 96-6510. (Benjamins Translation Library: Vol. 19). viii, 322p. 1997. lib. bdg. 79.00 (*1-55619-701-2*) J Benjamins Pubng Co.
Carr, Stephen. City Signs & Lights Prepared for the Boston Redevelopment Authority & U. S. Dept. of Housing & Urban Development. 1973. pap. text 21.95 (*0-262-02087-4*) MIT Pr.
Carr, Stephen, et al. Public Space. (Cambridge Series in Environment & Behavior). (Illus.). 416p. (C). 1993. text 85.00 (*0-521-35148-0*); pap. text 30.95 (*0-521-35960-0*) Cambridge U Pr.
Carr, Stephen J. Improving Cash Crops in Africa: Factors Influencing the Productivity of Cotton, Coffee, & Tea Grown by Smallholders. LC 93-5127. (Technical Paper, 0253-7494 Ser.: No. 216). 75p. 1993. pap. 22.00 (*0-8213-2509-4*, 12509) World Bank.
Carr, Stephen L. Historical Guide to Utah Ghost Towns. rev. ed. LC 72-91023. 174p. 1987. pap. 16.95 (*0-914740-30-X*) Western Epics.
Carr, Stephen L. & Edwards, Robert W. Utah Ghost Rails. LC 89-51670. (Illus.). 208p. (Orig.). 1990. pap. 19.95 (*0-914740-34-2*) Western Epics.
Carr, Steve. Married & How to Stay That Way: A Treasury of Practical Solutions Based Solely on Gods Word. 304p. 1998. pap. 12.99 (*0-9656749-3-2*) ACW Press.
Carr, Steven A., jt. ed. see Burlingame, A. L.
Carr, Stuart C. & Schumaker, John F., eds. Psychology & the Developing World. LC 95-43767. 248p. 1996. 75.00 (*0-275-95245-2*, Praeger Pubs) Greenwood.
Carr, Stuart C., et al. Psychology of Aid: Cassandra's Perspective. LC 97-35288. 256p. (C). 1998. 75.00 (*0-415-14207-5*) Routledge.
Carr, Tee. All Eyes up Here! A Portrait of Effective Teaching. LC 96-69548. (Illus.). 288p. (Orig.). 1996. pap. 14.95 (*0-9644760-3-7*) Phase II Publ.
— All Eyes Up Here! A Portrait of Effective Teaching. LC 96-69458. (Illus.). x, 276p. 1998. pap. 14.95 (*1-892897-00-8*) Carr Enterps.
— All Eyes Up Here! A Portrait of Effective Teaching. 2nd rev. ed. LC 96-69458. (Illus.). x, 276p. 1999. reprint ed. pap. 14.95 (*1-892897-02-4*) Carr Enterps.
— How Come the Wise Men Are in the Dempster Dumpster? LC 97-68540. (Illus.). 192p. 1997. pap. 10.95 (*0-9644760-4-5*) Phase II Publ.
— How Come the Wise Men Are in the Dempster Dumpster? A Celebration of Children. LC 97-68540. (Illus.). xiv, 146p. 1998. pap. 10.95 (*1-892897-01-6*) Carr Enterps.
Carr, Terry, ed. The Science Fiction Hall of Fame, Vol. IV. 432p. 1986. mass mkt. 4.95 (*0-380-89710-5*, Avon Bks) Morrow Avon.
Carr, Terry & Shaw, Bob. Between Two Worlds - Messages Found in an Oxygen Bottle. LC 86-61272. 171p. 1986. 15.00 (*0-915368-33-1*) New Eng SF Assoc.
Carr, Terry, ed. see Silverberg, Robert, et al.
Carr, Thomas H., jt. ed. see Dagenbach, Dale.
Carr, Thomas K. Newman & Gadamer: Toward a Hermeneutics of Religious Knowledge. LC 96-28988. (AAR Reflection & Theory in the Study of Religion Ser.). 214p. 1996. 34.95 (*0-7885-0303-0*, 01 10 10) OUP.
Carr, Thomas M., Jr. Descartes & the Resilience of Rhetoric: Varieties of Cartesian Rhetorical Theory. (Studies in Writing & Rhetoric). 224p. (C). 1989. text 26.95 (*0-8093-1557-2*) S Ill U Pr.
Carr, Tim. Antarctic Oasis: Under the Spell of South Georgia. LC 97-24636. 256p. 1998. 40.00 (*0-393-04605-2*) Norton.
Carr, Timothy W., ed. Plasma Chromatography. (Illus.). 274p. (C). 1984. text 102.00 (*0-306-41432-5*, Kluwer Plenum) Kluwer Academic.
Carr, Tony. Youth Soccer Coaching: A Complete Guide to Building a Successful Team. LC 98-115346. (Illus.). 160p. 1998. pap. 17.95 (*0-7063-7578-5*, Pub. by WrLock) Sterling.
Carr, Tyree. Ophthalmic Medical Assisting: An Independent Study Course. 3rd ed. LC 98-33325. 1999. write for info. (*1-56055-041-4*) Am Acad Ophthal.
Carr, Valerie, jt. auth. see Johns, Beverley.
Carr, Virginia. Your Home Color Guide: Making Color Work. Catalfio, Maria, ed. (Illus.). 206p. 1994. pap. 14.95 (*0-9640510-1-X*) Smart Home Moves.
***Carr, Virginia & Krueger, Anne.** ABC's of Budget Decorating Kit: Color Plans to Buying Furniture Direct. (Illus.). 2000. pap. 39.95 (*0-9640510-2-8*) Smart Home Moves.
Carr, Virginia S., ed. see Porter, Katherine Anne.
Carr, W. E. Statistical Problem Solving. (Quality & Reliability Ser.: Vol. 33). (Illus.). 224p. 1992. text 45.00 (*0-8247-8704-8*) Dekker.
Carr, W. J., Jr. AC Loss & Macroscopic Theory of Superconductors. xii, 158p. 1983. text 252.00 (*0-677-05700-8*) Gordon & Breach.
Carr, Waggoner & Varner, Byron D. Texas Politics in My Rearview Mirror. LC 92-30785. (Illus.). 168p. 1992. pap. 12.95 (*1-55622-314-5*, Rep of TX Pr) Wordware Pub.
Carr, Walt. Reflections of a Confused Middle Class Black Youth. 68p. (Orig.). 1996. pap. 10.00 (*0-911849-05-X*) Comptex Assocs Inc.
Carr, Walter H. The World & William Walker. LC 75-18354. (Illus.). 289p. 1975. reprint ed. lib. bdg. 59.75 (*0-8371-8328-6*, CAWWW, Greenwood Pr) Greenwood.
Carr, Wilford & Kemmis, Stephen. Becoming Critical: Education, Knowledge & Action Research. 240p. 1986. pap. 32.95 (*1-85000-090-5*, Falmer Pr) Taylor & Francis.
Carr, Wilfred. For Education: Towards Critical Educational Inquiry. LC 94-22209. 192p. 1995. pap. 31.95 (*0-335-19186-X*) OpUniv Pr.
— Quality in Teaching: Arguments for a Reflective Profession. 230p. 1989. 75.00 (*1-85000-546-X*, Falmer Pr); pap. 34.95 (*1-85000-547-8*, Falmer Pr) Taylor & Francis.
Carr, Wilfred & Hartnett, Anthony. Education & the Struggle for Democracy: The Politics of Educational Ideas. LC 95-24923. 256p. 1996. pap. 34.95 (*0-335-19520-2*) OpUniv Pr.
Carr, Wilfred & Kemmis, Stephen. Becoming Critical: Education, Knowledge, & Action Research. 249p. (C). 1995. pap. 40.00 (*0-7300-0437-6*, ECT432, Pub. by Deakin Univ) St Mut.
Carr, William. Aristocracy & People: A Study in German Foreign Policy, 1933-1939. 144p. pap. text. write for info. (*0-7131-5669-4*, Pub. by E A) Routldge.
— Arms, Autarky, & Aggression. (Foundations of Modern History Ser.). 136p. 1973. reprint ed. pap. text 1.95 (*0-393-09361-1*) Norton.
Carr, William. A History of Germany 1815-1990. 4th ed. LC 91-22908. 448p. 1995. pap. text 25.00 (*0-340-55930-6*, A6768, Pub. by E A) St Martin.
Carr, William. Hitler: A Study in Personality & Politics. 208p. 1995. pap. text 18.95 (*0-7131-6462-X*, Pub. by E A) St Martin.
Carr, William. Origins Wars German Unification. (Origins of Modern Wars Ser.). (Illus.). 256p. (C). 1995. pap. 39.06 (*0-582-49148-7*, 78818) Longman.
Carr, William C. KIS DC Electronics Laboratory Fundamentals. 1988. per. 16.00 (*0-88252-137-3*) Paladin Hse.
Carr, William G. The Conspiracy to Destroy All Governments & Religions. 1982. lib. bdg. 250.00 (*0-87700-358-0*) Revisionist Pr.
— The Continuing Education of William Carr: An Autobiography. LC 78-9918. 452p. reprint ed. pap. 140.20 (*0-608-15271-4*, 202952900061) Bks Demand.
— Pawns in the Game. 1978. pap. 10.00 (*0-911038-29-9*, 0004, Noontide Pr) Legion Survival.
— Pawns in the Game. 193p. 1997. reprint ed. pap. 10.00 (*0-913022-34-9*) CPA Bk Pub.
— Red Fog over America. 280p. 1996. reprint ed. pap. 10.00 (*0-913022-35-7*) CPA Bk Pub.
***Carr, William Guy.** The Conspiracy: To Destroy All Existing Governments & Religions. 31p. 1998. pap. 3.00 (*0-944379-34-6*) CPA Bk Pub.
— Pawns in the Game. unabridged ed. 230p. 1958. reprint ed. pap. 15.00 (*0-945001-15-0*) GSG & Assocs.
— The Red Fog over America. unabridged ed. 280p. 1989. reprint ed. pap. 15.00 (*0-945001-16-9*) GSG & Assocs.
Carr, William H. Up Another Notch. 1989. text 24.95 (*0-07-010159-0*) McGraw.
Carr, Williine. Health Expenditures in New York City 1983. (Papers: No. 1). 32p. 1985. 5.00 (*0-934459-09-6*) United Hosp Fund.
Carr, Williine, et al. Measuring Avoidable Deaths & Diseases in New York State. (Paper Ser.: No. 8). 56p. 1988. 5.00 (*0-934459-40-1*) United Hosp Fund.
***Carra, Diana.** Dawn at Dunnelson: Twelve Tales of the Anthracite Mountains. 132p. 1999. pap. 15.99 (*0-9676225-0-6*) Roberts Pubng.
Carra, Joseph S. & Cossu, Raffaello, eds. International Perspectives on Municipal Solid Wastes & Sanitary Landfilling. (International Solid Waste Professional Library). 234p. 1990. text 104.00 (*0-12-106355-0*) Acad Pr.
Carra, Lawrence, jt. auth. see Dean, Alexander.
Carra, Massimo. Carlo Carra: The Complete Paintings, 1900-1966, 3 vols. (ITA., Illus.). 1968. 795.00 (*1-55660-082-8*) A Wofsy Fine Arts.
— Carlo Carra's Graphic Work. (ITA.). 150p. 1976. 120.00 (*1-55660-116-6*) A Wofsy Fine Arts.
***Carracci, Annibale, et al.** The Drawings of Annibale Carracci. LC 99-28549. 1999. write for info. (*0-89468-243-1*) Natl Gallery Art.
Carracedo, A. & Brinkmann, B., eds. Advances in Forensic Haemogenetics Vol. 6: 16th Congress of the International Society for forensic Haemogenetics (Internationale Gesellschaft fur Forensische Hamogenetik e. V.), Santiage de Compostela, 12-16 September, 1995, Vol. 6. (Illus.). 704p. 1996. pap. 95.00 (*3-540-60492-8*) Spr-Verlag.
***Carrad, David Clayton.** The New QDRO Handbook: How to Divide Erisa, Military & Civil Service Pensions & Collect Child Support from Employee Benefit Plans. LC 00-30619. 2000. pap. write for info. (*1-57073-798-3*) Amer Bar Assn.
***Carrada-Bravo, Francisco.** Global Finance, Cases & Notes. LC HG3881.C3157 1999. 300p. 1999. text 78.95 (*1-85972-573-2*, Pub. by Ashgate Pub) Ashgate Pub Co.
Carradice, Ian. Greek Coins. (Illus.). 112p. (Orig.). 1995. pap. 19.95 (*0-292-71184-0*) U of Tex Pr.
Carradice, Ian, ed. The Lewis Collection, in Corpus Christi College, Cambridge Pt. II: The Greek Imperial Coins. (Sylloge Nummorum Graecorum Ser.: Vol. VI). (Illus.). 64p. 1992. text 115.00 (*0-19-726089-6*) OUP.
Carradice, Ian & Price, Martin J. Coinage in the Greek World. (Illus.). 154p. 1988. lib. bdg. 45.00 (*0-900652-82-9*) S J Durst.
***Carradine, Beverly.** Fish University: Jonah. 64p. 2000. pap. 5.99 (*0-88019-408-1*) Schmul Pub Co.
Carradine, Beverly. Graphic Scenes. 1990. reprint ed. pap. 10.99 (*0-88019-270-4*) Schmul Pub Co.
Carradine, Beverly. The Lottery. 72p. 1997. pap. 3.99 (*0-88019-363-8*) Schmul Pub Co.

C

— Mississippi Stories. 1989. reprint ed. pap. 11.99 (*0-88019-243-7*) Schmul Pub Co.

Carradine, Beverly. Pastoral Sketches. 1987. pap. 9.99 (*0-88019-218-6*) Schmul Pub Co.

— Remarkable Occurrences. unabridged ed. 176p. 1994. reprint ed. pap. 11.99 (*0-88019-323-9*) Schmul Pub Co.

***Carradine, Beverly.** Sanctification. 119p. 1998. pap. 7.99 (*0-88019-379-4*) Schmul Pub Co.

Carradine, Beverly. The Sanctified Life. unabridged ed. 286p. 1995. reprint ed. pap. 13.99 (*0-88019-339-5*) Schmul Pub Co.

Carradine, David. David Carradine's Intro To Chi Kung. LC 97-16271. 1997. pap. 12.95 (*0-8050-5100-7*) H Holt & Co.

— The Spirit of Shaolin: A Kung Fu Philosophy. (Illus.). 192p. 1993. pap. 14.95 (*0-8048-1828-2*) Tuttle Pubng.

Carradine, David & Nakahara, David. David Carradine's Tai Chi Workout: The Beginner's Program for a Healthier Mind & Body. (Illus.). 1995. pap. 11.95 (*0-8050-3767-5*, Owl) H Holt & Co.

Carradine, F. J. Runes & Riddles: The Empire of Elwolf. (Illus.). 378p. (Orig.). (YA). (gr. 7-12). 1993. pap. 9.99 (*0-88092-074-2*) Royal Fireworks.

Carradine, Frank. The Cretaceous Paradox. Kemnitz, Myrna, ed. (Illus.). 250p. (Orig.). (YA). (gr. 7 up). 1996. pap. 9.99 (*0-88092-042-4*, 0424) Royal Fireworks.

Carradini, Lawrence. Burning Heads. (Orig.). 1996. pap. 6.95 (*0-9636942-1-9*) VB Document.

Carradini, Lawrence, ed. see Fiore, Dolores.

Carradini, Lawrence, ed. & intro. see Willman, Mark.

Carrafiello, Michael L. Robert Parsons & English Catholicism, 1580-1610. LC 97-24182. 192p. 1998. 34.50 (*1-57591-012-8*) Susquehanna U Pr.

Carrafiello, Susan B. The Tombs of the Living: Prisons & Prison Reform in Liberal Italy. LC 97-8537. (Studies in Modern European History: Vol. 24). VIII, 138p. (C). 1998. text 38.95 (*0-8204-3778-6*) P Lang Pubng.

Carragher, Michael. A World Full of Places: And Other Stories. LC 97-163223. 176p. 1997. pap. 15.95 (*0-85640-595-7*, Pub. by Blackstaff Pr) Dufour.

Carragher, Michael, et al. The Second Blackstaff Book of Short Stories. 236p. (Orig.). 1991. pap. 14.95 (*0-85640-473-X*, Pub. by Blackstaff Pr) Dufour.

Carraher, C. E., jt. auth. see Gebelein, C. G.

Carraher, C. E., jt. auth. see Seymour, R. B.

Carraher, Charles E. Seymour - Carraher's Polymer Chemistry. 4th ed. LC 96-22846. (Undergraduate Chemistry Ser.: No. 13). (Illus.). 720p. 1996. text 59.75 (*0-8247-9752-3*) Dekker.

Carraher, Charles E., Jr., et al, eds. Advances in Organometallic & Inorganic Polymer Science. LC 82-5074. (Illus.). 465p. reprint ed. pap. 144.20 (*0-7837-0945-5*, 204124900019) Bks Demand.

Carraher, Charles E., Jr & Gabelein, Charles G. Biological Activities of Polymers. LC 82-3988. (ACS Symposium Ser.: Vol. 186). 304p. reprint ed. pap. 94.30 (*0-608-03111-9*, 206356400007) Bks Demand.

***Carraher, Charles E. & Seymour, Raymond Benedict.** Seymour/Carraher's Polymer Chemistry. 5th rev. ed. LC 00-24961. (Undergraduate Chemistry Ser.). 741p. 2000. 79.95 (*0-8247-0362-6*) Dekker.

Carraher, Charles E., Jr & Sperling, Leslie H., eds. Renewable - Resource Materials: New Polymer Sources. (Polymer Science & Technology Ser.: Vol. 33). 342p. 1986. 89.50 (*0-306-42271-9*, Plenum Trade) Perseus Pubng.

Carraher, Charles E. & Tsuda, Minoru, eds. Modification of Polymers. LC 79-28259. (ACS Symposium Ser.: No. 121). 1980. 54.95 (*0-8412-0540-X*) Am Chemical.

Carraher, Charles E., Jr & Tsuda, Minoru, eds. Modification of Polymers. LC 79-28259. (ACS Symposium Ser.: Vol. 121). 511p. 1980. reprint ed. pap. 158.50 (*0-608-03059-7*, 206351200007) Bks Demand.

Carraher, Charles E., jt. auth. see Seymour, Raymond B., Jr.

Carraher, Charles E., Jr., jt. ed. see Gebelein, Charles G.

Carraher, Charles E., Jr., jt. ed. see Millich, Frank.

Carraher, Charles E ., Jr. & Gebelein, Charles G., eds. Biological Activities of Polymers. LC 82-3988. (ACS Symposium Ser.: No. 186). 293p. 1982. 43.95 (*0-8412-0719-4*) Am Chemical.

Carral, Patricia, jt. ed. see Cepa, Jordi.

Carraminana, Alberto, jt. ed. see Franco, Jose.

Carranco, Lynwood. Redwood Country. (Illus.). 360p. (Orig.). 1986. pap. 19.95 (*0-89863-097-5*) Star Pub CA.

Carranco, Lynwood & Labbe, John T. Logging the Redwoods. LC 72-80989. (Illus.). 144p. 1975. pap. 29.95 (*0-87004-236-X*) Caxton.

Carrano, Carl J., jt. ed. see Winkelmann, Gunther.

Carrano, Frank M. Data Abstraction & Problem Solving with C++ Walls & Mirrors. 2nd ed. 816p. (C). 1997. text. write for info. (*0-201-34521-8*) Addison-Wesley.

***Carrano, Frank M. & Prichard, Janet.** Data Abstraction & Problem Solving with Java: Walls & Mirrors. 832p. 2000. 71.00 (*0-201-70220-7*) Addison-Wesley.

Carrano, Frank M., et al. Data Abstraction & Problem Solving with C++ Walls & Mirrors. 2nd ed. LC 97-30265. (Illus.). 800p. (C). 1997. 76.00 (*0-201-87402-4*) Addison-Wesley.

— Data Structures & Problem Solving with Turbo Pascal: Walls & Mirrors. LC 92-29450. 715p. (C). 1992. 76.00 (*0-8053-1217-X*) Addison-Wesley.

Carranza. Clinical Periodontology. 8th ed. 1998. text 14.29 (*0-8089-2156-8*, Grune & Strat) Harcrt Hlth Sci Grp.

***Carranza.** South American Free Trade Area or Free Trade Area. 2000. 70.95 (*1-84014-795-4*) Ashgate Pub Co.

Carranza, Elihu. Logic Workbook. Robbins, John W., ed. & intro. by. 140p. 1992. pap., student ed. 11.95 (*0-940931-34-6*) Trinity Found.

Carranza, Fermin A., Jr. & Perry, Dorothy A. Clinical Periodontology for the Dental Hygienist. (Illus.). 301p. 1986. pap. text 39.95 (*0-7216-1352-7*, W B Saunders Co) Harcrt Hlth Sci Grp.

Carranza, Fermin A., Jr., et al. Clinical Periodontology. 8th ed. (Illus.). 816p. 1995. text 85.00 (*0-7216-6728-7*, W B Saunders Co) Harcrt Hlth Sci Grp.

Carranza, Maria Luisa, ed. Cuando el Nino se Enferma, Que Hacer? (Children's Ailments, What to Do?) (SPA.). 192p. 1999. pap. write for info. (*0-939193-45-0*) Edit Concepts.

Carrar, Gianfranco & Kalay, Yehuda E., eds. Knowledge-Based Computer-Aided Architectural Design. LC 94-1201. 408p. 1994. 190.00 (*0-444-81759-X*) Elsevier.

Carrara, Alberto. Rivista. (C). 1997. pap. text 37.00 (*0-15-567327-0*) Harcourt Coll Pubs.

Carrara, Alberto & Guzzetti, Fausto, eds. Geographical Information Systems in Assessing Natural Hazards. LC 95-10770. (Advances in Natural & Technological Hazards Research Ser.: Vol. 5). 1995. text 184.00 (*0-7923-3502-3*) Kluwer Academic.

Carrara, Larry, jt. auth. see Wakefield, Pat A.

Carrara, Walter C., et al. Spotlight Synthetic Aperture Radar: Signal Processing Algorithms. LC 95-19078. 554p. 1995. 105.00 (*0-89006-728-7*) Artech Hse.

Carrard, Philippe. Poetics of the New History: French Historical Discourse from Braudel to Chartier. LC 91-20585. (Parallax: Re-Visions of Culture & Society Ser.). 272p. 1991. text 42.50 (*0-8018-4254-9*) Johns Hopkins.

— Poetics of the New History: French Historical Discourse from Braudel to Chartier. (Parallax). 220p. 1995. reprint ed. pap. text 17.95 (*0-8018-5233-1*) Johns Hopkins.

***Carraro, Carlo.** Efficiency & Equity of Climate Change Policy. LC 00-32706. (Economics, Energy & Environment Ser.). 2000. write for info. (*0-7923-6262-4*) Plenum.

Carraro, Carlo. International Environmental Agreements on Climate Change LC 98-46919. (Economics, Energy & Environment Ser.). 1999. write for info. (*0-7923-5515-6*) Kluwer Academic.

Carraro, Carlo, ed. The European Carbon Tax: An Economic Assessment. (FEEM-Kluwer International Series on Economics, Energy & Environment). 288p. (C). 1993. lib. bdg. 164.50 (*0-7923-2520-6*) Kluwer Academic.

— International Environmental Negotiations: Strategic Policy Issues. LC 96-41939. 208p. 1997. 80.00 (*1-85898-524-2*) E Elgar.

— Trade, Innovation, Environment. LC 94-3702. (Economics, Energy & Environment Ser.: Vol. 2). 416p. (C). 1994. lib. bdg. 166.50 (*0-7923-3033-1*) Kluwer Academic.

Carraro, Carlo, et al, eds. Environmental Management in a Transition to Market Economy, a Challenge to Governments & Business, Proceedings: International Conference on Environmental Management in a Transition to Market Economy (1993: University of Geneva) LC 95-152762. 456p. 1995. pap. 200.00 (*2-7108-0680-0*, Pub. by Edits Technip) Enfield Pubs NH.

— Environmental Policy & Market Structure. (FEEM/Kluwer International Series on Economics, Energy & Environment: Vol. 4). 256p. (C). 1996. lib. bdg. 144.00 (*0-7923-3656-9*) Kluwer Academic.

Carraro, Carlo & Hauri, Alain, eds. Operations Research & Environmental Management: The FEEN/KLUWER International Series on Economics, Energy & Environment. LC 95-40367. (Economics, Energy, & Environment Ser.). 304p. (C). 1996. lib. bdg. 136.00 (*0-7923-3767-0*) Kluwer Academic.

Carraro, Carlo & Levceque, Francois. Voluntary Approaches in Environmental Policy. LC 98-49930. (Economics, Energy & Environment Ser.). 1999. write for info. (*0-7923-5516-4*) Kluwer Academic.

Carraro, Carlo & Sartore, D., eds. Developments of Control Theory for Economic Analysis. (C). 1987. lib. bdg. 161.50 (*90-247-3345-6*) Kluwer Academic.

Carraro, Carlo & Siniscalco, Domenico, eds. Environmental Fiscal Reform & Unemployment. (FEEM/Kluwer International Series on Economics, Energy & Environment: Vol. 7). 272p. (C). 1996. text 107.00 (*0-7923-3750-6*) Kluwer Academic.

— New Directions in the Economic Theory of the Environment. LC 96-40021. 374p. (C). 1998. text 64.95 (*0-521-59089-2*) Cambridge U Pr.

Carraro, Carlo, jt. ed. see Filar, Jerzy A.

Carraro, Carlo E. & Filar, Jerzy A., eds. Game-Theoretic Models of the Environment. LC 95-22370. (Annals of the International Society of Dynamic Games Ser.: Vol. 2). 356p. 1995. 104.00 (*0-8176-3815-6*) Birkhauser.

***Carraro, Carlo E. & Metcalf, Gilbert E.** Behavorial & Distributional Effects of Environmental Policy. LC 00-41799. (National Bureau of Economic Research Conference Report Ser.). 2000. write for info. (*0-226-09481-2*) U Ch Pr.

Carraro, Francine. Jerry Bywaters: A Life in Art. LC 93-39098. (American Studies). (Illus.). 312p. (C). 1994. 34.95 (*0-292-71157-3*) U of Tex Pr.

Carraro, J. M., ed. see Rudner, Barry.

Carras, Costa, jt. auth. see Walker, Andrew.

Carras, Mary C. Indira Gandhi in the Crucible of Leadership. 289p. 1980. 18.95 (*0-318-36626-6*) Asia Bk Corp.

Carrasco. Assessment of Human Performance. (Standard Texts of Cosmetology Ser.). 1998. 39.95 (*0-8273-7522-0*) Delmar.

Carrasco, Alfonso. Agua, Energia y Desarrollo Rural. 288p. 1989. pap. 20.00 (*1-85339-377-0*, Pub. by Intermed Tech) Stylus Pub VA.

— Cambio Tecnologicco en Poblaciones Rurales Andinas. 134p. 1988. pap. 15.50 (*1-85339-362-2*, Pub. by Intermed Tech) Stylus Pub VA.

— La Electricida en el Peru. 100p. 1990. pap. 18.00 (*1-85339-380-0*, Pub. by Intermed Tech) Stylus Pub VA.

Carrasco, David. Aztec Ceremonial Landscapes. LC 99-18834. 1998. pap. 24.95 (*0-87081-509-1*) Univ Pr Colo.

***Carrasco, David.** City of Sacrifice: The Aztec Empire & the Role of Violence in Civilization. 2000. pap. 17.00 (*0-8070-4643-4*) Beacon Pr.

Carrasco, David. Quetzalcoatl & the Irony of Empire. xii, 248p. 1998. pap. text 16.95 (*0-226-09490-1*) U Ch Pr.

— Quetzalcoatl & the Irony of Empire: Myths & Prophecies in the Aztec Tradition. LC 91-46792. (Illus.). 247p. reprint ed. pap. 76.60 (*0-608-09013-1*, 206964800005) Bks Demand.

— Religions of Mesoamerica: Cosmovision & Ceremonial Centers. LC 89-45990. 208p. 1990. pap. 13.00 (*0-06-061325-4*, Pub. by Harper SF) HarpC.

— Religions of Mesoamerica: Cosmovision & Ceremonial Centers. (Illus.). 174p. (C). 1998. pap. text 11.95 (*1-57766-006-4*) Waveland Pr.

***Carrasco, David, ed.** The Oxford Encyclopedia of Mesoamerican Cultures, 3vols., Set. (Illus.). 1344p. 2000. text 395.00 (*0-19-510815-9*) OUP.

Carrasco, David, et al, eds. Mesoamerica's Classic Heritage: Teotihuacan to the Aztecs. LC 99-11257. (Illus.). 530p. 1999. 65.00 (*0-87081-512-1*) Univ Pr Colo.

Carrasco, David & Moctezuma, Eduardo M. Moctezuma's Mexico: Visions of the Aztec World. Sessions, Scott, ed. LC 92-11993. (Illus.). 200p. 1992. 49.95 (*0-87081-263-7*) Univ Pr Colo.

Carrasco, David & Sessions, Scott. Daily Life of the Ancient Aztecs: People of the Sun & Earth. LC 97-39721. (Greenwood Press "Daily Life Through History" Ser.). 304p. 1998. 45.00 (*0-313-29558-1*, Greenwood Pr) Greenwood.

Carrasco, David, ed. see Eliade, Mircea.

Carrasco, David L. The City of Sacrifice: Performing Violence in Pre-Modern Mexico. LC 99-23752. 304p. 1999. 27.50 (*0-8070-4642-6*) Beacon Pr.

***Carrasco, David L.** Quetzalcoatl & the Irony of Empire: Myths & Prophecies in the Aztec Tradition. rev. ed. (Illus.). 287p. 2001. pap. 24.95 (*0-87081-558-X*) U of Okla Pr.

Carrasco, Emma, jt. auth. see Cordova, Regina.

Carrasco, Felix, ed. see De Tormes, Lazarillo.

Carrasco, Gilbert P., jt. auth. see Boswell, Richard A.

Carrasco, Jose. Thoughts Wander Through. LC 88-63603. (Poetry Ser.). 1989. pap. 15.95 (*0-944109-05-5*) Margraf Pubns Grp.

Carrasco, L., et al. Regulation of Gene Expression in Animal Viruses. (NATO ASI Ser.: Vol. 240). (Illus.). 334p. (C). 1993. text 115.00 (*0-306-44408-9*, Kluwer Plenum) Kluwer Academic.

Carrasco, Luis. Mechanisms of Viral Toxicity in Animal Cells. 208p. 1987. 120.00 (*0-8493-6742-5*, CRC Reprint) Franklin.

Carrasco, Marta. El Cuaderno y la Ventana.Tr. of Window & the Notebook. (SPA.). (J). 1997. 17.95 (*84-233-2674-8*, Pub. by Destino) Continental Bk.

Carrasco, Patricia. Joven, Tu Vales!Tr. of You Are Valuable!. (SPA.). 96p. (J). 1995. pap. 5.99 (*0-311-12257-4*) Casa Bautista.

***Carrasco, Pedro.** Tenochca Empire of Ancient Mexico: The Triple Alliance of Tenochtitlan, Tetzcoco, & Tlacopan, Vol. 234. LC 99-26789. (Civilization of the American Indian Ser.). 1999. 49.95 (*0-8061-3144-6*) U of Okla Pr.

Carrasco, Pedro, ed. see Nutini, Hugo G.

Carrasco, R. C. & Oncina, Jose, eds. Grammatical Inference & Applications: Proceedings of the Second International Colloquium, ICGI-94, Alicante, Spain, September 21-23, 1994. (Lecture Notes in Computer Science: Lecture Notes in Artificial Intelligence: Vol. 862). viii, 290p. 1994. 44.95 (*3-540-58473-0*) Spr-Verlag.

Carrasco, Rafael C., et al, eds. Grammatical Inference & Applications: Proceedings of the Second International Colloquim, ICGI 94, Alicante, Spain, September 21-23, 1994. LC 94-34846. (Lecture Notes in Computer Science Ser.: Vol. 862). 1994. 42.00 (*0-387-58473-0*) Spr-Verlag.

Carrasco, Vincent N. & Pillsbury, Harold C., eds. Revision Otologic Surgery. LC 97-1120. (Illus.). 304p. 1997. text 99.00 (*0-86577-610-5*) Thieme Med Pubs.

Carrasquer, Francisco. Iman Y la Novella Historica de Sender. (Monagrafias A Ser.: Vol. XVII). (SPA.). 302p. (Orig.). (C). 1970. pap. 51.00 (*0-900411-15-5*, Pub. by Tamesis Bks Ltd) Boydell & Brewer.

Carrasquillo, Angela, et al, eds. Teaching the Bilingual Special Education Student. LC 90-37630. (Second Language Learning Ser.). 240p. (C). 1990. pap. 39.50 (*0-89391-712-5*); text 73.25 (*0-89391-623-4*) Ablx Pub.

Carrasquillo, Angela & Hedley, Carolyn N., eds. Whole Language & the Bilingual Learner. LC 92-10595. 240p. (C). 1993. text 73.25 (*0-89391-767-2*); pap. text 39.50 (*0-89391-861-X*) Ablx Pub.

Carrasquillo, Angela & Rodriguez, Judy. Measuring Success in Bilingual Education Programs: Case Studies of Bilingual Practices. 78p. (C). 1998. pap. text 17.00 (*1-883514-02-9*) Bastos Bk.

Carrasquillo, Angela & Segan, Philip, eds. The Teaching of Reading in Spanish to the Bilingual Student. 2nd ed. LC 97-44951. 256p. 1998. pap. write for info. (*0-8058-2462-6*) L Erlbaum Assocs.

Carrasquillo, Angela L. Teaching English As a Second Language: A Resource Guide. LC 93-41180. (Source Books on Education: Vol. 41). 240p. 1994. text 44.00 (*0-8153-0821-3*, SS750) Garland.

Carrasquillo, Angela L. & London, Clement B. Parents & Schools: A Source Book. LC 92-6699. 256p. 1993. text 46.00 (*0-8153-0820-5*, SS775) Garland.

Carrasquillo, Angela L. & Rodriguez, Vivian. Language Minority Students in the Mainstream Classroom. 208p. 1995. 69.00 (*1-85359-298-6*, Pub. by Multilingual Matters); pap. 24.95 (*1-85359-297-8*, Pub. by Multilingual Matters) Taylor & Francis.

Carratelli, G. Pugliese, ed. Greek World: Art & Civilization in Magna Graecia & Sicily. LC 96-68510. (Illus.). 800p. 1996. 85.00 (*0-8478-1980-9*, Pub. by Rizzoli Intl) St Martin.

Carratello. Duke the Blue Mule: Easy Phonics Reader. (Illus.). 16p. (J). (ps-1). 1996. pap. 2.49 (*1-57690-014-2*) Tchr Create Mat.

— Gail's Paint Pail: Easy Phonics Reader. (Illus.). 16p. (J). (ps-1). 1996. pap. 2.49 (*1-57690-015-0*) Tchr Create Mat.

— The Green Seed: Easy Phonics Reader. (Illus.). 16p. (J). (ps-1). 1996. pap. 2.49 (*1-57690-011-8*) Tchr Create Mat.

— Mice on Ice: Easy Phonics Reader. (Illus.). 16p. (J). (ps-1). 1996. pap. 2.49 (*1-57690-012-6*) Tchr Create Mat.

— Skate, Kate Skate: Easy Phonics Reader. (Illus.). 16p. (J). (ps-1). 1996. pap. 2.49 (*1-57690-010-X*) Tchr Create Mat.

— Will Bill? Easy Phonics Reader. (Illus.). 16p. (J). (ps-1). 1996. pap. 2.49 (*1-57690-018-5*) Tchr Create Mat.

Carratello, John. Multiplication - Long Division: Sing & Learn. 1994. pap. 9.95 incl. audio (*0-7604-0020-2*, JPC002) Wrner Bros.

— Political Action - Themes of Geography: Sing & Learn. 1994. pap. 9.95 incl. audio (*0-7604-0021-0*, JPC003) Wrner Bros.

— Punctuation - Parts of a Sentence: Sing & Learn. 1994. pap. 9.95 incl. audio (*0-7604-0019-9*, JPC001) Wrner Bros.

Carratello, John & Carratello, Patty. Animals. (Hands-On Minds-On Science Ser.). (Illus.). 96p. 1994. pap., teacher ed. 11.95 (*1-55734-626-7*) Tchr Create Mat.

— Beginning Charts, Graphs & Diagrams. (Illus.). 80p. (Orig.). (gr. 2-4). 1990. student ed. 9.95 (*1-55734-168-0*) Tchr Create Mat.

— Beginning Map Skills. (Illus.). 80p. (Orig.). (gr. 2-4). 1990. student ed. 9.95 (*1-55734-167-2*) Tchr Create Mat.

— Bridge to Terabithia: A Literature Unit. (Illus.). 48p. (Orig.). (gr. 5-8). 1991. pap., student ed. 7.95 (*1-55734-401-9*) Tchr Create Mat.

— Civil War: A Thematic Unit. (Thematic Units Ser.). (Illus.). 80p. (gr. 5-8). 1991. student ed. 9.95 (*1-55734-290-3*) Tchr Create Mat.

— Connecting Math & Literature. (Curriculum Connections Ser.). (Illus.). 144p. 1991. student ed. 14.95 (*1-55734-342-X*) Tchr Create Mat.

— Connecting Writing & Literature. (Curriculum Connections Ser.). (Illus.). 144p. (gr. k-3). 1992. student ed. 14.95 (*1-55734-344-6*) Tchr Create Mat.

— Dr. Seuss: Favorite Authors. (Favorite Authors Ser.). (Illus.). 112p. (Orig.). 1992. student ed. 11.95 (*1-55734-450-7*) Tchr Create Mat.

— Eric Carle: Favorite Authors. (Favorite Authors Ser.). (Illus.). 112p. (Orig.). 1992. student ed. 11.95 (*1-55734-451-5*) Tchr Create Mat.

— Focus on Composers. Goldfluss, Karen J., ed. (Focus Ser.). (Illus.). 112p. (Orig.). 1994. pap., student ed. 11.95 (*1-55734-492-2*) Tchr Create Mat.

— Great Americans. (Illus.). 112p. (J). (gr. 2-5). 1991. 11.95 (*1-55734-112-5*) Tchr Create Mat.

— The Hobbit: A Literature Unit. (Literature Units Ser.). (Illus.). 48p. 1992. student ed. 7.95 (*1-55734-405-1*) Tchr Create Mat.

— Literature Activities for Reluctant Readers: Intermediate. (Illus.). 112p. (J). (gr. 3-5). 1991. student ed. 11.95 (*1-55734-354-3*) Tchr Create Mat.

— Literature Activities for Reluctant Readers: Primary. (Illus.). 112p. (J). (gr. 1-3). 1991. student ed. 11.95 (*1-55734-353-5*) Tchr Create Mat.

— Maps, Charts, Graphs, & Diagrams. (Illus.). 80p. (gr. 3-6). 1990. student ed. 9.95 (*1-55734-169-9*) Tchr Create Mat.

— Revolutionary War: A Thematic Unit. (Thematic Units Ser.). (Illus.). 80p. (Orig.). (gr. 5-8). 1991. student ed. 9.95 (*1-55734-293-8*) Tchr Create Mat.

— The Sign of the Beaver: A Literature Unit. (Literature Units Ser.). (Illus.). 48p. (Orig.). (gr. 3-5). 1991. student ed. 7.95 (*1-55734-402-7*) Tchr Create Mat.

— United States Geography. (Illus.). 48p. (J). (gr. 3-6). 1989. student ed. 7.95 (*1-55734-160-5*) Tchr Create Mat.

— Where the Red Fern Grows: A Literature Unit. (Illus.). 48p. (Orig.). (gr. 5-8). 1991. student ed. 7.95 (*1-55734-400-0*) Tchr Create Mat.

— World Geography. (Illus.). 48p. (J). (gr. 3-6). 1989. student ed. 7.95 (*1-55734-161-3*) Tchr Create Mat.

— A Wrinkle in Time: A Literature Unit. (Illus.). 48p. (Orig.). (gr. 3-5). 1991. pap., student ed. 7.95 (*1-55734-403-5*) Tchr Create Mat.

— Write All about It: Activities for the Writing Process. (Illus.). 80p. (Orig.). (J). (gr. 1-3). 1993. pap., student ed. 9.95 (*1-55734-500-7*) Tchr Create Mat.

— Writing a Country Report. (Illus.). 48p. (J). (gr. 3-6). 1989. student ed. 7.95 (*1-55734-163-X*) Tchr Create Mat.

— Writing a State Report. (Illus.). 48p. (J). (gr. 3-6). 1989. student ed. 7.95 (*1-55734-162-1*) Tchr Create Mat.

Carratello, John, jt. auth. see Carratello, Patty.

Carratello, John, ed. see Riggs, Seth.

Carratello, Patricia. My Body. (Illus.). 38p. (J). (gr. 1-4). 1980. student ed. 7.95 (*1-55734-211-3*) Tchr Create Mat.

C

Carratello, Patty. Brett My Pet (Short E) Easy Phonics Reader. (Easy Reader Ser.). (Illus.). 16p. (J). (ps-1). 1996. pap., teacher ed. 2.49 (*1-57690-017-7*, TCM2017) Tchr Create Mat.
— Dot's Pot. (Easy Readers Ser.). 16p. (J). (gr. k-1). 1997. pap. 2.49 (*1-57690-019-3*) Tchr Create Mat.
— My Cap. (Easy Reader Ser.). (Illus.). 1996. teacher ed. 2.49 (*1-57690-016-9*, TCM2016) Tchr Create Mat.
— My Old Gold Boat. (Easy Readers Ser.). 16p. (J). (gr. k-1). 1997. pap. 2.49 (*1-57690-013-4*) Tchr Create Mat.
— My Truck & My Pup: Easy Reader. (Easy Readers Ser.). 16p. (J). (gr. k-1). 1997. pap. 2.49 (*1-57690-020-7*) Tchr Create Mat.
— This Is Fred. (Easy Reader Ser.). (Illus.). (J). 1996. pap., teacher ed. 2.49 (*1-57690-021-5*, TCM2021) Tchr Create Mat.
Carratello, Patty & Carratello, John. The Outsiders: A Literature Unit. (Literature Unit Ser.). (Illus.). 48p. (J). Date not set. student ed. 7.95 (*1-55734-406-X*, TCM406) Tchr Create Mat.
Carratello, Patty, jt. auth. see Carratello, John.
Carrau, Bob. Monsters & Aliens from George Lucas. (Illus.). 64p. 1996. reprint ed. pap. 9.98 (*0-8109-8139-4*, Pub. by Abrams) Time Warner.
Carrau, Bob, jt. auth. see Trimble, Irene.
Carrau, Ricardo L. & Murry, Thomas, eds. Comprehensive Management of Swallowing Disorders. LC 98-27803. (Illus.). 450p. 1998. pap. 174.95 (*1-56593-955-7*, 1884) Thomson Learn.
Carrau, Ricardo L., et al. Head & Neck Manifestations of Gastroesophageal Reflux. 2nd ed. LC 98-4058. (Self-Instructional Package Ser.). (Illus.). 60p. 1998. reprint ed. pap. text 25.00 (*1-56772-065-X*, 5506245) AAO-HNS.
Carravetta, Peter. Prefaces to the Diaphora: Rhetorics, Allegory, & the Interpretation of Postmodernity. LC 89-70239. (Illus.). 368p. 1991. 39.95 (*1-55753-004-1*) Purdue U Pr.
— The Sun & Other Things. LC 94-74389. (Essential Poets Ser.: No. 72). 150p. (C). 1995. pap. 12.00 (*1-55071-026-5*) Guernica Editions.
Carravetta, Peter, tr. see Oberto, Martio.
Carravetta, Peter, tr. see Pankiewicz, Flavia.
Carraway, Bill. Basic Christianity: A Study & Report from Inside the Church. LC 96-84257. (Illus.). 176p. 1996. 12.95 (*0-9633855-3-4*) BAC Pubns.
Carraway, Coralie A., jt. ed. see Carraway, Kermit L.
Carraway, Coralie A. Carothers, jt. ed. see Carraway, Kermit L.
***Carraway, Kermit L. & Carraway, Coralie A., eds.** Cytoskeleton: Signalling & Cell Regulation. 2nd ed. LC 99-41249. (The Practical Approach Ser.). (Illus.). 312p. 2000. pap. text 55.00 (*0-19-963781-4*) OUP.
***Carraway, Kermit L. & Carraway, Coralie A. Carothers, eds.** Cytoskeleton : Signalling & Cell Regulation: A Practical Approach. 2nd ed. LC 99-41249. (The Practical Approach Ser.: No. 221). (Illus.). 312p. 2000. text 110.00 (*0-19-963782-2*) OUP.
Carraway, Kermit L., et al. Signaling & the Cytoskeleton. LC 97-34514. (Molecular Biology Intelligence Unit Ser.). 225p. 1998. 159.00 (*3-540-64215-3*) Spr-Verlag.
Carraway, Leslie N., ed. A Morphological & Morphometric Analysis of the "Sorex Vagrans Species Complex" in the Pacific Coast Region. (C). 1990. pap. 14.00 (*0-89672-176-0*) Tex Tech Univ Pr.
Carraway, Leslie N., jt. auth. see Verts, B. J.
Carraway, W. B. A Call to Faith & Morality: A Time for Revolution. LC 92-90301. (Illus.). 360p. (Orig.). 1993. pap. 14.95 (*0-9633855-0-X*) BAC Pubns.
Carraway, W. B., ed. see Howell, Carlene M.
Carraway, W. B., ed. see Peterson, Gordon W.
Carraze, Alain. The Avengers Companion. LC 98-9188. 196p. 1998. pap. 19.95 (*0-912333-61-8*) BB&T Inc.
Carraze, Alain & Oswald, Helene. The Prisoner. (Illus.). 240p. (Orig.). 1996. pap. text 19.95 (*0-86369-557-4*, Pub. by Virgin Bks) London Brdge.
Carrdus, Anna. Classical Rhetoric & the German Poet. (Legenda Ser.). 275p. 1996. pap. 45.00 (*1-900755-02-5*, Pub. by E H R C) David Brown.
Carre, Abbe. The Travels of the Abbe Carre in India & the Near East, 1672 to 1674, 3 vols., Set. 1990. reprint ed. 120.00 (*81-206-0596-9*, Pub. by Asian Educ Servs) S Asia.
Carre, Alwar. Islam & the State in the World Today. (C). 1987. 30.00 (*81-85054-27-4*, Pub. by Manohar) S Asia.
Carre, Andree D. & Weil-Barais, Annick, eds. Tutelle et Mediation dans l'Education Scientifique. viii, 360p. 1998. pap. 47.95 (*3-906759-69-5*) P Lang Pubng.
Carre, Clive, jt. auth. see Bennett, Neville S.
Carre De Busserole, J. Dictionnaire Geographique, Historique et Biographique d'Indr. (FRE.). 1988. write for info. (*0-7859-8100-4*, 2-85554-031-3) Fr & Eur.
Carre, E. G. Praying Hyde: The Life of John "Praying" Hyde. LC 82-73972. 187p. 1983. pap. 9.99 (*0-88270-541-5*) Bridge-Logos.
Carre, Jacques, ed. The Crisis of Courtesy: Studies in the Conduct Book in Britain, 1600-1900. LC 94-5758. (Studies in Intellectual History: Vol. 51). vi, 202p. 1994. 92.50 (*90-04-10005-9*) Brill Academic Pubs.
Carre, Jean M. Frail Warrior: A Life of Robert Louis Stevenson. (BCL1-PR English Literature Ser.). 297p. 1992. reprint ed. lib. bdg. 79.00 (*0-7812-7671-3*) Rprt Serv.
— Robert Louis Stevenson: The Frail Warrior. Hard, Eleanor, tr. from FRE. LC 78-165619. (Select Bibliographies Reprint Ser.). 1977. reprint ed. 20.95 (*0-8369-5926-4*) Ayer.
— A Season in Hell: The Life of Arthur Rimbaud. Josephson, Hannah & Josephson, Matthew, trs. from FRE. LC 77-10254. reprint ed. 38.00 (*0-404-16309-2*) AMS Pr.
Carre, John Le, see Le Carre, John, pseud.
Carre, Kathy & Ansary, Mir Tamim. Natural Objects. LC 96-39409. (Cool Collections). (J). 1998. (*1-57572-115-5*) Heinemann Lib.
Carre, Kathy & Ansary, Mir Tamim. Model Cars. LC 96-39411. (Cool Collections). (J). 1998. 18.50 (*1-57572-116-3*) Heinemann Lib.
Carre, Kathy & Ansary, Mir Tamin. Insects. LC 96-39412. (Cool Collections). 1998. (*1-57572-117-1*) Heinemann Lib.
Carre, Marie. AA-1025: The Memoirs of an Anti-Apostle. LC 91-75254. 135p. 1994. reprint ed. pap. 6.00 (*0-89555-449-6*) TAN Bks Pubs.
Carre, Meyrick H., tr. & intro. see Herbert, Edward.
Carreau, Pierre J., et al. Rheology of Polymeric Systems: Principles & Applications. LC 96-36329. 1997. 197.50 (*1-56990-218-6*) Hanser-Gardner.
***Carreia, Joan.** Business Management in the Catholic School. 1998. pap. 8.00 (*1-55833-210-3*) Natl Cath Educ.
Carreiras, Manuel, et al, eds. Language Processing in Spanish. 384p. 1996. text 79.95 (*0-8058-1721-2*) L Erlbaum Assocs.
Carreiro, Carolyn. Hand-Print Animal Art. Williamson, Susan, ed. LC 96-51923. (Kids Can! Ser.). (Illus.). 144p. (Orig.). (J). (ps-5). 1997. pap. 14.95 (*1-885593-09-0*) Williamson Pub Co.
Carreiro, Mary E. Modern Education: One Size Fits All. LC 88-2861. (Gentle Wind Ser.: Vol. 3). (Illus.). 224p. 1988. reprint ed. pap. 14.95 (*0-89789-168-6*) Gentle Wind Proj.
— Modern Education: One Size Fits All. LC 88-2861. (Gentle Wind Ser.: Vol. 3). (Illus.). 224p. 1988. reprint ed. lib. bdg. 34.95 (*0-89789-169-4*) Gentle Wind Proj.
— Modern Religion & the Destruction of Spiritual Capacity. LC 87-24251. (Gentle Wind Ser.: Vol. 2). 160p. 1988. reprint ed. pap. 12.95 (*0-89789-141-4*); reprint ed. lib. bdg. 29.95 (*0-89789-140-6*) Gentle Wind Proj.
— The Psychology of Spiritual Growth. LC 86-20799. (Gentle Wind Ser.: Vol. 1). 160p. 1987. reprint ed. lib. bdg. 29.95 (*0-89789-123-6*) Gentle Wind Proj.
— The Psychology of Spiritual Growth. LC 86-20799. (Gentle Wind Ser.: Vol. 1). 160p. 1988. reprint ed. pap. 12.95 (*0-89789-124-4*) Gentle Wind Proj.
Carreiro, Paul. Tales of Thinking: Multiple Intelligences in the Classroom. LC 97-25733. (Illus.). viii, 216p. (C). 1998. pap. text 17.50 (*1-57110-061-X*) Stenhse Pubs.
Carreiro, Richard. Working with Families. Schulz, William, ed. (Options Ser.). 64p. (J). (gr. 1-8). 1989. pap. 8.00 (*0-920541-49-6*) Peguis Pubs Ltd.
Carreiro, Ron, jt. auth. see Wiesbauer, Marcia.
Carrel, Annette. It's the Law! A Young Person's Guide to Our Legal System. 219p. (Orig.). 1994. pap. 16.95 (*1-884244-06-8*) Volcano Pr.
— It's the Law! A Young Person's Guide to Our Legal System. LC 94-13552. 187p. (Orig.). (YA). (gr. 7-12). 1994. pap. 12.95 (*1-884244-01-7*) Volcano Pr.
Carrel-Billiard, Marc. Applying Visualage for C++ for Windows. LC 97-156774. 608p. (C). 1997. pap. text 49.95 (*0-13-618208-9*) P-H.
Carrel, Jeffrey M. & Sokoloff, Howard M. Complications in Foot & Ankle Surgery: Prevention & Management. 3rd ed. (Illus.). 486p. 1992. 80.00 (*0-683-01465-X*) Lppncott W & W.
Carrel, Mark. Alamo Jefferson. large type ed. 304p. 1992. pap. 16.99 (*0-7089-7149-0*, Linford) Ulverscroft.
— Comancheria. large type ed. (Linford Western Library). 1995. pap. 16.99 (*0-7089-7752-9*, Linford) Ulverscroft.
— Last of the Balfrys. large type ed. (Linford Western Library). 272p. 1995. pap. 16.99 (*0-7089-7760-X*, Linford) Ulverscroft.
— El Vengador! large type ed. (Linford Western Library).Tr. of Avenger!. 1995. pap. 16.99 (*0-7089-7757-X*, Linford) Ulverscroft.
— Wagon Train. large type ed. (Linford Western Library). 368p. 1995. pap. 16.99 (*0-7089-7700-6*, Linford) Ulverscroft.
Carrell. Fundamentals of Organizational Behavior. 1997. pap. text. write for info. (*0-13-568288-6*) P-H.
— Human Resource Management: Global Workplace. 6th ed. (C). 1999. text. write for info. (*0-03-026161-9*) Harcourt Coll Pubs.
Carrell, et al. Proceedings of the Nineteen Eighty-Four Vancouver Conference on Algebraic Geometry. LC 85-28720. (Proceedings, Canadian Mathematical Society Ser.: Vol. 6). 503p. 1986. reprint ed. pap. 72.00 (*0-8218-6010-0*, CMSAMS/6) Am Math.
Carrell, jt. auth. see Newsom.
Carrell, Al. Best Home Hints from the Super Handyman. LC 90-35324. (Illus.). 232p. 1990. pap. 12.95 (*0-87833-753-9*) Taylor Pub.
— 1000 Questions about Home Repair & Maintenance. LC 97-21210. 504p. 1997. pap. write for info. (*1-56530-267-2*) Summit TX.
Carrell, Bob, jt. auth. see Newsom, Doug.
Carrell, Bob J., jt. ed. see Newsom, Doug A.
Carrell, Jennifer, jt. auth. see Egli, Glenn.
***Carrell, Lori.** The Great American Sermon Survey. (Celebrate Jesus! Ser.). 253p. 1999. 25.00 (*1-57849-169-X*) Mainstay Church.
***Carrell, Michael & Heavrin, Christina.** Labor Relations & Collective Bargaining: Cases , Practices, & Law. 6th ed. 640p. 2000. 85.33 (*0-13-019474-3*, Prentice Hall) P-H.
Carrell, Michael & Heavrin, Christina. Labor Relations & Collective Bargaining: Cases, Practices & Law. 5th ed. LC 97-24221. 606p. (C). 1997. 87.00 (*0-13-768607-2*) P-H.
Carrell, Norman. Bach the Borrower. LC 79-26050. 396p. 1980. reprint ed. lib. bdg. 35.00 (*0-313-22205-3*, CABB, Greenwood Pr) Greenwood.
— Bach's Brandenburg Concerts. 1988. reprint ed. lib. bdg. 59.00 (*0-7812-0749-5*) Rprt Serv.
— Bach's Brandenburg Concerts. reprint ed. lib. bdg. 59.00 (*0-403-08968-9*) Scholarly.
Carrell, Patricia, et al, eds. Interactive Approaches to Second Language Reading. (Cambridge Applied Linguistics Ser.). (Illus.). 304p. 1988. pap. text 24.95 (*0-521-35874-4*) Cambridge U Pr.
Carrell, Peter R. Jesus & the Angels: Angelology & the Christology of the Apocalypse of John. (Society for New Testament Studies Monograph Ser.: Vol. 95). 292p. (C). 1997. text 59.95 (*0-521-59011-6*) Cambridge U Pr.
Carrell, Ross & Detz, Jim. For the Love of Justice. Miller, Marc, ed. 48p. 1999. pap. 15.00 (*0-9658694-4-X*) Jolly Roger.
Carrell, Susan. Group Exercises for Adolescents: A Manual for Therapists. LC 93-28206. (Illus.). 1993. pap. 21.50 (*0-8039-5292-9*) Sage.
Carrels, Peter. Uphill Against Water: The Great Dakota Water War. LC 98-24291. (Our Sustainable Future Ser.). (Illus.). 280p. 1999. text 45.00 (*0-8032-1496-0*) U of Nebr Pr.
***Carrels, Peter.** Uphill Against Water: The Great Dakota Water War. LC 98-24291. (Our Sustainable Future Ser.). (Illus.). 280p. 1999. pap. 25.00 (*0-8032-6397-X*) U of Nebr Pr.
Carreno, Antonio, ed. see de Vega, Lope.
Carreno, Jose. Cincuenta Testimonios Urgentes (Denuncias en Ginebra sobe violaciones de los Derechos Humanos-Presidio Politico Hist. Cubano) LC 87-8224. (Coleccion Cuba y sus Jueces). (SPA., Illus.). 171p. (Orig.). 1987. pap. 9.95 (*0-89729-459-9*) Ediciones.
— Cuba: Literatura Clandestina. LC 87-82224. (Coleccion Cuba y sus Jueces). (SPA., Illus.). 64p. (Orig.). 1987. pap. 5.00 (*0-89729-458-0*) Ediciones.
Carrera, Gustavo L. Salomon. (SPA.). 266p. 1993. pap. 18.99 (*980-01-0822-X*, Pub. by Fondo) Continental Bk.
Carrera-Hanley, Teresa, et al. Vistazos 1, Vol. 1. (SPA.). 158p. (C). 1986. pap. text 19.28 (*0-669-10290-3*) McDougal-Littell.
— Vistazos 2, Vol. 2. (SPA.). 197p. (C). 1986. pap. text 19.28 (*0-669-10291-1*) HM Trade Div.
Carrera, J. M. & Mandruzzato, G. P. Ultrasound & Fetal Growth. LC 99-16520. (Progress in Obstetric & Gynecological Sonography Ser.). (Illus.). 128p. 2000. 78.00 (*1-85070-618-2*) Prthnon Pub.
Carrera, John W. Immigrant Students: Their Legal Right of Access to Public Schools, a Guide for Advocates & Educators. rev. ed. 98p. 1992. reprint ed. pap. 12.00 (*1-880002-03-5*) Natl Coal Advocates.
***Carrera, Juliet.** Inside Out. LC 00-36968. 392p. 2000. lib. bdg. 49.95 (*1-56023-202-1*) Haworth Pr.
— Inside Out. LC 00-36968. 392p. 2000. pap. 19.95 (*1-56023-203-X*) Haworth Pr.
Carrera, Michael. Dictionary of Sexual Terms. (Reference Library). 1998. pap. 6.95 (*1-85326-353-2*, 3532WW, Pub. by Wrdsworth Edits) NTC Contemp Pub Co.
— The Language of Sex: An A to Z Guide. 192p. 1992. 24.95 (*0-8160-2397-2*) Facts on File.
***Carrera, Phyllis.** A Traveler's Journal: Beyond Fear into Freedom. Mitchell, Mardeene Burr, ed. (Illus.). 80p. 1999. spiral bd. 14.95 (*0-9675771-0-1*) Valley Graphics.
Carrera, Rosalina De La, see De la Carrera, Rosalina.
Carreras, B. A., jt. ed. see Alejaldre, C.
Carreras, F. J., et al, eds. Differential Geometry - Pensicola, 1989. (Lecture Notes in Mathematics Ser.: Vol. 1410). vi, 308p. 1989. 41.60 (*0-387-51885-1*, 3761) Spr-Verlag.
Carreras, J., et al. Diccionari de la Llengua Catalana. 2nd ed. (CAT.). 1677p. 1983. 37.50 (*0-8288-2083-X*, S40777) Fr & Eur.
— Shear Zones in Rocks: Papers Presented at the International Conference Held at the University of Barcelona, May 1979. 200p. 1980. pap. 48.00 (*0-08-026244-9*, Pergamon Pr) Elsevier.
Carreras, Joan. Marriage: Sex, Celebration & Law. 192p. 1999. pap. 18.00 (*1-85182-280-1*, Pub. by Four Cts Pr) Intl Spec Bk.
Carreras, Jose. Singing from the Soul: An Autobiography. Price, Walter, ed. Thomas et al, trs. from GER. LC 90-71130. (Library of Courage). (Illus.). 285p. 1991. 30.95 (*1-878756-89-3*) YCP Pubns.
Carreras, Jose, contrib. by. Jose Carreras: Collection. LC 96-753968. (CAT.). 64p. 1994. 19.95 (*0-7119-3604-8*, AM91348) Omnibus NY.
Carreras, Jose, frwd. Cancer: The Facts. 2nd ed. LC 98-107015. (Facts Ser.). (Illus.). 236p. 1996. pap. 19.95 (*0-19-261695-1*) OUP.
Carreras, Juan J., jt. ed. see Boyd, Malcolm.
Carrere. I Am Alive & You Are Dead. 1998. 16.00 (*0-8050-5464-2*); pap. 16.00 (*0-8050-5465-0*) H Holt & Co.
Carrere, Donna. Year of the Roasted Ear: Travels, Trials & Tribulations in South East Asia. (Illus.). 256p. 1999. pap. 11.99 (*1-84024-067-9*) Seven Hills Bk.
Carrere D'Encausse, Helene. Nicholas II. Holoch, George, tr. from FRE. LC 99-48898. 336p. 2000. 39.95 (*0-8419-1397-8*) Holmes & Meier.
***Carrere, Emmanuel.** The Adversary: A True Story of Murderous Deception. 224p. 2001. 23.00 (*0-8050-6583-0*, Metropol Bks) H Holt & Co.
Carrere, Emmanuel. Gothic Romance. 1990. 2.99 (*5-556-11499-4*) WP Pr.
— Hors d'Atteinte? (FRE.). 282p. 1989. pap. 10.95 (*0-7859-2131-1*, 2070382044) Fr & Eur.
— La Moustache. (FRE.). 192p. 1987. pap. 10.95 (*0-7859-2073-0*, 2070378837) Fr & Eur.
— Two by Carrere: Class Trip & the Mustache. Goodman, Lanie & Coverdale, Linda, trs. LC 97-43483. 318p. 1998. pap. 14.00 (*0-8050-5587-8*, Owl) H Holt & Co.
Carrere, Jean. Degeneration in the Great French Masters. McCabe, Joseph, tr. LC 67-26722. (Essay Index Reprint Ser.). 1977. 23.95 (*0-8369-0277-7*) Ayer.
— The Pope: An Analysis of the Office of the Pope & the Roman Church & City. 1977. lib. bdg. 59.95 (*0-8490-2453-6*) Gordon Pr.
Carrere, Jean & Dessaigne, Jacques. Lexique des Termes Usuels de Psychiatrie. (FRE.). 114p. 1976. pap. 39.95 (*0-8288-5738-5*, M6061) Fr & Eur.
Carrere, Ricardo & Lohmann, Larry. Pulping the South: Third World Tree Plantations in the Global Paper Economy. 256p. 1996. pap. 25.00 (*1-85649-438-1*, Pub. by Zed Books); text 65.00 (*1-85649-437-3*, Pub. by Zed Books) St Martin.
Carrero de Segarra, Teresa. Diccionario de la Taquigrafia: Gregg. (SPA.). 222p. 1992. pap. write for info. (*0-929441-27-3*) Pubns Puertorriquenas.
Carrero, Jaime. Los Nombres. (UPREX, Ficcion Ser.: No. 13). 167p. (C). 1972. pap. 1.50 (*0-8477-0013-5*) U of PR Pr.
Carrero, Josephine. Spanish Teacher's Book of Instant Word Games. LC 96-20549. (Illus.). 256p. 1996. pap., teacher ed. 28.50 (*0-87628-892-1*) Ctr Appl Res.
— Spanish Teacher's Book of Instant Word Games. LC 96-20549. (Illus.). 256p. 1996. spiral bd. 28.95 (*0-87628-757-7*) Ctr Appl Res.
Carrero, Luis Maria, see Maria Carrero, Luis.
Carrese, Marie A., jt. auth. see Araoz, Daniel L.
Carrese, Paul, ed. see Marshall, John.
Carret, Philip L. The Art of Speculation. LC 96-47487. 368p. 1997. 34.95 (*0-471-18187-0*); pap. 19.95 (*0-471-18188-9*) Wiley.
— The Art of Speculation. LC 84-73108. 364p. 1979. reprint ed. pap. 20.00 (*0-87034-050-6*) Fraser Pub Co.
— The Art of Speculation. rev. ed. LC 75-2625. (Wall Street & the Security Market Ser.). 1975. reprint ed. 34.95 (*0-405-06951-0*) Ayer.
— A Money Mind at Ninety. 248p. 1994. pap. 19.95 (*0-87034-118-9*) Fraser Pub Co.
Carrete, J. M., et al. A Roman Provincial Capital & Its Hinterland: The Survey of the Territory of Tarragona, Spain, 1985-1990. LC 96-161775. (JRA Supplementary Ser.: No. 15). (Illus.). 312p. 1995. 89.50 (*1-887829-15-6*) Jour Roman Arch.
Carrete Parrondo, Juan. El Grabado en Espana: Siglo XV al XVIII. (Summa Artis Ser.: Vol. 31). 600p. 1989. 295.00 (*84-239-5273-8*) Elliots Bks.
— El Grabado en Espana: Siglos XIX y XX. (Summa Artis Ser.: Vol. 32). 600p. 1989. 295.00 (*84-239-5274-6*) Elliots Bks.
Carreter, Fernando Lazaro, see Garcia Lorca, Federico & Lazaro Carreter, Fernando.
Carretero, Jose S. Analisis de Circuitos Electronicos Lineales. (SPA.). 304p. (C). 1994. pap. text 14.66 (*0-201-62577-6*) Addison-Wesley.
Carretero, Mario, et al, eds. Learning & Instruction Vol. 3: European Research in an International Context: Selected Proceedings of the 1989 European Conference for Research on Learning & Instruction. 614p. 1992. text 129.50 (*0-08-041039-1*, Pergamon Pr) Elsevier.
Carretero, Mario & Voss, James F., eds. Cognitive & Instructional Processes in History & the Social Sciences. 456p. 1994. pap. 45.00 (*0-8058-1565-1*) L Erlbaum Assocs.
— Cognitive & Instructional Processes in History & the Social Sciences. 456p. 1994. text 89.95 (*0-8058-1564-3*) L Erlbaum Assocs.
Carretta, Vincebt, jt. auth. see Cugoano, Ottobah.
Carretta, Vincent, ed. Unchained Voices: An Anthology of Black Authors in the English-Speaking World of the Eighteenth Century. LC 96-1019. (Illus.). 400p. 1996. pap. 19.95 (*0-8131-0884-5*); text 42.95 (*0-8131-1976-6*) U Pr of Ky.
Carretta, Vincent, ed. & intro. see Equiano, Olaudah.
Carrette, Jeremy, ed. see Foucault, Michel.
***Carrette, Jeremy R.** Foucault & Religion: Spiritual Corporality & Political Spirituality. LC 99-31682. 208p. 1999. pap. write for info. (*0-415-20260-4*) Routledge.
— Foucault & Religion: Spiritual Corporality & Political Spirituality. LC 99-31682. 208p. (C). 1999. text. write for info. (*0-415-20259-0*) Routledge.
Carretto, Carlo. Blessed Are You Who Believed.Tr. of Beata te Che Hai Creduto. 96p. (Orig.). 1994. pap. 21.00 (*0-86012-129-1*, Pub. by Srch Pr) St Mut.
— Blessed Are You Who Believed. Wall, Barbara, tr. from ITA. LC 82-22504.Tr. of Beata te Che Hai Creduto. (Illus.). 96p. (Orig.). 1983. reprint ed. pap. 10.50 (*0-88344-038-5*) Orbis Bks.
— Carlo Carretto. (Modern Spirituality Ser.). 96p. 1990. pap. 4.95 (*0-87243-179-7*) Templegate.
— Carlo Carretto - God's Name Is Love: Daily Reflections. Diele, Joseph, ed. (Christian Living Ser.). 136p. (Orig.). 1996. pap. 9.95 (*1-56548-079-1*) New City.
— Carlo Carretto Selected Writings. Ellsberg, Robert, ed. LC 93-42722. 200p. (Orig.). 1994. pap. 14.00 (*0-88344-956-0*) Orbis Bks.
— The Desert Journal: A Diary, 1954-55. Sibilla, Gian C., ed. Swaisland, Alison, tr. LC 92-24101. 191p. reprint ed. pap. 59.30 (*0-608-20256-8*, 207151500012) Bks Demand.
— The God Who Comes. Hancock, Rose M., tr. from ITA. LC 73-89358.Tr. of Il/Dio Che04492523x. (Illus.). 254p. (Orig.). 1974. pap. 10.50 (*0-88344-160-8*) Orbis Bks.
— I, Francis. Barr, Robert R., tr. from ITA. LC 81-16913. Orig. Title: Io Francesco. 144p. (Orig.). 1982. pap. 11.00 (*0-88344-200-0*) Orbis Bks.
— Letters from the Desert. Hancock, Rose, tr. from ITA. LC 72-85791. Orig. Title: Lettres dal deserto. 146p. (Orig.). 1982. pap. 11.00 (*0-88344-280-9*) Orbis Bks.

C

— Letters to Dolcidia, 1954-1983. Sibilia, Gian C., ed. Smith, Michael J., tr. LC 91-28836. 224p. reprint ed. pap. 69.50 (*0-608-20247-9*, 207150600012) Bks Demand.

— Summoned by Love. Neame, Alan, tr. LC 78-962. Orig. Title: Padre Mio me abbandono a Te. 144p. reprint ed. pap. 44.70 (*0-608-20196-0*, 207145500012) Bks Demand.

Carretto, Carlo & Board of St. Paul Editorial Staff. And God Saw That It Was Good. 142p. (C). 1996. pap. 39.95 (*0-85439-296-3*, Pub. by St Paul Pubns) St Mut.

Carrey, John, jt. auth. see Conley, Cort.

Carrez, Maurice. Dictionnaire de Culture Biblique. (FRE.). 356p. 1993. 79.95 (*0-7859-7795-3*, 2220034208) Fr & Eur.

Carrez, Maurice & Morel, Francois. Dictionnaire Grec-Francais du Nouveau Testament. 3rd ed. (FRE & GRE.). 270p. 1985. pap. 59.95 (*0-7859-4810-4*) Fr & Eur.

Carri, Robert L., ed. see International SAMPE Technical Conference Staff.

Carriage House Staff. Christmas Memories. deluxe ed. 17.95 (*0-89786-031-4*); 17.95 (*0-89786-032-2*) CHP Ltd Redding.

— My Family Heritage. 1993. 19.95 (*0-89786-144-2*); 19.95 (*0-89786-145-0*); 19.95 (*0-89786-146-9*); 19.95 (*0-89786-147-7*) CHP Ltd Redding.

— My Irish Heritage: The Story of My Family . . . an Exquisite Tribute to All Those of Irish Ancestry. 1993. 19.95 (*0-89786-149-3*) CHP Ltd Redding.

— School Years. 1993. 14.95 (*0-89786-140-X*); 14.95 (*0-89786-141-8*) CHP Ltd Redding.

— Treasured Recipes: An Organizer of Edible Nostalgia. 1993. 19.95 (*0-89786-148-5*) CHP Ltd Redding.

— What Every Family Should Know. 1993. 19.95 (*0-89786-098-5*); 19.95 (*0-89786-099-3*) CHP Ltd Redding.

Carriage Museum of America Staff. Conservation & Restoration of Horse-Drawn Vehicles. Green, Susan, ed. (Illus.). 258p. 1997. 20.00 (*1-880499-05-3*) Carriage Museum.

Carriazo, J., ed. see Menendez Pidal, Ramon.

Carrica, Jean L., jt. auth. see Birrer, G. Eddy.

Carricato, Annette M. Veterinary Notes for Dog Breeders. (Illus.). 256p. 1992. 25.95 (*0-87605-805-5*) Howell Bks.

Carrick, Carol. The Accident. LC 76-3532. (Illus.). 32p. (J). (ps-3). 1981. pap. 6.95 (*0-89919-041-3*, Clarion Bks) HM.

— Accident. (YA). 1976. 12.15 (*0-606-00359-2*, Pub. by Turtleback) Demco.

— Ben & the Porcupine. LC 80-214020. (Illus.). 32p. (J). (ps-3). 1985. pap. 6.95 (*0-89919-348-X*, Clarion Bks) HM.

— Big Old Bones: A Dinosaur Tale. 32p. (J). (ps-3). 1992. pap. 6.95 (*0-395-61582-8*, Clarion Bks) HM.

— Big Old Bones: A Dinosaur Tale. 1989. 12.15 (*0-606-01473-X*, Pub. by Turtleback) Demco.

— The Elephant. (Illus.). (J). write for info. (*0-318-62780-9*, Clarion Bks) HM.

— Elephant in the Dark. (Illus.). (J). write for info. (*0-318-62781-7*, Clarion Bks) HM.

Carrick, Carol. Left Behind. LC 88-1040. (Illus.). 32p. (J). (gr. k-3). 1988. text 16.60 (*0-89919-535-0*, Clarion Bks) HM.

Carrick, Carol. Lost in the Storm. (Illus.). 32p. (J). (ps-3). 1987. pap. 6.95 (*0-89919-493-1*, Clarion Bks) HM.

— Melanie. LC 94-15592. (Illus.). 32p. (J). (gr. k-3). 1996. 14.95 (*0-395-66555-8*, Clarion Bks) HM.

***Carrick, Carol.** Mothers Are Like That. LC 99-16587. (Illus.). 32p. (J). (ps-1). 2000. 15.00 (*0-395-88351-2*, Clarion Bks) HM.

Carrick, Carol. Patrick's Dinosaurs. LC 83-2049. (Illus.). 32p. (J). (gr. k-3). 1983. 15.00 (*0-89919-189-4*, Clarion Bks) HM.

— Patrick's Dinosaurs. LC 83-2049. (Illus.). 32p. (J). (gr. k-3). 1985. pap. 5.95 (*0-89919-402-8*, Clarion Bks) HM.

— Patrick's Dinosaurs. LC 83-2049. (Carry-Along Book & Cassette Favorites Ser.). 1p. (J). (ps-3). 1993. pap. 9.95 incl. audio (*0-395-66496-9*, 112725, Clarion Bks) HM.

— Patrick's Dinosaurs. (J). 1983. 11.15 (*0-606-00737-7*, Pub. by Turtleback) Demco.

— Patrick's Dinosaurs on the Internet. LC 97-47300. (Illus.). 32p. (J). (ps-3). 1999. 16.00 (*0-395-50949-1*, Clarion Bks) HM.

— Sleep Out. LC 72-88539. (Illus.). 32p. (J). (gr. 1-3). 1982. pap. 6.95 (*0-89919-083-9*, Clarion Bks) HM.

— Sleep Out. (J). 1973. 12.15 (*0-606-00576-5*, Pub. by Turtleback) Demco.

— Stay Away from Simon! LC 84-14289. (Illus.). 64p. (J). (gr. 4-7). 1989. pap. 5.95 (*0-89919-849-X*, Clarion Bks) HM.

— Stay Away from Simon. 1989. 11.40 (*0-606-12528-0*) Turtleback.

— Valentine. LC 93-35911. (Illus.). 32p. (J). 1995. 15.00 (*0-395-66554-X*, Clarion Bks) HM.

***Carrick, Carol.** Valentine. (Illus.). 32p. (J). (ps-3). 2001. pap. 5.95 (*0-618-05151-1*, Clarion Bks) HM.

Carrick, Carol. Whaling Days. (Illus.). 40p. (J). (gr. 4-7). 1993. 15.95 (*0-395-50948-3*, Clarion Bks) HM.

— Whaling Days. (Illus.). 40p. (J). (gr. k-3). 1996. pap. 6.95 (*0-395-76480-7*, Clarion Bks) HM.

Carrick, Carol. Whaling Days. 1993. 12.15 (*0-606-08896-2*, Pub. by Turtleback) Demco.

Carrick, Carol. What Happened to Patrick's Dinosaurs? LC 85-13989. (Illus.). 32p. (J). (gr. k-3). 1986. 16.00 (*0-89919-406-0*, Clarion Bks) HM.

— What Happened to Patrick's Dinosaurs? LC 85-13989. (Illus.). 32p. (J). (ps-3). 1988. pap. 5.95 (*0-89919-797-3*, Clarion Bks); pap. 9.95 incl. audio (*0-89919-838-4*, 111572, Clarion Bks) HM.

— What Happened to Patrick's Dinosaurs? (J). 1986. 11.15 (*0-606-03698-9*, Pub. by Turtleback) Demco.

***Carrick, Carol & Bouma, Paddy.** Upside-Down Cake. LC 98-52506. (Illus.). 64p. (J). (gr. 2-5). 1999. 14.00 (*0-395-84151-8*, Clarion Bks) HM.

Carrick, Edward, ed. Art & Design in the British Film: A Pictorial Directory of British Art Directors & Their Work. LC 76-169340. (Arno Press Cinema Program Ser.). (Illus.). 144p. 1972. reprint ed. 19.95 (*0-405-03913-1*) Ayer.

Carrick, Graham. Wood. (Craft Projects Ser.). (Illus.). 32p. (J). (gr. 2-6). 1990. lib. bdg. 11.95 (*0-685-36306-6*) Rourke Corp.

— Wood. (Craft Projects Ser.). (Illus.). 32p. (J). (gr. 2-6). 1990. lib. bdg. 22.60 (*0-86592-484-8*) Rourke Enter.

Carrick, J. C. Wycliffe & the Lollards. 1977. lib. bdg. 59.95 (*0-8490-2824-8*) Gordon Pr.

***Carrick, Jane.** Diamonds on the Lake. 288p. 2000. 18.99 (*0-7089-5659-9*) Ulverscroft.

***Carrick, Michael.** Caddie Sense. 2000. text 22.95 (*0-312-20286-5*) St Martin.

Carrick, Nancy & Finsen, Lawrence. Persuasive Pen: Reasoning & Writing. LC 96-43142. (Philosophy Ser.). 320p. 1997. pap. 35.00 (*0-7637-0234-X*) Jones & Bartlett.

Carrick, Noel. Belgium: Major World Nations. LC 99-19248. (Illus.). 144p. 1999. 19.95 (*0-7910-5379-2*) Chelsea Hse.

Carrick, Paul. Medical Ethics in Antiquity: Philosophical Perspectives on Abortion & Euthanasia. (Philosophy & Medicine Ser.: No. 18). 264p. 1985. pap. text 64.50 (*90-277-1915-2*); lib. bdg. 112.00 (*90-277-1825-3*) Kluwer Academic.

Carrick, Peter. Barbra Streisand: A Biography. large type ed. (Illus.). 288p. 1993. 27.99 (*0-7089-8693-5*, Charnwood) Ulverscroft.

— Liza Minnelli. large type ed. (Illus.). 416p. 1995. 27.99 (*0-7089-3254-1*) Ulverscroft.

— Mel Gibson. (Illus.). 208p. 1999. 24.95 (*0-7090-6088-2*, Pub. by R Hale Ltd) Seven Hills Bk.

Carrick, Tim. Color Coding EKGs. (Illus.). 29p. (C). 1994. text 14.95 (*0-943202-45-0*) H & H Pub.

Carrico, Bill. How to Live Your Life Without Experts. LC 91-90168. (Illus.). 144p. (Orig.). 1991. pap. 8.00 (*0-9629149-1-6*) Love Conn HI.

Carrico, C. J., ed. Operative Trauma Management Atlas. LC 97-20619. (Illus.). 335p. (C). 1998. pap. text 185.00 (*0-8385-7401-7*, A-7401-1, Apple Lange Med) McGraw.

Carrico, Clayton H. How to Close: A Guide to Residential Heating & Cooling Sales. 2nd ed. LC 92-44889. 1993. 14.95 (*0-912524-77-4*) Busn News.

— Refrigeration Licenses Unlimited. 2nd ed. LC 92-11928. 250p. 1992. 27.95 (*0-912524-72-3*) Busn News.

***Carrico, J. B.** Consolidated Guidance about Materials Licenses: Program-specific Guidance about Industrial Radiography Licenses, Final Report. 216p. 1998. per. 18.00 (*0-16-062759-1*) USGPO.

Carrico, J. De, see Nattinger, J. R. & De Carrico, J.

Carrico, Mara. The Ten Minute Yoga Work-In, Set. (Illus.). 1999. 17.95 incl. audio (*1-55927-563-4*) Audio Renaissance.

***Carrico, Mara.** Yoga. American Council on Exercise Staff, ed. (Illus.). 75p. 2000. pap. 14.95 (*1-890720-05-4*) Am Coun Exer.

Carrico, Mara & Yoga Journal Editors. Yoga Basics: The Essential Beginner's Guide to Yoga for a Lifetime of Health & Fitness. LC 97-11495. (Illus.). 224p. 1997. pap. 15.95 (*0-8050-4571-6*, Owl) H Holt & Co.

Carrico, Richard L. San Diego's Spirits: Ghosts & Hauntings in America's Southwest Corner. (Illus.). 95p. (Orig.). 1991. pap. text 9.95 (*0-9625788-1-9*) S Carrico.

Carrico, Richard L. Strangers in a Stolen Land: American Indians in San Diego. LC 86-63076. (Illus.). 130p. (C). 1987. reprint ed. pap. 10.95 (*0-940113-03-1*) Sierra Oaks Pub.

Carrico, Susan H. & Flanigan, Kathleen. San Diego's Historic Gaslamp Quarter: Then & Now. (Illus.). 90p. (Orig.). 1990. pap. 7.95 (*0-685-36271-X*) S Carrico.

Carrido, John. The Fitness Approach to Power Golf. 256p. 1997. pap. 13.95 (*0-399-52272-7*, Perigee Bks) Berkley Pub.

Carrie. Readings in Anthropolgy. 1998. 23.50 (*0-07-229198-2*) McGraw.

Carrie, Allan, jt. auth. see Bititci, Umit S.

Carrie, Christopher. Adventure in the Arctic Circle. (Crayola Color & Activity Ser.). (Illus.). 40p. (J). (gr. k up). 1990. 1.59 (*0-86696-249-2*) Binney & Smith.

— Alphabet. (Crayola Kinder Art BKs.). (Illus.). 12p. (Orig.). (J). (gr. 3-6). 1987. pap. 4.70 (*0-86696-204-2*) Binney & Smith.

— Amazing Animals. (Crayola Color & Activity Ser.). (Illus.). 40p. (J). (gr. k up). 1991. 1.49 (*0-86696-305-7*) Binney & Smith.

— Amazing Discoveries. (Crayola Color & Activity Ser.). (Illus.). 40p. (J). (gr. k up). 1991. 1.49 (*0-86696-308-1*) Binney & Smith.

— Amazing People. (Crayola Color & Activity Ser.). (Illus.). 40p. (J). (gr. k up). 1991. 1.49 (*0-86696-307-3*) Binney & Smith.

— Amazing Places. (Crayola Color & Activity Ser.). (Illus.). 40p. (J). (gr. k up). 1991. 1.49 (*0-86696-306-5*) Binney & Smith.

— Animals. (Crayola Kinder Art BKs.). (Illus.). 12p. (Orig.). (J). (gr. 3-6). 1987. pap. 4.70 (*0-86696-201-8*) Binney & Smith.

— Astronauts to Diving Ducks. (Crayola Encyclopedia of Coloring Fun Bks.). (Illus.). 40p. (Orig.). (J). (gr. k up). 1989. pap. 1.49 (*0-86696-219-0*) Binney & Smith.

— Chase Through the Desert Wilds. (Crayola Color & Activity Ser.). (Illus.). 40p. (J). (gr. k up). 1990. 1.59 (*0-86696-244-1*) Binney & Smith.

— Colorful Days Calendar. (Color & Activity Ser.). (Illus.). 32p. (Orig.). (YA). (gr. 5 up). 1989. pap. 1.99 (*0-86696-240-9*) Binney & Smith.

— Crazy Monster Mix-Ups. (Crayola Color & Activity Ser.). (Illus.). 32p. (J). (gr. k up). 1991. 1.49 (*0-86695-301-4*) Binney & Smith.

— Elephants to Haunted Houses. (Crayola Encyclopedia of Coloring Fun Bks.). (Illus.). 40p. (Orig.). (J). (gr. k up). 1989. pap. 1.49 (*0-86696-225-5*) Binney & Smith.

— Enchanted Toyland. (Crayola Coloring Storybks.). (Illus.). 32p. (J). (ps). 1991. 1.99 (*0-86696-314-6*) Binney & Smith.

— Everything Has a Shape. (Crayola So Big Bks.). (Illus.). 40p. (Orig.). (J). (ps up). 1989. pap. 1.99 (*0-86696-222-0*) Binney & Smith.

— Fun with Colors. (Crayola Color & Learn Series with Stickers). (Illus.). 28p. (J). (ps). 1991. 2.59 (*0-86696-312-X*) Binney & Smith.

— Fun with Letters. (Crayola Color & Learn Series with Stickers). (Illus.). 28p. (J). (ps). 1991. 2.59 (*0-86696-310-3*) Binney & Smith.

— Fun with Numbers. (Crayola Color & Learn Series with Stickers). (Illus.). 28p. (J). (ps). 1991. 2.59 (*0-86696-309-X*) Binney & Smith.

— Fun with Opposites. (Crayola Color & Learn Series with Stickers). (Illus.). 28p. (J). (ps). 1991. 2.59 (*0-86696-311-1*) Binney & Smith.

— Funny Animal Mix-Ups. (Crayola Color & Activity Ser.). (Illus.). 32p. (J). (gr. k up). 1991. 1.49 (*0-86696-302-2*) Binney & Smith.

— Going Places. (Crayola So Big Bks.). (Illus.). 40p. (Orig.). (J). (ps up). 1989. pap. 1.99 (*0-86696-221-2*) Binney & Smith.

— Growing Up. (Crayola So Big Bks.). (Illus.). 40p. (Orig.). (J). (ps up). 1989. pap. 1.99 (*0-86696-220-4*) Binney & Smith.

— Holiday Fun. (Crayola Holiday Fun Color & Activity Ser.). (Illus.). 32p. (Orig.). (J). (ps up). 1989. 1.99 (*0-685-27062-9*) Binney & Smith.

— Icebergs to Lazy Lizards. (Crayola Encyclopedia of Coloring Fun Bks.). (Illus.). 40p. (Orig.). (J). (gr. k up). 1989. pap. 1.49 (*0-86696-226-3*) Binney & Smith.

— Little Holiday Shop. (Coloring Storybook Ser.). (Illus.). 32p. (Orig.). (J). (gr. 2-5). 1989. pap. 1.99 (*0-86696-241-7*) Binney & Smith.

— The Magic Garden. (Crayola Coloring Storybks.). (Illus.). 32p. (J). (ps). 1991. 1.99 (*0-86696-313-8*) Binney & Smith.

— Measurement. (Crayola Kinder Art BKs.). (Illus.). 12p. (Orig.). (J). (gr. 3-6). 1987. pap. 4.70 (*0-86696-206-9*) Binney & Smith.

— Mission to the Space Station. (Crayola Color & Activity Ser.). (Illus.). 40p. (J). (gr. k up). 1990. 1.59 (*0-86696-247-6*) Binney & Smith.

— Mixed up Farm. (Crayola Coloring Storybks.). (Illus.). 32p. (Orig.). (J). (ps). 1990. 1.99 (*0-86696-236-0*) Binney & Smith.

— Monsters to Playful Penquins. (Crayola Encyclopedia of Coloring Fun Bks.). (Illus.). 40p. (Orig.). (J). (gr. k up). 1989. pap. 1.49 (*0-86696-227-1*) Binney & Smith.

— My Perfect Pet. (Crayola So Big Bks.). (Illus.) 40p. (Orig.). (J). (ps up). 1989. pap. 1.99 (*0-86696-218-2*) Binney & Smith.

— Mystery of the Forest Phantom. (Crayola Color & Activity Ser.). (Illus.). 40p. (J). (gr. k up). 1990. pap. 1.59 (*0-86696-243-3*) Binney & Smith.

— Numbers. (Crayola Kinder Art BKs.). (Illus.). 12p. (Orig.). (J). (ps). 1987. pap. 4.70 (*0-86696-203-4*) Binney & Smith.

— Over the Rainbow. (Crayola Coloring Storybks.). (Illus.). 32p. (Orig.). (J). (ps). 1990. 1.99 (*0-86696-239-5*) Binney & Smith.

— Playful Jungle Friends. (Crayola Coloring Storybks.). (Illus.). 32p. (Orig.). (J). (ps). 1990. 1.99 (*0-86696-238-7*) Binney & Smith.

— Quest for the Jungle City. (Crayola Color & Activity Ser.). (Illus.). 40p. (J). (gr. k up). 1990. 1.59 (*0-86696-245-X*) Binney & Smith.

— Quilts to Unusual Unicorns. (Crayola Encyclopedia of Coloring Fun Bks.). (Illus.). 40p. (Orig.). (J) (gr. k up). 1989. pap. 1.49 (*0-86696-229-8*) Binney & Smith.

— Search for the Sea Treasure. (Crayola Color & Activity Ser.). (Illus.). 40p. (J). (gr. k up). 1990. 1.59 (*0-86696-246-8*) Binney & Smith.

— Shapes. (Crayola Kinder Art BKs.). (Illus.). 12p. (Orig.). (J). (gr. 3-6). 1987. pap. 4.70 (*0-86696-202-6*) Binney & Smith.

— Silly People Mix-Ups. (Crayola Color & Activity Ser.). (Illus.). 32p. (J). (gr. k up). 1991. 1.49 (*0-86696-304-9*) Binney & Smith.

— Smiles, Giggles & Frowns. (Crayola So Big Bks.). (Illus.). 40p. (Orig.). (J). (ps up). 1989. pap. 1.99 (*0-86696-223-9*) Binney & Smith.

— So Big. (Crayola Crayons Ser.). (Illus.). 32p. (J). 1988. 2.70 (*0-86696-205-0*) Binney & Smith.

— Time. (Crayola Kinder Art BKs.). (Illus.). 12p. (Orig.). (J). (gr. 3-6). 1987. pap. 4.70 (*0-86696-207-7*) Binney & Smith.

— Tiny Town Tale. (Crayola Coloring Storybks.). (Illus.). 32p. (Orig.). (J). (ps). 1990. 1.99 (*0-86696-237-9*) Binney & Smith.

— Volcanoes to Zany Zebras. (Crayola Encyclopedia of Coloring Fun Bks.). (Illus.). 40p. (Orig.). (J). (gr. k up). 1989. pap. 1.49 (*0-86696-230-1*) Binney & Smith.

— Wacky Vehicle Mix-Ups. (Crayola Color & Activity Ser.). (Illus.). 32p. (J). (gr. k up). 1991. 1.49 (*0-86696-303-0*) Binney & Smith.

— Wild about Color. (Illus.). 40p. (J). (gr. k up). 1990. 1.99 (*0-86696-234-4*) Binney & Smith.

Carrie, Dennis. Precalculus. (C). 1990. pap. text 71.96 (*0-395-44464-0*); pap. text 3.96 (*0-395-53219-1*) HM.

— Precalculus. (C). 1990. pap. 2.76 (*0-395-44465-9*) HM.

— Precalculus. (C). 1990. pap. 5.16 (*0-395-52649-3*) HM.

Carrie, Doreen, jt. auth. see Comforti, Pat.

Carrie, Len E. S., et al. Understanding Anaesthesia. 3rd ed. LC 95-25188. 544p. 1996. pap. text 47.50 (*0-7506-2079-X*) Buttrwrth-Heinemann.

Carrie, Sean A., jt. auth. see Love-Eastham, Judith A.

Carrier. On Halloween. LC 98-74411. (Illus.). 40p. (YA). (ps-k). 1999. 7.95 (*0-694-01292-0*) HarpC Child Bks.

***Carrier.** Running after Antelope. 2000. 22.00 (*1-58243-111-6*, Pub. by Counterpt DC) HarpC.

Carrier. Ship & the Storm. (Illus.). 256p. 2000. pap. text 24.95 (*0-07-135526-X*) McGraw.

Carrier, et al. QRL Poetry Book Series. Vol. 36. 1997. pap. 12.00 (*1-888545-03-8*) Quarterly Rev.

Carrier, A. H. Structure & Process in a Melanesian Society: Ponam's Progress in the Twentieth Century. (Studies in Anthropology & History). xxii, 261p. 1991. text 77.00 (*3-7186-5149-1*, Harwood Acad Pubs) Gordon & Breach.

Carrier, Achsah H., jt. auth. see Carrier, James G.

Carrier Air Conditioning Co. Staff. Manual de Aire Acondicionado. (SPA.). 848p. 1977. 150.00 (*0-8288-5499-8*, S30875) Fr & Eur.

***Carrier, Arthur D.** The Beer-Barrel Waltz. 152p. 2000. 11.95 (*1-930498-01-2*) HedgehogCasino.

Carrier, Carol A., jt. ed. see Chapman, David W.

Carrier, Constance, tr. see Tibullus, Albius.

Carrier, David. The Aesthete in the City: The Philosophy & Practice of American Abstract Painting in the 1980s. (Illus.). 304p. (C). 1994. 47.50 (*0-271-00943-8*) Pa St U Pr.

— The Aesthetics of Comics. LC 99-17980. (Illus.). 152p. 2000. 45.00 (*0-271-01962-X*) Pa St U Pr.

— Artwriting. LC 86-24995. (Illus.). 176p. 1987. pap. 14.95 (*0-87023-562-1*) U of Mass Pr.

— High Art: Charles Baudelaire & the Origins of Modernist Painting. 224p. 1996. 45.00 (*0-271-01527-6*) Pa St U Pr.

— Poussin's Paintings: A Study in Art-Historical Methodology. (Illus.). 288p. 1993. 40.00 (*0-271-00816-4*) Pa St U Pr.

— Principles of Art History Writing. (Illus.). 264p. 1991. 35.00 (*0-271-00711-7*); pap. 18.95 (*0-271-00945-4*) Pa St U Pr.

— Robert Mangold: New Paintings. (Illus.). 42p. (Orig.). 1995. pap. write for info. (*1-878283-54-5*) PaceWildenstein.

— Warren Rohrer: New Painting. LC 93-79953. (Illus.). 36p. (Orig.). 1993. pap. text 20.00 (*1-879173-16-6*) Locks Gallery.

Carrier, David, comment. England & Its Aesthetes: Biography & Taste. (Critical Voices Ser.). 144p. (C). 1997. text 23.00 (*90-5701-211-1*); pap. text 18.00 (*90-5701-291-X*) Gordon & Breach.

Carrier, David & Tullis, Garner. Garner Tullis & the Art of Collaboration. (Illus.). 163p. 1998. 70.00 (*0-9630990-1-9*) G Tullis.

Carrier, David, jt. auth. see Roskill, Mark.

Carrier, David J. Industrial Restructuring, Financial Instability, & the Dynamics of the Postwar U. S. Economy. rev. ed. LC 96-49245. (Studies on Industrial Productivity). (Illus.). 240p. 1997. text 59.00 (*0-8153-2738-2*) Garland.

Carrier, Else H. Water & Grass: Study in the Pastoral Economy of Southern Europe. LC 77-87717. reprint ed. 49.50 (*0-404-16579-6*) AMS Pr.

Carrier, Franklin H. Begin to Keep Bees. (Illus.). 234p. 1981. text 20.75 (*0-9607550-0-4*) Carriers Bees.

— Behavior Traits of the Honeybee: Be As Smart As a Bee. large type ed. 73p. 1999. ring bd. 19.50 (*0-9607550-2-0*) Carriers Bees.

— Keeping Bees: A Handbook for the Hobbyist Beekeeper. (Illus.). (C). 1983. 22.50 (*0-9607550-1-2*) Carriers Bees.

— Tips & Tricks in Beekeeping. large type ed. 110p. 1999. ring bd. 22.50 (*0-9607550-3-9*) Carriers Bees.

Carrier, Fred. Ideas That Shaped the West & the Modern World. 2nd ed. 146p. (C). 1997. per. 23.95 (*0-7872-4236-5*, 41423601) Kendall-Hunt.

***Carrier, George B. & Christopherson, Dean.** Enforcing Security Interests in Personal Property - Action Guide - Fall 1999. Peyerwold, David, ed. 104p. 1999. ring bd. 58.00 (*0-7626-0366-6*, BU-11365) Cont Ed Bar-CA.

Carrier, George F. Partial Differential Equations. 2nd ed. 340p. 1988. text 48.00 (*0-12-160451-9*) Acad Pr.

Carrier, George F. & Pearson, Carl E. Ordinary Differential Equations. LC 91-2642. (Classics in Applied Mathematics Ser.: No. 6). x, 220p. 1991. pap. 34.50 (*0-89871-265-3*) Soc Indus-Appl Math.

Carrier, George F., et al. Functions of a Complex Variable: Theory & Technique. LC 83-80017. (C). 1983. reprint ed. text 34.95 (*0-9621973-0-0*) Hod Bks.

***Carrier, Helynn M., compiled by.** One Zumwalt Family: Many Descendants of the Eleven Children of Andrew Zumwalt & His Two Wives. LC 00-190740. 514p. 2000. pap. text 40.00 (*0-9607550-4-7*) Carriers Bees.

Carrier, Irene. James VI & I: King of Britain. (Topics in History Ser.). 160p. (C). 1998. pap. 17.95 (*0-521-49947-X*) Cambridge U Pr.

Carrier, James, ed. see Holenko, John & Ketchum, Hazel.

Carrier, James G. Gifts & Commodities: Exchange & Western Capitalism since 1700. LC 94-8920. 280p. (C). (gr. 13). 1995. 85.00 (*0-415-11752-6*, B4725) Routledge.

— Learning Disability: Social Class & the Construction of Inequality in American Education, 18. LC 86-400. (Contributions to the Study of Education Ser.: No. 18). 167p. 1986. 47.95 (*0-313-25396-X*, CLE/, Greenwood Pr) Greenwood.

Carrier, James G., ed. History & Tradition in Melanesian Anthropology. (Studies in Melanesian Anthropology: No. 10). (C). 1992. 48.00 (*0-520-07523-4*, Pub. by U CA Pr) Cal Prin Full Svc.

C

An Asterisk (*) at the beginning of an entry indicates that the title is appearing for the first time.

— Meanings of the Market. LC 97-202478. 1997. 55.00 (*1-85973-144-9*, Pub. by Berg Pubs); pap. 19.50 (*1-85973-149-X*, Pub. by Berg Pubs) NYU Pr.
— Occidentalism: Images of the West. 282p. 1995. pap. text 19.95 (*0-19-827979-5*) OUP.
Carrier, James G. & Carrier, Achsah H. Wage, Trade, & Exchange in Melanesia: A Manus Society in the Modern State. (Studies in Melanesian Anthropology). 160p. (C). 1989. 50.00 (*0-520-06389-9*, Pub. by U CA Pr) Cal Prin Full Svc.
Carrier, James G. & Miller, Daniel, eds. Virtualism: A New Political Economy. LC 99-178849. 256p. 1998. 55.00 (*1-85973-237-2*, Pub. by Berg Pubs); pap. 19.50 (*1-85973-242-9*, Pub. by Berg Pubs) NYU Pr.
Carrier, Jeffrey L. Jennifer Jones: A Bio-Bibliography, 11. LC 89-25834. (Bio-Bibliographies in the Performing Arts Ser.: No. 11). 155p. 1990. lib. bdg. 45.00 (*0-313-26651-4*, CJJ/, Greenwood Pr) Greenwood.
— Tallulah Bankhead: A Bio-Bibliography, 21. LC 91-24008. (Bio-Bibliographies in the Performing Arts Ser.: No. 21). 296p. 1991. lib. bdg. 49.95 (*0-313-27452-5*, CTB, Greenwood Pr) Greenwood.
Carrier, Jim. Letters from Yellowstone. 150p. 1987. 16.95 (*0-911797-37-8*); pap. 8.95 (*0-911797-38-6*) Roberts Rinehart.
— West of the Divide: Voices from a Ranch & Reservation. LC 91-58482. 192p. 1992. 19.95 (*1-55591-093-9*) Fulcrum Pub.
Carrier, Jim & Bekoff, Marc. Nature's Life Lessons: Everyday Truths from Nature. LC 95-49006. (Illus.). 112p. (Orig.). 1996. pap. 10.95 (*1-55591-248-6*) Fulcrum Pub.
Carrier, John. The Campaign for the Employment of Women As Police Officers. 275p. 1988. text 69.95 (*0-566-05486-8*, Pub. by Avebry) Ashgate Pub Co.
Carrier, John & Kendall, Ian. Health & the National Health Service. LC 97-18611. 420p. (C). 1997. pap. 34.95 (*0-485-80107-8*, Pub. by Athlone Pr) Transaction Pubs.
— Health & the National Health Service. LC 97-18611. 420p. (C). 1998. 90.00 (*0-485-80007-1*, Pub. by Athlone Pr) Transaction Pubs.
Carrier, John & Kendall, Ian, eds. Socialism & the NHS: Fabian Essays in Health Care. (Illus.). 120p. 1990. text 72.95 (*0-566-07110-X*, Pub. by Avebry) Ashgate Pub Co.
Carrier, John & Tomlinson, Dyland, eds. Asylum in the Community. LC 95-25158. 240p. (C). 1996. 80.00 (*0-415-10742-3*); pap. 27.99 (*0-415-10743-1*) Routledge.
Carrier, John V. I Hate Weddings: A Minister's & Couple's Guide to Sacred Weddings. 1993. pap. 8.95 (*1-55673-541-3*) CSS OH.
Carrier, Joseph. De los Otros: Intimacy & Homosexuality among Mexican Men. LC 95-6244. (Between Men - Between Women Ser.). (SPA.). 1995. 52.00 (*0-231-09692-5*); pap. 18.50 (*0-231-09693-3*) Col U Pr.
Carrier, Joseph R. Child Custody, Foster Care, & Adoptions. 372p. 1991. 37.00 (*0-669-27638-3*) Lxngtn Bks.
Carrier, Kimberli, jt. auth. see Goren, Ada H.
Carrier, Lark. A Christmas Promise. LC 86-12356. (Illus.). 36p. (J). (ps up). 1991. 15.95 (*0-88708-032-4*, Picture Book Studio) S&S Childrens.
— Do Not Touch. LC 87-32730. (Illus.). (J). (ps-12). 1991. pap. 15.95 (*0-88708-061-8*, Picture Book Studio) S&S Childrens.
— There Was a Hill . . . LC 84-25536. (Illus.). 40p. (J). (ps up). 1991. pap. 15.95 (*0-907234-70-4*, Picture Book Studio) S&S Childrens.
Carrier, Leonard S. Mortal Souls: A Neo-Aristotelian Theory of the Human Psyche. LC 95-53028. (San Francisco State University Series in Philosophy: Vol. 9). 1997. pap. write for info. (*0-8204-3111-7*) P Lang Pubng.
Carrier, Lois A. Illinois: Crossroads of a Continent. LC 92-31041. 296p. 1992. text 29.95 (*0-252-01991-1*) U of Ill Pr.
***Carrier, Lois A.** Illinois: Crossroads of a Continent. 296p. 1999. pap. text 19.95 (*0-252-06808-4*) U of Ill Pr.
Carrier, Lyman. Agriculture in Virginia, 1607-1699. LC S 0451.V8C37. (Jamestown 350th Anniversary Historical Booklet Ser.: No. 14). 43p. reprint ed. pap. 30.00 (*0-8357-5272-0*, 202622000048) Bks Demand.
— The Beginnings of Agriculture in America. 1976. lib. bdg. 59.95 (*0-8490-1485-9*) Gordon Pr.
Carrier, Martin. The Completeness of Scientific Theories: On the Derivation of Empirical Indicators Within a Theoretical Framework: The Case of Physical Geometry. LC 93-30527. (University of Western Ontario Series in Philosophy of Science). 296p. (C). 1993. lib. bdg. 164.50 (*0-7923-2475-7*, Pub. by Kluwer Academic) Kluwer Academic.
***Carrier, Martin, et al, eds.** Science at Century's End: Philosophical Questions on the Progress & Limits of Science. LC 99-50941. 384p. 2000. text 65.00 (*0-8229-4121-X*) U of Pittsburgh Pr.
Carrier, Martin & Machamer, Peter, eds. Mindscapes: Philosophy, Science, & the Mind. LC 98-116300. (Pittsburgh-Konstanz Series in the Philosophy & History of Science). 372p. (C). 1997. text 75.00 (*0-8229-3986-X*) U of Pittsburgh Pr.
Carrier, Martin & Mittelstrass, Juergen. Mind, Brain, Behavior: The Mind-Body Problem & the Philosophy of Psychology. x, 314p. (C). 1991. lib. bdg. 98.50 (*3-11-012876-4*, 159-91) De Gruyter.
— Mind, Brain, Behavior: The Mind-Body Problem & the Philosophy of Psychology. x, 314p. (C). 1995. pap. text 29.95 (*3-11-014954-0*) De Gruyter.
Carrier, Robert. Feasts of Provence. LC 92-85369. (Illus.). 224p. 1993. 40.00 (*0-8478-1661-3*, Pub. by Rizzoli Intl) St Martin.
— A Million Family Menus. 232p. 1996. 19.99 (*1-57215-194-3*, JG1194) World Pubns.
— A Taste of Morocco. 224p. 1997. pap. 19.95 (*0-7522-1039-4*, Pub. by Boxtree) Trafalgar.
Carrier, Roch. The Basketball Player. LC 96-60352. (Illus.). 24p. (J). (gr. 3 up). 1996. 15.95 (*0-88776-367-7*) Tundra Bks.
— Une Bonne et Heureuse Annee. LC 91-65366. (FRE., Illus.). 24p. (J). (gr. 3 up). 1991. 14.95 (*0-88776-268-9*) Tundra Bks.
— The Boxing Champion. LC 90-70133. Orig. Title: Un Champion. (Illus.). 24p. (J). (gr. 3 up). 1991. 15.95 (*0-88776-249-2*) Tundra Bks.
— The Boxing Champion. Orig. Title: Un Champion. (Illus.). 24p. (J). (gr. 3 up). 1993. pap. 7.95 (*0-88776-257-3*) Tundra Bks.
— Un Champion. LC 90-70134. (FRE., Illus.). 24p. (J). (gr. 3 up). 1991. 15.95 (*0-88776-250-6*) Tundra Bks.
— Un Champion. (FRE., Illus.). 24p. (YA). (gr. 3 up). 1996. pap. 7.95 (*0-88776-258-1*) Tundra Bks.
— Le Chandail de Hockey. (FRE., Illus.). 24p. (J). (gr. 1 up). 1985. 15.95 (*0-88776-171-2*); pap. 7.95 (*0-88776-176-3*) Tundra Bks.
— Floralie, Where Are You? Fischman, Sheila, tr. from FRE. 108p. (Orig.). 1971. pap. 6.95 (*0-88784-317-4*, Pub. by Hse of Anansi Pr) Genl Dist Srvs.
— The Garden of Delights. Fischman, Sheila, tr. from FRE. 173p. (Orig.). 1978. reprint ed. pap. 8.95 (*0-88784-066-3*, Pub. by Hse of Anansi Pr) Genl Dist Srvs.
— La Guerre, Yes Sir! Fischman, Sheila, tr. from FRE. (La Guerre Trilogy Ser.). 128p. 1970. reprint ed. pap. 8.95 (*0-88784-515-0*, Pub. by Hse of Anansi Pr) Genl Dist Srvs.
— A Happy New Year's Day. LC 91-65367. (Illus.). 24p. (J). (gr. 3 up). 1991. 14.95 (*0-88776-267-0*) Tundra Bks.
— The Hockey Sweater. Orig. Title: Le Chandail de Hockey. (Illus.). 24p. (J). (gr. 1 up). 1984. 15.95 (*0-88776-169-0*) Tundra Bks.
— The Hockey Sweater. Fischman, Sheila, tr. from FRE. Orig. Title: Le Chandail de Hockey. (Illus.). 24p. (J). (gr. 1 up). 1984. pap. 7.95 (*0-88776-174-7*) Tundra Bks.
— The Hockey Sweater: And Other Stories. Fischman, Sheila, tr. from FRE. (Illus.). 160p. 1979. pap. 11.95 (*0-88784-078-7*, Pub. by Hse of Anansi Pr) Genl Dist Srvs.
— El Jonron Mas Largo. Zeller, Beatriz, tr. LC 92-83961. (SPA., Illus.). 24p. (J). (gr. 3 up). 1993. 15.95 (*0-88776-304-9*) Tundra Bks.
— Le Joueur de Basket-ball. (FRE., Illus.). 24p. (J). 1996. 15.95 (*0-88776-368-5*) Tundra Bks.
— Lady with Chains. Fischman, Sheila, tr. from FRE. 151p. 1991. reprint ed. pap. 12.95 (*0-88784-511-8*, Pub. by Hse of Anansi Pr) Genl Dist Srvs.
— The Longest Home Run. Fischman, Sheila, tr. from FRE. LC 92-62364. Orig. Title: Le Plus Long Circuit. (Illus.). 24p. (J). (gr. 3 up). 1993. 15.95 (*0-88776-300-6*) Tundra Bks.
— Le Plus Long Circuit. LC 92-62362. (FRE., Illus.). 24p. (J). (gr. 2 up). 1993. 15.95 (*0-88776-301-4*) Tundra Bks.
— They Won't Demolish Me! Fischman, Sheila, tr. from FRE. 144p. 1974. reprint ed. pap. 7.95 (*0-88784-328-X*, Pub. by Hse of Anansi Pr) Genl Dist Srvs.
***Carrier, Roch & Fischman, Sheila.** Prayers of a Young Man. 192p. 1999. text. write for info. (*0-670-88587-8*) Studio Bks.
Carrier, S. G. Poetic Justice. 104p. 1999. pap. 11.00 (*0-8059-4637-3*) Dorrance.
***Carrier, Thomas J.** Historic Georgetown, DC: A Walking Tour. (Images of America Ser.). (Illus.). 128p. 1999. pap. 18.99 (*0-7385-0239-1*) Arcadia Publng.
Carrier, Thomas J. The Historic Walking Tour of Alexandria 1749. (Illus.). (Orig.). 1996. pap. 4.95 (*1-879295-15-6*) L B Prince.
***Carrier, Thomas J.** Washington, DC: A Historic Walking Tour. (Images of America Ser.). (Illus.). 128p. 1999. pap. 18.99 (*0-7385-0049-6*) Arcadia Publng.
— The White House, the Capitol & the Supreme Court: Historic Self-Guided Tours. (Images of America Ser.). (Illus.). 128p. 2000. pap. 18.99 (*0-7385-0557-9*) Arcadia Publng.
Carrier, Warren. Death of a Chancellor. large type ed. LC 94-1766. 274p. 1994. lib. bdg. 18.95 (*0-7862-0204-1*) Thorndike Pr.
— The Diver. (QRL Poetry Bks.: Vol. XXVI). 1986. 20.00 (*0-614-06414-7*) Quarterly Rev.
— An Honorable Spy. LC 92-83765. 248p. 1992. pap. 10.95 (*1-878044-11-7*) Mayhaven Pub.
— Murder at the Strawberry Festival. LC 93-77786. 295p. 1993. 19.95 (*1-878044-14-1*) Mayhaven Pub.
***Carrier, Warren.** Risking the Wind. LC 99-96301. (Illus.). 56p. 2000. pap. 13.50 (*0-913559-56-3*) Birch Brook Pr.
Carrier, Warren, et al. QRL Poetry Book Series, Vol. 36. 1997. 20.00 (*1-888545-02-X*) Quarterly Rev.
Carriera, Joanne, ed. see Clark, Gail I. & Boyer, William N.
Carriere, Albert. A Very Grammatical Family. 26p. 1940. pap. 3.50 (*0-87129-697-7*, V10) Dramatic Pub.
Carriere, Beate & Tanzberger, Renate. The Swiss Ball: Theory, Basic Exercises & Clinical Application. LC 97-36012. 1997. write for info. (*0-387-61144-4*) Spr-Verlag.
— The Swiss Ball: Theory, Basic Exercises & Clinical Application. LC 97-36012. xi, 300p. 1997. pap. write for info. (*3-540-61144-4*) Spr-Verlag.
Carriere, Fanie M., compiled by. Branch Genealogy. (Illus.). 60p. 1995. pap. 8.95 (*0-937242-16-0*) Scandia Pubs.
Carriere, G. Dictionary of Surface Active Agents, Cosmetics & Toiletries. (DUT, ENG, FRE, GER & ITA.). 198p. 1978. 127.50 (*0-444-99809-8*) Elsevier.
— Dictionary of Surface Active Agents, Cosmetics & Toiletries. (DUT, ENG, FRE, GER & ITA.). 198p. 1978. 175.00 (*0-8288-9220-2*, M15544) Fr & Eur.
— Lexicon of Detergents, Cosmetics & Toiletries. (DUT, ENG, FRE, GER & ITA.). 204p. 1966. 175.00 (*0-8288-9221-0*, M15543) Fr & Eur.
Carriere, Gaston. The Man Lowell Remembered: Andre Garin OMI, 1822-1895. Sawyer, Lucien, ed. & tr. by. from FRE. Orig. Title: L'Inoubliable Fondateur. (Illus.). vii, 107p. 1998. pap. 10.00 (*0-9665255-0-7*) Mssnry Oblates Mry Immac.
Carriere, Jose. Inverse Anchorage Technique in Fixed Orthodontic Treatment. (Illus.). 238p. 1991. text 95.00 (*0-86715-245-1*) Quint Pub Co.
Carriere, Joseph M. Tales from the French Folk-Lore of Missouri. LC 79-128989. (Northwestern University. Humanities Ser.: No. 1). reprint ed. 32.50 (*0-404-50701-8*) AMS Pr.
Carrieres, Joseph T. Mormon Controversies: A Balanced Approach. LC 88-90810. (Illus.). 156p. 1988. pap. 8.95 (*0-929251-00-8*) Sideris Pr.
***Carrieri.** Phenomena. 3rd ed. 2001. text. write for info. (*0-7216-8453-X*, W B Saunders Co) Harcrt Hlth Sci Grp.
Carrieri, et al. Pathophysiological Phenomena in Nursing: Human Responses to Illness. 2nd ed. (Illus.). 622p. (C). 1993. text 79.00 (*0-7216-3494-X*, W B Saunders Co) Harcrt Hlth Sci Grp.
***Carrieri, Joe R.** Joe Dimaggio - The Promise. (Illus.). 212p. 2000. 22.00 (*0-9644701-1-X*, Pub. by Carlyn Pubns) Bookazine Co Inc.
Carrieri, Joe R. Searching for Heroes Vol. 1: The Quest of a Yankee Batboy. (Illus.). 214p. 1998. 22.00 (*0-9644701-0-1*) Carlyn Pubns.
Carrieri, Joseph R. Foster Child: From Abandonment to Adoption, 1989. (Litigation & Administrative Practice Course Handbook, 1983-84 Ser.). 361p. 1989. 17.50 (*0-685-69438-0*) PLI.
Carriero, John. Descartes & the Autonomy of the Human Understanding. (Harvard Dissertations in Philosophy Ser.). 264p. 1990. reprint ed. text 10.00 (*0-8240-3184-9*) Garland.
Carriero, Nicholas & Gelernter, David. How to Write Parallel Programs: A First Course. 250p. 1990. 37.50 (*0-262-03171-X*) MIT Pr.
Carrig, Carol. The Re-Evaluation Counseling Community. 1972. pap. 2.00 (*0-911214-19-4*) Rational Isl.
Carrigan, Ana. The Palace of Justice: A Colombian Tragedy. LC 93-8704. (Illus.). 303p. 1993. 22.95 (*0-941423-82-4*) FWEW.
Carrigan, Andrew G. Sex Instructor, Retired. 18p. (Orig.). 1993. pap. 7.50 (*1-884763-02-2*) Ltd Mailing.
***Carrigan, Ann.** The Other Colombia: Conversations with Rebels, Warlords & Doves. (Open Media Pamphlet Ser.: Vol. 19). 80p. 2000. pap. 6.95 (*1-58322-043-7*, Pub. by Seven Stories) Publishers Group.
***Carrigan, Catherine.** Healing Depression: A Holistic Guide. LC 99-29136. 272p. 1999. pap. 15.95 (*1-56924-656-4*, Pub. by Marlowe & Co) Publishers Group.
Carrigan, Chris, ed. see Dickey, Terry.
Carrigan, Chris, ed. see Flanagan, Eileen & Scott, Jon.
Carrigan, Chris, ed. see Kindler, Herbert S. & Ginsburg, Marilyn.
Carrigan, Chris, ed. see Petrina, Bernard.
Carrigan, Christopher, ed. see Viale, J. David.
Carrigan, Henry, ed. see Lull, Ramon, pseud.
Carrigan, Henry L., Jr., ed. see Donne, John.
Carrigan, Henry L., Jr., ed. see Herbert, George.
Carrigan, Henry L., Jr., ed. see Mechthild of Magdeburg.
Carrigan, Henry L., Jr., ed. see St. Teresa of Avila.
Carrigan, J. A., ed. see DuPratz, M. L. & Fortier, Alcee.
Carrigan, J. A., ed. see Fortier, Alcee.
Carrigan, Jackie, jt. auth. see Bleakley, Ann.
Carrigan, Jo A. The Saffron Scourge: A History of Yellow Fever in Louisiana, 1796-1905. LC 93-73292. (Illus.). 480p. (C). 1993. 27.50 (*0-940984-86-5*) Univ LA Lafayette.
***Carrigan, Laura Ann Webb.** Best Friend's Guide to Getting Married. 2002. pap. write for info. (*0-06-039302-5*, ReganBks) HarperTrade.
Carrigan, Michael, jt. auth. see Walpole, Jeanne.
Carrigan, Nancy J., et al. Rabbinia Hopinska's Magic Music. 32p. (J). (gr. 2-5). 1998. pap. 6.95 (*1-890156-01-9*) Arbor Hill Pr.
Carrigan, R. & Ellison, J., eds. Relativistic Channeling. LC 87-7318. (NATO ASI Series B, Physics: Vol. 165). (Illus.). 538p. 1987. 120.00 (*0-306-42689-7*, Plenum Trade) Perseus Pubng.
Carrigan, Richard A., Jr. & Trower, W. Peter. Fundamental Particles & Forces. 227p. (C). 1989. pap. text 15.95 (*0-7167-2070-1*) W H Freeman.
Carrigan, Richard A., Jr. & Trower, W. Peter, eds. Particle Physics in the Cosmos. LC 88-32220. (Illus.). 228p. (C). 1989. pap. text 16.95 (*0-7167-1919-3*) W H Freeman.
Carrigg, Lise, et al. Girls on Film. LC 99-17079. (Illus.). 240p. (Orig.). 1999. pap. 13.95 (*0-06-095310-1*) HarpC.
***Carrighar, Sally.** Icebound Summer. LC 00-35836. (Illus.). 262p. 2000. pap. 18.95 (*1-58667-010-7*, Pub. by Derrydale Pr) Natl Bk Netwk.
Carriher, Shirley. Bakewise. write for info. (*0-688-16742-X*, Hearst) Hearst Commns.
Carriker, Kitti. Created in Our Image: The Miniature Body of the Doll As Subject & Object. LC 98-10777. 200p. 1998. 36.00 (*0-934223-54-8*) Lehigh Univ Pr.
Carriker, Robert C. Father Peter John de Smet: Jesuit in the West. LC 95-11891. (Oklahoma Western Biographies Ser.: Vol. 9). (Illus.). 288p. 1995. 26.95 (*0-8061-2750-3*) U of Okla Pr.
— Fort Supply, Indian Territory: Frontier Outpost on the Plains. LC 71-123345. (Illus.). 272p. 1990. pap. 13.95 (*0-8061-2790-2*) U of Okla Pr.
Carriker, Robert C., jt. auth. see Jesuits Staff.
Carriker, Robert C., jt. ed. see Lang, William L.
Carriker, S. David. North Carolina Railroads: The Common Carrier Railroads of North Carolina. 6th ed. 66p. 1998. pap. 20.00 (*0-936013-08-7*) Herit Pub NC.
— Railroading in the Carolina Sandhills, 5 vols. (Illus.). 812p. 1996. 140.00 (*0-936013-00-1*) Herit Pub NC.
— Railroading in the Carolina Sandhills Vol. 1: The 19th Century (1825-1900) (Illus.). 224p. 1985. 40.00 (*0-936013-01-X*) Herit Pub NC.
— Railroading in the Carolina Sandhills Vol. 2: The 20th Century (1900-1985) (Illus.). 272p. 1987. 40.00 (*0-936013-02-8*) Herit Pub NC.
— Railroading in the Carolina Sandhills Vol. 3: The Hoffman & Troy Railroad. (Illus.). 104p. 1992. pap. text 20.00 (*0-936013-03-6*) Herit Pub NC.
Carriker, S. David, ed. North Carolina Railroad Map: A History of North Carolina Railroads, 1830-1990. 6th rev. ed. (Illus.). 50p. (Orig.). 1998. pap. 20.00 (*0-936013-09-5*) Herit Pub NC.
— Railroading in the Carolina Sandhills Vol. 4: Sandhill Maps for Hiking & Study for North Carolina. (Illus.). 128p. 1992. pap. text 20.00 (*0-936013-04-4*) Herit Pub NC.
— Railroading in the Carolina Sandhills Vol. 5: Sandhill Maps for Hiking & Study for South Carolina. (Illus.). 84p. (Orig.). 1996. pap. text 20.00 (*0-936013-05-2*) Herit Pub NC.
Carril, Pete. The Smart Take from the Strong. LC 96-50904. 192p. 1997. 20.50 (*0-684-83510-X*) S&S Trade.
Carriles, Lazaro G., jt. auth. see Ronet, Jorge.
Carrill, John H., ed. see Douglas, Henry K.
Carrillo, Charles M. Hispanic New Mexican Pottery: Evidence of Craft Specialization 1790-1890. LC 97-70980. (Illus.). 288p. 1997. 37.95 (*0-9641542-3-4*); pap. 27.95 (*0-9641542-9-3*) LPD Pr.
Carrillo, Charles M., ed. see Salvador, Marilyn C., et al.
Carrillo, Fernando, jt. ed. see Jarquin, Edmundo.
Carrillo, Gilberto, ed. see International SAMPE Symposium & Exhibition Staff, et al.
Carrillo, Graciela. The Legend of Food Mountain (La Montana del Alimento) LC 81-71634. 24p. (J). (gr. k-8). 1982. 14.95 (*0-89239-022-0*) Childrens Book Pr.
Carrillo, Justo. A Cuba Le Toco Perder. LC 93-73083. (Coleccion Cuba y sus Jueces). (SPA., Illus.). 208p. (Orig.). 1993. pap. 19.00 (*0-89729-689-3*) Ediciones.
— Cuba, 1933: Students, Yankees, & Soldiers. LC 93-38233. (University of Miami North-South Center Ser.). 440p. (C). 1994. pap. 24.95 (*1-56000-690-0*, Pub. by U Miami N-S Ctr) L Rienner.
Carrillo, Louis. Oscar de la Renta. LC 95-19537. 48p. (J). (gr. 5-7). 1994. pap. 5.95 (*0-8114-9787-9*) Raintree Steck-V.
— Oscar de la Renta. (Contemporary Hispanic Americans Ser.). (Illus.). 48p. (J). (gr. 4-8). 1995. lib. bdg. 24.26 (*0-8172-3980-4*) Raintree Steck-V.
— Oscar de la Renta. large type ed. 54p. (J). (gr. 4-8). pap. 13.50 (*0-614-20573-5*, L-86297-00 APHB) Am Printing Hse.
Carrillo, Manuel J., et al. Pace-Forward: Policy Analytic & Computational Environment for Dutch Freight Transport. LC 96-37007. 72p. 1996. pap. 13.00 (*0-8330-2457-4*, MR-732/EAC/VW) Rand Corp.
Carrillo, Ricardo & Tello, Jerry, eds. Family Violence & Men of Color: Healing the Wounded Male Spirit. LC 97-51456. (Focus on Men Ser.). (Illus.). 8p. 1998. 43.95 (*0-8261-1173-4*) Springer Pub.
***Carrillo, Victor.** How to Kill a Marriage. 120p. 1999. pap. 12.95 (*0-7392-0469-6*, PO3785) Morris Pubng.
Carringer, Robert, jt. auth. see Allen, Nancy.
Carringer, Robert L. The Magnificent Ambersons: A Reconstruction. 318p. 1993. 42.50 (*0-520-07857-8*, Pub. by U CA Pr) Cal Prin Full Svc.
— The Making of Citizen Kane. rev. ed. LC 84-8777. 185p. (C). 1996. pap. 16.95 (*0-520-20567-7*, Pub. by U CA Pr) Cal Prin Full Svc.
Carrington. Introduction to Magnetic Resonance. 2nd ed. (Physics Ser.). Date not set. text 16.95 (*0-412-23830-6*) Chapman & Hall.
— Introduction to Magnetic Resonance. 2nd ed. (Physics Ser.). 1989. text 32.00 (*0-412-23820-9*) Chapman & Hall.
***Carrington, Arthur V., ed.** Human Rights: A Bibliography. 265p. 2000. lib. bdg. 49.00 (*1-56072-830-2*) Nova Sci Pubs.
Carrington, Betty. Judicial Carousel. LC 99-226702. 315p. (Orig.). 1996. pap. 18.95 (*0-9655838-0-5*) B Carrington.
Carrington, Bruce, jt. auth. see Troyna, Barry.
Carrington, Charles. Soldier from the Wars Returning. (Modern Revivals in Military History Ser.). 287p. 1992. 56.95 (*0-7512-0031-X*, Pub. by Gregg Revivals) Ashgate Pub Co.
Carrington, Charles E. An Exposition of Empire. LC 75-41051. (BCL Ser. II). reprint ed. 29.50 (*0-404-14650-3*) AMS Pr.
— A Subaltern's War: Being a Memoir of the Great War from the Point of View of a Romantic Young Man. LC 72-4273. (World Affairs Ser.: National & International Viewpoints). (Illus.). 236p. 1972. reprint ed. 23.95 (*0-405-04562-X*) Ayer.
***Carrington, Christopher.** No Place Like Home. 1998. pap. 17.00 (*0-226-09486-3*) U Ch Pr.
Carrington, Christopher. No Place Like Home: Domesticity, Family Life & Lesbian & Gay Relationships. LC 99-19780. (Worlds of Desire Ser.). 275p. 2000. 27.50 (*0-226-09485-5*) U Ch Pr.

C

Carrington, David K. & Stephenson, Richard W. Map Collections in the United States & Canada: A Directory. 3rd ed. LC 77-26685. 240p. 1978. reprint ed. pap. 74.40 (*0-608-14562-9*, 202496000040) Bks Demand.

Carrington, Delores, ed. see Haddock, Durwood & Miller, Ron.

Carrington, Dorothy. Granite Island. pap. 17.95 (*0-14-009524-1*, Pub. by Pnguin Bks Ltd) Trafalgar.

Carrington, Evelyn M., ed. Women in Early Texas. LC 94-21170. (Fred H. & Ella Mae Moore Texas History Reprint Ser.). (Illus.). 348p. 1994. pap. 19.95 (*0-87611-142-8*) Tex St Hist Assn.

Carrington, Fitzroy, ed. The Quiet Hour. LC 71-160901. (Granger Index Reprint Ser.). 1977. reprint ed. 19.95 (*0-8369-6264-8*) Ayer.

Carrington, FitzRoy, ed. The Quiet Hour. LC 78-74813. (Granger Poetry Library). (Illus.). 1979. reprint ed. 20.00 (*0-89609-131-7*) Roth Pub Inc.

Carrington, Frances C. My Army Life. LC 72-150173. (Select Bibliographies Reprint Ser.). 1977. 27.95 (*0-8369-5686-9*) Ayer.

Carrington, Gerald. Basic Thermodynamics. LC 93-34952. (Illus.). 396p. (C). 1994. text 67.95 (*0-19-851748-3*); pap. text 41.95 (*0-19-851747-5*) OUP.

Carrington, H. Death Deferred: How to Prolong Life & Postpone Death. 1991. lib. bdg. 250.00 (*0-87700-945-7*) Revisionist Pr.

Carrington, Henry B. Battle Maps & Charts of the American Revolution. LC 74-8018. 96p. 1974. reprint ed. 38.95 (*0-405-05540-4*) Ayer.

— Battles of the American Revolution. (American Revolution Ser.: Vol. 3). (Illus.). 370p. 1997. 25.95 (*1-58057-046-1*, BREV001B) Digital Antiq.

— Battles of the American Revolution, 1775-1781: Historical & Military Criticism, 2 vols., 1 bk. (Eyewitness Accounts of the American Revolution Ser.). 1968. 31.95 (*0-405-01107-5*) Ayer.

— Beacon Lights of Patriotism. LC 74-133068. (Granger Index Reprint Ser.). 1977. 25.95 (*0-8369-6196-X*) Ayer.

— The Indian Question. (Illus.). 1985. 16.95 (*0-914074-04-0*, J M C & Co) Amereon Ltd.

Carrington, Hereward. Death: The Causes & Phenomena with Special Reference to Immortality. Kastenbaum, Robert J., ed. LC 76-19563. (Death & Dying Ser.). 1977. lib. bdg. 30.95 (*0-405-09559-7*) Ayer.

— Death Deferred: How to Live Long & Happily, Defer Death, & Lose All Fear of It. 262p. 1993. reprint ed. spiral bd. 19.50 (*0-7873-0154-X*) Hlth Research.

— Death Deferred: How to Live Long & Happily, Defer Death, & Lose All Fear of It. 262p. 1996. reprint ed. pap. 18.95 (*1-56459-924-8*) Kessinger Pub.

— Fasting for Health & Long Life. 152p. 1996. pap. 14.00 (*0-7873-0156-6*) Hlth Research.

— The Hygienic Way of Life. 75p. 1996. reprint ed. spiral bd. 12.00 (*0-7873-0155-8*) Hlth Research.

— Laboratory Investigations into Psychic Phenomena. LC 75-7370. (Perspectives in Psychical Research Ser.). (Illus.). 1975. reprint ed. 23.95 (*0-405-07021-7*) Ayer.

— Loaves & Fishes: A Study of the Miracles, of the Resurrection, & of the Future Life in the Light of Modern Psychic Knowledge (1935) 260p. 1998. reprint ed. pap. 24.95 (*0-7661-0315-3*) Kessinger Pub.

— The Natural Food of Man. 286p. 1996. reprint ed. spiral bd. 20.00 (*0-7873-0153-1*) Hlth Research.

— The Natural Food of Man: Being an Attempt to Prove That the Original, Best, & Natural Diet of Man Is Fruits & Nuts. 286p. 1996. reprint ed. pap. 18.95 (*1-56459-683-4*) Kessinger Pub.

— Physical Phenomena of Spiritualism Fraudulent & Genuine (1920) 462p. 1998. reprint ed. pap. 29.95 (*0-7661-0512-1*) Kessinger Pub.

— Problems of Psychical Research & Theories in the Realm of the Supernormal (1921) 314p. 1998. reprint ed. pap. 24.95 (*0-7661-0528-8*) Kessinger Pub.

— Psychic Science & Survival. 90p. 1993. reprint ed. spiral bd. 10.50 (*0-7873-0152-3*) Hlth Research.

— Psychic Science & Survival: An Essay in Psychical Research. 90p. 1996. reprint ed. pap. 8.95 (*1-56459-702-4*) Kessinger Pub.

— The Story of Psychic Science (Psychical Research) 400p. 1992. reprint ed. pap. 35.00 (*1-56459-259-6*) Kessinger Pub.

— Vitality, Fasting & Nutrition. 648p. 1996. reprint ed. pap. 34.50 (*0-7873-0151-5*) Hlth Research.

— Vitality, Fasting & Nutrition. 690p. 1996. reprint ed. pap. 32.50 (*1-56459-915-9*) Kessinger Pub.

— Your Psychic Powers & How to Develop Them. (Occult Ser.). 390p. 1975. pap. 12.95 (*0-87877-033-X*, P-33) Newcastle Pub.

— Your Psychic Powers & How to Develop Them. 358p. 1996. reprint ed. spiral bd. 17.50 (*0-7873-0157-4*) Hlth Research.

— Your Psychic Powers & How to Develop Them (1920) 358p. 1996. reprint ed. pap. 16.95 (*1-56459-939-6*) Kessinger Pub.

Carrington, Hereward & Shelton, Herbert M. History of Natural Hygiene: The (Plus) Principles of Natural Hygiene. 95p. 1996. reprint ed. spiral bd. 10.00 (*0-7873-0158-2*) Hlth Research.

Carrington, Hereward, jt. auth. see Buckland, Raymond.

Carrington, Hereward, jt. auth. see Ernst, Bernard M.

Carrington, Hereward, jt. auth. see Muldoon, Sylvan.

Carrington, Hereward, jt. auth. see Muldoon, Sylvan J.

Carrington, Hereward, jt. auth. see Sweet, Marie P.

Carrington, Ildiko De Papp, see De Papp Carrington, Ildiko.

Carrington, Jackie. Romantic Wedding Destinations: Getaways in Hawaii. 3rd large type rev. ed. LC 97-70261. (Illus.). 44p. 1997. spiral bd. 14.95 (*1-888759-13-5*) Innovanna Pub Co Inc.

— Romantic Wedding Destinations: Getaways in the Caribbean. 3rd large type rev. ed. LC 97-70260. (Illus.). 76p. (Orig.). 1997. spiral bd. 19.95 (*1-888759-14-3*) Innovanna Pub Co Inc.

— Romantic Wedding Destinations: Guide to Wedding & Honeymoon Getaways Around the World. 2nd rev. ed. LC 96-76479. (Illus.). 154p. 1996. pap. 24.95 (*1-888759-11-9*) Innovanna Pub Co Inc.

— Romantic Wedding Destinations: Guide to Wedding & Honeymoon Getaways Around the World. 3rd large type rev. ed. LC 97-70259. (Illus.). 206p. 1997. pap. 24.95 (*1-888759-12-7*) Innovanna Pub Co Inc.

Carrington, John C. & Edwards, George T. Financing Industrial Investment. LC 78-65708. 299p. 1979. 75.00 (*0-275-90339-7*, C0339, Praeger Pubs) Greenwood.

Carrington, John F. Talking Drums of Africa. (Illus.). 96p. 1949. 15.00 (*0-317-00316-X*) G Vanderstoel.

— Talking Drums of Africa. LC 70-77195. (Illus.). 96p. 1969. reprint ed. lib. bdg. 35.00 (*0-8371-1292-3*, CDA&) Greenwood.

Carrington, Kerry. Offending Girls: Sex, Youth & Justice. 208p. 1994. pap. 21.95 (*1-86373-523-2*, Pub. by Allen & Unwin Pty) Paul & Co Pubs.

Carrington, L., intro. Fifteenth Century Illustrated Chinese Primer: Hsin-pien Tui-hsiang Szu Yen. 63p. (C). 1990. pap. text 17.95 (*962-209-256-X*, Pub. by HK Univ Pr) Coronet Bks.

Carrington, Lawarence D., ed. Dictionary of St. Lucian Creole, 2 pts. LC 92-10018. (Trends in Linguistics, Documentation Ser.: Vol. 7). xi, 626p. (C). 1992. lib. bdg. 229.25 (*3-11-012625-7*) Mouton.

Carrington, Leonora. Down Below. (Illus.). 56p. 1982. pap. 14.00 (*0-941194-17-5*) Black Swan Pr.

— The Hearing Trumpet. (Illus.). 240p. 1996. pap. 15.95 (*1-878972-19-7*) Exact Change.

Carrington, Lucinda. A Dangerous Game. 1999. mass mkt. 6.95 (*0-352-33432-0*) London Brdge.

— A Dangerous Lady. 1998. mass mkt. 5.95 (*0-352-33236-0*, Pub. by BLA4) London Brdge.

— The Master of Shilden. 256p. (Orig.). 1997. mass mkt. 5.95 (*0-352-33140-2*, Pub. by BLA4) London Brdge.

— The Ninety Days of Genevieve. (Black Lace Ser.). 288p. (Orig.). 1996. mass mkt. 5.95 (*0-352-33070-8*, Pub. by Virgin Bks) London Brdge.

Carrington, Margaret I. Absaraka: Home of the Crows. LC 83-6951. (Illus.). iv, 284p. 1983. reprint ed. pap. 12.00 (*0-8032-6315-5*, Bison Books) U of Nebr Pr.

Carrington, Mark & Languuth, Phillip. The Banking Revolution: Salvation or Slaughter? Unlocking the Real Role of Technology in Delivering Value. 1997. 104.50 (*0-273-63055-5*, Pub. by Pitman Pub) Trans-Atl Phila.

Carrington, Neville. A Fishkeeper's Guide to the Healthy Aquarium. rev. ed. 117p. 1991. 10.95 (*1-56465-161-4*, 16065) Tetra Pr.

— Mantenimiento Delacuario: Healthy Aquarium. (SPA.). 1995. 11.95 (*1-56465-180-0*) Tetra Pr.

Carrington, Neville, jt. auth. see Andrews, Chris.

Carrington, Norman. Shaw's Pygmalion. (Brodie's Notes Ser.). 70p. (Orig.). 1976. pap. 5.95 (*0-333-58194-6*, Pub. by Macmillan) Trans-Atl Phila.

Carrington, Norman T. George Bernard Shaw's Arms & the Man. rev. ed. (Brodie's Notes Ser.). 61p. 1993. pap. 5.95 (*0-333-58195-4*, Pub. by Macmillan) Trans-Atl Phila.

Carrington, Patricia. Book of Meditation: The Complete Guide to Modern Meditation. LC 98-9615. 1998. pap. 19.95 (*1-86204-236-5*, Pub. by Element MA) Penguin Putnam.

— Learn to Meditate Kit: The Complete Course in Modern Meditation. 128p. 1998. 39.95 (*1-86204-191-1*, Pub. by Element MA) Penguin Putnam.

— The Power of Letting Go: A Practical Approach to Releasing the Pressures in Your Life. LC 98-46434. 1999. pap. 14.95 (*1-86204-329-9*, Pub. by Element MA) Penguin Putnam.

Carrington, Paul. Stewards of Democracy: Law as Public Profession. LC 99-20269. (New Perspectives on Law, Culture & Society Ser.). 320p. 1999. 32.00 (*0-8133-6832-4*, Pub. by Westview) HarpC.

Carrington, Paul & Babcock, Barbara A. Civil Procedure: Cases & Comments on the Process of Adjudication. 3rd ed. 1250p. (C). 1983. 48.00 (*0-316-12988-7*, Aspen Law & Bus) Aspen Pub.

— Civil Procedure: Statutes & Rules the Court. 2nd ed. (C). 1983. pap. 20.00 (*0-316-12974-7*, Aspen Law & Bus) Aspen Pub.

Carrington, Peter L. Reflecting on Things Past. 1989. write for info. (*0-318-64757-5*) HM.

Carrington, Raye. Pearl Lakes Trout Club, Inc. A History. (Orig.). 1990. 25.00 (*0-9627071-0-4*) Kitty Creek.

Carrington, Raye, intro. Hooked: Funny Quotes from Serious Anglers. (Orig.). 1994. pap. 9.95 (*0-9627071-1-2*) Kitty Creek.

Carrington, Roslyn. Thirst for Rain, 1. 208p. 1999. text 22.00 (*1-57566-446-1*) Kensgtn Pub Corp.

***Carrington, Roslyn.** Thirst for Rain. 2000. pap. 12.00 (*1-57566-575-1*, Knsington) Kensgtn Pub Corp.

***Carrington, Ruth.** Dead Fish. 1998. pap. text 11.95 (*1-85702-877-5*, Pub. by Fourth Estate) Trafalgar.

— Dead Fish. large type ed. 368p. 1999. 31.99 (*0-7089-4057-9*) Ulverscroft.

Carrington, Selwyn H. H., jt. ed. see Cateau, Heather.

Carrington, Tori. Constant Craving. 1998. per. 3.75 (*0-373-25816-X*, 1-25816-9, Mira Bks) Harlequin Bks.

***Carrington, Tori.** For Her Eyes Only: The Magnificent McCoy Men, Vol. 789. (Temptation Ser.). 2000. mass mkt. 3.99 (*0-373-25889-5*, 1-25889-6) Harlequin Bks.

— Just Eight Months Old... (Special Edition Ser.: Bk. 1362). 2000. mass mkt. 4.50 (*0-373-24362-6*, 1-24362-5) Silhouette.

Carrington, Tori. License to Thrill: The Magnificent McCoy Men. (Temptation Ser.: Bk. 740). 1999. per. 3.75 (*0-373-25840-2*, 1-25840-9) Harlequin Bks.

***Carrington, Tori.** P. I. Who Loved Her. (Temptation Ser.: Vol. 776). 2000. per. 3.99 (*0-373-25876-3*) Harlequin Bks.

Carrington, Ulrich S. The Making of an American: An Adaptation of Memorable Tales by Charles Sealsfield. LC 74-77736. (Bicentennial Series in American Studies: No. 2). 223p. reprint ed. pap. 69.20 (*0-8357-8942-X*, 203343800086) Bks Demand.

Carrington, Vivian. Treasures of Inspiration. 70p. (Orig.). 1992. pap. 5.00 (*0-9628859-0-8*) V Carrington.

Carrington, W. G., ed. see Jarnigan, Jan G.

Carrington, W. G., ed. see Mountain, Rick.

***Carrington, Walter.** The Act of Living: Talks on the Alexander Technique. Sontag, Jerry, ed. 186p. 1999. 26.00 (*0-9644352-3-3*) Mornum Time.

Carrington, Walter. Thinking Aloud: Talks on Teaching the Alexander Technique. 176p. 1994. text 22.00 (*0-9644352-0-9*) Mornum Time.

Carrington, William C., ed. see Barnes, Nigel.

Carrington, William G. Tomorrow's Promise & Other Poems: Pieces of One Man's Heart. 2nd rev. ed. McKee, Sue, ed. LC 95-95350. 84p. (Orig.). 1995. pap. 9.95 (*1-888701-00-5*) Jarrett Pr.

— Tomorrow's Promise & Other Poems: Pieces of One Man's Heart. 2nd rev. ed. McKee, Sue, ed. LC 98-65112. 90p. (Orig.). 1998. pap. 11.95 (*1-888701-07-2*) Jarrett Pr.

Carrington, William G., ed. see Boylston, Raymond P., Jr.

Carrington, William G., ed. see Fortune, Gwen Y.

***Carrington, William Graham.** Cowboys with Chrome Horses: A Historical Explanation of America's Most Popular & Unique Phenomenon. LC 96-95508. 224p. 1999. pap. 14.95 (*1-888701-02-1*) Jarrett Pr.

Carrington-Windo, Tristam & Kohl, Katrin M. A Dictionary of Contemporary Germany. 456p. 1999. 60.00 (*1-57958-114-5*) Fitzroy Dearborn.

***Carrino, Deborah, compiled by.** The Spirit of Children: The Art & Life of Karen Carrino. (Illus.). 176p. 2000. 29.00 (*1-57392-811-9*) Prometheus Bks.

Carrino, Frank, jt. auth. see Robinson, Jerry.

Carrino, Frank G., ed. see Hernandez, Jose.

Carrino, Frank G., ed. see Hernandez, Jose, et al.

Carrino, Frank G., tr. see Hernandez, Jose.

Carrino, Michael. Some Rescues. 80p. 1994. 10.00 (*0-932616-48-8*) Brick Hse Bks.

— Under This Combustible Sky: Poems. LC 98-50955. 78p. 1999. pap. text 14.95 (*0-7734-3122-5*) E Mellen.

Carrio, Alejandro D. The Criminal Justice System of Argentina: (An Overview for American Readers) 216p. (Orig.). 1989. pap. 9.00 (*0-940448-18-1*) LSU Law Pubns.

Carrio, Genaro R., tr. see Silving, Helen.

Carrion, Antonio. The Great Seventh Number: Surviving Y2K & the New Millennium. 214p. 1999. pap. 12.95 (*0-9663101-1-X*) Carre Corp.

Carrion, Arturo M. Puerto Rico: A Political & Cultural History. (Illus.). 400p. (C). 1984. reprint ed. pap. text 18.25 (*0-393-30193-1*) Norton.

— Puerto Rico & the Non-Hispanic Caribbean: A Study in the Decline of Spanish Exclusivism. 160p. (C). 1974. pap. 2.50 (*0-8477-0835-7*) U of PR Pr.

Carrion, Beatriz L. Merino, see Garcia Cook, Angel & Merino Carrion, Beatriz L., compiled by.

Carrion de Fierro, Fanny. Where Light Was Born: Selected Poems by Fanny Cariron de Fierro. Bell, Sally C., tr. from SPA. 64p. 1999. pap. 14.95 (*1-882063-47-3*, Heritage Hse) Cottage Pr MA.

Carrion De Los Condes, Santob De, see De Carrion De Los Condes, Santob.

Carrion, Juan M., et al, eds. La Nacion Puertorriquena: Ensayos en Torno a Pedro Albizu Campos. (SPA.). 284p. 1993. pap. 12.50 (*0-8477-0203-0*) U of PR Pr.

Carrion, Philip. Inverse Problems & Tomography in Acoustics & Seismology. 1987. write for info. (*0-944573-00-2*) Penn Pub.

Carrion, Ramon. Guia de Inmigracion a Estados Unidos. 2nd ed. (Legal Survival Guides Ser.). (SPA.). 272p. 1999. pap. 19.95 (*1-57248-087-4*, Sphinx Pubng) Sourcebks.

— How to Attract (& Keep) the Foreign Buyer. 150p. 1995. write for info. (*0-937387-11-8*) Am Advisory.

— How to Get a Visa to the U. S. A. LC 86-70468. (Orig.). 1990. pap. 14.95 (*0-937387-00-2*) Am Advisory.

— Immigration & Visas to the U. S. A. 229p. 1995. 49.95 (*0-937387-10-X*) Am Advisory.

— U. S. A. Immigration Guide. 3rd ed. LC 98-16376. (Legal Survival Guides Ser.). 144p. 1998. pap. 19.95 (*1-57071-354-5*) Sourcebks.

Carris, Bill & Wolfe, Bob. Inside Commodore 64 BASIC. (Illus.). 192p. 12.95 (*0-317-13066-8*) P-H.

Carris, Joan. Hedgehogs in the Closet. LC 87-45309. (Illus.). 160p. (J). (gr. 5 up). 1988. 11.95 (*0-397-32233-X*); lib. bdg. 13.89 (*0-397-32234-8*) HarpC Child Bks.

***Carris, Joan.** Panic Plan for the SAT 2001. 4th ed. 314p. 2000. pap. text 9.95 (*0-7689-0503-6*) Petersons.

Carris, Joan. Pets, Vets, & Marty Howard. LC 84-47635. (Illus.). 192p. (J). (gr. 5 up). 1984. lib. bdg. 12.89 (*0-397-32093-0*) HarpC Child Bks.

— Rusty Timmons' First Million. LC 85-40096. (Illus.). 192p. (J). (gr. 5-9). 1985. 11.95 (*0-397-32154-6*) HarpC Child Bks.

***Carris, Joan.** SAT Word Flash 2001. 3rd ed. 147p. 2000. pap. 9.95 (*0-7689-0505-2*) Petersons.

Carris, Joan. Success with Words. 3rd ed. LC 98-5177. 390p. 1998. pap. text 11.95 (*0-7689-0049-2*) Petersons.

— When the Boys Ran the House. LC 82-47762. (Illus.). 160p. (J). (gr. 4-7). 1982. 12.95 (*0-397-32019-1*); lib. bdg. 12.89 (*0-397-32020-5*) HarpC Child Bks.

— Witch-Cat. LC 83-48448. (Illus.). 160p. (J). (gr. 5 up). 1984. lib. bdg. 11.89 (*0-397-32068-X*) HarpC Child Bks.

Carris, Joan & Crystal, Michael R. SAT Success: 1999 Edition. 6th ed. (Peterson's Test Success Ser.). (Illus.). 522p. 1998. pap. 14.95 incl. cd-rom (*0-7689-0014-X*) Petersons.

***Carris, Joan & Crystal, Michael R.** SAT Success 2001. 7th ed. 520p. 2000. pap. 16.95 (*0-7689-0417-X*) Petersons.

Carris, Joan D. Aunt Morbelia & the Screaming Skulls. (J). 1990. 8.09 (*0-606-02209-0*, Pub. by Turtleback) Demco.

— Just a Little Ham. MacDonald, Pat, ed. (Illus.). 144p. (J). (gr. 4-7). 1993. reprint ed. pap. 3.99 (*0-671-74783-5*, Minstrel Bks) PB.

— Panic Plan for the SAT. 3rd ed. LC 98-8129. 224p. 1998. pap. text 9.95 (*1-56079-848-3*) Petersons.

— Peterson's SAT Word Flash: Build Your Vocabulary in 30 Quick & Easy Lessons. 2nd rev. ed. Moscowitz, Mark, ed. LC 97-8917. 208p. (YA). 1997. pap. 8.95 (*1-56079-850-5*) Petersons.

— SAT Word Flash: The Quick Way to Build Verbal Power for the New SAT - & Beyond. LC 93-27328. 144p. (Orig.). 1993. pap. 7.95 (*1-56079-320-1*) Petersons.

Carris, Joan D. & Ordovensky, Pat. Success with Words: An Easy-to-Use Step-by-Step System That Gives You a More Powerful Vocabulary. 2nd ed. LC 87-29202. 390p. (Orig.). Date not set. pap. 11.95 (*1-56079-452-6*) Petersons.

Carris, Joan D., et al. SAT Success. 4th ed. LC 94-2714. 474p. 1994. pap. 12.95 (*1-56079-393-7*) Petersons.

— SAT Success. 4th rev. ed. LC 94-2714. 474p. 1994. pap. 18.95 incl. disk (*1-56079-469-0*) Petersons.

— SAT Success. 5th rev. ed. LC 96-25401. (Test Success Ser.). 512p. 1996. pap. 24.95 incl. disk (*1-56079-606-5*) Petersons.

Carris, Lori M., jt. ed. see Redlin, Scott C.

Carrison, Dan & Walsh, Rod. Semper Fi: Business Leadership the Marine Corps Way. LC 98-28370. 208p. 1998. 32.95 (*0-8144-0413-8*) AMACOM.

Carrison, Muriel P. Cambodian Folk Stories: From the Gatiloke. 140p. 1993. pap. 12.95 (*0-8048-1905-X*) Tuttle Pubng.

Carrithers, David W., ed. see De Montesquieu, Charles-Louis.

Carrithers, Gale H. Donne at Sermons: A Christian Existential World. LC 74-171183. 319p. (C). 1972. text 27.50 (*0-87395-122-0*) State U NY Pr.

— Mumford, Tate, Eiseley: Watchers in the Night. LC 91-11860. 257p. 1991. text 37.50 (*0-8071-1650-5*) La State U Pr.

Carrithers, Gale H., Jr. & Hardy, James D., Jr. Milton & the Hermeneutics Journey. LC 94-6781. 264p. 1994. text 37.50 (*0-8071-1876-1*) La State U Pr.

Carrithers, Gale H., Jr. & Hardy, Thomas D., Jr. Age of Iron: English Renaissance Tropologies of Love & Power. LC 98-13800. (Illus.). 344p. 1998. text 55.00 (*0-8071-2246-7*) La State U Pr.

Carrithers, Michael. The Buddha. LC 83-8004. (Past Masters Ser.). 112p. 1984. pap. text 9.95 (*0-19-287589-2*) OUP.

Carrithers, Michael, ed. Why Humans Have Cultures: Explaining Anthropology & Social Diversity. 228p. 1992. pap. text 17.95 (*0-19-289211-8*) OUP.

Carrithers, Michael, et al, eds. The Category of the Person. 319p. 1985. text 64.95 (*0-521-25909-6*); pap. text 23.95 (*0-521-27757-4*) Cambridge U Pr.

Carrithers, Russell L. The Making of God's Little Barber & Life in the Barber Shop. Rodman, John S., ed. (Illus.). 303p. 1998. pap. 12.95 (*0-9664085-0-0*) Barber-Shop.

Carritt, Edgar F. Ethical & Political Thinking. LC 73-3020. 186p. 1973. reprint ed. lib. bdg. 55.00 (*0-8371-6826-0*, CAET, Greenwood Pr) Greenwood.

Carritt, Edgar F., ed. Philosophies of Beauty, from Socrates to Robert Bridges. LC 76-5885. 334p. 1976. reprint ed. lib. bdg. 60.00 (*0-8371-8812-1*, CAPB, Greenwood Pr) Greenwood.

Carriuolo, Nancy, ed. School-College Collaboration: A Way of Redesigning the Educational Pipeline. (Freshman Year Experience Monograph: No. 16). 172p. (Orig.). 1996. pap. 35.00 (*1-889271-13-6*) Nat Res Ctr.

Carriveau, Gary W. & Chong, Dianne, eds. Nondestructive Evaluation Applied to Process Control of Composite Fabrication: Conference Proceedings. (Illus.). vi, 273p. (Orig.). 1994. pap. 50.00 (*1-890596-01-9*) TX Res Inst.

***Carrizales, Leonardo Martinez.** Juan Rulfo: Los Caminos de la Fama Publica. 1998. pap. 129.99 (*968-16-5161-8*) Fondo CA.

Carro, Daniel, et al, eds. Exodo. (Comentario Biblico Mundo Hispano Ser.: Vol. 2).Tr. of Exodus. (SPA.). 267p. 1993. pap. 8.50 (*0-311-03102-1*, Edit Mundo) Casa Bautista.

— Galatas, Colosenses y Filemon. (Comentario Biblico Mundo Hispano Ser.: Vol. 21).Tr. of Galatians, Collossians & Philemon. (SPA.). 338p. 1995. pap. 10.50 (*0-311-03121-8*, Edit Mundo) Casa Bautista.

Carro, Daniel, et al, eds. Genesis: Genesis. (Comentario Biblico Mundo Hispano Ser.: Vol. 1). (SPA.). 272p. 1994. pap. 8.99 (*0-311-03101-3*, Edit Mundo) Casa Bautista.

Carro, Daniel, et al, eds. Hechos. (Comentario Biblico Mundo Hispano Ser.: Vol. 18).Tr. of Acts. (SPA.). 237p. (Orig.). 1994. pap. 8.00 (*0-311-03118-8*, Edit Mundo) Casa Bautista.

— Isaias. (Comentario Biblico Mundo Hispano Ser.: Vol. 10).Tr. of Isaiah. (SPA.). 272p. 1993. pap. 8.50 (*0-311-03110-2*, Edit Mundo) Casa Bautista.

— 1 Samuel, 2 Samuel & 1 Cronras. (Comentario Biblico

C

Mundo Hispano Ser.: Vol. 5).Tr. of Samuel & I Chronicles. (SPA.). 440p. 1997. pap. text 13.50 (*0-311-03105-6*, Edit Mundo) Casa Bautista.

Carro, Daniel, et al, eds. Proverbios y Cantares. (Comentario Biblico Mundo Hispano Ser.).Tr. of Proverbs & Chants. (SPA.). 374p. (Orig.). 1995. pap. 8.99 (*0-311-03109-9*, Edit Mundo) Casa Bautista.

Carro, Daniel & Wilson, Richard F., eds. Contemporary Gospel Accents: Doing Theology in Africa, Asia, Southeast Asia, & Latin America. LC 96-32798. 192p. 1997. text 21.95 (*0-86554-505-7*, MUP/P144) Mercer Univ Pr.

Carro, Daniel, et al. Acerquemonos Al Calvario: Meditaciones Sobre la Pasion.Tr. of Drawing Near to Calvary: Meditations for Easter. (SPA.). 32p. 1996. pap. text 1.99 (*0-311-40062-0*) Casa Bautista.

Carro, Daniel, ed. see Bartley, James, et al.

Carroccia, Cara. The Architect's Geometry. (Illus.). 159p. (C). 1997. spiral bd. 22.80 (*0-87563-702-7*) Stipes.

Carrodeguas, andy, ed. see Bennett, Rita & Bennett, Dennis.

Carrodeguas, Angel, ed. see Fletcher, William M.

Carrodeguas, Angel, ed. see Hayford, Jack W.

Carrodeguas, Angel, tr. see Christenson, Larry & Hendricks, Howard.

Carroggio Staff. Enciclopedia Infantil, 10 vols., Set. (SPA.). 1974. 1395.00 (*0-8288-8230-4*, 8472541606) Fr & Eur.

Carrogio. Enciclopedia Infantil, 10 vols., Set. (SPA.). 2400p. (J). 1974. 495.00 (*0-8288-6033-5*, S50480) Fr & Eur.

— Enciclopedia Infantil, 10 vols., Set. (SPA.). 1978. 1395.00 (*0-8288-7575-8*, 8472541614) Fr & Eur.

Carrol. Caring for Older People. 1997. pap. 15.95 (*0-333-57295-5*) St Martin.

Carrol, B. F., jt. ed. see Morris, M. J.

Carrol, Frieda. Consumer Survival Notebook. rev. ed. LC 80-70456. 60p. 1993. ring bd. 29.95 (*0-939476-02-9*) Prosperity & Profits.

— Consumer Survival Notebook. rev. ed. LC 80-70456. (Illus.). 60p. 1993. ring bd. 26.95 (*0-9605246-2-2*) Prosperity & Profits.

— Continuing Education Alternatives. rev. ed. LC 80-68549. 1997. ring bd. 49.95 (*0-939476-14-2*); ring bd. 39.95 (*0-939476-15-0*) Prosperity & Profits.

— Continuing Education Alternatives Workbook. rev. ed. 75p. 1983. student ed., ring bd. 32.95 (*0-939476-85-1*) Prosperity & Profits.

— Creative Financing for Education, Housing, Automobiles, Vacations, Medical Care, Etc. A Self Paced Research Reference. 60p. (C). 1992. ring bd. 29.95 (*0-939476-58-4*) Prosperity & Profits.

— Factory Outlet Directories: A How to Find or Locate Workbook. 50p. 1983. ring bd. 25.95 (*0-939476-91-6*) Prosperity & Profits.

— Guide for the Unemployed Workbook. 60p. 1997. ring bd., wbk. ed. 24.95 (*0-939476-80-0*) Prosperity & Profits.

— The Joys of Saving & Economizing Encyclopedia. rev. ed. LC 80-70794. 1996. ring bd. 38.95 (*0-939476-08-8*) Prosperity & Profits.

— New & Useful Forms, Stationery & Greetings to Duplicate & Use. 50p. ring bd. 23.95 (*0-939476-84-3*) Prosperity & Profits.

— People's Money Pages at Your Own Pace Workbook. LC 80-70419. 50p. 1981. ring bd. 29.95 (*0-9605246-3-0*) Prosperity & Profits.

— Pick Your Own Fruits & Vegetables & More: A How to Find or Locate Workbook. LC 80-70861. 1981. ring bd. 25.95 (*0-939476-11-8*) Prosperity & Profits.

— Prescriptions for Survival with Workpages. LC 78-72312. 148p. 1981. ring bd. 26.95 (*0-9605246-1-4*) Prosperity & Profits.

— Survival Handbook for Small Business. rev. ed. LC 80-70496. 73p. 1992. ring bd. 35.95 (*0-9605246-4-9*) Prosperity & Profits.

— The Traveler's Workbook: Based on the People's Travel Book Index. 50p. (C). 1983. ring bd. 25.95 (*0-939476-52-5*) Prosperity & Profits.

— Unemployment Challenge Log Workbook. 60p. 1983. ring bd. 21.95 (*0-939476-86-X*) Prosperity & Profits.

Carrol, Frieda, compiled by. Barter Associations & Organizations & Businesses: An International Directory. rev. ed. LC 83-90672. 200p. 1997. ring bd. 39.95 (*0-911617-54-X*) Prosperity & Profits.

— Directory of Barter Directories. LC 83-90673. 100p. 1983. ring bd. 19.95 (*0-911617-55-8*) Prosperity & Profits.

— Meditation & Yoga Retreats: An International Directory. 200p. 1983. ring bd. 23.95 (*0-913597-06-6*) Prosperity & Profits.

— The People's Travel Book. rev. ed. LC 80-70869. 115p. 1992. pap. 29.95 (*0-939476-06-1*) Prosperity & Profits.

— The People's Travel Book. rev. ed. LC 80-70869. 115p. 1996. ring bd. 39.95 (*0-939476-05-3*) Prosperity & Profits.

— Private Postal Boxes, Mail Addresses & Mail Forwarding Services: A How to Find or Locate Workbook. 250p. 1983. ring bd. 29.95 (*0-913597-11-2*) Prosperity & Profits.

Carrol, Frieda, ed. Business Start-Up Fees: A Report: U. S. Edition. LC 83-90726. 50p. 1983. ring bd. 32.95 (*0-911569-13-8*) Prosperity & Profits.

— Business Start-up Fees: U. S. Edition. LC 83-90726. 160p. 1983. ring bd. 29.95 (*0-911569-08-1*) Prosperity & Profits.

Carrol, Frieda, Research Division Staff. Association, Club & Organization, Group Tours As a Travel Business: A Possibility Reference. rev. ed. 1992. ring bd. 21.95 (*0-317-04789-2*) Prosperity & Profits.

— Calligraphy As a Home Business. rev. ed. 78p. 1992. ring bd. 29.95 (*0-911569-74-X*) Prosperity & Profits.

— Catering Service Reference on Breads. rev. ed. 1992. ring bd. 22.95 (*0-317-04790-6*) Prosperity & Profits.

— Food Activities As Fundraisers: A Workbook. 1984. ring bd., wbk. ed. 29.95 (*0-318-04330-0*) Prosperity & Profits.

— Food Business Reference on Donut Shops & Other Pastry Shops. 1984. ring bd. 22.95 (*0-318-04331-9*) Prosperity & Profits.

— Freelance Writing As a Home Business - A Possibility Workbook. 1984. ring bd., wbk. ed. 29.95 (*0-318-04329-7*) Prosperity & Profits.

— Membership Applications for Clubs, Associations & Organizations: Samples to Duplicate & Use. 40p. 1984. ring bd. 23.95 (*0-318-04334-3*) Prosperity & Profits.

— Paying Office Expenses: Piggy-Backing, Cooperative, Sharing, Entrepreneural Services, Bartering: A Possibility Workbook. 1984. ring bd. 23.95 (*0-318-04335-1*) Prosperity & Profits.

— People's Money Pages: Fundraising Edition. 50p. 1984. ring bd. 32.95 (*0-318-04338-6*) Prosperity & Profits.

— Popcorn Use As Food, Crafts, Ornaments, Etc. & More with Select Recipes. rev. ed. 1992. student ed., ring bd. 24.95 (*0-911569-98-7*) Prosperity & Profits.

— Postage Stamp Recycling As Fundraising, Crafts & a Hobby. 1984. ring bd. 21.95 (*0-318-04346-7*) Prosperity & Profits.

— Telemarketing at Home - Finding Opportunities Workbook. rev. ed. 1991. ring bd. 25.95 (*0-317-04091-X*) Prosperity & Profits.

Carrol, Frieda, Staff. Home Business Telephone Survey & Sales Scripts. 60p. 1997. ring bd. 39.95 (*1-890928-27-5*) Frieda Carrol.

— Internet Marketing Telephone Survey & Sales Scripts. 60p. 1997. ring bd. 59.95 (*1-890928-28-3*) Frieda Carrol.

— School Products on Service Marketing Telephone Survey & Sales Scripts. 60p. 1997. ring bd. 39.95 (*1-890928-25-9*) Frieda Carrol.

— Trade Show Telephone Survey & Sales Scripts. 60p. 1997. ring bd. 39.95 (*1-890928-26-7*) Frieda Carrol.

Carrol, Terrence, et al. Communicate: A Video Course in English Viewer's Guides 1 & 2. (Illus.). (Orig.). 1986. write for info. (*0-318-60903-7*); pap. text 12.50 (*0-582-90704-7*, 75220) Longman.

— Communicate: A Video Course in English Viewer's Guides 1 & 2. (Communicate-A Video Course in English Ser.). (Illus.). (Orig.). 1986. pap. text 12.50 (*0-582-90703-9*, 75219) Longman.

Carroll. Bit of Seventh Cavalry History with Warts. 1976. pap. 14.95 (*0-8488-1600-5*, J M C & Co) Amereon Ltd.

— Civil War Custer. 1976. 10.00 (*0-685-71822-0*, J M C & Co) Amereon Ltd.

— Common Sense Philosophy. (International Archives of the History of Ideas Ser.: No. 77). 182p. 1975. lib. bdg. 99.50 (*90-247-1647-0*, Pub. by M Nijhoff) Kluwer Academic.

— Drugs in Modern Society. 4th ed. 1996. teacher ed. 15.31 (*0-697-22298-5*, WCB McGr Hill) McGrw-H Hghr Educ.

— Guide to History of Science. 1992. pap. text 26.00 (*0-934235-20-1*); lib. bdg. 39.00 (*0-934235-19-8*) U Ch Pr.

— Internet Handbook Educational Additional U.S. 1997. LC 98-162140. (C). 1997. pap. 40.67 (*0-13-851487-9*) P-H.

— Opening Arguments: Brief Rhetoric. (C). 1993. pap. text, teacher ed. 3.75 (*0-15-501510-9*) Harcourt Coll Pubs.

— Perspectives on Structure & Mechanism: Solutions Manual. (Chemistry Ser.). 1996. mass mkt., student ed. 16.50 (*0-534-34096-2*) Brooks-Cole.

— The Two Battles of Little Big Horn. 1976. pap. 15.95 (*0-685-71831-X*, J M C & Co) Amereon Ltd.

Carroll, ed. Emergency Planning. (Simulation Ser.: Vol. 15, No. 1). 156p. 1985. 40.00 (*0-911801-45-6*, SS15-1) Soc Computer Sim.

— Sexual Discourse. (C). 1998. text. write for info. (*0-321-01255-0*) Addson-Wesley Educ.

***Carroll & Buchholtz.** Business & Society: Ethics & Stake-Holder Management. 4th ed. 1999. pap. 91.95 (*0-324-00102-9*) Thomson Learn.

Carroll & Neft, David S. Total Football II: The Official Encyclopedia of the National Football League. 2nd ed. 1824p. 1999. 59.95 (*0-06-270174-6*, Harper Ref) HarpC.

Carroll & Wicklow, Donald T., eds. The Fungal Community: Its Organization & Role in the Ecosystem. 2nd ed. (Mycology Ser.: Vol. 9). (Illus.). 952p. 1992. text 275.00 (*0-8247-8605-X*) Dekker.

***Carroll, et al.** The Walrus & the Carpenter. (Other Literature Ser.). 1999. 8.00 (*1-55246-204-8*) Battered Silicon.

Carroll, jt. auth. see Phillip, John.

***Carroll, Karen M.** Entertaining with Southern Style. 184p. 2000. 35.00 (*0-8212-2688-6*) Bulfinch Pr.

***Carroll & Graf Staff.** Antarctic Adventure & Courage: South: A Memoir of the Endurance Voyage: Shackleton: The Worst. (Illus.). 1904p. 1999. pap. 49.85 (*0-7867-0652-X*) Carroll & Graf.

Carroll & Graf Staff. Pearl. 656p. 1999. mass mkt. 8.95 (*0-7867-0670-8*) Carroll & Graf.

— Venus Rising. 544p. 1999. mass mkt. 7.95 (*0-7867-0672-4*) Carroll & Graf.

— Wanton Women. 512p. 1999. mass mkt. 7.95 (*0-7867-0673-2*) Carroll & Graf.

***Carroll, A. J.** The Bluffer's Guide to Tax: Bluff Your Way in Tax. (Bluffer's Guides Ser.). 64p. 1999. pap. 5.95 (*1-902825-09-8*) Oval Bks.

Carroll, Aileen M. Bartlett, New Hampshire: In the Valley of the Saco. LC 90-7141. (Illus.). 240p. 1990. 22.00 (*0-914659-47-2*) Phoenix Pub.

Carroll, Alex L. Beat the Cops: The Guide to Fighting Your Traffic Ticket & Winning. 2nd rev. ed. Huijgen, Matthew & Russ, Adryan, eds. LC 94-71428. (Illus.). 125p. 1994. pap. 9.95 (*0-9634641-1-6*) Ace Co & Assocs.

Carroll, Alexander. Women of Early Christianity. 1978. 300.00 (*0-87968-268-X*) Gordon Pr.

Carroll, Amy & Brown, Denise. Baby Q & A. unabridged ed. LC 98-6874. 1999. write for info. (*0-307-44087-7*, Whitman Coin) St Martin.

— Storybook Knits. (Illus.). 64p. 1991. text 14.95 (*0-02-522111-6*) Macmillan.

Carroll, Andrew. Letters of a Nation: A Collection of Extraordinary American Letters. LC 98-38061. 496p. 1999. pap. 15.00 (*0-7679-0331-5*) Broadway BDD.

Carroll, Andrew, ed. Letters of a Nation: A Collection of Extraordinary American Letters. LC 97-25510. 512p. 1997. 27.00 (*1-56836-196-3*) Kodansha.

Carroll, Andrew, jt. auth. see Torricelli, Robert G.

Carroll, Andrew, jt. ed. see Torricelli, Robert G.

Carroll, Ann. Restrictions Imposed on Contaminated Sites: A Status of State Actions, Vols. One & Two. 2 vols., Set. Glass, Karen, ed. 472p. (Orig.). 1988. pap. text 20.00 (*1-55877-003-8*) Natl Governor.

— Rosie's Gift. 166p. 1997. pap. 8.95 (*1-85371-875-0*, Pub. by Poolbeg Pr) Dufour.

— Rosie's Quest. 134p. 1996. pap. 8.95 (*1-85371-281-7*, Pub. by Poolbeg Pr) Dufour.

— Rosie's Troubles. 204p. 1996. pap. 8.95 (*1-85371-681-2*, Pub. by Poolbeg Pr) Dufour.

— Together We Dance: A Teacher's Collection of Miracles & Memories. 64p. (Orig.). pap. 9.95 (*1-57736-010-9*) Providence Hse.

Carroll, Anna E. The Great American Battle. Whisker, James B., ed. & anno. by. LC 95-3014. 300p. 1995. write for info. (*0-7734-9019-1*) E Mellen.

Carroll, Anne K. Together Forever. 2000. 5.99 (*0-310-21502-1*) Zondervan.

Carroll, Anne Kristin. Together Forever. 256p. (Orig.). 1982. mass mkt. 9.99 (*0-310-45021-7*, 12051P) Zondervan.

Carroll, Anne W. Christ & the Americas. LC 96-61305. (Illus.). 423p. (YA). (gr. 9-12). 1997. pap. text 24.00 (*0-89555-594-8*, 1387) TAN Bks Pubs.

— Christ the King, Lord of History. LC 93-61594. 472p. (YA). (gr. 10-12). 1994. pap. text 24.00 (*0-89555-503-4*) TAN Bks Pubs.

Carroll, Archie B. Business & Society: Ethics & Stakeholder Management. 2nd ed. LC 92-12942. (SWC-Management). (C). 1992. pap. 64.95 (*0-538-82296-1*) S-W Pub.

— Business & Society: Ethics & Stakeholder Management. 3rd ed. LC 92-12942. (GO - Business & Society Ser.). 1995. text 75.95 (*0-538-85626-2*) S-W Pub.

Carroll, B. F., et al, eds. Turbulent Flows, 1995. LC 87-71097. (1995 ASME/JSME Fluids Engineering Conference Ser.: FED-Vol. 208). 128p. 1995. 72.00 (*0-7918-1463-7*, G00958) ASME.

Carroll, B. F., jt. ed. see Morris, M. J.

***Carroll, B. H.** Baptists & Their Doctrines. (Library of Baptist Classics). 1999. pap. text 19.99 (*0-8054-2059-2*) Broadman.

Carroll, B. H. Sermons with Life Sketch. 1986. reprint ed. 24.00 (*0-317-47643-2*) Church History.

Carroll, Barbara W. The Biases of Management. LC 93-7408. (Organizational Behaviour & Management Ser.). 208p. (C). (gr. 13). 1993. pap. 69.95 (*0-415-10196-4*) Thomson Learn.

Carroll, Barbara W. & Siegel, David. Service in the Field: The World of Front-Line Public Servants in Canada. 240p. 1998. text 60.00 (*0-7735-1795-2*) McG-Queens Univ Pr.

— Service in the Field: The World of Front-Line Public Servants in Canada. (Illus.). 251p. 1999. pap. 24.95 (*0-7735-1796-0*) McG-Queens Univ Pr.

Carroll, Barry J., et al, eds. Private Means - Public Ends: Private Business in Social Service Delivery. LC 86-25251. 204p. 1986. 55.00 (*0-275-92429-7*, C2429, Praeger Pubs) Greenwood.

Carroll, Bartholomew R., compiled by. Historical Collections of South Carolina: Embracing Many Rare & Valuable Pamphlets, & Other Documents, Relating to the History of That State, from Its First Discovery to Its Independence in the Year 1776. 2 vols. LC 72-14376. reprint ed. 155.00 (*0-404-11056-8*) AMS Pr.

Carroll, Benjamin, ed. Physical Methods in Macromolecular Chemistry, 1. LC 69-12679. 397p. 1969. reprint ed. pap. 123.10 (*0-608-08305-4*, 202710400001) Bks Demand.

— Physical Methods in Macromolecular Chemistry, 2. LC 69-12679. 381p. 1972. reprint ed. pap. 118.20 (*0-608-08306-2*, 202710400002) Bks Demand.

Carroll, Berenice A. Design for Total War: Arms & Economics in the Third Reich. LC 68-15527. (Studies in European History: Vol. 17). 1968. text 61.55 (*90-279-0299-2*) Mouton.

Carroll, Berenice A., ed. Liberating Women's History: Theoretical & Critical Essays. 448p. 1976. pap. text 14.95 (*0-252-00569-4*) U of Ill Pr.

Carroll, Berenice A., jt. auth. see Smith, Hilda L.

Carroll, Bernard J. & Barrett, James E., eds. Psychopathology & the Brain. (American Psychopathological Association Ser.). 312p. 1991. text 138.50 (*0-88167-802-3*) Lppncott W & W.

— Psychopathology & the Brain. LC 91-14227. (American Psychopathological Association Ser.). (Illus.). 315p. reprint ed. pap. 97.70 (*0-608-09744-6*, 206991300007) Bks Demand.

Carroll, Bill. Auto Mechanics Basic Engineering Guide. LC 70-102903. (Performance Engineering Handbooks Ser.). (Illus.). 228p. 1974. pap. 10.00 (*0-910390-19-3*) Coda Publications.

— Ford V8 Performance Guide. LC 76-16836. (Performance Engineering Handbooks Ser.). (Illus.). (Orig.). (YA). (gr. 7 up). 1993. pap. 15.00 (*0-910390-17-7*) Coda Publications.

— Honda Civic Guide. LC 74-75225. (Performance Engineering Handbooks Ser.). (Illus.). 214p. 1975. pap. 10.00 (*0-910390-21-5*) Coda Publications.

Carroll, Bob. Assessment in Physical Education: A Teacher's Guide to the Issues. LC 93-27227. 152p. 1994. 85.00 (*0-7507-0298-2*, Falmer Pr); pap. 29.95 (*0-7507-0299-0*, Falmer Pr) Taylor & Francis.

— Napoleon Bonaparte. LC 93-17852. (Importance of Ser.). 112p. (J). (gr. 5-8). 1994. lib. bdg. 22.45 (*1-56006-021-2*) Lucent Bks.

— Pancho Villa. LC 95-11707. (Importance of Ser.). (Illus.). 112p. (YA). (gr. 5-12). 1996. lib. bdg. 22.45 (*1-56006-069-7*) Lucent Bks.

Carroll, Bob, et al, eds. Total Football: The Official Encyclopedia of the National Football. LC 97-16987. 1664p. 1997. 55.00 (*0-06-270170-3*, Harper Ref) HarpC.

Carroll, Bob & Horrigan, Joe. Football Legends of All Times, Vol. 1. (Sports Legends Ser.). (Illus.). 216p. (J). (gr. k up). 1999. lib. bdg. 24.95 (*1-56674-284-6*) Forest Hse.

Carroll, Bob, et al. The Football Abstract. 1989. pap. 12.95 (*0-446-38731-2*) Warner Bks.

— The Hidden Game of Football. 416p. 1989. mass mkt. 12.95 (*0-446-39091-7*, Pub. by Warner Bks) Little.

— The Hidden Game of Football: The Next Edition. LC 98-86938. 320p. 1998. 21.95 (*1-892129-01-9*) Total Sprts.

Carroll, Bradley W. & Ostlie, Dale A. Introduction to Modern Astrophysics. Berisford, Julie, ed. LC 95-45144. 1326p. (C). 1995. 114.00 (*0-201-54730-9*) Addison-Wesley.

Carroll, Bradley W., jt. auth. see Ostile, Dale A.

Carroll, Brendan G. Erich Wolfgang Korngold, 1897-1957: His Life & Works. rev. ed. 43p. 1989. reprint ed. pap. 11.95 (*0-905075-15-3*, Pub. by Wilfion Bks) Dufour.

— The Last Prodigy: A Biography of Erich Wolfgang Korngold. LC 97-4963. (Illus.). 420p. 1997. 34.95 (*1-57467-029-8*, Amadeus Pr) Timber.

***Carroll, Bret E.** The Routledge Historical Atlas of American Religion. (Illus.). 2000. pap. 17.95 (*0-415-92137-6*); pap. 40.00 (*0-415-92131-7*) Routledge.

Carroll, Bret E. Spiritualism in Antebellum America. LC 97-7354. (Religion in North America Ser.). 227p. 1997. 35.00 (*0-253-33315-6*) Ind U Pr.

Carroll, Bruce. Sometimes Miracles Hide: Stirring Letters from Those Who Discovered God's Blessings in a Special Child. LC 99-31846. 127p. 1999. 14.99 (*1-58229-071-7*) Howard Pub LA.

***Carroll-Burke, Patrick.** Penal Correctionalism & the Colonial State in Ireland, 1763-1870. 256p. 1999. 55.00 (*1-85182-458-8*, Pub. by Four Cts Pr) Intl Spec Bk.

Carroll, C. Dennis, jt. auth. see Horn, Laura J.

Carroll, C. Dennis, ed. see Cuccaro-Alamin, Stephen & Choy, Susan P.

Carroll, C. Ronald, jt. auth. see Meffe, Gary K.

***Carroll, Cain & Kimata, Lori.** Partner Yoga: Making Contact for Physical, Emotional & Spiritual Growth. (Illus.). 2000. pap. 19.95 (*1-57954-271-9*, Rodale Reach) Rodale Pr Inc.

Carroll, Carleton W., ed. see de LaMarche, Olivier.

Carroll, Carleton W., tr. see De Troyes, Chretien.

Carroll, Cathryn & Mather, Susan M. Movers & Shakers: Deaf People Who Changed the World. 144p. 1998. pap. text, teacher ed. 14.95 (*0-915035-65-0*) Dawn Sign.

Carroll, Cathryn & Mozzer-Mather, Susan. Movers & Shakers: Deaf People Who Changed the World Storybook. LC 97-1408. 160p. 1997. 19.95 (*0-915035-64-2*, 9462B) Dawn Sign.

Carroll, Charles. Bet Right! A Guide to Odds & Betting for All Pari-Mutuel Sports. (Illus.). 65p. (Orig.). 2000. pap. 12.95 (*0-9658474-2-X*, HB105) Desert Sea.

— Drugs in Modern Society. 4th ed. LC 95-80770. 464p. (C). 1995. text 39.80 (*0-697-22297-7*) Brown & Benchmark.

***Carroll, Charles.** Drugs in Modern Society, with Annual Editions Online. 5th ed. (Illus.). 480p. 1999. pap. 52.81 (*0-07-235247-7*) McGraw.

Carroll, Charles. Handicapping Speed: The Thoroughbred & Quarter Horse Sprinters. (Illus.). 232p. 1996. pap. text 14.95 (*1-55821-497-6*) Lyons Pr.

— Legal Issues & Ethical Dilemmas in Respiratory Care. LC 95-44083. (Illus.). 163p. (C). 1996. pap. text 19.95 (*0-8036-0126-3*) Davis Co.

Carroll, Charles & Bock, William. Alcohol. 352p. 1995. pap. text. write for info. (*0-697-20018-3*) Brown & Benchmark.

Carroll, Charles, jt. auth. see Kayser, David.

Carroll, Charles F. The Timber Economy of Puritan New England. LC 73-7122. 235p. reprint ed. pap. 72.90 (*0-7837-2619-8*, 204295400006) Bks Demand.

Carroll, Charles H. Journal of Charles Carroll of Carrollton During His Visit to Canada in 1776, As One of the Commissioners from Congress. Mayer, Brantz & Decker, Peter, eds. LC 70-76557. (Eyewitness Accounts of the American Revolution Ser.). (Illus.). 1969. reprint ed. 14.95 (*0-405-01147-4*) Ayer.

— Negro a Beast. LC 74-89419. (Black Heritage Library Collection). 1977. 38.95 (*0-8369-8533-8*) Ayer.

— Organization of Debt into Currency: And Other Papers. Simmons, Edward C., ed. LC 70-172207. (Right Wing Individualist Tradition in America Ser.). 1972. reprint ed. 33.95 (*0-405-00418-4*) Ayer.

Carroll, Charles R. Drugs in Modern Society. 5th ed. LC 99-16250. 1999. pap. text 38.00 (*0-697-29448-X*) McGraw.

Carroll, Charles R. & Bock. Alcohol. 2nd ed. 2001. pap. text 22.00 (*0-697-29444-7*) McGraw.

Carroll, Clare. The Orlando Furioso: A Stoic Comedy. LC 97-11628. (Medieval & Renaissance Texts & Studies: Vo. 174). 256p. 1997. 26.00 (*0-86698-215-9*, MR174) MRTS.

An Asterisk (*) at the beginning of an entry indicates that the title is appearing for the first time.

Carroll, Clare & Carey, Vincent, eds. Richard Beacon, Solon His Follie (1594) LC 95-41147. (Medieval & Renaissance Texts & Studies: Vol. 154). 216p. 1996. 26.00 (*0-86698-194-2*, MR154) MRTS.

Carroll, Coleen, jt. auth. see Bergman, Ann.

Carroll, Colleen. Adrian the Angel, Incl. doll. LC 96-20891. (My Art Friends Ser.). (Illus.). 32p. (J). 1996. pap., bds. 19.95 (*0-7892-0109-7*, Abbeville Kids) Abbeville Pr.

***Carroll, Colleen.** Elements: Earth, Air, Fire & Water. (How Artists See Ser.). 1998. 10.95 (*0-7892-0476-2*) Abbeville Pr.

Carroll, Colleen. Gerlach the Gargoyle, Incl. doll. LC 96-8411. (My Art Friends Ser.). (Illus.). 32p. (J). 1996. pap., bds. 19.95 (*0-7892-0110-0*, Abbeville Kids) Abbeville Pr.

— How Artists See Animals. (J). 1998. 10.95 (*0-7892-0475-4*, Abbeville Kids) Abbeville Pr.

***Carroll, Colleen.** How Artists See Cities. LC 98-46583. (How Artists See Ser.). (Illus.). 48p. (J). 1999. 10.95 (*0-7892-0187-9*, Abbeville Kids) Abbeville Pr.

Carroll, Colleen. How Artists See Families: Mother, Father, Sister, Brother. LC 97-21325. (How Artists See Ser.). (Illus.). 48p. (YA). (gr. 3 up). 1997. 10.95 (*0-7892-0188-7*, Abbeville Kids) Abbeville Pr.

— How Artists See People: Woman, Boy, Girl, Man. LC 95-25796. 1996. 12.50 (*0-7892-0477-0*, Abbeville Kids) Abbeville Pr.

***Carroll, Colleen.** How Artists See Play. LC 98-46412. (How Artists See Ser.). (Illus.). 48p. (J). 1999. 10.95 (*0-7892-0393-6*, Abbeville Kids) Abbeville Pr.

Carroll, Colleen. How Artists See Work: Farm Factory Home Office. LC 97-20745. (How Artists See Ser.). (Illus.). 48p. (YA). (gr. 3 up). 1997. 10.95 (*0-7892-0185-2*, Abbeville Kids) Abbeville Pr.

— A Parents' & Teachers' Guide. (How Artist See Ser.). 1996. teacher ed. 10.95 (*0-7892-0271-9*, Abbeville Kids) Abbeville Pr.

— The Weather: Sun, Rain, Wind, Snow. (How Artists See Ser.). 1998. 10.95 (*0-7892-0478-9*) Abbeville Pr.

Carroll, D. Year of the Turtle. (Illus.). (J). 21.95 (*0-8048-7036-5*) Tuttle Pubng.

Carroll, D. Allen, ed. Greene's Groatsworth of Wit: Bought with a Million of Repentance (1592) LC 93-6276. (Medieval & Renaissance Texts & Studies: Vol. 114). 176p. 1994. 20.00 (*0-86698-167-5*, MR114) MRTS.

***Carroll, Daniel & Earp, Charles Albert.** Marylanders in Blue: The Artillery & the Cavalry. LC 99-70879. (Illus.). 176p. 1999. 34.95 (*0-9612670-8-9*) Toomey Pr.

Carroll, David. French Literary Fascism: Nationalism, Antisemitism & the Ideology of Culture. 310p. 1995. pap. text 17.95 (*0-691-05846-6*, Pub. by Princeton U Pr) Cal Prin Full Svc.

— George Eliot. LC 73-23395. (Critical Heritage Ser.). xv, 511 p. 1971. write for info. (*0-389-04073-8*) B&N Imports.

— Living with Dying. rev. ed. 389p. 1994. pap. 12.95 (*1-56924-998-9*) Marlowe & Co.

— Paraesthetics: Foucault, Lyotard, Derrida. 288p. 1987. 35.00 (*0-416-01721-5*, A0413) Routledge.

— Paraesthetics: Foucault, Lyotard, Derrida. 288p. (C). 1987. pap. 19.99 (*0-415-90291-6*, A0417) Routledge.

— The States of "Theory" History, Art & Critical Discourse. x, 316p. 1994. pap. 16.95 (*0-8047-2254-4*) Stanford U Pr.

— The Subject in Question: The Languages of Theory & the Strategies of Fiction. LC 82-1995. 240p. (C). 1982. pap. text 9.00 (*0-226-09494-4*) U Ch Pr.

— The Subject in Question: The Languages of Theory & the Strategies of Fiction. LC 82-1995. (Illus.). 239p. reprint ed. pap. 74.10 (*0-608-09282-7*, 205415600004) Bks Demand.

— Swampwalker's Journal: A Wetlands Year. LC 99-27342. (Illus.). 280p. 1999. 27.00 (*0-395-64725-8*) HM.

Carroll, David, intro. The States of "Theory" History, Art & Critical Discourse. (Irvine Studies in the Humanities). 320p. 1989. text 46.00 (*0-231-07086-1*) Col U Pr.

Carroll, David & Carroll, Susan R. How Smart Schools Get & Keep Community Support. LC 95-151605. (Illus.). 159p. (Orig.). 1994. pap. 24.95 (*1-879639-30-0*) Natl Educ Serv.

Carroll, David, jt. auth. see Feldman, B. Robert.

Carroll, David, jt. auth. see Moody, Harry R.

Carroll, David, ed. see Baron, W. R.

Carroll, David, ed. see Eliot, George, pseud.

Carroll, David, ed. see Sambrook, James.

Carroll, David, ed. & notes see Eliot, George, pseud.

Carroll, David D. New York - A Feast of Memories: A Re-Sampling of Times Past. LC 92-61110. (Illus.). 96p. 1994. 14.95 (*1-881554-01-5*) Skyward Pub.

Carroll, David L. How to Prepare Your Manuscript for a Publisher. 102p. 1995. pap. 10.95 (*1-56924-851-6*) Marlowe & Co.

— A Manual of Writer's Tricks. 127p. 1995. pap. 9.95 (*1-56924-877-X*) Marlowe & Co.

***Carroll, David L.** A Manual of Writer's Tricks: Essential Advice for Fiction & Nonfiction Writers. 144p. 2000. reprint ed. pap. 12.95 (*1-56924-607-6*) Marlowe & Co.

Carroll, David L. & Dorman, Jon. Living Well with Multiple Sclerosis: A Guide for Patient, Caregiver, & Family. LC 92-53396. 272p. (Orig.). 1993. pap. 13.00 (*0-06-096980-6*, Perennial) HarperTrade.

***Carroll, David L. & Karmally, Wahida.** Controlling High Blood Pressure the Natural Way. 2000. mass mkt. 6.99 (*0-345-43146-4*) Ballantine Pub Grp.

***Carroll, David M.** The Year of the Turtle: A Natural History. (Illus.). 172p. 1999. reprint ed. pap. text 18.00 (*0-7881-6534-8*) DIANE Pub.

Carroll, David W. Advanced Modula 2 Programming for the IBM PC, XT & AT. 300p. 1987. 39.00 (*0-444-01206-0*) Elsevier.

— Multiplan for Your Commodore 64. LC 84-22352. 200p. 1985. pap. 14.95 (*0-13-605130-8*) P-H.

— Psychology of Language. LC 85-22393. (Psychology Ser.). 467p. (C). 1985. mass mkt. 44.00 (*0-534-05640-7*) Brooks-Cole.

— Psychology of Language. 2nd ed. LC 93-26969. 1993. pap. 45.75 (*0-534-21300-6*) Brooks-Cole.

— Psychology of Language. 2nd ed. 1994. mass mkt., teacher ed. write for info. (*0-534-21301-4*) Brooks-Cole.

— Psychology of Language. 3rd ed. LC 98-28457. (Psychology Ser.). 24p. 1998. pap. 72.95 (*0-534-34973-0*) Brooks-Cole.

Carroll, Deborah. Teaching Your Children Life Skills. (Orig.). 1997. pap. 12.00 (*0-614-28118-0*) Berkley Pub.

— Teaching Your Children Life Skills: (While Having a Life of Your Own) LC 97-183792. 176p. 1997. pap. 12.00 (*0-425-15303-7*) Berkley Pub.

Carroll, Debra. Hot Copy. large type ed. (Black Satin Romance Ser.). 318p. 1997. 27.99 (*1-86110-026-4*) Ulverscroft.

— An Inconvenient Passion. (Temptation Ser.). 1996. per. 3.50 (*0-373-25697-3*, 1-25697-3) Harlequin Bks.

— Man under the Mistletoe. LC 96-3377. 217p. 1995. per. 3.25 (*0-373-25668-X*, 1-25668-4) Harlequin Bks.

— Obsession: (Secret Fantasies) LC 95-7075. (Temptation Ser.). 219p. 1995. per. 3.25 (*0-373-25630-2*, 1-25630-4) Harlequin Bks.

— One Enchanted Night. (It Happened One Night...Ser.). 1997. per. 3.50 (*0-373-25730-9*, 1-25730-2) Harlequin Bks.

— Prim & Improper. large type ed. (Black Satin Romance Ser.). 343p. 1997. 27.99 (*1-86110-023-X*) Ulverscroft.

— To Catch a Thief. (Temptation Ser.). 1996. per. 3.50 (*0-373-25678-7*, 1-25678-3) Harlequin Bks.

— Le Visiteur Sans Memoire. (Rouge Passion Ser.: Vol. 467). (FRE.). 1998. mass mkt. 3.50 (*0-373-37467-4*, 1-37467-7) Harlequin Bks.

Carroll, Denis. Unusual Suspects. 160p. 1998. pap. 54.95 (*1-85607-232-0*, Pub. by Columba Press) Intl Scholars.

Carroll, Dennis. Car$ense (TM) The "I Didn't Know That" Book for Saving Time & Money on Your Car. 2nd rev. ed. (Illus.). 120p. 1997. pap. 15.95 (*0-9654130-1-2*) C-Port Prods.

— The Man from God Knows Where. 286p. 1997. 74.95 (*1-85607-221-5*, Pub. by Columba Press); pap. 54.95 (*1-85607-130-8*, Pub. by Columba Press) Intl Scholars.

Carroll, Dennis J. Of Cops & Priests: Uses of Social & Moral Authority in Contemporary Irish-American Literature. LC 92-30422. (American University Studies: American Literature: Ser. XXIV, Vol. 40). IX, 131p. (C). 1993. text 39.95 (*0-8204-1967-2*) P Lang Pubng.

Carroll, Donald. Canada. (Traveler's Companion Ser.). 1999. pap. 24.95 (*0-7627-0356-3*) Globe Pequot.

***Carroll, Donald.** Traveler's Companion Guide to Florida. 2nd ed. (Illus.). 320p. 1999. pap. text 23.95 (*0-7627-0606-6*) Globe Pequot.

Carroll, Donald & Davies, Derek. Traveler's Turkey Companion. (Illus.). 318p. 1999. pap. 22.95 (*0-7627-0363-6*) Globe Pequot.

Carroll, Donald & Purdom, Laura. Traveler's Companion: Eastern Canada. (Illus.). 1998. pap. 22.95 (*0-7627-0357-1*) Globe Pequot.

— Traveler's Companion: Western Canada. (Illus.). 1998. pap. 22.95 (*0-7627-0366-0*) Globe Pequot.

Carroll, Douglas. Health Psychology: Stress, Behaviour & Disease. (Contemporary Psychology Ser.). 224p. 1992. pap. 29.95 (*1-85000-842-6*, Falmer Pr) Taylor & Francis.

***Carroll, Douglas.** An Interdisciplinary Study of Sport as a Symbolic Hunt: A Theory of the Origin & Nature of Sport Based on Paleolithic Hunting. LC 00-32881. 336p. 2000. pap. 99.95 (*0-7734-7685-7*) E Mellen.

Carroll, Douglas, jt. ed. see Cochrane, Raymond.

Carroll, Douglas, jt. ed. see Niven, Catherine A.

Carroll, Dyer E., et al. The ASME Code Simplified: Power Boilers. 2nd ed. (Illus.). 265p. 1996. 59.95 (*0-07-011636-9*) McGraw.

Carroll, E. Jean. A Dog in Heat Is a Hot Dog & Other Rules to Live By. 1997. per. 12.00 (*0-671-56814-0*, PB Trade Paper) PB.

Carroll, Eamon R. Understanding the Mother of Jesus. 106p. 1989. pap. 30.00 (*0-89453-101-8*, Pub. by Veritas Pubns) St Mut.

***Carroll, Eileen & Mackie, Karl.** The Art of Business Diplomacy: International Mediation. 204p. 1999. pap. 48.00 (*90-411-1290-1*) Kluwer Law Intl.

Carroll, Elizabeth. Ruby Tears of Edgecliff Manor. 1992. mass mkt. 3.99 (*0-8217-3665-5*, Zebra Kensgtn) Kensgtn Pub Corp.

Carroll, F. 101 Fun Bible Crosswords. 256p. 1989. mass mkt. 4.99 (*0-8423-0976-4*) Tyndale Hse.

Carroll, F. L. & Schwartz, P. Biographical Directory of National Librarians. 152p. 1989. text 99.50 (*0-7201-1875-1*) Continuum.

Carroll, Faye. South West Africa & the United Nations. LC 75-3984. 123p. 1975. reprint ed. lib. bdg. 49.50 (*0-8371-7441-4*, CASWA, Greenwood Pr) Greenwood.

Carroll, Felix A. Perspectives on Structure & Mechanism in Organic Chemistry. teacher ed. write for info. (*0-534-24949-3*) Brooks-Cole.

— Perspectives on Structure & Mechanism in Organic Chemistry. LC 95-37049. 876p. 1997. mass mkt. 110.95 (*0-534-24948-5*) Wadsworth Pub.

Carroll-Foster, Theodora. Guide to Agenda 21: Issues, Debates & Canadian Initiatives. 119p. 1993. pap. write for info. (*0-88936-687-X*) IDRC Bks.

Carroll, Frances. Book of Gifts: Traditional & Innovative Ways to Make Every Occasion Truly Speical. 224p. 1998. 14.95 (*0-8065-2053-1*, Citadel Pr); 89.70 (*0-8065-9847-6*, Citadel Pr) Carol Pub Group.

Carroll, Frances, tr. see Gombrowicz, Witold.

Carroll, Frances L. Brief Bible Studies for Busy People. LC 85-3470. 144p. 1985. 13.95 (*0-13-081993-X*) P-H.

— How to Talk with Your Children about God. 1985. pap. 6.95 (*0-317-18129-7*) P-H.

Carroll, Frances L., ed. International Biographical Directory of National Archivists, Documentalists, & Librarians. LC 96-31101. 256p. 1997. 45.00 (*0-8108-3223-2*) Scarecrow.

Carroll, Frances L. & Meacham, Mary. More Exciting, Funny, Scary, Short, Different, & Sad Books Kids Like about Animals, Science, Sports, Families, Songs, & Other Things. LC 92-11588. 180p. 1992. pap. text 22.00 (*0-8389-0585-4*) ALA.

Carroll, Frances L. & Meacham, Mary, eds. Exciting, Funny, Scary, Short, Different, & Sad Books Kids Like about Animals, Science, Sports, Families, Songs, & Other Things. LC 84-20469. 213p. reprint ed. pap. 66.10 (*0-7837-5907-X*, 204570500007) Bks Demand.

— More Exciting, Funny, Scary, Short, Different, & Sad Books Kids Like about Animals, Science, Sports, Families, Songs, & Other Things. LC 92-11588. 209p. 1992. reprint ed. pap. 64.80 (*0-608-02737-5*, 206340200004) Bks Demand.

Carroll, Frances L., jt. ed. see Harvey, John F.

Carroll, Frances L., tr. see Szechter, Szymon.

Carroll, Frances Laverne. Destination--Discovery! Activities for Studying Columbus & Other Explorers. LC 94-7035. 212p. (Orig.). 1994. pap. 30.00 (*0-8389-0634-6*) ALA.

Carroll, Francis M. & Raiter, Franklin R. The Fires of Autumn: The Cloquet-Moose Lake Disaster of 1918. LC 90-40688. (Illus.). xv, 246p. 1990. pap. 12.95 (*0-87351-258-8*) Minn Hist.

Carroll, Francis M., et al. Reflections of Our Past: A Pictorial History of Carlton County, Minnesota. LC 97-9724. 1997. write for info. (*0-89865-991-4*) Donning Co.

Carroll, Frank, ed. The Day Trader's Quick Reference to the Stock Market. viii, 108p. 1998. spiral bd. 14.95 (*0-9667136-0-5*) Alcor Pr.

***Carroll, Frank, ed.** Quick Reference to the Stock Market. 1999. write for info. (*0-9667136-4-8*) Alcor Pr.

Carroll, Frank, ed. The Stock Market Pocket Organizer. 100p. 1998. spiral bd. 14.95 (*0-9667136-1-3*) Alcor Pr.

Carroll, G. C. & Tudzynski, P., eds. Plant Relationships, Pt. A. (Mycota: Vol. 5). (Illus.). 250p. 1997. 169.00 (*3-540-58006-9*) Spr-Verlag.

— Plant Relationships, Pt. B. (Mycota: Vol. 5). (Illus.). 300p. 1997. 179.00 (*3-540-62018-4*) Spr-Verlag.

Carroll, Gary M. The Holy Spirit & the Keys to the Kingdom. (Illus.). 10.95 (*0-9673309-0-4*) Kingdom Keys.

***Carroll, George J.** Thoughts. 2000. write for info. (*1-58235-582-7*) Watermrk Pr.

Carroll, Gerald. No Place to Hide: A Novel of the Vietnam War. 1997. per. 6.99 (*0-671-86511-0*) PB.

Carroll, Gerald A. Project Seek: Onassis, Kennedy & the Gemstone Thesis. LC 94-2937. (Illus.). 310p. (Orig.). (C). 1994. pap. 16.95 (*0-9640104-0-2*) Bridger Hse.

Carroll, Gerald A., ed. see Nichols, James D., et al.

Carroll, Gerry. No Place to Hide. LC 94-45923. 432p. 1995. 23.00 (*0-671-86510-2*, PB Hardcover) PB.

— North SAR: A Novel of Navy Combat Pilots in Vietnam. McCarthy, Paul, ed. 416p. 1992. mass mkt. 5.99 (*0-671-73183-1*) PB.

Carroll, Gladys H. As the Earth Turns. 340p. 1995. pap. 10.95 (*0-942396-74-X*) Blackberry ME.

Carroll, Glenn R. Publish & Perish Vol. 8: The Organizational Ecology of Newspaper Industries. Bacharach, Samuel B., ed. LC 87-3267. (Monographs in Organizational Behavior & Industrial Relations: Vol. 8). 291p. 1987. 78.50 (*0-89232-440-6*) Jai Pr.

Carroll, Glenn R., ed. Ecological Models of Organizations. LC 87-19618. 304p. 1988. text 35.00 (*0-88730-208-4*, HarpBusn) HarpInfo.

***Carroll, Glenn R. & Hannan, Michael T.** The Demography of Corporations & Industries. LC 99-23937. (Illus.). 490p. 1999. 49.50 (*0-691-01030-7*, Pub. by Princeton U Pr) Cal Prin Full Svc.

Carroll, Glenn R. & Hannan, Michael T., eds. Organizations in Industry: Strategy, Structure & Selection. LC 94-9011. (Illus.). 400p. (C). 1995. text 59.95 (*0-19-508309-1*); pap. text 39.95 (*0-19-508310-5*) OUP.

Carroll, Glenn R. & Teece, David J., eds. Firms, Markets & Hierarchies: The Transaction Cost Perspective. LC 98-11411. (Illus.). 552p. 1999. text 55.00 (*0-19-511951-7*) OUP.

Carroll, Glenn R. & Vogel, David, eds. Organizational Approaches to Strategy. 224p. 1988. text 26.95 (*0-88730-267-X*, HarpBusn) HarpInfo.

Carroll, Grace. Environmental Stress & African Americans: The Other Side of the Moon. LC 97-5579. 160p. 1998. 49.95 (*0-275-95929-5*, Praeger Pubs) Greenwood.

***Carroll, H. Bailey.** Texas County Histories: A Bibliography. xxxii, 200p. 1999. reprint ed. 60.00 (*1-57898-175-1*) Martino Pubng.

Carroll, H. Bailey, jt. ed. see Webb, Walter Prescott.

Carroll, Harry. OS/2 Data Processing with Review of OS-VS. LC 74-2047. 298p. reprint ed. pap. 92.40 (*0-608-10300-4*, 201388100087) Bks Demand.

Carroll, Harry J. The Art of Greece & Rome. (Illus.). 12p. 1972. 1.00 (*0-915478-30-7*) Montgomery Gallery.

Carroll, Harry J., et al. The Development of Civilization: A Documentary History of Politics, Society & Thought, Vol. 2. LC 69-17828. 544p. reprint ed. pap. 168.70 (*0-7837-3010-1*, 204293000006) Bks Demand.

Carroll, Harvey F. Preview of General Chemistry. LC 88-5735. 432p. 1989. pap. 64.95 (*0-471-86002-6*) Wiley.

Carroll, Henry K. Report on the Island of Purto Rico. LC 74-14223. (Puerto Rican Experience Ser.). (Illus.). 817p. 1975. reprint ed. 65.95 (*0-405-06213-3*) Ayer.

Carroll, Holbert N. The House of Representatives & Foreign Affairs. LC 84-6718. 365p. 1984. reprint ed. lib. bdg. 75.00 (*0-313-24523-1*, CAHR, Greenwood Pr) Greenwood.

Carroll, Howard. Twelve Americans: Their Lives & Times. LC 70-37154. (Essay Index Reprint Ser.). 1977. reprint ed. 33.95 (*0-8369-2489-4*) Ayer.

Carroll, J. Introduction to Therapeutic Play: Working Together with Children, Young People, & Their Families. LC 96-40403. 1997. pap. 33.95 (*0-632-04148-X*) Blackwell Sci.

Carroll, J., jt. auth. see Duursma, E. K.

Carroll, J. B. & Freedle, R. O., eds. Language Comprehension & the Acquisition of Knowledge. LC 72-6708. 396p. reprint ed. 122.80 (*0-8357-9147-5*, 205070600082) Bks Demand.

Carroll, J. Douglas & Green, Paul E. Mathematical Tools for Applied Multivariate Analysis. 2nd rev. ed. (Illus.). 376p. 1997. text 69.95 (*0-12-160954-5*) Morgan Kaufmann.

Carroll, J. Douglas, et al. Mathematical Tools for Applied Multivariate Analysis. 2nd rev. ed. LC 97-74470. (Illus.). 376p. 1997. pap. text 39.95 (*0-12-160955-3*) Morgan Kaufmann.

Carroll, J. E. Rate Equations in Semiconductor Electronics. 192p. 1986. text 95.00 (*0-521-26533-9*) Cambridge U Pr.

— Rate Equations in Semiconductor Electronics. (Illus.). 185p. (C). 1990. pap. text 37.95 (*0-521-38866-X*) Cambridge U Pr.

Carroll, J. E., et al. Distributed Feedback Semiconductor Lasers. LC 99-159948. (Circuits, Devices & Systems Ser.: No. 10). 438p. 1998. 84.00 (*0-85296-917-1*, CS010) INSPEC Inc.

Carroll, J. Frank. Confederate Treasure in Danville. (Illus.). 140p. 1996. 24.95 (*0-933571-49-6*) Ure Pr.

— Meeting Singles: Where French Is Spoken. LC 85-50429. (Illus.). 60p. (Orig.). 1985. pap. 6.95 (*0-933571-00-3*) Ure Pr.

— Meeting Singles Where Spanish Is Spoken. LC 85-52049. (Illus.). 78p. (Orig.). pap. 6.95 (*0-933571-01-1*) Ure Pr.

Carroll, J. R. Harpoons to Harvest: The Story of Charles & John Mills Pioneers of Port Fairy. 300p. 1989. 90.00 (*0-949759-10-4*, Pub. by Deakin Univ) St Mut.

Carroll, Jackson W. As One with Authority: Reflective Leadership in Ministry. 192p. (Orig.). 1991. pap. 19.95 (*0-664-25168-4*) Westminster John Knox.

***Carroll, Jackson W.** Mainline to the Future: Congregations for the Twenty-First Century. 2000. pap. text 16.95 (*0-664-50122-2*) Westminster John Knox.

— Mainline to the Future: Congregations for the 21st Century. 220p. 2000. pap. 16.95 (*0-664-22253-6*, Pub. by Westminster John Knox) Presbyterian Pub.

Carroll, Jackson W., et al, eds. The Post-War Generation & Establishment Religion: Cross-Cultural Perspectives. LC 94-24178. 291p. (C). 1994. text 77.50 (*0-8133-8914-3*, Pub. by Westview) HarpC.

Carroll, Jackson W., et al. Being There: Culture & Formation in Two Theological Schools. LC 96-39062. (Religion in America Ser.). 320p. (C). 1997. 35.00 (*0-19-511493-0*) OUP.

Carroll, Jacqueline, jt. auth. see Ellis, Carol.

Carroll, James. Adventures of an Alaskan Missionary. (Illus.). 154p. 1997. pap. 14.92 (*1-891897-00-4*) Mission Evangelism.

— An American Requiem: God, My Father, & the War That Came between Us. 288p. 1997. pap. 13.00 (*0-395-85993-X*, Mariner Bks) HM.

***Carroll, James.** An American Requiem: God, My Father, & the War That Came between Us. large type ed. LC 99-41964. (American History Ser.). 1999. 26.95 (*0-7838-8765-5*, G K Hall & Co) Mac Lib Ref.

Carroll, James. The City Below. 422p. 1996. pap. 13.00 (*0-395-82522-9*) HM.

***Carroll, James.** Constantine's Sword: The Church Against the Jews: A History. (Illus.). 576p. 2001. 28.00 (*0-395-77927-8*) HM.

Carroll, James. Deliverance Out of the Valley of Decisions, Vol. 1. (Illus.). 176p. 1987. pap. 14.92 (*1-891897-15-2*) Mission Evangelism.

— Eleven Hundred Powerful Words. 107p. 1982. pap. 2.95 (*0-89826-008-6*) Natl Paperback.

— Firebird. large type ed. (General Ser.). 592p. 1989. lib. bdg. 20.95 (*0-8161-4845-7*, G K Hall Lrg Type) Mac Lib Ref.

— Going Home. (Illus.). 160p. 1997. pap. 14.92 (*1-891897-01-2*) Mission Evangelism.

— The Harmony of Your Body, Soul & Spirit, Vol. 12. (Illus.). 186p. 1995. pap. 14.92 (*1-891897-04-7*) Mission Evangelism.

— Helping Gifted Children Succeed at Home & School: A Comprehensive Resource for Parents & Teachers. 60p. 1997. pap. text 16.00 (*0-910609-34-9*) Gifted Educ Pr.

— How to Have a Wonderful New Life, Vol. 6. (Illus.). 138p. 1984. pap. 14.92 (*1-891897-10-1*) Mission Evangelism.

— How to Have an Abundance of Genuine Joy, Vol. 8. (Illus.). 202p. 1985. pap. 14.92 (*1-891897-08-X*) Mission Evangelism.

***Carroll, James.** How to Have the Most Important Thing on Planet Earth, No. 17. (Illus.). 182p. 1999. pap. 14.92 (*1-891897-17-9*) Mission Evangelism.

Carroll, James. How to Pray with Power, Vol. 5. 2nd ed. (Illus.). 188p. 1986. pap. 14.92 (*1-891897-11-X*) Mission Evangelism.

— Mortal Friends: A Novel. LC 91-41137. 608p. 1992. pap. 17.00 (*0-8070-6339-8*) Beacon Pr.

— Nature's Basic Law of Economics. 92p. 1982. pap. 2.95 (*0-89826-009-4*) Natl Paperback.

— The Power of Words. (Illus.). 192p. 1996. pap. 14.92 (*1-891897-02-0*) Mission Evangelism.

C

— The Prince of Peace. 544p. 1998. pap. 13.00 (*0-395-92619-X*) HM.

— The Purpose of Your Life on Planet Earth, Vol. 11. (Illus.). 294p. 1994. pap. 14.92 (*1-891897-05-5*) Mission Evangelism.

— The Secret of Happiness, Vol. 7. (Illus.). 182p. 1988. pap. 14.92 (*1-891897-09-8*) Mission Evangelism.

— Secret of Infinite Power, Vol. 9. (Illus.). 146p. 1991. pap. 14.92 (*1-891897-07-1*) Mission Evangelism.

— The Secrets of Victory, Vol. 4. (Illus.). 286p. 1983. pap. 14.92 (*1-891897-12-8*) Mission Evangelism.

— Seventeen Commandments Not from Heaven but Earth. 1985. pap. 3.95 (*0-89826-013-2*) Natl Paperback.

— Utopia Now. 160p. 1977. pap. 1.95 (*0-89826-001-9*) Natl Paperback.

— Who Am I? Book Series "E" (Illus.). 20p. 1991. pap. 1.95 (*1-891897-35-7*, 35) Mission Evangelism.

— Who Am I? Book Series "Z", Vol. 56. large type ed. (Illus.). 20p. 1991. pap. 1.95 (*1-891897-56-X*, 56) Mission Evangelism.

— Who Am I? No. 31: Book Series "A" (Illus.). 20p. 1991. pap. 1.95 (*1-891897-31-4*) Mission Evangelism.

— Who Am I? No. 32: Book Series "B" (Illus.). 20p. 1991. pap. 1.95 (*1-891897-32-2*) Mission Evangelism.

— Who Am I? No. 33: Book Series "C" (Illus.). 20p. 1991. pap. 1.95 (*1-891897-33-0*) Mission Evangelism.

— Who Am I? No. 34: Book Series "D" (Illus.). 20p. 1991. pap. 1.95 (*1-891897-34-9*) Mission Evangelism.

— Who Am I? No. 36: Book Series "F" (Illus.). 22p. 1991. pap. 1.95 (*1-891897-36-5*) Mission Evangelism.

— Who Am I? No. 37: Book Series "G" (Illus.). 22p. 1991. pap. 1.95 (*1-891897-37-3*) Mission Evangelism.

— Why? Oh Lord, Why?, Vol. 2. (Illus.). 316p. 1989. pap. 14.92 (*1-891897-14-4*) Mission Evangelism.

— Your Divine Ten with Love, Vol. 10. (Illus.). 134p. 1982. pap. 12.92 (*1-891897-06-3*) Mission Evangelism.

— Your Guardian Angel. (Illus.). 170p. 1995. pap. 12.92 (*1-891897-03-9*) Mission Evangelism.

— Your Ultimate Guidance to Permanent Wealth, Vol. 3. (Illus.). 158p. 1990. pap. 14.92 (*1-891897-13-6*) Mission Evangelism.

Carroll, James & Overton, Barbara. Be Sure Your Child Learns to Read. 160p. 1976. pap. 1.95 (*0-89826-000-0*) Natl Paperback.

Carroll, James, jt. auth. see El-Radhi, Sahib.

Carroll, James D. & Smith, Bruce L., eds. Improving the Accountability & Performance of Government. LC 82-71297. (Dialogues on Public Policy Ser.). 123p. 1982. pap. 12.95 (*0-8157-7993-3*) Brookings.

Carroll, James J. Effective Participation in Government: Instructor's Manual. 91p. (C). 1987. ring bd. 24.95 (*0-936826-29-0*) PS Assocs Croton.

— Our Constitutional Heritage. LC 98-179838. 67p. 1991. 15.75 (*1-56256-006-9*) Peoples Pub Grp.

Carroll, James J., jt. auth. see Greenfield, Richard P.

Carroll, James L. College Credit Without Classes: How to Obtain Academic Credit for What You Already Know. LC 96-489. 116p. 1996. pap. 12.95 (*0-89434-165-0*, F649) Ferguson.

Carroll, James M. Born Out of the Sun. 146p. 1998. pap. 7.95 (*0-89826-082-5*) Natl Paperback.

— Face to Face: A Guide for Government Employees Who Counsel Problem Employees. abr. ed. (Illus.). 132p. 1997. pap. text 14.95 (*0-936295-75-9*) FPMI Comns.

— Mixturism. rev. ed. 184p. (Orig.). 1996. pap. 7.95 (*0-89826-068-X*) Natl Paperback.

— The Problem with Public Education Is Administrative. 70p. 1984. pap. 3.95 (*0-89826-012-4*) Natl Paperback.

— Three Steps to Success. 86p. (Orig.). 1984. pap. 4.95 (*0-89826-011-6*) Natl Paperback.

— Why We Dream. 16p. (Orig.). 1996. pap. 9.95 (*0-89826-062-0*) Natl Paperback.

Carroll, James M. & Overton, Barbara. Words Every Good Reader Knows. 56p. (Orig.). (J). (gr. 1-6). 1992. pap. 9.95 (*0-89826-032-9*) Natl Paperback.

Carroll, James R., jt. auth. see Carroll, John T.

***Carroll, James T.** Seeds of Faith: Catholic Indian Boarding Schools. LC 00-26479. (Native Americans Ser.). (Illus.). 2000. write for info. (*0-8153-3811-2*) Garland.

Carroll, Jane. The Fly-Away Umbrella. LC 93-131. (Illus.). (J). 1994. write for info. (*0-383-03687-9*) SRA McGraw.

Carroll, Janet. Elegant Tatting Patterns. LC 96-11632. (Illus.). 32p. 1996. pap. 3.95 (*0-486-29149-9*) Dover.

Carroll, Janet, jt. auth. see Carroll, Malcolm.

Carroll, Janet R., jt. ed. see Andrle, Robert F.

Carroll, Jannell L. & Wolpe, Paul R. Sexuality & Gender in Society. 304p. (C). 1997. pap., student ed. 27.00 (*0-06-500873-1*) Addson-Wesley Educ.

Carroll, Jean. Growing in God's Garden. 180p. (Orig.). 1995. pap. write for info. (*1-885591-63-2*) Morris Pubng.

— Measuring & Managing Ambulatory Care Outcomes. 1996. 199.00 (*0-8342-0776-1*, S194) Aspen Pub.

Carroll, Jean, tr. see Metzi, Francisco.

Carroll, Jean G. Monitoring with Indicators: Evaluating the Quality of Patient Care. ring bd. 170.00 (*0-8342-0264-6*) Aspen Pub.

Carroll, Jeff. Jeff Carroll's Legendary Texas: Unsung Heritage. (Legendary Texas Ser.). (Illus.). 167p. 1998. pap. 22.95 (*0-9627034-6-X*) Wheelock Pr.

Carroll, Jennifer Y. The Conversational Classroom: Lesson Plans for Preschool Language Learning Through Interaction. Young, Dianne, ed. (Illus.). 610p. (Orig.). 1995. pap. text 49.95 (*0-9645202-0-6*) Commun Counts.

— The Pre-K Gourmet: Children's Recipes & Related Activities to Encourage Learning. Young, Dianne, ed. (Illus.). 140p. (J). 1998. pap. text 14.95 (*0-9645202-1-4*) Commun Counts.

Carroll, Jeri. The Complete Color Book. (Illus.). 112p. (J). (ps-3). 1991. 12.99 (*0-86653-585-3*, GP1300) Good Apple.

— Learning Centers for Little Kids. (Illus.). 64p. (J). (ps-2). 1983. student ed. 6.99 (*0-86653-103-3*, GA 458) Good Apple.

— Let's Learn about Magnificent Me. (Illus.). 64p. (J). (ps-2). 1987. pap. 8.99 (*0-86653-384-2*, GA1010) Good Apple.

Carroll, Jeri & Dunlavy, Kathy. My Very First Books to Make & Read. 144p. (J). (ps-2). 1990. 13.99 (*0-86653-557-8*, GA1163) Good Apple.

Carroll, Jeri & Kear, Dennis. Writing Fun with Phonics. (Illus.). 160p. (J). (ps-2). 1992. student ed. 12.99 (*0-86653-686-8*, 1420) Good Apple.

Carroll, Jeri & Wells, Candace B. Founders. (Famous Friends Ser.). (Illus.). 64p. (J). (ps-3). 1986. student ed. 7.95 (*0-86653-345-1*, GA 695) Good Apple.

Carroll, Jeri, et al. Back to School in January. (Illus.). 144p. (J). (gr. k-5). 1989. student ed. 10.99 (*0-86653-470-9*, GA1067) Good Apple.

Carroll, Jeri A. Centers for Early Learners Throughout the Year. 144p. 1991. 13.99 (*0-86653-615-9*, GA1334) Good Apple.

— Let's Learn about Getting Along with Others. 64p. (J). (ps-2). 1988. student ed. 8.99 (*0-86653-439-3*, GA1042) Good Apple.

***Carroll, Jeri A.** Meaningful Math: Creating an Environment with Math-Rich Experiences: Grades PS-2. Mitchell, Judy, ed. (Illus.). 128p. 1999. pap., teacher ed. 12.95 (*1-57310-191-5*) Teachng & Lrning Co.

— Meaningful Print: Creating an Environment with Print-Rich Experiences: Grades PS-2. Mitchell, Judy, ed. (Illus.). 128p. 1999. pap., teacher ed. 12.95 (*1-57310-192-3*) Teachng & Lrning Co.

Carroll, Jeri A. Transitions: Easy Ways to Adapt to Changes in Your Day. Mitchell, Judy, ed. (Illus.). 144p. (Orig.). (J). (ps-3). 1997. pap., teacher ed. 13.95 (*1-57310-070-6*) Teachng & Lrning Co.

Carroll, Jeri A. & Foster, Tom. The World of Work. (Focus On...Ser.). 112p. 7.99 (*0-86653-748-1*, GA1463) Good Apple.

Carroll, Jeri A. & Seaton, Marcia. Cooperative Learning Throughout the Year. (Illus.). 144p. 1992. 10.99 (*0-86653-663-9*, GA1395) Good Apple.

Carroll, Jeri A., et al. Character Building: Literature-Based Theme Units. (Illus.). 144p. (Orig.). (J). (ps-3). 1997. pap., teacher ed. 13.95 (*1-57310-071-4*) Teachng & Lrning Co.

— Compassion: Connecting Children's Favorite Stories to Meaningful Life Experiences. Mitchell, Judy, ed. (Illus.). 32p. (J). (ps-2). 1998. pap., teacher ed. 2.95 (*1-57310-120-6*) Teachng & Lrning Co.

— Friendship: Connecting Children's Favorite Stories to Meaningful Life Experiences. Mitchell, Judy, ed. (Illus.). 32p. (J). (ps-2). 1998. pap., teacher ed. 2.95 (*1-57310-121-4*) Teachng & Lrning Co.

— Giving: Connecting Children's Favorite Stories to Meaningful Life Experiences. Mitchell, Judy, ed. (Illus.). 32p. (J). (ps-2). 1998. pap., teacher ed. 2.95 (*1-57310-122-2*) Teachng & Lrning Co.

— Honesty: Connecting Children's Favorite Stories to Meaningful Life Experiences. Mitchell, Judy, ed. (Illus.). 32p. (J). (ps-2). 1998. pap., teacher ed. 2.95 (*1-57310-123-0*) Teachng & Lrning Co.

— Perseverance: Connecting Children's Favorite Stories to Meaningful Life Experiences. Mitchell, Judy, ed. (Illus.). 32p. (J). (ps-2). 1998. pap., teacher ed. 2.95 (*1-57310-124-9*) Teachng & Lrning Co.

— Respect: Connecting Children's Favorite Stories to Meaningful Life Experiences. Mitchell, Judy, ed. (Illus.). 32p. (J). (ps-2). 1998. pap., teacher ed. 2.95 (*1-57310-125-7*) Teachng & Lrning Co.

— Responsibility: Connecting Children's Favorite Stories to Meaningful Life Experiences. Mitchell, Judy, ed. (Illus.). 32p. (J). (ps-2). 1998. pap., teacher ed. 2.95 (*1-57310-126-5*) Teachng & Lrning Co.

— Self-Discipline: Connecting Children's Favorite Stories to Meaningful Life Experiences. Mitchell, Judy, ed. (Illus.). 32p. (J). (ps-2). 1998. pap., teacher ed. 2.95 (*1-57310-127-3*) Teachng & Lrning Co.

Carroll, Jeri A., jt. auth. see Dunlavy, Kathy.

Carroll, Jeri A., jt. auth. see Kear, Dennis J.

***Carroll, Jerry J.** Dog Eat Dog. 304p. 2000. mass mkt. 6.50 (*0-441-00740-6*) Ace Bks.

Carroll, Jerry J. Dog Eat Dog: A Novel. LC 99-173823. 272p. 1999. pap. 12.00 (*0-441-00597-7*) Ace Bks.

— Top Dog. 1998. mass mkt. 5.99 (*0-441-00513-6*) Ace Bks.

— Top Dog: A Novel. 320p. 1996. pap. text 12.00 (*0-441-00368-0*) Ace Bks.

Carroll, Jerry Jay. Inhuman Beings. LC 98-165578. 256p. 1998. pap. 12.00 (*0-441-00529-2*) Ace Bks.

— Inhuman Beings, 1 vol. 256p. 1999. reprint ed. mass mkt. 5.99 (*0-441-00612-4*) Ace Bks.

Carroll, Jim. The Basketball Diaries. 192p. 1995. pap. 11.95 (*0-14-024999-0*, Penguin Bks) Viking Penguin.

— Fear of Dreaming: The Selected Poems of Jim Carroll. LC 93-1719. 288p. (Orig.). 1993. pap. 15.95 (*0-14-058695-4*) Viking Penguin.

— Forced Entries: The Downtown Diaries, 1971-1973. 192p. 1987. pap. 11.95 (*0-14-008502-5*, Penguin Bks) Viking Penguin.

Carroll, Jim. Get on the Internet in Canada in 5 Minutes. 1996. pap. text 9.95 (*0-13-371204-4*) P-H.

Carroll, Jim. Living at the Movies. 100p. 1981. pap. 13.95 (*0-14-042290-0*, Penguin Bks) Viking Penguin.

— The Official Bad Golfers Test. (Illus.). 81p. 1999. pap. 8.95 (*0-9672841-0-4*) J Carroll.

***Carroll, Jim.** Permissive Bargaining & Congressional Intent: A Special Report. 2nd rev. ed. 131p. 1999. pap. 34.95 (*1-930542-04-6*) FPMI Comns.

Carroll, Jim. Void of Course: Poems, 1994-1997. LC 98-3495. (Poets Ser.). 96p. 1998. pap. 12.95 (*0-14-058909-0*) Viking Penguin.

***Carroll, Jim & Foose, Dennis.** Hollywood Dating Blunders: Rules, Questions, Baggage & Warning Signs. LC 00-41323. (Illus.). 2001. write for info. (*1-881554-06-6*) Skyward Pub.

Carroll, Joan. The Black College Career Guide. 140p. (YA). (gr. 9-12). 1992. pap. 6.95 (*1-881223-00-0*) Zulema Ent.

***Carroll, Joan.** Smile a Seven Step Journey Toward Self-Discovery & Leadership Empowerment. (Illus.). 100p. (YA). 2000. pap. 9.95 (*1-881223-18-3*) Zulema Ent.

Carroll, Joan. Where America's Black Leaders Learned to Lead: The Black College Career Guide. 144p. (YA). (gr. 9-12). 1995. pap. text 6.95 (*1-881223-05-1*) Zulema Ent.

Carroll, Joan, ed. see Stripling, Joe.

***Carroll, Joanne.** Dare to Dream. 1999. 7.95 (*1-56245-362-9*) Great Quotations.

Carroll, Jock. Falling for Marilyn: The Lost Niagara Collection. (Illus.). 112p. 1996. 25.00 (*1-56799-411-3*, Friedman-Fairfax) M Friedman Pub Grp Inc.

— Glenn Gould: Some Portraits of the Artist As a Young Man. (Illus.). 96p. 1999. 19.95 (*0-7737-2904-6*) Genl Dist Srvs.

Carroll, Joe, ed. see Lee, Lanny E., III.

Carroll, John. Applied Social Psychology & Organizational Settings. 240p. (C). 1990. text 49.95 (*0-8058-0541-9*) L Erlbaum Assocs.

— Buffalo Soldiers West. rev. ed. (Illus.). 1995. 26.95 (*0-8488-1519-X*, J M C & Co); pap. 17.95 (*0-8488-1518-1*, J M C & Co) Amereon Ltd.

— Catspaw. 190p. (C). 1990. 30.00 (*0-947087-16-8*, Pub. by Pascoe Pub) St Mut.

— Chopped Harleys. (Illus.). 112p. 1997. 14.99 (*0-517-18775-2*) Random Hse Value.

— Classic American Motorcycles. 96p. 1997. 12.98 (*0-7858-0837-X*) Bk Sales Inc.

— Classic Harley Davidson: A Celebration of an American Icon. LC 99-26499. (Illus.). 144p. 1999. 15.98 (*1-57145-208-7*, Thunder Bay) Advantage Pubs.

— Ego & Soul: The Modern West in Search of Meaning. 1999. pap. 15.95 (*0-7322-5990-8*, Pub. by HarpC) Consort Bk Sales.

— 4 x 4 Vehicles. LC 98-18098. (Illus.). 112p. (YA). (gr. 5 up). 1999. lib. bdg. 24.95 (*0-7910-5004-1*) Chelsea Hse.

***Carroll, John.** Harley Davidson, 1903-1965. (Illus.). 2000. 24.95 (*0-7509-2342-3*, Pub. by Sutton Publng) Intl Pubs Mktg.

Carroll, John. Harley Davidson 45: Warhorse & Workhorse. (Color Library). (Illus.). 128p. 1994. pap. 15.95 (*1-85532-444-X*, Pub. by Ospry) Motorbooks Intl.

— Intruders in the Bush: The Australian Quest for Identity. 1982. pap. 16.95 (*0-19-554308-4*) OUP.

***Carroll, John.** Jeep. (Illus.). 160p. 2000. 24.95 (*0-7509-2343-1*) Sutton Publng.

Carroll, John. A Little California Cookbook. (Illus.). 60p. 1992. 7.95 (*0-8118-0097-0*) Chronicle Bks.

— Measuring, Marking & Layout: A Builder's Guide. LC 98-18115. 1998. 34.95 (*1-56158-226-3*) Taunton.

***Carroll, John.** Pickup Trucks. LC 97-62276. (Illus.). 112p. 1998. 14.98 (*0-7651-9124-5*) Smithmark.

— The Return of Jesus in Early Christianity. Alexander, Patrick H., ed. 200p. (C). 2000. 19.95 (*1-56563-341-5*) Hendrickson MA.

Carroll, John. Trails of Two Cities: A Walker's Guide to Yokohama, Kamakura & Vicinity. Sagar, Hilary, ed. (Illus.). 320p. 1994. pap. 20.00 (*4-7700-1837-1*) Kodansha.

— Working Alone. LC 99-33471. (Illus.). 144p. 1999. write for info. (*1-56158-286-7*) Taunton.

***Carroll, John.** World of Tractors. 96p. 2000. pap. 9.95 (*0-7548-0471-2*) Anness Pub.

— World Of Tractors: An Illustrated History. 96p. 2000. 14.95 (*1-84215-060-X*) Anness Pub.

— World's Greatest Tractors. LC 97-62274. (Illus.). 112p. 1998. 14.98 (*0-7651-9123-7*) Smithmark.

Carroll, John & Green, Joel. The Death of Jesus in Early Christianity. 332p. 1995. 24.95 (*1-56563-151-X*) Hendrickson MA.

***Carroll, John & Stuart, Gary.** Classic Jeeps: The Jeep from World War II to the Present Day. (Illus.). 144p. 2000. 24.95 (*0-7603-0894-2*, 130164AP, Pub. by MBI Pubg) Motorbooks Intl.

Carroll, John, et al. Distributed Feedback Semiconductor Lasers, Vol. PM52. LC 99-159948. (Circuits, Devices & Systems Ser.: Vol. 10). 440p. 1998. 84.00 (*0-8194-2660-1*) SPIE.

Carroll, John, jt. auth. see Palm, Risa.

Carroll, John B. Human Cognitive Abilities: A Survey of Factor-Analytic Literature. LC 92-12453. (Illus.). 829p. (C). 1993. pap. text 31.95 (*0-521-38712-4*) Cambridge U Pr.

— Human Cognitive Abilities: A Survey of Factor-Analytic Literature. LC 92-12453. (Illus.). 829p. (C). 1993. text 80.00 (*0-521-38275-0*) Cambridge U Pr.

— Human Cognitive Abilities: A Survey of Factor-Analytic Literature. LC 92-12453. (Illus.). 600p. (C). 1993. disk 52.95 (*0-521-44787-9*) Cambridge U Pr.

Carroll, John B., jt. ed. see Anderson, Lorin W.

Carroll, John B., jt. ed. see Whorf, Benjamin L.

Carroll, John C., jt. auth. see Leech, Harper.

Carroll, John E. Acid Rain: An Issue in Canadian-American Relations. LC 82-82205. (Canadian-American Committee Ser.). 98p. (Orig.). (C). 1982. pap. 6.00 (*0-89068-064-7*) Natl Planning.

Carroll, John E., et al, eds. The Greening of Faith: God, the Environment, & the Good Life. LC 96-22547. (Illus.). 238p. 1997. pap. 19.95 (*0-87451-777-X*); text 45.00 (*0-87451-776-1*) U Pr of New Eng.

Carroll, John E. & Logan, Roderick M. The Garrison Diversion Unit: A Case Study in Canadian-U. S. Environmental Relations. (Canadian-U. S. Prospect Ser.). 60p. 1980. 5.00 (*0-88806-070-X*) Natl Planning.

Carroll, John E. & Warner, Keith. Ecology & Religion: Scientists Speak. LC 98-17882. 1998. 21.95 (*0-8199-0986-6*) Franciscan Pr.

Carroll, John J. Computers & Curriculum-Program Development. 250p. 2000. 49.95 (*0-938639-00-5*) Special Resc Pubns.

Carroll, John M. The Arrest & Killing of Sitting Bull. 1976. 22.95 (*0-8488-0949-1*) Amereon Ltd.

— Black Military Experience in America. 1976. 41.95 (*0-8488-0710-3*, J M C & Co) Amereon Ltd.

— Cavalry Scraps: The Writings of Frederick Benteen. 1985. 128.00 (*0-8488-0242-X*, J M C & Co) Amereon Ltd.

— Civil War Campaign Medal. 1976. 20.00 (*0-8488-0243-8*, J M C & Co) Amereon Ltd.

— Computer Security. 3rd ed. LC 95-4797. (Illus.). 540p. 1996. text 59.95 (*0-7506-9600-1*, Digital DEC) Buttrwrth-Heinemann.

— Confederate Roll of Honor. 1976. 21.95 (*0-8488-0049-4*); pap. 14.95 (*0-8488-0048-6*) Amereon Ltd.

— Confidential Information Sources: Public & Private. 2nd ed. 406p. 1991. 59.95 (*0-7506-9018-6*, BH Security) Buttrwrth-Heinemann.

— The Custer Autograph Album. (Illus.). 206p. 1993. 24.95 (*0-932702-97-X*) Creative Texas.

— Data Base & Computer Systems Security. LC 79-113523. (QED Monograph Series. Data Base Management: No. 4). 65p. reprint ed. pap. 30.00 (*0-608-15625-6*, 203175400076) Bks Demand.

— Fritz Pollard: Pioneer in Racial Advancement. (Sport & Society Ser.). (Illus.). 328p. 1992. text 32.50 (*0-252-01814-1*) U of Ill Pr.

— Fritz Pollard: Pioneer in Racial Advancement. (Sport & Society Ser.). 328p. 1999. pap. text 22.95 (*0-252-06799-1*) U of Ill Pr.

— Galveston, Gulf, Colorado & Santa Fe Railroad. 1976. 27.00 (*0-8488-0239-X*, J M C & Co) Amereon Ltd.

— History of Seventh Regiment U. S. Cavalry. Date not set. lib. bdg. 32.95 (*0-8488-0948-3*) Amereon Ltd.

— The Indian Wars Campaign Medal: Its History & Its Recipients. 73p. 1985. pap. 19.50 (*0-8488-1517-3*) Amereon Ltd.

— List of Field Officers of the Confederate Army. 29.95 (*0-8488-0010-9*, J M C & Co); pap. 19.95 (*0-8488-0044-3*, J M C & Co) Amereon Ltd.

***Carroll, John M.** Making Use: Scenario-Based Design of Human-Computer Interactions. LC 00-21621. (Illus.). 376p. 2000. 39.95 (*0-262-03279-1*) MIT Pr.

Carroll, John M. Medal of Honor: History & Recipients. 1976. 22.00 (*0-8488-1268-9*, J M C & Co) Amereon Ltd.

— The Medal of Honor: History & Recipients for the Indian Wars. 1985. pap. 19.00 (*0-317-28081-3*, J M C & Co) Amereon Ltd.

— Minimalism Beyond the Nurnberg Funnel. LC 97-36124. (Illus.). 428p. 1998. 49.50 (*0-262-03249-X*, 175-98) MIT Pr.

— The Nurenberg Funnel: Designing Minimalist Instruction for Practical Computer Skill. (Technical Communication Ser.). 362p. 1990. 48.50 (*0-262-03163-9*) MIT Pr.

— Red Grange & the Rise of Modern Football. LC 99-6056. (Sport & Society Ser.). (Illus.). 296p. 1999. 25.95 (*0-252-02384-6*) U of Ill Pr.

— Register of Officers of the Confederate States Navy 1861-1865. Date not set. pap. 19.95 (*0-8488-0046-X*, J M C & Co); lib. bdg. 29.95 (*0-8488-0011-7*, J M C & Co) Amereon Ltd.

— Roll Call on the Little Big Horn. 1976. 34.95 (*0-8488-0233-0*, J M C & Co) Amereon Ltd.

— Roster of General Officers of the Confederate Service During the Civil War. Date not set. 29.95 (*0-8488-0009-5*, J M C & Co); pap. 19.95 (*0-8488-0043-5*, J M C & Co) Amereon Ltd.

— Scenario-Based Design: Envisioning Work & Technology in System Development. LC 94-23772. 408p. 1995. 50.00 (*0-471-07659-7*) Wiley.

— The Seventh Cavalry's Own Colonel Tommy Tompkins: A Military Heritage & Tradition. (Illus.). 31.95 (*0-8488-0013-3*, J M C & Co) Amereon Ltd.

— Staff Officers of the Confederate States Army. Date not set. pap. 19.95 (*0-8488-0045-1*, J M C & Co); lib. bdg. 29.95 (*0-8488-0008-7*, J M C & Co) Amereon Ltd.

— Teepee Book, Pts. 1 & 2. 1976. 74.50 (*0-914074-10-5*, J M C & Co) Amereon Ltd.

— They Rode with Custer. Date not set. lib. bdg. 27.95 (*0-8488-0236-5*, J M C & Co) Amereon Ltd.

— They Rode with Custer. (Illus.). Date not set. pap. 17.95 (*0-8488-0237-3*, J M C & Co) Amereon Ltd.

— Toward a Structural Psychology of Cinema. (Approaches to Semiotics Ser.: No. 55). 224p. 1980. 43.10 (*90-279-3447-9*) Mouton.

Carroll, John M., ed. The Benteen-Goldin Letters on Custer & His Last Battle. (Illus.). 1985. 27.95 (*0-8488-0032-X*, J M C & Co) Amereon Ltd.

— The Benteen-Goldin Letters on Custer & His Last Battle. LC 90-20012. (Illus.). 336p. reprint ed. pap. 104.20 (*0-608-20013-1*, 207128900010) Bks Demand.

— Custer Civil War Unfinished Memoirs. pap. 23.95 (*0-8488-0025-7*, J M C & Co); text 27.95 (*0-89141-049-X*, J M C & Co) Amereon Ltd.

— General Custer & the Battle of the Little Big Horn: The Federal View. 1985. 32.00 (*0-8488-0017-6*, J M C & Co); pap. 17.00 (*0-8488-0018-4*, J M C & Co) Amereon Ltd.

— I, Varnum: The Autobiographical Reminiscences of Custer's Chief of Scouts. Including His Testimony at the Reno Court of Inquiry. 1985. pap. 22.95 (*0-8488-0027-3*, J M C & Co) Amereon Ltd.

An Asterisk (*) at the beginning of an entry indicates that the title is appearing for the first time.

— The Papers of the Order of the Indian Wars. (Illus.). 1975. 27.50 (*0-88342-040-6*) Old Army.

— The Two Battles of Little Big Horn. (Illus.). 1985. pap. 23.95 (*0-8488-0029-X*, J M C & Co) Amereon Ltd.

Carroll, John M., frwd. Official Army Register of the Volunteer Force of the United States Army. reprint ed. 178.00 (*0-8488-0038-9*, J M C & Co) Amereon Ltd.

Carroll, John M., intro. Cyclorama of Gen. Custer's Last Fight: A Reproduction of the Original Document Complete in All Respects. LC 88-50600. (Echoes of the Little Big Horn Ser.: Vol. 3). (Illus.). 104p. 1988. reprint ed. 30.00 (*0-912783-17-6*) Upton & Sons.

— The Sand Creek Massacre: A Documentary History, 1865-1867. 1985. 41.95 (*0-914074-03-2*, J M C & Co) Amereon Ltd.

Carroll, John M. & Aldrich, Robert, eds. The Reno Court of Inquiry: Proceedings of a Court of Inquiry in the Case of Major Marcus A. Reno, January 13, 1879, Chicago, Illinois, Concerning His Conduct at the Battle of the Little Big Horn River, June 25-26, 1876. (Illus.). 1985. 72.00 (*0-8488-0016-8*, J M C & Co) Amereon Ltd.

Carroll, John M. & Bjorklund, Lorence. The Benteen-Goldin Letters on Custer & His Last Battle. 1976. pap. 15.95 (*0-8488-0247-0*) Amereon Ltd.

Carroll, John M. & Herring, George C., eds. Modern American Diplomacy. rev. ed. LC 95-8681. (Illus.). 293p. 1995. pap. 17.95 (*0-8420-2555-3*); text 45.00 (*0-8420-2554-5*) Scholarly Res Inc.

Carroll, John M., ed. see Godfrey, Edward S.

Carroll, John M., jt. ed. see Moran, Thomas P.

Carroll, John M., ed. see Remsburg, John E. & Remsburg, George J.

Carroll, John M., ed. see United States Adjutant-General's Office.

Carroll, John P. Grilling. Wertz, Laurie, ed. LC 92-10316. (Williams-Sonoma Kitchen Library). (Illus.). 108p. 1992. lib. bdg. write for info. (*0-7835-0207-9*) Time-Life.

— Grilling. Wertz, Laurie, ed. LC 92-10316. (Williams-Sonoma Kitchen Library). (Illus.). 108p. (J). (gr. 11). 1999. 18.95 (*0-7835-0206-0*) Time-Life.

— Healthy Cooking. Williams, Chuck, ed. LC 96-24076. (Williams-Sonoma Kitchen Library). (Illus.). 108p. (J). (gr. 11). 1997. 18.95 (*0-7835-0319-9*) Time-Life.

— Muffins & Quick Breads. Wertz, Laurie, ed. LC 92-27837. (Williams-Sonoma Kitchen Library). (Illus.). 108p. 1993. lib. bdg. write for info. (*0-7835-0234-6*) Time-Life.

— Muffins & Quick Breads. Wertz, Laurie, ed. LC 92-27837. (Williams-Sonoma Kitchen Library). (Illus.). 108p. (J). (gr. 11). 1999. 18.95 (*0-7835-0233-8*) Time-Life.

— Outdoor Cooking. Williams, Chuck, ed. LC 96-24078. (Williams-Sonoma Kitchen Library). (Illus.). 108p. (J). (gr. 11). 1999. 18.95 (*0-7835-0320-2*) Time-Life.

— Pies & Tarts. Wertz, Laurie, ed. LC 92-10315. (Williams-Sonoma Kitchen Library). (Illus.). 108p. 1992. lib. bdg. write for info. (*0-7835-0201-X*) Time-Life.

— Pies & Tarts. Wertz, Laurie, ed. LC 92-10315. (Williams-Sonoma Kitchen Library). (Illus.). 108p. (gr. 11). 1999. 18.95 (*0-7835-0200-1*) Time-Life.

Carroll, John P. & Rainey, Virginia. California: The Beautiful Cookbook. (Illus.). 240p. 1991. 50.00 (*0-00-215931-7*) Collins SF.

Carroll, John R. A Carol for Tiny Tim. 1994. 5.50 (*0-87129-479-6*, C88) Dramatic Pub.

— Oh, What a Tangled Web. 1976. 3.50 (*0-87129-439-7*, O11) Dramatic Pub.

— Physical & Technical Aspects of Fire & Arson Investigation. (Illus.). 470p. 1982. pap. 56.95 (*0-398-06047-9*) C C Thomas.

— Physical & Technical Aspects of Fire & Arson Investigation. fac. ed. (Illus.). 470p. 1982. 71.95 (*0-398-03785-X*) C C Thomas.

Carroll, John S. & Johnson, Eric J. Decision Research: A Field Guide to Studying Decision Behavior. (Applied Social Research Methods Ser.: Vol. 22). (Illus.). 160p. (C). 1990. 42.00 (*0-8039-3268-5*); pap. 18.95 (*0-8039-3269-3*) Sage.

Carroll, John S. & Payne, John W. Cognition & Social Behavior. LC 76-48939. 290p. 1976. text 59.95 (*0-89859-111-2*) L Erlbaum Assocs.

Carroll, John T. & Carroll, James R. Preaching the Hard Sayings of Jesus. LC 96-15771. 174p. 1996. pap. 14.95 (*1-56563-230-3*) Hendrickson MA.

Carroll, John W. Laws of Nature. (Studies in Philosophy). (Illus.). 212p. (C). 1994. text 64.95 (*0-521-43334-7*) Cambridge U Pr.

Carroll-Johnson, Rose M., ed. Advanced Core Curriculum for Oncology Nursing. (Illus.). 430p. 1998. pap. write for info. (*0-7216-7394-5*, W B Saunders Co) Harcrt Hlth Sci Grp.

Carroll-Johnson, Rose Mary, et al, eds. Psychosocial Nursing Care along the Cancer Continuum. LC 98-65615. (Illus.). 502p. 1998. pap. text 29.95 (*1-890504-04-1*) Oncology Nursing.

Carroll, Jonathan. After Silence. LC 92-12698. 1993. 21.00 (*0-385-41974-0*) Doubleday.

— After Silence. LC 93-38874. 240p. 1994. pap. 12.00 (*0-385-47351-6*) Doubleday.

— Bones of the Moon. 224p. 1990. pap. 7.95 (*0-380-70688-1*, Avon Bks) Morrow Avon.

— Child Across the Sky. 224p. 1990. 18.95 (*0-385-26535-2*) Doubleday.

— From the Teeth of Angels. LC 93-22997. 224p. 1994. 22.00 (*0-385-46841-5*) Doubleday.

— From the Teeth of Angels. 224p. 1995. pap. 12.00 (*0-385-47646-9*) Doubleday.

***Carroll, Jonathan.** The Land of Laughs. 2001. text. write for info. (*0-312-87311-5*) St Martin.

— The Marriage of Sticks. 2000. pap. 14.95 (*0-312-87243-7*) St Martin.

— The Marriage of Sticks. 1999. mass mkt. write for info. (*0-8125-7618-7*) Tor Bks.

— The Marriage of Sticks. LC 99-33233. 256p. 1999. 23.95 (*0-312-87193-7*, Pub. by Tor Bks) St Martin.

Carroll, Jonathan. Outside the Dog Museum. 336p. 1993. mass mkt. 5.99 (*0-553-56164-2*) Bantam.

— Outside the Dog Museum. 256p. 1992. 20.00 (*0-385-41973-2*) Doubleday.

— Sleeping in Flames. 288p. 1989. 17.95 (*0-385-24957-8*) Doubleday.

— Sleeping in Flames. LC 89-40549. 288p. 1990. pap. 13.00 (*0-679-72777-9*) Vin Bks.

***Carroll, Jonathan.** The Wooden Sea. 2000. write for info. (*0-312-87823-0*) Tor Bks.

***Carroll, Jordan.** The Circle at the Top. LC 99-91580. 2000. 25.00 (*0-7388-0904-7*); pap. 18.00 (*0-7388-0905-5*) Xlibris Corp.

Carroll, Joseph. Evolution & Literary Theory. 512p. 1994. 44.95 (*0-8262-0979-3*) U of Mo Pr.

— How to Worship Jesus Christ. (Believer's Life System Ser.). 56p. 1997. pap. 7.99 (*0-8024-2683-2*) Moody.

Carroll, Joseph M. The Copernican Plan: Restructuring the American High School. (Orig.). 1989. pap. write for info. (*0-318-65833-X*) Reg Lab Educ IOT NE Isls.

— The Copernican Plan Evaluated: The Evolution of a Revolution. LC 94-94380. 168p. 1994. pap. 24.95 (*0-9641442-0-4*) Copernican.

Carroll, Joseph S. How to Worship Jesus Christ. pap. 7.99 (*0-8024-3424-X*, 175) Moody.

Carroll, Joseph T. Ireland in the War Years, 1939-1945. LC 97-15667. 190p. 1998. 74.95 (*1-57309-186-3*); pap. 54.95 (*1-57309-185-5*) Intl Scholars.

Carroll, Joyce A. The Best of Dr. Jac. 193p. 1998. pap. text 19.95 (*1-888842-10-5*) Absey & Co.

— Phonics Friendly Books: Teaching Phonics Through Children's Literature. 175p. 1998. pap. text 29.95 (*1-888842-11-3*) Absey & Co.

Carroll, Joyce A. & Habermas, Ron. Jesus Didn't Use Worksheets: A 2000 Year Old Model for Good Teaching. 202p. (Orig.). 1996. pap. 17.95 (*1-888842-00-8*, 11755) Absey & Co.

Carroll, Joyce A. & Wilson, Edward E. Acts of Teaching: How to Teach Writing: A Text, a Reader, a Narrative. (Illus.). 546p. 1993. pap. text 30.00 (*1-56308-039-7*) Teacher Ideas Pr.

Carroll, Joyce A. & Wilson, Edward E., eds. Poetry after Lunch: Poems to Read Aloud. 164p. (Orig.). 1997. pap. 17.95 (*1-888842-03-2*, 1040) Absey & Co.

Carroll, Juliet E. Fun with Fungi. (Four-H Ser.). (Illus.). 12p. (J). (gr. 6-10). 1989. pap. 2.75 (*1-57753-192-2*, 153J115) Corn Coop Ext.

— Know Your Tree Diseases. (Four-H Ser.). (Illus.). 28p. (YA). (gr. 8-12). 1988. pap. 3.25 (*1-57753-214-7*, 153J116) Corn Coop Ext.

— Learning Biology with Plant Pathology. 1994. 8.00 (*0-941212-16-5*) Natl Assn Bio Tchrs.

Carroll, K. K. Diet, Nutrition & Health. 368p. (C). 1990. text 65.00 (*0-7735-0733-7*, Pub. by McG-Queens Univ Pr); pap. text 29.95 (*0-7735-0741-8*, Pub. by McG-Queens Univ Pr) CUP Services.

Carroll, K. K., ed. Lipids & Tumors. (Progress in Biochemical Pharmacology Ser.: Vol. 10). (Illus.). 300p. 1975. 128.75 (*3-8055-1708-4*) S Karger.

Carroll, Karen J., ed. A Baby Is a Special Blessing. (Illus.). 32p. 1984. pap. 5.95 (*0-8378-2039-1*) Gibson.

***Carroll, Karen M. & Southern Accents Editors.** Entertaining with Southern Style. (Illus.). 184p. 2000. 35.00 (*0-8212-2638-X*) Bulfinch Pr.

Carroll, Kat, jt. auth. see Bullard, Barbara.

***Carroll, Kathleen.** Science for Every Learner: Brain-Compatible Pathways to Scientific Literacy. LC 99-57922. (Illus.). 208p. 2000. 39.00 (*1-56976-105-1*, 1105) Zephyr Pr AZ.

Carroll, Kathleen. Sing a Song of Science. LC 98-36097. 1998. 27.00 (*1-56976-090-X*) Zephyr Pr AZ.

***Carroll, Kathleen, ed.** Improving Compliance with Alcoholism Treatment. 104p. 2000. reprint ed. pap. text 20.00 (*0-7881-8471-7*) DIANE Pub.

***Carroll, Kathleen M.** Cognitive Behavioral Approach: Treating Cocaine Addiction. 140p. 1998. per. 12.00 (*0-16-061521-6*) USGPO.

Carroll, Kathryn B., ed. see Brown, John H.

Carroll, Kelly. The Pet Tracker: For Dog Owners. (Illus.). 40p. 1997. spiral bd. 23.00 (*0-9657256-0-X*) Falling Sun.

Carroll, Ken, Jr., jt. auth. see Mullican, Judy.

Carroll, Kenneth. So What! (For the White Dude Who Said This Ain't Poetry) 60p. 1995. pap. 10.00 (*0-938572-10-5*) Bunny Crocodile.

— Touched by God. 1998. write for info. (*0-87574-338-2*) Pendle Hill.

Carroll, Kenneth K., ed. Current Perspectives on Nutrition & Health. 312p. 1998. text 65.00 (*0-7735-1698-0*, Pub. by McG-Queens Univ Pr); pap. text 24.95 (*0-7735-1724-3*, Pub. by McG-Queens Univ Pr) CUP Services.

Carroll, Kenneth K., jt. ed. see Kritchevsky, David.

Carroll, Kevin. Architectures of Nigeria. 1996. text 45.00 (*0-905788-37-0*) St Martin.

Carroll, L. Alchemy of the Human Spirit: A Guide to Human Transition into the New Age, No. III. (Illus.). 376p. (Orig.). 1995. pap. 14.00 (*0-9636304-8-2*) Kryon Writings.

Carroll, L. Patrick. Where God May Be Found. LC 93-48993. 112p. (Orig.). 1994. pap. 7.95 (*0-8091-3472-1*) Paulist Pr.

Carroll, L. Patrick & Dyckman, Katharine M. Inviting the Mystic, Supporting the Prophet: An Introduction to Spiritual Direction. LC 81-80053. 112p. (Orig.). 1981. pap. 7.95 (*0-8091-2378-9*) Paulist Pr.

Carroll, Lavon B. Love, Sin & Survival: Three Women in 1930s Utah. LC 99-60983. 454p. 1999. pap. 12.95 (*1-888106-94-8*) Agreka Bks.

Carroll, Lawrence. Lawrence Carroll. (Illus.). 160p. 1999. pap. 39.95 (*3-89322-508-0*) Dr Cantz sche Druckerei GmbH.

Carroll, Lee. The Journey Home: The Story of Michael Thomas & the Seven Angels. LC 97-28197. 272p. 1997. 14.95 (*1-56170-399-0*, 814) Hay House.

— The Journey Home: The Story of Michael Thomas & the Seven Angels. 176p. 1998. pap. 11.95 (*1-56170-552-7*, 814T) Hay House.

— Kryon - Don't Think Like a Human! Vol. 2: Channelled Answers to Basic Questions. (Illus.). 288p. 1994. pap. 12.00 (*0-9636304-0-7*) Kryon Writings.

— Kryon - The End Times: New Information for Personal Peace. 176p. 1993. pap. 12.00 (*0-9636304-2-3*) Kryon Writings.

***Carroll, Lee.** Letters from Home: Loving Messages from the Family. Kramer, Jill, ed. 1999. pap. 14.00 (*1-888053-12-7*) Kryon Writings.

Carroll, Lee. The Parables of Kryon. LC 96-24695. (Illus.). 160p. 1996. 17.00 (*1-56170-364-8*, 850) Hay House.

***Carroll, Lee.** The Parables of Kryon. 176p. 2000. reprint ed. pap. 10.95 (*1-56170-663-9*, 850T) Hay House.

Carroll, Lee. Partnering with God: Practical Information for the New Millennium. Kramer, Jill, ed. (Book Six Ser.). 1997. pap. 14.00 (*1-888053-10-0*) Kryon Writings.

***Carroll, Lee.** Passing the Marker: Lightworker's Guide to the New Millennium Energy. Kramer, Jill, ed. (C). 2000. 13.50 (*1-888053-11-9*, Pub. by Kryon Writings) New Leaf Dist.

— Victim of the Game. rev. ed. 432p. 1999. pap. 19.95 (*1-58444-069-4*) DiscUs Bks.

Carroll, Lee & Tober, Jan. The Indigo Children: The New Kids Have Arrived. LC 99-19532. 272p. 1999. pap. 13.95 (*1-56170-608-6*, 580) Hay House.

***Carroll, Lee & Tober, Jan.** The Indigo Children: The New Kids Have Arrived. 224p. 2001. pap. 13.95 (*1-56170-801-1*) Hay House.

Carroll, Lenore. Abduction From Fort Union. 24.95 (*0-8027-4080-4*) Walker & Co.

Carroll, Lenore. Annie Chambers. 215p. 1990. pap. 8.50 (*0-922820-07-4*) Watermark Pr.

— One Hundred Girls' Mother. LC 98-23497. (Women of the West Ser.). 348p. 1998. 24.95 (*0-312-85994-5*, Pub. by Forge NYC) St Martin.

Carroll, Leo. Lawful Order: A Case Study of Correctional Crisis & Reform. McShane, Marilyn D. & Williams, Frank P., 3rd, eds. LC 97-39224. (Current Issues in Criminal Justice Ser.: Vol. 23). (Illus.). 384p. 1998. text 70.00 (*0-8153-1617-8*, SS949) Garland.

Carroll, Les. The Angel of Marye's Heights: Sergeant Richard Kirkland's Extraordinary Deed at the Battle of Fredericksburg. (Illus.). 87p. (YA). (gr. 10-12). 1994. 15.00 (*0-9623065-7-7*) Palmetto Bookworks.

— The Triplet's Big Switch. (Illus.). 154p. 1995. 13.95 (*0-9623065-8-4*); pap. 8.95 (*0-9623065-9-2*) Palmetto Bookworks.

Carroll, Lewis, jt. auth. see Center for Learning Network Staff.

Carroll, Lewis, jt. auth. see Fior, Jane.

Carroll, Lewis, jt. auth. see Lear, Edward.

Carroll, Lewis, jt. auth. see Sigler, Carolyn.

Carroll, Lewis Society of Canada Staff, jt. auth. see Bolster, Stephanie.

Carroll, Lewis, pseud. Alice: A One-Act Play. (Illus.). 36p. (J). (gr. 4-12). 1990. pap. 3.25 (*0-88680-336-5*) I E Clark.

— Alice au Pays des Merveilles. (FRE.). 1996. pap. 5.95 (*2-87714-315-5*, Pub. by Bookking Intl) Distribks Inc.

— Alice au Pays des Merveilles. (FRE.). (J). (gr. 3-8). 7.95 (*0-8288-6095-5*, M5497) Fr & Eur.

— Alice au Pays des Merveilles. (Folio - Junior Ser.: No. 437). (FRE., Illus.). 223p. (J). (gr. 5-10). 1987. pap. 9.95 (*2-07-033437-6*) Schoenhof.

— Alice Boxed Set--Alice's Adventures in Wonderland & Through the Looking-glass, 2 bks., Set. (Illus.). (J). (gr. 2 up). 1993. 32.00 (*0-688-12050-4*, Wm Morrow) Morrow Avon.

Carroll, Lewis, pseud. Alice in Wonderland. Date not set. lib. bdg. 16.95 (*0-8488-1262-X*) Amereon Ltd.

Carroll, Lewis, pseud. Alice in Wonderland. (Classics for Young Readers Ser.). 64p. (J). 1994. 5.98 (*0-86112-942-3*); 9.98 (*0-86112-457-X*) Brimax Bks.

— Alice in Wonderland. 12p. (J). 1992. pap. 14.00 (*0-440-80312-8*) Dell.

— Alice in Wonderland. LC 98-8401. (Children's Thrift Classics). (Illus.). 80p. (J). 1998. pap. 1.00 (*0-486-40345-9*) Dover.

— Alice in Wonderland. 124p. (J). (gr. 1 up). 1965. pap. 5.50 (*0-87129-241-6*, A13) Dramatic Pub.

— Alice in Wonderland. (Children's Classics Ser.). (Illus.). (J). 1992. write for info. (*0-89434-121-9*) Ferguson.

Carroll, Lewis, pseud. Alice in Wonderland. (Little Golden Bks.). (J). pap. 2.29 (*0-307-02149-1*, 98104) Gldn Bks Pub Co.

— Alice in Wonderland. 192p. (gr. 3 up). mass mkt. 8.95 (*0-06-440929-5*) HarpC.

Carroll, Lewis, pseud. Alice in Wonderland. 10p. 1999. 14.95 (*1-58117-037-8*) Intervisual Bks.

***Carroll, Lewis, pseud.** Alice in Wonderland. (GER., Illus.). (ps up). 1999. 12.95 (*3-499-20733-8*) Midwest European Pubns.

— Alice in Wonderland. LC 99-18975. (Illus.). 104p. (J). (gr. 4-7). 1999. 19.95 (*0-7358-1166-0*, Pub. by North-South Bks NYC) Chronicle Bks.

Carroll, Lewis, pseud. Alice in Wonderland. (Classics Ser.). (Illus.). 52p. (J). 1994. text 3.50 (*0-7214-1654-3*, Ladybrd) Penguin Putnam.

— Alice in Wonderland. LC 87-15289. (Illus.). 160p. (J). (gr. 4-7). 1988. pap. 3.50 (*0-590-42035-6*, Apple Classics) Scholastic Inc.

— Alice in Wonderland. 143p. 1993. pap. 3.95 (*0-460-87359-8*, Everyman's Classic Lib) Tuttle Pubng.

***Carroll, Lewis, pseud.** Alice in Wonderland. (Children's Library). 272p. (J). 1998. pap. 3.95 (*1-85326-002-9*, 0029WW, Pub. by Wrdsworth Edits) NTC Contemp Pub Co.

Carroll, Lewis, pseud. Alice in Wonderland. 215p. (J). 1981. reprint ed. lib. bdg. 15.95 (*0-89966-345-1*); reprint ed. lib. bdg. 12.95 (*0-89967-019-9*, Harmony Rain) Buccaneer Bks.

***Carroll, Lewis, pseud.** Alice in Wonderland. Carruth, Jane, ed. (Illus.). 93p. (J). (gr. 4-6). 2000. reprint ed. 25.00 (*0-7881-9229-9*) DIANE Pub.

Carroll, Lewis, pseud. Alice in Wonderland. 2nd ed. Grey, Donald J., ed. LC 91-12533. (Critical Editions Ser.). (Illus.). 408p. (C). 1992. pap. text 14.00 (*0-393-95804-3*) Norton.

— Alice in Wonderland & Through the Looking Glass. (Illustrated Junior Library). (Illus.). 320p. (J). (gr. 4-7). 1946. 15.99 (*0-448-06004-3*, G & D) Peng Put Young Read.

— Alice in Wonderland & Through the Looking Glass. abr. ed. (J). 1997. audio 16.99 (*0-553-47812-5*) Bantam.

— Alice in Wonderland & Through the Looking-Glass. large type ed. 270p. 1996. reprint ed. lib. bdg. 22.00 (*0-939495-07-4*) North Bks.

***Carroll, Lewis, pseud.** Alice in Wonderland Book & Charm. LC 99-42426. (Charming Classic Bks.). (Illus.). 176p. (J). (gr. 3-7). 2000. 5.95 (*0-694-01454-0*, HarpFestival) HarpC Child Bks.

Carroll, Lewis, pseud. Alice in Wonderland Coloring Book. 81st ed. (Illus.). 64p. (J). (gr. k-3). 1972. pap. 3.50 (*0-486-22853-3*) Dover.

***Carroll, Lewis, pseud.** Alice in Wonderland Jigsaw Book. (Illus.). 16p. (J). (gr. 2-6). 2000. 16.99 (*0-8037-2616-3*, Dial Yng Read) Peng Put Young Read.

— Alice in Wonderland; Through the Looking-Glass. 188p. 1998. reprint ed. lib. bdg. 22.00 (*1-58287-012-8*) North Bks.

Carroll, Lewis, pseud. Alice in Wonderland/Classic. LC 96-232489. (Illus.). 248p. (YA). Date not set. 14.95 (*1-884807-19-4*) Blushing Rose.

***Carroll, Lewis, pseud.** Alice Through the Looking Glass. Reed, Jeremy, ed. (Classic Portables Ser.). (Illus.). 192p. (J). 2000. reprint ed. pap. 10.95 (*1-84068-021-0*, Pub. by Creation Books) Subterranean Co.

Carroll, Lewis, pseud. Alice Through the Looking Glass: Musical. 1976. pap. 5.95 (*0-87129-215-7*, A01) Dramatic Pub.

— Alice's Abenteuer im Wunderland. Zimmermann, Antonie, tr. from GER. (Illus.). 178p. 1974. reprint ed. 6.95 (*0-486-20668-8*) Dover.

— Alice's Adventure in Wonderland. 2nd ed. (Illus.). 62p. 1993. pap. text 5.95 (*0-19-585274-5*) OUP.

Carroll, Lewis, pseud. Alice's Adventures in Wonderland. LC 96-24129. (Illus.). 152p. (J). 1996. 25.00 (*1-885183-47-X*) Artisan.

***Carroll, Lewis, pseud.** Alice's Adventures in Wonderland. Edens, Cooper, ed. LC 99-50816. (Illus.). (J). 2000. 19.95 (*0-8118-2274-5*) Chronicle Bks.

Carroll, Lewis, pseud. Alice's Adventures in Wonderland. LC 85-856. (Illus.). 128p. (J). (gr. 4-6). 1995. 19.95 (*0-8050-0212-X*, Bks Young Read) H Holt & Co.

— Alice's Adventures in Wonderland. Goodacre, Selwyn H., ed. 160p. (J). 1991. pap. 16.95 (*0-15-604426-9*, Harvest Bks) Harcourt.

***Carroll, Lewis, pseud.** Alice's Adventures in Wonderland. LC 00-40906. (Illus.). (J). 2001. lib. bdg. write for info. (*0-06-029498-1*) HarpC.

— Alice's Adventures in Wonderland. 192p. (YA). (gr. 3 up). Date not set. 19.95 (*0-06-029150-8*) HarpC Child Bks.

Carroll, Lewis, pseud. Alice's Adventures in Wonderland. LC 91-31482. (Illus.). 208p. (J). (gr. 2 up). 1992. 16.95 (*0-688-11087-8*, Wm Morrow) Morrow Avon.

— Alice's Adventures in Wonderland. (Classics for Young Readers Ser.). (Illus.). 156p. (YA). (gr. 4-7). 1994. pap. 3.99 (*0-14-036675-X*, PuffinBks) Peng Put Young Read.

— Alice's Adventures in Wonderland. LC 98-7216. (Illus.). 128p. (J). (gr. 4-7). 1998. 19.99 (*0-525-46094-2*, Dutton Child) Peng Put Young Read.

— Alice's Adventures in Wonderland. 304p. 1992. pap. 2.50 (*0-8125-0418-6*, Pub. by Tor Bks) St Martin.

— Alice's Adventures in Wonderland. (J). 1992. pap. 4.95 (*0-8167-2875-5*) Troll Communs.

— Alice's Adventures in Wonderland. LC 89-33889. (Illustrated Classics Ser.). (Illus.). 48p. (J). (gr. 3-6). 1997. pap. 5.95 (*0-8167-1862-8*) Troll Communs.

Carroll, Lewis, pseud. Alice's Adventures in Wonderland. (Illus.). (J). 1992. 8.34 (*0-606-18634-4*) Turtleback.

— Alice's Adventures in Wonderland. LC 99-28788. (Illus.). 206p. (J). (gr. 3-7). 1999. 24.99 (*0-7636-0804-1*) Candlewick Pr.

Carroll, Lewis, pseud. Alice's Adventures in Wonderland. large type ed. (Large Print Heritage Ser.). 140p. (YA). (gr. 7-12). 1997. lib. bdg. 24.95 (*1-58118-010-1*, 21962) LRS.

— Alice's Adventures in Wonderland. unabridged ed. 1994. lib. bdg. 18.95 incl. audio (*1-883049-46-6*) Sound Room.

Carroll, Lewis, pseud. Alice's Adventures in Wonderland, Set. unabridged ed. (Carroll Ser.). (J). 1994. 16.95 incl. audio (*1-883049-40-7*, 390330, Pub. by Sound Room) Lndmrk Audiobks.

C

Carroll, Lewis, pseud. Alice's Adventures in Wonderland, Vol. 1. (Selected Classic Fairy Tales Ser.). (Illus.). 20p. (J). (gr. k-6). 1999. lib. bdg. 13.95 (*1-56674-220-X*) Forest Hse.

— Alice's Adventures in Wonderland & Through the Looking Glass. (Illus.). 256p. (J). 1984. mass mkt. 3.95 (*0-553-21345-8*, Bantam Classics) Bantam.

— Alice's Adventures in Wonderland & Through the Looking Glass. LC 92-53181. (Illus.). 336p. (J). 1992. 14.95 (*0-679-41795-8*, Evryman's Lib Childs) Knopf.

— Alice's Adventures in Wonderland & Through the Looking Glass. (J). (gr. 4). 1960. mass mkt. 3.95 (*0-451-52320-2*, Sig Classics) NAL.

— Alice's Adventures in Wonderland & Through the Looking Glass. LC 88-33866. (Illus.). 160p. 1989. 29.95 (*0-922984-01-8*) Wellington IL.

*__Carroll, Lewis, pseud.__ Alice's Adventures in Wonderland & Through the Looking-Glass, 2 vols. LC 98-53263. (Illus.). 464p. (J). 1999. 34.95 (*0-15-202199-X*, Harvest Bks) Harcourt.

Carroll, Lewis, pseud. Alice's Adventures in Wonderland & Through the Looking-Glass. (Puffin Bks.). (Illus.). 336p. (J). (gr. 3-7). 1998. pap. 4.99 (*0-14-038351-4*, PuffinBks) Peng Put Young Read.

— Alice's Adventures in Wonderland & Through the Looking-Glass. (J). 1968. 9.05 (*0-606-03007-7*, Pub. by Turtleback) Demco.

— Alice's Adventures in Wonderland & Through the Looking Glass: And What Alice Found There. (Illus.). 448p. (J). 1992. pap. 4.99 (*0-440-40743-5*) Dell.

— Alice's Adventures in Wonderland & Through the Looking Glass: And What Alice Found There. Haughton, Hugh, ed. & intro. by. LC 99-178228. 1998. pap. 8.95 (*0-14-043317-1*) Viking Penguin.

— Alice's Adventures in Wonderland & Through the Looking-Glass: And What Alice Found There. Green, Roger L., ed. & intro. by. LC 98-204883. (Oxford World's Classics Ser.). (Illus.). 312p. 1998. pap. 6.95 (*0-19-283374-X*) OUP.

— Alice's Adventures in Wonderland, Through the Looking-Glass, & the Hunting of the Snark. (BCL1-PR English Literature Ser.). 351p. 1992. reprint ed. lib. bdg. 89.00 (*0-7812-7517-2*) Rprt Serv.

***Carroll, Lewis, pseud. Alice's Adventures Under-Ground. (Cottage Classics Ser.). (Illus.). 88p. (YA). (gr. 3-12). 2000. 29.95 (*1-892847-00-0*);pap. 17.95 (*1-892847-01-9*) Word Play Calif.**
Word Play Publications is proud to offer a unique edition of Alice's Adventures Under Ground. Previously available only in Facsimile form, this edition of Lewis Carroll's predecessor to Alice's Adventures in Wonderland is the first to be set in type as a single volume & the first published with drawings other than those by Carroll himself. All new art work by noted illustrator & former underground cartoonist Kim Deitch perfectly matches the spontaneity of Carroll's original. Using the image of the real Alice Liddell as his model is just one of the ingenious innovations that Deitch brings to this lively edition of Alice's Adventures Under Ground. In his perspective foreword, Mark Burstein, Vice President of the Lewis Carroll Society of North America & curator of one of the largest collections of Carrolliana in the world, relates the historic importance of this books revolutionary impact in expanding the horizons of children's literature. For ordering information; contact Word Play Publications, 1 Sutter St., San Francisco 94104, (415) 397-3716, wordplay@world passage.net, or BookPeople Distribution at (800) 999-4650. Libraries contact Unique Books (314) 776-6695 *Publisher Paid Annotation.*

Carroll, Lewis, pseud. Alice's Adventures under Ground: The Story That Became Alice in Wonderland. (Illus.). 120p. (J). 1999. 17.95 (*1-85145-471-3*, Pub. by Pavilion Bks Ltd) Trafalgar.

— Alice's Adventures Underground. 8th ed. (Illus.). 128p. (J). (gr. 4-9). 1965. pap. 4.95 (*0-486-21482-6*) Dover.

— Alicia en el Pais de las Maravillas.Tr. of Alice in Wonderland Coloring Book. (SPA., Illus.). (J). 1994. pap. 2.95 (*0-486-28177-9*) Dover.

*__Carroll, Lewis, pseud.__ The Annotated Alice: Alice's Adventures in Wonderland & Through the Looking Gass. LC 99-35647. 384p. 1999. 29.95 (*0-393-04847-0*) Norton.

— Anya V Strane Chudes (Alice in Wonderland), Set. Nabokov, Vladimir, tr. (RUS.). 1996. pap. 49.50 incl. audio (*1-58085-580-6*) Interlingua VA.

Carroll, Lewis, pseud. Anya V Stranye Chudes. Nabokov, Vladimir, tr. from RUS. LC 75-43371. (Illus.). 115p. 1976. reprint ed. pap. 4.95 (*0-486-23316-2*) Dover.

— Aventures D'Alice au Pays des Merveilles. Bue, Henri, tr. from ENG. (FRE., Illus.). 196p. (J). (gr. 4-8). 1972. reprint ed. pap. 6.95 (*0-486-22836-3*) Dover.

— Best of Lewis Carroll. 480p. (J). 1992. 7.98 (*0-89009-700-3*) Bk Sales Inc.

— The Collected Stories of Lewis Carroll. LC 94-18191. (Illus.). 304p. 1994. 9.95 (*0-8065-1552-X*, Citadel Pr) Carol Pub Group.

— Complete Illustrated Lewis Carroll. (Complete Classics Library). (Illus.). 1998. pap. 11.95 (*1-85326-897-6*, 8976WW, Pub. by Wrdsworth Edits) NTC Contemp Pub Co.

— The Complete Sylvie & Bruno: The Mercury House Edition. Christensen, Thomas, ed. LC 91-9958. (Illus.). 416p. 1991. 30.00 (*1-56279-009-9*) Mercury Hse Inc.

— The Complete Works of Lewis Carroll. 1993. 21.00 (*0-679-42575-6*) McKay.

*__Carroll, Lewis, pseud.__ The Complete Works of Lewis Carroll. (Illus.). 1166p. 1999. pap. 22.95 (*0-14-010542-5*, Pub. by Pnguin Bks Ltd) Trafalgar.

— Father William. deluxe limited ed. (Illus.). 16p. 1994. 20.00 (*0-614-10617-6*) Turtles Quill.

Carroll, Lewis, pseud. Humorous Verse of Lewis Carroll. Orig. Title: Collected Verse of Lewis Carroll. (Illus.). 446p. (J). (gr. 1 up). 1960. pap. 9.95 (*0-486-20654-8*) Dover.

— The Humorous Verse of Lewis Carroll. 30.95 (*0-89190-687-8*) Amereon Ltd.

— Hunting of Shark. LC 98-134194. 128p. 1998. pap. 9.95 (*0-14-043491-7*) Viking Penguin.

Carroll, Lewis, pseud. The Hunting of the Snark: A Musical Comedy. 36p. (J). (gr. 2 up). 1987. pap. 4.00 (*0-88680-273-3*) I E Clark.

Carroll, Lewis, pseud. The Hunting of the Snark: Essays on Lewis Carroll's Life & Art. LC 92-70826. (Illus.). 87p. 1992. 15.00 (*0-930326-07-5*) L Carroll Soc.

— Jabberwocky: From Through the Looking Glass. (Illus.). 32p. (J). 1989. 16.95 (*0-8109-1150-7*, Pub. by Abrams) Time Warner.

— Lewis Carroll. deluxe ed. (Illus.). 896p. 1995. 19.99 (*0-517-14781-5*) Random Hse Value.

— Lewis Carroll & the Kitchins. Cohen, Morton N., tr. LC 79-92406. (Carroll Studies: No. 4). (Illus.). 80p. (Orig.). pap. 10.00 (*0-930326-04-0*) L Carroll Soc.

— Lewis Carroll's Classic Photos of Children. 1998. pap. 4.95 (*0-486-29788-8*) Dover.

— Lewis Carroll's Games & Puzzles. 40th ed. (Illus.). 128p. (Orig.). 1992. pap. 4.95 (*0-486-26922-1*) Dover.

— Oeuvres de Jeunesse (Alice) (FRE.). 125.00 (*0-8288-3455-5*) Fr & Eur.

— Phantasmagoria. (Literary Classics Ser.). (Illus.). 70p. 1998. reprint ed. pap. 5.95 (*1-57392-252-8*) Prometheus Bks.

— Pillow Problems & a Tangled Tale. 261p. 1958. pap. 7.95 (*0-486-20493-6*) Dover.

— Poems of Lewis Carroll. Livingston, Myra C., ed. LC 73-7914. (Harper Poets Ser.). (Illus.). 128p. (YA). (gr. 7 up). 1986. lib. bdg. 11.89 (*0-690-04540-9*) HarpC Child Bks.

— Rediscovered Lewis Carroll Puzzles. Wakeling, Edward, ed. & compiled by by. LC 95-30151. 1996. pap. 4.95 (*0-486-28861-7*) Dover.

— Sylvie & Bruno. (Illus.). 448p. 1988. reprint ed. pap. 8.95 (*0-486-25588-3*) Dover.

— Symbolic Logic & the Game of Logic. 335p. 1958. pap. 8.95 (*0-486-20492-8*) Dover.

— A Tangled Tale. LC 74-82735. 1975. 15.00 (*0-89388-181-3*) Okpaku Communications.

— Through the Looking Glass. 176p. Date not set. 19.95 (*0-8488-2629-9*) Amereon Ltd.

— Through the Looking Glass. (Illus.). 176p. (YA). (gr. 5-9). 1996. pap. 4.99 (*0-14-036709-8*, PuffinBks) Peng Put Young Read.

— Through the Looking-Glass. LC 92-20642. (Books of Wonder). (Illus.). 240p. (J). (gr. 2 up). 1993. 16.95 (*0-688-12049-0*, Wm Morrow) Morrow Avon.

— Through the Looking Glass. large type ed. (Large Print Heritage Ser.). 161p. (YA). (gr. 7-12). 1997. lib. bdg. 26.95 (*1-58118-007-1*, 21495) LRS.

— Through the Looking Glass. (J). 1981. reprint ed. lib. bdg. 15.95 (*0-89966-419-9*) Buccaneer Bks.

— Through the Looking Glass: And What Alice Found There. LC 99-35222. (Dover Thrift Editions Ser.). 1999. pap. text 1.50 (*0-486-40878-7*) Dover.

— Through the Looking Glass & What Alice Found There. unabridged ed. 1994. lib. bdg. 18.95 incl. audio (*1-883049-47-4*) Sound Room.

— Through the Looking Glass & What Alice Found There. Set. unabridged ed. (J). 1994. 16.95 incl. audio (*1-883049-41-5*, Pub. by Sound Room) Lndmrk Audiobks.

— Thru the Looking Glass & What Alice Found There. 24p. (Orig.). (J). (gr. 3-8). 1993. pap. 3.00 (*1-57514-234-1*, 1071) Encore Perform Pub.

— The Walrus & the Carpenter. LC 85-7591. (Illus.). 32p. (J). (gr. k-3). 1998. pap. 9.95 (*1-56397-719-2*) Boyds Mills Pr.

Carroll, Lewis, pseud & Baker, Kyle. Through the Looking-Glass. (Classics Illustrated Ser.). (Illus.). 52p. (YA). pap. 4.95 (*1-57209-002-2*) Classics Int Ent.

Carroll, Lewis, pseud & Gave, Marc. Selected Classic Fairy Tales, 2 vols., Set. (Illus.). 40p. (J). (gr. k-6). 1999. 27.90 (*1-56674-945-X*) Forest Hse.

Carroll, Lewis, pseud & Mitchell, Kathy. Alice in Wonderland & Through the Looking Glass. LC 84-82525. (Golden Classics). 254p. (J). 1986. write for info. (*0-307-67111-9*, Whitman Coin) St Martin.

Carroll, Lewis, pseud & Tenniel, John. Alice's Adventures in Wonderland. LC 82-242973. (Illus.). (YA). (gr. 5 up). 1977. text 14.95 (*0-312-01821-5*) St Martin.

Carroll, Lilian. Quaker Memoirs: Recollections of Meetings at Hastings, Bedford, Allonby (Cumbria) & High Flatts (Yorkshire) 1995. pap. 45.00 (*1-85072-154-8*, Pub. by W Sessions) St Mut.

Carroll, Linda, ed. see Council of State Governments Staff.

Carroll, Lorraine. Beauty & the Groom. 1997. per. 3.99 (*0-373-24128-3*, 1-24128-0) Silhouette.

— Playing Daddy. LC 96-7298. 251p. 1996. per. 3.99 (*0-373-24020-1*, 1-24020-9) Silhouette.

Carroll, Louann. Journeys: The Adventures of Leaf. LC 92-13485. (Illus.). 64p. (J). (gr. 1-8). 1992. pap. 9.95 (*1-880090-03-1*) Galde Pr.

Carroll, Lynda, jt. auth. see Baram, Uzi.

Carroll, M. D. Contexts for Amos: Prophetic Poetics in Latin-American Perspective. (JSOT Supplement Ser.: No. 132). 362p. (C). 1992. 85.00 (*1-85075-297-4*, Pub. by Sheffield Acad) CUP Services.

Carroll, M. E. & Manners, Hazel K. Movement Education Leading to Gymnastics: A Session by Session Approach to Key Stage 1. 168p. (gr. 4-7). 1991. pap. 29.95 (*0-7507-0007-6*, Falmer Pr) Taylor & Francis.

Carroll, M. E. & Manners, Hazel K., eds. Gymnastics Seven-Eleven: A Session-by-Session Approach to Key Stage 2. rev. ed. 118p. 1992. pap. 27.95 (*0-7507-0002-5*, Falmer Pr) Taylor & Francis.

Carroll, M. M. & Hayes, M. A. Nonlinear Effects in Fluids & Solids, Vol. 45. (Mathematical Concepts & Methods in Science & Engineering Ser.: No. 45). (Illus.). 384p. (C). 1996. text 107.00 (*0-306-45179-4*, Kluwer Plenum) Kluwer Academic.

Carroll, M. R. & Holloway, J. R., eds. Volatiles in Magmas. (Reviews in Mineralogy Ser.: Vol. 30). 500p. 1994. per. 30.00 (*0-939950-36-7*) Mineralogical Soc.

Carroll, Malachy, tr. see Bricianer, Serge.

Carroll, Malachy, tr. see De Margerie, Bertrand.

Carroll, Malcolm & Carroll, Janet. French Extra. LC 98-65236. (Illus.). 256p. 1998. pap. 10.95 (*0-8442-3771-X*, Teach Yrslf) NTC Contemp Pub Co.

— French Extra, Set. (Teach Yourself Ser.). (FRE.). 256p. 1998. pap. 19.95 incl. audio (*0-8442-0296-7*, 02967, Teach Yrslf) NTC Contemp Pub Co.

Carroll, Malcolm E. Origins of the Whig Party: A Dissertation. LC 72-112705. (Law, Politics & History Ser.). 1970. reprint ed. lib. bdg. 37.50 (*0-306-71917-7*) Da Capo.

Carroll, Marcia, jt. auth. see Whittelsey, Frances C.

Carroll, Marcie, jt. ed. see Carroll, Rick.

Carroll, Margaret K. What Did You Do at School Today? A Guide to Schooling & School Success. LC 98-11121. 252p. 1998. text 51.95 (*0-398-06856-9*); pap. text 38.95 (*0-398-06857-7*) C C Thomas.

Carroll, Margaret Kelly & Smith, Kay Monroe. The Home As Learning Center: The Family As Educator. 144p. 1989. pap., per. 28.95 (*0-8403-5677-3*) Kendall-Hunt.

*__Carroll, Margie K. & Christopher, Tom.__ Both Sides of the Rainbow. LC 99-66054. 320p. 1999. pap. 15.95 (*0-9674998-0-1*) Arcangela Pr Inc.

Carroll, Marguerite R. & Wiggins, James D. Elements of Group Counseling. 2nd rev. ed. 112p. (Orig.). (C). 1997. pap. text 14.95 (*0-89108-247-6*, 9606) Love Pub Co.

Carroll, Marguerite R., et al. Group Leadership: A Manual for Group Counseling Leaders. 3rd rev. ed. 250p. (Orig.). (C). 1997. pap. text 36.00 (*0-89108-249-2*, 9608) Love Pub Co.

Carroll, Marilyn. Cocaine & Crack. LC 93-43451. (Drug Library Ser.). (Illus.). 112p. (YA). (gr. 6 up). 1994. lib. bdg. 20.95 (*0-89490-472-8*) Enslow Pubs.

— PCP: The Dangerous Angel. (Encyclopedia of Psychoactive Drugs Ser.: No. 1). (Illus.). 124p. (YA). (gr. 7 up). 1985. lib. bdg. 19.95 (*0-87754-753-X*) Chelsea Hse.

Carroll, Marisa. Before Thanksgiving Comes. (Superromance Ser.: No. 811). 1998. per. 4.25 (*0-373-70811-4*, 1-70811-4) Harlequin Bks.

— Crossroads. (Tyler Ser.: No. 10). 1999. mass mkt. 3.99 (*0-373-82510-2*, 0-82510-9) Harlequin Bks.

*__Carroll, Marisa.__ Une Famille à l'Epreuve. 1999. mass mkt. 5.50 (*0-373-38345-2*) Silhouette.

Carroll, Marisa. Keeping Christmas. 1992. per. 3.39 (*0-373-70529-8*, 1-70529-2) Harlequin Bks.

*__Carroll, Marisa.__ Last-Minute Marriage. (Superromance Ser.: Bk. 942). 2000. mass mkt. 4.50 (*0-373-70942-0*, 1-70942-7) Harlequin Bks.

Carroll, Marisa. Loveknot. (Tyler Ser.: No. 12). 1999. mass mkt. 3.99 (*0-373-82512-9*, 0-82512-5) Harlequin Bks.

— The Man Who Saved Christmas. 1996. per. 3.99 (*0-373-70718-5*, 1-70718-1) Harlequin Bks.

— Marry Me Tonight: Weddings, Inc. LC 95-7133. (Superromance Ser.). 297p. 1995. per. 3.75 (*0-373-70635-9*, 1-70635-7) Harlequin Bks.

— Megan. (Superromance Ser.: No. 742). 1997. per. 3.99 (*0-373-70742-8*, 1-70742-1) Harlequin Bks.

— Mission: Children. (Hometown Reunion Ser.). 1997. per. 4.50 (*0-373-82560-9*, Harlequin) Harlequin Bks.

— Natural Attraction. (Men Made in America Ser.). 1994. per. 3.59 (*0-373-45179-2*, 1-45179-8) Harlequin Bks.

— One to One, Bk. 35. (Born in the U. S. A. Ser.). 1997. mass mkt. 4.50 (*0-373-47185-8*, 1-47185-3) Harlequin Bks.

— Peacekeeper. LC 96-572. 296p. 1995. per. 3.75 (*0-373-70655-3*, 1-70655-5) Harlequin Bks.

— Sans Rime Ni Raison. (OR Ser.). (FRE.). 1994. pap. 4.50 (*0-373-38162-X*, 1-38162-3) Harlequin Bks.

— Unexpected Son. (Hometown Reunion Ser.). 1996. per. 4.50 (*0-373-82549-8*) Harlequin Bks.

— Wedding Invitation. 1994. per. 3.50 (*0-373-70598-0*, 1-70598-7) Harlequin Bks.

— Winter Soldier: In Uniform. (Superromance Ser.: Bk. 841). 1999. per. 4.25 (*0-373-70841-6*, 1-70841-1) Harlequin Bks.

Carroll, Mark. Organelles. LC 88-24625. (Molecular Cell Biology Ser.). 202p. 1989. pap. text 26.95 (*0-89862-526-2*) Guilford Pubns.

Carroll, Mark T., ed. see Institutional Staff.

Carroll, Martha E. Focus on Ability: Serving Girls with Special Needs. LC 98-193032. 111 p. 1998. write for info. (*0-88441-492-2*) Girl Scouts USA.

Carroll, Martin. Bait. large type ed. (Linford Mystery Library). 320p. 1987. pap. 16.99 (*0-7089-6392-7*, Linford) Ulverscroft.

— Begotten Murder. large type ed. (Linford Mystery Library). 262p. 1987. pap. 16.99 (*0-7089-6363-3*, Linford) Ulverscroft.

— Blood Vengeance. large type ed. (Linford Mystery Library). 240p. 1988. pap. 16.99 (*0-7089-6613-6*, Linford) Ulverscroft.

— Dead Trouble. large type ed. (Linford Mystery Library). 231p. 1988. pap. 16.99 (*0-7089-6560-1*, Linford) Ulverscroft.

— Goodbye Is Forever. large type ed. (Linford Mystery Library). 304p. 1987. pap. 16.99 (*0-7089-6454-0*, Linford) Ulverscroft.

— Hear No Evil. large type ed. (Linford Mystery Library). 273p. 1989. pap. 16.99 (*0-7089-6641-1*, Linford) Ulverscroft.

— Miranda Said Murder. large type ed. (Linford Mystery Library). 224p. 1988. pap. 16.99 (*0-7089-6620-9*, Linford) Ulverscroft.

— Too Beautiful to Die. large type ed. (Linford Mystery Library). 1988. pap. 16.99 (*0-7089-6509-1*) Ulverscroft.

Carroll, Martin D. & Ellis, Margaret A. Designing & Coding Reusable C++ LC 94-49369. 336p. (C). 1995. pap. 41.95 (*0-201-51284-X*) Addison-Wesley.

Carroll, Mary & Brue, L. Jane. A Nurse's Guide to Caring for Elders. 240p. (C). 1987. pap. 29.95 (*0-8261-5520-0*) Springer Pub.

Carroll, Mary & Long, Katie. Discovering Art: Art Activities with Children 8-12 Years Old. (Illus.). (J). 1997. pap. 14.95 (*0-9528068-0-0*, Pub. by Pineforest Arts) Intl Spec Bk.

— Starting Art: Art Activities with Children 4-8 Years Old. large type ed. LC 98-101785. (Illus.). 47p. (J). 1996. pap. 14.95 (*0-9528068-1-9*) Intl Spec Bk.

Carroll, Mary, jt. ed. see Becker, Angelika.

Carroll, Mary A. Catholic History of Alabama & the Floridas. LC 70-124228. (Select Bibliographies Reprint Ser.). 1977. 20.95 (*0-8369-5417-3*) Ayer.

Carroll, Mary C., jt. auth. see Bartle, Beth.

Carroll, Mary H. Streamlined Cooking for a Healthy Lifestyle. (Cole Group Ser.). 240p. (Orig.). 1995. pap. 18.95 (*1-56426-067-4*) Cole Group.

Carroll, Merle T. This Is Alabama. 3rd rev. ed. (Illus.). 336p. (J). (gr. 4). 1993. reprint ed. text 14.50 (*0-9632262-0-7*) J Y Carroll.

— This Is Alabama: Teacher's Guide - Student Activity Book. 3rd ed. (Illus.). 116p. 1993. pap. text 6.95 (*0-9632262-1-5*) J Y Carroll.

Carroll, Michael. Counseling Supervision: Theory, Skills, & Practice. (Counselor Trainer & Supervisor Ser.). (Illus.). 160p. 1997. 89.50 (*0-304-32936-3*) Continuum.

— Counseling Supervision: Theory, Skills, & Practice. (Counselor Trainer & Supervisor Ser.). (Illus.). 160p. 1997. pap. 35.00 (*0-304-32938-X*) Continuum.

*__Carroll, Michael.__ Dinosaurs. (Illus.). 47p. (J). (gr. 3-7). 2000. 15.99 (*0-7814-3366-5*) Chariot Victor.

Carroll, Michael. Lightning & Rainbows. (J). (gr. 1-5). 1997. write for info. (*1-56476-603-9*, Chariot Bks); 13.99 (*0-7814-3000-3*, Chariot Bks) Chariot Victor.

— Spinning Worlds. LC 96-204019. 32p. (J). (gr. 1-5). 1996. 13.99 (*1-56476-571-7*, 6-3571, Victor Bks) Chariot Victor.

— Volcanoes & Earthquakes: God's Power Beneath Our Feet. LC 97-214136. 32p. (J). (gr. 1-5). 1997. 13.99 (*1-56476-602-0*, Chariot Bks) Chariot Victor.

— Workplace Counselling: A Systematic Approach to Employee Care. 256p. 1996. 49.95 (*0-7619-5020-6*); pap. 22.95 (*0-7619-5021-4*) Sage.

Carroll, Michael & Downs, W. Scott. CyberStrategies: How to Build an Internet-Based Information System. (Communications Ser.). 286p. 1996. pap. 34.95 (*0-442-01988-2*, VNR) Wiley.

*__Carroll, Michael & Holloway, Elizabeth.__ Counseling Supervision in Context. LC 98-61426. (Counselling Supervision Ser.). 206 p. 1999. write for info. (*0-7619-5789-8*) Sage.

Carroll, Michael & Walton, Michael, eds. Handbook of Counselling in Organizations. 416p. 1997. 85.00 (*0-7619-5086-9*); pap. 32.95 (*0-7619-5087-7*) Sage.

Carroll, Michael, et al. Fundamentals of Organizational Behavior. LC 96-30614. 716p. (C). 1996. pap. text 79.00 (*0-02-319521-5*, Macmillan Coll) P-H.

Carroll, Michael L. CyberStrategies: How to Build an Internet-Based Information System. (Communications Ser.). 286p. 1995. pap. 34.95 (*0-471-28687-7*, VNR) Wiley.

Carroll, Michael P. Catholic Cults & Devotions: A Psychological Inquiry. (Illus.). 256p. 1989. 65.00 (*0-7735-0693-4*, Pub. by McG-Queens Univ Pr) CUP Services.

*__Carroll, Michael P.__ Irish Pilgrimage: Holy Wells & Popular Catholic Devotion. LC 99-24137. 248p. 1999. 38.00 (*0-8018-6190-X*) Johns Hopkins.

Carroll, Michael P. Madonnas that Maim: Popular Catholicism in Italy since the Fifteenth Century. (Illus.). 256p. 1992. text 39.95 (*0-8018-4299-9*) Johns Hopkins.

— Veiled Threats: The Logic of Popular Catholicism in Italy. LC 95-50982. (Illus.). 320p. 1996. text 39.95 (*0-8018-5290-0*) Johns Hopkins.

Carroll, Michael P., jt. auth. see Ritacco, Rochelle.

*__Carroll, Michael Thomas.__ Popular Modernity in America: Experience, Technology, Mythohistory. (C). 2000. text 57.50 (*0-7914-4713-8*) State U NY Pr.

— Popular Modernity in America: Experience, Technology, Mythohistory. 2000. pap. 18.95 (*0-7914-4714-6*) State U NY Pr.

*__Carroll, Michael Thomas & Tafoya, Eddie, eds.__ Phenomenological Approaches to Popular Culture. LC 99-45937. 2000. 51.95 (*0-87972-809-4*); pap. 25.95 (*0-87972-810-8*) Bowling Green Univ Popular Press.

Carroll, Michael W. Absolutely Awesome. LC 99-31845. 1999. pap. 10.99 (*0-8423-3043-7*) Tyndale Hse.

— Deserts & Jungles. LC 98-55557. 32p. 1999. 13.99 (*0-7814-3275-8*) Chariot Victor.

— Oceans & Rivers. LC 98-42132. (J). 1999. 13.99 (0-7814-3068-2) Chariot Victor.

Carroll, Mitchell. Greek Women. 1972. 250.00 (0-87968-326-0) Gordon Pr.

Carroll, Mollie R. Labor & Politics. LC 74-89723. (American Labor, from Conspiracy to Collective Bargaining Ser., No. 1: No. 1). 1974. reprint ed. 19.95 (0-405-02110-0) Ayer.

Carroll-Najder, Halina, tr. see Conrad, Joseph, et al.

Carroll, Nancy, jt. auth. see Kaplan, Lloyd S.

Carroll, Nancy J. Healing a Broken Heart: A Recovery Handbook for Relationship Loss. Orig. Title: New Beginnings - A Divorce Recovery Handbook. 91p. 1994. pap. 9.95 (0-9663204-1-7) Life Skills Dev.

— The Love Handbook for Singles: What Every Single Needs to Know about Love, Dating & Finding a Lifelong Partner. Orig. Title: Finding & Keeping a Loving Relationship. 179p. 1993. pap. 12.95 (0-9663204-0-9) Life Skills Dev.

Carroll, Nicholas. Dancing with Lawyers: How to Take Charge & Get Results. LC 90-64419. 192p. 1992. 19.95 (1-879435-03-9) Royce-Baker Pub.

Carroll, Nick, ed. The Next Wave: The World of Surfing. (Illus.). 240p. 1991. 29.98 (1-55859-162-1) Abbeville Pr.

Carroll, Noel. Interpreting the Moving Image. LC 97-22892. (Studies in Film). 384p. (C). 1998. text 59.95 (0-521-58039-0); pap. text 22.95 (0-521-58970-3) Cambridge U Pr.

***Carroll, Noel.** Philosophy of Art: Contemporary Introduction. LC 99-25928. (Contemporary Introductions to Philosophy Ser.). 1999. pap. 18.99 (0-415-15964-4) Routledge.

— Philosophy of Art: Contemporary Introduction. LC 99-25928. (Contemporary Introductions to Philosophy Ser.). 224p. (C). 1999. text. write for info. (0-415-15963-6) Routledge.

Carroll, Noel. The Philosophy of Horror: Paradoxes of the Heart. 288p. (C). (gr. 13). 1990. pap. 20.99 (0-415-90216-9, A3860) Routledge.

— The Philosophy of Mass Art. LC 97-25934. 438p. 1998. text 77.00 (0-19-871129-8); pap. text 18.95 (0-19-874237-1) OUP.

— Theorizing the Moving Image. (Studies in Film). 445p. (C). 1996. text 80.00 (0-521-46049-2) Cambridge U Pr.

— Theorizing the Moving Image. (Studies in Film). 445p. (C). 1996. pap. text 25.95 (0-521-46607-5) Cambridge U Pr.

Carroll, Noel, jt. ed. see Bordwell, David.

Carroll, Noel, ed. see Danto, Arthur C. & Bailey, George W. S.

Carroll, Norman V. Financial Management for Pharmacists: A Decision-Making Approach. LC 90-5886. 236p. 1991. pap. text 34.00 (0-8121-1341-1) Lppncott W & W.

— Financial Management for Pharmacists: A Decision-Making Approach. 2nd ed. LC 97-8492. 275p. 1997. pap. 39.00 (0-683-30119-5) Lppncott W & W.

Carroll, P. Free & Unfree. 1992. pap. 14.95 (0-14-016540-1, Viking) Viking Penguin.

Carroll, P. R., jt. ed. see Tanagho, Emil A.

Carroll, P. Thomas, ed. Annotated Calendar of the Letters of Charles Darwin in the Library of the American Philosophical Society. LC 75-29739. 233p. 1976. reprint ed. 50.00 (0-8420-2077-2) Scholarly Res Inc.

Carroll, P. Thomas, et al, eds. Guide to the History of Science, 1986. 318p. 1987. pap. text 19.00 (0-934235-07-4); lib. bdg. 35.00 (0-934235-06-6) Hist Sci Soc.

Carroll, Pamela S., ed. Using Literature to Help Troubled Teenagers Cope with Family Issues. LC 98-55348. (The Greenwood Press 'Using Literature to Help Troubled Teenagers' Ser.). 280p. 1999. 39.95 (0-313-30526-9) Greenwood.

Carroll, Pamela S., jt. ed. see Gregg, Gail P.

Carroll, Patricia, jt. ed. see Nash, David B.

Carroll, Patty, photos by. Spirited Visions: Portraits of Chicago Artists. (Illus.). 104p. 1991. 49.95 (0-252-01848-6); 24.95 (0-252-06220-5) U of Ill Pr.

***Carroll, Paul.** Baroque Woodwind Instruments: A Guide to Their History, Repertoire & Basic Technique. LC 98-45856. (Illus.). 256p. 1999. text 65.95 (1-85928-326-8, Pub. by Ashgate Pub) Ashgate Pub Co.

Carroll, Paul. The Garden of Earthly Delights. (Poetry Ser.). (Illus.). 40p. (Orig.). 1987. pap. 5.00 (0-938903-00-4) Cty of Chicago.

— New & Selected Poems. 1978. 7.95 (0-916328-11-2); pap. 3.50 (0-916328-10-4) Yellow Pr.

— The Road to Heaven, Bk. 1. 230p. (Orig.). 1997. pap. 9.00 (1-57502-455-1, PO1369) Morris Pubng.

— The Road to Heaven, Bk. 2. 230p. (Orig.). 1997. pap. 9.00 (1-57502-456-X, PO1370) Morris Pubng.

Carroll, Paul, ed. The Earthquake on Ada Street: An Anthology of Poems from the "Sculpture Factory" LC 79-20159. xii, 93p. (Orig.). 1979. pap. 20.00 (0-933104-06-5) Jupiter Pr.

Carroll, Paul, ed. see Younghans, Sam.

Carroll, Paul V. Goodbye to the Summer. (Lost Play Ser.). 1970. pap. 1.25 (0-912262-21-4) Proscenium.

— Irish Stories & Plays. 14.50 (0-8159-5818-8) Devin.

— Shadow & Substance: Manuscript Edition. 1948. pap. 13.00 (0-8222-1018-5) Dramatists Play.

— The Wise Have Not Spoken. 1954. pap. 5.25 (0-8222-1268-4) Dramatists Play.

Carroll, Paula N., ed. see Saxton, Harvey L.

Carroll, Peter. Liber Kaos. LC 92-6241. (Illus.). 224p. (Orig.). 1992. reprint ed. pap. 14.95 (0-87728-742-2) Weiser.

— Liber Null & Psychonaut. LC 86-24539. (Illus.). 222p. 1987. pap. 15.95 (0-87728-639-6) Weiser.

Carroll, Peter & Noble, David W. The Restless Centuries: A History of the American People. 2nd ed. LC 78-67974. 1979. pap. text 33.30 (0-8087-2920-9) Pearson Custom.

Carroll, Peter J. Psybermagick: Advanced Ideas in Chaos Magick. 2nd ed. LC 96-68644. 128p. 1996. pap. 12.95 (1-56184-092-0) New Falcon Pubns.

Carroll, Peter N. It Seemed Like Nothing Happened: America in the 1970s. 421p. 1990. reprint ed. pap. 17.00 (0-8135-1538-6) Rutgers U Pr.

— The Odyssey of the Abraham Lincoln Brigade: Americans in the Spanish Civil War. LC 93-21131. xviii, 440p. (C). 1994. 57.50 (0-8047-2276-5); pap. 18.95 (0-8047-2277-3) Stanford U Pr.

— The Other Samuel Johnson: A Psychohistory of Early New England. LC 77-74413. 247p. 1979. 34.50 (0-8386-2059-0) Fairleigh Dickinson.

Carroll, Peter N., jt. auth. see Horowitz, David.

Carroll, Peter N., jt. auth. see Horowitz, David A.

***Carroll, Peter R.** Prostate Cancer. (ACS Atlas of Clinical Oncology Ser.). 400p. 2000. boxed set 89.95 incl. cd-rom (1-55009-130-1) DEKR.

Carroll, Peter R., ed. see Williams, Richard D.

Carroll, Phidelia. Soul-Winning: A Problem & Its Solution. LC 92-62567. 108p. 1993. reprint ed. 10.95 (0-9605642-5-X) Messengers Hope.

***Carroll Publishing Staff, ed.** Government Phone Book U. S. A., 2000: A Comprehensive Guide to Federal, State, County, & Local Government Offices in the United States. 8th ed. 2000p. 1999. lib. bdg. 230.00 (0-7808-0345-0) Omnigraphics Inc.

— Government Phone Book USA 2001: A Comprehensive Guide to Federal, State, County, & Local Government Offices in the U. S. 9th ed. 3000p. 2000. lib. bdg. 240.00 (0-7808-0425-2) Omnigraphics Inc.

Carroll, Quigley. Anglo American Establishment. 354p. 1981. pap. 15.00 (0-913022-45-4) CPA Bk Pub.

Carroll, Quinn B. Evaluating Radiographs. LC 93-8350. (Illus.). 374p. (C). 1993. 44.95 (0-398-05878-4) C C Thomas.

***Carroll, Quinn B. & Fuchs, Arthur W.** Fuchs's Radiographic Exposure, Processing & Quality Control. 6th ed. LC 97-36977. (Illus.). 558p. 1998. text 49.95 (0-398-06830-5) C C Thomas.

Carroll, R., et al, eds. The Bible in Human Society: Essays in Honor of John Rogerson. (JSOT Supplement Ser.: Vol. 200). 479p. 1995. 90.00 (1-85075-568-X, Pub. by Sheffield Acad) CUP Services.

Carroll, R. A. The Printed Maps of Lincolnshire, 1576-1900 with an Appendix on Road-Books, 1675-1900: A Carto-Bibliography with an Appendix on Road-Books, 1675-1900. (Publications of Lincoln Record Society: Vol. 84). (Illus.). 502p. (C). 1996. 60.00 (0-901503-57-6) Boydell & Brewer.

Carroll, R. J., et al. Measurement Error in Nonlinear Models. (Illus.). 312p. (C). (gr. 13). 1995. boxed set 59.95 (0-412-04721-7, Chap & Hall CRC) CRC Pr.

Carroll, R. L., et al. Batrachosauria (Anthrosauria), Gephyrostegida-Chronlosuchide. (Encyclopedia of Paleoherpetology Ser.: Pt. 5-B). (Illus.). 81p. 1972. text 85.00 (3-437-30136-5) Lubrecht & Cramer.

Carroll, R. P. Jeremiah. (Old Testament Guides Ser.: No. 22). 128p. 1989. pap. 12.50 (1-85075-146-3, Pub. by Sheffield Acad) CUP Services.

Carroll, R. P. Text As Pretext: Essays in Honour of Robert Davidson. (JSOT Supplement Ser.: No. 138). 307p. (C). 1992. 85.00 (1-85075-295-8, Pub. by Sheffield Acad) CUP Services.

Carroll, R. W. Topics in Soliton Theory. (North-Holland Mathematics Studies: Vol. 167). xii, 428p. 1991. 141.00 (0-444-88869-1, North Holland) Elsevier.

Carroll, Raymond L. Electronic Media Programming: Strategies & Decision Making. 1993. 30.00 (0-07-010299-6) McGraw.

Carroll, Raymond L. & Davis, Donald M. Electronic Media Programming: Strategies & Decision Making. LC 92-46063. (Series in Mass Communication). 512p. (C). 1992. 63.44 (0-07-010298-8) McGraw.

Carroll, Raymonde. Cultural Misunderstandings: The French-American Experience. Volk, Carol, tr. 160p. 1990. pap. text 11.95 (0-226-09498-7) U Ch Pr.

— Cultural Misunderstandings: The French-American Experience. Volk, Carol, tr. 200p. 1992. 19.95 (0-226-09497-9) U Ch Pr.

Carroll, Raynor. Adagio - Allegro. 6p. 1996. pap. 4.95 (1-891188-15-1) Batterie Music.

— Allegro Marcato. 4p. 1996. pap. 3.95 (1-891188-07-0) Batterie Music.

— Brioso. 4p. 1996. pap. 3.95 (1-891188-12-7) Batterie Music.

— Chaccone. 6p. 1996. pap. 5.95 (1-891188-03-8) Batterie Music.

— Chorale. 4p. 1996. pap. 2.95 (0-9650322-9-9) Batterie Music.

— Dirge. 4p. 1996. pap. 2.95 (1-891188-00-3) Batterie Music.

— Exercises, Etudes & Solos for the Timpani. (Illus.). 160p. 1996. pap. 18.95 (0-9650322-0-5) Batterie Music.

— Fantasy. 4p. 1996. pap. 2.95 (1-891188-09-7) Batterie Music.

— Galop. 4p. 1996. pap. 3.95 (1-891188-01-1) Batterie Music.

— Kalimba. 4p. 1996. pap. 2.95 (1-891188-10-0) Batterie Music.

— Misterioso. 4p. 1996. pap. 2.95 (1-891188-06-2) Batterie Music.

— Modulation. 4p. 1996. pap. 2.95 (1-891188-08-9) Batterie Music.

— Orchestral Repertoire for Bass Drum & Cymbals. 90p. 1997. pap. 14.95 (0-9650322-5-6) Batterie Music.

— Orchestral Repertoire for the Glockenspiel, Vol. 1. 60p. 1996. pap. 12.95 (0-9650322-2-1) Batterie Music.

— Orchestral Repertoire for the Glockenspiel, Vol. 2. 60p. 1996. pap. 12.95 (0-9650322-3-X) Batterie Music.

— Orchestral Repertoire for the Snare Drum. 112p. 1997. pap. 16.95 (0-9650322-4-8) Batterie Music.

— Orchestral Repertoire for the Tambourine, Triangle & Castanets, Vol. II. 1998. pap. 16.95 (0-9650322-8-0) Batterie Music.

— Orchestral Repertoire for the Xylophone. 68p. 1998. pap. 16.95 (0-9650322-6-4); pap. 16.95 (0-9650322-7-2) Batterie Music.

— Pesante. 4p. 1996. pap. 3.95 (1-891188-11-9) Batterie Music.

— Prelude. 4p. 1996. pap. 3.95 (1-891188-13-5) Batterie Music.

— Rigoroso. 4p. 1996. pap. 2.95 (1-891188-04-6) Batterie Music.

— Scherzo. 4p. 1996. pap. 3.95 (1-891188-02-X) Batterie Music.

— Ten Progressive Etudes for the Marimba. 16p. 1996. pap. 6.95 (0-9650322-1-3) Batterie Music.

— Variations. 4p. 1996. pap. 2.95 (1-891188-05-4) Batterie Music.

— Waltz. 6p. 1996. pap. 4.95 (1-891188-14-3) Batterie Music.

Carroll, Rebecca, ed. Sugar in the Raw: Voices of Young Black Girls in America. LC 96-37527. 1997. pap. 12.00 (0-517-88497-6) Random Hse Value.

***Carroll, Rebecca F.** Broken Covenant: A Divorce Memoir. LC 00-8172. 144p. 2000. pap. 12.95 (1-56474-327-6) Fithian Pr.

Carroll, Richard. Finding God the Father: A Jubilee Retreat. 125p. Date not set. pap. text 9.95 (0-9643572-2-4) St Marg Mary Chur.

Carroll, Richard. The Triumph of Our Lady: Preparing for the Third Millennium. 325p. (Orig.). 1996. pap. text 9.95 (0-9643572-1-6) St Marg Mary Chur.

***Carroll, Richard G.** Desk Reference on the Economy. 2000. 49.95 (1-56802-526-2); pap. 29.95 (1-56802-525-4) CQ Pr.

Carroll, Richard J. The Economic Record of Presidential Performance: From Truman to Bush. LC 95-3334. 288p. 1995. 69.50 (0-275-94836-6, Praeger Pubs) Greenwood.

Carroll, Richard L. The Remnant Church. 173p. 1993. pap. text 9.95 (0-9643572-0-8) St Marg Mary Chur.

Carroll, Rick, compiled by. Hawaii's Best Spooky Tales: True Local Spine-Tinglers. LC 98-134387. (Illus.). 192p. (J). 1997. pap. 11.95 (1-57306-031-3) Bess Pr.

***Carroll, Rick, compiled by.** Hawaii's' Best Spooky Tales 4. 2000. pap. 11.95 (1-57306-114-X) Bess Pr.

— Hawaii's Best Spooky Tales 3: More True Local Spine-Tinglers. (Illus.). 160p. (J). 1999. pap. 11.95 (1-57306-100-X) Bess Pr.

Carroll, Rick, ed. Chicken Skin: True Spooky Stories of Hawaii. (Illus.). 144p. 1996. reprint ed. pap. 1 .95 (1-57306-055-0) Bess Pr.

— Hawaii's Best Spooky Tales 2: More True Local Spine-Tinglers. (Illus.). 144p. (J). 1998. pap. 11.95 (1-57306-040-2) Bess Pr.

***Carroll, Rick & Carroll, Marcie, eds.** Hawai'i: True Stories of the Island Spirit. (Travelers' Tales Ser.). 384p. 1999. pap. 17.95 (1-885211-35-X) Trvlers Tale.

Carroll, Ricki, jt. auth. see Carroll, Robert.

Carroll, Robert & Carroll, Ricki. Cheesemaking Made Easy: Sixty Delicious Varieties. LC 82-9300. (Illus.). 144p. 1983. pap. 14.95 (0-88266-267-8, Garden Way Pub) Storey Bks.

— Cheesemaking Made Easy: Sixty Delicious Varieties. LC 82-9300. (Illus.). 144p. 1987. 13.95 (0-88266-305-4, Garden Way Pub) Storey Bks.

Carroll, Robert & Gaskill, Pamela. The Order Microsauria. LC 78-56735. (Memoirs Ser.: Vol. 126). (Illus.). 1978. pap. 20.00 (0-87169-126-4, M126-CAR) Am Philos.

Carroll, Robert & Sangster-Wilson, Tom. Sons of Israel, Sons of God LC 87-174900. 128p. 1987. write for info. (0-551-01436-9, Pub. by M Pickering) Harper SF.

Carroll, Robert, tr. see Spaak, Torben.

Carroll, Robert F. Heat Lightning. rev. ed. (Read-along Radio Dramas Ser.). (YA). (gr. 7-12). 1983. ring bd. 38.00 (1-878298-05-4) Balance Pub.

Carroll, Robert L. Patterns & Processes of Vertebrate Evolution. LC 96-44161. (Cambridge Paleobiology Ser.: No. 2). (Illus.). 528p. (C). 1997. text 85.00 (0-521-47232-6); pap. text 39.95 (0-521-47809-X) Cambridge U Pr.

— Vertebrate Paleontology & Evolution. LC 86-31808. (Geology Ser.). (Illus.). 698p. (C). 1987. pap. text 66.95 (0-7167-1822-7) W H Freeman.

Carroll, Roberta, ed. see American Society for Healthcare Risk Management St.

Carroll, Roger. Lebanon, 1761-1994: The Evolution of a Resilient New Hampshire City. LC 94-24652. (Illus.). 320p. 1994. 38.00 (0-914659-71-5) Phoenix Pub.

***Carroll, S. & Abrahamse, A.** The Effects of a Choice Automobile Insurance Plan on Insurance Costs & Compensation. LC 99-52899. (Illus.). xix, 46p. (C). 1999. pap. 7.50 (0-8330-2784-0, MR-1134-ICJ) Rand Corp.

Carroll, S. & Leonardo, J. Introduction to PeopleSoft Development. 275p. 1999. write for info. (0-7615-1954-8) Prima Pub.

Carroll, S. G., et al. Preterm Prelabour Amniorrhexis. LC 95-15963. (Frontiers in Fetal Medicine Ser.). (Illus.). 176p. 1995. 65.00 (1-85070-692-1) Prthnon Pub.

Carroll, Sara, jt. auth. see Morgan, Michaela.

Carroll, Sarah M. & Beyerlein, Steve W. Learning Assessment Journal. 2nd ed. Wignall, Eric, ed. (Illus.). 144p. (C). 1996. pap. text 12.00 (1-878437-07-0) Pac Crest Soft.

Carroll, Servio A., jt. ed. see Canter, Andrea S.

Carroll, Sidney, jt. auth. see Inhaber, Herbert.

Carroll, Souzzann Y. Lasting Legacy: Scrapbooks & Photo Albums That Touch the Heart. LC 99-174069. 1998. pap. 19.95 (0-9663318-0-X) Living Vision.

Carroll Staff. Career Guide to Professional Associations: A Directory of Organizations by Occupational Field. 2nd ed. LC 80-13268. 288p. 1980. 19.95 (0-910328-06-4) Sulzburger & Graham Pub.

Carroll, Stephen, et al. Projecting California's Fiscal Future. 111p. (Orig.). 1996. pap. text 13.00 (0-8330-2364-0, MR-570-LE) Rand Corp.

Carroll, Stephen J. & Abrahamse, Allan F. The Effects of a Choice Automobile Insurance Plan on Insurance Costs & Compensation: An Updated Analysis. LC 98-16568. (Illus.). 86p. 1998. pap. text 9.00 (0-8330-2610-0, MR-970-ICJ) Rand Corp.

Carroll, Stephen J. & Gannon, Martin J. Ethical Dimensions of International Management. LC 96-25308. (Series in Business Ethics). 232p. 1996. 42.00 (0-8039-5543-X); pap. 18.95 (0-8039-5544-8) Sage.

Carroll, Stephen J., et al. The Fiscal & Demographic Environment of the California State University at Northridge. LC 96-205560. (Illus.). 56p. 1996. pap. text 13.00 (0-8330-2432-9, MR-624-CSUN) Rand Corp.

— Managing Organization Behavior. 3rd ed. LC 93-38203. 700p. 1994. pap. 50.95 (1-55786-551-5) Blackwell Pubs.

Carroll, Stephen J., jt. auth. see Abrahamse, Allan F.

Carroll, Steven & Miller, Mark. Fine Trails of Rockbridge. (Illus.). 120p. (Orig.). 1996. pap. 9.95 (0-9646692-3-4) Old Forge Prodns.

— Wilderness Virginia: A Guide to Hiking Virginia's National Forest Wilderness Area. LC 95-68417. (Illus.). (Orig.). 1995. pap. 12.95 (0-9646692-1-8) Old Forge Prodns.

Carroll, Stuart. Noble Power During the French Wars of Religion: The Guise Affinity & the Catholic Cause in Normandy. LC 97-38680. (Cambridge Studies in Early Modern History). (Illus.). 224p. (C). 1998. text 59.95 (0-521-62404-5) Cambridge U Pr.

Carroll, Sue. Breakfast at Nine, Tea at Four: Favorite Recipes from Cape May's Mainstay Inn. (Illus.). 200p. 1997. pap. 14.95 (1-896511-08-2, Pub. by Callawind) Firefly Bks Ltd.

Carroll, Susan. Black Lace & Linen. (Desire Ser.). 1994. per. 2.99 (0-373-05840-3, 5-05840-9) Silhouette.

— The Bride Finder. LC 97-47289. 352p. 1998. 17.95 (0-449-14927-7) Fawcett.

— The Bride Finder. 1999. mass mkt. 5.99 (0-449-00388-4, GM) Fawcett.

— The Bride Finder. large type ed. LC 98-29245. (Large Print Book Ser.). 1998. 25.95 (1-56895-585-5) Wheeler Pub.

— Love Power: Centerfolds. (Desire Ser.). 1994. per. 2.99 (0-373-05876-4, 1-05876-7) Silhouette.

— Magica Inocencia (Magical Innocence), No. 134. (Harlequin Deseo Ser.). (SPA.). 1998. mass mkt. 3.50 (0-373-35264-6, 1-35264-0) Harlequin Bks.

— The Night Drifter. LC PS3553.A7654N54 1999. 336p. 1999. 19.95 (0-345-43312-2) Ballantine Pub Grp.

***Carroll, Susan.** The Night Drifter. 2000. mass mkt. 6.99 (0-449-00585-2) Fawcett.

Carroll, Susan. Parker & the Gypsy. 1997. per. 3.50 (0-373-76068-X, 1-76068-5) Silhouette.

— Winterbourne. LC 99-31997. 1999. write for info. (1-56895-752-1) Wheeler Pub.

Carroll, Susan J. Women As Candidates in American Politics. 2nd ed. LC 93-41856. 256p. 1994. 31.50 (0-253-31319-8); pap. 13.95 (0-253-20877-7) Ind U Pr.

Carroll, Susan R., jt. auth. see Carroll, David.

Carroll, T. The Finance Director: A Changing Role. 1996. pap. 129.00 (1-85953-001-X, Pub. by Tech Comm) St Mut.

***Carroll, T.** The Role of the Finance Director. (Financial Times Management Briefings Ser.). 1998. pap. 89.50 (0-273-63725-8) F T P-H.

Carroll, T. L. & Pecora, L. M., eds. Nonlinear Dynamics in Circuits. 400p. 1995. text 102.00 (981-02-2438-9, N-PB2910) World Scientific Pub.

Carroll, Ted. Knights in Shining Tow Trucks. Carroll, Virginia, ed. 228p. 1995. pap. 9.95 (0-9648029-0-2) Ashby Kern.

— Live Debt Free. 180p. 1991. pap. 7.95 (1-55850-044-8) Adams Media.

Carroll, Terry. No Blood Relative. LC 95-175238. 1997. pap. 15.95 (1-55128-021-3, Pub. by Mercury Bk) LPC InBook.

Carroll, Thomas F. Intermediary NGOs: The Supporting Link in Grassroots Development. LC 92-6424. (Library of Management for Development). (Illus.). xiv, 274p. 1992. pap. 24.95 (1-56549-009-6) Kumarian Pr.

Carroll, Thomas F. & Montgomery, John D., eds. Supporting Grassroots Organizations. LC HN0981.V64S8. (Lincoln Institute of Land Policy Monograph: No. 87-1). 145p. reprint ed. pap. 45.00 (0-7837-5770-0, 204543500006) Bks Demand.

Carroll, Thomas F., jt. auth. see Montgomery, John D.

Carroll, Thomas K., intro. Jeremy Taylor: Selected Works. (Classics of Western Spirituality Ser.). 1990. 24.95 (0-8091-0438-5); pap. 17.95 (0-8091-3175-7) Paulist Pr.

Carroll, Thomas L. The Colony: A Novel for the Young Reader. LC 99-48827. 152p. (J). 2000. 18.95 (0-86534-295-4) Sunstone Pr.

Carroll, Tonya T. Traian Alexandru Filip: His Art & Life. LC 98-157520. (Illus.). 160p. 1998. 60.00 (0-9661111-0-9) Turner Carroll.

Carroll, Vern, ed. Adoption in Eastern Oceania. LC 77-89650. (Association for Social Anthropology in Oceania Monographs: No. 1). (Illus.). 436p. reprint ed. pap. 135.20 (0-8357-6006-5, 203463500090) Bks Demand.

— Pacific Atoll Populations. LC 75-1264. (Association for

C

Social Anthropology in Oceania Monographs: No. 3). (Illus.). 554p. reprint ed. pap. 171.80 (*0-8357-8531-9*, 203483300091) Bks Demand.

Carroll, Victoria M. Writing News for Television: Style & Format. LC 97-19031. 1997. pap. text 34.95 (*0-8138-2533-4*) Iowa St U Pr.

***Carroll, Vincent & Shiflett, David.** Christianity on Trial: Arguments Against Anti-Religious Bigotry. 204p. 2000. pap. 14.95 (*1-893554-15-5*) Encounter Bks.

Carroll, Vinette & Grant, Micki. Croesus & the Witch - Hansel & Gretel in the 1980's. 200p. (Orig.). 1984. pap. 19.95 (*0-88145-024-3*) Broadway Play.

Carroll, Virginia, ed. see Carroll, Ted.

Carroll, Virginia S. The Noble Gyn of Comedy in the Middle English Cycle Plays. (American University Studies: English Language & Literature: Ser. IV, Vol. 79). 248p. (C). 1989. text 34.95 (*0-8204-0714-3*) P Lang Pubng.

Carroll, W., et al. The Quest of the Individual: Roots of Western Civilization. LC 89-13615. XVI, 364p. (C). 1990. text 67.95 (*0-8204-1156-6*) P Lang Pubng.

Carroll, W. F. A Primer for Finite Elements in Elastic Structures. LC 98-13435. (Illus.). 512p. 1998. 85.00 (*0-471-28345-2*) Wiley.

Carroll, W. H., et al. Reasons for Hope. rev. ed. 254p. (C). 1982. pap. 6.95 (*0-931888-07-7*) Christendom Pr.

***Carroll, Warren.** Celebrating 2000 Years of Christian History: An Exhibit of Narrative Paintings by Gloria Thomas with Historical Articles Written by Warren Carroll, Ph.D. (Illus.). 43p. 2000. 5.00 (*1-892875-07-1*) New Hope Publicatns.

Carroll, Warren. Eagles Recalled: Pilot & Aircrew Wings of Canada, Great Britain & the British Commonwealth, 1913-1945. LC 96-71816. (Illus.). 352p. 1997. 79.95 (*0-7643-0244-2*) Schiffer.

Carroll, Warren H. The Building of Christendom. (History of Christendom Ser.: Vol. 2). 618p. 1987. 26.95 (*0-931888-24-7*) Christendom Pr.

— The Building of Christendom. (History of Christendom Ser.: Vol.2). 618p. 1987. pap. 16.95 (*0-931888-20-4*) Christendom Pr.

— The Founding of Christendom. (History of Christendom Ser.: Vol. 1). 605p. (C). 1985. 26.95 (*0-931888-21-2*); pap. 16.95 (*0-931888-18-2*) Christendom Pr.

— The Glory of Christendom. (History of Christendom Ser.: Vol. 3). 774p. (Orig.). 1993. 29.95 (*0-931888-55-7*); pap. 19.95 (*0-931888-54-9*) Christendom Pr.

— The Guillotine & the Cross. 204p. (Orig.). 1991. reprint ed. pap. 7.95 (*0-931888-45-X*) Christendom Pr.

— Isabel of Spain: The Catholic Queen. 386p. (Orig.). 1991. 26.95 (*0-931888-42-5*); pap. 14.95 (*0-931888-43-3*) Christendom Pr.

— 1917: Red Banners, White Mantle. 168p. (Orig.). (C). 1981. pap. 6.95 (*0-931888-05-0*) Christendom Pr.

— Our Lady of Guadalupe & the Conquest of Darkness. 123p. (Orig.). 1983. pap. 6.95 (*0-931888-12-3*) Christendom Pr.

— The Rise & Fall of the Communist Revolution. (Illus.). 852p. 1995. 34.95 (*0-931888-60-3*); pap. 24.95 (*0-931888-59-X*) Christendom Pr.

***Carroll, Willard & Fricke, John, eds.** 100 Years of Oz: A Century of Classic Images from the Wizard of Oz. LC 99-30777. (Illus.). 160p. 1999. 29.95 (*1-55670-940-4*) Stewart Tabori & Chang.

Carroll, William. Automotive Troubleshooting: Glossary. 144p. (Orig.). 1973. pap. 5.00 (*0-910390-18-5*, 118) Coda Publications.

— Beach & Park Access Guide for San Diego: Explore San Diego. (Explore San Diego County Ser.). Orig. Title: Beach Walking in San Diego: Park Walking in San Diego. (Illus.). 272p. (Orig.). 1996. pap. 16.95 (*0-910390-46-0*) Coda Publications.

— Beach Walking in San Diego County: Explore San Diego. LC 91-73239. (Illus.). 144p. (Orig.). 1992. pap. 10.00 (*0-910390-33-9*) Coda Publications.

— Free Things & More in San Diego Vol. II: Explore San Diego. 2nd rev. ed. LC 96-71675. (Explore San Diego County Ser.). (Illus.). 350p. 1997. pap. 9.95 (*0-910390-49-5*) Coda Publications.

— Hidden History in San Diego: Explore San Diego. (Illus.). 320p. 1998. reprint ed. pap. 16.95 (*0-910390-57-6*) Coda Publications.

— Los Angeles, 1939 . . . Street People & Friends. (Illus.). 144p. Date not set. pap. 25.00 (*0-910390-50-9*) Coda Publications.

— Mall Walking in San Diego County. LC 90-86355. (Explore San Diego County Ser.). (Illus.). 144p. (Orig.). 1990. pap. 10.00 (*0-910390-31-2*) Coda Publications.

— MUROC: When the Hot Rods Ran, May 15, 1938. LC 90-85257. (Illus.). 80p. (Orig.). 1991. pap. 20.00 (*0-910390-30-4*) Coda Publications.

— Museums, Gardens & More in San Diego County: Explore San Diego. (Illus.). 120p. (Orig.). 1994. pap. 10.00 (*0-910390-38-X*) Coda Publications.

— Park Walking in San Diego County. LC 91-73240. (Explore San Diego County Ser.). (Illus.). 144p. (Orig.). 1991. pap. 10.00 (*0-910390-32-0*) Coda Publications.

— Relocate in San Diego: Explore San Diego. LC 96-71676. (Illus.). 176p. (Orig.). 1997. pap. 16.95 (*0-910390-48-7*) Coda Publications.

— San Marcos: A Brief History. LC 75-26259. (Illus.). 1977. 25.00 (*0-910390-24-X*) Coda Publications.

— Secret Sites of Historic Trivia: Explore San Diego. (Explore San Diego County Ser.). (Illus.). 160p. (Orig.). 1994. pap. 10.00 (*0-910390-39-8*) Coda Publications.

— The Singles' Philosopher. (New Age Philosophy Ser.). 160p. (Orig.). 1990. pap. 10.00 (*0-910390-26-6*) Coda Publications.

— Streetwalking in San Diego County: Explore San Diego. LC 92-70341. (Illus.). 132p. (Orig.). 1992. pap. 10.00 (*0-910390-35-5*) Coda Publications.

— Superstitions: 10,000 You Really Need: Explore the World. rev. ed. LC 97-77399. (Illus.). 604p. 1998. pap. 24.95 (*0-910390-56-8*) Coda Publications.

— Two Wheels to Panama. (Illus.). 144p. (Orig.). 1995. pap. 20.00 (*0-910390-40-1*) Coda Publications.

— Walker's Guidebook to All San Diego: Explore San Diego. Orig. Title: Beach...Park...Mall Walking in San Diego. (Illus.). 410p. (Orig.). 1996. pap. 16.95 (*0-910390-47-9*) Coda Publications.

— Women Beware Women. 2nd ed. (New Mermaids Ser.). (C). 1994. pap. text 7.00 (*0-393-90069-X*, Norton Paperbks) Norton.

Carroll, William, ed. Kids Coloring Calendar: San Diego Old Town. (Anytime Calendars & More Ser.). (Illus.). 26p. (J). (gr. 2-6). 1998. pap. 8.95 (*0-910390-59-2*) Coda Publications.

Carroll, William A. & Prager, Susan W., intros. Estate Planning, 1991. LC 82-64082. 424p. 1992. pap. 90.00 (*0-88124-535-6*, ES-31601) Cont Ed Bar-CA.

Carroll, William A. & Smith, Norman B. American Constitutional Rights: Cases, Documents, & Commentary. 804p. (C). 1991. pap. text 56.00 (*0-8191-8260-5*); lib. bdg. 76.00 (*0-8191-8259-1*) U Pr of Amer.

Carroll, William C. Fat King, Lean Beggar: Representations of Poverty in the Age of Shakespeare. LC 95-37296. (Illus.). 256p. 1996. text 39.95 (*0-8014-3185-9*) Cornell U Pr.

— The Metamorphoses of Shakespearean Comedy. LC 84-42877. 303p. 1985. reprint ed. pap. 94.00 (*0-7837-9310-3*, 206005000004) Bks Demand.

Carroll, William C., selected by. Stories of Little Girls & Their Dolls: Classics from an Age of Remembered Joy. LC 98-70381. (Illus.). 196p. (YA). (gr. k up). 1998. 19.95 (*1-56397-738-9*) Boyds Mills Pr.

Carroll, William E., ed. see Weisheipl, James A.

Carroll, William J. & Furlong, John J., eds. Greek & Medieval Studies in Honor of Leo Sweeney. LC 93-31485. XXVIII, 302p. (C). 1995. text 65.95 (*0-8204-1641-X*) P Lang Pubng.

Carroll, William J., et al. Authentic Metaphysics in an Age of Unreality. 2nd ed. LC 93-981. 435p. 1993. pap. 35.95 (*0-8204-2278-9*) P Lang Pubng.

Carroll, William K., ed. Organizing Dissent: Dissenting Social Movements in Theory & Practice. 2nd ed. LC 97-190921. 350p. 1997. pap. 24.95 (*1-55193-002-1*) Garamond Pr.

***Carroll, Yvonne.** Leprechaun Tales. (Illus.). 64p. (J). (gr. k-5). 1999. 15.95 (*0-7171-2698-6*, Pub. by Gill & MacMill) Irish Bks Media.

— Very Little Leprechaun Book. (Illus.). 8p. (ps-3). 2000. 9.95 (*1-56554-781-0*) Pelican.

Carrollt & West, Cameron. Framework. Date not set. pap. text. write for info. (*0-582-03161-3*, Pub. by Addison-Wesley) Longman.

Carron. Morse Code: The Essential Language. 1991. pap. 8.00 (*0-87259-035-6*) Am Radio.

Carron, Albert V. & Hausenblas, Heather A. Group Dynamics in Sport. 2nd ed. LC 98-71185. (Illus.). 410p. (C). 1998. text 43.00 (*1-885693-12-5*) Fit Info Tech.

Carron, Andrew S. The Plight of the Thrift Institutions. LC 81-71434. (Studies in the Regulation of Economic Activity). 96p. 1982. 18.95 (*0-8157-1300-2*); pap. 8.95 (*0-8157-1299-5*) Brookings.

— Reforming the Bank Regulatory Structure. LC 84-45847. (Studies in the Regulation of Economic Activity). 52p. 1985. pap. 8.95 (*0-8157-1303-7*) Brookings.

— The Rescue of the Thrift Industry. LC 83-71590. (Studies in the Regulation of Economic Activity). 31p. 1983. pap. 7.95 (*0-8157-1301-0*) Brookings.

— Transition to a Free Market: Deregulation of the Air Cargo Industry. LC 81-10244. (Studies in the Regulation of Economic Activity). 45p. 1981. pap. 8.95 (*0-8157-1297-9*) Brookings.

Carron, Andrew S. & MacAvoy, Paul W. The Decline of Service in the Regulated Industries. LC 80-26081. (AEI Studies: No. 306). 87p. reprint ed. pap. 30.00 (*0-8357-4462-0*, 203730400008) Bks Demand.

Carron, Christian G. & Grand Rapids Public Museum Staff. Furniture: The Story of America's Furniture City. LC 98-96573. 244 p. 1998. write for info. (*0-9666524-0-1*) Pub Mus Grnd Rapids.

Carron, Gabriel & Chau, Ta N. Quality of Primary Schools in Different Development Contexts. 306p. 1992. pap. 35.00 (*0-614-31163-2*, U4591, Pub. by UNESCO) Bernan Associates.

Carron, Jean-Claude, ed. Francois Rabelais: Critical Assessments. 232p. 1995. text 38.50 (*0-8018-5028-2*) Johns Hopkins.

Carron, L. T. & Aken, K. M., eds. Breeding Technologies for Tropical Acacias. 132p. (Orig.). 1992. pap. 114.00 (*1-86320-056-8*) St Mut.

Carron, Peter, Jr. The World Below 500 Kilohertz. (Illus.). 64p. (Orig.). 1985. pap. 4.95 (*1-882123-00-X*) Universal Radio Rsch.

Carrondo, Manuel J., ed. Animal Cell Technology from Vaccines to Genetic Medicine. LC 96-48832. 816p. 1996. text 441.50 (*0-7923-4321-2*) Kluwer Academic.

Carrondo, Maria A. & Jeffrey, George A., eds. Chemical Crystallography with Pulsed Neutrons & Synchroton X-Rays. (C). 1987. text 278.50 (*90-277-2631-0*) Kluwer Academic.

Carroo, Ayodele T. Ancestral Rhythm. LC 91-91268. 100p. 1991. pap. write for info. (*0-9630695-0-0*) Sun Sum Pub.

Carroon, Robert G. From Freeman's Ford to Bentonville: The 61st Ohio Volunteer Infantry. LC 98-17945. (Civil War Heritage Ser.). 80p. 1999. pap. 7.95 (*1-57249-077-2*, Burd St Pr) White Mane Pub.

***Carroon, Robert G. & Shoaf, Dana.** Union Blue: The History of the Military Order of the Loyal Legion of the United States. 350p. 2000. 30.00 (*1-57249-190-6*, WM Books) White Mane Pub.

Carrothers, A. W., et al. Collective Bargaining Law in Canada. 2nd ed. 944p. 1986. 189.00 (*0-409-81879-8*, MICHIE) LEXIS Pub.

Carrothers, George E. The Physical Efficiency of Teachers: An Analytical Study of Some Factors Affecting the Health & Physical Efficiency of Public School Teachers. LC 76-176631. (Columbia University. Teachers College. Contributions to Education Ser.: No. 155). reprint ed. 37.50 (*0-404-55155-6*) AMS Pr.

Carrothers, Merlin R. Prison to Praise. unabridged ed. (Essential Christian Library Ser.). 252p. 1998. reprint ed. 9.97 (*1-57748-343-X*) Barbour Pub.

Carrothers, Scott, jt. auth. see Lacson, John M.

Carrothers, W. A. Emigration from the British Isles. 328p. 1965. reprint ed. 35.00 (*0-7146-1282-0*, Pub. by F Cass Pubs) Intl Spec Bk.

Carrouee, B., jt. contrib. by see Gatel, F.

Carrougher, Gretchen. Burn Care & Therapy. LC 98-10872. (Illus.). 496p. (C). (gr. 13). 1998. text 59.95 (*0-8151-1396-X*, 29559) Mosby Inc.

Carrow, Donald J., jt. ed. see Linde, Shirley.

Carrow, Milton M. Licensing Power in New York City. (Illus.). 223p. 1968. reprint ed. 25.00 (*0-8377-0401-4*, Rothman) W S Hein.

Carrow, Milton M., ed. see Cordes, Joseph J.

Carrow, R. N., jt. auth. see Duncan, R. R.

Carrow, Robert. Energy Systems for Residential Buildings. 1999. pap. text 39.95 (*0-07-014119-3*) McGraw.

— Put a Fan in Your Hat! Inventions, Contraptions, & Gadgets Kids Can Build. LC 96-41247. (Illus.). 160p. (YA). (gr. 5 up). 1996. pap. 14.95 (*0-07-011658-X*, Lrng Triangle) McGraw-Hill Prof.

— Turn on the Lights - From Bed! Electronic Inventions, Contraptions, & Gadgets Kids Can Build. LC 96-49657. (Illus.). 160p. (YA). (gr. 5 up). 1996. 24.95 (*0-07-011656-3*, Lrng Triangle); pap. 14.95 (*0-07-011659-8*, Lrng Triangle) McGraw-Hill Prof.

***Carrow, Robert.** Variable Electronic Speed Drives. (Electrical Trades Ser.). 2000. pap. 27.00 (*0-7668-1923-X*) Delmar.

Carrow, Robert N. & Duncan, Ronny R. Salt-Affected Turfgrass Sites: Assessment & Management. LC 97-46421. (Illus.). 185p. (C). 1998. 54.95 (*1-57504-091-3*) Sleepng Bear.

Carrow, Robert S. Electronic Drives: AC & DC Practical Applications Troubleshooting & Repair. (Illus.). 363p. 1996. 59.95 (*0-07-011611-3*) McGraw.

— Soft-Logic: A Guide to Using a Personal Computer As a Programmable Logic Controller. LC 97-22481. (Illus.). 368p. 1997. 60.00 (*0-07-014017-0*) McGraw.

— Technician's Guide to Industrial Electronics: How to Troubleshoot & Repair Automated Equipment. LC 95-3240. 1995. 47.95 (*0-07-011273-8*) McGraw-Hill Prof.

Carroy, P., et al. Chemistry & Technology for Uv & Eb Formulation for Coatings, Inks, & Paints Vol. V: Speciality Finishes. 350p. 1996. 225.00 (*0-471-97880-9*) Wiley.

— Chemistry & Technology for Uv & Eb Formulation for Coatings, Inks, & Paints Vol. Ii: Prepolymers & Reactive Diluents, Vol. II, Prepolymers & Reactive Diluents. 320p. 1997. 225.00 (*0-471-97891-4*) Wiley.

— Chemistry & Technology for Uv & Eb Formulation for Coatings, Inks, & Paints Vol. Iv: Formulation, Vol. IV, Formulation. 250p. 1997. 240.00 (*0-471-97893-0*) Wiley.

— Chemistry & Technology for Uv & Eb Formulation for Coatings, Inks, & Paints Vol. Vi: Test Methods for Uv & Eb Curable Systems. 300p. 1996. 240.00 (*0-471-97881-7*) Wiley.

Carrozza, Carl. Dr. Biology: How Thinking Like a Doctor Can Make You a Medical Detective. (Textworks Ser.). (Illus.). ix, 135p. (J). (gr. 4-8). 1995. ring bd. 39.95 (*1-58284-013-X*, Thoughtful Educ) Silver Strong.

— The Dust Bowl: The History, Ecology, & Echoes of 1930's America. (Textworks Ser.). (Illus.). ix, 77p. (YA). (gr. 6-12). 1995. ring bd. 39.95 (*1-58284-021-0*, Thoughtful Educ) Silver Strong.

— Every Breath You Take: The History, Biology, Chemistry, Ecology, & Mystery of Respiration. (Textworks Ser.). (Illus.). ix, 111p. (YA). (gr. 6-12). 1995. ring bd. 39.95 (*1-58284-018-0*, Thoughtful Educ) Silver Strong.

— From Puzzle to Paradox: Environmental Issues - A Problem Solving Approach. (Illus.). ix, 112p. (YA). (gr. 6-12). 1995. ring bd. 39.95 (*1-58284-020-2*, Thoughtful Educ) Silver Strong.

— How Things Work: An Interdisciplinary, Strategic Unit. (Textworks Ser.). (Illus.). ix, 161p. (YA). (gr. 6-12). 1995. ring bd. 39.95 (*1-58284-017-2*, Thoughtful Educ) Silver Strong.

— The Origin of Everything: The Cosmos, the Earth & You. (Textworks Ser.). (Illus.). ix, 91p. (YA). (gr. 6-12). 1995. ring bd. 39.95 (*1-58284-014-8*, Thoughtful Educ) Silver Strong.

Carrozza, John, ed. see Sussman, Ellen.

Carrozzi, Craig. City 'Scapes: A Fan's Eye View of the Game. 168p. 1999. pap. 8.95 (*0-9620286-2-2*) Suthrn Trails Pub.

***Carrozzi, Craig J.** Festival of Conception. (Illus.). 191p. 2000. pap. 15.00 (*0-9620286-3-0*, Pub. by Suthrn Trails Pub) Bookpeople.

Carrozzi, Craig J. The Road to El Dorado. Appiano, Len, ed. LC 97-91717. 450p. 1997. pap. 19.95 (*0-9620286-1-4*) Suthrn Trails Pub.

— Wedding of the Waters. LC 88-60526. (Illus.). 396p. (Orig.). (YA). 1988. pap. 9.95 (*0-9620286-0-6*) Suthrn Trails Pub.

Carrozzo, Anthony. Refounding: A Franciscan Provincial Experiment. (Spirit & Life Refounded Ser.). 135p. 1994. pap. 12.00 (*1-57659-037-2*) Franciscan Inst.

Carrozzo, Anthony M. Franciscan Leadership in Ministry. (Spirit & Life Ser.: No. 7). 245p. 1998. pap. 15.00 (*1-57659-132-8*) Franciscan Inst.

Carrozzo, Anthony M., ed. In Solitude & Dialogue: Contemporary Franciscans Theologize. (Theology Ser.). 195p. Date not set. pap. 18.00 (*1-57659-167-0*) Franciscan Inst.

Carruba, Michele O. & Blundell, John E., eds. Pharmacology of Eating Disorders: Theoretical & Clinical Developments. LC 85-32329. 192p. 1986. reprint ed. pap. 59.60 (*0-608-03394-4*, 206409100008) Bks Demand.

Carrubba, Paul A. Bank Operations Consolidation Manual: Combining & Streamlining Operations & Systems. 1991. 150.00 (*1-55738-305-7*, Irwn Prfssnl) McGraw-Hill Prof.

— UCC Revised Articles Three & Four: The Banker's Guide to Checks, Drafts & Other Negotiable Instruments. 250p. 1993. text 60.00 (*1-55738-351-0*, Irwn Prfssnl) McGraw-Hill Prof.

Carrubba, Robert W., tr. see Kaempfer, Engelbert.

Carruggi, Noelle. Marguerite Duras: Une Experience Interieure: "Le Gommage de l'Etre en Faveur du Tout, Vol. 6. (Francophone Cultures & Literatures Ser.). (FRE.). 170p. (C). 1995. 40.95 (*0-8204-2643-1*) P Lang Pubng.

Carruth, Alan A. & Oswald, Andrew J. Pay Determination & Industrial Prosperity. (Illus.). 224p. 1990. 65.00 (*0-19-828692-9*) OUP.

Carruth, Bruce, et al. Codependency Issues in Treatment. 1991. 39.95 (*0-86656-920-0*) Haworth Pr.

— Codependency Issues in Treatment. 1994. pap. 14.95 (*0-86656-942-1*) Haworth Pr.

***Carruth, Gordon.** What Happened When. 2nd ed. 2000. pap. 16.00 (*0-06-273250-1*) HarpC.

Carruth, Gorton. The Encyclopedia of American Facts & Dates 10th Edition. 10th ed. LC 97-5127. 1104p. 1997. 50.00 (*0-06-270192-4*, Harper Ref) HarpC.

Carruth, Gorton, ed. American Quotations. Orig. Title: Harper Book of American Quotations. 848p. 1992. reprint ed. 14.99 (*0-517-07361-7*) Random Hse Value.

Carruth, Gorton, ed. The Young Reader's Companion. LC 93-6662. 681p. (J). (gr. 4 up). 1993. 49.95 (*0-8352-2765-0*) Bowker.

Carruth Hager, Linda, jt. auth. see Hager, W. David.

Carruth, Harold B. Carruth Family: Brief Background & Genealogical Data of Twenty Branches in America. (Illus.). 273p. 1997. reprint ed. pap. 42.50 (*0-8328-7861-8*); reprint ed. lib. bdg. 52.50 (*0-8328-7860-X*) Higginson Bk Co.

Carruth, Hayden. Asphalt Georgics. LC 84-25499. 96p. 1985. 15.00 (*0-8112-0937-7*, Pub. by New Directions); pap. 6.95 (*0-8112-0938-5*, NDP591, Pub. by New Directions) Norton.

***Carruth, Hayden.** Beside the Shadow Tree. LC 99-6160. (Illus.). 154p. 1999. pap. 14.00 (*1-55659-099-7*, Pub. by Copper Canyon) SPD-Small Pr Dist.

Carruth, Hayden. Brothers, I Loved You All: Poems, 1969-1977. LC 77-95138. 110p. 1978. 15.95 (*0-8180-1543-8*, Pub. by Sheep Meadow) U Pr of New Eng.

— Collected Longer Poems. LC 93-11404. 240p. (Orig.). 1993. 25.00 (*1-55659-058-X*); pap. 14.00 (*1-55659-059-8*) Copper Canyon.

— Collected Shorter Poems. LC 92-3389. 352p. 1992. 28.00 (*1-55659-048-2*); pap. 14.00 (*1-55659-049-0*) Copper Canyon.

— Dark World. 1974. pap. 10.00 (*0-87711-052-2*) Story Line.

— Effluences from the Sacred Caves: More Selected Essays & Reviews. (Poets on Poetry Ser.). 280p. 1983. pap. 17.95 (*0-472-06349-9*, 06349) U of Mich Pr.

— For You. LC 71-122103. 1970. 5.95 (*0-8112-0256-9*, Pub. by New Directions); pap. 1.95 (*0-8112-0016-7*, NDP298, Pub. by New Directions) Norton.

— From Snow & Rock, from Chaos. LC 72-93973. 1973. pap. 2.25 (*0-8112-0469-3*, NDP349, Pub. by New Directions) Norton.

***Carruth, Hayden.** Hayden Carruth: A Listener's Guide. (Listener's Guides for Poetry Ser.). 32p. 1999. 12.00 incl. cd-rom (*1-55659-998-6*) Copper Canyon.

Carruth, Hayden. Reluctantly: Autobiographical Essays. LC 98-19742. 164p. 1999. pap. 15.00 (*1-55659-089-X*, Pub. by Copper Canyon) SPD-Small Pr Dist.

— Scrambled Eggs & Whiskey: Poems 1991-1995. LC 96-4487. 140p. 1996. 25.00 (*1-55659-109-8*); pap. 14.00 (*1-55659-110-1*) Copper Canyon.

— Selected Essays & Reviews. LC 95-4425. (Writing Re). 450p. 1995. pap. 18.00 (*1-55659-107-1*) Copper Canyon.

— Sitting In: Selected Writings on Jazz, Blues, & Related Topics. LC 93-1813. 239p. 1993. pap. 14.95 (*0-87745-423-X*) U of Iowa Pr.

— The Sleeping Beauty. rev. ed. LC 90-81353. 96p. 1990. reprint ed. pap. 10.00 (*1-55659-033-4*) Copper Canyon.

— Suicides & Jazzers. (Poets on Poetry Ser.). 256p. (C). 1993. text 39.50 (*0-472-09419-X*, 09419) U of Mich Pr.

— Tell Me Again How the White Heron Rises & Flies Across the Nacreous River at Twilight Toward the Distant Islands. LC 89-31603. Vol. 677. 96p. 1989. pap. 8.95 (*0-8112-1104-5*, NDP677, Pub. by New Directions) Norton.

— Voice That Is Great Within Us. 768p. 1983. mass mkt. 8.99 (*0-553-26263-7*) Bantam.

— Voice That Is Great Within Us: American Poetry of the Twentieth Century. (Bantam Classics Ser.). 1970. 13.09 (*0-606-02360-7*, Pub. by Turtleback) Demco.

An Asterisk (*) at the beginning of an entry indicates that the title is appearing for the first time.

Carruth, J. A. & McKenzie, A. Medical Lasers: Science & Clinical Practice. (Illus.). 280p. 1986. 116.00 (*0-85274-560-5*) IOP Pub.

Carruth, James H., jt. auth. see Eaves, Edgar D.

Carruth, Jane. My Giant Treasury of Fairy Tales. (J). 1988. 9.98 (*0-671-09118-2*) S&S Trade.

Carruth, Jane, ed. see Barrie, J. M.

Carruth, Jane, ed. see Carroll, Lewis, pseud.

Carruth, Mark, jt. auth. see Wier, Terry.

Carruth, Tom. Then Sings My Soul: Inspirational Hymn Arrangements for Piano. 40p. 1998. pap. 10.98 (*0-88290-629-1*, 2909) Horizon Utah.

Carruthers. Understanding Music. 1996. pap. text, student ed. 20.60 (*0-13-606260-1*) P-H.

Carruthers, Ann, ed. see Pan-Ling, Chen.

Carruthers, Annette. Edward Barnsley & His Workshop: Arts & Crafts in the Twentieth Century. 208p. 1994. pap. 29.95 (*1-873487-03-7*, Pub. by White Cockade) Paul & Co Pubs.

Carruthers, Annette, ed. The Scottish Home. (Illus.). 232p. 1996. 25.00 (*0-948636-72-6*, 6726, Pub. by Natl Mus Scotland) A Schwartz & Co.

Carruthers, Annette & Greensted, Mary, eds. Simplicity or Splendor: Arts & Crafts Living, Objects from the Cheltenham Collection. (Illus.). 184p. 1999. pap. 40.00 (*0-85331-779-8*, Pub. by Lund Humphries) Antique Collect.

***Carruthers, Bob.** Normandy Battles. (Illus.). 2000. 29.95 (*0-304-35396-5*) Continuum.

— Russian Front, 1941-1945. (Illus.). 2000. 29.95 (*0-304-35372-8*) Continuum.

Carruthers, Bruce G. City of Capital: Politics & Markets in the English Financial Revolution. LC 95-53190. 320p. (C). 1996. text 45.00 (*0-691-04455-4*, Pub. by Princeton U Pr) Cal Prin Full Svc.

***Carruthers, Bruce G.** City of Capital: Politics & Markets in the English Financial Revolution. 2000. pap. text 18.95 (*0-691-04960-2*) Princeton U Pr.

Carruthers, Bruce G. & Halliday, Terence C. Rescuing Business: The Making of Corporate Bankruptcy Law in England & the United States. LC 97-47443. 598p. 1998. text 85.00 (*0-19-826472-0*) OUP.

Carruthers, C. Ann, ed. see Aleotti, Vittoria.

Carruthers, Corine. Open the Lights. 1981. spiral bd. 40.13 (*0-201-10201-3*) Addison-Wesley.

Carruthers, Cynthia, ed. ATRA Annual in Therapeutic Recreation, Vol. 3. 95p. (Orig.). 1992. pap. 10.50 (*1-889435-01-5*) Am Therapeutic.

— ATRA Annual in Therapeutic Recreation, Vol. 4. 114p. (Orig.). 1993. pap. text 19.00 (*1-889435-04-X*) Am Therapeutic.

— ATRA Annual in Therapeutic Recreation, Vol. 5. 109p. (Orig.). 1994. pap. text 19.00 (*1-889435-06-6*) Am Therapeutic.

— ATRA Annual in Therapeutic Recreation, Vol. 6. 88p. (Orig.). 1996. pap. text 19.00 (*1-889435-08-2*) Am Therapeutic.

Carruthers, Douglas. Unknown Mongolia: A Record of Travel & Exploration in the North West Mongolia & Dzungaria. (C). 1994. reprint ed. 44.00 (*81-206-0857-7*, Pub. by Asian Educ Servs); reprint ed. write for info. (*81-206-0859-3*, Pub. by Asian Educ Servs) S Asia.

***Carruthers, George R. & Dymond, Kenneth F., eds.** Ultraviolet Atmospheric & Space Remote Sensing. 1999. pap. text 62.00 (*0-8194-3304-7*) SPIE.

***Carruthers, George S.** Highland Fling. unabridged ed. 40p. 2000. pap. 6.00 (*0-88734-759-2*) Players Pr.

Carruthers, Gregory H. The Uniqueness of Jesus Christ in the Theocentric Model of the Christian Theology of World Religions: An Elaboration & Evaluation of the Position of John Hick. 378p. (C). 1990. lib. bdg. 53.00 (*0-8191-7889-6*) U Pr of Amer.

Carruthers, Ian, ed. Social & Economic Perspectives on Irrigation. 100p. 1981. pap. 26.00 (*0-08-026780-7*, Pergamon Pr) Elsevier.

Carruthers, Ian, jt. auth. see Small, Leslie E.

Carruthers, Jacob. Essays in Ancient Egyptian Studies. 124p. 1984. pap. 10.95 (*0-943412-03-X*) Univ Sankore Pr.

Carruthers, Jacob, jt. auth. see Karenga, Maulana.

Carruthers, Jacob H. Intellectual Warfare. LC 97-29817. 310p. 1996. pap. 19.95 (*0-88378-180-8*) Third World.

— Intellectual Warfare. LC 97-29817. 310p. 1997. 32.95 (*0-88378-160-3*) Third World.

Carruthers, Jane. The Kruger National Park: A Social & Political History. LC 96-132522. (Illus.). 200p. (C). 1995. pap. 25.50 (*0-86980-915-6*, Pub. by Univ Natal Pr) Intl Spec Bk.

Carruthers, Lyn, jt. auth. see Baldwin, Norma.

***Carruthers, M.** Androgen Deficiency in the Aging Male. 2001. write for info. (*1-84214-032-9*) Prthnon Pub.

Carruthers, M., ed. see Annual Conference for Psychosomatic Research Staff.

Carruthers, Malcolm. Maximizing Manhood. 1998. pap. 13.00 (*0-7225-3532-5*) Thorsons PA.

***Carruthers, Margaret W. & Clinton, Susan.** Builders of Geology. LC 00-27011. (Lives in Science Ser.). 2001. write for info. (*0-531-11364-7*) Watts.

Carruthers, Mary. The Craft of Thought: Meditation, Rhetoric, & the Making of Images, 400-1200. LC 97-30143. (Cambridge Studies in Medieval Literature: No. 34). (Illus.). 452p. (C). 1998. text 59.95 (*0-521-58232-6*) Cambridge U Pr.

Carruthers, Mary J. The Book of Memory: A Study of Memory in Medieval Culture. (Studies in Medieval Literature: No. 10). (Illus.). 407p. (C). 1992. pap. text 25.95 (*0-521-42973-0*) Cambridge U Pr.

***Carruthers, Mary J.** The Craft of Thought: Meditation, Rhetoric & the Making of Images, 400-1200. (Cambridge Studies in Medieval Literature: Vol. 34). (Illus.). 426p. (C). 2000. pap. Price not set. (*0-521-79541-9*) Cambridge U Pr.

Carruthers, Mary J. & Kirk, Elizabeth D., eds. Acts of Interpretation: The Text in Its Context. LC 82-13148. 385p. 1982. 27.95 (*0-937664-60-X*) Pilgrim Bks OK.

Carruthers, Michael. Principles of Management for Quality Projects. (ITBP Textbooks Ser.). 1999. pap. 19.99 (*1-86152-522-2*) Thomson Learn.

Carruthers, N. Bermuda, 1985. (Fisher Annotated Travel Guides Ser.). 128p. 1984. 9.95 (*0-8116-0067-X*) NAL.

Carruthers, P. Hadronic Multiparticle Production. 708p. (C). 1988. text 91.00 (*9971-5-0558-4*); pap. text 46.00 (*9971-5-0559-2*) World Scientific Pub.

Carruthers, P. & Strottman, D. D., eds. Hadronic Matter in Collision: Proceedings of the Second International Workshop on Local Equilibrium in Strong Interaction Physics, Los Alamos, U. S. A., April 8-11, 1986. 450p. 1986. text 100.00 (*9971-5-0165-1*) World Scientific Pub.

Carruthers, P. A. & Rafelski, Johann, eds. Hadronic Matter in Collision. 860p. (C). 1989. text 166.00 (*9971-5-0849-4*) World Scientific Pub.

Carruthers, Peter. La Cuestion de los Animales - The Animals Issue: Teoria De la Moral Aplicada - Moral Theory in Practice. Perzaao, Jose M., tr. (SPA.). 258p. (C). 1995. pap. 14.95 (*0-521-47834-0*) Cambridge U Pr.

— Human Knowledge: A New Introduction to the Ancient Debate. 208p. 1992. pap. text 16.95 (*0-19-875102-8*) OUP.

— Introducing Persons: Theories & Arguments in the Philosophy of Mind. 288p. (C). 1991. pap. 24.99 (*0-415-04512-6*, A5711) Routledge.

— Language, Thought & Consciousness: An Essay in Philosophical Psychology. 308p. (C). 1998. reprint ed. pap. text 24.95 (*0-521-63999-9*) Cambridge U Pr.

***Carruthers, Peter.** Phenomenal Consciousness: A Naturalistic Theory. (Illus.). 358p. 2000. write for info. (*0-521-78173-6*) Cambridge U Pr.

Carruthers, Peter & Botterill, George. The Philosophy of Psychology. LC 98-33301. (Illus.). 312p. (C). 1999. 57.95 (*0-521-55111-0*) Cambridge U Pr.

Carruthers, Peter & Boucher, Jill, eds. Language & Thought: Interdisciplinary Themes. LC 97-35248. (Illus.). 338p. (C). 1998. text 59.95 (*0-521-63108-4*); pap. text 19.95 (*0-521-63758-9*) Cambridge U Pr.

Carruthers, Peter & Smith, Peter K., eds. Theories of Theories of Mind. (Illus.). 406p. (C). 1996. pap. text 20.95 (*0-521-55916-2*) Cambridge U Pr.

Carruthers, Peter, jt. auth. see Botterill, George.

Carruthers, Ruth R. Dr. Hugh Greer Carruthers: His Life & His Teachings. LC 94-76782. (Illus.). 325p. 1994. 29.50 (*0-9641194-0-4*) H G Carruthers.

Carruthers, S. W. The Everyday Work of the Westminster Assembly. Duncan, J. Ligon, III, ed. 284p. (C). 1995. reprint ed. pap. text 9.95 (*1-884416-06-3*) A Press.

— The Westminster Confession of Faith: The Preparation & Printing of Its Seven Leading Editions & a Critical Text. (C). 1995. pap. 9.95 (*1-884416-12-8*, Reformed Acad Pr) A Press.

***Carruthers, Susan L.** Media at War. LC 99-37492. 321p. 2000. text 55.00 (*0-312-22800-7*) St Martin.

— The Media at War: Communication & Conflict in the Twentieth Century. LC 99-37492. 2000. pap. 21.95 (*0-312-22801-5*) St Martin.

Carruthers, Susan L. Winning Hearts & Minds: British Governments, the Media & Colonial Counter-Insurgency 1944-1960. LC 95-7954. 320p. 1995. 85.00 (*0-7185-0027-X*); pap. 24.95 (*0-7185-0028-8*) Bks Intl VA.

Carruthers, Susan L., jt. ed. see Stewart, Ian.

Carruthers, V. C., jt. auth. see Passmore, N. I.

Carruthers, Vincent, ed. The Wildlife of Southern Africa. LC 97-173823. (Illus.). 320p. 1997. pap. 18.95 (*1-86812-675-7*) Menasha Ridge.

Carruthers, W. Cycloaddition Reactions in Organic Synthesis. (Tetrahedron Organic Chemistry Ser.: No. 8). (Illus.). 384p. 1990. pap. text 50.50 (*0-08-034712-6*) Elsevier.

— Cycloaddition Reactions in Organic Synthesis. (Tetrahedron Organic Chemistry Ser.: No. 8). (Illus.). 384p. 1990. text 128.50 (*0-08-034713-4*, Pergamon Pr) Elsevier.

— Some Modern Methods of Organic Synthesis. 3rd ed. (Cambridge Texts in Chemistry & Biochemistry Ser.). (Illus.). 538p. 1987. pap. text 44.95 (*0-521-31117-9*) Cambridge U Pr.

Carruthers, William L., jt. auth. see Craig, Marva E.

Carry, Julius J., III. The Alphabet Calendar Fun Book. (Illus.). 27p. (Orig.). (J). (gr. 1-4). 1997. pap. 6.95 (*0-9656962-1-9*) Alphabet Calendar.

Carryl, Charles E. River Syndicate & Other Stories. LC 70-106258. (Short Story Index Reprint Ser.). 1977. 20.95 (*0-8369-3295-1*) Ayer.

— The Walloping Window-Blind. LC 92-40338. (Illus.). (J). (gr. k-5). 1994. 16.00 (*0-688-12517-4*); lib. bdg. 15.93 (*0-688-12518-2*) Lothrop.

Carryl, Guy W. Grimm Tales Made Gay. LC 73-104428. (Illus.). reprint ed. lib. bdg. 22.75 (*0-8398-0253-6*) Irvington.

— Zut, & Other Parisians. LC 76-81266. (Short Story Index Reprint Ser.). 1977. 20.95 (*0-8369-3018-5*) Ayer.

***Cars & Parts Editors.** Ultimate Collector Car Price Guide, 1900-1990. 6th ed. (Illus.). 800p. 2000. pap. 15.95 (*1-880524-41-4*, 130553AP, Pub. by Cars & Parts) Motorbooks Intl.

Cars & Parts Magazine Editors Staff. Catalog of GTO I. D. Numbers, 1964-74. (Illus.). 320p. 1993. pap. text 19.95 (*1-880524-07-4*) Cars & Parts.

— Catalog of Mustang I. D. Numbers, 1964-5-1993. (Matching Number Ser.). (Illus.). 321p. 1993. pap. 19.95 (*1-880524-10-4*) Cars & Parts.

— Ultimate Collector Car Price Guide 1900-1990. 5th ed. (Illus.). 272p. 1999. pap. 15.95 (*1-880524-39-2*, Pub. by Cars & Parts) Motorbooks Intl.

Cars & Parts Magazine Staff. Catalog of American Car I. D. Numbers, 1950-59. (Matching Number Ser.). (Illus.). 460p. 1993. pap. 19.95 (*1-880524-04-X*) Cars & Parts.

— Catalog of American Car I. D. Numbers 1960-69. rev. ed. (Matching Number Ser.). (Illus.). 388p. 1996. pap. 19.95 (*1-880524-11-2*) Cars & Parts.

— Catalog of American Car I.D. Numbers, 1970-79. rev. ed. (Matching Number Ser.). (Illus.). 552p. (Orig.). 1991. pap. 19.95 (*0-87938-518-9*) Cars & Parts.

— Catalog of Camaro I.D. Number, 1967-1993. LC 98-117608. (Matching Number Ser.). (Illus.). 220p. 1995. pap. 19.95 (*1-880524-15-5*) Cars & Parts.

— Catalog of Chevelle, Malibu & El Camino I.D. Numbers, 1964-87. (Matching Number Ser.). (Illus.). 250p. 1993. pap. text 19.95 (*1-880524-06-6*) Cars & Parts.

— Catalog of Chevy Truck I. D. Numbers, 1946-1972. (Matching Number Ser.). (Illus.). 229p. 1992. pap. 19.95 (*1-880524-02-3*) Cars & Parts.

— Catalog of Chevy V-8 Engine Casting Numbers, 1955-1993. rev. ed. (Matching Number Ser.). (Illus.). 212p. (Orig.). 1996. pap. text 19.95 (*1-880524-13-9*) Cars & Parts.

— Catalog of Corvette I.D. Numbers, 1953-1993. rev. ed. (Matching Number Ser.). (Illus.). 255p. (Orig.). 1993. pap. 19.95 (*1-880524-08-2*) Cars & Parts.

— Catalog of Firebird I.D. Numbers, 1967-1993. LC 96-143195. (Matching Number Ser.). (Illus.). 179p. 1995. pap. text 19.95 (*1-880524-16-3*) Cars & Parts.

— Catalog of Ford Truck I. D. Numbers, 1946-1972. (Matching Number Ser.). (Illus.). 245p. 1992. pap. text 14.98 (*1-880524-03-1*) Cars & Parts.

— Catalog of Thunderbird I & D Numbers, 1955-93. LC 96-105630. (Matching Number Ser.). (Illus.). 283p. 1994. pap. text 19.95 (*1-880524-14-7*) Cars & Parts.

— Peggy Sue: 1957 Chevrolet Restoration: A Step by Step Restoration Guide. (Illus.). 248p. 1992. pap. text 12.95 (*1-880524-05-8*) Cars & Parts.

Cars & Parts Magazine Staff, ed. Suzy Q: Restoring a '63 Corvette Sting Ray. LC 96-210724. (Illus.). 257p. (Orig.). 1996. pap. 12.95 (*1-880524-19-8*) Cars & Parts.

Cars & Parts Staff. Salvage Yard Treasurers of America. (Illus.). 240p. 1998. pap. 19.95 (*1-880524-31-7*) Cars & Parts.

— Ultimate Muscle Car Price Guide, 1961-1990. (Illus.). 500p. 1998. pap. 12.95 (*1-880524-32-5*) Cars & Parts.

Cars, Goran, jt. ed. see Alterman, Rachelle.

***CARS '99 Staff & Lemke, H. U.** Cars '99: Computer Assisted Radiology & Surgery: Proceedings of the 13th International Congress & Exhibition, Paris, 23-26 June 1999. LC 99-35458. (International Congress Ser.). 1158p. 1999. 276.50 (*0-444-50290-4*, Excerpta Medica) Elsevier.

Carsaniga, Giovanni. Italiano Espresso. 256p. 1982. pap. text 22.95 (*0-521-28220-9*) Cambridge U Pr.

— Italiano Espresso, Set. 256p. audio 89.95 (*0-521-23777-7*) Cambridge U Pr.

— Just Listen 'n Learn Italian: Beginning. Hill, Brian, ed. LC 97-48940. (ITA.). (C). 1998. 17.95 (*0-8442-8450-5*, X8450-5) NTC Contemp Pub Co.

Carsberg, Bryan. Competition Regulation the British Way: Jaguar or Dinosaur? (IEA Occasional Paper Ser.: No. 97). 32p. 1996. pap. 9.95 (*0-255-36376-1*, Pub. by Inst Economic Affairs) Coronet Bks.

— Office of Telecommunications (OFTEL) Annual Report, 1994. 131p. 1995. pap. 30.00 (*0-10-234095-1*, HM40951, Pub. by Statnry Office) Bernan Associates.

— Office of Telecommunications (OFTEL) Annual Report, 1997. 131p. 1998. pap. 45.00 (*0-10-293198-4*, HM31984, Pub. by Statnry Office) Bernan Associates.

Carsberg, Bryan V. Introduction to Mathematical Programming for Accountants. LC 71-95609. xii, 108p. 1970. 29.50 (*0-678-06006-1*) Kelley.

Carscallen, William E., jt. auth. see Oosthuizen, P. H.

Carse, Adam. The History of Orchestration. (Illus.). 348p. 1964. pap. 9.95 (*0-486-21258-0*) Dover.

— Musical Wind Instruments: A History of the Wind Instruments Used in European Orchestras & Wind Bands, from the Later Middle Ages up to the Present Time. 2nd ed. LC 65-18502. (Music Ser.). 1975. reprint ed. 45.00 (*0-306-70906-6*); reprint ed. pap. 9.95 (*0-306-80005-5*) Da Capo.

— The Orchestra from Beethoven to Berlioz. 400p. (C). 1996. reprint ed. pap. text 35.00 (*0-87556-832-7*) Saifer.

— The Orchestra in the XVIIIth Century. (Illus.). 184p. 1941. lib. bdg. 27.50 (*0-8450-2551-1*) Broude.

Carse, Adam V. Musical Wind Instruments. (Music Book Index Ser.). 381p. 1992. reprint ed. lib. bdg. 89.00 (*0-7812-9496-7*) Rprt Serv.

Carse, Adam von Ahn. Orchestral Conducting: A Textbook for Students & Amateurs. LC 78-109716. (Illus.). 100p. 1971. reprint ed. lib. bdg. 59.50 (*0-8371-4206-7*, CAOC, Greenwood Pr) Greenwood.

Carse, Adam Von Ahn, see Von Ahn Carse, Adam.

Carse, James P. Breakfast at the Victory: The Mysticism of Ordinary Experience. LC 94-5010. 224p. 1995. pap. 11.00 (*0-06-251171-8*, Pub. by Harper SF); pap. 11.00 (*0-625-11718-2*) Harper SF.

— Finite & Infinite Games: A Vision of Life as Play & Possibility. 192p. 1987. mass mkt. 5.99 (*0-345-34184-8*) Ballantine Pub Grp.

— Finite & Infinite Games: A Vision of Life as Play & Possibility. 144p. 1986. 27.95 (*0-02-905980-1*) Free Pr.

— The Gospel of the Beloved Disciple. LC 97-17856. 1997. pap. 13.00 (*0-06-061577-X*) Harper SF.

— The Gospel of the Beloved Disciple. LC 97-17856. 144p. 1997. 18.00 (*0-06-061576-1*, Pub. by Harper SF) HarpC.

— The Silence of God: Meditations on Prayer. LC 95-10094. 128p. 1995. pap. 11.00 (*0-06-061410-2*, Pub. by Harper SF) HarpC.

Carse, Mary. Herbs of the Earth: A Self-Teaching Guide to Healing Remedies. 2nd expanded rev. ed. Carlson, Lisa, ed. (Illus.). 239p. (Orig.). 1998. pap. 12.95 (*0-942679-20-2*) Upper Access.

Carse-Slater. Payroll Accounting. 2nd ed. 1996. 53.44 (*0-256-25212-2*) McGraw.

— Payroll Accounting. 2nd ed. 1996. teacher ed. 39.37 (*0-256-25197-5*) McGraw.

Carse, Stephen, et al. The Financing Procedures of British Foreign Trade. LC 79-18146. 163p. reprint ed. pap. 46.50 (*0-608-15702-3*, 2031629) Bks Demand.

Carse, Timothy. Payroll Accounting. 2nd ed. LC 96-225197. 528p. (C). 1996. text 34.95 (*0-256-21754-8*, Irwn McGrw-H) McGrw-H Hghr Educ.

Carse, Timothy & Slater, Jeffrey. Directory of Vendors for Group Practice. 1993. text 75.00 (*0-07-413111-7*, Irwn McGrw-H) McGrw-H Hghr Educ.

— Healtcare Records Management, Disclosure & Retention: The Complete Legal Guide. 2nd rev. ed. (C). 1993. text 75.00 (*0-07-413117-6*, Irwn McGrw-H) McGrw-H Hghr Educ.

— M48 Financial Planning for Physician. 1995. text 35.00 (*0-07-413101-X*, Irwn McGrw-H) McGrw-H Hghr Educ.

— The 1995 Almanac of Hospital Financial & Operating Indicators. 2nd ed. 1996. text 350.00 (*0-07-413128-1*, Irwn McGrw-H) McGrw-H Hghr Educ.

— Patient Financial Services: Organizing & Managing a Cost-Effective Financial Services Operation. (C). 1993. text 65.00 (*0-07-413122-2*, Irwn McGrw-H) McGrw-H Hghr Educ.

— Transforming the Delivery of Health Care. 1995. text 95.00 (*0-07-413100-1*, Irwn McGrw-H) McGrw-H Hghr Educ.

Carse, Timothy F. & Slater, Jeffrey. Payroll Accounting. (Orig.). 1998. pap. text 59.95 (*0-89863-207-2*, 207-2) Star Pub CA.

***Carse, Timothy F. & Slater, Jeffrey. Payroll Accounting. 4th ed. (Orig.). 2000. pap. text 59.95 (*0-89863-222-6*) Star Pub CA.**

Payroll Accounting: A Practical Approach, reflects the authors' years of teaching payroll accounting! The authors simplify the discussion of employment & tax laws that affect payroll preparation, using clear, understandable language. The organization of the book matches the major steps a professional takes in calculating the payroll of a business. The book follows the payroll cycle for a company, within which various tasks & activities occur. *Publisher Paid Annotation.*

Carse, Timothy F. & Slater, Jeffrey. The Payroll Toolkit: Nuts & Bolts Techniques to Managing Your Payroll. LC 96-40919. 360p. 1996. 35.00 (*1-55623-848-7*, Irwn Prfssnl) McGraw-Hill Prof.

Carsella, P. J., jt. auth. see Schofield, William.

Carser, S. X. Motorcross Cycles. (Cruisin' Ser.). (Illus.). 48p. (J). (gr. 3-6). 1992. 19.00 (*0-516-35069-2*) Childrens.

***Carsetti, Arturo.** Functional Models of Cognition: Self-Organizing Dynamics & Semantic Structures in Cognitive Systems. LC 99-51949. (Theory & Decision Library Ser.). 312p. 1999. 125.00 (*0-7923-6072-9*) Kluwer Academic.

Carsey, Frank, ed. Microwave Remote Sensing of Sea Ice. LC 92-41032. (Geophysical Monograph Ser.: Vol. 68). 1993. 68.00 (*0-87590-033-X*) Am Geophysical.

***Carsey, Thomas M.** Campaign Dynamics: The Race for Governor. 232p. (C). 2000. text 49.50 (*0-472-11014-4*, 11014) U of Mich Pr.

Carskadden, Jeff & Gartley, Richard. China's Hand-Painted Marbles of the Late 19th Century. (Illus.). 100p. (Orig.). 1990. pap. 20.00 (*0-9626931-0-3*) Muskingum Val Arch.

Carskadden, Jeff & Morton, James. Where the Frolics & War Dances Are Held: The Indian Wars & the Early European Exploration & Settlement of Muskingum County & the Central Muskingum Valley. LC 97-68466. (Illus.). 543p. 1997. 30.00 (*0-9626931-5-4*) Muskingum Val Arch.

Carslallen, James. The Other Country: Patterns in the Writings of Alice Munro. 560p. (C). 1993. pap. text 40.00 (*1-55022-163-9*, Pub. by ECW) Genl Dist Srvs.

Carslaw, H. S., ed. see Bonola, Roberto.

Carslaw, Horatio S. & Jaeger, J. C. Conduction of Heat in Solids. 2nd ed. (Illus.). 520p. 1986. pap. text 74.95 (*0-19-853368-3*) OUP.

Carsola, Rita, ed. see Dorsey, Dayna R.

Carson. Abnormal Psychology & Modern Life. 10th ed. 85p. 1997. pap. 46.00 (*0-321-01830-3*) Addson-Wesley Educ.

— Abnormal Psychology & Modern Life: Study Guide. 11th ed. (C). 2000. pap. text 15.00 (*0-321-05453-9*) Addson-Wesley Educ.

— Abnormal Psychology & Modern Life Telecourse Study Guide. 11th ed. 256p. (C). 1999. pap. text, student ed. 21.00 (*0-321-05923-9*) Addson-Wesley Educ.

— African American Stories, American Lives. (C). 2000. pap. text Price not set. (*0-321-02586-5*) Addison-Wesley.

Carson. Black Panther Party. pap. text. write for info. (*0-312-07180-9*) St Martin.

Carson. Board of Registry Study Guide - Histotechnology. 1994. 40.00 (*0-89189-375-X*) Am Soc Clinical.

— Economic Issues. 5th ed. 2000. pap. text 24.00 (*0-312-13806-7*) St Martin.

C

— Hallelujah. 1994. pap. 8.99 (*0-85234-142-3*, Pub. by Evangelical Pr) P & R Pubng.

— Kid Biz. 1989. pap. text 13.95 (*0-9623168-0-6*) Kid Biz Pubns.

***Carson.** Knight of the Flaming Heart. (J). 2000. 27.95 (*0-385-40651-7*, Pub. by Transworld Publishers Ltd) Trafalgar.

Carson. Lost Woods. large type ed. LC 98-44509. 1999. 30.00 (*0-7862-1697-2*) Thorndike Pr.

— Mental Health Nursing. 2nd ed. LC 99-35203. (C). 1999. text. write for info. (*0-7216-8053-4*, W B Saunders Co) Harcrt Hlth Sci Grp.

— Multicultural Casebook to Accompany Abnormal Psychology & Modern Life e. 1998 Update. 10th ed. (C). 1998. pap. text. write for info. (*0-321-01729-3*) Addison-Wesley Educ.

— Philosophy of Medicine & Bioethicsa: Twenty-Year Retrospective & Critical Appraisal. LC 97-30020. 1997. text 117.50 (*0-7923-3545-7*) Kluwer Academic.

***Carson.** Prealgbera: Project Problem Manual. 2000. pap. 8.00 (*0-201-70404-8*) Addison-Wesley.

— Psychology Encyclopedia Lasderdisc III. 1998. 231.00 (*0-321-02092-8*) Addison-Wesley Educ.

Carson. The Safe Handling of Chemicals in Industries, Vol. 13. 1995. text. write for info. (*0-582-06307-8*, Pub. by Addison-Wesley) Longman.

— Spiritual Dimensions of Nursing Practice. 400p. 1989. pap. text 39.50 (*0-7216-2249-6*, W B Saunders Co) Harcrt Hlth Sci Grp.

— Stress & Coping in Mental Health. 221p. 1994. pap. 41.50 (*1-56593-330-3*, 0660) Singular Publishing.

— Treasure! Bonanzas Worth a Billion Bucks. 182p. 1996. pap. 10.00 (*0-918080-37-1*) Treas Chest Bks.

***Carson & Butcher.** Supplemental Abnormal Psychology & Modern Life. 11th ed. 2000. 85.00 incl. cd-rom (*0-205-32523-8*) Allyn.

***Carson & Cobelli.** Introduction to Modeling in Physiology & Medicine. 1999. 75.00 (*0-12-160240-0*) Morgan Kaufmann.

Carson & Mumford. Safe Handling of Chemicals, Vol. 1 & 2. 1988. text. write for info. (*0-582-00304-0*, Pub. by Addison-Wesley) Longman.

***Carson, et al.** Abnormal Psychology & Modern Life. 11th ed. LC 99-34830. 840p. (C). 1999. 88.00 (*0-321-03430-9*) Addison-Wesley.

Carson, et al. Late Roman Bronze Coinage. 1990. 25.00 (*0-942666-57-7*) S J Durst.

Carson & Carson. Management of Healthcare Organizations. (Swc-Management). Date not set. write for info. (*0-534-24036-4*) Brooks-Cole.

Carson, A. William. High Pitches & Other Tall Tales: A Mirror into the Soul of Housing. (Orig.). 1994. pap. write for info. (*0-9642731-0-1*) IN Builders Assn.

Carson, Aileen. Born to Exhale the Mundane. 24p. 1995. 6.95 (*1-885206-29-1*, Iliad Pr) Cader Pubng.

Carson, Alan. Inspecting a House. (Illus.). 268p. 1986. pap. 12.95 (*0-7737-5092-4*) Genl Dist Srvs.

Carson, Alan & Dunlop, Robert. Inspecting a House: A Guide for Buyers, Owners & Renovators. 1999. pap. text 16.95 (*0-7737-6037-7*, Pub. by Stoddart Publ) Genl Dist Srvs.

Carson, Allan. Trilogy. LC 97-186077. 96p. (Orig.). 1997. pap. 9.95 (*1-882897-06-4*) Lost Coast.

Carson, Andrew D. My Time in Hell: Memoir of an American Soldier Imprisoned by the Japanese in World War II. LC 97-23520. 264p. 1997. pap. 29.95 (*0-7864-0403-5*) McFarland & Co.

Carson, Angela. Sweet Illusion. large type ed. 358p. 1994. 27.99 (*0-7505-0634-2*, Pub. by Mgna Lrg Print) Ulverscroft.

Carson, Ann. The Memoirs of the Celebrated & Beautiful Mrs. Ann Carson, Daughter of an Officer of the U. S. Navy & Wife of Another, Whose Life Terminated in the Philadelphia Prison, 2 vols. rev. ed. Baxter, Annette K., ed. LC 79-8780. (Signal Lives Ser.). 1980. reprint ed. lib. bdg. 47.95 (*0-405-12829-0*) Ayer.

***Carson, Anne.** Autobiography of Red: A Novel in Verse. (Vintage Contemporaries Ser.). 160p. 1999. pap. 12.00 (*0-375-70129-X*) Vin Bks.

Carson, Anne. Canicula di Anna. (QRL Poetry Bks.: Vol. XXV). 1984. 20.00 (*0-614-06412-0*) Quarterly Rev.

***Carson, Anne.** Economy of the Unlost: Reading Simonides of Keos with Paul Celan. LC 98-49984. (Martin Classical Lectures). 147p. 1999. 29.95 (*0-691-03677-2*, Pub. by Princeton U Pr) Cal Prin Full Svc.

Carson, Anne. Eros the Bittersweet. LC 97-51954. 208p. 1998. reprint ed. pap. 12.95 (*1-56478-188-7*) Dalkey Arch.

— Eros the Bittersweet: An Essay. LC 85-43371. 202p. 1986. reprint ed. pap. 62.70 (*0-608-02740-5*, 206340500004) Bks Demand.

— Glass, Irony & God. LC 95-30637. 176p. 1995. pap. 14.00 (*0-8112-1302-1*, NDP808, Pub. by New Directions) Norton.

***Carson, Anne.** Men in the off Hours. 192p. 2000. 24.00 (*0-375-40803-7*) Knopf.

Carson, Anne. Plainwater: Essays & Poetry. 260p. 2000. pap. 13.00 (*0-375-70842-1*) Vin Bks.

— Short Talks. 64p. 1992. pap. 10.95 (*0-919626-58-0*, Pub. by Brick Bks) Genl Dist Srvs.

Carson, Anne, ed. Caretaking a New Soul: Writing on Parenting from Thich Nhat Hanh to Z. Budapest. LC 98-55282. Orig. Title: Spiritual Parenting in the New Age. 1999. pap. 14.95 (*1-58091-018-1*) Crossing Pr.

Carson, B. L., et al. Toxicology & Biological Monitoring of Metals in Humans--Including Feasability & Need. (Illus.). 360p. 1986. 190.00 (*0-87371-072-X*, RA1231, CRC Reprint) Franklin.

Carson, Barbara. The Governor's Palace: The Williamsburg Residence of Virginia's Royal Governor. LC 86-33413. (Illus.). 88p. (Orig.). 1987. 16.95 (*0-87935-120-9*); pap. 11.95 (*0-87935-121-7*) Colonial Williamsburg.

Carson, Barbara H. Eudora Welty: Two Pictures at Once in Her Frame. LC 91-75025. xxviii, 173p. 1992. 45.00 (*0-87875-422-9*) Whitston Pub.

Carson, Ben. Ben Carson. (Today's Heroes Ser.). 112p. (J). (gr. 3-9). 1992. pap. 4.99 (*0-310-58641-0*) Zondervan.

— Gifted Hands: The Ben Carson Story. 1990. 16.99 (*0-310-54650-8*) Zondervan.

— Gifted Hands: The Ben Carson Story. (Illus.). 232p. 1992. reprint ed. pap. 10.99 (*0-310-54651-6*) Zondervan.

Carson, Ben. Gifted Hands: 50 Minutes. 19.99 incl. VHS (*0-310-58129-X*) Zondervan.

Carson, Ben. Piense en Grande. 1994. pap. 10.99 (*0-88113-185-7*) Caribe Betania.

— Think Big. 1993. 4.99 (*0-310-96256-0*) Zondervan.

— Think Big: Discovering Your Gift of Excellence. LC 91-27217. 256p. 1992. 17.99 (*0-310-57410-2*) Zondervan.

Carson, Ben & Lewis, Greg. The Big Picture: Getting Perspective on What's Really Important in Life. LC 98-32033. 271p. 1999. 19.99 (*0-310-22583-3*) Zondervan.

Carson, Ben & Murphey, Cecil. Gifted Hands: The Ben Carson Story. 224p. 1997. mass mkt. 5.99 (*0-310-21469-6*) Zondervan.

Carson, Ben & Murphey, Cecil B. Think Big: Unleashing Your Potential for Excellence. 1996. pap. 5.99 (*0-310-21459-9*) Zondervan.

Carson, Ben & Smith, Jane B., eds. Renewal at the Schoolhouse: Management Ideas for Library Media Specialists & Administrators. LC 93-2997. (Illus.). xix, 156p. 1993. pap. text 25.00 (*0-87287-914-3*) Libs Unl.

Carson-Berndsen, Julie. Time Map Phonology Finite State Models & Event Logics in Speech Recognition Vol. 5: Text, Speech & Language Technology. LC 97-32527. 260p. 1998. text 117.50 (*0-7923-4883-4*) Kluwer Academic.

Carson, Betty J. Durbin & Logsdon Genealogy with Related Families, 1626-1991, Vol. 2. (Illus.). x, 253p. (Orig.). 1993. pap. text 21.00 (*1-55613-729-X*) Heritage Bk.

— Durbin & Logsdon Genealogy with Related Families, 1626-1994, 2 vols., rev. ed. (Illus.). 771p. (Orig.). 1995. pap. text 47.00 (*0-7884-0142-4*) Heritage Bk.

Carson, Betty J., compiled by. Durbin & Logsdon Genealogy: With Related Families, 1626-1991. (Illus.). 631p. (Orig.). 1991. pap. 36.50 (*1-55613-491-6*) Heritage Bk.

Carson, Betty J. & Wooley, Doris M. Our Ewing Heritage with Related Families, 2 vols., Set. LC 96-216331. 1057p. (Orig.). 1996. pap. 72.00 (*0-7884-0475-X*, C068) Heritage Bk.

Carson, Betty J. Durbin. Durbin & Logsdon Genealogy with Related Families, 1626-1998. 2nd ed. LC 98-231751. 1467 p. 1998. 23.00 (*0-7884-0964-6*) Heritage Bk.

***Carson, Bill.** Bill Carson: My Life & Times with Fender Musical Instruments. 1999. pap. text 14.95 (*1-884883-10-9*) Vintage Guitar.

Carson, Brian. Soil Conservation Strategies for Upland Areas of Indonesia. LC 89-12012. (East-West Environment & Policy Institute, Occasional Paper Ser.: Vol. 9). 134p. 1989. reprint ed. pap. 41.60 (*0-608-03575-0*, 206439800009) Bks Demand.

***Carson, Bruce & Llewellyn-Jones, Margaret, eds.** Frames & Fictions on Television: The Politics of Identity in TV Drama. 192p. 2000. pap. 34.95 (*1-84150-009-7*, Pub. by Intellect) Intl Spec Bk.

Carson, Bryce E., Sr., jt. auth. see Chuse, Robert.

Carson, Byrta R., et al. How You Plan & Prepare Meals. 3rd ed. (Illus.). 1980. text 28.00 (*0-07-010162-0*) McGraw.

Carson, Candice. High Country Wildflowers. Schwarz, Ann, ed. (Illus.). 68p. 1998. pap. 9.95 (*0-9651211-2-7*) Sage of Durango.

Carson, Carol. Bad Company. 320p. 1998. mass mkt. 4.99 (*0-8439-4448-X*, Leisure Bks) Dorchester Pub Co.

***Carson, Carol.** Family Man. 320p. 1999. mass mkt. 4.99 (*0-8439-4625-3*, Leisure Bks) Dorchester Pub Co.

Carson, Carol D., jt. auth. see Marzollo, Jean.

Carson, Carolyn L. Healing Body, Mind, & Spirit: The History of St. Francis Medical Center, Pittsburgh, Pennsylvania. LC 95-67955. 178p. (Orig.). 1996. pap. 19.95 (*0-88748-201-5*) Carnegie-Mellon.

Carson, Carrie, ed. see Cahill, Rick.

Carson, Cary. Becoming Americans: Our Struggle to Be Both Free & Equal: A Plan of Thematic Interpretation. LC 98-10785. 206p. 1998. 24.95 (*0-87935-167-5*) Colonial Williamsburg.

Carson, Charles. Mountain Troubadour. 1951. 5.95 (*0-87505-127-8*) Borden.

***Carson, Cheryl.** The Anguish - & Adventure - of Adversity. 3rd rev. ed. Carson, Michael, ed. 244p. 2000. reprint ed. pap. 13.95 (*0-9655150-2-8*, Pub. by TrueHeart Pub) Granite UT.

Carson, Cheryl. Forgiveness: The Healing Gift We Give Ourselves. 3rd rev. ed. iv, 163p. 1996. pap. 8.95 (*0-9655150-0-1*) TrueHeart Pub.

— His Law Is Love: Offering Unconditional Love Even to Those Who Don't Deserve It. unabridged ed. ix,312p. 1998. pap. 13.95 (*0-9655150-1-X*) TrueHeart Pub.

Carson, Cheryl L. Forgiveness: The Healing Gift We Give Ourselves. 90p. (Orig.). 1996. pap. 5.95 (*0-9651163-3-6*) Harkness Pubng.

Carson, Chris & McDonald, William, eds. A Guide to San Antonio Architecture. (Illus.). 136p. (Orig.). 1986. pap. 14.95 (*0-9616842-0-8*) AIA San Antonio Chap.

***Carson, Christie & Bratton, Jacky, eds.** Cambridge King Lear: Text & Performance Archive. (Illus.). (C). 2000. cd-rom Price not set. (*0-521-63640-X*) Cambridge U Pr.

Carson, Christopher. Kit Carson's Autobiography. (American Biography Ser.). 192p. 1991. reprint ed. lib. bdg. 59.00 (*0-7812-8061-3*) Rprt Serv.

Carson, Christopher, ed. When Ego Dies: A Compilation of Near-Death & Mystical Conversion Experiences. 196p. (Orig.). 1996. pap. 9.95 (*1-885373-07-4*) Emerald Ink.

Carson, Christopher, ed. see Pabst, William R.

***Carson, Ciaran.** Alexandrine Plan. 1998. pap. text. write for info. (*0-916390-83-7*) Wake Forest.

Carson, Ciaran. Belfast Confetti. LC 89-40527. 100p. 1989. 13.95 (*0-916390-41-1*); pap. 8.95 (*0-916390-40-3*) Wake Forest.

— First Language. LC 94-60031. 80p. 1994. 13.95 (*0-916390-61-6*); pap. 8.95 (*0-916390-60-8*) Wake Forest.

***Carson, Ciaran.** Fishing for Amber: A Long Story. viii, 360p. 2000. 19.95 (*1-86207-302-3*, Pub. by Granta) Midpt Trade.

Carson, Ciaran. The Irish for No. LC 87-50730. 64p. 1987. pap. 6.95 (*0-916390-29-2*) Wake Forest.

— Irish Traditional Music. (Pocket Guides Ser.). (Illus.). 72p. 1986. pap. 7.95 (*0-86281-168-6*) Irish Bks Media.

— Last Night's Fun: A Book about Irish Traditional Music. 1997. 21.00 (*0-86547-515-6*) N Point Pr.

— Last Night's Fun: In & Out of Time with Irish Music. 1998. 12.00 (*0-86547-531-8*) N Point Pr.

***Carson, Ciaran.** Last Night's Fun: In & Out of Time with Irish Music. 198p. 2000. reprint ed. text 21.00 (*0-7881-9087-3*) DIANE Pub.

Carson, Ciaran. The Star Factory. LC 98-24719. 304p. 1998. 23.95 (*1-55970-465-9*, Pub. by Arcade Pub Inc) Time Warner.

— The Twelfth of Never LC 99-174354. (Gallery Bks.). 91 p. 1998. write for info. (*1-85235-234-5*) Dufour.

***Carson, Ciaran.** Twelfth of Never. 1998. pap. text. write for info. (*0-916390-84-5*) Wake Forest.

Carson, Clara N., jt. auth. see Curran, Barbara A.

Carson, Clarence B. The American Tradition. 2nd ed. 306p. 1979. reprint ed. pap. 12.95 (*0-910614-17-2*) Foun Econ Ed.

Carson, Clarence B., frwd. The Foundations of American Constitutional Government. LC 95-61369. (Freeman Classics Ser.). 304p. (Orig.). 1995. pap. 14.95 (*1-57246-018-0*) Foun Econ Ed.

Carson, Clayborne. Guide to African-American History. 1999. pap. 16.95 (*0-14-017361-7*) Viking Penguin.

— Guide to American History. 1999. text 24.95 (*0-670-84699-6*) Viking Penguin.

— In Struggle: SNCC & the Black Awakening of the Nineteen Sixties. LC 80-16540. (Illus.). 373p. (C). 1982. pap. 15.50 (*0-674-44726-3*) HUP.

— In Struggle: SNCC & the Black Awakening of the 1960's. (Illus.). 384p. 1995. pap. text 17.95 (*0-674-44727-1*, CARSTY) HUP.

— Malcolm X: The FBI File. 1995. mass mkt. 6.99 (*0-345-40009-7*) Ballantine Pub Grp.

— Malcolm X: The FBI File. (Illus.). 512p. 1991. pap. 13.95 (*0-88184-758-5*) Carroll & Graf.

Carson, Clayborne, compiled by. The Autobiography of Martin Luther King, Jr. 1998. write for info. (*0-614-26130-9*) Warner Bks.

Carson, Clayborne, ed. The Autobiography of Martin Luther King, Jr. LC 98-35704. (Illus.). 400p. 1998. 25.00 (*0-446-52412-3*, Pub. by Warner Bks) Little.

***Carson, Clayborne, ed.** The Autobiography of Martin Luther King, Jr. 2000. pap. write for info. (*0-446-67650-0*) Warner Bks.

Carson, Clayborne, ed. The Movement, 1964-1970. LC 92-25745. 848p. 1993. lib. bdg. 215.00 (*0-313-28329-X*, CMO, Greenwood Pr) Greenwood.

— The Student Voice, 1960-1965: Periodical of the Student Nonviolent Coordinating Committee. LC 89-49690. 264p. 1990. lib. bdg. 135.00 (*0-313-28050-9*, CSY/, Greenwood Pr) Greenwood.

Carson, Clayborne, et al, eds. The Eyes on the Prize Civil Rights Reader: Documents, Speeches & Firsthand Accounts from the Black Freedom Movement, 1954-1990. LC 91-9507. 608p. 1991. pap. 16.95 (*0-14-015403-5*) Viking Penguin.

Carson, Clayborne & Holloran, Peter, eds. A Knock at Midnight: Inspiration from the Great Sermons of Reverend Martin Luther King, Jr. LC 98-84358. xx, 234p. 1998. 20.00 (*0-446-52346-1*, Pub. by Warner Bks) Little.

— A Knock at Midnight: Inspiration from the Great Sermons of Reverend Martin Luther King, Jr. 256p. 2000. mass mkt. 14.00 (*0-446-67554-7*, Pub. by Warner Bks) Little.

***Carson, Clayborne & Shepard, Kris, eds.** A Call to Conscience: The Landmark Speeches of Dr. Martin Luther King, Jr. 256p. 2001. 22.95 (*0-446-52399-2*) Warner Bks.

Carson, Clayborne, ed. see Harris, Robert.

Carson, Clayborne, jt. ed. see Hine, Darlene Clark.

Carson, Clayborne, ed. see King, Martin Luther, Jr.

Carson, Culley, et al. The Couples' Guide to Great Sex over 40. 1997. pap. 14.95 (*1-56333-543-3*, PCE) Masquerade.

Carson, Culley C., 3rd, ed. Complications of Interventional Techniques. LC 95-24468. (Topics in Clinical Urology Ser.). (Illus.). 256p. 1995. 69.50 (*0-89640-285-1*) Igaku-Shoin.

Carson, D. A. Basics for Believers: An Exposition of Philippians. LC 96-22499. 112p. (Orig.). (gr. 10). 1996. pap. 9.99 (*0-8010-5494-X*) Baker Bks.

— A Call to Spiritual Reformation: Encouragement from Paul & His Prayers. LC 92-11392. 232p. 1992. pap. 11.99 (*0-8010-2569-9*) Baker Bks.

***Carson, D. A.** The Difficult Doctrine of the Love of God. LC 99-47911. 112p. 1999. pap. 12.99 (*1-58134-126-1*) Crossway Bks.

Carson, D. A. Exegetical Fallacies. 2nd ed. LC 96-4156. 160p. 1996. pap. 8.99 (*0-8010-2086-7*) Baker Bks.

— For the Love of God: A Daily Companion for Discovering the Riches of God's Word. LC 98-26484. 384p. 1998. 19.99 (*1-58134-008-7*) Crossway Bks.

***Carson, D. A.** For the Love of God Vol. 2: A Daily Companion for Discovering the Treasures of God's Word. 400p. 1999. 19.99 (*1-58134-118-0*) Crossway Bks.

— From Sabbath to Lord's Day: A Biblical, Historical & Theological Investigation. 444p. 1999. pap. 32.00 (*1-57910-307-3*) Wipf & Stock.

— From Triumphalism to Maturity: An Exposition of Second Corinthians 10-13. 186p. 1996. reprint ed. mass mkt. 5.99 (*0-85364-751-8*, Pub. by Paternoster Pub) OM Literature.

Carson, D. A. The Gagging of God: Christianity Confronts Pluralism. 2nd ed. LC 95-36458. 400p. 1996. 27.99 (*0-310-47910-X*) Zondervan.

— God with Us: Themes from Matthew. 165p. 1995. reprint ed. write for info. (*0-9645014-0-6*) JKO Pub.

— Holy Sonnets of the Twentieth Century. 124p. (gr. 13). 1994. pap. 9.99 (*0-8010-2592-3*) Baker Bks.

— How Long, O Lord? Reflections on Suffering & Evil. LC 90-47788. 280p. 1990. pap. 16.99 (*0-8010-2556-7*) Baker Bks.

— The Inclusive-Language Debate: A Plea for Realism. LC 98-23473. 224p. (C). 1998. pap. 13.99 (*0-8010-5835-X*) Baker Bks.

***Carson, D. A.** Jesus' Sermon on the Mount: And His Confrontation with the World. 320p. 1999. pap. 16.25 (*1-58558-003-1*) Global Pubs.

— The King James Version Debate: A Plea for Realism. LC 79-50443. 128p. 1979. pap. 7.99 (*0-8010-2427-7*) Baker Bks.

— The Sermon on the Mount. (Biblical Classics Library: Vol. 2). 170p. 1998. reprint ed. mass mkt. 5.99 (*0-85364-607-4*, Pub. by Paternoster Pub) OM Literature.

Carson, D. A. The Sermon on the Mount: An Evangelical Exposition of Matthew 5-7. LC 77-93260. 160p. 1990. pap. 9.99 (*0-8010-2480-3*) Baker Bks.

Carson, D. A. Showing the Spirit: A Theological Exposition of I Corinthians 12-14. (Biblical & Theological Classics Library: Vol. 1). 229p. 1995. reprint ed. pap. 9.99 (*0-85364-636-8*, Pub. by Paternoster Pub) OM Literature.

Carson, D. A., ed. From Sabbath to Lord's Day. 432p. (Orig.). (C). 1982. pap. 21.99 (*0-310-44531-0*, 12035P) Zondervan.

***Carson, D. A., ed.** Telling the Truth. 2000. 27.99 (*0-310-23432-8*) Zondervan.

Carson, D. A., et al, eds. Hermeneutics, Authority & Canon. 480p. 1986. pap. 24.99 (*0-310-43991-4*, 12644P) Zondervan.

— Idiotypes in Biology & Medicine. (Chemical Immunology Ser.: Vol. 48). Orig. Title: Progress in Allergy. (Illus.). 214p. 1989. 154.00 (*3-8055-5000-6*) S Karger.

Carson, D. A. & Woodbridge, John D., eds. Scripture & Truth. 1983. pap. 20.95 (*0-310-43791-1*, 12643P) Zondervan.

— Scripture & Truth. LC 92-15722. 448p. 1992. reprint ed. pap. 24.99 (*0-8010-2570-2*) Baker Bks.

Carson, D. A., et al. The Expositor's Bible Commentary, Vol. 8. 1986. 41.99 (*0-88469-188-8*) BMH Bks.

— Introduction to the New Testament. 560p. 1991. 27.99 (*0-310-51940-3*) Zondervan.

Carson, D. A., ed. see Porter, Stanley E.

Carson, D. A., jt. ed. see Porter, Stanley E.

Carson, D. J., jt. auth. see Frost, K. A.

Carson, Dale. Native New England Cooking. 9th ed. (Illus.). 139p. (Orig.). 1980. reprint ed. pap. 5.95 (*0-933614-05-5*) Inst Amer Indian.

Carson, Dale B. How to Make Your Sales Explode with Television Advertising: The Small Business Television Advertising Manual. LC 91-90674. 280p. 1992. pap. 35.00 (*0-9632165-0-3*) D B Carson.

Carson, Daniel D. Embryo Implantation: Molecular, Cellular & Clinical Aspects. LC 99-19103. (Illus.). 312p. 1999. 140.00 (*0-387-98806-8*) Spr-Verlag.

Carson, Daniel H. Poems of Power & Praise. Carson, Mildred, ed. (Orig.). 1990. pap. 8.95 (*0-9627561-0-5*) Wordsmith NV.

Carson, Daniel H., jt. ed. see Wohlwill, Joachim F.

Carson, David. Lament: A Novel about How the West Was Blown. 192p. 1996. mass mkt. 7.95 (*1-56201-078-6*) Blue Moon Bks.

— Marketing & Entrepreneurship in SME's: An Innovative Approach. 296p. 1996. pap. text 35.00 (*0-13-150970-5*) P-H.

***Carson, David.** Rockin' down the Dial: The Detroit Sound of Radio from Jack the Bellboy. LC 99-59116. (Illus.). viii, 292p. 1999. pap. 24.95 (*1-879094-62-2*) Momentum Bks.

Carson, David. Second Sight: Grafik Design after the End of Print. 1997. pap. text 35.00 (*1-885254-80-6*) Monacelli Pr.

Carson, David & Blackwell, Lewis. The End of Print: The Graphic Design of David Carson. rev. ed. (Illus.). 160p. 2000. pap. 24.95 (*0-8118-1199-9*) Chronicle Bks.

— 2ndsight: David Carson Grafik Design at the End of Print. (Illus.). 192p. 50.00 (*1-885254-84-9*) Monacelli Pr.

Carson, David & Meggs, Philip. Fotografiks: Design by David Carson. (Illus.). 160p. 1999. pap. 35.00 (*1-58423-004-5*) Gingko Press.

Carson, David, jt. ed. see Bull, Ray.

Carson, David J., ed. see Minerals, Metals & Materials Society Staff.

Carson, David M. Pro Christo et Patria: A History of Geneva College. LC 97-28094. 1997. write for info. (*1-57864-006-7*) Donning Co.

An Asterisk (*) at the beginning of an entry indicates that the title is appearing for the first time.

Carson, Deane. Money & Finance: Readings in Theory, Policy & Institutions. 2nd ed. LC 70-37643. (Illus.). 510p. 1972. reprint ed. pap. 158.10 (*0-7837-3508-1*, 205784100008) Bks Demand.

Carson-Dellosa Staff. All about Me. (Home Workbooks Ser.). (Illus.). 64p. (Orig.). (J). (ps-1). 1995. wbk. ed. 2.49 (*0-88724-303-7*, CD-6800) Carson-Dellos.

Carson, Diane, ed. John Sayles: Interviews. (Conversations with Filmmakers Ser.). 232p. 1999. 45.00 (*1-57806-137-7*); pap. 18.00 (*1-57806-138-5*) U Pr of Miss.

Carson, Diane, et al, eds. Multiple Voices in Feminist Film Criticism. LC 93-13743. 560p. 1994. pap. 19.95 (*0-8166-2273-6*) U of Minn Pr.

Carson, Diane & Friedman, Lester D., eds. Shared Differences: Multicultural Media & Practical Pedagogy. LC 94-29251. 296p. 1995. text 49.95 (*0-252-02150-9*); pap. text 17.95 (*0-252-06450-X*) U of Ill Pr.

Carson, Diane, jt. auth. see Ware, Sue.

Carson, Dina C. The Genealogy & Local History Researcher's Self-Publishing Guide: How to Organize, Write, Print & Sell Your Family or Local History Book. 2nd ed. LC 92-71491. (Illus.). 204p. 1992. 21.95 (*1-879579-26-X*) Iron Gate Pub.

***Carson, Dina C., ed.** Directory of Genealogical & Historical Society Periodicals in the U. S. & Canada 2000. 500p. 2000. pap. 60.00 (*1-879579-20-0*); pap. 75.00 (*1-879579-19-7*) Iron Gate Pub.

— Directory of Genealogical Libraries, Archives & Collections in the U. S. & Canada 2000. 500p. 2000. pap. 50.00 (*1-879579-18-9*) Iron Gate Pub.

Carson, Donald A. The Gospel According to John. (The Pillar New Testament Commentary Ser.). 672p. 1990. 38.00 (*0-8028-3683-6*) Eerdmans.

***Carson, Donald W. & Johnson, James W.** Mo: The Life & Times of Morris K. Udall. LC 00-9255. 2001. write for info. (*0-8165-2049-6*) U of Ariz Pr.

Carson, Drew. Summer Discovery. Thatch, Nancy R., ed. LC 98-13429. (Books for Students by Students). (Illus.). 29p. (J). (gr. 2-4). 1998. lib. bdg. 15.95 (*0-933849-68-0*) Landmark Edns.

Carson, E. & Linkens, Derek A., eds. Modelling & Control in Biomedical Systems. LC 97-42725. (IFAC Postprint Ser.). 1997. pap. text. write for info. (*0-08-042601-8*, Pergamon Pr) Elsevier.

Carson, E. R., jt. auth. see Flood, R. L.

Carson, E. W., ed. see Virginia Polytechnic Institute on the Plant Root &.

Carson, Ed. Just Say No to Drug Tests: How to Beat the Whiz Quiz. 48p. 1991. 12.00 (*0-87364-624-X*) Paladin Pr.

Carson, Emmett. The Black Underclass: Critical Essays on Race & Unwantedness. Darity, William A. et al, eds. LC 94-31904. (Critical Studies in Black Life & Culture: No. 27). (Illus.). 304p. 1994. text 15.00 (*0-8153-1141-9*, SS875) Garland.

Carson, Ewart R. & Cramp, D. G., eds. Computers & Control in Clinical Medicine. 272p. 1985. 79.50 (*0-306-41892-4*, Plenum Trade) Perseus Pubng.

Carson, Ewart R., et al. The Mathematical Modeling of Metabolic & Endocrine Systems: Model Formulation, Identification & Validation. LC 82-13402. (Biomedical Engineering & Health Systems Ser.). 418p. reprint ed. pap. 129.60 (*0-7837-2834-4*, 205763800006) Bks Demand.

Carson, Ewart R., jt. ed. see Cramp, Derek.

Carson, Freida L. Histotechnology: A Self Assessment Workbook. 2nd ed. 97p. Date not set. 40.00 (*0-89189-412-8*) Am Soc Clinical.

— Histotechnology: A Self-Instructional Text. 2nd ed. LC 96-18880. 312p. 1996. 45.00 (*0-89189-411-X*) Am Soc Clinical.

— Histotechnology: A Self-Instructional Text, Set. 1990. sl. 250.00 (*0-89189-356-3*) Am Soc Clinical.

Carson, Frieda. Basics of Histotechnology: H & E Stain. 1992. 50.00 incl. VHS (*0-89189-351-2*) Am Soc Clinical.

Carson, Gary. Complete Book of Hold 'em Poker A Comprehensive Guide to Playing & Winning. LC 99-42085. 1999. pap. text 14.95 (*0-8184-0605-4*) Carol Pub Group.

Carson, Gayle. Winning Ways: How to Get to the Top & Stay There. Flowers, Charles, ed. 156p. (Orig.). (C). 1988. text 15.00 (*0-9621370-0-6*); pap. text 10.00 (*0-9621370-1-4*) Lane Pub.

Carson-Gentry, Martha. West Chester. (Images of America Ser.). 1997. pap. 16.99 (*0-7524-0865-8*) Arcadia Publng.

Carson, George B., jt. auth. see Brown, Louise F.

Carson, Gerald. Cornflake Crusade. LC 75-39240. (Getting & Spending: The Consumer's Dilemma Ser.). (Illus.). 1976. reprint ed. 28.95 (*0-405-08013-1*) Ayer.

— The Polite Americans: A Wide-Angle View of Our More or Less Good Manners over 300 Years. LC 80-11824. (Illus.). 346p. 1980. reprint ed. lib. bdg. 59.75 (*0-313-22417-X*, CAPO, Greenwood Pr) Greenwood.

Carson, Glenn T. Calling Out the Called: The Life & Work of Lee Rutland Scarborough. LC 95-35692. 160p. 1996. 19.95 (*1-57168-018-7*) Sunbelt Media.

Carson, Gordon, ed. see White, Gregory J.

Carson, H. G., jt. auth. see Boyd, L. M.

Carson, H. Glenn. Backroads to Adventure. (Illus.). 116p. (Orig.). 1986. pap. 7.95 (*0-941620-31-X*) Carson Ent.

— Coinshooting III. 64p. 1994. pap. 8.95 (*0-941620-62-X*) Carson Ent.

— A Guide to Treasure in Colorado. 224p. (Orig.). 1995. pap. 15.95 (*0-941620-63-8*) Carson Ent.

— Hedge Yourself Against Disaster. 47p. 1973. pap. 2.75 (*0-941620-25-5*) Carson Ent.

— Hunting the Ghost Towns. (Illus.). 1977. pap. 8.95 (*0-941620-08-5*) Carson Ent.

— Lost Ledges of the West. 96p. 1991. pap. 7.95 (*0-941620-43-3*) Carson Ent.

— The Malpais Gold. (Illus.). 148p. 1978. pap. 3.50 (*0-941620-09-3*) Carson Ent.

— A New Guide to Treasure Hunting. 160p. 1992. 12.95 (*0-941620-45-X*) Carson Ent.

— Pilar la Dura, Bk. One. 173p. (Orig.). 1993. pap. 9.95 (*0-941620-47-6*) Carson Ent.

— Some Paths to Sudden Wealth. 103p. 1992. pap. 9.95 (*0-941620-44-1*) Carson Ent.

— Southwest New Mexico Ghost Towns Sites. 40p. 1991. pap. 7.95 (*0-941620-41-7*) Carson Ent.

— Treasure Guide to Idaho. 127p. 1996. pap. 11.95 (*0-941620-64-6*) Carson Ent.

— Treasure Hunting: A Modern Search for Adventure. (Illus.). 82p. 1981. reprint ed. pap. 7.95 (*0-941620-05-0*) Carson Ent.

Carson, H. Glenn, compiled by. Treasure Hunting Annual, Vol. 1. (Illus.). 160p. 1979. pap. 7.95 (*0-941620-11-5*) Carson Ent.

— Treasure Hunting Annual, Vol. 2. (Illus.). 164p. 1980. pap. 7.95 (*0-941620-22-0*) Carson Ent.

Carson, Hampton L. The History of the Supreme Court of the United States with Biographies of All the Chief & Associate Justices, 2 vols., Set. LC 91-55436. xii, 656p. 1991. reprint ed. 145.00 (*0-912004-95-9*) Gaunt.

— Pedigrees in the Ownership of Law Books. Mersky, Roy M. & Jacobstein, J. Myron, eds. (Classics in Legal History Reprint Ser.: Vol. 2). 31p. 1968. reprint ed. lib. bdg. 36.00 (*0-89941-001-4*, 300130) W S Hein.

Carson, Haven. Illustrators' Reference File: Compositional Elements for Artists, Renderers, & Students. LC 92-42365. 1993. pap. 46.95 (*0-442-01197-0*, VNR) Wiley.

Carson, Haven. Illustrators Reference File: Compositional Elements for Artists, Renderers, & Students. (Architecture Ser.). 296p. 1993. pap. 54.95 (*0-471-28501-3*, VNR) Wiley.

Carson, Herbert M. Depression in the Christian Family. 1994. pap. 8.99 (*0-85234-313-2*, Pub. by Evangelical Pr) P & R Pubng.

— The Faith of the Vatican: A Fresh Look at Roman Catholicism. 192p. (Orig.). 1996. pap. 9.99 (*0-85234-345-0*, Pub. by Evangelical Pr) P & R Pubng.

Carson, J. W. Innovation: A Battle Plan for the 1990's. (Illus.). 208p. 1989. text 76.95 (*0-566-02785-2*, Pub. by Gower) Ashgate Pub Co.

Carson, James H. & Derby, George H. Bright Gem of the Western Seas: California, 1846-1852 - Includes: Early Recollections of the Mines, The Tulare Plains & Life in California by James H. Carson; Report of the Tulare Valley by George H. Derby. rev. ed. LC 91-4032. (Illus.). 224p. (C). 1991. pap. 12.95 (*0-944220-05-3*) Great West Bks.

Carson, James M. The Yosemite in Winter: An 1892 Account. Jones, William R., ed. (Illus.). 64p. 1979. reprint ed. pap. 2.00 (*0-89646-053-3*) Vistabooks.

Carson, James M. & Forster, Mark D. Life Insurance Analysis: Policy & Company Performance. (Illus.). 147p. 1996. 34.95 (*0-9656041-0-1*) Iona Pub.

Carson, James P., jt. auth. see Petigru, James L.

Carson, James Taylor. Searching for the Bright Path: The Mississippi Choctaws from Prehistory to Removal. LC 99-12949. (Indians of the Southeast Ser.). (Illus.). 200p. 1999. text 40.00 (*0-8032-1503-7*) U of Nebr Pr.

***Carson, Jana.** The Mighty Little Lion Hunter. (We Both Read Ser.). (Illus.). 44p. (J). (gr. k-1). 2000. 7.99 (*1-891327-21-6*); pap. 3.99 (*1-891327-22-4*) Treas Bay Inc.

Carson, Jane. James Innes & His Brothers of the F. H. C. LC 65-26594. (Williamsburg Research Studies). 184p. reprint ed. 57.10 (*0-8357-9804-6*, 201341400086) Bks Demand.

Carson, Janet. It's Art Time No. 2: A Guide for Beginning Art Teachers. (Illus.). 188p. (Orig.). 1990. pap. 11.95 (*0-9632017-0-0*) Wellington WI.

— Tell Me about Your Picture: Art Activities to Help Children Communicate. LC 94-160128. 1997. pap. 14.95 (*0-86651-550-X*) Seymour Pubns.

Carson, Jeffrey. Poems 1974-1996. LC 98-108716. 1997. pap. 24.95 (*3-7052-0085-2*, Pub. by Poetry Salzburg) Intl Spec Bk.

Carson, Jeffrey, tr. see Elytis, Odysseus, et al.

Carson, Jo. Daytrips. 1991. pap. 5.25 (*0-8222-0282-4*) Dramatists Play.

— The Last of the "The Waltz Across Texas" & Other Stories. LC 92-75359. 160p. (Orig.). 1993. pap. 13.50 (*0-917788-53-2*) Gnomon Pr.

— Pulling My Leg. LC 89-70978. (Illus.). 32p. (J). (ps-2). 1990. 15.95 (*0-531-05817-4*) Orchard Bks Watts.

— Pulling My Leg. LC 89-70978. (Illus.). 32p. (J). (ps-2). 1994. pap. 5.95 (*0-531-07046-8*) Orchard Bks Watts.

— Stories I Ain't Told Nobody Yet: Selections from the People Pieces. LC 90-29030. 96p. 1991. pap. 10.95 (*1-55936-027-5*) Theatre Comm.

— You Hold Me & I'll Hold You. LC 91-16370. (Illus.). 32p. (J). (ps-2). 1992. 15.95 (*0-531-05895-6*) Orchard Bks Watts.

— You Hold Me & I'll Hold You. LC 91-16370. (Illus.). 32p. (J). (ps-2). 1997. pap. 6.95 (*0-531-07088-3*) Orchard Bks Watts.

— You Hold Me & I'll Hold You. 1997. 12.05 (*0-606-12583-3*, Pub. by Turtleback) Demco.

Carson, Joan, jt. auth. see Carson, Peter.

Carson, Joan C. & Sykes, Dudley E. Behaviors of Preschoolers & Their Teachers: Little Children Draw Big Circles. 220p. 1991. pap. text 31.95 (*0-398-06629-9*) C C Thomas.

— Behaviors of Preschoolers & Their Teachers: Little Children Draw Big Circles. 220p. (C). 1991. text 47.95 (*0-398-05732-X*) C C Thomas.

Carson, John L. & Hall, David W., eds. To Glorify & Enjoy God: A Commemoration of the Westminster Assembly. 338p. 1994. 35.99 (*0-85151-668-8*) Banner of Truth.

Carson, Joseph J., jt. auth. see Grover, Margaret J.

Carson, Josephine. Dog Star & Other Stories. LC 98-60131. 160p. 1998. pap. 14.00 (*0-9655497-2-0*) SB Review Pubns.

Carson, Karen. Honey Harvest Quickmix Recipes & Poems: Baking Mix Recipes Using Natural Ingredients. (Illus.). 112p. (Orig.). 1991. pap. 11.95 (*0-9631417-0-8*) Sunflower Pr.

Carson, Karen, et al. The Lullaby & Goodnight Sleepkit: The Gift of Sweet Dreams & Family Memories. LC 91-67933. 32p. (J). (ps-3). 1992. pap. 2.95 (*1-880444-03-8*) Times to Treas.

Carson, Karen M., jt. auth. see Kamper, Karl G.

Carson, Kathy, jt. auth. see Carson, Tim.

Carson, Kay A. For Mother, with Love: A Little Treasury of Gold. 1994. 7.98 (*0-88486-092-2*) Arrowood Pr.

— For You with Love: A Little Treasury of Gold. 1995. 7.98 (*0-88486-105-8*) Arrowood Pr.

— Little Treasury of Gold: Poems of Love & Faith. 1992. 7.98 (*0-88486-062-0*) Arrowood Pr.

— Poems of Joy & Hope: A Little Treasury of Gold. 1993. 7.98 (*0-88486-072-8*) Arrowood Pr.

Carson, Kay Anne. Little Book of Cherished Poems: Beautiful Poetry to Treasure Always. 320p. 1999. 7.99 (*1-57866-060-2*) Galahad Bks.

Carson, Kelton. Simplified Computer Programming: Including the Easy RPG Way. LC 73-90739. (Illus.). 240p. 1974. pap. 8.95 (*0-8306-3676-5*, 676) McGraw-Hill Prof.

Carson, Kerry D. & Carson, Paula P. Defective Bosses: Working for the "Dysfunctional Dozen" LC 98-18463. (Illus.). 178p. 1998. pap. 14.95 (*0-7890-0581-6*); lib. bdg. 29.95 (*0-7890-0580-8*) Haworth Pr.

Carson, Kerry D., et al. The ABCs of Collaborative Change: The Manager's Guide to Library Renewal. LC 97-18779. 273p. 1997. pap. 37.00 (*0-8389-0699-0*) ALA.

Carson, Kim & Weil, Sherie M. Essence of Life: A Compilation of Inspiration & Poem. 50p. 1997. pap. 16.00 (*0-9659636-0-8*, 1) Carsonweil Pubs.

Carson, Kit. Kit Carson's Autobiography. Quaife, Milo M., ed. & intro. by. LC 66-4130. (Illus.). xxxii, 192p. 1966. pap. 9.00 (*0-8032-5031-2*, Bison Books) U of Nebr Pr.

Carson, Leonard C. Pursue & Destroy. (Illus.). 1978. text 19.95 (*0-913194-05-0*) Sentry.

Carson, Lillian. The Essential Grandparent: A Guide to Making a Difference. 200p. 1996. 22.00 (*1-55874-428-2*) Health Comm.

— The Essential Grandparent: A Guide to Making a Difference. 200p. 1996. pap. 10.95 (*1-55874-397-9*, 3979) Health Comm.

— Essential Grandparent's Guide to Divorce. LC 99-23526. 1999. pap. 10.95 (*1-55874-689-7*) Health Comm.

***Carson, Linda A., et al.** Mom's the Word. 112p. 2000. pap. 15.95 (*0-88922-431-5*, Pub. by Talonbks) SPD-Small Pr Dist.

Carson, Lois. Learning Poems for Children. (Illus.). 32p. (J). (gr. k-6). 1999. pap. 7.00 (*0-8059-4667-5*) Dorrance.

***Carson, Luke.** Consumption & Depression LC 98-8143. viii, 283 p. 1999. write for info. (*0-333-71451-2*) Trans-Atl Phila.

***Carson, Lyn & Martin, Brian.** Random Selection in Politics. LC 99-15399. 176p. 1999. 57.95 (*0-275-96702-6*) Greenwood.

Carson, M. L. & Martin, J. P., eds. Women & Human Rights: The Basic Documents. 251p. 1996. pap. 10.00 (*1-881482-03-0*) Columbia Ctr Stu Human Rts.

Carson, Margaret A., tr. see de Cuellar, Jose Tomas.

Carson, Marilynn. Exercise Your Mind. 72p. (Orig.). 1995. pap. text 10.95 (*0-9647509-2-9*) Expressway IL.

Carson, Mary. Handbook of Treasure Signs & Symbols. (Illus.). 60p. (Orig.). 1980. pap. 7.95 (*0-941620-33-6*) Carson Ent.

Carson, Mary, ed. see Koschmann, A. H. & Bergendahl, M. H.

Carson, Mary, ed. see Parker, Ben H., Jr.

Carson, Mary K. Epilepsy. LC 97-34160. (Diseases & People Ser.). (Illus.). 112p. (YA). (gr. 6 up). 1998. lib. bdg. 20.95 (*0-7660-1049-X*) Enslow Pubs.

— Space. 1996. pap. text 12.95 (*0-590-60344-2*) Scholastic Inc.

***Carson, Mary Kay.** Colonial America: A Complete Theme Unit Developed in Cooperation with the Colonial Williamsburg, 1. 64p. 1999. pap. text 11.95 (*0-590-96560-3*) SP Pubns.

— Great Weather Activites: All the Background Info & How-To's You Need for Teaching about the Wo. (Illus.). 64p. 2000. pap. 11.95 (*0-590-22181-7*) Scholastic Inc.

— Wow's & Why's of Weather. (Illus.). 80p. (J). 2000. pap. 12.95 (*0-590-36508-8*) Scholastic Inc.

Carson, Mary L. Guide to Treasure in Oklahoma, Vol. II. (Treasure Guide Ser.). 1988. pap. 9.95 (*0-941620-37-9*) Carson Ent.

— Guide to Treasure in Oklahoma, Vol. III. (Treasure Guide Ser.). 1988. pap. 9.95 (*0-941620-38-7*) Carson Ent.

— Tasty Recipes & Cherished Memories. 1989. 5.95 (*0-941620-40-9*) Carson Ent.

Carson, Meredith. Infinite Morning. LC 97-23690. 72p. 1997. pap. 12.95 (*0-8214-1212-4*); text 22.95 (*0-8214-1211-6*) Ohio U Pr.

Carson, Michael, ed. see Carson, Cheryl.

Carson, Mildred, ed. see Carson, Daniel H.

Carson, Mina. Settlement Folk: Social Thought & the American Settlement Movement, 1885-1930. LC 89-20319. 294p. 1990. 32.50 (*0-226-09501-0*) U Ch Pr.

Carson, Nancy & Fawcett, Allen. Kid Biz: How to Help Your Child Succeed in Show Business. Busnar, Gene, ed. 194p. (Orig.). 1989. reprint ed. pap. 13.95 (*0-685-26003-8*) Kid Biz Pubns.

Carson, Neil. A Companion to Henslowe's Diary. 168p. 1988. text 69.95 (*0-521-23545-6*) Cambridge U Pr.

— Harlequin in Hogtown: George Luscombe & Toronto Workshop Productions. (Illus.). 264p. 1995. text 50.00 (*0-8020-0680-9*); pap. text 19.95 (*0-8020-7633-5*) U of Toronto Pr.

Carson, P. & Mumford, Clive J. The Safe Handling of Chemicals in Industry, 3 vols., Vol. 3. 496p. 1996. text 199.00 (*0-470-23449-0*) Halsted Pr.

Carson, P. A. & Mumford, Clive J. Hazardous Chemicals Handbook. LC 93-7795. (Illus.). 400p. 1994. pap. 59.95 (*0-7506-0278-3*) Buttrwrth-Heinemann.

Carson, Patricia W. Peculiar Pain: A Close Look at Black on Black Sexual Harassment & Its Impact. Smith, Michelle, ed. (Illus.). 208p. 1995. 24.95 (*0-7872-1076-5*) Kendall-Hunt.

— The Wonderment: Ancestral Wisdom for Masterful Leadership. (Illus.). 125p. 1999. pap. text 12.00 (*1-928652-00-X*) Motivational OH.

Carson, Patti & Dellosa, Janet. Basics about Money. (Home Workbooks Ser.). (Illus.). 64p. (J). (gr. 1-2). 1995. pap., wbk. ed. 2.49 (*0-88724-353-3*, CD-6850) Carson-Dellos.

— Beginning Money Skills. (Home Workbooks Ser.). (Illus.). 64p. (J). (gr. k-1). 1995. pap., wbk. ed. 2.49 (*0-88724-352-5*, CD-6849) Carson-Dellos.

— Fun with Numbers. (Home Workbooks Ser.). (Illus.). 64p. (J). (gr. k-1). 1995. pap., wbk. ed. 2.49 (*0-88724-342-8*, CD-6839) Carson-Dellos.

***Carson, Paul L., et al.** Acoustic Output Measurement Standard for Diagnostic Ultrasound Equipment. (Illus.). 120p. 1998. pap. 44.00 (*1-930047-28-2*) Am Inst Ultrasound.

Carson, Paula P., et al. The Library Manager's Deskbook: 102 Expert Solutions to 101 Common Dilemmas. 212p. (Orig.). 1995. pap. 32.00 (*0-8389-0655-9*, 0655-9-2045) ALA.

Carson, Paula P., jt. auth. see Carson, Kerry D.

Carson, Peter & Carson, Joan. Don't Say You Can't When You Mean You Won't: How to Act in Your Own Best Interest. 163p. 1982. 12.95 (*0-685-03840-8*); pap. 5.95 (*0-685-03841-6*) P-H.

C

Carson, Phil. Across the Northern Frontier: Spanish Explorations in Colorado. LC 98-5316. (Illus.). 272p. 1998. 27.50 (*1-55566-215-3*); pap. 18.00 (*1-55566-216-1*) Johnson Bks.

— Among the Eternal Snows: The First Recorded Ascent of Pikes Peak, July 13-15, 1820. 1995. pap. text 7.95 (*0-9649473-0-7*) First Ascent.

***Carson, Phillip & Mumford, C. J.** Hazardous Chemicals Handbook. 2nd ed. 448p. 2001. 85.95 (*0-7506-4888-0*) Buttrwrth-Heinemann.

Carson, Philop, jt. auth. see Mumford, Clive J.

Carson, Phyllis M. Alive in Him. (Illus.). 32p. 1993. write for info. (*1-883331-01-3*) Anderie Poetry.

Carson Publications Staff. The 1997 International Who's Who of Institutions & Mutual Funds. 1997. ring bd. 500.00 (*0-9646311-4-8*) Carson Grp.

— The 1997 North American Who's Who of Institutions & Mutual Funds. 2000p. 1997. ring bd. 799.00 (*0-9646311-1-3*) Carson Grp.

— The 1996 International Who's Who of Institutions & Mutual Funds. Sax, Ian, ed. 700p. 1996. ring bd. 400.00 (*0-9646311-2-1*) Carson Grp.

— Who's Who of Institutions & Mutual Funds. Sax, Ian, ed. 1996. ring bd. write for info. (*0-614-32377-0*) Carson Grp.

Carson, R. A. The Geneva Forgeries. (Illus.). 1977. 4.75 (*0-915018-27-6*) Attic Bks.

— Scripta Nummaria Romana. (Illus.). 1978. lib. bdg. 40.00 (*0-932106-07-2*) S J Durst.

Carson, R. A. & Kraay, Colin M. Scripta Numaria Romana. 1979. 40.00 (*0-686-63876-X*) S J Durst.

Carson, R. A., jt. auth. see Sutherland, C. H.

Carson, Rachel Louise. The Edge of the Sea. 304p. 1998. pap. 14.00 (*0-395-92496-0*) HM.

***Carson, Rachel Louise.** The Edge of the Sea. 1999. 25.75 (*0-8446-7014-6*) Peter Smith.

Carson, Rachel Louise. Lost Woods: The Discovered Writing of Rachel Carson. Lear, Linda, ed. LC 98-20058. (Illus.). 288p. 1999. pap. 16.00 (*0-8070-8547-2*) Beacon Pr.

— The Sea Around Us Special Edition. (Illus.). 288p. 1991. reprint ed. pap. 13.95 (*0-19-506997-8*, 6464) OUP.

— The Sense of Wonder. LC 98-172587. (Illus.). 112p. 1998. 20.00 (*0-06-757520-X*) HarpC.

— Silent Spring. LC 95-109031. (Illus.). 400p. 1999. pap. 13.00 (*0-395-68329-7*) HM.

— Silent Spring. 1994. 18.10 (*0-606-05600-9*, Pub. by Turtleback) Demco.

— Silent Spring. large type ed. LC 96-49681. 437 p. 1997. write for info. (*0-7838-8053-7*, G K Hall Lrg Type) Mac Lib Ref.

— Silent Spring. 1994. reprint ed. lib. bdg. 27.95 (*1-56849-552-8*) Buccaneer Bks.

— Under the Sea Wind. (Illus.). 320p. 1996. pap. 11.95 (*0-14-025380-7*, Penguin Bks) Viking Penguin.

Carson, Ralph, ed. see International SAMPE Symposium & Exhibition Staff.

Carson, Ralph S. Radio Communications Concepts: Analog. LC 89-34210. 496p. 1990. 180.00 (*0-471-62169-2*) Wiley.

Carson, Randall L. The Information Superhighway: Strategic Alliances in Telecommunications & Multimedia. 160p. 1996. text 49.95 (*0-312-16068-2*) St Martin.

An Asterisk (*) at the beginning of an entry indicates that the title is appearing for the first time.

Carson, Ray F., ed. Championship Wrestling: An Anthology. LC 73-94015. (Illus.). 1974. 14.95 (*0-686-09318-6*) R Carson.

Carson, Richard B. The Olympian Cars: The Great American Luxury Automobiles of the Twenties & Thirties. 2nd rev. ed. (Illus.). 304p. 1998. 99.95 (*1-890676-02-0*) Beavers Pond.

Carson, Richard D. Taming Your Gremlin: A Guide to Enjoying Yourself. LC 86-45310. (Illus.). 128p. 1990. reprint ed. pap. 12.00 (*0-06-096102-3*, PL/6102, Perennial) HarperTrade.

Carson, Richard E., et al, eds. Quantitative Functional Brain Imaging with Positron Tomography. LC 98-85439. (Illus.). 504p. (C). 1998. boxed set 139.95 (*0-12-161340-2*) Acad Pr.

Carson, Richard L. Comparative Economic Systems, Three-Vol. Set. Three-Vol. Set. LC 89-10888. 752p. (C). (gr. 13). 1990. text 106.95 (*0-87332-583-4*); Set pap. text 89.95 (*0-87332-680-6*) M E Sharpe.

— Comparative Economic Systems, Vol. II. 2nd ed. Vol. II. (Illus.). 472p. (C). 1997. pap. text 39.95 (*1-56324-921-9*) M E Sharpe.

— Comparative Economic Systems: Market & State in Economic Systems, Vol. I. 2nd ed. LC 96-20587. Vol. I. 280p. (C). 1996. pap. text 40.95 (*1-56324-920-0*) M E Sharpe.

Carson, Richard T., jt. auth. see Mitchell, Robert C.

Carson, Rob. The Living Mountain. (Illus.). 72p. (Orig.). (J). (gr. k-8). 1992. pap. 10.95 (*0-9623072-9-7*) S Ink WA.

***Carson, Rob.** Mount St. Helens: The Eruption & Recovery of a Volcano. 20th anniversary ed. (Illus.). 160p. 2000. pap. 19.95 (*1-57061-248-X*) Sasquatch Bks.

Carson, Robert. Mental Health Nursing: The Nurse-Patient Journey: Instructor's Manual. 2nd ed. 205p. Date not set. pap. text, teacher ed. write for info. (*0-7216-8057-7*, W B Saunders Co) Harcrt Hlth Sci Grp.

Carson, Robert, jt. auth. see Babcock, Scott.

Carson, Robert B. Macroeconomic Issues Today: Alternative Approaches. 5th ed. 211p. (C). 1990. teacher ed. write for info. (*0-318-68118-8*) St Martin.

— Microeconomic Issues Today: Alternative Approaches. 5th ed. 207p. (C). 1990. teacher ed. write for info. (*0-318-68119-6*) St Martin.

Carson, Robert B., et al. Economic Issues Today: Alternative Approaches. 6th ed. LC 98-29530. 376p. (C). 1999. text 72.95 (*1-56324-631-7*); pap. text 35.95 (*1-56324-632-5*) M E Sharpe.

— Macroeconomic Issues Today: Alternative Approaches. 6th ed. LC 98-29532. 208p. 1999. pap. text 24.95 (*0-7656-0363-2*) M E Sharpe.

— Microeconomic Issues Today: Alternative Approaches. 6th ed. LC 98-29533. 200p. (C). (gr. 13). 1999. pap. text 23.95 (*0-7656-0364-0*) M E Sharpe.

Carson, Robert C. Abnormal Psychology & Modern Life. 11th ed. (C). 2000. text. write for info. (*0-321-03431-7*) Addson-Wesley Educ.

— Abnormal Psychology & Modern Life 1998. 10th ed. (C). 1997. pap. text, student ed. 30.00 (*0-321-02459-1*) Addison-Wesley.

— Psychology. 3rd ed. 688p. (C). 1999. pap. text. write for info. (*0-321-03433-3*) Addson-Wesley Educ.

Carson, Robert C. & Butcher, James N. Abnormal Psychology & Modern Life. 8th ed. (C). 1997. pap. text 21.00 (*0-673-18933-3*) Addson-Wesley Educ.

Carson, Robert S. & Butcher, James N. Abnormal Psychology. 9th ed. LC 91-20863. (C). 1991. pap. text 10.00 (*0-673-46617-5*, Harper Ref) HarpC.

Carson, Ronald A. & Rothstein, Mark A. Behavioral Genetics: The Clash of Culture & Biology. LC 98-43307. 1999. 39.95 (*0-8018-6069-5*) Johns Hopkins.

Carson, Russell. Peaks & People of the Adirondacks. 269p. 1993. reprint ed. lib. bdg. 79.00 (*0-7812-5120-6*) Rprt Serv.

Carson, Ruth, et al. The Adventures of Fifi's Honey Bears & the Big Bee Hive. (Illus.). 28p. (J). (gr. k-5). 1986. 8.95 (*0-935087-24-9*) Wright Pub Co.

Carson, Samuel. The Amazing Cross. 94p. 1997. pap. 7.99 (*1-898787-44-1*) Emerald House Group Inc.

— Desert House. 1997. pap. 7.99 (*1-898787-05-0*) Emerald House Group Inc.

— Genesis Brides. 1997. pap. 5.99 (*0-907927-79-3*) Emerald House Group Inc.

Carson, Sandra A., et al. Complete Guide to Fertility. LC 98-50746. (Illus.). 256p. 1999. pap. 16.95 (*0-8092-2862-9*, 286290, Contemporary Bks) NTC Contemp Pub Co.

***Carson, Shelly C.** Continuous Improvement in the History & Social Science Classroom. LC 00-22549. 2000. write for info. (*0-87389-433-2*) ASQ Qual Pr.

***Carson, Shirley.** Women of Warfare. (Illus.). 160p. 1999. pap. write for info. (*0-7392-0429-7*, PO3709) Morris Pubng.

Carson, Steven, jt. illus. see Rabinovitch, Leon.

Carson, Susan S. Joshua's Dream: A Town with Two Names. (Illus.). 168p. 1992. reprint ed. pap. 15.00 (*1-892444-03-8*) Southport Hist.

Carson, Susan S., ed. The Cemeteries of Southport (Smithville) & Surrounding Area. x, 94p. 1983. pap. 8.00 (*1-892444-01-1*) Southport Hist.

Carson, Terrance, jt. ed. see Sumara, Dennis J.

***Carson, Thomas.** Encyclopedia of U. S. Economic History LC 99-39623. 1999. write for info. (*0-7876-3889-7*) Gale.

Carson, Thomas, ed. Gale Encyclopedia of United States Economic History, 2 vols. LC 99-39623. (Illus.). 1250p. 1999. 195.00 (*0-7876-3888-9*, GML00299-113682, Gale Res Intl) Gale.

Carson, Thomas, tr. from LAT. Barbarossa in Italy: A Verse Translation of the Carmen de Gestis Federici I Imperatoris in Lombardia. LC 94-27071. (Illus.). 232p. (Orig.). 1994. pap. 14.50 (*0-934977-30-5*) Italica Pr.

Carson, Thomas L. The Status of Morality. (Philosophical Studies: No. 31). 216p. 1984. text 118.00 (*90-277-1691-9*, D Reidel) Kluwer Academic.

***Carson, Thomas L.** Value & the Good Life. LC 00-27542. 304p. 2000. 45.00 (*0-268-04352-3*); pap. 22.95 (*0-268-04353-1*) U of Notre Dame Pr.

Carson, Thomas L. & Moser, Paul K., eds. Morality & the Good Life. LC 96-44810. 528p. (C). 1997. text 58.00 (*0-19-510537-0*); pap. text 35.95 (*0-19-510538-9*) OUP.

Carson, Thomas L., jt. ed. see Moser, Paul K.

Carson, Tim & Carson, Kathy. So You're Thinking about Contemporary Worship. LC 97-19597. 104p. (Orig.). 1997. pap. 9.99 (*0-8272-3437-6*) Chalice Pr.

Carson, Timothy L. Liminal Reality & Transformational Power. LC 97-17052. 144p. 1997. 49.00 (*0-7618-0799-3*); pap. 27.50 (*0-7618-0800-0*) U Pr of Amer.

Carson, Tom. Twisted Kicks. LC 81-22901. 260p. 1982. pap. 5.95 (*0-915904-62-4*) And-Or Bks.

— Twisted Kicks. LC 81-67560. 264p. 1981. 12.95 (*0-934558-03-5*) Entwhistle Bks.

Carson, Verna B. & Arnold, Elizabeth N. EXAMaster for Mental Health Nursing: The Nurse-Patient Journey. Eoyang, Thomas, ed. 1997. pap. text. write for info. (*0-7216-6838-0*, W B Saunders Co) Harcrt Hlth Sci Grp.

Carson, Verna B. & Arnold, Elizabeth N., eds. Mental Health Nursing: The Nurse-Patient Journey. (Illus.). 1996. teacher ed. write for info. (*0-7216-6820-8*, W B Saunders Co) Harcrt Hlth Sci Grp.

Carson, W. E. Mexico, the Wonderland of the South. 1977. lib. bdg. 59.95 (*0-8490-2252-5*) Gordon Pr.

Carson, Wayne G. & Klinker, Richard L. Fire Protection Systems: Test, Inspection, & Maintenance Manual. 230p. 1993. pap. 64.50 (*0-87765-387-9*, FPS-93) Natl Fire Prot.

Carson, William G. Managers in Distress: The St. Louis Stage, 1840-1844. (Illus.). 1972. 23.95 (*0-405-08341-6*, Pub. by Blom Pubns) Ayer.

— Theatre on the Frontier: The Early Years of the St. Louis Stage. 2nd rev. ed. LC 65-16229. (Illus.). 1972. reprint ed. 35.95 (*0-405-08342-4*, Pub. by Blom Pubns) Ayer.

Carson, William S. Don't Drive Without It! Complete Car & Drivers Guidekit. (Illus.). 192p. 1987. pap. 12.95 (*0-940855-00-3*) Preparepak Pub.

Carson, Xanthus. Treasure! Bonanzas Worth a Billion Bucks. 182p. 1974. reprint ed. pap. 15.95 (*0-941620-66-2*) Carson Ent.

Carsons, Steven & Sciubba, James J., eds. The Sjogren's Syndrome Handbook: An Authoritative Guide for Patients Prepared by Specialists in the Diagnosis & Treatment of Sjogren's Syndrome. (Illus.). 237p. 1988. 24.95 (*0-685-44313-2*) Sjogrens Syndrome.

Carsons, Steven, ed. see Sjogren's Syndrome Foundation Staff.

Carsons, Steven E., ed. Fibronectin in Health & Disease. 320p. 1989. lib. bdg. 203.00 (*0-8493-5064-6*, QP552) CRC Pr.

Carspecken, Margaret. Sweet Treats: Dessert Recipes from the Kitchen of Marsha Redfox. deluxe ed. Benvenuto, Darrell, ed. (Illus.). 128p. 1998. pap. 18.95 (*1-887038-02-7*) Medsysts NY.

Carspecken, Phil F. Critical Ethnography in Educational Research: A Theoretical & Practical Guide. LC 95-30106. (Critical Social Thought Ser.). 256p. (C). 1995. pap. 19.99 (*0-415-90493-5*) Routledge.

— Voices from Downstream. 224p. 1998. pap. 12.95 (*0-9653988-3-8*) Wainsley Pr.

***Carspecken, Phil Francis.** Four Scenes for Posing the Question of Meaning & Other Essays in Critical Philosophy & Critical Methodology. LC 98-25585. (Counterpoints: Vol. 79). xii, 298p. (C). 1999. pap. 30.00 (*0-8204-3967-3*) P Lang Pubng.

***Carss, Bob & Birch, Stewart.** The Complete Guide to Tracking. LC 99-87669. (Illus.). 272p. 2000. pap. 19.95 (*1-58574-031-4*) Loyola Pr.

Carss, Marjorie, jt. auth. see Martin, Paula.

Carstairs, Carroll, ed. A Generation Missing. 240p. (C). 1988. 95.00 (*0-7855-2147-X*) St Mut.

Carstairs, Ian, jt. auth. see Birt, David.

Carstairs-McCarthy, Andrew. The Origins of Complex Language: An Inquiry into the Evolutionary Beginnings of Sentences, Syllables & Truth. (Illus.). 272p. 1999. text 80.00 (*0-19-823822-3*); pap. text 19.95 (*0-19-823821-5*) OUP.

Carstairs, Vera. Deprivation & Health in Scotland. 1991. pap. text 39.90 (*0-08-037979-6*, Pub. by Aberdeen U Pr) Macmillan.

Carstaphen, Meta G., ed. Framing the Word: A Festschrift in Honor of Turner S. Kobler: Essays on Literature & Film. (Illus.). 190p. (Orig.). 1996. pap. text 30.00 (*0-9635769-2-5*) Caxtons Mod Art.

Carstarphen. Maverick Sea Fare Caribbean Checkbook. 1983. pap. 6.95 (*0-916224-74-0*) Banyan Bks.

***Carstarphen, Dee.** The Conch Book: All You Ever Wanted to Know about the Queen Conch from Gestation to Gastronomy. 2nd ed. LC 99-96260. (Illus.). 80p. 2000. pap. 11.95 (*0-9607544-5-8*) Pen & Ink.

Carstarphen, Dee. Maverick Sea Fare: A Caribbean Cook Book. LC 78-107177. (Illus.). 60p. 1982. pap. 7.95 (*0-9607544-2-3*) Pen & Ink.

— Narrow Waters: An Artist's Memoir of Sailing Through Sound, Swamp, City, Forest, Marsh & Glade. LC 97-76110. (Illus.). v, 131p. 1998. pap. 19.95 (*0-9607544-4-X*) Pen & Ink.

— Windjammer Cooking. rev. ed. LC 89-91049. Orig. Title: Windjammer World. (Illus.). 158p. 1989. pap. 11.95 (*0-9607544-3-1*) Pen & Ink.

Carstarphen, James. My Trip to California in 1849. 8p. 1971. reprint ed. pap. 3.95 (*0-87770-038-9*) Ye Galleon.

Carstarphen, Meta G. & Zavoina, Susan G., eds. Sexual Rhetoric: Media Perspectives on Sexuality, Gender & Identity, 57. LC 99-21278. (Contributions to the Study of Mass Media & Communications Ser.: Vol. 57). 328p. 1999. 69.50 (*0-313-30788-1*, Greenwood Pr) Greenwood.

Carsten, F. L. Essays in German History. 400p. 1985. 60.00 (*0-907628-67-2*) Hambledon Press.

— The German Workers & the Nazis. LC 94-19955. 1994. 69.95 (*0-85967-998-5*, Pub. by Scolar Pr) Ashgate Pub Co.

— A History of the Prussian Junkers. 215p. 1989. text 55.95 (*0-85967-805-9*, Pub. by Scolar Pr) Ashgate Pub Co.

Carsten, Francis L. The Origins of Prussia. LC 81-17868. 309p. 1982. reprint ed. lib. bdg. 35.00 (*0-313-23220-2*, CAOP, Greenwood Pr) Greenwood.

— The Rise of Fascism. 2nd ed. LC 80-51592. 1980. pap. 17.95 (*0-520-04643-9*, Pub. by U CA Pr) Cal Prin Full Svc.

Carsten, Janet. The Heat of the Hearth: The Process of Kinship in a Malay Fishing Community. (Oxford Studies in Social & Cultural Anthropology). (Illus.). 330p. 1997. text 75.00 (*0-19-828045-9*); pap. text 32.00 (*0-19-828046-7*) OUP.

***Carsten, Janet, ed.** Cultures of Relatedness: New Approaches to the Study of Kinship. (Illus.). 232p. 2000. 54.95 (*0-521-65193-X*); pap. 19.95 (*0-521-65627-3*) Cambridge U Pr.

Carsten, M. E. & Miller, J. D. Uterine Function: Molecular & Cellular Aspects. LC 90-6882. (Illus.). 628p. (C). 1990. text 169.50 (*0-306-43446-6*, Kluwer Plenum) Kluwer Academic.

Carsten, Mary E., jt. ed. see Kao, C. Y.

Carsten Niebuhr Institute Staff, jt. ed. see Potts, Daniel T.

Carsten, Ron. Veterinary Contact Reflex Analysis: Applications in Clinical Veterinary Practice. (Illus.). 82p. (Orig.). 1996. pap. text 85.00 (*0-9649593-1-3*) Gran Farnum.

Carstens. Basic Instrumentation & Measuring Principles. (Electronics Technology Ser.). Date not set. pap., teacher ed. 14.00 (*0-8273-6330-3*) Delmar.

— Basic Instrumentation & Measuring Principles. (Electronics Technology Ser.). 1997. pap., lab manual ed. 18.95 (*0-8273-6331-1*); text 60.95 (*0-8273-6333-8*) Delmar.

Carstens, A. L., jt. auth. see Cronkite, E. P.

***Carstens, Cassie.** Linked to Jesus. 1999. pap. text 12.95 (*0-86997-768-7*) Lux Verbi.

Carstens, Diane V. Site Planning & Design for the Elderly. 1993. pap. 34.95 (*0-442-01351-5*, VNR) Wiley.

Carstens, Diane Y. Site Planning & Design for the Elderly: Issues, Guidelines, & Alternatives. 170p. 1993. pap. 49.95 (*0-471-28537-4*, VNR) Wiley.

Carstens, Harold, ed. Track Design. (Hobby Bks.: No. C88). (Illus.). 72p. 1996. pap. 11.95 (*0-911868-88-7*, C88) Carstens Pubns.

Carstens, Harold & Schopp, William. Complete Layout Plans. enl. rev. ed. (Hobby Bks.: No. C-73). (Illus.). 50p. 1991. pap. 7.95 (*0-911868-73-9*, C73) Carstens Pubns.

Carstens, Harold H. Circus Trains, Trucks & Models. (Illus.). 52p. 1990. pap. 12.95 (*0-911868-70-4*, C70) Carstens Pubns.

— Lionel Standard Gauge Era. LC 64-56883. (Hobby Bks.). (Illus.). 36p. 1987. pap. 4.00 (*0-911868-13-5*, C13) Carstens Pubns.

***Carstens, Harold H.** 150 Years of Train Models. (Illus.). 150p. 1999. 30.95 (*0-911868-95-X*, C95) Carstens Pubns.

Carstens, Harold H. Slim Gauge Cars. (Hobby Bks.: No. C-72). (Illus.). 116p. 1991. 19.95 (*0-911868-72-0*, C72) Carstens Pubns.

— Traction Planbook. 2nd ed. (Hobby Bks.: No. C-16). (Illus.). 100p. 1968. pap. 9.95 (*0-911868-16-X*, C16) Carstens Pubns.

Carstens, Harold H. & Mellander, Deane. Cumberland & Pennsylvania. (Illus.). 64p. 1989. pap. 9.95 (*0-911868-63-1*, C63) Carstens Pubns.

Carstens, James R. Automatic Control Systems & Components. 2nd ed. 400p. (C). 1989. text 62.25 (*0-13-054297-0*) P-H.

— Electrical Sensors & Transducers. 463p. (C). 1993. text 60.00 (*0-13-249632-1*) P-H.

Carstens, Johan L. St. Thomas in Early Danish Times. Highfield, Arnold R., ed. & tr. by. from DAN. LC 98-104326. (Orig.). 1997. pap. 15.00 (*1-886007-04-7*) VI Human Coun.

Carstens, Kenneth C. The Personnel of George Rogers Clark's Fort Jefferson: And the Civilian Community of Clarksville (Kentucky), 1780-1781. LC 99-219504. 189p. 1999. pap. 22.00 (*0-7884-1183-7*, C066) Heritage Bk.

Carstens, Kenneth C., ed. The Quartermaster Books of George Rogers Clark's Fort Jefferson, 1780-81: An Inventory of Quartermaster Activities in the Western Department in Support of George Rogers Clark's Illinois Battalion. LC 91-57966. (Studies in Social History: No. 12). 1993. 49.50 (*0-404-61612-7*) AMS Pr.

Carstens, Kenneth C. & Watson, Patty J., eds. Of Caves & Shell Mounds. LC 95-20772. (Illus.). 232p. (Orig.). 1996. pap. text 29.95 (*0-8173-0805-9*) U of Ala Pr.

Carstens, Peter. The Queen's People: A Study of Hegemony, Coercion, & Accommodation among the Okanagan of Canada. (Illus.). 416p. 1991. text 55.00 (*0-8020-5893-0*); pap. text 22.95 (*0-8020-6827-8*) U of Toronto Pr.

Carstens, R. W. The Medieval Antecedents of Constitutionalism. LC 91-16403. (American University Studies: History: Ser. IX, Vols. 115). 114p. (C). 1992. text 40.95 (*0-8204-1657-6*) P Lang Pubng.

— Notes on Humanity: Faith, Reason, Certainty. 142p. (Orig.). 1985. pap. text 15.00 (*0-8191-4885-7*) U Pr of Amer.

Carstens, Sharon A., ed. Cultural Identity in Northern Peninsular Malaysia. LC 83-11421. (Monographs in International Studies, Southeast Asia Ser.: No. 63). 108p. reprint ed. pap. 33.50 (*0-7837-1321-5*, 204146900021) Bks Demand.

Carstens, Torklid, jt. ed. see Wang, Sam S.

Carstens, W. Peter. The Social Structure of a Cape Coloured Reserve. LC 75-3985. (Illus.). 264p. 1975. reprint ed. lib. bdg. 65.00 (*0-8371-7431-7*, CACR, Greenwood Pr) Greenwood.

***Carstensen, Brenda.** Welcome to My Soul. LC 99-91455. 2000. 25.00 (*0-7388-0808-3*); pap. 18.00 (*0-7388-0809-1*) Xlibris Corp.

Carstensen, Edwin L. Biological Effects of Transmission Line Fields. LC 86-42117. 400p. 1987. 69.50 (*0-444-01018-1*) P-H.

Carstensen, Fred V., jt. ed. see Guroff, Gregory.

Carstensen, Frederick V., et al, eds. Outstanding in His Field: Perspectives on American Agricultural History in Honor of Wayne D. Rasmussen. LC 92-45889. (Henry A. Wallace Series on Agricultural History & Rural Studies). (Illus.). 176p. (C). 1993. text 44.95 (*0-8138-0739-5*) Iowa St U Pr.

Carstensen, Hans, ed. Steroid Hormone Analysis, Vol. 1. LC 67-17002. 507p. reprint ed. pap. 157.20 (*0-608-17066-6*, 202712100001) Bks Demand.

Carstensen, J. T. Modeling & Data Treatment in the Pharmaceutical Sciences. LC 96-60624. 235p. 1996. text 169.95 (*1-56676-440-8*) Technomic.

***Carstensen, Jakob & Gomilsek, Ivo.** Caldera Openlinux & Netfinity Server Integration Guide. 346p. 2000. pap. text 34.99 (*0-13-089771-X*) P-H.

— Suse Linux & Netfinity Server Integration Guide. 284p. 2000. pap. text 34.99 (*0-13-028675-3*) P-H.

***Carstensen, Jakob & Haskins, Jay.** Red Hat Linux & Netfinity Server Integration Guide. 340p. 2000. pap. 34.99 (*0-13-028674-5*) P-H.

Carstensen, Jens T. Drug Stability: Principles & Practices. 2nd expanded rev. ed. LC 95-12770. (Drugs & the Pharmaceutical Sciences Ser.: Vol. 68). (Illus.). 616p. 1995. text 185.00 (*0-8247-9635-7*) Dekker.

— Pharmaceutical Principles of Solid Dosage Forms. LC 92-64420. 255p. 1992. 99.95 (*0-87762-955-2*) Technomic.

Carstensen, J.T. Pharmaceutical Preformulation. 320p. 1998. 104.95 (*1-56676-690-7*) Technomic.

Carstensen, K. U., et al. Modelling Spatial Knowledge on a Linguistic Basis: Theory - Prototype - Integration. (Lecture Notes in Artificial Intelligence: Vol. 481). ix, 138p. 1991. 23.00 (*0-387-53718-X*) Spr-Verlag.

Carstensen, L. L., jt. ed. see Neale, John M.

Carstensen, Laura L., et al, eds. The Practical Handbook of Clinical Gerontology. LC 96-9986. 688p. 1996. 65.00 (*0-8039-5237-6*) Sage.

Carstensen, Laura L., ed. see Thomas, James H.

Carstensen, Vernon. Farms of Forests. Bruchey, Stuart, ed. LC 78-36706. (Management of Public Lands in the U. S. Ser.). (Illus.). 1979. reprint ed. lib. bdg. 15.95 (*0-405-11323-4*) Ayer.

Carstensen, Vernon, ed. The Public Lands: Studies in the History of the Public Domain. LC 62-21554. (Illus.). 538p. reprint ed. pap. 166.80 (*0-608-09848-5*, 206923600003) Bks Demand.

Carstensen, Vernon, jt. auth. see Curti, Merle E.

Carston, Rachel. Devil's Claw Root: And Other Natural Remedies for Arthritis. 3rd rev. ed. LC 94-910296. (Illus.). 110p. 1994. pap. 10.95 (*0-920470-36-X*) Alive Bks.

***Carston, Robyn.** Thoughts & Utterances: The Pragmatics of Verbal Communication. 350p. 1999. 64.95 (*0-631-17891-0*); pap. text 34.95 (*0-631-21488-7*) Blackwell Pubs.

Carston, Robyn & Uchida, Seiji, eds. Relevance Theory: Applications & Implications. LC 97-46673. (Pragmatics & Beyond New Ser.: No. 37). x, 300p. 1998. lib. bdg. 70.00 (*1-55619-330-0*) J Benjamins Pubng Co.

Carswell, Bob, jt. ed. see Gilmore, Gerry.

Carswell, Catherine. Lying Awake. 272p. 1997. pap. 12.95 (*0-86241-683-3*, Pub. by Canongate Books) Interlink Pub.

— Open the Door! 415p. 1997. pap. 12.95 (*0-86241-644-2*, Pub. by Canongate Books) Interlink Pub.

— The Savage Pilgrimage: A Narrative by D. H. Lawrence. 1988. reprint ed. lib. bdg. 49.00 (*0-7812-0593-X*) Rprt Serv.

Carswell, Catherine M. The Savage Pilgrimage: A Narrative by D. H. Lawrence. LC 75-144937. 307p. 1972. reprint ed. 39.00 (*0-403-01760-2*) Scholarly.

Carswell, Christine. The Complete Book of Fortune. 1989. 14.95 (*0-7011-3380-5*) Random.

Carswell, D. The Life of Sir Walter Scott. LC 70-176490. (English Biography Ser.: No. 31). 1971. lib. bdg. 75.00 (*0-8383-1365-5*) M S G Haskell Hse.

Carswell, Donald. Scott & His Circle. LC 72-175692. (Select Bibliographies Reprint Ser.). 1977. reprint ed. 21.95 (*0-8369-6607-4*) Ayer.

— Sir Walter: A Four-Part Study in Biography. (BCL1-PR English Literature Ser.). 292p. 1992. reprint ed. lib. bdg. 79.00 (*0-7812-7644-6*) Rprt Serv.

Carswell, Donald, ed. Trial of Guy Fawkes & Others: The Gunpowder Plot, No. 1. (Notable British Trials Ser.). 1995. reprint ed. 70.00 (*1-56169-113-5*) Gaunt.

— Trial of Ronald True. (Notable British Trials Ser.). x, 295p. 1995. reprint ed. 93.00 (*1-56169-170-4*, 15122) Gaunt.

Carswell, Evelyn & Bisignano, Judy. Living. (Illus.). 64p. (J). (gr. 3-8). 1985. student ed. 8.99 (*0-86653-332-X*, GA 679) Good Apple.

Carswell, John. Iznik Pottery LC 98-219903. (Eastern Art Ser.). 128p. 1998. write for info. (*0-7141-1482-0*, Pub. by British Mus Pr) Art Media Resources.

C

An Asterisk (*) at the beginning of an entry indicates that the title is appearing for the first time.

— Lives & Letters: A. R. Orage; Beatrice Hastings; Katherine Mansfield; John Middleton Murray; S. S. Koteliansky. LC 77-15986. (Illus.). 1978. 15.00 (*0-8112-0681-5*, Pub. by New Directions) Norton.
— South Sea Bubble. LC 92-164207. 1997. 33.95 (*0-86299-918-9*, Pub. by Sutton Pub Ltd) Intl Pubs Mktg.
Carswell, John, jt. auth. see Hourani, George F.
Carswell, Joseph C., jt. auth. see Watrous, Mitchell, Jr.
Carswell, Nicole H. A Matter of Pride: Horsemanship for Riders of Gaited Horses. (Illus.). 112p. 1998. pap. 25.00 (*0-9663262-0-2*) Seventh Heaven.
Carswell, Peter, jt. auth. see Nakamura, Shoichiro.
Carswell, Rodney. Rodney Carswell, Selected Works, 1975-1993: Selected Works: 1975-1993. (Illus.). 36p. 1993. pap. 20.00 (*0-941548-26-0*) Ren Soc U Chi.
***Carswell, Roger.** And Some... Evangelists: Growing Your Church Through Discovering & Developing Evangelists. 2000. 15.99 (*1-85792-512-2*) Christian Focus.
Carswell, Roger. Questions & Answers from the Bible. 1997. pap. text 8.99 (*1-898787-66-2*) Emerald House Group Inc.
— Why Believe? 160p. 1998. reprint ed. mass mkt. 7.99 (*1-85078-079-X*, Pub. by O M Pubng) OM Literature.
— Why Me? 95p. 1994. reprint ed. mass mkt. 4.99 (*1-85078-133-8*, Pub. by O M Pubng) OM Literature.
Carswell, Sue, ed. Spice World: The Movie: The Official Book of the Film. 1998. pap. 15.00 (*0-609-80338-7*, Crown) Crown Pub Group.
***Cart.** Paul Bowles. 1998. text. write for info. (*0-8057-1658-0*) Mac Lib Ref.
— What's So Funny? 288p. pap. 14.95 (*0-06-446170-X*) HarpC Child Bks.
Cart, Barbara J., et al, eds. Operation Desert Storm: Apache Helicopter Fratricide Incident. (Illus.). 100p. 1997. reprint ed. pap. text 40.00 (*0-7881-4115-5*) DIANE Pub.
Cart, Dorothy. Jail Bait: A Novel. LC 93-13562. 128p. (Orig.). 1994. pap. 10.95 (*0-86534-197-4*) Sunstone Pr.
Cart, Michael. From Romance to Realism: 50 Years of Growth & Change in Young Adult Literature. LC 95-31734. 320p. (YA). (gr. 7 up). 1996. 24.95 (*0-06-024289-2*) HarpC Child Bks.
— My Father's Scar. 208p. (YA). (gr. 7 up). 1996. mass mkt. 16.00 (*0-689-80749-X*) S&S Childrens.
— My Fathers Scar. LC 97-43657. 1998. pap. 11.95 (*0-312-18137-X*) St Martin.
— Presenting Robert Lipsyte. (Young Adult Authors Ser.). (YA). 1995. 28.00 (*0-8057-4151-8*, Twayne) Mac Lib Ref.
— Teenage Sex Anthology. 192p. (YA). (gr. 12 up). Date not set. lib. bdg. 15.89 (*0-06-027500-6*) HarpC.
— Teenage Sex Anthology. (Illus.). 192p. (YA). (gr. 12 up). 2000. 15.95 (*0-06-027499-9*) HarpC.
— What's So Funny? Wit & Humor in American Children's Literature. LC 94-15583. (Illus.). 256p. 1995. 25.00 (*0-06-024453-4*) HarpC.
Cart, Michael, ed. Tomorrowland: Ten Stories about the Future. LC 98-54832. 198p. (YA). (gr. 6-12). 1999. 15.95 (*0-590-37678-0*, Pub. by Scholastic Inc) Penguin Putnam.
Cart, Philip J., ed. see King, Lloyd.
Carta, Donatella, tr. see Seely, Contee & Romijn, Elizabeth.
CARTA Staff. The River Jordan: An Illustrated Guide from Bible Days to the Present. (Illus.). 48p. 1999. pap. 12.99 (*0-8254-2376-7*) Kregel.
CARTA Staff & Bruce, F. F. The Illustrated Bible Atlas. (Illus.). 32p. 1999. pap. 11.99 (*0-8254-2086-5*) Kregel.
— Illustrated Wall Maps of the Bible. (Illus.). 18p. 1999. 34.99 (*0-8254-2375-9*) Kregel.
Cartabruno, Leah. Breast Cancer. 21p. 1992. pap. write for info. (*1-58703-005-5*, CRB-92-004) CA St Libry.
Cartagena, Juan. Language Rights Survey of Legal Periodicals. LC 90-198063. 9p. 1989. 5.00 (*0-88156-098-7*) Comm Serv Soc NY.
Cartagena, Juntadel A. De, see De Cartagena, Juntadel A., ed.
Cartagena, Rafael. Una Agenda para la Excelencia Academica. LC 84-681. (Illus.). 128p. (Orig.). 1984. pap. 9.95 (*0-913480-60-6*) Inter Am U Pr.
Cartaino, Carol, jt. auth. see Aslett, Don.
Cartaino, Carol, ed. see Aslett, Don.
Cartaino, Carol, ed. see Aslett, Don A.
Cartaino, Carol, ed. see Aslett, Grant.
Cartalos, M. V., jt. ed. see Lecourtier, J.
Cartan, Elie. Elie Cartan - Albert Einstein: Letters on Absolute Parallelism, 1929-1932. Debever, Robert, ed. Leroy, Jules & Ritter, Jim, trs. LC 78-73832. (ENG & FRE.). 258p. reprint ed. pap. 80.00 (*0-8357-2925-7*, 203916400011) Bks Demand.
— Geometry of Riemannian Spaces. (LIE Groups Ser.: Vol. XIII). 506p. 1983. 75.00 (*0-915692-34-1*, 991600010) Math Sci Pr.
— The Theory of Spinors. 176p. (C). 1981. reprint ed. pap. 7.95 (*0-486-64070-1*) Dover.
Cartan, H. & Eilenberg, S. Homological Algebra. (Mathematical Ser.: Vol. 19). 408p. 1956. text 79.50 (*0-691-07977-3*, Pub. by Princeton U Pr) Cal Prin Full Svc.
Cartan, Henri. Elementary Theory of Analytic Functions of One or Several Complex Variables. Orig. Title: Theorie Elementaire des Fonctions Analytiques d'une ou Plusiers Variables Complexes. (Illus.). 228p. 1995. pap. text 8.95 (*0-486-68543-8*) Dover.
***Cartan, Henri.** Homological Algebra. (Landmarks in Mathematics Ser.). 2000. pap. text 19.95 (*0-691-04991-2*) Princeton U Pr.
Cartana, Luis. Poesias Completas. (SPA.). Date not set. pap. write for info. (*0-89729-541-2*) Ediciones.
***Cartano, David J.** Federal & State Taxation of Limited Liability Companies, 1. 800p. 1999. pap. text 165.00 (*0-7355-1073-3*) Panel Pubs.
— Taxation of Compensation & Benefits. 800p. 1999. pap. 145.00 (*0-7355-0407-5*) Panel Pubs.
Cartano, David J. Taxation of Limited Liability Companies. 500p. (Orig.). 1997. pap. text 48.00 (*0-9658184-0-3*) Internet Pubns.
Cartano, Tony. Blackbird. 1987. 18.95 (*0-02-529270-6*) Macmillan.
***Cartarescu, Mircea.** Bebop Baby. Sorkin, Adam J., tr. (Poetry New York Pamphlet Ser.: No. 19). 30p. 1999. pap. 5.00 (*0-923389-33-4*) Meet Eyes Bind.
Cartari, Vincenzo. The Fountaine of Ancient Fiction. Linche, Richard, tr. from ITA. LC 73-6109. (English Experience Ser.: No. 577). 206p. 1973. reprint ed. 20.00 (*90-221-0577-6*) Walter J Johnson.
Cartault, Augstin. Tibulle et les Auteurs du Corpus Tibullianum. 260p. 1981. reprint ed. 55.00 (*3-487-07131-2*) G Olms Pubs.
Carte. Carte Blanche: Le Calendrier. 1980. pap. text 34.40 (*0-201-18792-2*) Addison-Wesley.
— Carte Blanche: Le Corps. 1980. pap. text 34.40 (*0-201-18791-4*) Addison-Wesley.
— Carte Blanche: L'Ecole. 1980. pap. text 34.40 (*0-201-18797-3*) Addison-Wesley.
— Carte Blanche: Les Sports. 1980. pap. text 34.40 (*0-201-18798-1*) Addison-Wesley.
— Carte Blanche: Les Transports. 1980. pap. text 34.40 (*0-201-18799-X*) Addison-Wesley.
Cartee, Robert E., et al. Practical Veterinary Ultrasound. LC 94-44192. (Lea & Febiger Ser.). (Illus.). 352p. 1995. (*0-683-01483-8*) Lppncott W & W.
Cartee, Robert E., ed. see Nautrup, Cordula Poulsen & Tobias, Ralf.
Cartel, Michael. Disguise of Sanity: Serial Mass Murderers. LC 85-60605. (Illus.). 280p. 1985. 15.95 (*0-9614625-0-7*) Pepperbox.
Cartelier, Jean, jt. ed. see D'Autume, Antoine.
***Cartelli, Donna.** Black Mayonnaise. 88p. 2000. pap. 12.00 (*1-930330-01-4*) Ten Pell Bks.
Cartelli, Thomas. Marlowe, Shakespeare, & the Economy of Theatrical Experience. LC 91-21173. 264p. (C). 1991. text 39.95 (*0-8122-3102-3*) U of Pa Pr.
— Marlowe, Shakespeare, & the Economy of Theatrical Experience. LC 91-21173. reprint ed. pap. 80.30 (*0-608-07408-X*, 2067635) Bks Demand.
— Repositioning Shakespeare: National Formations, Postcolonial Appropriations. LC 98-30515. 1999. 85.00 (*0-415-19134-3*); pap. 25.99 (*0-415-19498-9*) Routledge.
Cartellieri, Otto. Court of Burgundy. LC 70-132437. (World History Ser.: No. 48). 1970. reprint ed. lib. bdg. 75.00 (*0-8383-1197-0*) M S G Haskell Hse.
Cartellieri, Ulrich & Greenspan, Alan. William Taylor Memorial Lectures 3: Global Risk Management. 42p. (Orig.). 1996. pap. 10.00 (*1-56708-098-7*) Grp of Thirty.
Carten, Jim. Pilgrims & Strangers on the Earth. LC 94-78461. (Illus.). 240p. (Orig.). 1994. pap. 17.50 (*0-9643069-0-5*) Heretic Pr.
— Pilgrims & Strangers on the Earth. limited ed. (Illus.). 240p. (Orig.). 1994. 32.50 (*0-9643069-1-3*) Heretic Pr.
Carter. Administrative Law & Politics: Cases & Comments. 3rd ed. LC 99-45951. 660p. (C). 1999. 72.00 (*0-321-03685-9*) Addison-Wesley Educ.
***Carter.** American Corporate Identity 2000. 2000. 45.00 (*0-688-17234-2*, Wm Morrow) Morrow Avon.
Carter. Ams Bugs Box 1 David Carter Fun Bug Pack Proprietary. (J). 1998. 17.97 (*0-689-82615-X*) S&S Childrens.
— Art & Science of War vs. Art of Fighting. (Guidon Monographs). 1976. 21.95 (*0-8488-1521-1*, J M C & Co) Amereon Ltd.
— Astrology of Accidents: Investigations & Research. 1978. pap. 10.00 (*0-7229-5059-4*) Theos Pub Hse.
— Baby Bug Pop up Book Colors. (J). 1997. 9.95 (*0-689-81970-6*) S&S Trade.
— Baby Bug Pop-up Book Counting. (J). 1997. 9.95 (*0-689-81971-4*) S&S Trade.
— Baby Bug Pop up Book in & Out. (J). 1997. 9.95 (*0-689-81972-2*) S&S Trade.
— Baby Bug Pop-up Book Opposites. (J). 1997. 9.95 (*0-689-81973-0*) S&S Trade.
— Basics for Success. 3rd ed. 1998. 18.74 (*0-07-428133-X*) McGraw.
— Brochures That Work. 1998. 35.00 (*0-688-16394-7*, Wm Morrow) Morrow Avon.
***Carter.** Brochures That Work. 1999. pap. 29.95 (*0-688-16601-6*, Wm Morrow) Morrow Avon.
Carter. Bug Riddle Flap Book. (J). (gr. k up). 2000. 6.99 (*0-689-80915-8*) S&S Bks Yung.
— Cambridge. 1986. pap. text. write for info. (*0-582-74907-7*, Pub. by Addison-Wesley) Longman.
— Career Toolkit & Graduating into the 90's Package. 2nd ed. 1998. 32.00 (*0-13-084094-7*) P-H.
***Carter.** Changing State of the Balkans. 2000. pap. text 25.00 (*0-8133-3631-7*, Pub. by Westview) HarpC.
— Classical & Statistical Thermodynamics. LC 00-27105. 448p. 2000. 91.33 (*0-13-779208-5*) P-H.
Carter. Company Uniforms. 1998. 35.00 (*0-688-15350-X*, Wm Morrow) Morrow Avon.
— Company Uniforms. 1999. pap. 29.95 (*0-688-16359-9*, Wm Morrow) Morrow Avon.
— Computer Applications & Accounting. (C). 1992. pap. 4.36 (*0-395-49450-8*) HM.
— Computer Programming Electronics. LC 98-33569. 465p. 1998. pap. text 95.00 (*0-13-442203-1*) P-H.
— Constitutional Interpretation. (Political Pampheleteer Ser.). (C). 1997. pap. text 7.86 (*0-673-99784-7*) Addson-Wesley Educ.
— Cool Cards. 1998. 35.00 (*0-688-16047-6*, Wm Morrow) Morrow Avon.
***Carter.** Cool Cards. 1999. pap. 29.95 (*0-688-16516-8*, Wm Morrow) Morrow Avon.
Carter. Cultural Memory. 1997. pap. 19.50 (*0-85315-860-6*, Pub. by Lawrence & Wishart) NYU Pr.
— Daniel Library User Guide. 3rd ed. 1998. 11.74 (*0-07-229247-4*) McGraw.
***Carter.** Dimensional Promotions. 2000. 35.00 (*0-688-16930-9*, Wm Morrow) Morrow Avon.
Carter. Ethical Journalist. (C). 2000. 29.33 (*0-205-28737-9*, Macmillan Coll) P-H.
— Exercises - Rinehard Guide to Grammar: Answer Key. 4th ed. (C). 1995. pap. text, suppl. ed. 3.00 (*0-15-503135-X*, Pub. by Harcourt Coll Pubs) Harcourt.
— Fun Fonts. 1997. 35.00 (*0-688-15345-3*, Wm Morrow) Morrow Avon.
— Hobbs Local History. (C). 1977. text 18.50 (*0-233-95615-8*) Westview.
— Job Order Cost Accounting Practice Case: Printwrite, Inc. 1998. pap. 30.95 (*0-87393-818-6*) Dame Pubns.
— Keys to Successful Spanish. 1997. pap. text 24.75 (*0-13-907437-6*) P-H.
***Carter.** Letterheads Gone Digital. 1999. 39.95 (*0-688-16476-5*, Wm Morrow) Morrow Avon.
Carter. Logos Go Digital. 1997. 35.00 (*0-688-15701-7*, Wm Morrow) Morrow Avon.
***Carter.** Logoware. 1998. 35.00 (*0-688-15348-8*, Wm Morrow) Morrow Avon.
Carter. Politics of Womens Rights. 1988. pap. text. write for info. (*0-582-29519-X*, Pub. by Addison-Wesley) Longman.
— Prep for TASP with Rinehart's Handbook. 4th ed. (C). 1995. pap. text 6.00 (*0-15-503606-8*, Pub. by Harcourt Coll Pubs) Harcourt.
— Process Cost Accounting Practice Case: PC Processors. 1998. pap. 30.95 (*0-87393-819-4*) Dame Pubns.
— Redesigning Logo & Letterheads. 1998. 35.00 (*0-688-16474-9*, Wm Morrow) Morrow Avon.
— The Relational Database. (C). 1994. mass mkt. 31.95 (*1-85032-255-4*) ITCP.
— The Rinehart Guide to Grammar: Exercises. 4th ed. (C). 1995. pap. text, suppl. ed. 7.00 (*0-15-503134-1*, Pub. by Harcourt Coll Pubs) Harcourt.
— The Rinehart Guide to Grammar & Style. 4th ed. (C). 1995. pap. text 13.50 (*0-15-503561-4*, Pub. by Harcourt Coll Pubs) Harcourt.
— The Rinehart Handbook for Writers. 4th ed. (C). 1996. pap. text 22.50 (*0-15-501984-8*, Pub. by Harcourt Coll Pubs) Harcourt.
— Rinehart Handbook Supplemental Excercises. 1993. pap. text 22.00 (*0-15-500755-6*) Harcourt.
— Shattering Illusions: West Indians in British Politics. (C). 1986. pap. 17.50 (*0-85315-674-3*, Pub. by Lawrence & Wishart) NYU Pr.
— Social Working. 1997. text 19.95 (*0-333-60911-5*, Pub. by Macmillan) St Martin.
— Sociology. (C). 1997. text, student ed. 20.00 (*0-06-502152-5*) Addson-Wesley Educ.
— Sounds Abound, 2 vols. (C). 1993. pap., teacher ed. 2.76 (*0-395-52931-X*) HM.
— Sources of Strength/Living Faith. 1999. boxed set 14.00 (*0-676-59269-4*, Times Bks) Crown Pub Group.
— Spreadsheet Skills Made Simple. 152p. Date not set. pap. text 19.95 (*0-7506-2679-8*) Buttrwrth-Heinemann.
Carter. Student's Guide Information Technology. 288p. 1997. pap. text 24.95 (*0-7506-3657-2*) Buttrwrth-Heinemann.
Carter. Symbolic Directions in Modern Astrology. 1984. pap. 9.95 (*0-7229-5145-0*) Theos Pub Hse.
— Testbank - The Rinehart Handbook, 3/e. 3rd ed. (C). 1993. pap. text 11.50 (*0-15-501350-5*) Harcourt Coll Pubs.
Carter, ed. Introduction to Administrative Law. (C). 1998. text. write for info. (*0-321-01355-7*) Addson-Wesley Educ.
Carter & Bishop. Keys to Success: Brief Edition. LC 98-33850. 311p. (C). 1998. pap. text 23.40 (*0-13-010798-0*) P-H.
Carter, et al. Cost Accounting. 12th ed. LC 98-70889. (SWC-Accounting). 1998. 82.95 (*0-87393-747-3*) Dame Pubns.
— First Amendment & the Fifth Estate: 1998 Supplement. 4th ed. 1998. write for info. (*1-56662-658-7*) Foundation Pr.
— Keys to Study Skills. LC 98-33550. 285p. (C). 1998. pap. text 28.60 (*0-13-917915-1*) P-H.
Carter, jt. auth. see Morgan.
Carter, jt. auth. see Seaburg.
Carter, ed. see Caesar.
***Carter, Dori.** Beautiful Wasps Having Sex. LC 00-38274. 336p. 2000. 24.00 (*0-688-17464-7*, Wm Morrow) Morrow Avon.
Carter, A. D. Mechanical Reliability & Design. LC 97-65. 240p. 1997. text 59.95 (*0-470-23719-8*) Halsted Pr.
Carter, A. Lee. Current Concepts in Carnitine Research. 288p. 1991. lib. bdg. 119.00 (*0-8493-0186-6*, QP772) CRC Pr.
***Carter, Abby.** Start a Club! (gr. 9-12). 1999. pap. text 1.95 (*1-56247-738-2*) Pleasant Co.
Carter, Abby, jt. auth. see Lindbergh, Reeve.
Carter, Al. Lifetimer Delivers Success: A Powerful Success Program That Actually Works! LC 91-92167. 283p. 1992. pap. 14.95 (*0-9625946-2-8*) Carter-Grove Pub.
Carter, Alan. A Radical Green Political Theory. LC 98-41317. 1999. write for info. (*0-415-20309-0*) Routledge.
Carter, Alan, jt. auth. see Solomon, James.
***Carter, Alan R.** Networking Essentials MCSE Study System. 544p. 1999. 49.99 (*0-7645-4604-X*) IDG Bks.
— Windows NT 4.0 Server in the Enterprise MCSE Study System. 900p. 1999. 49.99 (*0-7645-4605-8*) IDG Bks.
— Windows NT 4.0 Server MCSE Study System. 900p. 1999. 49.99 (*0-7645-4607-4*) IDG Bks.
— Windows NT 4.0 Workstation MCSE Study System. 900p. 1999. 49.99 (*0-7645-4606-6*) IDG Bks.
— Windows NT Server 4.0: MCSE Study Guide. LC QA76.3.C373 1998. 928p. 1998. pap., student ed. 49.99 (*0-7645-3250-2*) IDG Bks.
Carter, Alan R. Windows NT Workstation 4.0: MCSE Study Guide. LC QA76.3.C3734 1998. 864p. 1998. pap., student ed. 49.99 (*0-7645-3249-9*) IDG Bks.
***Carter, Alan R.** Windows 2000 Active Directory Services MCSE Study System. (Illus.). 700p. 2001. pap. text 39.99 (*0-7645-4734-8*) IDG Bks.
— Windows 2000 MCSE Study System. (Illus.). 1500p. 2000. pap. 89.99 (*0-7645-4701-1*) IDG Bks.
— Windows 2000 Network Infrastructure MCSE Study System. (Illus.). 700p. 2001. pap. text 39.99 (*0-7645-4735-6*) IDG Bks.
— Windows 2000 Professional MCSE Study System. (Illus.). 700p. 2001. pap. text 39.99 (*0-7645-4736-4*) IDG Bks.
— Windows 2000 Server MCSE Study System. (Illus.). 700p. 2001. pap. text 39.99 (*0-7645-4737-2*) IDG Bks.
Carter, Alan R. & Willingham, Thomas C. Windows NT 4.O MCSE Study Guide. LC 97-73384. (MCSE Certification Ser.). 1400p. 1997. 89.99 (*0-7645-3087-9*) IDG Bks.
Carter, Albert E. The Cancer Answer. 252p. write for info. (*0-9619041-1-9*) ALM Pubs.
— The Miracles of Minerals: The Human Need for 90 Plus Elements from a Cell's Point of View. 224p. (Orig.). 1995. pap. text 14.95 (*1-887995-00-5*) Amer Institute Res.
Carter, Albert H. First Cut: A Season in the Anatomy Lab. LC 97-20909. (Illus.). 352p. 1997. text 24.00 (*0-312-16840-3*) St Martin.
— Italo Calvino: Metamorphoses of Fantasy. LC 86-24957. (Studies in Speculative Fiction: No. 13). 192p. reprint ed. pap. 59.60 (*0-8357-1780-1*, 207060400005) Bks Demand.
Carter, Albert H. & Petro, Jane A. Rising from the Flames: The Experience of the Severely Burned. LC 97-46890. (Illus.). 229p. 1998. 23.00 (*0-8122-1517-6*) U of Pa Pr.
Carter, Albert Howard & Petro, Jane A. Rising from the Flames: The Experience of the Severely Burned. LC 97-46890. 229 p. 1998. write for info. (*0-8122-3264-X*) U of Pa Pr.
Carter, Albert T. History of English Legal Institutions. 302p. 1986. reprint ed. 47.50 (*0-8377-2007-9*, Rothman) W S Hein.
Carter, Alden R. The American Revolution: War for Independence. (First Bks.). (Illus.). 64p. (J). (gr. 5-8). 1993. pap. 6.95 (*0-531-15652-4*) Watts.
— American Revolution: War for Independence. (First Bks.). 1992. 11.15 (*0-606-05116-3*, Pub. by Turtleback) Demco.
— Between a Rock & a Hard Place. LC 94-39803. 240p. (YA). (gr. 7 up). 1995. 14.95 (*0-590-48684-5*, Scholastic Hardcover) Scholastic Inc.
— Between a Rock & a Hard Place. (Illus.). 224p. (J). (gr. 5-9). 1999. reprint ed. pap. 4.99 (*0-590-37486-9*) Scholastic Inc.
— Big Brother Dustin. LC 96-27301. (Illus.). 32p. (J). (gr. k-3). 1997. lib. bdg. 14.95 (*0-8075-0715-6*) A Whitman.
— Bull Catcher. LC 95-39538. 288p. (J). (gr. 7-12). 1997. 15.95 (*0-590-50958-6*) Scholastic Inc.
***Carter, Alden R.** Bull Catcher. (Illus.). 288p. (YA). (gr. 7-12). 2000. mass mkt. 4.99 (*0-590-50959-4*, Pub. by Scholastic Inc) Penguin Putnam.
Carter, Alden R. China Past - China Future. LC 93-13537. (International Affairs Ser.). 144p. (YA). (gr. 9-12). 1994. lib. bdg. 24.00 (*0-531-11161-X*) Watts.
— The Civil War: American Tragedy. (First Bks.). (Illus.). 64p. (J). (gr. 4-6). 1992. lib. bdg. 22.00 (*0-531-20039-6*) Watts.
— Civil War: American Tragedy. (First Bks.). 1992. 11.15 (*0-606-05207-0*, Pub. by Turtleback) Demco.
— The Civil War: American Tragedy. large type ed. (First Bks.). (Illus.). 64p. (J). (gr. 5-8). 1993. pap. 6.95 (*0-531-15653-2*) Watts.
— Colonial Wars: Clashes in the Wilderness. (First Bks.). (J). 1992. 12.15 (*0-606-05211-9*, Pub. by Turtleback) Demco.
***Carter, Alden R.** Crescent Moon. LC 99-24654. 208p. (YA). (gr. 5-9). 1999. 16.95 (*0-8234-1521-X*) Holiday.
Carter, Alden R. Crescent Moon. LC 98-23287. (J). 1999. 15.95 (*0-590-29882-8*) Scholastic Inc.
— Dancing on Dark Water. 144p. (YA). (gr. 7-9). 1994. pap. 3.25 (*0-590-45600-8*) Scholastic Inc.
— Dancing on Dark Water. (Point Ser.). (J). 1990. 8.35 (*0-606-05799-4*, Pub. by Turtleback) Demco.
— Dogwolf. LC 93-43518. 272p. (J). (gr. 7-9). 1994. 13.95 (*0-590-46741-7*) Scholastic Inc.
— Dogwolf. 272p. (YA). (gr. 7 up). 1996. mass mkt. 4.50 (*0-590-46742-5*, Scholastic Hardcover) Scholastic Inc.
— Dogwolf. LC 93-43518. 1994. 9.60 (*0-606-09200-5*, Pub. by Turtleback) Demco.
— Dustin's Big School Day. LC 98-29567. (Illus.). 32p. (J). (gr. k-3). 1999. lib. bdg. 14.95 (*0-8075-1741-0*) A Whitman.
— Seeing Things My Way. LC 98-5893. (Illus.). 32p. (J). (gr. 1-4). 1998. lib. bdg. 14.95 (*0-8075-7296-9*) A Whitman.
— The Spanish-American War: Imperial Ambitions. (First Bks.). (J). 1992. 11.15 (*0-606-05618-1*, Pub. by Turtleback) Demco.
— The Spanish-American War: Imperial Ambitions. large type ed. (First Bks.). (Illus.). 64p. (J). (gr. 5-8). 1993. pap. 6.95 (*0-531-15657-5*) Watts.
***Carter, Alden R.** Stretching Ourselves: Kids with Cerebral Palsy. (Concept Book Ser.). (Illus.). 40p. (J). (gr. k-4). 2000. lib. bdg. 14.95 (*0-8075-7637-9*) A Whitman.
Carter, Alden R. The War of 1812: Second Fight for Independence. (First Bks.). (J). 1992. 11.15 (*0-606-05686-6*, Pub. by Turtleback) Demco.

— The War of 1812: Second Fight for Independence. large type ed. (First Bks.). (Illus.). 64p. (J). (gr. 5-8). 1993. pap. 6.95 (*0-531-15659-1*) Watts.

Carter, Alden R., jt. auth. see Carter, Siri M.

Carter, Alexandra, ed. Routledge Dance Studies Reader. LC 97-46643. 304p. (C). 1998. pap. 24.99 (*0-415-16447-8*) Routledge.

— Routledge Dance Studies Reader. LC 97-46643. 336p. (C). 1998. 75.00 (*0-415-16446-X*) Routledge.

Carter, Alice A. The Art of National Geographic: A Century of Illustrations. LC 99-13167. 240p. 1999. per. 50.00 (*0-7922-7920-4*) Natl Geog.

***Carter, Alice A.** The Red Rose Girls: An Uncommon Story of Art & Love. LC 99-39866. (Illus.). 216p. 2000. 39.95 (*0-8109-4437-5*, Pub. by Abrams) Time Warner.

Carter, Alice E., jt. auth. see Thomas, William G.

Carter, Alicia, ed. see Carter, Mitch.

Carter, Amy, jt. auth. see Carter, Jimmy.

Carter, Andrew, jt. ed. see Blackwell, David.

***Carter, Andy & Saller, Carol.** George Washington Carver. LC 99-6825. (On My Own Biographies Ser.). (Illus.). 64p. (J). (ps-3). 2000. 19.93 (*1-57505-427-2*, Carolrhoda) Lerner Pub.

***Carter, Andy, et al.** George Washington Carver. LC 99-6825. (On My Own Biography Ser.). (Illus.). 64p. (J). (ps-3). 2000. pap. 5.95 (*1-57505-458-2*, Carolrhoda) Lerner Pub.

Carter, Angela. The Bloody Chamber. 128p. 1995. mass mkt. 5.99 (*0-09-958811-0*) Random Hse Value.

Carter, Angela. The Bloody Chamber. 128p. 1996. pap. 11.95 (*0-14-017821-X*) Viking Penguin.

Carter, Angela. Burning Your Boats. 480p. 1997. pap. 14.95 (*0-14-025528-1*) Viking Penguin.

— Burning Your Boats: The Collected Short Stories. 462p. 1995. 30.00 (*0-8050-4462-0*) H Holt & Co.

— Come unto These Yellow Sands. 1985. 35.00 (*0-906427-66-5*, Pub. by Bloodaxe Bks); pap. 16.95 (*0-906427-67-3*, Pub. by Bloodaxe Bks) Dufour.

— Fireworks: Nine Profane Pieces. 144p. 1987. pap. 11.95 (*0-14-010588-3*, Penguin Bks) Viking Penguin.

— Heroes & Villains. 160p. 1991. pap. 11.95 (*0-14-023464-0*, Penguin Bks) Viking Penguin.

— The Infernal Desire Machines of Doctor Hoffman. 224p. 1986. pap. 12.95 (*0-14-023519-1*, Penguin Bks) Viking Penguin.

— Love. 128p. 1988. pap. 10.95 (*0-14-010851-3*, Penguin Bks) Viking Penguin.

— The Magic Toyshop. LC 95-26415. 200p. 1996. pap. 11.95 (*0-14-025640-7*, Penguin Bks) Viking Penguin.

— Nights at the Circus. (Fiction Ser.). 304p. 1986. pap. 12.95 (*0-14-007703-0*, Penguin Bks) Viking Penguin.

— Saints & Strangers. 128p. 1987. pap. 11.95 (*0-14-008973-X*, Penguin Bks) Viking Penguin.

— Shadow Dance. 182p. 1996. pap. 10.95 (*0-14-025524-9*, Penguin Bks) Viking Penguin.

Carter, Angela. Shadow Dance. large type ed. 22.95 (*1-85695-229-0*, Pub. by ISIS Lrg Prnt) Transaction Pubs.

Carter, Angela. Shaking a Leg: Collected Writings. Uglow, Jenny, ed. LC 99-187160. 642p. 1998. pap. 15.95 (*0-14-027695-5*) Viking Penguin.

— Wise Children. 232p. 1992. 21.00 (*0-374-29133-0*) FS&G.

— Wise Children. 1991. write for info. (*0-316-13053-2*) Little.

— Wise Children. 240p. 1993. pap. 12.95 (*0-14-017530-X*, Penguin Bks) Viking Penguin.

Carter, Angela, ed. Strange Things Sometimes Still Happen: Fairy Tales from Around the World. (Illus.). 233p. 1994. pap. 13.95 (*0-571-19838-4*) Faber & Faber.

Carter, Angela & Uglow, Jennifer S. Shaking a Leg: Journalism & Writings LC 98-148778. (Collected Angela Carter Ser.). 641 p. 1997. write for info. (*0-7011-6336-4*) Chatto & Windus.

Carter, Angela M., ed. see Parenti, Jessica G.

Carter, Anjean B. & Brellochs, Christel. Building Primary Health Care in New York City's Low-Income Communities. LC 90-198029. 80p. 1990. pap. 9.00 (*0-88156-107-X*) Comm Serv Soc NY.

Carter, Ann, tr. see Tournier, Michel.

Carter, Anne. Mulberries & Prickly Pear. (Illus.). 161p. (Orig.). 1991. pap. 9.50 (*0-9632510-0-7*) A Carter.

— Tall in the Saddle. LC 99-61433. (Illus.). 32p. (J). (gr. k-3). 1999. 14.95 (*1-55143-154-8*) Orca Bk Pubs.

Carter, Anne, et al. Beauty & the Beast. LC 85-28125. 36p. (J). 1986. 0.00 (*0-517-56173-5*) Bell T.

Carter, Anne B. Strike Root. LC 97-61431. 80p. 1998. pap. 12.95 (*1-884800-21-1*) Four Way Bks.

***Carter, Anne Bryan.** Painting Indiana: Portraits of Indiana's 92 Counties. LC 99-48558. (Illus.). 216p. 2000. 39.95 (*0-253-33692-9*) Ind U Pr.

Carter, Anne P. Structural Change in the American Economy. LC 73-95516. (Studies in Technology & Society). 310p. 1970. 43.00 (*0-674-84370-3*) HUP.

Carter, Anthony. World Bayonets, 1800 to the Present: An Illustrated Reference Guide for Collectors. expanded rev. ed. (Illus.). 96p. 1996. 19.95 (*1-85409-344-4*, Pub. by Arms & Armour) Sterling.

Carter, Anthony, et al, eds. The Maternal Fetal Interface. LC 98-30167. (Trophoblast Research Ser.: Vol. 12). (Illus.). 448p. 1998. 120.00 (*1-58046-043-7*) Univ Rochester Pr.

Carter, April. Democratic Reform in Yugoslavia: The Changing Role of the Party. LC 81-47910. 295p. 1982. reprint ed. pap. 91.50 (*0-7837-9493-2*, 206023700004) Bks Demand.

— Mahatma Gandhi: A Bibliography, 2. LC 94-46929. (Bibliographies of World Leaders Ser.: No. 2). 184p. 1995. lib. bdg. 65.00 (*0-313-28296-X*, Greenwood Pr) Greenwood.

— Marshal Tito: A Bibliography, 1. LC 89-31984. (Bibliographies of World Leaders Ser.: No. 1). 160p. 1989. lib. bdg. 75.00 (*0-313-28087-8*, CMT/, Greenwood Pr) Greenwood.

— Success & Failure in Arms Control Negotiations. (SIPRI Publication). (Illus.). 320p. 1989. text 69.00 (*0-19-829128-0*) OUP.

Carter, April & Stokes, Geoff. Liberal Democracy & Its Critics: Perspectives in Contemporary Political Thought. LC 98-33638. 240p. 1998. 59.95 (*0-7456-1919-3*); pap. 26.95 (*0-7456-1920-7*) Blackwell Pubs.

***Carter, Arlan.** 19th Century Fishing Lures: A Collector's Guide to U. S. Lures Manufactures Prior to 1901. 304p. 2000. 29.95 (*1-57432-165-X*) Collector Bks.

Carter, Art. The Sporting Craftsmen: A Complete Guide to Contemporary Makers of Custom- Built Sporting Equipment. (Illus.). 256p. 1995. 49.00 (*0-924357-46-0*, 61100-A) Countrysport Pr.

— The Sporting Craftsmen: A Complete Guide to Contemporary Makers of Custom- Built Sporting Equipment. deluxe limited ed. (Illus.). 256p. 1994. lthr. 95.00 (*0-924357-47-9*, 61100-B) Countrysport Pr.

Carter, Art, photos by. Southeast Coast: Photos of Art Carter. LC 85-71193. (Illus.). 160p. 1985. 29.50 (*0-912856-95-5*) Gr Arts Ctr Pub.

Carter, Arthur. The Number: Manuscript Edition. 1952. pap. 13.00 (*0-8222-0833-4*) Dramatists Play.

Carter, Arthur B. The Tarnished Cavalier: Major General Earl Van Dorn, C. S. A. LC 98-40256. (Illus.). 264p. 1999. 42.00 (*1-57233-047-3*, Pub. by U of Tenn Pr) U Ch Pr.

Carter, Ashton B. Preventive Defense: A New Security Strategy for America. LC 98-51245. 1999. 24.95 (*0-8157-1308-8*) Brookings.

Carter, Ashton B., et al, eds. Managing Nuclear Operations. LC 86-32655. 751p. 1987. 52.95 (*0-8157-1314-2*); pap. 24.95 (*0-8157-1313-4*) Brookings.

Carter, Ashton B. & Perry, William J. Preventive Defense: An American Security Strategy for the 21st Century LC 98-51245. 1998. write for info. (*0-8157-1307-X*) Brookings.

Carter, Ashton B. & Schwartz, David N., eds. Ballistic Missile Defense. LC 83-24064. 455p. 1984. 42.95 (*0-8157-1312-6*); pap. 18.95 (*0-8157-1311-8*) Brookings.

Carter, Ashton B., et al. A New Concept of Cooperative Security. LC 92-74426. 65p. (C). 1993. pap. 8.95 (*0-8157-8145-8*) Brookings.

Carter, B. Child & Infant Pain: Principles of Nursing Care & Management. 176p. 1994. 39.95 (*1-56593-181-5*, 0496) Singular Publishing.

Carter, B. & Hartle, J. B., eds. Gravitation in Astrophysics: Cargese 1986. LC 87-7810. (NATO ASI Series B, Physical Sciences: Vol. 156). (Illus.). 418p. 1987. 95.00 (*0-306-42590-4*, Plenum Trade) Perseus Pubng.

Carter, Barbara B., tr. see Montessori, Maria.

Carter, Barbara J., jt. auth. see Taylor, Ronald L.

Carter, Barbara L., ed. Computed Tomography of the Head & Neck. LC 84-17565. (Contemporary Issues in Computed Tomography Ser.: No. 5). (Illus.). 351p. reprint ed. pap. 108.90 (*0-7837-6252-6*, 204596400010) Bks Demand.

Carter, Barbara R., jt. auth. see Carter, K. Codell.

Carter, Barry C. Infinite Wealth: A New World of Collaboration & Abundance in the Knowledge Era. LC 99-18730. (Illus.). 264p. 1999. pap. text 19.95 (*0-7506-7184-X*) Buttrwrth-Heinemann.

Carter, Barry E. International Law. 2nd ed. 1600p. 1995. 59.00 (*0-316-13297-7*, Aspen Law & Bus) Aspen Pub.

— International Law, 1995. 944p. 1995. 30.95 (*0-316-13300-0*, Aspen Law & Bus) Aspen Pub.

Carter, Barry E. & Trimble, Phillip R. International Law. 2nd ed. 1600p. 1995. teacher ed. write for info. (*0-316-13298-5*, 32985) Aspen Law.

— International Law. 3rd ed. LC 99-19138. 1999. boxed set 62.00 (*0-7355-0043-6*) Panel Pubs.

***Carter, Barry E. & Trimble, Phillip R.** International Law: Selected Documents. LC 99-200111. xvii, 951p. 1999. pap. text 35.95 (*0-7355-0042-8*) Panel Pubs.

Carter, Ben. Where to Buy Everything Wholesale: A Book of Lifetime Savings. 32p. 1997. pap. 7.95 (*0-934650-06-3*) Sunnyside.

Carter, Ben M. The Depersonalization of God: A Consideration of Soteriological Difficulties in High Calvinism. 72p. (C). 1989. lib. bdg. 33.00 (*0-8191-7512-9*) U Pr of Amer.

***Carter, Ben M.** The Making of Post-Protestant Christianity. LC 00-9578. 2000. pap. write for info. (*0-941037-87-8*, BIBAL Press) D & F Scott.

Carter, Ben M. Unity in Diversity. 102p. (C). 1991. lib. bdg. 36.00 (*0-8191-8314-8*) U Pr of Amer.

Carter, Benjamin F. & Carpenter, Jason D. History of Woodbury: From 1681 to 1936. With Biographical Sketches. (Illus.). 184p. 1997. reprint ed. pap. 24.00 (*0-8328-6885-X*); reprint ed. lib. bdg. 32.00 (*0-8328-6884-1*) Higginson Bk Co.

Carter, Benjamin H. Improving Staff Productivity: Great Ideas to Increase Profits. 113p. 1999. pap. 16.95 (*1-55571-456-0*, ISPRP, Oasis Pr) PSI Resch.

Carter, Bernadette, ed. Manual of Paediatric Intensive Care Nursing. LC 92-49068. 1993. 63.75 (*1-56593-042-8*, 0290) Thomson Learn.

— Perspectives on Pain: Mapping the Territory. (An Arnold Publication). (Illus.). 336p. 1998. pap. text 37.50 (*0-340-69254-5*) OUP.

Carter, Bernadette, et al. Child Health Care Nursing: Concepts, Theory & Practice. (Illus.). 800p. 1995. pap. 44.95 (*0-632-03689-3*) Blackwell Sci.

Carter, Bernie E., jt. auth. see Bull, Evelyn L.

Carter, Bette. Going It Alone: A Devotional Walk Through Philippians Without Your Spouse. LC 89-82582. 107p. 1990. pap. 3.25 (*0-88243-649-X*, 02-0649) Gospel Pub.

Carter, Betty. Best Books for Young Adults: The Selection, the History, the Romance. LC 94-2640. 214p. (Orig.). 1994. pap. 28.00 (*0-8389-3439-0*, 3439-0-2045) ALA.

Carter, Betty & Peters, Joan K. Love, Honor & Negotiate: Making Your Marriage Work. 320p. 1996. 23.00 (*0-671-89624-5*) PB.

— Marriage Ain't Easy: Love, Honor & Negotiate Your Way to Happiness. 352p. 1997. per. 14.00 (*0-671-89625-3*) PB.

***Carter, Betty, et al.** Best Books for Young Adults. 2nd ed. LC 00-35583. (Illus.). (YA). 2000. pap. write for info. (*0-8389-3501-X*) ALA.

Carter, Betty S. I Read It in the Wordless Book: A Novel. LC 95-39834. (Literary Fiction Ser.). 400p. (YA). (gr. 10). 1996. pap. 13.99 (*0-8010-5558-X*) Baker Bks.

— The Tower, the Mask & the Grave: A Mystery. LC 96-37643. (Orig.). 1997. pap. 12.99 (*0-87788-559-1*, H Shaw Pubs) Waterbrook Pr.

Carter, Betty W. I Can't Hear You in the Dark: How to Learn & Teach Lipreading. LC 97-15088. 226p. 1997. spiral bd. 34.95 (*0-398-06789-9*) C C Thomas.

Carter, Bill. The Late Shift: Letterman. 1996. pap. write for info. (*0-7868-8174-7*) Hyperion.

— The Late Shift: Letterman, Leno & the Network Battle for the Night. (Illus.). 336p. (J). 1995. pap. 12.45 (*0-7868-8089-9*, Pub. by Hyperion) Time Warner.

— The Late Shift: Letterman, Leno & the Network Battle for the Night. (Illus.). 512p. (J). 1996. mass mkt. 5.99 (*0-7868-8907-1*, Pub. by Hyperion) Time Warner.

Carter, Boake. Why Meddle in Europe & the Orient?, 2 vols., Set. 1972. 250.00 (*0-8490-1298-8*) Gordon Pr.

Carter, Bob. Best of Central California: Main Roads & Side Trips. LC 95-36952. (Illus.). 303p. (Orig.). 1995. pap. 14.95 (*1-881409-10-4*) Jhnstn Assocs.

— Food Festivals of Northern California: Traveler's Guide & Cookbook. LC 96-40514. (Illus.). 224p. (Orig.). 1997. pap. 14.95 (*1-56044-527-0*) Falcon Pub Inc.

— Food Festivals of Southern California: Travelers Guide & Cookbook. LC 97-402. (Illus.). 248p. (Orig.). 1997. pap. 14.95 (*1-56044-528-9*) Falcon Pub Inc.

***Carter, Bob.** Food Festivals of Texas: A Traveler's Guide & Cookbook. LC 98-50183. (Illus.). 304p. 1999. 14.95 (*1-56044-843-1*) Falcon Pub Inc.

— Realism & Racism: Concepts of Race in Sociological Research. LC 00-42480. (Critical Realism--Interventions Ser.). 2000. pap. write for info. (*0-415-23373-9*) Routledge.

Carter, Bob, jt. auth. see Hobbs, Gail.

***Carter, Bob L.** Joy is Here: Answers to Jealousy & Other Questions. 32p. 2000. pap. 7.99 (*0-9702182-0-6*) Filigreens.

Carter, Bonnie E. & Skates, Craig. The Rinehart Handbook for Writers. 800p. (C). 1990. teacher ed. write for info. (*0-03-032748-2*) Harcourt Coll Pubs.

— The Rinehart Handbook for Writers. 2nd ed. 800p. (C). 1990. teacher ed. write for info. (*0-03-032754-7*); disk. write for info. (*0-318-69144-2*) Harcourt Coll Pubs.

— The Rinehart Handbook for Writers. 2nd annot. ed. 800p. (C). 1990. text, teacher ed. write for info. (*0-03-032747-4*) Harcourt Coll Pubs.

Carter, Bonnie F., jt. ed. see Ginsburg, Benson E.

Carter, Brian. State Government in Iowa. 5th ed. Institute of Public Affairs Staff, ed. (Illus.). 1990. pap. text 7.00 (*0-317-02886-3*) U Iowa IPA.

Carter, Brian, jt. auth. see Wright, Frank Lloyd.

Carter, Brian, ed. see Diamond, A. J. & Donald Schmitt & Company Staff.

Carter, Brian, ed. see Patkau Architects Staff.

Carter, Brian J., jt. auth. see Bement, Leland C.

Carter, C. & Carter, S. A Genealogy of the Descendants of Samuel & Thomas, Sons of Rev. Samuel Carter, 1640-1886. 272p. 1989. reprint ed. pap. 41.00 (*0-8328-1315-X*); reprint ed. lib. bdg. 49.00 (*0-8328-1314-1*) Higginson Bk Co.

Carter, C. Allen. Kenneth Burke & the Scapegoat Process. LC 95-39958. (Oklahoma Project for Discourse & Theory Ser.: Vol. 17). 192p. (C). 1996. 34.95 (*0-8061-2824-0*, 2824) U of Okla Pr.

— Kenneth Burke & the Scapegoat Process. LC 95-39958. (Oklahoma Project for Discourse & Theory Ser.: Vol. 17). 192p. 1997. pap. 14.95 (*0-8061-2864-X*) U of Okla Pr.

***Carter, C. B., et al, eds.** Interfacial Engineering for Optimized Properties II Vol. 586: Materials Research Society Symposium Proceedings. 2000. text 90.00 (*1-55899-494-7*) Materials Res.

Carter, C. Barry, jt. auth. see Williams, David B.

Carter, C. E. Astrological Aspects. 1993. 15.00 (*0-86690-420-4*, C1034-014) Am Fed Astrologers.

— Essays of Foundation of Astrology. 1976. 15.95 (*0-7229-5131-0*) Theos Pub Hse.

— Zodiac & the Soul. 1972. 59.95 (*0-8490-1349-6*) Gordon Pr.

Carter, C. F. The Wedding Day in Literature & Art. 1972. 59.95 (*0-8490-1280-5*) Gordon Pr.

Carter, C. F. & Ford, J. L., eds. Uncertainty & Expectations in Economics: Essays in Honour of G. L. S. Shackle. LC 72-184239. ix, 299p. 1972. lib. bdg. 45.00 (*0-678-06277-3*) Kelley.

Carter, C. L., Jr. Quality Assurance, Quality Control & Inspection Handbook. 5th ed. LC 78-78394. (Illus.). 212p. 1991. pap. 16.50 (*1-879519-09-7*) C L Carter.

Carter, C. M. Redington: John Redington of Topsfield, Mass. & Some of His Descendants, with Notes on the Wales Family. Leach, J. G., ed. (Illus.). 86p. 1994. reprint ed. pap. 17.00 (*0-8328-4375-X*); reprint ed. lib. bdg. 27.00 (*0-8328-4374-1*) Higginson Bk Co.

Carter, C. Sue, et al, eds. The Integrative Neurobiology of Affiliation: Proceedings of a New York Academy of Sciences Conference, March 14-17, 1996, Vol. 807. LC 97-4325. 1996. 110.00 (*1-57331-058-1*) NY Acad Sci.

Carter, C. Sue, et al. The Integrative Neurobiology of Affiliation: Proceedings of a New York Academy of Sciences Conference, March 14-17, 1996. LC 97-4325. (Annals of the New York Academy of Sciences Ser.). 1997. pap. 110.00 (*1-57331-059-X*) NY Acad Sci.

Carter, Carmen. The Devil's Heart. Ryan, Kevin, ed. (Star Trek: The Next Generation Ser.). 320p. 1994. reprint ed. per. 5.99 (*0-671-79426-4*, Pocket Star Bks) PB.

— Dreams of the Raven. (Star Trek Ser.: No. 34). 1991. mass mkt. 5.50 (*0-671-74356-2*) PB.

Carter, Carol. Keys to Science Success. LC 99-30050. (Illus.). 332p. (C). 1999. pap. text 30.00 (*0-13-013305-1*) P-H.

— Majoring in High School: Survival Tips for Students. LC 94-41603. 224p. (Orig.). (gr. 7-12). 1995. pap. 10.00 (*0-374-52430-0*, Noonday) FS&G.

— Majoring in the Rest of Your Life: Career Secrets for College Students. rev. ed. LC 95-8346. 244p. 1995. pap. 10.00 (*0-374-52451-3*) FS&G.

***Carter, Carol.** Majoring in the Rest of Your Life: Career Secrets for College Students. 3rd rev. ed. LC 98-46504. (Illus.). 288p. 1999. pap. text 13.00 (*0-374-52602-8*) FS&G.

Carter, Carol, ed. Majoring in the Rest of Your Life. LC 99-15634. (Illus.). 332p. (C). 1999. pap. text 30.67 (*0-13-013154-7*) P-H.

***Carter, Carol & Bishop.** Keys to Effective Learning. 2nd ed. LC 99-39279. (Illus.). 544p. 1999. pap. text 32.67 (*0-13-012882-1*) P-H.

***Carter, Carol & Bishop, Joyce.** Keys to Preparing for College. 208p. 2000. pap. write for info. (*0-13-030806-4*) P-H.

***Carter, Carol & Block, Judy.** Corporate Skills Training Database: Achieving Success in Business. 288p. 1999. pap. 39.99 (*0-13-087400-0*) P-H.

Carter, Carol & Izumo, Gary. The Career Tool Kit: Skills for Success. 2nd ed. LC 97-37961. 316p. (C). 1997. pap. text 27.20 (*0-13-754359-X*) P-H.

***Carter, Carol & Izumo, Gary.** The Career Toolkit: Skills for Success. 3rd ed. 288p. 2000. pap. write for info. (*0-13-088418-9*) P-H.

— The Career Toolkit High School Students. 272p. 2000. pap. write for info. (*0-13-088417-0*) P-H.

Carter, Carol & June, Gary. Graduating into the Nineties: Getting the Most Out of Your First Job after College. LC 92-21945. 208p. 1993. 10.00 (*0-374-52359-2*) FS&G.

***Carter, Carol & Katz.** Keys to Nursing Success. 300p. 2000. pap. 25.33 (*0-13-019575-8*) P-H.

Carter, Carol & Kravits, Sarah. Keys to Effective Learning. 1997. pap. text 30.60 (*0-13-632191-7*) P-H.

— Keys to Success: How to Achieve Your Goals. 2nd ed. LC 97-25898. 425p. (C). 1997. pap. text 32.00 (*0-13-861089-4*) P-H.

Carter, Carol & Ozee, Carol. Keys to Career Success. LC 97-11419. 274p. 1997. pap. text 32.40 (*0-13-834277-6*) P-H.

Carter, Carol, et al. Keys to Success: How to Achieve Your Goals. 3rd ed. 464p. (C). 2000. pap. 30.67 (*0-13-012883-X*) P-H.

***Carter, Carol, et al.** Keys to Thinking & Learning: Creating Options & Opportunities. LC 99-48078. 329p. 2000. 26.67 (*0-13-086910-4*) P-H.

Carter, Carol, ed. see Katz, Janet R.

Carter, Carolle J. Mission to Yenan: American Liaison with the Chinese Communists, 1944-1947. LC 96-53110. (Illus.). 296p. 1997. 39.95 (*0-8131-2015-2*) U Pr of Ky.

— The Shamrock & the Swastika: German Espionage in Ireland in World War II. LC 76-14103. (Illus.). 287p. 1977. 23.95 (*0-87015-221-1*) Pacific Bks.

Carter, Carolyn L. Pennsylvania Consumer Law. 460p. 1999. ring bd. 95.00 (*1-887024-18-2*) Bisel Co.

Carter, Catherine, et al. The Healthy Home: Consumer Guide for Utah: Step-by-Step Guide for the Builder & Homeowner on the Principles of Healthy Home Building & Remodeling. (Healthy Home Ser.). 218p. 1996. pap. 24.95 (*0-9647263-0-0*) IHHE.

Carter, Cecile E. Caddo Indians: Where We Come From. LC 95-3395. (Illus.). 432p. 1995. 34.95 (*0-8061-2747-3*) U of Okla Pr.

Carter Center of Emory University Staff, jt. auth. see National Democratic Institute for International Af.

Carter, Charles. The Personal Social Services in an Unsuccessful Economy. (Younghusband Lectures: 1980). 1981. 25.00 (*0-7855-0835-X*, Pub. by Natl Inst Soc Work) St Mut.

Carter, Charles & Carter, Kimya M. Impact: A Book of Poetry. (Illus.). 50p. (Orig.). Date not set. pap. write for info. (*0-9648159-4-X*) Grampa C Pubns.

Carter, Charles & Meyers, Carol L., eds. Community, Identity, & Ideology: Social-Scientific Approaches to the Hebrew Bible. 1996. text 37.95 (*1-57506-005-1*) Eisenbrauns.

Carter, Charles, jt. auth. see Hardie, Martin.

Carter, Charles C. The Best of George Clinton. (Masters of Funk Ser.: Vol. 3). (Illus.). 92p. 1998. mass mkt. 24.95 (*1-888885-31-9*, JPMC-1507) JPMC.

Carter, Charles C., contrib. by. Stomp (Remix) Recorded by God's Property from Kirk Franklin's Nu Nation: Stomp. (Illus.). 8p. 1997. mass mkt. 3.95 (*1-888885-30-0*, JPMC-1506) JPMC.

Carter, Charles E. The Astrological Aspects. 190p. 1996. reprint ed. spiral bd. 15.00 (*0-7873-0160-4*) Hlth Research.

***Carter, Charles E.** The Emergence of Yehud in the Persian Period: A Social & Demographic Study. LC 99-491962. (Journal for the Study of the Old Testament Supplement Ser.: No. 294). 392p. 1999. 85.00 (*1-84127-012-1*, Pub. by Sheffield Acad) CUP Services.

Carter, Charles E. An Introduction to Political Astrology. (Illus.). 103p. 1999. pap. 11.95 (*0-8464-4949-8*) Beekman Pubs.

An Asterisk (*) at the beginning of an entry indicates that the title is appearing for the first time.

— Symbolic Directions in Modern Astrology. 88p. 1996. reprint ed. spiral bd. 9.00 (*0-7873-0159-0*) Hlth Research.

Carter, Charles F. Stories of the Old Missions of California. LC 71-116945. (Short Story Index Reprint Ser.). 1977. 17.95 (*0-8369-3447-4*) Ayer.

— The Wedding Day in Literature & Art: A Collection of the Best Descriptions of Wedding from the Works of the World's Leading Novelists & Poets. rev. ed. LC 89-71340. (Illus.). xii, 294p. 1990. reprint ed. lib. bdg. 38.00 (*1-55888-923-X*) Omnigraphics Inc.

Carter, Charles F., et al. The Measurement of Production Movements. LC 50-7304. (University of Cambridge, Dept. of Applied Economics, Occasional Papers: 1). 143p. reprint ed. pap. 40.80 (*0-608-12257-2*, 2024435) Bks Demand.

Carter, Charles F., jt. auth. see Barritt, Denis P.

Carter, Charles H., et al. Living with the Lake Erie Shore. LC 87-5398. (Living with the Shore Ser.). (Illus.). 276p. 1987. pap. 18.95 (*0-8223-0741-3*) Duke.

Carter, Charles W. As They Prayed: Great Bible Prayers. 1991. pap. 7.99 (*0-88019-275-5*) Schmul Pub Co.

— A Contemporary Wesleyan Theology, 2 vols., Set. 1992. reprint ed. pap. 48.99 (*0-88019-291-7*) Schmul Pub Co.

— From Revival to Evangelism. 1986. pap. 11.99 (*0-88019-205-4*) Schmul Pub Co.

— The Person & Ministry of the Holy Spirit. pap. 15.99 (*0-88019-094-9*) Schmul Pub Co.

Carter, Charles W., et al, eds. Contemporary Wesleyan Theology, 2 vols. 1200p. 1983. 46.95 (*0-310-45650-9*, 11626) Zondervan.

Carter, Charles W., Jr., et al, eds. Macromolecular Crystallography, Pt. B. (Methods in Enzymology Ser.: Vol. 277). (Illus.). 664p. 1997. text 99.95 (*0-12-182178-1*) Morgan Kaufmann.

Carter, Charles W. & Caldwell, Wayne E., eds. The Genius of the New Testament Church. unabridged ed. 251p. (Orig.). 1995. pap. 16.99 (*0-88019-334-4*) Schmul Pub Co.

Carter, Charles W. & Earle, Ralph. The Acts of the Apostles. 1988. pap. 10.99 (*0-88019-050-7*) Schmul Pub Co.

Carter, Charles W. & Thompson, R. Duane. The Biblical Ethic of Love. LC 90-35440. (American University Studies: Theology & Religion: Ser. VII, Vol. 79). XV, 250p. (C). 1990. text 51.95 (*0-8204-1365-8*) P Lang Pubng.

Carter, Charles W., jt. ed. see Bricogne, Gerard.

Carter, Charlotte. Coq au Vin: A Nanette Hayes Mystery. LC 98-22565. (Nanette Hayes Mystery Ser.). 200p. 1999. 22.00 (*0-89296-678-5*, Pub. by Mysterious Pr) Little.

— Coq au Vin: A Nanette Hayes Mystery. 224p. 2000. mass mkt. 6.50 (*0-446-60787-8*, Pub. by Warner Bks) Little.

— Drumsticks: A Nanette Hayes Mystery. LC 99-47073. 208p. 2000. 22.95 (*0-89296-679-3*, Pub. by Mysterious Pr) Little.

— Personal Effects. 92p. (Orig.). 1991. pap. 6.00 (*0-935992-16-2*) United Art Bks.

— Rhode Island Red. LC 96-71368. (Mask Noir Ser.). 176p. 1998. pap. 12.99 (*1-85242-591-1*) Serpents Tail.

— Rhode Island Red. 208p. 1999. mass mkt. 5.99 (*0-446-60664-2*, Pub. by Warner Bks) Little.

— Rhode Island Red, Vol. 1. LC 96-71368. (Mask Noir Ser.). 250p. 1997. 15.99 (*1-85242-564-4*, High Risk Bks) Serpents Tail.

Carter, Cheryl J., jt. auth. see McFarland, Peggy A.

Carter, Chris. The Art of the X-Files. LC 98-17943. (Illus.). 176p. 1998. 35.00 (*0-06-105037-7*, HarperPrism) HarpC.

Carter, Chris. Enfrentate Al Futuro. 1990. pap. text 7.95 (*84-241-3076-6*) Everest SP.

Carter, Chris. The X Files Encyclopedia. 2000. pap. 15.00 (*0-06-107310-5*) HarpC.

— The X-Files Film Novel. (Illus.). 224p. 1998. mass mkt. 5.99 (*0-06-105932-3*) HarpC.

— X-Files Film Novel The. (Illus.). 192p. 1998. 23.00 (*0-06-105067-9*) HarpC.

Carter, Chris, adapted by. X-Files Film Novel Adapted for Young Readers: Adapted for Young Readers. (Illus.). 160p. (J). (gr. 3-7). 1998. mass mkt. 3.99 (*0-06-105934-X*) HarpC.

Carter, Chris, creator. Goblins/Whirlwind. LC 96-15077. (X-Files Ser.). 416p. 1996. pap. 12.00 (*0-06-105347-3*, HarperPrism) HarpC.

***Carter, Chris & Spotnitz, Frank.** X-Files Feature Film Novel: Neville,&John, Set. abr. ed. 1998. audio 18.00 (*0-694-51964-2*, CC08R) HarperAudio.

Carter, Chris J., ed. Neuropharmacology of Polyamines. (Neuroscience Perspectives Ser.). (Illus.). 336p. 1994. text, boxed set 83.00 (*0-12-161640-1*) Acad Pr.

Carter, Christal. Holiday Happenings. LC 86-51627. (Illus.). 80p. (Orig.). 1999. reprint ed. pap. 18.95 (*0-943574-42-0*) Martingale & Co.

Carter, Christine. The Cairn Terrier, AKC Rank No. 45. (Illus.). 224p. 1996. 47.95 (*0-7938-0189-3*, TS216) TFH Pubns.

Carter, Christine, ed. The Other Side of Silence: Women Tell about Their Experiences with Date Rape. 257p. 1995. 19.95 (*0-9627671-9-0*) Avocus Pub.

Carter, Christine J., ed. The Diary of Dolly Lunt Burge, 1848-1879. LC 96-19304. 1997. 40.00 (*0-8203-1863-9*) U of Ga Pr.

Carter, Clarence E. Great Britain & the Illinois Country, 1763-1774. LC 79-164594. (Select Bibliographies Reprint Ser.). 1977. reprint ed. 21.95 (*0-8369-5878-0*) Ayer.

Carter, Clarence E., ed. Territorial Papers of the United States, 26 vols. in 25. LC 76-38840. reprint ed. lib. bdg. 3465.00 (*0-404-01450-X*) AMS Pr.

— Territorial Papers of the United States. General Introduction to the Series., Vols. 1 & 2. reprint ed. 138.60 (*0-404-01451-8*) AMS Pr.

— The Territory Northwest of the River Ohio, 1787-1803. (Territorial Papers of the United States: Vol. 3). reprint ed. 138.60 (*0-404-01453-4*) AMS Pr.

— The Territory of Alabama, 1817-1819. (Territorial Papers of the United States: Vol. 18). reprint ed. 138.60 (*0-404-01468-2*) AMS Pr.

— The Territory of Arkansas, 1819-1825. (Territorial Papers of the United States: Vol. 19). reprint ed. 138.60 (*0-404-01469-0*) AMS Pr.

— The Territory of Arkansas, 1825-1829. (Territorial Papers of the United States: Vol. 20). reprint ed. 138.60 (*0-404-01470-4*) AMS Pr.

— The Territory of Arkansas, 1829-1836. (Territorial Papers of the United States: Vol. 21). reprint ed. 138.60 (*0-404-01471-2*) AMS Pr.

— The Territory of Florida, 1834-1839. (Territorial Papers of the United States: Vol. 25). reprint ed. 138.60 (*0-404-01475-5*) AMS Pr.

— The Territory of Florida, 1839-1845. (Territorial Papers of the United States: Vol. 26). reprint ed. 138.60 (*0-404-01476-3*) AMS Pr.

— The Territory of Florida, 1828-1834. (Territorial Papers of the United States: Vol. 24). reprint ed. 138.60 (*0-404-01474-7*) AMS Pr.

— The Territory of Florida, 1824-1828. (Territorial Papers of the United States: Vol. 23). reprint ed. 138.60 (*0-404-01473-9*) AMS Pr.

— The Territory of Florida, 1821-1825. (Territorial Papers of the United States: Vol. 22). reprint ed. 138.60 (*0-404-01472-0*) AMS Pr.

— The Territory of Illinois, 1814-1818. (Territorial Papers of the United States: Vol. 17). reprint ed. 138.60 (*0-404-01467-4*) AMS Pr.

— The Territory of Illinois, 1809-1814. (Territorial Papers of the United States: Vol. 16). reprint ed. 138.60 (*0-404-01466-6*) AMS Pr.

— The Territory of Indiana, 1800-1810. (Territorial Papers of the United States: Vol. 7). reprint ed. 138.60 (*0-404-01457-7*) AMS Pr.

— The Territory of Indiana, 1810-1816. (Territorial Papers of the United States: Vol. 8). reprint ed. 138.60 (*0-404-01458-5*) AMS Pr.

— The Territory of Louisiana-Missouri, 1806-1814. (Territorial Papers of the United States: Vol. 14). reprint ed. 138.60 (*0-404-01464-X*) AMS Pr.

— The Territory of Louisiana-Missouri, 1815-1821. (Territorial Papers of the United States: Vol. 15). reprint ed. 138.60 (*0-404-01465-8*) AMS Pr.

— The Territory of Louisiana-Missouri, 1803-1806. (Territorial Papers of the United States: Vol. 13). reprint ed. 138.60 (*0-404-01463-1*) AMS Pr.

— The Territory of Michigan, 1805-1820. (Territorial Papers of the United States: Vol. 10). reprint ed. 138.60 (*0-404-01460-7*) AMS Pr.

— The Territory of Michigan, 1829-1837. (Territorial Papers of the United States: Vol. 12). reprint ed. 138.60 (*0-404-01462-3*) AMS Pr.

— The Territory of Michigan, 1820-1829. (Territorial Papers of the United States: Vol. 11). reprint ed. 138.60 (*0-404-01461-5*) AMS Pr.

— The Territory of Mississippi, 1809-1817. (Territorial Papers of the United States: Vol. 6). reprint ed. 138.60 (*0-404-01456-9*) AMS Pr.

— The Territory of Mississippi, 1798-1817. (Territorial Papers of the United States: Vol. 5). reprint ed. 138.60 (*0-404-01455-0*) AMS Pr.

— The Territory of Orleans, 1803-1812. (Territorial Papers of the United States: Vol. 9). reprint ed. 138.60 (*0-404-01459-3*) AMS Pr.

— The Territory South of the River Ohio, 1790-1796. (Territorial Papers of the United States: Vol. 4). reprint ed. 138.60 (*0-404-01454-2*) AMS Pr.

Carter, Claude. Working for a Loser!!!! Crazy Quotes, Jokes & Anecdotes of Corporate Chaos & Calamity. (Illus.). 130p. 1998. mass mkt. 7.95 (*0-9662624-4-1*) alotta edu.

Carter, Colin. Futures & Options Markets Today. (C). 2001. 79.00 (*0-13-598368-1*, Macmillan Coll) P-H.

Carter, Colin A., et al. China's Ongoing Agricultural Reform. LC 96-69840. 120p. (C). 1996. text 36.50 (*0-472-10814-X*, 10814) U of Mich Pr.

Carter, Craig. Your Handbook for Healing. 64p. 1981. pap. 7.95 (*0-911336-86-9*) Sci of Mind.

Carter, Craig, ed. Hockey Guide: 1998-99 Edition. 336p. 1998. 15.95 (*0-89204-599-X*) Sporting News.

— Official NBA Rules: 1998-99 Edition. 60p. 1998. 6.95 (*0-89204-602-3*) Sporting News.

— Pro Football Guide: 1998 Edition. 392p. 1998. 15.95 (*0-89204-596-5*) Sporting News.

Carter, Craig & Broussard, Mark, eds. Official NBA Guide: 1998-99 Edition. 684p. 1998. 15.95 (*0-89204-600-7*) Sporting News.

Carter, Craig, ed. see Sporting News Staff.

Carter, Craig A., ed. Property & Casualty General Insurance Primer. rev. ed. LC 95-61702. 240p. 1999. pap. text 24.95 (*1-884803-05-9*) Werbel Pub.

Carter, Craig R. Ethical Issues in Sourcing. LC 98-198507. 1998. write for info. (*0-945968-32-9*) Ctr Advanced Purchasing.

Carter, Curtis L., et al, eds. Skepticism & Moral Principles: Modern Ethics in Review. 28.95 (*0-913750-17-4*); pap. 9.95 (*0-685-04143-3*) Precednt Pub.

***Carter, Curtis L., et al.** Children in Art: A Century of Change LC 98-83162. 84p. 1999. write for info. (*0-945366-06-X*) MU Haggerty Mus.

Carter, Curtis L., et al. Matta: Surrealism & Beyond. LC 97-74576. 80 p. 1997. write for info. (*0-945366-03-5*) MU Haggerty Mus.

Carter, Cynthia, et al. News, Gender, & Power. LC 98-12179. (Illus.). 296p. (C). 1998. 75.00 (*0-415-17015-X*) Routledge.

— News, Gender, & Power. LC 98-12179. (Illus.). 296p. (C). 1998. pap. 24.99 (*0-415-17016-8*) Routledge.

Carter, D. Bruce. Psychology: The Foundations of Human Behavior Student Manual. 100p. (C). 1994. per. 8.95 (*0-8403-8974-4*) Kendall-Hunt.

Carter, D. Bruce, ed. Current Conceptions of Sex Roles & Sex Typing: Theory & Research. LC 87-13157. 273p. 1987. 69.50 (*0-275-92430-0*, C2430, Praeger Pubs) Greenwood.

Carter, D. C., et al. Atlas of General Surgery. 3rd ed. (Illus.). 1208p. 1996. text 100.00 (*0-412-72090-6*, Pub. by E A) OUP.

Carter, D. M., jt. ed. see Lin, A. N.

Carter, D. N. Robert Graves: The Lasting Poetic Achievement. LC 88-29245. 256p. (C). 1989. lib. bdg. 44.00 (*0-389-20818-3*) B&N Imports.

Carter, Dale, ed. Cracking the Ike Age: Aspects of Fifties America. (Dolphin Ser.: No. 23). (Illus.). 280p. (C). 1993. pap. 19.95 (*87-7288-373-1*, Pub. by Aarhus Univ Pr) David Brown.

Carter, Dale, tr. see Montemayor, Carlos.

Carter, Dan T. From George Wallace to Newt Gingrich: Race in the Conservative Counterrevolution, 1963-1994. LC 96-28201. 144p. 1996. 22.95 (*0-8071-2118-5*) La State U Pr.

— From George Wallace to Newt Gingrich: Race in the Conservative Counterrevolution, 1963-1994. LC 96-28201. 152p. 1999. pap. 14.95 (*0-8071-2366-8*) La State U Pr.

— George Wallace, Richard Nixon & the Transformation of American Politics. LC 92-81465. (Charles Edmondson Historical Lectures). 51p. (Orig.). 1992. pap. text 5.95 (*0-918954-58-4*) Baylor Univ Pr.

— The Politics of Rage: George Wallace, the Origins of the New Conservatism, & the Transformation of American Politics. LC 95-31477. (Illus.). 592p. 1996. pap. 17.95 (*0-8071-2113-4*) La State U Pr.

***Carter, Dan T.** The Politics of Rage: George Wallace, the Origins of the New Conservatism & the Transformation of American Politics. 2nd rev. ed. LC 99-54330. (Illus.). 608p. 2000. pap. 17.95 (*0-8071-2597-0*) La State U Pr.

Carter, Dan T. Scottsboro: Tragedy of the American South. rev. ed. LC 79-1090. (Illus.). 512p. 1979. pap. text 16.95 (*0-8071-0498-1*) La State U Pr.

— When the War Was Over: The Failure of Self-Reconstruction in the South, 1865-1867. LC 84-21315. 285p. 1985. pap. text 17.95 (*0-8071-1204-6*) La State U Pr.

Carter, Dan T., ed. see Mayo, Amory D.

Carter, Danella. Down-Home Wholesome: 300 Low-Fat Recipes from a New Soul Kitchen. 304p. 1998. pap. 15.95 (*0-452-27325-0*) NAL.

Carter, Daniel L., jt. auth. see Clark, John G.

Carter, Daniel R. Writing Localizable Software for the Macintosh. (C). 1991. pap. text 26.95 (*0-201-57013-0*) Addison-Wesley.

Carter, Daniela B., jt. auth. see Pease, Antonella.

Carter, Darerca. The Irish Language: An Informal History. 96p. (Orig.). 1997. pap. 11.95 (*0-9635738-1-0*) Irish Bks NY.

Carter, Darryl. Interpretation of Breast Biopsies. 3rd ed. LC 95-42587. (Biopsy Interpretation Ser.). 368p. 1996. text 102.00 (*0-397-51649-5*) Lppncott W & W.

Carter, Darryl & Patchefsky, Arthur S. Tumors & Tumor-Like Lesions of the Lung. LC 97-23526. (Illus.). 448p. (C). 1998. text 85.00 (*0-7216-3312-9*, W B Saunders Co) Harcrt Hlth Sci Grp.

Carter, David. Alpha Bugs. LC 94-235935. (Illus.). 26p. (J). (ps-2). 1994. 16.95 (*0-671-86631-1*) Litle Simon.

— Butterflies & Moths. LC 91-58221. (Eyewitness Handbooks Ser.). (Illus.). 304p. 1992. 29.95 (*1-56458-034-2*); pap. 18.95 (*1-56458-062-8*) DK Pub Inc.

— Butterflies & Moths in Britin & Europe. (Illus.). 192p. (Orig.). 1982. pap. 39.50 (*0-330-26642-X*, Pub. by Pan) Trans-Atl Phila.

— The Complete Book of Paint. LC 96-1177. 208p. 1996. 40.00 (*0-517-70451-X*) C Potter.

— George Santayana: Spanish Philosopher & Poet. (Hispanics of Achievement Ser.). (Illus.). 120p. (YA). (gr. 5 up). 1992. lib. bdg. 19.95 (*0-7910-1254-9*) Chelsea Hse.

— Hepatobiliary & Pancreatic Surgery. 5th ed. 1996. text 200.00 (*0-412-61930-X*, Pub. by E A) OUP.

— How to Write a Play. 192p. 1999. pap. 12.95 (*0-8442-0231-2*, 02312, Natl Textbk Co) NTC Contemp Pub Co.

— Judah Waten: Selected Works. LC 99-211194. 1998. pap. 24.95 (*0-7022-2859-1*, Pub. by Univ Queensland Pr) Intl Spec Bk.

— The Rolling Stones. (Illus.). 64p. 1994. write for info. (*1-57215-034-3*) World Pubns.

— Stinky Bugs. LC 99-166551. (Illus.). 12p. (J). (ps-1). 1998. 9.99 (*0-689-81866-1*) S&S Childrens.

Carter, David, creator. Finger Bugs Love Bug. (Finger Bugs Ser.). (Illus.). (J). (ps-3). 1997. 5.99 (*0-689-81738-X*) S&S Childrens.

Carter, David & O'Neil, Marnie H., eds. International Perspectives on Educational Reform & Policy Implementation, Vol. 1. 210p. 1995. 85.00 (*0-7507-0406-3*, Falmer Pr) Taylor & Francis.

Carter, David & O'Neill, Marnie H., eds. International Perspectives on Educational Reform & Policy Implementation, Vol. 1. 210p. 1995. pap. 27.95 (*0-7507-0407-1*, Falmer Pr) Taylor & Francis.

Carter, David, et al. The State of Police Education: Policy Direction for the 21st Century. LC 89-60695. 172p. (Orig.). (C). 1988. pap. text 11.50 (*1-878734-00-8*) Police Exec Res.

Carter, David, jt. auth. see Davis, Don.

Carter, David, jt. ed. see Hudson, Wayne.

Carter, David A. Bugs at Play. LC 99-165362. (Illus.). 12p. (J). (ps-k). 1997. 4.99 (*0-689-81344-9*) Atheneum Yung Read.

— Bugs at Work. (Illus.). 12p. (J). (ps-k). 1997. 4.99 (*0-689-81345-7*) Atheneum Yung Read.

— Bugs in Space: A Pop-Journey. LC 98-114644. (Illus.). 16p. (J). (ps-2). 1997. per. 14.95 (*0-689-81430-5*) Litle Simon.

— Bugs on the Go. (Illus.). 12p. (J). (ps-k). 1997. 4.99 (*0-689-81346-5*) Atheneum Yung Read.

— Bugs That Go Bump in the Night. (Illus.). 16p. (J). (ps-3). 1996. per. 14.95 (*0-689-80120-3*) S&S Bks Yung.

— Busy Bugs, Lazy Bugs. LC 99-165363. (Illus.). 12p. (J). (ps-k). 1997. 4.99 (*0-689-81347-3*) Atheneum Yung Read.

— Colors. (Bug Bks.). (Illus.). 14p. (J). (ps up). 1993. pap. 4.95 (*0-671-86875-6*) Litle Simon.

— Counting. (Bug Bks.). (Illus.). 14p. (J). (ps up). 1993. pap. 4.95 (*0-671-86876-4*) Litle Simon.

— The Elements of Pop-Up: A Pop-Up Book for Aspiring Paper Engineers. (Illus.). (YA). (gr. 3 up). 1999. per. 34.95 (*0-689-82224-3*) Litle Simon.

— Feely Bugs. LC 96-110934. (Illus.). 12p. (J). (ps-2). 1995. per. 13.95 (*0-689-80119-X*) Litle Simon.

— Finger Bugs: Frog Bug. (Illus.). (J). 1996. 5.99 (*0-689-81110-1*) S&S Childrens.

— Finger Bugs: Saw Bug. (Illus.). (J). 1996. 5.99 (*0-689-81111-X*) S&S Childrens.

— Finger Bugs Dracubug. (Finger Bugs Ser.). (Illus.). (J). 1997. mass mkt. 5.99 (*0-689-81737-1*) S&S Childrens.

***Carter, David A.** Giggle Bugs: A Lift-&-Laugh Book. (gr. k-3). 1999. per. 12.95 (*0-689-82717-2*) S&S Childrens.

Carter, David A. Giggle Bugs: A Lift-And-Laugh Book. (Illus.). 10p. (J). (ps-2). 1999. 12.95 (*0-689-81859-9*) S&S Childrens.

— Glitter Bugs: Make 6 Fab Bugs. (Illus.). 16p. (J). (ps-3). 1998. 7.99 (*0-689-81857-2*) S&S Childrens.

— How Many Bugs in a Box? (Illus.). 20p. (J). (ps-1). 1988. 13.95 (*0-671-64965-5*) S&S Bks Yung.

— If You'Re Happy & You Know It, Clap Your Hands! (Illus.). 16p. 1997. 14.95 (*0-590-93828-2*, Cartwheel) Scholastic Inc.

— I'm Shy: A Bashful Little Pop up Book. (Illus.). 14p. (J). (ps-1). 1993. pap. 7.95 (*0-671-72925-X*) S&S Trade.

— In a Dark, Dark Wood: An Old Tale with a New Twist. (Illus.). 28p. (J). (ps-3). 1991. 10.95 (*0-671-74134-9*) S&S Bks Yung.

— In & Out. (Bug Bks.). (Illus.). 14p. (J). (ps-k). 1993. pap. 4.95 (*0-671-86630-3*) Litle Simon.

Carter, David A. Jingle Bugs. (Illus.). 20p. (J). (gr. 4-6). 1992. per. 16.95 (*0-671-72924-1*) Litle Simon.

Carter, David A. Lazy Bugs. (Busy Bug Board Bks.). (J). (ps-k). 1997. bds. 4.99 (*0-614-29109-7*) Litle Simon.

— Love Bugs. LC 95-141692. (Bug Bks. : No. 1). (Illus.). 10p. (J). (ps-2). 1995. per. 12.95 (*0-671-86629-X*) Litle Simon.

— More Bugs in Boxes. (Illus.). 20p. (J). (ps-1). 1990. 13.95 (*0-671-69577-0*) S&S Trade.

— Opposites. (Bug Bks.). (Illus.). 14p. (J). (ps up). 1993. pap. 4.95 (*0-671-86877-2*) Litle Simon.

— Says Who? Pop up Book. (Illus.). 10p. (J). (ps-2). 1993. pap. 13.95 (*0-671-72923-3*) S&S Bks Yung.

— Says Who? Pop up Book. (J). 1999. per. 13.95 (*0-689-81864-5*) S&S Childrens.

— Sticker Bugs: Colors & Shapes. (Sticker Bugs Ser.). 20p. (J). (ps-1). 1996. 6.99 (*0-689-81042-3*) S&S Childrens.

— Sticker Bugs: Numbers. (Sticker Bugs Ser.). 12p. (J). 1996. 6.99 (*0-689-81041-5*) S&S Childrens.

***Carter, David A.** The 12 Bugs of Christmas: A Pop Up Christmas Counting Book. (Illus.). 26p. (J). (ps-k). 1999. per. 14.95 (*0-689-83104-8*) Litle Simon.

Carter, David A. What's in My Pocket? A Pop-Up & Peek-In Book. (Illus.). 10p. (J). (ps). 1989. 10.95 (*0-399-21685-5*, G P Putnam) Peng Put Young Read.

Carter, David A., et al, eds. Selecting, Preparing, & Developing the School District Superintendent. 176p. 1993. 85.00 (*0-7507-0170-6*, Falmer Pr); pap. 29.95 (*0-7507-0171-4*, Falmer Pr) Taylor & Francis.

Carter, David A., jt. auth. see Carter, Noelle.

Carter, David A., jt. auth. see Lackey, Mercedes.

Carter, David A., jt. ed. see Murphy, David.

Carter, David C., jt. auth. see Trede, M.

Carter, David E. American Corporate Identity, No. 6. LC 85-72864. (Illus.). 264p. 1991. text 42.50 (*0-88108-077-2*) Art Dir.

— American Corporate Identity, No. 10. LC 94-72169. (Illus.). 1994. text 49.95 (*0-88108-149-3*) Art Dir.

— American Corporate Identity, Vol. 11. LC 95-78481. (America Corporate Identity Ser.: No. 11). 1996. 59.95 (*0-88108-155-8*) Art Dir.

— American Corporate Identity 2. 1987. 39.95 (*0-88108-039-X*) Art Dir.

— Best Financial Advertising, No. 2. LC 79-50633. (Illus.). 424p. 1981. 35.00 (*0-910158-74-6*) Art Dir.

— Best Financial Advertising, No. 3. LC 79-50633. (Best Financial Advertising Ser.). 400p. 1984. 35.00 (*0-88108-013-6*) Art Dir.

— Best Financial Advertising, No. 4. 1986. 39.50 (*0-88108-032-2*) Art Dir.

— Branding: The Power of Market Identity. (Illus.). 184p. 1999. pap. text 35.00 (*0-8230-6631-2*) Watsn-Guptill.

— Brochures that Work. 1998. pap. 35.00 (*0-8230-6608-8*) Watsn-Guptill.

C

An Asterisk (*) at the beginning of an entry indicates that the title is appearing for the first time.

— Cool Cards: The Carter Library of Design. 1998. pap. text 35.00 (*0-8230-6604-5*) Watsn-Guptill.

***Carter, David E.** Creating Logo Families. 2000. pap. text 35.00 (*0-688-17975-4*, Hearst) Hearst Commns.

— Dimensional Promotions. (Illus.). 184p. 2000. pap. write for info. (*0-8230-6615-0*) Watsn-Guptill.

Carter, David E. Fun with Fonts. 1997. pap. text 34.95 (*0-8230-6586-3*) Watsn-Guptill.

— Fun with Fonts. (Illus.). 176p. 1997. pap. text 34.95 (*0-8230-1941-1*) Watsn-Guptill.

***Carter, David E.** Giant Graphics. 1999. pap. text 39.95 (*0-688-16927-9*, Hearst) Hearst Commns.

Carter, David E. How to Design Logos on Your Computer. LC 93-71361. (Illus.). 240p. 1993. pap. text 27.50 (*0-88108-117-5*) Art Dir.

— How to Improve Your Corporate Identity. LC 85-72865. 136p. 1986. pap. 12.95 (*0-88108-030-6*) Art Dir.

— Labels & Tags. 1998. pap. 35.00 (*0-8230-6623-1*) Watsn-Guptill.

— Letterheads, No. 3. LC 81-65825. (Illus.). 326p. 1981. 32.50 (*0-910158-71-1*) Art Dir.

— Letterheads, No. 5. LC 78-58439. 342p. 1985. 35.00 (*0-88108-018-7*) Art Dir.

— Letterheads, No. 6. LC 78-640636. 302p. 1987. 39.50 (*0-88108-038-1*) Art Dir.

— Letterheads, No. 7. LC 89-80318. 300p. 1989. 55.00 (*0-88108-065-9*) Art Dir.

— Letterheads Gone Digital. 1998. pap. 39.95 (*0-8230-6624-X*) Watsn-Guptill.

— Letterheads in the 3rd Dimension. (Illus.). 192p. 1997. pap. text 39.95 (*0-8230-2753-8*) Watsn-Guptill.

— LOGO International Two. (Illus.). 260p. 1986. 32.50 (*0-88108-033-0*) Art Dir.

— Logopower: Creating World-Class Logos & Effective Identities. 1998. pap. text 39.95 (*0-8230-6603-7*) Watsn-Guptill.

— Logos of American Restaurants. (Illus.). 176p. 1997. pap. text 35.00 (*0-8230-4541-2*) Watsn-Guptill.

***Carter, David E.** Logos of Bars & Restaurants. (Illus.). 184p. 2000. pap. 35.00 (*0-8230-7351-3*) Watsn-Guptill.

Carter, David E. Logoware: The 35 Best Programs for Creating Digital Logos. 1998. pap. text 35.00 (*0-8230-6602-9*) Watsn-Guptill.

***Carter, David E.** New Big Book of Logos. (Illus.). 384p. 2000. 45.00 (*0-688-17890-1*, Hearst) Hearst Commns.

— Power Packaging. 1999. pap. text 35.00 (*0-8230-4261-8*) Watsn-Guptill.

Carter, David E. Re-Design: Logo & Letterhead Makeovers. 1998. pap. 35.00 (*0-8230-6817-X*) Watsn-Guptill.

***Carter, David E.** 2 Cool Cards. (Illus.). 184p. 2000. pap. write for info. (*0-8230-7478-1*) Watsn-Guptill.

Carter, David E. World Corporate Identity, Vol. 3. LC 93-71473. 192p. 1993. 42.50 (*0-88108-120-5*) Art Dir.

Carter, David E., ed. American Corporate Identity, No. 3. LC 85-72864. 312p. 1988. text 39.95 (*0-88108-048-9*) Art Dir.

— American Corporate Identity, No. 4. LC 85-72864. 332p. 1989. text 39.95 (*0-88108-067-5*) Art Dir.

— American Corporate Identity, No. 5. LC 85-72864. 340p. 1990. text 39.95 (*0-88108-072-1*) Art Dir.

— American Corporate Identity, No. 8. LC 85-72864. 256p. 1992. text 44.95 (*0-88108-106-X*) Art Dir.

— Best Financial Advertising, No. 1. LC 79-50633. (Illus.). 1979. 35.00 (*0-910158-56-8*) Art Dir.

— The Book of American Trade Marks, Vol. 1. LC 72-76493. (Trade Marks Ser.). 1978. reprint ed. 17.50 (*0-88108-110-8*) Art Dir.

— The Book of American Trade Marks, Vol. 2. LC 72-76493. (Trade Marks Ser.). 1978. reprint ed. 18.50 (*0-910158-28-2*) Art Dir.

— The Book of American Trade Marks, Vol. 3. LC 72-76493. (Trade Marks Ser.). 1978. reprint ed. 18.50 (*0-910158-29-0*) Art Dir.

— Book of American Trade Marks, Vol. 4. LC 72-76493. (Illus.). 232p. 1976. 18.50 (*0-910158-30-4*) Art Dir.

— Book of American Trade Marks, Vol. 5. LC 72-76493. (Illus.). 1977. 18.50 (*0-910158-31-2*) Art Dir.

— Book of American Trademarks, Vol. 6. LC 72-76493. (Illus.). 208p. 1991. reprint ed. pap. text 18.50 (*0-88108-098-5*) Art Dir.

— Book of American Trademarks, Vol. 9. LC 72-76493. (Illus.). 1984. 18.50 (*0-88108-020-9*) Art Dir.

— Book of American Trademarks, Vol. 11. 1989. 24.75 (*0-88108-068-3*) Art Dir.

— Book of American Trademarks, Vol. 6. LC 72-76493. (Illus.). 1979. 18.50 (*0-910158-39-8*) Art Dir.

— Book of American Trademarks, Vol. 8. LC 72-76493. (Illus.). 1983. 18.50 (*0-910158-94-0*) Art Dir.

— Book of American Trademarks 10. 1987. 18.50 (*0-88108-034-9*) Art Dir.

— Company Uniforms. (Illus.). 176p. 1997. pap. 35.00 (*0-8230-6151-5*) Watsn-Guptill.

— Corporate Identity Manuals. LC 75-44679. (Illus.). 460p. 1978. reprint ed. 45.00 (*0-910158-33-9*) Art Dir.

— Designing Corporate Symbols. LC 74-29013. (Illus.). 1978. reprint ed. 10.95 (*0-910158-32-0*) Art Dir.

— Evolution of Design. LC 83-73399. 282p. 1985. 39.75 (*0-88108-005-5*) Art Dir.

— International Corporate Design Systems. LC 89-84878. 128p. 1989. text 39.50 (*0-88108-069-1*) Art Dir.

— Letterheads, No. 4. LC 78-58439. (Letterheads Ser.). 304p. 1984. 32.50 (*0-88108-002-0*) Art Dir.

— Letterheads: The International Annual of Letterhead Design, No. 1. LC 78-58439. (Illus.). 1977. 32.50 (*0-910158-42-8*) Art Dir.

— Letterheads: The Second International Annual of Letterhead Design, No. 2. LC 78-58439. (Letterheads Ser.). (Illus.). 1979. 32.50 (*0-910158-57-6*) Art Dir.

— Living Logos. LC 92-74314. (Illus.). 160p. 1993. text 22.95 (*0-88108-107-8*); pap. text 17.50 (*0-88108-108-6*) Art Dir.

— LOGO International One. LC 84-71451. 260p. 1984. 32.50 (*0-88108-012-8*) Art Dir.

— LOGO International Three. LC 84-71451. 192p. 1990. 49.50 (*0-88108-060-8*) Art Dir.

— Logos Go Digital. (Illus.). 176p. 1997. pap. 35.00 (*0-8230-6598-7*) Watsn-Guptill.

— Logos of America's Fastest Growing Corporations. LC 91-76054. (Illus.). 192p. 1992. text 39.50 (*0-88108-096-9*) Art Dir.

— Logos of America's Largest Corporations. LC 88-71637. 180p. 1988. text 39.50 (*0-88108-059-4*) Art Dir.

— Logos of Major World Corporations. LC 89-85962. 160p. 1989. text 39.50 (*0-88108-071-3*) Art Dir.

— World Corporate Identity, No. 1. LC 90-80342. 192p. 1990. text 39.95 (*0-88108-073-X*) Art Dir.

— World Corporate Identity, Vol. 2. LC 90-80342. (Illus.). 192p. 1992. 39.95 (*0-88108-102-7*) Art Dir.

Carter, David E., ed. see Annual of Trade Mark Design Staff.

Carter, David J. Pest Lepidopters of Europe. (Entomologica Ser.). 1984. text 303.50 (*90-6193-504-0*) Kluwer Academic.

Carter, David L. & Radelet, Louis A. The Police & the Community. 6th ed. LC 98-14531. 585p. 1998. 71.00 (*0-13-619677-2*) P-H.

Carter, David L. & Sapp, Allen D. Police Education & Minority Recruitment: The Impact of a College Requirement. LC 90-62532. 27p. (Orig.). 1991. pap. 4.00 (*1-878734-23-7*) Police Exec Res.

Carter, David L., et al. Toy Guns: Involvement in Crime & Encounters with the Police. LC 90-61772. (Illus.). 50p. (Orig.). 1990. pap. 5.50 (*1-878734-21-0*) Police Exec Res.

— Toy Guns: Involvement in Crime & Encounters with the Police. (Illus.). 47p. (Orig.). 1996. reprint ed. pap. text 25.00 (*0-7881-3671-2*) DIANE Pub.

Carter, David L., jt. auth. see Barker, Thomas.

Carter, David L., jt. auth. see Sapp, Allen D.

Carter, David L., jt. ed. see Moriarty, Laura J.

Carter, David M. Keeping Score: An Inside Look at Sports Marketing. Wait, Erin, ed. LC 95-40070. (Successful Business Library). 322p. 1996. pap. 18.95 (*1-55571-377-7*, Oasis Pr) PSI Resch.

— You Can't Play the Game If You Don't Know the Rules: Career Opportunities in Sports Management. LC 93-47435. 1994. pap. 14.95 (*1-57023-005-6*) Impact VA.

Carter, David S. & Vogt, Andrew. Collinearity-Preserving Functions Between Desarguesian Planes. LC 80-20427. (Memoirs Ser.: No. 27/235). 98p. 1980. pap. 16.00 (*0-8218-2235-7*, MEMO/27/235) Am Math.

Carter, David S.G. & O'Neill, Marnie H., eds. Case Studies in Educational Change. LC 94-36894. 1995. pap. 27.95 (*0-7507-0409-8*, Falmer Pr) Taylor & Francis.

Carter, David W. This Is My Life: Life Stories of David Carter As Told to Wanda Kay Steele. LC 96-97106. (Illus.). xix, 83p. (Orig.). 1996. pap. 10.00 (*0-9655009-0-X*) D Carter.

Carter, Davis B. The Story Uncle Minyard Told: A Family's 200-Year Migration Across the South. LC 94-3416. 518p. 1994. 35.00 (*0-87152-484-8*) Reprint.

Carter, Dawn, jt. auth. see Carter, Jonathan.

Carter, Debbie. Impressions: A Textbook Controversy. Kleinfeld, Judith, ed. (Teaching Cases in Cross-Cultural Education Ser.: No. 13). 34p. (Orig.). (C). 1994. pap. text 7.50 (*1-877962-30-9*) Univ AK Ctr CCS.

***Carter, Debra S.** An Eye Opener of Poems. 24p. 1999. pap. 6.00 (*0-8059-4620-9*) Dorrance.

Carter, Dennis. Teaching Poetry in the Primary School: Perspectives for a New Generation. 1998. pap. 25.95 (*1-85346-567-4*) Taylor & Francis.

***Carter, Dennis R. & Beaupre, Gary S.** Skeletal Function & Form: Mechanobiology of Skeletal Development, Aging, & Regeneration. (Illus.). 368p. 2000. write for info. (*0-521-79000-X*, Pub. by Cambridge U Pr) Cambridge U Pr.

Carter, Detra, jt. auth. see Lyna, Bill.

Carter, Dianne & Fisher, Karen. Intervening with Substance-Abusing Offenders: A Framework for Action. 159p. (C). 1998. reprint ed. pap. text 30.00 (*0-7881-4195-3*) DIANE Pub.

Carter, Dianne, jt. auth. see Coffey, Osa.

Carter, Dianne K., jt. auth. see Rawlings, Edna I.

Carter, Dilford C. & Dolan, Patricia G. Catalogue of Type Specimens of Neotropical Bats in Selected European Museums. (Special Publications: No. 15). 136p. 1978. pap. 8.00 (*0-89672-063-2*) Tex Tech Univ Pr.

Carter, Don. Intelligent Transportation Systems: 1995 Key Markets & Competitive Technology Assessment. Archdeacon, Tim, ed. 200p. 1995. 2400.00 (*1-883742-14-5*) Allied Busn.

Carter, Don, et al. Washington D. C. Running Guide. LC 98-40542. (City Running Guide Ser.). (Illus.). 136p. 1998. pap. 16.95 (*0-88011-726-5*, PCAR0726) Human Kinetics.

Carter, Donald E. & Baker, Barbara S. Concurrent Engineering: The Product Development Environment for the 1990s. (Illus.). 192p. (C). 1991. 58.00 (*0-201-56349-5*) Addison-Wesley.

Carter, Donald M. States of Grace: Senegalese in Italy & the New European Immigration. LC 97-25951. 1997. write for info. (*0-8166-2542-5*); pap. write for info. (*0-8166-2543-3*) U of Minn Pr.

Carter, Donna. Family Reunion Planner. LC 96-48657. 1997. 9.95 (*0-02-861193-4*) Macmillan.

Carter, Dorene E. Portraits of Historic St. Croix Before & after Hurricane Hugo. (Illus.). 88p. 1991. 39.95 (*0-9628507-0-5*) D E Carter.

Carter, Doris D. Robert Floyd Kennon: Reform Governor. LC 97-78331. (Illus.). 205p. 1998. 25.00 (*1-887366-20-2*) Univ LA Lafayette.

Carter, Doris V. Residential Real Estate: A Comprehensive Guide of the Profession: Dade County Edition. 700p. (Orig.). 1995. pap. 149.00 (*0-9649865-0-7*) Miami Daily.

Carter, Dorothy. Bye, Mis' Lela. LC 95-33516. (Frances Foster Book Ser.). (Illus.). 32p. (J). (gr. k-3). 1998. 16.00 (*0-374-31013-0*) FS&G.

— Wilhe'mina Miles: After the Stork Night. LC 98-3450. (Illus.). 32p. (J). (gr. k-3). 1999. 16.00 (*0-374-33551-6*) FS&G.

Carter, Dorothy S. His Majesty, Queen Hatshepsut. LC 85-45855. (Illus.). 256p. (J). (gr. 5 up). 1987. 13.95 (*0-397-32178-3*) HarpC Child Bks.

— His Majesty, Queen Hatsheput. LC 85-45855. (Illus.). 256p. (J). (gr. 5 up). 1987. lib. bdg. 15.89 (*0-397-32179-1*) HarpC Child Bks.

***Carter, Doug.** Big Picture People: Overcoming a Knothole View of Life. 120p. 2000. pap. 10.99 (*0-8341-1799-1*) Beacon Hill.

Carter, Doug. The Black Elvis - Jackie Wilson. (Illus.). 261p. 1998. 32.00 (*0-9669425-0-7*) Heyday Pub.

Carter, Douglas, pref. Beyond the Banks: Proceedings of the Third Biennial RMS Symposium on River Management & Planning. (Illus.). 272p. 1997. 15.00 (*0-9645866-0-6*) River Mgt Soc.

Carter-Douglas, Grace, ed. The Griot: An Anthology of African Necromancers. 224p. 1988. pap. 15.00 (*0-9619553-0-9*) Rumble Inc.

Carter, Dustin W. & Matthews, Birch J. Mustang: The Racing Thoroughbred. LC 91-60015. (Illus.). 208p. 1992. text 39.95 (*0-88740-391-3*) Schiffer.

***Carter, Dwayne.** The Best Man. 205p. 1999. pap. 14.00 (*1-892096-01-3*) Ishai Creat.

Carter, E. Brass Quintet 1974. 40p. 1986. pap. text 40.00 (*0-7935-2512-8*) H Leonard.

— Canon for 3 in Memoriam of Igor Stravinsky: For Three Equal Instrumental Voices. 1986. pap. 5.95 (*0-7935-1432-0*) H Leonard.

— Double Concerto: For Harpsichord & Piano with Two Chamber Orchestras 1961. 180p. 1986. per. 40.00 (*0-7935-3415-1*) H Leonard.

— Duo for Violin & Piano. 1986. pap. 40.00 (*0-7935-2062-2*) H Leonard.

— Eight Pieces: 4 Timpani 1 Player Includes Recitative & Improvisation. 24p. 1986. pap. 14.95 (*0-7935-4848-9*) H Leonard.

— Piano Concerto: Score. 1986. 45.00 (*0-7935-1130-5*) H Leonard.

— Sonata for Violin Cello & Piano, 1948. 48p. 1986. pap. 18.00 (*0-7935-1743-5*) H Leonard.

— String Quartet, Vol. 1. 236p. 1986. pap. text 35.00 (*0-7935-3785-1*) H Leonard.

— String Quartet No. 1, 1951: Score. 124p. 1987. per. 20.00 (*0-7935-3734-7*) H Leonard.

— Tarantella: For Men's Chorus & Piano Four Hands. 40p. 1986. pap. 8.95 (*0-7935-3023-7*) H Leonard.

— Three Poems of Robert Frost. 1987. pap. 8.95 (*0-7935-1326-X*) H Leonard.

— Variations for Orchestra: Corrected Edition 1967 Study Score. 152p. 1986. per. 60.00 (*0-7935-3121-7*) H Leonard.

— Woodwind Quintet, 1948: For Flute-Oboe-Clarinet-French Horn-Bassoon. 1986. pap. 18.95 (*0-7935-1573-4*) H Leonard.

— Woodwind Quintet, 1948: Score. 24p. 1988. pap. 15.00 (*0-7935-1572-6*) H Leonard.

Carter, E. Dale, Jr. & Bas, Joe, eds. Cuentos Argentinos de Misterio. LC 68-13434. (Orig.). (gr. 9 up). 1968. pap. text 11.95 (*0-89197-119-X*) Irvington.

Carter, Earl. No Apology Necessary: How Hidden Prophecies in the Old Testament Foretold the Tragedy of Slavery. 1997. pap. 10.99 (*0-88419-455-8*) Creation House.

***Carter, Earl W., Sr.** Trouble in the Barnyard: Hen Pecked Husband & Rooster Pecked Wife. LC 99-65699. 238p. 2000. pap. 14.99 (*1-57921-250-6*, Pub. by WinePress Pub) BookWorld.

Carter, Eatherly. Pre-Algebra: Teacher's Resource File. 1991. teacher ed. 395.00 (*0-538-61654-7*) Sth-Wstrn College.

Carter, Edward. Jesus, I Want to Talk with You: Contemporary Prayers. LC 73-75617. (Illus.). 1977. reprint ed. pap. 1.95 (*0-8189-1142-5*, Pub. by Alba Bks) Intl Spec Bk.

— The Mysticism of Everyday. LC 90-63487. 88p. (Orig.). (C). 1991. pap. 7.95 (*1-55612-410-4*, LL1410) Sheed & Ward WI.

Carter, Edward, ed. Prayer Perspectives. LC 86-28675. 108p. (Orig.). 1987. pap. 5.95 (*0-8189-0513-1*) Alba.

Carter, Edward C. Enterprise & Entrepreneurs in Nineteenth & Twentieth Century France. Forster, Robert & Moody, Joseph N., eds. LC 75-36936. (Illus.). 232p. reprint ed. pap. 72.00 (*0-8357-6605-5*, 203525000094) Bks Demand.

Carter, Edward C., II. One Grand Pursuit: A Brief History of the American Philosophical Society's First 250 Years, 1743-1993. LC 93-71157. (APS Ser.: No. 9). (Illus.). 118p. (C). 1993. pap. 15.00 (*0-87169-938-9*, APS9-CAE) Am Philos.

Carter, Edward C. Surveying the Record: North American Scientific Exploration to 1930 LC 98-50212. (Memoirs of the American Philosophical Society Ser.). 1999. 25.00 (*0-87169-231-7*) Am Philos.

Carter, Edward C., ed. see Latrobe, Benjamin.

Carter, Edward C., ed. see Latrobe, Benjamin H.

***Carter, Edward Carlos & American Philosophical Society Staff.** Three Journals of the Lewis & Clark Expedition 1804-1806: From the Collections of the American Philosophical Society. fac. ed. LC 00-38055. 2000. write for info. (*0-87169-354-2*) Am Philos.

Carter, Edward H., ed. New Past, & Other Essays on the Development of Civilization. LC 68-8446. (Essay Index Reprint Ser.). 1977. reprint ed. 19.95 (*0-8369-0278-5*) Ayer.

Carter, Edward R. The Black Side. LC 78-170692. (Black Heritage Library Collection). 1977. reprint ed. 36.95 (*0-8369-8882-5*) Ayer.

Carter, Eleanor-Jean. Doll Modes: Doll Fashions with Patterns. LC 72-76726. 105p. 1972. pap. 20.00 (*0-9604404-0-2*) Carter Craft.

Carter, Elizabeth. Excavations at Anshan (Tal-e Malyan) The Middle Elamite Period. LC 94-7555. (University Museum Monographs: No. 82, Report 2). xviii, 140p. 1996. 50.00 (*0-924171-22-7*) U Museum Pubns.

— A Hiking Guide to the Trails of Florida. (Illus.). 136p. (Orig.). 1998. pap. 12.95 (*0-89732-196-0*) Menasha Ridge.

— Letters from Mrs. Elizabeth Carter to Mrs. Montagu Between the Years 1755-1800, 3 vols., Set. LC 73-178402. reprint ed. 210.00 (*0-404-56720-7*) AMS Pr.

— Majorcan Food & Cookery. (Illus.). 228p. (Orig.). 1989. pap. 18.00 (*0-907325-43-2*, Pub. by Prospect) Food Words.

— Memoirs of the Life of Mrs. Elizabeth Carter, 2 vols., Set. 4th ed. Pennington, M., ed. LC 75-37674. reprint ed. 145.00 (*0-404-56727-4*) AMS Pr.

Carter, Elizabeth. Series of Letters Between Mrs. Elizabeth Carter & Miss Catherine Talbot from the Year 1741 to 1770, 4 vols. reprint ed. 295.00 (*0-404-56730-4*) AMS Pr.

Carter, Elizabeth & Pearce, John L. A Canoeing & Kayaking Guide to the Streams of Florida, Vol. I: North Central Peninsula & Panhandle. LC 85-11596. (Illus.). 216p. (Orig.). 1985. pap. 12.95 (*0-89732-033-6*) Menasha Ridge.

Carter, Elizabeth A., et al. The Expanded Family Life Cycle: Individual, Family & Social Perspectives. 3rd ed. LC 98-15208. 541p. (C). 1998. 73.00 (*0-205-20009-5*) Allyn.

Carter, Elliott. The Writings of Elliott Carter: An American Composer Looks at Modern Music. Stone, Else & Stone, Kurt, eds. LC 76-48539. 409p. reprint ed. pap. 126.80 (*0-7837-1761-X*, 205729900024) Bks Demand.

Carter, Elliott & Restagno, Enzo. Elliott Carter: In Conversation with Enzo Restagno for Settembre Musica 1989. Wolfthal, Katherine S., tr. from ITA. LC 91-75368. (I.S.A.M. Monographs: No. 32).Tr. of Carter. (Illus.). 116p. (Orig.). 1991. pap. 15.00 (*0-914678-35-3*) Inst Am Music.

***Carter, Emily.** Glory Goes & Gets Some. 192p. 2000. 20.95 (*1-56689-101-9*, Pub. by Coffee Hse) Consort Bk Sales.

Carter, Emily, ed. see Hines, Sedgwick D.

Carter, Eneida & Mikalac, Miriam. Break Dance: The Free & Easy Way! (Illus.). 32p. (YA). (gr. 7 up). 1984. pap. 9.95 (*0-916391-00-0*) Free & Easy Pubns.

Carter, Eric & Stansfield, Malcolm. British Farming: Changing Policies & Production Systems. (Illus.). 144p. 1994. text 29.95 (*0-85236-278-1*, Pub. by Farming Pr) Diamond Farm Bk.

Carter, Eric, jt. auth. see Soper, Mike.

Carter, Erica. How German Is She? Postwar West German Reconstruction & the Consuming Woman. 288p. (C). 1997. text 54.50 (*0-472-10755-0*, 10755) U of Mich Pr.

Carter, Erica, et al, eds. Cultural Remix: Theories of Politics & the Popular. LC 96-209571. 288p. (C). 1995. pap. 19.50 (*0-85315-794-4*, Pub. by Lawrence & Wishart) NYU Pr.

— Space & Place: Theories of Identity & Location. 256p. (C). 1993. pap. 21.50 (*0-85315-775-8*, Pub. by Lawrence & Wishart) NYU Pr.

Carter, Erica & Watney, Simon, eds. Taking Liberties: AIDS & Cultural Politics. 240p. 1991. pap. 14.95 (*1-85242-147-9*) Serpents Tail.

Carter, Erica, tr. see Theweleit, Klaus.

Carter, Eugenia G. Information Systems Policies. (Executive Briefing Ser.). 21p. 1996. pap. 59.00 (*1-889394-25-4*) Credit Union Execs.

Carter, Everett. The American Idea: The Literary Response to American Optimism. LC 76-13867. 286p. reprint ed. pap. 88.70 (*0-8357-4409-4*, 203722900008) Bks Demand.

Carter, Everett, ed. see Frederic, Harold.

Carter Ewel, Katherine & Odum, Howard T., eds. Cypress Swamps. LC 84-5230. (Center for Wetlands Research, University of Florida Ser.). (Illus.). 490p. 1985. 49.95 (*0-8130-0714-3*) U Press Fla.

Carter, F. D. H. Lawrence & the Body Mystical. LC 68-910. (Studies in D. H. Lawrence: No. 20). 1969. reprint ed. lib. bdg. 75.00 (*0-8383-0653-5*) M S G Haskell Hse.

Carter, F. L. Molecular Electronic Devices. 400p. 1982. 155.00 (*0-8247-8058-2*) Dekker.

Carter, F. W. Trade & Urban Development in Poland: An Economic Geography of Cracow, from Its Origins to 1795. LC 92-27971. (Cambridge Studies in Historical Geography: No. 20). (Illus.). 533p. (C). 1994. text 85.00 (*0-521-41239-0*) Cambridge U Pr.

***Carter, F. W. & Maik, W., eds.** Shock-Shift in an Enlarged Europe: The Geography of Socio-Economic Change in East Central Europe after 1989. LC 98-74443. 184p. 1999. 65.95 (*1-85972-303-9*, Pub. by Ashgate Pub) Ashgate Pub Co.

Carter, Forest L. Molecular Electronic Devices, Vol. 2. (Illus.). 560p. 1987. text 250.00 (*0-8247-7562-7*) Dekker.

Carter, Forrest. The Education of Little Tree. 20.95 (*0-8488-0955-6*) Amereon Ltd.

— The Education of Little Tree. 1986. 18.30 (*0-606-12272-9*) Turtleback.

— The Education of Little Tree. large type ed. (General Ser.). 327p. 1992. pap. 16.95 (*0-8161-5497-X*, G K Hall Lrg Type); lib. bdg. 20.95 (*0-8161-5496-1*, G K Hall Lrg Type) Mac Lib Ref.

— The Education of Little Tree. 216p. 1986. reprint ed. lib. bdg. 25.95 (*0-89966-536-5*) Buccaneer Bks.

— The Education of Little Tree. LC 85-28956. 216p. 1990. reprint ed. 19.95 (*0-8263-1233-0*); reprint ed. pap. 12.95 (*0-8263-0879-1*) U of NM Pr.

***Carter, Forrest.** The Education of Little Tree, Class Set. unabridged ed. (YA). 1998. boxed set 196.30 incl. audio (*0-7887-2547-5*, 46717) Recorded Bks.

— The Education of Little Tree, Homework Set. unabridged ed. (YA). 1998. boxed set 67.20 incl. audio (*0-7887-2242-5*, 40726) Recorded Bks.

Carter, Forrest. Gone to Texas. 1976. 20.95 (*0-8488-0954-8*) Amereon Ltd.

— Gone to Texas: The Rebel Outlaw, Josey Wales. 1985. lib. bdg. 29.95 (*0-89966-561-6*) Buccaneer Bks.

— Josey Wales. 431p. Date not set. 28.95 (*0-8488-2229-3*) Amereon Ltd.

— Josey Wales: Two Westerns by Forrest Carter. LC 89-16587. 419p. 1989. reprint ed. pap. 15.95 (*0-8263-1168-7*) U of NM Pr.

— Look for Me on the Mountain. 1976. 22.95 (*0-8488-1264-6*) Amereon Ltd.

— Vengeance Trail of Josey Wales. Date not set. 22.95 (*0-8488-2647-7*) Amereon Ltd.

— Watch for Me on the Mountain. 320p. 1990. pap. 12.95 (*0-385-30082-4*, Delta Trade) Dell.

— Watch for Me on the Mountain. large type ed. 1982. 15.95 (*0-7089-0771-7*) Ulverscroft.

Carter, Fran. On Teaching Genealogy. (Illus.). 53p. 1989. pap. 9.95 (*0-945433-05-0*) Herit Quest.

Carter, Fran. Searching American Land & Deed Records. 70p. pap. 7.95 (*0-945433-29-8*) Herit Quest.

— Searching American Military Records. 62p. pap. 7.95 (*0-945433-28-X*) Herit Quest.

— Searching American Probate Records. 60p. pap. 7.95 (*0-945433-27-1*) Herit Quest.

Carter, Frances. Hawaii for Free: Hundreds of Free Things to Do in Hawaii. 4th rev. ed. LC 96-49224. (Illus.). 128p. 1997. pap. 9.95 (*0-914457-82-9*) Mustang Pub.

***Carter, Francis W., et al, eds.** Central Europe After the Fall of the Iron Curtain: Geopolitical Perspectives, Spatial Patterns & Trends 2nd, Revised Edition. 346p. 1998. 51.95 (*3-631-33748-5*) P Lang Pubng.

— Central Europe after the Fall of the Iron Curtain: Geopolitical Perspectives, Spatial Patterns & Trends 2nd, Revised Edition. 2nd ed. Vol. 4. (Illus.). 346p. 1998. pap. 51.95 (*0-8204-3621-6*) P Lang Pubng.

Carter, Frank & Cheesman, Peter. Anxiety in Childhood & Adolescence: Encouraging Self-Help Through Relaxation Training. 144p. 1988. text 49.50 (*0-7099-4806-9*, A1479) Routledge.

Carter, Frank & Turnock, David, eds. Environmental Problems in Eastern Europe. 2nd rev. ed. (Illus.). 312p. (C). 1997. pap. 24.99 (*0-415-13757-8*) Routledge.

Carter, Frank B., Jr. Mendacity Without Scruples. Ashton, Sylvia, ed. LC 77-78384. 1978. 22.95 (*0-87949-093-4*) Ashley Bks.

Carter, Frank W. & Turnock, David, eds. The States of Eastern Europe, Vols. I & II. LC 97-26185. (Illus.). 500p. 1997. text 166.95 (*1-85521-512-8*, Pub. by Ashgate Pub) Ashgate Pub Co.

Carter, Franklin. Rails West No. 4: Sierra Passage. 272p. (Orig.). 1995. mass mkt. 4.99 (*0-515-11527-4*, Jove) Berkley Pub.

Carter, G., jt. ed. see Kiriakidis, G.

***Carter, G. B.** Chemical & Biological Defence at Porton Down 1916-2000. 192p. 2000. pap. 34.00 (*0-11-772933-7*, Pub. by Statnry Office) Balogh.

Carter, G. C. & Diamondston, B. I. Directory of International Compatible Environmental Data. 1990. 94.95 (*1-56032-059-1*) Hemisp Pub.

Carter, G. Clifford, intro. Coherence & Time Delay Estimation: An Applied Tutorial for Research, Development, Test, & Evaluation Engineers. LC 92-46209. (Illus.). 528p. (C). 1993. text 79.95 (*0-7803-1006-3*, PC03558) Inst Electrical.

Carter, G. M., jt. auth. see Quade, Edward S.

Carter, G. R. Essentials of Veterinary Bacteriology & Mycology. 4th ed. LC 90-42674. (Illus.). 280p. 1990. 46.00 (*0-8121-1369-1*) Lppncott W & W.

— Veterinarian's Guide to the Laboratory Diagnosis of Infectious Diseases. 326p. 1986. 29.95 (*0-935078-37-1*) Veterinary Med.

Carter, G. R. & Chengappa, M. M. Microbial Diseases: A Veterinarian's Guide to Laboratory Diagnosis. LC 92-35999. 318p. (C). 1993. text 49.95 (*0-8138-0671-2*) Iowa St U Pr.

Carter, G. R., et al. Essentials of Veterinary Microbiology. 5th ed. LC 94-29049. (Illus.). 394p. 1995. 46.95 (*0-683-01473-0*) Lppncott W & W.

Carter, G. S. A General Zoology of the Invertebrates. (Illus.). (C). 1965. 35.00 (*0-8464-1166-0*) Beekman Pubs.

Carter, Gale W. Let's Take a Walk: Discovering the Habitats, Adaptations, Uses & Folklore of Some Common Wild Plants of Eastern United States. LC 90-93571. (Illus.). 175p. (Orig.). 1991. pap. 14.95 (*0-9628153-0-6*) G W Carter.

Carter, Gari. Healing Myself: A Hero's Primer for Recovery from Tragedy. 208p. 1993. pap. 10.95 (*1-878901-75-3*) Hampton Roads Pub Co.

Carter, Gary & Hough, John, Jr. A Dream Season. (Illus.). 1987. 15.95 (*0-15-126571-2*) Harcourt.

Carter, Gary, jt. auth. see Chatterton, Mark.

Carter, Gary, jt. auth. see Overstreet, Robert M.

Carter, Gary R. & Cole, John R., Jr., eds. Diagnostic Procedures in Veterinary Bacteriology & Mycology. 5th ed. 620p. 1990. text 45.00 (*0-12-161775-0*) Acad Pr.

***Carter, Gary W.** J.K. Lasser's Taxes Made Easy for Your Home-Based Business. 3rd ed. 1999. pap. 15.95 (*0-471-38836-X*) Wiley.

Carter, Gelsomina C., jt. ed. see Uhlir, Paul F.

Carter, Gene R. & Cunningham, William G. The American School Superintendency: Leading in an Age of Pressure. LC 96-45874. 1997. 29.95 (*0-7879-0799-5*) Jossey-Bass.

Carter, Geoffrey W. The Electromagnetic Field in Its Engineering Aspects. 2nd ed. LC 79-355853. (Electrical Engineering Ser.). 388p. reprint ed. pap. 120.30 (*0-608-18553-1*, 200697800060) Bks Demand.

Carter, Geoffrey W. & Richardson, A. Techniques of Circuit Analysis. LC 79-183222. 556p. reprint ed. pap. 158.50 (*0-608-17576-5*, 2030584) Bks Demand.

Carter, George. Containers: Garden Project Workbook. LC 96-48045. (Illus.). 112p. 1997. 22.50 (*1-55670-545-X*) Stewart Tabori & Chang.

— Herbs: Garden Project Workbook. LC 96-49483. (Garden Project Workbooks). (Illus.). 112p. 1997. 22.50 (*1-55670-544-1*) Stewart Tabori & Chang.

***Carter, George.** Living with Plants. (Illus.). 2000. 29.95 (*1-84000-181-X*) Mitchell Beazley.

— The New London Garden. (Illus.). 208p. 2000. 45.00 (*1-84000-347-2*, Pub. by Mitchell Beazley) Antique Collect.

Carter, George W. Zoroastrianism & Judaism. LC 70-112489. 1970. reprint ed. 32.50 (*0-404-01396-1*) AMS Pr.

Carter, Gerald B. Data Entry Skills: Additional Problems. 2nd ed. 103p. (YA). (gr. 9-12). 1978. pap. text 14.00 (*0-9610582-1-8*) Apollo Com.

Carter, Gerald L. & Minkema, Douglas D. Data Entry Skills-Key Disk Machine. 3rd ed. (Data Entry Skills-Key Disk Machine & Additional Problems Ser.). 97p. (gr. 9-12). 1977. pap. text 14.50 (*0-9610582-0-X*) Apollo Com.

— Data Entry Skills Teacher's Guide. text 32.00 (*0-9610582-4-2*) Apollo Com.

Carter, Gerald L., jt. auth. see Minkema, Douglas D.

Carter, Gerard B. Australian Legal System. 292p. 1995. pap. 30.00 (*1-875114-42-4*, Pub. by Blackstone Pr) Gaunt.

Carter, Giles F. Principles of Physical & Chemical Metallurgy. LC 79-19184. 447p. reprint ed. pap. 138.60 (*0-608-12109-6*, 202514600042) Bks Demand.

— Solutions to the Problems in Principles of Physical & Chemical Metallurgy. LC TN0690.C292. (Illus.). 49p. reprint ed. pap. 30.00 (*0-608-16005-9*, 203308200083) Bks Demand.

Carter, Giles F., ed. Archaeological Chemistry, Vol. II. LC 78-26128. (Advances in Chemistry Ser.: No. 171). 389p. 1978. 60.95 (*0-8412-0397-0*) Am Chemical.

Carter, Giles F., ed. see Symposium on Archaeological Chemistry Staff.

Carter, Ginger Rudeseal. Stand! Public Relations. (C). pap. text 11.97 (*0-395-97781-9*) HM.

Carter, Gordon R. & Boyle, Stephen M. All You Need to Know about DNA, Genes & Genetic Engineering: A Concise, Comprehensive Outline. LC 98-3519. (Illus.). 146p. 1998. pap. text 22.95 (*0-398-06870-4*) C C Thomas.

Carter, Gordon R. & Rikihisa, Yasuko. Essentials of Veterinary Bacteriology & Mycology. 3rd ed. LC 85-10420. 270p. reprint ed. pap. 83.70 (*0-7837-1481-5*, 205717600023) Bks Demand.

Carter, Grace M. & Rogowski, Jeannette A. The Hospital Relative Value Method As An Alternative for Recalibrating DRG Relative Weights. LC 92-48505. 1993. pap. text 13.00 (*0-8330-1323-8*, MR-156-HCFA) Rand Corp.

***Carter, Graydon & Friend, David, eds.** Vanity Fair's Hollywood. (Illus.). 320p. 2000. 50.00 (*0-670-89141-X*, Viking) Viking Penguin.

***Carter, Grayson.** Anglican Evangelicals: Protestant Secessions from the Via Media, C. 1800-1850. (Oxford Theological Monographs). 350p. 2000. text 80.00 (*0-19-827008-9*) OUP.

Carter, Gregg, jt. auth. see Hesse-Biber, Sharlene.

Carter, Gregg L. Analyzing Contemporary Social Issues: A Workbook with Student CHIP Software. (C). 1995. teacher ed. write for info. (*0-205-19692-6*, H9692-8) Allyn.

***Carter, Gregg L.** Analyzing Contemporary Social Issues: A Workbook with Student Chip Software. 2nd ed. 272p. 2000. pap. text 29.00 (*0-205-32102-X*) Allyn.

Carter, Gregg L. Doing Sociology with Student Chip: Data Happy! 2nd ed. 285p. (C). 1997. pap. text 29.00 (*0-205-26479-4*) Allyn.

— Empirical Approaches to Sociology: Classic & Contemporary Readings. 2nd ed. LC 97-14949. 498p. (C). 1997. pap. text 40.00 (*0-205-26480-8*) Allyn.

— Perspectives on Current Social Problems. LC 96-29116. 368p. 1996. pap. text 35.00 (*0-205-19836-8*) Allyn.

Carter, Gregg Lee. Analyzing Contemporary Social Issues. LC 99-233004. 224p. 1995. pap. text 29.00 (*0-205-19134-7*) P-H.

***Carter, Gregg Lee.** Doing Sociology with Student Chip: Data Happy! 3rd ed. 256p. 2000. pap. text 29.00 (*0-205-30815-5*) Allyn.

Carter, Gregg Lee. Gun Control Movement. LC 97-6371. 1996. pap. 14.95 (*0-8057-3886-X*) Macmillan.

— Gun Control Movement. LC 97-6371. 1997. 33.00 (*0-8057-3885-1*) Macmillan.

Carter, Gregg Lee, jt. auth. see Hesse-Biber, Sharlene.

Carter, Gwendolen M. National Unity & Regionalism in Eight African States: Nigeria, Niger, the Congo, Gabon, Central African Republic. LC 66-12113. 581p. reprint ed. pap. 180.20 (*0-608-11575-4*, 200545700054) Bks Demand.

— Which Way Is South Africa Going? LC 79-3658. 174p. reprint ed. pap. 49.60 (*0-317-27941-6*, 2056026) Bks Demand.

Carter, Gwendolen M. & O'Meara, Patrick, eds. African Independence: The First Twenty-Five Years. LC 84-48457. 377p. 1985. reprint ed. pap. 116.90 (*0-7837-9645-5*, 205927800005) Bks Demand.

— Southern Africa: The Continuing Crisis. 2nd ed. LC 81-48324. 416p. reprint ed. pap. 129.00 (*0-608-18248-6*, 205669600081) Bks Demand.

Carter, Gwendolen M. & Paden, Ann, eds. Expanding Horizons in African Studies: Program of African Studies, Northwestern University, Proceedings of the Twentieth Anniversary Conference, 1968. LC 72-89823. 380p. reprint ed. pap. 117.80 (*0-608-14327-8*, 201670400004) Bks Demand.

Carter, Gwendolen M., ed. see Johns, Sheridan, III.

Carter, Gwendolen M., ed. see Karis, Thomas & Gerhart, Gail M.

Carter, Gwendolen M., jt. ed. see Karis, Thomas.

Carter, Gwendolyn, et al. South Africa's Transkei, the Politics of Domestic Colonialism. LC 67-15937. 214p. reprint ed. pap. 66.40 (*0-608-13055-9*, 201477300096) Bks Demand.

Carter, Gwendolyn M. Continuity & Change in Southern Africa. 117p. 1985. 9.95 (*0-918456-57-6*, Crossroads) African Studies Assn.

Carter, Gwendolyn M. & O'Meara, Patrick, eds. Southern Africa in Crisis. LC 76-48534. 279p. reprint ed. pap. 86.50 (*0-608-18626-0*, 205602700044) Bks Demand.

Carter, H. Adams, ed. The American Alpine Journal, 1989. LC 79-63733. (Illus.). 354p. 1989. pap. 25.00 (*0-930410-39-4*) Amer Alpine Club.

— The American Alpine Journal, 1980. 80th ed. (Illus.). 352p. 1980. pap. 25.00 (*0-930410-76-9*) Amer Alpine Club.

— The American Alpine Journal, 1981. 81st ed. (Illus.). 375p. 1981. pap. 25.00 (*0-930410-77-7*) Amer Alpine Club.

— The American Alpine Journal, 1983. 83rd ed. (Illus.). 367p. 1983. pap. 25.00 (*0-930410-21-1*) Amer Alpine Club.

— The American Alpine Journal, 1985. 85th ed. (Illus.). 407p. 1985. pap. 25.00 (*0-930410-24-6*) Amer Alpine Club.

— The American Alpine Journal, 1986. 86th ed. (Illus.). 356p. 1986. pap. 25.00 (*0-930410-27-0*) Amer Alpine Club.

— The American Alpine Journal, 1987. 87th ed. (Illus.). 387p. 1987. pap. 25.00 (*0-930410-29-7*) Amer Alpine Club.

— The American Alpine Journal, 1988. 88th ed. (Illus.). 362p. 1988. pap. 25.00 (*0-930410-33-5*) Amer Alpine Club.

— The American Alpine Journal, 1991. LC 79-63633. (Illus.). 378p. 1991. pap. 25.00 (*0-930410-46-7*) Amer Alpine Club.

— The American Alpine Journal, 1992. LC 79-63633. (Illus.). 325p. 1992. pap. 25.00 (*0-930410-51-3*) Amer Alpine Club.

— The American Alpine Journal, 1993. (Illus.). 364p. 1993. pap. 25.00 (*0-930410-55-6*) Amer Alpine Club.

— The American Alpine Journal, 1994. (Illus.). 360p. 1994. pap. 25.00 (*0-930410-58-0*) Amer Alpine Club.

— The American Alpine Journal, 1995. (Illus.). 410p. 1995. pap. 25.00 (*0-930410-61-0*) Amer Alpine Club.

— The American Alpine Journal, 1990. 90th ed. (Illus.). 385p. 1990. pap. 25.00 (*0-930410-43-2*) Amer Alpine Club.

— The American Alpine Journal, 1973. 73rd ed. (Illus.). 287p. 1973. pap. 15.00 (*0-930410-70-X*) Amer Alpine Club.

— The American Alpine Journal, 1974. 74th ed. (Illus.). 297p. 1974. pap. 15.00 (*0-930410-71-8*) Amer Alpine Club.

— The American Alpine Journal, 1975. 75th ed. (Illus.). 275p. 1975. pap. 15.00 (*0-930410-72-6*) Amer Alpine Club.

— The American Alpine Journal, 1976. 76th ed. (Illus.). 335p. 1976. pap. 15.00 (*0-930410-73-4*) Amer Alpine Club.

— The American Alpine Journal, 1979. 79th ed. (Illus.). 373p. 1979. pap. 15.00 (*0-930410-75-0*) Amer Alpine Club.

Carter, H. C. & Partington, I. Applied Economics in Banking & Finance. (C). 1989. 600.00 (*0-7855-4320-1*, Pub. by Witherby & Co) St Mut.

Carter, H. K., jt. ed. see Bemis, C. E.

Carter, H. W. A Genealogy of the Descendants of Thomas Carter of Mass. & Conn. Also Descendants of His Brothers, Grandson of Reverend Thomas Carter, Woburn, Mass., 1642. (Illus.). 341p. 1989. reprint ed. pap. 51.00 (*0-8328-0375-8*); reprint ed. lib. bdg. 59.00 (*0-8328-0374-X*) Higginson Bk Co.

Carter, H. W., et al. Clinical Applications of the Scanning Electron Microscope. Johari, Om & Becker, R. P., eds. (Illus.). 1980. pap. 10.00 (*0-931288-16-9*) Scanning Microscopy.

Carter, Harley. Diccionario de Electronica. (SPA.). 416p. 1962. 29.95 (*0-8288-6805-0*, S-33049) Fr & Eur.

Carter, Harlon B., ed. see Kukla, Robert J.

Carter, Harold. Social Areas in Cities: Past & Future. (Urban Studies: No. 3). 28p. 1984. pap. 3.00 (*0-913749-01-X*) U MD Urban Stud.

— The Study of Urban Geography. 4th ed. (Arnold Publications). (Illus.). 448p. 1995. pap. text 35.00 (*0-7131-6589-8*) OUP.

Carter, Harold & Lewis, C. Roy. An Urban Geography of England & Wales in the Nineteenth Century. (Illus.). 256p. 1990. pap. text 22.50 (*0-7131-6549-9*, A5497, Pub. by E A) Routldge.

Carter, Harold, jt. auth. see Aitchison, J. W.

Carter, Harold, jt. auth. see Aitchison, John.

***Carter, Harriet H. & Wells, Susan E.** Guided Tour to the Afterlife: The Remarkable First-Hand Account of One Woman's Death & Her Adventures in a New Life after Death. LC 00-101866. xi, 278p. 2000. pap. 16.95 (*0-9678939-3-3*) Hillbrook Pubng.

Carter, Harriet I., jt. auth. see Marrow, Raphael W.

Carter, Harry. Fire Fighting Strategies & Tactics. Murnane, Lynne, ed. LC 98-88706. (Illus.). 188p. 1998. pap. text 30.00 (*0-87939-160-X*, 36313) IFSTA.

Carter, Harry. The Real Munchhausen: Baron of Bodenwerder. 224p. (J). (gr. 6 up). 1960. 10.00 (*0-8159-6701-2*) Devin.

Carter, Harry & Rausch, Erwin. Management in the Fire Service. 3rd ed. Linville, Jim L., ed. LC 99-60368. 420p. 1999. text 64.50 (*0-87765-441-7*, MFS-89) Natl Fire Prot.

Carter, Harvey L. Dear Old Kit: The Historical Christopher Carson. LC 68-15681. (Illus.). 272p. 1990. pap. 16.95 (*0-8061-2253-6*) U of Okla Pr.

Carter, Harvey L., jt. auth. see Guild, Thelma S.

Carter, Hazel & Makoondekwa, Joao. Kongo Language Course - Maloongi Makikoongo: A Course in the Dialect of Zoombo, Northern Angola. LC 87-25433. (Publications in African Language Teaching: No. 1). (Orig.). 1987. pap. 25.00 (*0-942615-02-6*) U Wis African Stud.

Carter, Henry J. The Teachings of Mother Wit. LC 96-92386. (Illus.). 98p. 1996. pap. 14.00 (*0-7880-0691-6*, Fairway Pr) CSS OH.

Carter, Hilma O., ed. see Pavlovsky, Eduardo.

Carter, Hobart C. Modern Basic Mathematics. LC 63-19876. (Illus.). 1964. 32.00 (*0-89197-305-2*) Irvington.

Carter, Hodding, III. The Angry Scar: The Story of Reconstruction. LC 73-10751. 425p. 1974. reprint ed. lib. bdg. 49.75 (*0-8371-7022-2*, CAAS, Greenwood Pr) Greenwood.

— First Person Rural. LC 77-10014. 1977. reprint ed. lib. bdg. 59.75 (*0-8371-9727-9*, CAFI, Greenwood Pr) Greenwood.

Carter, Hodding. Westward Whoa. 1994. 21.00 (*0-671-79891-X*) S&S Trade.

Carter, Howard. Carter: History of the Isaac P. Carter Family & Their Descendants. 134p. 1997. reprint ed. pap. 21.00 (*0-8328-7872-3*); reprint ed. lib. bdg. 31.00 (*0-8328-7871-5*) Higginson Bk Co.

— First Cut. (Illus.). 320p. 1998. pap. 14.00 (*0-312-19546-X*, Picador USA) St Martin.

— Questions & Answers on Spiritual Gifts. 1997. pap. text 9.99 (*1-57794-065-2*) Harrison Hse.

— Spiritual Gifts & Their Operation. 96p. 1968. pap. 3.95 (*0-88243-593-0*, 02-0593) Gospel Pub.

Carter, Howard & Irvine, Gillian. Environmental Crime. (Environmental Law Ser.). 533p. 1999. 123.00 (*1-874698-40-6*, Pub. by Cameron May) Gaunt.

Carter, Howard & Mace, Arthur C. The Discovery of the Tomb of Tutankhamen. (Illus.). 1990. 21.25 (*0-8446-5562-7*) Peter Smith.

— The Discovery of the Tomb of Tutankhamen. LC 77-71042. (Illus.). 382p. 1977. reprint ed. pap. 8.95 (*0-486-23500-9*) Dover.

Carter, Howard M. Jurisdiction of Federal Courts: As Limited by the Citizenship & Residence of the Parties. xxviii, 303p. 1983. reprint ed. 42.50 (*0-8377-0445-6*, Rothman) W S Hein.

Carter, Hugh & Glick, Paul C. Marriage & Divorce: A Social & Economic Study. rev. ed. (Vital & Health Statistics Monographs, American Public Health Association). 483p. (C). 1970. 49.95 (*0-674-55076-5*) HUP.

— Marriage & Divorce: A Social & Economic Study. rev. ed. LC 79-105369. (Vital & Health Statistics Monographs, American Public Health Association). 483p. 1970. 12.00 (*0-674-55075-7*) HUP.

Carter, Huntly. The New Spirit in the Cinema. 1972. 59.95 (*0-8490-0724-0*) Gordon Pr.

— The New Spirit in the Cinema. LC 76-112580. (Literature of Cinema, Ser. 1). 1970. reprint ed. 21.95 (*0-405-01605-0*) Ayer.

— New Spirit in the Russian Theatre 1917-1928. LC 77-112583. (Literature of Cinema, Ser. 1). 1970. reprint ed. 19.95 (*0-405-01606-9*) Ayer.

— New Theatre & Cinema of Soviet Russia. LC 74-124001. (Literature of Cinema, Ser. 1). 1970. reprint ed. 19.95 (*0-405-01607-7*) Ayer.

— Theatre of Max Reinhardt. LC 64-14700. (Illus.). 1972. 24.95 (*0-405-08344-0*, Pub. by Blom Pubns) Ayer.

Carter, I., jt. auth. see Alexander, William.

***Carter, Ian.** Bomber Command 1939 - 1945. (Illus.). 2000. 34.95 (*0-7110-2699-8*, Pub. by Ian Allan) Combined Pub.

— A Measure of Freedom. LC 98-37478. 322p. 1999. text 70.00 (*0-19-829453-0*) OUP.

***Carter, Ira G.** The Life & Times of a Country Peddler. LC 99-93574. 117p. 1999. pap. 10.95 (*0-533-13070-0*) Vantage.

Carter, J. The Relational Database. 1994. mass mkt. 29.95 (*0-412-55090-3*, Chap & Hall NY) Chapman & Hall.

Carter, J., jt. auth. see Mason, K.

Carter, J. C. The Sculpture of the Sanctuary of Athena Polias at Priene. (Illus.). 448p. 1984. 39.98 (*0-85431-238-2*, Pub. by Soc Antiquaries) David Brown.

C

An Asterisk (*) at the beginning of an entry indicates that the title is appearing for the first time.

Carter, J. E., ed. Physical Structure of Olympic Athletes. (Medicine & Sport Science Ser.: Vol. 18). (Illus.). viii, 248p. 1984. 136.75 (3-8055-3871-5) S Karger.

Carter, J. E. & Ackland, Timothy R., eds. Kinanthropometry in Aquatic Sports: A Study of World Class Athletes. LC 93-42157. (Sport Science Monographs: Vol. 5). (Illus.). 184p. 1994. pap. text 19.00 (0-87322-658-5, BCAR0658) Human Kinetics.

Carter, J. E. & Heath, Barbara H. Somatotyping - Development & Applications. (Cambridge Studies in Biological Anthropology: No. 5). (Illus.). 448p. (C). 1990. text 159.95 (0-521-35117-0) Cambridge U Pr.

Carter, J. Edwin. Living Is Forever. 408p. 1992. pap. 12.95 (1-878901-42-7) Hampton Roads Pub Co.

Carter, J. H., et al. On Atmospheric Pollution: A Group of Contributions. (Meteorological Monograph: Vol. 1, No. 4). (Illus.). 55p. (Orig.). 1951. pap. 17.00 (0-933876-00-9) Am Meteorological.

Carter, J. J. & Withrington, D. J. Scottish Universities: Distinctiveness & Diversity. 250p. (C). 1997. text 50.00 (0-85976-375-7, Pub. by J Donald) St Mut.

Carter, J. M. Commercial Bank Liquidity Management, Discretionary Reserve Behavior, & the Allocation of Credit, 1863-1913. rev. ed. LC 92-22993. (Financial Sector of the American Economy Ser.). 200p. 1992. text 20.00 (0-8153-0962-7) Garland.

Carter, J. M., ed. Suetonius: Divus Augustus. 236p. 1982. 22.95 (0-906515-55-6, Pub. by Brist Class Pr) Focus Pub-R Pullins.

Carter, J. M., ed. see Caesar.

Carter, J. P. Racketeering in Medicine: The Suppression of Alternatives. 392p. 1992. pap. 12.95 (1-878901-32-X) Hampton Roads Pub Co.

Carter, J. R., ed. see Desikachar, T. K.

Carter, J. S. How Surfaces Intersect in Space: A Friendly Introduction to Topology. (Knots & Everything Ser.). 300p. 1993. text 40.00 (981-02-1050-7) World Scientific Pub.

— How Surfaces Intersect in Space: An Introduction to Topology. (Series on Knots & Everything). 336p. 1995. pap. text 23.00 (981-02-2066-9) World Scientific Pub.

Carter, J. Scott. How Surfaces Intersect in Space: An Introduction to Topology. (Series on Knots & Everything). 340p. 1995. text 48.00 (981-02-2082-0) World Scientific Pub.

Carter, J. Scott & Saito, Masahico. Knotted Surfaces & Their Diagrams. LC 97-34494. (Mathematical Surveys & Monographs Ser.). 258p. 1997. text 69.00 (0-8218-0593-2) Am Math.

Carter, J. Scott, et al. The Classical & Quantum 6j=Symbols. (Mathematical Notes Ser.: Vol. 43). 168p. 1996. pap. text 22.50 (0-691-02730-7, Pub. by Princeton U Pr) Cal Prin Full Svc.

Carter, J. Smyth. Story of Dundas: Being a History of the County of Dundas, 1784 to 1904. (Illus.). 462p. 1996. reprint ed. lib. bdg. 49.00 (0-8328-5154-X) Higginson Bk Co.

Carter, J. W. Contract Law in Australia. 2nd ed. 1991. 151.00 (0-409-30190-6, AT, MICHIE); pap. 106.00 (0-409-30191-4, AT, MICHIE) LEXIS Pub.

— Outline of Contract Law in Australia. 2nd ed. LC 94-169166. 328p. 1994. pap. 54.00 (0-409-30278-3, Austral, MICHIE) LEXIS Pub.

Carter, J. W. & Harland, D. J. Contract Law in Australia. 3rd ed. LC 96-166507. 944p. 1995. write for info. (0-409-30874-9, MICHIE) LEXIS Pub.

Carter, Jack. Elderly Cohort Migration Patterns: Methodological Prescriptions for Future Research. LC 93-48508. (Studies on the Elderly in America). 104p. 1994. text 20.00 (0-8153-1652-6) Garland.

Carter, Jack, jt. ed. see Entzinger, Han.

Carter, Jack L. Trees & Shrubs of Colorado: From Plains to Tundra. (Illus.). 165p. (Orig.). 1988. pap. 13.95 (0-9619945-0-9) Mimbres.

— Trees & Shrubs of New Mexico. (Illus.). vi, 520p. (Orig.). 1997. pap. 29.95 (0-9658404-0-9) Mimbres.

Carter, Jacqueline, ed. see Costello, Thomas.

Carter, Jaine & Carter, James D. He Works She Works: Successful Strategies for Working Couples. 2nd ed. (Illus.). 226p. 1995. reprint ed. pap. 17.95 (0-9663898-0-8, WC-1295) Carter & Carter.

***Carter, James.** Creating Writers: A Creative Writing Manual for Schools. LC 00-32214. 2000. write for info. (0-415-21691-5) Routledge.

Carter, James. Law: Its Origin, Growth & Function. LC 74-6413. (American Constitutional & Legal History Ser). 1974. reprint ed. lib. bdg. 42.50 (0-306-70631-8) Da Capo.

— The Other Theory of Nuclear Structure. LC 93-73894. (Illus.). 96p. (Orig.). (C). 1993. pap. 32.00 (0-9636592-0-0) Absolute Motion.

— The Other Theory of Physics: A Unified Non-Field Theory of Mass, Space, Time & Gravity. (Illus.). 208p. (Orig.). (C). 1994. pap. text 22.00 (0-9636592-1-9) Absolute Motion.

***Carter, James.** Talking Books: Children's Authors Talk about Craft, Creativity & Process of Writing. LC 98-32051. 1999. text 65.00 (0-415-19416-4) Routledge.

Carter, James. Talking Books: Children's Authors Talk about Craft Creativity & Process of Writing. LC 98-32051. 266p. 1999. pap. 21.99 (0-415-19417-2) Routledge.

— The Yin & Yang Universes. (Illus.). 256p. (Orig.). 1996. pap. 27.00 (0-9636592-2-7) Absolute Motion.

Carter, James, jt. ed. see Fraser, George C.

Carter, James C. Law: Its Origin Growth & Function: Being a Course of Lectures Prepared for Delivery Before the Law School of Harvard University. LC 94-75660. viii, 356p. 1994. reprint ed. 110.00 (1-56169-094-5) Gaunt.

Carter, James D., jt. auth. see Carter, Jaine.

Carter, James E. House upon a Rock Refurbished: A Sesquicentennial History of Louisiana Southern Baptists, 1973-1998. (Illus.). 160p. 1997. write for info. (1-57736-051-6) Providence Hse.

Carter, James E., jt. auth. see Trull, Joe E.

Carter, James G. Essays upon Popular Education. LC 70-89162. (American Education: Its Men, Institutions, & Ideas. Series 1). 1974. reprint ed. 12.95 (0-405-01399-X) Ayer.

— Letters to the Honorable William Prescott, LL.D., on the Free Schools of New England. LC 77-89161. (American Education: Its Men, Institutions, & Ideas. Series 1). 1975. reprint ed. 16.95 (0-405-01400-7) Ayer.

***Carter, James H.** Psychosocial Intervention with Aged African Americans--A Primer. LC 99-93821. 2000. pap. 10.95 (0-533-13157-X) Vantage.

Carter, James J. Nasty People: All You Ever Wanted to Know about SOB's but Were Afraid to Ask Them. (Illus.). 80p. 14.95 (0-937004-04-9); pap. 4.95 (0-937004-05-7) Unicorn PA.

Carter, James L. & Rankin, Ernest H., eds. North to Lake Superior: Journal of Charles W. Penny, 1840. LC 71-111886. 1970. 8.95 (0-938746-02-2) Marquette Cnty.

Carter, James L., ed. see Castle, Beatrice H.

Carter, James M. The Norman Conquest in English Historiography. 115p. (Orig.). 1980. pap. text 26.95 (0-89126-086-2) MA-AH Pub.

Carter, James R. Computer Mapping: Progress in the Eighties. LC 84-70007. (Resource Publications in Geography). 100p. 1984. pap. 15.00 (0-89291-175-1) Assn Am Geographers.

Carter, Jan. Day Services for Adults: Somewhere to Go. 1981. 80.00 (0-7855-0589-X, Pub. by Natl Inst Soc Work) St Mut.

Carter, Jan, jt. auth. see Edwards, Carol.

***Carter, Jane.** Heart & Soul of Nick Carter: Secrets Only a Mother Knows. 1998. pap. 9.50 (0-451-40895-0) NAL.

***Carter, Jane & Sagarese, Margaret.** Aaron Carter: The Little Prince of Pop: The Real Inside Scoop from His Mom. 1999. mass mkt. 9.95 (0-451-40920-5, Onyx) NAL.

Carter, Jane, jt. auth. see Kaplan, Joseph S.

Carter, Jane B. & Morris, Sarah P., eds. The Ages of Homer. (Illus.). 564p. (C). 1998. pap. 29.95 (0-292-71208-1, CARAGP) U of Tex Pr.

— The Ages of Homer: A Tribute to Emily Townsend Vermeule. LC 94-13817. (Illus.). xvii, 542 p. 1995. text 45.00 (0-292-71169-7) U of Tex Pr.

Carter, Jane F. If the Walls Could Talk: Colusa's Architectural Heritage. (Illus.). 350p. 1988. 40.00 (0-9620538-0-5) Heritage Preserv Comm.

Carter, Jane G. & Holmes, Susie P. Genealogical Record of the Dedham Branch of the Avery Family in America. (Illus.). 366p. 1988. reprint ed. pap. 58.00 (0-8328-0143-7); reprint ed. lib. bdg. 68.00 (0-8328-0142-9) Higginson Bk Co.

Carter, Janice. A Christmas Baby. LC 95-23077. 299p. 1995. per. 3.75 (0-373-70671-5, 1-70671-2) Harlequin Bks.

— Ghost Tiger. (Superromance Ser.). 1994. per. 3.50 (0-373-70593-X, 1-70593-8) Harlequin Bks.

— The Inheritance. (Superromance Ser.: Bk. 887). 1999. per. 4.25 (0-373-70887-4, 1-70887-4) Harlequin Bks.

— The Man She Left Behind. (Temptation Ser.). 1998. per. 4.25 (0-373-70779-7, 1-70779-3) Harlequin Bks.

Carter, Jared. After the Rain. LC 92-70728. (CSU Poetry Ser.: Vol. XXXVII). 98p. (Orig.). 1993. 17.50 (1-880834-03-0) Cleveland St Univ Poetry Ctr.

— After the Rain. LC 92-70728. (CSU Poetry Ser.: XXXVII). 98p. (Orig.). 1993. pap. 10.00 (0-914946-97-8) Cleveland St Univ Poetry Ctr.

— Les Barricades Mysterieuses. LC 98-72252. (CSU Poetry Ser.: No. XLVII). 48p. 1999. pap. 10.00 (1-880834-40-5) Cleveland St Univ Poetry Ctr.

— Blues Project. (City Ser.). 32p. 1991. pap. 3.00 (1-880649-27-6) Writ Ctr Pr.

— Pincushion's Strawberry. (Illus.). 31p. (Orig.). 1984. pap. 3.50 (0-914946-43-9) Cleveland St Univ Poetry Ctr.

— Situation Normal. 8p. 1991. pap. 2.00 (1-880649-26-8) Writ Ctr Pr.

— Work, for the Night Is Coming. 2nd ed. LC 95-70938. 47p. 1995. reprint ed. pap. 8.00 (1-880834-20-0) Cleveland St Univ Poetry Ctr.

Carter, Jay. Butterflies Don't Land on Manure: The Transformation of an Ordinary Man. Verhulst, Margaret, ed. (Illus.). 96p. 1998. pap. 9.95 (0-937004-12-X) Unicorn PA.

— Love: The "L" Word. 2nd rev. ed. Verhulst, Margaret, ed. (Illus.). 80p. Date not set. pap. 9.95 (0-937004-13-8) Unicorn PA.

— Nasty Men. (Illus.). 144p. 1993. pap. 7.95 (0-8092-3794-6, 379460, Contemporary Bks) NTC Contemp Pub Co.

— Nasty People. 96p. (Orig.). 1989. pap. 7.95 (0-8092-4406-3, 440630, Contemporary Bks) NTC Contemp Pub Co.

— Self-Analysis: A Kick-Butt Boot-Camp Approach. 2nd rev. ed. (Illus.). 96p. 1998. pap. 9.95 (0-937004-10-3) Unicorn PA.

Carter, Jay & Noll, Kathy. Taking the Bully by the Horns: Children's Version of Best-Selling Book Nasty People. (J). 1997. pap. 9.95 (0-937004-06-5) Unicorn PA.

Carter, Jay, ed. see Noll, Kathy.

Carter, Jean. Rural Harmony. 266p. 1997. 21.00 (0-8059-4009-X) Dorrance.

Carter, Jean G. Hospital Corporation Organization, Reorganization, & Joint Ventures. (Hospital Law in North Carolina Ser.: Chap. 15). 53p. 1991. ring bd. 10.50 (1-56011-182-8, 85.030) Institute Government.

Carter, Jean W. & Carter, Michael P. Sweet Grapes: How to Stop Being Infertile & Start Living Again. rev. ed. LC 89-34135. 160p. 1998. pap. 13.00 (0-944934-23-4) Perspect Indiana.

Carter, Jeanne Wilmot, see Dorson, Mercedes & Wilmot Carter, Jeanne, eds.

Carter, Jeannine K. Have Heart Will Travel: Personal Experiences & Practical Guidelines for Volunteer Mission Trips. LC 96-71626. (Illus.). 128p. (Orig.). 1996. pap. 11.95 (1-57736-024-9) Providence Hse.

Carter, Jeff. The New Frontier: Australia's Rising Northwest. LC 76-852106. 90p. 1971. write for info. (0-207-12146-X) Consort Bk Sales.

Carter, Jefferson. None of This Will Kill Me. 24p. (Orig.). 1987. pap. 5.00 (0-934910-01-4) Moon Pony.

Carter, Jennifer & Hirschhorn, Joel. Titanic Adventure: One Woman's True-Life Voyage down to the Legendary Ocean Liner. LC 98-66221. (Illus.). 288p. 1998. 26.95 (0-88282-170-9, Pub. by New Horizon NJ) Natl Bk Netwk.

Carter, Jennifer E. & Pittock, Joan. Aberdeen & the Enlightenment: Proceedings of a Conference Held at the University of Aberdeen. (Illus.). 272p. 1987. pap. text 30.00 (0-08-034524-7, Pub. by Aberdeen U Pr) Macmillan.

Carter, Jerilynn. Stand Fast in Liberty: An Expression of Freedom Through Music. 24p. 1996. pap. text 8.95 (1-57636-011-3) SunRise Pbl.

Carter, Jerry O. Tree of Spice. 1998. pap. write for info. (1-57553-649-8) Watermrk Pr.

***Carter, Jerry O. & Sharpe, Richard.** Teach Yourself Samba in 24 Hours. LC 98-83129. (Illus.). 490p. 1999. pap. 24.99 incl. cd-rom (0-672-31609-9) Sams.

Carter, Jill. Elimination Diet Cookbook: A 28-Day Plan for Detecting Allergies. LC 96-52049. 144p. 1997. pap. 9.95 (1-85230-946-6, Pub. by Element MA) Penguin Putnam.

— Embroidered Heirlooms to Make & Treasure. (Illus.). 128p. 1998. 29.95 (0-7134-7966-3, Pub. by B T B) Branford.

— Hardanger Embroidery: Over 20 Stunning Counted-Thread Projects. LC 98-56384. (Illus.). 128p. 1999. 27.50 (1-57990-094-1) Lark Books.

— Rotation Diet Cookbook: A 4-Day Plan for Relieving Allergies. LC 97-6977. 144p. 1997. pap. 9.95 (1-85230-965-2, Pub. by Element MA) Penguin Putnam.

***Carter, Jill, et al.** Planet Health: An Interdisciplinary Curriculum for Teaching Middle School Nutrition & Physical Activity. (Illus.). 312p. 2000. pap. write for info. (0-7360-3105-7) Human Kinetics.

Carter, Jimmy. Always a Reckoning: And Other Poems. 1994. 19.00 (0-8129-2434-7, Times Bks) Crown Pub Group.

— Always a Reckoning: And Other Poems. large type ed. LC 95-13851. (Illus.). 126p. 1995. lib. bdg. 20.95 (0-7838-1301-5, G K Hall Lrg Type) Mac Lib Ref.

— Atlanta. (Illus.). 1999. 49.95 (1-881096-73-4) Towery Pub.

— The Blood of Abraham: Insights into the Middle East. 1993. reprint ed. pap. 20.00 (1-55728-293-5) U of Ark Pr.

— A Government As Good As Its People. LC 95-23843. 248p. 1996. reprint ed. pap. 20.00 (1-55728-398-2) U of Ark Pr.

— Keeping Faith: Memoirs of a President. 640p. 1982. 350.00 (0-553-05028-1) Bantam.

— Keeping Faith: Memoirs of a President. LC 95-9691. 640p. 1995. pap. 32.00 (1-55728-330-3) U of Ark Pr.

— Letters to Hon. William Prescott. 1977. lib. bdg. 59.95 (0-8490-2156-1) Gordon Pr.

— Living Faith. 1996. 23.00 (0-8129-2736-2, Times Bks) Crown Pub Group.

— Living Faith. LC 99-204724. 1998. pap. 13.00 (0-8129-3034-7, Times Bks) Crown Pub Group.

— Living Faith. large type ed. 1996. pap. 24.00 (0-679-75902-6) Random Hse Lrg Prnt.

— Negotiation: The Alternative to Hostility. LC 84-10720. (Carl Vinson Memorial Lecture). (Illus.). xxxiii, 57p. 1984. 12.95 (0-86554-137-X, MUP/H128) Mercer Univ Pr.

— An Outdoor Journal: Adventures & Reflections: A Personal Memoir. rev. ed. LC 94-5845. 320p. 1994. reprint ed. pap. 22.00 (1-55728-354-0) U of Ark Pr.

— Sources of Strength. large type ed. LC 97-17771. (Large Print Ser.). 1997. pap. 23.00 (0-679-77453-X) Random.

***Carter, Jimmy.** Sources of Strength: Meditations on Scripture for a Living Faith. LC 97-27501. 272p. 1999. pap. 14.00 (0-8129-3236-6, Times Bks) Crown Pub Group.

Carter, Jimmy. Sources of Strength: Meditations on Scripture for a Living Faith. 272p. 1999. pap. 14.00 (1-57856-290-2) Waterbrook Pr.

— Sources of Strength: Meditations on Scripture for Daily Living. LC 97-27501. 256p. 1997. 23.00 (0-8129-2944-6, Times Bks) Crown Pub Group.

— Talking Peace. 1996. pap. 18.99 (0-525-45651-1) NAL.

— Talking Peace: A Vision for the Next Generation. (Illus.). 206p. (YA). (gr. 7 up). 1995. pap. 6.99 (0-14-037440-X, PuffinBks) Peng Put Young Read.

Carter, Jimmy. Talking Peace a Vison for the Next Generation. (J). 1995. 11.09 (0-606-08266-2, Pub. by Turtleback) Demco.

Carter, Jimmy. Turning Point: A Candidate, A State, & a Nation Come of Age. 1993. pap. 14.00 (0-8129-2299-9) Random.

— Turning Point: A Candidate, a State, & Nation Come of Age. large type ed. LC 93-13564. 283p. 1993. lib. bdg. 18.95 (1-56054-772-3) Thorndike Pr.

— The Virtues of Aging. LC 98-25298. 1998. 18.95 (0-345-42826-9) Ballantine Pub Grp.

— The Virtues of Aging. LC 98-25298. (Library of Contemporary Thought). 96p. 1998. pap. 9.95 (0-345-42592-8) Ballantine Pub Grp.

— Virtues of Aging. large type ed. LC 98-26244. 1998. pap. 14.95 (0-375-70460-4) Random.

— Why Not the Best? The First Fifty Years. LC 96-17579. 1996. pap. 20.00 (1-55728-418-0) U of Ark Pr.

***Carter, Jimmy & Boutros-Ghali, Boutros, eds.** Conference for Global Development Cooperation (1992) (Illus.). 90p. (C). 2000. pap. text 20.00 (0-7881-8487-3) DIANE Pub.

Carter, Jimmy & Carter, Amy. Little Baby Snoogle-Fleejer. LC 95-41408. (Illus.). 32p. (gr. 2 up). 1995. 17.00 (0-8129-2731-1, Times Bks) Crown Pub Group.

Carter, Jimmy & Carter, Rosalynn. Everything to Gain: Making the Most of the Rest of Your Life. 224p. 1995. pap. 20.00 (1-55728-388-5) U of Ark Pr.

Carter, Jimmy, jt. ed. see Pastor, Robert A.

Carter, Joan, ed. see Fong, Norman.

Carter, John. ABC for Book Collectors. 7th ed. Barker, Nicolas, ed. & rev. by. LC 94-29934. 224p. 1995. 25.00 (1-884718-05-1) Oak Knoll.

— The Arabian Desert: A Chronicle of Contrast. (Illus.). 112p. (C). 1995. 95.00 (0-907151-06-X, Pub. by IMMEL Pubng) St Mut.

***Carter, John.** Covert Operations as a Tool of Presidential Foreign Policy in American History from 1800 to 1920: Foreign Policy in the Shadows. LC 00-24441. (Studies in American History: 26). 240p. 2000. 89.95 (0-7734-7754-3) E Mellen.

Carter, John. Credit Repair & Debt Collection Practices. LC 95-67534. 120p. 1995. pap. 9.95 (0-9637515-4-9) Dageforde Pub.

— Postmodernity & the Fragmentation of Welfare. LC 97-26563. 304p. (C). 1998. pap. 27.99 (0-415-16392-7) Routledge.

— Postmodernity & the Fragmentation of Welfare. LC 97-26563. (Illus.). 304p. (C). 1998. 85.00 (0-415-16391-9) Routledge.

— Sex & Rockets: The Occult World of Jack Parsons. (Illus.). 240p. 1999. 24.95 (0-922915-56-3) Feral Hse.

— Tribes in Oman. 176p. (C). 1995. 96.00 (0-907151-02-7, Pub. by IMMEL Pubng) St Mut.

Carter, John, ed. New Paths in Book Collecting: Essays by Various Hands. LC 67-30179. (Essay Index Reprint Ser.). 1977. 18.95 (0-8369-0279-3) Ayer.

Carter, John, tr. Civil Wars. LC 96-232186. 480p. 1996. pap. 13.95 (0-14-044509-9, Viking) Viking Penguin.

Carter, John & Beall, Mary K. The Magnificent 7: The Sequel Teacher's Handbook: Great Composers in Song. 48p. 1999. pap., teacher ed. 19.95 (0-7390-0081-0, 18734) Alfred Pub.

— The Magnificent 7: The Sequel Teacher's Kit: Great Composers in Song. 1999. pap. 44.95 incl. audio compact disk (0-7390-0080-2, 18737) Alfred Pub.

Carter, John & Beall, Mary Kay. Christmas with the Classics: A School-Time, Yule-Time Journey. 1997. pap., student ed. 22.50 (0-7390-0765-3, 16388) Alfred Pub.

— The Magnificent Seven: Great Composers in Song. 1995. pap., student ed. 22.50 (0-7390-0696-7, 11694) Alfred Pub.

***Carter, John & Palihawadana, Mahinda, eds.** Dhammapada. (Oxford World's Classics Ser.). 120p. 2000. pap. 7.95 (0-19-283613-7) OUP.

Carter, John & Pollard. An Enquiry into the Nature of Nineteenth Century Pamphlets. LC 76-164659. (English Literature Ser.: No. 33). 1971. reprint ed. lib. bdg. 75.00 (0-8383-1261-6) M S G Haskell Hse.

Carter, John & Pollard, Graham. An Enquiry into the Nature of Certain Nineteenth Century Pamphlets. 2nd ed. Barker, Nicolas & Collins, John, eds. (Illus.). 432p. 1992. reprint ed. 55.00 (0-938768-31-X) Oak Knoll.

Carter, John, jt. auth. see Beall, Mary K.

Carter, John, jt. auth. see Narramore, Bruce S.

Carter, John, tr. & intro. see Caesar, Julius.

Carter, John E. Solomon D. Butcher: Photographing the American Dream. LC 85-5835. (Illus.). x, 142p. 1985. text 50.00 (0-8032-1404-9) U of Nebr Pr.

Carter, John E., jt. auth. see Vogel, Deanie.

Carter, John F. What We Are about to Receive. LC 68-29196. (Essay Index Reprint Ser.). 1977. reprint ed. 20.95 (0-8369-0280-7) Ayer.

Carter, John H. Log of Commodore Rollingpin: His Adventures Afloat & Ashore. LC 74-166690. (Illus.). 1971. reprint ed. 29.00 (0-403-01452-2) Scholarly.

Carter, John L. & Carter, Ruth C. Bibliography & Index of North American Carboniferous Brachiopoda 1898-1968. LC 74-129146. (Geological Society of America, Memoir Ser.: No. 128). 392p. reprint ed. pap. 121.60 (0-8357-7170-9, 202546000044) Bks Demand.

Carter, John M. Arms & the Man: Studies in Roman & Medieval Warfare & Society. 146p. 1984. pap. text 28.95 (0-89126-123-0) MA-AH Pub.

— Ludi Medi Aevi: Studies in the History of Medieval Sport. 1981. pap. text 30.95 (0-89126-102-8) MA-AH Pub.

— Medieval Games: Sports & Recreations in Feudal Society, 30. LC 91-785. (Contributions to the Study of World History Ser.: No. 30). 172p. 1992. 49.95 (0-313-26743-X, CRH, Greenwood Pr) Greenwood.

— Medieval Institutions: Study-Lecture Notes, Vol. 1. 205p. 1983. pap. text 35.95 (0-89126-125-7) MA-AH Pub.

— The Military & Social Significance of Ballad Singing in the English Civil War, 1642-1649. 95p. (Orig.). 1980. pap. text 25.00 (0-89126-095-1) MA-AH Pub.

Carter, John M., Sr. Rakke Nokuse (Big Bear) (Illus.). 112p. 1993. pap. 9.00 (0-934188-37-8) Evans Pubns.

Carter, John M. Sports & Games in the Middle Ages: An Annotated Bibliography. (Medieval Bibliographies Ser.: Vol. 12). 175p. 22.00 (0-8240-7184-0, H1369) Garland.

— War & Military Reform in the Roman Republic, 578-589 B. C. 95p. (Orig.). 1980. pap. 24.95 (0-89126-096-X) MA-AH Pub.

An Asterisk (*) at the beginning of an entry indicates that the title is appearing for the first time.

Carter, John M. & Kruger, Arnd, eds. Ritual & Record: Sports Records & Quantification in Pre-Modern Societies, 17. LC 89-78452. (Contributions to the Study of World History Ser.: No. 17). 184p. 1990. 57.95 (*0-313-25699-3*, CSE/, Greenwood Pr) Greenwood.

Carter, John R. On Understanding Buddhists: Essays on the Theravada Tradition in Sri Lanka. LC 92-10830. (SUNY Series in Buddhist Studies). 251p. 1993. text 19.50 (*0-7914-1413-2*) State U NY Pr.

Carter, John R. & Palihawadana, Mahinda, trs. The Dhammapada. 552p. 1998. pap. 24.95 (*0-19-510860-4*) OUP.

***Carter, John Ross, ed.** Religious Heritage of Japan: Foundations for Cross-Cultural Understanding in Religiously Plural World. (Illus.). 256p. (C). 2000. pap. 21.95 (*0-9647040-4-8*) Book East.

Carter, John S. American Traders in European Ports. LC 82-303. (Illus.). 56p. 1982. pap. 15.00 (*0-87577-068-1*, PEMP103, Peabody Museum) Peabody Essex Mus.

Carter, John S., ed. see Shirley, James.

Carter, John T. Louis Bromfield & the Malabar Farm Experience. Date not set. pap. 11.95 (*0-8488-1716-8*); lib. bdg. 21.95 (*0-8488-1813-X*) Amereon Ltd.

Carter, John W. Digital Designing with Programmable Logic Devices. LC 96-1547. 417p. 1996. 120.00 (*0-13-373721-7*) P-H.

Carter, John W., jt. auth. see Chappenden, W. J.

Carter, Jonathan & Carter, Dawn. Stock Journal. 90p. 1998. pap. 16.95 (*0-9669167-0-0*) Carter Pubg.

Carter, Jonathon. An Atlas of Transvaginal Sonography. LC 93-48347. 240p. 1994. text 135.00 (*0-397-51460-3*) Lppncott W & W.

Carter, Jonita B. Lord, I Got Much More Than I Asked For. 144p. (Orig.). 1993. pap. 12.00 (*0-9638881-0-2*) S E T H Pubs.

***Carter, Joseph C., ed.** The Choro of Metaporto Vols. 1 & 2: The Necropoleis, 2 vols. LC 97-36731. (Illus.). 909p. (C). 1998. 125.00 (*0-292-71211-1*, CARCHO) U of Tex Pr.

Carter, Joseph E. Shortcuts to Justice. LC 99-94516. (Illus.). vii, 212p. 1999. 18.95 (*0-9634357-4-4*); pap. 10.95 (*0-9634357-5-2*) S S I Pubns.

Carter, Joseph G. Skeletal Biomineralization: Patterns, Processes, & Evolutionary Trends, 2 vols., Set. (Illus.). 700p. (gr. 13). 1990. text 115.50 (*0-442-00667-5*) Chapman & Hall.

Carter, Joseph H. Never Met a Man I Didn't Like. 285p. Date not set. 23.95 (*0-8488-2230-7*) Amereon Ltd.

— Never Met Man Didn't Lik. LC 92-121146. 275p. 1991. pap. 11.00 (*0-380-76808-9*, Avon Bks) Morrow Avon.

Carter, Joseph R. Purchasing: Continued Improvement Through Integration. 270p. 1992. 45.00 (*1-55623-535-6*, Irwn Prfssnl) McGraw-Hill Prof.

Carter, Joseph R. & Narasimhan, Ram. Puchasing & Supply Management: Future Directions & Trends. LC 95-71340. 128p. (Orig.). 1996. pap. text 20.00 (*0-945968-24-8*) Ctr Advanced Purchasing.

— Purchasing & Materials Management's Role in Total Quality Management & Customer Satisfaction. Ketchum, Carol L., ed. LC 93-70434. 87p. (Orig.). (C). 1993. pap. text 20.00 (*0-945968-12-4*) Ctr Advanced Purchasing.

Carter, Juanita E. & Young. Electronic Calculators: A Mastery Approach, 3 vols. 3rd ed. (C). 1990. pap. 32.36 (*0-395-35926-0*) HM.

Carter, Juanita E. & Young. Electronic Calculators: A Mastery Approach, 3 vols. 3rd ed. (C). 1990. pap. text 4.76 (*0-395-52647-7*) HM.

Carter, Judith, jt. ed. see Bangalore, Nirmala.

Carter, Judith Q. & Carter, Richard D., compiled by. Herbert L. Fink: Graphic Artist. LC 80-39918. (Illus.). 158p. 1981. 31.95 (*0-8093-1016-3*) S Ill U Pr.

Carter, Judy. Homo Handbook. LC 96-20557. 224p. 1996. per. 12.00 (*0-684-81358-0*) S&S Trade.

— The Jesus Chronicles: Old Truth Uncovered. 1998. pap. 10.00 (*1-56411-205-5*) Untd Bros & Sis.

Carter, Judy. Malacwi: Wildlife, Parks & Reserves LC 89-161327. 176 p. 1987. write for info. (*0-333-43349-1*) Trans-Atl Phila.

Carter, Judy. Stand-up Comedy: The Book. 240p. 1989. pap. 13.95 (*0-440-50243-8*, Dell Trade Pbks) Dell.

Carter, Judy L., jt. auth. see Bruner, Charles.

Carter, June C. & Schmidt, Donald L., eds. Jose Agustin: "Onda" & Beyond. LC 86-6943. 136p. 1986. text 24.95 (*0-8262-0611-5*) U of Mo Pr.

Carter, K. Codell, tr. Essays of Robert Koch, 20. LC 87-19737. (Contributions in Medical Studies: No. 20). 160p. 1987. 49.95 (*0-313-25951-8*, CRK/, Greenwood Pr) Greenwood.

Carter, K. Codell & Carter, Barbara R. Childbed Fever: A Scientific Biography of Ignaz Semmelweis, 39. LC 93-32618. (Contributions in Medical Studies: No. 39). 144p. 1994. 45.00 (*0-313-29146-2*, Greenwood Pr) Greenwood.

Carter, K. Codell, tr. see Semmelweis, Ignaz.

Carter, K. Holly. The Asian Dilemma in United States Foreign Policy: National Interest vs. Strategic Planning. LC 88-3416. 250p. (C). 1989. pap. text 35.95 (*0-87332-544-3*, East Gate Bk) M E Sharpe.

Carter, K. Holly Maze. The Asian Dilemma in United States Foreign Policy: National Interest vs. Strategic Planning. LC 88-3416. 250p. (C). 1989. text 85.95 (*0-87332-512-5*, East Gate Bk) M E Sharpe.

Carter, K. N. Determining the Formula & Estimating the Dissociation Constant of a Complex Ion. Neidig, H. Anthony, ed. (Modular Laboratory Program in Chemistry Ser.). 16p. (C). 1994. pap. text 1.50 (*0-87540-438-3*, STOI 438-3) Chem Educ Res.

Carter, Karen. The Performance Budget Revisited: A Report on State Budget Reform. LC 97-186872. (Legislative Finance Papers: No. 91). 34p. 1994. 10.00 (*1-55516-553-2*, 5101-91) Natl Conf State Legis.

Carter, Karen, jt. auth. see Mackey, Scott R.

***Carter, Karen Rauch.** Move Your Stuff, Change Your Life: How to Use Feng Shui to Get Love, Money, Respect, & Happiness, LC 99-35705. 240p. 2000. per. 13.00 (*0-684-86604-8*) S&S Trade.

Carter, Kate. Mountain Bike! Vermont. LC 98-6082. (North America by Mountain Bike Ser.). 320p. 1998. pap. 15.95 (*0-89732-267-3*) Menasha Ridge.

Carter, Katharine J. Oceans. LC 81-17093. (New True Books Ser.). (Illus.). 48p. (J). (gr. 2-4). 1982. pap. 5.50 (*0-516-41639-1*) Childrens.

Carter, Katherine. Mighty Hand of God. 224p. 1991. pap. 8.95 (*0-89228-043-3*) Impact Christian.

Carter, Kathryn. Stagecoach Inns of Texas. LC 93-48190. 280p. 1994. 22.95 (*0-89015-914-9*) Sunbelt Media.

Carter, Kathryn & Presnell, Mick, eds. Interpretive Approaches to Interpersonal Communication. LC 93-7710. (SUNY Series, Human Communication Processes). 272p. (C). 1994. text 64.50 (*0-7914-1847-2*); pap. text 21.95 (*0-7914-1848-0*) State U NY Pr.

Carter, Kathryn, ed. see Dervin, Brenda.

Carter, Kaye E. Henry Perrine, Plant Pioneer of the Florida Frontier. (Southern Pioneer Ser.). (Illus.). 72p. 1998. pap. 14.95 (*0-9631241-7-X*) Tail Tours.

Carter, Keith. The Blue Man. LC 89-43350. (Illus.). 144p. 1990. 39.95 (*0-89263-272-0*) Tex A&M Univ Pr.

***Carter, Keith.** Ezekial's Horse. LC 00-29940. (Illus.). 168p. 2000. 50.00 (*0-292-71229-4*) U of Tex Pr.

Carter, Keith. Mojo. LC 92-50335. (Illus.). 1995. pap. 29.95 (*0-89263-335-2*) Tex A&M Univ Pr.

Carter, Keith, photos by. Bones. LC 96-3181. (Illus.). 120p. 1996. pap. 19.95 (*0-8118-1282-0*) Chronicle Bks.

— Bones. LC 96-3181. (Illus.). 120p. 1996. 35.00 (*0-8118-1258-8*) Chronicle Bks.

***Carter, Keith, photos by.** Keith Carter: Holding Venus. (Illus.). 2000. 65.00 (*1-892041-24-3*, Pub. by Arena Editions) Dist Art Pubs.

Carter, Keith, photos by. Keith Carter Photographs: Twenty-Five Years. LC 97-8052. (Wittliff Gallery of Southwestern & Mexican Photography Ser.). (Illus.). 168p. 1997. 50.00 (*0-292-71195-6*) U of Tex Pr.

Carter, Keith, jt. ed. see Delamont, Sarah.

Carter, Kent. The Dawes Commission & the Allotment of the Five Civilized Tribes, 1893-1914. LC 98-27344. 300p. 1998. pap. 29.95 (*0-916489-85-X*) Ancestry.

Carter, Kimya M., jt. auth. see Carter, Charles.

Carter, Kit, jt. auth. see Clark, I. E.

Carter, Kit C. & Mueller, Robert. The Army Air Forces in World War Two: Combat Chronology 1941-1945. Gilbert, James B., ed. LC 79-7235. (Flight: Its First Seventy-Five Years Ser.). 1980. reprint ed. lib. bdg. 88.95 (*0-405-12151-2*) Ayer.

Carter, Kit C. & Mueller, Robert, eds. Combat Chronology, 1941-1945. 991p. 1991. pap. text. write for info. (*0-912799-68-4*) AFH & MP.

Carter, Kyle. Animal Eating Habits. LC 94-46846. (Things Animals Do Discovery Library). 24p. (J). (gr. k-4). 1995. lib. bdg. 15.93 (*1-55916-111-6*) Rourke Bk Co.

— Animales Constructores de Casas. (Que Hacen los Animales?).Tr. of Animals That Build Homes. 24p. (J). (gr. k-4). 1995. lib. bdg. 17.97 (*1-55916-146-9*) Rourke Bk Co.

— Animales Viajeros. (Que Hacen los Animales?).Tr. of Animals That Travel. 24p. (J). (gr. k-4). 1995. lib. bdg. 17.97 (*1-55916-145-0*) Rourke Bk Co.

— Animals That Build Homes. LC 94-46845. (Things Animals Do Discovery Library). 24p. (J). (gr. k-4). 1995. lib. bdg. 15.93 (*1-55916-112-4*) Rourke Bk Co.

— Animals That Fight. LC 94-46854. (Things Animals Do Discovery Library). 24p. (J). (gr. k-4). 1995. lib. bdg. 15.93 (*1-55916-113-2*) Rourke Bk Co.

— Animals That Survive. LC 94-46847. (Things Animals Do Discovery Library). 24p. (J). (gr. k-4). 1995. lib. bdg. 15.93 (*1-55916-114-0*) Rourke Bk Co.

— Animals That Talk. LC 94-47362. (Things Animals Do Discovery Library). 24p. (J). (gr. k-4). 1995. lib. bdg. 15.93 (*1-55916-115-9*) Rourke Bk Co.

— Animals That Travel. LC 94-47360. (Things Animals Do Discovery Library). 24p. (J). (gr. k-4). 1995. lib. bdg. 15.93 (*1-55916-110-8*) Rourke Bk Co.

— At Home. LC 94-18133. (J). 1994. lib. bdg. 14.60 (*1-57103-080-8*) Rourke Pr.

— Athletes. LC 94-12386. (Performers Discovery Library). (J). 1994. lib. bdg. 14.60 (*1-57103-061-1*) Rourke Pr.

— Circus Stars. LC 94-12385. (Performers Discovery Library). (J). 1994. lib. bdg. 14.60 (*1-57103-066-2*) Rourke Pr.

— En el Agua. (Seguridad Ser.).Tr. of In Water. (Illus.). 24p. (J). (gr. k-4). 1989. lib. bdg. 10.95 (*0-86625-083-2*) Rourke Pubns.

— From Crime. LC 94-18132. (J). 1994. lib. bdg. write for info. (*1-57103-077-8*) Rourke Pr.

— Hunter-Killer Submarines. (Seguridad Ser.). (Illus.). 24p. (J). (gr. k-4). 1989. lib. bdg. 10.95 (*0-86625-086-7*) Rourke Pubns.

— In the Outdoors. LC 94-12677. (Safety Ser.). 1994. lib. bdg. 14.60 (*1-57103-079-4*) Rourke Pr.

— In Water. LC 94-19066. (J). 1994. lib. bdg. 14.60 (*1-57103-075-1*) Rourke Pr.

— El Lenguaje de los Animales. (Que Hacen los Animales?).Tr. of Animals That Talk. 24p. (J). (gr. k-4). 1994. lib. bdg. 17.27 (*1-55916-148-5*) Rourke Bk Co.

— Nuclear Carriers. (Seguridad Ser.). (Illus.). 24p. (J). (gr. k-4). 1989. lib. bdg. 10.95 (*0-86625-084-0*) Rourke Pubns.

— On Bicycles. LC 94-20174. (J). 1994. lib. bdg. 14.60 (*1-57103-078-6*) Rourke Pr.

— Las Peleas de los Animales. (Que Hacen los Animales?).Tr. of Animals That Fight. 24p. (J). (gr. k-4). 1995. lib. bdg. 17.27 (*1-55916-150-7*) Rourke Bk Co.

— Que Hacen los Animales para Sobrevivr. (Que Hacen los Animales?).Tr. of Animals That Survive. 24p. (J). (gr. k-4). Date not set. lib. bdg. 17.27 (*1-55916-149-3*) Rourke Bk Co.

— Sea Power Library, 6 bks., Set, Reading Level 5. (Seguridad Ser.). (Illus.). 24p. (J). (gr. k-4). 1989. lib. bdg. 10.95 (*0-86625-087-5*) Rourke Pubns.

— With Fire. LC 94-19067. (J). 1994. lib. bdg. 14.60 (*1-57103-076-X*) Rourke Pr.

Carter, L. L. & Cashwell, E. D. Particle-Transport Simulation with the Monte Carlo Method. LC 75-25993. (ERDA Critical Review Ser.). 124p. 1975. pap. 11.00 (*0-87079-021-8*, TID-26607); fiche 9.00 (*0-87079-382-9*, TID-26607) DOE.

Carter, L. Phillip & Spetzler, Robert F., eds. Neurovascular Surgery. 1446p. 1994. text 275.00 (*0-07-011020-4*) McGraw-Hill HPD.

Carter, Lamar C., et al, eds. Aspects of Hope: The Proceedings of a Seminar on Hope. LC 93-77736. 205p. (C). 1993. pap. 14.00 (*0-9636208-0-0*) ICIS Ctr Sci.

Carter, Lane, jt. auth. see Powell, Samuel.

Carter, Lanie & Ostrow, Lauren S. The Miracle Year: An Expectant Parents' Guide to the Miraculous Six Months Before - & after - the Birth of Their First Baby. 224p. 1992. pap. 8.00 (*0-671-70432-X*) PB.

Carter, Lark P., et al. Working in Plant Science: Activity Guide. Aaberson, Max, ed. (Illus.). (gr. 9-10). 1978. pap. text 12.96 (*0-07-000836-1*) McGraw.

Carter, Larry E. Health Care Reform: Policy Innovations at the State Level in the United States. LC 98-26539. (Health Care Policy in the United States Ser.). (Illus.). 110p. 1998. 39.00 (*0-8153-3135-5*) Garland.

Carter, Laura, ed. see Goldin, Stan M.

Carter, Laura, ed. see Goldin, Stan M. & Tankosic, Timothy.

Carter, Laura, jt. ed. see Raley, Nancy S.

Carter, Laurence. Foreign Direct Investment in Central & Eastern European Infrastructure. LC 96-217760. (Occasional Papers: No. 7). 38p. 1996. pap. 22.00 (*0-8213-3818-8*, 13818) World Bank.

— IFC's Experience in Promoting Emerging Market Investment Funds 1977-1995. LC 96-28502. (IFC Lessons of Experience Ser.: No. 2). xxp. 1996. pap. 22.00 (*0-8213-3676-2*, 13676) World Bank.

— Leasing in Emerging Markets, 1977-1995. LC 96-28074. (IFC Lessons of Experience Ser.: No. 3). 76p. 1996. pap. 22.00 (*0-8213-3675-4*, 13675) World Bank.

Carter, Lawrence E., ed. The Crises of the African-American Male: Dangers & Opportunities. 410p. 1995. pap. 24.95 (*0-931761-34-4*) Beckham Pubns.

Carter, Lawrence T. Eubie Blake: Keys of Memory. LC 79-12430. 1979. 8.00 (*0-913642-10-X*) Balamp Pub.

Carter, Lee. Lucifer's Handbook: A Simplified Critique of Popular Religion. LC 76-55893. 1977. pap. text 7.95 (*0-918260-01-9*) Acad Assoc.

Carter, Lee, jt. auth. see Micek, Greg.

Carter, Len J. & Bainum, Peter M., eds. Space: A Developing Role for Europe, 18th European Space Symposium, Jun. 6-9, 1983, London, England. (Science & Technology Ser.: Vol. 56). (Illus.). 278p. 1984. 45.00 (*0-87703-193-2*, Am Astronaut Soc); pap. 35.00 (*0-87703-194-0*, Am Astronaut Soc) Univelt Inc.

***Carter, Leon T., ed.** Arms Control & Non-Proliferation: Issues & Analysis. 267p. 2000. lib. bdg. 49.00 (*1-56072-818-3*) Nova Sci Pubs.

Carter, Les. Distant Partner: How to Tear Down Emotional Walls & Communicate with Your Husband. LC 96-47773. 1997. pap. 12.99 (*0-7852-7551-7*) Nelson.

— Getting the Best of Your Anger. 176p. 1997. mass mkt. 5.99 (*0-8007-8646-7*, Good [00d4]n[00d5] Angry, Spire) Revell.

***Carter, Les.** People Pleasers: Helping Others Without Hurting Yourself. LC 99-59090. 192p. 2000. 17.99 (*0-8054-2146-7*) Broadman.

Carter, Les & Minirth, Frank. Choosing to Forgive Workbook: A 12-Part Comprehensive Plan to Overcome Your Struggle to Forgive & Find Lasting Healing. LC 97-210045. 288p. (Orig.). 1997. pap. 15.99 (*0-7852-8255-6*, J Thoma Bks) Nelson.

— The Freedom from Depression Workbook. LC 96-121330. 256p. 1995. pap. 15.99 (*0-8407-6207-0*) Nelson.

Carter, Les & Underwood, Jim. The Significance Principle. LC 98-22599. 224p. 1998. pap. 19.00 (*0-8054-1664-1*) Broadman.

Carter, Les, et al. The Anger Workbook. LC 92-21048. (Minirth-Meier Clinic Ser.). 237p. 1993. pap., wbk. ed. 16.99 (*0-8407-4574-5*) Nelson.

Carter, Lewis F. Control & Charisma in Rajneeshpuram: The Role of Shared Values in the Creation of a Community. (ASA Rose Monographs). (Illus.). 338p. (C). 1990. text 69.95 (*0-521-38554-7*) Cambridge U Pr.

Carter, Lief, et al. New Perspectives on American Law: An Introduction to Private Law in Politics & Society. LC 97-69308. 488p. 1997. pap. 29.95 (*0-89089-709-3*) Carolina Acad Pr.

Carter, Lief H. Administrative Law & Politics: Cases & Commentaries. (C). 1983. text 29.95 (*0-316-13047-8*, Aspen Law & Bus) Aspen Pub.

— Contemporary Constitutional Lawmaking: The Supreme Court & the Art of Politics. (Government & Politics Ser.). (Illus.). 256p. 1985. text 55.00 (*0-08-030970-4*, Pergamon Pr); pap. text 19.95 (*0-08-030969-0*, Pergamon Pr) Elsevier.

— International Law: Selected Documents. 1991. 22.00 (*0-316-13043-5*, Aspen Law & Bus) Aspen Pub.

— Reason in Law. 3rd ed. (C). 1988. 23.80 (*0-673-39712-2*) Addson-Wesley Educ.

— Reason in Law. 5th ed. LC 97-35721. 295p. (C). 1997. pap. 34.60 (*0-321-01111-2*) Addson-Wesley Educ.

Carter, Lief H. & Harrington, Christine B. Administrative Law Politics. 2nd ed. 512p. (C). 1997. text 96.00 (*0-673-46031-2*) Addson-Wesley Educ.

Carter, Lief H., jt. auth. see Waite Group Staff.

***Carter, Lin.** Callisto, Vol. 1. 416p. 2000. per. 14.00 (*0-7434-0005-4*, Pub. by ibooks) S&S Trade.

Carter, Lin. Invisible Death. LC 75-9219. 173p. 1975. 25.00 (*0-385-08768-3*) Ultramarine Pub.

— Realms of Wizardry. LC 76-2761. xv, 269 p. (J). 1976. 7.95 (*0-385-11393-5*) Doubleday.

— Tara of the Twilight. (Orig.). 1979. mass mkt. 2.25 (*0-89083-428-8*, Zebra Kensgtn) Kensgtn Pub Corp.

— The Volcano Ogre. LC 75-21217. 177p. 1976. 25.00 (*0-385-08807-8*) Ultramarine Pub.

Carter, Lin, et al. The Xothic Legend Cycle: The Mythos Fiction of Lin Carter. (Call of Cthulhu Fiction Ser.). (Illus.). 1997. pap. 10.95 (*1-56882-078-X*, 6013) Chaosium.

Carter, Lisa & Marques, Lori. Child Safety Made Easy. 128p. 1996. pap. 5.95 (*0-9652770-0-3*) Screamin Mimi.

Carter, Lisa, jt. auth. see House, Thomas.

Carter, Lonnie. The Sovereign State of Boogedy Boogedy & Other Plays. LC 86-18503. (Illus.). 205p. (Orig.). 1986. pap. text 7.50 (*0-933951-04-3*) Locust Hill Pr.

Carter, Lorna M., ed. Proceedings of the Fourth Symposium on the Geology of Rocky Mountain Coal, 1980. (Resource Ser.: No. 10). (Illus.). 131p. (Orig.). 1980. pap. 3.00 (*1-884216-30-7*) Colo Geol Survey.

Carter, Louise. Basic Gardening: A Handbook for Beginning Gardeners. LC 94-37915. (Illus.). 160p. 1995. pap. 9.95 (*1-55591-173-0*) Fulcrum Pub.

Carter, Louise & Lawson, JoAnne. The New Three Year Garden Journal: With Regional Planning Guides. rev. ed. LC 98-20536. (Illus.). 114p. 1999. 29.95 (*1-55591-392-X*) Fulcrum Pub.

***Carter, Lucy R. & Lankford, Sara S.** Physician's Compensation: Measurement, Benchmarking & Implementation. 20p. 2000. 75.00 (*0-471-32361-6*) Wiley.

Carter, Lula M. Hold on to the Brass Ring. 480p. Date not set. 21.95 (*0-9649289-0-6*) Marshl Cartr Pub.

Carter, Luther F., et al, eds. Government in South Carolina, 4 vols. 918p. (Orig.). 1985. pap. 50.00 (*0-917069-00-5*) Univ SC Inst Pub Affairs.

Carter, Luther F. & Mann, David S., eds. Government in the Palmetto State: Toward the 21st Century. (Government in South Carolina Ser.). (Illus.). 176p. (Orig.). 1993. pap. 18.00 (*0-917069-07-2*) Univ SC Inst Pub Affairs.

Carter, Luther J. The Florida Experience: Land & Water Policy in a Growth State. LC 74-6816. 376p. 1976. pap. 12.95 (*0-8018-1896-6*) Johns Hopkins.

— Florida Experience: Land & Water Policy in a Growth State. 1975. 24.00 (*0-8018-1646-7*) Johns Hopkins.

— Nuclear Imperatives & Public Trust: Dealing with Radioactive Waste. LC 87-4706. 473p. 1987. pap. 22.95 (*0-915707-47-0*) Resources Future.

Carter, Lyn R., ed. see Schaffner, C. Beth & Buswell, Barbara E.

Carter, Lynn R. An Analysis of Pascal Programs. Stone, Harold, ed. LC 82-4925. (Computer Science: No. 6). 203p. 1982. reprint ed. pap. 63.00 (*0-8357-1331-8*, 207011300064) Bks Demand.

Carter, Lynn T., et al. The Thinking Skills Workbook: A Cognitive Skills Remediation Manual for Adults. 2nd ed. (Illus.). 234p. 1984. pap., spiral bd. 36.95 (*0-398-04992-0*) C C Thomas.

Carter, M. & Symons, M. V. Site Investigations & Foundations Explained. 342p. 1989. pap. text 33.50 (*0-7273-1907-8*, PP03) Am Soc Civil Eng.

***Carter, M. & Van Brunt, B.** The Lebesque-Stieltjes Integral. LC 00-20065. (Undergraduate Texts in Mathematics Ser.). (Illus.). 232p. 2000. 44.95 (*0-387-95012-5*) Spr-Verlag.

Carter, M. E. Brown, jt. auth. see Murdy, William H.

Carter, M. R. Conservation Tillage in Temperate Agroecosystems: Development & Adaptation to Soil, Climatic, & Biological Constraints. 400p. 1993. lib. bdg. 115.00 (*0-87371-571-3*, L571) Lewis Pubs.

Carter, M. R., ed. Soil Sampling & Methods of Analysis. 864p. 1993. lib. bdg. 95.00 (*0-87371-861-5*, L861) Lewis Pubs.

Carter, M. Tish, ed. see Cash-Dudley, E. F.

Carter, M. V. Phyto Paper No. 32: Status of Eutypa Lata as a Pathogen. (Illus.). 70p. (C). 1991. pap. text 38.00 (*0-85198-695-1*) C A B Intl.

Carter, Mack K. A Quest for Freedom: An African-American Odyssey. LC 94-195515. 269p. (Orig.). 1993. pap. 12.00 (*0-9625423-9-3*) Four-G Pubs.

Carter, Marcia H. Stephen's Moon: A Mother's Journey Through Grief. 1999. pap. 9.95 (*0-9671781-4-2*) Black Sands.

Carter, Marcia J., et al, eds. Designing Therapeutic Recreation Programs in the Community. (Illus.). 354p. (Orig.). (C). 1991. pap. 25.00 (*0-88314-518-9*, A5189) AAHPERD.

Carter, Marcia J., et al. Designing Instructional Swim Programs for Individuals with Disabilities. (Illus.). 124p. (Orig.). 1994. pap. text 25.00 (*0-88314-559-6*, A5596) AAHPERD.

— Therapeutic Recreation: A Practical Approach. 2nd rev. ed. (Illus.). 593p. (C). 1995. text 42.95 (*0-88133-822-2*) Waveland Pr.

Carter, Marcia J., jt. auth. see O'Morrow, Gerald S.

Carter, Margaret. Little Book of Herbs. 1994. 4.98 (*1-55521-988-8*) Bk Sales Inc.

— Shadow of the Beast: A Werewolf Novel. 256p. 1998. pap. 15.95 (*1-891946-03-X*) Design Image.

Carter, Margaret L. Dracula: The Vampire & the Critics. Scholes, Robert, ed. LC 88-17244. (Studies in Speculative Fiction: No. 19). 273p. reprint ed. 84.70 (*0-8357-1889-1*, 207066700016) Bks Demand.

— Specter or Delusion? The Supernatural in Gothic Fiction. 132p. 1987. pap. 49.95 (*0-7734-1984-5*) E Mellen.

— Vampirism in Literature: Shadow of a Shade. 1974. lib. bdg. 250.00 (*0-87968-225-6*) Gordon Pr.

Carter, Margaret L. & Scholes, Robert, eds. The Vampire in Literature: A Critical Bibliography. LC 89-31932. (Studies in Speculative Fiction: No. 21). 143p. reprint ed. 44.40 (*0-8357-1998-7*, 207070400004) Bks Demand.

Carter, Margie & Curtis, Deb. Spreading the News: Sharing the Stories of Early Childhood Education. LC 96-6995. 64p. 1996. pap. 13.95 (*1-884834-14-0*, 1327) Redleaf Pr.

— Training Teachers: A Harvest of Theory & Practice. LC 94-38144. (Illus.). 288p. (Orig.). 1995. pap. 34.95 (*0-934140-82-0*, 1311) Redleaf Pr.

Carter, Margie, jt. auth. see Curtis, Deb.

Carter, Margie, jt. auth. see Curtis, Debbie.

Carter, Marie P. The Great Kitchen Escape: How to: Cook Ahead, Save Time, Save Money & Make Money. Zanetti, Cynthia, ed. (Illus.). (Orig.). 1994. pap. text 19.95 (*0-9643449-0-4*) M Carters Cooks.

***Carter, Marie P.** The Light Behind Every Dark Cloud. 132p. (YA). 2000. pap. 12.00 (*1-881524-73-6*) Milligan Bks.

Carter, Marilyn. Dolls Dressmaking. (Illus.). 104p. 1993. pap. 12.95 (*1-86351-078-8*, Pub. by Sally Milner) Sterling.

Carter, Marina. Voices from Indenture: Experiences of Indian Migrants in the British Empire. LC 95-43296. (New Historical Perspectives on Migration Ser.). (Illus.). 224p. (C). 1996. 79.95 (*0-7185-0031-8*) Bks Intl VA.

Carter, Marina, ed. Servants, Sirdars & Settlers: Indians in Mauritius, 1834-1874. (Oxford University South Asian Studies Ser.). (Illus.). 360p. 1995. text 29.95 (*0-19-563296-6*) OUP.

Carter, Marion. The Flowering Season. large type ed. 560p. 1989. 27.99 (*0-7089-2006-3*) Ulverscroft.

Carter, Marion E. Role of the Symbol in French Romantic Poetry. LC 77-94178. (Catholic University of America. Studies in Romance Languages & Literatures: No. 32). reprint ed. 37.50 (*0-404-50332-2*) AMS Pr.

Carter, Marion P., jt. auth. see Caleff, George O.

Carter, Mark A. Using RICO to Take the Wind Out of a Corporate Campaign. 46p. 1998. pap. 12.50 (*0-9667568-0-0*) LPA Inc.

Carter, Mark B. & Pottle, Mark, eds. Lantern Slides: The Diaries & Letters of Violet Bonham Carter 1904-1914. (Illus.). 496p. 1997. pap. (*1-85799-860-X*) Phoenix Hse.

Carter, Mark B., ed. see Asquith, Margo.

Carter, Mark J. Jeffco Students Falling Behind. (Issue Papers: No. 24-93). 11p. 1993. pap. text 8.00 (*1-57655-065-6*) Independ Inst.

Carter, Marshall & Shipman, William. Promises to Keep: Saving Social Security's Dream. 302p. 1996. 24.95 (*0-89526-438-2*) Regnery Pub.

Carter, Marshall, jt. auth. see Skidmore, Max J.

Carter, Martha L., ed. A Treasury of Indian Coins. LC 94-901411. (C). 1994. 78.00 (*81-85026-25-4*, Pub. by Marg Publns) Art Media Resources.

Carter, Martin, et al, eds. The Economics of Marketing. LC 98-29701. (International Library of Critical Writings in Economics). 768p. 1998. 260.00 (*1-85898-795-4*) E Elgar.

Carter, Martin, jt. auth. see Greenwood, Malcolm.

Carter, Martin R. & Stewart, B. A., eds. Structure & Organic Matter Storage in Agricultural Soils. LC 95-38348. (Advances in Soil Science Ser.). 496p. 1995. lib. bdg. 99.95 (*1-56670-033-7*, L1033) Lewis Pubs.

Carter, Martin R., jt. auth. see Gregorich, E. G.

Carter, Mary. Reading for Comprehension Skills. (Illus.). (J). (gr. 2-7). 1982. student ed. 4.50 (*0-89525-177-9*) Ed Activities.

Carter, Mary C., ed. see Sandling, R. Harris.

Carter, Mary E. Electronic Highway Robbery: An Artist's Guide to Copyrights in the Digital Era. LC 96-191675. (Illus.). 248p. (C). 1996. pap. 18.95 (*0-201-88393-7*) Peachpit Pr.

Carter, Mary E. & McGarey, William A. Edgar Cayce on Healing. 208p. 1988. mass mkt. 3.95 (*0-446-35250-0*, Pub. by Warner Bks) Little.

Carter, Mary Ellen. Passage to Millennium, Vol. 1. 1998. 6.99 (*0-312-96743-8*, Pub. by Tor Bks) St Martin.

Carter, Mary J. The Insider's Guide to Planning the Perfect Wedding. 160p. 1994. pap. 13.95 (*1-883280-03-6*) Font & Ctr Pr.

Carter, Mary J. & Kaplan, Michael. The Ruling Passion: Reflections on a Society Under Siege. LC 98-44603. 286p. 1999. 22.95 (*1-883280-13-3*) Font & Ctr Pr.

Carter, Mary R. American Family Style. LC 87-18959. (Illus.). 280p. 1988. 24.95 (*0-670-81806-2*) Studio Bks.

— American Junk. 256p. 1997. pap. 19.95 (*0-14-024405-0*, Viking) Viking Penguin.

— American Junk: How to Hunt for, Haggle over, Rescue, & Transform America's Forgotten Treasures (from Five Dollar Chairs to Five Cent Swizzle Sticks) from Flea Markets, Tag Sales, Trash Heaps, Thrift Shops, Auctions, & Attics for a One-of-a-Kind Look for Your House, Apartment, Getaway, Kitchen, Bedroom - Home! (Illus.). 256p. 1994. 32.95 (*0-670-84400-4*) Studio Bks.

— Garden Junk. LC 97-8341. (Illus.). 256p. 1997. 29.95 (*0-670-86938-4*, Viking) Viking Penguin.

— Kitchen Junk. LC 98-53227. (Illus.). 252p. 1999. 29.95 (*0-670-88099-X*) Viking Penguin.

Carter, Mary R., jt. auth. see Miller, Mary C.

Carter, Mary Randolph. The Welcome Book: Guest Book. 2nd ed. (Illus.). 120p. Date not set. reprint ed. 15.95 (*0-926684-13-2*, Pub. by Eclectic Oregon) Cogan Bks.

Carter, Mia, jt. auth. see Harlow, Barbara.

Carter, Michael, jt. auth. see Burke, Edmund.

Carter, Michael C., jt. auth. see Jackson, Bobby L.

Carter, Michael D. Converting the Wasteplaces of Zion: The Maine Missionary Society (1807-1816) LC 90-46235. 185p. 1990. text 21.50 (*0-89341-633-9*, Longwood Academic) Hollowbrook.

Carter, Michael G., ed. Arab Linguistics: An Introductory Classical Text with Translation & Notes. (Studies in the History of Language Sciences: No. 24). x, 485p. 1981. 97.00 (*90-272-4506-1*) J Benjamins Pubng Co.

Carter, Michael G., jt. ed. see Versteegh, Kees.

Carter, Michael P., jt. auth. see Carter, Jean W.

Carter, Michael R., et al. Agro-Exports & the Rural Resource Poor in Latin America: Policy Options for Achieving Broadly Based Growth. (Research Papers: No. 125). (Illus.). 77p. 1995. 7.00 (*0-934519-38-2*, RP 125) U of Wis Land.

— Tenure Security for Whom? Differential Impacts of Land Policy in Kenya. (Research Paper Ser.: Vol. 106). ix, 38p. (C). 1991. pap. 4.00 (*0-934519-16-1*, RP106) U of Wis Land.

***Carter, Michael W. & Price, Camille C.** Operations Research: A Practical Introduction. LC 00-31144. 2000. write for info. (*0-8493-2256-1*) CRC Pr.

Carter, Michele. Marvel Super Dice: Avengers 12. 1998. 107.40 (*0-7869-0840-8*) TSR Inc.

Carter, Michelle & Dougherty, Barbara. The Artist's Guide to Successfully Exhibiting at Convention Center Shows & Other Fine Art Fairs: Powerful Venues for Broadening Your Client Base. Blakeslee, Carolyn, ed. (Art Calendar Guide Ser.). 21p. 1999. pap. 9.95 (*0-945388-11-X*) Art Calendar.

Carter, Mike & Williamson, David. Quantitative Modelling for Management & Business, w/disk. 320p. (Orig.). 1995. pap. 64.50 incl. disk (*0-273-60510-0*, Pub. by Pitman Pub) Trans-Atl Phila.

Carter, Mike, ed. see Gomes, Alan W.

***Carter, Mildred.** Como Mejorar la Salud Con la Reflexologia. (SPA.). 2000. pap. 14.00 (*0-7352-0192-7*) PH Pr.

— Hand Reflexology. 2nd expanded abr. rev. ed. LC 99-38511. (C). 1999. text 27.95 (*0-13-016230-2*) S&S Trade.

Carter, Mildred. Hand Reflexology: Key to Perfect Health. 256p. (C). 1988. pap. text 9.95 (*0-13-372343-7*) P-H.

***Carter, Mildred.** Hand Reflexology: Key to Perfect Health. rev. ed. LC 99-38511. (Illus.). 256p. 1999. pap. text 13.00 (*0-7352-0128-5*, Prentice Hall) P-H.

Carter, Mildred & Ringquist, Neil A., eds. 1997 Year-End Tax Strategies. 48p. 1997. pap. text 12.95 (*0-8080-0157-4*) CCH INC.

Carter, Mildred & Weber, Tammy. Body Reflexology: Healing at Your Fingertips. 2nd rev. ed. LC 94-15863. 272p. (C). 1994. reprint ed. text 29.95 (*0-13-299728-2*, Parker Publishing Co) P-H.

— Body Reflexology: Healing at Your Fingertips. 2nd rev. ed. LC 94-15863. (Illus.). 400p. (C). 1994. reprint ed. pap. text 11.95 (*0-13-299736-3*, Parker Publishing Co) P-H.

— Como Mejorar la Salud Con al Reflexologia. 2nd ed. (SPA., Illus.). 400p. (C). 1997. text 24.95 (*0-13-858044-8*) P-H.

— Como Mejorar la Salud Usando La Reflexologia. 2nd ed. (SPA., Illus.). 400p. 1997. pap. text 12.95 (*0-13-848730-8*) P-H.

— Healing Yourself with Foot Reflexology. 2nd expanded rev. ed. 288p. (C). 1996. pap. text 12.95 (*0-13-244120-9*) P-H.

Carter-Miller, Jocelyn, jt. auth. see Giovagnoli, Melissa.

***Carter, Mimi.** The Insider's Guide to Quality Child Care in Greater Washington: Detailed Descriptions of 42 Accredited Centers in DC, MD & VA. (Illus.). 192p. 2000. pap. 12.95 (*1-889324-19-1*) EPM Pubns.

Carter, Minnie I. Portraits in Black & White. 42p. (Orig.). 1996. pap. 10.00 (*0-9654392-0-8*) Carter Pubng.

Carter, Mitch. Spirit & Poverty. Carter, Alicia, ed. (Illus.). 124p. 1998. pap. 19.00 (*1-57502-907-3*, PO2497) Morris Pubng.

Carter, Morris. Isabella Stewart Gardner & Fenway Court. LC 72-5539. (Select Bibliographies Reprint Ser.). (Illus.). 1972. reprint ed. 34.95 (*0-8369-6901-4*) Ayer.

Carter, N., et al. The Relationship Between Expenditure-Based Plans & Development Plans: With Specific Reference to Housing. (Progress in Planning Ser.: Vol. 39). 69p. 1992. 70.00 (*0-08-042187-3*, Pergamon Pr) Elsevier.

Carter, N. F. History of Pembroke, New Hampshire, 1730-1895, 2 vols., Set. 1257p. 1976. reprint ed. 60.00 (*0-89725-032-X*, 1244) Picton Pr.

Carter, N. L., et al, eds. Mechanical Behavior of Crustal Rocks. (Geophysical Monograph Ser.: Vol. 24). 326p. 1981. 42.00 (*0-87590-024-0*) Am Geophysical.

Carter, Nancy. Study Guide to the Caribbean: Culture of Resistance, Spirit of Hope. 1993. pap. 5.95 (*0-377-00255-0*) Friendship Pr.

Carter, Nancy A. Keeping Covenant with the Poor: Study Guide on Poverty in North America. 48p. 1988. pap. 3.95 (*0-377-00184-8*) Friendship Pr.

Carter, Nancy C. Dragon Poems. LC 92-44223. 64p. 1993. pap. 14.95 (*0-7734-2768-6*, Mellen Poetry Pr) E Mellen.

Carter, Nancy M. & Cullen, John B. The Computerization of Newspaper Organizations: The Impact of Technology on Organizational Structuring. (Illus.). 146p. (Orig.). (C). 1983. pap. text 19.50 (*0-8191-3379-5*); lib. bdg. 47.00 (*0-8191-3378-7*) U Pr of Amer.

Carter, Nevada. Bear Paw. large type ed. (Linford Western Library). 256p. 1997. pap. 16.99 (*0-7089-5003-5*, Linford) Ulverscroft.

Carter, Nicala. Resources for Nonlawyers. 14p. 1985. pap. write for info. (*0-318-64282-4*) NCLS Inc.

***Carter, Nicholas.** King of Coins. 345p. 1999. 29.95 (*0-7528-1008-1*, Pub. by Orion Pubng Grp) Trafalgar.

— Knave of Swords. 442p. 29.95 (*0-7528-1009-X*, Pub. by Orion Pubng Grp) Trafalgar.

— Knave of Swords. 1999. pap. 13.95 (*0-7528-2679-4*, Pub. by Orion Pubng Grp) Trafalgar.

Carter, Nicholas. The Stolen Pay Train. LC 74-15733. (Popular Culture in America Ser.). 128p. 1975. reprint ed. 16.95 (*0-405-06368-7*) Ayer.

Carter, Nick, jt. auth. see Lewis, Dale.

Carter, Nicola, jt. auth. see Platt, Adam.

Carter, Nicole, et al. The Implementation of Infrastructure in Texas Colonias: Self-Help & the Small Towns. (Working Paper Ser.). 76p. 1997. pap. 7.00 (*0-89940-568-1*) LBJ Sch Pub Aff.

Carter, Noelle. I'm a Little Mouse. LC 90-80318. (Illus.). 12p. (J). (ps-2). 1995. 10.95 (*0-8050-1420-9*, Bks Young Read) H Holt & Co.

— Peek-a-Boo, Little Mouse. LC 91-78193. (Illus.). 12p. (J). (ps). 1995. 10.95 (*0-8050-2253-8*, Bks Young Read) H Holt & Co.

— Where's My Christmas Stocking? LC 96-175008. (Lift & Touch Bks.). (Illus.). 14p. (J). (ps-k). 1995. 6.95 (*0-590-56870-1*, Cartwheel) Scholastic Inc.

Carter, Noelle & Carter, David A. Merry Christmas, Little Mouse: A Lift-the-Flap, Scratch-the-Scent Book. (Illus.). 12p. (J). (ps). 1995. 11.95 (*0-8050-2712-2*, Bks Young Read) H Holt & Co.

Carter, Novella & Parker, Matthew, eds. Women to Women: Perspectives of Fourteen African-American Christian Women. 240p. 1996. pap. 12.99 (*0-310-20145-4*) Zondervan.

Carter, P. B. Work for the Night Is Coming. 1985. 10.95 (*0-02-522090-X*) Macmillan.

Carter, P. B. & Harrison, R. Offences of Violence. (Waterlow Criminal Law Library). 320p. 1991. 100.00 (*0-08-040138-4*) Macmillan.

Carter, P. B., jt. auth. see Rook, P. F.

Carter, Pam. Feminism, Breasts, & Breast Feeding. LC 95-12498. 1995. text 39.95 (*0-312-12625-5*) St Martin.

Carter, Patricia. An Allergy Cookbook: Recipes Free from Eggs, Milk, Cheese, Butter, Wheat Flour, Chocolate, Salt, Sugar, Baking Powder, & Cornflower. 4th ed. LC 98-37010. 124p. (Orig.). 1998. pap. 15.00 (*0-88734-629-4*) Players Pr.

— Art of Illumination. 1997. pap. 29.95 (*0-85532-783-9*, Pub. by Srch Pr) A Schwartz & Co.

— Illuminated Alphabets. (Illus.). 64p. (Orig.). 1992. pap. 16.95 (*0-85532-710-3*, 710-3, Pub. by Srch Pr) A Schwartz & Co.

— Illuminated Calligraphy. (Illus.). 64p. 1994. 29.00 (*0-85532-675-1*, Pub. by Srch Pr) St Mut.

— Illuminated Calligraphy: Borders & Letters. (Illus.). 64p. (Orig.). (J). 1992. pap. 16.95 (*0-85532-642-5*, 642-5, Pub. by Srch Pr) A Schwartz & Co.

— Illuminated Designs. (Illus.). 64p. (Orig.). 1994. pap. 20.00 (*0-85532-777-4*, Pub. by Srch Pr) St Mut.

— Illuminated Designs. (Illus.). 64p. (Orig.). 1994. pap. 16.95 (*0-85522-777-X*, 7774, Pub. by Srch Pr) A Schwartz & Co.

— Lady of the Rock. 1993. pap. 5.00 (*0-86025-417-8*, Pub. by I Henry Pubns) Empire Pub Srvs.

— Silver Point: The Ancient Art of Drawing in Solid Silver & How to Add Colour to It. (Illus.). 32p. (Orig.). 1996. pap. 10.95 (*0-85532-800-2*, 28002, Pub. by Srch Pr) A Schwartz & Co.

Carter, Patricia, jt. auth. see Adams, Nancy.

Carter, Patricia, jt. ed. see Alfred, Richard L.

Carter, Paul. Backstage Forms. 166p. 1990. pap. 15.00 (*0-911747-35-4*) Broadway Pr.

— Backstage Handbook: An Illustrated Almanac Or Technical Information. 3rd rev. ed. (Illus.). 320p. 1995. pap. 15.00 (*0-911747-29-X*) Broadway Pr.

— The Road to Botany Bay: An Exploration of Landscape & History. LC 89-33192. (Illus.). 412p. 1996. reprint ed. pap. 20.50 (*0-226-09516-9*) U Ch Pr.

— The Sound In-Between. (C). 1992. pap. 32.95 (*0-86840-109-9*, Pub. by New South Wales Univ Pr) Intl Spec Bk.

Carter, Paul A. Politics, Religion, & Rockets: Essays in Twentieth-Century American History. LC 90-21111. 224p. 1991. 43.00 (*0-8165-1213-2*) U of Ariz Pr.

— Revolt Against Destiny: An Intellectual History of the United States. 331p. 1989. text 44.00 (*0-231-06616-3*) Col U Pr.

— Spiritual Crisis of the Gilded Age. LC 72-156938. (Illus.). 295p. 1971. 30.00 (*0-87580-026-2*) N Ill U Pr.

— Twenties in America. 2nd ed. Eisenstadt, A. S. & Franklin, John H., eds. LC 74-26538. (American History Ser.). 144p. (C). 1975. pap. text 11.95 (*0-88295-717-1*) Harlan Davidson.

***Carter, Paula.** Deathday Party, 1 vol. 1999. mass mkt. 5.99 (*0-425-17121-3*) Berkley Pub.

Carter, Paula. Leading an Elegant Death. (Mysteries by Design Ser.: Vol. 1). 1999. pap. 5.99 (*0-425-16733-X*, Prime Crime) Berkley Pub.

***Carter, Paula.** Red Wine Goes with Murder. 2000. mass mkt. 5.99 (*0-425-17552-9*, Prime Crime) Berkley Pub.

Carter, Penny. Building a Business, Creating a Life: A Design for Personal Fulfillment & Professional Success. 200p. 1999. pap. 12.95 (*1-893075-06-0*) Spirit Pr OR.

Carter, Peter. Borderlands. (Aerial Fiction Ser.). (J). 1993. 10.05 (*0-606-05764-1*, Pub. by Turtleback) Demco.

— The Hunted. LC 93-34211. 320p. (J). 1994. 17.00 (*0-374-33520-6*) FS&G.

— Mies van der Rohe at Work. (Illus.). 192p. 1999. pap. 29.95 (*0-7148-3896-9*) Phaidon Pr.

Carter, Peter R. Reconstruction of the Child's Hand. LC 90-6068. (Illus.). 321p. 1990. text 89.00 (*0-8121-1350-0*) Lppncott W & W.

***Carter, Philip.** Mensa Logic Brainteasers. 1999. pap. text 9.95 (*1-85868-545-1*, Pub. by Carlton Bks Ltd) Natl Bk Netwk.

***Carter, Philip & Russell, Ken.** The IQ Workout Book. 112p. 1999. pap. text 21.95 incl. cd-rom (*0-7641-7299-9*) Barron.

Carter, Philip, jt. auth. see Russell, Ken.

Carter, Philip, jt. auth. see Russell, Kenneth.

Carter, Philip B., ed. see International Symposium on Yersinia Staff.

Carter, Philip J. & Russell, Ken A. The New IQ Test: Joint Editors of the Mensa UK Puzzle Group Journal. (Illus.). 128p. 1994. pap. 5.95 (*0-7063-7229-8*, Pub. by WrLock) Sterling.

— Young Genius Book of Brain Teasers. (Illus.). 128p. (J). 1993. pap. 5.95 (*0-7063-7102-X*, Pub. by WrLock) Sterling.

***Carter, Philip J. & Russell, Kenneth A.** The Little Giant Encyclopedia of IQ Tests. LC 00-28502. 2000. pap. 9.95 (*0-8069-2889-1*) Sterling.

Carter, Philip J., et al. Classic Brain Puzzlers. (Illus.). 128p. 1995. pap. 5.95 (*0-7063-7231-X*, Pub. by WrLock) Sterling.

Carter, Philip J., jt. auth. see Russell, Ken A.

***Carter, Philippa.** The Servant-Ethic in the New Testament. 2nd ed. (American University Studies VII: Vol. 196). 155p. 1999. pap. text 23.95 (*0-8204-4571-1*, 45711) P Lang Pubng.

Carter, Phillip L., jt. auth. see Melnyk, Steven A.

Carter, Pippa, jt. auth. see Jackson, Norman.

Carter, Polly. Harriet Tubman. Brook, Bonnie, ed. (Let's Celebrate Ser.). (Illus.). 32p. (J). (gr. k-2). 1990. lib. bdg. 6.95 (*0-671-69109-0*) Silver Burdett Pr.

— Harriet Tubman & Black History Month. 32p. (J). (ps-3). 1996. pap. text 4.95 (*0-382-39479-8*) Silver Burdett Pr.

— Harriet Tubman & Black History Month. LC 89-49538. (Let's Celebrate Ser.). 1990. 10.15 (*0-606-10205-1*, Pub. by Turtleback) Demco.

— Telescope. (J). 1996. 15.00 (*0-671-87310-5*) S&S Bks Yung.

Carter, R. A., et al, eds. Contributions to Econometric Theory & Application: A Volume in Honour of A. L. Nagar's Sixtieth Birthday. (Illus.). xiii, 366p. 1990. 54.00 (*0-387-97285-4*) Spr-Verlag.

Carter, R. G. Electromagnetismo para Ingenieria Electronica. (SPA.). 208p. (C). 1993. pap. text 12.66 (*0-201-60136-2*) Addison-Wesley.

Carter, R. L. C. I. I. Management Eleven Risk Management, No. 313. (C). 1981. suppl. ed. 230.00 (*0-7855-4278-7*, Pub. by Witherby & Co) St Mut.

— C. I. I. Practice of Reinsurance, No. 280. (C). 1981. suppl. ed. 265.00 (*0-7855-4268-X*, Pub. by Witherby & Co) St Mut.

— C. I. I. Reinsurance Market, No. 290. (C). 1981. 230.00 (*0-7855-4262-0*, Pub. by Witherby & Co) St Mut.

— Economics & Insurance. (C). 1981. 150.00 (*0-7855-4181-0*, Pub. by Witherby & Co) St Mut.

Carter, R. L. & Diacon, S. R. British Insurance Industry: Statistical Review. (C). 1989. 1350.00 (*0-7855-4315-5*, Pub. by Witherby & Co) St Mut.

Carter, R. M. The History of the 4th Armoured Brigade. 2nd rev. ed. (World War II Monograph: Vol. 303). (Illus.). 52p. 1997. reprint ed. 15.95 (*1-57638-066-1*, M303H); reprint ed. pap. 5.95 (*1-57638-018-1*, M303S) Merriam Pr.

Carter, R. M., jt. ed. see Bouma, A. H.

Carter, R. R. & Randolph, R. I. Carter: The Carter Tree, Tabulated & Indexed. 241p. 1991. reprint ed. pap. 38.00 (*0-8328-2111-X*); reprint ed. lib. bdg. 48.00 (*0-8328-2110-1*) Higginson Bk Co.

Carter, R. W. Coastal Environments: An Introduction to the Physical, Ecological & Cultural Systems of Ocean Sciences, Resources & Technology Coastlines. 617p. 1990. pap. text 75.00 (*0-12-161856-0*) Acad Pr.

Carter, R. W., et al, eds. Coastal Dunes: Geomorphology, Ecology & Management for Conservation - Proceedings of the Third European Congress, Galway, Ireland, 17-21 June 1991. (Illus.). 530p. (C). 1993. text 168.00 (*90-5410-058-3*, Pub. by A A Balkema) Ashgate Pub Co.

Carter, R. W. & Woodroffe, C. D., eds. Coastal Evolution: Late Quaternary Shoreline Morphodynamics. 538p. 1997. pap. text 39.95 (*0-521-59890-7*) Cambridge U Pr.

Carter, R. W., et al. Algebra IX: Group Representations, Finite-Dimensional Division Rings. Kostrikin, Alexei I. et al, eds. Cohn, P. M., tr. from RUS. (Encyclopedia of Mathematical Sciences Ser.: Vol. 77). (Illus.). 246p. 1996. 98.00 (*3-540-57038-1*) Spr-Verlag.

Carter, Ralph G., jt. auth. see Rourke, John T.

Carter, Randolph & Cole, Robert. Joseph Urban: Architecture, Theatre, Opera, Film. LC 92-15386. (Illus.). 272p. 1992. 65.00 (*0-89659-912-4*) Abbeville Pr.

Carter, Raphael. The Fortunate Fall. 288p. 1997. pap. 13.95 (*0-312-86327-6*) St Martin.

Carter, Ray H. Washburn, a Town History: Settlers of Salmon Brook, Maine. (Illus.). 192p. 1987. 25.00 (*0-933858-18-3*); pap. 17.50 (*0-933858-10-8*) Kennebec River.

Carter, Rebecca. Autumn Weather. (Illus.). 44p. 1998. 8.99 (*1-58050-029-3*, 40-6165) Provo Craft.

— A Claus for Celebration, 3 vols. (Illus.). 32p. 1998. 9.99 (*1-58050-043-9*, 40-6173) Provo Craft.

— Rebecca's Pattern Book for Teachers. (Illus.). 44p. 1997. 8.99 (*1-58050-009-9*, 40-6135) Provo Craft.

— Scrapbooking for the First Time. LC 99-31344. (Illus.). 112p. 1999. 19.95 (*0-8069-2047-5*, Chapelle) Sterling.

***Carter, Rebecca.** Stencilling for the First Time. LC 00-30818. (Illus.). 2000. pap. 19.95 (*0-8069-4485-4*) Sterling.

C

An Asterisk (*) at the beginning of an entry indicates that the title is appearing for the first time.

Carter, Reginald & Perry, Henry B. Alternatives in Health Care Delivery: Emerging Roles for Physician Assistants. (Allied Health Professions Monograph). 412p. 1984. 42.50 (*0-87527-327-0*) Green.

Carter, Reginald K. The Accountable Agency, Vol. 34. 152p. (Orig.). (C). 1983. reprint ed. pap. 10.00 (*0-9623984-0-3*) R K Carter.

***Carter, Reginald Webster.** The Black Whole. 275p. 2001. pap. 17.95 (*0-9676268-1-1*) Sire Pubng.

— Masks of the Darkest American Game. LC 99-97515. 243p. 2000. pap. 17.95 (*0-9676268-0-3*) Sire Pubng.

Carter, Renee H. A Good Work Begun. (Illus.). viii, 44p. 1997. pap. 8.00 (*1-891773-03-8*) Orman Pr.

***Carter, Reon.** Picture Perfect. 2000. pap. 8.95 (*1-58571-004-0*, Pub. by Genesis Press) BookWorld.

Carter, Richard. The Gentle Legions: National Voluntary Health Organizations in America. 332p. (C). 1992. 39.95 (*1-56000-053-8*) Transaction Pubs.

Carter, Richard B. Descartes' Medical Philosophy: The Organic Solution to the Mind-Body Problem. LC 82-14933. 317p. 1983. reprint ed. pap. 98.30 (*0-608-03644-7*, 206447000009) Bks Demand.

— Nurturing Evolution: The Family As a Social Womb. LC 92-33099. 248p. (C). 1993. pap. text 26.50 (*0-8191-8909-X*); lib. bdg. 54.00 (*0-8191-8908-1*) U Pr of Amer.

Carter, Richard B. Sailing on Spirit Wind: Midlife Reflections. LC 98-96745. 1998. pap. 12.00 (*0-9666891-0-0*) Spirit Wind Bks.

Carter, Richard B., tr. see Portmann, Adolf.

Carter, Richard D., ed. Future Challenges of Management Education. LC 81-11932. 166p. 1981. 47.95 (*0-275-90590-X*, C0590, Praeger Pubs) Greenwood.

Carter, Richard D., jt. compiled by see Carter, Judith Q.

Carter, Richard E. Cabin Fever: Dialogues with Nature. LC 95-12551. (Illus.). 192p. 1995. pap. 12.95 (*1-880090-20-1*) Galde Pr.

Carter, Richard G. Goodnight Sweetheart, Goodnight: The Story of the Spaniels. LC 94-78836. (Illus.). 224p. 1995. pap. 12.00 (*0-9635720-2-4*) August Pr.

Carter, Richard J., jt. auth. see Uhrig, Robert E.

Carter, Rick & Nicotra, Brooke. Better Living with Chronic Obstructive Pulmonary Disease: How Patients, Families & Care Givers Can Manage Emphysema & Asthmatic or Chronic Bronchitis. (Illus.). 192p. (Orig.). 1998. pap. 29.95 (*1-882431-04-9*) New Technology.

Carter, Rick, et al. Courage & Information for Life with Chronic Obstructive Pulmonary Disease: The Handbook for Patients, Families & Care Givers Managing COPD. (Illus.). 256p. (Orig.). 1999. pap. 29.95 (*1-882431-06-5*) New Technology.

Minimize the impact of COPD, feel better & enjoy a fuller, more satisfying life. People with COPD (COLD) can actively manage their own health care to maintain a less-restricted life-style. This comprehensive guide combines the experience & insights of a patient with the expertise of medical & rehabilitation professionals. Carter (rehabilitation physiology) & Nicotra (pulmonary medicine) have developed the COPD rehabilitation program at the Tyler Texas Health Center. The needs & feelings of the patient are seen from the perspective of Tucker, a founder & director of the Cape Cod COPD support group. Dr. Thomas Petty, MD, director of the NIH educational program in COPD, discusses prevention, education & early intervention. Dr. Brian Tiep, MD an authority on COPD rehabilitation, underscores the potential of patients to manage their disease. The authors explain medical & surgical treatment as well as how people with COPD can use rehabilitation to maintain & improve lung function, cardiovascular fitness & their emotional outlook & guide them to use medications, exercise, supplemental oxygen, nutrition & smoking cessation & review options for managing severe disease. In U.S.A. send $29.95 (MA residents add sales tax) per copy (includes Priority Mail delivery) to New Technology Publishing, Inc., POB 1737 Onset, MA 02558-1737. 508-291-1111, or 888-706-COPD; Fax: 800-452-7632. Distribution: Unique, Quality, Baker & Taylor, or direct by STOP order.<http://www.newtechpub.com> email <copd@newtechpub.com>. *Publisher Paid Annotation.*

Carter, Rick H. Car Sense: The Autobuyer's Guide to Purchasing & Financing New & Used Vehicles. Holder, Charmaine M., ed. 85p. (Orig.). 1996. pap., mass mkt. 19.95 (*0-9652133-0-7*, Car Sense) Spec Finance.

***Carter, Rita.** Mapping the Mind. LC 98-70490. (Illus.). 221p. 1999. 29.95 (*0-520-21937-6*, Pub. by U CA Pr) Cal Prin Full Svc.

— Mapping the Mind. 224p. 2000. pap. 22.95 (*0-520-22461-2*) U CA Pr.

Carter, Rob. American Typography Today. 1993. pap. 36.95 (*0-442-01457-0*, VNR) Wiley.

Carter, Rob. American Typography Today. 168p. 1993. pap. 36.95 (*0-471-28562-5*, VNR) Wiley.

Carter, Rob. Experimental Typography, Vol. 4. (Working with Computer Type Ser.). (Illus.). 160p. 1997. pap. 35.00 (*2-88046-279-7*) Watsn-Guptill.

Carter, Rob, et al. Typographic Design: Form & Communication. 2nd ed. 288p. 1993. pap. 49.95 (*0-471-28430-0*, VNR) Wiley.

Carter, Rob, jt. auth. see Meggs, Philip.

Carter, Robert. Armada. 1999. pap. 24.95 (*0-525-93715-3*) NAL.

— Talwar. (Orig.). 1999. pap. 25.00 (*0-525-93713-7*) NAL.

Carter, Robert & Wilkins, Leslie, eds. Probation, Parole & Community Corrections. 3rd ed. LC 83-23283. 432p. (C). 1984. text 26.50 (*0-471-87461-2*) P-H.

Carter, Robert A. Annotated List & Indexes of the New York State Legislative Document Series, 1919-1976, 7 vols., Set. 559p. 1986. 35.00 (*0-318-22978-1*) NYS Library.

— Annotated List of Indexes & Reports of New York State Governors Committees & Task Forces, 1925-1985. 33p. 1986. 5.00 (*0-318-22977-3*) NYS Library.

***Carter, Robert A.** Buffalo Bill Cody: The Man Behind the Legend. LC 00-20368. 400p. 2000. 30.00 (*0-471-31996-1*) Wiley.

Carter, Robert A. Casual Slaughters. 272p. 1994. mass mkt. 5.50 (*0-446-40302-4*, Pub. by Warner Bks) Little.

— Directory of Selected Automated Information Systems in New York State Government. 99p. 1984. 5.00 (*0-318-22979-X*) NYS Library.

— The Gun-Runners. large type ed. (Dales General Fiction Ser.). 188p. 1993. pap. 18.99 (*1-85389-414-1*, Dales) Ulverscroft.

— A Legal Definition of Death. 25p. 1982. 5.00 (*0-318-01522-6*) NYS Library.

— Legislative Intent in New York State. 57p. 1981. 5.00 (*0-318-01525-0*) NYS Library.

— New York State Constitution: Sources of Legislative Intent. ix, 204p. 1988. reprint ed. 40.00 (*0-8377-0459-6*, Rothman) W S Hein.

— The Official Compilation of Codes, Rules & Regulations of the State of New York & the State Register: Their History & Use. 36p. 1984. 5.00 (*0-318-22975-7*) NYS Library.

— Opportunities in Book Publishing. (Illus.). 160p. 1989. 13.95 (*0-8442-6139-4*, VGM Career) NTC Contemp Pub Co.

— Opportunities in Book Publishing. (Illus.). 160p. 1993. pap. 10.95 (*0-8442-6140-8*, VGM Career) NTC Contemp Pub Co.

***Carter, Robert A.** Publishing Careers. rev. ed. (Opportunities in . . . Ser.). 2000. 14.95 (*0-658-00483-2*, VGM Career) NTC Contemp Pub Co.

Carter, Robert A. Rent Control. 30p. 1982. 5.00 (*0-318-22974-9*) NYS Library.

— Sources of Published & Unpublished Administrative Opinions in New York State. 12p. 1985. 5.00 (*0-318-22976-5*) NYS Library.

Carter, Robert A., jt. auth. see Pattis, S. William.

Carter, Robert Allan. History of the Insanity Defense in New York State. LC 82-623135. 46p. 1982. 5.00 (*0-317-03159-7*) NYS Library.

Carter, Robert E. Becoming Bamboo: Western & Eastern Explorations of the Meaning of Life. 240p. 1992. 60.00 (*0-7735-0884-8*, Pub. by McG-Queens Univ Pr) CUP Services.

— Becoming Bamboo: Western & Eastern Explorations of the Meaning of Life. rev. ed. 140p. 1995. pap. 22.95 (*0-7735-1410-4*, Pub. by McG-Queens Univ Pr) CUP Services.

— The Damp Woods Greening: Poems. LC 92-6671. (Illus.). 64p. 1992. pap. 12.95 (*0-7734-9659-9*) E Mellen.

— Dimensions of Moral Education. 254p. 1984. pap. 15.95 (*0-8020-6540-6*) U of Toronto Pr.

— The Nothingness Beyond God: An Introduction to the Philosophy of Nishida Kitaro. 2nd expanded rev. ed. LC 97-32790. (Illus.). 256p. (C). 1998. pap. text 16.95 (*1-55778-761-1*) Paragon Hse.

— Wolf. 1990. 24.95 (*0-88946-033-7*) E Mellen.

Carter, Robert E. & Isenberg, Sheldon R., eds. The Ideal in the Worlds Religions: Essays on the Person, Family, Society & Environment. LC 97-49934. 446p. (Orig.). 1998. pap. 16.95 (*1-55778-750-6*) Paragon Hse.

Carter, Robert E., tr. see Tetsuro, Watsuji.

Carter, Robert F. A History of Missouri City. Koonce, Sandra & Cox, Betty, eds. 150p. (Orig.). 1986. 25.00 (*0-318-19649-2*); pap. 10.00 (*0-318-19650-6*) D Armstrong.

Carter, Robert G. The Old Sergeant's Story: Or Fighting Indians & Badmen in Texas. (Illus.). 1976. 32.95 (*0-8488-0000-1*, J M C & Co) Amereon Ltd.

— On the Border with Mackenzie: Winning West Texas from the Comanches. 1935th ed. 39.95 (*0-8488-0023-0*, J M C & Co) Amereon Ltd.

Carter, Robert G., jt. auth. see Parker, John L.

***Carter, Robert Goldthwaite.** Four Brothers in Blue, or, Sunshine & Shadows of the War of the Rebellion. LC 99-29049. 560p. 1999. pap. 18.95 (*0-8061-3185-3*) U of Okla Pr.

Carter, Robert L. A Dictionary of Dermatologic Terms. 4th ed. 408p. 1992. 24.95 (*0-683-14691-2*) Lppncott W & W.

— Molecular Symmetry & Group Theory. LC 97-25445. 320p. 1997. pap. 53.95 (*0-471-14955-1*) Wiley.

Carter, Robert L., et al. Obstacles to the Liberalization of Trade in Insurance. 208p. 1992. text 49.50 (*0-472-10318-0*, 10318) U of Mich Pr.

Carter, Robert M., jt. ed. see Tubbs, Stewart L.

Carter, Robert R. So You've Been Asked to... Develop a Worship Team. 24p. 1996. pap. 0.95 (*1-56212-215-0*) CRC Pubns.

Carter, Robert T. The Influence of Race & Racial Indentity in Psychotherapy: Toward a Racially Inclusive Model. LC 95-5145. 320p. 1995. 69.95 (*0-471-57111-3*) Wiley.

— The Influence of Race & Racial Indentity in Psychotherapy: Toward a Racially Inclusive Model. 312p. 1998. pap. 37.50 (*0-471-24533-X*) Wiley.

Carter, Robert T., jt. ed. see Thompson, Chalmer E.

Carter, Robin, ed. see Basham, Kimberley A. & Miracle, Vickie A.

Carter, Robin, ed. see Bucher, Linda & Melander, Sheila.

Carter, Robin, ed. see Copstead, Lee-Ellen C. & Banasik, Jacquelyn L.

Carter, Robin, ed. see Fahey, Victoria A.

Carter, Robin, ed. see Fenstermacher, Karen.

Carter, Robin, ed. see Hummel, John H., et al.

Carter, Robin, ed. see Ignatavicius, Donna D., et al.

Carter, Robin, ed. see Ignatavicius, et al.

Carter, Robin, ed. see Jairath, Nallini.

Carter, Robin, ed. see Kennedy, Elaine & Ignatavicius, Donna D.

Carter, Robin, ed. see Melander, Sheila & Bucher, Linda.

Carter, Robin, ed. see Obdlouk Darovic, Gloria & Franklin, Cory M.

Carter, Robin, ed. see Selfridge-Thomas, Judy, et al.

Carter, Robin, ed. see Zerwekh, JoAnn & Claborn, Jo C.

Carter, Robin, ed. see Zerwekh, JoAnn & Clayborn, Jo C.

Carter, Robin Borglum, see Borglum Carter, Robin.

Carter, Roger. Simple Groups of Lie Type. LC 72-39228. (Pure & Applied Mathematics Ser.: Vol. 28). 343p. reprint ed. pap. 106.40 (*0-608-12337-4*, 202427400036) Bks Demand.

Carter, Roger & Geck, Meinolf, eds. Representations of Reductive Groups. (Publications of the Newton Institute: No. 16). (Illus.). 200p. (C). 1999. text 59.95 (*0-521-64325-2*) Cambridge U Pr.

Carter, Roger & Gray, Jill. Spreadsheet Skills. (Made Simple Ser.). 200p. 1993. pap. text 19.95 (*0-7506-1567-2*) Buttrwrth-Heinemann.

Carter, Roger, et al. Lectures on Lie Groups & Lie Algebras. (London Mathematical Society Student Texts Ser.: No. 32). (Illus.). 198p. (C). 1995. text 69.95 (*0-521-49579-2*); pap. text 25.95 (*0-521-49922-4*) Cambridge U Pr.

Carter, Roger W. Finite Groups of Lie Type: Conjugacy Classes & Complex Characters. LC 84-13077. (Pure & Applied Mathematics Ser.). (Illus.). 556p. reprint ed. pap. 172.40 (*0-8357-4666-6*, 203761200008) Bks Demand.

— Simple Groups of Lie Type. 364p. 1989. pap. 139.95 (*0-471-50683-4*) Wiley.

Carter, Roger W. & Saxl, J. Algebraic Groups & Their Representations. LC 98-34659. (NATO ASI Series C). 1998. 173.00 (*0-7923-5251-3*) Kluwer Academic.

Carter, Ron. The Blackfoot Moonshine Rebellion of 1881: The Indian War That Never Was. (The Settlement Triology Ser.). 112p. 1997. 12.95 (*0-9643672-8-9*) Harbour Bks.

— Brigham's Ghost Brigade & the Case of the Deadly Counterfeiters. (Illus.). 144p. (Orig.). (J). (gr. 4 up). 1996. pap. 9.95 (*0-9643672-4-6*) Harbour Bks.

— The Case of the Golden Spike Kidnappers. LC 96-18601. (Brigham's Ghost Brigade Ser.). (J). 1996. pap. write for info. (*0-9643672-6-2*) Harbour Bks.

***Carter, Ron.** The Hand of Promise. LC 00-37943. (Prelude to Glory Ser.: Vol. 4). 2000. pap. 22.95 (*1-57345-783-3*) Deseret Bk.

Carter, Ron. Me & the Geezer: A True Story about Growing up in Little League Style. LC 95-51021. 176p. (Orig.). (J). 1996. pap. write for info. (*0-9643672-2-X*) Harbour Bks.

— Prelude to Glory Vol. 1: Our Sacred Honor. xv, 605p. 1998. 19.95 (*1-57008-431-9*) Bookcraft Inc.

— Rocky Mountain Salvation Company: How the West Was Conned. (The Settlement Trilogy Ser.). 104p. 1997. 12.95 (*0-9643672-7-0*) Harbour Bks.

— Settlement Trilogy Vol. 1: The Trial of Mary Lou. 1998. pap. 6.95 (*1-57008-556-0*) Bookcraft Inc.

— Settlement Trilogy Vol. 2: The Blackfoot Moonshine Rebellion. 1998. pap. 6.95 (*1-57008-557-9*) Bookcraft Inc.

— Settlement Trilogy Vol. 3: The Royal Maccabees Rocky Mountain Salvation Company. 1998. pap. 6.95 (*1-57008-581-1*) Bookcraft Inc.

— The Trial of Mary Lou. (Settlement Trilogy Ser.: Vol. 1). 98p. 1996. 12.95 (*0-9643672-5-4*) Harbour Bks.

— The Youngest Drover: One Man's True Story about Growing Up on a Real Cattle Drive. 1995. write for info. (*0-614-32136-0*) Harbour Bks.

Carter, Ronald. Investigating English Discourse: Language, Literacy, Literature. LC 98-117260. (Illus.). 272p. (C). 1997. pap. 27.99 (*0-415-14066-8*) Routledge.

— Investigating English Discourse: Language, Literacy, Literature. LC 98-117260. (Illus.). 272p. (C). 1997. 85.00 (*0-415-14065-X*) Routledge.

— Vocabulary: Applied Linguistic Perspectives. 2nd rev. ed. LC 98-15465. (Illus.). 304p. (C). 1998. pap. 25.99 (*0-415-16864-3*) Routledge.

— Vocabulary: Applied Linguistic Perspectives. 2nd rev. ed. (Illus.). 288p. (C). 1998. 85.00 (*0-415-16863-5*) Routledge.

Carter, Ronald & McCarthy, Michael. Exploring Spoken English. 160p. 1997. text 54.95 (*0-521-56049-7*) Cambridge U Pr.

Carter, Ronald & McRae, John. The Routledge History of Literature in English: Britain & Ireland. LC 96-41221. 608p. (C). 1997. 85.00 (*0-415-12342-9*); pap. 24.99 (*0-415-12343-7*) Routledge.

Carter, Ronald & Nash, Walter. Seeing Through Language: A Guide to Styles of English Language. (Language Library). 240p. (C). 1990. pap. text 24.95 (*0-631-15135-4*) Blackwell Pubs.

Carter, Ronald, ed. see Brazil, David.

Carter, Ronald, ed. see Channell, Joanna.

Carter, Ronald, ed. see Hoey, M. P.

Carter, Ronald, jt. ed. see Sanchez-Macarro, Antonio.

Carter, Ronald, ed. see Sinclair, John.

Carter, Ronald, ed. see Tsui, Amy.

Carter, Ronald A. Typographic Design. 2nd ed. 1993. pap. 41.95 (*0-442-00759-0*, VNR) Wiley.

— Vocabulary: Applied Linguistic Perspectives. (Aspects of English Ser.). 272p. 1987. text 49.95 (*0-04-418007-1*); pap. text 19.95 (*0-04-418008-X*) Routledge.

Carter, Ronald A., ed. Language & Literature: A Reader in Stylistics. (Aspects of English Ser.). 256p. (C). 1982. pap. text 16.95 (*0-04-407017-9*) Routledge.

Carter, Ronald A. & Simpson, Paul, eds. Language, Discourse & Literature: An Introductory Reader in Discourse Stylistics. LC 88-5678. 272p. (C). 1988. pap. text 22.95 (*0-04-445006-0*) Routledge.

Carter, Ronald A., jt. auth. see Brumfit, Christopher J.

Carter, Ronald A., jt. auth. see McCarthy, M. J.

Carter, Ronald D. Help! These Kids Are Driving Me Crazy. (Illus.). 118p. (Orig.). 1972. pap. text 9.95 (*0-87822-006-2*, 0062) Res Press.

Carter, Ronald G. The Beecher Incident. LC 95-26574. 188p. (Orig.). 1996. pap. 11.95 (*0-9643672-3-8*) Harbour Bks.

— The Youngest Drover: A True Story about Growing up on a Cattle Drive. 176p. 1995. 19.95 (*0-9643672-1-1*); pap. 14.95 (*0-9643672-0-3*) Harbour Bks.

***Carter, Rosalyn Y. & Thai, Khi V., eds.** Current Public Policy Issues. LC 94-17045. 222p. (C). 1999. pap. text 35.00 (*0-9668864-0-2*, 9901) PrAcademics Pr.

Carter, Rosalynn, jt. auth. see Carter, Jimmy.

Carter, Rosalynn W. First Lady from Plains. LC 94-20494. 320p. 1994. reprint ed. pap. 22.00 (*1-55728-355-9*) U of Ark Pr.

— Helping Someone with Mental Illness: Compassionate Guide for Family, Friends & Caregivers. LC 97-39218. 320p. 1998. 24.00 (*0-8129-2899-7*, Times Bks) Crown Pub Group.

Carter, Rosalynn W. & Golan. Helping Someone with Mental Illness: Learn the Newest Advances in Research & Treatment. 1998. 24.00 (*0-676-57569-2*, Times Bks); 24.00 (*0-676-57728-8*, Times Bks) Crown Pub Group.

Carter, Rosalynn W. & Golant, Susan K. Helping Someone with Mental Illness: The Newest Advances in Research & Treatment. 368p. 1999. pap. 15.00 (*0-8129-2898-9*, Times Bks) Crown Pub Group.

— Helping Yourself Help Others: A Book for Caregivers. 288p. 1995. pap. 14.00 (*0-8129-2591-2*, Times Bks) Crown Pub Group.

Carter, Rosann & Kirsch, Laurie. Crossing Boundaries: The Deployment of Global IT Solutions. (Practice-Driven Research in IT Management Ser.: No. 1). (Illus.). 125p. 1999. pap. 94.95 (*1-893673-01-4*) Pinnaflex Inc.

Carter, Rosemary. Father Found. (Harlequin Super Romance Ser.). 1978. per. 1.25 (*0-373-70763-0*, Harlequin) Harlequin Bks.

— A Husband Made in Texas. (Romance Ser.: No. 426). 1999. mass mkt. 3.50 (*0-373-17426-8*, 1-17426-7) Harlequin Bks.

— Safari Encounter. large type ed. (Linford Romance Library). 283p. 1984. pap. 16.99 (*0-7089-6013-8*) Ulverscroft.

***Carter, Rosemary.** A Wife & Child. 1999. mass mkt. 3.50 (*0-373-17441-1*) Harlequin Bks.

Carter, Rosemary A. Echoes in the Night. large type ed. 282p. 1994. 27.99 (*0-7505-0610-5*) Ulverscroft.

Carter, Ross S. Those Devils in Baggy Pants. 1976. 24.95 (*0-8488-1265-4*) Amereon Ltd.

— Those Devils in Baggy Pants. 280p. 1998. 28.95 (*1-886681-20-1*); pap. 22.95 (*1-886681-24-4*) Claymore Pub.

— Those Devils in Baggy Pants. 192p. 1987. reprint ed. lib. bdg. 25.95 (*0-89966-613-2*) Buccaneer Bks.

Carter, Roxanne. All-Star Sampler. LC 95-18283. (Illus.). 44p. 1995. pap. 9.95 (*1-56477-112-1*, B230) Martingale & Co.

— Easy Star Sampler. LC 97-31532. 1998. pap. 9.95 (*1-56477-208-X*) Martingale & Co.

Carter, Roy E., tr. see Schoenberg, Arnold.

Carter-Ruck, Peter F. Carter-Ruck on Libel & Slander. 5th ed. Elliott, Rupert, ed. 1997. write for info. (*0-406-99248-7*, CRLS5, MICHIE) LEXIS Pub.

***Carter, Ruth.** Amway Motivational Organizations: Behind the Smoke & Mirrors. LC 99-61374. 199p. 1999. pap. 14.95 (*0-9671070-2-4*) Backstreet FL.

— Women of the Dust. (Nick Hern Bks.). 96p. 2000. pap. 14.95 (*1-85459-448-6*) Theatre Comm.

— Yearning. (Nick Hern Bks.). 2000. pap. 14.95 (*1-85459-450-8*) Theatre Comm.

Carter, Ruth C., ed. Education & Training for Catalogers & Classifiers. LC 87-8535. (Cataloging & Classification Quarterly Ser.: Vol. 7, No. 4). 195p. 1987. text 49.95 (*0-86656-660-0*) Haworth Pr.

— The United States Newspaper Program: Cataloging Aspects. LC 86-4828. (Cataloging & Classification Quarterly Ser.: Vol. 6, No. 4). 119p. 1986. text 3.95 (*0-86656-576-0*) Haworth Pr.

Carter, Ruth C. & Hooks, James D., eds. Implementing Online Union Lists of Serials: The Pennsylvania Union List of Serials Experience. LC 88-24303. (Serials Librarian Supplement Ser.: No. 5). 218p. 1989. text 49.95 (*0-86656-802-6*) Haworth Pr.

Carter, Ruth C., jt. auth. see Carter, John L.

Carter, Ruth C., ed. see Lyttle, William H.

Carter, Ruth C., jt. ed. see Myall, Carolynne.

Carter, Ruth C., jt. ed. see Smith, Linda C.

Carter, S. Global Agricultural Marketing Management. LC 98-142645. (Marketing & Agribusiness Texts Ser.: Series 09005676, No. 3). 320p. 1998. 35.00 (*92-5-104013-3*, F40133, Pub. by FAO) Bernan Associates.

C

— New Succulent Spiny Euphorbias from East Africa. (Illus.). vi, 118p. 1982. pap. 20.00 (1-878762-72-9, Pub. by Royal Botnic Grdns) Balogh.

— Recuerdos de Nuestra Boda.Tr. of Our Wedding: A Keepsake Album. (SPA.). 31p. 1991. pap. 7.99 (1-56063-162-7, 497605) Editorial Unilit.

Carter, S., jt. auth. see Carter, C.

Carter, S., jt. auth. see Schuller, Robert H.

Carter, S. K., ed. New Anticancer Drugs. (Recent Results in Cancer Research Ser.: Vol. 70). (Illus.). 230p. 1980. 66.00 (0-387-09682-5) Spr-Verlag.

Carter, Samantha. Dateless in Dallas. (Yours Truly Ser.). 1996. per. 3.50 (0-373-52030-1, 1-52030-3) Silhouette.

— The Emergency Stand-By Date. 1998. per. 3.50 (0-373-52063-8, 1-52063-4) Silhouette.

Carter, Samuel. Carter: Descendants of Samuel Carter of Deerfield, Massachusetts, & Norwalk, Connecticut. (Illus.). 27p. 1997. reprint ed. pap. 6.00 (0-8328-7868-5) Higginson Bk Co.

Carter, Sarah. Lost Harvests: Prairie Indian Reserve Farmers & Government Policy. (McGill-Queen's Native & Northern Ser.). 352p. (C). 1990. text 65.00 (0-7735-0755-8, Pub. by McG-Queens Univ Pr) CUP Services.

— Lost Harvests: Prairie Indian Reserve Farmers & Government Policy. 352p. 1993. pap. 22.95 (0-7735-0999-2, Pub. by McG-Queens Univ Pr) CUP Services.

Carter, Sarah A. Capturing Women: The Manipulation of Cultural Imagery in Canada's Prairie West. Vol. 17. (Illus.). 264p. 1997. pap. 19.95 (0-7735-1656-5, Pub. by McG-Queens Univ Pr) CUP Services.

— Capturing Women: The Manipulation of Cultural Imagery in Canada's Prairie West. (Illus.). 248p. 1997. text 60.00 (0-7735-1655-7, Pub. by McG-Queens Univ Pr) CUP Services.

Carter, Scott, jt. auth. see Seifried, Richard.

***Carter-Scott, Cherie.** If High School Is a Game. (YA). 2001. mass mkt. (0-385-32796-X) BDD Bks Young Read.

Carter-Scott, Cherie. If Life Is a Game, These Are the Rules: 10 Rules for Being Human. LC 98-17458. 160p. 1998. 15.00 (0-7679-0238-6) Broadway BDD.

***Carter-Scott, Cherie.** If Success Is a Game, These Are the Rules: Ten Rules for a Fulfilling Career & Life. LC 99-49320. 224p. 2000. 17.50 (0-7679-0426-5) Broadway BDD.

Carter, Sebastian. Twentieth-Century Type Designers. rev. ed. (Illus.). 192p. 1995. 35.00 (0-393-70199-9) Norton.

Carter, Sharon & Monnig, Judith. Coping with a Hospital Stay. Rosen, Ruth C., ed. (Coping Ser.). 128p. (YA). (gr. 7-12). 1987. lib. bdg. 17.95 (0-8239-0682-5) Rosen Group.

Carter, Sharon & Wheeler, Joann. Brain Benders. (Enrichment & Gifted Ser.). (Illus.). 48p. (J). (gr. 4-6). 1982. pap. 6.95 (0-88160-048-2, LW234) Learning Wks.

Carter, Sharon, et al. Coping with Medical Emergencies. rev. ed. (Coping Ser.). 121p. (YA). (gr. 7-12). 1988. lib. bdg. 16.95 (0-8239-0782-1) Rosen Group.

Carter, Sharon, jt. auth. see Clayton, Lawrence.

Carter, Sharon N. Jomo: A Name to Be Proud. 1990. pap. 5.95 (0-913543-18-7) African Am Imag.

Carter, Simon. Rock Climbing in Australia. (Illus.). 176p. 1999. 49.95 (1-86436-340-1, Pub. by New Holland) BHB Intl.

Carter, Simon, jt. auth. see Clift, Stephen.

Carter, Siri M. & Carter, Alden R. I'm Tougher Than Asthma! (Concept Book Ser.). (Illus.). 32p. (J). (gr. k-4). 1996. lib. bdg. 14.95 (0-8075-3474-9) A Whitman.

— I'm Tougher Than Asthma! (Illus.). 32p. (J). (gr. k-4). 1999. pap. 6.95 (0-8075-3475-7) A Whitman.

Carter, Stephen. God's Name in Vain: The Wrongs & Rights of Religion in Politics. 256p. 26.00 (0-465-00886-0, Pub. by Basic) HarpC.

— Introducing Bar Chords. (Illus.). 1997. pap. 14.95 incl. audio compact disk (1-875726-91-8) Koala Pubns.

— Introducing Classical Guitar, Bk. 1. (Illus.). 1997. pap. text 14.95 incl. cd-rom (1-875726-23-3) Koala Pubns.

Carter, Stephen. The Politics of Solzhenitsyn. LC 76-28346. 161p. 1977. 22.00 (0-8419-0244-5) Holmes & Meier.

Carter, Stephen, jt. ed. see McCauley, Martin.

Carter, Stephen J. Living with Grief. (Master's Touch Bible Study Ser.). 1996. pap. 4.50 (0-570-09555-7, 20-2596) Concordia.

— My Daily Devotion: God's Promises for Joyful Living. 372p. (Orig.). 1988. pap. 14.99 (0-570-03077-3, 06-1192) Concordia.

Carter, Stephen K., jt. auth. see Broder, Lawrence E.

Carter, Stephen L. Civility: Manners, Morals & the Etiquette of Democracy. LC 97-44099. 338p. 1998. 25.00 (0-465-02384-3, Pub. by Basic); pap. write for info. (0-465-02385-1) Basic.

— Civility: Manners, Morals, & the Etiquette of Democracy. LC 98-44945. 352p. 1999. pap. 13.00 (0-06-097759-0) HarpC.

— The Culture of Disbelief: How American Law & Politics Trivialize Religious Devotion. LC 94-14781. 352p. 1994. pap. 15.95 (0-385-47498-9, Anchor NY) Doubleday.

— The Dissent of the Governed: A Meditation on Law, Religion & Loyalty. (History of American Civilization Ser.). 192p. 1999. pap. 12.95 (0-674-21266-5) HUP.

— The Dissent of the Governed: A Meditation on Law, Religion & Loyalty, Vol. 199. LC 97-39973. (William E. Massey, Sr. Lectures in the History of American Civilization). (Illus.). 192p. 1999. 20.50 (0-674-21265-7) HUP.

— Integrity. 288p. 1997. pap. 14.00 (0-06-092807-7, Perennial) HarperTrade.

— Reflections of an Affirmative Action Baby. LC 91-70054. 304p. 1992. pap. 14.50 (0-465-06869-3, Pub. by Basic) HarpC.

Carter, Steve. Nevis Mountain Dew. 1979. pap. 5.25 (0-8222-0812-1) Dramatists Play.

— Pecong. 1993. pap. 6.95 (0-88145-107-X) Broadway Play.

— Renaissance Management: The Rebirth of Learning Through People & Organizations. 1998. 22.95 (0-7494-2374-9) Kogan Page Ltd.

Carter, Steven. Bearing Across: Studies in Literature & Science. LC 98-25558. (Illus.). 150p. 1998. 74.95 (1-57309-328-9); pap. 54.95 (1-57309-327-0) Intl Scholars.

***Carter, Steven.** A Do-It-Yourself Dystopia: The Americanization of Big Brother. 184p. 2000. pap. 29.50 (0-7618-1729-8) U Pr of Amer.

Carter, Steven. Leopards in the Temple: Studies in American Popular Culture. LC 97-20352. 152p. 1997. 74.95 (1-57309-170-7); pap. 54.95 (1-57309-169-3) Intl Scholars.

— Leopards in the Temple: Studies in American Popular Culture. 2nd ed. LC 98-20478. 172p. 1998. 74.95 (1-57309-326-2, Cath Scholar Pr); pap. 54.95 (1-57309-325-4, Cath Scholar Pr) Intl Scholars.

— Men Like Women Who Like Themselves: And Other Secrets That the Smartest Women Know. 272p. 1997. pap. 11.95 (0-440-50615-8) Dell.

Carter, Steven & Sokol, Julia. Getting To Commitment: Overcoming the 8 Greatest Obstacles to Lasting Connection (And Finding the Courage to Love) LC 98-22533. 288p. 1998. 21.95 (0-87131-869-5) M Evans.

***Carter, Steven & Sokol, Julia.** Getting To Commitment: Overcoming the 8 Greatest Obstacles to Lasting Connection (And Finding the Courage to Love) 256p. 2000. pap. 14.95 (0-87131-905-5) M Evans.

Carter, Steven & Sokol, Julia. He's Scared, She's Scared: Understanding the Hidden Fears That Sabotage Your Relationships. 352p. 1995. pap. 12.95 (0-440-50625-5) Dell.

***Carter, Steven & Sokol, Julia.** He's Scared, She's Scared: Understanding the Hidden Fears That Sabotage Your Relationships. 352p. 2000. 7.98 (1-56731-370-1) Fine Comms.

Carter, Steven & Sokol, Julia. Men Who Can't Love. 336p. 1988. mass mkt. 6.99 (0-425-11170-9) Berkley Pub.

— Men Who Can't Love. 236p. 1994. 6.98 (1-56731-047-8, MJF Bks) Fine Comms.

***Carter, Steven & Sokol, Julia.** Men Who Can't Love: How to Recognize a Commitmentphobic Man Before He Breaks Your Heart. 336p. 2000. reprint ed. pap. 12.95 (0-425-17445-X) Berkley Pub.

Carter, Steven & Sokol, Julia. What Really Happens in Bed? A Demystification of Sex. LC 89-1561. 352p. 1989. 17.95 (0-87131-562-9) M Evans.

— What Smart Women Know: Wisdom for the Thinking Woman. LC 90-13826. 216p. 1991. pap. 11.95 (0-440-50389-2, Dell Trade Pbks) Dell.

***Carter, Steven & Sokol, Julia.** What Smart Women Know: Wisdom for the Thinking Woman. anniversary ed. 2000. pap. 14.95 (0-87131-906-3) M Evans.

Carter, Steven, jt. auth. see Levinson, Harold N.

***Carter, Steven D.** Medieval Japanese Writers. LC 98-51750. (Dictionary of Literary Biography Ser.: Vol. 203). 400p. 1998. text 155.00 (0-7876-3097-7) Gale.

Carter, Steven D. Regent Redux: A Life of the Statesman-Scholar Ichijo Kaneyoshi. LC 96-31597. (Michigan Monographs in Japanese Studies: Vol. 16). xv, 279p. 1996. 44.95 (0-939512-75-0) U MI Japan.

— The Road to Komatsubara: A Classical Reading of the Renga Hyakuin. LC 87-15713. (East Asian Monographs: No. 124). 311p. 1988. 30.00 (0-674-77385-3) HUP.

— Unforgotten Dreams: Poems by the Zen Monk Shotetsu. (Translations from the Asian Classics Ser.). 240p. 1996. 41.50 (0-231-10576-2); pap. 18.50 (0-231-10577-0) Col U Pr.

— Waiting for the Wind: Thirty-Six Poets of Japan's Late Medieval Age. 353p. 1994. pap. 19.00 (0-231-06855-7) Col U Pr.

Carter, Steven D., ed. Literary Patronage in Late Medieval Japan. LC 93-14920. (Michigan Papers in Japanese Studies: No. 23). ix, 175p. (C). 1993. pap. 13.95 (0-939512-60-2) U MI Japan.

Carter, Steven D., ed. from JPN. Traditional Japanese Poetry: An Anthology. (Illus.). 534p. (C). 1993. pap. 22.50 (0-8047-2212-9) Stanford U Pr.

Carter, Steven D., tr. from JPN. Traditional Japanese Poetry: An Anthology. (Illus.). 534p. 1991. 65.00 (0-8047-1562-9) Stanford U Pr.

Carter, Steven R. Hansberry's Drama: Commitment amid Complexity. (Illus.). 216p. 1991. 27.50 (0-252-01749-8) U of Ill Pr.

— James Jones: An American Literary Orientalist Master. LC 97-4887. 208p. 1998. text 32.50 (0-252-02371-4) U of Ill Pr.

Carter, Stewart. A Performer's Guide to Seventeenth-Century Music. LC 97-1310. (Early Music America Ser.). 1997. 42.00 (0-02-870492-4, Schirmer Books) Mac Lib Ref.

— Perspectives in Early Brass Scholarship: Proceedings of the 95 International Historic Brass Symposium 95. LC 97-33015. (Historic Brass Ser.: Vol. 2). 1997. text 54.00 (0-945193-97-1) Pendragon NY.

Carter, Stewart, ed. see Leonarda, Isabella.

Carter, Susan K. 1997 Comprehensive Guide to Idaho - Montana's Craft Fairs, Festivals & Bazaars. (Illus.). 125p. 1996. spiral bd. 23.00 (1-888651-04-0) Carters Guides.

— 1997 Comprehensive Guide to Washington's Craft Fairs, Festivals & Bazaars. 3rd ed. (Illus.). 232p. 1996. spiral bd. 23.00 (1-888651-03-2) Carters Guides.

— 1997 Comprehensive Guide to Oregon's Craft Fairs, Festivals & Bazaars. 5th ed. LC 95-96235. (Illus.). 248p. 1996. spiral bd. 23.00 (1-888651-02-4) Carters Guides.

Carter, Susanne. War & Peace Through Women's Eyes: A Selective Bibliography of Twentieth-Century American Women's Fiction, 14. LC 91-33399. (Bibliographies & Indexes in Women's Studies: No. 14). 336p. 1992. lib. bdg. 65.00 (0-313-27771-0, CWE, Greenwood Pr) Greenwood.

Carter, Susanne, compiled by. Mothers & Daughters in American Short Fiction: An Annotated Bibliography of Twentieth-Century Women's Literature, 19. LC 93-10822. 160p. 1993. lib. bdg. 59.95 (0-313-28511-X, Greenwood Pr) Greenwood.

Carter, Sydney. Lord of the Dance. LC 99-204375. 1999. write for info. (0-7459-3898-1) Lion USA.

Carter, Sylvester P. Writing for Your Peers: The Primary Journal Paper. LC 87-2513. 144p. 1987. pap. 13.95 (0-275-92229-4, B2229, Praeger Pubs) Greenwood.

— Writing for Your Peers: The Primary Journal Paper. LC 87-2513. 137p. 1987. 55.00 (0-275-92630-3, C2630, Praeger Pubs) Greenwood.

Carter, Sylvia. Eats NYC: A Guide to the Best, Cheapest, Most Interesting Restaurants in Brooklyn, Queens, & Manhattan. 192p. 1995. pap. 8.95 (0-8362-0809-9) Andrews & McMeel.

Carter, T. Images of an American Land: Vernacular Architecture in the Western United States. LC 95-41803. (Illus.). 337p. 1997. pap. 29.95 (0-8263-1730-8) U of NM Pr.

Carter, T., ed. Images of an American Land: Vernacular Architecture in the Western United States. LC 95-41803. (Illus.). 337p. 1997. 50.00 (0-8263-1729-4) U of NM Pr.

Carter, T. Barton & Franklin, Marc A. The First Amendment & the Fourth Estate: The Law of Mass Media. 6th ed. Wright, Jay B., ed. 1006p. 1994. text 42.50 (1-56662-147-X) Foundation Pr.

Carter, T. Barton, et al. The First Amendment & the Fifth Estate: Regulation of Electronic Mass Media. 3rd ed. 852p. 1992. text. write for info. (1-56662-039-2) Foundation Pr.

— The First Amendment & the Fifth Estate: Regulation of Electronic Mass Media, 1994 Supplement. 3rd ed. 169p. 1994. pap. text 7.95 (1-56662-216-6) Foundation Pr.

— The First Amendment & the Fifth Estate, Regulation of Electronic Mass Media. 4th ed. LC 96-21951. 977p. 1996. text. write for info. (1-56662-350-2) Foundation Pr.

— The First Amendment & the Fifth Estate, Regulation of Electronic Mass Media: 1997 Supplement. annuals 4th ed. 1080p. 1997. pap. text, suppl. ed. write for info. (1-56662-584-X) Foundation Pr.

— The First Amendment & the Fifth Estate, Regulation of Electronic Mass Media, Teacher's Manual to Accompany. 4th ed. 227p. (C). 1996. pap. text. write for info. (1-56662-525-4) Foundation Pr.

— The First Amendment & the Fourth Estate: The Law of Mass Media. 6th ed. 118p. 1994. teacher ed. write for info. (1-56662-229-8) Foundation Pr.

— The First Amendment & the Fourth Estate, the Law of Mass Media: The Law of Mass Media. 7th ed. LC 97-13314. 1040p. 1997. text. write for info. (1-56662-543-2) Foundation Pr.

— Supplement to the First Amendment & the Fifth Estate, Regulation of Electronic Mass Media. 3rd ed. 328p. 1995. pap. text, suppl. ed. 8.95 (1-56662-287-5) Foundation Pr.

— Teacher's Manual to Accompany the First Amendment & the Fifth Estate, Regulation of Electronic Mass Media. 3rd ed. 104p. 1993. pap. text. write for info. (1-56662-129-1) Foundation Pr.

Carter, T. P. Jokes, Notes, & Quotes. 240p. (Orig.). 1991. pap. 8.50 (0-932281-07-9) Quill Pubns GA.

Carter, Terry. Birmingham Pals: The 14th, 15th & 16th (Service) Battalions of the Royal Warwickshire Regiment. (Illus.). pap. 27.50 (0-85052-547-0) Leo Cooper.

***Carter, Terry Ann.** Waiting for Julia. LC 99-491986. 1999. write for info. (0-919581-99-4) Third Eye.

Carter, Terry G. The Journal & Selected Letters of William Carey. LC 99-14798. 320p. 1999. 27.00 (1-57312-197-5) Smyth & Helwys.

***Carter, Thomas.** First Lady of Tennis. LC 99-69685. 128p. 2000. pap. 13.95 (0-88739-334-9) Creat Arts Bk.

Carter, Thomas. Shakespeare & Holy Scripture. LC 74-113574. reprint ed. 41.50 (0-404-01398-8) AMS Pr.

— Shakespeare, Puritan & Recusant. LC 70-129386. reprint ed. 32.50 (0-404-01397-X) AMS Pr.

Carter, Thomas & Goss, Peter. Utah's Historic Architecture 1847-1940: A Guide. LC 87-34526. (Illus.). viii, 192p. (Orig.). 1988. reprint ed. pap. 19.95 (1-880351-00-5) Schl of Arch.

Carter, Thomas F. The Invention of Printing in China & Its Spread Westward. 2nd ed. LC 55-5418. 319p. reprint ed. pap. 98.90 (0-608-11313-1, 201240800081) Bks Demand.

Carter, Tim, jt. auth. see Peugeot, Roger.

Carter, Tim, jt. ed. see Fenlon, Iain.

Carter, Tim, ed. see Peri, Jacopo.

Carter, Tim, tr. see Fabbri, Paolo.

Carter, Timothy, jt. auth. see Parry, Martin.

Carter, Timothy E. The Accurate Angel: Heralding a Messiah Unlike Any Other. 212p. 1998. pap. 7.77 (1-57502-760-7, PO2098) Morris Pubng.

Carter, Timothy J., jt. ed. see Kricka, Larry J.

Carter, Tina. Collectible Teapots: A Reference & Price Guide. (Illus.). 208p. 2000. pap. 26.95 (1-58221-018-7, Antique Trader) Krause Pubns.

— Teapots: The Collector's Guide. 1998. 12.99 (0-7858-1021-8) Bk Sales Inc.

Carter, Tom. Day Hiking Grand Teton National Park. (Illus.). 88p. 1993. pap. 4.95 (0-9629536-1-X) Dayhiking Pr.

— Day Hiking the Wind River Range. (Illus.). 88p. (Orig.). 1997. pap. 4.95 (0-9629536-2-8) Dayhiking Pr.

— Day Hiking Yellowstone. rev. ed. (Illus.). 88p. 1998. pap. 4.95 (0-9629536-0-1) Dayhiking Pr.

— How to Buy & Sell Cars. LC 87-91429. (Illus.). 212p. 1993. pap. 14.95 (0-945162-00-6) Prof Pr NC.

— Nashville Wives: Country Music's Celebrity Wives Reveal the Truth about Their Husbands & Marriages. (Illus.). 320p. 1999. mass mkt. 6.50 (0-06-103006-6) HarpC.

— Promises by the Dozen. LC 87-71393. 160p. (Orig.). 1988. pap. 7.99 (0-88270-635-7) Bridge-Logos.

— 13 Crucial Questions Jesus Asked. LC 98-53734. 144p. 1999. pap. 9.99 (0-8254-2359-7) Kregel.

Carter, Tom, jt. auth. see Daly, Jackie.

Carter, Tom, jt. auth. see Emery, Ralph.

Carter, Tom, jt. auth. see Haggard, Merle.

Carter, Tom, jt. auth. see McEntire, Reba.

Carter, Tony. Contemporary Sales Force Management. LC 97-33155. (Illus.). 286p. 1997. 49.95 (0-7890-0113-6); pap. 29.95 (0-7890-0423-2) Haworth Pr.

Carter, Tony, ed. The Aftermath of Reengineering: Downsizing & Corporate Performance. LC 99-16947. 165p. (C). 1999. 34.95 (0-7890-0720-7) Haworth Pr.

Carter, Tonya, jt. auth. see Thompson, Paul B.

Carter, Tonya R. & Thompson, Paul B. Darkness & Light. LC 88-51718. (DragonLance Preludes Trilogy: Vol. 1). (Illus.). 352p. (Orig.). (J). 1989. pap. 5.99 (0-88038-722-X, Pub. by TSR Inc) Random.

Carter, Tonya R., jt. auth. see Thompson, Paul B.

Carter, Valerie. Machine Knits. LC 86-81960. (Illus.). 128p. (Orig.). 1987. pap. 17.95 (0-937274-29-1) Lark Books.

Carter, Violet B. Winston Churchill As I Knew Him. 495p. 1996. pap. 24.95 (0-297-81588-1, Pub. by Weidenfeld & Nicolson) Trafalgar.

Carter, Virginia B. A Handbook of Metal Threads for the Embroiderer. rev. ed. (Illus.). 50p. 1979. 8.00 (0-9603862-1-1) V B Carter.

Carter, W. A., ed. Selective Inhibitors of Viral Functions. LC 73-81479. (Uniscience Ser.). 377p. 1973. 70.50 (0-87819-027-9, CRC Reprint) Franklin.

Carter, W. Craig & Johnson, William C., eds. The Selected Works of John W. Cahn. LC 98-67360. 559p. 1998. 138.00 (0-87339-416-X) Minerals Metals.

Carter, W. D. & Engman, E. T., eds. Remote Sensing from Satellites: Proceedings of Workshops I & IX of the COSPAR Interdisciplinary Scientific Commission A (Meetings A2) of the COSPAR 25th Plenary Meeting Held in Graz, Austria 25 June - 7 July 1974. 264p. 1985. pap. 54.00 (0-08-032751-6, Pub. by PPL) Elsevier.

Carter, W. E., jt. ed. see McCarthy, D. D.

Carter, W. H. From Yorktown to Santiago with the Sixth U. S. Cavalry. limited ed. LC 89-19734. (Illus.). 343p. 1989. 60.00 (0-938349-43-0) State House Pr.

— From Yorktown to Santiago with the Sixth U. S. Cavalry. LC 89-19734. (Illus.). 343p. 1989. reprint ed. 24.95 (0-938349-42-2) State House Pr.

***Carter, W. Hodding.** An Illustrated Viking Voyage: Retracing Leif Eriksson's Journey in an Authentic Viking Knarr. (Illus.). 176p. 2000. 34.95 (0-7434-0702-4) PB.

— A Viking Voyage: In Which an Unlikely Crew of Adventurers Attempts an Epic Journey to the New World. 304p. 2000. 25.00 (0-345-42003-9, Ballantine) Ballantine Pub Grp.

Carter, W. Horace. Creatures & Chronicles from Cross Creek. LC 80-68460. (Illus.). 286p. (Orig.). 1981. pap. text 9.95 (0-937866-02-4) Atlantic Pub Co.

— Florida Nature Coast Tales & Truths. LC 93-70477. (Illus.). 444p. (Orig.). 1993. pap. 14.95 (0-937866-40-7) Atlantic Pub Co.

— A Man Called Raleigh. LC 87-83704. (Illus.). 264p. (Orig.). 1988. pap. 9.95 (0-937866-15-6) Atlantic Pub Co.

— Nature's Masterpiece at Homosassa. LC 81-69722. (Illus.). 288p. (Orig.). 1984. 9.95 (0-937866-07-5) Atlantic Pub Co.

— Return to Cross Creek. (Illus.). 308p. (Orig.). 1985. pap. text 9.95 (0-937866-09-1) Atlantic Pub Co.

— Tremblin' Earth. LC 94-93941. 260p. (Orig.). 1994. pap. 13.95 (0-937866-47-4) Atlantic Pub Co.

— Virus of Fear: Demise of the Carolinas Ku Klux Klan. (Illus.). 256p. 1991. 19.95 (0-937866-33-4) Atlantic Pub Co.

— W. Horace Carter's Crappie Secrets. LC 91-70622. (Illus.). 360p. (Orig.). 1991. pap. 12.95 (0-937866-24-5) Atlantic Pub Co.

— Wild & Wonderful Santee Cooper Country. LC 01-67210. (Illus.). 392p. (Orig.). 1983. pap. 9.95 (0-937866-03-2) Atlantic Pub Co.

Carter, W. Horace & Andrews, Bud. Headstart Fishing Handbook. LC 93-90829. (Illus.). 416p. (Orig.). 1993. pap. 16.95 (0-937866-42-3) Atlantic Pub Co.

Carter, W. Horace & Burleson, Scott. Coastal Carolinas Tales & Truths, Vol. 1. LC 96-92871. (Illus.). 500p. (Orig.). 1996. pap. 14.95 (0-937866-56-3) Atlantic Pub Co.

Carter, W. Horace & Mann, Don. Great Fishing Adventures. (Complete Angler's Library). 246p. 1990. write for info. (0-914697-35-8) N Amer Outdoor Grp.

Carter, W. Horace, jt. auth. see Andrews, Bud.

Carter, W. Horace, jt. auth. see Faircloth, Rudy.

Carter, W. Horace, jt. auth. see Hannon, Douglas.

Carter, W. Horace, jt. auth. see Hannon, R. Douglas.

Carter, W. Horace, ed. see Stone, C. R.

***Carter, W. Leslie, et al.** Overcoming Loneliness. 224p. 2000. mass mkt. 7.99 (0-8007-8689-0, Spire) Revell.

An Asterisk (*) at the beginning of an entry indicates that the title is appearing for the first time.

Carter, W. Nick. Procedures & Guidelines for Disaster Preparedness Planning. viii, 195p. 1985. pap. 12.25 (*0-86638-063-9*) EW Ctr HI.

Carter, W. R. History of the First Regiment of Tennessee Volunteer Cavalry in the Great War of the Rebellion. (Illus.). 432p. 1992. reprint ed. 24.95 (*0-932807-68-2*) Overmountain Pr.

Carter, Walter. The Complete History of Epiphone. 128p. 1996. per. 22.95 (*0-7935-4948-5*, 00330033) H Leonard.

— The History of the Ovation Guitar. 128p. 1996. per. 22.95 (*0-7935-5876-X*) H Leonard.

— Insects in Relation to Plant Disease. 2nd ed. LC 73-4362. 773p. reprint ed. pap. 200.00 (*0-608-13379-5*, 205573100034) Bks Demand.

— The Martin Book: A Complete History of Martin Guitars. (Illus.). 108p. 1995. 22.95 (*0-87930-354-9*) Miller Freeman.

— The Songwriters Guide to Collaboration. 2nd expanded rev. ed. LC 97-154769. 102p. 1998. pap. 14.95 (*0-918371-14-7*, HL00330296) Intertec Pub.

Carter, Walter, jt. auth. see Gruhn, George.

Carter, Walter H. & Wampler, Galen L. Regression Analysis of Survival Data in Cancer Chemotherapy. (Statistics Ser.: 44). (Illus.). 224p. 1983. text 125.00 (*0-8247-1736-8*) Dekker.

Carter, Wanda B. Elmendorf & Related Families: Including Tolle, Engelke, Kampmann, Dreiss, Jenull, Carter, Braun, Mueller, Boerner, Schmidt, Gloetzel, Kalteyer, Wefing, Hernandez, Rossy, Scrivener, Leighton, Lieck, Meyer, Irwin, Robertson & Others. (Illus.). 186p. 1990. pap. text 35.50 (*0-9625488-0-4*) June Pubns.

— The Morgan Family Vol. 1: Thomas Warren & Lue Ella & Their Descendants, 1866-1998. (Illus.). 276p. 1998. pap. 30.00 (*0-9625488-1-2*) June Pubns.

Carter-Ward, jt. auth. see Shea, Donna L.

Carter-Ward, Adrienne L., jt. auth. see Shea, Donna.

Carter, Warren. Households & Discipleship: A Study of Matthew 19-20. LC 94-212059. (JSNTS Ser.: Vol. 103). 249p. 1994. 70.00 (*1-85075-493-4*, Pub. by Sheffield Acad) CUP Services.

— Matthew: Storyteller, Interpreter, Evangelist. 322p. 1996. pap. 19.95 (*1-56563-153-6*) Hendrickson MA.

***Carter, Warren.** Matthew & the Margins: A Socio-Political & Religious Reading. (Bible & Liberation Ser.). 500p. 2000. pap. 35.00 (*1-57075-324-5*) Orbis Bks.

Carter, Warren. What Are They Saying about Matthew's Sermon on the Mount? LC 94-2720. (What Are They Saying about...Ser.). 160p. (Orig.). 1994. pap. 7.95 (*0-8091-3473-X*) Paulist Pr.

Carter, Warren & Heil, John P. Matthew's Parables: Audience-Oriented Perspectives. LC 97-44677. (Catholic Biblical Quarterly Monograph Ser.). 1998. write for info. (*0-915170-29-9*) Catholic Bibl Assn.

Carter-Wells, Jo Ann, jt. auth. see Hopper, Jane N.

Carter, Wendy. Communication Skills: The McGraw-Hill One-Day Workshop. 128p. 1995. 110.00 (*0-07-912090-3*) McGraw.

Carter, Wendy. Competitor Analysis. 118p. 1994. ring bd. 299.00 (*0-7494-1171-6*, Kogan Pg Educ); ring bd. 59.95 (*0-7494-1174-0*, Kogan Pg Educ) Stylus Pub VA.

Carter, Wendy. Customer Service. LC 94-13298. (McGraw-Hill One-Day Workshop Ser.). 121p. 1994. 110.00 (*0-07-011197-9*) McGraw.

— Discover Powerful Secrets of Retailing Never Revealed: An Invaluable Guide for the Beginning or Experienced Retailer. (Illus.). 128p. (Orig.). 1989. pap. text 14.95 (*0-926658-00-X*) Wencar.

— How to Successfully Advertise & Promote Your Retail Business. (Illus.). 135p. (Orig.). 1989. pap. text 16.95 (*0-926658-01-8*) Wencar.

— Managing Organizational Change. LC 94-10780. 126p. 1994. teacher ed. 110.00 (*0-07-011198-7*) McGraw.

***Carter, Will J., et al.** Casti Guidebook to ASME Section VIII Div. 1 Pressure Vessels. 2nd ed. LC 00-42386. (CASTI Guidebks.). 2000. write for info. (*0-07-136470-6*) McGraw.

Carter, Willaim K., jt. auth. see Center for Learning Network Staff.

***Carter, William.** Billy Carter: A Journey Through the Shadows. LC 99-61751. (Illus.). 288p. 1999. 22.00 (*1-56352-553-4*) Longstreet.

Carter, William. The Elements of Metaphysics. (Heritage Ser.). 200p. (C). 1989. pap. 29.38 (*0-07-557482-9*) McGraw.

— Illuminations. LC 96-85564. (Illus.). 120p. 1996. pap. 40.00 (*1-881529-14-2*) Custom & Limited.

***Carter, William.** Preservation Hall. 1999. pap. text. write for info. (*1-871478-01-4*) Cass Hill.

Carter, William. Preservation Hall. LC 81-70962. (Illus.). 315p. (C). 1998. pap. 24.95 (*0-304-70517-9*) Continuum.

— The Search for Savin' Sam. LC 97-76266. 186p. 1998. 20.00 (*1-56352-468-6*) Longstreet.

Carter, William, photos by. Illuminations. LC 96-85564. (Illus.). 120p. 1997. 65.00 (*1-881529-15-0*) Custom & Limited.

— Illuminations. limited ed. LC 96-85564. (Illus.). 160p. 1997. 350.00 (*1-881529-16-9*) Custom & Limited.

***Carter, William C.** Marcel Proust: A Life. LC 99-53701. (Illus.). 921p. 2000. 35.00 (*0-300-08145-6*) Yale U Pr.

Carter, William C. The Proustian Quest. (Illus.). 400p. (C). 1992. text 50.00 (*0-8147-1470-6*) NYU Pr.

— The Proustian Quest. (C). 1994. pap. text 19.50 (*0-8147-1502-8*) NYU Pr.

Carter, William C., ed. Conversations with Shelby Foote. LC 88-37292. (Literary Conversations Ser.). 296p. 1989. pap. 17.00 (*0-87805-386-7*); text 39.50 (*0-87805-385-9*) U Pr of Miss.

Carter, William C., ed. The UAB Marcel Proust Symposium: In Celebration of the 75th Anniversary of "Swann's Way" (1913-1988) LC 89-62847. 154p. 1989. lib. bdg. 25.95 (*0-917786-75-0*) Summa Pubns.

Carter, William G. Carter: Giles Carter of Virginia, a Genealogical Memoir. (Illus.). 134p. 1997. reprint ed. pap. 19.50 (*0-8328-7870-7*); reprint ed. lib. bdg. 29.50 (*0-8328-7869-3*) Higginson Bk Co.

— No Box Seats in the Kingdom: Sermons for the Sundays after Pentecost (Last Third): Gospel Texts. LC 96-11805. (Orig.). 1996. pap. 10.50 (*0-7880-0805-6*) CSS OH.

***Carter, William G.** Praying for a Whole New World: Gospel Sermons for Advent/Christmas/Epiphany, Cycle C. LC 00-35798. 126p. 2000. pap. 11.95 (*0-7880-1728-4*); disk 11.95 (*0-7880-1729-2*) CSS OH.

Carter, William G. Speaking of Stewardship: Model Sermons on Money & Possessions. LC 98-4050. 152p. 1998. pap. 14.95 (*0-664-50031-5*) Geneva Press.

— Water Won't Quench the Fire Cycle B: Sermons for the Sundays after Pentecost (First Third), Gospel Texts. LC 96-4985. 99p. 1996. pap. 9.95 (*0-7880-0797-1*) CSS OH.

Carter, William G., jt. ed. see Djedje, Jacqueline C.

Carter, William J. Team Spirituality: A Guide for Staff & Church. LC 96-32278. 160p. 1997. pap. 12.95 (*0-687-01604-5*) Abingdon.

Carter, William K. Graphic Calculator Applications for Pre-Algebra: Quick Start. (MA - Academic Math Ser.). 1994. mass mkt., wbk. ed. 12.95 (*0-538-62491-4*) S-W Pub.

Carter, William K. & Eatherly. Pre-Algebra. (MA - Academic Math Ser.). 1991. mass mkt. 54.95 (*0-538-61375-0*) S-W Pub.

Carter, William K. & Monczka, Robert M. Purchasing. LC 97-17872. (SB - Marketing Education Ser.). (C). 1997. mass mkt. 92.95 (*0-538-81495-0*) S-W Pub.

Carter, William L. The Angry Teenager. LC 94-38176. 250p. 1995. pap. 12.99 (*0-7852-8002-2*) Nelson.

Carter, William R. The Elements of Metaphysics. 208p. (C). 1989. 32.95 (*0-87722-619-9*) Temple U Pr.

Carter, William R., et al. The Way Things Are: Basic Readings in Metaphysics. LC 97-10598. 336p. 1997. pap. 19.38 (*0-07-010198-1*) McGraw.

Carter, William S. Anglo-Canadian Wartime Relations: RAF Bomber Command & No. 6 (Canadian) Group. Stansky, Peter, ed. LC 91-13395. (Modern European History Ser.). 224p. 1991. text 20.00 (*0-8153-0411-0*) Garland.

Carter, Youngman, jt. auth. see Allingham, Margery.

Carter, Yvonne & Thomas, Cathryn. Research Methods in Primary Care. LC 96-53628. 1997. write for info. (*1-85775-198-1*, Radcliffe Med Pr) Scovill Paterson.

Carteret, Carriede, jt. auth. see Bidgen, Richard.

Carterette, Edward C., et al, eds. Memory. 2nd ed. (Handbook of Perception & Cognition Ser.). (Illus.). 586p. 1998. reprint ed. pap. text 39.95 (*0-12-102571-3*) Morgan Kaufmann.

— Tasting & Smelling. 2nd ed. LC 97-22352. (Handbook of Perception & Cognition Ser.). (Illus.). 231p. 1997. text 75.00 (*0-12-161958-3*) Morgan Kaufmann.

Carterette, Edward C. & Jones, Margaret H. Informal Speech: Alphabetic & Phonemic Texts with Statistical Analyses & Tables. LC 73-92376. 660p. reprint ed. pap. 200.00 (*0-7837-4673-3*, 204441900003) Bks Demand.

Carterette, Edward C., jt. ed. see Friedman, Morton P.

Cartermill Publishing Staff. Financial Times: Mining International Yearbook, 1998. 500p. 1997. 280.00 (*1-85334-864-3*, 110959, Pub. by Cartermill Pubns) Gale.

— Financial Times: Oil & Gas International Yearbook, 1998. 500p. 1997. 280.00 (*1-85334-869-4*, 110958, Pub. by Cartermill Pubns) Gale.

CarterSouthard, Edna, ed. see Dietrich, Linnea S.

Cartes, Maria R., tr. see Garaway, Margaret K.

Cartes, Marie R., tr. see Garaway, Margaret.

Cartes, Rebeca, tr. see Kingsolver, Barbara.

Cartey, Ronald. Inspirational Training: How to Inspire Action. 200p. 1996. 69.95 (*0-566-07708-6*, Pub. by Gower) Ashgate Pub Co.

Cartey, Wilfred G. Black Images. LC 75-113096. (Columbia University, Center for Education in Asia, Publications). 200p. reprint ed. pap. 62.00 (*0-8357-7289-6*, 202599800048) Bks Demand.

— Whispers from the Caribbean: I Going Away, I Going Home. (Afro-American Culture & Society Monographs: Vol. 11). 504p. (C). 1991. 43.00 (*0-934934-35-5*); pap. text 25.95 (*0-934934-36-3*) CAAS Pubns.

Carthach. The Monastic Rule of St. Carthach: St. Mochuda the Younger. 1990. pap. 1.50 (*0-89981-059-4*) Eastern Orthodox.

Carthew & Webb. Aprobado. 1986. pap. text 17.04 (*0-582-33178-1*, 72067); audio 22.61 (*0-582-33177-3*, 72066) Longman.

Carthew, Annick H. Cadillac & the Dawn of Detroit. LC 94-19472. (Illus.). 278p. (Orig.). 1994. pap. 14.95 (*0-923568-38-7*) Wilderness Adventure Bks.

***Carthew, Annick Hivert.** Ghostly Lights Return: Great Lakes Lighthouse Fiends & Phantoms. (Illus.). 184p. 1999. pap. 14.95 (*0-923568-46-8*) Wilderness Adventure Bks.

Carthew, J. Robert. Carthew Family Records, 1994: Sort by Date. LC 94-70666. (Nineteen Ninety-Four Edition - Sort by Date Ser.). 461p. 1994. 59.95 (*1-885319-00-2*) Carthew Cnslt.

— Carthew Family Records, 1994: Sort by Name. LC 94-70666. (Nineteen Ninety-Four Edition - Sort by Name Ser.). 461p. 1994. 59.95 (*1-885319-01-0*) Carthew Cnslt.

— Carthew Family Records, 1994: Sort by Place. LC 94-70666. (Nineteen Ninety-Four Edition - Sort by Place Ser.). 461p. 1994. 59.95 (*1-885319-02-9*) Carthew Cnslt.

— Carthew Family Records, 1994: Sort by Relationship Number. LC 94-70666. (Nineteen Ninety-Four Edition - Sort by Relationship Number Ser.). 461p. 1994. 59.95 (*1-885319-03-7*) Carthew Cnslt.

Carthy, Brian. Football Captains: The All-Ireland Winners. (Illus.). 320p. 1997. 24.95 (*0-86327-394-7*, Pub. by Wolfhound Press) Irish Amer Bk.

Carthy, J. D. & Duddington, C. L., eds. Viewpoints in Biology, 4 vols., 1. LC 63-4816. 300p. 1962. pap. 93.00 (*0-608-08521-9*, 202576600001) Bks Demand.

— Viewpoints in Biology, 4 vols., 2. LC 63-4816. 258p. 1963. pap. 80.00 (*0-608-08522-7*, 202576600002) Bks Demand.

— Viewpoints in Biology, 4 vols., 3. LC 63-4816. 270p. 1964. pap. 83.70 (*0-608-08523-5*, 202576600003) Bks Demand.

— Viewpoints in Biology, 4 vols., 4. LC 63-4816. 266p. 1965. pap. 82.50 (*0-608-08524-3*, 202576600004) Bks Demand.

Carthy, Joe. An Introduction to Assembly Language Programming & Computer Architecture. (Illus.). 400p. 1995. mass mkt. 30.75 (*1-85032-129-9*) ITCP.

Carthy, Mary P. Old St. Patrick's: New York's First Cathedral. (Monographs: No. 23). (Illus.). 1947. 10.00 (*0-930060-05-9*) US Cath Hist.

Cartianu, Ana & Johnston, R. C., eds. Selected Works of Ion Creanga & Mihai Eminescu. LC 91-72148. (Classics of Romanian Literature Ser.: Vol. 1). 307p. 1993. text 49.00 (*0-88033-224-7*, Pub. by East Eur Monographs) Col U Pr.

Cartianu, Ana, tr. see Eliade, Mircea.

Cartier, Annee. Redemption. 320p. 1997. pap. 4.99 (*0-7860-0362-6*, Pinncle Kensgtn) Kensgtn Pub Corp.

— Surrender to the Dawn. 384p. 1999. pap. 4.99 (*0-7860-0228-X*, Pinncle Kensgtn) Kensgtn Pub Corp.

— Tradewinds. 416p. 1995. mass mkt. 4.99 (*0-8217-0099-5*, Zebra Kensgtn) Kensgtn Pub Corp.

— Tradewinds. large type ed. (Black Satin Romance Ser.). 455p. 1996. 27.99 (*1-86110-008-6*) Ulverscroft.

Cartier, Bresson. Fine Irish Crochet Lace. (Illus.). 54p. 1994. reprint ed. pap. text 3.95 (*0-486-27874-3*) Dover.

Cartier-Bresson, Anne. Paris Sous L'objectif 1885-1994. 1999. pap. text 27.95 (*2-85025-649-8*) Hazan.

Cartier-Bresson, Henri. America in Passing. (Illus.). 152p. 1996. pap. 37.50 (*0-8212-2332-1*, Pub. by Bulfinch Pr) Little.

— Europeans. LC 97-75772. (Illus.). 232p. 1998. 60.00 (*0-8212-2522-7*, Pub. by Bulfinch Pr) Little.

Cartier-Bresson, Henri. Henri Cartier-Bresson. 1976. 8.95 (*0-89381-000-2*) Aperture.

Cartier-Bresson, Henri. Henri Cartier-Bresson. 2nd ed. (Masters of Photography Ser.). (Illus.). 96p. 1997. reprint ed. 18.95 (*0-89381-744-9*) Aperture.

— Henri Cartier-Bresson: Photographer. (Illus.). 333p. 1992. 125.00 (*0-8212-1986-3*, Pub. by Bulfinch Pr) Little.

***Cartier-Bresson, Henri.** India: A Celebration of Independence, 1947-1997. (Illus.). 224p. 2000. pap. 35.00 (*0-89381-897-6*) Aperture.

— The Mind's Eye: Writings on Photography & Photographers. Sand, Michael L., ed. LC 99-64610. (Illus.). 112p. 1999. 19.95 (*0-89381-875-5*) Aperture.

Cartier-Bresson, Henri. Propos de Paris. (Illus.). 168p. 1998. pap. 35.00 (*0-8212-2496-4*, Pub. by Bulfinch Pr) Little.

— Tete a Tete: Portraits by Henri Cartier-Bresson, Vol. 1. LC TR680,C3824 1998. (Illus.). 144p. (gr. 8). 1998. 65.00 (*0-8212-2562-6*) Little.

Cartier-Bresson, Henri, photos by. Art Without Art. (Illus.). 1995. 75.00 (*0-614-96887-9*) Little.

— Henri Cartier-Bresson: Art Without Art. (Illus.). 320p. 1996. 75.00 (*0-8212-2285-6*, Pub. by Bulfinch Pr) Little.

— Henri Cartier-Bresson: Mexican Notebooks. LC 95-61576. (Illus.). 88p. 1996. 29.95 (*0-500-54199-X*, Pub. by Thames Hudson) Norton.

— Stern Portfolio: Henri Cartier-Bresson. (Illus.). 100p. 1998. pap. 19.95 (*3-570-19168-0*) te Neues.

***Cartier, Carolyn L.** Globalizing South China. 288p. 1999. 64.95 (*1-55786-887-5*); pap. text 32.95 (*1-55786-888-3*) Blackwell Pubs.

Cartier, Craig. Moscow Mutterings: The Collected Wit & Wisdom of the Former Soviet Leadership. LC 97-68962. 190p. (Orig.). 1997. pap. write for info. (*1-57502-564-7*, PO1633) Morris Pubng.

Cartier, Crystal. 4 - 1 - 1 Reality Check: Poetry & Song. 4th rev. ed. 300p. 1998. spiral bd. 19.99 (*1-883111-07-2*) Love Story.

— Immortal Obsession: Book One: The Prophecy. (Immortal Obsession Ser.). 500p. (C). 1993. pap. 24.95 (*1-883111-00-5*) Love Story.

Cartier, Francis A. & Todaro, Martin T. The Phonetic Alphabet. 3rd ed. 112p. (C). 1982. text. write for info. (*0-697-04218-9*) Brown & Benchmark.

Cartier, G. T. Deadlock at Walla Walla. 332p. (Orig.). (C). 1986. pap. 9.95 (*0-934129-00-2*) Somerton Pr.

Cartier, Jacques. A Shorte & Briefe Narration of the Two Navigations to Newe Fraunce. Florio, J., tr. LC 73-6110. (English Experience Ser.: No. 718). 1975. reprint ed. 25.00 (*90-221-0718-3*) Walter J Johnson.

***Cartier, Jacques.** A Vocabulary of Stadaconan: From the First & Second Relations of Jacques Cartier: Including a Word-List from Hochelaga. LC 99-28764. (American Language Reprints Ser.: Vol. 11). 53p. 1999. 15.00 (*1-889758-09-4*) Evol Pubng & Manuf.

Cartier, Jan, jt. auth. see Hall, John.

Cartier, Jean-Baptiste. L' Art du Violon: Troisieme Edition, Paris, c1885. (Monuments of Music & Music Literature in Facsimile I, Ser.: Vol. 14). (Illus.). 1973. lib. bdg. 75.00 (*0-8450-2014-5*) Broude.

Cartier, John O. Best Venison Ever: The Indispensable Guide for Big-Game Hunters Who Love Eating Wild Food. LC 96-104996. 114p. 1995. pap. 9.95 (*0-9647193-0-4*) Cartier Assocs.

Cartier, Lola, tr. see Boue, Andre, ed.

Cartier, M., ed. Le Travail et Ses Representations. 313p. 1984. pap. write for info. (*0-318-65450-4*) Gordon & Breach.

Cartier, M., ed. Le Travail et Ses Representations. (Ordres Sociaux Ser). (FRE.). 313p. 1984. pap. text 36.00 (*2-903928-01-0*, Harwood Acad Pubs) Gordon & Breach.

Cartier, N. R. Aquila, Vol. 3. (Aquila Chestnut Hill Studies in Modern Languages & Literatures Ser.). 1976. text 99.50 (*90-247-1797-3*) Kluwer Academic.

Cartier, N. R. & Boccaccio, Giovanni. Boccaccio's Revenge. 1977. pap. text 57.00 (*90-247-1961-5*) Kluwer Academic.

Cartier, Pierre. Algebraic Theory of Spinors & Clifford Algebras: Collected Works of Claude Chevalley. 240p. 1996. 54.00 (*3-540-57063-2*) Spr-Verlag.

Cartier, Pierre & Kosmann-Schwarzbach, Yvette. Integrable Systems: The Verdier Memorial Conference: Actes du Colloque International de Luminy. Babelon, Olivier et al, eds. LC 03-40972. (Progress in Mathematics Ser.: Vol. 115). xiii, 366p. 1993. 103.50 (*0-8176-3653-6*) Birkhauser.

Cartier, Pierre, et al. Grothendieck Festschrift: Articles in Honor of Alexander Grothendieck on His 60th Birthday, 3 vols., Set. (ENG & GER.). 1991. 279.50 (*0-8176-3429-0*) Birkhauser.

— Grothendieck Festschrift: Articles in Honor of Alexander Grothendieck on His 60th Birthday, 3 vols., Vol. I. (ENG & GER.). 1990. 114.50 (*0-8176-3427-4*) Birkhauser.

— Grothendieck Festschrift: Articles in Honor of Alexander Grothendieck on His 60th Birthday, 3 vols., Vol. II. (FRE & GER.). 1990. 113.50 (*0-8176-3428-2*) Birkhauser.

— Grothendieck Festschrift: Articles in Honor of Alexander Grothendieck on His 60th Birthday, 3 vols., Vol. III. (ENG & GER.). 1990. 113.50 (*0-8176-3487-8*) Birkhauser.

Cartier, R. Early Cultures & Rock Features of the Santa Teresa Hills: CA-SCI-64, CA-SCI-106 & CA-SCI-341. fac. ed. (Illus.). 285p. (C). 1980. reprint ed. pap. text 30.00 (*1-55567-780-0*) Coyote Press.

Cartier, Randi, ed. see Reed, Gary.

***Cartier, Wesley & Ruffins, Reynold.** Marco's Run. LC 00-9727. (Green Light Readers Series). (Illus.). (J). 2001. write for info. (*0-15-216249-6*) Harcourt.

Cartin, Thomas J. Principles & Practices of Organizational Performance Excellence. 2nd ed. LC 98-42726. 250p. 1997. 33.00 (*0-87389-428-6*, H0995) ASQ Qual Pr.

— Principles & Practices of TQM. 241p. (Orig.). 1993. pap. 28.00 (*0-87389-153-8*, H0691) ASQ Qual Pr.

Cartin, Thomas J. & Jacoby, Donald J. A Review of Managing Quality & a Primer for the Certified Quality Manager Exam. LC 97-2864. 333p. 1997. 29.00 (*0-87389-358-1*, H0917) ASQ Qual Pr.

Cartinhour, Gaines T. Digital Signal Processing: An Overview of Basic Principles. LC 98-53218. (Illus.). 416p. (C). 1999. 98.00 (*0-13-769266-8*, Macmillan Coll) P-H.

Cartinhour, Gaines T. & Westerfield, Ray B. Branch, Group & Chain Banking & Historical Survey of Branch Banking in the United States, 2 vols. Bruchey, Stuart, ed. LC 80-1139. (Rise of Commercial Banking Ser.). (Illus.). 1981. reprint ed. lib. bdg. 42.95 (*0-405-13639-0*) Ayer.

Cartland, Barbara. As Eagles Fly. 19.95 (*0-685-10840-6*) Amereon Ltd.

***Cartland, Barbara.** Bewildered in Berlin. large type ed. LC 00-39579. 206p. 2000. 23.95 (*0-7838-9103-2*, G K Hall & Co) Mac Lib Ref.

Cartland, Barbara. Beyond the Stars. large type ed. LC 96-30936. (Nightingale Ser.). 1997. pap. 18.95 (*0-7838-1894-7*, G K Hall Lrg Type) Mac Lib Ref.

***Cartland, Barbara.** The Cave of Love. large type ed. (Paperback Ser.). 2000. pap. 23.95 (*0-7838-9004-4*, G K Hall Lrg Type) Mac Lib Ref.

Cartland, Barbara. A Circus for Love. large type ed. 245p. 1992. 27.99 (*0-7505-0236-3*) Ulverscroft.

— The Dangerous Dandy. 1976. 20.95 (*0-685-10861-9*) Amereon Ltd.

— A Dream from the Night. large type ed. LC 98-5537. 210p. 1998. 19.95 (*0-7838-0127-0*, G K Hall Lrg Type) Mac Lib Ref.

— Drena & the Duke. 176p. 1992. 18.00 (*0-7278-4346-X*) Severn Hse.

— The Duke's Dilemma. 160p. 1994. 18.00 (*0-7278-4559-4*) Severn Hse.

— The Eyes of Love. (Camfield Ser.: No. 135). 176p. (Orig.). 1994. mass mkt. 3.99 (*0-515-11496-0*, Jove) Berkley Pub.

***Cartland, Barbara.** Forced to Marry. large type ed. LC 99-35305. 203p. (Orig.). 1999. pap. 23.95 (*0-7838-8720-5*, G K Hall Lrg Type) Mac Lib Ref.

Cartland, Barbara. The Frightened Bride. 20.95 (*0-89190-897-8*) Amereon Ltd.

— A Fugitive from Love. 416p. 1998. 7.99 (*0-517-18821-X*) Random Hse Value.

— The Ghost Who Fell in Love. large type ed. (Magna Large Print Ser.). 230p. 1996. 27.99 (*0-7505-0904-X*, Pub. by Mgna Lrg Print) Ulverscroft.

***Cartland, Barbara.** The Heart of the Clan. large type ed. LC 00-21195. (Thorndike Romance Ser.). 2000. 26.95 (*0-7862-2484-3*) Thorndike Pr.

— Hidden by Love. large type ed. LC 99-41718. (Thorndike Candlelight Romance Ser.). 183p. 1999. 20.95 (*0-7862-2196-8*) Thorndike Pr.

— The Hidden Evil. large type ed. 336p. 1999. 31.99 (*0-7505-1376-4*, Pub. by Mgna Lrg Print) Ulverscroft.

— Hiding. large type ed. (Candlelight Romance Ser.). 2000. 19.95 (*0-7862-2441-X*) Thorndike Pr.

C

Cartland, Barbara. I Reach for the Stars: An Autobiography. LC 00-4093. (Illus.). 197p. 1995. 23.95 (0-86051-924-4, Robson-Parkwest) Parkwest Pubns.

— I Seek the Miraculous LC 78-315166. 217 p. 1978. write for info. (0-85969-135-7) Sheldon Pr.

— The Incomparable. (Camfield Novel of Love Ser.: 137). 176p. 1995. mass mkt. 3.99 (0-515-11531-2, Jove) Berkley Pub.

— The Innocent Imposter. (Camfield Novel of Love Ser.: 138). 176p. (Orig.). 1995. mass mkt. 3.99 (0-515-11554-1, Jove) Berkley Pub.

*Cartland, Barbara. An Innocent in Russia. large type ed. LC 00-28638. 217p. 2000. 22.95 (0-7862-2579-3) Mac Lib Ref.

Cartland, Barbara. The Kiss of Life. large type ed. (Magna Large Print Ser.). 288p. 1998. 29.99 (0-7505-1110-9, Pub. by Mgna Lrg Print) Ulverscroft.

— Little Pretender. 286p. 1999. 10.95 (1-885478-72-0, Pub. by Genesis Press) BookWorld.

— Look, Listen & Love. large type ed. (Magna Large Print Ser.). 272p. 1996. 27.99 (0-7505-0905-8, Pub. by Mgna Lrg Print) Ulverscroft.

*Cartland, Barbara. Look with the Heart. large type ed. LC 00-27787. 172p. (Orig.). 2000. 27.95 (0-7838-9058-3) Mac Lib Ref.

— Love & Lucia. large type ed. 320p. 1999. 31.99 (0-7505-1419-1, Pub. by Mgna Lrg Print) Ulverscroft.

— Love & War. large type ed. LC 98-26225. 168 p. 1998. pap. write for info. (0-7540-3506-9, G K Hall Lrg Type) Mac Lib Ref.

— Love & War: A New Camfield Novel of Love. large type ed. LC 98-26225. 165p. 1998. 30.00 (0-7838-0311-7, G K Hall Lrg Type) Mac Lib Ref.

Cartland, Barbara. Love in the Ruins. 176p. (Orig.). 1995. mass mkt. 4.50 (0-515-11733-1, Jove) Berkley Pub.

— Love Leaves at Midnight. large type ed. (Magna Large Print Ser.). 288p. 1997. 27.50 (0-7505-1111-7) Thorndike Pr.

— The Loveless Marriage. (Camfield Ser.: No. 139). 176p. 1995. mass mkt. 3.99 (0-515-11572-X, Jove) Berkley Pub.

— The Loveless Marriage. large type ed. LC 97-32590. 220p. 1998. 19.95 (0-7838-1893-9, G K Hall Lrg Type) Mac Lib Ref.

*Cartland, Barbara. Lovers in Lisbon. large type ed. LC 99-54983. 2000. pap. 23.95 (0-7838-8929-1, G K Hall & Co) Mac Lib Ref.

— Lucky Logan Finds Love. LC 00-42583. .p. 2000. write for info. (0-7862-2787-7) Thorndike Pr.

Cartland, Barbara. The Magic of Love. 19.95 (0-89190-898-6) Amereon Ltd.

— A Magical Moment. (Camfield Novel of Love Ser.: 140). 176p. (Orig.). 1995. mass mkt. 3.99 (0-515-11594-0, Jove) Berkley Pub.

— The Magnificent Marriage. 20.95 (0-88411-247-0) Amereon Ltd.

— Miracle for a Madonna. large type ed. (Magna Large Print Ser.). 227p. 1997. 27.99 (0-7505-1108-7, Pub. by Mgna Lrg Print) Ulverscroft.

— Moonlight on the Sphinx. large type ed. (Magna Large Print Ser.). 304p. 1998. 29.99 (0-7505-1239-3, Pub. by Mgna Lrg Print) Ulverscroft.

— Never Lose Love. (Camfield Ser.: No. 133). 176p. (Orig.). 1994. mass mkt. 3.99 (0-515-11457-X, Jove) Berkley Pub.

*Cartland, Barbara. No Time for Love. LC 99-30988. (Thorndike Large Print Candlelight Series). 1999. 19.95 (0-7862-2029-5) Thorndike Pr.

— Paradise In Penang. large type ed. LC 99-46305. 190p. 1999. 23.95 (0-7838-8795-7, G K Hall Lrg Type) Mac Lib Ref.

Cartland, Barbara. Passage to Love. (Canfield Ser.: No. 147). 176p. 1995. mass mkt. 4.50 (0-515-11751-X, Jove) Berkley Pub.

— Passage to Love. large type ed. LC 98-14055. (Paperback Ser.). 194p. 1998. pap. 21.95 (0-7838-0147-5) Thorndike Pr.

— The Patient Bridegroom. (Camfield Ser.: No. 141). 176p. (Orig.). 1995. mass mkt. 3.99 (0-515-11615-7, Jove) Berkley Pub.

— The Protection of Love. (Camfield Ser.: No. 142). 176p. 1995. pap. text 3.99 (0-515-11640-8, Jove) Berkley Pub.

*Cartland, Barbara. Pure & Untouched. large type ed. 304p. 1999. 31.99 (0-7505-1420-5, Pub. by Mgna Lrg Print) Ulverscroft.

Cartland, Barbara. The Queen of Hearts. large type ed. LC 98-14058. 176p. 1998. 24.95 (0-7862-1455-4) Thorndike Pr.

— Safe in Paradise. large type ed. (Magna Large Print Ser.). 196p. 1997. 27.99 (0-7505-1109-5) Ulverscroft.

— Saved by a Saint. (Camfield Ser.: No. 136). 176p. (Orig.). 1994. mass mkt. 3.99 (0-515-11508-8, Jove) Berkley Pub.

— Someone to Love. 176p. (Orig.). 1995. mass mkt. 3.99 (0-515-11686-6, Jove) Berkley Pub.

— The Spirit of Love, No. 13. (Camfield Ser.: No. 134). 176p. (Orig.). 1994. mass mkt. 3.99 (0-515-11479-0, Jove) Berkley Pub.

— Tempted to Love. large type ed. (Magna Large Print Ser.). 240p. 1996. 27.99 (0-7505-0906-6, Pub. by Mgna Lrg Print) Ulverscroft.

— Three Complete Novels: A Night of Gaiety; A Duke in Danger; Secret Harbor. LC 94-17415. 336p. 1994. 7.99 (0-517-11929-3) Random Hse Value.

— Three Complete Novels of Courtly Love: The Prude & the Prodigal - Lies for Love - From Hate to Love. 480p. 1996. 7.99 (0-517-18238-6) Wings Bks.

— Three Complete Novels of Dukes & Their Ladies: Never Laugh at Love, The Disgraceful Duke, A Touch of Love. LC 95-47626. 448p. 1996. 7.99 (0-517-15046-8) Random Hse Value.

— Three Complete Novels of Earls & Their Ladies. LC 95-31433. 1996. 7.99 (0-517-14772-6) Wings Bks.

— Three Complete Novels of Royalty & Romance. LC 95-21906. 1995. pap. 7.99 (0-517-14678-9) Wings Bks.

— Three Complete Novels of Royalty & Romance. LC 95-21906. 464p. 1996. 7.99 (0-517-15045-X) Wings Bks.

— Three Days to Love No. 150: Camfield. (Camfield Ser.: No. 150). 176p. (Orig.). 1996. mass mkt. 4.50 (0-515-11812-5, Jove) Berkley Pub.

— Too Precious to Lose. LC 99-18828. 1999. 19.95 (0-7838-8594-6) Mac Lib Ref.

— A Virgin in Paris. large type ed. 368p. 1998. 29.99 (0-7505-1238-5) Ulverscroft.

— The Waltz of Hearts. large type ed. 239p. 1993. 27.99 (0-7505-0362-9) Ulverscroft.

— The Wild Cry of Love. large type ed. 268p. 1995. 27.99 (0-7505-0655-5) Ulverscroft.

— Winged Magic. large type ed. (Magna Romance Ser.). 229p. 1992. 27.99 (0-7505-0366-1) Ulverscroft.

*Cartland, Barbara. The Wings of Ecstasy. large type ed. LC 99-20125. 192p. 1999. pap. text 23.95 (0-7838-8609-8, G K Hall & Co) Mac Lib Ref.

Cartland, Barbara, pref. Diana: A Commemorative Biography, 1961-1997. 276p. 1997. mass mkt. 20.95 (1-55197-846-6) Picasso Publ.

Cartland, Barbara & Jove Books Publishing Staff. The Queen of Hearts. (Camfield Novel of Love Ser.: 119). 176p. 1993. mass mkt. 3.99 (0-515-11139-2, Jove) Berkley Pub.

Cartland, Doug. Ray Eliot: The Spirit & Legend of Mr. Illini. LC 95-69133. (Illus.). 255p. 1995. 19.95 (1-57167-015-7) Sports Pub.

Cartland, J. Henry. Twenty Years at Pemaquid: Sketches of Its History & Its Remains, Ancient & Modern. (Illus.). 224p. 1997. reprint ed. lib. bdg. 29.50 (0-8328-5890-0) Higginson Bk Co.

Cartledge, Bryan. Mind, Brain & the Environment, Vol. 199. LC 97-37602. (Linacre Lectures, 1995-1996). (Illus.). 198p. 1998. text 59.00 (0-19-854992-X) OUP.

Cartledge, Bryan, ed. Energy & the Environment. LC 92-43543. (Linacre Lectures: Vol. 1991-2). 184p. 1993. 45.00 (0-19-858413-X) OUP.

— Health & the Environment: The Linacre Lectures 1992-3. (Illus.). 240p. 1995. pap. text 24.95 (0-19-858417-2) OUP.

— Monitoring the Environment. (Linacre Lectures). (Illus.). 224p. 1992. pap. 16.95 (0-19-858412-1) OUP.

— Population & the Environment: The Linacre Lectures, 1993-94. LC 96-133283. (Illus.). 200p. 1995. text 45.00 (0-19-854842-7) OUP.

— Transport & the Environment: The Linacre Lectures, 1994-1995. (Illus.). 164p. 1996. 50.00 (0-19-854934-2) OUP.

Cartledge, Gwendolyn & Milburn, JoAnn F. Cultural Diversity & Social Skills Instruction: Understanding Ethnic & Gender Differences. LC 96-69184. 398p. (Orig.). 1996. pap. text 24.95 (0-87822-355-X, 4916) Res Press.

Cartledge, Gwendolyn & Milburn, JoAnne F., eds. Teaching Social Skills to Children. (General Psychology Ser.). 1980. 40.00 (0-08-024654-0, Pergamon Pr); pap. text 12.00 (0-08-024653-2, Pergamon Pr) Elsevier.

Cartledge, Gwendolyn & Milburn, JoAnne F., eds. Teaching Social Skills to Children & Youth: Innovative Approaches. 3rd ed. 384p. 1994. pap. text 50.00 (0-205-16507-9) Allyn.

Cartledge, Ned. Ned Cartledge. 1986. pap. 20.00 (0-932526-66-7) Nexus Pr.

— Ned Cartledge. 1986. 30.00 (0-932526-42-X) Nexus Pr.

Cartledge, P. Aristophanes & His Theatre of the Absurd. (Classical World Ser.). (Illus.). 100p. (C). 1990. pap. 18.95 (1-85399-114-7, Pub. by Brist Class Pr) Focus Pub-R Pullins.

Cartledge, Paul. The Greeks: A Portrait of Self & Others. LC 92-45898. (Illus.). 248p. 1993. pap. text 17.95 (0-19-289147-2) OUP.

*Cartledge, Paul. The Greeks: Crucible of Civilization. LC 99-89591. (Illus.). 280p. 2000. 25.00 (1-57500-093-8, Pub. by TV Bks) HarpC.

Cartledge, Paul, ed. The Cambridge Illustrated History of Ancient Greece. LC 96-51545. (Illustrated Histories Ser.). (Illus.). 400p. (C). 1998. 39.95 (0-521-48196-1) Cambridge U Pr.

— Kosmos: Essays in Order, Conflict & Community in Classical Athens. LC 97-27253. (Illus.). 284p. (C). 1998. 64.95 (0-521-57081-6) Cambridge U Pr.

Cartledge, Paul & Spawforth, Anthony. Hellenistic & Roman Sparta: A Tale of Two Cities. 256p. 1989. 35.00 (0-415-03290-3, A3288) Routledge.

Cartledge, Paul, et al. Hellenistic Constructs: Essays in Culture, History, & Historiography. LC 97-7317. (Hellenistic Culture & Society Ser.). 315p. 1997. 50.00 (0-520-20676-2, Pub. by U CA Pr) Cal Prin Full Svc.

Cartledge, Paul, tr. see Zaidman, Louise B. & Pantel, Pauline S.

Cartledge, Peter. Financial Arithmetic: A Practitioners Guide. 350p. 1993. pap. 170.00 (1-85564-209-3, Pub. by Euromoney) Am Educ Systs.

*Cartledge, Peter C. Hand Book of Financial Mathematics: Mathematics for Derivatives, Vol. 2. 3rd ed. 280p. 1999. pap. text 170.00 (1-85564-742-7, Pub. by Euromoney) Am Educ Systs.

— Hand Book of Financial Mathematics Vol. 3: Mathematics for Bond & Money Markets. 3rd ed. 300p. 2000. pap. text 170.00 (1-85564-741-9, Pub. by Euromoney) Am Educ Systs.

Cartledge, Tony W. Vows in the Hebrew Bible & the Ancient Near East. (Journal for the Study of the Old Testament Supplement Ser.: No. 147). 221p. 1992. 65.00 (1-85075-298-2, Pub. by Sheffield Acad) CUP Services.

Cartlidge, David R. & Dungan, David L., eds. Documents for the Study of the Gospels. enl. rev. ed. LC 93-42366. 344p. (Orig.). 1993. 21.00 (0-8006-2809-8, 1-2809) Augsburg Fortress.

Cartlidge, J. E. Newbold Astbury & Its History. 256p. (C). 1982. text 39.00 (0-947818-00-6, Pub. by Old Vicarage) St Mut.

Cartlidge, Michelle. Good Night, Teddy. LC 91-58732. (Illus.). 24p. (J). (ps). 1992. 5.95 (1-56402-076-2) Candlewick Pr.

— The Mice of Mousehold: A Moving Picture Book. LC 96-84673. (Illus.). 14p. (J). (ps). 1997. 14.99 (0-7636-0117-9) Candlewick Pr.

*Cartlidge, Michelle. Mouse Wedding. (J). 1999. 4.99 (0-525-46110-8, Dutton Child) Peng Put Young Read.

Cartlidge, Michelle. Mouse's Christmas House: A Press-Out Model House. (Illus.). 16p. (Orig.). (J). 1992. pap. 9.95 (0-8362-4500-8) Andrews & McMeel.

— Teddy's Friends. LC 91-58758. (Illus.). 24p. (J). (ps). 1992. 5.95 (1-56402-077-0) Candlewick Pr.

*Cartlidge, Patrick, et al. Revision Questions in Pediatrics: For Postgraduate Examinations. LC 99-28871. 1999. text. write for info. (0-443-06246-3) Church.

Cartmail, Keith St., see St. Cartmail, Keith.

Cartmel, Fred, jt. auth. see Furlong, Andy.

Cartmell. Sisterhoods: Feminists in Film & Fiction. 1998. 35.00 (0-7453-1223-3, Pub. by Pluto GBR) Stylus Pub VA.

— Trash Aesthetics: Popular Culture & Its Audience. LC 96-45671. (Film/Fiction Ser.). 1997. 49.95 (0-7453-1203-9) Pluto GBR.

Cartmell, B. Clay. Let's Go Fossil Shark Tooth Hunting: A Guide for Identifying Sharks & Where & How to Find Their Superbly Formed Fossilized Teeth. (Search Series Bk.). (Illus.). 76p. (Orig.). 1978. pap. 3.50 (0-930498-01-1) Nat Sci Res.

*Cartmell, Deborah. Interpreting Shakespeare on Screen. 2000. pap. 18.95 (0-312-23393-0); text 59.95 (0-312-23392-2) St Martin.

Cartmell, Deborah. Pulping Fictions: Consuming Culture Across the Literature-Media Divide. 168p. 1996. pap. 15.95 (0-7453-1070-2, Pub. by Pluto GBR) Stylus Pub VA.

— Sisterhoods: Feminists in Film & Fiction. 160p. 1998. pap. text 10.99 (0-7453-1218-7, Pub. by Pluto GBR) Stylus Pub VA.

— Trash Aesthetics. 1997. pap. text 15.95 (0-7453-1202-0, Pub. by Pluto GBR) Stylus Pub VA.

*Cartmell, Deborah, et al, eds. Alien Identities: Exploring Differences in Film & Fiction. LC 98-46720. 192p. 1999. 49.95 (0-7453-1405-8, Pub. by Pluto GBR) Stylus Pub VA.

— Alien Identities: Exploring Differences in Film & Fiction. 192p. 1999. pap. 18.95 (0-7453-1400-7, Pub. by Pluto GBR) Stylus Pub VA.

— Classics in Film & Fiction. 176p. 2000. pap. 19.95 (0-7453-1588-7, Pub. by Pluto GBR) Stylus Pub VA.

Cartmell, Deborah, et al, eds. Pulping Fictions: Consuming Culture Across the Literature-Media Divide. LC 95-52785. (Film - Fiction Ser.: Vol. 1). 168p. 1996. 49.95 (0-7453-1071-0) Pluto GBR.

*Cartmell, Deborah, et al. Classics in Film & Fiction. LC 00-20428. (Film/Fiction Ser.). (Illus.). 176p. 2000. 59.95 (0-7453-1593-3, Pub. by Pluto GBR) Stylus Pub VA.

Cartmell, Donald V. It's Because We're Family. 192p. 1998. pap. 12.95 (0-9664961-0-8) Toward Effect Mgmt.

Cartmell, E. Principles of Crystal Chemistry. 1989. 22.00 (0-85404-017-X) CRC Pr.

Cartmell, Robert. The Incredible Scream Machine. LC 87-70175. 252p. 1988. pap. 25.95 (0-87972-342-4) Bowling Green Univ Popular Press.

Cartmell, Stephen. Papal Whispers. 290p. 1998. 36.50 (1-85776-335-1, Pub. by Book Guild Ltd) Trans-Atl Phila.

Cartmell, T. K. Shenandoah Valley Pioneers & Their Descendants: A History of Frederick County, Virginia from Its Formation in 1733 to 1908 Compiled Mainly from Original Records of Old Frederick County, Now Hampshire, Berkeley, Shenandoah, Jefferson, Hardy, Clarke, Warren, Morgan & Frederick. (Illus.). 598p. 1989. reprint ed. pap. 60.00 (1-55613-243-3) Heritage Bk.

*Cartmell, T. K. Shenandoah Valley Pioneers & Their Descendants: A History of Frederick County, Virginia from Its Formation in 1738 to 1908. vii, 572p. 2000. reprint ed. pap. 62.50 (0-8063-4543-8, Pub. by Clearfield Co) ACCESS Pubs Network.

*Cartmell, Tim. Effortless Combat Throw. (Illus.). 194p. 1999. pap. 19.95 (0-86568-176-7) Unique Pubns.

— Effortless Combat Throws. 1998. pap. 19.95 (1-883175-06-2) High View Pubns.

Cartmell, Todd. The Parent Lifesaver: Practical Help for Everyday Childhood Problems. LC 98-24536. (Illus.). 208p. (Orig.). (C). (gr. 13). 1998. pap. 11.99 (0-8010-5826-0) Baker Bks.

Cartmell, Van H., ed. Plot Outlines of One Hundred Famous Plays. 1979. 16.50 (0-8446-0539-5) Peter Smith.

Cartmell, Van H. & Cerf, Bennett A., compiled by. Famous Plays of Crime & Detection: From Sherlock Holmes to Angel Street. LC 76-173621. (Play Anthology Reprint Ser.). 1977. reprint ed. 45.95 (0-8369-8220-7) Ayer.

Cartmell, Van H. & Cerf, Bennett A., eds. Twenty-Four Favorite One-Act Plays. LC 58-13274. 560p. 1963. pap. 14.95 (0-385-06617-1, C423) Doubleday.

Cartmell, Van H., ed. see Cerf, Bennett A.

Cartmell, Van H., jt. ed. see Cerf, Bennett A.

Cartmill, Matt. A View to a Death in the Morning: Hunting & Nature Through History. (Illus.). 384p. (C). 1993. text 29.95 (0-674-93735-X) HUP.

— A View to a Death in the Morning: Hunting & Nature Through History. (Illus.). 352p. 1996. pap. 15.95 (0-674-93736-8) HUP.

— A View to a Death in the Morning: Hunting & Nature Through History. (Illus.). 331p. 1999. reprint ed. pap. text 30.00 (0-7881-6301-9) DIANE Pub.

Cartmill, Matt, et al. Human Structure. LC 86-11982. (Illus.). 464p. 1987. 49.95 (0-674-41805-0) HUP.

Cartnell, E. Principles of Crystal Chemistry. 1971. pap. 10.00 (0-85404-018-8) CRC Pr.

Cartnell, Tim & Miller, Dan. Xing Yi Nei Gang: Xi Yi Health Maintenance & Internal Strength Development. (Illus.). 224p. (Orig.). 1994. pap. 19.95 (1-883175-04-6) High View Pubns.

Cartnell, Tim, tr. see Yun, Zhao D.

Cartner, Victoria Webb. Kennel Ideas: A Collection of Clever Ideas & Tricks of the Trade on Dog Kenneling that Will Save You Time, Trouble & Money. 4th rev. ed. LC 98-94797. (Illus.). 160p. (Orig.). 1999. pap. 19.95 (0-9618992-3-9) Farmington Pub.

Carto, W. A. Profiles in Populism. 1982. 12.95 (0-8159-6518-4); pap. 7.95 (0-8159-6519-2) Devin.

*Carton, Benedict. Blood from Your Children: The Colonial Origins of Generational Conflict in South Africa. (Illus.). 256p. 2000. 55.00 (0-8139-1931-2); pap. 19.50 (0-8139-1932-0) U Pr of Va.

Carton, Bernice. Beyond the Brooklyn Bridge: A Memoir. LC 97-38605. 160p. 1998. 18.95 (0-86534-269-5) Sunstone Pr.

Carton, Dana & Caprio, Anthony. En Francais: Practical Conversational French. 2nd ed. (C). 1987. pap. write for info. (0-442-21215-1) Thomson Learn.

— En Francais: Practical Conversational French. 2nd ed. (C). 1987. pap. write for info. (0-442-21218-6, VNR) Wiley.

Carton, Erik P. Dynamic Compaction of Ceramics & Composites. (Illus.). 164p. 1998. pap. 44.50 (90-407-1547-5, Pub. by Delft U Pr) Coronet Bks.

Carton, Evan. The Marble Faun: Hawthorne's Transformations. 170p. (C). 1992. 23.95 (0-8057-9448-4, Twyne) Mac Lib Ref.

— The Rhetoric of American Romance: Dialectic & Identity in Emerson, Dickinson, Poe, & Hawthorne. LC 84-27770. 301p. 1985. reprint ed. pap. 93.40 (0-608-03645-5, 206447100009) Bks Demand.

Carton, Evan & Friedman, Alan W., eds. Situating College English. LC 98-19216. (Series in Language & Ideology). 248p. 1999. 65.00 (0-89789-480-4, Bergin & Garvey) Greenwood.

— Situating College English: Lessons from an American University. LC 95-44323. (Series in Language & Ideology). 256p. 1996. 69.50 (0-89789-460-X, Bergin & Garvey); pap. 21.95 (0-89789-481-2, Bergin & Garvey) Greenwood.

Carton, Fernand & Poulet, Denise. Dictionnaire du Francais Regional du Nord-Pas-de-Calais. (FRE.). 125p. 1991. 50.00 (0-8288-9485-X) Fr & Eur.

Carton, J. Dictionary of French & International Acronyms. 3rd ed. (FRE.). 380p. 1987. pap. 55.00 (0-7859-7475-X, 2856080251) Fr & Eur.

Carton, Janis B., ed. see Barnitz, Jacqueline.

Carton, Jean-Paul. Poesie Francaise: Premiers Excercises d'Analyse. XII, 291p. (C). 1998. pap. text 29.95 (0-8204-4054-X) P Lang Pubng.

Carton, Lonnie. No Is a Love Word: How to Say "No" to Children of All Ages. LC 91-77338. 250p. 1992. pap. 12.95 (0-9627183-0-0) Learn Ctr MA.

Carton, Paul. Death of the Woodstock Generation. LC 94-94453. 80p. (Orig.). 1994. pap. 6.95 (0-9641889-0-2) V Cortlandt Bks.

*Carton, Sharon F. Sometimes You Get Killed, 1. 250p. 2000. pap. 9.95 (1-892614-30-8) Briarwood VA.

Cartoon Bank, Inc. Staff. E-mail.this.book! 1996. 17.00 incl. cd-rom (0-614-20691-X) Knopf.

Cartoon Bank Staff. E-Mail This Book. 96p. 1996. 18.50 (0-679-45085-8) McKay.

— Now That You Can Walk, Go Get Me a Beer. 128p. 1994. pap. 9.00 (0-671-87962-6, Fireside) S&S Trade Pap.

*Cartoon Network Staff. Bubblevicious. Vol. 2. (Illus.). 32p. (J). (ps-3). 2000. pap. 3.50 (0-439-17306-X) Scholastic Inc.

— Monkey See, Doggie Do. (Powerpuff Girls Ser.: Vol. 1). (Illus.). 32p. (J). (ps-3). 2000. pap. 3.50 (0-439-17305-1) Scholastic Inc.

Cartozian, Stephanie, jt. auth. see Holtorf, Kent.

Cartright. Handbook of Organizational Culture. text. write for info. (0-471-49126-8) Wiley.

Cartright, T., et al. Quantum Field Theory, Statistical Mechanics, Quantum Groups & Topology: NATO Advanced Research Workshop. 400p. 1992. text 109.00 (981-02-0959-2) World Scientific Pub.

Cartron, J. P. & Rouger, P., eds. Blood Cell Biochemistry Vol. 6: Molecular Basis of Human Blood Group Antigens. (Illus.). 512p. (C). 1995. text 120.00 (0-306-44853-X, Kluwer Plenum) Kluwer Academic.

Cartron, Jean-Pierre, jt. ed. see Agre, Peter C.

Cartstaff. 1998 Fedex Championship Series Media Guide. Bronder, Steve et al, eds. (Illus.). 368p. (Orig.). 1998. pap. 14.95 (0-9647598-2-9) Chmpship Auto.

Cartter, Allan. Ph.D.'s & the Academic Labor Market. LC 75-38700. 280p. reprint ed. pap. 86.80 (0-608-13900-9, 202088400020) Bks Demand.

Cartter, George R. Twilight of the Jackass Prospector: Death Valley Area Portraits of the 1930's. LC 82-62025. (Illus.). (Orig.). 1982. 10.95 (0-930704-13-4) Sagebrush Pr.

*Cartwheel Books Staff. Billy Goats Gruff. (Finger Puppet Theater Bks.). (Illus.). 16p. (ps-1). 2000. 14.95 (0-439-17679-4) Scholastic Inc.

— Sleeping Beauty. (Finger Puppet Theater Bks.). (Illus.). 16p. (ps-1). 2000. 14.95 (0-439-17680-8) Scholastic Inc.

C

Cartwright, Carol A., et al. Educating Special Learners. 4th ed. 648p. 1995. pap. 84.95 (0-534-17664-X) Wadsworth Pub.

Cartwright. Educating Special Learners. 2nd ed. 1984. pap. write for info. (0-534-03676-7) Wadsworth Pub.

— Educating Special Learners. 3rd ed. (Education Ser.). 1988. pap., teacher ed. write for info. (0-534-09571-2) Wadsworth Pub.

— Educating Special Learners. 4th ed. (Education Ser.). 1994. student ed. 17.75 (0-534-17665-8) Wadsworth Pub.

Cartwright. Educating Special Learners. 5th ed. (Special Education Ser.). 1919. pap. 60.50 (0-534-50783-2) Wadsworth Pub.

Cartwright. Storm of Passion. 1994. per. 2.99 (0-373-17168-4) Harlequin Bks.

— Training with Media: Designing & Producing Video & Multimedia. LC 99-18133. 232p. 1999. pap. text 44.95 (0-240-80325-6, Focal) Buttrwrth-Heinemann.

***Cartwright & Cooper.** HR Know-How in Mergers & Acquisitions. 230p. 2000. pap. 56.95 (0-8464-5175-1) Beekman Pubs.

Cartwright, et al. Laboratory Exercises in Biology. 3rd ed. 200p. (C). 1997. spiral bd. 26.95 (0-7872-3547-4) Kendall-Hunt.

Cartwright, Ann & Cartwright, Reg. Jackdaw. (Illus.). 32p. (J). (ps-2). 1995. 19.95 (0-09-176427-0, Pub. by Hutchnson) Trafalgar.

Cartwright, Ann & Smith, Christopher. Elderly People, Their Medicines, & Their Doctors. 240p. 1988. text 79.50 (0-415-00684-8) Routledge.

Cartwright, Ann, jt. auth. see Bowling, Ann.

Cartwright, Ann, jt. auth. see Seale, Clive.

Cartwright, Ann, jt. auth. see Whittaker, Mike.

Cartwright, B. O., tr. see Turpin, Francois H.

***Cartwright, Brenda E.** Encounters with Reality: 1,001 Interpreter Scenarios. LC 99-74403. 232p. 1999. per. 29.95 (0-916883-28-0) RID Pubns.

Cartwright, Carol A. & Cartwright, Phillip G. Developing Observation Skills. 2nd ed. Smith, Robert M., ed. (Special Education Ser.). 192p. (C). 1983. 44.06 (0-07-010185-X) McGraw.

Cartwright, Carrie, ed. see Cartwright, Gene.

Cartwright, Clyde. Computer User's Guide to Losing Weight & Gaining Fitness. LC 98-41974. 2000. 12.95 (1-56072-513-3) Nova Sci Pubs.

Cartwright, Colbert C. Candles of Grace. 112p. (Orig.). 1992. pap. 9.99 (0-8272-0461-2) Chalice Pr.

Cartwright, Colbert S. People of the Chalice. 112p. (Orig.). (C). 1987. pap. 7.99 (0-8272-2938-0) Chalice Pr.

Cartwright, Colbert S. & Harrison, O. I., eds. Chalice Worship. 512p. 1997. pap. 54.99 (0-8272-0470-1) Chalice Pr.

Cartwright, Colbert S. & Harrison, O. I., eds. Chalice Worship. deluxe ed. LC 95-48142. 512p. 1997. 39.99 (0-8272-0465-5) Chalice Pr.

Cartwright, Colbert S. & Harrison, O. I., eds. Chalice Worship: Library Edition. 512p. 1997. lthr. 46.99 (0-8272-0471-X) Chalice Pr.

Cartwright, D. E., tr. see Marchuk, Gurii I. & Kagan, B. A.

***Cartwright, D. J.** Underlying Principles of the Boundary Element Method. 300p. 2000. 135.00 (1-85312-839-2, Pub. by WIT Pr) Computational Mech MA.

Cartwright, D. J., ed. see Aliabaci, M. H., et al.

Cartwright, David & Warner, Rex. A Historical Commentary on Thucydides: A Companion to Rex Warner's Penguin Translation. LC 96-45789. 336p. (C). 1997. text 54.50 (0-472-10695-3, 10695); pap. text 20.95 (0-472-08419-4, 08419) U of Mich Pr.

Cartwright, David E. Tides: A Scientific History. LC 98-4660. (Illus.). 272p. (C). 1998. 69.95 (0-521-62145-3) Cambridge U Pr.

Cartwright, David E., tr. see Hubscher, Arthur.

Cartwright, Denise, ed. see George, Jeannette Clift.

***Cartwright, Derrick R.** Rivieres at Rivages: Les Artistes Americans, 1850-1900. Rose, Francesca, ed. (American Perspectives).Tr. of Waves & Waterways: American Perspectives, 1850-1900. (FRE., Illus.). 2000. pap. 13.00 (0-932171-14-1, Museed Art) Terra Found Arts.

— Waves & Waterways: American Perspectives, 1850-1900. Rose, Francesca, ed. (American Perspectives).Tr. of Rivieres et rivages: les artistes americans, 1850-1900. (Illus.). 2000. pap. 13.00 (0-932171-13-3, Museed Art) Terra Found Arts.

Cartwright, Derrick R. & Lovell, Margaretta M. The City & the Country: American Perspectives, 1870-1920. (Illus.). 56p. 1999. pap. 14.95 (0-932171-09-5, Museed Art) Terra Found Arts.

— Ville et Campagne (The City & the Country) Les Articles Americains, 1870-1920 (American Perspectives, 1870-1920) Waite, Alan, tr. (FRE., Illus.). 56p. 1999. pap. 85.00 (0-932171-10-9, Museed Art) Terra Found Arts.

Cartwright, Donald. Extensions of Positive Operators Between Banach Lattices. LC 75-19496. (Memoirs Ser.: No. 3/164). 48p. 1975. pap. 19.00 (0-8218-1864-3, MEMO/3/164) Am Math.

Cartwright, Donald I. Harmonic Functions on Trees & Buildings: Workshop on Harmonic Functions on Graphs, October 30-November 3, 1995, City University of New York. Koranyi, Adam, ed. LC 97-7967. (Contemporary Mathematics Ser.: Vol. 206). 181p. 1997. pap. 35.00 (0-8218-0605-X) Am Math.

Cartwright, Dorwin. Achieving Change in People: Some Applications of Group Dynamics Theory. (Reprint Series in Social Sciences). (C). 1993. reprint ed. pap. text 5.00 (0-8290-4163-X, S-39) Irvington.

Cartwright, Elizabeth, et al. Electro-epilation: A Practical Approach for NVQ Level 3. 280p. (Orig.). 1995. pap. 39.50 (0-7487-1915-6, Pub. by S Thornes Pubs) Trans-Atl Phila.

Cartwright, F. D., ed. see Cartwright, John.

***Cartwright, Frederick F. & Biddiss, Michael.** Disease & History. 2nd rev. exp. ed. (Illus.). 240p. 2000. 29.95 (0-7509-2315-6) Sutton Publng.

Cartwright, G. Phillip, et al. Educating Special Learners. 2nd ed. 499p. (C). 1984. pap. write for info. (0-534-03675-9) Wadsworth Pub.

— Educating Special Learners. 3rd ed. 575p. (C). 1988. pap. 39.25 (0-534-09570-4) Wadsworth Pub.

Cartwright, Gary. Blood Will Tell. Todd, Rebecca, ed. 488p. 1995. mass mkt. 5.99 (0-671-88330-5) PB.

— Dirty Dealing: Drug Smuggling on the Mexican Border & the Assasination of a Federal Judge - An American Parable. LC 98-11320. (Illus.). 400p. 1998. reprint ed. pap. 15.95 (0-938317-35-0) Cinco Puntos.

— Galveston: A History of the Island. LC 98-3289. (Chisholm Trail Ser.: No. 18). 338p. 1998. pap. 15.95 (0-87565-190-9) Tex Christian.

***Cartwright, Gary.** Turn Out the Lights: Chronicles of Texas During the 80s & 90s. LC 00-39297. (Southwestern Writers Collection Ser.). 320p. 2000. pap. 19.95 (0-292-71226-X) U of Tex Pr.

Cartwright, Gary. Turn Out the Lights: Chronicles of Texas During the 80s & 90s, Vol. 10. 320p. 1997. 39.95 (0-292-71199-9) U of Tex Pr.

Cartwright, Gary, anno. Heart Wiseguy: How to Live the Good Life after a Heart Attack, Vol. 1. LC 98-10193. 272p. 1998. text 22.95 (0-312-18591-X) St Martin.

Cartwright, Gene. A Family Gathering. Cartwright, Carrie, ed. 1999. 23.95 (0-9649756-1-0) Falcon Creek.

— I Never Played Catch with My Father. Ortman, Lisa, ed. 384p. 1996. 23.95 (0-9649756-0-2) Falcon Creek.

Cartwright, Hal V. Granny Boy & the Puny Warbler. LC 92-71096. (Illus.). 48p. (Orig.). (J). (gr. 4). 1992. pap. 8.50 (0-923687-16-5) Celo Valley Bks.

Cartwright, Howard E. Here Comes Doctor Ward: A Climb to Glory. (Illus.). 238p. 1995. 25.00 (1-886094-06-3) Chicago Spectrum.

Cartwright, Hugh M. Applications of Artificial Intelligence in Chemistry. (Oxford Chemistry Primers Ser.: No. 11). (Illus.). 96p. (C). 1994. pap. text 12.95 (0-19-855736-1) OUP.

***Cartwright, Hugh M., ed.** Intelligent Data Analysis in Science. (Oxford Chemistry Masters Ser.: Vol. 4). (Illus.). 224p. 2000. text 85.00 (0-19-850233-8) OUP.

Cartwright, J. & Critchley, J. Cruise, Pershing & SS-20: The Search for Consensus: Nuclear Weapons in Europe. 188p. 1985. text 45.00 (0-08-031201-2, Pergamon Pr); pap. text 23.75 (0-08-031202-0, Pergamon Pr) Elsevier.

Cartwright, Jennifer, jt. auth. see Mernagh, Dawn.

Cartwright, Jennifer, jt. auth. see Mernagh-Ward, Dawn.

Cartwright, Jim. Bed. (Methuen Modern Plays Ser.). 29p. (C). 1991. pap. write for info. (0-413-62230-4, A0419, Methuen Drama) Methn.

Cartwright, Jim. I Licked Slag's Deodorant. 1997. pap. 10.95 (0-413-71540-X) Methn.

Cartwright, Jim. Jim Cartwright: Plays One, Vol. 1. 1996. pap. 15.95 (0-413-70230-8, A0831, Methuen Drama) Methn.

— The Rise & Fall of Little Voice. LC 93-138999. 96p. (C). 1992. pap. 10.95 (0-413-67130-5, A0653, Methuen Drama) Methn.

— To. (Methuen Modern Plays Ser.). 49p. (Orig.). (C). 1991. pap. write for info. (0-413-63570-8, A0488, Methuen Drama) Methn.

— Two & Bed. 180p. 1994. pap. 13.95 (0-413-68330-3, A0697, Methuen Drama) Methn.

Cartwright, Jim, jt. auth. see Worth, Paul W.

***Cartwright, John.** Evolution & Human Behavior. LC 99-87600. (Illus.). 400p. (C). 2000. 60.00 (0-262-03281-3, Bradford Bks) MIT Pr.

— Evolution & Human Behavior: Darwinian Perspectives on Human Nature. LC 99-87600. (Illus.). 400p. 2000. pap. 24.95 (0-262-53170-4, Bradford Bks) MIT Pr.

Cartwright, John. Inside Harry's Brain Maze Book. (J). 1989. pap. 1.50 (0-8167-1222-0) Troll Communs.

— The Life & Correspondence of Major Cartwright, 2 Vols, Set. Cartwright, F. D., ed. LC 68-57728. 1969. reprint ed. 95.00 (0-678-00449-8) Kelley.

— More Amazing Dinosaurs Maze Book. 32p. (J). 1989. pap. 1.50 (0-8167-1221-2) Troll Communs.

— Road. rev. ed. (Methuen Modern Plays Ser.). 84p. (C). 1990. reprint ed. pap. write for info. (0-413-62390-4, A0410, Methuen Drama) Methn.

— Those Amazing Dinosaur Mazes. (J). 1989. pap. 1.50 (0-8167-1220-4) Troll Communs.

— Unequal Bargaining: A Study of Vitiating Factors in the Formation of Contracts. 288p. 1991. 75.00 (0-19-825243-9) OUP.

Cartwright, John, ed. see Hay, Gilbert.

Cartwright, John M. Farm & Ranch Real Estate Law. LC 70-189071. (Real Property-Zoning Ser.). 1970. 135.00 (0-685-59802-0) West Group.

Cartwright, John R. Political Leadership in Sierra Leone. LC 79-300056. 308p. reprint ed. pap. 95.50 (0-608-12846-5, 202360200033) Bks Demand.

— Politics in Sierra Leone, 1947-57. LC 71-18592. (Scholarly Reprint Ser.). 306p. reprint ed. pap. 94.90 (0-608-16264-7, 202651400050) Bks Demand.

Cartwright-Jones, Catherine. The Prolific Knitting Machine. LC 90-4592. (Illus.). 208p. (Orig.). 1990. pap. 17.95 (0-934026-58-0) Interweave.

Cartwright-Jones, Catherine & Jones, Roy. Enchanted Knitting: Charted Motifs for Hand & Machine Knitting. LC 96-46767. (Illus.). 96p. 1997. pap. 19.95 (1-883010-21-7) Interweave.

— The Tap-Dancing Lizard: Three Hundred Thirty-Seven Fanciful Charts for the Adventurous Knitter. (Illus.). 176p. (Orig.). 1992. pap. 18.95 (0-934026-78-5) Interweave.

Cartwright, Joseph H. The Triumph of Jim Crow: Tennessee Race Relations in the 1880s. LC 76-2009. 300p. reprint ed. pap. 93.00 (0-8357-8602-1, 203499800091) Bks Demand.

Cartwright, Julia. Beatrice D'Este: Duchess of Milan, 1475-1497; a Study of the Renaissance. LC 73-38345. (Select Bibliographies Reprint Ser.). 1977. 24.95 (0-8369-6762-3) Ayer.

— Botticelli (Sandro) His Art & Life. (Illus.). 90p. 1998. reprint ed. pap. 35.00 (0-87556-859-9) Saifer.

Cartwright, Justin. Leading the Cheers. 256p. 1999. 23.95 (0-7867-0658-9) Carroll & Graf.

— Masai Dreaming. LC 94-41335. 1995. 22.00 (0-614-32177-8) Random.

Cartwright, Keith. Saint-Louis: A Wool Strip-Cloth for Sekou Dabo. LC 98-216535. (Occasional Publications Ser.: No. 8). (Illus.). 41p. 1998. pap. 5.95 (1-883275-07-5) Xavier Rev.

Cartwright, Keith, ed. Meningococcal Disease. LC 94-32088. 324p. 1995. 245.00 (0-471-95259-1) Wiley.

Cartwright, Kent. Shakespearean Tragedy & Its Double: The Rhythms of Audience Response. 240p. 1991. 35.00 (0-271-00738-9) Pa St U Pr.

— Theatre & Humanism: English Drama in the Sixteenth Century. LC 98-37229. 336p. 1999. 59.95 (0-521-64075-X) Cambridge U Pr.

Cartwright, Kent, jt. ed. see Vaughan, Virginia M.

Cartwright, Lillian K., jt. auth. see Blackwell, Barbara L.

Cartwright, Lisa. Screening the Body: Tracing Medicine's Visual Culture. LC 94-30340. 1995. pap. 17.95 (0-8166-2290-6); text 49.95 (0-8166-2289-2) U of Minn Pr.

Cartwright, Lisa, et al, eds. The Visible Woman. LC 97-45325. 1998. text 55.00 (0-8147-1556-7); pap. text 19.00 (0-8147-1568-0) NYU Pr.

Cartwright, Lorin. Preparing for the Athletic Trainers' Certification Examination. LC 94-29306. 264p. (Orig.). 1994. pap. text 26.00 (0-87322-504-X, BCAR0504) Human Kinetics.

Cartwright, Lorin A. & Pitney, William A. Athletic Training for Student Assistants. LC 99-21226. (Illus.). 328p. 1999. spiral bd. 29.00 (0-88011-753-2, BCAR0753) Human Kinetics.

Cartwright, Madeline & O'Dorso, Michael. For the Children: Lessons from a Visionary Principal. LC 92-21194. 257p. 1999. reprint ed. 19.95 (0-9672812-0-2, 3729748'1-dc29) Berger-Cartwright.

Cartwright, Mason W., tr. & intro. see Chekhov, Anton.

Cartwright, Michael, jt. auth. see Drinnon, Bobby.

Cartwright, Michael, jt. auth. see Yoder, John H.

Cartwright, N. P. Candideces-Versos Spanish Poetry. LC 83-76. (ENG & SPA.). 91p. 1983. pap. text 5.00 (0-9601482-3-X) N P Cartwright.

***Cartwright, Nancy.** The Dappled World: A Study of the Boundaries of Science. LC 98-32176. (Illus.). 264p. (C). 1999. 54.95 (0-521-64336-8); pap. 19.95 (0-521-64411-9) Cambridge U Pr.

Cartwright, Nancy. How the Laws of Physics Lie. (Illus.). 230p. 1983. pap. text 26.00 (0-19-824704-4) OUP.

***Cartwright, Nancy.** My Life as a Ten-Year-Old Boy: Bart, the Simpsons & Me. (Illus.). 224p. (J). 2000. pap. 19.95 (0-7868-6696-9, Pub. by Hyprn Child) Time Warner.

Cartwright, Nancy. Nature's Capacities & Their Measurement. (Illus.). 278p. 1994. reprint ed. pap. text 21.00 (0-19-823507-0) OUP.

Cartwright, Nancy, et al. Otto Neurath: Philosophy Between Science & Politics. (Ideas in Context Ser.: No. 38). (Illus.). 304p. (C). 1996. text 59.95 (0-521-45174-4) Cambridge U Pr.

Cartwright, Nellie P. Bless the Nightingale: Ama Al ruisenor. rev. ed. LC 77-85799. (ENG & SPA.). 105p. 1977. pap. text 5.00 (0-9601482-2-1) N P Cartwright.

— Horizons - Horizontes. 50p. (Orig.). 1988. pap. 5.00 (0-9601482-5-6) N P Cartwright.

— New Moon - Luna Nueva. LC 70-38. (ENG & SPA.). 85p. (Orig.). 1982. pap. text 5.00 (0-9601482-4-8) N P Cartwright.

Cartwright, P. L. Quavers. 178p. 1997. pap. 10.00 (0-9658421-0-X) P L Cartwright.

Cartwright, Pauline. The Bird Chain. LC 93-20805. (Illus.). (J). 1994. 4.25 (0-383-03736-0) SRA McGraw.

— Home. LC 93-20062. (Illus.). (J). 1994. write for info. (0-383-03695-X) SRA McGraw.

— Jake Was a Pirate. LC 93-26216. (Illus.). (J). 1994. 4.25 (0-383-03754-9) SRA McGraw.

— Jimmy Parker's New Job. LC 93-20029. (Illus.). (J). 1994. pap. write for info. (0-383-03679-8) SRA McGraw.

— Taking Our Photo. LC 92-31950. (Voyages Ser.). (Illus.). (J). 1993. 3.75 (0-383-03595-3) SRA McGraw.

— The Troll in the Hole. LC 93-9282. (Illus.). (J). 1994. pap. write for info. (0-383-03722-0) SRA McGraw.

Cartwright, Peter. Autobiography of Peter Cartwright. 349p. 1986. pap. 9.95 (0-687-02319-X) Abingdon.

— Autobiography of Peter Cartwright: The Backwoods Preacher. Strickland, W. P., ed. LC 70-38344. (Select Bibliographies Reprint Ser.). 1977. 38.95 (0-8369-6761-5) Ayer.

Cartwright, Phillip G., jt. auth. see Cartwright, Carol A.

Cartwright, R. Y. & Hirsch, H. A., eds. Antifungals in Gynecology: Focus on Terconazole. (Journal: Gynaekologische Rundschau: Vol. 25, Suppl. 1). (Illus.). iv, 120p. 1985. pap. 33.25 (3-8055-4041-8) S Karger.

Cartwright, Reg. Peter & the Wolf. LC 86-27004. 32p. (J). (ps-2). 1995. pap. 5.95 (0-8050-1362-8, Bks Young Read) H Holt & Co.

Cartwright, Reg, jt. auth. see Cartwright, Ann.

Cartwright, Richard. Philosophical Essays. 312p. 1987. 30.00 (0-262-03130-2) MIT Pr.

Cartwright, Rita Cantos, jt. auth. see Conde, H. Victor.

Cartwright, Robert E. & Phillips, Jerry J. Products Liability with 1991 Cumulative Supplement, 3 vols., Set. 1986. text 240.00 (0-930273-41-9, 60815-10, MICHIE) LEXIS Pub.

Cartwright, Roger. Managing Yourself; A Competence Approach to Supervisory Management, Revised ed. LC 98-14602. 1998. pap. text 41.95 (0-631-20925-5) Blackwell Pubs.

Cartwright, Roger & Green, George. In Charge of Customer Satisfaction: A Competence Approach. LC 96-23266. (Illus.). 256p. (C). 1997. pap. 44.95 (0-631-20087-8) Blackwell Pubs.

Cartwright, Roger, et al. In Charge of Yourself: A Competency Approach to Personal Development. (In Charge Ser.). 236p. (C). 1996. pap. 26.95 (0-631-19761-3) Blackwell Pubs.

— Managing Operations. (In-Charge Ser.). 240p. (Orig.). (C). 1993. pap. text 40.95 (0-631-19011-2) Blackwell Pubs.

— Managing People: A Competence Approach to Supervisory Management. LC 97-45216. 200p. 1998. pap. 38.95 (0-631-20923-9) Blackwell Pubs.

— Managing Resources & Information. LC 97-45214. (Illus.). 256p. 1998. pap. 41.95 (0-631-20924-7) Blackwell Pubs.

Cartwright, Roger, jt. auth. see Baird, Carolyn.

Cartwright, Rosalind D. Fourier Methods. 1990. pap. write for info. (0-318-68281-8) P-H.

Cartwright, S. & Godlee, C. J. Churchill's Pocketbook of General Practice. 296p. 1998. pap. write for info. (0-443-04863-0) Church.

Cartwright, S., jt. auth. see Amery, H.

Cartwright, S., jt. auth. see Amery, Heather.

Cartwright, S., jt. auth. see Tyler, J.

***Cartwright, Stacey.** Charades for Experts. 360p. 2000. pap. 18.00 (0-7388-2162-4) Xlibris Corp.

Cartwright, Stephan & Zeff, Claudia. Find the Duck. (Usborne Kid Kits Ser.). (Illus.). (J). (ps). 1996. 10.95 (0-88110-732-8, Usborne) EDC.

— Find the Kitten. (Usborne Kid Kits Ser.). (Illus.). (J). (ps). 1996. 10.95 (0-88110-802-2, Usborne) EDC.

— Find the Piglet. (Usborne Kid Kits Ser.). (Illus.). (J). (ps). 1996. 10.95 (0-88110-800-6, Usborne) EDC.

— Find the Puppy. (Usborne Kid Kits Ser.). (Illus.). (J). (ps). 1996. 10.95 (0-88110-801-4, Usborne) EDC.

***Cartwright, Stephen.** Animal Babies. (Farmyard Tales Board Bks.). (Illus.). 12p. (J). (ps up). 2000. bds. 4.95 (0-7460-4105-5, Usborne) EDC.

— Animal Noises. (Farmyard Tales Board Bks.). (Illus.). 12p. (J). (ps up). 2000. bds. 4.95 (0-7460-4104-7, Usborne) EDC.

Cartwright, Stephen. Apple Tree Farm Cut-Out Model. (Cut Out Models Ser.). (J). (gr. 4 up). 1998. pap. 9.95 (0-7460-3286-2, Usborne) EDC.

— Going to School. (First Experiences Ser.). 16p. (J). (ps-3). 1986. pap. 4.50 (0-7460-1269-1) EDC.

— The New Baby. (First Experiences Ser.). 16p. (J). (ps-3). 1994. pap. 4.50 (0-7460-1271-3) EDC.

Cartwright, Stephen & Amery, Heather. The Usborne First Thousand Words in Russian. (Illus.). 47p. (J). (ps-7). lib. bdg. 20.95 (0-88110-574-0) EDC.

— The Usbourne Book of Christmas Carols. (Illus.). (J). (gr. 4-7). 1998. lib. bdg. 18.95 (1-58086-016-8, Usborne) EDC.

Cartwright, Stephen & Zeff, C. Find the Bird. (Find It Board Ser.). (Illus.). 12p. (J). (ps up). 1983. bds. 3.95 (0-86020-719-6, Usborne) EDC.

— Find the Duck. (Find It Board Ser.). (Illus.). 12p. (J). (ps up). 1984. bds. 3.95 (0-86020-714-5, Usborne) EDC.

— Find the Kitten. (Find It Board Ser.). (Illus.). 12p. (J). (ps). 1983. bds. 3.95 (0-86020-718-8, Usborne) EDC.

— Find the Piglet. (Find It Board Ser.). (Illus.). 12p. (J). (ps up). 1983. bds. 3.95 (0-86020-716-1, Usborne) EDC.

— Find the Puppy. (Find It Board Ser.). (Illus.). 12p. (J). (ps up). 1984. bds. 3.95 (0-86020-717-X, Usborne) EDC.

— Find the Teddy. (Find It Board Ser.). (Illus.). 12p. (J). (ps up). 1983. bds. 3.95 (0-86020-715-3, Usborne) EDC.

Cartwright, Stephen & Zeff, Claudia. Find the Teddy Kid Kit with Finger Puppets. (Usborne Kid Kits Ser.). (Illus.). (J). (ps-k). 1995. bds. 10.95 (0-88110-731-X, Usborne) EDC.

Cartwright, Stephen, jt. auth. see Amery, H.

Cartwright, Stephen, jt. auth. see Amery, Heather.

Cartwright, Stephen, jt. auth. see Ashman, I.

Cartwright, Stephen, jt. auth. see Civardi, Anne.

Cartwright, Stephen, jt. auth. see Miles, Lisa.

Cartwright, Steve R. Pre-Production Planning for Video, Film, & Multimedia. LC 96-17689. 224p. 1996. pap. 39.95 (0-240-80271-3, Focal) Buttrwrth-Heinemann.

— Secrets of Successful Video Training: The Training with Video Casebook. 164p. 1990. 44.95 (0-86729-281-4, Focal) Buttrwrth-Heinemann.

Cartwright, Susan, jt. auth. see Cooper, Cary L.

Cartwright, Terence. Animal Cells As Bioreactors. LC 93-33980. (Studies in Biotechnology: No. 11). (Illus.). 192p. (C). 1994. text 54.95 (0-521-41258-7) Cambridge U Pr.

Cartwright, Thomas. A Briefe Apologie Against M. Sutcliffe. LC 78-25890. (English Experience Ser.: No. 237). 28p. 1970. reprint ed. 20.00 (90-221-0237-8) Walter J Johnson.

— A Confutation of the Rhemists Translation, Glosses & Annotations on the New Testament. LC 71-171737. (English Experience Ser.: No. 364). 830p. 1971. reprint ed. 120.00 (90-221-0364-1) Walter J Johnson.

— Diary of Dr. Thomas Cartwright, Bishop of Chester 1686-1687. (Camden Society, London. Publications, First Ser.: No. 22). reprint ed. 32.00 (0-404-50122-2) AMS Pr.

C

Cartwright, Thomas & Blackburn, Harvey. Systems Analysis Applied to Livestock Production. 1995. text. write for info. (*0-8493-8751-5*) CRC Pr.

Cartwright, Timothy J. The Management of Human Settlements: Applications of the Use of Microcomputers. 304p. (C). 1990. text 74.95 (*0-415-03124-9*) Routledge.

— Modeling the World in a Spreadsheet: Environmental Simulation on a Microcomputer. 364p. (C). 1993. text 55.00 (*0-8018-4596-3*); pap. text 34.95 (*0-8018-4597-1*) Johns Hopkins.

***Cartwright, W., et al, eds.** Multimedia Cartography. LC GA139.5.M85 1999. (Illus.). xviii, 343p. 1999. 59.00 incl. cd-rom (*3-540-65818-1*) Spr-Verlag.

***Cartwright, William, ed.** Mexico, Facing the Challenges of Human Rights & Crime. LC 99-57634. 1999. text 125.00 (*1-57105-134-1*) Transnatl Pubs.

Cartwright, William & Hamilton, William B., eds. Duke University Centennial Conference on Teacher Training. LC 70-115993. (Duke University. Trinity College Historical Society. Historical Papers: No. 30). reprint ed. pap. text 30.00 (*0-404-51780-3*) AMS Pr.

Cartwright, William H. The Reinterpretation of American History & Culture. Watson, Richard L., ed. LC 73-84548. 574p. reprint ed. pap. 178.00 (*0-608-17166-2*, 205219200056) Bks Demand.

Cartwright, William H. & Goeden, Louise E. The Military District of Washington in the War Years, 1942-1945. abr. ed. Offutt, William M. et al, eds. 80p. (Orig.). 1995. pap. 4.00 (*0-9643819-1-5*) Innovat Game.

Carty. Padre Pio - Stigmatist. pap. 15.00 (*0-89555-355-4*, 0115) TAN Bks Pubs.

Carty, Alistair, jt. auth. see McCarthy, Martin.

Carty, Amy O. Positive Visualizations: For People with Cancer & Those Who Love Them. (Illus.). 40p. (Orig.). 1993. pap. 4.95 (*0-9635970-1-9*) Birchard Bks.

Carty, Anthony, ed. Law & Development. (International Library of Essays in Law & Legal Theory). 550p. (C). 1992. lib. bdg. 150.00 (*0-8147-1473-0*) NYU Pr.

— Post-Modern Law: Enlightenment, Revolution & the Death of Man. 166p. 1990. 70.00 (*0-7486-0156-2*, Pub. by Edinburgh U Pr) Col U Pr.

— Post-Modern Law: Enlightenment, Revolution, & the Death of Man. 166p. 1992. pap. 27.50 (*0-7486-0192-9*, Pub. by Edinburgh U Pr) Col U Pr.

Carty, Anthony & Danilenko, Gennady, eds. Perestroika & International Law: Current Anglo-Soviet Approaches to International Law. 288p. 1992. pap. 27.50 (*0-7486-0187-2*, Pub. by Edinburgh U Pr) Col U Pr.

***Carty, Anthony & Smith, Richard A.** Sir Gerald Fitzmaurice & the World Crisis of 1930-1945. 704p. 1999. text 225.00 (*90-411-1242-1*) Kluwer Law Intl.

Carty, Charles M. Bible Quizzes to a Street Preacher. (Radio Replies Quizzes to a Street Preacher Ser.). (Illus.). 32p. 1992. reprint ed. pap. 1.50 (*0-89555-109-8*) TAN Bks Pubs.

— Padre Pio: The Stigmatist. (Illus.). 1994. reprint ed. pap. 15.00 (*0-89555-054-7*, 115) TAN Bks Pubs.

— Stigmata & Modern Science. 31p. 1992. reprint ed. pap. 1.50 (*0-89555-104-7*) TAN Bks Pubs.

— Who Is Theresa Neumann? 1992. reprint ed. pap. 2.00 (*0-89555-093-8*) TAN Bks Pubs.

— Why Squander Illness? 1992. reprint ed. pap. 2.50 (*0-89555-051-2*) TAN Bks Pubs.

Carty, Charles M. & Rumble, Leslie. Birth Prevention Quizzes to a Street Preacher. (Radio Replies Quizzes to a Street Preacher Ser.). 32p. 1992. reprint ed. pap. 1.50 (*0-89555-110-1*) TAN Bks Pubs.

— Confession Quizzes to a Street Preacher. (Radio Replies Quizzes to a Street Preacher Ser.). 32p. 1992. reprint ed. pap. 1.50 (*0-89555-111-X*) TAN Bks Pubs.

— Eucharist Quizzes to a Street Preacher. (Radio Replies Quizzes to a Street Preacher Ser.). 32p. 1992. reprint ed. pap. 1.50 (*0-89555-112-8*) TAN Bks Pubs.

— Hell Quizzes to a Street Preacher. (Radio Replies Quizzes to a Street Preacher Ser.). 32p. 1992. reprint ed. pap. 1.50 (*0-89555-113-6*) TAN Bks Pubs.

— Indulgence Quizzes to a Street Preacher. (Radio Replies Quizzes to a Street Preacher Ser.). 32p. 1992. reprint ed. pap. 1.50 (*0-89555-114-4*) TAN Bks Pubs.

— Marriage Quizzes to a Street Preacher. (Radio Replies Quizzes to a Street Preacher Ser.). 32p. 1992. reprint ed. pap. 1.50 (*0-89555-115-2*) TAN Bks Pubs.

— Purgatory Quizzes to a Street Preacher. (Radio Replies Quizzes to a Street Preacher Ser.). 32p. 1992. reprint ed. pap. 1.50 (*0-89555-108-X*) TAN Bks Pubs.

— Quizzes to a Street Preacher, Set. (Radio Replies Quizzes to a Street Preacher Ser.). 32p. 1992. reprint ed. pap. 12.00 (*0-89555-356-2*) TAN Bks Pubs.

— True Church Quizzes to a Street Preacher. (Radio Replies Quizzes to a Street Preacher Ser.). 32p. 1992. reprint ed. pap. 1.50 (*0-89555-116-0*) TAN Bks Pubs.

— Virgin & Statue Worship: Quizzes to a Street Preacher. (Radio Replies Quizzes to a Street Preacher Ser.). 32p. 1991. reprint ed. pap. 1.50 (*0-89555-107-1*) TAN Bks Pubs.

Carty, Charles M., jt. auth. see O'Connell, Patrick.

Carty, Charles M., jt. auth. see Rumble, Leslie.

Carty, Ciaran. Confessions of a Sewer Rat: A Personal History of Censorship & the Irish Cinema. (Illus.). 190p. (Orig.). 1995. pap. write for info. (*1-874597-27-8*, Pub. by New Island Books) Irish Bks Media.

Carty, Ciaran, jt. ed. see Bolger, Dermot.

Carty, Dave. Born Again at the Laundromat: And Other Visions of the New West. 208p. 1994. 18.95 (*1-55821-200-0*) Lyons Pr.

Carty, Helen, et al, eds. Imaging Children, 2 vols. (Illus.). 2019p. 1994. text 380.00 (*0-443-04260-8*) Church.

Carty, Jay. Counter Attack: Taking Back Ground Lost to Sin. 3rd rev. ed. 277p. pap. 10.99 (*0-9652089-0-7*) Yes Ministries.

— O. Whillikers in the Hall of Champions: Portraits of Character. rev. ed. (Illus.). 113p. (J). (gr. 3-6). 1999. pap. 14.95 (*0-9652089-1-5*) Yes Ministries.

***Carty, Jay, et al.** O. Whillikers in the Hall of Champions. LC 00-24523. (Illus.). (J). 2000. pap. 12.99 (*0-8307-2634-9*, Gospel Light) Gospel Lght.

Carty, Joan, jt. auth. see Dale, Sheila.

***Carty, Joseph T.** Fragile Temple: A Book of Poetry by Joseph T. Carty. 61p. 1999. pap. 10.95 (*0-9663820-4-8*) Gerl Publishing.

Carty, Ken, ed. Politics, Policy, & Government in British Columbia. LC 96-221740. 396p. 1996. 65.00 (*0-7748-0582-X*) U of Wash Pr.

— Politics, Policy, & Government in British Columbia. LC 96-221740. 396p. 1997. pap. 26.95 (*0-7748-0583-8*) U of Wash Pr.

Carty, Linda, ed. And Still We Rise: Feminist Political Mobilizing in Contemporary Canada. 456p. pap. 20.95 (*0-88961-177-7*, Pub. by Womens Pr) LPC InBook.

Carty, Margaret F. Christmas in Vermont: Three Stories. LC 83-62750. (Illus.). 48p. (Orig.). (J). (gr. 5 up). 1983. pap. 2.95 (*0-933050-21-6*) New Eng Pr VT.

Carty, Mickey D. Searching in Indiana: A Reference Guide to Public & Private Records. LC 85-60284. (ISC State Search Bks.: No. 4). 278p. (Orig.). 1985. pap. text 14.95 (*0-942916-06-9*) ISC Pubns.

Carty, R. Kenneth, ed. Canadian Political Party Systems. 376p. 1992. pap. 19.95 (*0-921149-90-5*) Broadview Pr.

***Carty, R. Kenneth, et al.** Canadian Party Politics for the 21st Century. 265p. 2000. 75.00 (*0-7748-0777-6*) UBC Pr.

***Carty, Simon.** Criminal Practice & Procedure. 160p. 1999. pap. 37.50 (*1-901657-89-2*, 18421, Pub. by Blackhall Pub) Gaunt.

***Carty, T. J.** Dictionary of Literary Pseudonyms in the English Language. 2nd ed. 844p. 2000. pap. 49.95 (*0-7201-2383-6*) Continuum.

Carty, T.J., ed. Dictionary of Literary Pseudonyms in the English Language. 750p. 1995. lib. bdg. 85.00 (*1-884964-13-3*) Fitzroy Dearborn.

Carty, Winthrop P. & Lee, Elizabeth. The Rhino Man & Other Uncommon Environmentalists. LC 92-9166. 178p. 1992. pap. 12.95 (*0-929765-10-9*) Seven Locks Pr.

Cartz, Louis. Nondestructive Testing. 225p. 1995. 118.00 (*0-87170-517-6*, 6390) ASM.

Caruana, Carmen M. Education's Role in the Socioeconomic Development of Malta. LC 91-35026. 144p. 1992. 49.95 (*0-275-94065-9*, C4065, Praeger Pubs) Greenwood.

Caruana, Claudia M. The Abortion Debate. LC 92-22417. (Headliners Ser.). (Illus.). 64p. (YA). (gr. 5-8). 1992. lib. bdg. 23.40 (*1-56294-311-1*) Millbrook Pr.

Caruana, Edmund, jt. auth. see Braghin, Andrea.

Caruana, Russell A. Organizing a Healthcare Financial Services Division. 225p. 1989. 50.00 (*0-930228-36-7*, Irwn Prfssnl) McGraw-Hill Prof.

— Organizing a Healthcare Financial Services Division. 3rd ed. 170p. 1989. 50.00 (*0-930228-69-3*) Hlthcare Fin Mgmt.

Caruana, Vicki. Apples & Chalkdust. LC 99-218280. 208p. 1998. 14.99 (*1-56292-591-1*) Honor Bks OK.

— Apples & Chalkdust: A Little Book of Inspirational Stories & Encouragement for Teachers. 1998. 12.99 (*1-57757-028-6*) Trade Life.

***Caruana, Vicki.** Apples & Chalkdust for Teachers. 2000. 9.99 (*1-56292-626-8*) Honor Bks OK.

— Success in School: Building on Biblical Principles. 1999. pap. 12.95 (*1-885904-20-7*) Focus Pubng.

Caruana, Wally. Aboriginal Art. LC 92-62140. (World of Art Ser.). (Illus.). 216p. 1993. pap. 14.95 (*0-500-20264-8*, Pub. by Thames Hudson) Norton.

Caruana, Wally & Lendon, Nigel, eds. The Painters of the Wagilag Sisters Story, 1937-1997. LC 97-62503. (Illus.). 300p. 1998. pap. 34.95 (*0-500-97468-3*, Pub. by Thames Hudson) Norton.

Caruba, Glen. Afro-Cuban Drumming. (Illus.). 56p. 1996. pap. 19.95 (*1-57424-014-5*, 00000182) Centerstream Pub.

— Modern Percussion Grooves. (Illus.). 48p. (Orig.). 1998. pap. 19.95 incl. audio compact disk (*1-57424-042-0*) Centerstream Pub.

Carubba, E. R. & Gordon, R. D. Product Assurance Principles: Integrating Design Assurance & Quality Assurance. 278p. 1988. 53.00 (*0-07-010148-5*) McGraw.

Carucci, et al. Shared Spaces: Contexts of Interaction in Chicago's Ethnic Communities. LC 89-31161. (Immigrant Communities & Ethnic Minorities in the U. S. & Canada Ser.: No. 63). 1989. 49.50 (*0-404-19473-7*) AMS Pr.

Carucci, John. Capturing the Night With Your Camera: How to Take Great Photographs After Dark. (Illus.). 144p. 1995. pap. 24.95 (*0-8174-3661-8*, Amphoto) Watsn-Guptill.

— The New Media Guide to Creative Photography: Image Capture & Printing in the Digital Age. 144p. 1998. pap. 24.95 (*0-8174-5010-6*) Watsn-Guptill.

Carucci, Laurence M. Nuclear Nativity: Rituals of Renewal & Empowerment in the Marshall Islands. LC 96-30262. 210p. (C). 1997. lib. bdg. 32.00 (*0-87580-217-6*) N Ill U Pr.

***Carucci, Ron A. & Tetenbaum, Toby J.** The Value-Creating Consultant: How to Build & Sustain Lasting Client Relationships. LC 99-41185. (Illus.). 256p. 1999. 25.00 (*0-8144-0502-9*) AMACOM.

Carucci, Vic, jt. auth. see Chrebet, Wayne.

Caruf, Paul. Gospel of Buddha. 1995. pap. 13.99 (*1-85168-026-8*, Pub. by Onewrld Pubns) Penguin Putnam.

Carullo, Sylvia G. El Tetrato Literario en Sor Juana Ines de la Cruz. LC 91-23. (American University Studies: Romance Languages & Literature: Ser. II, Vol. 164). (SPA.). 232p. (C). 1991. text 38.95 (*0-8204-1468-9*) P Lang Pubng.

Carus. Higgelty Pigglety Pop! (J). 19.95 incl. audio (*0-8126-0057-6*); 15.95 (*0-8126-0056-8*) Open Court.

— Sing, Clap, & Dance with Ladybug. (J). 19.95 incl. audio (*0-8126-0053-3*); 15.95 (*0-8126-0083-5*) Open Court.

— Sing Together with Ladybug. (J). 19.95 incl. audio (*0-8126-0081-9*); 15.95 (*0-8126-0079-7*) Open Court.

— Teachings of Buddha. LC 98-53870. 1999. text 12.95 (*0-312-19586-9*) St Martin.

Carus, Carl G. Natur und Idee. (GER.). 1997. reprint ed. 108.00 (*3-487-05724-7*) G Olms Pubs.

— Symbolik der Menschlichen Gestalt. (GER.). 1997. 108.00 (*3-487-00266-3*) G Olms Pubs.

***Carus, Marianne.** That's Ghosts for You: 13 Scary Stories. (Illus.). 144p. (gr. 4-7). 2000. 15.95 (*0-8126-2675-3*) Front St-Cricket Bks.

Carus, Paul. Amitabha: A Story of Buddhist Theology. 1988. reprint ed. lib. bdg. 49.00 (*0-317-90092-7*) Rprt Serv.

— Amitabha: A Story of Buddhist Theology. 1977. reprint ed. 49.00 (*0-403-07255-7*) Scholarly.

— Chinese Thought: An Exposition of the Main Characteristic Features of the Chinese World Conception. LC 07-14567. (Illus.). 209p. reprint ed. pap. 64.80 (*0-608-11821-4*, 205091700070) Bks Demand.

— The Dharma: or the Religion of Enlightenment: An Exposition of Buddhism. 134p. 1996. pap. 11.00 (*0-89540-325-0*, SB-325) Sun Pub.

— The Dharma: or The Religious Enlightenment: An Exposition of Buddhism. 5th enl. rev. ed. LC 78-72393. reprint ed. 29.50 (*0-404-17253-9*) AMS Pr.

— The Ethical Problem: Three Lectures on Ethics As a Science. 2nd enl. ed. LC 75-3103. reprint ed. 32.50 (*0-404-59100-0*) AMS Pr.

— Goethe: With Special Consideration of His Philosophy. (Illus.). 376p. 1981. pap. 35.00 (*0-89540-121-5*, SB-121) Sun Pub.

— Gospel of Buddha. enl. rev. ed. LC 17-29837. (Illus.). 332p. 1973. pap. 15.95 (*0-87548-228-7*) Open Court.

— The Gospel of Buddha. (C). 1991. reprint ed. 17.50 (*81-206-0538-1*, Pub. by Asian Educ Servs) S Asia.

— The Gospel of Buddha. 295p. 1991. reprint ed. 13.95 (*0-910261-11-3*, Arcana Pubng) Lotus Pr.

— The History of the Devil & the Idea of Evil. (Illus.). 496p. 1988. pap. 13.95 (*0-87548-307-0*) Open Court.

— Nietzsche. LC 72-2039. (Studies in German Literature: No. 13). 1972. reprint ed. lib. bdg. 75.00 (*0-8383-1464-3*) M S G Haskell Hse.

— Nietzsche & Other Exponents of Individualism. LC 14-1736. (Illus.). 171p. reprint ed. pap. 53.10 (*0-608-10197-4*, 200907700070) Bks Demand.

— Nirvana: A Story of Buddhist Psychology. LC 98-904946. 93 p. 1997. 12.00 (*81-206-1301-5*, Pub. by Asian Educ Servs) S Asia.

— Nirvana, a Story of Buddhist Psychology. LC 78-72395. (Illus.). reprint ed. 32.50 (*0-404-15508-1*); reprint ed. 32.50 (*0-404-17254-7*) AMS Pr.

— The Philosophy of Form: An Expanded Reprint of the Author's Introduction to His "Philosophy As a Science" LC 80-12865. (Philosophy in America Ser.). reprint ed. 32.50 (*0-404-59104-3*) AMS Pr.

— The Pleroma: An Essay on the Origin of Christianity. 163p. 1997. pap. 12.00 (*0-89540-258-0*, SB-258) Sun Pub.

— The Principle of Relativity in the Light of the Philosophy of Science. LC 75-3109. reprint ed. 32.50 (*0-404-59105-1*) AMS Pr.

— The Soul of Man. 1972. 250.00 (*0-8490-1090-X*) Gordon Pr.

— The Venus of Milo: An Archaeological Study of the Goddess of Womanhood. 1977. lib. bdg. 59.95 (*0-8490-2796-9*) Gordon Pr.

— Whence & Whither. 1972. 59.95 (*0-8490-1289-9*) Gordon Pr.

***Carus, Paul, tr.** The Teachings of Lao-tzu. (Illus.). 144p. 2000. 16.95 (*0-312-26109-8*, Thomas Dunne) St Martin.

Carus, Paul, tr. see Kant, Immanuel.

Carus, Paul, tr. see Yin Chih Wen.

Carus, W. Seth. Ballistic Missiles in Modern Conflict, 146. LC 91-8731. (Washington Papers: No. 146). 128p. 1991. pap. 11.95 (*0-275-94077-2*, B4077, Praeger Pubs) Greenwood.

— Ballistic Missiles in the Third World: Threat & Response, 146. LC 90-7567. (Washington Papers: No. 146). 104p. 1990. 49.95 (*0-275-93749-6*, C3749, Praeger Pubs); pap. 14.95 (*0-275-93750-X*, B3750, Praeger Pubs) Greenwood.

Carus, W. Seth. Cruise Missile Proliferation in the 1990s, 159. LC 92-26115. (Washington Papers: No. 159). 184p. 1992. 49.95 (*0-275-94519-7*, C4519, Praeger Pubs); pap. 19.95 (*0-275-94520-0*, B4520, Praeger Pubs) Greenwood.

Carus, W. Seth. The Poor Man's Atomic Bomb? Biological Weapons in the Middle East. LC 91-10600. (Policy Papers: No. 23). 66p. 1991. pap. 8.00 (*0-944029-08-6*) Wash Inst NEP.

Carus, W. Seth, jt. auth. see Goodman, Hirsh.

Carus-Wilson, Eleanora M., ed. Essays in Economic History, 3 vols. Incl. Vol. 3. 1969. (*0-687-01188-4*); 1969. pap. write for info. (*0-318-55843-2*) St Martin.

Carusi, Andrea & Valsecchi, Giovanni B., eds. Dynamics of Comets: Their Origin & Evolution. (Astrophysics & Space Science Library). 1985. text 203.00 (*90-277-2047-9*) Kluwer Academic.

Caruso. Motor Speech Disorders in Children. LC 99-17630. (Illus.). 384p. 1999. 45.00 (*0-86577-762-4*) Thieme Med Pubs.

— Reading, Responding & Writing. 2nd ed. 1992. pap. text, teacher ed. 18.50 (*0-312-03606-X*) St Martin.

Caruso, Andy. Soccer Coaching. (Illus.). 102p. 1997. pap. 12.95 (*0-9651020-2-5*) Reedswain.

— Soccer's Dynamic Short Sided Games. (Illus.). 134p. 1998. pap. 14.95 (*0-9651020-0-9*) Reedswain.

Caruso, Beverly. Around the World. 378p. 1993. pap. 9.99 (*0-927545-46-2*) YWAM Pub.

Caruso, Domenick & Weidenborner, Stephen. Creating Contexts: A Practical Approach to Writing. LC 76-55159. (Illus.). (C). 1977. pap. text 33.50 (*0-393-09101-5*) Norton.

— Reading, Responding, Writing. 2nd ed. LC 91-67515. 256p. (C). 1992. pap. text, teacher ed. 5.00 (*0-312-07219-8*) St Martin.

Caruso, Donna & Quarrier, Ian, eds. Embassy's Complete Boating Guide: To Rhode Island & Massachusetts. 3rd rev. ed. LC 96-219522. (Illus.). 1996. spiral bd. 39.95 (*0-930527-39-9*) Maptech Inc.

Caruso, Dorian, ed. see Frank, Ojela.

Caruso, Doris D. Sevenity in Sandy Shoes. (Illus.). 80p. (Orig.). 1997. pap. 8.95 (*1-57502-497-7*, PO1478) Morris Pubng.

— Sleep Song: The Spell. 100p. 1998. pap. 12.95 (*1-57502-826-3*, P02278) Morris Pubng.

Caruso, Dorothy. Enrico Caruso: His Life & Death. LC 87-8506. (Illus.). 311p. 1987. reprint ed. lib. bdg. 62.50 (*0-313-25377-3*, CAEC, Greenwood Pr) Greenwood.

Caruso, Ellen M. Keeping Them Healthy, Keeping Them Home: How to Care for Your Loved Ones at Home. LC 98-26957. 1998. pap. 12.95 (*1-885987-13-7*, Health Info Pr) Practice Mgmt Info.

Caruso, Enrico, Jr. & Farkas, Andrew. Enrico Caruso: My Father & My Family. abr. ed. LC 96-38350. (Opera Biography Ser.: Vol. 2). (Illus.). 448p. 1997. pap. 24.95 (*1-57467-022-0*, Amadeus Pr) Timber.

Caruso, Enrico & Tetrazzini, Louisa. The Art of Singing: How to Sing, 2 vols. in 1. LC 74-23417. (Music Reprint Ser.). 1975. reprint ed. lib. bdg. 29.50 (*0-306-70674-1*) Da Capo.

Caruso, Enrico & Tetrazzini, Luisa. Caruso & Tetrazzini on the Art of Singing. LC 74-84048. 71p. 1975. reprint ed. pap. 4.95 (*0-486-23140-2*) Dover.

Caruso, Frank L. & Ramsdell, Donald C., eds. Compendium of Blueberry & Cranberry Diseases. (Disease Compendium Ser.). (Illus.). 126p. (Orig.). 1995. pap. 42.00 (*0-89054-173-6*) Am Phytopathol Soc.

Caruso, Gary. The Braves Encyclopedia. (Baseball Encyclopedias of North America Ser.). (Illus.). 533p. (C). 1995. 59.95 (*1-56639-384-1*) Temple U Pr.

— Turner Field: Rarest of Diamonds. Perry, Chuck, ed. LC 97-75690. (Illus.). 160p. 1998. 29.95 (*1-56352-450-3*) Longstreet.

***Caruso, George, Jr.** Oswego Speedway: The First Fifty Years. (Illus.). 542p. 2000. 49.95 (*0-9677438-1-8*) Speedway.

Caruso, George C., jt. auth. see Basile, Frank.

Caruso, Hank. Seabirds: An Unofficial Illustrated Encyclopedia of Naval Aviation. 96p. 1996. pap. 17.95 (*1-57427-046-X*) Howell Pr VA.

Caruso, Henry. Test Tailoring & Environmental Engineering - A Tutorial. LC 62-38584. 182p. 1988. pap. 100.00 (*0-915414-97-X*) IEST.

Caruso, James R., jt. auth. see Arthur, Mavis E.

Caruso, Joe. 12 Steps to Effective Meetings: Tips, Traps & Terrible Truths. 3rd rev. ed. (Illus.). 104p. (Orig.). 1997. write for info. (*1-885671-10-5*) Caruso Leader Inst.

Caruso, Joseph. The Priest. 1978. 20.95 (*0-405-10821-4*) Ayer.

— Success Strategies: Life's Simple Truths. 179p. 1995. 15.00 (*1-885671-07-5*) Caruso Leader Inst.

Caruso, Joseph & Fawcett, M. Temple. Supervision in Early Childhood Education: A Developmental Perspective. 2nd ed. LC 98-52823. 70. 264p. 1999. pap. 21.95 (*0-8077-3852-2*) Tchrs Coll.

Caruso, Joseph A. Five Ways to Get the Upper Hand Every Time. 105p. 1994. 15.00 (*1-885671-06-7*) Caruso Leader Inst.

— 12 Steps to Effective Meetings: Tips, Traps & Terrible Truths. 4th rev. ed. 93p. (Orig.). 1998. pap. 7.95 (*1-885671-11-3*) Caruso Leader Inst.

Caruso, Joseph G. Adam's Diary: A Musical Comedy. (Illus.). 26p. 1989. pap. 4.50 (*0-88680-313-6*) I E Clark.

— Happyville: A Comedy in 2 Acts. (Illus.). 24p. 1981. pap. 3.50 (*0-88680-079-X*) I E Clark.

— The Phantom of the Old Opera House: Comedy - Mystery in 3-Acts. 48p. (J). (gr. 4 up). 1982. pap. 4.00 (*0-88680-153-2*) I E Clark.

Caruso, Joseph J. & Fawcett, M. Temple. Supervision in Early Childhood Education. (Early Childhood Education Ser.). 256p. 1986. pap. text 18.95 (*0-8077-2802-0*) Tchrs Coll.

— Supervision in Early Childhood Education: A Developmental Perspective. 2nd ed. LC 98-52823. (Early Childhood Education Ser.). 1999. pap. write for info. (*0-8077-3853-0*) Tchrs Coll.

Caruso, Lane S. Selecting & Managing an Outsourcing Provider. (Innovations Ser.: Vol. 3). (Illus.). 36p. (Orig.). 1996. pap. 39.95 (*1-57963-001-4*, A0103) Am Compensation.

***Caruso, Mario.** North Plainfield. (Images of America Ser.). 128p. 1999. pap. 18.99 (*0-7385-0005-4*) Arcadia Publng.

***Caruso, Mary G.** Care of Favorite Dolls: Antique Bisque Conservation. (Illus.). 144p. 1999. pap. 24.95 (*0-87588-545-4*) Hobby Hse.

Caruso, Raymond P. & Power Play Technology Staff. Power Programming in HP Openview: Developing CMIS Applications. LC 96-24171. 400p. (C). 1996. pap. text 56.00 (*0-13-443011-5*) P-H.

An Asterisk (*) at the beginning of an entry indicates that the title is appearing for the first time.

Caruso, Richard. Mentoring & the Business Environment: Asset or Liability? 170p. 1992. 61.95 (*1-85521-317-6*, Pub. by Dartmth Pub) Ashgate Pub Co.

***Caruso, Robert.** Essential Guide to Windows, Word & Excel. (C). 1999. pap. 12.19 (*0-07-240016-1*) McGrw-H Hghr Educ.

Caruso, Robert & Travelstead, Will W., eds. Enhancing Campus Judicial Systems. LC 85-644751. (New Directions for Student Services Ser.: No. SS 39). 1987. pap. 22.00 (*1-55542-941-6*) Jossey-Bass.

Caruso, Sandra & Kosoff, Susan. The Young Actor's Book of Improvisation: Dramatic Situations from Shakespeare to Spielberg, Vol. 1. LC 97-50420. Vol. 1. 175p. (J). (gr. 2-6). 1998. pap. 19.95 (*0-325-00048-4*) Heinemann.

— The Young Actor's Book of Improvisation: Dramatic Situations from Shakespeare to Spielberg, Vol. 2. LC 97-46817. 259p. (YA). (gr. 7 up). 1998. pap. 22.95 (*0-325-00049-2*) Heinemann.

Carusone, Al. The Boy with Dinosaur Hands. LC 97-24616. 96p. (J). (gr. 5 up). 1998. 14.00 (*0-395-77515-9*, Clarion Bks) HM.

— Don't Open the Door after the Sun Goes Down: Tales of the Real & Unreal. LC 94-7406. (Illus.). 96p. (J). (gr. 4 up). 1994. 13.95 (*0-395-65225-1*) HM.

— Don't Open the Door after the Sun Goes Down: Tales of the Real & Unreal. LC 95-9737. (Illus.). 96p. (J). (gr. 3-7). 1995. pap. 3.95 (*0-7868-1086-6*, Pub. by Hypm Ppbks) Little.

— Don't Open the Door after the Sun Goes Down: Tales of the Real & Unreal. LC 95-9737. 1995. 9.05 (*0-606-09204-8*, Pub. by Turtleback) Demco.

— Scout's Honor: Mystery Jigsaw Puzzle Thriller. (Spider Tales Ser.). (Orig.). (J). (gr. 3-7). 1996. pap. 13.50 (*1-57561-011-6*, 00907HON) Bepuzzled.

— Time's Up: Mystery Jigsaw Puzzle Thriller. (Spider Tales Ser.). (Orig.). (J). (gr. 3-7). 1996. pap. 13.50 (*1-57561-010-8*, 00906TUP) Bepuzzled.

Caruth, Cathy. Empirical Truths & Critical Fictions: Locke, Wordsworth, Kant, Freud. LC 90-39243. 192p. 1991. text 34.00 (*0-8018-4080-5*) Johns Hopkins.

— Trauma: Explorations in Memory. LC 94-46167. 328p. 1995. text 48.50 (*0-8018-5009-6*) Johns Hopkins.

— Unclaimed Experience: Trauma, Narrative, & History. 152p. (C). 1996. text 33.50 (*0-8018-5246-3*) Johns Hopkins.

Caruth, Cathy & Esch, Deborah, eds. Critical Encounters: Reference & Responsibility in Deconstructive Writing. LC 93-39309. (Center for the Critical Analysis of Contemporary Culture Ser.). 340p. (C). 1994. text 50.00 (*0-8135-2085-1*); pap. text 20.00 (*0-8135-2086-X*) Rutgers U Pr.

Caruth, Donald L. & Handlogten, Gail D. Staffing the Contemporary Organization: A Guide to Planning, Recruiting & Selecting for Human Resource Professionals. 2nd ed. LC 97-8858. 336p. 1997. 79.50 (*1-56720-056-7*, Quorum Bks); pap. 25.95 (*0-275-95523-0*, Praeger Pubs) Greenwood.

Caruth, Donald L. & Stovall, Steven A., eds. Taking Care of Business: The Dictionary of Contemporary Business Terms. (Artful Wordsmith Ser.). (Illus.). 336p. 1996. pap. 14.95 (*0-8442-0902-3*, 09023) NTC Contemp Pub Co.

***Caruth, Jeannette.** In Search for the Pearl. McGuire, Deborah, ed. 2000. pap. 13.00 (*0-9670129-9-6*) Birthwrite.

Caruth, Jeannette. Song of My Life: A Journey to the Feet of Sathya Sai Baba. LC 96-76437. 128p. (Orig.). 1996. pap. 9.00 (*0-9629835-8-6*) Leela Pr.

Caruth, W. W., III, jt. auth. see Reynolds, Morgan O.

Caruthers, Clifford M., ed. Letters of Ring Lardner. rev. ed. LC 94-42459. (Illus.). 300p. 1995. reprint ed. 29.95 (*0-914061-52-6*) Orchises Pr.

Caruthers, Clifford M., ed. Ring Around Max: The Correspondence of Ring Lardner & Maxwell Perkins. LC 72-6919. (Illus.). 192p. 1973. pap. 15.00 (*0-87580-512-4*) N Ill U Pr.

Caruthers, Clifford M., ed. see Lardner, Ring, Jr.

Caruthers, J. M., et al. Handbook of Diffusion & Thermal Properties of Polymers & Polymer Solutions. LC 98-36293. 203p. 1998. 175.00 incl. disk (*0-8169-0762-5*, X-131) Am Inst Chem Eng.

Caruthers, John. Guitar Shop Set Up & Maintenance: The Player's Guide to Guitar Care. (Handy Guide Ser.). 48p. 1998. pap. 5.95 (*0-7390-0032-2*) Alfred Pub.

***Caruthers, Scott.** Truth Notes. (Illus.). 64p. 1999. 60.00 (*0-9673175-0-9*) Guinevere.

Caruthers, Terry. Kerry: A Natural History. LC 99-176154. (Illus.). 294p. 1998. 45.00 (*1-898256-45-4*, Pub. by Collins Press) Irish Bks Media.

Caruthers, William A. The Cavaliers of Virginia. LC 68-23715. (Americans in Fiction Ser.). reprint ed. pap. text 14.95 (*0-89197-693-0*); reprint ed. lib. bdg. 32.50 (*0-8398-0254-4*) Irvington.

***Caruthers, William A.** Fear Itself. LC 99-91958. 319p. 2000. 25.00 (*0-7388-1424-5*); pap. 18.00 (*0-7388-1425-3*) Xlibris Corp.

Caruthers, William A. The Kentuckian in New York. LC 68-23714. (Americans in Fiction Ser.). 219p. reprint ed. pap. text 8.50 (*0-89197-817-8*); reprint ed. lib. bdg. 16.50 (*0-8398-0255-2*) Irvington.

Caruzzi, Pamela. From New York City to Sunbury, Ohio: A Personal Memoir. LC 95-62006. (Illus.). 110p. (YA). 1996. lib. bdg. 12.95 (*1-883033-02-0*) Flats Pub.

Carvajal, Carol S., et al, eds. The Oxford Spanish Minidictionary. 2nd ed. LC 98-49688. 640p. 1999. pap. 6.50 (*0-19-860231-6*) OUP.

Carvajal, Carol S. & Horwood, Jane, eds. Diccionario Oxford Compacto: Espanol-Ingles, Ingles-Espanol. LC 97-3814. 992p. 1997. pap. 9.95 (*0-19-511885-5*) OUP.

— The Oxford Spanish Desk Dictionary. (SPA.). 992p. (C). 1997. 14.95 (*0-19-521352-1*) OUP.

— The Pocket Oxford Spanish Dictionary. LC 97-3814. 992p. 1997. pap. 9.95 (*0-19-521346-7*) OUP.

***Carvajal, Carol Styles & Harwood, Jane, eds.** El Diccionario Oxford: Espanol-Ingles/Ingles-Espanol. (SPA & ENG.). 1504p. 1999. 27.95 (*0-19-521585-0*) OUP.

***Carvajal, Carol Styles & Horwood, Jane, eds.** The Oxford College Spanish Dictionary. 2nd ed. LC 98-49985. (SPA.). 1024p. 2000. pap. 9.95 (*0-19-860281-2*) OUP.

Carvajal, Carol Styles & Horwood, Jane, eds. The Oxford Spanish Dictionary. (SPA.). 1504p. 1996. 25.00 (*0-19-864523-6*) OUP.

Carvajal, Carol Styles, jt. ed. see Horwood, Jane.

Carvajal, Francis F. Lukewarmness. rev. ed. 142p. 1992. pap. 9.95 (*0-933932-59-6*) Scepter Pubs.

Carvajal, Gaspar de. Discovery of the Amazon According to the Accounts of Friar Gaspar De Carvajal & Other Documents. Heaton, Harry C. & Lee, Bertram T., eds. LC 77-120567. reprint ed. 57.50 (*0-404-01404-6*) AMS Pr.

Carvajal, Manuel J. The Caribbean, 1975-1980: A Bibliography of Economic & Rural Development. LC 91-39695. 897p. 1993. 94.00 (*0-8108-2422-1*) Scarecrow.

Carvajal, Manuel J. & Geithman, David T. Family Planning & Family Size Determination: The Evidence from Seven Latin American Cities. LC 75-37700. (Latin American Monographs: Ser. 2, No. 18). 103p. reprint ed. pap. 32.00 (*0-7837-4910-4*, 204457500004) Bks Demand.

Carvajal, Pepe, ed. see Albert, Dalia N.

Carvalho, A., et al, eds. Advances in Artificial Intelligence: 12th Brazilian Symposium on Artificial Intelligence, SBIA '95, Campinas, Brazil, October 11-13, 1995 - Proceedings. (Lecture Notes in Computer Science Subseries: Lecture Notes in Artificial Intelligence: Vol. 991). xii, 342p. 1995. pap. 62.00 (*3-540-60436-7*) Spr-Verlag.

Carvalho, Barbara L., jt. auth. see Miringoff, Lee M.

Carvalho, E., et al, eds. Riemann Surfaces. 716p. (C). 1989. pap. 48.00 (*9971-5-0903-2*); text 161.00 (*9971-5-0902-4*) World Scientific Pub.

Carvalho, Franklin J., ed. Russian Defense Business Directory: St. Petersburg & Leningrad Oblast. 282p. (C). 1998. pap. text 45.00 (*0-7881-4993-8*) DIANE Pub.

Carvalho, Josely. Diary of Images: It's Still Time to Mourn. 62p. 1992. pap. 15.00 (*0-89822-100-5*) Visual Studies.

Carvalho, Joseph. Black Families in Hampden County, Massachusetts, 1650-1855. LC 83-22044. 211p. 1984. lib. bdg. 16.95 (*0-88082-006-3*) New Eng Hist.

Carvalho, Joseph, et al, eds. Dictionary of American Medical Biography, 2 vols., Set. LC 82-21110. 1028p. 1984. lib. bdg. 195.00 (*0-313-21378-X*, KDA/) Greenwood.

— Dictionary of American Medical Biography, 2 vols., Vol. 1. LC 82-21110. 600p. 1984. lib. bdg. 100.00 (*0-313-24333-6*, KDA/01) Greenwood.

— Dictionary of American Medical Biography, 2 vols., Vol. 2. LC 82-21110. 600p. 1984. lib. bdg. 100.00 (*0-313-24334-4*, KDA/02) Greenwood.

Carvalho, M. G., et al, eds. Heat Transfer in Radiating & Combusting Systems: Proceedings of EUROTHERM Seminar No. 17, 8-10 October 1990, Cascais, Portugal. (EUROTHERM Seminar Ser.: No. 17). (Illus.). 600p. 1992. 190.95 (*0-387-54709-6*) Spr-Verlag.

Carvalho, Maria De Graca, see De Graca Carvalho, Maria.

Carvalho, Maria Eulina P. De, see De Carvalho, Maria Eulina P.

Carvalho, Maria L. Novas Travessias: Contemporary Photography in Brazil. LC 96-163458. (Illus.). 224p. 1996. pap. 25.00 (*1-85984-088-4*, Pub. by Verso) Norton.

Carvalho, Maria Luiza Melo. Novas Travessias: Contemporary Photography in Brazil. LC 96-163458. (Illus.). 224p. (C). (gr. 13 up). 1996. 65.00 (*1-85984-963-6*, Pub. by Verso) Norton.

Carvalho, Michael. Skeletons in the Closet. 297p. 1999. pap. 11.95 (*1-891929-06-2*) Four Seasons.

Carvalho, Miriam Dreysse Passos de, see de Carvalho, Miriam Dreysse Passos.

***Carvalho, Silvia Maria de Magalhaes.** The Desire to Communicate: Reconsidering John Ashbery & the Visual Arts. (European University Studies: Vol. 367). 172p. 2000. pap. 34.95 (*0-8204-4390-5*) P Lang Pubng.

Carvalho, Solomon N. Incidents of Travel & Adventure in the Far West, with Colonel Fremont's Last Expedition Across the Rocky Mountains. LC 72-9434. (Far Western Frontier Ser.). 384p. 1973. reprint ed. 24.95 (*0-405-04964-1*) Ayer.

Carvalho, Soniya. Indicators for Monitoring Poverty Reduction. LC 94-3747. (Discussion Paper Ser.: Vol. 254). 68p. 1994. pap. 22.00 (*0-8213-2979-0*, 12979) World Bank.

Carvalho, Soniya & White, Howard. Combining the Quantitative & Qualitative Approaches to Poverty Measurement & Analysis: The Practice & the Potential, Vol. 366. LC 97-16992. (Technical Paper Ser.: No. 366). 40p. 1997. pap. 22.00 (*0-8213-3955-9*, 13955) World Bank.

— Implementing Projects for the Poor: What Has Been Learned? LC 96-3357. (Directions in Development Ser.). 96p. 1996. pap. 22.00 (*0-8213-3531-6*, 13531) World Bank.

Carvallo, Marc E. Nature, Cognition & System, No. I. (C). 1988. lib. bdg. 211.50 (*90-277-2740-6*) Kluwer Academic.

Carvallo, Marc E., ed. Nature, Cognition & System Two: Current Systems-Scientific Research on Natural & Cognitive Systems, Vol. 2: On Complementarity & Beyond. (Theory & Decision Library, Series D). 420p. (C). 1992. lib. bdg. 236.00 (*0-7923-1788-2*, Pub. by Kluwer Academic) Kluwer Academic.

Carvan, J. C. Social & Welfare Law. 232p. 1995. pap. write for info. (*0-409-30656-8*, MICHIE) LEXIS Pub.

Carvan, Jill. Pandas: A Portrait of the Animal World, 1. 1998. pap. text 10.98 (*1-880908-66-2*) Todtri Prods.

Carvan, John. Understanding the Australian Legal System: A Book for First Time Law Students. 2nd ed. 138p. 1994. pap. 20.00 (*0-455-21282-1*, Pub. by LawBk Co) Gaunt.

Carvan, John & Gooley, John. Essential Commercial Legislation - New South Wales. (Essential Legislation Ser.). 650p. 1995. pap. 45.00 (*0-455-21304-6*, Pub. by LawBk Co) Gaunt.

Carvell, H. T. & Svartvik, Jan. Computational Experiments in Grammatical Classification. LC 68-23805. (Janua Linguarum, Ser. Minor: No. 61). (Orig.). 1969. pap. text 72.35 (*90-279-0682-3*) Mouton.

Carvell, Peter, jt. auth. see Eldridge, Neville.

Carven, Chitamber. New Royal Hindustani & Hindustani English Dictionary. (ENG & HIN.). 706p. 1992. 95.00 (*0-8288-8427-7*) Fr & Eur.

Carver. Flying Dutchman, Vol. 1. 2000. text 23.95 (*0-312-85642-3*) St Martin.

— Take Ten, Vol. 1. 2000. pap. text. write for info. (*0-312-15712-6*); pap. text. write for info. (*0-312-15730-4*); pap. text, wbk. ed. write for info. (*0-312-15732-0*) St Martin.

— Take Ten, Vol. 2. 2000. pap. text. write for info. (*0-312-15713-4*); pap. text. write for info. (*0-312-15729-0*); pap. text, wbk. ed. write for info. (*0-312-15731-2*) St Martin.

— Take Ten Level 1A. 2000. pap. text. write for info. (*0-312-18916-8*); pap. text, wbk. ed. write for info. (*0-312-18919-2*) St Martin.

— Take Ten Level 1B. 2000. pap. text. write for info. (*0-312-18917-6*); pap. text, wbk. ed. write for info. (*0-312-18920-6*) St Martin.

— Take Ten Level 2A. 2000. pap. text, wbk. ed. write for info. (*0-312-18910-9*) St Martin.

— Take Ten Level 2B. 2000. pap. text, wbk. ed. write for info. (*0-312-18911-7*) St Martin.

— Take Ten Level 3B. 2000. pap. text. write for info. (*0-312-18961-3*) St Martin.

— Take Ten Basics. 2000. pap. text. write for info. (*0-312-18874-9*) St Martin.

Carver & Fotinos. Conversation. 3rd ed. 2000. pap. text, student ed. 27.53 (*0-13-728122-6*) P-H.

— Conversation, Book 2. 3rd ed. 288p. (C). 1997. pap. text 21.00 (*0-13-728114-5*) P-H.

Carver, jt. auth. see Bowles.

Carver, Ann C. & Chang, Sung-sheng Y., eds. Bamboo Shoots after the Rain: Contemporary Stories by Women Writers of Taiwan. LC 90-3665. 264p. 1990. 35.00 (*1-55861-017-0*); pap. 14.95 (*1-55861-018-9*) Feminist Pr.

Carver, Anthony F. Cori Spezzati, 2 vols. (Illus.). 168p. 1989. text 69.95 (*0-521-30399-0*) Cambridge U Pr.

Carver, Beth S. & Casey, Eleen M. Silver by Paul de Lamerie at the Clark Art Institute. (Illus.). 74p. 1978. 25.00 (*1-55660-185-9*) A Wofsy Fine Arts.

***Carver, Bill.** Branch Water Tales: Memories of a Mountain Family, 1. (Illus.). 221p. 1999. pap. 13.95 (*0-9671908-0-0*) Mtn Voices.

Carver, C. A. Chasing Rainbows. LC 96-68108. 136p. (Orig.). 1996. pap. text 11.95 (*1-883122-04-X*) Pearce Pub.

Carver, C. N. Carver Family of New England: Robert Carver of Marshfield & His Descendants. 204p. 1991. reprint ed. pap. 31.00 (*0-8328-2018-0*); reprint ed. lib. bdg. 41.00 (*0-8328-2017-2*) Higginson Bk Co.

Carver, Charles S. & Scheier, Michael F. Attention & Self Regulation: A Control-Theory Approach to Human Behavior. (Social Psychology Ser.). (Illus.). 403p. 1981. 80.00 (*0-387-90553-7*) Spr-Verlag.

— On the Self-Regulation of Behavior. LC 98-15204. (Illus.). 300p. (C). 1998. 49.95 (*0-521-57204-5*) Cambridge U Pr.

— Perspectives on Personality. 4th ed. LC 99-26281. 602p. (C). 1999. 85.00 (*0-205-29394-8*) Allyn.

Carver, Charles S., jt. auth. see Scheier, Michael F.

Carver, Craig M. American Regional Dialects: A Word Geography. (Illus.). 336p. 1987. pap. text 24.95 (*0-472-08103-9*, 08103) U of Mich Pr.

Carver, Deborah A., ed. see LAMA Development Committee Staff.

Carver, Dennie B., jt. auth. see Dillow, Louise B.

Carver, Donna J. & Weatherford, Sally E. The Ballet Book, Wkbk. I. (Ballet Workbook Ser.: No. 1). 80p. (J). (gr. 1-2). 1995. pap. text 12.00 (*1-887707-00-X*) Lewelyn & Co.

— The Ballet Book, Wkbk. II. (Ballet Workbook Ser.: No. 2). 88p. (J). (gr. 2-3). 1995. pap. text 12.00 (*1-887707-01-8*) Lewelyn & Co.

— The Ballet Book, Wkbk. III. (Ballet Workbook Ser.: No. 3). 100p. (YA). (gr. 5 up). 1995. pap. text 15.00 (*1-887707-02-6*) Lewelyn & Co.

— The Ballet Book, Wkbk. IV. (Ballet Workbook Ser.: No. 4). 100p. (YA). (gr. 6 up). 1996. pap. text 15.00 (*1-887707-03-4*) Lewelyn & Co.

— The Ballet Book, Wkbk. V. (Ballet Workbook Ser.: No. 5). 100p. (YA). (gr. 7 up). 1996. pap. text 15.00 (*1-887707-04-2*) Lewelyn & Co.

Carver, E. L., ed. Palsgrave's Acolastus. (EETS, OS Ser.: No. 202). 1974. reprint ed. 55.00 (*0-527-00202-X*) Periodicals Srv.

Carver, Elias. Carver: Genealogy of William Carver from Hertfordshire, England, in 1682. (Illus.). 146p. 1997. reprint ed. pap. 22.50 (*0-8328-7880-4*); reprint ed. lib. bdg. 32.50 (*0-8328-7879-0*) Higginson Bk Co.

Carver, F. Nuestra Victoria (Our Victory) (SPA.). 0.35 (*0-685-74963-0*, 540525) Editorial Unilit.

Carver, Frank G. The Cross & The Spirit. 124p. (Orig.). 1973. pap. 8.99 (*0-8341-1094-6*) Beacon Hill.

— Matthew Pt. I, Chapters 1-13: To Be a Disciple. Wolf, Earl C., ed. (Beacon Small-Group Bible Studies). 88p. (Orig.). 1984. pap. 4.99 (*0-8341-0870-4*) Beacon Hill.

— When Jesus Said Good-Bye. 136p. (Orig.). 1996. kivar 16.99 (*0-8341-1570-0*) Beacon Hill.

Carver, Frank G., ed. see Wolf, Earl C.

Carver, G. W. How to Grow Marijuana Indoors for Medicinal Use. (Illus.). 128p. (Orig.). 1997. pap. 19.95 (*0-930180-15-1*, Sun Magic) Homestead Bk.

***Carver, Gary L.** Out from the Ordinary: Sermons for Sundays after Pentecost, First Third. LC 99-32556. (First Lessons Ser.). 90p. 1999. pap. 9.25 (*0-7880-1382-3*) CSS OH.

Carver, George. The Catholic Tradition in English Literature. 1972. 59.95 (*0-87968-820-3*) Gordon Pr.

Carver, George, ed. Periodical Essays of the Eighteenth Century. LC 70-99621. (Essay Index Reprint Ser.). 1977. 28.95 (*0-8369-1555-0*) Ayer.

Carver, George W. Food Dispensers & Vending Machines: Index of New Information with Authors & Subjects. LC 96-15724. 1996. 47.50 (*0-7883-1154-9*) ABBE Pubs Assn.

Carver, George W. Food Dispensers & Vending Machines: Index of New Information with Authors & Subjects. LC 96-15724. 1996. pap. 44.50 (*0-7883-1155-7*) ABBE Pubs Assn.

Carver, Hartwell. Proposal for a Charter to Build a Railroad from Lake Michigan to the Pacific Ocean. 50p. 1987. pap. 6.95 (*0-87770-410-4*) Ye Galleon.

Carver, J., jt. auth. see Carver, John.

Carver, Jacob D. Life A-ta Z. pap. 12.95 (*1-893504-00-X*) ThirdEye Poet.

Carver, Jeffrey A. Dragon Rigger. 1994. mass mkt. 4.99 (*0-8125-3323-2*) Tor Bks.

— Dragons in the Stars. 352p. 1992. mass mkt. 4.99 (*0-8125-3303-8*, Pub. by Tor Bks) St Martin.

— Infinite Sea. 1997. mass mkt. 6.99 (*0-8125-3517-0*, Pub. by Tor Bks) St Martin.

— The Infinity Link. 544p. 1996. mass mkt. 4.95 (*0-8125-3327-5*, Pub. by Tor Bks) St Martin.

— Neptune Crossing. (Chaos Chronicles). 383p. 1995. mass mkt. 5.99 (*0-8125-3515-4*, Pub. by Tor Bks) St Martin.

— Panglor. 1996. mass mkt. 5.99 (*0-8125-5167-2*, Pub. by Tor Bks) St Martin.

— Star Rigger's Way. 1994. pap. 4.99 (*0-8125-3444-1*, Pub. by Tor Bks) St Martin.

— Strange Attractors. 352p. 1996. pap. write for info. (*0-614-05544-X*); mass mkt. 5.99 (*0-8125-3516-2*, Pub. by Tor Bks) St Martin.

Carver, Joan. Collage from Seeds, Leaves & Flowers. LC 97-204368. (Illus.). 176p. 1997. pap. text 16.95 (*1-86108-051-4*, Pub. by Guild Master) Sterling.

Carver, John. Board Assessment of the CEO. LC 97-4564. (CarverGuide Ser.: No. CG 07). 26p. 1997. pap. 10.95 (*0-7879-0834-7*) Jossey-Bass.

— Board Members As Fund Raisers, Advisors, & Lobbyists. LC 97-21104. (Carverguide Ser.: No. CG11). 1997. pap. 10.95 (*0-7879-1083-X*) Jossey-Bass.

— Board Self-Assessment. LC 97-4565. (CarverGuide Ser.: No. CG 08). 26p. 1997. pap. 10.95 (*0-7879-0833-9*) Jossey-Bass.

— Boards That Make a Difference: A New Design for Leadership in Nonprofit & Public Organizations. LC 89-77419. (Nonprofit Sector-Public Administration Ser.). 266p. 1990. text 28.95 (*1-55542-231-4*) Jossey-Bass.

— Boards That Make a Difference: A New Design for Leadership in Nonprofit & Public Organizations. 2nd ed. LC 97-4694. (Public Administration Ser.). 241p. 1997. 28.95 (*0-7879-0811-8*) Jossey-Bass.

— The Chairperson's Role as Servant-Leader to the Board. LC 96-35715. (CarverGuide Series on Policy Governance: No. CG 04). 26p. 1996. pap. 10.95 (*0-7879-0300-0*) Jossey-Bass.

— Creating a Mission That Makes a Difference. LC 96-45762. (CarverGuide Series on Policy Governance: No. CG 06). 26p. 1996. pap. 10.95 (*0-7879-0302-7*) Jossey-Bass.

— Planning Better Board Meetings. LC 96-45761. (CarverGuide on Policy Governance Ser.: No. CG 05). 26p. 1996. pap. 10.95 (*0-7879-0301-9*) Jossey-Bass.

— Strategies for Board Leadership. LC 97-21103. (Carverguide Ser.: No. 10). 1997. pap. 10.95 (*0-7879-1082-1*) Jossey-Bass.

— Three Steps to Fiduciary Responsibility. LC 96-10046. (CarverGuide Series on Policy Governance: No. CG 3). 26p. 1996. pap. 10.95 (*0-7879-0298-5*) Jossey-Bass.

— Winning. Fremming, Ali, ed. 490p. 1998. pap. 19.95 (*0-9663579-0-6*, 9801) Fountain Green.

Carver, John. Working with Your Board: Guidelines for CEOs. LC 97-21105. (Carverguide Ser.: No. CG 12). 24p. 1997. pap. 10.95 (*0-7879-1084-8*) Jossey-Bass.

Carver, John & Carver, J. Empowering Boards for Leadership. 1992. 29.95 incl. audio (*1-55542-447-3*) Jossey-Bass.

Carver, John & Carver, Miriam M. Basic Principles of Policy Governance. LC 96-10044. (CarverGuide Ser.: No. CG 01). 26p. 1996. pap. 10.95 (*0-7879-0296-9*) Jossey-Bass.

— Making Diversity Meaningful in the Boardroom. LC 97-4566. (CarverGuide Ser.: No. CG 09). 26p. 1997. pap. 10.95 (*0-7879-0835-5*) Jossey-Bass.

— Reinventing Your Board: A Step-by-Step Guide to Implementing Policy Governance. LC 97-4810. (Jossey-Bass Public Administration Ser.). 232p. 1997. 27.95 (*0-7879-0911-4*) Jossey-Bass.

C

Carver, John & Carver, Miriam M. Your Roles & Responsibilities As a Board Member. LC 96-10045. (CarverGuide Series on Effective Board Governance: No. CG 02). 26p. 1996. pap. 10.95 (*0-7879-0297-7*) Jossey-Bass.

Carver, John & Mayhew, Miriam. A New Vision of Board Leadership: Governing the Community College. 175p. 1994. 35.00 (*1-886237-01-8*) Assn Commun Coll.

Carver, John N. & Carver, Nellie E. The Family of the Retarded Child. LC 72-85384. (Segregated Settings & the Problems of Change Ser.: No. 2). 156p. 1972. 14.95 (*0-8156-8079-1*) Syracuse U Pr.

Carver, Jonathan. The Journals of Jonathan Carver & Related Documents, 1766-1770. Parker, John, ed. LC 76-2643. (Publications of the Minnesota Historical Society). (Illus.). 256p. 1976. reprint ed. pap. 79.40 (*0-608-06680-X*, 206687700009) Bks Demand.

Carver, Joseph. How to Grow the Finest Marijuana Indoors under Lights. 1996. pap. 22.95 (*0-930180-14-3*) Homestead Bk.

— How to Grow the Finest Marijuana Indoors under Lights. 2nd rev. ed. (Illus.). 128p. 1996. pap. 22.95 (*0-930180-16-X*) Homestead Bk.

Carver, Kevin G., jt. auth. see Steinman, Scott B.

Carver, Larry, ed. Essays in Honor of William B. Todd. (Illus.). 215p. 1991. pap. 20.00 (*0-87959-114-5*) U of Tex H Ransom Ctr.

Carver, Larry, jt. ed. see Oliphant, Dave.

Carver, Lee. Did I Just Kiss the Waiter. (Illus.). 170p. (Orig.). 1996. pap. 8.95 (*1-57502-104-8*) Morris Pubng.

Carver, Leland. The Ninetieth Aero Squadron, American Expeditionary Forces. (Great War Ser.: No. 4). (Illus.). 136p. 1990. reprint ed. 29.95 (*0-89839-146-6*) Battery Pr.

Carver, Leona P., ed. You Can't Get the Coons All up One Tree: True Life Story of John N. Jones. 244p. (Orig.). (C). 1980. pap. 7.95 (*0-686-36932-7*) Coltharp Pub.

Carver, Lisa. Dancing Queen: The Bawdy Adventures of Lisa Crystal Carver. 128p. (Orig.). 1995. pap. 12.00 (*0-8050-4392-6*, Owl) H Holt & Co.

Carver, M. O. Arguments in Stone: Archaeological Research & the European Town in the First Millennium. LC 94-141939. (Oxbow Monographs in Archaeology: No. 29). (Illus.). 134p. 1993. pap. 18.00 (*0-946897-57-3*, Pub. by Oxbow Bks) David Brown.

Carver, M. Robert. Understanding Statistics with Minitab. LC 98-223827. 1998. pap. text 21.95 (*0-534-35924-8*) PWS Pubs.

Carver, Martin. Sutton Hoo: Burial Ground of Kings. LC 98-16434. (Illus.). 224p. 1998. 29.95 (*0-8122-3455-3*) U of Pa Pr.

Carver, Martin, ed. In Search of Cult: Archaeological Investigations in Honour of Philip Rahtz. (Illus.). 256p. (C). 1993. 90.00 (*0-85115-337-2*) Boydell & Brewer.

— Sutton Hoo Research Committee: Bulletins, 1983-1993. (Illus.). 336p. (C). 1993. 75.00 (*0-85115-341-0*, Boydell Pr) Boydell & Brewer.

Carver, Miriam M., jt. auth. see Carver, John.

Carver, Nellie E., jt. auth. see Carver, John N.

Carver, Newton & Hare, Peter H., eds. Naturalism & Rationality. LC 86-20532. 289p. 1986. 38.95 (*0-87975-350-1*) Prometheus Bks.

Carver, Nona K. Bellyache Road, (An Excerpt from the Tarnish on the Golden Years) (Illus.). 24p. (Orig.). 1994. pap. 7.00 (*0-9641195-3-6*) Carver Cntry.

— Carver Country Cowboys. 62p. 1998. pap. 12.95 (*0-9641195-9-5*) Carver Cntry.

— Cowboy Poetry - Cowboys, Cookstoves & Catastrophies. LC 94-94483. (Illus.). 128p. (Orig.). 1995. pap. 12.95 (*0-9641195-6-0*) Carver Cntry.

— Memories, (An Excerpt from the Tarnish on the Golden Years) (Illus.). 32p. (Orig.). 1994. pap. 7.00 (*0-9641195-5-2*) Carver Cntry.

— Middle Age Spread, (An Excerpt of the Tarnish on the Golden Years) (Illus.). 24p. (Orig.). 1994. pap. 7.00 (*0-9641195-2-8*) Carver Cntry.

— Motorcycle Memories. 18p. (Orig.). 1994. pap. 5.00 (*0-9641195-7-9*) Carver Cntry.

— Retirement (An Excerpt from the Tarnish on the Golden Years) (Illus.). 22p. (Orig.). 1994. pap. 7.00 (*0-9641195-1-X*) Carver Cntry.

— Rocking Chair Rhapsodies, (An Excerpt from the Tarnish on the Golden Years) (Illus.). 24p. (Orig.). 1994. pap. 7.00 (*0-9641195-4-4*) Carver Cntry.

— The Tarnish on the Golden Years. LC 94-94371. 124p. 1994. pap. 12.95 (*0-9641195-0-1*) Carver Cntry.

Carver, Norman F. Angkor. (Illus.). 224p. 39.95 (*0-932076-16-5*); pap. 29.95 (*0-932076-17-3*) Documan.

Carver, Norman F., Jr. Form & Space in Japanese Architecture. (Illus.). 268p. 1993. reprint ed. 39.95 (*0-932076-10-6*); reprint ed. pap. 29.95 (*0-932076-11-4*) Documan.

— Greek Island Villages I. (Illus.). 224p. 1997. 42.95 (*0-932076-14-9*); pap. 32.95 (*0-932076-15-7*) Documan.

— Iberian Villages: Portugal & Spain. (Illus.). 192p. 1982. 34.95 (*0-932076-02-5*); pap. 27.95 (*0-932076-03-3*) Documan.

— Italian Hilltowns. rev. ed. (Illus.). 224p. 1994. pap. 29.95 (*0-932076-13-0*) Documan.

— Italian Hilltowns. 3rd ed. (Illus.). 224p. 1994. 39.95 (*0-932076-12-2*) Documan.

— Japanese Folkhouses. (Illus.). 200p. 1984. 34.95 (*0-932076-04-1*); pap. 27.95 (*0-932076-05-X*) Documan.

— North African Villages: Morocco, Algeria, & Tunisia. 200p. 1989. 34.95 (*0-932076-08-4*); pap. 27.95 (*0-932076-09-2*) Documan.

— Silent Cities of Mexico & the Maya. 2nd ed. (Illus.). 216p. 1986. 34.95 (*0-932076-06-8*); pap. 27.95 (*0-932076-07-6*) Documan.

Carver, Raymond. All of Us. 2000. pap. 14.00 (*0-375-70380-2*) Knopf.

— All of Us: The Collected Poems. LC 98-15880. 416p. 1998. 27.50 (*0-375-40398-1*) Knopf.

— Carver Country: The World of Raymond Carver. (Illus.). 160p. 1994. reprint ed. pap. 19.45 (*1-55970-255-9*, Pub. by Arcade Pub Inc) Time Warner.

— Cathedral. LC 84-40009. 1989. pap. 12.00 (*0-679-72369-2*) Random.

— Fires: Essays, Poems, Stories. 1989. pap. 11.00 (*0-679-72239-4*) Vin Bks.

— Jo Ann Callis: Object of Reverie, Selected Photographs 1977-1989. LC 88-71901. (Illus.). 63p. (Orig.). 1989. write for info. (*0-87685-756-X*) Edmundson.

— A New Path to the Waterfall. rev. ed. LC 88-34989. 160p. 1998. pap. 10.95 (*0-87113-374-1*, Atlntc Mnthly) Grove-Atltic.

Carver, Raymond. No Heroics, Please. 1992. pap. write for info. (*0-679-74031-7*) McKay.

— No Heroics, Please: Uncollected Writings. 1992. pap. 12.00 (*0-679-74007-4*) Vin Bks.

Carver, Raymond. Short Cuts: Selected Stories. LC 93-19747. (Contemporaries Ser.). 1993. pap. 10.00 (*0-679-74864-4*) Vin Bks.

— Les Trois Roses Jaunes. (FRE.). 189p. 1990. pap. 10.95 (*0-7859-2135-4*, 2070382257) Fr & Eur.

— Ultramarine. LC 87-40081. 160p. 1987. pap. 12.00 (*0-394-75535-9*) Random.

— What We Talk about When We Talk about Love. 168p. 1989. pap. 10.00 (*0-679-72305-6*) Vin Bks.

— Where I'm Calling From. (Contemporaries Ser.). 1989. pap. 14.00 (*0-679-72231-9*) Vin Bks.

***Carver, Raymond.** Where I'm Calling From: New & Selected Stories. 1998. 24.00 (*0-87113-721-6*, Atlntc Mnthly) Grove-Atltic.

Carver, Raymond. Where Water Comes Together with Other Water: Poems. 1986. pap. 11.00 (*0-394-74327-X*) Vin Bks.

— Will You Please Be Quiet, Please. 1992. pap. 12.00 (*0-679-73569-0*) McKay.

Carver, Raymond & Jenks, Tom, eds. American Short Story Masterpieces. 528p. 1989. mass mkt. 7.50 (*0-440-20423-2*, LE) Dell.

Carver, Raymond & Spector, Buzz. Jo Ann Callis: Object of Reverie, Selected Photographs 1977-1989. LC 88-71901. (Illus.). 63p. (Orig.). 1989. pap. 25.00 (*0-9614615-6-X*) Edmundson.

Carver, Raymond, jt. auth. see Gallagher, Tess.

Carver, Reginald & Bernstein, Lenny. Jazz Profiles: The Spirit of the Nineties. LC 98-30133. 320p. 1999. 21.95 (*0-8230-8338-1*) Watsn-Guptill.

Carver, Richard W. A History of Marshall. LC 93-2954. 1993. write for info. (*0-89865-854-3*) Donning Co.

***Carver, Robert.** The Accursed Mountains: Journeys in Albania. (Illus.). 338p. 1999. text 35.00 (*0-7195-5459-4*, Pub. by John Murray) Trafalgar.

— The Accursed Mountains: Journeys in Albania. 2000. reprint ed. pap. 16.95 (*0-00-655174-2*, Pub. by HarpC) Trafalgar.

***Carver, Ronald P.** The Causes of High & Low Reading Achievement. LC 99-53157. 2000. write for info. (*0-8058-3529-6*) L Erlbaum Assocs.

Carver, Ronald P. Writing a Publishable Research Report: In Education, Psychology, & Related Disciplines. (Illus.). 156p. (C). 1984. pap. text, spiral bd. 32.95 (*0-398-04986-6*) C C Thomas.

Carver, Sally S. The American Postcard Guide to Tuck. rev. ed. (Illus.). 1980. pap. 7.95 (*0-686-18747-4*) Carves.

— The American Postcard Guide to Tuck. rev. ed. (Illus.). 1982. pap. 10.95 (*0-686-38919-0*) Carves.

Carver, Terrel. Gender Is Not a Synonym for Women. LC 95-33095. 133p. 1995. lib. bdg. 15.95 (*1-55587-320-0*) L Rienner.

Carver, Terrell. The Postmodern Marx. LC 98-20426. 1999. 50.00 (*0-271-01867-4*); pap. 17.95 (*0-271-01868-2*) Pa St U Pr.

Carver, Terrell, ed. The Cambridge Companion to Marx. (Companions to Philosophy Ser.). 373p. (C). 1991. pap. text 22.95 (*0-521-36694-1*) Cambridge U Pr.

Carver, Terrell & Hyvarinen, Matti. Interpreting the Political: New Methodologies. LC 96-9857. 192p. (C). 1997. 85.00 (*0-415-13194-4*); pap. 25.99 (*0-415-13195-2*) Routledge.

Carver, Terrell & Mottier, V. Eronique. Politics of Sexuality. LC 98-21485. 224p. (C). 1998. 95.00 (*0-415-16953-4*) Routledge.

Carver, Terrell & Thomas, Paul, eds. Rational Choice Marxism. LC 94-41149. 350p. 1995. 50.00 (*0-271-01463-6*); pap. 18.95 (*0-271-01464-4*) Pa St U Pr.

Carver, Terrell, jt. auth. see Steger, Manfred B.

Carver, Terrell, ed. see Marx, Karl.

Carver, Thomas N. Essays in Social Justice. LC 79-105003. (Essay Index Reprint Ser.). 1977. 29.95 (*0-8369-1456-2*) Ayer.

— The Essential Factors of Social Evolution. LC 73-14151. (Perspectives in Social Inquiry Ser.). 580p. 1974. reprint ed. 36.95 (*0-405-05497-1*) Ayer.

Carver, Tina. Conversation, Bk. 1 Rev. 3rd rev. ed. 272p. (C). 1997. pap. text 21.00 (*0-13-792433-X*) P-H.

— Conversation, Bk. 1A Rev. 1. 3rd rev. ed. 160p. (C). 1997. pap. text 11.13 (*0-13-792458-5*) P-H.

— Conversation, Bk. 2A, Bk. 2. 3rd rev. ed. 176p. (C). 1998. pap. text 10.00 (*0-13-792508-5*) P-H.

— Conversation, Bk. 2B. 3rd rev. ed. 176p. (C). 1998. pap. text 10.00 (*0-13-792532-8*) P-H.

— Conversation, Bk.1 , Bk. 1B. 3rd rev. ed. 176p. (C). 1997. pap. text 10.00 (*0-13-792482-8*) P-H.

— Writing Book. 2nd ed. 1998. pap. 26.00 (*0-13-187972-3*) P-H.

Carver, Tom. Animal Flip Facts, Vol. I. 14p. (J). (ps up). 1996. 4.50 (*1-57846-023-9*) J N Hansen.

— Animal Flip Facts, Vol. II. 14p. (J). (ps up). 1996. 4.50 (*1-57846-024-7*) J N Hansen.

Carver, Ugly John. Mobius I Rulebook. 1990. 4.00 (*0-940244-86-1*) Flying Buffalo.

Carver, Vida. Social Workers & Their Workloads. Edwards, Les, ed. 1972. 25.00 (*0-7855-0995-X*, Pub. by Natl Inst Soc Work) St Mut.

Carver, Wayne, jt. auth. see Arc, Joan O.

Carver, William. The Job Hunter's Spiritual Companion. LC 97-44678. 144p. (Orig.). 1997. pap. 10.95 (*1-880913-30-5*) Innisfree Pr.

Carver, William F. Life of Dr. William F. Carver of California. (American Biography Ser.). 177p. 1991. reprint ed. lib. bdg. 59.00 (*0-7812-8062-1*) Rprt Serv.

Carvey, Paul M. Drug Action in the Central Nervous System. LC 97-14183. (Illus.). 432p. 1997. text 57.50 (*0-19-509333-X*); pap. text 32.50 (*0-19-509334-8*) OUP.

Carvic, Heron. Witch Miss Seeton. 192p. 1988. pap. 4.50 (*0-425-10713-2*) Berkley Pub.

Carvic, Heron, jt. auth. see Crane, Hamilton.

Carvill, Barbara, jt. auth. see Smith, David I.

Carvill, James. Mechanical Engineer's Data Handbook. LC 93-12482. 1993. 79.95 (*0-8493-7780-3*, TJ151) CRC Pr.

***Carville, Daragh.** Observatory. 2000. pap. 10.95 (*0-413-73910-4*, Methuen Drama) Methn.

Carville, Geraldine. The Occupation of Celtic Sites in Medieval Ireland by the Canons Regular of St Augustine & the Cistercians. (Cistercian Studies: Nbr. 56). (Illus.). 1983. pap. 9.00 (*0-87907-856-1*) Cistercian Pubns.

Carville, James. And the Horse He Rode In On: The People v. Kenneth Starr. 1998. 17.00 incl. audio (*0-671-04367-6*, Audioworks) S&S Audio.

— And the Horse He Rode in On: The People vs. Kenneth Starr. LC 98-45958. (Illus.). 176p. 1998. 14.95 (*0-684-85734-0*) S&S Trade.

***Carville, James.** Stickin' The Case for Loyalty. LC 99-58927. 224p. 2000. 16.45 (*0-684-85773-1*) S&S Trade.

— Stickin' The Case for Loyalty, 2 vols. 2000. audio 17.00 (*0-684-87237-4*) Simon & Schuster.

Carville, James. We're Right, They're Wrong: A Handbook for Spirited Progressives. LC 96-134063. (Illus.). 183p. 1996. pap. 10.00 (*0-679-76978-1*) Random.

Carville, Julie S. Hiking Tahoe's Wildflower Trails. Orig. Title: Lingering in Tahoe's Wild Gardens. (Illus.). 352p. 1997. reprint ed. pap. 11.95 (*1-55105-101-X*) Lone Pine.

Carville, Mike. Rock Climbing California's Lake Tahoe. rev. ed. LC 99-25924. (Illus.). 300p. 1998. pap. 25.00 (*1-57540-088-X*) Falcon Pub Inc.

Carville, Nippy. Delicious Heritage. 320p. 1988. pap., spiral bd. 9.95 (*0-935545-08-5*) Land & Land.

Carvin, Ruth. Color It Christmas: With Three Christmas Posters. (Illus.). 8p. (J). (gr. 3 up). 1987. write for info. (*0-318-62245-9*) Carvin Pub.

— A Visit to New Orleans: With Pictures to Color & Verses to Read. rev. ed. (Illus.). 32p. (J). (gr. k-4). 1988. ring bd. 3.50 (*0-9616390-2-4*) Carvin Pub.

— A Visit to New Orleans Coloring Book. (Illus.). 28p. (J). (gr. k-4). 1986. 3.50 (*0-9616390-0-8*) Carvin Pub.

Carvounis, Brinda Z., jt. auth. see Carvounis, Chris C.

Carvounis, C. P. Handbook of Biostatistics: A Review & Text. (Illus.). 160p. 2000. pap. 22.95 (*1-85070-749-9*) Prthnon Pub.

Carvounis, Chris C. The Debt Dilemma of Developing Nations: Issues & Cases. LC 84-1981. 189p. 1984. 57.95 (*0-89930-062-6*, CDD/, Quorum Bks) Greenwood.

— The Foreign Debt-National Development Conflict: External Adjustment & Internal Disorder in the Developing Nations. LC 86-630. 266p. 1986. 55.00 (*0-89930-155-X*, CBD/, Quorum Bks) Greenwood.

— The United States Trade Deficit of the 1980s: Origins, Meanings, & Policy Responses. LC 87-2561. 197p. 1987. 57.95 (*0-89930-219-X*, CTD/, Quorum Bks) Greenwood.

Carvounis, Chris C. & Carvounis, Brinda Z. U. S. Commercial Opportunities in the Soviet Union: Marketing, Production, & Strategic Planning Perspectives. LC 88-23666. 204p. 1989. 57.95 (*0-89930-351-X*, CAV/, Quorum Bks) Greenwood.

— United States Trade & Investment in Latin America: Opportunities for Business in the 1990s. LC 92-12719. 256p. 1992. 57.95 (*0-89930-786-8*, CUT/, Quorum Bks) Greenwood.

***Carwardine, Mark.** The Book of Dolphins. 160p. 1999. pap. text 17.95 (*1-85585-737-5*) Collins & Br.

— Great White Shark. (Natural World Ser.). (J). 2000. pap. 7.95 (*0-7398-2029-X*) Raintree Steck-V.

Carwardine, Mark. Killer Whale. 48p. (J). (gr. 4-7). 1999. pap. 7.95 (*0-7398-0949-0*) Raintree Steck-V.

— Whales & Dolphins. (Collins Gem Ser.). 1998. pap. text 8.00 (*0-00-472111-X*) Collins.

***Carwardine, Mark.** Whales & Dolphins. (Collins Gem Ser.). 256p. 2000. pap. 7.95 (*0-00-472273-6*, Pub. by HarpC) Trafalgar.

Carwardine, Mark. Whales, Dolphins & Porpoises. LC 92-7624. (See & Explore Library). (Illus.). 64p. (J). (gr. 3 up). 1992. 12.95 (*1-56458-144-6*) DK Pub Inc.

— Whales, Porpoises, & Dolphins. LC 94-33301. (Eyewitness Handbooks Ser.). (Illus.). 256p. 1995. 29.95 (*1-56458-621-9*); pap. 18.95 (*1-56458-620-0*) DK Pub Inc.

***Carwardine, Mark, contrib. by.** Killer Whale: Habitats, Life Cycles, Food Chains, Threats. LC 99-18099. (Natural World Ser.). (Illus.). 48p. (J). (gr. 4-7). 2000. lib. bdg. 25.69 (*0-7398-1058-8*) Raintree Steck-V.

Carwardine, Mark, et al. Whales, Dolphins & Porpoises. LC 97-37812. (Nature Company Guides Ser.). (Illus.). 288p. (gr. 9). 1998. 24.95 (*0-7835-5284-X*) Time-Life.

Carwardine, Mark, jt. auth. see Adams, Douglas.

Carwardine, Mark, jt. ed. see Bryden, Michael.

Carwardine, Richard. Transatlantic Revivalism: Popular Evangelicalism in Britain & America, 1790-1865, 75. LC 77-94740. (Contributions in American History Ser.: No. 75). 249p. 1978. 49.95 (*0-313-20308-3*, CTR/, Greenwood Pr) Greenwood.

Carwardine, Richard J. Evangelicals & Politics in Antebellum America. LC 96-38792. 512p. 1997. pap. text 25.00 (*0-87049-974-2*) U of Tenn Pr.

Carwardine, William H. Pullman Strike. 2nd ed. 160p. 1994. pap. 14.00 (*0-88286-224-3*) C H Kerr.

Carwell, Hattie. Blacks in Science: Astrophysicist to Zoologist. (Illus.). 96p. (YA). (gr. 8 up). 1988. reprint ed. 10.00 (*0-685-22950-5*); reprint ed. pap. 7.00 (*0-682-48911-5*) H Carwell.

Carwell, Steven, jt. auth. see Strebel, Paul.

Carwile, Karen, ed. Virginia Freedom of Information Act, Virginia Conflict of Interests Acts; Virginia Public Procurement Act: 1998 Edition. 163p. 1998. pap. write for info. (*0-327-06073-5*, 34436-13) LEXIS Pub.

Carwile, Mike, jt. auth. see Edwards, Bill.

Cary & Eisenberg. Corporations: 1998 Case Supplement. 7th unabridged ed. 1998. write for info. (*1-56662-633-1*) Foundation Pr.

— 1993 Case Supplement to Corporations. 1988. write for info. (*0-318-72442-1*) Foundation Pr.

Cary, jt. auth. see Jefferies, Chris.

Cary, Alice. Jean Craighead George. Welsh, Janet, ed. (Meet the Author Ser.). 132p. (J). (gr. 3-6). 1996. pap. 6.95 (*0-88160-283-3*, LW353) Learning Wks.

— Katherine Paterson. LC 97-668. (Meet the Author Ser.). 136p. (Orig.). (J). (gr. 3-6). 1997. pap. 6.95 (*0-88160-281-7*, LW351) Learning Wks.

— Parents' Guide to Outdoor Adventure: A Trailside Guide. LC 96-40320. (Illus.). 256p. 1997. pap. 18.95 (*0-393-31652-1*) Norton.

Cary, Alice & Cary, Phoebe. Ballads for Little Folk. LC 73-109136. (Granger Index Reprint Ser.). 1977. 17.95 (*0-8369-6120-X*) Ayer.

***Cary, Ann H. & Wharton, Chris, eds.** Quality Assurance Through Credentialing Vol. 1: Global Perspectives. 79p. 1999. write for info. (*1-55810-146-2*) Am Nurses Pub.

— Quality Assurance Through Credentialing Vol. 2: Concepts, Issues, & Trends. 85p. 1999. write for info. (*1-55810-147-0*) Am Nurses Pub.

Cary, Anna Marie, ed. see Azevedo Howard, Theresa M.

Cary, Anna Marie, ed. see Logan, Renne A.

***Cary, Barbara.** Meet Abraham Lincoln. (J). 2001. pap. 5.99 (*0-375-80396-3*) Random Bks Yng Read.

Cary, Barbara. Meet Abraham Lincoln. LC 88-19066. (Step-up Biographies Ser.). (Illus.). 72p. (J). (gr. 2-4). 1989. reprint ed. pap. 3.99 (*0-394-81966-7*, Pub. by Random Bks Yng Read) Random.

***Cary, Barbara.** Spirit of the Heart. 1999. 6.99 (*1-57343-013-7*) LionHearted.

Cary, Beth, tr. see Duus, Masayo U.

Cary, Beth, tr. see Gibney, Frank B., ed.

Cary, Beth, tr. see Shinbun, Asahi.

Cary, Beth, tr. see Tsujii, Takashi.

Cary, Bob. Born to Pull. LC 98-25471. (Illus.). 96p. 1998. 26.95 (*1-57025-146-0*) Pfeifer-Hamilton.

***Cary, Bob.** Ely Echoes: The Portages Grow Longer. LC 99-6706. (Illus.). 192p. 1999. pap. 14.95 (*1-57025-200-9*) Pfeifer-Hamilton.

Cary, Bob. Root Beer Lady: The Story of Dorothy Molter. LC 92-61331. (Illus.). 192p. 1993. pap. 14.95 (*0-938586-68-8*) Pfeifer-Hamilton.

— Tales from Jackpine Bob. Gustafson, Susan, ed. (Illus.). 208p. (Orig.). 1995. pap. 14.95 (*1-57025-086-3*) Pfeifer-Hamilton.

— Winter Camping. LC 78-58680. (Environmental Sport Bk.). 1979. 10.95 (*0-8289-0339-5*) Viking Penguin.

Cary, Bob, jt. auth. see Paull, Frankie.

Cary, Cecile W. & Limouze, Henry S., eds. Shakespeare & the Arts: A Collection of Essays from the Ohio Shakespeare Conference, Wright State University, Dayton, Ohio, 1981. LC 82-17486. (Illus.). 256p. (Orig.). 1983. lib. bdg. 56.00 (*0-8191-2819-8*) U Pr of Amer.

Cary, Cynthia. A Foxy Old Woman's Guide to Living with Friends. LC 98-24644. (Foxy Old Woman's Guides Ser.). 160p. 1998. pap. 10.95 (*0-89594-919-9*) Crossing Pr.

Cary, David. A Bit of Burlesque: A Brief History of Its Times & Stars. LC 97-26503. (Illus.). 70p. (Orig.). 1997. pap. 9.95 (*0-938711-47-4*) Tecolote Pubns.

***Cary, Devin.** The Winter Queen. 288p. 1999. mass mkt. 5.99 (*0-441-00681-7*) Ace Bks.

Cary, Diana S. The Hollywood Posse: The Story of a Gallant Band of Horsemen Who Made Movie History. LC 95-42374. (Illus.). 320p. (Orig.). 1996. pap. 16.95 (*0-8061-2835-6*) U of Okla Pr.

— Hollywood's Children: An Inside Account of the Child Star Era. LC 97-17376. (Illus.). 328p. 1997. reprint ed. pap. 14.95 (*0-87074-424-0*) SMU Press.

— Whatever Happened to Baby Peggy? The Autobiography of Hollywood's Pioneer Child Star. LC 96-23290. 352p. 1996. 25.95 (*0-312-14760-0*) St Martin.

Cary, Earnest. Roman Antiquities, 2. (Loeb Classical Library: No. 319, 347, 357, 364, 372, 378, 388). 538p. 1939. 18.95 (*0-674-99382-9*) HUP.

Cary, Earnest, tr. Roman Antiquities, 1. (Loeb Classical Library: No. 319, 347, 357, 364, 372, 378, 388). 602p. 1937. 18.95 (*0-674-99352-7*) HUP.

— Roman Antiquities, 3. (Loeb Classical Library: No. 319, 347, 357, 364, 372, 378, 388). 394p. 1940. 18.95 (*0-674-99394-2*) HUP.

— Roman Antiquities, 4. (Loeb Classical Library: No. 319, 347, 357, 364, 372, 378, 388). 392p. 1943. 18.95 (*0-674-99401-9*) HUP.

An Asterisk (*) at the beginning of an entry indicates that the title is appearing for the first time.

C

An Asterisk (*) at the beginning of an entry indicates that the title is appearing for the first time.

— Bluebonnet at the State Fair. (Bluebonnet Bks.: No. 3). (Illus.). 40p. (J). (gr. 4-5). 1995. pap. 5.95 (*1-57168-069-1*) Sunbelt Media.

— Bluebonnet at the Texas State Capitol. LC 97-11300. (Illus.). 32p. (J). (ps-3). Date not set. 14.95 (*1-56554-232-0*) Pelican.

— Bluebonnet of the Hill Country. (Illus.). 40p. (J). (gr. 4-5). 1995. pap. 5.95 (*1-57168-028-4*) Sunbelt Media.

Casad, Mary Brooke. Bluebonnet at Johnson Space Center. LC 92-37416. (Illus.). 32p. (gr. 4-7). 1993. 14.95 (*0-88289-963-5*) Pelican.

***Casad, Mary Brooke.** Bluebonnet at the Marshall Train Depot. LC 99-20920. (Illus.). 32p. (J). (gr. k-3). 1999. 14.95 (*1-56554-311-4*) Pelican.

Casad, Robert. Jurisdiction & Forum Selection, 1988-1990. 130.00 (*0-685-24498-9*) West Group.

Casad, Robert C. Civil Judgment Recognition & the Integration of Multiple-State Associations: Central America, the United States of America, & the European Economic Community. LC 81-11926. xiv, 258p. 1982. 29.95 (*0-7006-0218-6*) U Pr of KS.

— Jurisdiction in Civil Actions. 1370p. 1993. 185.00 (*0-88063-291-7*, 81309-10, MICHIE) LEXIS Pub.

Casad, Robert C. & Montagne, Rogelio S. Expropriation in Central America & Panama: Processes & Procedures. LC 74-21957. xiii, 188p. 1975. lib. bdg. 39.50 (*0-930342-10-0*, 300140) W S Hein.

Casad, Robert C. & Richman, William. Jurisdiction in Civil Action, Vol. 1. 3rd ed. LC 98-89531. 1600p. 1998. write for info. (*0-327-00795-8*, 8130911) LEXIS Pub.

— Jurisdiction in Civil Action, 2 vols., Vol. 1 & 2. 3rd ed. LC 98-89531. 1600p. 1998. 205.00 (*0-327-00714-1*, 8130911) LEXIS Pub.

— Jurisdiction in Civil Action, Vol. 2. 3rd ed. LC 98-89531. 1600p. 1998. write for info. (*0-327-00796-6*, 8130911) LEXIS Pub.

Casad, Robert C., et al. Civil Procedure: Cases & Materials. 2nd ed. (Contemporary Legal Education Ser.). 1153p. 1989. 48.00 (*0-87473-439-8*, 10741-10, MICHIE) LEXIS Pub.

Casada, Ann, jt. auth. see Casada, Jim.

Casada, James A. Sir Richard F. Burton: A Biobibliographical Study. 256p. 1990. 55.00 (*0-8161-9082-8*, Hall Reference) Macmillan.

***Casada, James A., ed.** Frederick Selous: A Hunting Legend. (Illus.). 187p. 2000. 75.00 (*1-57157-131-0*) Safari Pr.

Casada, James A., ed. see Selous, Frederick C.

Casada, Jim. Modern Fly Fishing. LC 93-84838. (Complete Angler's Library). 234p. 1993. write for info. (*0-914697-56-0*) N Amer Outdoor Grp.

Casada, Jim & Casada, Ann. The Complete Venison Cookbook: From Field to Table. LC 96-76699. 208p. 1996. pap. 12.95 (*0-87341-416-0*, CVC) Krause Pubns.

Casada, Jim & Rutledge, Archibald H., eds. America's Greatest Game Bird: Archibald Rutledge's Turkey-Hunting Tales. LC 93-39997. 222p. (YA). (gr. 10). 1994. 24.95 (*0-87249-983-9*) U of SC Pr.

Casada, Jim, ed. see Rutledge, Archibald.

Casada, Jim, ed. see Trout, John, Jr.

Casadevall, Arturo & Perfect, John R. Cryptococcus Neoformans. LC 98-8693. (Illus.). 450p. 1998. 99.95 (*1-55581-107-8*) ASM Pr.

Casadevall, T. J., ed. Volcanic Ash & Aviation Safety: Proceedings of the First International Symposium on Volcanic Ash & Aviation Safety. (Illus.). 450p. (Orig.). (C). 1995. pap. text 75.00 (*0-7881-1650-9*) DIANE Pub.

Casadio, Mariuccia. Emilio Pucci. 1998. pap. 18.95 (*0-7893-0250-0*, Pub. by Universe) St Martin.

Casado, Matt A. Conversational Spanish for Hospitality Managers & Supervisors: Basic Language Skills for Daily Operations. LC 94-37418. 304p. 1995. pap. 44.95 (*0-471-05959-5*) Wiley.

— Food & Beverage Service Manual. 144p. 1994. pap. 24.95 (*0-471-30464-6*) Wiley.

— Housekeeping Management. LC 99-22276. 304p. 1999. 44.95 (*0-471-25189-5*) Wiley.

— Spanish Cuisine: The Gourmet's Companion. LC 96-15478. 150p. 1997. pap. 16.95 (*0-471-13722-7*) Wiley.

Casado, Silvia, jt. auth. see Rodriguez, Gloria.

Casados, Janet, ed. see Fandre, Donovan J.

Casady. Fit for Fun Manual. 6th ed. 1988. teacher ed. 22.25 (*0-538-28623-7*) S-W Pub.

Casady, Cort, jt. auth. see Davidson, John.

Casady, Mona J. Fit for Fun: Document Processing. 6th ed. (C). 1988. text 31.00 (*0-538-20490-7*, T49) S-W Pub.

— Word-Information Processing: A System Approach. 2nd ed. 544p. (C). 1988. mass mkt. 49.95 (*0-538-70030-0*, WP40BA) S-W Pub.

— Word Processing. LC 94-31574. 1995. mass mkt. 20.95 (*0-538-63095-7*) S-W Pub.

— Word/Information Processing Concepts. 2nd ed. (DF - Computer Applications Ser.). (C). 1989. mass mkt., wbk. ed. 20.95 (*0-538-70031-9*) S-W Pub.

— Word/Information Processing Concepts. 3rd ed. (DF - Computer Applications Ser.). 1987. mass mkt. 20.95 (*0-538-23620-5*) S-W Pub.

Casady, R. B., et al. Commercial Rabbit Raising. (Lost Arts Ser.). (Illus.). 69p. reprint ed. pap. 10.00 (*0-8466-6054-7*, U54) Shoreys Bkstore.

Casaer, Paul, jt. ed. see Magnusson, David.

Casaer, Paul, jt. ed. see Rutter, Michael.

Casagranda, Brigitte. Creative Dough Crafts: 100 Delightful Designs to Make in Your Own Kitchen. Boswell, Holly, ed. Clifton, Mark, tr. LC 97-25164. 128p. 1997. 21.95 (*1-887374-49-3*, Pub. by Lark Books) Random.

— The Magic of Salt Dough. (Illus.). 96p. (Orig.). 1997. pap. 17.95 (*0-85532-830-4*, Pub. by Srch Pr) A Schwartz & Co.

Casagrande, Jean. The Sound System of French. fac. ed. LC 83-20594. 256p. 1984. reprint ed. pap. 79.40 (*0-7837-7801-5*, 204755700007) Bks Demand.

Casagrande, Peter J. Unity in Hardy's Novels: Repetitive Symmetries. xii, 252p. 1982. 29.95 (*0-7006-0209-7*) U Pr of KS.

Casagrande, Vivien A. & Shinkman, Paul, eds. Advances in Neural & Behavioral Development, Vol. 4. 264p. (C). 1994. text 78.50 (*0-89391-823-7*) Ablx Pub.

Casajuana, Carles. The Purity of a Pig. Denhard, Jennifer, tr. from SPA. (Catalan Studies: Vol. 19). 72p. (C). 1996. pap. text 24.95 (*0-8204-2793-4*) P Lang Pubng.

Casal, C. V., jt. ed. see Pullin, R. S.

Casal, F. G. Solar Thermal Power Plants: Achievements & Lessons Learned Exemplified by the SSPS Project in Almeria-Spain. (Illus.). 160p. 1987. 69.95 (*0-387-17458-3*) Spr-Verlag.

***Casal, Laura.** Noble Madness. (Illus.). 76p. 1999. pap. 15.00 (*0-9668545-0-0*) PeecaPress.

Casal, Lourdes. Los Fundadores, Alfonso y Otros Cuentos. (SPA.). 1973. pap. 7.95 (*0-89729-004-6*) Ediciones.

Casal, Mary. The Stone Wall: An Autobiography. LC 75-12307. (Homosexuality Ser.). 1975. reprint ed. 19.95 (*0-405-07404-2*) Ayer.

Casal, Pedro. Spanish Key Words: The Basic Two Thousand Word Vocabulary Arranged by Frequency in a Hundred Units with Comprehensive Italian & English Indexes. (Language & Literature Ser.: Vol. 14). 144p. (Orig.). 1992. pap. 13.50 (*0-906672-26-0*) Oleander Pr.

Casalbuoni, R. & Domokos, G. Theory Meets Experiment: Proceedings of the Johns Hopkins Workshop on Current Problems in Practice Theory. 300p. 1995. text 99.00 (*981-02-2235-1*) World Scientific Pub.

Casaldaliga, Pedro. In Pursuit of the Kingdom: Writings, 1968-1988. Berryman, Phillip, tr. LC 89-48235. 272p. 1990. reprint ed. pap. 84.40 (*0-7837-9844-X*, 206057300005) Bks Demand.

Casaldaliga, Pedro & Maria Vigil, Jose. The Spirituality of Liberation. 272p. 1994. pap. 40.00 (*0-86012-215-8*, Pub. by Srch Pr) St Mut.

Casaldaliga, Pedro & Vigil, Jose M. Political Holiness: A Spirituality of Liberation - Espiritialidad de la Liberacion. Burns, Paul & McDonagh, Francis, trs. from SPA. LC 94-22056. (Theology & Liberation Ser.). 275p. 1994. reprint ed. pap. 17.00 (*0-88344-979-X*) Orbis Bks.

Casale, Anne. Italian Family Cooking: Like Mama Used to Make. 384p. (Orig.). 1984. pap. 12.50 (*0-449-90133-5*, Columbine) Fawcett.

Casale, Anne. The Long Life Cookbook: Delectable Recipes for Two. (Illus.). 400p. 1991. pap. 12.50 (*0-345-37376-6*) Ballantine Pub Grp.

Casale, Dean. Writing at Kean: A Student Guide. 80p. (C). 1998. student ed., per. 11.95 (*0-7872-5361-8*, 41536101) Kendall-Hunt.

***Casale, Fernando & Katcheroff, Gustavo.** Manual de Creacion de Paginas Web en Espanol con CD-ROM: Crea, Publica y Promociona Tu Sitio Web en Internet. (Manuales PC Users Ser.). (SPA., Illus.). 223p. 1999. pap. 17.90 incl. cd-rom (*987-9131-54-1*, Pub. by MP Ediciones) Am Wholesale.

Casale, Mick. Elm Circle. 1984. pap. 5.25 (*0-8222-0358-8*) Dramatists Play.

Casale, Ottavio M., ed. & tr. see Leopardi, Giacomo.

Casale, R. Flood & Landslides: Integrated Risk Assessment. LC 98-32410. 1999. write for info. (*3-540-64981-6*) Spr-Verlag.

Casale, S. & Stockdale, Eric. Criminal Justice under Stress. 314p. 1992. 38.00 (*1-85431-222-7*, Pub. by Blackstone Pr) Gaunt.

Casale, Silvia. Women Inside: The Experience of Women Remand Prisoners in Holloway. (C). 1988. 39.00 (*0-7855-6069-6*, Pub. by NCCL) St Mut.

— Women Inside: The Experience of Women Remand Prisoners in Holloway. 136p. (C). 1989. pap. text 35.00 (*0-900137-30-4*, Pub. by NCCL) St Mut.

Casale, Theresa M. Evangelium Vitae - a Bible Study: How to: Proclaim Life, Serve Life, & Celebrate Life. (Evangelium Vitae Ser.). 117p. (Orig.). 1996. pap. 3.00 (*1-890712-03-5*, EV3) Amer Life League.

***Casale, Victor.** The Button Men. 342p. 1999. write for info. (*0-7541-0528-8*, Pub. by Minerva Pr) Unity Dist.

Casali, Roderic F. Resolving Hiatus. LC 98-8789. (Outstanding Dissertations in Linguistics Ser.). 230p. 1998. 59.00 (*0-8153-3149-5*) Garland.

Casalilla, Bartolome Y., jt. ed. see Thompson, I. A.

Casalini, Max, et al. Food: Its Evolution Through the Ages. (Illus.). 64p. (J). 1998. reprint ed. text 17.00 (*0-7881-5197-5*) DIANE Pub.

Casalis, Jacques. Dictionnaire Laitier: Francais, Allemand, Anglais. (ENG, FRE & GER.). 1963. 85.00 (*0-8288-6787-9*, M-6063) Fr & Eur.

Casals, A., ed. Sensor Devices & Systems for Robotics. (NATO Asi Series F: Vol. 52). ix, 362p. 1989. 89.00 (*0-387-50885-6*) Spr-Verlag.

Casals, A. & De Almeida, A. T., eds. Experimental Robotics V: Fifth International Symposium Barcelona, Catalonia, June 15-18, 1997. (Lecture Notes in Control & Information Sciences: Vol. 232). xx, 708p. 1998. pap. 129.00 (*3-540-76218-3*) Spr-Verlag.

Casals, Felipe G. The Syncretic Society. Daniels, Guy, tr. from FRE. LC 80-6455. 103p. reprint ed. pap. 32.00 (*0-608-18121-8*, 203277300081) Bks Demand.

Casals, Juana Julia, jt. auth. see Xicoy, Reyes Pujol.

Casals, Pablo. Joys & Sorrows. 316p. Date not set. 24.95 (*0-8488-2231-5*) Amereon Ltd.

— Joys & Sorrows: Reflections. 314p. reprint ed. lib. bdg. 59.00 (*0-685-14850-5*) Rprt Serv.

Casamada, Jose, tr. see Christophers.

Casamassima, Christy. Bar Excellence: Designs for Pubs & Clubs. LC 98-2843. 1998. pap. 45.00 (*0-86636-681-4*) PBC Intl Inc.

— Bar Excellence: Designs for Pubs & Clubs. LC 98-2843. 2000. 45.00 (*0-86636-680-6*) PBC Intl Inc.

— Restaurant 2000: Dining Design III. LC 97-22351. 1997. pap. write for info. (*0-86636-587-7*) PBC Intl Inc.

— Restaurant 2000: Dining Design III. LC 97-22351. (Illus.). 176p. 1998. 45.00 (*0-86636-586-9*) PBC Intl Inc.

Casamassimo, Paul S., ed. Bright Futures in Practice: Oral Health. LC 96-70897. (Illus.). 144p. 1996. pap. 12.50 (*1-57285-038-8*) Nat Ctr Educ.

Casanave, Christine P. Strategies for Readers: A Reading Communication Text for Students of ESL, Bk. 1. (Illus.). 160p. (C). 1986. pap. text 28.00 (*0-13-850728-7*) P-H.

Casanave, Christine P. & Schecter, Sandra R., eds. On Becoming a Language Educator: Personal Essays on Professional Development. LC 96-39504. 232p. 1997. 55.00 (*0-8058-2263-1*); pap. 24.95 (*0-8058-2264-X*) L Erlbaum Assocs.

Casanave, Suki. Natural Wonders of New Hampshire: A Guide to Parks, Preserves & Wild Places. LC 93-37652. (Natural Wonders Ser.). (Illus.). 200p. (Orig.). 1994. pap. 9.95 (*1-56626-043-4*, Cntry Rds Pr) NTC Contemp Pub Co.

***Casanave, Suki.** Natural Wonders of New Hampshire: Exploring Wild & Scenic Places. 2nd ed. LC 98-25158. (Natural Wonders of... Ser.). (Illus.). 256p. (Orig.). 1998. pap. 14.95 (*1-56626-140-6*, 61406) NTC Contemp Pub Co.

Casanegra De Jantscher, Milka, jt. ed. see Bird, Richard M.

***Casanellas, Antonio.** Great Discoveries & Inventions, 5 bks. Incl. Great Discoveries & Inventions That Advanced Industry & Technology. LC 99-53264. (Illus.). 32p. (J). (gr. 4 up). 2000. lib. bdg. 21.27 (*0-8368-2583-7*); Great Discoveries & Inventions That Helped Explore Earth & Space. LC 99-53262. (Illus.). 32p. (J). (gr. 4 up). 2000. lib. bdg. 21.27 (*0-8368-2584-5*); Great Discoveries & Inventions That Improved Human Health. LC 99-53261. (Illus.). 32p. (J). (gr. 4 up). 2000. lib. bdg. 21.27 (*0-8368-2585-3*); Great Discoveries & Inventions That Improved Our Daily Lives. LC 99-53260. (Illus.). 32p. (J). (gr. 4 up). 2000. lib. bdg. 21.27 (*0-8368-2586-1*); Great Discoveries & Inventions That Improved Transportation. LC 99-53259. (Illus.). 32p. (J). (gr. 4 up). 2000. lib. bdg. 21.27 (*0-8368-2587-X*); (Illus.). (J). (gr. 4 up). 2000. Set lib. bdg. 106.35 (*0-8368-2582-9*) Gareth Stevens Inc.

Casani, E. Kane & Vander Does, Mark A., eds. Space Sciencecraft Control & Tracking in the New Millennium. 284p. 1996. 66.00 (*0-8194-2198-7*) SPIE.

Casanova. Memoirs: Selections from Casanova's "Story of My Life" 400p. 1999. 30.00 (*1-56886-063-3*, Pub. by Marsilio Pubs) Consort Bk Sales.

Casanova, Angelo, jt. ed. see Braccesi, Lorenzo.

Casanova, Carlamaria. Tebaldi: The Voice of an Angel. De Caro, Connie, tr. (Great Voices Ser.). (Illus.). 265p. 1995. 35.00 (*1-880909-40-5*) Baskerville.

Casanova, Cynthia, ed. see Ramos, Jan C.

Casanova De Seingalt, Jacques. Casanova's "Icosameron", or the Story of Edward & Elizabeth Who Spent 81 Years in the Land of the Megamicres, Original Inhabitants of Protocosmos in the Interior of Our Globe. abr. ed. Zurer, Rachel, tr. from FRE. LC 83-82006. (Illus.). 260p. 1986. 17.95 (*0-941752-02-X*); pap. 10.95 (*0-941752-00-3*) Jenna Pr.

Casanova de Seingault, Jacques. Histoire de Ma Vie. (FRE.). 375p. 1986. pap. 13.95 (*0-7859-2043-9*, 2070377601) Fr & Eur.

***Casanova, Edward V.** Subprime Lending. rev. ed. 194p. (C). 1999. pap. 45.00 (*1-57599-064-4*, Real Est Fin Pr) Mortgage Bankers.

***Casanova, Edward V. & Casanova, Sharon L.** Sub-Prime Lending. (Illus.). x, 155p. 1998. pap. 79.95 (*1-928588-00-X*) Lenders Inst.

Casanova, Giacomo. The Quotable Casanova. Vitelli, Tom, ed. & intro. by. LC 97-77714. (Illus.). 280p. 1998. pap. 8.95 (*1-883696-04-6*) EveryWare Bks.

Casanova, Giacomo & De Seingalt, Chevalier. Philocalies sur les Sottises des Mortels: Documents Casanoviens. Vitelli, Tom, ed. & pref. by. LC 93-71713. (Cahier Ser.: No. 3). (FRE.). 71p. 1993. lib. bdg. 25.00 (*1-883696-00-3*) EveryWare Bks.

Casanova, Giacomo & Trask, Willard R. History of My Life Vols. 1 & 2: Giacomo Casanova, Chevalier de Seingalt, Vols. 1 & 2. LC 97-70304. (Illus.). 630p. 1997. reprint ed. pap. 15.95 (*0-8018-5662-0*) Johns Hopkins.

— History of My Life Vols. 3 & 4: Giacomo Casanova, Chevalier de Seingalt, Vols. 3 & 4. LC 97-70304. (Illus.). 704p. 1997. reprint ed. pap. 15.95 (*0-8018-5663-9*) Johns Hopkins.

— History of My Life Vols. 5 & 6: Giacomo Casanova, Chevalier de Seingalt, Vols. 5 & 6. LC 97-70304. (Illus.). 635p. 1997. reprint ed. pap. 15.95 (*0-8018-5664-7*) Johns Hopkins.

— History of My Life Vols. 7 & 8: Giacomo Casanova, Chevalier de Seingalt, Vols. 7 & 8. LC 97-70304. (Illus.). 658p. 1997. reprint ed. pap. 15.95 (*0-8018-5665-5*) Johns Hopkins.

— History of My Life Vols. 9 & 10: Giacomo Casanova, Chevalier de Seingalt, Vols. 9 & 10. LC 97-70304. (Illus.). 812p. 1997. reprint ed. pap. 15.95 (*0-8018-5666-3*) Johns Hopkins.

— History of My Life Vols. 11 & 12: Giacomo Casanova, Chevalier de Seingalt, Vols. 11 & 12. LC 97-70304. (Illus.). 812p. 1997. reprint ed. pap. 15.95 (*0-8018-5667-1*) Johns Hopkins.

Casanova, Humberto & Stam, Jeff. El Credo Apostolico: Basico. (SPA.). pap. 5.25 (*1-55955-169-0*, 6771-4551C) Libros Desafio.

— El Credo Apostolico: Basico y Superior. (SPA.). pap. 7.95 (*1-55955-172-0*, 6771-4612C) Libros Desafio.

— El Credo Apostolico: Superior. (SPA.). pap. 5.25 (*1-55955-171-2*, 6771-4511C) Libros Desafio.

Casanova, Humberto, ed. see Ridderbos, Herman.

Casanova, Humberto, tr. see Erdman, Charles.

Casanova, Humberto R., tr. see Harrison, Everett F., ed.

Casanova, J. Histoire de Ma Vie. (Folio Ser.: No. 1760). (FRE.). pap. 13.95 (*2-07-037760-1*) Schoenhof.

***Casanova, J. L., ed.** Remote Sensing in the 21st Century: Economic & Environmental Applications/Proceedings of the 19th EARSeL Symposium, Valladolid, Spain, 31 May - 2 June 1999. (Illus.). 624p. 2000. 99.00 (*90-5809-096-5*, Pub. by A A Balkema) Ashgate Pub Co.

Casanova, James E., ed. Faculty Practice Plans: Models for a New Health Care Age. LC 97-71052. 150p. 1997. pap. 48.00 (*0-924674-54-7*) Am Coll Phys Execs.

— Tools for the Task: The Role of Clinical Guidelines. LC 97-72633. 224p. 1997. 32.00 (*0-924674-55-5*) Am Coll Phys Execs.

Casanova, Jose. Public Religions in the Modern World. LC 93-37485. 330p. 1994. pap. text 18.00 (*0-226-09535-5*); lib. bdg. 49.95 (*0-226-09534-7*) U Ch Pr.

***Casanova, Joseph, ed.** The Borane, Carborane, Carbocation Continuum. LC 97-31255. 437p. 1998. 110.00 (*0-471-18075-0*, Wiley-Interscience) Wiley.

Casanova, Judith Boyce. From Sacred Lies to Holy Wisdom: A Faith Journey in a Postmodern World. LC 99-163016. 132p. 1998. pap. 14.95 (*0-9663255-7-5*) Pinch Pubns.

When all you've ever believed turns out to be a lie, when try as you might, you cannot hold on to what you have been taught, when you look for God & come up against brick walls, & when you still refuse to let it go, but struggle on until belief & life experience support & validate each other, then you move from sacred lies to holy wisdom, & you discover that the journey was worth the struggle, that all of life has become sacred, & that now, you are truly happy. This is a record of a faith that refused to give up, & quite possibly of a God who doesn't give up either. It calls attention to the harm done by Christian teaching, both as experienced personally at the hands of believers & as adopted by the wider culture, but the voice calling is unmistakably rooted in a living faith. John Cobb has called FROM SACRED LIES TO HOLY WISDOM "a book of uncompromising honesty & profound insight." Butch Henderson proclaims every page "a lived moment into meaning." Judith Merkel Riley says that "the reader who enters this lucid text" will come away "clearer in mind & closer to his or her own God." To order contact Pinch Publications, 691 W. 12th St., Claremont, CA 91711, Tel. 909-625-5994.

Publisher Paid Annotation.

***Casanova, Karen.** Letting Go of Debt: Meditations on Growing Richer One Day at a Time. 372p. 2000. pap. 12.00 (*1-56838-367-3*) Hazelden.

Casanova, M. A. The Concurrency Control Problem for Database Systems. (Lecture Notes in Computer Science Ser.: Vol. 116). 175p. 1981. 23.00 (*0-387-10845-9*) Spr-Verlag.

Casanova, Maria A., ed. Vocabulario Basico en la E. G. B. Ministerio de Educacion y Ciencia, 3 vols. (SPA.). 1940p. 1990. 295.00 (*84-239-5632-6*) Elliots Bks.

***Casanova, Mary.** The Hunter: A Chinese Folktale. LC 99-32166. (Illus.). (J). 2000. 16.95 (*0-689-82906-X*) S&S Childrens.

Casanova, Mary. Moose Tracks. LC 94-19907. (Illus.). 128p. (J). (gr. 4-7). 1995. 14.95 (*0-7868-0042-9*, Pub. by Hyprn Child); lib. bdg. 14.89 (*0-7868-2035-7*, Pub. by Hyprn Child) Little.

— Moose Tracks. (J). 1997. 10.05 (*0-606-13082-9*, Pub. by Turtleback) Demco.

— Moose Tracks. LC 94-19907. 128p. (J). (gr. 4-7). 1997. reprint ed. pap. 4.95 (*0-7868-1137-4*, Pub. by Hyprn Ppbks) Little.

***Casanova, Mary.** November Chill. 144p. (J). (gr. 3-7). 2000. 14.99 (*0-7868-0547-1*, Pub. by Disney Pr) Time Warner.

Casanova, Mary. One Dog Canoe. LC 98-47172. 1999. write for info. (*0-7894-2582-3*) DK Pub Inc.

— Riot. LC 96-6890. (Illus.). 128p. (J). (gr. 4-7). 1996. 13.45 (*0-7868-0215-4*, Pub. by Hyprn Child); lib. bdg. 13.89 (*0-7868-2204-X*, Pub. by Hyprn Child) Little.

— Riot. LC 96-6890. 128p. (J). (gr. 4-7). 1998. pap. 4.95 (*0-7868-1249-4*, Pub. by Hyprn Ppbks) Little.

— Riot. (J). 1998. 10.05 (*0-606-13743-2*, Pub. by Turtleback) Demco.

— Stealing Thunder. LC 98-40595. (J). 1999. lib. bdg. 15.49 (*0-7868-2268-6*, Pub. by Hyperion) Little.

***Casanova, Mary.** Stealing Thunder. LC 98-40595. 144p. (J). (gr. 3-7). 1999. 14.45 (*0-7868-0324-X*, Pub. by Hyperion) Time Warner.

— Stealing Thunder. 144p. (J). (gr. 3-7). 2000. pap. 5.99 (*0-7868-1480-2*, Pub. by Hyprn Child) Time Warner.

— Wolf Shadows. LC 97-7097. (Illus.). 144p. (J). (gr. 4 up). 1997. lib. bdg. 14.89 (*0-7868-2269-4*, Pub. by Hyprn Child) Time Warner.

— Wolf Shadows. LC 97-7097. (Illus.). 144p. (YA). (gr. 4 up). 1997. 14.95 (*0-7868-0325-8*, Pub. by Hyprn Child) Time Warner.

***Casanova, Mary.** Wolf Shadows. LC 97-7097. 144p. (J). (gr. 3-7). 1999. pap. 5.99 (*0-7868-1340-7*, Pub. by Hyprn Child) Time Warner.

An Asterisk (*) at the beginning of an entry indicates that the title is appearing for the first time.

— Wolf Shadows. 144p. (J). 1999. pap. 5.99 (*0-7868-1415-2*) Little.

Casanova, Nick. The Machiavellian's Guide to Womanizing. 128p. 1995. pap. 8.95 (*0-7867-0203-6*) Carroll & Graf.

— Machiavellian's Guide to Womanizing. 1999. pap. text 5.99 (*0-7858-1074-9*) Bk Sales Inc.

Casanova, Noelia R. Diccionario de Educacion Especial. (SPA.). 140p. 1995. pap. write for info. (*0-929441-00-1*) Pubns Puertorriquenas.

— Educacion Especial del Nino Excepcional. (SPA.). 486p. 1992. pap. write for info. (*0-929441-30-3*) Pubns Puertorriquenas.

— En Torno a Retardo Mental. (SPA.). 310p. 1997. pap. write for info. (*1-881713-03-2*) Pubns Puertorriquenas.

Casanova, Olga. La Charca de Manuel Zeno Gandia: Temas y Estilo. (SPA.). 160p. (Orig.). 1992. pap. text. write for info. (*1-56328-022-1*) Edit Plaza Mayor.

Casanova, Paul. Dictionnaire Tauromachique. (FRE.). 190p. 1982. pap. 75.00 (*0-7859-8126-8*, 2862760439) Fr & Eur.

Casanova, Richard L. & Ratkevich, Ronald P. Illustrated Guide to Fossil Collecting, Vol. 1. 3rd rev. ed. LC 81-18788. (Illus.). 240p. 1981. pap. 9.95 (*0-87961-113-8*) Naturegraph.

Casanova, Ron. Each One Teach One: Up & Out of Poverty: Memoirs of a Street Activist. 260p. 1996. 22.95 (*1-880684-37-3*) Curbstone.

Casanova, Sharon L., jt. auth. see Casanova, Edward V.

Casanova, Ursula. Elementary School Secretaries: The Women in the Principal's Office. LC 91-13613. 184p. 1991. 55.95 (*0-8039-3803-9*, D1478); pap. text 24.95 (*0-8039-3804-7*, D1478) Corwin Pr.

Casanova, Ursula, jt. auth. see Berliner, David C.

Casanova, Ursula, jt. ed. see Arias, M. Beatriz.

Casanova, Viviana, tr. see Erdman, Charles.

Casanovas, Joan. Bread or Bullets! Urban Labor & Spanish Colonialism in Cuba, 1850-1898. LC 98-25323. (Latin American Ser.). 340p. 1998. pap. 19.95 (*0-8229-5675-6*); text 45.00 (*0-8229-4070-1*) U of Pittsburgh Pr.

***Casanta, Isabelle.** Fickle Flights of Fancy. 2000. pap. write for info. (*1-58235-374-3*) Watermrk Pr.

Casarella, Peter & Gomez, Raul, eds. El Cuerpo de Cristo: The Hispanic Presence in the U. S. Catholic Church. LC 98-71206. 324p. 1998. pap. 19.95 (*0-8245-1741-5*, Herdr & Herdr) Crossroad NY.

Casarella, Peter J. & Schner, George P. Christian Spirituality & the Culture of Modernity: Essays in Conversation with Louis Dupre. LC 98-4440. 1999. 28.00 (*0-8028-3812-X*) Eerdmans.

Casarella, Peter J. & Schner, George P., eds. Christian Spirituality & the Culture of Modernity: The Thought of Louis Dupre. 359p. 1998. pap. 28.00 (*0-8028-4590-8*) Eerdmans.

Casares, Adolfo B. La Invencion de Morel (The Invention of Morel) (SPA.). 112p. 1997. pap. 10.95 (*0-14-026084-6*, Penguin Bks) Viking Penguin.

Casares, Adolfo Bioy, see Bioy Casares, Adolfo.

Casares, Angel J. Curso de Filosofia. 2nd rev. ed. 261p. (C). 1981. text 9.00 (*0-8477-2821-8*); pap. text 7.50 (*0-8477-2822-6*) U of PR Pr.

— Dos Palabras Sobre las Palabras: Apuntes sobre la traduccion y sus problemas. LC 82-4938. (SPA.). 118p. 1982. pap. 5.00 (*0-8477-3503-6*) U of PR Pr.

— Sobre la Esencia del Hombre. LC 78-15645. 104p. 1979. pap. 5.00 (*0-8477-2818-8*) U of PR Pr.

Casares Long, J. J., jt. ed. see Power, H.

***Casares, Margery Harkness.** Song of Innocence. Schulte, Colleen, ed. 1999. pap. 6.50 (*1-929613-02-4*) Avid MI.

Casares Sanchez, Julio. Diccionario Ideologico de la Lengua Castellana. 2nd ed. (SPA.). 1446p. 1992. 185.00 (*0-7859-4948-8*) Fr & Eur.

Casarett, George W. Radiation Histopathology, 2 vols., Vol. 1. 160p. 1981. 90.00 (*0-8493-5357-2*, RA1231, CRC Reprint) Franklin.

— Radiation Histopathology, 2 vols., Vol. 2. 176p. 1981. 89.00 (*0-8493-5358-0*, RA1231) CRC Pr.

Casarino, Cesare, jt. auth. see Makdisi, Saree.

Casarino, Cesare, jt. ed. see Makdisi, Saree.

Casarjian, Robin. Casas de Curacion: Una Guia Para el Presidiario Hacia el Poder Y la Libertad Interiores. Raiselle, Naomi, ed. Mellin, Marc, tr. LC 97-73488.Tr. of Houses of Healing: A Prisoner's Guide to Inner Power & Freedom. (SPA.). 278p. 1997. pap. 14.00 (*0-9644933-1-4*) Lionheart Found.

— Forgiveness: A Bold Choice for a Peaceful Heart. 256p. 1992. pap. 12.95 (*0-553-35236-9*) Bantam.

— Houses of Healing: A Prisoner's Guide to Inner Power & Freedom. Johnson, Jan et al, eds. 256p. (Orig.). 1995. pap. 12.00 (*0-9644933-0-6*) Lionheart Found.

Casaro, Jesus M. Las Sombras De La Caverna. 1998. pap. text 11.95 (*84-204-4801-X*) Santillana.

Casas. Paella Perfect! Date not set. pap. 15.95 (*0-8050-5624-6*, Owl) H Holt & Co.

***Casas-Alvero, E.** Singularities of Plane Curves. (London Mathematical Society Lecture Note Ser.). (Illus.). 350p. 2000. pap. write for info. (*0-521-78959-1*) Cambridge U Pr.

Casas-Alvero, E. & Xambo-Descamps, S. The Enumerative Theory of Conics after Halphen. (Lecture Notes in Mathematics Ser.: Vol. 1196). ix, 130p. 1986. 25.95 (*0-387-16495-2*) Spr-Verlag.

Casas, Arnoldo J., tr. see Johns, Helen.

Casas, Bartholome De Las. The Spanish Colonie, or Briefe Chronicle or the Acts & Gestes of the Spaniardes in the West Indies. LC 77-6866. (English Experience Ser.: No. 859). 1977. reprint ed. lib. bdg. 27.50 (*90-221-0859-7*) Walter J Johnson.

Casas, Bartholomew Las, see Las Casas, Bartholomew.

Casas, Bartolome de las, see De las Casas, Bartolome.

Casas, Celso A. De, see De Casas, Celso A.

Casas, Cristobal De Las, see De Las Casas, Cristobal.

Casas, Eduardo, ed. Control of Partial Differential Equations & Applications: Proceedings of the IFIP WG 7.2 International Conference, Laredo, Vol. 1. LC 95-34363. (Lecture Notes in Pure & Applied Mathematics Ser.: Vol. 174). (Illus.). 320p. 1995. pap. text 135.00 (*0-8247-9607-1*) Dekker.

Casas Internacional Editors. Best of Lofts. (Illus.). 216p. 1998. 35.00 (*950-9575-84-4*, Pub. by Libreria Tecnica) Spec Mrkting Grp.

Casas Internacionals Editors. Best of Bars & Restaurants. (Illus.). 216p. 1998. 35.00 (*950-9575-86-0*, Pub. by Libreria Tecnica) Spec Mrkting Grp.

Casas, J. Manuel, jt. auth. see Ponterotto, Joseph G.

Casas, Juan G. Anarchist Organisation: The History of the F. A. I. Bluestein, Abe, tr. from SPA. Orig. Title: Historia de la F. A. I.. 261p. 1986. 47.99 (*0-920057-40-3*, Pub. by Black Rose); pap. 18.99 (*0-920057-38-1*, Pub. by Black Rose) Consort Bk Sales.

Casas, Luis A. Cuentos Para la Medianoche. LC 91-78013. (Coleccion Caniqui). (SPA., Illus.). 189p. (Orig.). 1992. pap. 18.00 (*0-89729-632-X*) Ediciones.

— Trece Cuentos Nerviosos: Narraciones Burlescas y Diabolicas. LC 89-80763. (Coleccion Caniqui). (SPA.). 143p. (Orig.). 1990. pap. 12.00 (*0-89729-501-3*) Ediciones.

Casas, Luis Puig. Personal Memories of the Spanish Civil War: Luis Puig Casas. Puig, Idoya, ed. LC 99-23079. (Spanish Studies: Vol. 5). (CAT & ENG.). 280p. 1999. text 89.95 (*0-7734-7996-1*) E Mellen.

Casas, M., et al, eds. Condensed Matter Theories, Vol. 10. (Illus.). 551p. (C). 1995. lib. bdg. 195.00 (*1-56072-223-1*) Nova Sci Pubs.

Casas, M. & Wiley, M. Diagnosis Related Groups in Europe: Uses & Perspectives. LC 93-33225. 1993. 69.95 (*0-387-57168-X*) Spr-Verlag.

Casas, Myrna. La Trampa. (UPREX, Teatro y Cine Ser.: No. 36). 179p. (C). 1975. pap. 1.50 (*0-8477-0036-4*) U of PR Pr.

Casas, Penelope. Delicioso: The Regional Cooking of Spain. LC 95-34171. 448p. 1996. 35.00 (*0-679-43055-5*) Knopf.

— Delicioso! The Regional Cooking of Spain. 1996. 30.00 (*0-614-95772-9*) Knopf.

— Discovering Spain. 1992. pap. 23.50 (*0-394-57376-5*) Knopf.

— Discovering Spain. 608p. 1996. pap. 25.00 (*0-679-76569-7*) Random.

— Foods & Wines of Spain. LC 82-47830. (Illus.). 1982. 30.00 (*0-394-51348-7*) Knopf.

— Paella! Spectacular Rice Dishes from Spain. LC 98-34727. (Illus.). 226p. 1999. 30.00 (*0-8050-5623-8*) H Holt & Co.

— Tapas: The Little Dishes of Spain. LC 85-40160. (Illus.). 256p. (Orig.). 1985. pap. 19.95 (*0-394-74235-4*) Knopf.

Casas-Vazquez, J., et al, eds. Recent Developments in Nonequilibrium Thermodynamics: Fluids & Related Topics. (Lecture Notes in Physics Ser.: Vol. 253). x, 392p. 1986. 59.95 (*0-387-16489-8*) Spr-Verlag.

— Recent Developments in Nonequilibrium Thermodynamics: Proceedings of the Meeting Held at Bellaterra School of Thermodynamics, Autonomous University of Barcelona, Spain, Sept. 26-30, 1983. (Lecture Notes in Physics Ser.: Vol. 199). xiii, 485p. 1984. 47.95 (*0-387-12927-8*) Spr-Verlag.

Casas-Vazquez, J. & Jou, D., eds. Rheological Modelling: Thermodynamical & Statistical Approaches: Proceedings of the Meeting Held at the Bellatara School of Thermodynamics, Autonomous University of Barcelona, Sant Feliu de Gu, Catalonia, Spain, 24-28 Sept. 1990. x, 378p. 1991. 56.95 (*0-387-53996-4*) Spr-Verlag.

Casas, Walter M. De Las, see De Las Casas, Walter M.

Casasayas, Josefina & Llibre, Jaume. Qualitative Analysis of the Anistropic Kepler Problem. LC 84-18521. (Memoirs of the American Mathematical Society Ser.: No. 52/312). 115p. 1984. pap. 21.00 (*0-8218-2309-4*, MEMO/52/312) Am Math.

Casasent, David. Electronic Circuits. (Illus.). 400p. (C). 1982. pap. text 30.00 (*0-13-250233-X*) P-H.

Casasent, David, ed. Optical Data Processing: Applications. (Topics in Applied Physics Ser.: Vol. 23). (Illus.). 1978. 70.95 (*0-387-08453-3*) Spr-Verlag.

***Casasent, David P., ed.** Intelligent Robots & Computer Vision XVIII. 1999. pap. text 92.00 (*0-8194-3430-2*) SPIE.

Casasent, David P., ed. Intelligent Robots & Computer Vision XV Vol. 2904: Algorithms, Techniques, Active Vision & Materials Handling. 592p. 1996. 110.00 (*0-8194-2306-8*) SPIE.

— Intelligent Robots & Computer Vision XVI Vol. 3208: Algorithms, Techniques, Active Vision & Materials Handling. 572p. 1997. 99.00 (*0-8194-2640-7*) SPIE.

— Intelligent Robots & Computer Vision XVII Vol. 3522: Algorithms, Techniques & Active Vision. 1998. 99.00 (*0-8194-2983-X*) SPIE.

Casasent, David P. & Chao, Tien-Hsin, eds. Optical Pattern Recognition, No. 8. 55p. 1997. pap. 99.00 (*0-8194-2488-9*) SPIE.

— Optical Pattern Recognition IX, Vol. 3386. 410p. 1998. 99.00 (*0-8194-2835-3*) SPIE.

***Casasent, David P. & Chao, Tien-Hsin, eds.** Optical Pattern Recognition X. 424p. 1999. pap. text 92.00 (*0-8194-3189-3*) SPIE.

Casasent, David P. & Tescher, Andrew G., eds. Hybrid Image & Signal Processing VI. (Proceedings of SPIE Ser.: Vol. 3389). 244p. 1998. 59.00 (*0-8194-2838-8*) SPIE.

Casasola, Agustin V. Jefes, Heroes y Caudillos (Commanders, Heroes & Leaders) (SPA., Illus.). 109p. 1986. pap. 11.99 (*968-16-2204-9*, Pub. by Fondo) Continental Bk.

Casasus, Juan J. Jalones de Gloria Mambisa. (SPA.). 1969. pap. 9.95 (*0-89729-119-0*) Ediciones.

Casatelli-Vivenzio, Carol. Frankie Castle & the Crackers' Holiday Adventures. (Illus.). 94p. (Orig.). (J). 1994. pap. text. write for info. (*0-9641300-1-7*) Casatelli-Vivenzio.

— The Strangest Thing about Frankie Castle. (Illus.). 54p. (Orig.). (J). (gr. 4-5). 1994. pap. write for info. (*0-9641300-0-9*) Casatelli-Vivenzio.

Casati, G., ed. Chaotic Behavior in Quantum Systems: Theory & Applications. (NATO ASI Series B, Physics: Vol. 120). 380p. 1985. 89.50 (*0-306-41898-3*, Plenum Trade) Perseus Pubng.

***Casati, G., et al, eds.** New Directions in Quantum Chaos. (International School of Physics Enrico Fermi Ser.: Vol. 143). 530p. 2000. 126.00 (*1-58603-074-4*) IOS Press.

Casati, G., et al, eds. Quantum Chaos: Proceedings of the International School of Physics "Enrico Fermi," Course CXIX, 23 July-2 August, 1991. (Enrico Fermi International School of Physics Ser.: Vol. 119). 432p. 1993. 210.00 (*0-444-81588-0*, North Holland) Elsevier.

Casati, Giulio & Cerdeira, Hilda A., eds. Chaos in Mesoscopic Systems: Proceedings of the Miniworkshop on Nonlinearity: Chaos in Mesoscopic Systems & the Adriatico Research Conference on Mesoscopic Systems & Chaos: a Novel Approach ICTP, Trieste, Italy 26 July - 6 August 1993. (Series on Nonlinear Science: Series B). 220p. 1995. text 56.00 (*981-02-2171-1*, N-P2663) World Scientific Pub.

Casati, Giulio & Chirikov, Boris, eds. Quantum Chaos: Between Order & Disorder. LC 93-37135. (Illus.). 699p. (C). 1995. text 115.00 (*0-521-43291-X*) Cambridge U Pr.

Casati, Robert & Varzi, Achille C., eds. Fifty Years of Events: An Annotated Bibliography, 1947-1997. 402p. (C). 1997. 33.00 (*0-912632-66-6*) Philos Document.

Casati, Roberto & Tappolet, Christine, eds. European Review of Philosophy Vol. 3: Response-Dependence. 256p. (C). 1998. 59.95 (*1-57586-105-4*); pap. 22.95 (*1-57586-104-6*) CSLI.

Casati, Roberto & Varzi, Achille C. Holes & Other Superficialities. (Illus.). 288p. 1994. 40.00 (*0-262-03211-2*, Bradford Bks) MIT Pr.

— Holes & Other Superficialities. 1995. pap. text 16.50 (*0-262-53133-X*, Bradford Bks) MIT Pr.

— Parts & Places: The Structures of Spatial Representation. LC 98-51512. (Illus.). 429p. 1999. 35.00 (*0-262-03266-X*, Bradford Bks) MIT Pr.

Casati, Roberto, jt. ed. see Varzi, Achille C.

***Casatto, Giovanna.** Bitch in Heat, Vol. 1. (Illus.). 112p. 1999. pap. 18.95 (*1-56097-345-5*, Eros Comics) Fantagraph Bks.

Casaubon, Isaac. De Satyrica Graecorum Poesi & Romanorum Satira. LC 72-13784. (LAT.). 392p. 1973. reprint ed. lib. bdg. 60.00 (*0-8201-1115-5*) Schol Facsimiles.

Casaubon, Meric. A Letter of Meric Casaubon to Peter du Moulin Concerning Natural Experimental Philosophie. LC 76-47045. 600p. 1976. reprint ed. 90.00 (*0-8201-1284-4*) Schol Facsimiles.

— Treatise Concerning Enthusiasme. LC 77-119864. 324p. 1970. reprint ed. 50.00 (*0-8201-1077-9*) Schol Facsimiles.

Casaubon, Meric, jt. ed. see Dee, John.

Casaus, Victor, et al. Somos - We Are: Five Contemporary Cuban Poets. Whitney, Anita, ed. (Illus.). 48p. (Orig.). 1970. pap. 3.95 (*0-87810-000-8*) Times Change.

Casavant, Ken. Agricultural Economics & Management. LC 98-16481. 434p. (C). 1998. 96.00 (*0-13-660184-7*) P-H.

Casavant, Kenneth & Infanger, Craig. Agricultural Economics. (C). 1985. text 18.95 (*0-8359-0185-8*) P-H.

Casavant, T. & Singhal, M. Distributed Computing Systems (Readings in) LC 92-40164. 632p. 1993. 65.00 (*0-8186-3032-9*, 3032) IEEE Comp Soc.

Casavant, Thomas L., et al, eds. Parallel Computers: Theory & Practice. LC 95-10090. (Reprint Collection). 432p. 1995. 58.00 (*0-8186-5162-8*, BP05162) IEEE Comp Soc.

Casaverde, Mateo, jt. auth. see Forbush, Scott E.

Casazza, John A., jt. auth. see O'Mara, W. Paul.

Casazza, Martha E. & Silverman, Sharon L. Learning Assistance & Development Education: A Guide for Effective Practice. LC 95-45303. (Higher & Adult Education Ser.). 256p. 1996. 34.95 (*0-7879-0211-X*) Jossey-Bass.

Casazza, Ornella. Masaccio. (Grandes Maestros del Arte Ser.). (SPA., Illus.). 80p. 1993. pap. 12.99 (*1-878351-29-X*) Riverside NY.

— Masaccio: And the Brancacci Chapel. (Library of Great Masters). (Illus.). 80p. (Orig.). 1990. pap. 14.99 (*1-878351-11-7*) Riverside NY.

Casazza, Ornella, jt. auth. see Baldini, Umberto.

Casazza, P. G. & Shura, T. J. Tsirelson's Space. (Lecture Notes in Mathematics Ser.: Vol. 1363). 204p. 1989. pap. 21.10 (*0-318-41335-3*) Spr-Verlag.

Casberg, Melvin A. Death Stalks the Punjab. LC 80-23558. (Illus.). 240p. (Orig.). 1981. pap. 6.95 (*0-89407-045-2*) Strawberry Hill.

— Dowry of Death. (Illus.). 240p. (Orig.). 1984. pap. 6.95 (*0-89407-062-2*) Strawberry Hill.

— Five Rivers to Death. LC 82-5814. (Illus.). 240p. (Orig.). 1982. pap. 6.95 (*0-89407-051-7*) Strawberry Hill.

Casberg, Olivia. Around the World in Sixty Years. 1993. pap. 12.00 (*0-933380-14-3*) Olive Pr Pubns.

— Mission Through a Woman's Eyes. LC 84-27232. 120p. (Orig.). 1985. pap. 6.95 (*0-933380-31-3*) Olive Pr Pubns.

— My Sourdough Dad. LC 89-8644. 168p. (Orig.). 1989. pap. 8.00 (*0-933380-07-0*) Olive Pr Pubns.

— Wind Beneath His Wings. LC 99-217333. (Illus.). 200p. 1998. pap. 17.00 (*0-933380-34-8*) Olive Pr Pubns.

— Women of My Other Worlds. LC 84-27221. 100p. (Orig.). 1985. pap. 5.95 (*0-933380-30-5*) Olive Pr Pubns.

Cascadden, Edith V. History of Lapel & Fishersburg Indiana, from Pioneer Days to August, 1938. (Illus.). 201p. 1997. reprint ed. lib. bdg. 29.00 (*0-8328-7091-9*) Higginson Bk Co.

Cascardi, Andrea E. A Parent's Guide to Video & Audio Cassettes for Children. 1987. mass mkt. 7.95 (*0-446-38513-1*, Pub. by Warner Bks) Little.

Cascardi, Anthony J. The Bounds of Reason: Cervantes, Dostoevsky, Flaubert. LC 85-99994. 288p. 1986. text 57.50 (*0-231-06212-5*) Col U Pr.

— Consequences of Enlightenment. LC 98-21467. (Literature, Culture, Theory Ser.: No. 30). 280p. 1999. text 54.95 (*0-521-48149-X*) Cambridge U Pr.

— Consequences of Enlightenment. LC 98-21467. (Literature, Culture, Theory Ser.: No. 30). 280p. (C). 1999. pap. text 19.95 (*0-521-48490-1*) Cambridge U Pr.

— Ideologies of History in the Spanish Golden Age. LC 96-31045. (Penn State Studies in Romance Literatures). 1997. 55.00 (*0-271-01667-1*); pap. 19.95 (*0-271-01668-X*) Pa St U Pr.

Cascetta, Furio. Flowmeters: A Comprehensive Survey & Guide to Selection. rev. ed. LC 88-8871. (Illus.). 41p. reprint ed. pap. 30.00 (*0-608-20292-4*, 207155100001) Bks Demand.

Caschera, Louis G. Strictly Golf Balls: The Golf Ball Handbook. rev. ed. 1998. pap. 12.95 (*0-9644781-1-0*) StrictlyGolf.

Casci, Corrado, ed. Recent Advances in the Aerospace Sciences. 454p. 1985. 120.00 (*0-306-41079-6*, Plenum Trade) Perseus Pubng.

Cascia Hall Prepartory School Staff. Gourmet Our Way. 1995. 22.95 (*0-9643143-0-4*) Cascia Hall.

Casciani, Clement, jt. auth. see La Rue, Andre.

Casciani, Elizabeth. Oh, How We Danced! 152p. 1996. pap. 40.00 (*1-873644-29-9*, Pub. by Mercat Pr Bks) St Mut.

Casciani, Joseph M. & Rest, Stanley M. Aging & Mental Health: A Comprehensive Guide to Working with the Elderly. LC 87-73536. 520p. (C). 1988. pap. text 94.95 (*0-9619913-0-5*) Alliance Pr.

Casciani, Paul S. The Technique of Decorative Stained Glass. 120p. 1989. pap. 11.95 (*0-486-26157-3*) Dover.

Casciaro, J. M. & Monforte, J. M. God, the World & Man in the Message of the Bible. LC 96-229059. (ENG.). 464p. 1997. pap. 24.95 (*1-85182-148-1*, Pub. by Four Cts Pr) Intl Spec Bk.

Casciaro, Jose M., jt. auth. see Members of the Faculty of Theology of the Universi.

Casciati, Fabio. Civil Infrastructure Systems: Proceedings of the 3rd International Symposium on Intelligent Renewal. 1998. 68.00 (*981-02-3540-2*) World Scientific Pub.

— Dynamic Motion: Chaotic & Stochastic Behaviour. (CISM International Centre for Mechanical Sciences Ser.: No. 340). 325p. 1994. 76.95 (*0-387-82517-7*) Spr-Verlag.

Casciati, Fabio. Proceeding of 3rd World Conference on Structure. text. write for info. (*0-471-48980-8*) Wiley.

Casciati, Fabio & Roberts, J. B. Mathematical Models for Structural Reliability Analysis. LC 96-28018. 384p. 1996. lib. bdg. 95.00 (*0-8493-9631-X*) CRC Pr.

Casciati, Fabio & Roberts, J. B., eds. Reliability Problems: General Principles & Applications in Mechanics of Solids & Structures. (CISM International Centre for Mechanical Sciences Ser.: Vol. 317). (Illus.). vi, 271p. 1991. 71.95 (*0-387-82319-0*) Spr-Verlag.

Casciato, Arther D., ed. see Kromer, Tom.

Casciato, Dennis A. Manual of Bed Oncology. 1988. 10.95 (*0-316-13069-9*, Little Brwn Med Div) Lppncott W & W.

Casciato, Dennis A. & Lowitz, Barry B. Manual of Clinical Oncology. 4th ed. 704p. spiral bd. 39.95 (*0-7817-2159-8*) Lppncott W & W.

Casciato, Dennis A. & Lowitz, Barry B., eds. Manual of Clinical Oncology. 3rd ed. LC 95-9993. 720p. 1995. spiral bd. 37.95 (*0-316-13279-9*) Lppncott W & W.

Casciato, Jayne. Rock & Roll Survivors to Superstars. 1998. pap. write for info. (*1-57553-905-5*) Watermrk Pr.

— To You with Love. (Orig.). 1997. pap. write for info. (*1-57553-487-8*) Watermrk Pr.

Casciero, Albert J., jt. auth. see Sanjurjo, Annick.

Cascino, Gregory & Jack, Clifford R. Neuroimaging in Epilepsy: Principles & Practice. LC 96-32628. 289p. 1996. text 155.00 (*0-7506-9716-4*) Buttrwrth-Heinemann.

***Cascio.** The Cost Factor: Financial Impact of Human Resources in Corporation. 1999. pap. 27.95 (*0-324-02739-7*) Thomson Learn.

Cascio. Managing Human Resources. 6th ed. 2001. 64.00 (*0-07-231716-7*) McGraw.

Cascio, Chuck. School Daze & the Education Maze: A Teacher Talks to Parents. 173p. (Orig.). 1992. pap. 55.00 (*1-878907-39-5*) TechBooks.

Cascio, Danis. dBASE 5.0 for DOS. (C). Date not set. pap. write for info. (*0-395-78008-X*) HM.

Cascio, Danis & Podos, Arlene. Applying dBASE 5.0 for DOS: A Project Approach. 320p. (C). 1995. spiral bd. 30.76 (*0-395-73659-5*) HM.

— Applying dBASE 5.0 for DOS: A Project Approach. (C). 1996. text, teacher ed. 11.96 (*0-395-73661-7*) HM.

— Applying dBASE 5.0 for Windows: A Project Approach. 320p. (C). 1997. spiral bd. 33.16 (*0-395-73663-3*) HM.

— Applying dBASE 5.0 for Windows: A Project Approach. (C). 1998. text, teacher ed. 11.96 (*0-395-73665-X*) HM.

Cascio, Dorothy M., jt. auth. see Hodgetts, Richard M.

Cascio, Elena, tr. see Patin, Stanislav.

Cascio, J., et al. ISO 14000 Guide: The New International Environmental Management Standards. (Illus.). 221p. 1996. 54.95 (*0-07-011625-3*) McGraw.

***Cascio, Joseph, ed.** The ISO 14000 Handbook. (Illus.). 764p. 1999. 93.50 (*0-87389-440-5*) ASQ Qual Pr.

C

Cascio, Pat & McSweeney, John. SWAT Battle Tactics: How to Organize, Train, & Equip a SWAT Team for Law Enforcement or Self-Defense. LC 97-121314. (Illus.). 128p. 1996. pap. 17.00 (*0-87364-900-1*) Paladin Pr.

Cascio, Terese A. Holiday Bows for the Beginner. (Illus.). 32p. 1997. pap., spiral bd. 7.95 (*0-9664533-0-1*) Vashdom Pubng.

Cascio, Thomas S. Lo, see Lo Cascio, Thomas S.

Cascio, Toni, jt. auth. see Lipman, Bradford C.

Cascio, V. L., ed. see Besnier, P.

Cascio, Wayne F. Applied Psychology in Human Resource Management. 5th ed. LC 97-2914. 399p. (C). 1997. 82.00 (*0-13-834228-8*) P-H.

— Costing Human Resources. LC 82-15228. (SWC-Management). 224p. 1982. mass mkt. 15.50 (*0-534-01158-6*) PWS Pubs.

— Costing Human Resources. 2nd ed. (SWC-Management). 288p. (C). 1987. mass mkt. 17.75 (*0-534-08034-0*) PWS Pubs.

— Costing Human Resources. 3rd ed. 300p. (C). 1996. 29.95 (*0-534-91938-3*) S-W Pub.

Cascio, Wayne F. Guide to Responsible Restructuring. 39p. 1995. pap. 3.50 (*0-16-048025-6*) USGPO.

Cascio, Wayne F. Managing Human Resources: Productivity, Quality of Work Life, Profits. 3rd ed. 1992. pap. text, student ed. write for info. (*0-318-72596-7*) McGraw.

— Managing Human Resources: Productivity, Quality of Work Life, Profits. 4th ed. LC 94-3480. (Management Ser.). 660p. 1994. text 79.75 (*0-07-011154-5*) McGraw.

— Managing Human Resources: Productivity, Quality of Work Life, Profits. 4th ed. 1995. pap. text. write for info. incl. VHS (*0-07-911791-0*) McGraw.

— Managing Human Resources: Productivity, Quality of Work Life, Profits. 5th ed. LC 97-30865. 752p. 1997. 81.88 (*0-07-011944-9*) McGraw.

Cascio, Wayne F. & Sweet, Donald H., eds. Human Resource Planning, Employment & Placement. LC 89-31717. (ASPA/BNA Ser.: Vol. 2). 296p. 1989. reprint ed. pap. 91.80 (*0-608-00750-1*, 206154100010) Bks Demand.

Cascione, Joachim M. In Search of the Biblical Order: An Analysis of Coded Structure in the Book of Revelation. 222p. (Orig.). 1987. pap. 11.95 (*0-9620063-0-0*) Gods Word.

Cascone, A. G. Along Came a Spider. LC 96-228962. (Deadtime Stories Ser.). 128p. (Orig.). (J). (gr. 3-7). 1996. pap. 3.50 (*0-8167-4137-9*) Troll Communs.

— Beast of Baskerville. (J). 1997. pap. 3.50 (*0-8167-4294-4*) Troll Communs.

— Cyber Scare. 1997. pap. 3.50 (*0-8167-4396-7*) Troll Communs.

— Faerie Tale. 128p. 1997. pap. 3.50 (*0-8167-4398-3*, Dial Yng Read) Peng Put Young Read.

— Ghost Knight. LC 96-228963. (Deadtime Stories Ser.). 128p. (Orig.). (J). (gr. 3-7). 1996. pap. 3.50 (*0-8167-4138-7*) Troll Communs.

— Grandpa's Monster Movies. (Deadtime Stories Ser.: No. 10). (J). (gr. 3-7). 1997. pap. 3.50 (*0-8167-4261-8*) Troll Communs.

— Grave Secrets, Vol. 8. (Deadtime Stories Ser.). 1997. pap. 3.50 (*0-8167-4194-8*) Troll Communs.

— If He Hollers. 192p. (Orig.). (YA). 1995. mass mkt. 3.99 (*0-380-77753-3*, Avon Bks) Morrow Avon.

— Invasion of the Appleheads. (Deadtime Stories Ser.). 1996. pap. 1.75 (*0-8167-4259-6*) Troll Communs.

— Invasion of the Appleheads. LC 96-228957. (Deadtime Stories Ser.). 128p. (J). (gr. 3-7). 1996. pap. 3.50 (*0-8167-4136-0*) Troll Communs.

— It Came from the Deep, Vol. 7. (Deadtime Stories Ser.). 1997. pap. 3.50 (*0-8167-4216-2*) Troll Communs.

— Little Magic Shop of Horrors, Vol. 6. (Deadtime Stories Ser.). 1996. pap. 3.50 (*0-8167-4193-X*) Troll Communs.

— Mirror, Mirror, Vol. 9. (Deadtime Stories Ser.). 1997. pap. 3.50 (*0-8167-4260-X*) Troll Communs.

— Night of Pet Zombies. 1997. pap. 3.50 (*0-8167-4397-5*) Troll Communs.

— Nightmare on Planet X. (Deadtime Stories Ser.: No. 11). (J). (gr. 3-7). 1997. pap. 3.50 (*0-8167-4292-8*) Troll Communs.

— Revenge of Goblins. 1996. pap. 42.00 (*0-8167-4191-3*) Viking Penguin.

— Revenge of the Goblins. (Deadtime Stories Ser.). 128p. (Orig.). (J). (gr. 3-7). 1996. pap. 3.50 (*0-8167-4139-5*) Troll Communs.

— Terror in Tiny Town. (Deadtime Stories Ser.). 128p. (J). (gr. 3-7). 1996. pap. 3.50 (*0-8167-4135-2*) Troll Communs.

— Terror in Tiny Town. (Deadtime Stories Ser.: Vol. 1). 1996. pap. 1.75 (*0-8167-4258-8*) Troll Communs.

— There's No Place Like Home. (YA). (gr. 7 up). 1997. pap. 3.95 (*0-8167-4222-7*) Troll Communs.

— Trapped in a Tiny Town. 1997. pap. 3.50 (*0-8167-4395-9*) Troll Communs.

— Welcome to the Terror-Go-Round, Vol. 12. (Deadtime Stories Ser.). (J). 1997. pap. 3.50 (*0-8167-4293-6*) Troll Communs.

Cascorbi, Paul, jt. auth. see Heintze, Albert.

***Casdagli.** Trust & Power: Taking Care of Ourselves Through Drama. LC 99-160542. 1998. pap. 28.95 (*1-85302-556-9*) Jessica Kingsley.

Casdagli, Martin. Nonlinear Modeling & Forecasting. (C). 1992. 63.00 (*0-201-52764-2*) Addison-Wesley.

Casdagli, Penny, et al. Grief: The Play, Writings & Workshops. 160p. 1992. pap. 24.95 (*1-85346-212-8*, Pub. by David Fulton) Taylor & Francis.

Casden, Ron, jt. auth. see Mutchnick, Brenda.

Casdorph, H. Richard & Walker, Morton. Toxic Metal Syndrome: How Metal Poisonings Can Affect Your Brain. LC 94-28053. 430p. pap. 14.95 (*0-89529-649-7*, Avery) Penguin Putnam.

Casdorph, Paul D. Lee & Jackson. 448p. 1994. pap. 24.95 (*1-56924-985-7*) Marlowe & Co.

— Prince John Magruder: His Life & Campaigns. LC 96-16598. (Illus.). 400p. 1996. 30.00 (*0-471-15941-7*) Wiley.

Casdy, Mona J. Word-Information Processing Concepts. 3rd ed. 218p. (C). 1984. pap. text. write for info. (*0-538-23611-6*, W62U) S-W Pub.

Case. Principles of Macroeconomics. 4th ed. 1995. text, teacher ed. write for info. (*0-13-440926-4*) Allyn.

***Case.** Principles of Macroeconomics. 5th ed. 1999. 32.00 (*0-13-020498-6*) P-H.

— SNMP V3 Survival Guide: Practical Strategies for Integrated Network Management. 352p. 1999. 49.99 (*0-471-35646-8*) Wiley.

Case. Strength of Materials & Structures. 3rd ed. (Civil Engineering Ser.). 1994. 46.50 (*0-340-56829-1*, Pub. by E A) Routldge.

Case & Lawrence, eds. Collections. (Illus.). 312p. 1997. 49.95 (*1-885206-51-8*) Cader Pubng.

— Keepsakes. 196p. 1997. 49.95 (*1-885206-48-8*) Cader Pubng.

— Outstanding Achievement. (Illus.). 144p. 1997. text 49.95 (*1-885206-49-6*) Cader Pubng.

— Sensations. (Illus.). 261p. 1998. 49.95 (*1-885206-50-X*) Cader Pubng.

— Voices. 450p. (Orig.). 1995. 45.00 (*1-885206-25-9*, Iliad Pr) Cader Pubng.

Case & Nacubo. Expenditures in Fund Raising: Alumni Relations & Other Constituent (Public) Relations. 48p. 1990. 17.00 (*0-89964-276-4*, 24502) Coun Adv & Supp Ed.

Case, jt. auth. see Barrows.

Case, jt. auth. see Johnson.

Case, Adam. Who Tells the Truth? A Collection of Logical Puzzles to Make You Think. 39p. (J). 1991. pap. 5.50 (*0-906212-77-4*, Pub. by Tarquin Pubns) Parkwest Pubns.

Case, Alison A. Plotting Women: Gender & Narration in the Eighteenth- & Nineteenth-Century British Novel. LC 99-28818. 1999. 37.50 (*0-8139-1895-2*) U Pr of Va.

Case, Arthur E. Four Essays on Gulliver's Travels. 1990. 16.50 (*0-8446-1106-9*) Peter Smith.

Case, Arthur E., jt. ed. see Nettleton, George H.

Case, Barbara. World of Beads. (Illus.). 128p. 1998. pap. 14.95 (*0-7153-0712-6*, Pub. by D & C Pub) Sterling.

— A World of Beads: How to Make Your Own Unique Jewellery. (Illus.). 128p. 1996. 24.95 (*0-7153-0190-X*, Pub. by D & C Pub) Sterling.

Case, Barbara, ed. see Wilkins, Maureen.

Case, Bette. Career Planning for Nurses. LC 96-21218. (Professional Reference - Nursing Ser.). 384p. (C). 1996. pap. 41.95 (*0-8273-7165-9*) Delmar.

Case, Betty J. Exploring Twin Relationships: Is Being a Twin Always Fun? 197p. (Orig.). 1996. pap. 14.95 (*0-9629948-2-0*) Tibbutt Pub.

— Living Without Your Twin. 89p. (Orig.). 1994. pap. text 9.95 (*0-9629948-1-2*) Tibbutt Pub.

— We Are Twins: But Who Am I? LC 91-65981. 203p. 1991. 18.95 (*0-9629948-0-4*) Tibbutt Pub.

Case, Bettye A., ed. A Century of Mathematical Meetings. LC 95-40533. 332p. 1995. text 75.00 (*0-8218-0465-0*, MTGM) Am Math.

— You're the Professor What Next? Ideas & Resources for Preparing College Teachers. (Notes Ser.: Vol. 35). 362p. 1994. pap. 10.00 (*0-88385-091-5*, NTE-35) Math Assn.

Case, Brian. The Users. LC 97-200714. 190p. 1997. pap. 12.95 (*1-899344-05-5*) Dufour.

***Case, C.** Big Business. 1998. mass mkt. 6.95 (*0-7472-5955-0*, Pub. by Headline Bk Pub) Trafalgar.

Case, C., et al, eds. Low-Dielectric Constant Materials III: Materials Research Society Symposium Proceedings, Vol. 476. LC 97-48258. 300p. 1997. text 66.00 (*1-55899-380-0*) Materials Res.

Case, C. R. John Case of Ontario County, New York. (Illus.). 104p. 1989. reprint ed. pap. 20.00 (*0-8328-1325-7*); reprint ed. lib. bdg. 28.00 (*0-8328-1324-9*) Higginson Bk Co.

Case, Carleton B., ed. see Ali, Mohammed.

***Case, Carole.** The Right Blood: America's Aristocrats in Thoroughbred Racing. LC 00-25356. 224p. (C). 2001. 26.00 (*0-8135-2840-2*) Rutgers U Pr.

Case, Carole, jt. auth. see Farrell, Ronald A.

Case, Caroline & Dalley, Tessa, eds. Working with Children in Art Therapy. (Illus.). 272p. (C). 1990. pap. 27.99 (*0-415-01738-6*, A3879) Routledge.

Case, Caroline, jt. auth. see Dalley, Tessa.

Case, Carroll. The Slaughter: An American Atrocity. 300p. 1998. 25.95 (*0-9666499-0-7*) First Biltmore Corp.

Case, Cassandra. Run with Me, Nike! The Olympics in 420, B.C. LC 99-19244. (Smithsonian Odyssey Ser.: No. 12). (Illus.). 32p. (J). (gr. 2-5). 1999. 14.95 (*1-56899-604-7*); pap. 5.95 (*1-56899-605-5*) Soundprints.

Case, Charles. Tools of the Bear. 256p. 1997. 29.95 (*1-883272-20-3*) Traders Lib.

Case, Charles C. The Yankee Generations: A History of the Case Family in America. LC 81-40638. (Illus.). 338p. (Orig.). 1982. 60.00 (*0-8191-1947-4*) U Pr of Amer.

Case, Charles D., jt. auth. see Ellis, L. Neal, Jr.

Case, Charles W. & Matthes, William A., eds. Colleges of Education: Perspectives on Their Future. LC 84-61701. (National Society for the Study of Education Publication Ser.). 206p. (C). 1985. 35.75 (*0-8211-0230-3*) McCutchan.

Case, Charles W. & Norlander-Case, Kay A. Professional Teacher: Preparation & Nurturance of the Reflective Practioner. LC 99-6257. (Agenda for Education in a Democracy Ser.). 208p. 1999. pap. 39.95 (*0-7879-4560-9*) Jossey-Bass.

Case, Christine L. Telecourse Study Guide for Microbiology: An Introduction. 6th ed. 191p. (C). 1999. pap. text, student ed. 27.00 (*0-8053-2179-9*) Benjamin-Cummings.

Case, Christine L. & Johnson, Ted R. Microbiology: Lab Experiments. 350p. (C). 1984. pap. text 28.13 (*0-8053-5040-3*) Benjamin-Cummings.

Case, Christine L., jt. auth. see Johnson, Ted R.

Case, Christopher. The Ultimate Movie Thesaurus: The Only Book You'll Ever Need to Find the Movie You Want. LC 96-36427. 704p. 1995. pap. 22.50 (*0-8050-3496-X*, Owl) H Holt & Co.

Case, Clarence M. Essays in Social Values. LC 67-30201. (Essay Index Reprint Ser.). 1977. 18.95 (*0-8369-0281-5*) Ayer.

— Non-Violent Coercion: A Study in Methods of Social Pressure. LC 78-137530. (Peace Movement in America Ser.). viii, 423p. 1972. reprint ed. lib. bdg. 49.95 (*0-89198-058-X*) Ozer.

Case, Clifford J. How to Become a Merchant Seaman. (Illus.). 32p. (Orig.). 1990. pap. 5.00 (*0-939427-00-1*, 01135) Alpha Pubns OH.

Case Consulting Group Staff, ed. Introduction to CASE: The Best of CASE Outlook, 3 vols., Vol. 1. 99p. (Orig.). 1990. pap. 79.00 (*1-878806-00-9*) CASE Consulting.

— Introduction to CASE: The Best of CASE Outlook, 3 vols., Vol. 2. 65p. (Orig.). 1990. pap. 79.00 (*1-878806-01-7*) CASE Consulting.

— Introduction to CASE: The Best of CASE Outlook, 3 vols., Vol. 3. 154p. (Orig.). 1990. pap. 79.00 (*1-878806-02-5*) CASE Consulting.

Case, David. The Fighting Breed. (Orig.). 1979. mass mkt. 1.95 (*0-89083-541-1*, Zebra Kensgtn) Kensgtn Pub Corp.

— The Third Grave. LC 80-26818. (Illus.). 192p. 1981. 12.95 (*0-87054-089-0*) Arkham.

— Water Garden Plants: The Complete Guide. (Illus.). 160p. 1994. pap. 22.95 (*1-85223-812-7*, Pub. by Crolwood) Trafalgar.

Case, David A. Going Deeper: Insights Toward Intimacy in Christ. LC 99-94219. 226p. 1999. pap. 9.50 (*0-9662598-0-7*) Live Free KS.

Case, David B., et al, eds. Captopril & Hypertension. LC 80-23373. (Topics in Cardiovascular Disease Ser.). (Illus.). 248p. reprint ed. pap. 76.90 (*0-608-05438-0*, 206590700006) Bks Demand.

Case, David S. & Shinkwin, Anne D. Alaska Natives & American Laws. LC 79-603397. xxii, 586p. 1997. reprint ed. pap. 25.00 (*0-912006-09-9*) U of Alaska Pr.

Case, Deborah A., jt. ed. see Derderian, Robert L.

Case, Deborah A., jt. ed. see Lawrence, Robert.

Case, Dick. Good Guys, Bad Guys, Big Guys, Little Guys: Upstate New York Stories from the Syracuse Herald-Journal, Herald American. 1995. write for info. (*0-9629159-9-8*) Pine Tree NY.

Case, Dominic. Film Technology in Post Production. LC 97-192243. 160p. 1997. pap. text 29.95 (*0-240-51463-7*) Buttrwrth-Heinemann.

Case, Ed. We Have a Lift-Off: History of Shuttle Missions Photographs of Shuttle Launches. (Illus.). 1992. pap. 14.95 (*0-9633033-0-9*) Ed Case.

Case, Elinor. Humphrey, Wimsey & Doo. (Illus.). 48p. (Orig.). (J). (ps-6). 1984. pap. 5.95 (*0-910781-02-8*) G Whittell Mem.

Case, Evelyn C., jt. auth. see Volz, Jim.

Case, Evelyn C., jt. ed. see Volz, Jim.

Case, Everett N. & Case, Josephine Y. Owen D. Young & American Enterprise: A Biography. LC 80-83945. (Illus.). 992p. (C). 1986. 25.00 (*0-87923-360-5*) Godine.

Case, Fred E. Environmental Impact Review & Housing. LC 82-11272. 250p. 1982. 59.95 (*0-275-90770-8*, C0770, Praeger Pubs) Greenwood.

Case, Frederick W., Jr. Orchids of the Western Great Lakes Region. Bartz, Christine E., ed. LC 86-70869. (Bulletin Ser.: No. 48). (Illus.). 252p. 1987. reprint ed. 29.00 (*0-87737-036-2*) Cranbrook.

Case, Frederick W. & Case, Roberta B. Trilliums. LC 96-27583. 285p. 1997. 29.95 (*0-88192-374-5*) Timber.

Case, Gary & Rhoades-Baum, Patrice. How to Handle Difficult Customers. Bultema, Patrick et al, eds. 26p. (Orig.). pap. write for info. (*1-57125-020-4*) Help Desk Inst.

Case, George. Silence Descends: The End of the Information Age, 2000-2500. LC 97-204930. (Illus.). 120p. 1997. pap. 9.95 (*1-55152-041-9*, Pub. by Arsenal Pulp) LPC InBook.

Case, Gerard R. A Pictorial Guide to Fossils. 528p. (C). 1992. reprint ed. 62.50 (*0-89464-678-8*); reprint ed. pap. 45.50 (*0-89464-713-X*) Krieger.

Case, Howard E. Sussex County, New Jersey, Marriages. vi, 358p. (Orig.). 1993. pap. 24.00 (*1-55613-702-8*) Heritage Bk.

Case, J., jt. ed. see Dengo, G.

Case, J. Wickham, compiled by. Southold, New York Town Records (with Explanatory Notes), 1651-1787: With Appendix & Index, 2 vols. (Illus.). 1055p. 1997. reprint ed. lib. bdg. 99.00 (*0-8328-7147-8*) Higginson Bk Co.

Case, James L. Clinical Management of Voice Disorders. 3rd ed. LC 90-14313. 417p. 1995. text 41.00 (*0-89079-674-2*, 7311) PRO-ED.

Case, Jeremy. Here's Hanson. 96p. (J). pap. 7.95 (*0-14-130227-5*, Pub. by Pnguin Bks Ltd) Trafalgar.

Case, Joan S. Chester. LC 98-86141. (Images of America Ser.). (Illus.). 128p. 1998. pap. 16.99 (*0-7524-1274-4*) Arcadia Publng.

Case, John. The First Horseman. 373p. 1999. mass mkt. 6.99 (*0-345-43579-6*) Ballantine Pub Grp.

— The First Horseman. LC 98-18973. 325p. 1998. 25.00 (*0-449-91102-0*, Columbine) Fawcett.

— The First Horseman. large type ed. LC 98-35824. 597p. 1999. 30.00 (*0-7862-1619-0*, G K Hall Lrg Type) Mac Lib Ref.

— The Genesis Code. LC 97-97044. 467p. 1998. mass mkt. 6.99 (*0-345-42231-7*) Ballantine Pub Grp.

— The Genesis Code. large type ed. LC 97-18105. 761p. 1997. 25.95 (*0-7862-1205-5*) Thorndike Pr.

— Open-Book Experience: Lessons from Over 100 Companies Who Successfully Transformed Themselves. 256p. 1998. pap. text 14.00 (*0-7382-0040-9*) Perseus Pubng.

— Open-Book Management: The Coming Business Revolution. 224p. 1996. pap. 15.00 (*0-88730-802-3*) HarpC.

Case, John, jt. auth. see Kelly, Patrick.

Case, John, jt. auth. see Royer, James S.

Case, John, jt. ed. see Fulk, Mark.

***Case, John F.** Codigo Genesis. 1999. 29.95 (*84-08-02904-5*) Planeta.

Case, Josephine Y. At Midnight on the Thirty-First of March. (New York Classics Ser.). 144p. 1990. reprint ed. pap. text 14.95 (*0-8156-2492-1*) Syracuse U Pr.

— New & Selected Poems of Josephine Young Case. LC 92-17891. 104p. 1992. 18.00 (*0-915010-37-2*) Sutter House.

Case, Josephine Y., jt. auth. see Case, Everett N.

Case, Joyce, jt. auth. see Brohl, Kathryn.

Case, Justin. Clarence, the Talking Giraffe. (J). 1998. 13.95 (*1-890382-00-0*) Happy Face.

Case, Karl E. Economics & Tax Policy. LC 85-29843. 151p. (C). 1986. text 14.00 (*0-89946-209-X*) Lincoln Inst Land.

— Principles of Macroeconomics. 5th ed. LC 98-23825. 575p. 1998. pap. text 66.60 (*0-13-095733-X*) P-H.

— State & Local Tax Policy & the Telecommunications Industry. LC 92-43833. 1992. 13.95 (*0-934842-13-2*) CSPA.

Case, Karl E. & Fair, Ray C. Principles of Economics. 5th ed. LC 98-23823. 959p. (C). 1998. 92.00 (*0-13-095710-0*) P-H.

— Principles of Macroeconomics. 4th ed. LC 95-39055. 588p. 1995. pap. text 63.00 (*0-13-440843-8*) P-H.

— Principles of Macroeconomics. 5th ed. 1998. pap. text, student ed. write for info. (*0-13-095735-6*) P-H.

— Principles of Microeconomics. 5th ed. LC 98-23824. 607p. 1998. pap. text 66.60 (*0-13-095725-9*) P-H.

— Principles of Microeconomics. 5th ed. 1998. pap. text, student ed. write for info. (*0-13-095729-1*) P-H.

Case, Keith & Newman, Steven T., eds. Advances in Manufacturing Eight: Proceedings of the 10th National Conference on Manufacturing Research. 699p. 1994. pap. 99.00 (*0-7484-0254-3*, Pub. by Tay Francis Ltd) Taylor & Francis.

Case, L. W. The Goodrich Family in America: A Genealogy of the Descendants of John & William Goodrich of Wethersfield, Connecticut, Richard of Guilford, Conn., & William of Watertown, Mass., also a Short Account of the Family in England. (Illus.). 423p. 1989. reprint ed. pap. 63.50 (*0-8328-0606-4*); reprint ed. lib. bdg. 71.50 (*0-8328-0605-6*) Higginson Bk Co.

— Hollister Family in America; Lt. John Hollister of Wethersfield, Conn., & His Descendants. 805p. reprint ed. pap. 119.50 (*0-8328-0672-2*); reprint ed. lib. bdg. 127.50 (*0-8328-0671-4*) Higginson Bk Co.

Case, LeAnne. Fitness Aquatics. LC 96-369. (Fitness Spectrum Ser.). (Illus.). 176p. (Orig.). 1996. pap. 15.95 (*0-87322-963-0*, PCAS0963) Human Kinetics.

Case, Linda P. The Dog: Its Behavior, Nutrition & Health. LC 98-39307. (Illus.). 400p. (C). 1999. text 34.95 (*0-8138-1259-3*) Iowa St U Pr.

Case, Linda P. & Carey, Diane L. Canine & Feline Nutrition. LC 95-119829. (Illus.). 432p. (C). (gr. 13). 1994. text 65.00 (*0-8151-1536-9*, 25123) Mosby Inc.

Case, Linda W. Remodelers Business Basics. LC 88-62780. 232p. 1989. pap. 36.00 (*0-86718-300-4*) Home Builder.

— The Remodeler's Guide to Making & Managing Money. LC 95-92481. 140p. 1996. pap. 27.00 (*0-9648587-4-6*) Remodelers Advantage.

Case, Linda W. & Downing, Victoria L. Mastering the Business of Remodeling. LC 97-69352. 300p. 1997. pap. 35.00 (*0-9648587-5-4*) Remodelers Advantage.

— The Remodelers Marketing PowerPak. LC 95-92480. 300p. 1995. pap. 27.00 (*0-9648587-3-8*) Remodelers Advantage.

Case, Linda W. & Stoeppelwerth, Walter W. Remodeling Production. rev. ed. 172p. 1988. pap. 37.50 (*1-882379-07-1*) HomeTech Info Systs.

***Case, Lloyd A.** Building the Ultimate Game Machine: Configuring, Building, Troubleshooting & Maintaining Your Computer. 331p. 1999. pap. 19.99 (*0-7897-2204-6*) Que.

Case, Lynn & Sanderson, Page. Page: The Family of John Page of Haverhill, Massachusetts: A Comprehensive Genealogy from 1614 to 1977. (Illus.). 250p. 1991. reprint ed. pap. 37.50 (*0-8328-1936-0*); reprint ed. lib. bdg. 47.50 (*0-8328-1935-2*) Higginson Bk Co.

Case, Lynn M. Case. Descendants of Stephen Case of Marlboro NY, Including Allied Families. 82p. 1991. reprint ed. pap. 17.00 (*0-8328-1986-7*); reprint ed. lib. bdg. 27.00 (*0-8328-1985-9*) Higginson Bk Co.

— Franco-Italian Relations, 1860-1865. LC 75-121289. (BCL Ser. I). reprint ed. 49.50 (*0-404-01405-4*) AMS Pr.

Case, Lynn M., ed. European Pancreatic Club (EPC) 17th Meeting, Manchester, September 1985: Abstracts. (Illus.). 76p. 1985. pap. 50.50 (*3-8055-4203-8*) S Karger.

Case, Lynn M., tr. see De Bertier De Sauvigny, Guillaume.

***Case, Margaret.** Imagine If You Can. LC 98-89640. (Illus.). 60p. (J). (gr. 1-5). 1999. pap. 4.99 (*1-893181-12-X*, Simon & Northrop) Le Gesse Stevens.

C

An Asterisk (*) at the beginning of an entry indicates that the title is appearing for the first time.

Case, Margaret H. Seeing Krishna: The Religious World of A Brahmin Family in Vrindaban. LC 98-53863. (Illus.). 192p. 2000. pap. 17.95 (*0-19-513011-1*) OUP.
— Seeing Krishna: The Religious World of a Brahmin Family in Vrindaban. LC 98-53863. (Illus.). 192p. 2000. text 35.00 (*0-19-513010-3*) OUP.
— South Asian History, 1750-1950: A Guide to Periodicals, Dissertations, & Newspapers. LC 67-21019. 575p. reprint ed. pap. 178.30 (*0-8357-7029-X*, 203340600085) Bks Demand.

Case, Margaret H., ed. Govindadeva: A Dialogue in Stone. 1996. 140.00 (*81-85503-03-6*, Pub. by M Manoharial) S Asia.
— Heinrich Zimmer: Coming into His Own. LC 93-29645. 160p. (C). 1994. text 35.00 (*0-691-03337-4*, Pub. by Princeton U Pr) Cal Prin Full Svc.

Case, Margret H. & Barrier, N. Gerald, eds. Aspects of India. 1986. 20.00 (*81-85054-07-X*, Pub. by Manohar) S Asia.

Case, Marshall T. Look What I Found: The Young Conservationist's Guide to the Care & Feeding of Small Wildlife. 95p. 1983. pap. 9.95 (*0-8159-6119-7*) Devin.

Case, Mary. The Green Jellybean. (Illus.). 32p. (J). (ps-8). 1989. pap. text 4.95 (*1-877995-01-0*) Koala Pub Co.
— Katie Koala Bear Vol. 1: What Will Katie Wear to School? LC 89-83279. (Katie Koala Hear-Me-Read Bks.). (Illus.). 28p. (J). (gr. 2-4). 1989. pap. text 4.95 (*0-685-28857-9*) Koala Pub Co.
— Katie Koala Bear Vol. 2: Katie's Tree of Designs. (Katie Koala Hear-Me-Read Bks.). (Illus.). 28p. (J). (gr. 2-4). 1989. pap. text 4.95 (*1-877995-00-2*) Koala Pub Co.
— Katie Koala Bear Vol. 3: Katie & Karla Make Pizza. (Katie Koala Hear-Me-Read Bks.). (Illus.). 28p. (J). (gr. 2-4). 1989. pap. text 4.95 (*1-877995-05-3*) Koala Pub Co.
— Katie Koala Bear Vol. 4: Katie Loves Math. (Katie Koala Hear-Me-Read Bks.). (Illus.). 28p. (J). (gr. 2-4). 1989. pap. text 4.95 (*1-877995-13-4*) Koala Pub Co.
— Katie Koala Bear Vol. 5: Katie Learns to Read. (Katie Koala Hear-Me-Read Bks.). (Illus.). 28p. (J). (gr. 2-4). 1989. pap. text 4.95 (*1-877995-04-5*) Koala Pub Co.

***Case, Mary, ed.** The Specialized Scholarly Monograph in Crisis or How Can I Get Tenure If You Won't Publish My Book. (Illus.). 169p. 1999. pap. 40.00 (*0-918006-44-9*) Assn Res Lib.

Case, Mary & Shaffer, Dianna. Katie Koala Bear in What Will Katie Wear to School? (Illus.). 20p. (Orig.). (J). 1989. pap. 4.95 (*1-877995-06-1*) Koala Pub Co.

Case, Michael, jt. auth. see Eakin, David B.

Case, Nelly M. Introits for Two Ringers: Congregation-Quieting Service Starters. (Illus.). 14p. 1998. pap. 8.00 (*1-882508-06-8*) ABCs.

Case, Nelly M. & Ledoux, Stephen F. The Panda & Monkey King Christmas - A Family's Year in China. LC 97-72125. (Illus.). 200p. (Orig.). 1997. pap., spiral bd. 25.00 (*1-882508-10-6*) ABCs.

Case, Pamela & Alward, Gregory. Patterns of Demographic, Economic & Value Change in the Western United States. (Illus.). 52p. (C). 1998. pap. text 30.00 (*0-7881-7549-1*) DIANE Pub.

Case, Patricia A. How to Write Your Autobiography: Preserving Your Family Heritage. LC 77-72670. (Orig.). 1977. pap. 7.95 (*0-912800-38-0*) Woodbridge Pr.

Case, Paul F. The Book of Tokens: Tarot Meditations. enl. rev. ed. (Illus.). 200p. 1974. reprint ed. 16.00 (*0-938002-00-7*) Builders of Adytum.
— Das Buch der Siegel: Tarot Meditationen. (GER., Illus.). 192p. 1995. pap. 16.00 (*3-931089-00-2*) Builders of Adytum.
— Daniel, Master of Magicians & the Name of Names. 1981. 6.00 (*0-938002-04-X*) Builders of Adytum.
— La Doctrine Secrete du Tarot: Le Tarot, Clef de la Sagesse Eternelle. (FRE.). 1947. pap. 18.00 (*2-907941-01-1*) Builders of Adytum.
— The Great Seal of the United States. (Illus.). 1976. 6.00 (*0-938002-01-5*) Builders of Adytum.
— Highlights of Tarot. rev. ed. 72p. 1970. 5.00 (*0-938002-02-3*) Builders of Adytum.
— Le Livre des Signes et Temoignages: Kabbale et Meditation. (FRE., Illus.). 203p. Date not set. pap. 16.00 (*2-907941-02-X*) Builders of Adytum.
— The Masonic Letter G. 96p. 1994. pap. 8.50 (*0-88053-066-9*, M-326) Macoy Pub.
— Schlussel: Zur Ewigen Weisheit des "Tarot" (GER., Illus.). 196p. 1947. pap. 18.00 (*3-908644-87-9*) Builders of Adytum.
— The Tarot: A Key to the Wisdom of the Ages. (Illus.). 223p. 1975. 18.00 (*0-88053-767-1*) Builders of Adytum.
— El Tarot: Una Clave de la Sabiduria Eterna. rev. ed. (Illus.). 218p. 1975. reprint ed. 17.00 (*0-938002-08-2*) Builders of Adytum.
— The True & Invisible Rosicrucian Order. LC 85-3185. (Illus.). 342p. 1989. pap. 24.95 (*0-87728-709-0*) Weiser.

Case, Phil. Environmental Risk Management & Corporate Lending: A Global Perspective. 192p. 1999. 155.00 (*1-85573-436-2*) Am Educ Systs.

Case, Philip W. Yesterday This Hadn't Happened Yet. (Illus.). 175p. 1996. pap. 11.95 (*0-9653983-0-7*) Sloan Cnslting.

***Case, Pierre, ed.** Marino Marini. 332p. 2000. 45.00 (*88-8118-631-4*, Pub. by Skira IT) Abbeville Pr.

Case, R. H., ed. see Marlowe, Christopher.

Case, R. M., ed. Variations in Human Physiology. LC 84-11301. (Integrative Studies in Human Physiology). 241p. 1988. text 29.00 (*0-7190-1086-1*, Pub. by Manchester Univ Pr) St Martin.

***Case, Rebecca.** Jesus Now. 64p. 1999. (*1-58244-048-4*) Rutledge Bks.

Case, Richard M., et al, eds. Electrolyte & Water Transport Across Gastrointestinal Epithelia. LC 81-40606. 334p. 1982. reprint ed. pap. 103.60 (*0-608-00336-0*, 206105300007) Bks Demand.

Case, Riley B. Understanding Our New United Methodist Hymnal: What it Teaches Us about Our Faith & Ourselves. LC 89-60520. (Orig.). 1989. pap. 4.95 (*0-917851-31-5*) Bristol Hse.

Case, Robbie, ed. The Mind's Staircase: Stages in the Development of Human Intelligence. 424p. 1992. pap. 45.00 (*0-8058-1190-7*); text 79.95 (*0-8058-0324-6*) L Erlbaum Assocs.

Case, Robbie & Okamoto, Yukari. The Role of Central Conceptual Structures in the Development of Children's Thought. 225p. 1996. pap. text 19.50 (*0-226-09540-1*) U Ch Pr.

Case, Roberta B., jt. auth. see Case, Frederick W.

Case, Roland & Werner, Walter. Assessing Development - Global Education Programs: A Planning Model. 40p. (C). 1990. 5.00 (*0-944675-02-6*) Amer Forum.

Case, S. G., et al. Electronic Measurement & Control Applications, 3 vols. (Illus.). (C). 1981. ring bd. 595.00 (*0-87683-019-X*) GP Courseware.
— Electronic Measurement & Control Applications, 3 vols., Set. (Illus.). (C). 1981. 195.00 (*0-87683-015-7*) GP Courseware.
— Electronic Measurement & Control Applications, 3 vols., Vol. 1. (Illus.). 370p. (C). 1981. ring bd. 95.00 (*0-87683-016-5*) GP Courseware.
— Electronic Measurement & Control Applications, 3 vols., Vol. 2. (Illus.). 175p. (C). 1981. ring bd. 79.50 (*0-87683-017-3*) GP Courseware.
— Electronic Measurement & Control Applications, 3 vols., Vol. 3. (Illus.). 175p. (C). 1981. teacher ed., ring bd. 79.50 (*0-87683-018-1*) GP Courseware.

Case, S. T., et al, eds. Biomolecular Materials Vol. 292. (Materials Research Society Symposium Proceedings Ser.: Vol. 292). 287p. 1993. text 30.00 (*1-55899-187-5*) Materials Res.

Case, Sam. Big Profits from Small Stocks: How to Grow Your Investment Portfolio by Investing in Small Cap Companies. LC 94-19878. (Illus.). 160p. 1995. 18.95 (*1-55958-578-1*) Prima Pub.

Case, Samuel. Big Profits from Small Stocks: How to Grow Your Investment Portfolio by Investing in Small Cap Companies. (Illus.). 154p. 1998. text 19.00 (*0-7881-5240-8*) DIANE Pub.
— First Book of Investing: A Absolute Beginners Guide to Building Wealth Safely. 352p. 1995. pap. 14.95 (*0-7615-0008-1*) Prima Pub.

***Case, Samuel.** The First Book of Investing: An Absolute Beginner's Guide to Building Wealth Safely. 3rd rev. ed. LC 99-37477. 2000. pap. 15.95 (*0-7615-2133-X*) Prima Pub.

Case, Samuel. The First Book of Investing: The Absolute Beginner's Guide to Building Wealth Safely. LC 92-42949. 352p. 1993. 22.95 (*1-55958-292-8*) Prima Pub.
— The First Book of Investing: The Absolute Beginner's Guide to Building Wealth Safely. 2nd rev. ed. LC 96-51463. (Illus.). 352p. 1997. per. 15.00 (*0-7615-0838-4*) Prima Pub.
— The First Book of Small Stock Investing: How to Grow Your Investment Portfolio by Investing in Small Cap Companies. LC 98-15534. 160p. 1998. per. 12.95 (*0-7615-1439-2*) Prima Pub.

Case, Shirley J. Experience with the Supernatural in Early Christian Times. LC 75-174851. 341p. 1978. reprint ed. 29.95 (*0-405-08345-9*, Pub. by Blom Pubns) Ayer.
— Jesus: A New Biography. LC 68-57594. 452p. 1970. reprint ed. lib. bdg. 75.00 (*0-8371-0342-8*, CAJE, Greenwood Pr) Greenwood.
— Jesus, a New Biography. LC 70-95149. (BCL Ser. II). reprint ed. 39.50 (*0-404-01406-2*) AMS Pr.
— The Social Triumph of the Ancient Church. LC 76-164596. (Select Bibliographies Reprint Ser.). 1977. reprint ed. 20.95 (*0-8369-5880-2*) Ayer.

Case-Smith, Jane. Occupational Therapy: Making a Difference in School System Practice: a Self-Paced Clinical Course LC 99-178436. 1998. 463.00 (*1-56900-095-6*) Am Occup Therapy.
— Pediatric Occupational Therapy & Early Intervention. 2nd ed. LC 97-18094. 280p. 1997. text 52.50 (*0-7506-9780-6*) Buttrwrth-Heinemann.

Case-Smith, Jane, et al, eds. Occupational Therapy for Children. 3rd ed. (Illus.). 864p. (C). (gr. 13). 1995. text 63.00 (*0-8151-1541-5*, 24845) Mosby Inc.

Case-Smith, Jane & Pehoski, Charlane, eds. Development of Hand Skills in the Child. (Illus.). 150p. (C). 1992. pap. text 37.00 (*0-910317-78-X*) Am Occup Therapy.

Case-Smith, Jane & Semmler, Caryl J., eds. Pediatric Specialty Certification Examination Study Guide. 90p. (C). 1991. pap. text. write for info. (*0-910317-70-4*) Am Occup Therapy.

***Case-Speers, Barbara.** Victorious. 324p. 2000. pap. 15.95 (*0-595-00488-1*, Writers Club Pr) iUniversecom.

Case, Stanley R. The Poudre: A Photo History. (Illus.). 350p. 1994. write for info. (*0-9643000-0-1*) S R Case.

Case, Steve. It's My Choice: Junior Baptismal Guide LC 98-131774. 128 p. 1996. write for info. (*0-8280-1094-3*) Review & Herald.

Case, Steven T., ed. Structure, Cellular Synthesis, & Assembly of Biopolymers. LC 92-36490. (Results & Problems in Cell Differentiation Ser.: Vol. 19). 1992. 238.95 (*0-387-55549-8*) Spr-Verlag.

Case, Stevie. Buck Bumble: Official Strategy Guide. LC 98-67882. 96p. 1998. pap. text 12.99 (*0-7615-1910-6*) Prima Pub.
— Daikatana: Prima's Official Strategy Guide. LC 97-76272. (Illus.). 240p. 2000. pap. 19.99 (*0-7615-1483-X*) Prima Pub.
— Jazz Jackrabbit 2: Prima's Official Strategy Guide. LC 98-66505. 96p. 1998. pap. 14.99 (*0-7615-1709-X*) Prima Pub.

Case, Sue-Ellen. The Domain-Matrix: Performing Lesbian at the End of Print Culture. LC 96-8059. (Theories of Representation & Difference Ser.). (Illus.). 272p. 1997. 39.95 (*0-253-33226-5*); pap. 17.95 (*0-253-21094-1*) Ind U Pr.
— Feminism & Theatre. 160p. 1987. 32.50 (*0-416-01491-7*, 1190) Routledge.
— Feminism & Theatre. 160p. (C). 1988. pap. 17.99 (*0-416-01501-8*, 1195) Routledge.

Case, Sue-Ellen, ed. The Divided Home-Land: Contemporary German Women's Plays. (Illus.). 360p. (C). 1992. text 49.50 (*0-472-09406-8*, 09406); pap. text 21.95 (*0-472-06406-1*, 06406) U of Mich Pr.
— Performing Feminisms: Feminist Critical Theory & Theatre. LC 89-24602. 320p. 1990. pap. text 15.95 (*0-8018-3969-6*) Johns Hopkins.
— Split Britches: Lesbian Practice - Feminist Performance. LC 95-47164. (Illus.). 288p. (C). 1996. 85.00 (*0-415-12765-3*); pap. 22.99 (*0-415-12766-1*) Routledge.

Case, Sue-Ellen & Reinelt, Janelle, eds. The Performance of Power: Theatrical Discourse & Politics. LC 90-26750. (Studies in Theatre History & Culture). (Illus.). 306p. (C). 1991. pap. text 18.95 (*0-87745-318-7*) U of Iowa Pr.

***Case, Sue-Ellen, et al.** Decomposition: Post-Disciplinary Performance. LC 99-56968. (Illus.). 272p. 2000. pap. 19.95 (*0-253-21374-6*) Ind U Pr.
— Decomposition: Post-Disciplinary Performance. LC 99-56968. (Illus.). 272p. 2000. lib. bdg. 39.95 (*0-253-33723-2*) Ind U Pr.

Case, Susan. Aunt Charles' Surprise Visit. LC 94-45322. 96p. (Orig.). (J). 1995. pap. 3.99 (*1-56722-026-6*) Word Aflame.

Case, Suzanne J., ed. see David, C. A.

Case, Suzanne J., ed. see David, Charles Alexander, et al.

Case, Ted & Fisher, Robert. A Field Guide to Reptiles & Amphibians of Coastal Southern California. LC 97-92514. (Illus.). 50p. 1997. pap. write for info. (*0-9660059-0-2*) T Case.

Case, Ted J. An Illustrated Guide to Theoretical Ecology. LC 99-32309. (Illus.). 464p. (C). 1999. pap. text 49.95 (*0-19-508512-4*) OUP.

Case, Terrence D. Primer of Noninvasive Vascular Technology. LC 94-21978. 336p. 1994. pap. text 49.00 (*0-316-13035-4*) Lppncott W & W.

Case, Thomas. The Select Works of Thomas Case. 432p. 1993. reprint ed. 26.95 (*1-877611-58-1*) Soli Deo Gloria.

Case, Thomas & Smith, Larry. Managing Local Area Networks. 600p. (C). 1995. pap. 56.25 (*0-07-059225-X*) McGraw.

Case, Thomas W. Mind Forged Manacles: Cults & Spiritual Bondage. 277p. (Orig.). 1993. pap. 15.95 (*0-614-07026-0*) Fidelity Pr.
— Moonie-Buddhist-Catholic: A Spiritual Odyssey. LC 95-90655. 240p. (Orig.). 1995. pap. 12.95 (*0-9648310-0-7*, 8310-0-7) Whte Hrse Pr.
— The Shroud of Turin & the C-14 Dating Fiasco: A Scientific Detective Story. LC 96-60013. (Illus.). 104p. (Orig.). 1996. pap. 10.50 (*0-9648310-1-5*) Whte Hrse Pr.

Case, Victoria. We Called It Culture: The Story of Chautaugua. 272p. 1977. 18.95 (*0-8369-8051-4*) Ayer.

Case, W. R. & Sons Staff. W. R. Case & Sons Cookbook & Historical Companion. LC 96-92745. (Illus.). 160p. 1996. 19.95 (*0-9653124-0-2*) W R Case & Sons.

Case, Walter H. History of Long Beach & Vicinity, Vol. 1. LC 73-2901. (Metropolitan America Ser.). (Illus.). 692p. 1974. reprint ed. 47.95 (*0-405-05387-8*) Ayer.

Case, Walter H. & Harnett, Jane E. History of Long Beach & Vicinity, 2 vols. (Illus.). 1396p. 1997. reprint ed. lib. bdg. 135.00 (*0-8328-6607-5*) Higginson Bk Co.

Case Western Reserve University, Center for Crimin. Criminal Justice: Constitutional Provisions, Criminal Code with Comment, Juvenile Court Statutes, Controlled Substances, Rules of Criminal Procedure, Rules of Juvenile Procedure, Ohio Rules of Evidence, with Annotations & Complete Analysis of Elements of Crimes in Ohio. LC 83-174489. 1985. 35.00 (*0-317-00848-X*) Case Western.

Case Western Reserve University Staff. Die Casting of Copper Alloys. 115p. 1973. 17.25 (*0-317-34514-1*, 189) Intl Copper.

Casear, Paul. Postural Behavior in Newborn Infants. (Clinics in Developmental Medicine Ser.: Vol. 72). (Illus.). 112p. (C). 1991. text 29.95 (*0-521-41201-3*, Pub. by Mc Keith Pr) Cambridge U Pr.

Casebeer, Beverly B. Missiles to Learning: Beyond the Left/Right Brain. Kratoville, Betty Lou, ed. LC 96-208557. (Illus.). 206p. (Orig.). 1996. pap. 18.00 (*1-57128-018-9*, 018-9) Acad Therapy.

Casebeer, Macey. Acute Gout: The Devil's Curse. LC 95-68857. (Health Information Ser.). 72p. 1995. pap. 19.95 (*0-9645546-4-X*) Calgold Pubns.
— Bordello Stick Incident. LC 95-70152. (Gold Rush Novels Ser.). 214p. 1995. pap. 19.95 (*0-9645546-3-1*) Calgold Pubns.
— Indigestion, Heartburn & Stomach Ulcer: Bonfire in the Belly. LC 97-91637. (Health in Formation Ser.). 128p. (Orig.). 1997. pap. 19.95 (*0-9645546-5-8*) Calgold Pubns.
— The Quicksilver Incident: Murder at the Secret Ravine. LC 96-84770. (Goldrush Mystery Ser.). 139p. (Orig.). 1996. pap. 14.95 (*0-9645546-2-3*) Calgold Pubns.

Casebeer, MaryRuth. Discover California Wildflowers. LC 98-93219. (With Eyes of Wonder Ser.). (Illus.). vi, 70p. 1998. pap. 14.95 (*0-9665463-0-X*) Hooker Pr.

Casebier, Dennis, jt. auth. see King, Chester.

Casebier, Dennis G. Camp Beale's Springs & the Hualpai Indians. LC 79-92835. (Illus.). 240p. (Orig.). 1980. 18.50 (*0-914224-08-5*) Tales Mojave Rd.
— Guide to the East Mojave Heritage Trail - Fenner to Needles. (Illus.). 304p. 1990. 22.50 (*0-914224-19-0*) Tales Mojave Rd.
— Guide to the East Mojave Heritage Trail - Ivanpah to Rocky Ridge. (Illus.). 304p. 1988. 22.50 (*0-914224-16-6*) Tales Mojave Rd.
— Guide to the East Mojave Heritage Trail - Needles to Iuanpah. (Illus.). 320p. 1987. 22.50 (*0-914224-14-X*) Tales Mojave Rd.
— Guide to the East Mojave Heritage Trail - Rocky Ridge to Fenner. (Illus.). 304p. 1989. 22.50 (*0-914224-17-4*) Tales Mojave Rd.
— Mojave Road Guide. (Illus.). 232p. 1983. 18.50 (*0-914224-13-1*) Tales Mojave Rd.
— Nissan on the Mojave Road. LC 83-70971. (Illus.). 24p. 1983. 10.00 (*0-914224-11-5*) Tales Mojave Rd.

***Casebolt, Marjorie DeMoss.** Margarita: A Guatemalan Peace Corps Experience. 224p. (C). 2000. pap. 14.95 (*1-880222-38-8*) Red Apple Pub.

Casebooks Publishing Co., Inc. Staff. Taxation: Adaptable to Courses to Bittker, Clark & McCouch's Casenotes on Estate & Gift Taxation. Goldenberg, Norman S. et al, eds. (Legal Briefs Ser.). 1996. pap. write for info. (*0-87457-128-6*, 1217) Casenotes Pub.

Casel, Odo. The Mystery of Christ Made Present: Selected Texts for the Christian Year. Schilson, Arno, ed. Walls, Ronald, tr. from GER. LC 99-12918. Orig. Title: Gegenwart des Christus-Mysterium: Ausqewahlte Textezum Kirchenjahr. 101p. 1999. pap. 10.95 (*1-879007-38-X*, MYST) St Bedes Pubns.

Casel, Odo, jt. auth. see Cast, John.

Caseldine, Chris, jt. ed. see Maizels, Judith K.

Caseldine, Jennifer. Breast Disease for Radiographers. 1988. pap. 60.00 (*0-7236-1067-3*) Buttrwrth-Heinemann.

***Caseley, Judith.** Bully. (J). 2001. 15.95 (*0-688-17867-7*, Grenwillow Bks); lib. bdg. 15.89 (*0-688-17868-5*, Grenwillow Bks) HarpC Child Bks.

Caseley, Judith. Chloe in the Know. LC 92-14757. (Illus.). 144p. (J). (gr. 1 up). 1993. 14.00 (*0-688-11055-X*, Grenwillow Bks) HarpC Child Bks.
— Chloe in the Know. LC 92-14757. 1994. 10.05 (*0-606-06277-7*, Pub. by Turtleback) Demco.
— Chloe in the Know. Cohn, Amy, ed. LC 92-14757. (Illus.). (J). (gr. 3 up). 1994. reprint ed. pap. 4.95 (*0-688-13069-0*, Wm Morrow) Morrow Avon.
— Dear Annie. LC 90-39793. (Illus.). 32p. (J). (ps up). 1991. 16.00 (*0-688-10010-4*, Grenwillow Bks); lib. bdg. 15.93 (*0-688-10011-2*, Grenwillow Bks) HarpC Child Bks.
— Dear Annie. LC 90-39793. 1994. 10.15 (*0-606-06314-5*, Pub. by Turtleback) Demco.
— Dear Annie. Cohn, Amy, ed. LC 90-39793. (Illus.). 32p. (J). (ps-3). 1994. reprint ed. mass mkt. 5.95 (*0-688-13575-7*, Wm Morrow) Morrow Avon.
— Dorothy's Darkest Days. LC 96-39175. (Kane Family Ser.). (Illus.). 128p. (J). (gr. 3-7). 1997. 15.00 (*0-688-13422-X*, Grenwillow Bks) HarpC Child Bks.
— Field Day Friday. LC 98-45381. (Illus.). 32p. (J). (ps-3). 2000. 15.95 (*0-688-16761-6*, Grenwillow Bks); 15.89 (*0-688-16762-4*, Grenwillow Bks) HarpC Child Bks.
— Harry & Arney. LC 93-20787. 138p. (J). (ps-3). 1994. 14.00 (*0-688-12140-3*, Grenwillow Bks) HarpC Child Bks.
— Harry & Willy & Carrothead. LC 90-30291. (Illus.). 24p. (J). (ps-3). 1991. 15.95 (*0-688-09492-9*, Grenwillow Bks) HarpC Child Bks.
— Hurricane Harry. LC 93-6991. (Illus.). 112p. (J). (gr. 4-7). 1994. mass mkt. 5.95 (*0-688-12549-2*, Wm Morrow) Morrow Avon.

Caseley, Judith. Hurricane Harry. LC 93-6991. 1994. 10.05 (*0-606-06484-2*, Pub. by Turtleback) Demco.

Caseley, Judith. Jorah's Journal. LC 96-10411. (Illus.). 64p. (J). (gr. 2 up). 1997. 15.00 (*0-688-14879-4*, Grenwillow Bks) HarpC Child Bks.
— Losing Louisa. LC 98-19501. 235p. (YA). (gr. 8 up). 1999. pap. text 17.00 (*0-374-34665-8*) FS&G.
— Mama, Coming & Going. LC 92-29402. (Illus.). 32p. (J). (ps-3). 1994. 14.00 (*0-688-11441-5*, Grenwillow Bks) HarpC Child Bks.
— Mickey's Class Play. LC 97-33036. (Illus.). 32p. (J). (ps-3). 1998. 15.00 (*0-688-15405-0*, Grenwillow Bks) HarpC Child Bks.

***Caseley, Judith.** Mickey's Class Play. LC 97-33036. (Illus.). 32p. (J). (ps-3). 1998. 14.93 (*0-688-15406-9*, Grenwillow Bks) HarpC Child Bks.
— Mr. Green Peas. LC 93-24183. (Illus.). 32p. (J). (ps-3). 1995. 14.93 (*0-688-12860-2*, Grenwillow Bks) HarpC Child Bks.
— Mr. Green Peas. 1998. mass mkt. 4.95 (*0-688-16092-1*, Wm Morrow) Morrow Avon.

Caseley, Judith. Praying to A. L. LC 99-22045. 160p. (YA). (gr. 5-9). 2000. 15.95 (*0-688-15934-6*, Grenwillow Bks) HarpC Child Bks.
— Priscilla Twice. LC 94-12988. (Illus.). 32p. (J). (gr. k up). 1995. 15.00 (*0-688-13305-3*, Grenwillow Bks); lib. bdg. 14.93 (*0-688-13306-1*, Grenwillow Bks) HarpC Child Bks.
— Slumber Party! LC 95-963. (Illus.). 32p. (J). (ps up). 1996. 15.00 (*0-688-14015-7*, Grenwillow Bks); lib. bdg. 14.93 (*0-688-14016-5*, Grenwillow Bks) HarpC Child Bks.
— Sophie & Sammy's Library Sleepover. LC 91-48160. (Illus.). 32p. (J). (ps-3). 1993. 16.95 (*0-688-10615-3*, Grenwillow Bks) HarpC Child Bks.
— Starring Dorothy Kane. LC 90-24172. 154p. (J). (ps-3). 1992. 13.00 (*0-688-10182-8*, Grenwillow Bks) HarpC Child Bks.
— Starring Dorothy Kane. LC 93-6992. (Illus.). 160p. (J). (gr. 3 up). 1994. mass mkt. 4.95 (*0-688-12548-4*, Wm Morrow) Morrow Avon.

C

— Witch Mama. LC 95-35847. (Illus.). 32p. (J). (ps-3). 1996. 15.00 (*0-688-14457-8*, Grenwillow Bks); lib. bdg. 14.93 (*0-688-14458-6*, Grenwillow Bks) HarpC Child Bks.

Casella. Statistical Inference. 2nd ed. (Statistics Ser.). 2000. pap. 69.95 (*0-534-24312-6*) Wadsworth Pub.

***Casella, Cesare & Bishop, Jack.** Italian Cooking for Dummies. LC TX723.C2974 1998. (For Dummies Ser.). 400p. 1998. pap. 19.99 (*0-7645-5098-5*) IDG Bks.

Casella, Cesare & Daspin, Eileen. Diary of a Tuscan Chef: Recipes & Memories of Good Times & Great Food. LC 97-27743. (Illus.). 352p. 1998. 35.00 (*0-385-48547-6*) Doubleday.

Casella, G., jt. auth. see Lehmann, E. L.

Casella, G., ed. see Bilodeau, M. & Brenner, D.

Casella, G., ed. see Chow, Yuan S. & Teicher, Henry.

Casella, G., ed. see Durrett, R.

Casella, G., ed. see Kulkarni, Vidyadhar G.

Casella, G., ed. see Lehmann, E.

Casella, G., ed. see Nolan, D. J. & Speed, T. P.

Casella, G., ed. see Terrell, G. R.

Casella, George, jt. auth. see Robert, Christian P.

Casella, Jean, jt. ed. see Howe, Florence.

Casella, John. They Also Endure. (Illus.). 200p. 1998. pap. 14.95 (*1-884540-37-6*) Haleys.

Casella, John, ed. see Tucker, William H.

Casella, John W. Enduring Generations. (Illus.). 150p. (Orig.). 1997. pap. 14.95 (*1-884540-30-9*) Haleys.

Casella, L., jt. ed. see Montanari, F.

Caselli. Il Nuovo Dizionario Italiano-Inglese, Inglese-Italiano. (ENG & ITA.). 2427p. 1990. 125.00 (*0-7859-7476-8*, 8811103215) Fr & Eur.

Caselli, Giovanni. The First Civilizations. LC 84-6179. (History of Everyday Things Ser.). (Illus.). 48p. (YA). (gr. 5 up). 1985. 18.95 (*0-911745-59-9*, P Bedrick Books) NTC Contemp Pub Co.

— First Civilizations. (History of Everyday Things Ser.). (Illus.). 48p. (YA). (gr. 5 up). 1998. reprint ed. 10.95 (*0-87226-562-5*, 65625B, P Bedrick Books) NTC Contemp Pub Co.

— Greek Myths. LC 97-45899. (Myths of the World Ser.). (Illus.). 96p. (YA). (gr. 3-7). 1998. 22.50 (*0-87226-560-9*, 65609B, P Bedrick Books) NTC Contemp Pub Co.

— A Greek Potter. LC 85-30637. (Everyday Life of Ser.). (Illus.). 32p. (J). (gr. 3-6). 1991. lib. bdg. 12.95 (*0-87226-101-8*, P Bedrick Books) NTC Contemp Pub Co.

— An Ice Age Hunter. LC 91-33261. (Everyday Life of Ser.). (Illus.). 32p. (J). (gr. 3-6). 1992. lib. bdg. 12.95 (*0-87226-103-4*, P Bedrick Books) NTC Contemp Pub Co.

— In Search of Knossos: The Quest for the Minotaur's Labyrinth. LC 99-28013. (In Search of... Ser.). 48p. (J). 1999. 18.95 (*0-87226-544-7*, 65447B, P Bedrick Books) NTC Contemp Pub Co.

— In Search of Pompeii: Uncovering a Buried Roman City. LC 99-21352. (In Search of... Ser.). 48p. (J). 1999. 18.95 (*0-87226-545-5*, 65455B, P Bedrick Books) NTC Contemp Pub Co.

***Caselli, Giovanni.** In Search of Troy: One Man's Quest for Homer's Fabled City. LC 98-42579. (In Search of... Ser.). (Illus.). 48p. (J). (gr. 5-9). 1999. 18.95 (*0-87226-542-0*, 65420B, P Bedrick Books) NTC Contemp Pub Co.

Caselli, Giovanni. In Search of Tutankhamun: The Discovery of a King's Tomb. LC 98-44348. (In Search of... Ser.). (Illus.). 48p. (J). (gr. 5-9). 1999. 18.95 (*0-87226-543-9*, 65439B, P Bedrick Books) NTC Contemp Pub Co.

— Life Through the Ages. LC 92-52838. (See & Explore Library). (Illus.). 64p. (J). (gr. 3 up). 1992. 11.95 (*1-56458-143-8*) DK Pub Inc.

— The Middle Ages. 2nd ed. (History of Everyday Things Ser.). (Illus.). 48p. (YA). (gr. 5 up). 1998. reprint ed. pap. 10.95 (*0-87226-263-4*, 62634B, P Bedrick Books) NTC Contemp Pub Co.

— The Renaissance & the New World. (History of Everyday Things Ser.). (Illus.). 48p. (YA). (gr. 5 up). 1998. reprint ed. 10.95 (*0-87226-564-1*, 65641B, P Bedrick Books) NTC Contemp Pub Co.

— The Roman Empire & the Dark Ages. (History of Everyday Things Ser.). (Illus.). 48p. (YA). (gr. 4-7). 1998. reprint ed. 10.95 (*0-87226-563-3*, 65633B, P Bedrick Books) NTC Contemp Pub Co.

Caselli, Giovanni. Dotto & the Pharaoh's Mask: An Interactive Connect-the-Dots Adventure. 48p. (J). (gr. 3). 1997. pap. 10.95 (*0-8109-2783-7*, Pub. by Abrams) Time Warner.

Caselli, Graziella & Lopez, Alan D., eds. Health & Mortality among Elderly Populations. LC 95-49775. (International Studies in Demography). (Illus.). 376p. 1996. text 80.00 (*0-19-823337-X*, Clarendon Pr) OUP.

Caselli, R., jt. ed. see Capasso, V.

Caselmann, Wolfgang H., jt. ed. see Koshy, Rajen.

Caselton, Margaret. Beautiful Napkins: Stylish Ideas for Your Home. (Illus.). 152p. 1999. 17.95 (*0-7624-0440-X*) Running Pr.

— Gracious Table: The Art of Creating a Beautiful Table. LC 96-68513. (Illus.). 144p. 1996. 30.00 (*0-8478-1949-3*, Pub. by Rizzoli Intl) St Martin.

Casement, Ann. Post-Jungians Today: Key Papers in Contemporary Analytical Psychology. LC 98-9829. 248p. (C). 1998. 90.00 (*0-415-16154-1*); pap. 25.99 (*0-415-16155-X*) Routledge.

Casement, Charles, jt. auth. see Armstrong, Alison.

Casement, Gray, tr. see Fernandez Guardia, Ricardo.

Casement, Patrick. Invatand de la Pacient Vol. 1: Principii Fundamentale. Vladescu, F. V., ed. Dragolea, C. et al, trs.Tr. of Learning from the Patient: Fundamental Principles. (RUM.). 200p. 1996. pap. text 24.95 (*1-883881-20-X*, 20X) S Freud RT&PF.

Casement, Patrick J. Learning from the Patient. LC 90-14120. (Psychoanalysis Ser.). 384p. 1990. lib. bdg. 45.00 (*0-89862-559-9*) Guilford Pubns.

— Learning from the Patient. LC 90-14120. (Psychoanalysis Ser.). 384p. 1992. reprint ed. pap. text 25.00 (*0-89862-157-7*) Guilford Pubns.

— On Learning from the Patient. 232p. (Orig.). (C). 1985. pap. text 15.95 (*0-318-58396-8*, NO. 9235) Routledge.

Casement, Roger. Roger Casement's Diaries: 1910: The Black & the White. Sawyer, Roger, ed. 274p. 1999. pap. 19.95 (*0-7126-7375-X*) Barrie & Jenkins.

Casement, William. The Great Canon Controversy: The Battle of the Books in Higher Education. LC 95-13197. 172p. 1996. text 34.95 (*1-56000-276-X*) Transaction Pubs.

Casemore, Bob. South of the Gila. large type ed. (Linford Western Library Ser.). 272p. 1997. pap. 16.99 (*0-7089-5145-7*) Ulverscroft.

Casemore, Robert F. Splendid Morning. large type ed. LC 98-49016. 1999. 30.00 (*0-7838-8474-5*, G K Hall Lrg Type) Mac Lib Ref.

Casenotes Publishing Co., Inc. Staff. Administrative Law: Adaptable to Courses Utilizing Breyer & Stewart's Casebook on Administrative Law & Regulatory Policy. Goldenberg, Norman S. & Tenen, Peter, eds. (Legal Briefs Ser.). 1997. pap. write for info. (*0-87457-001-8*, 1263) Casenotes Pub.

— Administrative Law: Adaptable to Courses Utilizing Gellhorn, Byse, Strauss, Schotland, & Farina's Casebook on Administrative Law. Goldenberg, Norman S. & Tenen, Peter, eds. (Legal Briefs Ser.). 1995. pap. write for info. (*0-87457-003-4*, 1260) Casenotes Pub.

— Administrative Law: Adaptable to Courses Utilizing Mashaw & Merrill & Shane's Casebook on Administrative Law - the American Public Law System. Goldenberg, Norman S. & Tenen, Peter, eds. (Legal Briefs Ser.). (Orig.). 1998. pap. text. write for info. (*0-87457-154-5*, 1264) Casenotes Pub.

— Administrative Law: Adaptable to Courses Utilizing Schwartz's Casebook on Administrative Law. Goldenberg, Norman S. & Tenen, Peter, eds. (Legal Briefs Ser.). 1994. pap. write for info. (*0-87457-004-2*, 1262) Casenotes Pub.

— Administrative Law Adaptable to Courses Utilizing Bonfield, Asimow, & Levin's Casebook on State & Federal Administrative Law. Petertenen & Goldenberg, Norman S., eds. (Legal Briefs Ser.). 1998. pap. write for info. (*0-87457-161-8*, 1265) Casenotes Pub.

— Admiralty: Adaptable to Courses Utilizing Healy & Sharpe's Casebook on Admiralty. Goldenberg, Norman S. & Tenen, Peter, eds. (Legal Briefs Ser.). 1986. pap. write for info. (*0-87457-005-0*, 1290) Casenotes Pub.

— Agency & Partnership - Adaptable to Courses Utilizing Hynes' Casebook on Agency & Partnership. Goldenberg & Tenen Staff, ed. (Legal Briefs Ser.). 1994. pap. write for info. (*0-87457-168-5*, 1351) Casenotes Pub.

— Antitrust: Adaptable to Courses Utilizing Areeda & Kaplow's Casebook on Antitrust. Goldenberg, Norman S. & Tenen, Peter, eds. (Legal Briefs Ser.). 1998. pap. write for info. (*0-87457-008-5*, 1280) Casenotes Pub.

— Antitrust: Adaptable to Courses Utilizing Handler, Pitofsky, Goldschmid & Wood's Casebook on Trade Regulation. Goldenberg, Norman S. & Tenen, Peter, eds. (Legal Briefs Ser.). 1997. pap. write for info. (*0-87457-009-3*, 1281) Casenotes Pub.

— Banking Law: Adaptable to Courses Utilizing Symons & White's Casebook on Banking Law. Goldenberg, Norman S. & Tenen, Peter, eds. (Legal Briefs Ser.). (Orig.). 1991. pap. text. write for info. (*0-87457-153-7*, 1610) Casenotes Pub.

— Civil Procedure: Adaptable to Courses Utilizing Cound, Friedenthal, Miller & Sexton's Casebook on Civil Procedure. Goldenberg, Norman S. & Tenen, Peter, eds. (Legal Briefs Ser.). 1997. pap. write for info. (*0-87457-013-1*, 1040) Casenotes Pub.

— Civil Procedure: Adaptable to Courses Utilizing Field, Kaplan & Clermont's Casebook on Civil Procedure. Goldenberg, Norman S. & Tenen, Peter, eds. (Legal Briefs Ser.). 1997. pap. write for info. (*0-87457-014-X*, 1043) Casenotes Pub.

— Civil Procedure: Adaptable to Courses Utilizing Hazard, Tait & Fletcher Casebook on Pleading & Procedure. Goldenberg, Norman S. & Tenen, Peter, eds. (Legal Briefs Ser.). 1994. pap. write for info. (*0-87457-017-4*, 1041) Casenotes Pub.

— Civil Procedure: Adaptable to Courses Utilizing Rosenberg, Smit & Dreyfuss' Casebook on Civil Procedure. Goldenberg, Norman S. & Tenen, Peter, eds. (Legal Briefs Ser.). 1998. pap. write for info. (*0-87457-018-2*, 1044) Casenotes Pub.

— Civil Procedure: Adaptable to Courses Utilizing Yeazell's Casebook on Civil Procedure. Goldenberg, Norman S. et al, eds. (Legal Briefs Ser.). 1996. pap. write for info. (*0-87457-016-6*, 1046) Casenotes Pub.

— Civil Procedure Adaptable to Courses Utilizing Marcus, Redish & Sherman's Casebook on Civil Procedure. Goldenberg, Norman S. & Tenen, Peter, eds. (Legal Briefs Ser.). 1995. pap. write for info. (*0-87457-163-4*, 1047) Casenotes Pub.

— Commercial Law: Adaptable to Courses Utilizing Farnsworth, Honnald, Reitz, Harris & Mooney's Casebook on Commercial Law. Goldenberg, Norman S. & Tenen, Peter, eds. (Legal Briefs Ser.). 1993. pap. write for info. (*0-87457-019-0*, 1311) Casenotes Pub.

— Commercial Law: Adaptable to Courses Utilizing Jordan & Warren's Casebook on Commercial Law, Secured Transactions & Commercial Paper. Goldenberg, Norman S. & Tenen, Peter, eds. (Legal Briefs Ser.). 1992. pap. write for info. (*0-87457-020-4*, 1312) Casenotes Pub.

— Community Property: Adaptable to Courses Utilizing Bird's Casebook on California Community Property. Goldenberg, Norman S. & Tenen, Peter, eds. (Legal Briefs Ser.). 1994. pap. write for info. (*0-87457-022-0*, 1320) Casenotes Pub.

— Comparative Law: Adaptable to Courses Utilizing Schlesinger, Baade, Damska & Herzog's Casebook on Comparative Law, Casenote Legal Briefs. Goldenberg, Norman S. & Tenen, Peter, eds. (Orig.). (C). 1992. pap. text. write for info. (*0-87457-174-X*, 1630) Casenotes Pub.

— Conflicts: Adaptable to Courses Utilizing Cramton, Currie, Kay & Kramer's Casebook on Conflict of Laws. Goldenberg, Norman S. et al, eds. (Legal Briefs Ser.). 1993. pap. write for info. (*0-87457-023-9*, 1071) Casenotes Pub.

— Conflicts: Adaptable to Courses Utilizing Rosenberg, Hay & Weintraub Casebook on Conflict of Laws. Goldenberg, Norman S. et al, eds. (Legal Briefs Ser.). 1996. pap. write for info. (*0-87457-024-7*, 1070) Casenotes Pub.

— Constitutional Law: Adaptable to Courses Utilizing Brest & Levinson's Casebook on Processes of Constitutional Decision-Making. Goldenberg, Norman S. & Tenen, Peter, eds. (Legal Briefs Ser.). 1992. pap. write for info. (*0-87457-026-3*, 1086) Casenotes Pub.

— Constitutional Law: Adaptable to Courses Utilizing Cohen & Varat's Casebook on Constitutional Law. Goldenberg, Norman S. & Tenen, Peter, eds. (Legal Briefs Ser.). 1997. pap. write for info. (*0-87457-025-5*, 1082) Casenotes Pub.

— Constitutional Law: Adaptable to Courses Utilizing Gunther & Sullivan's Casebook on Constitutional Law. Goldenberg, Norman S. & Tenen, Peter, eds. (Legal Briefs Ser.). 1997. pap. write for info. (*0-87457-028-X*, 1080) Casenotes Pub.

— Constitutional Law: Adaptable to Courses Utilizing Lockhart, Kamisar Choper, Shiffrin & Fallon's Casebook on Constitutional Law. Goldenberg, Norman S. et al, eds. (Legal Briefs Ser.). 1996. pap. write for info. (*0-87457-030-1*, 1081) Casenotes Pub.

— Constitutional Law: Adaptable to Courses Utilizing Rotunda's Casebook on Modern Constitutional Law. Goldenberg, Norman S. & Tenen, Peter, eds. (Legal Briefs Ser.). 1997. pap. write for info. (*0-87457-031-X*, 1085) Casenotes Pub.

— Constitutional Law: Adaptable to Courses Utilizing Stone, Seidman, Sunstein & Tushnet's Casebook on Constitutional Law. Goldenberg, Norman S. et al, eds. (Legal Briefs Ser.). (Orig.). 1996. pap. text. write for info. (*0-87457-147-2*, 1087) Casenotes Pub.

— Contracts: Adaptable to Courses Utilizing Calamari, Perillo, & Bender's Casebook on Contracts, Cases & Problems. Goldenberg, Norman S. et al, eds. (Legal Briefs Ser.). 1989. pap. write for info. (*0-87457-033-6*, 1017) Casenotes Pub.

— Contracts: Adaptable to Courses Utilizing Dawson, Harvey & Henderson's Casebook on Contracts. Goldenberg, Norman S. & Tenen, Peter, eds. (Legal Briefs Ser.). 1998. pap. write for info. (*0-87457-034-4*, 1014) Casenotes Pub.

— Contracts: Adaptable to Courses Utilizing Farnsworth & Young's Casebook on Contracts. Goldenberg, Norman S. & Tenen, Peter, eds. (Legal Briefs Ser.). 1995. pap. write for info. (*0-87457-035-2*, 1010) Casenotes Pub.

— Contracts: Adaptable to Courses Utilizing Kessler, Gilmore & Kronman's Casebook on Contracts. Goldenberg, Norman S. & Tenen, Peter, eds. (Legal Briefs Ser.). 1986. pap. write for info. (*0-87457-037-9*, 1013) Casenotes Pub.

— Contracts: Adaptable to Courses Utilizing Knapp & Crystal's Casebook on Problems in Contract Law. Goldenberg, Norman S. & Tenen, Peter, eds. (Legal Briefs Ser.). 1993. pap. write for info. (*0-87457-038-7*, 1016) Casenotes Pub.

— Contracts: Adaptable to Courses Utilizing Murphy, Speidel & Ayres' Casebook on Contract Law. Goldenberg, Norman S. & Tenen, Peter, eds. (Legal Briefs Ser.). 1997. pap. write for info. (*0-87457-041-7*, 1012) Casenotes Pub.

— Contracts: Adaptable to Courses Utilizing Rosett's Casebook on Contracts Law & Its Application. Goldenberg, Norman S. & Tenen, Peter, eds. (Legal Briefs Ser.). 1994. pap. write for info. (*0-87457-040-9*, 1015) Casenotes Pub.

— Contracts: Adaptable to Courses Utilizing Vernon's Casebook on Contracts: Theory & Practice. Goldenberg, Norman S. & Tenen, Peter, eds. (Legal Briefs Ser.). 1981. pap. write for info. (*0-87457-043-3*, 1019) Casenotes Pub.

— Contracts - Adaptable to Courses Utilizing Crandall & Whaley's Casebook on Contracts. Goldenberg, Norman S. & Tenen, Peter, eds. (Legal Briefs Ser.). 1993. pap. write for info. (*0-87457-166-9*, 1101) Casenotes Pub.

— Copyright: Adaptable to Courses Utilizing Goldstein's Casebook on Copyright, Patent & Trademark Casenotes Legal Briefs. Goldenberg, Norman S. & Tenen, Peter, eds. (Legal Briefs Ser.). (Orig.). (C). 1997. pap. text. write for info. (*0-87457-173-1*, 1502) Casenotes Pub.

— Copyright: Adaptable to Courses Utilizing Nimmer, M, M & N's Casebook on Copyright & Other Aspects of Law Pertaining to Literary, Musical & Artistic Works. Goldenberg, Norman S. & Tenen, Peter, eds. (Legal Briefs Ser.). 1991. pap. write for info. (*0-87457-045-X*, 1501) Casenotes Pub.

— Corporations: Adaptable to Courses Utilizing Cary & Eisenberg's Casebook on Corporations. Goldenberg, Norman S. et al, eds. (Legal Briefs Ser.). 1995. pap. write for info. (*0-87457-046-8*, 1050) Casenotes Pub.

— Corporations: Adaptable to Courses Utilizing Choper, Coffee & Gilson's Casebook on Corporations. Goldenberg, Norman S. et al, eds. (Legal Briefs Ser.). 1995. pap. write for info. (*0-87457-047-6*, 1054) Casenotes Pub.

— Corporations: Adaptable to Courses Utilizing Hamilton's Casebook on Corporations-Including Partnerships & Limited Partnerships. Goldenberg, Norman S. et al, eds. (Legal Briefs Ser.). 1998. pap. write for info. (*0-87457-048-4*, 1053) Casenotes Pub.

— Corporations: Adaptable to Courses Utilizing Solomon, Schwartz, Bauman & Weiss' Casebook on Corporations. Goldenberg, Norman S. et al, eds. (Legal Briefs Ser.). 1998. pap. write for info. (*0-87457-158-8*, 1056) Casenotes Pub.

— Corporations: Adaptable to Courses Utilizing Vagt's Casebook on Basic Corporation Law. Goldenberg, Norman S. & Tenen, Peter, eds. (Legal Briefs Ser.). 1988. pap. write for info. (*0-87457-051-4*, 1052) Casenotes Pub.

— Creditors' Rights: Adaptable to Courses Utilizing Riesenfeld's Casebook on Creditors' Remedies & Debtors' Protection. Goldenberg, Norman S. & Tenen, Peter, eds. (Legal Briefs Ser.). 1987. pap. write for info. (*0-87457-052-2*, 1300) Casenotes Pub.

— Criminal Justice: Adaptable to Courses Utilizing Weinreb's Casebook on Criminal Justice. Goldenberg, Norman S. & Tenen, Peter, eds. (Legal Briefs Ser.). 1997. pap. write for info. (*0-87457-053-0*, 1550) Casenotes Pub.

— Criminal Law: Adaptable to Courses Utilizing Boyce & Perkin's Casebook on Criminal Law. Goldenberg, Norman S. & Tenen, Peter, eds. (Legal Briefs Ser.). 1989. pap. write for info. (*0-87457-058-1*, 1020) Casenotes Pub.

— Criminal Law: Adaptable to Courses Utilizing Johnson's Casebook on Criminal Law. Goldenberg, Norman S. et al, eds. (Legal Briefs Ser.). 1995. pap. write for info. (*0-87457-156-1*, 1027) Casenotes Pub.

— Criminal Law: Adaptable to Courses Utilizing LaFave's Casebook of Modern Criminal Law. Goldenberg, Norman S. & Tenen, Peter, eds. (Legal Briefs Ser.). 1988. pap. write for info. (*0-87457-057-3*, 1023) Casenotes Pub.

— Criminal Law: Adaptable to Kaplan, Weisberg & Binder Casebook on Criminal Law. Goldenberg, Norman S. et al, eds. (Legal Briefs Ser.). (Orig.). 1996. pap. text. write for info. (*0-87457-146-4*, 1026) Casenotes Pub.

— Criminal Procedure: Adaptable to Courses Utilizing Haddad, Zagel, Starkman, & Bauer's Casebook on Criminal Procedure. Goldenberg, Norman S. et al, eds. 1998. pap. write for info. (*0-87457-060-3*, 1202) Casenotes Pub.

— Criminal Procedure: Adaptable to Courses Utilizing Kamisar, LaFave & Israel's Casebook on Criminal Procedure. Goldenberg, Norman S. et al, eds. (Legal Briefs Ser.). 1994. pap. write for info. (*0-87457-062-X*, 1200) Casenotes Pub.

— Criminal Procedure: Adaptable to Courses Utilizing Weinreb's Casebook on Criminal Process. Goldenberg, Norman S. & Tenen, Peter, eds. (Legal Briefs Ser.). 1997. pap. write for info. (*0-87457-064-6*, 1203) Casenotes Pub.

— Debtor-Creditor: Adaptable to Courses Utilizing Warren & Westbrook's Casebook on the Law of Debtors & Creditors. Goldenberg, Norman S. et al, eds. (Legal Briefs Ser.). (Orig.). 1996. pap. text. write for info. (*0-87457-151-0*, 1304) Casenotes Pub.

— Decedents' Estates: Adaptable to Courses Utilizing Ritchie, Alford, Effland & Dobris' Casebook on Decedents' Estates & Trusts. Goldenberg, Norman S. & Tenen, Peter, eds. (Legal Briefs Ser.). 1998. pap. write for info. (*0-87457-069-7*, 1224) Casenotes Pub.

— Decedents' Estates: Adaptable to Courses Utilizing Scoles & Halbach's Casebook on Decedents' Estates & Trusts. Goldenberg, Norman S. & Tenen, Peter, eds. (Legal Briefs Ser.). 1993. pap. write for info. (*0-87457-070-0*, 1222) Casenotes Pub.

— Enterprise Organizations: Adaptable to Courses Utilizing Conard, Knauss & Siegel's Casebook on Enterprise Organizations. Goldenberg, Norman S. & Tenen, Peter, eds. (Legal Briefs Ser.). 1987. pap. write for info. (*0-87457-007-7*, 1350) Casenotes Pub.

— Environmental Law: Adaptable to Courses Utilizing Anderson, Mandelker & Tarlock's Casebook on Environmental Law. Goldenberg, Norman S. et al, eds. (Legal Briefs Ser.). (Orig.). (C). 1994. pap. text. write for info. (*0-87457-172-3*, 1342) Casenotes Pub.

— Environmental Law: Adaptable to Courses Utilizing Findley & Farber's Casebook on Environmental Law. Goldenberg, Norman S. et al, eds. (Legal Briefs Ser.). 1995. pap. write for info. (*0-87457-071-9*, 1341) Casenotes Pub.

— Ethics Adaptable to Courses Utilizing Giller's Casebook on Regulation of Lawyers. Goldenberg, Norman S. et al, eds. (Legal Briefs Ser.). (Orig.). (C). 1998. pap. text. write for info. (*0-87457-165-0*, 1091) Casenotes Pub.

— Evidence: Adaptable to Courses Utilizing Lempert, Saltzburg, Gross & Liebman Casebook on Test Problems, Transcripts & Cases. Goldenberg, Norman S. & Tenen, Peter, eds. (Legal Briefs Ser.). 1998. pap. write for info. (*0-87457-078-6*, 1063) Casenotes Pub.

— Evidence: Adaptable to Courses Utilizing Strong, Broun & Mosteller's Casebook on Evidence. Goldenberg, Norman S. et al, eds. (Legal Briefs Ser.). 1995. pap. write for info. (*0-87457-076-X*, 1064) Casenotes Pub.

— Evidence: Adaptable to Courses Utilizing Sutton & Wellborn's Casebook on Evidence. Goldenberg, Norman S. et al, eds. (Legal Briefs Ser.). 1996. pap. write for info. (*0-87457-081-6*, 1062) Casenotes Pub.

— Evidence: Adaptable to Courses Utilizing Waltz & Park's

Casebook on Evidence. Goldenberg, Norman S. et al, eds. (Legal Briefs Ser.). 1995. pap. write for info. (*0-87457-079-4*, 1061) Casenotes Pub.
— Evidence: Adaptable to Courses Utilizing Weinstein, Mansfield, Abrams & Berger's Casebook on Evidence. Goldenberg, Norman S. et al, eds. (Legal Briefs Ser.). 1997. pap. write for info. (*0-87457-080-8*, 1060) Casenotes Pub.
— Family Law: Adaptable to Courses Utilizing Areen's Casebook on Family Law. Goldenberg, Norman S. et al, eds. (Legal Briefs Ser.). (Orig.). 1992. pap. text. write for info. (*0-87457-152-9*, 1244) Casenotes Pub.
— Family Law: Adaptable to Courses Utilizing Clark & Glowinsky's Casebook on Domestic Relations. Goldenberg, Norman S. et al, eds. (Legal Briefs Ser.). 1998. pap. write for info. (*0-87457-082-4*, 1242) Casenotes Pub.
— Family Law: Adaptable to Courses Utilizing Krause, Oldman, Elrod & Garrison's Casebook on Family Law. Goldenberg, Norman S. & Tenen, Peter, eds. (Legal Briefs Ser.). 1998. pap. write for info. (*0-87457-084-0*, 1243) Casenotes Pub.
— Family Law: Adaptable to Courses Utilizing Wadlington's Casebook on Domestic Relations. Goldenberg, Norman S. et al, eds. (Legal Briefs Ser.). 1997. pap. write for info. (*0-87457-085-9*, 1240) Casenotes Pub.
— Federal Courts: Adaptable to Courses Utilizing Hart & Weschler's (Falcon et. al.) Casebook on the Federal Courts & the Federal System. Goldenberg, Norman S. et al, eds. (Legal Briefs Ser.). 1996. pap. write for info. (*0-87457-086-7*, 1360) Casenotes Pub.
— Federal Courts: Adaptable to Courses Utilizing McCormick, Chadbourn & Wright's Casebook on Federal Courts. Goldenberg, Norman S. & Tenen, Peter, eds. (Legal Briefs Ser.). 1992. pap. write for info. (*0-87457-088-3*, 1361) Casenotes Pub.
— Gratuitous Transfers: Adaptable to Courses Utilizing Clark, Lusky & Murphy's Casebook on Gratuitous Transfers, Wills, Intestate Succession, Trusts, Gifts, & Future Interests. Goldenberg, Norman S. & Tenen, Peter, eds. (Legal Briefs Ser.). 1985. pap. write for info. (*0-87457-089-1*, 1510) Casenotes Pub.
— Immigration Law Adaptable to Courses Courses Utilizing Aleinikoff, Martin & Motomura's Casebook on Immigration Laws. Goldenberg, Norman S. et al, eds. (Legal Briefs Ser.). (Orig.). (C). 1998. pap. text. write for info. (*0-87457-171-5*, 1640) Casenotes Pub.
— Insurance Law: Adaptable to Courses Utilizing Keeton's Casebook on Basic Insurance Law. Goldenberg, Norman S. & Tenen, Peter, eds. (Legal Briefs Ser.). 1983. pap. write for info. (*0-87457-090-5*, 1371) Casenotes Pub.
— Insurance Law: Adaptable to Courses Utilizing Young & Holmes' Casebook on Insurance. Goldenberg, Norman S. et al, eds. (Legal Briefs Ser.). 1985. pap. write for info. (*0-87457-091-3*, 1370) Casenotes Pub.
— Insurance Law Adaptable to Courses Utilizing York, Whelan & Martinez' Casebook on Insurance Law. Goldenberg, Norman S. et al, eds. (Legal Briefs Ser.). (Orig.). (C). 1994. pap. text. write for info. (*0-87457-167-7*, 1372) Casenotes Pub.
— International Law: Adaptable to Courses Utilizing Carter & Trimble's Casebook on International Law. Goldenberg, Norman S. et al, eds. (Legal Briefs Ser.). (Orig.). (C). 1995. pap. text. write for info. (*0-87457-170-7*, 1393) Casenotes Pub.
— International Law: Adaptable to Courses Utilizing Henkin, Pugh, Schacter & Smit's Casebook on International Law. Goldenberg, Norman S. et al, eds. (Legal Briefs Ser.). 1993. pap. write for info. (*0-87457-093-X*, 1392) Casenotes Pub.
— International Law: Adaptable to Courses Utilizing Oliver, Firmage, Blakesley, Scott & Williams Casebook on the International Legal System. Goldenberg, Norman S. et al, eds. (Legal Briefs Ser.). 1995. pap. write for info. (*0-87457-094-8*, 1390) Casenotes Pub.
— Labor Law: Adaptable to Courses Utilizing Harper & Estreicher's Casebook on Labor Law. Goldenberg, Norman S. et al, eds. (Legal Briefs Ser.). 1996. pap. write for info. (*0-87457-098-0*, 1332) Casenotes Pub.
— Labor Law: Adaptable to Courses Utilizing Leslie's Casebook on Labor Relations Law. Goldenberg, Norman S. & Tenen, Peter, eds. (Legal Briefs Ser.). 1992. pap. write for info. (*0-87457-097-2*, 1333) Casenotes Pub.
— Land Finance: Adaptable to Courses Utilizing Berger & Johnston's Casebook on Land Transfer & Finance. Goldenberg, Norman S. & Tenen, Peter, eds. (Legal Briefs Ser.). 1993. pap. write for info. (*0-87457-100-6*, 1471) Casenotes Pub.

Casenotes Publishing co., Inc. Staff. Land Finance: Adaptable to Courses Utilizing Penney, Broude & Cunningham's Casebook on Land Financing. Goldenberg, Norman S. & Tenen, Peter, eds. (Legal Briefs Ser.). 1985. pap. write for info. (*0-87457-101-4*, 1470) Casenotes Pub.

Casenotes Publishing Co., Inc. Staff. Local Government: Adaptable to Courses Utilizing Valente & McCarthy's Casebook on Local Government Law. Goldenberg, Norman S. & Tenen, Peter, eds. (Legal Briefs Ser.). 1992. pap. write for info. (*0-87457-105-7*, 1590) Casenotes Pub.
— Negotiable Instruments: Adaptable to Courses Utilizing Whaley's Casebook on Commercial Law. Goldenberg, Norman S. et al, eds. (Legal Briefs Ser.). 1997. pap. write for info. (*0-87457-108-1*, 1313) Casenotes Pub.
— Oil & Gas: Adaptable to Courses Utilizing Kuntz, Lowe, Anderson & Smith's Casebook on Oil & Gas Law. Goldenberg, Norman S. et al, eds. (Legal Briefs Ser.). (Orig.). 1993. pap. text. write for info. (*0-87457-155-3*, 1541) Casenotes Pub.
— Oil & Gas: Adaptable to Courses Utilizing Maxwell, Williams, Martin & Kramer's Casebook on Oil & Gas. Goldenberg, Norman S. & Tenen, Peter, eds. (Legal Briefs Ser.). 1992. pap. write for info. (*0-87457-110-3*, 1540) Casenotes Pub.
— Patent Law: Adaptable to Courses Utilizing Francis & Collins' Casebook on Patent Law. Goldenberg, Norman S. et al, eds. (Legal Briefs Ser.). 1995. pap. write for info. (*0-87457-111-1*, 1560) Casenotes Pub.
— Products Liability: Adaptable to Courses Utilizing Owen, Montgomery & Keeton's Casebook on Products Liability & Safety. Goldenberg, Norman S. et al, eds. (Legal Briefs Ser.). 1996. pap. write for info. (*0-87457-113-8*, 1431) Casenotes Pub.
— Professional Responsibility to Courses Utilizing Morgan & Rotunda. Goldenberg, Norman S. et al, eds. (Orig.). (C). 1995. pap. text. write for info. (*0-87457-169-3*, 1092) Casenotes Pub.
— Property: Adaptable to Courses Utilizing Casner & Leach's Casebook on Property. Goldenberg, Norman S. & Tenen, Peter, eds. (Legal Briefs Ser.). 1985. pap. write for info. (*0-87457-115-4*, 1030) Casenotes Pub.
— Property: Adaptable to Courses Utilizing Cribbet, Johnson, Findley & Smith's Casebook on Property. Goldenberg, Norman S. et al, eds. (Legal Briefs Ser.). 1996. pap. write for info. (*0-87457-116-2*, 1031) Casenotes Pub.
— Property: Adaptable to Courses Utilizing Dukeminier & Krier's Casebook on Property. Goldenberg, Norman S. et al, eds. (Legal Briefs Ser.). 1998. pap. write for info. (*0-87457-117-0*, 1035) Casenotes Pub.
— Property: Adaptable to Courses Utilizing Haar & Liebman's Casebook on Property & Law. Goldenberg, Norman S. & Tenen, Peter, eds. (Legal Briefs Ser.). 1985. pap. write for info. (*0-87457-118-9*, 1034) Casenotes Pub.
— Property: Adaptable to Courses Utilizing Nelson, Stoebuck & Whitman's Casebook on Basic Property Law. Goldenberg, Norman S. et al, eds. (Legal Briefs Ser.). 1996. pap. write for info. (*0-87457-114-6*, 1033) Casenotes Pub.
— Property: Adaptable to Courses Utilizing Rabin & Kwall's Casebook on Real Property Law. Goldenberg, Norman S. & Tenen, Peter, eds. (Legal Briefs Ser.). 1992. pap. write for info. (*0-87457-119-7*, 1032) Casenotes Pub.
— Real Estate Transfer & Finance Adaptable to Courses Utilizing Nelson & Whitman's Casebook on Real Estate Transfer, Finance, & Development. Goldenberg, Norman S. & Tenen, Peter, eds. (Legal Briefs Ser.). (Orig.). (C). 1998. pap. text. write for info. (*0-87457-157-X*, 1620) Casenotes Pub.
— Remedies: Adaptable to Courses Utilizing Leavell, Love, Nelson, & Kovacic-Fleisher's Casebook on Equitable Remedies & Restitution. Goldenberg, Norman S. et al, eds. (Legal Briefs Ser.). 1994. pap. write for info. (*0-87457-120-0*, 1253) Casenotes Pub.
— Remedies: Adaptable to Courses Utilizing Re & Re Casebook on Remedies. Goldenberg, Norman S. et al, eds. (Legal Briefs Ser.). 1996. pap. write for info. (*0-87457-121-9*, 1252) Casenotes Pub.
— Remedies: Adaptable to Courses Utilizing York, Bauman & Rendleman's Casebook on Remedies. Goldenberg, Norman S. & Tenen, Peter, eds. (Legal Briefs Ser.). 1992. pap. write for info. (*0-87457-122-7*, 1250) Casenotes Pub.
— Sales, Secured Trans. & Payment: Adaptable to Courses Utilizing Spiedel, Summers & White's Casebook on Sales & Secured Transactions. Goldenberg, Norman S. et al, eds. (Legal Briefs Ser.). 1993. pap. write for info. (*0-87457-021-2*, 1310) Casenotes Pub.
— Securities Regulations: Adaptable to Courses Utilizing Jennings, Marsh & Coffee's Casebook on Securities Regulation. Goldenberg, Norman S. & Tenen, Peter, eds. (Legal Briefs Ser.). 1998. pap. write for info. (*0-87457-123-5*, 1270) Casenotes Pub.
— Taxation: Adaptable to Courses Utilizing Freeland, Lind & Stephens' Casebook on Fundamentals of Federal Income Taxation. Goldenberg, Norman S. et al, eds. (Legal Briefs Ser.). 1998. pap. write for info. (*0-87457-129-4*, 1212) Casenotes Pub.
— Taxation: Adaptable to Courses Utilizing Graetz's Schenk's Casebook on Federal Income Taxation. Goldenberg, Norman S. et al, eds. (Legal Briefs Ser.). 1995. pap. write for info. (*0-87457-130-8*, 1211) Casenotes Pub.
— Taxation: Adaptable to Courses Utilizing Klein, Bankman, Bittker & Stone's Casebook on Federal Income Taxation. Goldenberg, Norman S. et al, eds. (Legal Briefs Ser.). 1997. pap. write for info. (*0-87457-127-8*, 1210) Casenotes Pub.
— Taxation: Adaptable to Courses Utilizing Lind, Schwarz, Lathrope & Rosenberg's Casebook on Fundamentals of Corporate Taxation. Goldenberg, Norman S. & Tenen, Peter, eds. (Legal Briefs Ser.). (Orig.). 1997. pap. text. write for info. (*0-87457-150-2*, 1218) Casenotes Pub.
— Torts: Adaptable to Courses Utilizing Dobbs' Casebook on Torts & Compensation. Goldenberg, Norman S. & Tenen, Peter, eds. (Legal Briefs Ser.). (Orig.). 1997. pap. text. write for info. (*0-87457-148-0*, 1006) Casenotes Pub.
— Torts: Adaptable to Courses Utilizing Epstein's Casebook on Torts. Tenen, Peter et al, eds. (Legal Briefs Ser.). 1995. pap. write for info. (*0-87457-134-0*, 1003) Casenotes Pub.
— Torts: Adaptable to Courses Utilizing Franklin & Rabin's Casebook on Tort Law & Alternatives. Tenen, Peter et al, eds. (Legal Briefs Ser.). 1996. pap. write for info. (*0-87457-135-9*, 1004) Casenotes Pub.
— Torts: Adaptable to Courses Utilizing Henderson, Pearson & Siliciano's Casebook on the Torts Process. Tenen, Peter et al, eds. (Legal Briefs Ser.). 1994. pap. write for info. (*0-87457-136-7*, 1001) Casenotes Pub.
— Torts: Adaptable to Courses Utilizing Keeton, Sargentich & Keating's Casebook on Torts. Tenen, Peter et al, eds. (Legal Briefs Ser.). 1998. pap. write for info. (*0-87457-137-5*, 1002) Casenotes Pub.
— Torts: Adaptable to Courses Utilizing Prosser, Wade, Schwartz, Kelly & Partlett's Casebook on Torts. Tenen, Peter et al, eds. (Legal Briefs Ser.). 1994. pap. write for info. (*0-87457-138-3*, 1000) Casenotes Pub.
— Torts: Adaptable to Courses Utilizing Shulman, James & Grey's Casebook on Torts. Tenen, Peter et al, eds. (Legal Briefs Ser.). 1979. pap. write for info. (*0-87457-139-1*, 1005) Casenotes Pub.
— Trusts: Adaptable to Courses Utilizing Bogert & Oak, Hansen & Hill's Casebook on Law of Trusts. Tenen, Peter, ed. (Legal Briefs Ser.). 1991. pap. write for info. (*0-87457-140-5*, 1230) Casenotes Pub.
— U.C.C. Adaptable to Courses Utilizing Epstein, Martin, Henning & Nickle's Casebook on Basic Uniform Commercial Code: Adaptable to Courses Utilizing Epstein & Martin's Casebook on Basic Uniform Commercial Code. Goldenberg, Norman S. & Tenen, Peter, eds. (Legal Briefs Ser.). 1988. pap. write for info. (*0-87457-142-1*, 1410) Casenotes Pub.
— Wills: Adaptable to Courses Utilizing Mechem & Atkinson's Casebook on Wills & Administration. Goldenberg, Norman S. et al, eds. (Legal Briefs Ser.). 1980. pap. write for info. (*0-87457-144-8*, 1220) Casenotes Pub.
— Wills & Trusts: Adaptable to Courses Utilizing Dukeminier & Johanson's Casebook on Family Wealth Transactions: Wills, Trusts, Future Interests & Estate Planning. Goldenberg, Norman S. et al, eds. (Legal Briefs Ser.). 1995. pap. write for info. (*0-87457-068-9*, 1223) Casenotes Pub.

Casenotes Publishing Co., Inc. Staff, et al. Complex Litigation: Adaptable to Courses Utilizing Marcus & Sherman's Casebook on Complex Litigation. Tenen, Peter & Goldenberg, Norman S., eds. (Legal Briefs Ser.). (Orig.). 1998. pap. text. write for info. (*0-87457-202-9*, 1048) Casenotes Pub.
— Contracts: Adaptable to Courses Utilizing Hamilton, Rau & Weintraub's Casebook on Contracts. Tenen, Peter & Goldenberg, Norman S., eds. LC 85-206453. 118p. 1993. write for info. (*0-87457-039-5*, 1100) Casenotes Pub.
— Corporations: Adaptable to Courses Utilizing O'Kelley & Thompson's Casebook on Corporations & Other Business Associations. Tenen, Peter & Goldenberg, Norman S., eds. (Legal Briefs Ser.). (Orig.). 1996. pap. text. write for info. (*0-87457-203-7*, 1057) Casenotes Pub.
— Employment Discrimination: Adaptable to Courses Utilizing Friedman & Strickler's Casebook on Employment Discrimination. Tenen, Peter & Goldenberg, Norman S., eds. (Legal Briefs Ser.). (Orig.). 1997. pap. text. write for info. (*0-87457-204-5*, 1670) Casenotes Pub.
— Evidence Adaptable to the Courses Utilizing Mueller & Kirkpatrick's Casebook on Evidence under the Rules. Goldenberg et al, eds. (Legal Briefs Ser.). 1996. pap. write for info. (*0-87457-160-X*, 1066) Casenotes Pub.
— Federal Courts Adaptable to Courses Utilizing Low & Jeffries Casebook on Federal Courts & the Law of Federal States Relations. Goldenberg, Norman S. et al, eds. (Legal Briefs Ser.). 1998. pap. write for info. (*0-87457-164-2*, 1363) Casenotes Pub.
— Property: Adaptable to Courses Utilizing Donohue, Kauper, & Martin's Casebook on Property. (Legal Briefs Ser.). (Orig.). 1993. pap. text. write for info. (*0-87457-208-8*, 1037) Casenotes Pub.
— Property Adaptable to Courses Utilizing Kurtz & Hovenkamps Casebook on American Property Law. Goldenberg, Norman S. et al, eds. (Legal Briefs Ser.). 1993. pap. write for info. (*0-87457-159-6*, 1036) Casenotes Pub.
— Real Estate Transactions: Adaptable to Courses Utilizing Goldstein & Korngold's Casebook on Real Estate Transactions. (Legal Briefs Ser.). (Orig.). 1997. pap. text. write for info. (*0-87457-207-X*, 1621) Casenotes Pub.
— Remedies: Adaptable to Courses Utilizing Laycock's Casebook on Modern American Remedies. Goldenberg, Norman S. & Tenen, Peter, eds. (Legal Briefs Ser.). (Orig.). 1994. pap. text. write for info. (*0-87457-149-9*, 1254) Casenotes Pub.
— Remedies: Adaptable to Courses Utilizing Shoben & Tabb's Casebook on Remedies. Goldenberg, Norman S. et al, eds. (Legal Briefs Ser.). 1995. pap. write for info. (*0-87457-162-6*, 1255) Casenotes Pub.
— Sales & Secured Transactions: Adaptable to Courses Utilizing Speidel, Summers & White's Casebook on Sales & Secured Transactions, Including the Companion Book on Payment Law. (Orig.). 1994. pap. text. write for info. (*0-318-72701-3*, 1310) Casenotes Pub.
— Securities Regulation: Adaptable to Courses Utilizing Cox, Hillman & Langevoort's Casebook on Securities Regulation. (Legal Briefs Ser.). (Orig.). 1997. pap. text. write for info. (*0-87457-206-1*, 1272) Casenotes Pub.

Casenotes Publishing Co., Ltd. Staff. Contracts: Adaptable to Courses Utilizing Fuller & Eisenberg's Casebook on Contracts. Goldenberg, Norman S. et al, eds. (Legal Briefs Ser.). 1996. pap. write for info. (*0-87457-036-0*, 1011) Casenotes Pub.

Caserio. The Novel in England. LC 98-35176. 441p. 1998. 33.00 (*0-8057-1662-9*, Twyne) Mac Lib Ref.

Caserio, Robert L. Plot, Story, & the Novel: From Dickens & Poe to the Modern Period. LC 79-4321. 326p. 1979. reprint ed. pap. 101.10 (*0-608-02538-0*, 206318200004) Bks Demand.

Caserta, Carmen & Nowitz, Marilyn. The Dog Ate My Homework. LC 94-75987. (Illus.). 32p. 1994. 9.95 (*1-880851-14-8*) Greene Bark Pr.

Caserta, Thomas G. Beyond the Darkness, into the Light: Thinking about Sin & Forgiveness Today. LC 93-19167. (Illus.). 67p. (Orig.). 1993. pap. 3.50 (*0-8198-1142-4*) Pauline Bks.
— Tablets of Stone, Hearts of Flesh: A Positive Approach to the Ten Commandments. 80p. 1996. pap. 3.50 (*0-8198-7387-X*) Pauline Bks.

Cases, J. M. & Thomas, F., eds. Waste Solidification-Stabilization Process: Proceedings of the International Congress, Nancy, November 28-December 1st, 1995. 536p. 1997. pap. 310.00 (*2-905015-32-2*, Pub. by Edits Technip) Enfield Pubs NH.

Casetti, Francesco. Inside the Gaze: The Fiction Film & Its Spectator. Andrew, Nell & O'Brien, Charles, trs. LC 98-34481. (Society for Cinema Studies Translation Ser.). 208p. 1998. 35.00 (*0-253-33443-8*); pap. 17.95 (*0-253-21232-4*) Ind U Pr.
— Theories of Cinema, 1945-1990. LC 98-58071. 462p. 1999. 50.00 (*0-292-71206-5*) U of Tex Pr.

Casetti, Franceso. Theories of Cinema, 1945-1990. LC 98-58071. 462p. 1999. pap. 24.95 (*0-292-71207-3*) U of Tex Pr.

Casetti, Pierre. Gibt es Ein Leben Vor Dem Tod? Eine Auslegung Von Psalm 49. (Orbis Biblicus et Orientalis Ser.: Vol. 44). 1982. text 61.50 (*3-7278-0254-5*, Pub. by Ed Univ Fri) Eisenbrauns.

Casetti, Pierre, et al, eds. Melanges Dominique Barthelemy. (Orbis Biblicus et Orientalis Ser.: Vol. 38). 1981. text 93.75 (*2-8271-0197-1*, Pub. by Ed Univ Fri) Eisenbrauns.

Casewit, Carla J., jt. auth. see Rappe, Anthony K.

Casewit, Curtis. Colorado: Off the Beaten Path: A Guide to Unique Places. 5th ed. LC 98-49500. (Off the Beaten Path Ser.). (Illus.). 225p. 1999. pap. text 10.95 (*0-7627-0403-9*) Globe Pequot.
— Graphology Handbook. (Illus.). 168p. 1980. pap. 14.95 (*0-914918-15-X*, Whitford) Schiffer.

Casewit, Curtis W. The Diary: A Complete Guide to Journal Writing. LC 81-69698. viii, 146 p. 1982. 2.95 (*0-89505-060-9*) Argus Comm.
— Handwriting Never Lies: What Personality Traits Your Handwriting Reveals. 192p. 1999. pap. 12.95 (*0-89529-995-X*, Avery) Penguin Putnam.
— Skiing Colorado: A Complete Guide to America's Number 1 Ski State. LC 75-21060. 160p. 1975. pap. 4.95 (*0-85699-123-6*) Chatham Pr.

Casewit, Jane, tr. see Radhu, Abdul W.

Casey. Hindu. 1994. pap. 24.00 (*0-9633858-1-X*) Dillard Pub.
— Making Country Style Curtains. (Country Wisdom Bulletin Ser.: Vol. A-98). 1988. pap. 2.95 (*0-88266-487-5*) Storey Bks.
— MHEG: International Standard for Multimedia Hypermedia. 1995. text 69.95 (*0-442-02201-8*, VNR) Wiley.
— Stained Glass Window Designs by Frank Lloyd Wright. 1998. pap. 4.50 (*0-486-29516-8*) Dover.

Casey, Aaron. Aviation Competitions: Effects on Consumers from Domestic Airline Alliances Vary. (Illus.). 68p. 1999. pap. text 20.00 (*0-7881-8093-2*) DIANE Pub.

Casey, Al. Casey's Law: If Something Can Go Right, It Should. LC 95-12716. 320p. 1998. pap. 14.45 (*1-55970-428-4*, Pub. by Arcade Pub Inc) Time Warner.

Casey, Albert V. Casey's Law: If Something Can Go Right, it Should. LC 95-12716. 256p. 1997. 25.45 (*1-55970-307-5*, Pub. by Arcade Pub Inc) Time Warner.

Casey, Alvin & Casey, Robert B. Shelton Wininger & Pace Families. LC 87-71662. (Illus.). 600p. 1987. 40.00 (*0-9619051-0-7*) Brooks TX.

Casey, Andrew. The Dr. Jekyll-Mr. Hyde Syndrome: Couples in Chaos. LC 92-91267. 1993. 16.95 (*0-533-10584-6*) Vantage.

Casey, B. Employers' Choice of Pension Schemes. (DSS Research Report Ser.). 1993. 10.00 (*0-11-762073-4*, Pub. by Statnry Office) Bernan Associates.

Casey, B., et al. Employers' Pension Provision, 1994. (DSS Research Report Ser.). 1996. write for info. (*0-11-762443-8*, Pub. by Statnry Office) Bernan Associates.

Casey, Barbara. New Radiance Metaphysical & Holistic Florida Directory. 1997. pap. 7.95 (*1-889131-35-0*) CasAnanda.

***Casey, Barbara & Dupas, Brenda, eds.** New Radiance Metaphysical & Holistic Florida Directory: Millennium Edition. 6th rev. ed. 208p. 1999. pap. 11.95 (*0-9645702-3-8*) New Radiance Dir.

***Casey, Bernard & Gold, Michael.** Social Partnership & Economic Performance: The Case of Europe. LC 99-88522. 176p. 2000. 75.00 (*1-84064-200-9*) E Elgar.

Casey, Bernice B., jt. auth. see Casey, Robert B.

Casey, Bert. Acoustic Guitar Primer. 6th ed. Hohwald, Geoff, ed. (Illus.). 80p. 1984. reprint ed. pap. text 14.95 (*1-893907-25-2*, AGP) Cassett & Video.
— Bass Guitar Primer. 4th ed. Hohwald, Geoff, ed. (Illus.). 56p. 1992. reprint ed. pap. text 14.95 (*1-893907-27-9*, BGP) Cassett & Video.

Casey, Bert. Bluegrass Fakebook. pap. text 14.95 (*1-893907-37-6*) Cassett & Video.

Casey, Bert. Electric Guitar Primer. 6th ed. Hohwald, Geoff, ed. (Illus.). 80p. 1992. reprint ed. pap. text 15.95 (*1-893907-26-0*, EGP) Cassett & Video.
— Mandolin Primer. 5th ed. Hohwald, Geoff, ed. (Illus.). 56p. 1988. reprint ed. pap. text 14.95 (*1-893907-33-3*, MP) Cassett & Video.

Casey, Bert, ed. see Hohwald, Geoff.

Casey, Bert, ed. see Tolles, Jim.

Casey, Bert, ed. see Vogl, Peter.

Casey, Bert, ed. see Vogler, Peter Z.

Casey, Bert, ed. see Wolf, Tom & Vogl, Peter.

Casey, Bert, ed. & illus. see Wimer, Tim.

An Asterisk (*) at the beginning of an entry indicates that the title is appearing for the first time.

Casey, Betty. Dance across Texas. (Illus.). 144p. 1985. pap. 11.95 (0-292-71551-X) U of Tex Pr.
Casey, Betty, ed. International Folk Dancing U.S.A. 1982. 22.50 (0-385-13308-1) Doubleday.
Casey, Betty, jt. auth. see Puglisi, Catherine R.
Casey, Betty, jt. auth. see Shay, Jack.
Casey, Betty, jt. auth. see Shay, Jack E.
Casey, Bill & McMullin, Rian E. Hablese con Sentido A Si Mismo: Una Guia de Terapia de Restructuracion Cognitiva. Navas, R. Jose, tr. from ENG. Orig. Title: Talk Sense to Yourself: A Guide to Cognitive Restructuring Therapy. (SPA., Illus.). 45p. (Orig.). 1975. pap. 4.00 (0-935205-04-7) Counseling Res.
Casey, Bill, jt. auth. see McMullin, Rian E.
Casey, Brenda, ed. Uncommon Numbers Vol. I: A Source Book for Artists. (Illus.). vi, 58p. (Orig.). 1996. pap. 13.95 (0-9651382-0-8) PenUltimates.
— The Uncommon Numbers Manual: A Guide to Harmonizing Beautiful Numbers & Letters. (Illus.). 80p. 1999. pap. 13.95 (0-9651382-1-6) PenUltimates.
Casey, C. Hebrews. 1989. pap. 40.00 (0-86217-033-8, Pub. by Veritas Pubns) St Mut.
Casey, Calvert. The Collected Stories. Stavans, Ilan, ed. Polt, John H., tr. LC 97-32272. 216p. 1998. pap. 16.95 (0-8223-2165-3) Duke.
Casey, Calvert & Stavans, Ilan. The Collected Stories. Polt, John H., tr. from SPA. LC 97-32272. 1998. 49.95 (0-8223-2153-X) Duke.
Casey, Caroline. Invoking the Invisible: Using. 1999. pap. 14.00 (0-609-80274-7) Harmony Bks.
Casey, Caroline W. Making the Gods Work for You: The Astrological Language of the Psyche. LC 98-6090. 272p. 1998. 23.00 (0-609-60058-3) Harmony Bks.
Casey, Catherine. Work, Self, & Society: After Industrialism. LC 94-44972. 240p. (C). (gr. 13). 1995. 90.00 (0-415-11202-8) Routledge.
— Work, Self, & Society: After Industrialization in Asia. 240p. (C). 1995. pap. 22.99 (0-415-11203-6) Routledge.
Casey-Celia, Shannon T. How to Be a Good Stepmom. LC 95-67416. 104p. 1995. pap. 9.95 (0-9643937-5-1) Rutledge Bks.
Casey, Chris. A Programming Approach to Formal Methods. LC 94-20022. (International Series in Software Engineering). 1994. 16.95 (0-07-707968-X) McGraw.
***Casey, Cindy.** Civil War Soldiers & Their Families. (Images of America Ser.). 128p. 1999. pap. 18.99 (0-7385-0269-3) Arcadia Publng.
Casey, Cindy, jt. auth. see Forsyth County Genealogical Society Staff.
Casey, Clyde. New Mexico Cooking: Southwestern Flavors of the Past & Present. LC 94-8949. (Illus.). 192p. (Orig.). 1994. reprint ed. pap. 12.95 (1-55561-059-5) Fisher Bks.
Casey, Clyde W. Sassy Southwest Cooking: Vibrant New Mexico Foods. LC 97-200921. (Illus.). 160p. 1997. pap. 9.95 (0-9659234-0-1) Pecos Valley Pepper.
Casey, Crysta. Heart Clinic. 67p. (Orig.). 1993. pap. 7.00 (0-944920-09-8) Bellowing Ark Pr.
Casey, Daniel. Benedict Kiely. (Irish Writers Ser.). 107p. 1975. 8.50 (0-8387-7936-0); pap. 1.95 (0-8387-7970-0) Bucknell U Pr.
Casey, Daniel E. & Gardos, George, eds. Tardive Dyskinesia & Neuroleptics: From Dogma to Reason. LC 86-10749. (Clinical Insights Ser.). 125p. reprint ed. pap. 38.80 (0-8357-2809-9, 203622500011) Bks Demand.
Casey, Daniel E., jt. ed. see Gardos, George.
Casey, Daniel J. Critical Essays on John Millington Synge. (Critical Essays on British Literature Ser.). 200p. 1994. 49.00 (0-7838-0006-1, Twyne) Mac Lib Ref.
Casey, Daniel J. & Rhodes, Robert E., eds. Irish-American Fiction: Essays in Criticism. LC 78-18944. (Studies in Modern Literature: No. 4). 1979. 34.50 (0-404-16036-0); pap. 11.95 (0-404-16037-9) AMS Pr.
— Modern Irish-American Fiction: A Reader. LC 88-32081. (Irish Studies). 336p. 1989. text 45.00 (0-8156-2462-X); pap. text 19.95 (0-8156-0234-0) Syracuse U Pr.
Casey, Daniel J., jt. ed. see Casey, Linda M.
Casey, David. Managing Learning in Organizations. LC 92-21156. (Managing Work & Organizations Ser.). 1993. pap. 34.95 (0-335-15657-6) OpUniv Pr.
Casey, Denise. Weather Everywhere. LC 92-23239. (Illus.). 40p. (J). (gr. k-3). 1995. mass mkt. 15.00 (0-02-717777-7, Mac Bks Young Read) S&S Childrens.
Casey, Denise, jt. ed. see Clark, Tim.
Casey, Denise, ed. & illus. see Clark, Tim W.
***Casey, Dennis J.** Art Glass Details Frank Lloyd Wright's Hollyhock House. (Illus.). 43p. 2000. spiral bd. 19.50 (0-615-11809-7, BK-5) Prairie Designs.
***Casey, Dermont.** Dealing with Scruples. 71p. 1999. reprint ed. pap. 15.95 (0-912141-76-X) Roman Cath Bks.
Casey, Don. The Aging Sailboat Checkup. LC 96-26741. (Illus.). 144p. 1996. 21.95 (0-07-013394-8) McGraw.
— Canvaswork & Sail Repair. (Illus.). 144p. 1996. 21.95 (0-07-013391-3) McGraw.
— Dragged Aboard: A Cruising Guide for the Reluctant Mate. LC 97-49571. (Illus.). 176p. 1998. 27.50 (0-393-04653-2) Norton.
— 50 Fast & Easy Boat Improvements. LC 97-32735. (Sailboat Library). (Illus.). 144p. 1998. pap. 21.95 (0-07-013402-2) Intl Marine.
— Sailboat Hull & Deck Repair. (International Marine Sailboat Library). (Illus.). 128p. 1996. 21.95 (0-07-013369-7) McGraw.
— Sailboat Refinishing: Painting, Varnishing, & Cosmetics. (International Marine Sailboat Library). (Illus.). 144p. 1995. 21.95 (0-07-013225-9) Intl Marine.
— This Old Boat. (Illus.). 480p. 34.95 (0-87742-262-1) Intl Marine.
— This Old Boat. 408p. 1991. 34.95 (0-07-157993-1) McGraw.
— This Old Boat: Powerboat Edition. 1996. text 34.95 (0-07-013241-0) McGraw.
Casey, Don & Hackler, Lew. Sensible Cruising: The Thoreau Approach, a Philosophic & a Practical Approach to Cruising. LC 86-60480. (Illus.). 364p. 1986. 24.95 (0-931595-01-0) Seascape Enters.
Casey, Don & Hackler, Lewis R. Sensible Cruising: The Thoreau Approach. (Illus.). 356p. 1990. pap. text 19.95 (0-87742-288-5) Intl Marine.
— Sensible Cruising: The Thoreau Approach. 356p. 1991. pap. 19.95 (0-07-158025-5) McGraw.
Casey, Douglas. Crisis Investing for the Rest of the '90s. LC 92-35971. 1993. 22.50 (1-55972-177-4, Birch Ln Pr) Carol Pub Group.
— Crisis Investing for the Rest of the 90's. enl. ed. 456p. (Orig.). 1995. pap. 14.95 (0-8065-1612-7, Citadel Pr) Carol Pub Group.
Casey, E. S., ed. see Carr, D.
Casey, Edward. The Fate of Place: A Philosophical History. LC 96-6411. (Centennial Bk.). (Illus.). 495p. 1997. 50.00 (0-520-20296-1, Pub. by U CA Pr) Cal Prin Full Svc.
— The Fate of Place: A Philosophical History. (Illus.). 495p. 1999. pap. 19.95 (0-520-21649-0, Pub. by U CA Pr) Cal Prin Full Svc.
Casey, Edward S. Getting Back into Place: Toward a Renewed Understanding of the Place-World. LC 93-16228. (Studies in Continental Thought). (Illus.). 432p. 1993. 47.50 (0-253-31331-7); pap. 24.95 (0-253-20837-8) Ind U Pr.
— Imagining: A Phenomenological Study. LC 76-12370. (Studies in Phenomenology & Existential Philosophy). 256p. 1976. 49.95 (0-253-32912-4) Ind U Pr.
— Spirit & Soul: Essays in Philosophical Psychology. LC 91-13223. xii, 314p. (Orig.). 1991. pap. 18.00 (0-88214-346-8) Spring Pubns.
Casey, Edward S. & Morano, Donald V., eds. The Life of the Transcendental Ego: Essays in Honor of William Earle. LC 86-5835. 217p. (C). 1986. pap. text 18.95 (0-88706-170-2) State U NY Pr.
Casey, Edward S., tr. see Dufrenne, Mikel.
Casey, Eileen. Maternity Leave: The Working Woman's Practical Guide to Combining Pregnancy, Motherhood & Career. LC 94-32059. 144p. (Orig.). 1995. pap. 10.00 (0-380-77810-6, Avon Bks) Morrow Avon.
Casey, Eileen L. Maternity Leave: The Working Woman's Practical Guide to Combining Pregnancy, Motherhood & Career. Lindau, Buff, ed. LC 91-45065. (Illus.). 144p. 1992. 19.95 (0-9631555-1-2); pap. 12.95 (0-9631555-0-4); lib. bdg. 19.95 (0-685-51619-9) Green Mtn Pub.
Casey, Eleen M., jt. auth. see Carver, Beth S.
Casey, Elizabeth T. The Lucy Truman Aldrich Collection of European Porcelain Figures of the Eighteenth Century. LC 65-28229. (Illus.). 157p. 1965. 9.00 (0-911517-26-X) Mus of Art RI.
***Casey, Eoghan.** Digital Evidence & Computer Crime. 450p. 1999. 69.95 (0-12-162885-X) Acad Pr.
Casey, Erika, tr. see Paul, Jean.
Casey, Frank, jt. auth. see Donovan, Graeme.
Casey, G. J. & Miller, Elizabeth, eds. Tempered Days: A Century of Newfoundland Short Fiction. LC 96-950158. 234p. 1996. pap. 12.95 (1-895387-73-6) Creative Bk Pub.
Casey, Gerard. Echoes. 130p. 1990. 29.50 (1-869887-60-3) S Perennis.
Casey, Glenn F. Unity of Man's Trinity. 68p. (Orig.). 1992. pap. text 5.95 (0-9633714-0-1) G F Casey.
Casey, H. Craig. Devices for Integrated Circuits: Silicon & III-V Compound Semiconductors. LC 98-6992. 544p. 1998. text 100.95 (0-471-17134-4) Wiley.
Casey, Harry F. Land of the Eagle. 400p. 1997. pap. 12.95 (0-9659184-0-8) Scribe Pub.
Casey, Helen M. & Morgante, Amy, eds. Abolishing War. LC 98-74360. 144p. 1998. pap. text 5.00 (1-887917-03-9) Boston RCFT-FC.
— Human Rights, Environmental Law & the Earth Charter, Vol. 3. LC 98-74359. 106p. 1998. pap. text 3.00 (1-887917-06-3) Boston RCFT-FC.
— Women's Views on the Earth Charter, Vol. 2. 65p. 1997. pap. text 3.00 (1-887917-05-5) Boston RCFT-FC.
Casey, Jack. The Trial of Bat Shea. (Illus.). 372p. 19.95 (0-9639886-0-3) Diamond Rock.
— The Trial of Bat Shea. limited ed. (Illus.). 372p. 29.95 (0-9639886-1-1) Diamond Rock.
Casey, Jackie, jt. auth. see Peacock, Judith.
***Casey, James.** Early Modern Spain: A Social History. LC 98-31118. 1999. write for info. (0-415-13813-2); pap. 32.99 (0-415-20687-1) Routledge.
Casey, James. They Died in Silence: A Woman Steps Forward. Gilliss, Doug, ed. 400p. (Orig.). 1992. reprint ed. pap. text 19.00 (0-9633858-0-1) Dillard Pub.
***Casey, James & Abeyaratne, Rohan, eds.** Finite Thermoelacticity: Proceedings ASME International Mechanical Engineering Congress & Exposition, Nasheville, Tennessee, 1999. LC 99-76074. (AMD Ser.: Vol. 236). 131p. 1999. 70.00 (0-7918-1654-0) ASME Pr.
Casey, James & Crochet, Marcel J., eds. Theoretical, Experimental & Numerical Contributions to the Mechanics of Fluids & Solids: A Collection of Papers in Honor of Paul M. Naghdi. LC 95-20143. (ZAMP Special Issue Ser.: Vol. 46). 847p. 1995. 365.00 (0-8176-5139-X) Birkhauser.
Casey, James F. Fire Service Hydraulics. 2nd ed. (Illus.). 1970. 30.00 (0-912212-05-5) Fire Eng.
— Fire Service Hydraulics. 2nd ed. (Illus.). 1970. student ed. 14.95 (0-912212-03-9) Fire Eng.
Casey, James F., ed. The Fire Chief's Handbook. 4th ed. (Illus.). 1978. 25.00 (0-87814-907-4) Fire Eng.
Casey, James P. Casey's Reports on Paper & the Paper Industry No. 1: Chemical & Mechanical Pulping. LC 83-25217. 136p. reprint ed. pap. 42.20 (0-7837-4305-X, 204399600012) Bks Demand.
— Pigment-Coated Papers: A Critical Assessment of the Processes, Technical Developments, & Economics. LC 85-6836. (Series of Special Reports: No. 13). (Illus.). 115p. reprint ed. pap. 35.70 (0-7837-0860-2, 204116800019) Bks Demand.
Casey, James P., ed. Pulp & Paper: Chemistry & Chemical Technology, 4 vols. 3rd ed. 2649p. 1983. 975.00 (0-471-88186-4) Wiley.
— Pulp & Paper Vol. 1: Chemistry & Chemical Technology, 4 vols., Vol. 1. 3rd ed. LC 79-13435. 820p. 1980. 310.00 (0-471-03175-5) Wiley.
— Pulp & Paper Vol. 2: Chemistry & Chemical Technology, 4 vols., Vol. 2. 3rd ed. LC 79-13435. 576p. 1980. 298.00 (0-471-03176-3) Wiley.
— Pulp & Paper Vol. 3: Chemistry & Chemical Technology, 4 vols., Vol. 3. 3rd ed. LC 79-13435. 592p. 1981. 275.00 (0-471-03177-1) Wiley.
— Pulp & Paper Vol. 4: Chemistry & Chemical Technology, 4 vols., Vol. 4. 3rd ed. 640p. 1983. 275.00 (0-471-03178-X) Wiley.
Casey, Jane A., ed. see Nalin, David R.
Casey, Jane C. Millard Fillmore. LC 87-35183. (Encyclopedia of Presidents Ser.). (Illus.). 100p. (J). (gr. 3 up). 1988. lib. bdg. 24.00 (0-516-01353-X) Childrens.
— William Howard Taft. LC 88-8675. (Encyclopedia of Presidents Ser.). (Illus.). 100p. (J). (gr. 5-8). 1989. lib. bdg. 24.00 (0-516-01366-1) Childrens.
Casey, Janet G. Dos Passos & the Ideology of the Feminine. LC 97-47264. (Cambridge Studies in American Literature & Culture Ser.: No. 115). (Illus.). 248p. (C). 1998. text 59.95 (0-521-62025-2) Cambridge U Pr.
***Casey, Jean M.** Creating the Early Literacy Classroom: Activities for Using Technology to Empower Elementary Students. 150p. 2000. pap. 25.00 (1-56308-712-X) Libs Unl.
— Early Literacy: The Empowerment of Technology. LC 96-28987. 178p. 1997. lib. bdg. 25.00 (1-56308-458-9) Libs Unl.
***Casey, Jean M.** Early Literacy: The Empowerment of Technology. 200p. 2000. pap. 27.50 (1-56308-865-7) Libs Unl.
Casey, Joan D. Bordeaux, Colonial Port of Nineteenth Century France. Bruchey, Stuart, ed. LC 80-2798. (Dissertations in European Economic History Ser.). 1981. lib. bdg. 42.95 (0-405-13982-9) Ayer.
Casey, Joan F. & Wilson, Lynn. The Flock: The Autobiography of a Multiple Personality. 320p. 1992. pap. 10.00 (0-449-90732-5, Columbine) Fawcett.
Casey, John. The Half-Life of Happiness. 352p. 1998. 25.00 (0-679-40978-5) Knopf.
— The Half-Life of Happiness. 528p. 1999. pap. 14.00 (0-375-70608-9) Vin Bks.
— Pagan Virtue: An Essay in Ethics. 254p. 1991. reprint ed. pap. text 26.00 (0-19-824003-1) OUP.
— Spartina. 384p. 1990. pap. 12.00 (0-380-71104-4, Avon Bks) Morrow Avon.
— Spartina. 1998. pap. 13.00 (0-375-70268-7) Vin Bks.
— Supper at the Black Pearl. deluxe ed. 45p. 1996. 50.00 (0-935716-65-3) Lord John.
***Casey, John, et al, eds.** Imaging Humanity: Immagine Dell'Umanita. (VIA Folios Ser.: Vol. 25). (ITA & ENG., Illus.). 238p. (C). 2000. pap. 18.00 (1-884419-38-0) Bordighera.
Casey, John L. Ethics in the Financial Marketplace: Building Your Own. 140p. (Orig.). (C). 1988. pap. 10.00 (0-317-90964-9) Scudder Stevens Clark.
— Values Added: Making Ethical Decisions in the Financial Marketplace. McCandless, Bruce, 3rd, ed. LC 96-46347. 264p. 1996. 57.50 (0-7618-0610-5); pap. 32.50 (0-7618-0609-1) U Pr of Amer.
Casey, Joseph. Tool & Die Design & Construction. (C). 2002. 57.33 (0-13-436445-7, Macmillan Coll) P-H.
Casey, Joseph H. God Is: From Question to Proof to Embracing the Truth. LC 98-27044. 288p. 1998. pap. 29.50 (0-7618-1207-5) U Pr of Amer.
Casey, Joseph J. Personal Names in Hening's Statutes at Large of Virginia & Shepherd's Continuation. 159p. 1995. reprint ed. pap. 17.50 (0-8063-0068-X, 910) Clearfield Co.
Casey, Joy. Estate Planning for Middle & Large Income Earners: Save Thousands to Millions of Dollars Through Proper Estate Planning! LC 98-178881. 112 p. 1998. write for info. (0-9641627-0-9) JC Insurance.
Casey, Juanita. Eternity Smith & Other Poems. 56p. 1985. pap. 10.95 (0-85105-431-5, Pub. by Smyth) Dufour.
— Horse of Selene. 168p. 1985. pap. 14.95 (0-85105-251-7, Pub. by Smyth) Dufour.
— A Sampling. (Chapbooks Ser.). 1981. pap. 2.95 (0-912262-72-9) Proscenium.
***Casey, Judi C. & O'Leary, Susan M.** The Corporate Imperative: A Business Guide for Implementing Strategic Education Partnerships. (Illus.). 84p. (C). 2000. pap. text 20.00 (0-7881-8192-0) DIANE Pub.
Casey, Juliana. Food for the Journey: Theological Foundations of the Catholic Healthcare Ministry. 140p. 1991. pap. 10.00 (0-87125-194-9, 250) Cath Health.
Casey, Karen. Daily Meditations for Practicing the Course. LC 95-12829. 384p. 1995. pap. 13.00 (0-06-255276-7, Pub. by Harper SF) HarpC.
— Daily Meditations for Practicing the Course. 400p. 1996. pap. text 12.00 (1-56838-043-7) Hazelden.
***Casey, Karen.** Girl to Girl: Finding Our Voices: Daily Thoughts on Living for Girls Ages 11-15. LC 99-86566. 366p. 2000. pap. 12.00 (1-56838-372-X) Hazelden.
Casey, Karen. Girls Only! Daily Thoughts for Young Girls, Ages 7 to 10. LC 99-40711. 380p. 1999. pap. text 12.00 (0-930100-92-1, Pub. by Holy Cow) Consort Bk Sales.
— If Only I Could Quit: Recovering from Nicotine Addiction. 320p. pap. 10.95 (0-89486-438-6, 5031A) Hazelden.
— Keepers of the Wisdom: Reflections from Lives Well-Lived. 400p. pap. 12.00 (1-56838-117-4) Hazelden.
— A Life of My Own: Daily Meditations on Hope & Acceptance. 400p. (Orig.). pap. 10.00 (0-89486-863-2, 1070A) Hazelden.
***Casey, Karen.** The Miracle of Sponsorship: Recovery Stories of Hope & Renewal. 250p. 2000. pap. 15.00 (1-56838-553-6) Hazelden.
Casey, Karen. Worthy of Love. (Meditation Ser.). (Illus.). 106p. pap. 10.00 (0-89486-339-8, 5005A) Hazelden.
Casey, Karen & Vanceburg, Martha. The Promise of a New Day. (Illus.). 400p. (Orig.). pap. 10.00 (0-89486-203-0) Hazelden.
— The Promise of a New Day: A Book of Daily Meditations. LC 96-188316. 416p. (Orig.). 1996. pap. 5.99 (0-06-255268-6, Pub. by Harper SF) HarpC.
Casey, Karen, et al. Promise of a New Day/Night Light. LC 97-75630. 784p. 1998. reprint ed. 8.98 (1-56731-261-6, MJF Bks) Fine Comms.
Casey, Kathleen. I Answer with My Life: Life Histories of Women Teachers Working for Social Change. LC 92-27507. (Critical Social Thought Ser.). 256p. (C). (gr. 13). 1993. pap. 19.99 (0-415-90403-X, A5296) Routledge.
Casey, Kathleen M., et al. ANAC's Core Curriculum for HIV-AIDs Nursing. (Illus.). 500p. (Orig.). 1995. pap. 40.00 (0-9637042-2-2) N Am Nursing.
Casey, Kathryn. The Rapist's Wife. 376p. (Orig.). 1995. mass mkt. 5.50 (0-380-77456-9, Avon Bks) Morrow Avon.
***Casey, Kathryn.** A Warrant to Kill: A True Story of Obsession, Lies, & a Killer Cop. 384p. 2000. mass mkt. 6.99 (0-380-78041-0) Morrow Avon.
Casey, Kenneth F. & Weigel, George. "Striking Back!" The Trigeminal Neuralgia Handbook. LC 99-47204. 2000. pap. 15.95 (0-9672393-0-3) Trigeminal Neuralgia Assoc.
Casey, Kenneth L., ed. see Bristol-Myers Squibb Symposium on Pain Research St.
Casey, Kevin. Judo. LC 94-4090. (Illustrated History of Martial Arts Ser.). 32p. (J). (gr. 3-8). 1994. lib. bdg. 14.95 (0-86593-369-3) Rourke Corp.
— Karate. LC 94-4094. (Illustrated History of Martial Arts Ser.). 32p. (J). (gr. 3-8). 1994. lib. bdg. 14.95 (0-86593-366-9) Rourke Corp.
— Kung Fu. LC 94-4087. (Illustrated History of Martial Arts Ser.). 32p. (J). (gr. 3-8). 1994. lib. bdg. 14.95 (0-86593-368-5) Rourke Corp.
Casey, Kevin, et al. A Community-Based System for the Mentally Retarded: The ENCOR Experience. LC 84-13126. 233p. 1985. reprint ed. pap. 72.30 (0-608-01848-1, 206249800003) Bks Demand.
Casey, Kevin K. Costumes. LC 96-21652. (Customs, Costumes, & Cultures Ser.). 32p. (J). (gr. 3-6). 1996. lib. bdg. 18.60 (0-86625-596-6) Rourke Pubns.
— Jewelry. LC 96-26593. (Customs, Costumes, & Cultures Ser.). 32p. (J). (gr. 3-6). 1996. lib. bdg. 18.60 (0-86625-597-4) Rourke Pubns.
— Masks. LC 96-11394. (Customs, Costumes, & Cultures Ser.). 32p. (J). (gr. 3-6). 1996. lib. bdg. 18.60 (0-86625-592-3) Rourke Pubns.
Casey, Lillian. Inspirational Word Find Puzzles, Questions & Answers Book. 70p. 1998. pap. 2.99 (1-889732-11-7) Word-For-Word.
Casey, Linda M. & Casey, Daniel J., eds. Stories by Contemporary Irish Women. LC 89-29523. (Irish Studies). 160p. 1990. pap. 16.95 (0-8156-0249-9); text 45.00 (0-8156-2489-1) Syracuse U Pr.
Casey, Lynn, ed. see Fishell, Dave.
Casey, Marion R. & Shea, Ann M., eds. The Irish Experience in New York City: A Select Bibliography. 140p. 1995. 29.95 (0-8156-8121-6) Syracuse U Pr.
Casey, Mary. The Clear Shadow. 208p. 1992. 29.50 (1-869887-12-3) S Perennis.
— A Net in Water: A Selection from the Journals of Mary Casey. Lang, J. M. & De Bruin, Louise, eds. (Illus.). 229p. (Orig.). 1994. pap. 18.95 (1-874559-10-4) S Perennis.
— Sparkley, the Tooth Fairy: The Story of Susie & Scotty in Toothdom. Pettigrew, M. E., ed. LC 95-94501. (Illus.). 32p. (J). (ps up). 1996. 14.95 (0-9647073-0-6) MECK & Co.
Casey, Mary C., jt. auth. see Bate, Marjorie D.
***Casey, Maud.** Untitled Stories. 2002. write for info. (0-688-17696-8) Morrow Avon.
Casey, Maude. Over the Water. 88p. (J). 1995. write for info. (0-8050-3276-2) H Holt & Co.
— Over the Water. 1996. 10.09 (0-606-08841-5, Pub. by Turtleback) Demco.
Casey, Maurice. Aramaic Sources of Mark's Gospel. LC 98-13839. (Society for New Testament Studies Monograph Ser.: No. 102). 288p. (C). 1998. text 59.95 (0-521-63314-1) Cambridge U Pr.
— From Jewish Prophet to Gentile God: The Origins & Development of New Testament Christology. 197p. 1991. text 24.95 (0-664-21960-8) Westminster John Knox.
— Is John's Gospel True? 280p. (C). 1996. 90.00 (0-415-14630-5) Routledge.
Casey, Michael. Bernard of Clairvaux: Man, Monk, Mystic. 123p. 1991. pap. 49.95 incl. audio (0-87907-199-0) Cistercian Pubns.
***Casey, Michael.** The Million Dollar Hole. 80p. 2001. pap. 12.95 (0-914061-86-0) Orchises Pr.
— Millrat. enl. ed. 54p. 1999. pap. 6.00 (0-938566-81-4, Pub. by Adastra Pr) SPD-Small Pr Dist.
Casey, Michael. Sacred Reading: The Ancient Art of Lectio Divina. LC 95-44569. 160p. (Orig.). 1996. pap. 12.95 (0-89243-891-6, Liguori Triumph) Liguori Pubns.

An Asterisk (*) at the beginning of an entry indicates that the title is appearing for the first time.

— Toward God: The Ancient Wisdom of Western Prayer. LC 95-46093. 192p. 1996. pap. 12.95 (*0-89243-890-8*, Liguori Triumph) Liguori Pubns.
— Towards God: The Western Tradition of Contemplation. 182p. 1991. reprint ed. 12.95 (*0-85924-716-3*) Harper SF.
— Truthful Living: Saint Benedict's Teaching on Humility. LC 98-44023. 256p. 1999. pap. 15.95 (*1-879007-35-5*) St Bedes Pubns.
— The Undivided Heart: The Western Monastic Approach to Contemplation. LC 94-6259. 217p. 1994. pap. 19.95 (*1-879007-04-5*) St Bedes Pubns.
Casey, Michael, et al. Flags into Battle. Boston Publishing Company Editors, ed. (Vietnam Experience Ser.). (Illus.). 192p. 1987. 16.30 (*0-201-11676-6*) Addison-Wesley.
— Word & Spirit No. 12: St. Bernard of Clairvaux (1090-1153) (Word & Spirit Ser.: No. 12). 192p. 1990. pap. 8.00 (*0-932506-84-4*) St Bedes Pubns.
Casey, Michael, tr. see Bernard of Clairvaux.
Casey, Michael W. The Battle over Hermeneutics in the Stone-Campbell Movement, 1800-1870. LC 98-28604. (Studies in American Religion: Vol. 67). 320p. 1998. text 99.95 (*0-7734-8314-4*) E Mellen.
— Saddlebags, City Streets & Cyberspace: A History of Preaching in the Churches of Christ. LC 95-78970. (Illus.). 215p. 1995. pap. 14.95 (*0-89112-017-3*) Abilene Christ U.
Casey, Mike & Herbst, Judith. Red Lace, Yellow Lace. LC 95-39550. (Illus.). 24p. (J). 1996. spiral bd. 10.95 (*0-8120-6553-0*) Barron.
Casey, Moe. The Most Excellent Book of Dress Up. LC 96-48290. (Most Excellent Book of...Ser.). (Illus.). 32p. (J). (gr. 4-6). 1997. lib. bdg. 19.90 (*0-7613-0550-5*, Copper Beech Bks) Millbrook Pr.
— The Most Excellent Book of Dress Up. (Most Excellent Book of...Ser.). (Illus.). 32p. (J). (gr. 4-6). 1997. pap. 6.95 (*0-7613-0575-0*, Copper Beech Bks) Millbrook Pr.
***Casey, Nell.** Unholy Ghost. 2000. write for info. (*0-688-17031-5*, Wm Morrow) Morrow Avon.
Casey, P. A., tr. see Freuler, F., et al.
Casey, P. A., tr. see Henche, H. R.
***Casey, P. Bradley.** The Quickening Begins. 116p. 1999. pap. 14.95 (*0-7392-0366-5*, PO3570) Morris Pubng.
Casey, P. J. Roman Coinage in Britain. (Archaeology Ser.: Vol. 12). (Illus.). 54p. pap. write for info. (*0-7478-0231-9*, Pub. by Shire Pubns) Parkwest Pubns.
Casey, Patricia. Beep! Beep! Oink! Oink! Animals in the City. LC 96-44369. (Illus.). 48p. (J). (ps-3). 1997. 16.99 (*0-7636-0306-6*) Candlewick Pr.
— My Cat Jack. LC 93-39669. (Illus.). (J). (ps-3). 1996. pap. 5.99 (*1-56402-660-4*) Candlewick Pr.
— My Cat Jack. (Read & Wonder Ser.). 1996. 11.19 (*0-606-08827-X*, Pub. by Turtleback) Demco.
Casey, Patricia, jt. ed. see Tyrer, Peter.
Casey, Patricia R. A Guide to Psychiatry in Primary Care. 2nd rev. ed. LC 97-7979. 320p. 1997. 39.00 (*1-871816-33-5*, Pub. by Wrightson Biomed) Taylor & Francis.
Casey, Patrick J. & Buss, Janice E., eds. Lipid Modifications of Proteins. (Methods in Enzymology Ser.: Vol. 250). (Illus.). 754p. 1995. text 104.00 (*0-12-182151-X*) Acad Pr.
Casey, Paula, jt. auth. see Vine, Peter.
Casey, Philip. The Fabulists. LC 94-228973. 240p. 1994. pap. 18.95 (*1-874675-30-9*) Dufour.
Casey, Phillip. The Fabulists. 240p. 1998. pap. 14.95 (*1-897959-18-4*, Pub. by Serif) IPG Chicago.
Casey, R. & Davies, D. R., eds. Peas: Genetics, Molecular Biology & Biotechnology. (Biotechnology in Agriculture Ser.: No. 10). (Illus.). 336p. 1993. text 110.00 (*0-85198-863-6*) OUP.
Casey, R., jt. auth. see Thompson, R.
Casey, R., ed. see International Symposium on the Boreal Lower Cretac.
Casey, Ralph D., ed. The Press in Perspective. LC 63-16657. 235p. reprint ed. pap. 72.90 (*0-608-14446-0*, 20518760013) Bks Demand.
Casey, Richard E., ed. Siliceous Microfossil & Microplankton Studies of the Monterey Formation & Modern Analogs. (Illus.). 154p. (Orig.). 1986. pap. 8.00 (*1-878861-27-1*) Pac Section SEPM.
Casey, Richard J., et al. Abdominal Wound Infections. (Illus.). 137p. 1994. text 19.95 (*1-880906-01-5*) IDI Pub.
Casey-Richmond, Susan M. Money, Astrology & You (In the Driver's Seat) (Illus.). 54p. 1997. pap. 10.00 (*1-885201-23-0*) Mandala CA.
Casey, Robert. Journey to the High Southwest: A Traveler's Guide to Santa Fe & the Four Corners Region of Arizona, Colorado, New Mexico, & Utah. 5th rev. ed. LC 96-52215. (Illus.). 464p. 1997. pap. 19.95 (*0-7627-0069-6*) Globe Pequot.
Casey, Robert B. & Casey, Bernice B. Olliff Family History: Descendants of John Shears Olliff & Johannah (Jackson) Olliff of Bulloch County, Georgia. (Illus.). 384p. (C). text 25.00 (*0-9619051-3-1*) Brooks TX.
Casey, Robert B., jt. auth. see Casey, Alvin.
***Casey, Robert L.** Journey to the High Southwest: A Traveler's Guide. 6th ed. LC 99-87386. (Illus.). 480p. 2000. pap. 19.95 (*0-7627-0499-3*) Globe Pequot.
Casey, Robert P. Fighting for Life. (Illus.). 320p. 1996. 21.99 (*0-8499-1224-5*) Word Pub.
Casey, Robert P., ed. see Serapion.
Casey, Robert W. Best Practices for Nonprofit Boards: Managing Finances & Investments. 256p. 1996. text 40.00 (*1-57660-004-1*) Bloomberg NJ.
Casey, Robin. How to Find a Job. LC 93-4503. 1993. 8.99 (*0-8407-9243-3*) Nelson.
Casey, Rod, jt. ed. see Shewry, Peter R.
Casey, Roger N. Textual Vehicles: The Automobile in American Literature. LC 97-39730. (Studies in American Popular History & Culture). 250p. 1997. text 53.00 (*0-8153-3050-2*) Garland.
Casey, Samuel B. Christian Leadership: The Source of the Vision. 24p. (Orig.). 1992. pap. text 4.00 (*0-944561-21-7*) Chr Legal.
Casey, Silas. U. S. Infantry Tactics, 3 vols. in 1. (Illus.). 810p. 1991. 50.00 (*0-89029-085-7*) Morningside Bkshop.
Casey, Stephen, jt. auth. see Listokin, David.
Casey, Steven M. Set Phasers on Stun: And Other True Tales of Design, Technology, & Human Error. 2nd ed. LC 97-77875. 256p. 1998. 29.00 (*0-9636178-8-5*) Aegean Pub.
Casey, Susan. The Weekend Was Murder: Homicide As Entertainment. 240p. (Orig.). 1987. pap. 5.95 (*0-15-695300-5*, Harvest Bks) Harcourt.
— Women Invent: Two Centuries of Discoveries That Have Shaped Our World. LC 97-18870. (Illus.). 144p. (J). (gr. 4-7). 1997. pap. 14.95 (*1-55652-317-3*) Chicago Review.
Casey, T. J. Water & Wastewater Engineering Hydraulics. (Illus.). 288p. 1992. 75.00 (*0-19-856360-4*); pap. 45.00 (*0-19-856359-0*) OUP.
Casey, T. J., et al, eds. Methods of Characterization of Sewage Sludge. 164p. 1984. text 90.50 (*90-277-1782-6*) Kluwer Academic.
Casey, Terri. Pride & Joy: The Lives & Passions of Women Without Children. LC 98-7952. 224p. 1998. pap. 14.95 (*1-885223-82-X*) Beyond Words Pub.
Casey, Theresa M. & Hernandez, Pedro, eds. Research Guide to the Records of MALDEF: Mexican American Legal Defense & Education Fun & PRLDEF Puerto Rican Legal Defense & Education Fund. 148p. (Orig.). 1996. pap. 15.00 (*0-911221-16-6*) Stanford U Libraries.
Casey, Therese. PMS & Alcoholism. 20p. (Orig.). (C). 1984. pap. 2.00 (*0-89486-247-2*, 1377B) Hazelden.
Casey, Thomas A. Color Atlas of Corneal Dystrophies & Degenerations. (Illus.). 126p. (C). (gr. 13). 1991. text 90.00 (*0-8151-1445-1*, 21948) Mosby Inc.
Casey, Thomas A., et al. Corneal Grafting: Principles & Practice. 2nd ed. (Illus.). 352p. 1984. text 180.00 (*0-7216-2448-0*, W B Saunders Co) Harcrt Hlth Sci Grp.
***Casey, Thomas F.** Social Manual for Seminarians. 162p. 1999. reprint ed. 21.95 (*0-912141-74-3*) Roman Cath Bks.
Casey, Thomas M. Meaning in Myth. LC 89-61931. 160p. (Orig.). (C). 1989. pap. 14.95 (*1-55612-253-5*) Sheed & Ward WI.
Casey, Thompson L. Seven Four, & Three. 320p. 1995. 45.00 (*1-887189-07-6*); pap. text 29.50 (*1-887189-08-4*) Symi Pub.
***Casey, Timothy.** ISP Liability Survival Guide: For Managing Copyright, Spam, Cache & Privacy Regulations. 256p. 2000. pap. 39.99 (*0-471-37748-1*) Wiley.
Casey, Timothy & Embree, Lester, eds. Lifeworld & Technology. LC 89-39437. (Current Continental Research Ser.: No. 009). (Illus.). 326p. (C). 1990. lib. bdg. 50.50 (*0-8191-7626-5*) U Pr of Amer.
Casey, Timothy J., ed. see Paul, Jean.
Casey, Tina. Creating Extraordinary Beads from Ordinary Materials. LC 97-3649. (Illus.). 128p. 1997. pap. 22.99 (*0-89134-763-1*, North Lght Bks) F & W Pubns Inc.
— Fabulous Fashion Doll Clothing You Can Make. LC 98-40868. (Illus.). 128p. 1999. pap. 22.99 (*0-89134-890-5*, 31355, North Lght Bks) F & W Pubns Inc.
Casey, Tom. Human Error. LC 96-20775. 272p. 1996. 21.95 (*0-312-14622-1*) St Martin.
— Last Call: Selections from the Best of "Down to Cases" Ronald, Jack, ed. 180p. 1997. pap. 14.95 (*0-9661729-0-6*) Graphic Printing.
Casey, W. Wilson. TV Trivia Teasers. (Illus.). 260p. 1984. pap. 29.50 (*0-87650-164-1*) Popular Culture.
Casey, Watt M., Jr., jt. auth. see Lasater, Annette N.
Casey, William & Colman, Alfredo, eds. Thomas Robinson's New Citharen Lessons (1609) 189p. 1998. pap. text 24.95 (*0-918954-65-7*) Baylor Univ Pr.
Casey, William J. & Institute for Business Planning, Inc., Staff. Estate Planning. write for info. (*0-318-62384-6*, Inst Busn Plan) P-H.
Casgrain & Laverdiere, Eugene, eds. Le Journal des Jesuites. (French-Canadian Civilization Ser.). (FRE.). reprint ed. lib. bdg. 46.00 (*0-697-00050-8*) Irvington.
Cash & Maples. Making of the Bahamas. Date not set. pap. text. write for info. (*0-582-02805-1*, Pub. by Addison-Wesley) Longman.
Cash, jt. auth. see Stewart.
***Cash, Adam.** Getting Started in the Underground Economy. 1999. pap. text 14.95 (*1-893626-20-2*) Breakout Prods Inc.
Cash, Alan. Crosswords Daily Express, Vol. 1. 144p. pap. 8.95 (*0-14-009802-X*, Pub. by Pnguin Bks Ltd) Trafalgar.
— Crosswords Daily Express, Vol. 2. 144p. pap. 7.95 (*0-14-009803-8*, Pub. by Pnguin Bks Ltd) Trafalgar.
Cash, Annette G., tr. see De Berceo, Gonzalo.
Cash, Annette Grant & Keller, John E. Daily Life Depicted in the Cantigas de Santa Maria. LC 98-17601. (Studies in Romance Languages). (Illus.). 120p. (C). 1998. 55.00 (*0-8131-2050-0*) U Pr of Ky.
Cash, Annette Grant, et al. A Que Si. (College Spanish). (SPA.). (C). 1993. pap. 38.95 (*0-8384-3546-7*) Heinle & Heinle.
Cash, Anthony, compiled by. The Russian Revolution. 39.00 (*1-56696-060-6*) Jackdaw.
Cash, Arthur H. Laurence Sterne: The Early & Middle Years. LC 75-18378. (Illus.). 1975. 85.00 (*0-416-82210-X*, NO. 2126) Routledge.
— Laurence Sterne: The Later Years. 400p. 1986. 60.00 (*0-416-32930-6*, 9922) Routledge.
Cash-Callahan & Company, Inc. Staff. Accessible Design Handbook: The ADA Troubleshooter Guide & Workbook. 100p. 1991. ring bd. 129.95 (*0-9633145-0-5*) Race Pt Pr.
Cash, Carol, jt. auth. see Cash, Ron.
Cash, Catherine. The Slipper Orchids. LC 90-39595. (Illus.). 304p. 1991. 49.95 (*0-88192-183-1*) Timber.
Cash, Connacht. The Medicare Answer Book. 2nd ed. LC 98-65682. 304p. 1998. pap. 19.95 (*0-9633145-4-8*) Race Pt Pr.
***Cash, Connacht.** The Medicare Answer Book. 3rd ed. LC 98-89280. 304p. 1999. pap. 19.95 (*0-9633145-5-6*) Race Pt Pr.
Cash, David. Negotiate: Winning Strategies for Builders & Developers. LC 91-14075. 1991. write for info. (*0-86718-364-0*) Home Builder.
Cash, David & Kraskouskas, Jeffrey. Stock Market Basics: Insider's Guide for the Online Investor. (Basics Ser.). (Illus.). 51p. 1999. pap. 14.95 (*0-9672745-0-8*) Krackhead Ent.
Cash-Dudley, E. F. Tips on Grandparent Rights in California. Carter, M. Tish, ed. LC 98-231754. 152p. 1998. pap. 15.95 (*0-9665469-0-3*) E F Cash-Dudley.
Cash, E. A. John A. Williams: The Evolution of a Black Writer. LC 73-92796. 1974. 20.00 (*0-89388-142-2*) Okpaku Communications.
Cash, Edith K. A Mycological English-Latin Glossary, 1965. (Mycologia Memoirs Ser.: No. 1). 152p. 1965. pap. text 12.50 (*0-945345-37-2*) Lubrecht & Cramer.
Cash, Grady. Spend Yourself Rich! A Value-Based Approach to Help You Reach Your Financial Dreams. LC 97-61519. (Illus.). 108p. 1998. pap. 10.95 (*0-9659638-2-9*) Fin Literacy.
Cash, J. Grady & Cash, Kathy K. Conquer the Seven Deadly Money Mistakes: The No-Math, No-Hassle, Values-Based Way to Reach Your Financial Dreams. (Illus.). 224p. pap. 16.95 (*1-884121-21-7*) Ctr Fin Well-Being.
Cash, J. R. & Gladwell, I., eds. Computational Ordinary Differential Equations: Based on the Proceedings of a Conference on Computational Ordinary Differential Equations Held at Imperial College of Science & Technology, University of London, in July 1989. LC 92-22635. (Institute of Mathematics & Its Applications Conference Series, New Ser.: New Series 39). (Illus.). 480p. 1992. text 95.00 (*0-19-853659-3*, Clarendon Pr) OUP.
Cash, James B. Unsung Heroes: Ohioans in the White House: A Modern Appraisal. LC 98-23600. (Illus.). 322p. 1998. pap. 19.95 (*1-882203-22-4*) Orange Frazer.
Cash, James I. Building the Information-Age Organization: Structure Control & Information Technologies. LC 93-40865. 512p. (C). 1994. text 73.25 (*0-256-12458-2*, Irwn McGrw-H) McGrw-H Hghr Educ.
— CPS Building the Information-Age Organization, Chapter 8. 32p. (C). 1995. text 5.00 (*0-256-21156-6*, Irwn McGrw-H) McGrw-H Hghr Educ.
Cash, James I., et al. Building the Information-Age Organization Corporate Information Systems Management. (C). 1994. text 84.50 (*0-256-19065-8*, Irwn McGrw-H) McGrw-H Hghr Educ.
— Corporate Information Systems Management: Text & Cases. 3rd ed. 704p. (C). 1992. text 73.25 (*0-256-08705-9*, Irwn McGrw-H) McGrw-H Hghr Educ.
Cash, John A., et al. Seven Firefights in Vietnam. (Illus.). 159p. (Orig.). (C). 1993. pap. text 20.00 (*1-56806-563-9*) DIANE Pub.
Cash, John D. Identity, Idology & Conflict: The Structuration of Politics in Northern Ireland. 240p. (C). 1996. text 54.95 (*0-521-55052-1*) Cambridge U Pr.
Cash, John D., ed. Progress in Transfusion Medicine, No. 3. (Illus.). 232p. 1988. text 144.00 (*0-443-03721-3*) Church.
Cash, John J., et al. Rheumatology: Diagnosis & Therapeutics. LC 97-42809. 559p. 1998. pap. 37.95 (*0-683-30014-8*) Lppncott W & W.
Cash, Johnny. Cash: The Autobiography. LC 98-227899. (Illus.). 448p. 1998. mass mkt. 6.50 (*0-06-101357-9*, Pub. by Harper SF) HarpC.
Cash, Johnny & Carr, Patrick. Cash. large type ed. LC 97-50593. (Core Ser.). 440p. 1998. 26.95 (*0-7838-8424-9*, G K Hall & Co) Mac Lib Ref.
***Cash, Jonathan M.** Age of Antichrist. LC 00-9793. 400p. 2000. pap. 14.99 (*0-88368-629-5*) Whitaker Hse.
Cash, Jonathan M. The Age of the Antichrist. LC 97-77315. 352p. 1999. 21.95 (*0-8158-0534-9*) Chris Mass.
Cash, Joseph H. & Hoover, Herbert T., eds. To Be an Indian: An Oral History. LC 94-39879. (Illus.). xxiv, 239p. 1995. pap. 11.95 (*0-87351-306-1*, Borealis Book) Minn Hist.
Cash, Kathy. Designing & Using Simulations for Training. (Technical Notes Ser.: No. 20). 34p. (Orig.). (C). 1982. pap. 2.00 (*0-932288-66-9*) Ctr Intl Ed U of MA.
Cash, Kathy K. How to Add Sparkle & Pizzazz to Your Health Promotion Program: Powerful Programming Tips to Attract & Motivate Participants. LC 98-8965. 1998. pap. 29.95 (*0-965725-168-1*) Whole Person.
Cash, Kathy K., jt. auth. see Cash, J. Grady.
Cash, Marie R. Built of Earth & Song: Churches of Northern New Mexico. (Illus.). 184p. 1993. pap. 14.95 (*1-878610-30-9*) Red Crane Bks.
— Living Shrines: Home Alters of New Mexico. LC 98-26816. (Illus.). 124p. 1998. 45.00 (*0-89013-369-7*); pap. 24.95 (*0-89013-370-0*) Museum NM Pr.
***Cash, Marie R.** Santos: Enduring Images of Northern New Mexican Village Churches. LC 99-10288. (Illus.). 296p. 1999. 39.95 (*0-87081-494-X*) Univ Pr Colo.
Cash, Martin. Winnipeg: A Prairie Portrait. LC 98-6721. (Illus.). 256p. 1998. 39.00 (*1-885352-88-3*) Community Comm.
Cash, Martin, et al. Winnipeg, a Prairie Portrait. LC 98-6721. 1998. pap. write for info. (*1-885352-89-1*) Community Comm.
***Cash, Megan Montague.** Way to Yo! (American Girl Backpack Bks.: Vol. 28). (Illus.). 32p. (YA). (gr. 3). 2000. 1.95 (*1-58485-065-5*) Pleasant Co.
***Cash, Mel.** Pocket Atlas of the Moving Body: For All Students of Human Biology, Medicine, Sports & Physical Therapy. (Illus.). 68p. 2000. spiral bd. 15.95 (*0-09-186512-3*, Pub. by Ebury Pr) Trafalgar.
Cash, Mel. Sport & Remedial Massage Therapy. (Illus.). 288p. 1997. pap. 24.95 (*0-09-180956-8*, Pub. by Ebury Pr) Trafalgar.
Cash, Mel, jt. auth. see Ylinen, Jari.
Cash, Paul & Smith, Timothy, eds. Paul Brunton: Essential Readings. 1991. pap. 12.95 (*1-85274-080-9*, Pub. by Aqrn Pr) Harper SF.
Cash, Paul, ed. see Brunton, Paul.
Cash, Paul, ed. see Kircher, Pamela M.
Cash, Paul, ed. see Toms, Michael.
Cash, Paul, ed. see Wile, Mary L.
Cash, Paul, ed. & pref. see Brunton, Paul, et al.
Cash, Philip, et al, eds. Medicine in Colonial Massachusetts, 1620-1820. LC 80-68589. (Illus.). xxiv, 425p. 1980. text 35.00 (*0-8139-0908-2*) U Pr of Va.
Cash, Phyllis. Case Worker. 11th ed. LC 97-81095. Vol. 11. 272p. 1998. 14.95 (*0-02-862507-2*, Arc) IDG Bks.
— How to Develop & Write a Research Report. 2nd ed. 112p. 1988. pap. 8.00 (*0-671-87939-1*) S&S Trade.
Cash, Phyllis, et al. Holiday Open House. 128p. 1998. pap. 9.95 (*0-942249-03-8*) Starr-Toof.
Cash, R. Patrick, et al. Management of Retail Buying. 3rd ed. 424p. 1995. 110.00 (*0-471-07640-6*) Wiley.
Cash, Ron & Cash, Carol. The New Complete Keeshond. 2nd ed. LC 87-3881. (Illus.). 304p. 1987. pap. 25.95 (*0-87605-199-9*) Howell Bks.
Cash, Rosanne. Bodies of Water. 144p. 1996. 19.45 (*0-7868-6083-9*, Pub. by Hyperion) Time Warner.
Cash, Rosanne. Bodies of Water. 144p. 1997. pap. 10.00 (*0-380-72944-X*, Avon Bks) Morrow Avon.
— Penelope Jane: A Fairy's Tale. LC 98-41512. (Illus.). 32p. (J). (ps-3). 2000. 15.95 (*0-06-027543-X*) HarpC Child Bks.
***Cash, Rosanne.** Songs Without Rhyme: Prose by Celebrated Songwriters. (Illus.). 288p. 2001. 19.95 (*0-7868-6277-7*, Pub. by Hyperion) Time Warner.
— Songs Without Rhyme: Short Stories by Songwriters. 304p. Date not set. pap. 14.95 (*0-7868-8390-1*, Pub. by Disney Pr) Time Warner.
Cash, Sarah. American Art: Paintings from the Amon Carter Museum. LC 92-54538. (Illus.). 60p. 1992. pap. 10.00 (*0-88360-070-6*) Amon Carter.
Cash, Terry. Bricks. Stefoff, Rebecca, ed. LC 90-40249. (Threads Ser.). (Illus.). 32p. (J). (gr. 3-5). 1990. lib. bdg. 15.93 (*0-944483-68-2*) Garrett Ed Corp.
Cash, Terry. 175 More Science Experiments to Amuse & Amaze Your Friends: Experiments! Tricks! Things to Mak. 1991. 20.09 (*0-606-04852-9*, Pub. by Turtleback) Demco.
Cash, Terry & Taylor, Barbara. One Hundred Seventy-Five More Science Experiments to Amuse & Amaze Your Friends. LC 90-39250. (Illus.). 176p. (Orig.). (J). (gr. 4-7). 1991. pap. 14.99 (*0-679-80390-4*, Pub. by Random Bks Yng Read) Random.
Cash, Thomas F. Body Image Workbook. 224p. 1998. pap., wbk. ed. 8.98 (*1-56731-271-3*) Fine Comms.
— The Body Image Workbook: An 8-Step Program for Learning to Like Your Looks. LC 97-171686. 224p. 1997. pap. 18.95 (*1-57224-062-8*) New Harbinger.
Cash, Thomas F. & Pruzinsky, Thomas, eds. Body Images: Development, Deviance & Change. LC 90-3405. 361p. 1990. lib. bdg. 45.00 (*0-89862-438-X*) Guilford Pubns.
Cash, W. J. The Mind of the South. 1992. 26.00 (*0-8446-6632-7*) Peter Smith.
— The Mind of the South. LC 91-50042. 464p. 1991. pap. 14.00 (*0-679-73647-6*) Vin Bks.
Cash, William. Educating William: Memoirs of a Hollywood Correspondent. large type ed. 22.95 (*1-85695-119-7*, Pub. by ISIS Lrg Prnt) Transaction Pubs.
***Cash, William.** The Third Woman: The Secret Passion That Inspired "The End of the Affair" 336p. 2000. 25.00 (*0-7867-0812-3*, Pub. by Carroll & Graf) Publishers Group.
Cash, William B., jt. auth. see Stewart, Charles J.
Cashdan, Asher & Overall, Lyn. Teaching in Primary Schools. LC 99-182781. 1998. 75.00 (*0-304-70360-5*); pap. 24.95 (*0-304-70361-3*) Continuum.
Cashdan, Linda. It's Only Love. large type ed. LC 92-29407. 619p. 1993. reprint ed. lib. bdg. 21.95 (*1-56054-551-8*) Thorndike Pr.
Cashdan, Liz. Laughing All the Way. LC 96-140109. 72p. (Orig.). (YA). (gr. 10). 1995. pap. 12.98 (*0-907123-46-5*, Pub. by Five Leaves) AK Pr Dist.
Cashdan, Rochelle, ed. Indians of the Northwest. LC 97-77591. (Perspectives on History Ser.: Pt. III). (Illus.). 64p. 1998. pap. 6.95 (*1-57960-014-X*) Disc Enter Ltd.
Cashdan, Sheldon. Object Relations Therapy: Using the Relationship. 1988. 25.00 (*0-393-70059-3*) Norton.
— The Witch Must Die: How Fairy Tales Shape Our Lives. LC 99-32619. 304p. 1999. 25.00 (*0-465-09148-2*, Pub. by Basic) HarpC.
***Cashdan, Sheldon.** Witch Must Die: How Fairy Tales Shape Our Lives. 2000. pap. 15.00 (*0-465-00896-8*, Pub. by Basic) HarpC.
Cashdollar & Hertzberg, eds. Industrial Dust Explosions, Vol. STP 958. 372p. 1987. 49.00 (*0-8031-0957-1*, STP958) ASTM.
***Cashdollar, Charles D.** A Spiritual Home: Life in British & American Reformed Congregations, 1830-1915. LC 99-42595. 2000. text. write for info. (*0-271-02015-6*) Pa St U Pr.

C

Cashdollar, Charles D. The Transformation of Theology, 1830-1890: Positivism & Protestant Thought in Britain & America. LC 88-25442. 501p. 1989. reprint ed. pap. 155.40 (*0-608-03305-7*, 206401700008) Bks Demand.

Cashel Diocesan Library Staff. Catalog of the Cashel Diocesan Library. 1994. 175.00 (*0-7838-2275-8*, G K Hall & Co) Mac Lib Ref.

Cashell, E. M., ed. Durability & Fracture. 200p. 1988. text 66.00 (*0-87849-573-8*, Pub. by Trans T Pub) Enfield Pubs NH.

Cashen, J. Larry, et al. Kentucky Health Law. 2nd ed. xvii, 778p. 1995. 87.00 (*1-58757-011-4*, DH025) Univ of KY.

Cashen, William R. Farthest North College President. LC 72-91700. 387p. 1972. 10.00 (*0-912006-10-2*) U of Alaska Pr.

Cashet, Thomas. A Breviary of Torment. Hanley, John, ed. (Illus.). 109p. (Orig.). 1991. 18.95 (*1-879194-04-X*); pap. 13.95 (*1-879194-03-1*) GLB Pubs.

Cashford, Jules, jt. auth. see Baring, Anne.

***Cashill, Jack.** 2006: The Chatauqua Rising. 2000. 23.95 (*0-9672357-1-5*) O Frederick Inc.

***Cashin, Arthur D., Jr.** A View of Wall Street from the Seventh Floor: Prepared & Served by the Stock Exchange Luncheon Club. LC 99-68224. (Illus.). 96p. 1999. write for info. (*0-944641-39-3*) Greenwich Pub Group.

Cashin, Chris, et al, eds. Intense: Graduate Literary Magazine of Saint Mary's College of California, Vol. 2. 100p. 1998. pap. 8.00 (*0-9653764-1-9*) Sufi Warrior.

Cashin, Edward, intro. The Market Place. (Illus.). 1986. 8.95 (*0-9615980-0-X*) Augusta Jr Womans.

Cashin, Edward J. General Sherman's Girl Friend & Other Stories about Augusta. LC 93-40903. (Illus.). 1993. 18.00 (*0-87152-477-5*) Reprint.

***Cashin, Edward J.** The King's Ranger: Thomas Brown & the American Revolution on the Southern Frontier. LC 98-56007. 250p. 1999. reprint ed. 34.00 (*0-8232-1907-0*); reprint ed. pap. 19.95 (*0-8232-1908-9*) Fordham.

Cashin, Edward J. Lachlan McGillivray, Indian Trader: The Shaping of the Southern Colonial Frontier. LC 91-12479. 352p. 1992. 45.00 (*0-8203-1368-8*) U of Ga Pr.

— Old Springfield: Race & Religion in Augusta, Georgia. LC 95-72536. (Illus.). 134p. 1996. 20.00 (*0-9649511-5-0*) Sprngfield Village.

— The Story of Augusta. 2nd ed. (Illus.). 334p. 1991. reprint ed. 35.00 (*0-87152-452-X*) Richmond Cty Hist Soc.

— William Bartram & the American Revolution on the Southern Frontier. LC 99-6278. (Illus.). 360p. 2000. 39.95 (*1-57003-325-0*) U of SC Pr.

Cashin, Edward J., ed. Setting Out to Begin a New World: Colonial Georgia. (Documentary History Ser.). 248p. 1995. 35.00 (*0-88322-014-8*) Beehive GA.

— A Wilderness Still the Cradle of Nature: Frontier Georgia. (Documentary History Ser.). 204p. 1994. 35.00 (*0-88322-015-6*) Beehive GA.

Cashin, Herschel V. Under Fire with the Tenth U. S. Cavalry. 1993. 32.50 (*0-87081-280-7*) Univ Pr Colo.

Cashin, Herschel V., et al. Under Fire with the Tenth U. S. Cavalry. LC 69-18550. (American Negro: His History & Literature. Series 2). 378p. 1969. reprint ed. 32.95 (*0-405-01854-1*) Ayer.

Cashin, James A. & Owens, Garland C. Auditing. 2nd ed. LC 63-9246. 857p. reprint ed. pap. 200.00 (*0-8357-5872-9*, 201239300081) Bks Demand.

Cashin, James A., et al. Schaum's Outline of Intermediate Accounting. 2nd rev. ed. (Schaum's Outline Ser.). 288p. 1989. pap. text 12.95 (*0-07-010204-X*) McGraw.

Cashin, James A., jt. auth. see Lerner, Joel J.

Cashin, Jerry. Client/Server Operating Systems: Evaluation & Implementation. LC 95-15397. (Illus.). 227p. 1995. pap. 290.00 (*1-56607-049-X*) Comput Tech Res.

Cashin, Jerry. Client/Server Technology: The New Direction in Computer Networking. LC 93-12133. (Illus.). 188p. 1995. pap. 220.00 (*1-56607-008-2*) Comput Tech Res.

Cashin, Jerry. Developing Second Generation Client/Server Applications. LC 95-43369. (Illus.). 252p. 1996. pap. 280.00 (*1-56607-958-6*) Comput Tech Res.

— Distributed Systems: Future Trends & Technologies. LC 97-24161. (Illus.). 230p. 1997. pap. 280.00 (*1-56607-991-8*) Comput Tech Res.

— E-Commerce Success: Building a Global Business Architecture. LC 99-13886. 225p. 1999. pap. 290.00 (*1-56607-071-6*) Comput Tech Res.

— Implementing & Managing Client/Server Systems. LC 96-11464. (Illus.). 220p. 1996. pap. 295.00 (*1-56607-972-1*) Comput Tech Res.

— Intranets: Strategies & Technologies for Building Effective Enterprisewide Intranet Systems. LC 97-49562. (Illus.). 225p. 1998. 280.00 (*1-56607-996-9*) Comput Tech Res.

— Messaging Technologies for Global Communications. LC 98-2758. (Illus.). 236p. 1998. pap. 290.00 (*1-56607-055-4*) Comput Tech Res.

— Object Technology: The New Approach to Application Development. LC 96-30867. (Illus.). 231p. 1996. pap. 270.00 (*1-56607-977-2*) Comput Tech Res.

— Web Commerce: Developing & Implementing Effective Business Solutions. LC 98-26735. (Illus.). 251p. 1999. pap. 270.00 (*1-56607-062-7*) Comput Tech Res.

Cashin, Joan E. A Family Venture: Men & Women in the Southern Frontier. (Illus.). 216p. 1991. text 55.00 (*0-19-505344-3*, 6577) OUP.

— A Family Venture: Men & Women in the Southern Frontier. LC 94-14544. 208p. 1994. reprint ed. pap. text 14.95 (*0-8018-4964-0*) Johns Hopkins.

Cashin, Joan E., ed. Our Common Affairs: Texts from Women in the Old South. LC 95-51431. (Illus.). 352p. (C). 1996. text 39.95 (*0-8018-5306-0*) Johns Hopkins.

***Cashion, D. S.** The Official Bbmak Scrapbook. (Illus.). 48p. (YA). (gr. 5 up). 2000. pap. 9.99 (*0-7868-1516-7*) Hyprn Ppbks.

Cashion, David, ed. see RuPaul.

Cashion, Deena D. The Master Potter & His Clay. 62p. 1992. pap. text 5.00 (*1-882411-00-5*) Walk Faith Minist.

Cashion, Gerald. Thirteenth Summer: An Adirondack Adventure. (Illus.). 156p. (Orig.). (J). (gr. 5-8). 1996. pap. 11.50 (*0-9654280-0-1*) Sunset Ent.

Cashion, Gerald, ed. see O'Keeffe, Daniel, 2nd.

Cashion, Ty. Pigskin Pulpit: A Social History of Texas High School Football Coaches. LC 98-20976. (Illus.). 300p. 1998. 29.95 (*0-87611-168-1*) Tex St Hist Assn.

— A Texas Frontier: The Clear Fork Country & Fort Griffin, 1849-1887. LC 95-41192. (Illus.). 384p. (C). 1996. 24.95 (*0-8061-2791-0*) U of Okla Pr.

— A Texas Frontier: The Clear Fork Country & Fort Griffin, 1849-1887. LC 95-41192. (Illus.). 384p. 1997. pap. 17.95 (*0-8061-2855-0*) U of Okla Pr.

Cashlla, Richard P., tr. see Teresa, Madre.

Cashman. Groundwater Lowering in Construction. (Illus.). 384p. 1998. pap. 119.95 (*0-419-21110-1*) Thomson Learn.

Cashman, jt. auth. see Shelly.

Cashman, Aileen. Money Matters for Women. (C). 1989. 65.00 (*0-946211-75-2*) St Mut.

Cashman, Dennis. Prohibition: The Lie of the Land. 1981. 17.95 (*0-317-30516-6*) Free Pr.

Cashman, Diane C. Wilmington: Cape Fear Adventure. 1989. 22.95 (*0-89781-057-0*) Am Historical Pr.

Cashman, Greer F. & Frankel, Alona. Jewish Days & Holidays. LC 86-70789. (Illus.). 64p. (J). (ps up). 1986. 11.95 (*0-915361-58-2*) Lambda Pubs.

Cashman, Greg. What Causes War? An Introduction to Theories of International Conflict. LC 92-40643. 360p. 1993. pap. 19.95 (*0-669-21215-6*) Lxngtn Bks.

***Cashman, Greg.** What Causes War? An Introduction to Theories of International Conflict. 272p. 2000. pap. 24.95 (*0-7391-0112-9*) Lxngtn Bks.

Cashman, Holly, tr. see Riera, Carme.

Cashman, J. N., jt. ed. see Adams, A. P.

***Cashman, John R.** Emergency Response to Chemical & Biological Agents. LC 99-43796. 347p. 1999. 79.95 (*1-56670-355-7*) Lewis Pubs.

Cashman, John R. Hazardous Materials Emergencies: The Professional Response Team. 3rd rev. ed. LC 95-61048. 330p. 1995. 99.95 (*1-56676-322-3*) Technomic.

Cashman, Jude, ed. see Duncan, William.

Cashman, Jude, ed. see Ruckle, Gene.

Cashman, Jude, ed. see Santucci, Robert M.

***Cashman, Kevin.** Leadership from the Inside Out: Becoming a Leader for Life. 224p. 1999. pap. 15.95 (*1-890009-31-8*) Exec Excell.

Cashman, Kevin. Leadership from the Inside Out: Becoming a Leader for Life. (Illus.). 224p. 1999. 24.95 (*1-890009-29-6*) Exec Excell.

Cashman, Richard. The Demon Spofforth. 275p. 1990. 37.95 (*0-86840-004-1*, Pub. by New South Wales Univ Pr) Intl Spec Bk.

***Cashman, Richard & Hughes, Anthony, eds.** Staging the Olympics: The Event & Its Impact. 224p. 1999. pap. 29.95 (*0-86840-729-1*, Pub. by New South Wales Univ Pr) Intl Spec Bk.

Cashman, Richard, jt. auth. see Weaver, Amanda.

Cashman, Sean D. African Americans & the Quest for Civil Rights, 1900-1990. (Illus.). 360p. (C). 1991. text 45.00 (*0-8147-1440-4*) NYU Pr.

— African-Americans & the Quest for Civil Rights, 1900-1990. (Illus.). 321p. (C). 1992. pap. text 19.50 (*0-8147-1441-2*) NYU Pr.

— America Ascendant: From Theodore Roosevelt to FDR in the Century of American Power, 1901-1945. LC 97-45320. (Illus.). 520p. 1998. text 65.00 (*0-8147-1565-6*); pap. text 22.50 (*0-8147-1566-4*) NYU Pr.

— America in the Age of the Titans: From the Rise of Theodore Roosevelt to the Death of FDR. (Illus.). 450p. (C). 1988. text 50.00 (*0-8147-1410-2*) NYU Pr.

— America in the Gilded Age: From the Death of Lincoln to the Rise of Theodore Roosevelt. 3rd ed. LC 93-12999. (Illus.). 450p. (C). 1993. text 55.00 (*0-8147-1494-3*); pap. text 19.50 (*0-8147-1495-1*) NYU Pr.

— America in the Twenties & Thirties: The Olympian Age of Franklin Delano Roosevelt. (Illus.). 450p. (C). 1989. pap. text 18.50 (*0-8147-1413-7*) NYU Pr.

— America, Roosevelt, & World War II. 416p. (C). 1989. text 50.00 (*0-8147-1430-7*) NYU Pr.

Cashman, Shelly. DOS 6.0. (C). 1994. text. write for info. (*0-318-70358-0*) S-W Pub.

— Lotus for Windows 2.4. (C). 1994. text. write for info. (*0-318-70359-9*) S-W Pub.

— Microsoft PowerPoint. (C). 1994. text. write for info. (*0-318-70360-2*) S-W Pub.

— Microsoft Visual Basic. (C). 1994. text. write for info. (*0-318-70361-0*) S-W Pub.

***Cashman, Shelly.** Ms Office 2000 Advanced Concepts & Techniques (C). 1999. ring bd. (*0-7895-5947-1*) Course Tech.

Cashman, Shelly. Paradox 4.0. (C). 1994. text. write for info. (*0-318-70362-9*) S-W Pub.

— Quattro Pro 5.O. (C). 1994. text. write for info. (*0-318-70363-7*) S-W Pub.

— Quattro Pro for Windows 2.O. (C). 1994. text. write for info. (*0-318-70364-5*) S-W Pub.

— Visual Basic (C). 1996. spiral bd. 25.95 (*0-7895-2844-4*) Course Tech.

— WordPerfect 6.0. (C). 1994. text. write for info. (*0-318-70365-3*) S-W Pub.

***Cashman, Shelly & Forsythe.** Microsoft Windows 98 Complete Concepts & Techniques. (C). 1998. pap. 44.95 (*0-7895-4746-5*) Course Tech.

Cashman, T. & Shelly, Gary B. Exploring Computers - Activity Book. (Shelly Cashman Ser.). 1996. mass mkt. 12.00 (*0-7895-0741-2*) Course Tech.

Cashman, T., jt. auth. see Shelly, Gary B.

Cashman, Thomas J. & Shelly, Gary B. Brief Introduction to Computers. 2nd ed. (C). 1997. pap. 7.50 (*0-7895-4323-0*) Course Tech.

Cashman, Thomas J., jt. auth. see Shelly.

Cashman, Thomas J., jt. auth. see Shelly, Gary B.

Cashmore, E. Ellis. Dictionary of Race & Ethnic Relations. 320p. 1989. pap. 14.95 (*0-415-02511-7*, A3547) Routledge.

— Having To: The World of One Parent Families. 1985. pap. text 12.95 (*0-04-301099-7*) Routledge.

— The Logic of Racism. 288p. 1986. pap. text 16.95 (*0-04-301256-6*) Routledge.

— United Kingdom? 208p. 1989. text 44.95 (*0-04-305014-X*) Routledge.

Cashmore, E. Ellis & Troyna, Barry. Introduction to Race Relations. 256p. (Orig.). 1983. pap. 10.95 (*0-7100-9930-4*, Routledge Thoemms) Routledge.

— Introduction to Race Relations. 2nd ed. (Orig.). 1990. 85.00 (*1-85000-759-4*, Falmer Pr); pap. 29.95 (*1-85000-760-8*, Falmer Pr) Taylor & Francis.

Cashmore, Ellis. And There Was Television. LC 93-33670. (Illus.). 288p. (C). 1994. pap. 22.99 (*0-415-09131-4*, B3525) Routledge.

— Dictionary of Race & Ethnic Relations. 4th ed. LC 96-42215. 432p. (C). 1996. pap. 27.99 (*0-415-13822-1*) Routledge.

— Dictionary of Race & Ethnic Relations, 4 vols., Set. 4th ed. 432p. (C). 1996. 110.00 (*0-415-15167-8*) Routledge.

— Making Sense of Sport. 2nd ed. LC 95-25971. 304p. (C). 1996. 80.00 (*0-415-13306-8*); pap. 24.99 (*0-415-13307-6*) Routledge.

***Cashmore, Ellis.** Sports Culture: An A-Z Guide. LC 99-16891. 452p. 2000. 85.00 (*0-415-18169-0*); pap. 30.00 (*0-415-22335-0*) Routledge.

Cashmore, Ellis & Rojek, Chris, eds. The Dictionary of Cultural Theorists. LC 98-36502. 384p. 1999. text 75.00 (*0-340-64549-0*, Pub. by E A) OUP.

— The Dictionary of Cultural Theorists. LC 98-36502. (Illus.). 384p. 1999. pap. text 19.95 (*0-340-64548-2*, Pub. by E A) OUP.

Cashmore, Ernest. The Black Culture Industry. LC 96-48116. 216p. (C). 1997. 75.00 (*0-415-12082-9*); pap. 22.99 (*0-415-12083-7*) Routledge.

Cashmore, R. J. & Myatt, G. Perkins Conference - Meeting in Honor of the Retirement of Professor D H Perkins. 216p. 1994. text 74.00 (*981-02-1561-4*) World Scientific Pub.

Cashorali, Peter. Fairy Tales: Traditional Stories Retold by Gay Men. 1997. pap. 11.00 (*0-614-27335-8*) Harper SF.

— Fairy Tales: Traditional Tales Retold for Gay Men. LC 95-14185. 192p. 1997. pap. 13.00 (*0-06-251309-5*, Pub. by Harper SF) HarpC.

— Gay Fairy & Folk Tales: More Traditional Stories Retold for Gay Men. LC 97-10787. 176p. 1997. 19.95 (*0-571-19926-7*) Faber & Faber.

Cashore, Benjamin W. & University of Maine at Orono Staff. Flights of the Phoenix: Explaining the Durability of Canada-U.S. Softwood Lumber Dispute. (Canadian-America Public Policy Ser.). 63p. 1997. (*1-882582-21-7*) Canadian-Amer Ctr.

Cashwell, E. D., jt. auth. see Carter, L. L.

Cashwell, Roberta E. Working in Light. unabridged ed. 248p. 1998. pap. 12.00 (*0-9659834-0-4*); lib. bdg. 12.00 (*0-9659834-1-2*) Cornell Farm.

***Casiani, Santa & Kleinhenz, Christopher, trs.** The Fiore & the Detto d'Amore. (William & Katherine Devers Series in Dante Studies: Vol. 4). 552p. 2000. pap. text 45.00 (*0-268-00893-0*, Pub. by U of Notre Dame Pr) Chicago Distribution Ctr.

Casiati, F., jt. ed. see Bellomo, N.

Casida, John E., ed. Pyrethrum Flowers: Production, Chemistry, Toxicology & Uses. (Illus.). 384p. 1995. text 70.00 (*0-19-508210-9*) OUP.

Casida, John E., jt. auth. see Yamamoto, Izuru.

CASIE Committee. CASIE Compendium, Vol. IV. 1997. pap. text 20.00 (*1-56318-055-3*) Assn Natl Advertisers.

— CASIE Glossary of Internet Advertising Terms & Interactive Media Measurement Guidelines. 1997. pap. text 15.00 (*1-56318-054-5*) Assn Natl Advertisers.

Casier, Tom & Malfliet, Katlijn, eds. Is Russia a European Power? The Position of Russia in a New Europe. 150p. 1998. pap. 36.50 (*90-6186-906-4*, Pub. by Leuven Univ) Coronet Bks.

Casil, Kathleen L. Hawaiian Baby Book. Losch, Naomi N., tr. (ENG & HAW., Illus.). 48p. 1986. 14.95 (*0-935848-33-9*) Bess Pr.

Casilla. Going to a New School. 1996. 14.00 (*0-689-80468-7*) S&S Childrens.

Casilla, Robert, photos by. Daddy Poems. LC 99-63735. (Illus.). 32p. (gr. k-7). 2000. 15.95 (*1-56397-735-4*, Wordsong) Boyds Mills Pr.

Casilla, Robert, jt. auth. see Wing, Natasha.

Casimir, Jean. La Invencion del Caribe. (Coleccion Caribena Ser.). (SPA.). 292p. 1997. pap. 14.95 (*0-8477-0222-7*) U of PR Pr.

Casimir, John. Postcards from the Net. 1997. pap. text 16.95 (*1-86448-280-X*, Pub. by Allen & Unwin Pty) IPG Chicago.

Casimir, Louis. Easy Chemistry. 6th ed. (Illus.). 247p. 1997. pap. text 19.95 (*0-87563-765-5*) Stipes.

— Unique Chemical Labs. 107p. 1994. pap. text 8.95 (*0-87563-511-3*) Stipes.

Casimir, Michael J. & Rao, Aparna, eds. Mobility & Territoriality: Social & Spatial Boundaries among Foragers, Fishers, Pastoralists & Peripatetics. 256p. 1991. 39.50 (*0-85496-739-7*) Berg Pubs.

Casimjee, Farida. An Autosegmental Analysis of Venda Tonology. LC 92-31752. (Outstanding Dissertations in Linguistics Ser.). 368p. 1992. text 25.00 (*0-8153-0706-3*) Garland.

Casin, John. Illustrations: Of the Birds of California, Texas, Oregon, British & Russian America. (Illus.). xxx, 298p. 1991. 29.95 (*0-87611-106-1*) Tex St Hist Assn.

— Illustrations: Of the Birds of California, Texas, Oregon, British & Russian America. limited ed. (Illus.). xxx, 298p. 1991. boxed set 75.00 (*0-87611-107-X*) Tex St Hist Assn.

Casini, G. Plasma Physics for Thermonuclear Fusion Reactors, Vol. 1. (Ispra Courses on Nuclear Engineering & Technology Ser.). vi, 492p. (C). 1981. text 349.00 (*3-7186-0091-9*) Gordon & Breach.

Casini, G., ed. Engineering Aspects of Thermonuclear Fusion Reactors, Vol. 2. (Ispra Courses on Nuclear Engineering & Technology Ser.). vi, 640p. 1982. text 497.00 (*3-7186-0090-0*) Gordon & Breach.

Casjens, Sherwood. Virus Structure & Assembly. 290p. (C). 1985. 100.00 (*0-86720-044-8*) Jones & Bartlett.

Caskey, Deborah. Geology. 352p. (C). 1994. spiral bd., lab manual ed. 27.95 (*0-8403-7570-0*) Kendall-Hunt.

Caskey, Gregory M. Caskey's Bench Guide to California Search & Seizure Cases: A Summary of Recent California Decisions. 2nd ed. 1995. ring bd. 124.95 (*1-883952-08-5*) Hse of Steno.

Caskey, James E., Jr., ed. A Century of Weather Progress: A Collection of Addresses Presented at a Joint Symposium Commemorating the Centennial of the U. S. Weather Service & the Golden Anniversary of the AMS. (Illus.). 170p. 1970. 15.00 (*0-933876-36-X*) Am Meteorological.

Caskey, Jefferson D., compiled by. Index to Poetry in Popular Periodicals: 1960-1964. LC 87-32277. 247p. 1988. lib. bdg. 59.95 (*0-313-24810-9*, CIT/, Greenwood Pr) Greenwood.

— Index to Poetry in Popular Periodicals, 1955-1959. LC 83-22584. 269p. 1984. lib. bdg. 47.95 (*0-313-22227-4*, CIP/, Greenwood Pr) Greenwood.

Caskey, Jefferson D. & Stapp, Melinda M., eds. Samuel Taylor Coleridge: A Selective Bibliography of Criticism, 1935-1977. LC 78-57765. 174p. 1978. lib. bdg. 42.95 (*0-313-20564-7*, CCO/, Greenwood Pr) Greenwood.

Caskey, John H. The Life & Works of Edward Moore. LC 72-8823. (Yale Studies in English: No. 75). iv, 197p. 1973. reprint ed. 59.50 (*0-208-01125-0*) Elliots Bks.

Caskey, John L. & Blackburn, E. T. Lerna in the Argolid. 2nd rev. ed. LC 98-161669. (Illus.). 32p. 1997. pap. text 4.00 (*0-87661-680-5*) Am Sch Athens.

Caskey, John P. Fringe Banking: Check-Cashing Outlets, Pawnshops, & the Poor. 156p. 1994. 29.95 (*0-87154-195-5*) Russell Sage.

— Fringe Banking: Check-Cashing Outlets, Pawnshops, & the Poor. 192p. (C). 1996. pap. text 14.95 (*0-87154-180-7*) Russell Sage.

— Lower Income Americans, Higher Cost Financial Services. 75p. 1997. pap. 100.00 (*1-880572-26-5*) Filene Res.

***Caskey, John P. & Humphrey, David B.** Credit Unions & Asset Accumulation by Lower-Income Households. 79p. (Orig.). 1999. pap. 100.00 (*1-880572-39-7*, 1752-51) Filene Res.

Caskey, Larry. Rim of the Wheel. LC 97-65964. 326p. 1997. 24.95 (*1-57197-061-4*) Pentland Pr.

***Caskey, Margret.** The Third Choice. LC 99-75014. 220p. 1999. pap. 15.95 (*0-9661657-7-2*) Mead.

Caskey, Marie. Chariot of Fire: Religion & the Beecher Family. LC 77-5291. (Yale Historical Publications: Miscellany: No. 117). 457p. reprint ed. pap. 141.70 (*0-7837-3287-2*, 205768900006) Bks Demand.

Caskey, Michael Mac, see Haas, Cathy, contrib. by.

Caskey, Miriam E. The Temple at Ayia Irini: The Statues. LC 85-15713. (Keos Ser.: Vol. 2, Pt. 1). (Illus.). xxviii, 130p. 1986. 45.00 (*0-87661-702-X*) Am Sch Athens.

Caskey, Owen L. Suggestive-Accelerative Learning & Teaching. Langdon, Danny G., ed. LC 79-26386. (Instructional Design Library). 136p. 1980. 27.95 (*0-87778-156-7*) Educ Tech Pubns.

***Caskey, Susan.** Debt Free - For Life! Strategies to Eliminate Debt for Good. 120p. 1999. pap. 12.95 (*0-9656994-1-2*) Blue Sky PA.

Caskie, Donald. The Tartan Pimpernel. 1999. pap. 13.95 (*1-84158-014-7*) Birlinn Ltd.

Caskie, Jason, ed. see Abendroth, John & Juricich, Mitch.

Casler, Carlton C. Arizona Landlord's Deskbook. 3rd rev. ed. 384p. 1998. pap. text 34.95 (*1-881436-05-5*) Consumer Law Bks.

— Tenant's Survival Guide. 2nd rev. ed. 208p. 1998. pap. 14.95 (*1-881436-03-9*) Consumer Law Bks.

Casler, Dave. Fox Hunt Adventure. 2nd ed. 136p. (J). (gr. 3-12). 1992. reprint ed. pap. 7.95 (*1-891237-08-X*, MFJ-3101) MFJ Ent.

Casler, Jennifer R., et al. The Path to Enlightenment: Masterpieces of Buddhist Sculpture from the National Museum of Asian Arts/Musee Guimet, Paris. LC 96-75653. (Illus.). 72p. (Orig.). 1996. pap. 12.95 (*0-912804-32-7*) Kimbell Art.

Casler, Jennifer R., jt. auth. see Berger, Patricia.

Casler, Ken & Palmer, David. Business Assignments. 126p. 1989. pap. text 7.95 (*0-19-451381-5*) OUP.

— Business Assignments Deskwork. (Illus.). 108p. 1989. pap. text 8.95 (*0-19-451374-2*) OUP.

— Business Assignments Info File. (Illus.). 152p. 1989. pap. text 13.95 (*0-19-451373-4*) OUP.

***Casler, Kristin.** Asthma. 256p. 2000. mass mkt. 5.99 (*0-380-73291-2*, HarpTorch) Morrow Avon.

Casler, Kristin. Asthma: Questions You Have... Answers You Need. rev. ed. LC 98-20353. 1998. pap. 12.95 (*1-882606-42-6*) Peoples Med Soc.

Casler, Melyer. A Journal Giving the Incidents of a Journey to California in the Summer of 1859, by the Over-Land Route. 64p. 1969. reprint ed. 24.95 (*0-87770-039-7*) Ye Galleon.

*Casler, Michael M. Steamboats of the Fort Union Fur Trade: An Illustrated Listing of Steamboats on the Upper Missouri River, 1831-1867. (Illus.). 150p. 1999. write for info. (0-9672251-0-8) Ft Union Assn.

Casler, Nelie H. Cape Vincent & Its History. (Illus.). 240p. 1997. reprint ed. lib. bdg. 32.00 (0-8328-6109-X) Higginson Bk Co.

Casler, Stephen D. HCO Intro to Economi. LC 91-55388. (College Outline Ser.). 480p. (C). 1992. pap. 16.00 (0-06-467113-5, Harper Ref) HarpC.

Casley, D. J. & Lury, D. A. Data Collection in Developing Countries. 2nd ed. 256p. 1987. 65.00 (0-19-877283-1) OUP.

*Casley, Dennis. Death under Par. 480p. 2000. 18.99 (0-7089-5736-6) Ulverscroft.

— Death Understates. large type ed. 456p. 2000. pap. 18.99 (0-7089-5677-7, Linford) Ulverscroft.

Casley, Dennis J. & Kumar, Krishna. The Collection, Analysis, & Use of Monitoring & Evaluation Data. LC 87-46375. (Illus.). 184p. 1988. reprint ed. pap. 57.10 (0-608-07332-6, 206756000009) Bks Demand.

— Project Monitoring & Evaluation in Agriculture. LC 87-22632. 174p. 1987. reprint ed. pap. 54.00 (0-608-03653-6, 206447900009) Bks Demand.

*Caslione, John A. & Thomas, Andrew R. Growing Your Business in Emerging Markets: Promise & Perils. LC 99-56359. 2000. write for info. (1-56720-339-6, Quorum Bks) Greenwood.

Caslow. Cisco Certification in Box. 1998. pap. text 145.00 (0-13-011929-6) P-H.

*Caslow, Andrew Bruce. Cisco Certification: Bridges, Routers & Switches for CCIEs. Pavlichenko, Valerly, ed. LC 98-31189. 840p. 1998. pap. text 69.99 (0-13-082537-9) P-H.

— Cisco Routing Illustrated: A Workbook for Ccies & Concepts. (Illus.). 500p. 2001. 59.99 (0-13-085266-X) P-H.

*Caslow, Andrew Bruce & Huitema. CCIE Resource Library, Year 2000 Update. 2nd ed. 1999. pap. text 137.00 (0-13-087695-X) P-H.

Caslow, Bruce, et al. The CCIE Resource Library. 1998. pap. 154.00 (0-13-083829-2) P-H.

*Caslte, Helen. Modernism & Modernization. LC 99-203743. 128p. 1999. pap. 65.00 (0-471-98469-8) Wiley.

CASM Seminar Staff, et al. A New Agenda for Interdisciplinary Survey Research Methods: Proceedings of the Casm Li Seminar. LC 99-11314. 1999. write for info. (0-8406-0552-8) Natl Ctr Health Stats.

*Casmier, Susan B., et al, eds. A Deadly Dozen. LC 00-102195. 224p. 2000. pap. 13.00 (0-9663473-2-3) UglyTown Prods.

Casmir, Fred, ed. Intercultural & International Communication. LC 78-61912. (Illus.). 834p. 1978. reprint ed. pap. 200.00 (0-608-08287-2, AU0036100079) Bks Demand.

Casmir, Fred L. Communication in Development. Dervin, Brenda, ed. LC 90-19861. (Communication & Information Science Ser.). 368p. (C). 1991. pap. 39.50 (0-89391-770-2); text 73.25 (0-89391-642-2) Ablx Pub.

Casmir, Fred L., ed. Building Communication Theories: A Socio/Cultural Approach. (LEA's Communication Ser.). 320p. 1994. text 69.95 (0-8058-1516-3) L Erlbaum Assocs.

— Communication in Eastern Europe: The Role of History, Culture, & Media in Contemporary Conflicts. (Communication Ser.). 360p. 1995. text 69.95 (0-8058-1625-9) L Erlbaum Assocs.

Casmir, Fred L., et al, eds. Communication & International & Intercultural Ethics. LC 97-46380. (Communication Ser.). 300p. 1997. write for info. (0-8058-2352-2); pap. write for info. (0-8058-2353-0) L Erlbaum Assocs.

Casner. Estate Planning. LC 94-76926. 1994. 145.00 (0-316-13259-4, Aspen Law & Bus) Aspen Pub.

— Estate Planning. 5th ed. 1992. 35.00 (0-316-13267-5, Aspen Law & Bus) Aspen Pub.

— Estate Planning: 1995. 1995. 295.00 (0-316-13305-1, Aspen Law & Bus) Aspen Pub.

— Supplement to Estate Planning, 1994. 1994. suppl. ed. 295.00 (0-316-12960-7) Little.

Casner, A. James. American Law of Property, No. 1. 1952. 135.00 (0-316-13090-7, Aspen Law & Bus) Aspen Pub.

— American Law of Property, No. 2. 1952. 135.00 (0-316-13091-5, Aspen Law & Bus) Aspen Pub.

— American Law of Property, No. 3. 1952. 135.00 (0-316-13092-3, Aspen Law & Bus) Aspen Pub.

— American Law of Property, No. 4. 1952. 135.00 (0-316-13093-1, Aspen Law & Bus) Aspen Pub.

— American Law of Property, No. 5. 1952. 135.00 (0-316-13095-8, Aspen Law & Bus) Aspen Pub.

— American Law of Property, No. 6. 1952. 135.00 (0-316-13096-6, Aspen Law & Bus) Aspen Pub.

— American Law of Property, No. 6A. 1954. 135.00 (0-316-13099-0, Aspen Law & Bus) Aspen Pub.

— American Law of Property, No. 7. 1952. 135.00 (0-316-13097-4, Aspen Law & Bus) Aspen Pub.

— Estate Planning, 9 vols., Set. 4th ed. 4503p. 1998. ring bd. 1295.00 (0-316-13154-7, Aspen Law & Bus) Aspen Pub.

— Estate Planning, Vol. 1. 5th ed. 1984. 135.00 (0-316-13197-0, Aspen Law & Bus) Aspen Pub.

— Estate Planning, Vol. 2. 5th ed. 1985. 135.00 (0-316-13200-4, Aspen Law & Bus) Aspen Pub.

— Estate Planning, Vol. 2A. 5th ed. 1985. 135.00 (0-316-13201-2, Aspen Law & Bus) Aspen Pub.

— Estate Planning, Vol. 3. 5th ed. 1986. 135.00 (0-316-13220-9, Aspen Law & Bus) Aspen Pub.

— Estate Planning, Vol. 3A. 5th ed. 1986. 135.00 (0-316-13221-7, Aspen Law & Bus) Aspen Pub.

— Estate Planning, Vol. 4. 5th ed. 1987. 135.00 (0-316-13233-0, Aspen Law & Bus) Aspen Pub.

— Estate Planning, Vol. 4A. 5th ed. 1987. 135.00 (0-316-13232-2, Aspen Law & Bus) Aspen Pub.

— Estate Planning, Vol. 5. 5th ed. 1983. 135.00 (0-316-13163-6, Aspen Law & Bus) Aspen Pub.

— Estate Planning, Vol. 6. 5th ed. 1987. 135.00 (0-316-13228-4) Aspen Pub.

— Estate Planning: Student Edition. 4th ed. 1150p. 1979. 38.00 (0-316-13173-3, Aspen Law & Bus) Aspen Pub.

— 1982 Supplement to Estate Planning. 4th ed. 1982. pap., student ed. 16.00 (0-316-13171-7, Aspen Law & Bus) Aspen Pub.

— A Proposed Estate Plan for Mr. & Mrs. Richard Harry Black III. rev. ed. (C). 1983. ring bd. 26.00 (0-316-13162-8, Aspen Law & Bus) Aspen Pub.

— Supplement to American Law of Property '89. 1360p. 1989. 15.95 (0-316-13238-1, Aspen Law & Bus) Aspen Pub.

Casner, A. James, ed. American Law of Property, 8 vols., Set. LC 52-10235. 1952. 550.00 (0-316-13145-8, Aspen Law & Bus) Aspen Pub.

Casner, A. James & Leach, W. Barton. Cases & Text on Property. 1360p. 1984. teacher ed. write for info. (0-316-13186-5, 31865) Aspen Law.

— Cases & Text on Property. LC 83-82695. 1427p. (C). 1984. suppl. ed. 12.00 (0-316-13205-5, Aspen Law & Bus) Aspen Pub.

— Cases & Text on Property. 3rd ed. LC 83-82695. 1360p. (C). 1984. 57.00 (0-316-13183-0, Aspen Law & Bus) Aspen Pub.

Casner, A. James, ed. see Institutional Staff.

Casner, James A., ed. see Institutional Staff.

Casner, Jan, jt. auth. see Caneda, Marion.

Casner-Lotto, Jill & Work in America Associates Staff. Successful Training Strategies. LC 88-42781. (Management Ser.). 450p. 32.95 (1-55542-101-6) Work in Amer.

Casner-Lotto, Jill, jt. auth. see Rosow, Jerome M.

Casner-Lotto, Jill, ed. see Rosow, Jerome M. & Zager, Robert.

Casner-Lotto, Jill, ed. see Rosow, Jerome M., et al.

Caso, A. Reyes y Reinos de la Mixteca I. (SPA.). 32.99 (968-16-1787-8, Pub. by Fondo) Continental Bk.

— Reyes y Reinos de la Mixteca II. (SPA.). 41.99 (968-16-1788-6, Pub. by Fondo) Continental Bk.

Caso, A., ed. Barbra - An Actress Who Sings Vol. I: Unauthorized Biography of Barbra Streisand. (Illus.). 465p. 1989. 22.95 (0-8283-1923-5) Branden Bks.

— Cinderfella & the Slam Dunk Contest. (Illus.). 32p. (J). (gr. 2-6). 1994. pap. 13.95 (0-8283-1966-9) Branden Bks.

Caso, A., ed. see Borges, Jorge Luis, et al.

Caso, A., ed. see Campbell, Lisa.

Caso, A., ed. see Carisella, P. J.

Caso, A., ed. see Elkhart, Mary.

Caso, A., ed. see Francis, Charles E.

Caso, A., ed. see Johnson, K. & Rasche, John.

Caso, A., jt. ed. see Kimbrell, Cheri.

Caso, A., ed. see Schofield, W.

Caso, Adolfo, ed. see Angiolieri, Cecco.

Caso, Adolfo, ed. see Damioli, Carol.

Caso, Adolfo, ed. see Fagan, Patricia M.

Caso, Adolfo, ed. see Manaster, Benjamin.

Caso, Adolfo, ed. see Marks, Kathy.

Caso, Adolfo, ed. see Robin, Harry.

Caso, Adolfo, ed. see Zubritsky, John.

Caso, Adolph. Alfieri's Ode to America's Independence. LC 76-6244. 1976. pap. 11.95 (0-8283-1667-8) Branden Bks.

— America's Italian Founding Fathers. 1975. 25.95 (0-8283-1610-4) Branden Bks.

— Issues in Foreign Language & Bilingual Education. LC 77-94784. 1979. pap. 11.95 (0-8283-1721-6) Branden Bks.

— Lives of Italian Americans: Fifty Biographies. (Illus.). 1979. 19.95 (0-8283-1699-6) Branden Bks.

Caso, Adolph. Mass Media vs. the Italian Americans. 1984. pap. 11.95 (0-8283-1831-X) Branden Bks.

Caso, Adolph. The Straw Obelisk. (Illus.). 390p. 1995. 24.95 (0-8283-2005-5) Branden Bks.

Caso, Adolph. Water & Life: Poetry in English & Italian. 1976. pap. 11.95 (0-8283-1682-1) Branden Bks.

Caso, Adolph. We, the People: Formative Documents of America's Democracy. (Illus.). 336p. (C). 1995. 22.95 (0-8283-2006-3) Branden Bks.

Caso, Adolph, jt. auth. see Francis, Charles E.

Caso, Adolph, jt. auth. see Kinney, Joseph.

Caso, Adolph, ed. see Berkley, George E.

Caso, Adolph, ed. see Berman, Joel A.

Caso, Adolph, ed. see Bertini, Tullio B.

Caso, Adolph, ed. see Bodie, Neil & Bodie, Renee.

Caso, Adolph, ed. see Burton, Elizabeth.

Caso, Adolph, ed. see Cagle, Gerry.

Caso, Adolph, ed. see Caso, Laura M.

Caso, Adolph, ed. see Courtnay, Eileen.

Caso, Adolph, ed. see Cummings, Martha T.

Caso, Adolph, ed. see Di Plan Carpini, Giovanni.

Caso, Adolph, ed. see Flynn, George L.

Caso, Adolph, ed. see Grigg, Martha L.

Caso, Adolph, ed. see Hopkins, Roland.

Caso, Adolph, ed. see Kayworth, Alfred E.

Caso, Adolph, ed. see Kranz, Marian R.

Caso, Adolph, ed. see Masterton, William L.

Caso, Adolph, ed. see Moliere.

Caso, Adolph, ed. see Mosher, Eunice D.

Caso, Adolph, ed. see Myers, Robert.

Caso, Adolph, ed. see Paisley, Melvyn & Paisley, Vicki.

Caso, Adolph, ed. see Pergolizzi, Carl Milo.

Caso, Adolph, ed. see Seguin, Marilyn Weymouth.

Caso, Adolph, ed. see Spurling, Emma C.

Caso, Adolph, ed. see Tambini, Anthony J.

Caso, Adolph, ed. see Tanger, Woody.

Caso, Adolph, ed. see Turk, Ruth.

Caso, Adolph, ed. see Walkowski, Paul J. & Connoly, William M.

Caso, Adolpho, ed. see Seguin, Marilyn Weymouth.

Caso, Adolph, ed. see Tambini, Anthony J.

Caso, Alfonso. El Pueblo del Sol (The People of the Sun) (SPA., Illus.). 154p. 1983. pap. 5.99 (968-16-2901-9, Pub. by Fondo) Continental Bk.

Caso, Jose M., ed. see Cadalso, Jose.

*Caso, Laura M. Chicken Pox Explosion! Caso, Adolph, ed. (Illus.). 32p. (J). (gr. 2-5). 2000. pap. 7.95 (0-8283-2054-3) Branden Bks.

Casofret, Vaslie V. Pharmaceutical Applications of Membrane Sensors. 448p. 1992. lib. bdg. 129.00 (0-8493-4406-9, R857) CRC Pr.

Casolaro, Nancy. Gifted & Talented Math Workbook. (Illus.). 96p. (J). (gr. 1-3). 1993. pap. 4.95 (1-56565-039-5, 00395W, Pub. by Lowell Hse) NTC Contemp Pub Co.

Casolaro, Nancy, jt. auth. see Furlong, Kaye.

Casoli, F., jt. ed. see Combes, F.

Cason, Clarence. 90 Degrees in the Shade. LC 83-1249. (Library of Alabama Classics). (Illus.). 216p. 1983. reprint ed. pap. 19.95 (0-8173-0170-4) U of Ala Pr.

Cason, Debra, ed. see American College of Emergency Physicians Staff.

*Cason, James. Things Remembered. LC 00-100849. 608p. 2000. 25.95 (1-58244-070-0) Rutledge Bks.

Cason, Jeff. Photo Gallery & Workshop Handbook. 192p. 1991. pap. 19.95 (0-929667-08-5, 10251) Images NY.

— Photo Marketing Handbook. 3rd ed. (Orig.). 1992. pap. 21.95 (0-929667-11-5) Images NY.

Cason, Jeff & Lawrence, Peter. Photomarketing Handbook. 156p. 1989. pap. 19.95 (0-929667-05-0) Images NY.

Cason, Jeffrey. Photo Marketing Handbook. Lawrence, Peter, ed. 200p. (Orig.). 1988. pap. 18.95 (0-317-91257-7) Images NY.

Cason, Jeffrey W., jt. auth. see Barrett, Christopher B.

Cason, Jim, ed. see Tilton, Douglas J.

*Cason, John & Punchard, Neville A., eds. Human Genital Papillomaviruses. 350p. 2000. 99.50 (0-89603-619-7) Humana.

Cason, Kathryn, jt. auth. see Jaques, Elliott.

Cason, Mabel Earp. Spotted Boy & the Commanches. LC 63-21050. (Kids' Klassics Ser.). (Illus.). 155p. (YA). (gr. 4 up). 1999. pap. 5.99 (0-8163-1331-8) Pacific Pr Pub Assn.

Cason-Reiser, G., et al. Dying 101: A Short Course on Living for the Terminally ill. LC 96-92022. 224p. 1996. 19.95 (0-9649938-0-5) Push the Envelope.

Cason, Robert. Writing for the Business World. LC 96-35424. 268p. (C). 1996. pap. text 37.33 (0-13-440264-2) P-H.

Casona, Alejandro. Barca Sin Pescador. Balseiro, Jose A. & Owre, J. Riis, eds. 176p. (YA). (gr. 9 up). 1975. pap. 18.95 (0-19-501984-9) OUP.

— Caballero de las Espuelas de Oro - Retablo Jovial. 216p. 1991. pap. 12.95 (0-7859-5209-8) Fr & Eur.

— El Caballero de las Espuelas de Oro. Retablo Jovial. Marcos Sanchez, Maria D., ed. (Nueva Austral Ser.: Vol. 223). (SPA.). 1991. pap. text 15.95 (84-239-7223-2) Elliots Bks.

— La Dama de Alba. (SPA.). pap. 13.95 (84-376-0465-6, Pub. by Ediciones Catedra) Continental Bk.

— Flor de Levendas - Francisco Pizarro. 7th ed. 256p. 1991. 14.95 (0-7859-5149-0) Fr & Eur.

— Flor de Leyendas. (SPA.). 18.95 (0-8288-2558-0, S15217) Fr & Eur.

— Flor de Leyendas. Vida de Francisco Pizarro. (Nueva Austral Ser.: Vol. 233). (SPA.). 1991. pap. text 16.95 (84-239-7233-X) Elliots Bks.

— Lady of the Dawn by Alejandro Casona. unabridged ed. Gibbs, Donald B., tr. from SPA. LC 98-60107. 90p. 1998. pap. 16.00 (0-938972-29-4) Spanish Lit Pubns.

— Otra Vez . . . - Prohibido . . . - Arboles . . . (SPA.). 172p. 1985. 7.95 (0-8288-7030-6, S30189) Fr & Eur.

— Otra Vez el Diablo Nuestra Natacha: Arboles Mueren de Pie. (SPA.). pap. 8.95 (968-432-252-6, Pub. by Porrua) Continental Bk.

— La Sirena Varada. Los Arboles Mueren de Pie. Diaz Castanon, Carmen, ed. (Nueva Austral Ser.: Vol. 121). (SPA.). 1991. pap. text 24.95 (84-239-1921-8) Elliots Bks.

Casona, Alejandro & Castellano, Juan R. La Dama del Alba. 207p. (C). 1972. pap. text 21.00 (0-13-521642-7) P-H.

Casona, Alejandro Rodriguez, see Rodriguez Casona, Alejandro.

Caspall, John. Fire & Light in the Home Pre-1820. (Illus.). 280p. 1992. reprint ed. 49.50 (1-85149-021-3) Antique Collect.

Caspar, Franz. Plan Analysis: Toward Optimizing Therapy. (Illus.). 294p. 1995. text 35.00 (0-88937-117-2) Hogrefe & Huber Pubs.

Caspard, Pierre, ed. Guide International de la Recherche en Histoire de l'Education: En Coedition avec l'Institut National de Recherche Pedagogique, Service d'Histoire de l'Education, Paris. 2nd ed. (FRE.). 275p. 1995. 18.95 (3-906754-27-8, Pub. by P Lang) P Lang Pubng.

Casparek-Turkann, Erika. Das Grosse Lexikon der Guten Kuche. (GER.). 504p. 1992. 75.00 (0-7859-8554-9, 3924678308) Fr & Eur.

Caspari, Conrad. Processed Foodstuffs, Vol. I-7. (Single Market Review Ser.). 1998. 80.00 (0-7494-2311-0) Kogan Page Ltd.

Caspari, Gregor, ed. Nucleic Acid Amplification Techniques for Virus Detection in Transfusion Medicine. (Infusionstherapie und Transfusionsmedizin Ser.: Vol. 25, No. 2-3). (Illus.). 140p. 1998. pap. 58.25 (3-8055-6717-0) S Karger.

Caspari, Rachel, jt. auth. see Wolpoff, Milford.

Caspari, W. A., ed. see Buening, K. R.

Casparie. Chronic Diseases in the Year 2005 Vol. 3: Scenarios on Rheumatoid Arthritis 1990-2005 Scenario Report Commissioned by the Steering Committee on Future Health Scenarios, Vol. 3. (Future Health Scenarios Ser.). 271p. (C). 1995. pap. text 92.50 (0-7923-3367-5) Kluwer Academic.

Casparie, A. F., et al. Competitive Health Care in Europe: Future Prospects. 429p. 1990. text 82.95 (1-85521-186-6, Pub. by Dartmth Pub) Ashgate Pub Co.

Casparie, A. F., jt. auth. see Chronic Diseases Scenario Committee Staff.

Casparie, W. A., jt. ed. see Bartstra, G. J.

Casparie, W. A., ed. see Kempers, A. J.

Casparie, Willem A., ed. see Stuyts, Inge-Lise M.

Caspary, Vera. Laura. 1955. pap. 5.25 (0-8222-0646-3) Dramatists Play.

— Laura. 216p. 1977. reprint ed. lib. bdg. 23.95 (0-89244-066-X, Queens House) Amereon Ltd.

— Laura. 1993. reprint ed. lib. bdg. 29.95 (1-56849-193-X) Buccaneer Bks.

— The Man Who Loved His Wife. large type ed. 496p. 1986. 27.99 (0-7089-1400-4) Ulverscroft.

Caspary, W. F., jt. auth. see Becker, H. D.

*Caspary, William R. Dewey on Democracy. LC 99-54584. 2000. 39.95 (0-8014-3705-9) Cornell U Pr.

Caspel, Paul Van, see Van Caspel, Paul.

Casper & Davies. 500 Years Exploring American Trade. 2nd ed. 296p. (C). 1997. pap. text 29.00 (0-536-00157-X) Pearson Custom.

Casper & Kurland, Philip B., eds. Landmark Briefs & Arguments of the Supreme Court of the United States: Constitutional Law 1974 Term Supplement, Vol. 81-82. LC 75-15202. 2000p. 1974. 305.00 (0-89093-130-5) U Pubns Amer.

— Landmark Briefs & Arguments of the Supreme Court of the United States: Constitutional Law 1975 Term Supplement, Vol. 83-90. LC 75-15202. 8000p. 1975. 1215.00 (0-89093-131-3) U Pubns Amer.

— Landmark Briefs & Arguments of the Supreme Court of the United States: Constitutional Law 1976 Term Supplement, Vol. 91-98. LC 75-15202. 8000p. 1976. 1215.00 (0-89093-185-2) U Pubns Amer.

— Landmark Briefs & Arguments of the Supreme Court of the United States: Constitutional Law 1977 Term Supplement, 99-105. LC 75-15202. 1977. 1065.00 (0-89093-197-6) U Pubns Amer.

— Landmark Briefs & Arguments of the Supreme Court of the United States: Constitutional Law 1977 Term Supplement, Vols. 99-100. LC 75-15202. 2000p. 1977. 115.00 (0-685-57793-7) U Pubns Amer.

— Landmark Briefs & Arguments of the Supreme Court of the United States: Constitutional Law 1977 Term Supplement, Vols. 101-105. LC 75-15202. 5000p. 1977. 290.00 (0-89093-277-8) U Pubns Amer.

— Landmark Briefs & Arguments of the Supreme Court of the United States: Constitutional Law 1978 Term Supplement, Vol. 106-112. LC 75-15202. 7000p. 1978. 1065.00 (0-89093-299-9) U Pubns Amer.

— Landmark Briefs & Arguments of the Supreme Court of the United States: Constitutional Law 1979 Term Supplement, Vol. 113-119. LC 75-15202. 7000p. 1980. 1065.00 (0-89093-474-6) U Pubns Amer.

Casper & Pinchback, eds. Geothermal Scaling & Corrosion - STP 717. 268p. 1980. 29.50 (0-8031-0705-6, STP717) ASTM.

*Casper, Barry M. Lost in Washington: Finding the Way Back to Democracy in America. 416p. 2000. 60.00 (1-55849-246-1); pap. 19.95 (1-55849-247-X) U of Mass Pr.

Casper, Barry M. & Noer, Richard J. Revolutions in Physics. (Illus.). 479p. (C). 1972. text 39.00 (0-393-09992-X) Norton.

Casper, Barry M. & Wellstone, Paul D. Powerline: The First Battle of America's Energy War. LC 80-25903. (Illus.). 328p. 1981. lib. bdg. 35.00 (0-87023-320-3) U of Mass Pr.

Casper, Claudia. The Reconstruction. LC 96-29245. 1996. 22.95 (0-312-15199-3) St Martin.

— The Reconstruction. 1998. pap. 12.95 (0-312-18164-7) St Martin.

Casper, Daniel S., et al. Orbital Disease: Imaging & Analysis. LC 92-49784. (Illus.). 1992. 142.00 (0-86577-430-7) Thieme Med Pubs.

Casper, Des, jt. ed. see Apthorpe, Raymond.

Casper, Dorothy. Come Fly with Me. (Magic of Love Ser.). (Illus.). 16p. (J). (gr. k-6). 1997. pap. 12.95 (0-9662488-0-5) Bee & Cee.

Casper, Geraldine J. Glass Paperweights in the Art Institute of Chicago. Junker, Peter, ed. LC 90-86374. (Illus.). 120p. (Orig.). 1991. pap. 24.95 (0-86559-091-5) Art Inst Chi.

Casper, Gerhard. Separating Power: Essays on the Founding Period. LC 96-36353. 208p. 1996. 29.00 (0-674-80140-7); pap. write for info. (0-674-80141-5) HUP.

Casper, Gerhard & Hutchinson, Dennis J., eds. The Supreme Court Review, 1989. LC 60-14353. 360p. 1990. lib. bdg. 51.00 (0-226-09571-1) U Ch Pr.

— The Supreme Court Review, 1990. 328p. 2000. lib. bdg. 49.00 (0-226-09573-8) U Ch Pr.

Casper, Gerhard & Posner, Richard A. The Workload of the Supreme Court. xiii, 118p. 1986. 25.00 (0-910058-78-4, 305460) W S Hein.

C

— The Workload of the Supreme Court. LC 76-49801. 134p. reprint ed. pap. 41.60 (*0-608-16207-8*, 202714000054) Bks Demand.

Casper, Gerhard, jt. auth. see Kurland, Philip B.

Casper, Gerhard, jt. ed. see Kurland, Philip B.

Casper, Gretchen. Fragile Democracies: Legacies & Authoritarian Rule. (Pitt Series in Policy & Institutional). (Illus.). 235p. (C). 1995. pap. 19.95 (*0-8229-5540-7*); text 49.95 (*0-8229-3857-X*) U of Pittsburgh Pr.

Casper, Gretchen & Taylor, Michelle M. Negotiating Democracy: Transitions from Authoritarian Rule. LC 96-3224. (Pitt Series in Policy & Institutional). 288p. 1996. pap. 19.95 (*0-8229-5588-1*); text 44.95 (*0-8229-3931-2*) U of Pittsburgh Pr.

Casper, Janina K. & Colton, Raymond H. Clinical Manual for Laryngectomy & Head & Neck Cancer Rehabilitation. (Clinical Competence Ser.). (Illus.). 214p. (Orig.). (C). 1992. pap. text 34.95 (*1-879105-61-6*, 0326) Thomson Learn.

— Clinical Manual for Laryngectomy & Head/Neck Cancer Rehabilitation. 2nd ed. LC 98-17724. (Illus.). 250p. 1998. pap. 49.95 (*1-56593-959-X*, 1892) Thomson Learn.

Casper, Janina K., jt. auth. see Colton, Raymond H.

Casper, John A. Stanley Donen. LC 83-2913. (Filmmakers Ser.: No. 5). 300p. 1983. 30.00 (*0-8108-1615-6*) Scarecrow.

Casper, Jonathan D. Lawyers Before the Warren Court: Civil Liberties & Civil Rights, 1957-1966. LC 74-186342. 231p. reprint ed. pap. 71.70 (*0-608-30523-5*, 201502900092) Bks Demand.

— Lawyers Before the Warren Court: Civil Liberties & Civil Rights, 1957-66. LC 74-186342. 232p. 1972. text 24.95 (*0-252-00244-X*) U of Ill Pr.

Casper, K. N. Her Brother's Keeper: Family Man, 839. (Harlequin Super Romance Ser.). 1999. per. 4.25 (*0-373-70839-4*) Harlequin Bks.

***Casper, K. N.** Major Comes to Texas, (Superromance Ser.: Vol. 915). 2000. mass mkt. 4.50 (*0-373-70915-3*) Harlequin Bks.

Casper, K. N. A Man Called Jesse: Love That Man! (Superromance Ser.). 1998. per. 4.25 (*0-373-70806-8*, 1-70806-4) Harlequin Bks.

— The Texan. (Superromance Ser.: Bk. 884). 1999. per. 4.25 (*0-373-70884-X*, 1-70884-1) Harlequin Bks.

Casper, Kathleen, jt. auth. see Casper, Paul.

Casper, Kurland, ed. Landmark Briefs & Arguments of the Supreme Court of the United States: Constitutional Law, 1982, Vols. 134-142. LC 75-15202. (Term Supplement 1982 Ser.). 1984. 1370.00 (*0-89093-652-8*) U Pubns Amer.

Casper, Lawrence A., ed. Microelectronics Processing: Inorganic Materials Characterization. LC 85-30648. (ACS Symposium Ser.: No. 295). (Illus.). x, 440p. 1986. 87.95 (*0-8412-0934-0*, Pub. by Am Chemical) OUP.

— Microelectronics Processing: Inorganic Materials Characterization. LC 85-30648. (ACS Symposium Ser.: Vol. 295). 454p. 1986. reprint ed. pap. 140.80 (*0-608-03922-5*, 206436900009) Bks Demand.

Casper, Lawrence A. & Powell, Cedric J., eds. Industrial Applications of Surface Analysis. LC 82-16290. (ACS Symposium Ser.: No. 199). 438p. 1982. lib. bdg. 60.95 (*0-8412-0735-6*) Am Chemical.

— Industrial Applications of Surface Analysis: Based on a Symposium. LC 82-16290. (ACS Symposium Ser.: No. 199). (Illus.). 447p. 1982. reprint ed. pap. 138.60 (*0-608-04333-8*, 206511300001) Bks Demand.

***Casper, Lawrence E.** Falcon Brigade: Combat & Command in Somalia & Haiti. 225p. 2000. 35.00 (*1-55587-945-4*) L Rienner.

Casper, Leonard. Blood-Marriage of Earth & Sky: Robert Penn Warren's Later Novels. LC 97-20271. (Southern Literary Studies). 128p. 1997. text 25.00 (*0-8071-2155-X*) La State U Pr.

— Firewalkers: Literary Celebrations, 1964-1984. 184p. (Orig.). 1987. pap. 12.50 (*971-10-0289-2*, Pub. by New Day Pub) Cellar.

— In Burning Ambush: Essays 1985-90. viii, 111p. (Orig.). (C). 1992. pap. 8.75 (*971-10-0436-4*, Pub. by New Day Pub) Cellar.

— New Writing from the Philippines: A Critique & Anthology. LC 66-18506. 429p. reprint ed. pap. 133.00 (*0-608-15205-6*, 202739700055) Bks Demand.

— Robert Penn Warren: The Dark & Bloody Ground. LC 71-90479. 212p. 1969. reprint ed. lib. bdg. 55.00 (*0-8371-2131-0*, CAPW, Greenwood Pr) Greenwood.

Casper, Lionel I. The Agreement: The Epic Struggle for the Temple Mount. 384p. 1996. 24.95 (*965-229-157-9*) Gefen Bks.

Casper, Lynne M., et al. Who's Minding the Kids? Child Care Arrangements, Fall 1991. (Illus.). 61p. (Orig.). (C). 1994. pap. text 25.00 (*0-7881-0867-0*) DIANE Pub.

Casper, Mary K. & Ashley, Mabel E. Ashley Family History. (Illus.). 153p. 1997. reprint ed. pap. 23.50 (*0-8328-7299-7*); reprint ed. lib. bdg. 33.50 (*0-8328-7298-9*) Higginson Bk Co.

Casper, Max. Kepler. Hellman, C. Doris & Gingerich, Owen, trs. from GER. LC 93-14292. 448p. 1993. reprint ed. pap. 11.95 (*0-486-67605-6*) Dover.

Casper, Max, jt. ed. see Alissi, Albert.

***Casper, Michele L., et al.** Women & Heart Disease: An Atlas of Racial & Ethnic Disparities in Mortality. (Illus.). 245p. 1999. pap. text. write for info. (*0-9665085-1-3*) Prevention Ctr.

Casper, Monica J. The Making of the Unborn Patient: A Social Anatomy of Fetal Surgery. LC 97-39331. (Illus.). 267p. (C). 1998. text 50.00 (*0-8135-2515-2*); pap. text 20.00 (*0-8135-2516-0*) Rutgers U Pr.

Casper, Paul & Casper, Kathleen. Chicago Home Book: A Comprehensive Hands-On Guide to Building, Remodeling, Decorating, Furnishing & Landscaping a Home in Chicago & Its Suburbs. 3rd ed. (Illus.). 764p. 1998. 34.95 (*0-9642057-2-6*, Pub. by Ashley Group) IPG Chicago.

***Casper, Paul A.** Chicago Home Book: A Comprehensive Hands-On Guide to Building, Remodeling, Decorating, Furnishing & Landscaping a Home in Chicago & Its Suburbs. 4th ed. (Illus.). 784p. 2000. 39.95 (*0-9642057-5-0*, Pub. by Ashley Group) IPG Chicago.

***Casper, Peggy Wiedman.** Terri Lee Identification & Price Guide. (Illus.). 128p. 2000. pap. 24.95 (*0-87588-566-7*) Hobby Hse.

Casper, Regina C., ed. Women's Health: Hormones, Emotions & Behavior. LC 97-3022. (Psychiatry & Medicine Ser.). (Illus.). 344p. (C). 1997. text 74.95 (*0-521-56341-0*) Cambridge U Pr.

Casper, Regina C., jt. ed. see Williams, Katherine E.

Casper, Rosa E., tr. see Ramirez, Rafael L.

Casper, S. J. & Krausch, H. D. Suesswasserflora von Mitteleuropa Band 23: Pteridophyta und Antophyta: 1 - Lycopodiaceae bis Orchidaceae. Pascher, A. et al, eds. (GER., Illus.). 403p. 1980. lib. bdg. 85.00 (*3-437-30309-0*, Pub. by Gustav Fischer) Balogh.

Casper, S. Jost, ed. Lake Stachlin. (Monographiae Biologicae). 1985. text 366.50 (*90-6193-512-1*) Kluwer Academic.

Casper, Scott E. Constructing American Lives: Biography & Culture in Nineteenth-Century America. LC 98-22056. (Illus.). 456p. 1999. lib. bdg. 49.95 (*0-8078-2462-3*) U of NC Pr.

— Constructing American Lives: Biography & Culture in Nineteenth-Century America. LC 98-22056. (Illus.). 456p. (C). 1999. pap. 19.95 (*0-8078-4765-8*) U of NC Pr.

— Of Sagebrush & Slot Machines: This Curious Place. 104p. (C). 1997. pap. 15.00 (*0-536-00089-1*, Macmillan Coll) P-H.

Casper, Scott E. & Davies, Richard. Five Hundred Years of Exploring American Tradition. 260p. (C). 1995. text 35.00 (*0-536-58943-7*) Pearson Custom.

Casper, Virginia & Schultz, Steven. Gay Parents/Straight Schools: Building Communication & Trust. LC 99-24052. 240p. 1999. text 44.00 (*0-8077-3825-5*) Tchrs Coll.

Casper, Virginia & Schultz, Steven B. Gay Parents/Straight Schools: Building Communication & Trust. LC 99-24052. 1999. pap. text 19.95 (*0-8077-3824-7*) Tchrs Coll.

Casper, Wayne & Price, Pat. Scott Numer Index & Cachetmaker Index for First Days, Vols. 1-41. 3rd rev. ed. (Illus.). 36p. 1997. pap. 8.95 (*1-879390-22-1*) AFDCS.

Caspers, Rod, jt. auth. see Berghammer, Gretta.

Caspers, W. J. Spin Systems. 232p. (C). 1989. text 40.00 (*9971-5-0788-9*) World Scientific Pub.

Casperson, Dana M. Power Etiquette: What You Don't Know Can Kill Your Career. LC 98-49831. 150p. 1999. pap. 21.95 (*0-8144-7998-7*) AMACOM.

— The Story of Tea. (Illus.). 1997. pap. 5.00 (*0-9659587-1-X*) Everyones Cup of Tea.

Casperson, Lana. Shelter from the Storm. LC 98-75470. 256p. (YA). (gr. 7-12). 1999. pap. 7.95 (*0-9621392-1-1*) Lighthouse Christian.

Casperson, Ralph A. Biblio - the Intimate Confessions of a Used-Book Dealer. (Illus.). 271p. (Orig.). 1997. pap. 16.50 (*1-883228-15-8*) Invictus MI.

— A Northern Boyhood. 500p. 1993. 27.95 (*1-883228-00-X*) Invictus MI.

***Caspery, Vera.** Laura. 240p. 2000. per. 14.00 (*0-7434-0010-0*, Pub. by ibooks) S&S Trade.

Caspi, Dan. Media Decentralization: The Case of Israel's Local Newspapers. (Illus.). 150p. (C). 1985. 44.95 (*0-88738-055-7*) Transaction Pubs.

Caspi, Dan & Limor, Yehiel. The In - Outsiders: The Mass Media in Israel. LC 98-44567. (Communication Ser.). 352p. 1999. pap. 28.50 (*1-57273-174-5*); pap. text 75.00 (*1-57273-173-7*) Hampton Pr NJ.

Caspi, M. M., ed. Jewish Tradition in the Diaspora: Studies in Memory of Professor Walter J. Fischel. 314p. 1981. 19.95 (*0-943376-16-5*) Magnes Mus.

Caspi, Mischael M. The Book of Ruth: An Annotated Bibliography. Thompson, Henry O., ed. LC 94-21346. (Books of the Bible: Vol. 7). 152p. 1994. text. write for info. (*0-8240-4632-3*, H1410) Garland.

Caspi, Mishael & Cohen, Sascha B. The Binding (Aqedah) & Its Transformations in Judaism & Islam: The Lambs of God. LC 94-30514. (Biblical Press Ser.: Vol. 32). 188p. 1995. 79.95 (*0-7734-2389-3*, Mellen Biblical Pr) E Mellen.

Caspi, Mishael M., ed. Oral Tradition & Hispanic Literature: Essays in Honor of Samuel G. Armistead, Vol. 15. LC 95-7724. (Albert Bates Lord Studies in Oral Tradition: Vols. 15 & 1919). 647p. 1995. text 75.00 (*0-8153-2062-0*, H1919) Garland.

Caspi, Mishael M. & Blessing, Julia A. Weavers of the Songs: The Oral Poetry of Arab Women in Israel & the West Bank. 158p. (Orig.). 1991. pap. 14.00 (*0-89410-651-1*, Three Contnts); text 28.00 (*0-89410-650-3*, Three Contnts) L Rienner.

Caspi, Mishael M. & Cohen, Sascha B. Still Waters Run Deep: Five Women of the Bible Speak. LC 99-30246. 256p. 1999. 52.00 (*0-7618-1430-2*); pap. 32.50 (*0-7618-1431-0*) U Pr of Amer.

Caspi, Mishael M. & Havrelock, Rachel S. Women on the Biblical Road: Ruth, Naomi, & the Female Journey. (C). 1996. pap. text 28.00 (*0-7618-0280-0*); lib. bdg. 47.00 (*0-7618-0279-7*) U Pr of Amer.

Caspi, Mishael M. & Waltsch, Jerome D. From Slumber to Awakening: Culture & Identity of Arab Israeli Literati. LC 98-26465. 296p. 1998. 57.00 (*0-7618-1192-3*); pap. 37.50 (*0-7618-1193-1*) U Pr of Amer.

Caspian-Kaufman, Jonatha. Sid Meier's Civnet Official Secrets & Solutions. 1996. pap. text 12.95 (*0-7615-0140-1*) Prima Pub.

***Caspit, Ben, ed.** Israel 50. 300p. 2000. pap. 35.00 (*1-56799-678-7*, Friedman-Fairfax) M Friedman Pub Grp Inc.

Cass, jt. auth. see Davis.

Cass, A. E., ed. Biosensors: A Practical Approach. (Practical Approach Ser.: No. 107). (Illus.). 288p. 1990. pap. 49.95 (*0-19-963047-X*) OUP.

Cass, Alvah R., jt. auth. see Krug, Ronald S.

Cass, Angelica W. Letters for Everyday Use. pap. write for info. (*0-671-09224-3*, Arco) Macmillan Gen Ref.

— Reading Power, Bk. 1. 128p. 1985. pap. 8.00 (*0-668-05968-0*, Arc) IDG Bks.

— Reading Power, Bk. 2. 176p. 1985. pap. 8.00 (*0-668-05969-9*, Arc) IDG Bks.

— Reading Power, Bk. 3. 160p. 1983. pap. 8.00 (*0-668-05970-2*, Arc) IDG Bks.

— Reading Power, Bk. 4. 192p. 1985. pap. 8.00 (*0-668-05971-0*, Arc) IDG Bks.

Cass, Annie. Notes from the Colorado Rockies: Living in a Small Town, Today & Yesterday. large type ed. 93p. 1996. pap. 9.95 (*0-9649137-0-4*) Oldham Pubng.

Cass-Beggs, Barbara. Your Baby Needs Music. (C). 1990. pap. text. write for info. (*0-201-54669-8*) Addison-Wesley.

Cass, Bettina, jt. ed. see Smyth, Paul.

***Cass, Bruce & Robinson, Jancis, eds.** Oxford Companion to the Wines of North America. 320p. 2000. 45.00 (*0-19-860114-X*) OUP.

Cass, Caroline. Elton John Flower Fantasies. (Illus.). 144p. 1997. 35.00 (*0-8212-2467-0*, Pub. by Bulfinch Pr) Little.

***Cass, Caroline.** Elton John's Flower Fantasies: An Intimate Tour of His Houses & Garden. (Illus.). 144p. 2000. reprint ed. pap. text 22.00 (*0-7881-6920-3*) DIANE Pub.

Cass, Caroline. Grand Illusions: Contemporary Interior Murals. (Illus.). 160p. (C). 1993. reprint ed. pap. 24.95 (*0-7148-2947-1*, Pub. by Phaidon Press) Phaidon Pr.

— Joy Adamson: Behind the Mask. large type ed. (Charnwood Ser.). (Illus.). 432p. (Orig.). 1994. 11.50 (*0-7089-8761-3*, Charnwood) Ulverscroft.

Cass Co. Historical Commission, ed. Historical Reflections of Cass County. (Illus.). 147p. 1981. pap. text 12.00 (*0-9615358-2-2*) Cass County His.

Cass, Cynthia. Success after Teen Pregnancy: Against All Odds. LC 98-93652. 150p. (YA). 1998. pap. 9.95 (*1-57502-961-8*, PO2639) Morris Pubng.

Cass, D. A. Negro Freemasonry. 18.95 (*0-685-22057-5*) Wehman.

Cass, David B. & Floss, Michael M. Alexandre Gabriel Decamps, 1803-1860. LC 84-50229. (Illus.). 68p. (Orig.). 1983. pap. 5.95 (*0-931102-11-1*) S & F Clark Art.

Cass, David B. & Wetenhall, John. Italian Paintings, 1850-1910 from Collections in the Northeastern United States. (Illus.). 64p. (Orig.). 1982. pap. 6.95 (*0-931102-10-3*) S & F Clark Art.

Cass, Devon. DoubleTake. LC 97-14913. (Illus.). 304p. 1998. pap. 24.00 (*0-06-098806-1*, ReganBks) HarperTrade.

Cass, Don. Negro Freemasonry & Segregation. 17.00 (*0-911164-27-8*) Powner.

Cass, Earle M. Cass, Ancestry of Ada Ball Cass. (Illus.). 93p. 1997. reprint ed. pap. 17.00 (*0-8328-7888-X*); reprint ed. lib. bdg. 27.00 (*0-8328-7887-1*) Higginson Bk Co.

Cass, Edward H. Hidden Treasures: The Story of the Ohio River & Western Railway. Schnell, Philip H., ed. (Illus.). 248p. 1997. 44.95 (*0-9650213-3-5*, Pub. by TimberTimes) Partners-West.

Cass, Hyla. All about St. John's Wort. (FAQs All about Health Ser.). 96p. 1998. mass mkt. 2.99 (*0-89529-893-7*, Avery) Penguin Putnam.

— Frequently Asked Questions All about Herbs. (FAQs All about Health Ser.). 96p. 1998. mass mkt. 2.99 (*0-89529-938-0*, Avery) Penguin Putnam.

— St. John's Wort: Nature's Blues Buster. 1997. pap. text 9.95 (*0-89529-843-0*, Avery) Penguin Putnam.

— St. John's Wort: Nature's Blues Buster. LC 98-154528. 208p. 1997. pap. 9.95 (*0-89529-834-1*, Avery) Penguin Putnam.

Cass, Hyla & McNally, Terrence. Kava: Nature's Answer to Stress, Anxiety & Insomnia. LC 98-25977. 274p. 1998. per. 12.95 (*0-7615-1667-0*) Prima Pub.

Cass, James, ed. Education, U. S. A. LC 73-8866. (Great Contemporary Issues Ser.). 1973. 27.95 (*0-405-01292-6*) Ayer.

Cass, James, jt. ed. see Woodring, Paul.

Cass, Jim, ed. & des. see Pulley, Dean.

***Cass, Joan.** The Dance: A Handbook for the Appreciation of the Choreographic Experience. LC 99-39737. (Illus.). 245p. 1999. boxed set 36.50 (*0-7864-0147-8*) McFarland & Co.

Cass, Joan. Dancing Through History. LC 93-106. 368p. 1993. pap. text 44.00 (*0-13-204389-0*) P-H.

Cass, Joan E. The Role of the Teacher in the Nursery School. 97p. 1975. 43.00 (*0-08-018282-8*, Pub. by Pergamon Repr) Franklin.

Cass, Julia, jt. auth. see Chestnut, J. L., Jr.

Cass, Lewis. Considerations on the Present State of the Indians, & Their Removal to the West of the Mississippi. LC 75-91. (Mid-American Frontier Ser.). 1980. reprint ed. 16.95 (*0-405-06858-1*) Ayer.

Cass, Linda, jt. auth. see Cass, Noel.

Cass, Marque & Cass, Melvin. Thoughts: A Mini Anthology. 50p. 1998. pap. write for info. (*1-57502-881-6*, PO2400) Morris Pubng.

Cass, Maxine & Gebhardt, Fred. On the Road Around California. 352p. 1994. pap. 14.95 (*0-8442-9015-7*, Passprt Bks) NTC Contemp Pub Co.

***Cass, Maxine & Gebhart, Fred.** Signpost Guide: California. 2000. pap. 22.95 (*0-7627-0676-7*) Globe Pequot.

— Signpost Guide: Vancouver & British Columbia. 2000. pap. 22.95 (*0-7627-0692-9*) Globe Pequot.

Cass, Maxine & Gebhart, Fred. Touring the Canadian Rockies: Fly-Drive Holidays & Rail Journeys in Alberta & British Columbia. (Touring... Ser.). 372p. 1998. 18.95 (*0-8442-9998-7*, 99987, Passprt Bks) NTC Contemp Pub Co.

Cass, Maxine, et al. On the Road Around Florida: The Complete Fly - Drive Guide. LC 96-233497. (Illus.). 352p. 1995. pap. 14.95 (*0-8442-9014-9*, Passprt Bks) NTC Contemp Pub Co.

Cass, Melvin, jt. auth. see Cass, Marque.

Cass, Noel & Cass, Linda. Pharmacology for Anaesthetists. LC 93-7322. 208p. 1995. pap. text 25.00 (*0-443-04639-5*) Church.

Cass, Patricia J. & O'Connor, Elizabeth R. Fundamentals With Elements Of Algebra. (Math). 448p. (C). 1990. mass mkt. 43.00 (*0-534-92464-6*) PWS Pubs.

— Fundamentals with Elements of Algebra: A Bridge to College Mathematics. 3rd ed. (C). 1997. pap. text, teacher ed. write for info. (*0-534-95020-5*) Brooks-Cole.

— Fundamentals with Elements of Algebra: A Bridge to College Mathematics. 3rd ed. LC 96-51832. (Mathematics Ser.). 688p. (C). 1997. mass mkt. 74.95 (*0-534-95604-1*) Brooks-Cole.

Cass, R. Michael, et al. Reinsurance Practices, Vols. 1 & 2. 2nd ed. LC 97-77839. 209p. 1997. pap. text 41.00 (*0-89462-121-1*, 14202) IIA.

Cass, Richard W., ed. The Honorable Right Side. 140p. 1994. pap. 9.50 (*0-9643866-0-7*) Ethics Grp.

Cass, Ronald A. Administrative Law. 2nd ed. LC 93-80777. 1208p. 1994. lib. bdg. 55.00 (*0-316-13263-2*, Aspen Law & Bus) Aspen Pub.

Cass, Ronald A. & Diver, Colin S. Administrative Law: Case & Materials. 1024p. 1987. 45.00 (*0-316-13222-5*, Aspen Law & Bus) Aspen Pub.

Cass, Ronald A. & Haring, John R. International Trade in Telecommunications: Monopoly, Competition, & Trade Strategy. LC 97-47741. (AEI Studies in Telecommunications Deregulation). 128p. 1998. 32.50 (*0-262-03234-1*) MIT Pr.

Cass, Ronald A., et al. Administrative Law: Cases & Materials. 2nd ed. 1208p. 1994. teacher ed. write for info. (*0-316-13281-0*, 32810) Aspen Law.

— Administrative Law: Cases & Materials. 2nd ed. LC 97-45762. 1998. boxed set 60.00 (*1-56706-742-5*) Aspen Law.

Cass, Stephen P., jt. auth. see Furman, Joseph M.

Cass, Victoria. Dangerous Women: Warriors, Grannies & Geishas of the Ming. LC 99-19011. 184p. 1999. text 59.00 (*0-8476-9394-5*) Rowman.

— Dangerous Women: Warriors, Grannies & Geishas of the Ming. LC 99-19011. 184p. 1999. pap. 24.95 (*0-8476-9395-3*) Rowman.

Cass, William. Return to the Summit of Scouting: A Mid-Life Journey Back to Philmont. LC 93-12448. (Illus.). 384p. (Orig.). 1993. pap. 12.95 (*0-923568-29-8*) Wilderness Adventure Bks.

Cass, Zoe. The Silver Leopard. large type ed. 379p. 1980. 27.99 (*0-7089-0554-4*) Ulverscroft.

— A Twist in the Silk. large type ed. 320p. 1983. 27.99 (*0-7089-0969-8*) Ulverscroft.

Cassa, Yvonne & Sanders, Joanne. How to Form a Parish Liturgy Board. rev. ed. 92p. 1987. reprint ed. pap. 10.00 (*0-930467-67-1*, LITBD) Liturgy Tr Pubns.

Cassabois, Jacques. Port Englouti. (Folio - Cadet Rouge Ser.: No. 204). (FRE., Illus.). 79p. (J). (gr. 3-7). 1989. pap. 8.95 (*2-07-031204-6*) Schoenhof.

Cassada, Jackie. The Court of All Kings: The Immortal Eyes, Bk. III. (Changeling: The Dreaming Ser.). (Orig.). 1996. pap. 5.99 (*1-56504-862-8*, 11403, Wrld of Darkness) White Wolf.

— The Hierarchy. (Wruith Ser.). 1995. pap. 12.00 (*1-56504-614-5*, 6009) White Wolf.

***Cassada, Jackie.** Mage Storytellers Companion. (Mage Storyteller's Guide Ser.). 2000. pap. 14.95 (*1-56504-406-1*) White Wolf.

Cassada, Jackie. Rage Across Appalachia. (Werewolf Ser.). 1995. 18.00 (*1-56504-313-8*, 3107) White Wolf.

— Shadows on the Hill: The Immortal Eyes, Bk. II. (Orig.). 1996. pap. 5.99 (*1-56504-861-X*, 11402, Wrld of Darkness) White Wolf.

***Cassada, Jackie.** War in Concordia. (Changeling: The Dreaming Ser.). 2000. pap. 18.00 (*1-56504-724-9*) White Wolf.

Cassada, Jackie & Rea, Nicky. Kingdom of Willows. (Changeling: The Dreaming Ser.). (Illus.). 1998. pap. 18.00 (*1-56504-720-6*, 7306) White Wolf.

— Rage Across the Heavens. (Werewolf Ser.). (Illus.). 128p. 1999. pap. 17.95 (*1-56504-309-X*, 3110) White Wolf.

— Uktena: Tribebook. (Werewolf Ser.). (Illus.). 1998. pap. 10.00 (*1-56504-333-2*, 3062) White Wolf.

— World of Darkness: Hong Kong. (Vampire Ser.). (Illus.). 1998. pap. 18.00 (*1-56504-222-0*, 2009) White Wolf.

***Cassada, Jackie, et al.** Sorcerers Crusade Companion. (Mage Ser.). (Illus.). 160p. 1999. pap. 19.95 (*1-56504-494-0*, 4805) White Wolf.

Cassada, Jackie, jt. auth. see Rea, Nicky.

Cassaday, Kelly, text. Fellowships That Shape the Future: The ISAAA Biotechnology Fellowship Program. (Illus.). 16p. 1996. pap. write for info. (*1-892456-08-7*) Agri-Biotech.

***Cassadean, Shandale.** Expressions of Love: A Diary of Songs. 64p. 1999. pap. 3.50 (*1-891877-04-6*) Sheron Ent.

Cassady, Carolyn. Off the Road: My Years with Cassady, Kerouac, & Ginsberg. (Illus.). 448p. 1991. pap. 14.95 (*0-14-015390-X*, Penguin Bks) Viking Penguin.

Cassady, Carolyn, et al. A Different Beat Vol. 1: Early Work by Women of the Beat Generation. Peabody, Richard, ed. LC 96-72581. (High Risk Ser.). 275p. (Orig.). 1997. pap. 13.99 (*1-85242-431-1*) Serpents Tail.

Cassady, David. EHRGEIZ Official Fighter's Guide: God Bless the Ring, 1. (Illus.). 142p. 1999. pap. 11.99 (*1-56686-876-9*) Brady Pub.

***Cassady, David.** Final Fantasy Anthology. (Final Fantasy Ser.). (Illus.). (YA). 1999. pap. text. write for info. (*1-56686-925-0*, BradyGAMES) Brady Pub.

— Final Fantasy VIII. (Strategy Guides Ser.). (Illus.). (J). 1999. pap. text 14.99 (*1-56686-903-X*, BradyGAMES) Brady Pub.

Cassady, David. Final Fantasy VII Official Guide. 208p. 1997. 14.99 (*1-56686-714-2*) Brady Pub.

— Official Guide to Turok: Dinosaur Hunter. 128p. 1997. 11.99 (*1-56686-681-2*) Brady Pub.

— Parasite Eve: Official Strategy Guide, 1. LC 98-73580. (Brady Games Strategy Guides Ser.). 1998. pap. text 14.99 (*1-56686-824-6*) Brady Pub.

***Cassady, David.** The Unauthorized Nintendo 64 Games Guides (1996) Bartley, David, ed. (Illus.). 112p. 1999. pap. text 10.00 (*0-7881-6791-X*) DIANE Pub.

Cassady, David, jt. auth. see Brady Games Staff.

Cassady-Dorian, Luke. Industrial Strength Java. LC 97-3456. 1000p. 1997. pap. text 55.00 incl. cd-rom (*1-56205-634-4*) New Riders Pub.

Cassady, J. Robert, ed. see Ang, K. Kian, et al.

Cassady, Jim & Calhoun, Fryar. California Whitewater: A Guide to the Rivers. 3rd rev. ed. (Illus.). 315p. 1995. pap. 19.95 (*0-9613650-2-1*) North Fork Pr.

Cassady, Jim & Dunlap, Dan. World Whitewater: A Global Guide for River Runners. LC 98-53524. (Illus.). 304p. 1998. pap. 22.95 (*0-07-011962-7*) Intl Marine.

Cassady, Jim, et al. Western Whitewater from the Rockies to the Pacific: A River Guide for Raft, Kayak, & Canoe. LC 93-93680. (Illus.). 590p. (Orig.). 1994. pap. 34.95 (*0-9613650-4-8*) North Fork Pr.

Cassady, John, jt. auth. see Mariotte, Jeff.

Cassady, Marsh. Acting Games: Improvisations & Exercises. Zapel, Theodore O., ed. LC 93-37322. (Illus.). 192p. (YA). (gr. 9 up). 1993. pap. 15.95 (*0-916260-92-5*, B168) Meriwether Pub.

— The Art of Storytelling: Creative Ideas for Preparation & Performance. Zapel, Theodore O., ed. LC 94-12938. 288p. (Orig.). (YA). (gr. 9 up). 1994. pap. 14.95 (*1-56608-002-9*, B139) Meriwether Pub.

— Book of Monologues for Aspiring Actors. (Illus.). 204p. 1994. pap. 16.95 (*0-8442-5771-0*, 57710, Passprt Bks) NTC Contemp Pub Co.

— Book of Scenes for Aspiring Actors. (Illus.). 204p. 1995. pap. 16.95 (*0-8442-5769-9*, 57699, Passprt Bks) NTC Contemp Pub Co.

— Creating Stories for Storytelling. LC 91-3627. 158p. 1992. pap. 9.95 (*0-89390-205-5*, Pub. by Resource Pubns) Empire Pub Srvs.

— Funny Business: An Introduction to Comedy with Royalty-Free Plays & Sketches. Zapel, Theodore O., ed. LC 97-45060. 336p. (YA). (gr. 9 up). 1997. pap. 14.95 (*1-56608-037-1*, B212) Meriwether Pub.

— Great Scenes from Women Playwrights: Classic & Contemporary Selections for One to Six Actors. Zapel, Theodore O., ed. LC 95-35597. 368p. (Orig.). (YA). (gr. 9 up). 1995. pap. 14.95 (*1-56608-016-9*, B119) Meriwether Pub.

— The Music of Tree Limbs. (Amelia Chapbooks Ser.). 20p. (Orig.). 1993. pap. 5.00 (*0-936545-18-6*) Amelia.

— Playwriting Step by Step. LC 92-3406. 114p. 1990. pap. 11.95 (*0-89390-056-7*, Pub. by Resource Pubns) Empire Pub Srvs.

— Storytelling Step by Step. LC 90-37986. 140p. (Orig.). (C). 1990. pap. 9.95 (*0-89390-183-0*) Resource Pubns.

— The Theatre & You: A Beginning. Zapel, Arthur L., ed. LC 92-14993. (Illus.). 256p. (Orig.). 1992. pap. 15.95 (*0-916260-83-6*, B115) Meriwether Pub.

Cassady, Marsh & Zapel, Theodore O., eds. Great Scenes from Minority Playwrights: Seventy-Four Scenes of Cultural Diversity. LC 97-298. 352p. (Orig.). (YA). (gr. 8-12). 1997. pap. 15.95 (*1-56608-029-0*, B207) Meriwether Pub.

Cassady, Marsh, jt. auth. see Anderson, John.

Cassady, Marsh, jt. auth. see Anderson, John P.

Cassady, Marshall. Book of Cuttings for Acting & Directing. (Illus.). 208p. 1994. pap. 17.95 (*0-8442-5120-8*, 51208, Natl Textbk Co) NTC Contemp Pub Co.

— The Book of Scenes for Acting Practice. (Illus.). 128p. 1994. pap. 17.95 (*0-8442-5125-9*, 51259, Natl Textbk Co) NTC Contemp Pub Co.

— Characters in Action: Playwriting the Easy Way. Zapel, Theodore O., ed. LC 95-7721. 216p. (Orig.). (YA). (gr. 9 up). 1995. pap. 14.95 (*1-56608-010-X*, B106) Meriwether Pub.

— Introduction to Modern One-Act Plays. LC 90-61971. (Illus.). 352p. (Orig.). 1991. pap. 25.33 (*0-8442-5113-5*, Natl Textbk Co) NTC Contemp Pub Co.

— Introduction to Modern One-Act Plays. LC 90-61971. (Illus.). 352p. (Orig.). 1991. pap. text, teacher ed. 6.60 (*0-685-74320-9*, Natl Textbk Co) NTC Contemp Pub Co.

— An Introduction to Modern One-Act Plays. pap., teacher ed. 6.99 (*0-8442-5114-3*) NTC Contemp Pub Co.

— Introduction to Theatre Drama. 624p. 1985. pap. 26.60 (*0-8442-5100-3*) NTC Contemp Pub Co.

Cassady, Michael J., jt. ed. see Buczala, George S.

Cassady, Neal. The First Third & Other Writings. LC 74-88229. 1971. pap. 12.95 (*0-87286-005-1*) City Lights.

— Grace Beats Karma, 1958-1960: Letters from Prison. 192p. 1993. 24.95 (*0-922233-08-X*) Blast Bks.

— Grace Beats Karma, 1958-1960: Letters from Prison. (Illus.). 192p. 1993. pap. 12.95 (*0-922233-07-1*) Blast Bks.

Cassady, Ralph, Jr., jt. auth. see Waite, Warren C.

Cassady, Stephen. Spanning the Gate: Building the Golden Gate Bridge. rev. ed. (Illus.). 144p. 1987. pap. 18.95 (*0-916290-36-0*) Squarebooks.

Cassady, William A. A Short Course in Permanent Magnet Materials. (Illus.). 192p. 1993. pap. text 39.95 (*1-882637-34-8*) SJL Pub.

Cassady, William A., ed. & illus. see Brinsbury, Wolf.

Cassagio. Accounting, Ch. 1-9. annot. ed. LC 96-101125. Date not set. text. write for info. (*0-314-07094-X*) West Pub.

— Accounting, Ch 1-15. Date not set. pap. text, student ed. write for info. (*0-314-06308-0*) West Pub.

— Accounting, Chapters 1-9. annot. ed. LC 96-101143. Date not set. text. write for info. (*0-314-07093-1*) West Pub.

— Accounting, Chapters 16-28. Date not set. pap. text, student ed. write for info. (*0-314-07704-9*) West Pub.

— College Accounting. Date not set. pap. text, teacher ed. write for info. (*0-314-06313-7*) West Pub.

— College Accounting. annot. ed. Date not set. text. write for info. (*0-314-07095-8*) West Pub.

Cassagio, Janet. College Accounting: The Frame Up Practice Set. 2nd ed. 160p. (C). 1995. text 16.95 (*0-256-17101-7*, Irwn McGrw-H) McGrw-H Hghr Educ.

Cassagio, Janet, et al. College Accounting, Chapters 1-28. LC 95-38501. 800p. (C). 1996. mass mkt. 80.95 (*0-314-06307-2*) West Pub.

Cassagnac, Adolphe G. De, see De Cassagnac, Adolphe G.

Cassagnau, Pascale & Pillet, Christophe, texts. Starck's School. (Illus.). 128p. 1999. pap. text 23.50 (*2-906571-84-9*, Pub. by Editions Dis Voir) Dist Art Pubs.

Cassagne, J. M. 101 French Proverbs: Understanding French Language & Culture Through Common Savings. (ENG & FRE., Illus.). 160p. 1998. pap. 6.95 (*0-8442-1291-1*, 12911, Passprt Bks) NTC Contemp Pub Co.

Cassagne, Jean-Marie. 101 Spanish Idioms. (ENG & SPA.). 128p. 1995. pap. 6.95 (*0-8442-7217-5*, 72175) NTC Contemp Pub Co.

Cassagne, Jean-Marie & Nisset-Raidon, Lucques. 101 French Idioms. (101...Idioms Ser.). (Illus.). 128p. 1995. pap. 6.95 (*0-8442-1290-3*, 12903, Passprt Bks) NTC Contemp Pub Co.

Cassagneres, Ev. The New Ryan: The ST's & SC's. 195p. 1995. pap. 24.95 (*0-911139-20-6*) Flying Bks.

Cassagnol Chierici, Rose-Marie. Making It - Migration & Adaptation among Haitian Boat People in the United States. (Immigrant Communities & Ethnic Minorities in the U. S. & Canada Ser.: No. 70). 1990. 49.50 (*0-404-19480-X*) AMS Pr.

Cassals, J. A. Christ & Antichrist. unabridged ed. 348p. 1994. reprint ed. 24.95 (*0-923309-16-0*) Hartland Pubns.

Cassam, Quassim. Self & World. 216p. (C). 1997. text 49.95 (*0-19-823540-2*) OUP.

— Self & World. 216p. 1999. pap. text 19.95 (*0-19-823895-9*) OUP.

— Self-Knowledge. (Oxford Readings in Philosophy Ser.). 232p. 1994. text 55.00 (*0-19-875115-X*); pap. text 19.95 (*0-19-875116-8*) OUP.

Cassanda, J. & Cassanda, Rea N. Reunion. 1998. 9.95 (*0-7869-1196-4*, Pub. by TSR Inc) Random.

Cassanda, Rea N., jt. auth. see Cassanda, J.

Cassandra, Kathleen A., jt. auth. see Opperman, Cathleen S.

Cassandras, Christos. Discrete Event Systems: Modeling & Performance Analysis. 450p. (C). 1993. text 72.75 (*0-256-11212-6*, 19-3766-01, Irwn McGrw-H) McGrw-H Hghr Educ.

Cassanelli, Lee V. The Shaping of Somali Society: Reconstructing the History of a Pastoral People, 1600 to 1900. LC 81-43520. (Ethnohistory Ser.). 328p. reprint ed. pap. 101.70 (*0-7837-3007-1*, 204293400006) Bks Demand.

Cassanelli, Rino. El Cosmos de Fernando Arrabal: Lo Cosmicocidico en El Arquitecto y el Emperador de Asiria. LC 90-34853. (American University Studies: Romance Languages & Literature: Ser. II, Vol. 143). (SPA.). 149p. (C). 1991. text 32.95 (*0-8204-1302-X*) P Lang Pubng.

Cassanetti, Michelle L., ed. James Carter. LC 89-84655. (Illus.). 168p. 1990. 30.00 (*0-941393-18-6*) Lublin Graph.

Cassanetti, Michelle L., ed. see Boulanger, Graciela R.

Cassanetti, Michelle L., ed. see Delacroix, Michel.

Cassanetti, Michelle L., ed. see Kaiko Moti.

Cassani, J. R., ed. Managing Aquatic Vegetation with Grass Carp. LC 96-78895. 194p. 1996. pap. 25.00 (*1-888569-02-6*, 530.26) Am Fisheries Soc.

Cassano, Alberto E., jt. ed. see Whitaker, Stephen.

Cassano, Angelo, jt. auth. see Salazar, Marivel.

Cassano, Angelo, jt. auth. see Schwartz, Karl.

Cassano, D. Rosemary, ed. Social Work with Multi-Family Groups. 107p. 1989. 29.95 (*0-86656-882-4*) Haworth Pr.

Cassano, Giovanni B., ed. see Akiskal, Hagop S.

Cassano, Mauro. Algebraic Concepts. 416p. (C). 1995. pap. text, per. 41.95 (*0-7872-1353-5*) Kendall-Hunt.

Cassanve, Christine P. & Williams, Diane. The Active Reader: An Introductory Reading-Communication Text for Students of ESL-EFL. (Illus.). 224p. (C). 1987. pap. text 20.40 (*0-13-003740-0*) P-H.

***Cassanya, Vicente.** El Gran Libro de la Luna. 1999. 22.95 (*84-270-2435-5*) E Martinez Roca.

Cassar, et al. Survey of Western Civilization, Vol. I. 2nd ed. (C). 1997. pap. 46.86 (*0-07-022616-4*) McGraw.

— Survey of Western Civilization, Vol. 2. 2nd ed. (C). 1997. pap., student ed. 46.86 (*0-07-011231-2*) McGraw.

Cassar, Ann, et al. Favorite Recipes. (Illus.). 100p. 1992. spiral bd. 6.00 (*0-939016-21-4*) Johannes Schwalm Hist.

Cassar, Ann, ed. see Schwalm, Mark A., et al.

Cassar, George H. Asquith As War Leader. LC 94-28401. 1994. 55.00 (*1-85285-117-1*) Hambledon Press.

— The Forgotten Front: Britain & the Italian Campaign, 1917-1918. LC 97-32575. 1998. 55.00 (*1-85285-166-X*) Hambledon Press.

— The Tragedy of Sir John French. LC 82-49302. (Illus.). 320p. 1985. 42.50 (*0-87413-241-X*) U Delaware Pr.

Cassar, Mario-Paul. Easy Home Massage. LC 99-26882. (Health Factfiles Ser.). (Illus.). 112p. (J). (gr. 11). 1999. pap. 12.95 (*0-7370-1613-2*) T-L Custom Pub.

***Cassar, Mario-Paul.** Handbook of Massage Therapy: A Complete Guide for the Student & Professional Massage Therapist. LC 99-21301. 222p. 1999. pap. text 65.00 (*0-7506-4000-6*) Buttrwrth-Heinemann.

Cassar, Mario-Paul. Massage Made Easy. 160p. 1995. pap. 16.95 (*1-882606-17-5*) Peoples Med Soc.

Cassar, May. Environmental Management Guidelines: For Museums & Galleries. LC 94-7776. (Illus.). 208p. (C). (gr. 13). 1994. 65.00 (*0-415-10559-5*, B3478) Routledge.

Cassar, May, ed. Museums Environment Energy. 100p. 1994. pap. 30.00 (*0-11-290519-6*, HM05196, Pub. by Statnry Office) Bernan Associates.

Cassara, Beverly, ed. Adult Education in a Multicultural Society. (Theory & Practice of Adult Education in North America Ser.). 256p. (C). 1994. pap. 25.99 (*0-415-90913-9*) Routledge.

Cassara, Beverly B., ed. Adult Education Through World Collaboration: Adult Education Through World Collaboration. LC 93-49527. 288p. (C). 1995. 34.50 (*0-89464-828-4*) Krieger.

Cassara, Ernest. The Enlightenment in America. (Illus.). 208p. (C). 1988. reprint ed. pap. text 22.00 (*0-8191-6769-X*) U Pr of Amer.

— Murder on Beacon Hill. LC 95-80566. 201p. (Orig.). 1995. pap. 10.00 (*0-9625794-6-7*) A Miniver Pr.

— Murder on Boston Common: A Father Ballou & His Dog Spot Mystery. LC 98-72219. 174p. 1998. pap. 9.95 (*0-9662870-0-2*) Cambridge Crnrstone.

Cassara, Ernest, ed. Universalism in America. 1997. pap. 15.00 (*0-933840-21-7*, Skinner Hse Bks) Unitarian Univ.

Cassara, Ernest, jt. auth. see Schurz, Carl.

Cassara, Silvio. Richard Meier. (Works & Projects Ser.). (Illus.). 200p. 1996. pap. text 19.95 (*84-252-1593-1*) Watsn-Guptill.

Cassareau, Kristen, ed. see Greenberg, Seth.

Cassaro, James P. Gaetano Donizetti: A Guide to Research. Marco, Guy A., ed. (Composer Resource Manuals Ser.). 300p. 1998. text 45.00 (*0-8153-2350-6*) Garland.

Cassaro, James P., compiled by. Space Utilization in Music Libraries. (Music Library Association Index & Bibliography Ser.: No. 20). 140p. 1991. pap. 30.00 (*0-914954-44-X*) Scarecrow.

Cassaro, Michael A., ed. Lifeline Earthquake Engineering. LC 91-23493. (Technical Council on Lifeline Earthquake Engineering, Monographs: No. 4). 1192p. 1991. pap. text 82.00 (*0-87262-821-3*) Am Soc Civil Eng.

Cassaro, Michael A. & Cooper, James D., eds. Seismic Design & Construction of Complex Civil Engineering Systems. 112p. 1988. 5.00 (*0-87262-678-4*) Am Soc Civil Eng.

Cassaro, Michael A. & Romero, Enrique M., eds. Mexico Earthquakes, 1985: Factors Involved & Lessons Learned. 488p. 1987. 40.00 (*0-87262-579-6*) Am Soc Civil Eng.

Cassart, C. & Moirant, R. Dictionary of Horse & Rider: Dictionnaire du Cheval et du Chevalier. (ENG & FRE.). 288p. 1979. 69.95 (*0-8288-4795-9*, M6064) Fr & Eur.

Cassat, Julie. What I Like Best about Christmas. (Illus.). 14p. (J). (gr. 4-7). 1989. pap. text 5.95 (*0-927106-02-7*) Prod Concept.

***Cassata, Mary.** Mary Cassatt Notebook. (Illus.). (J). 1999. pap. 1.00 (*0-486-40836-1*) Dover.

Cassata, Mary & Skill, Thomas D. Life on Daytime Television: Tuning in American Serial Drama. Voigt, Melvin J., ed. LC 84-2853. (Communication & Information Science Ser.). 272p. (C). 1982. text 73.25 (*0-89391-138-0*); pap. text 39.50 (*0-89391-180-1*) Ablx Pub.

Cassatella, A. & Viotti, Roberto, eds. Physics of Classical Novae: Proceedings of Colloquium No. 122 of the International Astronomical Union Held in Madrid, Spain, on 27-30 June 1989. (Lecture Notes in Physics Ser.: Vol. 369). xii, 462p. 1991. 67.95 (*0-387-53500-4*) Spr-Verlag.

Cassatella, Marco A. Cytokines Produced by Polymorphonuclear Neutrophils: Molecular & Biological Aspects. LC 96-24469. (Molecular Biology Intelligence Unit Ser.). 204p. 1996. 99.00 (*1-57059-378-7*) Landes Bioscience.

Cassatt, Mary. Cassatt, 1 vol. 1998. pap. 1.00 (*0-486-40390-4*) Dover.

— A Child Is Born. (Miniature Editions Ser.). (Illus.). 160p. (Orig.). (C). 1994. pap. 8.95 (*0-7148-3253-7*, Pub. by Phaidon Press) Phaidon Pr.

— A Child's Book of Lullabies. 32p. (J). 1997. 14.95 (*0-7894-1507-0*) DK Pub Inc.

— The Mary Cassatt Datebook. (Illus.). 32p. 1998. 12.50 (*1-55595-006-X*, Pub. by Hudson Hills) Natl Bk Netwk.

— Mary Cassatt-Postcards. 1989. pap. 4.95 (*0-486-26135-2*) Dover.

Cassatt, Mary. Lullabies & Good Night. 32p. (J). 1989. 13.95 (*0-8249-8441-2*, Ideals Child); 17.95 incl. audio (*0-8249-7351-8*, Ideals Child) Hambleton-Hill.

Cassatt, Mary, et al. Mary Cassatt, Modern Woman. LC 98-7306. 1998. write for info. (*0-86559-166-0*) Abrams.

***Cassavetes, John & Carney, Ray.** John Cassavetes: The Adventure of Insecurity--An Illustrated Pocket Guide. Shaw, Sam & Shaw, Larry, trs. (Studies in Contemporary Film). (Illus.). 68p. 2000. pap. 10.00 (*0-9674170-0-7*) Company C.

Casscells, S. Ward. Arthroscopy: Diagnostic & Surgical Practice. LC 83-11289. 206p. reprint ed. pap. 63.90 (*0-7837-2694-5*, 204307200006) Bks Demand.

Casse, L. R., ed. Combinatorial Mathematics X. (Lecture Notes in Mathematics Ser.: Vol. 1036). xi, 419p. 1983. 49.95 (*0-387-12708-9*) Spr-Verlag.

Casse, L. R. & Wallis, W. D., eds. Combinational Mathematics, IV: Proceedings of the Australian Conference, 4th, University of Adelaide, Aug. 27-29, 1976. (Lecture Notes in Mathematics Ser.: Vol. 560). 1976. pap. 17.00 (*3-540-08053-8*) Spr-Verlag.

Cassebaum. American Culture & Media. (C). 1997. pap. 33.96 (*0-395-72770-7*); pap. text 32.76 (*0-395-72769-3*) HM.

Cassedy, David, et al. William Sidney Mount: Annotated Bibliography & Listings of Archival Holdings of the Museums at Stony Brook. (Illus.). (Orig.). 1983. pap. 3.00 (*0-943924-05-7*) Mus Stony Brook.

— William Sidney Mount: Works in the Collection of the Museums at Stony Brook. LC 83-23646. (Illus.). 96p. (Orig.). 1983. pap. 8.00 (*0-943924-06-5*) Mus Stony Brook.

Cassedy, Edward S. Prospects for Sustainable Energy: A Critical Assessment. LC 99-11969. (Illus.). 345p. (C). 2000. 69.95 (*0-521-63120-3*) Cambridge U Pr.

Cassedy, Edward S. & Grossman, Peter Z. Introduction to Energy: Resources, Technology, & Society. 2nd ed. LC 98-17413. (Illus.). 400p. (C). 1998. 74.95 (*0-521-63106-8*); pap. 29.95 (*0-521-63767-8*) Cambridge U Pr.

Cassedy, Ellen, jt. auth. see Bravo, Ellen.

Cassedy, James H. American Medicine & Statistical Thinking, 1800-1860. LC 83-12831. (Illus.). 312p. 1984. 44.00 (*0-674-02560-1*) HUP.

Cassedy, James H. Medicine & American Growth, 1800-1860. LC 86-40047. (Publications in the History of Science & Medicine: Vol. 5). (Illus.). 317p. reprint ed. pap. 98.30 (*0-608-20417-X*, 207167000002) Bks Demand.

Cassedy, James H. Medicine in America: A Short History. LC 91-7058. (American Moment Ser.). 204p. 1991. pap. text 14.95 (*0-8018-4208-5*) Johns Hopkins.

***Cassedy, Patrice.** Flowers for Algernon. LC 00-9157. (Understanding Great Literature Ser.). 2000. write for info. (*1-56006-784-5*) Lucent Bks.

Cassedy, Steven. Flight from Eden: The Origins of Modern Literary Criticism & Theory. 260p. 1990. 45.00 (*0-520-06863-7*, Pub. by U CA Pr) Cal Prin Full Svc.

— To the Other Shore: The Russian Jewish Intellectuals Who Came to America. 320p. 1997. text 29.95 (*0-691-02975-X*, Pub. by Princeton U Pr) Cal Prin Full Svc.

Cassedy, Sylvia. Behind the Attic Wall. LC 82-45922. 320p. (J). (gr. 3-7). 1983. 12.95 (*0-690-04336-8*); lib. bdg. 15.89 (*0-690-04337-6*) HarpC Child Bks.

— Behind the Attic Wall. (J). (gr. 4-7). 1998. 19.25 (*0-8446-6965-2*) Peter Smith.

— Behind the Attic Wall. 1985. 9.60 (*0-606-00763-6*, Pub. by Turtleback) Demco.

— Behind the Attic Wall. 320p. (J). (gr. 4-7). 1985. reprint ed. mass mkt. 4.99 (*0-380-69843-9*, Avon Bks) Morrow Avon.

— In Your Own Words: A Beginner's Guide to Writing. rev. ed. LC 89-78079. 240p. (J). (gr. 5 up). 1990. lib. bdg. 13.89 (*0-690-04823-8*) HarpC Child Bks.

— In Your Own Words: A Beginner's Guide to Writing. rev. ed. LC 89-78079. 240p. (J). (gr. 5 up). 1990. 13.95 (*0-690-04821-1*) HarpC Child Bks.

— In Your Own Words: A Beginner's Guide to Writing. rev. ed. LC 89-78079. (Trophy Nonfiction Bk.). 240p. (YA). (gr. 5 up). 1990. pap. 7.95 (*0-06-446102-5*, HarpTrophy) HarpC Child Bks.

— Lucie Babbidge's House. 256p. (J). 1993. pap. 4.50 (*0-380-71812-X*, Avon Bks) Morrow Avon.

— Me & Morton. LC 85-48251. (Trophy Bk.). 320p. (J). (gr. 4-7). 1989. pap. 3.95 (*0-06-440306-8*, HarpTrophy) HarpC Child Bks.

Cassee, E. & Reuland, R., eds. The Management of Hospitality. LC 82-18610. (International Series in Hospitality Management). (Illus.). 236p. 1983. 109.00 (*0-08-028107-9*, Pub. by Pergamon Repr) Franklin.

Cassel. Psychology & Criminal Behavior. (C). 2000. 60.00 (*0-205-28040-4*, Macmillan Coll) P-H.

— Source 1 - Computing Essentials DBase IV 1.5. pap. text 5.00 (*0-685-70923-X*) P-H.

Cassel, C. K., et al, eds. Geriatric Medicine. 2nd ed. (Illus.). xxvii, 697p. 1989. 110.00 (*0-387-96977-2*) Spr-Verlag.

— Geriatric Medicine. 3rd ed. (Illus.). 1070p. 1997. 130.00 (*0-387-94692-6*) Spr-Verlag.

Cassel, C. K. & Walsh, J. R., eds. Geriatric Medicine Vol. 1: Medical, Psychiatric & Pharmacological Topics. (Illus.). 590p. 1984. 105.00 (*0-387-90944-3*) Spr-Verlag.

— Geriatric Medicine Vol. 2: Fundamentals of Geriatric Care. (Illus.). 415p. 1984. 99.00 (*0-387-90958-3*) Spr-Verlag.

***Cassel, Christine, ed.** The Practical Guide to Aging: What Everyone Needs to Know. 2001. pap. 17.95 (*0-8147-1516-8*) NYU Pr.

Cassel, Christine, ed. see Abraham, Henry.

Cassel, Christine K., ed. The Practical Guide to Aging: What Everyone Needs to Know. LC 97-21571. (Illus.). 352p. (C). 1999. 24.95 (*0-8147-1515-X*) NYU Pr.

Cassel, Christine K., et al, eds. Geriatric Medicine. LC 96-13736. 1996. write for info. (*0-614-14601-1*) Spr-Verlag.

C

***Cassel, Christine K. & Foley, Kathleen M.** Principles for Care of Patients at the End of Life: An Emerging Consensus among the Specialities of Medicine. 32p. 1999. pap. write for info. (*1-887748-34-2*) Milbank Memorial.

Cassel, Christine K., ed. see Committee on Care at the End of Life, Institute of.

Cassel, Claes-Magnus, et al. Foundations of Inference in Survey Sampling. LC 91-35698. (Probability & Mathematical Statistics Applied Prob). 206p. (C). 1993. reprint ed. lib. bdg. 54.95 (*0-89464-667-2*) Krieger.

Cassel, D. K. Genealogical History of the Cassel Family in America, Being the Descendants of Julius Kassel or Yelles Cassel, of Kriesheim, Baden, Germany. 465p. 1993. reprint ed. pap. 71.50 (*0-8328-3767-9*); reprint ed. lib. bdg. 81.50 (*0-8328-3766-0*) Higginson Bk Co.

Cassel, Daniel K. Kolb. Genealogical History of the Kolb, Kulp or Culp Family & Its Branches in America, with Biographical Sketches of Their Descendants from the Earliest Available Records from 1707 to the Present Time, Including Dielman Kolb in Germany. (Illus.). 584p. 1997. reprint ed. pap. 88.50 (*0-8328-9455-9*); reprint ed. lib. bdg. 98.50 (*0-8328-9454-0*) Higginson Bk Co.

Cassel, Don. The dBASE II Simplified for the IBM Personal Computer. (Illus.). 176p. 1986. 16.50 (*0-13-195934-4*); pap. text 24.33 (*0-13-195942-5*) P-H.

— dBASE IV. (C). 1993. 6.67 (*0-13-045634-9*) P-H.

— DOS 4.0. (C). 1993. 9.33 (*0-13-045642-X*) P-H.

— EasyWriter Simplified for the IBM Personal Computer. 208p. 1986. text 23.33 (*0-13-222449-6*) P-H.

— Excel 4.0. (Source 1 Ser.). (C). 1993. pap. 9.33 (*0-13-834318-7*) P-H.

— Lotus 1-2-3. 114p. (C). 1993. pap. 9.33 (*0-13-013657-3*) P-H.

— Lotus 1-2-3 Simplified for the IBM PC. 272p. 1985. pap. 53.95 (*0-671-93843-6*) S&S Trade.

— Lotus 2.4. (Source 1 Ser.). (C). 1993. pap. 9.33 (*0-13-834300-4*) P-H.

— Microsoft Access 7.0. LC 97-158754. 112p. 1997. pap. text 7.00 (*0-13-236879-X*) P-H.

— Paradox. (Source 1 Ser.). (C). 1993. pap. 9.33 (*0-13-834292-X*) P-H.

— Qbasic. (Source 1 Ser.). (C). 1994. pap. text 9.40 (*0-13-834326-8*) P-H.

— Quattro. 122p. (C). 1993. pap. 9.33 (*0-13-013665-4*) P-H.

— Quattro Pro. 122p. (C). 1993. pap. 9.33 (*0-13-013673-5*) P-H.

— Source 1 - Computing Essentials Lotus 1-2-3. (C). 1993. pap. text 9.33 (*0-13-106535-1*) P-H.

— Source 1 - Lotus 3.1. (C). 1994. pap. text 9.33 (*0-13-101494-3*) P-H.

— Source 1 - Paradox 4.0. 104p. (C). 1994. pap. 9.33 (*0-13-101502-8*) P-H.

— Source 1 - Quattro Pro 5.0. 138p. (C). 1994. pap. 9.33 (*0-13-101528-1*) P-H.

— Source 1 - Word for Windows. 128p. (C). 1994. pap. 9.33 (*0-13-101536-2*) P-H.

— Source 1 - WordPerfect 6.0. 1994. pap. text 5.00 (*0-685-70619-2*) P-H.

— Using WordPerfect 5.1. 160p. (C). 1993. pap. text 12.00 (*0-13-951666-2*) P-H.

— Windows. (Source 1 Ser.). 96p. (C). 1993. pap. 9.33 (*0-13-834334-9*) P-H.

— WordPerfect 5.1. 96p. (C). 1993. pap. 9.33 (*0-13-013699-9*) P-H.

— WordStar Simplified for the IBM Personal Computer. (Illus.). 160p. 1984. pap. 13.50 (*0-13-963612-9*) P-H.

— WordStar Simplified with WordStar 3.3: MailMerge, Spellstar & StarIndex. 176p. (C). 1986. 15.50 (*0-13-963646-3*); text 24.33 (*0-13-963638-2*) P-H.

Cassel, Gary H., et al. The Eye Book: A Complete Guide to Eye Disorders & Health. LC 97-35348. (Johns Hopkins Press Health Bks.). (Illus.). 348p. 1998. pap. 18.95 (*0-8018-5847-X*); text 39.95 (*0-8018-5835-6*) Johns Hopkins.

***Cassel, Gary H., et al.** Eye Book: A Complete Guide to Eye Disorders & Health. large type ed. (Health Book Ser.). (Illus.). 528p. 2000. pap. 19.95 (*0-8018-6520-4*) Johns Hopkins.

Cassel, Gudrun. Cyanide & the Central Nervous System: Foreign Countries' Approaches to High-Level Waste Storage & Disposal. (Illus.). 101p. (Orig.). (C). 1994. pap. text 40.00 (*0-7881-1132-9*) DIANE Pub.

Cassel, Gustav. Downfall of the Gold Standard. 262p. 1966. 30.00 (*0-7146-1213-8*, Pub. by F Cass Pubs) Intl Spec Bk.

— Economic Essays in Honour of Gustav Cassel: October 20, 1933. 720p. 1967. 47.00 (*0-7146-1214-6*, Pub. by F Cass Pubs) Intl Spec Bk.

— Foreign Investments. Wilkins, Mira, ed. LC 78-3902. (International Finance Ser.). 1979. reprint ed. lib. bdg. 23.95 (*0-405-11207-6*) Ayer.

— Money & Foreign Exchange after 1914. LC 72-4266. (World Affairs Ser.: National & International Viewpoints). 294p. 1972. reprint ed. 21.95 (*0-405-04563-8*) Ayer.

Cassel, J., et al. Education & Training of Engineers for Environmental Health. 152p. 1970. pap. text 20.00 (*92-4-156004-5*, 1150038) World Health.

Cassel, Jay. The Secret Plague: Venereal Disease in Canada, 1838-1939. 1987. pap. 17.95 (*0-8020-6617-8*); text 35.00 (*0-8020-2593-5*) U of Toronto Pr.

Cassel, Jeris F. & Congleton, Robert J. Critical Thinking: An Annotated Bibliography. LC 92-35306. 413p. 1992. 50.00 (*0-8108-2635-6*) Scarecrow.

Cassel, Katrina L. The Junior High Survival Manual. LC 98-2643. 128p. (J). (gr. 7-9). 1998. 6.99 (*0-570-05062-6*) Concordia.

***Cassel, Katrina L.** On the Homefront: A Family Survival Guide. LC 99-47327. (Illus.). 128p. (gr. 7-12). 2000. 6.99 (*0-570-07000-7*) Concordia.

Cassel, Paul. Sams Teach Yourself Access 97 in 21 Days. 5th ed. 563p. 1998. pap. text 29.99 (*0-672-31298-0*) Sams.

— Using Windows NT Workstation 4. 2nd ed. 1998. pap. text 29.99 (*0-7897-1648-8*) Que.

Cassel, Paul & Palmer, Pamela. Sam's Teach Yourself Microsoft Access 2000 in 21 Days. (Sams Teach Yourself... in 21 Days Ser.). (Illus.). 785p. 1999. pap. 29.99 (*0-672-31292-1*) Sams.

Cassel, Paul, et al. Windows NT 4 Workstation Unleashed. 2nd ed. LC 97-65460. 926p. 1997. pap. 49.99 incl. cd-rom (*0-672-31081-3*) Sams.

Cassel, Paul, jt. auth. see Hart, Michael.

Casselberry, L. & Candy, F. Love Lists: What Every Woman Wants Her Man Can Know. Lehman, Barbara & Morgan, G., eds. (Illus.). 144p. 1998. pap. 14.95 (*0-9660772-0-2*) Access Ability.

Cassell & the Publishers Association Staff. Cassell Directory of Publishing, 1997. 22nd rev. ed. 544p. 1996. pap. 95.00 (*0-304-33823-0*) Continuum.

— Directory of Publishing: United Kingdom, Commonwealth & Overseas, 1998. 514p. 1997. pap. 95.00 (*0-304-70172-6*) Continuum.

***Cassell & the Publishers Association Staff, ed.** Directory of Publishing: United Kingdom, Commonwealth & Overseas, 2000. 535p. 1999. 99.00 (*0-304-70646-9*) Continuum.

Cassell, A. C., ed. see Kleiber, Michael & Breitkopf, Piotr.

Cassell, Abayomi. Liberia: History of the First African Republic, 2 vols., 1. (Illus.). 1988. 37.50 (*0-8290-1307-5*) Irvington.

— Liberia: History of the First African Republic, 2 vols., 2. (Illus.). 1988. 39.50 (*0-8290-1308-3*) Irvington.

— Liberia: History of the First African Republic, Vol. 1. (Illus.). 457p. 15.00 (*0-685-41741-7*) Fountainhead.

Cassell Academic Staff. Cassell Dictionary of Chemistry. 1998. pap. text 27.95 (*0-304-35039-7*) Continuum.

Cassell, Anthony K. Lectura Dantis Americana: Inferno I. Hollander, Robert & Creagh, Patrick, trs. LC 89-4751. (Lectura Dantis Americana Ser.). 280p. (C). 1989. text 39.95 (*0-8122-8176-4*) U of Pa Pr.

Cassell, Anthony K., ed. & tr. see Boccaccio, Giovanni.

Cassell, Carol & Wilson, Pamela M. Sexuality Education: A Resource Book. LC 88-16994. (Source Books on Education: Vol. 19). 470p. 1989. text 81.00 (*0-8240-7899-3*, SS416) Garland.

Cassell, Cathy & Symon, Gillian, eds. Qualitative Research Methods in Organizational Psychology: A Practical Guide. LC 94-66701. 272p. 1994. 69.95 (*0-8039-8769-2*); pap. 26.95 (*0-8039-8770-6*) Sage.

***Cassell, Dana K. & Gleaves, David H.** The Encyclopedia of Obesity & Eating Disorders. 2nd ed. LC 99-40824. (Illus.). 304p. 2000. 55.00 (*0-8160-4042-7*) Facts on File.

— Food for Thought: The Sourcebook for Obesity & Eating Disorders. (Illus.). 256p. 2000. pap. 16.95 (*0-8160-4147-4*, Checkmark) Facts on File.

Cassell, Dana K. & Larocca, Felix E. Encyclopedia of Obesity & Eating Disorders. 272p. 1994. lib. bdg. 45.00 (*0-8160-1985-1*) Facts on File.

Cassell, David. The Lifeskills Arithmetic File. 1986. pap. 7.95 (*0-906212-50-2*, Pub. by Tarquin Pubns) Parkwest Pubns.

Cassell, Eric J. Doctoring: The Nature of Primary Care Medicine. 224p. (C). 1997. 27.50 (*0-19-511323-3*) OUP.

— The Healer's Art. 240p. 1985. pap. text 16.00 (*0-262-53062-7*) MIT Pr.

— The Place of the Humanities in Medicine. 1984. 7.00 (*0-916558-19-3*) Hastings Ctr.

— Talking with Patients Vol. 1: The Theory of Doctor-Patient Communication. (Illus.). 240p. 1985. pap. text 13.50 (*0-262-53055-4*) MIT Pr.

— Talking with Patients Vol. 2: Clinical Technique. 215p. 1985. pap. text 13.50 (*0-262-53056-2*) MIT Pr.

Cassell, Eric J. & Siegler, Mark, eds. Changing Values in Medicine. LC 85-10033. 221p. 1979. pap. 24.95 (*0-313-27060-0*, P7060, Greenwood Pr); lib. bdg. 59.95 (*0-313-27050-3*, U7050, Greenwood Pr) Greenwood.

Cassell, Frank A. Merchant Congressman in the Young Republic: Samuel Smith of Maryland, 1752-1839. LC 79-157390. (Illus.). 303p. reprint ed. pap. 94.00 (*0-8357-6784-1*, 203546100095) Bks Demand.

Cassell, Frank A., jt. ed. see Rury, John L.

Cassell, Frank H. Public Employment Service: Organization in Change. LC 68-27448. (Orig.). (C). 1968. pap. 5.00 (*0-87736-310-2*) U of Mich Inst Labor.

Cassell, Jack L. & Mulkey, S. Wayne. Rehabilitation Caseload Management: Concepts & Practice. LC 85-3385. 350p. 1985. pap. text 34.00 (*0-936104-67-8*, 1275) PRO-ED.

Cassell, Jay, ed. The Best of Sports Afield: The Greatest Outdoor Writing of the 20th Century. LC 96-20432. 336p. 1996. 25.00 (*0-87113-644-9*, Atlntc Mnthly) Grove-Atltic.

Cassell, Jay & Fiduccia, Peter, eds. The Quotable Hunter. LC 99-34850. 1999. 20.00 (*1-55821-955-2*) Lyons Pr.

Cassell, Jay, jt. auth. see Ross, John E.

Cassell, Jenna. Bravo ASL! Curriculum Instructor's Guide. Holland, Karla & Cox, Dian, eds. (Illus.). 924p. (Orig.). 1996. pap. text 180.00 (*1-882872-98-3*, ASL-IG) Sign Enhancers.

— Bravo ASL! Curriculum Student Workbook. Holland, Karla & Cox, Dian, eds. (Illus.). 350p. (Orig.). 1996. pap. text 34.00 (*1-882872-97-5*, ASL-SW) Sign Enhancers.

Cassell, Jenna & McCaffrey, Eileen. ASL Grammatical Aspects Vol. 1: Comparative Translations: Course 2001: Instructional Guide. 113p. (C). 1995. pap. text 39.95 (*1-882872-99-1*, 2001G) Sign Enhancers.

Cassell, Jo Anne. Carry the Flame: The History of the American Dietetic Association. LC 88-72202. 509p. (Orig.). 1990. pap. text 32.95 (*0-88091-038-0*, 0175) Am Dietetic Assn.

Cassell, Joan. Expected Miracles: Surgeons at Work. 259p. 1991. 59.95 (*0-87722-804-3*); pap. 22.95 (*0-87722-838-8*) Temple U Pr.

— The Woman in the Surgeon's Body. LC 97-47091. 267p. 1998. 35.00 (*0-674-95467-X*) HUP.

***Cassell, Joan.** Woman in the Surgeon's Body. 288p. 2000. pap. 17.95 (*0-674-00407-8*) HUP.

Cassell, Joan, ed. Children in the Field: Anthropological Experiences. LC 86-23160. (Illus.). 288p. 1987. 32.95 (*0-87722-477-3*) Temple U Pr.

— Children in the Field: Anthropological Experiences. LC 86-23160. 288p. 1994. pap. 22.95 (*1-56639-206-3*) Temple U Pr.

***Cassell, Julian.** Easy Bathroom Improvements: The Essential Guide to Home Decoration. LC 99-89110. (Do-It-Yourself Factfile Ser.). (Illus.). 112p. (gr. 8). 2000. spiral bd. 12.95 (*0-7370-0309-X*) T-L Custom Pub.

— Easy Home Improvements: The Essential Guide to Home Decoration. LC 99-89111. (Do-It-Yourself Factfile Ser.). (Illus.). 112p. (gr. 8). 2000. spiral bd. 12.95 (*0-7370-0311-1*) T-L Custom Pub.

— Tiling: The Essential Guide to Home Decoration. LC 99-89112. (Do-It-Yourself Factfile Ser.). (Illus.). 112p. (gr. 8). 2000. spiral bd. 12.95 (*0-7370-0312-X*) T-L Custom Pub.

Cassell, Julian & Parham, Peter. Decorating Hints & Tips. LC 97-34411. (Hints & Tips Ser.). (Illus.). 144p. 1998. pap. 19.95 (*0-7894-2393-6*) DK Pub Inc.

***Cassell, Julian & Parham, Peter.** Papering & Painting: The Essential Guide to Home Decorating. LC 99-89109. (Do-It-Yourself Factfile Ser.). (Illus.). 112p. (gr. 8). 2000. spiral bd. 12.95 (*0-7370-0310-3*) Time-Life.

***Cassell, Justine, et al, eds.** Embodied Conversational Agents. LC 99-89951. (Illus.). 438p. 2000. 45.00 (*0-262-03278-3*) MIT Pr.

Cassell, Justine & Jenkins, Henry, eds. From Barbie to Mortal Kombat: Gender & Computer Games. LC 98-23562. (Illus.). 380p. 1998. 35.00 (*0-262-03258-9*) MIT Pr.

***Cassell, Justine & Jenkins, Henry, eds.** From Barbie to Mortal Kombat: Gender & Computer Games. (Illus.). 380p. 2000. pap. 17.95 (*0-262-53168-2*) MIT Pr.

Cassell, Justine & Jenkins, Henry, eds. The Integrative Neurobiology of Affiliation: Proceedings of a New York Academy of Sciences Conference, March 14-17, 1996. LC 98-36500. (Illus.). 300p. 1999. 40.00 (*0-262-53158-5*) MIT Pr.

Cassell, Kay & Futas, Elizabeth. Developing Public Library Collections, Policies & Procedures: A How-to-Do-It Manual for Small & Medium Sized Public Libraries. (How-to-Do-It Ser.). 143p. 1991. pap. text 45.00 (*1-55570-060-8*) Neal-Schuman.

***Cassell, Kay Ann.** Developing Reference Collections & Services in an Electronic Age: A How-to-Do-It Manual for Librarians. 128p. 1999. pap. 55.00 (*1-55570-363-1*) Neal-Schuman.

Cassell, Nancy. An Easygoing Guide to Astrology. 80p. (Orig.). 1992. pap. 6.95 (*0-9625402-1-8*) Altan Pub.

— Rebirth: My Transplant Experience. 64p. (Orig.). 1993. pap. 4.95 (*0-9625402-3-4*) Altan Pub.

Cassell, Philip, ed. The Giddens Reader. LC 93-83193. 368p. (C). 1993. 47.50 (*0-8047-2202-1*); pap. 17.95 (*0-8047-2204-8*) Stanford U Pr.

Cassell Publishing Staff. The Popular Carol Book: Music Edition, Words Edition. Coleman et al, eds. (Illus.). 1998. pap. text 23.95 (*0-264-67481-2*) A R Mowbray.

Cassell, Richard A. Ford Madox Ford: A Study of His Novels. LC 76-57731. 307p. 1977. reprint ed. lib. bdg. 38.50 (*0-8371-9465-2*, CAFF, Greenwood Pr) Greenwood.

Cassell, Richard A., ed. Critical Essays on Ford Madox Ford. (Critical Essays Ser.). 208p. 1987. 49.00 (*0-8161-8761-4*, Hall Reference) Macmillan.

Cassell, Robert P. Echoes of Love: An Appalachian Story. LC 93-61736. 160p. (Orig.). 1993. pap. 12.95 (*1-881692-08-6*) Trillium WV.

Cassell, Ronald D. Medical Charities, Medical Politics: The Irish Dispensary System & the Poor Law, 1836-1872. LC 97-3751. (Royal Historical Society Studies in History). 192p. 1997. 60.00 (*0-86193-228-5*, Royal Historical Soc) Boydell & Brewer.

Cassell Staff. Cassell Directory of Publishing, 1999: U. K., Commonwealth & Overseas. 528p. 1998. pap. 99.00 (*0-304-70412-1*) Continuum.

— Cassell's German & English Dictionary. (ENG & GER.). 541p. 1986. pap. text 6.00 (*0-02-024850-4*) Macmillan.

— Cassell's Latin & English Dictionary. (ENG & LAT.). 379p. 1987. pap. 4.95 (*0-02-013340-5*, Pub. by Macmillan) S&S Trade.

— Cassell's Spanish & English Dictionary. (ENG & SPA.). 464p. 1986. pap. 4.95 (*0-02-013690-0*, Pub. by Macmillan) S&S Trade.

Cassell Staff, et al, compiled by. Cassell's Italian Dictionary: Italian-English, English-Italian. LC 77-7405. (ENG & ITA.). 1152p. 1977. pap. 21.00 (*0-02-522530-8*) Macmillan.

— Cassell's Italian Dictionary: Italian-English, English-Italian. LC 77-7405. (ENG & ITA.). 1152p. 1994. 24.95 (*0-02-522540-5*, Pub. by Macmillan) S&S Trade.

Cassell, Stephen. Final Voyage of the S.S.N. Skate. 1989. mass mkt. 3.95 (*1-55817-157-6*, Pinncle Kensgtn) Kensgtn Pub Corp.

— Strike of the China Falcon. 1992. mass mkt. 4.50 (*1-55817-584-9*, Pinncle Kensgtn) Kensgtn Pub Corp.

Cassell, Stuart K., Jr., jt. auth. see Schetz, Katherine F.

Cassella, J. P., et al. The Rat Nervous System: An Introduction to Preparatory Techniques. LC 96-30347. 116p. 1997. pap. 125.00 (*0-471-96967-2*) Wiley.

Cassella, Maggie, jt. auth. see Delaria, Lea.

Casselli, Joseph & Winn, Paul. Tax Planning from the Heart: Increase Income, Reduce Taxes & Benefit Your Favorite Charity. LC 98-24655. 160p. 1998. text 24.95 (*1-58008-047-2*) Ten Speed Pr.

Cassells, A. C. Pathogen & Microbial Contamination Management in Micropropagation. LC 97-31344. (Development in Plant Pathology Ser.). 384p. 1997. text 200.50 (*0-7923-4784-6*) Kluwer Academic.

Cassells, Alan C. The Methodology of Plant Genetic Manipulation: Criteria for Decision Making. Jones, Peter W., ed. (Developments in Plant Breeding Ser.: Vol. 3). 486p. (C). 1995. text 257.50 (*0-7923-3687-9*) Kluwer Academic.

Cassells, Cyrus. Beautiful Signor. LC 97-4699. 112p. 1997. pap. text 14.00 (*1-55659-124-1*) Copper Canyon.

***Cassells, Cyrus.** Mud Actor. (Classic Contemporaries Ser.). 2000. pap. text 12.95 (*0-88748-325-9*) Carnegie-Mellon.

Cassells, Cyrus. Soul Make a Path Through Shouting. LC 94-9842. 96p. 1994. 22.00 (*1-55659-066-0*); pap. 12.00 (*1-55659-065-2*) Copper Canyon.

Cassells, E. Steve. The Archaeology of Colorado. rev. ed. LC 97-1761. (Illus.). 432p. 1997. pap. 19.00 (*1-55566-193-9*) Johnson Bks.

Cassells Editors. Cassell's New Dutch Dictionary: English-Dutch, Dutch-English. 2nd rev. ed. (DUT & ENG.). 729p. 1982. pap. 55.00 (*0-02-522940-0*) Macmillan.

Cassells, J. S., ed. see Institute of Medicine Staff.

Cassells, Vic. For Those in Peril... 1996. pap. text 24.95 (*0-86417-734-8*, Pub. by Kangaroo Pr) Seven Hills Bk.

Casselman, Barbie. Barbie Casselman's Good-for-You Cooking. 1993. text 16.96 (*0-394-22327-6*) Random.

Casselman, J. M., jt. auth. see Crossman, Edward J.

***Casselman, Karen D.** Lichen Dyes: The New Source Book. 2000. pap. 6.95 (*0-486-41231-8*) Dover.

Casselman, Karen D., jt. auth. see Dean, Jenny.

Casselman, Karen L. Craft of the Dyer: Colour from Plants & Lichens. 2nd rev. ed. LC 93-8110. Orig. Title: Craft of the Dyer: Colour from Plants & Lichens of the Northeast. (Illus.). 256p. 1993. reprint ed. pap. 8.95 (*0-486-27606-6*) Dover.

Casselman, Lucy. Bridge Love. 1980. per. 1.50 (*0-373-58047-9*) Harlequin Bks.

Casselman, W., jt. ed. see Borel, Armand.

Casselman, William, et al. Dictionary of Medical Derivations: The Real Meaning of Medical Terms. LC 97-26856. (Illus.). 436p. 1998. 41.95 (*1-85070-771-5*) Prthnon Pub.

Cassels, A. Aid Instruments & Health Systems Development: An Analysis of Current Practice No. 3: Forum on Health Sector Reform, Discussion Paper. 27p. 1995. pap. 10.80 (*0-614-32412-2*, 1933076) World Health.

— Health Sector Reform: Key Issues in Less Developed Countries No. 1: Forum on Health Sector Reform, Discussion Paper. 23p. 1995. pap. 10.80 (*0-614-32409-2*, 1931076) World Health.

Cassels, A. & Janovsky, Katja. Strengthening Health Management in Districts & Provinces: Handbook for Facilitators. 121p. 1991. pap. text 18.00 (*0-614-08047-9*, 1930027) World Health.

Cassels, Alan. Fascism. LC 73-13716. (Illus.). 416p. (C). 1975. pap. text 19.95 (*0-88295-718-X*) Harlan Davidson.

— Fascist Italy. 2nd ed. LC 84-214850. (Europe since 1500 Ser.). 160p. (C). 1985. pap. text 11.95 (*0-88295-828-3*) Harlan Davidson.

— Ideology & International Relations in the Modern World. (New International History Ser.). 320p. (C). 1996. 80.00 (*0-415-11926-X*); pap. 25.99 (*0-415-11927-8*) Routledge.

Cassels, Alan, ed. Italian Foreign Policy, 1918-1945: A Guide to Research & Research Materials. rev. ed. LC 90-31288. (European Diplomatic History Ser.). 261p. 1991. 65.00 (*0-8420-2307-0*) Scholarly Res Inc.

Cassels, Andrew & Janovsky, Katja. Strengthening Health Management in Districts & Provinces. (FRE & SPA.). vi, 75p. (C). 1995. pap. text 20.00 (*92-4-154483-X*, 1150428) World Health.

Cassels, Bruce K., tr. see Breitmaier, Eberhard & Bauer, Gerhard.

Cassels, J. M. Basic Quantum Mechanics. 2nd ed. (Illus.). 220p. (C). 1995. reprint ed. 28.50 (*0-89464-906-X*) Krieger.

Cassels, J. W. An Introduction to the Geometry of Numbers. LC 96-51827. (Classics in Mathematics Ser.). 375p. 1997. pap. 35.00 (*3-540-61788-4*) Spr-Verlag.

— Lectures on Elliptic Curves. (London Mathematical Society Student Texts Ser.: No. 24). (Illus.). 143p. (C). 1991. pap. text 27.95 (*0-521-42530-1*) Cambridge U Pr.

— Local Fields. (London Mathematical Society Student Texts Ser.: No. 4). 360p. 1986. pap. text 31.95 (*0-521-31525-5*) Cambridge U Pr.

Cassels, J. W. & Flynn, V. Prolegomena to a Middlebrow Arithmetic of Curves of Genus 2. (London Mathematical Society Lecture Note Ser.: No. 230). (Illus.). 232p. (C). 1996. pap. text 42.95 (*0-521-48370-0*) Cambridge U Pr.

***Cassels, Jamie.** Remedies: The Law of Damages. (Essentials of Canadian Law Ser.). 400p. 2000. pap. 35.95 (*1-55221-037-5*, Pub. by Irwin Law) Gaunt.

Cassels, Jamie. The Uncertain Promise of Law: Lessons from Bhopal. 364p. 1993. text 45.00 (*0-8020-2841-1*); pap. text 19.95 (*0-8020-7722-6*) U of Toronto Pr.

Cassels, Jean, jt. auth. see Robinson, Fay.

Cassels, John M. A Study of Fluid Milk Prices. LC 75-39237. (Getting & Spending: Tthe Consumer's Dilemma Ser.). (Illus.). 1976. reprint ed. 28.95 (*0-405-08014-X*) Ayer.

Cassels, Julia. How to Capture Movement in Your Paintings. (Illus.). 144p. 1996. 27.99 (*0-89134-734-8*, North Lght Bks) F & W Pubns Inc.

Cassels, Nancy G., ed. Orientalism, Evangelicalism, & the Military Cantonment in Early Nineteenth Century India. LC 91-34611. 164p. 1991. lib. bdg. 79.95 (*0-7734-9686-6*) E Mellen.

Cassem, Ned H., ed. see Massachusetts General Hospital Staff.

Cassen, R. H. India: Population, Economy, Society. LC 77-16217. 419p. (C). 1978. 49.50 (*0-8419-0300-X*); pap. 19.50 (*0-8419-0648-3*) Holmes & Meier.

Cassen, Robert. Does Aid Work? 2nd ed. (Illus.). 334p. 1994. pap. text 19.95 (*0-19-877386-2*) OUP.

Cassen, Robert. Population Policy: A New Consensus. LC 94-28294. (Policy Essay Ser.: Vol. 12). 128p. (Orig.). 1994. pap. 13.95 (*1-56517-017-2*) Overseas Dev Council.

Cassen, Robert, ed. Fictions, Factions, & Facts: The Population & Development Debate. LC 94-11399. (U. S. Third World Policy Perspectives Ser.: No. 19). 304p. (C). 1994. pap. 17.95 (*1-56000-740-0*) Transaction Pubs.

— Fictions, Factions, & Facts: The Population & Development Debate. LC 94-11399. (U. S. Third World Policy Perspectives Ser.: No. 19). 304p. (C). 1994. text 39.95 (*1-56000-165-8*) Transaction Pubs.

— Soviet Interests in the Third World. LC 85-61574. 341p. reprint ed. pap. 105.80 (*0-8357-4773-5*, 203771000009) Bks Demand.

Cassen, Robert & Joshi, Vijay, eds. India: The Future of Econonic Reform. (Illus.). 384p. 1995. text 29.95 (*0-19-563719-4*) OUP.

Cassena, R. G., ed. Muscle Biology, Vol. 1. LC 72-81501. 311p. reprint ed. pap. 96.50 (*0-608-16730-4*, 202782200001) Bks Demand.

Cassens, B. Preventive Medicine & Public Health. 2nd ed. (National Medical Series for Independent Study). (Illus.). 497p. 1992. 26.00 (*0-683-06262-X*) Lppncott W & W.

Cassens, Daniel L., et al. Selection & Use of Preservative-Treated Wood. (Illus.). 104p. 1995. pap. 24.95 (*0-935018-75-1*, 7299) Forest Prod.

Cassens, Kenneth H. Screwball Express: A Meaningful Tribute to the 8th Air Force, the 379th Bomb Group & the Screwball Express. LC 92-85015. (Illus.). 160p. 1992. 29.95 (*1-56311-095-4*) Turner Pub KY.

Cassens, Robert G. Meat Preservation: Preventing Losses & Assuring Safety. LC 94-70368. (Publications in Food & Nutrition). 133p. 1994. 72.00 (*0-917678-34-6*) Food & Nut Pr.

— Nitrite-Cured Meat: A Food Safety Issue in Perspective. 176p. 1990. 67.00 (*0-917678-27-3*) Food & Nut Pr.

Casser. Appleton & Lange's Quick Review: Optometry. 5th ed. (C). 1998. pap. 35.95 (*0-8385-0343-8*, A-0343-2) Appleton & Lange.

Casser & Fingeret, Murray. Atlas of Primary Eyecare Procedures. 2nd ed. LC 96-40178. (Illus.). 494p. (C). 1997. 115.00 (*0-8385-0257-1*, A-0257-4, Apple Lange Med) McGraw.

Casser, Linda. Optometry Examination Review (MEPC) 4th ed. (Illus.). 416p. (C). 1999. pap. text 36.95 (*0-8385-7449-1*, A7449-0, Apple Lange Med) McGraw.

Casseres, Benjamin de, see De Casseres, Benjamin.

Casserley, J. V. Langmead & Keyes, C. Don. No Faith of My Own & Graceful Reason: The Contribution of Reason to Theology. 408p. 1984. reprint ed. pap. text 29.00 (*0-8191-3793-6*) U Pr of Amer.

Casserley, Julian. Evil & Evolutionary Eschatology: Two Essays. LC 90-37596. (Toronto Studies in Theology: Vol. 39). 136p. 1991. lib. bdg. 69.95 (*0-88946-978-4*) E Mellen.

Casserly, Catherine M. African-American Women & Poverty: Can Education Alone Change the Status Quo? rev. ed. LC 98-9414. (Children of Poverty Ser.). (Illus.). 224p. 1998. text 50.00 (*0-8153-3055-3*) Garland.

Casserly, Constance D. A Fine Line. LC 93-70368. 218p. (YA). (gr. 8-12). 1993. pap. 7.95 (*0-943864-71-2*) Davenport.

Casserly, Dominic. Facing up to the Risks. 224p. 1991. 25.00 (*0-685-49785-2*, HarpBusn) HarpInfo.

— Facing up to the Risks: How Financial Institutions Can Survive & Prosper. LC 92-40871. 336p. 1993. 29.95 (*0-471-59219-6*) Wiley.

— Racing up to the Risks: Reclaiming the Fundamental Challenge of the Financial Industry. 1992. 27.00 (*0-88730-514-8*, HarpBusn) HarpInfo.

Casserly, Dominic, et al. Banking in Asia: The End of Entitlement. LC 99-12956. (Wiley Frontiers in Finance Ser.). 438p. (C). 1999. 69.95 (*0-471-83192-1*) Wiley.

Casserly, Jack. Once upon a Time in Italy: The Vita Italiana of an American Journalist. (Illus.). 284p. 1995. pap. 12.95 (*1-57098-019-5*) Roberts Rinehart.

Casserly, Jack, jt. auth. see Hearst, William R., Jr.

Casserly, John J. The Ford White House: The Diary of a Speechwriter. LC 77-82185. (Illus.). 388p. reprint ed. pap. 120.30 (*0-8357-5496-0*, 203511000093) Bks Demand.

Casserly, Patrick S. Learn Latin for English Speakers. (ENG & LAT.). pap. 20.95 (*0-87557-051-8*) Saphrograph.

Cassese, A. Self-Determination of Peoples: A Legal Reappraisal. (Hersch Lauterpacht Memorial Lectures: No. 12). 393p. (C). 1998. reprint ed. pap. text 39.95 (*0-521-63752-X*) Cambridge U Pr.

Cassese, A., ed. Legal Restraints on the Use of Force 40 Years after the U. N. Charter. (C). 1986. lib. bdg. 191.00 (*90-247-3247-6*) Kluwer Academic.

Cassese, Antonio. Inhuman States: Imprisonment, Detention & Torture in Europe Today. 141p. (Orig.). 1996. 60.95 (*0-7456-1721-2*, Pub. by Polity Pr); pap. 22.95 (*0-7456-1722-0*, Pub. by Polity Pr) Blackwell Pubs.

— International Law in a Divided World. LC 86-16456. 446p. 1989. pap. text 45.00 (*0-19-876233-X*) OUP.

— Parliamentary Control over Foreign Policy. 216p. 1980. lib. bdg. 75.50 (*90-286-0019-1*) Kluwer Academic.

— Terrorism, Politics & Law: The Achille Lauro Affair. LC 89-3971. 174p. 1989. reprint ed. pap. 54.00 (*0-7837-9494-0*, 206023800004) Bks Demand.

— Violence & Law in the Modern Age. Greenleaves, S. J., tr. LC 88-3642. 200p. 1988. reprint ed. pap. 62.00 (*0-7837-9495-9*, 206023900004) Bks Demand.

Cassese, Antonio, ed. U. N. Law-Fundamental Rights: Two Topics in International Law. 268p. 1979. lib. bdg. 87.50 (*90-286-0828-1*) Kluwer Academic.

Cassese, Antonio & Roling, B. V., eds. The Tokyo Trial & Beyond. 152p. 1994. pap. 25.95 (*0-7456-1485-X*, Pub. by Polity Pr) Blackwell Pubs.

Cassese, Antonio & Weller, Joseph H., eds. Change & Stability in International Law-Making. (European University Institute, Series A (Law): No. 9). 214p. (C). 1988. lib. bdg. 73.10 (*3-11-011494-1*) De Gruyter.

Casset, Mama. Les Precurseurs de la Photographie au Senegal, 1950. (Illus.). 96p. 1996. pap. 96.00 (*2-909571-07-6*, 610603, Pub. by Revue Noire) Dist Art Pubs.

Casseus, Maurice. Viejo. (B. E. Ser.: No. 45). (FRE.). 1935. 25.00 (*0-8115-2996-7*) Periodicals Srv.

Cassford, G., jt. auth. see Hollingum, Jack.

Cassian, John. John Cassian: Conferences. Luibheid, Colm, tr. (Classics of Western Spirituality Ser.). 201p. 1985. pap. 19.95 (*0-8091-2694-X*) Paulist Pr.

— Teachings of St. John Cassian. 1977. pap. 5.95 (*0-89981-102-7*) Eastern Orthodox.

Cassian, Nina. Blue Apple. Barkan, Stanley H., ed. Feiler, Eva, tr. (Cross-Cultural Review Chapbook Ser.: No. 13: Romanian Poetry 1). (ENG & RUM.). 16p. 1981. 15.00 (*0-685-01272-7*, CCC140); pap. 5.00 (*0-89304-812-7*); audio 10.00 (*0-89304-837-2*) Cross-Cultrl NY.

— Call Yourself Alive? The Love Poems of Nina Cassian. Deletant, A. & Walker, B., trs. LC 87-83570. (Illus.). 80p. 1989. reprint ed. pap. 16.95 (*0-948259-38-8*, Pub. by Forest Bks) Dufour.

— Cheerleader for a Funeral: Poems. Walker, B., tr. from ROM. LC 92-72468. (ENG & RUM., Illus.). 67p. 1993. pap. 15.95 (*1-85610-013-8*, Pub. by Forest Bks) Dufour.

— Life Sentences: Selected Poems. 1991. pap. 8.95 (*0-393-30721-2*) Norton.

— Take My Word for It: Poems. LC 97-49190. 96p. 1998. 21.00 (*0-393-04654-0*) Norton.

Cassiana, Mother. Come Follow Me - Orthodox Monasticism in Moldavia. 1991. 10.95 (*0-9694927-1-5*) Light&Life Pub Co MN.

Cassianus, Joannes. Spiritual Life, a Guide for Those Seeking Perfection. 1977. pap. 5.95 (*0-89981-098-5*) Eastern Orthodox.

Cassiday, Bruce. Who Should Melissa Marry? LC 94-12616. 224p. 1994. 18.95 (*1-55972-259-2*) Carol Pub Group.

Cassiday, Bruce, jt. auth. see Adler, Bill, Jr.

***Cassiday, Julie A.** The Enemy on Trial: Early Soviet Courts on Stage & Screen. LC 00-25544. (Illus.). 200p. 2000. write for info. (*0-87580-266-4*, 266-4) N Ill U Pr.

Cassidi, Deborah, ed. Favourite Prayers: Chosen by People from All Walks of Life. 192p. 1998. pap. 16.50 (*0-304-70315-X*) Continuum.

Cassidy. Dental Team Management of Medical Emergency. 1999. text. write for info. (*0-7216-5259-X*, W B Saunders Co) Harcrt Hlth Sci Grp.

— Heart-Lung Interactions in Health & Disease. Scharf, Steven M., ed. (Lung Biology in Health & Disease Ser.: Vol. 42). (Illus.). 1168p. 1989. text 295.00 (*0-8247-7986-X*) Dekker.

— The 1998-1999 Scholarship Book. 6th ed. (C). 1998. pap. 24.95 (*0-13-095093-9*, Macmillan Coll) P-H.

***Cassidy.** When the Dow Breaks. LC 99-28705. 208p. 1999. 24.95 (*0-07-134768-2*) McGraw.

Cassidy, Bridget. Don't Look Back. LC 98-67427. 144p. 1999. 18.95 (*1-57197-133-5*) Pentland Pr.

Cassidy, Anita. A Practical Guide to Information System Strategic Planning. LC 98-13359. 304p. 1998. boxed set 44.95 (*1-57444-133-7*) St Lucie Pr.

***Cassidy, Anita & Guggenberger, Keith.** A Practical Guide to Information Systems Process Improvement. LC 00-9370. 2000. write for info. (*1-57444-281-3*) St Lucie Pr.

Cassidy, Anne. No Through Road. large type ed. (J). 1997. pap. 16.95 (*0-7540-6005-5*, Galaxy Child Lrg Print) Chivers N Amer.

Cassidy, Anne. Parents Who Think Too Much. LC 97-50127. 288p. 1998. pap. 12.95 (*0-440-50812-6*) Doubleday.

***Cassidy, Anne.** Patsy Kelly Investigates: A Family Affair. large type ed. (J). 1998. pap. 16.95 (*0-7540-6028-4*, Galaxy Child Lrg Print) Chivers N Amer.

***Cassidy, B.** Danny Boy. 1998. mass mkt. 6.95 (*0-7472-5971-2*, Pub. by Headline Bk Pub) Trafalgar.

Cassidy, Brendan, ed. Iconography at the Crossroads: Papers from the Colloquim Sponsored by the Index of Christian Art, Princeton University, 23-24 March 1990. LC 93-16268. (Index of Christian Art, Occasional Papers: No. 2). (Illus.). 265p. reprint ed. pap. 82.20 (*0-608-09580-X*, 205438200006) Bks Demand.

— Iconography at the Crossroads: Papers from the Colloquium Sponsored by the Index of Christian Art, Princeton University. LC 93-16268. (Illus.). 265p. 1993. text 55.00 (*0-691-03212-2*) Princeton A & A.

— The Ruthwell Cross: Papers from the Colloquium Sponsored by the Index of Christian Art, Princeton University, 8 December 1989. LC 92-34870. (Occasional Papers - Index of Christian Art). (Illus.). 220p. 1992. 55.00 (*0-691-03211-4*); pap. 19.95 (*0-691-00038-7*) Princeton A & A.

***Cassidy, Carla.** Un Amor Sin Futuro (A Love Without Future) (Bianca Ser.). (SPA.). 2000. mass mkt. 3.50 (*0-373-33582-2*, 1-33582-7) Harlequin Bks.

Cassidy, Carla. Anything for Danny: (Fabulous Father, under the Mistletoe) (Romance Ser.). 1994. per. 2.75 (*0-373-19048-4*, 1-19048-7) Silhouette.

— Behind Closed Doors. 1997. per. 3.99 (*0-373-07778-5*, 1-07778-3) Silhouette.

— Code Name: Cowboy (Mustang Montana) (Silhouette Intimate Moments Ser.: Vol. 902). 1998. per. 4.25 (*0-373-07902-8*, 1-07902-9, Mira Bks) Harlequin Bks.

— Daddy on the Run. (Romance Ser.). 1996. per. 3.25 (*0-373-19158-8*, 1-19158-4) Silhouette.

— Deputy Daddy (The Baker Brood) LC 96-7282. (Romance Ser.). 185p. 1996. per. 3.25 (*0-373-19141-3*, 1-19141-0) Silhouette.

— En Cas de Doutes... (Rouge Passion Ser.: Vol. 502). (FRE.). 1999. mass mkt. 3.50 (*0-373-37502-6*, 1-37502-1) Harlequin Bks.

— A Father's Love: Lost & Found. 1998. per. 3.99 (*0-373-22498-2*, 1-22498-9, Mira Bks) Harlequin Bks.

— A Fleeting Moment. (Desire Ser.). 1993. per. 2.89 (*0-373-05784-9*, 5-05784-9) Silhouette.

— Fugitive Father. 1994. per. 3.50 (*0-373-07604-5*, 1-07604-1) Harlequin Bks.

— Getting It Right: Jessica. (Loop Ser.). 1994. per. 3.50 (*0-373-20202-4*, 1-20202-7) Silhouette.

— Golden Girl. 1993. pap. 2.69 (*0-373-08924-4*, 5-08924-8) Silhouette.

— Her Counterfeit Husband: Mustang, Montana. (Intimate Moments Ser.: No. 885). 1998. per. 4.25 (*0-373-07885-4*, 1-07885-6) Harlequin Bks.

***Cassidy, Carla.** Imminent Danger. (Intimate Moments Ser.: Bk. 1018). 2000. mass mkt. 4.50 (*0-373-27088-7*, 1-27088-3) Silhouette.

Cassidy, Carla. An Impromptu Proposal. (Romance Ser.). 1996. per. 3.25 (*0-373-19152-9*, 1-19152-7) Silhouette.

***Cassidy, Carla.** In a Heartbeat. Vol. 1005. 2000. mass mkt. 4.50 (*0-373-27075-5*) Harlequin Bks.

Cassidy, Carla. The Littlest Matchmaker: Under the Mistletoe. (Romance Ser.). 1993. per. 2.75 (*0-373-08978-3*, 5-08978-4) Silhouette.

— The Marriage Scheme. (Romance Ser.). 1994. per. 2.75 (*0-373-08996-1*, 5-08996-6) Silhouette.

— Midnight Wishes. (Cheyenne Nights Ser.). 1997. per. 3.75 (*0-373-22415-X*, 1-22415-3) Harlequin Bks.

— Mom in the Making (The Baker Brood) (Romance Ser.). 1996. per. 3.25 (*0-373-19147-2*, 1-19147-7) Silhouette.

— Mystery Child. (Shadows Ser.). 1996. per. 3.50 (*0-373-27061-5*, 1-27061-0) Silhouette.

***Cassidy, Carla.** One of the Good Guys. 2000. mass mkt. 4.50 (*0-373-82223-5*, 1-82223-8) Harlequin Bks.

Cassidy, Carla. One of the Good Guys. (Intimate Moments Ser.). 1993. per. 3.50 (*0-373-07531-6*, 5-07531-2) Silhouette.

— Le Passe pour Temoin. (Rouge Passion Ser.: No. 518). (FRE.). 1999. mass mkt. 3.99 (*0-373-37518-2*, 1-37518-7) Harlequin Bks.

— Passion in the First Degree. (Harlequin Intrigue Ser.: No. 379). 1996. per. 3.75 (*0-373-22379-X*, 1-22379-1) Harlequin Bks.

— Un Petit Frere pour Billy. (Horizon Ser.: Vol.502). (FRE.). 1999. mass mkt. 3.50 (*0-373-39502-7*, 1-39502-9) Harlequin Bks.

— Pixie Dust: Fabulous Father. (Romance Ser.). 1993. per. 2.75 (*0-373-08958-9*, 5-08958-6) Silhouette.

— Pop Goes the Question. (Yours Truly Ser.). 1997. per. 3.50 (*0-373-52037-9*, 1-52037-8) Silhouette.

— Pregnant with His Child. 1997. per. 3.25 (*0-373-19259-2*, 1-19259-0) Silhouette.

— The Princess's White Knight: Royally Wed. (Romance Ser.: Vol. 1415). 1999. per. 3.50 (*0-373-19415-3*, 1-19415-8) Silhouette.

— Reluctant Dad. 1998. per. 4.25 (*0-373-07856-0*, 1-07856-7) Silhouette.

— Reluctant Wife (Sisters) 1998. per. 4.25 (*0-373-07850-1*, 1-07850-0) Silhouette.

— Rodeo Dad: Mustang, Montana. (Intimate Moments Ser.: No. 934). 1999. per. 4.25 (*0-373-07934-6*, 1-07934-2) Silhouette.

— Something New. (Romance Ser.). 1993. per. 2.75 (*0-373-08942-2*, 5-08942-0) Silhouette.

***Cassidy, Carla.** Strangers When We Married. 2001. mass mkt. 4.50 (*0-373-27116-6*, 1-27116-2) Silhouette.

Cassidy, Carla. Sunrise Vows. (Cheyenne Nights Ser.). 1997. per. 3.75 (*0-373-22419-2*, 1-22419-5) Harlequin Bks.

— Sunset Promises: Cheyenne Nights. (Intrigue Ser.). 1997. per. 3.75 (*0-373-22411-7*, 1-22411-2) Harlequin Bks.

— Swamp Secrets. 1993. mass mkt. 3.50 (*0-373-27004-6*, 5-27004-6) Silhouette.

— Les Terreurs du Passe. (Amours d'Aujourd'Hui Ser.: Vol. 295). (FRE.). 1998. mass mkt. 4.99 (*0-373-38295-2*, 1-38295-1) Harlequin Bks.

— Their Only Child. (Intrigue Ser.: No. 447). 1997. per. 3.75 (*0-373-22447-8*, 1-22447-6) Harlequin Bks.

— Try to Remember. (Intimate Moments Ser.). 1994. per. 3.50 (*0-373-07560-X*, 5-07560-1) Silhouette.

— Under the Boardwalk. (Desire Ser.). 1994. per. 2.99 (*0-373-05882-9*, 1-05882-5) Silhouette.

***Cassidy, Carla.** Waiting for the Wedding. (Romance Ser.: Vol. 142). 2000. mass mkt. 3.50 (*0-373-19426-9*) Silhouette.

Cassidy, Carla. Whatever Alex Wants. (Romance Ser.: No. 856). 1992. per. 2.69 (*0-373-08856-6*, 5-08856-2) Silhouette.

— Whatever Alex Wants. large type ed. 217p. 1992. reprint ed. lib. bdg. 13.95 (*1-56054-460-0*) Thorndike Pr.

— Wife for a Week: Mustang, Montana. (Romance Ser.: No. 1400). 1999. per. 3.50 (*0-373-19400-5*, 1-19400-0) Silhouette.

— Will You Give My Mommy a Baby? (Romance Ser.). 1998. per. 3.50 (*0-373-19315-7*, 1-19315-0) Silhouette.

***Cassidy, Carol.** Girls in America: Their Stories, Their Words. LC 99-40418. (Illus.). 256p. 1999. 25.00 (*1-57500-084-9*, Pub. by TV Bks) HarpC.

Cassidy, Carol-June. Inside Law Schools. 7th ed. LC 97-38139. 384p. 1998. pap. 16.95 (*0-452-27946-1*, Plume) Dutton Plume.

Cassidy, Carole, ed. see Cassidy, Pete.

Cassidy, Christine, jt. ed. see Grier, Barbara.

Cassidy, Christine, ed. see Naiad Press Staff.

Cassidy, D. Going Back to School: Deciding to Return. Keppler, Kay, ed. LC 91-58540. (Fifty-Minute Ser.). (Illus.). 84p. (Orig.). 1992. pap. 10.95 (*1-56052-142-2*) Crisp Pubns.

Cassidy, Dan. Liability Exposures. 150p. (C). 1989. pap. 250.00 (*0-948691-75-1*, Pub. by Witherby & Co) St Mut.

***Cassidy, Daniel J.** Dan Cassidy's Worldwide College Scholarship Directory: Thousands of Top Scholarships Throughout the United States & Around the World. 5th rev. ed. 600p. 2000. pap. 23.99 (*1-56414-466-6*) Career Pr Inc.

— Dan Cassidy's Worldwide Graduate Scholarship Directory: Thousands of Top Scholarships Throughout the United States & Around the World. 5th rev. ed. 600p. 2000. pap. 26.99 (*1-56414-467-4*) Career Pr Inc.

— Last Minute College Financing: It's Never Too Late to Prepare for the Future. 128p. 2000. pap. 10.99 (*1-56414-468-2*) Career Pr Inc.

Cassidy, Daniel J. Scholarship Book: 2000 Edition. 1999. 35.95 (*0-13-020732-2*) P-H.

***Cassidy, Daniel J.** The Scholarship Book 2001: The Complete Guide to Private-Sector Scholarships, Fellowships, Grants, & Loans for the Undergraduate. 592p. 2000. pap. 25.00 (*0-7352-0165-X*); pap. 30.00 incl. cd-rom (*0-7352-0196-X*) PH Pr.

— Scholarship Book 2001. 2000. 48.00 (*0-13-027561-1*); 43.00 (*0-13-088008-6*) P-H.

Cassidy, Daniel J. & Alves, Michael J. The Scholarship Book: For Student Care Center. 1988. text 19.95 (*0-13-855677-6*) P-H.

— The Scholarship Book: The Complete Guide to Private-Sector Scholarships, Grants, & Loans for Undergraduates. 2nd ed. 1987. 29.95 (*0-13-792425-9*); 19.95 (*0-13-792417-8*) P-H.

Cassidy, David. Einstein & Our World. LC 94-17472. (Control of Nature Ser.). 112p. (C). 1995. pap. 12.50 (*0-391-03875-3*) Humanities.

Cassidy, David & Baker, Martha, compiled by. Werner Heisenberg: A Bibliography of His Writings. LC 82-60498. (Berkeley Papers in History of Science: No. 9). 153p. (Orig.). 1984. pap. 10.00 (*0-918102-10-3*) U Cal Hist Sci Tech.

Cassidy, David & Deffaa, Chip. C'mon Get Happy: Fear & Loathing on the Partridge Family Bus. 256p. (Orig.). 1994. mass mkt. 11.99 (*0-446-39531-5*, Pub. by Warner Bks) Little.

Cassidy, David C. Einstein & Our World. LC 98-52946. 1998. write for info. (*1-57392-714-7*); pap. write for info. (*1-57392-540-3*) Prometheus Bks.

— Uncertainty: The Life & Science of Werner Heisenberg. LC 91-13818. 1993. pap. text 21.95 (*0-7167-2503-7*) W H Freeman.

Cassidy, Dawn, jt. auth. see Powell, Lane H.

Cassidy, Donald L. It's When You Sell That Counts. 2nd rev. ed. LC 96-41901. 312p. 1996. text 24.95 (*0-7863-1129-0*, Irwn Prfssnl) McGraw-Hill Prof.

— It's When You Sell That Counts: A Must-Have Book for Anyone Who Owns Stocks. 1994. pap. 19.95 (*1-55738-596-3*, Irwn Prfssnl) McGraw-Hill Prof.

— Plugging into Utilities: A Safe & Sound Way to Superior Returns in the Stock Market. 250p. 1993. text 24.95 (*1-55738-498-3*, Irwn Prfssnl) McGraw-Hill Prof.

Cassidy, Donna M. Painting the Musical City: Jazz & Cultural Identity in American Art, 1910-1940. LC 96-44169. (Illus.). 240p. 1997. text 45.00 (*1-56098-677-8*) Smithsonian.

Cassidy, Ed. Hawaii Trivia. 192p. (Orig.). 1996. pap. 6.95 (*1-55853-422-9*) Rutledge Hill Pr.

Cassidy, Eoin, jt. auth. see Murphy, Anne.

Cassidy, Eric, jt. auth. see Dixon, Joan B.

Cassidy, F. G. The Place-Names of Dane County, Wisconsin. (Publications of the American Dialect Society: No. 7). 255p. 1947. pap. text 23.50 (*0-8173-0607-2*) U of Ala Pr.

Cassidy, F. J. & Ringler, R. Bright's Old English Grammar. 3rd ed. LC 76-179921. (C). 1972. text 51.50 (*0-03-084713-3*, Pub. by Harcourt Coll Pubs) Harcourt.

Cassidy, Frank. Reaching Just Settlements: Land Claims in British Columbia. 153p. 1991. pap. text 15.95 (*0-88645-122-1*, Pub. by Inst Res Pub) Ashgate Pub Co.

Cassidy, Frank, ed. Aboriginal Self-Determination. 296p. 1991. pap. text 15.95 (*0-88982-111-9*, Pub. by Oolichan Bks) Genl Dist Srvs.

— Aboriginal Title in British Columbia: Delgamuukw Versus The Queen. 320p. 1992. text 18.95 (*0-88982-115-1*, Pub. by Oolichan Bks) Genl Dist Srvs.

Cassidy, Frank & Seward, Shirley B., eds. Alternatives to Social Assistance in Indian Communities. 120p. 1993. pap. 17.00 (*0-88645-137-X*, Pub. by Inst Res Pub) Ashgate Pub Co.

Cassidy, Frederic G. Modern American Plays. 501p. 1977. 26.95 (*0-8369-8201-0*) Ayer.

Cassidy, Frederic G., ed. Dictionary of American Regional English, Vol. 1 A-C. (Illus.). 1056p. 1985. text 75.00 (*0-674-20511-1*) Belknap Pr.

Cassidy, Frederic G. & Duckert, Audrey R. The ADS Dictionary - How Soon?; The Linguistic Atals of New England Revisited. (Publications of the American Dialect Society: No. 39). 27p. 1963. pap. 2.70 (*0-8173-0639-0*) U of Ala Pr.

C

— A Method for Collecting Dialect. 2nd ed. (Publications of the American Dialect Society: No. 20). 96p. 1970. reprint ed. pap. text 9.60 (0-8173-0620-X) U of Ala Pr.

Cassidy, Frederic G. & Hall, Joan H., eds. Dictionary of American Regional English, Vol. 2 D-H. 1175p. (C). 1991. text 70.00 (0-674-20512-X) Belknap Pr.

— Dictionary of American Regional English, Vol. III. (Illus.). 960p. 1996. 75.00 (0-674-20519-7) Belknap Pr.

Cassidy, Frederic G., jt. auth. see Wood, Gordon R.

Cassidy, Harold G. Knowledge, Experience & Action: An Essay on Education. LC 70-81590. 219p. reprint ed. pap. 67.90 (0-608-14960-8, 202599900048) Bks Demand.

Cassidy, Harold G., jt. auth. see Haskell, Edward F.

Cassidy, Hope & Brady-Thomas, Marilyn. T. H. E. ASN Clinical Practice Laboratory Handbook. (Illus.). 128p. (C). 1999. pap. text 149.00 (1-884591-47-7) T H E Educ.

— T. H. E. BSN Clinical Practice Laboratory Handbook. (Illus.). 71p. (C). 1999. pap. text 149.00 (1-884591-46-9) T H E Educ.

Cassidy, J. J., jt. auth. see Hejelmfelt, A. T., Jr.

Cassidy, J. J., ed. see Hejelmfelt, A. T., Jr.

Cassidy, Jack, et al. A Shortcut Through Adventureland, Vol. I. write for info. (0-318-58217-1) P-H.

***Cassidy, James & Bissett, D.** Oxford Handbook of Oncology. (Illus.). 2000. pap. text 29.95 (0-19-263035-0) OUP.

Cassidy, James, ed. see Isaac, James.

Cassidy, James A. Study of Browning's Ring & the Book. LC 74-117581. (Studies in Browning: No. 4). 1970. reprint ed. lib. bdg. 75.00 (0-8383-1014-1) M S G Haskell Hse.

***Cassidy, James G.** Ferdinand V. Hayden: Entrepreneur of Science. LC 99-58427. (Illus.). 416p. 2000. text 55.00 (0-8032-1507-X) U of Nebr Pr.

Cassidy, James T. Textbook of Pediatric Rheumatology. LC 82-4951. (Illus.). 700p. reprint ed. pap. 200.00 (0-8357-6572-5, 203595300097) Bks Demand.

Cassidy, James T. & Petty, Ross E. Textbook of Pediatric Rheumatology. 2nd ed. LC 89-22236. (Illus.). 619p. reprint ed. pap. 191.90 (0-7837-6713-7, 204634000011) Bks Demand.

— Textbook of Pediatric Rheumatology. 3rd ed. LC 94-33337. (Illus.). 622p. 1994. text 145.00 (0-7216-5244-1, W B Saunders Co) Harcrt Hlth Sci Grp.

C

Cassidy, Janet. Civil War: Literature Units, Projects & Activities. 128p. 1993. pap. 10.95 (0-590-49509-7) Scholastic Inc.

— Homecoming: A Study Guide. Friedland, J. & Kessler, R., eds. (Novel-Ties Ser.). (J). (gr. 6-8). 1993. pap. text, student ed. 15.95 (0-88122-907-5) Lrn Links.

— The House with a Clock in Its Walls: A Study Guide. Friedland, J. & Kessler, R., eds. (Novel-Ties Ser.). (J). (gr. 3-5). 1992. pap. text, student ed. 15.95 (0-88122-728-5) Lrn Links.

Cassidy, John. Earthsearch: A Kids' Geography Museum in a Book. LC 95-124635. 110p. (J). 1994. spiral bd. 19.95 (1-878257-74-9) Klutz.

— The Klutz Book of Knots. (Illus.). 21p. (Orig.). 1985. pap. 10.95 (0-932592-10-4) Klutz.

— Night Cries. 1982. pap. 12.95 (0-906427-45-2, Pub. by Bloodaxe Bks) Dufour.

— The Official Icky-Poo Book. (Illus.). 70p. (Orig.). 1990. pap. 10.95 (0-932592-90-2) Klutz.

— The Time Book. (Illus.). 32p. (J). (ps-8). 1991. spiral bd. 10.95 (1-878257-08-0) Klutz.

— The Unbelievable Bubble Book. 138p. (Orig.). 1987. pap. 12.95 (0-932592-15-5) Klutz.

— Walking on Frogs. LC 89-84279. 64p. 1990. pap. 11.95 (1-85224-089-X, Pub. by Bloodaxe Bks) Dufour.

Cassidy, John & Rimbeaux, B. C. Juggling for the Complete Klutz. 3rd rev. ed. (Illus.). 75p. (YA). 1978. pap. 10.95 (0-932592-00-7) Klutz.

Cassidy, John, et al. Zap Science: A Scientific Playground in a Book. (Illus.). 66p. (J). (gr. 2 up). 1997. spiral bd. 19.95 (1-57054-108-6) Klutz.

Cassidy, John, jt. auth. see Blake, Quentin.

Cassidy, John, jt. auth. see Cassidy, Nancy.

Cassidy, John, jt. auth. see Doherty, Paul.

Cassidy, John, jt. auth. see Exploratorium Staff.

Cassidy, John, jt. auth. see Hurd, Thacher.

Cassidy, John, jt. auth. see Stroud, Mike.

Cassidy, John J., ed. Waterpower, '95: Proceedings; International Conference on Hydropower (1995: San Francisco, Calif.), 3 vols. LC 95-24175. 2868p. 1995. pap. 209.00 (0-7844-0099-7) Am Soc Civil Eng.

Cassidy, John J. & Lettenmaier, Dennis P., eds. A Critical Assessment of Forecasting in Water Quality Goals in Western Water Resources Management: Proceedings of a Symposium Held in Seattle, Washington. LC 85-71659. (American Water Resources Association Technical Publication Ser.: No. TPS-84-1). (Illus.). 189p. reprint ed. pap. 58.60 (0-8357-3167-7, 203943000012) Bks Demand.

***Cassidy, Jude & Shaver, Phillip R., eds.** Handbook of Attachment: Theory, Research & Clinical Applications. LC 98-53527. 925p. 1999. 85.00 (1-57230-087-6) Guilford Pubns.

Cassidy, Jules, jt. auth. see Stewart-Park, Angela.

Cassidy, Julie. Concise Corporations Law. 350p. 1995. pap. 39.00 (1-86287-166-3, Pub. by Federation Pr) Gaunt.

— Concise Corporations Law. 2nd ed. 360p. 1999. pap. 44.00 (1-86287-326-7, Pub. by Federation Pr) Gaunt.

— Manual of Income Tax. 332p. 1997. pap. 49.00 (1-86287-261-9, Pub. by Federation Pr) Gaunt.

Cassidy, Kevin A. Fire Safety & Loss Prevention. (Illus.). 198p. 1992. 56.95 (0-7506-9039-9) Buttrwrth-Heinemann.

Cassidy, Kevin J. & Bischak, Gregory A., eds. Real Security: Converting the Defense Economy & Building Peace. LC 93-32011. (SUNY Series, Global Conflict & Peace Education). 308p. (C). 1993. pap. text 21.95 (0-7914-1608-9) State U NY Pr.

— Real Security: Converting the Defense Economy & Building Peace. LC 93-32011. (SUNY Series, Global Conflict & Peace Education). 308p. (C). 1993. text 64.50 (0-7914-1607-0) State U NY Pr.

Cassidy, Laura. Judith's Place. large type ed. 350p. 1996. 23.99 (0-263-14527-1, Pub. by Mills & Boon) Ulverscroft.

— A Remembered Love. large type ed. 350p. 1995. 23.99 (0-263-14191-8, Pub. by Mills & Boon) Ulverscroft.

Cassidy, Laurence L. The Thinking Self. 133p. (Orig.). 1993. pap. 28.00 (0-9626761-3-6) Al H Morrison.

— The Thinking Self. LC 97-21573. 168p. (Orig.). 1997. pap. 24.50 (0-7618-0793-4) U Pr of Amer.

Cassidy, Maggie B. Taking Students Abroad: A Complete Guide for Teachers. rev. ed. (Illus.). 176p. 1988. pap. text 2.00 (0-86647-028-X) Pro Lingua.

Cassidy, Marsh. Acting Step by Step. LC 88-8500. (Illus.). 186p. (C). 1990. pap. text 10.00 (0-89390-120-2, Pub. by Resource Pubns) Empire Pub Srvs.

Cassidy, Marsh, jt. auth. see Sturkie, Joan.

***Cassidy, Michael.** Christianity for the Open-Minded, Vol. 5. 1999. pap. 4.95 (0-8308-6570-5) InterVarsity.

Cassidy, Michael A., jt. ed. see Becker, Scott.

Cassidy, Nancy. Kids' Songs Jubilee. (Illus.). 50p. (J). 1990. spiral bd. 11.95 incl. audio (0-932592-84-8) Klutz.

— KidsSongs Sleepyheads. 50p. (J). spiral bd. 11.95 incl. audio (1-878257-11-0) Klutz.

— Patterns of History Through Cycles of Time, 2 vols. Incl. Vol. I. World Events. 299p. 1997. pap. 22.00 (0-89540-355-2, Sun Bks); Vol. II. American Presidents. 288p. 1998. pap. 22.00 (0-89540-356-0, Sun Bks); 1997. pap. write for info. (0-89540-357-9, Sun Bks) Sun Pub.

Cassidy, Nancy & Cassidy, John. The Book of Kids' Songs: A Holler-Along Handbook. (Illus.). 86p. (J). (ps-6). 1986. spiral bd. 11.95 incl. audio (0-932592-13-9) Klutz.

— The Book of Kids' Songs 2: Another Holler-Along Handbook. (Illus.). 70p. (J). (ps-6). 1988. spiral bd. 11.95 incl. audio (0-932592-20-1) Klutz.

Cassidy, Norma C. Favorite Novenas & Prayers, New Edition. LC 90-36453. 144p. 1972. pap. 6.95 (0-8091-3205-2, DEUS) Paulist Pr.

Cassidy, Patrick E. Thermally Stable Polymers: Syntheses & Properties. LC 80-18571. (Illus.). 413p. reprint ed. pap. 128.10 (0-608-08916-8, 206955100005) Bks Demand.

***Cassidy, Paul R.** Verifiable Adjunct to the Christian Theological System. 2000. pap. 16.00 (0-8059-4994-1) Dorrance.

Cassidy, Pete. Pete Cassidy's Oracle Cookbook for SQL Plus. Cassidy, Carole, ed. (Illus.). 228p. (Orig.). 1995. pap. 29.95 (0-9656696-0-2) Chef Pierre.

***Cassidy, Peter.** A Guide to European Financial Markets. 350p. 2001. pap. 35.00 (1-86076-134-8, Pub. by Oak Tr) Midpt Trade.

Cassidy, Richard J. Jesus, Politics & Society: A Study of Luke's Gospel. LC 78-735. 240p. reprint ed. pap. 74.40 (0-8357-4075-7, 203676500005) Bks Demand.

Cassidy, Richard J. & Scharper, Philip J., eds. Political Issues in Luke - Acts. LC 82-19060. 192p. (Orig.). reprint ed. pap. 59.60 (0-8357-2669-X, 204020500015) Bks Demand.

Cassidy, Robert C. & Fleischman, Alan R., eds. Pediatric Ethics - From Principles to Practice. (Mongraphs in Clinical Pediatrics Ser). 224p. 1996. text 36.00 (3-7186-5756-2, Harwood Acad Pubs) Gordon & Breach.

Cassidy, S. B., ed. Prader-Willi Syndrome & Other Chromosome 15q Deletion Disorders. (NATO ASI Series H: Cell Biology: Vol. 61). (Illus.). xvi, 265p. 1992. 181.95 (0-387-53095-9) Spr-Verlag.

Cassidy, Samuel M., ed. Elements of Practical Coal Mining. LC 72-86921. 622p. 1973. reprint ed. pap. 192.90 (0-608-14284-0, 201741900005) Bks Demand.

Cassidy, Sheila. Good Friday People. 1991. pap. 13.50 (0-88344-741-X) Orbis Bks.

— The Loneliest Journey. pap. write for info. (0-232-52120-4) S Asia.

— Sharing the Darkness: The Spirituality of Caring. LC 91-28462. 1992. pap. 12.50 (0-88344-779-7) Orbis Bks.

Cassidy, Sheila, ed. Remembering Jack & Bobby: An Anthology. LC 92-70109. 108p. (Orig.). 1992. pap. 12.95 (0-9630485-2-X) In Print.

Cassidy, Steven. Building the Future: Jewish Immigrant Intellectuals & the Making of TSUKUNFT. LC 98-44814. (New Perspectives Ser.). (Illus.). 1999. 39.50 (0-8419-1372-2) Holmes & Meier.

Cassidy, Steven, jt. auth. see Harrington, Jonathan.

Cassidy, Susan J., pseud, et al. We Have Lived & Loved Before. LC 91-77037. (Illus.). 64p. (Orig.). 1992. pap. 7.95 (1-879559-05-6) Galaxy OH.

Cassidy, T. K. Dolphin, Dolphin. Maeshino, Hiroshi, tr. (ENG & JPN., Illus.). 32p. (J). (gr. 3 up). 1997. pap. 8.00 (0-9660152-1-5) Cassidy Wdsmith.

— The Stone-Shaper's Daughter. Kang, Toyoko, tr. (ENG & JPN., Illus.). 32p. (J). (gr. 3 up). 1996. pap. 8.00 (0-9660152-0-7) Cassidy Wdsmith.

Cassidy, Thomas M. Elder Care: What to Look for... What to Look Out For. 188p. 1999. pap. 14.95 (0-88282-153-9) New Horizon NJ.

Cassidy, Tony. Environmental Psychology: Behaviour & Experience in Context. LC 97-202071. (Illus.). vi, 282p. 1997. write for info. (0-86377-480-6, Pub. by Psychol Pr) Taylor & Francis.

— Immobilized Biomolecules in Analysis: A Practical Approach. LC 99-214745. 198. 240p. 1999. pap. text 49.95 (0-19-963636-2) OUP.

***Cassidy, Tony.** Immobilized Biomolecules in Analysis: A Practical Approach. LC 99-214745. 198. 240p. 1999. text 105.00 (0-19-963637-0) OUP.

Cassidy, Vincent & Simpson, Amos. Traveling Man: The Life Story of Henry Watkins Allen. (J). 1967. 6.50 (0-87511-017-7) Claitors.

Cassidy, Virginia, jt. ed. see Stevens, Kathleen R.

Cassidy, William. Complete Book of Knife Fighting. (Illus.). 136p. 1993. pap. 25.00 (0-87364-029-2) Paladin Pr.

— Memorial of William Cassidy. LC 73-125684. (American Journalists Ser.). 1978. reprint ed. 19.95 (0-405-01661-1) Ayer.

Cassidy, William, ed. Bioengineering & Cabin Ecology (AAS/AAAS Symposium) Dec. 30, 1968, Dallas, TX: AAS/AAAS Symposium, Dallas, TX, Dec. 30, 1968. (Science & Technology Ser.: Vol. 20). (Illus.). 162p. 1969. 20.00 (0-87703-048-0, Am Astronaut Soc) Univelt Inc.

***Cassie, Brian.** Amphibians. LC 98-40931. (National Audubon Society First Field Guides Ser.). (Illus.). 160p. (YA). (gr. 3-7). 1999. 17.95 (0-590-63982-X, Pub. by Scholastic Inc); vinyl bd. 11.95 (0-590-64008-9, Pub. by Scholastic Inc) Penguin Putnam.

— Butterfly Alphabet Book. LC 95-7066. 1995. 12.15 (0-606-09121-1, Pub. by Turtleback) Demco.

— Say It Again. LC 99-13394. (Illus.). 32p. (J). (ps-3). 2000. 16.95 (0-88106-341-X); pap. 6.95 (0-88106-342-8) Charlesbridge Pub.

— Shells. LC 99-46831. (National Audubon Society First Field Guides Ser.). (Illus.). 160p. (gr. 4-7). 2000. pap. 8.95 (0-590-64258-8) Scholastic Inc.

Cassie, Brian & Burns, Marjorie. National Audubon Society First Field Guide. LC 98-21855. (Illus.). 159p. (J). (gr. 3-7). 1999. 17.95 (0-590-05472-4); pap. 11.95 (0-590-05490-2) Scholastic Inc.

***Cassie, Brian & National Audubon Society Staff.** Shells. LC 99-46831. (Illus.). 160p. (J). (gr. 4-7). 2000. 17.95 (0-590-64233-2) Scholastic Inc.

Cassie, Brian & Pallotta, Jerry. The Butterfly Alphabet Book. LC 95-7066. (Jerry Pallotta's Alphabet Bks.). (Illus.). 32p. (J). (ps-3). 1995. 15.95 (0-88106-895-0); pap. 6.95 (0-88106-894-2) Charlesbridge Pub.

Cassie, Noel A. Statistics for Spatial Data. 2nd rev. ed. 928p. 1993. 126.00 (0-471-00255-0) Wiley.

Cassie, Vivienne. A Contribution to the Study of New Zealand Diatoms. (Bibliotheca Diatomologica Ser.: Vol. 17). (Illus.). iv, 266p. 1989. pap. text 77.00 (3-443-57008-9, Pub. by Gebruder Borntraeger) Balogh.

Cassie, W. F. Structural Analysis: The Solution of Statically Indeterminate Structures. 3rd ed. LC 67-72611. 295p. reprint ed. pap. 91.50 (0-608-11637-8, 200491400047) Bks Demand.

Cassileth, Barrie. The Alternative Medicine Handbook: The Complete Reference Guide to Alternative & Complementary Therapies. LC 97-16268. 352p. 1998. 25.00 (0-393-04566-8) Norton.

Cassileth, Barrie R. The Alternative Medicine Handbook: The Complete Reference Guide to Alternative & Complementary Therapies. (Illus.). 352p. 1999. pap. 19.95 (0-393-31816-8, Norton Paperbks) Norton.

Cassileth, Barrie R., ed. The Cancer Patient: Social & Medical Aspects of Care. LC 79-11338. (Illus.). 344p. reprint ed. pap. 106.70 (0-8357-7641-7, 205696500096) Bks Demand.

Cassileth, Barrie R. & Cassileth, Peter A., eds. Clinical Care of the Terminal Cancer Patient. LC 82-15222. 286p. reprint ed. pap. 88.70 (0-7837-1482-3, 205717700023) Bks Demand.

Cassileth, Peter A., jt. ed. see Cassileth, Barrie R.

***Cassill & Bausch.** Anthology of Short Fiction. 6th ed. LC 99-47447. 2000. pap. text 35.00 (0-393-97508-8) Norton.

Cassill, R. Norton Anthology of Contemporary Fiction. 2nd ed. (C). 1997. pap., teacher ed. write for info. (0-393-96834-0) Norton.

Cassill, R. V. Clem Anderson. 1990. pap. 12.95 (0-916366-61-8, Pub. by Pushcart Pr) Norton.

— Late Stories (Chapbook) 50p. 1995. pap. 5.00 (0-916092-23-2) Tex Ctr Writers.

Cassill, R. V. Norton Anthology of Contemporary Fiction. (Orig.). (C). 1987. pap. text 33.50 (0-393-95619-9) Norton.

Cassill, R. V. Three Stories. LC 82-82012. 75p. (Orig.). 1982. pap. 4.50 (0-9605008-1-2) Hermes Hse Pr.

Cassill, R. V., ed. The Norton Anthology of Short Fiction. 5th ed. LC 94-42761. 1718p. (C). 1995. pap. 33.00 (0-393-96663-1); pap. 37.00 (0-393-96664-X) Norton.

— The Norton Anthology of Short Fiction. 5th ed. (C). 1995. pap. text, teacher ed. write for info. (0-393-96703-4) Norton.

***Cassill, R. V. & Bausch, Richard.** The Anthology of Short Fiction. 6th ed. LC 99-45756. 2000. 27.50 (0-393-97509-6) Norton.

Cassill, R. V. & Oates, Joyce Carol. The Norton Anthology of Contemporary Fiction. 2nd ed. LC 96-51171. 556p. (C). 1997. pap. text 37.50 (0-393-96833-2) Norton.

Cassill, R. V. & White, James. Two Short Novels. 180p. 1991. 25.00 (0-685-40747-0); pap. 9.95 (0-685-40748-9) Soft Teach Inc.

— Two Short Novels: Unknown Soldier by R. V. Cassill - Clara's Call by James White. 154p. (Orig.). 1993. pap. 9.95 (0-916092-12-7) Tex Ctr Writers.

Cassill, R. V. & White, James P. Two Short Novels: The Unknown Soldier & Clara's Call. 161p. (Orig.). (C). 1991. text 19.95 (0-916092-14-3) Tex Ctr Writers.

Cassill, Ronald V. The Happy Marriage & Other Stories. LC 66-63480. 122p. 1966. 49.95 (0-911198-11-3) Purdue U Pr.

— In an Iron Time: Statements & Reiterations. LC 69-11273. 140p. 1969. 49.95 (0-911198-17-2) Purdue U Pr.

Cassils, J. Anthony. The Financial Services Industry & Sustainable Development: Managing Information & Risk in Canada. 30p. (Orig.). 1996. pap. text 35.00 (0-7881-2800-0) DIANE Pub.

Cassiman, Bart, et al. The Sublime Void: On the Memory of the Imagination. (Illus.). 280p. 55.00 (90-5544-002-7) Dist Art Pubs.

Cassimatis, Jack. The Super Stain Remover Book. LC 96-25720. 80p. 1996. pap. 5.95 (0-8069-9483-5) Sterling.

Cassimatis, Louis P. American Influence in Greece, 1917-1929. LC 88-3012. (Illus.). 320p. 1988. 25.00 (0-87338-357-5) Kent St U Pr.

Cassimatis, P. A Concise Introduction to Engineering Economics. 288p. 1988. text 60.00 (0-04-445038-9); pap. text 29.95 (0-04-445047-8) Routledge.

— A Concise Introduction to Engineering Economics. (Illus.). 384p. (C). 1988. pap. 39.99 (0-419-15910-X, E & FN Spon) Routledge.

Cassimatis, Peter. Introduction to Managerial Economics. LC 95-22195. 1995. pap. 90.95 (0-415-12754-8); pap. 23.99 (0-415-12755-6) Thomson Learn.

Cassin, Barbara. Fundamentals for Ophthalmic Technical Personnel. Hamed, Latif M., ed. (Illus.). 464p. 1995. text 54.00 (0-7216-4931-9, W B Saunders Co) Harcrt Hlth Sci Grp.

Cassin, Barbara & Solomon, Sheila A. Dictionary of Eye Terminology. 3rd rev. ed. Rubin, Melvin L., ed. (Illus.). 288p. 1997. spiral bd. 24.95 (0-937404-44-6) Triad Pub FL.

Cassin, Craig. Optical Designs in Motion: With 3 Different Moire Screens. LC 96-54604. (Clip-Art Ser.). (Illus.). 1997. pap. 8.95 (0-486-29571-0) Dover.

Cassin, Elena & Glassner, Jean-Jacques. Anthroponymie et Anthropologie de Nuzi: Les Anthroponymes, Vol. 1. (FRE.). 187p. 1977. 52.00 (0-89003-024-3) Undena Pubns.

Cassin, John. United States Exploring Expedition During the Years 1838, 1839, 1840, 1841, 1842 under the Command Charles Wilkes, U.S.N., 2 vols., Vol. 8. Sterling, Keir B., ed. LC 77-81079. (Biologists & Their World Ser.). (Illus.). 1979. reprint ed. lib. bdg. 52.95 (0-405-10656-4) Ayer.

Cassin, John D. How to Lead So Others Follow: A Guide to Leading the Diverse Workforce of Today & Tomorrow. 120p. 1997. pap. 13.95 (0-9660766-0-5) JDC Solns.

Cassin, Maxine. The Other Side of Sleep: Selected Poems of Maxine Cassin. 2nd ed. LC 95-71175. (Illus.). 144p. 1995. pap. 11.00 (0-916620-50-6) Portals Pr.

Cassin, Maxine, et al, eds. The Maple Leaf Rag: An Anthology of New Orleans Poetry. (Illus.). 116p. (Orig.). 1980. pap. 25.00 (0-938498-01-0) New Orleans Poetry.

Cassin, Maxine, ed. see Black, Charles.

Cassin, Maxine, ed. see DeGravelles, Charles.

Cassin, Maxine, ed. see Favorite, Malaika.

Cassin, Maxine, ed. see Maddox, Everette.

Cassin, Maxine, ed. see McFerren, Martha.

Cassin, Maxine, ed. see Miller, Raeburn.

Cassin, Maxine, ed. see Miller, Vassar.

Cassin, Michael. More Than Meets the Eye. (National Gallery Publications). (Illus.). 1990. pap. 16.00 (0-300-06161-7) Yale U Pr.

Cassin-Scott, Jack. The Greek & Persian Wars 500-323 B.C. (Men-at-Arms Ser.: No. 69). (Illus.). 48p. pap. 11.95 (0-85045-271-6, 9015, Pub. by Ospry) Stackpole.

— The Illustrated Encyclopedia of Costume & Fashion: From 1066 to the Present. (Illus.). 192p. 1994. 27.95 (0-289-80093-5, Pub. by SVista Bks) Sterling.

— Stage Costume Sourcebook. 1999. 29.95 (0-304-35068-0, Pub. by Cassell) Sterling.

Cassinari, Ramon P. The Legend of Little Nessie. (Illus.). 24p. (J). (gr. k-4). 1997. 14.95 (0-9654002-0-4) Little Lochness.

Cassinari, Valentino & Pagni, Carlo A. Central Pain: A Neurosurgical Survey. LC 68-54017. (Illus.). 102p. 1969. 21.50 (0-674-10540-0) HUP.

Cassinelli, Dennis. Gathering Traces of the Great Basin Indians. LC 96-60066. (Illus.). 160p. (Orig.). 1996. pap. 19.95 (0-936029-45-5) Western Bk Journ.

Cassinelli, Joseph P., jt. auth. see Lamers, Henry.

Cassinelli, Mary E., jt. ed. see Eller, Peter M.

Cassingham, Barbee J. & O'Neil, Sally M. And Then I Met This Woman: Previously Married Women's Journeys into Lesbian Relationships. 2nd rev. ed. LC 98-60940. 281p. 1999. pap. 14.95 (0-9658844-1-4) Soar Eagle.

Cassingham, R. C. The Dvorak Keyboard: The Ergonomically Designed Typewriter Keyboard. (Illus.). 96p. 1986. pap. 12.95 (0-935309-10-1) Freelance Comm.

Cassingham, Randy. Artificial Intelligence Like Real Thing: And 500 Other Bizarre-but-True Stories & Headlines from the World's Press. (This Is True Ser.: Vol. 4). 158p. 1998. pap. 11.00 (0-935309-24-1) Freelance Comm.

— This is True: Deputy Kills Man with Hammer: And 500 Other Bizarre-but-True Stories & Headlines from the World's Press. LC 95-61330. (This Is True Ser.: Vol. 1). 160p. (Orig.). 1995. pap. 11.00 (0-935309-21-7) Freelance Comm.

— This is True: Glow-in-the-Dark Plants Could Help Farmers: And 500 Other Bizarre-but True Stories & from the World's Press. LC 98-111239. (This Is True Ser.: Vol. 2). 160p. (Orig.). 1996. pap. 11.00 (0-935309-22-5) Freelance Comm.

— This is True: Pit Bulls Love You, Really: And 500 Other Bizarre-but-True Stories & Headlines from the World's Press. LC 99-173664. (This Is True Ser.: No. 3). 158p. 1998. pap. 11.00 (0-935309-23-3) Freelance Comm.

Cassini. Cassini on Compositae III: From Journal de Physique, de Chimie, d'Histoire Naturelle et des Arts... 507p. 1995. 48.00 (0-915279-32-0, MSB-55) Miss Botan.

— Cassini on Compositae II: Collected from the Bulletin Des Sciences Par la Societe Philomatique de Paris. rev. ed. (Monographs in Systematic Botany from the Missouri Botanical Garden: No. 54). (FRE.). 190p. 1995. pap. 24.00 (*0-915279-31-2*) Miss Botan.

Cassini, J. Now You Can Dance. (Ballroom Dance Ser.). 1986. lib. bdg. 69.95 (*0-8490-3264-4*) Gordon Pr.

Cassini, Kathleen K. & Rogers, Jacqueline L. Death & the Classroom: A Teacher's Guide to Assist Grieving Students. LC 89-85498. 108p. (C). 1996. reprint ed. pap. text 17.95 (*0-9627002-1-5*) Griefwrk OH.

Cassini, Oleg. A Thousand Days of Magic: Dressing Jacqueline Kennedy for the White House. LC 95-15119. (Illus.). 224p. 1995. 42.50 (*0-8478-1900-0*, Pub. by Rizzoli Intl) St Martin.

Cassinis, R., et al, eds. Digital Seismology & Fine Modeling of the Lithosphere. (Ettore Majorana International Science Series, Life Sciences: Vol. 42). (Illus.). 432p. 1989. 115.00 (*0-306-43211-0*, Plenum Trade) Perseus Pubng.

Cassir, Chris, jt. auth. see Bell, Michael G. H.

Cassirer, Bruce. Travel & the Single Male: The World's Best Destinations for the Single Male. 256p. 1992. pap. 14.95 (*0-9634234-0-1*) TSM Pub.

Cassirer, E. Las Ciencias de la Cultura. (Breviarios Ser.). (SPA.). pap. 8.99 (*968-16-0613-2*, Pub. by Fondo) Continental Bk.

Cassirer, Ernst. Das Erkenntnisproblem in der Philosophie und Wissenschaft der Neuren Zeit. (GER.). 1997. 498.00 (*3-487-04061-1*) G Olms Pubs.

— Essay on Man: An Introduction to a Philosophy of Human Culture. (C). 1962. pap. 16.00 (*0-300-00034-0*, Y52) Yale U Pr.

***Cassirer, Ernst.** The Individual & the Cosmos in Renaissance Philosophy. 2000. pap. 7.95 (*0-486-41438-8*) Dover.

Cassirer, Ernst. Kant, Vida y Doctrina. (Breviarios Ser.). (SPA.). pap. 6.99 (*968-16-0571-3*, Pub. by Fondo) Continental Bk.

— Kant's Life & Thought. Haden, James, tr. from GER. LC 81-3354. 464p. (C). 1981. 60.00 (*0-300-02358-8*) Yale U Pr.

— Kant's Life & Thought. Haden, James, tr. from GER. LC 81-3354. 464p. (C). 1983. pap. 20.00 (*0-300-02982-9*) Yale U Pr.

— Language & Myth. Langer, Susanne K., tr. 103p. 1953. pap. 4.95 (*0-486-20051-5*) Dover.

— Leibniz' System in Seinen Wissenschaftlichen Grundlagen. (GER.). 1980. reprint ed. write for info. (*3-487-00318-X*) G Olms Pubs.

***Cassirer, Ernst.** The Logic of the Cultural Sciences: Five Studies. Lofts, S. G., tr. & intro. by. LC 00-25024. 208p. 2000. 30.00 (*0-300-08114-6*) Yale U Pr.

Cassirer, Ernst. The Myth of the State. (C). 1961. pap. 15.00 (*0-300-00036-7*, y33) Yale U Pr.

— The Myth of the State. LC 82-18392. 303p. 1983. reprint ed. lib. bdg. 38.50 (*0-313-23790-5*, CAMO, Greenwood Pr) Greenwood.

— Philosophy of Symbolic Forms, Vol. 1, Language. Manheim, Ralph, tr. Vol. 1. (C). 1965. pap. 20.00 (*0-300-00037-5*, Y146) Yale U Pr.

— Philosophy of Symbolic Forms, Vol. 2, Mythical Thought. Manheim, Ralph, tr. Vol. 2. (C). 1965. pap. 18.00 (*0-300-00038-3*, Y147) Yale U Pr.

— The Philosophy of Symbolic Forms, Vol. 3, The Phenomenology Of Knowledge. Manheim, Ralph, tr. 1965. pap. 22.00 (*0-300-00039-1*, Y148) Yale U Pr.

***Cassirer, Ernst.** The Philosophy of Symbolic Forms Vol. 4: The Metaphysics of Symbolic Forms. Krois, John M., ed. & tr. by. Verene, Donald Phillip, ed. 272p. 1998. pap. 16.00 (*0-300-07433-6*) Yale U Pr.

Cassirer, Ernst. The Philosophy of Symbolic Forms Vol. 4: The Metaphysics of Symbolic Forms with an Essay On... LC 52-13969. 272p. 1996. 40.00 (*0-300-06278-8*) Yale U Pr.

— The Philosophy of the Enlightenment. Koelin, F. & Pettegrove, J., trs. from FRE. 384p. 1951. pap. text 18.95 (*0-691-01963-0*, Pub. by Princeton U Pr) Cal Prin Full Svc.

— Platonic Renaissance in England. LC 71-128186. 207p. (C). 1970. reprint ed. 50.00 (*0-87752-128-X*) Gordian.

— Problem of Knowledge: Philosophy, Science, & History Since Hegel. Woglom, William H. & Hendel, Charles W., trs. 1969. pap. 18.00 (*0-300-01098-2*, Y211) Yale U Pr.

— Symbol, Myth & Culture: Essays & Lectures of Ernst Cassirer, 1935-1945. Verene, Donald Phillip, ed. LC 78-9887. 316p. reprint ed. pap. 98.00 (*0-8357-3742-X*, 203646800003) Bks Demand.

Cassirer, Ernst, et al, eds. Renaissance Philosophy of Man: Petrarca, Valla, Ficino, Pico, Pomponazzi, Vives. LC 48-9358. 405p. 1956. pap. text 15.00 (*0-226-09604-1*, P1) U Ch Pr.

***Cassirer, Ernst & Lofts, Steve G.** The Logic of the Cultural Sciences: Five Studies. LC 00-25024. 208p. 2000. pap. 15.00 (*0-300-08115-4*) Yale U Pr.

Cassirer, Ernst, jt. auth. see Bayer, Thora I.

Cassirer, Heinrich W. God's New Covenant: A New Testament Translation. LC 89-23653. 512p. (Orig.). reprint ed. pap. 158.80 (*0-7837-6408-1*, 204638800012) Bks Demand.

— Grace & Law: St. Paul, Kant & the Hebrew Prophets. LC 88-16365. 192p. reprint ed. pap. 59.60 (*0-7837-6556-8*, 204612100011) Bks Demand.

Cassirer, Thomas, tr. see Diderot, Denis.

Cassirer, Thomas, tr. see Gregoire, Henri.

Cassis, jt. auth. see Cottrell.

Cassis, A. F. Graham Greene: An Annotated Bibliography of Criticism. LC 81-770. (Author Bibliographies Ser.: No. 55). 423p. 1981. 45.00 (*0-8108-1418-8*) Scarecrow.

Cassis, A. F., ed. see Greene, Graham.

Cassis, G. & Gross, G. F. Zoological Catalogue of Australia Vol. 27.3A: Hemiptera: Heteroptera I. 524p. 1995. 79.95 (*0-643-05704-8*, Pub. by CSIRO) Accents Pubns.

Cassis, Youssef. Big Business: The European Experience in the Twentieth Century. LC 99-31582. (Illus.). 292p. 1999. pap. text 24.95 (*0-19-829606-1*) OUP.

— Big Business: The European Experiences in the Twentieth Century. LC 97-3698. (Illus.). 292p. (C). 1997. text 75.00 (*0-19-828965-0*) OUP.

— City Bankers, 1890-1914. Rocques, Margaret, tr. LC 93-30566. (Illus.). 366p. (C). 1994. text 69.95 (*0-521-44188-9*) Cambridge U Pr.

Cassis, Youssef, ed. Business Elites. (International Library of Critical Writings in Business History: Vol. 8). 720p. 1994. 265.00 (*1-85278-781-3*) E Elgar.

Cassis, Youssef, et al, eds. The Evolution of Financial Institutions & Markets in Twentieth-Century Europe. LC 94-15195. (Illus.). 345p. 1995. 86.95 (*1-85928-127-3*, Pub. by Scolar Pr) Ashgate Pub Co.

— Management & Business in Britain & France: The Age of the Corporate Economy (1850-1990) (Illus.). 254p. 1995. text 49.95 (*0-19-828940-5*) OUP.

Cassis, Youssef, jt. auth. see Van Helten, Jean-Jacques.

Cassis, Yves, ed. Finance & Financiers in European History, 1880-1960. 461p. (C). 1992. text 80.00 (*0-521-40024-4*) Cambridge U Pr.

Cassistre, Debra. Activity Ideas for the Budget Minded. LC 94-70600. 120p. 1994. pap. 10.95 (*0-943873-15-0*) Elder Bks.

— Free Things for Activity Directors. LC 94-70727. 120p. 1995. pap. 10.95 (*0-943873-16-9*) Elder Bks.

Cassity, Brad & Combs, Gary B. Fisher-Price Toys 1931-1990. 192p. 1999. pap. 19.95 (*1-57432-142-0*) Collector Bks.

***Cassity, Don.** Discovering America. (Rugrats (tv) Ser.). Orig. Title: Rugrats Discover America. 32p. (J). (ps-3). 2000. pap. 5.99 (*0-689-83272-9*, Simon Spot) Litle Simon.

Cassity, Julia E., jt. auth. see Cassity, Michael D.

Cassity, Kevin, ed. The Alaska Adventure Book. LC 87-70492. 120p. (Orig.). 1987. pap. 13.95 (*0-9617945-0-X*) Alaska Illus.

Cassity, Martin M., Jr. Fifty-Nine Front Street. LC 93-44783. 1993. pap. 13.95 (*1-881399-09-5*) Beaver Pond P&P.

Cassity, Michael. Defending a Way of Life: An American Community in the Nineteenth Century. LC 88-12324. (SUNY Series in American Labor History). 259p. (C). 1989. text 64.50 (*0-88706-868-5*); pap. text 21.95 (*0-88706-869-3*) State U NY Pr.

Cassity, Michael D. & Cassity, Julia E. Multimodal Psychiatric Music Therapy for Adults, Adolescents, & Children: A Clinical Manual. 250p. 1993. pap. text 30.00 (*0-9643602-0-9*) MMB Music.

— Multimodal Psychiatric Music Therapy for Adults, Adolescents, & Children: A Clinical Manual. 2nd ed. LC 95-45524. 1996. 24.95 (*0-918812-85-2*) MMB Music.

Cassity, Michael J. Chains of Fear: American Race Relations since Reconstruction, 3. LC 82-21092. (Grass Roots Perspectives on American History Ser.: No. 3). 253p. 1984. 65.00 (*0-313-21324-0*, CRR/, Greenwood Pr) Greenwood.

— Legacy of Fear: American Race Relations to 1900, 4. LC 84-8981. (Grass Roots Perspectives on American History Ser.: No. 4). (Illus.). 248p. 1985. 59.95 (*0-313-24553-3*, CLF/, Greenwood Pr) Greenwood.

Cassity, Turner. Between the Chains. (Phoenix Poets Ser.). 96p. 1991. pap. 10.95 (*0-226-09617-3*) U Ch Pr.

— Between the Chains. (Phoenix Poets Ser.). 96p. 1991. lib. bdg. 26.50 (*0-226-09616-5*) U Ch Pr.

— The Defense of the Sugar Islands. 28p. 1979. 25.00 (*0-936576-01-4*) Symposium Pr.

— The Destructive Element: New & Selected Poems. LC 97-37649. 260p. 1998. pap. 15.95 (*0-8214-1222-1*); text 29.95 (*0-8214-1221-3*) Ohio U Pr.

— Hurricane Lamp. LC 85-20873. (Phoenix Poets Ser.). vii, 80p. (C). 1986. pap. 8.50 (*0-226-09615-7*) U Ch Pr.

— Hurricane Lamp. LC 85-20873. (Phoenix Poets Ser.). vii, 68p. (C). 1986. lib. bdg. 18.00 (*0-226-09614-9*) U Ch Pr.

— Watchboy, What of the Night? 1991. pap. 15.00 (*0-936576-15-4*) Symposium Pr.

***Cassizzi, Vic.** The Elijah Chronicles: A Dangerous Challenge Pits an Entire Kingdom Against One Fearless Prophet. 320p. 2000. 21.95 (*1-57090-100-7*, Pub. by Alexander Dist) Midpt Trade.

Cassler, Robert. Second in the Realm. 65p. (Orig.). 1996. pap. 4.00 (*1-57514-183-3*, 1164) Encore Perform Pub.

Cassola. La Raggaza di Bube: C Level. text 8.95 (*0-88436-284-1*) EMC-Paradigm.

Cassola, Carlo. Un Coeur Aride. (FRE.). 1975. pap. 10.95 (*0-7859-1796-9*, 2070366456) Fr & Eur.

Casson, A. & Bleiler, S. Automorphisms of Surfaces after Nielsen & Thurston. (London Mathematical Society Student Texts Ser.: No. 9). 112p. 1988. pap. text 22.95 (*0-521-34985-0*) Cambridge U Pr.

Casson, Allan. AP English Literature & Composition: Preparation Guide. (Cliffs Test Preparation Ser.). (Illus.). 308p. 1993. pap. 10.95 (*0-8220-2305-9*, Cliff) IDG Bks.

Casson, Allan & Cliffs Notes Staff. SAT II Writing Preparation Guide: Scholastic Assessment Test. (Cliffs Test Preparation Ser.). 354p. (Orig.). (YA). (gr. 11-12). 1996. pap. text, student ed. 14.95 (*0-8220-2325-3*, Cliff) IDG Bks.

Casson, H. History of the Telephone. 1977. lib. bdg. 250.00 (*0-8490-2007-7*) Gordon Pr.

Casson, Herbert N. Cyrus Hall McCormick: His Life & Work. LC 74-152977. (Select Bibliographies Reprint Ser.). 1977. reprint ed. 26.95 (*0-8369-5729-6*) Ayer.

Casson, Herbert N., Jr. Factory Efficiency: How to Increase Output, Wages, Dividends & Good-Will. Chandler, Alfred D., ed. LC 79-7537. (History of Management Thought & Practice Ser.). 1980. reprint ed. lib. bdg. 19.95 (*0-405-12322-1*) Ayer.

Casson, Herbert N. The History of the Telephone. LC 76-175693. (Select Bibliographies Reprint Ser.). 1977. reprint ed. 30.95 (*0-8369-6608-2*) Ayer.

— The Romance of Steel: Story of a Thousand Millionaires. LC 72-179510. (Select Bibliographies Reprint Ser.). 1977. reprint ed. 41.95 (*0-8369-6639-2*) Ayer.

Casson, Hugh. Hugh Casson's Cambridge. (Illus.). 96p. 1998. pap. 14.95 (*0-7148-3811-X*) Phaidon Pr.

— Hugh Casson's Cambridge. (Illus.). 96p. 1997. 24.95 (*0-7148-2459-3*, Pub. by Phaidon Press) Phaidon Pr.

— Hugh Casson's Oxford. (Illus.). 96p. 1990. text 29.95 (*0-7148-2458-5*, Pub. by Phaidon Pr) Phaidon Pr.

— Hugh Casson's Oxford. LC 99-185562. (Illus.). 96p. 1998. 14.95 (*0-7148-3810-1*) Phaidon Pr.

Casson, L. F., ed. The Romance of Sir Degrevant. (EETS Original Ser.: Vol. 221). 1970. reprint ed. 30.00 (*0-19-722221-8*, Pub. by EETS) Boydell & Brewer.

Casson, Les. My Uncle Max. (Annikins Ser.: Vol. 10). (Illus.). 32p. (Orig.). (J). (ps-2). 1990. pap. 0.99 (*1-55037-130-4*, Pub. by Annick) Firefly Bks Ltd.

Casson, Lionel. The Ancient Mariners: Seafarers & Sea Fighters of the Mediterranean in Ancient Times. 2nd ed. (Illus.). 299p. 1991. pap. text 16.95 (*0-691-01477-9*, Pub. by Princeton U Pr) Cal Prin Full Svc.

— Ancient Trade & Society. LC 83-19880. 285p. reprint ed. pap. 88.40 (*0-608-06271-5*, 206660000008) Bks Demand.

— Daily Life in Ancient Egypt. (PaperBook Series in History). (Illus.). 128p. (Orig.). 1994. pap. text 2.25 (*1-877891-13-4*) Paperbook Pr Inc.

— Everyday Life in Ancient Rome. LC 98-19972. (Illus.). 144p. 1998. 39.95 (*0-8018-5991-3*) Johns Hopkins.

— Everyday Life in Ancient Rome. rev. ed. LC 98-19972. 144p. 1998. pap. 14.95 (*0-8018-5992-1*) Johns Hopkins.

— The Periplus Maris Erythraei: Text with Introduction, Translation, & Commentary. LC 88-15178. (Illus.). 338p. reprint ed. pap. 104.80 (*0-608-06382-7*, 206674300008) Bks Demand.

— Ships & Seafaring in Ancient Times. (Illus.). 160p. (Orig.). 1994. pap. 27.95 (*0-292-71162-X*) U of Tex Pr.

— Ships & Seamanship in the Ancient World. LC 95-20034. (Illus.). 469p. 1995. pap. text 19.95 (*0-8018-5130-0*) Johns Hopkins.

— Ships & Seamanship in the Ancient World. LC 78-112996. (Illus.). 577p. reprint ed. pap. 178.90 (*0-7837-0564-6*, 204090800019) Bks Demand.

— Travel in the Ancient World. LC 93-30502. 400p. 1994. pap. 16.95 (*0-8018-4808-3*) Johns Hopkins.

Casson, Lionel, ed. Amphitryon & Two Other Plays. 1971. pap. 11.95 (*0-393-00601-8*) Norton.

Casson, Lionel, et al, eds. The Athlit Ram. LC 90-10804. (Nautical Archaeology Ser.: No. 3). (Illus.). 112p. 1991. 75.00 (*0-89096-451-3*) Tex A&M Univ Pr.

Casson, Lionel & Price, Martin, eds. Coins, Culture, & History in the Ancient World: Numismatic & Other Studies in Honor of Bluma L. Trell. LC 81-10491. (Illus.). 205p. reprint ed. pap. 63.60 (*0-7837-3590-1*, 204345400009) Bks Demand.

Casson, M. Introduction to Mathematical Economics. 1973. pap. 31.95 (*0-442-30718-7*, VNR) Wiley.

Casson, M. C., ed. Multinational Corporations. (International Library of Critical Writings in Economics: Vol. 1). 640p. 1990. text 270.00 (*1-85278-192-0*) E Elgar.

Casson, Mark. The Economics of Business Culture: Game Theory, Transaction Costs, & Economic Performance. (Illus.). 298p. 1994. reprint ed. pap. text 24.95 (*0-19-828888-3*) OUP.

***Casson, Mark.** Economics of International Business: A New Research Agenda. LC 99-45194. 2000. write for info. (*1-84064-355-2*) E Elgar.

Casson, Mark. Enterprise & Competitiveness: A Systems View of International Business. (Illus.). 244p. 1995. pap. text 24.00 (*0-19-828957-X*) OUP.

***Casson, Mark.** Enterprise & Leadership: Studies on Firms, Markets & Networks. LC 99-86199. 2000. write for info. (*1-84064-354-4*) E Elgar.

Casson, Mark. Entrepreneurship & Business Culture: Studies in the Economics of Trust, Vol. 1. LC 94-48413. (Illus.). 292p. 1995. 95.00 (*1-85898-229-4*) E Elgar.

— Entrepreneurship & the Industrial Revolution. 7 vols., Set. 1792p. (C). 1997. 660.00 (*0-415-15086-8*) Routledge.

— The Firm & the Market: Studies on the Multinational Enterprise & the Scope of the Firm. LC 86-27199. 295p. 1987. 37.50 (*0-262-03129-9*) MIT Pr.

— Information & Organization: A New Perspective on the Theory of the Firm. (Illus.). 328p. 1997. text 79.00 (*0-19-829232-5*) OUP.

— Multinationals & World Trade. 1986. text 60.00 (*0-04-338125-1*) Routledge.

— The Organization of International Business: Studies in the Economics of Trust, Vol. 2. LC 94-48432. (Illus.). 224p. 1995. 85.00 (*1-85898-230-8*) E Elgar.

— Unemployment: A Disequilibrium Approach. (Modern Revivals in Economics Ser.). 280p. 1993. 63.95 (*0-7512-0216-9*, Pub. by Gregg Revivals) Ashgate Pub Co.

Casson, Mark, ed. Culture, Social Norms & Economics, 2 vols., Set. LC 97-33595. (Reference Collection Critical Writings in Economics). 1224p. 1997. 455.00 (*1-85898-617-6*) E Elgar.

— Entrepreneurship. (International Library of Critical Writings in Economics: Vol. 3). 640p. 1990. text 265.00 (*1-85278-209-9*) E Elgar.

— The Growth of International Business. 288p. (C). 1983. text 45.00 (*0-04-330333-1*) Routledge.

— The Railway Revolution, 8 vols. (Origins of Business Economics Ser.). 2000p. (C). 1998. 785.00 (*0-415-15088-4*) Routledge.

— The Rise of Big Business. (Origins of Business Economics Ser.). 2154p. (C). 1997. 785.00 (*0-415-15087-6*) Routledge.

— The Theory of the Firm. LC 96-8724. (International Library of Critical Writings in Economics: Vol. 72). 768p. 1996. 280.00 (*1-85278-715-5*) E Elgar.

Casson, Mark, ed. International Competitiveness: Productivity & Technological Progress, 8 vols. fac. ed. (Origins of Business Economics Ser.). 2328p. (C). (gr. 13). 1999. 865.00 (*0-415-19109-2*, D5978) Routledge.

Casson, Mark & Creedy, John, eds. Industrial Concentration & Economic Inequality: Essays in Honour of Peter Hart. 256p. 1993. 90.00 (*1-85278-648-5*) E Elgar.

Casson, Mark & Rose, Mary B., eds. Institutions & the Evolution of Modern Business. LC 97-28112. 208p. (C). 1998. 42.50 (*0-7146-4845-0*, Pub. by F Cass Pubs); pap. 19.50 (*0-7146-4400-5*, Pub. by F Cass Pubs) Intl Spec Bk.

Casson, Mark, jt. ed. see Beamish, Paul W.

Casson, Mark, jt. ed. see Buckley, Peter J.

Casson, Mark, jt. ed. see Engelhoff, William G.

Casson, Mark, jt. ed. see Foreman-Peck, James.

Casson, Mark, jt. ed. see Milner, Chris R.

Casson, Michael. The Craft of the Potter. LC 78-15013. (Illus.). (gr. 10-12). 1979. pap. 16.95 (*0-8120-2028-6*) Barron.

Casson, Paul. Decoys Simplified. (Illus.). 132p. 1973. 14.95 (*0-88395-016-2*) Freshet Pr.

Casson, Peter D. Company Share Options. LC 99-59515. 228p. 2000. text 95.00 (*0-471-96659-2*) Wiley.

Casson, Stanley. Ancient Cyprus, Its Art & Archaeology. (Illus.). 1976. 30.00 (*0-916710-29-7*) Obol Intl.

— Some Modern Sculptors. LC 67-28746. (Essay Index Reprint Ser.). 1977. 15.95 (*0-8369-0282-3*) Ayer.

— Twentieth Century Sculptors. LC 67-23189. (Essay Index Reprint Ser.). 1977. 15.95 (*0-8369-0283-1*) Ayer.

Casson, Stanley, ed. Essay in Aegean Archaeology: Presented to Sir Arthur Evans in Honor of His 75th Birthday. LC 72-309. (Essay Index Reprint Ser.). 1977. reprint ed. 22.95 (*0-8369-2791-5*) Ayer.

Casson, Steve. Culture Change for Total Quality: An Action Guide for Managers in Social & Health Care Services LC 99-215404. ix, 137p. 1996. pap. text 60.95 (*0-471-97227-4*) Wiley.

Casson, Thomas. Lecture on the Pedal Organ. 1988. reprint ed. lib. bdg. 49.00 (*0-7812-0145-4*) Rprt Serv.

***Casson, Thomas.** Reform in Organ Building. 151p. 2000. reprint ed. lib. bdg. 59.00 (*0-7812-9310-3*) Rprt Serv.

Cassone, Diane, jt. auth. see Cassone, Philip.

Cassone, Philip & Cassone, Diane. Hand Jobs. (Illus.). 56p. (Orig.). 1982. pap. 6.95 (*0-9610082-0-2*) Cassone Pr.

***Cassou, Michelle.** Creativity Without Limits. 2001. pap. 16.95 (*1-58542-085-9*, Tarcher Putnam) Putnam Pub Group.

Cassou, Michelle & Cubley, Stewart. Life, Paint & Passion: Reclaiming the Magic of Spontaneous Expression. (Illus.). 208p. (Orig.). 1996. pap. 16.95 (*0-87477-810-7*, Tarcher Putnam) Putnam Pub Group.

Casstevens, Frances H. The Civil War & Yadkin County, North Carolina: A History, with Contemporary Photographs & Letters; New Evidence Regarding Home Guard Activity & the Shootout at the Bond School House; a Roster of Militia Officiers; the Names of Yadkin Men at Appomattox; & 1200 Confederate Army & Navy Service Records with Parents, Vital Dates, & Place of Burial for Most. LC 97-18931. (Illus.). 304p. 1997. boxed set 45.00 (*0-7864-0288-1*) McFarland & Co.

Casstevens, Francis H. Yadkin County, North Carolina: The First One Hundred Years. (Images of America Ser.). (Illus.). 128p. 1996. pap. 16.99 (*0-7524-0522-5*) Arcadia Publng.

Casstevens, Martha, jt. auth. see Adams, Kevin.

Casstevens, Thomas W. Politics, Housing & Race Relations: California's Rumford Act & Proposition 14. LC 67-64842. 103p. reprint ed. pap. 32.00 (*0-608-15396-6*, 202942100060) Bks Demand.

Cassuto. From Noah to Abraham: A Commentary on the Book of Genesis 6-11. 1992. 30.00 (*965-223-481-8*, Pub. by Magnes Pr) Gefen Bks.

Cassuto, David N. Cold Running River. 168p. (C). 1994. text 34.50 (*0-472-10474-8*, 10474) U of Mich Pr.

***Cassuto, David N.** Dripping Dry: Literature, Politics & Water in the Desert Southwest. (Studies in Literature & Science). 240p. (C). 2000. pap. text 19.95 (*0-472-06756-7*) U of Mich Pr.

— Dripping Dry: Literature, Politics & Water in the Desert Southwest. (Studies in Literature & Science). (Illus.). 240p. (C). 2000. text 49.50 (*0-472-09756-3*, 09756) U of Mich Pr.

Cassuto, George, ed. see Hedberg, Betsy & Porter, Evan.

Cassuto, Leonard. The Inhuman Race: The Racial Grotesque in American Literature & Culture. LC 96-16785. (Illus.). 288p. 1996. pap. 18.50 (*0-231-10337-9*) Col U Pr.

Cassuto, Leonard & Reesman, Jeanne C., eds. Rereading Jack London. LC 96-17052. 308p. 1996. 55.00 (*0-8047-2634-5*) Stanford U Pr.

— Rereading Jack London. 308p. 1998. pap. 19.95 (*0-8047-3516-6*) Stanford U Pr.

Cassuto, Leonard, ed. see Poe, Edgar Allan.

Cassuto, Leonare. The Inhuman Race: The Racial Grotesque in American Literature & Culture. LC 96-16785. (Illus.). 288p. 1996. 52.00 (*0-231-10336-0*) Col U Pr.

Cassuto, Nelda, ed. see Eis, Ruth.

C

Cassuto, U. Biblical & Oriental Studies -- Selected Writings, Vol. 1. Abrahams, I., tr. ix, 309p. 1973. text 25.00 (*965-223-476-1*, Pub. by Magnes Pr) Eisenbrauns.

— Biblical & Oriental Studies -- Selected Writings, Vol. 2. Abrahams, I., tr. xi, 286p. 1975. text 25.00 (*0-685-54095-2*, Pub. by Magnes Pr) Eisenbrauns.

— A Commentary on the Book of Exodus. 3rd ed. Abrahams, I., tr. from HEB. xvi, 509p. (C). 1967. text 30.00 (*965-223-456-7*, Pub. by Magnes Pr) Eisenbrauns.

— A Commentary on the Book of Genesis Pt. I & II: From Adam to Noah: From Noah to Abraham. (HEB.). 251p. 1996. reprint ed. text 22.00 (*965-223-502-4*, Pub. by Magnes Pr) Eisenbrauns.

— From Adam to Noah: A Commentary on the Book of Genesis I-VI. 3rd ed. Abrahams, I., tr. from HEB. xviii, 323p. (C). 1961. text 30.00 (*965-223-480-X*, Pub. by Magnes Pr) Eisenbrauns.

— From Noah to Abraham: A Commentary on the Book of Genesis VI-XI. 3rd ed. Abrahams, I., tr. from HEB. xiv, 386p. (C). 1964. text 30.00 (*965-223-540-7*, Pub. by Magnes Pr) Eisenbrauns.

— The Goddess Anath: Canaanite Epics of the Patriarchal Age (Texts, Hebrew Translation, Commentary & Introduction) Abrahams, I., tr. from HEB. (Illus.). xii, 202p. 1971. text 20.00 (*965-223-482-6*, Pub. by Magnes Pr) Eisenbrauns.

***Cassutt.** Missing Man. 448p. 2000. mass mkt. 6.99 (*0-8125-7786-8*, Pub. by Tor Bks) St Martin.

Cassutt, Michael. Missing Man. LC 98-22541. 352p. 1998. 24.95 (*0-312-86620-8*, Pub. by Forge NYC) St Martin.

***Cassutt, Michael.** Red Moon. 2001. text 27.95 (*0-312-87440-5*) St Martin.

Cassutt, Michael. Who's Who in Space: The First Twenty-Five Years. (Illus.). 336p. 1987. text 40.00 (*0-8161-8801-7*, Hall Reference) Macmillan.

— Who's Who in Space: The International Space Station Edition. 3rd ed. LC 98-35587. 496p. 1998. 115.00 (*0-02-864965-6*) Macmillan.

Cassutt, Michael, jt. auth. see Slayton, Deke.

***Cassutto, George H.** Internet Guide for Teachers. (Illus.). 96p. 1999. pap. write for info. (*1-890911-11-9*) Genium Pub.

Cassvan, Arminius, et al. Cumulative Trauma Disorders. LC 97-2667. 264p. 1997. text 70.00 (*0-7506-9570-6*) Buttrwrth-Heinemann.

Cassway, Esta. The Five Books of Moses for Young People. LC 92-8013. 248p. (J). 1992. 40.00 (*0-87668-451-7*) Aronson.

— The Five Books of Moses for Young People. LC 92-8013. (Illus.). 248p. (J). 1995. reprint ed. pap. 30.00 (*1-56821-518-5*) Aronson.

— The Prophets for Young People. LC 94-2498. 376p. (J). 1994. 50.00 (*1-56821-148-1*) Aronson.

Cast, C. Vance. Where Did the Dinosaurs Go? (Clever Calvin Ser.). (Illus.). 40p. (J). (ps-2). 1994. pap. 4.95 (*0-8120-1573-8*) Barron.

— Where Does Electricity Come From? (Clever Calvin Ser.). (Illus.). 40p. (J). (ps-2). 1992. pap. 5.95 (*0-8120-4835-0*) Barron.

— Where Does Electricity Come From? (Clever Calvin Ser.). (J). 1992. 11.15 (*0-606-01653-8*, Pub. by Turtleback) Demco.

— Where Does Oil Come From? (Clever Calvin Ser.). 1993. 10.15 (*0-606-06091-X*, Pub. by Turtleback) Demco.

— Where Does Paper Come From? (Clever Calvin Ser.). (Illus.). 40p. (J). (ps-2). 1993. pap. 4.95 (*0-8120-1468-5*) Barron.

— Where Does Pollution Come From? (Clever Calvin Ser.). (Illus.). 40p. (J). (ps-2). 1994. pap. 5.95 (*0-8120-1571-1*) Barron.

— Where Does Water Come From? (Clever Calvin Ser.). (Illus.). 40p. (J). (ps-2). 1992. pap. 5.95 (*0-8120-4642-0*) Barron.

— Where Does Water Come From? (J). 1992. 11.15 (*0-606-01654-6*, Pub. by Turtleback) Demco.

Cast, C.Vance. Where Does Pollution Come From? (Clever Calvin Ser.). 1994. 10.15 (*0-606-06871-6*, Pub. by Turtleback) Demco.

Cast, John. All Change. LC 99-58109. 1999. pap. text 3.99 (*0-85953-569-X*) Childs Play.

***Cast, John.** Animal Bluff. LC 99-57501. 1999. pap. text 3.99 (*0-85953-567-3*) Childs Play.

Cast, John. Art of Therapy & the Therapy of Art, 1. 1998. 49.99 (*0-9665870-0-6*) Crane Pubg.

— Children of the Sun. 1999. 3.99 (*0-85953-933-4*) Childs Play.

— Concrete Beams with Openings: Analysis & Design. LC 98-51792. 1998. 89.95 (*0-8493-7435-9*) CRC Pr.

***Cast, John.** Dearest Freshness Deep Down: An Introduction to Metaphysics. LC 99-31417. 1999. pap. text 17.95 (*0-8245-1794-6*) Crossroad NY.

— Hide & Seek. LC 99-58108. 1999. pap. text 3.99 (*0-85953-566-5*) Childs Play.

Cast, John. Little Mouse. 1999. 6.99 (*0-85953-694-7*) Childs Play.

***Cast, John.** Magic Mouse. 1999. pap. text 3.99 (*0-85953-568-1*) Childs Play.

Cast, John. Rulemaking: How Government Agencies Write Law & Make Policy. 2nd ed. LC 98-31571. 1998. pap. text 29.95 (*1-56802-418-5*) Congr Quarterly.

— Shorty: The Other Malcom: A Sequel to the Autobiography of Malcom X. Date not set. 28.95 (*0-940121-49-2*) Cross Cultural Pubns.

— Time Tunnel. 1999. 3.99 (*0-85953-928-8*) Childs Play.

Cast, John & Casel, Odo. The Mystery of Christian Worship. Neunheuser, Burkhard, ed. LC 99-11630. 99p. 1999. pap. 12.95 (*0-8245-1808-X*) Crossroad NY.

Cast, John & Franklin Covey Company Staff. Loving Reminders for Couples: 60 Affectionate Notes for Those Close to Your Heart. 1998. pap. 9.95 (*1-883219-92-2*) Franklin Covey.

Cast, John, jt. ed. see Hamilton, Richard J.

***Casta, Laetitia.** Laetitia: Gorgeous, Sexy, Up Close & Personal. (Illus.). 128p. 1999. 30.00 (*0-670-88819-2*) Viking Penguin.

Castafero, Jeanne C. Summer Smarts: Activities & Skills to Prepare You Child for the 2nd Grade. 100p. 1998. pap. 9.95 (*0-395-91381-0*) HM.

— Summer Smarts: Activities & Skills to Prepare You Child for the 3nd Grade. 100p. 1998. pap. 9.95 (*0-395-91382-9*) HM.

— Summer Smarts: Activities & Skills to Prepare Your Child for the Fifth Grade. (Illus.). 100p. 1999. pap. 9.95 (*0-395-98492-0*) HM.

— Summer Smarts: Activities Skills to Prepare Your Child for the 4th Grade. 100p. 1998. pap. 9.95 (*0-395-91384-5*) HM.

Castafero, Jeanne C. & Van Roden, Janet. Summer Smarts Activities & Skills to Prepare Your Child for the Fifth Grade. (Summer Smarts Ser.). 100p. 1999. pap. 9.95 (*0-669-46944-0*) HM Schl Div.

— Summer Smarts Activities & Skills to Prepare Your Child for the First Grade. (Summer Smarts Ser.). 100p. 1999. pap. 9.95 (*0-669-46943-2*) HM Schl Div.

Castafero, Jeanne Crane & Van Roden, Janet. Summer Smarts First Grade: Activities & Skills to Prepare Your Child for the First Grade. (Illus.). 100p. 1999. pap. 9.95 (*0-395-98491-2*) HM.

Castagna, Debbie, et al. Get Paid for Your Services: Simple, Sensible Payment Arrangements That Work! 106p. 1998. ring bd. 89.00 incl. disk (*0-910167-54-0*, Dental Commun) Comm Unltd CA.

Castagna, G. Object Oriented Programming: A Unified Foundation. 355p. 1996. 69.50 (*0-8176-3905-5*) Birkhauser.

Castagna, Giuseppe. Object Oriented Programming: A Unified Foundation. LC 96-33163. (Progress in Theoretical Computer Science Ser.). 394p. 1996. write for info. (*3-7643-3905-5*) Birkhauser.

Castagna, Harry F. Life: His Acronyms Really Refresh You. 96p. 1997. pap. 9.95 (*0-9661950-0-0*) HP Pub.

Castagna, John P. & Backus, Milo M., eds. Offset-Dependent Reflectivity: Theory & Practice of AVO Analysis. LC 93-14279. (Investigations in Geophysics Ser.: No. 8). (Illus.). 345p. 1993. text 120.00 (*1-56080-059-3*, 108A) Soc Expl Geophys.

Castagna, M., jt. ed. see Manzi, J. J.

Castagnara. Karel Teige, 1900-1951. (ITA., Illus.). 270p. 1996. pap. 50.00 (*88-435-5457-3*, Pub. by Art Bks Intl) Partners Pubs Grp.

Castagnaro, R. Anthony. A Portuguese Primer. (American University Studies: Foreign Language Instruction: Ser. VI, Vol. 9). (ENG & POR.). 415p. (C). 1989. text 47.95 (*0-8204-0870-0*) P Lang Pubng.

Castagner, Claude, jt. auth. see Mayer, Margaret M.

Castagnera, Elizabeth, et al. Deciding What to Teach & How to Teach It: Connecting Students Through Curriculum & Instruction. (Connecting Sudents Ser.). 1998. pap. 13.00 (*1-884720-09-9*) PEAK Parent.

Castagnera, James O. Employment Law Answer Book: Forms & Checklists. rev. ed. 728p. 1994. pap. text 96.00 (*1-56706-016-1*) Panel Pubs.

— How to Prepare an Employee Handbook. 2nd ed. LC 87-37843. 350p. 1988. ring bd. 79.95 (*0-916592-73-1*) Panel Pubs.

— PA Labor & Employment Law Forms Kit. 1997. ring bd. 89.50 incl. disk (*1-887024-75-1*) Bisel Co.

— Personnel Law Answer Book, 1991 Supplement. Walton, Richard K., ed. 1990. text 49.00 (*1-878375-25-3*) Panel Pubs.

Castagnera, James O. & Derewicz, Kristine G. Personnel Law Answer Book: Special Supplement, Forms & Checklists. Persons, Mark D., ed. 350p. 1991. pap. 49.00 (*1-878375-66-0*) Panel Pubs.

Castagnera, James O. & Haffeman, JoAnne S. Personnel Law Answer Book. 315p. 1988. text 79.00 (*0-916592-89-8*) Panel Pubs.

— Personnel Law Answer Book. 400p. 1991. pap. text, suppl. ed. 49.99 (*1-878375-65-2*) Panel Pubs.

Castagnera, James O. & Ryan, Edward, eds. Job Descriptions for Law Firms & Corporate Legal Departments. 1996. ring bd. 155.00 (*1-888286-03-2*) Altman Weil.

Castagnera, James O. & Ryan, John. PA Employee Handbook Forms Kit. 1997. ring bd. 89.50 incl. disk (*1-887024-76-X*) Bisel Co.

***Castagnera, James O., et al.** Pennsylvania Labor & Employment Lawsource: Collected Labor & Employment Federal & State Statutes, Regulations, Cases & Commentary. LC 99-73296. 448p. 1999. pap. 64.50 (*1-887024-77-8*) Bisel Co.

Castagnera, James O., jt. auth. see Cihon, Patrick J.

Castagnera, James O., jt. auth. see Sprang, Kenneth A.

Castagnetta, L., jt. auth. see Nenci, Italo.

***Castagnetto, Jesus, et al.** Professional PHP Programming. (Professional Ser.). (Illus.). 850p. 1999. pap. 49.99 (*1-86100-296-3*) Wrox Pr Inc.

Castagno, John. American Artists: Signatures & Monograms, 1800-1989. LC 89-28371. (Illus.). 843p. 1990. 152.50 (*0-8108-2249-0*) Scarecrow.

— Artists As Illustrators: An International Directory with Signatures & Monograms, 1800-Present. LC 88-34832. (Illus.). 645p. 1989. 134.00 (*0-8108-2168-0*) Scarecrow.

— Artists' Monograms & Indiscernible Signatures: An International Directory, 1800-1991. LC 91-23003. (Illus.). 558p. 1991. 134.00 (*0-8108-2415-9*) Scarecrow.

— European Artists: Signatures & Monograms, 1800-1990 Including Selected Artists from Other Parts of the World. LC 90-41504. (Illus.). 914p. 1990. 152.50 (*0-8108-2313-6*) Scarecrow.

— Latin American Artists' Signatures & Monograms: Colonial Era to 1996. LC 97-12178. 600p. 1997. 145.00 (*0-8108-3293-3*) Scarecrow.

— Old Masters Signatures & Monograms, 1400-Born 1800. 396p. 1996. 110.00 (*0-8108-3082-5*) Scarecrow.

Castagno, Paul C. The Early "Commedia Dell'arte (1550-1621) The Mannerist Context. LC 91-39538. (American University Studies, XXVI, Theatre Arts: Vol. 13). (Illus.). XXVI, 290p. (C). 1994. text 39.95 (*0-8204-1794-7*) P Lang Pubng.

Castagno, Paul C., ed. Theatre Symposium Vol. 4: A Journal of the Southeastern Theatre Conference - Theatrical Spaces & Dramatic Places - The Reemergence of the Theatre Building in the Renaissance. 151p. 1996. pap. text 20.00 (*0-8173-0854-7*) U of Ala Pr.

Castagno, Paul C., jt. ed. see Hill, Philip G.

Castagnola, George S., as told by. Cooking Italian in Hawaii. LC 91-66826. (Illus.). 128p. 1991. write for info. (*0-9631154-0-5*) Watermark.

Castagnola, Larry. Heroes, Rebels & Survivors: Mostly True Tales about Growing Up. LC 95-51520. (Illus.). 112p. (Orig.). (J). 1996. pap. 10.95 (*0-89390-365-5*) Resource Pubns.

Castagnola, Lawrence. Parables for Little People. LC 86-60029. (Illus.). 104p. (J). (gr. 4 up). 1982. pap. 99.95 (*0-89390-034-6*) Resource Pubns.

Castagnoli, G. Cini & Provenzale, A., eds. Past & Present Variability of the Solar-Terrestrial System: Measurement, Data Analysis & Theoreticcal Models. (International School of Physics Enrico Fermi Ser.: Vol. 133). 600p. Date not set. 145.00 (*90-5199-358-7*) IOS Press.

Castagnoli, Neal, et al, eds. Molecular Basis of the Action of Drugs & Toxic Substances: Proceedings International Symposium San Francisco, CA, April 23-26, 1987. x, 318p. (C). 1988. lib. bdg. 203.85 (*3-11-011290-6*) De Gruyter.

Castagnoli, William, et al. Medicine Avenue: The Story of Medical Advertising in America. (Illus.). 128p. 1998. 60.00 (*0-9667793-0-4*) Med Ad Hall Fame.

Castain, Jose N., et al. Atlas of Seville: The Form of the Historic Center. LC 92-62374. (Illus.). 280p. 1993. boxed set 175.00 (*0-941419-90-8*) Marsilio Pubs.

Castaing, J., jt. ed. see Looney, C.

Castalanas, Guadalupe, tr. see Mozeleski, Peter A.

Castaldi, Basil. Educational Facilities: Planning, Modernization, & Management. 4th ed. LC 93-126022. 448p. 1993. 82.00 (*0-205-15201-5*) Allyn.

Castaldi, C. R., et al, eds. Safety in Ice Hockey. LC 89-35946. (Special Technical Publication Ser.: Vol. 2, No. STP 1212). (Illus.). 230p. 1993. text 94.00 (*0-8031-1873-2*, STP1212) ASTM.

***Castaldi, Patricia.** Basic Nursing: A Critical Thinking Approach. 4th ed. (Illus.). 432p. (C). 1998. text, student ed. write for info. (*0-323-00100-9*) Mosby Inc.

Castaldi, Thomas E. Cicott's Mill on the Upper Wabash. large type ed. (Illus.). 24p. 1991. pap. write for info. (*1-928835-02-3*) Castaldi.

— Wabash & Erie Canal: Cass Carroll & Tippecanoe Counties. (Illus.). 115p. 1998. pap. write for info. (*1-928835-01-5*) Castaldi.

— Wabash & Erie Canal Notebook: Allen & Huntington Counties. (Illus.). 76p. 1995. pap. write for info. (*1-928835-00-7*) Castaldi.

Castaldo, Debra D. Assessing Foster & Adoptive Families for Placement of Sexually Abused Children: Practice Guidelines. 32p. 1996. pap. 5.95 (*0-87304-299-9*) Manticore Pubs.

Castaldo, George, ed. see Von Normann, Bob.

Castaldo, Meg. Shop NY Downtownstyle. LC 97-152840. (Illus.). 240p. (Orig.). 1996. pap. 15.95 (*1-885492-32-4*) City & Co.

Castaldo, Nancy F. The Little Hands Nature Book: Earth, Sky, Critters & More. Williamson, Susan, ed. LC 97-13774. (Little Hands Ser.: Vol. 7). Orig. Title: Sunny Days & Starry Nights, a Little Hands Nature Book. (Illus.). 144p. (Orig.). (J). (ps-1). 1997. pap. 12.95 (*1-885593-16-3*) Williamson Pub Co.

— Rainy Day Play! Explore, Create, Discover, Pretend. Williamson, Susan, ed. LC 95-50477. (Little Hands Bks.: No. 6). (Illus.). 144p. (Orig.). (J). (ps-12). 1996. pap. 12.95 (*1-885593-00-7*) Williamson Pub Co.

Castamans, Raymond, tr. see Levy, Maurice, et al, eds.

Castan, C., jt. auth. see Cayon, J.

Castan, Fran. The Widow's Quilt. LC 96-83170. 84p. 1996. pap. 12.00 (*1-886435-04-9*) Canios Edit.

Castandea, Deborah, jt. auth. see Geib, Pam.

Castaneda. A History of the Natural Gas Industry. LC 99-27714. (Twayne's Evolution of Modern Business Ser.). 1999. 23.95 (*0-8057-9830-7*, Twyne); per. 14.95 (*0-8057-9831-5*, Twyne) Mac Lib Ref.

Castaneda, Aldo R., et al. Cardiac Surgery of the Neonate & Infant. LC 93-22880. (Illus.). 528p. 1994. text 205.00 (*0-7216-4301-9*, W B Saunders Co) Harcrt Hlth Sci Grp.

Castaneda, Alfredo, et al, eds. Mexican Americans & Educational Change. LC 73-14196. (Mexican American Ser.). 424p. 1976. 31.95 (*0-405-05671-0*) Ayer.

Castaneda, Carlos. The Active Side of Infinity. LC 98-19980. 288p. 1999. 25.00 (*0-06-019220-8*) HarpC.

***Castaneda, Carlos.** The Active Side of Infinity. 288p. 2000. pap. 13.00 (*0-06-092960-X*, Perennial) HarperTrade.

— Active Side of Infinity: Smith,&Cotter, Set. 1999. audio 18.00 (*0-694-52124-8*) HarperAudio.

Castaneda, Carlos. The Art of Dreaming. LC 92-56194. 272p. 1994. pap. 14.00 (*0-06-092554-X*, Perennial) HarperTrade.

— El Arte de Ensonar. LC 95-31332.Tr. of Art of Dreaming. (SPA.). 304p. 1995. pap. 11.00 (*0-06-095155-9*) HarperTrade.

— The Eagle's Gift. Rosenman, Jane, ed. 320p. 1991. pap. 14.00 (*0-671-73251-X*, WSP) PB.

— Ensenanzas de Don Juan. (SPA.). 1991. pap. 9.99 (*968-16-0169-6*) Fondo.

— The Fire from Within. 300p. 1991. per. 14.00 (*0-671-73250-1*, WSP) PB.

— El Fuego Interno. (SPA.). 351p. 1997. pap. 22.98 (*968-890-018-4*) Edivision Comp.

Castaneda, Carlos. Journey to Ixtlan. LC 72-83221. 268p. 1991. pap. 14.00 (*0-671-73246-3*) S&S Trade.

Castaneda, Carlos. Journey to Ixtlan. 1994. reprint ed. lib. bdg. 32.95 (*1-56849-259-6*) Buccaneer Bks.

— Magical Passes: Practical Wisdom of the Shamans of Ancient Mexico. LC 97-26884. (Illus.). 240p. 1998. 25.00 (*0-06-017584-2*) HarpC.

— Magical Passes: The Practical Wisdom of the Shamans of Ancient Mexico. (Illus.). 240p. (Orig.). 1999. pap. 14.00 (*0-06-092882-4*) HarpC.

— Mexican Side of the Texan Revolution. 1993. reprint ed. lib. bdg. 75.00 (*0-7812-5920-7*) Rprt Serv.

— Our Catholic Heritage in Texas, 1519-1936, 7 vols., Set. 1993. reprint ed. lib. bdg. 525.00 (*0-7812-5963-0*) Rprt Serv.

— The Power of Silence. Rosenman, Jane, ed. 288p. 1991. 14.00 (*0-671-73248-X*, WSP) PB.

— Una Realidad Aparte. (SPA.). 1992. pap. 11.99 (*968-16-0218-8*) Fondo.

— Relatos de Poder. (SPA.). 1992. pap. 11.99 (*968-16-0341-9*) Fondo.

***Castaneda, Carlos.** La Rueda del Tiempo. (SPA.). 1999. pap. 15.95 (*0-553-06103-8*) Bantam.

— La Rueda del Tiempo los Chaman. (SPA.). 1999. pap. 15.95 (*84-01-01222-8*) Plaza.

Castaneda, Carlos. The Second Ring of Power. 328p. (YA). (gr. 10-12). 1991. per. 14.00 (*0-671-73247-1*) PB.

— A Separate Reality. Rosenman, Jane, ed. 272p. 1991. pap. 14.00 (*0-671-73249-8*, WSP) PB.

— Tales of Power. LC 91-5122. 295p. 1991. pap. 14.00 (*0-671-73252-8*, WSP) PB.

— Tales of Power. 1994. reprint ed. lib. bdg. 32.95 (*1-56849-260-X*) Buccaneer Bks.

— Teachings of Don Juan. 1985. per. 6.99 (*0-671-60041-9*, WSP) PB.

— The Teachings of Don Juan. 1998. mass mkt. 14.00 (*0-671-01908-2*, PB Trade Paper) PB.

— The Teachings of Don Juan: A Yaqui Way of Knowledge. 30th anniversary deluxe ed. LC 98-204322. 215p. 1998. pap. 14.95 (*0-520-21757-8*, Pub. by U CA Pr) Cal Prin Full Svc.

— Teachings of Don Juan: A Yaqui Way of Knowledge. 30th anniversary deluxe ed. LC 98-204322. 215p. 1998. 29.95 (*0-520-21755-1*, Pub. by U CA Pr) Cal Prin Full Svc.

— Viaje a Ixtlan. (SPA.). 1992. pap. 12.99 (*968-16-0335-4*) Fondo.

— The Wheel of Time: The Shamans of Ancient Mexico, Their Thoughts about Life, Death & the Universe. 300p. 1998. 25.00 (*0-9664116-0-9*) LA Eidolona.

***Castaneda, Carlos E., et al.** Wilderness Mission: Preliminary Studies of the Texas Catholic Historical Society II. De La Teja, Jesus F., ed. (Studies in Southwestern Catholic History: Vol. 2). viii, 237p. 1999. pap. 19.95 (*0-9660966-1-4*) TX Cath Hist.

Castaneda, Carlos E., jt. auth. see Foik, Paul J.

Castaneda, Carlos E., ed. see Morfi, Fray J.

Castaneda, Carlos E., tr. & anno. see Morfi, Fray J.

Castaneda, Christopher J. & Pratt, Joseph A. From Texas to the East: A Strategic History of Texas Eastern Corporation. LC 93-3073. (Illus.). 310p. (C). 1993. 36.95 (*0-89096-551-X*) Tex A&M Univ Pr.

Castaneda, Christopher J. & Smith, Clarance M. Gas Pipelines & the Emergence of America's Regulatory State: A History of Panhandle Eastern Corporation, 1928-1993. LC 96-197025. (Studies in Economic History & Policy: The United States in the Twentieth Century). (Illus.). 316p. (C). 1996. text 47.95 (*0-521-56166-3*) Cambridge U Pr.

Castaneda, Christopher J., jt. auth. see Pratt, Joseph A.

***Castaneda, Elisa.** I Bid You to... "Come into My Garden" Garden of Eden, the Simplicity of God. (Illus.). 58p. 2000. pap. 9.95 (*0-615-11601-9*) Heavn on Earth Inspir.

Castaneda, Flavio, et al, eds. Therapeutic Alternatives in Management of Benign Prostatic Hyperplasia. LC 92-49924. 1993. 105.00 (*0-86577-440-4*) Thieme Med Pubs.

Castaneda, Flavio, et al. Therapeutic Alternatives in the Management of Benign Prostatic Hyperplasia. LC 92-49924. 1992. write for info. (*3-13-783201-2*) Thieme Med Pubs.

Castaneda, Gonzalo. Macroeconomic Consequences of the 1986-87 Boom in the Mexican Stock Exchange & Treasury Bill Markets. LC 91-28444. (Developing Economies of the Third World Ser.). 136p. 1991. text 10.00 (*0-8153-0734-9*) Garland.

Castaneda, Hector-Neri. Action, Knowledge & Reality: Studies in Honor of Wilfrid Sellars. LC 74-8419. 374p. (C). 1975. text. write for info. (*0-672-61213-5*, Bobbs) Macmillan.

***Castaneda, Hector-Neri.** The Phenomeno-Logic of the I: Essays on Self-Consciousness. Hart, James G. & Kapitan, Tomis, eds. LC 98-50153. (Illus.). 384p. 1999. text 45.00 (*0-253-33506-X*) Ind U Pr.

Castaneda, Jorge. The Mexican Shock: Its Meaning for the U. S. 256p. 1995. 23.00 (*1-56584-311-8*, Pub. by New Press NY) Norton.

— The Mexican Shock: Its Meaning for the U. S. 288p. 1996. pap. 13.00 (*1-56584-312-6*, Pub. by New Press NY) Norton.

***Castaneda, Jorge.** Perpetuating Power. Smithies, Padraic Arthur, tr. from SPA. 2000. 30.00 (*1-56584-616-8*) New Press NY.

C

An Asterisk (*) at the beginning of an entry indicates that the title is appearing for the first time.

Castaneda, Jorge, et al. Leandro Katz: Two Projects/A Decade. (Illus.). 24p. (Orig.). 1996. pap. 20.00 (*1-882454-04-9*) El Museo Barrio.

Castaneda, Jorge G. Companero: La Vida Y Muerte de Che Guevara.Tr. of Companero: The Life & Death of Che Guevara. (SPA.). 1997. pap. 16.00 (*0-679-78161-7*) Vin Bks.

— Companero: The Life & Death of Che Guevara. LC 98-26441. (Illus.). 496p. pap. 16.00 (*0-679-75940-9*) Vin Bks.

***Castaneda, Jorge G.** La Herencia: Arqueologia de la Sucesion Presidencial en Mexico. (Extra Alfaguara Ser.). (SPA.). 2000. pap. 21.95 (*968-19-0573-3*) Aguilar.

Castaneda, Jorge G. Utopia Unarmed: The Latin American Left after the Cold War. 512p. 1994. pap. 15.00 (*0-679-75141-6*) Vin Bks.

Castaneda, Laura & Castellanos, Laura. The Latino Guide to Personal Money Management. LC 99-13522. (Illus.). 311p. 1999. pap. 16.95 (*1-57660-058-0*, Pub. by Bloomberg NJ) Norton.

Castaneda, Luis A. 52 Semanas de Virtudes. (SPA.). 1997. pap. text 6.98 (*968-38-0569-8*) Panorama Edit.

Castaneda, Marcia, ed. see Edelman, Ellis S., et al.

Castaneda, Margaret Runyan. A Magical Journey with Carlos Castaneda. (Illus.). 204p. 1996. pap. write for info. (*0-9696960-1-9*) Mil2enia Pr.

Castaneda, Marina, tr. see Shein, Max.

Castaneda-Mendez, Kicab. The Baldrige Assessor's Workbook: How to Perform the Examiner's Role for Internal & External Assessments. LC 97-26526. 239p. 1997. spiral bd. 39.95 (*0-527-76325-X*) Productivity Inc.

— Value-Based Cost Management for Healthcare: Linking Costs to Quality & Delivery. 189p. 1996. 32.95 (*0-527-76304-7*) Productivity Inc.

Castaneda, Omar. Among the Volcanoes. (J). 1996. pap. 4.50 (*0-440-91118-4*) BDD Bks Young Read.

Castaneda, Omar S. Abuela's Weave. LC 92-71927. (Illus.). 32p. (J). (gr. k-4). 1993. 15.95 (*1-880000-00-8*) Lee & Low Bks.

— Abuela's Weave. LC 92-71927. (Illus.). 32p. (J). (ps-3). 1995. pap. 6.95 (*1-880000-20-2*) Lee & Low Bks.

Castaneda, Omar S. Abuela's Weave. 1993. 12.15 (*0-606-08912-8*, Pub. by Turtleback) Demco.

Castaneda, Omar S. Among the Volcanoes. 192p. (J). (ps-3). 1992. pap. 4.50 (*0-440-40746-X*) Dell.

Castaneda, Omar S. Among the Volcanoes. (J). 1991. 9.09 (*0-606-02481-6*, Pub. by Turtleback) Demco.

Castaneda, Omar S. Remembering to Say "Mouth" or "Face" Stories. (Winner of the Nineteen Ninety-Three Charles H. & N. Mildred Nilon Award for Excellence in Minority Fiction Ser.). 156p. 1993. 18.95 (*0-932511-80-5*); pap. 8.95 (*0-932511-81-3*) Fiction Coll.

— El Tapiz de Abuela. Marcuse, Aida E., tr. LC 93-38628. (SPA., Illus.). 32p. (J). (ps-4). 1994. 15.95 (*1-880000-08-3*); pap. 6.95 (*1-880000-11-3*) Lee & Low Bks.

Castaneda, Omar S. El Tapiz De Abuela. 1993. 11.15 (*0-606-08919-5*, Pub. by Turtleback) Demco.

Castaneda, Pedro. Journey of Coronado. 1990. pap. 8.95 (*0-486-26308-8*) Dover.

Castaneda, Quetzil. In the Museum of Maya Culture: Touring Chichen Itza. LC 96-4583. 1996. pap. 21.95 (*0-8166-2673-1*); text 54.95 (*0-8166-2672-3*) U of Minn Pr.

Castaneda, Rosalva, tr. see Subcommittee for the Third Millennium/Jubilee Year.

Castaneda, Rosolva, tr. see US Catholic Conference Staff.

Castaneda, Tarsicio. Combating Poverty: Innovative Social Reforms in Chile During the 1980's. 275p. 1992. 34.95 (*1-55815-192-3*); pap. 19.95 (*1-55815-154-0*) ICS Pr.

Castaneda-Zuniga, Wilfrido R. Interventional Radiology, 2 vols. 3rd ed. 1816p. write for info. (*0-7817-2117-2*) Lppncott W & W.

Castaneda-Zuniga, Wilfrido R. & Tadavarthy, S. Murthy. Interventional Radiology, 2 vols., Set. 2nd ed. (Illus.). 1568p. 1991. 250.00 (*0-683-01476-5*) Lppncott W & W.

Castaneda-Zuniga, Wilfrido R., et al. Interventional Radiology, 2 vols. 3rd ed. LC 95-51106. (Illus.). 2080p. 1996. 275.00 (*0-683-01477-3*) Lppncott W & W.

Castanede, Marina G., tr. see Fuentes, Carlos.

Castanias, Richard P., jt. auth. see Griffin, Paul A.

Castanien, Pliny. To Protect & Serve: A History of the San Diego Police Department & Its Chiefs, 1889-1989. LC 92-47133. (Illus.). 130p. (Orig.). 1993. pap. 14.95 (*0-918740-14-2*) San Diego Hist.

Castano, Silvana. Database Security. 480p. (C). 1994. 54.95 (*0-201-59375-0*) Addison-Wesley.

Castano, Silvana, et al. Database Security Vol. 10: Status & Prospects; Proceedings. (Illus.). 456p. 1999. reprint ed. text 25.00 (*0-7881-6542-9*) DIANE Pub.

Castanon, Santiago G., tr. see Villanueva, Dario.

Castanos, Octavio, et al. Latin-American School of Physics: XXX ELAF. (AIP Press Conference Proceedings Ser.: No. 365). (Illus.). 432p. 1996. 145.00 (*1-56396-567-4*, CP 365, AIP Pr) Spr-Verlag.

Castans, R. Grand Dictionnaire des Mots D'Esprit. (FRE.). 1998. 19.95 (*0-320-00369-8*) Fr & Eur.

Castans, Raymond. Dictionnaire de l'Esprit: Deaux Mille Citations de Rabelias a Coluche. (FRE.). 344p. 1991. pap. 39.95 (*0-7859-8179-9*, 2877061167) Fr & Eur.

— Marcel Pagnol M'a Raconte. (FRE.). 1976. pap. 10.95 (*0-7859-1826-4*, 2070367932) Fr & Eur.

Castany, Gilbert. Dictionnaire Francais d'Hydrogeologie. (FRE.). 250p. 1977. 95.00 (*0-7859-9276-6*) Fr & Eur.

Castanza, Philip. The Complete Films of Jeanette MacDonald & Nelson Eddy. (Illus.). 224p. 1981. pap. 14.95 (*0-8065-0771-3*, Citadel Pr) Carol Pub Group.

Castberg, A. Didrick. Japanese Criminal Justice. LC 90-32792. 168p. 1990. 45.00 (*0-275-93355-5*, C3355, Praeger Pubs) Greenwood.

Castberg, C., jt. auth. see Adler, Lillian W.

Caste, Nicholas J., jt. auth. see Kiersky, James H.

Castedo, Elena. Paradise. LC 89-25640. 336p. 1995. pap. 13.00 (*0-8021-3427-0*, Grove) Grove-Atltic.

Casteel, Bette D., et al. Old Town-Albuquerque in the 1940's & a Little Beyond. (Illus.). 52p. 1996. per. 8.00 (*0-9654431-9-1*) Chaparral Press.

***Casteel, David A. & Moss, Steven D.** Basic Collision Analysis & Scene Documentation. 2nd ed. LC 99-53288. 160p. 2000. spiral bd. 45.00 (*0-913875-82-1*, 5821-N) Lawyers & Judges.

Casteel, Herbert C. The Drums of Moloch. LC 90-55602. 164p. (Orig.). 1990. pap. 6.99 (*0-89900-384-2*) College Pr Pub.

Casteel, J. Doyle, et al. Cross-Cultural Models of Teaching: Latin American Examples. LC 76-13369. 173p. reprint ed. pap. 53.70 (*0-7837-4915-5*, 204458000004) Bks Demand.

Casteel, Richard W. & Quimby, George I., eds. Maritime Adaptations of the Pacific. (World Anthropology Ser.). x, 320p. 1975. 60.00 (*90-279-7619-8*) Mouton.

Casteel, Rick. Poop with Flies Drawing Contest! (Illus.). 112p. 1998. per. 10.95 (*0-9663633-0-2*) Cream Corn.

Casteels, Kristina. 1,25-Dihydroxyvitamin D3 & Its Analogues As Immunomodulators in Autoimmune Type 1 Diabetes: Mechanisms of Action & Preclinical Applications. (Acta Biomedica Lovaniensia Ser.). (Illus.). 160p. 1998. pap. 39.50 (*90-6186-876-9*, Pub. by Leuven Univ) Coronet Bks.

Castegnaro, M., et al, eds. Laboratory Decontamination & Destruction of Carcinogens in Laboratory Wastes: Some Aromatic Amines & 4-Nitrobiphenyl. (IARC Scientific Publications: No. 64). 100p. 1985. pap. 12.95 (*0-19-723064-4*) OUP.

— Laboratory Decontamination & Destruction of Carcinogens in Laboratory Wastes: Some Mycotoxins. (IARC Scientific Publications: No. 113). (Illus.). 68p. 1992. pap. text 30.00 (*92-832-2113-3*) OUP.

— Laboratory Decontamination & Destruction of Carcinogens in Laboratory Wastes: Some Polycyclic Heterocyclic Hydrocarbons. (IARC Scientific Publications: No. 114). (Illus.). 58p. 1992. pap. text 20.00 (*92-832-2114-1*) OUP.

Castegnaro, M. & Sansone, Eric B. Chemical Carcinogens. 130p. 1986. 23,00 (*0-387-16719-6*) Spr-Verlag.

Castegnaro, M., et al. Mycotoxins, Nephropathy & Urinary Tract Tumors. (IARC Scientific Publications: No. 115). (Illus.). 358p. 1992. pap. text 98.00 (*92-832-2115-X*) OUP.

Castegnaro, M., ed. see International Agency for Research on Cancer Staff.

Castel. Canadian Conflict of Laws. 2nd ed. 824p. 1986. pap., suppl. ed. 50.00 (*0-409-89377-3*, MICHIE) LEXIS Pub.

— Introduction to Conflict of Laws. 2nd ed. 240p. 1986. pap. 49.00 (*0-409-80592-0*, MICHIE) LEXIS Pub.

Castel, Albert. The Campaign for Atlanta. (Civil War Ser.). (Illus.). 56p. 1996. pap. 4.95 (*0-915992-94-9*) Eastern National.

— Civil War Kansas: Reaping the Whirlwind. LC 97-21546. (Modern War Studies). (Illus.). 266p. 1997. pap. 15.95 (*0-7006-0872-9*) U Pr of KS.

— Decision in the West. LC 92-10882. (Modern War Studies). (Illus.). 688p. (Orig.). (C). 1995. pap. 19.95 (*0-7006-0748-X*) U Pr of KS.

— Decision in the West: The Atlanta Campaign of 1864. LC 92-10882. (Modern War Studies). (Illus.). xviii, 668p. (Orig.). 1992. 34.95 (*0-7006-0562-2*) U Pr of KS.

— A Frontier State at War: Kansas, 1861-1865. (Illus.). 251p. (C). 1992. reprint ed. pap. 15.95 (*1-878882-03-1*) KS Heritage Pr.

— General Sterling Price & the Civil War in the West. LC 68-21804. (Illus.). 300p. (C). 1993. pap. 18.95 (*0-8071-1854-0*) La State U Pr.

— The Presidency of Andrew Johnson. LC 79-11050. (American Presidency Ser.). x, 262p. 1979. 29.95 (*0-7006-0190-2*) U Pr of KS.

***Castel, Albert.** Tom Taylor's Civil War. 2000. 29.95 (*0-7006-1049-9*) U Pr of KS.

Castel, Albert. Winning & Losing in the Civil War: Essays & Stories. LC 95-40947. 220p. 1996. 29.95 (*1-57003-074-X*) U of SC Pr.

Castel, Albert & Goodrich, Thomas. Bloody Bill Anderson: The Short, Savage Life of a Civil War Guerrilla. LC 98-34144. (Illus.). 192p. 1998. 24.95 (*0-8117-1506-X*) Stackpole.

Castel, Albert E. A Frontier State at War: Kansas, Eighteen Sixty-One to Eighteen Sixty-Five. LC 78-26281. 251p. 1979. reprint ed. lib. bdg. 35.00 (*0-313-20863-8*, CAFS, Greenwood Pr) Greenwood.

Castel, Alberte. William Clarke Quantrill: His Life & Times. LC 98-49039. 1999. pap. text 13.95 (*0-8061-3081-4*) U of Okla Pr.

Castel, B. & O'Donnell, P. J., eds. Symmetry Violations in Subatomic Physics: Proceedings of the 6th Summer Institute in Theoretical Physics. 240p. (C). 1989. text 93.00 (*9971-5-0908-3*) World Scientific Pub.

Castel, B. & Towner, Ian S. Modern Theories of Nuclear Moments. (Oxford Studies in Nuclear Physics: No. 12). (Illus.). 282p. 1990. text 75.00 (*0-19-851728-9*) OUP.

Castel, Boris, jt. auth. see El-Baz, Edgard.

Castel, Christine Du, see Du Castel, Christine.

Castel, Francoise, et al. The Psychiatric Society. Goldhammer, Arthur, tr. from FRE. LC 81-15504. (European Perspectives Ser.). 368p. 1982. text 67.00 (*0-231-05244-8*) Col U Pr.

Castel, Nico. The Complete Puccini Libretti, Vol. 1. (Illus.). xv, 579p. (Orig.). (C). 1993. pap. text 55.00 (*1-878617-08-7*) Leyerle Pubns.

— The Complete Puccini Libretti, Vol. 2. (Illus.). xvi, 434p. (Orig.). (C). 1994. pap. text 50.00 (*1-878617-09-5*) Leyerle Pubns.

— The Complete Verdi Libretti, Vol. 1. (Illus.). xv, 438p. (C). 1995. text 60.00 (*1-878617-10-9*) Leyerle Pubns.

— The Complete Verdi Libretti, Vol. 2. (Illus.). (C). 1995. text 65.00 (*1-878617-11-7*) Leyerle Pubns.

— The Complete Verdi Libretti, Vol. 3. (Illus.). xv, 484p. (C). 1996. text 60.00 (*1-878617-12-5*) Leyerle Pubns.

— The Complete Verdi Libretti, Vol. 4. (Illus.). xv, 523p. (C). 1996. text 60.00 (*1-878617-13-3*) Leyerle Pubns.

— French Opera Libretti, Vol. I. (ENG & FRE., Illus.). xviii, 700p. 1999. text 75.00 (*1-878617-27-3*) Leyerle Pubns.

— A Singer's Manual of Spanish Lyric Diction. LC 94-6333. (ENG & SPA., Illus.). 164p. (Orig.). (C). 1994. 15.95 (*0-9627226-9-3*) Excalibur Pub.

Castelain, Daniel. A Sentimental Talk & an Unlikely Meeting. Bowles, Patrick, tr. from FRE. LC 79-131217. (French Ser.).Tr. of Ed de Minuit & Un Rencontre Improbable. 128p. 1971. 4.95 (*0-87376-014-X*) Red Dust.

Casteldine, George & McGee, Paula. Advanced & Specialist Nursing Practice. LC 98-25008. 1998. 36.95 (*0-632-04248-6*) Blackwell Sci.

Castelfranchi, Cristiano & Werner, Eric, eds. Artificial Social Systems: 4th European Workshop on Modelling Autonomous Agents in a Multi-Agent World MAAMAW '92, S. Martino al Cimino, Italy, July 29-31 1992. LC 94-3556. (Lecture Notes in Computer Science Ser.: Vol. 830). 1994. 55.95 (*0-387-58266-5*) Spr-Verlag.

Castelijn, Boudewijn. USFHA Coaches Manual. 100p. 1988. 19.00 (*0-318-49983-5*) US Field Hockey.

Castelijns, J. A., jt. ed. see Mukherji, S. K.

Castelino, Mark G., jt. auth. see Powers, Mark J.

Castelino, Meher. Fashion Kaleidoscope. (C). 1994. 72.00 (*81-7167-155-1*, Pub. by Rupa) S Asia.

Castelino, Noel, tr. see Henriot, Christian.

Castell. The Business of Data Broadcasting. (Computer Science Ser.). Date not set. text 60.50 (*0-412-39660-2*) Chapman & Hall.

— Cassell's Dictionary of Spanish Language: Diccionario de la Lengua Espanalo. (ENG & SPA.). 1036p. 1986. 34.95 (*0-8288-2033-3*, S15304) Fr & Eur.

***Castell, Adrian M.** Synergy Matters: Working with Systems in the 21st Century. LC 99-33091. 657p. 1999. write for info. (*0-306-46186-2*, Kluwer Plenum) Kluwer Academic.

***Castell, Alburey & Borchert, Donald M.** Introduction to Modern Philosophy: Examining the Human Condition. 7th ed. 672p. 2000. pap. 50.67 (*0-13-019458-1*) P-H.

Castell, Alburey, et al. An Introduction to Modern Philosophy: Examining the Human Condition. 6th ed. LC 93-6964. (Illus.). 656p. (C). 1993. 75.33 (*0-02-320092-8*, Macmillan Coll) P-H.

Castell, Alburey, ed. see Huxley, Thomas Henry.

Castell, Alburey, ed. see James, William.

Castell, Alburey, ed. see Mill, John Stuart.

Castell, Donald, jt. ed. see Dubois, Andre.

Castell, Donald O., ed. The Esophagus. 2nd ed. LC 94-45588. 832p. 1995. text 199.95 (*0-316-15842-9*, Little Brwn Med Div) Lppncott W & W.

Castell, Donald O. & Richter, Joel E., eds. Esophagus. 3rd ed. 22p. 1999. 200.00 (*0-7817-1535-0*) Lppncott W & W.

Castell, Hazel & Griffin, Kathleen. Out of the Frying Pan: Seven Women Who Changed the Course on Postwar Cookery (In Britain) (Illus.). 183p. 1998. text 22.00 (*0-7881-5755-8*) DIANE Pub.

Castell, J. V. & Gomez-Lechon, M. J., eds. In Vitro Methods in Pharmaceutical Research. (Illus.). 480p. 1996. boxed set 80.00 (*0-12-163390-X*) Acad Pr.

Castell, Suzanne De, see De Castell, Suzanne.

Castella, Robert De, see De Castella, Robert.

Castellan. Los Arboles Mueren de Pie. (C). 1995. pap. text 23.50 (*0-15-504248-3*) Harcourt Coll Pubs.

Castellan, Georges. History of the Balkans from Mohammed the Conqueror to Stalin. 493p. 1991. text 75.50 (*0-88033-222-0*, Pub. by East Eur Monographs) Col U Pr.

— A History of the Romanians. (East European Monographs: No. 257). 268p. 1989. text 62.00 (*0-88033-154-2*, Pub. by East Eur Monographs) Col U Pr.

Castellan, Gilbert W. Physical Chemistry. 3rd ed. LC 82-22754. (Chemistry Ser.). (Illus.). 1040p. (C). 1983. text 69.00 (*0-201-10386-9*) Addison-Wesley.

Castellan, N. J., jt. auth. see Siegel, Sidney.

Castellan, N. J., Jr., jt. ed. see Restle, Frank.

Castellan, N. John, Jr., ed. Individual & Group Decision Making: Current Issues. 328p. 1993. text 79.95 (*0-8058-1090-0*) L Erlbaum Assocs.

Castellan, Yvone. La Familia. (Breviarios Ser.). (SPA.). pap. 6.99 (*968-16-1952-8*, Pub. by Fondo) Continental Bk.

Castellaneta, P. J. Together Alone: The Text of the Internationally Acclaimed Film. (Illus.). 100p. (Orig.). pap. 9.95 (*0-9646504-0-1*) PJ Party Prodns.

Castellani, A., ed. DNA Damage & Repair. (Illus.). 382p. 1988. 110.00 (*0-306-43083-5*, Plenum Trade) Perseus Pubng.

Castellani, Amleto, ed. Lymphocyte Stimulation: Differential Sensitivity to Radiation, Biochemical, & Immunological Processes. LC 80-19883. (Illus.). 196p. 1980. reprint ed. pap. 60.80 (*0-608-05440-2*, 206590900006) Bks Demand.

Castellani, Brian. Pathological Gambling: The Making of a Medical Problem. LC 99-40431. (C). 2000. text 57.50 (*0-7914-4521-6*); pap. text 18.95 (*0-7914-4522-4*) State U NY Pr.

Castellani, C., et al, eds. Disordered Systems & Localization: Proceedings. (Lecture Notes in Physics Ser.: Vol. 149). 308p. 1981. 33.95 (*0-387-11163-8*) Spr-Verlag.

Castellani, Elena. Interpreting Bodies: Classical & Quantum Objects in Modern Physics. LC 98-17178. 344p. 1998. text 65.00 (*0-691-01724-7*, Pub. by Princeton U Pr); pap. text 19.95 (*0-691-01725-5*, Pub. by Princeton U Pr) Cal Prin Full Svc.

Castellani, L. & Wess, J., eds. Quantum Groups & Their Applications in Physics. LC 95-8172. (International School of Physics Enrico Fermi Ser.: Vol. 127). 629p. (YA). (gr. 12). 1996. pap. 176.00 (*90-5199-247-5*, 247-5) IOS Press.

Castellani, L., et al. Supergravity & Superstrings: A Geometric Perspective, 3 vols. 2216p. 1991. text 205.00 (*9971-5-0037-X*); pap. text 113.00 (*9971-5-0038-8*) World Scientific Pub.

Castellano, Aldo, intro. Zeidler Roberts Partnership: Architecture & Culture. (I Talenti Ser.). (FRE, ITA & KOR., Illus.). 144p. 1998. pap. 40.00 (*88-7838-031-8*) Rockport Pubs.

Castellano, Bernardo, ed. see Berta, Alez G.

Castellano, C. Electrocardiografia Clinica. (C). 1996. text 34.00 (*84-8174-133-7*) Mosby Inc.

Castellano, Carmine C. & Seitz, Clifford P. You Fix It: Washing Machines LC 72-86423. 192 p. 1975. 4.95 (*0-668-02704-5*) Macmillan.

Castellano, Carol & Kosman, Dawn. The Bridge to Braille: Reading & School Success for the Young Blind Child. large type ed. LC 97-18720. (Illus.). 214p. 1997. spiral bd. 12.00 (*1-885218-08-7*) Natl Fed Blind.

Castellano-Giron, Hernan. Twilights of Anthony Wayne Drive. Efthimides, Emil, tr. from SPA. (Illus.). 60p. (Orig.). 1984. pap. 6.00 (*0-931081-00-9*) Operation DOME.

Castellano, Joseph A. Handbook of Display Technology. (Illus.). 341p. 1992. text 100.00 (*0-12-163420-5*) Acad Pr.

Castellano, Juan R., jt. auth. see Casona, Alejandro.

Castellano, Marcello, et al, eds. New Trends in Fuzzy Logic II: Proceedings of the WILF '97 - Italian Workshop on Fuzzy Logic, 1997 Bari, Italy, 19-20 March, 1997. 300p. 1998. 78.00 (*981-02-3309-4*) World Scientific Pub.

Castellano, Michael A., et al. Key to Spores of the Genera of Hypogeous Fungi of North Temperate Forests with Special Reference to Animal Mycophagy. (Illus.). 196p. (Orig.). 1989. pap. text 24.95 (*0-916422-77-1*) Mad River.

Castellano, Robert N. Semiconductor Device Processing: Technology Trends in the VLSI Era. LC 91-36127. 234p. 1992. text 72.00 (*2-88124-516-1*) Gordon & Breach.

Castellano, Rocco. The H. I. T. Fitness System. 1997. pap. 34.95 incl. audio compact disk (*1-890923-02-8*) Castleco Pub.

— The H. I. T. Fitness System. Brzycki, Matt, ed. (Illus.). 65p. 1997. 5.95 (*1-890923-00-1*, 1-0011-1) Castleco Pub.

Castellano, Thomas C., jt. ed. see Auerbach, Barbara J.

Castellanos, A., ed. Electrohydrodynamics. (CISM International Centre for Mechanical Sciences Ser.: No. 380). (Illus.). viii, 363p. 1998. pap. 82.95 (*3-211-83137-1*) Spr-Verlag.

Castellanos, Agustin. Historia de Mi Vida. LC 87-80406. (Coleccion Cuba y sus Jueces). (SPA., Illus.). 152p. (Orig.). 1987. pap. 15.00 (*0-89729-437-8*) Ediciones.

Castellanos, Gabriela. Laughter, War & Feminism Vol. 11: Elements of Carnival in Three of Jane Austen's Novels. LC 93-42550. (Writing about Women Ser.: Vol. 11). XI, 241p. (C). 1995. text 43.95 (*0-8204-2351-3*) P Lang Pubng.

Castellanos, Henry C. New Orleans As It Was. LC 89-26568. (Illus.). 364p. 1990. pap. 10.95 (*0-88289-787-X*) Pelican.

Castellanos, Isabel & Inclan, Josefina, eds. En Torno a Lydia Cabrera. LC 86-83361. (Coleccion Ebano y Canela). (SPA., Illus.). 335p. (Orig.). 1988. pap. 30.00 (*0-89729-432-7*) Ediciones.

Castellanos, Isabel & Llorenc. Diccionario. (FRE & CAT.). 624p. 1997. 69.95 (*0-320-02189-0*) Fr & Eur.

— Diccionario. 2nd ed. (FRE & CAT.). 632p. 1997. 69.95 (*0-320-02056-8*) Fr & Eur.

Castellanos, Isabel, jt. auth. see Castellanos, Jorge.

Castellanos, Isabel, ed. see Cabrera, Lydia.

Castellanos, Javier, tr. see Piaget, Jean, et al.

Castellanos, Jorge. Placido, Poeta Social y Politico. LC 83-82303. (SPA.). 141p. (Orig.). 1984. pap. 10.00 (*0-89729-341-X*) Ediciones.

— 24 de Febrero de 1895: Un Programa Vigente. (SPA.). 1995. pap. 18.00 (*0-89729-752-0*) Ediciones.

Castellanos, Jorge & Castellanos, Isabel. Cultura Afrocubana No. 1: El Negro en Cuba, 1492-1844. LC 87-83071. (Coleccion Ebano y Canela). (SPA.). 369p. (Orig.). 1989. pap. 39.00 (*0-89729-463-7*) Ediciones.

— Cultura Afrocubana No. 2: El Negro en Cuba, 1845-1959. LC 87-83071. (Coleccion Ebano y Canela). (SPA.). 482p. (Orig.). 1990. pap. 39.00 (*0-89729-506-4*) Ediciones.

— Cultura Afrocubana No. 4: Letras - Musica - Arte. LC 87-83071. (Coleccion Ebano y Canela). (SPA.). 511p. (Orig.). 1994. pap. 39.00 (*0-89729-618-4*) Ediciones.

— Cultura Afrocubana, No. 3: Las Religiones y las Lenguas. LC 87-83071. (Coleccion Ebano y Canela). (SPA., Illus.). 456p. (Orig.). 1992. pap. 39.00 (*0-89729-507-2*) Ediciones.

***Castellanos, Jose A. & Tardos, Juan D.** Mobile Robot Localization & Map Building - A Multisensor Fusion Approach. 224p. 2000. 125.00 (*0-7923-7789-3*) Kluwer Academic.

Castellanos, Laura, jt. auth. see Castaneda, Laura.

Castellanos, Laura, ed. see Moroso, Pam.

Castellanos, Linda & Kunz, Cindy. Foster Penguin: A Story about a Foster Child. LC 95-81934. (Illus.). 40p. (J). (ps-1). 1996. 10.95 (*1-57543-003-7*) Mar Co Prods.

C

An Asterisk (*) at the beginning of an entry indicates that the title is appearing for the first time.

Castellanos Llorenc, Carles & Castellanos Llorenc, Rafael. Diccionario Catala-Frances, Frances-Catala, 2 vols.Tr. of Catalan-French, French-Catalan Dictionary. (SPA.). 1090p. 1983. 150.00 (*0-7859-5032-X*) Fr & Eur.

Castellanos Llorenc, Rafael, jt. auth. see Castellanos Llorenc, Carles.

Castellanos, Rosario. Balun Canan. 1991. pap. 10.99 (*968-16-0729-5*) Fondo.

— The Book of Lamentations. Allen, Esther, tr. from SPA. 400p. 1996. 24.00 (*1-56886-038-2*) Marsilio Pubs.

— Book of Lamentations. Allen, Esther, tr. & afterword by by. LC 98-11868. xiii, 381p. 1998. pap. 13.95 (*0-14-118003-X*) Viking Penguin.

— City of Kings. Miller, Yvette E., ed. Rudder, Robert S. & Chacon de Arjona, Gloria, trs. from SPA. LC 92-21223. (Discoveries Ser.). 143p. 1992. pap. 14.95 (*0-935480-63-3*) Lat Am Lit Rev Pr.

***Castellanos, Rosario.** Ciudad Real. 1998. pap. 19.95 (*968-19-0332-3*) Santillana.

Castellanos, Rosario. Meditacion en el Umbral (Meditation on the Threshold) (SPA.). 232p. 1985. pap. 8.99 (*968-16-1888-2*, Pub. by Fondo) Continental Bk.

— Meditation on the Threshold: A Bilingual Anthology of Poetry. Palley, Julian, tr. LC 87-73552. (ENG & SPA.), 176p. 1988. pap. 15.00 (*0-916950-80-8*) Biling Rev-Pr.

— Mujer Que Sabe Latin (Woman Who Speaks Latin) (SPA.). 216p. 1992. reprint ed. pap. 14.99 (*968-16-1673-1*, Pub. by Fondo) Continental Bk.

— Nine Guardians. Nicholson, Irene, tr. from SPA. 272p. 1992. pap. 14.95 (*0-930523-90-3*) Readers Intl.

— Obras I (Complete Works I) Narrativa (Prose) (SPA.). 983p. 1989. 31.99 (*968-16-3213-3*, Pub. by Fondo) Continental Bk.

— Oficio de Tinieblas. 368p. 1998. pap. 13.95 (*0-14-026833-2*) Viking Penguin.

— Poesia No Eres Tu (Poetry . . . It's Not You!) 2nd ed. (SPA.). 336p. 1975. pap. 16.99 (*968-16-1004-0*, Pub. by Fondo) Continental Bk.

***Castellanos, Rosario.** Rito de Iniciacion. 1998. pap. 19.95 (*968-19-0333-1*) Santillana.

Castellanos, Rosario. A Rosario Castellanos Reader. Ahern, Maureen, tr. from SPA. (Texas Pan American Ser.). 400p. 1988. 34.95 (*0-292-77039-1*); pap. 17.95 (*0-292-77036-7*) U of Tex Pr.

Castellarin, Loretta & Roberts, Ken. Spike. (Degrassi Book Ser.). 117p. (J). (gr. 7-9). 1995. mass mkt. 4.95 (*1-55028-113-5*); bds. 16.95 (*1-55028-115-1*) Formac Dist Ltd.

Castelle, Kay, jt. auth. see Nurkse, Dennis.

Castelle, Kay, jt. ed. see Nurkse, Dennis.

Castellet, George C. Cine-Lit: Essays on Peninsular Film & Fiction. Marti-Olivella, Jaume & Wood, Guy H., eds. 240p. 1992. pap. text 10.00 (*0-9631927-0-1*) G H Wood.

Castellet, M. & Dicks, W., eds. Collected Works of Pere Menal. 656p. 1996. 69.00 (*0-8176-5147-0*) Birkhauser.

Castellet, M., jt. ed. see Casacuberta, C.

Castelli, A. C. & Castelli, C. A. The Sensuous Artichoke: Magic of the Artichoke. (Illus.). 294p. 1998. 24.95 (*0-9669552-2-6*) A C Castelli.

Castelli, C. A., jt. auth. see Castelli, A. C.

Castelli, Jim. People Power. 1995. pap. 14.95 (*0-8050-4299-7*) H Holt & Co.

Castelli, Jim, ed. How I Pray. 208p. 1994. pap. 9.00 (*0-345-38331-1*) Ballantine Pub Grp.

Castelli, Joseph R. Basques in the Western United States: A Functional Approach to Determination of Cultural Presence in the Geographical Landscape. Cordasco, Francesco, ed. LC 80-844. (American Ethnic Groups Ser.). 1981. lib. bdg. 23.95 (*0-405-13408-8*) Ayer.

Castelli, Leo. Jasper Johns. (Illus.). 80p. 1997. text 18.95 (*0-7893-0085-0*) St Martin.

— Jasper Johns. (Universe of Art Ser.). 1997. 18.95 (*0-614-28066-4*) Vendome.

Castelli, Michael G. Thermomechanical Fatigue Behavior of Materials, Vol. 2, No. 1263. Verrilli, Michael J., ed. LC 96-19174. (Special Technical Publication Ser.). (Illus.). 390p. text 79.00 (*0-8031-2001-X*, STP1263) ASTM.

Castelli Theisen, Vera, tr. see Martini, Carlo M.

Castelli, William P. & Griffin, Glen C. Good Fat, Bad Fat: Lower Your Cholesterol & Reduce Your Odds of a Heart Attack. 2nd rev. ed. LC 96-37278. 300p. 1997. pap. 12.95 (*1-55561-117-6*) Fisher Bks.

Castellini, Michael A., et al. Annual Cycles of Diving Behavior & Ecology of the Weddell Seal. LC 92-21717. (Bulletin of the Scripps Institute of Oceanography Ser.: Vol. 28). 1992. pap. 10.00 (*0-520-09779-3*, Pub. by U CA Pr) Cal Prin Full Svc.

***Castellino, Joshua.** International Law & Self-Determination: The Interplay of the Politics Of Territorial Possession With Formulations of Post-Colonial National Identity. LC 00-41095. (Developments in International Law Ser.). 2000. write for info. (*90-411-1409-2*) Kluwer Law Intl.

Castellino, Nicolo, et al. Inorganic Lead Exposure: Metabolism & Intoxication. 544p. 1994. lib. bdg. 104.95 (*0-87371-997-2*, L997) Lewis Pubs.

Castellino, Robert L. Colorado: Heart & Soul. (Illus.). 136p. 1999. write for info. (*1-879914-52-2*); pap. write for info. (*1-879914-53-0*) Whispering River.

***Castellino, Robert L.** Denver: Gateway to the Rockies. LC 00-132991. 180p. 2001. 59.95 (*1-879914-93-X*) Whispering River.

Castelliz, K., tr. see Grohmann, Gerbert.

Castelliz, K., tr. see Lauer, Hans E.

Castelliz, K., tr. see Remer, Nicolaus.

Castelliz, K., tr. see Steiner, Rudolf.

Castello, Charles G. Symptoms of Schizophrenia. LC 93-16759. (Series on Personality Processes). 336p. 1993. 99.95 (*0-471-54875-8*) Wiley.

Castello, Dario. Dario Castello: Selected Ensemble Sonatas I. Selfridge-Field, Eleanor, ed. (Recent Researches in Music of the Baroque Era Ser.: Vol. RRB23). (Illus.). xiii, 103p. 1977. pap. 30.00 (*0-89579-091-2*) A-R Eds.

Castello, Elena R. & Kapon, Uriel M. The Jews & Europe: 2000 Years of History. LC 94-16970. 1995. 50.00 (*0-8050-3526-5*) H Holt & Co.

Castello, Elena Romero. Jews & Europe. 1998. 29.99 (*0-7858-0954-6*) Bk Sales Inc.

***Castello, Gerald M., ed.** Our Sunday Visitor's Treasury of Catholic Stories. LC 99-70510. 400p. 1999. 24.95 (*0-87973-947-9*) Our Sunday Visitor.

Castello, Marsha K. Mothers Apple Pie: A Collection of Treasured Words & Recipes. Enos, Herbert A., ed. (Illus.). 140p. (Orig.). 1997. pap. 10.95 (*1-57502-536-1*, P01576) Morris Pubng.

Castello, R. Random House Timetables of History. 2nd rev. ed. 320p. 1996. pap. 6.99 (*0-679-76960-9*) Random Ref & Info.

Castello, Sergio & Ozawa, Terutomo. Globalization of Small Economies as Strategic Behavior in International Business. LC 99-30105. (Transnational Business & Corporate Culture Ser.). 155p. 1999. 50.00 (*0-8153-3307-2*) Garland.

Castellon, Carol, et al. Mathematics for Health Careers. LC 93-15623. (C). 1993. pap. 26.50 (*0-8273-5569-6*) Delmar.

— Mathematics for Health Careers: Instructor's Guide. 52p. 1994. teacher ed. 12.95 (*0-8273-6357-5*) Delmar.

Castellon, Ninoska Perez. Dulcamara (Bittersweet) LC 82-82596. (Coleccion Espejo de Paciencia). (ENG & SPA.). 77p. (Orig.). 1982. pap. 9.00 (*0-89729-317-7*) Ediciones.

Castells. Guia Practica del Adolescente. 1999. pap. text 24.95 (*84-08-02382-9*) Planeta Edit.

— Mosaicos. 2nd ed. 280p. (C). 1997. pap. text, wbk. ed. 14.67 (*0-13-915893-6*) P-H.

— Mosaicos. 2nd ed. 168p. (C). 1998. pap. text, lab manual ed. 14.67 (*0-13-915885-5*) P-H.

***Castells, Manuel.** The Castells Reader on Cities. Susser, Ida, ed. 2001. 64.95 (*0-631-21932-3*); pap. 27.95 (*0-631-21933-1*) Blackwell Pubs.

Castells, Manuel. The Economic Crisis & American Society. LC 79-3194. 301p. reprint ed. pap. 93.40 (*0-8357-8866-0*, 203338800085) Bks Demand.

***Castells, Manuel.** End of Millennium. 2nd ed. (Information Age Ser.: Vol. 3). 560p. 2000. pap. 27.95 (*0-631-22139-5*) Blackwell Pubs.

Castells, Manuel. End of Millennium: The Information Age: Economy, Society & Culture, Vol. III. LC 97-20968. (Illus.). 352p. 1997. text 73.95 (*1-55786-871-9*) Blackwell Pubs.

— End of Millennium: The Information Age: Economy, Society & Culture, Vol. III. LC 97-20968. (Illus.). 352p. 1998. pap. text 27.95 (*1-55786-872-7*) Blackwell Pubs.

— The Information Age: Economy, Society, & Culture, 3 vols. 1296p. 1999. pap. 64.95 (*0-631-21594-8*) Blackwell Pubs.

— Informational City: Economic Restructuring & Urban Development. 1991. pap. 29.95 (*0-631-17937-2*) Blackwell Pubs.

— The Power of Identity Vol. 2: The Information Age: Economy, Society & Culture. LC 96-36317. (Information Age Ser.). (Illus.). 352p. 1997. pap. text 27.95 (*1-55786-874-3*) Blackwell Pubs.

***Castells, Manuel.** Rise of the Network Society. 2nd ed. (Information Age Ser.: Vol. 1). 272p. 2000. pap. 27.95 (*0-631-22140-9*) Blackwell Pubs.

Castells, Manuel. The Rise of the Network Society: The Information Age: Economy, Society & Culture. (Illus.). 480p. (C). 1996. pap. 27.95 (*1-55786-617-1*) Blackwell Pubs.

— Technopoles of the World: Making of 21st Century Industrial Complexes. (Illus.). 320p. (C). 1994. pap. 27.99 (*0-415-10015-1*) Routledge.

Castells, Manuel, ed. High Technology, Space, & Society. LC 84-24876. (Urban Affairs Annual Reviews Ser.: No. 28). (Illus.). 320p. 1985. reprint ed. pap. 99.20 (*0-7837-4561-3*, 204409000003) Bks Demand.

Castells, Manuel & Kiselyova, Emma. The Collapse of Soviet Communism: A View from the Information Society. LC 95-13474. (Exploratory Essays Ser.: No. 2). xi, 97p. (Orig.). 1995. pap. text 9.50 (*0-87725-704-3*) U of Cal IAS.

Castells, Manuel, et al. Critical Education in the New Information Age. LC 98-29543. (Critical Perspectives Ser.). 224p. (C). 1998. reprint ed. pap. 60.00 (*0-8476-9011-3*) Rowman.

***Castells, Manuel, et al.** Critical Education in the New Information Age. LC 98-29543. (Critical Perspectives Ser.). 224p. (C). 1998. reprint ed. 18.95 (*0-8476-9010-5*) Rowman.

Castells, Manuel, jt. auth. see Borja, Jordi.

Castells, Manuel, jt. auth. see Mollenkopf, John H.

Castells, Manuel, jt. ed. see Henderson, Jeffrey.

Castells, Manuel, jt. ed. see Mollenkopf, John H.

***Castells, Paulino.** Guia Practica De La Salud Y Psicologia Del Nino. 1999. 32.95 (*84-08-02876-6*) Planeta.

Castells, Ricardo. Calisto's Dream & the Celestinesque Tradition: A Rereading of Celestina. LC 95-8444. (Romance Languages & Literatures Ser.: No. 249). 150p. (C). 1995. pap. text 24.95 (*0-8078-9253-X*) U of NC Pr.

***Castells, Ricardo.** Fernando de Rojas & the Renaissance Vision. LC 99-53721. (Studies in Romance Literatures). 2000. 45.00 (*0-271-01984-0*) Pa St U Pr.

Castells, Ricardo, jt. auth. see De Castells, Matilda O.

Castellucci, F., et al. Coherent Raman Spectroscopy - Applications & New Developments: XI European Cars Workshop. 280p. 1993. text 109.00 (*981-02-1125-2*) World Scientific Pub.

Castellucci, Marion, jt. auth. see Throop, Robert K.

***Castelluccio, Frank.** Other Side of Ethel Mertz. 2000. mass mkt. 6.99 (*0-425-17609-6*) Blvd Books.

Castelluccio, Frank & Walker, Alvin. The Other Side of Ethel Mertz: The Life Story of Vivian Vance. (Illus.). 300p. 1998. 24.95 (*1-879198-26-6*) Knwldg Ideas & Trnds.

***Castelluci, Bardi.** Pasta & More! 1999. 24.95 (*0-7370-0071-6*) T-L Custom Pub.

Castelman, Harry & Niewoehner, Christopher. Going to Law School? Everything You Need to Know to Choose & Pursue a Degree in Law. LC 96-51993. 224p. 1997. pap. 14.95 (*0-471-14907-1*) Wiley.

Castelnuovo, Sheri, et al, intros. Wisconsin Triennial, 1993. (Illus.). (Orig.). (C). 1993. pap. 10.00 (*0-913883-20-4*) Madison Art.

Castelnuovo, Sheri & Rodgers, Sandy. Making Connections: Integrating Art into the Classroom: a Handbook of Lesson Plans for Kindergarten Through Grade Five. (Illus.). 1995. pap. write for info. (*0-913883-22-0*) Madison Art.

***Castelnuovo, Sheri, et al.** Wisconsin Triennial 1999. (Illus.). 64p. 1999. pap. 10.00 (*0-913883-26-3*) Madison Art.

Castelnuovo, Sheri, et al. Wisconsin Triennial, 1996. (Illus.). 64p. (Orig.). 1996. pap. 15.00 (*0-913883-23-9*) Madison Art.

Castelnuovo, Shirley & Guthrie, Sharon R. Feminism & the Female Body: Liberating the Amazon Within. LC 97-49323. (Gender & Political Theory Ser.). 182p. 1998. lib. bdg. 39.95 (*1-55587-439-8*) L Rienner.

Castelnuovo-Tedesco, Pietro. Dynamic Psychiatry: Explorations in Psychotherapy, Psychoanalysis, & Psychosomatic Medicine. LC 90-4927. (Emotions & Behavior Monographs: No. 10). 450p. 1991. 70.00 (*0-8236-1515-4*) Intl Univs Pr.

— The Twenty-Minute Hour: A Guide to Brief Psychotherapy for the Physician. LC 86-7890. 195p. reprint ed. pap. 60.50 (*0-608-20022-0*, 207129400010) Bks Demand.

Castelnuovo-Tedesco, Pietro & Lichtenberg, Joseph D., eds. Change & Therapeutic Effectiveness in Psychoanalysis & Psychotherapy. (Psychoanalytic Inquiry Ser.: Vol. 9, No. 1). 1995. 20.00 (*0-88163-959-1*) Analytic Pr.

Castelo, M. J. Mapfre Dictionary of Insurance: Trilingual Glossary in Spanish, English, & French. 3rd ed. (ENG, FRE & SPA.). 1992. 150.00 (*0-7859-8956-0*) Fr & Eur.

Castelot, Andre. King of Rome. LC 74-6778. (Illus.). 396p. 1974. reprint ed. lib. bdg. 79.50 (*0-8371-7571-2*, CAKR, Greenwood Pr) Greenwood.

— Turbulent City: Paris 1783 to 1871. Folliot, Denise, tr. LC 76-117867. (Select Bibliographies Reprint Ser.). 1977. 28.95 (*0-8369-5320-7*) Ayer.

Castelvecchi, Stefano, ed. see Verdi, Giuseppe.

Castelvetro, Lodovico. Castelvetro on the Art of Poetry: An Abridged Translation of Lodovico Castelvetro's "Poetica d'Aristotele Vulgarizzata et Sposta" LC 83-17386. (Medieval & Renaissance Texts & Studies: Vol. 29). 432p. 1984. 40.00 (*0-86698-063-6*, MR29) MRTS.

Castelyn, Mary & Webb, Sylvia. Promoting Excellence: Personnel Management & Staff Development in Libraries. 300p. 1993. lib. bdg. 63.00 (*0-86291-606-2*) Bowker-Saur.

Casten, Carole M. Aqua Aerobics Today. Perlee, Clyde, ed. 200p. (C). 1993. mass mkt. 19.25 (*0-314-93454-5*) West Pub.

Casten, Carole M. & Jordan, Peg. Aerobics Today. Perlee, Clyde, ed. 151p. (C). 1990. mass mkt. 19.25 (*0-314-68953-2*) West Pub.

Casten, R. F., et al. Perspectives for the Interacting Boson Model: Proceedings on the Occasion of Its 20th Anniversary. 780p. 1994. text 162.00 (*981-02-2071-5*) World Scientific Pub.

Casten, Richard F. Nuclear Structure from a Simple Perspective. (Oxford Studies in Nuclear Physics). (Illus.). 400p. 1990. text 85.00 (*0-19-504599-8*) OUP.

***Casten, Richard F.** Nuclear Structure from a Simple Perspective. 2nd ed. (Oxford Studies in Nuclear Physics: Vol. 23). (Illus.). 432p. 2000. pap. text 60.00 (*0-19-850724-0*) OUP.

Casten, Richard F., ed. Algebraic Approaches to Nuclear Structure: Interacting Boson & Fermion Models. LC 92-26649. (Contemporary Concepts in Physics Ser.: Vol. 6). 500p. 1993. text 118.00 (*3-7186-0537-6*); pap. text 51.00 (*3-7186-0538-4*) Gordon & Breach.

Casten, Richard F., et al, eds. Contemporary Topics in Nuclear Structure Physics: Proceedings of the International Conference, Cocoyoc, Mexico. 768p. 1988. text 138.00 (*9971-5-0685-8*) World Scientific Pub.

Casten, Thomas R. Turning off the Heat: Why America Must Double Energy Efficiency to Save Money & Reduce Global Warming. LC 98-28272. 230p. 1998. 26.95 (*1-57392-269-2*) Prometheus Bks.

Castenada, Carlos E. Our Catholic Heritage in Texas, 1519-1936, 7 vols., Set. LC 76-1471. (Chicano Heritage Ser.). (Illus.). 1976. reprint ed. 272.95 (*0-405-09488-4*) Ayer.

Castenada, Carlos E., tr. see Cortes, Carlos E., ed.

***Casteneda, Carlos.** Wheel of Time. 2001. pap. 13.95 (*0-7434-1280-X*, WSP) PB.

Castenell, Louis A., Jr. & Pinar, William F., eds. Understanding Curriculum As Racial Text: Representations of Identity & Difference in Education. LC 92-38899. (SUNY Series, Feminist Theory in Education). 312p. (C). 1993. text 59.50 (*0-7914-1661-5*); pap. text 19.95 (*0-7914-1662-3*) State U NY Pr.

Castenell, Louis A. & Tarule, Jill M. The Minority Voice in Educational Reform: An Analysis by Minority & Women College of Education Deans. LC 96-52286. (Social & Policy Issues in Education). 1997. 73.25 (*1-56750-318-7*); pap. 24.95 (*1-56750-319-5*) Ablx Pub.

Castenell, Louis A., Jr., et al. Essays on Emerging Assessment Issues. 1993. 18.00 (*0-89333-113-9*) AACTE.

Castenell, Louis A., Jr., jt. ed. see Valverde, Leonard A.

Castenholz, B. J. Field Guide to Revenue Stamped Paper Pt. 3: The Central States. LC 88-92684. (C. & S. Revenue Ser.). (Illus.). 96p. 1989. pap. 14.95 (*0-9603498-6-3*) Castenholz Sons.

— Field Guide to Revenue Stamped Paper, Pt. 2: The Southern States. LC 89-90940. (C. & S. Revenue Ser.). (Illus.). 96p. 1989. pap. 14.95 (*0-9603498-5-5*) Castenholz Sons.

Castenholz, B. J., ed. Field Guide to Revenue Stamp Paper Pt. 5: Eastern States. LC 88-92684. (C. & S. Revenue Ser.). (Illus.). 128p. 1990. pap. 17.45 (*0-9603498-8-X*) Castenholz Sons.

— Field Guide to Revenue Stamped Paper Pt. 1: The Western States. rev. ed. LC 96-96402. (Series on Revenue Stamps). (Illus.). 128p. 1996. pap. 20.00 (*1-879767-05-8*) Castenholz Sons.

— Field Guide to Revenue Stamped Paper Pt. 4: Eastern Central States. (C. & S. Revenue Ser.). (Illus.). 112p. 1990. pap. 15.95 (*0-9603498-7-1*) Castenholz Sons.

— Field Guide to Revenue Stamped Paper Pt. 6: New York State. (C. & S. Revenue Ser.). (Illus.). 128p. 1991. pap. 17.45 (*1-879767-00-7*) Castenholz Sons.

— Field Guide to Revenue Stamped Paper Pt. 7. LC 88-92684. (C. & S. Revenue Ser.). (Illus.). 128p. 1992. pap. 17.45 (*1-879767-01-5*) Castenholz Sons.

Castenholz, Bill J. An Introduction to Revenue Stamps. LC 93-90966. (C. & S. Revenue Ser.). (Illus.). 96p. 1994. pap. 6.50 (*1-879767-04-X*) Castenholz Sons.

Castenholz, Richard W., jt. auth. see Boone, David B., Jr.

Caster, Andrew. The Complete Guide to Better Vision. LC 96-49572. 1997. pap. 11.00 (*0-345-40951-5*) Ballantine Pub Grp.

Caster, Harriet. Fat Puss & Slimpup. (Illus.). pap. 7.95 (*0-14-036631-8*, Pub. by Pnguin Bks Ltd) Trafalgar.

Caster, J. L., ed. Aquatic Oligochaete Biology: Proceedings of the 4th International Symposium on Aquatic Oligochaete Biology. (Developments in Hydrobiology Ser.). 264p. (C). 1989. reprint ed. text 266.50 (*0-7923-0283-4*) Kluwer Academic.

Caster, Kenneth E. Palaeontographica Americana: A New Jellyfish (Kirklandia Texana Caster) from the Lower Cretaceous of Texas, No. 18. 1945. 3.00 (*0-87710-319-4*) Paleo Res.

Caster, Lillie D. The Classifier's Guide to LC Class H: Subdivision Techniques for the Social Sciences. LC 85-28459. 143p. (C). 1986. pap. text 49.95 (*0-918212-99-5*) Neal-Schuman.

Caster, Paul. Reunion in Hell. LC 82-62274. (Illus.). 80p. 1983. pap. 25.00 (*0-937486-02-7*) Perimeter Pr.

Caster, Pierre-Georges, ed. see Balzac, Honore de.

Caster, Wendy. The Lesbian Sex Book: A Guide for Women Who Love Women. LC 93-71122. (Illus.). 192p. 1998. pap. 15.95 (*1-55583-211-3*) Alyson Pubns.

***Castera, Georges.** Alarive Lezanfan. (Illus.). 46p. 1998. pap. write for info. (*2-9805796-3-7*) Edit Memo.

— Jean Le Menuiser: Bos Jan. (FRE., Illus.). 11p. 1999. pap. write for info. (*1-58437-010-6*) Edit Memo.

— Le Pere et L'Enfant: Pitit Papa L. (FRE., Illus.). 11p. 1999. pap. write for info. (*1-58437-011-4*) Edit Memo.

Casteras, Susan P. English Pre-Raphaelitism & Its Reception in America in the Nineteenth-Century. LC 87-46421. (Illus.). 216p. 1990. 65.00 (*0-8386-3328-5*) Fairleigh Dickinson.

— James Smetham (1821-1889) LC 94-27581. 1995. 69.95 (*1-85928-103-6*, Pub. by Scolar Pr) Ashgate Pub Co.

— Pocket Cathedrals: Pre-Raphaelite Book Illustration. LC 91-65082. (Illus.). 112p. 1991. pap. 18.95 (*0-930606-65-5*) Yale Ctr Brit Art.

Casteras, Susan P. & Denney, Colleen, eds. The Grosvenor Gallery: A Palace of Art in Victorian England. LC 95-50255. 209p. 1996. 55.00 (*0-300-06752-6*) Yale U Pr.

Casteras, Susan P. & Faxon, Alicia C. Pre-Raphaelite Art in Its European Context. LC 92-55114. 248p. 1995. 80.00 (*0-8386-3539-3*) Fairleigh Dickinson.

Casteras, Susan P. & Faxon, Alicia C., eds. Pre-Raphaelite Art in Its European Context. LC 94-15619. 1995. write for info. (*0-8386-4850-9*) Fairleigh Dickinson.

Casteras, Susan P. & Parkinson, Ronald. Richard Redgrave. LC 87-51378. (Illus.). 224p. (C). 1988. 45.00 (*0-300-04221-3*) Yale U Pr.

Casteras, Susan P. & Peterson, Linda H. A Struggle for Fame: Victorian Women Artists & Authors. LC 94-60143. (Illus.). 104p. (Orig.). 1994. pap. 14.95 (*0-930606-72-8*) Yale Ctr Brit Art.

Casteras, Susan P., et al. The Grosvenor Gallery: A Palace of Art in Victorian England. LC 95-50255. 1996. 8.00 (*0-930606-77-9*) Yale Ctr Brit Art.

— John Ruskin & the Victorian Eye. LC 92-30289. (Illus.). 223p. 1993. 39.95 (*0-910407-27-4*) Phoenix Art.

Casteret, Norbert. Ten Years under the Earth. Massey, Burrows, tr. LC 75-26892. (Illus.). 255p. 1975. reprint ed. pap. 6.95 (*0-914264-07-9*) Cave Bks MO.

Casterline, Charlotte L. The Asthma Attack by Bo B. Bear. (Illus.). (Orig.). (J). (ps-6). 1988. pap. 5.95 (*0-9617218-2-0*) Info All Bk.

— My Friend Has Asthma. (Illus.). 24p. (Orig.). (J). (ps-6). 1985. pap. 4.95 (*0-9617218-0-4*) Info All Bk.

— Sam the Allergen. (Illus.). 26p. (Orig.). (J). (ps-6). 1985. pap. 4.95 (*0-9617218-1-2*) Info All Bk.

Casterline, Gail F., jt. auth. see Darling, Sharon S.

An Asterisk (*) at the beginning of an entry indicates that the title is appearing for the first time.

Casterline, J. B., et al. Fertility in the United States: New Patterns, New Theories. LC 96-44636. 1996. pap. 20.00 (*0-87834-086-6*) Population Coun.

Castetter, Edward F. & Underhill, Ruth M. The Ethnobiology of the Papago Indians. LC 76-43676. (University of New Mexico Bulletin Biological Ser.: Vol. 4). reprint ed. 30.00 (*0-404-15509-X*) AMS Pr.

Castetter, Edward F., et al. Pima & Papago Indian Agriculture. LC 76-43674. reprint ed. 42.50 (*0-404-15510-3*) AMS Pr.

***Castetter, William Benjamin & Young, Ila Phillip.** The Human Resource Function in Educational Administration. 7th ed. LC 99-21248. (Illus.). 400p. 2000. 71.00 (*0-13-927112-0*, Merrill Coll) P-H.

Castex, et al. Hispanic Young People & the Church's Pastoral Response, Vol. 1. Cervantes, Carmen M., ed. Wood, Richard, tr. from SPA. (Prophets of Hope Ser.). (Illus.). 296p. 1994. pap. 14.95 (*0-88489-325-1*) St Marys.

Castex, ed. see Balzac, Honore de.

Castex, ed. see Castex, Pierre-Georges.

Castex, Pierre-G., jt. auth. see Balzac, Honore de.

Castex, Pierre-Georges. La Maison du Chat-qui-pelote. Castex, ed. Incl. Bal de Sceaux. Vendetta. (Class. Garnier Ser.). Set pap. 29.95 (*0-685-23883-0*) Fr & Eur.

Castex, Pierre-Georges & Surer, P. Manuel Des Etudes Litteraires Francaises, 6 tomes, Tome 1: Moyen Age. (Illus.). 5.95 (*0-685-11344-2*) Fr & Eur.

— Manuel Des Etudes Litteraires Francaises, 6 tomes, Tome 2: 16e Siecle. (Illus.). 14.95 (*0-685-11345-0*) Fr & Eur.

— Manuel Des Etudes Litteraires Francaises, 6 tomes, Tome 3: 17e Siecle. (Illus.). 14.95 (*0-685-11346-9*) Fr & Eur.

— Manuel Des Etudes Litteraires Francaises, 6 tomes, Tome 4: 18e Siecle. (Illus.). 14.95 (*0-685-11347-7*) Fr & Eur.

— Manuel Des Etudes Litteraires Francaises, 6 tomes, Tome 5: 19e Siecle. (Illus.). 15.95 (*0-685-11348-5*) Fr & Eur.

— Manuel Des Etudes Litteraires Francaises, 6 tomes, Tome 6: 20e Siecle. (Illus.). 16.95 (*0-685-11349-3*) Fr & Eur.

— Manuel des Etudes Litteraires Francaises, 6 tomes, Vol. 1. 13.95 (*0-8288-7640-1*, F13980) Fr & Eur.

Castex, Pierre-Georges, et al. Manuel des Etudes de la Litterature Francaise - 17th. 261p. 1966. 19.95 (*0-8288-7441-7*) Fr & Eur.

Castex, Pierre-Georges, jt. auth. see Auguste de Villiers de l'Isle, Adam.

Castex, Pierre-Georges, ed. see Balzac, Honore de.

Castex, Pierre-Georges, ed. see Villiers de l'Isle-Adam, Auguste de.

Castex, Raoul. Strategic Theories. Kiesling, Eugenia C., tr. & intro. by. LC 93-1840. (Classics of Sea Power Ser.). 479p. 1993. 39.95 (*1-55750-100-9*) Naval Inst Pr.

Casthasaigh, Aindrias O., jt. auth. see Connolly, James.

Casthely, Pierre, et al. Update in Critical Care Medicine: Management of the Critical Care Patient. LC 89-91693. (Illus.). 200p. (Orig.). 1989. 59.00 (*0-9623083-0-7*) P A Casthely.

***Casti.** Borderline. 2000. 25.00 (*0-7382-0097-2*, Pub. by Perseus Pubng) HarpC.

Casti, jt. auth. see Larson, Robert Edward.

Casti, John. The Cambridge Quintet: A Work of Scientific Speculation. (Helix Bks.). 208p. 1999. pap. text 13.00 (*0-7382-0138-3*, Pub. by Perseus Pubng) HarpC.

Casti, John L. Alternate Realities: Mathematical Models of Nature & Man. LC 88-22337. 493p. 1989. 115.00 (*0-471-61842-X*) Wiley.

— Complexification: Explaining a Paradoxical World Through the Science of Surprise. LC 93-36049. 336p. 1995. pap. 14.00 (*0-06-092587-6*, Perennial) HarperTrade.

— Five Golden Rules: Great Theories of 20th- Century Mathhematics & Why They Matter. LC 94-44470. (Illus.). 256p. 1997. pap. 16.95 (*0-471-19337-2*) Wiley.

— Five Golden Rules: Great Theories of 20th-Century Mathematics--& Why They Matter. LC 94-44470. 235p. 1995. 26.95 (*0-471-00261-5*) Wiley.

***Casti, John L.** Five More Golden Rules: Gordian Knots, Secret Codes, & the Importance of Being Nonlinear - More Great Theories of 20th Century Mathematics. LC 99-39544. 256p. 2000. 27.95 (*0-471-32233-4*) Wiley.

— Godel: A Life of Logic, the Mind & Mathematics. 224p. 2000. text 25.00 (*0-7382-0274-6*, Pub. by Perseus Pubng) HarpC.

Casti, John L. Mission to Abisko: Stories & Myths in the Creation of Scientific "Truth" Karlqvist, Anders, ed. 1998. 25.00 (*0-7382-0002-6*) Perseus Pubng.

— Paradigms Lost: Tackling the Unanswered Mysteries of Modern Science. 1990. pap. 14.00 (*0-380-71165-6*, Avon Bks) Morrow Avon.

***Casti, John L.** Paradigms Regained: A Further Exploration of the Mysteries of Modern Science. LC 99-45972. (Illus.). 256p. 2000. 25.00 (*0-688-16115-4*, Wm Morrow) Morrow Avon.

Casti, John L. Reality Rules: Picturing the World in Mathematics, 2 vols. 864p. 1992. 175.00 (*0-471-57797-9*) Wiley.

— Reality Rules: Picturing the World in Mathematics, Vol. 1. 96p. 1992. pap. text 19.95 (*0-471-58941-1*) Wiley.

— Reality Rules: Picturing the World in Mathematics, 2 vols., Vol. 2. LC 92-12213. 864p. 1997. pap. 99.95 (*0-471-18437-3*, Wiley-Interscience) Wiley.

— Reality Rules: Picturing the World in Mathematics - The Frontier, Vol. 2. LC 92-12213. 448p. 1997. pap. 54.95 (*0-471-18436-5*, Wiley-Interscience) Wiley.

— Reality Rules: Picturing the World in Mathematics - The Fundamentals, Vol. 1. LC 92-12213. 416p. 1997. pap. 54.95 (*0-471-18435-7*, Wiley-Interscience) Wiley.

— Reality Rules Vol. 1: Picturing the World in Mathematics, the Fundamentals. 2nd ed. LC 92-12213. 416p. 1992. 115.00 (*0-471-57021-4*) Wiley.

— Reality Rules Vol. 2: Picturing the World in Mathematics, The Frontier, Vol. 2. LC 92-12213. 448p. 1992. 105.00 (*0-471-57798-7*) Wiley.

— Science As Storytelling. 1998. write for info. (*0-201-36086-1*) Addison-Wesley.

***Casti, John L.** Would-Be Worlds: How Simulation Is Changing the Frontiers of Science. 256p. 1998. 14.95 (*0-471-19693-2*) Wiley.

Casti, John L. Would-Be Worlds: How the New Science of Simulation Is Breaking the Complexity Barrier. LC 96-16841. 256p. 1996. 24.95 (*0-471-12308-0*) Wiley.

Casti, John L., ed. Beyond Belief: Randomness, Prediction & Explanation - Science. 330p. 1990. boxed set 104.95 (*0-8493-4291-0*, Q174) CRC Pr.

Casti, John L. & Karlqvist, Anders. Newton to Aristotle: Towards a Theory of Models for Living Systems. (Mathematical Modeling Ser.: No. 4). 296p. 1989. 73.00 (*0-8176-3435-5*) Birkhauser.

***Casti, John L. & Karlqvist, Anders, eds.** Art & Complexity: At the Interface. 304p. 2000. text 35.00 (*0-7382-0236-3*) Perseus Pubng.

Casti, John L. & Karlqvist, Anders, eds. Complexity, Language, & Life: Mathematical Approaches. (Biomathematics Ser.: Vol. 16). x, 284p. 1986. 107.95 (*0-387-16180-5*) Spr-Verlag.

— Cooperation & Conflict in General Evolutionary Processes. 435p. 1994. 115.00 (*0-471-59487-3*) Wiley.

***Casti, John L. & Karlqvist, Anders, eds.** Mission to Abisko: Stories & Myths in the Creation of Scientific "Truth" 208p. 1999. pap. text 13.00 (*0-7382-0167-7*, Pub. by Perseus Pubng) HarpC.

Casti, John L., jt. auth. see Larson, Robert E.

Castiello, Umberto, jt. ed. see Bennett, Keree M. B.

Castiglia, Christopher. Bound & Determined: Captivity, Culture-Crossing & the White Womanhood from Mary Rowlandson to Patty Hearst. LC 95-20049. (Women in Culture & Society Ser.). (Illus.). 268p. 1995. pap. text 13.95 (*0-226-09654-8*) U Ch Pr.

— Bound & Determined: Captivity, Culture-Crossing & the White Womanhood from Mary Rowlandson to Patty Hearst. LC 95-20049. (Women in Culture & Society Ser.). (Illus.). 268p. 1996. lib. bdg. 38.00 (*0-226-09652-1*) U Ch Pr.

Castiglia, Julie. Margaret Mead. (Pioneers in Change Ser.). (Illus.). 144p. (J). (gr. 5-9). 1989. lib. bdg. 13.95 (*0-382-09525-1*) Silver Burdett Pr.

Castiglia, Patricia T. & Harbin, Richard E., eds. Child Health Care: Process & Practice. LC 91-46703. (Illus.). 1134p. reprint ed. pap. 200.00 (*0-608-07315-6*, 206754300009) Bks Demand.

Castiglia, Paul, ed. Archie Americana Series: Best of the Fifties. (Illus.). 96p. (Orig.). pap. 8.95 (*1-879794-01-2*) Archie Comic.

— Archie Americana Series: Best of the Sixties. (Illus.). 96p. (Orig.). 1995. pap. 9.95 (*1-879794-02-0*) Archie Comic.

Castiglione, Baldassare. The Book of the Courier. 304p. 1994. 8.50 (*0-460-87502-7*, Everyman's Classic Lib) Tuttle Pubng.

— The Book of the Courtier. Bull, George, tr. (Classics Ser.). 368p. 1976. pap. 13.95 (*0-14-044192-1*, Penguin Classics) Viking Penguin.

— Book of the Courtier. Hoby, Thomas, tr. LC 01-7785. (Tudor Translations, First Ser.: No. 23). reprint ed. 57.50 (*0-404-51854-0*) AMS Pr.

Castiglione, Dario & Sharpe, Lesley, eds. Shifting the Boundaries: Transformation of the Languages of Public & Private in the 18th Century. 272p. 1995. text 59.95 (*0-85989-444-4*, Pub. by Univ Exeter Pr) Northwestern U Pr.

Castiglione, Dennis J. Fundamentals of Self-Promotion. 63p. 90.00 (*0-614-25582-1*, 00SM44341) Print Indus Am.

***Castiglione, Janice.** Musical Twinkle, Twinkle, Little Star. (Rub-a-Dub-Tub Musical Bks.). (Illus.). (J). 2000. pap. 5.99 (*1-883043-18-2*) Straight Edge.

— Wheels on the Bus, 1. 1999. pap. text 5.00 (*1-883043-14-X*) Straight Edge.

Castiglione, Janice, jt. illus. see Stuchly, Judith.

Castiglione, Mary M. & Johnson, Cynthia C. Brain Attack: Mapping Out Early Recovery from Stroke. Hollingsworth, Anna, ed. LC 95-3305. (Illus.). 48p. (Orig.). 1995. pap. text 8.95 (*0-939838-40-0*) Pritchett & Hull.

— Waiting to Clear: Brain Injury: Early Stages of Recovery. LC 93-37557. (Illus.). 48 + 40p. 1994. pap. text 9.50 (*0-939838-35-4*) Pritchett & Hull.

Castiglione, Pierina B. Italian Phonetics, Diction & Intonation. (ITA.). 103p. 1957. reprint ed. pap. 12.95 (*0-913298-48-4*) S F Vanni.

Castiglioni, Arturo. Adventures of the Mind. (Illus.). 402p. 1997. 38.95 (*0-8369-2984-5*) Ayer.

— Encantamiento y Magia (Enchantment & Magic) 2nd ed. (SPA.). 395p. 1947. pap. 12.99 (*968-16-0540-3*, Pub. by Fondo) Continental Bk.

— The Renaissance of Medicine in Italy. LC 79-114967. 1979. 17.95 (*0-405-10587-8*) Ayer.

Castiglioni, Marco & Benco, Argeo A., eds. Advanced Techniques for Radiotherapy. LC 92-49636. (Eurocourses: Advanced Scientific Techniques Ser.: Vol. 2). 144p. (C). 1992. text 95.00 (*0-7923-1588-X*) Kluwer Academic.

Castilaw-Palliser, Diane. A Court Reporting: Grammar & Punctuation. (C). 1987. text 29.95 (*0-538-11610-2*, K61) S-W Pub.

Castilawpalliser, Diane. Court Reporting: Grammar & Punctuation. 2nd ed. (KK - Legal Secretary Studies). (C). 1992. mass mkt. 23.25 (*0-538-70577-9*) S-W Pub.

Castile. To Show Heart: Native American Self-Determination & Federal Indian Policy, 1960-1975. LC 97-33775. 216p. 1998. 35.00 (*0-8165-1837-8*) U of Ariz Pr.

Castile, George P. To Show Heart: Native American Self-Determination & Federal Indian Policy, 1960-1975. LC 97-33775. 227p. 1999. pap. 16.95 (*0-8165-1838-6*) Univ of Arizona Graduate Library.

Castile, George P. & Bee, Robert L., eds. State & Reservation: New Perspectives on Federal Indian Policy. LC 92-8229. 259p. (Orig.). (C). 1992. 42.00 (*0-8165-1319-8*); pap. text 21.50 (*0-8165-1325-2*) U of Ariz Pr.

Castile, Rand. Ikeda & Idea: Two New Japanese Printmakers. (Illus.). 43p. 1995. pap. 3.50 (*0-913304-03-4*, 034X) Japan Soc.

Castilejo, Jose. The War of Ideas in Spain: Philosophy, Politics & Education. 1976. lib. bdg. 59.95 (*0-8490-2806-X*) Gordon Pr.

Castilho, Lydia. Believing in Angels. 64p. (Orig.). 1997. 8.95 (*0-9658433-0-0*) Poetry & Prose.

Castilla, Constanza De, see De Castilla, Constanza.

Castilla, Greg S. Struggles from Both Shores. (Illus.). 267p. (Orig.). 1995. pap. text 11.95 (*0-9636557-1-X*) Paperworks.

Castilla, Julia M., tr. see Baca, Ana.

Castilla, Julia M., tr. see Gonzales Bertrand, Diane.

Castilla, Julia Mercedes. Emilio. LC 99-29481. 160p. (gr. 4-7). 1999. pap. 9.95 (*1-55885-271-9*, Pinata Bks) Arte Publico.

Castilla, Julia Mercedes, tr. see Chavarria-Chairez, Becky.

Castilla, Lara. Aprender a Volar. (SPA.). 1997. pap. 7.98 (*968-13-2951-1*, Pub. by Edit Diana) Libros Fronteras.

— Aprender a Volar 2. (SPA.). 1997. pap. 7.98 (*968-13-3008-0*, Pub. by Edit Diana) Libros Fronteras.

— Busqueda La. (SPA.). 1997. pap. text 11.98 (*968-13-1119-1*) Libros Fronteras.

— Caminos de Amor. (SPA.). 1997. pap. 7.98 (*968-13-2835-3*, Pub. by Edit Diana) Libros Fronteras.

— Vive. (SPA.). 1997. pap. text 9.98 (*968-13-1545-6*) Libros Fronteras.

— Vuelve Maestro Vuelve. (SPA.). 1997. pap. text 11.98 (*968-13-1833-1*) Libros Fronteras.

Castilla, Ramon, tr. see Gomez, Luis O. & Torretti, Roberto, eds.

Castillejo, Irene Claremont De, see Claremont de Castillejo, Irene.

Castillo. Antologia Sobre Manuel Gomez Morin. (SPA.). pap. 16.99 (*968-16-4430-1*, Pub. by Fondo) Continental Bk.

Castillo. Cuentos y Microcuentos. (SPA.). 1995. pap. text 28.00 (*0-03-017208-X*) HarBrace.

— Instructor's Manual for Strategies, Techniques & Approaches to Thinking: Case Studies in Clinical Nursing. Eoyang, Thomas, ed. (Illus.). 159p. 1999. teacher ed. write for info. (*0-7216-7649-9*, W B Saunders Co) Harcrt Hlth Sci Grp.

Castillo. Nursing Issues, Trends & Portents. (Nursing Education Ser.). 1997. pap. 26.50 (*0-8273-6270-6*) Delmar.

— Spanish English Dictionary (Export) 1991. per. 3.50 (*0-671-74172-1*) PB.

— Spanish-English English-Spanish Dictionary. 1997. mass mkt. 3.50 (*0-671-01956-2*) PB.

— The University Of Chicago Spanish Dictionary: Bolivia Edition. (SPA.). 1997. 4.99 (*0-671-02345-4*, Pocket Books) PB.

— The University of Chicago Spanish Dictionary: Mexico Edition. (SPA.). 1997. 4.99 (*0-671-02344-6*, Pocket Books) PB.

Castillo & Bond. University of Chicago Spanish Dictionary: A New Concise Spanish-English & English-Spanish Dictionary of Words & Phrases Basic to the Written & Spoken Language of Today, 7 vols. large type ed. (ENG & SPA.). 1740p. (YA). (gr. 9 up). 1967. reprint ed. 434.00 (*0-317-01954-6*, J-23870-00) Am Printing Hse.

Castillo, ed. see Ibstedt, Henry.

Castillo, Abelardo. El Que Tiene Sed. (SPA.). 257p. 1985. pap. 9.00 (*0-317-46764-6*) Ediciones Norte.

Castillo, Adelaida Del, see Del Castillo, Adelaida, ed.

Castillo, Amelia del. Agua y Espejos: Imagenes. LC 86-80921. (Coleccion Espejo de Paciencia). (SPA., Illus.). 69p. (Orig.). 1986. pap. 9.00 (*0-89729-402-5*) Ediciones.

***Castillo, Ana.** Carmen la Coja. 2000. pap. 12.00 (*0-375-72468-0*) Knopf.

— La Diosa de las Americas. 288p. 2000. pap. 13.00 (*0-375-70369-1*) Vin Bks.

Castillo, Ana. Loverboys. LC 96-29904. 224p. 1997. pap. 11.95 (*0-452-27773-6*, Plume) Dutton Plume.

— Loverboys. 220p. 1996. 21.00 (*0-393-03959-5*) Norton.

— Massacre of the Dreamers: Essays on Xicanisma. LC 95-12412. 258p. 1995. pap. 14.95 (*0-452-27424-9*, Plume) Dutton Plume.

***Castillo, Ana.** Mi Hija, Mi Hijo, el Aguila, la Paloma. (SPA., Illus.). 48p. (J). 2000. 12.99 (*0-525-45867-0*, Dutton Child) Peng Put Young Read.

Castillo, Ana. The Mixquiahuala Letters. LC 86-70701. 132p. 1986. 20.00 (*0-916950-67-0*) Biling Rev-Pr.

— The Mixquiahuala Letters. 144p. 1992. pap. 11.00 (*0-385-42013-7*, Anchor NY) Doubleday.

— The Mixquiahuala Letters & Sapogonia. 368p. 1994. pap. 13.00 (*0-385-47080-0*, Anchor NY) Doubleday.

***Castillo, Ana.** My Daughter, My Son, the Eagle, the Dove: An Aztec Chant. (Illus.). 48p. (J). 2000. 12.99 (*0-525-45856-5*, Dutton Child) Peng Put Young Read.

Castillo, Ana. My Father Was a Toltec & Selected Poems. 192p. 1996. pap. 12.00 (*0-393-31354-9*) Norton.

— Peel My Love Like an Onion. LC 99-25057. 240p. 1999. 23.95 (*0-385-49676-1*) Doubleday.

***Castillo, Ana.** Peel My Love Like an Onion. 256p. 2000. reprint ed. pap. 12.00 (*0-385-49677-X*, Anchor NY) Doubleday.

Castillo, Ana. Sapogonia. LC 89-933. 320p. 1990. 27.00 (*0-916950-95-6*); pap. 17.00 (*0-916950-96-4*) Biling Rev-Pr.

— So Far from God: A Novel. LC 93-45382. 258p. 1994. pap. 12.95 (*0-452-27209-2*, Plume) Dutton Plume.

***Castillo, Ana.** Tan Lejos de Dios. 1999. pap. 14.95 (*0-452-28004-4*) NAL.

Castillo, Ana, ed. Goddess of the Americas: Writings on the Virgin of Guadalupe. 256p. 1997. reprint ed. pap. 14.00 (*1-57322-630-0*, Riverhd Trade) Berkley Pub.

Castillo, Ana, ed. from ENG. Esta Puente, Mi Espalda: Voces de Mujeres Tercermundistas en los Estados Unidos. rev. ed. Alarcon, Norma, tr. from ENG. LC 88-13481. (SPA., Illus.). 268p. 1988. 16.00 (*0-910383-20-0*); pap. 10.00 (*0-910383-19-7*) Ism Pr.

Castillo, Ana Hernandez Del, see Hernandez del Castillo, Ana.

Castillo, Andres V. Spanish Mercantilism: Geronimo de Uztariz-Economist. LC 79-20392. ix, 193p. 1980. reprint ed. lib. bdg. 35.00 (*0-87991-858-6*) Porcupine Pr.

Castillo, Bernal D. De, see De Castillo, Bernal D.

Castillo, Carlo. University of Chicago Spanish-English, English-Spanish Dictionary. (ENG & SPA.). 1977. 10.09 (*0-606-02029-2*, Pub. by Turtleback) Demco.

Castillo, Carlos. Spanish-English Dictionary. 4th ed. (SPA & ENG.). 1991. per. 4.99 (*0-671-74348-1*) PB.

Castillo, Carlos & Bond, Otto F. University of Chicago Spanish Dictionary. 3rd enl. rev. ed. (SPA.). 1977. pap. 6.95 (*0-226-09674-2*) U Ch Pr.

— University of Chicago Spanish Dictionary. 3rd enl. rev. ed. (SPA.). 1977. 16.95 (*0-226-09673-4*) U Ch Pr.

— University of Chicago Spanish-English, English-Spanish Dictionary. 3rd ed. 1987. pap. 3.95 (*0-317-56745-4*) PB.

Castillo, Carlos E., tr. see Johnson, Diana F.

Castillo, Cecilia R., jt. ed. see Grasso, Kenneth L.

Castillo, Celerino, III & Harmon, Dave. Powder Burns: Cocain, Contras & the Drug War. 224p. 1994. pap. 16.95 (*0-88962-578-6*) Mosaic.

Castillo-Chavez, C. Mathematical & Statistical Approaches to AIDS Epidemiology. (Lecture Notes in Biomathematics Ser.: Vol. 83). ix, 405p. 1990. 69.95 (*0-387-52174-7*) Spr-Verlag.

Castillo-Chavez, C., et al, eds. Mathematical Approaches to Problems in Resource Management & Epidemiology. (Lecture Notes in Biomathematics Ser.: Vol. 81). vii, 327p. 1989. 60.95 (*0-387-51820-7*) Spr-Verlag.

Castillo-Chavez, C. & Cooke, K. Differential Equations & Applications to Biology & to Industry: Proceedings of the Claremont International Conference Dedicated to the Memory of Stavros Busenberg, 1941-1993, June 1-4, 1994. Martelli, Mario, ed. LC 95-44987. 550p. 1995. text 147.00 (*981-02-2233-5*) World Scientific Pub.

Castillo, Cicelia R. Liberty under Law: American Constitutionalism, Yesterday, Today & Tomorrow. 2nd ed. Grasso, Kenneth L., ed. LC 97-25976. 254p. (C). 1997. pap. 20.95 (*0-7618-0852-3*) U Pr of Amer.

Castillo, Daisy, jt. auth. see Bueno, Maria de Los Reyes Castillo.

Castillo De Mayada, Maruja Del, see Ackerman, James D. & Del Castillo De Mayada, Maruja.

Castillo, Debra A. Easy Women: Sex & Gender in Modern Mexican Fiction. LC 97-40102. 1998. 47.95 (*0-8166-3112-3*); pap. 18.95 (*0-8166-3113-1*) U of Minn Pr.

— Talking Back: Toward a Latin American Feminist Literary Criticism. LC 91-27789. (Reading Women Writing Ser.). (Illus.). 376p. 1992. text 45.00 (*0-8014-2608-1*); pap. text 17.95 (*0-8014-9912-7*) Cornell U Pr.

— The Translated World: A Postmodern Tour of Libraries in Literature. LC 84-17200. x, 358p. 1985. pap. 29.95 (*0-8130-0792-5*) U Press Fla.

Castillo, Debra A., tr. see Campbell, Federico.

Castillo, Diego Del, see Del Castillo, Diego.

Castillo, Edmund, ed. see DeQuoy, Alfred.

Castillo, Edward D. The Pomo. LC 99-23200. (Indian Nations Ser.). (Illus.). 48p. (ps-3). 1999. 25.69 (*0-8172-5455-2*) Raintree Steck-V.

Castillo, Edward D., ed. Native American Perspectives on the Hispanic Colonization of Alta California. LC 91-45780. (Spanish Borderlands Sourcebooks Ser.: Vol. 26). 520p. 1992. text 30.00 (*0-8240-2348-X*) Garland.

Castillo, Edward D., jt. auth. see Jackson, Robert H.

Castillo, Eloise, et al. Feasibility of Small System Restructuring to Facilitate SDWA Compliance. LC 97-211485. (Illus.). 190p. 1996. pap. 195.00 (*0-89867-900-1*, 90720) Am Water Wks Assn.

Castillo, Enrique. Functional Networks with Applications: A Neural-Based Paradigm. LC 98-42556. (International Series In Engineering & Computer Science). 308p. 1998. 132.00 (*0-7923-8332-X*) Kluwer Academic.

Castillo, Enrique & Ruiz-Cobo, Maria Reyes, eds. Functional Equations & Modelling in Science & Engineering. (Pure & Applied Mathematics Ser.: Vol. 161). (Illus.). 352p. 1992. text 155.00 (*0-8247-8717-X*) Dekker.

Castillo, Enrique, et al. Expert Systems & Probabilistic Network Models. LC 96-33161. (Monographs in Computer Science). 605p. 1996. 59.95 (*0-387-94858-9*) Spr-Verlag.

***Castillo, Enrique, et al.** Orthogonal Sets & Polar Methods in Linear Algebra: Applications to Matrix Calculations, Systems of Equations, Inequalities, & Linear Programming. LC 98-38391. (Pure & Applied Mathematics: A Wiley-Interscience Series of Texts, Monographs & Tracts). 422p. 1999. 99.95 (*0-471-32889-8*) Wiley.

Castillo, Enrique C. UFOs: A Great New Dawn for Humanity. Castro, Hugo A., tr. from SPA. LC 97-11568. (Illus.). 272p. 1997. pap. 19.95 (*1-57733-000-5*) B Dolphin Pub.

Castillo-Feliu, Guillermo I. Cuentos y Microcuentos. LC 77-12972. 227p. (C). 1978. pap. text 20.75 (*0-03-021796-2*) Harcourt Coll Pubs.

C

An Asterisk (*) at the beginning of an entry indicates that the title is appearing for the first time.

***Castillo-Feliu, Guillermo I.** Culture & Customs of Chile. LC 99-58879. (Culture & Customs of Latin America & the Caribbean Ser.). 192p. 2000. 45.00 (0-313-30783-0, Greenwood Pr) Greenwood.

Castillo-Feliu, Guillermo I. LECTURAS BAS 4/E. 4th ed. LC 88-15589. (SPA., Illus.). 96p. (C). 1989. pap. text 32.50 (0-03-013338-6) Harcourt Coll Pubs.

Castillo-Feliu, Guillermo I., ed. The Creative Process in the Works of Jose Donoso. (Winthrop College: Studies on Major Modern Writers). 161p. 1982. pap. 8.00 (0-938972-22-7) Spanish Lit Pubns.

Castillo-Feliu, Guillermo I., jt. auth. see Varela, Felix.

Castillo-Feliu, Guillermo I., tr. see Palma, Clemente.

Castillo-Feliu, Guillermo I., tr. see Prado, Pedro.

Castillo, George R. & Bayse, Daniel J. My Life Between the Cross & the Bars. unabridged ed. LC 96-230393. (Illus.). 295p. 1996. 21.95 (0-9649916-0-8) G & M Pubns.

Castillo, Glenna D., ed. see DeQuoy, Alfred.

Castillo, Hazel M. The Nurse Assistant in Long-Term Care: A Rehabilitative Approach. (Illus.). 528p. (gr. 13). 1992. pap. text 27.00 (0-8016-0945-3, 00945) Mosby Inc.

Castillo, Jessie. Garifuna Folk Tales. (Illus.). 44p. (Orig.). (J). (gr. k-5). 1994. pap. text 10.00 (1-878433-11-3) Caribbean Diaspora Pr.

Castillo, Jesus M. & Gonzales, Manuel. Three-Space Problems in Banach Space Theory, Vol. 166. Dold, A. & Takens, F., eds. LC 97-29902. (Lecture Notes in Mathematics Ser.: Vol. 1667). xii, 267p. 1997. pap. 48.00 (3-540-63344-8) Spr-Verlag.

Castillo, Jose E., ed. Mathematical Aspects of Numerical Grid Generation. LC 91-14973. (Frontiers in Applied Mathematics Ser.: No. 8). xiv, 157p. 1991. pap. 33.00 (0-89871-267-X) Soc Indus-Appl Math.

Castillo, Laurie & Endahl, Carol, eds. St. Anthony's HCPCS Level II Codebook - Short Version: HBIN. (C). 1997. write for info. (1-56329-390-0) St Anthony Pub.

— St. Anthony's HCPCS Level II Codebook: HBK. (C). 1997. 75.00 (1-56329-389-7) St Anthony Pub.

Castillo, Laurie & Hopkins, Catherine, eds. St. Anthony's Color-Coded Compact ICD-9-CM Code Book for Physician Payment, 2 vols. 1418p. 1996. 49.95 (1-56329-356-0) St Anthony Pub.

— St. Anthony's Illustrated ICD-9-CM Code Book for Physician Payment. (Illus.). 1110p. 1997. pap. 79.95 (1-56329-424-9) St Anthony Pub.

— St. Anthony's Softbound ICD-9-CM Code Book for Physician Payment, 2 vols. 982p. 1996. 59.95 (1-56329-353-6) St Anthony Pub.

— St. Anthony's Spiral ICD-9-CM Code Book for Physician Payment, 2 vols. 982p. 1996. 59.95 (1-56329-354-4) St Anthony Pub.

— St. Anthony's Illustrated ICD-9-CM Code Book, 2 vols. (Illus.). 1110p. 1996. write for info. (1-56329-350-1) St Anthony Pub.

— St. Anthony's Illustrated ICD-9-CM Code Book, 2 vols. (Illus.). 1110p. 1997. write for info. (1-56329-423-0) St Anthony Pub.

— St. Anthony's Updatable ICD-9-CM Code Book for Physician Payment, 2 vols. 982p. Date not set. 129.00 (1-56329-420-6) St Anthony Pub.

— St. Anthony's Updatable ICD-9-CM Code Book for Physician Payment, 2 vols. 982p. 1996. 129.00 (1-56329-352-8) St Anthony Pub.

— St. Anthony's Updatable ICD-9-CM Code Book for Physician Payment, 2 vols. 982p. 1997. pap. 59.95 (1-56329-421-4); spiral bd. 59.95 (1-56329-422-2) St Anthony Pub.

Castillo, Laurie, jt. ed. see Hart, Anita.

***Castillo, Linda.** Remember the Night. 248p. 2000. mass mkt. 4.50 (0-373-27078-X) Harlequin Bks.

Castillo, Luis F. Del, see Del Castillo, Luis F.

***Castillo, Lydia.** Poetic Thoughts. 2000. write for info. (1-58235-572-X) Watermrk Pr.

Castillo, M. Teresa, ed. A Proposito del Formativo. 136p. 1993. pap. 6.00 (968-29-5114-3, IN060) UPLAAP.

Castillo, Mauricio. Neuroradiology Companion: Methods, Guidelines, & Imaging Fundamentals. LC 94-34493. (Illus.). 384p. 1994. pap. text 54.00 (0-397-51472-7) Lppncott W & W.

— Neuroradiology Companion: Methods, Guidelines & Imaging Fundamentals. 2nd ed. LC 98-26851. 416p. 1998. pap. text. write for info. (0-7817-1695-0) Lppncott W & W.

Castillo, Mauricio & Harris, John H., Jr. Imaging of the Spine: A Teaching File. LC 97-44168. (Illus.). 400p. 1998. 89.00 (0-683-30244-2) Lppncott W & W.

Castillo, Mauricio & Mukherji, Suresh K. Imaging of the Pediatric Head, Neck, & Spine. LC 95-44623. (Illus.). 743p. 1995. text 165.00 (0-397-51577-4) Lppncott W & W.

Castillo, Mauricio, jt. auth. see Mukherji, Suresh K.

***Castillo, Nahum Boone.** Before & after Time. LC 99-96677. 2000. pap. 7.95 (0-533-13291-6) Vantage.

***Castillo, Obdulia R.** Raindrops. Dubois, Christine, ed. 240p. 2000. pap. 14.95 (0-9700198-0-7) O G Zapata.

Castillo, Otto R. Let's Go. Randall, Margaret, tr. LC 84-9397. 96p. 1996. pap. 11.95 (0-915306-44-1) Curbstone.

Castillo Parker, Tamarra C. & Schaefer, Mary. Unearthing James Madison's Boyhood Home: Archaeology at Mount Pleasant, Monpelier Station, Virginia. Phillips, John T., II, ed. (Illus.). 64p. (Orig.). 1999. per. 17.75 (0-9656758-6-6) Goose Creek.

Castillo, Patricia. La Alimentacion de Tu Hijo. 1999. 32.95 (84-08-01601-6) Planeta Edit.

— La Expresion Simbolica del Tajin. (SPA., Illus.). 524p. 1995. pap. 16.00 (968-29-5217-4, IN71, Pub. by Dir Gen Pubicaiones) UPLAAP.

Castillo, Pedro, jt. auth. see Rios-Bustamante, Antonio.

Castillo, Rafael. Distant Journeys. LC 91-8477. 112p. 1991. pap. 10.00 (0-927534-15-0) Biling Rev-Pr.

Castillo, Richard G. Del, see Del Castillo, Richard G.

Castillo, Richard L. Culture & Mental Illness. LC 96-41263. (Miscellaneous/Catalogs Ser.). 348p. (C). 1996. mass mkt. 49.95 (0-534-34558-1) Brooks-Cole.

— The Meanings of Madness: Readings in Culture & Mental Illness. LC 97-19078. (Miscellaneous/Catalogs Ser.). 240p. (C). 1997. pap. 49.95 (0-534-34560-3) Brooks-Cole.

***Castillo, Roberto.** The Bugler: Bilingual Edition. Hood, Edward Waters, tr. LC 99-89764.Tr. of Corneta. (SPA.). 144p. 2000. pap. 27.50 (0-7618-1608-9) U Pr of Amer.

***Castillo, Roger, ed.** Not with My Child: Combating What Predators Do to Sexually Abuse & Silence Children. 376p. 1999. pap. 29.95 (0-9665882-9-0) United Youth Security.

Castillo, Rose & Castle, Holly. Homeopathy. 160p. 1999. per. 9.99 (0-7615-1758-8) Prima Pub.

***Castillo, Salvador.** Dramas y Poemas Para Actividades Cristianas. LC 99-94780. (SPA.). 84p. 2000. write for info. (0-9644410-2-0) Salvador Castillo.

Castillo, Salvador. Esencias de Cristo: (Poesia Cristiana) LC 94-93980. (SPA.). 168p. 1995. write for info. (0-9644410-0-4) Salvador Castillo.

— Romances (La Poesia del Amor) LC 95-92257. (SPA.). 202p. Date not set. write for info. (0-9644410-1-2) Salvador Castillo.

***Castillo, Sandra.** Strategies, Techniques & Approaches to Thinking: Case Studies in Clinical Nursing. Eoyang, Thomas, ed. LC 98-55263. 415p. 1999. text. write for info. (0-7216-7648-0, W B Saunders Co) Harcrt Hlth Sci Grp.

***Castillo, Sara, et al.** Getting Face to Face with Your Fears: A Kid's Guide to Understanding & Coping with Fears & Phobias. LC 00-100779. (Illus.). 72p. (J). 2000. pap. text 11.95 (1-930572-00-X) Ed Media Corp.

Castillo Solorzano, Alonso De, see De Castillo Solorzano, Alonso.

Castillo Solorzano, Alonso del. Lisardo Enamorado. Julia y Martinez, Eduardo, ed. (SPA.). 333p. 1968. pap. 100.00 (0-614-00225-7) Elliots Bks.

Castillo-Speed, Lillian, ed. Latina: Women's Voices from the Borderlands. 288p. 1995. per. 13.00 (0-684-80240-6) S&S Trade Pap.

Castillo-Speed, Lillian, ed. The Chicana Studies Index: Twenty Years of Gender Research, 1971-1991. LC 92-10870. (Ethnic Studies Library Publications: No. 18). 450p. (C). 1992. lib. bdg. 90.00 (0-918520-21-5) Ethnic Stud Lib.

Castillo-Speed, Lillian, et al, eds. Chicano Periodical Index (ChPI) A Comprehensive Subject, Author & Title Index for 1992-93. (Ethnic Studies Library Publications: No. 12). 884p. 1995. lib. bdg. 150.00 (0-918520-10-X) Ethnic Stud Lib.

Castillo, Steve. Maximum Happiness: Jack & Jill Discover True Love. (Illus.). 58p. (Orig.). (YA). (gr. 9). 1989. 5.95 (0-317-93187-3) Paisley Bks.

Castillo, Susan. Notes from the Periphery: Marginality in North American Literature & Culture, Vol. 63. (American University Studies: American Literature: No. XXIV). XIII, 196p. (C). 1995. pap. 29.95 (0-8204-2757-8) P Lang Pubng.

Castillo, Vincent J., jt. ed. see Beadle, Edward R.

Castillo, Yuriria Blanco, tr. see Jackins, Harvey & Laud, Catherine.

Castillon, David A. Conservation of Natural Resources. 448p. (C). 1995. text, suppl. ed. write for info. (0-697-34187-9, WCB McGr Hill) McGrw-H Hghr Educ.

— Conservation of Natural Resources. 3rd ed. 2000. 61.50 (0-07-303644-7) McGraw.

— Conservation of Natural Resources: A Resource Management Approach. 448p. (C). 1992. text. write for info. (0-697-11229-2, WCB McGr Hill) McGrw-H Hghr Educ.

— Conservation of Natural Resources: A Resource Management Approach. 2nd ed. 400p. (C). 1996. text. write for info. (0-697-15782-2, WCB McGr Hill) McGrw-H Hghr Educ.

Castilonia, Raymnond R. Nuggets in the Ground: A Beginner's Guide to Aoinagi Karate. LC 96-75886. (Illus.). 175p. 1996. pap., lab manual ed. write for info. (0-9636817-4-5) Intl Univ Line.

Castine Historical Society Staff. Castine. (Images of America Ser.). 128p. 1996. pap. 16.99 (0-7524-0269-2) Arcadia Publng.

Castine, Jacqueline. Recovery from Rescuing. 1989. pap. 7.95 (1-55874-016-3) Health Comm.

Castine, Joseph, et al. The Foreign Language Teacher's Handbook: Aiming for Proficiency in German. (GER., Illus.). 200p. (Orig.). 1991. teacher ed. 28.95 (1-879279-06-1) Proficiency Pr.

Castine, Peter. Set Theory Objects: Abstractions for Computer-Aided Design Analysis & Compostion of Serial & Atonal Music. LC 94-33468. (European University Studies Series XXXVI: Vol. 121). (Illus.). 211p. 1994. write for info. (3-631-47897-6) P Lang Pubng.

Castino & Harmathy, Tibor Z., eds. Fire Risk Assessment - STP 762. 112p. 1982. pap. 19.00 (0-8031-0724-2, STP762) ASTM.

Castino, G. T., ed. see American Society for Testing & Materials Staff.

Castino, Tony. Cost Effective In-House Training. 50p. 50.00 (0-614-25560-0, OOSM44340) Print Indus Am.

Castle. The Twentieth Century House Book. pap. text. write for info. (0-471-49127-6) Wiley.

Castle, Gilbert H., ed. GIS in Real Estate: Integrating, Analyzing, & Presenting Locational Information. LC 98-47198. 206p. 1998. 35.00 (0-922154-52-X) Appraisal Inst.

Castle, A. F., tr. see Laue, Kurt & Stenger, Helmut.

Castle, Alfred L. A Century of Philanthropy: A History of the Samuel N. & Mary Castle Foundation. LC 98-128776. (Illus.). 384p. 1992. pap. text 25.00 (0-8248-1470-3) HI Hist Soc.

— Diplomatic Realism: William R. Castle, Jr., & American Foreign Policy, 1919-1953. MacMillan, Michael E., ed. (Illus.). 240p. 1997. text 32.00 (0-8248-2009-6) UH Pr.

Castle, Anthony. A Treasury of Quips, Quotes, & Anecdotes for Preachers & Teachers. LC 97-62562. 624p. 1998. pap. 29.95 (0-89622-920-3) Twenty-Third.

Castle, Barbara. The Castle Diaries, 1974-1976. 788p. 1981. 55.00 (0-8419-0689-0) Holmes & Meier.

Castle, Beatrice H. The Grand Island Story. Carter, James L., ed. LC 71-11186. 1974. 8.95 (0-938746-01-4) Marquette Cnty.

Castle, Brenda. Mysterious Stranger. large type ed. (Linford Romance Library). 240p. 1997. pap. 16.99 (0-7089-5008-6, Linford) Ulverscroft.

— Whispers of Fear. large type ed. (Dales Large Print Ser.). 245p. 1996. pap. 18.99 (1-85389-668-3, Dales) Ulverscroft.

***Castle, Caroline.** Gorgeous. LC 99-42666. 32p. (J). 2000. lib. bdg. 16.99 (0-517-80084-5, Pub. by Crown Bks Yng Read) Random.

— Gorgeous. LC 99-42666. (Illus.). 32p. (J). (ps). 2000. 14.95 (0-517-80083-7, Pub. by Crown Bks Yng Read) Random.

Castle, Caroline. Phoebe & the Monster Maze. (Illus.). 32p. (J). (ps-2). 1998. 19.95 (0-09-176714-8, Pub. by Hutchnson) Trafalgar.

Castle, Coralie. Soup. 2nd ed. LC 92-30791. (One Hundred One Productions Ser.). (Illus.). 192p. 1993. reprint ed. pap. 11.95 (1-56426-552-8, One Hund One Prods) Cole Group.

Castle, Coralie & Kourik, Robert. Cooking from the Gourmet's Garden: Edible Ornamentals, Herbs & Flowers. 2nd ed. LC 92-3220. Orig. Title: Gourmet Garden: Edible Ornamentals for the Cook. 224p. 1994. pap. 12.95 (1-56426-563-3) Cole Group.

Castle, Coralie, jt. auth. see Baylis, Maggie.

Castle, David. Living with the Sages: Rashi & the Tosafists, Vol. I. 1996. 19.95 (0-87306-762-2) Feldheim.

Castle, David J. Psychosis in the Inner City: The Camberwell First Episode Study. LC 99-159356. (Maudsley Monographs Ser.). 1998. 44.95 (0-86377-516-0, Pub. by Psychol Pr) Taylor & Francis.

***Castle, David J., et al, eds.** Women & Schizophrenia. (Illus.). 112p. (C). 2000. pap. write for info. (0-521-78617-7) Cambridge U Pr.

Castle, Dian K., et al. High-Performance Learning Communities. Herman, Jerry J. & Herman, Janice L., eds. LC 94-23861. (Road Maps to Success Ser.). (Illus.). 80p. 1995. pap. 14.95 (0-8039-6180-4) Corwin Pr.

Castle, Diane L. Telephone Strategies: A Technical & Practical Guide for Hard-of-Hearing People. (Illus.). 55p. 1988. 6.50 (0-935473-04-1) SHHH.

Castle, Dorothy R. The Diabolical Game to Win Man's Soul: A Rhetorical & Structural Approach to Mankind. LC 89-13662. (American University Studies: English Language & Literature: Ser. IV, Vol. 70). VI, 215p. (C). 1990. text 41.50 (0-8204-1237-6) P Lang Pubng.

Castle, Eduard. Der Grosse Unbekannte. (Samtliche Werke - Supplement Series: Vol. 25). (GER., Illus.). iv, 727p. 1993. reprint ed. write for info. (3-487-08344-2) G Olms Pubs.

Castle, Emery N. Agricultural Industrialization in the American Countryside. unabridged ed. (Policy Studies Report: No. 11). (Illus.). 43p. 1998. pap. 10.00 (1-893182-18-5) H A Wallace Inst.

Castle, Emery N., ed. The Changing American Countryside: Rural People & Places. LC 95-8076. (Rural America Ser.). 584p. (C). 1995. 45.00 (0-7006-0724-2); pap. 25.00 (0-7006-0725-0) U Pr of KS.

Castle, Emery N. & Price, Kent A., eds. U. S. Interests & Global Natural Resources: Energy, Minerals, Food. LC 83-42905. 147p. 1983. 20.00 (0-8018-3099-0); pap. 12.95 (0-8018-3106-7) Resources Future.

Castle, Emery N., et al. Farm Business Management. 3rd ed. 456p. (C). 1986. reprint ed. text 69.00 (0-02-320200-9, Macmillan Coll) P-H.

— U. S.-Japanese Agricultural Trade Relations. LC 82-7832. 436p. 1982. 35.00 (0-8018-2815-5); pap. 21.95 (0-8018-2814-7) Resources Future.

Castle, Fiona. Rainbows Through the Rain. 1998. pap. 4.99 (0-340-70980-4, Pub. by Hodder & Stought Ltd) Trafalgar.

Castle, Frederick & Crum, Katherine B. Richards Ruben. 54p. 1994. pap. 20.00 (0-9638030-1-8) Mills Art Gal.

Castle, Frederick T. Anticipation. LC 83-14931. 352p. 1984. 22.50 (0-914232-60-6) McPherson & Co.

— Anticipation. LC 83-14931. 352p. 1996. pap. 14.00 (0-914232-65-7) McPherson & Co.

— Anticipation. limited ed. LC 83-14931. 352p. 1984. 50.00 (0-914232-61-4) McPherson & Co.

— Gilbert Green: The Real Right Way to Dress for Spring. LC 86-2634. 241p. 1986. 16.95 (0-914232-76-2) McPherson & Co.

— Gilbert Green: The Real Right Way to Dress for Spring. deluxe ed. LC 86-2634. 241p. 1986. 50.00 (0-914232-77-0) McPherson & Co.

— Gilbert Green: The Real Right Way to Dress for Spring. LC 86-2634. 241p. 1993. reprint ed. pap. 11.00 (0-929701-23-2) McPherson & Co.

Castle, Frederick T. & Sonmez, Necmi. Dogansay: Walls. Duben, Ipek A., tr. from TUR. (Illus.). 60p. (Orig.). 1993. pap. write for info. (0-932169-25-2) Tenth Ave Edit.

***Castle, George.** The Million-to-One Team: Why the Chicago Cubs Haven't Won a Pennant since World War II. 2000. 29.95 (1-888698-31-4) Diamond Communications.

Castle, George. Sammy Sosa: Clearing the Vines. Associated Press Staff, ed. (Illus.). 200p. 1998. pap. 14.95 (1-58261-024-X) Sprts Pubng.

— Sammy Sosa: Slammin' Sammy. Rains, Rob, ed. (Super Star Ser.). (Illus.). 96p. (J). 1999. pap. 4.95 (1-58261-029-0) Sprts Pubng.

Castle, George & Rygelski, Jim. The I-55 Series: Cubs vs. Cardinals. (The ISS Ser.). (Illus.). 200p. 1999. pap. 14.95 (1-58261-032-0) Sprts Pubng.

Castle, George & Wolfe, Rich. I Remember Harry Caray. (Illus.). 220p. 1998. 22.95 (1-58261-002-9) Sprts Pubng.

— I Remember Harry Caray. (Illus.). 225p. 1999. pap. 12.95 (1-58261-040-1) Sprts Pubng.

Castle, Gilbert H., III, ed. Profiting from a Geographic Information System. (Illus.). 414p. 1993. pap. 37.95 (0-9625063-7-0) GIS World Bks.

***Castle, Gilbert H., III, ed.** Profiting from a Geographic Information System. 415p. 1998. pap. 90.00 (0-471-32984-3) Wiley.

Castle, Gladys C., jt. auth. see Gunn, Jack W.

Castle, Grace Elting, ed. Advanced Forensic Civil Investigations. LC 97-6362. 745p. 1997. 99.00 (0-913875-39-2, 5392-N) Lawyers & Judges.

Castle, Grace Elting, jt. ed. see Ciolino, Paul J.

Castle, Holly, jt. auth. see Castillo, Rose.

Castle, Ian. Eggmuhl, 1809. (Campaign Ser.). (Illus.). 96p. 1999. pap. 16.95 (1-85532-708-2, Pub. by Ospry) Stackpole.

— Majuba, 1881. (Illus.). 96p. 1996. pap. 14.95 (1-85532-503-9, Pub. by Ospry) Stackpole.

— Wagram, 1809. (Campaign Ser.). (Illus.). 96p. 1994. pap. 14.95 (1-85532-366-4, 9532, Pub. by Ospry) Stackpole.

Castle, Ian & Knight, Ian. British Army: Zulu War to the Boer War. Newark, Tim, ed. (Brassey's History of Uniforms Ser.). (Illus.). 144p. 1999. 32.95 (1-85753-284-8, Pub. by Brasseys) Brasseys.

— Fearful Hard Times: The Siege & Relief of Eshowe, 1879. 256p. 1994. 34.95 (1-85367-180-0, 5412) Stackpole.

Castle, Irene. My Husband. LC 78-12730. (Series in Dance). (Illus.). 1979. reprint ed. lib. bdg. 29.50 (0-306-79505-1) Da Capo.

Castle, J. E. & Kelly, M. J., eds. Advanced Materials in the Market Place: Proceedings of the Symposium Held at the University of Surrey on 22 September 1994. 198p. 1995. 110.00 (0-901716-92-8, Pub. by Inst Materials) Ashgate Pub Co.

***Castle, Jayne, pseud.** After Dark. 2000. mass mkt. 6.99 (0-515-12902-X, Jove) Berkley Pub.

Castle, Jayne, pseud. Amaryllis. 328p. 1996. mass mkt. 6.50 (0-671-56903-1) PB.

— Amaryllis. 1998. per. 3.99 (0-671-02143-5, Pocket Books) PB.

— Amaryllis. large type ed. LC 98-15773. 1998. 24.95 (1-57490-139-7, Beeler LP Bks) T T Beeler.

— Orchid. 327p. 1998. per. 6.99 (0-671-56902-3) PB.

***Castle, Jayne, pseud.** Orchid. LC 98-48130. 1999. write for info. (1-57490-174-5) T T Beeler.

Castle, Jayne, pseud. Zinnia. 1997. per. 6.50 (0-671-56901-5) PB.

— Zinnia. large type ed. LC 97-39085. 1997. 23.95 (1-57490-130-3, Beeler LP Bks) T T Beeler.

Castle, Jayne, pseud, et al. Charmed. 352p. 1999. mass mkt. 5.99 (0-425-17129-9) Berkley Pub.

Castle, Joseph. Christmas Songs-Classic Guitar. 32p. 1981. pap. 5.95 (0-87166-005-9, 93789) Mel Bay.

Castle, Joseph. Complete Anthology of Elementary Classic Guitar Solos. 192p. 1997. spiral bd. 22.95 incl. audio compact disk (0-7866-2932-0, 94641BCD) Mel Bay.

Castle, Joseph. Deluxe Album of Classic Guitar Music. 96p. 1971. spiral bd. 10.95 (0-87166-942-0, 93284) Mel Bay.

— Favorite Hymns for Classical Guitar. 32p. 1978. pap. 5.95 (0-87166-730-4, 93409) Mel Bay.

— Folio of Great Classic Guitar Solos. 32p. 1971. pap. 5.95 (1-56222-313-5, 93213) Mel Bay.

Castle, Joseph, jt. auth. see Bay, Mel.

Castle, Joseph, jt. auth. see Bay, Mel, Publications, Inc. Staff.

Castle, Kate. Ballet. LC 96-5986. (Illus.). 64p. (J). (gr. 1-7). 1996. 16.95 (0-7534-5001-1, Kingfisher) LKC.

— My Ballet Book: An Introduction to the Magical World of Ballet. LC 98-22803. (Illus.). 61p. (J). (gr. 1-6). 1998. pap. 15.95 (0-7894-3432-6) DK Pub Inc.

Castle, Kathryn. Cool Junk. LC 98-71331. (Think-Kids Book Collection). (Illus.). 16p. (J). (gr. 1-4). 1998. pap. 2.95 (1-58237-014-1) Creat Think.

— Games Rule. LC 98-71341. (Think-Kids Book Collection). (Illus.). 16p. (J). (gr. 1-4). 1998. pap. 2.95 (1-58237-020-6) Creat Think.

***Castle, Kathryn.** Reglas Para Juegos. Alvarado, Ana M., tr. (Think-Kids Book Collection).Tr. of Games Rule. (SPA., Illus.). 16p. (J). 2000. pap. 2.95 (1-58237-047-8) Creat Think.

— Todavia Sirven! Alvarado, Ana M., tr. (Think-Kids Book Collection).Tr. of Cool Junk. (SPA., Illus.). 16p. (J). 2000. pap. 2.95 (1-58237-057-5) Creat Think.

Castle, Ken. Foghorn Outdoors: Tahoe: The Complete Guide to Year-Around Recreation, Lodging & Dining in the Greater Lake Tahoe Region. 2nd ed. (Complete Guide Ser.). (Illus.). 700p. 1997. pap. 20.95 (1-57354-024-2, Foghorn Outdoors) Avalon Travel.

***Castle, Ken.** Moon Handbooks - Tahoe: Including Reno & Carson Valley. 3rd rev. ed. (Moon Handbks.). (Illus.). 680p. 2000. pap. 19.95 (1-56691-211-3, Pub. by Avalon Travel) Publishers Group.

Castle, Kit & Bechtel, Stefan. Katherine, It's Time. 384p. 1990. mass mkt. 5.99 (0-380-71198-2, Avon Bks) Morrow Avon.

Castle, Lana R. Style Meister: The Quick-Reference Custom Style Guide. LC 98-159723. (Illus.). xii, 314p. 1998. pap. 29.95 (0-9662926-1-8) Castle Com.

An Asterisk (*) at the beginning of an entry indicates that the title is appearing for the first time.

Castle, Larry & Peterson, Marlow. Collectable Machine-Made Marbles: Identification & Price Guide. (Illus.). 34p. (Orig.). (C). 1989. pap. 7.95 (*0-9624185-0-1*) UT Marble Connection.
— Marbles: A Guide to Machine-Made Marbles. (Illus.). 75p. (Orig.). 1991. pap. 15.00 (*0-9624185-1-X*) UT Marble Connection.
— Marbles: The Guide to Cat's-Eyes Marbles. (Illus.). 32p. 1998. pap. 8.95 (*0-9624185-3-6*) UT Marble Connection.
— Marbles: The Guide to Machine-Made Marbles. 2nd ed. LC 95-60961. (Illus.). 118p. 1995. pap. 19.95 (*0-9624185-2-8*) UT Marble Connection.
Castle, Leila, ed. Earthwalking Sky Dancers: Women's Pilgrimages to Sacred Places. LC 96-4353. (Illus.). 250p. 1996. pap. 16.95 (*1-883319-33-1*) Frog Ltd CA.
Castle, Linda. Abbie's Child. (Historical Ser.). 1996. per. 4.99 (*0-373-28921-9*, 1-28921-4) Harlequin Bks.
— Fearless Hearts: (March Madness) LC 95-7082. (Historical Ser.). 299p. 1995. per. 4.50 (*0-373-28861-1*, 1-28861-2) Harlequin Bks.
— Heart of the Lawman. 1999. per. 4.99 (*0-373-29073-X*, 1-29073-3) Harlequin Bks.
— The Return of Chase Cordell. 1997. per. 4.99 (*0-373-28948-0*, 1-28948-7) Silhouette.
— Temple's Prize. (Historical Ser.: No. 394). 1997. per. 4.99 (*0-373-28994-4*, 1-28994-1) Harlequin Bks.
— Territorial Bride. (Historical Ser.: No. 441). 1998. per. 4.99 (*0-373-29041-1*, 1-29041-0) Harlequin Bks.
Castle, Lynn. Quetzalcoatl Legends from Mexico & Central America Set: Picture Books & Teacher's Guides, 9 bks., Set. (ENG & SPA.). (J). (gr. k-5). 75.99 (*1-56417-771-8*, FE0059) Fearon Teacher Aids.
— A Quetzalcoatl Tale of Chocolate: Picture Book. (SPA.). 48p. (J). (gr. k-5). 8.99 (*0-86653-958-1*, FE0958) Fearon Teacher Aids.
— A Quetzalcoatl Tale of the Ball Game. (SPA.). 48p. (J). (gr. k-5). 8.99 (*0-86653-961-1*, FE0961) Good Apple.
— A Teacher's Guide to a Quetzalcoatl Tale of Chocolate, Incl. student work sheets. (ENG & SPA.). 48p. 8.99 (*0-86653-957-3*, FE0957) Fearon Teacher Aids.
— A Teacher's Guide to a Quetzalcoatl Tale of Corn, Incl. student work sheets. (ENG & SPA.). 48p. teacher ed. 8.99 (*0-86653-963-8*, FE0963) Good Apple.
Castle, Lynn P., jt. auth. see Hobbs, Robert.
Castle, Lynn P., ed. see Hyland, Douglas, et al.
Castle, Lynn P., ed. see Tully, Judd.
Castle, Marrietta, jt. ed. see Cramer, Eugene H.
Castle, Mary & Ajemian, Elizabeth. Hospital Infection Control: Principles & Practice. 2nd ed. 1989. text 33.10 (*0-8273-4222-5*) Delmar.
***Castle, Michael N., ed.** Computer Generated Check Fraud: Congressional Hearing. (Illus.). 96p. 2000. reprint ed. pap. text 20.00 (*0-7881-8730-9*) DIANE Pub.
Castle, Michael N., ed. Federal Payment System. 313p. (C). 1999. pap. text 35.00 (*0-7881-7839-3*) DIANE Pub.
***Castle, Michael N., ed.** The Federal Role in Electronic Authentication: Congressional Hearing. 174p. (C). 2000. reprint ed. pap. text 30.00 (*0-7881-8822-4*) DIANE Pub.
Castle, Michael N., ed. Funding Requests for the International Monetary Fund: Congressional Hearing. 65p. 1999. pap. text 20.00 (*0-7881-7527-0*) DIANE Pub.
***Castle, Mike N., ed.** School Violence: Protecting Our Children - Congressional Hearing. 110p. 2000. pap. text 25.00 (*0-7567-0101-5*) DIANE Pub.
***Castle, Mort.** In Memoriam: Papa, Blake & HPL. deluxe ed. 40p. 1999. pap. 8.99 (*0-9672029-2-2*) Darktales Pubns.
Castle, Mort, ed. Writing Horror: A Handbook by the Horror Writers Association. LC 97-17493. 256p. 1997. 17.99 (*0-89879-798-5*, Wrtrs Digest Bks) F & W Pubns Inc.
Castle, Mort, et al. Nukes: Four Horror Writers on the Ultimate Horror. Maclay, John, ed. & intro. by. LC 85-63719. 100p. (Orig.). 1986. pap. 4.95 (*0-940776-22-7*) Maclay Assoc.
Castle, Nick, jt. ed. see Hodgetts, Tim.
Castle, Pamela. Integrated Pollution Control. (Environmental Law Ser.). 270p. 1996. 115.00 (*1-874698-80-5*, Pub. by Federation Pr) Gaunt.
Castle, Robert L. van de, see Van de Castle, Robert L.
Castle, Shari, jt. ed. see Livingston, Carol.
Castle, Sue. Mother Knows Best? The Truth about Mom's Well Meaning (but Not Always Accurate) Advice. (Illus.). 160p. 1995. pap. 8.95 (*0-8065-1631-3*, Citadel Pr) Carol Pub Group.
— Old Wives' Tales: The Truth Behind Common Notions. (Illus.). 144p. 1992. pap. 7.95 (*0-8065-1378-0*, Citadel Pr) Carol Pub Group.
Castle, Suzi. Suzi Castle's Deliciously Healthy Favorite Foods Cookbook: Over 250 Mouth-Watering Recipes Low-Fat, Sugar-Free & Quick & Easy. LC 95-94689. (Illus.). 132p. 1997. pap. 14.95 (*0-9647423-2-2*) Hlth Cookbks.
Castle, Ted & Ballerini, Julia. Carolee Schneemann: Early & Recent Work. limited ed. LC 82-72833. (Illus.). 52p. 1983. 100.00 (*0-914232-57-6*, Documentext) McPherson & Co.
Castle, Terry. The Apparitional Lesbian: Female Homosexuality & Modern Culture. 307p. 1995. pap. 18.50 (*0-231-07653-3*) Col U Pr.
— Clarissa's Ciphers: Meaning & Disruption in Richardson's "Clarissa" fac. ed. LC 82-2460. 205p. 1982. reprint ed. pap. 63.60 (*0-608-01011-1*, 206186900012) Bks Demand.
— Masquerade & Civilization: The Carnivalesque in Eighteenth-Century English Culture & Fiction. LC 86-1942. (Illus.). 416p. 1986. pap. 18.95 (*0-8047-1468-1*) Stanford U Pr.
— Noel Coward & Radclyffe Hall: Kindred Spirits. LC 96-22750. 1996. pap. write for info. (*0-231-10597-5*) Col U Pr.
— Noel Coward & Radclyffe Hall: Kindred Spirits. LC 96-22750. (Illus.). 160p. 1996. 21.00 (*0-231-10596-7*) Col U Pr.
Castle, Timothy. At War in the Shadow of Vietnam: United States Military Aid to the Royal Lao Government, 1955-1975. 210p. 1995. pap. 18.00 (*0-231-07977-X*) Col U Pr.
Castle, Timothy J. Castle: Perfect Cup. (C). 1992. pap. text. write for info. (*0-201-53850-4*) Addison-Wesley.
— Perfect Cup: A Coffee Lover's Guide to Buying, Brewing, & Tasting. 1991. pap. 13.00 (*0-201-57048-3*) Addison-Wesley.
Castle, Timothy J. & Nielsen, Joan. The Great Coffee Book. LC 99-50069. 160p. 1999. pap. text 15.95 (*1-58008-122-3*) Ten Speed Pr.
Castle, Timothy N. One Day Too Long: Top Secret Site 85 & the Bombing of North Vietnam. LC 98-43117. (Illus.). 352p. 1999. 24.95 (*0-231-10316-6*) Col U Pr.
***Castle, Timothy N.** One Day Too Long: Top Secret Site 85 & the Bombing of North Vietnam. 368p. 2000. pap. text 15.95 (*0-231-10317-4*) Col U Pr.
Castle, Tony. Gateway to the Trinity: Meditations on Rublev's Icon. 112p. (C). 1996. pap. 39.95 (*0-85439-273-4*, Pub. by St Paul Pubns) St Mut.
Castle, Tony, ed. The Catholic Prayer Book. 273p. (Orig.). 1986. pap. 10.99 (*0-89283-283-5*, Charis) Servant.
— The Catholic Prayer Book. deluxe ed. 280p. (Orig.). 1986. bond lthr. 29.99 (*0-89283-314-9*) Servant.
— Young People's Mass Book. (Illus.). 64p. (Orig.). 1989. pap. 3.95 (*0-8146-1844-8*) Liturgical Pr.
Castle, Tony, ed. & compiled by see John Paul, II, pseud.
Castle, Vernon. Modern Dancing. (Ballroom Dance Ser.). 1986. lib. bdg. 250.00 (*0-8490-3325-X*) Gordon Pr.
— Modern Dancing. (Ballroom Dance Ser.). 1985. lib. bdg. 79.95 (*0-87700-758-6*) Revisionist Pr.
— Modern Dancing, 1914. (Illus.). 176p. 1998. pap. 18.00 (*0-916896-99-4*, LE54) Lacis Pubns.
Castle, Wanda. The Vicarious Image. Ingraham, Steve, ed. 108p. (Orig.). 1985. pap. 1.45 (*0-916835-00-6*, 600) C & I Pubns.
Castle, Wendell & Hunter-Stiebel, Penelope. The Fine Art of the Furniture Maker. Bayer, Patricia, ed. LC 81-83164. (Illus.). 1981p. (Orig.). 1984. pap. 17.95 (*0-295-96209-7*) U of Wash Pr.
Castle, Win M. & North, Philip M. Statistics in Small Doses. 3rd ed. LC 95-9992. 1995. pap. text 21.00 (*0-443-04542-9*) Church.
Castle, Winifred M. Statistics in Small Doses. 2nd rev. ed. LC 76-8430. (Illus.). 226p. (C). 1977. pap. text 23.00 (*0-443-01491-4*) Church.
Castleberry, jt. auth. see McGivney, Glenn P.
Castleberry, Barbara M., et al. Board of Registry Study Guide for Clinical Laboratory Certification Examinations. 4th ed. LC 96-2826. 1996. 40.00 (*0-89189-416-0*) Am Soc Clinical.
Castleberry, Edith. Punkin's Night Out. LC 96-27279. (Illus.). (J). 1997. write for info. (*1-56763-247-5*); pap. write for info. (*1-56763-248-3*) Ozark Pub.
Castleberry, Guy A. The AGV Handbook: A Handbook for the Selection of Automated Guided Vehicle Systems. LC 90-82031. (Illus.). 288p. 1991. 110.00 (*0-9627038-1-8*) AGV Decisions.
— AGV System Specification, Procurement, & Implementation Guide: A Step-by-Step Guide to Selecting & Installing an Automated Guided Vehicle System. LC 90-83341. (Illus.). 227p. 1992. 250.00 (*0-9627038-2-6*) AGV Decisions.
Castleberry, Haynes H. Gasoline: Index of New Information & Research Bible. 150p. 1994. 47.50 (*0-7883-0080-6*); pap. 44.50 (*0-7883-0081-4*) ABBE Pubs Assn.
Castleberry, May. Perpetual Mirage: Photographic Narratives of the Desert West. LC 95-25999. (Illus.). 1996. write for info. (*0-87427-100-2*) Whitney Mus.
Castleberry, Michael S., jt. ed. see Wald, Penelope J.
Castleberry, Rosalie, jt. auth. see Rozmajzl, Michon.
Castleberry, Stephen B. & Castleberry, Susan L. Call Her Blessed. (Illus.). 103p. 1998. pap. 6.00 (*1-891907-08-5*) Castleberry.
Castleberry, Stephen B. & Castleberry, Susie L. The Courtship of Sarah McLean. 2nd ed. (Courtship Ser.). 173p. 1997. reprint ed. pap. 7.50 (*1-891907-00-X*) Castleberry.
***Castleberry, Stephen B. & Castleberry, Susie L.** The Delivery. 220p. 1999. pap. 9.00 (*1-891907-09-3*) Castleberry.
Castleberry, Stephen B. & Castleberry, Susie L. Footprints in the Barn. (Farm Mystery Ser.). 168p. 1996. 12.00 (*1-891907-01-8*) Castleberry.
— In the Spring of the Year. (Orchard Lane Ser.). (Illus.). 141p. (J). (gr. k-4). 1999. pap. 8.00 (*1-891907-07-7*) Castleberry.
— Jeff McLean: His Courtship. (Courtship Ser.). 175p. 1998. pap. 7.50 (*1-891907-05-0*) Castleberry.
— Midnight Sky. (Farm Mystery Ser.). 160p. (YA). 1998. pap. 7.50 (*1-891907-06-9*) Castleberry.
— The Mysterious Message. (Farm Mystery Ser.). 160p. 1997. pap. 7.50 (*1-891907-04-2*) Castleberry.
— Our Homestead Story: The First Years. 210p. 1996. pap. 7.50 (*1-891907-02-6*) Castleberry.
— Waiting for Her Isaac. (Courtship Ser.). 155p. 1997. pap. 7.50 (*1-891907-03-4*) Castleberry.
Castleberry, Susan L., jt. auth. see Castleberry, Stephen B.
Castleberry, Susie L., jt. auth. see Castleberry, Stephen B.
Castleberry, Vivian A. Daughters of Dallas. 550p. 1994. 35.00 (*0-9623216-8-0*) Odenwald Pr.
Castleden, Rodney. Atlantis Destroyed. LC 97-45656. (Illus.). 240p. (C). 1998. 35.00 (*0-415-16539-3*) Routledge.
***Castleden, Rodney.** King Arthur: Truth Behind the Legend. LC 99-29051. (Illus.). 288p. 2000. 29.95 (*0-415-19575-6*) Routledge.
Castleden, Rodney. The Making of Stonehenge. LC 93-12736. 320p. (C). (gr. 13). 1994. 65.00 (*0-415-08513-6*) Routledge.
— Minoans: Life in Bronze Age Crete. (Illus.). 272p. (C). 1993. pap. 22.99 (*0-415-08833-X*, B0410) Routledge.
— The Stonehenge People: An Exploration of Life in Neolithic Britain, 4700-2000 B.C. (Illus.). 224p. 1987. text 29.50 (*0-7102-0968-1*, Routledge Thoemms) Routledge.
— The Stonehenge People: An Exploration of Life in Neolithic Britain 4700-2000 BC. LC 89-70136. (Illus.). 296p. (Orig.). (C). (gr. 13). 1992. pap. 24.99 (*0-415-04065-5*, A4660) Routledge.
Castledine, Annie. Plays by Women, Vol. 10. 256p. (Orig.). 1993. pap. 17.95 (*0-413-68000-2*, A0690, Methuen Drama) Methn.
Castlehaven, James T. The Earl of Castlehaven's Memoirs of the Irish Wars with the Earl of Anglesey's: A Letter from a Person of Honour in the Country. LC 74-3345. 332p. 1974. reprint ed. lib. bdg. 50.00 (*0-8201-1128-7*) Schol Facsimiles.
Castlehaven, James T., jt. auth. see Trusky, Tom.
Castleman, Barry I. Asbestos: Medical & Legal Aspects. 3rd ed. 798p. 1995. boxed set 95.00 (*0-13-048414-8*) Aspen Law.
Castleman, Barry I. & Berger, Stephen L. Asbestos: Medical & Legal Aspects, 1. 4th ed. LC 95-47681. 940p. 1996. boxed set 120.00 (*1-56706-275-X*) Panel Pubs.
Castleman, Craig. Getting Up: Subway Graffitti in New York. (Illus.). 209p. 1984. reprint ed. pap. text 14.00 (*0-262-53051-1*) MIT Pr.
Castleman, Deke. Compass American Guide to Las Vegas. 6th ed. (Guides Ser.). 1999. pap. 19.95 (*0-679-00370-3*, Compass Amrcn) Fodors Travel.
— Las Vegas. 2nd ed. Parr, Barry, ed. LC 93-1244. (Compass American Guides Ser.). (Illus.). 320p. 1998. pap. 18.95 (*1-878867-47-4*, Compass Amrcn) Fodors Travel.
— Moon Handbooks: Nevada. 5th rev. ed. (Illus.). 560p. 1998. pap. 18.95 (*1-56691-116-8*, Moon Handbks) Avalon Travel.
Castleman, Deke, et al. Foghorn Outdoors: Utah & Nevada Camping: The Complete Guide to More Than 25,000 Campsites. 380p. 1997. pap. 18.95 (*1-57354-012-9*, Foghorn Outdoors) Avalon Travel.
Castleman, Deke, jt. auth. see Pitcher, Don.
Castleman, Deke, ed. see Parr, Barry.
Castleman, Harry & Podrazik, Walter J. The Beatles Again. LC 77-92320. (Rock & Roll Reference Ser.: No. 2). 280p. 1977. 34.50 (*0-87650-089-0*) Popular Culture.
Castleman, Heidi, II & Koob, Joseph E. The Tonal Application of Finger Patterns to Viola Technique. 50p. 1990. lib. bdg. write for info. (*0-929918-04-5*) Midstates Pub.
Castleman, Kenneth R. Digital Image Processing. LC 95-11113. 667p. (C). 1995. 105.00 (*0-13-211467-4*) P-H.
Castleman, Michael. An Aspirin a Day: What You Can Do to Prevent Heart Attack, Stroke, & Cancer. LC 92-36368. 192p. 1993. pap. 7.70 (*1-56282-880-0*, Pub. by Hyperion) Time Warner.
***Castleman, Michael.** Blended Medicine: The Best Choices in Healing. LC 99-48384. (Illus.). 512p. 2000. text 31.95 (*0-87596-520-2*) Rodale Pr Inc.
Castleman, Michael. The Healing Herbs. 656p. 1995. mass mkt. 7.50 (*0-553-56988-0*) Bantam.
— The Healing Herbs: The Ultimate Guide to the Curative Power of Nature's Medicines. LC 91-6400. 436p. 1991. text 27.95 (*0-87857-934-6*, 05-968-0) Rodale Pr Inc.
— The Healing Herbs Spanish Edition. (SPA.). 448p. 1995. text 26.95 (*0-87596-267-X*) Rodale Pr Inc.
— Hierbas Milagrosas (Miracle Herbs) La Guia de las 50 Hierbas Mas Poderosas del Mundo (The Guide to the World's 50 Most Powerful Herbs) LC 98-22475. (SPA., Illus.). 192p. 1998. pap. 12.95 (*1-57954-031-7*) Rodale Pr Inc.
— Nature's Cures. 608p. 1997. mass mkt. 6.99 (*0-553-57696-8*) Bantam.
— Nature's Cures: From Acupressure & Aromatherapy to Walking & Yoga--The Ultimate Guide to the Best, Scientifically Proven, Drug-Free Healing Methods. 528p. 1995. text 27.95 (*0-87596-301-3*) Rodale Pr Inc.
— Remedios de la Naturaleza: Desde la Aromaterapia Hasta Layoga, la Gu la Maxima de Los Mejores Tratamientos Sin Medicamentos Todos Comprobados. LC 97-24241. 1997. write for info. (*0-87596-502-4*) Rodale Pr Inc.
— Sexual Solutions: A Guide for Men & the Women Who Love Them. rev. ed. 304p. 1989. per. 12.00 (*0-671-66488-3*, Touchstone) S&S Trade Pap.
Castleman, Michael, et al. There's Still a Person in There: The Complete Guide to Treating & Coping with Alzheimer's. LC 99-34745. 384p. 2000. 22.95 (*0-399-14571-0*, G P Putnam) Peng Put Young Read.
Castleman, Nancy, jt. auth. see Eisenson, Marc.
Castleman, Nancy, ed. see Eisenson, Adam.
Castleman, Riva. Art of the Forties. (Illus.). 160p. 1991. pap. 19.95 (*0-87070-189-4*) Mus of Modern Art.
— Art of the Forties. (Illus.). 160p. 1991. 39.95 (*0-87070-188-6*, 0-8109-6089-3) Mus of Modern Art.
— A Century of Artists Books. (Illus.). 264p. 1994. 55.00 (*0-8109-6124-5*, Pub. by Abrams) Time Warner.
— A Century of Artists Books. (Illus.). 264p. 1997. pap. 29.95 (*0-8109-6181-4*, Pub. by Abrams) Time Warner.
— A Century of Artists Books. LC 94-76019. (Illus.). 264p. 1994. 55.00 (*0-87070-151-7*, 0-8109-6124-5, Pub. by Mus of Modern Art); pap. 29.95 (*0-87070-152-5*, 0-8109-4181-4, Pub. by Mus of Modern Art) Abrams.
— Jasper Johns: A Print Retrospective. (Illus.). 148p. 1990. 40.00 (*0-87070-401-X*); pap. 25.00 (*0-87070-402-8*, 0-8109-6109-1) Mus of Modern Art.
— Prints of the Twentieth Century: A History. rev. ed. LC 87-51289. (World of Art Ser.). (Illus.). 192p. 1988. pap. 14.95 (*0-500-20228-1*, Pub. by Thames Hudson) Norton.
— Seven Master Printmakers: Innovations in the Eighties. (Illus.). 120p. 1991. 37.50 (*0-87070-194-0*); pap. 19.95 (*0-87070-190-8*) Mus of Modern Art.
Castleman, Riva, ed. Art of the Forties. (Illus.). 160p. 1991. 39.95 (*0-8109-6089-3*, Pub. by Abrams) Time Warner.
Castleman, Riva, et al. Toulouse-Lautrec: Posters & Prints from the Collection of Irene & Howard Stein. LC 97-46141. 1998. 35.95 (*0-939802-83-X*); pap. 24.95 (*0-939802-84-8*) High Mus Art.
Castleman, Riva, jt. auth. see Matisse, Henri.
Castleman, Robbie. David: Man after God's Own Heart, 2 vols., Vol. 1. (Fisherman Bible Studyguide Ser.). 80p. 1973. pap. 4.99 (*0-87788-164-2*, H Shaw Pubs) Waterbrook Pr.
***Castleman, Robbie.** David - Chinese Edition Vol. I: Man after God's Own Heart. 68p. 1999. pap. 6.00 (*1-56582-130-0*) Christ Renew Min.
— David - Chinese Edition Vol. II: Man after God's Own Heart. 60p. 1999. pap. 6.00 (*1-56582-131-9*) Christ Renew Min.
Castleman, Robbie. Elijah: Obedience in a Threatening World. (Fisherman Bible Studyguide Ser.). 64p. (Orig.). 1986. pap. 4.99 (*0-87788-218-5*, H Shaw Pubs) Waterbrook Pr.
— King David: Trusting God for a Lifetime, 2 vols., Vol. 2. (Fisherman Bible Studyguide Ser.). 63p. 1981. pap. 4.99 (*0-87788-165-0*, H Shaw Pubs) Waterbrook Pr.
— Miracles. 80p. 1996. pap. 4.99 (*0-87788-555-9*, H Shaw Pubs) Waterbrook Pr.
— Parenting in the Pew: Guiding Your Children into the Joy of Worship. LC 92-40659. 125p. (Orig.). 1993. pap. 8.99 (*0-8308-1627-5*, 1627) InterVarsity.
***Castleman, Robbie.** Peter. 1999. pap. 4.99 (*0-8308-3088-X*) InterVarsity.
Castleman, Robbie. True Love in a World of False Hope: Sex, Romance & Real People. LC 96-16813. 178p. (Orig.). 1996. pap. 9.99 (*0-8308-1958-4*, 1958) InterVarsity.
***Castleman, Terry L.** Death Investigation: A Handbook for Police Officers. LC 00-42304. 2000. pap. write for info. (*0-398-07105-5*) C C Thomas.
***Castleman, Vivian Rochelle Grant.** As a Man in Sports I'm Coming Out of the Closet to Confess There Is Not One. large type ed. Delin, Marilyn, ed. 50p. 2000. pap. write for info. (*1-930577-00-1*) Grant Prod.
Castles, et al, eds. Australia's Italians: Culture & Community in a Changing Society. 272p. 1992. pap. text 19.95 (*1-86373-170-9*, Pub. by Allen & Unwin Pty) Paul & Co Pubs.
Castles, Alex. Annotated Bibliography of Printed Materials on Australian Law (1788-1900) 464p. 1994. 120.00 (*0-455-21299-6*, Pub. by LawBk Co) Gaunt.
— Shark Arm Murders: The Thrilling True Story of a Tiger Shark & a Tattooed Arm. LC 95-199170. 1999. pap. text 9.95 (*1-86254-335-6*) Wakefield Pr.
Castles, Alex C. An Australian Legal History. xx, 553p. 1982. pap. 62.00 (*0-455-19609-5*, Pub. by LawBk Co) Gaunt.
Castles, Alex C., jt. auth. see Bennett, J. M.
Castles, Cheryl. Carving Card-Carrying Critters with Power. LC 97-65634. (Schiffer Book for Woodcarvers Ser.). (Illus.). 72p. 1997. pap. 14.95 (*0-7643-0274-4*) Schiffer.
Castles, Elaine E. "We're People First" The Social & Emotional Lives of Individuals with Mental Retardation. LC 95-34409. 224p. 1996. 39.95 (*0-275-95243-6*, Praeger Pubs) Greenwood.
Castles, Francis, et al, eds. The Great Experiment: Labor Parties & Public Policy Transformation in Australia & New Zealand. 272p. 1996. pap. 24.95 (*1-86448-003-3*, Pub. by Allen & Unwin Pty) Paul & Co Pubs.
Castles, Francis G. Comparative Public Policy: Patterns of Post-War Transformation. LC 98-13443. 368p. 1998. 95.00 (*1-85898-816-0*) E Elgar.
— Comparative Public Policy: Patterns of Post-War Transformation. 368p. 1999. pap. 30.00 (*1-85898-823-3*) E Elgar.
— The Social Democratic Image of Society: A Study of the Achievements & Origins of Scandinavian Social Democracy in Comparative Perspective. 1978. 22.50 (*0-7100-8870-1*, Routledge Thoemms) Routledge.
— The Working Class & Welfare: Reflections of the Political Development & the Welfare State in Australia & New Zealand, 1890-1980. 128p. 1985. text 29.95 (*0-86861-669-9*) Routledge.
Castles, Francis G., ed. Australia Compared: People, Politics, & Policies. 224p. (Orig.). 1992. pap. text 19.95 (*0-04-442339-X*, Pub. by Allen & Unwin Pty) Paul & Co Pubs.
— Families of Nations: Patterns of Public Policy in Western Democracies. 377p. 1993. 77.95 (*1-85521-345-1*, Pub. by Dartmth Pub) Ashgate Pub Co.
Castles, Francis G., et al, eds. The Future of Party Government Vol. 3: Managing Mixed Economics. (European University Institute, Series C (Political & Social Science): No. 5.3). 320p. (C). 1987. lib. bdg. 77.70 (*3-11-010941-7*) De Gruyter.
Castles, Francis G. & Wildenmann, Rudolf, eds. The Future of Party Government Vol. 1: Visions & Realities of Party Government. (European University Institute, Series C (Political & Social Science): No. 5-1). x, 246p. 1986. 83.85 (*3-11-010651-5*) De Gruyter.
Castles, Francis G., jt. ed. see Pierson, Christopher.
Castles, Mary R. Primer of Nursing Research. (Illus.). 208p. 1987. pap. text 29.00 (*0-7216-1713-1*, W B Saunders Co) Harcrt Hlth Sci Grp.

C

— Primer of Nursing Research. 1987. pap. text, teacher ed. write for info. (*0-03-013054-9*) SCP.

Castles, Stephen & Miller, Mark J. The Age of Migration: International Population Movements in the Modern World. 2nd ed. LC 98-16000. 352p. 1998. pap. text 24.95 (*1-57230-382-4*, C0382); lib. bdg. 45.00 (*1-57230-381-6*) Guilford Pubns.

Castles, Stephen, et al. Immigration & Australia. LC 99-204585. 208p. 1998. pap. 29.95 (*1-86448-851-4*, Pub. by Allen & Unwin Pty) Paul & Co Pubs.

Castles, Stephen, jt. auth. see Vasta, Ed E.

Castleton, K., et al. Journal of California & Great Basin Anthropology. fac. ed. (Malki Museum, Journal of California & Great Basin Anthropology Ser.: Vol. 3:2). (Illus.). 146p. (C). 1981. reprint ed. pap. text 16.25 (*1-55567-768-1*) Coyote Press.

Castleton, Kenneth B. Petroglyphs & Pictographs of Utah, Vol. I. 1984. pap. 24.95 (*0-940378-29-9*) U of Utah Pr.

— Petroglyphs & Pictographs of Utah, Vol. II. 1987. pap. 24.95 (*0-940378-30-2*) U of Utah Pr.

— Petroglyphs & Pictographs of Utah, Vol. 2. (Illus.). 1980. 15.00 (*0-686-26976-4*) Utah Mus Natural Hist.

Castley, Andrew. Business Situation German. (ENG & GER.). 97p. 1980. pap. 19.95 (*0-8288-4685-5*, M9206) Fr & Eur.

Castley, Andrew & Wagener, Debbie. Business German: A Complete Course for Beginners. (Teach Yourself Ser.). (GER., Illus.). 224p. 1994. pap. 12.95 (*0-8442-3783-3*, Teach Yrslf) NTC Contemp Pub Co.

— Teach Yourself Business German. (Teach Yourself Ser.). (GER.). 224p. 1994. pap. 24.95 incl. audio (*0-8442-3891-0*, Teach Yrslf) NTC Contemp Pub Co.

— Teach Yourself German Business. (Teach Yourself Ser.). 1992. 19.95 (*0-8288-8334-3*); 45.00 incl. audio (*0-8288-8345-9*) Fr & Eur.

Castley, Anna. Practical Spelling. LC 97-39166. (Basics Made Easy Ser.). 208p. 1998. pap. 13.95 (*1-57685-083-8*) LrningExprss.

Castley, Robert. Korea's Economic Miracle: The Crucial Role of Japan. LC 96-9306. 396p. 1997. text 59.95 (*0-312-16056-9*) St Martin.

Castner, Charles. Louisville & Nashville: The Old Reliable. (Illus.). 240p. 1996. 29.95 (*1-883089-19-0*) TLC VA.

— Nashville, Chattanooga & St. Louis. (Hobby Bks.: No. C87). (Illus.). 100p. 1995. 26.95 (*0-911868-87-9*, C87) Carstens Pubns.

***Castner, Charles B., et al.** Louisville & Nashville Passenger Trains: The Pan American Era, 1921-1971. (Illus.). 240p. 2000. 33.95 (*1-883089-49-2*, Pub. by TLC VA) Motorbooks Intl.

Castner, David G. & Grainger, David W. Fluorinated Surfaces, Coatings & Film. (ACS Symposium Ser). 130.00 (*0-8412-3623-2*, Pub. by Am Chemical) OUP.

Castner, David G., jt. ed. see Ratner, Buddy D.

Castner, Don. Keep Your Drawers Clean. 1992. pap. write for info. (*0-9632203-0-6*) D L Castner.

Castner, Harvey R., jt. ed. see Balchin, Nigel C.

Castner, Henry W. Discerning New Horizons: A Perceptual Approach to Geographic Education. LC 96-175589. (Pathways Ser.: No. 13). (Illus.). 245p. 1995. pap. 18.00 (*1-884136-07-9*) NCFGE.

— Seeking New Horizons: A Perceptual Approach to Geographic Education. 224p. (C). 1990. 65.00 (*0-7735-0728-0*, Pub. by McG-Queens Univ Pr) CUP Services.

Castner, James L. The Amazon Rainforest: An Exploration of Countries, Cultures & Creatures. LC 98-94792. 104p. 1999. pap. 15.00 (*0-9625150-9-4*) Feline Pr.

***Castner, James L.** Explorama's Amazon: A Journey Through the Rainforest of Peru. (Illus.). 192p. 2000. pap. 35.00 (*0-9625150-5-1*) Feline Pr.

Castner, James L. Rainforests: A Guide to Research & Tourist Facilities at Selected Tropical Forest Sites in Central & South America. LC 89-81847. (Illus.). 416p. (Orig.). 1990. pap. 21.95 (*0-9625150-2-7*) Feline Pr.

***Castner, James L. & Byrd, Jason H.** Forensic Insect Identification Cards. (Illus.). 60p. 2000. pap. 25.00 (*0-9625150-8-6*) Feline Pr.

Castner, James L., et al. A Field Guide to Medicinal & Useful Plants of the Upper Amazon. LC 97-77509. (Illus.). 160p. 1998. pap. 35.00 (*0-9625150-7-8*) Feline Pr.

Castner, James L., jt. auth. see Byrd, Jason H.

***Castner, James Lee.** Amazon Insects: A Photo Guide. (Illus.). 160p. 2000. pap. 15.00 (*0-9625150-1-9*) Feline Pr.

Casto. American Government Internet Activities. 2nd ed. (Political Science Ser.). 1999. 13.50 (*0-534-55315-X*) Wadsworth Pub.

Casto, B., jt. auth. see Hughes, T.

Casto, James E. Towboat on the Ohio. (Illus.). 208p. 1995. 24.95 (*0-8131-1916-2*) U Pr of Ky.

— West Virginia: Mountain Majesty. Sullivan, Ken, ed. (Illus.). 256p. 1996. 49.95 (*0-9651580-0-4*) Publns Mgmt Assoc.

***Casto, L. Dalton.** African Embrace. (Illus.). 256p. 1999. pap. 15.95 (*0-9659830-1-3*) African Ways Publishing.

Casto, L. Dalton. The Dilemmas of Africanization: Choices & Dangers for Sub-Saharan Africa. LC 97-94407. (Illus.). 280p. 1998. 27.50 (*0-9659830-0-5*) African Ways Publishing.

Casto, M. L. Get Smart! About Modern Romantic Relationships: Your Personal Guide to Right & Real Love. LC 99-61942. 65p. 1999. 25.00 (*0-7388-0380-4*); pap. 15.00 (*0-7388-0381-2*) Xlibris Corp.

***Casto, Marilyn Dee.** Actors, Audiences & Historic Theaters of Kentucky. LC 99-49116. (Illus.). 192p. 2000. 29.95 (*0-8131-2162-0*) U Pr of Ky.

***Casto, Michelle L.** Get Smart! About Modern Career Development: Your Personal Guide to Creating Your Life's Work. LC 00-92181. (Learning Book Ser.). 240p. 2000. pap. 15.95 (*0-9674704-5-5*) Get Smart.

— Get Smart! About Modern Romantic Relationships: Your Personal Guide to Finding Right & Real Love. LC 99-61942. 225p. 1999. 15.95 (*0-9674704-0-4*) Get Smart.

Casto, William R. Oliver Ellsworth & the Creation of the Federal Republic. LC 97-27882. (Illus.). 145p. (Orig.). 1997. pap. write for info. (*0-9618400-2-1*) Second Circuit Committee on Bicentennial.

— The Supreme Court in the Early Republic: The Chief Justiceships of John Jay & Oliver Ellsworth. LC 94-18750. (Chief Justiceships of the United States Supreme Court Ser.). 292p. 1995. text 39.95 (*1-57003-033-2*) U of SC Pr.

Caston, Anne. Flying Out with the Wounded. LC 96-45903. 96p. 1997. pap. 12.95 (*0-8147-1560-5*); text 25.00 (*0-8147-1561-3*) NYU Pr.

Caston, Art, jt. auth. see Tapscott, Don.

Caston, Catherine. Burnout in African American Family Caregivers: Nursing Interventions. rev. ed. LC 96-37839. (Studies on the Elderly in America). (Illus.). 160p. 1997. text 53.00 (*0-8153-2647-5*) Garland.

Caston, Richard J. Life in a Business-Oriented Society: A Sociological Perspective. LC 97-25014. 344p. 1997. pap. text 46.00 (*0-205-15975-3*) Allyn.

Castonguay, C. Meaning & Existence in Mathematics. LC 72-96052. (Library of Exact Philosophy: Vol. 9). 159p. 1973. 52.95 (*0-387-81110-9*) Spr-Verlag.

Castonguay, Russell. A Comparative Guide to Classification Schemes for Local Government Document Collections. LC 83-26594. xv, 143p. 1984. 42.95 (*0-313-24208-9*, CCG/, Greenwood Pr) Greenwood.

Castor, Graham & Cave, Terence, eds. Neo-Latin & the Vernacular in Renaissance France. (Illus.). 1984. 55.00 (*0-19-815780-0*) OUP.

Castor, H. Dinosaurs Next Door. (Reading for Beginners Ser.). (Illus.). 24p. (J). (gr. k-4). 1995. lib. bdg. 12.95 (*0-88110-744-1*, Usborne) EDC.

Castor, H. Ella's Last Dance. (Illus.). (J). 1996. mass mkt. 7.95 (*0-340-65132-6*, Pub. by Hodder & Stought Ltd) Trafalgar.

Castor, H. Incredible Present. (Reading for Beginners Ser.). (Illus.). 24p. (J). (gr. k-4). 1995. pap. 4.95 (*0-7460-1535-6*, Usborne); lib. bdg. 12.95 (*0-88110-745-X*, Usborne) EDC.

Castor, H. Pippa on Pointe. (Illus.). (J). 1996. mass mkt. 7.95 (*0-340-65131-8*, Pub. by Hodder & Stought Ltd) Trafalgar.

— Sadie's Ballet. (Illus.). (J). 1996. mass mkt. 7.95 (*0-340-65129-6*, Pub. by Hodder & Stought Ltd) Trafalgar.

Castor, H. Starting Needlecraft. (First Skills Ser.). (Illus.). 32p. (J). (gr. k-3). 1994. text 4.95 (*0-7460-1664-6*, Usborne); lib. bdg. 12.96 (*0-88110-706-9*, Usborne) EDC.

Castor, Harriet. Ballet Magic. (Illus.). 64p. (J). pap. 7.95 (*0-14-038479-0*, Pub. by Pnguin Bks Ltd) Trafalgar.

— Ballet Magic on Stage. 2nd ed. (Illus.). 64p. (J). pap. 7.95 (*0-14-038480-4*, Pub. by Pnguin Bks Ltd) Trafalgar.

Castor, Harriet. Ballet Stories. LC 96-34093. (Story Library). (Illus.). 260p. (J). (gr. 1 up). 1997. 7.95 (*0-7534-5073-9*, Kingfisher) LKC.

Castor, Harriet. Confident Readers Milly's Golden Goal. (Illus.). 96p. (J). pap. 7.95 (*0-14-038478-2*, Pub. by Pnguin Bks Ltd) Trafalgar.

— Fat Puss & Friends. 96p. (J). (gr. 3). 1985. pap. 7.95 (*0-14-031658-2*, Pub. by Pnguin Bks Ltd) Trafalgar.

— Fat Puss on Wheels. (Illus.). 96p. (J). (gr. 3-6). 1989. pap. 7.95 (*0-14-032402-X*, Pub. by Pnguin Bks Ltd) Trafalgar.

— Milly of the Rovers. (Illus.). 96p. (J). 1998. pap. 7.95 (*0-14-037839-1*, Pub. by Pnguin Bks Ltd) Trafalgar.

Castor, Harriet. Starting Chess. (First Skills Ser.). (Illus.). 32p. (J). (gr. k-3). 1995. pap. 4.95 (*0-7460-1386-8*, Usborne) EDC.

Castor, Harriet. Starting Chess. (First Skills Ser.). (Illus.). 32p. (J). (gr. k-3). 1995. lib. bdg. 12.95 (*0-88110-768-9*, Usborne) EDC.

Castor, Harriet. Starting Chess. (Usborne Kid Kits Ser.). (Illus.). (J). (gr. k up). 1996. 13.95 (*0-88110-833-2*, Usborne) EDC.

— Trucks: Truck Board Book. (Machines Board Bks.). (Illus.). 32p. (J). (ps up). 1993. bds. 4.95 (*0-7460-1098-2*, Usborne) EDC.

Castor, Harriet, et al. Read It Yourself Stories. (Reading for Beginners Ser.). (Illus.). 96p. (J). (ps-3). 1995. 14.95 (*0-7460-2313-8*, Usborne) EDC.

Castor, Harriet, jt. auth. see Young, Caroline.

***Castor, Helen.** The King, the Crown & the Duchy of Lancaster. (Illus.). 340p. 2000. text 89.00 (*0-19-820622-4*) OUP.

Castoriadis, Cornelius. The Imaginary Institution of Society. (Illus.). 432p. 1998. reprint ed. pap. text 19.00 (*0-262-53155-0*) MIT Pr.

— Philosophy, Politics & Autonomy: Essays in Political Philosophy. Curtis, David A., ed. (Odeon Ser.). 320p. (C). 1991. pap. text 23.95 (*0-19-506963-3*) OUP.

— Political & Social Writings Vol. 1: From the Critique of Bureaucracy to the Positive Content of Socialism. 347p. 1988. pap. 19.95 (*0-8166-1617-5*) U of Minn Pr.

— Political & Social Writings Vol. 2: From the Worker's Struggle Against Bureaucracy to Revolution in the Age of Modern Capitalism. LC 87-10893. 384p. 1988. pap. 19.95 (*0-8166-1619-1*) U of Minn Pr.

— Political & Social Writings Vol. 3: Recommencing the Revolution: From Socialism to the Autonomous Society, 1961-1979. Curtis, David A., tr. from FRE. 544p. (C). 1992. pap. 19.95 (*0-8166-2168-3*); text 49.95 (*0-8166-2069-5*) U of Minn Pr.

— Political & Social Writings Vol. 3: Recommencing the Revolution: From Socialism to the Autonomous Society, 1961-1979, 3 vols., Set. Curtis, David A., tr. from FRE. 1318p. (C). 1992. pap. 45.00 (*0-8166-2264-7*) U of Minn Pr.

— World in Fragments: Writings on Politics, Society, Psychoanalysis, & the Imagination. Curtis, David A., ed. & tr. by. from FRE. LC 96-37014. (Deridian Ser.). 1997. write for info. (*0-8047-2762-7*) Stanford U Pr.

Castorillo, Noel T., ed. see Viloria, Jose B., Jr.

Castorina, Edward P., jt. auth. see Berger, Joseph C.

Castoro, Michael, Sr. Faith Doctrine of Eternal Life: What Are the Commandments of Christ? What Purpose Do They Serve? 2nd rev. ed. (Illus.). 40p. 1997. pap. 3.99 (*0-9660781-2-8*) St Michael Archangel Soc.

— Genesis Interpretation. 15p. 1998. 3.99 (*0-9660781-3-6*) St Michael Archangel Soc.

— Interpretation Thereof: Interpretation of the Bible. (Illus.). 350p. 1998. 24.95 (*0-9660781-0-1*) St Michael Archangel Soc.

***Castoro, Michael.** Interpretation Theteof. 2nd rev. ed. 130p. 1999. pap. 24.95 (*0-9660781-1-X*) St Michael Archangel Soc.

Castoro, Michael, Sr. New Testament Scriptures. 1998. 3.99 (*0-9660781-6-0*) St Michael Archangel Soc.

— Old Testament Scriptures. Date not set. 3.99 (*0-9660781-5-2*) St Michael Archangel Soc.

— Revelation Interpretation: The Book of Revelations. 50p. 1998. 3.99 (*0-9660781-4-4*) St Michael Archangel Soc.

***Castoro, Michael, Jr.** Tutor f-o-r Inactive Christians. 200p. 1999. pap. 2.00 (*0-9660781-9-5*) St Michael Archangel Soc.

Castorri, Alexis. Exercise Your Mind: 36 Mental Workouts for Peak Performance. (Illus.). 112p. 1996. pap. text 9.95 (*0-8065-1815-4*, Citadel Pr) Carol Pub Group.

Castorri, Alexis & Heller, Jane. Mental Aerobics: Exercises for a Stronger, Healthier Mind. (Illus.). 112p. 1992. pap. 7.95 (*0-8065-1362-4*, Citadel Pr) Carol Pub Group.

Castranova, Vincent, et al, eds. Silica & Silica-Induced Lung Diseases: Current Concepts. 432p. 1995. boxed set 244.95 (*0-8493-4709-2*, 4709) CRC Pr.

Castranova, Vincent, jt. ed. see Van Dyke, Knox.

Castree, Noel, jt. auth. see Braun, Bruce.

Castrejon, Pilar. Kinientos - New Pictures of an Old World: An Anthology Commemorating the Last 500 Years. LC 92-61833. 85p. (Orig.). 1992. pap. 4.95 (*0-945530-07-2*) Wordsworth KS.

Castren, M. Alexander. Grammatik Der Samojedischen Sprachen. LC 66-64409. 608p. 1966. write for info. (*0-87750-017-7*) Curzon Pr Ltd.

Castri, Francesco Di, see Di Castri, Francesco, ed.

***Castria, Francesca.** Vincent Van Gogh. (Quadrifolios Ser.). (Illus.). 16p. 2000. 35.00 (*0-8478-2311-3*) Rizzoli Intl.

Castria, Francesca, jt. auth. see Zuffi, Stefano.

Castrilli, Anna Maria, tr. see Ardizzi, Maria.

Castriota, David. The Ara Pacis Augustae & the Imagery of Abundance in Later Greek & Early Roman Imperial Art. LC 94-23503. 300p. 1995. text 47.50 (*0-691-03715-9*, Pub. by Princeton U Pr) Cal Prin Full Svc.

— Myth, Ethos, & Actuality: Official Art in Fifth-Century B. C. Athens. LC 92-50247. (Studies in Classics). (Illus.). 354p. (C). 1992. pap. 24.95 (*0-299-13354-0*) U of Wis Pr.

— Myth, Ethos, & Actuality: Official Art in Fifth-Century B.C. Athens. LC 92-50247. (Studies in Classics). (Illus.). 354p. (Orig.). (C). 1992. lib. bdg. 50.00 (*0-299-13350-8*) U of Wis Pr.

Castriota, David, ed. Artistic Strategy & the Rhetoric of Power: Political Uses of Art from Antiquity to the Present. LC 85-27764. (Illus.). 280p. (C). 1986. text 31.95 (*0-8093-1289-1*) S Ill U Pr.

Castro. English-Spanish, Spanish-English Dictionary of Business, Economics & Law. (ENG & ITA.). 1734p. 1990. 275.00 (*0-7859-7477-6*, 8487532004) Fr & Eur.

— Iberia in Prehistory. (History of Spain Ser.). (Illus.). 320p. (C). 1995. text 88.95 (*0-631-16794-3*) Blackwell Pubs.

— Marine Biology. 4th ed. 2002. 49.00 (*0-07-029421-6*) McGraw.

— Restaurant Rose Pasadena. (Illus.). 1996. 8.95 (*0-9624023-3-8*) J C West Prodns.

***Castro, A., et al, eds.** Understanding Granites: Integrating New & Classical Techniques. (Special Publication Ser.: No. 168). 288p. 2000. 117.00 (*1-86239-058-4*, Pub. by Geol Soc Pub Hse) AAPG.

***Castro, A. & Haya, J.** La Terapia Hormonal Sustitutiva en Esquemas. (Illus.). 64p. 2000. write for info. (*1-84214-002-7*) Prthnon Pub.

Castro, Adam. Halloween & Beyond. 1999. 14.95 (*0-671-01197-9*) S&S Trade.

Castro, Adam-Troy. Spider-Man: The Gathering of the Sinister Six. 320p. (Orig.). 1999. mass mkt. 6.99 (*0-425-16774-7*) Berkley Pub.

***Castro, Adam-Troy.** Spider-Man Bk. 2: The Revenge of the Sinister Six. 2000. mass mkt. 6.99 (*0-425-17337-2*) Berkley Pub.

Castro, Adam-Troy, jt. auth. see Defalco, Tom.

Castro, Adrian. Cantos to Blood & Honey. LC 97-16016. 110p. (Orig.). 1997. pap. 12.95 (*1-56689-067-5*) Coffee Hse.

Castro, Alberto, et al, eds. International Integration & Labour Market Organization. (Illus.). 268p. 1992. text 77.00 (*0-12-163870-7*) Acad Pr.

Castro, Alfonso Peter. Facing Kirinyaga: A Social History of Forest Commons in Southern Mount Kenya. LC 95-219356. 166p. 1995. pap. 29.95 (*1-85339-253-7*, Pub. by Intermed Tech) Stylus Pub VA.

Castro-Amaya, Roselio A. & Kattan-Zablah, Jorge. Dos Amigos: Viajando por Hispanoamerica. 1986. pap. 9.95 (*0-910286-66-3*) Boxwood.

Castro, Ana A. Jarreta de, see De Mattos Bicudo, Carlos E. & Jarreta de Castro, Ana A.

Castro, Angel. Cubano..., Go Home! 1972. pap. 3.00 (*0-685-48631-1*) E Torres & Sons.

— Cuentos De Nueva York. 1973. pap. 2.50 (*84-399-0644-7*) Ediciones.

— Cuentos Yanquis. 1972. pap. 2.50 (*0-89729-137-9*) Ediciones.

— Refugiados. 1971. pap. text 4.00 (*0-685-48630-3*) E Torres & Sons.

Castro, Ann, jt. auth. see Gittleman, Ann Louise.

Castro, Anthony J. Mosby's USMLE Step 1 Reviews: Neuroscience. LC 96-22065. (Ace the Boards Ser.). (Illus.). 496p. (C). (gr. 13). 1996. pap. text 30.00 (*0-8151-1479-6*, 27046); pap. text 30.00 (*0-8151-1480-X*, 28956) Mosby Inc.

Castro, Barry. Business & Society: A Reader in the History, Sociology & Ethics of Business. (Illus.). 288p. 1996. pap. text 33.95 (*0-19-509566-9*) OUP.

Castro, Brenda, jt. ed. see Farhart, Sandy.

***Castro, Brian.** Looking for Estrellita. 264p. 2000. pap. 19.95 (*0-7022-3115-0*, Pub. by Univ Queensland Pr) Intl Spec Bk.

— Looking for Estrillita. 1999. pap. 24.95 (*0-7022-3114-2*, Pub. by Univ Queensland Pr) Intl Spec Bk.

— Stepper. LC 97-159133. 1997. write for info. (*0-09-183502-X*) Trafalgar.

Castro, C. Fernandez de, see De Castro, C. Fernandez.

Castro, Claudio D., ed. La Educacion en la Era de la Informatica. (SPA.). 238p. 1998. pap. text 21.00 (*1-886938-48-2*) IADB.

Castro, Claudio De Moura, see De Moura Castro, Claudio, ed.

Castro, Claudio De Moura, see Espinola, Viola & De Moura Castro, Claudio, eds.

Castro, Concepcion Obon de, see Obon de Castro, Concepcion.

Castro, D., ed. The Facial Nerve. LC 89-24517. (Illus.). 579p. 1990. lib. bdg. 148.50 (*90-6299-058-4*, Pub. by Kugler) Kugler Pubns.

Castro, Daniel. In That Stillness... LC 79-92054. 201p. (Orig.). 1980. pap. 4.95 (*0-918038-12-X*) Journey Pubns.

Castro, Daniel, ed. Revolution & Revolutionaries: Guerrilla Movements in Latin America. LC 99-12775. (Jaguar Books on Latin America: No. 17). 234p. 1999. pap. 18.95 (*0-8420-2626-6*) Scholarly Res Inc.

***Castro, Daniel, ed.** Revolution & Revolutionaries: Guerrilla Movements in Latin America. LC 99-12775. (Jaguar Books on Latin America: No. 17). 234p. 1999. 55.00 (*0-8420-2625-8*) Scholarly Res Inc.

***Castro, David.** Keoua, Father of Kings. rev. ed. Orig. Title: Keoua, Father of Hawaiian Kings. (Illus.). 68p. 2000. 9.95 (*0-9669586-2-4*) Ke Ali i.

Castro, David A. High Chief Kalokuokamaile: The Older Brother of Kamehameha 1st LC 98-94237. 86 p. 1998. write for info. (*0-9669586-0-8*) Ke Ali i.

— Understanding Supernatural Dreams According to the Bible. Irish, Eddie Joe, ed. 286p. 1994. reprint ed. pap. 11.95 (*0-9637001-0-3*) D A Castro.

— Understanding Supernatural Visions According to the Bible. Irish, Eddie Joe, ed. 122p. (Orig.). 1994. pap. 14.95 (*0-9637001-3-8*) D A Castro.

Castro De Davila, Maria D. Arquitectura en San Juan de Puerto Rico (Siglo XIX) LC 78-21582. (Illus.). 424p. 1980. 15.00 (*0-8477-2110-8*) U of PR Pr.

Castro, Diane R. De, see Harvey, Ruth B.

Castro, Diane R. De, see Harvey, Ruth B. & De Castro, Diane R.

Castro, Dom J. De, see De Castro, Dom J.

Castro, Donald S. The Argentine Tango as Social History, 1880-1955: The Soul of the People. LC 90-20558. (Latin American Studies: Vol. 3). 284p. 1990. lib. bdg. 89.95 (*0-7734-9923-7*) E Mellen.

— The Development & Politics of Argentine Immigration Policy, 1852-1914: To Govern Is to Populate. LC 91-30100. 324p. 1991. lib. bdg. 99.95 (*0-7734-9980-6*) E Mellen.

Castro, E. A., jt. auth. see Fernandez, F. M.

Castro, E. G. Spanish-English - English-Spanish Dictionary of Economic, Business & Legal Terminology. (ENG & SPA.). 1734p. 1990. 275.00 (*84-87532-00-4*) IBD Ltd.

Castro, Eduardo A., jt. auth. see Fernandez, Francisco M.

Castro, Elizabeth. HTML 4 for the World Wide Web: Visual QuickStart Guide. 3rd ed. Davis, Nancy, ed. LC 98-216979. 336p. (C). 1998. pap. text 17.95 (*0-201-69696-7*, Pub. by Peachpit Pr) Addison-Wesley.

***Castro, Elizabeth.** HTML 4 for the World Wide Web: Visual QuickStart Guide. 4th ed. (Visual QuickStart Guide Ser.). 384p. 1999. pap. 19.99 (*0-201-35493-4*) Peachpit Pr.

Castro, Elizabeth. Netscape Communicator 4 for Macintosh: Visual QuickStart Guide. LC 98-123575. 360p. (C). 1997. pap. text 17.95 (*0-201-68886-7*, Pub. by Peachpit Pr) Addison-Wesley.

— Netscape Communicator 4 for Windows: Visual QuicksSart Guide. LC 98-104769. 368p. (C). 1997. pap. text 17.95 (*0-201-68864-6*) Peachpit Pr.

— Netscape 3 for Windows: Visual Quickstart Guide. LC 96-229975. 288p. (C). 1996. pap. text 16.95 (*0-201-69409-3*) Peachpit Pr.

— Netscape 2 for Windows: Visual QuickStart Guide. LC 96-167903. (Illus.). 256p. (C). 1996. pap. text 16.95 (*0-201-88615-4*) Peachpit Pr.

***Castro, Elizabeth.** Perl & CGI for the World Wide Web: Visual QuickStart Guide. LC 99-190538. (Visual QuickStart Guide Ser.). (Illus.). 272p. (C). 1998. pap. 18.99 (*0-201-35358-X*, Pub. by Peachpit Pr) Addison-Wesley.

Castro, Ellen. Spirited Leadership: 52 Ways to Build Trust on the Job. (Illus.). 136p. 1998. pap. 10.95 (*0-88347-363-1*) T More.

Castro, Emilio. Freedom in Mission: The Perspective of the Kingdom of God: An Ecumenical Inquiry. LC 85-206199. (Oikoumene Ser.). 356p. 1985. reprint ed. pap. 110.40 (*0-608-00211-9*, 206099400006) Bks Demand.

Castro, Emilio G. Diccionario Terminologico de Economia, Comercio y Derecho, 2 vols., Set. 1768p. 1990. 595.00 (*0-7859-6423-1*, 8487532020) Fr & Eur.

— Diccionario Terminologico de Economia, Comercio y Derecho, Vol. 1. (SPA.). 1768p. 1990. 395.00 (*0-7859-6421-5*, 8487532004) Fr & Eur.

— Diccionario Terminologico de Economia, Comercio y Derecho, Vol. 2. (SPA.). 900p. 1990. 300.00 (*0-7859-6422-3*) Fr & Eur.

Castro, Emilio g. Muniz. Routledge Spanish Dictionary of Telecommunications/Diccionario Ingles de Telecomunicaciones: Spanishenglish/Englishspanish. LC 98-232709. (Routledge Bilingual Specialist Dictionaries Ser.). (ENG & SPA.). xx, 547p. (C). 1998. 140.00 (*0-415-15266-6*) Routledge.

Castro, Fernando. Five Rolls of Plus-X: An Urban Photography Vision of Peru.Tr. of Cinco rollos de plus-X. (ENG & SPA.). 1983. 8.00 (*0-934840-08-3*) Studia Hispanica.

Castro, Fernando, et al. Image & Memory: Photography from Latin America, 1866-1994. Watriss, Wendy & Zamora, Lois, eds. LC 94-35532. (ENG & SPA., Illus.). 468p. 1998. 65.00 (*0-292-79118-6*) U of Tex Pr.

Castro, Fidel. Cancelar la Deuda De America Latina! (SPA.). 43p. 1987. pap. 3.50 (*0-87348-494-0*) Pathfinder NY.

— Che: En la Memoria de Fidel Castro. Deutschmann, David, ed. (SPA., Illus.). 174p. 1998. pap. 13.95 (*1-875284-83-4*, Pub. by Ocean Pr NJ) LPC InBook.

— Cuba at the Crossroads. La Riva, Gloria, tr. from SPA. 179p. (Orig.). 1996. pap. 15.95 (*1-875284-94-X*) Ocean Pr NJ.

— Cuba Will Never Adopt Capitalist Methods. 30p. 1988. reprint ed. pap. 3.00 (*0-87348-538-6*) Pathfinder NY.

— Fidel: My Early Years. Tabio, Pedro A. & Shnookal, Deborah, eds. (Illus.). 148p. 1998. pap. 14.95 (*1-876175-07-9*) Ocean Pr NJ.

— Fidel by Fidel: An Interview with Dr. Fidel Castro Ruz, President of the Republic of Cuba. LC 85-25551. (Great Issues of the Day Ser.: No. 3). 120p. 1996. pap. 17.00 (*0-89370-430-X*) Millefleurs.

— Fidel Castro at the UN: "We Represent the Immense Majority of Humanity" 46p. 1979. reprint ed. 3.50 (*0-87348-427-4*) Pathfinder NY.

— Fidel Castro on Chile. 158p. 1982. pap. 12.00 (*0-87348-678-1*) Pathfinder NY.

— Fidel Castro Speeches: Building Socialism in Cuba, Vol. 2. Taber, Michael, ed. LC 81-80717. 367p. (C). 1983. pap. 20.95 (*0-87348-650-1*); lib. bdg. 50.00 (*0-87348-624-2*) Pathfinder NY.

— Fidel Castro Speeches Vol. 1: Cuba's Internationalist Foreign Policy 1975-80. LC 81-80717. 391p. 1981. reprint ed. pap. 20.95 (*0-87348-609-9*); reprint ed. lib. bdg. 55.00 (*0-87348-610-2*) Pathfinder NY.

— Fidel Castro Speeches, 1984-1985: War & Crisis in the Americas. Taber, Michael, ed. LC 85-61641. (Fidel Castro Speeches Ser.: Vol. 3). 239p. (Orig.). 1985. pap. 17.95 (*0-87348-657-9*); lib. bdg. 50.00 (*0-87348-656-0*) Pathfinder NY.

— El Guerrerismo de EUA y la Crisis Economica Mundial: Fidel Castro Se Dirige a los Sindicalistas. 32p. 1983. pap. 3.00 (*0-87348-480-0*) Pathfinder NY.

— In Defense of Socialism: Four Speeches on the 30th Anniversary of the Cuban Revolution. LC 89-61061. (Illus.). 142p. (Orig.). (C). 1989. pap. 13.95 (*0-87348-539-4*); lib. bdg. 40.00 (*0-87348-542-4*) Pathfinder NY.

— Selected Speeches of Fidel Castro. 2nd ed. (Illus.). 134p. 1992. pap. 14.00 (*0-87348-700-1*) Pathfinder NY.

— Tomorrow Is Too Late: Development & the Environmental Crisis in the Third World. 54p. 1993. pap. 6.95 (*1-875284-73-7*) Ocean Pr NJ.

— The U. S. War Drive & the World Economic Crisis. 31p. 1982. pap. 2.50 (*0-87348-447-9*) Pathfinder NY.

— Verdum Eins Og Che. (ICE., Illus.). 30p. pap. 3.00 (*0-87348-498-3*) Pathfinder NY.

— Why Socialism Works in Cuba. 26p. 1988. pap. 0.50 (*0-89567-092-5*) World View Forum.

Castro, Fidel & Alarcon, Ricardo. E. E. U. U. Fuera del Oriente Medio! Cuba Habla en Naciones Unidas. LC 90-63781. (SPA., Illus.). 135p. (Orig.). (C). 1990. pap. 10.95 (*0-87348-625-0*) Pathfinder NY.

— U. S. Hands off the Mideast! Cuba Speaks Out at the United Nations. 2nd ed. LC 90-63931. (Illus.). 126p. (Orig.). (C). 1990. pap. 10.95 (*0-87348-629-3*); lib. bdg. 35.00 (*0-87348-630-7*) Pathfinder NY.

Castro, Fidel & Borge, Tomas. Face to Face with Fidel Castro: A Conversation with Tomas Borge. (Illus.). 183p. 1994. pap. 13.95 (*1-875284-72-9*) Ocean Pr NJ.

Castro, Fidel & Guevara, Ernesto. To Speak the Truth: Why Washington's 'Cold War' against Cuba Doesn't End. LC 91-75347. (Illus.). 232p. (C). 1992. pap. 16.95 (*0-87348-633-1*); lib. bdg. 50.00 (*0-87348-634-X*) Pathfinder NY.

Castro, Fidel, et al. Fidel Castro: Nothing Can Stop the Course of History. LC 86-61524. 258p. 1986. reprint ed. pap. 18.95 (*0-87348-661-7*); reprint ed. lib. bdg. 50.00 (*0-87348-660-9*) Pathfinder NY.

Castro, Fidel, jt. auth. see Bishop, Maurice.

Castro, Fidel, jt. auth. see Che Guevara, Ernesto.

Castro, Fidel, jt. auth. see Guevara, Ernesto.

Castro, Fidel, jt. auth. see Harnecker, Marta.

Castro, Fidel, jt. auth. see Mandela, Nelson.

Castro, Fidel O. Mammary Gland Transgenesis: Therapeutic Protein Production. LC 97-44557. (Biotechnology Intelligence Unit (SV) Ser.). 192p. 1997. 129.00 (*1-57059-518-6*) Landes Bioscience.

Castro, Fidel O., ed. Mammary Gland Transgenesis: Therapeutic Protein Production. LC 97-44557. (Biotechnology Intelligence Unit (SV) Ser.). 192p. 1998. 129.00 (*3-540-63712-5*) Spr-Verlag.

Castro, Fred. A Quick Easy to Learn . . . Geography: Europe. Kohlenberg, Leah & Roach, Paul, eds. LC 92-71431. (Illus.). (Orig.). 1992. pap. text 9.95 (*1-881314-03-0*) Creat Tour Mgmt Dev.

— A Quick Easy Way to Learn . . . Geography: Africa. Kohlenberg, Leah & Roach, Paul, eds. LC 92-71431. (Illus.). (Orig.). 1992. pap. text 9.95 (*1-881314-05-7*) Creat Tour Mgmt Dev.

— A Quick Easy Way to Learn . . . Geography: Central & South America. Kohlenberg, Leah & Roach, Paul, eds. LC 92-71431. (Illus.). (Orig.). 1992. pap. text 9.95 (*1-881314-02-2*) Creat Tour Mgmt Dev.

— A Quick Easy Way to Learn . . . Geography: North America & Canada. Kohlenberg, Leah & Roach, Paul, eds. LC 92-71431. (Illus.). (Orig.). 1992. pap. text 9.95 (*1-881314-01-4*) Creat Tour Mgmt Dev.

— A Quick Easy Way to Learn . . . Geography: The Caribbean. Kohlenberg, Leah & Roach, Paul, eds. LC 92-71431. (Illus.). (Orig.). 1992. pap. text 9.95 (*1-881314-06-5*) Creat Tour Mgmt Dev.

— A Quick Easy Way to Learn . . . Geography: The Middle East. Kohlenberg, Leah & Roach, Paul, eds. LC 92-71431. (Illus.). (Orig.). 1992. pap. text 9.95 (*1-881314-07-3*) Creat Tour Mgmt Dev.

— A Quick Easy Way to Learn . . . World Geography. Kohlenberg, Leah & Roach, Paul, eds. LC 92-71431. (Illus.). 310p. (Orig.). 1992. pap. text 24.95 (*1-881314-00-6*) Creat Tour Mgmt Dev.

— A Quick Easy Way to Learn Geography... The World: Asia & the Pacific. 2nd rev. ed. Roach, Paul & Kohlenberg, Leah, eds. LC 92-71431. (Illus.). 264p. (Orig.). 1992. pap. text 24.95 (*1-881314-04-9*) Creat Tour Mgmt Dev.

Castro, G. R. & Cardona, M., eds. Lectures on Surface Science. (Illus.). 240p. 1987. 73.95 (*0-387-17318-8*) Spr-Verlag.

Castro, Ginette. American Feminism: A Contemporary History. 300p. (C). 1990. pap. text 19.00 (*0-8147-1448-X*) NYU Pr.

Castro, Guillen De, see De Castro, Guillen.

Castro, Hugo A., tr. see Castillo, Enrique C.

Castro, I. P. An Introduction to the Digital Analysis of Stationary Signals. (Illus.). 146p. 1989. pap. text 39.00 (*0-85274-254-1*) IOP Pub.

Castro, I. P. & Rockliffe, N. J., eds. Stably Stratified Flows: Flows & Dispersion over Topography. (Illus.). 376p. 1994. text 95.00 (*0-19-853698-4*) OUP.

Castro, Ida L., ed. What Works! The Working Women Count Honor Roll Report. 164p. (C). 1998. pap. text 30.00 (*0-7881-7184-4*) DIANE Pub.

— The Working Women Count Honor Roll Report: A Selection of Programs & Policies That Make Work Better. 163p. (C). 1998. pap. text 25.00 (*0-7881-7101-1*) DIANE Pub.

Castro, Isabel C. & Phillips, Antonia. A Guide to the Birds of the Galapagos Islands. LC 96-3194. 144p. 1997. text 24.95 (*0-691-01225-3*, Pub. by Princeton U Pr) Cal Prin Full Svc.

Castro, J. De, see De Castro, J.

Castro, J. Ridley. Mary's Plan: The Madonna Comes to Santa Maria. LC 93-83223. 180p. 1993. pap. 2.00 (*1-882972-08-2*, 3011) Queenship Pub.

Castro, Jaime C., jt. auth. see McQuade, Margaret C.

Castro, Jan G. Art & Life of G. O'Keefe. 1995. pap. 27.50 (*0-517-88387-2*) Random.

Castro, Jan G., jt. ed. see Van Spanckeren, Kathryn.

Castro, Jan W. Restaurant Rose - The Menu Guide to Greater Pasadena. 8th rev. ed. 88p. (Orig.). 1996. pap. 7.95 (*0-9624023-0-3*) J C West Prodns.

— Restaurant Rose Six: The Menu Guide to Greater Pasadena. 1992. pap. 8.95 (*0-9624023-4-6*) J C West Prodns.

— Sweets 'n Eats: The Goodie Guide to Greater Pasadena. 1992. pap. 6.95 (*0-9624023-2-X*) J C West Prodns.

Castro, Jorge Q., jt. auth. see Brehm, Monica R.

Castro, Jose Rodriguez De, see Rodriguez De Castro, Jose.

Castro, Josue De, see De Castro, Josue.

Castro, Juan M., tr. see Ferguson, V. S.

Castro, Juan M., tr. see Pope, Judi, ed.

Castro, Juan M., tr. see Ramtha.

Castro, Juan M., tr. see Weinberg, Steven L., ed.

Castro, Juan M., tr. see Whitworth, Eugene E.

Castro, Juan M., tr. see Zion, Judi P., ed.

Castro, Karen G., tr. see Ferreiro, Emilia & Teberosky, Ana.

Castro, Kathleen M. & DeAlteris, Joseph. The Atlantic Coast Fishing Vessel Safety Manual. (Illus.). 320p. (Orig.). (C). 1991. pap. text 25.00 (*1-882027-03-5*) URI ICMRD.

Castro, Kathleen M., ed. see DeAlteris, Joseph T.

Castro-Klaren, Sara. Understanding Mario Vargas Llosa. Hardin, James, ed. LC 89-70449. (Understanding Modern European & Latin American Literature Ser.). 258p. 1992. pap. 12.95 (*0-87249-848-4*) U of SC Pr.

Castro-Leal, Florencia. Who Benefits from Public Education Spending in Malawi? Results from the Recent Education Reform. LC 96-48247. (World Bank Discussion Papers: No. 350). 60p. 1996. pap. 22.00 (*0-8213-3837-4*, 13837) World Bank.

Castro, Lee, ed. see Hamlin, V. T.

***Castro, Leonard E., et al.** Selecting & Forming Business Entities: May 2000 Update. Peyerwold, David, ed. LC 96-85264. (California Business Start-Up-Series). 476p. 2000. 60.00 (*0-7626-0433-6*, BU-32574) Cont Ed Bar-CA.

— Selecting & Forming Business Entities - 6/98 Update. Briggs, Donald R., ed. LC 96-85264. (California Business Start-Up Ser.). 334p. 1998. ring bd. 50.00 (*0-7626-0244-9*, BU-32572) Cont Ed Bar-CA.

Castro, Leonard E., jt. auth. see Briggs, Donald R.

Castro, M. D. Luque De, see Valcarcel, M. & Luque de Castro, M. D.

Castro, Margarida, jt. auth. see Erzini, Karim.

Castro, Maria de los A., et al. Los Primeros Pasos: Una Bibliografia Para Empezar A Investigar la Historia De Puerto Rico. rev. ed. (SPA.). 204p. (C). 1994. pap. text 8.50 (*0-929157-29-X*) Ediciones Huracan.

Castro, Maria-Rosario. La Vision de Espana de Julian Marias. LC 90-34651. (American University Studies: Romance Languages & Literature: Ser. II, Vol. 152). X, 161p. (C). 1991. text 33.95 (*0-8204-1364-X*) P Lang Pubng.

Castro-Marin, A., et al. Esperan do a su Bebe' Vol. 1: Guia Completa del Embarazo y Alumbramiento. LC RG551.C3801993. (Salud y Comportamiento Ser.). (SPA., Illus.). 112p. 1993. pap. 10.00 (*0-9637512-0-4*) Quinto Centenario.

Castro, Mary G., jt. ed. see Chaney, Elsa M.

Castro, Max J., ed. Free Markets, Open Societies, Closed Borders? Trends in International Migration Policy in the Americas. LC 99-14109. 304p. 1999. pap. 27.95 (*1-57454-053-X*, Pub. by U Miami N-S Ctr) L Rienner.

Castro, Mercedes. Noche Callada (Poemas) (SPA., Illus.). 79p. (Orig.). pap. 3.75 (*0-9604748-0-3*) Castro.

Castro, Michael. Ghost Hiways & Other Homes. 1976. 2.50 (*0-918476-03-8*) Cornerstone Pr.

— Interpreting the Indian: Twentieth-Century Poets & the Native American. LC 90-50684. 242p. 1991. reprint ed. pap. 15.95 (*0-8061-2351-6*) U of Okla Pr.

Castro, Miranda. The Complete Homeopathy Handbook: A Guide to Everyday Health Care. (Illus.). 258p. (Orig.). 1990. pap. 37.50 (*0-333-55581-3*, Pub. by Pan) Trans-Atl Phila.

— The Complete Homeopathy Handbook: Safe & Effective Ways to Treat Fevers, Coughs, Colds & Sore Throats, Childhood Ailments, Food Poisoning, Flu, & a Wide Range of Everyday Complaints. (Illus.). 272p. (Orig.). 1991. pap. 15.95 (*0-312-06320-2*) St Martin.

***Castro, Miranda.** Homeopathic Guide to Stress: Safe & Effective Natural Ways to Alleviate. 399p. 1999. reprint ed. pap. text 19.00 (*0-7881-6798-7*) DIANE Pub.

Castro, Miranda. Homeopathic Remedies for Stress. LC 96-37350. 1997. pap. 18.95 (*0-312-15140-3*) St Martin.

— Homeopathy for Pregnancy, Birth, & Your Baby's First Year. LC 92-28880. 1993. pap. 16.95 (*0-312-08809-4*) St Martin.

Castro, Norma G. & Soberon, Cecilia A. Lo Mejor de la Literatura Para Ninos (The Best of Literature for Children) (Illus.). 312p. (J). 1998. pap. 16.95 (*970-03-0823-5*) Hispanic Bk Dist.

Castro, Oscar. Teachers Manual Three. 2nd ed. 1992. pap. text 14.95 (*0-8013-1028-8*) Longman.

Castro, Oscar & Kimbrough, Victoria F. In Touch: Color Editions, 3 vols. (Beginning American English Ser.). 1992. pap. text 12.95 (*0-685-59056-9*) Longman.

— In Touch: English As a Second Language. Incl. T/M IN TOUCH LEVEL 1. 1980. pap. text 18.95 (*0-582-79743-8*, 74997); T/M 2 IN TOUCH LEVEL 2. 1980. pap. text 18.50 (*0-582-79747-0*, 75001); T/M 3 IN TOUCH LEVEL 3. 1980. pap. text 18.95 (*0-582-79753-5*, 75007); WRKBK LEV1 IN TOUCH. 1980. pap. text 8.95 (*0-582-79744-6*, 74998); WRKBK LEV2 IN TOUCH. 1980. pap. text 8.95 (*0-582-79748-9*, 75002); Bk. 2. In Touch Student. 1980. pap. text 13.95 (*0-582-79746-2*, 75000); 1980. 13.95 (*0-582-79750-0*, 75004); (Beginning American English Ser.). (Illus.). 1980. pap. text. write for info. (*0-318-54107-6*) Longman.

— In Touch: Revised, 3 vols., Bk. 1. (Beginning American English Ser.). 1992. pap. text, student ed. 19.13 (*0-8013-0918-2*, 79179) Longman.

— In Touch: Revised, 3 vols., Bk. 2. (Beginning American English Ser.). 128p. 1992. pap. text, student ed. 19.13 (*0-8013-0919-0*, 79180) Longman.

— In Touch: Revised, 3 vols., Bk. 3. (Beginning American English Ser.). 1992. pap. text, student ed. 19.13 (*0-8013-0920-4*, 79181) Longman.

— Workbook Three Updated, 3 vols., Bk. 3. 2nd ed. (Beginning American English Ser.). 1992. pap. text, student ed. 12.26 (*0-8013-1031-8*, 79336) Longman.

— Workbook 1 Updated, 3 vols. 2nd ed. (Beginning American English Ser.). 1992. pap. text, student ed. 12.26 (*0-8013-1029-6*, 79334) Longman.

— Workbook 2 Updated, 3 vols., Bk. 2. 2nd ed. (Beginning American English Ser.). 1992. pap. text, student ed. 12.26 (*0-8013-1030-X*, 79335) Longman.

***Castro-Paniagua, Francisco.** English-Spanish Translation, Through a Cross-Cultural Interpretation Approach. 176p. 2000. 49.00 (*0-7618-1711-5*); pap. 27.50 (*0-7618-1712-3*) U Pr of Amer.

Castro, Percio B. De, see De Castro, Percio B.

Castro, Peter & Huber, Michael. Marine Biology. 2nd ed. LC 95-78746. 480p. (C). 1996. text. write for info. (*0-697-24360-5*, WCB McGr Hill) McGrw-H Hghr Educ.

Castro, Peter & Huber, Michael E. Marine Biology. 3rd ed. LC 98-53832. 464p. 1999. 62.50 (*0-07-012197-4*) McGraw.

Castro, Peter & Huber, Miichael. Marine Biology 2nd ed. 480p. (C). 1996. write for info. (*0-697-31312-3*, WCB McGr Hill) McGrw-H Hghr Educ.

Castro, Rafael Fernandez de, see Pastor, Robert A. & Fernandez de Castro, Rafael, eds.

Castro, Rafael L., jt. ed. see De Rojo, Alba C.

***Castro, Ramon.** Uncle Moncho's Treasure Chest. LC 99-66802. (Illus.). 100p. (J). (gr. 2-6). 1999. pap. 7.99 (*1-893181-31-6*) Le Gesse Stevens.

Castro, Raoul. Corporate Aviation Management. LC 94-7933. (Southern Illinois Universtiy Press Series in Aviation Management). (Illus.). 344p. (C). 1995. 34.95 (*0-8093-1911-X*) S Ill U Pr.

Castro, Rene & De Cadenet, J.J. Welding Metallurgy of Stainless & Heat-Resisting Steels. LC 74-76582. 200p. reprint ed. pap. 57.00 (*0-608-18614-7*, 2024434) Bks Demand.

Castro, Rick, et al. Castro. (Illus.). 120p. (Orig.). 1991. 45.00 (*1-879055-26-0*, DPR Pr); pap. 25.00 (*1-879055-27-9*, DPR Pr) Tom Finland.

Castro, Rosalia de. Poems. Gantt, Barbara N., ed. & tr. by. from GAE. Aldaz, Anna-Marie et al, trs. from GAE. LC 90-9895. (SUNY Series, Women Writers in Translation). 216p. (C). 1991. pap. text 19.95 (*0-7914-0583-4*) State U NY Pr.

***Castro, Ruy.** Bossa Nova: The Story of the Brazilian Music That Seduced the World. (Illus.). 352p. 2000. 26.00 (*1-55652-409-9*, Pub. by A Cappella Bks) IPG Chicago.

***Castro, Sallie.** Self-Disclosure. 1999. pap. write for info. (*1-58235-265-8*) Watermrk Pr.

***Castro-Urioste, Jose.** Dramaturgia Peruana. Latinoamericana Editores, ed. (SPA., Illus.). 438p. (Orig.). 1999. pap. text 20.00 (*0-9640795-7-7*, Pub. by Latinoam Edit) Intl Assn Peruvianists.

Castro, Vanessa & Prevost, Gary, eds. The Nineteen Ninety Elections in Nicaragua & Their Aftermath. 1992. pap. 24.50 (*0-8476-7766-4*) Rowman.

— The Nineteen Ninety Elections in Nicaragua & Their Aftermath. 240p. (C). 1992. text 60.00 (*0-8476-7761-3*) Rowman.

Castro, W. M. & Jerosch, J. Examination & Diagnosis of Muskuloskeletal Disorders: History - Physical Examination - Imaging Techniques. (Illus.). 400p. 2000. 119.00 (*0-86577-741-1*) Thieme Med Pubs.

Castro, Walter E., ed. see Benjamin, Laura L.

Castro, Wendy. Welfare Reform & Abstinence Education: An Issue Brief. LC 99-165725. 1998. pap. 8.95 (*0-87868-713-0*, 7130, CWLA Pr) Child Welfare.

***Castrone, Linda & Lipsher, Steve.** The Insiders' Guide to Colorado's Mountains. 2nd ed. (Insiders' Guide Travel Ser.). (Illus.). 392p. 1999. pap. 15.95 (*1-57380-135-6*, The Insiders Guide) Falcon Pub Inc.

Castronovo. Edmund Wilson. LC 97-31613. 1998. 32.00 (*0-8057-1642-4*) Mac Lib Ref.

Castronovo, David. Richard Yates. large type ed. LC 96-38515. 1996. 32.00 (*0-8057-4031-7*, Twyne) Mac Lib Ref.

Castronovo, David, ed. see Wilson, Edmund.

Castronovo, Joseph P., ed. Pipeline Crossings. LC 91-7788. 1991p. 1991. pap. text 7.00 (*0-87262-800-0*) Am Soc Civil Eng.

Castronovo, Joseph P., et al. Pipelines in the Constructed Environment. LC 98-35557. 824p. 1998. 89.00 (*0-7844-0372-4*) Am Soc Civil Eng.

Castronovo, Michelle. My Daddy Likes to Be with Me. LC 95-92266. (Kids Comfort Inc. Ser.: No. 2). (Illus.). 16p. (Orig.). (J). 1995. pap. 9.95 (*1-887453-17-2*) Kids Comfort.

— My Daddy's Going Working. LC 95-92265. (Kids Comfort Inc. Ser.: No. 1). (Illus.). 16p. (Orig.). (J). 1995. pap. 9.95 (*1-887453-09-1*) Kids Comfort.

— My Mommy Likes to Be with Me. LC 95-92267. (Kids Comfort Inc. Ser.: No. 3). (Illus.). 16p. (Orig.). (J). 1995. pap. 9.95 (*1-887453-08-3*) Kids Comfort.

— My Mommy's Going Working. LC 95-92268. (Kids Comfort Inc. Ser.: No. 4). 16p. (Orig.). (J). 1995. pap. 9.95 (*1-887453-02-4*) Kids Comfort.

Castronovo, Russ. Fathering the Nation: American Genealogies of Slavery & Freedom. LC 94-42959. (Illus.). 287p. 1996. 38.00 (*0-520-08901-4*, Pub. by U CA Pr) Cal Prin Full Svc.

Castronuovo, David, tr. see Bianchini, Angela.

Castroviejo, Concha. Los Dias de Lina. 2nd ed. (Punto Juvenil Ser.). (SPA.). (J). 1971. 10.05 (*0-606-05445-6*, Pub. by Turtleback) Demco.

Castroviejo, Ignacio P. Spinal Tumors in Children & Adolescents. LC 89-10646. (International Review of Child Neurology Ser.). 314p. 1990. reprint ed. pap. 97.40 (*0-608-03437-1*, 206413800008) Bks Demand.

Castuera, Ignacio, ed. Dreams on Fire - Embers of Hope: From the Pulpits of Los Angeles after the Riots. 128p. (Orig.). 1992. pap. 10.99 (*0-8272-0620-8*) Chalice Pr.

Casty, Alan H. Act of Writing & Reading: A Combined Text. 1966. pap. text 24.85 (*0-13-003780-X*) P-H.

***Casullo, Albert, ed.** A Priori Knowledge. LC 98-45963. (International Research Library of Philosophy). 560p. 1999. text 194.95 (*1-85521-983-2*, Pub. by Ashgate Pub) Ashgate Pub Co.

Casurella, Anthony. Bibliography of Literature on First Peter. LC 95-53248. (New Testament Tools & Studies: Vol. 23). xviii, 170p. 1996. 64.50 (*90-04-10488-7*) Brill Academic Pubs.

— The Johannine Paraclete in the Church Fathers. 272p. 1983. lib. bdg. 57.50 (*3-16-144648-8*, Pub. by JCB Mohr) Coronet Bks.

Caswall, Henry. America, & the American Church. LC 77-83413. (Religion in America, Ser.). 1980. reprint ed. 23.95 (*0-405-00234-3*) Ayer.

Caswell, Austin, ed. see Rossini, Gioachino, et al.

Caswell, Austin B., ed. Bacilly: A Commentary Upon the Art of Proper Singing. (Musical Theorists in Translation Ser.: Vol. 7). 1968. lib. bdg. 67.00 (*0-912024-27-5*) Inst Mediaeval Mus.

Caswell, Brian. Deucalion. (YA). 1995. 12.95 (*0-7022-2865-6*, Pub. by Univ Queensland Pr) Intl Spec Bk.

— Dreamslip. LC 95-111948. (J). 1994. pap. 12.95 (*0-7022-2641-6*, Pub. by Univ Queensland Pr) Intl Spec Bk.

C

— Gargantua. LC 98-229280. (Alien Zone Ser.: Bk. 4). (J). 1998. 8.95 (*0-7022-3025-1*, Pub. by Univ Queensland Pr) Intl Spec Bk.

— Gladiators in the Holo-Colosseum. LC 98-229257. (Alien Zone Ser.: Bk. 3). (J). 1998. 8.95 (*0-7022-3024-3*, Pub. by Univ Queensland Pr) Intl Spec Bk.

— Maddie. (Storybridge Ser.). (J). 1995. pap. 9.95 (*0-7022-2735-8*, Pub. by Univ Queensland Pr) Intl Spec Bk.

— Messenges of the Great Orff. LC 98-229292. (Alien Zone Ser.: Bk. 2). (J). 1998. 8.95 (*0-7022-2989-X*, Pub. by Univ Queensland Pr) Intl Spec Bk.

— Relax Max! LC 97-192236. (Storybridge Ser.). 86p. (J). 1997. pap. 10.95 (*0-7022-2897-4*, Pub. by Univ Queensland Pr) Intl Spec Bk.

— Tee Dee & the Collectors. LC 98-229299. (Alien Zone Ser.: Bk. 1). (J). 1998. 8.95 (*0-7022-2988-1*, Pub. by Univ Queensland Pr) Intl Spec Bk.

***Caswell, Brian.** The View from Ararat. (J). 1999. pap. 14.95 (*0-7022-3067-7*, Pub. by Univ Queensland Pr) Intl Spec Bk.

Caswell, Brian. What Were the Gremholz's Dimensions Again? LC 99-217321. (Alien Zones Ser.: No. 5). 1998. pap. 8.95 (*0-7022-3090-1*) Intl Spec Bk.

— Whispers from the Sibboleth. LC 99-232888. (Alien Zones Ser.: No.6). 1998. pap. 8.95 (*0-7022-3091-X*) Intl Spec Bk.

Caswell, Brian & Chiem, David P. Only the Heart. LC 98-210377. 198p. (YA). 1997. pap. 12.95 (*0-7022-2927-X*, Pub. by Univ Queensland Pr) Intl Spec Bk.

Caswell, C. Wayne & Clark, Arthur E., Jr., eds. Dental Implant Prosthodontics. LC 90-6332. (Illus.). 351p. 1991. reprint ed. pap. 108.90 (*0-608-07246-X*, 206747100009) Bks Demand.

Caswell, Caroline P. A Study of Thumos in Early Greek Epic. (Mnemosyne Ser.: Supplement 114). ix, 85p. 1990. pap. 36.50 (*90-04-09260-9*) Brill Academic Pubs.

Caswell, Christopher. Illustrated Book of Basic Boating. 1990. pap. 15.00 (*0-688-08931-3*, Wm Morrow) Morrow Avon.

Caswell, Deborah L., jt. auth. see Grady, Robert B.

C

Caswell, Donald. Three Legged Dog. 128p. 1999. 21.00 (*0-938078-59-3*); pap. 12.00 (*0-938078-58-5*) Anhinga Pr.

Caswell, Donald, ed. see Seeman, Julianne.

Caswell, Frances P. Growing Through Faith: A History of the United Methodist Church of Brunswick, Maine. (Illus.). x, 135p. (Orig.). 1997. pap. 30.00 (*0-9655456-0-1*) UMC of Brunswick.

Caswell, Hal. Evolutionary Demography: Matrix Models & Their Interpretation. 300p. 1985. write for info. (*0-318-57713-5*) Macmillan.

— Matrix Population Models. 2nd rev. ed. 328p. (Orig.). (C). 1999. text 49.95 (*0-87893-096-5*) Sinauer Assocs.

Caswell, Hal, jt. auth. see Tuljapurkar, Shripad.

Caswell, Helen. Daniel & His Friends. 6.00 (*0-687-08285-4*) Abingdon.

Caswell, Helen. Daniel & His Friends. LC 93-25305. 24p. (J). 1993. 11.95 (*0-687-10085-2*) Abingdon.

— God Is Always with Me. LC 89-41. 1989. pap. 5.95 (*0-687-14974-6*) Abingdon.

— God Makes Us Different. LC 87-33466. (J). (ps-3). 1988. pap. 5.95 (*0-687-15336-0*) Abingdon.

— God Makes Us Different. 1996. pap. text 5.95 (*0-687-06706-5*) Abingdon.

— God Must Like to Laugh. LC 87-1362. (Illus.). (J). (ps-3). 1987. pap. 5.95 (*0-687-15188-0*) Abingdon.

— God's Love Is for Sharing. LC 87-11580. (Illus.). (J). (gr. k-3). 1987. text 5.95 (*0-687-15335-2*) Abingdon.

— God's World Makes Me Feel So Little. LC 84-14545. (Illus.). 32p. (J). (gr. k-3). 1985. pap. 5.95 (*0-687-15510-X*) Abingdon.

— I Can Talk to God. 1996. pap. text 5.95 (*0-687-06714-6*) Abingdon.

— I Can Talk with God. LC 88-30629. 1989. pap. 5.95 (*0-687-18686-2*) Abingdon.

— I Know Who Jesus Is. rev. ed. 1995. pap. text 5.95 (*0-687-02079-4*) Abingdon.

— Know Who Jesus Is. LC 89-52. 1989. pap. 5.95 (*0-687-18229-8*) Abingdon.

— Loaves & Fishes. LC 93-25308. 24p. (J). 1993. 11.95 (*0-687-22526-4*) Abingdon.

— The Lord's Prayer. 24p. (J). 1995. pap. 5.95 (*0-687-01589-8*) Abingdon.

— My Big Family at Church. LC 88-30630. (J). 1989. pap. 5.95 (*0-687-27533-4*) Abingdon.

— Parable of the Bridesmaids. (Illus.). 24p. (J). (ps-3). 1992. 11.95 (*0-687-30022-3*) Abingdon.

— Parable of the Lost Coin. LC 92-33875. (Growing in Faith Library). (Illus.). 24p. (J). (gr. 1-3). 1993. pap. 5.95 (*0-687-30026-6*) Abingdon.

— Parable of the Lost Sheep. LC 92-33876. (Growing in Faith Library). (Illus.). 24p. (Orig.). 1993. pap. 5.95 (*0-687-30027-4*) Abingdon.

— Parable of the Sower. LC 90-23200. (J). (ps-3). 1991. 11.95 (*0-687-30020-7*) Abingdon.

— Parable of the Vineyard. LC 90-23228. (J). (ps-3). 1991. 11.95 (*0-687-30021-5*) Abingdon.

— Twenty-Third Psalm. 1995. pap. 5.95 (*0-687-01172-8*) Abingdon.

— Whom God Has Joined Together: Words to Stay Married By. LC 97-170469. (Illus.). 48p. 1997. 10.00 (*0-687-01009-8*) Dimen for Liv.

Caswell, Helen. The Lord's Prayer. LC 95-5369. 1995. 5.95 (*0-687-01173-6*) Abingdon.

Caswell, Helen R. Growing in Faith: Seven Stories for Children. (Illus.). 160p. (J). (ps-3). 1998. pap. 15.95 (*0-687-05616-0*) Abingdon.

— Parables of Jesus: The Mustard Seed & Other Stories. (Illus.). 96p. (J). (ps-3). 1998. pap. 10.95 (*0-687-05606-3*) Abingdon.

Caswell, Hollis L. City School Surveys: An Interpretation & Appraisal. LC 70-176632. (Columbia University. Teachers College. Contributions to Education Ser.: No. 358). reprint ed. 37.50 (*0-404-55358-3*) AMS Pr.

Caswell, J., jt. auth. see Sadovsky, M. C.

Caswell, Lucy S., compiled by. Guide to Sources in American Journalism History, 2. LC 89-11857. (Bibliographies & Indexes in Mass Media & Communications Ser.: No. 2). 326p. 1989. lib. bdg. 65.00 (*0-313-26178-4*, CGJ/, Greenwood Pr) Greenwood.

Caswell, Lucy S. & Loomis, George A., Jr. Billy Ireland. LC 81-119198. (Illus.). 235p. (Orig.). 1980. pap. 20.00 (*0-88215-051-0*) Friends Ohio St U Lib.

Caswell, M. F., et al. Agricultural Biotechnology: An Economic Perspective. 52p. (Orig.). (C). 1994. pap. text 35.00 (*0-7881-1282-1*) DIANE Pub.

Caswell, Maurice. Kakadu: And Other National Parks. 72p. (C). 1990. 90.00 (*0-86439-068-8*, Pub. by Boolarong Pubns) St Mut.

Caswell Publishing Staff. God Must Like to Laugh. 1987. pap. text 5.95 (*0-687-01869-2*) Abingdon.

Caswell, Robert. Scales of Justice. 176p. (C). 1993. pap. 17.95 (*0-86819-097-7*, Pub. by Currency Pr) Accents Pubns.

Caswell, Robert W. The Compass of the Heart. 1978. 20.00 (*0-913028-59-2*); pap. 12.00 (*0-913028-52-5*) North Atlantic.

Caswell, Sharon. New Perspectives on the Internet Using Netscape Navigator Software: Introductory. (New Perspectives Ser.). 300p. (C). 1997. pap. 31.95 (*0-7600-4078-6*) Course Tech.

— New Perspectives on the Internet Using Netscape Navigator Software - Introductory. 300p. 1997. teacher ed. write for info. (*0-7600-4080-X*) Course Tech.

Caswell, W. E. & Snow, G. A. Particles & Fields, APS-DPF, University of Maryland, 1982: AIP Conference Proceedings No. 98, Particles & Fields Subseries, 29th. LC 83-70807. 413p. 1983. lib. bdg. 37.75 (*0-88318-197-5*) Am Inst Physics.

Casy, A. F. The Steric Factor in Medicinal Chemistry: Dissymmetric Probes of Pharmacological Receptors. (Illus.). 590p. (C). 1994. text 135.00 (*0-306-44289-2*, Kluwer Plenum) Kluwer Academic.

Casy, A. F. & Parfitt, R. T. Opioid Analgesics: Chemistry & Receptors. LC 86-1520. (Illus.). 534p. (C). 1986. text 145.00 (*0-306-42130-5*, Kluwer Plenum) Kluwer Academic.

Casy, G., ed. see Roberts, Stanley M.

Cat, Christopher & Cullen, Countee. My Lives & How I Lost Them. LC 92-46738. (Illus.). 174p. (J). (gr. 3-5). 1993. pap. 7.95 (*0-8136-7209-0*) Silver Burdett Pr.

Cat Fanciers' Association Inc. Staff, ed. Cat Fanciers' Association Cat Encyclopedia: Authorative Illustrated Guide 40 Breeds. 220p. 1995. 30.00 (*0-684-80186-8*) S&S Trade.

***Cat, Ivan.** The Burning Heart of Night. 2000. 6.99 (*0-88677-789-5*, Pub. by DAW Bks) Penguin Putnam.

Cat, Ivan. Eyes of Light & Darkness. 240p. 1996. mass mkt. 5.99 (*0-88677-726-7*, Pub. by DAW Bks) Penguin Putnam.

Catach. L' Orthographe Francaise a l'Epoque de la Renaissance. (Publ. Romanes et Franc.). 87.40 (*0-685-36649-9*, F134160) Fr & Eur.

— L' Orthographe Francaise a l'Epoque de la Renaissance. (FRE.). 498p. 1968. pap. 150.00 (*0-7859-5219-5*) Fr & Eur.

Catach, N. Dictionnaire Historique de l'Orthographe Francaise. (FRE.). 1994. 135.00 (*0-7859-9805-5*) Fr & Eur.

Catacosinos, Paul A. & Daniels, P. A., Jr., eds. Early Sedimentary Evolution of the Michigan Basin. (Special Papers: No. 256). (Illus.). 270p. 1991. pap. 20.00 (*0-8137-2256-X*) Geol Soc.

Catacosinos, Paul A. & Daniels, Paul A., eds. Early Sedimentary Evolution of the Michigan Basin. LC 90-25692. (Geological Society of America, Special Paper: No. 156). (Illus.). 256p. Date not set. reprint ed. pap. 79.40 (*0-608-20646-6*, 207208200003) Bks Demand.

Catacosinos, Paul A., jt. ed. see Van der Plujim, Ben A.

Catagnus, Julia M., jt. auth. see Lee, Jarene Frances.

Catala, Francisco. Democracia Obrera: Autogestion o Privatizacion? 176p. 1996. pap. 12.95 (*0-929157-34-6*) Ediciones Huracan.

Catala, Rafael. Cienciapoesia. LC 83-62040. (Serie de Poesia Guampara: No. 1). (SPA.). 128p. (Orig.). 1984. pap. text 5.95 (*0-910235-04-X*) Prisma Bks.

— Copulantes. LC 83-62039. (Serie de Poesia Guampara: No. 2). (SPA.). 80p. (Orig.). 1984. pap. text 5.95 (*0-910235-03-1*) Prisma Bks.

— Mysticism of Now. LC 97-41081. 1998. pap. 13.95 (*1-889051-19-5*, Awakening) Acrpls Bks CO.

— Para una Lectura Americana del Barroco Mexicano: Sor Juana y Siguenza y Gongora. (SPA.). 200p. (Orig.). 1987. pap. text 8.95 (*0-910235-07-4*) Prisma Bks.

Catala, Rafael, et al, eds. Index of American Periodical Verse: 1988. LC 73-3060. 549p. 1990. 65.00 (*0-8108-2334-9*) Scarecrow.

— Index of American Periodical Verse, 1990. LC 73-3060. 670p. 1992. 72.00 (*0-8108-2587-2*) Scarecrow.

Catala, Rafael & Anderson, James D. American Periodical Verse Index: 1989. LC 73-3060. 606p. 1991. 72.00 (*0-8108-2456-6*) Scarecrow.

— Index of American Periodical Verse: 1981. LC 73-3060. 406p. 1983. 21.00 (*0-8108-1602-4*) Scarecrow.

— Index of American Periodical Verse: 1984. 14th ed. LC 73-3060. 808p. 1986. 21.00 (*0-8108-1918-X*) Scarecrow.

— Index of American Periodical Verse: 1985. LC 73-3060. 579p. 1987. 21.00 (*0-8108-2038-2*) Scarecrow.

— Index of American Periodical Verse: 1991. LC 73-3060. 631p. 1993. 72.00 (*0-8108-2724-7*) Scarecrow.

— Index of American Periodical Verse: 1992. 647p. 1994. 72.00 (*0-8108-2911-8*) Scarecrow.

***Catala, Rafael & Anderson, James D.** Index of American Periodical Verse: 1997. 696p. 1999. 75.00 (*0-8108-3721-8*) Scarecrow.

Catala, Rafael & Anderson, James D. Index of American Periodical Verse, 1995. 650p. 1997. 72.00 (*0-8108-3391-3*) Scarecrow.

— Index of American Periodical Verse, 1996. 680p. 1998. 75.00 (*0-8108-3545-2*) Scarecrow.

— Index of American Periodical Verse 1993. (Index of American Periodical Verse Ser.). 686p. 1995. 72.00 (*0-8108-3066-3*) Scarecrow.

— Index of American Periodical Verse 1994. 632p. 1996. 72.00 (*0-8108-3227-5*) Scarecrow.

— Index of American Periodical Versei: 1986. LC 73-3060. 540p. 1988. 21.00 (*0-8108-2149-4*) Scarecrow.

Catala, Rafael & Anderson, James D., eds. Index of American Periodical Verse: 1982. LC 73-3060. 669p. 1984. 21.00 (*0-8108-1731-4*) Scarecrow.

Catala, Rafael & Lugo, Roberto, eds. Soles Emellis. LC 83-61864. (SPA.). 160p. (Orig.). 1983. pap. text 6.95 (*0-910235-02-3*) Prisma Bks.

Catala, Rafael, et al. Index of American Periodical Verse: 1983. LC 73-3060. 711p. 1985. 21.00 (*0-8108-1832-9*) Scarecrow.

— Index of American Periodical Verse: 1987. LC 73-3060. 575p. 1989. 65.00 (*0-8108-2243-1*) Scarecrow.

Catala, Victor. Solitude. Rosenthal, David, tr. from CAT. 226p. (Orig.). 1992. 19.95 (*0-930523-91-1*); pap. 11.95 (*0-930523-92-X*) Readers Intl.

Catalan, J., et al, eds. Psychological Medicine of HIV Infection. (Illus.). 316p. 1996. text 85.00 (*0-19-262202-1*) OUP.

Catalan, Jose. Mental Health Problems & HIV Infection. (Social Aspects of AIDS Ser.). 256p. 1999. pap. 25.95 (*1-85728-171-3*, Pub. by UCL Pr Ltd) Taylor & Francis.

Catalan, Jose, ed. Mental Health Problems & HIV Infection. (Social Aspects of AIDS Ser.). 256p. 1999. 74.00 (*1-85728-170-5*, Pub. by UCL Pr Ltd) Taylor & Francis.

Catalan, Jose, et al, eds. The Impact of AIDS: Psychological & Social Aspects of HIV Infection. 272p. 1997. text 45.00 (*90-5702-040-8*, Harwood Acad Pubs); pap. text 18.00 (*90-5702-041-6*, Harwood Acad Pubs) Gordon & Breach.

Catalan Lafuente, Jose. Diccionario Tecnico del Agua: Technical Dictionary of Water. (SPA.). 301p. 1977. pap. 39.95 (*0-8288-5365-7*, S50098) Fr & Eur.

Catalanello, Ralph F., jt. auth. see Redding, John C.

Catalani, J. Christine & McAuliffe, Cathleen F. Let the Kids Do It! Using Rebus Task Cards. 176p. (J). (ps-3). 1996. 14.99 (*1-56417-858-7*, FE7858) Fearon Teacher Aids.

Catalani, M. S. & Clerico, G. F. Decision Making Structures: Dealing with Uncertainty within Organizations. (Contributions to Management Science Ser.). 167p. 1996. 59.00 (*3-7908-0895-4*) Spr-Verlag.

Catalani, Michael. Subfiles for RPG Programmers: A Comprehensive User Guide. (Illus.). 505p. (Orig.). 1994. pap. 99.00 (*1-883884-18-7*, 517) Midrange Comput.

Catalano. Getting Established in Las Vegas. 1996. pap. 7.95 (*1-881895-10-6*) Info & Assist Netwk.

***Catalano, Dominic.** Santa & the Three Bears. LC 99-69853. (Illus.). 32p. (J). (ps-3). 2000. 15.95 (*1-56397-864-4*) Boyds Mills Pr.

Catalano, Dominic. The Frog Went A-Courting. LC 97-77908. 32p. (J). (gr. k-3). 1998. 14.95 (*1-56397-637-4*) Boyds Mills Pr.

***Catalano, Ellen M.** Seals! (Know-It-Alls Ser.). (Illus.). 24p. (J). (ps). 2000. mass mkt. 2.79 (*0-7681-0212-X*, McClanahan Book) Learn Horizon.

Catalano, Ellen M. & Hardin, Kimeron N. The Chronic Pain Control Workbook: A Step-by-Step Guide for Coping with & Overcoming Pain. 2nd rev. ed. LC 96-67938. (Illus.). 252p. 1996. pap. 18.95 (*1-57224-050-4*) New Harbinger.

Catalano, Ellen M. & Sonenberg, Nina. Consuming Passions: Help for Compulsive Shoppers. LC 93-83369. 224p. (Orig.). 1993. pap. 11.95 (*1-879237-38-5*) New Harbinger.

Catalano, Gary. Fresh Linen. LC 87-30070. (Poetry Ser.). 68p. (Orig.). 1988. pap. text 14.95 (*0-7022-2114-7*, Pub. by Univ Queensland Pr) Intl Spec Bk.

***Catalano, Gary.** Jigsaw. 80p. 1999. pap. text 15.95 (*0-9586482-5-5*) Gordon & Breach.

Catalano, Gary. Selected Poems, 1973-1992. 158p. 1993. pap. 19.95 (*0-7022-2542-8*, Pub. by Univ Queensland Pr) Intl Spec Bk.

— The Years of Hope: Australian Art & Criticism, 1959-1968. (Illus.). 1981. 45.00 (*0-19-554220-7*) OUP.

Catalano, Grace. Bryan White. LC 98-41712. 144p. (YA). 1999. mass mkt. 4.99 (*0-440-22826-3*) BDD Bks Young Read.

— Freddie Prinze: Jr. He's All That. LC 99-222918. 144p. 1999. mass mkt. 4.99 (*0-440-22863-8*) Dell.

— LeAnn Rimes: Teen Country Queen. 128p. (YA). 1997. mass mkt. 4.99 (*0-440-22737-2*) Dell.

Catalano, Grace. Leonardo DiCaprio: Modern Day Romeo. LC 97-127572. 144p. (YA). 1997. mass mkt. 4.99 (*0-440-22701-1*) Dell.

Catalano, Grace, jt. auth. see Doubleday Publishing Staff.

***Catalano, John.** Francis Lieber: Hermeneutics & Practical Reason. 160p. 2000. 34.50 (*0-7618-1691-7*) U Pr of Amer.

Catalano, Joseph S. A Commentary of Jean-Paul Sartre's "Being & Nothingness" LC 79-21234. xvi, 256p. 1985. reprint ed. pap. text 22.00 (*0-226-09699-8*) U Ch Pr.

— A Commentary on Jean-Paul Sartre's Critique of Dialectical Reason: Theory of Practical Ensembles, Vol. 1. LC 86-11323. 352p. 1987. pap. text 19.50 (*0-226-09701-3*); lib. bdg. 40.00 (*0-226-09700-5*) U Ch Pr.

— Good Faith & Other Essays: Perspective on a Sartrean Ethics. 198p. (C). 1995. pap. text 24.95 (*0-8476-8088-6*); lib. bdg. 58.50 (*0-8476-8082-7*) Rowman.

***Catalano, Joseph S.** Thinking Matter: Consciousness from Aristotle to Putnam & Sartre. LC 99-49935. 240p. (C). 2000. text. write for info. (*0-415-92664-5*) Routledge.

— Thinking Matter: Consciousness from Aristotle to Putnam & Sartre. LC 99-49935. 224p. 2000. pap. write for info. (*0-415-92665-3*) Routledge.

Catalano, Joseph T. American Nursing Review for Critical Care Nursing Certification. 2nd ed. LC 97-46905. 320p. 1998. pap. text 32.95 (*0-87434-928-1*) Springhouse Corp.

***Catalano, Joseph T.** Davis's Pharmacology Review for the NCLEX-RN. LC 99-17377. (Illus.). 357p. 1999. pap. 27.95 (*0-8036-0404-1*, C3922) Davis Co.

— Nursing Now: Today's Issues, Tomorrow's Trends. 2nd ed. LC 99-40516. (Illus.). 536p. 1999. pap. text 31.95 (*0-8036-0496-3*) Davis Co.

Catalano, Julie. The Mexican Americans. LC 95-14181. (Immigrant Experience Ser.). 120p. (YA). (gr. 5 up). 1995. lib. bdg. 19.95 (*0-7910-3359-7*) Chelsea Hse.

— The Mexican Americans. LC 95-14181. (Immigrant Experience Ser.). 120p. (YA). (gr. 5 up). 1995. pap. 9.95 (*0-7910-3381-3*) Chelsea Hse.

***Catalano, Julie.** Women's Pharmacy: An Essential Guide to What Women Should Know about Prescription Drugs. 384p. 2000. mass mkt. 6.99 (*0-440-23537-5*) Dell.

Catalano, L. Optimum Inventory Levels. 34p. 1990. reprint ed. pap. 28.50 (*0-938648-24-1*) T-C Pr CA.

***Catalano, Mike.** Face of a Thousand Wisdoms. 1999. pap. 7.00 (*1-930714-01-7*) Good SAMAR.

***Catalano, Nick.** Clifford Brown: The Life & Art of the Legendary Jazz Trumpeter. LC 99-27887. (Illus.). 232p. 2000. 25.00 (*0-19-510083-2*) OUP.

Catalano, Pete, ed. see Heath, Maya.

Catalano, Robert A. Guide to ECG Analysis. 430p. 1993. pap. text 32.00 (*0-397-55015-4*) Lppncott W & W.

Catalano, Robert A., ed. When Autism Strikes: Families Cope with Childhood Disintegrative Disorder. LC 98-12011. (Illus.). 244p. (C). 1998. pap. 19.95 (*0-306-45789-X*, Plenum Trade) Perseus Pubng.

Catalano, Robert A. & Nelson, Leonard B. Pediatric Ophthalmology: A Text Atlas. (Illus.). 1099p. (C). 1994. 150.00 (*0-8385-7817-9*, A7817-8, Apple Lange Med) McGraw.

Catalano, Robert A., jt. auth. see Nelson.

Catalano, S. Children's Dreams in Clinical Practice. LC 89-28470. (Illus.). 240p. (C). 1990. 45.00 (*0-306-43308-7*, Plenum Trade) Perseus Pubng.

Catalano, S. & Stauffer, J. R., eds. Angular Momentum Evolution of Young Stars. (C). 1991. text 234.00 (*0-7923-1316-X*) Kluwer Academic.

Catalano, Tom. Poetry 'n Motion: Rhymes for All Times. 96p. (Orig.). 1996. pap. 9.95 (*1-882646-03-7*) Wordsmith Bks.

— Rhyme & Reason: A Collection of Poems. 96p. (Orig.). 1993. pap. 9.95 (*1-882646-07-X*) Wordsmith Bks.

***Catalano, Tom.** Rhymes for Kids! Poems Children Can Enjoy. 48p. (J). (gr. k-6). 2000. pap. 6.95 (*1-882646-05-3*) Wordsmith Bks.

Catalano, Tom. Tall Tales & Short Stories: A Collection of Short Fiction. (Illus.). 176p. (Orig.). 1994. pap. 10.95 (*1-882646-16-9*) Wordsmith Bks.

— Verse Things First: A Collection of Poems. 96p. 1998. pap. 9.95 (*1-882646-43-6*) Wordsmith Bks.

Catalanotto, Peter. Christmas Always... LC 90-28712. (Illus.). 32p. (J). (ps-1). 1996. pap. 6.95 (*0-531-07066-2*) Orchard Bks Watts.

— Christmas Always-- LC 90-28712. 1995. 11.15 (*0-606-09145-9*, Pub. by Turtleback) Demco.

***Catalanotto, Peter.** Dad & Me. LC 99-11504. (Illus.). 40p. (J). (gr. 1-2). 1999. text 16.95 (*0-7894-2584-X*) DK Pub Inc.

Catalanotto, Peter. Dylan's Day Out. LC 88-36440. (Illus.). 32p. (J). (ps-1). 1989. lib. bdg. 16.99 (*0-531-08429-9*) Orchard Bks Watts.

— Dylan's Day Out. LC 88-36440. (Illus.). 32p. (J). (ps-1). 1993. pap. 5.95 (*0-531-07034-4*) Orchard Bks Watts.

— Dylan's Day Out. LC 88-36440. 1989. 11.15 (*0-606-09220-X*, Pub. by Turtleback) Demco.

***Catalanotto, Peter.** Emily's Art. LC 00-29293. (Illus.). (J). 2001. write for info. (*0-689-83831-X*) Atheneum Yung Read.

Catalanotto, Peter. Mr. Mumble. LC 89-48940. (Illus.). 32p. (J). (ps-2). 1990. 16.95 (*0-531-05880-8*) Orchard Bks Watts.

— Mr. Mumble. LC 89-48940. (Illus.). 32p. (J). (ps-2). 1994. pap. 5.95 (*0-531-07052-2*) Orchard Bks Watts.

— The Painter. LC 94-48808. (Illus.). 32p. (J). (ps-2). 1996. 15.95 (*0-531-09465-0*); lib. bdg. 16.99 (*0-531-08765-4*) Orchard Bks Watts.

— The Painter. LC 94-48808. (Illus.). 32p. (J). (ps-2). 1999. pap. 5.95 (*0-531-07116-2*) Orchard Bks Watts.

Catalci, Anna. Letters from Sarajevo: Voices under Siege. 1994. text 19.95 (*1-85230-500-2*, Pub. by Element MA) Penguin Putnam.

Cataldi, Lee, jt. auth. see Napaljarri, Peggy R.

Cataldi, Lee, jt. tr. see Napaljarri, Peggy R.

***Cataldi, Raffaele, et al.** Stories from a Heated Earth: Our Geothermal Heritage. LC 99-71835. (Illus.). 588p. 1999. pap. 70.00 (*0-934412-19-7*) Geothermal.

An Asterisk (*) at the beginning of an entry indicates that the title is appearing for the first time.

Cataldi, Sue L. Emotion, Depth, & Flesh: A Study of Sensitive Space: Reflections on Merleau-Ponty's Philosophy of Embodiment. LC 92-36052. 215p. (C). 1993. text 20.50 (*0-7914-1651-8*) State U NY Pr.

Cataldo. Nutrition & Diet. 2nd ed. Date not set. pap. text, student ed. 18.50 (*0-314-50888-0*) West Pub.

***Cataldo, et al.** Nutrition & Diet Therapy. 5th ed. LC 98-42478. (Health Sciences Ser.). 1998. pap. 69.95 (*0-534-54594-7*) Wadsworth Pub.

Cataldo, jt. auth. see Whitney.

Cataldo, Christine Z. Infant & Toddler Programs: A Guide to Very Early Childhood Education. LC 82-11418. (Illus.). 240p. 1983. pap. text 15.95 (*0-201-11020-2*) Addison-Wesley.

— Parent Education for Early Childhood: Child-Rearing Concepts & Program Content for the Student & Practicing Professional. LC 86-14573. 288p. reprint ed. pap. 89.30 (*0-7837-6483-9*, 204651000001) Bks Demand.

Cataldo, Corinne B., et al. Fundamentals of Normal & Clinical Nutrition. LC 95-3813. 700p. (C). 1996. pap. 60.95 (*0-314-04449-3*) West Pub.

— Nutrition & Diet Therapy: Principles & Practice. 3rd ed. Marshall, ed. 613p. (C). 1992. pap. 52.50 (*0-314-93359-X*) West Pub.

— Nutrition & Diet Therapy: Principles & Practice. 4th ed. LC 95-16288. 750p. (C). 1995. 57.95 (*0-314-04448-5*) West Pub.

— Understanding Clinical Nutrition. Marshall, ed. 382p. (C). 1992. pap. text 52.00 (*0-314-20865-8*) West Pub.

Cataldo, Corinne Balog, jt. auth. see Whitney, Eleanor Noss.

Cataldo, Joseph & Quirin, William L. Essex County Country Club: New Jersey's First Country Club. LC 97-36413. 1997. write for info. (*1-57864-012-1*) Donning Co.

Cataldo, Leonard & Pelletier, Robert. The Cosmic Informer. 256p. (Orig.). 1984. pap. 14.95 (*0-316-13198-9*) Little.

— A Look at Tomorrow Today. LC 89-50770. (Illus.). 500p. 1989. pap. 18.95 (*0-914918-94-X*, Whitford) Schiffer.

Cataldo, Nicci, ed. see Cerlo, Nick.

Cataldo, Peter A., jt. ed. see MacKeigan, John M.

Cataldo, Peter J., ed. The Dynamic Character of Christian Culture: Essays on Dawsonian Themes. 242p. (Orig.). (C). 1984. pap. text 20.50 (*0-8191-3960-2*); lib. bdg. 49.50 (*0-8191-3959-9*) U Pr of Amer.

Cataldo, Peter J. & Moraczewski, Albert S., eds. The Fetal Tissue Issue: Medical & Ethical Aspects. LC 94-6927. 1994. pap. 19.95 (*0-935372-37-7*) NCBC.

Cataldo, Susan. Brooklyn-Queens Day. Owen, Maureen, ed. (Summer Ser.). 48p. (Orig.). 1982. pap. 3.00 (*0-916382-30-3*) Telephone Bks.

Cataleno, Ellen M., et al. The Chronic Pain Control Workbook. 2nd ed. 256p. 1997. 8.98 (*1-56731-210-1*, MJF Bks) Fine Comms.

Catalfamo, Jamie S. Nathan's Fear: Book One of the Creation. 104p. (Orig.). 1994. pap. 6.95 (*0-9641739-0-5*) J S Catalfamo.

Catalfio, Maria, ed. see Carr, Virginia.

Catalfo, Jaclyn. Clarence Honeybear Shines His Inner Light. LC 94-79318. (Illus.). (YA). 1995. pap. 7.95 (*0-918915-00-7*) Inner Light Found.

Catalfo, Jaclyn, jt. auth. see Bethards, Betty.

Catalfo, Phil. Raising Spiritual Children in a Material World: Introducing Spirituality into Family Life. LC 97-157027. 272p. 1997. pap. 12.95 (*0-425-14954-4*); pap. 12.00 (*0-614-27489-3*) Berkley Pub.

Cataliotti, Robert H. The Music in African American Fiction: Representing Music in African American Fiction. rev. ed. LC 95-35215. (Studies in African American History & Culture). 272p. 1995. text 70.00 (*0-8153-2330-1*) Garland.

***Catalla, Rebecca.** Beyond Research Methods: Capacity Building for Research & Social Analysis & Disseminating Research Findings for Policy Making & Development Practice, 6 vols., Vol. 2. Ngin, Navirak, tr. 65p. 2000. pap. 4.00 (*0-910082-38-3*) Am Fr Serv Comm.

***Catalla, Rebecca, et al.** Bins of Gold: Livelihoods of Young People in the Tonle Bassac Squatter Area, Phnom Penh, 6 vols., Vol. 6. Liv, Leang Hy, tr. 56p. 2000. pap. 4.00 (*0-910082-42-1*) Am Fr Serv Comm.

— Choices from the Peripheries: Vulnerable People's Responses to Adversity & Change, 6 vols., Vol. 1. 78p. 2000. pap. 4.00 (*0-910082-37-5*) Am Fr Serv Comm.

— Crossing Borders, Crossing Norms: Vulnerability & Coping in Battambang Province (Cambodia), 6 vols., Vol. 5. 72p. 2000. pap. 4.00 (*0-910082-41-3*) Am Fr Serv Comm.

— My Heart Is Not Disabled: People with Disabilities in Kampot Province, 6 vols., Vol. 4. 63p. 2000. pap. 4.00 (*0-910082-40-5*) Am Fr Serv Comm.

Catalla, Rebecca, et al. On the Edge of Forest, On the Edge of Roads: People Dependent on Forest Resources in Kim Kong Province, 6 vols., Vol. 3. 55p. 2000. pap. 4.00 (*0-910082-39-1*) Am Fr Serv Comm.

Catalod, jt. auth. see Billon.

Catalog Age Editors, ed. The Catalog Management Handbook. 2nd rev. ed. 350p. 1999. pap. 79.95 (*0-918110-28-9*) Primedia Intertec.

Cataloging Policy & Support Office, Collections Se. Library of Congress Classification: R, Medicine. LC 95-13948. 1995. write for info. (*0-614-05431-1*) Lib Congress.

Cataloging Policy & Support Office, Collections Se, contrib. by. Library of Congress Classification: H Social Studies. 1994. write for info. (*0-614-32031-3*) Lib Congress.

— Library of Congress Classification: T Technology. LC 95-36131. 1995. write for info. (*0-614-08623-X*) Lib Congress.

— Library of Congress Classification: 1995 Edition. 1995. write for info. (*0-614-08609-4*) Lib Congress.

Catalogue Raisonne Staff. Liudmila Kondakova. (Illus.). 32p. Date not set. pap. write for info. (*0-9648085-1-X*) Jenkintwn Pr.

Catalogues of the Library of the Marine Biological. Marine Biological Association of the United Kingdom, Library. 1978. 1890.00 (*0-8161-0076-4*, G K Hall & Co) Mac Lib Ref.

***Catalon, Katie B.** Down Home. 112p. 1999. pap. 10.00 (*0-8059-4791-4*) Dorrance.

Catalona, William J. & Ratliff, T., eds. Urologic Oncology. (Cancer Treatment & Research Ser.). 1984. text 187.00 (*0-89838-628-4*) Kluwer Academic.

Catalona, William J., jt. ed. see Ratliff, Timothy L.

***Catalonia Staff.** Catalonia. 2000. 19.95 (*3-8290-2703-6*) Konemann.

Catalysis Society of India Staff, et al. Recent Advances in Basic & Applied Aspects of Industrial Catalysis: Proceedings of the 13th National Symposium & Silver Jubilee Symposium of Catalysis Society of India, Dehradun, India, April 2-4, 1997, Vol. 113. LC 97-51600. (Studies in Surface Science & Catalysis). 1998. 431.00 (*0-444-82920-2*) Elsevier.

Catalyst. Creating Women's Networks: A How-to-Guide for Women & Companies. (Business & Management Ser.). 208p. 1999. 24.00 (*0-7879-4014-3*) Jossey-Bass.

***Catalyst, Clint.** Cottonmouth Kisses. 160p. 1999. pap. 12.95 (*0-916397-65-3*) Manic D Pr.

Catalyst Institute Staff. U. S. Treasury Securities Market: The Scholars' Assesment. LC 94-26475. 1994. write for info. (*0-7863-0355-7*, Irwn McGrw-H) McGrw-H Hghr Educ.

Catalyst Institute Staff, ed. Securities Transaction Taxes: False Hopes & Unintended Consequences. LC 94-18464. 204p. 1994. text 75.00 (*0-7863-0354-9*, Irwn Prfssnl) McGraw-Hill Prof.

Catalyst Research Staff. Women Entrepreneurs: Why Companies Lose Female Talent & What They Can Do about It. (Illus.). 44p. 1998. pap. text 90.00 (*0-89584-202-5*) Catalyst.

Catalyst Staff. Advancing Women in Business, the Catalyst Guide: Best Practices from the Corporate Leaders. LC 97-45394. 245p. 1998. mass mkt. 26.00 (*0-7879-3966-8*) Jossey-Bass.

— Child Care Centers: Quality Indicators. 31p. 1993. 20.00 (*0-89584-159-2*) Catalyst.

— Child Care in Corporate America: Model Programs & Practices. 102p. 1993. 60.00 (*0-89584-158-4*) Catalyst.

— Cracking the Glass Ceiling: Strategies for Success. 108p. 1998. 90.00 (*0-89584-185-1*) Catalyst.

— Flexible Work Arrangements II: Succeed with Part-Time Options. 58p. 1993. 60.00 (*0-89584-157-6*) Catalyst.

Catan, John R., ed. see Owens, Joseph.

Catan, John R., ed. & tr. see Kramer, Hans J.

Catan, John R., ed. & tr. see Reale, Giovanni.

Catan, John R., tr. see Reale, Giovanni.

Catan, Omero C. Secrets of Shuffleboard Strategy. 2nd enl. ed. LC 72-91761. (Illus.). 224p. 1973. lib. bdg. 6.00 (*0-9600618-1-9*) Catan.

Catana, Leo. Vico & Literary Mannerism: A Study in the Early Vico & His Idea of Rhetoric & Ingenuity. LC 97-40824. (Emory Vico Studies: Vol. 6). XII, 142p. (C). 1999. text 40.95 (*0-8204-3963-0*, 39630) P Lang Pubng.

Cataneo, David. Hornsby Hit One over My Head: A Fan's Oral History of Baseball. LC 96-39518. 320p. 1997. pap. 14.00 (*0-15-600218-3*) Harcourt.

— Peanuts & Crackerjacks: A Treasury of Baseball Legends & Lore. (Illus.). 304p. 1994. pap. 11.95 (*0-15-671568-6*) Harcourt.

Catanese, Anthony. Haitians: Migration & Diaspora. LC 99-37267. 160p. 1999. 60.00 (*0-8133-3543-4*) Westview.

Catanese, Anthony J. Planners & Local Politics: Impossible Dreams. LC 73-94287. (Sage Library of Social Research: No. 7). 189p. reprint ed. pap. 58.60 (*0-8357-4774-3*, 203771100009) Bks Demand.

— The Politics of Planning & Development. LC 84-8334. (Sage Library of Social Research: No. 156). 231p. 1984. reprint ed. pap. 71.70 (*0-608-01500-8*, 205954400001) Bks Demand.

— Scientific Methods of Urban Analysis. LC 71-160384. 352p. reprint ed. pap. 109.20 (*0-7837-5733-6*, 204539400006) Bks Demand.

Catanese, Anthony J. & Snyder, James C. Introduction to Urban Planning. (Illus.). 1979. text. write for info. (*0-07-010228-7*) McGraw.

Catanese, Anthony J. & Synder, J. C. Urban Planning. 2nd ed. 386p. (C). 1988. 90.63 (*0-07-010229-5*) McGraw.

Catanese, Anthony J., jt. auth. see McClendon, Bruce W.

Catanese, Anthony V. Rural Poverty & Environmental Degradation in Haiti. Conway, Dennis, ed. (Series on Environment & Development). 40p. (Orig.). 1991. pap. 1.75 (*1-881157-07-5*) In Ctr Global.

Catanese, F., ed. Arithmetic Geometry. (Symposia Mathematica Ser.: Vol. 37). 310p. (C). 1997. text 69.95 (*0-521-59133-3*) Cambridge U Pr.

Catanese, F., et al, eds. Symposia Mathematica Vol. 32: Problems in the Theory of Surfaces & Their Classification. 410p. 1992. text 123.00 (*0-12-612232-6*) Acad Pr.

Catanese, Lynn A. Women's History: A Guide to Sources at Hagley Museum & Library, 26. LC 97-39753. (Bibliographies & Indexes in Women's Studies: Vol. 26). (Illus.). 352p. 1997. lib. bdg. 77.95 (*0-313-30270-7*, Greenwood Pr) Greenwood.

Catanese, Lynn A., compiled by. Guide to Records of the Court of Quarter Sessions, Chester County, Pennsylvania, 1681-1969. (Illus.). iii, 80p. (Orig.). 1988. pap. 25.00 (*0-929706-04-8*) Chester Co Hist Soc.

Catania, A. Charles. Learning. 4th ed. LC 97-9015. 462p. 1997. 74.00 (*0-13-235250-8*) P-H.

Catania, A. Charles & Harnad, Stevan R., eds. The Selection of Behavior: The Operant Behaviorism of B. F. Skinner: Comments & Consequences. (Illus.). 592p. 1988. pap. text 42.95 (*0-521-34861-7*) Cambridge U Pr.

Catania, Clifford P. Boudoir Art: The Celebration of Life. LC 94-65629. (Illus.). 144p. 1994. 59.95 (*0-88740-615-7*) Schiffer.

Catania, Cliford P., jt. auth. see Holland, William R.

Catania, Louis J. Primary Care of the Anterior Segment. 2nd ed. (Illus.). 552p. (C). 1996. pap. text 129.95 (*0-8385-7911-6*, A7911-9, Apple Lange Med) McGraw.

Catania, Louis J., ed. Ocular Disease Update Manual. 180p. 1991. 39.95 (*1-879040-12-3*) Scovill Paterson.

— Ocular Disease Update 2. 296p. 1991. 49.95 (*1-879040-13-1*) Scovill Paterson.

Catania, Patrick & Rosner, Martin M., eds. Home Health Care Practice. 2nd ed. LC 93-79105. (Illus.). 352p. (C). 1994. pap. 60.00 (*0-9627640-4-3*) Hlth Mrkts Res.

Catania, Patrick J., et al, eds. Commodity Trading Manual. rev. ed. 400p. (C). 1993. 45.95 (*0-917456-04-1*) Chicago Bd Trade.

Catania, Patrick J. & Whaley, Robert E., eds. Selected Writings on Futures Markets: Interrelations among Futures, Options, & Futures Option Markets. (Readings in Futures Markets Ser.: Bk. VI). 416p. (C). 1992. 15.00 (*0-917456-03-3*) Chicago Bd Trade.

Catania, Patrick J., ed. see Chicago Board of Trade, Education & Marketing Depa.

Catania, Patrick M. Getting the Most from Your Insurance Claim. 75p. 1998. pap. 39.95 (*0-9667675-0-0*) Insurance Info Srvc.

Catania, Patrick N., jt. auth. see King, James C.

Catanio, Kathleen. HIS Love Song. 34p. (Orig.). 1997. pap. 6.00 (*1-890413-00-3*) HIS Sceptre.

Catano, James V. Language, History, Style: Leo Spitzer & the Critical Tradition. 216p. 1988. text 25.95 (*0-252-01530-4*) U of Ill Pr.

Catanoy, Nicholas. Modern Romanian Poetry: An Anthology. 144p. 1989. 15.95 (*0-88962-046-6*); pap. 8.95 (*0-88962-045-8*) Mosaic.

Catany, Tony. Tony Catany: Life & Still Life. (Illus.). 108p. 1998. 50.00 (*1-899235-41-8*, 811031, Pub. by Dewi Lewis) Dist Art Pubs.

Catanzarite, Anne M. Managing the Chemically Dependent Nurse: A Guide to Identification, Intervention & Retention. 203p. 1992. pap. 25.00 (*1-886624-09-7*) Creative Nursing.

Catanzarite, Gina, jt. auth. see Treganowan, Lucille.

Catanzarite, Valerian A. & Duff, W. Patrick. Obstetric Infections: Amnionitis & Endometritis. 1989. write for info. (*0-683-17956-X*) Lppncott W & W.

— Obstetric Infections: Clinical Cases. 1989. write for info. (*0-683-17958-6*) Lppncott W & W.

Catanzariti, John, ed. The Papers of Robert Morris 1781-1784 Vol. 7: November 1, 1782 - May 4, 1783. LC 72-91107. (Illus.). 968p. (C). 1989. text 55.00 (*0-8229-3592-9*) U of Pittsburgh Pr.

— The Papers of Thomas Jefferson Vol. 24: June 1-December 31, 1792, Vol. 24. (Illus.). 928p. (Orig.). 1990. text 85.00 (*0-691-04776-6*, Pub. by Princeton U Pr) Cal Prin Full Svc.

Catanzariti, John & Ferguson, E. James. The Papers of Robert Morris, 1781-1784 Vol. 6: July 22-October 31, 1782, Vol.6. LC 72-91107. (Robert Morris Papers). (Illus.). 824p. 1984. text 55.00 (*0-8229-3485-X*) U of Pittsburgh Pr.

Catanzariti, John, jt. ed. see Ferguson, E. James.

Catanzariti, John, ed. see Jefferson, Thomas.

Catanzaro, jt. ed. see Einstein.

Catanzaro, Antonio, jt. ed. see Einstein, Hans E.

Catanzaro, B. J., ed. The SPARC Technical Papers. (Sun Technical Reference Library). (Illus.). 416p. 1991. 58.95 (*0-387-97634-5*) Spr-Verlag.

***Catanzaro, Frank J.** It's Only a Step! From This Life to the Next. 1999. write for info. (*0-9677052-0-7*) CEA Inc.

Catanzaro, Marci, jt. auth. see Kraft, George H.

Catanzaro, R., jt. ed. see Sabetti, Filippo.

Catanzaro, Raimondo. Men of Respect: A Social History of the Sicilian Mafia. 256p. 1992. 24.95 (*0-02-905225-0*) Free Pr.

Catanzaro, Thomas E. Building the Successful Veterinary Practice: Leadership Tools, Vol. 1. LC 97-374. (Illus.). 180p. (Orig.). (C). 1997. pap. text 24.95 (*0-8138-2819-8*) Iowa St U Pr.

— Building the Successful Veterinary Practice Vol. 2: Programs & Procedures, Vol. 2. LC 97-374. (Illus.). 368p. 1997. pap. 44.95 (*0-8138-2399-4*) Iowa St U Pr.

— Building the Successful Veterinary Practice Vol. 3: Innovation & Creativity, Vol. 3. LC 97-374. (Illus.). 200p. 1998. pap. text 34.95 (*0-8138-2984-4*) Iowa St U Pr.

***Catanzaro, Thomas E.** Veterinary Management in Transition: Preparing for the Twenty-first Century. LC 99-58668. (Illus.). 265p. 2000. 49.95 (*0-8138-2626-8*) Iowa St U Pr.

***Catanzaro, Thomas E., et al.** Beyond the Successful Veterinary Practice: Succession Planning & Other Legal Issues. LC 00-39679. (Illus.). 228p. 2000. 49.95 (*0-8138-1209-7*) Iowa St U Pr.

— Veterinary Healthcare Services: Options in Delivery. LC 99-59177. (Illus.). 182p. 2000. pap. 34.95 (*0-8138-0929-0*) Iowa St U Pr.

— Veterinary Practice Management Secrets. LC 00-23118. (Secrets Ser.). 2000. write for info. (*1-56053-400-1*) Hanley & Belfus.

Catanzaro, Thomas E., jt. ed. see Jevring, Caroline.

Catapano, A. L., et al, eds. Drugs Affecting Lipid Metabolism. LC 93-5111. (Medical Science Symposia Ser.: Vol. 2). 544p. (C). 1993. lib. bdg. 200.00 (*0-7923-2232-0*) Kluwer Academic.

Catapano, Alberico L., et al, eds. High-Density Lipoproteins: Physiopathological Aspects & Clinical Significance. LC 87-4902. (Atherosclerosis Reviews Ser.: Vol. 16). 229p. 1987. reprint ed. pap. 71.00 (*0-608-00296-8*, 205932400009) Bks Demand.

— High Density Lipoproteins: Physiopathology & Clinical Relevance. LC 92-49482. (Atherosclerosis Reviews Ser.: No. 24). (Illus.). 251p. 1993. reprint ed. pap. 77.90 (*0-608-05843-2*, 205980900007) Bks Demand.

Catapult, Inc., Staff. Microsoft Access for Windows 95 Step by Step. (Step by Step Ser.). 352p. 1995. 29.95 incl. disk (*1-55615-876-9*) Microsoft.

— Microsoft Access 2000 Step by Step. LC 98-48188. (Step by Step Ser.). 940p. 1999. pap. text 29.99 (*1-57231-976-3*) Microsoft.

— Microsoft Excel 5 for Windows Step by Step. 3rd ed. LC 93-23634. (Step by Step Ser.). 368p. 1994. pap. 29.95 incl. disk (*1-55615-587-5*) Microsoft.

— Microsoft Excel for Windows 95 Step by Step. (Step by Step Ser.). 368p. 1995. 29.95 incl. disk (*1-55615-825-4*) Microsoft.

— Microsoft Excel 97 Step by Step, Advanced Topics. LC 97-10658. 300p. 1997. pap. text 29.99 (*1-57231-564-4*) Microsoft.

— Microsoft Excel 97 Step by Step, Complete Course, 2 Vols. LC 97-221618. 672p. 1997. pap. text 49.99 incl. cd-rom (*1-57231-580-6*) Microsoft.

Catapult, Inc. Staff. Microsoft Excel 97 Step by Step. LC 96-38988. (Step by Step Ser.). (Illus.). 269p. pap. 29.95 (*1-57231-314-5*) Microsoft.

Catapult, Inc., Staff. Microsoft Excel 2000 Step by Step. (Step by Step Ser.). 432p. 1998. pap. text 34.99 (*1-57231-974-7*) Microsoft.

Catapult Inc. Staff. Microsoft Exchange 5.0 Step-by-Step. LC 97-11549. 336p. 1997. 29.99 incl. cd-rom (*1-57231-627-6*) Microsoft.

Catapult, Inc., Staff. Microsoft Exchange Step by Step: For Windows 95. (Step by Step Ser.). 336p. 1996. pap. 29.95 incl. disk (*1-55615-853-X*) Microsoft.

— Microsoft Frontpage 97 Step by Step. LC 96-38985. 336p. 1996. pap. text 29.99 incl. cd-rom (*1-57231-336-6*) Microsoft.

— Microsoft Internet Explorer 4.0 Step by Step. LC 97-31137. 208p. 1996. pap. text 24.99 incl. 3.5 hd (*1-57231-514-8*) Microsoft.

— Microsoft MS-DOS Step by Step, Revised for Version 6.2: Versions 6.0 & 6.2. LC 93-41595. (Step by Step Ser.). 304p. 1994. 29.95 incl. disk (*1-55615-635-9*) Microsoft.

— Microsoft Office for Windows Step by Step. LC 94-31277. (Step by Step Ser.). 328p. 1994. pap. 39.95 incl. audio compact disk (*1-55615-648-0*) Microsoft.

Catapult, Inc. Staff. Microsoft Office 97 Integration Step by Step. LC 96-44274. 336p. 29.95 (*1-57231-317-X*) Microsoft.

— Microsoft Office 97 Professional, 6 in 1 Step by Step. LC 97-27386. 800p. 1997. pap. text 39.99 incl. cd-rom (*1-57231-703-5*) Microsoft.

Catapult Inc. Staff. Microsoft Office 2000 8-1 Step by Step. LC 99-13767. 1999. pap. 44.99 (*1-57231-984-4*) Microsoft.

Catapult, Inc. Staff. Microsoft Outlook 98 Step by Step. LC 98-11186. (Step by Step Ser.). 320p. 29.99 (*1-57231-717-5*) Microsoft.

Catapult, Inc., Staff. Microsoft Outlook 2000 Step by Step. LC 98-48190. (Step by Step Ser.). 304p. 1999. pap. text 29.99 (*1-57231-982-8*) Microsoft.

Catapult, Inc. Staff. Microsoft Project 98 Step by Step. LC 97-27389. (Step by Step Ser.). (Illus.). 292p. 1997. pap. 29.99 incl. cd-rom (*1-57231-605-5*) Microsoft.

— Microsoft Team Manager 97 Step by Step. LC 96-44281. 336p. 29.95 incl. cd-rom (*1-57231-217-3*) Microsoft.

— Microsoft Windows NT Workstation Version 4.0 Step by Step. LC 96-31376. 288p. 29.95 (*1-57231-225-4*) Microsoft.

***Catapult Inc. Staff.** Microsoft Windows Step by Step, Millennium. 2000. pap. 19.99 (*0-7356-0990-X*) Microsoft.

Catapult, Inc. Staff. Microsoft Windows 98 Step by Step. LC 98-13999. 320p. 1997. 29.99 incl. 3.5 hd (*1-57231-683-7*) Microsoft.

Catapult, Inc., Staff. Microsoft Word 97 Developer's Handbook. Date not set. 39.99 (*1-57231-453-2*) Microsoft.

— Microsoft Word 97 Step by Step, Advanced Topics. LC 97-10663. 300p. 1997. pap. text 29.99 (*1-57231-563-6*) Microsoft.

— Microsoft Word 97 Step by Step, Complete Course, 2 Vols. 672p. 1997. pap. text 49.99 incl. cd-rom (*1-57231-579-2*) Microsoft.

Catapult, Inc. Staff. Microsoft Word 97 Step by Step. LC 96-44021. 320p. 29.95 (*1-57231-313-7*) Microsoft.

Catapult, Inc., Staff. Microsoft Word 6 for the Macintosh Step by Step. LC 94-15138. (Step by Step Ser.). 336p. 1994. pap. text 29.95 incl. disk (*1-55615-643-X*) Microsoft.

Catapult Inc. Staff. Microsoft Word 2000 Step by Step. LC 98-48194. 432p. 1999. pap. 34.99 (*1-57231-970-4*) Microsoft.

Catapult, Inc., Staff. More Microsoft Windows 95 Step by Step. (Step by Step Ser.). 304p. 1996. 29.95 incl. disk (*1-55615-888-2*) Microsoft.

— MS Outlook 97 Step by Step. 368p. 1996. pap. text 29.99 (*1-57231-382-X*) Microsoft.

— Upgrading the Microsoft Windows 95 Step by Step. (Step by Step Ser.). 224p. 1995. pap. 19.95 (*1-55615-816-5*) Microsoft.

— Windows 95 par Etapes. (FRE.). 336p. 1995. 95.00 incl. cd-rom (*0-7859-9849-7*) Fr & Eur.

Catapult, Inc., Staff & Microsoft Corporation Staff. Microsoft Access 97 Step by Step. (Illus.). 276p. 1997. pap. 29.95 incl. disk (*1-57231-316-1*) Microsoft.

Catapult, Inc., Staff & Sagman, Stephen W. Microsoft Project for Windows 95 Step by Step. LC 95-35792. (Step by Step Ser.). 400p. 1995. 29.95 incl. disk (*1-55615-866-1*) Microsoft.

Catarci, T., et al. Advanced Visual Interfaces (AVI '92) Proceedings of the International Workshop. (Computer Science Ser.). 436p. 1992. text 116.00 (*981-02-1123-6*) World Scientific Pub.

Catarci, Tiziana, jt. auth. see Arisawa, Hiroshi.

Catarroja, Dolores, tr. see Tebo, Mary E.

Catasus, S., et al. Cuban Women: Changing Roles & Population Trends. (Women, Work & Development Ser.: No. 17). xi, 125p. (Orig.). 1988. pap. 18.00 (*92-2-106387-9*) Intl Labour Office.

Catau, Dan. In the Thrill of the Night: Fishing the Michigan Hex. (Illus.). 112p. 1999. pap. 20.50 (*0-9669306-0-6*) Brook Trout.

Cataudella, Joe, et al. Creating Stores on the Web: Insider's Guide to Setting up a Profitable Cybershop. Collins, Corbin, ed. LC 98-187157. 560p. (C). 1998. pap. text 32.95 (*0-201-69681-9*, Pub. by Peachpit Pr) Addison-Wesley.

Catches, Cynthia L., ed. see Catches, Pete S., Sr. & Catches, Retek V.

Catches, Pete S., Sr. & Catches, Retek V. Oceti Wakan. Catches, Cynthia L., ed.Tr. of Sacred Fireplace. (Illus.). xi, 214p. (Orig.). 1997. pap. 28.00 (*0-9658626-7-4*) Oceti Wakan.

Catches, Peter, Sr. Sacred Fireplace: Life & Teachings of a Lakota Medicine Man. Catches, Peter, Jr., ed. LC 99-38800. (Illus.). 250p. 1999. pap. 14.95 (*1-57416-036-2*) Clear Light.

— Sacred Fireplace: Life & Teachings of a Lakota Medicine Man. 1995. per. write for info. (*0-671-89812-4*) S&S Trade.

Catches, Peter, Jr., ed. see Catches, Peter, Sr.

Catches, Retek V., jt. auth. see Catches, Pete S., Sr.

Catchings, James. Catching on to Reading. (Illus.). 60p. 1998. pap. 18.95 (*1-57502-673-2*, PO1908) Morris Pubng.

— Catching on to Reading: Read for a Brighter Future. 90p. 1998. pap. write for info. (*1-57502-916-2*, PO2512) Morris Pubng.

— Catching on to Reading for Kids. 48p. (J). (ps-3). 1998. pap. 14.95 (*1-57502-728-3*, PO2039) Morris Pubng.

Catchings, T. C. & Torrey. Catchings & Holliday Families, & Various Related Families in Virginia, Georgia, Mississippi & Other Southern States. (Illus.). 190p. 1997. reprint ed. pap. 28.00 (*0-8328-7894-4*); reprint ed. lib. bdg. 38.00 (*0-8328-7893-6*) Higginson Bk Co.

Catchpole, Barbara. Spirals Stories: Nick! Jackson, Anita, ed. 1998. pap. 22.00 (*0-7487-3653-0*, Pub. by S Thornes Pubs) Trans-Atl Phila.

***Catchpole, Brian.** The Korean War. (Illus.). 320p. 2000. 26.00 (*0-7867-0780-1*, Pub. by Carroll & Graf) Publishers Group.

Catchpole, Brian. A Map History of the United States. (YA). (gr. 7). 1972. pap. text 15.00 (*0-435-31158-1*, 31158) Heinemann.

Catchpole, C. K. & Slater, P. J. Bird Song: Biological Themes & Variations. (Illus.). 256p. (C). 1995. text 36.95 (*0-521-41799-6*) Cambridge U Pr.

Catchpole, David. The Quest for Q. 256p. 1993. text 49.95 (*0-567-09616-5*, Pub. by T & T Clark) Bks Intl VA.

Catchpole, L. T. Lynton & Barnstaple Railway. 84p. (C). 1985. 45.00 (*0-85361-363-X*) St Mut.

***Catchpole, Mark.** Employee Share Schemes. 200p. 2000. pap. write for info. (*1-902558-19-7*, Pub. by Palladian Law) Gaunt.

Catcott, E. J., ed. Animal Health Technology. 2nd ed. LC 77-85491. (Illus.). 480p. 1991. text 44.95 (*0-939674-10-6*) Am Vet Pubns.

Cate, Curtis. Andre Malraux: A Biography. LC 96-27987. (Illus.). 480p. 1997. 29.95 (*0-88064-171-1*) Fromm Intl Pub.

— Andre' Malraux: A Biography. (Illus.). 480p. 1998. reprint ed. pap. 17.00 (*0-88064-197-5*) Fromm Intl Pub.

Cate, Curtis, tr. see Saint-Exupery, Antoine de.

Cate, Folkert J. Ten, see Ten Cate, Folkert J.

Cate, Fred H. The Internet & the First Amendment: Schools & Sexually Explicit Expressions. LC 97-75653. 109p. 1998. pap. 12.00 (*0-87367-398-0*) Phi Delta Kappa.

— Privacy in the Information Age. LC 97-21114. 248p. 1997. 39.95 (*0-8157-1316-9*); pap. 16.95 (*0-8157-1315-0*) Brookings.

Cate, George A. John Ruskin: A Reference Guide. 1988. 50.00 (*0-8161-8908-0*, Hall Reference) Macmillan.

Cate, H. J. Houwink Ten, see Bittel, K.

***Cate, Hollis L.** At the Beach & Elsewhere. LC 00-32440. 2000. write for info. (*0-7734-1262-X*, Mellen Poetry Pr) E Mellen.

Cate, J. M. Ten, see Ten Cate, J. M.

Cate, J. M. Ten, see Curzon, M. E. & Ten Cate, J. M., eds.

Cate, James L., jt. auth. see Craven, Wesley F.

Cate, Margaret D. Our Todays & Yesterdays: A Story of Brunswick, Ga., & the Coastal Islands. rev. ed. (Illus.). 302p. 1997. lib. bdg. 36.00 (*0-8328-7063-3*) Higginson Bk Co.

Cate, Michael. Scott County, Arkansas. (Illus.). 354p. 1991. 60.00 (*0-88107-183-8*) Curtis Media.

Cate, Michael & Coogan, Harold. Mena Centennial History: A Photographic History of Mena, Arkansas. LC 96-77840. (Illus.). 288p. 1996. 45.00 (*1-886130-04-3*) Cate Media.

Cate, Michael & Hoofman, Judy. DeQueen Centennial History: A Pictorial History of DeQueen, Arkansas. LC 96-77844. (Illus.). 260p. 1997. 45.00 (*1-886130-05-1*) Cate Media.

Cate, Michael, et al. Port Arthur Centennial History: Official Pictorial History of Port Arthur, Texas, 1898-1998, 2 vols. 2nd ed. Brown, Dub, ed. LC 96-77840. 488p. 1997. 65.00 (*1-886130-06-X*) Cate Media.

Cate, Michael, ed. & tr. see Burton, Paul.

Cate, Phillip D. The Spirit of Montmartre: Cabarets, Humor, & the Avant-Garde, 1875-1905. Shaw, Mary, ed. (Illus.). 240p. (C). 1996. pap. 29.95 (*0-8135-2324-9*) Rutgers U Pr.

Cate, Phillip D., ed. The Graphic Arts & French Society, 1871-1914. (Illus.). 194p. (C). 1988. text 40.00 (*0-8135-1278-6*) Rutgers U Pr.

***Cate, Phillip Dennis, et al.** Prints Abound: Paris in the 1890s: From the Collections of Virginia & Ira Jackson & the National Gallery of Art. LC 00-33261. (Illus.). 2000. write for info. (*0-89468-277-6*) Natl Gallery Art.

Cate, Robert L. Introduccion al Estudio del Antiguo Testamento. Zorzoli, Ruben O., tr.Tr. of An Introduction to the Old Testament & Its Study. (SPA.). 496p. (Orig.). 1990. pap. 16.99 (*0-311-04034-9*) Casa Bautista.

— Introduction to the Old Testament & Its Study. 1999. pap. text 24.99 (*0-8054-1998-5*) Broadman.

— Teologia del Antiguo Testamento, Raices para la Fe Neotestamentaria. Fricke, Roberto, tr. from ENG.Tr. of Old Testament Roots for New Testament Faith. (SPA.). 264p. 1989. pap. 14.50 (*0-311-09110-5*) Casa Bautista.

Cate, Rodney M. Courtship. (Series on Close Relationships: Vol. 2). 160p. (C). 1992. text 42.00 (*0-8039-3708-3*); pap. text 17.95 (*0-8039-3709-1*) Sage.

Cate, Thomas, et al, eds. An Encyclopedia of Keynesian Economics. LC 96-23171. 672p. 1997. 250.00 (*1-85898-145-X*) E Elgar.

Cate, Weston A., Jr. Up & Doing: The Vermont Historical Society, 1838-1970. 123p. 1988. pap. 14.95 (*0-934720-32-0*) VT Hist Soc.

Cate, Wirt A. Lucius Q. C. Lamar, Secession & Reunion. (History - United States Ser.). 594p. 1993. reprint ed. lib. bdg. 99.00 (*0-7812-4907-4*) Rprt Serv.

***Cateau, Heather & Carrington, Selwyn H. H., eds.** Capitalism & Slavery Fifty Years Later: Eric Eustace Williams--a Reassessment of the Man & His Work. LC 98-42972. 272p. 2000. text 49.95 (*0-8204-4171-6*) P Lang Pubng.

Catedra, Manuel F. & Perez-Arriaga, Jesus. Cell Planning for Wireless Communications. LC 99-10825. (Mobile Communications Library). 264p. 1999. 83.00 (*0-89006-601-9*) Artech Hse.

Catedra, Manuel F., et al. The CG-FFT Method: Application of Signal Processing Techniques to Electromagnetics. LC 94-5746. 361p. 1994. 37.00 (*0-89006-634-5*) Artech Hse.

Catedra, Maria. This World, Other Worlds: Sickness, Suicide, Death, & the Afterlife among the Vaqueiros De Alzada of Spain. Christian, William A., Jr., tr. (Illus.). 402p. 1992. pap. text 22.00 (*0-226-09716-1*); lib. bdg. 69.00 (*0-226-09715-3*) U Ch Pr.

Cateforis, David, ed. see Ross, Novelene.

Catel, Jean. Walt Whitman: La Naissance Du Poete. (BCL1-PS American Literature Ser.). 483p. 1992. reprint ed. lib. bdg. 99.00 (*0-7812-6920-2*) Rprt Serv.

— Walt Whitman: La Naissance Du Poete. 1971. reprint ed. 39.00 (*0-403-00900-6*) Scholarly.

***Catelani, Angelo J.** In Bocca al Lupo: In the Mouth of the Wolf. LC 99-75604. (Illus.). 256p. 1999. pap. 19.95 (*0-936029-53-6*) Western Bk Journ.

Catena, Liu, ed. Gravitational Waves: Proceedings of the 2nd Edoardo Amaldi Conference. (Edoardo Amaldi Foundation Ser.: Vol. 4). 700p. 1998. 128.00 (*981-02-3565-8*) World Scientific Pub.

Cateora. International Marketing/Global Marketing. 9th ed. 1998. 82.50 (*0-256-22438-2*) McGraw.

Cateora & Maidment. International Marketing/International Business 96-97. 9th ed. 1995. 73.25 (*0-256-21154-X*) McGraw.

Cateora, Philip. International Marketing Cases. 8th ed. (C). 1993. pap. text 6.00 (*0-256-16665-X*, Irwn McGrw-H) McGraw-H Hghr Educ.

Cateora, Philip & Graham, John. International Marketing. 10th ed. LC 98-21048. 752p. (C). 1998. 84.38 (*0-256-25982-8*) McGraw.

Cateora, Philip R. International Marketing. 9th ed. LC 95-9132. (Series in Marketing). 800p. (C). 1995. text 70.95 (*0-256-13950-4*, Irwn Prfssnl) McGraw-Hill Prof.

Cateora, Philip R. & Richardson, Lee, eds. Readings in Marketing: The Qualitative & Quantitative Areas. LC 67-10928. (Illus.). (Orig.). 1967. pap. text 12.95 (*0-89197-373-7*) Irvington.

Cater, jt. auth. see Russell.

Cater, Charles K., jt. auth. see Cousens, Elizabeth M.

Cater, Douglas J. As It Was: Reminiscences of a Soldier of the Third Texas Calvary & the Nineteenth Louisiana... LC 90-9967. 266p. 1990. reprint ed. 24.95 (*0-938349-47-3*) State House Pr.

Cater, Douglass & Nyhan, Michael J., eds. The Future of Public Broadcasting. LC 76-8889. 382p. 1976. pap. 18.95 (*0-275-64590-8*, Praeger Pubs) Greenwood.

Cater, Douglass & Strickland, Stephen P. TV Violence & the Child: The Evolution & Fate of the Surgeon General's Report. LC 74-83207. 168p. 1975. 25.00 (*0-87154-203-X*) Russell Sage.

Cater, Earl M., jt. ed. see Caldwell, Brian J.

Cater, Erlet & Lowman, Gwen, eds. Ecotourism: A Sustainable Option? LC 94-15985. 230p. 1994. 110.00 (*0-471-94896-9*) Wiley.

Cater, John & Jones, Trevor. Social Geography: An Introduction to Contemporary Issues. 256p. 1989. 49.50 (*0-7131-6486-7*, Pub. by E A); pap. 18.95 (*0-7131-6474-3*, Pub. by E A) Routldge.

Cater, Joseph H. The Awesome Life Force. 479p. 1984. pap. 25.00 (*0-7873-0161-2*) Hlth Research.

Cater, Ralph F. The Great Entrapment: A Biblical Model of a Workable Church in Any Community of a Cross Cultural World. LC 96-61988. 360p. 1998. pap. 14.95 (*0-9654818-1-6*) Tanglewood Hill.

***Cater, Steve.** New River Gorge & Summersville Lake Rock Climbers' Guidebook. 2nd rev. ed. (Illus.). 200p. 1999. 19.95 (*0-9678270-1-9*) King Coal.

— New River Gorge Select Rock Climbs. (Illus.). 86p. 1997. 11.95 (*0-9678270-0-0*) King Coal.

— New River Gorge Trail Guide. 2nd ed. (Illus.). 2000. 11.95 (*0-9678270-2-7*) King Coal.

Caterette, Edward C., et al, eds. Perception & Cognition at Century's End. 2nd ed. (Handbook of Perception & Cognition Ser.). (Illus.). 487p. (C). 1998. boxed set 99.95 (*0-12-301160-4*) Acad Pr.

***Caterino, Michael S.** The Taxonomy & Phylogenetics of the Coenosus Group of Hister Linnaeus (Coleoptera:Histeridae) LC 98-51373. (Publications in Entomology: Vol. 119). 104p. 1999. pap. 20.00 (*0-520-09831-5*, Pub. by U CA Pr) Cal Prin Full Svc.

Caterson, Lucile P. Handbook of Florida Flowers. 48p. (Orig.). 1959. pap. 2.95 (*0-8200-0405-7*) Great Outdoors.

Cates. The Far Fetched Story Quilt. (J). 2000. mass mkt. 16.00 (*0-689-81964-1*) S&S Childrens.

Cates, et al. Biology - Zoology. 5th ed. 300p. (C). 1999. spiral bd., lab manual ed. 33.95 (*0-7872-5719-2*, 41571901) Kendall-Hunt.

Cates, Alison. Great Barrier Reef. 1998. 49.95 (*1-86436-218-9*) Stikk Co.

Cates, Ayn W. Consider This... Recovering Harmony & Balance Naturally. (Illus.). (Orig.). 1995. pap. 12.95 (*1-899171-40-1*, Pub. by Findhorn Pr) Words Distrib.

Cates, Bill. Unlimited Referrals: Secrets That Turn Your Business Relationships to Gold! 200p. 1996. 24.95 (*1-888970-07-3*) Thndr Hill Pr.

Cates, Bill, ed. see Whalen, Nana.

Cates, Christopher, et al. Brand Building & Communication: Power Strategies for the 21st Century. Elliott, Susan, ed. (Illus.). 163p. 1999. spiral bd. 495.00 (*1-928593-12-7*) Am Prodtv Qual.

Cates, Claudia. Heart of an Angel. (Illus.). 74p. 1998. pap. write for info. (*1-57502-722-4*, PO2027) Morris Pubng.

Cates, Cynthia L., jt. auth. see Mcintosh, Wayne V.

Cates, David. Unconditional Money: A Magical Journey into the Heart of Abundance. 256p. (Orig.). 1996. pap. 14.95 (*0-9647578-7-7*) Buffalo Pr OR.

Cates, Diana F. Choosing to Feel: Virtue, Friendship, & Compassion for Friends. LC 95-50517. 304p. (C). 1996. text 32.00 (*0-268-00814-0*) U of Notre Dame Pr.

Cates, Donald W. Index to J. C. Flanigan's Vol. II: History of Gwinnett County, Georgia 1818-1960. McCabe, Alice S., ed. 120p. 1985. 10.00 (*0-914923-06-4*) Gwinnett Hist.

Cates, Dudley F. Blossoms of the Nile. LC 97-69237. 128p. 1999. pap. 11.95 (*1-57197-083-5*) Pentland Pr.

— Portents of the Coming Millennium. LC 98-65629. 64p. 1999. pap. 9.95 (*1-57197-107-6*) Pentland Pr.

— The Rise & Fall of King Nimrod. LC 97-67139. 68p. (Orig.). 1998. pap. 10.95 (*1-57197-068-1*) Pentland Pr.

Cates, Janis E. Depression-Free Living: A 21st Century Guide to Beating the Blues on Your Own. unabridged ed. LC 97-95110. 240p. 1998. pap. 15.00 (*0-9662514-0-7*) Reflection Hse.

— Today You Can Stop Dieting . . . Forever: A Simple, Natural Solution to Permanent Weight Control. unabridged ed. LC 98-91675. 128p. 1998. pap. 11.95 (*0-9662514-1-5*) Reflection Hse.

Cates, Jean, jt. auth. see Cunningham, Sue.

Cates, Jerry R. Insuring Inequality: Administrative Leadership in Social Security, 1935-1954. 200p. 1983. text 39.50 (*0-472-10026-2*, 10026) U of Mich Pr.

Cates, Jo A. Journalism: A Guide to Reference Literature. 2nd ed. LC 96-48335. (Reference Sources in the Humanities Ser.). 265p. 1997. lib. bdg. 55.00 (*1-56308-374-4*) Libs Unl.

Cates, Judith N. & Sussman, Marvin B., eds. Family Systems & Inheritance Patterns. LC 82-15790. (Marriage & Family Review Ser.: Vol. 5, No. 3). 116p. 1982. pap. text 14.95 (*0-86656-214-1*) Haworth Pr.

— Family Systems & Inheritance Patterns. LC 82-15790. (Marriage & Family Review Ser.: Vol. 5, No. 3). 116p. 1983. text 39.95 (*0-86656-158-7*) Haworth Pr.

Cates, Karin. The Far-Fetched Story Quilt. (J). 2000. 15.95 (*0-688-15938-9*, Grenwillow Bks); lib. bdg. 15.89 (*0-688-15939-7*, Grenwillow Bks) HarpC Child Bks.

Cates, Kim. A Father's Claim. (Intimate Moments Ser.). 1994. per. 3.50 (*0-373-07580-4*, 1-07580-3) Harlequin Bks.

— Uncertain Angels. (Intimate Moments Ser.). 1994. per. 3.50 (*0-373-07550-2*, 5-07550-2) Silhouette.

Cates, Kimberly. Angel's Fall. 1996. mass mkt. 5.99 (*0-671-56872-8*) PB.

— Briar Rose. 1999. mass mkt. 6.50 (*0-671-01495-1*) PB.

— Crown of Dreams. Marrow, Linda, ed. 400p. (Orig.). 1993. mass mkt. 5.99 (*0-671-79601-1*) PB.

***Cates, Kimberly.** Fly Away Home. 400p. 2000. per. 6.99 (*0-671-02823-5*, Pocket Books) PB.

Cates, Kimberly. Gather the Stars. 1996. pap. 5.99 (*0-614-98086-0*, Pocket Books) PB.

— Gather the Stars. 336p. 1996. per. 5.99 (*0-671-89746-2*) S&S Trade.

***Cates, Kimberly.** Lily Fair. 1999. per. 6.50 (*0-671-02822-7*, Sonnet Bks) PB.

Cates, Kimberly. Magic. 328p. 1998. per. 6.50 (*0-671-01494-3*) PB.

— Morning Song. 1997. per. 5.99 (*0-671-56873-6*) PB.

— Only Forever. 1992. mass mkt. 5.99 (*0-671-74083-0*) PB.

— The Raider's Bride. Marrow, Linda, ed. 320p. (Orig.). 1994. mass mkt. 5.50 (*0-671-75508-0*) PB.

— Raider's Daughter. Marrow, Linda, ed. 320p. (Orig.). 1994. mass mkt. 5.50 (*0-671-75509-9*) PB.

— Restless Is the Wind. 1989. mass mkt. 5.99 (*0-671-63395-3*) PB.

— Stealing Heaven. (Illus.). (J). 1995. mass mkt. 5.99 (*0-671-89745-4*) PB.

— To Catch a Flame. Marrow, Linda, ed. 320p. (Orig.). 1991. mass mkt. 5.99 (*0-671-68494-9*) PB.

Cates, Kimberly, et al. A Gift of Love. 1997. 4.99 (*0-681-06799-3*) Waldenbooks Co Inc.

Cates, Lori, ed. see Bendaly, Leslie.

Cates, Lori, ed. see Kursmark, Louise.

Cates, Lori, ed. see Wolfinger, Anne.

Cates, Robert B. Joshua Tree National Park: A Visitor's Guide. 2nd rev. ed. LC 94-73488. (Illus.). 100p. 1994. pap. 6.95 (*0-9619128-1-2*) Live Oak Pr of Chatsworth.

Cates, Rosalie. Branded. LC 79-19211. 1981. 19.95 (*0-87949-147-7*) Ashley Bks.

Cates, Timothy G. Confessions of a Dandy. LC 98-65644. 240p. 1998. pap. 15.95 (*1-57197-124-6*) Pentland Pr.

***Cates, Timothy G.** A Dandy's Quest. 182p. 2000. pap. text 14.95 (*0-9677815-0-7*) Tiger Sea.

Cates, Truett, jt. tr. see Knowlton, James.

Cates, W. L., tr. see Merle d'Augbine, Jean H.

Catesby, D. Setting a Course for Health. 236p. 1995. pap. 45.00 (*1-85609-077-9*, Pub. by Witherby & Co) St Mut.

Catesby, Mark. Catesby's Birds of Colonial America. Feduccia, Alan, ed. LC 85-1176. (Fred W. Morrison Series in Southern Studies). 208p. reprint ed. pap. 64.50 (*0-608-02058-3*, 206271100003) Bks Demand.

Cateura, Linda. Oil Painting Secrets from a Master. (Illus.). 144p. 1995. pap. 24.95 (*0-8230-3279-5*) Watsn-Guptill.

Catford, J. C. A Practical Introduction to Phonetics. (Illus.). 255p. (C). 1988. pap. text 24.00 (*0-19-824217-4*) OUP.

Catford, Lorna & Ray, Michael. The Path of the Everyday Hero: Drawing on the Power of Myth to Meet Life's Most Important Challenges. (Illus.). 256p. (Orig.). 1991. pap. 14.95 (*0-87477-630-9*, Tarcher Putnam) Putnam Pub Group.

Cath, Stanley H., et al, eds. On Stepfathers & Stepfathering. Date not set. write for info. (*0-88163-176-0*) Analytic Pr.

Cath, Stanley H., jt. ed. see Berezin, Martin A.

Cath, Stanley H., ed. see Gurwitt, Alan R. & Gunsberg, Linda.

Cathaoir, Brendan O. Famine Diary. 216p. 1999. 27.95 (*0-7165-2655-7*, Pub. by Irish Acad Pr) Intl Spec Bk.

Cathart, Michael. Manning Clarks's History of Australia: Special Anniversary Edition. abr. ed. LC 98-222510. 592p. 1997. 85.00 (*0-522-84779-X*, Pub. by Melbourne Univ Pr) Paul & Co Pubs.

Cathcart, jt. auth. see Liddell, Sharon.

Cathcart, Alex. The Missionary. LC 88-61440. 256p. (Orig.). 1988. pap. 12.95 (*0-948275-48-0*) Dufour.

Cathcart, Brian. Test of Greatness: Britain's Struggle for the Atom Bomb. (Illus.). 301p. 1995. 45.00 (*0-7195-5225-7*, Pub. by John Murray) Trafalgar.

***Cathcart, Brian.** Were You Still up for Portillo? 160p. 1998. pap. 11.95 (*0-14-027237-2*, Pub. by Pnguin Bks Ltd) Trafalgar.

Cathcart, David A., et al. The Civil Rights Act of 1991. LC 93-71601. 478p. 1993. text 38.00 (*0-8318-0696-6*, B696) Am Law Inst.

Cathcart, Edgar S., jt. ed. see Newcombe, David S.

***Cathcart, George, et al.** Learning Mathematics in Elementary & Middle Schools. LC 99-33271. (Illus.). 417p. (C). 1999. pap. text 63.00 (*0-13-011681-5*) P-H.

Cathcart, Jim. The Acorn Principle: Discover, Explore & Grow the Seeds of Your Greatest Potential. LC 98-21123. (Illus.). 214p. 1998. 22.95 (*0-312-19652-0*) St Martin.

— The Acorn Principle: Discover, Explore & Grow the Seeds of Your Greatest Potential. 240p. 1999. pap. 12.95 (*0-312-24284-0*) St Martin.

Cathcart, K. J. & Healey, J. F., eds. Back to the Sources: Biblical & Near Eastern Studies in Honour of Dermot Ryan. (Distributed Books in Biblical Studies). 191p. 1989. 57.50 (*0-907606-61-X*, Pub. by Sheffield Acad) CUP Services.

Cathcart, Kevin & Gordon, Robert. The Targum of the Minor Prophets. (Aramaic Bible Ser.: Vol. 14). 259p. 1989. 65.00 (*0-8146-5489-4*) Liturgical Pr.

Cathcart, Kevin J. & Maher, Michael, eds. Targumic & Cognate Studies: Essays in Honour of Martin McNamara. (JSOTS Ser.: No. 230). 250p. 1996. 70.00 (*1-85075-632-5*, Pub. by Sheffield Acad) CUP Services.

Cathcart, Linda. The Martha Jackson Collection at the Albright-Knox Art Gallery. LC 75-24230. (Illus.). 1976. pap. 4.95 (*0-914782-04-5*) Buffalo Fine-Albrght-Knox.

Cathcart, Linda, jt. auth. see Tucker, Marcia.

Cathcart, Linda L. American Painting of the Seventies. LC 78-21790. (Illus.). 1978. 22.00 (*0-914782-22-3*) Buffalo Fine-Albrght-Knox.

— Nancy Graves: A Survey 1969 to 1980. LC 80-13227. (Illus.). 1980. pap. 15.00 (*0-914782-34-7*) Buffalo Fine-Albrght-Knox.

Cathcart, Linda L., text. American Still Life, 1945-1985. (Illus.). 144p. 1983. pap. 19.95 (*0-936080-12-4*) Cont Arts Museum.

— The Americans: The Landscape. (Illus.). 44p. 1981. pap. 10.00 (*0-936080-03-5*) Cont Arts Museum.

— Extensions: Jennifer Bartlett, Lynda Benglis, Robert Long, Judy Pfaff. (Illus.). 34p. 1980. pap. 8.50 (*0-936080-00-0*) Cont Arts Museum.

— Robert Rauschenberg, Work from Four Series: A Sesquicentennial Exhibition. (Illus.). 86p. 1985. pap. 22.95 (*0-936080-15-9*) Cont Arts Museum.

Cathcart, Michael, abr. Manning Clark's History of Australia: An Abridgement. 588p. 1993. 45.00 (*0-522-84523-1*, Pub. by Melbourne Univ Pr) Paul & Co Pubs.

Cathcart, Michael, ed. Great Australian Speeches. 352p. 1996. 59.95 (*0-522-84681-5*, Pub. by Melbourne Univ Pr) Paul & Co Pubs.

Cathcart, Pamela B. History Hunt at Cold Harbor. (Illus.). 95p. (Orig.). (J). 1994. 19.95 (*0-931563-15-1*); pap. 6.95 (*0-931563-14-3*) Wishing Rm.

Cathcart, Robert. Post Communication: Criticism & Evaluation. LC 66-19701. (Orig.). 1966. pap. 5.95 (*0-672-61073-6*, SC2, Bobbs) Macmillan.

— Small Group Communication: A Reader. 7th ed. 432p. (C). 1995. text 32.50 (*0-697-20437-5*) Brown & Benchmark.

***Cathcart, Robert, et al, eds.** Small Group Communication: An Anthology. 8th ed. 437p. (C). 2001. pap. text. write for info. (*1-891487-50-7*) Roxbury Pub Co.

***Cathcart, Robert H.** A Yankee Peddler Nutmeg Cookbook. (Illus.). 120p. 2000. pap. 12.97 (*0-615-11865-8*) Nutmeg Cookbk.

Cathcart, Robert S., jt. auth. see Drucker, Susan J.

Cathcart, Yvonne, jt. auth. see Liddell, Sharen.

***Cathedral Choir.** Let the Children Sing. 1999. pap. text 14.98 (*5-555-32727-7*) ISNM.

***Cathedral Choir Staff.** Let the Children Sing. 1999. pap. text 16.98 (*5-550-00644-8*) Nairi.

Cathedral Church of St. Paul Staff. Bookcheck. 2nd ed. 1993. pap. 2.95 (*0-9627253-1-5*) VT Kitchen.

Cathell, D. W. The Physician Himself & What He Should Add to His Scientific Acquirements. 2nd ed. LC 70-180562. (Medicine & Society in America Ser.). 216p. 1972. reprint ed. 18.95 (*0-405-03941-7*) Ayer.

Cather, Flavius J. The Jasper Cather Family of Frederick Co VA. 42p. 1999. reprint ed. 18.50 (*0-8328-9761-2*); reprint ed. pap. 8.50 (*0-8328-9762-0*) Higginson Bk Co.

Cather, Sharon, ed. The Conservation of Wall Paintings: Proceedings of a Symposium Organized by the Courtauld Institute of Art & the Getty Conservation Institute, London, July 1987. LC 91-16526. 130p. 1991. pap. 42.50 (*0-89236-162-X*, Pub. by J P Getty Trust) OUP.

Cather, Steven M., jt. ed. see Keller, G. Randy.

Cather, Willa. Alexander's Bridge. Lindemann, Marilee, ed. & intro. by. (The World's Classics Ser.). 152p. 1997. pap. 8.95 (*0-19-283214-X*) OUP.

— Alexander's Bridge. LC 96-42550. 1998. 21.50 (*0-684-81907-4*) S&S Trade.

— Alexander's Bridge. 1977. reprint ed. lib. bdg. 19.95 (*0-89190-520-0*, Queens House) Amereon Ltd.

— Alexander's Bridge. 1990. reprint ed. lib. bdg. 16.95 (*0-89968-491-2*) Buccaneer Bks.

— Alexander's Bridge. (Collected Works of Willa Cather). 174p. 1998. reprint ed. lib. bdg. 88.00 (*1-58201-566-X*) Classic Bks.

— Alexander's Bridge. LC 76-56439. 140p. 1977. reprint ed. pap. 9.95 (*0-8032-5863-1*, Bison Books) U of Nebr Pr.

— April Twilights. 1976. 18.95 (*0-88411-127-X*) Amereon Ltd.

— April Twilights. 1990. reprint ed. lib. bdg. 15.95 (*0-89968-492-0*) Buccaneer Bks.

— April Twilights. rev. ed. Slote, Bernice, ed. LC 76-14216. (Landmark Edition Ser.). xlviii, 88p. 1990. text 40.00 (*0-8032-1448-0*) U of Nebr Pr.

— April Twilights: And Other Poems. (Collected Works of Willa Cather). 66p. 1998. reprint ed. lib. bdg. 88.00 (*1-58201-567-8*) Classic Bks.

— The Autobiography of S. S. McClure. LC 96-43609. (Illus.). xxvi, 298p. 1997. pap. 15.00 (*0-8032-6373-2*, Bison Books) U of Nebr Pr.

— Collected Stories of Willa Cather. LC 92-5006. 544p. 1992. pap. 15.00 (*0-679-73648-4*) Vin Bks.

— Coming, Aphrodite! And Other Stories. O'Connor, Margaret A., ed. & notes by. LC 98-40654. (Penguin Twentieth-Century Classics Ser.). 1999. pap. 12.95 (*0-14-118156-7*) Viking Penguin.

— Death Comes for the Archbishop. 1976. 24.95 (*0-8488-0448-1*) Amereon Ltd.

— Death Comes for the Archbishop. 1992. 15.00 (*0-679-41319-7*) Everymns Lib.

— Death Comes for the Archbishop. (Vintage Classics). 1971. 15.10 (*0-606-01551-5*, Pub. by Turtleback) Demco.

— Death Comes for the Archbishop. LC 98-26107. (Willa Cather Scholarly Edition Ser.). (Illus.). xiii, 559p. 1999. text 60.00 (*0-8032-1429-4*) U of Nebr Pr.

— Death Comes for the Archbishop. LC 89-40540. (Vintage Classics Ser.). 297p. 1990. pap. 10.00 (*0-679-72889-9*) Vin Bks.

— Death Comes for the Archbishop. 1992. reprint ed. lib. bdg. 19.95 (*0-89966-978-6*) Buccaneer Bks.

— Death Comes for the Archbishop. 19th ed. LC 92-34349. 320p. 1993. 14.95 (*0-679-60050-7*) Modern Lib NY.

— Early Novels & Stories: The Troll Garden; O Pioneers!; The Song of the Lark; My Antonia; One of Ours. O'Brien, Sharon, ed. LC 87-10704. 1336p. 1987. 40.00 (*0-940450-39-9*, Pub. by Library of America) Penguin Putnam.

— Early Stories of Willa Cather. 1976. 23.95 (*0-8488-0956-4*) Amereon Ltd.

— Five Stories. 1976. 21.95 (*0-8488-0449-X*) Amereon Ltd.

— The Kingdom of Art: Willa Cather's First Principles & Critical Statements, 1893-1896. Slote, Bernice, ed. LC 65-15275. (Illus.). xiv, 489p. 1967. text 50.00 (*0-8032-0012-9*) U of Nebr Pr.

— Later Novels: A Lost Lady; The Professor's House; Death Comes for the Archbishop; Shadows on the Rock; Lucy Gayheart; Sapphira & the Slave Girl. O'Brien, Sharon, ed. LC 89-61430. 988p. 1990. 35.00 (*0-940450-52-6*, Pub. by Library of America) Penguin Putnam.

— A Lost Lady. 1976. 19.95 (*0-8488-0450-3*) Amereon Ltd.

— A Lost Lady. LC 98-34211. 160p. 1999. mass mkt. 4.95 (*0-451-52720-8*, Sig Classics) NAL.

— A Lost Lady. Mignon, Charles W. et al, eds. LC 96-20642. (Willa Cather Scholarly Edition Ser.). (Illus.). xii, 371p. 1997. text 60.00 (*0-8032-1427-8*) U of Nebr Pr.

— A Lost Lady. 174p. 1990. pap. 9.00 (*0-679-72887-2*) Vin Bks.

— A Lost Lady. 1990. reprint ed. lib. bdg. 19.95 (*0-89966-650-7*) Buccaneer Bks.

— A Lost Lady. (Collected Works of Willa Cather). 173p. 1998. reprint ed. lib. bdg. 88.00 (*1-58201-569-4*) Classic Bks.

— Lucy Gayheart. 1976. 21.95 (*0-8488-0451-1*) Amereon Ltd.

— Lucy Gayheart. 240p. 1995. pap. 12.00 (*0-679-72888-0*) Random.

— Lucy Gayheart. large type ed. 225p. 1992. reprint ed. lib. bdg. 19.95 (*1-56054-483-X*) Thorndike Pr.

— My Antonia. 24.95 (*0-88411-287-X*) Amereon Ltd.

— My Antonia. 320p. 1994. mass mkt. 4.95 (*0-553-21418-7*, Bantam Classics) Bantam.

— My Antonia. (Barron's Book Notes Ser.). 1985. pap. 2.50 (*0-8120-3528-3*) Barron.

— My Antonia. LC 95-30223. (Illus.). 244p. 1995. pap. 5.95 (*0-395-75514-X*) HM.

— My Antonia. 288p. 1994. mass mkt. 4.95 (*0-451-52579-5*, Sig Classics) NAL.

— My Antonia. (Critical Editions Ser.). (C). 1997. pap. text. write for info. (*0-393-96790-5*, Norton Paperbks) Norton.

— My Antonia. 1996. 15.95 (*0-679-60205-4*) Random.

— My Antonia. LC 96-223945. 1996. 16.00 (*0-679-44727-X*) Random.

— My Antonia. (Signet Classics). 1994. 10.05 (*0-606-05933-4*, Pub. by Turtleback) Demco.

Cather, Willa. My Antonia. LC 94-20031. (Enriched Classics Ser.). 1994. 10.60 (*0-606-06588-1*, Pub. by Turtleback) Demco.

Cather, Willa. My Antonia. 240p. 1997. pap. 5.95 (*0-460-87723-2*, Everyman's Classic Lib) Tuttle Pubng.

— My Antonia. Mignon, Charles W. & Ronning, Kari, eds. LC 93-50941. (Willa Cather Scholarly Edition Ser.). (Illus.). xx, 415p. 1997. pap. 14.95 (*0-8032-6372-4*, Bison Books) U of Nebr Pr.

— My Antonia. LC 93-2491. (Illus.). 304p. 1994. pap. 9.95 (*0-14-018764-2*, Penguin Classics) Viking Penguin.

— My Antonia. 1997. pap. write for info. (*0-14-771198-3*) Viking Penguin.

— My Antonia. (C). 1999. pap. 10.95 (*0-14-028327-7*) Viking Penguin.

— My Antonia. 1999. audio 16.95 (*0-14-086313-3*) Viking Penguin.

— My Antonia. 256p. 1994. pap. 9.00 (*0-679-74187-9*) Vin Bks.

Cather, Willa. My Antonia. LC 95-206306. 125 p. 1994. write for info. (*0-573-69499-0*) S French Trade.

— My Antonia. large type ed. 352p. 2000. pap. 22.00 (*0-06-095694-1*, HarpCollins) HarperTrade.

Cather, Willa. My Antonia. large type ed. 400p. 1996. reprint ed. lib. bdg. 24.00 (*0-939495-05-8*) North Bks.

— My Antonia. 1992. reprint ed. lib. bdg. 25.95 (*0-89966-977-8*) Buccaneer Bks.

— My Antonia. (Collected Works of Willa Cather). 418p. 1998. reprint ed. lib. bdg. 108.00 (*1-58201-570-8*) Classic Bks.

— My Antonia. 240p. 1998. reprint ed. lib. bdg. 24.00 (*1-58287-051-9*) North Bks.

— My Antonia. O'Brien, Sharon, ed. & intro. by. 344p. 1994. reprint ed. mass mkt. 5.50 (*0-671-89086-7*, WSP) PB.

— My Antonia. Mignon, Charles W. & Ronning, Kari A., eds. LC 93-50941. (Willa Cather Scholarly Edition Ser.: Vol. 2). (Illus.). xxv, 543p. 1995. reprint ed. text 65.00 (*0-8032-1468-5*) U of Nebr Pr.

— My Antonia. unabridged ed. 176p. 1994. pap. text 2.00 (*0-486-28240-6*) Dover.

— My Mortal Enemy. 1976. 17.95 (*0-8488-0452-X*) Amereon Ltd.

— My Mortal Enemy. LC 90-50169. (Vintage Classics Ser.). 144p. 1990. pap. 8.95 (*0-679-73179-2*) Vin Bks.

— Not Under Forty. LC 88-14282. vii, 149p. 1988. pap. 10.00 (*0-8032-6331-7*, Bison Books) U of Nebr Pr.

— Not Under Forty. (Collected Works of Willa Cather). 147p. 1998. reprint ed. lib. bdg. 88.00 (*1-58201-571-6*) Classic Bks.

— Novels & Stories, 1905-1918: The Troll Garden; O Pioneers; The Song of Lark; My Antonia. LC 99-20131. (Library of America College Editions Ser.). 975p. (C). 1999. pap. text 13.95 (*1-883011-74-4*, Pub. by Library of America) Penguin Putnam.

— O Pioneers! lib. bdg. 24.95 (*0-8488-0454-6*) Amereon Ltd.

— O Pioneers! 224p. 1989. mass mkt. 4.95 (*0-553-21358-X*, Bantam Classics) Bantam.

— O Pioneers!, 001. 208p. 1988. pap. 4.95 (*0-395-08365-6*) HM.

***Cather, Willa.** O Pioneers! Lindemann, Marilee, ed. LC 98-35944. (Oxford World's Classics Ser.). 224p. 1999. pap. 7.95 (*0-19-283216-6*) OUP.

Cather, Willa. O Pioneers! (Illus.). 544p. 1992. write for info. (*0-614-32001-1*) Random Hse Value.

— O Pioneers! 1992. mass mkt. 3.99 (*0-8125-2076-9*, Pub. by Tor Bks) St Martin.

— O Pioneers! (Signet Classics). 1988. 10.05 (*0-606-04107-9*, Pub. by Turtleback) Demco.

— O Pioneers! 1989. 10.05 (*0-606-13671-1*, Pub. by Turtleback) Demco.

— O Pioneers! Rosowski, Susan J. et al, eds. LC 96-47330. (Willa Cather Scholarly Edition Ser.). (Illus.). vii, 295p. 1997. pap. 12.95 (*0-8032-6371-6*, Bison Books) U of Nebr Pr.

— O Pioneers! 224p. 1994. pap. 8.95 (*0-14-018775-8*, Penguin Classics) Viking Penguin.

— O Pioneers! LC 92-53878. (Vintage Classics Ser.). 176p. 1992. pap. 9.00 (*0-679-74362-6*) Vin Bks.

— O Pioneers! 1998. lib. bdg. write for info. (*1-56723-027-X*) Yestermorrow.

— O Pioneers ! (C). 1989. mass mkt. 4.95 (*0-451-52285-0*) NAL.

— O Pioneers! abr. ed. (Classics on Cassette Ser.). 1994. 16.00 incl. audio (*0-453-00876-3*, 391292, Pub. by Penguin-HghBrdg) Penguin Putnam.

— O Pioneers! large type ed. (Large Print Heritage Ser.). 259p. 1997. lib. bdg. 28.95 (*1-58118-018-7*, 21493) LRS.

— O Pioneers! 1992. reprint ed. lib. bdg. 25.95 (*0-89966-976-X*) Buccaneer Bks.

— O Pioneers! (Collected Works of Willa Cather). 308p. 1998. reprint ed. lib. bdg. 98.00 (*1-58201-572-4*) Classic Bks.

— O Pioneers! 128p. 1993. reprint ed. pap. text 1.00 (*0-486-27785-2*) Dover.

— O Pioneers! Rosowski, Susan J. et al, eds. LC 91-31149. (Willa Cather Scholarly Edition Ser.). (Illus.). xi, 392p. 1992. reprint ed. text 55.00 (*0-8032-1457-X*) U of Nebr Pr.

— O Pioneers! - Musical. 77p. 1996. pap. 5.95 (*0-87129-617-9*, O07) Dramatic Pub.

— Obscure Destinies. 1976. 21.95 (*0-8488-0453-8*) Amereon Ltd.

***Cather, Willa.** Obscure Destinies: Willa Cather Scholarly Edition. LC 98-13549. (Illus.). 424p. 1998. text 65.00 (*0-8032-1430-8*) U of Nebr Pr.

Cather, Willa. One of Ours. LC 91-50236. (Vintage Classics Ser.). 391p. 1991. pap. 13.00 (*0-679-73744-8*) Vin Bks.

— One of Ours. (Collected Works of Willa Cather). 459p. 1998. reprint ed. lib. bdg. 108.00 (*1-58201-573-2*) Classic Bks.

— Paul's Case & Other Stories. LC 95-49595. (Thrift Editions Ser.). 64p. (Orig.). 1996. pap. text 1.00 (*0-486-29057-3*) Dover.

— Pionniers. Orig. Title: Oh Pioneers!. (FRE.). 310p. 1989. pap. 12.95 (*0-7859-2117-6*, 2070381382) Fr & Eur.

***Cather, Willa.** The Professor's House. Link, Frederick M., ed. (Willa Cather Scholarly Edition Ser.). (Illus.). 2001. text 75.00 (*0-8032-1428-6*) U of Nebr Pr.

Cather, Willa. Professor's House. 1976. 23.95 (*0-8488-0456-2*) Amereon Ltd.

— Professor's House. LC 90-50269. (Vintage Classics Ser.). 283p. 1990. pap. 11.00 (*0-679-73180-6*) Vin Bks.

— The Professor's House. large type ed. (All-Time Favorites Ser.). 299p. 1993. reprint ed. lib. bdg. 19.95 (*1-56054-484-8*) Thorndike Pr.

— The Professor's House. (Collected Works of Willa Cather). 283p. 1998. reprint ed. lib. bdg. 88.00 (*1-58201-574-0*) Classic Bks.

— Sapphira & the Slave Girl. LC 74-20797. 1975. pap. 10.00 (*0-394-71434-2*) Vin Bks.

— Sapphira & the Slave Girl. large type ed. 295p. 1992. reprint ed. lib. bdg. 20.95 (*1-56054-482-1*, G K Hall Lrg Type) Mac Lib Ref.

— Shadows on the Rock. 1976. 23.95 (*0-8488-0455-4*) Amereon Ltd.

— Shadows on the Rock. LC 95-8915. 288p. 1995. pap. 12.00 (*0-679-76404-6*) Vin Bks.

— The Song of the Lark. 34.95 (*0-88411-288-8*) Amereon Ltd.

— The Song of the Lark, 001. LC 87-22822. 480p. 1983. pap. 5.95 (*0-395-34530-8*) HM.

— The Song of the Lark. LC PS3505.A87S6 1999b. 480p. 1999. pap. 12.00 (*0-375-70645-3*) Knopf.

— The Song of the Lark. large type ed. 667p. 1991. reprint ed. lib. bdg. 21.95 (*1-56054-281-0*) Thorndike Pr.

— The Song of the Lark. 1990. reprint ed. lib. bdg. 31.95 (*0-89968-493-9*) Buccaneer Bks.

— The Song of the Lark. (Collected Works of Willa Cather). 489p. 1998. reprint ed. lib. bdg. 108.00 (*1-58201-575-9*) Classic Bks.

— The Song of the Lark: The Sleeper-McCann House. 432p. 1991. mass mkt. 5.95 (*0-451-52533-7*, Sig Classics) NAL.

— Stories, Poems, & Other Writings. O'Brien, Sharon, ed. 1039p. 1992. 35.00 (*0-940450-71-2*, Pub. by Library of America) Penguin Putnam.

— Three Novels: O Pioneers!, The Song of the Lark & My Antonia. 816p. 1998. pap. 17.95 (*0-7867-0598-1*) Carroll & Graf.

***Cather, Willa.** Troll Garden. (Illus.). (J). 2000. pap. 12.00 (*0-8032-6403-8*) U of Nebr Pr.

Cather, Willa. The Troll Garden: A Definitive Edition. Woodress, James L., ed. LC 82-20138. xxx, 176p. 1983. text 25.00 (*0-8032-1417-0*) U of Nebr Pr.

***Cather, Willa.** The Troll Garden & Selected Stories. LC 99-49990. 300p. 1999. 27.95 (*1-56000-470-3*) Transaction Pubs.

Cather, Willa. Uncle Valentine & Other Stories: Willa Cather's Uncollected Short Fiction, 1915-1929. Slote, Bernice, ed. LC 72-83755. xxx, 183p. 1973. reprint ed. pap. 11.95 (*0-8032-6317-1*, Bison Books) U of Nebr Pr.

— Willa Cather in Europe: Her Own Story of the First Journey. LC 88-1125. xiv, 178p. 1988. pap. 9.00 (*0-8032-6333-3*, Bison Books) U of Nebr Pr.

— Willa Cather in Person: Interviews, Speeches, & Letters. Bohlke, L. Brent, ed. LC 86-19161. (Illus.). xxxiii, 202p. 1986. reprint ed. pap. 12.95 (*0-8032-6326-0*, Bison Books); reprint ed. text 35.00 (*0-8032-1184-8*) U of Nebr Pr.

— Willa Cather on Writing: Critical Studies on Writing As an Art. LC 87-30078. xxvi, 126p. 1988. pap. 12.00 (*0-8032-6332-5*, Bison Books) U of Nebr Pr.

— Willa Cather's Collected Short Fiction, 1892-1912. rev. ed. Faulkner, Virginia, ed. LC 73-126046. xlii, 601p. 1970. text 55.00 (*0-8032-0770-0*) U of Nebr Pr.

— The World & the Parish: Willa Cather's Articles & Reveiws, 1893-1902, Vol. 2. Curtin, William M., ed. LC 79-21110. 548p. reprint ed. pap. 169.90 (*0-7837-8104-0*, 204790700002) Bks Demand.

— The World & the Parish: Willa Cather's Articles & Reviews, 1893-1902, Vol. 1. Curtin, William M., ed. LC 79-21110. 524p. 1970. reprint ed. pap. 162.50 (*0-7837-8103-2*, 204790700001) Bks Demand.

— Youth & the Bright Medusa. (Collected Works of Willa Cather). 303p. 1998. reprint ed. lib. bdg. 98.00 (*1-58201-576-7*) Classic Bks.

Cather, Willa & Dickstein, Morris. A Lost Lady. LC 98-11660. (Penguin Twentieth-Century Classics Ser.). 1999. 8.95 (*0-14-118131-1*) Viking Penguin.

Cather, Willa & Harbison, Sherrill. The Song of the Lark. LC 98-41698. (Penguin Twentieth-Century Classics Ser.). 400p. 1999. pap. 9.95 (*0-14-118104-4*) Viking Penguin.

Cather, Willa & Milmine, Georgine. The Life of Mary Baker G. Eddy & the History of Christian Science. LC 92-37437. (Illus.). xxvii, 520p. (C). 1993. pap. 14.95 (*0-8032-6349-X*, Bison Books); text 45.00 (*0-8032-1453-7*) U of Nebr Pr.

— The Life of Mary Baker G. Eddy & the History of Christian Science. (Collected Works of Willa Cather). 495p. 1998. reprint ed. lib. bdg. 108.00 (*1-58201-568-6*) Classic Bks.

Cather, Willa, et al. Willa Cather's University Days: The University of Nebraska, 1890-1895. (Illus.). 40p. 1995. pap. text 10.00 (*0-938932-07-1*) U Nebr CFGPS.

Catherall, John. Real Estate Tax Digest. 3rd ed. LC 98-85393. 1998. write for info. (*0-7913-3459-7*) Warren Gorham & Lamont.

Catherall, John, jt. auth. see Feld, Daniel E.

***Catherine & Noffke, Suzanne.** The Letters of Catherine of Siena: Vol. 1: Letters 1-70. 2nd ed. LC 99-54886. (Medieval & Renaissance Texts & Studies: Vol. 202). 1999. write for info. (*0-86698-244-2*) MRTS.

Catherine, Jenna. Conversing with the Future: Visions of 2020. LC 97-38504. 210p. 1998. per. 15.00 (*0-926524-45-3*) Granite Pub.

***Catherine, Mary.** Peru. LC 99-42409. (Illus.). (J). 2000. lib. bdg. write for info. (*1-56766-739-2*) Childs World.

Catherine, Susan. Overhead in London Snack Bars. (Overheard Ser.: No. 6). (Illus.). 64p. (Orig.). 1987. pap. 2.50 (*0-944617-06-9*) Cherry Stone Pr.

— Overheard at America's Lunch Counters, No. 7. (Overheard Ser.). (Illus.). 64p. (Orig.). 1987. pap. 2.50 (*0-944617-07-7*) Cherry Stone Pr.

— Overheard in Seattle Donut Shops. (Overheard Ser.: No. 8). (Illus.). 64p. (Orig.). 1988. pap. 2.98 (*0-944617-08-5*) Cherry Stone Pr.

Catherine Yi-yu Chu Woo. Luster of Jade: Poetry, Painting, & Music. (University Research Lectures: No. 7). (Illus.). 86p. 1992. 30.00 (*1-879691-10-8*) SDSU Press.

Cathers, David. Stickley Style: Arts & Crafts Homes in the Craftsman Tradition. LC 99-24774. (Illus.). 224p. 1999. 40.00 (*0-684-85603-4*) S&S Childrens.

Cathers, David M. Furniture of the American Arts & Crafts Movement: Furniture Made by Gustav Stickley, L. & J. G. Stickley & the Roycroft Shop. rev. ed. (Illus.). 256p. (Orig.). 1996. pap. 27.50 (*0-940326-19-1*) Turn of Cent.

Cathers, David M., jt. auth. see Clark, Robert J.

Catherwood, Benjamin F. Basic Theories of Distribution. LC 71-121454. (Essay Index Reprint Ser.). 1977. 23.95 (*0-8369-1700-6*) Ayer.

Catherwood, C. Five Evangelical Leaders. 11.99 (*1-85792-065-1*, Pub. by Christian Focus) Spring Arbor Dist.

Catherwood, Christopher. Crash Course on Christian Teaching. 1998. 10.99 (*0-340-71018-7*, Pub. by Hodder & Stought Ltd) Trafalgar.

— Crash Course on Church History. (Illus.). 208p. 1998. pap. 13.95 (*0-340-71014-4*, Pub. by Hodder & Stought Ltd) Trafalgar.

***Catherwood, Christopher.** Five Leading Reformers: Lives at a Watershed of History; Martin Luther, Thomas Cranmer, John Cal. 2000. pap. text 10.99 (*1-85792-507-6*) Christian Focus.

Catherwood, Christopher. Martyn Lloyd Jones: From Wales To Westminster. 1999. pap. text 5.99 (*1-85792-349-9*) Christian Focus.

— Why the Nations Rage: Killing in the Name of God. 271p. 1998. pap. 14.95 (*0-340-69062-3*, Pub. by Hodder & Stought Ltd) Trafalgar.

Catherwood, Di, jt. ed. see Boulton-Lewis, Gillian.

Catherwood, E., ed. Twelve Baskets Full. 16.99 (*1-85792-008-2*, Pub. by Christian Focus) Spring Arbor Dist.

Catherwood, F., jt. auth. see Burford, Robert.

Catherwood, Mary. Chase of Saint-Castin, & Other Stories of the French in the New World. LC 77-128723. (Short Story Index Reprint Ser.). 1977. 19.95 (*0-8369-3614-0*) Ayer.

— Romance of Dollard. LC 75-137725. (American Fiction Reprint Ser.). 1977. 20.95 (*0-8369-7024-1*) Ayer.

Catherwood, Mary H. Mackinac & Lake Stories. 1972. reprint ed. lib. bdg. 19.50 (*0-8422-8023-5*) Irvington.

— The Queen of the Swamp & Other Plain Americans. 1972. reprint ed. lib. bdg. 30.00 (*0-8422-8024-3*) Irvington.

Cathey, Boyt H. Cathey Family History & Genealogy (1700-1900), Vol. 1. LC 93-79588. (Illus.). 600p. 1993. lib. bdg. 32.50 (*1-881851-03-6*) Genealogy Pub.

C

Cathey, Cornelius O. Agriculture in North Carolina Before the Civil War. (Illus.). viii, 46p. 1974. pap. 4.00 (*0-86526-073-7*) NC Archives.

Cathey, Gerald M. Dental Anatomy. (Dental Laboratory Technology Manuals Ser.). viii, 236p. 1972. pap. 34.95 (*0-8078-7905-3*) U of NC Pr.

Cathey, J. J. Schaum's Outline of Electronic Devices & Circuits. 352p. (C). 1989. pap. 14.95 (*0-07-010274-0*) McGraw.

Cathey, J. J. & Nasar, Syed A. Schaum's Outline of Basic Electrical Engineering. 304p. (C). 1983. pap. 14.95 (*0-07-010234-1*) McGraw.

Cathey, Jimmy J., ed. see Nasar, Syed A.

Cathey, Marc. Successful Summer Gardening: Heat Zone Gardening. LC 97-31250. (Illus.). 192p. (gr. 11). 1999. pap. 24.95 (*0-7835-5279-3*) Time-Life.

Cathey, Oliver, et al. Public Golf in Orange County California. 80p. 1994. pap. text. write for info. (*0-9641557-0-2*) R Limmers Golf.

***Cathey, Patrice.** Nubian Princess. 4p. 1999. pap. 3.00 (*0-9673501-0-7*) Onya Pubg.

Cathey, W. Thomas. Optical Information Processing & Holography. 414p. (C). 1974. text 54.50 (*0-471-14078-3*) Krieger.

Cathiard, Yvette. Dimey Ou la Blessure De l'Ogre: Dimey or the Ogre's Wound. (FRE.). 220p. 1995. pap. 54.95 (*2-86808-074-X*) Intl Scholars.

— La Morsure de L'Ange. 200p. 59.95 (*2-86808-091-X*) Intl Scholars.

Cathie, Bruce. The Bridge to Infinity. 220p. 1997. pap. 14.95 (*0-932813-05-4*) Adventures Unltd.

— The Energy Grid. 255p. 1997. reprint ed. pap. 15.95 (*0-932813-44-5*) Adventures Unltd.

— The Harmonic Conquest of Space. (Illus.). 248p. 1998. pap. 16.95 (*0-932813-62-3*) Adventures Unltd.

Cathie, Bruce L. The Bridge to Infinity - Harmonic 371244. rev. ed. LC 88-33299. (Illus.). 200p. (C). 1989. pap. 11.95 (*0-922356-00-9*) Amer West Pubs.

— The Energy Grid: Harmonic Six Hundred Ninety-Five & the Pulse of the Universe. (Illus.). 242p. (Orig.). (C). 1990. pap. 13.95 (*0-922356-20-3*) Amer West Pubs.

Cathie, John. European Food Aid Policy. LC 97-70895. (Illus.). 160p. 1997. text 55.95 (*1-85972-599-6*, Pub. by Ashgate Pub) Ashgate Pub Co.

C

Cathie, John & Dick, Hermann. Food Security & Macroeconomic Stabilization: A Case Study of Botswana, 1965-1984. 172p. 1987. lib. bdg. 53.75 (*3-16-345261-2*, Pub. by JCB Mohr) Coronet Bks.

Cathie, Kate. Secondary Fibre Treatment. 100p. Date not set. pap. 100.00 (*1-85802-033-6*, Pub. by Pira Internatl) Bks Intl VA.

Cathie, Kate & Guest, David. PIRA Guide to Wastepaper. 134p. 1991. 65.00 (*0-902799-81-9*, Pub. by Pira Internatl) Bks Intl VA.

Cathles, Lawrence M. The Viscosity of the Earth's Mantle. LC 74-16162. 362p. 1975. reprint ed. pap. 112.30 (*0-608-03321-9*, 206403300008) Bks Demand.

Catholic. Liturgy of Hours Supplmt. 1990. pap. 2.50 (*0-89942-405-8*, 405) Catholic Bk Pub.

Catholic. Way of the Cross. (Saint Joseph Picture Bks.). (Illus.). (J). 1992. pap. 1.25 (*0-89942-497-X*, 497-00) Catholic Bk Pub.

Catholic. Works of Mercy. (Saint Joseph Picture Bks.). (Illus.). (J). 1987. pap. 1.25 (*0-89942-305-1*, 305-00) Catholic Bk Pub.

Catholic Bishops of England & Wales Staff. A Catechism of Christian Doctrine. LC 82-50599. 72p. 1988. reprint ed. pap. 2.50 (*0-89555-176-X*) TAN Bks Pubs.

Catholic Book Publishers Staff. St. Joseph Millennium Prayer Book. (Illus.). 192p. 1998. 5.95 (*0-89942-930-0*, 930/04) Catholic Bk Pub.

— St. Joseph Missal Set - Blk Imt L. 1992. pap. text 8.25 (*0-89942-741-3*) Catholic Bk Pub.

Catholic Book Publishers Staff, ed. St. Joseph Christian Prayer Guide, 2000 ed. 1997. pap. 1.75 (*0-89942-430-9*) Catholic Bk Pub.

Catholic Book Publishing Staff. Every Day Is a Gift. (Spiritual Life Ser.). 192p. 1984. vinyl bd. 6.25 (*0-89942-195-4*, 195/09) Catholic Bk Pub.

***Catholic Book Publishing Staff.** St. Joseph Missal Guide 2000. (St. Joseph Liturgy Guides for 2000 Ser.). 1999. pap. 1.75 (*0-89942-431-7*) Catholic Bk Pub.

Catholic Book Publishing Staff, ed. Dictionary of Mary. expanded rev. ed. 1998. 17.95 (*0-89942-368-X*, 367/22) Catholic Bk Pub.

***Catholic Book Publishing Staff, ed.** Libro de Bolsillo de Oraciones Catolicas.Tr. of Pocket Book of Catholic Prayers. 2000. pap. 4.95 (*0-89942-332-9*) Catholic Bk Pub.

Catholic Book Publishing Staff, ed. St. Rita: Saint of the Impossible. 128p. 1998. 2.95 (*0-89942-127-X*, 128/04) Catholic Bk Pub.

Catholic Book Publishing Staff, ed. see Lovasik.

Catholic Book Publishing Staff, ed. see Winkler, Jude.

Catholic Book Staff. Liturgy of the Hours Annual Guide, 2000 Edition. 1.75 (*0-89942-429-5*, 400-G) Catholic Bk Pub.

— St. Joseph Children's Missal Boxed Gift Set. 1992. pap. text 17.25 (*0-89942-744-8*, B806/82W); pap. text 17.25 (*0-89942-745-6*, B806/82B) Catholic Bk Pub.

— St. Joseph Children's Missal Boxed Gift Set. 1996. pap. text 10.50 (*0-89942-743-X*, B806/42B) Catholic Bk Pub.

Catholic Book Staff & Donaghy, Thomas J. Lives of the Saints II, Vol. 2. large type ed. (Illus.). 528p. 1993. 7.95 (*0-89942-875-4*, 875/22) Catholic Bk Pub.

Catholic Charities Refugee Services Staff, ed. The First Supper: A Collection of Stories & Recipes from the Women Refugees of Memphis. 126p. 1997. pap. write for info. (*0-9659923-0-6*) Cath Charities.

Catholic Charities USA Staff, jt. auth. see Catholic Health Association of the United States Staff.

Catholic Church, jt. auth. see Lutheran World Federation Staff.

Catholic Church Clergy Staff & Cleveland Museum of Art Staff. Vatican Treasures: Early Christian, Renaissance, & Baroque Art from the Papal Collections: An Exhibition in Honor of the Sesquicentenary of the Diocese of Cleveland. LC 97-38598. 1998. write for info. (*0-940717-44-1*); pap. write for info. (*0-940717-45-X*) Cleveland Mus Art.

Catholic Church Staff. Equipped for the Work of Ministry: A Reflection & Planning Guide for the Continuing Formation of Priests. LC 96-152559. (United States Catholic Conference Publications). iv, 32 p. 1996. write for info. (*1-57455-029-2*) US Catholic.

— Norms for Priestly Formation, 2 vols. LC 97-146505. (United States Catholic Conference Publications). 1994. write for info. (*1-55586-619-0*) US Catholic.

Catholic Church Staff & Path to Peace Foundation Staff. The United Nations: A Family of Nations?: A Seminar on the Address of His Holiness Pope John Paul II to the United Nations Organization: Trusteeship Council Chamber, United Nations Headquarters, New York City, Wednesday, 8 May 1996. LC 96-28118. 1996. pap. 20.00 (*0-9651613-1-5*) Path to Peace.

Catholic Church Staff & United States Catholic Conference Staff. Called to Global Solidarity: International Challenges for U. S. Parishes: A Statement of the National Conference of Catholic Bishops with Parish Resources. LC 98-158688. 42p. 1998. pap. write for info. (*1-57455-118-3*) US Catholic.

Catholic Church Staff, jt. auth. see Melina, Livio.

Catholic Edition. PM-My First Book: Prayer Boy-Baptist. 1996. 12.95 (*0-88271-323-X*) Regina Pr.

Catholic Health Association of the United States Staff. Medicare & Medicaid Managed Care: A Strategic Guide to Serving Dually Eligible Persons Throughout the Continuum. LC 98-221767. (Mission in Action Ser.). xv, 131 p. 1998. write for info. (*0-87125-244-9*) Cath Health.

***Catholic Health Association of the United States Staff & Catholic Charities USA Staff.** Ministry Partners in Senior Housing: A Shared Vision for Service: Principles for Catholic-Sponsored Assisted Living & Senior Housing. LC 99-203064. 8 p. 1998. pap. write for info. (*0-87125-250-3*) Cath Health.

Catholic Human Services Staff. The Nuts & Bolts of Open Adoption. 1995. 150.00 (*0-9641035-3-2*) R-Squared Pr.

Catholic Institute of Education Staff. Learning for Living - A Catholic Contribution to the Culture of Learning & Teaching in South Africa. 64p. 1999. pap. 14.95 (*0-7021-4630-7*, Pub. by Juta & Co) Intl Spec Bk.

Catholic Mirror Staff. Rome's Challenge. LC 95-70520. 32p. 1995. pap. 0.99 (*1-57258-052-6*) Teach Servs.

Catholic News Service Staff, ed. John Paul II Speaks to Youth! World Youth Day. LC 93-61455. 130p. 1993. 19.95 (*0-89870-479-0*); pap. 11.95 (*0-89870-480-4*) Ignatius Pr.

***Catholic PM Staff.** Precious Moments Bible for Catholics. 1999. pap. text 24.99 (*0-7852-0054-1*) Word Pub.

Catholic Publication Society Staff. Manresa: or The Spiritual Exercises of St. Ignatius. 394p. 1996. reprint ed. pap. 21.95 (*1-56459-923-X*) Kessinger Pub.

— St. Joseph Missal Set - White Vinyl. 1993. pap. text 6.95 (*0-89942-738-3*) Catholic Bk Pub.

***Catholic Reader Staff, ed.** Catholic Reader's Text Bible. 1632p. 2000. pap. text 19.99 (*0-19-528265-5*); pap. text 12.99 (*0-19-528266-3*) OUP.

Catholic Treasures Staff, ed. Letter to a Fallen Away Catholic. 2nd ed. (Illus.). 109p. 1994. reprint ed. pap. 4.95 (*0-9620994-5-7*) Cath Treas.

Catholic Truth Society London Staff. Catecismo Basico de la Doctrina Cristiana: Spanish Basic Catechism (Pocket)Tr. of Spanish Basic Catechism (Pocket). (SPA.). 67p. 1992. 0.25 (*1-56036-028-3*, 35704) AMI Pr.

Catholic University of America, Music Education Wo. Music Pedagogy: The Proceedings of the Workshop on Music Pedagogy, Conducted at the Catholic University of America, June 15-16, 1962. Werder, Richard H., ed. LC 64-66051. 96p. reprint ed. pap. 30.00 (*0-608-10887-1*, 200535900053) Bks Demand.

Catholic University of America, School of Law Staff. Jubilee Law Lectures. LC 71-134067. (Essay Index Reprint Ser.). 1977. 19.95 (*0-8369-1907-6*) Ayer.

Catholic University of America Staff. Catholic University Studies in German, 19 vols. reprint ed. 712.50 (*0-404-50220-2*) AMS Pr.

— Catholic University Studies in Romance Languages & Literatures, 60 vols. reprint ed. 2275.00 (*0-404-50300-4*) AMS Pr.

— New Catholic Encyclopedia, 19 vols., Set. LC 66-22292. 1989. suppl. ed. 940.00 (*0-07-010235-X*) J Heraty Assocs.

— Psychological Counseling of Adolescents: The Proceedings. Steimel, Raymond J., ed. LC 62-6111. 176p. reprint ed. pap. 54.60 (*0-608-11308-5*, 200521200051) Bks Demand.

— Studies in American Church History, 25 vols. reprint ed. 958.00 (*0-404-57750-4*) AMS Pr.

Catholic University of America, Washington, D. C. Catalog of the Oliveira Lima Library, 2 vols., Set. 1970. 255.00 (*0-8161-0873-0*, G K Hall & Co) Mac Lib Ref.

— Proceedings of the Catholic University of America, Washington, D. C., Plasma Space Science Symposium, June 11-14, 1963. Chang, C. C. & Huang, S. S., eds. (Astrophysics & Space Science Library: No.3). 377p. 1965. text 192.50 (*90-277-0112-1*) Kluwer Academic.

Catholic Women of Cincinnati Staff. A Feast in Eden: A Garden of Culinary Delights. (Illus.). 286p. 1997. spiral bd. 17.50 (*0-9660278-0-9*) Catholic Women.

***Catholic Womens Devotional Bible Staff.** Catholic Women's Devotional Bible. 2000. 24.99 (*0-310-90061-1*); pap. 19.99 (*0-310-90057-3*) Zondervan.

Catholicon Anglicum Staff. An English Latin Wordbook. (EETS, OS Ser.: No. 75). 1972. reprint ed. 70.00 (*0-527-00074-4*) Periodicals Srv.

Catholicus. DOA: The Ambush of the Universal Cathechism. 170p. 1995. pap. 13.95 (*1-883357-12-8*, Crisis Bks) Dumb Ox Bks.

Cathy, Robert, ed. see Thorndike, Karl.

Caticchio, John A. Putting Humpty Back Together. Goren, Eileen, ed. 152p. 1990. pap. 9.95 (*0-9625876-0-5*) Vivere Pub.

Catich, Edward M. The Origin of the Serif: Brush Writings & Roman Letters. Gilroy, Mary W., ed. (Illus.). 311p. 1991. write for info. (*0-9629740-0-5*); pap. write for info. (*0-9629740-1-3*) St Ambrose U.

Catignani, Emile, jt. auth. see Kozar, Andy.

Cativiela, A., tr. see Bonnet, L. & Schroeder, A.

Cativiela, A., tr. see Schroeder, A. & Bonnet, L.

Cativiela, A., tr. see Schroeder, L. Bonnet.

Catlett & Libbin. Investing in Futures. LC 98-33925. (Agriculture Ser.). (C). 1998. text 72.95 (*0-8273-8570-6*) Delmar.

Catlett, Autumn. Black Butterfly. LC 98-96490. 219p. 1998. write for info. (*0-9666709-0-6*) Black & Blue Pub.

Catlett, Charles T. Home for Sale by Owner. 1991. pap. 9.00 (*0-9619946-0-6*) Catlett Bks.

Catlett, Estell. Track down Your Ancestors. large type ed. 192p. 1990. 19.95 (*1-85089-380-2*, Pub. by ISIS Lrg Prnt) Transaction Pubs.

***Catlett, Estelle.** Track down Your Ancestors: Draw up Your Family Tree. 3rd ed. (Illus.). 160p. 2001. pap. 7.95 (*0-7160-2082-3*, Pub. by Elliot RW Bks) Midpt Trade.

***Catlett, J. Stephen.** Martin's & Miller's Greensboro. (Images of America Ser.). (Illus.). 128p. 1999. pap. 18.99 (*0-7385-0315-0*) Arcadia Publng.

Catlett, J. Stephen. A New Guide to the Collections in the Library of the American Philosophical Society. LC 86-71834. (Memoirs Ser.: Vol. 66S). (C). 1987. 20.00 (*0-87169-660-6*, M66S-CAS) Am Philos.

Catlett, Joyce, jt. auth. see Firestone, Robert.

Catlett, Joyce, jt. auth. see Firestone, Robert W.

Catlett, Lowell B., et al. Cash Flow Planning in Agriculture. LC 93-45684. (Illus.). 214p. (C). 1994. pap. text 39.95 (*0-8138-0642-9*) Iowa St U Pr.

Catlett, Robert H., ed. Readings of Biological Concern. LC 72-6695. 84p. 1972. pap. text 7.75 (*0-8422-0239-0*) Irvington.

Catlett, Ruel D. Guest Editorial. 62p. (Orig.). 1989. pap. 3.95 (*0-940999-46-3*, C-2159) Star Bible.

Catlette, Bill & Hadden, Richard. Contented Cows Give Better Milk: The Plain Truth about Employee Relations & Your Bottom Line. (Illus.). 224p. 1998. 30.00 (*1-890651-04-4*, Saltillo Press) Williford Communs.

Catleugh, Jon. William De Morgan Tiles. (Illus.). 134p. 1991. pap. 20.00 (*0-903685-27-2*, Pub. by R Dennis) Antique Collect.

Catley, Alison. Rabbit. (Illus.). 32p. (J). (ps-1). 1993. 15.95 (*0-09-174408-3*, Pub. by Hutchnson) Trafalgar.

Catley, Bob. Globalising Australian Capitalism. (Illus.). 272p. (C). 1996. text 69.95 (*0-521-56246-5*) Cambridge U Pr.

Catley, Bob & Cristaudo, Wayne. This Great Beast: Progress & the Modern State. LC 97-74439. (Avebury Series in Philosophy). 430p. 1997. text 91.95 (*1-84014-300-2*, Pub. by Ashgate Pub) Ashgate Pub Co.

Catley, Bob & Dugis, Vinsensio. Australian Indonesian Relations since 1945: The Garuda & the Kangaroo. LC 98-72800. 356p. 1998. text 78.95 (*1-84014-837-3*, Pub. by Ashgate Pub) Ashgate Pub Co.

Catley, Bob & Keliat, Makmur. Spratlys: The Dispute in the South China Sea. LC 97-23846. 232p. (C). 1997. text 77.95 (*1-85521-995-6*, Pub. by Dartmth Pub) Ashgate Pub Co.

Catley, Bob, jt. auth. see Mosler, David.

Catley, Bryan. Art Deco & Other Figures. (Illus.). 348p. 1978. 89.50 (*0-902028-57-X*) Antique Collect.

***Catlin.** International Business Cultural Sourcebook & Case Studies. 2nd ed. (SWC-General Business Ser.). 2001. pap. 18.00 (*0-324-05573-0*) Thomson Learn.

Catlin, Alan. Shelley & the Romantics. limited ed. LC 95-120114. 20p. (Orig.). 1994. pap. 7.00 (*0-938566-64-4*) Adastra Pr.

***Catlin, Alan.** Under the Volcano. 24p. 2000. pap. 3.95 (*0-9676660-5-8*, Pick Pocket Pr) Phony Lid Pubns.

Catlin, Alan. Visiting Day on the Psychiatric Ward. limited ed. 24p. 1984. pap. 7.95 (*0-944754-04-X*) Pudding Hse Pubns.

Catlin, Amy, jt. auth. see Dunnigan, Timothy.

Catlin, Avery. Standard BASIC Programming with True BASIC. (Illus.). 400p. (C). 1987. pap. text 34.00 (*0-13-841578-1*) P-H.

Catlin, Barbara. Shotgun Wedding. (Special Edition Ser.: No. 724). 1992. per. 3.29 (*0-373-09724-7*, 5-09724-1) Harlequin Bks.

Catlin, Brian. Programming the Microsoft WIN32 Driver Model. 1998. pap. 44.99 (*1-57231-850-3*) Microsoft.

Catlin, Cynthia. More Toddlers Together: The Complete Planning Guide for a Toddler Curriculum, Vol. II. LC 96-26582. (Illus.). 272p. (Orig.). 1996. pap. 24.95 (*0-87659-179-9*) Gryphon Hse.

— Toddlers Together: The Complete Planning Guide to a Toddler Curriculum. (Illus.). 319p. (Orig.). 1998. pap. text 24.95 (*0-87659-171-3*) Gryphon Hse.

Catlin, Cynthia G. The Calusa Indians of Florida, Vol. 1. LC 96-208076. 40p. (Orig.). (J). (gr. 4 up). 1996. pap. 8.95 (*0-9648842-2-4*) M S Gilliland.

Catlin, D. E. Estimation, Control, & the Discrete Kalman Filter. (Applied Mathematical Sciences Ser.: Vol. 71). (Illus.). xiii, 274p. 1988. 76.95 (*0-387-96777-X*) Spr-Verlag.

Catlin, David T. A Naturalist's Blue Ridge Parkway. LC 83-26003. 234p. 1984. pap. 16.95 (*0-87049-430-9*) U of Tenn Pr.

Catlin, George. The Breath of Life or Mal-Respiration. (Works of George Catlin). 1990. reprint ed. lib. bdg. 79.00 (*0-7812-2250-8*) Rprt Serv.

— Catlin's Letters & Notes on the North American Indians. 290p. 1995. write for info. (*1-57215-195-1*) World Pubns.

— Catlin's North American Indian Portfolio. (Works of George Catlin). 1990. reprint ed. lib. bdg. 198.00 (*0-7812-2248-6*) Rprt Serv.

— Catlin's Notes on Eight Years Travels & Residence in Europe. (Works of George Catlin). 1990. reprint ed. lib. bdg. 79.00 (*0-7812-2249-4*) Rprt Serv.

— Cry of the Thunderbird: The American Indian's Own Story. Hamilton, Charles, ed. LC 70-177336. (Civilization of the American Indian Ser.: Vol. 119). (Illus.). 283p. 1977. pap. 18.95 (*0-8061-1292-1*) U of Okla Pr.

— Dress & Decoration Of The American Indian, 1. 1999. 19.95 (*1-885440-49-9*) First Glance.

— Episodes from "Life among the Indians" & "Last Rambles" unabridged ed. Ross, Marvin C., ed. & intro. by. LC 97-31062. (Illus.). 368p. 1998. reprint ed. pap. 14.95 (*0-486-29934-1*) Dover.

— Last Rambles Amongst the Indians of the Rocky Mountains & the Andes. (Works of George Catlin). 1990. reprint ed. lib. bdg. 79.00 (*0-685-44759-6*) Rprt Serv.

— Last Rambles Amongst the Indians of the Rocky Mountains & the Andes. (LC History-America-E). 361p. 1999. reprint ed. lib. bdg. 89.00 (*0-7812-4245-2*) Rprt Serv.

— Letters & Notes on the Manners, Customs & Conditions of the North American Indians, Vol. 1. LC 64-18844. (Illus.). 264p. 1973. reprint ed. pap. 9.95 (*0-486-22118-0*) Dover.

— Letters & Notes on the Manners, Customs & Conditions of the North American Indians, Vol. 2. LC 64-18844. (Illus.). 266p. 1973. reprint ed. pap. 9.95 (*0-486-22119-9*) Dover.

***Catlin, George.** Letters & Notes on the North American Indians. (Illus.). 290p. 1999. reprint ed. text 30.00 (*0-7881-6659-X*) DIANE Pub.

Catlin, George. Letters Notes, on the Manners, Customs & Condition of the North American Indians. (Works of George Catlin). 1990. reprint ed. lib. bdg. 79.00 (*0-7812-2247-8*) Rprt Serv.

***Catlin, George.** Life Amongst the Indians. A Book for Youth. (LC History-America-E). 339p. 1999. reprint ed. lib. bdg. 89.00 (*0-7812-4246-0*) Rprt Serv.

— North & South American Indians. (LC History-America-E). 99p. 1999. reprint ed. lib. bdg. 69.00 (*0-7812-4247-9*) Rprt Serv.

Catlin, George. O-Kee-Pa, a Religious Ceremony & Other Customs of the Mandans. (Works of George Catlin). 1990. reprint ed. lib. bdg. 79.00 (*0-7812-2253-2*) Rprt Serv.

— The Story of the Political Philosophers, 2 vols, Set. 1976. 500.00 (*0-87968-436-4*) Gordon Pr.

Catlin, George & Matthiessen, Peter. North American Indians. (Illus.). 560p. 1989. pap. 13.95 (*0-14-025267-3*, Penguin Bks) Viking Penguin.

Catlin, George B., jt. auth. see Ross, Robert B.

Catlin, Linda B. & White. Cross-Cultural Sourcebook for Business. (C). 1994. mass mkt. 21.95 (*0-538-83518-4*, GN71AA) S-W Pub.

Catlin, Mark G. The Art of Soccer: A Better Way to Play. rev. ed. (Illus.). 206p. (Orig.). 1993. pap., per. 19.95 (*0-9626834-2-6*) Soccer Bks.

— Good N Fun Soccer Manual. (Illus.). 91p. 1994. pap. text 11.95 (*0-9626834-8-5*) Soccer Bks.

— Player Picker Software. 1993. pap. 24.95 (*0-9626834-3-4*) Soccer Bks.

Catlin, Robert A. Land Use Planning, Environmental Protection & Growth Management: The Florida Experience. LC 97-22724. 270p. (C). 1997. ring bd. 54.95 (*1-57504-042-5*, 042-5) CRC Pr.

— Racial Politics & Urban Planning: Gary, Indiana, 1980-1989. LC 92-43016. (Illus.). 256p. (C). 1993. text 35.00 (*0-8131-1798-4*) U Pr of Ky.

Catlin, Robin J., ed. Appleton & Lange's Review for the USMLE Step 2. 2nd ed. LC 95-50682. 331p. (C). 1996. pap. 36.95 (*0-8385-0266-0*, A0266-5, Apple Lange Med) McGraw.

Catlin, Steven. Work Less & Play More. rev. ed. LC 96-50307. (Illus.). 200p. 1997. pap. 14.00 (*0-9654188-0-4*) Kimberlite Pub.

Catlin, Warren B. The Progress of Economics: A History of Economic Thought. LC 61-15681. 788p. 1962. text 67.50 (*0-8290-0200-6*) Irvington.

Catling, Chris. Florence & Tuscany. LC 93-34986. (Eyewitness Travel Guides Ser.). (Illus.). 312p. 1994. pap. 22.95 (*1-56458-502-6*) DK Pub Inc.

Catling, Christopher. Amsterdam. (Illustrated Travel Guides from Thomas Cook Ser.). (Illus.). 192p. 1993. pap. 12.95 (*0-8442-9043-2*, Passprt Bks) NTC Contemp Pub Co.

— Amsterdam. 2nd rev. ed. (Passport's Illustrated Travel Guides Ser.). (Illus.). 192p. 1996. pap. 14.95 (*0-8442-4832-0*, 48320, Passprt Bks) NTC Contemp Pub Co.

— Crete. (Thomas Cook Illustrated Guides Ser.). (Illus.). 192p. (Orig.). 1996. pap. 12.95 (*0-8442-9164-1*, Passprt Bks) NTC Contemp Pub Co.

— Madeira. LC 94-68478. (Illustrated Travel Guides from Thomas Cook Ser.). (Illus.). 192p. (Orig.). 1994. pap. 12.95 (*0-8442-9071-8*, Passprt Bks) NTC Contemp Pub Co.

***Catling, Christopher.** Passport's Illustrated Guide to Amsterdam. 3rd ed. (Passport's Illustrated Travel Guides from Thomas Cook Ser.). 192p. 2000. pap. 14.95 (*0-658-00151-5*, 001515) NTC Contemp Pub Co.

Catling, Christopher. Umbria, the Marches & San Marino. (Regional Guides of Italy Ser.). (Illus.). 192p. 1994. pap. 16.95 (*0-8442-9964-2*, 99642, Passprt Bks) NTC Contemp Pub Co.

Catling, Christopher, ed. On the Road around Northern Italy: Driving Holidays & Tours in Tuscany, Umbria, the Italian Lakes & Rivieria, Veneto & the South Tyrol. LC DG416.O5 1998. (On the Road Around...Ser.). (Illus.). 372p. 1998. pap. 17.95 (*0-8442-9994-4*, 99944, Passprt Bks) NTC Contemp Pub Co.

Catling, H. W. Some Problems in Aegean Prehistory, 1450-1380 BC. 7.00 (*0-904920-16-X*) David Brown.

Catling, Ian, ed. Advanced Technology for Road Transport: IVHS & ATT. LC 93-38272. 376p. 1993. 89.00 (*0-89006-613-2*) Artech Hse.

Catling, J. M., ed. A History of Women's Writing in Germany, Austria & Switzerland. 408p. (C). 2000. 64.95 (*0-521-44482-9*); pap. 24.95 (*0-521-65628-1*) Cambridge U Pr.

Catling, Joanna M., tr. see Haug, Walter.

Catling, Linda, jt. auth. see Hollender, Jeffrey.

Catling, Patrick. The Chocolate Touch. 96p. (J). 1995. pap. 4.99 (*0-440-41289-7*) BDD Bks Young Read.

Catling, Patrick. The Chocolate Touch. 87p. (J). (gr. 3-5). pap. 4.99 (*0-8072-1454-X*) Listening Lib.

Catling, Patrick S. The Chocolate Touch. (J). 1996. pap. 4.99 (*0-440-91162-1*) BDD Bks Young Read.

Catling, Patrick S. The Chocolate Touch. LC 78-31100. (Illus.). 96p. (J). (gr. 4-6). 1979. reprint ed. 14.89 (*0-688-32187-9*, Wm Morrow) Morrow Avon.

Catling, Patrick Skene. The Chocolate Touch. 1996. 9.19 (*0-606-02063-2*, Pub. by Turtleback) Demco.

Catling, S. Mapstart 2. Date not set. pap. text. write for info. (*0-582-00187-0*, Pub. by Addison-Wesley) Longman.

Catlow, C. R. Molecular Modelling of High Tc Materials. 76p. 1995. pap. text 130.00 (*2-88124-968-X*) Gordon & Breach.

— New Trends in Materials Chemistry. LC 97-29915. (NATO ASI, Series C, Mathematical & Physical Sciences). 1997. text 264.50 (*0-7923-4714-5*) Kluwer Academic.

Catlow, C. R., ed. Advances in Solid-State Chemistry, Vol. 1. 333p. 1989. 109.50 (*0-89232-867-3*) Jai Pr.

— Advances in Solid-State Chemistry, Vol. 2. 394p. 1991. 109.50 (*0-89232-954-8*) Jai Pr.

— Advances in Solid-State Chemistry, Vol. 3. 285p. 1993. 109.50 (*1-55938-271-6*) Jai Pr.

— Advances in Solid-State Chemistry, Vol. 4. Date not set. 109.50 (*1-55938-792-0*) Jai Pr.

— Defects & Disorder in Crystalline & Amorphous Solids: Proceedings of the NATO ASI on Defects & Disorder in Crystalline & Amorphous Solids, Madrid, Spain, September 15-28, 1991. (NATO Advanced Science Institutes Series C: Mathematical & Physical Sciences). 520p. (C). 1994. text 281.00 (*0-7923-2610-5*) Kluwer Academic.

— High Resolution Powder Diffraction. (Material Science Forum Ser.: Vol. 9). 200p. (C). 1986. pap. text 66.00 (*0-87849-553-3*, Pub. by Trans T Pub) Enfield Pubs NH.

Catlow, C. R., et al, eds. Computer Modelling of Fluids Polymers & Solids: Proceedings of the NATO Advanced Study Institute Held in Bath, United Kingdom, September 4-17, 1988. (C). 1989. text 282.00 (*0-7923-0549-3*) Kluwer Academic.

— Quantum Mechanical Cluster Calculations in Solid State Studies. 450p. (C). 1992. text 114.00 (*981-02-0750-6*) World Scientific Pub.

Catlow, C. R. & Greaves, G. N., eds. Applications of Synchrotron Radiation. 388p. 1991. 145.00 (*0-412-02001-7*, A3597, Chap & Hall NY) Chapman & Hall.

Catlow, C. R. & Mackrodt, eds. Localization, Vol. 51, No. 3. 1985. 42.00 (*0-85066-973-1*) Taylor & Francis.

Catlow, C. R., jt. auth. see Agullo-Lopez, F.

Catlow, C. R. A., et al, eds. New Methods of Modelling Processes Within Solids & at Their Surfaces. LC 92-42240. (Illus.). 192p. 1994. text 55.00 (*0-19-853988-6*) OUP.

Catlow, C. R. A., jt. auth. see Wright, Kate.

Catlow, Richard, ed. Computer Modelling in Inorganic Crystallography. (Illus.). 320p. 1997. text 99.95 (*0-12-164135-X*) Morgan Kaufmann.

Catlow, Richard, jt. ed. see Day, Peter.

Cato. Guilty Men. 160p. pap. 13.95 (*0-14-118098-6*, Pub. by Pnguin Bks Ltd) Trafalgar.

Cato. On Farming. LC 99-177125. (Illus.). 243p. 1998. pap. 24.00 (*0-907325-80-7*) Food Words.

***Cato.** User Centered Interface Design. 272p. (C). 2000. pap. text 34.95 (*0-201-39860-5*) Addison-Wesley.

Cato, jt. auth. see Mobley.

Cato, Allen E. Clinical Trials & Tribulations. (Drugs & the Pharmaceutical Sciences Ser.: Vol. 34). (Illus.). 432p. 1988. text 210.00 (*0-8247-7854-5*) Dekker.

Cato, Bertha, et al, eds. Youth at Risk. 140p. (Orig.). 1994. pap. text 31.00 (*0-697-25752-5*, 300-10005) AAHPERD.

Cato, Bob, jt. auth. see Meyer, Barbara F.

Cato, Charles. Restitution in Australia & New Zealand. LC 97-207090. lxiii, 368p. 1997. pap. 63.00 (*1-876213-23-X*, Pub. by Cavendish Pubng) Gaunt.

Cato, D. Mark. Arbitration Practice & Procedure: Interlocutory & Hearing Problems. 554p. 1992. 170.00 (*1-85044-440-4*) LLP.

Cato, D. Mark. Arbitration Practice & Procedure: Interlocutory & Hearing Problems. 2nd ed. LC 98-171844. lxxxiii, 1728 p. 1997. write for info. (*1-85978-150-0*) LLP.

Cato, D. Mark. Arbitration Workbook: The Sanctuary House File, 2 vols., Set. 500p. 1995. pap. 225.00 (*1-85044-853-1*) LLP.

Cato, Fred, Jr. Words of Inspiration. Cato, William T., ed. 150p. (Orig.). 1996. pap. write for info. (*1-57502-204-4*, PO841) Morris Pubng.

Cato, Ingemar, jt. ed. see Olausson, Eric.

Cato Institute Staff, ed. Cato Handbook for Congress. 554p. 1997. spiral bd. 25.00 (*1-882577-51-5*) Cato Inst.

Cato Institute Staff, jt. auth. see Palmer, Tom G.

Cato, Jimmy E. Speaking with a Thesis. 256p. (C). 1993. per. 27.95 (*0-8403-8618-4*) Kendall-Hunt.

Cato, Ken. Cato Design. 160p. 1995. 34.99 (*1-56496-085-4*) Rockport Pubs.

***Cato, Ken.** Design by Thinking. 2000. 35.00 (*0-06-019843-5*) HarpC.

***Cato, Ken, ed.** Hindsight. (Illus.). 160p. 1998. text 40.00 (*90-5703-341-0*, Harwood Acad Pubs) Gordon & Breach.

Cato, Leigh. The Other Woman: True Stories of Love, Betrayal, & the Men Women Have Shared as Husbands & Lovers. 240p. 1996. pap. 12.95 (*1-56352-336-1*) Longstreet.

Cato, Leigh, ed. The Business of Ecology: Australian Organizations Tackling Evnironmental Issues. (Illus.). 192p. 1996. pap. 24.95 (*1-86373-733-2*, Pub. by Allen & Unwin Pty) Paul & Co Pubs.

Cato-Louis, Cassandra & Dejongh, Monique J. How to Marry a Black Man. (Illus.). 256p. 1997. pap. 9.95 (*0-385-48247-7*, Main St Bks) Doubleday.

Cato, Nancy. Marigold. large type ed. (Charnwood Ser.). 240p. 1994. 27.99 (*0-7089-8753-2*, Charnwood) Ulverscroft.

— North-West by South. large type ed. 416p. 1987. 15.95 (*0-7089-8391-X*, Charnwood) Ulverscroft.

Cato, Nathaniel J. Le, see Le Cato, Nathaniel J.

Cato, Paisely S. Guidelines for Managing Bird Collections. (Museology Ser.: No. 7). (Illus.). 78p. 1986. pap. 16.00 (*0-89672-145-0*) Tex Tech Univ Pr.

Cato, Paisley S., et al, eds. Developing Staff Resources for Managing Collections. (Special Publications: No. 4). (Illus.). 72p. (Orig.). 1996. pap. text 15.00 (*1-884549-04-7*) VA Mus Natl Hist.

Cato, Paisley S. & Jones, Clyde. Natural History Museums. 200p. 1990. 25.00 (*0-89672-240-6*) Tex Tech Univ Pr.

Cato, Phillip. All the Way to Memphis: A Glamodyssey. 160p. (Orig.). 1996. pap. 12.95 (*1-898928-60-6*, Pub. by S T Pubng) AK Pr Dist.

— Crash Course for the Ravers: A Glamodyssey. 136p. (Orig.). 1997. pap. 14.95 (*1-898927-65-0*, Pub. by S T Pubng) AK Pr Dist.

Cato, Ruth & Towne, Jonathan B. Techniques of Peripheral Arterial Sonography. Date not set. text. write for info. (*0-941022-31-5*); VHS. write for info. (*0-941022-34-X*) Davies Pubng.

Cato, Sheila. Addition. LC 98-15725. (Question of Math Book Ser.). (Illus.). 32p. (J). (gr. 1-4). 1998. 25.26 (*1-57505-320-9*, Carolrhoda) Lerner Pub.

— Counting & Numbers. LC 98-15724. (Question of Math Book Ser.). (Illus.). 32p. (J). (gr. 1-4). 1999. 25.26 (*1-57505-322-5*, Carolrhoda) Lerner Pub.

— Division. LC 98-6354. (Question of Math Book Ser.). (Illus.). 32p. (J). (gr. 1-4). 1999. 25.26 (*1-57505-319-5*, Carolrhoda) Lerner Pub.

— Measuring. LC 98-16123. (Question of Math Bks.). (Illus.). 32p. (J). (gr. 1-4). 1999. 25.26 (*1-57505-323-3*, Carolrhoda) Lerner Pub.

— Multiplication. LC 98-6377. (Question of Math Book Ser.). (Illus.). 32p. (J). (gr. 1-4). 1999. 25.26 (*1-57505-321-7*, Carolrhoda) Lerner Pub.

— Subtraction. LC 98-6355. (Question of Math Bks.). (Illus.). 32p. (J). (gr. 1-4). 1999. 25.26 (*1-57505-318-7*, Carolrhoda) Lerner Pub.

Cato, William T., ed. see Cato, Fred, Jr.

Catoe, Kaye, ed. see Barrier, Jean & Kennedy, Alice.

Catoir, Barbara, et al. Conversations with Antoni Tapies. (Illus.). 168p. (Orig.). 1991. pap. 25.95 (*3-7913-1149-2*, Pub. by Prestel) te Neues.

— Miro on Mallorca. (Pegasus Library). (Illus.). 128p. 1995. 25.00 (*3-7913-1483-1*, Pub. by Prestel) te Neues.

Catoir, John T. Dios Se Complace En Ti: Una Introduccion a la Espiritualidad Del Evangelio. LC 92-34571. Orig. Title: God Delights in You. (SPA.). 1992. pap. 7.95 (*0-8189-0658-8*) Alba.

— Enjoy the Lord: A Path to Contemplation. LC 88-22127. 113p. 1988. pap. 5.95 (*0-8189-0538-7*) Alba.

— Enjoy the Lord: A Path to Contemplation. large type ed. (Large Print Inspirational Ser.). 224p. 1986. pap. 9.95 (*0-8027-2553-8*) Walker & Co.

— God Delights in You: An Introduction to Gospel Spirituality. LC 90-41425. 172p. (Orig.). 1990. pap. 7.95 (*0-8189-0594-8*) Alba.

— Vamos a Orar: Oraciones para Diferentes Ocasiones. (SPA.). 90p. 1991. pap. 2.95 (*0-8189-0610-3*) Alba.

— Where Do You Stand with the Church? The Dilemma of Divorced Catholics. LC 96-33124. 124p. (Orig.). 1996. pap. 7.95 (*0-8189-0776-2*) Alba.

— World Religions. LC 91-45842. 146p. (Orig.). 1992. pap. 7.95 (*0-8189-0640-5*) Alba.

— World Religions: Beliefs Behind Today's Headlines. rev. ed. xxiii, 148p. 1992. pap. 5.00 (*0-939055-00-7*) Chrstphrs NY.

***Catoir, John T. & De Vinck, Catherine.** Stations of the Cross for the New Millennium. (Illus.). 64p. (YA). 2000. pap. 3.75 (*0-8189-0885-8*, Saint Pauls) Alba.

Catoire, B., ed. Electron Spin Resonance (ESR) Applications in Organic & Bioorganic Materials: Proceedings of the First European Meeting January 1990, Lyon, France. (Illus.). 314p. (C). 1992. 130.95 (*0-387-55024-0*) Spr-Verlag.

Catolica Editorial Staff. Diccionario Rioduero: Geologia y Mineralogia. 2nd deluxe ed. (SPA.). 1978. 35.00 (*0-8288-5151-4*, S50168) Fr & Eur.

— Diccionario Rioduero: Zoologia. (SPA.). 432p. 1979. 35.00 (*0-8288-4780-0*, S50171) Fr & Eur.

Catolicas por el Derecho a Decidir Staff, ed. see Hume, Maggie.

Caton, Barbara & Cleveland, Alexandra. Games for All Seasons. (Illus.). 1999. pap. text 16.95 (*0-943452-29-5*) Building Blocks.

Caton, Bill. Josh & the Flat Cows. (Illus.). (J). (gr. 2-5). 1994. pap. 7.95 (*0-9642606-0-3*) Hand Made Eks.

Caton, Bill, ed. Fighting Words: Words on Writing from 21 of the Heart of Dixie's Best Contemporary Authors. 200p. 1995. 22.00 (*1-881320-36-7*, Black Belt) Black Belt Communs.

Caton, Carol L. Homeless in America. 256p. 1990. text 35.00 (*0-19-503918-1*) OUP.

Caton, Charles E. Philosophy & Ordinary Language. LC 63-7250. 260p. reprint ed. pap. 80.60 (*0-608-10774-3*, 202086000020) Bks Demand.

Caton, Chris. Dolphins. 1995. text 24.95 (*0-312-13241-7*) St Martin.

Caton, Donald. What a Blessing She Had Chloroform: The Medical & Social Response to the Pain of Childbirth from 1800 to the Present. LC 98-36869. (Illus.). 287p. 1999. 30.00 (*0-300-07597-9*) Yale U Pr.

Caton, G. J. Lumen: Food for a New Age. LC 86-62413. (Illus.). 245p. 1986. pap. 4.95 (*0-939955-00-8*) Grand Union.

***Caton, Helen, et al.** Fertility Plan: A Holistic Program to Conceiving a Healthy Baby. (Illus.). 144p. 2000. per. 15.00 (*0-684-86944-6*) S&S Trade.

Caton, Hilda. Specifications for Selecting a Vocabulary & Teaching Method for Beginning Braille Readers. LC HV1669.. (AFB Research Report). 84p. reprint ed. pap. 30.00 (*0-7837-3076-4*, 204315000006) Bks Demand.

Caton, Hiram. The AIDS Mirage. (Frontlines Ser.). 64p. 1995. pap. 9.95 (*0-86840-342-3*, Pub. by New South Wales Univ Pr) Intl Spec Bk.

— The Origin of Subjectivity: An Essays on Descartes. LC 72-91291. 264p. reprint ed. pap. 81.90 (*0-608-10173-7*, 201055700069) Bks Demand.

— The Politics of Progress: The Origins & Development of the Commercial Republic, 1600-1835. LC 86-30886. 639p. 1988. 49.95 (*0-8130-0847-6*) U Press Fla.

Caton, Hiram, compiled by. The Bibliography of Human Behavior, 7. LC 93-3066. (Bibliographies & Indexes in Anthropology Ser.: No. 7). 600p. 1993. lib. bdg. 125.00 (*0-313-27897-0*, CBJ) Greenwood.

Caton, Hiram, ed. The Samoa Reader: Anthropologists Take Stock. 366p. (Orig.). (C). 1990. pap. text 31.00 (*0-8191-7721-0*) U Pr of Amer.

Caton, J. A. Proceedings of the 17th Annual Fall Technical Conference of the ASME Internal Combustion Engine Division Vol. 25-2: New Technology & Design. LC 95-80398. 156p. 1995. pap. 84.00 (*0-614-16881-3*, G0980B) ASME.

— Proceedings of the 17th Annual Fall Technical Conference of the ASME Internal Combustion Engine Division Vol. 25-3: New Technology & Design. LC 95-80398. 132p. 1995. 76.00 (*0-614-16878-3*, G0980C) ASME.

Caton, J. A., ed. Proceedings of the 17th Annual Fall Technical Conference of the ASME Internal Combustion Engine Division Vol. 25-1: New Technology & Design, 4 vols., Set. LC 95-80398. 132p. 1995. pap. 76.00 (*0-7918-1485-8*, G0980A) ASME.

— 17th Annual Fall Technical Conference of the ASME Internal Combustion Engine Division Vol. 25-3: Alternate Fuels & Natural Gas. 132p. 76.00 (*0-614-97060-1*, G0980C) ASME.

— 17th Annual Fall Technical Conference of the ASME Internal Combustion Engine Division Vol. 25-4: Combustion & Emissions. 128p. 76.00 (*0-614-97061-X*, G0980D) ASME.

— 17th Annual Fall Technical Conference of the ASME Internal Combustion Engine Division Vol. 25-2: Simulations, Controls, & Lubrication. 156p. 84.00 (*0-614-97059-8*, G098B) ASME.

Caton, J. A. & Webb, H. A., eds. Coal-Fueled Diesel Engines - 1993. (ICE Ser.: Vol. 19). 72p. 1993. 35.00 (*0-7918-0947-1*, 100352) ASME.

Caton, Jacolyn. The Potter. (Illus.). 32p. (J). (ps-3). 1992. 10.95 (*1-55050-037-6*, Pub. by Coteau) Genl Dist Srvs.

Caton, Jerald A., ed. Combustion Engine Conference: Proceedings 18th Fall Technical Conference of the ASME Internal Combustion Engine Division, Fairborn, Ohio 1996, 5 vols. LC 96-86515. 1996. pap. 360.00 (*0-7918-1516-1*, TJ1075) ASME Pr.

Caton, John D. The Antelope & Deer of America: A Scientific Treatise upon the Natural History, Habits, Affinities & Capacity for Domestication of the Antilocapra & Cervidae of North America. LC 73-17896. (Natural Sciences in America Ser.). (Illus.). 428p. 1974. reprint ed. 33.95 (*0-405-05723-7*) Ayer.

Caton, Joseph H. The Utopian Vision of Moholy-Nagy. Kirkpatrick, Diane, ed. LC 83-18182. (Studies in Photography: No. 5). 200p. reprint ed. 62.00 (*0-8357-1528-0*, 207044000089) Bks Demand.

***Caton, Mary Anne.** Fooles & Fricassees: Food in Shakespeare's England. (Illus.). 128p. 2000. pap. 26.95 (*0-295-97926-7*) U of Wash Pr.

Caton, Patrick. The Candy Counter: A Daily Collection of Confections. 365p. 1996. 6.50 (*1-56245-236-3*) Great Quotations.

— The Cornerstones of Success. LC 96-78972. 168p. 1997. pap. 5.95 (*1-56245-279-7*) Great Quotations.

***Caton, Patrick.** Essence of Great Women. 1999. pap. 6.50 (*1-56245-388-2*) Great Quotations.

Caton, Patrick. Graduation is Just the Beginning: Lessons to Take with You. LC 98-71846. 168p. 1998. pap. 5.95 (*1-56245-347-5*) Great Quotations.

— Kid Stuff. 365p. 1997. pap., spiral bd. 6.50 (*1-56245-314-9*) Great Quotations.

— Midwest Wisdom: The Character of the Heartland. LC 97-71654. 168p. 1997. pap. 5.95 (*1-56245-306-8*) Great Quotations.

— Older Than Dirt: 365 Ways to Show You're over the Hill! 365p. 1998. 6.50 (*1-56245-350-5*) Great Quotations.

— The Passion of Chocolate. LC 96-76127. 68p. 1996. 6.50 (*1-56245-272-X*) Great Quotations.

— Passions: Glimpses of Romance. LC 96-76126. 68p. 1996. 6.50 (*1-56245-273-8*) Great Quotations.

— Quick Tips for Home Improvement. (Day Riser Ser.). 366p. 1995. spiral bd. 6.50 (*1-56245-220-7*) Great Quotations.

— The Secrets in Your Face: Revealing Your Hidden Mysteries. LC 97-77653. (Illus.). 168p. 1998. pap. 5.95 (*1-56245-337-8*) Great Quotations.

— Stretching Your Dollars: A Daily Guide to Smart Spending. (Day Riser Ser.). 366p. 1995. 6.50 (*1-56245-219-3*) Great Quotations.

— Words from the Coach: The Man Behind the Champion. LC 97-77655. 168p. 1998. pap. 5.95 (*1-56245-339-4*) Great Quotations.

Caton, Patrick, ed. Caring Thoughts: Seeds for the Spirit. 80p. (Orig.). 1996. pap. 7.95 (*1-56245-250-9*) Great Quotations.

— I'm Here: And I've Just Started to Turn Your Life Upside Down. 80p. 1997. spiral bd. 7.95 (*1-56245-291-6*) Great Quotations.

— Over the Hill. 80p. 1997. spiral bd. 7.95 (*1-56245-289-4*) Great Quotations.

— Over the Hill Test: How Far over the Hill Are You? 80p. 1997. spiral bd. 7.95 (*1-56245-288-6*) Great Quotations.

— Pillow Talk: Humorous Quotes on Love & Marriage. 80p. 1997. spiral bd. 7.95 (*1-56245-292-4*) Great Quotations.

— Retirement: Beginning Your Best Years. 80p. 1997. spiral bd. 7.95 (*1-56245-287-8*) Great Quotations.

Caton, Patrick & Hansen, Debbie. Grandma, I Love You. LC 96-76131. 168p. (Orig.). 1996. pap. 5.95 (*1-56245-262-2*) Great Quotations.

Caton, Patrick, jt. auth. see Hansen, Debbie.

Caton, Patrick, ed. see Allen, Kimberly B.

Caton, Patrick, ed. see Anderson, Mac & Ryan, Michael.

Caton, Patrick, ed. see Be, Be.

Caton, Patrick, ed. see Blaurock, Donna.

Caton, Patrick, ed. see Chambers, Kimberly.

Caton, Patrick, ed. see Cofield, Lisa & Dongerson, Debbie.

Caton, Patrick, ed. see Cofield, Lisa, et al.

Caton, Patrick, ed. see Davis, Kathy.

Caton, Patrick, ed. see Down, Heather.

Caton, Patrick, ed. see Duran, Cathi.

Caton, Patrick, ed. see Eggers, John.

Caton, Patrick, ed. see Fink, Joanne.

Caton, Patrick, ed. see Frei, Edward.

Caton, Patrick, ed. see Gall, Morris.

Caton, Patrick, ed. see Hansen, Debbie.

Caton, Patrick, ed. see Hansen, Deborah.

Caton, Patrick, ed. see Honegger, Roy.

Caton, Patrick, ed. see Hudson, Selma.

Caton, Patrick, ed. see Johnson, Jane.

Caton, Patrick, ed. see Leimann, Dan.

Caton, Patrick, ed. see Mackiney, Millie.

Caton, Patrick, ed. see MacKiney, Millie.

Caton, Patrick, ed. see Martin, Patricia.

Caton, Patrick, ed. see Mauk, Laura.

Caton, Patrick, ed. see McCauley, Mark.

Caton, Patrick, ed. see McKenzie, Sandra.

Caton, Patrick, ed. see McLellan, Vernon.

Caton, Patrick, ed. see Miller, Merry.

Caton, Patrick, ed. see Neely, Joseph L.

Caton, Patrick, ed. see Ortman, Mark.

Caton, Patrick, ed. see Otlewis, Julie.

Caton, Patrick, ed. see Reyes, Simone.

Caton, Patrick, ed. see Reyes, Simone & Compton, Ken.

Caton, Patrick, ed. see Rimler, Marlene.

Caton, Patrick, ed. see Ryan, Michael.

Caton, Patrick, ed. see Schaffer, Peggy.

Caton, Patrick, ed. see Stark, Susanne.

Caton, Patrick, ed. see Von Ehrenfels, Greg.

Caton, Patrick, ed. see Voreis, Diane & Henderson, Cheryl.

Caton, Patrick, ed. see Weaver, Sherri.

Caton, Patrick, ed. see Weaver, Sherrie.

Caton, Peggy, compiled by. The Wisdom of the Master: Words of 'Abdu'l-Baha. (Illus.). 1997. 17.00 (*0-933770-81-2*) Kalimat.

Caton, Peggy, ed. Equal Circles: Women & Men in the Baha'i Community. (Orig.). 1987. pap. 14.95 (*0-933770-60-X*) Kalimat.

Caton, Sandra, ed. see McKee, Judy.

Caton, Steven C. Lawrence of Arabia: A Film's Anthropology. LC 98-3621. 1999. 50.00 (*0-520-21082-4*, Pub. by U CA Pr); 19.95 (*0-520-21083-2*, Pub. by U CA Pr) Cal Prin Full Svc.

— Peaks of Yemen I Summon: Poetry As Cultural Practice in a North Yemeni Tribe. LC 89-20524. 330p. 1990. 55.00 (*0-520-06766-5*, Pub. by U CA Pr); pap. 18.95 (*0-520-08261-3*, Pub. by U CA Pr) Cal Prin Full Svc.

Caton-Thompson, Gertrude. The Zimbabwe Culture: Ruins & Reactions. 2nd ed. LC 72-175986. (Library of African Studies). 299p. 1971. write for info. (*0-7146-1886-1*) F Cass Pubs.

C

An Asterisk (*) at the beginning of an entry indicates that the title is appearing for the first time.

Caton-Thompson, Gertrude & Gardner, Elinor W. The Desert Fayum, 2 vols., Set. LC 77-86428. (Royal Anthropological Institute of Great Britain & Ireland. Publication Ser.). reprint ed. 65.00 (*0-404-16630-X*) AMS Pr.

Caton-Thompson, Gertrude, jt. auth. see Brunton, Guy.

Catone, Guy A. & Alling, Charles C., 3rd, eds. Laser Applications in Oral & Maxillofacial Surgery. LC 95-45035. 1997. text 99.00 (*0-7216-5020-1*, W B Saunders Co) Harcrt Hlth Sci Grp.

Catovsky, D., ed. The Leukemic Cell. 2nd ed. (Methods in Hematology Ser.). (Illus.). 428p. 1991. text 152.00 (*0-443-03867-8*) Church.

Catovsky, D., jt. auth. see Polliack, Aaron.

Catovsky, Daniel, ed. The Leukemic Cell. LC 80-41107. (Methods in Hematology Ser.: No. 2). (Illus.). 293p. reprint ed. pap. 90.90 (*0-8357-3065-4*, 203932100012) Bks Demand.

Catran. Onager. 1998. pap. 6.95 (*0-7322-5700-X*) HarpC.

Catran, Jack. How to Speak English Without a Foreign Accent, 20 vols. 1986. 49.95 (*0-937399-01-9*); audio. write for info. (*0-318-60713-1*) Jade Pubns.

Catran, Jack. How to Speak English Without a Foreign Accent: Arabic. 1986. 49.95 incl. audio (*0-937399-04-3*) Jade Pubns.

Catran, Jack. How to Speak English Without a Foreign Accent: Arabic Edition. 1986. audio. write for info. (*0-318-60986-X*) Jade Pubns.

Catran, Jack. How to Speak English Without a Foreign Accent: Black English. 1986. 49.95 incl. audio (*0-937399-05-1*) Jade Pubns.

Catran, Jack. How to Speak English Without A Foreign Accent: Black English Edition. 1986. audio. write for info. (*0-318-60987-8*) Jade Pubns.

— How to Speak English Without a Foreign Accent: Chinese Edition. pap. 49.95 incl. audio (*0-937399-21-3*) Jade Pubns.

Catran, Jack. How to Speak English Without a Foreign Accent: Filipino. 1986. 49.95 incl. audio (*0-937399-12-4*) Jade Pubns.

Catran, Jack. How to Speak English Without a Foreign Accent: Filipino Edition. 1986. audio. write for info. (*0-318-60993-2*) Jade Pubns.

Catran, Jack. How to Speak English Without a Foreign Accent: French. 1986. 49.95 incl. audio (*0-937399-14-0*) Jade Pubns.

Catran, Jack. How to Speak English Without a Foreign Accent: French Edition. 1986. audio. write for info. (*0-318-60996-7*) Jade Pubns.

Catran, Jack. How to Speak English Without a Foreign Accent: German. 1986. 49.95 incl. audio (*0-937399-13-2*) Jade Pubns.

Catran, Jack. How to Speak English Without a Foreign Accent: German Edition. 1986. audio. write for info. (*0-318-60994-0*) Jade Pubns.

Catran, Jack. How to Speak English Without a Foreign Accent: Hispanic. 54p. 1986. 49.95 incl. audio (*0-937399-02-7*) Jade Pubns.

Catran, Jack. How to Speak English without a Foreign Accent: Hispanic Edition. 54p. 1986. audio. write for info. (*0-318-60860-X*) Jade Pubns.

Catran, Jack. How to Speak English Without a Foreign Accent: Indian. 1986. 49.95 incl. audio (*0-937399-09-4*) Jade Pubns.

Catran, Jack. How to Speak English Without a Foreign Accent: Indian Edition. 1986. audio. write for info. (*0-318-60991-6*) Jade Pubns.

Catran, Jack. How to Speak English Without a Foreign Accent: Iranian. 1986. 49.95 incl. audio (*0-937399-08-6*) Jade Pubns.

Catran, Jack. How to Speak English Without a Foreign Accent: Iranian Edition. 1986. audio. write for info. (*0-318-60990-8*) Jade Pubns.

— How to Speak English Without a Foreign Accent: Irish Edition. 1986. 49.95 (*0-685-14210-8*); audio. write for info. (*0-318-60995-9*) Jade Pubns.

Catran, Jack. How to Speak English Without a Foreign Accent: Israeli. 1986. 49.95 incl. audio (*0-937399-06-X*) Jade Pubns.

Catran, Jack. How To Speak English Without a Foreign Accent: Israeli Edition. 1986. audio. write for info. (*0-318-60988-6*) Jade Pubns.

Catran, Jack. How to Speak English Without a Foreign Accent: Italian. 1986. 49.95 incl. audio (*0-937399-10-8*) Jade Pubns.

Catran, Jack. How to Speak English Without a Foreign Accent: Italian Edition. 1986. audio. write for info. (*0-318-60992-4*) Jade Pubns.

— How to Speak English Without a Foreign Accent: Japanese Edition. pap. 49.95 incl. audio (*0-937399-20-5*) Jade Pubns.

Catran, Jack. How to Speak English Without a Foreign Accent: Korean. 1988. 49.95 incl. audio (*0-937399-19-1*) Jade Pubns.

— How to Speak English Without a Foreign Accent: New York. 1986. 49.95 incl. audio (*0-937399-16-7*) Jade Pubns.

Catran, Jack. How to Speak English Without a Foreign Accent: New York Edition. 1986. audio. write for info. (*0-318-60998-3*) Jade Pubns.

Catran, Jack. How to Speak English Without a Foreign Accent: Oriental. 1986. 49.95 incl. audio (*0-937399-03-5*) Jade Pubns.

Catran, Jack. How to Speak English Without a Foreign Accent: Oriental Edition. 1986. audio. write for info. (*0-318-60985-1*) Jade Pubns.

— How to Speak English Without a Foreign Accent: Pygmalion Edition (all accents) 1986. 49.95 incl. audio (*0-937399-43-4*) Jade Pubns.

Catran, Jack. How to Speak English without a Foreign Accent: Russian. 1986. 49.95 incl. audio (*0-937399-07-8*) Jade Pubns.

Catran, Jack. How to Speak English Without a Foreign Accent: Russian Edition. 1986. audio. write for info. (*0-318-60989-4*) Jade Pubns.

Catran, Jack. How to Speak English Without a Foreign Accent: Scandinavian. 1986. 49.95 incl. audio (*0-937399-15-9*) Jade Pubns.

Catran, Jack. How to Speak English Without a Foreign Accent: Scandinavian Edition. 1986. audio. write for info. (*0-318-60997-5*) Jade Pubns.

— How to Speak English Without a Foreign Accent: Vietnamese. 1986. pap. 49.95 incl. audio (*0-937399-17-5*) Jade Pubns.

— How to Speak English Without a Foreign Accent: Vietnamese Edition. 1986. audio. write for info. (*0-318-61707-2*) Jade Pubns.

— Is There Intelligent Life on Earth? LC 80-80016. 220p. 1980. 12.95 (*0-936162-29-5*, L42, Lidiraven Bks) Jade Pubns.

— The Plot to Win the White House: And How It Succeeded. 200p. (Orig.). 1994. pap. 14.95 (*0-937399-22-1*) Jade Pubns.

— Walden Three. 432p. (Orig.). 1989. pap. 14.95 (*0-936162-30-9*) Jade Pubns.

Catravas, J. D., et al, eds. Vascular Endothelium: Physiological Basis of Clinical Problems. (NATO ASI Ser.: Vol. 208). (Illus.). 318p. (C). 1991. text 126.00 (*0-306-44012-1*, Kluwer Plenum) Kluwer Academic.

— Vascular Endothelium: Receptors & Transduction Mechanisms. (NATO ASI Series A, Life Sciences: Vol. 175). (Illus.). 320p. 1989. 89.50 (*0-306-43253-6*, Plenum Trade) Perseus Pubng.

— Vascular Endothelium: Responses to Injury. (NATO ASI Ser.: Vol. 281). (Illus.). 364p. 1996. 115.00 (*0-306-45282-0*, Kluwer Plenum) Kluwer Academic.

Catravas, J. D., et al. Vascular Endothelium Vol. 2: Physiological Basis of Clinical Problems. (NATO ASI Ser.: Vol. 257). (Illus.). 240p. (C). 1993. text 95.00 (*0-306-44633-2*, Kluwer Plenum) Kluwer Academic.

— Vascular Endothelium Vol. 4: Pharmacologic & Genetic Manipulations. LC 98-9865. (NATO ASI Ser.: No. 294). (Illus.). 308p. (C). 1998. text 110.00 (*0-306-45819-5*, Kluwer Plenum) Kluwer Academic.

Catrice, R., jt. auth. see Lane, A.

Catrillon, Laura V. Memoria Natural y Artificial. (Ciencia para Todos Ser.). (SPA.). pap. 6.99 (*968-16-3481-0*, Pub. by Fondo) Continental Bk.

Catrina, Christian, jt. auth. see Frei, Daniel.

Catron. Journey Through the Old Testment. 1997. pap. 10.99 (*1-85792-234-4*, Pub. by Christian Focus) Spring Arbor Dist.

Catron, Bayard L., jt. ed. see Kass, Henry D.

Catron, Carol & Parks, Barbara. Super Story Telling. (Preschool-Toddler Ser.). 239p. (J). (ps). 1986. 15.95 (*0-513-01793-3*) Denison.

Catron, Carol E. & Allen, Jan. Early Childhood Curriculum: A Creative Play Model. 2nd ed. LC 98-6057. 431p. (C). 1998. pap. text 52.00 (*0-13-080406-1*, Merrill Coll) P-H.

Catron, Donald G. Code-Som: Composite Diagnostic Evaluation of Somatoform Disorders. 192p. 1995. pap. text 30.00 (*0-9651214-3-7*) Somnos Programs.

— The Stress Management Handbook: Strategies for Effective Problem Solving. 175p. 1996. pap. 14.50 (*0-9651214-4-5*) Somnos Programs.

Catron, Linda S., jt. auth. see Chiriboga, David A.

Catron, Louis E. The Director's Vision: Play Direction from Analysis to Production. LC 88-32582. xix, 358p. (C). 1989. text 55.95 (*0-87484-760-5*, 760) Mayfield Pub.

— The Elements of Playwriting. LC 93-31653. 256p. 1994. per. 10.00 (*0-02-069291-9*) Macmillan Gen Ref.

— Playwriting: Writing, Producing & Selling Your Play. Orig. Title: Writing, Producing & Selling Your Play. 272p. (C). 1990. reprint ed. pap. text 16.95 (*0-88133-564-9*) Waveland Pr.

***Catron, Louis E.** Power of One: The Solo Play for Playwrights, Actors & Directors. LC 99-49233. 240p. 2000. pap. 18.95 (*0-325-00153-7*, Pub. by Heinemann) Natl Bk Netwk.

Catron, Rhonda, ed. see Bland, Bill.

Catroux, G., jt. auth. see Hucker, T. W.

Catrow, Dave. That's Good! That's Bad! 1999. text 16.95 (*0-8050-5975-X*) St Martin.

Catrow, David. Why Lapin's Ears Are Long & Other Tales from the Louisiana Bayou. LC 96-53304. 64p. (J). (gr. k up). 1997. 18.95 (*0-531-30041-2*) Orchard Bks Watts.

— Why Lapin's Ears Are Long & Other Tales of the Louisiana Bayou. LC 96-53304. 64p. (J). (gr. k up). 1997. lib. bdg. 19.99 (*0-531-33041-9*) Orchard Bks Watts.

Catrow, David, jt. illus. see Dorros, Arthur.

Catrow, David, jt. illus. see Katz, Alan.

Catrow, David, jt. illus. see Policoff, Stephen P.

Cats. Information Technology & Management. 1996. pap. text, teacher ed. 29.50 (*0-256-22558-3*) McGraw.

Cats & Baril. Information Technology & Management. 2nd ed. 2000. 58.50 (*0-07-231532-6*) McGraw.

Cats-Baril, JoAnne B. & Martin, Rux, eds. Simmering Suppers: Classic & Creative One-Pot Meals. (Illus.). 240p. (Orig.). 1988. pap. 16.95 (*0-920656-69-2*, Pub. by Camden Hse) Firefly Bks Ltd.

Cats-Baril, William & Thompson, Ronald. Information Technology & Management. LC 96-20202. 576p. (C). 1996. text 59.95 (*0-256-17618-3*, Irwn McGrw-H) McGrw-H Hghr Educ.

Catsadorakis, George, jt. ed. see Crivelli, Alain J.

Catsimpoolas, Nicholas, ed. Cell Analysis, Vol. 1. LC 82-5289. 350p. 1982. 75.00 (*0-306-40864-3*, Plenum Trade) Perseus Pubng.

— Methods of Cell Separation, 3 vols. LC 77-11018. (Biological Separations Ser.). (Illus.). 1977. 59.50 (*0-306-34604-4*, Plenum Trade) Perseus Pubng.

— Methods of Cell Separation, 3 vols. LC 77-11018. (Biological Separations Ser.). (Illus.). 1979. 59.50 (*0-306-40094-4*, Plenum Trade) Perseus Pubng.

— Methods of Cell Separation, 3 vols. LC 77-11018. (Biological Separations Ser.). (Illus.). 1980. 55.00 (*0-306-40377-3*, Plenum Trade) Perseus Pubng.

Catsimpoolas, Nicholas, ed. see International Conference on Electrophoresis (1978:.

Catsis, John R. Sports Broadcasting. LC 95-1215. (Mass Communication Ser.). 1996. pap. text 35.95 (*0-8304-1379-0*) Thomson Learn.

Catsky, J., jt. ed. see Sestak, Z.

Catt. Practical Building Conservation. (Illus.). 192p. 1997. text. write for info. (*0-419-21660-X*, E & FN Spon) Routledge.

Catt, Helena. Democracy in Practice. LC 98-35093. vii, 166p. 1999. pap. write for info. (*0-415-16840-6*) Routledge.

***Catt, Helena.** Democracy in Practice. LC 98-35093. 13p. 1999. 85.00 (*0-415-16839-2*) Routledge.

Catt, Helena. Voting Behaviour: A Radical Critique. (Critical Political Studies). 192p. (C). 1997. pap. 21.95 (*0-7185-2232-X*); text 69.50 (*0-7185-1473-4*) Bks Intl VA.

***Catt, Hilton.** Power Of Networking: It's Not What You Know, I'ts Who You Know. 1999. pap. text 17.95 (*0-7494-2975-5*, Kogan Pg Educ) Stylus Pub VA.

Catt, Ivor. Electromagnetics, Vol. 1. (Illus.). xvi, 76p. (Orig.). (C). 1995. pap. 9.80 (*0-906340-10-1*, Pub. by Westfields) M Gibson.

Catt, J. A. Soils & Quaternary Geology: A Handbook for Field Scientists. (Monographs on Soil & Resources Survey: No. 11). (Illus.). 300p. 1986. 89.00 (*0-19-854568-1*) OUP.

Catt, John A. Quaternary Geology for Scientists & Engineers. 312p. 1988. text 73.95 (*0-470-21135-0*) P-H.

Cattabriga, L. & Bony, J. M., eds. Microlocal Analysis & Applications. (Lecture Notes in Mathematics Ser.: Vol. 1495). vii, 349p. 1992. pap. 52.00 (*0-387-54948-X*) Spr-Verlag.

Cattan, Henry. The Palestine Question. 320p. 1987. lib. bdg. 57.50 (*0-7099-4860-3*, Pub. by C Helm) Routldge.

Cattanach, Ann. Children's Stories in Play Therapy. LC 97-197797. 240p. 1997. pap. write for info. (*1-85302-362-0*, Pub. by Jessica Kingsley) Taylor & Francis.

— Drama for People with Special Needs. rev. ed. (Illus.). 172p. 1997. pap. 16.95 (*0-89676-144-4*, Drama Pubs) QSMG Ltd.

— Play Therapy: From the Sky to the Underworld. LC 93-44030. 1994. 75.00 (*1-85302-250-0*); pap. 25.00 (*1-85302-211-X*) Taylor & Francis.

— Play Therapy with Abused Children. (Illus.). 160p. 1993. write for info. (*1-85302-193-8*, Pub. by Jessica Kingsley) Taylor & Francis.

— Process in the Arts Therapies. LC 98-45891. 1999. pap. 26.95 (*1-85302-625-5*) Jessica Kingsley.

***Cattanach, Ann, ed.** Process in the Arts Therapies. LC 98-45891. 224p. 1999. 69.95 (*1-85302-624-7*, Pub. by Jessica Kingsley) Taylor & Francis.

Cattanach, David. The School Leader in Action: Discovering the Golden Mean. LC 95-61925. 538p. 1996. text 39.95 (*1-56676-343-6*) Scarecrow.

Cattanach, Robert E., Jr. Encyclopedia of Environmental Law: Clauses, Definitions & Forms. 1993. ring bd. 85.00 (*0-317-05395-7*, 00622) NY Law Pub.

Cattanach, Robert E., et al. The Handbook of Environmentally Conscious Manufacturing: From Design & Production to Labeling & Recycling. LC 94-33053. 300p. 1994. text 75.00 (*0-7863-0147-3*, Irwn Prfssnl) McGraw-Hill Prof.

***Cattanach, Wayne.** Handcrafting Bamboo Fly Rods. rev. ed. LC 99-44885. (Illus.). 2000. 50.00 (*1-55821-769-X*) Lyons Pr.

Cattaneo, Antonio & Biocca, Silvia. Intracellular Antibodies: Ectopic Antibody Expression for Intracellular & Intercellular Immunization. LC 97-20286. (Biotechnology Intelligence Unit Ser.). 157p. 1997. text 99.95 (*1-57059-462-7*) Landes Bioscience.

Cattaneo, Antonio & Biocca, Silvia, eds. Intracellular Antibodies: Ectopic Antibody Expression for Intracellular & Intercellular Immunization. LC 97-20286. (Biotechnology Intelligence Unit Ser.). (Illus.). 157p. 1997. 99.95 (*3-540-63191-7*) Spr-Verlag.

Cattaneo, Pietro, jt. auth. see Morgan, Lee.

Cattani, E., et al, eds. Hodge Theory. (Lecture Notes in Mathematics Ser.: Vol. 1246). vii, 175p. 1987. 34.95 (*0-387-17743-4*) Spr-Verlag.

Cattani, Mary H., tr. see Ferry, Luc & Renaut, Alain.

Cattarulla, Kay, ed. Texas Bound: Nineteen Texas Stories. LC 93-45385. (Southwest Life & Letters Ser.). 262p. 1994. 22.50 (*0-87074-367-8*); pap. 10.95 (*0-87074-368-6*) SMU Press.

— Texas Bound Bk. II: 22 Texas Stories. LC 97-48345. 280p. 1998. 22.50 (*0-87074-426-7*); pap. 12.95 (*0-87074-427-5*) SMU Press.

Cattaui, Georges. Marcel Proust. Hall, Ruth, tr. from FRE. 125p. 1967. 17.95 (*0-8464-1159-8*) Beekman Pubs.

Catteau, Jacques. Dostoyevsky & the Process of Literary Creation. Littlewood, Audrey, tr. (Cambridge Studies in Russian Literature). 576p. 1989. text 99.95 (*0-521-32436-X*) Cambridge U Pr.

Cattell, Albert & Cattell, Maria. Old Age in Global Perspective. LC 93-18773. (Reference Ser.). 304p. 1993. 26.95 (*0-8161-7393-1*, Hall Reference); 15.95 (*0-8161-1604-0*, Hall Reference) Macmillan.

Cattell, Catherine. From Bamboo to Mango: An Autobiography of Missionary Catherine Cattell. 1976. pap. 4.50 (*0-913342-23-8*) Barclay Pr.

— From Bamboo to Mango: An Autobiography of Missionary Catherine Cattell. (Illus.). 218p. 1978. 8.95 (*0-913342-05-X*) Barclay Pr.

Cattell, Catherine D. Over the Teacup. 98p. (Orig.). 1983. pap. 4.50 (*0-913342-41-6*) Barclay Pr.

Cattell, Edward V., Jr. Parks Vol. 1: Law of Tug, Tow & Pilotage. 3rd ed. 1994. 192.00 (*0-421-52370-0*, Pub. by Sweet & Maxwll) Gaunt.

Cattell, Edward V., Jr., jt. auth. see Parks, Alex L.

Cattell, Heather B. The Sixteen PF: Personality in Depth. 1989. pap. 21.00 (*0-918296-20-X*) Inst Personality & Ability.

Cattell, Heather B. & Cattell, Heather E. 16PF Cattell Comprehensive Personality Interpretation Manual. (Illus.). 56p. (Orig.). 1997. pap. text 25.00 (*0-918296-30-7*) Inst Personality & Ability.

Cattell, Heather E., jt. auth. see Cattell, Heather B.

Cattell, Hudson & Miller, Lee. Wine East of the Rockies. LC 82-90971. (Illus.). 160p. 1982. 17.50 (*0-911301-00-3*) L&H Photojrnl.

Cattell, Hudson & Miller, Lee S. Native American Grapes. (Wines of the East Ser.). (Illus.). 28p. (Orig.). 1981. pap. 2.75 (*0-911301-03-8*) L&H Photojrnl.

— The Vinifera. (Wines of the East Ser.). (Illus.). 28p. (Orig.). 1979. pap. 2.75 (*0-911301-02-X*) L&H Photojrnl.

Cattell, Hudson & Stauffer, H. Lee. The Hybrids. (Wines of the East Ser.). (Illus.). 28p. (Orig.). 1978. pap. 2.75 (*0-911301-01-1*) L&H Photojrnl.

Cattell, J. McKeen. University Control. Metzger, Walter P., ed. LC 76-55179. (Academic Profession Ser.). 1977. reprint ed. lib. bdg. 40.95 (*0-405-10007-8*) Ayer.

Cattell, Maria, jt. auth. see Cattell, Albert.

***Cattell, N. R.** Children's Language: Consensus & Controversy LC 99-38234. 256p. 2000. pap. 26.95 (*0-304-70681-7*) Continuum.

Cattell, Psyche. Raising Children with Love & Limits. LC 77-187810. 240p. 1972. text 28.95 (*0-911012-20-6*) Burnham Inc.

Cattell, R. B., jt. auth. see Nesselroade, J. R.

Cattell, R. G. G. Object Data Management: Object-Oriented & Extended Relational Database Systems. LC 93-39690. 416p. (C). 1994. 47.95 (*0-201-54748-1*) Addison-Wesley.

Cattell, Raymond B. Beyondism: Religion from Science. LC 87-17885. 335p. 1987. 59.95 (*0-275-92431-9*, C2431, Praeger Pubs) Greenwood.

— How Good Is Your Country? What You Should Know. (Mankind Quarterly Monographs: No. 5). 128p. 1994. pap. 20.00 (*0-941694-44-5*) Inst Study Man.

— Human Motivation & the Dynamic Calculus. LC 84-15153. 164p. 1985. 49.95 (*0-275-90071-1*, C0071, Praeger Pubs) Greenwood.

— The Inheritance of Personality & Ability: Research Methods & Findings. LC 80-70667. (Personality & Psychopathology Ser.). (Illus.). 476p. 1982. reprint ed. pap. 147.60 (*0-608-05388-0*, AU0048700006) Bks Demand.

— Intelligence: Its Structure, Growth & Action. (Advances in Psychology Ser.: No. 35). xxii,694p. 1987. 269.50 (*0-444-87922-6*, North Holland) Elsevier.

— Personality & Mood by Questionnnaire. LC 73-1853. (Jossey-Bass Behavioral Science Ser.). 552p. reprint ed. pap. 171.20 (*0-608-12258-0*, 202378300034) Bks Demand.

— Psychotherapy by Structured Learning Theory. (Illus.). 192p. 1987. 37.95 (*0-8261-5080-2*) Springer Pub.

— Structured Personality Learning Theory: A Holistic Multivariate Research Approach. LC 83-16103. (Centennial Psychology Ser.). 466p. 1983. 69.50 (*0-275-90958-1*, C0958, Praeger Pubs) Greenwood.

Cattell, Raymond B., et al, eds. Human Affairs. LC 70-128219. (Essay Index Reprint Ser.). 1977. 28.95 (*0-8369-1943-2*) Ayer.

Cattell, Raymond B. & Butcher, H. J. The Prediction of Achievement & Creativity. LC 67-18662. 1968. 39.50 (*0-672-60641-0*); pap. text 14.95 (*0-89197-900-X*) Irvington.

Cattell, Raymond B. & Schuerger, James M. Personality Theory in Action: Handbook for the Objective-Analytic (O-A) Battery. LC 78-50146. 1978. 58.75 (*0-918296-11-0*) Inst Personality & Ability.

Cattell, Raymond B., Jr., ed. see Lerner, Barbara & Vining, Daniel R.

Cattell, R.G.G., et al, eds. The Object Database Standard: ODMG 2.0. LC 97-17031. 200p. (C). 1997. pap. text 36.95 (*1-55860-463-4*) Morgan Kaufmann.

Cattell, Rick. JDBC Database Access with Java: A Tutorial Annotated Reference. (Java Ser.). 1995. pap. text 36.53 (*0-201-92454-4*) Addison-Wesley.

***Cattell, Rick.** The Object Database Standard: ODMG. 288p. (C). 2000. pap. text 39.95 (*1-55860-647-5*) Morgan Kaufmann.

Cattell, Roderic. Formalization & Automatic Derivation of Code Generators. LC 82-4802. (Computer Science. Systems Programming Ser.: No. 3). (Illus.). 158p. 1982. reprint ed. pap. 49.00 (*0-8357-1316-4*, 207033700085) Bks Demand.

Cattell, W. R., ed. Infections of the Kidney & Urinary Tract. (Oxford Clinical Nephrology Ser.). (Illus.). 360p. (C). 1996. text 99.00 (*0-19-262441-5*) OUP.

Cattell, W. R., et al. Clinical Renal Imaging. LC 89-5398. (Illus.). 232p. 1989. reprint ed. pap. 72.00 (*0-608-01629-2*, 206221400002) Bks Demand.

Catterall, A., ed. Recent Advances in Orthopaedics 6. (Illus.). 175p. (Orig.). 1992. pap. text 65.00 (*0-443-04386-8*) Church.

Catterall, Claire, jt. ed. see Frayling, Christopher.

Catterall, Eric. Begonias: The Complete Guide. (Illus.). 216p. 1996. pap. 22.95 (*1-85223-969-7*, Pub. by Cro1wood) Trafalgar.

An Asterisk (*) at the beginning of an entry indicates that the title is appearing for the first time.

Catterall, H. T. & Hayden, J. J., eds. Judicial Cases Concerning American Slavery & the Negro, 5 vols., Set. 2949p. 1968. 250.00 (*0-7165-0564-9*, Pub. by Irish Acad Pr) Intl Spec Bk.

Catterall, Helen, ed. Judicial Cases Concerning American Slavery & the Negro, 5 vols. LC 97-80914. 1998. reprint ed. 375.00 (*1-57588-411-9*, 311540) W S Hein.

***Catterall, Miriam, et al.** Marketing & Feminism: Current Issues & Research. LC 00-20069. (Interpretive Marketing Research Ser.). 2000. pap. write for info. (*0-415-21973-6*) Routledge.

Catterall, Peter. British History, 1945-1987: An Annotated Bibliography. 900p. (C). 1991. text 184.95 (*0-631-17049-9*) Blackwell Pubs.

— The Making of Channel 4. LC 98-29722. 160p. 1999. 22.50 (*0-7146-4485-4*, Pub. by F Cass Pubs); 45.00 (*0-7146-4926-0*, Pub. by F Cass Pubs) Intl Spec Bk.

***Catterall, Peter.** Northcliffe's Legacy. LC 99-89311. 210p. 2000. text 65.00 (*0-312-23256-X*) St Martin.

Catterall, Peter & McDougall, Sean, eds. The Northern Ireland Question in British Politics. LC 95-53126. 256p. 1996. text 65.00 (*0-312-12982-3*) St Martin.

Catterall, Peter & Morris, C. J., eds. Britain & the Threat to Stability in Europe, 1918-47. 240p. 1994. 59.00 (*0-7185-1483-1*, Pub. by Leicester U Pr) Cassell & Continuum.

Catterall, Peter & Preston, Virginia, eds. Contemporary Britain: An Annual Review 1995. (Illus.). 500p. 1996. text 94.95 (*1-85521-645-0*, Pub. by Dartmth Pub) Ashgate Pub Co.

— Contemporary Britain: An Annual Review 1996. (Illus.). 448p. 1997. 91.95 (*1-85521-900-X*, Pub. by Ashgate Pub) Ashgate Pub Co.

***Catterall, Peter, et al.** Reforming the Constitution: Debates in 20th-Century Britain. LC 00-31541. (British Politics & Society Ser.). 2000. write for info. (*0-7146-8107-5*, Pub. by F Cass Pubs) Intl Spec Bk.

Catterall, Peter, jt. ed. see Obelkevich, James.

Catterall, Ross & Aldcroft, Derek H. Exchange Rate Regimes & Economic Policy in the 20th Century. 94.95 (*1-84014-264-2*) Ashgate Pub Co.

Catterall, Ross, jt. ed. see Aldcroft, Derek H.

Catterberg, Edgardo. Argentina Confronts Politics: Political Culture & Public Opinion in the Argentine Transition to Democracy. LC 90-42450. 136p. 1991. lib. bdg. 32.00 (*1-55587-248-4*) L Rienner.

Cattermole, Peter. Building Planet Earth: Five Billion Years of Earth History. LC 98-36460. (Illus.). 304p. 2000. 39.95 (*0-521-58278-4*) Cambridge U Pr.

— Earth & Other Planets: Geology & Space Research. (New Encyclopedia of Science Ser.). (Illus.). 160p. 1995. 39.95 (*0-19-521138-3*) OUP.

— Planetary Volcanism: A Study of Volcanic Activity in the Solar System. 1990. text 72.95 (*0-470-21602-6*) P-H.

— Venus: A New Geology. (Illus.). 256p. (C). 1996. reprint ed. pap. text 19.95 (*0-8018-5418-0*) Johns Hopkins.

— Venus, a New Geology. LC 93-11636. 256p. (C). 1994. 49.95 (*0-8018-4787-7*) Johns Hopkins.

Cattermole, Peter & Moore, Patrick. Atlas of Venus. (Illus.). 160p. (C). 1997. 29.95 (*0-521-49652-7*) Cambridge U Pr.

— The Story of the Earth. (Illus.). 224p. 1985. text 44.95 (*0-521-26292-5*) Cambridge U Pr.

Catterns, David, ed. see Bogulavsky, M. M.

Catterwell, Thelma. Sebastian Lives in a Hat. (Illus.). 32p. (J). (ps-1). 1990. 13.95 (*0-916291-30-8*) Kane-Miller Bk.

Catthoor, Francky. Custom Memory Management Methodology: Exploration of Memory Organisation for Embedded Multimedia System Design. LC 98-39842. 344p. 1998. 128.00 (*0-7923-8288-9*) Kluwer Academic.

Catthoor, Francky, ed. Application-Driven Architecture Synthesis. 256p. (C). 1993. text 138.00 (*0-7923-9355-4*) Kluwer Academic.

Catthoor, Francky, jt. ed. see Moonen, Marc.

Cattle, Dorothy J. & Schwerin, Karl H., eds. Food Energy in Tropical Ecosystems. (Food & Nutrition in History & Anthropology Ser.: Vol. 4). xxvi, 290p. 1985. text 134.00 (*2-88124-036-4*) Gordon & Breach.

Cattle, Edward, tr. see Elwenspoek, Curt.

Cattley, S. R., ed. see Foxe, John.

Catto, Bonnie & Lucretius. Lucretius Selections from de Rerum Natura. LC 97-43158. 304p. 1997. pap. 26.00 (*0-86516-399-5*) Bolchazy-Carducci.

Catto, G. D., ed. Clinical Transplantation: Current Practice & Future Prospects. (Immunology & Medicine Ser.). 296p. (C). 1987. text 176.50 (*0-85200-960-7*) Kluwer Academic.

Catto, G. R. D. & Thomson, Angus W., eds. Immunology of Renal Transplantation. 336p. 1993. text 95.00 (*0-340-55162-3*, Pub. by E A) OUP.

Catto, Graeme R. Drugs & the Kidney. 176p. 1990. text 107.00 (*0-7923-8918-2*) Kluwer Academic.

— Glomerulonephritis. 176p. 1990. text 107.00 (*0-7462-0109-5*) Kluwer Academic.

Catto, Graeme R., ed. Calculus Disease. (New Clinical Applications - Nephrology Ser.). (C). 1988. text 95.50 (*0-7462-0074-9*) Kluwer Academic.

— Chronic Renal Failure. (New Clinical Applications - Nephrology Ser.). (C). 1988. text 134.50 (*0-7462-0048-X*) Kluwer Academic.

— Haemodialysis. (New Clinical Applications Nephrology Ser.). (C). 1989. text 95.50 (*0-7462-0100-1*) Kluwer Academic.

— Multisystem Diseases. (New Clinical Applications Nephrology Ser.). (C). 1989. text 91.00 (*0-7462-0060-9*) Kluwer Academic.

— Pregnancy & Renal Disorders. (New Clinical Applications Nephrology Ser.). (C). 1988. text 95.50 (*0-7462-0057-9*) Kluwer Academic.

— Transplantation. (New Clinical Applications Nephrology Ser.). (C). 1989. text 121.50 (*0-7462-0116-8*) Kluwer Academic.

— Urinary Tract Infections. (New Clinical Applications Nephrology Ser.). (C). 1989. text 111.00 (*0-7462-0115-X*) Kluwer Academic.

Catto, Graeme R., et al. Diagnostic Picture Tests in Renal Disease. (Illus.). 128p. 1994. pap. 21.00 (*0-7234-1973-6*) Mosby Inc.

Catto, Henry E., Jr. Ambassadors at Sea: The High & Low Adventures of a Diplomat. LC 98-23612. (Illus.). 384p. 1998. 29.95 (*0-292-71212-X*) U of Tex Pr.

Catto, Isabelle, et al. Mathematical Theory of Thermodynamic Limits: Thomas--Fermi Type Models. (Oxford Mathematical Monographs). (Illus.). 292p. 1998. text 115.00 (*0-19-850161-7*) OUP.

Catto, J. I. The History of the University of Oxford Vol. I: The Early Oxford Schools, Vol. 1. (Illus.). 728p. 1984. text 150.00 (*0-19-951011-3*) OUP.

Catto, J. I., ed. The History of the University of Oxford Vol. II: Late Medieval Oxford, Vol. 2. (Illus.). 866p. 1993. text 180.00 (*0-19-951012-1*) OUP.

Catto, Mike. Art in Ulster 2: 1957-1977. (Illus.). 190p. 1991. reprint ed. pap. 29.00 (*0-85640-129-3*, Pub. by Blackstaff Pr) Dufour.

Catto, S. & Rocha, A., eds. Differential Geometric Methods in Theoretical Physics: Twentieth International Conference, 2 vols., Set. 1300p. 1992. text 239.00 (*981-02-0993-2*) World Scientific Pub.

Catto, Susan, jt. auth. see Lechmere, Adam.

Catto, Susan, jt. auth. see Lechunere, Adam.

Catto, William T. Semi-Centenary Discourse. LC 78-154073. (Black Heritage Library Collection). 1977. 19.95 (*0-8369-8784-5*) Ayer.

Catton, Bruce. America Goes to War. 126p. Date not set. 17.95 (*0-8488-2581-0*) Amereon Ltd.

— America Goes to War: An Introduction to the Civil War & Its Meaning to Americans Today. (Illus.). 128p. 1992. 7.98 (*1-56731-006-0*, MJF Bks) Fine Comms.

— America Goes to War: The Civil War & Its Meaning in American Culture. LC 58-13602. (Illus.). 128p. 1992. reprint ed. pap. 11.95 (*0-8195-6016-2*, Wesleyan Univ Pr) U Pr of New Eng.

— The American Heritage, Short History of the Civil War. 286p. Date not set. 23.95 (*0-8488-2232-3*) Amereon Ltd.

— Banners at Shenandoah: A Story of Sheridan's Fighting Cavalry. 254p. reprint ed. lib. bdg. 22.95 (*0-89244-019-8*) Amereon Ltd.

— The Bold & Magnificent Dream: America's Founding Years, 1492-1815. LC 98-33250. 1999. 9.99 (*0-517-20375-8*) Random Hse Value.

— Civil War. (American Heritage Library). 1985. 21.10 (*0-606-00907-8*, Pub. by Turtleback) Demco.

— The Civil War. LC 85-3969. (American Heritage Library). (Illus.). 382p. 1985. pap. 16.00 (*0-8281-0305-4*) HM.

— The Civil War. 1998. 27.00 (*0-8446-6937-7*) Peter Smith.

— Gettysburg: The Final Fury. 128p. 1990. pap. 12.95 (*0-385-41145-6*) Doubleday.

— Grant Moves South. 576p. Date not set. 33.95 (*0-8488-2234-X*) Amereon Ltd.

— Grant Moves South. (Illus.). 1960. 27.95 (*0-316-13207-1*) Little.

— Michigan, a History. 1984. pap. 13.95 (*0-393-30175-3*) Norton.

— Never Call Retreat. (Centennial History of the Civil War Ser.: Vol. 3). 572p. 1976. 33.95 (*0-8488-1266-2*) Amereon Ltd.

— Never Call Retreat. (Centennial History of the Civil War Ser. : Vol. 3). 450p. 1991. reprint ed. lib. bdg. 31.95 (*0-89966-800-3*) Buccaneer Bks.

— A New History of the Civil War. 1996. pap. write for info. (*0-670-78082-0*) Viking Penguin.

— Reflections on the Civil War. Leekley, John, ed. 272p. 1987. mass mkt. 6.99 (*0-425-10495-8*) Berkley Pub.

— Reflections on the Civil War. Leekley, John, ed. LC 94-148995. 272p. 1994. reprint ed. pap. 12.00 (*0-425-14141-1*) Berkley Pub.

— A Stillness at Appomattox. 1992. 25.50 (*0-8446-6550-9*) Peter Smith.

— A Stillness at Appomattox, Vol. III. 448p. 1953. pap. 14.95 (*0-385-04451-8*, Anchor NY) Doubleday.

— This Hallowed Ground. 1998. pap. 12.99 (*1-85326-696-5*) NTC Contemp Pub Co.

— This Hollowed Ground. 448p. Date not set. 29.95 (*0-8488-2233-1*) Amereon Ltd.

— U. S. Grant & the American Military Tradition. 1985. 20.95 (*0-8488-0279-9*, J M C & Co) Amereon Ltd.

— Waiting for the Morning Train: An American Boyhood. LC 87-10613. (Illus.). 278p. 1987. reprint ed. 29.95 (*0-8143-1884-3*, Great Lks Bks); reprint ed. pap. 16.95 (*0-8143-1885-1*, Great Lks Bks) Wayne St U Pr.

— War Lords of Washington. LC 70-90481. 313p. 1969. reprint ed. lib. bdg. 35.00 (*0-8371-2149-3*, CAWL, Greenwood Pr) Greenwood.

Catton, Chris & Gray, James. Sex in Nature. LC 85-236716. 224p. reprint ed. pap. 69.50 (*0-8357-3489-7*, 203974800013) Bks Demand.

Catton, I., ed. Heat & Mass Transfer in Porous Media. (HTD Ser.: Vol. 216). 68p. 1992. 27.50 (*0-7918-1057-7*, G00701) ASME.

Catton, I. & Torrance, K. E., eds. Natural Convection in Enclosures. (HTD Ser.: Vol. 26). 113p. 1983. pap. text 24.00 (*0-317-02635-6*, H00270) ASME.

Catton, I., ed. see National Heat Transfer Conference Staff.

Catton, Margaret M. Social Service in Hawaii. LC 58-14378. (Illus.). xx, 308p. 1959. 24.95 (*0-87015-088-X*) Pacific Bks.

Catton, Theodore. Inhabited Wilderness: Indians Eskimos & National Parks in Alaska. LC 97-4873. (New American West Ser.). 287p. 1997. 55.00 (*0-8263-1826-6*); pap. 22.95 (*0-8263-1827-4*) U of NM Pr.

Catton, William R., Jr. Overshoot: The Ecological Basis of Revolutionary Change. LC 80-13443. 320p. 1980. text 29.95 (*0-252-00818-9*) U of Ill Pr.

— Overshoot: The Ecological Basis of Revolutionary Change. LC 80-13443. 320p. 1982. pap. text 16.95 (*0-252-00988-6*) U of Ill Pr.

Cattoni, Ernesto. Good News of Jesus. 63p. (C). 1990. 35.00 (*0-85439-408-7*, Pub. by St Paul Pubns) St Mut.

Cattou, George. The Destiny of the World Between Socialism & Free Enterprise: The Worlds New Order. 135p. (Orig.). pap. text 7.00 (*0-9637473-0-4*) Euros Amer.

Cattrall, Robert W. Chemical Sensors. LC 97-20150. (Oxford Chemistry Primers: Vol. 52). (Illus.). 78p. 1997. pap. text 12.95 (*0-19-850090-4*) OUP.

Cattrell, Claire. Food: Design & Culture. (Illus.). 176p. 1999. pap. 35.00 (*1-85669-163-2*, Pub. by L King Pubng) Antique Collect.

Catts & Kamhi. Language & Reading Disabilities. LC 98-34364. 328p. 1998. pap. text 46.00 (*0-205-27088-3*) Allyn.

Catts, E. Paul, jt. ed. see Haskell, Neal.

Catts, Hugh & Olsen, Tina. Sounds Abound: Listening, Rhyming & Reading. 190p. 1993. student ed., spiral bd. 37.95 (*1-55999-394-4*) LinguiSystems.

Catty, D., ed. Antibodies: A Practical Approach, Vol. 1. (Practical Approach Ser.: 38). 220p. 1988. 85.00 (*0-947946-86-1*); pap. 45.00 (*0-947946-85-3*) OUP.

— Antibodies: A Practical Approach, Vol. 2. (Practical Approach Ser.: 44). (Illus.). 280p. 1989. pap. 45.00 (*0-19-963019-4*) OUP.

Catty, F. B., tr. see Guth, Wilfried.

***Catty, Jocelyn.** Writing Rape, Writing Women in Early Modern England: Unbridled Speech. LC 99-18661. 260p. 1999. text 65.00 (*0-312-22181-9*) St Martin.

Catucci, Stefano. Bach & Baroque Music. LC 98-72303. (Masters of Music Ser.). (Illus.). 64p. (YA). (gr. 6 up). 1998. 14.95 (*0-7641-5130-4*) Barron.

***Catudal, Jacques N.** Privacy & Rights to the Visual: The Internet Debate. (Philosophy & the Global Context Ser.). 1999. pap. 22.95 (*0-8476-8800-3*) Rowman.

Catullus, Gaius Valerius. Carmina. Mynors, Roger A., ed. (Oxford Classical Texts Ser.). 130p. 1958. text 16.95 (*0-19-814604-3*) OUP.

— Catullus. Thomson, D. F., ed. LC 97-181192. (Phoenix Supplementary Volumes Ser.: Vol. 34). 736p. 1996. text 95.00 (*0-8020-0676-0*) U of Toronto Pr.

— Catullus. Merrill, Elmer T., ed. (College Classical Ser.). (LAT.). 1988. reprint ed. text 32.50 (*0-89241-023-X*); reprint ed. pap. text 17.50 (*0-89241-381-6*) Caratzas.

— Catullus. Merrill, Elmer T., ed. 273p. 1965. reprint ed. 36.50 (*0-674-10350-5*) HUP.

— Catullus: Advanced Placement Edition. Bender, Henry V. & Forsyth, Phyllis Y., eds. LC 96-43616. (Illus.). 105p. (Orig.). 1997. pap. text, student ed. 19.00 (*0-86516-275-1*) Bolchazy-Carducci.

— Catullus: Advanced Placement Edition. Bender, Henry V. & Forsyth, Phyllis Y., eds. (Illus.). 95p. (Orig.). (YA). (gr. 9-12). 1997. pap., teacher ed. 20.00 (*0-86516-276-X*) Bolchazy-Carducci.

— Catullus: Love & Hate: Selected Short Poems Series. Kaiser, Leo M., ed. & tr. by. (ENG & LAT.). 42p. (Orig.). 1986. pap. 9.00 (*0-86516-180-1*) Bolchazy-Carducci.

— Catullus: Poems. Williamson, A. G., ed. & selected by by. 1996. pap. 20.95 (*0-86292-211-9*, Pub. by Brist Class Pr) Focus Pub-R Pullins.

— Catullus: Poems. rev. ed. Quinn, Kenneth, ed. (LAT.). 334p. (C). 1996. pap. text 33.95 (*1-85399-497-9*, Pub. by Brist Class Pr) Focus Pub-R Pullins.

— Catullus: Poems II, 61-8. Godwin, John, ed. & tr. by. from LAT. (Classical Texts Ser.). 240p. 1995. 59.99 (*0-85668-670-0*, Pub. by Aris & Phillips); pap. 23.00 (*0-85668-671-9*, Pub. by Aris & Phillips) David Brown.

***Catullus, Gaius Valerius.** Catullus: The Shorter Poems. Godwin, John, ed. & tr. by. from LAT. (Classical Texts Ser.). 240p. 1999. pap. text 28.00 (*0-85668-715-4*, Pub. by Aris & Phillips) David Brown.

— Catullus: The Shorter Poems. Godwin, John, ed. & tr. by. from LAT. (Classical Texts Ser.). 240p. (C). 1999. text 59.95 (*0-85668-714-6*, Pub. by Aris & Phillips) David Brown.

Catullus, Gaius Valerius. Catullus Redivivus. Hamill, Sam, tr. 96p. (Orig.). 1986. pap. 23.00 (*0-911287-10-8*) Blue Begonia.

— Catullus, Tibullus & Pervigilium Veneris. Warmington, E. H., ed. Cornish, Francis W. et al, trs. (Loeb Classical Library: No. 6). (ENG & LAT.). 394p. 1950. 18.55 (*0-674-99007-2*) HUP.

— Catullus's Complete Poetic Works. Rabinowitz, Jacob, tr. from LAT. & anno. by. LC 91-11173. (Dunquin Ser.: No. 20). 150p. (Orig.). 1991. pap. 15.00 (*0-88214-220-8*) Spring Pubns.

— The Poems of Catullus. Martin, Charles, tr. from LAT. LC 89-45486. 208p. 1989. pap. 13.95 (*0-8018-3926-2*); text 35.00 (*0-8018-3925-4*) Johns Hopkins.

— The Poems of Catullus. 224p. 1998. pap. 10.95 (*0-19-283587-4*) OUP.

— The Poems of Catullus. Whigham, Peter, tr. from LAT. (Classics Ser.). 254p. 1966. pap. 16.99 (*0-14-044180-8*, Penguin Classics) Viking Penguin.

— Poems of Catullus. Michie, James, tr. 240p. 1989. pap. 18.95 (*1-85399-129-5*, Pub. by Brist Class Pr) Focus Pub-R Pullins.

— Selections from Catullus. Lyne, R. O., ed. (Cambridge Latin Texts Ser.). 31p. 1973. pap. text 9.95 (*0-521-20267-1*) Cambridge U Pr.

— The Student's Catullus. annuals 2nd ed. Garrison, Daniel H., ed. LC 95-1280. (Oklahoma Series in Classical Culture: Vol. 5). (LAT., Illus.). 248p. 1995. pap. text 15.95 (*0-8061-2763-5*) U of Okla Pr.

Caturano, Terry, ed. see Buttram, Nora.

***CatWatch Editors.** The Best of CatWatch Vols. I & II: The Newsletter for Cat People. (Illus.). 187p. 2000. 19.95 (*1-929942-04-4*) Torstar.

Catz, Rebecca. Christopher Columbus & the Portuguese, 1476-1498, Vol. 39. LC 93-18141. (Contributions to the Study of World History Ser.: No. 39). 144p. 1993. 49.95 (*0-313-28867-4*, GM8867) Greenwood.

Catz, Rebecca D., ed. & tr. see Pinto, Fernao Mendes.

Catz, Sylvester L. Joints & Bones of Humans-Afflictions, Conditions & Treatments: Index of New Information. 160p. Date not set. 47.50 (*0-7883-1936-1*); pap. 44.50 (*0-7883-1937-X*) ABBE Pubs Assn.

Cau, A., jt. auth. see Zedan, Hussein.

Cau, Jean. La Pitie de Dieu. (FRE.). 384p. 1974. pap. 10.95 (*0-7859-1780-2*, 2070365565) Fr & Eur.

Caubang, Ted C. & Economic Development Foundation Staff. Readings on Production Planning & Control. (Illus.). 178p. 1972. text 15.75 (*92-833-1017-9*, 310179); pap. text 12.00 (*92-833-1018-7*, 310187) Productivity Inc.

Caubarreaux, Eric R. America's Most Decorated: A Reference Book Profiling the Most Decorated People in the U. S. Military. rev. ed. Caubarreaux, Peggy A., ed. LC 97-92929. (Illus.). 90p. 1997. pap. 39.95 (*0-9652924-1-X*) Medals Pr.

— America's Most Decorated Vol. 1: A Reference Book Profiling the Most Decorated People in the U. S. Military. Caubarreaux, Peggy A., ed. LC 96-94523. (Illus.). x, 98p. (Orig.). 1996. 34.95 (*0-9652924-0-1*) Medals Pr.

— America's Most Decorated Vol. 2: A Reference Book Profiling the Most Decorated People in the U. S. Military. Caubarreaux, Peggy A., ed. LC 97-92929. (Illus.). 90p. (Orig.). 1997. pap. 39.95 (*0-9652924-2-8*) Medals Pr.

— America's Most Decorated Vol. 3: A Reference Book Profiling the Most Decorated People in the U. S. Military. Caubarreaux, Peggy A., ed. LC 96-94523. (Illus.). 90p. 1997. pap. 24.95 (*0-9652924-3-6*) Medals Pr.

— Decorations & Awards of Heroes of the U. S. Military. LC 99-70520. (Illus.). 200p. 1999. spiral bd. 99.95 (*0-9652924-5-2*) Medals Pr.

Caubarreaux, Peggy A., ed. see Caubarreaux, Eric R.

Caubet. Ancient Near East. 1998. pap. 27.50 (*2-87939-152-0*) Stewart Tabori & Chang.

Caubet, Annie & Bernus-Taylor, Marthe. The Louvre: Near Eastern Antiquities. (Illus.). 96p. 1991. 30.00 (*1-870248-80-5*) Scala Books.

Caubi, Luis F. Apuntes Sobre la Nacionalidad Cubana. LC 96-83780. (Coleccion Cuba y Sus Jueces Ser.). (SPA.). 141p. (Orig.). 1996. pap. 15.00 (*0-89729-798-9*) Ediciones.

— Cuba Justicia y Terror. LC 94-70487. (Coleccion Cuba y sus Jueces). 124p. 1994. pap. 13.00 (*0-89729-730-X*) Ediciones.

Cauble, Chris, ed. Montana: The Last Best Place. LC 92-72803. (Illus.). 120p. 1992. 29.95 (*1-56044-151-8*) Falcon Pub Inc.

Cauble, Chris, ed. see Graham, Gary.

Cauble, Chris, ed. see Gray, Mary T.

Cauble, Chris, ed. see Knue, Joseph.

Cauble, Chris, ed. see Roe, Charles.

Cauble, Chris, ed. see Seng, Phil T. & Chase, David J.

Cauble, Frank P. Biography of Wilmer McLean, May 3, 1814 - June 5, 1882. (Illus.). 114p. 1987. 12.95 (*0-930919-39-4*) H E Howard.

— The Surrender Proceedings, April 9, 1865, Appomattox Court House. (Illus.). 141p. 1987. 12.95 (*0-930919-40-8*) H E Howard.

Cauble, John, ed. see Klain, James.

Cauble, Karen. 33 Days Hath September: A Travel Adventure Cookbook on Alaska's Yukon River. (Illus.). 100p. 1992. pap. 9.95 (*0-940055-74-0*) Vanessapress.

Cauble, R. S. Echoes. 70p. 1997. pap. write for info. (*1-57502-640-6*, P01818) Morris Pubng.

Cauchi, Francesca. Zarathustra Contra Zarathustra: The Tragic Buffoon. (Avebury Series in Philosophy). 196p. 1998. text 63.95 (*1-84014-351-7*, Pub. by Ashgate Pub) Ashgate Pub Co.

Cauchi, Patrick & Carbone, Joyce. Sleeping with Our Sons & Daughters. LC 92-90015. (Orig.). 1992. pap. 8.95 (*1-878116-12-6*) JVC Bks.

Cauchi, Patrick J. Concessions. LC 91-90087. (Illus.). 84p. (Orig.). 1991. pap. 7.95 (*1-878116-07-X*) JVC Bks.

Cauchi, Patrick S. Upon Your Sword. (Illus.). 92p. (Orig.). 1993. pap. 8.95 (*1-878116-18-5*) JVC Bks.

Cauchi, Simon, ed. see Virgil.

Cauchie, Maurice. Thematic Index of the Works of Francois Couperin. LC 74-24057. reprint ed. 37.50 (*0-404-12879-3*) AMS Pr.

Cauchois, Y., et al, eds. Wavelengths of X-Ray Emission Lines & Absorption Edges. LC 78-40419. 1978. pap. text 80.00 (*0-685-04017-8*, Pub. by Pergamon Repr) Franklin.

***Cauchon, Janet Wirth.** Women & Borderline Personality Disorder: Symptoms & Stories. LC 00-39037. 192p. 2001. text 52.00 (*0-8135-2890-9*); pap. text 22.00 (*0-8135-2891-7*) Rutgers U Pr.

Caudell, Thomas, jt. auth. see Barfield, Woodrow.

Caudell, Thomas, jt. ed. see Barfield, Woodrow.

Caudery, Tim, ed. New Thinking in TEFL. (The Dolphin Ser.: No. 21). 192p. (C). 1992. pap. 19.95 (*87-7288-371-5*, Pub. by Aarhus Univ Pr) David Brown.

Caudill. Did You Carry the Flag Today? (J). 1995. 16.95 (*0-8050-4400-0*) H Holt & Co.

C

An Asterisk (*) at the beginning of an entry indicates that the title is appearing for the first time.

Caudill, David S. Lacan & the Subject of Law: Toward a Psychoanalytic Critical Legal Theory. LC 96-24792. 200p. (C). 1997. pap. 15.00 (*0-391-04010-3*); text 49.95 (*0-391-04009-X*) Humanities.

Caudill, David S. & Gold, Steven J., eds. Radical Philosophy of Law: Contemporary Challenges to Mainstream Legal Theory & Practice. LC 94-18238. 386p. (C). 1995. pap. 18.50 (*0-391-03862-1*) Humanities.

— Radical Philosophy of Law: Contemporary Challenges to Mainstream Legal Theory & Practice. LC 94-18238. 386p. (C). 1995. text 49.95 (*0-391-03861-3*) Humanities.

Caudill, Ed, ed. Darwinism in the Press: The Evolution of an Idea. 184p. (C). 1990. text 36.00 (*0-8058-0521-4*) L Erlbaum Assocs.

Caudill, Edward. Darwinian Myths: The Legends & Misuses of a Theory. LC 97-4691. 208p. (C). 1997. text 35.00 (*0-87049-984-X*) U of Tenn Pr.

***Caudill, Edward, intro.** The Scopes Trial: A Photographic History. LC 99-50735. (Illus.). 112p. 2000. 45.00 (*1-57233-080-5*); pap. 18.95 (*1-57233-081-3*) U of Tenn Pr.

Caudill, Gertrude. Monkey on a Bellrope. 1992. pap. 8.95 (*0-9626441-1-0*) Drift Creek Pr.

Caudill, Gertrude, jt. auth. see Caudill, Rebecca.

Caudill, Gil & Croteau, James. Guiding Images: Helping Gifted & Talented & Creative Children. (Orig.). 1993. pap. 14.99 (*0-89824-529-X*) Trillium Pr.

Caudill, H. Edwin. Traditional Episcopal. 44p. 1990. pap. write for info. (*1-889711-05-5*) Cathedral Direct.

Caudill, Harry. Slender Is the Thread: Tales from a Country Law Office. LC 87-1983. 192p. (C). 1987. reprint ed. pap. 16.00 (*0-8131-0811-X*) U Pr of Ky.

Caudill, Harry M. Dark Hills to Westward: The Saga of Jenny Wiley. LC 94-19890. 256p. 1994. reprint ed. 22.00 (*0-945084-45-5*) J Stuart Found.

— A Darkness at Dawn: Appalachian Kentucky & the Future. LC 74-7871. (Kentucky Bicentennial Bookshelf Ser.). 88p. reprint ed. pap. 30.00 (*0-8357-4293-8*, 203709100007) Bks Demand.

— Lester's Progress. LC 86-82569. 106p. (Orig.). 1986. pap. 6.95 (*0-935680-29-2*) Kentucke Imprints.

— Mountain, the Miner & the Lord, & Other Tales from a Country Law Office. LC 80-51012. 192p. 1980. pap. 16.00 (*0-8131-0195-6*) U Pr of Ky.

— Night Comes to the Cumberlands: Biography of a Depressed Area. 394p. 1964. pap. 15.95 (*0-316-13212-8*) Little.

— The Senator from Slaughter County. LC 97-31650. (Illus.). 1997. reprint ed. pap. 14.95 (*0-945084-66-8*) J Stuart Found.

— Theirs Be the Power: The Moguls of Eastern Kentucky. LC 83-5771. 224p. reprint ed. pap. 69.50 (*0-7837-5734-4*, 204539500006) Bks Demand.

Caudill, Kathy. Landscapes in Watercolor. (How to Draw & Paint Ser.). (Illus.). 32p. (Orig.). 1995. pap. 6.95 (*1-56010-144-X*, HT245) W Foster Pub.

Caudill, L. Susan, jt. auth. see Caudill, Steven W.

Caudill, Margaret A. Managing Pain Before It Manages You. LC 94-17730. 224p. 1994. pap. text 19.95 (*0-89862-224-7*, 2224) Guilford Pubns.

Caudill, Maureen. Understanding Neural Networks: Computer Explorations, 2 vols., Vol. 1. LC 92-224098. Vol. 1. 1992. 52.50 (*0-262-53102-X*, Bradford Bks) MIT Pr.

— Understanding Neural Networks: Computer Explorations, 2 vols., Vol 1: Basic Networks, IBM. LC 92-224098. Vol. 1. (Illus.). 1992. 52.50 (*0-262-53099-6*, Bradford Bks) MIT Pr.

— Understanding Neural Networks: Computer Explorations, 2 vols., Vol. 2. LC 92-224098. Vol. 2. (Illus.). 1992. 52.50 (*0-262-53103-8*, Bradford Bks) MIT Pr.

Caudill, Maureen, ed. Proceedings of the Winter, 1990, International Joint Conference on Neural Networks, 2 Vols., Set. 1590p. (C). 1990. pap. text 220.00 (*0-8058-0754-3*) L Erlbaum Assocs.

Caudill, Maureen & Butler, Charles. Naturally Intelligent Systems. (Illus.). 320p. 1992. reprint ed. pap. text 17.50 (*0-262-53113-5*, Bradford Bks) MIT Pr.

***Caudill, O. Brandt, Jr. & Pope, Kenneth S.** L&MHP: California, 1999 Supplement. 1999. 24.95 (*1-55798-550-2*) Am Psychol.

Caudill, O. Brant & Pope, Kenneth S. Law & Mental Health Professionals: California. LC 94-40248. 630p. 1995. text 59.95 (*1-55798-276-7*, 431-5100) Am Psychol.

Caudill, R. A Certain Small Shepherd. (J). 1971. 9.05 (*0-606-12217-6*, Pub. by Turtleback) Demco.

Caudill, R. Paul. The Mountain Preacher, Vol. 1. LC 84-71992. 1984. pap. 2.98 (*0-938980-02-5*) Blue Ridge.

— The Mountain Preacher, Vol. 2. LC 84-71992. (Illus.). 165p. 1985. pap. 3.00 (*0-938980-03-3*) Blue Ridge.

— The Mountain Preacher, Vol. 3. LC 84-71992. (Illus.). 165p. 1986. pap. 3.00 (*0-938980-05-X*) Blue Ridge.

— Philippians: A Translation with Notes. LC 80-70403. (Orig.). 1981. pap. 2.25 (*0-938980-00-9*) Blue Ridge.

— Seeds of Faith, Vol. I. (Illus.). 175p. (Orig.). 1987. pap. 3.00 (*0-317-65700-3*) Blue Ridge.

— Seeds of Faith, Vol. II. (Illus.). 210p. (Orig.). 1988. pap. 3.00 (*0-938980-07-6*) Blue Ridge.

Caudill, Rebecca. The Best-Loved Doll. (Illus.). 1997. pap. 6.95 (*0-8050-5467-7*) H Holt & Co.

— The Best-Loved Doll. 1997. 12.05 (*0-606-13197-3*, Pub. by Turtleback) Demco.

— Did You Carry the Flag Today, Charley? LC 66-11422. (Illus.). 96p. (J). (gr. 2-4). 1995. 16.95 (*0-8050-1201-X*, Bks Young Read); 3.95 (*0-03-086620-0*, Bks Young Read) H Holt & Co.

— Did You Carry the Flag Today, Charley? (J). 1966. 8.60 (*0-606-02815-3*, Pub. by Turtleback) Demco.

— Did You Carry the Flag Today, Charley? 96p. (J). (gr. k-6). 1988. reprint ed. pap. 3.99 (*0-440-40092-9*) Dell.

— A Pocketful of Cricket. LC 64-12617. (Illus.). 48p. (J). (gr. k-2). 1995. pap. 5.95 (*0-8050-1275-3*, Bks Young Read) H Holt & Co.

Caudill, Rebecca & Caudill, Gertrude. A Certain Small Shepherd. (Illus.). 48p. (J). (ps-3). 1997. pap. 6.95 (*0-8050-5392-1*) H Holt & Co.

Caudill, Rebecca & Pene Du Bois, William. A Certain Small Shepherd. LC 65-17604. (Illus.). 88p. (J). (gr. 2-4). 1995. 14.95 (*0-8050-1323-7*, Bks Young Read) H Holt & Co.

Caudill, Roy. A Christmas Classic Celebration: Candlelight Service for Christmas Eve. 20p. 1998. pap. 3.95 (*0-7880-1291-6*) CSS OH.

— Funeral Service for Jesus/He Is Not Here: A Service for Good Friday/An Easter Sunrise Service. 24p. 1997. pap. 4.50 (*0-7880-1137-5*) CSS OH.

Caudill-Slosberg, Margaret. Controle el Dolor Antes de Que el Dolor le Controle a Usted. Custodio, Isabel, tr. 256p. 1997. pap. text 19.95 (*1-57230-357-3*) Guilford Pubns.

Caudill, Steven W. & Caudill, L. Susan. Couponing for Wealth: The Only Couponing & Money Guide that Shows You How to Quickly Organize & Turn Cents-off Coupons into Thousands of Extra Dollars. LC 90-61928. 140p. 1990. pap. 9.95 (*0-9627101-0-5*) Money Watchers Pub.

Caudle, Ann. Guide to Cisco Routing. (Networking Ser.). (C). 2000. pap. text 60.95 (*0-619-00092-9*) Course Tech.

Caudle, Brad & Caudle, Melissa. Animals. (Rock 'N Learn Ser.). (Illus.). 32p. (J). (ps-k). 1995. pap. 12.99 incl. audio (*1-878489-49-6*, RL949) Rock N Learn.

— The Little Red Hen. unabridged ed. (Rock 'N Read Ser.). (Illus.). 20p. (J). (gr. 1 up). 1996. pap. 7.95 incl. audio (*1-878489-69-0*, RL969) Rock N Learn.

Caudle, Brad & Caudle, Melissa. Oceans. (Rock 'n Learn Ser.). (J). 7.98 incl. audio NewSound.

Caudle, Brad & Caudle, Melissa. Oceans. unabridged ed. (Rock 'N Learn Ser.). (Illus.). 32p. (J). (gr. 2 up). 1998. pap. 12.99 incl. audio (*1-878489-75-5*, RL975) Rock N Learn.

— Solar System. unabridged ed. (Rock 'N Learn Ser.). (Illus.). 24p. (J). (gr. 2 up). 1997. pap. 12.99 incl. audio (*1-878489-60-7*, RL960) Rock N Learn.

***Caudle, Brad & Caudle, Melissa.** Spiders & Insects. unabridged ed. (Rock 'n Learn Ser.). (Illus.). 32p. (J). (gr. 2-6). 1999. pap. 12.99 incl. audio (*1-878489-55-0*, RL955) Rock N Learn.

Caudle, Brad & Caudle, Richard. Addition & Subtraction Country. (Rock 'N Learn Ser.). (Illus.). 24p. (J). (gr. 1 up). 1995. pap. 12.99 incl. audio (*1-878489-33-X*, RL933) Rock N Learn.

— Addition & Subtraction Rock. unabridged ed. (Rock 'N Learn Ser.). (Illus.). 28p. (J). (gr. 1 up). 1993. pap. 12.99 incl. audio (*1-878489-06-2*, RL906) Rock N Learn.

— Addition Rap. unabridged ed. (Rock 'N Learn Ser.). (Illus.). 24p. (J). (gr. 1 up). 1992. 12.99 incl. audio (*1-878489-09-7*, RL909) Rock N Learn.

— Building Self-Esteem. unabridged ed. (Rock 'N Learn Ser.). (Illus.). 18p. (J). (gr. 1 up). 1994. pap. 9.95 incl. audio (*1-878489-43-7*, RL943) Rock N Learn.

— Division Rap. unabridged ed. (Rock 'N Learn Ser.). (Illus.). 24p. (J). (gr. 3 up). 1992. pap. 12.99 incl. audio (*1-878489-08-9*, RL908) Rock N Learn.

— Division Rock. unabridged ed. (Rock 'N Learn Ser.). (Illus.). 22p. (J). (gr. 3 up). 1994. pap. 12.99 incl. audio (*1-878489-41-0*, RL941) Rock N Learn.

— French, Vol. 1. unabridged ed. (Rock 'N Learn Ser.). (Illus.). 16p. (YA). (gr. 1 up). 1993. pap. 12.99 incl. audio (*1-878489-26-7*, RL926) Rock N Learn.

— Grammar, Vol. 1. unabridged ed. (Rock 'N Learn Ser.). (Illus.). 24p. (J). (gr. 1-5). 1994. pap. 12.99 incl. audio (*1-878489-29-1*, RL929) Rock N Learn.

— Letter Sounds - Phonics for Beginners. rev. ed. (Rock 'N Learn Ser.). (Illus.). 28p. (J). (gr. k-2). 1997. pap. 12.99 incl. audio (*1-878489-11-9*, RL911) Rock N Learn.

— Multiplicacion Rap in Spanish. unabridged ed. (Rock 'N Learn Ser.). (SPA., Illus.). 20p. (J). (gr. 3 up). 1994. pap. 9.95 incl. audio (*1-878489-27-5*, RL927) Rock N Learn.

— Multiplication Rap. unabridged ed. (Rock 'N Learn Ser.). (Illus.). 24p. (J). (gr. 3 up). 1991. pap. 12.99 incl. audio (*1-878489-07-0*, RL907) Rock N Learn.

— Multiplication Rap. unabridged ed. (Rock n' Learn Ser.). (Illus.). 24p. (J). (gr. 3 up). 1994. pap. 12.95 incl. audio compact disk (*1-878489-37-2*, RL937) Rock N Learn.

— Multiplication Rock. unabridged ed. (Rock 'n Learn Ser.). (Illus.). 24p. (J). (gr. 3 up). 1992. pap. 12.99 incl. audio (*1-878489-05-4*, RL905) Rock N Learn.

— Phonics, Vol. I. unabridged ed. (Rock 'N Learn Ser.). (Illus.). 16p. (J). (gr. 1-12). 1994. pap. 9.95 incl. audio (*1-878489-30-5*, RL930) Rock N Learn.

— Phonics, Vol. II. unabridged ed. (Rock 'N Learn Ser.). (Illus.). 16p. (J). (gr. 1-12). 1994. pap. 9.95 incl. audio (*1-878489-31-3*, RL931) Rock N Learn.

— Phonics, Vols. I & II. (Rock 'N Learn Ser.). (Illus.). 24p. (J). (gr. 1 up). 1990. pap. 15.95 incl. audio (*1-878489-00-3*, RL900) Rock N Learn.

— Spanish, Vol. I. unabridged ed. (Rock 'N Learn Ser.). (Illus.). 28p. (J). (gr. 1-12). 1993. pap. 12.99 incl. audio (*1-878489-19-4*, RL919) Rock N Learn.

— States & Capitals Rap. unabridged ed. (Rock 'N Learn Ser.). (Illus.). 24p. (J). (gr. 4-12). 1993. 12.99 incl. audio (*1-878489-15-1*, RL915) Rock N Learn.

— Subtraction Rap. unabridged ed. (Rock 'N Learn Ser.). (Illus.). 24p. (J). (gr. 1 up). 1992. pap. 12.99 incl. audio (*1-878489-10-0*, RL910) Rock N Learn.

Caudle, C. Edd. Motivation for Greatness. Brotherton, Velda, ed. LC 96-161560. 1969. 4.50 (*0-9652493-0-1*) E C Publishing.

Caudle, David J., jt. auth. see Green, Suzanne Disheroon.

Caudle, Iris. Amazing Paragons. 1998. pap. write for info. (*1-57553-989-6*) Watermrk Pr.

— I Am a Poet. 1998. pap. write for info. (*1-57553-864-4*) Watermrk Pr.

Caudle, Melissa. Phonics Easy Readers, 4 bks. (Rock 'N Learn Ser.). (Illus.). 40p. (J). (gr. k-2). 1997. pap. 11.95 (*1-878489-65-8*, RL965) Rock N Learn.

Caudle, Melissa & Herbert, Trey. Spanish, Vol. II. unabridged ed. (Rock 'N Learn Ser.). (ENG & SPA., Illus.). 32p. (J). (gr. 1-12). 1995. pap. 12.99 incl. audio (*1-878489-34-8*, RL934) Rock N Learn.

Caudle, Melissa, jt. auth. see Caudle, Brad.

Caudle, Melissa, jt. auth. see Caudle, Richard.

Caudle, Neil, jt. auth. see Woodall, Brad.

Caudle, Richard & Caudle, Melissa. Jack & the Beanstalk. unabridged ed. (Rock 'N Read Ser.). (Illus.). 20p. (J). (gr. 1 up). 1996. pap. 7.95 incl. audio (*1-878489-66-6*, RL966) Rock N Learn.

Caudle, Richard, et al. The Three Little Pigs. unabridged ed. (Rock 'N Read Ser.). (Illus.). 20p. (J). (gr. 1 up). 1996. pap. 7.95 incl. audio (*1-878489-67-4*, RL967) Rock N Learn.

— The Ugly Duckling: Rock 'n Read. unabridged ed. (Rock 'N Read Ser.). (Illus.). 20p. (J). (gr. 1 up). 1996. pap. 7.95 incl. audio (*1-878489-68-2*, RL968) Rock N Learn.

Caudle, Richard, jt. auth. see Caudle, Brad.

Caudle, Todd. Colorado Seasons. (Illus.). 160p. 1994. pap. 14.95 (*0-9632012-4-7*) Skyline Pr.

— Colorado Wet & Wild. (Illus.). 80p. 1995. 14.95 (*0-9632012-6-3*) Skyline Pr.

***Caudle, Todd.** Garden of the Gods. (Colorado Souvenir Ser.). (Illus.). 64p. 1998. pap. 9.95 (*1-888845-05-8*) Skyline Pr.

— Magnificent Colorado. (Colorado Souvenir Ser.). (Illus.). 64p. 1998. pap. 9.95 (*1-888845-06-6*) Skyline Pr.

— Pikes Peak & Garden of the Gods: Two Worlds, One Vision. (Illus.). 96p. 1997. 25.00 (*1-888845-00-7*) Skyline Pr.

Caudron, Andre, ed. see Mayeur, Jean-Marie & Hilaire, Yves-Marie.

***Caudron, Cordell.** Perihelion. 85p. 2000. 17.95 (*0-7541-1294-2*, Pub. by Minerva Pr) Unity Dist.

Caudron, Shari. Lifestyle: Butte County. (Illus.). (Orig.). 1989. pap. 6.50 (*0-685-29406-4*) Busn Ctr Chico.

Caudwell, Christopher. Romance & Realism: A Study in English Bourgeois Literature. Hynes, Samuel, ed. LC 78-120752. 148p. 1970. reprint ed. pap. 45.90 (*0-7837-8578-X*, 204939300011) Bks Demand.

— Studies & Further Studies in a Dying Culture. LC 77-142989. 544p. 1972. reprint ed. pap. 11.00 (*0-85345-218-0*, Pub. by Monthly Rev) NYU Pr.

Caudwell, Christopher, et al. Scenes & Actions: Unpublished Manuscripts. (Illus.). 224p. 1987. pap. 19.95 (*0-7102-0985-1*, 09851, Routledge Thoemms) Routledge.

Caudwell, Sarah L. The Shortest Way to Hades. 320p. 1995. mass mkt. 5.99 (*0-440-21233-2*) Dell.

***Caudwell, Sarah L.** The Sibyl in Her Grave. LC 99-59212. 304p. 2000. 23.95 (*0-385-29934-6*) Delacorte.

Caudwell, Sarah L. Thus Was Adonis Murdered. 320p. 1994. mass mkt. 5.99 (*0-440-21231-6*) Dell.

Caudy, Don W., jt. auth. see Hackman, Donald J.

Cauer, Paul. Grundfragen der Homerkritik. (GER.). v, 709p. 1971. reprint ed. 150.00 (*0-318-70899-X*) G Olms Pubs.

Cauet, Fernand, jt. auth. see Bornecque, Henri.

Caufagno, G. Farmland Preservation Directory. 180p. 1986. 12.00 (*0-318-23276-6*) Natl Resources Defense Coun.

Cauffiel, Lowell. Dark Rage. 352p. 1997. mass mkt. 5.99 (*0-7860-0355-3*, Pinncle Kensgtn) Kensgtn Pub Corp.

— Eye of the Beholder. 512p. 1995. mass mkt. 5.99 (*0-8217-0121-5*, Zebra Kensgtn); mass mkt. 5.99 (*0-7860-0121-6*, Pinncle Kensgtn) Kensgtn Pub Corp.

— Forever & Five Days. 544p. 1993. mass mkt. 4.99 (*0-8217-4213-2*, Zebra Kensgtn) Kensgtn Pub Corp.

— Forever & Five Days. 544p. 1997. mass mkt. 5.99 (*0-7860-0469-X*, Pinncle Kensgtn) Kensgtn Pub Corp.

— House of Secrets. LC 97-71645. 320p. 1997. 23.00 (*1-57566-221-3*, Knsington) Kensgtn Pub Corp.

— House of Secrets. 432p. 1998. mass mkt. 5.99 (*0-7860-0579-3*, Pinncle Kensgtn) Kensgtn Pub Corp.

***Cauffiel, Lowell.** House of Secrets. 1999. pap. 6.50 (*0-7860-1185-8*, Pinncle Kensgtn) Kensgtn Pub Corp.

Cauffiel, Lowell. Marker. LC 97-9111. 1997. text 23.95 (*0-312-15583-2*) St Martin.

— Marker. 1998. mass mkt. 6.50 (*0-312-96497-8*) St Martin.

— Masquerade. 1989. mass mkt. 4.95 (*0-8217-2833-4*, Zebra Kensgtn) Kensgtn Pub Corp.

— Masquerade. 480p. 1997. mass mkt. 5.99 (*0-7860-0468-1*, Pinncle Kensgtn) Kensgtn Pub Corp.

Cauffiel, William, jt. auth. see Esiason, Boomer.

Cauffield, Joyce V., et al, eds. The River Book: Cincinnati & the Ohio. 2nd ed. LC 81-83675. (Illus.). 228p. (gr. 7-12). 1982. reprint ed. 29.95 (*0-9608200-0-0*) Prog Cincinnati.

Caufield, Catherine. In the Rainforest: Report from a Strange, Beautiful, Imperiled World. LC 85-24620. xii, 320p. 1986. pap. 15.95 (*0-226-09786-2*) U Ch Pr.

— Masters of Illusion: The World Bank & the Poverty of Nations. LC 96-16804. 384p. 1995. 27.50 (*0-8050-2875-7*) H Holt & Co.

— Multiple Exposures: Chronicles of the Radiation Age. (Illus.). 312p. 1990. pap. 16.95 (*0-226-09785-4*) U Ch Pr.

Caufield, Gregory M., jt. auth. see Schwartz, Barbara K.

Caufield, Jack & Wells, Harold C. One Hundred Ways to Enhance Self-Concept in the Classroom. 2nd ed. 250p. 1993. pap. text 34.99 (*0-205-15415-8*, Longwood Div) Allyn.

Caufield, Sue Ann. In Defense of Honor: Sexual Morality, Modernity & Nation in Early Twentieth Century Brazil. LC 99-28323. 320p. 1999. pap. 19.95 (*0-8223-2398-2*) Duke.

Caufriez, A. & Forest, M. G., eds. Recent Advances in the Pharmcological Control of Gonadal Function. (Journal: Hormone Research Ser.: Vol. 28, No. 2-4, 1987). vi, 212p. 1988. pap. 108.00 (*3-8055-4822-2*) S Karger.

***Caughey, Bruce & Whitehead, Doug.** Colorado's Best: The Essential Guide to Favorite Places. (Illus.). 240p. 2000. pap. 16.95 (*1-55591-435-7*) Fulcrum Pub.

Caughey, Bruce & Winstanley, Dean. The Colorado Guide. 4th rev. ed. LC 97-465. (Illus.). 608p. 1997. pap. 19.95 (*1-55591-329-6*) Fulcrum Pub.

Caughey, C. A. Depositional Systems in the Paluxy Formation (Lower Cretaceous), Northeast Texas--Oil, Gas, & Ground-Water Resources. (Geological Circular Ser.: GC 77-8). (Illus.). 59p. 1977. reprint ed. pap. 2.50 (*0-686-29327-4*) Bur Econ Geology.

Caughey, D. A. & Hafez, M. M. Frontiers of Computational Fluid Dynamics 1998 LC 98-46926. 1998. 101.00 (*981-02-3707-3*) World Scientific Pub.

Caughey, D. A. & Hafez, M. M., eds. Frontiers of Computational Fluid Dynamics, 1994. (Computational Methods in Mechanics & Aerodynamics Ser.). 654p. 1995. 125.00 (*0-471-95334-2*) Wiley.

***Caughey, Ellen.** Eric Liddell. 208p. 2000. pap. 3.97 (*1-57748-667-6*) Barbour Pub.

— Eric Liddell: Gold Medal Missionary. (Young Reader's Christian Library). (Illus.). 224p. (J). 2000. pap. 1.39 (*1-57748-721-4*) Barbour Pub.

Caughey, Ellen. Samuel. (Young Reader's Christian Library). (Illus.). 220p. (YA). (gr. 8-12). 1999. pap. 1.39 (*1-57748-516-5*) Barbour Pub.

***Caughey, Ellen.** Zacchaeus Meets Jesus. (Little Bible Bks.). (Illus.). 24p. (J). (ps-1). 2000. 1.99 (*1-57748-683-8*) Barbour Pub.

Caughey, Ellen, ed. Promises of the Psalms. LC 98-119958. 192p. 1997. lthr. 4.97 (*1-57748-077-5*) Barbour Pub.

Caughey, Ellen W. Daniel. (Young Reader's Christian Library). (Illus.). 192p. (J). (gr. 3-7). 1998. pap. 1.39 (*1-57748-366-9*) Barbour Pub.

Caughey, George H. Mast Cell Proteases in Immunology & Biology, No. 6. (Clinical Allergy & Immunology Ser.: Vol. 6). (Illus.). 352p. 1995. text 170.00 (*0-8247-9484-2*) Dekker.

***Caughey, James.** Arrows from My Quiver: Selected from the Private Papers of the Reverend James Caughey. (Illus.). 336p. 1999. reprint ed. pap. 14.99 (*0-88019-388-3*) Schmul Pub Co.

— Earnest Christianity Illustrated: Selections from the Journal of the Rev. James Caughey. 2nd rev. ed. (Illus.). 328p. 1997. pap. 16.99 (*0-88019-368-9*) Schmul Pub Co.

Caughey, James, et al. Holiness Readings: A Selection of papers on the Doctrine, Experience & Practice of Holiness. 1984. pap. 9.99 (*0-88019-045-0*) Schmul Pub Co.

Caughey, John & Caughey, LaRee, eds. Los Angeles: Biography of a City. LC 75-17300. 1976. pap. 18.95 (*0-520-03410-4*, Pub. by U CA Pr) Cal Prin Full Svc.

Caughey, John L. Imaginary Social Worlds: A Cultural Approach. LC 83-6702. viii, 280p. 1984. text 45.00 (*0-8032-1421-9*) U of Nebr Pr.

Caughey, John W., ed. see Wilson, B. D.

Caughey, LaRee, jt. ed. see Caughey, John.

Caughey, Mildred. Through the Eyes of a Child. 83p. 1979. 9.95 (*0-87770-224-1*) Ye Galleon.

Caughie, J. Theories of Authorship: Reader. 318p. (C). 1981. pap. 21.99 (*0-415-02552-4*) Routledge.

***Caughie, John.** Television Drama: Realism, Modernism, & British Culture. (Oxford Television Studies). 272p. 2000. pap. 24.95 (*0-19-874218-5*); text 42.00 (*0-19-874219-3*) OUP.

Caughie, John, ed. Theories of Authorship. (BFI Readers in Film Ser.). (Illus.). 320p. 1981. pap. 15.95 (*0-7100-0650-0*, Routledge Thoemms) Routledge.

Caughie, John, ed. see British Film Institute Staff.

Caughie, Pamela L. Passing & Pedagogy: The Dynamics of Responsibility. LC 98-58007. 304p. 1999. pap. text 18.95 (*0-252-06770-3*) U of Ill Pr.

— Passing & Pedagogy: The Dynamics of Responsibility. LC 98-58007. (Illus.). 286p. 1999. 42.50 (*0-252-02466-4*) U of Ill Pr.

— Virginia Woolf & Postmodernism: Literature in Quest & Question of Itself. 256p. 1991. text 39.95 (*0-252-01763-3*) U of Ill Pr.

***Caughie, Pamela L., ed.** Virginia Woolf in the Age of Mechanical Reproduction. LC 99-50393. (Border Crossings Ser.: Vol. 6). 336p. 1999. 70.00 (*0-8153-2761-7*, H2045) Garland.

Caughlan, Larry. Yoga: The Spirit of Union. 3rd ed. 112p. (C). 1996. pap. text, per. 17.50 (*0-7872-2115-5*) Kendall-Hunt.

Caughley, Graeme. Analysis of Vertebrate Populations. LC 76-913. 244p. reprint ed. pap. 75.70 (*0-8357-5442-1*, 203146700074) Bks Demand.

Caughley, Graeme & Gunn, Anne. Conservation Biology in Theory & Practice. LC 95-1616. (Illus.). 459p. 1995. pap. 56.95 (*0-86542-431-4*) Blackwell Sci.

Caughley, Graeme & Sinclair, J. Wildlife Ecology & Management. LC 93-41589. (Illus.). 324p. 1994. pap. 56.95 (*0-86542-144-7*) Blackwell Sci.

***Caughman, Ginger Morris.** Teaching with Rhythm & Rhyme: Resources & Activities for Preschoolers Through Grade Two. (Illus.). 208p. 2000. 38.50 (*0-7864-0811-1*) McFarland & Co.

Caughman, Jennifer T., ed. California Museum Directory: A Guide to Museums, Zoos, Botanic Gardens, & Historic Buildings Open to the Public. 2nd ed. LC 91-9748. (California Information Guides Ser.). 192p. (Orig.). 1991. pap. 25.00 (*0-912102-96-9*) Cal Inst Public.

Caughman, Joyce L. Real Estate Prospecting. 2nd ed. 226p. 1994. pap. 24.95 (*0-7931-0945-0*, 19130702) Dearborn.

Caugtenvto, Peggy. Mastering Viavoice Gold. large type ed. (Illus.). 110p. 1997. pap. 25.00 (*0-9662486-0-0*, BSI1297001.0) SunBeach Intl.

Cauis, J. F. The Medicinal & Poisonous Legumes of India. (C). 1988. 200.00 (*0-7855-3340-0*, Pub. by Scientific) St Mut.

Cauisi, J. F. The Medicinal & Poisonous Legumes of India. 187p. (C). 1989. 140.00 (*81-85046-74-3*, Pub. by Scientific) St Mut.

Caujolle, Christian, text. End Time City. 144p. 1999. 49.95 (*3-908247-13-6*, Pub. by Scalo Pubs) Dist Art Pubs.

Caujolle, Christian, jt. text see Valtorta, Roberta.

Caujolle, Claude, jt. auth. see Price, Betty G.

Caulaincourt, Armand A. No Peace with Napoleon. Hanoteau, Jean, ed. Libaire, George, tr. LC 74-29631. 286p. 1975. reprint ed. lib. bdg. 35.00 (*0-8371-7984-X*, CANP, Greenwood Pr) Greenwood.

— With Napoleon in Russia: The Memoirs of General De Caulaincourt, Duke of Vicenza. Hanoteau, Jean & Libaire, George, eds. LC 75-40914. 422p. 1976. reprint ed. lib. bdg. 35.00 (*0-8371-8689-7*, CAWN, Greenwood Pr) Greenwood.

Caulcutt, R. Achieving Quality Improvement: A Practical Guide. (Illus.). 240p. (C). (gr. 13). 1995. per. 77.95 (*0-412-55930-7*, Chap & Hall CRC) CRC Pr.

— Data Analysis in the Chemical Industry: Basic Techniques, Vol. 1. (Ellis Horwood Series in Inorganic Chemistry). 1989. text 74.95 (*0-470-21492-9*) P-H.

Caulder, Inglath. L' Inavouable Verite. (Amours d'Aujourd'Hui Ser.: No. 309). (FRE.). 1998. mass mkt. 4.99 (*0-373-38309-6*, 1-38309-0) Harlequin Bks.

— Truths & Roses. (Superromance Ser.). 1994. per. 3.50 (*0-373-70609-X*, 1-70609-2) Harlequin Bks.

Cauldrette. Romans of Partenay or of Lusignen. Skeat, Walter W., ed. (EETS, OS Ser.: No. 22). 1974. reprint ed. 50.00 (*0-527-00022-1*) Periodicals Srv.

Cauldwell, Rex. Safe Home Wiring Projects. LC 97-5789. (Illus.). 160p. 1997. pap. 19.95 (*1-56158-164-X*, 070295) Taunton.

— Wiring a House. LC 96-22821. (Illus.). 248p. 1996. 34.95 (*1-56158-113-5*, 070244) Taunton.

Cauldwell, Samuel M. Chocolate Cake & Black Sand & Two Other Plays. LC 79-50021. (One-Act Plays in Reprint Ser.). 1980. reprint ed. 20.00 (*0-8486-2045-3*) Roth Pub Inc.

Cauldwell, Samuel M., ed. see Ansell, Dorothy I.

Cauldwell, Sarah L. The Sirens Sang of Murder. 288p. 1990. mass mkt. 5.99 (*0-440-20745-2*) Dell.

Cauley. Educational Psychology. 9th ed. 1994. 12.74 (*1-56134-273-4*) McGraw.

Cauley, et al. Educational Psychology 1995/96. 10th annot. ed. 1996. teacher ed. 13.12 (*0-697-31556-8*, WCB McGr Hill) McGrw-H Hghr Educ.

Cauley, Elizabeth, et al. College Level Academikc Skills Test (CLAST) Study Guide for Mathematics. 2nd ed. 400p. (C). 1994. per. 20.95 (*0-8403-7879-3*) Kendall-Hunt.

Cauley, Helen, jt. auth. see Wantuck, Karen.

Cauley, Kate, jt. ed. see Grayson, Paul A.

Cauley, Kathleen, et al, eds. Annual Editions: Educational Psychology, 95-96. 10th rev. ed. (Illus.). 256p. (C). 1995. text 12.95 (*1-56134-398-6*, Dshkn McG-Hill) McGrw-H Hghr Educ.

Cauley, Kathleen & Linder. Annual Editions: Educational Psychology, 97-98. 12th ed. 256p. (C). 1997. text. write for info. (*0-697-37261-8*) Brown & Benchmark.

Cauley, Kathleen & Linder, Fredric. Educational Psychology, 1996-1997. annuals 11th ed. 256p. (C). 1996. text. write for info. (*0-697-31555-X*) Brown & Benchmark.

Cauley, Kathleen M., et al. Educational Psychology, 98-99. 13th ed. (Annual Ser.). (Illus.). 240p. 1998. pap. text 12.25 (*0-697-41284-9*, Dshkn McG-Hill) McGrw-H Hghr Educ.

Cauley, Lorinda B. Clap Your Hands. (Illus.). 32p. (J). (ps-1). 1992. lib. bdg. 16.95 (*0-399-22118-2*, G P Putnam) Peng Put Young Read.

— Clap Your Hands. (Illus.). 32p. (J). (ps-1). 1997. pap. 5.99 (*0-698-11428-0*, PapStar) Peng Put Young Read.

— Puss in Boots. LC 86-7629. (Illus.). 32p. (J). (ps-3). 1988. pap. 3.95 (*0-15-264228-5*, Harcourt Child Bks) Harcourt.

— The Trouble with Tyrannosaurus Rex. LC 86-33637. (Illus.). 32p. (J). (ps-3). 1990. pap. 7.00 (*0-15-290881-1*, Voyager Bks) Harcourt.

Cauley, Lorinda Bryan. Ugly Duckling: A Tale from Hans Christian Andersen. LC 79-12340. (J). 1979. 11.20 (*0-606-03694-6*, Pub. by Turtleback) Demco.

***Cauley, Lorinda Bryan.** What Do You Know! LC 00-38231. (Illus.). (J). 2001. write for info. (*0-399-23573-6*) Putnam Pub Group.

Cauley, Lorinda Bryan. The Ugly Duckling. LC 79-12340. 48p. (J). (gr. k up). 1979. pap. 6.00 (*0-15-692528-1*, Voyager Bks) Harcourt.

Cauley, Margaret L. Managing a Successful Global Alliance. 220p. (C). 1994. 31.88 (*0-201-42771-0*) Addison-Wesley.

Caulfeild, S. F. & Saward, Blanche. Encyclopedia of Victorian Needlework, 2 vols., 1. 1972. reprint ed. pap. 14.95 (*0-486-22800-2*) Dover.

— Encyclopedia of Victorian Needlework, 2 vols., 2. 1972. reprint ed. pap. 14.95 (*0-486-22801-0*) Dover.

Caulfield. Infants. (C). 1998. text 33.75 (*0-15-503951-2*, Pub. by Harcourt Coll Pubs) Harcourt.

Caulfield, Anna B. Quakers in Fiction: Annotated Bibliography, Indexed. 170p. 1993. pap. 13.95 (*0-938875-29-9*) Pittenbruach Pr.

Caulfield, Annie. Kingdom of the Film Stars: Journey into Jordan. LC 97-141782. 272p. 1997. pap. text 10.95 (*0-86442-461-2*) Lonely Planet.

***Caulfield, Annie.** The Winners Enclosure. LC 99-47398. 352p. 2000. per. 14.00 (*0-684-86955-1*) S&S Trade.

Caulfield, Carlota. Thirty-Fourth Street & Other Poems. Allen, Chris, tr. LC 87-80166. (Poetry Ser.). (ENG & SPA.). 56p. (Orig.). 1987. pap. 5.00 (*0-932367-08-9*) Ed El Gato Tuerto.

Caulfield, Carlota, et al, eds. Literary & Cultural Journeys: Selected Letters to Arturo Torres-Rioseco. 2nd ed. Torres-Rioseco, Rosalie & Passalacqua, Rose, trs. (ENG & SPA., Illus.). 231p. (Orig.). 1995. pap. 20.00 (*0-9648938-1-9*) Mills Coll Ctr Bk.

Caulfield, Caspar. Only a Beginning: The Passionists in China, 1921-31. LC 90-61190. (Illus.). xvi, 296p. (Orig.). (C). 1990. pap. 14.95 (*0-9626119-0-5*) Passionist Pr.

Caulfield, Charles R. & Goldberg, Billi. The Anarchist AIDS Medical Formulary: A Guide to Guerrilla Immunology. LC 93-43598. (Illus.). 155p. (Orig.). (C). 1994. pap. 12.95 (*1-55643-175-9*) North Atlantic.

Caulfield, D., et al, eds. Materials Interactions Relevant to the Pulp, Paper, & Wood Industries. (Symposium Proceedings Ser.: Vol. 197). 357p. 1990. text 17.50 (*1-55899-086-0*) Materials Res.

Caulfield, Deborah. Population Change & Crime Change. 15p. (Orig.). 1982. pap. 1.50 (*1-55719-040-2*) U NE CPAR.

Caulfield, Ernest. Disease & Society in Provincial Massachusetts: Collected Accounts 1736-1939. (Medicine & Society in America Ser.). 1979. 25.95 (*0-405-03948-4*, 15700) Ayer.

Caulfield, Gary J. Proudly We Serve: A Guide for Waiters & Waitresses. (Illus.). 48p. (Orig.). 1987. pap. 3.95 (*0-912661-11-9*) Woodsong Graph.

Caulfield, H. John, ed. Handbook of Optical Holography. LC 79-51672. 1979. text 159.00 (*0-12-165350-1*) Acad Pr.

Caulfield, H. John & Chen, Su-Shing, eds. Adaptive Computing Vol. 2824: Mathematical & Physical Methods for Complex Environments. 224p. 1996. 66.00 (*0-8194-2212-6*) SPIE.

Caulfield, H. John & Gheen, Gregory, eds. Selected Papers on Optical Computing, Vol. 1142. (Milestone Series of Selected Reprints). (Illus.). 636p. 1989. pap. text 50.00 (*0-8194-0178-1*) SPIE.

Caulfield, H. John, jt. ed. see Abushagur, Mustafa A.

Caulfield, H. John, jt. ed. see Robillard, Jean.

Caulfield, H. John, jt. ed. see Tocci, Christopher.

Caulfield, James, jt. ed. see Sperelakis, Nicholas.

Caulfield, John H., jt. ed. see Chen, Su-Shing.

Caulfield, Jon. City Form & Everyday Life: Toronto's Centrification & Critical Social Practice. (Illus.). 256p. (C). 1994. text 55.00 (*0-8020-2997-3*); pap. text 17.95 (*0-8020-7448-0*) U of Toronto Pr.

Caulfield, Jon & Peake, Linda, eds. City Lives & City Forms: Critical Research & Canadian Urbanism. LC 97-123137. 347p. 1996. text 60.00 (*0-8020-0514-4*); pap. text 21.95 (*0-8020-6950-9*) U of Toronto Pr.

Caulfield, Leslie J. Shake, Rattle & Rot: The Zombie Musical. LC 99-170345. 29p. (YA). (gr. 7 up). 1997. pap. 5.95 (*0-87129-749-3*, SB7) Dramatic Pub.

Caulfield, Max. The Easter Rebellion. LC 74-5550. 375p. 1975. reprint ed. lib. bdg. 35.00 (*0-8371-7507-0*, CAER, Greenwood Pr) Greenwood.

— The Easter Rebellion. 2nd ed. LC 95-69277. (Illus.). 328p. 1995. pap. 16.95 (*1-57098-042-X*) Roberts Rinehart.

Caulfield, Myra, jt. ed. see Austen, Kay.

Caulfield, Norman. Mexican Workers & the State: From the Porifiriato to NAFTA. LC 98-16392. (Illus.). 224p. 1998. 24.95 (*0-87565-192-5*) Tex Christian.

Caulfield, Patricia. Capturing the Landscape with Your Camera. (Illus.). 160p. 1987. pap. 22.50 (*0-8174-3658-8*, Amphoto) Watsn-Guptill.

Caulfield, Patricia. Photographing Wildlife. LC 87-31929. (Illus.). 144p. 1988. pap. 18.95 (*0-8174-5443-8*, Amphoto) Watsn-Guptill.

Caulfield, Richard, ed. see Davies, Rowland.

Caulfield, Richard A. Greenlanders, Whales, & Whaling: Sustainability & Self-Determination in the Arctic. LC 97-522. (Arctic Visions Ser.). (Illus.). 219p. 1997. text 35.00 (*0-87451-810-5*) U Pr of New Eng.

Caulfield, Sean. The God of Ordinary People. LC 88-60115. 128p. (Orig.). 1988. pap. 6.95 (*1-55612-129-6*) Sheed & Ward WI.

Caulfield, Thomas B. The Story of a Cancer Cure, Bk. I. 224p. 1983. lib. bdg. 27.95 (*0-9611788-0-9*) Ctr Adv Psychic Res.

***Caulfield, Timothy A. & Williams-Jones, Bryn.** The Commercialization of Genetic Research: Ethical, Legal & Policy Issues. LC 99-50371. 208p. 1999. write for info. (*0-306-46287-7*, Kluwer Acad) Kluwer Academic.

Caulfield, Tom, ed. see Klain, James.

Caulier, Hilde. An Animal Experimental Study to Improve the Success Rate of Oral Implants in Bone of Low Density: The Influence of CA-P Coatings. (Acta Biomedica Lovaniensia Ser.: No. 136). (Illus.). 177p. (Orig.). 1996. pap. 46.50 (*90-6186-762-2*, Pub. by Leuven Univ) Coronet Bks.

***Caulkins, Craig S.** High Rise Window Cleaning Techniques & Equipment. 167p. 1999. pap. 38.00 (*0-944352-36-7*) Cleaning Cons.

Caulkins, Fannie M. History of Norwich, from Its Settlement in 1660 to January, 1845. With Index. (Illus.). 401p. 1997. reprint ed. lib. bdg. 42.00 (*0-8328-5679-7*) Higginson Bk Co.

Caulkins, Frances M. The History of New London, Connecticut: From the First Survey of the Coast in 1612, to 1860. 714p. 1988. reprint ed. lib. bdg. 71.50 (*0-8328-0008-2*, CT0034) Higginson Bk Co.

— History of Norwich, Connecticut: From Its Possession by the Indians, to the Year 1866. (Illus.). 704p. 1992. reprint ed. lib. bdg. 70.00 (*0-8328-2267-1*) Higginson Bk Co.

— The Stone Records of Groton, Ct. Gilman, E. S., ed. 96p. 1994. reprint ed. pap. 18.00 (*0-8328-4404-7*) Higginson Bk Co.

Caulkins, Jonathan, et al. An Ounce of Prevention, a Pound of Uncertainty: The Cost-Effectiveness of School-Based Drug Prevention Programs. LC 99-19931. (Illus.). 150p. 1999. pap. 15.00 (*0-8330-2560-0*, MR-923-RWJ, Pub. by Rand Corp) Natl Bk Netwk.

Caulkins, Jonathan P. Developing Price Series for Cocaine. LC 94-7504. 1994. pap. text 13.00 (*0-8330-1518-4*, MR-317-DPRC) Rand Corp.

Caulkins, Jonathan P., et al. Mandatory Minimum Drug Sentences: Throwing Away the Key or the Taxpayer's Money? LC 97-8234. (Illus.). 220p. 1997. pap. 15.00 (*0-8330-2453-1*, MR-827-DPRC) Rand Corp.

— Preventing Drug Use among Youth Through Community Outreach: The Military's Pilot Programs. LC 94-24075. 1994. pap. text 13.00 (*0-8330-1618-0*, MR-536-OSD) Rand Corp.

Caulkins, Mary, jt. auth. see Helderman, Jennie M.

Caullery, Maurice. French Science & Its Principle Discoveries since the Seventeenth Century. LC 74-26256. (History, Philosophy & Sociology of Science Ser.). (Illus.). 1979. reprint ed. 23.95 (*0-405-06584-1*) Ayer.

— Universities & Scientific Life in the United States. LC 74-26257. (History, Philosophy & Sociology of Science Ser.). 1975. reprint ed. 26.95 (*0-405-06585-X*) Ayer.

Caullery, Maurice J. Universities & Scientific Life in the United States. LC 72-94312. (American Scientific Community, 1790-1920 Ser.). 1973. reprint ed. lib. bdg. 30.00 (*0-8420-1677-5*) Scholarly Res Inc.

Caulton, Regina & Tressenwriter, Gary. Captive Hearts: Breaking the Cycle of Unhealthy Relationships. 131p. (C). 1998. reprint ed. pap. text. write for info. (*0-9666226-0-X*) Captive Hrts.

Caulton, Sonia. The Man Hunt. Whitaker, Ginger, ed. 1997. pap. 12.95 (*0-9655545-0-3*) SistahGirl Pub.

— Voodoo Love. Whitaker, Ginger, ed. (Illus.). 299p. 1999. pap. 14.95 (*0-9655545-1-1*) SistahGirl Pub.

Caulton, Tim. Hands-On Exhibitions: Managing Interactive Museums & Science Centres. LC 97-17886. (Illus.). 168p. (C). 1998. 85.00 (*0-415-16521-0*); pap. 25.99 (*0-415-16522-9*) Routledge.

Caum, E. L. Check-List of Hawaiian Land & Freshwater Mollusca. (BMB Ser.: No. 56). 1972. reprint ed. 25.00 (*0-527-02162-8*) Periodicals Srv.

Caum, E. L., jt. auth. see Christophersen, E.

Cauman, Leigh S. First-Order Logic: An Introduction. LC 98-27510. 336p. 1998. pap. 30.00 (*3-11-015766-7*) De Gruyter.

Caumartin, Francois. Now You See Them, Now You Don't. Homel, David, tr. (Illus.). 24p. (J). (ps-3). 1996. pap. 4.95 (*1-55209-007-8*) Firefly Bks Ltd.

Caumette, Pierre, ed. Coastal Lagoon Eutropnication & Anaerobic Processes: Nitrogen & Sulfur Cycles & Population Dynamics in Coastal Lagoons. LC 96-28457. 256p. (C). 1996. text 242.50 (*0-7923-4165-1*) Kluwer Academic.

Caumette, Pierre, jt. ed. see Stal, Lucas J.

Caumont, Jacques, jt. auth. see Gough-Cooper, Jennifer.

Caunce, Stephen. Oral History. LC 93-26417. (Approaches to Local History Ser.). 1994. pap. text. write for info. (*0-582-07295-6*, Pub. by Addison-Wesley) Longman.

— Oral Hst & Local Historian. LC 93-26417. (Approaches to Local History Ser.). (C). 1994. text 52.50 (*0-582-07294-8*, Pub. by Addison-Wesley) Longman.

Cauneau, I. Hoeren - Brummen - Sprechen: Angewandte Phonetik im Unterricht Deutsch als Fremdsprache: Handbuch. (GER.). 80p. (C). 1992. pap. text 22.50 (*3-12-675352-3*, Pub. by Klett Edition); audio 38.00 (*3-12-675353-1*, Pub. by Klett Edition) Intl Bk Import.

Caunes, Antoine De, see De Caunes, Antoine.

Caunitz, William J. Chains of Command. LC 99-28778. 352p. 1999. 23.95 (*0-525-94514-8*, Dutt) Dutton Plume.

***Caunitz, William J.** Chains of Command. 2000. mass mkt. 6.99 (*0-451-40918-3*, Onyx) NAL.

Caunitz, William J. Cleopatra Gold. 352p. 1994. mass mkt. 6.99 (*0-425-14394-5*) Berkley Pub.

— Pigtown. 352p. 1996. mass mkt. 6.99 (*0-7860-0293-X*, Pinncle Kensgtn) Kensgtn Pub Corp.

— Pigtown. 1996. pap. 5.99 (*0-614-98083-6*, Onyx) NAL.

Caunt, David, jt. auth. see Hackett, Graham.

Cauper, Eunice. Martin Luther King, Jr. & Our January 15th Holiday for Children. (Illus.). 32p. (Orig.). (J). (gr. k-3). 1991. pap. text 6.00 (*0-9617551-3-X*) E Cauper.

— The Story of Christopher Columbus & Our October 12th Holiday for Kindergarten Children. (Kindergarten Holiday Bks.). (Illus.). 16p. (Orig.). (J). (gr. k-3). 1985. pap. 3.95 (*0-9617551-0-5*) E Cauper.

— The Story of the Pilgrims & Their Indian Friends: A Thanksgiving Story for Children. 5th ed. (Illus.). 15p. (J). (gr. k). 1990. pap. 4.95 (*0-9617551-1-3*) E Cauper.

Cauquelin, Josiane, et al. Asian Values: Encounter with Diversity. 288p. 1998. text 48.00 (*0-7007-1096-5*, Pub. by Curzon Pr Ltd) UH Pr.

CAUR Staff. Demographic Survey of the Omaha Jewish Community. 80p. (Orig.). 1976. pap. 6.50 (*1-55719-055-0*) U NE CPAR.

— Employment in the Omaha SMSA: Estimates & Projections by Industry & Occupation. 125p. (Orig.). 1977. pap. 7.50 (*1-55719-064-X*) U NE CPAR.

— A Guide Toward Residential Land Development in the City of Norfolk. 56p. (Orig.). 1978. pap. 3.00 (*1-55719-071-2*) U NE CPAR.

— An Inventory of Housing, Vacant Land & Neighborhood Conditions: Lincoln, Nebraska. 133p. (Orig.). 1985. pap. 9.00 (*1-55719-094-1*) U NE CPAR.

— Juveniles in Nebraska Jails & Lockups. 110p. (Orig.). 1985. pap. 7.00 (*1-55719-042-9*) U NE CPAR.

— Land Use Development in Gretna, Nebraska: A Cost Analysis. 76p. (Orig.). 1976. pap. 5.00 (*1-55719-072-0*) U NE CPAR.

— A Study of Alcohol Prevention Grants in the State of Nebraska, 1973-1979. 40p. (Orig.). 1980. pap. 3.00 (*1-55719-090-9*) U NE CPAR.

— Survey of Cable Subscribers: Viewing Preferences for Channels 4, 13, & 19. 25p. (Orig.). 1985. pap. 2.50 (*1-55719-037-2*) U NE CPAR.

Caur Staff & Hauswald, Edward L. Identification of Prime Residential Land in Rural Nebraska. 76p. (Orig.). 1978. pap. 5.00 (*1-55719-039-9*) U NE CPAR.

Causa-Steindler, Mariangela, ed. & tr. see Boccaccio, Giovanni.

Causa-Steindler, Mariangela, tr. see Boccaccio, Giovanni.

Cause, Sue. Wilmington City Business Profiles: Wilmington, NC. 1996. pap. text 19.95 (*1-885352-35-2*) Community Comm.

Causer, H. Phillip. M. I. A. (Missing in Action) 2nd ed. LC 77-88747. (Illus.). 1995. pap. 12.95 (*0-918442-00-1*) Phipps Pub.

Causey, jt. auth. see Chiras/Causey.

Causey, Andrew. Poet & Painter. 280p. (C). 1989. 85.00 (*1-872971-15-6*, Pub. by Redcliffe Pr Ltd) St Mut.

— Sculpture since 1945. (Oxford History of Art Ser.). (Illus.). 300p. 1998. 39.95 (*0-19-284255-2*); pap. 16.95 (*0-19-284205-6*) OUP.

Causey, Beth. Euripides' Bacchae. (Greek Commentaries Ser.). 28p. 1995. pap. text 4.00 (*0-929524-85-3*) Bryn Mawr Commentaries.

Causey, C. Harry. If Only I Could Read Music. (Illus.). 128p. 1991. pap. 15.00 (*0-9620795-1-0*) Music Revelatn.

— Things They Didn't Tell Me about Being a Minister of Music. (Illus.). 234p. (Orig.). 1988. pap. 12.00 (*0-9620795-0-2*) Music Revelatn.

— Things They Didn't Tell Me about Being a Minister of Music. (Illus.). 234p. (Orig.). 1988. pap. 14.00 (*0-317-91233-X*) Music Revelatn.

Causey, Cindy U. Cherish the Gift: A Congregational Guide to Earth Stewardship. LC 96-14561. 160p. 1996. pap. 15.00 (*0-8170-1246-X*) Judson.

Causey, Denzil Y., Jr. & Causey, Sandra A. Duties & Liabilities of Public Accountants. 5th ed. LC 94-47392. 510p. 1995. lib. bdg. 109.95 (*0-930001-09-5*) Accountants Pr.

— Duties & Liabilities of Public Accountants. 6th rev. ed. LC 98-50358. 568p. 1999. lib. bdg. 125.00 (*0-930001-11-7*) Accountants Pr.

Causey, Denzil Y., Jr. & Causey, Sandra A., eds. Supplement to Duties & Liabilities of Public Accountants. 6th ed. 1999. ring bd. 79.95 (*0-930001-12-5*) Accountants Pr.

Causey, Dorothy, jt. auth. see Stollsteimer, Robert S.

Causey, Fred. No Rooms in Tara & Other Red Clay Stories. LC 95-73044. 121p. (Orig.). 1996. pap. text 8.95 (*1-884778-13-5*) Old Mountain.

Causey, James, jt. auth. see Burk, Robin.

Causey, Kimberly. The Furniture Factory Outlet Guide. (Illus.). 350p. 1999. pap. 24.95 (*1-888229-41-1*) Home Decor.

— The Insider's Guide to Buying Home Furnishings. 356p. 1996. pap. 24.95 (*1-888229-21-7*) Home Decor.

— The 1997 Decorative Fabrics Cross-Reference Guide. 194p. (Orig.). 1997. pap. 39.95 (*1-888229-02-0*) Home Decor.

***Causey, Max.** The Jack Ruby Trial Revisited: The Diary of Jury Foreman Max Causey. Dempsey, John Mark, ed. (Illus.). 200p. 2000. 29.95 (*1-57441-121-7*, Pub. by UNTX Pr) Tex A&M Univ Pr.

Causey, Michael, jt. auth. see Pfaff, Eugene E., Jr.

Causey, Robert L. Logic, Sets, & Recursion. LC 93-6375. 416p. 1994. 57.50 (*0-86720-463-X*) Jones & Bartlett.

— Unity of Science. (Synthese Library: No. 109). 192p. 1977. text 106.00 (*90-277-0779-0*, D Reidel) Kluwer Academic.

Causey, Sandra A., jt. auth. see Causey, Denzil Y., Jr.

Causey, Sandra A., jt. ed. see Causey, Denzil Y., Jr.

Causin, Susan, jt. auth. see Dillard, Elsie.

***Causland, Robert.** A Tale to Tell - A Time to Remember: Robert H. Causland...His Early Memories & War Years. (Illus.). 151p. 1999. pap. write for info. (*1-882194-56-X*) TN Valley Pub.

Causley, Charles. Figure of 8: Narrative Poems. LC 71-459088. 86p. 1969. write for info. (*0-333-10488-9*) Macmlln Intrctve.

— Quack! Said the Billy-Goat. LC 85-23856. (Illus.). 24p. (J). (ps-2). 1986. lib. bdg. 11.89 (*0-397-32192-9*) HarpC Child Bks.

— Secret Destinations. LC 87-46301. 1989. 9.95 (*0-87923-739-2*) Godine.

Causley, Charles, compiled by. Poetry Please! (Everyman's Poetry Ser.). 116p. 1997. pap. 1.95 (*0-460-87824-7*, Everyman's Classic Lib) Tuttle Pubng.

Causley, Charles, ed. Modern Folk Ballads. (Pocket Poet Ser.). 1968. pap. 3.95 (*0-8023-9043-9*) Dufour.

Causley, Charles & Firth, Barbara. "Quack!" Said the Billy-Goat. LC 98-21932. (Illus.). 24p. (J). (ps-k). 1999. pap. 5.99 (*0-7636-0692-8*, Pub. by Candlewick Pr) Penguin Putnam.

Causley, Marguerite. An Introduction to Benesh: Movement Notation. LC 79-7755. (Dance Ser.). (Illus.). 1980. reprint ed. lib. bdg. 18.95 (*0-8369-9280-6*) Ayer.

Causley, Monroe, jt. auth. see Madison Public Library Staff.

Caussade, Jean Pierre. A Treatise on Prayer from the Heart: A Christian Mystical Tradition Recovered for All. McKeon, Robert M., tr. from FRE. LC 98-70159. (Series I: Vol. 17).Tr. of Traite sur l'Oraison du Coeur, Instructions Spirituelles. vi, 249p. 1998. pap. 17.95 (*1-880810-31-X*) Inst Jesuit.

C

An Asterisk (*) at the beginning of an entry indicates that the title is appearing for the first time.

Caussade, Jean-Pierre de, see De Caussade, Jean-Pierre.

Causseaux, R. N. Search for a Beginning. LC 98-93188. 172p. 1998. pap. 6.75 (*0-9665412-0-0*) R N Causseaux.

Caussy, Fernand, ed. see Voltaire.

Causton, David R. A Biologist's Advanced Mathematics. (Illus.). 288p. (C). 1987. pap. 37.95 (*0-04-574037-2*) Routledge.

— An Introduction to Vegetation Analysis. 320p. 1988. text 100.00 (*0-04-581024-9*); pap. text 29.95 (*0-04-581025-7*) Routledge.

Causton, Eric E. Militarism & Foreign Policy in Japan. LC 78-63658. (Studies in Fascism: Ideology & Practice). reprint ed. 32.50 (*0-404-16918-X*) AMS Pr.

Causton, Linda. The Adventures of Gladly, the Cross-Eyed Bear. (Illus.). 50p. (J). (ps-5). 1996. pap. 10.00 (*0-9649922-3-X*) Deforest Pr.

Cautela, Joseph R. & Groden, June. Relaxation: A Comprehensive Manual for Adults, Children, & Children with Special Needs. LC 78-62906. (Illus.). 108p. 1978. spiral bd. 14.95 (*0-87822-186-7*, 1867) Res Press.

Cautela, Joseph R. & Ishaq, Waris, eds. Contemporary Issues in Behavior Therapy: Improving the Human Condition. (Applied Clinical Psychology Ser.). (Illus.). 432p. (C). 1996. 69.50 (*0-306-45168-9*, Plenum Trade) Perseus Pubng.

Cautela, Joseph R., et al. Forms for Behavior Analysis with Children. LC 82-62572. 208p. 1983. spiral bd. 39.95 (*0-87822-267-7*, 2677) Res Press.

Cauter, E. Van, see Van Cauter, E., ed.

Cauter, Eve Van, see Copinschi, Georges & Van Cauter, Eve, eds.

Cauthen, jt. auth. see Palkovic.

Cauthen, Irby B., Jr., ed. see Norton, Thomas.

***Cauthen, Joyce H.** With Fiddle & Well-Rosined Bow: A History of Old-Time Fiddling in Alabama. 2000. pap. 19.95 (*0-8173-1066-5*) U of Ala Pr.

Cauthen, Kenneth. The Ethics of Assisted Death: When Life Becomes a Burden Too Hard to Bear. LC 98-44910. 102p. 1999. pap. 9.95 (*0-7880-1332-7*) CSS OH.

— The Many Faces of Evil: Reflections on the Sinful, the Tragic, the Demonic & the Ambiguous. LC 96-38674. (Orig.). 1997. pap. 14.95 (*0-7880-1004-2*) CSS OH.

— The Many Faces of Evil: The Study Guide. 1997. 8.95 (*0-7880-1070-0*) CSS OH.

— The Passion for Equality. 208p. 1987. 55.00 (*0-8476-7544-0*) Rowman.

— Process Ethics: A Constructive System. LC 84-16662. (Toronto Studies in Theology: Vol. 18). 365p. 1983. lib. bdg. 99.95 (*0-88946-764-1*) E Mellen.

— Systematic Theology: A Modern Protestant Approach. LC 86-23807. (Toronto Studies in Theology: Vol. 25). 520p. 1986. lib. bdg. 119.95 (*0-88946-769-2*) E Mellen.

— Theological Biology: The Case for a New Modernism. LC 91-41520. (Toronto Studies in Theology: Vol. 62). 320p. 1991. lib. bdg. 99.95 (*0-7734-9655-6*) E Mellen.

— Toward a New Modernism. 184p. 1996. pap. text 24.50 (*0-7618-0521-4*) U Pr of Amer.

— Toward a New Modernism. 184p. 1997. lib. bdg. 44.00 (*0-7618-0520-6*) U Pr of Amer.

Cauthen, Paul, ed. see Toeschi, Carl J.

Cauthen, Steve. Northern Kentucky: Looking to the New Millennium, a 100-Year Reflection. LC 99-49625. (Illus.). 1999. 49.95 (*1-881096-74-2*) Towery Pub.

Cauthery, Philip & Stanway, Andrew. The Complete Guide to Sexual Fulfillment. LC 86-61822. (Illus.). 349p. (Orig.). 1986. pap. 21.95 (*0-87975-356-0*) Prometheus Bks.

***Cauthorn, Dan & Lewis, S. Peter.** Climbing: From Gym to Crag, Building Skills for Real Rock. LC 00-8885. (Illus.). 224p. 2000. pap. 19.95 (*0-89886-682-0*) Mountaineers.

Cauthorn, Henry S. A History of the City of Vincennes, Indiana from 1702 to 1901. (Illus.). 220p. 1993. reprint ed. lib. bdg. 29.50 (*0-8328-3474-2*) Higginson Bk Co.

Cauthorne-Burnette, Tamera & Estes, Mary E. Clinical Companion for Health Assessment & Physical Examination. LC 97-24664. 384p. (C). 1998. text 30.95 (*0-8273-8243-X*) Delmar.

Cautley, Patricia W. New Foster Parents: The First Experience. LC 80-10937. 287p. 1980. 45.95 (*0-87705-495-9*, Kluwer Acad Hman Sci) Kluwer Academic.

Cautrey, Peter, ed. see Darwin, Charles.

***Cauvain, Stanley P. & Young, Linda S.** Bakery Food Manufacture & Quality: Water Control & Effects. LC 99-49521. 2000. write for info. (*0-632-05327-5*) Blackwell Sci.

Cauvain, Stanley P., jt. auth. see Young, Linda S.

Cauveren, Sydney. A. L. Rowse: A Bibliophile's Extensive Bibliography. LC 99-15195. (Scarecrow Author Bibliographies Ser.: No. 103). (Illus.). 336p. 2000. 60.00 (*0-8108-3641-6*) Scarecrow.

Cauvier, Denis. How to Hire the Right Person. 1993. text 24.95 (*0-87425-230-X*) HRD Press.

Cauvier Seminars Staff. Keep Your Staff Productive. 208p. 1995. pap., per. 24.95 (*0-7872-0572-9*) Kendall-Hunt.

Cauvin, jt. auth. see Baker.

Cauvin, Sylvie, jt. ed. see Dhurjati, P. S.

***Cauvin, Jacques.** Birth of the Gods & the Origins of Agriculture: A Symbolic Interpretation. Watkins, Trevor, tr. (New Studies in Archaeology). (Illus.). 276p. (C). 2000. 59.95 (*0-521-65135-2*) Cambridge U Pr.

Cauvin, Jean-Pierre, tr. see Breton, Andre.

Cauwels, Janice M. Imbroglio: Rising to the Challenge of Borderline Personality Disorder. 448p. 1992. 31.95 (*0-393-03349-X*) Norton.

Cauwenberge, P. Van, see Bernstein, J. M. & Van Cauwenberge, P., eds.

Cauwenberge, P. Van, see Van Cauwenberge, P., ed.

Cauwenberge, P. Van, see Ars, B. & Van Cauwenberge, P., eds.

Cauwenberge, P. Van, see Van Cauwenberge, P.

Cauwenberghe, A. Van, see Van Cauwenberghe, A.

Cauwenberghe, Marc Van, see Kushi, Michio & Van Cauwenberghe, Marc.

***Cauwenberghs, Gert & Bayoumi, Magdy A.** Learning on Silicon: Adaptive VLSI Neural Systems. LC 99-30265. (International Series In Engineering & Computer Science). 1999. write for info. (*0-7923-8555-1*) Kluwer Academic.

CAV '94 Staff. Computer Aided Verification: Proceedings of the Sixth International Conference, CAV '94, Stanford, California, U.S.A., June 21-23, 1994. Dill, David L., ed. LC 94-21760. (Lecture Notes in Computer Science Ser.: Vol. 818). 1994. 65.95 (*0-387-58179-0*) Spr-Verlag.

Cava, John, jt. ed. see Frampton, Kenneth.

Cava, Olha D., compiled by. A Guide to the Archives, Vol. III. 38p. 1979. pap. 9.95 (*0-913256-52-8*) CMS.

Cava, Olha D., ed. Guide to the Archives Vol. 1, Vol. I. 38p. 1974. 9.95 (*0-913256-18-8*) CMS.

***Cava, Pete.** 50 Great Backyard Games. 160p. 2000. pap. 12.95 (*1-58382-034-5*, Pub. by Sports Masters) Partners-West.

— Mom's Handy Book of Backyard Games. (Illus.). 192p. 2000. pap. write for info. (*1-930546-43-2*) Wish Pub.

— Tales from the Cubs Dugout. (Illus.). 224p. 2000. 19.95 (*1-58382-044-2*) Sports Pub.

Cava, Roberta, pseud. Before Tying the Knot - Questions Couples Must Ask Each Other Before They Marry! 1995. pap. 9.95 (*1-895632-18-8*) Cava Mgmt Consult.

— Dealing with Difficult Spouses & Children: How to Handle Difficult Family Problems. 1994. pap. 14.95 (*1-895632-16-1*) Cava Mgmt Consult.

— Difficult People: How to Deal with Impossible Clients, Bosses & Employees. 192p. 1997. pap. text 14.95 (*1-55209-125-2*) Firefly Bks Ltd.

— What Am I Going to Do with the Rest of My Life? Facing Dismissal? Forced Retirement? Company Downsizing? Hate Your Job - Want a Change? LC 96-24635. 176p. 1995. 14.95 (*1-895632-14-5*) Cava Mgmt Consult.

Cavaco-Paulo, Arthur, jt. auth. see Eriksson, Karl-Erik.

Cavada, F. F. Libby Life: Experiences of a Prisoner of War in Richmond, VA, 1863-64. (Illus.). 232p. (Orig.). 1994. pap. text 20.00 (*0-7884-0051-7*) Heritage Bk.

Cavadas, Athenagoras. World Beyond the Grave. Andres, Constantine, tr. from GRE. 98p. (Orig.). 1988, pap. 3.95 (*0-917651-52-9*, Pub. by Holy Cross Orthodox) BookWorld.

Cavadini, John C. The Last Christology of the West: Adoptionism in Spain & Gaul, 785-820. LC 93-9444. (Middle Ages Ser.). 248p. (C). 1993. text 39.95 (*0-8122-3186-4*) U of Pa Pr.

Cavadini, John.C., ed. Gregory the Great: A Symposium. LC 95-18780. (Notre Dame Studies in Theology: Vol. 2). (C). 1996. text 34.95 (*0-268-01030-7*) U of Notre Dame Pr.

— Miracles in Jewish & Christian Antiquity: Imagining Truth. LC 99-35187. (Notre Dame Studies in Theology: Vol. 3). 240p. 1999. 35.00 (*0-268-01217-2*, Pub. by U of Notre Dame Pr) Chicago Distribution Ctr.

***Cavadini, John C., ed.** Miracles in Jewish & Christian Antiquity: Imagining Truth. LC 99-35187. (Notre Dame Studies in Theology: Vol. 3). 256p. 2000. reprint ed. pap. 25.00 (*0-268-03453-2*, Pub. by U of Notre Dame Pr) Chicago Distribution Ctr.

Cavadino, Michael. Mental Health Law in Context: Doctors Orders. (Medico-Legal Issues Ser.). (Illus.). 192p. 1989. text 78.95 (*1-85521-024-X*, Pub. by Dartmth Pub) Ashgate Pub Co.

Cavadino, Michael & Digan, James. The Penal System: An Introduction. (Illus.). 288p. (C). 1992. 55.00 (*0-8039-8343-3*); pap. 25.95 (*0-8039-8344-1*) Sage.

Cavadino, Michael & Dignan, James. The Penal System: An Introduction. 2nd ed. 352p. (C). 1997. 69.95 (*0-7619-5327-2*, 53272); pap. 27.95 (*0-7619-5328-0*, 53280) Sage.

***Cavadino, Michael, et al.** Criminal Justice 2000: Strategies for a New Century. (Criminal Policy Ser.). 224p. 1999. pap. 25.00 (*1-872870-77-5*, 18467, Pub. by Waterside Pr) Gaunt.

Cavadino, Paul & British Juvenile & Family Courts Society Staff. Children Who Kill: An Examination of the Treatment of Juveniles Who Kill in Different European Countries. LC 98-211783. 224p. 1996. write for info. (*1-872870-29-5*) Waterside Pr.

Cavafy, C. P. C. P. Cavafy: Collected Poems. Savidis, George, ed. Keeley, Edmund & Sherrard, Philip, trs. from GRE. LC 74-2977. (Lockert Library of Poetry in Translation). 508p. 1975. pap. 12.95 (*0-691-01320-9*, Pub. by Princeton U Pr) Cal Prin Full Svc.

— C. P. Cavafy: Collected Poems. rev. ed. Keeley, Edmund & Sherrard, Philip, trs. (Lockert Library of Poetry in Translation). 278p. 1992. 45.00 (*0-691-06984-0*, Pub. by Princeton U Pr); pap. 14.95 (*0-691-01537-6*, Pub. by Princeton U Pr) Cal Prin Full Svc.

— The Complete Poems of Cavafy. expanded ed. Dalven, Rae, tr. LC 76-22804. 336p. 1976. pap. 14.00 (*0-15-619820-7*, Harvest Bks) Harcourt.

— The Essential Cavafy. Keeley, Edmund & Sherrard, Philip, trs. LC 95-8451. (Essential Poets Ser.: Vol. 21). 160p. 1995. 16.00 (*0-88001-426-1*) HarpC.

— Essential Cavafy. Keeley, Edmund, ed. (Essential Poets Ser.: No. 22). 80p. 1996. reprint ed. pap. 10.00 (*0-88001-516-0*) HarpC.

— The Greek Poems of C. P. Cavafy As Translated by Memas Kolaitis, 2 vols. Kolaitis, Memas, tr. from GRE. 1989. 55.00 (*0-89241-400-6*) Caratzas.

— The Greek Poems of C. P. Cavafy As Translated by Memas Kolaitis, 2 vols., Set. Kolaitis, Memas, tr. from GRE. 320p. 1995. pap. 25.00 (*0-89241-580-0*) Caratzas.

— The Greek Poems of C. P. Cavafy As Translated by Memas Kolaitis, 2 vols., Vol. 1. Kolaitis, Memas, tr. from GRE. xvi, 187p. 1989. 35.00 (*0-89241-426-X*) Caratzas.

— The Greek Poems of C. P. Cavafy As Translated by Memas Kolaitis, 2 vols., Vol. 2. Kolaitis, Memas, tr. from GRE. xiv, 130p. 1989. 25.00 (*0-89241-427-8*) Caratzas.

Cavafy, C. P., et al. Quarterly Review of Literature: The 1970s Poetry, Vol. XVIII, Nos. 1-2. 1970. pap. 10.00 (*1-888545-15-1*) Quarterly Rev.

Cavage, Betty. The Elegant Onion: The Art of Allium Cookery. LC 87-45011. (Illus.). 160p. (Orig.). 1987. pap. 9.95 (*0-88266-460-3*, Garden Way Pub) Storey Bks.

Cavagnaro, David, jt. auth. see Geary, Ida.

Cavagnaro, David, jt. photos by see Lanting, Frans.

Cavaiani, Mabel. Cholesterol-Free Cakes & Cookies: All-Time Favorite Recipes Adapted for a Low-Cholesterol Diet. LC 92-8664. 320p. 1995. pap. 14.95 (*0-8050-1739-9*, Owl) H Holt & Co.

— Desserts for Diabetics. 176p. (Orig.). 1992. pap. 13.00 (*0-399-51734-0*, Perigee Bks) Berkley Pub.

— The New Diabetic Cookbook. rev. ed. 384p. 1989. reprint ed. pap. 14.95 (*0-8092-4251-6*) NTC Contemp Pub Co.

— The New Diabetic Cookbook. 4th rev. ed. 432p. 1996. pap. 14.95 (*0-8092-3164-6*, 316460, Contemporary Bks) NTC Contemp Pub Co.

— The New Diabetic Cookbook: More than 200 Delicious Recipes for a Low-Fat, Low-Sugar, Low-Cholesterol, Low-Salt, High-Fiber Diet. 384p. 1994. pap. write for info. (*0-8092-3547-1*) NTC Contemp Pub Co.

Cavaignac, Godegroy, jt. auth. see Lemaitre, Jules.

Cavaille, Marie-Dominique. Rudolf Breitscheid et la France, 1919-1933. (Publications Universitaires Europeennes Ser.: Series 3, Vol. 660). (FRE.). 538p. 1995. 74.95 (*3-631-48795-9*) P Lang Pubng.

Cavaioli, Frank J. & Lagumina, Salvatore J. The Peripheral Americans. LC 82-14019. 268p. (C). 1984. pap. 16.00 (*0-89874-542-X*) Krieger.

Cavajoni, Giuseppe A., ed. Supplementum Adnotationum Super Lucanum III: Libri viii-x. (Classical & Byzantine Monographs: No. 16). (LAT.). viii, 165p. (Orig.). 1990. pap. 56.00 (*90-256-0982-1*, Pub. by AM Hakkert) BookLink Distributors.

Cavalcante. English Portuguese Dictionary of Economic & Commercial Terms. 5th ed. (ENG & POR.). 408p. 1988. pap. 49.95 (*0-7859-7478-4*) Fr & Eur.

Cavalcanti, Clovis de Vasconcelos, ed. The Environment, Sustainable Development, & Public Policies: Building Sustainability in Brazil. LC 99-12142. 232p. 2000. 90.00 (*1-84064-018-9*) E Elgar.

Cavalcanti, Guido. The Complete Poems. Cirigliano, Marc A., tr. from ITA. & intro. by. LC 92-12123. 200p. (Orig.). 1992. pap. 14.50 (*0-934977-27-5*) Italica Pr.

Cavalcanti, Guido & Anderson, David. Pound's Cavalcanti: An Edition of the Translations, Notes, & Essays. LC 82-47581. 335p. 1983. reprint ed. pap. 103.90 (*0-7837-9293-X*, 206003200004) Bks Demand.

Cavalcaselle, Giovanni B., jt. auth. see Crowe, Joseph A.

Cavalchini, Mariella, ed. see Tasso, Torquato.

***Cavalconte, Cheryl.** Barley Cakes: Parables for the 21st Century. (Illus.). 100p. 2000. pap. 10.00 (*0-9658137-5-4*) Woven Word.

Cavaleri, Steven & Fearon, David, eds. Managing in Organizations That Learn. (Developmental Management Ser.). (Illus.). 650p. 1996. pap. 44.95 (*1-55786-660-0*) Blackwell Pubs.

***Cavaleri, Steven A.** Designing Knowledge-Creating Systems: An Autognomic Approach. 224p. 2001. pap. 21.95 (*0-7506-7340-0*) Buttrwrth-Heinemann.

Cavaletto, M., et al. Dizionario Italiano-Bulgaro: Italian-Bulgarian Dictionary. deluxe ed. (BUL & ITA.). 967p. 1979. 95.00 (*0-8288-4730-4*, M9835) Fr & Eur.

***Cavalheiro, E. A., et al, eds.** Excitatory Amino Acids: Ten Years Later. (Biomedical & Health Research Ser.: Vol. 45). 300p. 2000. 100.00 (*1-58603-072-8*) IOS Press.

Cavalheiro, E. A., et al. Molecular Neurobiology of Epilepsy. Engel, J., Jr. et al, eds. LC 92-18550. (Epilepsy Research Supplements Ser.: No. 9). xvi,412p. 1992. 289.50 (*0-444-89711-9*) Elsevier.

Cavalie. Blues Keyboard Basics, Step 1 & 2. (Ultimate Beginner Ser.). 1997. pap. 12.95 (*1-57623-689-7*) Wrner Bros.

— Le Mystere des Caves Saint Emilion. text 4.25 (*0-8219-1032-9*) EMC-Paradigm.

Cavalier & Covey. Right to Die: Dax Cowart Case. 96p. (C). 1997. pap., teacher ed. 20.99 (*0-415-15274-7*) Routledge.

Cavalier, Debbie. Keyboard Basics, Steps 1 & 2. 1997. pap. 9.95 (*1-57623-429-0*) Wrner Bros.

Cavalier, Debbie, ed. Adventures in Music Listening: Level 1. (Orig.). (J). 1996. audio 19.95 (*1-57623-370-7*, BMR08201AT) Wrner Bros.

— Canadian Folk Dances. (Illus.). 28p. (Orig.). (YA). 1995. pap. text 19.95 (*1-57623-719-2*, BMR05119) Wrner Bros.

— The Complete Rhythm Section. (Contemporary Rhythm Section Ser.). 76p. (Orig.). (YA). 1997. pap. text 24.95 (*1-57623-990-X*, 0047B) Wrner Bros.

— Five Spirituals for Chorus: Student Book. 28p. (C). 1994. pap. text, student ed. 2.95 (*0-7692-1779-6*, EL03969SB) Wrner Bros.

— Folk Dances from France. (Illus.). 48p. (Orig.). (YA). 1997. pap. text 19.95 (*1-57623-725-7*, BMR05122) Wrner Bros.

— Folk Dances of Latin America. (World Dance Ser.). (Illus.). (YA). 1994. 19.95 incl. cd-rom (*0-89898-980-9*, BMR65115) Wrner Bros.

— General MIDI Sampler Book. (Dan Coates for All Methods Ser.). 24p. (Orig.). (YA). 1996. pap. text 29.95 (*1-57623-361-8*, ITB0700G) Wrner Bros.

— Kurzweil Sampler Book. (Dan Coates for All Methods Ser.). 24p. (Orig.). (YA). 1996. pap. text 29.95 (*1-57623-360-X*, ITB0700K) Wrner Bros.

— Lamb Chop's Play-Along. (Illus.). (Orig.). (J). 1996. pap. text 16.95 (*1-57623-354-5*, PF9612) Wrner Bros.

— Lamb Chop's Special Chanukah. (Illus.). 80p. (Orig.). (J). 1996. pap. 14.95 (*0-7604-0088-1*; PF9634) Wrner Bros.

— Let's Sing, Listen & Learn, Bk. 1. 16p. (Orig.). (YA). 1992. pap. text 9.95 (*1-57623-721-4*, BSM1001) Wrner Bros.

— Let's Sing, Listen & Learn, Bk. 2. 16p. (Orig.). (YA). 1992. pap. text 9.95 (*1-57623-722-2*, BSM1002) Wrner Bros.

— Let's Sing, Listen & Learn, Bk. 3. 16p. (Orig.). (YA). 1992. pap. text 9.95 (*1-57623-723-0*, BSM1003) Wrner Bros.

— Let's Sing, Listen & Learn, Bk. 4. 16p. (Orig.). (YA). 1992. pap. text 9.95 (*1-57623-724-9*, BSM1004) Wrner Bros.

— Master Musician. (YA). 1995. pap. text 24.95 (*1-57623-718-4*, BMR06101) Wrner Bros.

— Mexican Folk Dances. 2nd ed. (World Dance Ser.). (Illus.). 20p. (YA). 1994. pap. text 19.95 incl. cd-rom (*0-89898-947-7*, BMR05117) Wrner Bros.

— Shari's Passover Surprise. (Illus.). (Orig.). (J). 1997. pap. text 19.95 (*1-57623-982-9*, PF9713) Wrner Bros.

— The Sounds of Christmas. (Shari Lewis Presents...Ser.). 96p. (C). 1997. pap. text 14.95 (*0-7692-1546-7*, PF9728) Wrner Bros.

— Traditional Songs from Latin America. 28p. (Orig.). 1995. pap. text 5.95 (*0-89724-671-3*, AF9526) Wrner Bros.

— Yakko's World: Animaniacs. 72p. (Orig.). (YA). 1995. pap. text 9.95 (*0-89724-581-4*, PF9513) Wrner Bros.

— You Write the Songs. 32p. (Orig.). (J). 1994. pap. 9.95 (*0-89898-910-8*, JPC006) Wrner Bros.

Cavalier, Debbie, ed. see Brimhall, John.

Cavalier, Debbie, ed. see Burton, Leon, et al.

Cavalier, Debbie, ed. see Feldstein, Sandy.

Cavalier, Debbie, ed. see Giese, Gayle.

Cavalier, Debbie, ed. see Goodkin, Doug.

Cavalier, Debbie, ed. see Houghton, Steve.

Cavalier, Debbie, ed. see Kleiner, Lynn & Riddell, Cecilia.

Cavalier, Debbie, ed. see Molineaux, Othello.

Cavalier, Debbie, ed. see Most, Sam.

Cavalier, Debbie, ed. see Nicholl, Matthew.

Cavalier, Debbie, ed. see Rainer, Tom.

Cavalier, Debbie, ed. see Saliba, Konnie.

Cavalier, Debbie, ed. see Stoehr, Judy.

Cavalier, Debbie, ed. see Strid, George L. & Donnelly, Mary.

Cavalier, Debbie, ed. see Viapiano, Paul.

Cavalier, Debbie, ed. see Warrington, Tom.

Cavalier, Debbie, ed. see White, Jack N.

Cavalier, Debbie, ed. see Yurko, Michiko.

Cavalier, Robert P. Personal Motivation: A Model for Decision Making. LC 99-34426. 176p. 2000. 55.00 (*0-275-96168-0*) Greenwood.

Cavalier, Tom M., jt. auth. see Ignizio, James P.

Cavalier, Victoria. America's Favorites Naturally. LC 86-50166. (Illus.). 176p. 1987. pap. 10.95 (*0-9610130-5-2*) Melius Pub.

Cavaliere, Alfredo, ed. see Raimon, Peire.

Cavaliere, Anne. Private Lessons. (Desire Ser.: No. 693). 1992. per. 2.79 (*0-373-05693-1*, 5-05693-2) Harlequin Bks.

Cavaliere, Barbara. Theodoros Stamos. Bush, Martin, ed. Cress, Alan, tr. (Illus.). 63p. (Orig.). 1991. pap. 30.00 (*0-925315-98-2*) ACA Galleries.

Cavaliere, Barbara, ed. see Joans, Ted, et al.

Cavaliere, Lorraine A. & Sgroi, Angela, eds. Learning for Personal Development. LC 85-644750. (New Directions for Adult & Continuing Education Ser.: No. ACE 53). 130p. 1992. pap., student ed. 22.00 (*1-55542-747-2*) Jossey-Bass.

Cavaliere, Michael, tr. see Virilio, Paul.

Cavaliere, Robert. Plato for Beginners. (for Beginners Ser.). (Illus.). 176p. (Orig.). 1996. pap. 11.95 (*0-86316-039-5*) Writers & Readers.

Cavalieri, Felicia. La Petite Fille Aux Allumettes. (Best-Sellers Ser.).Tr. of Little Match Girl. (FRE., Illus.). 40p. (J). (ps-2). 2000. pap. 9.95 incl. audio (*2-921997-31-2*) Coffragants.

Cavalieri, Grace. Heart on a Leash. 36p. 1998. pap. 5.00 (*1-891387-01-4*) Red Dragon VA.

***Cavalieri, Grace.** Pinecrest Resthaven. LC 97-61901. (Capital Collection). 60p. 1998. pap. 10.00 (*0-915380-39-0*) Word Works.

Cavalieri, Grace. Poems: New & Selected. Comitz, Cindy & Sargent, Robert, eds. 100p. (Orig.). 1994. pap. 10.00 (*0-938572-06-7*) Bunny Crocodile.

— Trenton: Poems. Ward, Herman M., ed. 66p. (Orig.). 1990. pap. 10.00 (*0-9610346-0-2*) Belle Mead Pr.

Cavalieri, Grace, ed. WPFW 89.3FM Poetry Anthology: The Poet & the Poem. LC 91-78328. 340p. (Orig.). 1992. pap. 18.00 (*0-938572-03-2*) Bunny Crocodile.

— WPFW 89.3FM Poetry Anthology: The Poet & the Poem. 2nd ed. 340p. (Orig.). 1993. pap. 17.95 (*0-938572-19-9*) Bunny Crocodile.

Cavalieri, Grace, et al. True Stories: Fiction by Uncommon Women. LC 96-70943. 84p. 1997. pap. 11.95 (*0-9637704-6-2*) Red Dragon VA.

Cavalieri, Grace, ed. see Barras, Jonetta R.

Cavalieri, Grace, ed. see Becker, Anne.

Cavalieri, Grace, ed. see Darr, Ann.

Cavalieri, Grace, ed. see Emerson, Jean.

Cavalieri, Grace, ed. see James, Sonja.

Cavalieri, Grace, ed. see Lalonde Alenier, Karren.

Cavalieri, Grace, ed. see Morland, Margaret W.

Cavalieri, Grace, ed. see Sargent, Robert.

Cavalieri, Grace, ed. see Tuthill, Stacy.

Cavalieri, Liebe F. The Double-Edged Helix: Genetic Engineering in the Real World. Anshen, Ruth N., ed. LC 84-17890. (Convergence Ser.). 208p. 1984. pap. 12.95 (0-275-91783-5, B1783, Praeger Pubs) Greenwood.
— The Double-Edged Helix: Science in the Real World. Anshen, Ruth N., ed. LC 81-2213. (Convergence Ser.: Vol. II). 207p. 1981. text 49.00 (0-231-05306-1) Col U Pr.
***Cavaliero, Glen.** The Alchemy of Laughter: Comedy in English Fiction. LC 99-15265. 256p. 2000. text 65.00 (0-312-22551-2) St Martin.
Cavaliero, Glen. Charles Williams, Poet of Theology. LC 82-11420. 209p. reprint ed. 64.80 (0-608-16662-6, 202753800055) Bks Demand.
— A Reading of E. M. Forster. 187p. 1979. 38.00 (0-8476-6191-1) Rowman.
— Steeple on a Hill. 57p. 1997. 19.95 (1-872621-23-6, Pub. by Tartarus Pr) Firebird Dist.
Cavaliero, Roderick. Admiral Satan: The Life & Campaigns of Suffren, Scourge of the Royal Navy. 224p. 1994. text 49.50 (1-85043-686-X, Pub. by I B T) St Martin.
Cavalla, David, et al. Modern Strategy for Preclinical Pharmaceutical R & D: Towards the Virtual Research Company. LC 96-37234. 228p. 1997. 139.95 (0-471-97117-0) Wiley.
***Cavallar, Georg.** Kant & the Critique of International Law. 200p. 1999. (0-7083-1509-7, Pub. by Univ Wales Pr); pap. (0-7083-1508-9, Pub. by Univ Wales Pr) Paul & Co Pubs.
Cavallar, Osvaldo, et al. A Grammar of Signs: Bartolo da Sassoferrato's Tract on Insignia & Coats of Arms. Kirshner, Julius, ed. (Studies in Comparative Legal History). (Illus.). 200p. (C). 1994. text 30.00 (1-882239-07-5) Robbins Collection.
***Cavallaro, Claire C. & Haney, Michele.** Preschool Inclusion. LC 99-11264. 320p. 1999. 45.00 (1-55766-419-6) P H Brookes.
Cavallaro, Dan, jt. auth. see Grauer, Ken.
***Cavallaro, Dani.** Cyberpunk & Cyberculture: Science Fiction & the Work of William Gibson. 256p. 2000. 95.00 (0-485-00412-7, Pub. by Athlone Pr) Transaction Pubs.
— Cyberpunk & Cyberculture: Science Fiction & the Work of William Gibson. LC 00-36345. 256p. 2000. pap. 18.95 (0-485-00607-3) Transaction Pubs.
Cavallaro, Dani, jt. auth. see Warwick, Alexandra.
***Cavallaro, Daniel.** Art for Beginners. (Illus.). 192p. 1999. pap. 11.95 (0-86316-265-7) Writers & Readers.
— The Body for Beginners. 1999. pap. 11.00 (0-86316-266-5) Writers & Readers.
Cavallaro, Daniel. Kristeva for Beginners. (Illus.). 192p. 1999. pap. 11.95 (0-86316-267-3) Writers & Readers.
***Cavallaro, Eleonora.** Real & Financial Dynamics in a Macroeconomic Growth Model with Endogenous Cycles. (Dynamische Wirtschaftstheorie Ser.: Bd. 20). 196p. 1999. pap. 39.95 (3-631-35033-3) P Lang Pubng.
— Real & Financial Dynamics in a Macroeconomic Growth Model with Endogenous Cycles. LC 99-41029. (Dynamische Wirtschaftstheorie Ser.: Vol. 20). 196p. (C). 1999. pap. text 39.95 (0-8204-4345-X) P Lang Pubng.
Cavallaro, Harold E., jt. auth. see Srikanth, Mokshagundam L.
Cavallaro, Karen, ed. see Sohn, Anton P.
Cavallaro, Lenny, jt. auth. see Kortchnoi, Viktor.
Cavallerano, Anthony A. & Gutner, Rodney K. Macular Disorders: An Illustrated Diagnostic Guide. LC 96-39906. (Illus.). 304p. 1997. text 97.50 (0-7506-9224-3) Buttrwrth-Heinemann.
Cavalleri, Stephen J. & Monif, Gilles R. G. A Physician's Guide for the Collection of Bacteriogical & Viral Specimens. (Illus.). 52p. 1995. pap. 6.95 (1-880906-41-4) IDI Pub.
Cavalletti, Sofia. History's Golden Thread: The History of Salvation. Rojcewicz, Rebekah, tr. from ITA. LC 99-29190. 163p. 1999. pap. 10.00 (1-56854-261-5, GOLDEN) Liturgy Tr Pubns.
— Living Liturgy: Elementary Reflections. LC 98-65273. 96p. 1998. pap. 10.00 (1-56854-241-0) Liturgy Tr Pubns.
— The Religious Potential of the Child: Experiencing Scripture & Liturgy with Young Children. Coulter, Patricia M. & Coulter, Julie M., trs. LC 92-19804. 251p. 1992. pap. 16.00 (0-929650-67-0, CHILD) Liturgy Tr Pubns.
Cavalletti, Sofia, et al. The Good Shepherd & the Child: A Joyful Journey. LC 96-9874. 1995. pap. 16.00 (1-56854-157-0, GSHEP) Liturgy Tr Pubns.
Cavalli, Alessandro & Galland, Olivier, eds. Youth in Europe. LC 94-45076. (Social Change in Western Europe Ser.). 160p. 1995. 79.50 (1-85567-305-3); pap. 19.95 (1-85567-306-1) Bks Intl VA.
Cavalli, Ana & Sarma, Amardeo. SDL '97: Time for Testing SDL, MSC & Trends: Proceedings of the Eighth SDL Forum, Evry, France, 23-26 September, 1997. LC 97-26512. 564p. 1997. 215.50 (0-444-82816-8) Elsevier.
Cavalli-Bjorkman, Gorel. Dutch & Flemish Painting: 1400-1600, Vol. 1. (Illus.). 128p. 1986. 79.00 (91-7100-304-5) Coronet Bks.
Cavalli-Bjorkman, Gorel, ed. Rembrandt & His Pupils. (Illus.). 233p. 1993. 57.50 (91-7100-463-7) Coronet Bks.
Cavalli-Bojorkman, Gorel & Lindwall, Bo, eds. The World of Carl Larsson. Rice, Allan L., tr. LC 93-23754. (J). 1991. 39.95 (0-671-75264-2) S&S Trade.
Cavalli, F., ed. Endocrine Therapy of Breast Cancer, No. III. (ESO Monographs). (Illus.). xii, 65p. 1989. 51.95 (0-387-50819-8) Spr-Verlag.
Cavalli, F., et al, eds. Malignant Lymphomas & Hodgkin's Disease: Experimental & Therapeutic Advances. (Developments in Oncology Ser.). 1986. text 253.50 (0-89838-727-2) Kluwer Academic.
Cavalli, Franco, et al. Textbook of Medical Oncology. 550p. 1997. write for info. (1-85317-290-1) Martin Dunitz.
Cavalli-Sforza, Francesco, jt. auth. see Cavalli-Sforza, Luigi L.
Cavalli-Sforza, L. L. & Bodmer, W. F. The Genetics of Human Population. unabridged ed. LC 99-27328. 984p. 1999. pap. text 29.95 (0-486-40693-8) Dover.
Cavalli-Sforza, L. L. & Feldman, Marcus W. Cultural Transmission & Evolution: A Quantitative Approach. Robert, M., ed. LC 80-8539. (Monographs in Population Biology: No. 16). (Illus.). 368p. 1981. pap. text 26.95 (0-691-08283-9, Pub. by Princeton U Pr) Cal Prin Full Svc.
Cavalli-Sforza, L. L., et al. On Evolutionary Anthropology: In Honor of Harry Hoijer 1983. LC 85-51127. (Other Realities Ser.: Vol 7). 104p. 1986. 26.00 (0-89003-170-3); pap. 16.00 (0-89003-171-1) Undena Pubns.
Cavalli-Sforza, L. L., jt. auth. see Ammerman, Albert J.
Cavalli-Sforza, L. Luca. History & Geography of Human Genes. 428p. 1996. pap. text 35.00 (0-691-02905-9, Pub. by Princeton U Pr) Cal Prin Full Svc.
Cavalli-Sforza, Luigi L. Genes, Peoples, & Languages. Seielstad, Mark, tr. from ITA. LC 98-26360. 224p. 2000. 24.00 (0-86547-529-6) N Point Pr.
Cavalli-Sforza, Luigi L. & Cavalli-Sforza, Francesco. The Great Human Diasporas: The History of Diversity & Evolution. (Illus.). 300p. (C). 1998. text 27.00 (0-7881-5624-1) DIANE Pub.
Cavalli-Sforza, Luigi L., et al. The Great Human Diasporas: The History of Diversity & Evolution. Mimnaugh, Heather, ed. 320p. (C). 1995. pap. 17.00 (0-201-44231-0) Addison-Wesley.
— The History & Geography of Human Genes. LC 93-19339. (Illus.). 522p. 1994. text 175.00 (0-691-08750-4, Pub. by Princeton U Pr) Cal Prin Full Svc.
Cavallin, Jens. Content & Objest: Husswerl, Twardowski & Psychologism, Vol. 142. LC 97-28856. (Phaenomenologica Ser.: No. 142). 268p. 1997. text 124.00 (0-7923-4734-X) Kluwer Academic.
Cavalline, Jo Jo & O'Donnell, Jo Anne. Recycled Container Arts & Crafts Activities: Week-by-Week Projects Using All Kinds of Containers. Mitchell, Judy, ed. (Illus.). 112p. (Orig.). 1996. pap., teacher ed. 10.95 (1-57310-040-4) Teachng & Lrning Co.
Cavallini & Company Staff. Bee Journal. 1995. 24.00 (1-57489-000-X); 16.00 (1-57489-001-8) Cavallini.
— Palmist Hand Journal. 1995. 16.00 (1-57489-005-0); 24.00 (1-57489-006-9) Cavallini.
— Sunflower Journal. 1995. 24.00 (1-57489-002-6) Cavallini.
— Voyage Journal. 1995. 16.00 (1-57489-003-4); 24.00 (1-57489-004-2) Cavallini.
Cavallini, Doriano, ed. see International Meeting on Low Molecular Weight Sulf.
Cavallini, Ernesto. Thirty Caprices for the Clarinet. 64p. 1909. pap. 10.95 (0-8258-0238-5, 0106) Fischer Inc NY.
Cavallini, Giuliana. Catherine of Siena. LC 99-192043. (Outstanding Christian Thinkers Ser.). 154p. 1998. 60.00 (0-225-66767-3, Pub. by G Chapman); pap. 21.50 (0-225-66765-7, Pub. by G Chapman) Cassell & Continuum.
— St. Martin de Porres - Apostle of Charity. Holland, Caroline, tr. from ITA. LC 79-65530. (Cross & Crown Series of Spirituality). 1979. reprint ed. pap. 12.50 (0-89555-092-X) TAN Bks Pubs.
— Things Visible & Invisible: Images in the Spirituality of St. Catherine of Siena. Jeremiah, Mary, tr. from ITA. LC 95-51322. 153p. (Orig.). 1996. pap. 5.50 (0-8189-0733-9) Alba.
Cavallo. Widowhood in Medieval & Early Modern Europe. LC 98-52954. 288p. (C). 1999. 72.95 (0-582-31747-9) Longman.
— Widowhood in Medieval Early Modern England. LC 98-52954. 288p. 1999. pap. 29.06 (0-582-31748-7) Addison-Wesley.
Cavallo, jt. see Marek, Michael F.
Cavallo, Adolfo Salvatore. Unicorn Tapestries. LC 98-4153. (Illus.). 128p. 1998. 35.00 (0-8109-3947-9, Pub. by Abrams) Time Warner.
Cavallo, Adolph S. Textiles - Isabella Stewart Gardner Museum. LC 85-51863. (Illus.). 223p. 1986. 29.95 (0-914660-09-8); pap. 8.00 (0-914660-10-1) I S Gardner Mus.
Cavallo, Adolph S. & Metropolitan Museum of Art (New York, N. Y.) Staff. The Unicorn Tapestries at the Metropolitan Museum of Art. LC 98-4153. 1998. 35.00 (0-87099-868-4); pap. 25.00 (0-87099-869-2) Metro Mus Art.
Cavallo, Albert. Using MATLAB, Simulink & Control Toolbox: A Practical Approach. (MATLAB Curriculum Ser.). 512p. 1996. pap. 65.00 (0-13-261058-2) P-H.
Cavallo, Barbara L., ed. see Abramchik, Lois.
Cavallo, Diana. A Bridge of Leaves. LC 96-78719. 244p. 1997. reprint ed. pap. 12.00 (1-55071-051-6) Guernica Editions.
Cavallo, Dominick. A Fiction of the Past: The Sixties in American History. LC 98-46179. 282p. 1999. 26.95 (0-312-21930-X) St Martin.
Cavallo, Guglielmo, et al, contrib. by. Codex Purpureus Rossanensis. (Codices Selecti A Ser.: Vol. LXXXI). (ENG, GER & ITA., Illus.). 1985. 190.00 (3-201-01400-1, Pub. by Akademische Druck-und) Balogh.
— Codex Purpureus Rossanensis. fac. limited ed. (Codices Selecti A Ser.: Vol. LXXXI). (ENG, GER & ITA., Illus.). 386p. 1985. lthr. 5859.00 (3-201-01273-4, Pub. by Akademische Druck-und) Balogh.
Cavallo, Guglielmo, ed. The Byzantines. LC 96-19671. 296p. 1997. pap. text 20.00 (0-226-09792-7); lib. bdg. 48.00 (0-226-09791-9) U Ch Pr.
Cavallo, Guglielmo & Chartier, Roger, eds. A History of Reading in the West. Cochrane, Lydia G., tr. from FRE. LC 99-22447. (Studies in Print Culture & the History of the Book). Orig. Title: Histoire de la Lecture dans le Mode Occidental. 488p. 1999. 40.00 (1-55849-213-5) U of Mass Pr.
Cavallo, Jo A. Boiardo's Orlando Innamorato: An Ethics of Desire. LC 92-37288. (C). 1993. 34.50 (0-8385-3534-2) Assoc Univ Prs.
Cavallo, Jo Ann & Ross, Charles S., eds. Fortune & Romance: Boiardo in America. LC 98-11569. Medieval & Renaissance Texts & Studies: Vol. 183). 352p. 1998. 30.00 (0-86698-225-6, MR183) MRTS.
***Cavallo, John.** Aberrant: Elites. 2000. pap. 14.95 (1-56504-692-7) White Wolf.
Cavallo, Margaret S. Loss Control: If Disaster Strikes We're Ready. (Illus.). 1997. 3.5 ld. write for info. (0-9658375-5-6) O-Hill Pub.
— Loss Control: If Disaster Strikes We're Ready. unabridged ed. (Illus.). 75p. 1997. ring bd. write for info. (0-9658375-4-8) O-Hill Pub.
— Loss Control: If Disaster Strikes We're Ready. unabridged ed. (Illus.). 200p. 1997. ring bd. write for info. (0-9658375-3-X) O-Hill Pub.
Cavallo, Roger. The Role of Systems Methodology in Social Science Research. (Frontiers in Systems Research Ser.: Vol. 1). 1979. lib. bdg. 73.50 (0-89838-005-7) Kluwer Academic.
— Systems Methodology in Social Science Research: Recent Developments. (Frontiers in Systems Research Ser.). 1982. lib. bdg. 138.50 (0-89838-044-8) Kluwer Academic.
Cavallo, Sandra. Charity & Power in Early Modern Italy: Benefactors & Their Motives in Turin, 1541-1789. (Cambridge History of Medicine Ser.). (Illus.). 298p. (C). 1995. text 69.95 (0-521-46091-3); pap. text 29.95 (0-521-48333-6) Cambridge U Pr.
Cavallo, Susana, et al, eds. Estudies en Honor de Janet Perez No. 129: El Sugeto Feminino en Escritosas Hispanicas. (SPA.). 200p. (C). 1998. 59.95 (1-882528-19-0) Scripta.
Cavalloro, R., ed. Aphid Antagonists: Proceedings of a Meeting of the EC Experts' Group, Portici, Italy, 23-24 November 1982. 152p. 1983. 91.00 (90-6191-505-8, Pub. by A A Balkema) Ashgate Pub Co.
— European Research on Varroatosis Control: Proceedings of the EC Experts' Group Meeting, Bad Homburg, 15-17 October 1986. 272p. (C). 1988. text 97.00 (90-6191-846-4, Pub. by A A Balkema) Ashgate Pub Co.
— Fruit Flies of Economic Importance: Proceedings of the International Symposium Organized Jointly by the CEC & the IOBC, Athens, Greece, 16-19 November 1983. 656p. (C). 1983. text 168.00 (90-6191-503-1, Pub. by A A Balkema) Ashgate Pub Co.
— Fruit Flies of Economic Importance, 1984: Proceedings of the CEC-IOBC "Ad Hoc Meeting", Hamburg, 23 August 1984. 224p. (C). 1986. text 97.00 (90-6191-636-4, Pub. by A A Balkema) Ashgate Pub Co.
— Fruit Flies of Economic Importance 87: Proceedings of the CEC - IOBC International Symposium, Rome, 7 - 10 April 1987. (Illus.). 640p. (C). 1989. text 123.00 (90-6191-869-3, Pub. by A A Balkema) Ashgate Pub Co.
— Influence of Environmental Factors on the Control of Grape Pests, Diseases & Weeds: Proceedings of a Meeting of the EC Experts Group, Thessaloniki, Greece, 6 - 8 October 1987. (Illus.). 352p. (C). 1990. text 97.00 (90-6191-870-7, Pub. by A A Balkema) Ashgate Pub Co.
— Integrated & Biological Control in Protected Crops: Proceedings of a Meeting of the EC Experts' Group, Heraklion, 24-26 April 1985. 270p. (C). 1987. text 97.00 (90-6191-790-5, Pub. by A A Balkema) Ashgate Pub Co.
— Integrated Pest Control in Viticulture: Proceedings of a Meeting of the EC Experts' Group, Portoferraio, 26-28 September 1985. 405p. 1987. 97.00 (90-6191-749-2, Pub. by A A Balkema) Ashgate Pub Co.
— Integrated TSE-TSE Fly Control & Strategies: Proceedings of the CEC International Symposium, Ispra, 4-6 March 1986. 210p. (C). 1987. text 91.00 (90-6191-702-6, Pub. by A A Balkema) Ashgate Pub Co.
— Statistical & Mathematical Methods in Population Dynamics & Pest Control: Proceedings of a Meeting of the EC Experts Group, Parma, 26-28th October 1983. 256p. (C). 1984. text 110.00 (90-6191-548-1, Pub. by A A Balkema) Ashgate Pub Co.
— Varroa Jacobsoni Oud. Affecting Honey Bees: Present Status & Needs: Proceedings of a Meeting of the EC Experts' Group, Wageningen, 7-9 February 1983. 129p. 1983. 110.00 (90-6191-524-4, Pub. by A A Balkema) Ashgate Pub Co.
Cavalloro, R. & Crovetti, A., eds. Integrated Pest Control in Olive-Groves: Proceeedings of the CEC-FAO-IOBC International Joint Meeting, Pisa, 3-6 April 1984. 528p. (C). 1985. text 168.00 (90-6191-609-7, Pub. by A A Balkema) Ashgate Pub Co.
Cavalloro, R. & DiMartino, E., eds. Integrated Pest Control in Citrus-Groves. (Proceedings of the Experts' Meeting Acireale, 26-29 March 1985 Ser.). 612p. (C). 1985. 168.00 (90-6191-678-X, Pub. by A A Balkema) Ashgate Pub Co.
Cavalloro, R. & El Titi, A., eds. Weed Control in Vegetable Production: Proceedings of the EC Experts' Group Meeting, Stuttgart, 28-31 October 1986. 316p. (C). 1988. text 97.00 (90-6191-845-6, Pub. by A A Balkema) Ashgate Pub Co.
Cavalloro, R. & Pelereants, C., eds. Integrated Pest Management in Protected Vegetable Crops: Proceedings of the CEC/IOBC Experts' Group Meeting, Cabrils, 27-29 May 1987. 430p. 1989. 110.00 (90-6191-874-X, Pub. by A A Balkema) Ashgate Pub Co.
Cavalloro, R. & Pelerents, C., eds. Progress on Pest Management in Field Vegetables: Proceedings of the CEC-IOBC Experts' Group Meeting, Rennes, November 20-22, 1985. (Illus.). 312p. 1988. lib. bdg. 97.00 (90-6191-759-X, Pub. by A A Balkema) Ashgate Pub Co.
Cavalloro, R. & Robinson, D. W., eds. Weed Control on Vine & Soft Fruits: Proceedings. 176p. 1987. text 91.00 (90-6191-691-7, Pub. by A A Balkema) Ashgate Pub Co.
Cavalloro, R. & Sunderland, K. D., eds. Integrated Crop Protection in Cereals: Proceedings of a Meeting of the EC Experts Group, Littlehampton, November 25-27, 1986. (Illus.). xi, 333p. 1988. lib. bdg. 97.00 (90-6191-844-8, Pub. by A A Balkema) Ashgate Pub Co.
Cavallucci, Fabio. Tuscia Electa 1997: Itineraries of Contemporary Art in Chianti. (Illus.). 96p. 1998. pap. 24.95 (88-7757-079-2, Pub. by Hopefulmonster Editore) Dist Art Pubs.
***Cavalola, Alan A. & Lavender, Neil J.** Toxic Coworkers: How to Deal with Dysfunctional People on the Job. 176p. 2000. pap. 13.95 (1-57224-219-1, Pub. by New Harbinger) Publishers Group.
Cavan, Ruth S. & Ranck, Katherine H. Family & the Depression: A Study of One Hundred Chicago Families. LC 79-102229. (Select Bibliographies Reprint Ser.). 1977. 24.95 (0-8369-5114-X) Ayer.
— The Family & the Depression: A Study of one Hundred Chicago Families. 1976. 19.95 (0-405-03096-7) Ayer.
Cavan, Ruth S., et al. Personal Adjustment in Old Age. Kastenbaum, Robert J., ed. LC 78-22188. (Aging & Old Age Ser.). (Illus.). 1979. reprint ed. lib. bdg. 19.95 (0-405-11806-6) Ayer.
Cavan, Seamus. Daniel Boone & the Opening of the Ohio Country. Goetzmann, William H., ed. (World Explorers Ser.). (Illus.). 120p. (YA). (gr. 5 up). 1991. lib. bdg. 19.95 (0-7910-1309-X) Chelsea Hse.
***Cavan, Seamus.** Euthanasia. LC 00-9392. (Focus on Science & Society Ser.). 2000. lib. bdg. write for info. (0-8239-3215-X) Rosen Group.
Cavan, Seamus. The Irish-American Experience. LC 92-7512. (Coming to America Ser.). (Illus.). 64p. (J). (gr. 4-6). 1993. lib. bdg. 22.40 (1-56294-218-2) Millbrook Pr.
— Lewis & Clark & the Route to the Pacific. (World Explorers Ser.). (J). 1991. 15.15 (0-606-07784-7) Turtleback.
— Thurgood Marshall & Equal Rights. LC 92-12995. (Gateway Civil Rights Ser.). (Illus.). 32p. (J). (gr. 2-4). 1993. pap. 4.95 (1-56294-793-1) Millbrook Pr.
— Thurgood Marshall & Equal Rights. (Gateway Civil Rights Ser.). 1993. 10.15 (0-606-06813-9, Pub. by Turtleback) Demco.
— W. E. B. Du Bois & Racial Relations. LC 92-33015. (Gateway Civil Rights Ser.). (Illus.). 32p. (J). (gr. 2-4). 1993. pap. 4.95 (1-56294-794-X); lib. bdg. 20.90 (1-56294-288-3) Millbrook Pr.
Cavan, Sherri. Twentieth Century Gothic: America's Nixon. LC 79-65722. (Illus.). 1979. 20.00 (0-934594-00-7) Wigan Pier.
Cavanagh. British Theatre, a Bibliography 1901 to 1985. 1992. 170.00 (0-8161-0573-1, G K Hall & Co) Mac Lib Ref.
Cavanagh, Clare. Osip Mandelstam & the Modernist Creation of Tradition. LC 94-11248. 376p. 1995. text 49.50 (0-691-03682-9, Pub. by Princeton U Pr) Cal Prin Full Svc.
Cavanagh, Clare, jt. ed. see Baranczak, Stanislaw.
Cavanagh, Clare, tr. see Szymborska, Wislawa.
Cavanagh, Clare, tr. see Zagajewski, Adam.
Cavanagh, D. & Brown, T. D., eds. Coronaviruses & Their Diseases. (Advances in Experimental Medicine & Biology Ser.: Vol. 276). (Illus.). 670p. 1990. 149.50 (0-306-43664-7, Plenum Trade) Perseus Pubng.
***Cavanagh, Dermot & Kirk, Tim, eds.** Subversion & Scurrility: Popular Discourse in Europe from 1500 to the Present. (Illus.). 350p. 2000. text 78.95 (1-84014-643-5, Pub. by Ashgate Pub) Ashgate Pub Co.
Cavanagh, Eileen, jt. auth. see Harelson, Randy.
Cavanagh, G. S. The Panorama of Vesalius: A Lost Design from Titian's Studio. (Illus.). 38p. 1996. 275.00 (0-937543-54-3) Sacrum Pr.
Cavanagh, Gerald F. American Business Values. 4th ed. LC 97-2915. 314p. 1997. pap. text 38.60 (0-13-518234-4) P-H.
Cavanagh, Gerald F. & McGovern, Arthur F. Ethical Dilemmas in the Modern Corporation. (Illus.). 224p. 1988. pap. text 45.00 (0-13-290058-0) P-H.
Cavanagh, Helen. The Last Piper. LC 95-44423. (Illus.). 128p. (J). (gr. 3-7). 1996. mass mkt. 16.00 (0-689-80481-4) S&S Bks Yung.
— Panther Glade. LC 92-23406. 160p. (J). (gr. 5-9). 1993. mass mkt. 16.00 (0-671-75617-6) S&S Bks Yung.
Cavanagh, Helen, tr. see Vatromanolakis, Voryis.
Cavanagh, Helen, tr. see Yatromanolakis, Yoryis.
Cavanagh, James P. ATM in Action: Scenarios for Success. Clark, Dave, ed. (Networking Ser.). 350p. 1999. pap. 49.95 (1-55860-468-5) Morgan Kaufmann.
Cavanagh, James P., ed. Multimedia Networking Handbook. 560p. 1995. 154.00 (0-7913-2480-X) Warren Gorham & Lamont.
Cavanagh, Jim. Frame Relay Applications. LC 97-31803. 400p. (C). 1997. text 49.95 (1-55860-399-9) Morgan Kaufmann.
— Standard Catalog of Piper Single Engine Aircraft. Sakrison, David C., ed. (Illus.). 528p. (Orig.). 1993. pap. 49.95 (1-879825-08-2) Jones Publish.
— Standard Catalog of Piper Twin Engine Aircraft. Sakrison, David C., ed. LC 95-169006. (Illus.). 248p. (Orig.). 1994. pap. 29.95 (1-879825-10-4) Jones Publish.
Cavanagh, Jim, compiled by. Cessna Single Engine Aircraft. (Illus.). 830p. 69.95 (0-614-13199-5, 21-31835) EAA Aviation.

An Asterisk (*) at the beginning of an entry indicates that the title is appearing for the first time.

— Piper Single Engine Aircraft. (Illus.). 525p. 49.95 (*0-614-13201-0*, 21-31836) EAA Aviation.

Cavanagh, John, et al. Beyond Bretton Woods: Alternatives to the Global Economic Order. LC 94-20615. (Transnational Institute Ser.). 256p. (C). 1994. 54.95 (*0-7453-0890-2*, Pub. by Pluto GBR); pap. 18.95 (*0-7453-0889-9*, Pub. by Pluto GBR) Stylus Pub VA.

— Trade's Hidden Costs: Worker Rights in a Changing World Economy. 66p. 1988. pap. 3.95 (*1-880103-00-1*) Intl Labor Rghts.

— Trading Freedom: How Free Trade Affects Our Lives, Work & Environment. 130p. (C). 1992. pap. 10.00 (*0-685-60300-8*) Inst Policy Stud.

Cavanagh, John C. Decision at Fayetteville: The North Carolina Ratification Convention & General Assembly of 1789. (North Carolina & the Constitution Ser.). (Illus.). 41p. (Orig.). 1989. pap. 4.00 (*0-86526-239-X*) NC Archives.

Cavanagh, K. My First Mass Book: Little Angel. (J). (ps-3). Date not set. pap. text 1.25 (*0-88271-200-4*) Regina Pr.

— My First Prayer Book: Little Angel. (J). (ps-3). Date not set. pap. text 1.25 (*0-88271-204-7*) Regina Pr.

— The Sacraments: Little Angel. (J). (ps-3). Date not set. pap. text 1.25 (*0-88271-210-1*) Regina Pr.

— Ten Commandments: Little Angel. (J). (ps-3). Date not set. pap. text 1.25 (*0-88271-205-5*) Regina Pr.

— Way of the Cross: Little Angel. (J). (ps-3). Date not set. pap. text 1.25 (*0-88271-211-X*) Regina Pr.

Cavanagh, Karen, ed. The Christmas Story. (Illus.). 32p. (J). (ps-3). 1990. 19.50 (*0-88271-209-8*, 1811) Regina Pr.

Cavanagh, Kate & Cree, Viviene. Working with Men: Feminism & Social Work. LC 95-16148. (The State of Welfare Ser.). 240p. (C). 1995. pap. 25.99 (*0-415-11185-4*) Routledge.

— Working with Men: Feminism & Social Work. LC 95-16148. (The State of Welfare Ser.). 240p. (C). (gr. 13). 1995. 85.00 (*0-415-11184-6*) Routledge.

Cavanagh, Michael E. Before the Wedding: Look Before You Leap. 224p. 1994. pap. 18.95 (*0-664-25440-3*) Westminster John Knox.

— The Counseling Experience: A Theoretical & Practical Approach. 383p. (C). 1990. reprint ed. pap. text 25.95 (*0-88133-531-2*) Waveland Pr.

— The Counseling Experience: Understanding & Living It. LC 81-17050. (Psychology-Counseling Ser.). 552p. (C). 1982. text 24.50 (*0-8185-0509-5*) Brooks-Cole.

Cavanagh, Peter. The Running Shoe Book. LC 80-20365. (Illus.). 400p. 1980. pap. 11.95 (*0-89037-182-2*) Anderson World.

— The Running Shoe Book. 1980. pap. 11.95 (*0-02-499730-7*, Macmillan Coll) P-H.

Cavanagh, Sean. Transportation Conformity. 5p. 1995. 15.00 (*0-614-10576-5*, 7302-2005) Natl Conf State Legis.

Cavanagh, Sheila M., ed. see Goldman, Marshall I., et al.

Cavanagh, Sheila T. Wanton Eyes & Chaste Desires: Female Sexuality in The Faerie Queene. LC 93-40515. 1994. 27.95 (*0-253-31367-8*); pap. 15.95 (*0-253-20889-0*) Ind U Pr.

Cavanagh, Terri. Lesson of the 1965 Indonesian Coup. 58p. 1995. reprint ed. 3.00 (*1-875639-00-4*) Mehring Bks.

Cavanagh, Terry. Public Sculpture of Liverpool. LC 96-225806. (Public Sculpture of Britain Ser.: Vol. 1). 58.95 (*0-85323-701-8*, Pub. by Liverpool Univ Pr) Intl Spec Bk.

— Public Sculpture of Liverpool. LC 96-225806. (Public Sculpture of Britain Ser.: Vol. 1). (Illus.). 1998. pap. 25.95 (*0-85323-711-5*, Pub. by Liverpool Univ Pr) Intl Spec Bk.

Cavanagh, W. G., et al, eds. Post-Minoan Crete. (BSA Studies: Vol. 2). (Illus.). 143p. 1998. lib. bdg. 35.00 (*0-904887-29-4*, Pub. by Brit Sch Athens) David Brown.

Cavanagh, W. G. & Walker, Susan, eds. Sparta in Laconia: The Archaeology of a City & Its Countryside. (BSA Studies: Vol. 4). (Illus.). 185p. 1999. lib. bdg. 42.50 (*0-904887-36-7*, Pub. by Brit Sch Athens) David Brown.

Cavanagh, William & Mee, Christopher. A Private Place: Death in Prehistoric Greece. (Studies in Mediterranean Archaeology: Vol. CXXV). (Illus.). 262p. 1998. pap. 99.50 (*91-7081-178-4*, Pub. by P Astroms) Coronet Bks.

Cavanaugh. Adult Developing & Aging. 2nd ed. (Psychology Ser.). 1993. pap., student ed. 19.95 (*0-534-17253-9*) Brooks-Cole.

— Adult Development. (Adaptable Courseware Ser.). 1997. reprint ed. pap. 11.00 (*0-534-49806-X*) Brooks-Cole.

— Lettering & Alphabets. (Illus.). 121p. pap. 6.95 (*0-486-20053-1*) Dover.

Cavanaugh, jt. auth. see Kail.

Cavanaugh, Arthur, jt. auth. see Horn, Geoffrey.

Cavanaugh, Bonita M. Nurse's Manual of Laboratory & Diagnostic Tests. 3rd rev. ed. LC 98-50920. (Illus.). 1056p. 1999. pap. 35.95 (*0-8036-0363-0*) Davis Co.

Cavanaugh, Brian. Fresh Packet of Sower's Seeds: Third Planting. 128p. 1994. pap. 7.95 (*0-8091-3491-8*) Paulist Pr.

— Sower's Seeds: One Hundred Inspiring Stories for Preaching, Teaching, & Public Speaking. 112p. 1990. pap. 7.95 (*0-8091-3138-2*) Paulist Pr.

— Sower's Seeds Aplenty: Fourth Planting. 99p. 1996. pap. 6.95 (*0-8091-3629-5*, 3629-5) Paulist Pr.

— Sower's Seeds of Encouragement: Fifth Planting. 5th ed. LC 98-18581. (Sower's Seeds Ser.). 128p. 1998. pap. 7.95 (*0-8091-3811-5*) Paulist Pr.

— Sower's Seeds of Virtue: Stories of Faith, Hope & Love. LC 96-6812. (Spiritual Samplers Ser.). 96p. (Orig.). 1997. pap. 1.95 (*0-8091-3722-4*) Paulist Pr.

— Sower's Seeds Pack. 1996. pap. 24.95 (*0-8091-3688-0*) Paulist Pr.

***Cavanaugh, Brian.** Sower's Seeds That Nurture Family Values: Sixth Planting. 128p. 2000. pap. 8.95 (*0-8091-3938-3*) Paulist Pr.

Cavanaugh, Brian, ed. More Sower's Seeds: Second Planting. rev. ed. LC 92-12675. 128p. 1992. pap. 7.95 (*0-8091-3324-5*) Paulist Pr.

Cavanaugh, Cam. In Lights & Shadows: Morristown in Three Centuries. (Illus.). 320p. 1994. 35.00 (*0-940631-02-4*) JFP Lib Morristown.

— Saving the Great Swamp: The People, the Power Brokers & an Urban Wilderness. LC 78-8132. (Illus.). 1978. 11.95 (*0-914366-11-4*) Columbia Pub.

Cavanaugh, Carole, jt. ed. see Washburn, Dennis.

Cavanaugh, Catherine. Love & Forgiveness in Yeats's Poetry. LC 85-20692. (Studies in Modern Literature: No. 57). (Illus.). 186p. reprint ed. pap. 57.70 (*0-8357-1728-3*, 207053700001) Bks Demand.

Cavanaugh, Catherine, jt. auth. see Cavanaugh, Terrence.

Cavanaugh, Catherine, jt. auth. see Feinstein, Barbara.

Cavanaugh, Cecelia J. Lorca's Drawings & Poems: Forming the Eye of the Reader. LC 95-4099. (Illus.). 208p. 1995. 39.50 (*0-8387-5302-7*) Bucknell U Pr.

Cavanaugh, Christopher. AA to Z: Addictionary to the 12-Step Culture. LC 97-25139. 208p. 1998. pap. 12.95 (*0-385-48340-6*) Doubleday.

***Cavanaugh, Dan.** Preparing Visual Aids for Presentations. 2nd ed. 24p. 1999. pap. text 3.00 (*0-205-30482-6*) Allyn.

Cavanaugh, Francis X. The Truth about the National Debt: Five Myths & One Reality. LC 96-4074. 192p. 1996. 22.95 (*0-87584-734-X*) Harvard Busn.

Cavanaugh, George L. Beyond the Pearly Gates. 128p. (Orig.). 1989. pap. 7.95 (*0-945767-01-3*) Write Place.

Cavanaugh, Gerald J., ed. Drafting Manual Pocket Companion. (Illus.). 73p. (Orig.). 1991. pap. text 14.95 (*0-931690-36-6*) Genium Pub.

Cavanaugh, Helen. The Last Piper. (J). 15.00 (*0-671-88421-2*) S&S Bks Yung.

Cavanaugh, Jack. The Adversaries. (American Family Portrait Ser.). 500p. 1996. pap. 11.99 (*1-56476-535-0*, 6-3535, Victor Bks) Chariot Victor.

— The Allies. LC 97-169632. (American Family Portrait Ser.). 475p. 1997. pap. 11.99 (*1-56476-588-1*, Victor Bks) Chariot Victor.

— The Colonists. (American Family Portrait Ser.). 500p. (Orig.). 1995. pap. 11.99 (*1-56476-346-3*, 6-3346, Victor Bks) Chariot Victor.

— Daughter of Two Nations: Boston Colonies in the Early 1700s. A Native Princess & Printer's Son Are Caught Between Conflicting Loyalties. 300p. 1998. pap. 10.99 (*0-8024-0864-8*) Moody.

— Glimpses of Truth. LC 98-51956. 1999. pap. 10.99 (*0-310-21574-9*) Zondervan.

— The Patriots. (American Family Portrait Ser.). 475p. 1995. pap. 11.99 (*1-56476-428-1*, 6-3428, Victor Bks) Chariot Victor.

— The Peacemakers. LC 99-18695. (American Family Portrait Ser.: Vol. 8). 512p. 1999. pap. 11.99 (*1-56476-681-0*, Victor Bks) Chariot Victor.

— The Pioneers. LC 96-22940. (American Family Portrait Ser.). 500p. 1996. pap. 11.99 (*1-56476-587-3*) Chariot Victor.

— The Pride & the Passion: A Determined People Forge a New Destiny in South Africa. (African Covenant Ser.: No. 1). pap. 10.99 (*0-8024-0862-1*, 257) Moody.

— Puritans: An American Family Portrait. 432p. 1994. pap. text 11.99 (*1-56476-440-0*, Victor Bks) Chariot Victor.

— Quest for the Promised Land: Oppressed by British Rule, the Van der Kemps Cross a Hostile Wilderness to Find a Home. (African Covenant Ser.: No. 2). 288p. 1997. pap. 10.99 (*0-8024-0863-X*, 261) Moody.

— The Victors. LC 97-39652. 500p. 1997. 11.99 (*1-56476-589-X*, Victor Bks) Chariot Victor.

— When the Lamp Flickers. 2000. 10.99 (*0-310-21576-5*) Zondervan.

***Cavanaugh, Jack.** While Mortals Sleep. 384p. 2000. pap. 11.99 (*0-7642-2307-0*) Bethany Hse.

Cavanaugh, James. Basics. (Illus.). 68p. 1989. write for info. (*0-318-64776-1*) CFAOA.

Cavanaugh, James J. The Basics: A Program Designed to Help You Recognize & Enhance Your Child's Abilities. 256p. 1991. 18.95 (*1-55972-085-9*, Birch Ln Pr) Carol Pub Group.

***Cavanaugh, Jan.** Out Looking In: Early Modern Polish Art, 1890-1918 LC 99-35618. 403p. 2000. 60.00 (*0-520-21190-1*) U CA Pr.

Cavanaugh, Jim. Multimedia Networking Handbook: 1999 Edition. LC 98-37258. 19p. 1998. lib. bdg. 175.00 (*0-8493-9949-1*) Lewis Pubs.

Cavanaugh, Joan & Forseth, Pat. More of Jesus, Less of Me. LC 76-23361. 144p. 1976. pap. 6.99 (*0-88270-176-6*) Bridge-Logos.

***Cavanaugh, Joe.** Jungle Hunter. limited ed. (Illus.). 406p. 2000. 70.00 (*1-57157-127-2*) Safari Pr.

Cavanaugh, Joe & Dorn, Katie. Healing Hearts: A Young Person's Guide to Discovering the Goodness Within. Wright, Wendy, ed. (Illus.). 64p. (Orig.). (YA). (gr. 6 up). 1994. pap. text 10.99 (*0-9640435-0-5*) Nantucket Pubng.

Cavanaugh, John, et al. Protein NMR Spectroscopy: Principles & Practice. LC 95-12822. (Illus.). 587p. 1995. text 70.00 (*0-12-164490-1*) Acad Pr.

Cavanaugh, John, jt. auth. see Ravenscroft, Peter J.

Cavanaugh, John C. Adult Development & Aging. 587p. (C). 1989. mass mkt. 45.50 (*0-534-11640-X*) Brooks-Cole.

— Adult Development & Aging. 2nd ed. LC 92-2316. (C). 1993. text 47.50 (*0-534-17250-4*) Brooks-Cole.

— Adult Development & Aging. 3rd ed. 1996. mass mkt., teacher ed. write for info. (*0-534-34424-0*) Brooks-Cole.

— Adult Development & Aging. 3rd ed. (Psychology Ser.). 560p. (C). 1996. mass mkt. 83.95 (*0-534-34423-2*) Brooks-Cole.

Cavanaugh, John C. & Whitbourne, Susan K., eds. Gerontology: An Interdisciplinary Perspective. LC 98-22404. (Illus.). 480p. (C). 1999. text 55.00 (*0-19-511546-5*) OUP.

Cavanaugh, John C., jt. auth. see Kail, Robert V.

Cavanaugh, John C., jt. ed. see Sinnott, Jan D.

Cavanaugh, John T., ed. see Braly, Scott A. & Kay, Robert S.

Cavanaugh, John W. Media Effects on Voters: A Panel Study of the 1992 Presidential Election. 194p. (C). 1995. lib. bdg. 39.00 (*0-8191-9942-7*) U Pr of Amer.

Cavanaugh, Karen B. A Genealogist's Guide to the Allen County Public Library. rev. ed. 100p. 1989. pap. text 16.95 (*0-318-43234-X*) Watermill IN.

Cavanaugh, Kate. Hope for the Best. (Illus.). 232p. 1993. pap. 11.95 (*0-9622353-5-0*) KAC.

— I Can't Sleep with Those Elves Watching Me. (Illus.). 24p. (J). (ps-8). 1990. pap. text 4.95 (*0-9622353-1-8*) KAC.

— Mother's Day. (Illus.). 228p. (Orig.). 1989. pap. 9.95 (*0-9622353-0-X*) KAC.

— Pete & His Elves Series, Set. (Illus.). 28p. (J). 1992. pap. write for info. (*0-9622353-4-2*) KAC.

— Pete Goes to Grand Island. (Illus.). 24p. (J). 1992. pap. 5.95 (*0-9622353-3-4*) KAC.

— Pete's Lost. (Illus.). 24p. (Orig.). (J). 1991. pap. 4.95 (*0-9622353-2-6*) KAC.

Cavanaugh, Leah. Graphics & Sound Reference Book: Course Code 183-2. Doheny, Cathy & Schroeder, Bonnie, eds. (Illus.). 65p. (gr. 5). 1989. reprint ed. pap. text 8.00 (*0-917531-50-7*) CES Compu-Tech.

— Graphics & Sound Reference Book Teacher Edition: Course Code 183-2R. rev. ed. Doheny, Cathy & Schroeder, Bonnie, eds. (Illus.). 61p. 1989. reprint ed. 12.50 (*0-917531-08-6*) CES Compu-Tech.

Cavanaugh, M. Llamado de Dios Al Adulto Soltero.Tr. of God's Call to the Single Adult. (SPA.). 128p. 1992. pap. 4.99 (*0-8297-0336-5*) Vida Pubs.

Cavanaugh, M. P. The History of Holistic Literacy: Five Major Educators. LC 93-50067. 176p. 1994. 57.95 (*0-275-94789-0*, Praeger Pubs) Greenwood.

Cavanaugh, Maureen B. Eleusis & Athens: Documents in Finance, Religion & Politics in the Fifth Century B. C. LC 94-23331. (American Philological Association American Classical Studies: Vol. 35). 238p. 1996. pap. 29.95 (*0-7885-0032-5*, 400435) OUP.

Cavanaugh, Merry. The Metropolitan Washington Preschool & Daycare Guidebook: A Descriptive Guide to Preschool & Daycare Programs in Washington, Maryland & Virginia. 5th ed. (Illus.). 208p. 1998. pap. text 12.95 (*0-9614212-4-X*) Cavanaugh.

Cavanaugh, Michael. Biotheology: A New Synthesis of Science & Religion. 362p. (Orig.). (C). Date not set. lib. bdg. 68.00 (*0-7618-0104-9*) U Pr of Amer.

— Biotheology: A New Synthesis of Science & Religion. 362p. (Orig.). 1995. pap. 37.00 (*0-7618-0160-X*) U Pr of Amer.

— Memoirs of General Thomas Francis Meagher. 534p. 35.00 (*1-56013-006-7*) Olde Soldier Bks.

Cavanaugh, Michael & McCarthy, Susan. God's Call to the Single Adult: Study Guide. (Illus.). 84p. (Orig.). 1988. student ed. 4.95 (*0-9621231-0-2*) Elim Fellowship.

Cavanaugh, Michael A. The Otey, Ringgold & Davidson Virginia Artillery. (Virginia Regimental Histories Ser.). (Illus.). 118p. 1993. 19.95 (*1-56190-045-1*) H E Howard.

— Sixth Virginia Infantry. (Virginia Regimental Histories Ser.). (Illus.). 143p. 1988. 19.95 (*0-930919-57-2*) H E Howard.

Cavanaugh, Nadine. Whirlwind Love by the River. 184p. 1998. pap. 8.95 (*1-890622-27-3*) Leathers Pub.

Cavanaugh-O'Keefe, John. Evangelium Vitae - the Gospel of Life: A Study Guide for Pro-Life Americans. (Evangelium Vitae Ser.). 231p. (Orig.). 1996. pap. 3.00 (*1-890712-02-7*, EV2) Amer Life League.

Cavanaugh, Peggy & Spontak, Margaret. Protecting Paradise: Three Hundred Ways to Protect Florida's Environment. 160p. 1992. pap. 11.95 (*0-9632566-5-3*) Phoenix Fla.

Cavanaugh, Robert W., ed. see Tomkins, Thomas.

Cavanaugh, S. W. & Barnes, S. Consumer Credit Law in Australia. 1988. 55.00 (*0-409-49449-6*, AT, MICHIE) LEXIS Pub.

Cavanaugh, S. W. & Phegan, C. S. Product Liability in Australia. 1983. 82.00 (*0-409-49101-2*, AT, MICHIE) LEXIS Pub.

Cavanaugh, Sean. Digital Type Design Guide: The Page Designer's Guide to Working with Type. LC 95-77735. 288p. 1995. 45.00 (*1-56830-190-1*) Hayden.

Cavanaugh, Susan. The Good Sense of a Bird. Warren, Shirley, ed. 28p. 1994. pap. 5.00 (*1-877801-24-0*) Still Waters.

Cavanaugh, Terrence & Cavanaugh, Catherine. Learning Science with Science Fiction Films. 238p. 1996. spiral bd. 29.95 (*0-7872-2463-4*, 41246301) Kendall-Hunt.

***Cavanaugh, William J. & Wilkes, Joseph A., eds.** Architectural Acoustics: Principles & Practice. LC 98-6418. 352p. 1998. 85.00 (*0-471-30682-7*) Wiley.

Cavanaugh, William T. Torture & Eucharist: Theology, Politics, & the Body of Christ. LC 98-7113. (Challenges in Contemporary Theology Ser.). 288p. 1998. 64.95 (*0-631-21119-5*); pap. 26.95 (*0-631-21199-3*) Blackwell Pubs.

Cavanaush, Michael A. & Marvel, William. The Petersburg Campaign the Battle of the Crater, "the Horrid Pit," June 25-August 6, 1864. (Virginia Civil War Battles & Leaders Ser.). (Illus.). 1989. 19.95 (*0-930919-77-7*) H E Howard.

Cavander, Jeff, jt. auth. see Stanley, Dave.

Cavander, Kenneth. The Children's Crusade - Musical. 47p. 1998. pap. 5.95 (*0-87129-611-X*, CO8) Dramatic Pub.

Cavanee, W. K., jt. ed. see Kleihues, P.

Cavagh, Jim. Standard Catalog of Cessna Single Engine Aircraft. 2nd rev. ed. LC 95-77239. (Illus.). 840p. 1959. pap. text 49.95 (*1-879825-18-X*) Jones Publish.

Cavanilles, A. J. Icones & Descriptiones Plantarum Quae Aut Sponte in Hispania Crescunt Aut in Hortis Hospitantur 1791-1801, 6 pts. in 1 vol. 1965. 650.00 (*3-7682-0292-5*) Lubrecht & Cramer.

Cavanna, Agustin M. Desden Con el Desden. 2nd ed. 268p. 1978. pap. 14.95 (*0-7859-5183-0*) Fr & Eur.

— El Lindo Don Diego. 5th ed. 152p. 1987. pap. 9.95 (*0-7859-5210-1*) Fr & Eur.

Cavanna, Betty. The Black Spaniel Mystery. (J). 1995. reprint ed. lib. bdg. 21.95 (*1-56849-591-9*) Buccaneer Bks.

— The Boy Next Door. 1924. pap. write for info. (*0-688-16657-1*, Wm Morrow) Morrow Avon.

— Going on Sixteen. 188p. (J). (gr. 6-9). 1992. pap. 2.50 (*0-8167-1266-2*) Troll Communs.

***Cavanna, Betty.** Going on Sixteen. LC 85-4877. 192p. (YA). (gr. 7-12). 1998. reprint ed. mass mkt. 5.95 (*0-688-16324-6*, Wm Morrow) Morrow Avon.

Cavanna, Betty. Paintbox Summer. 212p. (J). 1981. reprint ed. lib. bdg. 27.95 (*0-89966-357-5*); reprint ed. lib. bdg. 16.95 (*0-89967-031-8*, Harmony Rain) Buccaneer Bks.

Cavanna, Francois. Four, Rue Choron. (FRE.). 203p. 1978. pap. 10.95 (*0-7859-1867-1*, 2070370038) Fr & Eur.

— Le Saveiz-Vous? (FRE.). 316p. 1990. pap. 16.95 (*0-7859-2138-9*, 2070382354) Fr & Eur.

Cavanna, Henry, ed. Challanges to the Welfare State: Internal & External Dynamics for Change. LC 97-17945. 224p. 1998. 80.00 (*1-85898-636-2*) E Elgar.

***Cavanna, Henry, ed.** The New Citizenship of the Family: Comparative Perspectives. 232p. 2000. text 69.95 (*0-7546-1222-8*, Pub. by Ashgate Pub) Ashgate Pub Co.

Cavanna, Roberto, ed. PSI Favorable States of Consciousness: Proceedings of an International Conference on Methodology in Psi Research, France, Sept. 2-6, 1968. LC 75-97821. 1970. 16.00 (*0-912328-17-7*) Parapsych Foun.

Cavanna, Roberto & Servadio, Emilio. ESP Experiments with LSD Twenty-Five & Psilocybin. LC 64-24271. (Parapsychological Monographs: No. 5). 1964. pap. 5.00 (*0-912328-08-8*) Parapsych Foun.

Cavanna, Roberto, ed. see International Conference on Hypnosis, Drugs, Dream.

Cavanos. An Introduction to Modern Business Statistics. (Business Statistics Ser.). 1993. pap., student ed. 20.95 (*0-534-16843-4*) Wadsworth Pub.

Cavanuagh, John C., jt. auth. see Kail, Robert V.

Cavarero, Adriana. The Figurative Body. (Illus.). (C). pap. text. write for info. (*0-472-06674-9*) U of Mich Pr.

Cavarero, Adriana. In Spite of Plato: A Feminist Rewriting of Ancient Philosophy. LC 97-155114. 135p. (C). 1995. pap. 18.99 (*0-415-91447-7*) Routledge.

— In Spite of Plato: A Feminist Rewriting of Ancient Philosophy. LC 97-155114. 135p. (C). (gr. 13 up). 1995. 60.00 (*0-415-91446-9*) Routledge.

***Cavarero, Adriana.** Relating Narratives: Storytelling & Selfhood. LC 99-46437. (Warwick Studies in European Philosophy Ser.). 176p. 2000. pap. 22.99 (*0-415-20058-X*) Routledge.

— Relating Narratives: Storytelling & Selfhood. Kottman, Paul, tr. LC 99-46437. (Warwick Studies in European Philosophy Ser.). 192p. (C). 2000. text 75.00 (*0-415-20057-1*) Routledge.

Cavaretta, A., et al. Stationary Subdivision. LC 91-22743. (Memoirs Ser.). 186p. 1991. pap. 25.00 (*0-8218-2507-0*, MEMO/93/453) Am Math.

Cavaretta, Vito. Imputato Alzalev! Ovvoro Ritorne le Caccia Alle Stregha: Italian Essays. (ITA.). 55p. 1984. pap. 5.00 (*0-89304-574-8*) Cross-Cultrl NY.

Cavarnos, Constantine. Anchored in God: Life, Art, & Thought on the Holy Mountain of Athos. 3rd ed. LC 75-35432. (Illus.). 230p. 1991. reprint ed. pap. 9.50 (*0-914744-31-3*) Inst Byzantine.

— Biological Evolutionism: A Lecture Dealing with Lamarckian & Darwinian Evolutionism That Was Delivered at Clark University in Worcester Massachusetts Published in Considerably Augmented Form & Amply Documented. LC 97-71023. (Illus.). 93p. 1997. 15.00 (*1-884729-24-X*); pap. 6.50 (*1-884729-25-8*) Inst Byzantine.

— Byzantine Chant: A Sequel to the Monograph Byzantine Sacred Music, Containing a Concise Discussion of the Origin of Byzantine Chant, Its Modes, Tempo, Notation, Prologoi, Prasomoi, Style, & Other Features. LC 98-71925. (Illus.). 102p. 1998. 15.00 (*1-884729-38-X*); pap. 6.95 (*1-884729-39-8*) Inst Byzantine.

— Byzantine Churches of Thessaloniki: An Illustrated Account of the Architecture & Iconographic Decoration of Seven Byzantine Churches of Thessaloniki, Together with Important Historical Data. LC 95-78036. (Illus.). 88p. 1995. pap. 6.50 (*1-884729-08-8*) Inst Byzantine.

— Byzantine Sacred Music: The Traditional Music of the Orthodox Church: It's Nature, Purpose, & Execution. 31p. 1996. pap. 2.00 (*0-914744-23-2*) Inst Byzantine.

— Byzantine Thought & Art: A Collection of Essays. LC 68-21884. (Illus.). 139p. 1988. pap. 6.95 (*0-914744-22-4*) Inst Byzantine.

— The Classical Theory of Relations: A Study in the Metaphysics of Plato, Aristotle, & Thomism. LC 75-2659. 116p. 1975. pap. 8.00 (*0-914744-28-3*) Inst Byzantine.

— The Concept of Christian Love: A Lecture Delivered at Columbia University, Together with a Swedish Version of It. LC 95-81782. 64p. 1996. pap. 5.95 (*1-884729-09-6*) Inst Byzantine.

— Cultural & Educational Continuity of Greece: From Antiquity to the Present, a Discussion of a Lecture Which Was Delivered at the Institute for Byzantine & Modern Greek Studies by the Distinguished Argentine

Philosopher, Philologist, & Hellenist Dr. Saul A. Tovar, Discussed by Constantine Cavarnos. LC 94-93908. (Illus.). 75p. 1995. pap. 5.95 (*1-884729-03-7*) Inst Byzantine.

— A Dialogue Between Bergson, Aristotle, & Philologos: A Comparative & Critical Study of Some Aspects of Henri Bergson's Theory of Knowledge & of Reality with a Preface by John Wild. 3rd enl. ed. LC 88-80318. 80p. 1988. pap. 6.50 (*0-914744-79-8*) Inst Byzantine.

— A Dialogue on G. E. Moore's Ethical Philosophy: Together with an Account of Three Talks with Moore on Diverse Philosophical Questions. LC 79-65479. 68p. 1979. 12.00 (*0-914744-43-7*); pap. 5.00 (*0-914744-44-5*) Inst Byzantine.

— Dostoivsky's Philosophy of Man: A General Discussion of Dostoievsky's View of Man's Nature & Destiny, Together with Pertinent Discussion-Reviews of Six of His Works. LC 98-75223. (Illus.). 88p. 1998. 15.00 (*1-884729-44-4*); pap. 6.95 (*1-884729-45-2*) Inst Byzantine.

— Ecumenism Examined: A Concise Analytical Discussion of the Contemporary Ecumenical Movement, an Introduction to It By Reference to Earlier Discussion of It By the Author, an Attempt to Define It & Distinguish It's Varieties, & an Extensive Treatment of "Orthodox Exumenism" & Its Fruits. LC 96-79018. (Illus.). 64p. 1996. pap. 6.50 (*1-884729-19-3*) Inst Byzantine.

— Ecumenism Examined: A Concise Analytical Discussion of the Contemporary Ecumenical Movement, an Introduction to It By Reference to Earlier Discussion of It By the Author, an Attempt to Define It & Distinguish Its Varieties & an Extensive Treatment of "Orthodox Exumenism" & Its Fruits. LC 96-79018. (Illus.). 64p. 1996. 12.50 (*1-884729-18-5*) Inst Byzantine.

— Fine Arts As Therapy: Plato's Teaching Organized & Discussed. LC 98-70118. (Illus.). 91p. 1998. 15.00 (*1-884729-32-0*); pap. 7.00 (*1-884729-33-9*) Inst Byzantine.

— Guide to Byzantine Iconography Vol. 1: Detailed Explanation of the Distinctive Characteristics of Byzantine Iconography, of the Traditional Pattern of Decorating Eastern Orthodox Churches with Panel Icons, Wall Paintings, & Mosaics, & of the Chief Doctrinal, Liturgical, & Festal Icons; Together with a Concise Systematic Exposition of St. John Damascene's Defense of Holy Icons. LC 93-77765. (Illus.). 264p. 1993. pap. 20.00 (*0-914744-90-9*) Inst Byzantine.

— The Hellenic-Christian Philosophical Tradition. LC 89-85717. 137p. 1989. pap. 7.95 (*0-914744-84-4*) Inst Byzantine.

— The Hellenic-Christian Philosophical Tradition: Four Lectures Delivered at Boston University, an Original Discussion of the Legacy of Socrates, Plato & Aristotle in the Hellenic East from Ancient to Modern Times of Stoic Elements in the Greek Church Fathers & of the Concept of Philosophy in Ancient Greece, Byzantium, & Modern Greece. LC 89-85717. 137p. 1989. 15.00 (*0-914744-83-6*) Inst Byzantine.

— The Holy Mountain: Two Lectures on Mount Athos, of Which the First Deals with Its Scholars, Missionaries & Saints & the Second with Its Music, Musicians, & Hymnographers, Together with an Account of a Recent Visit to Athos. 2nd ed. LC 73-84103. (Illus.). 172p. 1988. pap. 7.95 (*0-914744-38-0*) Inst Byzantine.

— Immortality of the Soul: The Testimony of the Old & New Testaments, Orthodox Iconography & Hymnography, & the Works of Eastern Fathers & Other Writers of the Orthodox Church. LC 93-77138. (Illus.). 96p. 1993. pap. 5.95 (*0-914744-96-8*) Inst Byzantine.

— Meetings with Kontoglou: Enlightening, Lively Discussions on Byzantine Iconography & Music, Diverse Writers, Philosophers & Theologians, & Contemporary Events & Trends, Between the Author & the Great Icon Painter, Writer, & Philosopher Photios Kontoglou. LC 92-74877. (Illus.). 216p. 1993. pap. 12.00 (*0-914744-95-X*) Inst Byzantine.

— Modern Greek Philosophers on the Human Soul: Selections from the Writings of Seven Representative Thinkers of Modern Greece - Benjamin of Lesvos, Vrailas - Armenis, Skaltsounis, St. Nectarios, Louvaris, Kontoglou, & Theodorakopoulos on the Nature & Immortality of the Soul. 2nd enl. rev. ed. LC 86-83011. (Illus.). 140p. 1987. pap. 6.95 (*0-914744-77-1*) Inst Byzantine.

— Modern Greek Thought: Three Essays Dealing with Philosophy, Critique of Science, & Views of Man's Nature & Destiny. LC 71-93095. 115p. 1986. pap. 5.95 (*0-914744-11-9*) Inst Byzantine.

— Modern Orthodox Saints: St. Nikephoros of Chios, Vol. 4. 2nd rev. ed. LC 86-82207. (Illus.). 124p. 1986. pap. 6.95 (*0-914744-74-7*) Inst Byzantine.

— Modern Orthodox Saints Vol. 1: St. Cosmas Aitolos. enl. rev. ed. LC 85-80440. (Illus.). 118p. 1995. pap. 6.95 (*0-914744-65-8*) Inst Byzantine.

Cavarnos, Constantine. Modern Orthodox Saints Vol. 2: St. Macarios of Corinth. 3rd ed. LC 72-85116. (Illus.). 120p. 1993. pap. 6.95 (*0-914744-97-6*) Inst Byzantine.

Cavarnos, Constantine. Modern Orthodox Saints Vol. 3: St. Nicodemos the Hagiorite Great Theologian & Teacher of the Orthodox Church, Reviver of Hesychasm, Moralist, Canonist, Hagiologist & Writer of Liturgical Poetry, an Account of His Life, Character & Message, Together with a Comprehensive List of His Writings & Selections from Them. 2nd ed. LC 78-71478. (Illus.). 167p. 1994. pap. 7.50 (*0-914744-41-0*) Inst Byzantine.

— Modern Orthodox Saints Vol. 6: St. Arsenios of Paros. 2nd rev. ed. LC 88-80496. (Illus.). 124p. 1988. pap. 6.95 (*0-914744-80-1*) Inst Byzantine.

— Modern Orthodox Saints Vol. 7: St. Nectarios of Aegina. rev. ed. LC 87-83600. (Illus.). 222p. 1995. pap. 7.95 (*0-914744-78-X*) Inst Byzantine.

— Modern Orthodox Saints Vol. 8: St. Savvas the New. LC 85-60117. (Illus.). 144p. 1996. pap. 6.95 (*0-914744-62-3*) Inst Byzantine.

— Modern Orthodox Saints Vol. 9: St. Methodia of Kimolos. LC 86-82479. (Illus.). 123p. 1987. 15.00 (*0-914744-75-5*) Inst Byzantine.

— Modern Orthodox Saints Vol. 10: Sts. Raphael, Nicholas & Irene of Lesvos. LC 90-80711. (Illus.). 200p. 1994. 17.50 (*0-914744-87-9*); pap. 7.95 (*0-914744-88-7*) Inst Byzantine.

— Modern Orthodox Saints Vol. 11: Blessed Elder Philotheos Zervakos. LC 93-79586. (Illus.). 240p. 1993. 17.50 (*0-914744-93-3*); pap. 9.50 (*0-914744-94-1*) Inst Byzantine.

— Modern Orthodox Saints Vol. 12: Blessed Hermit Philaretos of the Holy Mountain. LC 96-80495. (Illus.). 109p. 1997. 15.95 (*1-884729-20-7*); pap. 7.50 (*1-884729-21-5*) Inst Byzantine.

***Cavarnos, Constantine.** Modern Orthodox Saints Vol. 13: Blessed Elder Gabriel Dionysiatis (1886-1993) 238p. 1999. pap. 9.95 (*1-884729-48-7*) Inst Byzantine.

— Modern Orthodox Saints Vol. 13: Blessed Elder Gabriel Dionysiatis (1886-1993) LC 99-783339. (Illus.). 238p. 1999. 16.50 (*1-884729-47-9*) Inst Byzantine.

Cavarnos, Constantine. New Library Vol. 1: Reviews & Discussions of Over Fifty Books of Modern Greek, Russian & Other Writers - Ancient, Byzantine & Modern Greek - Eastern Orthodox Christianity, Byzantine Art & Hellenism. LC 89-80265. 176p. 1989. 15.00 (*0-914744-81-X*); pap. 7.95 (*0-914744-82-8*) Inst Byzantine.

— New Library Vol. 2: Summaries & Discussions of Thirty Books of or about Byzantine & Modern Writers, Greeks & Russians, in the Fields of Philosophy, Literature & Christian Religion. LC 89-80265. (Illus.). 211p. 1992. pap. 9.50 (*1-884729-12-6*) Inst Byzantine.

— Orthodox Christian Terminology: A Discussion of the Subject of Developing a Satisfactory, Acceptable, Standardised English Language Terminology in Eastern Orthodox Theology, Hagiology, Church Services, & the Sacred Arts, Together with Greek-English & English Greek Glossaries. LC 94-77265. 80p. 1997. pap. 5.95 (*0-914744-98-4*) Inst Byzantine.

— Orthodox Iconography: Four Essays Dealing with the History of Orthodox Iconography, the Iconographic Decoration of Churches, the Functions of Icons, & the Theology & Aesthetics of Byzantine Iconography, in Addition Three Appendices Containing Early Christian Texts on Icons, Etc. 3rd ed. LC 77-74606. (Illus.). 100p. 1992. pap. 5.95 (*0-914744-37-2*) Inst Byzantine.

— Plato's Theory of Fine Art: "He Who Knows Not the Truth, but Pursues Opinions, Will, It Seems, Attain an Art Which Is Ridiculous, & Not an Art at All" - Plato's Phaedrus, 262C. 107p. 1998. 15.00 (*1-884729-34-7*) Inst Byzantine.

— Plato's Theory of Fine Art: "He Who Knows Not the Truth, but Pursues Opinions, Will, It Seems, Attain an Art Which Is Ridiculous, & Not an Art at All" - Plato's Phaedrus, 262C. 2nd ed. LC 98-70395. 107p. 1998. pap. 7.00 (*1-884729-35-5*) Inst Byzantine.

— Plato's View of Man: Two Bowen Prize Essays Dealing with the Problem of the Destiny of Man & the Individual Life, Together with Selected Passages from Plato's Dialogues on Man & the Human Soul. LC 74-27242. 95p. 1982. pap. 5.00 (*0-914744-26-7*) Inst Byzantine.

— Pythagoras on the Fine Arts As Therapy: A Lecture Delivered in 1993 at Wellesley College. LC 94-75725. (Illus.). 80p. 1994. pap. 6.00 (*1-884729-00-2*) Inst Byzantine.

— St. Photios the Great: Philosopher & Theologian. LC 98-72482. (Illus.). 84p. 1998. 15.00 (*1-884729-42-8*); pap. 6.95 (*1-884729-43-6*) Inst Byzantine.

— The Seven Sages of Ancient Greece: The Lives & Teachings of the Earliest Greek Philosophers: Thales, Pittacos, Bias, Solon, Cleobulos, Myson, & Chilon. LC 96-77300. (Illus.). 64p. 1996. 12.00 (*1-884729-16-9*); pap. 6.50 (*1-884729-17-7*) Inst Byzantine.

— Spiritual Beauty: A Discussion, in English & Greek, of the Concept of Spiritual Beauty by Reference to Philosophic, Religious, & Literary Writings That Date from Antiquity to the Present. LC 96-75550. (Illus.). 62p. 2000. pap. 5.95 (*1-884729-13-4*) Inst Byzantine.

— Victories of Orthodoxy: Homilies in Which Are Discussed in a Forthright & Analytical Manner Iconoclasm, Orthodox Mysticism, the False Union of Florence, the Calendar Change, Traditional Iconography, Sacred Music, & Eaimenism, & the Stand of the Orthodox Christian Church Regarding These. LC 97-74684. (Illus.). 109p. 1997. 15.00 (*1-884729-30-4*); pap. 7.00 (*1-884729-31-2*) Inst Byzantine.

Cavarnos, Constantine, ed. see Cavarnos, John P.

Cavarnos, Constantine, ed. see Whiteman, Cedric H.

Cavarnos, Constantine, tr. see Damascene, John & Seventh Oecumenical Synod Staff.

Cavarnos, Constantine, tr. & compiled by see Kontoglou, Photios.

***Cavarnos, Constatine.** The Hellenic Heritage: Two Lecures Dealing with Greek Culture: Ancient, Byzantine & Modern. LC 99-75590. (Illus.). 128p. 2000. 15.00 (*1-884729-50-9*) Inst Byzantine.

Cavarnos, Constatine & Zeldin, Mary B. Modern Orthodox Saints Vol. 5: St. Seraphim of Sarov, Widely Beloved Mystic, Healer, Comforter, & Spiritual Guide, an Account of His Life, Character & Message, Together with a Very Edifying Conversation with His Disciple Motovilor on the Acquisition of the Grace of the Holy Spirit, & the Saint's Spiritual Counsels. LC 80-80124. (Illus.). 167p. 1993. pap. 7.50 (*0-914744-48-8*) Inst Byzantine.

Cavarnos, John P. The Dramatic Poetry of Demetrios N. Vernardakis: An Analytical, Comprehensive, & Critical Study of Seven Tragedies of the Foremost Greep Playwright of the Nineteenth Century. (GRE.). 244p. 1962. pap. 8.50 (*0-914744-67-4*) Inst Byzantine.

— New Library: Seventeen Discussion-Reviews of Books, Vol. 3. Cavarnos, Constantine, ed. LC 95-75903. (Illus.). 120p. 1995. 15.00 (*1-884729-05-3*); pap. 7.50 (*1-884729-06-1*) Inst Byzantine.

— St. Gregory of Nyssa on the Origin & Destiny of the Soul. rev. ed. 12p. 1996. pap. 2.00 (*0-914744-60-7*) Inst Byzantine.

Cavarozzi, Marcelo. Argentina. 1999. pap. 30.00 (*0-8133-0343-5*) Westview.

Cavasina, Richard G. Codependency Communicat on Skills Training. rev. ed. 1994. 14.95 (*1-55691-162-9*) Learning Pubns.

Cavata, C., jt. auth. see Hughes, V. W.

Cavaye, Douglas M. & White, Rodney A. Intravascular Ultrasound Imaging. LC 92-49652. 144p. 1992. text 62.00 (*0-88167-971-2*) Lppncott W & W.

— Intravascular Ultrasound Imaging. LC 92-49652. (Illus.). 137p. reprint ed. pap. 42.50 (*0-608-09767-5*, 206994000007) Bks Demand.

Cavaye, Ronald. Kabuki: A Pocket Guide. (Illus.). 184p. 1993. pap. 12.95 (*0-8048-1730-8*) Tuttle Pubng.

Cavazos, Amado F. Zachry: The Man & His Companies. LC 92-83993. (Illus.). 525p. 1993. 30.00 (*0-9635379-0-3*) Metro Pr TX.

***Cavazos, Bobby.** The Cowboy from the Wild Horse Desert: A Story of the King Ranch. LC 99-31453. 270p. 1999. 14.95 (*0-89896-453-9*) R J Cavazos.

Cavazos, Edward A. & Morin, Gavino. Cyberspace & the Law: Your Rights & Duties in the On-Line World. LC 94-12356. 215p. 1994. pap. text 21.50 (*0-262-53123-2*) MIT Pr.

Cavazos-Gaither, A. E., jt. auth. see Gaither, C. C.

Cavazos-Gaither, Alma E., jt. auth. see Gaither, Carl C.

Cavazos, Israel. Breve Historia de Nuevo Leon (Concise History of Nuevo Leon) (Breves Historias de los Estados de Mexico Ser.). (SPA.). 1995. pap. 13.99 (*968-16-4541-3*, Pub. by Fondo) Continental Bk.

Cavazos, Josie. Corporate Intercession: Empowering the Local Church. 62p. 1998. pap. 4.95 (*0-9635014-2-9*) Jubilee Ridge.

***Cavazos, Lauro, frwd.** One on One: A Guide for Establishing Mentor Programs. (Illus.). 56p. (C). 2000. reprint ed. pap. text 20.00 (*0-7881-8211-0*) DIANE Pub.

Cavazza, Albertina & Barrile, Anna R., eds. Livius Andronicus - Lexicon Livianum et Naevianum. (Alpha-Omega, Reihe A Ser.: Bd. XIII). 201p. 1981. 55.00 (*3-487-07077-4*) G Olms Pubs.

Cavazzoni, Marco Antonio. Recerchari, Motetti, Canzoni, Libro Primo. fac. ed. (Monuments of Music & Music Literature in Facsimile, I Ser.: Vol. 12). 1974. lib. bdg. 35.00 (*0-8450-2012-9*) Broude.

Cave & Riddell. Emperor's Grucklehound. (Illus.). (J). 1996. pap. text 8.95 (*0-340-65599-2*, Pub. by Hodder & Stought Ltd) Trafalgar.

Cave, Alfred A. Jacksonian Democracy & the Historians. LC 64-63899. (University of Florida Monographs: Social Sciences: No. 22). 95p. reprint ed. pap. 30.00 (*0-7837-4983-X*, 204465000004) Bks Demand.

— The Pequot War. LC 95-47282. (Native Americans of the Northeast Ser.). 232p. 1996. pap. 15.95 (*1-55849-030-2*); text 45.00 (*1-55849-029-9*) U of Mass Pr.

Cave, Anne G. Balloons for Trevor: Understanding Death. LC 98-162154. (Comforting Little Hearts Ser.). (ps-1). 1998. 6.99 (*0-570-05040-5*, 56-1864) Concordia.

***Cave, Bryan, ed.** Business Law of the Middle East: The United Arab Emirates. 1300p. 1999. ring bd. 900.00 (*90-411-1259-6*) Kluwer Law Intl.

Cave, C. H., tr. see Jeremias, Joachim.

Cave, Dorothy. Beyond Courage: One Regiment Against Japan, 1941-1945. rev. ed. LC 95-60801. (Illus.). 480p. 1996. pap. 18.95 (*1-881325-14-8*) Yucca Tree Pr.

— Four Trails to Valor. LC 97-61181. (Illus.). 448p. 1998. 22.95 (*1-881325-22-9*) Yucca Tree Pr.

— Mountains of the Blue Stone: A Novel. LC 98-79 5. Orig. Title: Go Find the Mountain. 304p. 1998. 26.95 (*0-86534-272-5*) Sunstone Pr.

Cave, Edward. The Boy Scout's Hike Book. 243p. (YA). (gr. 10). 1992. pap. 12.95 (*0-9632054-0-4*) Stevens Pub.

Cave, Eric M. Preferring Justice: Rationality, Self-Transformation & the Sense of Justice. LC 98-119238. 200p. (C). 1997. text 69.00 (*0-8133-2808-X*, Pub. by Westview) HarpC.

Cave, Ernie, jt. auth. see Wilkinson, Cyril.

Cave, F. H., tr. see Jeremias, Joachim.

Cave, George A. An Intelligent Approach to Buying Real Estate: Using Your Ingenuity in Place of Money. Rasmussen, James, ed. LC 97-91730. (Illus.). 200p. 1999. write for info. (*1-57502-470-5*, P01405) Morris Pubng.

Cave, H. W. The Ruined Cities of Ceylon. (Illus.). 136p. 1986. reprint ed. 44.00 (*0-8364-1745-3*, Pub. by Chanakya) S Asia.

Cave, Henry W. Golden Tips: A Description of Ceylon & Its Great Tea Industry. (C). 1994. text 47.00 (*81-206-0940-9*, Pub. by Asian Educ Servs) S Asia.

***Cave, Hugh B.** The Dawning. 368p. 2000. pap. 5.50 (*0-8439-4739-X*, Leisure Bks) Dorchester Pub Co.

Cave, Hugh B. Death Stalks the Night. Wagner, Karl E., ed. & intro. by. (Illus.). 500p. 1995. 27.00 (*1-878252-15-1*) Fedogan & Bremer.

— Death Stalks the Night. limited ed. Wagner, Karl E., ed. & intro. by. (Illus.). 500p. 1995. 90.00 (*1-878252-17-8*) Fedogan & Bremer.

— The Door Below. 336p. 1997. 27.00 (*1-878252-30-5*) Fedogan & Bremer.

— The Door Below. limited ed. 336p. 1997. 95.00 (*1-878252-31-3*) Fedogan & Bremer.

— Long Were the Nights: The Saga of a PT Squadron in the Solomons. 1981. reprint ed. 17.95 (*0-89201-091-6*) Zenger Pub.

— Lucifer's Eye. 1991. pap. 3.95 (*0-8125-1079-8*, Pub. by Tor Bks) St Martin.

***Cave, Hugh B.** Officer Coffey Stories. unabridged ed. 64p. 2000. 40.00 (*1-892284-72-3*); pap. 12.00 (*1-892284-71-5*) Subtrrnean Pr.

Cave, Hugh B., jt. auth. see Miller, Norman M.

Cave, Hugh B., jt. auth. see Morris, Colton G.

Cave, Jane, jt. ed. see Frankel, Mark S.

Cave, Jane, tr. see Lopinski, Maciej, et al.

***Cave, Janet.** Encyclopedia of Gardening & Landscaping. (gr. 11). 1999. pap. 14.95 (*0-7835-5330-7*, Pub. by Mouse Works) Time Warner.

Cave, Janet, ed. Death & Celebrity. (True Crime Ser.). (Illus.). 176p. 1993. lib. bdg. 17.45 (*0-7835-0026-2*) Time-Life.

Cave, Janet, ed. see Time-Life Books Editors.

Cave, John. Technology in School: A Handbook of Practical Approaches & Ideas. (Education Bks.). (Illus.). 160p. (C). 1986. pap. text 12.95 (*0-7102-0732-8*, Routledge Thoemms) Routledge.

Cave, John D. Mircea Eliade's Vision for a New Humanism. 232p. 1993. text 55.00 (*0-19-507434-3*) OUP.

Cave, K. Horatio Happened. pap. text 11.95 (*0-340-71515-4*, Pub. by Hodder & Stought Ltd) Trafalgar.

— Horatio Happened. (J). text 22.95 (*0-340-72268-1*, Pub. by Hodder & Stought Ltd) Trafalgar.

— Similon. 1996. mass mkt. 8.95 (*0-340-65354-X*, Pub. by Hodder & Stought Ltd) Trafalgar.

***Cave, Kathryn.** The Boy Who Became an Eagle. LC 00-35897. (Illus.). 32p. (J). (ps-3). 2000. 15.95 (*0-7894-2666-8*) DK Pub Inc.

Cave, Kathryn. Something Else. LC 97-42258. (Illus.). (J). (gr. 1-5). 1998. pap. 5.95 (*1-57255-563-7*) Mondo Pubng.

— W Is for World: Around the World ABC. LC 97-50515. (J). 1999. write for info. (*0-382-42113-2*); write for info. (*0-382-42114-0*) Silver Press.

***Cave, Kathryn & Hendra, Sue.** Henry's Song. LC 99-37942. 26p. (J). 2000. 16.00 (*0-8028-5198-3*) Eerdmans.

Cave, Kathryn, ed. see Farington, Joseph.

Cave, Kent, ed. see Coggins, Allen R.

Cave, M. Donald, jt. auth. see Burns, E. Robert.

Cave, Martin. Computers & Economic Planning, the Soviet Experience. LC 79-7659. (Soviet & East European Studies). 236p. reprint ed. pap. 67.30 (*0-608-17577-3*, 2030585) Bks Demand.

Cave, Martin, et al, eds. Output & Performance Measurement in Government: The State of the Art. 160p. 1990. 49.95 (*1-85302-521-6*) Taylor & Francis.

Cave, Martin, et al. Regulating Utilities: Understanding the Issues. (Readings Ser.: Vol. 48). 279p. 1998. pap. 39.50 (*0-255-36418-0*) Inst Economic Affairs.

— The Use of Performance Indicators in Higher Education: A Critical Analysis of Developing Practice. LC 97-104701. (Higher Education Policy Ser.: No. 34). 160p. 1996. pap. 34.95 (*1-85302-345-0*, Pub. by Jessica Kingsley) Taylor & Francis.

Cave, Martin, jt. auth. see Baldwin, Robert.

Cave, Martin, jt. ed. see Estrin, Saul.

Cave, Maxine. The BHSAI PTT Companion. 1997. pap. 50.00 (*0-85131-685-9*, Pub. by J A Allen) Trafalgar.

— BHS11 Course Companion. 200p. 1998. pap. 75.00 (*0-85131-712-X*, Pub. by J A Allen) Trafalgar.

— Horse Talks. 206p. 1994. 17.95 (*0-85131-596-8*, Pub. by J A Allen) Trafalgar.

***Cave, Michael.** A Cross by the Road. 1999. pap. write for info. (*1-58235-173-2*) Watermrk Pr.

— Fabulous Places of Myth. (Illus.). 48p. 2000. 14.95 (*0-85091-839-1*, Pub. by Lothian Pub) Star Brght Bks.

Cave, Nick. King Ink. 161p. 1990. pap. 12.00 (*1-880985-08-X*) Two Thirteen Sixty-one.

— King Ink II. 160p. 1997. pap. 12.00 (*1-880985-49-7*) Two Thirteen Sixty-one.

Cave, Nigel. Beaumont Hamel. (Battleground Europe Ser.). (Illus.). 112p. 1994. pap. 13.95 (*0-85052-398-2*, Pub. by Leo Cooper) Trans-Atl Phila.

***Cave, Nigel.** Delville Wood: Somme. (Battleground Europe Ser.). 1998. pap. text 16.95 (*0-85052-584-5*, Pub. by Leo Cooper) Trans-Atl Phila.

— Field-Marshall Sir Douglas Haig: Seventy Years On. 1999. 45.00 (*0-85052-698-1*) Pen & Sword Bks Ltd.

— Hill 60: The Battle of Ypres. 1998. pap. text 16.95 (*0-85052-559-4*, Pub. by Leo Cooper) Trans-Atl Phila.

— Mons - 1914. (Battleground Europe Ser.). 1999. pap. write for info. (*0-85052-677-9*) Pen & Sword Bks Ltd.

Cave, Nigel. Passchendaele: Ypres. (Illus.). 1998. pap. 16.95 (*0-85052-558-6*) Leo Cooper.

Cave, Oenoen. Cut-Work Embroidery & How to Do It. (Illus.). 96p. 1982. pap. 5.95 (*0-486-24267-6*) Dover.

Cave, Peter. Fatal Inheritance. 224p. 1995. pap. 10.95 (*1-85158-628-8*, Pub. by Mainstream Pubng) Trafalgar.

— Forbidden Fruit. 221p. 1995. pap. 11.95 (*1-85158-627-X*, Pub. by Mainstream Pubng) Trafalgar.

— Invasion Earth: The Last Echo. 288p. 1999. pap. 9.95 (*1-57500-032-6*, Pub. by TV Bks) HarpC.

Cave, Philip. Creating Japanese Gardens. (Illus.). 176p. 1996. pap. 21.95 (*0-8048-3100-9*) Tuttle Pubng.

Cave, Richard. Charles Ricketts' Stage Designs. (Theatre in Focus Ser.). 1987. pap. write for info. incl. sl. (*0-85964-195-3*) Chadwyck-Healey.

— Terence Gray & the Cambridge Festival Theatre. (Theatre in Focus Ser.). (Illus.). 90p. 1980. pap. text. write for info. incl. sl. (*0-85964-069-8*) Chadwyck-Healey.

Cave, Richard, et al, eds. Ben Jonson & the Theatre: A Critical & Practical Introduction. LC 98-29160. (Illus.). 240p. (C). 1999. pap. 24.99 (*0-415-17981-5*, D6028) Routledge.
— Ben Jonson & the Theatre: A Critical & Practical Introduction. LC 98-29160. (Illus.). 240p. (C). (gr. 13). 1999. 75.00 (*0-415-17980-7*, D6024) Routledge.
Cave, Richard, jt. auth. see Pine, Richard.
Cave, Richard A. A Study of the Novels of George Moore. (Irish Literary Studies: Vol. # 3). 272p. 1978. 40.00 (*0-901072-58-3*, Pub. by Smyth) Dufour.
Cave, Richard A., ed. The Romantic Theatre: An International Symposium. LC 86-26492. 144p. (C). 1987. 45.00 (*0-389-20697-0*) B&N Imports.
Cave, Richard A., jt. ed. see Genet, Jacqueline.
Cave, Richard A., ed. see Moore, George.
Cave, Richard Allen, ed. see Murray, T. C.
Cave, Roderick. Chinese Paper Offerings. (Images of Asia Ser.). (Illus.). 80p. 1998. 16.95 (*0-19-590356-0*) OUP.
— Rare Book Librarianship. 2nd fac. rev. ed. LC 82-220919. 178p. 1982. reprint ed. pap. 55.20 (*0-7837-8202-0*, 204796000009) Bks Demand.
Cave, Roy C. & Coulson, Herbert H. Source Book for Medieval Economic History. LC 64-25840. 1936. 30.00 (*0-8196-0145-4*) Biblo.
Cave, S. & Harper, D. R. Introduction to Fermentation Practices. 2nd ed. LC 97-49308. 160p. 1998. pap. 34.95 (*0-387-91557-5*) Spr-Verlag.
Cave, Sue. Therapeutic Approaches in Psychology. LC 98-45311. (Modular Psychology Ser.). 1999. pap. write for info. (*0-415-18871-7*) Routledge.
***Cave, Sue.** Therapeutic Approaches in Psychology. LC 98-45311. (Routledge Modular Psychology Ser.). 1999. write for info. (*0-415-18870-9*) Routledge.
Cave, Sydney. Redemption, Hindu & Christian: The Religious Quest of India. LC 73-102230. (Select Bibliographies Reprint Ser.). 1977. 26.95 (*0-8369-5115-8*) Ayer.
Cave, Terence. The Cornucopian Text: Problems of Writing in the French Renaissance. (Illus.). 416p. 1985. pap. text 29.95 (*0-19-815835-1*) OUP.
— Recognitions: A Study in Poetics. 544p. 1990. reprint ed. pap. text 35.00 (*0-19-815163-2*) OUP.
Cave, Terence, jt. ed. see Castor, Graham.
Cave, Terence, ed. & intro. see Eliot, George, pseud.
Cave, V., jt. auth. see Borton, P.
Cave, Vicky, jt. auth. see Borton, Paula.
Cave, William C. & Maymon, Gilbert W. Software Lifecycle Management: The Incremental Method. LC 84-11264. (Atre Ser.). 300p. 1984. 34.95 (*0-02-949210-6*) Free Pr.
Cave, Yvonne. The Succulent Garden: A Practical Gardening Guide. LC 96-34044. (Illus.). 100p. (Orig.). 1997. pap. 19.95 (*0-88192-378-8*) Timber.
***Cave, Yvonne & Paddison, Valda.** Gardener's Encyclopedia of New Zealand Native Plants. (Illus.). 2000. 39.95 (*1-86962-043-7*, Pub. by Godwit Pubg) Timber.
***Cavedo, Keith, et al, eds.** Men's & Boy's Wear Buyers, 2000. 731p. 1999. 220.00 (*0-87228-131-0*, Salesmn Gde) Douglas Pubns.
— Women's & Children's Wear & Fashion Accessories Buyers. 913p. 1999. write for info. (*0-87228-130-2*) Douglas Pubns.
Cavedon, Lawrence, et al. Intelligent Agent Systems Vol. 120: Theoretical & Practical Issues: Based on a Workshop Held at Pricai '96, Cairns, Australia, August 26-30, 1996. LC 97-6051. (Lecture Notes in Artificial Intelligence Ser.). 188p. 1997. pap. 37.00 (*3-540-62686-7*) Spr-Verlag.
Caveglia, Rico. Real Food Real Fast: Delicious & Nutritious Meals in 12 Minutes or Less. Cullins, Judy, ed. (Illus.). 168p. (Orig.). 1997. pap., per. 12.95 (*1-890904-02-3*) Ageless Living.
Cavel, Michael P. Nebraska Legal Forms: Workers' Compensation. 160p. 1994. ring bd. 69.95 incl. disk (*0-614-05916-X*, MICHIE) LEXIS Pub.
— Workers' Compensation Forms, 1981-1988. (Nebraska Legal Forms Ser.). 160p. ring bd. 69.95 (*0-86678-023-8*, 82015-10, MICHIE); ring bd. 85.00 incl. disk (*0-685-70859-4*, MICHIE) LEXIS Pub.
Cavel, Michael P., jt. auth. see Liebo, Stephen L.
Cavelaris, Athina. Rachel, Crying for Her Children: Secrets of the Third Reich. (Illus.). 257p. 1994. pap. write for info. (*0-9642706-3-3*) A Cavelaris.
***Cavele, Keith.** Storm Child. (Illus.). (J). (gr. 4-7). 1999. pap. 14.95 (*1-894155-01-7*) C&B Co.
Cavell, Lily. About Angels. (Illus.). 1986. spiral bd. 7.95 (*1-885038-00-3*) Uriel Press.
— A Blessing Is. (Illus.). 24p. (J). 1993. spiral bd. 8.95 (*1-885038-03-8*); audio 4.00 (*1-885038-06-2*) Uriel Press.
— Life's Greatest Miracle. (Illus.). 20p. 1991. spiral bd. 7.95 (*1-885038-02-X*) Uriel Press.
— Our Father. (Illus.). 24p. 1990. spiral bd. 7.95 (*1-885038-01-1*) Uriel Press.
Cavell, Marcia. The Psychoanalytic Mind. 288p. 1996. pap. text 17.00 (*0-674-72096-2*) HUP.
— The Psychoanalytic Mind: From Freud to Philosophy. LC 93-7325. 288p. 1993. 37.95 (*0-674-72095-4*) HUP.
Cavell, Stanley. The Claim of Reason: Wittgenstein, Skepticism, Morality & Tragedy. 2nd ed. LC 98-31557. 511p. 1999. pap. 19.95 (*0-19-513107-X*) OUP.
— Conditions Handsome & Unhandsome: The Constitution of Emersonian Perfectionism. LC 89-49128. (Paul Carus Lectures). 190p. (C). 1991. 49.95 (*0-8126-9149-0*) Open Court.
— Conditions Handsome & Unhandsome: The Constitution of Emersonian Perfectionism. (Carus Lectures, 1988). 120p. 1997. 14.95 (*0-226-09820-6*) U Ch Pr.
— Conditions Handsome & Unhandsome: The Constitution of Emersonian Perfectionism: The Carus Lectures. 192p. 1991. pap. 11.95 (*0-226-09821-4*) U Ch Pr.
— Contesting Tears: The Hollywood Melodrama of the Unknown Woman. 208p. 1996. pap. 14.95 (*0-226-09816-8*) U Ch Pr.
— Contesting Tears: The Hollywood Melodrama of the Unknown Woman. LC 96-23834. 208p. (C). 1996. lib. bdg. 39.95 (*0-226-09814-1*) U Ch Pr.
— Disowning Knowledge: In Six Plays of Shakespeare. 238p. 1987. pap. text 21.95 (*0-521-33890-5*) Cambridge U Pr.
— In Quest of the Ordinary: Lines of Romanticism & Skepticism. 184p. 1995. 23.95 (*0-226-09817-6*) U Ch Pr.
— In Quest of the Ordinary: Lines of Skepticism & Romanticism. xiii, 213p. 1994. pap. text 12.95 (*0-226-09818-4*) U Ch Pr.
— Must We Mean What We Say? LC 75-32911. 394p. 1976. pap. text 35.95 (*0-521-29048-1*) Cambridge U Pr.
— Philosophical Passages: Wittgenstein, Emerson, Austen, Derrida. LC 94-15838. (Bucknell Lectures in Literary Theory Ser.: Vol. 12). 208p. 1995. pap. 26.95 (*0-631-19271-9*) Blackwell Pubs.
— A Pitch of Philosophy: Autobiographical Exercises. LC 93-47642. (Jerusalem-Harvard Lectures). 282p. (C). 1994. text 26.00 (*0-674-66980-0*) HUP.
— A Pitch of Philosophy: Autobiographical Exercises. 216p. 1996. pap. 15.95 (*0-674-66981-9*) HUP.
— Pursuits of Happiness: The Hollywood Comedy of Remarriages. (Harvard Film Studies). 296p. 1984. pap. text 16.95 (*0-674-73906-X*) HUP.
— The Senses of Walden. LC 91-35306. 168p. 1992. pap. 13.95 (*0-226-09813-3*) U Ch Pr.
— Themes Out of School: Effects & Causes. 282p. 1988. pap. 19.00 (*0-226-09788-9*) U Ch Pr.
— This New Yet Unapproachable America: Essays after Emerson after Wittgenstein. 108p. 1989. 19.95 (*0-945953-01-1*, Pub. by Living Batch Bks); pap. 9.95 (*0-945953-00-3*, Pub. by Living Batch Bks) U Ch Pr.
— The World Viewed: Reflections on the Ontology of Film. enl. ed. 278p. 1980. pap. 15.50 (*0-674-96196-X*) HUP.
— The World Viewed: Reflections on the Ontology of Film. enl. ed. (Harvard Film Studies: No. 151). 278p. 1980. 32.00 (*0-674-96197-8*) HUP.
***Cavell, Timothy A.** Working with Parents of Aggressive Children: A Practitioner's Guide. LC 99-45997. (Division 16 (School Psychology) Ser.: Vol. 3). 256p. 2000. text 39.95 (*1-55798-637-1*) Am Psychol.
Cavelle, Simon. The Encyclopedia of Decorative Paint Techniques. LC 93-85510. (Illus.). 176p. 1994. 24.95 (*1-56138-212-4*) Running Pr.
***Cavelletti, Carlo.** Chopin & Romantic Music. (Masters of Music Ser.). 64p. (J). 2000. 14.95 (*0-7641-5136-3*) Barron.
Cavello, James, jt. auth. see Almeida, Margarite.
***Cavelos, Jeanne.** Science of Star Wars: An Astrophysicist's Independent Examination of Space Travel, Aliens, Planets & Robots. 2000. pap. 14.95 (*0-312-26387-2*) St Martin.
— The Science of Star Wars: An Astrophysicist's Independent Examination of Space Travel, Aliens, Planets, & Robots As Portrayed in the Star Wars Films & Books. LC 99-22007. 224p. 1999. text 22.95 (*0-312-20958-4*) St Martin.
Cavelos, Jeanne. The Science of "The X-Files" LC 98-227316. 256p. 1998. pap. 12.00 (*0-425-16711-9*) Blvd Books.
Caven. Essentials of Word Perfect for Windows. (C). 1996. spiral bd. write for info. (*0-201-83040-X*) Addison-Wesley.
— Essentials of Word 7.0 Windows 95. (C). 1996. spiral bd. write for info. (*0-201-58872-2*) Addison-Wesley.
— Word 7.0 Complete Windows 95. (C). 1996. spiral bd. write for info. (*0-201-58873-0*) Addison-Wesley.
Caven, Jean, et al. Wordperfect 6.1 for Windows. (C). 1996. spiral bd. write for info. (*0-201-83045-0*) Addison-Wesley.
Cavenagh, Thomas D., jt. auth. see Ponte, Lucille M.
Cavenar, Jesse O., Jr., et al, eds. Psychiatry, 6 vols., Vol. V. 1986. 60.00 (*0-317-52307-4*) Basic.
***Cavenaugh, Thomas D.** Business Dispute Resolution. LC 99-30343. 218p. 1999. pap. 24.95 (*0-324-01597-6*) Thomson Learn.
Cavender, jt. auth. see Kahane, Howard.
Cavender, Bruce. Mineral Production Costs Vol. I: Analysis & Management. LC 98-54796. 192p. 1999. 69.00 (*0-87335-174-6*, 174-6) SMM&E Inc.
Cavender, Gary L. & Falgout, Marshall. Algebra I: Written by Teachers for Students. (Power Algebra Ser.). (Illus.). 520p. (YA). (gr. 8-12). 1995. 30.00 (*0-9645613-0-1*) Power Pubs.
Cavender, Gray, jt. ed. see Fishman, Mark.
Cavender, Jeff, ed. see Zeller, Bob.
Cavender, Nancy, jt. auth. see Kahane, Howard.
Cavendish, Clare. Hospital in Danger. large type ed. (Linford Romance Library). 384p. 1995. pap. 16.99 (*0-7089-7722-7*, Linford) Ulverscroft.
Cavendish, Clare A. Sister at Rivermead. large type ed. 244p. 1994. pap. 18.99 (*1-85389-453-2*, Dales) Ulverscroft.
Cavendish, George. The Life & Death of Cardinal Wolsey. 1962. write for info. Yale U Pr.
Cavendish, K. Impulse. 1997. mass mkt. 6.95 (*0-7472-5473-7*, Pub. by Headline Bk Pub) Trafalgar.
— Liaison Heatwave. 1997. mass mkt. 6.95 (*0-7472-5652-7*, Pub. by Headline Bk Pub) Trafalgar.
— Possession. mass mkt. 6.95 (*0-7472-5244-0*, Pub. by Headline Bk Pub) Trafalgar.
Cavendish, M., ed. Great Writers. 1993. 24.98 (*1-55521-963-2*) Bk Sales Inc.
Cavendish, Margaret. The Blazing World & Other Writings. Lilley, Kate, ed. & intro. by. 272p. 1994. pap. 12.95 (*0-14-043372-4*, Penguin Classics) Viking Penguin.
— The Description of New Blazing World & Other Writings. Lilley, Kate, ed. LC 92-16908. (Women's Classics Ser.). 250p. (C). 1992. text 55.00 (*0-8147-1475-7*) NYU Pr.
Cavendish, Margaret L. Grounds of Natural Philosophy. LC 96-12960. (Women in the Sciences Ser.: Vol. 2). 311p. (C). 1996. reprint ed. lib. bdg. 38.00 (*0-933951-66-3*) Locust Hill Pr.
***Cavendish, Marshall.** Cultures of the World Group 18, 6 vol set (J). 1999. 213.86 (*0-7614-0950-5*) Marshall Cavendish.
Cavendish, Marshall. The Encyclopedia of North American Indians, 11 vols., Set. LC 96-7700. 1536p. (J). 1996. lib. bdg. 657.07 (*0-7614-0227-6*) Marshall Cavendish.
Cavendish, Mavis. Cassell Handbook of Copyright in British Publishing Practice. 3rd rev. ed. 240p. 1993. text 70.00 (*0-304-32635-6*) Continuum.
Cavendish Newcastle, Margaret. Convent of Pleasure & Other Plays. LC 98-48352. 1999. 47.50 (*0-8018-6099-7*) Johns Hopkins.
***Cavendish Newcastle, Margaret.** Convent of Pleasure & Other Plays. LC 98-48352. 1999. pap. text 15.95 (*0-8018-6100-4*) Johns Hopkins.
Cavendish, Patricia. Always & Forever. large type ed. 548p. 1992. 27.99 (*0-7505-0440-4*, Pub. by Mgna Lrg Print) Ulverscroft.
Cavendish Publishing Limited Staff. Student Law Review, 1993 Yearbook. 174p. (C). 1994. pap. write for info. (*1-874241-07-4*, Pub. by Cavendish Pubng) Gaunt.
Cavendish, Richard. The World of Ghosts & the Supernatural: The Occult, the Unexplained & the Mystical Around the Globe. LC 94-15743. (Illus.). 160p. 1994. 22.95 (*0-8160-3209-2*) Facts on File.
Cavendish, Richard, ed. Man, Myth & Magic: The Illustrated Encyclopedia of Mythology, Religion & the Unknown, 21 vols. rev. ed. LC 94-10784. (Illus.). 2976p. 1994. lib. bdg. 714.21 (*1-85435-731-X*) Marshall Cavendish.
Cavendish, Richard, et al. Journeys of the Great Explorers. LC 92-9195. (Illus.). 224p. 1992. 34.95 (*0-8160-2840-0*) Facts on File.
Cavendish, Susan, et al. Assessing Science in the Primary Classroom: Observing Activities. (Assessing Science in the Primary Classroom Ser.). (Illus.). 128p. 1990. pap., teacher ed. (*1-85396-076-4*) Corwin Pr.
Cavendish, Thomas. The Last Voyage of Thomas Cavendish, 1591-1592. Quinn, David B., ed. LC 74-11619. (Studies in the History of Discoveries). x, 182p. (C). 1976. lib. bdg. 48.00 (*0-226-09819-2*) U Ch Pr.
Cavendish, William. The Country Captain. Johnson, Anthony, ed. 162. (Illus.). 120p. 1999. text 35.00 (*0-19-729038-8*) OUP.
— Des Weltberuhmten Hertzog Wilhelms von Newcastle Neu-Eroffnete Reit-Bahn - Nouvelle Methode Pour Dresser les Chevaux. (Deutsch-Franzosische Parallelausgabe, Documenta Hippologica Ser.). 301p. 1994. reprint ed. 240.00 (*3-487-08052-4*) G Olms Pubs.
— Dramatic Works by William Cavendish. Hulse, E Lynn, ed. LC 97-205987. (Malone Society Reprints Ser.: No. 158). (Illus.). 172p. 1997. text 45.00 (*0-19-729034-5*) OUP.
Cavenee, Webster, et al, eds. Recessive Oncogenes & Tumor Suppression. (Current Communications in Molecular Biology Ser.). (Illus.). 234p. (C). 1989. pap. text 24.00 (*0-87969-332-0*) Cold Spring Harbor.
Caveney, Gail, ed. see Fernandez, Ilana.
Caveney, Graham. Gentleman Junkie: The Life & Legacy of William S. Burroughs. LC 97-76356. (Illus.). 224p. (gr. 8). 1998. 27.95 (*0-316-13725-1*) Little.
— Screaming with Joy: The Life of Allen Ginsberg. LC 99-18075. 224p. 1999. 27.50 (*0-7679-0278-5*) Bantam.
Caveney, Graham, jt. auth. see Young, Elizabeth.
Caveney, Mike, jt. auth. see Lewis, Eric C.
Caveney, Philip. Burn down Easy. 416p. 1997. pap. 11.95 (*0-7472-5209-2*, Pub. by Headline Bk Pub) Trafalgar.
— Skin Flicks. 512p. 1996. mass mkt. 11.95 (*0-7472-4419-7*, Pub. by Headline Bk Pub) Trafalgar.
— The Tarantula Stone. large type ed. 528p. 1986. 27.99 (*0-7089-8362-6*) Ulverscroft.
— Tiger, Tiger. large type ed. 576p. 1985. 11.50 (*0-7089-8294-8*) Ulverscroft.
***Cavens, Travis.** Being a Pediatrician: The Struggles & Rewards of Caring for Children. (Illus.). 96p. 2000. 21.95 (*0-9659385-2-2*) Lake Pub.
Cavens, Travis. Lake Sacajawea: Longview's Treasure. LC 97-74061. (Illus.). 96p. 1997. pap. 20.00 (*0-9659385-0-6*) Lake Pub.
Cavera, Anthony La, see Thomas, George & La Cavera, Anthony.
Caverly, A. M. Historical Sketch of Troy, N. H. (Illus.). 299p. 1993. reprint ed. lib. bdg. 35.00 (*0-8328-2870-X*) Higginson Bk Co.
— History of the Town of Pittsford, Vt., with Biographical Sketches & Family Records. (Illus.). 756p. 1995. reprint ed. lib. bdg. 75.00 (*0-8328-4482-9*) Higginson Bk Co.
Caverly, Carol. All the Old Lions. 214p. 1994. 18.95 (*1-885173-00-8*) Write Way.
***Caverly, Carol.** Dead in Hog Heaven. 272p. 2000. 22.95 (*1-885173-83-0*, Pub. by Write Way) Midpt Trade.
Caverly, Carol. Frogskin & Muttonfat. 250p. 1996. 20.95 (*1-885173-24-5*); mass mkt. 5.95 (*1-885173-42-3*) Write Way.
Caverly, D. J., jt. auth. see Eagle, D. J.
Caverly, David. Clarisworks 4.0 for Elementary School Teachers. 86p. (C). 1998. spiral bd. 20.95 (*0-7872-4700-6*, 41470001) Kendall-Hunt.
— Clarisworks 4.0 for Secondary School Teachers. 86p. (C). 1998. spiral bd. 20.95 (*0-7872-4755-3*, 41475501) Kendall-Hunt.
Caverly, David C., jt. ed. see Flippo, Rona F.
Caverly, R. B. Annals of the Boodeys in New England. (Illus.). 297p. 1988. reprint ed. pap. 46.50 (*0-8328-0281-6*); reprint ed. lib. bdg. 56.50 (*0-8328-0280-8*) Higginson Bk Co.
— Caverly Family Genealogy 1116-1880. (Illus.). 201p. 1989. reprint ed. pap. 33.00 (*0-8328-1327-3*); reprint ed. lib. bdg. 43.00 (*0-8328-1326-5*) Higginson Bk Co.
Caverly, R. B., jt. auth. see Jewett, Jeremiah P.
Cavern, Brian. Dionysiusi: War-Lord of Sicily. LC 89-50651. 272p. 1989. 32.00 (*0-300-04507-7*) Yale U Pr.
Caverni, Jean-Paul, et al, eds. Cognitive Biases. (Advances in Psychology Ser.: No. 68). iv,576p. 1990. 201.50 (*0-444-88413-0*, North Holland) Elsevier.
Caverni, Jean-Paul, ed. see Research Conference on Subjective Probability, Uti, et al.
Cavers, Amy, jt. auth. see Hazen, Kari.
Cavers, David F. The Choice-of-Law Process. LC 65-21050. (Michigan Legal Publications). xiv, 336p. 1983. reprint ed. lib. bdg. 75.00 (*0-89941-316-1*, 303090) W S Hein.
Cavert, Chris. Affordable Portables: A Working Book of Initiative Activities & Problem Solving Elements. rev. expanded ed. 182p. 1999. spiral bd. 27.95 (*1-885473-40-0*) Wood N Barnes.
— E. A. G. E. R. Curriculum: Experiential Activities Games & Educational Recreation. (Illus.). 274p. 1996. ring bd. 49.95 (*1-885473-12-5*) Wood N Barnes.
— Games (& Other Stuff) for Group: Activities to Initiate Group Discussion. rev. ed. (Illus.). 128p. 1999. pap. 19.95 (*1-885473-39-7*) Wood N Barnes.
— Games (And Other Stuff) for Group Bk. 2: More Activities to Initiate Group Discussions. (Illus.). 116p. 1998. pap. 24.95 (*1-885473-21-4*) Wood N Barnes.
***Cavert, Chris.** What Would It Be Like? 1,001 Anytime Questions for Anysize Answers. (Pocket Prompters Ser.: Bk. 2). 150p. 2000. pap. 9.95 (*1-885473-33-8*) Wood N Barnes.
Cavert, Chris & Frank, Laurie. Games (And Other Stuff) for Teachers: Classroom Activities that Promote Pro-Social Learning. (Illus.). 168p. 1999. pap. 27.95 (*1-885473-22-2*) Wood N Barnes.
Cavert, Chris & Sikes, Sam. 50 Ways to Use Your Noodle: Loads of Land Games with Foam Noodle Toys. (Illus.). 200p. 1997. pap. 15.97 (*0-9646541-1-3*) Lrning Unltd.
Caves. Strategic Airport Planning. LC 99-10050. 468p. 1999. text 98.50 (*0-08-042764-2*, Pergamon Pr) Elsevier.
Caves & Jones Staff. World Trade & Payments + Sg. 7th ed. (C). 1997. pap. write for info. (*0-673-52549-X*) Addison-Wesley.
Caves, Richard, & Associates Staff. Industrial Efficiency in Six Nations. (Illus.). 520p. 1992. 60.00 (*0-262-03193-0*) MIT Pr.
Caves, Richard E. American Industry: Structure, Conduct, Performance. 7th ed. 144p. (C). 1992. pap. text 51.93 (*0-13-029893-X*) P-H.
***Caves, Richard E.** Creative Industries: Contracts Between Arts & Commerce. LC 99-86569. 2000. text 45.00 (*0-674-00164-8*) HUP.
Caves, Richard E. Multinational Enterprise & Economic Analysis. 2nd ed. (Surveys of Economic Literature Ser.). (Illus.). 336p. (C). 1996. pap. text 20.95 (*0-521-47858-8*) Cambridge U Pr.
— Trade & Economic Structure: Models & Methods. LC 60-5389. (Economic Studies: No. 115). (Illus.). 325p. 1960. 22.50 (*0-674-89881-8*) HUP.
Caves, Richard E., et al, eds. Britain's Economic Performance. LC 79-3773. 404p. reprint ed. pap. 125.30 (*0-8357-7414-7*, 202796400057) Bks Demand.
Caves, Richard E. & Krause, Lawrence B., eds. The Australian Economy: A View from the North. LC 84-17074. 415p. 1984. 39.95 (*0-8157-1326-6*); pap. 18.95 (*0-8157-1325-8*) Brookings.
— Britain's Economic Performance. 388p. 1980. 38.95 (*0-8157-1320-7*); pap. 16.95 (*0-8157-1319-3*) Brookings.
Caves, Richard E. & Reuber, Grant L. Canadian Economic Policy & the Impact of International Capital Flows. LC 77-443977. (Canada in the Atlantic Economy Ser.: No. 10). 92p. reprint ed. pap. 30.00 (*0-8357-4018-8*, 203670800005) Bks Demand.
— Capital Transfers & Economic Policy: Canada, 1951-1962. LC 79-129123. (Economic Studies: No. 135). 452p. 1971. 27.50 (*0-674-09485-9*) HUP.
Caves, Richard E. & Uekusa, Masu. Industrial Organization in Japan. LC 75-44509. 183p. reprint ed. pap. 56.80 (*0-608-17111-5*, 202774000056) Bks Demand.
Caves, Richard E., et al. Competition in the Open Economy: A Model Applied to Canada. LC 79-23908. (Economic Studies: No. 150). (Illus.). 452p. 1980. 30.00 (*0-674-15425-8*) HUP.
— World Trade & Payments: An Introduction. 6th ed. LC 92-24764. (C). 1992. text 43.00 (*0-673-52274-1*) Addson-Wesley Educ.
Caves, Robert E., jt. auth. see Kazda, Antonbin.
Caves, Roger W. Land Use Planning: The Ballot Box Revolution. (Library of Social Research: Vol. 187). 260p. (C). 1992. text 59.95 (*0-8039-3824-1*); pap. text 26.00 (*0-8039-3825-X*) Sage.
— Readings in Urban Studies: An Introduction. 1994. 65.00 (*0-8039-5637-1*); pap. 29.95 (*0-8039-5638-X*) Sage.
Cavet, J., jt. auth. see Hogg, J.
Cavet, J., jt. ed. see Hogg, J.
Cavet, Judith. People Don't Understand: Children, Young People & Their Families Coping with a Hidden Disability. LC 98-200463. 80p. 1998. pap. 18.00 (*1-900990-24-5*, Pub. by Natl Childrens Bur) Paul & Co Pubs.

An Asterisk (*) at the beginning of an entry indicates that the title is appearing for the first time.

Cavett. Music of Mozart. (C). Date not set. write for info. (*0-415-03352-7*) Routledge.

Cavett, Dorcas. My First 81 Years. Dageforde, Linda J., ed. (Illus.). 224p. 1999. pap. 16.95 (*1-886225-33-8*, 2000) Dageforde Pub.

Cavey, Christopher. Gems & Jewels: Fact & Fable. 1992. 17.98 (*1-55521-745-1*) Bk Sales Inc.

Cavey, Robert D., jt. auth. see Nelson, Charles A.

Caviani, Mabel & Urbashich, Muriel. Simplified Quantity Recipes: Nursing-Convalescent Homes & Hospitals. 310p. 1986. pap. 37.70 (*0-317-57875-8*, FP783) Natl Restaurant Assn.

Cavicchi, Daniel. Tramps Like Us: Music & Meaning among Springsteen Fans. (Illus.). 240p. 1998. pap. 18.95 (*0-19-512564-9*); text 55.00 (*0-19-511833-2*) OUP.

Cavicchi, Daniel & Keil, Charles, eds. My Music. LC 92-56907. (Music - Culture Ser.). 244p. 1993. pap. 17.95 (*0-8195-6264-5*, Wesleyan Univ Pr) U Pr of New Eng.

Cavicchio, Carolyn, et al. Improving Public Policy: States & Grantmakers Working Together. LC 92-10523. 1992. pap. 16.95 (*0-934842-74-4*) CSPA.

Caviedes, Cesar. The Southern Cone: Realities of the Authoritarian State in South America. LC 83-17842. 222p. (C). 1984. text 59.00 (*0-86598-109-4*, R3907) Rowman.

Caviedes, Cesar & Knapp, Gregory W. South America. 1995. write for info. (*0-614-32055-0*) P-H.

Caviedes, Cesar N. Elections in Chile: The Road Toward Redemocratization. LC 91-7296. 156p. 1991. lib. bdg. 32.00 (*1-55587-218-2*) L Rienner.

***Caviezel, Kurt.** Red Light. (Illus.). 280p. 2000. pap. 45.00 (*3-905509-21-0*, Pub. by Patrick Frey) Dist Art Pubs.

Caviezel, Sandy. Directory of Summer Music Programs, 1995. 105p. 1995. pap. 17.95 (*1-885383-02-9*) Music Resources.

— The Directory of Summer Music Programs, 1996. 135p. 1996. pap. 16.95 (*1-885383-03-7*) Music Resources.

Caviglia, G. & Morro, A. Inhomogeneous Waves in Solids & Fluids. (Series in Theoretical & Applied Mechanics: Vol. 12). 150p. (C). 1992. text 61.00 (*981-02-0804-9*) World Scientific Pub.

***Caviglia, Jill L.** Sustainable Agriculture in Brazil: Economic Development & Deforestations. LC 99-22086. (New Horizons in Environmental Economics Ser.). 160p. 1999. write for info. (*1-84064-145-2*) E Elgar.

Cavileer, Carol. Feminine Resistance. 20p. (Orig.). 1994. pap. 3.00 (*0-916397-35-1*) Manic D Pr.

Cavilier, Debbie. Congatown. (Illus.). 32p. (Orig.). (YA). 1995. pap. text 12.95 (*0-89724-903-8*, BMR08002) Wrner Bros.

***Cavill, Paul.** Anglo-Saxon Christianity: Exploring the Earliest Roots of Christian Spirituality in England. LC 99-491019. 176p. 1999. pap. 14.95 (*0-00-628112-5*, Pub. by HarpC) Trafalgar.

— Maxims in Old English Poetry. LC 98-46866. 256p. 1999. 75.00 (*0-85991-541-7*) Boydell & Brewer.

Cavin, Diantha S. Scripture by Picture: Make Memorizing the Bible Fun & Easy. (Illus.). 78p. (Orig.). (J). (ps-6). 1992. pap. 10.95 (*0-9628012-3-2*) Dexter KS.

Cavin, Gene. View from the Hills. 119p. 1995. boxed set 16.95 (*0-9657025-1-0*) Hanover Pub.

Cavin, Lee. The Dam & 50 Years Beyond. (Illus.). 52p. 1988. pap. 4.50 (*1-879377-02-0*) Truax Print.

— The Dream Makers. 517p. 1995. boxed set 22.95 (*0-9657025-0-2*) Hanover Pub.

— The Edge of Paradise. (Illus.). 1994. 29.95 (*1-879377-01-2*) Truax Print.

— The Great Depression. 183p. 1997. boxed set 17.95 (*0-9657025-2-9*) Hanover Pub.

— Tales of the Mohican Country. 138p. 1984. boxed set 7.50 (*1-879377-00-4*) Truax Print.

— They Rose from the Valley. (Illus.). 127p. 1990. boxed set 9.95 (*1-879377-03-9*) Truax Print.

Cavin, Susan. Lesbian Origins. rev. ed. LC 85-18158. Orig. Title: An Hystorical & Cross-Cultural Analysis of Sex Ratios, Female Sexuality, & Homosexual Segregation Versus Heterosexual Integration Patterns in Relation to the Liberation of Women. (Illus.). 288p. 1985. 18.00 (*0-910383-16-2*); pap. 12.00 (*0-910383-15-4*) Ism Pr.

Cavin, Vicky. A Chair Full of Heart. LC 97-78247. (Illus.). 60p. 1998. 16.95 (*1-883697-25-5*) Hara Pub.

Cavina, Anna O. Felice Giani. (ITA., Illus.). 576p. 1997. 310.00 (*88-435-5390-9*, Pub. by Art Bks Intl) Partners Pubs Grp.

Cavina, Kristan. Critical Thinking & Writing: A Developing Writer's Guide with Readings. 429p. 1995. 32.50 (*0-534-24294-4*) Wadsworth Pub.

— Making Advanced Grammar Work: Grammar in Context for ESL Students. LC 98-92677. xiv, 322p. 1998. pap. 24.00 (*1-889850-06-3*) De Anza Pr.

— Making Advanced Grammar Work: Instructor's Manual. 52p. 1997. pap. text, teacher ed. write for info. (*1-889850-07-1*) De Anza Pr.

— Making Intermediate Grammar Work: Grammar in Context for ESL Students. LC 97-91562. 264p. (Orig.). 1997. pap. text 22.00 (*1-889850-04-7*) De Anza Pr.

— Making Intermediate Grammar Work: Instructor's Manual. 52p. 1997. pap. text, teacher ed. write for info. (*1-889850-05-5*) De Anza Pr.

— Reading & Writing in English Bk. 1: An Interactive Text for Intermediate ESL Students. LC 96-92732. 175p. 1996. pap. text 18.00 (*1-889850-00-4*) De Anza Pr.

— Reading & Writing in English Bk. 1: An Interactive Text for Intermediate ESL Students. 44p. 1996. teacher ed. 10.00 (*1-889850-01-2*) De Anza Pr.

— Reading & Writing in English Bk. 2: An Interactive Text for Intermediate ESL Students. LC 97-91561. 170p. (Orig.). 1997. pap. text 18.00 (*1-889850-02-0*) De Anza Pr.

— Reading & Writing in English Bk. 2: Instructor's Manual. 44p. 1997. pap. text, teacher ed. write for info. (*1-889850-03-9*) De Anza Pr.

***Cavina, Kristan.** Regarding the United States: Reading & Writing for Advanced ESL Students. LC 99-94700. (Illus.). xiv, 212p. 1999. pap. text 24.00 (*1-889850-08-X*) De Anza Pr.

Cavinato, Joseph L. Purchasing & Materials Management: Integrative Strategies. (Illus.). 475p. (C). 1984. pap. text, teacher ed. write for info. (*0-314-77870-5*) West Pub.

Cavinder, Fred D. Amazing Tales from Indiana. LC 89-46005. (Illus.). 176p. 1990. 25.00 (*0-253-31329-5*); pap. 12.95 (*0-253-20658-8*, MB-658) Ind U Pr.

— The Indiana Book of Records, Firsts, & Fascinating Facts. LC 84-43155. (Illus.). 374p. 1985. pap. 16.95 (*0-253-28320-5*) Ind U Pr.

Caviness, B. F. EUROCAL '85: Proceedings: Research Contributions, Vol. 2. (Lecture Notes in Computer Science Ser.: Vol. 204). xvi, 650p. 1985. 68.00 (*0-387-15984-3*) Spr-Verlag.

Caviness, Bob F. & Johnson, J. R. Quantifier Elimination & Cylindrical Algebraic Decomposition. LC 96-43590. (Texts & Monographs in Symbolic Computation Ser.). 430p. 1996. 79.95 (*3-211-82794-3*) Spr-Verlag.

Caviness, Cheryl T. Choices: Quick & Healthy Cooking. LC 95-131121. 144p. 1994. ring bd. 12.99 (*0-8280-0847-7*) Review & Herald.

— Fabulous Food for Family & Friends. Harvey, Susan, ed. 128p. 1990. pap. 12.99 (*0-8280-0567-2*) Review & Herald.

— Quick & Easy Cooking. 112p. (Orig.). 1988. ring bd. 12.99 (*0-8280-0445-5*) Review & Herald.

Caviness, Madeline, et al. Stained Glass Before 1700 in American Collections: Corpus Vitrearum Checklists, 4 vols. Bieber, Margarete, ed. (Studies in the History of Art: Vols. I-IV). (Illus.). 1056p. 1991. reprint ed. boxed set 195.00 (*0-8150-0018-9*) Wittenborn Art.

Caviness, Madeline H. Paintings on Glass: Studies in Romanesque & Gothic Monumental Art. LC 97-843. (Variourm Collected Studies: Vol. 573). (Illus.). 304p. 1997. 175.95 (*0-86078-638-2*, Pub. by Ashgate Pub) Ashgate Pub Co.

Caviness, Madeline H., et al, eds. Stained Glass Before 1700 in American Collections: New England & New York - Corpus Vitrearum Checklist I. LC 72-600309. (Illus.). 219p. 1985. pap. 40.00 (*0-89468-078-1*) Wittenborn Art.

Caviness, Madeline H., ed. see National Gallery of Art Staff.

Caviness, Mary H., et al, eds. Therapeutic Drug Monitoring: A Guide to Clinical Application. LC 85-71233. (Illus.). 438p. 1987. spiral bd. 35.00 (*0-9614903-1-4*, 9520-56) Abbott Laboratories.

Caviola, H. In the Zone: Perception & Presentation of Space in German & American Postmodernism. (International Cooper Series in English Language & Literature). 224p. 1992. 50.50 (*0-8176-2696-4*) Birkhauser.

Caviris, George & Moore, Sophie. Physical Science Lab Manual. 2nd ed. 320p. 1995. pap. text, ring bd. 31.95 (*0-7872-1389-6*) Kendall-Hunt.

Cavis, jt. compiled by see Mitchell.

Cavitation & Polyphase Flow Forum Staff. Cavitation & Polyphase Flow Forum, 1980: Proceedings of the Cavitation & Polyphase Flow Forum, New Orleans, 1980. Hoyt, J. W., ed. LC TC0171.C316. 52p. reprint ed. pap. 30.00 (*0-608-15134-3*, 202314800032) Bks Demand.

Cavitch. Spring Reader, Now I Get It. 1998. pap. text 31.50 (*0-312-20138-9*) St Martin.

— Springfield Reader. 1997. pap. text 20.00 (*0-312-19159-6*) St Martin.

— Springfield Reader with Easy Writer. 1998. pap. text 23.40 (*0-312-20063-3*) St Martin.

Cavitch, David. Life Studies. 5th ed. 1995. pap. text, teacher ed. 22.00 (*0-312-10339-5*) St Martin.

— Life Studies. 6th ed. LC 97-74957. 525p. 1998. pap. 35.95 (*0-312-15714-2*); pap. text 23.00 (*0-312-17071-8*) St Martin.

— Life Studies Rules. 3rd ed. 1996. pap. text 30.60 (*0-312-14962-X*) St Martin.

— Springfield Reader. LC 96-86770. 197p. 1997. pap. 24.95 (*0-312-14912-3*); pap. text 5.00 (*0-312-15041-5*); pap. text 12.50 (*0-312-15040-7*) St Martin.

Cavitch, Susan M. The Natural Soap Book: Making Herbal & Vegetable-Based Soaps. (Illus.). 144p. 1995. pap. 14.95 (*0-88266-888-9*, Storey Pub) Storey Bks.

— The Soapmaker's Companion: A Comprehensive Guide with Recipes, Techniques & Know-How. LC 97-5139. (Illus.). 256p. (Orig.). 1997. pap. 18.95 (*0-88266-965-6*) Storey Bks.

Cavitch, Zolman. Business Organizations with Tax Planning, 16 vols. 1963. ring bd. 2570.00 (*0-8205-1165-X*) Bender.

— Ohio Corporation Law with Federal Tax Analysis, 2 vols. 1961. ring bd. 240.00 (*0-8205-1190-0*) Bender.

— Tax Planning for Corporations & Shareholders: Forms. 1985. ring bd. 200.00 (*0-8205-1430-6*) Bender.

Cavitch, Zolman & Belden, Thomas G. Ohio Transaction Guide: Legal Forms, 16 vols. 1975. ring bd. 1340.00 (*0-8205-1538-8*) Bender.

Cavitch, Zolman, jt. auth. see Schmidt, Robert M.

Cavitch, Zolman, jt. auth. see Smith, James W.

Cavitt, Opal. Flight for Life: A Matter of Life & Death. Hassell, Marie, ed. (Illus.). 157p. 1990. 29.95 (*1-878394-12-6*) Sanuk.

***Cavnar, Cindy.** Saints from A to Z. (Inspirational Dictionary Ser.). 2000. pap. 11.99 (*1-56955-190-1*) Servant.

Cavnar, Cindy, ed. Prayers & Meditations of Therese of Lisieux. 186p. 1993. pap. 9.99 (*0-89283-749-7*, Charis) Servant.

Cavoleau, Pierre. Soviet Industrial Terminology: Terminologie Industrielle Sovietique: Lexique Russe-Francais d'Organization. 2nd ed. (FRE & RUS.). 72p. 1983. pap. 19.95 (*0-8288-2131-3*, F53070) Fr & Eur.

***Cavolina, Mary Jane Frances, et al.** Growing up Catholic. (Illus.). 208p. 2000. 12.00 (*0-7679-0597-0*) Broadway BDD.

Cavolo, Sally W., jt. auth. see Shrake, Mary I.

Cavonius, C. R., ed. Colour Vision Deficiencies Vol. XIII: Proceedings of the International Symposium, Fau 1995. (Documenta Opthalmologica Proceedings Ser.). 544p. (C). 1997. text 234.00 (*0-7923-4224-0*) Kluwer Academic.

Cavoski, Kosta, jt. auth. see Kostunica, Vojislav.

Cavoukian, Ann & Tapscott, Don. Who Knows: Safeguarding Your Privacy in a Networked World. (Illus.). 233p. 1996. 24.95 (*0-07-063320-7*) McGraw.

Cavuoto, James. Laser Print It! A Desktop Publishing Guide to Reports, Resumes, Newsletters, Directories, Business Forms, & More. 208p. 1986. pap. 16.95 (*0-201-11349-X*) Addison-Wesley.

— Laser Write It. 1986. pap. 16.95 (*0-201-11327-9*) Addison-Wesley.

— Laserwrite It! write for info. (*0-318-60210-5*) Addison-Wesley.

Cavuoto, James & Beale, Stephen. The Color Scanner Book. 2nd ed. 224p. 1995. pap. 27.95 (*0-941845-11-7*) Micro Pub Pr.

Cavuoto, James, jt. auth. see Beale, Stephen.

Cavusgil, S. T. & Horn, Nancy E., eds. Internationalizing Doctoral Education in Business: Viewpoints & Proposals for Change. 250p. 1997. 45.95 (*0-87013-424-8*) Mich St U Pr.

Cavusgil, S. Tamer, ed. Advances in International Marketing Vol. 9: From Marketing-Mix to Relationships & Networks. Date not set. 78.50 (*0-7623-0318-2*) Jai Pr.

— Internationalizing Business Education: Meeting the Challenge. 220p. (C). 1993. 39.95 (*0-87013-332-2*) Mich St U Pr.

Cavusgil, S. Tamer, et al, eds. Advances in International Marketing, Vol. 1. 300p. 1986. 78.50 (*0-89232-275-6*) Jai Pr.

— Advances in International Marketing, Vol. 2. 277p. 1987. 78.50 (*0-89232-646-8*) Jai Pr.

— Advances in International Marketing, Vol. 3. 336p. 1989. 78.50 (*0-89232-891-6*) Jai Pr.

— Advances in International Marketing, Vol. 4. 241p. 1991. 78.50 (*1-55938-128-0*) Jai Pr.

— Advances in International Marketing, Vol. 7. 1995. 78.50 (*1-55938-839-0*) Jai Pr.

— Advances in International Marketing Vol. 5: Industrial Networks. 261p. 1993. 78.50 (*1-55938-407-7*) Jai Pr.

— Advances in International Marketing Vol. 6: Export Marketing: International Perspective. 229p. 1994. 78.50 (*1-55938-645-2*) Jai Pr.

Cavusgil, S. Tamer & Czinkota, Michael R., eds. International Perspectives on Trade Promotion & Assistance. LC 89-10713. 264p. 1990. 67.95 (*0-89930-485-0*, CTA/, Greenwood Pr) Greenwood.

Cavusgil, S. Tamer & Li, Tiger, eds. International Marketing: An Annotated Bibliography. 220p. pap. 26.00 (*0-87757-223-2*) Am Mktg.

Cavusgil, Sharon. Looking Ahead Bk. 1: Introduction to Academic Writing. LC 98-158909. 256p. (J). 1998. pap. 29.95 (*0-8384-7884-0*) Heinle & Heinle.

Cavusgil, Sharon L. The Road to Healthy Living. 144p. 1995. pap., teacher ed. 13.95 (*0-472-08324-4*, 08324); pap. text 16.95 (*0-472-08294-9*, 08294) U of Mich Pr.

Cavusgil, Sharon L. The Road to Healthy Living. LC 94-61574. (Illus.). 144p. (C). 1996. audio 15.00 (*0-472-00254-6*, 00254) U of Mich Pr.

Cavvadas, Adv J., ed. Consolidated Cape Provincial Ordinances - Gekonsolideerde Kaapse Provinsiale Ordonnansies, 3 vols., Set. (AFR & ENG.). 288.00 (*0-7021-0122-2*, Pub. by Juta & Co) Gaunt.

Caw, James I. Veterinary Nursing Questions. pap. text 18.00 (*0-7506-4795-7*) Buttrwrth-Heinemann.

Cawdrey, Robert. A Treasurie: or Store-House of Similies. LC 75-171738. (English Experience Ser.: No. 355). 880p. 1971. reprint ed. 150.00 (*90-221-0365-X*) Walter J Johnson.

Cawdry, Robert. Table Alphabetical of Hard Usual English Words. LC 66-12119. 144p. 1977. reprint ed. 50.00 (*0-8201-1007-8*) Schol Facsimiles.

Cawein, Madison, ed. Book of Love. LC 79-116395. (Granger Index Reprint Ser.). (Illus.). 1977. 19.95 (*0-8369-6136-6*) Ayer.

Cawein, Wanda. What about Religion? An Exploratory View. LC 92-60737. (Illus.). 208p. 1992. pap. 10.00 (*0-9633488-1-7*) Midngt Oil.

— What about Religion? An Exploratory View. 2nd rev. expanded ed. (Illus.). 192p. (YA). 1999. per. 14.95 (*0-9633488-7-6*) Midngt Oil.

Cawelti, G. Scott & Duncan, Jeffrey L. The Inventive Writer: A Discovery-Based Rhetoric. LC 92-26824. xv, 256p. 1993. pap. text 33.95 (*1-55934-060-6*, 1060) Mayfield Pub.

— The Inventive Writer: Instructor's Manual. LC 92-26824. 1993. pap. text. write for info. (*1-55934-061-4*, 1061) Mayfield Pub.

Cawelti, Gordon, ed. Challenges & Achievements of American Education. 216p. 1993. pap. 23.95 (*0-87120-200-X*) ASCD.

Cawelti, Gordon, jt. auth. see Roberts, Arthur D.

Cawelti, John, jt. auth. see Snyder, Joel.

Cawelti, John G. Adventure, Mystery & Romance: Formula Stories as Art & Popular Culture. LC 75-5077. (Phoenix Ser.). 336p. 1977. reprint ed. pap. 18.95 (*0-226-09867-2*) U Ch Pr.

— Apostles of the Self-Made Man. 296p. 1999. pap. text 18.00 (*0-226-09870-2*, Midway Reprint) U Ch Pr.

— Leon Forrest: Introductions & Interpretations. LC 96-39151. 322p. 1997. 44.95 (*0-87972-733-0*); pap. 19.95 (*0-87972-734-9*) Bowling Green Univ Popular Press.

— The Six Gun Mystique. 2nd ed. LC 84-72052. 155p. 1984. 18.95 (*0-87972-313-0*); pap. 9.95 (*0-87972-314-9*) Bowling Green Univ Popular Press.

***Cawelti, John G.** The Six-Gun Mystique Sequel. 2nd expanded rev. ed. LC 98-47399. 7p. 1999. 49.95 (*0-87972-785-3*); pap. 16.95 (*0-87972-786-1*) Bowling Green Univ Popular Press.

Cawelti, John G. & Rosenberg, Bruce A. The Spy Story. LC 86-30716. x, 272p. 1987. 27.00 (*0-226-09868-0*) U Ch Pr.

Cawelti, John O. Apostles of the Self-Made Man. LC 65-25123. 1965. lib. bdg. 15.00 (*0-226-09864-8*) U Ch Pr.

Cawkell, A. E. Encyclopaedic Dictionary of Information Technology & Systems. LC 93-25291. 350p. 1993. 95.00 (*1-85739-036-9*) Bowker-Saur.

— A Guide to Picture Management & Image Processing. LC 94-2390. 1994. 96.95 (*0-566-07546-6*, Pub. by Gower) Ashgate Pub Co.

Cawkell, A. E., ed. World Information Technology Manual, 2 vols. 1010p. 1991. 165.00 (*0-685-50930-3*, North Holland) Elsevier.

Cawkell, Tony. The Multimedia Handbook. LC 96-6079. (Illus.). 480p. (C). 1996. 165.00 (*0-415-13666-0*) Routledge.

Cawkwell, George. Thucydides & the Peloponnesian War. LC 96-37755. 176p. (C). 1997. 65.00 (*0-415-16430-3*); pap. 20.99 (*0-415-16552-0*) Routledge.

Cawley, A. C., ed. Everyman & Medieval Miracle Plays. 266p. 1993. pap. 5.95 (*0-460-87280-X*, Everyman's Classic Lib) Tuttle Pubng.

Cawley, A. C. & Stevens, Martin. The Towneley Cycle: A Facsimile of Huntington MSHM I. LC 75-42854. 332p. 1976. pap. 12.00 (*0-87328-113-6*) Huntington Lib.

Cawley, A. C., ed. & intro. see Chaucer, Geoffrey.

Cawley, Anne, ed. see O'Brian, Ellen G.

Cawley, Catherine B. A Rainy Afternoon with God. LC 97-50235. 64p. 1998. pap. 5.95 (*0-8091-3779-8*) Paulist Pr.

Cawley, Clifford C. Chamru: A World State from the Nucleus of a China-America-Russia Federation. LC 88-23456. 203p. 1989. 16.95 (*0-936339-13-6*); pap. 11.95 (*0-936339-14-4*) Circa Pr Portland.

Cawley, Edward T., jt. auth. see Johnson, George B.

Cawley, Frederick D., jt. ed. see Waite, Diana S.

Cawley, J. C., jt. auth. see Burthem, J.

Cawley, James & Cawley, Margaret. Along the Delaware & Raritan Canal. LC 79-85760. (Illus.). 128p. 1975. 14.50 (*0-8386-7529-8*) Fairleigh Dickinson.

— Exploring the Little Rivers of New Jersey. rev. ed. LC 93-1113. (Illus.). 250p. (C). 1993. pap. 14.95 (*0-8135-2014-2*) Rutgers U Pr.

— The First New York-Philadelphia Stage Road. LC 78-75175. (Illus.). 120p. 1980. 24.50 (*0-8386-2331-X*) Fairleigh Dickinson.

Cawley, James, jt. auth. see Edgcomb, Elaine.

Cawley, James, jt. ed. see Edgcomb, Elaine.

Cawley, Jennifer. Relative Sizes & Amounts of Things. 1991. 3.00 (*0-932526-76-4*) Nexus Pr.

Cawley, John. The Animated Films of Don Bluth. (Illus.). 200p. (Orig.). 1991. pap. 14.95 (*0-685-50334-8*) Retro Vision.

Cawley, John C., jt. ed. see Galvani, David W.

Cawley, Linda A. Legal Beagle: Diary of a Canine Counselor. LC 96-68928. 256p. 1996. 21.95 (*0-88282-146-6*) New Horizon NJ.

Cawley, Lucinda R., et al. Saved for the People of Pennsylvania: Quilts from the Collection of the State Museum of Pennsylvania. LC 97-196062. (Illus.). 67p. 1997. pap. 14.95 (*0-89271-073-X*, 0203) Pa Hist & Mus.

Cawley, Margaret, jt. auth. see Cawley, James.

Cawley, R. McGreggor. Federal Land, Western Anger: The Sagebrush Rebellion & Environmental Politics. LC 93-10690. (Development of Western Resources Ser.). 208p. 1996. pap. 14.95 (*0-7006-0804-4*) U Pr of KS.

— Federal Land, Western Anger: The Sagebrush Rebellion & Environmental Politics. LC 93-10690. (Development of Western Resources Ser.). 208p. (C). 1996. 29.95 (*0-7006-0613-0*) U Pr of KS.

Cawley, R. McGreggor, jt. ed. see Brick, Philip.

Cawley, Rhya N. Pongee Goes to Paris. (Illus.). 70p. (Orig.). (J). 1996. pap. 4.95 (*1-57502-282-6*, PO985) Morris Pubng.

Cawley, Richard. Easy & Artful Asian Cooking. LC 93-37457. (Creative Cook Ser.). 64p. 1993. 16.95 (*1-56426-654-0*) Cole Group.

— Fast Fab Food. (Illus.). 128p. 1998. 29.95 (*0-7472-2098-0*, Pub. by Headline Bk Pub) Trafalgar.

— Outdoor Affairs: Picnics & Barbecues. LC 93-39689. (Creative Cook Ser.). 64p. 1994. 16.95 (*1-56426-657-5*) Cole Group.

Cawley, Robert R. Milton & the Literature of Travel. LC 72-114095. (Princeton Studies in English: No. 32). 163p. (C). 1970. reprint ed. 45.00 (*0-87752-015-1*) Gordian.

— Milton's Literary Craftsmanship: A Study of a Brief History of Muscovia. LC 65-25136. (Princeton Studies in English: No. 24). 103p. 1965. reprint ed. 45.00 (*0-87752-016-X*) Gordian.

Cawley, Sherry. Around Walterboro, South Carolina. (Postcard History Ser.). (Illus.). 128p. 1999. pap. 18.99 (*0-7524-0989-1*) Arcadia Publng.

Cawley, William A. & Morand, James M., eds. Environmental Engineering. (Conference Proceedings Ser.). 552p. 1986. 59.00 (*0-87262-544-3*) Am Soc Civil Eng.

C

Cawley, William K., jt. auth. see Ames, Charlotte A.
Cawood, Charles L. Vintage Tractors. (Album Ser.: No. 256). (Illus.). 32p. 1989. pap. 4.75 (*0-85263-499-4*, Pub. by Shire Pubns) Parkwest Pubns.
Cawood, Chris. Carp. Seale, Gaynell, ed. LC 97-93523. 312p. (Orig.). 1997. pap. 9.95 (*0-9642231-4-7*) Magnolia Hill.
— How to Live to 100 (& Enjoy It!) Stories of Tennessee Centenarians. Seale, Gaynell, ed. LC 96-94049. (Illus.). 110p. (Orig.). 1996. pap. 8.95 (*0-9642231-1-2*) Magnolia Hill.
— The Jimmy Streater Story: The Saga of an All-American. (Illus.). 250p. 1999. pap. 12.95 (*0-9642231-3-9*) Magnolia Hill.
— Legacy of the Swamp Rat: Tennessee Quarterbacks Who Just Said No to Alabama. LC 94-76938. 224p. 1994. 15.95 (*0-9642231-6-3*) Magnolia Hill.
— 1998: The Year of the Beast. Seale, Gaynell, ed. LC 96-94050. 312p. (Orig.). 1996. pap. 12.95 (*0-9642231-9-8*) Magnolia Hill.
— Tennessee's Coal Creek War: Another Fight for Freedom. Seale, Gaynell, ed. LC 95-76607. (Illus.). 272p. (Orig.). 1995. pap. 12.95 (*0-9642231-0-4*) Magnolia Hill.
Cawood, Diana. Assertiveness for Managers: Learning Effective Skills for Managing People. 3rd rev. ed. (Business Ser.). (Illus.). 168p. 1992. pap. 12.95 (*0-88908-996-5*, 9568) Self-Counsel Pr.
Cawood, Frank W., jt. auth. see Failes, Janice M.
***Cawood, Ian & McKinnon-Bell, David.** The First World War. LC 00-24298. 2000. write for info. (*0-415-22276-1*) Routledge.
Cawrtney, Sue, et al, eds. Gracing Tables of Whitefish, Montana. (Illus.). 219p. 1995. 16.95 (*0-9652913-0-8*) CCC PTF.
Caws & Prendergast. Issues in World Literature. 1997. 15.73 (*0-06-502265-3*) P-H.
Caws, Ian. The Feast of Fools. 56p. pap. write for info. (*3-7052-0810-1*, Pub. by Poetry Salzburg) Intl Spec Bk.
Caws, Ian, ed. Herrick's Women. 1997. pap. 8.95 (*3-7052-0972-8*, Pub. by Poetry Salzburg) Intl Spec Bk.
Caws, M. A. City Images: Perspectives from Literature, Philosophy, & Film. iiv, 278p. 1991. text 64.00 (*2-88124-426-2*); pap. text 27.00 (*2-88124-464-5*) Gordon & Breach.
Caws, Marry Ann & Prendergast, Christopher, eds. Harper Collins World Reader, Vol. 1. 1472p. (C). 1997. pap. 50.00 (*0-06-501382-4*) Addson-Wesley Educ.
Caws, Mary A. Andre Breton. rev. ed. 1996. 32.00 (*0-8057-4623-4*, Twyne) Mac Lib Ref.
— Ecritures De Femmes: Nouvelles Cartographies. LC 95-49489. 413p. 1996. 30.00 (*0-300-06412-8*) Yale U Pr.
— A Metapoetics of the Passage: Architextures in Surrealism & After. LC 80-54468. (Illus.). 218p. reprint ed. pap. 67.60 (*0-8357-6511-3*, 203588200097) Bks Demand.
— Perspectives on Perception: Philosophy, Art & Literature. (Reading Plus Ser.: Vol. 3). XII, 265p. (C). 1989. text 49.00 (*0-8204-0469-1*) P Lang Pubng.
— Reading Frames in Modern Fiction. LC 84-16092. 327p. reprint ed. pap. 101.40 (*0-7837-0243-4*, 204055200017) Bks Demand.
— Rene Char. (Twayne's World Authors Ser.). (C). 1977. lib. bdg. 20.95 (*0-8057-6268-X*) Irvington.
— Robert Motherwell: What Art Holds. LC 95-20819. (Interpretations in Art Ser.). (Illus.). 215p. 1996. 38.50 (*0-231-09644-5*) Col U Pr.
— The Surrealist Look: An Erotics of Encounter. LC 96-44541. (Illus.). 366p. 1997. 44.00 (*0-262-03244-9*) MIT Pr.
Caws, Mary A., ed. About French Poetry from Dada to "Tel Quel" Text & Theory. LC 74-10962. 299p. reprint ed. pap. 92.70 (*0-7837-3665-7*, 204353700009) Bks Demand.
— Textual Analysis: Some Readers Reading. LC 85-18808. viii, 327p. 1986. pap. text 8.00 (*0-87352-141-2*, T121P); lib. bdg. 12.00 (*0-87352-140-4*, T121C) Modern Lang.
— Writing in a Modern Temper: Essays on French Literature & Thought, in Honor of Henri Peyre. (Stanford French & Italian Studies: Vol. 33). 286p. 1984. pap. 56.50 (*0-915838-04-4*) Anma Libri.
Caws, Mary A., et al, eds. Contre-Courants: Les femmes s'ecrivent a travers les siecles. LC 94-12379. (FRE.). 304p. 1994. pap. text 50.00 (*0-13-042920-1*) P-H.
— Surrealism & Women. (Illus.). 246p. 1991. pap. text 17.00 (*0-262-53098-8*) MIT Pr.
Caws, Mary A. & Nicole, Eugene, eds. Reading Proust Now. LC 90-6063. (Reading Plus Ser.: Vol. 8). (Illus.). XII, 316p. (C). 1991. text 89.00 (*0-8204-1239-2*) P Lang Pubng.
Caws, Mary A. & Riffaterre, Hermine, eds. The Prose Poem in France: Theory & Practice. LC 82-20691. 256p. 1983. text 69.00 (*0-231-05434-3*); pap. text 23.00 (*0-231-05435-1*) Col U Pr.
Caws, Mary A., jt. auth. see DeSalvo, Donna.
Caws, Mary A., ed. see Galand, Rene.
Caws, Mary A., ed. see Perse, Saint-John, pseud.
Caws, Mary A., ed. see Tison-Braun, Micheline.
Caws, Mary A., ed. & intro. see Mallarme, Stephane.
Caws, Mary A., tr. see Breton, Andre.
Caws, Mary A., tr. see Char, Rene.
***Caws, Mary Ann.** Joseph Cornell's Theater of the Mind: Selected Diaries, Letters & Files. 2nd ed. LC 92-80750. (Illus.). 496p. 2000. reprint ed. pap. 27.50 (*0-500-28243-9*, Pub. by Thames Hudson) Norton.
— Picasso's Weeping Woman: The Life & Art of Dora Maar. (Illus.). 224p. 2000. 50.00 (*0-8212-2693-2*) Bulfinch Pr.
Caws, Mary Ann. The Surrealist Look: An Erotics of Encounter. (Illus.). 1999. pap. text 22.00 (*0-262-53162-3*) MIT Pr.
***Caws, Mary Ann.** Surrealist Painters & Poets: An Anthology. LC 00-32888. 2001. write for info. (*0-262-03275-9*) MIT Pr.
***Caws, Mary Ann, ed.** Manifesto: A Century of Isms. 768p. 2000. pap. 35.00 (*0-8032-6407-0*, Bison Books) U of Nebr Pr.
Caws, Mary Ann & Bird Wright, Sarah. Bloomsbury & France: Art & Friends. LC 98-54638. (Illus.). 448p. 1999. 35.00 (*0-19-511752-2*) OUP.
Caws, Mary Ann & Terry, Patricia, trs. from FRE. Roof Slates & Other Poems of Pierre Reverdy. LC 80-26806. 293p. 1981. pap. text 17.95 (*0-930350-52-9*) NE U Pr.
Caws, Mary Ann, ed. & tr. see Mallarme, Stephane.
Caws, Mary Ann, tr. see Breton, Andre.
Caws, Mary Anne m, ed. see Prendergast, Christopher.
Caws, Peter. The Capital Connection: Business, Science & Government. (Philip Morris Lectures on Business & Society Ser.). 108p. 1993. pap. write for info. (*1-884663-00-1*) Baruch Coll Cty U.
— Ethics from Experience. (Philosophy Ser.). (C). 1996. 37.95 (*0-534-54246-8*) Wadsworth Pub.
— Sartre. (Arguments of the Philosophers Ser.). 224p. 1984. pap. 11.95 (*0-7102-0233-4*, Routledge Thoemms) Routledge.
— Structuralism: A Philosophy for the Human Science. LC 96-52015. (Contemporary Sudies in Philosophy & the Human Science Ser.). 1997. pap. 19.95 (*0-391-04044-8*) Humanities.
***Caws, Peter.** Structuralism Updated. rev. ed. 1999. pap. 26.00 (*1-57392-438-5*) Prometheus Bks.
Caws, Peter. Yorick's World: Science & the Knowing Subject. LC 92-31834. (C). 1993. 55.00 (*0-520-07919-1*, Pub. by U CA Pr) Cal Prin Full Svc.
Cawsey, Alison. The Essence of Artificial Intelligence. LC 97-11460. 240p. (C). 1997. pap. text 19.95 (*0-13-571779-5*) P-H.
— Explanation & Interaction: The Computer Generation of Explanatory Dialogues. LC 92-35405. (Natural Language Processing Ser.). (Illus.). 220p. 1993. 35.00 (*0-262-03202-3*, Bradford Bks) MIT Pr.
Cawson. Path of Tumors of Oral Tissue. 5th ed. (C). 1998. text 195.00 (*0-443-03990-9*) Church.
Cawson, Alan, ed. Organized Interests & the State: Studies in Neo-Corporatism. 192p. (Orig.). (C). 1985. pap. text 20.95 (*0-8039-9719-1*) Sage.
Cawson, Alan, et al. Hostile Brothers: Competition & Closure in the European Electronics Industry. (Government-Industry Relations Ser.: No. 4). (Illus.). 418p. 1990. text 82.00 (*0-19-827568-4*) OUP.
— The Shape of Things to Consume. 289p. 1995. 77.95 (*1-85972-052-8*, Pub. by Avebry) Ashgate Pub Co.
Cawson, R. A. & Odell, E. W. Essentials of Oral Pathology & Oral Medicine. 6th ed. LC 97-28646. 1998. pap. text 65.00 (*0-443-05348-0*) Church.
— Oral Pathology. 2nd ed. LC 99-11698. (Colour Guide Ser.). (Illus.). 1999. write for info. (*0-443-06171-8*, W B Saunders Co) Harcrt Hlth Sci Grp.
Cawson, R. A. & Odell, J. W. Oral Pathology. (Colour Guide Ser.). (Illus.). 152p. 1993. pap. text 16.95 (*0-443-04800-2*) Harcrt Hlth Sci Grp.
Cawson, R. A. & Spector, R. G. Clinical Pharmacology in Dentistry. 5th ed. (Illus.). 250p. 1989. pap. text 36.00 (*0-443-04043-5*) Church.
***Cawson, R. A., et al.** Surgical Pathology of the Mouth & Jaws. (Illus.). 326p. 2000. pap. text 85.00 (*0-7236-1083-5*, Pub. by John Wright) Buttrwrth-Heinemann.
Cawson, R. A., jt. auth. see Scully, Crispian.
Cawson, Roderick A., et al. Pathology No. 2: The Mechanisms of Disease. 2nd ed. (Illus.). 592p. (C). (gr. 13). 1989. pap. text 49.95 (*0-8016-1246-2*, 01246) Mosby Inc.
— Surgical Pathology of the Mouth & Jaws. (Illus.). 326p. 1996. text 220.00 (*0-7236-0840-7*) Buttrwrth-Heinemann.
Cawte, Alice. Atomic Australia. 220p. 1992. pap. 24.95 (*0-86840-388-1*, Pub. by New South Wales Univ Pr) Intl Spec Bk.
Cawte, John. Healers of Arnhem Land. LC 97-145841. 160p. 1996. pap. 29.95 (*0-86840-351-2*, Pub. by New South Wales Univ Pr) Intl Spec Bk.
— The Last of the Lunatics. 272p. 1998. pap. 24.95 (*0-522-84804-4*, Pub. by Melbourne Univ Pr) Paul & Co Pubs.
— The Universe of the Warramirri. 1992. 22.95 (*0-86840-013-0*, Pub. by New South Wales Univ Pr) Intl Spec Bk.
Cawte, John, tr. see Grillmeier, Aloys & Hainthaler, Theresia.
Cawthon, Elisabeth A. Job Accidents & the Law in England's Early Railway Age: Origins of Employer Liability & Workmen's Compensation. LC 96-37775. (Studies in British History: Vol. 43). 244p. 1997. text 89.95 (*0-7734-8735-2*) E Mellen.
Cawthon, Elisabeth A. & Narrett, David E., eds. Essays on English Law & the American Experience. LC 93-34549. (Walter Prescott Webb Memorial Lectures: Vol. 27). 152p. 1994. 25.95 (*0-89096-581-1*) Tex A&M Univ Pr.
Cawthon, Elisabeth A., jt. ed. see Reinhardt, Steven G.
Cawthon, Kathy L. Getting Out: An Escape Manual for Abused Women. LC 95-75954. 224p. 1995. pap. 10.99 (*1-56384-093-6*) Huntington Hse.
Cawthon, Thomas. Proceedings of the 1994 DOE/NREL Hydrogen Program Review (April 18-21, 1994) National Renewable Energy Laboratory Staff, ed. (Hydrogen Fuel Information Ser.: Vol. I). (Illus.). 476p. 1996. lib. bdg. 195.00 (*0-89934-262-0*, BT938) Bus Tech Bks.
Cawthorn, C. P. & Warnell, N. L. Pioneer Baptist Church Records of South-Central Kentucky & the Upper Cumberland of Tennessee. 1987. reprint ed. 34.00 (*0-685-30502-3*) Church History.
Cawthorn, John. Cawthorn: Residential Estate Conveyancing. 2nd ed. 1995. write for info. (*0-406-14822-8*, MICHIE) LEXIS Pub.
Cawthorn, R. Grant, ed. Layered Intrusions. LC 96-9423. (Developments in Petrology Ser.: Vol. 15). 542p. 1996. pap. 86.00 (*0-444-82518-5*) Elsevier.
— Layering Intrusions. LC 96-9423. (Developments in Petrology Ser.: Vol. 15). (Illus.). 542p. 1996. text 184.00 (*0-444-81768-9*) Elsevier.
Cawthorn, Todd. Jerry Jones & the "New Regime" Memoirs, Recollections, Times & Travels with "America's Team" & Its Most Notorious Cowboy. (Illus.). 240p. 1995. 22.95 (*0-9649652-9-1*) TTHORN Pubg.
***Cawthorne.** Sex Lives of the Great Artists. 1998. pap. text 13.95 (*1-85375-295-9*, Pub. by Prion) Trafalgar.
— Sex Lives of the Great Composers. 1999. pap. text 13.95 (*1-85375-294-0*) Key Porter.
Cawthorne, Barbara. Instant Success for Classroom Teachers: New & Substitute Teachers (K-8) LC 81-82947. (Illus.). 112p. (Orig.). 1981. pap. 8.50 (*0-9606666-0-5*) Greenfield Pubns.
Cawthorne, James & Moorcock, Michael. Fantasy: The One Hundred Best Books. 224p. 1991. pap. 8.95 (*0-88184-708-9*) Carroll & Graf.
Cawthorne, Nigel. The Art of India, 6 vols. LC 97-28571. (Art of Ser.). (Illus.). 96p. 1997. 22.00 (*1-57145-631-7*, Laurel Glen Pub) Advantage Pubs.
— The Art of Japanese Prints, 6 vols. LC 97-13778. (Art of Ser.). (Illus.). 96p. 1997. 22.00 (*1-57145-606-6*, Laurel Glen Pub) Advantage Pubs.
— The Art of Native North America, 6 vols. LC 97-22073. (Art of Ser.). (Illus.). 96p. 1997. 22.00 (*1-57145-630-9*, Laurel Glen Pub) Advantage Pubs.
— The Art of the Aztecs. LC 98-49125. (Art of Ser.). (Illus.). 96p. 1999. 22.00 (*1-57145-639-2*, Laurel Glen Pub) Advantage Pubs.
***Cawthorne, Nigel.** The Art of the Icon. (Art of Ser.). (Illus.). 2000. 22.00 (*1-57145-681-3*, Laurel Glen Pub) Advantage Pubs.
Cawthorne, Nigel. Images of the Cat. LC 99-30653. (Images of Ser.). (Illus.). 96p. 1999. 22.00 (*1-57145-642-2*, Laurel Glen Pub) Advantage Pubs.
— The Man in the Bamboo Cage. (Illus.). 1991. 30.95 (*0-85052-148-3*) Leo Cooper.
— New Look: The Dior Revolution. 1998. 19.99 (*0-7858-0963-5*) Bk Sales Inc.
— Satanic Murder: Chilling True Stories of Sacrificial Slaughter. LC 97-105387. 288p. (Orig.). 1996. mass mkt. 5.95 (*0-86369-978-2*, Pub. by Virgin Bks) London Brdge.
— Sex Lives of Hollywood Idols. 288p. 1997. pap. 13.95 (*1-85375-249-5*) Prion.
— Sex Lives of the Great Dictators. 288p. 1996. pap. 11.95 (*1-85375-210-X*) Prion.
— Sex Lives of the Hollywood Goddesses. 288p. 1997. pap. 13.95 (*1-85375-250-9*) Prion.
— Sex Lives of the Popes. 280p. 1996. pap. 11.95 (*1-85375-207-X*) Prion.
— Sex Lives of the Presidents: From Washington to Clinton. 1998. mass mkt. 5.99 (*0-312-96838-8*) St Martin.
— '60's Source Book. 25.98 (*1-55521-529-7*) Bk Sales Inc.
Cawthorne, Nigel, jt. auth. see Turner, Ike.
Cawthra, Gavin. Policing South Africa: The SAP & the Transition from Apartheid. LC 93-37608. 240p. (C). 1993. text 59.95 (*1-85649-065-3*, Pub. by Zed Books); text 22.50 (*1-85649-066-1*, Pub. by Zed Books) St Martin.
— Securing South Africa's Democracy. LC 96-46508. 208p. 1997. text 65.00 (*0-312-17419-5*) St Martin.
Cawthra, Gavin, jt. ed. see Moller, Bjorn.
***Cawthra, Lin Y.** Primus Three. Cawthra, Seth E., ed. LC 99-93091. (Space Voyagers Ser.: Vol. 1). 288p. 1999. pap. 7.99 (*1-893906-00-0*) Maze Pubg.
Cawthra, Seth E., ed. see Cawthra, Lin Y.
***Cawthron, John.** Poems by the Dozen. (Illus.). 57p. (J). (gr. 2-4). 1999. 12.95 (*1-888565-06-3*) Trinity Rivrs.
— Poems by the Dozen. LC 99-62973. (Illus.). 57p. (J). (gr. 2-4). 1999. pap. 9.95 (*1-888565-07-1*) Trinity Rivrs.
Cawthron, P. Butterworths Student Companions: Trade Practices. 101p. 1989. pap. 17.00 (*0-409-49379-1*, Austral, MICHIE) LEXIS Pub.
Cawyer, Shirley B. Death Records of Earth County, Texas (1903-1917), Vol. 1. LC 92-75273. 50p. (C). 1993. pap. 10.00 (*0-9622746-3-1*) Datatrace Systems.
Caxton, Guy, et al, eds. Liberating the Learner: Lessons for Professional Development in Education. LC 95-36543. (Educational Management Ser.). 304p. (C). 1996. pap. 27.99 (*0-415-13127-8*) Routledge.
Caxton, William. Begin Two A. LC 72-5980. (English Experience Ser.: No. 508). 1973. reprint ed. 70.00 (*90-221-0508-3*) Walter J Johnson.
— Dialogues in French & English. Bradley, H., ed. (EETS, ES Ser.: No. 79). 1972. reprint ed. pap. 35.00 (*0-527-00281-X*) Periodicals Srv.
— The Prologue & Epilogues of William Caxton. Crotch, W. J., ed. (EETS, OS Ser.: No. 176). 1974. reprint ed. 45.00 (*0-527-00173-2*) Periodicals Srv.
Caxton, William, tr. The Book of the Order of Chivalry. LC 76-57359. (English Experience Ser.: No. 778). 1977. reprint ed. lib. bdg. 25.00 (*90-221-0778-7*) Walter J Johnson.
— Here Begynneth a Lityll Treatise Spekynge of the Arte & Crafte to Knowe Well to Dye. LC 72-169. (English Experience Ser.: No. 221). 28p. 1970. reprint ed. 20.00 (*90-221-0221-1*) Walter J Johnson.
Caxton, William, jt. auth. see Lull, Ramon, pseud.
Caxton, William, ed. & tr. see Aesop.
Caxton, William, tr. see De Deguilleville, Guillaume.
Caxton, William, tr. see De Voragine, Jacobus.
Caxton, William, tr. see Heraclius.
Caxton, William, tr. see Herrtage, S. J., ed.
Caxton, William, tr. see Jerome, S.
Caxton, William, tr. see Lefevre, Raoul.
Caxton, William, tr. see Lull, Ramon, pseud.
Caxton, William, tr. see Vincentius, Bellovacensis.
***Cay, Robin, photos by.** Fetish Art. (Illus.). 160p. 2000. 29.95 (*3-908163-15-3*, Pub. by Edit Stemmle) Abbeville Pr.
Caya, Rene & Montcalm, Henriette. Le Principe du Phenix: Le Reve Comme Processus de Transformation Selon la Psychologie de C. G. Jung. (FRE.). 1994. 22.95 (*2-920083-85-6*) Edns Roseau.
Cayace, Charles T., ed. see Fuller, John G.
Cayce, Charles T. & Cayce, Leslie G. Love Relationships: A Moving Sea. LC 95-30994. (Edgar Cayce's Wisdom for the New Age Ser.). 215p. 1995. pap. 12.95 (*0-87604-347-3*, 457) ARE Pr.
Cayce, Charles T., ed. see Campbell, Dan.
Cayce, Charles T., ed. see Cochran, Lin.
Cayce, Charles T., ed. see Langley, Noel.
Cayce, Charles T., ed. see Reed, Henry.
Cayce, Charles T., ed. see Smith, Robert C.
***Cayce, Charles Thomas & Thomas, Jeanette M., eds.** The Work of Edgar Cayce As Seen Through His Letters. LC 99-41418. 350p. 2000. 19.95 (*0-87604-407-0*) ARE Pr.
Cayce, Edgar. Auras: An Essay on the Meaning of Colors. 20p. 1973. pap. 3.50 (*0-87604-012-1*, 206) ARE Pr.
— Edgar Cayce: The Modern Prophet. 640p. 1990. 10.99 (*0-517-69702-5*) Random Hse Value.
— My Life As a Seer: The Lost Memoirs. Smith, A. Robert, ed. & compiled by by. LC 99-31180. 400p. 1999. text 25.95 (*0-312-20419-1*) St Martin.
— Revelation: A Commentary on the Book, Based on the Study of Twenty Four Psychic Discourses of Edgar Cayce. (Twenty-Six Interpretive Readings Ser.). 214p. 1969. pap. 14.95 (*0-87604-003-2*, 215) ARE Pr.
Cayce, Edgar, et al. No Death: God's Other Door. LC 98-37645. 195p. 1999. pap. 12.95 (*0-87604-417-8*, 531) ARE Pr.
Cayce, Edgar, jt. auth. see Daily, Dick.
Cayce, Edgar E. Edgar Cayce on Atlantis. Cayce, Hugh L., ed. 176p. 1988. reprint ed. mass mkt. 5.99 (*0-446-35102-4*, Pub. by Warner Bks) Little.
— Search for God Bks. 1 & 2: Anniversary Edition. (Illus.). 257p. 1992. text 24.95 (*0-87604-290-6*, 370) ARE Pr.
— Think on These Things: Selections from the Edgar Cayce Readings. 125p. 1981. pap. 4.50 (*0-87604-132-2*, 308) ARE Pr.
Cayce, Edgar E., et al. Mysteries of Atlantis Revisited. LC 97-138785. 212p. 1997. mass mkt. 5.99 (*0-312-96153-7*) St Martin.
Cayce, Hugh L. Venture Inward. LC 95-43166. 238p. 1995. reprint ed. pap. 13.95 (*0-87604-354-6*, 467) ARE Pr.
Cayce, Hugh L., ed. Edgar Cayce Reader, Vol. 1. 192p. 1988. mass mkt. 3.95 (*0-446-35112-1*, Pub. by Warner Bks) Little.
Cayce, Hugh L., et al. Dreams, Language of the Unconscious. rev. ed. 94p. 1971. pap. 6.95 (*0-87604-047-4*, 218) ARE Pr.
Cayce, Hugh L., ed. see Bro, Harmon H.
Cayce, Hugh L., ed. see Cayce, Edgar E.
Cayce, Leslie G., jt. auth. see Cayce, Charles T.
***Cayce, Martin.** Elixir. 1999. pap. write for info. (*1-57553-887-3*) Watermrk Pr.
Caycedo, Bernardo J. The Life & Times of Juan Jose d'Elhuyar: Discoverer of Tungston in 18th Century New Granada. (Illus.). 290p. 1981. 25.00 (*0-87291-149-7*) Coronado Pr.
Caycedo Garner, Lucia, et al. Claro Que Si! (C). 1990. 31.96 (*0-395-52912-3*) HM.
— Claro Que Si! (C). 1990. pap. text, teacher ed. 4.76 (*0-395-52916-6*) HM.
— Claro Que Si! (C). 1990. pap. text, teacher ed. 4.76 (*0-395-52915-8*) HM.
— Claro Que Si! An Integrated Skills Approach, Activities Manual. 3rd ed. (SPA.). (C). 1996. pap. text 33.96 (*0-395-74555-1*) HM.
Caycedo, Julio C. Conversational Sociology: An Intercultural Bridge Where East Meets West. LC 95-10145. 216p. (C). 1995. text 39.95 (*0-391-03937-7*) Humanities.
***Caye, Billi.** Nothing More Than Question Marks. 24p. 1999. 3.50 (*1-57688-016-8*, 80168) Branch & Vine.
Caye, Leslie, ed. see Page, Jennifer.
Cayen, Ron, jt. auth. see Dalton, David.
Cayer, N. Joseph. Public Personnel Administration in the U. S. 2nd ed. LC 85-61242. 175p. (C). 1986. pap. text 25.00 (*0-312-65521-5*) St Martin.
— Public Personnel Administration in the U. S. 3rd ed. 214p. 1995. pap. 36.95 (*0-312-11611-X*) St Martin.
Cayford, Joel. Computer Media: Living & Working with Computers. 110p. 1987. pap. 10.95 (*1-85178-001-7*, Pub. by Comedia) Routldge.
Cayford, John E. Fort Knox-Fortress in Maine. LC 83-71723. (Illus.). 114p. (YA). (gr. 6 up). 1995. pap. 9.95 (*0-941216-14-4*) Cay-Bel.
— Maine's Hall of Fame, Vol. 1. (Illus.). 208p. (Orig.). 1987. pap. 9.95 (*0-941216-22-5*) Cay-Bel.
— Maine's Hall of Fame, Vol. 2. LC 88-62792. (Illus.). 214p. (Orig.). (YA). (gr. 6 up). 1995. pap. 9.95 (*0-941216-43-8*, 0-941216-43-8) Cay-Bel.
— Underwater Work: A Manual of Scuba Commercial, Salvage, & Construction Operations. 2nd ed. LC 66-28081. (Illus.). 244p. reprint ed. pap. 75.70 (*0-7837-6298-4*, 204601300010) Bks Demand.
Cayford, John E. & Scott, Ronald E. Underwater Logging. LC 64-18585. (Illus.). 93p. reprint ed. pap. 30.00 (*0-7837-6297-6*, 204601200010) Bks Demand.
Caygill, David, jt. auth. see Abbey, J. L.
Caygill, Howard. Introducing Walter Benjamin. 176p. 1998. pap. 10.95 (*1-874166-87-0*, Pub. by Totem Bks) Natl Bk Netwk.

An Asterisk (*) at the beginning of an entry indicates that the title is appearing for the first time.

— A Kant Dictionary. (Philosopher Dictionaries Ser.). (Illus.). 400p. (C). 1995. pap. 29.95 (0-631-17535-0) Blackwell Pubs.

— Walter Benjamin: The Colour of Experience. LC 97-16700. 184p. (C). 1998. 70.00 (0-415-08958-1); pap. 24.99 (0-415-08959-X) Routledge.

Caygill, Howard, jt. ed. see Ansell-Pearson, Keith.

***Caygill, John C. & Mueller-Harvey, Irene, eds.** Secondary Plant Products Considerations for Animal Feeds. 136p. 1999. pap. 75.00 (1-897676-28-X, Pub. by Nottingham Univ Pr) St Mut.

Caygill, Wayne M., jt. ed. see Kimura, Samuel J.

Cayla, Edward & LaFray, Joyce. The Hunt for Unclaimed Cash. 96p. 1990. pap. 16.95 (0-942084-83-7) SeaSide Pub.

Cayla, X. Protein Phosphatases of Xenopus Oocytes: Phosphotyrosyl Phosphatase Activation of the PCS Phosphatases. No. 19. 133p. (Orig.). 1990. pap. 32.50 (90-6186-355-4, Pub. by Leuven Univ) Coronet Bks.

Caylan, Refik, jt. auth. see Sanna, M.

***Cayleff, Susan.** Babe Didrikson: The Greatest All-Sport Athlete of All Time. LC 00-23561. (Barnard Biography Ser.: Vol. 4). (Illus.). 168p. (YA). (gr. 7-12). 2000. pap. 8.95 (1-57324-194-6) Conari Press.

Cayleff, Susan. Wash & Be Healed: The Water-Cur Movement & Women's Health. (Health, Society, & Policy Ser.). 257p. 1991. pap. 22.95 (0-87722-859-0) Temple U Pr.

Cayleff, Susan E. Babe: The Life & Legend of Babe Didrikson Zaharias. (Illus.). Date not set. 29.95 (0-614-17658-1) U of Ill Pr.

— Babe: The Life & Legend of Babe Didrikson Zaharias. (Women in American History & Sport in Society Ser.). (Illus.). 370p. 1996. 14.95 (0-252-06593-X) U of Ill Pr.

— Babe: The Life & Legend of Babe Didrikson Zaharis. (Illus.). pap. 14.95 (0-614-19270-6) U of Ill Pr.

***Cayleff, Susan E.** Babe Didrikson: The Greatest All-Sport Athlete of All Time. (Illus.). (J). 2000. 14.30 (0-606-18829-0) Turtleback.

Cayleff, Susan E. The Life & Legend of Babe Didrikson Zaharias. LC 94-35584. (Women in American History; Sport & Society Ser.). (Illus.). 370p. 1995. 29.95 (0-252-01793-5) U of Ill Pr.

Cayleff, Susan E., jt. ed. see Bair, Barbara.

***Cayley, David.** The Expanding Prison: The Crisis in Crime & Punishment & the Search for Alternatives. 400p. (Orig.). 1999. pap. 25.95 (0-8298-1333-0) Pilgrim OH.

Cayley, David. George Grant in Conversation. 208p. 1995. pap. 13.95 (0-614-17722-7, Pub. by Hse of Anansi Pr) Genl Dist Srvs.

— George Grant in Conversation. LC 97-163808. (In Conversation Ser.). 208p. 1996. pap. text 16.95 (0-88784-553-3) Stoddart Publ.

— Ivan Illich in Conversation. (In Conversation Ser.). 320p. (Orig.). 1992. pap. 16.95 (0-88784-524-X, Pub. by Hse of Anansi Pr) Genl Dist Srvs.

— Northrop Frye in Conversation. (In Conversation Ser.). 240p. 1996. pap. 13.95 (0-88784-525-8) Stoddart Publ.

— Northrup Frye in Conversation. 240p. (Orig.). 1992. pap. 13.95 (0-614-17723-5, Pub. by Hse of Anansi Pr) Genl Dist Srvs.

Cayley, David, tr. see Poerksen, Uwe.

Caylor, David. Screams in America. LC 98-89798. 170p. 2000. pap. 13.95 (0-88739-230-X) Creat Arts Bk.

Caylor, H. W. H. W. Caylor, Frontier Artist. LC 80-6112. (Illus.). 130p. 1981. 29.50 (0-89096-108-5) Tex A&M Univ Pr.

Caylor, Lawrence M., ed. Leander by Walter Hawkesworth: A Variorum Edition with Translation. LC 92-37051. (Renaissance Imagination Ser.). 304p. 1993. text 25.00 (0-8153-0462-5) Garland.

Cayne, Bernard S., ed. The New Lexicon Webster's Dictionary of the English Language: Deluxe Encyclopedia Edition. (Illus.). 2064p. 1987. 14.95 (0-7172-4546-2) Lexicon Pubns.

— The New Lexicon Webster's Dictionary of the English Language: Encyclopedia Edition, 2 vols., Set, Vols. 1 & 2. (Illus.). 1987. write for info. (0-7172-4547-0) Lexicon Pubns.

— The New Lexicon Webster's Dictionary of the English Language: One Volume Encyclopedia Edition. (Illus.). 1504p. 1987. write for info. (0-7172-4535-7) Lexicon Pubns.

Cayne, Bernard S., ed. see Tesar, Jenny.

Cayne, Bernard S., ed. see Tesar, Jenny E.

***Cayon, J. & Castan, C.** Las Monedas Hispano del Tremis al Euro (411AD to Present) (Illus.). 1998. lib. bdg. 95.00 (84-920980-3-1) S J Durst.

Cayre, Raul O., jt. auth. see Valdes-Cruz, Lilliam V.

Cayrol, Jean. Le Froid Du Soleil. (FRE.). 192p. 1974. pap. 10.95 (0-7859-1777-2, 2070365514) Fr & Eur.

Cayrol, Pierre. Hong Kong: In the Mouth of the Dragon. Pratl, Carol, tr. from FRE. 172p. 1998. pap. 16.95 (0-8048-2115-1) Tuttle Pubng.

Cayten, C. Gene, et al. Principles & Practice of Emergency Medicine, 2 vols., Set. 3rd ed. Mayer, Thom & Mangelsen, Mary A., eds. (Illus.). 1992. text 199.00 (0-8121-1373-X) Lppncott W & W.

Cayten, Gene C., jt. ed. see Ivatury, Rao R.

Cayton, Andrew R. Frontier Indiana. LC 95-26443. (History of the Trans-Appalachian Frontier Ser.). (Illus.). 360p. 1998. pap. 18.95 (0-253-21217-0) Ind U Pr.

— Frontier Indiana. LC 95-26443. (History of the Trans-Appalachian Frontier Ser.). (Illus.). 360p. (C). 1998. 35.00 (0-253-33048-3) Ind U Pr.

— The Frontier Republic: Ideology & Politics in the Ohio Country, 1780-1825. LC 86-4706. 209p. 1989. pap. 10.50 (0-87338-409-1) Kent St U Pr.

Cayton, Andrew R. & Onuf, Peter S. The Midwest & the Nation: Rethinking the History of an American Region. LC 89-45479. (Midwestern History & Culture Ser.). 192p. 1990. 10.95 (0-253-31525-5) Ind U Pr.

Cayton, Andrew R. & Teute, Fredrika J., eds. Contact Points: American Frontiers from the Mohawk Valley to the Mississippi, 1750-1830. LC 97-49510. (Published for the Omohundro Institute of Early American History & Culture, Williamsburg, Virginia Ser.). (Illus.). 408p. (C). 1998. 49.95 (0-8078-2427-5); pap. 18.95 (0-8078-4734-8) U of NC Pr.

***Cayton, Andrew R., et al.** America: Pathways to the Present: America in the Twentieth Century LC 99-192552. xxii, 1032 p. 1998. teacher ed. write for info. (0-13-432386-6) P-H.

Cayton, Andrew R., jt. ed. see Brown, Jeffrey P.

Cayton, Horace R. & Mitchell, George S. Black Workers & the New Unions. 18.95 (0-405-18493-X) Ayer.

Cayton, Horace R., jt. auth. see Drake, St. Clair.

Cayton, Mary K. Emerson's Emergence: Self & Society in the Transformation of New England, 1800-1845. LC 89-32663. xiv, 308p. (C). 1992. pap. 19.95 (0-8078-4392-X) U of NC Pr.

Cayton, Mary K., et al, eds. Encyclopedia of American Social History, 3 vols., Set. LC 92-10577. (Scribner American Civilization Ser.). 2632p. 1993. 375.00 (0-684-19246-2, Scribners Ref) Mac Lib Ref.

Cayuga County Bicentennial Publications Committee, jt. auth. see Itzin, Charles.

Cayuga Nature Center Staff & Lang, Susan S. Nature in Your Backyard: Simple Activities for Children. (Illus.). 48p. (J). (gr. 2-4). 1995. pap. 7.95 (1-56294-893-8); lib. bdg. 22.90 (1-56294-451-7) Millbrook Pr.

Caywood, Clarke L. International Handbook of Public Relations & Corporate Communications. 600p. 1995. 55.00 (1-55738-820-2, Irwn Prfssnl) McGraw-Hill Prof.

Caywood, Clarke L., ed. The Handbook of Strategic Public Relations & Integrated Communications. LC 96-36234. 528p. 1997. text 50.00 (0-7863-1131-2, Irwn Prfssnl) McGraw-Hill Prof.

Caywood, Cynthia & Overing, Gillian R., eds. Teaching Writing: Pedagogy, Gender, & Equity. LC 86-14520. 238p. (C). 1986. pap. text 24.95 (0-88706-353-5) State U NY Pr.

— Teaching Writing: Pedagogy, Gender, & Equity. LC 86-14520. 238p. (C). 1986. text 67.50 (0-88706-352-7) State U NY Pr.

Caywood, Nancy L., jt. ed. see Houck, Rudolph S., III.

Caywood, Paul & Chekhov, Anton. The Marriage Proposal. (Half Hour Classics Ser.). 1997. pap. 2.50 (1-57514-316-X, 3106) Encore Perform Pub.

Caywood, Paul & Moliere. The Imaginary Invalid. (Half Hour Classics Ser.). 1997. pap. 2.50 (1-57514-317-8, 3107) Encore Perform Pub.

Caywood, Paul & Shakespeare, William. Pyramus & Thisby: A Cutting of a Midsummer Nights Dream. (Half Hour Classics Ser.). (YA). 1997. pap. 2.50 (1-57514-300-3, 3099) Encore Perform Pub.

Caywood, Paul, ed. see Shakespeare, William.

Caywood, Paul, tr. see Sophocles.

Caywood, Pual & Moliere. The Would Be Gentleman. (Half Hour Classics Ser.). (YA). 1997. pap. 2.50 (1-57514-301-1, 3101) Encore Perform Pub.

Caywood, Zoe. Arkansas Celebration. 1990. write for info. (0-9616521-2-8) War Eagle Cks.

— War Eagle Wholegrain & Honey Cookbook. 1991. write for info. (0-9616521-1-X) War Eagle Cks.

Caywood, Zoe M. Lowfat Wholegrain Cookbook. (Illus.). 175p. (Orig.). 1993. pap. write for info. (0-9616521-3-6) War Eagle Cks.

Cayzer, Elizabeth. Changing Perceptions: Milestones in Twentieth-Century British Portraiture. LC 98-39847. 1998. pap. 30.00 (1-898595-30-5, Pub. by Alpha Pr Ltd) Intl Spec Bk.

— Changing Perceptions: Milestones in Twentieth-Century British Portraiture. LC 98-39847. (Illus.). 127p. 1998. 50.00 (1-898595-29-1, Pub. by Alpha Pr Ltd) Intl Spec Bk.

Caza, A. Margaret. Walk Alone Together: Portrait of a French-English Marriage. 208p. 1990. 22.95 (0-7737-2430-3); pap. 9.95 (0-7737-5371-0) Sh1oreline.

Caza, A. Margaret, tr. see Caza, J. Euclide.

Caza, J. Euclide. The Lights of Lancaster: Letters to Rome. Caza, A. Margaret, tr. (Illus.). 160p. pap. 13.95 (0-9698752-7-4) Sh1oreline.

Caza, Shawn. Soviet Tactical Doctrine in WWII, as Found in-Hand Book on U. S. S. R. Military Forces, TM-30-340. (Illus.). 146p. 1998. pap. 19.95 (1-58545-030-8) Nafziger Collection.

Cazabon, Michel J. Views of Trinidad. (Illus.). reprint ed. 80.00 (0-910938-92-X) McGilvery.

Cazacu, C. A., et al, eds. Complex Analysis-Fifth Romanian--Finnish Seminar, Pt. I. (Lecture Notes in Mathematics Ser.: Vol. 1013). 393p. 1983. 49.95 (0-387-12682-1) Spr-Verlag.

— Complex Analysis-Fifth Romanian--Finnish Seminar, Pt. II. (Lecture Notes in Mathematics Ser.: Vol. 1014). 338p. 1983. 46.95 (0-387-12683-X) Spr-Verlag.

Cazade, Enrique. Cuba, una Isla que Cubrieron de Sangre. (SPA.). pap. 12.00 (0-89729-047-X) Ediciones.

Cazals, Remy, ed. see Dougados, Venance.

Cazals, Remy, ed. see Folcher, Gustave.

Cazals, Y., et al. Auditory Physiology & Perception: Proceedings of the Ninth International Symposium on Hearing, Carcens, France, 9-14 June 1991. (Advances in the Biosciences Ser.: No. 83). (Illus.). 590p. 1992. 210.50 (0-08-041847-3, Pergamon Pr) Elsevier.

Cazaly, O. H. W. Common Snakes of India & Burma & How to Recognize Them. 1984. pap. 125.00 (81-7089-016-0, Pub. by Intl Bk Distr) St Mut.

Cazaly, O. W. Common Snakes of India & Burma & How to Recognize Them. 1984. reprint ed. 85.00 (0-7855-3064-9, Pub. by Intl Bk Distr) St Mut.

Cazamian, Louis. Development of English Humor, 2 pts. in 1. LC 75-181925. reprint ed. 27.50 (0-404-01441-0) AMS Pr.

Cazarre, Lourenco. La Espada del General (The General's Sword) Mansour, Monica, tr. (SPA., Illus.). 168p. (J). (gr. 5-6). 1992. reprint ed. pap. 5.99 (968-16-3661-9, Pub. by Fondo) Continental Bk.

Cazden, Courtney. Classroom Discourse: The Language of Teaching & Learning. LC 87-11874. 230p. (Orig.). (C). (ps). 1988. pap. text 26.00 (0-435-08445-3, 08445) Heinemann.

Cazden, Courtney B. Whole Language Plus: Essays on Literacy in the United States & New Zealand. LC 92-17657. (Language & Literacy Ser.). 328p. (C). 1992. text 46.00 (0-8077-3210-9); pap. text 21.95 (0-8077-3209-5) Tchrs Coll.

Cazden, Courtney B., ed. Language in Early Childhood Education. rev. ed. LC 81-82158. (Illus.). 170p. 1981. pap. text 6.00 (0-912674-74-1, NAEYC #131) Natl Assn Child Ed.

— Review of Research in Education, Vol. 16. LC 72-89719. 424p. 1990. text. write for info. (0-935302-11-5) Am Educ Res.

Cazden, Courtney B., ed. see Review of Research in Education Staff.

Cazden, Elizabeth. Antoinette Brown Blackwell: A Biography. LC 82-4986. (Illus.). 328p. (C). 1983. 29.95 (0-935312-00-5); pap. 12.95 (0-935312-04-8) Feminist Pr.

Cazden, Norman, et al, eds. Folk Songs of the Catskills: Notes & Sources. LC 81-14565. 650p. (C). 1983. pap. text 24.95 (0-87395-581-1) State U NY Pr.

Cazden, Robert. German Exile Literature in America, 1933-1960: A History of the Free German Press & Book Trade. LC 76-98639. 262p. reprint ed. pap. 81.30 (0-608-12788-4, 202420000035) Bks Demand.

Cazden, Robert E. A History of the German Book Trade in America to the Civil War. LC 81-70545. (GERM Ser.: Vol. 1). (Illus.). xviii, 802p. 1984. 75.00 (0-938100-09-2) Camden Hse.

Cazeau, C. J. Science Trivia: From Anteaters to Zeppelins. (Illus.). 296p. (C). 1986. 19.95 (0-306-42353-7, Plenum Trade) Perseus Pubng.

Cazeau, C. J. & Scott, S. D., Jr. Exploring the Unknown: Great Mysteries Reexamined. LC 78-27413. (Illus.). 294p. 1979. 18.95 (0-306-40210-6); pap. 11.95 (0-306-80139-6) Da Capo.

***Cazeau, Charles J.** Test Your Science IQ. 350p. 2000. pap. 20.00 (1-57392-851-8) Prometheus Bks.

***Cazeaux, Clive.** The Continental Aesthetics Reader. 504p. 2000. 90.00 (0-415-20053-9); pap. 27.99 (0-415-20054-7) Routledge.

Cazelles, Brigitte. La Faiblesse Chez Gautier De Coinci. (Stanford French & Italian Studies: No. 14). (FRE.). viii, 180p. 1978. pap. 56.50 (0-915838-27-3) Anma Libri.

— The Unholy Grail: A Social Reading of Chretien de Troyes's 'Conte du Graal' LC 95-1781. (Figurae Ser.). 414p. 1995. 42.50 (0-8047-2481-4) Stanford U Pr.

Cazelles, Brigitte, ed. The Lady As Saint: A Collection of French Hagiographic Romances of the Thirteenth Century. LC 91-21158. (Middle Ages Ser.). 346p. 1991. pap. 107.30 (0-608-04819-4, 206547600004) Bks Demand.

Cazelles, Brigitte & Girard, Rene, eds. Alphonse Juilland: D'une passion l'autre. (Stanford French & Italian Studies: No. 53). 290p. 1987. pap. 56.50 (0-915838-69-9) Anma Libri.

Cazemajou, Jean. Stephen Crane. LC 74-625287. (University of Minnesota Pamphlets on American Writers Ser.: No. 76). 47p. (Orig.). reprint ed. pap. 30.00 (0-7837-2894-8, 205756100006) Bks Demand.

Cazemier, Jacques A., et al. Security Management. (IT Infrastructure Library Ser.). 124p. 90.00 (0-11-330014-X, Pub. by Statnry Office) Balogh.

Cazenave, Anny, ed. Earth Rotation: Solved & Unsolved Problems. 1986. text 161.50 (90-277-2333-8) Kluwer Academic.

Cazenave, M. Dictionnaire Ignorance aux Frontieres de la Science. (FRE.). 1998. 55.00 (0-320-00360-4) Fr & Eur.

Cazenave, Odile. Rebellious Women: The New Generation of Female African Novelists. LC 99-34821. (Three Continents Ser.). 260p. 1999. lib. bdg. 55.00 (0-89410-884-0) L Rienner.

Cazenave, Thierry & Haraux, Alain. An Introduction to Semi-Linear Evolution Equations. LC 99-196876. (Lecture Series in Mathematics & Its Applications: Vol. 13). (Illus.). 200p. 1999. text 75.00 (0-19-850277-X) OUP.

Cazeneuve. Cross Country Skiing. (Trailside Series Guide). 192p. 1995. pap. write for info. (0-393-31351-4, Norton Paperbks) Norton.

Cazeneuve, Brian. Cross-Country Skiing: A Complete Guide. LC 95-5529. (Trailside Series Guide). (Illus.). 192p. 1995. pap. 17.95 (0-393-31335-2) Norton.

Cazenove, Theophile. Cazenove Journal, 1794: A Journey Through New Jersey & Pennsylvania. Kelsey, Rayner W., ed. (Haverford Coll. Studies: No. 13). 1922. 30.00 (0-686-17388-0) R S Barnes.

Cazerres, et al. Supplement au Dictionnaire de la Bible, 9 vols., Set. (FRE.). 1967. 1995.00 (0-8288-6691-0, M-6065) Fr & Eur.

Cazes, J. Liquid Chromatography of Polymers & Related Materials, Part III. (Chromatographic Science Ser.: Vol. 19). (Illus.). 312p. 1981. text 165.00 (0-8247-1514-4) Dekker.

Cazes, J. & Delamare. Liquid Chromatography of Polymers & Related Materials, Pt. II. (Chromatographic Science Ser.: Vol. 13). (Illus.). 272p. 1980. text 145.00 (0-8247-6985-6) Dekker.

Cazes, Jack, ed. see International Symposium on Liquid Chromatographic.

Cazet. Minnie & Moo Go Dancing. (J). (gr. 1-3). Date not set. 3.95 (0-7894-2536-X) DK Pub Inc.

Cazet, Denys. Are There Any Questions? (Illus.). 32p. (J). (ps-2). 1992. 15.95 (0-531-30121-4) Orchard Bks Watts.

— Are There Any Questions? LC 91-42977. (Illus.). 32p. (J). (ps-2). 1998. pap. 6.95 (0-531-07109-X) Orchard Bks Watts.

— Born in the Gravy. LC 92-44523. (Illus.). 32p. (J). (ps-1). 1993. 15.95 (0-531-05488-8) Orchard Bks Watts.

— Born in the Gravy. LC 92-44523. (Illus.). 32p. (J). (ps-1). 1997. pap. 5.95 (0-531-07096-4) Orchard Bks Watts.

— Christmas Moon. LC 87-37434. (Illus.). 32p. (J). (ps-2). 1988. pap. 4.95 (0-689-71259-6) Aladdin.

— Dancing. LC 94-45920. (Illus.). 32p. (J). (ps-1). 1995. 15.95 (0-531-09466-9); lib. bdg. 16.99 (0-531-08766-2) Orchard Bks Watts.

— A Fish in His Pocket. LC 87-5462. (Illus.). 32p. (J). (ps-2). 1987. 15.95 (0-531-05713-5) Orchard Bks Watts.

— A Fish in His Pocket. LC 87-5462. (Illus.). 32p. (J). (ps-2). 1991. pap. 5.95 (0-531-07021-2) Orchard Bks Watts.

— "I'm Not Sleepy" LC 91-15958. (Illus.). 32p. (J). (ps-1). 1992. 15.95 (0-531-05898-0); lib. bdg. 16.99 (0-531-08498-1) Orchard Bks Watts.

***Cazet, Denys.** Minnie & Moo & the Musk of Zorro. LC 00-21280. (Illus.). 48p. (J). (ps-3). 2000. pap. 3.95 (0-7894-2653-6) DK Pub Inc.

— Minnie & Moo & the Musk of Zorro. LC 00-21280. (Illus.). 48p. (ps-3). 2000. 12.95 (0-7894-2652-8) DK Pub Inc.

— Minnie & Moo & the Thanksgiving Tree. LC 00-21278. (Illus.). 48p. (ps-3). 2000. pap. 3.95 (0-7894-2655-2) DK Pub Inc.

— Minnie & Moo & the Thanksgiving Tree. LC 00-21278. (Illus.). 48p. (ps-3). 2000. 12.95 (0-7894-2654-4) DK Pub Inc.

Cazet, Denys. Minnie & Moo Go Dancing. LC 97-39416. (Illus.). 47p. (J). (gr. 1-3). 1998. 12.95 (0-7894-2515-7) DK Pub Inc.

***Cazet, Denys.** Minnie & Moo Go to Paris. LC 98-47421. 48p. (J). 1999. pap. 3.95 (0-7894-3928-X) DK Pub Inc.

— Minnie & Moo Go to Paris, Vol. 4. LC 98-47421. 48p. (J). 1999. 12.95 (0-7894-2595-5) DK Pub Inc.

Cazet, Denys. Minnie & Moo Go to the Moon. (J). (gr. 1-3). 1998. write for info. (0-7894-2537-8) DK Pub Inc.

— Minnie & Moo Go to the Moon. LC 97-39417. (Illus.). 48p. (J). (gr. 1-3). 1998. 3.95 (0-7894-2516-5) DK Pub Inc.

— Minnie & Moo Save the Earth, Vol. 3. LC 98-47394. 48p. (J). 1999. 12.95 (0-7894-2594-7); pap. 3.95 (0-7894-3929-8) DK Pub Inc.

— "Never Spit on Your Shoes" LC 89-35164. (Illus.). 32p. (J). (ps-1). 1990. 16.95 (0-531-05847-6) Orchard Bks Watts.

— "Never Spit on Your Shoes" LC 89-35164. (Illus.). 32p. (J). (ps-1). 1993. pap. 6.95 (0-531-07039-5) Orchard Bks Watts.

— Never Spit on Your Shoes. 1993. 12.15 (0-606-05952-0, Pub. by Turtleback) Demco.

— Night Lights: 24 Poems to Sleep On. LC 96-42282. (Illus.). 32p. (J). (ps-1). 1997. 15.95 (0-531-30010-2); lib. bdg. 16.99 (0-531-33010-9) Orchard Bks Watts.

— The Non-Coloring Book: A Drawing Book for Mind Stretching & Fantasy Building. 64p. 1973. pap. 5.95 (0-88316-501-5) Chandler & Sharp.

— Nothing at All. LC 93-25204. (Illus.). 32p. (J). (ps-1). 1993. 15.95 (0-531-06822-6) Orchard Bks Watts.

— Nothing at All. LC 93-25204. (Illus.). 32p. (J). (ps-1). 1994. lib. bdg. 16.99 (0-531-08672-0) Orchard Bks Watts.

Cazimero, Momi, ed. see Belknap, Jodi P.

Cazoria, Angelina, jt. auth. see Vasquez, Milton.

Cazorla, Hazel, tr. see Mediero, Manuel M.

Cazorla, Nathalie M., jt. auth. see Williams, Stuart.

Cazort, Douglas. Under the Grammar Hammer. 2nd ed. 144p. Date not set. pap. 14.00 (1-56565-647-4, 06474W, Pub. by Lowell Hse) NTC Contemp Pub Co.

— Under the Grammar Hammer: The Twenty-Five Most Common Mistakes & How to Avoid Them. 128p. 1992. pap. 12.00 (0-929923-75-8) Lowell Hse.

Cazort, Jean E. & Hobson, Constance T. Born to Play: The Life & Career of Hazel Harrison, 3. LC 82-12169. (Contributions to the Study of Music & Dance Ser.: No. 3). (Illus.). 171p. 1983. 52.95 (0-313-23643-7, CBO/, Greenwood Pr) Greenwood.

Cazort, Mimi. The Ingenious Machine of Nature: Four Centuries of Art & Anatomy. (Illus.). 240p. 1997. pap. 49.95 (0-88884-657-6) U Ch Pr.

Cazort, Mimi, ed. Bella Pittura: The Art of the Gandolfi. 80p. 1996. pap. 24.95 (0-88884-629-0, Pub. by Natl Gallery) U Ch Pr.

Cazotte, Jacques. The Devil in Love. Sartarelli, Stephen, tr. from FRE. LC 92-82640. 220p. 1994. 28.00 (0-941419-78-9); pap. 14.00 (0-941419-79-7) Marsilio Pubs.

— The Devil in Love. 2nd ed. Stableford, Brian, ed. Landry, Judith, tr. from FRE. (European Classics). 109p. 1997. reprint ed. pap. 9.99 (0-946626-73-1, Pub. by Dedalus) Subterranean Co.

— Le Diable Amoureux. (FRE.). 1981. pap. 10.95 (0-7859-1934-1, 2070372723) Fr & Eur.

— Oeuvres Badines et Morales, Historiques et Philosophiques, 4 vols., Set. cxxix, 2118p. 1976. reprint ed. 400.00 (3-487-06149-X) G Olms Pubs.

Cazri, Jodhpur, ed. see Prakash, Ishwar & Ghosh, P. K.

Cazzaroli, Gianni. Dictionnaire de la Navigation: Dictionary of Navigation. (FRE.). 392p. 1973. 39.95 (0-7859-0730-0, M-4650) Fr & Eur.

C

An Asterisk (*) at the beginning of an entry indicates that the title is appearing for the first time.

Cazzulio, C. L., ed. Etiopathogenetic Hypotheses of Schizophrenia. 208p. (C). 1987. text 124.00 (*0-85200-843-0*) Kluwer Academic.

Cazzulio, C. L., et al, eds. Plasticity & Morphology of the Central Nervous System. (C). 1989. text 152.50 (*0-7462-0094-3*) Kluwer Academic.

Cazzullo, C. L., et al, eds. Symposium on Trazodone. (Journal: Neuropsychobiology: Vol. 15, Suppl. 1, 1986). (Illus.). iv, 52p. 1986. pap. 24.50 (*3-8055-4338-7*) S Karger.

CBA Service Corp. Staff. Current Christian Books, 1990. 1990. 79.95 (*0-317-03836-2*) Chr Bksellers.
— Suppliers Directory, 1990. 1990. 67.95 (*0-317-03835-4*) Chr Bksellers.

Cbardenas, Marbia Luz, jt. auth. see Cornish-Bowden, Athel.

CBC Editorial Staff. Modern Workers Compensation, 3 vols. LC 93-71460. 1993. ring bd. 395.00 (*0-685-68853-4*) West Group.
— Nichols Debtor-Creditor Practice Forms, 3 vols. (Commercial Law Ser.). 1993. 320.00 (*0-685-68856-9*) West Group.
— Worker's Compensation Claims Management, 3 vols., Set. LC 94-69181. 1994. ring bd. 495.00 (*0-614-07301-4*) West Group.

CBC Radio Staff. Words on Waves: Selected Radio Plays of Earle Birney. 320p. 1985. 22.95 (*0-919627-71-4*, Pub. by Quarry Pr); pap. 15.95 (*0-919627-73-0*, Pub. by Quarry Pr) LPC InBook.

CBE Style Manual Committee. Scientific Style & Format: The CBE Manual for Authors, Editors, & Publishers. 6th rev. ed. LC 83-7172. (Council of Biology Editors Manual Ser.). (Illus.). 825p. (C). 1995. text 39.95 (*0-521-47154-0*) Coun Biology Eds.

CBEMA Staff. The Information Technology Industry Data Book, 1960-2004. Sayadian, Helga F., ed. 138p. (Orig.). 1994. pap. 59.50 (*0-912797-32-0*) Info Tech Indust.

CBI Industries, Inc. Staff. The Bridge Works: A History of Chicago Bridge & Iron. Harper, Graham, ed. LC 86-63855. 224p. 1987. 10.00 (*0-916371-05-0*) Mobium Pr.

CBL Staff, ed. see Wenzel, George, Jr.

CBMC Staff. Operation Timothy, Set, Bks. 1-4. rev. ed. (Illus.). 1995. wbk. ed. write for info. (*0-945292-07-4*) Christ Busn Mens Committee.
— Operation Timothy: Series & Leader's Guide, Set, Bks. 1-4. rev. ed. (Illus.). 1995. teacher ed., wbk. ed. write for info. (*0-945292-08-2*) Christ Busn Mens Committee.
— Operation Timothy Bk. 1: Finding the Way. (Illus.). 1995. wbk. ed. write for info. (*0-945292-01-5*) Christ Busn Mens Committee.
— Operation Timothy Bk. 2: Knowing the Truth. (Illus.). wbk. ed. write for info. (*0-614-11411-X*) Christ Busn Mens Committee.
— Operation Timothy Bk. 3: Living with Power. rev. ed. (Illus.). wbk. ed. write for info. (*0-945292-03-1*) Christ Busn Mens Committee.
— Operation Timothy Bk. 4: Making a Difference. (Illus.). 1995. wbk. ed. write for info. (*0-945292-05-8*) Christ Busn Mens Committee.

CBO Staff, ed. China's Automotive Industry - Annual Report. 300p. (Orig.). 1998. pap. 395.00 (*0-9650671-5-7*, C B U) China Business.

CBOT Market & Product Development Department Staff, ed. see Burghardt, Galen.

CBS, Inc. Staff. Sixty Minutes Verbatim. LC 80-23836. (Illus.). 1981. lib. bdg. 23.95 (*0-405-13723-0*) Ayer.

CBS Masterworks Staff. Carnaval. (All Time Favorites Ser.). 128p. (Orig.). 1989. pap. 16.95 (*0-8258-0402-7*, ATF114) Fischer Inc NY.

CBS News & New York Times. CBS News-New York Times National Surveys, 1981. LC 84-219135. 1983. write for info. (*0-89138-919-9*) ICPSR.

CBS News Staff & New York Times Staff. CBS News-New York Times National Surveys 1983. 2nd ed. LC 85-60276. 1985. write for info. (*0-89138-891-5*) ICPSR.
— CBS News-The New York Times Election Day Surveys. 2nd ed. LC 84-81926. 1984. write for info. (*0-89138-895-8*) ICPSR.
— CBS News-The New York Times Election Surveys 1980, 2 vols. LC 82-81160. 1982. write for info. (*0-89138-931-8*, ICPSR 7812) ICPSR.
— CBS News-The New York Times Election Surveys 1980, 2 vols., II. LC 82-81160. 1982. write for info. (*0-89138-932-6*) ICPSR.
— CBS News-The New York Times National Surveys. LC 84-81221. 1984. write for info. (*0-89138-897-4*) ICPSR.

CBS News Staff, jt. auth. see New York Times Staff.

CBS Staff. Health: Nutrition Concern Quarterly, 5. (C). 1995. text 67.00 (*0-03-016413-3*) Harcourt.

CBS Staff. Quarterly Concerns: Human Behavior & Education. (C). 1995. 84.00 (*0-15-503120-1*, Pub. by Harcourt Coll Pubs) Harcourt.

***CBS Staff & HMG Staff.** Census of Manufacturing Establishments Nepal 1996-1997 National Level, Regional Level, District Level, Directory, 4 vols. 1998. pap. 110.00 (*0-7855-7527-8*) St Mut.
— A Compendium on Environment Statistics 1998 Nepal. 1998. pap. 55.00 (*0-7855-7528-6*) St Mut.

CBS Staff, jt. auth. see HMG Staff.

CBU Staff, ed. CBU Directory of Foreign Invested Automotive Companies in China. 100p. (Orig.). 1997. pap. 95.00 (*0-9650671-4-9*, C B U) China Business.
— China's Long-Term Strategies for Automotive Related Industries. unabridged ed. 180p. (Orig.). 1997. pap. 595.00 (*0-9650671-3-0*, C B U) China Business.

***CC Pace Systems Staff.** Technology Handbook for Mortgage Executives. 135p. (C). 1998. pap. 125.00 (*1-57599-054-7*, PB2-110118-BK-P, Real Est Fin Pr) Mortgage Bankers.

***CCAI Staff, ed.** SAP R/3 Implementation Guide: A Manager's Guide to Understanding SAP. 1999. pap. 39.99 (*0-672-31576-9*) Sams.

CCAR Committee on Interreligious Activities Staff, ed. Workbook on Interreligious Affairs. 24p. 1982. pap. text 1.50 (*0-916694-72-0*) Central Conf.

Ccar Press Staff. The Union Prayerbook, 1. 365p. 1977. 16.00 (*0-916694-09-7*) Central Conf.

CCAST (World Laboratory) Symposium/Workshop Staff, et al. Charm Physics. LC 87-19781. (China Center of Advanced Science & Technology Ser.). xi, 561p. 1988. write for info. (*2-88124-275-8*) Gordon & Breach.

***CCC (Ruhle) Staff.** Instructor's Manual to Accompany Geology Laboratory Manual for Distance Learning. 80p. (C). 1998. pap. text. write for info. (*0-7872-5734-6*) Kendall-Hunt.

CCC of America Staff. Nicholas: The Boy Who Became Santa. (Illus.). 35p. (J). (ps-4). 1989. 14.99 incl. VHS (*1-56814-003-7*) CCC of America.
— Nicholas: The Boy Who Became Santa. (Illus.). 35p. (J). (ps-6). 1989. pap. text 1.49 (*0-685-62400-5*) CCC of America.

CCC Staff, jt. auth. see Karol, Jim.

CCGS Staff, compiled by. Camas Funeral Home Records, 1912-1943. (Clark County Washington Mortuary/Funeral Home Records Ser.: No. 1). (Illus.). v, 300p. 1993. 20.00 (*1-892685-26-4*) Clark Cnty Gene.
— Clark County Death Records, 1891-1903. 29p. 1986. 3.00 (*1-892685-36-1*) Clark Cnty Gene.
— Clark County Pioneers: Through the Turn of the Century. LC 96-177875. (Illus.). iv, 911p. 1993. 55.00 (*1-892685-00-0*) Clark Cnty Gene.
— Clark County Washington Cemetery Records, Vol. 2. (Illus.). xiv, 217p. 1982. 15.00 (*1-892685-02-7*) Clark Cnty Gene.
— Clark County Washington Cemetery Records, Vol. 3. (Illus.). viii, 272p. 1987. 15.00 (*1-892685-03-5*) Clark Cnty Gene.
— Clark County Washington Cemetery Records, Vol. 4. (Illus.). viii, 274p. 1987. 15.00 (*1-892685-04-3*) Clark Cnty Gene.
— Clark County Washington Cemetery Records, Vol. 5. iii, 346p. 1989. 17.50 (*1-892685-05-1*) Clark Cnty Gene.
— Clark County Washington Cemetery Records Vol. 1: Old City Cemetery of Vancouver. x, 184p. 1981. 15.00 (*1-892685-01-9*) Clark Cnty Gene.
— Clark County Washington Cemetery Records Vol. 6: Camas Cemetery. xiv, 351p. 1989. 17.50 (*1-892685-06-X*) Clark Cnty Gene.
— Clark County, Washington 1880 Census. (Clark County Washington Census Records Ser.: No. 3). 121p. 1986. 15.00 (*1-892685-24-8*) Clark Cnty Gene.
— Clark County Washington Marriages, Vol. 1. x, 244p. 1982. 15.00 (*1-892685-09-4*) Clark Cnty Gene.
— Clark County Washington Marriages, 1897-1904, Vol. 2. vii, 289p. 1984. 15.00 (*1-892685-10-8*) Clark Cnty Gene.
— Clark County Washington Marriages, 1920. 421p. 1993. 17.50 (*1-892685-18-3*) Clark Cnty Gene.
— Clark County Washington Marriages, 1905-1909, Vol. 3. vi, 300p. 1987. 15.00 (*1-892685-11-6*) Clark Cnty Gene.
— Clark County Washington Marriages, 1914-1915, Vol. 5. i, 500p. 1990. 17.50 (*1-892685-13-2*) Clark Cnty Gene.
— Clark County Washington Marriages, 1916, Vol. 6. i, 217p. 1990. 15.00 (*1-892685-14-0*) Clark Cnty Gene.
— Clark County Washington Marriages, 1917, Vol. 7. i, 429p. 1991. 17.50 (*1-892685-15-9*) Clark Cnty Gene.
— Clark County Washington Marriages, 1918, Vol. 8. i, 485p. 1992. 17.50 (*1-892685-16-7*) Clark Cnty Gene.
— Clark County Washington Marriages, 1919, Vol. 9. ii, 429p. 1994. 17.50 (*1-892685-17-5*) Clark Cnty Gene.
— Clark County Washington Marriages, 1921, Vol. 11. iv, 383p. 1995. 17.50 (*1-892685-19-1*) Clark Cnty Gene.
— Clark County Washington Marriages, 1922, Vol. 12. 276p. 1994. 17.50 (*1-892685-20-5*) Clark Cnty Gene.
— Clark County Washington Marriages, 1923, Vol. 13. 311p. 1995. 17.50 (*1-892685-21-3*) Clark Cnty Gene.
— Clark County Washington Marriages, 1910-1913, Vol. 4. vi, 397p. 1989. 17.50 (*1-892685-12-4*) Clark Cnty Gene.
— Clark County, Washington 1900 Census. (Clark County Washington Census Records Ser.: No. 4). ii, 234p. 1991. 20.00 (*1-892685-25-6*) Clark Cnty Gene.
— Diary of Cyrus Shepard, March 4, 1834-December 20, 1835. 120p. 1986. 10.00 (*1-892685-39-6*) Clark Cnty Gene.
— Early Land Records of Clark County, Washington. 39p. 1980. reprint ed. 5.00 (*1-892685-35-3*) Clark Cnty Gene.
— Evergreen Memorial Gardens Cemetery: Vol. 1: A-L; Vol. 2: M-Z, 2 vols. (Washington Cemetery Records Ser.: No. 7 & 8). viii, 952p. 1994. 38.50 (*1-892685-07-8*) Clark Cnty Gene.
— Hamilton Funeral Records, 1917-1929. (Clark County Washington Mortuary/Funeral Home Records Ser.: No. 2). (Illus.). xvi, 104p. 1993. 10.00 (*1-892685-27-2*) Clark Cnty Gene.
— Index to the Annuals of the Fort Vancouver Historical Society, 1960-1985. ii, 107p. 1987. 7.50 (*1-892685-34-5*) Clark Cnty Gene.
— Knapp Mortuary Funerals, 1907-1925, 2 vols. (Washington Mortuary/Funeral Home Records Ser.: No. 3). xvi, 360p. 1992. 20.00 (*1-892685-28-0*) Clark Cnty Gene.
— Knapp Mortuary Funerals, 1926-1940. (Clark County Washington Mortuary/Funeral Home Records Ser.: No. 4). vi, 418p. 1994. 20.00 (*1-892685-29-9*) Clark Cnty Gene.
— The Long Trail to Paradise: Linus Brooks - Founder of Brooks, Oregon Journal of 1850. (Illus.). 162p. 1986. 15.00 (*1-892685-38-8*) Clark Cnty Gene.
— Park Hill Cemetery: Vol. 1: A-G; Vol. 2: H-Q; Vol. 3: R-Z, 3 vols. (Clark County Washington Cemetery Records Ser.: No. 9, 10 & 11). 1267p. 1995. 58.00 (*1-892685-08-6*) Clark Cnty Gene.
— St. Luke's Parish Register: The Diaries of Rev. John McCarty (1853-1868) & Rev. Albert S. Nicholson (1868-1886) xii, 66p. 1987. 7.50 (*1-892685-37-X*) Clark Cnty Gene.
— Skamania County Washington Births, 1893-1926: Deeds & Miscellaneous Records, 1855-1894. (Skamania County Washington Records Ser.: No. 1). ix, 106p. 1987. 10.00 (*1-892685-30-2*) Clark Cnty Gene.
— Skamania County Washington Cemetery Records. (Skamania County Washington Records Ser.: No. 2). (Illus.). xii, 153p. 1987. 15.00 (*1-892685-31-0*) Clark Cnty Gene.
— Skamania County Washington Census Records, 1860, 1870, 1880, 1885, 1887. (Skamania County Washington Records Ser.: No. 4). x, 101p. 1987. 15.00 (*1-892685-33-7*) Clark Cnty Gene.
— Skamania County Washington Marriage Records. (Skamania County Washington Records Ser.: No. 3). viii, 188p. 1987. 15.00 (*1-892685-32-9*) Clark Cnty Gene.
— United States Census of 1870, Washington Counties: Clark, Chehalis, Cowlitz, Island & Jefferson. (Clark County Washington Census Records Ser.: No. 2). (Illus.). xii, 48p. 1983. 15.00 (*1-892685-23-X*) Clark Cnty Gene.
— United States Census of Oregon Territory, 1850 Washington Territory 1860 Clark County. (Clark County Washington Census Records Ser.: No. 1). 68p. 1982. 7.50 (*1-892685-22-1*) Clark Cnty Gene.

CCH Business & Finance Editors. Cost Accounting Standards Board Regulations, Jan. 1, 1997. rev. ed. 240p. 1997. text 24.00 (*0-8080-0141-8*, 000-4753-1) CCH INC.
— Department of Defense FAR Supplement. rev. ed. 1048p. 1997. text 44.00 (*0-8080-0142-6*, 04754101) CCH INC.

CCH Business Law Editors. NASD Manual As of 1/99. 1999. pap. text 49.00 (*0-8080-0357-7*) CCH INC.
— SEC Handbook: Rules & Forms for Financial Statements & Related Discourses. 1200p. 1999. pap. text 48.00 (*0-8080-0353-4*) CCH INC.

CCH Business Owner's Toolkit Editorial Staff. Hire Manage & Retain Employees for Your Small Business. 2nd rev. ed. Handelsman, Joel, ed. (CCH Business Owner's Toolkit Ser.). (Illus.). 304p. 1998. pap. 19.95 (*0-8080-0155-8*) CCH INC.
— Start Run & Grow & Successful Business. 2nd rev. ed. Jacksach, Susan, ed. LC 98-150912. (CCH Business Owner's Toolkit Ser.). (Illus.). 704p. 1998. pap. 24.95 (*0-8080-0156-6*) CCH INC.

CCH Canadian Limited Staff. Canadian Stock Exchanges Manual. 1994. 300.00 (*1-55141-928-9*) CCH Canad.

CCH Editoral Staff Publication. 1998 Social Security Benefits: Including Medicare. rev. ed. 56p. 1998. pap. 10.00 (*0-8080-0217-1*) CCH INC.

***CCH Editorial Staff.** CCH State Payroll Law Handback. 500p. 2000. pap. 125.00 (*0-8080-0485-9*) CCH INC.

CCH Editorial Staff. CCH State Payroll Law Handbook. 2nd ed. LC 98-176384. 450p. (Orig.). 1998. pap. 125.00 (*0-8080-0224-4*) CCH INC.
— CCH State Payroll Law Handbook. 3rd ed. LC 99-461771. (Payroll Management Professional Ser.). 500p. (Orig.). 1999. pap. 125.00 (*0-8080-0310-0*) CCH INC.
— Facsimile Tax Return: Problems & Forms - 1998 Edition. 88p. 1998. wbk. ed. 13.95 (*0-8080-0233-3*) CCH INC.

***CCH Editorial Staff.** Federal Estate & Gift Taxes: Code & Regulations: Including Related Income Tax Provisions. rev. ed. 1475p. 2000. pap. text 47.00 (*0-8080-0480-8*) CCH INC.
— Federal Estate & Gift Taxes - Code & Regulations: Including Related Income Tax Provisions, As of March 9, 1999. rev. ed. 1400p. (C). 1999. pap. text 44.95 (*0-8080-0359-3*) CCH INC.

CCH Editorial Staff. Highlights of IRS Restructuring & Reform Act of 1998. 32p. 1998. pap. text 7.00 (*0-8080-0282-1*) CCH INC.
— Hire, Manage & Retain Employees for Your Small Business. Handelsman, Joel, ed. (CCH Business Owner's Toolkit Ser.). (Illus.). 312p. (Orig.). 1997. pap. 24.95 (*0-8080-0175-2*) CCH INC.
— Income Tax Regulations: Including Proposed Regulations As of January 11, 1999, 6 vols. rev. ed. 10000p. 1999. pap. text 92.00 (*0-8080-0344-5*) CCH INC.

***CCH Editorial Staff.** Income Tax Regulations: Including Proposed Regulations as of January 11, 2000. rev. ed. 10,000p. 2000. pap. text 99.00 (*0-8080-0468-9*) CCH INC.

CCH Editorial Staff. Income Tax Regulations: Including Proposed Regulations As of January 13, 1998. rev. ed. 1998. pap. text 82.95 (*0-8080-0226-0*) CCH INC.
— Internal Revenue Code, 2 vols. rev. ed. 4200p. 1998. pap. text 59.00 (*0-8080-0312-7*) CCH INC.
— Medicare & Choice Interim Final Rule: Regulations Effective July 27, 1998 Including CCH Executive Summary & Medicare & Choice Provisions from the Balanced Budget Act of 1997. (Health Law Professional Ser.). 320p. 1998. pap. 49.95 (*0-8080-0283-X*) CCH INC.
— New York State Tax Law. 1150p. 1998. pap. 37.95 (*0-8080-0251-1*) CCH INC.
— 1998 Guidebook to Massachusetts Taxes. 1998. pap. 37.95 (*0-8080-0231-7*) CCH INC.
— 1998 Guidebook to New Jersey Taxes. 1998. pap. 37.95 (*0-8080-0230-9*) CCH INC.
— 1998 Guidebook to New York Taxes. 1998. pap. 37.95 (*0-8080-0232-5*) CCH INC.
— 1998 U. S. Master Tax Guide. 688p. Date not set. pap. 37.95 (*0-8080-0162-0*) CCH INC.
— 1999 Federal Witholding Tables with Highlights, Effective January 1, 1999. (Payroll Professional Management Ser.). 40p. 1998. pap. 17.50 (*0-8080-0300-3*) CCH INC.
— 1999 Fee Schedule & Payment Policies for Physician's Medicare Services. rev. ed. 300p. 1998. pap. 45.00 (*0-8080-0303-8*) CCH INC.
— 1999 Medicare & Medicaid Benefits. rev. ed. 48p. 1999. pap. 10.00 (*0-8080-0308-9*) CCH INC.
— 1999 Medicare Explained. 224p. 1999. pap. 25.00 (*0-8080-0307-0*) CCH INC.
— 1999 New York State Sales & Use Tax Law & Regulations. rev. ed. 1400p. 1999. pap. text 89.00 (*0-8080-0314-3*) CCH INC.
— 1999 New York State Tax Law. rev. ed. 700p. 1999. pap. text 79.00 (*0-8080-0315-1*) CCH INC.
— 1999 Social Security Benefits Including Medicare. rev. ed. 64p. 1999. pap. 10.00 (*0-8080-0309-7*) CCH INC.
— 1999 U. S. Master Tax Guide. 720p. 1998. text 59.95 (*0-8080-0293-7*); pap. text 42.95 (*0-8080-0294-5*) CCH INC.
— 1999 U. S. Master Tax Guide CCH Federal Tax Service Edition. 720p. 1998. pap. text 42.95 (*0-8080-0311-9*) CCH INC.
— 1997 Investment Allocation Percentages. 600p. 1998. pap. 29.95 (*0-8080-0252-X*) CCH INC.
— 1997 Medicare & Medicaid Legislation: Law & Explanation. 900p. Date not set. pap. text 85.00 (*0-8080-0169-8*) CCH INC.
— NY State Corporation Tax Law & Regulations. 484p. 1998. pap. 99.95 (*0-8080-0258-9*) CCH INC.
— NY State Sales & Use Tax Law & Regulations. LC 98-174985. 952p. 1998. pap. 89.95 (*0-8080-0259-7*) CCH INC.
— Occupational Safety & Health Standards for General Industry: With Amendments As of February 1, 1999. (Illus.). 864p. 1999. pap. 42.95 (*0-8080-0350-X*) CCH INC.
— Occupational Safety & Health Standards for General Industry - As of February 1, 1998. rev. ed. (Safety Professional Ser.). 850p. 1998. pap. 39.50 (*0-8080-0245-7*) CCH INC.
— Occupational Safety & Health Standards for the Construction Industry: With Amendments As of February 1, 1999. 615p. 1999. pap. 34.95 (*0-8080-0351-8*) CCH INC.
— Pension & Employee Benefit Changes under 1997 Tax & Budget Acts. 272p. Date not set. pap. text 39.00 (*0-8080-0161-2*) CCH INC.
— Pension & Employee Benefits Code - ERISA - Regulations Vol. 3: Preambles to Final & Temporary Regulations. rev. ed. 1216p. 1998. pap. 30.00 (*0-8080-0236-8*) CCH INC.
— Pension & Employee Benefits Code ERISA Regulations Vol. 1: Internal Revenue Code & Regulations. rev. ed. 2000p. 1998. pap. 39.50 (*0-8080-0234-1*) CCH INC.
— Pension & Employee Benefits, Code, ERISA, Regulations as of January 1, 1999 Vol. 1: Internal Revenue Code & Regulations. 2300p. 1999. pap. 54.50 (*0-8080-0341-0*) CCH INC.
— Pension & Employee Benefits, Code, ERISA, Regulations as of January 1, 1999 Vol. 2: ERISA Laws & Regulations Related Laws Proposed Regulations. 1450p. 1999. pap. 54.50 (*0-8080-0342-9*) CCH INC.
— Pension & Employee Benefits, Code, ERISA, Regulations as of January 1, 1999 Vol. 3: Preambles to Final & Temporary Regulations. 1250p. 1999. pap. 30.00 (*0-8080-0343-7*) CCH INC.
— SEC Handbook: Rules & Forms for Financial Statements & Related Disclosures. Tavares, Carlos, ed. 1048p. 1996. pap. text 42.00 (*0-8080-0132-9*, 04805001) CCH INC.
— Start, Run & Grow a Successful Small Business. Jacksack, Susan, ed. (CCH Business Owner's Toolkit Ser.). (Illus.). 720p. (Orig.). 1997. pap. 39.95 (*0-8080-0176-0*) CCH INC.
— State Individual Rights Laws: Labor Relations, Employee Leave, Employee Rights & Protections. 2nd ed. LC 99-462512. (Employment & Human Resources Professional Ser.). 1200p. 1999. pap. 125.00 (*0-8080-0361-5*) CCH INC.
— Tax & Relief Extension Act of 1998: Law & Explanation. LC 99-159587. 120p. 1998. pap. text 26.95 (*0-8080-0298-8*) CCH INC.

***CCH Editorial Staff.** Tax Relief Extension Act of 1999: Explanation. 40p. 2000. pap. text 12.00 (*0-8080-0467-0*) CCH INC.

CCH Editorial Staff. U. S. Master Excise Tax Guide. LC 98-214976. 304p. 1998. pap. text 45.95 (*0-8080-0280-5*) CCH INC.

CCH Editorial Staff, ed. CCH State Payroll Law Handbook. LC 98-106661. 400p. (Orig.). 1997. pap. 125.00 (*0-8080-0144-2*) CCH INC.
— 1998 Guidebook to Pennsylvania Taxes. rev. ed. 320p. 1998. pap. 37.95 (*0-8080-0219-8*) CCH INC.
— 1998 U. S. Master Depreciation Guide. 1998. pap. text 37.95 (*0-8080-0253-8*) CCH INC.

CCH Editorial Staff, ed. 1999 Investment Allocation Percentages. rev. ed. pap. text 35.00 (*0-8080-0488-3*) CCH INC.

CCH Editorial Staff, ed. 1999 New York State Corporation Tax Law & Regulations. rev. ed. 600p. 1999. pap. text 99.00 (*0-8080-0313-5*) CCH INC.
— 1999 Pocketax for Returns of 1998 Income. rev. ed. 85p. 1998. pap. text 7.50 (*0-8080-0319-4*) CCH INC.
— 1997 Medicare Explained. rev. ed. 192p. 1997. pap. text 22.00 (*0-8080-0147-7*, 4750) CCH INC.
— 1997 U. S. Master Depreciation Guide. 560p. 1997. pap. text 32.95 (*0-8080-0150-7*) CCH INC.
— Occupational Safety & Health Standards for the

C

Construction Industry - As of February 1, 1998. LC 98-160157. (Safety Professional Ser.). 560p. 1998. pap. 29.50 (*0-8080-0246-5*) CCH INC.
— Prospective Payment Systems for Inpatient Hospital Services Fiscal Year 1998 Regulations & Rates: Final Rule with Provider Reimbursement Provisions from the Balanced Budget Act of 1997. LC 98-170465. 256p. 1997. pap. 18.00 (*0-8080-0158-2*) CCH INC.
— Securities, Commodities & Banking: 1998 Year in Review. 150p. 1998. pap. text 55.00 (*0-8080-0295-3*) CCH INC.
CCH Editorial Staff, ed. Federal Estate & Gift Tax-Explained. 30th rev. ed. 512p. 1997. pap. text 26.00 (*0-8080-0145-0*) CCH INC.
— Federal Estate & Gift Taxes - Code & Regulations: Including Related Income Tax Provisions, As of April 18, 1997. rev. ed. 1384p. (C). 1997. pap. text 34.00 (*0-8080-0197-3*) CCH INC.
CCH Editorial Staff, ed. Federal Estate & Gift Taxes - Code & Regulations: Including Related Income Tax Provision As of January 1, 1998. rev. ed. 1400p. (C). 1998. pap. text 42.95 (*0-8080-0238-4*) CCH INC.
CCH Editorial Staff & Brown, Eric, eds. Federal Estate & Gift Taxes Explained. rev. ed. 512p. 1998. pap. text 37.95 (*0-8080-0250-3*) CCH INC.
CCH Editorial Staff Publication. 1998 Medicare Explained. (Health Law Professional Ser.). 200p. 1998. pap. 25.00 (*0-8080-0215-5*) CCH INC.
— 1998 Social Security Explained. rev. ed. 320p. 1998. pap. 30.00 (*0-8080-0216-3*) CCH INC.
— Pension & Employee Benefits Code - ERISA - Regulations: ERISA Law & Regulations - Related Laws - Proposed Regulations. rev. ed. 4550p. 1998. pap. 39.50 (*0-8080-0235-X*) CCH INC.
CCH Editorial Staff Publication, ed. 1998 Medicare & Medicaid Benefits. rev. ed. (Health Law Professional Ser.). 340p. 1998. pap. text 10.00 (*0-8080-0214-7*) CCH INC.
CCH Editorial Staff Publication, ed. OSHA Standards for the construction Industry. (Safety Professional Series). 700p. pap. text 37.50 (*0-8080-0474-3*) CCH INC.
— OSHA Standards for the General Industry. (Safety Professional Series). 1100p. 2000. pap. 45.95 (*0-8080-0473-5*) CCH INC.
CCH Editors. CCH Federal Tax Service 1998 U. S. Master Tax Guide: 1998 Edition. 684p. 1997. pap. text 37.95 (*0-8080-0174-4*) CCH INC.
***CCH Editors.** Commodity Exchange Act Regulations & Forms: December 1999. rev. ed. 968p. 1999. pap. text 46.50 (*0-8080-0458-1*) CCH INC.
— Corporation Partnership Fiduciary: Filled-In Tax Return Forms. rev. ed. 144p. 2000. pap. text 31.00 (*0-8080-0451-4*) CCH INC.
CCH Editors. Corporation Partnership Fiduciary: Filled-In Tax Return Forms, 1999. rev. ed. 144p. 1999. pap. text 21.50 (*0-8080-0337-2*) CCH INC.
***CCH Editors.** Federal Income Taxes of Decedents, Estates & Trusts. 19th ed. 210p. 1999. pap. text 45.00 (*0-8080-0414-X*, 0-5220-100) CCH INC.
CCH Editors. Guide to Limited Liability Companies. 4th ed. LC 98-123511. 269p. 1997. pap. 37.95 (*0-8080-0170-1*) CCH INC.
— Income Tax Regulations: Including Proposed Regulations As of June 10, 1998, 6 vols. rev. ed. 10000p. 1998. pap. text 82.95 (*0-8080-0277-5*) CCH INC.
***CCH Editors.** Income Tax Regulations: Including Proposed Regulations as of June 10, 1999, 6 vols. rev. ed. 1999. pap. text 95.00 (*0-8080-0379-8*) CCH INC.
— Internal Revenue Code: Income, Estate, Gift, Employment & Excise Taxes As of November, 1999. rev. ed. 4900p. (C). 1999. pap. text 65.00 (*0-8080-0447-6*) CCH INC.
— Medicare & Medicaid Laws & Regulations As of January 1, 2000, 2 vols. 2650p. 2000. pap. text 160.00 (*0-8080-0462-X*) CCH INC.
CCH Editors. 1998 Federal Tax Withholding Tables with Highlights, Effective January 1, 1998. LC 99-202854. 40p. 1998. pap. 17.50 (*0-8080-0209-0*) CCH INC.
— 1998 Fee Schedule & Payment Policies for Physicians' Medicare Services. (Health Law Professional Ser.). 300p. 1997. pap. 45.00 (*0-8080-0200-7*) CCH INC.
— 1998 Tax Year in Review. 260p. 1999. pap. text 42.95 (*0-8080-0339-9*) CCH INC.
— 1998 U. S. Master Tax Guide. 98th ed. 684p. 1997. text 54.95 (*0-8080-0173-6*) CCH INC.
***CCH Editors.** 1999 Federal Tax Forms for Individuals & Businesses: Including Sample Filled-In Tax Returns. 1568p. 2000. pap. text 99.00 (*0-8080-0465-4*) CCH INC.
CCH Editors. 1999 U. S. Master Depreciation Guide. rev. ed. 560p. Date not set. pap. text 41.95 (*0-8080-0349-6*) CCH INC.
***CCH Editors.** Pension & Employee Benefits Code - ERISA - Regulations, Vol. 2. 2200p. 2000. pap. 57.50 (*0-8080-0460-3*) CCH INC.
— Pension & Employee Benefits Code - ERISA - Regulations Vol. 1: Internal Revenue Code & Regulations. 2300p. 2000. pap. 57.50 (*0-8080-0461-1*) CCH INC.
— Pension & Employee Benefits Code - ERISA - Regulations Vol. 3: Preambles. 1300p. 2000. pap. 32.00 (*0-8080-0459-X*) CCH INC.
— State Compensation Laws: Minimum Wage/Overtime - Prevailing Wage - Wage Payment. 2350p. 2000. pap. 125.00 (*0-8080-0463-8*) CCH INC.
CCH Editors. State Compensation Laws & Regulations: Minimum Wage/Overtime, Prevailing Wage, Wage Payment. Shipley, Sharon A., ed. LC 98-135805. (Employment & Human Resources Professional Ser.). 2400p. 1997. pap. 125.00 (*0-8080-0202-3*) CCH INC.
— State Individual Employment Rights Laws. LC 99-164445. 2000p. 1998. pap. 125.00 (*0-8080-0273-2*) CCH INC.
***CCH Editors.** State Individual Employment Rights Laws. 1500p. 2000. pap. 125.00 (*0-8080-0464-6*) CCH INC.
— State Tax Handbook. 380p. (C). 1999. pap. text 44.00 (*0-8080-0448-4*) CCH INC.
— 2000 Medicare & Medicaid Benefits. pap. 10.00 (*0-8080-0443-3*) CCH INC.
— 2000 Medicare Explained. pap. 25.00 (*0-8080-0444-1*) CCH INC.
— 2000 Pocketax: For Returns of 1999 Income. rev. ed. 85p. 1999. pap. text 8.00 (*0-8080-0434-4*) CCH INC.
— 2000 U. S. Master Depreciation Guide. rev. ed. 560p. 2000. pap. text 45.00 (*0-8080-0435-2*) CCH INC.
***CCH Editors, ed.** CCH Federal Tax Service U. S. Master Tax Guide, 2000. 720p. 1999. pap. text 46.00 (*0-8080-0423-9*) CCH INC.
— CCH Guide to Record Retention Requirements. 406p. 1999. pap. 49.95 (*0-8080-0425-5*) CCH INC.
— Facsimile Tax Return Problems & Forms. 87p. 2000. pap. text 14.00 (*0-8080-0469-7*) CCH INC.
CCH Editors, ed. 1997 Security Transactions: Taxation of Your Stock & Bond Transactions. 64p. 1997. pap. text 7.75 (*0-8080-0206-6*) CCH INC.
***CCH Editors, ed.** Internal Revenue Code & Income Estate, Gift, Employment & Excise Taxes, as of June 1999. rev. ed. 4900p. (C). 1999. pap. text 62.00 (*0-8080-0384-4*) CCH INC.
***CCH Editors & Brown, Eric, eds.** Federal Estate & Gift Taxes Explained. 32nd rev. ed. 544p. 1999. pap. text 42.95 (*0-8080-0375-5*) CCH INC.
CCH Inc. Staff. Benequick 2.0. 5th rev. ed. 1996. 4.49 (*0-943293-03-0*) ViewPlan.
— Factuary 1.0. 6th rev. ed. 1994. 4.49 (*0-943293-08-1*) ViewPlan.
— Progeny 2.0. 5th rev. ed. 1992. 4.49 (*0-943293-01-4*) ViewPlan.
— Vista 2.0. 5th rev. ed. 1997. 8.49 (*0-943293-09-X*) ViewPlan.
CCH Inc. Staff, jt. auth. see View Plan Staff.
CCH Incorporated Staff. NASD Manual April, 1998. 1500p. 1998. pap. text 44.00 (*0-8080-0279-1*) CCH INC.
— 1997 Tax Year in Review. LC 98-147328. 200 p. 1998. write for info. (*0-8080-0237-6*) CCH INC.
CCH Incorporated Staff. Office of the Comptroller of the Currency: Laws & Regulations. LC 94-213090. 339p. 1994. write for info. (*0-8080-0023-3*) CCH INC.
***CCH Staff.** Car, Travel & Entertainment & Home Office Deductions. rev. ed. 190p. 1999. pap. text 42.00 (*0-8080-0426-3*) CCH INC.
CCH Staff. Facsimile Tax Return Problems & Forms (1999 Edition) rev. ed. 1998. pap. text 13.95 (*0-8080-0345-3*) CCH INC.
— Federal Tax Course. (C). 1997. pap. text, teacher ed. write for info. (*0-8080-0182-5*) CCH INC.
— Federal Tax Course: Study Guide. (C). 1997. pap. text, student ed. 30.00 (*0-8080-0183-3*) CCH INC.
— Federal Tax Course (General Edition) (C). 1997. text 105.00 (*0-8080-0181-7*) CCH INC.
— Federal Tax Course (General Edition) 1998. text 112.00 (*0-8080-0255-4*) CCH INC.
— Federal Tax Course Instructor's Guide. (C). 1998. pap. text 77.50 (*0-8080-0256-2*) CCH INC.
— Federal Tax Course (School Edition) (C). 1997. text 77.50 (*0-8080-0180-9*) CCH INC.
— Federal Tax Course (School Edition) (C). 1998. text 79.00 (*0-8080-0254-6*) CCH INC.
***CCH Staff.** Individuals' Filled-In Tax Return Forms (1999 Edition) rev. ed. 1999. pap. text 29.50 (*0-8080-0338-0*) CCH INC.
CCH Staff. Medicare & Medicaid Laws & Regulations As of August 20, 1998, 2 vols. (Vol. 1: Laws). 2958p. 1998. pap. 199.00 (*0-8080-0289-9*) CCH INC.
— 1998 Tax Legislation Law, Explanation & Analysis: IRS Restructuring & Reform. 816 p. 1998. pap. text 34.95 (*0-8080-0281-3*) CCH INC.
***CCH Staff.** Tax Angles for Special Taxpayers, 2000. rev. ed. 1999. pap. text 75.00 (*0-8080-0427-1*) CCH INC.
CCH Staff. 2000 Federal Tax Course: General Edition. rev. ed. (C). 1999. text 117.00 (*0-8080-0365-8*) CCH INC.
— 2000 Federal Tax Course: Instructor's Guide. rev. ed. 1999. teacher ed. write for info. (*0-8080-0366-6*) CCH INC.
— 2000 Federal Tax Course: School Edition. rev. ed. (C). 1999. 83.00 (*0-8080-0364-X*) CCH INC.
***CCH Staff.** 2001 Federal Tax Course: School Edition. rev. ed. (C). 2000. text 86.00 (*0-8080-0489-1*) CCH INC.
— 2001 Federal Tax Guide: General Edition. rev. ed. (C). 2000. text 123.00 (*0-8080-0490-5*) CCH INC.
CCH Staff, ed. Internal Revenue Code, Vol. 1. 1998. pap. text 56.95 (*0-8080-0261-9*) CCH INC.
CCH Tax Law Editors. California Income Tax Laws & Regulations: 1998 Edition. annot. ed. 1600p. 1998. pap. 95.00 (*0-8080-0210-4*) CCH INC.
***CCH Tax Law Editors.** California Income Tax Laws & Regulations: 2000 Edition. annot. ed. 1648p. 2000. pap. 115.00 (*0-8080-0453-0*) CCH INC.
CCH Tax Law Editors. California Income Tax Laws & Regulations Annotated - 1997 Edition. 1700p. 1997. pap. 89.00 (*0-8080-0139-6*) CCH INC.
— California Income Tax Laws & Regulations Annotated - 1999 Edition. 1552p. 1999. pap. 105.00 (*0-8080-0346-1*) CCH INC.
— Federal Tax Forms for Individuals & Business, Including Sample Filled-In Forms. 1500p. 1999. pap. text 99.00 (*0-8080-0355-0*) CCH INC.
***CCH Tax Law Editors.** Guide Book to New Jersey Taxes, 2000. 256p. 2000. 44.00 (*0-8080-0399-2*) CCH INC.
— Guide Book to California Taxes, 2000. 688p. pap. 44.00 (*0-8080-0401-8*) CCH INC.
— Guide Book to Connecticut Taxes, 2000. 256p. 2000. pap. 44.00 (*0-8080-0403-4*) CCH INC.
— Guide Book to Florida Taxes, 2000. 240p. 2000. pap. 44.00 (*0-8080-0406-9*) CCH INC.
— Guide Book to Illinois Taxes, 2000. 272p. 2000. pap. 44.00 (*0-8080-0409-3*) CCH INC.
— Guide Book to Indiana Taxes, 2000. 256p. 2000. pap. 44.00 (*0-8080-0402-6*) CCH INC.
— Guide Book to Massachusetts Taxes, 2000. 240p. 2000. pap. 44.00 (*0-8080-0411-5*) CCH INC.
— Guide Book to Michigan Taxes, 2000. 288p. 2000. pap. 44.00 (*0-8080-0408-5*) CCH INC.
— Guide Book to New York Taxes, 2000. 464p. 2000. pap. 44.00 (*0-8080-0400-X*) CCH INC.
— Guide Book to North Carolina Taxes, 2000. 288p. 2000. pap. 44.00 (*0-8080-0405-0*) CCH INC.
— Guide Book to Pennsylvania Taxes, 2000. 288p. 2000. pap. 44.00 (*0-8080-0407-7*) CCH INC.
— Guide Book to Texas Taxes, 2000. 256p. 2000. pap. 44.00 (*0-8080-0404-2*) CCH INC.
— Guide to Limited Liability Companies. 5th ed. 300p. 1999. pap. text 45.00 (*0-8080-0429-8*) CCH INC.
— Guide to Ohio Taxes, 2000. 304p. 2000. pap. 44.00 (*0-8080-0410-7*) CCH INC.
CCH Tax Law Editors. Guidebook to California Taxes. 388p. 1999. pap. 41.95 (*0-8080-0328-3*) CCH INC.
— Guidebook to Florida Taxes. 202p. 1998. pap. 37.95 (*0-8080-0163-9*) CCH INC.
— Guidebook to Florida Taxes. 208p. 1999. pap. 41.95 (*0-8080-0330-5*) CCH INC.
— Guidebook to Illinois Taxes. 256p. 1998. pap. 37.95 (*0-8080-0167-1*) CCH INC.
— Guidebook to Illinois Taxes. 256p. 1999. pap. 41.95 (*0-8080-0324-0*) CCH INC.
— Guidebook to Massachusetts Taxes. 208p. 1999. pap. 41.95 (*0-8080-0329-1*) CCH INC.
— Guidebook to Michigan Taxes. 272p. 1997. pap. 41.95 (*0-8080-0327-5*) CCH INC.
— Guidebook to Michigan Taxes. 272p. 1998. pap. 37.95 (*0-8080-0166-3*) CCH INC.
— Guidebook to New Jersey Taxes. 256p. 1999. pap. 41.95 (*0-8080-0326-7*) CCH INC.
— Guidebook to New York Taxes. 496p. 1998. pap. 41.95 (*0-8080-0325-9*) CCH INC.
— Guidebook to North Carolina Taxes. 1998. pap. 37.95 (*0-8080-0165-5*) CCH INC.
— Guidebook to North Carolina Taxes. 256p. 1999. pap. 41.95 (*0-8080-0331-3*) CCH INC.
— Guidebook to Ohio Taxes. 288p. 1998. pap. 37.95 (*0-8080-0164-7*) CCH INC.
— Guidebook to Ohio Taxes. 304p. 1999. pap. 41.95 (*0-8080-0332-1*) CCH INC.
***CCH Tax Law Editors.** Guidebook to Pennsylvania Taxes. 288p. 1999. pap. 41.95 (*0-8080-0333-X*) CCH INC.
— New York State Corporation Tax Law & Regulations: 2000 Edition. 544p. 2000. pap. 99.00 (*0-8080-0456-5*) CCH INC.
— New York State Personal Income Tax Law & Regulations: 2000 Edition. 624p. 2000. pap. 99.00 (*0-8080-0457-3*) CCH INC.
— New York State Sales & Use Tax Law & Regulations: 2000 Edition. 1120p. 2000. pap. 95.00 (*0-8080-0454-9*) CCH INC.
— New York State Tax Law: 2000 Edition. 1248p. 2000. pap. 80.00 (*0-8080-0455-7*) CCH INC.
CCH Tax Law Editors. 1998 Guidebook to California Taxes. 49th ed. 648p. 1998. pap. 37.50 (*0-8080-0207-4*) CCH INC.
— 1998 Investment Allocation Percentages for New York State & New York City. 680p. 1999. pap. text 32.95 (*0-8080-0356-9*) CCH INC.
— 1998 State Tax Handbook. Sotelo, Victor & Plunkett, Brian, eds. 388p. 1998. pap. 39.95 (*0-8080-0211-2*) CCH INC.
— 1999 Guidebook to California Taxes. 50th ed. (Illus.). 672p. 1999. text 41.95 (*0-8080-0286-4*) CCH INC.
***CCH Tax Law Editors.** 1999 Tax Year in Review. 268p. 2000. pap. text 42.00 (*0-8080-0471-9*) CCH INC.
CCH Tax Law Editors. U. S. Master Sales Tax Guide. 800p. 1998. pap. 49.95 (*0-8080-0168-X*) CCH INC.
***CCH Tax Law Editors.** U.S. Master Multistate Corporate Tax Guide. 1100p. 2000. pap. text 67.00 (*0-8080-0493-X*) CCH INC.
— U.S. Master Sales & Use Tax Guide. 2000th ed. 928p. 2000. pap. 57.00 (*0-8080-0479-4*) CCH INC.
CCH Tax Law Editors. Use Tax Guide. 944p. 1999. pap. text 52.95 (*0-8080-0360-7*) CCH INC.
***CCH Tax Law Editors.** Year-End Tax Strategies, 1999. 48p. 1999. pap. text 15.00 (*0-8080-0419-0*) CCH INC.
CCH Tax Law Editors, ed. New York State Law Including Law Provisions Imposing Admissions & Sales Tax December 1998. (Orig.). pap. 65.00 (*0-8080-0143-4*) CCH INC.
***CCM Staff.** Avalon. LC 99-44487. (Story Behind the Music Ser.). 128p. 1999. pap. 8.99 (*0-7369-0275-9*) Harvest Hse.
— Caedmon's Call. (Lifelines Ser.). 128p. Date not set. pap. 8.99 (*0-7369-0344-5*) Harvest Hse.
— Jaci Velasquez. (Lifelines Ser.). 128p. 2000. pap. 8.99 (*0-7369-0444-1*) Harvest Hse.
— Lifelines: Audio Adrenaline. (Lifelines Ser.). 128p. 2000. pap. 8.99 (*0-7369-0430-1*) Harvest Hse.
— Lifelines: Sixpence None the Richer. (Story Behind the Music Ser.). 128p. Date not set. pap. 7.99 (*0-7369-0248-1*) Harvest Hse.
— Point of Grace. (Lifelines Ser.). 128p. 2001. pap. 8.99 (*0-7369-0443-3*) Harvest Hse.
— Steven Curtis Chapman. LC 99-57613. 128p. 2000. pap. 8.99 (*0-7369-0272-4*) Harvest Hse.
***CCM Staff, et al.** CCM Presents: The 100 Greatest Albums in Christian Music. 300p. 2001. pap. 12.99 (*0-7369-0281-3*) Harvest Hse.
CCN Editorial Staff. 1997 Tax Legislation Law, Explanation & Analysis: Taxpayer Relief Act of 1997. LC 97-211656. 1200p. 1997. pap. text 42.50 (*0-8080-0152-3*) CCH INC.
Ccotbe, Roger A. & College of American Pathologists Staff. Snomed International: The Systematized Nomenclature of Human & Veterinary Medicine, 4 vols. 3rd ed. LC 98-221770. 1993. write for info. (*0-930304-48-9*) Coll Am Pathol.
CCPS, AIChE. Guidelines for Evaluating Process Plant Buildings for External Explosion or Fire. LC 94-24458. 1996. 140.00 (*0-8169-0646-7*, G-26) Am Inst Chem Eng.
CCS Center for Health & Human Services Staff, jt. auth. see North Manhattan Health Action Group Report Staff.
CCS Inc. Staff. Eastern Fairfield County. (Street Directions Without a Map Ser.). 187p. 1992. pap. 14.95 (*1-881638-00-6*) CCS Inc.
— Eastern New Haven County. (Street Directions Without a Map Ser.). 145p. 1992. pap. 14.95 (*1-881638-05-7*) CCS Inc.
— Litchfield County. (Street Directions Without a Map Ser.). 150p. 1992. pap. 14.95 (*1-881638-03-0*) CCS Inc.
— Southern Fairfield County. (Street Directions Without a Map Ser.). 180p. 1992. pap. 14.95 (*1-881638-02-2*) CCS Inc.
— Southern New Haven County. (Street Directions Without a Map Ser.). 143p. 1992. pap. 14.95 (*1-881638-06-5*) CCS Inc.
— Western Fairfield County. (Street Directions Without a Map Ser.). 100p. 1992. pap. 14.95 (*1-881638-01-4*) CCS Inc.
— Western New Haven County. (Street Directions Without a Map Ser.). 144p. 1992. pap. 14.95 (*1-881638-04-9*) CCS Inc.
CCS Staff. Bloodborne Pathogen Exposure Control Guidelines. 1993. pap. 25.00 (*0-944352-07-3*) Cleaning Cons.
CCS Staff. Diccionario de Catequetica. (SPA.). 850p. 1987. 150.00 (*0-7859-3443-X*, 847043456X) Fr & Eur.
***CCTA Staff.** Acquisition. (IS Management Guides Ser.). (Illus.). 74p. 2000. 50.00 (*1-903091-03-9*, Pub. by Format Pubg Ltd) Balogh.
CCTA Staff. Capacity Management. (IT Infrastructure Library Ser.). 200p. 1991. pap. 80.00 (*0-11-330544-3*, Pub. by Statnry Office) Sftware Mgmt Network.
— Change Management. (IT Infrastructure Library Ser.). 54p. 1989. pap. 80.00 (*0-11-330525-7*, Pub. by Statnry Office) Sftware Mgmt Network.
— Configuration Management. (IT Infrastructure Library Ser.). 77p. 1990. pap. 80.00 (*0-11-330530-3*, Pub. by Statnry Office) Sftware Mgmt Network.
— Contingency Planning. (IT Infrastructure Library Ser.). 64p. 1989. pap. 80.00 (*0-11-330524-9*, Pub. by Statnry Office) Sftware Mgmt Network.
— Cost Management for Information Technology Services. (IT Infrastructure Library Ser.). 76p. 1991. pap. 80.00 (*0-11-330547-8*, Pub. by Statnry Office) Sftware Mgmt Network.
— Data Management. (IT Infrastructure Library Ser.). 1994. pap. 70.00 (*0-11-330634-2*, Pub. by Statnry Office) Sftware Mgmt Network.
— Data Management Standards. (IT Infrastructure Library Ser.). 94p. 1995. pap. 75.00 (*0-11-330670-9*, Pub. by Statnry Office) Sftware Mgmt Network.
— Help Desk. (IT Infrastructure Library Ser.). 76p. 1989. pap. 80.00 (*0-11-330522-2*, Pub. by Statnry Office) Sftware Mgmt Network.
— Information Technology Infrastructure Library Practices for Small Information Technology Units. (IT Infrastructure Library Ser.). 110p. 1995. pap. 75.00 (*0-11-330674-1*, Pub. by Statnry Office) Sftware Mgmt Network.
— Information Technology Infrastructure Support Tools. (IT Infrastructure Library Ser.). 166p. 1992. pap. 85.00 (*0-11-330586-9*, HM05869, Pub. by Statnry Office) Sftware Mgmt Network.
— Information Technology Service Management Case Studies. (IT Infrastructure Library Ser.). 166p. 1996. pap. 100.00 (*0-11-330676-8*, Pub. by Statnry Office) Sftware Mgmt Network.
— Information Technology Services Organization. (IT Infrastructure Library Ser.). 110p. 1993. pap. 70.00 (*0-11-330563-X*, Pub. by Statnry Office) Sftware Mgmt Network.
— An Introduction to Information Technology Infrastructure Planning. (IT Infrastructure Library Ser.). 70p. 1995. pap. 65.00 (*0-11-330617-2*, Pub. by Statnry Office) Sftware Mgmt Network.
— Introduction to Managing Project Risk. 52p. 1995. pap. 45.00 (*0-11-330671-7*, HM06717, Pub. by Statnry Office) Bernan Associates.
***CCTA Staff.** IS Strategy: Process & Products. (IS Practice Guides Ser.). (Illus.). 105p. 2000. 50.00 (*1-903091-00-4*, Pub. by Format Pubg Ltd) Balogh.
CCTA Staff. Justifying Investment in Information Systems. 94p. 1989. pap. text 112.00 (*0-471-92529-2*) Wiley.
***CCTA Staff.** Managing Change. (IS Management Guides Ser.). (Illus.). 81p. 2000. 50.00 (*1-903091-01-2*, Pub. by Format Pubg Ltd) Balogh.
CCTA Staff. Managing Facilities Management. (IT Infrastructure Library Ser.). viii, 67p. 1990. pap. 80.00 (*0-11-330526-5*, Pub. by Statnry Office) Sftware Mgmt Network.
***CCTA Staff.** Managing Performance. (IS Management Guides Ser.). (Illus.). 99p. 2000. 50.00 (*1-903091-05-5*, Pub. by Format Pubg Ltd) Balogh.
— Managing Services. (IS Management Guides Ser.). (Illus.). 82p. 2000. 50.00 (*1-903091-04-7*, Pub. by Format Pubg Ltd) Balogh.

— Managing Successful Projects with PRINCE 2. 336p. 1998. ring bd. 110.00 (0-11-330855-8, Pub. by Statnry Office) Balogh.

— Managing Successful Projects with PRINCE 2: Manual. 336p. 1998. pap. 110.00 (0-11-330018-2, Pub. by Statnry Office) Balogh.

— Passing the Prince 2 Examinations: Project Management. 53p. 1999. 20.00 (0-11-330013-1, Pub. by Statnry Office) Balogh.

CCTA Staff. Planning & Control for Information Technology Services. (Information Technology Infrastructure Library (ITIL)). 135p. 1994. pap. 87.00 (0-11-330548-6, HM5413, Pub. by Statnry Office) Sftware Mgmt Network.

— Problem Management. (IT Infrastructure Library Ser.). 74p. 1990. pap. 80.00 (0-11-330527-3, Pub. by Statnry Office) Sftware Mgmt Network.

— Service Delivery Tools. (IT Infrastructure Library Ser.). 86p. 1990. pap. 80.00 (0-11-330633-4, HM06334, Pub. by Statnry Office) Bernan Associates.

— Service Level Management. 2nd ed. (IT Infrastructure Library Ser.). 74p. 1997. pap. 95.00 (0-11-330691-1, Pub. by Statnry Office) Sftware Mgmt Network.

— Software Control & Distribution. (IT Infrastructure Library Ser.). 70p. 1990. pap. 80.00 (0-11-330537-0, Pub. by Statnry Office) Balogh.

— Software Lifecycle Support. (IT Infrastructure Library Ser.). 112p. 1993. pap. 80.00 (0-11-330559-1, Pub. by Statnry Office) Sftware Mgmt Network.

— Surviving Information Technology Infrastructure Transitions. (Information Technology Infrastructure Library (ITIL)). 146p. 1995. 79.00 (0-11-330678-4, Pub. by Statnry Office) Sftware Mgmt Network.

CCTA Staff, et al. Customer Liaison. (IT Infrastructure Library Ser.). 124p. 1990. pap. 80.00 (0-11-330546-X, Pub. by Statnry Office) Sftware Mgmt Network.

— Network Services Management. (IT Infrastructure Library Ser.). 200p. 1994. pap. 80.00 (0-11-330558-3, Pub. by Statnry Office) Sftware Mgmt Network.

CCTP Staff. Warbonnets. (Illus.). 17p. 1995. pap. 6.00 (0-9624883-6-4) Reddick Enterp.

Cd Inc Pro. Free Phone. 1994. 17.04 (0-9637458-3-2) Pro CD.

CDA-Wiesenberger Staff. Investment Companies Yearbook, 1994. 54th ed. 1995. write for info. (1-883593-01-8) CDA-Wiesenberger.

CDC Staff & DHHS Staff. Health Information for International Travel 1996-97. (Illus.). 220p. 1997. pap. 14.95 (1-883205-33-6) Intl Med Pub.

CDE Communication Group Staff. Advanced User's & System Administrator's Guide. LC 95-11126. (Common Desktop Environment 1.0 Ser.). 320p. (C). 1995. pap. 29.95 (0-201-48952-X) Addison-Wesley.

CDI Staff. SAP R/3 Controlling: Financial Systems. 1997. pap. 39.95 (1-55851-498-8, M&T Bks) IDG Bks.

— SAP R/3 Finanzwessen: System Administration. 1997. pap. 39.95 (1-55851-499-6, M&T Bks) IDG Bks.

— SAP R/3 Systems: Basissystem. 1997. pap. 39.95 (1-55851-501-1, M&T Bks) IDG Bks.

— SAP R/3 Systems Materialswirtschaft: Inventory Management. 1997. pap. 39.95 (1-55851-497-X, M&T Bks) IDG Bks.

CDL Institute Inc. Staff. Commercial Driver's License General Knowledge Study Program. (Adult Education Ser.). 1991. pap. 18.50 (0-8273-4779-0) Delmar.

CDL Institute, Inc., Staff. The Complete Commercial Driver's License (CDL) Study Program, 2 bks., Set, Bks. 1-2. 1991. pap. 69.50 (0-8273-4778-2) Delmar.

Cea, J., ed. Optimization Techniques: Modeling & Optimization in the Service of Man, Pt. 1. LC 76-9857. (Lecture Notes in Computer Science Ser.: Vol. 40.). 1976. 46.00 (0-387-07622-0) Spr-Verlag.

Cea, J., et al, eds. Partial Differential Equations & Functional Analysis: In Memory of Pierre Grisvard. LC 96-1384. (Progress in Nonlinear Differential Equations & Their Applications Ser.: Vol. 22). 263p. 1996. 84.50 (0-8176-3839-3) Birkhauser.

Cea, J., jt. auth. see Haug, Edward J.

CEAC Staff. Diccionario de la Contruccion. (SPA.). 622p. 1991. pap. 59.95 (0-7859-5906-8, 8432926086) Fr & Eur.

Ceadel, Eric B. Japanese-English Dictionary, Romanized, 2 vols. (ENG & JPN.). 49.50 (0-87557-048-8) Saphrograph.

Ceadel, Martin. Pacifism in Britain, 1914-1945: The Defining of a Faith. (Oxford Historical Monographs). 1980. 55.00 (0-19-821882-6) OUP.

Cearley, Buster, jt. auth. see Cope, Eddie.

Cearley, Jack E., jt. auth. see Coryell, John W.

Cearnal, Christine, et al. A Thin Line. (Illus.). 32p. 1998. pap. 5.00 (0-941276-42-2) Bard Coll Pubns.

Ceasar, Lisbeth D. Big Fearon Book of Comprehension Capers. 1986. pap. 17.99 (0-8224-1479-1) Fearon Teacher Aids.

Cease, Cheryl & Bruno, Susan. The Insiders' Guide to Williamsburg. 9th rev. ed. (Insiders' Guide Travel Ser.). (Illus.). 1999. pap. 15.95 (1-57380-092-9, The Insiders Guide) Falcon Pub Inc.

Ceaser, James. American Government. 656p. (C). 1995. pap. text 46.95 (0-7872-1046-3) Kendall-Hunt.

— American Government: Origins, Institutions & Public Policy. 5th ed. LC 98-125270. 704p. (C). 1998. per. 58.95 (0-7872-4643-3, 41464301) Kendall-Hunt.

Ceaser, James W. Liberal Democracy & Political Science. LC 89-27310. 224p. 1990. text 39.95 (0-8018-3985-8) Johns Hopkins.

— Liberal Democracy & Political Science. LC 89-27310. 224p. 1992. reprint ed. pap. text 15.95 (0-8018-4511-4) Johns Hopkins.

— Presidential Selection: Theory & Development. LC 78-70282. 392p. 1979. pap. text 19.95 (0-691-02188-0, Pub. by Princeton U Pr) Cal Prin Full Svc.

Ceaser, James W. Reconstructing America: The Symbol of America in Modern Thought. LC 96-52890. 304p. 1997. 35.00 (0-300-07053-5) Yale U Pr.

***Ceaser, James W.** Reconstructing America: The Symbol of America in Modern Thought. 304p. 2000. pap. 16.00 (0-300-08453-6) Yale U Pr.

Ceaser, James W. & Busch, Andrew. Losing to Win: The 1996 Elections & American Politics. LC 97-1579. (Illus.). 198p. 1997. 51.00 (0-8476-8405-9); pap. 16.95 (0-8476-8406-7) Rowman.

Ceaser, James W., jt. auth. see David, Paul T.

***Ceaser, Jennifer.** Everything You Need to Know about Acne. LC 00-26928. (Need to Know Library). 2000. write for info. (0-8239-3222-2) Rosen Group.

***Ceaser, Jonathan.** Essential Deer Hunting for Teens. (High Interest Bks.). (Illus.). (YA). 2000. 19.00 (0-516-23354-8) Childrens.

— Essential Deer Hunting for Teens. (High Interest Bks.). (Illus.). 48p. (J). (gr. 4-7). 2000. pap. 6.95 (0-516-23554-0) Childrens.

Ceaser, Lisbeth. Reciprocal Teaching Interactivities. 262p. (C). 1997. pap. text, per. 35.95 (0-7872-3486-9, 41348601) Kendall-Hunt.

Ceasor, Ebraska D. Black Achievers (1880-1920) Laney, Dolores & Rambo, Dorothy, eds. (Black History Bks.: No. III). (Illus.). (Orig.). (J). (gr. 4-8). 1995. pap. 8.00 (0-913678-28-7) New Day Pr.

— A Galaxy of Cleveland's Black Stars--1796-1996. (Illus.). 40p. (Orig.). (J). (gr. 2-7). 1996. pap. 5.95 (0-913678-30-9) New Day Pr.

— Mae C. Jemison: First Black Female Astronaut. Durant, Charlotte T. & Pye, Ethel, eds. (Illus.). 40p. (Orig.). (J). (ps-1). 1992. pap. 4.00 (0-913678-22-8) New Day Pr.

Ceasor, Frank, Sr. & Gaines, Edith M. Can You Count?; Carpetbaggers in Action; Mr. Impossible. 2nd ed. McCluskey, John A., ed. (Stories from Black History Series II: Vol. 3). (Illus.). (J). (gr. 4-7). 1993. pap. 2.00 (0-913678-27-9) New Day Pr.

Ceasor, Frank G., Sr. Stories from Black History: Nine Stories, 4 vols. Incl. Can You Count, Bound with Carpetbaggers in Action. 1975. (0-913678-11-2, 204); (Series 2). (Illus.). (Orig.). (J). (gr. 5 up). 1975. Set pap. 3.20 (0-913678-07-4) New Day Pr.

***Ceaton, P. F.** Oneness: Synthesis of Souls. LC 99-65229. 125p. 2000. pap. 14.95 (1-58501-056-1, Pub. by CeShore Pubg) Natl Bk Netwk.

Ceaton, Peter F. Vestures of Brotherhood. (Illus.). xii, 103p. 1999. pap. 14.95 (0-9672721-0-6) Golden Threads.

Ceaucescu, Ilie, et al. A Turning Point in World War II: August 23, 1944 in Rumania. 235p. 1985. 51.00 (0-88033-084-8, Pub. by East Eur Monographs) Col U Pr.

Ceausescu, Ilie. Romanian Military Doctrine: Past & Present. 246p. 1988. text 61.00 (0-88033-135-6, Pub. by East Eur Monographs) Col U Pr.

— War, Revolution, & Society in Romania: The Road to Independence. (East European Monographs: No. 135). 298p. 1983. text 63.00 (0-88033-023-6, Pub. by East Eur Monographs) Col U Pr.

CEB Attorneys Staff. Estate Planning: 1987. LC 82-640282. 328p. 1988. 75.00 (0-88124-166-0, ES-39540) Cont Ed Bar-CA.

CEB Attorneys Staff, ed. see Astle, Ruth S., et al.

***Ceballos Gomez, Diana L.** Zauberei und Hexerei. 2000. 45.95 (3-631-35952-7) P Lang Pubng.

Ceballos-Lascurain, Hector. Tourism, Ecotourism & Protected Areas. LC 97-105698. 301p. (Orig.). 1996. pap. 35.00 (2-8317-0124-4, Pub. by IUCN) World Resources Inst.

Ceballos-Picot, Irene. Oxidative Stress in Neuronal Death. LC 97-19204. (Medical Intelligence Unit Ser.). 196p. 1997. 99.00 (1-57059-454-6) Landes Bioscience.

***Cebe, Peggy, et al.** Scattering from Polymers: Characterization by X-rays, Neutrons & Light. LC 99-35339. (Symposium Ser.). 576p. 1999. write for info. (0-8412-3644-5, Pub. by Am Chemical) OUP.

Cebeci, T. Solutions Manual & Computer Programs for Physical & Computational Aspects of Convective Heat Transfer by T. Cebeci & P. Bradshaw. (Illus.). 130p. 1988. 29.95 (0-387-96825-3) Spr-Verlag.

Cebeci, T., ed. Numerical & Physical Aspect of Aerodynamic Flows III. 490p. 1986. 118.95 (0-387-96281-6) Spr-Verlag.

— Numerical & Physical Aspects of Aerodynamic Flows, Pt. II. (Illus.). 500p. 1983. 131.00 (0-387-12659-7) Spr-Verlag.

— Numerical & Physical Aspects of Aerodynamic Flows IV. (Illus.). xii, 420p. 1990. 121.95 (0-387-52259-X) Spr-Verlag.

Cebeci, T. & Bradshaw, P. Physical & Computational Aspects of Convective Heat Transfer. (Illus.). 345p. 1984. 82.50 (0-387-12097-1) Spr-Verlag.

— Physical & Computational Aspects of Convective Heat Transfer: Springer Study Edition. (Illus.). xii, 487p. 1991. 79.95 (0-387-96821-0) Spr-Verlag.

***Cebeci, Tuncer.** An Engineering Approach to the Calculation of Aerodynamic Flows: Laminar, Turbulent & Transitional Boundary Layer Methods, Inviscid Methods & Stability/Transition Methods. LC 99-35756. (Illus.). xv, 396p. 1999. 96.00 (3-540-66181-6) Spr-Verlag.

Cebeci, Tuncer. Legacy of a Gentle Genius: The Life of A. M. O. Smith LC 99-24379. 1999. write for info. (0-9668461-1-7) Horizons Pubg.

***Cebeci, Tuncer.** Modeling & Computation of Boundary-Layer Flows: Laminar, Turbulent & Transitional Boundary Layers in Incompressible Flows LC 98-45815. 1998. pap. text 95.00 (3-540-65010-5) Spr-Verlag.

Cebeci, Tuncer & Cousteix, J. Modeling & Computation of Boundary-Layer Flows: Laminar, Turbulent & Transitional Boundary Layers in Incompressible Flows LC 98-45815. 1998. write for info. (0-9668461-0-9) Horizons Pubg.

Cebes. Cebes' Tablet. Sider, Sandra, ed. & intro. by. (Renaissance Text Ser.: No. 6). (Illus.). iv, 230p. 1979. 9.95 (0-9602696-2-2) Renaiss Society Am.

Cebik, L. B. Nonaesthetic Issues in the Philosophy of Art: Art As a Social Realm. LC 94-44818. 376p. 1995. text 99.95 (0-7734-8999-1) E Mellen.

Cebik, L. B., et al, eds. Advances in Bioethics Vol. 1: Violence, Neglect, & the Elderly. LC 96-208085. 251p. 1996. 128.50 (0-7623-0096-5) Jai Pr.

Cebollero, Pedro A. A School Language Policy for Puerto Rico. LC 74-14224. (Puerto Rican Experience Ser.). (Illus.). 148p. 1974. reprint ed. 12.95 (0-405-06214-1) Ayer.

Cebon, D. & Mitchell, C. G., eds. Heavy Vehicles & Roads: Technology, Safety & Policy. 451p. 1992. 21.00 (0-7277-1903-3) Am Soc Civil Eng.

***Cebon, David.** Handbook of Vehicle-Road Interaction: Vehicle Dynamics, Suspension Design & Road Damage. LC 99-16701. (Advances in Engineering Ser.: Vol. 2). (Illus.). 612p. 1999. 118.00 (90-265-1554-5) Swets.

Cebon, David. Interaction Between Heavy Vehicles & Roads, 39th Buckendale Lecture. 88p. 1993. 15.00 (1-56091-336-3, SP-951) Soc Auto Engineers.

***Cebon, David & Ashby, Michael.** Case Studies in Materials Selection. 256p. 1999. pap. 47.95 (0-7506-3604-1, Newnes) Buttrwrth-Heinemann.

Cebon, Jonathan, ed. Colorectal Cancer. (Journal Ser.: Vol. 4, No. 2-3, 1995). (Illus.). 84p. 1995. pap. 47.00 (3-8055-6150-4) S Karger.

Cebon, Peter, et al, eds. Views from the Alps: Regional Perspectives on Climate Change. LC 98-3946. (Politics, Science & the Environment Ser.). (Illus.). 536p. 1998. 60.00 (0-262-03252-X) MIT Pr.

Cebrian, Jose, ed. see De la Cueva, Juan.

Cebuhar, Jo K. Principles of Tax-Deferred Exchanging. 2nd rev. ed. (Illus.). x, 298p. 1997. pap., spiral bd. 85.00 (0-9661851-0-2) XPr.

Cebul, Randall D. & Beck, Lawrence H., eds. Teaching Clinical Decison Making: A Handbook for Instructors. LC 85-3532. 192p. 1985. 37.50 (0-275-91333-3, C1333, Praeger Pubs) Greenwood.

Cebula. Public Finance. (Miscellaneous/Catalogs Ser.). 2002. mass mkt. 55.95 (0-538-86948-8) S-W Pub.

Cebula, et al. Economic Thinking. 628p. (C). 1993. pap. text 47.72 (1-56226-138-X) CAT Pub.

— Economics Alive: Macroeconomics. 1998. 29.95 (0-538-86850-3) Sth-Wstrn College.

Cebula-Hung, Richard J. The Savings & Loan Crisis. 128p. (C). 1992. pap. text 13.95 (0-8403-7620-0) Kendall-Hunt.

Cebula, Richard J., jt. auth. see Belton, Willie.

Cebulak, M., jt. auth. see Hudlicky, Thomas.

Cebulak, Mary, jt. auth. see Hudlicky, Thomas.

Cebulash, Mel. Bases Loaded: Great Baseball of the Twentieth Century, Reading Level 3-5. 1993. 4.95 (0-88336-742-4); 9.95 incl. audio (0-88336-899-4) New Readers.

— Catnapper. (Author's Signature Collection). (Illus.). 40p. (J). (gr. 3-8). 1993. lib. bdg. 12.79 (0-89565-878-X) Childs World.

— Dirty Money: A Sully Gomez Mystery. LC 93-29071. 1993. 3.95 (1-56420-002-7) New Readers.

Cebulash, Mel. Dirty Money: A Sully Gomez Mystery. LC 93-29071. (J). 1993. audio 10.00 (1-56420-003-5) New Readers.

Cebulash, Mel. Kid with the Left Hook. (FastBack Sports Ser.). (J). 1985. 11.27 (0-606-00326-6, Pub. by Turtleback) Demco.

— Knockout Punch: A Sully Gomez Mystery. LC 93-29072. 1993. 3.95 (1-56420-008-6); audio 9.95 (1-56420-009-4) New Readers.

— Muscle Bound. (Author's Signature Collection). (Illus.). 40p. (J). (gr. 3-8). 1993. lib. bdg. 12.79 (0-89565-883-6) Childs World.

— Set to Explode: A Sully Gomez Mystery. LC 93-29069. 1993. 3.95 (1-56420-004-3) New Readers.

Cebulash, Mel. Set to Explode: A/Sully Gomez Mystery. LC 93-29069. (J). 1993. audio 10.00 (1-56420-005-1) New Readers.

Cebulash, Mel. A Sucker for Redheads: A Sully Gomez Mystery. LC 93-29070. 1993. 3.95 (1-56420-006-X); audio 9.95 (1-56420-007-8) New Readers.

— Third & Goal: Great Football of the Twentieth Century, Reading Level 3-5. LC 93-433. 1993. 9.95 incl. audio (0-88336-900-1); pap. 4.95 (0-88336-743-2) New Readers.

— Willie's Wonderful Pet. LC 91-44270. (Hello Reader! Ser.). (Illus.). 32p. (J). (ps-3). 1993. pap. 3.50 (0-590-45787-X) Scholastic Inc.

Cebulesh, Mel. Fast Break: Great Basketball of the Twentieth Century, Reading Level 3-5. LC 93-6897. 1993. 4.95 (0-88336-744-0); audio 9.95 (0-88336-928-1) New Readers.

— Lights Out: Great Fights of the Twentieth Century, Reading Level 3-5. LC 93-6899. 1993. 4.95 (0-88336-741-6); digital audio 9.95 (0-88336-898-6) New Readers.

Cebulska, Marcia. Time for a Change. (Literacy Volunteers of America Readers Ser.). 32p. (Orig.). 1988. pap. text 3.00 (0-8428-9606-6) Cambridge Bk.

Cebulski, C. B., tr. see Taniguchi, Tomoko.

Cebulski, Frank. Corm. 1974. 5.00 (0-685-48373-8); pap. 2.50 (0-685-48374-6) Oyez.

— Mediterranean Sonnets. 152p. 1988. 20.00 (1-55643-022-1); pap. 8.95 (1-55643-020-5) North Atlantic.

Cec. Fusion Technology, 1984, 2 vols., Vol. 1-2. (International School of Fusion Reactor Technology). 1985. pap. 200.00 (0-08-032562-9, Pergamon Pr) Elsevier.

Cec. A Guide to Higher Education Systems & Qualifications in the European Community. 544p. 1991. pap. 39.95 (0-7494-0387-X, Kogan Pg Educ) Stylus Pub VA.

CEC IAPCO, Staff. Congress Terminology. (ENG, FRE, GER, ITA & SPA.). 172p. 1987. pap. 75.00 (0-8288-7642-8) Fr & Eur.

***CEC Public Policy Unit Staff.** IDEA 1997 - Let's Make It Work: Preliminary Analysis: The Law & Regulations. 97p. 1999. pap. 14.95 (0-86586-303-2) Coun Exc Child.

***CECAFEC/UNICEF Ecuador Staff.** Convencion Sobre los Derechos de los Ninos: Un Instrumento para Conocer. (SPA.). 43p. 1999. write for info. (92-806-3523-9) U N I C E.

Cecala, Kathy. Secret Vow. 1998. mass mkt. 6.99 (0-451-19227-3, Onyx) NAL.

Cecava, Michael, jt. ed. see Perry, Tilden W.

Ceccaldi, Mathieu. Dictionnaire Corse-Francais, Pierre d'Evisa. 2nd ed. (COR & FRE.). 464p. 1988. pap. 115.00 (0-7859-4811-2, M6066) Fr & Eur.

Ceccanese, Mary, jt. ed. see Slemeod, Joel.

Ceccarelli, B., ed. see NATO Advanced Study Institute Staff.

Ceccarelli, G., jt. ed. see Axenrod, T.

***Ceccarelli, Marco.** International Symposium on History of Machines & Mechanisms: Proceedings of the HMM2000. LC 00-33063. (Illus.). 2000. write for info. (0-7923-6372-8) Plenum.

Ceccato, Bebbe. Brazil. LC 97-68225. (Places & History Ser.). 272p. 1998. 24.95 (1-55670-691-X) Stewart Tabori & Chang.

Ceccato, Silvio, ed. Linguistic Analysis & Programming for Mechanical Translation. (Illus.). 246p. 1961. text 190.00 (0-677-00110-X) Gordon & Breach.

Ceccerallo, Julius, jt. auth. see Brobyn, Anne.

Cecchetti, Giovanni. Contrappunti/Counterpoints: Selected Prose of Giovanni Cecchetti. Petrillo, Raymond, tr. from ITA. LC 96-52150. (Studies in Southern Italian & Italian/American Culture: Vol. 9). X, 325p. (C). 1997. pap. text 35.95 (0-8204-3134-6) P Lang Pubng.

Cecchetti, Grazioso. Classical Dance: A Complete Manual for the Cecchetti Method. 1997. 24.95 (88-7301-072-5, Pub. by Gremese Intl) Natl Bk Netwk.

— Classical Dance: A Complete Manual of the Cecchetti Method, Vol. 2. 1998. pap. text 24.95 (88-7301-199-3, Pub. by Gremese Intl) Natl Bk Netwk.

Cecchettini, Philip A., ed. see Ferretti, Louis.

***Cecchi, A., et al.** Italian Paintings of the Uffizi. (Illus.). 2000. pap. 29.99 (3-8228-5999-0) Taschen Amer.

Cecchi, Alessandro. Bronzino. Evans, Christopher, tr. from ITA. (Library of Great Masters). (Illus.). 80p. (Orig.). 1996. pap. 14.99 (1-878351-52-4) Riverside NY.

— Bronzino. (Grandes Maestros del Arte Ser.). (SPA., Illus.). 80p. (Orig.). 1997. pap. 14.99 (1-878351-42-7) Riverside NY.

Cecchi, Anna. La Struttura del Sistema Bancario Toscano Dal, 1815 Al 1859, 2 vols. Bruchey, Stuart, ed. LC 80-2804. (Dissertations in European Economic History Ser.).Tr. of Structures of the Tuscan Banking System from the Restoration to Italian Unification. (Illus.). 1981. lib. bdg. 39.95 (0-405-13988-8) Ayer.

Cecchi, Dario. Titian. Wydenbruck, Nora, tr. from ITA. LC 72-13188. (Biography Index Reprint Ser.). 1977. reprint ed. 22.95 (0-8369-8143-X) Ayer.

Cecchi, F., et al. Anaerobic Digestion of Solid Waste. (Water Science & Technology Ser.: Vol. 27). 298p. 1993. 174.00 (0-08-042200-4, Pergamon Pr) Elsevier.

Cecchi, Giovan M. The Horned Owl. Eisenbichler, Konrad, tr. 114p. 1998. pap. text 6.95 (0-88920-116-1, PDH46, Pub. by Dovehouse) Sterling.

— The Slave Girl. Ferraro, Bruno, ed. & tr. by. (Carleton Renaissance Plays in Translation Ser.: No. 28). 118p. (C). 1996. pap. text 8.00 (1-895537-29-0, Pub. by Dovehouse) Sterling.

Cecchi, Giovanna, et al, eds. Earth Surface Remote Sensing. (Europto Ser.: Vol. 3222). 576p. 1997. 107.00 (0-8194-2654-7) SPIE.

***Cecchi, Giovanna, et al, eds.** Remote Sensing for Earth Science, Ocean & Sea Ice Applications. 1999. pap. text 120.00 (0-8194-3463-9) SPIE.

Cecchi, Giovanna, et al, eds. Remote Sensing of Vegetation & Water, & Standardization of Remote Sensing Methods. LC 97-197226. (Europto Ser.: Vol. 3107). 326p. 1997. 69.00 (0-8194-2528-1) SPIE.

Cecchin, Gianfranco, et al. The Cybernetics of Prejudices in the Practice of Psychotherapy. 96p. 1994. pap. text 22.00 (1-85575-056-2, Pub. by H Karnac Bks Ltd) Other Pr LLC.

— Irreverence: A Strategy for Therapists' Survival. 96p. 1993. pap. text 22.00 (1-85575-031-7, Pub. by H Karnac Bks Ltd) Other Pr LLC.

Cecchine, Glenn. 101 Championship Baseball Drills. (101 Drills Ser.). 1999. pap. text. write for info. (1-57167-361-X) Coaches Choice.

***Cecchini, Marie E.** Exploring Weather: Primary. (Illus.). 80p. 2000. pap., teacher ed. 9.95 (1-57690-611-6, TCM 2611) Tchr Create Mat.

Cecchini, Paolo, et al. The European Challenge, 1992: The Benefits of a Single Community. Robinson, John, tr. 150p. 1988. pap. text 22.95 (0-7045-0613-0) Ashgate Pub Co.

Cecchini, Tina. Enciclopedia de las Hierbas y de las Plantas Medicinales: Encyclopedia of Medicinal Herbs & Plants. 4th ed. (SPA.). 536p. 1990. write for info. (0-7859-5053-2) Fr & Eur.

***Ceccio, Cathy M., et al.** An Introduction to Orthopaedic Nursing. 2nd ed. LC 99-462575. (Illus.). 148p. 1999. pap. 52.00 (1-892665-03-4) Natl Assn Ortho Nurse.

Cecco, John P. De, see Klein, Fritz.

C

An Asterisk (*) at the beginning of an entry indicates that the title is appearing for the first time.

Cecco, John P. De, see De Cecco, John P., ed.

Cecco, John P. De, see Klein, Fritz, ed.

Cecco, John P. De, see Parker, David A., ed.

Cecco, John P. De, see Parker, David A. & De Cecco, John P., eds.

Cecco, Marcello De, see De Cecco, Marcello, ed.

***Ceccola, Russ.** Crazy Taxi: Prima's Official Strategy Guide. LC 00-10014. (Illus.). 80p. 2000. pap. 12.99 (*0-7615-2781-8*) Prima Pub.

— Heroes of Might & Magic III: The Shadow of Death. (Official Strategy Guides Ser.). (Illus.). 240p. 2000. pap. 19.99 (*0-7615-2840-7*) Prima Pub.

— Tomba 2. LC 00-100023. (Official Strategy Guides Ser.). (Illus.). 127p. (YA). 2000. pap. 14.99 (*0-7615-2776-1*) Prima Pub.

***Cecconi, Antonio.** Betty Crocker's Italian Cooking: 200 Easy Recipes That Celebrate the Food & Culture of Italy. (Illus.). 304p. 2000. 23.95 (*0-7645-6078-6*) IDG Bks.

Cecconi, L., et al. MRI Atlas of Central Nervous System Tumors. Tettamanti, E., ed. & contrib. by. (Illus.). 280p. 1992. 274.00 (*0-387-82304-2*) Spr-Verlag.

***Cecelski, David.** A Historian's Coast: Adventures into the Tidewater Past. (Illus.). 130p. 2000. pap. 16.95 (*0-89587-189-0*) Blair.

Cecelski, David, ed. Flowers in the Desert Die: Have the Central American Wars Come Home to the South? (Illus.). 64p. (Orig.). 1988. pap. 5.00 (*0-943810-39-6*) Southern Exposure.

Cecelski, David S. Along Freedom Road: Hyde County, North Carolina & the Fate of Black Schools in the South. LC 93-32687. (Illus.). xii, 236p. (C). 1994. pap. 17.95 (*0-8078-4437-3*) U of NC Pr.

Cecelski, David S. & Tyson, Timothy B., eds. Democracy Betrayed: The Wilmington Race Riot of 1898 & Its Legacy. LC 98-3467. 320p. 1998. 45.00 (*0-8078-2451-8*); pap. 18.95 (*0-8078-4755-0*) U of NC Pr.

Cecelski, David S., ed. see Singleton, William Henry.

Cecelski, Elizabeth, et al. Household Energy & the Poor in the Third World. LC 79-4863. 160p. reprint ed. pap. 49.60 (*0-7837-5948-7*, 204574700007) Bks Demand.

— Household Energy & the Poor in the Third World: Domestic Energy Consumption for Low-Income Groups in Development Areas. LC 79-4863. (Resources for the Future Ser.). 1979. pap. 10.00 (*0-8018-2283-1*) Johns Hopkins.

***Cecere, Cathy, ed.** Meeting the Competency Challenge in Behavioral Health Care. 240p. 2000. 117.00 (*0-9679474-0-5*) C & R Pubns.

Cech, Donna & Martin, Suzanne T. Functional Movement Development Across the Life Span. LC 93-37402. 1994. text 39.00 (*0-7216-3174-6*, W B Saunders Co) Harcrt Hlth Sci Grp.

Cech, John. Angels & Wild Things: The Archetypal Poetics of Maurice Sendak. LC 92-39709. (Illus.). 296p. 1996. 35.00 (*0-271-00949-7*) Pa St U Pr.

— Django. LC 93-46782. (Illus.). 40p. (J). (ps-3). 1994. mass mkt. 15.95 (*0-02-765705-1*) S&S Bks Yung.

— First Snow, Magic Snow. LC 91-42988. (Illus.). 40p. (J). (gr. k-2). 1992. lib. bdg. 14.95 (*0-02-717971-0*, Mac Bks Young Read) S&S Childrens.

— My Grandmother's Journey. LC 90-35731. (Illus.). 40p. (J). (ps-4). 1991. lib. bdg. 16.00 (*0-02-718135-9*, Bradbury S&S) S&S Childrens.

— My Grandmother's Journey. (Illus.). 40p. (J). (ps-4). 1998. per. 5.99 (*0-689-81890-4*) S&S Childrens.

— My Grandmother's Journey. 1998. 11.15 (*0-606-13633-9*, Pub. by Turtleback) Demco.

— Rush of Dreamers: The Remarkabe Story of Norton I, Emperor of the United States & Protector of Mexico. LC 97-30231. (Illus.). 192p. 1997. 20.00 (*1-56924-775-7*) Marlowe & Co.

— The Southernmost Cat. LC 93-40671. (Illus.). 40p. (J). (ps-3). 1996. mass mkt. 16.00 (*0-689-80510-1*) S&S Bks Yung.

— The Southernmost Cat. 11th ed. LC 93-40671. (Illus.). (J). 1995. text 14.00 (*0-02-717885-4*) S&S Bks Yung.

Cech, John, ed. American Writers for Children, 1900-1960. LC 83-14199. (Dictionary of Literary Biography Ser.: Vol. 22). (Illus.). 432p. 1983. text 155.00 (*0-8103-1146-1*) Gale.

Cech, Joseph J., et al. Multiple Stresses in Ecosystems. LC 97-49109. 224p. 1998. lib. bdg. 59.95 (*1-56670-309-3*) CRC Pr.

Cech, Joseph J., jt. auth. see Moyle, Peter B.

Cech, Maureen. Globalchild: Multicultural Resources for Young Children. LC 91-202692. 240p. 1991. pap. text, teacher ed. 19.95 (*0-201-29822-8*) Addison-Wesley.

***Cech, Maureen.** Globalchild: Multicultural Resources for Young Children. (Illus.). 240p. 1999. reprint ed. pap. text 20.00 (*0-7881-6374-4*) DIANE Pub.

***Cech, Richard A.** Making Plant Medicine. (Illus.). 296p. 2000. pap. 14.98 (*0-9700312-0-3*) Horizon Herbs.

Ceci. Children & the Law. 2nd ed. 1998. 49.00 (*0-07-230563-0*) McGraw.

Ceci, Lynn. The Effect of European Contact & Trade on the Settlement Pattern of Indians in Coastal New York, 1524-1665. LC 90-14073. (Evolution of North American Indians Ser.). 360p. 1991. text 10.00 (*0-8240-2363-3*) Garland.

Ceci, S. J., et al, eds. Perspectives on Children's Testimony. (Illus.). 270p. 1989. 90.95 (*0-387-96864-4*) Spr-Verlag.

Ceci, Stephen J. On Intelligence: A Bio-Ecological Treatise on Intellectual Development. (Illus.). 288p. 1996. pap. 19.50 (*0-674-63456-X*) HUP.

Ceci, Stephen J., ed. Handbook of Cognitive, Social, & Neuropsychological Aspects of Learning Disabilities, 2 vols., 1. 555p. (C). 1986. text 99.95 (*0-89859-682-3*) L Erlbaum Assocs.

— Handbook of Cognitive, Social, & Neuropsychological Aspects of Learning Disabilities, 2 vols., Vol. 2. 432p. (C). 1986. text 99.95 (*0-89859-797-8*) L Erlbaum Assocs.

Ceci, Stephen J., et al, eds. Children's Eyewitness Memory. LC 86-24852. 1987. 46.00 (*0-387-96429-0*) Spr-Verlag.

— Cognitive Social Factors in Early Deception. 192p. 1992. text 39.95 (*0-8058-0953-8*) L Erlbaum Assocs.

Ceci, Stephen J. & Bruck, Maggie. Jeopardy in the Courtroom: A Scientific Analysis of Children's Testimony. LC 95-14433. (Illus.). 336p. 1995. pap. 24.95 (*1-55798-632-0*) Am Psychol.

Ceci, Stephen J. & Hembrooke, Helene, eds. Expert Witnesses in Child Sexual Abuse Cases: What Can & Should Be Said in Court. LC 98-13683. 299p. 1998. 39.95 (*1-55798-515-4*) Am Psychol.

Ceci, Steven, ed. The Nature-Nurture Debate: The Essential Readings. LC 99-16941. (Essential Readings in Developmental Psychology Ser.). 256p. (C). 1999. 59.95 (*0-631-21738-X*) Blackwell Pubs.

Ceci, Steven J., ed. The Nature-Nurture Debate: The Essential Readings. LC 99-16941. (Essential Readings in Developmental Psychology Ser.). 256p. (C). 1999. pap. 24.95 (*0-631-21739-8*) Blackwell Pubs.

Cecil, ed. Carboniferous Geology of the Eastern United States. (IGC Field Trip Guidebooks Ser.). 168p. 1989. 35.00 (*0-87590-647-8*, T143) Am Geophysical.

Cecil, jt. auth. see Matacia, Louis J.

Cecil, Andrew R. Moral Values the Challenge of the Twenty-First Century. LC 96-60491. 253p. 1996. 16.50 (*0-292-71192-1*) U of Tex Pr.

Cecil, Andrew R., et al. Moral Values in Liberalism & Conservatism. Taitte, Lawson, ed. LC 95-60717. (Andrew R. Cecil Lectures on Moral Values in a Free Society: Vol. 16). 1995. text 16.50 (*0-292-78139-3*) U of Tex Pr.

Cecil, Anthony C. The Theological Development of Edwards Amasa Park, Last of the Consistent Calvinists. LC 74-83338. (American Academy of Religion, Dissertation Ser.: Vol. 1). 354p. reprint ed. pap. 109.80 (*0-608-08682-7*, 206920500003) Bks Demand.

Cecil, C. B., jt. ed. see Cobb, J. C.

Cecil, C. W. The Perfect Gay Pre-Nuptial Agreement. 100p. 2000. pap. 10.00 (*1-886383-86-3*) Pride & Imprints.

— The Perfect Lesbian Pre-Nuptial Agreement. 100p. 2000. pap. 10.00 (*1-886383-87-1*) Pride & Imprints.

Cecil, David. Hardy: The Novelist (1946) 235p. 12.00 (*0-614-09420-8*) Appel.

— Melbourne. LC 54-9486. (Illus.). 450p. 1974. 8.95 (*0-672-52038-9*, Bobbs) Macmillan.

Cecil, David R., jt. auth. see Albert, Stan.

Cecil, Edward. A Journall & Relation of the Action Which E. Lord Cecil Did Vndertake Vpon the Coast of Spaine. LC 68-54643. (English Experience Ser.: No. 27). 1968. reprint ed. 20.00 (*90-221-0027-8*) Walter J Johnson.

Cecil-Fronsman, Bill. Common Whites: Class & Culture in Antebellum North Carolina. LC 91-34867. (Illus.). 288p. 1992. 36.00 (*0-8131-1777-1*) U Pr of Ky.

Cecil, Grayson, ed. Restoration of Lost Human Uses of the Environment. LC 98-43870. (Illus.). 1999. pap. 60.00 (*1-880611-21-X*) SETAC.

Cecil, H. C., jt. auth. see Bakst, M. R.

Cecil, Henry. According to the Evidence. 160p. 1988. pap. 5.95 (*0-89733-295-4*) Academy Chi Pubs.

Cecil, Henry. The Asking Price. 143p. 1990. reprint ed. pap. 5.95 (*0-89733-355-1*) Academy Chi Pubs.

— Cross Purposes. LC 76-363922. 186 p. 1976. 3.75 (*0-7181-1442-6*, M Joseph) Viking Penguin.

— Daughters in Law. 187p. 1991. pap. 8.95 (*1-55882-105-8*) Intl Polygonics.

— The English Judge. LC 75-325733. 190 p. 1972. 0.30 (*0-09-905830-8*) Seven Hills Bk.

— Hunt the Slipper. LC 77-362960. 151 p. 1977. 3.75 (*0-7181-1578-3*, M Joseph) Viking Penguin.

— Independent Witness. 172p. 1989. reprint ed. pap. 5.95 (*0-89733-325-X*) Academy Chi Pubs.

— Just Within the Law. LC 76-369224. 220 p. 1975. 4.00 (*0-09-123070-5*) Trafalgar.

— Settled Out of Court. 184p. 1992. pap. 8.95 (*1-55882-104-X*) Intl Polygonics.

— Tell You What I'll Do. LC 77-447582. 216 p. 1969. write for info. (*0-7181-0354-8*, M Joseph) Viking Penguin.

— Truth with Her Boots on. LC 74-194524. 191 p. 1974. 2.20 (*0-7181-1167-2*, M Joseph) Viking Penguin.

— A Woman Named Anne. 261p. 1993. reprint ed. pap. 5.95 (*0-89733-338-1*) Academy Chi Pubs.

Cecil, Hugh. Facing Armageddon: The First World War Experienced. 1996. pap. text 39.95 (*0-85052-525-X*, Pub. by Leo Cooper) Trans-Atl Phila.

Cecil, Hugh. The Flower of Battle: How Britain Won the Great War. rev. ed. LC 96-5030. (Illus.). 440p. 1996. 32.00 (*1-883642-05-1*) Steerforth Pr.

Cecil, Hugh, jt. auth. see Liddle, Peter.

Cecil, Ivon. Kirby Kelvin & the Not Laughing Lessons. LC 97-30994. (Illus.). (J). (ps-4). 1998. 14.95 (*1-879085-95-X*, Whispering Coyote); pap. 5.95 (*1-879085-39-9*, Whispering Coyote) Charlesbridge Pub.

Cecil, John, et al. Tug Hill: A Four Season Guide to the Natural Side. McNamara, Robert, ed. & illus. by. LC 99-50099. 272p. 2000. pap. 19.95 (*0-925168-76-9*) North Country.

Cecil, John, jt. auth. see Guyhn, Nguyen.

Cecil, Lamar. The German Diplomatic Service, 1871-1914. LC 76-3250. 367p. 1976. reprint ed. pap. 113.80 (*0-7837-9312-X*, 206005200004) Bks Demand.

— Wilhelm II: Prince & Emperor, 1859-1900. LC 88-27798. (Illus.). xxii, 464p. (C). 1989. 49.95 (*0-8078-1828-3*) U of NC Pr.

— Wilhelm II Vol. 2: Emperor & Exile, 1900-1941. 448p. (C). 1996. 49.95 (*0-8078-2283-3*) U of NC Pr.

Cecil, Larry & Beckwith, Jack. Glossary of Standard Finishing Terminology. Deemer, Betty, ed. LC 91-60453. 98p. 1991. pap. text 5.80 (*0-87263-403-5*) SME.

Cecil, Laura. The Frog Princess, Vol. VII. LC 94-4573.Tr. of Tsarevna Liagushka. (Illus.). 32p. (J). (gr. 1 up). 1995. 16.00 (*0-688-13506-4*, Grenwillow Bks) HarpC Child Bks.

— Noah & the Space Ark. LC 97-12428. (Illus.). 32p. (J). (ps-3). 1998. lib. bdg. 19.85 (*1-57505-255-5*, Carolrhoda) Lerner Pub.

***Cecil, Laura & Chichester Clark, Emma.** Kingfisher Book of Toy Stories. LC 99-49921. (Illus.). 80p. (J). (gr. k-2). 2000. 17.95 (*0-7534-5184-0*, Kingfisher) LKC.

Cecil, Mirabel. Ruby, the Christmas Donkey. LC 98-19627. (J). 1999. pap. text 3.99 (*0-7636-0716-9*) Candlewick Pr.

Cecil, Nancy L. The Art of Inquiry: Questioning Strategies for K-6 Classrooms. (Illus.). 164p. 1995. pap., teacher ed. 17.00 (*1-895411-74-2*) Peguis Pubs Ltd.

— Developing Environmental Awareness Through Children's Literature: A Guide for Teachers & Librarians, K-8. LC 96-2361. 188p. (J). (gr. k-8). 1996. pap. 28.50 (*0-7864-0221-0*) McFarland & Co.

— Freedom Fighters: Affective Teaching of the Language Arts. 2nd ed. LC 94-197880. (Illus.). 232p. (C). 1994. pap. text 15.95 (*1-879215-22-5*) Sheffield WI.

— Literacy & the Arts for the Integrated Classroom. 2nd ed. (C). 1998. pap. text. write for info. (*0-8013-1860-2*) Addison-Wesley.

— Striking a Balance: Positive Practices for Early Literacy. LC 98-50862. 1999. pap. 32.95 (*1-890871-21-4*) Holcomb Hath.

— Teaching to the Heart: An Affective Approach to Literacy Instruction. 2nd ed. 153p. (C). 1992. pap. text 15.50 (*1-879215-13-6*) Sheffield WI.

Cecil, Nancy L. & Roberts, Patricia L. Families in Children's Literature: A Resource Guide. LC 97-33635. 125p. (J). (gr. 4-8). 1998. pap. 18.50 (*1-56308-313-2*) Libs Unl.

Cecil, Nancy L., jt. auth. see Roberts, Patricia L.

***Cecil, Nancy Lee.** Activities for Striking a Balance in Early Literacy. 160p. 2000. pap. 18.95 (*1-890871-31-1*) Holcomb Hath.

Cecil, Nancy Lee & Lauritzen, Phyllis. Literacy & the Arts for the Integrated Classroom: Alternative Ways of Knowing. 192p. (C). 1994. pap. text 40.31 (*0-8013-1096-2*, 79549) Longman.

Cecil, Paul F. Herbicidal Warfare: The Ranch Hand Project in Vietnam. LC 85-30779. 302p. 1986. 55.00 (*0-275-92007-0*, C2007, Praeger Pubs) Greenwood.

Cecil, R. John Newton. 1997. pap. 11.99 (*1-85792-284-0*, Pub. by Christian Focus) Spring Arbor Dist.

Cecil, Randy. Dusty Locks & the Three Bears. 1999. 15.95 (*0-8050-5862-1*) H Holt & Co.

Cecil, Richard. Alcatraz. LC 91-23326. 82p. 1992. pap. 14.95 (*1-55753-015-7*) Purdue U Pr.

— Einstein's Brain. LC 86-1607. (University of Utah Press Poetry Ser.). 87p. (Orig.). reprint ed. pap. 30.00 (*0-7837-5540-6*, 204531400005) Bks Demand.

— In Search of the Great Dead: Poems. LC 98-40993. 1999. pap. 11.95 (*0-8093-2260-9*) S Ill U Pr.

Cecil, Robert. Cults in 19th Century Britain. 20p. 1988. pap. 7.00 (*0-904674-15-0*, Pub. by Octagon Pr) ISHK.

— Cultural Imperialism. 7p. 1971. pap. 6.00 (*0-904674-06-1*, Pub. by Octagon Pr) ISHK.

— Education & Elitism in Nazi Germany. 6p. 1971. pap. 6.00 (*0-904674-05-3*, Pub. by Octagon Pr) ISHK.

Cecil, Robert & Wade, David, eds. Cultural Encounters. 241p. 1990. 30.00 (*0-86304-050-0*, Pub. by Octagon Pr) ISHK.

Cecil, Rosanne, ed. The Anthropology of Pregnancy Loss: Comparative Studies in Miscarriage, Stillbirth & Neo-natal Death. LC 96-9158. 226p. 1996. 49.50 (*1-85973-120-1*, Pub. by Berg Pubs); pap. 19.50 (*1-85973-125-2*, Pub. by Berg Pubs) NYU Pr.

Cecil, Russell L., et al, eds. Cecil Textbook of Medicine, 2 vols., Vol. 1. 20th ed. LC 94-43773. 1996. write for info. (*0-7216-3574-1*, W B Saunders Co) Harcrt Hlth Sci Grp.

— Cecil Textbook of Medicine, 2 vols., Vol. 2. 20th ed. LC 94-43773. 1996. write for info. (*0-7216-3575-X*, W B Saunders Co) Harcrt Hlth Sci Grp.

***Cecil, Sam K.** Evolution of the Bourbon Whiskey Industry in Kentucky. 1999. 34.95 (*1-56311-508-5*) Turner Pub KY.

Cecil, T. E. Lie Sphere Geometry: With Applications to Submanifolds. (Universitext Ser.). (Illus.). xii, 207p. 1991. 47.95 (*0-387-97747-3*) Spr-Verlag.

Cecil, Thomas E. & Chern, Shiing-Shen, eds. Tight & Taut Submanifolds. LC 98-108271. (Mathematical Sciences Research Institute Publications: Vol. 32). 368p. (C). 1997. text 47.95 (*0-521-62047-3*) Cambridge U Pr.

Cecil, Tom. I Want My Turn in the Shower. LC 96-97136. (Illus.). 150p. (Orig.). 1996. pap. 13.95 (*0-925436-14-3*) Cam-Tech Pub.

Cecil, William. A Declaration of the Favourable Dealing of Her Maiesties Commissioners Appointed for the Examination of Certaine Traitours. LC 73-25637. (English Experience Ser.: No. 113). 1969. reprint ed. 15.00 (*90-221-0113-4*) Walter J Johnson.

Cecil, William W. The List. (Illus.). 7.95 (*0-9602766-0-2*) Whitten Pub Co.

Cecile, Jean-Jacques. Encyclopedia of Special Forces. (Special Operations Ser.). (Illus.). 450p. 1999. pap. text 24.95 (*2-908182-92-0*) Histoire.

Cecilia, Cesar A. Enciclopedia de la Avicultura. 2nd ed. (SPA.). 990p. 1964. 125.00 (*0-8288-6771-2*, S14560) Fr & Eur.

Cecilio, Bob, ed. see Neusom, Daniel.

Cecilione, Michael. Domination. 448p. 1993. mass mkt. 4.50 (*0-8217-4406-2*, Zebra Kensgtn) Kensgtn Pub Corp.

— Easy Prey. 320p. 1995. mass mkt. 4.99 (*0-8217-4860-2*, Zebra Kensgtn) Kensgtn Pub Corp.

— Muse. 320p. 1999. text 23.95 (*1-57566-313-9*) Kensgtn Pub Corp.

***Cecilione, Michael.** Muse. 2000. mass mkt. 6.99 (*0-7860-1134-3*) Kensgtn Pub Corp.

— Thirst. 2000. mass mkt. 5.99 (*0-7860-1091-6*, Pinncle Kensgtn) Kensgtn Pub Corp.

Cecilione, Micheal. Tell Me No Lies. 1996. pap. 5.99 (*1-57566-061-X*) Kensgtn Pub Corp.

Cecilione, Mike. Thirst. 480p. 1999. mass mkt. 5.99 (*0-8217-5143-3*, Zebra Kensgtn) Kensgtn Pub Corp.

Cecille, L. & Simon, R., eds. Acid Digestion Process for Radioactive Waste. LC 83-10792. (Radioactive Waste Management Ser.: Vol. 11). (Illus.). x, 108p. 1983. text 147.00 (*3-7186-0174-5*) Gordon & Breach.

Cecio, S. L., et al, eds. Cavitation & Gas-Liquid Flow in Fluid Machinery & Devices - 1995. LC 94-71579. (1995 ASME/JSME Fluids Engineering Conference Ser.: FED-Vol. 226). 168p. 1995. 90.00 (*0-7918-1481-5*, G00976) ASME.

Cecire, Kenneth. Multiple Choice Questions in Preparation for the AP Physics ("B" & "C") Examination. 80p. (YA). (gr. 11-12). 1991. teacher ed. write for info. (*1-878621-11-4*); student ed. 15.95 (*1-878621-10-6*) D & S Mktg Syst.

Cecka, J. M., jt. ed. see Terasaki, Paul I.

Cecka, J. Michael & Terasaki, Paul I. Clinical Transplants, 1997. (Illus.). 650p. 1998. 90.00 (*1-880318-06-7*) UCLA Tissue.

Cecka, J. Michael, jt. ed. see Terasaki, Paul I.

Cecotti, Loralie. Pacific Northwest Writers Conference Story. (Illus.). 60p. (Orig.). 1983. pap. 6.95 (*0-933992-27-0*) Coffee Break.

— Seattle Center. (Color-A-Story Ser.). (Illus.). 24p. (Orig.). (J). (gr. 1-4). 1983. pap. 2.75 (*0-933992-30-0*) Coffee Break.

— Washington Wildlife. (Color-A-Story Ser.). (Illus.). 24p. (Orig.). (J). (gr. k-5). 1984. pap. text 2.75 (*0-318-04105-7*) Coffee Break.

Cecrle, Ruth F. George Jacob Straub Comes to Plainview. LC 85-63403. 68p. 1986. pap. write for info. (*0-9616159-0-7*) R F S Cecrle.

CEDA Staff. Atlas of Nepal (on Sample Basis) 1997. pap. 23.00 (*0-7855-7522-7*) St Mut.

— Contemporary Argumentation & Debate: The Journal of the Cross. 116p. 1998. per. 8.50 (*0-7872-5555-6*, 41555501) Kendall-Hunt.

Cedar Bog Symposium Staff. Proceedings of the Cedar Bog Symposium, Urbana College, Nov. 3, 1973. King, Charles C. & Frederick, Clara M., eds. (Informative Circular Ser.: No. 4). 1974. pap. text 3.00 (*0-86727-071-3*) Ohio Bio Survey.

Cedar, Nick. Farm Tractor Collectibles. (Illus.). 160p. 1998. 29.95 (*0-7603-0385-1*) MBI Pubg.

Cedar, P. James, I & II Peter, Jude. (Mastering the Old & New Testament Ser.: Vol. 11). pap. 14.99 (*0-8499-3327-7*) Word Pub.

Cedar, Paul A. James, I & II Peter, Jude. (Communicator's Commentary Ser.: Vol. 11). 262p. 22.99 (*0-8499-0164-2*) Word Pub.

— A Life of Prayer: Cultivating the Inner Life of the Christian Leader. LC 98-15084. (Swindoll Christian Leadership Library). 262p. 1998. 24.99 (*0-8499-1355-1*) Word Pub.

***Cedar, Paul A.** Life of Prayer: Cultivating the Inner Life of the Christian Leader, Supersaver Edition. (Swindoll Leadership Library). 1998. 19.97 (*0-8499-1564-3*) Tommy Nelson.

Cedar Rapids Community School District Staff. Improving Spelling Performance: Administrator's Guide Block Five. 3rd ed. 192p. 1991. ring bd. 24.90 (*0-8403-6581-0*) Kendall-Hunt.

— Improving Spelling Performance: Administrator's Guide Block Four. 3rd ed. 192p. 1991. ring bd. 24.90 (*0-8403-6579-9*) Kendall-Hunt.

***Cedar-Southworth, Donna Marie.** The Catholic Marriage Wisdom Book. LC 00-130463. 160p. 2000. pap. 14.95 (*0-87973-410-8*) Our Sunday Visitor.

***Cedar, William J.** A Window into My Soul. 36p. 2000. pap. 10.95 (*1-58535-021-4*) In His Steps.

Cedard, Lise & Firth, Anthony, eds. Placental Signals: Autocrine & Paracine Control of Pregnancy. (Trophoblast Research Ser.: Vol. 6). (Illus.). 400p. (C). 1993. 90.00 (*1-878822-27-7*) Univ Rochester Pr.

Cedarleaf, Jay. Plant Layout & Flow Improvement. LC 94-4207. (Illus.). 240p. 1997. reprint ed. pap. 29.00 (*0-9658416-1-8*) Bluecreek Publ.

Cedarmont, Ninos. Cantemos y Juguemos. 1999. 7.99 (*0-7601-2853-7*) Brentwood Music.

— Cantos Biblicos: 16 Cantos Biblicos Clasicos Para Ninos. 1999. 7.99 (*0-7601-2850-2*) Brentwood Music.

— Cantos de Escuela Dominical. 1999. 7.99 (*0-7601-2852-9*) Brentwood Productions.

— Cantos Escolares. 1999. 7.99 (*0-7601-2855-3*) Brentwood Music.

— Cantos Pre-Escolares. 1999. 7.99 (*0-7601-2856-1*) Brentwood Music.

Cedars, Mary. Stories Rocks Tell: An Introduction to Rocks, Fossils & Soils for Children. (Illus.). 34p. (J). (gr. k-7). 1993. reprint ed. pap. 5.00 (*0-939132-04-4*) Hermione Hse.

CEDC Federal Credit Union Staff. Head Start to Success. 48p. 1994. pap., per. 12.95 (*0-7872-0211-8*) Kendall-Hunt.

***CEDCO Publishing Staff.** Austin Powers Sticker Book. (Illus.). (J). 2000. pap. 8.95 (*0-7683-2225-1*) CEDCO Pub.

— Big Dogs Sticker Book. (Illus.). (J). 2000. pap. 8.95 (*0-7683-2173-5*) CEDCO Pub.

— Blue Kitty Journal. 2000. 6.95 (*0-7683-2137-9*) CEDCO Pub.

— Blue Kitty Journal. large type ed. 2000. 8.95 (*0-7683-2131-X*) CEDCO Pub.
— Bubblegum Sticker Book: An Alter-Ego Trip. (Illus.). (J). 2000. pap. 8.95 (*0-7683-2172-7*) CEDCO Pub.
— .com Internet @ddress Book. 2000. 14.95 (*0-7683-2218-9*) CEDCO Pub.
— Gerbera Daisies Journal. 2000. 6.95 (*0-7683-2139-5*) CEDCO Pub.
— Gerbera Daisies Journal. large type ed. 2000. 8.95 (*0-7683-2133-6*) CEDCO Pub.
— Girl Thangs: Big Sticker Book. (Illus.). (J). 2000. pap. 8.95 (*0-7683-2168-9*) CEDCO Pub.
— Inspired Words. 2000. pap. 8.95 (*0-7683-2171-9*) CEDCO Pub.
— Inspired Words Sticker Book. (Illus.). 22p. (J). 2000. pap. 8.95 (*0-7683-2170-0*) CEDCO Pub.
— Internet @ddress Book. 2000. 14.95 (*0-7683-2219-7*) CEDCO Pub.
— IPO & Palm Tree Journal. 2000. 6.95 (*0-7683-2134-4*) CEDCO Pub.
— IPO & Palm Tree Journal, 1. large type ed. 2000. 8.95 (*0-7683-2128-X*) CEDCO Pub.
— IPO on a Pedestal Journal. 2000. 6.95 (*0-7683-2135-2*) CEDCO Pub.
— IPO on a Pedestal Journal. large type ed. 2000. 8.95 (*0-7683-2129-8*) CEDCO Pub.
— Power Puff Sticker Book. (Illus.). (J). 2000. pap. 8.95 (*0-7683-2227-8*) CEDCO Pub.
— Powerpuff Girls. (Illus.). (J). 2000. 14.95 (*0-7683-2229-4*) CEDCO Pub.
— Shagwell, CIA: Confidential. (Austin Powers Bks.). 2000. pap. text 9.95 (*0-7683-2146-8*) CEDCO Pub.
— Shar-Pei with Apples. 2000. 6.95 (*0-7683-2138-7*) CEDCO Pub.
— Shar-Pei with Apples Journal. large type ed. 2000. 8.95 (*0-7683-2132-8*) CEDCO Pub.
— South Park Sticker Book. (Illus.). (J). 2000. pap. 8.95 (*0-7683-2226-X*) CEDCO Pub.
— Why Must I Be Surrounded by Idiots? 2000. pap. text 9.95 (*0-7683-2145-X*) CEDCO Pub.
— WWJD Sticker Book. (Illus.). (J). 2000. pap. 8.95 (*0-7683-2169-7*) CEDCO Pub.
— Xtreme Sticker Book. (Illus.). (J). 2000. pap. 8.95 (*0-7683-2158-1*) CEDCO Pub.
— Yellow Daisies Journal. 2000. 6.95 (*0-7683-2136-0*) CEDCO Pub.
— Yellow Daisies Journal. large type ed. 2000. 8.95 (*0-7683-2130-1*) CEDCO Pub.

Cedefop Staff, jt. auth. see Eurydice Staff.

Cedel Staff. Diccionario de los Alimentos. (SPA.). 1988. 65.00 (*0-7859-5974-2*, 8435203387) Fr & Eur.
— Diccionario de Medicina de Urgencia: Dictionary of Emergency Medicine. 2nd ed. (SPA.). 208p. 1977. 9.95 (*0-8288-5318-5*, S13672) Fr & Eur.

Cedeno, Christine L., jt. ed. see Clevinger, Mary A.

Cedeno, Maria E. Cesar Chavez: Labor Leader. LC 92-22620. (Hispanic Heritage Ser.). (Illus.). 32p. (J). (gr. 2-4). 1993. pap. 4.95 (*1-56294-808-3*) Millbrook Pr.

Cedeno, Maria E. Cesar Chavez: Labor Leader. LC 92-22620. (Hispanic Heritage Ser.). 1993. 10.15 (*0-606-06271-8*, Pub. by Turtleback) Demco.

Cederbaums, Juris. Wiretapping & Electronic Eavesdropping: The Law & Its Implications - A Comparative Study. (N. Y. U. Criminal Law Education & Research Center, Monograph Ser.: Vol. 2). 77p. 1969. reprint ed. pap. 18.50 (*0-8377-0402-2*, Rothman) W S Hein.

Cederberg, Donna, et al. Breast Cancer? Let Me Check My Schedule! 250p. 1994. pap. 12.95 (*0-9641386-0-3*) Innovat Med.

Cederberg, Fred. The Long Road Home: The Autobiography of a Canadian Soldier in Italy in World War II. LC 99-203982. (Illus.). 257p. 1985. pap. 13.95 (*0-7737-5050-9*) Genl Dist Srvs.

***Cederberg, Fred.** The Long Road Home: The Autobiography of a Canadian Soldier in Italy in World War II. (Illus.). 262p. 2000. pap. 19.95 (*0-7737-6105-5*) Stoddart Publ.

Cederberg, Goran, et al. The Complete Book of Trout Flyfishing. (Illus.). 200p. (Orig.). 1995. pap. 21.95 (*0-88317-191-0*) Stoeger Pub Co.

Cederberg, Herbert. An Economic Analysis of English Settlement in North America (1583-1635) Bruchey, Stuart, ed. LC 76-39825. (Continuing Series for American Dissertations). (Illus.). 1977. reprint ed. lib. bdg. 35.95 (*0-405-09905-3*) Ayer.

Cederberg, J. N. A Course in Modern Geometries. Ewing, J. H. et al, eds. (Undergraduate Texts in Mathematics Ser.). (Illus.). xii, 232p. 1995. reprint ed. 49.95 (*0-387-96922-5*) Spr-Verlag.

***Cederberg, Judith N.** A Course in Modern Geometries. 2nd ed. LC 99-57465. (Undergraduate Texts in Mathematics Ser.). (Illus.). 285p. 2000. 59.95 (*0-387-98972-2*) Spr-Verlag.

Cederberg, William E. On the Solution of the Differential Equations of Motion of a Double Pendulum. LC 24-3604. (Augustana College Library Publications: No. 9). 62p. 1923. pap. 1.00 (*0-910182-06-X*) Augustana Coll.

Cederblom. Critical Reasoning. 3rd ed. (Philosophy Ser.). 1990. text, teacher ed. write for info. (*0-534-14689-9*) Wadsworth Pub.
— Critical Reasoning. 5th ed. (Philosophy Ser.). 2000. pap. 39.75 (*0-534-51940-7*) Wadsworth Pub.

Cederblom, Jerry & Paulsen, David W. Critical Reasoning: Understanding & Criticizing Arguments & Theories. 2nd ed. 290p. (C). 1985. mass mkt. 21.00 (*0-534-05616-4*) Wadsworth Pub.
— Critical Reasoning: Understanding & Criticizing Arguments & Theories. 4th ed. LC 95-18557. 440p. (C). 1995. 55.95 (*0-534-50410-8*) Wadsworth Pub.

Cedercrans, Lucille. The Nature of the Soul. 614p. pap. text 16.95 (*1-883493-02-1*) Wisdom Impress.
— The Nature of the Soul. 614p. 1993. 3.5 hd 24.95 (*1-883493-03-X*) Wisdom Impress.
— Soul & Its Instrument. 200p. 1994. disk 24.95 (*1-883493-19-6*) Wisdom Impress.
— Soul & Its Instrument. (Path of Initiation Ser.). 250p. 1995. text 24.95 (*1-883493-20-X*); pap. text 18.95 (*1-883493-21-8*) Wisdom Impress.

Cedergren, Harry R. Drainage of Highway & Airfield Pavements. LC 86-21018. 306p. 1987. reprint ed. lib. bdg. 49.50 (*0-89874-986-7*) Krieger.

***Cedergren, Sten.** The Adventurous Life of a Vagabond Hunter. limited aut. num. ed. (Illus.). 300p. 2000. boxed set 70.00 (*1-57157-159-0*) Safari Pr.

Cederholm, Theresa. Afro-American Artists: A Bio-Bibliographical Directory. 1973. 10.00 (*0-89073-007-5*, 101) Boston Public Lib.

Cedering, Siv. Letters from the Floating World: Selected & New Poems. LC 84-5222. (Pitt Poetry Ser.). 195p. 1984. pap. 60.50 (*0-608-05083-0*, 206563700005) Bks Demand.

Cedering, Siv, jt. auth. see Barkan, Stanley H.

Cedering, Siv, jt. ed. see Barkan, Stanley H.

Cedering, Siv, tr. see Aspenstrom, Werner.

Cederlof, Gunnel. Bond Lost: Subordination, Conflict & Mobilisation in Rural South India c. 1900-70. LC 97-906098. (C). 1997. 36.00 (*81-7304-193-8*, Pub. by Manohar) S Asia.

Cederlof, Mikael. The Element - Stow in the History of English. LC 98-171826. (Studia Anglistica Upsaliensia Ser.: Vol. 103). 220p. 1998. pap. 42.50 (*91-554-4218-8*) Coronet Bks.

Cederman, Lars-Erik. Emergent Actors in World Politics: How States & Nations Develop & Dissolve. LC 96-45562. (Princeton Studies in Complexity). 290p. 1997. pap. text 19.95 (*0-691-02148-1*, Pub. by Princeton U Pr) Cal Prin Full Svc.

***Cederman, Lars-Erik, ed.** Constructing Europe's Identity: The External Dimension. 280p. 2000. lib. bdg. 55.00 (*1-55587-872-5*) L Rienner.

Cederquist, Natalie, jt. auth. see Levin, James.

Cederroth, Sven. Survival & Profit in Rural Java: The Case of an East Javanese Village. (SIAS Monographs: No. 63). 330p. (C). 1996. text 49.00 (*0-7007-0294-6*, Pub. by Curzon Pr Ltd) UH Pr.

Cederroth, Sven, jt. auth. see Antlov, Hans.

Cederroth, Sven, jt. auth. see Syed Hassan, Sharifah Z.

Cederstrom, Lorelei. Fine-Tuning the Feminine Psyche: Jungian Patterns in the Novels of Doris Lessing. LC 89-13242. (American University Studies: English Language & Literature: Ser. IV, Vol. 99). 249p. 1990. text 44.95 (*0-8204-1047-0*) P Lang Pubng.

Cederstrom, Ritva, tr. see Joenpelto, Eeva.

***Cederwall, Sandraline & Riney, Hal.** Spratling Silver: Centennial Edition. (Illus.). 2000. pap. 50.00 (*0-8118-2954-5*) Chronicle Bks.

Cedex, Pierre B., jt. auth. see Bouysset, M.

Cedolin, Luigi, jt. auth. see Bazant, Zdenek P.

Cedoline, Anthony J. Job Burnout in Public Education: Symptoms, Causes & Survival Skills. LC 81-23289. 270p. reprint ed. pap. 83.70 (*0-8357-5546-0*, 203516400093) Bks Demand.

Cedor, Jean, jt. auth. see Aresenault, Jane.

Cedor, Jean, jt. auth. see Arsenault, Jane.

Cedra, C. Lexique Illustre du Machinisme et des Equipements Agricoles. (FRE.). 350p. 1991. 85.00 (*0-8288-7258-9*, 2852067390) Fr & Eur.

Cedric Willson Symposium on Expansive Cement Staff. Cedric Willson Symposium on Expansive Cement. LC 80-67065. (American Concrete Institute Publication: No. SP-64). (Illus.). 333p. 1980. reprint ed. pap. 103.30 (*0-608-07960-X*, 206793200012) Bks Demand.

Cedrins, Inara, ed. Contemporary Latvian Poetry. LC 84-8800. (Iowa Translations Ser.). 216p. (Orig.). reprint ed. pap. 67.00 (*0-7837-1619-2*, 204191200024) Bks Demand.

Cedrins, Inara, tr. see Ivask, Astrud.

Cedrone, Stuart. Righteousness Inside Out: The Believer's Guide to Experiencing the Righteousness of Christ. LC 95-46991. 1996. pap. 1.97 (*0-8163-1307-5*) Pacific Pr Pub Assn.

Cedronio, M. Francois Simiand: Methode Historique et Sciences Sociales. 541p. 1987. write for info. (*2-903928-28-2*) Gordon & Breach.
— Francois Simiand: Methode Historique et Sciences Sociales. vi, 534p. 1987. pap. text 72.00 (*2-88124-188-3*) Gordon & Breach.

Cee, Gary. Classic Rock. 1995. text 17.98 (*1-56799-168-8*, MetroBooks) M Friedman Pub Grp Inc.

Ceely, Jonatha, et al. Writing a Research Paper. rev. ed. (C). 1983. pap. text 5.25 (*0-88334-108-5*) Longman.
— Writing a Research Paper. 4th ed. 87p. 1992. pap. 10.99 (*0-8013-0698-1*, 78725) Longman.

***Ceely, Jonatha, et al.** Writing a Research Paper. 5th ed. 138p. (YA). (gr. 7-12). 1999. pap. text 13.33 (*1-877653-66-7*) Wayside Pub.

CEEM Information Services Staff. Aboveground Tank State Regulatory Guide. 483p. 1992. pap. 195.00 (*1-883337-00-3*) Ctr Energy Envir.
— The ISO 9000 Registered Company Directory. 240p. 1992. pap. text 195.00 (*1-883337-50-X*) Ctr Energy Envir.

CEF Staff. Child Evangelism Handbook. 218p. 1987. text 35.99 (*1-55976-200-4*) CEF Press.
— How to Lead a Child to Christ. 1962. 0.25 (*0-685-74177-X*) CEF Press.

CEF Staff, ed. Growing Songs for Children. 60p. (J). (gr. k-6). 1978. pap. text 2.99 (*1-55976-205-5*) CEF Press.

***Cefali, Leslie.** Cook-a-Book: Reading Activities for Grades Pk to 6. 2nd ed. LC 99-22697. (Illus.). 127p. 1999. pap. 17.95 (*1-57950-001-3*) Highsmith Pr.

Cefalo, Robert C., ed. Clinical Decisions in Obstetrics & Gynecology. LC 89-17573. (Illus.). 399p. 1990. reprint ed. pap. 123.70 (*0-608-05844-0*, 205981000007) Bks Demand.

Cefalo, Robert C. & Moos, Merry K. Preconceptional Health Care: A Practical Guide. 2nd ed. LC 94-10569. (Illus.). 276p. (C). (gr. 13). 1994. pap. text 50.95 (*0-8151-1638-1*, 24064) Mosby Inc.

Cefalo, Robert C., jt. auth. see Kuller, Jeffrey A.

***Cefola, Francine R.** Tell It to the Future: Have I Got a Story for You... about the Twentieth Century. Benkler, Marilyn, ed. (Illus.). 2000. pap. 14.95 (*0-9676256-8-8*) Gold Quill.

Cegarra, J., et al. The Dyeing of Textile Materials. 1993. pap. 90.00 (*1-870812-58-1*, Pub. by Textile Inst) St Mut.

Cegielka, Francis A. Toward a New Spring of Humankind. LC 84-72170. 1987. 8.95 (*0-8158-0427-X*) Chris Mass.

Cegielski, Jim. The Howard Stern Book: An Unauthorized, Unabashed, Uncensored Fan's Guide. LC 93-43798. 1994. pap. 12.95 (*0-8065-1505-8*, Citadel Pr) Carol Pub Group.

Cegla, Wojciech, ed. see Third Max Born Symposium Staff.

Ceglie, Domenico Di, see Freedman, D. & Di Ceglie, Domenico, eds.

Ceglowski, Deborah. Inside a Head Start Center: Developing Policies from Practice. LC 98-17077. (Early Childhood Education Ser.). 1998. pap. 19.95 (*0-8077-3748-8*) Tchrs Coll.
— Inside a Head Start Center: Developing Policies from Practice. LC 98-17077. (Early Childhood Education Ser.). 176p. 1998. 19.95 (*0-8077-3749-6*) Tchrs Coll.

Cegrell, Torsten. Power System Control Technology. (Illus.). 352p. 1986. text 46.00 (*0-13-688433-4*) P-H.

Ceh, Nick & Harder, Jeffery. The Golden Apple: War & Democracy in Croatia & Bosnia. 140p. 1996. 20.00 (*0-88033-347-2*, 450, Pub. by East Eur Monographs) Col U Pr.

Ceh, Nick, jt. ed. see Schelbert, Leo.

Cehovic, G. & Robison, G. A. Cyclic Nucleotides & Therapeutic Perspectives. (Advances in the Biosciences Ser.: 24). 256p. 1979. 55.00 (*0-08-023760-6*, Pergamon Pr) Elsevier.

Cei, Jose M. A New Species of Liolaemus: Sauria: Iguanidae, from the Andean Mountains of the Southern Mendoza Volcanic Region of Argentina. (Occasional Papers: No. 76). 6p. 1978. 1.00 (*0-317-04841-4*) U KS Nat Hist Mus.
— A New Species of Tropidurus (Sauria, Iguanidae) from the Arid Chacoan & Western Regions of Argentina. (Occasional Papers: No. 97). 10p. 1982. 1.00 (*0-317-04843-0*) U KS Nat Hist Mus.

Ceidigh, P. O., jt. ed. see Keegan, B. F.

Ceirin, Cyril O., jt. auth. see Ceirin, Kit O.

Ceirin, Kit O. & Ceirin, Cyril O. Women of Ireland: A Biographic Dictionary. (Illus.). 228p. (Orig.). 1996. pap. 19.95 (*0-937702-16-1*) Irish Bks Media.

Ceisel, Hans, jt. auth. see Kuprianczyk, George.

Ceitin, G. S., et al. Five Papers on Logic & Foundations. LC 51-5559. (Translations Ser.: Series 2, Vol. 99). 275p. 1972. text 45.00 (*0-8218-1799-X*, TRANS2/99) Am Math.
— Five Papers on Logic & Foundations. LC 51-5559. (Translations Ser.: Series 2, Vol. 98). 288p. 1972. text 49.00 (*0-8218-1798-1*, TRANS2/98) Am Math.
— Fourteen Papers on Logic, Geometry, Topology & Algebra. LC 72-2350. (Translations Ser. 2: Vol. 100). 316p. 1972. 67.00 (*0-8218-3050-3*, TRANS2/100) Am Math.

Cejador y Frauca, Julio. Historia de la Lengua y Literatura Castellana, 7 vols. limited ed. (SPA.). 1993. 750.00 (*84-249-1940-8*) Elliots Bks.
— Vocabulario Medieval Castellano. xii, 414p. 1996. reprint ed. 105.00 (*3-487-03378-X*) G Olms Pubs.

Cejas, Jose M. Montse, a Fun Loving Teenager. 256p. 1998. pap. 9.95 (*0-906138-46-9*) Scepter Pubs.

Cejka, Jaroslav, et al. The New Czech Poetry. LC 88-51309. 64p. 1988. pap. 13.95 (*1-85224-066-0*, Pub. by Bloodaxe Bks) Dufour.

Cejka, Joyce, jt. auth. see Wedemeyer, Avaril.

Cekada, Anthony. The Problems with the Prayers of the Modern Mass. 44p. (Orig.). 1993. pap. 4.00 (*0-89555-447-X*) TAN Bks Pubs.

Cekada, Anthony, tr. see Ottaviani, Alfredo C. & Bacci, Antonio C.

Cekala, Sharon, ed. Military Retirement: Possible Changes Merit Further Evaluation. (Illus.). 53p. (C). 1999. reprint ed. pap. text 20.00 (*0-7881-7857-1*) DIANE Pub.

Cekala, Sharon, et al. Military Attrition: DOD Could Save Millions by Better Screening Enlisted Personnel. (Illus.). 64p. (C). 1998. reprint ed. pap. text 20.00 (*0-7881-4334-4*) DIANE Pub.

Cekala, Sharon A. General & Flag Officers: Number Required Is Unclear Based on DOD's Draft Report. (Illus.). 46p. (C). 1998. pap. text 20.00 (*0-7881-4780-3*) DIANE Pub.
— Telemedicine: Federal Strategy Is Needed to Guide Investments. (Illus.). 103p. (C). 1999. pap. text 30.00 (*0-7881-4372-7*) DIANE Pub.

Cekala, Sharon A., et al. Defense Ammunition: Significant Problems Left Unattended Will Get Worse. (Illus.). 92p. (Orig.). (C). 1996. pap. text 25.00 (*0-7881-3695-X*) DIANE Pub.

Cekalska, K., tr. see Bienkowska, B., ed.

Cekanovskii, E. R., et al. Five Papers on Functional Analysis. LC 51-5559. (Translations Ser.: Series 2, Vol. 62). 284p. 1967. pap. 50.00 (*0-8218-1762-0*, TRANS2/62) Am Math.

Cela, Camillo Jose. La Colmena (The Hive)Tr. of Hive. 330p. 1996. pap. 14.95 (*0-679-76753-3*) Random.

Cela, Camilo J. Familia de Pascual Duarte. (SPA.). pap. 12.95 (*84-233-0732-8*, Pub. by Destino) Continental Bk.
— Mazurca para Dos Muertos. (SPA.). 1983. pap. 8.50 (*84-322-0484-6*, 3014) Ediciones Norte.

***Cela, Camilo Jose.** La Familia de Pascal Duarte. 1998. pap. text 8.95 (*84-8328-013-2*) E Martinez Roca.

Cela, Camilo Jose. Journey to the Alcarria. Lopez-Morillas, Frances M., tr. from SPA. LC 64-22235. 160p. (C). 1964. reprint ed. 12.95 (*0-299-03250-7*) U of Wis Pr.
— Loveless Fables. 1994. 19.95 (*0-02-523330-0*) Macmillan.
— Mazurka for Two Dead Men. Haugaard, Patricia, tr. from SPA. LC 92-12618.Tr. of Mazurca para Dos Muertos. 272p. 1992. 21.95 (*0-8112-1222-X*, Pub. by New Directions) Norton.
— Mazurka for Two Dead Men. Haugaard, Patricia, tr. from SPA. LC 92-12618.Tr. of Mazurca para Dos Muertos. 272p. 1994. reprint ed. pap. 10.95 (*0-8112-1277-7*, NDP789, Pub. by New Directions) Norton.
— Mrs. Caldwell Speaks to Her Son. Bernstein, J. S., tr. from SPA. LC 68-16379. 232p. 1990. reprint ed. 35.00 (*0-8014-0073-2*); reprint ed. pap. 12.95 (*0-8014-9783-3*) Cornell U Pr.
— Paginas Escogidas. Villanueva, Dario, ed. (Nueva Austral Ser.: Vol. 229). (SPA.). 1991. pap. text 24.95 (*84-239-7229-1*) Elliots Bks.
— San Camilo, 1936: The Eve, Feast, & Octave of St. Camillus of the Year 1936 in Madrid. Polt, John H., tr. LC 91-13388. 327p. 1991. pap. 17.95 (*0-8223-1196-8*); lib. bdg. 49.95 (*0-8223-1179-8*) Duke.
— Viaje a la Alcarria. (Nueva Austral Ser.: Vol. 131). (SPA.). 1991. pap. text 24.95 (*84-239-1931-5*) Elliots Bks.

Cela, Camilo Jose, et al, eds. La Familia de Pascula Duarte. 175p. (C). 1990. pap. text 19.33 (*0-13-528307-8*) P-H.

Cela, Camilo Jose & Lock, Penelope. Of Genes, Gods & Tyrants. 208p. (C). 1987. pap. text 58.50 (*1-55608-036-0*, D Reidel); lib. bdg. 110.00 (*1-55608-024-7*, D Reidel) Kluwer Academic.

Cela, Eranda. The Quadratic Assignment Problem: Theory & Algorithms. LC 97-43113. (Combinatorial Optimization Ser.). 287p. 1998. text 147.00 (*0-7923-4878-8*) Kluwer Academic.

Celada, F. & Pernis, B. T Lymphocytes: Structure, Function & Choices. LC 92-49284. (NATO ASI Ser.: Vol. 233). (Illus.). 268p. (C). 1992. text 95.00 (*0-306-44258-2*, Kluwer Plenum) Kluwer Academic.

Celalettin Bugday, M. Dizionario Italiano-Turco-Italiano. (ITA & TUR.). 1980. 14.95 (*0-8288-1646-8*, F58090) Fr & Eur.

***Celan, Paul.** Breathturn.Tr. of Atemwende. 300p. 2000. pap. 12.95 (*1-892295-76-8*) Green Integer.

Celan, Paul. Breathturn. Joris, Pierre, tr. from GER. (Sun & Moon Classics Ser.: No. 74).Tr. of Atemwende. 272p. 1995. 21.95 (*1-55713-217-8*) Sun & Moon CA.
— Breathturn. Joris, Pierre, tr. from GER. LC 95-206527. (Sun & Moon Classics Ser.: No. 74).Tr. of Atemwende. 272p. 1998. pap. 12.95 (*1-55713-218-6*, Pub. by Sun & Moon CA) Consort Bk Sales.

***Celan, Paul.** Collected Prose. 68p. 2000. pap. 14.95 (*1-85754-469-2*, Pub. by Carcanet Pr) Paul & Co Pubs.

Celan, Paul. Collected Prose. Waldrop, Rosmarie, tr. LC 90-30112. 77p. 1990. 15.95 (*0-935296-92-1*, Pub. by Sheep Meadow) U Pr of New Eng.
— Poems of Paul Celan. Hamburger, Michael, tr. from GER. & intro. by. (ENG & GER.). 350p. 1989. 24.95 (*0-89255-140-2*) Persea Bks.
— Poems of Paul Celan. Hamburger, Michael, tr. from GER. LC 88-22567. 350p. 1990. reprint ed. pap. 16.95 (*0-89255-134-8*) Persea Bks.

***Celan, Paul.** Romanian Poems. 2000. pap. 9.95 (*1-892295-41-5*) Green Integer.

Celan, Paul. Sprachgitter/Die Niemandsrose: Gedichte. (GER.). 158p. 1986. 18.00 (*3-10-010504-4*, Pub. by S Fischer) Intl Bk Import.
— Threadsuns. Joris, Pierre, tr. & intro. by. (Classics Ser.: No. 122). 272p. 2000. pap. 13.95 (*1-55713-294-1*, Pub. by Sun & Moon CA) Consort Bk Sales.

Celan, Paul & Sachs, Nelly. Paul Celan, Nelly Sachs: Correspondence. Wiedemann, Barbara, ed. Clark, Christopher, tr. from GER. LC 95-26058. (Illus.). 126p. 1995. text 24.95 (*1-878818-37-6*, Pub. by Sheep Meadow) U Pr of New Eng.
— Paul Celan, Nelly Sachs: Correspondence. Wiedemann, Barbara, ed. Clark, Christopher, tr. from GER. LC 94-24548. (Illus.). 126p. 1998. pap. 13.95 (*1-878818-71-6*, Pub. by Sheep Meadow) U Pr of New Eng.

***Celan, Paul, et al.** Glottal Stop: 101 Poems. LC 00-9307. (Poetry Ser.). 2000. 24.95 (*0-8195-6448-6*, Wesleyan Univ Pr) U Pr of New Eng.

Celani, David P. The Illusion of Love: Why the Battered Woman Returns to Her Abuser. 224p. 1995. 42.00 (*0-231-10036-1*) Col U Pr.
— The Illusion of Love: Why the Battered Woman Returns to Her Abuser. 240p. 1996. pap. 18.50 (*0-231-10037-X*) Col U Pr.
— The Treatment of the Borderline Patient: Applying Fairbairn's Object Relations Theory in the Clinical Setting. LC 92-1699. 200p. 1993. 30.00 (*0-8236-6644-1*) Intl Univs Pr.

Celano, Anthony, jt. auth. see Smith, Eugene.

***Celano, Thomas.** The First Life of St. Francis. Stace, Christopher, tr. 2000. pap. 12.95 (*0-281-05245-X*, Pub. by Society Prom Christ Know) Intl Pubs Mktg.

Celano, Thomas. St. Francis of Assisi: First & Second Life of St. Francis with Selections from the Treatise on the Miracles of Blessed Francis. 405p. 1963. pap. 15.00 (*0-8199-0554-2*, Frncscn Herld) Franciscan Pr.

Celant, Geramo, et al. Art-Fashion. (Illus.). 350p. 1997. pap. 45.00 (*1-881616-85-1*) Dist Art Pubs.

Celant, Germano. Aquattromani. 56p. 1996. pap. 25.95 (*88-7757-044-X*, Pub. by Hopefulmonster Editore) Dist Art Pubs.
— Arte Povera. (Illus.). 266p. 1998. 65.00 (*88-422-0810-8*, Pub. by U Allemandi) Antique Collect.
***Celant, Germano.** Dennis Oppenheim. 1999. 65.00 (*88-8158-219-8*) Charta.
Celant, Germano. Gilberto Zorio. (Illus.). 208p. (Orig.). 1991. pap. 40.00 (*88-7757-038-5*) Dist Art Pubs.
— Italian Metamorphosis, 1943-1968. 1994. 85.00 (*0-89207-115-X*) S R Guggenheim.
— Joel Peter Witkin: A Retrospective. (Illus.). 224p. 1995. 75.00 (*1-881616-20-7*, Pub. by Scalo Pubs) Dist Art Pubs.
***Celant, Germano.** Merce Cunningham. 317p. 1999. 45.00 (*88-8158-216-3*) Charta.
Celant, Germano. Michael Heizer. 1997. pap. 85.00 (*88-87029-02-4*, Pub. by Fondazione Prada) Dist Art Pubs.
— Rebecca Horn. 1993. 59.95 (*0-89207-110-9*) S R Guggenheim.
— Tony Cragg. LC 96-60053. (Illus.). 352p. 1996. 65.00 (*0-500-23723-9*, Pub. by Thames Hudson) Norton.
Celant, Germano, contrib. by. Biennale di Venezia XLVII: The 47th International Art Exhibition. LC 97-190587. (Illus.). 700p. 1997. pap. 59.95 (*88-435-6152-9*, Pub. by Electa) Gingko Press.
— Biennale Venezia XLVII: Future, Present, Past. LC 97-217477. (Illus.). 700p. 1997. pap. 79.95 (*88-435-6154-5*, Pub. by Electa) Gingko Press.
Celant, Germano, ed. Looking at Fashion: The Catalogue of the Florence Biennial. (Illus.). 684p. 1999. 75.00 (*88-8118-208-4*, Pub. by Skira IT) Abbeville Pr.
Celant, Germano, ed. Keith Haring. (Illus.). 208p. 1993. pap. 35.00 (*3-7913-1234-0*, Pub. by Prestel) te Neues.
Celant, Germano, et al, texts. Italian Painting. (Illus.). 220p. 1998. pap. 45.00 (*88-8158-125-6*, 810922) Dist Art Pubs.
— Piero Manzoni. LC 98-155335. (Illus.). 265p. 1998. pap. 49.95 (*88-8158-141-8*, 810921, Pub. by Charta) Dist Art Pubs.
Celant, Germano & Cacciari, Massimo, texts. Anselm Kiefer. (Illus.). 428p. 1998. pap. 55.00 (*88-8158-130-2*, 700024, Pub. by Charta) Dist Art Pubs.
***Celant, Germano & Koda, Harold.** Giorgio Armani. (Illus.). 400p. 2000. 75.00 (*0-8109-6927-0*, Pub. by Abrams) Time Warner.
Celant, Germano, et al. Claes Oldenburg: An Anthology. (Illus.). 592p. 1995. pap. 75.00 (*0-8109-6887-8*, Pub. by Abrams) Time Warner.
— Jim Dine: Walking Memory, 1959-1969. 1999. 55.00 (*0-8109-6918-1*, Pub. by Abrams) Time Warner.
— Richard Artschwager: PUBLIC (public) LC 91-75567. (Illus.). 80p. 1992. 19.95 (*0-932900-28-3*) Elvejhem Mus.
Celarie, Henriette. Behind Moroccan Walls. Morris, Constance L., tr. LC 74-106259. (Short Story Index Reprint Ser.). (Illus.). 1977. 21.95 (*0-8369-3296-X*) Ayer.
Celati, Gianni. Appearances. Hood, Stuart, tr. from ITA. 160p. (Orig.). 1992. pap. 14.99 (*1-85242-212-2*) Serpents Tail.
— Voices from the Plains. 144p. 1990. pap. 10.95 (*1-85242-143-6*) Serpents Tail.
Celaya, G., jt. ed. see Turnbull, P.
Celaya, Gabriel. Espacios de Chillida. (SPA., Illus.). 194p. 1993. 100.00 (*84-343-0184-9*) Elliots Bks.
***Celbridge, Yolanda.** Police Ladies. 2000. mass mkt. 6.95 (*0-352-33489-4*) Nexus.
Celbridge, Yolanda. Sandra's New School. 2000. mass mkt. 6.95 (*0-352-33454-1*) London Brdge.
***Celcasun, Merih.** State-Owned Enterprises in the Middle East & North Africa: Privatization, Performance & Reform. LC 00-32208. 2000. write for info. (*0-415-23609-6*) Routledge.
Celce-Murcia, Marianne. Teaching English As a Second or Foreign Language. 1994. pap. 75.00 (*963-05-6770-9*, Pub. by Akade Kiado) St Mut.
Celce-Murcia, Marianne, ed. Teaching English As a Second or Foreign Language. 2nd ed. 567p. (J). 1991. pap. 33.95 (*0-8384-2860-6*) Heinle & Heinle.
Celce-Murcia, Marianne & Hilles, Sharon L. Teaching Techniques in English as a Second Language: Techniques & Resources in Teaching Grammar. Campbell, Russel N. & Rutherford, William E., eds. (Illus.). 200p. 1988. pap. text 13.50 (*0-19-434191-7*) OUP.
***Celce-Murcia, Marianne & Olshtain, Elite.** Discourse & Context in Language Teaching. 352p. (C). 2000. 69.95 (*0-521-64055-5*); pap. 26.95 (*0-521-64837-8*) Cambridge U Pr.
Celce-Murcia, Marianne, et al. Teaching Pronunciation: A Course for Teachers of English to Speakers of Other Languages. LC 96-20132. (Illus.). 447p. (C). 1996. text 69.95 (*0-521-40504-1*); pap. text 30.95 (*0-521-40694-3*) Cambridge U Pr.
Celcemurcia. The Grammar Book. 2nd ed. LC 98-218133. (Teaching Methods Ser.). 800p. (J). 1998. pap. 54.95 (*0-8384-4725-2*) Heinle & Heinle.
Celebrar, Para. Mil Voces: Blue. 11.00 (*0-687-43183-2*) Abingdon.
— Mil Voces: Red. 11.00 (*0-687-43185-9*) Abingdon.
Celebrate Jesus Inc. Staff. Celebrate Jesus! The Commemorative Bible of the Millennium. 1999. 29.99 (*1-55819-795-8*) Broadman.
Celebrating the Lectionary. 24 Intergenerational Liturgies of the Word. 92p. 1999. pap. text 19.95 (*0-89390-460-0*) Resource Pubns.
***Celebration Staff, ed.** Struggle for Democracy Brief Edition 99 Update. 2nd ed. (C). 1999. (*0-321-06801-7*) Benjamin-Cummings.
Celebre, Dionne M. Let's Talk: A Resource Guide to Good Speaking. 1996. 10.00 (*1-878276-24-7*) Educ Systs Assocs Inc.
Celebrity Collection of Recipes Staff. Toastin' the Dogs: Recipes of the Famous & Distinguished. Bresticker, Lane et al, eds. (Illus.). (Orig.). 1994. pap. text 16.95 (*0-9643198-0-2*) Paws With A Cause.
Celebuski, Carin. Nutrition Education in Public Elementary & Secondary Schools. 65p. 1996. pap. 4.25 (*0-16-048755-2*) USGPO.
— Nutrition Education in Public Elementary School Classrooms, K-5. 76p. 2000. pap. 7.00 (*0-16-050280-2*) USGPO.
— Status of Education Reform in Public Elementary & Secondary Schools: Principals' Perspectives. LC 98-156669. 92p. 1998. pap. 7.50 (*0-16-049521-0*) USGPO.
Celebuski, Carin & Farris, Elizabeth. Nutrition Education in Public Elementary & Secondary Schools. (Illus.). 57p. (C). 1998. pap. text 20.00 (*0-7881-4839-7*) DIANE Pub.
— Status of Education Reform in Public Elementary & Secondary Schools: Principals' Perspectives. (Illus.). 82p. (C). 1999. pap. text 20.00 (*0-7881-8152-1*) DIANE Pub.
Celebuski, Carin, jt. auth. see Cherlin, Andrew J.
Celecia, Deneen. Ancient Egypt Photo Fun Activities. Milliken, Linda, ed. (Illus.). 8p. (J). (gr. 3-6). 1994. pap. 6.95 (*1-56472-039-X*) Edupress Inc.
— Colonial American Photo Fun Activities. Milliken, Linda, ed. (Illus.). 8p. (J). (gr. 3-6). 1994. pap. 6.95 (*1-56472-040-3*) Edupress Inc.
— Frontier American Photo Fun Activities. Milliken, Linda, ed. (Illus.). 8p. (J). (gr. 3-6). 1994. pap. 6.95 (*1-56472-041-1*) Edupress Inc.
— Native American Photo Fun Activities. Milliken, Linda, ed. (Illus.). 8p. (J). (gr. 3-6). 1994. pap. 6.95 (*1-56472-042-X*) Edupress Inc.
Celecia, Deneen, ed. see Brown, Karen.
Celecia, Deneen, ed. see Brown, Karen & Engel, Holly.
Celecia, Deneen, ed. see Engel, Holly.
Celecia, Deneen, ed. see Engel, Holly & Brown, Karen.
Celecia, Deneen, ed. see Keller, Mary J.
Celecia, Deneen, ed. see Milliken, Linda.
Celek, Tim & Willow Creek Resources Staff. How to Rally Teams for Ministry. (Defining Moments Ser.: Vol. 8). 1994. audio 12.99 (*0-310-21049-6*) Zondervan.
Celek, Tim, et al. Inside the Soul of a New Generation: Insights & Strategies for Reaching Busters. 160p. 1996. pap. 9.99 (*0-310-20594-8*) Zondervan.
— Relating to Baby Busters. (Defining Moments Ser.: Vol. 11). 1995. audio 12.99 (*0-310-21079-8*) Zondervan.
Celender, Donald. Donald Celender: 28 Years of Writings, Questions & Answers. 500p. Date not set. pap. 29.95 (*0-923183-25-6*, Pub. by ART Pr NY) Dist Art Pubs.
Celenko, Theodore, ed. Egypt in Africa. (Illus.). 1997. 39.95 (*0-253-33269-9*) Ind U Pr.
Celentano, Dare. Essential Blues Guitar. (Illus.). 86p. 1998. pap. 19.95 incl. audio compact disk (*1-57424-060-9*) Centerstream Pub.
Celentano, Dave. The Art of Transcribing for Guitar. 76p. 1991. pap. text 16.95 incl. audio (*0-931759-56-0*) Centerstream Pub.
— Flying Fingers: The Technique of Speed Picking on the Guitar. 58p. (C). 1987. 15.95 incl. audio compact disk (*0-931759-20-X*) Centerstream Pub.
Celentano, Dave. Killer Pentatonics. (Illus.). 86p. (Orig.). 1992. pap. text 16.95 incl. audio (*0-931759-66-8*) Centerstream Pub.
Celentano, Dave. The Magic Touch: Two Hand Rock Technique. 48p. 1986. pap. text 14.95 incl. audio (*0-931759-16-1*) Centerstream Pub.
— Modal Jams & Theory: Using the Modes for Solo Guitar. (Illus.). 40p. (Orig.). 1993. pap. text 17.95 incl. cd-rom (*0-931759-76-5*) Centerstream Pub.
— Monster Scales & Modes. 48p. 1992. pap. 7.95 (*0-931759-59-5*) Centerstream Pub.
Celentano, Dave. Over the Top: Advance Two Hand Tapping for the Guitar. 50p. 1994. pap. 17.95 incl. audio compact disk (*0-931759-82-X*) Centerstream Pub.
Celentano, Dave. Rock Around the Classics: Innovative Ways of Playing Some of the Most Popular Classical Songs Ever. (Illus.). 80p. (Orig.). 1996. pap. text 19.95 incl. audio compact disk (*1-57424-039-0*) Centerstream Pub.
— Rock Licks: 40 of the Newest Rock Licks from Heavy Metal, Blues, Two-Handed & Basic Licks, Vol. 1. (Illus.). 32p. 1998. pap. 15.95 incl. audio (*0-931759-26-9*) Centerstream Pub.
— Rockin Christmas - Guitar. (Illus.). 68p. (YA). (gr. 9-12). 1994. pap. 17.95 (*0-931759-88-9*) Centerstream Pub.
— Speed Metal. 48p. 1989. pap. text 16.95 incl. audio (*0-931759-34-X*) Centerstream Pub.
Celentano, Suzanne C. & Marshall, Kevin. Theatre Management: A Successful Guide to Producing Plays on Commercial & Non-Profit Stages. LC 98-5835. 1998. pap. 29.00 (*0-88734-684-7*) Players Pr.
Celente, Gerald. Trends 2000: How to Prepare for & Profit from the Changes of the 21st Century. 352p. 1998. mass mkt. 14.99 (*0-446-67331-5*, Pub. by Warner Bks) Little.
Celente, Gerald & Milton, Tom. Trend Tracking. 1991. mass mkt. 12.99 (*0-446-39287-1*, Pub. by Warner Bks) Little.
Celente, Mary A. Fairy Tale at Forty: Curing My Incurable Disease, a True Story. 283p. (Orig.). 1995. pap. 25.00 (*0-9648167-1-7*) Trends Res Inst.
Celenza, Christopher S. Renaissance Humanism & the Papal Curia: Lapo da Castigliochio the Younger's "De Curia Commodis" LC 99-6686. (Papers & Monographs of the American Academy in Rome). (Illus.). 264p. 2000. text 47.50 (*0-472-10994-4*, 10994) U of Mich Pr.
***Celenza, Anna.** The Farewell Symphony. LC 99-47970. (Illus.). 32p. (J). (ps-4). 2000. 19.95 (*1-57091-406-0*) Charlesbridge Pub.
***Celenza, Gaetano Joseph.** Biological Processes. LC 99-66876. 216p. 1999. text 99.95 (*1-56676-768-7*) Technomic.
— Specialized Treatment Systems. (Industrial Waste Treatment Process Engineering Ser.: Vol. 3). 216p. 1999. text 99.95 (*1-56676-769-5*) Technomic.
Celenza, L. C. & Shakin, C. M. Relativistic Nuclear Physics: Theories of Structure & Scattering. (Lecture Notes in Physics Ser.: Vol. 2). 300p. 1986. text 54.00 (*9971-5-0010-8*); pap. text 30.00 (*9971-5-0011-6*) World Scientific Pub.
Celer, H. L., ed. Mercury in Liquids, Compressed Gases, Molten Salts & Other Elements. (Illus.). 271p. 1987. 120.00 (*0-317-66355-0*, Pergamon Pr) Elsevier.
Celeste, Emily, jt. auth. see Courtney, Elise.
Celeste, Marie. The Church & Love: A Treatise on the Love of Christ for the People of God. LC 98-17863. 196p. 1998. 49.00 (*0-7618-1131-1*); pap. 29.50 (*0-7618-1132-X*) U Pr of Amer.
— Elizabeth Ann Seton - A Self-Portrait: A Study of Her Spirituality. LC 85-72765. (Illus.). 305p. 1986. 18.95 (*0-913382-33-7*, 101-33); pap. 14.50 (*0-913382-53-1*, 101-33SC) Marytown Pr.
***Celeste, Marie.** The Intimate Friendships of Elizabeth Ann Bayley Seton: First Native Born American Saint (1774-1821) 232p. 2000. pap. 28.50 (*0-7618-1786-7*) U Pr of Amer.
***Celeste, Marie, ed.** Elizabeth Ann Seton - A Woman of Prayer: Meditation, Reflections & Poems Taken from Her Writings. 160p. 2000. pap. 19.50 (*0-7618-1785-9*) U Pr of Amer.
Celestial Arts Publishing Co. Staff. Princess Diana: The Book of Love. 1997. pap. 6.95 (*0-89087-866-8*) Celestial Arts.
Celestin, J. B., ed. see Haan, H.
Celestin, Julio. HCO French Grammar. LC 90-56018. (HarperCollins College Outline Ser.). 336p. 1991. pap. 15.00 (*0-06-467128-3*, Harper Ref) HarpC.
Celestin, L. R. Color Atlas of the Surgery & Management of Intestinal Stomas. (Illus.). 96p. (C). (gr. 13). 1987. 89.95 (*0-8151-1484-2*, 09093) Mosby Inc.
Celestin, Roger. From Cannibals to Radicals: Figures & Limits of Exoticism. 1996. pap. 21.95 (*0-8166-2605-7*); text 54.95 (*0-8166-2604-9*) U of Minn Pr.
***Celestine.** Fortune Telling: The Complete Guide to Predicting Fate & Fortune in the Stars & Other Mystic Arts. (Illus.). 533p. 2000. reprint ed. pap. text 15.00 (*0-7881-6894-0*) DIANE Pub.
Celestine. The Mammoth Book of Fortune Telling. LC 97-20113. (Illus.). 512p. 1997. pap. 10.95 (*0-7867-0429-2*) Carroll & Graf.
Celestri, John. The Christian Crusader: Plague of Evil. (Illus.). 80p. (Orig.). (J). (gr. 3-6). 1994. pap. 4.99 (*0-9634183-3-5*) CC Comics.
— The Christian Crusader: The Quest Begins. rev. ed. (Illus.). 80p. (J). (gr. 3-6). 1992. pap. 4.99 (*0-9634183-1-9*) CC Comics.
— The Christian Crusader: Web of Lies...Chains of Sin. (Illus.). 80p. (Orig.). (J). (gr. 3-6). 1993. pap. 4.99 (*0-9634183-2-7*) CC Comics.
Celi, Louis J. & Rutizer, Barry. Global Cash Management: How Top Companies Structure International Financial Transactions. 504p. 1991. 65.00 (*0-88730-468-0*, HarpBusn) HarpInfo.
Celia, George. The Triumph of Ideals: Love Affair with Every Day. (Illus.). 120p. 1998. 17.00 (*0-9621057-3-2*) G Celia.
— Ultimate You: With the Personal Magna Carta. LC 88-92579. (Illus.). 120p. (Orig.). 1989. 13.95 (*0-9621057-0-8*); pap. 7.95 (*0-9621057-2-4*); lib. bdg. 12.95 (*0-9621057-1-6*) G Celia.
Celia, Jean, ed. see Pearson, Judy C.
Celia, Michael A. & Gray, William G. Numerical Methods for Differential Equations: Fundamental Concepts for Scientific & Engineering Applications. 464p. (C). 1991. 69.80 (*0-13-626961-3*, 540801) P-H.
Celic, I., et al, eds. Experimental & Computational Aspects of Validation of Multiphase Flow CFD Codes. LC 94-71259. (Fluid Engineering Division Conference Ser.: Vol. 180). 1994. pap. 35.00 (*0-7918-1363-0*) ASME.
***Celichowska, Renata & Dlugoszewski, Lucia.** The Erick Hawkins Modern Dance Technique. (Illus.). 176p. 2000. pap. 24.95 (*0-87127-213-X*, Pub. by Princeton Bk Co) IPG Chicago.
Celicia, Deneen, ed. see Keller, Mary Jo.
Celidze, V. G. & Davarseisvili, A. G., eds. The Theory of the Denjoy Integral & Some Applications. 334p. (C). 1989. text 58.00 (*981-02-0021-8*) World Scientific Pub.
Celieres, Andre. The Prose Style of Emerson. 1972. 59.95 (*0-8490-0903-0*) Gordon Pr.
— The Prose Style of Emerson. (BCL1-PS American Literature Ser.). 87p. 1993. reprint ed. lib. bdg. 59.00 (*0-7812-6962-8*) Rprt Serv.
Celik, I., et al, eds. Quantification of Uncertainty in Computational Fluid Dynamics. LC 93-71641. (FED Ser.: Vol. 158). 121p. 1993. pap. 35.00 (*0-7918-0966-8*, H00798) ASME.
Celik, Vladislav. Piano & Organ Without a Teacher, Bk. 1. LC 92-80239. (Music Instructional Ser.). (Illus.). 80p. pap. text 9.95 (*0-9624062-3-6*) Music Inst CA.
— Piano & Organ Without a Teacher One. (Music Instructional Ser.). (Illus.). 80p. pap. 12.95 incl. audio (*0-9624062-4-4*) Music Inst CA.
— You Too Can Play Piano & Organ Without Teacher, Vol. 1. (Music Instructional Ser.). (Illus.). 96p. pap. text 12.95 incl. audio (*0-9624062-1-X*) Music Inst CA.
Celik, Yasemin. Contemporary Turkish Foreign Policy. LC 99-21270. 208p. 1999. 59.95 (*0-275-96590-2*) Greenwood.
Celik, Zeynep. Displaying the Orient: Architecture of Islam at Nineteenth-Century World's Fairs. 255p. 1996. 40.00 (*0-614-21575-7*, 207) Kazi Pubns.
— Displaying the Orient: Architecture of Islam at Nineteenth-Century World's Fairs. (Comparative Studies on Muslim Societies: No. 12). (C). 1992. 50.00 (*0-520-07494-7*, Pub. by U CA Pr) Cal Prin Full Svc.
— The Remaking of Istanbul: Portrait of an Ottoman City in the Nineteenth Century. LC 92-31825. 201p. 1993. 19.95 (*0-520-08239-7*, Pub. by U CA Pr) Cal Prin Full Svc.
— Urban Forms & Colonial Confrontations: Algiers under French Rule. LC 96-37606. (Illus.). 245p. 1997. 45.00 (*0-520-20457-3*, Pub. by U CA Pr) Cal Prin Full Svc.
Celik, Zeynep, et al, eds. Streets: Critical Perspectives on Public Space. LC 93-42658. 1994. 55.00 (*0-520-08550-7*, Pub. by U CA Pr) Cal Prin Full Svc.
— Streets: Critical Perspectives on Public Space. (Illus.). 300p. 1996. pap. 22.50 (*0-520-20528-6*, Pub. by U CA Pr) Cal Prin Full Svc.
Celine, Louis-Ferdinand. Ballets Sans Musique. 1959. pap. 8.95 (*0-7859-0658-4*, F91880) Fr & Eur.
— Ballets Without Music, Without Dancers, Without Anything. Christensen, Thomas & Christensen, Carol, trs. (Green Integer Bks.: No. 18). 192p. 1999. pap. text 10.95 (*1-892295-06-7*, Pub. by Green Integer) SPD-Small Pr Dist.
— Casse-Pipe. (Folio Ser.: No. 666). (FRE.). 1975. pap. 6.95 (*2-07-036666-9*) Schoenhof.
— Casse-Pipe: Carnet de Cuirassier Destouches. (FRE.). 1975. pap. 10.95 (*0-8288-3669-8*, M3188) Fr & Eur.
— Castle to Castle. Manheim, Ralph, tr. from FRE. LC 96-51792.Tr. of D'un Chateau l'Autre. 360p. 1997. reprint ed. pap. 13.95 (*1-56478-150-X*) Dalkey Arch.
***Celine, Louis-Ferdinand.** Church: A Comedy in Five Acts. 156p. 2000. pap. 12.95 (*1-892295-78-4*) Green Integer.
Celine, Louis-Ferdinand. Conversations with Professor Y. LC 85-40932. (ENG & FRE.). 180p. reprint ed. pap. 55.80 (*0-608-09073-5*, 206970700005) Bks Demand.
— Death on the Installment Plan. Manheim, Ralph, tr. from FRE. LC 48-6410. 1971. reprint ed. pap. 15.95 (*0-8112-0017-5*, NDP330, Pub. by New Directions) Norton.
— D'un Chateau l'Autre. (FRE.). 1976. pap. 13.95 (*0-7859-0645-2*, M3189) Fr & Eur.
— D'un Chateau l'Autre. (Folio Ser.: No. 776). (FRE.). 1973. pap. 10.95 (*2-07-036776-2*) Schoenhof.
— L' Eglise. 1952. pap. 15.95 (*0-7859-0927-3*, F92110) Fr & Eur.
— Feerie Pour une Autre Fois. (Folio Ser.). (FRE.). pap. 8.95 (*2-07-036918-8*) Fr & Eur.
— Feerie Pour une Autre Fois. (FRE.). 1977. pap. 10.95 (*0-8288-3671-X*, M11013); pap. 10.95 (*0-7859-1847-7*, 2070369188) Fr & Eur.
— Guignol's Band. LC 54-10186. 1969. pap. 12.95 (*0-8112-0018-3*, NDP278, Pub. by New Directions) Norton.
— Guignol's Band I & II. (Folio Ser.: No. 2112). (FRE.). 1972. pap. 17.95 (*2-07-038148-X*) Schoenhof.
— Guignol's Bande 1, Guignol's Bande 2. (FRE.). 1989. pap. 19.95 (*0-8288-3672-8*, F92031) Fr & Eur.
— Journey to the End of the Night. Manheim, Ralph, tr. from FRE. LC 82-7970. 1983. pap. 12.95 (*0-8112-0847-8*, NDP542, Pub. by New Directions) Norton.
— Line Letters to Elizabeth. Juilland, Alphonse, ed. (Illus.). 104p. (Orig.). (C). 1990. pap. 24.00 (*1-884868-04-5*) Montparnasse.
***Celine, Louis-Ferdinand.** London Bridge. Di Bernardi, Dominic, tr. from FRE. LC 94-25168. 390p. 1999. reprint ed. pap. 14.50 (*1-56478-175-5*, Pub. by Dalkey Arch) SPD-Small Pr Dist.
Celine, Louis-Ferdinand. London Bridge: Guignol's Band II. Di Bernardi, Dominic, tr. from FRE. LC 94-25168. 449p. 1995. 23.95 (*1-56478-071-6*) Dalkey Arch.
— Mort a Credit. (FRE.). pap. 17.95 (*0-8288-3673-6*, F92033) Fr & Eur.
— Mort a Credit. (Folio Ser.: No. 1692). (FRE.). 1972. pap. 14.95 (*2-07-037692-3*) Schoenhof.
— Nord. (FRE.). 1976. pap. 16.95 (*0-8288-3625-6*, F92041) Fr & Eur.
— Nord. (Folio Ser.: No. 851). (FRE.). 1972. pap. 13.95 (*2-07-036851-3*) Schoenhof.
— Normance. (Feerie Pour une Autre Fois Ser.: Vol. II). (FRE.). 463p. 1989. pap. 11.95 (*0-7859-1877-9*, 2070370534) Fr & Eur.
— Normance: Feerie pour une Autre Fois 2. (FRE.). 1977. pap. 13.95 (*0-8288-3674-4*, F92050) Fr & Eur.
— Normance (Feerie . . . 2) (Folio Ser.: No. 1053). (FRE.). 463p. (Orig.). 1954. pap. 10.95 (*2-07-037053-4*) Schoenhof.
— North. Manheim, Ralph, tr. from FRE. LC 96-15668. 454p. 1996. reprint ed. pap. 13.95 (*1-56478-142-9*) Dalkey Arch.
— Rigadoon. Manheim, Ralph, tr. from FRE. LC 97-23297. 296p. 1997. reprint ed. pap. 13.50 (*1-56478-162-3*) Dalkey Arch.
— Rigodon. (FRE.). 1987. pap. 11.95 (*0-8288-3626-4*, M3190) Fr & Eur.
— Rigodon. (Folio Ser.: No. 481). (FRE.). 9.95 (*0-685-57722-8*); pap. 8.95 (*2-07-036481-X*) Schoenhof.
— Romans. Godard, Henri, ed. 1981. lib. bdg. 125.00 (*0-7859-3875-3*) Fr & Eur.
— Romans. Godard, Henri, ed. 1988. lib. bdg. 140.00 (*0-7859-3885-0*) Fr & Eur.
— Romans, 3 tomes, Vol. I: Voyage au Bout de la Nuit. deluxe ed. (Pleiade Ser.). (FRE.). 83.95 (*2-07-011000-1*) Schoenhof.
— Romans, Vol. 2. Godard, J., ed. (FRE.). 1974. lib. bdg. 110.00 (*0-7859-3827-3*) Fr & Eur.

C

— Romans, 3 tomes, Vol. II: D'un Chateau l'Autre. deluxe ed. (Pleiade Ser.). (FRE.). 71.95 (*0-685-37272-3*) Schoenhof.
— Romans, 3 tomes, Vol. III. deluxe ed. (Pleiade Ser.). (FRE.). 89.95 (*2-07-011155-5*) Schoenhof.
— Romans: D'un Chateau l'Autre; Nord; Rigodon, Tome 2. deluxe ed. (Pleiade Ser.). (FRE.). 1272p. 1974. 71.95 (*2-07-010797-3*) Schoenhof.
— Le Style Contre les Idees: Rabelais, Zola, Sartre et les Autres. (FRE.). 1987. pap. 23.95 (*0-7859-3310-7*, 2870272189) Fr & Eur.
— Voyage au Bout de la Nuit. (FRE.). 1972. pap. 16.95 (*0-8288-3627-2*, F92100) Fr & Eur.
— Voyage au Bout de la Nuit. (Folio Ser.: No. 28). (FRE.). pap. 13.95 (*2-07-036028-8*) Schoenhof.
Celio, Marco, ed. Guidebook to the Calcium-Binding Proteins. LC 97-114948. (Guidebook Ser. A Sambrook & Tooze Publication at Oxford University Press)). (Illus.). 254p. (C). 1996. text 65.00 (*0-19-859951-X*); pap. text 34.95 (*0-19-859950-1*) OUP.
Celio, Mary B., jt. auth. see Hill, Paul T.
Celis. Cell Biology, Vol. 1. 2nd ed. LC 97-80300. 1997. pap. text 79.95 (*0-12-164726-9*) Acad Pr.
— Cell Biology, Vol. 2. 2nd ed. LC 97-80300. 1997. pap. text 79.95 (*0-12-164727-7*) Acad Pr.
— Cell Biology, Vol. 3. 2nd ed. LC 97-80300. 1997. pap. text 79.95 (*0-12-164728-5*) Harcourt.
— Cell Biology, Vol. 4. 2nd ed. LC 97-80300. 1997. pap. text 79.95 (*0-12-164729-3*) Harcourt.
Celis, Julio E., ed. Cell Biology: A Laboratory Handbook, 4 vols. 2nd ed. (Factsbooks Ser.). 2400p. 1997. spiral bd., lab manual ed. 179.95 (*0-12-164725-0*) Morgan Kaufmann.
Celiz, B., et al. Educacion Cristiana. (SPA.). 1992. pap. 7.95 (*1-55955-063-5*, 6761-1110C) Libros Desafio.
Celiz, Fray F. Diary of the Alarcon Expedition into Texas 1718-1719. Hoffman, Fritz L., ed. LC 67-24717. (Quivira Society Publications, Vol. 5). 1967. reprint ed. 19.95 (*0-405-00075-8*) Ayer.
Celizic, Michael, jt. auth. see Ruettiger, Rudy.
Celko, Joe. Instant SQL Programming. 350p. 1995. pap. 29.95 incl. disk (*1-874416-50-8*) Wrox Pr Inc.
— Joe Celko's Data & Databases: Concepts in Practice. LC 99-30307. 400p. (C). 1999. pap. text 39.95 (*1-55860-432-4*, Pub. by Morgan Kaufmann) Harcourt.
***Celko, Joe.** Joe Celko's SQL for Smarties: Advance SQL Programming. 2nd ed. Gray, Jim, ed. LC 99-46068. (Data Management Systems Ser.). 450p. 1999. pap. text 44.95 (*1-55860-576-2*, Pub. by Morgan Kaufmann) Harcourt.
Celko, Joe. Joe Celko's SQL for Smarties: Advanced SQL Programming. 467p. 1998. pap. text 42.00 (*1-55860-323-9*) Morgan Kaufmann.
— Joe Celko's SQL Puzzles & Answers. LC 97-3991. 265p. 1997. pap. text 22.95 (*1-55860-453-7*) Morgan Kaufmann.
Celko, Joe & MacDonald, Michael. Sybase SQL Anywhere: Secrets of the Watcom SQL Masters: PowerBuilder Developer's Journal. (SQL Training Ser.: No. I). (Illus.). 480p. (Orig.). 1996. pap. 37.75 (*1-886141-05-3*) SYS-Con Pubns.
***Cell.** Newfoundland Discovered English Attempts at Colonial. 1998. 52.95 (*0-904180-13-1*) Ashgate Pub Co.
Cell, Edward. Learning to Learn from Experience. LC 83-9283. 245p. (C). 1984. text 49.50 (*0-87395-832-2*); pap. text 16.95 (*0-87395-833-0*) State U NY Pr.
— Organizational Life: Learning to Be Self-Directed. LC 98-16033. 352p. (C). 1998. 62.00 (*0-7618-1112-5*); pap. 34.50 (*0-7618-1113-3*) U Pr of Amer.
Cell, Edward, ed. Daily Readings in Quaker Spirituality. 96p. 1987. pap. 4.95 (*0-87243-160-6*) Templegate.
Cell, George C. The Rediscovery of John Wesley. LC 83-6505. 438p. (C). 1983. reprint ed. pap. text 27.00 (*0-8191-3222-5*) U Pr of Amer.
Cell, John W. Hailey: A Study in British Imperialism, 1872-1969. (Illus.). 350p. (C). 1992. text 52.95 (*0-521-41107-6*) Cambridge U Pr.
Cell, John W., ed. By Kenya Possessed: The Correspondence of J. H. Oldham & Norman Leys, 1918-1926. LC 75-27894. (Studies in Imperialism). 382p. 1976. lib. bdg. 28.00 (*0-226-09971-7*) U Ch Pr.
Cella, Alexander. Massachusetts Practice: Administrative Law & Practice, 3 vols. 2136p. 1986. 172.50 (*0-317-52113-6*) West Pub.
Cella, Catherine. Great Videos for Kids: A Parent's Guide to Choosing the Best. 144p. 1992. pap. 7.95 (*0-8065-1377-2*, Citadel Pr) Carol Pub Group.
Cella, Charles P. & Lane, Rodney, eds. Basic Issues in Coordinating Family & Child Welfare Programs. 1964. 39.50 (*0-317-27416-3*) Elliots Bks.
Cella, Edward, et al. Thresholds No. 7: Viewing Culture. Gomes, Dan et al, eds. (Illus.). 166p. 1993. pap. 10.00 (*1-892751-01-1*) Thresholds.
Cella, Edward, ed. see Barringer, Carol E.
Cella, Len. Things to Worry About (In Case You Run Out) A Definitive Guide to the Ultimate in Worries, Phobias & Fears. (Illus.). 96p. (Orig.). 1987. pap. 6.95 (*0-930753-03-8*) Spect Ln Pr.
Cellar, Paula & Sieff, Janet. Celebration of Life: A Journal for the Living. 1997. 8.95 (*1-56123-100-2*) Centering Corp.
Cellard, Jacques. Dictionary of Non-Conventional French: Dictionnaire de Francais Nonconventionnel. rev. ed. (ENG & FRE.). 893p. 1991. 95.00 (*0-8288-1931-9*, M9313) Fr & Eur.
— Le Subjonctif. 3rd rev. ed. (FRE.). 88p. 1983. pap. 19.95 (*0-8288-3354-0*) Fr & Eur.
Cellarius, Andreas. Harmonia Macrocosmica Seu Atlas Universalis et Novus. (Mapping of the Stars Ser.). (LAT., Illus.). 128p. 1998. reprint ed. pap. 1050.00 (*1-85297-024-3*, Pub. by Archival Facs) St Mut.
Celler, G. K., et al, eds. Proceedings of the International Symposium on Ultra Large Scale Integration Science & Technology, 4th. LC 93-70066. (Proceedings Ser.: Vol. 93-13). 320p. 1993. 42.00 (*1-56677-063-7*) Electrochem Soc.
Celler, G. K. & Maldonado, J. R., eds. Materials Aspects of X-Ray Lithography. (Symposium Proceedings Ser.: Vol. 306). 291p. 1993. text 30.00 (*1-55899-202-2*) Materials Res.
Celletti, Rodolfo. A History of Bel Canto. Fuller, Frederick, tr. (Illus.). 224p. 1997. reprint ed. pap. text 26.00 (*0-19-816641-9*) OUP.
Celley, David. Woodruff's Firebase. 520p. mass mkt. 6.99 (*1-896329-16-0*) Picasso Publ.
Celli. Merger Control in the United Kingdom & European Union. LC 98-121484. 1997. 125.00 (*90-411-0652-9*) Kluwer Law Intl.
Celli, Angelo. The History of Malaria in the Roman Campagna from Ancient Times. Celli-Fraentzel, Anna, ed. LC 75-23694. reprint ed. 39.50 (*0-404-13243-X*) AMS Pr.
Celli-Fraentzel, Anna, ed. see Celli, Angelo.
Celli, L., ed. The Elbow: Traumatic Lesions. Warr, A., tr. from ITA. (Illus.). ix, 194p. 1991. 182.00 (*0-387-82244-5*) Spr-Verlag.
— The Shoulder: Periarticular Degenerative Pathology. Notini, S., tr. (Current Concepts in Orthopedic Surgery Ser.: Vol. 1). (Illus.). 144p. 1991. 135.00 (*0-387-82219-4*) Spr-Verlag.
Celli, Michelangelo. Words Are Dogs Barking at Windmills. LC 97-91162. 52p. 1998. pap. 8.95 (*0-533-12586-3*) Vantage.
Celli, Rose, tr. A Ghost, a Witch & a Goblin. (J). (gr. k-3). 1970. reprint ed. pap. 1.50 (*0-590-04447-8*) Scholastic Inc.
Cellier. Languages for Continuous System Simulation, 1986 Conference. 148p. 1986. pap. 32.00 (*0-911801-08-1*, MC-86-1) Soc Computer Sim.
Cellier & Granda, eds. 1995 International Conference on Bond Graph Modeling & Simulation. 310p. 1995. 100.00 (*1-56555-037-4*, SS-27-1) Soc Computer Sim.
Cellier, jt. ed. see Granda.
Cellier, Elizabeth. Malice Defeated & the Matchless Rogue. LC 92-22035. (Augustan Reprints Ser.: Nos. 249-250). 1988. reprint ed. 21.50 (*0-404-70249-X*) AMS Pr.
Cellier, F. E. Continuous System Modeling. (Illus.). xxviii, 775p. 1995. 79.95 (*0-387-97502-0*) Spr-Verlag.
Cellier, Francois & Bridgeman, Cunningham. Gilbert & Sullivan & Their Operas. LC 72-91479. (Illus.). 1972. 36.95 (*0-405-08346-7*, Pub. by Blom Pubns) Ayer.
Cellier, Francois E., jt. ed. see Granda, Jose J.
Cellier, Leon, ed. see Sand, George.
Cellina, A., et al, eds. Methods of Nonconvex Analysis: Lectures Given at the 1st Session of the Centro Internazionale Estivo Matematico (C. I. M. E.) Held at Varenna, Italy, June 15-23, 1989. (Lecture Notes in Mathematics Ser.: Vol. 1446). v, 206p. 1990. 41.95 (*0-387-53120-3*) Spr-Verlag.
Cellina, A., jt. auth. see Aubin, Jean P.
Cellini, Alva, tr. & intro. see Galdos, Benito Perez.
***Cellini, Benvenuto.** Autobiography. Bull, George, tr. & intro. by. 496p. 2000. pap. 11.95 (*0-14-044718-0*, Penguin Classics) Viking Penguin.
Cellini, Benvenuto. Due Trattati. fac. ed. (Documents of Art & Architectural History Ser.: Series II, Vol. 3). (ITA., Illus.). 148p. 1981. lib. bdg. 37.50 (*0-89371-203-5*) Broude Intl Edns.
— The Life of Benvenuto Cellini. Symonds, John A., tr. (Arts & Letters Ser.). (Illus.). 496p. (C). 1995. pap. 14.95 (*0-7148-3364-9*, Pub. by Phaidon Press) Phaidon Pr.
Cellini, Henry R., jt. ed. see Schwartz, Barbara K.
Cellman, Carol. On Course: Student Book 1. (Illus.). 96p. 1989. pap. text, student ed. 9.95 (*0-19-434285-9*) OUP.
— On Course: Teacher's Book 1. (Illus.). 108p. 1989. pap. text, teacher ed. 15.95 (*0-19-434286-7*) OUP.
— Open Sesame: Stage E: Open Sesame Multilevel Book Duplicating Masters. (Illus.). 64p. 1989. pap. text 23.95 (*0-19-434264-6*) OUP.
Celly, Jean-Jacques. The Sleepwalker with Eyes of Clay. Gallagher, Katherine, tr. from FRE. LC 93-71943. (ENG & FRE., Illus.). 79p. 1994. pap. 14.95 (*1-85610-029-4*, Pub. by Forest Bks) Dufour.
Celment, Richard W. The Book in America: With Images from the Library of Congress. (Library of Congress Ser.). (Illus.). 160p. 1996. 39.95 (*1-55591-234-6*) Fulcrum Pub.
Celmer, Al. Federal Labor Relations 1996 Desk Book. abr. ed. 1992. pap. 57.50 (*0-934753-69-5*) LRP Pubns.
Celmer, Al & Creo, Robert A. Federal Arbitration Advocate's Handbook. 1991. 25.00 (*0-934753-48-2*) LRP Pubns.
Celmer, Marc A. Terrorism, U. S. Strategy & Reagan Policies, 173. LC 86-33647. (Symposium Papers IX: Vol. 22). 142p. 1987. 49.95 (*0-313-25632-2*, Greenwood Pr) Greenwood.
Celmins, Martin. Peter Green: The Biography. (Illus.). 240p. pap. 14.95 (*1-898141-13-4*, SG 00603, Pub. by Sanctuary Pubng) Music Sales.
Celmins, Vija, contrib. by. Vija Celmins: A Survey Exhibition. LC 79-92204. (Illus.). 96p. 1980. pap. 16.00 (*0-911291-04-0*, Pub. by Fellows Cont Art) RAM Publications.
Celmrauga, I. German-Russian Polytechnical Dictionary. 3rd ed. (GER & RUS.). 1984. write for info. (*0-8288-2136-4*, M15077) Fr & Eur.
Celmrauga, I., et al. German-Latvian Dictionary: Deutsch-Lettisches Woerterbuch. 4th ed. (GER & LAV.). 1984. 39.95 (*0-8288-1623-9*, F58220) Fr & Eur.
Celnik, Max, ed. Physician's Book Compendium, 1969-1970: The Medical Book Reference for Physicians. LC Z 6658.. 872p. reprint ed. pap. 200.00 (*0-608-16971-4*, 202710600054) Bks Demand.
Celoria, Francis. Archeology. LC 76-154855. (All-Color GuideSer.: No. 43). 159 p. 1973. write for info. (*0-448-00885-8*, G & D) Peng Put Young Read.
Celorio, Jose M., jt. auth. see Jalkh, Alexandre E.
Celorio, Marta & Barlow, Annette C. Handbook of Spanish Idioms. 460p. 1974. pap. text 7.75 (*0-88345-216-2*, 18112) Prentice ESL.
Celotta, Robert, et al, eds. Experimental Methods in the Physical Sciences Vol. 30: Laser Ablation & Desorption. LC 97-220327. (Illus.). 647p. 1997. text 95.00 (*0-12-475975-0*) Morgan Kaufmann.
— Methods in Experimental Physics Vol. 28: Statistical Methods for Physical Science. (Illus.). 542p. 1994. text write for info. (*0-12-475973-4*) Acad Pr.
— Methods of Experimental Physics: Scanning Tunneling Microscopy, Vol. 27. (Illus.). 459p. 1993. text 111.00 (*0-12-475972-6*) Acad Pr.
Celotta, Robert J., ed. see Wong, Po-Zen.
Celotti, G., jt. ed. see Tampieri, A.
Celoza, Albert F. Ferdinand Marcos & the Philippines: The Political Economy of Authoritarianism. LC 96-37732. 152p. 1997. 55.00 (*0-275-94137-X*, Praeger Pubs) Greenwood.
Celsi, Teresa. Fourth Little Pig. (J). (ps-3). 1993. pap. 4.95 (*0-8114-6740-6*) Raintree Steck-V.
— The Fourth Little Pig. LC 90-8059. (Ready-Set-Read Ser.). (Illus.). 32p. (J). (ps-3). 1992. lib. bdg. 21.40 (*0-8172-3577-9*) Raintree Steck-V.
— Golf: The Lore of the Links. (Illus.). 80p. 1992. 4.95 (*0-8362-3019-1*) Andrews & McMeel.
— Jesse Jackson & Political Power. (Gateway Civil Rights Ser.). (Illus.). 32p. (J). (gr. 2-4). 1991. pap. 4.95 (*1-878841-70-X*) Millbrook Pr.
— Ralph Nader: The Consumer Revolution. (New Directions Ser.). (Illus.). 104p. (YA). (gr. 7 up). 1991. lib. bdg. 21.90 (*1-56294-044-9*) Millbrook Pr.
— Rosa Parks & the Montgomery Bus Boycott. (Gateway Civil Rights Ser.). (Illus.). 32p. (J). (gr. 2-4). 1991. pap. 4.80 (*1-878841-34-3*); lib. bdg. 20.90 (*1-878841-14-9*) Millbrook Pr.
Celsi, Teresa N. Squanto & the First Thanksgiving. (Real Readers Ser.: Level Red). (Illus.). 32p. (J). (gr. 1-4). 1989. pap. 4.95 (*0-8114-6710-4*) Raintree Steck-V.
Celsi, Teresa Noel. Ralph Nader the Consumer Revolution. (New Directions Ser.). 1991. 11.15 (*0-606-08053-8*, Pub. by Turtleback) Demco.
— Rosa Parks & the Montgomery Bus Boycott. (Gateway Civil Rights Ser.). 1991. 11.15 (*0-606-01458-6*, Pub. by Turtleback) Demco.
Celsing, Peter. The Architecture of Peter Celsing. (Illus.). 165p. 1998. 65.00 (*91-86050-36-2*) Gingko Press.
Celsnak, Marlene. Country Club Cuisine: Culinary Specialties from Prestigious Golf Clubs. Kempers, Christian, ed. LC 97-94797. (Illus.). 284p. 1998. 19.95 (*0-9659747-0-7*) C&C Enter.
Celso, Garrido N., jt. auth. see Motamen-Samadian, Sima.
Celsus. De Medicina, 3 vols., 3. (Loeb Classical Library: No. 292, 304, 336). 656p. 1938. 18.95 (*0-674-99370-5*) HUP.
Celsus, Cornelius. Uber die Arzneiwissensschaft (De Medicina, Deutscsh) xlii, 862p. 1967. reprint ed. 190.00 (*0-318-71087-0*) G Olms Pubs.
Celt, Marek. Biali Kurierzy. (POL., Illus.). 384p. (Orig.). 1997. pap. 11.95 (*0-9635004-1-4*) Flying Heart.
— Koncert: Opowiadanie Cichociemnego. (POL., Illus.). 100p. (Orig.). 1997. pap. 5.95 (*0-9635004-0-6*) Flying Heart.
— Raport z Podziemia, 1942. (POL., Illus.). 409p. (Orig.). 1997. pap. 11.95 (*0-9635004-2-2*) Flying Heart.
CEMA Staff. Belt Conveyors No. 402: ANSI/CEMA 402-1992. 1992. reprint ed. pap. 15.00 (*1-891171-06-2*) Conveyor Equip Mfrs.
— Belt Conveyors for Bulk Materials: The CEMA Belt Book. 5th ed. (Illus.). 1997. 125.00 (*1-891171-18-6*) Conveyor Equip Mfrs.
— Belt Driven Live Rollers No. 403: ANSI/CEMA 403-1997. (Illus.). 16p. 1997. pap. 15.00 (*1-891171-07-0*) Conveyor Equip Mfrs.
— CEMA Standard No. 502-1998: Bulk Material Belt Conveyor Troughing & Return Idlers (Selection & Dimensions) rev. ed. (Illus.). 34p. 1998. pap. 20.00 (*1-891171-22-4*) Conveyor Equip Mfrs.
— Chain Driven Live Roller Conveyors No. 404: ANSI/CEMA 404-1985. (Illus.). 12p. 1985. reprint ed. pap. 15.00 (*1-891171-08-9*) Conveyor Equip Mfrs.
— Conveyor Installation Standards: For Belt Conveyors Handling Bulk Materials. 2nd ed. (Illus.). 1990. pap. 10.00 (*1-891171-19-4*) Conveyor Equip Mfrs.
— Conveyor Terms & Definitions No. 102: ANSI/CEMA 102-1994. (Illus.). 73p. 1994. pap. 20.00 (*1-891171-00-3*) Conveyor Equip Mfrs.
— Electrical Terms & Definitions No. 110: CEMA 110-1995. 14p. 1995. pap. 10.00 (*1-891171-01-1*) Conveyor Equip Mfrs.
— Roller Conveyors-Non Powered No. 401: ANSI/CEMA 401-1994. (Illus.). 17p. 1994. pap. 15.00 (*1-891171-05-4*) Conveyor Equip Mfrs.
— Safety Label Brochure No. 201: CEMA 201-1995. (Illus.). 36p. 1995. pap. 10.00 (*1-891171-02-X*) Conveyor Equip Mfrs.
***CEMA Staff.** Screw Conveyor Dimensional Standards No. 300: CEMA 300-1999. (Illus.). 36p. 1999. pap. 10.00 (*1-891171-27-5*) Conveyor Equip Mfrs.
CEMA Staff. Specifications for Welded Steel Conveyor Pulleys with Compression Type Hubs: ANSI/CEMA B105.1. (Illus.). 12p. 1992. pap. 10.00 (*1-891171-21-6*) Conveyor Equip Mfrs.
— Specifications for Welded Steel Wing Pulleys: ANSI/CEMA 501.1-1988 (R1996) (Illus.). 6p. 1996. pap. 10.00 (*1-891171-20-8*) Conveyor Equip Mfrs.
Cemagref Staff. Diccionario Tecnologico: Maquinaria y Equipos Agricoles. (SPA.). 1295p. 1990. pap. 325.00 (*0-7859-6124-0*, 8471142805) Fr & Eur.
Cember. Radiation Biology. 1994. write for info. (*0-8493-8856-2*, CRC Reprint) Franklin.
Cember, H. Herbert. Introduction to Health Physics. 3rd ed. 1993. text 45.00 (*0-07-105453-7*) McGraw-Hill HPD.
***Cember, Herman & Johnson, Thomas E.** The Health Physics Solutions Manual: Introduction to Health Physics Problems Made Easy. LC 98-68614. 442p. 1999. pap. 39.95 (*0-9625963-6-1*) Bartleby Pr.
Cember, Herman H. Introduction to Health Physics. 3rd ed. LC 95-25269. 752p. 1996. text 45.00 (*0-07-105461-8*) McGraw-Hill HPD.
Cembranos, Pilar & Mendoza, Jose. Banach Spaces of Vector-Valued Functions. LC 97-39141. (Lecture Notes in Mathematics Ser.: Vol. 1676). viii, 118p. 1997. pap. 27.00 (*3-540-63745-1*) Spr-Verlag.
Cembrowski, George S. & Carey, R. Neill. Laboratory Quality Management: QC & QA. LC 89-6729. (Illus.). 264p. 1989. text 45.00 (*0-89189-277-X*) Am Soc Clinical.
Ceminchuk, Barry. How I Learned to Shoot 75, Occassionally. mass mkt. 14.95 (*0-646-13115-X*) Picasso Publ.
Cempel, Czes A., jt. auth. see Naptke, H. G.
Cempel, Czes A., jt. auth. see Natke, H. G.
Cempura, E. Rosalie. Springboards for Today's Children. LC 92-74214. 222p. (Orig.). 1993. pap. 14.95 (*0-9633919-9-2*) Hells Canyon.
Cen-Cenelec & Etsi Staff, ed. Conformance Testing & Certification in Information Technology & Telecommunications. LC 90-84753. 399p. (gr. 12). 1991. 130.00 (*90-5199-038-3*, Pub. by IOS Pr) IOS Press.
Cen Yuefang. Chinese Qigong Essentials. (Illus.). 189p. 1996. 16.95 (*7-80005-300-8*, Pub. by New World Pr) China Bks.
Cena, Resty M., jt. auth. see Ramos, Teresita V.
Cena, Valentin, jt. ed. see Soria, Bernat.
Cenac, Arnaud, et al. Dictionnaire des Urgences Medicales de l'Adulte. 2nd ed.Tr. of Dictionary of Adult Emergency Medicine. (FRE.). 416p. 1989. ring bd. 85.00 (*0-7859-4621-7*, F126640) Fr & Eur.
— Practical Dictionary of Adult Emergency Medicine: Diccionario Practico de Urgencias Medicas del Adulto. (SPA.). 368p. 1982. 69.95 (*0-8288-1864-9*, S39898) Fr & Eur.
Cenacle Staff, ed. The Myth of Papal Infallibility. (Illus.). 112p. (Orig.). 1990. pap. 5.00 (*0-912927-41-0*, X041) St John Kronstadt.
Cence, Robert J. Pion-Nucleon Scattering. LC 66-11964. (Investigations in Physics Ser.: Vol. 11). 148p. 1969. reprint ed. pap. 45.90 (*0-7837-9313-8*, 206005300004) Bks Demand.
Cencini, Alvaro. Monetary Theory: National & International. LC 94-33804. 400p. (C). (gr. 13). 1995. 110.00 (*0-415-11054-8*, C0182) Routledge.
— Monetary Theory: National & International. LC 96-40351. 400p. (C). 1997. pap. 29.99 (*0-415-11055-6*) Routledge.
— Money, Income & Time: A Quantum Theoretical Approach. 232p. 1988. text 55.00 (*0-86187-943-0*) St Martin.
Cencini, Alvaro & Baranzini, Mauro, eds. Inflation & Unemployment: Contributions to a New Macroeconomic Approach. LC 95-46208. (Studies in the Modern World Economy). (Illus.). 200p. (C). 1996. 80.00 (*0-415-11822-0*) Routledge.
Cencini, Alvaro & Schmitt, Bernard. The Vicious Circle of External Debt Servicing. 1991. text 59.00 (*0-86187-185-5*, Pub. by P P Pubs) Cassell & Continuum.
Cencov, N. N. Statistical Decision Rules & Optimal Inference. LC 81-15039. (Translations of Mathematical Monographs: Vol. 53). 499p. 1982. text 119.00 (*0-8218-4502-0*, MMONO/53) Am Math.
Cenczyk, Mark. Guildbook: Spooks & Oracles. (Wruith Ser.). 1998. pap. 18.00 (*1-56504-666-8*) White Wolf.
— Technocrary: Syndicate. (Mage). (Illus.). (Orig.). 1997. pap. 10.00 (*1-56504-421-5*, 4206) White Wolf.
Cenczyk, Mark, jt. auth. see Ditchburn, Elizabeth.
Cendant. Jumpstart: Kindergarten, 1. 1996. cd-rom 28.40 (*1-56997-203-6*) Knowledge Adv.
Cendejas, Deena L., jt. auth. see Smith, M. Sherry.
Cendenen, Gray & Kern, Julie. Fundamental College Mathematics. 160p. (C). 1997. pap., student ed. 25.00 (*0-06-501964-4*) Addson-Wesley Educ.
***Cender, Stephen.** Serial Killers - An American Focus Vols. 1 & 2: Poetry & Writings Written from Prison by David Berkowitz. deluxe ed. 160p. 1998. 65.00 (*1-877858-80-3*) Amer Focus Pub.
CENDIT (Centre for Development of Instructional Te. Indian Social & Economic Development, 1994: An Index to the Literature. (Indian Social & Economic Development Ser.: Vol. 8). 204p. 1995. 25.95 (*0-8039-9226-2*) Sage.
CENDIT (Centre for Development of Instructional Te & CAPART (Council for Advancement of People's Action. Indian Social & Economic Development, 1989: An Index to the Literature. (Indian Social & Economic Development Ser.: Vol. 3). 216p. (C). 1989. text 25.00 (*0-8039-9629-2*) Sage.
Cendrars, Blaise. The African Saga. Bianco, Margery, tr. LC 75-97359. 378p. 1969. reprint ed. lib. bdg. 35.00 (*0-8371-2419-0*, CEA&) Greenwood.
— Anthologie Negre. (FRE.). 1985. pap. 12.95 (*0-7859-3105-8*) Fr & Eur.

C

An Asterisk (*) at the beginning of an entry indicates that the title is appearing for the first time.

— Au Coeur du Monde, Feuilles de Route: Sud-Americaines, Poemes Divers. (FRE.). 1979. pap. 10.95 (0-8288-3818-6, F92191) Fr & Eur.
— Bourlinguer. (FRE.). 1974. pap. 11.95 (0-7859-1789-6, 2070366022) Fr & Eur.
— Christmas at the Four Corners of the Earth. Mathieu, Bertrand, tr. (American Reader Ser.: Vol. 1). 60p. 1994. 16.95 (1-880238-16-0) BOA Edns.
— Complete Poems: A Bilingual Edition. (C). 1993. pap. 17.95 (0-520-06580-8, Pub. by U CA Pr) Cal Prin Full Svc.
— Confessions of Dan Yack. Rootes, Nina, tr. 120p. 1990. 30.00 (0-7206-0766-3) Dufour.
— Du Monde Entier: Poesies Completes, 1912-1924. (FRE.). 1966. pap. 14.95 (0-7859-2758-1) Fr & Eur.
— Emmene-Moi Au Bout De Monde. (FRE.). 1972. pap. 10.95 (0-7859-1685-7, 2070360156) Fr & Eur.
— Emmene-moi au Bout du Monde! (Folio Ser.: No. 15). (FRE.). pap. 8.95 (2-07-036015-6) Schoenhof.
— Hollywood: Mecca of the Movies. White, Garrett, tr. LC 93-37426. (Illus.). 1995. 32.50 (0-520-07807-1, Pub. by U CA Pr) Cal Prin Full Svc.
— Homme Foudroye. (Folio Ser.: No. 467). (FRE.). pap. 10.95 (2-07-036467-4) Schoenhof.
— L' Homme Foudroye. (FRE.). 1973. pap. 11.95 (0-7859-1759-4, 2070364674) Fr & Eur.
— Lice. Rootes, Nina, tr. from FRE. 189p. 1973. pap. 17.95 (0-7206-0634-9, Pub. by P Owen Ltd) Dufour.
— Le Lotissement du Ciel. (FRE.). 1976. pap. 11.95 (0-7859-2209-1, 207036724X) Fr & Eur.
— La Main Coupee. (FRE.). 448p. 1975. pap. 11.95 (0-7859-1792-6, 2070366197) Fr & Eur.
— Modernities & Other Writings. Chefdor, Monique, ed. & tr. by. from FRE. Allen, Esther, tr. from FRE. LC 91-43824. (French Modernist Library). xxvi, 134p. 1992. text 40.00 (0-8032-1439-1) U of Nebr Pr.
— Moravagine. Brown, Alan, tr. from FRE. 250p. 1990. pap. 9.95 (0-922233-04-7) Blast Bks.
— Moravagine. (Illus.). 236p. 1968. 24.00 (0-7206-5202-2, Pub. by P Owen Ltd) Dufour.
— Moravigne. (FRE.). 1983. pap. 19.95 (0-7859-3044-2) Fr & Eur.
— L' Or. (FRE.). 1973. pap. 10.95 (0-7859-1733-0, 2070363317) Fr & Eur.
— Panorama de la Pegre. (FRE.). 1986. pap. 16.95 (0-7859-3189-9, 2264007605) Fr & Eur.
— Planus. 208p. 1989. reprint ed. pap. 17.95 (0-7206-0740-X, Pub. by P Owen Ltd) Dufour.
— Rhum: L'aventure de Jean Galmot. (FRE.). 1990. pap. 19.95 (0-7859-3110-4) Fr & Eur.
— Selected Writings of Blaise Cendrars. Albert, Walter, ed. LC 78-14223. 273p. 1978. reprint ed. lib. bdg. 35.00 (0-313-21020-9, CESW, Greenwood Pr) Greenwood.
— Shadow. Brown, Marcia, tr. from FRE. & illus. by. LC 81-9424. 40p. (J). (gr. 2 up). 1982. 17.00 (0-684-17226-7) Scribner.
— Shadow. 2nd ed. Brown, Marcia, tr. from FRE. & illus. by. LC 94-792. 40p. (J). (gr. 4 up). 1995. mass mkt. 4.95 (0-689-71875-6) Aladdin.
— To the End of the World. 251p. 1991. reprint ed. 30.00 (0-7206-0819-8, Pub. by P Owen Ltd) Dufour.
— La Vie Dangereuse. (FRE.). 1987. pap. 23.95 (0-7859-3052-3) Fr & Eur.
Cendrero, A., et al, eds. Planning the Use of the Earth's Surface. (Lecture Notes in Earth Sciences Ser.: Vol. 42). (Illus.). ix, 556p. 1992. 131.95 (0-387-55353-3) Spr-Verlag.
Ceneco Staff. Le Dixeco de l'Enterprise: Dictionnaire des Principaux Termes Financiers. 5th ed. 292p. 1991. pap. 39.95 (0-7859-4929-1) Fr & Eur.
CENECO Staff. Dixeco of Business.Tr. of Dixeco de l'Enterprise. 208p. 1985. 19.95 (0-8288-1265-9, M7867) Fr & Eur.
— Dixeco of the Economy.Tr. of Dixeco de l'Economie. 216p. 1985. 19.95 (0-8288-1264-0, M7099) Fr & Eur.
Cengel. Thermodynamics. 3rd ed. 1056p. 1997. 91.88 (0-07-913238-3) McGraw.
***Cengel.** Thermodynamics. 4th ed. 2001. 72.50 (0-07-238332-1) McGraw.
Cengel. Thermodynamics: Property, Tables. 2nd ed. 1994. 7.50 (0-07-011222-3) McGraw.
Cengel, Unus & Boles, Michael A. Thermodynamics: An Engineering Approach. 2nd ed. (C). 1993. pap. text 31.25 (0-07-011062-X) McGraw.
Cengel, Yanus A. & Boles, Michael A. Thermodynamics: An Engineering Approach. 2nd ed. 1994. text. write for info. (0-07-011061-1) McGraw.
Cengel, Yunis A. & Boles, Michael A. Thermodynamics: An Engineering Approach, 2 vols., Set. (Mechanical Engineering Ser.). (C). 1989. text 72.50 (0-07-909389-2) McGraw.
Cengel, Yunus A. Heat Transfer: A Practical Approach. LC 97-6640. 1997. write for info. (0-07-011506-0); 72.00 (0-07-011505-2) McGraw.
— Introduction to Thermodynamics & Heat Transfer. LC 96-36053. (Mcgraw-Hill Series in Mechanical Engineering). 1996. write for info. (0-07-011499-4) McGraw.
Cengel, Yunus A. & Boles, Michael A. Thermodynamics: An Engineering Approach. 2nd ed. (C). 1993. text 72.50 incl. 5.25 hd (0-07-911651-5); text 69.25 incl. 3.5 hd (0-07-911652-3) McGraw.
— Thermodynamics: An Engineering Approach. 3rd ed. LC 97-28300. 1997. 66.50 (0-07-011927-9) McGraw.
Cenini, Sergio. Catalytic Reductive Carbonylation of Organic Nitro Compounds. LC 96-36618. (Catalysis by Metal Complexes Ser.). 352p. (C). 1996. text 191.50 (0-7923-4307-7) Kluwer Academic.
Ceniza, Sherry. Walt Whitman & 19th-Century Women Reformers. LC 97-24621. 296p. 1998. text 34.95 (0-8173-0893-8) U of Ala Pr.
Cenkl, Mila, et al, eds. The Cech Centennial: A Conference on Homotopy Theory, June 22-26, 1993, Northeastern University. LC 94-43164. (Contemporary Mathematics Ser.: Vol. 181). 422p. 1995. pap. 63.00 (0-8218-0296-8, CONM/181) Am Math.
Cenkner, William. Evil & the Response of World Religions. LC 96-37024. (IRFWP Congress Ser.). 1997. 29.95 (1-55778-758-1) Paragon Hse.
— The Hindu Personality in Education: Tagore - Gandhi - Aurobindo. (C). 1995. reprint ed. 18.00 (81-7304-040-0, Pub. by Manohar) S Asia.
Cenkner, William, ed. Evil & the Response of World Religions. LC 96-37024. ix, 256p. 1997. pap. 16.95 (1-55778-753-0) Paragon Hse.
— The Multicultural Church: A New Landscape in U. S. Theologies. LC 95-31265. 208p. (Orig.). 1996. pap. 14.95 (0-8091-3607-4) Paulist Pr.
Cenlit Ediciones Staff, ed. see Pedraza Jimenez, Felipe B. & Rodriguez Caceres, Milagros.
Cenn, Robert C., Jr. Electronic Servicing Data & Procedures: A Complete Manual & Guide. 384p. 1988. 16.95 (0-13-251919-4) P-H.
Cennamo, G. Ultrasonography in Ophthalmology 15. LC 97-231. (Documenta Ophthalmologicia Proceedings Ser.). 624p. 1997. text 314.50 (0-7923-4464-2) Kluwer Academic.
Cennamo, James. Grey Matter: A Humorous View of Life on Nantucket & Other Cartoons. Daub, Suzanne, ed. (Illus.). 88p. (Orig.). 1990. pap. 6.95 (0-9623188-0-9) Yesterdays Island.
Cennini, Cennino A. Craftsman's Handbook. (Illus.). 142p. 1954. pap. 6.95 (0-486-20054-X) Dover.
Cenotto, Larry. Historical Jackson Guide Book. (Illus.). 32p. (Orig.). 1986. pap. 3.00 (0-938121-02-2) Cenotto Pubns.
— Logan's Alley: Amador County Yesterdays in Picture & Prose, Vol. 3. (Illus.). 280p. 1999. pap. 29.95 (0-938121-13-8) Cenotto Pubns.
Cenoweth, Candace, ed. see Taylor, Blaine.
Cenoz, Guillermina, tr. see McClelland, I. L.
Cenoz, Jasone & Genesee, Fred. Beyond Bilingualism: Multilingualism & Multilingual Education, Vol. 110. LC 98-22406. (Multilingual Matters Ser.). 1998. pap. 39.95 (1-85359-420-2, Pub. by Multilingual Matters) Taylor & Francis.
— Beyond Bilingualism: Multilingualism & Multilingual Education, Vol. 110. LC 98-22406. (Multilingual Matters Ser.). 1998. 3.00 (1-85359-421-0) Taylor & Francis.
Cenrzyk, Mark, jt. auth. see Baugh, Bruce.
Censer, Jack. The French Press in the Age of Enlightenment. LC 93-44377. (Illus.). 272p. (C). (gr. 13). 1994. 80.00 (0-415-09730-4, B3828) Routledge.
Censer, Jack R. Prelude to Power: The Parisian Radical Press, 1789-1791. LC 76-7968. 206p. reprint ed. pap. 63.90 (0-608-14684-6, 202584100046) Bks Demand.
***Censer, Jack Richard & Hunt, Lynn Avery.** Liberty, Equality, Fraternity: Exploring the French Revolution. LC 00-33653. 2001. write for info. (0-271-02088-1) Pa St U Pr.
Censer, Jane T. North Carolina Planters & Their Children, 1800-1860. LC 83-19960. 191p. 1990. pap. text 15.95 (0-8071-1634-3) La State U Pr.
Censer, Jane T., ed. The Papers of Frederick Law Olmsted Vol. 4: Defending the Union: The Civil War & the U. S. Sanitary Commission, 1861-1863. LC 85-24044. 770p. 1986. text 59.50 (0-8018-3067-2) Johns Hopkins.
Censer, Jane T., jt. ed. see Schuyler, David.
Censoni. Humorous Christmas Designs. 1998. pap. text 1.00 (0-486-27476-4) Dover.
— Humorous Valentine Mofifs. 1998. pap. 1.00 (0-486-27831-X) Dover.
Censoni, Bob. Baseball-Sticker Book. (Illus.). (J). 1991. pap. 1.00 (0-486-26603-6) Dover.
Censoni, Bob. Football Stickers. (Illus.). (J). (gr. k-3). 1993. pap. 1.00 (0-486-27453-5) Dover.
Censoni, Bob. Hockey Sticker Book. (Little Activity Bks.). (Illus.). (J). 1993. pap. 1.00 (0-486-26989-2) Dover.
Censoni, Bob. Karate Stickers. (Illus.). (J). (gr. k-3). 1994. pap. 1.00 (0-486-27984-7) Dover.
— Monster Faces Stickers. (Illus.). (J). (gr. k-3). 1998. pap. 1.00 (0-486-27751-8) Dover.
— Ready-to-Use Humorous Christmas Illustrations. (Clip Art Ser.). (Illus.). 64p. 1992. text 4.95 (0-486-27152-8) Dover.
— Ready-to-Use Humorous Cuts with Message Balloons. (Clip Art Ser.). (Illus.). 64p. 1992. text 5.95 (0-486-27251-6) Dover.
— Ready-to-Use Humorous Family Illustrations: 96 Different Copyright-Free Designs Printed One Side. (Clip Art Ser.). (Illus.). 64p. 1993. text 4.95 (0-486-27812-3) Dover.
— Ready-to-Use Humorous Food Shopping Illustrations. (Clip Art Ser.). (Illus.). 64p. 1991. pap. text 4.50 (0-486-26815-2) Dover.
— Ready-to-Use Humorous Four Seasons Illustrations. (Clip Art Ser.). (Illus.). 64p. (Orig.). 1991. pap. 4.95 (0-486-26656-7) Dover.
— Ready-to-Use Humorous Halloween Illustrations. (Clip Art Ser.). (Illus.). 64p. 1990. text 4.95 (0-486-26392-4) Dover.
— Ready-to-Use Humorous Illustrations of Children. (Clip Art Ser.). (Illus.). 64p. 1990. pap. text 5.95 (0-486-26247-2) Dover.
— Ready-to-Use Humorous Illustrations of Children's Recreations: 96 Different Copyright-Free Designs Printed One Side. (Clip Art Ser.). (Illus.). 64p. 1994. text 4.95 (0-486-28195-7) Dover.
— Ready-to-Use Humorous Illustrations of Trades & Services: 96 Different Copyright-Free Designs Printed One Side. (Clip Art Ser.). (Illus.). 1993. text 5.95 (0-486-27536-1) Dover.
— Ready-to-Use Humorous Office Spot Illustrations. (Clip Art Ser.). (Illus.). 64p. 1987. pap. text 5.95 (0-486-25307-4) Dover.
— Ready-to-Use Humorous Seasonal & Holiday Illustrations. (Clip Art Ser.). (Illus.). 64p. 1986. pap. 5.95 (0-486-25075-X) Dover.
— Ready-to-Use Humorous Sports Illustrations. 81st ed. (Illus.). 64p. 1989. pap. 5.95 (0-486-25955-2) Dover.
— Ready to Use Humourous Mortise. 81st ed. 1985. pap. 4.95 (0-486-25041-5) Dover.
— Ready-to-Use Silhouette Spot Illustrations. 64p. 1984. pap. 4.95 (0-486-24711-2) Dover.
Censoni, Bob. Soccer Sticker Book. (Little Activity Bks.). (Illus.). (J). 1992. pap. 1.00 (0-486-27256-7) Dover.
Censoni, Bob. Ready-to-Use Humorous Spot Illustrations. (Clip Art Ser.). 64p. 1984. pap. 4.95 (0-486-24644-2) Dover.
Censor, Yair & Zenios, Stavros A. Parallel Optimization: Theory, Algorithms & Applications. LC 96-46388. (Numerical Mathematics & Scientific Computation Ser.). (Illus.). 576p. 1998. text 85.00 (0-19-510062-X) OUP.
Censor, Yair Al & Reich, Simeon. Recent Developments in Optimization Theory & Nonlinear Analysis: AMS IMU Special Session on Optimization & Nonlinear Analysis, May 24-26, 1995, Jerusalem, Vol. 204. LC 96-29934. (Contemporary Mathematics Ser.). 278p. 1997. pap. 49.00 (0-8218-0515-0, CONM/204) Am Math
Censored, Project, jt. auth. see Phillips, Peter.
Censorinus. Censorini De die Natali Liber. xxiv, 109p. 1965. reprint ed. 25.00 incl. 3.5 hd (0-318-71088-9) G Olms Pubs.
Centa, Mary A., ed. see Kalibabky, Mike.
Centa, Mary Ann, ed. see Kalibabky, Mike.
Centala, Sandy, ed. see Daytrade Technologies Staff.
Centaur Press, Ltd. Staff, ed. The Dialectics of Diotima. 176p. 1970. 25.00 (0-8464-0325-0) Beekman Pubs.
Centeio, Tara Jaye. Mommy Lovers Her Baby. 32p. (ps-1). pap. 5.95 (0-06-443715-9) HarpC.
— Mommy Loves Her Baby. 32p. (ps-1). pap. 15.95 (0-06-029077-3); lib. bdg. 15.89 (0-06-029078-1) HarpC.
Centellas, Miguel. E. Bonell/J. M. Gil/F. Ruis. (Illus.). 76p. 1996. pap. text 30.00 (0-8230-6574-X) Watsn-Guptill.
— Enric Miralles. (Illus.). 76p. 1996. pap. text 30.00 (0-8230-6570-7) Watsn-Guptill.
— Jeronimo Junquera/E. Peres Pita. (Illus.). 76p. 1996. pap. text 30.00 (0-8230-6572-3) Watsn-Guptill.
— Jose Antonio Carrales-Ramon Vazquez Molezum. (Illus.). 76p. 1996. pap. text 30.00 (0-8230-6569-3) Watsn-Guptill.
Centenary Committee. Champion of Liberty: Charles Bradlaugh. LC 75-161323. (Atheist Viewpoint Ser.). (Illus.). 384p. 1972. reprint ed. 28.95 (0-405-03626-4) Ayer.
Centennial Colloquim on Thomas Mann Staff. Thomas Mann in Context: Proceedings of the Centennial Colloquium on Thomas Mann, Clark University, 1975. Hughes, Kenneth, ed. LC 77-26366. 138p. 1978. reprint ed. pap. 42.80 (0-608-13142-3, 201554500001) Bks Demand.
***Centennial Committee.** Centennial of the Settlement of Upper Canada by the United Empire Loyalists 1784-1884. 334p. 1999. reprint ed. pap. 26.00 (0-7884-1234-5, C157) Heritage Bk.
Centennial Committee, ed. Centennial History of Mt. Vernon, 1847-1947. (Illus.). 236p. 1997. reprint ed. lib. bdg. 32.00 (0-8328-6692-X) Higginson Bk Co.
Centennial Committee Sons of the Revolution in the & Woodall, Norman, frwds. Sons of the Revolution in the State of Alabama: Centennial Register. LC 93-74916. (Illus.). 214p. (C). 1994. 25.00 (0-9640149-0-4) Sons Revolution AL.
Centennial Committee Staff. Our Church: The 100th Anniversary Osman Immanuel Lutheran Church. LC 95-60510. (Illus.). 334p. 1995. pap. 17.95 (1-878044-25-7, Wld Rose) Mayhaven Pub.
***Centennial Historical Committee.** Granite City: A Pictorial History. 3rd ed. (Illinois Pictorial History Ser.) (Illus.). 200p. 1998. reprint ed. write for info. (0-943963-47-8) G Bradley.
Centeno, Barbara A. & Pitman, Martha Bishop. Fine Needle Aspiration Biopsy of the Pancreas. LC 97-52016. 200p. 1998. text 160.00 (0-7506-9725-3) Buttrwrth-Heinemann.
Centeno, Christopher J. The Spine Dictionary. LC 98-3975. 1998. 25.00 (1-56053-270-X) Hanley & Belfus.
***Centeno, Jesse.** Moontime Stories. large type ed. Flanagan, Patricia A., ed. 14p. 1999. pap. 5.00 (0-923242-84-8) Sparrowgrass Poetry.
Centeno, Jesse. Strange Nights & Weird Things. large type ed. Teri, Peggy, ed. (Illus.). 60p. 1998. pap. 6.50 (1-57553-706-0) Watermrk Pr.
Centeno, Miguel A. Democracy Within Reason: Technocratic Revolution in Mexico. LC 93-4485. (Illus.). 256p. (C). 1994. lib. bdg. 40.00 (0-271-01020-7) Pa St U Pr.
— Democracy Within Reason: Technocratic Revolution in Mexico. 2nd ed. 1997. pap. 16.95 (0-271-01701-5) Pa St U Pr.
— Liberian Dreams: Back-to-Africa Narratives from the 1850's. Moses, Wilson J., ed. LC 97-37112. 272p. 1998. 50.00 (0-271-01710-4) Pa St U Pr.
— Mexico in the 1990s: Government & Opposition Speak Out. (Current Issue Briefs Ser.: No. 1). 37p. 1991. pap. 7.50 (1-878367-01-3, CIB01) UCSD Ctr US-Mex.
Centeno, Miguel A. & Font, Mauricio, eds. Toward a New Cuba? Legacies of a Revolution. LC 96-32581. 245p. 1997. lib. bdg. 52.00 (1-55587-632-3, 876323) L Rienner.
— Toward a New Cuba: Legacies of a Revolution. LC 96-32581. 245p. 1998. pap. 19.95 (1-55587-814-8) L Rienner.
Centeno, Miguel A., et al. The Politics of Expertise in Latin America. LC 97-29474. (Latin American Studies). 224p. 1998. text 65.00 (0-312-21026-4) St Martin.
***Centeno, Miguel Angel.** Other Mirror: Grand Theory Through the Lens of Latin America. (Illus.). 360p. 2001. 59.50 (0-691-05016-3) Princeton U Pr.
***Centeno, Miguel Angel & Lopez-Alves, Fernando.** The Other Mirror: Grand Theory Through the Lens of Latin America. LC 00-32625. 360p. 2000. 15.95 (0-691-05017-1) Princeton U Pr.
Centeno-Roman, Jose M. Enciclopedia de la Cocina, 1. 6th ed. 1986. pap. 110.00 (0-7859-5740-5) Fr & Eur.
— Enciclopedia de la Cocina, 2. 6th ed. 1986. pap. 110.00 (0-7859-5741-3) Fr & Eur.
— Enciclopedia de la Cocina, 3. 6th ed. 1986. pap. 110.00 (0-7859-5742-1) Fr & Eur.
***Center & Moore.** NASCAR 50 Greatest Drivers. 2000. 40.00 (0-06-105125-X) HarpC.
Center, Allen H. Public Relations Practices: Managerial Case Studies & Problems. 5th ed. 574p. (C). 1995. pap. text 59.00 (0-13-098153-2) P-H.
***Center, Bill.** Ultimate Stock Car. (Illus.). 192p. 2000. write for info. (0-7894-5967-1, Pub. by DK Pub Inc) Pub Resources Inc.
***Center, Bill & Moore, Bob.** NASCAR 50 Greatest Drivers. LC 98-12421. (Illus.). 112p. (J). 1998. pap. 20.00 (0-06-107330-X, HarperHorizon) HarpC.
Center, Bill, jt. auth. see Hembree, Michael F.
Center, Candy & Nadeau, Jean-Pau. Public Speaking. 176p. (C). 1995. per. 25.95 (0-7872-1254-7, 41125401) Kendall-Hunt.
Center, E. Public Relations Practices. 6th ed. 2000. text 46.67 (0-13-613803-9) P-H.
Center for Afro-American & African Studies Staff. Black Immigration & Ethnicity in the United States: An Annotated Bibliography, 2. University of Michigan Staff, ed. LC 84-12886. (Bibliographies & Indexes in Afro-American & African Studies: No. 2). 170p. 1985. lib. bdg. 59.95 (0-313-24366-2, SBI/) Greenwood.
Center for American Places, Harrisonburg, Va. Staf, jt. auth. see Shore, Stephen.
***Center for Applied Gerontology Staff, ed.** Quality Care Management of the Elderly: A Cost Effective Approach. 97p. 2000. pap. text 29.95 (0-9677434-1-9) Ctr for Applied Gerontology.
Center for Applied Linguistics Staff. Bilingual Education, Vols. 1-5: Current Perspectives, 5 vols., Vol. 1: Social Science. LC 77-80381. 153p. reprint ed. pap. 47.50 (0-8357-3383-1, 203964300001) Bks Demand.
— Bilingual Education, Vols. 1-5: Current Perspectives, 5 vols., Vol. 2: Linguistics. LC 77-80381. 199p. reprint ed. pap. 61.70 (0-8357-3384-X, 203964300002) Bks Demand.
— Bilingual Education, Vols. 1-5: Current Perspectives, 5 vols., Vol. 3: Law. LC 77-80381. 89p. reprint ed. pap. 30.00 (0-8357-3385-8, 203964300003) Bks Demand.
— Bilingual Education, Vols. 1-5: Current Perspectives, 5 vols., Vol. 4: Education. LC 77-80381. 161p. reprint ed. pap. 50.00 (0-8357-3386-6, 203964300004) Bks Demand.
— Bilingual Education, Vols. 1-5: Current Perspectives, 5 vols., Vol. 5: Synthesis. LC 77-80381. 152p. reprint ed. pap. 47.20 (0-8357-3387-4, 203964300005) Bks Demand.
— English-Spanish (Cuban) unabridged ed. (Survival English Ser.). 1989. pap. 49.50 incl. audio (0-88432-417-6, AFE555) Audio-Forum.
— Handbook for Staff Development Workshops in Indian Education. LC 76-27562. 64p. reprint ed. pap. 30.00 (0-8357-3336-X, 203956200013) Bks Demand.
— Languages of Southeast Asia & the Pacific. LC 76-44595. (Survey of Materials for the Study of the Uncommonly Taught Languages Ser.: No. 7). 73p. reprint ed. pap. 30.00 (0-8357-3365-3, 203960400013) Bks Demand.
Center for Applied Linguistics Staff, et al. Languages of Eastern Asia. LC 76-44593. (Survey of Materials for the Study of the Uncommonly Taught Languages Ser.: No. 5). 51p. reprint ed. pap. 30.00 (0-8357-3366-1, 203960500013) Bks Demand.
— Languages of Eastern Europe & the Soviet Union. LC 76-44589. (Survey of Materials for the Study of the Uncommonly Taught Languages Ser.: No. 2). 53p. reprint ed. pap. 30.00 (0-8357-3367-X, 203960600013) Bks Demand.
— Languages of Sub-Saharan Africa. LC 76-44594. (Survey of Materials for the Study of the Uncommonly Taught Languages Ser.: No. 6). 93p. reprint ed. pap. 30.00 (0-8357-3368-8, 203960800013) Bks Demand.
Center for Applied Research in Education Staff, jt. auth. see Stowe, Cynthia.
Center for Applied Urban Research Staff. Housing & Business Investment in Nebraska. 161p. (Orig.). 1976. pap. 10.50 (1-55719-022-4) U NE CPAR.
— Identification & Analysis of Growth Occupations & Entry Level Positions in the Omaha SMSA with Special Attention to Minimal Training. 51p. (Orig.). 1977. pap. 4.00 (1-55719-062-3) U NE CPAR.
— Incentive Study. (Illus.). 72p. (Orig.). 1973. pap. 5.00 (1-55719-011-9) U NE CPAR.
— Job Match: Together for Good Business: Accommodating Individuals with Special Needs in the Workplace, Module III. 156p. (Orig.). 1987. 9.00 (1-55719-175-1) U NE CPAR.
— Job Match: Together for Good Business: Building Effective Partnerships: A Win-Win Approach, Module II. 116p. (Orig.). 1987. 6.50 (1-55719-174-3) U NE CPAR.
— Job Match: Together for Good Business: Business Practices & Resources. 124p. (Orig.). 1987. 7.00 (1-55719-177-8) U NE CPAR.
— Job Match: Together for Good Business: Inside & Outside the Corporation: Human Relations Factors, Module IV. 24p. (Orig.). 1987. 2.00 (1-55719-176-X) U NE CPAR.

C

— Job Match: Together for Good Business: Introductory Guide. 28p. (Orig.). 1987. 1.00 (*1-55719-172-7*) U NE CPAR.

— Job Match: Together for Good Business: Workers with Special Needs: An Overview, Module I. 52p. (Orig.). 1987. 3.50 (*1-55719-173-5*) U NE CPAR.

— Omaha Awareness Tours: The Near South Side. (Illus.). 16p. (Orig.). 1979. pap. 2.00 (*1-55719-104-2*) U NE CPAR.

— Omaha Public Schools: Opinion Surveys of a Parent & Taxpayer Group. 56p. (Orig.). 1987. pap. 3.50 (*1-55719-112-3*) U NE CPAR.

— Omaha's Traditional Business Districts: Their Impact & Proposals for Revitalization. 267p. (Orig.). 1976. pap. 16.00 (*1-55719-003-8*) U NE CPAR.

— Patterns & Prospects of Development in Downtown Kearney. 100p. (Orig.). 1982. pap. 6.00 (*1-55719-059-3*) U NE CPAR.

— The Sanitary Improvement District As a Mechanism for Urban Development. 126p. 1975. pap. 9.00 (*1-55719-027-5*) U NE CPAR.

— Saudi Arabia Sociological Research Project. 52p. (Orig.). 1977. pap. 3.50 (*1-55719-070-4*) U NE CPAR.

Center for Attitudinal Healing Staff. Another Look at the Rainbow. LC 82-12951. (Illus.). 96p. (J). (gr. 1-5). 1995. pap. 8.95 (*0-89087-341-0*) Celestial Arts.

Center for Attitudinal Healing Staff, jt. auth. see Jampolsky, Gerald G.

Center for Attitudinal Healing Staff, ed. see Jampolsky, Gerald G.

Center for Auto Safety Staff & Goodman, Richard M. Automobile Design Liability, 3 vols., Set. 3rd ed. LC 91-76912. 1991. ring bd. 370.00 (*0-685-59882-9*) West Group.

Center for Biblical Leadership Staff. Evangelism & Assimilation. (Equipped to Serve Ser.). (Illus.). 132p. (Orig.). 1996. pap. text 4.95 (*0-934942-96-X*) White Wing Pub.

Center for Bioethics & Human Dignity Staff. The Changing Face of Health Care: A Christian Appraisal of Managed Care, Resource Allocation & Patient-Caregiver Relationships. Kilner, John F. et al, eds. LC 98-22481. (Horizons in Bioethics Ser.). 240p. 1997. pap. 19.00 (*0-8028-4533-9*) Eerdmans.

C

Center for Black Music Research, Columbia College Staff, jt. ed. see Floyd, Samuel A., Jr.

Center for Chemical Process Safety of the American. Guidelines for Auditing Process Safety Management Systems. LC 92-40116. 1992. 99.00 (*0-8169-0556-8*, G-20) Am Inst Chem Eng.

— Guidelines for Safe Storage & Handling of Reactive Materials. LC 95-40831. 364p. 1995. 130.00 (*0-8169-0629-7*, G-30) Am Inst Chem Eng.

Center for Chemical Process Safety Staff. Contractor & Client Relations to Assure Process Safety. LC 96-21287. 81p. 1996. 49.00 (*0-8169-0667-X*, G-34) Am Inst Chem Eng.

— Guidelines for Preventing Human Error in Process Safety. LC 94-2481. 1994. 140.00 (*0-8169-0461-8*, G-15) Am Inst Chem Eng.

— Tools for Making Acute Risk Decisions: With Chemical Process Applications. LC 94-2462. 472p. 1995. 140.00 (*0-8169-0557-6*, G-21) Am Inst Chem Eng.

— Understanding Atmospheric Dispersion of Accidental Releases. 64p. 1995. 50.00 (*0-8169-0681-5*, G-37) Am Inst Chem Eng.

Center for Chemical Process Safety Staff, compiled by. Guidelines for Evaluating the Characteristics of Vapor Cloud Explosives, Flash Fires, & Bleves. 1994. 159.00 (*0-8169-0474-X*, G-9) Am Inst Chem Eng.

— Plant Guidelines for Technical Management of Chemical Process Safety. 393p. 1992. 120.00 (*0-8169-0499-5*, G-10) Am Inst Chem Eng.

— Safety, Health & Loss Prevention in Chemical Processes: Problems for Undergraduate Engineering Curriculum. 479p. 1990. pap., teacher ed. 69.00 (*0-8169-0421-9*, G-16) Am Inst Chem Eng.

— Safety, Health & Loss Prevention in Chemical Processes: Problems for Undergraduate Engineering Curriculum, Student Problems. 180p. 1990. pap. 18.00 (*0-8169-0473-1*, G-17) Am Inst Chem Eng.

Center for Chemical Process Safety Staff, ed. Guidelines for Design Solutions to Process Equipment Failures. LC 97-20538. (CCPS Guidelines Ser.). 254p. 1998. 140.00 (*0-8169-0684-X*, G-39) Am Inst Chem Eng.

— Guidelines for Pressure Relief & Emergency Handling Systems. LC 97-36450. (CCPS Guidelines Ser.). 1998. 199.00 (*0-8169-0476-6*, G-11) Am Inst Chem Eng.

— Guidelines for Safe Warehousing of Chemicals. LC 97-30661. (CCPS Guidelines Ser.). 1997. 120.00 (*0-8169-0659-9*, G-33) Am Inst Chem Eng.

— International Conference & Workshop on Risk Analysis in Process Safety. 856p. 1997. 100.00 (*0-8169-0737-4*, P-86) Am Inst Chem Eng.

Center for Child & Family Studies, Far West Labora. Module II, Group Care: Trainer's Manual. (Program for Infant - Toddler Caregivers Ser.). (Illus.). 158p. 1993. pap. 20.00 (*0-8011-1076-9*) Calif Education.

Center for Child & Family Studies Staff. Visions for Infant-Toddler Care: Guidelines for Professional Caregiving. (Program for Infant - Toddler Caregivers Ser.). (Illus.). 48p. 1988. pap. 6.50 (*0-8011-0758-X*) Calif Education.

Center for Co-operation with the Economies in Tran. Promoting Cleaner & Safer Industrial Production in Central & Eastern Europe. LC 96-177020. 144p. (Orig.). 1995. pap. 22.00 (*92-64-14589-3*, Pub. by Org for Econ) OECD.

Center for Communication & Social Policy Staff, ed. National Television Violence Study, Vol. 3. 368p. 1998. 79.95 (*0-7619-1653-9*) Sage.

Center for Communication, Inc. Staff, ed. Career Guide for Jobs in Communications. (Orig.). 1990. pap. 15.00 (*0-9625891-0-1*) Ctr Communication.

Center for Competitive, Sustainable Economies Staf. Setting Priorities, Getting Results: A New Direction for EPA. 221p. (Orig.). 1995. pap. 20.00 (*0-9646874-5-3*) Nat Acad Public Admin.

Center for Composite Materials Staff. Delaware Composites Design Encyclopedia: Index. Carlsson, Leif A. & Gillespie, John W., eds. 40p. 1991. pap. 26.95 (*0-87762-705-3*) Technomic.

Center for Conflict Resolution Staff. A Manual for Group Facilitators. 89p. 1978. 12.95 (*0-318-17938-5*, E03A) NASCO.

Center for Contemporary Arts Staff, ed. see Renner, Eric.

Center for Creative Leadership Staff. Job Challenge Profile: Facilitator's Guide. 72p. 1999. pap. text 24.95 (*0-7879-4506-4*) Jossey-Bass.

— Job Challenge Profile: Participant's Workbook. 48p. 1999. pap. text 12.95 (*0-7879-4505-6*) Jossey-Bass.

— Learning Tactics Inventory: Facilitator's Guide. 48p. 1999. pap. text 24.95 (*0-7879-4841-1*) Jossey-Bass.

— Learning Tactics Inventory: Participant's Workbook. 48p. 1999. pap. text 12.95 (*0-7879-4842-X*) Jossey-Bass.

Center for Creative Leadership Staff, et al. Breaking the Glass Ceiling: Can Women Reach the Top of America's Largest Corporations? LC 87-1853. 224p. 1987. 17.95 (*0-201-15787-X*) Addison-Wesley.

Center for Creative Leadership Staff, jt. auth. see Bracken, David.

Center for Creative Leadership Staff, jt. auth. see Mayer, Pamela S.

Center for Critical European Studies Staff, ed. Requiem for a Grand Design: The Demise of the European Union. 350p. 1996. 80.00 (*90-5711-001-6*, Pub. by NeXed Edits) Intl Spec Bk.

Center for Defense Studies Staff. Brassey's Defence Yearbook. 1998. 55.00 (*1-85753-277-5*, Pub. by Brasseys) Brasseys.

Center for Design Planning Staff. Streetscape Equipment Sourcebook 2: Lighting; Paving & Fixtures; Traffic Safety & Control; Housekeeping & Amenity; Signage; Communications & Safety Devices; Shelters; Recreation & Play; Miscellaneous. LC 79-56221. 244p. reprint ed. pap. 75.70 (*0-608-14614-5*, 202324100032) Bks Demand.

Center for Development of Instructional Technology, compiled by. Indian Social & Economic Development, 1993: An Index to the Literature. (Indian Social & Economic Development Ser.: Vol. 25). 200p. (C). 1993. text 33.50 (*0-8039-9167-3*) Sage.

Center for Disease Control Editors. Author-Title & Subject Catalogs of the Centers for Disease Control Library. 1983. 990.00 (*0-8161-0395-X*, G K Hall & Co) Mac Lib Ref.

Center for Disease Control Editors & Latham, Barbara. Promoting Physical Activity: A Guide for Community Action. LC 99-17119. (Illus.). 17p. 1999. pap. text 32.00 (*0-7360-0152-2*, BCDC0152) Human Kinetics.

Center for Disease Control Staff, et al. Proceedings of the International Collaborative Effort on Injury Statistics: Papers & Workshop Findings Presented at the International Symposium on Injury Statistics, May, 1994, Bethesda, Maryland. LC 94-45553. (Department of Health & Human Services Publications: PHS 95-1252). 1994. write for info. (*0-8406-0503-X*) Natl Ctr Health Stats.

Center for Economic Research on Africa Staff. Managing the Economic Transition in South Africa. (CERAF Conference Proceedings Ser.). 108p. 1994. pap. 9.50 (*0-944572-07-3*) MSU Ctr Econ Res Africa.

Center for Educational Research Staff. Best Mailbox for Kindergarten. (Illus.). (J). 1997. pap. text 32.00 (*1-56234-145-6*) Educ Ctr.

Center for Emergency Medicine Staff. Pharmacology. 96p. (gr. 13). 1996. pap. text 9.95 (*0-8151-7951-0*) Mosby Inc.

Center for Emergency Medicine Staff, jt. auth. see Stoy, Walt A.

Center for Environmental & Consumer Justice Staff. Discrimination in Private Employment in Puerto Rico (Color, Sex, & National Origin) LC 79-16965. 1987. pap. write for info. (*0-8477-2454-9*) U of PR Pr.

Center for Environmental Education Staff. The Ocean: Consider the Connections. Maraniss, Linda & Bierce, Rose, eds. (Illus.). 104p. (Orig.). (J). (gr. 2-6). 1985. pap., student ed. 8.95 (*0-9615294-0-7*) Ctr Env Educ.

Center for Food Safety & Applied Nutrition, U.S. F. Everything Added to Food in the United States. 160p. 1993. boxed set 141.95 (*0-8493-8723-X*, TX553) Smoley.

Center for Futures Education Staff. A Guide to Futures & Option Market Terminology. 50p. 1997. pap. 3.95 (*0-915513-80-3*) Ctr Futures Ed.

— Securities Broker Home Study Course (Series 7) 884p. 1998. pap. 175.00 (*0-915513-96-X*) Ctr Futures Ed.

— Understanding Commodity Futures. 53p. 1997. pap. 3.00 (*0-915513-77-3*) Ctr Futures Ed.

Center for Gifted Education Staff. Autobiographies: A Language Arts Unit for High-Ability Learners. 388p. (C). 1998. boxed set 65.95 (*0-7872-5337-5*, 41533701) Kendall-Hunt.

***Center for Gifted Education Staff.** Guide to Teaching a Language Arts Curriculum for High-Ability Learners. 116p. (C). 1999. per. 32.95 (*0-7872-5349-9*) Kendall-Hunt.

Center for Gifted Education Staff. Guide to Teaching a Science Curriculum. LC 98-156458. 128p. (C). 1997. pap. text, per. 32.95 (*0-7872-3328-5*, 41332801) Kendall-Hunt.

— Hot Rods: A Problem-Based Unit. 248p. 1996. pap. text, per. 32.95 (*0-7872-2813-3*, 41281301) Kendall-Hunt.

— Literary Reflection: A Language Arts Unit for High-Ability Learning. 346p. (C). 1998. boxed set 65.95 (*0-7872-5287-5*) Kendall-Hunt.

— Literature Packet for Persuasion. 42p. (C). 1998. 65.95 (*0-7872-5342-1*) Kendall-Hunt.

***Center for Gifted Education Staff.** The 1940's. 364p. 1998. boxed set 65.95 (*0-7872-5343-X*, 41534301) Kendall-Hunt.

— The 1940s: A Decade of Change: A Language Arts Unit for High-ability Learners. 332p. (C). per. 28.95 (*0-7872-5344-8*) Kendall-Hunt.

Center for Gifted Education Staff. Pak: Journeys & Destinations. 3rd ed. (C). 1998. 65.95 (*0-7872-5166-6*) Kendall-Hunt.

— Pak: Threads of Change in 19th Century Literature. 900p. (C). 1998. boxed set 65.95 (*0-7872-5346-4*, 41534601) Kendall-Hunt.

— Persuasion: A Language Arts Unit for High-Ability Learners. 340p. (C). 1998. per. 28.95 (*0-7872-5341-3*, 41534101); boxed set 65.95 (*0-7872-5340-5*, 41534001) Kendall-Hunt.

— Text: Threads of Change in 19th Century Literature. 340p. (C). 1998. per. 28.95 (*0-7872-5347-2*, 41534701) Kendall-Hunt.

Center for Gifted Staff. Acid, Acid Everywhere. 176p. (C). 1996. pap. text, per. 26.95 (*0-7872-2468-5*) Kendall-Hunt.

Center for Health & Human Services, jt. auth. see North Manhattan Health Action Group & CSS.

Center for Health Economics Research Staff. Access to Health Care. (Key Indicators for Policy Ser.). (Illus.). 96p. (Orig.). 1993. pap. write for info. (*0-942054-09-1*) R W Johnson Found.

Center for Healthcare Industry Performance Studies. The Procedures Resource Book. 235p. 1995. pap. 295.00 (*1-882733-03-7*) Ctr Hlthcare IPS.

Center for Holocaust Studies Staff, jt. auth. see Gurewitsch, Brana.

Center for Human Resources Management Staff. Alternatives for Federal Agencies: A Summary Report. (Implementing Real Change in Human Resources Management Ser.). 41p. (Orig.). 1995. pap. 15.00 (*0-9646874-7-X*) Nat Acad Public Admin.

— Effective Downsizing: A Compendium of Lessons Learned for Government Organizations. (Implementing Real Change in Human Resources Management Ser.). 60p. (Orig.). 1995. pap. 15.00 (*0-9646874-6-1*) Nat Acad Public Admin.

— Innovative Approaches to Human Resources Management. (Implementing Real Change in Human Resources Management Ser.). 340p. (Orig.). 1995. pap. 15.00 (*0-9646874-4-5*) Nat Acad Public Admin.

— Modernizing Federal Classification: Operational Broad-Banding Systems Alternatives. (Implementing Real Change in Human Resources Management Ser.). 113p. (Orig.). 1995. pap. 15.00 (*0-9646874-9-6*) Nat Acad Public Admin.

— Strategies & Alternatives for Transforming Federal Human Resources Management. (Implementing Real Change in Human Resources Management Ser.). 115p. (Orig.). 1995. pap. 15.00 (*0-9646874-3-7*) Nat Acad Public Admin.

Center for Human Values, CIS Committee for Statist, compiled by. Statistical Handbook of Social & Economic Indicators for the Former Soviet Union. LC 94-33435. 312p. 1996. lib. bdg. 75.00 (*0-88354-378-8*) N Ross.

Center for Info. Management Staff. Economic Report on Veterinarians & Veterinary Practices. 3rd ed. (Illus.). 229p. (Orig.). 1996. pap. 96.00 (*1-882691-10-5*) Am Veterinary Med Assn.

— The U. S. Livestock Market for Veterinary Medical Services & Products. 2nd ed. Orig. Title: The U. S. Market for Food Animal Veterinary Medical Services. (Illus.). 103p. (Orig.). 1995. pap. 74.50 (*1-882691-08-3*) Am Veterinary Med Assn.

— U. S. Pet Ownership & Demographics Sourcebook. 2nd ed. LC 97-72094. (Illus.). (Orig.). 1997. pap. 79.50 (*1-882691-02-4*) Am Veterinary Med Assn.

— Veterinary Demographic Annual Reports, 4 vols. 5th ed. Incl. Pt. 1: National Distribution of U. S. Veterinarians. 5th ed.Tr. of Veterinary Demographic Data Resource, Chaps. 2 & 3. (Illus.). 31p. (Orig.). 1996. pap. 25.00 (*1-882691-04-0*); Pt. 2: Distribution of U. S. Veterinarians by Primary Employment. 5th ed. Orig. Title: Veterinary Demographic Data Resource, Chap. 4. (Illus.). 55p. (Orig.). 1996. pap. 25.00 (*1-882691-05-9*); Pt. 4: Distribution of U. S. Veterinarians by State. 5th ed. Orig. Title: Veterinary Demographic Data Resource, Chap. 6. (Illus.). 107p. (Orig.). 1996. pap. 125.00 (*1-882691-07-5*); 295.00 (*1-882691-03-2*) Am Veterinary Med Assn.

Center for Innovation & Business Development Staff. The Business Plan. 200p. 1988. 49.95 (*0-930204-26-3*) Lord Pub.

Center for Innovation in Education Staff. Beyond the Book: Activities & Projects from Classrooms Like Yours. Brill, Patricia et al, eds. (Mathematics Their Way Ser.). (Illus.). 72p. (Orig.). (J). (gr. k-4). 1996. pap. 15.95 (*0-201-49334-9*) Supplementary Div.

Center for International & Strategic Affairs, Univ. Soviet - U. S. Cooperation in Africa: A Report on the Moscow Workshop, December, 1987. (Research Note Ser.). 1988. 10.00 (*0-86682-081-7*) Ctr Intl Relations.

Center for International Education & Center for Co, ed. Participatory Research: An Annotated Bibliography. 56p. 1991. spiral bd. 8.00 (*0-932288-88-X*) Ctr Intl Ed U of MA.

Center for International Education Staff, ed. see Kindervatter, Suzanne.

Center for International Legal Studies Staff. International Execution Against Judgment Debtors, 3 vols. Campbell, Dennis & Rodriguez, Susan, eds. LC 98-20740. 1998. ring bd. 375.00 (*0-379-01253-7*, 1344013) Oceana.

— International Public Procurement, 2 vols. Campbell, Dennis, ed. LC 98-27426. 1998. ring bd. 395.00 (*0-379-01252-9*, 1343114) Oceana.

Center for International Legal Studies Staff, jt. auth. see Campbell, Dennis.

Center for International Legal Studies Staff, ed. see Campbell, Dennis.

Center for International Legal Studies Staff, jt. ed. see Campbell, Dennis.

Center for International Security & Arms Control S, et al. Compliance & the Future of Arms Control. 272p. 1988. text 34.95 (*0-88730-277-7*, HarpBusn); pap. text 14.95 (*0-88730-280-7*, HarpBusn) HarpInfo.

Center for Investigative Reporting Staff & Moyers, Bill. Global Dumping Ground: The International Traffic in Hazardous Waste. LC 90-43079. (Illus.). 152p. 1990. pap. 11.95 (*0-932020-95-X*) Seven Locks Pr.

***Center for Japanese Studies Staff, ed.** Japan in the World, the World in Japan: Fifty Years of Japanese Studies at Michigan. 200p. 1999. pap. 11.95 (*0-939512-95-5*) U MI Japan.

Center for Justice & International Law Staff, jt. auth. see Human Rights Watch Americas Staff.

Center for Labor Education & Research Staff. Emergency Responder Training Manual for the Hazardous Materials Technician. Andrews, Lori P., ed. (Industrial Health & Safety Ser.). 528p. 1992. 84.95 (*0-471-28442-4*, VNR) Wiley.

Center for Labor Education & Research Staff. Worker Protection During Hazardous Waste Remediation. Andrews, Lori P., ed. 391p. 1990. text 70.95 (*0-442-23899-1*, VNR) Wiley.

Center for Labor Education & Research Staff. Worker Protection During Hazardous Waste Remediation. Andrews, Lori P., ed. 416p. 1990. 89.95 (*0-471-28916-7*, VNR) Wiley.

Center for Land Use Interpretation Staff. 100 Places in Washington: From the Center for Land Use Interpretation Archives. (Illus.). 112p. 1999. pap. write for info. (*0-9650962-2-X*) Ctr Land Use Interpret.

Center for Land Use Interpretation Staff, photos by. Hinterland: A Voyage into Exurban Southern California. (Illus.). 100p. 1997. pap. 10.00 (*0-937225-13-4*) LA Contemp Exhib.

Center for Law & Religious Freedom Staff. What Is a Church? The Dilemma of the Parachurch. 73p. (Orig.). (C). 1979. pap. text 3.00 (*0-944561-00-4*) Chr Legal.

***Center for Learning Network Staff.** Absolutely Normal Chaos/Chasing Redbird: Curriculum Unit. (Novel - Drama Ser.). 79p. 1998. teacher ed., spiral bd. 18.95 (*1-56077-569-6*) Ctr Learning.

Center for Learning Network Staff. Adam of the Road - Catherine, Called Birdy: Curriculum Unit. (Novel - Drama Ser.). 84p. 1997. teacher ed., spiral bd. 18.95 (*1-56077-526-2*) Ctr Learning.

— Advanced Placement U. S. History 2 - Student Edition: Twentieth-Century Challenges 1914-1996. (Social Studies Ser.). 233p. 1996. pap. text, wbk. ed. 10.95 (*1-56077-501-7*) Ctr Learning.

Center for Learning Network Staff. Advanced Composition: Student Edition. (YA). (gr. 9-11). spiral bd. 8.95 (*1-56077-376-6*) Ctr Learning.

— Advanced Compostition. 235p. (YA). (gr. 9-11). spiral bd. 37.95 (*1-56077-375-8*) Ctr Learning.

— Advanced Placement English 1: Practical Approaches to Literary Analysis. (English Ser.). 220p. (YA). (gr. 11-12). 1997. spiral bd. 37.95 (*1-56077-532-7*) Ctr Learning.

— Advanced Placement English 2: In-depth analysis of Literary Forms. 266p. (YA). (gr. 11-12). 1997. spiral bd. 37.95 (*1-56077-533-5*) Ctr Learning.

— Advanced Placement European History I: The Modern World: New Direction. 255p. (YA). (gr. 11-12). 1988. spiral bd. 37.95 (*1-56077-419-3*) Ctr Learning.

— Advanced Placement European History I: The Modern World: New Direction. (YA). (gr. 11-12). 1992. student ed. 12.95 (*1-56077-420-7*) Ctr Learning.

— Advanced Placement European History II: Westerniaing the World. 255p. (YA). (gr. 11-12). 1991. spiral bd. 37.95 (*1-56077-421-5*) Ctr Learning.

— Advanced Placement European History II: Westernizing the World. (YA). (gr. 11-12). 1992. student ed. 12.95 (*1-56077-422-3*) Ctr Learning.

— Advanced Placement Poetry. 245p. (YA). (gr. 11-12). spiral bd. 37.95 (*1-56077-379-0*) Ctr Learning.

— Advanced Placement Short Story. 212p. (YA). (gr. 11-12). spiral bd. 37.95 (*1-56077-380-4*) Ctr Learning.

Center for Learning Network Staff. Advanced Placement U. S. History 1 - Student Edition: The Evolving American Nation-State, 1607-1914. (Social Studies Ser.). 254p. (YA). (gr. 11-12). 1996. student ed., spiral bd., wbk. ed. 10.95 (*1-56077-500-9*) Ctr Learning.

— Advanced Placement U. S. History 1: The Evolving American Nation-State 1607-1914. rev. ed. (Social Studies Ser.). 254p. 1996. teacher ed., spiral bd. 37.95 (*1-56077-485-1*) Ctr Learning.

— Advanced Placement U. S. History 2: Twentieth-Century Challenges 1914-1996. rev. ed. (Social Studies Ser.). 233p. 1996. teacher ed., spiral bd. 37.95 (*1-56077-486-X*) Ctr Learning.

Center for Learning Network Staff. Advanced Placement United States Government & Politics: Institutions, Policy & Politics. 226p. (YA). (gr. 12). spiral bd. 37.95 (*1-56077-423-1*) Ctr Learning.

— Advanced Placement United States Government & Politics - Student Edition: Institutions, Policy & Politics. 118p. (YA). (gr. 12). 8.95 (*1-56077-424-X*) Ctr Learning.

An Asterisk (*) at the beginning of an entry indicates that the title is appearing for the first time.

— Advanced Placement Writing 2: Strategies for Honors, Gifted & AP Students. (English - AP). 267p. (YA). (gr. 11-12). 1999. spiral bd. 37.95 (*1-56077-603-X*) Ctr Learning.

Center for Learning Network Staff. Aging & the Parish Community: Adult Workshops. (Adult Workshops Ser.). 103p. 1990. pap. text 15.95 (*1-56077-054-6*) Ctr Learning.

***Center for Learning Network Staff.** America in Upheaval: The 1960s: Primary Sources in U.S. History. (Social Studies Primary Sources). 94p. (YA). (gr. 9-12). 1999. spiral bd. 27.95 (*1-56077-587-4*) Ctr Learning.

— America in World War II: The 1940s - Primary Sources in U. S. History. (Social Studies). 100p. 1999. teacher ed., spiral bd. 27.95 (*1-56077-573-4*) Ctr Learning.

— The American Family. (Social Issues Ser.). 64p. 1998. teacher ed., spiral bd. 19.95 (*1-56077-563-7*) Ctr Learning.

— American Social Issues: An Interactive Encyclopedia. 239p. (YA). (gr. 9-12). spiral bd. 37.95 (*1-56077-425-8*) Ctr Learning.

Center for Learning Network Staff. Animal Farm by George Orwell & The Book of the Dun Cow by Walter Wangerin: Curriculum Unit. (Novel Ser.). 107p. 1992. spiral bd. 18.95 (*1-56077-150-X*) Ctr Learning.

***Center for Learning Network Staff.** Antebellum America & Civil War: 1840-1865 (Primary Sources in U.S. History) (Social Studies Primary Sources). 104p. (YA). (gr. 9-12). 2000. spiral bd. 27.95 (*1-56077-614-5*) Ctr Learning.

— Anthropology. (Social Studies). 260p. 1999. teacher ed., spiral bd. 37.95 (*1-56077-590-4*) Ctr Learning.

Center for Learning Network Staff. April Morning by Howard Fast: Curriculum Unit. (Novel - Drama Ser.). 76p. 1996. teacher ed., spiral bd. 18.95 (*1-56077-507-6*) Ctr Learning.

— Archetypes in Life, Literature, & Myth: Curriculum Unit. (Language Arts - English Ser.). 82p. 1996. teacher ed., spiral bd. 19.95 (*1-56077-487-8*) Ctr Learning.

— Babbitt by Sinclair Lewis: Curriculum Unit. (Novel Ser.). 61p. 1992. teacher ed., spiral bd. 18.95 (*1-56077-210-7*) Ctr Learning.

Center for Learning Network Staff. Basic Composition. 218p. (YA). (gr. 7-9). spiral bd. 37.95 (*1-56077-385-5*) Ctr Learning.

— Basic Composition - Student Editioni. (YA). (gr. 7-9). spiral bd. 8.95 (*1-56077-386-3*) Ctr Learning.

Center for Learning Network Staff. Belief & Practice: Adult Workshops. (Adult Workshops Ser.). 119p. 1989. pap. text 15.95 (*1-56077-038-4*) Ctr Learning.

— Black Boy by Richard Wright: Curriculum Unit. (Novel - Drama Ser.). 83p. 1997. reprint ed. spiral bd. 18.95 (*1-56077-527-0*) Ctr Learning.

— Blended Families - Intermediate - Leader Manual: A Guided Support Program for Intermediate Grades. 40p. 1996. teacher ed., spiral bd. 3.95 (*1-56077-462-2*) Ctr Learning.

— Blended Families - Intermediate - Student Edition: A Guided Support Program for Intermediate Grades. 68p. (J). (gr. 4-6). 1996. pap. text, wbk. ed. 5.95 (*1-56077-461-4*) Ctr Learning.

Center for Learning Network Staff. Blended Families - Leader Manual: A Guided Suppored Prograrn for Primary Grades. (Elementary). 39p. 1996. pap. 3.95 (*1-56077-460-6*) Ctr Learning.

— Blended Families - Student: A Guided Support Progarm for Primary Grades. (Elementary). 65p. 1996. 5.95 (*1-56077-459-2*) Ctr Learning.

Center for Learning Network Staff. Brave New World by Aldous Huxley: Curriculum Unit. (Novel Ser.). 85p. 1993. teacher ed., spiral bd. 18.95 (*1-56077-281-6*) Ctr Learning.

— Building Peace & Justice: Adult Workshops. (Adult Workshops Ser.). 122p. 1990. pap. text 15.95 (*1-56077-052-X*) Ctr Learning.

***Center for Learning Network Staff.** Catechists: 8 Spiritual Formation Sessions. (Religion Ser.). 102p. 2000. spiral bd. 19.95 (*1-56077-611-0*) Ctr Learning.

— Cathechetical Ministry. (Adult Workshops Ser.). 99p. 1989. spiral bd. 15.95 (*1-56077-049-X*) Ctr Learning.

— Catholic Teaching on Authority, Obedience & Freedom. (Religion). 51p. 1999. pap. text 2.95 (*1-56077-578-5*) Ctr Learning.

— Catholic Teaching on Life Commitments. (Religion). 51p. 1999. pap. 2.95 (*1-56077-579-3*) Ctr Learning.

— Catholic Teaching on Life Issues. (Religion - Catholic Teaching Ser.). 57p. 1998. pap. text 2.95 (*1-56077-544-0*) Ctr Learning.

— Catholic Teaching on Mary. (Religion - Catholic Teaching Ser.). 41p. 1998. pap. text 2.95 (*1-56077-543-2*) Ctr Learning.

— Catholic Teaching on Ministry. (Religion - Catholic Teaching Ser.). 51p. 1998. pap. text 2.95 (*1-56077-542-4*) Ctr Learning.

Center for Learning Network Staff. Catholic Teaching on Morality. (Catholic Teaching Ser.). 42p. 1997. pap. text 2.95 (*1-56077-519-X*) Ctr Learning.

— Catholic Teaching on Sin & Grace. (Catholic Teaching Ser.). 31p. 1997. pap. text 2.95 (*1-56077-521-1*) Ctr Learning.

— Catholic Teaching on Social Justice. (Catholic Teaching Ser.). 44p. 1997. pap. text 2.95 (*1-56077-522-X*) Ctr Learning.

***Center for Learning Network Staff.** Catholic Teaching on the Christian Scriptures. (Religion). 43p. 1999. spiral bd. 2.95 (*1-56077-599-8*) Ctr Learning.

— Catholic Teaching on the End Times. (Religion). 34p. 1999. spiral bd. 2.95 (*1-56077-570-X*) Ctr Learning.

Center for Learning Network Staff. Catholic Teaching on the Eucharist. (Catholic Teaching Ser.). 39p. 1997. pap. text 2.95 (*1-56077-523-8*) Ctr Learning.

— Catholic Teaching on the Hebrew Scriptures. (Catholic Teaching Ser.). 47p. 1997. pap. text 2.95 (*1-56077-518-1*) Ctr Learning.

— Catholic Teaching on the Sacraments. (Catholic Teaching Ser.). 46p. 1997. pap. text 2.95 (*1-56077-520-3*) Ctr Learning.

***Center for Learning Network Staff.** Catholic Teaching on the Saints. (Religion - Catholic Teaching Ser.). 40p. 1998. pap. text 2.95 (*1-56077-550-5*) Ctr Learning.

Center for Learning Network Staff. Celebrating Reconciliation: 10 Penitential Services. (Religion Ser.). 95p. 1996. teacher ed., spiral bd. 15.95 (*1-56077-456-8*) Ctr Learning.

— The Chosen by Chaim Potok: Curriculum Unit. (Novel Ser.). 82p. 1994. reprint ed. teacher ed., spiral bd. 18.95 (*1-56077-295-6*) Ctr Learning.

Center for Learning Network Staff. Christian Scriptures: Responding to the good News - Parish Edition. (Parish Religion Series). 69p. (YA). (gr. 9-12). 1996. spiral bd. 12.95 (*1-56077-411-8*) Ctr Learning.

— Christian Scriptures - Teacher: Responding to the Good News. (Religion). 136p. (YA). (gr. 9-12). 1999. spiral bd. 9.95 (*1-56077-589-0*) Ctr Learning.

Center for Learning Network Staff. Christian Service: Workshop Models. (Junior High Religion Ser.). 101p. 1992. teacher ed., spiral bd. 15.95 (*1-56077-182-8*) Ctr Learning.

Center for Learning Network Staff. The Chronicles of Narnia: Curriculum Unit. (Novel Ser.). 88p. (YA). (gr. 9-12). 1996. spiral bd. 18.95 (*1-56077-327-8*) Ctr Learning.

— Church: Tracing Our Pilgrimage - Parish Edition. (Parish Religion Series). 77p. (YA). (gr. 9-12). 1996. spiral bd. 12.95 (*1-56077-374-X*) Ctr Learning.

— Church - Teacher Manual: Tracing Our Pilgrimage. (Discipleship Ser.). spiral bd. 9.95 (*1-56077-351-0*) Ctr Learning.

— Colonization 1521-1763: Primary Sources in U.S. History. (Social Studies Primary Sources). 100p. (YA). (gr. 9-12). 1999. spiral bd. 27.95 (*1-56077-601-3*) Ctr Learning.

— The Color of Water: Curriculum Unit. (Novel - Drama Ser.). 73p. (YA). (gr. 9-12). 1999. spiral bd. 18.95 (*1-56077-600-5*) Ctr Learning.

— Coming to Terms with Divorce: A Guided Support Program for Intermediate Grades. 134p. (J). (gr. 4-6). 1991. 6.95 (*1-56077-148-8*); spiral bd. 8.95 (*1-56077-149-6*) Ctr Learning.

Center for Learning Network Staff. Coming to Terms with Divorce: A Guided Support Program for Primary Grades Leader's Manual. 75p. 1992. pap., teacher ed. 8.95 (*1-56077-147-X*) Ctr Learning.

— Coming to Terms with Divorce: A Guided Support Program for Primary Grades Workbook. 98p. 1992. pap. text, student ed. 6.95 (*1-56077-146-1*) Ctr Learning.

— Commitments: Growing in the Catholic Lifestyle: Parish Edition. (Discipleship Ser.). 73p. (YA). (gr. 9-12). 1997. teacher ed., spiral bd. 12.95 (*1-56077-540-8*) Ctr Learning.

— Commitments - Student Book: Growing in the Catholic Lifestyle. (Discipleship Ser.). 167p. (YA). (gr. 11-12). 1997. pap. text, wbk. ed. 7.95 (*1-56077-475-4*) Ctr Learning.

— Commitments - Teacher Guide: Growing in the Catholic Lifestyle. (Discipleship Ser.). 119p. 1997. teacher ed., spiral bd. 9.95 (*1-56077-476-2*) Ctr Learning.

— Connections: A Summer Bible Program for Children. 78p. (J). (gr. 1-3). 1990. pap. text 6.95 (*1-56077-053-8*) Ctr Learning.

Center for Learning Network Staff. Conscience: Developing Skills for Moral Decision making - Student Text. (Discipleship Ser.). 193p. (YA). (gr. 11-12). 1996. 7.95 (*1-56077-471-1*) Ctr Learning.

— Conscience: Developing Skills for Moral Decision making - Teacher Manual. 181p. (YA). (gr. 11-12). spiral bd. 9.95 (*1-56077-472-X*) Ctr Learning.

Center for Learning Network Staff. Conscience - Parish Edition: Developing Skills for Moral Decision Making. (Discipleship Ser.). 85p. 1996. teacher ed., spiral bd. 12.95 (*1-56077-479-7*) Ctr Learning.

***Center for Learning Network Staff.** Consensus & Conformity: The 1950s - Primary Sources in U. S. History. (Social Studies Ser.). 102p. 1999. teacher ed., spiral bd. 27.95 (*1-56077-574-2*) Ctr Learning.

— Contemporary Issues. 226p. (YA). (gr. 9-12). spiral bd. 37.95 (*1-56077-430-4*) Ctr Learning.

— The Count of Monte Cristo: Curriculum. (Novel Ser.). 93p. (YA). (gr. 9-12). 1996. spiral bd. 18.95 (*1-56077-331-6*) Ctr Learning.

— Creating a Values-Based Literature Program: Novel - Drama Curriculum Units. 48p. 1999. pap. text, teacher ed. 5.00 (*1-56077-585-8*) Ctr Learning.

Center for Learning Network Staff. Creative Dramatics in the Classroom: Curriculum Unit. (English - Language Arts Ser.). 104p. (YA). (gr. 6-9). 1996. teacher ed., spiral bd. 19.95 (*1-56077-491-6*) Ctr Learning.

— Crime & Punishment by Fyodor Dostoevsky: Curriculum Unit. (Novel Ser.). 79p. 1991. reprint ed. spiral bd. 18.95 (*1-56077-176-3*) Ctr Learning.

Center for Learning Network Staff. Current Issues in Global Education. 231p. (YA). (gr. 9-12). spiral bd. 37.95 (*1-56077-431-2*) Ctr Learning.

Center for Learning Network Staff. Cyrano de Bergerac by Edmond Rostand: Curriculum Unit. (Drama Ser.). 78p. 1992. reprint ed. teacher ed., spiral bd. 18.95 (*1-56077-209-3*) Ctr Learning.

Center for Learning Network Staff. Daily Writing Topics. (YA). (gr. 7-12). spiral bd. 29.95 (*1-56077-390-1*) Ctr Learning.

Center for Learning Network Staff. Death Comes for the Archbishop by Willa Cather: Curriculum Unit. (Novel - Drama Ser.). 62p. (YA). (gr. 11-12). 1996. teacher ed., spiral bd. 18.95 (*1-56077-499-1*) Ctr Learning.

— The Deficit & National Debt. 72p. 1998. teacher ed., spiral bd. 19.95 (*1-56077-546-7*) Ctr Learning.

— The Divine Comedy by Dante Alighieri: Curriculum Unit. (Novel Ser.). 125p. 1994. teacher ed., spiral bd. 18.95 (*1-56077-280-8*) Ctr Learning.

— Divorce: Adjusting to Change: Looking at Life. 12p. (YA). (gr. 7-12). 1992. pap. text 0.80 (*1-56077-223-9*) Ctr Learning.

— A Doll's House & Hedda Gabler by Henrik Ibsen: Curriculum Unit. (Drama Ser.). 71p. 1991. reprint ed. spiral bd. 18.95 (*1-56077-174-7*) Ctr Learning.

— Dubliners by James Joyce: Curriculum Unit. (Novel - Drama Ser.). 80p. 1996. teacher ed., spiral bd. 18.95 (*1-56077-337-5*) Ctr Learning.

Center for Learning Network Staff. Economics Book I: Microeconomics & The American Economy. (Economics). 233p. (YA). (gr. 11-12). spiral bd. 37.95 (*1-56077-432-0*) Ctr Learning.

— Economics Book II: Macroeconomics & The American Economy. (Economics). 189p. (YA). (gr. 11-12). spiral bd. 37.95 (*1-56077-433-9*) Ctr Learning.

— The Egypt Game; The Bronze Bow: Curriculum Unit. (Novel - Drama Ser.). 92p. 1999. teacher ed., spiral bd. 18.95 (*1-56077-595-5*) Ctr Learning.

Center for Learning Network Staff. Emma by Jane Austen: Curriculum Unit. (Novel - Drama Ser.). 98p. 1997. teacher ed., spiral bd. 18.95 (*1-56077-541-6*) Ctr Learning.

***Center for Learning Network Staff.** The Environment. (Social Issues Ser.). 84p. 1998. pap. text, teacher ed. 19.95 (*1-56077-513-0*) Ctr Learning.

— Eucharistic Ministers: 8 Spriitual Formation Session. 125p. 1999. spiral bd. 19.95 (*1-56077-592-0*) Ctr Learning.

— Exploring the Catechism of the Catholic Church - Facilitator's Guide: A Guide for Facilitating Adult discussion & Prayer. (Religion Ser.). 45p. (YA). 1996. pap. 3.50 (*1-56077-503-3*) Ctr Learning.

— Exploring the Catechism of the Catholic Church - Facilitator's Guide: A Guide for Facilitating Adult discussion & Prayer. (Religion Ser.). 44p. (YA). 1997. pap. 5.50 (*1-56077-502-5*) Ctr Learning.

— Faith: Developing an Adult Spirituality - Parish Edition. (Parish Religion). 81p. (YA). (gr. 9-12). 1995. spiral bd. 12.95 (*1-56077-354-5*) Ctr Learning.

Center for Learning Network Staff. Faith & Belief: Workshop Models. (Junior High Religion Ser.). 95p. 1992. teacher ed., spiral bd. 15.95 (*1-56077-181-X*) Ctr Learning.

Center for Learning Network Staff. Faith: Developing an Adult Spirituality: Student Text. 157p. (YA). (gr. 12). 1994. spiral bd. 7.95 (*1-56077-312-X*) Ctr Learning.

— Faith: Developing an Adult Spirituality: Teacher Manual. 147p. (YA). (gr. 12). 1994. spiral bd. 9.95 (*1-56077-313-8*) Ctr Learning.

Center for Learning Network Staff. A Farewell to Arms by Ernest Hemingway: Curriculum Unit. (Novel Ser.). 64p. (YA). (gr. 9-12). 1993. teacher ed., spiral bd. 13.95 (*1-56077-274-3*) Ctr Learning.

***Center for Learning Network Staff.** Formula Writing Basics: Beginning a Writing Proficiency Program. (English - Language Arts Ser.). 149p. 1998. teacher ed., spiral bd. 19.95 (*1-56077-568-8*) Ctr Learning.

— Formula Writing 1: Building Toward Writing Proficiency. 145p. (YA). (gr. 7-10). 1999. pap. text, student ed. 10.95 (*1-56077-610-2*) Ctr Learning.

— Formula Writing 1: Building Toward Writing Proficiency. rev. ed. (English Ser.). 111p. (YA). (gr. 7-10). 1997. spiral bd. 19.95 (*1-56077-529-7*) Ctr Learning.

— Formula Writing 2: Diverse Writing Situations. (English Ser.). 101p. (YA). (gr. 8-12). 1996. spiral bd. 23.95 (*1-56077-483-5*) Ctr Learning.

Center for Learning Network Staff. From the Mixed-Up Files of Mrs. Basil E. Frankweiler - The Westing Game: Curriculum Unit. (Novel - Drama Ser.). 110p. 1997. teacher ed., spiral bd. 18.95 (*1-56077-525-4*) Ctr Learning.

— Fundamentalism: A Catholic Response. 98p. 1992. spiral bd. 5.95 (*1-56077-062-7*) Ctr Learning.

Center for Learning Network Staff. A Gathering of Flowers: Stories about Being Young in America. (Novel Ser.). 84p. (YA). (gr. 9-12). 1996. spiral bd. 18.95 (*1-56077-451-7*) Ctr Learning.

— Grammar Mastery - for Better Writing - Level 1 Curriculum Unit. (English Ser.). 159p. (YA). (gr. 7-9). 1997. 7.95 (*1-56077-510-6*) Ctr Learning.

— Grammar Mastery - for Better Writing - Level 2 Curriculum Unit. (English Ser.). 123p. (YA). (gr. 8-10). 1997. 7.95 (*1-56077-511-4*) Ctr Learning.

— Grammar Mastery - for Better Writing - Teacher Guide: Curriculum Unit. (English Ser.). 121p. (YA). (gr. 7-10). 1997. spiral bd. 7.95 (*1-56077-509-2*) Ctr Learning.

— Grammar Power: The Essential Elements. (Intermediate Social Studies Activities). 138p. 1999. teacher ed., spiral bd. 10.95 (*1-56077-594-7*) Ctr Learning.

— Grammar Power: The Essential Elements. 171p. (YA). (gr. 6-9). 1999. pap. text, student ed. 10.95 (*1-56077-593-9*) Ctr Learning.

— Hebrew Scriptures: Growing in Faith - Student Text. (Discipleship Ser.). 182p. (YA). (gr. 9-10). 1996. 7.95 (*1-56077-465-7*) Ctr Learning.

— Hebrew Scriptures: Growing in Faith - Teacher Manual. (Discipleship Ser.). 152p. (YA). (gr. 9-10). 1996. spiral bd. 9.95 (*1-56077-466-5*) Ctr Learning.

— Hebrew Scriptures: Grwoing in Faith (Parish) (Religion). 82p. (YA). (gr. 9-12). 1996. spiral bd. 12.95 (*1-56077-480-0*) Ctr Learning.

— Hiking Into Whole Language. 225p. (J). (gr. 1-3). 1992. spiral bd. 19.95 (*1-56077-235-2*) Ctr Learning.

Center for Learning Network Staff. Hiroshima by John Hersey - On the Beach by Nevil Shute: Curriculum Unit. (Novel Ser.). 82p. 1992. spiral bd. 18.95 (*1-56077-153-4*) Ctr Learning.

Center for Learning Network Staff. The Human Comedy/My Name is Aram: Curriculum Unit. (Novel Ser.). 65p. (YA). (gr. 4-12). 1995. spiral bd. 18.95 (*1-56077-319-7*) Ctr Learning.

Center for Learning Network Staff. Hunger. LC 97-156728. (Social Studies Ser.). 270p. 1997. teacher ed., spiral bd. 24.95 (*1-56077-506-8*) Ctr Learning.

Center for Learning Network Staff. International Biographies Book 1: Africa & the Middle East. (International Biographies). 147p. (J). (gr. 4-8). 1992. spiral bd. 19.95 (*1-56077-192-5*) Ctr Learning.

— International Biographies Book 2: Asia, Australia & Oceania. (International Biographies). 141p. (J). (gr. 4-8). 1992. spiral bd. 19.95 (*1-56077-193-3*) Ctr Learning.

— International Biographies Book 3: Europe (Central & Southern) (International Biographies). 140p. (J). (gr. 4-8). 1992. spiral bd. 19.95 (*1-56077-194-1*) Ctr Learning.

— International Biographies Book 4: Europe (Eastern) (International Biographies). 125p. (J). (gr. 4-8). 1992. spiral bd. 19.95 (*1-56077-195-X*) Ctr Learning.

— International Biographies Book 5: Europe (Northern & Western) (International Biographies). 137p. (J). (gr. 4-8). 1992. spiral bd. 19.95 (*1-56077-196-8*) Ctr Learning.

— International Biographies Book 6: Latin America (Central & South) (International Biographies). 140p. (J). (gr. 4-8). spiral bd. 19.95 (*1-56077-197-6*) Ctr Learning.

— International Biographies Book 7: North America (U.S. & Canada) (International Biographies). 148p. (J). (gr. 4-8). 1992. spiral bd. 19.95 (*1-56077-198-4*) Ctr Learning.

— Interwar America, 1920-1940: Primary Sources in U. S. History. (Social Studies Ser.). 99p. 1999. teacher ed., spiral bd. 27.95 (*1-56077-591-2*) Ctr Learning.

Center for Learning Network Staff. Invitations from God. 96p. 1995. pap. text 6.95 (*1-56077-353-7*) Ctr Learning.

Center for Learning Network Staff. Issues in Our Changing World. spiral bd. 37.95 (*1-56077-434-7*) Ctr Learning.

— Issues in the Workplace. (Social Issues Ser.). 79p. 1998. teacher ed., spiral bd. 19.95 (*1-56077-562-9*) Ctr Learning.

— Johnny Tremain. (J). spiral bd. Price not set. (*1-56077-498-3*) Ctr Learning.

— Jubal Sackett & the Walking Drum: Curriculum Unit. (Novel Ser.). 67p. (YA). (gr. 9-12). 1996. spiral bd. 18.95 (*1-56077-372-3*) Ctr Learning.

Center for Learning Network Staff. Julie of the Wolves by Jean Graighead George - Island of the Blue Dolphins by Scott O'Dell: Curriculum Unit. (Novel Ser.). 93p. 1993. teacher ed., spiral bd. 18.95 (*1-56077-282-4*) Ctr Learning.

Center for Learning Network Staff. Junior High Language Arts. 174p. (YA). (gr. 7-10). spiral bd. 34.95 (*1-56077-394-4*) Ctr Learning.

Center for Learning Network Staff. Justice & Peace: Workshop Models. (Junior High Religion (Grades 7-8) Ser.). 79p. 1992. teacher ed., spiral bd. 15.95 (*1-56077-183-6*) Ctr Learning.

— Juvenile Justice: In the Hands of the Law. (Social Issues Ser.). 90p. 1998. pap., teacher ed. 19.95 (*1-56077-556-4*) Ctr Learning.

— Killer Angels by Michael Shaara: Curriculum Unit. (Novel Ser.). 1994. teacher ed., spiral bd. 18.95 (*1-56077-293-X*) Ctr Learning.

Center for Learning Network Staff. Let's Talk to Teens about Chastity: For Public School Audience. (Molly Kelly Ser.). 42p. 1994. pap. text, teacher ed. 5.95 (*1-56077-559-9*) Ctr Learning.

— Let's Talk to Teens about Chastity: Molly Kelly Catholic Program. 57p. 1998. pap. text, teacher ed. 5.95 (*1-56077-560-2*) Ctr Learning.

— Let's Talk to Teens about Chastity: Molly Kelly Christian Program. 57p. 1998. pap. text, teacher ed. 5.95 (*1-56077-558-0*) Ctr Learning.

Center for Learning Network Staff. Little House in the Big Woods: Curriculum Unit. (Novel Ser.). 96p. 1994. teacher ed., spiral bd. 18.95 (*1-56077-291-3*) Ctr Learning.

***Center for Learning Network Staff.** Little Women by Louisa May Alcott: Curriculum Unit. (Novel - Drama Ser.). 53p. (YA). (gr. 6-9). 1998. teacher ed., spiral bd. 18.95 (*1-56077-557-2*) Ctr Learning.

Center for Learning Network Staff. Liturgy Models. (Parish Ministry Manuals Ser.). 127p. 1991. spiral bd. 15.95 (*1-56077-032-5*) Ctr Learning.

— Marriage: A Shared Sacrament. 65p. (YA). (gr. 9-12). 1993. teacher ed., spiral bd. 12.95 (*1-56077-286-7*) Ctr Learning.

Center for Learning Network Staff. Marriage - The Early Years. (Religion Ser.). 44p. 1995. 6.00 (*1-56077-340-5*) Ctr Learning.

— Marriage - The Early Years (Leader's Guide) (Religion Ser.). 20p. 1995. spiral bd. 3.00 (*1-56077-339-1*) Ctr Learning.

— The Meaning of Faith: Spirituality for Adult Christians. (Religion Ser.). 52p. 1999. pap. text 3.95 (*1-56077-580-7*) Ctr Learning.

— The Meaning of Hope: Spirituality for adult Christians. (Religion Ser.). 46p. 1999. pap. text 3.95 (*1-56077-581-5*) Ctr Learning.

— Medea/The Lion in Winger: Curriculum Unit. (Drama Ser.). 115p. (YA). (gr. 9-12). 1996. spiral bd. 18.95 (*1-56077-329-4*) Ctr Learning.

Center for Learning Network Staff. Ministry & Leadership: Adult Workshops. (Adult Workshops Ser.). 88p. 1989. pap. text 15.95 (*1-56077-039-2*) Ctr Learning.

C

— Much Ado about Nothing by William Shakespeare: Curriculum Unit. (Novel - Drama Ser.). 95p. 1997. teacher ed., spiral bd. 18.95 (*1-56077-505-X*) Ctr Learning.
— Multicultural Literature: Essays, Fiction, & Poetry. (English - Language Arts Ser.). 100p. 1996. teacher ed., spiral bd. 19.95 (*1-56077-474-6*) Ctr Learning.
— My Journey, My Prayer. 96p. (YA). (gr. 9-12). 1991. reprint ed. pap. text 5.95 (*1-56077-128-3*) Ctr Learning.
Center for Learning Network Staff. Mythology. 269p. (YA). (gr. 9-12). spiral bd. 37.95 (*1-56077-395-2*) Ctr Learning.
— Nectar in a Sieve & The Woman Warrior: Curriculum Unit. (Novel Ser.). 93p. (YA). (gr. 9-12). 1996. spiral bd. 18.95 (*1-56077-410-X*) Ctr Learning.
Center for Learning Network Staff. 1984 by George Orwell: Curriculum Unit. (Novel - Drama Ser.). 89p. 1996. teacher ed., spiral bd. 18.95 (*1-56077-323-5*) Ctr Learning.
Center for Learning Network Staff. Nonfiction: A Critical Approach. 275p. spiral bd. 37.95 (*1-56077-396-0*) Ctr Learning.
Center for Learning Network Staff. O Pioneers! - The Country of the Pointed Firs: Curriculum Unit. (Novel - Drama Ser.). 118p. 1997. teacher ed., spiral bd. 18.95 (*1-56077-524-6*) Ctr Learning.
— Oedipus the King by Sophocles: Curriculum Unit. (Drama Ser.). 116p. 1991. spiral bd. 18.95 (*1-56077-167-4*) Ctr Learning.
Center for Learning Network Staff. Ohio History & Geography. 280p. (YA). (gr. 7). spiral bd. 34.95 (*1-56077-435-5*) Ctr Learning.
Center for Learning Network Staff. The Old Man & the Sea by Ernest Hemingway - Ethan Frome by Edith Wharton: Curriculum Unit. (Novel Ser.). 83p. (YA). (gr. 9-12). 1993. teacher ed., spiral bd. 18.95 (*1-56077-279-4*) Ctr Learning.
Center for Learning Network Staff. Once & Future King: Curriculum Unit. (Novel Ser.). 122p. (YA). (gr. 9-12). 1994. spiral bd. 18.95 (*1-56077-287-5*) Ctr Learning.
— Ordinary Time: Praying with Children & Families. (Religion Ser.). 179p. 1996. spiral bd. 19.95 (*1-56077-458-4*) Ctr Learning.
Center for Learning Network Staff. Our Town by Thornton Wilder: Curriculum Unit. (Drama Ser.). 84p. 1991. reprint ed. spiral bd. 18.95 (*1-56077-172-0*) Ctr Learning.
Center for Learning Network Staff. Parent Meeting Models 1. rev. ed. (Parish Ministry Manuals Ser.). 108p. 1989. spiral bd. 15.95 (*1-56077-033-3*) Ctr Learning.
— Parent Seminars. (Parish Ministry Manuals Ser.). 160p. 1985. spiral bd. 15.95 (*1-56077-034-1*) Ctr Learning.
— Peer mediation: Training Students in Conflict Resolution. (Communication). 67p. (YA). (gr. 7-12). 1996. spiral bd. 15.95 (*1-56077-368-5*) Ctr Learning.
— Peer Ministry: Empowering Teens to Be Salt for the Earth. (Religion Ser.). 127p. 1998. pap. text, teacher ed. 19.95 (*1-56077-545-9*) Ctr Learning.
— Pentacost, Peanuts, Popcorn & Prayer. rev. ed. 128p. 1988. spiral bd. 15.95 (*1-56077-027-9*) Ctr Learning.
Center for Learning Network Staff. Personal Growth. (Junior High Religion Ser.). 72p. (J). (gr. 7-8). 1992. student ed., per. 5.95 (*1-56077-233-6*) Ctr Learning.
— Personal Growth: Workshop Models for Gr. 7-8. (Junior High Religion (Grades 7-8) Ser.). 45p. 1992. teacher ed., spiral bd. 7.95 (*1-56077-184-4*) Ctr Learning.
Center for Learning Network Staff. Personhood: Growing in Wholeness & Holiness. (Religion). 60p. (YA). (gr. 9-12). 1996. spiral bd. 12.95 (*1-56077-481-9*) Ctr Learning.
— Personhood: Growing in Wholeness & Holiness - Student Text. (Discipleship Ser.). 122p. (YA). (gr. 9-10). 1996. 7.95 (*1-56077-469-X*) Ctr Learning.
— Personhood: Growing in Wholeness & Holiness -Teacher Manual. (Discipleship Ser.). 117p. (YA). (gr. 9-10). 1996. spiral bd. 9.95 (*1-56077-470-3*) Ctr Learning.
Center for Learning Network Staff. Prayer & Spirituality: Adult Workshops. (Adult Workshops Ser.). 88p. 1989. spiral bd. 15.95 (*1-56077-037-6*) Ctr Learning.
— Prayer & Worship: Workshop Models for Gr. 7-8. (Junior High Religion Ser.). 111p. 1992. teacher ed., spiral bd. 15.95 (*1-56077-185-2*) Ctr Learning.
Center for Learning Network Staff. Prayer Service Models. (Parish Ministry Manuals Ser.). 108p. 1989. spiral bd. 15.95 (*1-56077-035-X*) Ctr Learning.
Center for Learning Network Staff. Praying with Children, Bk. 1. 119p. (J). (gr. 1-3). 1991. spiral bd. 12.95 (*1-56077-028-7*) Ctr Learning.
— Praying with Children, Bk. 2. 107p. (J). (gr. 4-6). 1991. spiral bd. 12.95 (*1-56077-029-5*) Ctr Learning.
— Praying with Scriptures. (Spiritual Growth Ser.). 61p. 1993. teacher ed., spiral bd. 15.95 (*1-56077-273-5*) Ctr Learning.
— Preparing for Marriage. 116p. 1993. teacher ed., spiral bd. 15.95 (*1-56077-276-X*) Ctr Learning.
— Psychology: Cirruculum Unit. (Social Studies). 268p. 1998. teacher ed., spiral bd. 37.95 (*1-56077-547-5*) Ctr Learning.
— A Raisin in the Sun by Lorraine Hansberry: Curriculum Unit. (Drama Ser.). 90p. (YA). (gr. 9-12). 1992. reprint ed. teacher ed., spiral bd. 18.95 (*1-56077-214-X*) Ctr Learning.
***Center for Learning Network Staff.** Reconstruction 1865-1877: Primary Sources in U.S. History. (Social Studies Primary Sources). 111p. (YA). (gr. 9-12). 1999. spiral bd. 27.95 (*1-56077-586-6*) Ctr Learning.
Center for Learning Network Staff. Relationships. (Junior High Religion Ser.). 88p. 1992. student ed., per. 5.95 (*1-56077-232-8*) Ctr Learning.
— Relationships: Journal for Gr. 7-8. (Junior High Religion Ser.). 48p. 1992. teacher ed., spiral bd. 7.95 (*1-56077-186-0*) Ctr Learning.
***Center for Learning Network Staff.** Research 1: Information Literacy. rev. ed. (English Ser.). 211p. (YA). (gr. 9-12). 1999. spiral bd. 37.95 (*1-56077-597-1*) Ctr Learning.
— Research 2: The Research Paper. (English Ser.). 238p. (YA). (gr. 11-12). 1999. spiral bd. 37.95 (*1-56077-619-6*) Ctr Learning.
— Retreat Models. rev. ed. (Parish Ministry Manuals Ser.). 124p. 1989. spiral bd. 15.95 (*1-56077-036-8*) Ctr Learning.
— Revolution & Constitution, 1763-1791. (Primary Sources in U. S. History Ser.). 109p. 1999. teacher ed., spiral bd. 27.95 (*1-56077-571-8*) Ctr Learning.
— Richard III: Curriculum Unit. (Shakespeare Ser.). 75p. (YA). 1994. spiral bd. 18.95 (*1-56077-304-9*) Ctr Learning.
Center for Learning Network Staff. A River Runs Through It by Norman Maclean: Curriculum Unit. (Novel - Drama Ser.). 72p. 1997. teacher ed., spiral bd. 18.95 (*1-56077-528-9*) Ctr Learning.
Center for Learning Network Staff. Sacraments - Student Text: Living Our Faith. (Discipleship Ser.). 170p. (YA). (gr. 10-11). 1997. pap. text 7.95 (*1-56077-477-0*) Ctr Learning.
— Sacraments - Teacher Manual: Living Our Faith. (Discipleship Ser.). 131p. (YA). (gr. 10-11). 1997. spiral bd. 9.95 (*1-56077-478-9*) Ctr Learning.
Center for Learning Network Staff. Saint Maybe by Anne Tyler: Curriculum Unit. (Novel - Drama Ser.). 71p. 1997. teacher ed., spiral bd. 18.95 (*1-56077-548-3*) Ctr Learning.
Center for Learning Network Staff. Saints: A Lively, Loving People, 2. (Elementary Resources). 199p. (J). (gr. 4-8). 1995. spiral bd. 19.95 (*1-56077-358-8*) Ctr Learning.
— Saints: A Lively, Loving People: Curriculum Unit. 213p. (YA). (gr. 9-12). 1992. spiral bd. 19.95 (*1-56077-253-0*) Ctr Learning.
— Science Fiction 19th Century: Curriculum Unit. 126p. (YA). (gr. 10-12). spiral bd. 19.95 (*1-56077-482-7*) Ctr Learning.
— Scientists & Inventors. 245p. (J). (gr. 4-8). 1992. spiral bd. 24.95 (*1-56077-226-3*) Ctr Learning.
— Scripture & the Truth of our Identity: Spirituality for Adult Christians. (Religion Ser.). 52p. 1999. pap. text 3.95 (*1-56077-577-7*) Ctr Learning.
Center for Learning Network Staff. Searching for Yourself: A Journey to Discover Values. rev. ed. (Values Ser.). 212p. 1992. teacher ed., spiral bd. 30.00 (*1-56077-152-6*) Ctr Learning.
Center for Learning Network Staff. Seasonal Liturgies. (Youth Ministry). (Illus.). 108p. (YA). (gr. 9-12). 1987. spiral bd. 15.95 (*1-56077-021-X*) Ctr Learning.
Center for Learning Network Staff. Senior High Retreats. 150p. 1992. reprint ed. teacher ed., spiral bd. 15.95 (*1-56077-216-6*) Ctr Learning.
— Sexuality: Connecting Mind, Body, & Spirit. (Centering Faith Ser.). 121p. 1992. teacher ed., spiral bd. 9.95 (*1-56077-219-0*); per. 7.95 (*1-56077-220-4*) Ctr Learning.
Center for Learning Network Staff. Sexuality: Connecting Mind, Body & Spirit (Parish Edition) (Centering Faith Ser.). 65p. (YA). (gr. 9-12). 1992. spiral bd. 12.95 (*1-56077-227-1*) Ctr Learning.
— Shabanu: Daughter of the Wind/Havel I: Curriculum Unit. (Novel - Drama Ser.). 80p. (YA). (gr. 9-12). 1997. spiral bd. 18.95 (*1-56077-517-3*) Ctr Learning.
Center for Learning Network Staff. Shane - The Ox-Bow Incident by Jack Schaefer & Walter Van Tilburg Clark: Curriculum Unit. (Novel - Drama Ser.). 79p. 1996. teacher ed., spiral bd. 18.95 (*1-56077-330-8*) Ctr Learning.
Center for Learning Network Staff. Short Poems: Their Vitality & Versatility. 224p. (YA). (gr. 7-12). spiral bd. 37.95 (*1-56077-400-2*) Ctr Learning.
— The Short Story: Understanding, analysis & Appreciation. 215p. (YA). (gr. 9-12). spiral bd. 37.95 (*1-56077-401-0*) Ctr Learning.
— The Signet Classic Book of Southern Short Stories. (Novel Ser.). 100p. (YA). (gr. 9-12). 1996. spiral bd. 18.95 (*1-56077-412-6*) Ctr Learning.
— Silas Marner & the Elephant Man: Curriculum Unit. (Novel - Drama Ser.). 67p. (YA). (gr. 9-12). 1999. spiral bd. 18.95 (*1-56077-617-X*) Ctr Learning.
Center for Learning Network Staff. The Slave Dancer by Paula Fox & I, Juan De Pareja by Elizabeth Borton de Trevino: Curriculum Unit. (Novel Ser.). 89p. 1992. spiral bd. 18.95 (*1-56077-180-1*) Ctr Learning.
— Sociology: Curriculum Unit. (Social Studies Ser.). 201p. (YA). (gr. 9-12). 1996. teacher ed., spiral bd. 37.95 (*1-56077-494-0*) Ctr Learning.
Center for Learning Network Staff. Speech: Skill, Process & Practice. 215p. (YA). (gr. 7-12). spiral bd. 37.95 (*1-56077-402-9*) Ctr Learning.
Center for Learning Network Staff. Stepfamilies: Personal Adjustment: Looking at Life. 12p. (YA). (gr. 7-12). 1992. pap. text 0.80 (*1-56077-224-7*) Ctr Learning.
— The Stranger - The Plague by Albert Camus: Curriculum Unit. (Novel Ser.). 72p. 1994. teacher ed., spiral bd. 18.95 (*1-56077-294-8*) Ctr Learning.
— A Streetcar Named Desire by Tennessee Williams: Curriculum Unit. (Drama Ser.). 87p. 1992. spiral bd. 18.95 (*1-56077-169-0*) Ctr Learning.
Center for Learning Network Staff. Supervisor/Student Teacher Manual. 176p. spiral bd. 29.95 (*1-56077-403-7*) Ctr Learning.
Center for Learning Network Staff. Tale of Two Cities by Charles Dickens: Curriculum Unit. (Novel Ser.). 73p. 1991. spiral bd. 18.95 (*1-56077-173-9*) Ctr Learning.
— The Taming of the Shrew by William Shakespeare: Curriculum Unit. 2nd rev. ed. (Shakespeare Ser.). 115p. 1992. spiral bd. 18.95 (*1-56077-170-4*) Ctr Learning.
***Center for Learning Network Staff.** Tara Road & The Return Journey: Curriculum Unit. (Novel - Drama Ser.). 65p. (YA). (gr. 9-12). 1999. spiral bd. 18.95 (*1-56077-636-6*) Ctr Learning.
Center for Learning Network Staff. Tartuffe by Moliere: Curriculum Unit. (Drama Ser.). 68p. 1994. reprint ed. teacher ed., spiral bd. 18.95 (*1-56077-290-5*) Ctr Learning.
— Teens & Alcohol. LC 98-204740. (Social StudiesSocial Studies Ser.). 98p. 1998. teacher ed., spiral bd. 19.95 (*1-56077-549-1*) Ctr Learning.
— Thematic Approaches to British Poetry: Curriculum Unit. 71p. (YA). (gr. 9-12). 1998. pap., teacher ed. 19.95 (*1-56077-488-6*) Ctr Learning.
Center for Learning Network Staff. Things Fall apart & No Longer at Ease: Curriculum Unit. (Novel Ser.). 66p. (YA). (gr. 9-12). 1996. spiral bd. 18.95 (*1-56077-413-4*) Ctr Learning.
Center for Learning Network Staff. Time Apart: Reflection Models for Parish Ministers. 120p. 1992. teacher ed., spiral bd. 15.95 (*1-56077-207-7*) Ctr Learning.
— Today Is: An Ecumenical Prayer Journal for Young Teens. rev. ed. 80p. (J). (gr. 6-9). 1992. pap. text 3.95 (*1-56077-217-4*) Ctr Learning.
— Transforming Parish Life: A Spirituality of Parish Leadership for the Twenty-First Century. 99p. 1996. teacher ed., spiral bd. 15.95 (*1-56077-373-1*) Ctr Learning.
— Transforming Parish Life Bk. 2: Reclaiming a Baptismal Mentality. LC 98-148112. (Religion Ser.). 124p. 1997. teacher ed., spiral bd. 15.95 (*1-56077-531-9*) Ctr Learning.
Center for Learning Network Staff. Travels with Charley: Curriculum Unit. (Novel Ser.). 56p. (YA). (gr. 9-12). 1996. spiral bd. 18.95 (*1-56077-344-8*) Ctr Learning.
— A Tree Grows in Brooklyn by Betty Smith: Curriculum Unit. (Novel Ser.). 88p. (YA). (gr. 9-12). 1993. teacher ed., spiral bd. 18.95 (*1-56077-277-8*) Ctr Learning.
Center for Learning Network Staff. Tuck Everlasting by Natalie Babbitt - Bridge to Terabithia by Katherine Patterson: Curriculum Unit. (Novel Ser.). 96p. 1993. teacher ed., spiral bd. 18.95 (*1-56077-278-6*) Ctr Learning.
— Twelfth Night by William Shakespeare: Curriculum Unit. 2nd rev. ed. (Shakespeare Ser.). 111p. 1992. spiral bd. 18.95 (*1-56077-171-2*) Ctr Learning.
— U. S. Biographies: Beginning to 1800, Bk. 1. 48p. 1992. pap. text, student ed. 3.95 (*1-56077-200-X*); teacher ed., spiral bd. 19.95 (*1-56077-160-7*) Ctr Learning.
— U. S. Biographies, 1850-1890, Bk. 4. 56p. 1992. pap. text, student ed. 3.95 (*1-56077-203-4*); teacher ed., spiral bd. 19.95 (*1-56077-163-1*) Ctr Learning.
— U. S. Biographies, 1800-1830, Bk. 2. 56p. 1992. pap. text, student ed. 3.95 (*1-56077-201-8*); teacher ed., spiral bd. 19.95 (*1-56077-161-5*) Ctr Learning.
— U. S. Biographies, 1890-1930, Bk. 5. 54p. 1992. pap. text, student ed. 3.95 (*1-56077-204-2*); teacher ed., spiral bd. 19.95 (*1-56077-164-X*) Ctr Learning.
— U. S. Biographies, 1830-1850, Bk. 3. 56p. 1992. pap. text, student ed. 3.95 (*1-56077-202-6*); teacher ed., spiral bd. 19.95 (*1-56077-162-3*) Ctr Learning.
— U. S. Biographies, 1960-1990, Bk. 7. 139p. 1992. teacher ed., spiral bd. 19.95 (*1-56077-166-6*) Ctr Learning.
— U. S. Biographies, 1960-1990, Bk. 7. 56p. (J). (gr. 4-8). 1992. pap. text, student ed. 3.95 (*1-56077-206-9*) Ctr Learning.
— U. S. Biographies, 1930-1960, Bk. 6. 54p. 1992. pap. text, student ed. 3.95 (*1-56077-205-0*); teacher ed., spiral bd. 19.95 (*1-56077-165-8*) Ctr Learning.
— U. S. History & Geography Bk. 1: Beginnings to 1877. (Intermediate Social Studies Activities). 192p. (J). (gr. 5-8). 1992. spiral bd. 24.95 (*1-56077-119-4*) Ctr Learning.
— U. S. History & Geography Bk. 2: 1878 to the Present. (Intermediate Social Studies Activities Ser.). 194p. (J). (gr. 5-8). 1992. spiral bd. 24.95 (*1-56077-120-8*) Ctr Learning.
— U. S. History (Grade 8) Bk. 1: Beginnings to 1876. 235p. 1997. teacher ed., spiral bd. 37.95 (*1-56077-514-9*) Ctr Learning.
— Uncle Tom's Cabin by Harriet Beecher Stowe: Curriculum Unit. (Novel Ser.). 102p. 1992. spiral bd. 18.95 (*1-56077-151-8*) Ctr Learning.
— Understanding Scripture: Adult Workshop. (Adult Workshops Ser.). 97p. 1992. teacher ed., spiral bd. 15.95 (*1-56077-199-2*) Ctr Learning.
Center for Learning Network Staff. U.S. Governemnt Book 2: Government of the People & by the People. (U.S. Government: 2). 275p. spiral bd. 37.95 (*1-56077-437-1*) Ctr Learning.
— U.S. Government Book 1: We the People. (U.S. Government). 259p. spiral bd. 37.95 (*1-56077-436-3*) Ctr Learning.
— U.S. History Book 1: America: Creating the Dream, Beginnings - 1865. 233p. (YA). (gr. 9-12). spiral bd. 37.95 (*1-56077-438-X*) Ctr Learning.
— U.S. History Book 2: The Emergence of Modern american, 1866-1920. 205p. (YA). (gr. 9-12). spiral bd. 37.95 (*1-56077-439-8*) Ctr Learning.
— U.S. History Book 3: Prelud to Present, 1920-1960. 231p. (YA). (gr. 9-12). spiral bd. 37.95 (*1-56077-440-1*) Ctr Learning.
— U.S. History Book 4: Seeking New Directions, 1960-1990. 229p. (YA). (gr. 9-12). spiral bd. 37.95 (*1-56077-441-X*) Ctr Learning.
Center for Learning Network Staff. Valuing Others: A Journey to Discover Values. rev. ed. (Values Ser.). 199p. 1992. teacher ed., spiral bd. 34.95 (*1-56077-141-0*) Ctr Learning.
— Walden - A Different Drummer by William Melvin Kelley: Curriculum Unit. (Novel - Drama Ser.). 120p. 1997. teacher ed., spiral bd. 18.95 (*1-56077-508-4*) Ctr Learning.
Center for Learning Network Staff. Walk Humbly With Your god. (Religion Ser.). 176p. 1995. spiral bd. 7.95 (*1-56077-338-3*) Ctr Learning.
Center for Learning Network Staff. Watership Down by Richard Adams: Curriculum Unit. (Novel Ser.). 88p. 1989. teacher ed., spiral bd. 18.95 (*1-56077-352-9*) Ctr Learning.
***Center for Learning Network Staff.** The Watsons Go to Birmingham, 1964; The View from Saturday: Curriculum Unit. (Novel - Drama Ser.). 89p. 1999. teacher ed., spiral bd. 18.95 (*1-56077-598-X*) Ctr Learning.
Center for Learning Network Staff. When the Legends Die by Hal Borland: Curriculum Unit. (Novel Ser.). 1994. reprint ed. teacher ed., spiral bd. 18.95 (*1-56077-288-3*) Ctr Learning.
— World Cultures & Geography: Curriculum Unit, Grade 7. rev. ed. (Social Studies Ser.). 240p. (YA). (gr. 7). 1996. teacher ed., spiral bd. 34.95 (*1-56077-489-4*) Ctr Learning.
Center for Learning Network Staff. World History & Geography Book 1: The East. (Intermediate Social Studies Activities). 136p. (J). (gr. 4-8). 1990. spiral bd. 24.95 (*1-56077-066-X*) Ctr Learning.
— World History & Grography book 2: The West. (Intermediate Social Studies Activities). 175p. 1990. spiral bd. 24.95 (*1-56077-067-8*) Ctr Learning.
— World History Book 1: Beginnings to A.D. 1200. 283p. (YA). (gr. 10-12). spiral bd. 37.95 (*1-56077-445-2*) Ctr Learning.
— World History Book 3: 1815-1919. 288p. (YA). (gr. 10-12). spiral bd. 37.95 (*1-56077-447-9*) Ctr Learning.
— World History Book 4: 1920-1992. 288p. (YA). (gr. 10-12). spiral bd. 37.95 (*1-56077-448-7*) Ctr Learning.
— World Religions: Reverencing Faith Traditions (Parish Edition) (Centering Faith Ser.). 98p. (YA). (gr. 9-12). 1990. spiral bd. 12.95 (*1-56077-126-7*) Ctr Learning.
— World Religions: Sensing in the 21st Centrury. (Centering Faith Ser.). 169p. (YA). (gr. 9-12). 1990. pap. text 7.95 (*1-56077-068-6*) Ctr Learning.
— World Religions: Sensing in the 21st Century. (Centering Faith Ser.). 183p. (YA). (gr. 9-12). 1990. spiral bd. 9.95 (*1-56077-069-4*) Ctr Learning.
Center for Learning Network Staff. A Wrinkle in Time by Madeleine L'Engle - The Lion, the Witch & the Wardrobe by C. S. Lewis: Curriculum Unit. (Novel Ser.). 87p. 1993. teacher ed., spiral bd. 18.95 (*1-56077-283-2*) Ctr Learning.
— Writing Short Stories. (English Ser.). 63p. 1997. teacher ed., spiral bd. 19.95 (*1-56077-538-6*) Ctr Learning.
***Center for Learning Network Staff.** Writing 1: Learning the Process. (English Ser.). 211p. (YA). (gr. 7-9). 1999. spiral bd. 37.95 (*1-56077-607-2*) Ctr Learning.
Center for Learning Network Staff. Year of Impossible Goodbyes - So Far from the Bamboo Grove by Sook Nyul Choi & Yoko Kawashima Watkins: Curriculum Unit. (Novel - Drama Ser.). 83p. 1997. teacher ed., spiral bd. 18.95 (*1-56077-537-8*) Ctr Learning.
Center for Learning Network Staff. Youth to Youth Ministry. (Youth Ministry). (Illus.). 111p. 1987. spiral bd. 15.95 (*1-56077-023-6*) Ctr Learning.
Center for Learning Network Staff & Anaya, Rudolfo A. Bless Me, Ultima: Curriculum Unit. (Novel Ser.). (YA). (gr. 9-12). 1996. spiral bd. 18.95 (*1-56077-370-7*) Ctr Learning.
Center for Learning Network Staff & Anderson, Sherwood. Winesburg, Ohio: Curriculum Unit. (Novel Ser.). 72p. (YA). (gr. 9-12). 1995. spiral bd. 18.95 (*1-56077-334-0*) Ctr Learning.
Center for Learning Network Staff & Arnow, Harriette. The Dollmaker: Curriculum Unit. (Novel Ser.). 74p. (YA). (gr. 8-12). 1996. spiral bd. 18.95 (*1-56077-490-8*) Ctr Learning.
Center for Learning Network Staff & Bolt, Robert. A Man for All Seasons: A Curriculum Unit. (Drama Ser.). 105p. (YA). (gr. 9-12). 1990. spiral bd. 18.95 (*1-56077-118-6*) Ctr Learning.
Center for Learning Network Staff & Bradbury, Ray. Fahrenheit 451: Curriculum Unit. (Novel Ser.). 84p. (YA). (gr. 9-12). 1990. 18.95 (*1-56077-105-4*) Ctr Learning.
— The martian Chronicles: Curriculum Unit. (Novel Ser.). 94p. (YA). (gr. 9-12). 1995. spiral bd. 18.95 (*1-56077-317-0*) Ctr Learning.
***Center for Learning Network Staff & Bradford, Richard.** Red Sky at Morning: Curriculum Unit. (Novel - Drama Ser.). 91p. 1999. teacher ed., spiral bd. 18.95 (*1-56077-582-3*) Ctr Learning.
Center for Learning Network Staff & Bronte, Charlotte. Jane Eyre: Curriculum Unit. (Novel Ser.). 112p. (YA). (gr. 9-12). 1990. spiral bd. 18.95 (*1-56077-136-4*) Ctr Learning.
Center for Learning Network Staff & Bronte, Emily Jane. Wuthering Heights: Curriculum Unit. (Novel Ser.). 84p. (YA). (gr. 9-12). 1991. reprint ed. spiral bd. 18.95 (*1-56077-145-3*) Ctr Learning.
Center for Learning Network Staff & Burns, Olive Ann. Cold Sassy Tree: Curriculum Unit. (Novel Ser.). 97p. (YA). (gr. 9-12). 1991. spiral bd. 18.95 (*1-56077-188-7*) Ctr Learning.
Center for Learning Network Staff & Carroll, Lewis. Alice's Adventures in Wonderland & Through the Looking Glass: Curriculum Unit. (Novel Ser.). 61p. (YA). (gr. 4-9). 1992. spiral bd. 18.95 (*1-56077-260-3*) Ctr Learning.

C

An Asterisk (*) at the beginning of an entry indicates that the title is appearing for the first time.

Center for Learning Network Staff & Carter, Willaim K. My Antonia: Curriculum Unit. (Novel Ser.). 71p. (YA). (gr. 9-12). 1990. spiral bd. 18.95 (*1-56077-357-X*) Ctr Learning.

Center for Learning Network Staff & Chaucer, Geoffrey. The Canterbury Tales: Curriculum Unit. (Novel Ser.). 95p. (YA). (gr. 9-12). reprint ed. spiral bd. 18.95 (*1-56077-134-8*) Ctr Learning.

Center for Learning Network Staff & Conrad, Joseph. Heart of Darkness: Curriculum Unit. (Novel Ser.). 84p. (YA). (gr. 9-12). 1991. reprint ed. spiral bd. 18.95 (*1-56077-143-7*) Ctr Learning.

Center for Learning Network Staff & Crane, Stephen. The Red Badge of courage: Curriculum Unit. (Drama Ser.). 75p. (YA). (gr. 9-12). 1992. reprint ed. spiral bd. 18.95 (*1-56077-218-2*) Ctr Learning.

Center for Learning Network Staff & de Maurier, Daphne. Rebecca: Curriculum Unit. (Novel Ser.). 79p. (YA). (gr. 9-12). 1995. spiral bd. 18.95 (*1-56077-320-0*) Ctr Learning.

***Center for Learning Network Staff & Delany, Delany & Hearth/Gaines Staff.** Having Our Say/A Gathering of Old Men: Curriculum Unit. (Novel - Drama Ser.). 71p. 1999. teacher ed., spiral bd. 18.95 (*1-56077-575-0*) Ctr Learning.

Center for Learning Network Staff & Dickens, Charles. The Christmas Box by Richard Paul Evans - A Christmas Carol by Charles Dickens: Curriculum Unit. (Novel - Drama Ser.). 46p. (YA). (gr. 7-12). 1996. teacher ed., spiral bd. 18.95 (*1-56077-496-7*) Ctr Learning.

Center for Learning Network Staff & Dickens, Charles. David Copperfield: Curriculum Unit. (Novel Ser.). 83p. (YA). (gr. 9-12). 1995. spiral bd. 18.95 (*1-56077-349-9*) Ctr Learning.

— Great Expectations: Curriculum Unit. (Novel Ser.). 76p. (YA). (gr. 9-12). 1990. reprint ed. spiral bd. 18.95 (*1-56077-133-X*) Ctr Learning.

— Hard Times: Curriculum Unit. (Novel Ser.). 69p. (YA). (gr. 9-12). 1992. spiral bd. 18.95 (*1-56077-261-1*) Ctr Learning.

Center for Learning Network Staff & Doyle, Arthur Conan. The Hound of the Baskervilles: Curriculum Unit. (Novel Ser.). 92p. (YA). (gr. 9-12). 1990. spiral bd. 18.95 (*1-56077-110-0*) Ctr Learning.

Center for Learning Network Staff & Eliot, T. S. Murder in the Cathedral/Galileo: Curriculum Unit. (Drama Ser.). 102p. (YA). (gr. 9-12). 1995. spiral bd. 18.95 (*1-56077-345-6*) Ctr Learning.

***Center for Learning Network Staff & Ellison, Ralph.** Invisible Man: Curriculum Unit. 63p. 1998. teacher ed., spiral bd. 18.95 (*1-56077-561-0*) Ctr Learning.

Center for Learning Network Staff & Faulkner, William. The Sound & the Fury: Curriculum Unit. (Novel Ser.). 95p. (YA). (gr. 9-12). 1990. spiral bd. 18.95 (*1-56077-113-5*) Ctr Learning.

Center for Learning Network Staff & Fitzgerald, F. Scott. The Great Gatsby: Curriculum Unit. (Novel Ser.). 75p. (YA). (gr. 9-12). 1990. reprint ed. spiral bd. 18.95 (*1-56077-124-0*) Ctr Learning.

Center for Learning Network Staff & Frank, Anne. Anne Frank: The Diary of a Young Girl: Curriculum Unit. (Novel Ser.). 95p. (YA). (gr. 9-12). 1992. reprint ed. spiral bd. 18.95 (*1-56077-230-1*) Ctr Learning.

Center for Learning Network Staff & Gardner, John. Beowulf/Grendel: Curriculum Unit. (Novel Ser.). 86p. (YA). (gr. 9-12). 1991. spiral bd. 18.95 (*1-56077-139-9*) Ctr Learning.

***Center for Learning Network Staff & Gibbons, Kaye.** Ellen Foster/A Virtuous Woman: Curriculum Unit. (Novel - Drama Ser.). 55p. 1999. teacher ed., spiral bd. 18.95 (*1-56077-584-X*) Ctr Learning.

Center for Learning Network Staff & Gibson, William. The Miracle Worker: Curriculum Unit. (Drama Ser.). 84p. (YA). (gr. 9-12). 1990. spiral bd. 18.95 (*1-56077-117-8*) Ctr Learning.

Center for Learning Network Staff & Golding, William. Lord of the Flies: Curriculum Unit. (Novel Ser.). 60p. (YA). (gr. 9-12). 1991. reprint ed. spiral bd. 18.95 (*1-56077-144-5*) Ctr Learning.

Center for Learning Network Staff & Greene, Graham. The Power & the Glory: Curriculum Unit. (Novel Ser.). 68p. (YA). (gr. 9-12). 1991. spiral bd. 18.95 (*1-56077-168-2*) Ctr Learning.

***Center for Learning Network Staff & Guterson, David.** Snow Falling on Cedars: Curriculum Unit. (Novel - Drama Ser.). 81p. 1998. teacher ed., spiral bd. 18.95 (*1-56077-564-5*) Ctr Learning.

Center for Learning Network Staff & Hansberry, Lorraine. A Raisin in the Sun: Curriculum Unit. (Novel - Drama Ser.). 88p. (YA). (gr. 9-12). 1997. spiral bd. 18.95 (*1-56077-536-X*) Ctr Learning.

Center for Learning Network Staff & Hardy, Thomas. The Return of the Native: Curriculum Unit. (Novel Ser.). 71p. (YA). (gr. 9-12). 1994. spiral bd. 18.95 (*1-56077-298-0*) Ctr Learning.

— Tess of the D'Urbervilles: Curriculum Unit. (Novel Ser.). 73p. (YA). (gr. 9-12). 1993. spiral bd. 18.95 (*1-56077-244-1*) Ctr Learning.

Center for Learning Network Staff & Harriot, James. All Creatures Great & Small by James Herriot: Curriculum Unit. (Novel - Drama Ser.). 94p. (YA). (gr. 6-12). 1996. teacher ed., spiral bd. 18.95 (*1-56077-492-4*) Ctr Learning.

Center for Learning Network Staff & Hawthorne, Nathaniel. The Scarlet Letter: Curriculum Unit. (Novel Ser.). 94p. (YA). (gr. 9-12). 1990. reprint ed. spiral bd. 18.95 (*1-56077-125-9*) Ctr Learning.

Center for Learning Network Staff & Hesse, Hermann. Siddhartha: Curriculum Unit. (Novel Ser.). 69p. (YA). (gr. 9-12). 1995. spiral bd. 18.95 (*1-56077-360-X*) Ctr Learning.

Center for Learning Network Staff & Hillerman, Tony. Talking God/A Thief of Time: Curriculum Unit. (Novel Ser.). 101p. (YA). (gr. 7-12). 1994. spiral bd. 18.95 (*1-56077-310-3*) Ctr Learning.

Center for Learning Network Staff & Homer. The Odyssey: Curriculum Unit. (Novel Ser.). 104p. (YA). (gr. 9-12). 1990. spiral bd. 18.95 (*1-56077-112-7*) Ctr Learning.

Center for Learning Network Staff & Hugo, Victor. Les Miserables: Curriculum Unit. (Novel Ser.). 98p. (YA). (gr. 9-12). 1992. reprint ed. spiral bd. 18.95 (*1-56077-255-7*) Ctr Learning.

Center for Learning Network Staff & Hunt, Irene. Across five Aprils: Curriculum Unit. (Novel Ser.). 85p. (YA). (gr. 9-12). 1990. spiral bd. 18.95 (*1-56077-108-9*) Ctr Learning.

Center for Learning Network Staff & Hurston, Zora Neale. Their Eyes Were Watching God: Curriculum unit. (Novel Ser.). 56p. (YA). (gr. 9-12). 1996. spiral bd. 18.95 (*1-56077-467-3*) Ctr Learning.

Center for Learning Network Staff & Irving, John. A Prayer for Owen meany: Curriculum Unit. (Novel Ser.). 86p. (YA). (gr. 9-12). 1996. spiral bd. 18.95 (*1-56077-414-2*) Ctr Learning.

Center for Learning Network Staff & James, Henry. The Turn of the Screw/Daisy Miller: Curriculum Unit. (Novel Ser.). 69p. (YA). (gr. 9-12). 1994. spiral bd. 18.95 (*1-56077-305-7*) Ctr Learning.

Center for Learning Network Staff & Joyce, James. A Portrait of the Artist As a Young Man: Curriculum Unit. (Novel Ser.). 75p. (YA). (gr. 9-12). 1991. spiral bd. 18.95 (*1-56077-189-5*) Ctr Learning.

***Center for Learning Network Staff & Kelly, Molly.** Chastity: The Only Choice. 12p. 1998. pap. text 0.80 (*1-56077-566-1*) Ctr Learning.

Center for Learning Network Staff & Kennedy, John F. Profiles in Courage: Curriculum Unit. (Novel Ser.). 104p. (YA). (gr. 9-12). 1990. spiral bd. 18.95 (*1-56077-127-5*) Ctr Learning.

Center for Learning Network Staff & Knowles, John. A Seperate Peace: Curriculum Unit. rev. ed. (Novel Ser.). 86p. (YA). (gr. 9-12). 1990. spiral bd. 18.95 (*1-56077-103-8*) Ctr Learning.

Center for Learning Network Staff & Koestler, Arthur. Darkness at Noon: Curriculum Unit. (Novel Ser.). 89p. (YA). (gr. 9-12). 1995. spiral bd. 18.95 (*1-56077-324-3*) Ctr Learning.

Center for Learning Network Staff & Lee, Harper. To Kill a Mockingbird: Curriculum Unit. rev. ed. (Novel Ser.). 103p. (YA). (gr. 9-12). 1990. spiral bd. 18.95 (*1-56077-122-4*) Ctr Learning.

Center for Learning Network Staff & London, Jack. The Call of the Wild & White Fang: Curriculum Unit. (Novel Ser.). 102p. (YA). (gr. 7-12). 1992. spiral bd. 18.95 (*1-56077-241-7*) Ctr Learning.

Center for Learning Network Staff & Lowry, Lois. The Giver: Curriculum Unit. (Novel Ser.). 68p. (YA). (gr. 9-12). 1995. spiral bd. 18.95 (*1-56077-348-0*) Ctr Learning.

Center for Learning Network Staff & Malamud, Bernard. The Asistant & The Fixer: Curriculum Unit. (Novel Ser.). 84p. (YA). (gr. 9-12). 1995. spiral bd. 18.95 (*1-56077-359-6*) Ctr Learning.

Center for Learning Network Staff & Marshall, Vance. Walkabout: Curriculum Unit. (Novel Ser.). 85p. (YA). (gr. 6-12). 1990. spiral bd. 18.95 (*1-56077-367-7*) Ctr Learning.

Center for Learning Network Staff & Melville, Herman. Billy Budd & Moby Dick: Curriculum Unit. (Novel Ser.), 86p. (YA). (gr. 9-12). 1991. spiral bd. 18.95 (*1-56077-187-9*) Ctr Learning.

Center for Learning Network Staff & Miller, Arthur. The Crucible: Curriculum Unit. (Drama Ser.). 88p. (YA). (gr. 9-12). 1990. reprint ed. spiral bd. 18.95 (*1-56077-132-1*) Ctr Learning.

— Death of a Salesman: Curriculum Unit. (Drama Ser.). 94p. (YA). (gr. 9-12). 1992. reprint ed. spiral bd. 18.95 (*1-56077-234-4*) Ctr Learning.

Center for Learning Network Staff & Montgomery, L. M. Anne of Green Gables: Curriculum Unit. (Novel Ser.). 89p. (YA). (gr. 4-12). 1995. spiral bd. 18.95 (*1-56077-333-2*) Ctr Learning.

Center for Learning Network Staff & Morrison, Toni. Song of Solomon: Curriculum Unit. (Novel Ser.). 60p. (YA). 1987. 18.95 (*1-56077-355-3*) Ctr Learning.

Center for Learning Network Staff & O'Neill, Eugene. Long Day's Journey Into Night: Curriculum Unit. (Drama Ser.). 67p. (YA). (gr. 9-12). 1993. spiral bd. 18.95 (*1-56077-245-X*) Ctr Learning.

***Center for Learning Network Staff & Orczy, Emmuska.** The Scarlet Pimpernel: Curriculum Unit. (Novel - Drama Ser.). 77p. 1999. teacher ed., spiral bd. 18.95 (*1-56077-583-1*) Ctr Learning.

Center for Learning Network Staff & Pasternak, Boris. Dr. Zhivago: Curriculum Unit. (Novel Ser.). 90p. (YA). (gr. 9-12). 1990. spiral bd. 18.95 (*1-56077-135-6*) Ctr Learning.

Center for Learning Network Staff & Paterson, Katherine. The Sign of the Chrysanthemum/The Master Puppeteer: Curriculum unit. (Novel Ser.). 111p. (J). (gr. 4-8). 1996. spiral bd. 18.95 (*1-56077-473-8*) Ctr Learning.

Center for Learning Network Staff & Paton, Alan. Cry the Beloved Country. (Novel Ser.). 78p. (YA). (gr. 9-12). 1992. reprint ed. spiral bd. 18.95 (*1-56077-213-1*) Ctr Learning.

Center for Learning Network Staff & Peck, Rob. A Day No Pigg Would Die: Curriculum Unit. (Novel Ser.). (YA). (gr. 7-12). 1994. reprint ed. spiral bd. 18.95 (*1-56077-289-1*) Ctr Learning.

***Center for Learning Network Staff & Potok, Chaim.** Davita's Harp: Curriculum Unit. (Novel - Drama Ser.). 107p. 1998. teacher ed., spiral bd. 18.95 (*1-56077-576-9*) Ctr Learning.

Center for Learning Network Staff & Remarque, Erich-Maria. All Quiet on the Western Front: Curriculum Unit. (Novel Ser.). 91p. (YA). (gr. 9-12). 1992. reprint ed. spiral bd. 18.95 (*1-56077-231-X*) Ctr Learning.

Center for Learning Network Staff & Richter, Conrad. The Light in the Forest & A Country of Strangers: Curriculum Unit. (Novel Ser.). 100p. (YA). (gr. 9-12). 1990. spiral bd. 18.95 (*1-56077-121-6*) Ctr Learning.

Center for Learning Network Staff & Salinger, J. D. The Catcher in the Rye: Curriculum Unit. (Novel Ser.). 78p. (YA). (gr. 9-12). 1991. reprint ed. spiral bd. 18.95 (*1-56077-142-9*) Ctr Learning.

Center for Learning Network Staff & Shakespeare, William. As You Like It: Curriculum Unit. (Shakespeare Ser.). 69p. (YA). (gr. 9-12). 1993. spiral bd. 18.95 (*1-56077-257-3*) Ctr Learning.

— Hamlet: Curriculum Unit. rev. ed. (Shakespeare Ser.). 100p. (YA). (gr. 9-12). 1990. spiral bd. 18.95 (*1-56077-101-1*) Ctr Learning.

— Henry V: Curriculum Unit. (Shakespeare Ser.). 65p. (YA). (gr. 9-12). 1992. spiral bd. 18.95 (*1-56077-258-1*) Ctr Learning.

— Henry IV, Part I: Curriculum Unit. (Shakespeare Ser.). 68p. (YA). (gr. 9-12). 1995. spiral bd. 18.95 (*1-56077-322-7*) Ctr Learning.

— Julius Caesar: Curriculum Unit. rev. ed. (Shakespeare Ser.). 78p. (YA). (gr. 9-12). 1997. spiral bd. 18.95 (*1-56077-535-1*) Ctr Learning.

— King Lear: Curriculum Unit. (Shakespeare Ser.). 92p. (YA). (gr. 9-12). 1992. spiral bd. 18.95 (*1-56077-263-8*) Ctr Learning.

— A Midsummers Night's Dream: Curriculum Unit. (Shakespeare Ser.). 69p. (YA). (gr. 9-12). 1992. spiral bd. 18.95 (*1-56077-262-X*) Ctr Learning.

— Othello: Curriculum Unit. (Shakespeare Ser.). 83p. (YA). (gr. 9-12). 1992. reprint ed. spiral bd. 18.95 (*1-56077-254-9*) Ctr Learning.

— Romeo & Juliet: Curriculum Unit. (Shakespeare Ser.). 89p. (YA). (gr. 4-12). 1991. reprint ed. spiral bd. 18.95 (*1-56077-191-7*) Ctr Learning.

— The Tempest: Curriculum Unit. (Shakespeare Ser.). 80p. (YA). (gr. 9-12). 1990. spiral bd. 18.95 (*1-56077-138-0*) Ctr Learning.

Center for Learning Network Staff & Shaw, George Bernard. Arms & The Man/Saint Joan: Curriculum Unit. (Drama Ser.). 63p. (YA). (gr. 9-12). 1992. spiral bd. 18.95 (*1-56077-212-3*) Ctr Learning.

— Pygmalion: Curriculum Unit. (Drama Ser.). 100p. (YA). (gr. 9-12). 1990. spiral bd. 18.95 (*1-56077-115-1*) Ctr Learning.

Center for Learning Network Staff & Shelley, Mary V. Frankenstein: Curriculum Unit. (Novel Ser.). (YA). (gr. 9-12). 1991. 18.95 (*1-56077-190-9*) Ctr Learning.

Center for Learning Network Staff & Sophocles. Antigons: Curriculum Unit. (Drama Ser.). 84p. (YA). (gr. 9-12). 1990. reprint ed. spiral bd. 18.95 (*1-56077-131-3*) Ctr Learning.

Center for Learning Network Staff & Steinbeck, John. East of Eden: Curriculum Unit. (Novel Ser.). 80p. (YA). (gr. 9-12). 1996. spiral bd. 18.95 (*1-56077-484-3*) Ctr Learning.

— The Grapes of Wrath: Curriculum Unit. (Novel Ser.). 91p. (YA). (gr. 9-12). 1990. reprint ed. spiral bd. 18.95 (*1-56077-129-1*) Ctr Learning.

Center for Learning Network Staff & Swift, Johnathan. Gulliver's Travels: Curriculum Unit. (Novel Ser.). 65p. (YA). (gr. 6-12). 1993. spiral bd. 18.95 (*1-56077-242-5*) Ctr Learning.

Center for Learning Network Staff & Synge, John Millington. The Playboy of the Western World/Riders to the Sea: Curriculum Unit. (Drama Ser.). 75p. (YA). (gr. 11 up). 1994. spiral bd. 18.95 (*1-56077-302-2*) Ctr Learning.

Center for Learning Network Staff & Tan, Amy. The Joy Luck Club: Curriculum Unit. (Novel Ser.). 113p. (YA). (gr. 9 up). 1994. spiral bd. 18.95 (*1-56077-301-4*) Ctr Learning.

Center for Learning Network Staff & Taylor, Mildred D. Roll of Thunder, Hear My Cry/Let the Circle Be Unbroken: Curriculum Unit. (Novel Ser.). 105p. (YA). (gr. 7-12). 1992. spiral bd. 18.95 (*1-56077-256-5*) Ctr Learning.

Center for Learning Network Staff & Taylor, Theodore. The Cay & Timothy of the Cay: Curriculum Unit. (Novel Ser.). 86p. (YA). (gr. 4-12). 1995. spiral bd. 18.95 (*1-56077-346-4*) Ctr Learning.

Center for Learning Network Staff & Tolkien, J. R. R. Lord of the Rings: Curriculum Unit. (Novel Ser.). 96p. (YA). 1991. spiral bd. 18.95 (*1-56077-137-2*) Ctr Learning.

Center for Learning Network Staff & Tolstoy, Leo. Anna Karenina: Curriculum Unit. (Novel Ser.). 95p. (YA). (gr. 9-12). 1995. spiral bd. 18.95 (*1-56077-328-6*) Ctr Learning.

Center for Learning Network Staff & Twain, Mark. The Adventures of Huckleberry Finn: Curriculum Unit. (Novel Ser.). 83p. (YA). (gr. 9-12). 1990. reprint ed. spiral bd. 18.95 (*1-56077-123-2*) Ctr Learning.

— The Adventures of Tom Sawyer: Curriculum Unit. (Novel Ser.). 59p. (YA). (gr. 7-12). 1994. spiral bd. 18.95 (*1-56077-306-5*) Ctr Learning.

Center for Learning Network Staff & Twain, Mark. The Prince & the Pauper by Mark Twain: Curriculum Unit. (Novel - Drama Ser.). 54p. (YA). (gr. 8-12). 1996. teacher ed., spiral bd. 18.95 (*1-56077-493-2*) Ctr Learning.

Center for Learning Network Staff & Warren, Robert Penn. All the King's Man: Curriculum Unit. (Novel Ser.). 82p. (YA). (gr. 9-12). 1990. spiral bd. 18.95 (*1-56077-109-7*) Ctr Learning.

Center for Learning Network Staff & Wiesel, Elie. Night: Curriculum Unit. (Novel Ser.). 101p. (YA). (gr. 9-12). 1992. spiral bd. 18.95 (*1-56077-225-5*) Ctr Learning.

Center for Learning Network Staff & Wilde, Oscar. The Importance of Being Earnest: Curriculum Unit. (Drama Ser.). 82p. (YA). (gr. 9-12). 1990. spiral bd. 18.95 (*1-56077-114-3*) Ctr Learning.

Center for Learning Network Staff & Wilder, Thornton. The Bridge of San Luis Rey: Curriculum Unit. (Novel Ser.). 104p. (YA). (gr. 9-12). 1990. spiral bd. 18.95 (*1-56077-104-6*) Ctr Learning.

Center for Learning Network Staff & Williams, Tennessee. The Glass Menagerie: Curriculum Unit. (Drama Ser.). 68p. (YA). (gr. 9-12). 1990. spiral bd. 18.95 (*1-56077-106-2*) Ctr Learning.

Center for Learning Network Staff & Zindel, Paul. The Pigman/The Pigman's Legacy: Curriculum Unit. (Novel Ser.). 87p. (YA). (gr. 6-12). 1993. spiral bd. 18.95 (*1-56077-246-8*) Ctr Learning.

Center for Learning Network Staff, et al. December Stillness & Willy-Nilly: Curriculum Unit. (Novel Ser.). 115p. (J). (gr. 4-8). 1996. spiral bd. 18.95 (*1-56077-363-4*) Ctr Learning.

— Farewell to Manzanar/Black Like Me: Curriculum unit. (Novel Ser.). 78p. (YA). (gr. 9-12). 1996. spiral bd. 18.95 (*1-56077-468-1*) Ctr Learning.

— Inherit the Wind: Curriculum Unit. (Novel Ser.). 73p. (YA). (gr. 9-12). 1990. spiral bd. 18.95 (*1-56077-356-1*) Ctr Learning.

— Journey of the Sparrows & the Honorable Prison: Curriculum Unit. (Novel Ser.). 70p. (YA). (gr. 4-12). 1995. spiral bd. 18.95 (*1-56077-347-2*) Ctr Learning.

— Life with Father & I Remember Mama & You Can't Take It with You: Curriculum Unit. (Drama Ser.). 62p. (YA). (gr. 9-12). 1995. spiral bd. 18.95 (*1-56077-321-9*) Ctr Learning.

— The Matchmaker & She Stoops to Conquer: Curriculum Unit. (Drama Ser.). 64p. (YA). (gr. 9-12). 1995. spiral bd. 18.95 (*1-56077-325-1*) Ctr Learning.

— Missing May & The Summer of the Swans: Curriculum Unit. (Novel Ser.). 64p. (YA). (gr. 4-9). 1994. spiral bd. 18.95 (*1-56077-314-6*) Ctr Learning.

— Mrs. Mike & I Heard the Owl Call My Name: Curriculum Unit. (Novel Ser.). 76p. (YA). (gr. 7-12). 1994. spiral bd. 18.95 (*1-56077-300-6*) Ctr Learning.

— The Night Thoreau Spent in Jail: Curriculum Unit. (Novel Ser.). 72p. (YA). (gr. 9-12). 1990. spiral bd. 18.95 (*1-56077-371-5*) Ctr Learning.

— A Night to Remember & Streams to the river, River to the Sea: Curriculum Unit. (Novel Ser.). 91p. (YA). (gr. 4-12). 1995. spiral bd. 18.95 (*1-56077-318-9*) Ctr Learning.

— Number the Stars & Friedrich: Curriculum Unit. (Novel Ser.). 96p. (YA). (gr. 6-9). 1994. spiral bd. 18.95 (*1-56077-315-4*) Ctr Learning.

— Ordinary People & The tin Can Tree: Curriculum Unit. (Novel Ser.). 62p. (YA). (gr. 9-12). 1996. spiral bd. 18.95 (*1-56077-369-3*) Ctr Learning.

— The Picture of Dorian Gray & Dr. Jekyll & Mr. Hyde: Curriculum Unit. (Novel Ser.). 83p. (YA). (gr. 9-12). 1992. spiral bd. 18.95 (*1-56077-211-5*) Ctr Learning.

— The Prince & Utopia: Curriculum Unit. (Novel Ser.). 93p. (YA). 1994. spiral bd. 18.95 (*1-56077-308-1*) Ctr Learning.

— 1776: Curriculum Unit. (Drama Ser.). 95p. 1990. spiral bd. 18.95 (*1-56077-116-X*) Ctr Learning.

— Summer of My German Soldier & Waiting for the rain: Curriculum Unit. (Novel Ser.). 97p. (YA). (gr. 7-12). 1994. spiral bd. 18.95 (*1-56077-303-0*) Ctr Learning.

— Waiting for Godot & Rosencrantz & Guildenstern Are Dead: Curriculum Unit. (Drama Ser.). 91p. (YA). (gr. 9-12). 1993. spiral bd. 18.95 (*1-56077-243-3*) Ctr Learning.

— Where the Lilies Bloom & No Promises in the Wind: Curriculum Unit. (Novel Ser.). 103p. (YA). (gr. 7-12). 1994. spiral bd. 18.95 (*1-56077-307-3*) Ctr Learning.

— The Witch of Blackbird Pond & My Brother Sam is Dead. (Novel Ser.). 93p. (YA). (gr. 6-9). 1992. spiral bd. 18.95 (*1-56077-259-X*) Ctr Learning.

— The yearling & the Red Pony: Curriculum Unit. (Novel Ser.). 122p. (YA). (gr. 7-12). 1992. spiral bd. 18.95 (*1-56077-228-X*) Ctr Learning.

Center for Learning Network Staff, jt. auth. see Buck, Pearl Synderstricker.

Center for Learning Network Staff, jt. auth. see Malory, Thomas.

Center for Learning Network Staff, jt. auth. see Rutherford, Edward, pseud.

Center for Learning Network Staff, jt. auth. see Shakespeare, William.

Center for Learning Network Staff, jt. auth. see Tolkien, J. R. R.

Center for Learning Network Staff, jt. auth. see Voigt, Cynthia.

Center for Marine Conservation Staff. The Ocean Book: Aquarium & Seaside Activities & Ideas for All Ages. 113p. 1989. 22.95 (*0-471-50973-6*) Wiley.

— The Ocean Book: Aquarium & Seaside Activities & Ideas for All Ages. 128p. (J). (gr. k-6). 1989. pap. 12.95 (*0-471-62078-5*) Wiley.

Center for Mathematics, Science, & Technology, Illinois State University Staff, contrib. by. Integrated Mathematics, Science & Technology: Energy Transformation. (Illus.). (YA). (gr. 6-12). 1999. student ed. 14.99 (*0-02-647846-3*) Glencoe.

C

— Integrated Mathematics, Science & Technology: Food Production. (Illus.). (YA). (gr. 6-12). 1999. student ed. 14.99 (*0-02-647840-4*) Glencoe.
— Integrated Mathematics, Science & Technology: Waste Management. (Illus.). (YA). (gr. 6-12). 1999. student ed. 14.99 (*0-02-647843-9*) Glencoe.
— Integrated Mathematics, Science & Technology: Wellness Module. (Illus.). (YA). (gr. 6-12). 1998. student ed. 14.99 (*0-02-647837-4*) Glencoe.

Center for Mobility Resources Staff, ed. Mobility Plus . . . A Reference Guide. 2nd ed. 773p. 1999. pap. 259.60 (*0-9643934-0-9*, D5503; D5504) Ctr Mobility Res.

Center for Occupational Research & Development Staff. Applications in Biology - Chemistry: A Workshop Presenter's Guide for Teacher Training. (Illus.). 1993. pap. text. write for info. (*1-55502-483-1*) CORD Commns.
— Applications in Biology - Chemistry: "Air & Other Gases" (Illus.). 1996. pap. write for info. (*1-55502-404-1*) Thomson Learn.
— Applications in Biology - Chemistry: "Animal Life Processes" (Illus.). 1996. pap. write for info. (*1-55502-477-7*) Thomson Learn.
— Applications in Biology - Chemistry: "Continuity of Life" (Illus.). 1996. pap. write for info. (*1-55502-390-8*) Thomson Learn.
— Applications in Biology - Chemistry: "Disease & Wellness" (Illus.). 260p. 1996. pap. write for info. (*1-55502-388-6*) Thomson Learn.
— Applications in Biology - Chemistry: "Microorganisms" (Illus.). 1996. pap. write for info. (*1-55502-472-6*) Thomson Learn.
— Applications in Biology - Chemistry: "Natural Resources" (Illus.). 212p. 1996. pap. write for info. (*1-55502-364-9*) Thomson Learn.
— Applications in Biology - Chemistry: Nutrition. (Illus.). 1996. pap. write for info. (*1-55502-400-9*); pap. write for info. (*1-55502-402-5*) Thomson Learn.
— Applications in Biology - Chemistry: "Plant Growth & Reproduction" (Illus.). 1996. pap. write for info. (*1-55502-406-8*) Thomson Learn.
— Applications in Biology - Chemistry Series. (Illus.). 1992. pap. text. write for info. (*1-55502-363-0*) CORD Commns.

Center for Occupational Research & Development Staff. Applications in Biology & Chemistry. 1996. pap. 60.75 (*1-55502-558-7*) Thomson Learn.

Center for Occupational Research & Development Staff. Applications in Biology-Chemistry: "Synthetic Materials" (Illus.). 1996. pap. write for info. (*1-55502-479-3*) Thomson Learn.
— Applied Mathematics Student Resource Book. (CORD Co-published Titles). (Illus.). 1996. pap. write for info. (*1-55502-370-3*) Thomson Learn.
— Applied Mathematics, Unit A: "Getting to Know Your Calculator" (Illus.). 1996. pap. write for info. (*1-55502-337-1*) Thomson Learn.
— Applied Mathematics, Unit B: "Naming Numbers in Different Ways" (Illus.). 1996. pap. write for info. (*1-55502-339-8*) Thomson Learn.
— Applied Mathematics, Unit C: "Finding Answers with Your Calculator" (Illus.). 1996. pap. write for info. (*1-55502-341-X*) Thomson Learn.
— Applied Mathematics, Unit 1: "Learning Problem-Solving Techniques" (Illus.). 1996. pap. write for info. (*1-55502-297-9*) Thomson Learn.
— Applied Mathematics, Unit 10: "Working with Scale Drawings" (Illus.). 1996. pap. write for info. (*1-55502-311-8*) Thomson Learn.
— Applied Mathematics, Unit 11: "Using Signed Numbers & Vectors" (Illus.). 1996. pap. write for info. (*1-55502-313-4*) Thomson Learn.
— Applied Mathematics, Unit 12: "Using Scientific Notation" (Illus.). 1996. pap. write for info. (*1-55502-315-0*) Thomson Learn.
— Applied Mathematics, Unit 13: "Precision, Accuracy, & Tolerance" (Illus.). 1996. pap. write for info. (*1-55502-317-7*) Thomson Learn.
— Applied Mathematics, Unit 14: "Solving Problems with Powers & Roots" (Illus.). 1996. pap. write for info. (*1-55502-319-3*) Thomson Learn.
— Applied Mathematics, Unit 15: "Using Formulas to Solve Problems" (Illus.). 1996. pap. write for info. (*1-55502-321-5*) Thomson Learn.
— Applied Mathematics, Unit 16: "Solving Problems That Involve Linear Equations" (Illus.). 1996. pap. write for info. (*1-55502-323-1*) Thomson Learn.
— Applied Mathematics, Unit 17: "Graphing Data" (Illus.). 1996. pap. write for info. (*1-55502-325-8*) Thomson Learn.
— Applied Mathematics, Unit 18: "Solving Problems That Involve Nonlinear Equations" (Illus.). 1996. pap. write for info. (*1-55502-327-4*) Thomson Learn.
— Applied Mathematics, Unit 19: "Working with Statistics" (Illus.). 1996. pap. write for info. (*1-55502-329-0*) Thomson Learn.
— Applied Mathematics, Unit 2: "Estimating Answers" (Illus.). 1996. pap. write for info. (*1-55502-299-5*) Thomson Learn.
— Applied Mathematics, Unit 20: "Working with Probabilities" (Illus.). 1996. pap. write for info. (*1-55502-331-2*) Thomson Learn.
— Applied Mathematics, Unit 21: "Using Right-Triangle Relationships" (Illus.). 1996. pap. write for info. (*1-55502-333-9*) Thomson Learn.
— Applied Mathematics, Unit 22: "Using Trigonometric Functions" (Illus.). 1996. pap. write for info. (*1-55502-335-5*) Thomson Learn.
— Applied Mathematics, Unit 23: Factoring. (Illus.). 53p. 1996. pap., student ed. write for info. (*1-55502-442-4*) Thomson Learn.
— Applied Mathematics, Unit 24: Patterns & Functions. (Illus.). 60p. 1996. pap., student ed. write for info. (*1-55502-443-2*) Thomson Learn.
— Applied Mathematics, Unit 25: Quadratics. (Illus.). 59p. 1996. pap., student ed. write for info. (*1-55502-444-0*) Thomson Learn.
— Applied Mathematics, Unit 26: "Systems of Equations" (Illus.). 1996. pap. write for info. (*1-55502-445-9*) Thomson Learn.
— Applied Mathematics, Unit 27: "Inequalities" (Illus.). 1996. pap. write for info. (*1-55502-446-7*) Thomson Learn.
— Applied Mathematics, Unit 28: "Geometry in the Workplace I" (Illus.). 1996. pap. write for info. (*1-55502-447-5*) Thomson Learn.
— Applied Mathematics, Unit 29: "Geometry in the Workplace II" (Illus.). 1996. pap. write for info. (*1-55502-448-3*) Thomson Learn.
— Applied Mathematics, Unit 3: Measuring in English & Metric Units. (Illus.). 1996. pap. write for info. (*1-55502-301-0*) Thomson Learn.
— Applied Mathematics, Unit 30: Solving Problems with Computer Spreadsheets. (Illus.). 1996. pap. write for info. (*1-55502-449-1*) Thomson Learn.
— Applied Mathematics, Unit 31: Solving Problems with Computer Graphics. (Illus.). 1996. pap. write for info. (*1-55502-450-5*) Thomson Learn.
— Applied Mathematics, Unit 32: Quality Assurance & Process Control 1. (Illus.). 1996. pap. write for info. (*1-55502-451-3*) Thomson Learn.
— Applied Mathematics, Unit 33: Quality Assurance & Process Control 2. (Illus.). 1996. pap. write for info. (*1-55502-452-1*) Thomson Learn.
— Applied Mathematics, Unit 4: "Using Graphs, Charts, & Tables" (Illus.). 1996. pap. write for info. (*1-55502-303-7*) Thomson Learn.
— Applied Mathematics, Unit 5: "Dealing with Data" (Illus.). 1996. pap. write for info. (*1-55502-292-8*) Thomson Learn.
— Applied Mathematics, Unit 6: "Working with Lines & Angles" (Illus.). 1996. pap. write for info. (*1-55502-305-3*) Thomson Learn.
— Applied Mathematics, Unit 7: "Working with Shapes in Two Dimensions" (Illus.). 1996. pap. write for info. (*1-55502-293-6*) Thomson Learn.
— Applied Mathematics, Unit 8: "Working with Shapes in Three Dimensions" (Illus.). 1996. pap. write for info. (*1-55502-307-X*) Thomson Learn.
— Applied Mathematics, Unit 9: "Using Ratios & Proportions" (Illus.). 1996. pap. write for info. (*1-55502-309-6*) Thomson Learn.

Center for Occupational Research & Development Staff. Community of Life. 1996. pap. 6.75 (*1-55502-576-5*) Thomson Learn.

Center for Occupational Research & Development Staff. CORD Applied Mathematics - Metric Version, Unit A: "Getting to Know Your Calculator" (Illus.). 1994. teacher ed. write for info. (*1-55502-522-6*); pap. text. write for info. (*1-55502-521-8*) CORD Commns.
— CORD Applied Mathematics - Metric Version, Unit B: "Naming Numbers in Different Ways" (Illus.). 1994. pap. text. write for info. (*1-55502-523-4*) CORD Commns.
— CORD Applied Mathematics - Metric Version, Unit C: "Finding Answers with Your Calculator" (Illus.). 1994. pap. text. write for info. (*1-55502-525-0*) CORD Commns.
— CORD Applied Mathematics - Metric Version, Unit 1: "Learning Problem-solving Techniques" (Illus.). 1994. pap. text. write for info. (*1-55502-527-7*) CORD Commns.
— CORD Applied Mathematics - Metric Version, Unit 10: "Working with Scale Drawings" (Illus.). 1994. teacher ed. write for info. (*1-55502-546-3*); pap. text. write for info. (*1-55502-545-5*) CORD Commns.
— CORD Applied Mathematics - Metric Version, Unit 11: "Using Signed Numbers & Vectors" (Illus.). 1994. pap. text. write for info. (*1-55502-547-1*) CORD Commns.
— CORD Applied Mathematics - Metric Version, Unit 12: "Using Scientific Notation" (Illus.). 1994. pap. text. write for info. (*1-55502-549-8*) CORD Commns.
— CORD Applied Mathematics - Metric Version, Unit 13: "Precision, Accuracy, & Tolerance" (Illus.). 1994. pap. text. write for info. (*1-55502-551-X*) CORD Commns.
— CORD Applied Mathematics - Metric Version, Unit 14: "Solving Problems with Powers & Roots" (Illus.). 1994. pap. text. write for info. (*1-55502-553-6*) CORD Commns.
— CORD Applied Mathematics - Metric Version, Unit 15: "Using Formulas to Solve Problems" (Illus.). 1994. pap. text. write for info. (*1-55502-555-2*) CORD Commns.
— CORD Applied Mathematics - Metric Version, Unit 2: "Estimating Answers" (Illus.). 1994. pap. text. write for info. (*1-55502-529-3*) CORD Commns.
— CORD Applied Mathematics - Metric Version, Unit 3: "Measuring in English & Metric Units" (Illus.). 1994. pap. text. write for info. (*1-55502-531-5*) CORD Commns.
— CORD Applied Mathematics - Metric Version, Unit 4: "Using Graphs, Charts, & Tables" (Illus.). 1994. pap. text. write for info. (*1-55502-533-1*) CORD Commns.
— CORD Applied Mathematics - Metric Version, Unit 5: "Dealing with Data" (Illus.). 1994. pap. text. write for info. (*1-55502-535-8*) CORD Commns.
— CORD Applied Mathematics - Metric Version, Unit 6: "Working with Lines & Angles" (Illus.). 1994. pap. text. write for info. (*1-55502-537-4*) CORD Commns.
— CORD Applied Mathematics - Metric Version, Unit 7: "Working with Shapes in Two Dimensions" (Illus.). 1994. pap. text. write for info. (*1-55502-539-0*) CORD Commns.
— CORD Applied Mathematics - Metric Version, Unit 8: "Working with Shapes in Three Dimensions" (Illus.). 1994. pap. text. write for info. (*1-55502-541-2*) CORD Commns.
— CORD Applied Mathematics - Metric Version, Unit 9: "Using Ratios & Proportions" (Illus.). 1994. pap. text. write for info. (*1-55502-543-9*) CORD Commns.
— Course I: Introduction to Lasers. 2nd ed. LC 84-71821. (Laser-Electro-Optics Technology Ser.). (Illus.). 292p. (C). 1986. pap. text 28.00 (*1-55502-019-4*) CORD Commns.
— Drives. (Mechanical Technology Ser.). (Illus.). 267p. (C). 1983. pap. text 28.00 (*1-55502-152-2*) CORD Commns.
— Electronic Devices & Systems Bk. II: Digital Circuits. (High Technology Ser.). (Illus.). 316p. (C). 1985. pap. text 30.00 (*1-55502-030-5*) CORD Commns.
— Electronic Devices & Systems, Book I: Analog Circuits. (High Technology Ser.). (Illus.). 474p. (C). 1985. pap. text 35.00 (*1-55502-029-1*) CORD Commns.
— Electronic Devices & Systems I. (EUTEC Instrumentation & Control Curriculum Ser.). (Illus.). 474p. (C). 1985. pap. text. write for info. (*1-55502-182-4*) CORD Commns.
— Electronic Devices & Systems II. (EUTEC Instrumentation & Control Curriculum Ser.). (Illus.). 312p. (C). 1985. pap. text. write for info. (*1-55502-183-2*) CORD Commns.
— Electrostatic Precipitators. (EUTEC Power Plant Operator Curriculum Ser.). (Illus.). 28p. (C). 1987. pap. text. write for info. (*1-55502-234-0*) CORD Commns.
— Evaluating Your Tech Prep Program. (Illus.). 1993. pap. text. write for info. (*1-55502-517-X*) CORD Commns.
— Experimental Optical Methods, Course 4. (Laser-Electro-Optics Technology Ser.). (Illus.). 300p. (C). 1980. pap. text 28.00 (*1-55502-022-4*) CORD Commns.
— Fundamentals of Electricity & Electronics. (High Technology Ser.). (Illus.). 236p. (C). 1985. pap. text 25.00 (*1-55502-028-3*) CORD Commns.
— Geometric Optics, Course 2. rev. ed. (Laser-Electro-Optics Technology Ser.). (Illus.). 200p. (C). 1987. pap. text 22.00 (*1-55502-020-8*) CORD Commns.
— Geometric Optics: Light Sources & Wave Optics, Course 2-5. (Laser-Electro-Optics Technology Ser.). 472p. 1987. pap. text 37.00 (*1-55502-350-9*) CORD Commns.
— Graphics for Technicians. 362p. 1988. pap. text 35.00 (*1-55502-356-8*) CORD Commns.
— Graphics for Technicians. (Illus.). 96p. 1992. pap. text, teacher ed. 15.00 (*1-55502-473-4*) CORD Commns.
— Hazardous Materials Technology Report. 1990. pap. text 10.00 (*1-55502-468-8*) CORD Commns.
— Heat Transfer & Fluid Flow. (EUTEC Power Plant Operator Curriculum Ser.). (Illus.). 250p. (C). 1985. pap. text. write for info. (*1-55502-194-8*) CORD Commns.
— Heating & Cooling. (High Technology Ser.). (Illus.). 248p. (C). 1985. pap. text 28.00 (*1-55502-025-9*) CORD Commns.
— Implementation Guidebook to Principles of Technology. (CORD Co-published Titles). (Illus.). 400p. 1996. pap. 40.00 (*1-55502-367-3*) Thomson Learn.
— Instrumental Analysis I. (EUTEC Environmental & Chemical Analysis Curriculum Ser.). (Illus.). 330p. (C). 1985. pap. text. write for info. (*1-55502-202-2*) CORD Commns.
— Instrumental Analysis II. (EUTEC Environmental & Chemical Analysis Curriculum Ser.). (Illus.). 238p. (C). 1985. pap. text. write for info. (*1-55502-203-0*) CORD Commns.
— Instrumentation & Control. (High Technology Ser.). (Illus.). 256p. (C). 1985. pap. text 28.00 (*1-55502-026-7*) CORD Commns.
— Laser-Electro-Optic Devices, Course 7. (Laser-Electro-Optics Technology Ser.). (Illus.). 336p. (C). 1986. pap. text 35.00 (*1-55502-050-X*) CORD Commns.
— Laser-Electro-Optic Measurements, Course 10. (Laser Electro-Optics Technology Ser.). (Illus.). 160p. (C). 1980. pap. text 22.00 (*1-55502-053-4*) CORD Commns.
— Laser-Electro-Optics. (Technology Ser.). (Illus.). 3771p. (C). 1980. pap. text 250.00 (*1-55502-017-8*) CORD Commns.
— Laser-Electro-Optics Curriculum Planning Guide. (Laser-Electro-Optics Technology Ser.). (Illus.). 130p. 1985. pap. text 20.00 (*1-55502-018-6*) CORD Commns.
— Laser Technology, Course 3. LC 85-71925. (Laser-Electro-Optics Technology Ser.). (Illus.). 356p. (C). 1985. pap. text 32.00 (*1-55502-021-6*) CORD Commns.
— Laser Technology: Applications in Manufacturing. (Laser Electro-Optics Technology Ser.). 246p. 1991. pap. text 25.00 (*1-55502-454-8*) CORD Commns.
— Laser Technology: Applications in Medicine & Surgery. (Laser Electro-Optics Technology Ser.). 214p. 1991. pap. text 25.00 (*1-55502-456-4*) CORD Commns.
— Laser Technology: Applications in Photonics & Telecommunications. (Laser Electro-Optics Technology Ser.). 226p. 1991. pap. text 25.00 (*1-55502-455-6*) CORD Commns.
— Light Sources & Wave Optics, Course 5. rev. ed. (Laser-Electro-Optics Technology Ser.). (Illus.). 268p. (C). 1987. pap. text 28.00 (*1-55502-023-2*) CORD Commns.
— Linkages. (Mechanical Technology Ser.). (Illus.). 258p. (C). 1983. pap. text 28.00 (*1-55502-153-0*) CORD Commns.
— Machines. (Mechanical Technology Ser.). (Illus.). 142p. (C). 1983. pap. text 22.00 (*1-55502-154-9*) CORD Commns.
— Matematica Aplicada; Aprendizaje de Tecnicas de Resolvcion de Problemas. (Illus.). 1993. teacher ed. write for info. (*1-55502-493-9*); pap. text. write for info. (*1-55502-492-0*) CORD Commns.
— Matematica Aplicada: Conozca Su Calculadora. (Illus.). 1993. teacher ed. write for info. (*1-55502-487-4*); pap. text. write for info. (*1-55502-486-6*) CORD Commns.
— Matematica Aplicada: Diferentes Formas de Llamar a los Numeros. (Illus.). 1993. teacher ed. write for info. (*1-55502-489-0*); pap. text. write for info. (*1-55502-488-2*) CORD Commns.
— Matematica Aplicada: Encontramos Respuestas Con la Calculadora. (Illus.). 1993. teacher ed. write for info. (*1-55502-491-2*); pap. text. write for info. (*1-55502-490-4*) CORD Commns.
— Matematica Aplicada: Estimacion y Calculo de Respuestas. (Illus.). 1993. teacher ed. write for info. (*1-55502-495-5*); pap. text. write for info. (*1-55502-494-7*) CORD Commns.
— Matematica Aplicada: Medidas en Unidades Inglesas y Metricas. (Illus.). 1993. pap. text. write for info. (*1-55502-496-3*) CORD Commns.
— Matematica Aplicada: Nos Ocupamos de los Datos. (Illus.). 1993. pap. text. write for info. (*1-55502-500-5*) CORD Commns.
— Matematica Aplicada: Trabajo Con Dibujos a Escala. (Illus.). 1993. pap. text. write for info. (*1-55502-510-2*) CORD Commns.
— Matematica Aplicada: Trabajo Con Formas en Tres Dimensiones. (Illus.). 1993. pap. text. write for info. (*1-55502-506-4*) CORD Commns.
— Matematica Aplicada: Trabajo Con Formas on Dos Dimensiones. (Illus.). 1993. teacher ed. write for info. (*1-55502-505-6*); pap. text. write for info. (*1-55502-504-8*) CORD Commns.
— Matematica Aplicada: Trabajo Con Rectas y Angulos. (Illus.). 1993. pap. text. write for info. (*1-55502-502-1*) CORD Commns.
— Matematica Aplicada: Use de Notacion Cientifica. (Illus.). 1993. pap. text. write for info. (*1-55502-514-5*) CORD Commns.
— Matematica Aplicada: Uso de Graficos, Cuadrosy Tablas. (Illus.). 1993. pap. text. write for info. (*1-55502-498-X*) CORD Commns.
— Matematica Aplicada: Uso de Numeros Con Su Signoy Vectores. (Illus.). 1993. pap. text. write for info. (*1-55502-512-9*) CORD Commns.
— Matematica Aplicada: Uso de Razones y Proporciones. (Illus.). 1993. pap. text. write for info. (*1-55502-508-0*) CORD Commns.
— Materials. (Mechanical Technology Ser.). (Illus.). 148p. (C). 1983. pap. text 22.00 (*1-55502-155-7*) CORD Commns.
— Mechanical & Fluid Devices & Systems. (EUTEC Instrumentation & Control Curriculum Ser.). (Illus.). 222p. (C). 1985. pap. text. write for info. (*1-55502-184-0*) CORD Commns.
— Mechanical Devices & Systems. (High Technology Ser.). (Illus.). 200p. (C). 1989. pap. text 25.00 (*1-55502-361-4*) CORD Commns.
— Mechanical Devices & Systems Teacher's Guide. (High Technology Ser.). (Illus.). 37p. 1990. pap. text 10.00 (*1-55502-369-X*) CORD Commns.
— Nondestructive Examination (NDE) Techniques II, Course 32. (Nuclear Technology Ser.). pap. text 30.00 (*1-55502-121-2*) CORD Commns.
— Personal Computers. 26p. 1992. teacher ed. 10.00 (*1-55502-465-3*); pap. text 15.00 (*1-55502-464-5*) CORD Commns.
— Physics for Technicians - A Systems Approach. (Illus.). 997p. 1988. text 45.00 (*1-55502-272-3*) CORD Commns.
— Physics for Technicians - A Systems Approach. (Illus.). 1993. write for info. (*1-55502-516-1*) CORD Commns.
— Physics for Technicians - A Systems Approach: Instructor's Manual. (Illus.). 103p. 1988. pap. text 15.00 (*1-55502-462-9*) CORD Commns.
— Physics for Technicians - A Systems Approach: Laboratory Exercises. 366p. 1989. pap. text 28.00 (*1-55502-362-2*) CORD Commns.

Center for Occupational Research & Development Staff. Principles of Technology. 1996. pap., student ed. 4.75 (*1-55502-386-X*) Thomson Learn.

Center for Occupational Research & Development Staff. Principles of Technology, Unit 10: Energy Convertors. (Illus.). 1985. pap. text. write for info. (*1-55502-010-0*) CORD Commns.
— Principles of Technology, Unit 11: Transducers. (Illus.). 1985. pap. text. write for info. (*1-55502-011-9*) CORD Commns.
— Principles of Technology, Unit 12: Radiation. (Illus.). 1985. pap. text. write for info. (*1-55502-012-7*) CORD Commns.
— Principles of Technology, Unit 13: Optics & Optical Systems. (Illus.). 1985. pap. text. write for info. (*1-55502-013-5*) CORD Commns.
— Principles of Technology, Unit 14: Time Constants. (Illus.). 1985. pap. text. write for info. (*1-55502-014-3*) CORD Commns.
— Principles of Technology, Unit 2: Work. 2nd ed. (Illus.). 102p. 1996. pap., student ed. write for info. (*1-55502-373-8*) Thomson Learn.
— Principles of Technology, Unit 3: Rate. (Illus.). 1985. pap. text. write for info. (*1-55502-003-8*) CORD Commns.
— Principles of Technology, Unit 3: Rate. 2nd ed. (Illus.). 134p. 1996. pap., student ed. write for info. (*1-55502-374-6*) Thomson Learn.
— Principles of Technology, Unit 4: Resistance. (Illus.). 1985. pap. text. write for info. (*1-55502-004-6*) CORD Commns.
— Principles of Technology, Unit 4: Resistance. 2nd ed. (Illus.). 142p. 1996. pap., student ed. write for info. (*1-55502-375-4*) Thomson Learn.

C

— Principles of Technology, Unit 5: Energy. (Illus.). 1985. pap. text. write for info. (*1-55502-005-4*) CORD Commns.

— Principles of Technology, Unit 5: Energy. 2nd ed. (Illus.). 146p. 1996. pap., student ed. write for info. (*1-55502-376-2*) Thomson Learn.

— Principles of Technology, Unit 6: Power. (Illus.). 1985. pap. text. write for info. (*1-55502-006-2*) CORD Commns.

— Principles of Technology, Unit 6: Power. 2nd ed. (Illus.). 106p. 1996. pap., student ed. write for info. (*1-55502-377-0*) Thomson Learn.

— Principles of Technology, Unit 7: Force Transformers. (Illus.). 1985. pap. text. write for info. (*1-55502-007-0*) CORD Commns.

— Principles of Technology, Unit 7: Force Transformers. 2nd ed. (Illus.). 144p. 1996. pap., student ed. write for info. (*1-55502-378-9*) Thomson Learn.

— Principles of Technology, Unit 8: Momentum. (Illus.). 1985. pap. text. write for info. (*1-55502-008-9*) CORD Commns.

— Principles of Technology, Unit 9: Vibrations & Waves. (Illus.). 1985. pap. text. write for info. (*1-55502-009-7*) CORD Commns.

— Tech Prep Bridge: Preparing Adult Students to Enter a Two-Year Degree Program. (Illus.). 1993. pap. text. write for info. (*1-55502-518-8*) CORD Commns.

— Technical Communications. (High Technology Ser.). (Illus.). 228p. (C). 1985. pap. text 25.00 (*1-55502-164-6*) CORD Commns.

— Unified Technical Concepts in Physics. (Unified Technical Concepts Ser.). 171p. 1991. pap. text 20.00 (*1-55502-415-7*) CORD Commns.

— Unified Technical Concepts in Physics. 3rd ed. (Illus.). 520p. 1990. text, suppl. ed. 30.00 (*1-55502-353-3*) CORD Commns.

— Unified Technical Concepts in Physics--Laboratory Exercises Manual. 3rd ed. (Unified Technical Concepts Ser.). (Illus.). 1990. pap. text 35.00 (*1-55502-393-2*) CORD Commns.

Center for Occupational Research & Development Staff. Waste & Waste Management. 1996. pap. 6.75 (*1-55502-582-X*) Thomson Learn.

— Working with Equations: Unit 15bg. 1996. pap. 1.95 (*1-55502-829-2*) Thomson Learn.

Center for Occupational Research & Development Staff. Worksheets-Air & Other Gases. (Cord Communications). (YA). 1996. pap. 12.75 (*1-55502-733-4*) Thomson Learn.

Center for Ocean Management Studies Staff. Impact of Marine Pollution on Society. (Illus.). 320p. 1981. 59.95 (*0-275-90733-3*, C0733, Praeger Pubs) Greenwood.

Center for Ocean Management Studies Staff, ed. Comparative Marine Policy: Perspectives from Europe, Scandinavia, Canada & the United States. LC 80-21455. 260p. 1981. 59.95 (*0-275-90591-8*, C0591, Praeger Pubs) Greenwood.

Center for Pastoral Life & Ministry of the Diocese, jt. des. see Morseth, Ellen.

Center for Photographic Images of Medicine & Healt. Illustrated Catalogue of the Slide Archive of Historical Medical Photographs at Stonybrook. LC 83-22626. (Illus.). 442p. 1984. lib. bdg. 99.50 (*0-313-24169-4*, FCM/, Greenwood Pr) Greenwood.

Center for Policy Development Staff. Adrift in a Sea of Change: California's Public Libraries Struggle to Meet the Information Needs of Multicultural Communities. (Partnerships for Change Ser.: No. 2). 125p. 1990. pap. text 20.00 (*0-929722-44-2*) CA State Library Fndtn.

Center for Policy Research on the Impact of General & Special Education Reform Staff. Charter Schools & Students with Disabilities. 2nd ed. 20p. 1996. pap. 7.50 (*1-58434-032-0*) NASBE.

— Standards-Based School Reform & Students with Disabilities. 2nd ed. 12p. 1996. pap. 6.00 (*1-58434-033-9*) NASBE.

— What Will It Take? Standards-Based Education Reform for All Students. 2nd ed. 30p. 1996. pap. 10.00 (*1-58434-034-7*) NASBE.

Center for Political Studies Staff. American National Election Series: 1972, 1974, 1976, 5 vols., 1. LC 79-84172. 1979. write for info. (*0-89138-976-8*) ICPSR.

— American National Election Series: 1972, 1974, 1976, 5 vols., 2. LC 79-84172. 1979. write for info. (*0-89138-975-X*) ICPSR.

— American National Election Series: 1972, 1974, 1976, 5 vols., 3. LC 79-84172. 1979. write for info. (*0-89138-974-1*) ICPSR.

— American National Election Series: 1972, 1974, 1976, 5 vols., 4. LC 79-84172. 1979. write for info. (*0-89138-973-3*) ICPSR.

— American National Election Series: 1972, 1974, 1976, 5 vols., 5. LC 79-84172. 1979. write for info. (*0-89138-972-5*) ICPSR.

— American National Election Series: 1972, 1974, 1976, 5 vols., Set. LC 79-84172. 1979. write for info. (*0-89138-977-6*) ICPSR.

— American National Election Study, 1970. 1972. write for info. (*0-89138-051-5*) ICPSR.

Center for Popular Economics Staff. Economic Report of the People: An Alternative to the Economic Report of the President. LC 85-30342. 260p. 1986. 30.00 (*0-89608-316-0*); pap. 11.00 (*0-89608-315-2*) South End Pr.

Center for Popular Economics Staff, jt. auth. see Folbre, Nancy.

Center for Preventive Action Staff & Rubin, Barnett R. Toward Comprehensive Peace in Southeast Europe: Preventing Conflict in the South Balkans: Report of the South Balkans Working Group. LC 96-27647. 1996. 9.95 (*0-87078-402-1*) Century Foundation.

Center for Professional Responsibility Staff. Annotated Model Rules of Professional Conduct. 3rd ed. 704p. 1996. pap. 74.95 (*0-89707-736-9*, 561-0102) Amer Bar Assn.

— Definitions of Practice of Law Survey. 16p. 1984. pap. 7.95 (*0-685-19029-3*, 561-0067-01) Amer Bar Assn.

— Formal & Informal Ethics Opinions. 655p. 1985. 49.95 (*0-685-14423-2*, 561-0047) Amer Bar Assn.

— The Judicial Response to Lawyer Misconduct. 180p. 1989. ring bd. 29.95 (*0-685-14424-0*, 561-0042) Amer Bar Assn.

— Model Federal Rules of Disciplinary Enforcement. 15p. 1978. pap. 7.95 (*0-685-19032-3*, 720-0012-01) Amer Bar Assn.

— Model Rules of Professional Conduct. LC 95-80482. 176p. 1995. pap. 15.95 (*1-57073-235-3*, 561-0120) Amer Bar Assn.

Center for Professional Responsibility Staff, jt. auth. see American Bar Association Staff.

***Center for Public Integrity Staff.** Citizen Muckraking: How to Investigate & Right the Wrongs in Your Community. 200p. 2000. lib. bdg. 29.95 (*1-56751-189-9*, Pub. by Common Courage) LPC InBook.

— Citizen Muckraking: How to Investigate & Right Wrongs in Your Community. 208p. 2000. pap. 11.96 (*1-56751-188-0*, Pub. by Common Courage) LPC InBook.

Center for Public Integrity Staff. The Trading Game: Inside Lobbying for the North American Free Trade. 108p. 1995. pap. 10.00 (*1-882583-02-7*) U Pr of Amer.

— Under the Influence: Presidential Candidates & Their Campaign Advisers. 80p. 1995. pap. 10.00 (*0-9629012-5-3*) U Pr of Amer.

Center for Public Integrity Staff, jt. auth. see Green, Alan.

Center for Public Integrity Staff, jt. auth. see Lewis, Charles.

Center for Public Policy Staff. Part of the Solution: Innovative Approaches to Nonprofit Funding. 140p. (Orig.). 1988. pap. 15.00 (*1-886949-12-3*) Union Inst.

Center for Public Representation Staff. Counseling the Elderly Client in Minnesota. Klobucher, Lynn K., ed. LC 92-37263. 1992. 160.00 (*0-317-05374-4*) West Group.

— Counseling the Elderly Client in Virginia, 2 vols., Set. Wagner, Laura L. & Wagner, Robert, eds. LC 92-29603. 1992. ring bd. 165.00 (*0-317-05371-X*) West Group.

Center for Quality of Management Staff, et al. Voices into Choices: Acting on the Voice of the Customer. 1997. 49.95 (*1-884731-13-9*) Oriel Inc.

Center for Research & Documentation on World Langu, contrib. by. Esperanto, Interlinguistics, & Planned Language, Vol. 5. LC 97-25060. (Papers of the Center for Research & Documentation on World Language Problems). (CHI & GER.). 256p. (C). 1997. 42.50 (*0-7618-0847-7*) U Pr of Amer.

Center for Research in Ambulatory Health Care Admi, ed. see Knutson, Karen, et al.

Center for Resource Management Staff, jt. auth. see Wann, David.

Center for Self-Sufficiency, Research Division Sta. Almost Coffee: Coffee Substitutes Poetry Book. 11p. 1983. pap. text 8.95 (*0-910811-66-0*) Ctr Self Suff.

— The Alternative Cooking Facilities Cookbook. LC 83-90718. 50p. 1983. ring bd. 25.95 (*0-910811-08-3*) Ctr Self Suff.

— Beauty Products from Fruits, Flowers, Vegetables & Other Sources: A Researcher's Guide & Workbook. rev. ed. (Illus.). 60p. 1997. ring bd. 25.95 (*0-910811-54-7*) Ctr Self Suff.

— Cleaning Products from Nature: Vinegar, Baking Soda, Lemon Juice, & More - A Report. 68p. 1986. ring bd. 29.95 (*0-910811-55-5*) Ctr Self Suff.

— Considering a Secretarial Service? An Income Possibility Workbook. rev. ed. 131p. 1992. ring bd. 31.95 (*0-910811-63-6*) Ctr Self Suff.

Center for Self Sufficiency, Research Division Sta. Creativity, Productivity & Positivity: A Poetry Book. 21p. 1993. pap. text 7.95 (*0-910811-15-6*) Ctr Self Suff.

— Finding Bargains by Using the Newspapers & or Telephone Directory: A Workbook. 53p. (YA). (gr. 11-12). ring bd. 31.95 (*0-910811-87-3*) Ctr Self Suff.

Center For Self-Sufficiency, Research Division Sta. Food Self-Sufficiency Seminar-Workshop Workbook. 62p. 1984. ring bd. 35.95 (*0-910811-94-6*) Ctr Self Suff.

Center for Self-Sufficiency, Research Division Sta. For Baby Kimono Basic Pattern with use Poem. 1985. pap. text 9.95 (*0-317-00979-6*) Ctr Self Suff.

Center for Self Sufficiency, Research Division Sta. Home Plans: Three Basics for Beginners. 10p. 1985. pap. text 19.95 (*0-910811-47-4*) Ctr Self Suff.

— Honey for Many Reasons, Uses As Cosmetics, Medicinal Uses & More: A Poem. 30p. 1983. pap. text 7.95 (*0-910811-72-5*) Ctr Self Suff.

Center for Self-Sufficiency, Research Division Sta. Ideas for Becoming Self Sufficient: An at Your Own Pace Workbook. LC 83-90723. 90p. 1983. ring bd. 25.95 (*0-910811-29-6*) Ctr Self Suff.

— Made from Scratch: A Report on Cooking, Crafts, Etc. LC 83-90712. 50p. 1985. ring bd. 25.95 (*0-910811-07-5*) Ctr Self Suff.

— Making a Change from City Living to Country Living & from Country Living to City Living: A Report. LC 83-90713. 55p. 1985. ring bd. 39.95 (*0-910811-05-9*) Ctr Self Suff.

— Natural Foods & Nutrition: A Report. 50p. 1983. ring bd. 25.95 (*0-910811-67-9*) Ctr Self Suff.

— One Kettle Cookbook with Make It Tasty Spice Blends. 55p. 1985. ring bd. 21.95 (*0-910811-06-7*) Ctr Self Suff.

Center for Self Sufficiency, Research Division Sta. Pick Your Own Apples, Oranges, & Pear Locations: A How to Find or Locate Workbook. 50p. 1985. ring bd. 24.95 (*0-910811-48-2*) Ctr Self Suff.

Center for Self-Sufficiency, Research Division Sta. Pick Your Own Blueberries, Raspberries & Other Berries Locations: A How to Find or Locate Workbook. 50p. 1985. ring bd. 24.95 (*0-910811-50-4*) Ctr Self Suff.

Center for Self Sufficiency, Research Division Sta. Pick Your Own Peaches, Melons & Grapes Locations: A How to Find or Locate Workbook. 50p. 1985. ring bd. 24.95 (*0-910811-60-1*) Ctr Self Suff.

Center for Self-Sufficiency, Research Division Sta. Pick Your Own Tomatoes, Plums & Avocadoes Locations: A How to Find or Locate Workbook. 50p. 1985. ring bd. 24.95 (*0-910811-57-1*) Ctr Self Suff.

Center for Self Sufficiency, Research Division Sta. Recipes Free & Almost Free: A One Thousand & More Possibilities Workbook. 200p. 1983. ring bd. 21.95 (*0-910811-13-X*) Ctr Self Suff.

Center for Self-Sufficiency, Research Division Sta. Recycling: How to Find or Locate Information on Recycling Workbook. 80p. 1992. student ed., ring bd. 24.95 (*0-910811-91-1*) Prosperity & Profits.

— Recycling Businesses: Suggestions for Types of Recycling Businesses. rev. ed. 50p. 1991. 19.95 (*0-685-48413-0*) Ctr Self Suff.

— Recycling Businesses: Suggestions for Types of Recycling Businesses. rev. ed. 108p. 1992. ring bd. 39.95 (*0-910811-34-2*) Ctr Self Suff.

— Recycling Seminar-Workshop: Workbook. 25p. 1984. student ed., ring bd. 31.95 (*0-910811-90-3*) Ctr Self Suff.

— Select Your Own Tree & Shrubbery Locations with a Tree & Shrubbery Care Information Locator Guide: A How to Find or Locate Workbook. 50p. 1984. ring bd. 21.95 (*0-910811-58-X*) Ctr Self Suff.

Center For Self Sufficiency, Research Division Sta. Self Employment, Self Starter, & Start Your Own: A Report. LC 83-90708. 200p. 1983. ring bd. 35.95 (*0-910811-12-1*) Ctr Self Suff.

Center for Self-Sufficiency, Research Division Sta. Self Sufficiency Continuing Education Alternatives: A Report. rev. ed. 200p. 1996. ring bd. 24.95 (*0-910811-73-3*) Ctr Self Suff.

— Self-Sufficiency Encyclopaedia. LC 83-90715. 75p. 1983. ring bd. 34.95 (*0-910811-00-8*) Ctr Self Suff.

Center for Self Sufficiency, Research Division Sta. Sewing Publications, Pattern Companies, Fabric Outlets, Etc. A How to Find or Locate Workbook. LC 83-90722. 60p. 1983. ring bd. 24.95 (*0-910811-30-X*) Ctr Self Suff.

Center for Self-Sufficiency, Research Division Sta. Shelter, Home & Housing Self-Sufficiency References in American History: A Report. 60p. 1985. pap. text 35.95 (*0-910811-41-5*) Ctr Self Suff.

Center for Self Sufficiency, Research Division Sta. Small Business Possibilities for At Your Own Pace Research. 60p. 1984. ring bd. 25.95 (*0-317-03486-3*) Ctr Self Suff.

Center for Self-Sufficiency, Research Division Sta. Solar Education Home Plan Kits, Solar Related Companies & Information: A Report. rev. ed. 100p. 1993. ring bd. 31.95 (*0-910811-35-0*) Ctr Self Suff.

— Telephone Repair Service & Recycling Possibilities: A Report. rev. ed. 1996. ring bd. 24.95 (*0-910811-40-7*) Ctr Self Suff.

Center for Self-Sufficiency, Research Division Sta, compiled by. The Food Preservation Index: A Report. LC 83-90716. 50p. 1982. ring bd. 32.95 (*0-910811-10-5*) Ctr Self Suff.

— Soybeans & Their Uses with Recipe Ingredient Replacements. LC 83-90709. 50p. 1985. ring bd. 19.95 (*0-910811-03-2*) Ctr Self Suff.

Center for Self-Sufficiency, Research Division Sta, ed. The Barter Index: How to Find or Locate Information on Barter. LC 83-90717. 60p. 1985. ring bd. 25.95 (*0-910811-09-1*) Ctr Self Suff.

Center for Self Sufficiency Staff. Be Somebody, Be Yourself Letterheads to Duplicate & Use. Doyle, A. C., ed. 1992. ring bd. 25.95 (*0-910811-74-1*) Ctr Self Suff.

— Considering a Referral Service? Referral Service Suggestions: A Business Workbook. rev. ed. (Illus.). 108p. 1993. ring bd. 29.95 (*0-910811-64-4*) Ctr Self Suff.

— Creative Suggestions on Obtaining Company Benefits for a Small Business: A Report. rev. ed. 117p. 1992. ring bd. 29.95 (*0-910811-21-0*) Ctr Self Suff.

— Domestic Help Services: Suggestive Ideas for Services Plus Work Pages. rev. ed. 114p. 1992. student ed., ring bd. 29.95 (*0-910811-49-0*) Ctr Self Suff.

Center for Self Sufficiency Staff. Health Care Alternatives: A Report. rev. ed. 90p. 1993. ring bd. 27.95 (*0-910811-37-7*) Ctr Self Suff.

Center for Self-Sufficiency Staff. Home Business - How to Find or Locate Information on Home Business: An at Your Own Pace Workbook. rev. ed. 60p. 1993. ring bd. 29.95 (*0-910811-92-X*) Ctr Self Suff.

Center for Self Sufficiency Staff. Home Business Possibility Encyclopedia. Orig. Title: Home Business Encyclopedia; Two Hundred-Fifty Plus Home Business Possibilities. 100p. 1991. ring bd. 59.95 (*0-910811-78-4*) Prosperity & Profits.

— Housing Alternatives: Self Paced Workbook. 1983. ring bd. 21.95 (*0-317-00664-9*) Ctr Self Suff.

Center for Self-Sufficiency Staff. Jobs, Business & Industry Creating with Recycling: Seminar Workshop Workbook. rev. ed. 60p. 1993. ring bd. 29.95 (*0-910811-39-3*) Ctr Self Suff.

— Recycling Projects for Creating Summer & Year Around Jobs-Possibilities. rev. ed. 78p. 1992. ring bd. 39.95 (*0-910811-42-3*) Ctr Self Suff.

— Rent Almost Free, Mortgage Almost Free Housing: A Report. 65p. 1992. ring bd. 29.95 (*0-910811-22-9*) Ctr Self Suff.

— Sewing As a Home or Small Business: Possibilities. rev. ed. 83p. 1992. ring bd. 25.95 (*0-910811-65-2*) Ctr Self Suff.

Center for Self Sufficiency Staff. Small Business Possibility Encyclopaedia: Word Mapping Edition. Orig. Title: The A to Z Small Business Reference Encyclopaedia: Word Mapping Edition. 100p. (C). 1991. ring bd. 149.00 (*0-910811-17-2*) Ctr Self Suff.

Center for Self-Sufficiency Staff. Suggestions for Making Money Addressing & Stuffing Envelopes or How to Start a Lettershop Business: A Workbook. rev. ed. 78p. 1992. ring bd. 25.95 (*0-910811-20-2*) Prosperity & Profits.

— Suggestions for Starting a Business from Businesses That Are Going Out of Business: A Business Workbook. rev. ed. (Illus.). 67p. 1992. ring bd. 29.95 (*0-910811-25-3*) Ctr Self Suff.

— Thrift Stores & Resale Shops - Suggestive Ideas for Specialized Thrift Shops: A Business Workbook. rev. ed. (Illus.). 128p. 1992. ring bd. 29.95 (*0-910811-46-6*) Ctr Self Suff.

— Unemployed? Laid Off? Survival Possibilities for the Unemployed & Similar Situations. rev. ed. 70p. 1993. ring bd. 25.95 (*0-910811-11-3*) Ctr Self Suff.

Center for Social Research on Old Textiles Staff, jt. ed. see Siegelaub, Seth.

Center for Social Research Staff. The Source Book: A Presentation of Demographic & Social Data for Nashville/Davidson County. 69p. 1995. spiral bd. 29.95 (*1-888334-02-9*) Coun Commun Serv.

Center for Strategic & International Studies Staff. The Congress & Mexico, Bordering on Change: A Report of the CSIS Congressional Study Group on Mexico. LC 89-15890. (Significant Issues Ser.: Vol. 11, No. 8). 65p. reprint ed. pap. 30.00 (*0-7837-6149-X*, 204587100009) Bks Demand.

— United States - Japanese Political Relations: The Critical Issues Affecting Asia's Future, No. 7. LC 80-12143. (Center for Strategic Studies, Georgetown University Special Report: No. 7). 104p. 1980. reprint ed. lib. bdg. 55.00 (*0-313-22376-9*, CSUS) Greenwood.

— United States China Policy: Building a New Consensus. LC E 0183.8.C5U. (Asian Studies Report). 117p. 1994. reprint ed. pap. 36.30 (*0-608-00206-2*, 206098900006) Bks Demand.

Center for Strategic & International Studies Staff, ed. World Trade Competition: Western Countries & Third World Markets. LC 81-11930. 464p. 1981. 79.50 (*0-275-90600-0*, C0600, Praeger Pubs) Greenwood.

Center for Strategic & International Studies Staff, jt. auth. see MacGregor, Douglas A.

Center for Strategic & International Studies Staff, jt. auth. see MacGregor, Douglas A.

Center for Studies in Criminal Justice, University of Chicago Law School Staff, tr. Greenland Criminal Code. (American Series of Foreign Penal Codes: Vol. 16). ix, 47p. 1970. 20.00 (*0-8377-0036-1*, Rothman) W S Hein.

Center for Study of the American Experience Staff. The Yankee Mariner & Sea Power: America's Challenge of Ocean Space. Bartell, Joyce J., ed. 300p. 1982. 44.95 (*0-88474-105-2*) Transaction Pubs.

Center for Study of the American Experience Staff, ed. Energy in America: Fifteen Views. 285p. 1980. 39.95 (*0-88474-103-6*) Transaction Pubs.

Center for the Blind Friends Staff. Jumbo Print Cookbook. 256p. (Orig.). 1989. pap. 11.95 (*0-685-29426-9*) Friends Ctr Blind.

Center for the Child Care Staff. Creating Better Child Care Jobs: Model Work Standards for Teaching Staff in Center-Based Child Care. 32p. 1998. pap. text 10.00 (*1-889956-15-5*) Natl Ctr EC.

Center for the Evaluative Clinical Sciences Staff. The Dartmouth Atlas of Health Care 1998. (Illus.). 328p. 1998. 350.00 (*1-55648-217-5*) OUP.

Center for the Study & Practice of Survival at Sea. A Practical Guide to Lifeboat Survival. Jeffs, David S. & Keating, David, trs. from FRE. LC 95-50503. (ENG., Illus.). 160p. 1997. 29.95 (*1-55750-121-1*) Naval Inst Pr.

Center for the Study of Democratic Institutions St. Challenges to Democracy: The Next Ten Years. Reed, Edward, ed. LC 78-156709. (Essay Index Reprint Ser.). 1977. reprint ed. 20.95 (*0-8369-2293-X*) Ayer.

— Natural Law & Modern Society. LC 73-156626. (Essay Index Reprint Ser.). 1977. reprint ed. 19.95 (*0-8369-2388-X*) Ayer.

Center for the Study of Law & Politics Staff. Energy, Efficiency & Production: Building Sustainable Communities, an Environmental Guide for Local Government. 258p. 1991. 40.00 (*1-880386-06-2*) Ctr Study Law.

— Open Space, Preservation & Acquisition: Building Sustainable Communities, an Environmental Guide for Local Government. 162p. 1991. 40.00 (*1-880386-05-4*) Ctr Study Law.

— Solid Waste, Reduction, Reuse & Recycling: Building Sustainable Communities, an Environmental Guide for Local Government. 144p. 1991. 40.00 (*1-880386-02-X*) Ctr Study Law.

— Toxics, Management & Reduction: Building Sustainable Communities, an Environmental Guide for Local Government. 182p. 1991. 40.00 (*1-880386-03-8*) Ctr Study Law.

— Transportation, Efficiency & Alternatives: Building Sustainable Communities, an Environmental Guide for Local Government. 92p. 1991. 40.00 (*1-880386-04-6*) Ctr Study Law.

C

— Urban Forestry: Building Sustainable Communities, an Environmental Guide for Local Government. 112p. 1991. 40.00 (*1-880386-07-0*) Ctr Study Law.

— Water, Conservation & Reclamation: Building Sustainable Communities, an Environmental Guide for Local Government. 135p. 1990. 40.00 (*1-880386-01-1*) Ctr Study Law.

Center for the Study of Pharmacy & Therapeutics for the Elderly Staff, et al. Prescription Drugs for People over 50. LC 98-119623. 576p. 1997. write for info. (*0-7853-2465-8*) Pubns Intl Ltd.

***Center for the Study of Services Checkbook Magazine Staff.** Guide to Top Doctors. 320p. 2000. pap. 19.95 (*1-888124-06-7*) Ctr Study Serv.

Center for Transnational Law Staff, jt. auth. see Berger, Klaus P.

Center for Waste Reduction & American Institute fo, jt. auth. see CWRT Staff.

***Center Foundation Staff.** Foundation Directory Supplement. 2000. pap. 125.00 (*0-87954-896-7*) Foundation Ctr.

— Grants for Film Media & Commun. 1999. pap. text 75.00 (*0-87954-834-7*) Foundation Ctr.

Center Foundation Staff. Guide to U.S. Foundations: Their Trustees, Officers, & Donors 2 Vols., 1999 Edition, 2 Vols. 4235p. 1999. pap. text 215.00 (*0-87954-872-X*) Foundation Ctr.

Center of Learning Network Staff. Sacraments: Living Our Faith: Parish Edition. (Discipleship Ser.). 82p. (YA). (gr. 9-12). 1997. teacher ed., spiral bd. 12.95 (*1-56077-539-4*) Ctr Learning.

Center of Military History Staff. The War Against Germany: Europe & Adjacent Areas. LC 93-34602. (Association of the U. S. Army Book Ser.). (Illus.). 464p. 1994. 30.00 (*0-02-881093-7*) Brasseys.

— The War Against Germany: Europe & Adjacent Areas. (World War II Commemorative, Association of the U. S. Army Book Ser.). (Illus.). 464p. 1999. pap. 27.95 (*1-57488-101-9*) Brasseys.

— The War Against Japan: Pictorial Record. (World War II Commemorative, Association of the U. S. Army Book Ser.). (Illus.). 496p. 1994. 30.00 (*0-02-881101-1*) Brasseys.

— The War Against Japan: Pictorial Record. LC 98-154054. (World War II Commemorative, Association of the U. S. Army Book Ser.). (Illus.). 496p. 1998. pap. 27.95 (*1-57488-102-7*) Brasseys.

— The War in the Mediterranean: A WWII Pictorial History. LC 97-23500. (World War II Commemorative, Association of the U. S. Army Book Ser.). Orig. Title: The War Against Germany & Italy. (Illus.). 480p. 1998. 32.95 (*1-57488-130-2*) Brasseys.

***Center of Strategic Emirates Staff.** Air/missile Defense, Counterproliferation & Security Policy Planning: Implications for Collabo. 1999. 55.00 (*1-86064-491-0*, Pub. by I B T) St Martin.

Center on Education & Training for Employment Staf. Job Placement Assistance Kit (Job-Pak) 1989. 10.00 (*0-317-03899-0*, SN59A) Ctr Educ Trng Employ.

— Strengthening Work-Related Education & Training Through Improved Guidance Programs in the 1990s. 1989. 3.00 (*0-317-04617-9*, SN58) Ctr Educ Trng Employ.

Center Women Staff. A Celebration Everyday: Traditional Jewish & Contemporary American Cooking. LC 97-69784. 288p. 1997. 18.95 (*0-9660382-0-7*) Jewish Comun Ctr.

Centers for Disease Control & Prevention Staff & U. S. Department of Health & Human Services Editor. 1998 Guidelines for Treatment of Sexually Transmitted Diseases. (C). 1998. pap. 7.95 (*1-883205-45-X*) Intl Med Pub.

Centers for Disease Control & Prevention Staff, jt. auth. see U. S. Department of Health & Human Services Editor.

***Centers for Disease Control Staff, ed.** Health Information for International Travel 1999-2000. (Illus.). 2000. pap. text 14.95 (*1-883205-76-X*) Intl Med Pub.

***CenterWatch Editorial Staff.** The Directory of Drugs in Clinical Trials. (Focus on Heart Disease Ser.). 150p. 1999. pap. 31.99 (*0-9673029-3-5*) CenterWatch.

***Centi, G., et al.** Selective Oxidation by Heterogeneous Catalysis. LC 99-55323. (Fundamental & Applied Catalysis Ser.). 2000. write for info. (*0-306-46265-6*, Kluwer Plenum) Kluwer Academic.

***Centilli, Barbara.** Finding Our Father: In the Gospels & Catholic Catechism. (Illus.). 84p. 2000. pap. 6.95 (*1-891903-12-8*) St Andrew Prodns.

Centilli, Barbara. The Prodigal Children. 104p. 1998. pap. 4.95 (*1-891903-11-X*) St Andrew Prodns.

— Seeing with the Eyes of the Soul Vol. 2: Revelation from God the Father to Barbara Centilli. 3 vols. (Illus.). 124p. 1999. pap. 3.00 (*1-891903-10-1*) St Andrew Prodns.

***Centilli, Barbara.** Seeing with the Eyes of the Soul Vol. 3: Revelations from God the Father to Barbara Centilli. (Illus.). 128p. 2000. pap. 3.00 (*1-891903-20-9*) St Andrew Prodns.

Centinela Hospital Medical Center Staff, ed. Exercise Guide to Better Golf: A Scientifically Based Exercise Program for Golfers! LC 94-2257. (Illus.). 92p. (Orig.). 1994. 9.95 (*0-936691-06-9*) Champ Pr Inglewood.

***Centis, Devin.** Thy Brother's Reaper. 450p. 2000. pap. 24.99 (*0-9674196-9-7*, 010) Renaissance Alliance.

***Centlives, P.** Chroniques Afghanes 1965-1993. (Ordres Sociaux Ser). (FRE.). 272p. 1998. pap. text 32.00 (*90-5709-006-6*, edit archives) Gordon & Breach.

Centlivre, Susanna. A Bold Stroke for a Wife. Stathas, Thalia, ed. LC 67-12640. (Regents Restoration Drama Ser.: No. BB267). 138p. reprint ed. pap. 42.80 (*0-8357-7335-3*, 203160700075) Bks Demand.

— A Bold Stroke for a Wife. 2nd ed. Copeland, Nancy, ed. (Broadview Literary Texts Ser.). 195p. 1998. pap. 12.95 (*1-55111-021-0*) Broadview Pr.

— Dramatic Works of the Celebrated Mrs. Centlivre, 3 vols. LC 69-20425. reprint ed. 230.00 (*0-404-01480-1*) AMS Pr.

Centner, Jacques, et al. Atlas of Immuno-Allergology: An Illustrated Primer for Health Care Professionals. 3rd ed. De Weck, Christine, tr. from FRE. LC 95-9994.Tr. of Atlas d'Immuno-Allergologie. (Illus.). 200p. 1995. text 54.00 (*0-88937-142-3*); text 54.00 (*0-88937-143-1*); text 54.00 (*0-88937-144-X*); text 54.00 (*0-88937-145-8*) Hogrefe & Huber Pubs.

***Cento Bull, Anna, et al.** Feminisms & Women's Movements in Contemporary Europe. LC 00-33305. 2000. write for info. (*0-312-23522-4*) St Martin.

Centofante, Jane, ed. see Coryell, Deborah Morris.

Centola, Grace M. & Ginsburg, Kenneth, eds. Evaluation & Treatment of the Infertile Male. (Illus.). 335p. (C). 1996. text 85.00 (*0-521-45059-4*) Cambridge U Pr.

Centola, Ron. Playing Bar Chords. Stang, Aaron, ed. 68p. (Orig.). (C). 1985. pap. text 10.00 (*0-7692-1278-6*, EL02803) Wrner Bros.

Centola, Steven R., ed. The Achievement of Arthur Miller: New Essays. LC 95-34103. 1995. write for info. (*0-935061-75-4*) Contemp Res.

Centola, Steven R., ed. see Miller, Arthur.

Centolella, Thomas. Lights & Mysteries. LC 95-32542. 84p. 1995. pap. 12.00 (*1-55659-106-3*) Copper Canyon.

— Terra Firma. LC 89-81835. (National Poetry Ser.). 80p. (Orig.). 1990. pap. 10.00 (*1-55659-030-X*) Copper Canyon.

Centore, F. F. Being & Becoming: A Critique of Post-Modernism, 44. LC 90-45070. 304p. 1991. 65.00 (*0-313-27616-1*, CBM, Greenwood Pr) Greenwood.

— Confusions & Clarifications: An Introduction to Philosophy for the Twenty-First Century. LC 97-41756. 288p. 1997. pap. 24.50 (*0-7618-0968-6*) U Pr of Amer.

— Persons: A Comparative Account of the Six Possible Theories, 13. LC 78-74653. (Contributions in Philosophy Ser.: No. 13). 329p. 1979. 65.00 (*0-313-20817-4*, CPE/, Greenwood Pr) Greenwood.

***Centore, F. F.** Two Views of Virtue: Absolute Relativism & Relative Absolutism, 76. LC 99-56461. (Contributions in Political Science Ser.: Vol. 76). 216p. 2000. 65.00 (*0-313-31412-8*, Greenwood Pr) Greenwood.

Centra, John A. Determining Faculty Effectiveness. LC 79-88776. 224p. reprint ed. pap. 69.50 (*0-7837-6508-8*, 204562000007) Bks Demand.

— Reflective Faculty Evaluation: Enhancing Teaching & Determining Faculty Effectiveness. LC 93-19504. (Higher Education Ser.). 266p. 1993. text 35.45 (*1-55542-579-8*) Jossey-Bass.

Centra, John A., jt. auth. see Baez, Benjamin.

Central American Refugees & Children Breaking the. Stories from Central American Refugees & from Children Breaking the Cycle of Violence. (Common Ground Ser.: Vol. 1). (Illus.). 44p. (Orig.). 1985. pap. 5.00 (*1-884478-00-X*) Common Grnd.

Central Book Supply Inc Staff. Environmental Laws in the Philippines. LC 98-947605. vi, 306 p. 1998. write for info. (*971-16-0361-6*) New Day Pub.

Central Conference of American Rabbis Staff, jt. ed. see Commission on Synagogue Affiliation of Union of Am.

Central Conference of American Rabbis Staff, tr. see Stern, Chaim.

Central Electric Railfans' Association Staff. Indiana Railroad System: Bulletin No. 91. (Illus.). 72p. 1975. pap. 7.00 (*0-915348-92-6*) Central Electric.

Central Electricity Generating Board Staff. Modern Power Station Practice, 8 vols. Incl. Nuclear Power Generation., 8 vols. 2nd ed. 1971. 480.00 (*0-08-016436-6*); Vol. 1. Planning & Layout. 1971. 76.00 (*0-08-006454-X*); Vol. 2. Mechanical (Boilers Fuel & Ash-Handling Plant) 1971. 68.00 (*0-08-016060-3*); Vol. 3. Mechanical (Turbines & Auxiliary Equipment) 1971. 58.00 (*0-08-006606-2*); Vol. 4. Electrical (Generator & Electrical Plant) 1971. 76.00 (*0-08-016061-1*); Vol. 5. Chemistry & Metallurgy. 1971. 76.00 (*0-08-015568-5*); Vol. 6. Instrumentation Controls & Testing. 1971. 90.00 (*0-08-006872-3*); Vol. 7. Operation & Efficiency. 1971. 90.00 (*0-08-016062-X*); Vol. 8. Nuclear Power Generation. 1971. 58.00 (*0-08-006871-5*); 1971. write for info. (*0-318-55182-9*) Elsevier.

Central Instruc Media Inst. Staff. Welder Trade Practicals. 1995. write for info. (*81-224-0737-4*, Pub. by Wiley Estrn) Franklin.

Central Intelligence Agency Staff. CIA World Factbook, 1994. 1995. pap. 29.00 (*0-614-30786-4*, CWOR94) Claitors.

Central Intelligence Agency Staff. The Laotian National Liberation Government Organization. 72p. 1964. reprint ed. text 15.00 (*0-923135-39-1*) Dalley Bk Service.

— Selected Intelligence Monographs. v, 101p. 2000. pap. 22.80 (*0-89412-287-8*, I-20) Aegean Park Pr.

— The World Factbook: 2000 Edition. 2000. 29.95 (*1-57488-266-X*) Brasseys.

Central Intelligence Agency Staff. World Factbook, '95. 1995. pap. 40.00 (*0-614-30823-2*, CWDR95) Claitors.

— World Factbook, '96. 1997. pap. 45.00 (*1-57980-009-2*, CWOR96) Claitors.

***Central ME Power Co. Staff.** The Light from the River: Central Maine Power Company's First Century of Service, 1899-1999. unabridged ed. Irwin, Clark, ed. (Illus.). 80p. 1999. pap. 15.00 (*0-9665645-1-0*) Ctrl ME Power.

Central Missouri State University Staff. Academic Libraries & Research: Mastering the Maze. 2nd ed. LC 97-214678. 192p. (C). 1997. per. 26.95 (*0-7872-3732-9*) Kendall-Hunt.

Central Office of Info. The Aerospace Industry. (Aspects of Britain Ser.). (Illus.). 111p. 1997. pap. 10.00 (*0-11-701727-2*, HM17272, Pub. by Statnry Office) Bernan Associates.

— The Arts. (Aspects of Britain Ser.). (Illus.). 76p. 1997. pap. 9.00 (*0-11-701742-6*, HM17426, Pub. by Statnry Office) Bernan Associates.

— Britain & Africa: Aspects of Britain. (Aspects of Britain Ser.). (Illus.). 92p. 1997. pap. 10.00 (*0-11-701731-0*, HM17310, Pub. by Statnry Office) Bernan Associates.

— Britain & Development Aid. (Aspects of Britain Ser.). (Illus.). 82p. 1995. pap. 13.00 (*0-11-701928-3*, HM19283, Pub. by Statnry Office) Bernan Associates.

— Britain & Hong Kong: Aspects of Britain. (Aspects of Britain Ser.). (Illus.). 88p. 1997. pap. 12.00 (*0-11-701697-7*, HM16977, Pub. by Statnry Office) Bernan Associates.

— Britain & the Commonwealth: Aspects of Britain. LC 93-117238. (Aspects of Britain Ser.). (Illus.). 100p. 1997. pap. 12.00 (*0-11-701675-6*, HM16756, Pub. by Statnry Office) Bernan Associates.

— Britain & the Falkland Islands. (Aspects of Britain Ser.). (Illus.). 1997. pap. 8.95 (*0-11-701757-4*, Pub. by Statnry Office) Bernan Associates.

— Britain & the Gulf Crisis. (Aspects of Britain Ser.). (Illus.). 85p. 1997. pap. 10.00 (*0-11-701734-5*, HM17345, Pub. by Statnry Office) Bernan Associates.

— Britain & the United Nations. LC 95-183836. (Aspects of Britain Ser.). (Illus.). 75p. 1995. pap. 12.00 (*0-11-701866-X*, HM1866X, Pub. by Statnry Office) Bernan Associates.

— Britain, NATO & European Security. (Aspects of Britain Ser.). (Illus.). 83p. 1997. pap. 12.00 (*0-11-701781-7*, HM17817, Pub. by Statnry Office) Bernan Associates.

— Britain's Overseas Trade. LC 96-201102. (Aspects of Britain Ser.). (Illus.). 88p. 1997. pap. 12.00 (*0-11-701826-0*, HM18260, Pub. by Statnry Office) Bernan Associates.

— British System of Government. 3rd ed. LC 97-178141. (Aspects of Britain Ser.). (Illus.). 151p. 1997. pap. 15.00 (*0-11-702042-7*, HM020427, Pub. by Statnry Office) Bernan Associates.

— Broadcasting. (Aspects of Britain Ser.). (Illus.). 91p. 1997. pap. 9.00 (*0-11-701761-2*, HM17612, Pub. by Statnry Office) Bernan Associates.

— Civil Service. LC 95-189754. (Aspects of Britain Ser.). (Illus.). 152p. 1997. pap. 12.00 (*0-11-701856-2*, Pub. by Statnry Office) Bernan Associates.

— Conservation. (Aspects of Britain Ser.). (Illus.). 90p. 1997. pap. 10.00 (*0-11-701726-4*, HM17264, Pub. by Statnry Office) Bernan Associates.

— Criminal Justice. 2nd ed. LC 96-209266. (Aspects of Britain Ser.). (Illus.). 102p. 1997. pap. 11.95 (*0-11-701981-X*, Pub. by Statnry Office) Bernan Associates.

— Education. 2nd ed. (Aspects of Britain Ser.). (Illus.). 103p. 1996. pap. 12.00 (*0-11-702025-7*, HM20257, Pub. by Statnry Office) Bernan Associates.

— Education after 16. (Aspects of Britain Ser.). (Illus.). 67p. 1995. pap. 12.00 (*0-11-701868-6*, HM18686, Pub. by Statnry Office) Bernan Associates.

— Education Reforms in School. (Aspects of Britain Ser.). (Illus.). 66p. 1994. pap. 12.00 (*0-11-701789-2*, HM17892, Pub. by Statnry Office) Bernan Associates.

— Employment. (Aspects of Britain Ser.). (Illus.). 90p. 1997. pap. 12.00 (*0-11-701788-4*, HM17884, Pub. by Statnry Office) Bernan Associates.

— Energy & Natural Resources. (Aspects of Britain Ser.). (Illus.). 70p. 1997. pap. 12.00 (*0-11-701700-0*, HM17000, Pub. by Statnry Office) Bernan Associates.

— European Union. LC 95-129480. (Aspects of Britain Ser.). (Illus.). 95p. 1994. pap. 12.00 (*0-11-701794-9*, HM17949, Pub. by Statnry Office) Bernan Associates.

— Financial Services. (Aspects of Britain Ser.). (Illus.). 94p. 1995. pap. 12.00 (*0-11-701874-0*, HM18740, Pub. by Statnry Office) Bernan Associates.

— Functions of Government Departments. (Aspects of Britain Ser.). (Illus.). 1997. pap. 10.00 (*0-11-701766-3*, Pub. by Statnry Office) Bernan Associates.

— Government & Industry. LC 96-201623. (Aspects of Britain Ser.). (Illus.). 115p. 1995. pap. 13.00 (*0-11-701881-3*, HM18813, Pub. by Statnry Office) Bernan Associates.

— Government & the Individual: The Citizen's Means of Redress. LC 96-201472. (Aspects of Britain Ser.). (Illus.). 110p. 1996. pap. 12.00 (*0-11-701595-4*, HM15954, Pub. by Statnry Office) Bernan Associates.

— Honours & Titles: Aspects of Britain. 2nd ed. (Aspects of Britain Ser.). (Illus.). 159p. 1996. pap. 12.00 (*0-11-702027-3*, HM020273, Pub. by Statnry Office) Balogh.

— Housing. (Aspects of Britain Ser.). (Illus.). 84p. 1997. pap. 10.00 (*0-11-701729-9*, HM17299, Pub. by Statnry Office) Bernan Associates.

— Human Rights. 2nd ed. LC 96-209269. (Aspects of Britain Ser.). (Illus.). 174p. 1996. pap. 12.00 (*0-11-701593-8*, HM15938, Pub. by Statnry Office) Bernan Associates.

— Immigration & Nationality. (Aspects of Britain Ser.). (Illus.). 64p. 1997. pap. 9.00 (*0-11-701741-8*, HM17418, Pub. by Statnry Office) Bernan Associates.

— Northern Ireland. 2nd ed. LC 96-201614. (Aspects of Britain Ser.). (Illus.). 131p. 1997. pap. 12.95 (*0-11-702009-5*, Pub. by Statnry Office) Bernan Associates.

— Organisation of Political Parties. 2nd ed. LC 95-140361. (Aspects of Britain Ser.). (Illus.). 66p. 1997. pap. 11.95 (*0-11-701838-4*, HM18384, Pub. by Statnry Office) Bernan Associates.

— Parliament. 3rd ed. (Aspects of Britain Ser.). (Illus.). 171p. 1996. pap. 15.00 (*0-11-702046-X*, HM02046X, Pub. by Statnry Office) Bernan Associates.

— Parliamentary Elections. 2nd ed. LC 95-204049. (Aspects of Britain Ser.). (Illus.). 86p. 1995. pap. 11.95 (*0-11-701939-9*, HM19399, Pub. by Statnry Office) Bernan Associates.

— Planning. (Aspects of Britain Ser.). (Illus.). 1997. pap. 10.00 (*0-11-701723-X*, Pub. by Statnry Office) Bernan Associates.

— Pollution. (Aspects of Britain Ser.). (Illus.). 1997. pap. 10.00 (*0-11-701777-9*, Pub. by Statnry Office) Bernan Associates.

— Population. LC 96-162400. (Aspects of Britain Ser.). (Illus.). 105p. 1995. pap. 12.00 (*0-11-702007-9*, Pub. by Statnry Office) Bernan Associates.

— Pressure Groups. LC 95-189767. (Aspects of Britain Ser.). (Illus.). 84p. 1997. pap. 12.00 (*0-11-701849-X*, HM1849X, Pub. by Statnry Office) Bernan Associates.

— Religion: Aspects of Britain. (Aspects of Britain Ser.). (Illus.). 84p. 1997. pap. 12.00 (*0-11-701704-3*, HM17043, Pub. by Statnry Office) Bernan Associates.

— Science & Technology. (Aspects of Britain Ser.). (Illus.). 115p. 1995. pap. 12.00 (*0-11-701947-X*, Pub. by Statnry Office) Bernan Associates.

— Social Welfare. 2nd ed. LC 96-201642. (Aspects of Britain Ser.). (Illus.). 138p. 1997. pap. 13.00 (*0-11-701931-3*, Pub. by Statnry Office) Bernan Associates.

— Sport & Leisure. (Aspects of Britain Ser.). (Illus.). 115p. 1997. pap. 12.00 (*0-11-701740-X*, HM1740X, Pub. by Statnry Office) Bernan Associates.

— Telecommunications. LC 94-233690. (Aspects of Britain Ser.). (Illus.). 90p. 1994. pap. 12.00 (*0-11-701784-1*, Pub. by Statnry Office) Bernan Associates.

— Transport & Communications: Aspects of Britain. (Aspects of Britain Ser.). (Illus.). 88p. 1997. pap. 12.95 (*0-11-701698-5*, HM16985, Pub. by Statnry Office) Bernan Associates.

— Urban Regeneration. LC 97-121021. (Aspects of Britain Ser.). (Illus.). 85p. 1995. pap. 12.00 (*0-11-701927-5*, HM19275, Pub. by Statnry Office) Bernan Associates.

— Wales. (Aspects of Britain Ser.). (Illus.). 88p. 1997. pap. 9.95 (*0-11-701754-X*, HM1754X, Pub. by Statnry Office) Bernan Associates.

— Women in Britain. 2nd ed. LC 96-212602. (Aspects of Britain Ser.). (Illus.). 131p. 1996. pap. 11.95 (*0-11-701982-8*, HM19828, Pub. by Statnry Office) Bernan Associates.

Central Office of Information Staff. When Peace Broke Out: Britain, 1945. LC 98-146608. (Illus.). 148p. 1994. pap. 19.95 (*0-11-701860-0*, Pub. by Statnry Office) Balogh.

Central Society Of Education London Staff. Papers, First, Second & Third Series, 3 Vols. LC 74-5890. (Social History of Education Series 1). 1969. reprint ed. 150.00 (*0-678-08456-4*) Kelley.

Central State University Ohio Editors. Hallie Q. Brown Memorial Library, Index to Periodical Articles by & about Blacks, 1977. 1978. 185.00 (*0-8161-0256-2*, G K Hall & Co) Mac Lib Ref.

— Index to Periodical Articles by & About Blacks, Annual, 1978. 1979. 190.00 (*0-8161-0323-2*, G K Hall & Co) Mac Lib Ref.

— Index to Periodical Articles by & about Negroes, Annual, 1972. 826p. 1978. 175.00 (*0-8161-1106-5*, G K Hall & Co) Mac Lib Ref.

— Index to Periodical Articles by & about Negroes, Decennial Cumulation, 1950-1959. 1970. 100.00 (*0-8161-0503-0*, G K Hall & Co) Mac Lib Ref.

— Index to Periodical Articles by & about Negroes, 1971. 1977. 215.00 (*0-8161-0869-2*, G K Hall & Co) Mac Lib Ref.

Central State University Ohio Editors, et al, compiled by. Index to Periodical Articles by & about Blacks: 1983. (Library Reference Ser.). 300p. 1986. 210.00 (*0-8161-0442-5*, G K Hall & Co) Mac Lib Ref.

Central State University Ohio Editors & Hallie Q. Brown Memorial Library Staff, eds. Index to Black Periodicals: 1984. 200p. 1988. 115.00 (*0-8161-0454-9*, Hall Reference) Macmillan.

Central Statistical Office Staff. United Kingdom Balance of Payments: The Pink Book, 1996. 80p. 1996. pap. 60.00 (*0-11-620776-0*, HM07760, Pub. by Statnry Office) Bernan Associates.

Centre. The Revelation of Ramala. (Ramala Trilogy Ser.). 188p. 1978. pap. 17.95 (*0-85978-035-X*, Pub. by C W Daniel) Natl Bk Netwk.

— Vision of Ramala. (Ramala Trilogy Ser.). 191p. 1991. pap. 17.95 (*0-85207-231-7*, Pub. by C W Daniel) Natl Bk Netwk.

— Wisdom of Ramala. (Ramala Trilogy Ser.). 191p. 1986. pap. 15.95 (*0-85435-185-X*, Pub. by C W Daniel) Natl Bk Netwk.

Centre County Historical Society Staff, ed. The Notable Trees of Centre County. (Illus.). 40p. 1992. pap. 8.00 (*1-887315-06-3*) Centre Cty Hist Soc.

Centre Culturel Americain, Paris Staff. Annees Vingt: Les Ecrivains Americains a Paris et Leurs Amis, 1920-1930. (FRE., Illus.). 1959. pap. 9.50 (*0-910664-09-9*) Gotham.

Centre de Documentation de l'Armement Staff. Lexique Thematique des Descripteurs et Identificateurs. (FRE.). 151p. 1976. pap. 35.00 (*0-8288-5740-7*, M6371) Fr & Eur.

Centre de Documentation de l'Armement Staff, ed. Lexique des Mots-Cles, Descripteurs et Identificateurs, Francais et Anglais, a Utiliser Pour la Recherche Documentaire, 3 vols., Set. (ENG & FRE.). 2001p. 1976. pap. 95.00 (*0-8288-5737-7*, M6360) Fr & Eur.

Centre de Recherche Pour un Tresor de la Langue Fr. Tresor de la Francaise: Dictionnaire du XIXe et du XXe Siecles (1789-1960), 4 vols. 175.00 (*0-685-36650-2*) Fr & Eur.

An Asterisk (*) at the beginning of an entry indicates that the title is appearing for the first time.

Centre de Recherche Pour un Tresor de la Langue Fr, ed. Dictionnaire des Frequences, Vocabulaire Litteraire des 19 et 20 Siecles, 4 vols. (FRE.). 2284p. 1976. pap. 110.00 (*0-8288-5641-9*, M6620) Fr & Eur.

Centre de Recherches Metallurgiques Staff. Stahleisen-Woerterbuch: German-French, French-German. 3rd ed. (FRE & GER.). 555p. 1991. 75.00 (*0-7859-7101-7*) Fr & Eur.

— Stahleisen Woerterbuch: German-Spanish, Spanish-German. 3rd ed. (GER & SPA.). 569p. 1991. 75.00 (*0-7859-6945-4*) Fr & Eur.

Centre de Recherches pour le Developpement Interna, contrib. by. Un Brevet pour la Vie: La Propriete Intellectuelle et Ses Effets sur le Commerce, la Biodiversite et le Monde Rural. (FRE., Illus.). xxvii, 136p. 1994. pap. 20.00 (*0-88936-734-5*, Pub. by IDRC Bks) Stylus Pub VA.

Centre de Terminologie de Bruxelles Staff. Elsevier's Dictionary of Office Automation. (DUT, ENG, FRE & GER.). 484p. 1991. 174.00 (*0-444-88065-8*) Elsevier.

— Elsevier's Dictionary of Office Automation in English, French, German & Dutch. (DUT, ENG, FRE & GER.). 462p. 1991. 250.00 (*0-8288-9227-X*) Fr & Eur.

Centre de Traduction & de Documentation Juridiques. Lexique des Lois & des Reglements de l'Ontario. LC 89-90449. (FRE.). 976p. 1989. reprint ed. pap. 200.00 (*0-608-01996-8*, 206265200003) Bks Demand.

***Centre d'Etude de Recherche de Droit International et de Relations Internationales Staff, ed.** Centre d'Etude et de Recherche de Droit International et de Relations Internationales 1998 (Centre for Studies & Research in International Law & International Relations 1998) Vol. 12: Incidences Juridiques des Telecommunicaitons Globales (Legal Implications of Global Telecommunications) 116p. 1999. pap. text 35.00 (*90-411-1241-3*) Kluwer Law Intl.

Centre d'Etude et de Recherche de Droit Internatio. Centre for Studies & Research in International Law & International Relations, 1992, Vol. CERD 9.Tr. of Centre d' Etude et Recherche de Droit International et de Relations. 1997. 35.00 (*90-411-0311-2*) Kluwer Law Intl.

Centre d'Etude et de Recherche de Droit Internatio, ed. Centre d'Etude et de Recherche de Droit International et de Relations Internationales 1987. (C). 1988. pap. text 35.00 (*90-247-3691-9*) Kluwer Academic.

— Transfrontier Pollution & International Law. 1986. pap. text 35.00 (*90-247-3394-4*) Kluwer Academic.

Centre d'Etude et de Recherched de Droit Internati, ed. State Succession: Codification Tested Against the Facts. LC 98-118039. (Center Studies Research, 1996 VIO Ser.). 180p. 1998. text 35.00 (*90-411-0530-1*) Kluwer Law Intl.

Centre d'Etude et de Recherchede Droit Internation, ed. Centre for Studies & Research in International Law & International Relations, 1992. Internationales de l'Academie de Droit Internation, tr.Tr. of Centre d' Etude et de Recherche de Droit International et de Relations Internationales, 1992. 108p. (C). 1993. pap. text 35.00 (*0-7923-2249-5*) Kluwer Academic.

Centre d'Etudes Superieures de la Renaissance Univ. Emotion in the Theatre (L'Emotion au Theatre) Vol. 3: Table Ronde V. LC 95-167635. (THETA Ser.: Vol. 3). (FRE.). 212p. 1996. 35.95 (*3-906754-49-9*, Pub. by P Lang) P Lang Pubng.

— Narrative & Drama (Le Narratif et le Dramatique) Vol. 2: Table Ronde IV. LC 95-167635. (THETA Ser.: Vol. 2). (FRE.). 180p. 1995. 31.95 (*3-906754-30-8*, Pub. by P Lang) P Lang Pubng.

— The Problematics of Text & Character (Le Texte et le Personnage en Question(s)) Vol. 1. LC 95-167635. (THETA Ser.: Vol. 1). (FRE.). 286p. 1994. 42.95 (*3-906752-57-7*, Pub. by P Lang) P Lang Pubng.

Centre d'Etudes Superieures de la Renaissance Universite Francois Rabelais, Tours Staff, ed. Tudor Theatre. (THETA: Vol. 4). (Illus.). xxi, 277p. 1998. pap. 42.95 (*3-906760-02-2*) P Lang Pubng.

***Centre d'Etudes Superieures de la Renaissance Universite Francois Rabelais, Tours Staff, ed.** Tudor Theatre: Allegory in the Theatre/L'Allegorie au Theatre Actes de la Table Ronde VII. (THETA: Vol. 5). 278p. 2000. pap. text 44.95 (*3-906760-08-1*) P Lang Pubng.

Centre for Civil Engineering Research & Codes Staf. Structural Behaviour of Concrete with Coarse Lightweight Aggregates. LC 99-227199. (CUR Report Ser.: No. 173). (Illus.). 76p. (C). 1995. text 110.00 (*90-5410-625-5*, Pub. by A A Balkema) Ashgate Pub Co.

Centre for Co-Operation with Economies in Transiti, jt. auth. see OECD Staff.

***Centre for Construction Ecology at BSRIA Staff.** Environmentally Friendly Cooling Products. 86p. 1998. pap. 160.00 (*0-86022-508-9*, Pub. by Build Servs Info Assn) St Mut.

— Environmentally Friendly Heating Products. 1998. pap. 160.00 (*0-86022-509-7*, Pub. by Build Servs Info Assn) St Mut.

— Environmentally Friendly Lighting Products. 1998. pap. 160.00 (*0-86022-510-0*, Pub. by Build Servs Info Assn) St Mut.

— Environmentally Friendly Water Systems. 73p. 1998. pap. 160.00 (*0-86022-511-9*, Pub. by Build Servs Info Assn) St Mut.

Centre for Defence Studies. Brassey's Defence Yearbook 1993. 1993. 64.00 (*1-85753-092-6*, Pub. by Brasseys) Brasseys.

Centre for Defence Studies Staff. Brassey's Defence Yearbook 1994. 400p. 1994. 64.00 (*1-85753-033-0*, Pub. by Brasseys) Brasseys.

— Brassey's Defence Yearbook 1995. Clarke, Michael, ed. 350p. 1995. 55.00 (*1-85753-131-0*, Pub. by Brasseys) Brasseys.

Centre for Development of Instructional Technology. Indian Social & Economic Development 1990: An Index to Literature. (Indian Social Economic Development Ser.: No. 4). (Illus.). 220p. 1991. text 27.50 (*0-8039-9676-4*) Sage.

Centre for Disarmament Affairs Staff. The United Nations Disarmament Yearbook, 1996. 367p. 1997. pap. 50.00 (*92-1-142222-1*, JX1901) UN.

Centre for European Economic Research Staff, ed. Environmental & Resource Economics. write for info. (*0-614-20358-9*) Spr-Verlag.

***Centre for European Law Staff.** Democratic & Legal Problems in the European Community. (IUSEF Ser.: No. 12). 148p. (C). 1999. pap. 22.00 (*82-00-03954-4*, Pub. by Scand Univ Pr) IBD Ltd.

— State & Nation: Current Legal & Political Problems Before the 1996 Intergovernment. 83p. (C). 1995. pap. 16.00 (*82-00-22682-4*, Pub. by Scand Univ Pr) IBD Ltd.

Centre for European Policy Studies Staff. The Annual Review of European Community Affairs, 1990. Ludlow, Peter, ed. 348p. 1991. 59.95 (*0-08-040968-7*, Pub. by Brasseys) Brasseys.

— The Annual Review of European Community Affairs, 1991, Vol. 3. 400p. 1992. 59.95 (*1-85753-085-3*, Pub. by Brasseys) Brasseys.

— Setting European Community Priorities, 1991-92. 154p. 1991. pap. 39.95 (*0-08-040969-5*, Pub. by Brasseys) Brasseys.

Centre for European Policy Studies Staff, ed. The Annual Review of European Community Affairs, 1991. 1992. pap. 59.95 (*0-08-041313-7*, Pergamon Pr) Elsevier.

Centre for Hazards & Risk Management, Loughborough, ed. Tolley's Office Health & Safety Handbook. 280p. 1995. pap. 105.00 (*0-85459-998-3*, Pub. by Tolley Pubng) St Mut.

Centre for Hazards & Risk Management Staff. Tolley's Office Health & Safety Handbook Second Edition. 2nd rev. ed. 1998. pap. write for info. (*1-86012-794-0*, Pub. by Tolley Pubng) St Mut.

Centre for Industrial Economics Staff, jt. auth. see Martin, Stephen.

***Centre for Public Law at the University of Cambridge Staff.** The Human Rights Act & the Criminal Justice & Regulatory Process. 224p. 1999. pap. 45.00 (*1-84113-050-8*) Hart Pub.

Centre for Study of Australia-Asia Relations Staff, compiled by. The Asia-Australia Survey, 1994. 300p. 1994. 79.95 (*0-7329-2795-1*, Pub. by Macmill Educ) Paul & Co Pubs.

Centre for the Independence of Judges & Lawyers Staff. CIJL Yearbook Vol. 4: The Media & Judiciary, December, 1995. LC 94-645018. 167p. Date not set. reprint ed. pap. 51.80 (*0-608-20623-7*, 206180300004) Bks Demand.

— The Independence of the Judiciary & the Legal Profession in English-Speaking Africa: A Report of Seminars Held in Lusaka from 10 to 14 November 1986 & in Banjul from 6 to 10 April 1987 Convened Jointly by the Centre for the Independence of Judges & Lawyers, African Bar Association, International Commission of Jurists. LC 92-194626. 185p. (Orig.). Date not set. reprint ed. pap. 57.40 (*0-608-20635-0*, 207207100003) Bks Demand.

Centre for Theology & Public Issues Staff. Capital: A Moral Instrument? 96p. (C). 1992. pap. 50.00 (*0-86153-149-3*, Pub. by St Andrew) St Mut.

— The End of Punishment: Christian Perspectives on the Crisis in Criminal Justices. 160p. (C). 1992. pap. 39.00 (*0-86153-145-0*, Pub. by St Andrew) St Mut.

Centre For Tomorrow Staff. Inclusive Approach & Business Success. 24p. 1997. pap. 43.95 (*0-566-08096-6*) Ashgate Pub Co.

***Centre for Women's Development Staff.** Shifting Sands: Women's Live & Globalization. 2000. 34.00 (*81-85604-09-6*, Pub. by Stree) S Asia.

Centre Informatique et Bible (Maredsous, Belgique). Dictionnaire Encyclopedique de la Bible. (FRE.). 1987. 295.00 (*0-7859-7909-3*, 2-503-59002-0) Fr & Eur.

Centre Informatique et Bible Staff. Petit Dictionnaire de la Bible. (FRE.). 949p. 1992. pap. 125.00 (*0-7859-7904-2*, 2503502466) Fr & Eur.

Centre International d' Etudes Liturgigue Staff. Altar & Sacrifice: Proceedings of the 3rd International Colleium on the Liturgy. 192p. 1998. pap. 22.95 (*1-901157-85-7*) St Augustines Pr.

Centre, Michael. In Search of God-the Solar Connection. LC 78-73706. (Illus.). (C). 1978. 9.95 (*0-932876-00-5*); pap. 5.95 (*0-932876-01-3*) Centre Ent.

Centre National d'Etudes Spatiales Staff. Dictionary of Astronautics Vol. 1: Terms & Definitions. 3rd ed. (ENG, GER, RUS & SPA.). 332p. 1992. 125.00 (*0-7859-4705-1*, F71240) Fr & Eur.

Centre Nautique de G. Dictionnaire de la Plaisance. (FRE.). 140p. 1993. pap. 36.95 (*0-7859-5574-7*, 2020197170) Fr & Eur.

Centrello, Gina, ed. see Pinsky, Laura, et al.

Centrello, Gina, ed. see Spock, Benjamin M. & Rothenberg, Michael B.

Centric Media, Inc. Staff. Centric Bicycle Link: The Ultimate Bicycle Source. Karp, Jack, ed. 600p. 1998. 12.99 (*0-9667679-1-8*) Orton Developmnt.

Centro de Estudios Cientificos de Santiago, Chile. The Black Hole, Twenty-Five Years After. Teitelboim, Claudio & Zanelli, Jorge, eds. LC 98-28357. 326p. 1998. 54.00 (*981-02-3341-8*) World Scientific Pub.

Centro de las Letras Staff. Diccionario de Autores: Quien es Quien an las Letras Espanolas. (SPA.). 288p. 1988. 55.00 (*0-7859-5979-3*, 8436804473) Fr & Eur.

Centro Espagnol de Logistica Staff, tr. Dicionario-7a Edicion.Tr. of APICS Dictonary. (POR.). 260p. (Orig.). 1994. pap. 11.50 (*1-55822-114-X*) Am Prod & Inventory.

Centro Estudios Estrategicos Staff. Entendiendo el TLC (Understanding NAFTA) (SPA.). 229p. 1994. pap. 9.99 (*968-16-4447-6*, Pub. by Fondo) Continental Bk.

Centro Internationale Mathematico Estivo Staff. Bifurcation Theory & Applications: Lectures Given at the Second Session of the Centro Internationale Mathematico Estivo Held at Montecatini, Italy, June 24-July 2, 1983. Salvadori, L., ed. (Lecture Notes in Mathematics Ser.: Vol. 1057). vii, 223p. 1984. 35.95 (*0-387-12931-6*) Spr-Verlag.

Centro Internazionale Matematico Estivo Staff, jt. auth. see Cockburn, B.

Centro Nuclear de Puerto Rico Staff. Simposio Sobre Energia Nuclear y el Desarrollo de Latinoamerica. 167p. 1969. pap. 3.00 (*0-8477-2304-6*) U of PR Pr.

***Centro Studi Industria Leggera Staff.** The Furniture Industry in China. LC 99-46661. (Illus.). 175p. 1999. pap. text 1000.00 (*0-921577-99-0*) AKTRIN.

Centro Studi Industria Leggera Staff. Furniture Industry in Russia. 2nd ed. (Illus.). 97p. 1998. spiral bd. 1000.00 (*0-921577-96-6*) AKTRIN.

— The Furniture Industry in Saudi Arabia, United Arab Emirates & Kuwait. LC 98-44417. 85p. 1998. spiral bd. 450.00 (*0-921577-86-9*) AKTRIN.

***Centro Studi Industria Leggera Staff.** The Furniture Industry in South East Asia, Korea & Taiwan. 2nd ed. LC 99-21006. (Illus.). 195p. 1998. spiral bd. 1000.00 (*0-921577-93-1*) AKTRIN.

Centro Studi Industria Leggera Staff. The U. S. Market for Upholstered Furniture. LC 99-33820. (Illus.). 164p. 1998. spiral bd. 1900.00 (*0-921577-95-8*) AKTRIN.

Centro Studi Industria Leggera Staff, jt. auth. see AKTRIN Furniture Information Center Staff.

Centro Studi Industria Leggera Staff, jt. auth. see Aktrin Research Institute Staff.

***Centro Studi Industrial Leggera Staff.** The Furniture Industry in the European Union. (Illus.). 258p. 1998. spiral bd. 1000.00 (*0-921577-90-7*) AKTRIN.

Centro Tecnico de la Sociedad Staff, ed. see Albertos, Jose L. & Suarez, Luisa S.

Centuori, Walter J., tr. see Jovine, Francesco.

***Century Architectural Co.** Late Victorian Houses & Cottages: Floor Plans & Illustrations for 40 House Designs. LC 98-43893. 1999. pap. text 7.95 (*0-486-40490-0*) Dover.

Century Association, New York Staff. Robert Henri & Five of His Pupils: Loan Exhibition of Paintings, April 5, to June 1, 1946. LC 74-160918. (Biography Index Reprint Ser.). 1977. reprint ed. 18.95 (*0-8369-8081-6*) Ayer.

Century, Douglas. Street Kingdom: Five Years Inside the Franklin Avenue Posse. LC 98-15083. 418p. 1999. 25.00 (*0-446-52266-X*, Pub. by Warner Bks) Little.

***Century, Douglas.** Street Kingdom: Five Years Inside the Franklin Avenue Posse. 432p. 2000. mass mkt. 14.95 (*0-446-67563-6*, Pub. by Warner Bks) Little.

Century, Douglas. Toni Morrison: Author. Huggins, Nathan I., ed. LC 93-31166. (Black Americans of Achievement Ser.). (Illus.). 124p. (YA). (gr. 5 up). 1994. pap. 8.95 (*0-7910-1906-3*); lib. bdg. 19.95 (*0-7910-1877-6*) Chelsea Hse.

***Century Foundation Staff.** Medicare Reform: Beyond the Basics: A Century Foundation Report. LC 99-88500. 2000. 10.95 (*0-87078-446-3*) Century Foundation.

Century Foundation Staff, jt. auth. see Citizens for Independent Courts Staff.

Century 21 Editors & Rejnis, Ruth. The Century 21 Guide to Buying a Second Home: For Vacation, Retirement, Investment & More! LC 97-41250. 208p. (Orig.). 1998. pap. 15.95 (*0-7931-2711-4*, 1940-0801, Real Estate Ed) Dearborn.

Century 21 Staff & Hogan, Patrick. The Century 21 Guide to Buying Your First Home. LC 96-52848. (Century 21 Guide to Ser.). 208p. 1997. pap. 14.95 (*0-7931-2424-7*, 1940-0701) Dearborn.

Cenzer, Pamela S. & Gozzi, Cynchia I., eds. Evaluating Acquisitions & Collection Management. LC 91-15299. (Acquisitions Librarian Ser.: Vol. 6). 162p. 1991. lib. bdg. 49.95 (*1-56024-160-8*) Haworth Pr.

CEO Solutions Staff, ed. see Reilly, Mary A.

Ceodick, Denis. Zero Leaks. Geshwiler, Mildred, ed. (Illus.). 234p. 1997. pap. text 48.00 (*1-883413-51-6*, 90394) Am Heat Ref & Air Eng.

Ceolin, David. The Idea Guide: The Step-by-Step Guide for Planning & Starting Your Own Business. McGee, Tom, ed. 120p. 1997. pap. text. write for info. (*0-9699498-0-4*) Envsn Commns.

CEP Inc., Staff. Corel Quattro Pro 7.0 for Windows 95: Quicktorial. 1997. wbk. ed. 22.95 (*0-538-67855-0*) Thomson Learn.

CEP Inc., Staff, jt. auth. see Newberry.

CEP Inc., Staff, jt. auth. see Skintak.

CEP Incorporated Staff, jt. auth. see Skintir, C.

***Cepa, Jordi & Carral, Patricia, eds.** Star Formation in Early-Type Galaxies, Vol. 163. LC 99-61291. (ASP Conference Series Proceedings). 299p. (C). 1999. text 52.00 (*1-886733-84-8*) Astron Soc Pacific.

CEPAL Staff & BID (Banco Interamericano De Desarrollo) Staff, eds. La Liberalizacion Del Comercio en el Hemisferio Occidental. (SPA.). 656p. (C). 1995. pap. text. write for info. (*0-9645938-1-5*) ECLAC.

Cepeda, Claudio. Concise Guide to the Psychiatric Interview of Children & Adolescents. LC 99-26053. 2000. 22.95 (*0-88048-330-X*) Am Psychiatric.

Cepeda, Diana. Dominican Republic: Technical Assistance Project Final Report, March 1993-July 1994. (Illus.). ii, 450p. 1994. pap. text 47.00 (*1-879720-47-7*) Intl Fndt Elect.

Cepeda, Joe, jt. auth. see Schotter, Roni.

Cepeda, Joe, jt. illus. see Schotter, Roni.

Cepeda, Joseph C. Introduction to Minerals & Rocks. LC 93-31893. (Illus.). 217p. (Orig.). (C). 1993. pap. text 44.00 (*0-02-320452-4*, Macmillan Coll) P-H.

Cepeda, Orlando & Fagen, Herb. Baby Bull: From Hardball to Hard Time & Back. LC 98-38639. (Illus.). 256p. 1999. 22.95 (*0-87833-212-X*) Taylor Pub.

***Cepeda, Rebecca.** A Garden for Allegra. Yarak, Jo Ann, ed. (Illus.). 260p. 1998. pap. 12.95 (*1-893963-00-4*) YarakWorks Pub.

Cepeda Samudio, Alvaro. La Casa Grande: A Novel. Menton, Seymour & Garcia Marquez, Gabriel, trs. (Texas Pan American Ser.). (SPA., Illus.). 112p. (Orig.). 1991. pap. 9.95 (*0-292-74673-3*) U of Tex Pr.

Cepero, Nilda. Lil' Havana Blues. (Illus.). 60p. 1998. pap. 8.00 (*1-890953-03-2*, 98LHB) LS Pr.

— Sugar Cane Blues. (Illus.). 61p. 1997. pap. 8.00 (*1-890953-02-4*, 97SCB) LS Pr.

Cephalas, Paphnutius. Paphnutius: Histories of the Monks of Upper Egypt & the Life of Onnophrius. Vivian, Tim, tr. & intro. by. LC 92-39032. (Cistercian Studies: No. 140). (COP & ENG.). (Orig.). 1993. 34.95 (*0-87907-440-X*); pap. 16.95 (*0-87907-540-6*) Cistercian Pubns.

***Cephas, Judith, et al.** John Brown Mysteries. Libby, Jean, ed. LC 99-70466. (Illus.). 124p. 1999. pap. 11.95 (*1-57510-059-2*) Pictorial Hist.

Ceplair, Larry. Charlotte Perkins Gilman: A Nonfiction Reader. 320p. 1991. text 84.00 (*0-231-07616-9*) Col U Pr.

— A Great Lady: A Life of the Screenwriter Sonya Levien. LC 95-43945. (Filmmakers Ser.: No. 50). 176p. 1996. 34.50 (*0-8108-3092-2*) Scarecrow.

— The Public Years of Sarah & Angelina Grimke. 400p. 1991. pap. text 22.00 (*0-231-06801-8*) Col U Pr.

— Under the Shadow of War: Fascism, Anti-Fascism, & Marxists, 1918-1939. LC 86-32652. 272p. 1987. text 57.50 (*0-231-06532-9*) Col U Pr.

Ceplair, Larry, ed. see Gilman, Charlotte Perkins.

Ceplitis, L. Orthographic Dictionary of the Lettish (Latvian) Language. (LAV.). 358p. 1981. 14.95 (*0-8288-1624-7*, F58240) Fr & Eur.

Ceponkus, Alex & Hoodbhoy, Faraz. Applied XML: A Toolkit for Programmers. LC 99-29984. 496p. 1999. pap. 49.99 incl. cd-rom (*0-471-34402-8*) Wiley.

Cera, Deanna F. Amazing Gems: An Illustrated Guide to the World's Most Dazzling Costume Jewelry. Leister, Elizabeth, tr. from ITA. LC 96-38617. (Illus.). 256p. 1997. 19.95 (*0-8109-3147-8*, Pub. by Abrams) Time Warner.

— Costume Jewellery. (Illus.). 256p. 1997. 19.95 (*1-85149-265-8*) Antique Collect.

— The Jewels of Miriam Haskell. (Antique Collectors' Club Ser.). (Illus.). 200p. 1997. 49.50 (*1-85149-263-1*) Antique Collect.

Cera, Deanna F., ed. Jewels of Fantasy: Costume Jewelry of the 20th Century. (Illus.). 408p. 1992. 95.00 (*0-8109-3178-8*) Abrams.

***Cera, Deanna Farneti.** Amazing Gems: An Illustrated Guide to the World's Most Dazzling Costume Jewelry. (Illus.). 256p. 2000. reprint ed. text 30.00 (*0-7881-9073-3*) DIANE Pub.

Cera, Enrico Di, see Di Cera, Enrico, ed.

Cera, Mary J. Living with Death - Primary. 64p. (J). (gr. 1-4). 1991. 7.99 (*0-86653-588-8*, GA1316) Good Apple.

Cera, Mary J. & Bisignano, Judith. Creating Your Future: Level 1. (Illus.). 72p. 1982. 6.95 (*0-910141-00-2*, KP107) Kino Pubns.

Ceracini, Marc. The Twelve Labors of Hercules. LC 97-10010. (Step into Reading Ser.: A Step 3 Book). (J). (gr. 1-4). 1997. lib. bdg. 11.99 (*0-679-98393-7*, Pub. by Random Bks Yng Read) Random.

Cerael, Larche, jt. auth. see Miller, Miamon.

Ceram, C. W. Gods, Graves & Scholars: The Story of Archaeology. 568p. 1986. pap. 14.00 (*0-394-74319-9*) Knopf.

Cerami, Anthony & Washington. Sickle Cell Anemia. LC 72-93681. 1973. 25.95 (*0-89388-068-X*) Okpaku Communications.

Cerami, Bob. To the Ends of the Earth Pt. I: A Spiritual Journey to God's Holy Mountain. LC 96-92490. 176p. (Orig.). 1997. pap. 9.95 (*0-9655658-0-7*) SS Pub Co.

— To the Ends of the Earth Pt. II: Ascending the Mountain. LC 96-93119. 148p. (Orig.). 1997. pap. 9.95 (*0-9655658-3-1*) SS Pub Co.

Cerami, Charles A., ed. A Marshall Plan for the 1990s: An International Roundtable on World Economic Development. LC 88-27503. 276p. 1989. 59.95 (*0-275-93137-4*, C3137, Praeger Pubs) Greenwood.

Cerami, Ethan. Delivering Push. LC 97-46599. 400p. 1998. pap. 49.95 incl. cd-rom (*0-07-913693-1*) McGraw.

— Delivering Push. 1997. 49.95 (*0-07-012024-2*) Osborne-McGraw.

Cerami, Pietro, jt. auth. see Aoolloni, Ignazio.

Cerami, Vicenzo, jt. auth. see Benigni, Roberto.

Ceramic Powder Science & Technology: Synthesis, Pr. Ceramic Powder Science. Messing, Gary L. et al, eds. LC 87-1317. (Advances in Ceramics Ser.: Vol. 21). 837p. 1987. reprint ed. pap. 200.00 (*0-608-00719-6*, 206149300009) Bks Demand.

Cerar, K. Melissa. Teenage Refugees from Nicaragua Speak Out. LC 94-23653. (In Their Own Voices Ser.). (Illus.). 64p. (YA). (gr. 7-12). 1997. lib. bdg. 16.95 (*0-8239-1849-1*) Rosen Group.

Cerard, Jean, ed. see Ronsard, Pierre De.

Cerasano, S. P. & Wynne-Davies, Marion. Readings in Renaissance Women's Drama: Criticism, History, & Performance, 1594-1998. LC 98-6670. 320p. (C). 1998. 80.00 (*0-415-16442-7*); pap. 24.99 (*0-415-16443-5*) Routledge.

C

An Asterisk (*) at the beginning of an entry indicates that the title is appearing for the first time.

Cerasano, Susan & Wynne-Davies, Marion. Renaissance Drama by Women: Texts & Documents. LC 95-14783. (Illus.). 256p. (C). (gr. 13). 1996. 90.00 (0-415-09806-8); pap. 24.99 (0-415-09807-6) Routledge.

Cerasano, Susan, jt. ed. see Pitcher, John.

Cerasano, Susan P. & Wynne-Davies, Marion, eds. Gloriana's Face: Women, Public & Private, in the English Renaissance. (Illus.). 248p. (C). 1992. text 34.95 (0-8143-2426-6) Wayne St U Pr.

Cerasano, Susan P., jt. ed. see Barroll, J. Leeds.

Cerasini, M., jt. auth. see Lees, J. D.

Cerasini, Marc. Big Machines, Cars & Trucks. 24p. (J). (ps-1). 1997. pap. 2.25 (1-56293-905-X, McClanahan Book) Learn Horizon.

— Diana: Queen of Hearts. 1997. lib. bdg. 11.99 (0-679-99214-6) Random.

— Godzilla & the Lost Continent. (Godzilla Ser.). (J). 2000. pap. 5.99 (0-679-88829-2, Pub. by Random Bks Yng Read) Random.

— Godzilla at World's End. LC 97-75899. (J). (gr. 9-12). 1998. pap. 5.99 (0-679-88827-6) Random.

Cerasini, Marc. Godzilla 2000. LC 97-66656. (Illus.). 320p. (J). (gr. 3-7). 1997. pap. 5.99 (0-679-88751-2, Pub. by Random Bks Yng Read) Random.

Cerasini, Marc. Godzilla Vs. the Robot Monsters. (Godzilla Ser.). (YA). (gr. 9 up). 1998. pap. 5.99 (0-679-88828-4) Random.

— The Mask: A Weird New Adventure! (J). (gr. 3-7). 1997. pap. 3.99 (0-614-28923-8) Random Bks Yng Read.

***Cerasini, Marc.** Thomas & the Big Big Bridge. 24p. (J). 2001. mass mkt. 2.99 (0-375-81151-6, Pub. by Random Bks Yng Read) Random.

Cerasini, Marc. The Twelve Labors of Hercules. LC 97-10010. (Step into Reading Ser.: A Step 3 Book). (Illus.). 48p. (J). (gr. 2-3). 1997. pap. 3.99 (0-679-88393-2, Pub. by Random Bks Yng Read) Random.

Cerasini, Marc. The Twelve Labors of Hercules. (Step into Reading Ser.: A Step 3 Book). (J). (gr. 2-3). 1997. 9.19 (0-606-12834-4, Pub. by Turtleback) Demco.

Cerasini, Marc A. Fighter Pilots. (J). 1997. lib. bdg. write for info. (0-679-98244-2, Bullseye Bks) Random Bks Yng Read.

— Fighter Pilots. (YA). 1997. pap. write for info. (0-679-88244-8, Bullseye Bks) Random Bks Yng Read.

— Godzilla Returns. LC 96-67480. (Godzilla Sprinter Ser.). (Illus.). 233p. (J). (gr. 9-12). 1996. pap. 4.99 (0-679-88221-9, Pub. by Random Bks Yng Read) Random.

— The Hunchback of Notre Dame. LC 95-1267. (Bullseye Step into Classics Ser.). 1995. 9.09 (0-606-09442-3, Pub. by Turtleback) Demco.

— I Am a Droid. LC 98-68611. (Star Wars). (Illus.). (YA). (ps-3). 1999. pap. 3.99 (0-375-80025-5, Pub. by Random Bks Yng Read) Random.

***Cerasini, Marc A.** I am a Jedi. (Star Wars). (YA). (gr. 1 up). 1999. 3.99 (0-375-80026-3) Random House.

Cerasini, Marc A. Navy Seals: Undersea Commandoes. (YA). 1997. pap. write for info. (0-679-88245-6, Bullseye Bks) Random Bks Yng Read.

— O. J. Simpson: American Hero, American Tragedy. LC 94-197868. 352p. 1994. mass mkt. 4.99 (0-7860-0118-6, Pinncle Kensgtn) Kensgtn Pub Corp.

— Star Wars: Anakin's Fate. LC 98-48534. (Step into Reading Ser.: A Step 4 Book). (Illus.). (J). (gr. 2-4). 1999. pap. 4.99 (0-375-80029-8) Random.

***Cerasini, Marc A.** Star Wars: Anakin's Fate. LC 98-48534. (Step into Reading Ser.: A Step 4 Book). (Illus.). (J). (gr. 2-4). 1999. lib. bdg. 11.99 (0-375-90029-2) Random.

Cerasini, Marc A. The Ugly Duckling. (Storyshapes Ser.). (Illus.). 24p. (Orig.). (J). (ps-1). 1996. pap. 2.25 (1-56293-906-8, McClanahan Book) Learn Horizon.

Cerasini, Marc A. & Hoffman, Charles E. Robert E. Howard. Schlobin, Roger C., ed. LC 85-17161. (Starmont Reader's Guide Ser.: Vol. 35). vi, 156p. 1987. pap. 21.00 (0-930261-27-5) Millefleurs.

***Ceraso, Melanie, et al.** Friends of ED: Digitial Divas Design Studio. 350p. 2001. pap. 39.99 (1-903450-09-8) Wrox Pr Inc.

Ceravolo, Joseph. The Green Lake Is Awake: Selected Poems. Padgett, Ron et al, eds. LC 93-23692. 150p. (Orig.). 1994. pap. 11.95 (1-56689-021-7) Coffee Hse.

— Transmigration Solo. LC 79-1068. 45p. (Orig.). 1979. pap. 8.00 (0-915124-21-1) Coffee Hse.

Cerberus, Damien R. Vampiric Verses. LC 94-67174. (Illus.). 120p. (Orig.). 1994. pap. 10.95 (0-9642180-0-3) Sunset Pubng.

Cerbone, John, jt. auth. see Monte, Peter.

Cerboni, Giuseppe. Primi Saggi di Logismografia Presentati, All' XI Congresso Degli Scienziati Italiani in Roma. Brief, Richard P., ed. LC 80-1477. (Dimensions of Accounting Theory & Practice Ser.). (ITA.). 1980. reprint ed. lib. bdg. 17.95 (0-405-13507-6) Ayer.

Cerbus, jt. auth. see Rice.

Cerbus, Deborah P. & Rice, Cheryl F. Connecting Holidays & Literature. (Curriculum Connections Ser.). (Illus.). 144p. (Orig.). 1992. student ed. 12.95 (1-55734-348-9) Tchr Create Mat.

— Connecting Science & Literature. (Curriculum Connections Ser.). (Illus.). 144p. 1991. student ed. 14.95 (1-55734-341-1) Tchr Create Mat.

— Connecting Social Studies & Literature. (Curriculum Connections Ser.). (Illus.). 144p. 1992. student ed. 14.95 (1-55734-345-4) Tchr Create Mat.

— Early Childhood Units for Science. (Whole Language Units Ser.). (Illus.). 144p. (J). (ps-1). 1993. pap., student ed. 14.95 (1-55734-201-6) Tchr Create Mat.

— Early Childhood Units for Social Studies. (Whole Language Units Ser.). (Illus.). 144p. (J). (ps-1). 1993. pap., student ed. 14.95 (1-55734-203-2) Tchr Create Mat.

***Cerbus, Deborah P. & Rice, Cheryl Feichtenbiner.** Social Studies Through the Year. (Illus.). 384p. (J). 1999. pap., teacher ed. 24.95 (1-57690-467-9, TCM2467) Tchr Create Mat.

Cerbus, Deborah P., jt. auth. see Rice.

Cerchione, Angelo J., et al, eds. Master Planning the Aviation Environment. LC 74-125171. 224p. reprint ed. pap. 69.50 (0-608-13351-5, 202555300044) Bks Demand.

Cercignani, C. Mathematical Methods in Kinetic Theory. 2nd ed. (Illus.). 263p. (C). 1990. 59.50 (0-306-43460-1, Plenum Trade) Perseus Pubng.

Cercignani, C. & Sattinger, D. Scaling Limits & Models in Physical Processes. LC 98-37005. (DMV Ser.: Vol. 28). (Illus.). 200p. 1998. pap. 39.50 (3-7643-5985-4) Birkhauser.

Cercignani, Carlo. The Boltzmann Equation & Its Applications. (Applied Mathematical Sciences Ser.: Vol. 67). (Illus.). xiii, 455p. 1987. 79.95 (0-387-96637-4) Spr-Verlag.

— Ludwig Boltzmann: The Man Who Trusted Atoms. (Illus.). 348p. 1998. text 49.95 (0-19-850154-4) OUP.

***Cercignani, Carlo.** Rarefied Gas Dynamics: From Basic Concepts to Actual Calculations. (Cambridge Texts in Applied Mathematics Ser.: No. 21). (Illus.). 328p. 2000. pap. text 29.95 (0-521-65992-2) Cambridge U Pr.

— Rarefied Gas Dynamics: From Basic Concepts to Actual Calculations. (Cambridge Texts in Applied Mathematics Ser.: No. 21). (Illus.). 328p. (C). 2000. text 74.95 (0-521-65008-9) Cambridge U Pr.

Cercignani, Carlo, ed. Kinetic Theories & the Boltzmann Equation: Lectures Given at the 1st Session of the Centro Interrrazionale Matematico Estivo (C. I. M. E.) Held at Montecatini, Italy, June 10-18, 1981. (Lecture Notes in Mathematics Ser.: Vol. 1048). vii, 248p. 1984. 38.95 (0-387-12899-9) Spr-Verlag.

— Kinetic Theory & Gas Dynamics. (CISM International Centre for Mechanical Sciences Ser.: Vol. 293). vii, 215p. 1989. 51.95 (0-387-82090-6) Spr-Verlag.

Cercignani, Carlo & Pulvirenti, Mario, eds. Nonequilibrium Problems in Many-Particle Systems. (Lecture Notes in Mathematics Ser.: Vol. 1551). (Illus.). 158p. 1993. pap. write for info. (3-540-56945-6) Spr-Verlag.

Cercignani, Carlo & Sattinger, David. Scaling Limits & Models in Physical Processes. LC 98-37005. (DMV Seminar Ser.). 1998. pap. 39.50 (0-8176-5985-4) Birkhauser.

Cercignani, Carlo, et al. Many-Particle Dynamics & Kinetic Equations. Petrina, K. & Gredzhuk, V., trs. from RUS. LC 97-23958. (Mathematics & Its Applications Ser.: Vol. 420). 244p. 1997. text 164.00 (0-7923-4696-3) Kluwer Academic.

— The Mathematical Theory of Dilute Gases. LC 94-10086. (Applied Mathematical Sciences Ser.). (Illus.). vii, 347p. 1994. 64.95 (0-387-94294-7) Spr-Verlag.

Cercone, Karen R. Blood Tracks. (American Historical Mystery Ser.). 1998. mass mkt. 5.99 (0-425-16241-9, Prime Crime) Berkley Pub.

— Coal Bones. 288p. 1999. mass mkt. 5.99 (0-425-16698-8, Prime Crime) Berkley Pub.

— Steel Ashes. 272p. 1997. mass mkt. 5.99 (0-425-15856-X, Prime Crime) Berkley Pub.

Cercone, N. J. Practical Artificial Intelligence Systems. (Computers & Mathematics with Applications Ser.). 1985. pap. 30.00 (0-08-032598-X, Pergamon Pr) Elsevier.

Cercone, N. J., ed. Computational Linguistics. (International Series in Modern Applied Mathematics & Computer Science: Vol. 5). (Illus.). 200p. 1983. pap. 45.00 (0-08-030253-X, Pergamon Pr) Elsevier.

Cercone, N. J. & Maccalla, G., eds. The Knowledge Frontier. (Symbolic Computation Ser.). (Illus.). 550p. 1987. 82.95 (0-387-96557-2) Spr-Verlag.

Cercone, Phyllis. Amanda's Secret Wish. (Amanda Stories Ser.). (Illus.). 24p. (Orig.). (J). (ps-3). 1996. pap. 6.99 (0-9643728-3-5) Perry Pubng.

Cerda, Alfredo G. Peregrinos del Amazonas (Pilgrims of the Amazons) (SPA.). 133p. (YA). 1994. pap. 6.99 (968-16-4071-3, Pub. by Fondo) Continental Bk.

— La Princesa y el Pirata (The Princess & the Pirate) (SPA.). 32p. (J). (gr. 1-3). 1991. 12.99 (968-16-3654-6, Pub. by Fondo) Continental Bk.

Cerda, Carlos. To Die in Berlin. Labinger, Andrea G., tr. from SPA. LC 99-16678. (Discoveries Ser.).Tr. of Morir en Berlin. 176p. 1999. pap. 15.95 (1-891270-02-8, Pub. by Lat Am Lit Rev Pr) Consort Bk Sales.

Cerda, Diego De La, see De La Cerda, Diego.

Cerda, Gina. Angels Come & Sleep with Me: A Children's Prayer. (Illus.). 20p. (J). (gr. k-4). 1998. 17.95 (0-9665153-0-7) Gina Designs.

Cerda, Jose G. El Comunismo Frente a los Trabajadores. (SPA., Illus.). 305p. (Orig.). 1986. pap. 10.00 (0-917049-03-9) Saeta.

Cerda, M. A., jt. auth. see Goberna, M. A.

Cerda, Martha. Cohabitants - Cohabitantes. Hernandez, Juan, tr. from SPA. 96p. 1995. pap. text 8.00 (1-57139-028-6) Hernandez Translat.

— Senora Rodriguez & Other Worlds. Jimenez-Anderson, Sylvia, tr. from SPA. LC 96-33336. (Latin America in Translation Ser.). 128p. 1997. pap. 12.95 (0-8223-1890-3); lib. bdg. 35.00 (0-8223-1886-5) Duke.

Cerda-Olmedo, Enrique & Lipson, Edward D., eds. Phycomyces. LC 86-30982. (Illus.). 420p. 1987. text 88.00 (0-87969-199-9) Cold Spring Harbor.

Cerda, Sandra. Incest: The Curse of Destruction...Reversed. 102p. 1994. write for info. (0-614-14023-4); pap. 8.00 (0-9643649-0-5) N Life Minist.

— War of the Spirits. (Orig.). 1996. pap. 5.00 (0-9643649-1-3) N Life Minist.

Cerda, Victor & Ramis, Guillermo. An Introduction to Laboratory Automation. LC 90-35305. (Chemical Analysis: A Series of Monographs on Analytical Chemistry & Its Applications). 336p. 1990. 125.00 (0-471-61818-7) Wiley.

Cerdeira, Hilda A., ed. Quantum Chaos. 480p. (C). 1991. text 128.00 (981-02-0621-6) World Scientific Pub.

Cerdeira, Hilda A., et al, eds. Quantum Fluctuations in Mesoscopic & Macroscopic Systems. 300p. (C). 1991. text 89.00 (981-02-0629-1) World Scientific Pub.

Cerdeira, Hilda A., et al. Path Integration: Lectures on Trieste, 1991. 600p. 1993. text 114.00 (981-02-1070-1) World Scientific Pub.

Cerdeira, Hilda A., jt. ed. see Casati, Giulio.

Cerdeira, Hilda A., jt. ed. see Lundqvist, S. O.

Cerdic Colloquium Staff. Liberation Theology & the Message of Salvation: Proceedings of the Cerdic Colloquium, 4th, Strasbourg, May 10-12, 1973. Metz, Rene & Schlick, Jean, eds. Gelzer, David G., tr. LC 78-7540. (Pittsburgh Theological Monographs: No. 20). 1978. pap. 8.75 (0-915138-26-3) Pickwick.

Cerdonio, M., et al, eds. General Relativity & Gravitational Physics: Proceedings of the 8th Italian Conference. 648p. (C). 1989. text 138.00 (9971-5-0844-3) World Scientific Pub.

Cerdonio, M., et al. General Relativity & Gravitational Physics: Proceedings of the Xth International Conference. 692p. 1994. text 109.00 (981-02-1734-X) World Scientific Pub.

— Introductory Biophysics. 224p. 1986. text 38.00 (9971-966-33-6) World Scientific Pub.

Cerebellum. Wrinkle Free World English. 1998. VHS 20.95 (0-205-29896-6, Longwood Div) Allyn.

Cereijido, Marcelino. The Tight Junction. (Illus.). 384p. 1991. lib. bdg. 195.00 (0-8493-8850-3, QH603) CRC Pr.

Cereijido, Marcelino & Rotunno, Catalina A. Introduction to the Study of Biological Membranes. x, 262p. 1970. text 218.00 (0-677-02410-X) Gordon & Breach.

Cerek. Water Flowing over Stone. LC 98-75007. 144p. 1999. pap. 13.00 (0-9667513-9-6) Yggdrasil Bks.

— Water Flowing over Stone. deluxe limited ed. LC 98-75007. 144p. 1999. 45.00 (0-9667513-8-8) Yggdrasil Bks.

Cerel, Lon. How to Blow up Animals: A Beginner's Guide to Fun with Balloons. (Illus.). 48p. (Orig.). (YA). (gr. 5 up). 1996. pap. 9.95 (0-924771-66-6, Covered Brdge Pr) Douglas Charles Ltd.

Ceren, Sandra Levy. Prescription for Terror. LC 99-94664. 240p. 1999. pap. 11.95 (0-9669861-0-5) Andrw Scott.

Cerenio, Virginia. Trespassing Innocence. 72p. 1989. pap. 8.95 (0-9609630-5-7) Kearny St Wkshop.

Cerepak, John, ed. Principles of Accounting. (C). 1999. write for info. (0-13-709239-3, Macmillan Coll) P-H.

Ceres. Ecstasy to Agony Through the Plan 2000. (Phoenix Journals). pap. 7.95 (1-56935-007-8) Phoenix Source.

— Herbal Teas for Health & Healing. (Illus.). 96p. (Orig.). 1996. reprint ed. pap. 9.95 (0-89281-646-5, Heal Arts VT) Inner Tradit.

— The Last Great Plague: AIDS & Related Murder Tools. (Phoenix Journals). 255p. 1993. pap. 7.95 (1-56935-004-3) Phoenix Source.

— The Ultimate Psychopolitics, Mass Mind Control & the Global Control System. (Phoenix Journals). 248p. 1993. pap. 7.95 (1-56935-005-1) Phoenix Source.

Ceres, Gerald V. Holmdel & Pleasant Valley. LC 97-133977. (Images of America Ser.). 1999. pap. 16.99 (0-7524-0473-3) Arcadia Publng.

Ceresa, R. J. Block & Graft Copolymerization, Vol. 1. LC 72-5713. 389p. reprint ed. pap. 120.60 (0-8357-7323-X, 202400100001) Bks Demand.

Ceresa, R. J., ed. Block & Graft Copolymerization, Vol. 2. LC 72-5713. 420p. reprint ed. pap. 130.20 (0-8357-7324-8, 202480800002) Bks Demand.

Ceresko, Anthony. Introduction to Old Testament Wisdom: A Spirituality for Liberation. LC 99-31688. (Illus.). 192p. 1999. pap. 18.00 (1-57075-277-X) Orbis Bks.

— Introduction to the Old Testament: A Liberation Perspective. LC 92-17486. (Illus.). 325p. (Orig.). (C). 1992. pap. 21.00 (0-88344-821-1) Orbis Bks.

Cereta, Laura & Robi, Diana M. Collected Letters of a Renaissance Feminist. LC 96-45730. (The Other Voice in Early Modern Europe Ser.). 1997. pap. text 19.95 (0-226-10013-8) U Ch Pr.

Cereta, Laura & Robin, Diana M. Collected Letters of a Renaissance Feminist. LC 96-45730. (The Other Voice in Early Modern Europe Ser.). 1997. lib. bdg. 45.00 (0-226-10011-1) U Ch Pr.

Cereteli, Grigorij F. Sokrascenija V'Greceskich' Rukopisjach' Preimuscestvenno Po Datirovannym' Rukopisjam' S. Petersburga i Moskvy. lvii, 226p. 1969. reprint ed. 90.00 (0-318-71750-6) G Olms Pubs.

***Cerexhe, Peter & Ashton, John.** Risky Food, Safer Choices: Avoiding Food Poisoning. 188p. 1999. pap. 24.95 (0-86840-522-1, Pub. by NSW U Pr) Intl Spec Bk.

Cerezo, Antonio M. Diccionario de Banca. 8th ed. (SPA.). 208p. 1988. write for info. (0-7859-5083-4) Fr & Eur.

Cerezo, German A. & Clonts, Howard A. Economic Analysis of Effluent Control from Catfish Ponds. (Illus.). 51p. (Orig.). (C). 1994. pap. text 30.00 (0-7881-1345-3) DIANE Pub.

Cerezo, Maria, jt. ed. see Angelelli, Igancio.

Cerf, Aleeza. Say It in Modern Hebrew. (Orig.). 1953. pap. 3.95 (0-486-20805-2) Dover.

Cerf, Bennett. Riddles & More Riddles. LC 99-20133. (J). 1999. lib. bdg. 11.99 (0-679-98970-6) Random.

— Try & Stop Me. Date not set. lib. bdg. 26.95 (0-8488-1963-2) Amereon Ltd.

Cerf, Bennett & Palen, Debbie. Riddles & More Riddles! LC 99-20133. (Illus.). 48p. 1999. 7.99 (0-679-88970-1) Random.

Cerf, Bennett A. At Random: The Reminiscences of Bennett Cerf. LC 77-1867. 1977. 24.00 (0-394-47877-0) Random.

— Bennett Cerf's Book of Riddles. LC 60-13492. (Illus.). 72p. (J). (gr. 1-2). 1960. 7.99 (0-394-80015-X) Beginner.

— Famous Ghost Stories. reprint ed. lib. bdg. 26.95 (0-88411-146-6) Amereon Ltd.

— Modern American Short Stories. (BCL1-PS American Literature Ser.). 384p. 1993. reprint ed. lib. bdg. 89.00 (0-7812-6934-2) Rprt Serv.

— Sixteen Famous British Plays. Cartmell, Van H., ed. 46.95 (0-88411-265-9) Amereon Ltd.

— Sixteen Famous European Plays. 1976. 48.95 (0-8488-0957-2) Amereon Ltd.

— Stories Selected from the Unexpected. 1976. 20.95 (0-8488-1277-8) Amereon Ltd.

Cerf, Bennett A. & Cartmell, Van H., eds. Twenty Four Favorite One Act Plays. 29.95 (0-88411-264-0) Amereon Ltd.

Cerf, Bennett A., jt. compiled by see Cartmell, Van H.

Cerf, Bennett A., jt. ed. see Cartmell, Van H.

Cerf, Christopher B. & Navasky, Victor. The Experts Speak: The Definitive Compendium of Authoritative Misinformation. rev. ed. LC 98-11252. 445p. 1998. pap. 16.95 (0-679-77806-3) Villard Books.

Cerf, Muriel. L' Antivoyage. (FRE.). 224p. 1978. pap. 11.95 (0-7859-1888-4, 2070371069) Fr & Eur.

— Le Diable Vert. (FRE.). 288p. 1981. pap. 10.95 (0-7859-1943-0, 2070373355) Fr & Eur.

— Maria Tiefenthaler. (FRE.). 1984. pap. 15.95 (0-7859-2003-X, 2070376168) Fr & Eur.

— Les Rois et les Voleurs. (FRE.). 212p. 1977. pap. 10.95 (0-7859-1837-X, 2070368807) Fr & Eur.

— Street Girl. Di Bernardi, Dominic, tr. from FRE. LC 88-23694. 200p. 1988. 19.95 (0-916583-33-3) Dalkey Arch.

CERF Staff. Dictionnaire Culturel de la Bible. (FRE.). 302p. 1990. 45.00 (0-7859-7763-5, 2204040282) Fr & Eur.

— Dictionnaire Encyclopedique du Christianisme Ancien. (FRE.). 1200p. 1990. 795.00 (0-8288-9495-7) Fr & Eur.

— High-Performance Construction Materials & Systems: A Ten-Year Plan & Implementation Strategy. LC 94-31335. 172p. 1994. 82.00 (0-7844-0059-8) Am Soc Civil Eng.

Cerf, Walter, ed. see Hegel, Georg Wilhelm Friedrich.

Cerfolli, Fulvio. Adapting to the Environment. LC 97-51394. (Everyday Life of Animals Ser.). (Illus.). (J). 1999. 27.12 (0-8172-4196-5) Raintree Steck-V.

— The Animal Atlas. (Everyday Life of Animals Ser.). (Illus.). 64p. (YA). 1998. lib. bdg. 27.12 (0-8172-4198-1) Raintree Steck-V.

Ceri, Federico. Dino Pedriali: Photographs. (Illus.). 120p. 1994. 55.00 (3-905514-38-9, Pub. by Edit Stemmle) Dist Art Pubs.

Ceri, S., et al. Logic Programming & Databases. (Surveys in Computer Science Ser.). (Illus.). 368p. 1990. 56.95 (0-387-51728-6) Spr-Verlag.

Ceri, Stefano & Tanaka, Katsumi, eds. Deductive & Object-Oriented Databases: Third International Conference, DOOD '93, Phoenix, Arizona, U. S. A., December 6-8, 1993: Proceedings. LC 93-39552. (Lecture Notes in Computer Science Ser.: Vol. 760). 1993. 65.00 (0-387-57530-8) Spr-Verlag.

Ceri, Stefano, jt. ed. see Widom, Jennifer.

Ceriani, R. L. Antigen & Antibody Molecular Engineering in Breast Cancer Diagnosis & Treatment: Diagnosis & Treatment. (Advances in Experimental Medicine & Biology Ser.: Vol. 353). (Illus.). 234p. (C). 1994. text 85.00 (0-306-44720-7, Kluwer Plenum) Kluwer Academic.

Ceriani, Roberto L., ed. Breast Cancer Immunodiagnosis & Immunotherapy. (Illus.). 272p. 1989. 85.00 (0-306-43338-9, Plenum Trade) Perseus Pubng.

— Breast Epithelial Antigens. (Illus.). 256p. (C). 1991. text 114.00 (0-306-44009-1, Kluwer Plenum) Kluwer Academic.

— Immunological Approaches to the Diagnosis & Therapy of Breast Cancer. LC 87-15373. (Illus.). 282p. 1987. 69.50 (0-306-42601-3, Plenum Trade) Perseus Pubng.

— Monoclonal Antibodies & Breast Cancer. (Developments in Oncology Ser.). 1985. text 127.00 (0-89838-739-6) Kluwer Academic.

Ceric, Mustafa. Roots of Synthetic Theology in Islam. 286p. (C). 1997. text 18.00 (0-934905-88-6, Library of Islam) Kazi Pubns.

Ceriello, Vincent R. & Freeman, Christine. Human Resource Management Systems: Strategies, Tactics, & Techniques. LC 98-20009. (Business & Management Ser.). 832p. reprint ed. pap. 41.95 (0-7879-4536-6) Jossey-Bass.

Cerier, Leslie. The Quick & Easy Organic Gourmet: Quick & Delicious, Healthy Meals Without Meat, Wheat, Dairy or Sugar. LC 95-15667. (Illus.). 352p. 1995. pap. 17.95 (1-886449-00-7) Barrytown Ltd.

Cerillo, Augustus, Jr. Reform in New York City: A Study in Urban Progressivism. (Modern American History Ser.). 272p. 1991. text 20.00 (0-8240-1893-1) Garland.

Cerimele, Decio. Kaposi's Sarcoma. LC 84-13423. (Illus.). 168p. 1985. text 35.00 (0-88331-155-0) R B Luce.

Cerino, Deborah A., jt. auth. see Clapp, Judith A.

Cerio, R. Genital Skin Disorders: A Guide to Non-Sexually Transmitted Conditions. (Illus.). 104p. 1995. text 75.00 (0-412-55020-2, Pub. by E A) OUP.

Cerio, Rino & Archer, C., eds. Clinical Investigation of Skin Disorders. (Illus.). 192p. 1997. text 75.00 (0-412-59230-4, Pub. by E A) OUP.

Cerio, Steven. Steven Cerio's ABC Book: A Drug Primer. LC 99-159405. (Illus.). 64p. 1998. 12.95 (1-889539-07-4) Heck Editions.

An Asterisk (*) at the beginning of an entry indicates that the title is appearing for the first time.

C

— You're a Stepparent . . . Now What? A Supportive Guide for Stepmothers & Stepfathers. LC 94-66761. 192p. 1994. pap. 12.95 (*0-88282-129-6*) New Horizon NJ.

Cerra, Charles La, see La Cerra, Charles.

Cerra, Frank B. & Shoemaker, William c., eds. Critical Care: State of the Art, Vol. 8. 1987. write for info. (*0-936145-10-2*) SCCM Fullerton.

Cerra, Frank B., jt. auth. see Irwin, Richard S.

Cerra, Frank B., jt. ed. see Abrams, Jerome H.

Cerra, Frank B., jt. ed. see Bihari, David.

Cerra, Joseph M. The Sales Associate Book, Version 3: How to Use the PC in Sales. rev. ed. (Illus.). 250p. 1994. spiral bd. 29.95 incl. disk (*0-927701-04-9*) Evergreen Ventures.

Cerra, Julie L. Fire Burn & Cauldron Bubble: A Collection of Well-Used, Time Sensitive Recipes Reflecting the Diversity on an American Family & That Family's Friends. LC 98-86090. (Illus.). 224p. 1998. pap. 16.00 (*1-879415-27-5*) Mtn n Air Bks.

Cerrada, M., jt. auth. see Aguilar-Benitez, M.

Cerrah, Ibrahim. Crowds & Public Order Policing: An Analysis of Crowds & Interpretations of Their Behaviour Based on Observational Studies in England, Wales & Turkey. LC 97-22752. (Illus.). 268p. 1997. text 82.95 (*1-84014-004-6*, Pub. by Ashgate Pub) Ashgate Pub Co.

Cerrato, jt. auth. see Pooler.

Cerretelli, P., et al, eds. High Altitude Deterioration. (Medicine & Sport Science Ser.: Vol. 19). (Illus.). xvi, 228p. 1985. 126.25 (*3-8055-3972-X*) S Karger.

Cerretti, Elena R., jt. auth. see Schanne, Otto F.

Cerri, Giovanni, jt. auth. see Gentili, Bruno.

***Cerri, Pierluigi.** Coating. (Rassegna Ser.: Vol. 73). 1999. pap. 35.00 (*88-85322-36-0*) Birkhauser.

Cerri, Stefano A. & Whiting, John, eds. Learning Technology in the European Communities. 760p. 1991. lib. bdg. 283.50 (*0-7923-1473-5*) Kluwer Academic.

Cerri, Stefano A., jt. ed. see Verdejo, Felisa M.

Cerrina, F. & Marrian, Christie, eds. Materials - Fabrication & Patterning at the Nanoscale. (Symposium Proceedings Ser.: Vol. 380). 203p. 1995. text 83.00 (*1-55899-283-9*) Materials Res.

Cerrito, Joann. Nineteenth Century Literary Criticism: Excerpts from Criticism of the Works of Novelists, Poets, Playwrights, Short Story Writers, Philosophers & Other Creative Writers Who Died Between 1800 & 1899, from the First Published Critical Appraisals to Current Evaluations, Vol. 45. (Nineteenth Century Literary Criticism Ser.). 472p. 1994. text 150.00 (*0-8103-8936-3*) Gale.

— Twentieth-Century Literary Criticism: Excerpts from Criticism of Various Topics in Twentieth-Century Literature, Including Literary & Critical Movements, Prominent Themes & Genres, Anniversary Celebrations, & Surveys of National Literatures, Vol. 58. 500p. 1995. text 150.00 (*0-8103-2440-7*) Gale.

Cerrito, Joann, ed. Contemporary Artists. 4th ed. LC 95-34088. (Contemporary Arts Ser.). (Illus.). 1340p. 1995. 160.00 (*1-55862-183-0*) St James Pr.

— Nineteenth Century Literary Criticism, Vol. 38. 507p. 1993. 150.00 (*0-8103-9191-0*, 100600) Gale.

— Nineteenth Century Literary Criticism: Excerpts from Criticism of the Works of Novelists, Poets, Playwrights, Short Story Writers, Philosophers & Other Creative Writers Who Died Between 1800 & 1899, from the First Published Critical Appraisals to Current Evaluations. (Nineteenth Century Literary Criticism Ser.: Vol. 46). 499p. 1994. text 140.00 (*0-8103-8937-1*) Gale.

Cerrito, Joann, ed. Nineteenth Century Literary Criticism & Cumulative Index, Vol. 42. (Nineteenth Century Literary Criticism Ser.). 600p. 1994. text 150.00 (*0-8103-9290-9*) Gale.

— Twentieth-Century Literary Criticism: Excerpts from Criticism of the Works of Novelists, Poets, Playwrights, Short Story Writers, & Other Creative Writers Who Lived Between 1900 & 1960, from the First Published Critical Appraisals to Current Evaluations, Vol. 57. 500p. 1995. text 150.00 (*0-8103-2439-3*) Gale.

— Twentieth-Century Literary Criticism Vol. 56: Excerpts from Criticism of the Work of Novelists, Poets, Playwrights, Short Story Writers & Other Creative Writers who Lived Between 1900 & 1960, from the First Published Appraisals to Current Evaluations, Vol. 56. 497p. 1994. text 150.00 (*0-8103-2438-5*) Gale.

Cerrito, Joann & Lazzari, Marie, eds. Nineteenth Century Literary Criticism: Excerpts from Criticism of the Works of Novelists, Poets, Playwrights, Short Story Writers, Philosophers & Other Creative Writers Who Died Between 1800 & 1899, from the First Published Critical Appraisals to Current Evaluations. (Nineteenth Century Literary Criticism Ser.: Vol. 46). 499p. 1994. text 140.00 (*0-8103-9293-3*) Gale.

Cerro, Ana M., tr. see Ada, Alma F.

Cerro, Ana M., tr. see Flor Ada, Alma.

Cerro Copper & Brass Company Staff. Investigation of Materials for Use in Copper Alloy Die Casting Dies. 150p. 1966. 22.50 (*0-317-34533-8*, 59) Intl Copper.

Cerro, Luis Farinas del, see Farinas del Cerro, Luis, ed.

Cerrolaza, M., et al, eds. Numerical Methods in Engineering Simulation. LC 96-83299. 424p. 1996. 175.00 (*1-85312-475-3*, 4753) Computational Mech MA.

— Simulation Modelling in Bioengineering: Proceedings of the BIOSIM '96 Conference. LC 96-83652. 328p. 1996. 147.00 (*1-85312-455-9*, 4559) Computational Mech MA.

Cerroni-Long, E. L. Anthropological Theory in North America. LC 99-15406. 304p. 1999. 65.00 (*0-89789-684-X*, Bergin & Garvey); pap. 24.95 (*0-89789-685-8*, Bergin & Garvey) Greenwood.

Cerroni-Long, E. L., ed. Insider Anthropology. 1995. write for info. (*0-913167-73-8*) Am Anthro Assn.

Cerroni, Lorenzo, et al. An Illustrated Guide to Skin Lymphoma Diagnosis. (Illus.). 176p. 1998. 199.95 (*0-632-05082-9*) Blackwell Sci.

Cerrudo, Jose. Spanish for Police & Firefighters, Set. 55p. pap. 59.50 incl. audio (*0-88432-072-3*, SSP450) Audio-Forum.

— Spanish for the Health Professional, Set 4. 40p. pap. 49.50 incl. audio (*0-88432-650-0*, SSP300) Audio-Forum.

***Cersole, A., et al, eds.** Quantum Aspects of Gauge Theories, Supersymmetry & Unification: Proceedings of the 2nd International Conference Held in Corfu, Greece, September 20-26, 1998. LC 99-36318. (Lecture Notes in Physics Ser.: Vol. 525). xx, 511p. 1999. 94.00 (*3-540-66005-4*) Spr-Verlag.

Cerstrik Nolan, Anne, ed. see Whitmore, Marilyn P.

Certa, Rolando. Love Song for Sicily. Barkan, Stanley H., ed. Scammacca, Nina & Scammacca, Nat, trs. (Review Chapbook Ser.: No. 30: Italian (Sicilian Poetry) 1).Tr. of Ital. & Sicilian & Eng.. (Illus.). 16p. 1982. 15.00 (*0-89304-879-8*, CCC153); pap. 5.00 (*0-89304-854-2*) Cross-Cultrl NY.

Certeau, Michel de, see Materne, Yves, ed.

Certification Insider Press Staff. A+ Practice Test Exam Cram. LC 99-31034. (Exam Cram / Coriolis' Certification Insi Ser.). 184p. 1999. pap. text 19.99 (*1-57610-477-X*) Coriolis Grp.

— MCSD Architectures Exam Cram. LC 99-23865. (Exam Cram / Coriolis' Certification Insi Ser.). 328p. 1999. pap. text 29.99 (*1-57610-378-1*) Coriolis Grp.

***Certification Insider Press Staff.** MCSE NT Server 4 Prep & Cram Pack: Customized MCSE Training System for the Busy NT 4 Professional. (Illus.). 1998. pap. 64.99 (*1-57610-307-2*) Coriolis Grp.

Certo. Experient Ex. Workbook Modern. 7th ed. 1997. pap. text. write for info. (*0-13-577503-5*) P-H.

— Modern Management. 7th ed. 1996. text. write for info. (*0-13-260522-8*); text. write for info. (*0-13-260555-4*) Allyn.

— Modern Management. 7th ed. 1996. pap. text, teacher ed. write for info. (*0-13-260498-1*) Allyn.

— Modern Management. 7th ed. 1996. text. write for info. (*0-13-260514-7*); pap. text, teacher ed. write for info. incl. cd-rom (*0-13-260480-9*); pap. text, teacher ed. write for info. (*0-13-260472-8*) Allyn.

— Modern Management. 7th ed. 144p. (C). 1997. pap. text, student ed. 20.00 (*0-13-902694-0*) P-H.

— Supervision. 3rd ed. LC 99-15439. 608p. 1999. pap. 67.81 (*0-07-228404-8*) McGraw.

Certo, Dominic N. Success - Pure & Simple: How to Make It in Business, Sports & the Arts. LC 83-90470. (Self-Help Bks.). (Illus.). 200p. (Orig.). 1983. reprint ed. pap. 12.95 (*0-915755-00-9*) Hillside Pubns.

Certo, Samuel C. Human Relations Today: Concepts & Skills. 528p. 1995. pap. write for info. (*0-614-32239-1*, Irwn McGrw-H) McGrw-H Hghr Educ.

***Certo, Samuel C.** Modern Management: Diversity, Quality, Ethics & the Global Environment. 8th ed. LC 99-12570. 608p. 1999. pap. 80.00 incl. disk (*0-13-013307-8*) P-H.

Certo, Samuel C. Supervision: Quality & Diversity Through Leadership. 2nd ed. 608p. (C). 1996. text 54.50 (*0-256-20805-0*, Irwn McGrw-H) McGrw-H Hghr Educ.

Certo, Samuel C. & Husted, Stewart. Business. 3rd ed. 1990. pap. text, student ed. 22.40 (*0-205-12355-4*) Allyn.

Certo, Samuel C. & Peter, J. Paul. Strategic Management: A Focus on Process. 2nd ed. LC 92-36103. 384p. (C). 1993. text 47.95 (*0-256-14120-7*, Irwn McGrw-H) McGrw-H Hghr Educ.

Certo, Samuel C., et al. Business. 2nd ed. 672p. 1987. text 36.00 (*0-205-11450-4*, H1450-9) Allyn.

— Business: Foundations of Our Business System. 3rd ed. 720p. 1989. teacher ed. write for info. (*0-318-66329-5*, H23500) Allyn.

— Business: Foundations of Our Business System. 3rd ed. 720p. 1989. student ed. 17.00 (*0-685-29825-6*, H23559); write for info. (*0-318-66330-9*, H22189); write for info. (*0-318-66332-5*, H23534); VHS. write for info. (*0-318-66331-7*, H23518) P-H.

— Business: Foundations of Our Business System. 3rd annot. ed. 720p. 1989. teacher ed. write for info. (*0-318-66328-7*, H22189) P-H.

— Cases in Strategic Management. 2nd ed. 848p. (C). 1992. text 53.95 (*0-256-14124-X*, Irwn McGrw-H) McGrw-H Hghr Educ.

Certo, Samuel C., jt. auth. see Graf, Lee A.

Certoma, G. L. The Italian Legal System. 540p. 1985. write for info. (*0-409-49084-9*, MICHIE) LEXIS Pub.

— The Law of Succession in New South Wales. 2nd ed. 307p. 1992. 85.00 (*0-455-21082-9*, Pub. by LawBk Co); pap. 65.00 (*0-455-21083-7*, Pub. by LawBk Co) Gaunt.

Certoma, G. L., jt. auth. see Wood, Olive.

Certon, M. J. & Davidson, H. F. Industrial Technology Transfer, No. 19. (NATO Advanced Study, Applied Science Ser.). 480p. 1977. lib. bdg. 148.50 (*90-286-0426-X*) Kluwer Academic.

Cerulean, Susan & Morrow, Ann. Florida Wildlife Viewing Guide. LC 98-18370. (Watchable Wildlife Ser.). (Illus.). 168p. 1998. 10.95 (*1-56044-353-7*) Falcon Pub Inc.

Cerulean, Susan, jt. ed. see Ripple, Jeff.

Cerulli, Dom, et al, eds. The Jazz Word. (Illus.). 248p. 1987. pap. 9.95 (*0-306-80288-0*) Da Capo.

Cerulli, Francette. The Spirits Need to Eat. 1999. pap. 12.95 (*0-9669473-0-4*, 1) Nine Patch.

Cerullo, Bob. What's Wrong with My Car? A Quick & Easy Guide to the Most Common Symptoms of Car Trouble. 160p. (Orig.). 1993. pap. 12.95 (*0-452-26993-8*, Plume) Dutton Plume.

***Cerullo, David.** Turn Off the Darkness: Changing the World for Good. 160p. 1999. 16.95 (*1-887600-15-9*) INSP-Direct.

Cerullo, Mary M. Dolphins: What They Can Teach Us. LC 97-34424. (Illus.). 42p. (J). (gr. 4-7). 1999. 16.99 (*0-525-65263-9*, Dutton Child) Peng Put Young Read.

— Lobsters: Gangsters of the Sea. LC 93-1288. (Illus.). 64p. (J). (gr. 4 up). 1994. 16.99 (*0-525-65153-5*, Dutton Child) Peng Put Young Read.

***Cerullo, Mary M.** Ocean Detectives: Solving the Mysteries of the Sea. LC 99-20406. (Turnstone Ocean Explorer Bks.). 64p. (J). 1999. 27.12 (*0-7398-1236-X*) Raintree Steck-V.

Cerullo, Mary M. Ocean Detectives: Solving the Mysteries of the Sea. (Turnstone Ocean Explorer Ser.). 64p. (YA). (gr. 5-9). 1999. pap. 8.95 (*0-7398-1237-8*) Raintree Steck-V.

— The Octopus. LC 96-13971. (Illus.). 64p. (YA). (gr. 5). 1997. 16.99 (*0-525-65199-3*) NAL.

— Reading the Environment: Children's Literature in the Science Classroom. LC 97-8894. 152p. 1997. pap. text 19.00 (*0-435-08383-X*) Heinemann.

— Sea Soup: Phytoplankton. LC 99-39210. 40p. (J). (gr. 3-6). 1999. 16.95 (*0-88448-208-1*) Tilbury Hse.

***Cerullo, Mary M.** Sea Soup: Phytoplankton. (Illus.). 40p. (J). (gr. 3-7). 2000. 16.95 (*0-88448-219-7*) Tilbury Hse.

Cerullo, Mary M. Sharks: Challengers of the Deep. LC 92-14206. (Illus.). 64p. (J). (gr. 4 up). 1993. 16.99 (*0-525-65100-4*, Dutton Child) Peng Put Young Read.

***Cerullo, Mary M.** The Truth about Great White Sharks. (Truth about Ser.). (Illus.). 48p. (J). (gr. 3-7). 2000. 14.95 (*0-8118-2467-5*) Chronicle Bks.

Cerullo, Mary M., text. Sharks: Challengers of the Deep. large type ed. 78p. (J). (gr. 6). 19.50 (*0-614-20618-9*, L-38205-00 APHB) Am Printing Hse.

Cerullo, Morris. Last Great Anointing. LC 99-20264. 216p. 1999. 18.99 (*0-8307-2473-7*) Gospel Lght.

***Cerullo, Morris.** The Last Great Anointing. LC 99-20264. 216p. 1999. pap. 9.99 (*0-8307-2472-9*, Regal Bks) Gospel Lght.

Cerulo, Karen A. Deciphering Violence: The Cognitive Structure of Right & Wrong. LC 97-37670. 201p. (C). 1998. pap. 19.99 (*0-415-91799-9*) Routledge.

— Deciphering Violence: The Cognitive Structure of Right & Wrong. LC 97-37670. (Illus.). 201p. (C). 1998. 75.00 (*0-415-91798-0*) Routledge.

— Identity Designs: The Sights & Sounds of a Nation. LC 95-4326. (Rose Series of the American Sociological Association). 264p. (C). 1995. text 50.00 (*0-8135-2211-0*) Rutgers U Pr.

Cerulo, Karen A., jt. auth. see Ruane, Janet M.

Ceruti, Mauro. Constraints & Possibilities Vol. 8: The Evolution of Knowledge & Knowledge of Evolution. (World Futures General Evolution Studies). 208p. 1994. text 49.00 (*2-88449-123-6*) Gordon & Breach.

Ceruti, Mauro, jt. auth. see Bocchi, Gianluca.

Cerutti, Peter A., et al, eds. Anticarcinogenesis & Radiation Protection, No. 1. LC 87-36133. (Illus.). 524p. 1988. 135.00 (*0-306-42785-0*, Plenum Trade) Perseus Pubng.

Cerutti, Stephen. The Official Fantasy Hockey Guide, 1998-1999: Definitive Hockey Pool Reference. 2nd ed. Morrison, Scott, ed. (Illus.). 288p. 1998. pap. 14.95 (*1-57243-272-1*) Triumph Bks.

Cerutti, Steven M. Cicero's Accretive Style: Rhetorical Strategies in the Exordia of the Judicial Speeches. LC 96-23758. 202p. 1996. lib. bdg. 36.00 (*0-7618-0438-2*) U Pr of Amer.

Cerutti, Steven M. & Cicero, Marcus Tullius. Cicero Pro Archia Poeta Oratio: A Syntactic Analysis of the Speech & Companion to the Commentary. LC 99-21314. 1999. 20.00 (*0-86516-439-8*) Bolchazy-Carducci.

Cerutti, Vincent. Cacti. 1998. 19.99 (*3-8228-7760-3*) Taschen Amer.

***Cerutti, Vincent.** Cactos (Cactus) 1998. 25.99 (*3-8228-8035-3*) Benedikt Taschen.

Ceruzzi, Paul. Beyond the Limits: Flight Enters the Computer Age. (Illus.). 284p. (Orig.). 1989. 42.50 (*0-262-03143-4*); pap. 19.95 (*0-262-53082-1*) MIT Pr.

— A History of Modern Computing. LC 98-22856. (Illus.). 408p. 1998. 35.00 (*0-262-03255-4*) MIT Pr.

***Ceruzzi, Paul.** The History of Modern Computing. (Illus.). 416p. 2000. reprint ed. pap. 18.95 (*0-262-53169-0*) MIT Pr.

Ceruzzi, Paul. The Information Revolution. (ABC-CLIO Companions Ser.). 225p. 1996. lib. bdg. 57.00 (*0-87436-713-1*) ABC-CLIO.

Ceruzzi, Paul E. Reckoners: From Relays to the Stored Program Concept, 1935-1945, 1. LC 82-20980. (Contributions to the Study of Computer Science Ser.: No. 1). (Illus.). 181p. 1983. 45.00 (*0-313-23382-9*, CED/, Greenwood Pr) Greenwood.

Ceruzzi, Paul E., jt. auth. see Kidwell, Peggy A.

Cerva, Victor La, see La Cerva, Victor.

Cervantes. Don Quijote de la Mancha, Primera parte: Level D Books. 8.95 (*0-88436-056-3*) EMC-Paradigm.

— Don Quijote de la Mancha, Segunda parte: Level D Books. text 8.95 (*0-88436-887-4*) EMC-Paradigm.

Cervantes, Carmen, et al, eds. En Alianza con Dios. Wood, Richard, tr. (Forjadores de Esperanza Ser.). (SPA., Illus.). 200p. (YA). 1998. pap. 9.95 (*0-88489-438-X*) St Marys.

— In Covenant with God. Wood, Richard, tr. (Builders of Hope Ser.). (Illus.). 200p. (YA). 1998. pap. 9.95 (*0-88489-437-1*) St Marys.

Cervantes, Carmen, et al. El Modelo Profetas de Esperanza. (Profetas de Esperanza Ser.: Vol. 3). (SPA., Illus.). 72p. 1997. pap. text 4.95 (*0-88489-515-7*) St Marys.

— The Prophets of Hope Model: A Weekend Workshop. LC 96-71261. (Prophets of Hope Ser.: Vol. 3).Tr. of Modelo Profetas de Esperanza. (Illus.). 72p. (Orig.). 1997. pap. 4.95 (*0-88489-451-7*) St Marys.

Cervantes, Carmen M. Amanecer en el Horizonte: Creando Pequenas Communidades. Diaz-Vilar, Juan & Arnouil, Eduardo, eds. Brancatelli, Robert, tr. (Promotores de Esperanza Ser.). (SPA., Illus.). 200p. 1996. pap. 9.95 (*0-88489-430-4*) St Marys.

Cervantes, Carmen M., et al. La Juventud Hispana y la Respuesta Pastoral de la Iglesia, Vol. 1. (Profetas de Esperanza Ser.). (SPA., Illus.). 296p. 1994. pap. 14.95 (*0-88489-326-X*) St Marys.

Cervantes, Carmen M., jt. auth. see De Cervantes Saavedra, Miguel.

Cervantes, Carmen M., ed. see Castex, et al.

Cervantes, Carmen M., ed. see De Cervantes Saavedra, Miguel.

Cervantes, Carmen M., ed. see Sanchez, Maria A., et al.

Cervantes, Carmen Maria, ed. Followers of Jesus. (Builders of Hope Ser.: Bk. 2). (Illus.). 208p. (YA). pap. 9.95 (*0-88489-439-8*); pap. 9.95 (*0-88489-440-1*) St Marys.

Cervantes, Carmen Maria, et al, eds. Dawn on the Horizon: Creating Small Communities. Brancatelli, Robert, tr. LC 96-68232. (Agents of Hope Ser.). (Illus.). 192p. (Orig.). (YA). 1996. pap. 9.95 (*0-88489-429-0*) St Marys.

Cervantes de Salazar, Francisco. Life in the Imperial & Loyal City of Mexico in New Spain. Shepard, Minnie L., tr. LC 79-100224. 113p. 1970. reprint ed. lib. bdg. 55.00 (*0-8371-3033-6*, CELM, Greenwood Pr) Greenwood.

Cervantes, Edgar J. Basic Laboratory Exercises for Physiology, Vol. I. 100p. (C). 1996. pap. text, ring bd. 21.95 (*0-7872-2676-9*) Kendall-Hunt.

Cervantes, Ellen, et al. The Paraprofessional in Home Health & Long-Term Care: Training Modules for Working with Older Adults. LC 95-11564. 272p. 1995. pap. text 30.00 (*1-878812-25-4*) Hlth Prof Pr.

Cervantes, Esther D. Barrio Ghosts: Reading Level 4. 1993. 8.75 (*1-56256-315-7*) Peoples Pub Grp.

Cervantes, Fernando. Devil in the New World: The Impact of Diabolism in New Spain. LC 94-60191. (Illus.). 192p. 1994. 30.00 (*0-300-05975-2*) Yale U Pr.

— The Devil in the New World: The Impact of Diabolism in New Spain. (Illus.). 192p. 1997. pap. 14.00 (*0-300-06889-1*) Yale U Pr.

Cervantes, Fernando, jt. ed. see Griffiths, Nicholas.

Cervantes, Gabriel, jt. auth. see Porter, Dahlia.

Cervantes, Gabriel, jt. auth. see Porter, Dahlia.

Cervantes Gimeno, Fernando, ed. see Laplanche, Jean & Pontalis, Jean-Bertrand.

Cervantes, Hermes T., jt. auth. see Baca, Leonard.

Cervantes, James, jt. ed. see Wright, Leilani.

Cervantes, Jesse & DiMartino, David R. Alcoholism Research Project of Mexican Americans in Scottsbluff, Nebraska. 35p. (Orig.). 1980. pap. 3.00 (*1-55719-051-8*) U NE CPAR.

Cervantes, John R. My Moline: An Illegal Immigrant Dreams. LC 86-71156. (Illus.). 192p. 1986. pap. 7.95 (*0-942568-12-5*) Canyon Pub Co.

Cervantes, Jorge & Clark, Robert C. Indoor Marijuana Horticulture. (Illus.). 400p. 1993. pap. 21.95 (*1-878823-17-5*) Van Patten Pub.

Cervantes, Jose Ramas & Walls, Alfonso V. The Cervantes-Walls Spanish-English Dictionary of the Americas. LC 98-44707. (SPA & ENG., Illus.). 560p. 1994. 11.95 (*0-8442-7974-9*, 79749, Natl Textbk Co); pap. 8.95 (*0-8442-7973-0*, 79730, Natl Textbk Co) NTC Contemp Pub Co.

Cervantes, Lorna D. Emplumada. LC 80-54063. (Poetry Ser.). 80p. 1981. pap. 10.95 (*0-8229-5327-7*) U of Pittsburgh Pr.

— From the Cables of Genocide: Poems on Love & Hunger. LC 91-8721. 78p. (Orig.). 1991. pap. 7.00 (*1-55885-033-3*) Arte Publico.

Cervantes, Richard C., ed. Substance Abuse & Gang Violence. (Focus Editions Ser.: Vol. 147). (Illus.). 208p. (C). 1992. 59.95 (*0-8039-4283-4*); pap. 26.00 (*0-8039-4284-2*) Sage.

Cervantez, Ernesto E. Once upon the 1950s. LC 97-66795. 128p. 1997. 14.95 (*1-887750-65-7*) Rutledge Bks.

Cerve, Wishar S. Lemuria: The Lost Continent of the Pacific. LC 31-34377. 197p. 1931. pap. 12.95 (*0-912057-97-1*, 510728) GLELJ AMORC.

Cervelli, Roseann. Voices of Love. 286p. (Orig.). 1986. pap. 10.00 (*0-87418-024-4*, 159) Coleman Pub.

Cervello, Mike. Heart of a Killer. LC 98-92816. (Illus.). 530p. 1998. pap. 16.00 (*0-9654364-1-1*) C V K Publishing.

— The Refuge of Night Vol. 1: A Modern Vampire Myth with a Bonus Tale of Renaissance Terror. LC 96-96817. (Illus.). 70p. (Orig.). 1996. pap. 4.95 (*0-9654364-0-3*) C V K Publishing.

Cervenka, Edward J., jt. auth. see Saitz, Robert L.

Cervenka, Exene. Virtual Unreality. (Illus.). 128p. (Orig.). 1993. pap. 10.00 (*1-880985-15-2*) Two Thirteen Sixty-one.

Cervenka, Jarda. Mal d'Afrique. LC 94-67069. (Minnesota Voices Project Ser.: Vol. 66). 120p. 1995. pap. 11.95 (*0-89823-158-2*) New Rivers Pr.

— Revenge of Underwater Man. LC 99-89196. (Richard Sullivan Prize in Short Fiction Ser.). 176p. 2000. 25.00 (*0-268-04000-1*, Pub. by U of Notre Dame Pr) Chicago Distribution Ctr.

Cervenka, Jaroslav. The Revenge of Underwater Man: Winner of the 2000 Richard Sullivan Prize in Short Fiction. LC 99-89196. (Richard Sullivan Prize in Short Fiction Ser.). 176p. 2000. pap. 16.00 (*0-268-04001-X*, Pub. by U of Notre Dame Pr) Chicago Distribution Ctr.

Cervenka, Patricia A. Briefs in Law Librarianship Series Vol. 1: Survey on Job Descriptions. Studwell, Roberta, ed. LC 97-1733. (AALL Publications: No. 56 Vol. 1). 56p. 1997. 20.00 (*0-8377-9315-7*, Rothman) W S Hein.

An Asterisk (*) at the beginning of an entry indicates that the title is appearing for the first time.

Cervenka, Tom. Internet & Intranet Applications with Power Builder 6. LC 98-29940. 300p. 1998. pap. 43.95 (*1-884777-60-0*) Manning Pubns.

Cervenka, Zdenek. African National Congress Meets Eastern Europe: A Dialog on Common Experiences. (Scandinavian Institute of African Studies: No. 15). 40p. (Orig.). 1992. pap. 4.95 (*91-7106-337-4*) Coronet Bks.

— Land-Locked Countries of Africa. (Seminar Proceedings Ser.: No. 9). 368p. 1973. write for info. (*91-7106-065-0*, Pub. by Nordic Africa) Transaction Pubs.

Cervenka, Zdenek, ed. Vit Makt i Zimbabwe: En Rasistregim i Sodra Afrika. 51p. 1974. write for info. (*91-7106-074-X*, Pub. by Nordic Africa) Transaction Pubs.

Cervenka, Zdenek & Legum, Colin. Can National Dialogue Break the Power of Terror in Burundi? LC 95-201078. (Current African Issues Ser.: No. 17). 29p. 1994. 6.95 (*91-7106-353-6*, Pub. by Nordic Africa) Transaction Pubs.

— Le Dialogue National Peut - Il Briser la Puissance de la Terreur au Burundi? 36p. 1994. 6.95 (*91-7106-358-7*, Pub. by Nordic Africa) Transaction Pubs.

Cervenka, Zdenek, jt. auth. see Widstrand, Carl G.

Cervenkova, Exene, ed. see Maybe, Ellyn.

Cerveny, George. Mark the Wind's Power. 299p. 1982. 10.95 (*0-87770-272-1*); pap. 5.95 (*0-87770-273-X*) Ye Galleon.

Cerveny, L. K., jt. auth. see Marshall, C. A.

Cerveny, Robert P. Strategic Information Systems for Strategic, Manufacturing, Operations, Marketing, Sales, Financial & Human Resources Management. Pegels, C. Carl et al, eds. LC 93-33185. (Monographs in Organizational Behavior & Industrial Relations: Vol. 16). 307p. 1993. 78.50 (*1-55938-716-5*) Jai Pr.

Cerveny, Vlastislav, et al. Seismic Waves in Laterally Inhomogeneous Media, Pt. I. LC 96-48399. (Pageoph Topical Volumes Ser.: Vol. 148, Nos. 1 & 2, 1996). 342p. 1997. pap. 34.50 (*3-7643-5648-0*) Birkhauser.

Cerver, Francisco. The New International House. (Illus.). 208p. 55.00 (*0-8230-3167-5*) Watsn-Guptill.

Cerver, Francisco A. Charming Hotels. (Illus.). 176p. 1999. pap. 35.00 (*0-8230-0618-2*) Watsn-Guptill.

— Dream Apartments. (Illus.). 176p. 1999. pap. 35.00 (*0-8230-6637-1*) Watsn-Guptill.

— Remarkable Restaurants. (Illus.). 160p. 1998. pap. 35.00 (*0-8230-6816-1*) Watsn-Guptill.

Cerver, Francisco A., ed. Exclusive Houses. (Illus.). 240p. 1999. pap. 39.95 (*84-8185-041-1*) St Martin.

Cerver, Francisco Asenio. Landscape of Recreation I: Sports Facilities. (World of Environmental Designs Ser.). (Illus.). 256p. 1998. text 80.00 (*84-8185-009-8*) Arco Edit.

Cerver, Francisco Asensio. An Architectural Promenade. (Illus.). 192p. 1998. 45.00 (*0-8230-0288-8*) Watsn-Guptill.

— Business & Corporation Parks: Roof Gardens. (World of Environmental Designs Ser.). (Illus.). 256p. 1998. 80.00 (*84-8185-008-X*) Watsn-Guptill.

— Civil Engineering: Nature Conservation & Land Reclamation. (Illus.). 256p. 1999. text 80.00 (*84-8185-000-4*, Pub. by Arco Edit) Watson Guptill.

— Contemporary Architectural Images. (Illus.). 192p. 1998. 45.00 (*0-8230-0932-7*) Watsn-Guptill.

— Dream Pools & Gardens. LC 99-10489. (Illus.). 208p. 1999. text 50.00 (*1-55670-907-2*) Stewart Tabori & Chang.

— Extraordinary Offices. (Illus.). 160p. 1998. pap. 35.00 (*0-8230-6616-9*) Watsn-Guptill.

— Landscape of Recreation II: Amusement Parks. (World of Environmental Designs Ser.). (Illus.). 256p. 1998. 80.00 (*84-8185-010-1*) Watsn-Guptill.

— Lofts: Living & Working Spaces. 1999. pap. text 35.00 (*0-8230-6632-0*) Watsn-Guptill.

— Selected Architecture. (Illus.). 192p. 1998. pap. 45.00 (*0-8230-4780-6*) Watsn-Guptill.

— Spectacular Swimming Pools. 1999. pap. text 35.00 (*0-8230-6633-9*) Watsn-Guptill.

Cervera, Alejo De, see De Cervera, Alejo.

Cervera, Neil & Videka-Sherman, Lynn, eds. Working with Pregnant & Parenting Teenage Clients. 256p. 1990. pap. 18.95 (*0-87304-248-4*) Manticore Pubs.

Cervera, Neil, jt. auth. see Carlson, Bonnie E.

Cervera, Ricard. Antibodies to Endothelial Cells & Vascular Damage. 208p. 1993. lib. bdg. 179.00 (*0-8493-4914-1*, RC694) CRC Pr.

Cervera Tomas, Vicente, tr. Enciclopedia Internacional de las Ciencias Sociales, 11 vols., 11 vols. (SPA.). 1977. 1295.00 (*0-8288-8232-0*, 8403189966) Fr & Eur.

Cervera Vera, L. Plazas Mayores de Espana, I. (SPA., Illus.). 408p. 1993. 295.00 (*84-239-5285-1*) Elliots Bks.

Cervero, F., jt. ed. see Belmonte, C.

Cervero, Robert B. Paratransit in America: Jitneys, Vans & Minibuses. LC 96-21246. 320p. 1997. 59.95 (*0-275-95725-X*, Praeger Pubs) Greenwood.

— The Transit Metropolis: A Global Inquiry. LC 98-34096. (Illus.). 400p. 1998. pap. text 45.00 (*1-55963-591-6*) Island Pr.

Cervero, Robert B., jt. auth. see Bernick, Michael S.

*__Cervero, Ronald M.__ Power in Practice: Adult Education & the Struggle for Knowledge & Power in Society. 2000. 34.95 (*0-7879-4729-6*) Jossey-Bass.

Cervero, Ronald M. & Wilson, Arthur L. Planning Responsibly for Adult Education: A Guide to Negotiating Power & Interests. LC 93-43174. (Higher & Adult Education Ser.). 228p. 1994. text 32.95 (*1-55542-628-X*) Jossey-Bass.

Cervero, Ronald M., et al. Visions for the Future of Continuing Professional Education. (Illus.). (Orig.). (C). 1990. pap. text 14.95 (*0-9619031-2-0*) U GA GA Ctr Cnt Educ.

Cervetti, Nancy. Scenes of Reading: Transforming Romance in Bronte, Eliot, & Woolf. Vol. 24. LC 97-8513. (Writing about Women Ser.). XII, 173p. (C). 1998. text 42.95 (*0-8204-3805-7*) P Lang Pubng.

Cervigni, Dino S., tr. see Dante Alighieri.

Cervin, David R., ed. see Frey, Albert R.

Cervin, Tina, jt. ed. see Ito, Susan.

Cervinka, Otakar. Evantioselective Reactions in Organic Chemistry. 300p. (C). 1996. 61.00 (*0-13-276239-0*) P-H.

Cervinskas, J., et al, eds. Growth Promotion for Child Development. 280p. 1993. pap. write for info. (*0-88936-676-4*) IDRC Bks.

*__Cervone, Daniel & Shoda, eds.__ The Coherence of Personality: Social-Cognitive Bases of Consistency, Variability & Organization. LC 98-52114. 1p. 1999. lib. bdg. 45.00 (*1-57230-436-7*) Guilford Pubns.

Cervone, Daniel, jt. auth. see Caprara, Gian Vittorio.

*__Cervone, Ed.__ Der Mann in der Kinst, Band 5. 1998. pap. 24.95 (*3-925443-55-X*) Janssen.

Cervone, Ed. Phantasies of Gay Sex: Drawings & Water Colour. 1998. 79.95 (*3-925443-69-X*) Janvid Pubs.

Cervone, Frank H. AIX/6000 System Guide. LC 95-23306. (J. Ranade Workstation Ser.). 501p. 1996. pap. 40.00 (*0-07-024129-5*) McGraw.

*__Cervone, Frank H.__ Red Hat Linux Performance Administration Tools. (Illus.). 2000. pap. 39.99 (*0-07-212214-5*) McGrw-H Intl.

— Solaris 7 Performance Administration Tools. (Illus.). 2000. pap. 39.99 (*0-07-212211-0*) McGrw-H Intl.

Cervone, H. Frank. Solaris Performance Adminisration. (Illus.). 352p. 1998. pap. 44.95 (*0-07-011768-3*) McGraw.

Cervone, John & Fleagle, Arnold. Foundations I: Basic Blocks for Building a Life of Faith. (Walking with the Word Ser.: Vol. I). 55p. (Orig.). 1996. pap. 5.99 (*0-87509-684-0*) Chr Pubns.

Cervone, John C. & Fleagle, Arnold R. Foundations II: Basic Blocks for Building a Life of Faith. (Walking with the Word Ser.: Vol. 2). 80p. 1998. pap. 5.99 (*0-87509-780-4*) Chr Pubns.

Cervos-Navarro, Jorge, et al, eds. Pathology of Cerebrospinal Microcirculation. fac. ed. LC 77-84125. (Advances in Neurology Ser.: No. 20). (Illus.). 632p. pap. 196.00 (*0-7837-7256-4*, 204704900005) Bks Demand.

Cervos-Navarro, Jorge & Ferszt, Ron, eds. Stroke & Microcirculation. LC 86-45980. 609p. 1987. reprint ed. pap. 188.80 (*0-608-00327-1*, 206104400007) Bks Demand.

Cervos-Navarro, Jorge & Fritschka, Emmanuel, eds. Cerebral Microcirculation & Metabolism. fac. ed. LC 80-5444. (Illus.). 499p. pap. 154.70 (*0-7837-7511-3*, 204699400005) Bks Demand.

Cervos-Navarro, Jorge & Sarkander, H. I., eds. Brain Aging: Neuropathology & Neuropharmacology. LC 82-15111. (Aging Ser.: No. 21). (Illus.). 454p. reprint ed. pap. 140.80 (*0-608-00618-1*, 206120500007) Bks Demand.

Cervos-Navarro, Jorge & Urich, Henry, eds. Metabolic & Degenerative Diseases of the Central Nervous System: Pathology, Biochemistry, & Genetics. (Illus.). 873p. 1995. text 129.95 (*0-12-165250-5*) Acad Pr.

Cervos-Navarro, Jorge, ed. see Erwin Riesch Symposium on the Cerebral Vessel Wall.

Cerwinske, Laura. In a Spiritual Style: The Home As Sanctuary. LC 98-60337. (Illus.). 112p. 1998. 24.95 (*0-500-01873-1*, Pub. by Thames Hudson) Norton.

Cerwinske, Laura. Russian Imperial Style. (Illus.). 224p. 1997. 9.99 (*0-517-18705-1*) Random Hse Value.

— Writing as a Healing Art: The Transforming Power of Self-Expression. LC 99-39285. 1999. pap. 14.00 (*0-399-52542-4*, Perigee Bks) Berkley Pub.

*__Cerwinske, Laura & Chase, Linda.__ In the Romantic Style: Creating Intimacy, Fantasy & Charm in the Contemporary Home. 2nd ed. LC 90-70067. (Illus.). 160p. 2000. reprint ed. pap. 24.95 (*0-500-28244-7*, Pub. by Thames Hudson) Norton.

Cerwinske, Laura, jt. auth. see Brooke, Steven.

Cerwinske, Laura, jt. auth. see Chase, Linda.

Cerwinski, Laura. Miami: Hot & Cool. 240p. 1998. pap. 25.00 (*0-609-80382-4*) Crown Pub Group.

Cerza, Alphonse. The Courts & Freemasonry. 105p. 1986. 12.50 (*0-935633-03-0*) Anchor Comm.

Cerza, June. When Will I Stop Hurting? Dealing with a Recent Death. 62p. 1990. pap. 5.99 (*0-8010-5487-7*) Baker Bks.

Cerza, Mary K., ed. see Woman's Club Staff.

CES Industries, Inc. Staff. Ed-Lab Eight Hundred Exercise Manual: Interfaces, Unit 2. (Illus.). (Orig.). (gr. 9-12). 1982. write for info. (*0-86711-030-9*) CES Industries.

— Ed-Lab Eight Hundred Exercise Manual: Programming for Ohm's Law, Unit 1. (Illus.). (Orig.). (C). 1982. write for info. (*0-318-57823-9*) CES Industries.

— Ed-Lab Eight Hundred Experiment & Exercise Manual: Programming in BASIC. rev. ed. (Illus.). 1983. write for info. (*0-318-57822-0*) CES Industries.

— Ed-Lab Eight Hundred Experiment Manual: Contactor Sensor Operation. (Illus.). (Orig.). (YA). (gr. 9-12). 1983. write for info. (*0-86711-048-1*) CES Industries.

— Ed-Lab Eight Hundred Experiment Manual: EPROM Programming. (Illus.). (Orig.). 1984. pap. write for info. (*0-86711-084-8*) CES Industries.

— Ed-Lab Eight Hundred Experiment Manual: Infra-Red Sensor. (Illus.). (Orig.). (YA). (gr. 9-12). 1983. write for info. (*0-86711-047-3*) CES Industries.

— Ed-Lab Eight Hundred Experiment Manual: Photocell Sensor. (Illus.). (Orig.). (gr. 9-12). 1983. write for info. (*0-86711-049-X*) CES Industries.

— Ed-Lab Eight Hundred Experiment Manual: Printer Interfacing. (Illus.). (Orig.). (YA). (gr. 9-12). 1984. write for info. (*0-86711-070-8*) CES Industries.

— Ed-Lab Eight Hundred Experiment Manual: Robotics Interfacing. (Illus.). (Orig.). (gr. 9-12). 1983. write for info. (*0-86711-046-5*) CES Industries.

— Ed-Lab Eight Hundred Experiment Manual: Talker Interfacing. (Illus.). (Orig.). (YA). (gr. 9-12). 1983. write for info. (*0-86711-069-4*) CES Industries.

— Ed-Lab Eight Hundred Experiment Manual: Thermal Probe Sensor. (Illus.). (Orig.). 1983. pap. write for info. (*0-86711-073-2*) CES Industries.

— Ed-Lab Eight Hundred Experiment Manual: Touch Sensor. (Illus.). (Orig.). (YA). (gr. 9-12). 1983. write for info. (*0-86711-068-6*) CES Industries.

— Ed-Lab Eight Hundred Series Reference Manual Operations & BASIC. (Illus.). (Orig.). (C). 1983. write for info. (*0-86711-067-8*) CES Industries.

— Ed-Lab Eighty Exercise Manual: DC-AC Electronics Programming. (Illus.). (gr. 9-12). 1982. write for info. (*0-86711-062-7*) CES Industries.

— Ed-Lab Eighty Exercise Manual: Interfaces, Unit 2. (Illus.). (gr. 9-12). 1982. write for info. (*0-86711-057-0*) CES Industries.

— Ed-Lab Eighty Exercise Manual: Programming for Ohm's Law. (Illus.). (YA). (gr. 9-12). 1982. write for info. (*0-86711-058-9*) CES Industries.

— Ed-Lab Eighty Experiment Manual: Contactor Sensor Operation. (Illus.). (gr. 9-12). 1982. write for info. (*0-86711-063-5*) CES Industries.

— Ed-Lab Eighty Experiment Manual: Infra-Red Sensor. (Illus.). (Orig.). 1983. write for info. (*0-86711-065-1*) CES Industries.

— Ed-Lab Eighty Experiment Manual: Photocell Sensor. (Illus.). (Orig.). (gr. 9-12). 1983. write for info. (*0-86711-036-8*) CES Industries.

— Ed-Lab Eighty Experiment Manual: Printer Interfacing. (Illus.). (Orig.). (gr. 9-12). 1983. write for info. (*0-86711-033-3*) CES Industries.

— Ed-Lab Eighty Experiment Manual: Thermal Probe Sensor. (Illus.). (Orig.). 1983. write for info. (*0-86711-041-4*) CES Industries.

— Ed-Lab Eighty Experiment Manual: Touch Sensor. (Illus.). (Orig.). (gr. 9-12). 1983. write for info. (*0-86711-040-6*) CES Industries.

— Ed-Lab Eighty Reference Manual: Using the Ed-Lab 80 & the Basic Language. (Illus.). (gr. 9-12). 1982. write for info. (*0-86711-061-9*) CES Industries.

— Ed-Lab Experiment Manual: CES 211 Breadboard Lab Manual. (Illus.). 1983. write for info. (*0-86711-066-X*) CES Industries.

— Ed-Lab Experiment Manual: CES 303 Synchro-Servo Mechanism. (Illus.). (gr. 9-12). 1981. write for info. (*0-86711-012-0*) CES Industries.

— Ed-Lab Experiment Manual: CES 307 Torque Synchros. (Illus.). (gr. 9-12). 1981. write for info. (*0-86711-011-2*) CES Industries.

— Ed-Lab Experiment Manual: CES 308 Resolvers. (Illus.). (gr. 9-12). 1981. write for info. (*0-86711-013-9*) CES Industries.

— Ed-Lab Experiment Manual: CES 309 Motor Speed Control Servo. (Illus.). (gr. 9-12). 1981. write for info. (*0-86711-009-0*) CES Industries.

— Ed-Lab Experiment Manual: CES 310 Potentiometer Position Servo. (Illus.). (gr. 9-12). 1981. write for info. (*0-86711-010-4*) CES Industries.

— Ed-Lab Experiment Manual: CES 311 Transducers. (Illus.). (gr. 9-12). 1982. write for info. (*0-86711-050-3*) CES Industries.

— Ed-Lab Experiment Manual: CES 318 Relay Module. (Illus.). (gr. 9-12). 1981. write for info. (*0-86711-024-4*) CES Industries.

— Ed-Lab Experiment Manual: CES 349 Counter Timer Module; Troubleshooting System. (Illus.). (gr. 9-12). 1982. write for info. (*0-318-56867-5*); write for info. (*0-86711-031-7*) CES Industries.

— Ed-Lab Experiment Manual: CES 380 Microprocessors. (Illus.). 162p. (gr. 9-12). 1980. 11.50 (*0-86711-007-4*) CES Industries.

— Ed-Lab Experiment Manual: CES 380-85 Microprocessors. (Illus.). (Orig.). (J). (gr. 9-12). 1984. pap. write for info. (*0-86711-076-7*) CES Industries.

— Ed-Lab Experiment Manual: CES 6010 Microwave Training System. (Illus.). (Orig.). (J). (gr. 9-12). 1984. pap. write for info. (*0-86711-083-X*) CES Industries.

— Ed-Lab Experiment Manual: CES 6016 Telephone Modem. (Illus.). (Orig.). (J). (gr. 9-12). 1984. pap. write for info. (*0-86711-085-6*) CES Industries.

— Ed-Lab Experiment Manual: Instructor Guide to Troubles: TV Trainer. (Illus.). (Orig.). (C). 1983. write for info. (*0-86711-045-7*) CES Industries.

— Ed-Lab Experiment Manual: Mechanical Module. Nesenoff, Norman, ed. (Illus.). (Orig.). (gr. 9-12). 1980. write for info. (*0-86711-037-6*) CES Industries

— Ed-Lab Experiment Manual: Microprocessor; Student Guide. (Illus.). (gr. 9-12). 1981. write for info. (*0-86711-018-X*) CES Industries.

— Ed-Lab Experiment Manual: Optics Trainer. (Illus.). (Orig.). 1983. write for info. (*0-86711-042-2*) CES Industries.

— Ed-Lab Experiment Manual: Student Guide to Test Points; TV Trainer. (Illus.). (Orig.). (J). (gr. 9-12). 1983. write for info. (*0-86711-044-9*) CES Industries.

— Ed-Lab Instructor's Guide: I-O Module CES 342; A-D Converter Latch-Module CES 343. (Illus.). (gr. 9-12). 1982. write for info. (*0-86711-060-0*) CES Industries.

— Ed-Lab Nine Hundred & Eighty: Microprocessor Concepts, Unit 1. (Illus.). (gr. 9-12). 1981. 9.50 (*0-86711-021-X*) CES Industries.

— Ed-Lab Nine Hundred & Eighty Appendicies: Microcomputer Technology. (Illus.). (gr. 9-12). 1981. 11.50 (*0-86711-023-6*) CES Industries.

— Ed-Lab Nine Hundred & Eighty Experiment: Projects & Interfacing. (Illus.). (gr. 9-12). 1982. 9.50 (*0-86711-025-2*) CES Industries.

— Ed-Lab Nine Hundred & Eighty Experiment Manual: Microcomputer Technology, Unit 2. (Illus.). (gr. 9-12). 11.50 (*0-86711-022-8*) CES Industries.

— Ed-Lab Nine Hundred Experiment Manual: Advanced Digital Systems. (Illus.). (gr. 9-12). 1981. 12.50 (*0-86711-008-2*) CES Industries.

— Ed-Lab Seven Hundred Experiment Manual: Digital Systems. (Illus.). 304p. (gr. 9-12). 1979. 12.50 (*0-86711-001-5*) CES Industries.

— Ed-Lab Six Hundred & Fifty Experiment Manual: Basic Electronics Concepts, Book O. (Illus.). 206p. (gr. 9-12). 1980. 11.50 (*0-86711-002-3*) CES Industries.

— Ed-Lab Six Hundred & Fifty Experiment Manual: Communications, Bk. III. (Illus.). (gr. 9-12). 1982. 11.50 (*0-86711-026-0*) CES Industries.

— Ed-Lab Six Hundred & Fifty Experiment Manual: Electricity-Electronics AC-DC, Bk. I. (Illus.). 288p. (gr. 9-12). 1981. 12.50 (*0-86711-015-5*) CES Industries.

— Ed-Lab Six Hundred & Fifty Experiment Manual: Electricity-Electronics Solid-State, Bk. II. (Illus.). 304p. (gr. 9-12). 1981. 12.50 (*0-86711-014-7*) CES Industries.

— Ed-Lab Six Hundred & Fifty Experiment Manual: Operational Amplifiers, Bk. IV. (Illus.). 148p. (gr. 9-12). 1979. 9.50 (*0-86711-016-3*) CES Industries.

— Ed-Lab Six Hundred & Fifty Experiment Manual: Pulses & Waveshaping, Bk.V. (Ed-Lab 650 Experiment Manual Ser.). (Illus.). (gr. 9-12). 1982. student ed. 11.50 (*0-86711-052-X*) CES Industries.

— Ed-Lab Sixty Three Experiment Manual: Basic Electronics; User's Manual. (Illus.). (gr. 9-12). 1982. write for info. (*0-86711-028-7*) CES Industries.

CES Industries, Inc. Staff & Nesenoff, Norman. Ed-Lab Eighty Experiment Manual: EPROM Programming. (Illus.). 1983. write for info. (*0-86711-038-4*) CES Industries.

— Ed-Lab Eighty Experiment Manual: Robotics Interfacing. (Illus.). (Orig.). 1983. write for info. (*0-86711-034-1*) CES Industries.

CE's Terminology Office Staff, contrib. by. Population: French-English Glossary & Glossaire Anglais-Francais. 500p. (Orig.). 1994. pap. 56.00 (*92-871-2506-6*, Pub. by Council of Europe) Manhattan Pub Co.

C

Cesa, Margaret. The World of Flower Blue: Pop Chalee: An Artistic Biography. LC 97-18137. (Illus.). 288p. 1997. 49.95 (*1-878610-65-1*) Red Crane Bks.

Cesaire, Aime. Les Armes Miraculeuses. (Poesie Ser.). pap. 7.95 (*2-07-030063-3*) Schoenhof.

— Cadastre. pap. 8.95 (*0-8288-9082-X*, 2020016672) Fr & Eur.

— Cadastre. Snyder, Emile, tr. from FRE. LC 75-169155. 160p. 1973. 15.95 (*0-89388-070-1*); pap. 9.95 (*0-89388-085-X*) Okpaku Communications.

— Cahier d'un Retour au Pays Natal. (FRE.). 93p. pap. 22.95 (*0-7859-9262-6*) Fr & Eur.

*__Cesaire, Aime.__ Cahier d'un Retour au Pays Natal. 2nd ed. Irele, Abiola, ed. LC 99-32570. 240p. (C). 2000. pap. text 24.95 (*0-8142-5020-3*) Ohio St U Pr.

Cesaire, Aime. Discours sur le Colonialisme. pap. 13.95 (*0-8288-9083-8*, 2708705318) Fr & Eur.

Cesaire, Aime. Discourse on Colonialism. text 30.00 (*1-58367-024-6*); pap. text 14.00 (*1-58367-025-4*) Monthly Rev.

Cesaire, Aime. Discourse on Colonialism. Pinkham, Joan, tr. LC 72-178714. 96p. 1972. pap. 10.00 (*0-85345-226-1*) Monthly Rev.

— Et les Chiens se Taisaient. pap. 14.95 (*0-8288-9084-6*, 2708705296) Fr & Eur.

— Ferrements. pap. 29.95 (*0-8288-9085-4*, 2020016656) Fr & Eur.

— Lost Body. Eshleman, Clayton & Smith, Annette, trs. from FRE. LC 86-1001. (Illus.). 132p. 1986. pap. 14.95 (*0-8076-1148-4*) Braziller.

— Lost Body. Eshleman, Clayton & Smith, Annette, trs. from FRE. LC 86-1001. (Illus.). 132p. 1986. 25.00 (*0-8076-1147-6*, Pub. by Braziller) Norton.

— Moi, Laminaire. (FRE.). 1991. pap. 10.95 (*0-7859-2724-7*) Fr & Eur.

— Notebook of a Return to a Native Land. 86p. 1997. pap. text 14.95 (*1-56886-046-3*) Marsilio Pubs.

— Une Saison au Congo. 1975. pap. 10.95 (*0-8288-9086-2*) Fr & Eur.

— The Tempest. LC 74-82723. 1974. 5.95 (*0-89388-174-0*); pap. 2.95 (*0-89388-175-9*) Okpaku Communications.

— A Tempest. rev. ed. Miller, Richard, tr. from FRE. LC 92-63019. 72p. 1993. pap. 11.95 (*0-913745-40-5*) Ubu Repertory.

— Une Tempete. 1975. pap. 10.95 (*0-8288-9087-0*) Fr & Eur.

— Textes. Mercier, R. et al, eds. (Classiques du Monde, Litterature Africaine Ser.). pap. 8.95 (*0-685-35627-2*) Fr & Eur.

— La Tragedie du Roi Christophe. (FRE.). 160p. 1970. pap. 12.95 (*0-7859-3452-9*) Fr & Eur.

Cesal, Barbara P. Heart to Heart: Family Reading for Home & School. 1997. pap. 12.95 (*0-201-45500-5*) Addison-Wesley.

*__Cesana, Luisa.__ MCSD Visual Basic 6 Desktop Applications. LC 98-88946. (Microsoft Certified Professional Ser.). (Illus.). 592p. 1999. student ed. 44.99 incl. cd-rom (*0-7821-2438-0*) Sybex.

*__Cesana, Luisa, et al.__ Windows CE Developer's Handbook. LC 99-61299. (Developer's Handbks.). (Illus.). 640p. 1999. pap. 49.99 incl. cd-rom (*0-7821-2414-3*) Sybex.

Cesana, Luisa, ed. see Tolstoy, Leo.

Cesar, Ana C. Intimate Diary. 128p. 1997. pap. 14.95 (*1-899460-50-0*, Pub. by Boulevard-Babel) Paul & Co Pubs.

Cesar, Bruno, jt. auth. see D'Herbemont, Olivier.

Cesar, Edison M. Strategies for Defining the Army's Objective Vision of Command & Control for the 21st Century. LC 95-8471. xxiv, 56p. 1995. pap. text 9.00 (*0-8330-1643-1*, MR-487-A) Rand Corp.

***Cesar, Erlie.** What God Did for Me, He Can Also Do for You. 1999. pap. 10.99 (*1-56043-328-0*, Treasure Hse) Destiny Image.

Cesar, H. S. Control & Games Models of the Greenhouse Effect: Economics Essays on the Comedy & Tragedy of the Commons. LC 94-21966. (Lecture Notes in Economics & Mathematical Systems Ser.: Vol. 416). 1994. 49.95 (*0-387-58220-7*); write for info. (*3-540-58220-7*) Spr-Verlag.

Cesar, Jasiel. Walter Benjamin on Experience & History: Profane Illumination. LC 92-3641. 240p. 1992. lib. bdg. 89.95 (*0-7734-9812-5*) E Mellen.

Cesar, Julio C. Comentarios de la Guerra de las Galias, No. 121. (SPA.). 248p. 1964. write for info. (*0-8288-8576-1*) Fr & Eur.

— Guerre Des Gaules. (FRE.). 480p. 1981. pap. 11.95 (*0-7859-1939-2*, 2070373150) Fr & Eur.

Cesar, Waldo, jt. auth. see Shaull, Richard.

Cesarani, Antonio, et al. Vertigo & Dizziness Rehabilitation: The MCS Method. (Illus.). x, 243p. 1999. pap. 49.00 (*3-540-64084-3*) Spr-Verlag.

***Cesarani, David.** Arthur Koestler: The Homeless Mind. LC 99-13114. 656p. 1999. 30.00 (*0-684-86720-6*) Free Pr.

Cesarani, David, ed. Final Solution: Origins & Implementation. 328p. (C). 1996. pap. 27.99 (*0-415-15232-1*) Routledge.

— Genocide & Rescue: The Holocaust in Hungary 1944. LC 98-115343. 1997. 55.00 (*1-85973-121-X*, Pub. by Berg Pubs); pap. 19.50 (*1-85973-126-0*, Pub. by Berg Pubs) NYU Pr.

Cesarani, David & Fulbrook, Mary, eds. Citizenship, Nationality, & Migration in Europe. LC 95-38744. 240p. (C). 1996. pap. 22.99 (*0-415-13101-4*) Routledge.

Cesarani, David & Kushner, Tony, eds. The Internment of Aliens in Twentieth Century Britain. LC 92-21176. 1993. 39.50 (*0-7146-3466-2*, Pub. by F Cass Pubs); pap. 22.50 (*0-7146-4095-6*, Pub. by F Cass Pubs) Intl Spec Bk.

C

Cesare. Organic Chemistry. 1999. lab manual ed. 12.49 (*0-07-228897-3*) McGraw.

Cesare, Angelo De, see De Cesare, Angelo.

Cesare, Marc. Fragrances & Their Applications. LC 98-120754. 123p. 1997. 2850.00 (*1-56965-370-4*, C-206) BCC.

Cesare, Mario A. Di, see Di Cesare, Mario A., ed.

Cesareo, Francesco C. Humanism & Catholic Reform: The Life & Work of Gregorio Cortese (1483-1548) LC 89-13009. (Renaissance & Baroque Studies & Texts: Vol. 2). (Illus.). XVIII, 205p. (C). 1990. text 45.50 (*0-8204-0907-3*) P Lang Pubng.

— A Shepherd in Their Midst: The Episcopacy of Girolame Seripardo (1554-1563) LC 98-49786. (Augustinian Ser.: Vol. 21). 166p. 1999. pap. 14.95 (*1-889542-08-3*) Augustinian Pr.

Cesareo, Mario. Cruzados, Martires y Beatos: Emplazamientos del Cuerpo Colonial. LC 95-30211. (Purdue Studies in Romance Literatures: Vol. 9). (SPA.). 213p. 1995. 39.95 (*1-55753-075-0*) Purdue U Pr.

Cesareo, Roberto, jt. auth. see Moro, Renata.

Cesaresco, Evelyn M. Cavour. LC 76-150174. (Select Bibliographies Reprint Ser.). 1977. 18.95 (*0-8369-5687-7*) Ayer.

— Liberation of Italy, 1815-1870. LC 72-2563. (Select Bibliographies Reprint Ser.). 1980. reprint ed. 26.95 (*0-8369-6850-6*) Ayer.

Cesaretti, Charles A. & Vitale, Joseph T., eds. Rumors of War: A Moral & Theological Perspective on the Arms Race. 128p. (Orig.). 1984. 6.95 (*0-8164-2365-2*) Harper SF.

Cesari, Cecile. Strengthen Your Performance in Psychological Tests. 96p. 1996. pap. text 18.95 (*0-572-02208-5*, Pub. by W Foulsham) Trans-Atl Phila.

Cesari, F. Economics & Finance Dictionary. 400p. 1988. 75.00 (*0-8288-4033-4*, F128013) Fr & Eur.

Cesari, Lamberto. Optimization Theory & Applications: Problems with Ordinary Differential Equations. (Applications of Mathematics Ser.: Vol. 17). (Illus.). 544p. 1983. 161.95 (*0-387-90676-2*) Spr-Verlag.

— Surface Area. (Annals of Mathematics Studies: No. 35). 1956. 45.00 (*0-527-02752-9*) Periodicals Srv.

Cesari, Lamberto, et al, eds. Nonlinear Functional Analysis & Differential Equations. (Lecture Notes in Pure & Applied Mathematics Ser.: Vol. 19). (Illus.). 368p. 1976. pap. text 175.00 (*0-8247-6452-8*) Dekker.

Cesarini, F. & Salza, S., eds. Database Machine Performance: Modeling Methodologies & Evaluation Strategies. (Notes in Computer Science Ser.: Vol. 257). ix, 250p. 1987. 36.00 (*0-387-17942-9*) Spr-Verlag.

Cesarini, Jeanie, et al. Secrets Vol. 3: The Best in Women's Sensual Fiction. 224p. 1997. pap. 12.99 (*0-9648942-2-X*) Red Sage.

— Secrets Vol. 4: The Best in Women's Sensual Fiction. 248p. 1998. pap. 12.99 (*0-9648942-4-6*, 04) Red Sage.

Cesarini, N., jt. auth. see Alpini, D.

Cesario, Lee. Modeling, Analysis, & Design of Water Distribution Systems. (Illus.). 328p. 1995. 84.00 (*0-89867-758-0*, 20296) Am Water Wks Assn.

Cesarone, John, jt. auth. see Brauer, Douglas C.

Cesbron, G. Il Est Minuit Docteur Schweitzer. (FRE.). 1985. pap. 10.95 (*0-7859-3250-X*, 2266046098) Fr & Eur.

Cescinsky, Herbert & Webster. English Domestic Clocks. (Illus.). 354p. 1976. reprint ed. 69.50 (*0-902028-37-5*) Antique Collect.

Cescotti, R. German/English/German Glossary Aerospace Definitions. 2nd ed. (ENG & GER.). 298p. 1993. 85.00 (*0-320-00592-5*) Fr & Eur.

Cescotti, Roderich. Aerospace Dictionary: English-German, German-English. (ENG & GER.). 382p. 1994. 95.00 (*0-7859-6971-3*) Fr & Eur.

— Glossary of Aeronautical Definitions: English-German, German-English. 2nd ed. (ENG & GER.). 298p. 1993. 85.00 (*0-7859-9998-1*) Fr & Eur.

Cesena, Robert R. Residential Child Care in America, National Edition, 1995-96: A Comprehensive Guide to Residential Treatment Options for Children in Need. 400p. (Orig.). 1994. pap. 44.00 (*1-878817-02-7*) Services West Pub.

Cesena, Robert R., ed. Residential Child Care in America: Western Edition, 93-94. 2nd ed. 387p. 1993. per. 36.00 (*1-878817-01-9*) Services West Pub.

Ceserani, Jonne. Innovation & Creativity. 1997. pap. text 19.95 (*0-7494-1593-2*) Kogan Page Ltd.

Ceserani, Victor & Kinton, Ronald. Practical Cookery. 7th ed. 570p. 1993. text 39.95 (*0-470-23351-6*) Halsted Pr.

Ceserani, Victor, et al. Contemporary Cookery. (Illus.). 336p. (C). 1988. text 17.95 (*0-7131-7752-7*, Pub. by E A) Routldge.

— Contemporary Cookery. 323p. 1993. text 39.95 (*0-470-23350-8*) Halsted Pr.

Cesereanu, Ruxandra. Schizoid Ocean: Poems. unabridged ed. Litvinchievici, Claudia, tr. from RUM. 96p. 1997. pap. 10.95 (*1-883881-23-4*, 234) S Freud RT&PF.

Cesher, Tonya, ed. see Garrett, Ottie.

Cesnakova, E. & Kodlova, A. Slovensky Jazyk - Cvicenia a Diktaty Na Prijimacie Skusky Na Stredne Skoly (Slovak - Exercises & Dictations for Admittance Examinations for Secondary Schools) (SLO.). 152p. 1996. pap. write for info. (*80-08-02453-4*, Pub. by Slov Pegagog Naklad) IBD Ltd.

Cesoni, Bob. Basketball Stickers. (Illus.). (J). (gr. k-3). 1992. pap. 1.00 (*0-486-26987-6*) Dover.

Cespedes. Concurrent Marketing. 1995. 29.95 (*0-07-103630-X*) McGraw.

Cespedes, Alba de. Remorse. Weaver, William, tr. from ITA. LC 78-14003. 1979. lib. bdg. 75.00 (*0-313-20731-3*, CERE, Greenwood Pr) Greenwood.

Cespedes, Frank V. Concurrent Marketing: Integrating Product, Sales, & Service. LC 95-4325. 336p. 1995. 29.95 (*0-87584-444-8*) Harvard Busn.

Cespedes, Frank V. Managing Marketing Linkages: Text, Cases & Readings. 403p. 1995. pap. text 38.20 (*0-13-234923-X*) P-H.

Cess, R. D., jt. auth. see Sparrow, E. M.

Cessario, Romanus. Christian Faith & the Theological Life. LC 96-15512. 195p. (C). 1996. text 34.95 (*0-8132-0868-8*); pap. text 17.95 (*0-8132-0869-6*) Cath U Pr.

— The Godly Image. LC 89-62742. (Studies in Historical Theology). 214p. 1990. pap. 19.95 (*0-932506-74-7*, 6747) St Bedes Pubns.

— The Moral Virtues & Theological Ethics. LC 90-70854. (C). 1992. pap. text 13.00 (*0-268-01389-6*) U of Notre Dame Pr.

— Perpetual Angelus: As the Saints Pray the Rosary. LC 94-42253. 1995. pap. 9.95 (*0-8189-0722-3*) Alba.

Cessario, Romanus, jt. ed. see Cameron, Peter J.

Cessenat, M. Mathematical Methods in Electromagnetism: Linear Theory & Applications. (Series on Advances in Mathematics for Applied Sciences). 384p. 1996. text 68.00 (*981-02-2467-2*, Ma-B2938) World Scientific Pub.

***Cessna, Cornelia B., et al, eds.** Energy: Shortage, Glut or Enough? 10th rev. ed. (Reference Ser.). (Illus.). 180p. (YA). (gr. 9-12). 1999. pap. text 26.95 (*1-57302-085-0*) Info Plus TX.

Cessna, H. Cessna: The House of Cessna. 2nd ed. (Second Ser.). (Illus.). 199p. 1992. reprint ed. pap. 31.00 (*0-8328-2367-8*); reprint ed. lib. bdg. 41.00 (*0-8328-2366-X*) Higginson Bk Co.

— House of Cessna. (Illus.). 120p. 1989. reprint ed. pap. 25.00 (*0-8328-1329-X*); reprint ed. lib. bdg. 33.00 (*0-8328-1328-1*) Higginson Bk Co.

Cesta, Toni G., et al. The Case Manager's Survival Guide: Winning Strategies for Clinical Practice. LC 99-208413. (Illus.). 288p. (C). (gr. 13). 1997. pap. text 32.95 (*0-8151-1771-X*, 30312) Mosby Inc.

Cesta, Toni G., jt. auth. see Cohen, Elaine L.

Cestaro, Nicholas G., jt. auth. see Smith, Timothy K.

Cestero, Emmett. All about Guinea Pigs: Animal Care Booklet. Mathews-Danzer, R., ed. (Illus.). 1999. pap. 12.95 (*1-888417-71-4*) Dimefast.

— Lories & Lorikeets. (Illus.). 1999. pap. 12.50 (*1-888417-77-3*) Dimefast.

— Parrotlets. (Illus.). 1999. pap. 12.50 (*1-888417-75-7*) Dimefast.

Cestero, Emmett, jt. auth. see Mathews-Danzer, R.

Cesti, Antonio. Antonio Cesti: Il Pomo D'Oro. Schmidt, Carl B., ed. (Recent Researches in Music of the Baroque Era Ser.: Vol. RRB42). (Illus.). xv, 80p. 1982. pap. 35.00 (*0-89579-168-4*) A-R Eds.

***Cestnick, Tim.** Winning the Tax Game in 2000: A Year-Round Tax & Investing Guide for Canadians. 288p. 1999. pap. write for info. (*0-13-025480-0*, Prentice Hall) P-H.

Cestre, Charles. La Litterature Americaine. (BCL1-PS American Literature Ser.). 218p. 1993. reprint ed. lib. bdg. 79.00 (*0-7812-6565-7*) Rprt Serv.

Ceta Group Staff. Optilex Chinese - English General Dictionary Database. 1993. cd-rom 425.00 (*1-881265-03-X*) Dunwoody Pr.

Cetas, T. C., et al. Methods of Hyperthermia Control. (Clinical Thermology Ser.: Vol. 3). (Illus.). 120p. 1990. 125.00 (*0-387-50978-X*) Spr-Verlag.

***Cethial & Bossche Publishing Staff.** Fairy Tale Garden Castle Games: Cinderella & Dracula. (Illus.). (J). 1999. 29.95 (*1-55274-036-6*) C&B Co.

— Fairy Tale Garden Song Book. (Illus.). (J). 2000. 14.95 (*1-55274-054-4*) C&B Co.

— Voyages of Noah's Ark. (Illus.). (J). 1999. 12.95 (*1-55274-004-8*) C&B Co.

Cetina, Karin K. Epistemic Cultures: How the Sciences Make Knowledge. LC 98-30277. (Illus.). 320p. 1998. 45.00 (*0-674-25893-2*) HUP.

— Epistemic Cultures: How the Sciences Make Knowledge. LC 98-30277. (Illus.). 320p. 1999. text 22.95 (*0-674-25894-0*) HUP.

Cetnar, Jean, jt. auth. see Cetnar, William.

Cetnar, William. Questions for Jehovah's Witnesses. 1983. pap. 7.99 (*0-685-73959-7*) Chr Lit.

Cetnar, William & Cetnar, Jean. Questions for Jehovah's Witnesses. 1983. pap. 5.99 (*0-87552-162-2*) P & R Pubng.

***Cetojevic, Igor & Pinoni, Francesca.** Your Health: It's a Question of Balance. 2000. 12.95 (*1-56718-121-X*) Llewellyn Pubns.

Cetron, M. & Goldhar, J. D. The Science of Managing Organized Technology, 4 vols. Lvi, 1698p. 1970. text 704.00 (*0-677-02320-0*) Gordon & Breach.

Cetron, Marvin. American Renaissance. 1990. pap. 10.95 (*0-312-05050-X*) St Martin.

Cetron, Marvin & Davies, Owen. Cheating Death: The Promise & the Future Impact of Trying to Live Forever. LC 97-35510. 224p. 1997. text 21.95 (*0-312-18065-9*) St Martin.

— Probable Tomorrows: How Science & Technology Will Transform Our Lives in the Next Twenty Years. LC 96-54503. 352p. 1997. text 24.95 (*0-312-15429-1*) St Martin.

Cetron, Marvin J. Technological Forecasting: A Practical Approach. xxx, 346p. (C). 1969. text 229.00 (*0-677-02140-2*) Gordon & Breach.

Cetron, Marvin J. & Davies, Owen. Mastering Information in the New Century. LC 94-208421. 100p. 1994. reprint ed. pap. 31.00 (*0-608-03812-1*, 206466200009) Bks Demand.

Cetrulo, Curtis L., et al, eds. The Problem-Oriented Medical Record for High-Risk Obstetrics. LC 83-17712. 510p. 1984. 110.00 (*0-306-41325-6*, Plenum Trade) Perseus Pubng.

Cetrulo, Larry. Toxic Torts: A Complete Personal Injury Guide, 2 vols. 1993. ring bd. 240.00 (*0-685-68855-0*) West Group.

Cetti, Charles L. Money Management for Young Adults: A Practical Guide to Financial Independence. LC 92-73383. 160p. (Orig.). 1992. pap. 14.95 (*0-9633856-0-7*) Baron Pub FL.

Cetti, Nicholas & Kirby, Roger S. Trauma to the Genito-Urinary Tract: A Practical Guide to Management. LC 96-39334. 96p. 1997. pap. text 63.00 (*0-7506-1587-7*) Buttrwrth-Heinemann.

Cetto, Ana M. La Luz. (Ciencia para Todos Ser.). (SPA.). pap. 6.99 (*968-16-2565-X*, Pub. by Fondo) Continental Bk.

Cetto, Ana M., jt. auth. see De La Pena, Luis.

Cetto, Bruno. Enzyklopaedie der Pilze, Vol. 1, 1987.Tr. of Nomenclature & Systematic Description. (GER., Illus.). 662p. 1987. text 70.00 (*3-405-13474-9*) Lubrecht & Cramer.

— Enzyklopaedie der Pilze, Vol. 2, 1987.Tr. of Nomenclature & Systematic Description. (GER., Illus.). 450p. 1987. text 70.00 (*3-405-13475-7*) Lubrecht & Cramer.

— Enzyklopaedie der Pilze: Registerband. Gerhardt, Ewald, ed. (GER.). 93p. 1989. lib. bdg. 20.00 (*3-405-13478-1*, Pub. by BLV Verlagsgesellschaft) Lubrecht & Cramer.

— Enzyklopaedie der Pilze: Taeublinge, Milchlinge, Etc., Vol. 4. (GER., Illus.). 607p. 1988. lib. bdg. 70.00 (*3-405-13477-3*) Lubrecht & Cramer.

Cetuk, Virginia S. Theological Education As Spiritual Formation. LC 98-35777. 240p. 1997. pap. 19.95 (*0-687-01728-9*) Abingdon.

***Ceurter, J. S., et al.** The Barkhausen Noise Inspection Method for Detecting Grinding Damage in Gears. (Technical Papers: Vol. 99FTM1). 10p. 1999. pap. 30.00 (*1-55589-739-8*) AGMA.

Ceusters, W. & Spyns, P., eds. Syntactic-Semantic Tagging of Medical Texts: The Multitale Project. LC 97-77952. (Studies in Health Technology & Informatics: Vol. 47). 200p. Date not set. 75.00 (*90-5199-384-6*, Pub. by IOS Pr) IOS Press.

Cevallos-Candau, Francisco J., et al, eds. Coded Encounters: Writing, Gender, & Ethnicity in Colonial Latin America. LC 93-24562. (Illus.). 312p. 1994. pap. 18.95 (*0-87023-886-8*); lib. bdg. 45.00 (*0-87023-885-X*) U of Mass Pr.

Cevallos, Elena E. Puerto Rico. (World Bibliographical Ser.: No. 52). 193p. 1985. lib. bdg. 45.00 (*0-903450-89-5*) ABC-CLIO.

Cevallos, Jorge. The New York Labor Pool: Alucinaciones de un Immigrante. (SPA., Illus.). 174p. 1997. pap. 19.95 (*0-9654237-2-7*) Town Compass.

Cevallos, Juan C. Tesalonicenses: El Senor Viene. (Estudios Biblicos Basicos Ser.).Tr. of Thessalonians: the Lord Is Coming. (SPA.). 160p. 1991. pap. 7.99 (*0-311-04361-5*) Casa Bautista.

***Cevasco, G. A.** The Breviary of the Decadence: J. K. Huysmans's a Rebours & English Literature. LC 99-59859. (Studies in the Nineteenth Century). 2000. write for info. (*0-404-64455-4*) AMS Press.

Cevasco, G. A. The Sitwells: Edith, Osbert, & Sacheverell. (Twayne's English Authors Ser.). 176p. 1987. 24.95 (*0-8057-6953-6*) Macmillan.

Cevasco, George A. Three Decadent Poets: Ernest Dowson, John Gray, Lionel Johnson - An Annotated Bibliography. LC 89-23712. 412p. 1990. text 20.00 (*0-8240-3149-0*, H968) Garland.

Cevasco, George A., ed. The Eighteen Nineties: An Encyclopedia of British Literature, Art, & Culture. LC 92-42341. 736p. 1993. text 40.00 (*0-8240-2585-7*, H1237) Garland.

Cevc, Gregor. Phospholipids Handbook. (Illus.). 992p. 1993. text 275.00 (*0-8247-9050-2*) Dekker.

Ceve, G. & Paltauf, F., eds. Phospholipids: Characterization, Metabolism & Novel Biological Applications. 400p. 1995. 95.00 (*0-935315-62-4*) Am Oil Chemists.

Cevese, P. G. Surgery of the Neck. (Illus.). 422p. 1988. text 275.00 (*88-299-0232-2*, Pub. by Piccin Nuova) Gordon & Breach.

Cevese, P. G., et al. Surgery of the Neck. (Surgical Technique Ser.: Vol. XII). 422p. 1988. text 250.00 (*1-57235-037-7*) Piccin Nuova.

Cevolan. Cross: Way to Resurrection. 94p. 1994. pap. 1.75 (*0-8198-1529-2*) Pauline Bks.

Ceylan, Yasin. Theology & Tafsir in the Major Works of Al-Razi. 240p. (C). 1997. text 33.00 (*0-934905-83-5*, Library of Islam) Kazi Pubns.

Ceynar, Marvin. Writing for the Religious Market. 1986. 2.50 (*0-89536-804-8*, 6822, Fairway Pr) CSS OH.

Ceynar, Marvin E., et al, eds. Creativity in the Communicative Arts: A Selected Bibliography, 1960-1970. LC 74-18202. xii, 134p. 1975. 25.00 (*0-87875-062-2*) Whitston Pub.

Ceyp, Michael H. Okologieorientierte Profilierung im Vertikalen Marketing: Dargestellt am Beispiel der Elektrobranche. (GER., Illus.). XXII, 284p. 1996. 57.95 (*3-631-30996-1*) P Lang Pubng.

***Cezair-Thompson, Margaret.** True History of Paradise. 2000. pap. 13.95 (*0-452-28075-3*, Plume) Dutton Plume.

Cezairliyan, Ared, ed. Recent Developments in Thermophysical Properties Research: Presented at the Winter Annual Meeting of the ASME, Washing, D. C., Dec. 1, 1971. LC 76-180675. (American Society of Mechanical Engineers, Applied Mechanics Division Ser.: Vol. 3). 20p. reprint ed. pap. 30.00 (*0-608-30778-5*, 201690200005) Bks Demand.

Cezairliyan, Ared, ed. see Symposium on Thermophysical Properties Staff.

***Cezanne, Paul.** Art Mini-Cezanne. (Illus.). 96p. 2000. pap. text 4.95 (*3-8290-2929-2*) Konemann.

— Cezanne: Finished - Unfinished. 408p. 2000. 65.00 (*3-7757-0879-0*) Gerd Hatje.

— Cezanne Paintings Book: 24 Full-Color Cards. (Illus.). (J). 1999. pap. 4.95 (*0-486-40823-X*) Dover.

Cezanne, Paul. A Cezanne Sketchbook: Figures, Portraits, Landscapes & Still Lives. (Fine Art Ser.). (Illus.). 144p. 1985. reprint ed. pap. 7.95 (*0-486-24790-2*) Dover.

***Cezanne, Paul.** Conversations with Cezanne. Doran, Michael, ed. Cochran, Julie Lawrence, tr. LC 00-28716. (Documents of Twentieth Century Art Ser.). (Illus.). 256p. 2000. 40.00 (*0-520-22517-1*, Pub. by U CA Pr); pap. 15.95 (*0-520-22519-8*, Pub. by U CA Pr) Cal Prin Full Svc.

Cezanne, Paul. Drawings of Cezanne. Longstreet, Stephen, ed. (Master Draughtsman Ser.). (Illus.). 1964. pap. 4.95 (*0-87505-154-5*) Borden.

— Paul Cezanne, Letters. Rewald, John, ed. LC 83-45728. (Illus.). reprint ed. 49.50 (*0-404-20053-2*) AMS Pr.

— Paul Cezanne, Letters. 4th ed. Rewald, John, ed. Kay, Marguerite, tr. from FRE. (Illus.). 470p. 1995. reprint ed. pap. 15.95 (*0-306-80630-4*) Da Capo.

Cezzar, Ruknet. A Guide to Programming Languages: Overview & Comparison. LC 95-19080. 496p. 1995. 39.00 (*0-89006-812-7*) Artech Hse.

Cezzar, Ruknet, jt. auth. see Research & Education Association Staff.

Cfalin, Marin C., et al. Values & Education in Romania Today. LC 99-37505. (Cultural Heritage & Contemporary Change). pap. write for info. (*1-56518-134-4*) Coun Res Values.

CFFP Staff. Selected Readings in Advanced Estate Planning. 376p. 1987. per. 37.15 (*1-55623-013-3*, Irwn Prfssnl) McGraw-Hill Prof.

— Selected Readings in Financial Planning for the Retired. 608p. 1987. per. 41.18 (*1-55623-012-5*, Irwn Prfssnl) McGraw-Hill Prof.

CFKR Career Materials Staff. Children's Occupational Outlook Handbook. (Illus.). 240p. (Orig.). (J). (gr. k-6). 1998. pap. 18.95 (*0-934783-71-3*) CFKR Career.

— Children's Occupational Outlook Handbook Activities. (Illus.). 26p. (J). (gr. k-6). 1994. 20.25 (*0-934783-79-9*) CFKR Career.

— The College Major Handbook. (Illus.). 72p. (YA). (gr. 9-12). 1996. reprint ed. pap. 13.95 (*0-934783-12-8*) CFKR Career.

CFKR Career Materials Staff. Explore the World of Work. (Illus.). 6p. (J). (gr. 2-7). 1991. pap. 1.38 (*0-934783-14-4*) CFKR Career.

CFKR Career Materials Staff. Explore the World of Work: Adult Spanish. Aguirre, Sylvia, tr. (Illus.). 4p. (YA). (gr. 7 up). 1998. reprint ed. pap. 1.38 (*0-934783-63-2*) CFKR Career.

— Explore the World of Work - Adult. (Illus.). 4p. (YA). (gr. 9 up). 1998. reprint ed. pap. 0.85 (*0-934783-54-3*) CFKR Career.

CFKR Career Materials Staff. High School Career Course Planner. 6p. (YA). (gr. 6-10). 1990. pap. 1.38 (*0-934783-16-0*) CFKR Career.

CFKR Career Materials Staff. Job-O Enhanced: Spanish. Cutler, Art et al, eds. (Job-O Ser.). (SPA.). 16p. (J). (gr. 7-10). 1998. pap. 4.50 (*0-934783-87-X*, 115) CFKR Career.

— Job-O Enhanced, 1995. 21p. (YA). (gr. 6 up). 1995. reprint ed. pap. 4.20 (*0-934783-65-9*) CFKR Career.

— Looking at Myself, Form I Booklet & Answer Folder. Kauk, Robert, ed. (Illus.). 20p. (J). (gr. 2-5). 1998. reprint ed. pap. 4.20 (*0-934783-55-1*) CFKR Career.

CFKR Career Materials Staff. Major Minor Finder. 16p. (YA). (gr. 7 up). 1995. pap. 4.20 (*0-934783-08-X*) CFKR Career.

An Asterisk (*) at the beginning of an entry indicates that the title is appearing for the first time.

CFKR Career Materials Staff. Students Occupational Outlook Handbook. 2nd rev. ed. Ferry, Francis, ed. (Illus.). 296p. (YA). (gr. 6 up). 1998. pap. 17.95 (*1-887481-03-6*, SK94) CFKR Career.
— Voc-Tech Quick Screener. 6p. (YA). (gr. 9 up). 1998. reprint ed. pap. 1.38 (*0-934783-18-7*) CFKR Career.
CFKR Career Materials Staff, ed. Job-O Dictionary. rev. ed. 1998. pap. 4.86 (*1-887481-15-X*) CFKR Career.
CFL Staff. Question & Answer Financial Management. (C). 1984. pap. write for info. (*0-03-910497-4*) Harcourt Coll Pubs.
CFNPP Staff & Canagarajah, R. Sudarshan. Participation Rates, Efficiency, & Characteristics of Workers. (Working Papers). (C). 1992. pap. 7.00 (*1-56401-130-5*) Cornell Food.
CFNPP Staff & Lynch, Sarah. Income Distribution, Poverty, & Consumer Preferences in Cameroon. (Working Papers). (C). 1991. pap. text 7.00 (*1-56401-116-X*) Cornell Food.
CFNPP Staff & Quinn, Victoria. A User's Manual for Conducting Child Nutrition Surveys in Developing Countries. (Working Papers). (C). 1992. pap. text 7.00 (*1-56401-121-6*) Cornell Food.
CFNPP Staff & Sarris, Alexander H. Household Welfare During Crisis & Adjustment in Ghana. (Working Papers). (C). 1992. pap. 7.00 (*1-56401-133-X*) Cornell Food.
CFNPP Staff & Schnepf, Randall. Nutritional Status of Rwandan Households: Survey Evidence on the Role of Household Consumpiton Behavior. (Working Papers). (C). 1992. pap. 7.00 (*1-56401-123-2*) Cornell Food.
CFNPP Staff & Shekar, Meera. The Tamil Nedu Integrated Nutrition Program: A Review of the Project with Special Emphasis on the Monitoring & Information System. (Working Papers). (C). 1991. pap. text 7.00 (*1-56401-114-3*) Cornell Food.
CFNPP Staff & Younger, Stephen D. Exchange Rate Management in Ghana. (Working Papers). (C). 1993. pap. 7.00 (*1-56401-138-0*) Cornell Food.
— Testing the Link Between Devaluation & Inflation: Time Series Evidence from Ghana. (Working Papers). (C). 1992. pap. 7.00 (*1-56401-124-0*) Cornell Food.
CFNPP Staff, et al. The Adverse Nutrition Effects of Taxing Export Crops in Malawi. (Working Papers). (C). 1992. pap. 7.00 (*1-56401-129-1*) Cornell Food.
— Agricultural Growth Linkages in Madagascar. (Working Papers). (C). 1992. pap. text 7.00 (*1-56401-122-4*) Cornell Food.
— Agricultural Input Policies under Structural Adjustment: Their Distributional Implications. (Working Papers: No. 31). (C). 1992. pap. 7.00 (*1-56401-131-3*) Cornell Food.
— Consequences of Permanent Lay-off from the Civil Service: Results from a Survey of Retrenched Workers in Ghana. (Working Papers). (C). 1993. pap. 7.00 (*1-56401-135-6*) Cornell Food.
— Constraints on Rice Production in Madagascar: The Farmer's Perspective. (Working Papers). (C). 1993. pap. 7.00 (*1-56401-134-8*) Cornell Food.
— The Enclosures Revisited: Privatization Titling, & the Quest for Advantage in Africa. (Working Papers). (C). 1992. pap. text 7.00 (*1-56401-119-4*) Cornell Food.
— External Shocks, Policy Reform & Income Distribution to Niger. (Working Papers). (C). 1993. pap. 7.00 (*1-56401-140-2*) Cornell Food.
— Food & Nutritional Adequacy in Ghana. (Working Paper Ser.). (C). 1992. pap. 7.00 (*1-56401-127-5*) Cornell Food.
— A General Equilibrium Analysis of the Effect of Macroeconomic Adjustment on Poverty in Africa. (Working Papers). (C). 1993. pap. 7.00 (*1-56401-139-9*) Cornell Food.
— Labor & Women's Nutrition: A Study of Energy Expenditure, Fertility & Nutritional Status in Ghana. (Working Papers). (C). 1993. pap. 7.00 (*1-56401-137-2*) Cornell Food.
— The Microeconomics of an Indigenous African Credit Institution: Rotating Savings & Credit Associations. (Working Papers). (C). 1991. pap. text 7.00 (*1-56401-115-1*) Cornell Food.
— The Political Economy of Economic Decline & Reform in Africa: The Role of the State, Markets, & Civil Institutions. (Working Papers). (C). 1992. pap. 7.00 (*1-56401-125-9*) Cornell Food.
— Short Term Consumption Behavior, Seasonality, & Labor Market Uncertainty in Rural India. (Working Papers). (C). 1993. pap. 7.00 (*1-56401-136-4*) Cornell Food.
— A Social Accounting Matrix for Niger: Methodology & Results. (Working Papers). (C). 1991. pap. text 7.00 (*1-56401-118-6*) Cornell Food.
— Tolerating the Private Sector: Grain Trade in Tanzania after Adjustment. (Working Papers). (C). 1992. pap. 7.00 (*1-56401-132-1*) Cornell Food.
CFNPP Staff, jt. auth. see Alderman, Harold.
CGE (Van Tassel-Baska) Staff. What a Find! Using Archaeology to Unearth a System. 184p. (C). 1996. pap. text, per. 26.95 (*0-7872-2608-4*) Kendall-Hunt.
CGE (VanTassel-Baska) Staff. Electricity City: A Problem-Based Unit. 184p. 1996. pap. text, per. 32.95 (*0-7872-2916-4*, 41291601) Kendall-Hunt.
— No Quick Fix: A Problem-Based Unit. 184p. (C). 1996. per. 32.95 (*0-7872-2846-X*, 41284601) Kendall-Hunt.
CGI Staff. Evangelistic Letters: Reaching Your Community for Christ. Spear, Cindy G. & Pierce, Timothy J., eds. 65p. 1994. teacher ed., ring bd. 39.95 incl. disk (*1-57052-025-9*) Chrch Grwth VA.
— Special Occasion Letters: Recognizing Important Times in Your Members' Lives. Spear, Cindy G. & Norton, Christine B., eds. 66p. 1995. ring bd. 39.95 incl. disk (*1-57052-033-X*) Chrch Grwth VA.
CGS Magazine Staff. The Best Action & Arcade Games Strategies & Secrets. 1996. 19.99 incl. cd-rom (*0-614-20331-7*, Strategies & Secrets) Sybex.
— The Best Strategy & War Games Strategies & Secrets. 1996. 19.99 incl. cd-rom (*0-614-20332-5*, Strategies & Secrets) Sybex.
CGS Staff. Systems - Agriculture, Pollution, & Politics: How They Interact Within the Chesapeake Bay. 192p. (C). 1996. per. 32.95 (*0-7872-2518-5*, 41251801) Kendall-Hunt.
Ch Lai & Ladwai, Z. Ideals & Realities: Selected Essays of Abdus Salam. 3rd ed. 530p. (C). 1989. text 55.00 (*981-02-0080-3*); pap. text 18.00 (*981-02-0081-1*) World Scientific Pub.
***Cha, Soyoung S., et al, eds.** Optical Diagnostics for Fluids, Heat, Combustion & Photomechanics for Solids. 1999. pap. text 103.00 (*0-8194-3269-5*) SPIE.
Cha, Soyoung S., et al, eds. Optical Technology in Fluid, Thermal & Combustion Flow III, Vol. 3172. LC 98-122619. 740p. 1997. 124.00 (*0-8194-2594-X*) SPIE.
Cha, Dia. Dia's Story Cloth: The Hmong People's Journey of Freedom. LC 95-41465. (Illus.). 24p. (YA). (gr. 1 up). 1996. 15.95 (*1-880000-34-2*) Lee & Low Bks.
— Dia's Story Cloth: The Hmong People's Journey of Freedom. LC 95-41465. (Illus.). 24p. (YA). (gr. 1 up). 1998. pap. 6.95 (*1-880000-63-6*) Lee & Low Bks.
***Cha, Dia & Livo, Norma.** Teaching with Folk Stories of the Hmong: An Activity Book. (Learning Through Folklore Ser.). 2000. pap. 20.00 (*1-56308-668-9*) Libs Unl.
Cha, Dia, jt. auth. see Livo, Norma J.
Cha Jian Yin. The Glacier in the Forest. (CHI.). pap. 12.95 (*7-5387-0919-3*, Pub. by China Intl Bk) Distribks Inc.
***Cha-Jua, Sundiata K.** America's First Black Town. LC 99-6776. 2000. write for info. (*0-252-02537-7*) U of Ill Pr.
***Cha, Philip D., et al.** Fundamentals of Modeling & Analyzing Engineering Systems. LC 99-31144. (Illus.). 488p. (C). 2000. 100.00 (*0-521-59443-X*); pap. 44.95 (*0-521-59463-4*) Cambridge U Pr.
Cha, Shou C., jt. auth. see Hones, Donald F.
Cha, Soyoung S., et al. Optical Techniques in Fluid, Thermal & Combustion Flow, 10-13 July, 1995, San Diego, California. LC 95-68561. xi, 590p. 1995. write for info. (*0-8194-1905-2*) SPIE.
Cha, Victor D. Alignment Despite Antagonism: The United States - Korea - Japan Security Triangle. LC 98-35015. (Illus.). 385p. 1998. 49.50 (*0-8047-3191-8*) Stanford U Pr.
Cha, Y. K., jt. auth. see Pollack, Jonathan.
Cha, Young K. Northeast Asian Security: A Korean Perspective. LC 88-2842. (Significant Issues Ser.: Vol. 10, No. 1). (Illus.). 67p. (Orig.). reprint ed. pap. 30.00 (*0-8357-6640-3*, 203530700094) Bks Demand.
Chaaban, Ahmad, ed. ICPVT-8: International Conference on Pressure Vessel Technology. 995p. 1996. pap. text 300.00 (*0-7918-1789-X*, TS283) ASME Pr.
Chaabane, Sadok. Ben Ali on the Road to Pluralism in Tunisia. LC 97-37520. 1997. write for info. (*0-937165-07-7*) Am Educ Trust.
Chaad, J. M. Free Boundary Problems in Fluid Flow with Applications. LC 96-960216. (Illus.). 253p. 1993. lib. bdg. 64.95 (*0-582-21567-6*) Longman.
Chaadaev, Peter Y. Philosophical Letters & Apology of a Madman. LC 79-88186. 219p. reprint ed. pap. 67.90 (*0-608-30623-1*, 201967500014) Bks Demand.
Chabal, Patrick, ed. The Post-Colonial Literature of Lusophone Africa. LC 95-53848. 314p. (C). 1996. pap. 17.95 (*0-8101-1423-2*); text 49.95 (*0-8101-1422-4*) Northwestern U Pr.
Chabal, Patrick & Daloz, Jean-Pascal. Africa Works: The Political Instrumentalisation of Disorder. LC 98-38855. (African Issues Ser.). 192p. 1999. pap. 18.95 (*0-253-21287-1*); text 39.95 (*0-253-33525-6*) Ind U Pr.
Chaballe, L. Y. Elsevier's Sugar Dictionary. (DUT, ENG, FRE, GER & LAT., Illus.). 336p. 1984. 175.50 (*0-444-42376-1*, I-410-84) Elsevier.
— Elsevier's Sugar Dictionary in English - American, French, Spanish, Dutch, German & Latin. (DUT, ENG, FRE, GER & LAT.). 322p. 1984. 250.00 (*0-8288-9203-2*) Fr & Eur.
Chaballe, L. Y. & Vandenberghe, J. P. Elsevier's Dictionary of Building Tools & Materials. (DUT, ENG, FRE, GER & SPA.). 734p. 1982. 269.00 (*0-444-42047-9*, I-261-82) Elsevier.
— Elsevier's Dictionary of Building Tools & Materials. (DUT, ENG, FRE & GER.). 722p. 1982. 350.00 (*0-8288-9265-2*, M14276) Fr & Eur.
Chaballe, L. Y., et al. Elsevier's Oil & Gas Field Dictionary. LC 86-60136. (ARA, DUT, ENG, FRE & GER.). 684p. 1980. 260.50 (*0-444-41833-4*) Elsevier.
— Elsevier's Oil & Gas Field Dictionary. (ARA, DUT, ENG, FRE & GER.). 672p. 1980. 350.00 (*0-8288-9266-0*, M7963) Fr & Eur.
Chaban, Joel. Practical Food Service Spreadsheets with Lotus 1-2-3. 2nd ed. LC 93-3346. 1993. text 44.95 (*0-442-01304-3*, VNR) Wiley.
— Practical Foodservice Spreadsheets with LOTUS 1-2-3. 2nd ed. 256p. 1993. 54.95 (*0-471-29011-4*, VNR) Wiley.
Chaban, Michele. The Life Work of Dr. Elisabeth Kubler-Ross & Its Impact on the Death Awareness Movement. LC 98-8630. (Symposium Ser.: Vol. 49). 406p. 1998. text 109.95 (*0-7734-8302-0*) E Mellen.
Chabaneix, Gilles De, see D'Arnoux, Alexandra & De Chabaneix, Gilles.
Chabaneix, Gilles De, see De Chabaneix, Gilles, photos by.
Chabat, Pierre. Victorian Brick & Terra-Cotta Architecture in Full Color. (Illus.). 168p. 1989. pap. 26.95 (*0-486-26164-6*) Dover.
***Chabay.** Matter & Interaction. 1999. pap. text 10.00 (*0-471-37388-5*) Wiley.
Chabay. Matter & Interactions. pap. text. write for info. (*0-471-35491-0*) Wiley.
Chabay, Ruth W. & Sherwood, Bruce A. Electric & Magnetic Interactions. 672p. 1994. pap. 43.95 (*0-471-07847-6*) Wiley.
Chabert, Jean-Luc, ed. A History of Algorithms: From the Pebble to the Micro-Chip. Weeks, C., tr. from FRE. LC 98-20468. (Illus.). viii, 586p. 1999. pap. 59.95 (*3-540-63369-3*) Spr-Verlag.
Chabert, Jean-Luc, jt. auth. see Cahen, Paul-Jean.
Chabert, Joelle, et al. Tell Me the Bible. 110p. (Orig.). 1991. 14.95 (*0-8146-2064-7*) Liturgical Pr.
***Chabert, Sally C.** The Jacks Book & the Jacks. LC 99-13139. (Illus.). 176p. (YA). (gr. k up). 1999. pap. 9.95 (*0-7611-1627-3*) Workman Pub.
Chabert, Sally C., jt. auth. see Brallier, Jess.
Chabert, Sally C., jt. auth. see Brallier, Jess M.
Chabner. Language of Medicine. 1996. 150.00 (*0-7216-6839-9*) Harcourt.
***Chabner.** Medical Language. 2000. pap. text. write for info. (*0-7216-8582-X*, W B Saunders Co) Harcrt Hlth Sci Grp.
Chabner, Bruce A. Cancer Chemotherapy: Principles & Practice. Collins, Jerry M., ed. (Illus.). 576p. 1990. text 105.00 (*0-397-50900-6*) Lppncott W & W.
Chabner, Bruce A. Cancer Chemotherapy & Biotherapy: Principles & Practice. 3rd ed. 800p. text 139.00 (*0-7817-2269-1*) Lppncott W & W.
Chabner, Bruce A. The Language of Medicine: Exam/Testbank. 5th ed. 1996. pap., suppl. ed. 200.00 (*0-7216-3339-0*, W B Saunders Co) Harcrt Hlth Sci Grp.
— Medical Terminology: A Short Course. (Illus.). 240p. 1990. text 17.95 (*0-7216-2939-3*, W B Saunders Co) Harcrt Hlth Sci Grp.
Chabner, Bruce A. & Longo, Dan L., eds. Cancer Chemotherapy & Biotherapy: Principles & Practice. 2nd ed. 848p. 1995. text 124.00 (*0-397-51418-2*) Lppncott W & W.
Chabner, Davi-Ellen. The Language of Medicine. 5th ed. (Illus.). 1996. pap., teacher ed. write for info. (*0-7216-6027-4*, W B Saunders Co) Harcrt Hlth Sci Grp.
— The Language of Medicine: A Write-in Text Explaining Medical Terms. 5th ed. Biblis, Margaret, ed. LC 95-5451. (Illus.). 880p. 1996. pap. text 39.95 (*0-7216-6026-6*, W B Saunders Co) Harcrt Hlth Sci Grp.
***Chabner, Davi-Ellen.** The Language of Medicine: A Write-In Text Explaining Medical Terms. 6th ed. LC 99-89410. (Illus.). 895p. Date not set. pap. text. write for info. (*0-7216-8569-2*, W B Saunders Co) Harcrt Hlth Sci Grp.
Chabner, Davi-Ellen. Medical Terminology: A Short Course. (Illus.). 238p. (C). 1991. pap. text, teacher ed. write for info. (*0-7216-3508-3*, W B Saunders Co) Harcrt Hlth Sci Grp.
— Medical Terminology: Short Course. 2nd ed. Allan, Andrew, ed. LC 98-48477. (Illus.). 300p. (C). 1998. text 17.95 (*0-7216-8124-7*, W B Saunders Co) Harcrt Hlth Sci Grp.
Chaboche, Jean-Louis, jt. auth. see Lemaitre, Jean P.
Chabod, Federico. A History of Italian Fascism. Grindrod, Muriel, tr. from ITA. LC 74-12405. 192p. 1995. reprint ed. 35.00 (*0-86527-095-3*) Fertig.
— Italian Foreign Policy: The Statecraft of the Founders, 1870-1896. 616p. (C). 1996. pap. text 29.95 (*0-691-04450-3*, Pub. by Princeton U Pr) Cal Prin Full Svc.
— Italian Foreign Policy: The Statecraft of the Founders, 1870-1896. McCuaig, William, tr. from ITA. LC 95-489. (Storia Della Politica Estera Italiana dal 1870 al 1896). 616p. 1996. text 65.00 (*0-691-04451-1*, Pub. by Princeton U Pr) Cal Prin Full Svc.
Chabon, Michael. The Amazing Adventures of Kavalier & Clay: A Novel. LC 00-29063. 736p. 2000. 26.95 (*0-679-45004-1*) Random.
— Model World & Other Co. 208p. 1992. reprint ed. pap. 12.00 (*0-380-71099-4*, Avon Bks) Morrow Avon.
— The Mysteries of Pittsburgh. LC 88-45708. 304p. 1989. reprint ed. pap. 12.00 (*0-06-097212-2*, PL 7212, Perennial) HarperTrade.
— Werewolves in Their Youth. LC 98-18980. 224p. 1999. 22.95 (*0-679-41587-4*) Random.
***Chabon, Michael.** Werewolves in Their Youth: Stories. LC 99-54101. 224p. 2000. pap. 12.00 (*0-312-25438-5*, Picador USA) St Martin.
— Wonder Boys. 2000. pap. write for info. (*0-312-26508-5*) St Martin.
Chabon, Michael. Wonder Boys. large type ed. 1995. 24.95 (*1-56895-257-0*, Compass) Wheeler Pub.
— Wonder Boys. 2nd ed. LC 95-39997. 384p. 2000. pap. 13.00 (*0-312-14094-0*, Picador USA) St Martin.
Chabot, C. Barry. Freud on Schreber: Psychoanalytic Theory & the Critical Act. LC 81-16476. 192p. 1982. lib. bdg. 27.50 (*0-87023-348-3*) U of Mass Pr.
***Chabot, C. Barry.** Writers for the Nation: American Literary Modernism. 290p. 1999. pap. text 19.95 (*0-8173-1011-8*) U of Ala Pr.
Chabot, Christian. Understanding the Euro. LC 98-18356. (Illus.). 300p. 1998. 29.95 (*0-07-064762-3*) Osborne-McGraw.
***Chabot, Christian.** Understanding the Euro: The Clear & Concise Guide to the New Trans-European Economy. LC 98-49945. (Illus.). 189p. 1998. 29.95 (*0-07-134388-1*) McGraw.
Chabot, Daniel. Wisdom of Pleasure: Pleasure Experienced Here & Now Is the Basis of Happiness & Health. Orig. Title: La Sagesse Du Plaisir. (Illus.). 332p. Date not set. pap. 14.95 (*1-880396-39-4*, JP9639-4) Jalmar Pr.
Chabot, Frederick C. Perote Prisoners. 1993. reprint ed. lib. bdg. 75.00 (*0-7812-5921-5*) Rprt Serv.
Chabot, Gregoire. Jacques Cartier Errant: Jacques Cartier Discovers America. (Editions Reveil Ser.). (FRE.). 309p. (Orig.). 1996. pap. 12.95 (*0-89101-087-4*) U Maine Pr.
Chabot, H. T. Kinship, Status & Gender in South Celebes. (KITLV Translation Ser.: No. 26).Tr. of Vervantschap, Stand en Sexe in Zuid-Celebes. (DUT., Illus.). 281p. (Orig.). 1996. 37.00 (*90-6718-074-2*, Pub. by KITLV Pr) Cellar.
Chabot, John A. A New Lease on Life: Facing the World after a Suicide Attempt. LC 96-35265. 224p. 1997. pap. 14.95 (*1-57749-009-6*) Fairview Press.
Chabot, Joseph F. Development of Plastics Processing: Machinery & Methods. LC 91-20433. (Society of Plastics Engineers Monographs). 216p. 1992. 105.00 (*0-471-54716-6*) Wiley.
Chabot-Long, Lynn. A Gift of Life: A Page from the Life of a Living Organ Donor. Jenkins, Paul, ed. (Illus.). 184p. 1996. per. 9.99 (*0-9650555-5-8*) Je-Lynn Pubns.
Chabout, Rene. Weather: Drama of the Heavens. Paris, I. Mark, tr. (Discoveries Ser.). (Illus.). 160p. 1996. pap. text 12.95 (*0-8109-2878-7*, Pub. by Abrams) Time Warner.
Chabra, Bashamber N. The Ultimate Particle of the Universe - The Raton. 1998. pap. 10.95 (*0-533-12118-3*) Vantage.
***Chabram-Dernerse, Angie.** Chicana/O Latina/O Cultural Studies: Transnational & Transdiciplinary Movements. (Cultural Studies: Vol. 13). 1999. pap. 16.99 (*0-415-19796-1*) Routledge.
Chabran, Melissa, et al. The Provision of Health Care Services to the Undocumented Population in Bexar County, Texas. (Working Paper Ser.: No. 75). 54p. (C). 1994. pap. 5.50 (*0-89940-570-3*) LBJ Sch Pub Aff.
Chabreck, Robert H. Coastal Marshes: Ecology & Wildlife Management. LC 88-1168. (Wildlife Habitats Ser.). (Illus.). xiii, 138p. (Orig.). 1988. pap. 15.95 (*0-8166-1663-9*) U of Minn Pr.
Chabrier, jt. auth. see Dukas.
Chabrier, Emmanuel. Works for Piano. 128p. 1995. pap. 10.95 (*0-486-28574-X*) Dover.
Chabrier, Gilles & Schatzman, Evry L., eds. The Equation of State in Astrophysics No. 147: IAU Colloquium. (Illus.). 639p. (C). 1994. text 85.00 (*0-521-47260-1*) Cambridge U Pr.
Chabrier, Gwendolyn. Faulkner's Families: A Southern Saga. LC 93-49606. 1994. 25.00 (*0-87752-241-3*) Gordian.
Chabris, Christopher, ed. American Chess Journal, Vol. 4. (Illus.). 144p. (Orig.). Date not set. pap. 14.95 (*1-888281-05-7*, Am Chess Jrnl) HThree.
— American Chess Journal 1. (Illus.). 128p. 1995. pap. 14.95 (*1-888281-00-6*) HThree.
— American Chess Journal 2. (Illus.). 128p. 1995. pap. 14.95 (*1-888281-01-4*) HThree.
— American Chess Journal 3. (Illus.). 128p. 1996. pap. 14.95 (*1-888281-02-2*) HThree.
Chabrol, Guillaume-Michel. Dictionnaire Historique des Fiefs, Chatellenies et Paroisses. (FRE.). 1973. write for info. (*0-7859-8054-7*, 2-85023-006-5) Fr & Eur.
Chabrol, Jean-Pierre. Le Bout-Galeux. (FRE.). 1978. pap. 11.95 (*0-7859-1865-5*, 2070369927) Fr & Eur.
— La Chatte Rouge. (FRE.). 1976. pap. 10.95 (*0-7859-1828-0*, 2070367967) Fr & Eur.
— Fleur d'Epine. (FRE.). 480p. 1975. pap. 11.95 (*0-7859-1802-7*, 2070366804) Fr & Eur.
— La Folie Des Miens. (FRE.). 1984. pap. 13.95 (*0-7859-1987-2*, 2070375285) Fr & Eur.
— Les Fous De Dieu. (FRE.). 1972. pap. 12.95 (*0-7859-1716-0*, 2070362574) Fr & Eur.
— Un Homme De Trop. (FRE.). 256p. 1972. pap. 10.95 (*0-7859-1700-4*, 2070361217) Fr & Eur.
Chabrowe, Leonard. Ritual & Pathos: The Theater of O'Neill. (Illus.). xxiii, 226 p. 1976. 32.50 (*0-8387-1575-3*) Bucknell U Pr.
Chabrowski, J. The Dirichlet Problem with L2-Boundary Data for Elliptic Linear Equations. Dold, A. et al, eds. (Lecture Notes in Mathematics Ser.: Vol. 1482). vi, 173p. 1991. 35.95 (*0-387-54486-0*) Spr-Verlag.
Chabrowski, Jan. Variational Methods for Potential Operator Equations: With Applications to Nonlinear Elliptic Equations. LC 97-8060. (Studies in Mathematics: Vol. 24). ix, 290p. (C). 1997. text 99.95 (*3-11-015269-X*) De Gruyter.
***Chabrowski, Jan.** Weak Convergence Methods for Semilinear Elliptic Equations. 230p. 2000. 44.00 (*981-02-4076-7*) World Scientific Pub.
Chabrowski, O. Waclaw. Madonny. 46p. 1965. 2.50 (*0-940962-13-6*) Polish Inst Art & Sci.
Chabrowski, T., jt. auth. see Waclaw, O.
Chabyn, Jerome. Margot: Queen of the Night. 1996. 14.95 (*1-882931-15-7*) Heavy Metal Magazine.
Chacalos, Elias H. Dialogues on Time, Being & Awareness. LC 75-25220. 1976. 18.95 (*0-917262-01-8*) Potomac Pr Cir.
— Time & Change: Short but Different Philosophies. LC 88-63739. 367p. (C). 1989. text 24.95 (*0-917262-03-4*) Potomac Pr Cir.
Chace, Amanda, ed. see Levine, Victoria L.
Chace, Charles, jt. auth. see Shima, Miki.
Chace, Charles, tr. see Bowei, Qin.
Chace, Charles, tr. see Flaws, Bob, ed.
***Chace, Daniella.** The What to Eat If You Have Heart Disease Cookbook. LC 00-31478. (Illus.). 2000. 14.95 (*0-8092-9709-4*, Contemporary Bks) NTC Contemp Pub Co.
***Chace, Daniella & Keane, Maureen.** Smoothies for Life: Yummy, Fun & Nutritious. LC 98-2552. 228p. 2000. pap. 14.95 (*0-7615-1340-X*) Prima Pub.
Chace, Daniella, jt. auth. see Keane, Maureen.
Chace, Daniella, jt. auth. see Keane, Maureen B.
Chace, Daniella B. & Keane, Maureen B. Pressure Cooking the Meatless Way: Over 125 Delicious & Nutritious Recipes for Today's Busy Cooks. 216p. 1996. per. 14.95 (*0-7615-0032-4*) Prima Pub.

C

An Asterisk (*) at the beginning of an entry indicates that the title is appearing for the first time.

Chace, Daniella B., jt. auth. see Keane, Maureen B.

Chace, Fenner A. The Atya-Like Shrimps of the Indo-Pacific Region: Decapoda: Atyidae. LC 83-600083. (Smithsonian Contributions to Zoology Ser.: No. 384). 58p. reprint ed. pap. 30.00 (*0-8357-5870-2*, 202186600023) Bks Demand.

— The Caridean Shrimps: Crustacea: Decapoda, of the Albatross Philippine Expedition, 1907-1910, Part 3. LC 83-600061. (Smithsonian Contribution to Zoology Ser.: No. 411). 147p. reprint ed. pap. 45.60 (*0-608-14830-X*, 202617700048) Bks Demand.

— The Caridean Shrimps: Crustacea: Decapoda, of the Albatross Philippine Expedition, 1907-1910, Pt. 2: Families Glyphocrangonidae & Crangonidae. LC 83-600061. (Smithsonian Contributions to Zoology Ser.: No. 397). 67p. reprint ed. pap. 25.00 (*0-608-11950-4*, 2023164) Bks Demand.

— The Caridean Shrimps (Crustacea: Decapoda) of the Albatross Philippine Expedition, 1907-1910, Pt. 7. LC 83-600061. (Smithsonian Contributions to Zoology Ser.: Vol. 587). (Illus.). 114p. reprint ed. pap. 35.40 (*0-608-07973-1*, 206794500007) Bks Demand.

Chace, Fenner A., ed. Contributions on the Biology of the Gulf of Mexico. LC 71-135998. (Texas A & M University Oceanographic Studies: No. 1). (Illus.). 288p. reprint ed. pap. 89.30 (*0-608-18171-4*, 20328810081) Bks Demand.

Chace, Fenner A. & Bruce, A. J. The Caridean Shrimps, Crustacea, Decapoda of the Albatross Philippine Expedition, 1907-1910, Pt. 6: Superfamily Palaemonoidea. LC 83-600061. (Smithsonian Contributions to Zoology Ser.: No. 543). 160p. reprint ed. pap. 49.60 (*0-7837-6417-0*, 204639700006) Bks Demand.

Chace, Fenner A., jt. auth. see Manning, Raymond B.

Chace, Henry R. (Providence) Owners & Occupants of the Lots, Houses & Shops in the Town of Providence in 1798: With Maps of Providence, 1650-1765-1770. (Illus.). 66p. 1997. reprint ed. pap. 12.00 (*0-8328-6485-4*) Higginson Bk Co.

Chace, Isobel. A Canopy of Rose Leaves. large type ed. (Linford Romance Library). 363p. 1984. pap. 16.99 (*0-7089-6044-8*, Linford) Ulverscroft.

— The Cornish Hearth. large type ed. (Linford Romance Library). 333p. 1984. pap. 16.99 (*0-7089-6024-3*) Ulverscroft.

Chace, James. Acheson: The Secretary of State Who Created the American World. 528p. 1999. pap. 17.95 (*0-674-00081-1*) HUP.

— Acheson: The Secretary of State Who Created the American World. LC 98-3801. (Illus.). 512p. 1998. 30.00 (*0-684-80843-9*) S&S Trade.

***Chace, Joel.** Heisenberg's Uncertainties. large type ed. LC 00-131411. (Illus.). 56p. 2000. pap. 13.50 (*0-913559-60-1*) Birch Brook Pr.

Chace, Joel. The Melancholy of Yorick. (Illus.). 64p. 1998. pap. 12.50 (*0-913559-44-X*) Birch Brook Pr.

— Twentieth Century Deaths. 64p. 1997. pap. 9.00 (*1-880286-26-2*) Singular Speech Pr.

Chace, Paul G., jt. auth. see Yohe, Robert, 2nd.

***Chace, Rebecca.** Capture the Flag. LC 99-24078. 288p. 1999. 22.50 (*0-684-85758-8*) Simon & Schuster.

Chace, Rebecca. Chautauqua Summer: Adventures of a Late-Twentieth-Century Vaudevillian. LC 92-33104. 1993. 21.95 (*0-15-117012-6*) Harcourt.

Chace, Reeve. Northeast Indians Fact Cards: Indians of New England & the Northeast Coast. (Illus.). 70p. (J). 1998. ring bd. 29.00 (*1-884925-59-6*) Toucan Valley.

Chace, Sharon R. When Baby Jesus Grows Up: A Children's Christmas Program. 8p. 1998. pap. 3.25 (*0-7880-1289-4*) CSS OH.

Chace, William M. The Political Identities of Ezra Pound & T. S. Eliot. LC 73-80620. 256p. 1973. 32.50 (*0-8047-0843-6*) Stanford U Pr.

— The Political Identities of Ezra Pound & T. S. Eliot. LC 73-80620. 256p. 1973. reprint ed. pap. 30.00 (*0-608-00552-5*, 206143500008) Bks Demand.

Chace, William M. & Collier, Peter. An Introduction to Literature. 1097p. (C). 1985. pap. text, teacher ed. 4.00 (*0-15-543035-1*) Harcourt Coll Pubs.

Chacel, Rosa. The Maravillas District. Demers, D. A., tr. from SPA. LC 92-8098. (European Women Writers Ser.). 286p. 1992. pap. 14.95 (*0-8032-6353-8*, Bison Books) U of Nebr Pr.

— Memoirs of Leticia Valle. Maier, Carol, tr. & afterword by by. LC 93-25205. (European Women Writers Ser.). v, 201p. 1994. pap. 12.95 (*0-8032-6360-0*, Bison Books) U of Nebr Pr.

Chach, Maryann, ed. see Matheson, Katy & Duclow, Geraldine.

Chachage, Chachage S., et al. Mining & Structural Adjustment: Studies on Zimbabwe & Tanzania. (Research Report Ser.: No. 92). 112p. 1993. 16.95 (*91-7106-340-4*, Pub. by Nordic Africa) Transaction Pubs.

Chachere, Tony. The Basics of Creole Cooking. (Illus.). 32p. 1982. pap. 2.95 (*0-9604580-6-9*) T Chacheres.

— Tony Chachere's Cajun Country Cookbook. Gomez, Griffin L., ed. (Illus.). 196p. 1972. pap. 9.95 (*0-9604580-1-8*) T Chacheres.

— Tony Chachere's Second Helping: A Lifetime Collection of the Ole Master's Favorite Cajun & Creole Recipes. (Illus.). 240p. 1995. 22.95 (*0-9604580-3-4*) T Chacheres.

Chachich, Alan C. & De Vries, Marten J., eds. Transporation Sensors & Controls Vol. 2902: Collision Avoidance, Traffic Management & ITS. LC 96-69754. 318p. 1997. 66.00 (*0-8194-2304-1*) SPIE.

Chachulski, Bogdan, jt. ed. see Nowakowski, Antoni.

Chackerian, Richard. Florida Public Policy Management System: Growth & Reform. 2nd ed. LC 98-214633. 600p. 1998. per. 39.96 (*0-7872-5138-0*) Kendall-Hunt.

Chackerian, Richard, ed. see Bradley, Robert D., et al.

Chacko, Chirakaikaran J. International Joint Commission Between the United States of America & the Dominion of Canada. LC 68-58554. (Columbia University. Studies in the Social Sciences: No. 358). reprint ed. 30.00 (*0-404-51358-1*) AMS Pr.

Chacko, George K. Computer-aided Decision-making. LC 72-169839. xv, 373p. 1972. write for info. (*0-444-00115-8*) Elsevier.

— Decision-Making under Uncertainty: An Applied Statistics Approach. LC 89-78157. 272p. 1990. 65.00 (*0-275-93569-8*, C35569, Praeger Pubs) Greenwood.

— Dynamic Program Management: From Defense Experience to Commercial Application. LC 88-26044. 253p. 1989. 65.00 (*0-275-92885-3*, C2885, Praeger Pubs) Greenwood.

— India: Toward an Understanding. pap. 16.95 (*0-8084-0402-4*) NCUP.

— The Systems Approach to Problem Solving from Corporate Markets to National Missions. LC 89-3925. 227p. 1989. 59.95 (*0-275-93203-6*, C3203, Praeger Pubs) Greenwood.

— Technology Management: Applications for Corporate Markets & Military Missions. LC 88-12029. 213p. 1988. 55.00 (*0-275-92941-8*, C2941, Praeger Pubs) Greenwood.

Chacko, George K., ed. Reducing Cost of Space Transportation: Proceedings of the Goddard Memorial Symposium, 7th, Washington, D.C., 1969. (Science & Technology Ser.: Vol. 21). (Illus.). 1969. 25.00 incl. fiche (*0-87703-049-9*) Univelt Inc.

Chacko, K. C. Economic Development of India & Experiences from Other Major Economically Developed Countries. (C). 1997. 38.00 (*81-259-0214-7*, Pub. by Vikas) S Asia.

— Economic Development of India & Japan. (C). 1993. 38.00 (*0-7069-7053-5*, Pub. by Vikas) S Asia.

Chacko, Ranjit C., ed. The Chronic Mental Patient in a Community Context. LC 84-24542. (Clinical Insights Ser.). 96p. reprint ed. pap. 30.00 (*0-8357-7829-0*, 203620300002) Bks Demand.

Chacon. Architectural Stone: Fabrication, Installation & Selection. LC 99-25460. 240p. 1999. 85.00 (*0-471-24659-X*) Wiley.

***Chacon, Daniel.** Chicano Chicanery: Short Stories. 152p. 2000. pap. 11.95 (*1-55885-280-8*, Pub. by Arte Publico) SPD-Small Pr Dist.

Chacon de Arjona, Gloria, tr. see Castellanos, Rosario.

***Chacon, Hernan.** Tractado de la Caulleria de la Ginate. (SPA.). 1999. pap. 24.95 (*0-85989-652-8*) Univ Exeter Pr.

Chacon, J., et al, eds. Landslides: Proceedings of the 8th International Conference & Field Workshop. Granada, Spain, 27-28 September 1996. (Illus.). 408p. (C). 1996. 123.00 (*90-5410-832-0*, Pub. by A A Balkema) Ashgate Pub Co.

Chacon, Jeff & Reynoso, Anthony. E-Male: Of Mouse & Men. LC 98-86744. 252p. 1998. pap. 12.95 (*0-9665406-4-6*, 9801) Acumen Hse LLC.

Chacon, Joaquin Armando. Las Amarras Terrestres. (SPA.). 149p. 1982. pap. 9.00 (*0-910061-08-4*, 1107) Ediciones Norte.

Chacon, Rafael. Legacy of Honor: The Life of Rafael Chacon, a Nineteenth-Century New Mexican. Meketa, Jacqueline D., ed. LC 86-16018. (Illus.). 451p. 1986. reprint ed. pap. 139.90 (*0-608-04125-4*, 206485800011) Bks Demand.

***Chaconas, Doris J.** On a Wintry Morning. LC 99-89535. (Illus.). 32p. (J). (ps-k). 2000. 15.99 (*0-670-89245-9*, PuffinBks) Peng Put Young Read.

Chaconas, Spiro J. Orthodontics. 2nd ed. (Illus.). 356p. 1989. boxed set. write for info. (*0-8151-1612-8*) Mosby Inc.

Chaconas, Stephen G. Adamantios Korais: A Study in Greek Nationalism. LC 68-58555. (Columbia University. Studies in the Social Sciences: No. 490). reprint ed. 29.50 (*0-404-51490-1*) AMS Pr.

Chacornac, P. Simple Life of Rene Guenon. 1996. pap. 16.00 (*0-614-21611-7*, 1139) Kazi Pubns.

Chacour, Elias & Hazard, David. Blood Brothers. LC 84-9510. 226p. (gr. 10). 1987. pap. 8.99 (*0-8007-9096-0*) Chosen Bks.

***Chacour, Elias & Jensen, Mary E.** We Belong to the Land: The Story of a Palestinian Israeli Who Lives for Peace & Reconciliation. (The Erma Konya Kess Lives of the Just & Virtuous Ser.). 240p. 2000. reprint ed. pap. 15.00 (*0-268-01963-0*, Pub. by U of Notre Dame Pr) Chicago Distribution Ctr.

Chad, J. & Wheal, H., eds. Cellular & Molecular Neurobiology: A Practical Approach, 2 vols., Set. (Practical Approach Ser.). (Illus.). 568p. 1991. pap. text 85.00 (*0-19-963254-5*) OUP.

— Cellular Neurobiology: A Practical Approach. (Practical Approach Ser.: 78). (Illus.). 312p. 1991. 79.00 (*0-19-963106-9*); pap. 49.95 (*0-19-963107-7*) OUP.

— Molecular Neurobiology: A Practical Approach. (Practical Approach Ser.: 74). (Illus.). 256p. 1991. 59.00 (*0-19-963108-5*); pap. 49.95 (*0-19-963109-3*) OUP.

Chad, Norman. Hold on, Honey, I'll Take You to the Hospital at Half-Time: Confessions of a TV Sports Junkie. LC 93-30252. 256p. 1994. pap. 11.00 (*0-87113-584-1*, Atlntc Mnthly) Grove-Atltic.

Chada, Narender, jt. auth. see Van Willigan, John K.

Chadabe, Joel. Electric Sound: The Past & Promise of Electronic Music. LC 96-29349. 370p. (C). 1996. pap. text 47.00 (*0-13-303231-0*) P-H.

Chadam, J. M. Emerging Applications in Free, 001. 1993. lib. bdg. 67.95 (*0-582-08768-6*, Pub. by Addison-Wesley) Longman.

Chadam, John, et al, eds. Pattern Formation: Symmetry Methods & Applications. LC 95-33706. (Fields Institute Communications Ser.: Vol. 5). 358p. 1995. text 99.00 (*0-8218-0256-9*, FIC/5) Am Math.

Chadan, Knosrow & Sabatier, Pierre C. Inverse Problems in Quantum Scattering Theory. (Texts & Monographs in Physics). 545p. 1989. 101.95 (*0-387-18731-6*) Spr-Verlag.

Chadan, Knosrow, et al. An Introduction to Inverse Scattering & Inverse Spectral Problems. LC 96-52459. (SIAM Monographs on Mathematical Modeling & Computation: Vol. 2). (Illus.). x, 198p. 1997. pap. text 42.50 (*0-89871-387-0*, MM0002) Soc Indus-Appl Math.

Chadarevain. Molecularizing Biology & Medicine: New Practices & Alliances, 1930s to 1970s. 292p. 1998. text 38.00 (*90-5702-293-1*) Gordon & Breach.

Chadarevain, Soraya De, see De Chadarevain, Soraya.

Chadbourn. Wigmore, Vol. 2. 4th ed. 1979. 145.00 (*0-316-13567-4*, Aspen Law & Bus) Aspen Pub.

— Wigmore, Vol. 3. 4th ed. 1970. 145.00 (*0-316-13560-7*, Aspen Law & Bus) Aspen Pub.

— Wigmore, Vol. 3A. 4th ed. 1970. 145.00 (*0-316-13561-5*, Aspen Law & Bus) Aspen Pub.

— Wigmore, Vol. 4. 4th ed. 1972. 145.00 (*0-316-13562-3*, Aspen Law & Bus) Aspen Pub.

— Wigmore, Vol. 5. 4th ed. 1974. 145.00 (*0-316-13563-1*, Aspen Law & Bus) Aspen Pub.

— Wigmore, Vol. 7. 4th ed. 1978. 145.00 (*0-316-13566-6*, Aspen Law & Bus) Aspen Pub.

— Wigmore, Vol. 9. 4th ed. 1981. 145.00 (*0-316-13568-2*, Aspen Law & Bus) Aspen Pub.

Chadbourne, Ava H. The Beginnings of Education in Maine. LC 73-176633. (Columbia University. Teachers College. Contributions to Education Ser.: No. 336). reprint ed. 37.50 (*0-404-55336-2*) AMS Pr.

Chadbourne, Bruce D., jt. auth. see Wells, Alexander T.

Chadbourne, Eugene. Bye Bye DDR. (Illus.). 110p. (Orig.). 1998. pap. 12.00 (*1-56439-037-3*) Ridgeway.

— I Hate the Man Who Runs This Bar: The Survival Guide for Real Musicians. LC 97-73715. 1997. pap. 29.95 (*0-918371-19-8*, MixBooks) Intertec Pub.

Chadbourne, Janice, ed. The Boston Art Club Exhibition Record: 1873-1909. 480p. 1991. boxed set 64.00 (*0-932087-18-3*) Sound View Pr.

***Chadbourne, Joseph H. & Chadbourne, Mary M.** Common Groundwork: A Practical Guide to Protecting Rural & Urban Land: A Handbook for Making Land-Use Decisions. 3rd rev. ed. 2000. pap. 28.50i (*1-930156-00-6*) Chadbourne Inc.

Chadbourne, Kathryn, et al, eds. Proceedings of the Harvard Celtic Colloquium XV (1995) (Illus.). viii, 306p. (C). Date not set. 32.50 (*0-9642446-9-1*, PHCC15); pap. write for info. (*0-9642446-8-3*, PHCC15) Celtic Studies.

Chadbourne, Mary M., jt. auth. see Chadbourne, Joseph H.

Chadbourne, Richard M. Ernest Renan. LC 67-25197. (Twayne's World Authors Ser.). 1968. lib. bdg. 20.95 (*0-8057-2754-X*) Irvington.

Chadbourne, Rod, jt. auth. see Ingvarson, Lawrence.

Chadd, Charles M. & Bowman, Jerome K. Practice under the Occupational Safety & Health Act. 3rd ed. (Corporate Practice Ser.: No. 9). 1992. ring bd. 95.00 (*1-55871-289-5*) BNA.

Chadd, Charles M., et al. Avoiding Liability for Hazardous Waste: RCRA, CERCLA & Related Corporate Law Issues. (Corporate Practice Ser.: No. 57). 1991. 92.00 (*1-55871-198-8*) BNA.

***Chadd, David, ed.** The Ordinal of the Abbey of the Holy Trinity Fecamp: Fecamp, Musee de la Benedictine, MS 186, Pt. 1. (Henry Bradshaw Society Ser.). 256p. 2000. 60.00 (*1-870252-13-6*, Henry Bradshaw Soc) Boydell & Brewer.

Chadda, H. C., ed. Seeing Is Above All: Sant Darshan Singh's First Indian Tour. (Illus.). 117p. 1977. pap. 5.00 (*0-918224-04-7*) S K Pubns.

***Chadda, Maya.** Building Democracy in South Asia: India, Nepal, Pakistan. LC 99-89666. 260p. 2000. pap. 19.95 (*1-55587-859-8*) L Rienner.

— Building Democracy in South Asia: India, Nepal, Pakistan. LC 99-89666. 260p. 2000. lib. bdg. 49.95 (*1-55587-748-6*) L Rienner.

Chadda, Maya. Ethnicity, Security & Separatism in India. LC 96-48962. 1997. 52.00 (*0-231-10736-6*); pap. 19.50 (*0-231-10737-4*) Col U Pr.

Chadde, Steve W. A Great Lakes Wetland Flora: An Illustrated Guide to the Aquatic & Wetland Plants of the Great Lakes Region. LC 98-96155. (Pocketflora Guide Ser.: Vol. 3). (Illus.). 550p. 1998. pap. 40.00 (*0-9651385-2-6*) PocketFlora.

— Plants of Pictured Rocks National Lakeshore: A Complete, Illustrated Guide to the Plants of America's First National Lakeshore. (Pocketflora Guide Ser.: Vol. 2). (Illus.). 104p. (Orig.). 1996. pap. 8.95 (*0-9651385-1-8*) PocketFlora.

— Plants of the Copper Country: An Illustrated Guide to the Vascular Plants of Houghton & Keweenaw Counties, Michigan & Isle Royale National Park. (Pocketflora Guide Ser.: Vol. 1). (Illus.). 112p. (Orig.). 1996. pap. 8.95 (*0-9651385-0-X*) PocketFlora.

— Sedges of North America: A Comprehensive Guide to the Genus Carex in the United States. (Illus.). (C). 2000. write for info. (*0-9651385-3-4*) PocketFlora.

***Chadde, Steve W.** Wisconsin Flora. (Illus.). (C). 2000. pap. write for info. (*0-9651385-4-2*) PocketFlora.

Chadder, Roger. Accounts & Audit of Leases. 1995. boxed set. write for info. (*0-406-02013-2*, UK, MICHIE) LEXIS Pub.

Chadderton, D. Building Services Engineering. (Illus.). 300p. 1997. pap. 47.95 (*0-419-16910-5*, E & FN Spon) Routledge.

Chadderton, David V. Air Conditioning: Practical Introduction. 2nd ed. LC 98-168077. (Illus.). 328p. (C). 1998. pap. 39.99 (*0-419-22610-9*, E & FN Spon) Routledge.

***Chadderton, David V.** Building Services Engineering. 3rd ed. LC 99-86245. 2000. pap. write for info. (*0-419-25740-3*) Chapman & Hall.

— Building Services Engineering. 3rd ed. LC 99-86245. (Illus.). 352p. 2000. 110.00 (*0-419-25730-6*, E & FN Spon) Routledge.

Chadderton, David V. Building Services Engineering Spreadsheets. LC 97-66255. (Illus.). 328p. (C). (gr. 13). 1998. pap. 49.99 (*0-419-22620-6*, D5575, E & FN Spon) Routledge.

Chaddha, Asha. Export Structure & Management in India. (C). 1991. 40.00 (*81-7041-490-3*, Pub. by Anmol) S Asia.

Chaddock, D. H. Introduction to Fastening Systems. (Engineering Design Guides Ser.). (Illus.). 1974. pap. 5.95 (*0-19-859128-4*) OUP.

Chaddock, Diane K. Wild Flowers of the Dunes: A Guide to the Flowering Plants of the Michigan & Indiana Dunes. Woodland, Dennis, ed. LC 97-91136. 120p. 1998. pap. 12.95 (*0-9660311-0-5*) Sand Cress.

Chaddock, Robert E. Ohio Before 1850. LC 08-18567. (Columbia University. Studies in the Social Sciences: No. 82). reprint ed. 34.50 (*0-404-51082-5*) AMS Pr.

— Ohio Before 1850. 1993. reprint ed. lib. bdg. 89.00 (*0-7812-5349-7*) Rprt Serv.

***Chaddock, Robin.** The Proverbial Woman. LC 00-100228. 128p. 2000. pap. 10.95 (*1-57921-267-0*) WinePress Pub.

Chadeayne, Leander. The Chadeayne Family in America. 65p. 1984. 15.00 (*0-318-17306-9*) Huguenot Hist.

Chadeayne, Lee, tr. see Luthi, Max.

***Chadenet, Sylvia.** French Furniture: From Louis XIII to Art Deco. 2000. pap. 25.00 (*0-8212-2683-5*) Bulfinch Pr.

Chader, G. J., jt. ed. see Osborne, Neville N.

Chader, Gerald J., jt. ed. see Osborne, Neville N.

Chadha, Ajanta. Industrial Pollution & Plants, 2 vols., Set. (C). 1992. 74.00 (*81-7024-502-8*, Pub. by Ashish Pub Hse) S Asia.

Chadha, G. K. Employment, Earnings & Poverty: A Study of Rural India & Indonesia. (Indo-Dutch Studies on Development Alternatives: Vol. 13). (Illus.). 300p. 1994. 36.00 (*0-8039-9169-X*) Sage.

Chadha, G. K., ed. Policy Perspectives in Indian Economic Development: Essays in Honour of Professor G. S. Bhana. (C). 1994. 27.50 (*81-241-0142-6*, Pub. by Har-Anand Pubns) S Asia.

Chadha, G. K. & Sharma, Alakh N., eds. Growth, Employment & Poverty: Change & Continuity in Rural India. LC 97-902741. (C). 1997. 38.00 (*81-259-0343-7*, Pub. by Vikas) S Asia.

Chadha, P. N. Hindu Law. abr. ed. 354p. 1982. 75.00 (*0-7855-1406-6*) St Mut.

— Hindu Law: (Shorter Edition) 6th ed. (C). 1982. 20.00 (*0-7855-5541-2*) St Mut.

— Law of Partnership. 828p. 1982. 330.00 (*0-7855-1405-8*) St Mut.

— Law of Partnership. (C). 1989. 63.00 (*0-7855-5271-5*) St Mut.

Chadha, Rajender K., jt. ed. see Gupta, Harsh K.

Chadha, Rajesh, et al. The Impact of Trade & Domestic Policy Reforms in India: A CGE Modeling Approach. 184p. (C). 1998. text 47.50 (*0-472-10933-2*, 10933) U of Mich Pr.

Chadha, Rajni. Social Realism in the Novels of John Steinbeck. 1991. text 30.00 (*81-85151-31-8*) Advent Bks Div.

Chadha, Ramesh. Cross-Cultural Interaction in Indian-English Fiction. (C). 1988. 24.00 (*81-85135-32-0*, Pub. by Natl Bk Orgn) S Asia.

Chadha, S. K. Environmental Crisis in India. 154p. 1992. pap. 225.00 (*81-7089-179-5*, Pub. by Intl Bk Distr) St Mut.

— Himachal Himalaya Ecology & Environment. (Progress in Ecology Ser.: Vol. IX). (Illus.). 140p. 1987. 39.00 (*1-55528-146-X*, Pub. by Today Tomorrow) Scholarly Pubns.

— Himalayas, Environmental Problems. 1990. 27.50 (*81-7024-354-8*, Pub. by Ashish Pub Hse) S Asia.

— Kashmir: Ecology & Environment. (C). 1991. 16.00 (*81-7099-327-X*, Pub. by Mittal Pubs Dist) S Asia.

Chadha, S. K., ed. Ecology of Kashmir. 1990. 32.00 (*81-7024-280-0*, Pub. by Ashish Pub Hse) S Asia.

— Environmental Holocaust in Himalaya. (C). 1989. 34.00 (*81-7024-266-5*, Pub. by Ashish Pub Hse) S Asia.

— Himalayas: Ecology & Environment. (C). 1988. 26.00 (*81-7099-072-6*, Pub. by Mittal Pubs Dist) S Asia.

Chadha, Yogesh. Gandhi: A Life. LC 97-37406. (Illus.). 546p. 1998. 30.00 (*0-471-24378-7*) Wiley.

Chadi, J. D. & Harrison, W. A., eds. Proceedings of the Seventeenth International Conference on the Physics of Semiconductors. (Illus.). 1600p. 1985. 219.00 (*0-387-96108-9*) Spr-Verlag.

Chadiali, Dinshah P. Spectro-Chrome Metry Encyclopedia. 3rd ed. (Illus.). 240p. 1992. 14.00 (*0-933917-08-2*) Dinshah Hlth Soc.

Chadirji. Social Life in the Middle East. (Illus.). 84p. 1995. text 49.50 (*1-85043-837-4*, Pub. by I B T) St Martin.

— Social Life in the Middle East, Vol. 1. (Illus.). 84p. 1995. text 24.95 (*1-85043-860-9*, Pub. by I B T) St Martin.

Chadirji, Rifat. Concepts & Influences: Towards a Regionalized International Architecture. (Illus.). 192p. 1986. 87.50 (*0-7103-0180-4*, 01804) Routledge.

Chadler, Louis A., jt. auth. see Gibson, Janice T.

Chadman, Charles E. A Treatise on Criminal Law & Criminal Procedure. LC 77-156008. (Foundations of Criminal Justice Ser.). reprint ed. 72.50 (*0-404-09108-3*) AMS Pr.

Chadman, Charles E., ed. White House Hand-Book of Oratory. LC 77-88075. (Granger Poetry Library). 1977. reprint ed. 25.00 (*0-89609-062-0*) Roth Pub Inc.

Chadney, James G. The Sikhs of Vancouver. LC 83-45350. (Immigrant Communities & Ethnic Minorities in the U. S. & Canada Ser.: No. 1). (Illus.). 1984. 71.50 (*0-404-19403-6*) AMS Pr.

Chadour Sampson, Beatriz. Ancient Finger Rings. (Illus.). 192p. 135.00 (*3-927806-20-X*, Pub. by Prahistorische Staatssammlung) Antique Collect.

Chadraba, Petr, ed. Central & Eastern European Markets: Guideline for New Business Ventures. 120p. 1995. 39.95 (*1-56024-712-6*, Intl Busn Pr) Haworth Pr.

***Chadrow, Jordan.** Singles' Scene Quotables. 60p. 1999. spiral bd. 7.95 (*0-9670500-0-6*, 040) Singular Impressions.

Chads, Diana. World of Dogs: Fox Terrier. (Illus.). 240p. 1997. 35.95 (*1-85279-020-2*, GB-007) TFH Pubns.

Chadsey, Charles E. Struggle Between President Johnson & Congress over Reconstruction. LC 79-181926. (Columbia University. Studies in the Social Sciences: No. 19). reprint ed. 24.50 (*0-404-51019-1*) AMS Pr.

— Struggle Between President Johnson & Congress over Reconstruction. (History - United States Ser.). 142p. 1992. reprint ed. lib. bdg. 69.00 (*0-7812-6202-X*) Rprt Serv.

Chadukov. Der Rav. (YID.). 258p. 1985. 10.00 (*0-8266-0437-4*) Kehot Pubn Soc.

Chadwell. Illustrated Guide to Venemous Snakes. (Illus.). 1995. write for info. (*0-8069-0335-X*) Sterling.

Chadwell, David W. Beware of the Leaven of the Pharisees. 1985. pap. 7.15 (*0-89137-566-X*) Quality Pubns.

— Christian Perspectives on Dating & Marriage. 1980. pap. 7.15 (*0-89137-523-6*) Quality Pubns.

Chadwell, Sandra S., jt. auth. see Collins, Linda B.

Chadwick-Jones, J. K. & Brown, Colin. Social Psychology of Absenteeism. LC 81-23395. 161p. 1982. 31.95 (*0-275-90771-6*, C0771, Praeger Pubs) Greenwood.

Chadwick. Encyclopedia of Applied Ethics. 1997. text 157.00 (*0-12-227066-5*); text 156.00 (*0-12-227067-3*); text 156.00 (*0-12-227068-1*); text 156.00 (*0-12-227069-X*) Acad Pr.

— History of Christianity. 1998. pap. 19.95 (*0-312-18723-8*) St Martin.

***Chadwick.** Management Accounting, Vol. 1. 2nd ed. (ITBP Textbooks Ser.). 1998. pap. 16.99 (*1-86152-260-6*) Thomson Learn.

— Warden: (trollope 1995) 1995. 32.00 (*1-870587-40-5*) Ashgate Pub Co.

Chadwick, jt. auth. see Drake.

Chadwick, A. F. The Role of the Museum & Art Gallery in Community Education. (C). 1980. 45.00 (*0-902031-44-9*, Pub. by Univ Nottingham); text 45.00 (*0-7855-3196-3*, Pub. by Univ Nottingham) St Mut.

Chadwick, A. F., jt. auth. see Jones, D. J.

Chadwick, A. V. & Terenzi, M., eds. Defects in Solids: Modern Techniques. LC 85-25417. (NATO ASI Series B, Physics: Vol. 147). 470p. 1986. 120.00 (*0-306-42474-6*, Plenum Trade) Perseus Pubng.

Chadwick, A.J. Hydraulics in Civil & Environmental Engineering. 3rd ed. LC 98-214458. (Illus.). 632p. (C). 1998. pap. 37.99 (*0-419-22580-3*, E & FN Spon) Routledge.

Chadwick, Alex. Illustrated History of Baseball. 1995. 17.98 (*0-7858-0223-1*) Bk Sales Inc.

***Chadwick, Andrew.** Augmenting Democracy: Political Movements & Constitutional Reform During the Rise of Labour, 1900-1924. LC 99-76345. 285p. 1999. text 74.95 (*0-7546-1030-6*, Pub. by Ashgate Pub) Ashgate Pub Co.

Chadwick, Andrew & Morfett, John C. Hydraulics in Civil Engineering. (Illus.). 512p. 1986. text 90.00 (*0-04-627003-5*); pap. text 29.95 (*0-04-627004-3*) Routledge.

Chadwick, Andrew J. & Morfett, J. C. Hydraulics in Civil & Environmental Engineering Solutions Manual. 3rd ed. (Illus.). 64p. (C). 1998. pap. write for info. (*0-419-23490-X*, E & FN Spon) Routledge.

Chadwick, Annie & Norman, Wallace. Showbiz Bookkeeper: The Tax Record-Keeping System for Professionals Working in the Arts. rev. ed. 120p. (Orig.). 1992. pap., spiral bd. 16.95 (*0-933919-22-0*) Theatre Directories.

Chadwick, Annie H., jt. ed. see Chadwick, John W.

Chadwick, Bruce. Baltimore Orioles: Memories & Memorabilia of the Lords of Baltimore. (Major League Memories Ser.). (Illus.). 132p. 1995. 29.95 (*1-55859-862-6*) Abbeville Pr.

— Baseball's Hometown Teams: The Story of the Minor Leagues. (Illus.). 192p. 1997. 14.98 (*0-89660-090-4*) Abbeville Pr.

— Brother Against Brother: The Lost Civil War Diary of Lt. Edmund Halsey. LC 97-7214. (Illus.). 288p. 1997. 24.95 (*1-55972-401-3*, Birch Ln Pr) Carol Pub Group.

— The Chicago Cubs: Memories & Memorabilia of the Wrigley Wonders. LC 93-21376. (Major League Memories Ser.). (Illus.). 132p. 1994. 29.95 (*1-55859-513-9*) Abbeville Pr.

— The Cincinnati Reds: Memories & Memorabilia of the Big Red Machine. LC 93-37735. (Major League Memories Ser.). (Illus.). 132p. 1994. 29.95 (*1-55859-514-7*) Abbeville Pr.

— Deion Sanders. LC 95-30122. (Football Legends Ser.). (Illus.). 96p. (J). (gr. 3 up). 1996. lib. bdg. 15.95 (*0-7910-2460-1*) Chelsea Hse.

— Dodgers: Memories & Memorabilia from Brooklyn to L. A. LC 92-37341. (Major League Memories Ser.). (Illus.). 132p. 1993. 24.95 (*1-55859-380-2*) Abbeville Pr.

— The Giants: Memories & Memorabilia from a Century of Baseball. LC 92-32272. (Major League Memories Ser.). (Illus.). 132p. 1993. 9.98 (*1-55859-379-9*) Abbeville Pr.

— Infamous Trials. LC 96-40311. (Crime, Justice, & Punishment Ser.). 100p. (YA). (gr. 8 up). 1997. lib. bdg. 19.95 (*0-7910-4293-6*) Chelsea Hse.

— John Madden. LC 96-34788. (Football Legends Ser.). (Illus.). 96p. (J). (gr. 3 up). 1997. lib. bdg. 15.95 (*0-7910-4399-1*) Chelsea Hse.

— The St. Louis Cardinals: Over 100 Years of Baseball Memories & Memorabilia. (Major League Memories Ser.). (Illus.). 132p. 1995. 29.95 (*1-55859-861-8*) Abbeville Pr.

— Traveling the Underground Railroad: A Visitor's Guide to More Than 300 Sites. LC 98-53474. (Illus.). 224p. 1999. pap. 16.95 (*0-8065-2093-0*, Citadel Pr) Carol Pub Group.

— Two American Presidents: A Dual Biography of Abraham Lincoln & Jefferson Davis. LC 97-51193. (Illus.). 288p. 1998. 24.95 (*1-55972-462-5*, Birch Ln Pr) Carol Pub Group.

— When the Game Was Black & White: The Illustrated History of Baseball's Negro Leagues. (Illus.). 192p. 1997. 14.98 (*0-89660-091-2*, Artabras) Abbeville Pr.

Chadwick, Bruce, jt. auth. see Top, Brent L.

Chadwick, Bruce A. & Heaton, Tim B. Statistical Handbook on Adolescents in America. LC 96-10514. (Illus.). 344p. 1996. boxed set 65.00 (*0-89774-922-7*) Oryx Pr.

— Statistical Handbook on the American Family. 2nd ed. LC 98-42669. (Illus.). 344p. 1998. 65.00 (*1-57356-169-X*) Oryx Pr.

Chadwick, Charles. Symbolism. (Critical Idiom Ser.). 1971. pap. 8.95 (*0-416-60910-4*, 2129) Routledge.

Chadwick, Charley G. Wall Framing. Harrington, Lois G., ed. (Illus.). (YA). (gr. 10-12). 1989. 5.00 (*0-89606-335-6*, 701TK) Am Assn Voc Materials.

Chadwick, Charley G., et al. Floor Framing. Harrington, Lois G., ed. (Illus.). 28p. 1988. teacher ed. 5.00 (*0-89606-336-4*); pap. text 9.00 (*0-89606-261-9*, 700) Am Assn Voc Materials.

Chadwick, Charley G., et al. Roof Framing. Harrington, Lois G., ed. (Basic Carpentry Skills Ser.). (Illus.). 24p. (Orig.). 1991. teacher ed. 5.00 (*0-89606-292-9*, 703TK); pap. text 11.00 (*0-89606-287-2*, 703) Am Assn Voc Materials.

Chadwick, Charley G., et al. Wall Framing. Harrington, Lois G., ed. (Basic Carpentry Skills Ser.). (Illus.). 72p. (YA). (gr. 10-12). 1989. pap. text 9.00 (*0-89606-266-X*, 701) Am Assn Voc Materials.

Chadwick, Cleo. A Lakeside Season. 384p. 1995. mass mkt. 3.99 (*0-8217-4817-3*, Pinncle Kensgtn) Kensgtn Pub Corp.

Chadwick, Cydney. Enemy Clothing. (Five Fingers Book Ser.: No. 5). 60p. (Orig.). 1992. pap. 7.95 (*0-9618409-9-4*) Five Fingers.

— The Gift Horse's Mouth. 15p. 1994. pap. 4.00 (*0-9632544-7-2*) Stand Stones.

— Interims. 26p. 1997. pap. 5.00 (*0-9646017-4-5*) Thirty-Three Hund Pr.

— Oeuvres. limited ed. 40p. (Orig.). 1995. pap. 10.00 (*0-9641837-4-9*) Texture Pr.

***Chadwick, Cydney.** Persistent Disturbances. 3rd rev. ed. (Texture Chapbook Ser.: No. 22). 48p. (Orig.). 1999. reprint ed. pap. 5.00 (*0-9641837-5-7*, Pub. by Texture Pr) SPD-Small Pr Dist.

Chadwick, Cydney, ed. see Bromige, David.

Chadwick, Cydney, ed. see Moriarty, Laura.

Chadwick, Cydney, ed. see Moriarty, Laura, et al.

Chadwick, Cydney, ed. see Palmer, Michael, et al.

Chadwick, Cydney, ed. see Parshchikov, Alexei.

Chadwick, D. Understanding X.500: The Directory. LC 94-72023. 412p. 1994. pap. 49.95 (*0-412-43020-7*) Chapman & Hall.

***Chadwick, David.** Crooked Cucumber: The Life & Zen Teaching of Shunryu Suzuki. 464p. 2000. pap. 15.00 (*0-7679-0105-3*) Broadway BDD.

Chadwick, David. Thank You & OK! An American Zen Failure in Japan. 464p. (Orig.). 1994. pap. 13.95 (*0-14-019457-6*, Arkana) Viking Penguin.

— Twelve Leadership Principles of Dean Smith. (Illus.). 256p. 1999. pap. text 23.95 (*1-892129-08-6*) Total Sprts.

Chadwick, David, et al. Medical Neurology. (Illus.). 506p. 1989. pap. text 59.95 (*0-443-03051-0*) Church.

Chadwick, David W., et al, eds. A Textbook of Epilepsy. 4th ed. LC 92-12309. 768p. 1992. text 205.00 (*0-443-04473-2*) Church.

Chadwick, David W., jt. auth. see Porter, Roger J.

Chadwick, Derek & Cardew, Gail. Bacterial Responses to PH. LC 98-46836. (Novartis Foundation Symposium Ser.). 264p. 1999. 128.00 (*0-471-98599-6*) Wiley.

***Chadwick, Derek & Cardew, Gail.** Epigenetics, Vol. 214. LC 97-43770. (Novartis Foundation Symposium Ser.). 201p. 1998. 145.00 (*0-471-97771-3*) Wiley.

Chadwick, Derek & Cardew, Gail. Novartis Foundation Symposium 217 Genetics & Tuberculosis, Vol. 217. LC 98-23836. (Novartis Foundation Symposium Ser.). 280p. 1998. 128.00 (*0-471-98261-X*) Wiley.

— Telomeres & Telomerase, Vol. 211. LC 97-41703. (CIBA Foundation Symposium Ser.). 250p. 1998. 128.00 (*0-471-97278-9*) Wiley.

Chadwick, Derek J., et al, eds. The Molecular Basis of Smell & Taste Transduction - Symposium No. 179. LC 93-28783. (CIBA Foundation Symposium Ser.: No. 179). 298p. 1993. 128.00 (*0-471-93946-3*) Wiley.

Chadwick, Derek J. & Cardew, Gail. Oligonucleotides As Therapeutic Agents, Vol. 209. LC 97-24989. (CIBA Foundation Symposium Ser.). 260p. 1997. 128.00 (*0-471-97279-7*) Wiley.

Chadwick, Derek J. & Goode, Jamie. Antibiotic Resistance: Origins, Evolution, Selection & Spread, Vol. 207. LC 96-29697. (CIBA Foundation Symposium Ser.). 260p. 1997. 147.95 (*0-471-97105-7*) Wiley.

Chadwick, Derek J. & Goode, Jamie A., eds. P2 Purinoceptors: Localization, Function, & Transduction Mechanisms. LC 96-1089. (Ciba Foundation Symposium Ser.: No. 198). 346p. 1996. 128.00 (*0-471-96125-6*) Wiley.

Chadwick, Derek J. & Marsh, Joan, eds. Crop Protection & Sustainable Agriculture - Symposium No. 177. LC 93-22791. (CIBA Foundation Symposium Ser.: Vol. 177). 296p. 1993. 140.00 (*0-471-93944-7*) Wiley.

— Functional Anatomy of the Neuroendocrine Hypothalamus - Symposium No. 168. LC 92-5731. (CIBA Foundation Symposium Ser.: Vol. 168). 310p. 1992. 128.00 (*0-471-93440-2*) Wiley.

Chadwick, Derek J., et al. Ethnobotany & the Search for New Drugs. LC 94-28300. (Ciba Foundation Symposium Ser.: 185). (Illus.). 290p. 1994. 128.00 (*0-471-95024-6*) Wiley.

Chadwick, Donna, jt. compiled by see Clark, Cynthia.

Chadwick, Douglas. The Company We Keep: America's Endangered Species. 162p. 1997. per. 16.00 (*0-7922-7132-7*) Natl Geog.

— Enduring America. LC 94-49542. 200p. 1995. 12.95 (*0-7922-2733-6*) Natl Geog.

— Enduring America: Lands Untouched by Time. 200p. 1996. 30.00 (*0-7922-3330-1*) Natl Geog.

Chadwick, Douglas H. The Fate of the Elephant. LC 92-4520. (Sierra Club Guides Ser.). 512p. 1992. 25.00 (*0-87156-635-4*, Pub. by Sierra) Random.

— The Fate of the Elephant. LC 92-4520. 512p. 1994. reprint ed. pap. 14.00 (*0-87156-495-5*, Pub. by Sierra) Random.

***Chadwick, Douglas H.** Yellowstone to Yukon. (National Geographic Destinations Ser.). (Illus.). 200p. 2000. per. 15.00 (*0-7922-7690-6*, Pub. by Natl Geog) S&S Trade.

Chadwick, E. M., ed. Water, Science, & the Public: The Miramichi Ecosystem. (Canadian Special Publication of Fisheries & Aquatic Sciences Ser.: No. 123). (Illus.). 300p. 1995. pap. 50.00 (*0-660-15903-1*, Pub. by NRC Res Pr) Accents Pubns.

Chadwick, Edward W. Pastoral Teaching of Paul. LC 84-7123. 416p. 1984. pap. 15.99 (*0-8254-2325-2*, Kregel Class) Kregel.

Chadwick, Edwin. Report on the Sanitary Condition of the Labouring Population of Great Britain, 1842. Flinn, M., ed. 443p. 1979. 28.00 (*0-85224-145-3*, Pub. by Edinburgh U Pr) Col U Pr.

— Self-Determination, Terrorism, & the International Humanitarian Law of Armed Conflict. rev. ed. LC 96-2672. 1996. lib. bdg. 77.00 (*90-411-0122-5*, Pub. by M Nijhoff) Kluwer Academic.

Chadwick, Elizabeth. The Champion. LC 98-41425. 512p. 1998. text 26.95 (*0-312-19246-0*) St Martin.

— First Knight - Movie Tie-In. 1995. mass mkt. 5.99 (*0-671-53532-3*) PB.

— The Love Knot. 474p. 1999. text 27.95 (*0-312-24407-X*) St Martin.

***Chadwick, Elizabeth.** Marsh King's Daughter. 416p. 2000. 25.95 (*0-312-26491-7*) St Martin.

Chadwick, Elizabeth. Shields of Pride. large type ed. LC 94-33627. 471p. 1995. 22.95 (*0-7838-1154-3*, G K Hall Lrg Type) Mac Lib Ref.

Chadwick, Enid M. At God's Altar: Rite One. Schuler, Eugenia, ed. (Illus.). 1978. pap. 1.50 (*0-934502-01-3*) Thursday Pubs.

Chadwick, Esther A. In the Footsteps of the Brontes. LC 70-159488. (English Literature Ser.: No. 33). 1971. reprint ed. lib. bdg. 75.00 (*0-8383-1272-1*) M S G Haskell Hse.

Chadwick, Eva, jt. auth. see Farr, Dennis.

Chadwick, Francis E. The Ninth Marine Defense & AAA Battalions. LC 90-70003. (Illus.). 120p. 1990. 65.00 (*0-938021-85-0*) Turner Pub KY.

***Chadwick, Frank.** Cloud Captains of Mars & Conklin's Atlas of the Worlds: Sourcebooks for Space: 1889. (Illus.). 144p. 2000. pap. 21.95 (*1-930658-00-1*) Heliograph Inc.

Chadwick, Frank A. Desert Shield Fact Book. 1991. pap. 10.00 (*1-55878-093-9*) Game Designers.

— Space, 1889: Role-Playing in a Gentler Age. (Illus.). 216p. 1988. 30.00 (*0-943580-80-3*) Game Designers.

Chadwick, Frank A. Twilight - 2000: Post Holocaust Role-Playing (V2.0) (Illus.). 280p. (Orig.). (YA). 1990. pap. 30.00 (*1-55878-070-X*) Game Designers.

Chadwick, Frank A. & Caffrey, Matt. Gulf War Fact Book. 1991. pap. 10.00 (*1-55878-094-7*) Game Designers.

Chadwick, French E. Relations of the United States & Spain: The Spanish-American War, 2 vols., Set. (History - United States Ser.). 1992. reprint ed. lib. bdg. 150.00 (*0-7812-6210-0*) Rprt Serv.

Chadwick, French E., ed. Graves Papers & Other Documents Relating to the Naval Operations of the Yorktown Campaign, July to October 1781. LC 76-29044. (Eyewitness Accounts of the American Revolution Ser.). 1968. reprint ed. 27.95 (*0-405-01108-3*) Ayer.

Chadwick, Gary, jt. auth. see Dunn, Cynthia.

Chadwick, George. Harmony: A Course of Study, 2 vols. in 1. Incl. Key to Chadwick's Harmony. LC 74-36316. vii, 103p. 1975. LC 74-36316. (Music Reprint Ser.). xiv, 231p. 1975. reprint ed. Set lib. bdg. 45.00 (*0-306-70663-6*) Da Capo.

Chadwick, George W. Horatio Parker. LC 72-1392. reprint ed. 20.00 (*0-404-08304-8*) AMS Pr.

— Songs to Poems by Arlo Bates. LC 79-18584. (Earlier American Music Ser.). 1980. 29.50 (*0-306-77316-3*) Da Capo.

— Symphony No. 2: In B Flat, Opus 21. LC 71-170930. (Earlier American Music Ser.: No. 3). 216p. 1972. reprint ed. 35.00 (*0-306-77304-X*) Da Capo.

Chadwick, Gloria. Discovering Your Past Lives. 224p. (Orig.). 1988. pap. 11.95 (*0-8092-4546-9*, 454690, Contemporary Bks) NTC Contemp Pub Co.

***Chadwick, Gloria.** Exploring Your Past Lives: A Guide into & Through Your Past-Life Memories. LC 99-93242. 260p. 2000. pap. 14.95 (*1-883717-63-9*) Myst Mndscapes.

Chadwick, Gloria. Happy Ways to Heal the Earth. LC 99-93099. 150p. 1999. pap. 12.95 (*1-883717-22-1*) Myst Mndscapes.

— Images & Inner Journeys: Meditations & Musings. LC 96-94422. 150p. 2000. pap. 12.95 (*1-883717-27-2*) Myst Mndscapes.

— The Key to Self-Empowerment: Open the Magic Inside Your Mind. rev. ed. LC 97-91336. 178p. 1999. pap. 13.95 (*1-883717-38-8*) Myst Mndscapes.

***Chadwick, Gloria.** Life Is Just a Dream. 70p. 2000. pap. 9.95 (*1-883717-24-8*) Myst Mndscapes.

Chadwick, Gloria. Looking into Your Future Lives. 1996. pap. write for info. (*0-8092-3412-2*) NTC Contemp Pub Co.

***Chadwick, Gloria.** Psychic Senses: How to Develop Your Innate Powers. LC 00-90910. 110p. 2000. pap. 11.95 (*1-883717-30-2*) Myst Mndscapes.

— Really Good Recipes. LC 99-96061. 142p. 2000. spiral bd. 9.95 (*1-883717-15-9*, Cozy Kitchens) Myst Mndscapes.

Chadwick, Gloria. Somewhere over the Rainbow: A Soul's Journey Home. LC 93-91601. 248p. 1995. pap. 12.95 (*1-883717-33-7*) Myst Mndscapes.

***Chadwick, Gloria.** Soul Shimmers: Awakening Your Spiritual Self. LC 99-70664. 76p. 1999. pap. 11.00 (*1-883717-83-3*) Myst Mndscapes.

Chadwick, Gloria. Spirituality & Self-Empowerment. LC 95-32765. 224p. 1995. pap. 12.95 (*0-8092-3441-6*, 344160, Contemporary Bks) NTC Contemp Pub Co.

— You've Been There Before. LC 98-38292. 1999. 5.99 (*0-517-20496-7*) Random Hse Value.

Chadwick, Gloria, ed. see Amberson, Cynthia.

Chadwick, Gloria, ed. see Bolduc, Henry Leo.

Chadwick, Gloria, ed. see Jordan, Vicki.

Chadwick, Gloria, ed. see Michaels, Laura.

Chadwick, Gloria, ed. see Raemer, Jillian.

Chadwick, H. M. & Chadwick, Nora K. The Growth of Literature, 3 vols., Vols. I-II. 1792p. 1986. pap. text 110.00 (*0-521-20831-9*) Cambridge U Pr.

Chadwick, H. Munro. The Origin of the English Nation. 232p. (C). 1983. reprint ed. pap. 18.00 (*0-941694-09-7*) Cliveden Pr.

Chadwick, Harold, ed. see Murray, Andrew.

Chadwick, Harold J. We Shall Judge Angels. LC 94-70064. 348p. (Orig.). 1994. pap. 9.99 (*0-88270-706-X*) Bridge-Logos.

Chadwick, Harold J., ed. see Brother Lawrence.

Chadwick, Harold J., ed. see Drummond, Henry.

Chadwick, Harold J., ed. see Freeman, James M.

Chadwick, Harold J., ed. see Price, Charles.

Chadwick, Harold J., ed. see Sheldon, Charles M.

Chadwick, Harold J., ed. see Smith, Hannah W.

Chadwick, Harold J., ed. see Thomas, a Kempis.

***Chadwick, Helen Sell.** Redeeming Choices: A Work of Fiction. LC 99-75682. 468p. 1999. pap. 24.95 (*0-936029-52-8*) Western Bk Journ.

Chadwick, Henry. Augustine. (Past Masters Ser.). 128p. 1986. pap. text 9.95 (*0-19-287534-5*) OUP.

— Early Christian Thoughts & the Classical Tradition: Studies in Justin, Clement & Origan. 182p. 1984. reprint ed. pap. text 24.00 (*0-19-826673-1*) OUP.

— The Early Church. 1993. pap. 13.95 (*0-14-023199-4*) Viking Penguin.

— Heresy & Orthodoxy in the Early Church. (Collected Studies: No. CS342). 350p. 1991. text 109.95 (*0-86078-294-8*, Pub. by Variorum) Ashgate Pub Co.

— History & Thought of the Early Church. (Collected Studies: No. CS164). 344p. (C). 1982. reprint ed. lib. bdg. 109.95 (*0-86078-112-7*, Pub. by Variorum) Ashgate Pub Co.

— Tradition & Exploration: Collected Papers on Theology & the Church. 1995. 58.00 (*1-85311-082-5*, 860, Pub. by Canterbury Press Norwich) Morehouse Pub.

Chadwick, Henry, intro. A Canny Lad: The Early Life of Thomas Moffett. LC 99-205443. 144p. 1998. pap. 100.00 (*1-85297-052-9*, Pub. by Erskine Press) St Mut.

Chadwick, Henry & Evans, Gillian. Atlas of the Christian Church. (Cultural Atlas Ser.). (Illus.). 240p. 1987. 45.00 (*0-8160-1643-7*) Facts on File.

Chadwick, Henry, tr. see Augustine, Saint.

Chadwick, Henry, tr. see Lessing, Gotthold Ephraim.

Chadwick, Henry, tr. & intro. see Augustine, Saint.

***Chadwick, Hollee.** A Dictionary of Christian Terms & Phrases. 2000. pap. 11.99 (*0-88270-799-X*) Bridge-Logos.

Chadwick, Irene. Dawn Pearl: Poems. (Illus.). 48p. (Orig.). 1994. pap. 9.50 (*0-9642725-0-4*) Ietje Kooi Pr.

— Images from Iowa: Keuken Kinderen Kerk (Kitchen Children Church) (Illus.). 1999. pap. write for info. (*0-9642725-3-9*) Ietje Kooi Pr.

Chadwick, J., tr. see Lloyd, G. E., ed.

Chadwick, James M. Chadwick on Subjective Landscaping. Minor, Hinda R., ed. (Illus.). (Orig.). 1989. pap. text 29.95 (*0-685-27002-5*) J Chadwick.

Chadwick, Janet. The Busy Person's Guide to Preserving Food: Easy Step-by-Step Instructions for Freezing, Drying & Canning. (Illus.). 224p. 1995. pap. 14.95 (*0-88266-900-1*, Garden Way Pub) Storey Bks.

— The No-Time-To-Cook Book: An Afternoon of Cooking... A Week of Meals. LC 85-70194. (Illus.). 192p. 1986. pap. 14.95 (*0-88266-393-3*, Garden Way Pub) Storey Bks.

— The No-Time-To-Cook Book: An Afternoon of Cooking... A Week of Meals. LC 85-70194. (Illus.). 192p. 1986. 14.95 (*0-88266-394-1*, Garden Way Pub) Storey Bks.

C

Chadwick, Jeff. Logarithms Without a Calculator. 123p. 1995. pap. text 12.95 (*0-9646272-0-5*) Alpine Pub OR.

Chadwick, Jeffrey L. New Testament Greek I Study Sheets. 65p. 1998. pap. text 14.95 (*0-9646272-2-1*); ring bd., wbk. ed. 14.95 (*0-9646272-1-3*) Alpine Pub OR.

***Chadwick, Jerah.** Story Hunger. 64p. 2000. pap. 12.95 (*1-897648-56-1*, Pub. by Salmon Poetry) Dufour.

Chadwick, John. The Decipherment of Linear B. (Canto Book Ser.). (Illus.). 173p. (C). 1990. pap. 12.95 (*0-521-39830-4*) Cambridge U Pr.

— Lexicographica Graeca: Contributions to the Lexicography of Ancient Greek. LC 96-13436. 350p. 1997. text 85.00 (*0-19-814970-0*, Clarendon Pr) OUP.

— Linear B & Related Scripts. (Reading the Past Ser.: Vol. 1). 64p. (Orig.). (C). 1987. pap. 13.95 (*0-520-06019-9*, Pub. by U CA Pr) Cal Prin Full Svc.

— The Mycenaean World. (Illus.). 218p. 1976. text 69.95 (*0-521-21077-1*); pap. text 22.95 (*0-521-29037-6*) Cambridge U Pr.

Chadwick, John, et al. Corpus of Mycenaean Inscriptions from Knossos. (Illus.). 296p. (C). 1999. 250.00 (*0-521-32025-9*) Cambridge U Pr.

— Corpus of Mycenaean Inscriptions from Knossos Vol. 3: (5000-7999), Vol. 3. (Illus.). 284p. (C). 1998. text 250.00 (*0-521-32024-0*) Cambridge U Pr.

— Corpus of Mycenaean Inscriptions from Knossos, 1-1063, Vol. I. (Illus.). 452p. 1987. text 275.00 (*0-521-32022-4*) Cambridge U Pr.

— Corpus of Mycenaean Inscriptions from Knossos, 1064-4495, Vol. II. (Illus.). 253p. (C). 1992. text 185.00 (*0-521-32023-2*) Cambridge U Pr.

Chadwick, John, jt. auth. see Szathmary, Louis.

Chadwick, John W. Theodore Parker: Preacher & Reformer. LC 72-144939. 1971. reprint ed. 39.00 (*0-403-00925-1*) Scholarly.

Chadwick, John W. & Chadwick, Annie H., eds. Lovers' Treasury of Verse. LC 70-139758. (Granger Index Reprint Ser.). 1977. 18.95 (*0-8369-6212-5*) Ayer.

— Out of the Heart. LC 70-86795. (Granger Index Reprint Ser.). 1977. 19.95 (*0-8369-6072-6*) Ayer.

— Treasury of Helpful Verse. LC 73-76933. (Granger Index Reprint Ser.). 1977. 19.95 (*0-8369-6007-6*) Ayer.

***Chadwick-Jones, John.** Developing a Social Psychology of Monkeys & Apes. (Illus.). 208p. 2000. pap. 24.95 (*0-86377-821-6*) Psychol Pr.

Chadwick, Joseph T., Sr. The Pension Investment Guidebook. Persons, Mark D., ed. (Illus.). 800p. 1991. 79.00 (*1-878375-78-4*) Panel Pubs.

Chadwick-Joshua, Jocelyn. The Jim Dilemma: Reading Race in "Huckleberry Finn" LC 98-25226. 183p. 1998. pap. 17.00 (*1-57806-061-3*); text 45.00 (*1-57806-060-5*) U Pr of Miss.

Chadwick, K. H. & Leenhouts, H. P. The Molecular Theory of Radiation Biology. (Monographs on Theoretical & Applied Genetics: Vol. 5). (Illus.). 377p. 1981. 119.95 (*0-387-10297-3*) Spr-Verlag.

Chadwick, Kamilla C. The War According to Anna. 132p. (Orig.). 1986. pap. 8.95 (*0-940249-00-6*) Seven Stones Pr.

***Chadwick, Kay & Unwin, Timothy, eds.** New Perspectives on the Fin de Siecle in Nineteenth- & Twentieth-Century France. LC 99-59020. (Studies in French Civilization: Vol. 15). 296p. 2000. text 89.95 (*0-7734-7786-1*) E Mellen.

Chadwick, Kenneth E. A Hear Do'n Sing Book: Little Bitty You Little Bitty Me. (Illus.). (J). (ps). 1979. 4.25 (*0-9603698-0-5*) Bet-Ken Prods.

Chadwick, L. The Myths & Realities of Managerial Accounting & Finance. (Financial Times Management Briefings Ser.). 1997. pap. 94.50 (*0-273-63262-0*, Pub. by F T P-H) Trans-Atl Phila.

Chadwick, L. C., et al. Guide for Plant Appraisal. 8th ed. (C). 1992. pap. 125.00 (*1-881956-00-8*) Int Soc Arboricult.

Chadwick, Leigh, tr. see Stumpke, Harald.

Chadwick, Leigh E., tr. see Von Frisch, Karl.

Chadwick, Leslie. The Essence of Financial Accounting. 2nd ed. (Essence of Management Ser.). 192p. (C). 1996. pap. text 19.95 (*0-13-356510-6*) P-H.

— The Essence of Management Accounting. 2nd ed. (Essence of Management Ser.). 172p. (C). 1996. pap. text 19.95 (*0-13-552340-0*) P-H.

***Chadwick, Leslie.** Essential Financial Accounting. LC 00-55155. 2001. write for info. (*0-273-64659-1*) F T P H.

Chadwick, Leslie. Management Accounting. Weir, David, ed. LC 92-23921. (Elements of Business Ser.). (Illus.). 288p. 1993. pap. 64.95 (*0-415-07084-8*) Thomson Learn.

— Management Accounting. Weir, David, ed. LC 92-23921. (Elements of Business Ser.). (Illus.). 128p. (C). 1993. pap. 26.95 (*0-415-07085-6*, B0106) Thomson Learn.

Chadwick, Leslie & Kirkby, Donald. Financial Management. LC 94-44801. (Elements of Business Ser.). 216p. (C). 1995. pap. 17.99 (*0-415-11067-X*) Thomson Learn.

— Financial Management. LC 94-44801. (Bus Press-Previous Routledge). 216p. (C). (gr. 13). 1995. pap. 72.95 (*0-415-11066-1*) Thomson Learn.

Chadwick, M. H., jt. ed. see Goodman, G. T.

Chadwick, M. J. & Kristoferson, Lars A., eds. Renewable Energy Technologies. 1986. 146.00 (*0-08-034061-X*, Pub. by PPL) Franklin.

Chadwick, M. J. & Lindman, N., eds. Environmental Implications of Expanded Coal Utilization. LC 81-23560. (Illus.). 304p. 1982. 67.00 (*0-08-028734-4*, Pergamon Pr) Elsevier.

Chadwick, Mary, et al. Anima. (Illus.). 96p. (Orig.). 1988. pap. 5.00 (*1-880306-00-X*) SF Women Writs.

Chadwick, Nora K. The Druids. 120p. 1997. pap. 19.95 (*0-7083-1416-3*, Pub. by Univ Wales Pr) Paul & Co Pubs.

— The Druids. 119p. 1998. 49.50 (*0-7083-1435-X*, Pub. by Univ Wales Pr) Paul & Co Pubs.

Chadwick, Nora K., jt. auth. see Chadwick, H. M.

Chadwick, Norah K. The Beginnings of Russian History: An Enquiry into Sources. LC 75-41052. (BCL Ser. II). reprint ed. 20.00 (*0-404-14651-1*) AMS Pr.

— An Early Irish Reader. LC 78-72634. (Celtic Language & Literature Ser.: Goidelic & Brythonic). reprint ed. 27.50 (*0-404-17559-7*) AMS Pr.

Chadwick, O., et al. Solvent Abuse: A Population-Based Neuropsychological Study. (Recent Research in Psychology Ser.). xi, 150p. 1991. 63.95 (*0-387-97607-8*) Spr-Verlag.

Chadwick, Owen. Acton & History. 288p. (C). 1998. text 49.95 (*0-521-57074-3*) Cambridge U Pr.

— Christian School Curriculum. 15.99 (*0-88469-228-0*) BMH Bks.

— History of Christianity. 304p. 1996. text 35.00 (*0-312-13807-5*) St Martin.

— A History of the Popes 1830-1914. LC 97-47470. (Oxford History of the Christian Church Ser.). 624p. 1998. text 135.00 (*0-19-826922-6*) OUP.

***Chadwick, Owen.** Michael Ramsey: A Life. 1998. pap. 25.00 (*0-334-02736-5*) S C M Pr Ltd.

Chadwick, Owen. The Popes & European Revolution. (Oxford History of the Christian Church Ser.). 656p. 1981. 105.00 (*0-19-826919-6*) OUP.

— Prince Albert & the University: The Prince Albert Sesquicentennial Lecture. LC 97-42161. (Illus.). 32p. 1998. pap. text 8.95 (*0-521-63756-2*) Cambridge U Pr.

— Professor Lord Acton. 56p. 1995. pap. 5.00 (*1-880595-04-4*) Acton Inst Stu Rel.

— Reformation. (Orig.). 1990. pap. 14.95 (*0-14-013757-2*, Viking) Viking Penguin.

— The Secularization of the European Mind in the Nineteenth Century. (Canto Book Ser.). 292p. (C). 1990. pap. 12.95 (*0-521-39829-0*) Cambridge U Pr.

— The Spirit of the Oxford Movement: Tractarian Essays. 334p. (C). 1992. pap. text 23.95 (*0-521-42440-2*) Cambridge U Pr.

— Victorian Miniature. (Canto Book Ser.). 189p. (C). 1991. pap. 11.95 (*0-521-42251-5*) Cambridge U Pr.

Chadwick, P. Continuum Mechanics: Concise Theory & Problems. 2nd enl. ed. LC 99-38303. 200p. 1998. pap. 9.95 (*0-486-40180-4*) Dover.

Chadwick, Paul. Concrete: Complete Short Stories 1986-1989. deluxe limited ed. Stradley, Randy, ed. (Illus.). 128p. 39.95 (*1-56971-012-0*) Dark Horse Comics.

— Concrete: Fragile Creature. (Illus.). 164p. 1994. pap. 15.95 (*1-56971-022-8*) Dark Horse Comics.

— Concrete: Killer Smile. (Illus.). 1995. pap. 16.95 (*1-56971-080-5*) Dark Horse Comics.

— Concrete: Short Stories 1990-1995. unabridged ed. (Illus.). 112p. (Orig.). (YA). (gr. 7 up). 1996. pap. 14.95 (*1-56971-099-6*) Dark Horse Comics.

— Concrete Complete Short Stories 1986-1989, Bk. 1. 2nd ed. (Illus.). 114p. 1995. pap. 15.95 (*1-56971-114-3*) Dark Horse Comics.

Chadwick, Paul, et al. Cognitive Therapy for Delusions, Voices & Paranoia. LC 96-1475. (Clinical Psychology Ser.). 230p. 1996. 195.00 (*0-471-93888-2*) Wiley.

— Cognitive Therapy for Delusions, Voices & Paranoia. LC 96-1475. (Series in Clinical Psychology). 1999. pap. text 46.50 (*0-471-96173-6*) Wiley.

Chadwick, Peter K. Schizophrenia: The Positive Perspective, in Search of Dignity for Schizophrenic People. LC 96-40143. 240p. (C). 1997. 85.00 (*0-415-14287-3*); pap. 25.99 (*0-415-14288-1*) Routledge.

Chadwick, Priscilla. Schools of Reconciliation: Issues in Joint Roman Catholic-Anglican Education. LC 94-6804. 1994. 59.95 (*0-304-33140-6*) Continuum.

— Shifting Alliances: Church & State in English Schools. LC 98-118716. viii, 184p. 1997. pap. 31.95 (*0-304-70124-6*) Continuum.

Chadwick, R. M. Spon's Grounds Maintenance Contract Handbook. 190p. 1990. 44.95 (*0-442-31235-0*) Chapman & Hall.

Chadwick, Roger. Bureaucratic Mercy: The Home Office & the Treatment of Capital Cases in Victorian Britain. LC 91-45919. (Modern European History Ser.). 424p. 1992. text 35.00 (*0-8153-0740-3*) Garland.

Chadwick, Roxane. Felt Board Story Times. LC 96-43671. (Illus.). 115p. 1997. pap. 15.95 (*0-917846-82-6*, Alleyside) Highsmith Pr.

— Once upon a Felt Board. (Illus.). 128p. (J). (gr. k-4). 1986. student ed. 12.99 (*0-86653-338-9*, GA 798) Good Apple.

Chadwick, Roxanne. Amelia Earhart: Aviation Pioneer. (Achievers Biographies Ser.). (Illus.). 56p. (J). (gr. 4-8). 1987. pap. 4.95 (*0-8225-9515-X*, First Ave Edns) Lerner Pub.

Chadwick, Ruth. Ethics & the Professions. (Avebury Series in Philosophy). 176p. 1994. 73.95 (*1-85628-632-0*, Pub. by Avebury) Ashgate Pub Co.

— Immanuel Kant: Critical Assessments, 4 vols., Set. LC 92-2188. (Critical Assessments Ser.). (Illus.). 1400p. (C). (gr. 13). 1992. 655.00 (*0-415-02143-X*, A7936) Routledge.

Chadwick, Ruth, ed. The Encyclopedia of Applied Ethics, 4 vols. LC 97-74395. (Illus.). 3101p. 1997. text 625.00 (*0-12-227065-7*) Morgan Kaufmann.

— Ethics, Reproduction & Genetic Control. rev. ed. (Illus.). 224p. (C). 1994. pap. 25.99 (*0-415-08979-4*, B0338) Routledge.

Chadwick, Ruth, et al, eds. The Right to Know & the Right Not to Know. LC 96-79376. (Avebury Series in Philosophy). 112p. 1997. text 61.95 (*1-85972-424-8*, Pub. by Avebury) Ashgate Pub Co.

Chadwick, Ruth & Belsey, Andrew, eds. Ethical Issues in Journalism & the Media. LC 92-4869. 208p. (C). 1994. pap. 24.99 (*0-415-06927-0*, A7937) Routledge.

Chadwick, Ruth F. The Ethics of Genetic Screening LC 99-10447. 22p. 1999. write for info. (*0-7923-5614-4*) Kluwer Academic.

Chadwick, Ruth F., ed. Ethics, Reproduction & Genetic Control. 224p. 1987. lib. bdg. 49.95 (*0-7099-3472-6*, Pub. by C Helm) Routldge.

Chadwick, Ruth F., jt. ed. see Thompson, A. K.

Chadwick, Samuel. Humanity & God. pap. 7.99 (*0-88019-071-X*) Schmul Pub Co.

Chadwick, Tim. Cabbage Moon. LC 93-28952. (Illus.). 32p. (J). (ps-2). 1994. 15.95 (*0-531-06827-7*) Orchard Bks Watts.

Chadwick, Tom & Rajogopal, Shan. Strategic Supply Management: An Implementation Toolkit. (Illus.). 288p. 1995. 54.95 (*0-7506-2253-9*) Buttrwrth-Heinemann.

Chadwick, Vernon, ed. In Search of Elvis: Music, Race, Art, Religion. LC 96-46837. 1996. text 75.00 (*0-8133-2986-8*, Pub. by Westview) HarpC.

— In Search of Elvis: Music, Race, Art, Religion. (C). 1996. pap. text 30.00 (*0-8133-2987-6*, Pub. by Westview) HarpC.

Chadwick, Vernon, tr. see Haverkamp, Anselm.

Chadwick, W. R. The Battle for Berlin, Ontario: An Historical Drama. (Illus.). 192p. (C). 1992. pap. 19.95 (*0-88920-226-5*) W Laurier U Pr.

***Chadwick, Whitney.** Amazons in the Drawing Room: The Art of Romaine Brooks. (Illus.). 128p. 2000. 50.00 (*0-520-22565-1*, Pub. by U CA Pr); pap. 24.95 (*0-520-22567-8*, Pub. by U CA Pr) Cal Prin Full Svc.

Chadwick, Whitney. Audrey Flack: Sketchbook, 1985-1989. LC 92-80435. (Illus.). 80p. 1992. pap. 14.95 (*0-940979-20-9*) Natl Museum Women.

— Myth in Surrealist Painting, 1929-1939. LC 79-26713. (Studies in the Fine Arts: The Avant-Garde: No. 1). (Illus.). 261p. 1980. reprint ed. pap. 81.00 (*0-8357-1907-3*, 207068500017) Bks Demand.

— Women, Art, & Society. 2nd rev. ed. LC 96-60233. (World of Art Ser.). (Illus.). 448p. (Orig.). 1997. pap. 16.95 (*0-500-20293-1*, Pub. by Thames Hudson) Norton.

— Women Artists & the Surrealist Movement. LC 90-71450. (Illus.). 256p. 1991. reprint ed. pap. 24.95 (*0-500-27622-6*, Pub. by Thames Hudson) Norton.

Chadwick, Whitney, ed. Mirror Images: Women, Surrealism & Self-Representation. LC 97-46576. (Illus.). 154p. 1998. pap. text 35.00 (*0-262-53157-7*) MIT Pr.

Chadwick, Whitney & De Courtivron, Isabelle, eds. Significant Others: Creativity & Intimate Partnership. LC 92-62321. (Interplay Ser.). (Illus.). 256p. 1996. pap. 17.95 (*0-500-27874-1*, Pub. by Thames Hudson) Norton.

Chadwick, Whitney, et al. American Dreamer: The Art of Philip C. Curtis. LC 99-34201. (Illus.). 180p. 1999. 45.00 (*1-55595-166-X*) Hudson Hills.

***Chadwin, Dean.** Those Damn Yankees: The Secret History of America's Greatest Franchise. (Illus.). 272p. 2000. pap. 15.00 (*1-85984-283-6*, Pub. by Verso) Norton.

Chadwin, Dean. Those Damn Yankees: The Secret Life of America's Greatest Franchise. LC 99-25369. (Illus.). 264p. 1999. 25.00 (*1-85984-713-7*, Pub. by Verso) Norton.

— Wahine Ball: The Story of Hawai'i's Most Beloved Team. (Illus.). 224p. 1997. pap. 12.95 (*1-56647-153-2*) Mutual Pub HI.

Chadwin, Mark L., et al. Ocean Container Transportation: An Operations Perspective. (Illus.). 300p. (C). 1990. text 90.00 (*0-8448-1628-0*) Taylor & Francis.

Chadwyck-Healey, Charles, intro. Catalogue of British Official Publications Not Published by HMSO, 1980. 256p. 1981. lib. bdg. write for info. (*0-85964-101-5*) Chadwyck-Healey.

Chadwyck-Healey, Charles, pref. Catalogue of British Official Publications Not Published by HMSO, 1981. 303p. 1983. lib. bdg. write for info. (*0-85964-102-3*) Chadwyck-Healey.

— Catalogue of British Official Publications Not Published by HMSO, 1982. xxiii, 437p. 1983. lib. bdg. write for info. (*0-85964-114-7*) Chadwyck-Healey.

Chadwyck-Healey Staff, jt. auth. see National Security Archive Staff.

Chadwyck-Healey Staff, ed. see National Security Archive Staff.

Chadzis, Athina. Die Expressionistischen Maskentanzer Lavinia Schulz und Walter Holdt. Deutschen Tanzarchiv Koln Staff, ed. (Stidien und Dokumente Zur Tanzwissenschaft: Bd. 1). (Illus.). 176p. 1998. pap. 39.95 (*3-631-33057-X*) P Lang Pubng.

Chae, Daniel J.-S. Paul as Apostle to the Gentiles: His Apostolic Self-Awareness & Its Influence on the Soteriological Argument in Romans. (Biblical & Theological Monographs). xiv, 378p. 1997. reprint ed. pap. 40.00 (*0-85364-829-8*, Pub. by Paternoster Pub) OM Literature.

Chae-Jin Lee, ed. The Korean War: 40-Year Perspectives. (Keck Center for International & Strategic Studies: No. 1). viii, 131p. 1991. pap. 10.95 (*0-930607-12-0*) Regina Bks.

— The United States & Japan: Changing Relations. (Keck Center for International & Strategic Studies: No. 2). viii, 75p. 1992. pap. 9.95 (*0-930607-13-9*) Regina Bks.

Chae, K., jt. ed. see Park, E. K.

Ch'ae, Man-Sik. Peace under Heaven: A Modern Korean Novel. Kyung-Ja, Chun, tr. from KOR. LC 92-31807. 272p. (C). 1993. 51.95 (*1-56324-112-9*, East Gate Bk) M E Sharpe.

Chae, Soo Bong. Holomorphy & Calculus in Normed Spaces. (Pure & Applied Mathematics Ser.: Vol. 92). (Illus.). 440p. 1985. text 175.00 (*0-8247-7231-8*) Dekker.

Chae, Soo-Bong. Lebesque Integration. 2nd ed. LC 94-27962. 1994. 43.95 (*0-387-94357-9*) Spr-Verlag.

Chae, Young. Successful COBOL Upgrades: Highlights & Programming Techniques. LC 99-17181. (Illus.). 287p. (C). 1999. pap. 49.99 incl. cd-rom (*0-471-33011-6*) Wiley.

Chaet, Bernard. The Art of Drawing. 3rd ed. LC 82-15404. (C). 1983. pap. text 61.50 (*0-03-062028-7*, Pub. by Harcourt Coll Pubs) Harcourt.

— An Artists Notebook. LC 78-11274. 254p. (C). 1979. pap. text 53.00 (*0-03-040726-5*, Pub. by Harcourt Coll Pubs) Harcourt.

Chafe, Eric. Analyzing Bach Cantatas. LC 98-15109. (Illus.). 304p. 2000. text 55.00 (*0-19-512099-X*) OUP.

— Monteverdi's Tonal Language. 442p. 1992. 55.00 (*0-02-870495-9*, Schirmer Books) Mac Lib Ref.

— Tonal Allegory in the Vocal Music of J. S. Bach. LC 90-40050. (Illus.). 460p. 1991. 89.95 (*0-520-05856-9*, Pub. by U CA Pr) Cal Prin Full Svc.

Chafe, Eric T. The Church Music of Heinrich Biber. LC 86-30866. (Studies in Musicology: No. 95). 317p. 1987. reprint ed. pap. 98.30 (*0-8357-1770-4*, 2070651) Bks Demand.

Chafe, Kabiru S. State & Economy in Sokoto Caliphate: Policies & Practices in the Metropolitan Districts, 1804-1903. (Making of Modern Africa Ser.). (Illus.). 234p. 1998. text 68.95 (*1-84014-534-X*, Pub. by Ashgate Pub) Ashgate Pub Co.

Chafe, L. Seneca Thanksgiving Rituals, No. 25. (Bureau of American Ethnology Bulletins Ser.). 302p. 1995. lib. bdg. 99.00 (*0-7812-4183-9*) Rprt Serv.

Chafe, Paul. Mission Critical: Death of the Phoenix: A Novel. 264p. 1996. mass mkt. 5.99 (*0-7615-0234-3*) Prima Pub.

Chafe, Wallace L. Discourse, Consciousness, & Time: The Flow & Displacement of Conscious Experience in Speaking & Writing. LC 93-50610. (Illus.). 392p. 1994. pap. text 25.00 (*0-226-10054-5*) U Ch Pr.

— Discourse, Consciousness, & Time: The Flow & Displacement of Conscious Experience in Speaking & Writing. LC 93-50610. (Illus.). 392p. 1994. lib. bdg. 75.00 (*0-226-10053-7*) U Ch Pr.

— Meaning & Structure of Language. LC 79-114855. x, 360p. 1975. pap. text 11.00 (*0-226-10056-1*) U Ch Pr.

— Seneca Thanksgiving Rituala. 1988. reprint ed. lib. bdg. 75.00 (*0-7812-0079-2*) Rprt Serv.

Chafe, Wallace L., ed. The Pear Stories - Cognitive, Cultural & Linguistic Aspects of Narrative Production. (Advances in Discourse Processes Ser.: Vol. 3). (Illus.). 352p. 1980. text 78.50 (*0-89391-032-5*) Ablx Pub.

Chafe, Wallace L., et al, eds. Evidentiality - The Linguistic Coding of Epistemology. LC 86-10873. (Advances in Discourse Processes Ser.: Vol. 20). 368p. 1986. text 78.50 (*0-89391-203-4*) Ablx Pub.

Chafe, Wallace L., jt. ed. see Garfield, Viola E.

Chafe, William H. America since 1945. 2nd expanded rev. ed. (New American History Essays Ser.). 19p. (C). 1997. reprint ed. pap. 5.00 (*0-87229-084-0*) Am Hist Assn.

— Civilities & Civil Rights: Greensboro, North Carolina, & the Black Struggle for Freedom. (Illus.). 288p. 1981. pap. text 12.95 (*0-19-502919-4*) OUP.

— Never Stop Running: Allard Lowenstein & the Struggle to Save American Liberalism. LC 98-26621. 556p. 1998. pap. text 19.95 (*0-691-05973-X*, Pub. by Princeton U Pr) Cal Prin Full Svc.

— The Paradox of Change: American Women in the 20th Century. 272p. 1992. pap. text 11.95 (*0-19-504419-3*) OUP.

— The Road to Equality: American Women since 1962, Vol. 10. (Young Oxford History of Women in the United States Ser.). (Illus.). 144p. (J). 1998. reprint ed. pap. 10.95 (*0-19-512408-1*) OUP.

— The Unfinished Journey: America since World Ward II. LC 97-49385. (Illus.). 592p. (C). 1998. text 59.95 (*0-19-511617-8*) OUP.

— The Unfinished Journey: America since World Ward II. 4th ed. LC 97-49385. (Illus.). 592p. (C). 1998. pap. text 29.95 (*0-19-511618-6*) OUP.

— Women & Equality: Changing Patterns in American Culture. LC 76-42639. 207p. 1978. reprint ed. pap. text 10.95 (*0-19-502365-X*) OUP.

Chafe, William H. & Isserman, Maurice. Main Problems in American History Vol. 8: American Political History, 1960-1987 & American Social History, 1960-1987. abr. ed. (PaperBook Series in History). (Illus.). 128p. (C). 1996. pap. text 2.25 (*1-877891-39-8*) Paperbook Pr Inc.

Chafe, William H. & Sitkoff, Harvard. A History of Our Time: Readings on Postwar America. 5th ed. LC 98-22735. 512p. (C). 1999. pap. text 24.95 (*0-19-511619-4*) OUP.

Chafee, Claire. Why We Have a Body. 57p. 1996. pap. 5.60 (*0-87129-690-X*, W79) Dramatic Pub.

Chafee, John H., ed. Brownfield Liability & Resource Issues: Hearing Before the U. S. Senate. (Illus.). 255p. (C). 1998. pap. text 35.00 (*0-7881-7364-2*) DIANE Pub.

***Chafee, John H., ed.** Child Care: Congressional Hearing. (Illus.). 188p. (C). 2000. reprint ed. pap. text 30.00 (*0-7567-0039-6*) DIANE Pub.

— Children's SSI Policy: Congressional Hearing. (Illus.). 166p. (C). 2000. reprint ed. pap. text 30.00 (*0-7567-0037-X*) DIANE Pub.

— Endangered Species Recovery Act: Congressional Hearings. 225p. (C). 1999. reprint ed. pap. text 35.00 (*0-7881-8432-6*) DIANE Pub.

— Enforcement of Environmental Laws: Congressional Hearing. 260p. (C). 1999. reprint ed. pap. text 35.00 (*0-7881-8329-X*) DIANE Pub.

— Environmental Tobacco Smoke: Congressional Hearing. 101p. (C). 2000. reprint ed. pap. text 20.00 (*0-7881-8769-4*) DIANE Pub.

— Global Climate Change: Congressional Hearings. (Illus.). 276p. (C). 2000. reprint ed. pap. text 35.00 (*0-7881-8772-4*) DIANE Pub.

An Asterisk (*) at the beginning of an entry indicates that the title is appearing for the first time.

***Chafee, Zechariah.** Free Speech in the United States. 1967. LC 99-8731?. 2000. write for info. (*1-58477-085-6*) Lawbk Exchange.

Chafee, Zechariah, Jr. Freedom of Speech. LC 96-75738. vii, 431p. 1996. reprint ed. 85.00 (*1-57588-075-X*, 310510) W S Hein.

Chafee, Zechariah. The Inquiring Mind. LC 74-699. (American Constitutional & Legal History Ser.). 276p. 1974. reprint ed. lib. bdg. 32.50 (*0-306-70641-5*) Da Capo.

Chafee, Zechariah, Jr. Some Problems of Equity. LC 51-630. (Michigan Legal Publications). xiv, 441p. 1990. 45.00 (*1-57588-363-5*, 300160) W S Hein.

Chafee, Zechariah. The Zechariah Chafee, Jr. Papers. LC 89-892142. (American Legal Manuscripts from the Harvard). 8? p. 1987. write for info. (*0-89093-817-2*) U Pubns Amer.

Chafee, Zechariah, Jr., et al. Third Degree: Report to the National Commission on Law Observance & Enforcement. LC 70-90169. (Mass Violence in America Ser.). 1973. reprint ed. 28.95 (*0-405-01304-3*) Ayer.

Chafel, Judith A., ed. Child Poverty & Public Policy. LC 93-27329. (Illus.). 350p. (C). 1993. pap. text 30.50 (*0-87766-610-5*); lib. bdg. 69.50 (*0-87766-609-1*) Urban Inst.

Chafer. French Colonial Empire Popular. LC 98-37554. 2p. 1999. text 65.00 (*0-312-21826-5*) St Martin.

Chafer, Lewis Sperry. The Epistle to the Ephesians. LC 90-20617. Orig. Title: The Ephesian Letter: Doctrinally Considered. 60p. 1991. reprint ed. pap. 9.99 (*0-8254-2342-2*) Kregel.

— Grace: An Exposition of God's Marvelous Gift. LC 94-37813. 272p. 1995. pap. 11.99 (*0-8254-2341-4*) Kregel.

— He That Is Spiritual. 152p. 1983. pap. 12.90 (*0-310-22345-5*, 6307P) Zondervan.

— El Hombre Espiritual.Tr. of He That is Spiritual. (SPA.). 176p. 1973. mass mkt. 4.99 (*0-8254-1122-X*, Edit Portavoz) Kregel.

— Salvation: God's Marvelous Work of Grace. LC 91-24545. 128p. 1991. reprint ed. pap. 8.99 (*0-8254-2343-0*) Kregel.

— Satan: His Motives & Methods. LC 90-20616. 144p. 1991. reprint ed. pap. 9.99 (*0-8254-2344-9*) Kregel.

— Systematic Theology, 8 vols. in 4. LC 92-34956. 2880p. 1993. 160.00 (*0-8254-2340-6*) Kregel.

— True Evangelism. 1980. pap. 6.70 (*0-310-22381-4*, 6312P) Zondervan.

— True Evangelism: Winning Souls by Prayer. LC 92-44075. 112p. 1993. pap. 7.99 (*0-8254-2345-7*) Kregel.

Chafer, Lewis Sperry, jt. auth. see Walvood, John F.

Chafer, Tony & Jenkins, Brian, eds. France: From the Cold War to the New World Order. 230p. 1996. text 65.00 (*0-312-12588-7*) St Martin.

Chafets, Zev. The Bookmakers. 261p. 1995. 21.00 (*0-614-32287-1*) Random Hse Value.

— Hang Time. 256p. 1997. mass mkt. 6.99 (*0-446-60411-9*, Pub. by Warner Bks) Little.

— The Project. 272p. 1998. mass mkt. 6.50 (*0-446-60542-5*, Pub. by Warner Bks) Little.

— The Project. large type ed. LC 97-12439. (Core Ser.). 286p. 1997. lib. bdg. 25.95 (*0-7838-8207-6*, G K Hall Lrg Type) Mac Lib Ref.

Chafetz, Glenn, et al, eds. Origins of National Interests. LC 99-38155. (Series on Security Studies). 400p. 1999. 57.50 (*0-7146-4985-6*, Pub. by F Cass Pubs); pap. 19.50 (*0-7146-8048-6*, Pub. by F Cass Pubs) Intl Spec Bk.

Chafetz, Glenn R. Gorbachev, Reform, & the Brezhnev Doctrine: Soviet Policy Toward Eastern Europe, 1985-1990. LC 92-31848. 168p. 1993. 52.95 (*0-275-9448?-0*, C4484, Praeger Pubs) Greenwood.

Chafetz, Janet S. Gender Equity: An Integrated Theory of Stability & Change. (Library of Social Research: Vol. 176). (Illus.). 224p. (C). 1989. text 59.95 (*0-8039-3401-7*); pap. text 26.00 (*0-8039-3402-5*) Sage.

— Gender Equity An Integrated Theory of Stability & Change. LC 89-10720. (Sage Library of Social Research: No. 176). (Illus.). 256p. 1990. reprint ed. pap. 79.40 (*0-608-04304-4*, 206508300012) Bks Demand.

***Chafetz, Janet S.** Handbook of the Sociology of Gender. LC 99-13097. (Handbooks of Sociology & Social Research). xii, 630 p. 1999. write for info. (*0-306-45978-7*) Kluwer Academic.

Chafetz, Janet S. Sex & Advantage: A Comparative, Macro-Structural Theory of Sex Stratification. LC 83-19077. 142p. (C). 1984. 41.00 (*0-86598-159-0*); pap. 20.00 (*0-86598-161-2*) Rowman.

Chafetz, Janet S., jt. auth. see Ebaugh, Helen R. F.

Chafetz, Janet Saltzman, jt. auth. see Ebaugh, Helen Rose.

Chafetz, Lester. The Ill Tempered String Quartet: A Vademecum for the Amateur Musician. LC 88-27354. 180p. 1989. lib. bdg. 28.50 (*0-89950-398-5*) McFarland & Co.

Chafetz, Linda, ed. A Nursing Perspective on Severe Mental Illness. LC 87-646993. (New Directions for Mental Health Services Ser.: No. MHS 58). 107p. (Orig.). 1993. pap. 25.00 (*1-55542-695-6*) Jossey-Bass.

Chafetz, M. E., jt. ed. see Blane, Howard T.

Chafetz, Marion C. Health Education: An Annotated Bibliography on Lifestyle, Behavior, & Health. 272p. 1981. 65.00 (*0-306-40754-X*, Plenum Trade) Perseus Pubng.

Chafetz, Marion C., jt. auth. see Chafetz, Morris E.

Chafetz, Morris, jt. auth. see O'Brien, Robert.

Chafetz, Morris E. The Tyranny of Experts: Blowing the Whistle on the Cult of Expertise. 173p. 1996. 19.95 (*1-56833-06?-2*) Madison Bks UPA.

Chafetz, Morris E. & Chafetz, Marion C. Drink Moderately & Live Longer: Understanding the Good of Alcohol. LC 95-94. 1995. pap. 9.95 (*0-8128-8560-0*) Madison Bks UPA.

Chafetz, Morris E., jt. ed. see O'Brien, Robert.

Chaff, Lin, jt. auth. see Blackwell, Mary Alice.

***Chaff, Linda F.** Health & Safety Management for Medical Practices 2000. 2000. pap. 70.00 (*1-57947-083-1*) AMA.

Chaff, Linda F. Safety Guide for Health Care Institutions. 5th ed. LC 94-29435. 196p. (Orig.). 1994. pap. 52.00 (*1-55648-126-8*, 181149) AHPI.

Chaffee. Thinkers College Success. (C). Date not set. 34.76 (*0-395-90547-8*); 45.56 (*0-395-90549-4*) HM.

— Thinkers College Success: Dictionary. (C). Date not set. 37.16 (*0-395-90548-6*) HM.

***Chaffee.** Thinking Critically. 6th ed. 1999. pap. text 30.87 (*0-395-95931-4*) HM.

Chaffee, Clarence L. & Penrod, James T. Licensure & the L. A. R. E. 1993. 44.95 incl. VHS (*1-882998-04-9*) Coun Lndscape.

Chaffee, Clarence L., et al. The Road to Licensure & Beyond: Including Understanding the L. A. R. E. 4th ed. Isbell, Elizabeth A., ed. 290p. 1997. pap. text 129.95 (*1-882998-06-5*) Coun Lndscape.

Chaffee, David. The Rewiring of America: The Fiber Optics Revolution. 1996. 49.95 (*0-614-18442-8*, B01023) Info Gatekeepers.

Chaffee, Ellen D. Songs from the Stone House. 38p. (Orig.). 1993. pap. 10.00 (*1-884824-07-2*, Timonier Bks) Tryon Pubng.

Chaffee, Ellen E. & Sherr, Lawrence A. Quality: Transforming Postsecondary Education. Fife, Jonathan D., ed. LC 92-62286. (ASHE-ERIC Higher Education Reports: No. 92-3). 114p. (Orig.). 1993. pap. text 24.00 (*1-878380-16-8*) GWU Grad Schl E&HD.

Chaffee, Ellen E., et al. Collegiate Culture & Leadership Strategies. LC 88-1517. (American Council on Education-Oryx Press Series on Higher Education). 288p. (C). 1993. 27.95 (*0-02-905291-2*) Oryx Pr.

Chaffee, Graham. The Big Wheels. 56p. 1993. pap. 6.95 (*1-56097-136-3*) Fantagraph Bks.

— The Most Important Thing & Other Stories. 64p. 1995. pap. 7.95 (*1-56097-193-2*) Fantagraph Bks.

***Chaffee, Janice.** One Silent Night: Stories of Christmas Through Women's Eyes. 160p. 2000. pap. 9.99 (*0-7369-0496-4*) Harvest Hse.

Chaffee, Janice. Sisters: The Story Goes On. 192p. 1995. pap. 12.99 (*0-7852-7601-7*) Nelson.

***Chaffee, John.** The Thinker's Guide to College Success. 2nd ed. LC 98-72007. xx, 352p. 1999. write for info. (*0-395-93427-3*) HM.

— The Thinker's Way: Tag: Create the Life You Want. 432p. 2000. pap. 14.95 (*0-316-13333-7*, Back Bay) Little.

Chaffee, John. The Thinker's Way: 8 Steps to a Richer Life. LC 98-18513. 432p. (gr. 8). 1998. 25.00 (*0-316-13317-5*, Back Bay) Little.

— Thinking Critically, 4 vols. (C). 1994. pap., teacher ed. 3.96 (*0-395-69070-6*) HM.

— Thinking Critically, 4 vols. 4th ed. (C). 1993. pap. text 37.16 (*0-395-67546-4*) HM.

— Thinking Critically, 5 vols. 5th ed. (C). 1996. pap. text 37.16 (*0-395-83105-9*) HM.

— Thinking Critically, 5 vols. 5th ed. (C). 1997. pap. text, teacher ed. 11.96 (*0-395-83106-7*) HM.

— Thinking Thru Writing. LC 96-76877. (C). 1998. pap. text 28.36 (*0-395-73766-4*) HM.

— Thinking Thru Writing. (C). 1999. pap. text 11.96 (*0-395-73767-2*) HM.

— The Thorny Gates of Learning in Sung China, New Edition: A Social History of Examinations. LC 94-18315. 280p. (C). 1995. pap. text 20.95 (*0-7914-2424-3*) State U NY Pr.

***Chaffee, John W.** Branches of Heaven: A History of the Imperial Clan of Sung China. LC 99-28564. (East Asia Monographs). 350p. 1999. 45.00 (*0-674-08049-1*) HUP.

Chaffee, John W., jt. auth. see De Bary, William T.

Chaffee, Lyman G. Political Protest & Street Art: Popular Tools for Democratization in Hispanic Countries, 40. LC 92-45084. (Contributions to the Study of Mass Media & Communications Ser.: No. 40). 208p. 1993. 62.95 (*0-313-28808-9*, GM8808, Greenwood Pr) Greenwood.

Chaffee, Paul. Accountable Leadership: A Resource Guide for Sustaining Legal, Financial & Ethical Integrity in Today's Congregations. LC 96-45857. (Religion in Practice Ser.). 1997. 20.95 (*0-7879-0364-7*) Jossey-Bass.

Chaffee, Paul, ed. see McKenney, James B.

Chaffee, Robert. From Within. LC 97-75572. 64p. 1998. pap. 8.70 (*1-882792-57-2*) Proctor Pubns.

***Chaffee, Roy.** The Quit Claim: Pioneering in Minnesota, 1880-1940. Howe, Ray, ed. (Illus.). 320p. 2000. pap. 16.95 (*1-883477-44-1*) Lone Oak MN.

Chaffee, Steven H. Explication. (Communication Concepts Ser.: Vol. 1). 118p. (C). 1991. text 28.00 (*0-8039-4474-8*); pap. text 11.95 (*0-8039-4475-6*) Sage.

Chaffee, Steven H., ed. Political Communication: Issues & Strategies for Research. LC 75-14629. (Sage Annual Reviews of Communication Research Ser.: No. 4). 319p. reprint ed. pap. 98.90 (*0-7837-1122-0*, 204165200022) Bks Demand.

Chaffee, Steven H., jt. ed. see Berger, Charles R.

Chaffee, Steven H., ed. see Schramm, Wilbur L.

Chaffee, W. H. The Chaffee Genealogy: Descendants of Thomas Chaffee of Hingham, Hull, Rehoboth & Swansea, Mass, 1635-1909. (Illus.). 663p. 1989. reprint ed. pap. 83.00 (*0-8328-0381-2*); reprint ed. lib. bdg. 93.00 (*0-8328-0380-4*) Higginson Bk Co.

Chaffee, Wilber A. Desenvolvimento: Politics & Economy in Brazil. LC 97-21301. (Critical Perspectives LA Ser.). 232p. 1997. 49.95 (*1-55587-747-8*) L Rienner.

Chaffee, Wilber A., Jr. The Economics of Violence in Latin America: A Theory of Political Competition. LC 92-4200. 184p. 1992. 49.95 (*0-275-94298-8*, C4298, Praeger Pubs) Greenwood.

Chaffee, Wilber A. & Griffin, Honor M. Dissertations on Latin America by U. S. Historians, 1960-1970: A Bibliography. LC 72-96194. (Guides & Bibliographies Ser.: 7). 72p. reprint ed. pap. 30.00 (*0-608-17154-6*, 202732000055) Bks Demand.

Chaffee, Wilber A., jt. ed. see Ross, Stanley R.

Chaffee, Wilbur R., Jr. & Prevost, Gary, eds. Cuba: A Different America. 200p. (C). 1991. 62.00 (*0-8476-7503-3*, RR 7503); pap. text 23.95 (*0-8476-7694-3*) Rowman.

Chaffer, J. & Taylor, Lawrence. History & the History Teacher. 136p. 1975. 17.95 (*0-8464-1260-8*); pap. 12.95 (*0-685-00724-3*) Beekman Pubs.

Chaffers. Concise Marks & Monograms on Pottery & Porcelain. (Reference Library). 272p. 1998. pap. 6.95 (*1-85326-324-9*, 3249WW, Pub. by Wrdsworth Edits) NTC Contemp Pub Co.

Chaffers, William. Marks & Monograms on European & Oriental Pottery & Porcelain. 1983. 45.00 (*0-87505-067-0*) Borden.

Chaffetz, David. A Journey Through Afghanistan: A Memorial. LC 84-2623. (Illus.). xviii, 254p. 1984. pap. 9.95 (*0-226-10063-4*) U Ch Pr.

Chaffetz, David & Rapoport, Mitchell, eds. The Middle East: Issues & Events of 1978 from The New York Times Information Bank. LC 78-32140. (News in Print Ser.). 300p. 1979. lib. bdg. 30.95 (*0-405-12875-4*) Ayer.

Chaffey, Dave. Groupware & Workflow Management Systems: Selection, Design. LC 98-3741. 280p. 1998. pap. text 36.95 (*1-55558-184-6*) Buttrwrth-Heinemann.

Chaffey, Dave, jt. auth. see Bocij, Paul.

Chaffey, P. Norwegian-English Legal Dictionary (Plus E-N Vocabulary) 2nd ed. (ENG & NOR.). 176p. 1997. pap. 78.00 (*82-00-22602-6*, Pub. by Scand Univ Pr) IBD Ltd.

Chaffey, Patrick N. Norsk - Engelsk Administrativ Ordbok. (ENG & NOR.). 192p. lib. bdg. 150.00 (*0-7859-3674-2*, 8200077586) Fr & Eur.

— Norwegian-English Law Dictionary: Criminal Law & Procedure & Miscellaneous Terms. (ENG & NOR.). 188p. 1992. 65.00 (*0-7859-8910-2*) Fr & Eur.

Chaffin, Bethany. Caring for Those You Love: A Guide to Compassionate Care for the Aged. LC 84-63125. 107p. 1985. 12.98 (*0-88290-270-9*) Horizon Utah.

— Whence Comes the Rain. LC 83-81724. 114p. 1983. 8.98 (*0-88290-230-X*) Horizon Utah.

Chaffin, C. E. Elementary. LC 97-25486. 64p. 1997. pap. 14.95 (*0-7734-2832-1*, Mellen Poetry Pr) E Mellen.

Chaffin, Christopher. Olympiodorus of Thebes & the Sack of Rome: A Study of the Historikoi Logoi, with Translated Fragments, Commentary & Additional Material. LC 93-11697. 392p. 1993. text 99.95 (*0-7734-9321-2*) E Mellen.

Chaffin, Don B., et al. Occupational Biomechanics 3e. 3rd ed. LC 98-28797. 600p. 1999. 74.95 (*0-471-24597-2*) Wiley.

Chaffin, Gary J. How to Become a Land Baron or Baroness on a Janitors Pay: A Guide to Tax-Defaulted Real Estate Auctions. (Illus.). 304p. (Orig.). 1997. pap. 19.95 (*0-9654389-6-1*) Ama-Tor Pubng.

Chaffin, Glenn M., Jr. & Peterson, Ernst. I'm in the Dog House. 1954. pap. 1.50 (*0-87517-037-4*) Dietz.

— Sittin' & a Thinkin' 1952. pap. 1.50 (*0-87517-036-6*) Dietz.

Chaffin, Marian S., ed. Thomas Bartlett Sears, Jr. (1834-1925), the Journals of a Plymouth Seaman. 58p. 1989. pap. 5.00 (*0-940628-50-3*) Pilgrim Soc.

Chaffin, R., jt. ed. see Herrmann, D. J.

Chaffin, Tom. Fatal Glory: Narciso Lopez & the First Clandestine U. S. War Against Cuba. LC 96-12978. 368p. (C). 1996. 37.50 (*0-8139-1673-9*) U Pr of Va.

Chaffin, W. L. History of Robert Chaffin & His Descendants & Other Chaffins in America. (Illus.). 337p. 1989. reprint ed. pap. 51.00 (*0-8328-0383-9*); reprint ed. lib. bdg. 59.00 (*0-8328-0382-0*) Higginson Bk Co.

Chaffin, William L. History of the Town of Easton, Massachusetts. (Illus.). 838p. 1997. reprint ed. lib. bdg. 85.00 (*0-8328-7118-4*) Higginson Bk Co.

Chafin, Ann & Hymes, Donald L. The Changing Face of Testing & Assessment: Problems & Solutions. Gonder, Peggy O., ed. LC 91-61874. (Critical Issues Report Ser.). 102p. 1991. pap. 14.95 (*0-87652-164-2*, 321-00338) Am Assn Sch Admin.

***Chafin, Donald G. & Hoepner, Paul H.** Commodity Marketing: From a Producer's Perspective. 2nd ed. (Illus.). 334p. 2001. 43.75 (*0-8134-3179-4*) Interstate.

Chafin, Kenneth L. I & II Corinthians. (Mastering the Old & New Testament Ser.: Vol. 7). pap. 14.99 (*0-8499-3323-4*) Word Pub.

— I, II Samuel. (Communicator's Commentary Ser.: Vol. 8). 404p. 22.99 (*0-8499-0413-7*); pap. 14.99 (*0-8499-3547-4*) Word Pub.

Chafin, Kenneth L., jt. auth. see Ogilvie, Lloyd J.

Chafin, M. B., jt. auth. see Moore, Clancy.

Chafin, Raymond & Sherwood, Topper. Just Good Politics: The Life of Raymond Chafin, Appalachian Boss. (Illus.). 224p. (C). 1994. text 24.95 (*0-8229-3789-1*) U of Pittsburgh Pr.

— Just Good Politics: The Life of Raymond Chafin. Appalachian Boss. (Illus.). 224p. (C). 1996. pap. 12.95 (*0-8229-5577-6*) U of Pittsburgh Pr.

Chag, Eugene B., et al. Gastrointestinal, Hepatobiliary & Nutritional Physiology. LC 95-43188. (Lippincott-Raven Series in Physiology). 320p. 1996. pap. text 37.00 (*0-7817-0262-3*) Lppncott W & W.

Chagall, Bella. Burning Lights. 4th expanded ed. Guterman, Norbert, tr. LC 96-22870. (Illus.). 288p. 1996. reprint ed. pap. 10.95 (*0-930395-26-3*) Biblio NY.

Chagall, David. Diary of a Deaf Mute. 1971. pap. 5.95 (*0-916538-01-X*) Millenium Hse.

***Chagall, David.** Target: Special Victims of the Holocaust. LC 99-90686. 1998. 25.00 (*0-7388-0486-X*); pap. 18.00 (*0-7388-0487-8*) Xlibris Corp.

***Chagall, Marc.** Chagall Drawings: 42 Works. 2000. pap. 5.95 (*0-486-41222-9*) Dover.

Chagall, Marc. Drawings for the Bible. LC 94-44646. (Illus.). 136p. 1995. reprint ed. pap. text 13.95 (*0-486-28575-8*) Dover.

— Marc Chagall: Daphnis & Chloe. (Pegasus Library). (Illus.). 152p. 1994. 25.00 (*3-7913-1373-8*, Pub. by Prestel) te Neues.

— Marc Chagall: Paintings. Exhibition Catalogue. (Illus.). 24p. 1980. pap. 15.00 (*0-8150-0004-9*) Wittenborn Art.

— Marc Chagall Postcard Book. 1998. pap. 5.99 (*3-8228-7968-1*) Taschen Amer.

— My Life. (Illus.). 192p. 1996. pap. 29.95 (*0-7206-0969-0*, Pub. by P Owen Ltd) Dufour.

— My Life. (Illus.). 227p. 1994. reprint ed. pap. 14.95 (*0-306-80571-5*) Da Capo.

— My Life. (Illus.). 173p. 1985. reprint ed. boxed set 30.00 (*0-685-18787-X*, Pub. by P Owen Ltd) Dufour.

Chagall, Marc. The Wisdom of Judaism. LC 96-16439. 56p. 1996. 8.95 (*0-7892-0236-0*) Abbeville Pr.

Chagall, Marc, jt. ed. see Asher, Sandy.

Chagall, Mark. Marc Chagall: The Lithographs; La Collection Sorlier. Gauss, Ulrike, ed. (Illus.). 415p. 1999. 125.00 (*1-891024-07-8*) Dist Art Pubs.

Chaganti, Rajeswararao, et al. High Performance Management Strategies for Entrepreneurial Companies: Research Findings from over 500 Firms. LC 91-8375. 208p. 1991. 49.95 (*0-89930-561-X*, CSL/, Quorum Bks) Greenwood.

Chaganti, Rajeswararao, jt. auth. see Sherman, Hugh.

Chagas, Carlos, ed. see Canuto, V.

Chaghtai, Mirza S. & Lafar, Uz, eds. Advances in Atomic & Molecular Physics. (Illus.). 300p. 1991. 69.00 (*1-55528-255-5*, Pub. by Today Tomorrow) Scholarly Pubns.

***Chagme, Karma.** Naked Awareness: Practical Instructions on the Union of Mahamudra & Dzogchen. Steele, Linda, ed. Wallace, B. Alan, tr. from TIB. LC 00-23802. 300p. 2000. pap. 19.95 (*1-55939-146-4*) Snow Lion Pubns.

Chagme, Karma. Spacious Path to Freedom: Practical Instructions on the Union of Mahamudra & AtiYoga. Wallace, B. Alan, tr. from TIB. LC 97-33447. 250p. 1997. pap. 18.95 (*1-55939-071-9*) Snow Lion Pubns.

Chagnollaud, Dominique. Dictionnaire de la Vie Politique et Sociale. (FRE.). 251p. 1993. pap. 24.95 (*0-7859-7778-3*, 2218003155) Fr & Eur.

Chagnon, Lucille. Voice Hidden, Voice Heard: A Reading & Writing Anthology. 164p. (C). 1998. per. 36.95 (*0-7872-5432-0*, 41543201) Kendall-Hunt.

Chagnon, Napoleon A. The Yanomamo. 5th ed. LC 96-78476. 304p. (C). 1996. pap. text 25.00 (*0-15-505327-2*) Harcourt Coll Pubs.

— Yanomamo: The Fierce People. 4th ed. 145p. (C). 1992. pap. text. write for info. (*0-318-69118-3*) Harcourt Coll Pubs.

— Yanomamo: The Last Days of Eden. LC 92-1630. (Illus.). 332p. 1992. pap. 18.00 (*0-15-699682-0*, Harvest Bks) Harcourt.

— Yanomamo Interactive CDROM. 1997. cd-rom 31.00 (*0-15-505428-7*, Pub. by Harcourt Coll Pubs) Harcourt.

Chagrov, Alexander & Zakharyaschev, Michael. Modal Logic. LC 97-185365. (Oxford Logic Guides Ser.: No. 35). (Illus.). 624p. (C). 1997. 140.00 (*0-19-853779-4*) OUP.

Chagtai, Nadeem, jt. auth. see Sant'Angelo, Rick.

Chah, Ajahn. A Taste of Freedom. 1988. 3.75 (*955-24-0033-3*, Pub. by Buddhist Pub Soc) Vipassana Res Pubns.

Chahal, D. S. Food, Feed & Fuel from Biomass. (C). 1991. text 52.00 (*81-204-0499-8*, Pub. by Oxford IBH) S Asia.

Chahal, J. S. Topics in Number Theory. (University Series in Mathematics). (Illus.). 206p. (C). 1988. text 75.00 (*0-306-42866-0*, Kluwer Plenum) Kluwer Academic.

Chahal, S. K. Environment & the Moral Life: Towards a New Paradigm. vii, 136p. 1994. 15.00 (*81-7024-615-6*, Pub. by Ashish Pub Hse) Nataraj Bks.

Chahal, S. S. Achievements & Prospects in Mycology & Plant Pathology. LC 98-901269. (Illus.). 173p. 1997. pap. 110.00 (*81-7089-249-X*, Pub. by Intl Bk Distr) St Mut.

Chahin, M. The Kingdom of Armenia. (Illus.). 368p. (C). 1987. text 110.00 (*0-7099-4800-X*, Pub. by C Helm) Routldge.

Chahl, L. A., et al. Antidromic Vasodilatation & Neurogenic Inflammation. 352p. (C). 1984. 120.00 (*963-05-3996-9*, Pub. by Akade Kiado) St Mut.

Chahroudi, Martha, et al. New Art on Paper No. 2: Acquired with Funds from the Hunt Manufacturing Co., 1989-1995. LC 96-2426. (Illus.). 92p. 1996. 26.00 (*0-87633-102-9*) Phila Mus Art.

***Chahrour, Janet.** Flash! Bang! Pop! Fizz! Exciting Science for Curious Minds. LC 99-45295. (Illus.). 144p. (J). (gr. 5-9). 2000. 14.95 (*0-7641-1142-6*) Barron.

Chai, Arlene J. Eating Fire & Drinking Water. LC 98-10090. 368p. 1998. pap. 13.00 (*0-449-91143-8*) Fawcett.

— The Last Time I Saw Mother. 1997. pap. 10.00 (*0-449-91234-5*) Fawcett.

— The Last Time I Saw Mother. large type ed. (Ulverscroft Large Print Ser.). 406p. 1997. 27.99 (*0-7089-3751-9*) Ulverscroft.

Chai, B. H., et al, eds. New Materials for Advanced Solid-State Lasers Vol. 329: Materials Research Society Symposium Proceedings. LC 94-6659. 299p. 1994. text 30.00 (*1-55899-228-6*) Materials Res.

C

Chai, Bruce H. Handbook of Crystalline Optical Materials. (Laser & Optical Science & Technology Ser.). 1999. 149.95 (*0-8493-3789-5*) CRC Pr.

***Chai, C. H.** The Economic Development of Modern China. LC 00-39301. (Reference Collection). 2000. write for info. (*1-84064-054-5*) E Elgar.

Chai, C. L. & Faltings, Gerd. Degeneration of Abelian Varieties. Serre, Jean-Pierre et al, eds. (Ergebnisse der Mathematik und Ihrer Grenzgebiete Ser.). 320p. 1990. 79.95 (*0-387-52015-5*) Spr-Verlag.

Chai, Chu & Chai, Winberg. The Story of Chinese Philosophy. LC 75-17196. (Illus.). 252p. 1975. reprint ed. lib. bdg. 35.00 (*0-8371-8289-1*, CHSC, Greenwood Pr) Greenwood.

Chai, Joseph C. China: Transition to a Market Economy. LC 96-36785. (Studies in Contemporary China). (Illus.). 244p. (C). 1997. text 65.00 (*0-19-829067-5*) OUP.

— China: Transition to a Market Economy. (Studies on Contemporary China). (Illus.). 244p. 1998. reprint ed. pap. text 19.95 (*0-19-829430-1*) OUP.

Chai, Joseph C., et al. China & the Asia Pacific Economy. 327p. 1997. 75.00 (*1-56072-523-0*) Nova Sci Pubs.

Chai, Joseph C., jt. ed. see Tisdell, Clement A.

***Chai, Joseph C. H.** Economic History of Modern China. (Priorities for Development Economics Ser.). 256p. 2000. pap. 22.99 (*0-415-09567-0*); text 75.00 (*0-415-09566-2*) Routledge.

Chai, Julie. Somewhere Between Double Trouble & Infinity: Walking My Soul Path. Charles, Rodney & Hubert, Isabelle, eds. LC 97-61875. 250p. 1999. pap. 18.95 (*1-887472-42-8*) Sunstar Pubng.

Chai, Leon. Aestheticism: The Religion of Art in Post-Romantic Literature. 352p. 1990. text 44.00 (*0-231-07224-4*) Col U Pr.

— Jonathan Edwards & the Limits of Enlightenment Philosophy. 192p. (C). 1998. text 39.95 (*0-19-512009-4*) OUP.

— The Romantic Foundations of the American Renaissance. LC 87-5428. 456p. (C). 1987. pap. text 18.95 (*0-8014-9715-9*) Cornell U Pr.

Chai Lin Sien, jt. auth. see Leinbach, Thomas R.

Chai, Mary A. Herb Walk: Medicinal Guide. (Illus.). 127p. 1992. per. 7.95 (*0-935596-01-1*) LM Pubns.

Chai, Mary-Lee, jt. auth. see Chai, Winberg.

Chai, May-Lee. My Lucky Face. 272p. 2000. 13.00 (*1-56947-181-9*) Soho Press.

Chai, Michele. Wet Behind the Ears: Young Lesbian & Bisexual Women in Canada. In Your Space Collective Staff, ed. 200p. 1999. pap. text. write for info. (*0-88961-236-6*) Womans Pr.

Chai, Poh C. Law of Insurance. xxi, 289p. 1986. 54.00 (*9971-70-048-4*, MICHIE) LEXIS Pub.

Chai-Shin Yu. Early Buddhism & Christianity: A Comparative Study of the Founders' Authority, the Community, & Discipline. 241p. 1986. 8.50 (*0-317-60570-4*, Pub. by Motilal Bnarsidass) S Asia.

Chai-Shin, Yu. Early Buddhism & Christianity: A Comparative Study of the Founders' Authority, the Community & the Discipline. xv, 241p. 1986. reprint ed. 17.50 (*81-208-0050-8*, Pub. by Motilal Bnarsidass) S Asia.

Chai, Sun-Ki. Re-examining Development: The Cognitive Basis for Rational Action. (Illus.). 328p. (C). text 47.50 (*0-472-10701-1*, 10701) U of Mich Pr.

Chai, Sun-Ki, ed. see Wildawsky, Aaron.

***Chai, T. Y., et al, eds.** Manufacturing, Social Effects, Scheduling. Vol. A. 506p. 1999. pap. 126.00 (*0-08-043212-3*) Elsevier.

— Robotics Automation, Vol. B. 556p. 1999. pap. 126.00 (*0-08-043213-1*) Elsevier.

Chai, T. Y., jt. auth. see Chen, Z. Y.

Chai, Winberg & Chai, Mary-Lee. Chinese Mainland & Taiwan: A Study of Historical, Cultural, Economic, & Political Relations. 328p. (C). 1996. pap. text, per. 35.95 (*0-7872-2694-7*, 41269401) Kendall-Hunt.

Chai, Winberg & Clark, Cal, eds. Political Stability & Economic Growth. 1991. write for info. (*0-318-68599-X*) Third Wrld Inst.

Chai, Winberg, jt. auth. see Chai, Chu.

Chai, Winberg, jt. ed. see Hsiung, James C.

Chai Yeh. Handbook of Fiber Optics: Theory & Applications. 382p. 1990. text 116.00 (*0-12-770455-8*) Acad Pr.

Chaianov, Aleksandr. Istoriia Parikmakherskoi Kukly I Drugie Sochineniia Botanika Kh. LC 82-60919. 450p. (C). 1982. pap. 15.00 (*0-89830-028-2*) Russica Pubs.

Chaichian, M. & Demichev, A. P. Introduction to Quantum Groups. LC 96-25942. 300p. 1996. 48.00 (*981-02-2623-3*) World Scientific Pub.

Chaichian, M. & Hagedorn, R. Symmetries in Quantum Mechanics: From Angular Momentum to Supersymmetry. LC 97-48375. (Graduate Student Series in Physics). 1997. 150.00 (*0-7503-0407-3*); pap. 50.00 (*0-7503-0408-1*) IOP Pub.

Chaichian, M. & Nelipa, N. F. Introduction to Gauge Field Theories. Estrin, J., tr. (Texts & Monographs in Physics). (Illus.). 350p. 1984. 117.95 (*0-387-13008-X*) Spr-Verlag.

Chaichian, M., et al. Future Physics & Accelerators. 500p. 1995. text 128.00 (*981-02-2360-9*) World Scientific Pub.

***Chaiet, Donna.** Safe Zone: A Kid's Guide to Personal Safety. (Illus.). (J). 1998. 10.30 (*0-606-15824-3*, Pub. by Turtleback) Demco.

Chaiet, Donna. Staying Safe at Home. (Get Prepared Library of Violence Prevention for Young Women). (Illus.). 64p. (YA). (gr. 7-12). 1998. lib. bdg. 16.95 (*0-8239-2740-7*) Rosen Group.

— Staying Safe at School. LC 95-8493. (Get Prepared Library of Violence Prevention for Young Women). (Illus.). 64p. (YA). (ps-3). 1995. lib. bdg. 16.95 (*0-8239-1864-5*) Rosen Group.

— Staying Safe at Work. LC 95-8481. (Get Prepared Library of Violence Prevention for Young Women). (Illus.). 64p. (YA). (gr. 7-12). 1995. lib. bdg. 16.95 (*0-8239-1867-X*) Rosen Group.

— Staying Safe on Dates. LC 95-8475. (Get Prepared Library of Violence Prevention for Young Women). (Illus.). 64p. (YA). (gr. 7-12). 1996. lib. bdg. 16.95 (*0-8239-1862-9*) Rosen Group.

— Staying Safe on Dates. (Get Prepared Library of Violence Prevention for Young Women). (Illus.). 64p. (YA). (gr. 7-12). 1998. lib. bdg. 16.95 (*0-8239-2739-3*) Rosen Group.

— Staying Safe on Public Transportation. LC 95-8476. (Get Prepared Library of Violence Prevention for Young Women). (Illus.). 64p. (YA). (gr. 7-12). 1995. lib. bdg. 16.95 (*0-8239-1866-1*) Rosen Group.

— Staying Safe on the Streets. (Get Prepared Library). (Illus.). 64p. (YA). (gr. 7-12). 1995. lib. bdg. 16.95 (*0-8239-1865-3*) Rosen Group.

— Staying Safe on the Streets. (Get Prepared Library of Violence Prevention for Young Women). (Illus.). 64p. (YA). (gr. 7-12). 1998. lib. bdg. 16.95 (*0-8239-2741-5*) Rosen Group.

— Staying Safe While Shopping. LC 95-8478. (Get Prepared Library of Violence Prevention for Young Women). (Illus.). 64p. (YA). (gr. 7-12). 1995. lib. bdg. 16.95 (*0-8239-1869-6*) Rosen Group.

— Staying Safe While Traveling. LC 95-8477. (Get Prepared Library of Violence Prevention for Young Women). (Illus.). 64p. (YA). (gr. 7-12). 1995. lib. bdg. 16.95 (*0-8239-1868-8*) Rosen Group.

Chaiet, Donna & Russell, Francine. The Safe Zone: A Kid's Guide to Personal Safety. 160p. (YA). (gr. 6 up). 1998. mass mkt. 4.95 (*0-688-15308-9*, Wm Morrow) Morrow Avon.

— The Safe Zone: A Kid's Guide to Personal Safety. LC 97-36309. (Illus.). 160p. (J). (gr. 5-9). 1998. 16.00 (*0-688-15307-0*, Wm Morrow) Morrow Avon.

Chaiffetz, Shelley. Designing Children. 102p. 1991. pap. 14.95 (*0-9641897-0-4*) Design Child.

Chaigne, Louis. Paul Claudel: The Man & the Mystic. LC 78-5951. 280p. 1978. reprint ed. lib. bdg. 65.00 (*0-313-20465-9*, CHCL, Greenwood Pr) Greenwood.

Chaigneau, P. Dictionnaire des Relations Internationales. (FRE.). 1998. 125.00 (*0-320-00402-3*) Fr & Eur.

Chaij, Fernando. Preparation for the Final Crisis. LC 66-29118. 1966. pap. 9.99 (*0-8163-0939-6*, 16510-0) Pacific Pr Pub Assn.

Chaika, Elaine O. Language, the Social Mirror. 3rd ed. LC 93-42854. 376p. (J). 1994. mass mkt. 27.95 (*0-8384-4731-7*) Heinle & Heinle.

***Chaiken, Andrew.** A Man on the Moon , 3 Vols., Set. (YA). (gr. 7). 1999. 99.95 (*0-7835-5679-9*) Little.

Chaiken, Irwin M. Analytical Affinity Chromatography. 208p. 1987. 120.00 (*0-8493-5658-X*, QP519, CRC Reprint) Franklin.

Chaiken, Irwin M., et al, eds. Macromolecular Biorecognition: Principles & Methods. LC 87-29304. (Experimental Biology & Medicine Ser.: Vol. 19). (Illus.). 850p. (C). 1988. 125.00 (*0-89603-141-1*) Humana.

Chaiken, Irwin M. & Janda, Kim D., eds. Molecular Diversity & Combinatorial Chemistry: Libraries & Drug Discovery. (ACS Conference Proceedings Ser.). (Illus.). 336p. 1996. text 115.00 (*0-8412-3450-7*, Pub. by Am Chemical) OUP.

Chaiken, J., ed. Laser Chemistry of Organometallics. LC 93-7877. (ACS Symposium Ser.: No. 530). (Illus.). 334p. 1993. text 85.00 (*0-8412-2687-3*, Pub. by Am Chemical) OUP.

Chaiken, Jan M., et al. The Impact of Fiscal Limitation on California's Criminal Justice System. LC 83-3392. 198p. 1981. pap. text 15.00 (*0-8330-0494-8*, R-2675-NIJ) Rand Corp.

Chaiken, Marcia R. Identifying & Responding to New Forms of Drug Abuse: Lessons Learned from "Crack" & "Ice" 62p. (Orig.). (C). 1994. pap. text 30.00 (*0-7881-1303-8*) DIANE Pub.

— Kids, Cops & Communities. 48p. (C). 1999. pap. text 20.00 (*0-7881-7628-5*) DIANE Pub.

Chaiken, Marcia R., ed. see Kleiman, Mark A., et al.

Chaiken, Shelly & Trope, Yaacov, eds. Dual-Process Theories in Social Psychology. LC 98-54246. 657p. 1999. lib. bdg. 82.00 (*1-57230-421-9*) Guilford Pubns.

Chaiken, Shelly, jt. auth. see Eagly, Alice.

Chaiken, Stacie. A Wish Book. 1993. 21.00 (*0-517-59429-3*, Crown) Crown Pub Group.

Chaikin, Andrew. A Man on the Moon: The Voyages of the Apollo Astronauts. 704p. 1998. pap. 15.95 (*0-14-027201-1*) Viking Penguin.

***Chaikin, Andrew.** A Man on the Moon Vol. 1: One Giant Leap. Hassig, Lee, ed. LC 99-15449. (Illus.). 368p. 1999. write for info. (*0-7835-5675-6*) Time-Life.

— A Man on the Moon Vol. 2: The Odyssey Continues. Hassig, Lee, ed. LC 99-15449. (Illus.). 256p. 1999. write for info. (*0-7835-5676-4*) Time-Life.

Chaikin, Andrew. A Man on the Moon Vol. 3: Lunar Explorers. Hassig, Lee, ed. LC 99-15449. (Illus.). 336p. 1999. write for info. (*0-7835-5677-2*) Time-Life.

***Chaikin, Andrew & Smith, Sonian.** Air & Space: The National Air & Space Museum Story of Flight. 318p. 2000. pap. 29.95 (*0-8212-2670-3*, Pub. by Bulfinch Pr) Little.

Chaikin, Andrew, jt. auth. see Smithsonian Institute Staff.

Chaikin, Andrew, jt. ed. see Beatty, J. Kelly.

Chaikin, Ira, jt. auth. see Cole, Douglas.

Chaikin, Joseph. The Presence of the Actor. LC 91-22915. 176p. 1991. reprint ed. pap. 10.95 (*1-55936-030-5*) Theatre Comm.

Chaikin, Judy, ed. see Hurwitz, Sadie W.

***Chaikin, L. L.** Captive Heart. LC 00-32601. 2000. write for info. (*0-7862-2719-2*) Thorndike Pr.

Chaikin, Linda. Captive Heart. LC 97-32029. (Trade Wind Ser.: No. 1). 221p. 1998. pap. 8.99 (*1-56507-755-5*) Harvest Hse.

— Endangered. LC 97-4708. (Portraits Ser.). 256p. 1997. pap. 8.99 (*1-55661-977-4*) Bethany Hse.

— Endangered. large type ed. LC 99-16093. 1999. pap. 23.95 (*0-7862-2059-7*) Mac Lib Ref.

— The Everlasting Flame: A Tale of Undying Love for Each Other & God's Word in a Dangerous Time. LC 95-167927. 244p. pap. 10.99 (*0-8024-2339-6*, 135) Moody.

— For Whom the Stars Shine. LC 99-6623. (Jewel of the Pacific Ser.). 256p. 1999. pap. 9.99 (*1-55661-647-3*) Bethany Hse.

— Island Bride. LC 98-41743. (Trade Wind Ser.: Vol. 3). 260p. 1999. pap. 8.99 (*0-7369-0004-7*) Harvest Hse.

— Jamaican Sunset. (Buccaneers Ser.: No. 3). 1997. pap. 10.99 (*0-8024-1073-1*, 6) Moody.

— The Lions of the Desert. LC 97-27848. 454p. 1997. pap. 9.99 (*1-57673-114-6*, Multnomah Bks) Multnomah Pubs.

***Chaikin, Linda.** Monday's Child. LC 99-20926. (Day to Remember Ser.). 1999. pap. 10.99 (*0-7369-0067-5*) Harvest Hse.

Chaikin, Linda. Silver Dreams. LC 98-15188. (Trade Wind Ser.). 1998. pap. 8.99 (*1-56507-756-3*) Harvest Hse.

***Chaikin, Linda.** Tuesday's Child. LC 99-57069. (Day to Remember Ser.: Bk. 2). 400p. 2000. pap. 10.99 (*0-7369-0068-3*) Harvest Hse.

Chaikin, Linda. Valiant Hearts. LC 98-13065. 377p. 1998. pap. 11.99 (*1-57673-240-1*) Multnomah Pubs.

***Chaikin, Linda.** Wednesday's Child. (Day to Remember Ser.). 350p. 2000. pap. 10.99 (*0-7369-0069-1*) Harvest Hse.

Chaikin, Linda L. Arabian Winds: Lions of the Desert, Palisads Premier. LC 96-53685. (Egypt Trilogy Ser.: Bk. 1). 393p. 1997. pap. 11.99 (*1-57673-105-7*, Palisades OR) Multnomah Pubs.

— Behind the Veil. LC 97-33845. (Royal Pavilions Ser.). 256p. 1998. pap. 9.99 (*1-55661-513-2*) Bethany Hse.

— Empire Builders. LC 94-25696. (Great Northwest Ser.). 336p. 1994. pap. 9.99 (*1-55661-441-1*) Bethany Hse.

— Golden Palaces. LC 96-25295. (Royal Pavilions Ser.: No. 2). 352p. 1996. pap. 9.99 (*1-55661-865-4*) Bethany Hse.

— Golden Palaces. large type ed. LC 98-4363. 1998. 23.95 (*0-7862-1467-8*) Thorndike Pr.

— Heart of India, Vol. 1-3. 1994. boxed set 29.99 (*1-55661-783-6*) Bethany Hse.

— Kingscote. LC 94-6788. (Heart of India Ser.: No. 3). 4p. 1994. pap. 9.99 (*1-55661-378-4*) Bethany Hse.

— The Pirate & His Lady. LC 97-147217. (Buccaneers Ser.: No. 2). 384p. 1997. pap. 11.99 (*0-8024-1072-3*, 251) Moody.

— Port Royal. LC 96-207804. (Buccaneers Ser.: No. 1). pap. 11.99 (*0-8024-1071-5*, 252) Moody.

— Silk. (Heart of India Ser.: Bk. 1). 352p. (Orig.). 1993. pap. 9.99 (*1-55661-248-6*) Bethany Hse.

— Swords & Scimitars. LC 96-45768. (Royal Pavilions Ser.: No. 1). 288p. 1996. pap. 9.99 (*1-55661-881-6*) Bethany Hse.

— Swords & Scimitars. large type ed. LC 97-35680. (Christian Fiction Ser.). 430p. 1997. 22.95 (*0-7862-1236-5*) Thorndike Pr.

— Under the Eastern Stars. LC 93-25160. (Heart of India Ser.: Bk. 2). 384p. 1993. pap. 9.99 (*1-55661-366-0*) Bethany Hse.

— Winds of Allegiance. LC 95-45788. (Great Northwest Ser.: Vol. 2). 34p. (Orig.). 1996. pap. 9.99 (*1-55661-442-X*) Bethany Hse.

Chaikin, Miriam. Clouds of Glory: Legends & Stories about Bible Times. LC 97-237. (Illus.). 118p. (J). (gr. 4 up). 1998. 19.00 (*0-395-74654-X*, Clarion Bks) HM.

***Chaikin, Miriam.** Dancing with the Moon. 2001. text 16.95 (*0-8050-6384-6*) St Martin.

Chaikin, Miriam. Esther. LC 86-20183. (Illus.). 32p. (J). (gr. 2-6). 1987. pap. 4.95 (*0-8276-0508-0*) JPS Phila.

— Exodus. LC 85-27361. (Illus.). 32p. (J). (gr. k-3). 1987. lib. bdg. 15.95 (*0-8234-0607-5*) Holiday.

— Feathers in the Wind. LC 88-10978. (Charlotte Zolotow Bk.). (Illus.). 64p. (J). (gr. 3-5). 1989. 10.95 (*0-06-021162-8*) HarpC Child Bks.

— Friends Forever. LC 86-45777. (Charlotte Zolotow Bk.). (Illus.). 128p. (J). (gr. 3-6). 1988. 11.95 (*0-06-021203-9*) HarpC Child Bks.

***Chaikin, Miriam.** Haiku. 2001. text 15.95 (*0-8050-6474-5*) H Holt & Co.

Chaikin, Miriam. Joshua in the Promised Land. (Illus.). 96p. (J). (gr. 3-6). 1990. reprint ed. pap. 7.95 (*0-395-54797-0*, Clarion Bks) HM.

— Lower! Higher! You're a Liar! LC 83-48445. (Charlotte Zolotow Bk.). (Illus.). 160p. (J). (gr. 3-7). 1984. 12.95 (*0-06-021186-5*) HarpC Child Bks.

— Menorahs, Mezuzas, & Other Jewish Symbols. (Illus.). 96p. (J). (gr. 5 up). 1990. 17.00 (*0-89919-856-2*, Clarion Bks) HM.

— A Nightmare in History: The Holocaust 1933-1945. (Illus.). 160p. 1992. pap. 10.00 (*0-395-61580-1*, Clarion Bks) HM.

— Nightmare in History: The Holocaust, 1933-1945. 1987. 15.10 (*0-606-01476-4*, Pub. by Turtleback) Demco.

— Yossi Asks the Angels for Help. LC 84-48351. (Charlotte Zolotow Bk.). (Illus.). 64p. (J). (gr. 3-5). 1985. 11.95 (*0-06-021195-4*) HarpC Child Bks.

— Yossi Tries to Help God. LC 85-45848. (Charlotte Zolotow Bk.). (Illus.). 80p. (J). (gr. 3-5). 1987. 11.95 (*0-06-021197-0*) HarpC Child Bks.

Chaikin, P. M. & Lubensky, T. C. Principles of Condensed Matter Physics. LC 93-44244. (Illus.). 719p. (C). 1995. text 59.95 (*0-521-43224-3*) Cambridge U Pr.

***Chaikin, P. M. & Lubensky, T. C.** Principles of Condensed Matter Physics. (Illus.). 720p. 2000. pap. write for info. (*0-521-79450-1*) Cambridge U Pr.

***Chaikin, Rosalind B.** The Perfect Starfish. LC 98-52876. 115p. 1999. pap. 15.00 (*0-912526-80-7*) Lib Res.

Chaikin, Rosalind B. To My Memory Sing: A Memoir Based on Letters & Poems from Sol Chick Chaikin, an American Soldier in China, India, Burma During World War II. LC 96-29627. (Illus.). 300p. 1997. 30.00 (*0-912526-77-7*) Lib Res.

***Chaiklin, Seth, et al, eds.** Activity Theory & Social Practice: Cultural-Historical Approaches. 381p. 1999. 34.95 (*87-7288-811-3*, Pub. by Aarhus Univ Pr) David Brown.

Chaiklin, Seth & Lave, Jean, eds. Understanding Practice: Perspectives on Activity & Context. LC 92-10606. (Learning in Doing: Social, Cognitive & Computational Perspectives Ser.). (Illus.). 426p. (C). 1993. text 64.95 (*0-521-39263-2*) Cambridge U Pr.

— Understanding Practice: Perspectives on Activity & Context. (Learning in Doing: Social, Cognitive & Computational Perspectives Ser.). (Illus.). 424p. (C). 1996. pap. text 19.95 (*0-521-55851-4*) Cambridge U Pr.

Chaiklin, Sharon, ed. Dance - Movement Therapy Abstracts Vol. 2: Doctoral Dissertations, Masters' Theses, & Special Projects. 250p. (C). 1998. pap. 10.00 (*1-881766-04-7*) M Chace Mem Fund.

Chaiko, David J., jt. ed. see Liddell, Knona C.

Chaiko, Lev. Helicopter Construction in the U. S. S. R. Jones, Steve, ed. 116p. (Orig.). 1985. pap. text 75.00 (*1-55831-005-3*) Delphic Associates.

Chailakhyan, M. K. & Khrianin, V. N. Sexuality in Plants & Its Hormonal Regulation. (Illus.). 175p. 1987. 159.00 (*0-387-96488-6*) Spr-Verlag.

Chaille, Christine & Britain, Lory. The Young Child as Scientist: A Constructive Approach to Early Childhood Science Educations. 2nd ed. LC 96-20745. 192p. (C). 1997. pap. 44.00 (*0-673-99091-5*) Longman.

Chaille, Francois. The Book of Ties. (Illus.). 180p. 45.00 (*2-08-013568-6*) Abbeville Pr.

***Chaille, Francois.** Cartier: Creative Writing. (Illus.). 2000. 45.00 (*2-08-013683-6*, Pub. by Flammarion) Abbeville Pr.

Chailley, Jacques. The Magic Flute Unveiled: Esoteric Symbolism in Mozart's Masonic Opera. (Illus.). 368p. (Orig.). 1992. pap. 14.95 (*0-89281-358-X*) Inner Tradit.

Chaillou. The Roman de Fauvel in the Edition of Mesire Chaillou de Pesstain: Facsimile of Paris, Bibliotheque Nationale Manuscript. fac. ed. (Illus.). 1990. lib. bdg. 575.00 (*0-8450-0007-1*) Broude.

Chaillou, Jacques. Hyperbolic Differential Polynomials & Their Singular Perturbations. Nienhuys, J. W., tr. from FRE. (Mathematics & Its Applications Ser.: No. 3). 1979. text 144.00 (*90-277-1032-5*) Kluwer Academic.

Chaillou, Michel. Jonathamour. (FRE.). 189p. 1991. pap. 14.95 (*0-7859-2240-7*, 207038344X) Fr & Eur.

— Le Reve de Saxe. (FRE.). 245p. 1988. pap. 11.95 (*0-7859-2090-0*, 2070380335) Fr & Eur.

Chailloux, J. & Queinnec, Christian, eds. LISP Standardization & Evolution: Proceedings of the 1st International Workshop, Paris, France, 1988. (Frontiers in Artificial Intelligence & Applications Ser.: Vol. 2). 86p. (gr. 12). 1988. pap. 37.00 (*90-5199-008-1*, Pub. by IOS Pr) IOS Press.

Chaillu, Paul E. Du, see Du Chaillu, Paul E.

Chaim, B. A Bibliography of Mutualism & Individualist Anarchism. 1979. lib. bdg. 42.95 (*0-686-25748-0*) Mutualist Pr.

Chaim, Bezalel. Against the Tide: Jewish Nonconformist Views of Israel & Zionism. 1979. lib. bdg. 42.95 (*0-686-24783-3*) M Buber Pr.

— Hugo Bilgram & Louis Levy: The Battle Against the Money Monopoly. 1980. lib. bdg. 49.95 (*0-686-26596-3*) Mutualist Pr.

Chaim, Bezalel, ed. A Bio-Bibliographical Dictionary of Mutualist & Individualist Anarchist Authors. 1980. lib. bdg. 49.95 (*0-686-26595-5*) Mutualist Pr.

— Toward Jewish-Arab Rapprochement: A History of Ihud. 1979. lib. bdg. 44.95 (*0-686-24785-X*) M Buber Pr.

Chaim, Chafetz, pseud. Ahavath Chesed: The Love of Kindness As Required by G-D. Oschry, Leonard, tr. from HEB. 1994. 9.95 (*0-87306-167-5*) Feldheim.

Chaim-Chofet. Mishna Berurah Vol. 2C: Covering Chapters 202-241 of Shulchan Aruch Orach Chaim. Orenstein, Aviel, tr. from HEB. 458p. 1989. 22.95 (*0-87306-503-4*) Feldheim.

— Mishna Berurah Vol. 2C: Covering Chapters 202-241 of Shulchan Aruch Orach Chaim. large type ed. Orenstein, Aviel, tr. from HEB. 458p. 1989. 26.95 (*0-87306-502-6*) Feldheim.

Chaim, Daphna Ben, see Ben Chaim, Daphna.

Chaim Press Staff. The Future Festival: Laws, Traditions, & Customs of the Three Weeks & Tisha B'Av. 178p. 1996. 16.95 (*1-56871-103-4*, Pub. by Targum Pr) Feldheim.

Chaine, Jacques. The Orphee Data-Base of Guitar Records. Ophee, Matanya, ed. LC 89-80418. 1990. 25.00 (*0-936186-30-5*, RTFT-6); pap. 15.00 (*0-936186-35-6*, RTFT-6A) Edit Orphee.

— The Orphee Data-Base of Guitar Records: 1991 Supplement. Ophee, Matanya, ed. LC 89-80418. 128p. (Orig.). 1991. pap. 8.00 (*0-936186-58-5*, RTFT-6-91) Edit Orphee.

Chainey, Barbara. Essential Quilter: Tradition, Techniques, Design, Patterns & Projects. (Illus.). 144p. 1997. pap. 19.95 (*0-7153-0569-7*) Sterling.

— Essential Quilter Project Book: 20 Projects. LC 97-192237. (Illus.). 128p. 1997. 27.95 (*0-7153-0485-2*) Sterling.

***Chainey, Barbara.** Quilt It! Quilting Ideas & Inspiration for Patchwork & Applique. (Illus.). 192p. 1999. pap. 29.95 (*1-56477-276-4*, DB397) Martingale & Co.

Chainey, Peter. Legal Time Limits. 100p. (C). 1991. text 30.00 (*1-85431-140-9*, Pub. by Blackstone Pr) Gaunt.

Chaintrier, Louis. Balloon Post of the Siege of Paris, Eighteen Seventy to Eighteen Seventy-One. (ENG.). 163p. 1981. 12.50 (*0-939429-09-8*) Am Air Mail.

Chaio-Hui & Liu, Jenny. Ancient China Treasure Chest. LC 96-67139. (Illus.). 32p. (J). (gr. 4-7). 1996. pap. 19.95 (*1-56138-785-1*) Running Pr.

Chairanya, Krishna. Freedom & Transcendence. 1983. 28.00 (*0-8364-0953-1*, Pub. by Manohar) S Asia.

Chaison, Gary N. Union Mergers in Hard Times: The View from Five Countries. LC 96-28101. (IRL Press Book/Cornell International Reports: No. 31). (Illus.). 256p. 1996. text 42.50 (*0-8014-3330-4*); pap. text 16.95 (*0-8014-8380-8*) Cornell U Pr.

Chaisson, Christine F. Understanding Pesticides in Food. LC 92-230714. 12p. 1991. reprint ed. pap. 30.00 (*0-608-03031-7*, 206348200006) Bks Demand.

***Chaisson, Eric & McMillan, Steve.** Astronomy: A Beginners Guide to the Universe, 2000 Media Update Edition. 2nd ed. 564p. (C). 1999. pap. text 68.00 incl. audio compact disk (*0-13-085848-X*) P-H.

— Astronomy Today, 2000 Media Update Edition. 3rd ed. 693p. 1999. 76.00 incl. cd-rom (*0-13-085863-3*, Prentice Hall) P-H.

Chaisson, Eric J. Astronomy: A Beginner's Guide to the Universe. 2nd ed. LC 97-38104. 556p. 1997. pap. text 69.00 (*0-13-733916-X*) P-H.

***Chaisson, Eric J.** Cosmic Evolution: The Rise of Complexity in Nature. (Illus.). 320p. 2001. 27.95 (*0-674-00342-X*) HUP.

Chaisson, Eric J. Hubble Wars: Astrophysics Meets Astropolitics in the Two-Billion-Dollar Struggle over the Hubble Telescope. LC 98-156757. 424p. 1998. pap. text 17.95 (*0-674-41255-9*) HUP.

— Relatively Speaking: Relativity, Black Holes, & the Fate of the Universe. 1990. pap. 14.95 (*0-393-30675-5*) Norton.

— Space Trials: The Hubble Space Telescope Story. 512p. 1993. 28.00 (*0-393-03604-9*) Norton.

— Universe. (Illus.). 544p. (C). 1988. text 54.00 (*0-13-938391-3*) P-H.

Chaisson, Eric J. & Kim, Tae-Chang, eds. The Thirteenth Labor: Improving Science Education. 346p. 1999. text 48.00 (*90-5700-538-7*); pap. text 26.00 (*90-5700-539-5*) Gordon & Breach.

***Chaisson, Reba L.** For Entertainment Purposes Only? An Analysis of the Struggle to Control Filmic Representations. 272p. 2000. 50.00 (*0-7391-0156-0*) Lxngtn Bks.

Chait, A. M. Butterworths Tax Diary, 1995. ring bd. write for info. (*0-409-07560-4*, SA, MICHIE) LEXIS Pub.

Chait, Baruch. The Thirty-Nine Av Melachoth of Shabbath. 1992. 25.95 (*0-87306-586-7*) Feldheim.

— The Thirty-Nine Av Melachoth of Shabbath. large type ed. 1993. 33.95 (*1-58330-135-6*) Feldheim.

Chait, Richard, et al, eds. Twentieth Army Science Conference: Award-Winning Papers, Norfolk, Virginia, 24-27 June 1996. 150p. 1997. 38.00 (*981-02-3178-4*) World Scientific Pub.

Chait, Richard P. Como Ajudar Seu Conselho Director a Governor Mais e Administar Menos.Tr. of How to Govern More & Manage Less. (POR.). 16p. (Orig.). 1996. pap. write for info. (*0-925299-61-8*) Natl Ctr Nonprofit.

— How to Help Your Board Govern More & Manage Less. (Nonprofit Governance Ser.: No. 49). 16p. 1993. pap. text 12.00 (*0-925299-26-X*) Natl Ctr Nonprofit.

Chait, Richard P. & Ford, Andrew T. Beyond Traditional Tenure: A Guide to Sound Policies & Practices. LC 81-23606. (Jossey-Bass Series in Higher Education). 317p. reprint ed. pap. 98.30 (*0-8357-4935-5*, 203786500009) Bks Demand.

Chait, Richard P., et al. The Effective Board of Trustees. LC 92-43362. 144p. 1991. boxed set 27.95 (*0-89774-806-9*) Oryx Pr.

— Improving the Performance of Governing Boards. LC 96-39056. (Ace-Oryx Series on Higher Education). 176p. 1996. boxed set 34.95 (*1-57356-037-5*) Oryx Pr.

Chait, Thelma. Call of Africa. (Illus.). 64p. (J). (gr. 4-8). 1998. pap. 10.95 (*1-880812-29-0*) S Ink WA.

Chaitanya, Deva B. An Introduction to Indian Music. 149p. 1992. 14.95 (*0-317-12340-8*, Pub. by Pubns Div) Asia Bk Corp.

Chaitanya, Krishana. A Profile of Indian Culture. 1975. 15.95 (*0-318-36956-7*) Asia Bk Corp.

Chaitanya, Krishna. Arts of India: Architecture, Sculpture, Painting, Music, Dance & Handicraft. (Illus.). 107p. (C). 1987. 80.00 (*81-7017-209-8*, Pub. by Abhinav) S Asia.

— The Betrayal of Krishna: Vicissitudes of a Great Myth. (C). 1991. 42.50 (*81-85120-39-0*, Pub. by Clarion) S Asia.

— A History of Arabic Literature. 1983. 18.00 (*0-8364-1045-9*, Pub. by Manohar) S Asia.

— History of Indian Painting: The Modern Period. (C). 1994. text 128.00 (*81-7017-310-8*) S Asia.

— A History of Indian Painting: The Mural Tradition. LC 76-900494. 1976. 28.50 (*0-88386-786-9*) S Asia.

— Latin Literature of the Christian Epoch. (C). 1994. text 18.50 (*81-220-0342-7*, Pub. by Konark Pubs) S Asia.

— The Mahabharata: A Literary Study. 462p. 1993. 39.95 (*81-85120-04-8*) Asia Bk Corp.

— Sociology of Freedom. 1978. 18.50 (*0-8364-0008-9*) S Asia.

Chaitanya, Ramakrishna, ed. see Amritaswarupananda, Swami.

Chaitanyo, ed. & illus. see Hu, Ra Uru.

Chaithiraphan, S. Current Concept in the Therapy of Hypertension with Beta-Blockers. (Journal: Cardiology: Vol. 66, Suppl. 1). (Illus.). vi, 62p. 1980. pap. 28.50 (*3-8055-0912-X*) S Karger.

Chaitin, G. J. Algorithmic Information Theory. (Cambridge Tracts in Theoretical Computer Science Ser.: No. 1). 192p. 1987. text 54.95 (*0-521-34306-2*) Cambridge U Pr.

— Information, Randomness & Incompleteness. 284p. (C). 1987. text 90.00 (*9971-5-0479-0*); pap. text 47.00 (*9971-5-0480-4*) World Scientific Pub.

— Information, Randomness & Incompleteness. (Series in Computer Science: Vol. 8). 324p. (C). 1990. pap. text 36.00 (*981-02-0171-0*) World Scientific Pub.

— Information, Randomness & Incompleteness. 2nd ed. (Series in Computer Science: Vol. 8). 324p. (C). 1990. text 74.00 (*981-02-0154-0*) World Scientific Pub.

Chaitin, Gilbert D. Rhetoric & Culture in Lacan. (Literature, Culture, Theory Ser.: No. 19). 290p. (C). 1996. text 59.95 (*0-521-49728-0*); pap. text 19.95 (*0-521-49765-5*) Cambridge U Pr.

Chaitin, Gregorg J. The Limits of Mathematics: A Course on Information Theory & the Limits of Formal Reasoning. LC 97-36103. (Springer Series in Discrete Mathematics & Theoretical Computer Science). (Illus.). 160p. 1998. 32.00 (*981-3083-59-X*, Pub. by Spr-Verlag) Spr-Verlag.

Chaitin, Gregory J. Information-Theoretic Incompleteness. LC 92-30891. 240p. 1992. text 61.00 (*981-02-1208-9*) World Scientific Pub.

***Chaitin, Gregory J.** The Unknowable. LC 99-29345. x, 122p. 1999. 32.95 (*981-4021-72-5*, Pub. by U Auckland) Spr-Verlag.

***Chaitin, Joy & Stevens-Estabrook, Sarah.** Henny Penny (Musical) 1999. pap. 3.50 (*0-87129-916-X*, H07) Dramatic Pub.

Chaitin, Joy & Stevens-Estabrook, Sarah. On Time - Musical. 1994. 5.50 (*0-87129-468-0*, O05) Dramatic Pub.

Chaitin, Joy, et al. The Fourth Wise Man - Play with Music. 27p. (J). (gr. 1 up). 1998. pap. 5.60 (*0-87129-881-3*, F09) Dramatic Pub.

Chaitin, Joy, jt. auth. see Stevens-Estabrook, Sarah.

Chaitin, Rebecca, jt. auth. see Knowlton, Judith.

Chaitin, Rebecca D., jt. auth. see Knowlton, Judith M.

Chaitin, Rebecca D., ed. see Knowlton, Judith M.

***Chaitkin, Anton.** Treason in America: From Aaron Burr to Averell Harriman. 2nd ed. 608p. 1999. reprint ed. pap. 20.00 (*0-943235-15-4*) Exec Intel Review.

Chaitkin, Anton. Treason in America: From Aaron Burr to Averell Harriman. 2nd ed. (Illus.). 608p. 1999. reprint ed. pap. 20.00 (*0-943235-01-4*) Exec Intel Review.

Chaitkin, Carol. Barron's English Power Pack. 2nd rev. ed. (YA). 1999. pap. 14.95 (*0-7641-7215-8*) Barron.

— English. 2nd rev. ed. LC 98-42411. (Let's Review Ser.). 280p. (YA). 1999. pap. 11.95 (*0-7641-0100-5*) Barron.

***Chaiton, Sam & Swinton, Terry.** Lazarus & the Hurricane: The Freeing of Rubin "Hurricane" Carter. 384p. 2000. pap. 14.95 (*0-312-25397-4*, St Martin Griffin) St Martin.

Chaitow. Modern Neuromuscular Technique. 1996. text 45.00 (*0-443-05298-0*, W B Saunders Co) Harcrt Hlth Sci Grp.

— Muscle Energy Techniques. 1996. text 44.00 (*0-443-05297-2*, W B Saunders Co) Harcrt Hlth Sci Grp.

— Positional Release Technique. (C). 1998. pap. text 95.00 (*0-443-06129-7*) Church.

— Positional Release Techniques. 1996. text 38.95 (*0-443-05299-9*, W B Saunders Co) Harcrt Hlth Sci Grp.

— Recipes for Health: Arthritis. 1998. 11.00 (*0-7225-3317-9*) Thorsons PA.

— Your Control Cholesterol Cookbook. 1998. pap. 11.00 (*0-7225-3476-0*, 902670Q) Thorsons PA.

Chaitow, Alkimini. Greek Vegetarian Cooking. 128p. (Orig.). 1998. pap. 10.95 (*0-89281-340-7*) Inner Tradit.

***Chaitow, L.** Cranial Manipulation Theory & Practice: Osseous & Soft Tissue Approaches. 1999. text 99.00 (*0-443-06439-3*) Harcrt Hlth Sci Grp.

Chaitow, L. Modern Neuromuscular Techniques. 24p. 1997. pap. write for info. (*0-443-05977-2*) Church.

Chaitow, Leon. Acupuncture Treatment of Pain: Safe & Effective Methods for Using Acupuncture in Pain Relief. 192p. (Orig.). 1990. pap. text 19.95 (*0-89281-383-0*) Inner Tradit.

— Amino Acids in Therapy: A Guide to the Therapeutic Application of Protein Constituents. 112p. (Orig.). 1985. pap. 12.95 (*0-89281-287-7*, Heal Arts VT) Inner Tradit.

— The Antibiotic Crisis: Antibotic Alternatives. 240p. 1998. 19.95 (*0-7225-3772-7*) Thorsons PA.

— Aromatherapy for Back Pain. 1998. 14.95 (*1-85833-957-X*) Quadrillion Pubng.

***Chaitow, Leon.** Arthritis: Safe Alternatives Without Drugs. rev. ed. 1998. pap. 7.00 (*0-7225-3562-7*) Thorsons PA.

Chaitow, Leon. Asthma & Hay Fever: Proven Drug-Free Methods to Combat the Causes. 112p. 1990. pap. 4.99 (*0-7225-1899-4*) Thorsons PA.

— Candida Albicans: Could Yeast Be Your Problem? 1989. pap. 8.95 (*0-89281-247-8*, Heal Arts VT) Inner Tradit.

— Candida Albicans: Could Yeast Be Your Problem? rev. ed. LC 98-18448. (SPA.). 160p. 1998. pap. 10.95 (*0-89281-795-X*, Heal Arts VT) Inner Tradit.

***Chaitow, Leon.** Cranial Manipulation Theory & Practice: Osseous & Soft Tissue Approaches. LC 99-36445. 1999. write for info. (*0-443-05803-2*) Church.

Chaitow, Leon. Fibromyalgia & Muscle Pain: What Causes It, How It Feels & What to Do about It. 220p. 1996. pap. 11.95 (*0-7225-3098-6*) Harper SF.

— Fibromyalgia & Muscle Pain: What Causes It, How It Feels & What to Do about It. 1. 1999. pap. 11.00 (*0-7225-3735-2*) Thorsons PA.

***Chaitow, Leon.** High Blood Pressure: Safe Alternatives Without Drugs. (Natural Health Ser.). 1998. pap. 7.00 (*0-7225-3563-5*) Thorsons PA.

Chaitow, Leon. Hydrotherapy: Water Therapy for Health & Beauty. LC 99-20224. (Health Essentials Ser.). 128p. (J). 1999. pap. 9.95 (*1-86204-445-7*, Pub. by Element MA) Penguin Putnam.

— Palpation Skills: Assessment & Diagnosis Through Touch. LC 96-37078. 1996. pap. text 39.95 (*0-443-05320-0*) Church.

— Soft-Tissue Manipulation: A Practitioner's Guide to the Diagnosis & Treatment of Soft-Tissue Dysfunction & Reflex Activity. 192p. 1988. text 44.95 (*0-89281-276-1*) Inner Tradit.

— Vaccination & Immunisation: Dangers, Delusions & Alternatives (What Every Parent Should Know) 5th ed. 192p. pap. 20.95 (*0-8464-4308-2*) Beekman Pubs.

— Vaccination & Immunization. 64p. 1988. pap. 13.95 (*0-85207-191-4*, Pub. by C W Daniel) Natl Bk Netwk.

— You Don't Have to Die: Unraveling the AIDS Myth. LC 94-72701. 325p. 1994. pap. 14.95 (*0-9636334-4-9*) AlternMed Bks.

Chaix, Dominique & Williams, Roger L. The Letters of Dominique Chaix, Botanist-Cur E. LC 97-19829. (International Archives of the History of Ideas Ser.). 1997. lib. bdg. 174.00 (*0-7923-4615-7*) Kluwer Academic.

Chaix-Ruy, Jules. La Formation de la Pensee Philosophique de G. B. Vico. Mayer, J. P., ed. LC 78-67339. (European Political Thought Ser.). (FRE.). 1980. reprint ed. lib. bdg. 25.95 (*0-405-11684-5*) Ayer.

Chaiyana, Samorn, ed. see Allyn, E. G.

Chajes, Saul. Thesaurus Pseudonymorum. xiv, 415p. 1967. reprint ed. 130.00 (*0-318-71891-X*) G Olms Pubs.

Chajet, Clive. Image by Design: For Corporate Vision to Business Reality. 1991. 23.99 (*0-201-55042-3*) Addison-Wesley.

Chakabarty, S. K. Q. T., MIS & Data Processing, Vol. II. (C). 1989. 125.00 (*0-89771-440-7*, Pub. by Current Dist) St Mut.

Chakalov, G. Elsevier's Dictionary of Science & Technology. (ENG & RUS.). 1144p. 1995. 258.50 (*0-444-81955-X*) Elsevier.

— English-Russian Dictionary of Science & Technology. (ENG & RUS.). 1134p. 1996. 395.00 (*0-7859-9369-X*) Fr & Eur.

Chakalov, G., compiled by. Elsevier's Dictionary of Science & Technology. LC 92-46539. (ENG & RUS.). 1256p. 1993. 273.00 (*0-444-88924-8*) Elsevier.

Chakalov, G. G. Elsevier's Dictionary of Science & Technology: Russian - English. (ENG & RUS.). 1243p. 1993. 450.00 (*0-8288-9267-9*, 444889248) Fr & Eur.

Chakbabarti, Dilip K. The External Trade & the Indus Civilization. 180p. 1990. reprint ed. 27.50 (*81-215-0485-6*, Pub. by M Manoharial) Coronet Bks.

Chakela, Qualabane K. Soil Erosion & Reservoir Sedimentation in Lesotho. 208p. 1981. write for info. (*91-7106-186-X*, Pub. by Nordic Africa) Transaction Pubs.

Chaker, Victor, ed. Corrosion Effect of Stray Currents & the Technique for Evaluating Corrosion of REBARS in Concrete-STP 906. LC 85-30618. (Illus.). 145p. 1986. text 29.00 (*0-8031-0468-5*, STP906) ASTM.

— Corrosion Forms & Control for Infrastructure. LC 92-35015. (Special Technical Publication Ser.: Vol. 1137). (Illus.). 430p. 1992. text 55.00 (*0-8031-1432-X*, STP1137) ASTM.

— Innovative Ways for Controlling the Decaying Infrastructure. LC 95-74995. 300p. 1995. pap. 74.00 (*1-877914-83-5*) NACE Intl.

Chaker, Victor & Palmer, David J., eds. Effects of Soil Characteristics on Corrosion. LC 88-38337. (Special Technical Publication Ser.: No. STP 1013). (Illus.). 175p. 1989. pap. text 29.00 (*0-8031-1189-4*, STP1013) ASTM.

Chakeres, Donald W. Fundamentals of MRI. (Illus.). 320p. 1991. 70.00 (*0-683-01666-0*) Lppncott W & W.

Chakerian, G. D., et al. Geometry: A Guided Inquiry. 557p. (C). 1984. teacher ed. 18.50 (*0-916327-09-4*) Davis Math Pr.

— Geometry: A Guided Inquiry. rev. ed. 557p. (C). 1984. text 16.50 (*0-916327-08-6*); student ed. 6.00 (*0-916327-10-8*); student ed. 4.00 (*0-916327-11-6*) Davis Math Pr.

Chakerian, G. D., jt. auth. see Kreith, Kurt.

Chaki-Sircar, Manjusri, jt. auth. see Rohner, Ronald P.

Chakkour, Mario H. Painting with Computers: The Step by Step Guide & Showcase. (Illus.). 144p. 1995. 29.99 (*1-56496-212-1*) Rockport Pubs.

— Painting with Computers: The Step-by-Step Guide & Showcase. (Illus.). 144p. 29.99 (*1-56496-284-9*) Rockport Pubs.

***Chakkour, Mario H.** Virtual Pose. (Illus.). 80p. 1999. pap. 34.99 incl. cd-rom (*0-9666383-1-X*) Design Books.

Chakladar, Haran C. Social Life in Ancient India: Studies in Vatsysayana's Kama Sutra. 1990. 20.00 (*81-206-0524-1*, Pub. by Asian Educ Servs) S Asia.

Chakladar, Snehamoy. Minority Rights: A Socio-Linguistic Analysis of Group Conflicts in Eastern Region of India. (C). 1987. 14.00 (*81-7074-011-8*, Pub. by KP Bagchi) S Asia.

Chaklader, A. C. & Lund, J. A., eds. Sintering '91. 680p. 1992. text 216.00 (*0-87849-638-6*, Pub. by Trans T Pub) Enfield Pubs NH.

Chaklader, Snehamoy. Sociolinguistics: A Guide to Language Problems in India. 1990. 37.50 (*81-7099-194-3*, Pub. by Mittal Pubs Dist) S Asia.

Chakma, Amit, et al, eds. Enhanced Oil Recovery. (Symposium Ser.: No. 280). 148p. 1991. pap. 35.00 (*0-8169-0541-X*) Am Inst Chem Eng.

Chako, K. C. Metaphysical Implications of Gandhian Thought. 1986. 15.00 (*0-8364-1901-4*, Pub. by Mittal Pubs Dist) S Asia.

Chakotin, Serge. Rape of the Masses: The Psychology of Totalitarian Political Propaganda. LC 77-157553. (Studies in Philosophy: No. 40). 1971. lib. bdg. 75.00 (*0-8383-1264-0*) M S G Haskell Hse.

Chakrabarthi, N. M. Disease of Cultivable Freshwater Fishes & Their Control. 180p. 1994. pap. 175.00 (*0-7855-0405-2*, Pub. by Intl Bks & Periodicals) St Mut.

Chakrabarti. Social Welfare. 61.95 (*1-84014-187-5*) Ashgate Pub Co.

Chakrabarti, A. K., ed. see Metallurgical Society of AIME Staff.

Chakrabarti, Alok K., jt. auth. see Baily, Martin N.

Chakrabarti, Aloknath, jt. auth. see Mandal, Birendra N.

Chakrabarti, Amaresh, jt. auth. see Blessing, Lusienne T. M.

Chakrabarti, Arindam. Denying Existence: The Logic, Epistemology & Pragmatics of Negative Existentials & Fictional Discourse. LC 96-52725. (Synthese Library). 1997. text 151.00 (*0-7923-4388-3*) Kluwer Academic.

Chakrabarti, Asim P. Muslim Identity & Community Consciousness. (C). 1993. 22.00 (*81-85195-58-7*, Pub. by Minerva) S Asia.

— Studies on the Development of Economical Drainage Systems for Multi-Storeyed Buildings. (C). 1986. 15.00 (*0-317-68062-5*, Pub. by Oxford IBH) S Asia.

Chakrabarti, B. K., et al. Quantum Ising Phases & Transitions in Traverse Ising Models. LC 96-4092. (Lecture Notes in Physics Ser.: Vol. 41). 204p. 1996. 49.00 (*3-540-61033-2*) Spr-Verlag.

Chakrabarti, Bidyut. Subhas Chandra Bose & Middle Class Radicalism: A Study in Indian Nationalism, 1928-1940. 200p. 1990. text 59.50 (*1-85043-149-3*, Pub. by I B T) St Martin.

Chakrabarti, Bikas K. & Benuigui, L. Gilles. Statistical Physics of Fracture & Breakdown in Disordered Systems. LC 97-30388. (Monographs on the Physics & Chemistry of Materials: No. 55). (Illus.). 172p. 1997. text 85.00 (*0-19-852056-5*) OUP.

Chakrabarti, Byomkes. Comparative Study of Santali & Bengali. (C). 1994. 28.50 (*81-7074-128-9*, Pub. by KP Bagchi); 28.00 (*0-614-00718-6*, Pub. by KP Bagchi) S Asia.

Chakrabarti, C. L. Progress in Analytical Atomic Spectroscopy, 2 vols., Set. (Illus.). 282p. 1981. 100.00 (*0-08-027126-X*, Pergamon Pr) Elsevier.

Chakrabarti, C. L., ed. Progress in Analytical Atomic Spectroscopy, Vol. 1, Pt. 1. 1978. 44.00 (*0-08-022924-7*, Pergamon Pr) Elsevier.

— Progress in Analytical Atomic Spectroscopy, Vol. 3. 368p. 1981. 92.00 (*0-08-029081-7*, E130, Pergamon Pr) Elsevier.

— Progress in Analytical Atomic Spectroscopy, Vol. 4. 440p. 1982. 125.00 (*0-08-029659-9*, Pergamon Pr) Elsevier.

— Progress in Analytical Atomic Spectroscopy, Vol. 5. (Illus.). 470p. 1983. 125.00 (*0-08-030418-4*, Pergamon Pr) Elsevier.

Chakrabarti, C. L. & Sturgeon, R. E., eds. Progress in Analytical Atomic Spectroscopy, Vol. 6. (Illus.). 444p. 1985. 145.00 (*0-08-032307-3*, Pergamon Pr) Elsevier.

— Progress in Analytical Atomic Spectroscopy, Vol. 7. (Illus.). 426p. 1986. 132.00 (*0-08-034141-1*, Pub. by PPL) Elsevier.

Chakrabarti, Dilip K. Ancient Bangladesh: A Study of the Archaeological Sources. (Illus.). 224p. 1993. 27.00 (*0-19-562879-9*) OUP.

— The Archaeology of Ancient Indian Cities. (Illus.). 344p. 1995. 38.00 (*0-19-563472-1*) OUP.

— Archaeology of Eastern India: Chhotanagpur Plateau & West Bengal. (C). 1993. 42.00 (*81-215-0601-8*, Pub. by M Manoharial) Coronet Bks.

— Colonial Indology: Sociopolitics of the Ancient Indian Past. (C). 1997. 30.00 (*81-215-0750-2*, Pub. by M Manoharial) Coronet Bks.

— The Early Use of Iron in India. (Illus.). 232p. (C). 1993. 28.00 (*0-19-562992-2*) OUP.

— The External Trade of the Indus Civilization. 1990. 36.00 (*0-685-40170-7*, Pub. by M Manoharial) S Asia.

— A History of Indian Archaeology. 1988. 44.00 (*81-215-0079-6*, Pub. by M Manoharial) Coronet Bks.

— India: An Archaeological History; Palaeolithic Beginnings to Early Historic Foundations. (Illus.). 400p. 2000. text 29.95 (*0-19-564573-1*) OUP.

— Issues in East Indian Archaeology. LC 98-903900. 1998. 24.00 (*81-215-0804-5*, Pub. by M Manoharial) Coronet Bks.

— Theoretical Issues in Indian Archaeology. (C). 1989. 21.50 (*0-685-30706-9*, Pub. by M Manoharial) S Asia.

Chakrabarti, Dilip K., jt. auth. see Rakshit, Mihir.

Chakrabarti, Dilip K., jt. ed. see Allchin, F. R.

Chakrabarti, Jayanta, et al. The Santiniketan Murals. LC 98-900589. xii, 96 p. 1995. write for info. (*81-7046-116-2*) Seagull Bks.

Chakrabarti, Jyoti P., jt. auth. see Khasnabis, Ratan.

Chakrabarti, Kisor K. Definition & Induction: A Historical & Comparative Study. LC 95-7339. (Society for Asian & Comparative Philosophy Ser.: No. 13). 248p. (C). 1995. pap. text, teacher ed. 12.75 (*0-8248-1658-7*) UH Pr.

Chakrabarti, Kisor Kumar. Classical Indian Philosophy of Mind: The Nyaya Dualist Tradition. LC 98-47027. 309p. (C). 1999. pap. text 22.95 (*0-7914-4172-5*) State U NY Pr.

— Classical Indian Philosophy of Mind: The Nyaya Dualist Tradition. LC 98-47027. 288p. (C). 1999. text 68.50 (*0-7914-4171-7*) State U NY Pr.

Chakrabarti, Kunal. Religious Processes: The Puranas & the Making of a Regional Tradition in South Asia. 400p. 2000. text 45.00 (*0-19-564989-3*) OUP.

Chakrabarti, Mohit. Gandhian Humanism. (Ghandhian Studies & Peace Research Ser.: No. 5). (C). 1992. 19.00 (*81-7022-383-0*, Pub. by Concept) S Asia.

C

— Gandhian Philosophy of Man. LC 95-901598. (C). 1995. 10.00 (*81-7223-181-4*, Pub. by Indus Pub) S Asia.
— Gandhian Religion. (C). 1994. 18.50 (*81-212-0446-1*, Pub. by Gian Publng Hse) S Asia.
— Gandhian Socio-Aesthetics. 130p. 1997. pap. 100.00 (*81-7533-048-1*, Pub. by Print Hse) St Mut.
*__Chakrabarti, Mohit.__ A Hundred Devotional Songs of Tagore. 104p. 1999. 125.00 (*81-208-1505-X*, Pub. by Motilal Bnarsidass); pap. 75.00 (*81-208-1687-0*, Pub. by Motilal Bnarsidass) St Mut.
— Swami Vivekananda: Poetic Visionary. LC 99-931669. xi, 209p. 1998. pap. 100.00 (*81-7533-075-9*, Pub. by Print Hse) St Mut.
Chakrabarti, Mohit, ed. Mahatma Gandhi: A Revaluation. (C). 1994. 17.50 (*81-7024-635-0*, Pub. by Ashish Pub Hse) S Asia.
Chakrabarti, N. K. Administration of Criminal Justice: The Correctional Services, 5 vols. 1200p. 1997. 900.00 (*81-7100-873-9*, Pub. by Print Hse) St Mut.
— Environment Protection & the Law. (Illus.). xxii, 652p. 1994. 59.00 (*81-7024-642-3*, Pub. by Ashish Pub Hse) Nataraj Bks.
Chakrabarti, P. K. Coal Industry in West Bengal. 1989. 19.00 (*81-85119-61-9*, Pub. by Northern Bk Ctr) S Asia.
— Geometrical Optics. (C). 1989. 60.00 (*0-89771-401-6*, Pub. by Current Dist) St Mut.
— Text Book of Waves & Acoustics. (C). 1989. 75.00 (*0-89771-402-4*, Pub. by Current Dist) St Mut.
Chakrabarti, P. N., jt. ed. see Ray, N. R.
Chakrabarti, Prafulla. Social Profile of Tarakeswar. 1984. 14.00 (*0-8364-1244-3*, Pub. by Mukhopadhyaya) S Asia.
Chakrabarti, Pranab J. Problems of Cooperative Development in India, with Special Reference to West Bengal. 1983. text 22.00 (*0-685-14093-8*) Coronet Bks.
Chakrabarti, S., et al, eds. Proceedings of the 16th International Conference on Offshore Mechanics & Arctic Engineering, Yokohama, Japan, April 13-17, 1997 Vol. I, Pts. A & B: Offshore Technology. 684p. 1997. 230.00 (*0-7918-1799-7*, HX1080) ASME Pr.
Chakrabarti, S. K. Hydrodynamics of Offshore Structures. rev. ed. LC 87-71235. 464p. (C). 1994. 195.00 (*0-931215-16-1*, 166X) Computational Mech MA.
— Nonlinear Methods in Offshore Engineering. (Developments in Marine Technology Ser.: No. 5). xviii,544p. 1990. 228.00 (*0-444-88457-2*) Elsevier.
Chakrabarti, S. K., ed. Fluid Structure Interaction in Offshore Engineering. 256p. 1994. 117.00 (*1-85312-280-7*) Computational Mech MA.
Chakrabarti, S. K., ed. Fluid Structure Interaction in Offshore Engineering. LC 94-70413. (Advances in Fluid Mechanics Ser.: Vol. 1). 256p. 1994. 117.00 (*1-56252-204-3*, 2807) Computational Mech MA.
Chakrabarti, S. K., et al, eds. 1995 Offshore Mechanics & Arctic Engineering Conference Vol. 1, Pt. A: Offshore Technology Symposium. LC 82-70515. (OMAE 1995 Ser.). 524p. 1995. 170.00 (*0-7918-1306-1*, H00938) ASME.
— 1995 Offshore Mechanics & Arctic Engineering Conference Vol. 1, Pt. B: Offshore Technology Symposium. 540p. 1995. 170.00 (*0-7918-1307-X*, H93839) ASME.
— Offshore Mechanics & Arctic Engineering, 1993 Vol. 1: Offshore Technology. LC 82-70515. 550p. 1993. pap. 95.00 (*0-7918-0783-5*, G00677) ASME.
Chakrabarti, S. P. Studies on the Development of Economical Drainage Systems for Multi-Storeyed Buildings. 114p. (C). 1987. text 91.00 (*90-6191-474-4*, Pub. by A A Balkema) Ashgate Pub Co.
Chakrabarti, Sandip. Observational Evidence for Black Holes in the Universe. LC 98-41434. (Astrophysics & Space Science Library). 1998. 162.00 (*0-7923-5298-X*) Kluwer Academic.
Chakrabarti, Sandip K. Theory of Transonic Astrophysical Flows. 212p. (C). 1990. text 48.00 (*981-02-0204-0*) World Scientific Pub.
Chakrabarti, Subir Kumar, jt. auth. see Aliprantis, Charalambos D.
Chakrabarti, Subrata. Offshore Structure Modeling. (Advanced Series in Ocean Engineering). 400p. 1994. text 78.00 (*981-02-1512-6*); pap. text 40.00 (*981-02-1513-4*) World Scientific Pub.
Chakrabarti, Subrata, et al, eds. Offshore Mechanics & Arctic Engineering Vol. 1: Offshore Technology: Proceedings - International Conference (15th: 1996: Florence, Italy), 2 pts. 991p. Date not set. pap. 270.00 (*0-7918-1490-4*, TN871) ASME.
Chakrabarti, Vibhuti. Indian Architectural Theory: Contemporary Uses of Vastu Vidya. 288p. 1998. text 48.00 (*0-7007-1113-9*, Pub. by Curzon Pr Ltd) UH Pr.
Chakrabaty, Alok. A Textbook of Physics, 2 vols. 1985. text 100.00 (*0-7855-0753-1*, Pub. by Current Dist) St Mut.
Chakrabarty, Ananda M. Genetic Engineering Benefits & Biohazards. (Uniscience Ser.). 208p. 1978. 75.00 (*0-8493-5259-2*, QH442, CRC Reprint) Franklin.
Chakrabarty, Ananda M., ed. Biodegradation & Detoxification of Environmental Pollutants. 160p. 1982. 85.00 (*0-8493-5524-9*, QR88, CRC Reprint) Franklin.
Chakrabarty, Ananda M., jt. ed. see Moo-Young, M.
Chakrabarty, Aneeta B. Roses & Thorns: A Synopsis of Life Between Two Worlds. 297p. (Orig.). 1993. pap. 9.99 (*0-9637198-0-7*) Chakra Pubns.
Chakrabarty, Bidyut. Local Politics & Indian Nationalism: Midnapur, 1919-1944. (C). 1997. 30.00 (*81-7304-158-X*, Pub. by Manohar) S Asia.
Chakrabarty, Bidyut, ed. Whither India's Democracy? 1993. 22.00 (*81-7074-126-2*, Pub. by KP Bagchi) S Asia.
Chakrabarty, D. K. & Gupta, S. P., eds. Middle Atmosphere: Changes & Electrodynamics. (Advances in Space Research Ser.: 20/11). 160p. 1997. pap. 100.50 (*0-08-043308-1*, Pergamon Pr) Elsevier.
*__Chakrabarty, Dipesh.__ Provincializing Europe: Postcolonial Thought & Historical Difference. LC 99-87722. (Studies in Culture - Power - History). (Illus.). 336p. 2000. pap. 16.95 (*0-691-04909-2*, Pub. by Princeton U Pr) Cal Prin Full Svc.
— Provincializing Europe: Postcolonial Thought & Historical Difference. LC 99-87722. (Reprints of Economics Classics Ser.). (Illus.). 336p. 2000. 55.00 (*0-691-04908-4*) Princeton U Pr.
— Rethinking Working-Class History: Bengal, 1890-1940. (Illus.). 2000. pap. 18.95 (*0-691-07030-X*) Princeton U Pr.
Chakrabarty, Dipesh. Rethinking Working-Class History: Bengal, 1890-1940. LC 88-19954. (Illus.). 265p. reprint ed. pap. 82.20 (*0-608-06362-2*, 206672300008) Bks Demand.
Chakrabarty, Dipesh, jt. ed. see Amin, Shahid.
Chakrabarty, J. Applied Plasticity. LC 99-17361. (Mechanical Engineering Ser.). (Illus.). 704p. 1999. 98.00 (*0-387-98812-2*) Spr-Verlag.
Chakrabarty, Rameswar P. American Housing Survey: A Quality Profile. 108p. 1996. per. 7.50 (*0-16-061063-X*) USGPO.
Chakrabarty, S. K. Q. T., MIS & Data Processing, Vol. I. (C). 1989. 100.00 (*0-89771-439-3*, Pub. by Current Dist) St Mut.
Chakraberty, C. Racial Basis of Indian Culture: Including Pakistan, Bangladesh, Sri Lanka, & Nepal. (C). 1997. 88.00 (*81-7305-110-0*, Pub. by Aryan Bks Intl) S Asia.
Chakraberty, Chandra. Comparative Hindu Materia Medica. (C). 1993. text 9.00 (*81-85557-01-2*, Pub. by Low Price) S Asia.
— An Interpretation of Ancient Hindu Medicine. (C). 1988. 100.00 (*0-7855-2286-7*, Pub. by Scientific) St Mut.
— An Interpretation of Ancient Hindu Medicine. (C). 1993. reprint ed. 15.00 (*81-85418-97-7*, Pub. by Low Price) S Asia.
Chakrabirti, Mohit. Ghandhian Spiritualism: A Quest for the Essence of Excellence. (Ghandhian Studies & Peace Research Ser.: No. 7). 1993. 20.00 (*81-7022-457-8*, Pub. by Concept) S Asia.
Chakraborti, Diplab. Pessimism & Contemporary Bengali Literature. 1985. 12.00 (*0-8364-1459-4*) S Asia.
Chakraborti, Haripada. Asceticism in Ancient India in Brahmanical, Buddhist, Jaina & Ajivika Societies. (C). 1993. text 52.00 (*81-85094-69-1*, Pub. by Punthi Pus) S Asia.
— Sakta Tantrik Cult in India. (C). 1997. 52.00 (*81-86791-01-9*, Pub. by Punthi Pus) S Asia.
Chakraborti, Subh, jt. ed. see Gibbons, Jean.
Chakraborti, Tridib. India & Kampuchea: A Phase in Their Relations, 1978-81. 1985. 11.50 (*0-8364-1438-1*, Pub. by Minerva) S Asia.
Chakrabortty, Krishna. Conflicting Worlds of Working Mothers. 305p. 1978. 17.95 (*0-318-37050-6*) Asia Bk Corp.
— The University Student: Background Profile & Stance. 1985. 10.00 (*0-8364-1480-2*, Pub. by KP Bagchi) S Asia.
Chakrabortty, Krishna & Bhattacharyya, Swapan K. Leadership, Factions & Panchayati Raj. (C). 1993. 22.00 (*81-7033-192-7*, Pub. by Rawat Pubns) S Asia.
Chakraborty, Ajita. Social Stress & Mental Health: Social Psychiatric Field Study of Calcutta Ser. (Illus.). 200p. (C). 1990. 25.00 (*0-8039-9633-0*) Sage.
Chakraborty, B. K. Child Health & Disease. (C). 1989. 60.00 (*0-89771-378-8*, Pub. by Current Dist) St Mut.
— Constitution & Constitutional Law of India. (C). 1989. 35.00 (*0-89771-458-X*, Pub. by Current Dist) St Mut.
— Human Physiology. 1985. 160.00 (*0-7855-0737-X*, Pub. by Current Dist) St Mut.
Chakraborty, Basanti D. Education of the Creative Children. 1993. text 25.00 (*81-220-0282-X*, Pub. by Konark Pubs) Advent Bks Div.
Chakraborty, Bhaktivenode. Platonic Bearings in Rabindranath. 1986. 9.00 (*0-8364-1580-9*, Pub. by KP Bagchi) S Asia.
Chakraborty, Bimal. The United Nations & the Third World: Shifting Paradigms. LC 99-938609. 1997. write for info. (*0-07-462059-2*) McGrw-H Hghr Educ.
Chakraborty, Bishwanath. Principles of Plasma Mechanics. 2nd ed. LC 90-26596. 612p. 1991. text 105.00 (*0-470-21729-4*) Halsted Pr.
Chakraborty, C., et al, eds. Pasture & Forage Crop Pathology. LC 96-84970. 653p. 1996. 42.00 (*0-89118-129-6*) Am Soc Agron.
Chakraborty, Chandana, jt. auth. see Diwan, Romesh.
Chakraborty, Gayatri. Espionage in Ancient India. 1991. 22.00 (*81-85195-31-5*, Pub. by Minerva) S Asia.
Chakraborty, Kanad, jt. auth. see Mazumder, Pinaki.
Chakraborty, Kishore, jt. auth. see Skinner, Wickham.
Chakraborty, Mriganka S. Indian Musicology: Melodic Structure. (C). 1992. 24.00 (*0-8364-2777-7*, Pub. by Firma KLM) S Asia.
Chakraborty, Phani B. & Bhattacharya, Brojen. News Behind Newspapers: A Study of the Indian Press. (C). 1989. 17.50 (*81-85195-16-1*, Pub. by Minerva) S Asia.
Chakraborty, Ranajit, jt. ed. see Rao, C. R.
Chakraborty, S. K. Ethics in Management: Vedantic Perspectives. (Illus.). 308p. 1995. text 24.00 (*0-19-563656-2*) OUP.
— Ethics in Management: Vedantic Perspectives. (Illus.). 308p. 1996. pap. text 14.95 (*0-19-564092-6*) OUP.
— Management by Values: Towards Cultural Congruence. 340p. 1993. pap. text 14.95 (*0-19-563218-4*) OUP.
— Managerial Transformation by Values: A Corporate Pilgrimage. LC 92-42609. (Illus.). 250p. (C). 1993. text 33.50 (*0-8039-9464-8*) Sage.
— Values & Ethics for Organizations: Theory & Practice. LC 98-902979. (Illus.). 274p. (C). 1998. text 27.50 (*0-19-564307-0*) OUP.
Chakraborty, S. K., et al, eds. Applied Ethics in Management: Towards New Perspectives. LC 99-26103. (Studies in Economic Ethics & Philosophy). (Illus.). x, 298p. 1999. 89.00 (*3-540-65724-X*) Spr-Verlag.
*__Chakraborty, Sudip.__ Rural Poverty & IRDP: Search of a New Model LC 99-932152. xxii, 194 p. 1999. write for info. (*81-7211-097-9*) S Asia.
Chakraborty, Tapash & Pietil-Ainen, Pekka. The Fractional Quantum Hall Effect: A Survey of the Incompressible Quantum Fluid Including the Integer Quantum Hall Effect. 2nd ed. LC 95-14465. 1995. write for info. (*0-387-58515-X*) Spr-Verlag.
Chakraborty, Tapash & Pietilainen, P. The Fractional Quantum Hall Effect. (Solid-State Sciences Ser.: Vol. 85). 205p. 1988. 46.00 (*0-387-19111-9*) Spr-Verlag.
— The Quantum Hall Effects. 2nd ed. (Illus.). 300p. 1995. 48.95 (*3-540-58515-X*) Spr-Verlag.
Chakradhar, Srimat T., et al. Neural Models & Algorithms for Digital Testing. (C). 1991. text 95.00 (*0-7923-9165-9*) Kluwer Academic.
Chakrapani, C. & Kumar, S. Vijaya, eds. Changing Status & Role of Women in Indian Society. 361p. 1994. pap. 250.00 (*81-85880-27-1*, Pub. by Print Hse) St Mut.
Chakrapani, Chuck. How to Measure Service Quality & Customer Satisfaction: The Informal Field-Guide for Tools & Techniques. LC 97-28835. 300p. 1997. 44.95 (*0-87757-267-4*) Am Mktg.
*__Chakrapani, Chuck, et al.__ Marketing Research: State-of-the-Art Perspectives: Handbook of the American Marketing Association & the Professional Marketing Research Society. LC 00-35565. 2000. write for info. (*0-87757-283-6*) Am Mktg.
*__Chakravarthy.__ Conversations & Cultural Reflections. LC 99-936620. 1999. 5.50 (*81-7646-077-X*, Pub. by BR Pub) S Asia.
Chakravarthy, R. S., tr. see Kontrimavichus, V. L., ed.
Chakravarthy, R. S., tr. see Rozova, A. V.
Chakravarthy, R. S., tr. see Skarlato, O. A., ed.
Chakravarthy, Sharma. Fundamentals of Active Database Systems. 500p. 1998. text 54.95 (*1-55860-378-6*) Morgan Kaufmann.
Chakravarthy, Srinivas R. & Alfa, Attahiru S., eds. Matrix-Analytic Methods in Stochastic Models. LC 96-31577. (Lecture Notes in Pure & Applied Mathematics Ser.: Vol. 183). (Illus.). 398p. 1996. pap. text 165.00 (*0-8247-9766-3*) Dekker.
Chakravarthy, Srinivas R., jt. ed. see Alfa, Attahiru S.
*__Chakravarti.__ Tantras: Studies on Their Religion & Literature. 2nd ed. 1999. reprint ed. 32.00 (*81-86791-19-1*, Pub. by Punthi Pus) S Asia.
Chakravarti, Arauna. Ruth Prawer Jhabvala: A Study in Empathy & Exile. LC 98-904092. (Indian Writers Ser.). xii, 285 p. 1998. write for info. (*81-7018-961-6*) BR Pub.
Chakravarti, Aruna, jt. auth. see Gangopadhyaya, Sunil.
Chakravarti, K. P. Administrative Tribunal Law & Procedure. (C). 1989. 138.00 (*0-7855-4817-3*) St Mut.
Chakravarti, Mahadev. The Concept of Rudra-Siva Through the Ages. (Illus.). xiii, 219p. (C). 1995. reprint ed. 26.00 (*81-208-0053-2*, Pub. by Motilal Bnarsidass) S Asia.
Chakravarti, Neimichandra S. Gomatsara Karma-Kanda, Pt. II. 1991. reprint ed. 55.00 (*0-685-59959-0*) Scholarly Pubns.
Chakravarti, Nemichandra S. Gommatsara Jiva Kanda: The Soul. 400p. 1990. reprint ed. 60.00 (*0-685-59957-4*) Scholarly Pubns.
Chakravarti, Phanindra N. Trans-Himalayan Trade - A Retrospect (1774-1914) In Quest of Tibet's Identity. (C). 1990. 20.00 (*81-85132-10-0*, Pub. by Classics India Pubns) S Asia.
Chakravarti, Ranabir. Warfare for Wealth: Early Indian Perspective. 1986. 34.00 (*0-8364-1570-1*) S Asia.
*__Chakravarti, Ranabir, ed.__ Trade in Early India. (Oxford in India Readings). 480p. 2000. text 29.95 (*0-19-564795-5*) OUP.
Chakravarti, Robin, jt. auth. see Bains, Richard.
Chakravarti, S., jt. auth. see Nath, Bholeshwar.
Chakravarti, Saranjan. Domestic Tribunals & Administrative Jurisdiction. (C). 1965. 35.00 (*0-7855-5650-8*) St Mut.
Chakravarti, Sitansu S. Hinduism: A Way of Life. 1991. 14.00 (*81-208-0927-0*, Pub. by Motilal Bnarsidass); pap. 8.50 (*81-208-0899-1*, Pub. by Motilal Bnarsidass) S Asia.
Chakravarti, Sri N. Gommatsara Karma-Kanda, Pt. I. 324p. 1991. reprint ed. 55.00 (*0-685-59958-2*, Pub. by Today Tomorrow) Scholarly Pubns.
Chakravarti, Sri S. Be Your Own Guru. 1971. pap. 2.50 (*0-685-58384-8*) Ranney Pubns.
— Samadhi & Beyond. LC 74-79444. 1974. pap. 3.50 (*0-87707-135-7*) Ranney Pubns.
— Scientific Yoga for the Man of Today. 1971. pap. 3.50 (*0-685-58385-6*) Ranney Pubns.
Chakravarti, Sri S., ed. Hidden Treasure of the Gospel of Sri Ramakrishna. 1975. reprint ed. 6.25 (*0-685-58386-4*) Ranney Pubns.
Chakravarti, Suranjan. Administrative Law & Tribunals. 2nd ed. (C). 1988. 100.00 (*0-7855-3561-6*) St Mut.
— Domestic Tribunals & Administrative Jurisdiction. (C). 1965. 40.00 (*0-7855-5396-7*) St Mut.
Chakravarti, Uma. Rewriting History: The Life & Times of Pandita Ramabai LC 98-902425. xiii, 370p. 1998. write for info. (*81-85107-79-3*, Pub. by Kali for Women) S Asia.
— The Social Dimensions of Early Buddhism. (C). 1996. 24.00 (*81-215-0749-9*, Pub. by M Manoharial) Coronet Bks.
Chakravartinayanan, A., tr. see Kundakunda Acharya.
*__Chakravarty, Ajanta.__ Teachings of Buddha. 1998. pap. 6.95 (*0-7126-7177-3*, Pub. by Random) Trafalgar.
— Teachings of Hinduism. 1998. pap. 6.95 (*0-7126-7182-X*, Pub. by Random) Trafalgar.
— Teachings of Jesus Christ. 1998. pap. 6.95 (*0-7126-7192-7*, Pub. by Random) Trafalgar.
— Teachings of Mohammad. 1998. pap. 6.95 (*0-7126-7187-0*, Pub. by Random) Trafalgar.
Chakravarty, Amiya. The Indian Testimony. (C). 1953. pap. 4.00 (*0-87574-072-3*) Pendle Hill.
Chakravarty, Amiya, ed. see Tagore, Rabindranath.
*__Chakravarty, Arati.__ An Introduction to Hindustani Music. LC 99-939391. 175p. 1999. 24.00 (*81-241-0428-X*, Pub. by Har-Anand Pubns) Nataraj Bks.
Chakravarty, Kalyan K. Early Buddhist Art of Bodh-Gaya. LC 97-904605. (Illus.). (C). 1997. 40.00 (*81-215-0723-5*, Pub. by M Manoharial) Coronet Bks.
Chakravarty, Kalyan Kumar, et al. Indian Rock Art & Its Global Context. LC 98-900826. 228 p. 1997. write for info. (*81-208-1464-9*) Motilal Bnarsidass.
Chakravarty-Kaul, Minoti. Common Lands & Customary Law: Institutional Change in North India over the Past Two Centuries. LC 96-902125. (Illus.). 332p. 1996. text 35.00 (*0-19-563862-X*) OUP.
Chakravarty, Nilima. Indian Philosophy the Pathfinders & the System Builders 700 BC-1000 AD. (C). 1992. 30.00 (*81-7023-151-5*, Pub. by Allied Pubs) S Asia.
Chakravarty, R., tr. see Frolova, T. I., et al.
Chakravarty, R., tr. see McHedlidze, G. A.
Chakravarty, R., tr. see Preobrazhensky, B. V.
Chakravarty, S. C., et al. Problems of Space Science Education & the Role of Teachers. (Advances in Space Research Ser.: Vol. 20/7). 106p. 1997. pap. 100.50 (*0-08-043304-9*) Elsevier.
Chakravarty, S. R. Bangladesh: The Nineteen Seventy-Nine Elections. (C). 1988. 16.00 (*81-7003-088-9*, Pub. by S Asia Pubs) S Asia.
— Bangladesh under Mujib, Zia & Ershad. (C). 1995. text 30.00 (*81-241-0309-7*, Pub. by Har-Anand Pubns) S Asia.
— Society, Polity, & Economy of Bangladesh. (C). 1994. text 22.00 (*81-241-0237-6*, Pub. by Har-Anand Pubns) S Asia.
Chakravarty, S. R., ed. Foreign Policy of Bangladesh. (C). 1994. text 34.00 (*81-241-0238-4*, Pub. by Har-Anand Pubns) S Asia.
Chakravarty, S. R. & Hussain, Mazhar, eds. Partision of India: Literary Responses. 1998. 26.00 (*81-241-0583-9*) Har-Anand Pubns.
Chakravarty, S. R. & Narain, N. V., eds. Bangladesh: Domestic Politics, Vol. 2. xvi, 218p. 1986. 18.00 (*81-7003-068-4*, Pub. by S Asia Pubs) S Asia.
Chakravarty, S. R. & Narain, Virendra, eds. Bangladesh: Domestic Policies, Vol. 2. xvi, 218p. 1986. 15.00 (*0-685-67624-2*, Pub. by S Asian Pubs) Nataraj Bks.
— Bangladesh: Global Politics, Vol. 3. (C). 1989. 24.00 (*81-7003-096-X*, Pub. by S Asia Pubs) S Asia.
— Bangladesh: History & Culture, Vol. 1. xvi, 220p. 1986. 15.00 (*0-685-58182-9*, Pub. by S Asian Pubs) Nataraj Bks.
Chakravarty, Sarat C. Nag Mahasaya: A Saintly Householder Disciple of Sri Ramakrishna. 1978. pap. 3.95 (*81-7120-238-1*) Vedanta Pr.
— Talks with Swami Vivekananda. (Illus.). pap. 4.95 (*81-7505-153-1*, Pub. by Advaita Ashrama) Vedanta Pr.
Chakravarty, Satya. Issues in Industrial Economics. 183p. (C). 1995. text 72.95 (*1-85972-018-8*, Pub. by Avebry) Ashgate Pub Co.
Chakravarty, Sreejit & Thadikaran, Paul J. Introduction to IDDQ Testing. LC 97-16861. (Frontiers in Electronic Testing Ser.). 1997. text 125.00 (*0-7923-9945-5*) Kluwer Academic.
Chakravarty, Suhash. From Khyber to Oxus: A Study in Imperial Expansion. 286p. 1976. text 18.95 (*0-86125-077-X*) Apt Bks.
Chakravarty, Sukhamoy. Development Planning: The Indian Experience. 150p. 1987. 49.95 (*0-19-828555-8*) OUP.
— Development Planning: The Indian Experience. 156p. 1993. reprint ed. pap. 5.95 (*0-19-562346-0*) OUP.
— Selected Economic Writings. 618p. (C). 1993. 39.95 (*0-19-562803-9*, 5966) OUP.
— Writings on Development. Rakshit, Mihir, ed. LC 96-912038. 316p. 1997. text 21.95 (*0-19-564093-4*) OUP.
Chakravarty, Sumantra, ed. see Gnedenko, Boris, et al.
Chakravarty, Sumita S. National Identity in Indian Popular Cinema, 1947-1987. Schatz, Thomas G., ed. LC 93-16985. (Film Studies). (Illus.). 368p. (Orig.). 1994. text 50.00 (*0-292-75551-1*) U of Tex Pr.
Chakravarty, Uma. Indra & Other Vedic Deities: A Euhemeristic Study. (C). 1997. 28.00 (*81-246-0080-5*, Pub. by DK Pubs Ind) S Asia.
Chakravarti, Suranjan. Cases & Materials on Code of Civil Procedure. 1717p. 1985. 495.00 (*0-7855-1400-7*) St Mut.
— Domestic Tribunals & Administrative Jurisdiction. 115p. 1965. pap. 30.00 (*0-7855-1403-1*) St Mut.
Chakraverty, A. Biotechnology & Other Alternative Technologies for Utilization of Biomass-Agricultural Wastes. (C). 1989. 15.00 (*81-204-0418-1*, Pub. by Oxford IBH) S Asia.
— Post Harvest Technology of Cereals: Pulses & Oilseeds. rev. ed. (C). 1988. 9.50 (*81-204-0289-8*, Pub. by Oxford IBH) S Asia.
Chakraverty, B. K. Critical Trends in HTC Superconductivity. 300p. (C). 1995. text 73.00 (*981-02-0195-8*) World Scientific Pub.
Chakraverty, Chiranjit. Environment for Everyone. (Illus.). xiv, 160p. 1996. 19.00 (*81-86545-01-8*, Pub. by Augustan Pubs) Nataraj Bks.
Chakraverty, R., ed. see Razvalyaev, A. V.

An Asterisk (*) at the beginning of an entry indicates that the title is appearing for the first time.

Chakravorty. Color Atlas of Bone & Joint Disease in the Elderly. 160p. 60.00 (*0-8151-1613-6*) Mosby Inc.

Chakravorty, Basuda. Jyotindra Nath Mukherjee: The Humanist Revolutionary. 1982. 8.00 (*0-8364-0919-1*, Pub. by Minerva) S Asia.

Chakravorty, Birendra C. British Relations with the Hill Tribes of Assam Since Eighteen Fifty-Eight. 1981. 12.50 (*0-8364-0705-9*, Pub. by Mukhopadhyaya) S Asia.

Chakravorty, N. K. Visual Aids to the MRCP Examination. LC 94-40907. 1900. lib. bdg. write for info. (*0-7923-8873-9*) Kluwer Academic.

Chakravorty, Swapan. Society & Politics in the Plays of Thomas Middleton. (Oxford English Monographs). 242p. 1996. text 55.00 (*0-19-818266-X*) OUP.

Chakroff, Marilyn. Fresh Water Fish Pond Culture & Management. (C). 1987. text 165.00 (*81-85046-64-6*, Pub. by Scientific Pubs) St Mut.

— Freshwater Fish Pond Culture: Appropriate Technologies for Development. Druben, Laurel, ed. (Illus.). 197p. (Orig.). (C). 1994. pap. text 35.00 (*0-7881-1459-X*) DIANE Pub.

— Freshwater Fish Pond Culture & Management. (Illus.). 196p. 1979. pap. 19.95 (*0-86619-056-2*) Vols Tech Asst.

— Freshwater Fish Pond Culture & Management. Druben, Laurel, ed. (Information Collection & Exchange Manual M1B. VITA Publications Manual Ser.: No. 36E). (Illus.). 207p. 1989. reprint ed. pap. 16.00 (*0-16-006533-X*, S/N 056-000-00013-5) USGPO.

Chakroff, Marilyn, ed. Freshwater Fish Pond Culture & Management. (C). 1988. 200.00 (*0-7855-3339-7*, Pub. by Scientific) St Mut.

Chalabian, Antranig. Armenia after the Coming of Islam. large type ed. (Illus.). 600p. 1999. write for info. (*0-9622741-3-5*) A Chalabian.

— General Andranik & the Armenian Revolutionary Movement. abr. rev. ed. Bogart, Margot, ed. (Illus.). 588p. 1988. 40.00 (*0-9622741-1-9*); pap. 30.00 (*0-9622741-0-0*) A Chalabian.

— Revolutionary Figures (in Armenian) Mihran Damadian, Hambartzum Boyajian, Serob Aghbiur, Hrair-Dzhoghk, Gevorg Chavush, Sebastatsi Murad, Nigol Tuman. (Illus.). 464p. 1991. 25.00 (*0-9622741-2-7*) A Chalabian.

Chalaguina, I. Dicionario de Bolso Portugues-Russo. (POR & RUS.). 343p. 1976. 9.95 (*0-8288-5626-5*, M9103) Fr & Eur.

Chalam, K. S. Suddha (Nectar) Contemporary Telegu Poetry. JSRI Narayanana Moorthy, tr. 1990. 22.50 (*81-208-0614-X*, Pub. by Motilal Bnarsidass) S Asia.

Chalam, K. S., ed. Relevance of Ambedkarism in India. (C). 1993. 22.00 (*81-7033-216-8*) S Asia.

Chalam, V. V. Adaptive Control Systems: Techniques & Applications. (Electrical Engineering & Electronics Ser.: Vol. 39). (Illus.). 544p. 1987. text 195.00 (*0-8247-7650-X*) Dekker.

Chalat, Nan. Seashells & Sunsets. Weller, Don & Hampshire, David, eds. LC 86-50559. (Illus.). 72p. 1986. write for info. (*0-916873-51-X*); pap. write for info. (*0-916873-52-8*) Weller Inst.

Chalberg. Essays in American History. 1996. 6.50 (*0-07-217647-4*) McGraw.

Chalberg, John C. Emma Goldman: American Individualist. LC 90-20170. 200p. (C). 1997. pap. 21.20 (*0-673-52102-8*) Addson-Wesley Educ.

***Chalberg, John C.** Rickey & Robinson: The Preacher, the Player & America's Game. (Illus.). 250p. 2000. pap. 16.95 (*0-88295-952-2*) Harlan Davidson.

Chalberg, John C., ed. Isolationism: Opposing Viewpoints. LC 94-5112. (American History Ser.). (Illus.). 312p. 1995. pap. text 16.20 (*1-56510-222-3*, 2223); lib. bdg. 26.20 (*1-56510-223-1*, 2231) Greenhaven.

Chalcidensis, Iamblichus. In Platonis Dialogos Commentariorum Fragmenta. Dillon, J. M., ed. & tr. by. 1973. pap. 78.00 (*90-04-03578-8*, PHA, 23) Brill Academic Pubs.

Chalcraft, Anthony, et al. Walford's Guide to Reference Material Vol. 3: Generalia, Language & Literature, the Arts. 7th ed. Day, Alan, ed. 1186p. 1998. 279.00 (*1-85604-300-2*, LAP43002, Pub. by Library Association) Bernan Associates.

Chalcraft, C. The Justification & Costing of Information Systems. (Financial Times Management Briefings Ser.). 1997. pap. 89.50 (*0-273-63216-7*, Pub. by F T P-H) Trans-Atl Phila.

Chalcraft, C. The Justification & Costing of Information Systems. 1996. pap. 129.00 (*1-85953-022-2*, Pub. by Tech Comm) St Mut.

Chalcraft, David J., ed. Social-Scientific Old Testament Criticism: A Sheffield Reader. (Biblical Seminar Ser.: Vol. 47). 395p. 1997. pap. 19.95 (*1-85075-813-1*, Pub. by Sheffield Acad) CUP Services.

Chalcroft, Anthony, et al, eds. Walford's Concise Guide to Reference Material. 2nd ed. xiv, 496p. 1993. write for info. (*3-598-07605-3*) K G Saur Verlag.

Chalder, Trudie. Coping with Chronic Fatigue. large type ed. 96p. 1997. text 19.95 (*1-85695-078-6*, Pub. by ISIS Lrg Prnt) Transaction Pubs.

Chaleby, Kutaiba S. & Racy, John C. Psychotherapy with the Arab Patient. LC 98-89893. 1999. pap. 25.00 (*0-9669830-0-9*) Q S O V.

Chaleff, Ira. The Courageous Follower: Standing up to & for Our Leaders. LC 95-6952. 212p. 1998. reprint ed. pap. 17.95 (*1-57675-036-1*) Berrett-Koehler.

Chalem, Denise. The Sea Between Us. Brunon, Danielle et al, trs. from FRE. 64p. (Orig.). 1986. pap. text 8.95 (*0-913745-26-X*) Ubu Repertory.

***Chalet, Francois.** Chalet. 2000. pap. text 42.00 (*3-931126-39-0*) Die Gestalten.

Chalfant, Edward. Better in Darkness: A Biography of Henry Adams: His Second Life, 1862-1891. LC 93-10202. (Illus.). xiv, 927p. (C). 1994. lib. bdg. 47.50 (*0-208-02041-1*, Archon Bks) Shoe String.

— Both Sides of the Ocean: A Biography of Henry Adams, His First Life, 1838-1862. LC 82-6805. 475p. (C). 1982. lib. bdg. 39.50 (*0-208-01901-4*, Archon Bks) Shoe String.

***Chalfant, Edward.** Improvement of the World: A Biography of Henry Adams, His Last Life, 1891-1918. LC 00-33147. 2000. lib. bdg. write for info. (*0-208-02232-5*, Archon Bks) Shoe String.

Chalfant, Edward, ed. Sketches for "The North American Review" by Henry Adams. LC 86-10901. (Illus.). xiii, 262p. (C). 1986. lib. bdg. 35.00 (*0-208-02115-9*, Archon Bks) Shoe String.

Chalfant, Frank E. Galveston Island of Chance. LC 97-90783. (Illus.). 182p. 1997. 27.95 (*0-9659566-0-1*) Treas Nost.

Chalfant, H. Paul. Sociology of Poverty in the United States: An Annotated Bibliography, 3. LC 84-25191. (Bibliographies & Indexes in Sociology Ser.). 187p. 1985. lib. bdg. 65.00 (*0-313-23929-0*, CHS/, Greenwood Pr) Greenwood.

Chalfant, H. Paul & Roper, Brent S., compiled by. Social & Behavioral Aspects of Female Alcoholism: An Annotated Bibliography. LC 80-1021. 145p. 1980. lib. bdg. 55.00 (*0-313-20947-2*, CAL/, Greenwood Pr) Greenwood.

Chalfant, H. Paul, et al. Religion in Contemporary Society. 3rd ed. LC 93-86173. 502p. (C). 1994. boxed set 40.00 (*0-87581-382-8*, RCS3) F E Peacock Pubs.

Chalfant, Henry & Prigoff, James. Spraycan Art. LC 87-50389. (Illus.). 96p. (Orig.). 1987. pap. 15.95 (*0-500-27469-X*, Pub. by Thames Hudson) Norton.

Chalfant, Henry, jt. auth. see Cooper, Martha.

Chalfant, John W. Abandonment Theology: The Clergy & the Decline of American Christianity - An Action Guide to Save America. LC 99-213865. (Illus.). 238p. 1996. pap. 14.95 (*0-9656074-0-2*) Am - A Call To Greatness.

Chalfant, Richard D. The Education of an Architect Bk. 1: The Verdict. 115p. 1997. pap. write for info. (*1-86106-182-X*, Pub. by Minerva Pr) Unity Dist.

***Chalfant, Richard David.** The Education of an Architect Bk. 2: An Architectural Rendering. LC 00-130509. (Illus.). 136p. 2000. pap. write for info. (*1-57197-222-6*, Pub. by Pentland Pr) Assoc Pubs Grp.

Chalfant, William Y. Cheyennes & Horse Soldiers: The 1857 Expedition & the Battle of Solomon's Fork. LC 89-32203. (Illus.). 432p. 1989. 29.95 (*0-8061-2194-7*) U of Okla Pr.

— Dangerous Passage: The Santa Fe Trail & the Mexican War. LC 93-38605. (Illus.). 336p. 1994. 32.95 (*0-8061-2613-2*) U of Okla Pr.

— Without Quarter: The Wichita Expedition & the Fight on Crooked Creek. LC 91-50300. (Illus.). 192p. 1991. 22.95 (*0-8061-2367-2*) U of Okla Pr.

Chalfant, Willie A. Gold, Guns & Ghost Towns, 1868-1943. reprint ed. pap. 9.95 (*0-912494-33-6*) Commun Print.

— The Story of Inyo. LC 33-19367. 1975. reprint ed. pap. 18.95 (*0-912494-35-2*) Commun Print.

— The Story of Inyo. 1992. reprint ed. lib. bdg. 75.00 (*0-7812-5011-0*) Rprt Serv.

Chalfen, Israel. Paul Celan: A Biography of His Youth. Bleyleben, Maximilian, tr. from GER. LC 91-25855. 176p. 1991. 24.95 (*0-89255-162-3*) Persea Bks.

Chalfen, Richard. Snapshot Versions of Life. LC 87-70258. (Illus.). 213p. 1987. 23.95 (*0-87972-387-4*) Bowling Green Univ Popular Press.

— Turning Leaves: The Photograph Collections of Two Japanese American Families. LC 90-43793. (Illus.). 288p. 1991. reprint ed. pap. 89.30 (*0-608-04146-7*, 206487900011) Bks Demand.

Chalfie, Martin & Kain, Steven. Green Fluorescent Proteins: Properties, Applications & Protocols. LC 97-38102. 400p. 1998. pap. 65.00 (*0-471-17839-X*, Wiley-Liss) Wiley.

Chalfont, William Y. Cheyennes at Dark Water Creek: The Last Fight of the Red River War. LC 96-46290. (Illus.). 256p. 1997. 27.95 (*0-8061-2875-5*) U of Okla Pr.

Chalfonte, Jessica. I Am Muslim, 8 vols., Set. LC 96-732. (Religions of the World Ser.). (Illus.). 24p. (J). (gr. k-4). 1996. lib. bdg. 15.93 (*0-8239-2375-4*, PowerKids) Rosen Group.

Chalford, Ginger. Inner Personalities of the Chart. LC 82-73124. 128p. 1982. 15.00 (*0-86690-040-3*, C2648-014) Am Fed Astrologers.

— Pluto, Planet of Magic & Power. LC 83-73607. 200p. 1984. 18.50 (*0-86690-270-8*, C2524-014) Am Fed Astrologers.

Chalfoun, Michelle. Roustabout: A Novel. 240p. 1997. pap. 13.00 (*0-06-092799-2*, Perennial) HarperTrade.

Chaliand. Minority Peoples Age Ntn States. (C). 49.95 (*0-7453-0276-9*); pap. 15.95 (*0-7453-0286-6*, Pub. by Pluto GBR) Stylus Pub VA.

Chaliand, G. Dictionnaire de la Strategie Militaire. (FRE.). 1998. 120.00 (*0-320-00275-6*) Fr & Eur.

Chaliand, Gerard. Armed Struggle in Africa: With the Guerrillas in "Portuguese" Guinea. LC 72-81789. 160p. 1969. pap. 10.00 (*0-85345-179-6*, Pub. by Monthly Rev) NYU Pr.

— Guerrilla Strategies: An Historical Anthology from the Long March to Afghanistan. LC 81-16347. 808p. 1982. pap. 18.95 (*0-520-04443-6*, Pub. by U CA Pr) Cal Prin Full Svc.

— The Kurdish Tragedy. LC 94-142896. 192p. (C). 1994. text 19.95 (*1-85649-100-5*, Pub. by Zed Books) St Martin.

— Mirrors of Disaster: A Chronicle of the Spanish Military Conquest of America. Berrett, A. M., tr. from FRE. LC 93-30414. (Illus.). 300p. 1994. 35.00 (*0-9628715-6-7*) Blue Crane Bks.

— The Stubborn March. Demir, Andre, tr. LC 92-28719. (ENG & FRE.). 112p. (Orig.). 1992. pap. 15.95 (*0-9628715-3-2*) Blue Crane Bks.

— Terrorism: From Popular Struggle to Media Spectacle. 139p. 1998. pap. text 17.00 (*0-7881-5476-1*) DIANE Pub.

— Terrorism: From Popular Struggle to Media Spectacle. pap. 9.95 (*0-86356-083-0*, Pub. by Saqi) Intl Spec Bk.

Chaliand, Gerard, ed. Minority People in the Age of Nation States. (C). 1989. 22.50 (*81-202-0275-9*, Pub. by Ajanta) S Asia.

Chaliand, Gerard & Rageau, Jean-Pierre. The Penguin Atlas of Diasporas. Berrett, A. M. et al, trs. 203p. 16.95 (*0-614-26613-0*) Penguin Putnam.

— The Penguin Atlas of Diasporas. 1997. pap. 22.95 (*0-14-017814-7*) Viking Penguin.

Chaliand, Gerard, ed. see Ghassemlou, A. R., et al.

Chaliapin, Lydia. Glazami Docheri - Through the Eyes of the Daughter. unabridged ed. Darsky, Joseph, ed. LC 96-92737. (RUS., Illus.). 169p. (Orig.). 1997. pap. 20.00 (*0-9655131-0-6*) J Stremlin.

Chalidze, Valerii. Brain Code & Paleolinguistic. (ENG & RUS.). 88p. 1986. pap. write for info. (*1-56541-170-6*) Chalidze.

— Hierarchical Instinct & Human Evolution. 211p. 1992. pap. 15.00 (*1-56541-168-4*) Chalidze.

— On the Possibility of a Vortex Theory of Matter. 20p. 1992. pap. 7.00 (*1-56541-179-X*) Chalidze.

— The Soviet Human Rights Movement: A Memoir. LC 84-72146. xii, 50p. 1984. pap. 2.50 (*0-87495-064-3*) Am Jewish Comm.

Chalidze, Valerii & Schifter, Richard. Glasnost & Social & Economic Rights. McColm, R. Bruce, ed. LC 88-30426. (Occasional Paper Ser.). 48p. (Orig.). 1989. pap. 3.50 (*0-932088-31-7*) Freedom Hse.

Chalifour, Martin, tr. see Moore, Shirley, ed.

Chalifour, Paul. Wilmington. (Images of America Ser.). 1998. pap. 16.99 (*0-7524-0857-7*) Arcadia Publng.

Chalifoux, Paul R. Keep Your Smile Beautiful! A Guide to Quality Dentistry. Leslie, Richard, ed. (Illus.). (Orig.). 1990. pap. text 30.00 (*0-9625549-0-1*) Chalifoux Pub.

Chaliha, Jaya, jt. auth. see Joly, Edward L.

Chaliha, Jaya, jt. auth. see Le Joly, Edward.

Chaline, Eric. Gay Planet. 2000. text 24.95 (*0-312-25297-8*) St Martin.

***Chaline, Eric.** Gay Planet: All Things for (Gay) Men. LC 99-49315. 2000. text 24.95 (*0-312-25322-2*) St Martin.

Chaline, Eric. Tai Chi for Body, Mind & Spirit. LC 98-48407. (Illus.). 128p. 1998. pap. 14.95 (*0-8069-6321-2*) Sterling.

Chaline, Eric, ed. see Ikenami, Shotaro.

Chaline, Eric, jt. ed. see Stevens, John.

Chaline, Eric, ed. see Yoshikawa, Eiji.

Chaline, Jean. Paleontology of Vertebrates. (Illus.). 200p. 1990. 42.95 (*0-387-51755-3*) Spr-Verlag.

Chaline, Jean, jt. auth. see Devillers, Charles.

Chaline, Jean, jt. auth. see Dvillers, C.

Chalip, Laurence, et al, eds. National Sports Policies: An International Handbook. LC 95-25327. 456p. 1996. lib. bdg. 105.00 (*0-313-28481-4*, Greenwood Pr) Greenwood.

Chalip, Laurence, jt. auth. see Thoma, James E.

Chalk, B. T., jt. auth. see Scheuer, Paul J.

Chalk, Frank & Jonassohn, Kurt. The History & Sociology of Genocide: Analyses & Case Studies. LC 89-27381. 624p. (C). 1990. 25.00 (*0-300-04445-3*); pap. 26.00 (*0-300-04446-1*) Yale U Pr.

***Chalk, Gary.** The Forebears: 1000 Years of Bearly Factual History LC 99-34326. (Illus.). (J). 1999. write for info. (*0-7894-4937-4*) DK Pub Inc.

Chalk, Gary. Hide & Seek in History. (Illus.). 24p. (J). 1997. 14.95 (*0-7894-1500-3*) DK Pub Inc.

Chalk, Gary, jt. auth. see Dever, Joe.

Chalk, H. The Devil Sits among the Congregation. 88p. (C). 1989. 60.00 (*0-7223-2221-6*, Pub. by A H S Ltd) St Mut.

Chalk, Jane, tr. see French Ramblers Association Staff.

Chalk, John, ed. see Garrod, Stan.

Chalk, Nigel Andrew, et al. Kuwait: From Reconstruction Toward Accumulation for Future Generations. LC 97-171688. (Occasional Papers). 1996. 15.00 (*1-55775-623-6*) Intl Monetary.

***Chalk, Peter.** Non-military Security & Global Order: The Impact of Extremism Violence. LC 00-21169. 272p. 2000. text 69.95 (*0-312-23167-9*) St Martin.

Chalk, Peter. West European Terrorism & Counter-Terrorism: The Evolving Dynamic. 256p. 1997. text 59.95 (*0-312-12971-8*) St Martin.

Chalk, Rosemary, et al, eds. Violence in Families: Assessing Prevention & Treatment Programs. LC 97-45375. 416p. (C). 1997. 39.95 (*0-309-05496-6*) Natl Acad Pr.

Chalk, Rosemary, ed. see National Research Council Staff.

Chalke, F. C. R., ed. see Roberts, Charles A., et al.

Chalker. Ladders Dream. 1987. mass mkt. write for info. (*0-8125-3310-0*) Tor Bks.

Chalker, Christopher S. Effective Alternative Education Programs: Best Practices from Planning Through Evaluating. LC 96-60271. 225p. 1997. pap. text 39.95 (*1-56676-412-2*) Scarecrow.

Chalker, Christopher S. & Brown, Kimila S. Effective Alternative Education Programs: Teachers for K-8 Students. LC 99-63650. 264p. 1999. pap. text 32.50 (*1-56676-732-6*) Scarecrow.

Chalker, Dennis C., et al. The United States Navy Seals Workout Guide: The Exercise And Fitness Programs Based On The U.s. Navy Seals And Bud/s Training. LC 97-35393. (Illus.). 192p. 1998. pap. 18.00 (*0-688-15862-5*, Wm Morrow) Morrow Avon.

Chalker, Donald M. Leadership for Rural Schools: Lessons for All Educators. LC 98-87453. xvi, 308p. 1998. 39.95 (*1-56676-695-8*) Scarecrow.

Chalker, Donald M., jt. auth. see Haynes, Richard M.

***Chalker, Jack.** Balshazzars Serpent. 304p. 2000. 22.00 (*0-671-57880-4*) PB.

Chalker, Jack Bridger. Burma Railway Artist: An Artist at War in Singapore, Thailand & Burma, 1942-45. (Illus.). 176p. 1994. 29.95 (*0-85052-337-0*, Pub. by Leo Cooper) Trans-Atl Phila.

Chalker, Jack L. And the Devil Will Drag You Under. 1984. mass mkt. 4.95 (*0-345-32334-3*, Del Rey) Ballantine Pub Grp.

— The Birth of Flux & Anchor. (Soul Rider Ser.: Bk. 4). 384p. (Orig.). 1992. mass mkt. 3.99 (*0-8125-2292-3*) Tor Bks.

— The Changewinds. 832p. 1996. 15.00 (*0-671-87734-8*) PB.

— Charon: A Dragon at the Gate. (Four Lords of the Diamond Ser.: Bk. 3). (Orig.). 1982. mass mkt. 3.95 (*0-345-29370-3*, Del Rey) Ballantine Pub Grp.

— Children of Flux & Anchor. (Soul Rider Ser.: Bk. 5). 352p. 1993. mass mkt. 3.99 (*0-8125-2340-7*) Tor Bks.

— The Demons at Rainbow Bridge. (Quintara Marathon Ser.: Bk. 1). 1990. mass mkt. 4.99 (*0-441-69992-8*) Ace Bks.

— The Demons at Rainbow Bridge. (Quintara Marathon Ser.: Bk. 1). 384p. 1998. per. 5.99 (*0-671-87887-5*) S&S Trade.

— Downtiming the Night Side. 288p. 1993. reprint ed. mass mkt. 4.99 (*0-671-72170-4*) Baen Bks.

— Echoes of the Well of Souls. (Watchers at the Well Ser.: Bk. 1). 320p. 1994. mass mkt. 5.99 (*0-345-38686-8*, Del Rey) Ballantine Pub Grp.

— Ghost of the Well of Souls. 2000. mass mkt. 6.99 (*0-345-39485-2*, Del Rey) Ballantine Pub Grp.

— Gods of the Well of Souls. (Watchers at the Well Ser.: Bk. 3). 1995. mass mkt. 5.99 (*0-345-38850-X*, Del Rey) Ballantine Pub Grp.

— Horrors of the Dancing Gods. (Dancing Gods Ser.: Bk. 5). 1995. mass mkt. 5.99 (*0-345-37692-7*, Del Rey) Ballantine Pub Grp.

— Hotel Andromeda. 256p. (Orig.). 1994. mass mkt. 4.99 (*0-441-00010-X*) Ace Bks.

— The Identity Matrix. 320p. 1989. mass mkt. 4.99 (*0-671-69854-0*) Baen Bks.

— A Jungle of Stars. (Military Science Fiction Promotion). 1986. mass mkt. 4.99 (*0-345-34190-2*, Del Rey) Ballantine Pub Grp.

— The Labyrinth of Dreams. (G. O. D. Inc. Ser.: Bk. 1). 1992. mass mkt. 3.99 (*0-8125-1928-0*, Pub. by Tor Bks) St Martin.

— Lords of the Middle Dark. (Rings of the Master Ser.: Bk. 1). 1986. mass mkt. 4.99 (*0-345-32560-5*, Del Rey) Ballantine Pub Grp.

— The March Hare Network. (Wonderland Gambit Ser.: Bk. 2). 1996. pap. 11.00 (*0-614-97803-3*, Del Rey) Ballantine Pub Grp.

— The March Hare Network. (Wonderland Gambit Ser.: Bk. 2). 1996. mass mkt. 5.99 (*0-345-38848-8*, Del Rey) Ballantine Pub Grp.

— Masks of the Martyrs. (Rings of the Master Ser.: Bk. 4). 352p. 1988. mass mkt. 4.95 (*0-345-34309-3*, Del Rey) Ballantine Pub Grp.

— Masks of the Martyrs. (Rings of the Master Ser.). 1988. pap. write for info. (*0-318-62998-4*) Random.

— The Maze in the Mirror. (G. O. D. Inc. Ser.: Bk. 3). 416p. 1992. mass mkt. 3.99 (*0-8125-2069-6*) Tor Bks.

— Medusa: A Tiger by the Tail. (Four Lords of the Diamond Ser.: Bk. 4). 304p. (Orig.). 1983. mass mkt. 4.95 (*0-345-29372-X*, Del Rey) Ballantine Pub Grp.

— The Moreau Factor. 2000. mass mkt. 6.99 (*0-345-40296-0*, Del Rey) Ballantine Pub Grp.

— The Ninety Trillion Fausts. (Quintara Marathon Ser.: Bk. 3). 368p. 1992. mass mkt. 4.99 (*0-441-58103-X*) Ace Bks.

— The Ninety Trillion Fausts. 416p. 1999. per. 6.99 (*0-671-57830-8*) S&S Trade.

— Pirates of the Thunder. (Rings of the Master Ser.: Bk. 2). (Orig.). 1987. mass mkt. 5.99 (*0-345-32561-3*, Del Rey) Ballantine Pub Grp.

— Priam's Lens. 1999. 6.99 (*0-345-40294-4*) Ballantine Pub Grp.

— The Run to Chaos Keep. (Quintara Marathon Ser.: Bk. 2). 1992. mass mkt. 4.99 (*0-441-69348-2*) Ace Bks.

— The Run to Chaos Keep. (Quintara Marathon Ser.: Bk. 2). 336p. 1999. mass mkt. 6.99 (*0-671-57799-9*) Baen Bks.

— The Sea is Full of Stars. 2000. mass mkt. 6.99 (*0-345-39486-0*) Ballantine Pub Grp.

— The Shadow Dancers. 2nd ed. (G. O. D. Inc. Ser.: Bk. 2). 1992. mass mkt. 3.99 (*0-8125-2073-4*, Pub. by Tor Bks) St Martin.

— Spirits of Flux & Anchor. (Soul Rider Ser.: Bk. 1). 1988. pap. 3.95 (*0-8125-3320-8*) Tor Bks.

— Warriors of the Storm. (Rings of the Master Ser.: Bk. 3). 352p. (Orig.). 1987. mass mkt. 4.95 (*0-345-32562-1*, Del Rey) Ballantine Pub Grp.

Chalker, John. The English Georgic: A Study in the Development of a Form. LC 79-97053. (Ideas & Forms in English Literature Ser.). 235p. reprint ed. pap. 72.90 (*0-608-14685-4*, 202584200046) Bks Demand.

Chalker, John, ed. see Swift, Jonathan.

***Chalker, Rebecca.** The Clitoral Truth: The World at Your Fingertips. (Illus.). 244p. 2000. 19.95 (*1-58322-038-0*, Pub. by Seven Stories) Publishers Group.

Chalker, Rebecca & Downer, Carol. A Woman's Book of Choices: Abortion, Menstrual Extraction, RU-486. LC 92-13956. (Illus.). 192p. (Orig.). 1992. pap. 13.95 (*1-888363-28-2*) Seven Stories.

Chalker, Rebecca & Whitmore, Kristene E. Overcoming Bladder Disorders: Compassionate, Authoritative, Medical & Self-Help Solutions. LC 89-45789. 352p. 1991. pap. 14.00 (*0-06-092083-1*, Perennial) HarperTrade.

C

Chalker, S. The Parentalk Guide to the Childhood Years. 11.95 (*0-340-72168-5*, Pub. by Hodder & Stought Ltd) Trafalgar.

Chalker, Slyvia & Weiner, Edmund, eds. The Oxford Dictionary of English Grammar. LC 98-11436. (Oxford Paperback Reference Ser.). (Illus.). 464p. (Orig.). 1998. pap. 12.95 (*0-19-280087-6*) OUP.

***Chalker, Sylvia.** The Little Oxford Dictionary of English Grammar. 2nd ed. (Illus.). 304p. 1998. pap. 7.95 (*0-19-860210-3*) OUP.

Chalker, Sylvia. Student's Grammar of English Language. 300p. (C). 1995. pap. text, student ed. 26.24 (*0-582-08819-4*) Longman.

Chalker, Sylvia, ed. The Little Oxford Dictionary of English Grammar. (Illus.). 282p. (C). 1995. 12.95 (*0-19-861315-6*) OUP.

Chalker, Sylvia, jt. ed. see Weiner, Edmund S.

Chalker-Tennant, Nancy. Secret Wing. (Illus.). 12p. 1991. pap. 10.00 (*0-89822-068-8*) Visual Studies.

Chalkin, Christopher. English Counties & Public Building, 1650-1830. LC 97-32534. 288p. 1997. 60.00 (*1-85285-153-8*) Hambledon Press.

Chalkley, John F. Zach Lamar Cobb: El Paso Customs & Intelligence During the Mexican Revolution, 1913-1918. LC 96-61730. (Southwestern Studies Ser.). 1997. pap. text 12.50 (*0-87404-199-6*) Tex Western.

Chalkley, M. E., et al, eds. International Symposium on Tailings & Effluent Management. (Proceedings, Metallurgical Society of the Canadian Institute of Mining & Metallurgy Ser.: Vol. 14). 350p. 1989. 176.00 (*0-08-037289-9*, Pergamon Pr) Elsevier.

Chalkley, Richard, ed. Professional Conduct: A Handbook for Chartered Surveyors. (C). 1991. 110.00 (*0-7855-6631-7*, Pub. by Surveyors Pubns) St Mut.

Chalkley, Thomas. The Journal of Thomas Chalkley. LC 75-31088. reprint ed. 45.00 (*0-404-13506-4*) AMS Pr.

***Chalkley, Thomas.** Your Eyes. 4th ed. LC 99-58325. (Illus.). 140p. 2000. 4.95 (*0-398-07048-2*) C C Thomas.

***Chalkley, Tom, et al.** Charmed Life. LC 00-40856. 2000. write for info. (*1-891521-09-8*) Woodholme Hse.

Chalklin, Christopher W. The Provincial Towns of Georgian England: A Study of the Building Process, 1740-1820. LC 74-82919. (Studies in Urban History: No. 3). 405p. reprint ed. pap. 125.60 (*0-7837-1037-2*, 204134800020) Bks Demand.

Chalklin, Christopher W. & Wordie, J. R., eds. Town & Countryside: The English Landowner in the National Economy, 1660-1860. 220p. 1989. 55.00 (*0-04-445353-1*) Routledge.

***Chall, Jeanne S.** The Academic Achievement Challenge: What Really Works in the Classroom? LC 99-86150. 210p. 2000. lib. bdg. 25.00 (*1-57230-500-2*, CO500) Guilford Pubns.

Chall, Jeanne S. Learning to Read: The Great Debate. 2nd ed. (C). 1995. text 38.50 (*0-15-503080-9*, Pub. by Harcourt Coll Pubs) Harcourt.

— Qualitative Assessment of Text Difficulty: A Practical Guide for Teachers & Writers. LC 96-24405. 112p. 1996. pap. 19.95 (*1-57129-023-0*) Brookline Bks.

— Stages of Reading Development. 2nd ed. (C). 1995. text 38.50 (*0-15-503081-7*, Pub. by Harcourt Coll Pubs) Harcourt.

Chall, Jeanne S. & Conard, Sue S. Should Textbooks Challenge Students? The Case for Easier or Harder Books. 176p. (C). 1991. text 41.00 (*0-8077-3065-3*); pap. text 18.95 (*0-8077-3064-5*) Tchrs Coll.

Chall, Jeanne S. & Dale, Edgar. Manual for Use of the New Dale-Chall Readability Formula. 40p. (Orig.). 1994. pap. text 14.95 (*1-57129-012-5*) Brookline Bks.

— Readability Revisited: The New Dale-Chall Readability Formula. LC 95-16034. 104p. 1995. pap. text 29.95 (*1-57129-008-7*) Brookline Bks.

Chall, Jeanne S. & Popp, Helen M. Teaching & Assessing Phonics: Why, What, When, How - A Guide for Teachers. Noon, Jen, ed. LC 98-150893. (Orig.). 1996. pap. text 18.00 (*0-8388-2314-9*) Ed Pub Serv.

Chall, Jeanne S. & Roswell, Florence G. Roswell - Chall Auditory Blending Test: Manual of Instructions. Noon, Jen, ed. 5p. (Orig.). 1997. pap. text 5.25 (*0-8388-2316-5*, 2316) Ed Pub Serv.

— Roswell - Chall Diagnostic Reading Test of Word Analysis Skills: Manual of Instruction. Noon, Jen, ed. 14p. (Orig.). 1997. pap. text 6.00 (*0-8388-2318-1*, 2318) Ed Pub Serv.

— Roswell - Chall Diagnostic Reading Test of Word Analysis Skills: Technical Supplement. Noon, Jen, ed. 16p. (Orig.). 1997. pap. text 5.60 (*0-8388-2317-3*, 2317) Ed Pub Serv.

Chall, Jeanne S., et al. The Reading Crisis: Why Poor Children Fall Behind. (Illus.). 208p. (C). 1991. pap. 17.00 (*0-674-74885-9*) HUP.

Chall, Jeanne S., ed. see Menyuk, Paula.

Chall, Marsha W. Happy Birthday, America. LC 93-49820. (Illus.). 32p. (YA). (ps-3). 2000. lib. bdg. 15.89 (*0-688-13052-6*) Morrow Avon.

— Rupa Raises the Sun. LC 97-47294. (Illus.). (J). (gr. k-3). 1998. 15.95 (*0-7894-2496-7*) DK Pub Inc.

— Up North at the Cabin. LC 91-3035. (J). (ps-8). 1992. 16.00 (*0-688-09732-4*) Lothrop.

***Chall, Marsha W. & Halperin, Wendy A.** Bonaparte. LC 00-21282. 32p. (J). (ps-3). 2000. 16.95 (*0-7894-2617-X*) DK Pub Inc.

Chall, Miriam & Owen, Terry. Sociological Abstracts: User's Reference Manual. 4th ed. LC 89-63306. v, 175p. 1989. 60.00 (*0-930710-07-X*) Soc Abstracts.

Chall, Miriam, jt. auth. see Blackman, Michelle.

Chall, Sally Lehman. Que Los Ninos Vengan a Mi.Tr. of Making God Real to Your Children. (SPA.). 176p. 1995. pap. 8.99 (*0-8297-1826-5*) Vida Pubs.

Chall, Sally Leman, see Leman Chall, Sally.

Challa, G. S. World Economy in Transition: An Indian Perspective. (C). 1994. 22.00 (*81-241-0173-6*, Pub. by Har-Anand Pubns) S Asia.

Challa, Ger. Polymer Chemistry: An Introduction. 170p. (C). 1993. 50.00 (*0-13-682519-2*) P-H.

Challa, Krishna. Investment & Returns in Exploration & the Impact on the Supply of Oil & Natural Gas Reserves. Bruchey, Stuart, ed. LC 78-22667. (Energy in the American Economy Ser.). (Illus.). 1979. lib. bdg. 18.95 (*0-405-11971-2*) Ayer.

Challa, Ram. Soyem, Sanskar. 12p. 1991. 1.50 (*0-317-03095-7*) Samisdat.

Challa, Sudha & Hoh, Carl K. Nuclear Medicine Self-Study Program: Nuclear Medicine Oncology: PET Tumor Imaging, 8 vols. Haynie, Thomas P., ed. LC 99-34619. 1999. write for info. (*0-932004-62-8*, Pub. by Soc Nuclear Med) Matthews Medical Bk Co.

Challacombe, J. R. Games the Mind Plays: Tips, Tricks, Traps & Timing. 96p. (Orig.). 1996. pap. 12.95 (*1-886287-43-0*) Clair Studies.

— Life of the Mind: The Vision Cry. LC 95-92533. 262p. (Orig.). (C). 1995. pap. 19.95 (*1-886287-13-9*) Clair Studies.

— Opening Hidden Frontiers: The Dragons of Time. LC 94-68854. Orig. Title: Everyman His Own Frontier. 204p. 1994. pap. 17.95 (*1-886287-03-1*) Clair Studies.

— Organize the Chaos! The Achiever Ethic. LC 95-92531. 173p. (Orig.). (C). 1995. pap. 17.95 (*1-886287-33-3*) Clair Studies.

— Upon the Fields of Time: Four Minds of Man. LC 95-92532. 257p. (Orig.). (C). 1995. pap. 19.95 (*1-886287-23-6*) Clair Studies.

Challacombe, S. J., jt. ed. see Kemeny, D. M.

Challamel, Augustin. Les Clubs Contre-Revolutionnaires. LC 72-38038. (Collection de documents relatifs a l'histoire de Paris pendant la Revolution francaise). reprint ed. 135.00 (*0-404-52552-0*) AMS Pr.

Challancin, James. The Assembly Celebrates: Gathering the Community for Worship. 1989. pap. 5.95 (*0-8091-3096-3*) Paulist Pr.

Challand, Gerard, compiled by. The Art of War in World History: From Antiquity to the Nuclear Age. LC 92-20153. 1996. pap. 40.00 (*0-520-07964-7*, Pub. by U CA Pr) Cal Prin Full Svc.

Challand, Helen J. Experiments with Electricity. LC 85-30887. (New True Books Ser.). (Illus.). 48p. (J). (gr. 3-5). 1986. pap. 5.50 (*0-516-41276-0*) Childrens.

— Experiments with Electricity. LC 85-30887. (New True Books Ser.). (Illus.). 48p. (J). (ps-3). 1986. lib. bdg. 21.00 (*0-516-01276-2*) Childrens.

— Experiments with Magnets. LC 85-30851. (New True Books Ser.). (Illus.). 48p. (J). (gr. 3-5). 1986. pap. 5.50 (*0-516-41279-5*); lib. bdg. 21.00 (*0-516-01279-7*) Childrens.

Challand, Richard & Young, Robert J. Antiviral Chemotherapy. (Biochemical & Medicinal Chemistry Ser.). (Illus.). 136p. 1998. reprint ed. pap. text 21.95 (*0-19-850480-2*) OUP.

***Challand, S. R. & Agrofoglio, L. A.** Acylic, Carbocyclic & L-Nucleosides. 393p. 1998. write for info. (*0-7514-0434-9*) Kluwer Academic.

Challeen, Dennis A. The NORP Think Factor. (Illus.). 216p. 1994. pap. text 24.95 (*0-9641375-0-X*) Staige Prods.

Challem, Jack. ABCs of Hormones. (Good Health Guides Ser.). 48p. 1999. pap. 3.95 (*0-87983-902-3*, 39023K, Keats Publng) NTC Contemp Pub Co.

— Frequently Asked Questions All about Carotenoids. (FAQs All about Health Ser.). Date not set. mass mkt. 2.99 (*0-89529-936-4*, Avery) Penguin Putnam.

— Frequently Asked Questions All about Chromium Picolinate. (FAQs All about Health Ser.). 1998. mass mkt. 2.99 (*0-89529-876-7*, Avery) Penguin Putnam.

Challem, Jack & Dolby, Victoria. Homocysteine: The New "Cholesterol" (Good Health Guides Ser.). 48p. (Orig.). 1996. pap. 3.95 (*0-87983-722-5*, 37225K, Keats Publng) NTC Contemp Pub Co.

Challem, Jack J. Spirulina. (Good Health Guide Ser.). 30p. 1982. pap. 3.50 (*0-87983-262-2*, 32622K, Keats Publng) NTC Contemp Pub Co.

Challem, Jack J. & Dolby, Victoria. The Health Benefits of Soy. (Good Health Guides Ser.). 48p. (Orig.). 1996. pap. 3.95 (*0-87983-727-6*, 37276K, Keats Publng) NTC Contemp Pub Co.

Challem, Jack J., jt. auth. see Huemer, Richard P.

Challen, Bernard, jt. auth. see Baranescu, Rodica.

Challen, D. W., et al. Unemployment & Inflation in the UK: An Introduction to Macroeconomics LC 82-20882. ix, 394 p. 1984. pap. write for info. (*0-582-29618-8*) Longman.

Challen, Paul. The Book of Isiah: The Rise of a Basketball Legend. LC 97-138307. (Illus.). 280p. 1996. 25.95 (*1-55022-300-3*, Pub. by ECW) Genl Dist Srvs.

— Isiah: The Rise of a Basketball Legend. rev. ed. (Illus.). 336p. 1997. pap. 8.99 (*0-7704-2770-7*) Bantam.

— A Sociological Analysis of Southern Regionalism: The Contributions of Howard W. Odum. LC 93-1724. 92p. 1993. 49.95 (*0-7734-9161-9*) E Mellen.

***Challen, Ray.** Institutions, Transaction Costs & Environmental Policy: Institutional Reform for Water Resources. LC 99-49033. (New Horizons in Environmental Economics Ser.). 256p. 2000. 90.00 (*1-84064-250-5*) E Elgar.

Challener, Daniel D. Stories of Resilience in Childhood: The Narratives of Maya Angelou, Maxine Hong Kingston, Richard Rodriguez, John Edgar Wideman, & Tobias Wolff. rev. ed. LC 97-11822. (Children of Poverty Ser.). 216p. 1997. text 54.00 (*0-8153-2800-1*) Garland.

Challener, Richard D. Admirals, Generals, & American Foreign Policy, 1898-1914. LC 72-732. 443p. 1973. pap. 137.40 (*0-7837-0556-5*, 204090000019) Bks Demand.

Challener, Richard D., ed. The Legislative Origins of American Foreign Policy, 5 vols. Incl. Vol. 1. Proceedings, April 7, 1913 to March 7, 1923. 415p. 1979. lib. bdg. 53.00 (*0-8240-3030-3*); Vol. 2. Proceedings, December 3, 1923 to March 3, 1933. 279p. 1979. lib. bdg. 37.00 (*0-8240-3031-1*); Vol. 3. Legislative Origins of the Truman Doctrine, March to April, 1947. 235p. 1979. 30.00 (*0-8240-3032-X*); Vol. 4. Foreign Relief Aid, 1947. 401p. 1979. lib. bdg. 48.00 (*0-8240-3033-8*); Vol. 5. Foreign Relief Assistance Act of 1948. 809p. 1979. lib. bdg. 86.00 (*0-8240-3034-6*); 1979. write for info. (*0-318-52530-5*) Garland.

Challener, Richard D., jt. ed. see Schmitz, David F.

Challenger, Douglas F. Durkheim Through the Lens of Aristotle: Durkheimian, Postmodernist, & Communitarian Responses to the Enlightenment. 246p. (C). 1995. pap. text 22.95 (*0-8476-7973-X*); lib. bdg. 59.50 (*0-8476-7972-1*) Rowman.

Challenger, James E. The Challenger Guide. LC 99-12026. 224p. 1999. 19.95 (*0-8092-2669-3*, 266930, Contemporary Bks) NTC Contemp Pub Co.

***Challenger, James E.** Challenger Guide: Job-Hunting Success for Mid-Career Professionals. 224p. 2000. pap. 14.95 (*0-8092-9875-9*, Contemporary Bks) NTC Contemp Pub Co.

Challenger, Robert James. Eagle's Reflection & Other Westcoast Stories. 48p. 1995. pap. 9.95 (*1-895811-07-4*) Heritage Hse.

— Orca's Family: And More Northwest Coast Stories. 48p. 1997. pap. 9.95 (*1-895811-39-2*) Heritage Hse.

— Raven's Call: And Other Northwest Coast Stories. 48p. 1999. pap. 9.95 (*1-895811-91-0*, Pub. by Heritage Hse) Midpt Trade.

***Challes, Robert, et al.** A Critical Edition of Penelope Aubin's Translation of Robert Challe's les Illustres Franpcaises the Illustrious French Lovers. De Sola, Anne, ed. Aubin, Penelope, tr. LC 00-33871. (Studies in French Literature: Vol. 44). (Illus.). 476p. 2000. 109.95 (*0-7734-7701-2*) E Mellen.

Challet, Gilbert L. & Keller, Justine, eds. Directory of Mosquito Control Agencies in the United States & Canada, 1981. 2nd ed. 39p. 1981. 20.00 (*0-9606210-3-2*) Am Mosquito.

Challeyssin, Patrick. James McNeill Whistler: The Strident Cry of the Butterfly. (Great Painters Ser.). (Illus.). 176p. 1996. 40.00 (*1-85995-019-1*) Parkstone Pr.

Challgren, Crafer, ed. see Lohr, Andrew.

Challgren, Patricia, jt. auth. see Kennedy, Belle C.

Challice, Annie E. Illustrious Women of France, Seventeen Ninety to Eighteen Seventy-Three. 1977. 19.95 (*0-8369-7212-0*, 8011) Ayer.

Challinger, D., ed. Bail or Remand? (Australian Institute Conference Proceedings Ser.: Vol. 6). 148p. 1991. pap. 20.00 (*0-642-15368-X*, Pub. by Aust Inst Criminology) Advent Bks Div.

— Intellectually Disabled Offenders. 148p. 1987. pap. 15.00 (*0-642-11934-1*, Pub. by Aust Inst Criminology) Advent Bks Div.

Challinor, A. M. The Alternative Shakespeare: A Modern Introduction. LC 97-151810. 247p. 1996. 42.50 (*1-85776-049-2*, Pub. by Book Guild Ltd) Trans-Atl Phila.

Challinor, David, jt. auth. see Robinson, Michael H.

Challinor, Joan R. & Beisner, Robert L., eds. Arms at Rest: Peacemaking & Peacekeeping in American History, 121. LC 86-14954. (Contributions in American History Ser.: No. 121). 238p. 1987. 62.95 (*0-313-24642-4*, BEW/, Greenwood Pr) Greenwood.

Challinor, Joan R., jt. auth. see Lichtman, Allan J.

Challinor, Paul & Sedgewick, John. Principles & Practice of Renal Nursing. (Illus.). 1998. pap. 59.50 (*0-7487-3331-0*, Pub. by S Thornes Pubs) Trans-Atl Phila.

Challinor, Raymond. A Radical Lawyer in Victorian England: W. P. Roberts & the Struggle for Workers' Rights. 256p. 1990. text 59.50 (*1-85043-150-7*) I B T.

Challiol, Paul, tr. see Schalliol, Willis L.

Challis. Organising Public Social Services. 1990. pap. 34.95 (*0-582-06302-7*) Ashgate Pub Co.

Challis, et al. Case Management in Social & Primary Health Care. 56.95 (*1-85742-206-6*) Ashgate Pub Co.

Challis, Bob, jt. auth. see Bagley, Bill.

Challis, Bradford H. Stratification in Cognition & Consciousness. Velichkovsky, Boris M., ed. LC 99-29157. (Advances in Consciousness Research Ser.: Vol. 15). viii, 293p. 1999. pap. 34.95 (*1-55619-195-2*) J Benjamins Pubng.

Challis, C. E., ed. A New History of the Royal Mint. (Illus.). 830p. (C). 1993. text 175.00 (*0-521-24026-3*) Cambridge U Pr.

Challis, Christopher. Are They Really So Awful? A Cameraman's Chronicle. (Illus.). 266p. 1995. 16.95 (*1-85756-193-7*, Pub. by Janus Pubng) Paul & Co Pubs.

Challis, David, et al, eds. Community Care: New Agendas & Challenges from the U. K. & Overseas. 336p. 1994. 83.95 (*1-85742-208-2*, Pub. by Arena) Ashgate Pub Co.

— Community Care, Secondary Health Care & Care Management. LC 98-73022. (Personal Social Services Research Unit Ser.). 184p. 1998. text 50.95 (*1-84014-581-1*, Pub. by Ashgate Pub) Ashgate Pub Co.

Challis, David & Davies, Bleddyn. Case Management in Community Care. 289p. 1989. pap. text 31.95 (*0-566-05816-2*, Pub. by Arena) Ashgate Pub Co.

Challis, David, et al. Care Management & Health Care of Older People: The Darlington Community Care Project. 384p. 1995. 72.95 (*1-85742-184-1*, Pub. by Arena) Ashgate Pub Co.

— Care Management & Health Care of Older People: The Darlington Community Care Project. 384p. 1996. pap. 36.95 (*1-85742-190-6*, Pub. by Arena) Ashgate Pub Co.

Challis, David, jt. auth. see Davies, Bleddwyn.

Challis, David, jt. auth. see Samson, Danny.

Challis, Evelyn. Jumping, Laughing, Resting. (Illus.). 128p. 1984. pap. 14.95 (*0-8256-0158-4*, AM38621) Music Sales.

Challis, John K. & Scott, John G., eds. Riches of Eternity: Twelve Fundamental Doctrines from the Doctrine & Covenants. LC 93-29480. 258p. 1993. 14.95 (*1-56236-210-0*, Pub. by Aspen Bks) Origin Bk Sales.

— Riches of Faith: The First Principle of the Gospel in the Lives of the Prophets & Saints. LC 95-6363. 276p. 1995. pap. 9.95 (*1-56236-214-3*, Pub. by Aspen Bks) Origin Bk Sales.

Challis, K. M. & Davies, R. A., compiled by. Index Kewensis - Supplementum XX. ix, 338p. 1996. 140.00 (*1-900347-10-5*, Pub. by Royal Botnic Grdns) Balogh.

Challis, Linda & Bartlett, Helen, eds. Old & Ill. (C). 1989. 40.00 (*0-86242-059-8*, Pub. by Age Concern Eng) St Mut.

Challis, Simon. Death on a Quiet Beach. large type ed. (Linford Mystery Library). 304p. 1989. pap. 16.99 (*0-7089-6724-8*, Linford) Ulverscroft.

Challiss, R. A. John, ed. Receptor Signal Transduction Protocols. (Methods in Molecular Biology Ser.: Vol. 83). 296p. 1997. 99.50 (*0-89603-495-X*) Humana.

— Receptor Signal Transduction Protocols. LC 97-12424. (Methods in Molecular Biology Ser.: Vol. 83). (Illus.). 296p. 1997. 79.50 (*0-89603-418-6*) Humana.

Challoner, H. K. The Path of Healing: Finding Your Soul's Potential. LC 76-3660. 175p. 1990. pap. 9.95 (*0-8356-0662-7*, Quest) Theos Pub Hse.

— Regents of the Seven Spheres. (Illus.). 1976. pap. 10.00 (*0-7229-5009-8*) Theos Pub Hse.

— What of Tomorrow: The Problem of Fear. 1976. pap. 4.95 (*0-7229-5046-2*) Theos Pub Hse.

Challoner, J. What's the Big Idea? Alien Life. (J). mass mkt. 8.95 (*0-340-72263-0*, Pub. by Hodder & Stought Ltd) Trafalgar.

Challoner, Jack. Big & Small. (Start-Up Science Ser.). (Illus.). 32p. (J). (gr. 1-4). 1996. lib. bdg. 21.40 (*0-8172-4319-4*) Raintree Steck-V.

— Energy. LC 92-54479. (Eyewitness Books). (Illus.). 64p. (J). (gr. 4-7). 1993. 15.95 (*1-56458-232-9*) DK Pub Inc.

***Challoner, Jack.** Energy. (Eyewitness Books). 64p. (J). (gr. 4-7). 2000. 15.95 (*0-7894-5576-5*, D K Ink) DK Pub Inc.

Challoner, Jack. Eyewitness Visual Dictionary: Chemistry. 64p. (J). 1996. 18.95 (*0-7894-0444-3*) DK Pub Inc.

— Fast & Slow. LC 95-50268. (Illus.). 32p. (J). (gr. 1-4). 1996. lib. bdg. 21.40 (*0-8172-4320-8*) Raintree Steck-V.

— Floating & Sinking. LC 95-40152. (Start-Up Science Ser.). (Illus.). 32p. (J). (gr. 1-4). 1996. lib. bdg. 21.40 (*0-8172-4317-8*) Raintree Steck-V.

— Floating & Sinking. (Start-Up Science Ser.). (Illus.). 32p. (J). (gr. 2-4). 1997. pap. 5.95 (*0-8172-6486-8*) Raintree Steck-V.

— Hot & Cold. LC 95-30013. (Start-up Science Ser.). (Illus.). 32p. (J). (gr. 1-4). 1996. lib. bdg. 21.40 (*0-8172-4323-2*) Raintree Steck-V.

— Hot & Cold. (Start-Up Science Ser.). (Illus.). 32p. (J). (gr. 2-4). 1997. pap. 5.95 (*0-8172-6492-2*) Raintree Steck-V.

— Human Wonders: Detective Files. (Illus.). 32p. (J). (gr. 2-6). 1998. 19.95 (*1-57145-324-5*, Silver Dolph) Advantage Pubs.

— Light & Dark. LC 95-30023. (Start-up Science Ser.). (Illus.). 32p. (J). (gr. 1-4). 1996. lib. bdg. 21.40 (*0-8172-4321-6*) Raintree Steck-V.

— Loud & Quiet. LC 95-48339. (Illus.). 32p. (J). (gr. 1-4). 1996. lib. bdg. 21.40 (*0-8172-4318-6*) Raintree Steck-V.

— My First Batteries & Magnets. LC 92-52825. (Illus.). 48p. (J). (gr. k-4). 1992. 12.95 (*1-56458-133-0*) DK Pub Inc.

— The Visual Dictionary of Physics. LC 95-11937. (Eyewitness Visual Dictionaries Ser.). (Illus.). 64p. (J). (gr. 4 up). 1995. 18.95 (*0-7894-0239-4*, 5-70647) DK Pub Inc.

— Wet & Dry. LC 95-30014. (Start-up Science Ser.). (Illus.). 32p. (J). (gr. 1-4). 1996. lib. bdg. 21.40 (*0-8172-4322-4*) Raintree Steck-V.

Challoner, Jack, et al. Let's Build an Invention. LC 97-12560. (Illus.). (J). (gr. k up). 1997. write for info. (*0-7894-1558-5*) DK Pub Inc.

Challoner, Richard. Life of St. Simon Stylites. 1991. pap. text 1.95 (*0-89981-051-9*) Eastern Orthodox.

Challoner, Richard, tr. see Gibbons, James, ed.

Challoner, Richard, tr. see Thomas, a Kempis.

Chalmel, Loic. La Petite Ecole dans l'Ecole: Origine Pietiste-Morave de l'Ecole Maternelle Francaise. (Exploration Ser.). (FRE.). xiv, 354p. 1996. 42.95 (*3-906754-58-8*, Pub. by P Lang) P Lang Pubng.

Chalmer, Bruce J. Understanding Statistics. (Statistics: Textbooks & Monographs). (Illus.). 448p. 1986. text 85.00 (*0-8247-7322-5*) Dekker.

Chalmer, Judith. Out of History's Junk Jar. LC 95-31079. 100p. 1995. pap. 12.50 (*1-56809-017-X*) Time Being Bks.

— Out of History's Junk Jar: Poems of a Mixed Inheritance. LC 95-31079. 100p. 1995. 18.95 (*1-56809-016-1*) Time Being Bks.

***Chalmer, Judith, ed.** Close to My Heart: Three Generations Reflect upon the Holocaust. LC 99-46554. (Illus.). 96p. 1999. pap. 14.95 (*0-9673921-0-1*) Parent Teachers.

Chalmer, Lawrence R., et al. NATO, 1997: Year of Change. LC 98-39243. 1998. write for info. (*1-57906-013-7*) Natl Defense.

Chalmers. 100 Hill Walks Around Edinburgh. pap. 15.95 (*1-85158-537-0*, Pub. by Mainstream Pubng) Trafalgar.

Chalmers, ed. Buddha's Teachings: Being the Sutta-Nipata or Discourse Collection. (C). 1997. 36.00 (*81-208-1355-3*, Pub. by Motilal Bnarsidass) S Asia.

Chalmers, A., jt. auth. see Miles, R. E.

Chalmers, Alan. Science & Its Fabrication. 160p. (C). 1990. pap. 14.95 (*0-8166-1888-7*) U of Minn Pr.

C

***Chalmers, Alan A.** International Pharmaceutical Registration. LC 99-86387. 2000. 249.00 (*1-57491-103-1*) Interpharm.

Chalmers, Alan D. Jonathan Swift & the Burden of the Future. LC 94-44075. 176p. 1995. 32.50 (*0-87413-554-0*) U Delaware Pr.

Chalmers, Alan F. Science & Its Fabrication. 160p. 1990. 37.50 (*0-335-09318-3*); pap. 11.99 (*0-335-09317-5*) OpUniv Pr.

***Chalmers, Alan F.** What is This Thing Called Science? An Assessment of the Nature & Status of Science & Its Meaning. 3rd ed. (Illus.). 1999. pap. 24.95 (*0-335-20109-1*) OpUniv Pr.

Chalmers, Alan F. What Is This Thing Called Science? An Assessment of the Nature & Status of Science & Its Methods. 2nd ed. 200p. 1982. pap. 11.99 (*0-335-10107-0*) OpUniv Pr.

— What Is This Thing Called Science? An Assessment of the Nature & Status of Science & Its Methods. 3rd ed. LC 99-71498. 200p. 1999. pap. 12.95 (*0-87220-452-9*); lib. bdg. 34.95 (*0-87220-453-7*) Hackett Pub.

Chalmers, Alaxander. Minor English Poets, 1660-1780: A Selection from Alexander Chalmer's "The Works of the English Poets" 1810. 1972. 60.95 (*0-405-12601-8*) Ayer.

Chalmers, Aldie. Fantastic Book of In-Line Skating. LC 97-10590. (Fantastic Book of . . . Ser.). (Illus.). 32p. (J). 1997. 10.95 (*0-7613-0638-2*, Copper Beech Bks); lib. bdg. 22.40 (*0-7613-0623-4*, Copper Beech Bks) Millbrook Pr.

Chalmers, Alexander. Minor English Poets, 1660-1780: A Selection from Alexander Chalmer's "The Works of the English Poets" 1810. 1972. 60.95 (*0-405-12602-6*); 60.95 (*0-405-12603-4*); 60.95 (*0-405-12605-0*); 60.95 (*0-405-12606-9*); 60.95 (*0-405-12607-7*); 60.95 (*0-405-12608-5*); 60.95 (*0-405-12609-3*) Ayer.

— The Works of English Poets, from Chaucer to Cowper, 21 Vols, Set. 1970. reprint ed. 2385.00 (*3-487-02603-1*) G Olms Pubs.

— The Works of English Poets, From Chaucer to Cowper, 21 vols., Set. (BCL1-PR English Literature Ser.). 1992. reprint ed. lib. bdg. 1890.00 (*0-7812-7129-0*) Rprt Serv.

Chalmers, Alexander, ed. General Biographical Dictionary, 32 vols., Set. rev. ed. LC 54-51862. reprint ed. 2640.00 (*0-404-01490-9*) AMS Pr.

— Works of the English Poets from Chaucer to Cowper, 21 vols., Set. Incl. Vol. 1. LC 69-13853. 1969. lib. bdg. 32.50 LC 69-13853. 1969. reprint ed. 605.00 (*0-8371-0344-4*, CHEP, Greenwood Pr) Greenwood.

Chalmers, Alexander & French, David P. Minor English Poets, 1660-1780: A Selection from Alexander Chalmer's "The Works of the English Poets" 1810. 1972. 60.95 (*0-405-12604-2*) Ayer.

Chalmers, Alexander, jt. auth. see French, David P.

Chalmers, Andrew, et al, eds. Fibromyalgia, Chronic Fatigue Syndrome, & Repetitive Strain Injury: Current Concepts in Diagnosis, Management, Disability, & Health Economics. LC 95-30842. (Journal of Musculoskeletal Pain: Vol. 3, No. 2). 1995. 49.95 (*1-56024-744-4*, Hawrth Medical) Haworth Pr.

Chalmers, Annie C. Rites of Passage. 1998. pap. write for info. (*1-57553-940-3*) Watermrk Pr.

Chalmers, B. Progress in Materials Science, Vol. 14. 1969. pap. 45.00 (*0-08-006404-3*, Pergamon Pr) Elsevier.

— Progress in Materials Science, Vol. 14. 1971. 115.00 (*0-08-016136-7*, Pergamon Pr) Elsevier.

Chalmers, B., ed. Progress in Materials Science, Vol. 23. 280p. 1980. 115.00 (*0-08-024846-2*, Pergamon Pr) Elsevier.

Chalmers, B. & King, R. Progress in Metal Physics. (Progress in Materials Science Ser.: Vol. 5). 1954. 156.00 (*0-08-009012-5*, Pub. by Pergamon Repr) Franklin.

Chalmers, Benita R. When Love Calls. 192p. (Orig.). 1998. pap. 6.99 (*0-9669658-0-9*) Poole & Smith.

Chalmers, Bruce. Physical Metallurgy. LC 59-14983. (Wiley Series on the Science & Technology of Materials). 468p. reprint ed. pap. 145.10 (*0-608-11262-3*, 205514000008) Bks Demand.

Chalmers, D. R., jt. auth. see Kenkel, James L.

Chalmers, Dalzell & Barnes, L. H. Student's Guide to Roman Law (Justinian & Gaius) LC 93-79704. 367p. 1994. reprint ed. 90.00 (*1-56169-062-7*) Gaunt.

Chalmers, Dalzell R. Legal Studies for Tasmania. 3rd ed. 1992. pap. 47.00 (*0-409-30489-1*, Austral, MICHIE) LEXIS Pub.

Chalmers, Dalzell R. & Paliwala, A. H. An Introduction to the Law in Papua New Guinea. 2nd ed. xxiv, 236p. 1984. pap. 29.00 (*0-455-20380-6*, Pub. by LawBk Co) Gaunt.

Chalmers, Damian. European Union Law Vol. I(H) Law & EU Government. LC 98-73151. 611p. 1998. text 102.95 (*1-85521-680-9*, Pub. by Dartmth Pub) Ashgate Pub Co.

Chalmers, Damian & Szyszczak, Erika. European Union Law: Towards a European Polity?, Vol. II. LC 98-73151. 750p. 1998. pap. 55.95 (*1-84014-479-3*, Pub. by Dartmth Pub); text 110.95 (*1-84014-473-4*, Pub. by Dartmth Pub) Ashgate Pub Co.

— European Union Law Vol. I: Law & EU Government, 2 vols. LC 98-73151. 650p. 1998. pap. 50.95 (*1-85521-693-0*, Pub. by Dartmth Pub) Ashgate Pub Co.

Chalmers, David. And the Crooked Places Made Straight: The Struggle for Social Change in the 1960s. LC 91-11021. (American Moment Ser.). (Illus.). 272p. 1991. text 38.95 (*0-8018-4173-9*); pap. text 13.95 (*0-8018-4174-7*) Johns Hopkins.

— And the Crooked Places Made Straight: The Struggle for Social Change in the 1960s. 2nd ed. LC 95-45588. (The American Moment Ser.). 264p. (C). 1996. text 38.50 (*0-8018-5333-8*); pap. text 14.95 (*0-8018-5334-6*) Johns Hopkins.

Chalmers, David, et al. Otitus Media with Effusion in Children. (Clinics in Developmental Medicine Ser.: No. 108). (Illus.). 167p. (C). 1991. text 49.95 (*0-521-41224-2*, Pub. by Mc Keith Pr) Cambridge U Pr.

Chalmers, David John. The Conscious Mind: In Search of a Fundamental Theory. (Philosophy of Mind Ser.). (Illus.). 432p. (Orig.). 1996. 35.00 (*0-19-510553-2*) OUP.

— The Conscious Mind: In Search of a Fundamental Theory. (Philosophy of Mind). (Illus.). 432p. (Orig.). 1997. reprint ed. pap. 16.95 (*0-19-511789-1*) OUP.

Chalmers, David M. Hooded Americanism: The History of the Ku Klux Klan. LC 86-29133. xii, 477p. 1987. reprint ed. pap. text 19.95 (*0-8223-0772-3*) Duke.

— The Muckrake Years. LC 79-22780. (Anvil Ser.). 176p. 1980. reprint ed. pap. 10.50 (*0-89874-066-5*) Krieger.

— Neither Socialism nor Monopoly: Theodore Roosevelt & the Decision to Regulate the Railroads. LC 85-18147. 132p. 1985. reprint ed. pap. 9.50 (*0-89874-878-X*) Krieger.

— Social & Political Ideas of the Muckrakers. LC 70-117765. (Essay Index Reprint Ser.). 1977. 18.95 (*0-8369-1745-6*) Ayer.

Chalmers, Don, jt. auth. see Pont, Gino D.

Chalmers, Donald R., et al. Criminal Law & Practice of Papua New Guinea. 2nd ed. xxxiv, 807p. 1985. 67.00 (*0-455-20398-9*, Pub. by LawBk Co) Gaunt.

Chalmers, Doug A. The United States & Anastasio Somoza: Dealing with Friendly Dictators Who Are Losing Authority. (Pew Case Studies in International Affairs). 50p. (C). 1992. pap. text 3.50 (*1-56927-105-4*) Geo U Inst Dplmcy.

Chalmers, Douglas A., et al, eds. The New Politics of Inequality in Latin America: Rethinking Participation & Representation. (Oxford Studies in Democratization). (Illus.). 662p. 1997. pap. text 28.00 (*0-19-878183-0*) OUP.

— The New Politics of Inequaltiy in Latin America: Rethinking Participation & Representation. LC 96-29002. (Oxford Studies in Democratization). (Illus.). 664p. 1997. text 85.00 (*0-19-878184-9*) OUP.

— The Right & Democracy in Latin America. LC 91-22940. 336p. 1992. 55.00 (*0-275-93822-0*, C3822, Praeger Pubs) Greenwood.

***Chalmers, Elden M.** Healing the Broken Brain: Science & the Bible Reveal How the Brain Works, Vol. 1. (Illus.). 219p. 1998. pap. 11.99 (*0-9669314-0-8*, RP1009, Pub. by E M Chalmers) Remnant Pubns.

Chalmers, F. Graeme. Celebrating Pluralism: Art, Education, & Cultural Diversity. LC 96-8712. (Occasional Paper Ser.: Vol. 5). (Illus.). 112p. 1996. pap. 15.00 (*0-89236-393-2*, Pub. by J P Getty Trust) OUP.

— Women in the Nineteenth-Century Art World: Schools of Art & Design for Women in London & Philadelphia, 5. LC 97-46521. (Contributions to the Study of Art & Architecture: Vol. 5). 160p. 1998. 55.00 (*0-313-30604-4*, Greenwood Pr) Greenwood.

Chalmers, George. Another Account of the Incidents, from Which the Title, & a Part of the Story of Shakspeare's Tempest Were Derived. LC 72-1051. reprint ed. 29.50 (*0-404-01442-9*) AMS Pr.

— Considerations on Commerce, Bullion, & Coin, Circulation & Exchanges. LC 68-55502. (Reprints of Economic Classics Ser.). 237p. 1969. reprint ed. 39.50 (*0-678-00431-5*) Kelley.

— Eighteenth Century Shakespeare, Vol. 25. 628p. 1971. reprint ed. 45.00 (*0-7146-2531-0*, Pub. by F Cass Pubs) Intl Spec Bk.

— An Estimate of the Comparative Strength of Great Britain: During the Present & Four Preceeding Reigns. LC 67-29496. (Reprints of Economic Classics Ser.). cxliv, 289p. 1969. reprint ed. 57.50 (*0-678-00415-3*) Kelley.

— Introduction to the History of the Revolt of the American Colonies. LC 70-141083. (Research Library of Colonial Americana). 1972. reprint ed. 72.95 (*0-405-03278-1*) Ayer.

— An Introduction to the History of the Revolt of the American Colonies, 2 vols. LC 75-119049. (Era of the American Revolution Ser.). 1971. reprint ed. lib. bdg. 85.00 (*0-306-71948-7*) Da Capo.

— Opinions of Eminent Lawyers on Various Points of English Jurisprudence. LC 87-80148. (Historical Writings in Law & Jurisprudence Ser.: No. 13). xxvii, 718p. 1987. reprint ed. lib. bdg. 52.00 (*0-89941-545-8*, 305110) W S Hein.

— Supplemental Apology for the Believers in the Shakespeare-Papers. 656p. 1971. reprint ed. 45.00 (*0-7146-2536-1*, Pub. by F Cass Pubs) Intl Spec Bk.

— A Supplemental Apology for the Believers in the Shakespeare-Papers: Being a Reply to Mr. Malone's Answer. LC 70-96374. (Eighteenth Century Shakespeare Ser.: No. 26). viii, 656p. 1971. reprint ed. lib. bdg. 42.50 (*0-678-05141-0*) Kelley.

Chalmers, George, ed. see Henryson, Robert.

Chalmers, Helena. Clothes, on & off the Stage: A History of Dress from the Earliest Times to the Present Day. LC 89-61542. (Illus.). xx, 312p. 1989. reprint ed. 48.00 (*1-55888-820-9*) Omnigraphics Inc.

Chalmers-Hunt, B. L., jt. auth. see Haynes, J. H.

Chalmers-Hunt, B. L, jt. auth. see Haynes, J. H.

Chalmers, Iain & Altman, Douglas, eds. Systematic Reviews. (Illus.). 128p. (Orig.). 1995. pap. text 27.00 (*0-7279-0904-5*, Pub. by BMJ Pub) Login Brothers Bk Co.

Chalmers, Iain & Hadiz, Vedi R. The Politics of Economic Development in Indonesia: Contending Perspectives. LC 96-25077. 304p. (C). 1997. 90.00 (*0-415-14502-3*) Routledge.

***Chalmers, Irena.** The Creative Cook, 3 vols. (Illus.). 1100p. 1999. reprint ed. pap. text 35.00 (*0-7881-6035-4*) DIANE Pub.

Chalmers, Irena. Food Professional's Guide. 325p. 1990. 35.00 (*0-471-52460-3*) Wiley.

— Good Old Food: A Taste from the Past. 320p. 1993. pap. 16.95 (*0-8120-1725-0*) Barron.

— The Great American Baby Almanac: A Complete Compendium of Facts, Fancies, & Traditions. 1989. 24.95 (*0-318-41507-0*) Viking Penguin.

— The Working Family's Cookbook. (Illus.). 336p. 1993. pap. 12.95 (*0-8120-1566-5*) Barron.

Chalmers, J. 100 Hill Walks Around Glasgow. pap. 15.95 (*1-85158-536-2*, Pub. by Mainstream Pubng) Trafalgar.

Chalmers, J. & Terr Haar, D. Atmospheric Electricity. 2nd ed. LC 66-29669. (International Series of Monographs in Natural Philosophy: Vol. 11). 1967. 240.00 (*0-08-012005-9*, Pub. by Pergamon Repr) Franklin.

***Chalmers, J. M., ed.** Polymer Spectroscopy Macromolecular Symposia Volume 141. 312p. 1999. 140.00 (*3-527-29809-6*) Wiley.

Chalmers, J. M. & Dent, G. Industrial Analysis with Vibrational Spectroscopy. (RCS Analytical Spectroscopy Monographs). 392p. 1997. 134.00 (*0-85404-563-1*) Am Chemical.

***Chalmers, James.** Achieving Personal Well-Being How to Discover & Balance Your Physical & Emotional Needs. 2nd ed. (Self-Development Ser.). (Illus.). 144p. 1999. pap. 19.95 (*1-85703-532-1*, Pub. by How To Bks) Trans-Atl Phila.

Chalmers, James. Organising Effective Training: How to Plan & Run Successful Courses & Seminars. (Business Basics Ser.). 127p. 1996. pap. 19.95 (*1-85703-229-9*, Pub. by How To Bks) Trans-Atl Phila.

Chalmers, Jan A., ed. International Symposium on Microwave Signatures in Remote Sensing: Special Issue of the International Journal of Remote Sensing. 156p. 1988. pap. 42.00 (*0-85066-901-4*) Taylor & Francis.

Chalmers, Jennifer H., jt. auth. see Harley, Willard F., Jr.

Chalmers, John, Jr. Divisions of the Tetrachord: A Prolegomenon to the Construction of Musical Scales. 234p. (C). 1993. pap. 35.00 (*0-945996-04-7*) Frog Peak Music.

Chalmers, John I., jt. ed. see Chalmers, Patrick.

***Chalmers, John M.** Spectroscopy in Process Analysis. LC 99-39057. 1999. write for info. (*0-8493-9747-2*) CRC Pr.

Chalmers, John W. Laird of the West, Vol. 1. 289p. 1981. 19.95 (*0-920490-18-2*) Temeron Bks.

Chalmers, Joseph, jt. auth. see Smith, Elizabeth.

***Chalmers, Karen Hanson & Peterson, Amy A.** 15 Myths of a Diabetic Diet. LC 99-44966. 224p. 1999. pap. 14.95 (*1-58040-031-0*, 00310Q, Pub. by Am Diabetes) NTC Contemp Pub Co.

Chalmers, Kenneth. Bela Bartok. LC 95-210377. (20th Century Composers Ser.). (Illus.). 240p. (Orig.). (C). 1995. pap. 19.95 (*0-7148-3164-6*, Pub. by Phaidon Press) Phaidon Pr.

Chalmers, Kenneth E., jt. auth. see Biron, Henry C.

Chalmers, Liz, jt. auth. see Hale, M. Fellenstein.

Chalmers, Lynne. Modifying Curriculum for the Special Needs Student in the Regular Classroom. 48p. (C). 1992. pap. text 9.95 (*1-886979-00-6*) Practicl Pr.

***Chalmers, Lynne.** Modifying Curriculum for the Special Needs Student in the Regular Classroom. 2nd ed. (Illus.). 60p. (C). 2000. pap. 11.95 (*1-886979-14-6*) Practicl Pr.

Chalmers, Lynne & Olson, Myrna. Collaboration Handbook for Educators Working Toward Inclusion of Special Needs Students. 64p. 1995. pap. text 11.95 (*1-886979-04-9*) Practicl Pr.

Chalmers, Lynne & Wasson, Barbara. Successful Inclusion: Assistance for Teachers of Adolescents with Mild Disabilities. 64p. (C). 1993. pap. text 12.95 (*1-886979-01-4*) Practicl Pr.

Chalmers, M., et al. An Illustrated Catalogue of Airborne Microbiota from the Maritime Antarctic. (Illus.). 182p. 1996. 70.00 (*0-85665-179-6*, Pub. by Brit Antarctic Surv) Balogh.

***Chalmers, M. D., ed.** The Negotiable Instruments Act (Act XXVI of 1881) Being an Act to Define & Amend the Law Relating to Promissory Notes, Bills of Exchange & Cheques. xxxvi, 167p. 1999. reprint ed. 65.00 (*1-56169-565-3*) Gaunt.

***Chalmers, Malcolm.** Sharing Security: The Politics of OECD Burdensharing. LC 00-33303. 2000. write for info. (*0-312-23596-8*) St Martin.

Chalmers, Margaret T. Colonial Fireplace Cooking & Early American Recipes. (Illus.). 96p. (Orig.). 1979. pap. 7.95 (*0-932296-04-1*) Eberly Pr.

Chalmers, Martin, tr. see Enzensberger, Hans M.

Chalmers, Martin, tr. see Fichte, Hubert.

Chalmers, Martin, tr. see Jelinek, Elfriede.

Chalmers, Martin, tr. see Weiss, Ernst.

Chalmers, Martin, tr. & pref. see Klemperer, Victor.

Chalmers, Mary. Be Good, Harry. LC 67-16230. (Trophy Picture Bk.). (Illus.). 32p. (J). (ps-3). 1981. pap. 1.50 (*0-06-443027-8*, HarpTrophy) HarpC Child Bks.

— A Christmas Story. LC 56-8143. (Illus.). 24p. (J). (ps-1). 1956. reprint ed. 12.95 (*0-06-021190-3*) HarpC Child Bks.

— Come to the Doctor, Harry. LC 80-7910. (Illus.). 32p. (J). (ps-1). 1981. 10.95 (*0-06-021178-4*) HarpC Child Bks.

— Merry Christmas, Harry. LC 90-27516. (Illus.). 32p. (J). (ps-2). 1992. lib. bdg. 12.89 (*0-06-022742-7*) HarpC Child Bks.

— Take a Nap, Harry. LC 64-11838. (Trophy Picture Bk.). (Illus.). 32p. (J). (ps-3). 1981. pap. 1.50 (*0-06-443028-6*, HarpTrophy) HarpC Child Bks.

— Take a Nap, Harry. LC 89-77655. (Illus.). 32p. (J). (ps-2). 1991. 13.95 (*0-06-021243-8*) HarpC Child Bks

— Throw a Kiss, Harry. LC 58-5294. (Trophy Picture Bk.). (Illus.). 32p. (J). (ps-3). 1981. pap. 1.50 (*0-06-443030-8*, HarpTrophy) HarpC Child Bks.

— Throw a Kiss, Harry. LC 89-49064. (Illus.). 32p. (J). (ps-2). 1990. 12.95 (*0-06-021246-2*) HarpC Child Bks.

Chalmers, Mary A., et al. Damaged Parents: An Anatomy of Child Neglect. LC 80-22793. (Illus.). xii, 284p. 1983. pap. 11.95 (*0-226-67222-0*) U Ch Pr.

***Chalmers, Michelle.** Passages: A Journal for Growing Home. (Illus.). 151p. (YA). (gr. 7 up). 1999. 15.00 (*0-9637696-4-2*) Human Srv Assocs.

Chalmers, N., jt. auth. see Redhead, D. N.

Chalmers, Patrick. Ancient Sculptured Monuments of the County of Angus. LC 72-1052. (Bannatyne Club, Edinburgh. Publications: No. 88). reprint ed. 175.00 (*0-404-52818-X*) AMS Pr.

Chalmers, Patrick & Chalmers, John I., eds. Registrum Episcopatus Brechinensis, 2 vols. LC 72-39524. (Bannatyne Club, Edinburgh. Publications: No. 102). reprint ed. 155.00 (*0-404-52855-4*) AMS Pr.

Chalmers, Patrick, ed. see Arbroath Abbey Staff.

Chalmers, R. A. Microprocessors in Analytical Chemistry, Vol. 27, No. 7b. 64p. 1982. pap. 28.00 (*0-08-026284-8*, Pergamon Pr) Elsevier.

Chalmers, R. A., ed. Gains & Losses: Errors in Trace Analysis. 90p. 1983. pap. 30.00 (*0-08-030239-4*, Pergamon Pr) Elsevier.

Chalmers, R. A. & Lawson, A. M. Organic Acids in Man. LC 81-11342. 1982. 82.50 (*0-412-14890-0*, NO. 6573) Chapman & Hall.

Chalmers, R. A., tr. see Buffle, Jacques.

Chalmers, Robert A. Multilingual Dictionary of Analytical Terms. LC 94-11359. 288p. 1994. 75.00 (*0-86542-859-X*) Blackwell Sci.

Chalmers, Robert A., ed. Multilingual Dictionary of Analytical Terms: English, French, German, Spanish, Russian, Chinese & Japanese. LC 94-11359. 1994. write for info. (*0-08-654285-0*, Pergamon Pr) Elsevier.

Chalmers, Ronald. Questions from the Shadows. Iddings, Kathleen, ed. LC 92-61837. 100p. (Orig.). 1992. per. 10.00 (*0-931289-12-2*) San Diego Poet Pr.

Chalmers, Thomas. On Political Economy: In Connection with the Moral State & Moral Aspects of Society. LC 67-19707. (Reprints of Economic Classics Ser.). viii, 566p. 1968. reprint ed. 57.50 (*0-678-00370-X*) Kelley.

Chalmers, W. Ellison. Racial Negotiations: Potentials & Limitations. LC 74-78509. 1974. 15.00 (*0-87736-321-8*) U of Mich Inst Labor.

Chalmers, W. Ellison & Cormick, G. W., eds. Racial Conflict & Negotiations: Perspectives & First Case Studies. LC 72-634167. (Orig.). 1971. 12.00 (*0-87736-313-7*); pap. 5.95 (*0-87736-314-5*) U of Mich Inst Labor.

Chalmers, William. No More Worthy. 176p. 1996. text 14.95 (*0-88982-157-7*, Pub. by Oolichan Bks) Genl Dist Srvs.

Chalmin, P. The Making of a Sugar Giant: Tate & Lyle, 1859-1989. xviii, 782p. 1990. text 160.00 (*3-7186-0434-5*) Gordon & Breach.

Chalmin, Philippe. International Commodity Markets Handbook, 1994. 512p. 1993. pap. 145.00 (*1-85573-141-X*, Pub. by Woodhead Pubng) Am Educ Systs.

— Traders & Merchants: An Introduction to International Commodity Trading. xii, 310p. (C). 1987. text 132.00 (*3-7186-0435-3*) Gordon & Breach.

Chalmlee-Wright, Emily. The Cultural Foundations of Economic Development: Urban Female Entrepreneurship in Ghana. LC 97-3704. (Foundations of the Market Economy Ser.). 224p. (C). 1997. 75.00 (*0-415-16994-1*) Routledge.

Chalofsky, N. & Lincoln, C. I. Up the HRD Ladder: A Guide to Professional Growth. 1983. 16.76 (*0-201-04998-8*) Addison-Wesley.

Chalofsky, Barry. The Home & Land Buyer's Guide to the Environment. LC 97-7684. (Illus.). 140p. (Orig.). 1997. pap., per. 16.95 (*0-88285-158-6*) Ctr Urban Pol Res.

Chalofsky, Barry & Finestine, Joel. The Real Estate Guide to the Environment. LC 97-69402. (Illus.). 160p. 1997. pap. 29.95 (*0-9660660-0-6*) Prof Educ Assocs.

Chalofsky, Margie. Changing Places: A Kid's View of Shelter Living. 61p. 1992. pap. 5.95 (*0-87659-161-6*) Gryphon Hse.

Chalofsky, Neal & Bianco-Mathis, Virginia. The Full-Time Faculty Handbook. LC 98-40062. 1998. pap. 32.00 (*0-7619-1223-1*) Sage.

Chalofsky, Neal, jt. auth. see Bianco-Mathis, Virginia.

Chalofsky, Neal, jt. ed. see Bianco-Mathis, Virginia.

Chalofsky, Neal E. & Reinhart, Carlene. Effective Human Resource Development: How to Build a Strong & Responsive HRD Function. LC 87-46334. (Management Ser.). 164p. 1988. text 39.95 (*1-55542-081-8*) Jossey-Bass.

Chalom Des Cordes, J., jt. auth. see Chalom Des Cordes, V.

Chalom Des Cordes, V. & Chalom Des Cordes, J. Bugatti (Rembrandt) Catalogue Raisonne of the Sculptures. (FRE., Illus.). 336p. 1987. 250.00 (*1-55660-192-1*) A Wofsy Fine Arts.

Chalon, Jean. St. Therese of Lisieux: A Life of Love. 296p. 1997. pap. 65.00 (*0-86012-275-1*, Pub. by Srch Pr) St Mut.

— Therese of Lisieux: A Life of Love. Rehill, Anne C., tr. from ENG. LC 97-9983. 288p. (Orig.). 1997. pap. 16.00 (*0-7648-0111-2*) Liguori Pubns.

***Chaloner, Chris & Coffey, Michael.** Forensic Mental Health Nursing: Current Approaches LC 99-34311. 1999. write for info. (*0-632-05031-4*) Blackwell Sci.

Chaloner, Penny A. Homogeneous Hydrogenation. LC 93-20972. (Catalysis by Metal Complexes Ser.). 288p. (C). 1994. text 166.50 (*0-7923-2474-9*) Kluwer Academic.

Chaloner, W. H., tr. see Engels, Friedrich.

Chaloner, William H. People & Industries. (Illus.). 151p. 1963. 24.00 (*0-7146-1284-7*, Pub. by F Cass Pubs) Intl Spec Bk.

Chaloner, William H., jt. auth. see Engels, Friedrich.

C

Chaloner, William H., ed. see Bamford, Samuel.

Chaloner, William H., ed. see Redford, Arthur.

Chaloner, William H., tr. see Hoffmann, Walther G.

Chalos, Peter. Managing Cost in Today's Manufacturing Environment. 1992. write for info. (*0-318-69292-9*) P-H.

Chalou, George C., ed. The Secret War: The Office of Strategic Services in World War II. (Illus.). 376p. 1995. text 55.00 (*0-7881-2598-2*) DIANE Pub.

— Secrets War: The Office of Strategic Services in World War II. LC 91-45158. (Illus.). 376p. (C). 1992. text 25.00 (*0-911333-91-6*, 100021) National Archives & Recs.

Chalouh & Malette, Louise, eds. The Montreal Massacre. 184p. 1994. pap. 12.95 (*0-921881-14-2*, Pub. by Gynergy-Ragweed) U of Toronto Pr.

Chaloupka, Frank J. The Economic Analysis of Substance Use & Abuse: An Integration of Econometric & Behavioral Economic Research LC 99-17554. (A National Bureau of Economic Research Conference Report). 352p. 1999. 53.00 (*0-226-10047-2*) U Ch Pr.

Chaloupka, Frank J., jt. auth. see Jha, Prabhat.

Chaloupka, Frank J., jt. ed. see Jha, Prabhat.

Chaloupka, J. & Krumphanzl, V., eds. Extracellular Enzymes of Microorganisms. LC 87-14102. (Illus.). 226p. 1987. 65.00 (*0-306-42609-9*, Plenum Trade) Perseus Pubng.

Chaloupka, William. Everybody Knows: Cynicism in America. LC 99-21025. 256p. 1999. 25.95 (*0-8166-3310-X*, Pub. by U of Minn Pr) Chicago Distribution Ctr.

— Knowing Nukes: The Politics & Culture of the Atom. 192p. (C). 1992. pap. 14.95 (*0-8166-2076-8*); text 39.95 (*0-8166-2074-1*) U of Minn Pr.

Chaloupka, William, jt. ed. see Bennett, Jane.

Chaloupka, William, jt. ed. see Stearns, William.

Chaloupkia, William. Everybody Knows: Cynicism in America. LC 99-21025. 1999. write for info. (*0-8166-3311-8*) U of Minn Pr.

Chalres, Celestin, et al. Oeuvre d'Henri de Saint-Simon & Saint Simon und die Okonomische Geschichtstehorie, 2 vols. Mayer, J. P., ed. LC 78-67334. (European Political Thought Ser.). (FRE & GER.). 1979. reprint ed. lib. bdg. 28.95 (*0-405-11682-9*) Ayer.

C

Chalupa, Leo M. & Finlay, Barbara L., eds. Development & Organization of the Retina from Molecules to Function: Proceedings of a NATO ASI Held in Crete, Greece, June 18-28, 1997. LC 98-21939. (NATO ASI Ser.: Vol. 299). (Illus.). 356p. (C). 1998. text 125.00 (*0-306-45906-X*, Kluwer Plenum) Kluwer Academic.

Chalupa, V. John. An A-B-C-D of Politics at the End of a Road. 379p. 1997. pap. 17.00 (*1-887567-10-0*) CBCCU Amer.

Chalus, Elaine, jt. auth. see Barker, Hannah.

Chalutz, Edo, jt. ed. see Fuchs, Yoram.

Chalvet, O., ed. Localization & Delocalization in Quantum Chemistry: Ionized & Excited States: Proceedings, Vol.2. 1976. text 199.50 (*90-277-0661-1*) Kluwer Academic.

Chalvet, O., et al, eds. Localization & Delocalization in Quantum Chemistry: Atoms & Molecules in the Ground State, Vol. 1. LC 75-2437. vii, 350p. 1975. text 211.50 (*90-277-0559-3*) Kluwer Academic.

Chalvon-Demersay, Sabine. A Thousand Screenplays. LC 98-37985. 208p. 1999. pap. 15.00 (*0-226-10069-3*); lib. bdg. 30.00 (*0-226-10068-5*) U Ch Pr.

Chalyi, A. V. Physics Reviews Vol. 16, Pt. 2.1: Non-Homogeneous Liquids Near the Critical Point & the Boundary of Stability, Vol. 16. (Soviet Scientific Reviews Ser.: Section A). 125p. 1992. pap. text 136.00 (*3-7186-5219-6*, Harwood Acad Pubs) Gordon & Breach.

Cham, Kit M., et al. Computer Aided Design & VLSI Device Development. 1985. text 98.00 (*0-89838-204-1*) Kluwer Academic.

Cham, Kit Man, et al. Computer-Aided Design & VLSI Device Development. 2nd ed. (C). 1988. text 140.50 (*0-89838-277-7*) Kluwer Academic.

Cham, Mbye, ed. Ex-iles: Essays on Caribbean Cinema. LC 91-76983. (Illus.). 432p. 1992. 49.95 (*0-86543-274-0*); pap. 18.95 (*0-86543-275-9*) Africa World.

Cham, Mbye & Andrade-Watkins, Claire. Black Frames: Critical Perspectives on Independent Black Cinema. (Celebration of Black Cinema Ser.). (Illus.). 116p. (Orig.). 1988. pap. text 10.95 (*0-262-53080-5*) MIT Pr.

Cham, Mbye, jt. ed. see Bakari, Imruh.

Chamala, Shankariah, jt. auth. see Coughenour, C. Milton.

Chamala, Shankarish, jt. ed. see Crouch, Bruce R.

Chamalambous, S., et al, eds. Antiproton '86: Proceedings of the VIII European Symposium on Nucleon-Antinucleon Interactions. 448p. 1987. text 144.00 (*9971-5-0313-1*) World Scientific Pub.

Chamallas, Martha. Introduction to Feminist Legal Theory. LC 98-30396. 360p. 1998. pap. text 30.95 (*0-7355-0045-2*) Panel Pubs.

***Chamallas, Stan, et al.** Extended Stability Data for Parenteral Drugs. Bing, Caryn, ed. 150p. 2000. pap. write for info. (*1-58528-011-9*) Am Soc Hlth-Syst.

Chaman, Jain L. A Managerial Guide to Judgmental Forecasting. 107p. (C). 1987. 24.95 (*0-932126-13-8*) Graceway.

***Chaman, Lal.** Hindu America, Revealing the Story of the Romance of the Surya Vanshi Hindus & Depicting the Imprints of Hindu Culture on the Two Americas. 3rd ed. (LC History-America-E). 273p. 1999. reprint ed. lib. bdg. 79.00 (*0-7812-4286-X*) Rprt Serv.

Chamaria, Pradeep. Kailash Manasarovar on the Rugged Road to Revelation. (C). 1996. 82.00 (*81-7017-336-1*, Pub. by Abhinav) S Asia.

Chamarro, A., ed. Stroke Treatment & Prevention: From Clinical Trials to Daily Practice: 51st Meeting of the Spanish Society of Neurology Barcelona, December 1998. (Cerebrovascular Diseases Ser.: Vol. 9, Suppl. 3). (Illus.). iv, 50p. 1999. pap. 25.25 (*3-8055-6926-2*) S Karger.

Chambadal, L. Dictionary of Mathematics: Dictionnaire des Mathematiques. (ENG & FRE.). 312p. 1982. 69.95 (*0-8288-1896-7*, M6625) Fr & Eur.

Chambard, Claude. The Maquis: A History of the French Resistance Movement. Halperin, Elaine P., tr. from FRE. LC 75-6400. (Illus.). 372p. 1976. 15.00 (*0-672-52156-3*, Bobbs) Macmillan.

Chamber, John. A Treatise Against Judicial Astrology, 2 pts. LC 77-6872. (English Experience Ser.: No. 860). 1977. reprint ed. lib. bdg. 20.00 (*90-221-0860-0*) Walter J Johnson.

Chamber, Karen, jt. tr. see Perlman, Ian.

Chamber, Mary E., jt. auth. see Humphrey, Robert L.

Chamber of Mines of the Philippines Staff. The Critical Years of the Philippine Mining Industry, 1993-1995. LC 96-946187. 48, p. 1995. write for info. (*971-91691-0-9*) New Day Pub.

Chamber of Princes Staff. British Crown & Indian States. (C). 1988. reprint ed. 32.50 (*81-212-0141-1*, Pub. by Gian Publng Hse) S Asia.

Chamberas, Peter, ed. & tr. see Papadopoulos, Gerasimos, et al.

Chamberas, Peter A., tr. Nicodemos of the Holy Mountain: A Handbook of Spiritual Counsel. (Classics of Western Spirituality Ser.). 1989. pap. 12.95 (*0-8091-3038-6*) Paulist Pr.

Chamberas, Peter A., jt. auth. see Papadopoulos, Gerasimos.

Chamberlai. Turnbulls Obstetrics. 2nd ed. 1995. text 175.00 (*0-443-04998-X*, W B Saunders Co) Harcrt Hlth Sci Grp.

Chamberlain. Milk Production in the Tropic. 1990. pap. text. write for info. (*0-582-77513-2*, Pub. by Addison-Wesley) Longman.

— Narratives of Exile & Return. LC 96-41006. 248p. 1997. text 39.95 (*0-312-16484-X*) St Martin.

— Oceanography: An Introduction to the Marine Science. 480p. 1994. 48.50 (*0-8016-6344-X*) Mosby Inc.

— Oceanography: Introduction Marine. 1999. 16.50 (*0-697-21704-3*) McGraw.

— Oceanography: Introduction to Marine Science. 1999. 43.50 (*0-697-21702-7*) McGraw.

Chamberlain & Ryan, Mark. Teach Yourself . . . Visual Age for Java in 21 Days. 1997. 39.99 (*1-57521-359-1*) Sams.

Chamberlain, jt. auth. see Boas.

Chamberlain, A. C. Radioactive Aerosols. (Cambridge Environmental Chemistry Ser.). (Illus.). 265p. (C). 1991. text 100.00 (*0-521-40121-6*) Cambridge U Pr.

Chamberlain, Alan & Steele, Ross. Guide Pratique de la Communication. (FRE.). 191p. 1991. pap. 38.95 incl. audio (*2-278-04177-0*, Pub. by Edns Didier) Hatier Pub.

***Chamberlain, Alexander F.** The Contributions of the American Indian to Civilization. (LC History-America-E). 36p. 1999. reprint ed. lib. bdg. 69.00 (*0-7812-4248-7*) Rprt Serv.

Chamberlain, Andrew. Human Remains. LC 93-47200. (Interpreting the Past Ser.). (C). 1994. pap. 13.95 (*0-520-08834-4*, Pub. by U CA Pr) Cal Prin Full Svc.

Chamberlain, Ann. Reign of Favored Women. LC 98-19412. 384p. 1998. 25.95 (*0-312-86592-9*, Pub. by Forge NYC) St Martin.

Chamberlain, Anne. Meat Pies & Puddings. (Illus.). 96p. (Orig.). 1979. pap. 9.95 (*0-572-01039-7*) Trans-Atl Phila.

— Practical Herb Gardening. (Illus.). 128p. (Orig.). 1993. pap. 15.95 (*0-572-01701-4*, Pub. by W Foulsham) Trans-Atl Phila.

— The Tall Dark Man. 216p. 1986. reprint ed. pap. 5.95 (*0-89733-195-8*) Academy Chi Pubs.

Chamberlain, Arthur B. George Romney. LC 70-157329. (Select Bibliographies Reprint Ser.). 1977. reprint ed. 42.95 (*0-8369-5789-X*) Ayer.

Chamberlain, Ava, jt. auth. see Edwards, Jonathan.

Chamberlain, B. H. Ainu Folktales. 1976. lib. bdg. 250.00 (*0-8490-1407-7*) Gordon Pr.

Chamberlain, Basil H. Aino Folk Tales. (Folk-Lore Society, London Monographs: Vol. 22). 1972. reprint ed. pap. 25.00 (*0-8115-0509-X*) Periodicals Srv.

— Japanese Things: Being Notes on Various Subjects Connected with Japan. LC 76-87791. 576p. 1970. pap. 16.95 (*0-8048-0713-2*) Tuttle Pubng.

Chamberlain, Basil H., tr. from JPN. The Kojiki: Records of Ancient Matters. LC 81-52934. 512p. 1982. reprint ed. pap. 16.95 (*0-8048-1439-2*) Tuttle Pubng.

Chamberlain, Beverly, jt. auth. see Bates, Virginia T.

Chamberlain, Bobby J. Jorge Amado (Brazi) (Twayne's World Authors Ser.: No. 767). 152p. 1990. 32.00 (*0-8057-8261-3*) Macmillan.

— Portuguese Dictionary. 1991. pap. 6.99 (*0-679-40060-5*) McKay.

— Portuguese Language & Luso-Brazilian Literature: An Annotated Guide to Selected Reference Works. LC 88-8409. (Selected Bibliographies in Language & Literature Ser.: No. 6). x, 95p. 1989. pap. 18.00 (*0-87352-957-X*, SB06P); lib. bdg. 32.00 (*0-87352-956-1*, SB06C) Modern Lang.

Chamberlain, Bobby J. & Harmon, Ronald M. A Dictionary of Informal Brazilian Portuguese: With English Index. LC 84-13735. (ENG & POR.). 720p. (C). 1984. text 29.95 (*0-87840-091-5*) Georgetown U Pr.

***Chamberlain, Brenda.** Selected Readings. 114p. 1999. pap. 25.00 (*1-58692-001-4*) Copyright Mgmt.

Chamberlain, Brenda. Tide-Race. (Illus.). 228p. 1996. pap. 14.95 (*0-907476-65-1*, Pub. by Seren Bks) Dufour.

Chamberlain, Catherine E. Easy Does It for Voice: A Program for Detecting & Reducing Vocal Abuse, 2 bks. 197p. 1992. spiral bd. 41.95 (*1-55999-900-4*) LinguiSystems.

Chamberlain, Catherine E., jt. auth. see Strode, Robin.

Chamberlain, Cathi. How to Succeed in Singles' Bars (For Men Only!) Carle, Cliff, ed. (Illus.). 64p. (Orig.). 1986. pap. 3.95 (*0-918259-04-5*) CCC Pubns.

Chamberlain, Clint. Marinas: Recommendations for Design, Construction & Management, Vol. 1. 169p. 35.00 (*0-318-17794-3*) Natl Marine Mfrs.

Chamberlain, Colin E. Tolley's Practical Guide to Employees Share Schemes. 250p. (C). 1994. 105.00 (*0-85459-818-9*, Pub. by Tolley Pubng) St Mut.

Chamberlain Corp. Staff. A Sketch, the Original 1905 Biography of Joshua Lawrence Chamberlain. (Illus.). 70p. Date not set. text. write for info. (*0-9649433-1-X*) N P S.

Chamberlain, D. A., jt. ed. see Sleight, P.

Chamberlain, D. F. Subgenus Hymenanthes, Vol. 39, No. 2. (Revision of Rhododendron Ser.). (Illus.). 1982. 7.50 (*0-11-491994-1*, Pub. by Royal Botanic Edinburgh) Balogh.

Chamberlain, D. F. & Rae, S. J. Subgenus Tsutsusi, Vol. 47, No. 2. (Revision of Rhododendron Ser.). 1990. 40.00 (*0-11-494113-0*, Pub. by Royal Botanic Edinburgh) Balogh.

Chamberlain, Daniel F. Narrative Perspective in Fiction: A Phenomenological Mediation of Reader, Text, & World. 272p. 1990. text 45.00 (*0-8020-5838-8*) U of Toronto Pr.

Chamberlain, Darrel. The Glory of the Temple. LC 97-68804. 1997. 39.95 (*1-57008-326-6*) Bookcraft Inc.

Chamberlain, David. The Mind of Your Newborn Baby. 3rd ed. LC 97-46583. Orig. Title: Babies Remember Birth. 225p. 1998. reprint ed. pap. 14.95 (*1-55643-264-X*) North Atlantic.

Chamberlain, David, ed. New Readings of Late Medieval Love Poems. LC 92-32018. 204p. (Orig.). (C). 1993. pap. text 26.00 (*0-8191-8912-X*); lib. bdg. 49.50 (*0-8191-8911-1*) U Pr of Amer.

Chamberlain, David, et al. The Genus Rhododendron: Its Classification & Synonymy. iii, 184p. 1996. pap. 23.00 (*1-872291-66-X*, Pub. by Royal Botanic Edinburgh) Balogh.

Chamberlain, David, jt. auth. see Sweeney, Patrick.

Chamberlain, David E., et al. Wireless Communications: Critical New Links on the Info-Highway. DeSonne, Marcia L., ed. (Illus.). 94p. 1996. pap. 149.95 (*0-89324-238-1*, 3817) Natl Assn Broadcasters.

Chamberlain, Denis, ed. Automation & Robotics in Construction XI: Proceedings of the Eleventh International Symposium on Automation & Robotics in Construction--ISARC, Brighton, UK, 24-26 May, 1994. LC 94-14975. 730p. 1994. 351.50 (*0-444-82044-2*, North Holland) Elsevier.

Chamberlain, Diane. Brass Ring. large type ed. LC 94-41568. 677p. 1995. 23.95 (*0-7862-0377-3*) Thorndike Pr.

— Breaking the Silence. 416p. 1999. per. 5.99 (*1-55166-484-4*, 1-66484-6, Mira Bks) Harlequin Bks.

***Chamberlain, Diane.** The Courage Tree. 2001. 22.95 (*1-55166-799-1*, Mira Bks) Harlequin Bks.

Chamberlain, Diane. The Escape Artist. large type ed. LC 96-53101. (Basic Ser.). 590p. 1997. 25.95 (*0-7862-1039-7*) Thorndike Pr.

— Fire & Rain. large type ed. 1993. 90.95 (*0-7862-9997-5*, G K Hall Lrg Type) Mac Lib Ref.

— Reflection. large type ed. 586p. 1996. lib. bdg. 24.95 (*0-7838-1836-X*, G K Hall Lrg Type) Mac Lib Ref.

***Chamberlain, Diane.** Summer's Child. 416p. 2000. per. 5.99 (*1-55166-509-3*, 1-66509-0, Mira Bks) Harlequin Bks.

Chamberlain, Donald, jt. auth. see Lieberman, Betsy.

Chamberlain, Donald, jt. ed. see Putnam, Mark.

Chamberlain, Dorothy, ed. see Ferguson, Otis.

Chamberlain, Dorothy, ed. see Ferguson, Otis, et al.

Chamberlain, E. R. Florence in the Time of the Medici. Reeves, Marjorie, ed. (Then & There Ser.). (Illus.). 96p. (Orig.). (J). (gr. 7-12). 1982. reprint ed. pap. 8.76 (*0-582-20489-5*, 70771) Longman.

***Chamberlain, Ellsworth T.** Trapped in Paradise. LC 98-91000. 1999. pap. 11.95 (*0-533-13005-0*) Vantage.

Chamberlain, Elwyn M. Gates of Fire. 313p. 1984. reprint ed. 20.00 (*0-938190-21-0*); reprint ed. pap. 9.95 (*0-938190-20-2*) North Atlantic.

— Hound Dog. 320p. 1984. 16.95 (*0-938190-25-3*) North Atlantic.

Chamberlain, Eric, compiled by. Catalogue of the Pepys Library at Magdalene College, Cambridge Vol. III: Prints & Drawings: ii. Portraits. 284p. (C). 1994. 215.00 (*0-85991-332-5*, DS Brewer) Boydell & Brewer.

Chamberlain, Franc, ed. Rod Wooden Smoke & Moby Dick. (Contemporary Theatre Review). 174p. 1997. pap. text 21.00 (*90-5702-022-X*, Harwood Acad Pubs) Gordon & Breach.

***Chamberlain, G.** Victor Bonney: Gynaecological Surgeon of the Century. (Illus.). 250p. 2000. 45.00 (*1-85070-712-X*) Prthnon Pub.

Chamberlain, G. W. Glidden: The Descendants of Charles Glidden. Strong, Lucia G., ed. (Illus.). 420p. 1991. reprint ed. pap. 65.00 (*0-8328-2142-X*); reprint ed. lib. bdg. 75.00 (*0-8328-2141-1*) Higginson Bk Co.

Chamberlain, Gary L., jt. auth. see Howell, Patrick J.

Chamberlain, Geoffrey. ABC of Antenatal Care. (Illus.). 84p. 1992. pap. text 25.00 (*0-7279-0313-6*, Pub. by BMJ Pub) Login Brothers Bk Co.

— ABC of Antenatal Care. 2nd ed. 92p. 1994. pap. text 30.00 (*0-7279-0884-7*, Pub. by BMJ Pub) Login Brothers Bk Co.

— ABC of Autenatal Care. 3rd ed. (Illus.). 91p. 1997. pap. 26.00 (*0-7279-1103-1*, Pub. by BMJ Pub) Login Brothers Bk Co.

Chamberlain, Geoffrey, et al, eds. Home Births: The Report of the 1994 Confidential Inquiry by the National Birthday Trust. (Illus.). 310p. 1997. 32.00 (*1-85070-934-3*) Prthnon Pub.

Chamberlain, Geoffrey & Broughton-Pipkin, Fiona. Clinical Physiology in Obstetrics. 3rd ed. LC 97-42723. 510p. 1998. 195.00 (*0-86542-948-0*) Blackwell Sci.

Chamberlain, Geoffrey & Friend, J. A Practice of Obstetrics & Gynecology. 3rd ed. LC 98-32449. (Illus.). 250p. 1998. pap. write for info. (*0-443-05103-8*) Church.

Chamberlain, Geoffrey & Hamilton-Fairly, Diana. Lecture Notes on Obstetrics & Gynaecology. LC 98-39642. 1999. pap. 29.95 (*0-632-04957-X*) Blackwell Sci.

Chamberlain, Geoffrey, jt. ed. see Turnbull, Alec.

Chamberlain, Geoffrey V. P., ed. Gynaecology by Ten Teachers. 16th ed. 320p. 1995. pap. text 29.50 (*0-340-57315-5*, Pub. by E A) OUP.

Chamberlain, Geoffrey V.P. Airships - Cardington. 244p. 1990. 55.00 (*0-86138-025-8*, Pub. by T Dalton) St Mut.

Chamberlain, Geoffrey V.P. Lecture Notes in Obstetrics. 7th ed. (Illus.). 296p. (Orig.). 1996. pap. text 29.95 (*0-86542-681-3*) Blackwell Sci.

Chamberlain, Geoffrey V.P., ed. Obstetrics by Ten Teachers. 16th ed. (Illus.). 384p. 1995. pap. text 29.50 (*0-340-57313-9*, Pub. by E A) OUP.

Chamberlain, Geoffrey V.P. & Dewhurst, C. J. A Practice of Obstetrics & Gynecology. (Illus.). 271p. 1977. 34.95 (*0-8464-1120-2*) Beekman Pubs.

Chamberlain, Geoffrey V.P. & Gunn, Philippa, eds. Birthplace: Report of the Confidential Enquiry into Facilities Available at the Place of Birth Conducted by the National Birthday Trust. LC RG0964.G7. (Wiley Medical Publication). (Illus.). 305p. 1987. reprint ed. pap. 94.60 (*0-608-01637-3*, 206222200002) Bks Demand.

Chamberlain, Geoffrey V.P. & Lumley, Judith, eds. Prepregnancy Care: A Manual for Practice. LC 85-13983. (Wiley-Medical Publication). 289p. reprint ed. pap. 89.60 (*0-7837-3234-1*, 204325300007) Bks Demand.

Chamberlain, Geoffrey V.P., et al. Lecture Notes on Gynaecology. 7th rev. ed. (Lecture Notes Ser.). (Illus.). 275p. 1996. pap. 29.95 (*0-632-03111-5*) Blackwell Sci.

Chamberlain, George W. Babson Genealogy, 1637-1930. 104p. 1995. reprint ed. pap. 19.00 (*0-8328-4738-0*); reprint ed. lib. bdg. 29.00 (*0-8328-4737-2*) Higginson Bk Co.

— Soldiers of the American Revolution of Lebanon. (Illus.). 48p. 1997. reprint ed. pap. 10.00 (*0-8328-5866-8*) Higginson Bk Co.

— York County Marriage Returns, 1771-1794. 14p. 1986. reprint ed. pap. 2.50 (*0-935207-34-1*) Danbury Hse Bks.

Chamberlain, George W., ed. Lebanon Vital Records, to the Year 1892: Volume I, Births; Volume III, Deaths. (Illus.). 317p. 1997. reprint ed. pap. 39.00 (*0-8328-5865-X*) Higginson Bk Co.

— Vital Records of Lebanon, Maine to the Year 1892 Vol. 1: Births. 1986. reprint ed. pap. 6.00 (*0-935207-51-1*) Danbury Hse Bks.

Chamberlain, George W., jt. auth. see Chase, John C.

Chamberlain, Hope S. History of Wake County: With Sketches of Those Who Have Most Influenced Its Development. (Illus.). 302p. 1997. reprint ed. lib. bdg. 35.00 (*0-8328-6909-0*) Higginson Bk Co.

Chamberlain, Houston S. Foundations of the Nineteenth Century, 2 vols., Set. LC 67-29735. 1968. reprint ed. 119.00 (*0-86527-069-4*) Fertig.

— Political Ideals. Jacob, Alexander, tr. from GER. Orig. Title: Politische Ideale. 135p. (Orig.). 1996. pap. 15.00 (*0-937944-08-4*) Natl Vanguard.

Chamberlain, Isabel C., jt. auth. see Williams, Pierce.

Chamberlain, Izanna L. Prairie Memories: An Eighteen Ninety-One Iowa Album in Painting & Verse. Chamberlain, Lowell & Sherinian, Mary, eds. LC 91-66691. (Illus.). 64p. 1991. 35.00 (*0-945213-04-2*) Rudi Pub.

Chamberlain, J. M., et al, eds. Electronic Properties of Multilayers & Low-Dimensional Semiconductor Structures. LC 90-44242. (NATO ASI Ser.: Vol. 231). (Illus.). 490p. (C). 1990. text 174.00 (*0-306-43662-0*, Kluwer Plenum) Kluwer Academic.

Chamberlain, J. M. & Miles, R. E., eds. New Directions in Terahertz Technology. LC 97-6835. (NATO ASI Series: Vol. 334). 424p. 1997. text 234.00 (*0-7923-4537-1*) Kluwer Academic.

***Chamberlain, J. Martyn, ed.** Terahertz Spectroscopy & Applications II. 45p. 1999. pap. text 111.00 (*0-8194-3314-4*) SPIE.

Chamberlain, Jacob C. A Bibliography of the First Editions in Book Form of the Writings of Henry Wadsworth Longfellow. LC 72-3116. (American Literature Ser.: No. 49). 1972. reprint ed. lib. bdg. 75.00 (*0-8383-1513-5*) M S G Haskell Hse.

***Chamberlain, James R., ed.** The Ram Khamaeng Controversy: Collected Papers. (Illus.). 592p. (C). 1999. pap. text 42.50 (*0-472-53051-8*) Ctr S&SE Asian.

***Chamberlain, Jane & Ree, Jonathan, eds.** The Kierkegaard Reader. 2001. 64.95 (*0-631-20467-9*); pap. 26.95 (*0-631-20468-7*) Blackwell Pubs.

Chamberlain, Jane, jt. auth. see Ree, Jonathan.

Chamberlain, Jeffrey & Borland, Lee. Alarm Company Client Agreements. (Illus.). vi, 565p. 1992. ring bd. 225.00 (*1-892594-02-1*) Security Pr Inc.

Chamberlain, Jeffrey, jt. auth. see Thomas, Lee O.

Chamberlain, Jeffrey S. Accommodating High Churchmen: The Clergy of Sussex, 1700-1745. LC 96-25377. 216p. 1997. text 32.50 (*0-252-02308-0*) U of Ill Pr.

Chamberlain, Jeffrey T., jt. auth. see Gaeng, Paul A.

An Asterisk (*) at the beginning of an entry indicates that the title is appearing for the first time.

Chamberlain, Jocelyn & Moss, Sue, eds. Evaluation of Cancer Screening. LC 95-23890. (Focus on Cancer Ser.). 204p. 1995. 42.95 (*3-540-19957-8*) Spr-Verlag.

Chamberlain, John. The Enterprising Americans: A Business History of the United States. 282p. 1991. reprint ed. 14.95 (*0-930464-41-9*) Inst Christian.

— Gondolas & Dooms Day Flotilla. Wright, Charles, ed. (Illus.). 47p. 1991. pap. 20.00 (*0-944521-21-5*) Dia Ctr Arts.

— Letters Written by John Chamberlain During the Reign of Queen Elizabeth. Williams, Sarah, ed. (Camden Society, London. Publications, First Ser.: No. 79). reprint ed. 45.00 (*0-404-50179-6*) AMS Pr.

***Chamberlain, John.** Medieval Arts Doctrines on Ambiguity & Their Place in Langland's Poetics. 176p. 2000. 55.00 (*0-7735-2073-2*, Pub. by McG-Queens Univ Pr) CUP Services.

Chamberlain, John. The Roots of Capitalism. LC 76-58035. 1977. reprint ed. 10.00 (*0-913966-23-1*) Liberty Fund.

— The Turnabout Years: American Cultural Life, 1900-1950. 254p. (Orig.). 1992. pap. 12.95 (*0-915463-61-X*) Jameson Bks.

Chamberlain, John B., et al. The Sea Urchin: Molecular Biology, 3 vols., Vol. 2. 188p. (C). 1973. text 31.50 (*0-8422-7121-X*) Irvington.

Chamberlain, Jonathan. Fighting Cancer: A Survival Guide. 342p. 1998. pap. 19.95 (*0-7472-7728-1*, Pub. by Headline Bk Pub) Trafalgar.

Chamberlain, Jonathan M. Student Handbook for Eliminating Your SDBs: Self-Defeating Behaviors. 3rd ed. (Illus.). ix, 134p. (C). 1979. pap. text, wbk. ed. 5.50 (*0-8425-1763-4*, Friends of the Library) Brigham.

Chamberlain, Joseph. Analysis of Drugs in Biological Fluids. 320p. 1985. 161.00 (*0-8493-5144-8*, RB52) CRC Pr.

— Analysis of Drugs in Biological Fluids. 2nd ed. LC 95-19022. 368p. 1995. boxed set 139.95 (*0-8493-2492-0*, 2492) CRC Pr.

Chamberlain, Joseph, ed. Chemistry & Physics of the Stratosphere. 171p. 1976. pap. 3.00 (*0-87590-221-9*) Am Geophysical.

— Reviews of Lunar Sciences. (Illus.). 540p. 1977. reprint ed. pap. 5.00 (*0-87590-220-0*) Am Geophysical.

Chamberlain, Joseph P. Regime of the International Rivers: Danube & Rhine. LC 68-57565. (Columbia University. Studies in the Social Sciences: No. 237). reprint ed. 29.50 (*0-404-51237-2*) AMS Pr.

Chamberlain, Joseph P., et al, eds. Judicial Function in Federal Administrative Agencies. LC 79-128875. (Select Bibliographies Reprint Ser.). 1977. 21.95 (*0-8369-5495-5*) Ayer.

Chamberlain, Joseph W. Physics of the Aurora & Airglow. LC 95-25022. 1995. pap. 55.00 (*0-87590-857-8*) Am Geophysical.

Chamberlain, Joseph W. & Hunten, Donald M. Theory of Planetary Atmospheres: An Introduction to Their Physics & Chemistry. 2nd ed. (International Geophysics Ser.). 481p. 1989. reprint ed. pap. text 62.00 (*0-12-167252-2*) Acad Pr.

Chamberlain, Joshua J. Passing of the Armies. 1997. reprint ed. 30.00 (*1-56515-022-8*) Collect Reprints.

Chamberlain, Joshua J. Through Blood & Fire: Selected Civil War Papers of Major General Joshua Chamberlain. LC 95-25430. (Illus.). 240p. 1996. 19.95 (*0-8117-1750-X*) Stackpole.

Chamberlain, Joshua L. Bayonet! Forward: My Civil War Reminiscences. (Illus.). 328p. 1994. pap. 17.95 (*1-879664-22-4*) Stan Clark Military.

–Bayonet! Forward: My Civil War Reminiscences. LC 94-233618. (Illus.). 328p. 1994. 25.00 (*1-879664-21-6*) Stan Clark Military.

BAYONET! FORWARD: MY CIVIL WAR REMINISCENCES by Joshua Lawrence Chamberlain is a compilation of the General's most substantial Civil War addresses & writings. This collection contains chapters on the campaigns of Fredericksburg, Gettysburg, Petersburg, the White Oak Road, Five Forks, Appomattox, as well as Chamberlain's personal account of the surrender of the Confederate Army & the Grand Review of the Army of the Potomac. As a prominent member of the Fifth Army Corps, Chamberlain's reminiscences also serve as a history of that Corps' service from Fredericksburg through the end of the war at Appomattox. Also contained in this informative assemblage are appendices including official battle reports of the Gettysburg & Appomattox campaigns, a moving account of the last salute to the Army of Northern Virginia, monument dedication exercises on the Gettysburg Battlefield, & a stirring memorial address on the life of President Abraham Lincoln. BAYONET! FORWARD is further enhanced with photographs, maps, a bibliography, index & full color covers. Anyone interested in General Joshua Lawrence Chamberlain, the Fifth Army Corps or the American Civil War, will find this reading insightful & entertaining. A masterful publishing event. Order from: Stan Clark Military Books, 915 Fairview Ave., Gettysburg, PA 17325; Phone: 717-337-1728; Fax: 717-337-0581. *Publisher Paid Annotation.*

— Passing of the Armies. 368p. 1992. mass mkt. 6.99 (*0-553-29992-1*) Bantam.

— The Passing of the Armies: An Account of the Final Campaign of the Army of the Potomac, Based upon Personal Reminiscences of the Fifth Army Corps. LC 98-35167. (Illus.). xxxvii, 407p. 1998. pap. 16.95 (*0-8032-6390-2*, Bison Books) U of Nebr Pr.

–The Passing of the Armies: The Last Campaign of the Armies. (Illus.). 402p. 1995. reprint ed. 25.00 (*1-879664-18-6*); reprint ed. pap. 17.95 (*1-879664-19-4*) Stan Clark Military.

"THE PASSING OF THE ARMIES is essential reading for those who wish to touch the mind & character of Joshua Lawrence Chamberlain."--John Peterson. "There is real human depth & critical judgement in some of his original opinions of Grant & Lee, formed on the field. His account of the arrival at the front of the news of Lincoln's assassination is a masterly stroke."--Springfield Republican. "...the best study by a contemporary on the last days of the Civil War."--Willard Wallace. "Chamberlain had a most successful military career capped by his being chosen to command the Union troops who were present when the Army of Northern Virginia laid down their arms. His account of the final Virginia campaign is superb. He was as great a writer as he was a fighter...One of the classics of Civil War literature."--The Union Bookshelf. "The fullest account of the surrender of the Army of Northern Virginia, written by the generous Federal general who commanded at the laying down of arms."--Clifford Dowdey. "The climax of Chamberlain's readable reminiscences is his moving description of the surrender ceremonies at Appomattox."--Civil War Books. Stan Clark Military Books, 915 Fairview Avenue, Gettysburg, PA 17325; Phone: 717-337-1728; Fax: 717-337-0581. *Publisher Paid Annotation.*

Chamberlain, Jules K. Disasters (Earthquakes, Hurricanes, Floods & Droughts) & Relief Work: Index of New Information. (Illus.). 160p. 1998. 47.50 (*0-7883-1646-X*); pap. 44.50 (*0-7883-1647-8*) ABBE Pubs Assn.

***Chamberlain, Kathleen P.** Under Sacred Ground: A History of Navajo Oil, 1920s-1970s. LC 00-8608. (Illus.). 2000. 35.00 (*0-8263-2043-0*) U of NM Pr.

Chamberlain, Kathryn A., jt. auth. see Hamner, Candace J.

Chamberlain, Kerry, jt. auth. see Reker, Gary T.

Chamberlain, Kerry, jt. ed. see Reker, Gary T.

Chamberlain, Lawrence. The Work of the Bond House. LC 75-2626. (Wall Street & the Security Market Ser.). 1975. reprint ed. 20.95 (*0-405-06952-9*) Ayer.

Chamberlain, Lawrence H. President, Congress & Legislation. LC 72-181927. (Columbia University. Studies in the Social Sciences: No. 523). reprint ed. 32.50 (*0-404-51523-1*) AMS Pr.

Chamberlain, Lesley. The Festive Food of Russia. (Illus.). 64p. 1996. 9.95 (*1-85626-195-6*, Pub. by Cathie Kyle) Trafalgar.

— Nietzsche in Turin: An Intimate Biography. LC 98-51549. 272p. 1998. pap. 13.00 (*0-312-19938-4*) St Martin.

— The Practical Encyclopedia of East European Cooking: The Definitive Collection of Traditional Recipes, from the Baltic to the Black Sea. (Illus.). 256p. 1999. 40.00 (*0-7548-0071-7*, Lorenz Bks) Anness Pub.

Chamberlain, Linda L., jt. auth. see Butz, Michael R.

Chamberlain, Linda L., jt. auth. see McCown, William G.

Chamberlain, Logan V. Using Herbs: Choose the Best Manufactured Products, Understand Herb Supplement Labels, Design Your Own Herbal Program. LC 98-8457. (Illus.). 96p. 1998. pap. 9.95 (*1-883010-49-7*) Interweave.

Chamberlain, Lorna, jt. auth. see Preece, Rod.

Chamberlain, Lowell, ed. see Chamberlain, Izanna L.

Chamberlain, Lyn & Chamberlain, Tony. Cross-Country Skiing in New England: Recommended Ski Touring-Touring Facilities & Trails. 4th ed. LC 85-17561. (Illus.). 224p. 1995. pap. 12.95 (*1-56440-837-X*) Globe Pequot.

Chamberlain, M. Pequeno Libro de la Navidad.Tr. of Little Christmas Concertina Book. (SPA.). 30p. (J). 1986. 2.99 (*1-56063-270-4*, 494010) Editorial Unilit.

Chamberlain, M., ed. & tr. see Fabri, Friedrich.

Chamberlain, M. Anne, et al, eds. Traumatic Brain Injury Rehabilitation: Services, Treatments & Outcomes. 286p. 1995. pap. 45.00 (*1-56593-307-9*, 0631) Singular Publishing.

Chamberlain, M. Anne, ed. see Goodwill, C. John.

Chamberlain, M. E. The Scramble for Africa. LC 74-177119. (Seminar Studies in History). 163p. (C). 1989. pap. text 15.80 (*0-582-35204-5*) Longman.

Chamberlain, Margaret, jt. auth. see Umansky, Kaye.

Chamberlain, Mariam K. Women in Academe: Progress & Prospects. (Illus.). 448p. 1991. pap. 14.95 (*0-87154-218-8*) Russell Sage.

Chamberlain, Mariam K., ed. Women in Academe: Progress & Prospects. LC 88-37217. 400p. 1989. 45.00 (*0-87154-204-8*) Russell Sage.

Chamberlain, Mariam K. & Fiol-Matta, Liza, eds. Women of Color & the Multicultural Curriculum: Transforming the College Classroom. LC 94-8242. 390p. (C). 1994. 35.00 (*1-55861-082-0*); pap. 18.95 (*1-55861-083-9*) Feminist Pr.

Chamberlain, Marisha. Scheherazade. 1985. pap. 5.25 (*0-8222-0996-9*) Dramatists Play.

Chamberlain, Marjorie D. Johannes Dyckman of Fort Orange & His Descendants Vol. 1: The First Five Generations. LC 88-92677. (Illus.). 150p. 1988. write for info. (*0-9621789-0-X*) M D Chamberlain.

***Chamberlain, Mark.** Wanting More: The Challenge of Enjoyment in the Age of Addiction. 2000. pap. 15.95 (*1-57345-817-1*, Shadow Mount) Deseret Bk.

***Chamberlain, Mark D.** Kids Are from Jupiter: A Guide for Puzzled Parents. LC 99-53916. 160p. 2000. pap. 14.95 (*1-57345-575-X*, Shadow Mount) Deseret Bk.

Chamberlain, Mark D., jt. auth. see Byrd, A. Dean.

Chamberlain, Martha & Adams, Mary. Hymn Devotions for All Seasons. 64p. 1989. pap. 1.98 (*0-687-18120-8*) Abingdon.

Chamberlain, Mary. Caribbean Migration: Globalised Identities. LC 97-45099. 272p. (C). 1998. 85.00 (*0-415-16580-6*) Routledge.

— Fenwomen: A Portrait of Women in an English Village. 3.95 (*0-7043-3806-8*, Pub. by Quartet) Charles River Bks.

Chamberlain, Mary & Thompson, Paul R., eds. Narrative & Genre. LC 97-13178. 224p. (C). 1998. 75.00 (*0-415-15198-8*) Routledge.

Chamberlain, Mellen. A Documentary History of Chelsea, Including the Boston Precincts of Wimmisimmet, Rumney Marsh & Pullen Point, 1624-1824, Vol. I. (Illus.). 712p. 1989. reprint ed. lib. bdg. 74.00 (*0-8328-0816-4*, MA0193) Higginson Bk Co.

— A Documentary History of Chelsea, Including the Boston Precincts of Wimmisimmet, Rumney Marsh & Pullen Point, 1624-1824, Vol. II. (Illus.). 793p. 1989. reprint ed. lib. bdg. 81.00 (*0-8328-0817-2*, MA0194) Higginson Bk Co.

Chamberlain, Mildred M. The Rhode Island 1777 Military Census. LC 84-82485. 181p. 1985. 14.00 (*0-8063-1107-X*) Genealog Pub.

Chamberlain, Muriel. Longman Companion to European Decolonization in the 20th Century. LC 98-14251. (C). 1998. 73.13 (*0-582-07774-5*) Addison-Wesley.

— Longman Companion to European Decolonization in the 20th Century. LC 98-14251. 360p. (C). 1998. pap. text 25.50 (*0-582-07773-7*) Longman.

— Lord Palmerston. LC 87-28827. (Political Portraits Ser.). 135p. 1988. 22.95 (*0-8132-0663-4*); pap. 9.95 (*0-8132-0664-2*) Cath U Pr.

Chamberlain, Muriel E. Pax Britainnica. (Studies in Modern European History). (Illus.). 224p. (C). 1989. text 37.95 (*0-582-03079-X*, 78199) Longman.

— Pax Britannica? British Foreign Policy 1789-1914 (Studies in Modern History) (Illus.). 224p. (C). 1989. pap. text 23.95 (*0-582-49442-7*, 78199) Longman.

Chamberlain, Nancy & Power, John. A Structure for Intercommunity Governance of North Central Victoria, Vol. 5. 1993. pap. 60.00 (*0-7300-2011-8*, PTSSSO, Pub. by Deakin Univ) St Mut.

Chamberlain, Narcissa G. & Kingsland, Jane F. The Prints of Samuel Chamberlain N. A. 1984. 100.00 (*0-89073-095-4*, 300) Boston Public Lib.

Chamberlain, Narcissa G., jt. auth. see Chamberlain, Samuel.

Chamberlain, Neil W. Intellectual Odyssey - An Economist's Ideological Journey. LC 96-67504. 224p. 1996. 19.95 (*1-57197-020-7*) Pentland Pr.

Chamberlain, Neil W. & Schilling, Jane M. Impact of Strikes: Their Social & Economic Costs. LC 73-11841. 257p. 1973. reprint ed. lib. bdg. 65.00 (*0-8371-7066-4*, CHIS, Greenwood Pr) Greenwood.

Chamberlain, Neville. In Search of Peace. LC 77-156627. (Essay Index Reprint Ser.). 1977. reprint ed. 20.95 (*0-8369-2274-3*) Ayer.

***Chamberlain, Neville & Self, Robert C.** The Neville Chamberlain Diary Letters. LC 00-26601. 2000. write for info. (*1-84014-691-5*, Pub. by Ashgate Pub) Ashgate Pub Co.

Chamberlain, Newell D. The Call of Gold. LC 81-50164. (Illus.). 187p. 1981. reprint ed. pap. 4.95 (*0-934136-12-2*) Good Life.

Chamberlain, Nugent F. & Reed, J. J. The Analytical Chemistry of Sulfur & Its Compounds: Nuclear Magnetic Resonance Data of Sulfur Compounds, Pt. 3. Karchmer, J. H., ed. LC 77-84969. (Chemical Analysis Ser.: Vol. 29). 320p. reprint ed. pap. 99.20 (*0-8357-5450-2*, 201243300081) Bks Demand.

Chamberlain of the Lews Staff, jt. auth. see MacKenzie, John M.

Chamberlain of the Lews Staff, jt. auth. see Mackenzie, John M.

Chamberlain, Patricia. Being Somebody: Spring the Mind-Traps That Keep You Fat & Frustrated With Your Life. Kyper, Barbara, ed. (Illus.). 1991. pap. text 14.99 (*0-685-49324-5*); 19.99 (*1-880011-01-8*); audio 9.99 (*1-880011-02-6*) Dundas-Devonhills Assoc.

— Family Connections, Vol. 5. 2nd ed. Patterson, Scot, ed. (Illus.). 141p. 1998. reprint ed. pap. 24.95 (*1-892194-00-7*) NW Media.

Chamberlain, Paul. Can We Be Good Without God? A Conversation about Truth, Morality, Culture, & a Few Other Things That Matter. LC 95-50077. 202p. (Orig.). 1996. pap. 12.99 (*0-8308-1686-0*, 1686) InterVarsity.

***Chamberlain, Paul.** Final Wishes: A Cautionary Tale on Death, Dignity & Physician-Assisted Suicide. LC 99-86866. 228p. 2000. pap. 12.99 (*0-8308-2259-3*) InterVarsity.

***Chamberlain, Peter.** Encyclopedia of German Tanks of World War Two: The Complete Illustrated Dictionary of German Bat. 272p. 1999. pap. text 19.95 (*1-85409-518-8*) Arms & Armour.

Chamberlain, Peter & Ellis, Christopher. British & American Tanks of World War II. LC 69-13591. (Illus.). 1981. 15.00 (*0-668-01867-4*, Arco) Macmillan Gen Ref.

Chamberlain, R. Early Loading Tools & Bullet Moulds. 1988. 7.50 (*0-913150-62-2*) Pioneer Pr.

Chamberlain, R. H. & Quigley, Tom. Cartridge Reloading Tools of the Past. (Illus.). 100p. 1997. pap. 25.00 (*0-9661334-0-4*) T Quigley.

Chamberlain, R. L. Computer Systems Validation for the Pharmaceutical & Medical Device Industries. 216p. 1994. 235.00 (*0-9631489-0-7*) Alaren Pr.

— Computer Systems Validation for the Pharmaceutical & Medical Device Industries. 2nd ed. 350p. 1994. 247.00 incl. disk (*0-9631489-5-8*) Alaren Pr.

Chamberlain, Ronald. The Surgical Intern Pocket Survival Guide. 78p. 1993. pap. text 7.50 (*0-9634063-5-3*) Intl Med Pub.

Chamberlain, Rudolph W. There Is No Truce. LC 74-124229. (Select Bibliographies Reprint Ser.). 1977. 25.95 (*0-8369-5418-1*) Ayer.

Chamberlain, Russel. Florence & Tuscany. (Illustrated Travel Guides from Thomas Cook Ser.). (Illus.). 192p. 1994. pap. 12.95 (*0-8442-9055-6*, Passprt Bks) NTC Contemp Pub Co.

***Chamberlain, Safford.** An Unsung Cat: The Life & Music of Warne Marsh. (Studies in Jazz). 440p. 2000. 59.50 (*0-8108-3718-8*) Scarecrow.

Chamberlain, Samuel. Domestic Architecture in Rural France. (Illus.). 96p. (Orig.). 1986. reprint ed. pap. 7.95 (*0-8038-1578-6*) Archit CT.

— My Confession: The Recollections of a Rogue. limited ed. LC 96-31788. (Illus.). 400p. 1996. 165.00 (*0-87611-157-6*, Pub. by Tex St Hist Assn) Tex A&M Univ Pr.

— The New England Image. (Illus.). 192p. 1994. 42.50 (*0-942655-08-7*) Archit CT.

Chamberlain, Samuel & Chamberlain, Narcissa G. New England Rooms (1639-1863) (Illus.). 192p. 1993. 40.00 (*0-942655-06-0*) Archit CT.

Chamberlain, Samuel E. My Confession: The Recollections of a Rogue. Goezman, William H., ed. LC 96-31788. (Illus.). 400p. 1996. 60.00 (*0-87611-156-8*) Tex St Hist Assn.

Chamberlain, Shannin. My ABC Book of Cancer. (Illus.). 40p. (J). 1991. pap. 6.95 (*0-912184-07-8*) Synergistic Pr.

Chamberlain, Stephen C., ed. see Fauer, Jon.

Chamberlain, Susan. Beyond the Psychic Line. (Illus.). 192p. 1998. pap. 14.75 (*0-9663990-1-3*) Ancora Pubns.

— Birds! LC 98-24682. (Fun & Care Bks.). (Illus.). 112p. 1998. pap. 16.95 (*1-889540-07-2*) Bowtie Press.

***Chamberlain, Ted.** Spring 1999 Syllabus & Study Guide for ER130. 1998. pap. 6.67 (*0-13-021557-0*) Prntice Hall Bks.

***Chamberlain, Theodore.** Earth Science System: Syllabus & Study Guide. 174p. 1999. pap. write for info. (*0-13-027368-6*) P-H.

Chamberlain, Thomas H. The Generals & the Admirals, Some Leaders of the United States Forces in World War II. 1977. 22.95 (*0-8369-2362-6*) Ayer.

Chamberlain, Timothy J., ed. Eighteenth Century German Criticism: Johann Gottfried Herder, Jakob M R Lenz, Gotthold Ephraim Lessing & Others. (German Library: Vol. 11). 324p. 1992. 39.50 (*0-8264-0700-5*); pap. 19.95 (*0-8264-0701-3*) Continuum.

Chamberlain, Tony, jt. auth. see Chamberlain, Lyn.

Chamberlain, Trevor & Gair, Angela. Trevor Chamberlain: A Personal View: Light & Atmosphere in Watercolor. LC 99-494992. (Illus.). 128p. 1999. 29.95 (*0-7153-0845-9*, Pub. by D & C Pub) Sterling.

Chamberlain, V. B., jt. ed. see Rogers, Robert S.

Chamberlain, Valerie M. Teen Guide. 7th ed. 544p. 1989. text 30.00 (*0-07-007847-5*) McGraw.

— Teen Guide to Homemaking. 5th ed. 1982. text 31.08 (*0-07-007843-2*) McGraw.

Chamberlain, Valerie M., et al. Teen Guide. 6th ed. O'Neill, Martha, ed. (Illus.). 528p. (YA). 1985. text 30.00 (*0-07-007842-4*); pap. text, teacher ed. 11.68 (*0-07-007831-9*) McGraw.

Chamberlain, Valerie M., jt. auth. see Kelly, Joan B.

Chamberlain, Von Del, see Del Chamberlain, Von.

Chamberlain, Von Del, jt. ed. see Hanle, Paul A.

Chamberlain, William. Multidisciplinary Child Abuse & Neglect Team Manual. 77p. 3.50 (*0-318-16356-X*, B10) Regional Inst Social Welfare.

Chamberlain, Wilt. Who's Running the Asylum? Inside the Insane World of Sports Today. (Illus.). 350p. (Orig.). 1996. pap. 12.95 (*1-57901-005-9*) Intl Promotions.

— Wilt Chamberlain: A View from Above. (Illus.). 304p. 1992. mass mkt. 6.99 (*0-451-17493-3*, Sig) NAL.

Chamberlaine, Sally, jt. auth. see Prince, Jan.

Chamberland, Luc. Programming VisualAge for Java Version 2. 1998. pap. text 49.99 (*0-471-31730-6*) Wiley.

Chamberland, Paul. The Courage of Poetry. 88p. pap. 8.00 (*0-919349-75-7*) Guernica Editions.

Chamberlaon, Anne. Chicken Dishes from Around the World. 144p. 1995. pap. text 9.95 (*0-572-02139-9*, Pub. by W Foulsham) Trans-Atl Phila.

***Chamberlayne, C. G.** The Vestry Book of Kingston Parish: Mathews County Virginia 1679-1796. (Illus.). 187p. 1999. pap. 18.50 (*0-7884-1323-6*, C309) Heritage Bk.

Chamberlayne, C. G., ed. The Vestry Book of Blisland (Blissland) Parish, New Kent & James City Counties, Virginia, 1721-1786. LC 79-16401. lxii, 277p. 1979. reprint ed. 15.00 (*0-88490-030-4*) Library of VA.

C

Chamberlayne, Churchill G. Births from the Bristol Parish Register of Henrico, Prince George & Dinwiddie Counties, Virginia, 1720-1798. LC 74-8784. 133p. 1998. reprint ed. pap. 16.00 (0-8063-0627-0) Clearfield Co.

***Chamberlayne, Churchill G.** Colonial Virginia Parish Records: The Vestry Book & Register of Bristol Parish, Virginia, 1720-1789. 419p. 1999. reprint ed. pap. 29.50 (0-8063-4843-7) Clearfield Co.

Chamberlayne, Churchill G. The Vestry Book & Register of Bristol Parish, VA, 1720-1789. LC 98-227821. 419p. 1998. pap. 32.00 (0-7884-0919-0, C304) Heritage Bk.

***Chamberlayne, Churchill G.** The Vestry Book of Blisland (Blissland) Parish, New Kent & James City Counties, Virginia, 1721-1786. 277p. 1999. reprint ed. pap. 28.50 (0-8063-4848-8) Clearfield Co.

— The Vestry Book of Kingston Parish: Matthews County, Virginia, 1679-1796. 161p. 1999. reprint ed. pap. 20.00 (0-8063-4842-9) Clearfield Co.

— The Vestry Book of Petsworth Parish, Glouster County, Virginia, 1677-1793. 429p. 1999. reprint ed. pap. 31.50 (0-8063-4845-3) Clearfield Co.

— The Vestry Book of St. Paul's Parish, Hanover County, Virginia, 1706-1786. 672p. 1999. reprint ed. pap. 52.50 (0-8063-4847-X) Clearfield Co.

— The Vestry Book of Stratton Major Parish, King & Queen County, Virginia, 1729-1783. 257p. 1999. reprint ed. pap. 25.00 (0-8063-4846-1) Clearfield Co.

Chamberlayne, John H. China & Its Religious Inheritance. 175p. (Orig.). pap. 17.95 (1-85756-052-3, Pub. by Janus Pubng) Paul & Co Pubs.

— Ham Chamberlayne-Virginian: Letters & Papers of an Artillery Officer in the War for Southern Independence, 1861-1865. (Illus.). 440p. 1992. 45.00 (1-56837-045-8) Broadfoot.

Chamberlayne, Prue. Welfare & Culture in Europe, Vol. 1. 1999. pap. 34.95 (1-85302-700-6) Jessica Kingsley.

***Chamberlayne, Prue, et al, eds.** Turn to Biographical Methods in Social Science: Comparative Issues & Examples. LC 99-48261. 368p. (C). 2000. text. write for info. (0-415-22837-9) Routledge.

***Chamberlayne, Prue, et al.** The Turn to Biographical Methods in Social Science. LC 99-48261. (Social Research Today Ser.). 256p. 2000. pap. 24.99 (0-415-22838-7) Routledge.

Chamberlayne Staff. The Vestry Book of Christ Church Parish Middlesex County, Virginia, 1663-1767. LC 98-205972. 379p. 1998. reprint ed. pap. 28.50 (0-7884-0806-2, C305) Heritage Bk.

Chamberlin. A Glossary of West Worcestershire Words. (English Dialect Society Publications: No. 36). 1969. reprint ed. pap. 25.00 (0-8115-0461-1) Periodicals Srv.

Chamberlin, Joseph P., tr. see North, Thomas J., et al.

Chamberlin, Al. Circle of Courage. 1991. 17.95 (0-533-09092-X) Vantage.

***Chamberlin, Ann.** Joan of Arc Novel 2. 2000. text 24.95 (0-312-87284-4) St Martin.

— Leaving Eden. 240p. 2000. pap. 13.95 (0-312-87511-8) Forge NYC.

Chamberlin, Ann. Leaving Eden. LC 99-22072. 240p. 1999. text 23.95 (0-312-86550-3) Forge Pr.

***Chamberlin, Ann.** Leaving Eden. 2000. mass mkt. 6.99 (0-8125-9001-5) Tor Bks.

— The Merlin of St. Gilles' Well. 2000. pap. 13.95 (0-312-87591-6) St Martin.

— The Merlin of St. Gilles' Well. 2000. mass mkt. 6.99 (0-8125-9002-3) Tor Bks.

— The Merlin of St. Gilles' Well. 2nd ed. LC 99-22204. 320p. 1999. 23.95 (0-312-86551-1, Pub. by Tor Bks) St Martin.

— Reign of the Favored Women. pap. write for info. (0-312-87684-X) St Martin.

Chamberlin, Ann. Sofia. 1998. mass mkt. 6.99 (0-8125-5386-1, Pub. by Tor Bks) St Martin.

— The Sultan's Daughter. LC 96-44192. 1997. text 24.95 (0-312-86203-2) St Martin.

— The Sultan's Daughter. 1998. mass mkt. 6.99 (0-8125-5385-3, Pub. by Tor Bks) St Martin.

— Tamar. 448p. 1994. pap. 5.99 (0-8125-2370-9, Pub. by Tor Bks) St Martin.

Chamberlin, Anthony & Stenburg, Kurt. Play & Practice! Graded Games for English Language Teaching. 128p. 1979. pap. 14.06 (0-8442-5213-1) NTC Contemp Pub Co.

Chamberlin, Ballantyne. Animal Physiology. (Biology Ser.). 2000. pap. text 48.00 (0-534-53064-8) Brooks-Cole.

Chamberlin, Bill F., jt. auth. see Middleton, Kent R.

Chamberlin, Bonita E. & Bowersox, Gary W. Gemstones of Afghanistan. LC 95-75921. (Illus.). 240p. 1995. 60.00 (0-945005-19-9) Geoscience Pr.

Chamberlin, Brewster, jt. ed. see Foner, Philip S.

Chamberlin, David C. The Conceptual Approach to Genealogy: Essential Methodology for Organizing & Compiling Genealogical Records. Stewart, Brad, ed. (Illus.). 264p. 1998. 24.95 (1-877677-87-6) Herit Quest.

Chamberlin, Don. A Complete Guide to DB2 Universal Database: IBM's Object-Relational Database Systems, Database 2. 2nd ed. LC 98-16057. 840p. 1998. pap. 59.95 (1-55860-482-0) Morgan Kaufmann.

Chamberlin, Donald. Using the New DB2: IBM's Object-Relational Database System. 708p. 1996. pap. text 49.95 (1-55860-373-5) Morgan Kaufmann.

Chamberlin, E. R. The Black Death. (Illus.). 1995. reprint ed. student ed. 39.00 (1-56696-043-6) Jackdaw.

Chamberlin, E. R., compiled by. Martin Luther. 39.00 (1-56696-070-3) Jackdaw.

Chamberlin, Edward H. Theory of Monopolistic Competition: A Re-Orientation of the Theory of Value. 8th ed. LC 63-649. (Economic Studies: No. 38). 410p. 1962. 27.50 (0-674-88125-7) HUP.

— Towards a More General Theory of Value. LC 82-6259. 318p. 1982. reprint ed. lib. bdg. 69.50 (0-313-23590-2, CHTO, Greenwood Pr) Greenwood.

Chamberlin, Everett. Chicago & Its Suburbs. LC 73-2902. (Metropolitan America Ser.). (Illus.). 474p. 1977. reprint ed. 31.95 (0-405-05388-6) Ayer.

Chamberlin, F. The Balearics. 1976. lib. bdg. 59.95 (0-8490-1473-5) Gordon Pr.

Chamberlin, Henry H., tr. see Horace.

Chamberlin, Ida. The Story of Alice. LC 96-11605. (Illus.). 56p. (J). 1997. pap. 12.00 (1-880158-13-2) J N Townsend.

Chamberlin, J. Allen, jt. auth. see McCormick, Carlynn L.

Chamberlin, J. Edward. Come Back to Me My Language: Poetry & the West Indies. LC 92-21910. 328p. (C). 1993. text 44.95 (0-252-01973-3); pap. text 17.95 (0-252-06297-3) U of Ill Pr.

Chamberlin, J. Gordon. Church vs. Education: A Battle Lost. viii, 140p. (Orig.). 1994. pap. 13.95 (0-915481-02-2) Ed Pr.

— I Don't Have No Education & Other Reflections. LC 83-25491. 138p. 1984. 11.75 (0-915481-01-4); pap. 7.75 (0-915481-00-6) Ed Pr.

***Chamberlin, J. Gordon.** Upon Whom We Depend: The American Poverty System. LC 98-26799. (Counterpoints: Vol. 98). 200p. (C). 1999. pap. text 24.95 (0-8204-4151-1) P Lang Pubng.

Chamberlin, Jane. Cool Grey City of Love: A Celebration of San Francisco. Leer, Dustin, ed. LC 96-61193. (Illus.). 56p. (Orig.). 1997. pap., per. 10.95 (0-9653987-0-6) Tinkachew Pr.

Chamberlin, John, ed. see Saint Benedict of Nursia.

Chamberlin, John H., jt. auth. see Gellings, Clark W.

Chamberlin, Jonathan M. Eliminate Your SDBs: Self-Defeating Behaviors. rev. ed. LC 77-27634. (Illus.). xiv, 193p. 1978. pap. 12.95 (0-8425-0998-4, Friends of the Library) Brigham.

Chamberlin, Joseph. Nomads & Listeners. Waxman, Samuel M., ed. LC 68-22905. (Essay Index Reprint Ser.). 1977. 19.95 (0-8369-0287-4) Ayer.

Chamberlin, Joseph E. Boston Transcript: A History of Its First Hundred Years. LC 76-103646. (Select Bibliographies Reprint Ser.). 1977. 29.95 (0-8369-5146-8) Ayer.

Chamberlin, Kate. The Night Search. large type ed. LC 96-39005. (Turtle Bks.). (Illus.). 32p. (J). (gr. k-3). 1997. pap. 8.95 (0-944727-31-X); lib. bdg. 14.95 (0-944727-32-8) Jason & Nordic Pubs.

— The Night Search, Print & Braille Ed. braille large type ed. (Turtle Bks.). (Illus.). 32p. (J). (gr. k-3). 1997. lib. bdg. 24.95 (0-944727-33-6) Jason & Nordic Pubs.

Chamberlin, Kathy & Hoffman, Debby. Find Something Nice to Say: The Power of Compliments. (Creating Happiness Ser.). 230p. 1999. pap. 15.95 (0-9669105-0-8) Two Frnds Pubg.

Chamberlin, M., jt. ed. see Losick, R.

***Chamberlin, M. E.** Decolonization: The Fall of the European Empires. 2nd ed. LC 99-33570. (Historical Association Studies Ser.). 2000. pap. 24.95 (0-631-21602-2) Blackwell Pubs.

— Decolonization: The Fall of the European Empires. 2nd rev. ed. LC 99-33570. (Historical Association Studies Ser.). 2000. 54.95 (0-631-21804-1) Blackwell Pubs.

Chamberlin, Neil W. Social Strategy & Corporate Structure. 192p. 1982. 32.95 (0-02-905810-4) Free Pr.

Chamberlin, R. M., et al, eds. Mogollon Slope: West-Central New Mexico & East-Central Arizona. (Guidebook Ser.: No. 45). (Illus.). 335p. 1994. pap. 50.00 (1-58546-080-X) NMex Geol Soc.

Chamberlin, Ralph V. Ethno-Botany of the Gosiute Indians of Utah. LC 14-11549. (American Anthropological Association Memoirs Ser.: Vol. 11). 1911. 25.00 (0-527-00510-X) Periodicals Srv.

Chamberlin, Richard A. Chamberlin: Trusts in Commercial & Financial Transactions. 1997. write for info. (0-406-04981-5, CTCF, MICHIE) LEXIS Pub.

***Chamberlin, Robert.** Of Love & Pain. 2000. write for info. (1-58235-512-6) Watermrk Pr.

Chamberlin, Robert, jt. auth. see Hymovich, Debra P.

Chamberlin, Roxanna, ed. see Shell, Harvey.

Chamberlin, Russell. Florence & Tuscany. 3rd ed. (Passport's Illustrated Travel Guides from Thomas Cook Ser.). (Illus.). 192p. 1999. pap. 14.95 (0-658-00031-4, 000314, Passprt Bks) NTC Contemp Pub Co.

Chamberlin, Shirley S. A History of Cuba, Tennessee with Family Accounts & Genealogy. (Illus.). 318p. 1986. boxed set 29.00 (0-685-51182-0) S S Chamberlin.

***Chamberlin, Taylor M., et al.** The Waterford News: An Underground Union Newspaper Published by Three Quaker Maidens in Confederate Virginia 1864-65. (Illus.). 47p. 1999. pap. 6.95 (0-9660485-3-9) Waterford Found.

***Chamberlin, Thomas C.** The Geologic Relations of the Human Relics of Lansing, Kansas, with an Editorial on the Antiquity of Man in America & a Review on Kakabikansing. (LC History-America-E). 793p. 1999. reprint ed. lib. bdg. 169.00 (0-7812-4317-3) Rprt Serv.

Chamberlin, Vernon A. Galdos & Beethoven: Fortunata y Jacinta. (Monagrafias A Ser.: Vol. LXII). 123p. (C). 1977. 41.00 (0-7293-0031-5, Pub. by Tamesis Bks Ltd) Boydell & Brewer.

Chamberlin, W. H. The Russian Revolution, 2 vols. 130p. 1992. pap. text 35.00 (0-691-00816-7, Pub. by Princeton U Pr) Cal Prin Full Svc.

Chamberlin, Willard J. Entomological Nomenclature & Literature. 3rd enl. rev. ed. LC 79-108387. 141p. 1970. reprint ed. lib. bdg. 65.00 (0-8371-3810-8, CHNO, Greenwood Pr) Greenwood.

Chamberlin, William C. Economic Development of Iceland Through World War Two. LC 73-76653. (Columbia University. Studies in the Social Sciences: No. 531). reprint ed. 20.00 (0-404-51531-2) AMS Pr.

Chamberlin, William H. America's Second Crusade. 1962. pap. 2.00 (0-87926-000-9) R Myles.

— The Russian Revolution, Nineteen Seventeen to Nineteen Twenty-One, Vol. II: 1918-1921: From the Civil War to the Consolidation of Power. Koenker, Diane P., ed. 612p. 1987. pap. text 26.95 (0-691-00815-9, Pub. by Princeton U Pr) Cal Prin Full Svc.

— The Russian Revolution, Nineteen Seventeen to Nineteen Twenty-One, Vol. 1: 1917-1918: From the Overthrow of the Tsar to the Assumption of Power by the Bolsheviks. Koenker, Diane P., ed. 536p. 1987. pap. text 26.95 (0-691-00814-0, Pub. by Princeton U Pr) Cal Prin Full Svc.

— Russia's Iron Age. LC 73-115517. (Russia Observed, Series I). 1970. reprint ed. 25.95 (0-405-03013-4) Ayer.

— Soviet Planned Economic Order. LC 70-107342. (BCL Ser.: No. I). 1970. reprint ed. 27.50 (0-404-00595-0) AMS Pr.

— Soviet Planned Economic Order. LC 77-95088. 1970. reprint ed. lib. bdg. 75.00 (0-8371-2544-8, CHSE, Greenwood Pr) Greenwood.

Chamberlin, William J. Catalogue of English Bible Translations: A Classified Bibliography of Versions & Editions Including Books, Parts, & Old & New Testament Apocrypha & Acpocryphal Books, 21. LC 91-27497. (Bibliographies & Indexes in Religious Studies: No. 21). 960p. 1991. lib. bdg. 195.00 (0-313-28041-X, CTJ/, Greenwood Pr) Greenwood.

Chamberlyne, C. G., ed. The Vestry Book of Stratton Major Parish, King & Queen County, Virginia, 1729-1783. LC 80-14672. xxi, 257p. 1980. reprint ed. 15.00 (0-88490-087-8) Library of VA.

Chamberod, A. & Hillairet, J., eds. Metallic Multilayers. 648p. (C). 1990. text 183.00 (0-87849-609-2, Pub. by Trans T Pub) Enfield Pubs NH.

Chamberos, Peter, tr. see Papadopoulos, Gerasimos.

Chambers. Alchemy & the Alchemists. 50p. 1992. reprint ed. pap. 9.95 (1-56459-005-4) Kessinger Pub.

— American Slavery & Color. 216p. 1969. lib. bdg. 45.00 (0-8371-0345-2, Greenwood Pr) Greenwood.

— Case Studies on Anaesthesia. 1995. pap. text 72.95 (0-443-05070-8, W B Saunders Co) Harcrt Hlth Sci Grp.

— College Algebra with Technology. (C). 1999. write for info. (0-321-01594-0) Addison-Wesley.

— Compatible PCJr SF. 1985. 19.95 (0-13-154220-6) P-H.

***Chambers.** Finding Recruiting & Keep. 2000. pap. 15.00 (0-7382-0289-4, Pub. by Perseus Pubng) HarpC.

Chambers. Gerard de Nerval et la Poetique du Voyage. 34.95 (0-7859-0621-5, F70010) Fr & Eur.

— Marisol y Magdelena, Bk. 2. (J). 1998. 15.00 (0-689-81025-3) S&S Childrens.

***Chambers.** Social Policy & Social Programs. 3rd ed. LC 98-45316. 272p. 1999. pap. text 40.00 (0-205-29148-1) Allyn.

Chambers. The Tyranny of Change. 3rd ed. 1995. pap. text. write for info. (0-312-11209-2) St Martin.

— Western Experience, Vol. 1. 6th ed. 1995. pap., student ed. 22.81 (0-07-011073-5) McGraw.

— Western Experience, Vol. 2. 6th ed. 1995. pap., student ed. 22.81 (0-07-011074-3) McGraw.

Chambers, ed. Aristotelis. (GRE.). 1994. pap. 21.95 (3-8154-1113-0, T1113, Pub. by B G Teubner) U of Mich Pr.

— Chambers Dictionary 98. 2020p. 1998. 40.00 (0-550-14005-0) LKC.

— Hellenica Oxyrhynchia. (GRE.). 1993. 47.50 (3-8154-1365-6, T1365, Pub. by B G Teubner) U of Mich Pr.

Chambers & Natali, Patricia. The Call of the Prophets. 24p. 1996. pap. text 2.95 (1-55612-303-5, LL1303) Sheed & Ward WI.

Chambers, A. Our Life after Death. 1972. 59.95 (0-8490-0784-4) Gordon Pr.

Chambers, A., et al. Basic Vacuum Technology. 2nd ed. LC 98-20304. (Illus.). 235p. 1998. 45.00 (0-7503-0495-2) IOP Pub.

Chambers, A. B. Andrew Marvell & Edmund Waller: Seventeenth-Century Praise & Restoration Satire. 208p. 1991. 35.00 (0-271-00703-6) Pa St U Pr.

— Transfigured Rites in Seventeenth-Century English Poetry. 296p. (C). 1992. text 39.95 (0-8262-0808-8) U of Mo Pr.

Chambers, A. B., et al, eds. The Works of John Dryden Vol. IV: Poems: 1693-1699. 1974. 80.00 (0-520-02120-7, Pub. by U CA Pr) Cal Prin Full Svc.

Chambers, A. C. Has Technology Been Considered? A Guide for IEP Teams. 50p. 1997. pap. 15.95 (0-86586-298-2) Coun Exc Child.

Chambers, A. D. Internal Auditing. (International Library of Management). (Illus.). 704p. 1996. text 259.95 (1-85521-547-0, Pub. by Dartmth Pub) Ashgate Pub Co.

Chambers, Ada & Chambers, Anna. Guides for Hire. 197p. (Orig.). 1988. pap. 10.95 (0-9621954-1-3) A Cataldo.

— Pod Run. 2nd ed. 228p. 1989. reprint ed. pap. 10.95 (0-9621954-0-5) A Cataldo.

Chambers, Aidan. Booktalk: Occasional Writing on Literature & Children. LC 85-45389. (Charlotte Zolotow Bk.). 192p. (J). 1986. 13.95 (0-06-021249-7) HarpC Child Bks.

— Breaktime. LC 78-19472. 192p. (YA). (gr. 7 up). 1979. 13.95 (0-06-021256-X) HarpC Child Bks.

— Dance On My Grave: A Life & a Death in Four Parts ... LC 82-48258. 256p. (YA). (gr. 12 up). 1995. pap. 5.95 (0-06-440579-6, HarpTrophy) HarpC Child Bks.

— Dance On My Grave: A Life & a Death in Four Parts ... 1995. 11.05 (0-606-07408-2, Pub. by Turtleback) Demco.

— Introducing Books to Children. 2nd ed. 224p. 1983. 16.95 (0-87675-284-9) Horn Bk.

— NIK: Now I Know. LC 87-30836. (Charlotte Zolotow Bk.). 288p. (YA). (gr. 7 up). 1988. 13.95 (0-06-021208-X) HarpC Child Bks.

— The Reading Environment: How Adults Help Children Enjoy Books. LC 96-26384. 96p. 1996. pap. text 10.00 (1-57110-029-6) Stenhse Pubs.

— Tell Me: Children, Reading, & Talk. 128p. (C). 1996. pap. text 10.00 (1-57110-030-X) Stenhse Pubs.

Chambers, Aidan, ed. A Haunt of Ghosts. LC 86-45486. (Charlotte Zolotow Bk.). 192p. (YA). (gr. 7 up). 1987. 12.95 (0-06-021206-3) HarpC Child Bks.

— Shades of Dark. LC 85-45840. (Charlotte Zolotow Bk.). 128p. (YA). (gr. 7 up). 1986. 11.95 (0-06-021247-0) HarpC Child Bks.

Chambers, Aiden. The Toll Bridge. LC 94-36602. (Illus.). (gr. 8 up). mass mkt. 4.95 (0-06-440605-9) HarpC.

Chambers, Alec & Roberts, Stanley. Chem-Bio: Frequently Asked Questions. Graves, Barbara, ed. (Illus.). 164p. 1998. pap. 18.00 (0-9665437-1-8) Tempest Publ.

***Chambers, Alf.** Battlers of the Barkly. 1998. pap. 19.95 (1-875998-44-6, Pub. by Central Queensland) Accents Pubns.

***Chambers, Alice.** Taming Angelica. 320p. 2000. mass mkt. 4.99 (0-8439-4682-2, Leisure Bks) Dorchester Pub Co.

Chambers, Andrew D. & Rand, G. K. The Operational Auditing Handbook: Auditing Business Processes. LC 96-41459. 546p. 1997. 149.00 (0-471-97060-3) Wiley.

Chambers, Andrew J., jt. auth. see Chambers, Margaret W.

***Chambers, Ann.** Merchant Power: A Basic Guide. LC 99-39983. 220p. 1999. 89.95 (0-87814-766-7) PennWell Bks.

Chambers, Ann. Natural Gas & Electric Power in Nontechnical Language. LC 99-13897. 258p. 1999. 64.95 (0-87814-761-6) PennWell Bks.

— Power Branding. LC 98-30379. 1998. 74.95 (0-87814-745-4) PennWell Bks.

***Chambers, Ann.** Power Primer: A Nontechnical Guide from Generation to End Use. LC 98-54440. 262p. 1999. 64.95 (0-87814-756-X) PennWell Bks.

Chambers, Ann & Kerr, Susan D. Power Industry Dictionary. LC 96-19937. 1996. 69.95 (0-87814-605-9) PennWell Bks.

Chambers, Anna, jt. auth. see Chambers, Ada.

Chambers, Anna R. & Laird, Winona I. Have You Ever Lived in a Mining Town: The Life & Spirit of a Wonderful Woman. LC 99-60974. 86p. 1999. pap. 9.95 (1-892298-14-7) Abique.

— Have You Ever Lived in a Mining Town: The Life & Spirit of a Wonderful Woman. LC 99-60974. (Illus.). 1999. 14.95 (1-892298-13-9) Abique.

Chambers, Anne. The Geraldine Conspiracy. 452p. 1997. pap. 13.95 (1-86023-034-2, Pub. by Martello Bks) Irish Amer Bk.

— Granuaile: The Life & Times of Grace O'Malley. (Illus.). 224p. 1998. pap. 12.95 (0-86327-631-8, Pub. by Wolfhound Press) Irish Amer Bk.

— Marbling on Fabric. (Illus.). 48p. 1995. pap. 12.95 (0-85532-788-X, 2788X, Pub. by Srch Pr) A Schwartz & Co.

— Marbling on Paper Using Oil Paints. 64p. (Orig.). 1993. pap. 15.95 (0-85532-709-X, 709-X, Pub. by Srch Pr) A Schwartz & Co.

Chambers, Anthony H., jt. ed. see Boscaro, Adriana.

Chambers, Anthony H., jt. ed. see Gatten, Aileen.

Chambers, Anthony H., tr. see Tanizaki, Jun'ichiro.

Chambers, Antonia. Sow the Wind. LC 93-18512. 48p. 1993. pap. 14.95 (0-7734-0025-7, Mellen Poetry Pr) E Mellen.

Chambers, Arthur. Our Life after Death: The Teaching of the Bible Concerning the Unseen World. 239p. 1996. reprint ed. spiral bd. 16.50 (0-7873-0162-0) Hlth Research.

Chambers, B., et al. To the Hands of the Poor, Water & Trees. (C). 1989. 24.00 (81-204-0428-9, Pub. by Oxford IBH) S Asia.

Chambers, B. Keith. Computer Applications for School Administrators. LC 94-60911. 155p. 1994. pap. text 24.95 (1-56676-174-3) Scarecrow.

Chambers, Barry & Powell, Mary. Willy the Hit Man. 94p. (J). (gr. 4-7). 1992. pap. 4.95 (1-880384-01-9) Coldwater Pr.

***Chambers-Belida, Candace.** The Secret Codes of Conduct for Marriage - Mission Accomplished. 144p. 2000. pap. 8.95 (0-9679782-0-3) Ewe Babe.

Chambers-Benjamin, Carol, ed. see Johnson, Charisse, et al.

Chambers-Benjamin, Carol, ed. see Johnson, Loren G., et al.

Chambers, Bill. FoxPro 2 MIS Applications. Leventhal, Lance A., ed. LC 91-53068. (Lance A. Leventhal Microtrend Ser.). 400p. (Orig.). 1992. pap. 27.95 (0-915391-46-5) Slawson Comm.

Chambers, Brenda, et al. Forest Plants of Central Ontario. LC 96-172116. (Illus.). 448p. 1996. pap. 19.95 (1-55105-061-7) Lone Pine.

Chambers, Cally, jt. auth. see Peacock, Graham.

Chambers, Carl D. & Brill, Leon, eds. Methadone: Experiences & Issues. LC 72-6122. 411p. 1973. 52.00 (0-87705-072-4, Kluwer Acad Hman Sci) Kluwer Academic.

Chambers, Carl D., jt. ed. see Inciardi, James A.

Chambers, Catherine. Africa. LC 96-1723. (Origins Ser.). (J). (gr. 5-8). 1997. lib. bdg. 19.30 (0-531-14416-X) Watts.

— All about Maps. (Hello Out There Ser.). (Illus.). 32p. 1998. pap. 6.95 (0-531-15348-7) Watts.

C

An Asterisk (*) at the beginning of an entry indicates that the title is appearing for the first time.

— All Saints, All Souls & Halloween. LC 96-34334. (World of Holidays Ser.). (Illus.). 32p. (J). 1997. lib. bdg. 22.88 (*0-8172-4606-1*) Raintree Steck-V.

***Chambers, Catherine.** All Saints, All Souls & Halloween. 32p. (J). (gr. 2-5). 1999. pap. 6.95 (*0-7398-1383-8*) Raintree Steck-V.

— All Saints, All Souls & Halloween. (Illus.). (J). 2000. 12.40 (*0-606-18476-7*) Turtleback.

Chambers, Catherine. Bark. (Would You Believe It! Ser.). (Illus.). 32p. (J). (gr. 1-6). 1996. lib. bdg. 21.40 (*0-8172-4100-0*) Raintree Steck-V.

— Carnival. LC 97-18329. (World of Holidays Ser.). (J). 1998. 22.83 (*0-8172-4613-4*) Raintree Steck-V.

— Chinese New Year. 32p. 1997. pap. text 6.95 (*0-8172-3884-0*) Raintree Steck-V.

— Chinese New Year. LC 96-34426. (World of Holidays Ser.). (Illus.). 32p. (J). 1997. lib. bdg. 22.83 (*0-8172-4605-3*) Raintree Steck-V.

— Christmas. LC 96-33583. (World of Holidays Ser.). (Illus.). 32p. (J). (gr. 2-5). 1997. lib. bdg. 22.83 (*0-8172-4608-8*) Raintree Steck-V.

— Christmas. (World of Holidays Ser.). (Illus.). 32p. (J). (gr. 2-5). 1998. pap. 7.95 (*0-8172-8104-5*) Raintree Steck-V.

***Chambers, Catherine.** Computer. LC 97-31456. (Look Inside Ser.). (Illus.). 24p. 1998. 19.92 (*1-57572-622-X*) Heinemann Lib.

— Deserts. LC 99-43375. (Mapping Earthforms Ser.). (Illus.). 2000. lib. bdg. write for info. (*1-57572-522-3*) Heinemann Lib.

— Drought. LC 00-20025. (Disasters in Nature Ser.). (Illus.). 2000. lib. bdg. write for info. (*1-57572-426-X*) Heinemann Lib.

— Earthquakes. LC 00-20026. (Disasters in Nature Ser.). (Illus.). 2000. lib. bdg. write for info. (*1-57572-427-8*) Heinemann Lib.

Chambers, Catherine. Easter. LC 97-18328. (World of Holidays Ser.). (J). 1998. 22.83 (*0-8172-4615-0*) Raintree Steck-V.

— Easter. 1999. pap. text 6.95 (*0-8172-3886-7*) Raintree Steck-V.

***Chambers, Catherine.** The Elephants' Ears. (Illus.). 32p. (J). (ps-k). 2000. 15.95 (*1-84148-052-5*) Barefoot Bks NY.

— Floods. LC 00-20022. (Disasters in Nature Ser.). (Illus.). 2000. lib. bdg. write for info. (*1-57572-428-6*) Heinemann Lib.

Chambers, Catherine. Grasses. LC 95-33270. (Would You Believe It! Ser.). (Illus.). 32p. (J). (gr. 1-6). 1996. lib. bdg. 21.40 (*0-8172-4103-5*) Raintree Steck-V.

***Chambers, Catherine.** Hurricanes. LC 00-20023. (Disasters in Nature Ser.). (Illus.). 2000. lib. bdg. write for info. (*1-57572-429-4*) Heinemann Lib.

— Islands. LC 99-43373. (Mapping Earthforms Ser.). (Illus.). 2000. lib. bdg. write for info. (*1-57572-523-1*) Heinemann Lib.

— Lakes. LC 99-43374. (Mapping Earthforms Ser.). (Illus.). 2000. lib. bdg. write for info. (*1-57572-524-X*) Heinemann Lib.

Chambers, Catherine. Light. (Illus.). (J). 1997. 24.95 (*0-237-51773-6*) EVN1 UK.

***Chambers, Catherine.** Mountains. LC 99-46852. (Mapping Earthforms Ser.). 2000. lib. bdg. write for info. (*1-57572-525-8*) Heinemann Lib.

Chambers, Catherine. Nuts. (Would You Believe It! Ser.). (Illus.). 32p. (J). (gr. 1-6). 1996. lib. bdg. 21.40 (*0-8172-4104-3*) Raintree Steck-V.

***Chambers, Catherine.** Oceans & Seas. LC 99-44189. (Mapping Earthforms Ser.). (Illus.). 2000. lib. bdg. write for info. (*1-57572-526-6*) Heinemann Lib.

Chambers, Catherine. Personal Stereo. LC 97-31458. (Look Inside Ser.). (Illus.). 24p. 1998. write for info. (*1-57572-623-8*) Heinemann Lib.

***Chambers, Catherine.** Rivers. LC 99-46853. (Mapping Earthforms Ser.). 2000. lib. bdg. write for info. (*1-57572-527-4*) Heinemann Lib.

Chambers, Catherine. Shells. (Would You Believe It! Ser.). (Illus.). 32p. (J). (gr. 1-6). 1996. lib. bdg. 21.40 (*0-8172-4101-9*) Raintree Steck-V.

— Sneaker. LC 97-31455. (Look Inside Ser.). (Illus.). 24p. 1998. 18.50 (*1-57572-624-6*) Heinemann Lib.

— Speaking Through Pictures. (Hello Out There Ser.). (Illus.). 32p. 1998. pap. 6.95 (*0-531-15347-9*) Watts.

— Speaking Through Pictures. LC 97-44436. (Hello Out There Ser.). (Illus.). 32p. (J). 1998. lib. bdg. 18.00 (*0-531-14469-0*) Watts.

— Stones. (Would You Believe It! Ser.). (Illus.). 32p. (J). (gr. 1-6). 1996. lib. bdg. 21.40 (*0-8172-4105-1*) Raintree Steck-V.

— Telephone. LC 97-31457. (Look Inside Ser.). (Illus.). 24p. 1998. write for info. (*1-57572-625-4*) Heinemann Lib.

***Chambers, Catherine.** Tornadoes. LC 00-20024. (Disasters in Nature Ser.). (Illus.). 2000. lib. bdg. write for info. (*1-57572-430-8*) Heinemann Lib.

Chambers, Catherine. West African States: 15th Century to the Colonial Era. LC 98-21840. (Looking Back Ser.). (Illus.). 64p. (J). (gr. 6-9). 1998. 25.69 (*0-8172-5427-7*) Raintree Steck-V.

— Wood. LC 95-21400. (Illus.). 32p. (J). (gr. 1-6). 1996. lib. bdg. 21.40 (*0-8172-4102-7*) Raintree Steck-V.

Chambers, Catherine, ed. see Coleman, Kenneth.

Chambers, Catherine D., et al. In Situ Treatment of Hazardous Waste-Contaminated Soils. 2nd ed. LC 90-23060. (Pollution Technology Review Ser.: No. 199). (Illus.). 533p. 1991. 79.00 (*0-8155-1263-5*) Noyes.

Chambers, Catherine E. California Gold Rush: Search for Treasure. (Adventures in Frontier America Ser.). (Illus.). 32p. (J). (gr. 4-8). 1998. pap. 3.95 (*0-8167-4556-0*) Troll Communs.

— Daniel Boone & the Wilderness Road. LC 83-18291. (Adventures in Frontier America Ser.). (Illus.). 32p. (J). (gr. 4-8). 1984. pap. text 3.50 (*0-8167-0038-9*) Troll Communs.

— Daniel Boone & the Wilderness Road. (Adventures in Frontier America Ser.). (Illus.). 32p. (J). (gr. 4-8). 1998. pap. 3.95 (*0-8167-4888-8*) Troll Communs.

— Flatboats on the Ohio: Westward Bound. LC 83-18278. (Adventures in Frontier America Ser.). (Illus.). 32p. (J). (gr. 4-8). 1984. pap. text 3.50 (*0-8167-0050-8*) Troll Communs.

— Flatboats on the Ohio: Westward Bound. (Adventures in Frontier America Ser.). (Illus.). 32p. (J). (gr. 4-8). 1998. pap. 3.95 (*0-8167-4890-X*) Troll Communs.

— Frontier Farmer: Kansas Adventures. LC 83-18279. (Adventures in Frontier America Ser.). (Illus.). 32p. (J). (gr. 5-9). 1984. pap. text 3.50 (*0-8167-0054-0*) Troll Communs.

— Frontier Village: A Town Is Born. LC 83-18271. (Adventures in Frontier America Ser.). (Illus.). 32p. (J). (gr. 5-9). 1984. pap. text 3.50 (*0-8167-0046-X*) Troll Communs.

— Frontier Village: A Town Is Born. (Adventures in Frontier America Ser.). (Illus.). 32p. (J). (gr. 4-8). 1999. pap. 3.95 (*0-8167-5040-8*) Troll Communs.

— Indiana Days: Life in a Frontier Town. LC 83-18283. (Adventures in Frontier America Ser.). (Illus.). 32p. (J). (gr. 5-9). 1984. pap. text 3.50 (*0-8167-0056-7*) Troll Communs.

— Log Cabin Home: Pioneers in the Wilderness. LC 83-18277. (Adventures in Frontier America Ser.). (Illus.). 32p. (J). (gr. 4-8). 1984. pap. text 3.50 (*0-8167-0042-7*) Troll Communs.

— Log Cabin Home: Pioneers in the Wilderness. (Adventures in Frontier America Ser.). (Illus.). 32p. (J). (gr. 4-8). 1998. pap. 3.95 (*0-8167-4889-6*) Troll Communs.

— Texas Roundup: Life on the Range. LC 83-18281. (Adventures in Frontier America Ser.). (Illus.). 32p. (J). (gr. 5-9). 1984. pap. text 3.50 (*0-8167-0048-6*) Troll Communs.

***Chambers, Catherine E.** Texas Roundup: Life on the Range. (Adventures in Frontier America Ser.). (Illus.). 32p. (J). (gr. 4-8). 1999. pap. 3.95 (*0-8167-5039-4*) Troll Communs.

Chambers, Catherine E. Wagons West: Off to Oregon. LC 83-18276. (Adventures in Frontier America Ser.). (Illus.). 32p. (J). (gr. 4-8). 1984. pap. text 3.50 (*0-8167-0044-3*) Troll Communs.

***Chambers, Catherine E.** Wagons West: Off to Oregon. (Illus.). 32p. (J). (gr. 5-9). 1999. pap. text 3.95 (*0-8167-6294-5*) Troll Communs.

Chambers, Catherine E. & Lawn, John. Indiana Days: Life in a Frontier Town. (Adventures in Frontier America Ser.). (Illus.). 32p. (J). (gr. 4-8). 1999. pap. 3.95 (*0-8167-4891-8*) Troll Communs.

Chambers, Catherine M., jt. auth. see Chambers, Edna C.

Chambers, Charles M., ed. see American Institute of Biological Sciences.

Chambers, Charlotte, et al. The Good Management Development Guide. 128p. (Orig.). 1990. pap. 23.95 (*0-8464-1343-4*) Beekman Pubs.

Chambers, Christine, et al. Celebrating Identity. 64p. 1996. pap. 15.00 (*1-85856-068-3*, Trentham Bks) Stylus Pub VA.

Chambers, Clarke A. Descriptive Inventories of Collections in the Social Welfare History Archives Center. LC 73-102265. 846p. 1970. lib. bdg. 150.00 (*0-8371-3270-3*, SWH/, Greenwood Pr) Greenwood.

— Paul U. Kellogg & the Survey: Voices for Social Welfare & Social Justice. LC 77-172931. (Illus.). 297p. reprint ed. pap. 92.10 (*0-608-16070-9*, 203321000084) Bks Demand.

— Seedtime of Reform: American Social Service & Social Action, 1918 to 1933. LC 80-36788. 326p. 1980. reprint ed. lib. bdg. 69.50 (*0-313-22666-0*, CHRE, Greenwood Pr) Greenwood.

— Seedtime of Reform: American Social Service & Social Action, 1918-1933. LC 63-23058. 346p. reprint ed. pap. 107.30 (*0-608-14091-0*, 205584700039) Bks Demand.

Chambers, Colin. Peggy: The Life of Margaret Ramsay, Play Agent. LC 97-42554. 383p. 1998. text 27.95 (*0-312-17713-5*) St Martin.

— The Story of Unity Theatre. (Illus.). 446p. 1990. 39.95 (*0-685-31436-7*) St Martin.

***Chambers, Colin, ed.** Companion to Twentieth Century Theatre. 928p. 2000. write for info. (*0-7201-2366-6*) Continuum.

Chambers, Colin, ed. see Nelson, Richard & Jones, David.

Chambers, Cullen. The Movie Extras Guidebook: How to Make Good Money As a Hollywood Extra. 8th ed. 1997. pap. text 19.95 (*0-9624577-5-2*) C G Chambers.

Chambers, Cullen G. The Movie Extras Guidebook: How to Make Good Money As a Background Actor. rev. ed. (Illus.). 320p. 1996. pap. 19.95 (*0-9624577-2-8*) C G Chambers.

Chambers, D. The Reinvention of the World: English Writing, 1650-1750. LC 95-36365. (Writing History Ser.). 232p. 1996. pap. text 19.95 (*0-340-58478-5*, Pub. by E A) OUP.

— The Reinvention of the World: English Writing, 1650-1750. LC 95-36365. (Writing History Ser.). 232p. 1996. text 49.95 (*0-340-66242-5*, Pub. by E A) OUP.

Chambers, D. S. Individuals & Institutions in Renaissance Italy. LC 98-23627. (Variorum Collected Studies Ser.: Vol. 619). (Illus.). 370p. 1998. text 110.95 (*0-86078-699-4*, DG445.C47, Pub. by Variorum) Ashgate Pub Co.

— Renaissance Cardinals & Their Worldly Problems. LC 96-33155. (Collected Studies: No. CS559). 384p. 1997. 109.95 (*0-86078-614-5*, Pub. by Ashgate Pub) Ashgate Pub Co.

Chambers, Dave. Coaching: Winning Strategies for Every Level of Play. LC 97-931993. (Illus.). 152p. 1998. pap. 19.95 (*1-55209-208-9*) Firefly Bks Ltd.

— Complete Hockey Instruction. (Illus.). 224p. 1994. pap. 16.95 (*0-8092-3511-0*, 351100, Contemporary Bks) NTC Contemp Pub Co.

— The Incredible Hockey Drill Book. LC 95-30788. (Illus.). 160p. 1995. pap. 13.95 (*0-8092-3254-5*, 325450, Contemporary Bks) NTC Contemp Pub Co.

Chambers, David. Joan Hassall Engravings & Drawings. 160p. 1985. 48.00 (*0-900002-54-9*, Pub. by Priv Lib Assn) Oak Knoll.

Chambers, David, et al. Morris Cox & the Gogmagog Press. 184p. 1991. 90.00 (*0-900002-25-5*, Pub. by Priv Lib Assn) Oak Knoll.

Chambers, David L. Making Fathers Pay: The Enforcement of Child Support. LC 79-11953. 380p. 1979. 39.00 (*0-226-10077-4*) U Ch Pr.

— Metre of Macbeth. LC 78-113575. reprint ed. 24.50 (*0-404-01443-7*) AMS Pr.

Chambers, David S., et al, eds. War, Culture, & Society in Renaissance Venice: Essays in Honour of John Hale. LC 93-27448. 276p. 1993. 65.00 (*1-85285-090-6*) Hambledon Press.

Chambers, David S. & Dean, Trevor. Clean Hands & Rough Justice: An Investigating Magistrate in Renaissance Italy. LC 96-45861. 344p. (C). 1997. text 54.50 (*0-472-10748-8*, 10748, Ann Arbor Bks) U of Mich Pr.

Chambers, David W. Beasts & Other Illusions. 68p. (C). 1982. pap. 45.00 (*0-7300-0158-X*, HUS204, Pub. by Deakin Univ) St Mut.

— Imagining Landscapes. 76p. (C). 1982. 75.00 (*0-7300-0156-3*, Pub. by Deakin Univ) St Mut.

— Imagining Nature. (C). 1982. 75.00 (*0-7300-0154-7*, Pub. by Deakin Univ) St Mut.

— On the Social Analysis of Science. 102p. (C). 1979. 33.00 (*0-86828-065-8*, Pub. by Deakin Univ) St Mut.

— Putting Nature in Order. 60p. (C). 1992. pap. 45.00 (*0-7300-0155-5*, HUS204, Pub. by Deakin Univ) St Mut.

— A Worm in the Bud. 242p. (C). 1979. 44.00 (*0-86828-296-0*, Pub. by Deakin Univ) St Mut.

Chambers, David W. & Abrams, Ronald G. Dental Communication. 295p. (C). 1992. pap. text 24.00 (*0-9632599-0-3*) Ohana Grp.

Chambers, David W., et al. Liberating & Control: Leader: The Uses of Knowledge & Power. 276p. (C). 1984. 44.00 (*0-86828-273-1*, Pub. by Deakin Univ); student ed. 44.00 (*0-7855-6751-8*, Pub. by Deakin Univ) St Mut.

Chambers, David W., jt. auth. see Watson, Helen.

Chambers, Dennis. The Agile Manager's Guide to Writing to Get Action. LC 97-81355. (Agile Manager Ser.). (Illus.). 96p. 1998. pap. 9.95 (*1-58099-008-8*) Velocity Busn.

Chambers, Diane. Solo Parenting: Raising Strong & Happy Families. 192p. (Orig.). 1997. pap. 12.95 (*1-57749-008-8*) Fairview Press.

Chambers, Donald L. Guide to Curriculum Planning in Mathematics. 330p. (C). 1986. pap. text 33.00 (*1-57337-009-6*) WI Dept Pub Instruct.

Chambers, Donald R., ed. Modern Corporate Finance. 2nd ed. 736p. (C). 1998. 96.00 (*0-321-01447-2*) Addson-Wesley Educ.

Chambers, Donald R. & Lacey, Nelson J. Modern Corporate Finance: Theory & Practice. LC 93-5470. 688p. (C). 1997. pap. 88.00 (*0-06-501004-3*); pap., student ed. 33.00 (*0-06-501005-1*) Addson-Wesley Educ.

Chambers, Donald R., jt. auth. see Bukics, Rose Marie.

Chambers, Donald R., jt. ed. see Nawalkha, Sanjay K.

Chambers, Douglas. The Planters of the Landscape Garden: Botany, Trees, & the Georgics. LC 92-35695. (Paul Mellon Centre for Studies in British Art). (Illus.). 224p. (C). 1993. 60.00 (*0-300-05464-5*) Yale U Pr.

Chambers, Edgar, 4th & Baker Wolf, Mona, eds. Sensory Testing Methods. 2nd ed. LC 96-32386. (Manual Ser.: Vol. 26). (Illus.). 120p. 1996. pap. text 36.00 (*0-8031-2068-0*, MNL26) ASTM.

Chambers, Edith K. Claggett: Genealogical Narrative, History of the Claggett-Irvine Clans. (Illus.). 150p. 1997. reprint ed. pap. 24.00 (*0-8328-7934-7*); reprint ed. lib. bdg. 34.00 (*0-8328-7933-9*) Higginson Bk Co.

Chambers, Edmund. Index to 'The Elizabethan Stage' & 'William Shakespeare' by Sir Edmund Chambers. White, Beatrice, ed. LC 64-14701. 1972. reprint ed. 21.95 (*0-405-09067-6*) Ayer.

Chambers, Edmund K. Early English Lyrics, Amorous, Divine, Moral & Trivial. LC 70-178518. reprint ed. 49.50 (*0-404-56531-X*) AMS Pr.

— Early English Lyrics, Amorous, Divine, Moral & Trivial. (BCL1-PR English Literature Ser.). 384p. 1992. reprint ed. lib. bdg. 89.00 (*0-7812-7134-7*) Rprt Serv.

— The English Folk Play. 248p. (C). 1966. reprint ed. lib. bdg. 75.00 (*0-8383-0521-0*) M S G Haskell Hse.

— English Pastorals. LC 70-76943. (Granger Index Reprint Ser.). 1977. 20.95 (*0-8369-6008-4*) Ayer.

— The Mediaeval Stage. unabridged ed. LC 96-14913. (Illus.). 960p. 1996. reprint ed. pap. text 19.95 (*0-486-29229-0*) Dover.

— Samuel Taylor Coleridge: A Biographical Study. LC 78-19152. 373p. 1978. reprint ed. lib. bdg. 69.50 (*0-313-20539-6*, CHST, Greenwood Pr) Greenwood.

— Sheaf of Studies. LC 74-99622. (Essay Index Reprint Ser.). 1977. 20.95 (*0-8369-1398-1*) Ayer.

— Sir Thomas Wyatt & Some Collected Studies. (BCL1-PR English Literature Ser.). 227p. 1992. reprint ed. lib. bdg. 79.00 (*0-7812-7010-3*) Rprt Serv.

— William Shakespeare: A Study of Facts & Problems, Vol. I. (Illus.). 594p. 1989. text 95.00 (*0-19-811773-6*) OUP.

— William Shakespeare: A Study of Facts & Problems, Vol. II. (Illus.). 460p. 1989. text 82.00 (*0-19-811774-4*) OUP.

Chambers, Edmund K. & Sidgwick, F. Early English Lyrics. 1967. 8.95 (*0-8079-0039-7*); pap. 4.95 (*0-8079-0040-0*) October.

Chambers, Edmund K. & Sidgwick, F., eds. Early English Lyrics: Amorous, Divine, Moral & Trivial. LC 76-173857. 384p. 1972. reprint ed. 26.95 (*0-405-08347-5*, Pub. by Blom Pubns) Ayer.

Chambers, Edna C. & Chambers, Catherine M. Eldercare Planner: An Easy-to-Use Planning System for Managing Eldercare Responsibilities. 100p. 1993. student ed. 24.95 (*0-9637011-2-6*) Chambers Care.

Chambers, Edward L., jt. auth. see Chambers, Robert.

Chambers, Elnora. Kid-Friendly Computer Book. (Illus.). 96p. (J). 1997. pap. 11.95 (*1-57612-011-2*, MM2039) Monday Morning Bks.

— Kid-Friendly Computer Start-Ups: Activity Cards for Writing-Geography-Math. (Illus.). 96p. 1998. pap. 11.95 (*1-57612-047-3*, MM2061) Monday Morning Bks.

***Chambers, Emma.** An Indolent & Blundering Art? The Etching Revival & the Redefinition of Etching in England. LC 98-53574. (Illus.). 300p. 1999. text 86.95 (*1-85928-444-2*) Ashgate Pub Co.

Chambers, Ephraim. Cyclopaedia, 5 vols., Set. write for info. incl. 3.5 hd (*0-318-71751-4*) G Olms Pubs.

Chambers, Eric. Reproduction Photography for Lithography. LC TR0940.C431. 339p. reprint ed. pap. 105.10 (*0-7837-0362-7*, 204068400018) Bks Demand.

Chambers, Eric G. Psychology & the Industrial Worker. LC 53-5436. 199p. reprint ed. pap. 56.80 (*0-608-11142-2*, 2050766) Bks Demand.

Chambers, Erve. Applied Anthropology: A Practical Guide. rev. ed. 258p. (C). 1989. reprint ed. pap. text 15.95 (*0-88133-449-9*) Waveland Pr.

***Chambers, Erve.** Native Tours: The Anthropology of Travel & Tourism. 137p. (C). 1999. pap. 10.95 (*1-57766-089-7*) Waveland Pr.

Chambers, Erve, ed. Tourism & Culture: An Applied Perspective. LC 96-41497. (SUNY Series in Advances in Applied Anthropology). 221p. (C). 1997. text 59.50 (*0-7914-3427-3*); pap. text 19.95 (*0-7914-3428-1*) State U NY Pr.

Chambers, Everett. Producing TV Movies. (Illus.). 229p. (C). 1988. reprint ed. pap. 12.00 (*0-9620587-0-X*) ECP Inc.

Chambers, F. M., ed. Climate Change & Human Impact on the Landscape. 304p. 1992. 79.95 (*0-412-46200-1*, A9444) Chapman & Hall.

Chambers, Frances. Guyana. LC 90-157550. (World Bibliographical Ser.: No. 96). 224p. 1989. lib. bdg. 55.00 (*1-85109-070-3*) ABC-CLIO.

— Trinidad & Tobago. LC 88-150894. (World Bibliographical Ser.: No. 74). 232p. 1987. lib. bdg. 55.00 (*1-85109-020-7*) ABC-CLIO.

Chambers, Frances, compiled by. Paris, Vol. 206. LC 99-218231. (World Biographical Series). 142p. 1998. lib. bdg. 54.00 (*1-85109-271-4*) ABC-CLIO.

Chambers, Frank. Hayden & His Men: A Selection of 108 Photographs by William Henry Jackson of the United States Geological & Geographical Survey of the Territories for the Years 1870-1878. (Illus.). (Orig.). 1988. pap. 27.50 (*0-9624110-0-0*) F PAUL geo lit.

Chambers, Frank M. An Introduction to Old Provencal Versification. LC 84-45898. (Memoirs Ser.: Vol. 167). 300p. 1985. 20.00 (*0-87169-167-1*, M167-CHF) Am Philos.

Chambers, Frank P. The War Behind the War, 1914-1918: A History of the Political & Civilian Fronts. LC 72-4267. (World Affairs Ser.: National & International Viewpoints). (Illus.). 638p. 1972. reprint ed. 39.95 (*0-405-04564-6*) Ayer.

Chambers, Frederick, compiled by. Black Higher Education in the United States: A Selected Bibliography on Negro Higher Education & Historically Black Colleges & Universities. LC 77-91100. 268p. 1978. lib. bdg. 42.95 (*0-313-20037-8*, CBH/, Greenwood Pr) Greenwood.

Chambers, Frederick P. Death & Injury at Work. 104p. 1995. pap. 30.00 (*1-85811-032-7*, Pub. by CLT Prof) Gaunt.

— Health & Safety at Work. 96p. 1995. pap. 30.00 (*1-85811-030-0*, Pub. by CLT Prof) Gaunt.

— Negligence at Work. 96p. 1995. pap. 30.00 (*1-85811-031-9*, Pub. by CLT Prof) Gaunt.

Chambers, G. B. Folksong Plainsong: A Study in Musical Origins. 2nd ed. (C). 1972. text 9.95 (*0-85036-178-8*, Pub. by MRLN) Paul & Co Pubs.

Chambers, Gary N. Motivating Language Learners. LC 99-22423. (Modern Languages in Practice Ser.). 1999. 27.95 (*1-85359-448-2*) Taylor & Francis.

Chambers, George. The Last Man Standing. 142p. 1990. 16.95 (*0-932511-19-8*); pap. 8.95 (*0-932511-20-1*) Fiction Coll.

— Null Set. LC 76-47788. 1977. 15.95 (*0-914590-34-0*); pap. 6.95 (*0-914590-35-9*) Fiction Coll.

— The Scourging of W. H. D. Wretched Hutchinson. Lyons, Richard, ed. LC 95-68861. 162p. (Orig.). 1995. pap. 14.00 (*0-9638099-1-1*) SPSHR.

Chambers, Gerald, jt. auth. see Smith, David J.

Chambers, Gerald, jt. ed. see McCrudden, Christopher.

Chambers, Ginger. Bachelor's Puzzle. (Tyler Ser.: No. 8). 1992. per. 3.99 (*0-373-82508-0*, 0-82508-3) Harlequin Bks.

— Born in Texas. (Superromance Ser.). 1999. mass mkt. 4.25 (*0-373-70862-9*, 1-70862-7) Harlequin Bks.

— Courthouse Steps. (Tyler Ser.: No. 11). 1999. mass mkt. write for info. (*0-373-82511-0*, 0-82511-7) Harlequin Bks.

— Daddy Next Door. (Hometown Reunion Ser.). 256p. 1997. per. 4.50 (*0-373-82554-4*, 1-82554-6) Harlequin Bks.

— Une Famille en Heritage. (FRE.). 1998. mass mkt. 4.99 (*0-373-38303-7*, 1-38303-3) Harlequin Bks.

C

— Father Takes a Wife. LC 95-13688. (Superromance Ser.). 296p. 1995. per. 3.75 (*0-373-70647-2*, 1-70647-2) Harlequin Bks.

***Chambers, Ginger.** Hidden in Texas: The West Texans. (Superromance Ser.: Bk. 907). 2000. per. 4.50 (*0-373-70907-2*, 1-70907-0) Harlequin Bks.

Chambers, Ginger. A Match Made in Texas. LC 96-2343. (Superromance Ser.). 299p. 1996. per. 3.99 (*0-373-70680-4*, 1-70680-3) Harlequin Bks.

— Puppy Love. (Hometown Reunion Ser.). 1997. per. 4.50 (*0-373-82558-7*, 1-82558-7) Harlequin Bks.

— Texas Lawman: The West Texans. (Superromance Ser.). 1998. per. 4.25 (*0-373-70778-9*, 1-70778-5) Harlequin Bks.

— Till September. 1994. per. 3.50 (*0-373-70601-4*, 1-70601-9) Harlequin Bks.

— West Texas Weddings: The West Texans. 1997. per. 3.99 (*0-373-70730-4*, 1-70730-6) Harlequin Bks.

Chambers, Ginger, ed. Twilight, Texas: The/West Texans. (West Texans Ser.: No. 820). 1998. per. 4.25 (*0-373-70820-3*, 1-70820-5) Harlequin Bks.

Chambers, Glen, jt. auth. see Fisher, Gene.

Chambers, Graham, jt. auth. see Peacock, James.

Chambers, Harry. Getting Promoted: Real Strategies for Advancing Your Career. LC 98-83276. 242p. 1999. pap. 13.00 (*0-7382-0102-2*, Pub. by Perseus Pubng) HarpC.

Chambers, Harry & Craft, Robert. No Fear Management: Rebuilding Trust, Performance & Commitment in the New American Workplace. (Illus.). 1997. lib. bdg. 39.95 (*1-57444-119-1*) St Lucie Pr.

Chambers, Harry E. The Bad Attitude Survival Guide: Essential Tools for Managers. LC 97-40871. 224p. 1998. pap. 15.00 (*0-201-31146-1*) Addison-Wesley.

***Chambers, Harry E.** Effective Communication Skills for Scientific & Technical Professionals. 256p. 2000. pap. text 15.00 (*0-7382-0287-8*, Pub. by Perseus Pubng) HarpC.

Chambers, Helen, ed. Co-Existent Contradictions: Joseph Roth in Retrospect. (Studies in Austrian Literature, Culture, & Thought). 246p. 1991. 33.50 (*0-929497-32-5*); pap. 26.50 (*0-929497-33-3*) Ariadne CA.

Chambers, Helen, tr. see Fontane, Theodor.

Chambers, Helen E., ed. The Changing Image of Theodor Fontane. LC 97-1360. (LCGERM Ser.). 172p. 1997. 55.00 (*1-57113-084-5*) Camden Hse.

Chambers, Henry E. Constitutional History of Hawaii. LC 78-63846. (Johns Hopkins University. Studies in the Social Sciences. Thirtieth Ser. 1912: 1). reprint ed. 37.50 (*0-404-61103-6*) AMS Pr.

— Mississippi Valley Beginnings: An Outline of the Early History of the Earlier West. (Illus.). 389p. 1997. reprint ed. lib. bdg. 42.50 (*0-8328-6821-3*) Higginson Bk Co.

— Mississippi Valley Beginnings: An Outline of the Early History of the Earlier West. (BCL1 - United States Local History Ser.). 389p. 1991. reprint ed. text 89.00 (*0-7812-6303-4*) Rprt Serv.

Chambers, I. Mench. Devil of Today: His Play Between the False & the Good (1906) 516p. 1998. reprint ed. pap. 33.00 (*0-7661-0498-2*) Kessinger Pub.

Chambers, Iain. Migrancy, Culture, Identity. LC 93-7863. (Illus.). 192p. (C). 1994. pap. 19.99 (*0-415-08802-X*) Routledge.

— Popular Culture. 1986. pap. 10.95 (*0-416-37680-0*) Routledge.

— Popular Culture: The Metropolitan Experience. (Communication Ser.). (Illus.). 256p. (C). 1986. pap. 18.99 (*0-415-02551-6*, 1022) Routledge.

Chambers, Iain & Curti, Lidia, eds. The Post-Colonial Question: Common Skies, Divided Horizons. LC 95-475. (Illus.). 288p. (C). 1996. pap. 20.99 (*0-415-10858-6*) Routledge.

Chambers, J. Graphical Methods for Data Analysis. 336p. (C). (gr. 13). 1983. per. 59.95 (*0-412-05271-7*) Chapman & Hall.

— Thomas Pynchon. (Twayne's United States Authors Ser.). 150p. 1992. 28.95 (*0-8057-3960-2*) Macmillan.

Chambers, J., jt. auth. see Crawshaw, J.

Chambers, J., ed. see Gentle, J. E.

Chambers, J., ed. see Lange, Kenneth.

Chambers, J., ed. see Loader, C.

Chambers, J., ed. see Wilkinson, L.

Chambers, J. A. & Rickwood, David, eds. Biochemistry Labfax. (Labfax Ser.). (Illus.). 357p. 1993. boxed set 63.00 (*0-12-167340-5*) Acad Pr.

Chambers, J. D., jt. auth. see Bell, I. E.

Chambers, J. E., jt. auth. see Narahashi, T.

Chambers, J. K. Sociolinguistic Theory: Linguistic Variation & Its Social Significance. (Language in Society Ser.). 256p. 1995. pap. 26.95 (*0-631-18326-4*) Blackwell Pubs.

Chambers, J. K. & Trudgill, Peter. Dialectology. 2nd rev. ed. LC 97-40830. (Cambridge Textbooks in Linguistics). (Illus.). 216p. (C). 1998. text 59.95 (*0-521-59378-6*) Cambridge U Pr.

— Dialectology. 2nd rev. ed. LC 97-40830. (Cambridge Textbooks in Linguistics). (Illus.). 216p. (C). 1998. pap. text 22.95 (*0-521-59646-7*) Cambridge U Pr.

Chambers, J. M. Programming with Data. LC 98-13049. (Illus.). 480p. 1998. pap. 44.95 (*0-387-98503-4*) Spr-Verlag.

Chambers, Jack. Milestones: The Music & Times of Miles Davis. LC 98-28958. (Illus.). 816p. 1998. reprint ed. pap. 23.00 (*0-306-80849-8*) Da Capo.

Chambers, James. Christopher Wren. LC 98-229718. (Pocket Biographies Ser.). 1998. pap. 9.95 (*0-7509-1852-7*, Pub. by Sutton Pub Ltd) Intl Pubs Mktg.

— Genghis Kahn. 1999. pap. text 9.95 (*0-7509-2064-5*) Sutton Pub Ltd.

Chambers, James. The Norman Kings. LC 82-112904. 224p. 1981. write for info. (*0-297-77964-8*, Pub. by Weidenfeld & Nicolson) Trafalgar.

Chambers, James, ed. From Dusk till Dawn: The Graphic Novel. (Illus.). 48p. (Orig.). 1996. 4.96 (*0-9645175-3-1*) Big Enter Inc.

Chambers, James, ed. see Nimoy, Leonard.

Chambers, James A. Blacks & Crime: A Function of Class. LC 94-8338. 368p. 1995. 65.00 (*0-275-94937-0*, Praeger Pubs) Greenwood.

Chambers, Jane. Burning. LC 94-62041. (Classic Novels Ser.). (Illus.). 157p. 1995. pap. 9.95 (*1-886586-00-4*) T n T Class.

— Chasin' Jason. LC 86-21456. (Classic Novels Ser.). 224p. (Orig.). 1987. pap. 9.95 (*0-935672-13-3*) T n T Class.

— Last Summer at Bluefish Cove. deluxe limited ed. LC 81-86655. (Gay Play Script Ser.). (Illus.). 107p. (Orig.). 1982. 35.00 (*0-935672-04-4*) T n T Class.

— My Blue Heaven. LC 81-83856. (Gay Play Script Ser.). (Illus.). 91p. 1986. pap. 7.95 (*0-935672-03-6*) T n T Class.

Chambers, Jane. Quotable Cat. 9.95 (*1-85479-728-X*, Pub. by M OMara) Trafalgar.

Chambers, Jane. Quotable Cats. 100p. 1995. 4.98 (*0-7858-0427-7*) Bk Sales Inc.

— Two from Chambers: Last Summer at Bluefish Cove; A Late Snow. LC 97-60649. (Illus.). 193p. 1998. pap. 13.95 (*1-886586-04-7*) T n T Class.

— Warrior at Rest: A Collection of Poetry by Jane Chambers. LC 84-4377. 72p. 1984. pap. 6.95 (*0-935672-12-5*) T n T Class.

Chambers, Janice E. & Levi, Patricia E., eds. Organophosphates: Chemistry, Fate, & Effects. (Illus.). 443p. 1992. text 94.00 (*0-12-167345-6*) Acad Pr.

Chambers, Janice E. & Yarbrough, James D., eds. Effects of Chronic Exposures to Pesticides on Animal Systems. fac. ed. LC 81-40894. (Illus.). 262p. 1982. pap. 81.30 (*0-7837-7197-5*, 204710200005) Bks Demand.

***Chambers, Jay C., et al.** Measuring Inflation in Public Libraries: A Comparison of Two Approcahes, the Input Cost & the Cost of Services Index. 88p. 2000. pap. text 20.00 (*0-7881-8400-8*) DIANE Pub.

***Chambers, Jay G.** Measuring Inflation in Public Libraries: A Comparison of Two Approaches, the Input Cost Index & Cost of Services Index. 100p. 1999. pap. text 8.50 (*0-16-050001-X*) USGPO.

Chambers, Jeanne H. Life Is Too Short to Be Ordinary: 365 Ways to Live More Creatively at Home, at Work & Everywhere in Between. LC 96-90701. 160p. (Orig.). 1996. pap. 9.95 (*1-889771-07-4*) Full Moon Ink.

Chambers, Jim. The Police Community: Theory & Practice Alternatives, Preliminary Edition. 164p. (C). 1994. per. 22.95 (*0-8403-9284-2*) Kendall-Hunt.

Chambers, Joan. Picture the Past: Art Ideas to Recreate History for Children Ages 5-11. (Kids' Stuff Ser.). (Illus.). (J). 1995. 15.95 (*0-947882-22-7*) Belair Pubns Ltd.

Chambers, Joanna F. Art for Writing. 1999. pap. text 15.95 (*0-947882-54-5*) Incent Lrning.

— Hey, Miss! You Got a Book for ME? A Model Multicultural Resource Collection. rev. ed. LC 81-135242. 91p. 1981. pap. 12.95 (*0-940048-01-9*) Austin Bilingual Lang Ed.

Chambers, Joanna F. Simply Artistic. 1995. 15.95 (*0-947882-08-1*) Incentive Pubns.

Chambers, John. Conversations with Eternity: The Forgotten Masterpiece of Victor Hugo. LC 98-65689. 272p. 1998. pap. 13.95 (*1-892138-01-8*, Pub. by New Para Bks) ACCESS Pubs Network.

— Echocardiography in Primary Care. (Illus.). 78p. 1996. 45.00 (*1-85070-909-2*) Prthnon Pub.

Chambers, John & Monaghan, M. J., eds. Echocardiography: An International Review. (Illus.). 226p. (C). 1994. 98.00 (*0-19-262091-6*) OUP.

Chambers, John, jt. auth. see Rimmington, Helen.

Chambers, John B., ed. Clinical Echocardiography. 260p. 1995. text 51.00 (*0-7279-0810-3*, Pub. by BMJ Pub) Login Brothers Bk Co.

Chambers, John H. The Achievement of Education: An Examination of Key Concepts in Educational Practice. 206p. (C). 1989. reprint ed. pap. text 22.50 (*0-8191-7503-X*) U Pr of Amer.

— Empiricist Research on Teaching: A Philosophical & Practical Critique of Its Scientific Pretensions. LC 92-17197. (Philosophy & Education Ser.). 296p. (C). 1992. lib. bdg. 152.50 (*0-7923-1848-X*, Pub. by Kluwer Academic) Kluwer Academic.

— A Travellers' History of Australia. LC 99-10052. 1999. pap. 14.95 (*1-56656-323-2*) Interlink Pub.

Chambers, John M. Computational Methods for Data Analysis. LC 77-9493. (Wiley Series in Probability & Mathematical Statistics). (Illus.). 282p. reprint ed. pap. 87.50 (*0-8357-6067-7*, 203433100089) Bks Demand.

Chambers, John M. & Hastie. Statistical Models in S. 608p. (C). (gr. 13). 1991. per. 62.95 (*0-412-05301-2*, Chap & Hall CRC) CRC Pr.

Chambers, John W. Marisol y Magdelena Book, No. 1. LC 97-34365. (J). 1998. 15.00 (*0-689-81024-5*) S&S Trade.

Chambers, John W., II. To Raise an Army: The Draft Comes to Modern America. LC 87-15150. 448p. 1987. 40.00 (*0-02-905820-1*) Free Pr.

Chambers, John W., II, intro. The Eagle & the Dove: The American Peace Movement & United States Foreign Policy, 1900-1922. rev. ed. (Studies on Peace & Conflict Resolution). 296p. (C). 1991. reprint ed. pap. text 17.95 (*0-8156-2519-7*) Syracuse U Pr.

— The Eagle & the Dove: The American Peace Movement & United States Foreign Policy, 1900-1922. 2nd rev. ed. (Studies on Peace & Conflict Resolution). 296p. (C). 1991. reprint ed. text 45.00 (*0-8156-2518-9*) Syracuse U Pr.

Chambers, John W., 2nd & Culbert, David. World War II, Film, & History. (Illus.). 208p. 1996. pap. 15.95 (*0-19-509967-2*); text 30.00 (*0-19-509966-4*) OUP.

***Chambers, John W. & Piehler, G. Kurt.** Major Problems in American Military History: Documents & Essays. LC 98-72009. (Major Problems in American History Ser.). xx, 488p. (C). 1999. write for info. (*0-669-33538-X*) HM Trade Div.

Chambers, John W., jt. ed. see Moskos, Charles C., II.

***Chambers, John Whiteclay.** The Tyranny of Change: America in the Progressive Era, 1890-1920. LC 99-54338. 350p. 2000. pap. text 22.00 (*0-8135-2799-6*) Rutgers U Pr.

Chambers, John Whiteclay, ed. The Oxford Companion to American Military History. LC 99-21181. (Illus.). 960p. 2000. 60.00 (*0-19-507198-0*) OUP.

Chambers, Jonathan D. Nottinghamshire in the Eighteenth Century. 377p. 1966. 35.00 (*0-7146-1285-5*, Pub. by F Cass Pubs) Intl Spec Bk.

Chambers, Joseph. A Palace for the Antichrist. LC 96-69688. 296p. 1996. pap. 11.95 (*0-89221-333-7*) New Leaf.

Chambers, Joyce. How Anyone Can Create Fashion Jewelry at Home for Fun or Profit: January 1999 Edition. (Illus.). 19p. 1999. 8.95 (*0-9646693-0-7*) Paper Art Orig.

Chambers, Julie. Baby Bunny's Busy Day. (Illus.). 16p. (J). (ps-k). 1996. 7.95 (*0-694-00694-7*, HarpFestival) HarpC Child Bks.

— Santa's Busy Christmas. LC 96-230446. (Illus.). 14p. (J). (ps-3). 1996. 7.95 (*0-694-00905-9*, HarpFestival) HarpC Child Bks.

Chambers, Kareen S. Glass from Ancient Craft to Contemporary Art: 1962-1992 & Beyond. Bedula, Jane, ed. LC 92-61733. 83p. 1992. 9.00 (*0-9613046-8-5*) Morris Mus.

Chambers, Karen & Watson-Guptill Publishing Staff. Artist's Resource: The Watson-Guptill Guide to Academic Programs, Artists' Colonies & Artist-in-Residence Programs, Conferences, Workshops. (Getting Your Act Together Ser.). (Illus.). 240p. 1999. pap. text 19.95 (*0-8230-7657-1*) Watsn-Guptill.

Chambers, Karen S. Trompe l'Oeil at Home: Faux Finishes & Fantasy Settings. LC 91-52799. (Illus.). 224p. 45.00 (*0-8478-1420-3*, Pub. by Rizzoli Intl) St Martin.

Chambers, Kate. The Case of the Dog-Lover's Legacy. LC 99-60493. (Diana Winthrop Detective Ser.). 200p. (YA). (gr. 5-12). 1999. reprint ed. pap. 16.00 (*1-892323-43-5*, Pierce Harris Pr) Vivisphere.

— Danger in the Old Fort. LC 99-60494. (Diana Winthrop Detective Ser.). 200p. (YA). (gr. 5-12). 1999. reprint ed. pap. 16.00 (*1-892323-42-7*, Pierce Harris Pr) Vivisphere.

— The Legacy of Lucian Van Zandt. LC 99-60491. (Diana Winthrop Detective Ser.). 200p. (YA). (gr. 5-12). 1999. reprint ed. pap. 16.00 (*1-892323-45-1*) Vivisphere.

— The Secret of the Singing Strings. LC 99-60495. (Diana Winthrop Detective Ser.). 200p. (YA). (gr. 5-12). 1999. reprint ed. pap. 16.00 (*1-892323-41-9*, Pierce Harris Pr) Vivisphere.

— Secrets on Beacon Hill. LC 99-60492. (Diana Winthrop Detective Ser.). 200p. (YA). (gr. 5-12). 1999. reprint ed. pap. 16.00 (*1-892323-44-3*, Pierce Harris Pr) Vivisphere.

— The Threat of the Pirate Ship. LC 99-60490. (Diana Wintrop Detective Ser.). 200p. (YA). (gr. 5-12). 1999. reprint ed. pap. 16.00 (*1-892323-46-X*) Vivisphere.

Chambers, Kate & Natali, Patricia. Choose Life: Consistent Life Ethic & Political Responsibility. 32p. (Orig.). 1988. pap. text 2.95 (*1-55612-150-4*) Sheed & Ward WI.

Chambers, Kate, jt. auth. see Reardon, Anne M.

Chambers, Keith. Teach Yourself Beginner's Spanish. (Teach Yourself Beginner's Grammar Ser.). 224p. 1999. pap. 9.95 (*0-8442-2687-4*, Teach Yrslf) NTC Contemp Pub Co.

Chambers, Kevin. Culture Shock! Succeed in Business: Taiwan. (Culture Shock! Ser.). 1999. pap. text 12.95 (*1-55868-421-2*) Gr Arts Ctr Pub.

Chambers, Kevin, jt. auth. see Baguley, Kitt.

Chambers, Kimberly. Coffee Breaks. Caton, Patrick, ed. 365p. 1997. pap., spiral bd. 6.50 (*1-56245-303-3*) Great Quotations.

— Erasing My Sanity: A Humorous Look at a Teacher's Stress. Caton, Patrick, ed. LC 98-71847. 168p. 1998. pap. 5.95 (*1-56245-346-7*) Great Quotations.

***Chambers, Kimberly.** Mom's Homemade Jams. (Illus.). 1999. pap. 5.95 (*1-56245-383-1*) Great Quotations.

Chambers, Kimberly. Teacher Zone. Caton, Patrick, ed. 365p. 1996. 6.50 (*1-56245-235-5*) Great Quotations.

***Chambers, Kristin & Riley, Jan.** Malcolm Cochran Collection: (Re) Collections. (Illus.). 48p. 1999. pap. 20.00 (*1-880353-10-5*) Cleveland Ctr.

***Chambers, Kristin, et al.** Christa Donner: Pretty on the Insides. (Illus.). 24p. 1999. pap. 12.00 (*1-880353-14-8*) Cleveland Ctr.

Chambers, Lance D. Practical Handbook of Genetic Algorithm Complex Coding System. 592p. 1998. boxed set 84.95 (*0-8493-2539-0*) CRC Pr.

Chambers, Lance D., ed. Practical Handbook of Genetic Algorithms Vol. 2: New Frontiers, Vol. II. 448p. 1995. boxed set 94.95 (*0-8493-2529-3*, 2529) CRC Pr.

— Practical Handbook of Genetic Algorithms (GAs) Applications. 568p. 1995. boxed set 99.95 (*0-8493-2519-6*, 2519) CRC Pr.

Chambers, Lance D. & Taylor, Michael A. Strategic Planning: Processes, Tools & Outcomes. LC 98-70148. (Urban & Regional Planning & Development Ser.). 262p. 1998. text 65.95 (*1-84014-515-3*, Pub. by Ashgate Pub) Ashgate Pub Co.

Chambers, Larry. Death in the A Shau Valley. LC 98-92823. 1998. mass mkt. 6.99 (*0-8041-1575-3*) Ivy Books.

***Chambers, Larry.** Financial Success in the Year 2000 & Beyond. LC 99-46798. 301p. 1999. boxed set 39.95 (*1-57444-258-9*) St Lucie Pr.

Chambers, Larry. The First Time Investor: How to Start Safe, Invest Smart & Sleep Well. 2nd ed. (Illus.). 297p. 1998. pap. 19.95 (*0-07-013070-1*) McGraw.

— Guide to Financial Public Relations: How to Stand Out in the Midst of Competitive Clutter. LC 99-25238. 1999. 49.95 (*0-910944-12-1*) St Lucie Pr.

***Chambers, Larry.** The Online Trading & Brokerage Directory. LC 99-37786. 250p. 1999. pap. 19.95 (*0-07-135425-5*) McGraw.

Chambers, Larry. Recondo: LRRPs in the 101st Airborne. (Orig.). 1992. mass mkt. 5.99 (*0-8041-0843-9*) Ivy Books.

Chambers, Larry & Miller, Kenn. The First Time Investor: How to Start Safe, Invest Smart & Sleep Well! 275p. 1994. per. 19.95 (*1-55738-515-7*, Irwn Prfssnl) McGraw-Hill Prof.

Chambers, Larry, jt. auth. see Bott, Daniel R.

Chambers, Larry, jt. auth. see Bowen, John.

Chambers, Larry, jt. auth. see Lane, Michael F.

Chambers, Larry, jt. auth. see Miller, Jeffrey M.

Chambers, Leila & Hayes, Robyn. Specialized SOPs for OGBYNs. 1998. ring bd. 50.00 incl. disk (*0-910167-57-5*) Comm Unltd CA.

— Specialized SOPs for Pediatricians. 52p. 1998. ring bd. 45.00 incl. disk (*0-910167-44-3*, Dental Commun) Comm Unltd CA.

— Specialized SOPs for Primary Care Physicians. 44p. 1998. ring bd. 45.00 incl. disk (*0-910167-56-7*, Dental Commun) Comm Unltd CA.

Chambers, Leila, jt. auth. see Freeman, Robyn.

Chambers, Leland, tr. see Stamadianos, Jorge.

Chambers, Leland H., jt. ed. see Levi, Enrique J.

Chambers, Leland H., tr. see Boullosa, Carmen.

Chambers, Leland H., tr. see Campos, Julieta.

Chambers, Leland H., tr. see Estrada, Ezequiel M.

Chambers, Leland H., tr. see Leviq, Enrique J.

Chambers, Lenoir & Leidholdt, Alexander S. Standing Before the Shouting Mob: Lenoir Chambers & Virginia's Massive Resistance to Public-School Integration. LC 96-19043. 208p. 1997. text 29.95 (*0-8173-0858-X*) U of Ala Pr.

Chambers, Liam. Rebellion in Kildare, 1790-1803. LC 98-192066. 176p. 1998. pap. 19.95 (*1-85182-363-8*, Pub. by Four Cts Pr); boxed set 45.00 (*1-85182-362-X*, Pub. by Four Cts Pr) Intl Spec Bk.

Chambers, Linda A. & Issitt, Linda A., eds. Supporting the Pediatric Transfusion Recipient. LC 94-32346. (Illus.). 161p. (C). 1994. 50.00 (*1-56395-032-4*) Am Assn Blood.

Chambers, Linda A., jt. ed. see Capon, Stephen M.

Chambers, Linda A., jt. ed. see Kasprisin, Christina A.

Chambers, Lori. Married Women & the Law of Property in Nineteenth-Century Ontario. LC 97-210553. 272p. 1997. pap. text 18.95 (*0-8020-7839-7*) U of Toronto Pr.

— Married Wowen & the Law of Property in Nineteenth-Century Ontario. LC 97-210553. 272p. 1997. text 55.00 (*0-8020-0854-2*) U of Toronto Pr.

Chambers, M. Western Experience, Vol. 1. 7th ed. 1998. 40.00 (*0-07-013065-5*) McGraw.

— Western Experience, Vol. 2. 7th ed. 1998. 40.00 (*0-07-013066-3*) McGraw.

— Western Experience, Vol. C. 7th ed. 1998. 35.00 (*0-07-013069-8*) McGraw.

— Western Experience, Vol. B. 7th ed. 1998. 35.00 (*0-07-013068-X*) McGraw.

Chambers, M. M., jt. ed. see Elliott, Edward C.

Chambers, Maggie. Love Beyond the Stars: Spiritual Warriors. Miller, David & Miller, Linda, eds. (Illus.). 106p. (Orig.). 1990. pap. 8.95 (*0-9624206-1-1*) Inner Mind Dynamics.

Chambers, Marcia. The Unplayable Lie: The Untold Story of Women & Discrimination in American Golf. 240p. 1996. pap. 12.00 (*0-671-50155-0*) S&S Trade.

***Chambers, Marcia.** The Unplayable Lie: The Untold Story of Women & Discrimination in American Golf. 228p. 2000. reprint ed. text 21.00 (*0-7881-9051-2*) DIANE Pub.

Chambers, Marcus. Works Wonders: Rallying & Racing with BMC, Rootes & Chrysler. (Illus.). 320p. 1995. 32.95 (*0-947981-94-2*, Pub. by Motor Racing) Motorbooks Intl.

***Chambers, Margaret.** The Surgical Nursing of Children. (Illus.). 256p. 2001. pap. 40.50 (*0-7506-4807-4*) Buttrwrth-Heinemann.

Chambers, Margaret W. & Chambers, Andrew J. Recollections & Reminiscences. 1975. 16.95 (*0-87770-156-3*) Ye Galleon.

Chambers, Marjorie B. The Battle for Civil Rights: Or How Los Alamos Became a County. Storms, Barbara G., ed. & intro. by. LC 99-27401. (Los Alamos Story Ser.). (Illus.). 60p. 1999. pap. 10.00 (*0-941232-23-9*) Los Alamos Hist Soc.

***Chambers, Marjorie B.** Los Alamos, New Mexico: A Survey to 1949. Aldrich, Linda K., ed. LC 99-25047. (Los Alamos Story Ser.). (Illus.). 45p. 1999. pap. 10.00 (*0-941232-21-2*) Los Alamos Hist Soc.

***Chambers, Mark.** Computer Gamer's Bible. LC 99-38314. 672p. 2000. pap. 34.99 (*0-7645-3373-8*) IDG Bks.

Chambers, Mark. Running a Perfect BBS. 2nd ed. 608p. 1995. pap. 49.99 (*0-7897-0664-4*) Que.

Chambers, Mark L. Building a PC for Dummies. LC 97-81234. (For Dummies Ser.). 384p. 1998. pap. 24.99 incl. cd-rom (*0-7645-0348-0*) IDG Bks.

***Chambers, Mark L.** Building a PC for Dummies. 2nd ed. (For Dummies Ser.). 432p. 1999. pap. 24.99 incl. cd-rom (*0-7645-0571-8*) IDG Bks.

— Hewlett-Packard Official Printer Handbook. LC 98-52380. (Hewlett-Packard Press Ser.). (Illus.). 408p. 1999. pap. 19.99 (*0-7645-3289-8*) IDG Bks.

An Asterisk (*) at the beginning of an entry indicates that the title is appearing for the first time.

— Hewlett-Packard Official Recordable CD Handbook. (Illus.). 312p. 2000. pap. text 19.99 (*0-7645-3474-2*) IDG Bks.

— Teach Yourself the iMac Visually. (Illus.). 320p. 2000. pap. 29.99 (*0-7645-3453-X*) IDG Bks.

Chambers, Mark L. The Windows 98 Optimizing & Troubleshooting Little Black Book: The Hands-On Reference Guide. LC 98-8324. 400p. 1998. pap. text 29.99 (*1-57610-295-5*) Coriolis Grp.

Chambers, Marlene, ed. see Chanzit, Gwen Finkel.

Chambers, Marlene, ed. see Curry, David P.

Chambers, Marlene, ed. see Daley, Ann S.

Chambers, Marlene, ed. see Griffin, Gillett G. & Stroessner, Robert.

Chambers, Mary. Church Is Stranger Than Fiction. LC 90-37194. (Illus.). 104p. (Orig.). 1990. pap. 6.99 (*0-8308-1326-8*, 1326) InterVarsity.

— Faith in Orbit: A Spaced Odyssey. LC 95-12633. (Illus.). 104p. (Orig.). 1995. pap. 6.99 (*0-8308-1612-7*) InterVarsity.

— Motherhood Is Stranger Than Fiction. (Illus.). 104p. 1995. pap. 6.99 (*0-8308-1603-8*, 1603) InterVarsity.

Chambers, Mary D. Secret of Better Baking. (Illus.). 1975. pap. 2.00 (*0-89166-007-0*) Cobblesmith.

Chambers, Mary-Lynn. A Time for Training Wheels: Family Devotions for Three to Eight Year Olds. (Illus.). 87p. (J). (ps-2). 1995. pap. 11.95 (*0-921788-22-3*) Kindred Prods.

***Chambers, Melvett G.** Black History Quiz Book: A Look Back at the Past 100 Years; 1900-1999. Halstied, Evelyn F., ed. (Illus.). 186p. 2000. pap. 16.95 (*1-890994-18-9*, Pub. by M Chambers) Baker & Taylor.

Chambers, Merritt M., jt. ed. see Elliott, Edward C.

Chambers, Mortimer, et al. The Western Experience. 6th ed. LC 94-17442. 1216p. (C). 1994. 76.56 (*0-07-011066-2*) McGraw.

— The Western Experience. 7th ed. LC 98-18172. 1133p. 1999. write for info. (*0-07-012954-1*, McGrw-H College) McGrw-H Hghr Educ.

— The Western Experience Vol. 1: To the Eighteenth Century, Vol. 2. 6th ed. (C). 1994. pap. 54.38 (*0-07-011068-9*) McGraw.

— The Western Experience Vol. C: The Modern Era, Vol. 6. 6th ed. (C). 1994. pap. 45.63 (*0-07-011072-7*) McGraw.

— The Western Experience Vol. A: Antiquity & the Middle Ages, Vol. 4. 6th ed. (C). 1994. pap. 45.63 (*0-07-011070-0*) McGraw.

— The Western Experience Vol. B: The Early Modern Era, Vol. 5. 6th ed. (C). 1994. pap. 45.63 (*0-07-011071-9*) McGraw.

Chambers, Mortimer, tr. see Polybius.

Chambers, Mortimer H. Georg Busolt: His Career in His Letters. LC 89-71202. (Mnemosyne Ser.: Supplement 113). (ENG & GER., Illus.). xii, 232p. 1990. pap. 64.00 (*90-04-09225-0*) Brill Academic Pubs.

***Chambers, Muriel Evelyn.** Scramble for Africa. 2nd ed. LC 98-54665. 160p. 1999. pap. 14.66 (*0-582-36881-2*) Addison-Wesley.

Chambers, Nancy, ed. The Signal Approach to Children's Books. LC 81-8824. 352p. 1981. 29.00 (*0-8108-1447-1*) Scarecrow.

Chambers, Nancy K., et al. Growth Through Nature: A Preschool Program for Children with Disabilities. Loomis, Harvey, ed. LC 99-21559. 1999. pap. 25.00 (*0-89831-042-3*, Pub. by Sagapr) Timber.

Chambers, Naomi. Nurse Practitioners in Primary Care. LC 98-198331. 130 p. 1998. write for info. (*1-85775-298-8*) Scovill Paterson.

***Chambers, Neil, ed.** The Letters of Sir Joseph Banks. LC 99-89844. 200p. 2000. 46.00 (*1-86094-204-0*) World Scientific Pub.

Chambers, O. En Pos de Lo Supremo.Tr. of My Utmost for His Highest. (SPA.). pap. 6.95 (*958-9149-03-0*, 498599) Editorial Unilit.

Chambers, Oswald. Approved unto God. 1991. pap. 10.95 (*0-87508-329-3*) Chr Lit.

— Approved unto God. 1980. pap. write for info. (*0-551-05148-5*) M Pickering.

— Approved unto God with, Facing Reality: The Spiritual Life of the Christian Worker. LC 97-19061. 128p. 1997. pap. 10.99 (*1-57293-003-9*) Discovery Hse Pubs.

— Baffled to Fight Better. 1990. pap. 9.95 (*0-87508-304-8*) Chr Lit.

— Baffled to Fight Better: Job & the Problem of Suffering. LC 96-17994. 144p. 1990. pap. 9.99 (*0-929239-19-9*) Discovery Hse Pubs.

— Biblical Ethics. 359p. 1998. pap. 13.95 (*0-87508-493-1*, 493) Chr Lit.

— Biblical Ethics; Moral Foundations of Life; the Philosophy of Sin: Ethical Principles of the Christian Life, 2 vols. in 1. LC 98-27275. 368p. 1998. pap. 14.99 (*1-57293-035-7*) Discovery Hse Pubs.

— Biblical Psychology. rev. ed. 240p. (Orig.). 1995. pap. 12.95 (*0-87508-089-8*, 089) Chr Lit.

— Biblical Psychology: Christ-Centered Solutions for Daily Problems. rev. ed. LC 95-32209. 240p. 1995. pap. 12.99 (*0-929239-60-1*) Discovery Hse Pubs.

— Bringing Sons into Glory. 224p. (Orig.). 1990. pap. 10.95 (*0-87508-301-3*, 301) Chr Lit.

— Bringing Sons into Glory - Making All Things New. 224p. 1990. pap. 11.99 (*0-929239-24-5*) Discovery Hse Pubs.

— Christian Disciplines. 222p. 1995. pap. 12.95 (*0-87508-090-1*, 090) Chr Lit.

— Christian Disciplines. LC 94-30010. 224p. 1995. pap. 12.99 (*0-929239-64-4*) Discovery Hse Pubs.

— Classic Writings of Oswald Chambers: Daily Meditations for Morning & Evening. 1994. 14.99 (*0-88486-102-3*) Arrowood Pr.

***Chambers, Oswald.** Complete Works of Oswald Chambers. 2000. 39.95 (*1-57293-039-X*) Discovery Hse Pubs.

Chambers, Oswald. Conformed to His Image: Servant As His Lord. rev. ed. 1996. pap. 12.99 (*0-87508-327-7*, 327, Discov Hse) Chr Lit.

— Conformed to His Image & the Servant as His Lord: Lessons Jesus on Living Like Jesus. LC 96-34431. 224p. 1996. pap. 12.99 (*1-57293-020-9*) Discovery Hse Pubs.

— Daily Thoughts for Disciples. LC 94-13451. 384p. 1994. 16.99 (*0-929239-47-4*) Discovery Hse Pubs.

— Daily Thoughts for Disciples. 208p. 1986. 12.95 (*0-310-30470-9*, 6450) Zondervan.

— Daily Thoughts for Disciples. 256p. 1992. pap. 9.99 (*0-310-58481-7*) Zondervan.

— Devotions for a Deeper Life: A Daily Devotional. 240p. 1986. 14.99 (*0-310-38710-8*, 17070) Zondervan.

***Chambers, Oswald.** Disciplinas Cristanas. 1999. pap. text 8.99 (*0-8297-0619-4*) Vida Pubs.

Chambers, Oswald. En Pos de Lo Supremo. 1994. 13.95 (*84-7645-706-5*) Libros Clie.

***Chambers, Oswald.** Faith: A Holy Walk. Link, Julie, ed. LC 99-46084. 160p. 1999. 12.99 (*1-57293-053-5*, Pub. by Discovery Hse Pubs) Barbour Pub.

Chambers, Oswald. God's Workmanship. 1979. 13.95 (*0-87508-331-5*) Chr Lit.

— God's Workmanship. write for info. (*0-551-05517-0*) Zondervan.

— God's Workmanship & He Shall Glorify Me: The Holy Spirit & the Life of the Believer. LC 97-17066. 352p. 1997. reprint ed. pap. 13.99 (*1-57293-029-2*) Discovery Hse Pubs.

Chambers, Oswald. The Highest Good & the Shadow of an Agony. 240p. (Orig.). 1992. pap. 10.95 (*0-87508-307-2*, 307) Chr Lit.

Chambers, Oswald. If You Will Ask. 1985. pap. 7.95 (*0-87508-292-0*) Chr Lit.

— If You Will Ask: Reflections on the Power of Prayer. LC 96-33345. 96p. 1989. pap. 7.99 (*0-929239-06-7*) Discovery Hse Pubs.

— In the Presence of His Majesty. LC 96-221567. 72p. 1996. 17.99 (*1-57673-125-1*) Multnomah Pubs.

— The Love of God. 1986. pap. 8.95 (*0-87508-293-9*) Chr Lit.

— The Love of God. 128p. 1988. pap. 8.99 (*0-929239-04-0*) Discovery Hse Pubs.

— Meditaciones Vida Mas Profundo. (SPA.). 1998. pap. 10.99 (*0-8297-0487-6*) Vida Pubs.

— My Utmost for His Highest. (Essential Christian Library Ser.). 384p. 1998. 9.97 (*1-57748-264-6*) Barbour Pub.

***Chambers, Oswald.** My Utmost for His Highest. (Deluxe Christian Classics). 384p. 2000. 9.97 (*1-57748-914-4*) Barbour Pub.

Chambers, Oswald. My Utmost for His Highest. anniversary ed. (Christian Library Ser.). 282p. 1987. reprint ed. bond lthr. 9.97 (*1-55748-054-0*) Barbour Pub.

— My Utmost for His Highest. deluxe ed. 1988. bond lthr. 14.97 (*1-55748-059-1*) Barbour Pub.

— My Utmost for His Highest. large type ed. 384p. 1999. pap. 12.97 (*1-57748-589-0*) Barbour Pub.

— My Utmost for His Highest. large type ed. (Christian Library Ser.). 282p. 1987. reprint ed. bond lthr. 14.97 (*0-916441-83-0*) Barbour Pub.

— My Utmost for His Highest. anniversary ed. (Christian Library Ser.). 384p. 2000. reprint ed. lthr. 4.97 (*0-916441-82-2*) Barbour Pub.

— My Utmost for His Highest: An Updated Edition in Today's Language - the Golden Book of Oswald Chambers. Reimann, James, ed. LC 95-18752. 400p. 1995. 14.99 (*0-929239-99-7*) Discovery Hse Pubs.

— My Utmost for His Highest: An Updated Edition in Today's Language:The Golden Book of Oswald Chambers. rev. ed. LC 92-15394. 395p. 1992. 14.99 (*0-929239-57-1*) Discovery Hse Pubs.

— My Utmost for His Highest: Prayer Edition. 384p. 1999. 12.97 (*1-57748-590-4*) Barbour Pub.

— My Utmost for His Highest Journal. 1995. bond lthr. 19.97 (*1-55748-737-5*) Barbour Pub.

— My Utmost for His Highest, Updated Language: An Updated Edition in Today's Language. large type ed. LC 98-7253. 384p. 1998. pap. 14.99 (*1-57293-037-3*) Discovery Hse Pubs.

— A New Testment Walk with Oswald Chambers. LC 97-37467. 208p. 1998. 14.99 (*0-8007-1753-8*) Revell.

— Not Knowing Where. 1989. pap. 8.95 (*0-87508-302-1*) Chr Lit.

— Not Knowing Where: A Spiritual Journey Through the Book of Genesis. LC 96-33343. 208p. 1989. pap. 10.99 (*0-929239-15-6*) Discovery Hse Pubs.

— Our Brilliant Heritage. 334p. 1999. pap. 13.95 (*0-87508-494-X*, 494) Chr Lit.

— Our Brilliant Heritage: And, If You Will Be Perfect, with Disciples Indeed. LC 98-26759. 336p. 1998. pap. 14.99 (*1-57293-042-X*) Discovery Hse Pubs.

— The Place of Help. 1979. pap. 10.95 (*0-87508-303-X*) Chr Lit.

— The Place of Help: God's Provision for Our Daily Needs. 256p. 1989. pap. 10.99 (*0-929239-18-0*) Discovery Hse Pubs.

— Prayer: A Holy Occupation. LC 92-35949. 192p. 1993. 12.99 (*0-929239-59-8*) Discovery Hse Pubs.

***Chambers, Oswald.** Selections from My Utmost for His Highest. 96p. 2000. 9.97 (*1-57748-716-8*) Barbour Pub.

Chambers, Oswald. Shade of His Hand. 1979. pap. 10.95 (*0-87508-295-5*) Chr Lit.

— Shade of His Hand. 176p. 1991. pap. 10.99 (*0-929239-28-8*) Discovery Hse Pubs.

— Shadow of an Agony - The Highest Good. 240p. 1992. pap. 11.99 (*0-929239-53-9*) Discovery Hse Pubs.

— So Send I You - Workmen of God. 1993. pap. 10.95 (*0-87508-308-0*) Chr Lit.

— So Send I You - Workmen of God: Recognizing & Answering God's Call to Service. LC 93-395. 240p. 1993. pap. 11.99 (*0-929239-74-1*) Discovery Hse Pubs.

— Still Higher for His Highest. LC 75-120048. 1970. reprint ed. 10.95 (*0-310-22410-1*, 6494) Zondervan.

— Studies in the Sermon on the Mount. 96p. 1995. pap. 7.95 (*0-87508-310-2*, 310) Chr Lit.

— Studies in the Sermon on the Mount: God's Character & the Believer's Conduct. LC 95-47654. 96p. 1996. reprint ed. pap. 7.99 (*1-57293-009-8*) Discovery Hse Pubs.

— Treasures from My Utmost for His Highest. Harmon, Dan, ed. LC 99-176686. 128p. 1997. 7.97 (*1-57748-078-3*) Barbour Pub.

Chambers, Oswald & Bargain Books Staff. My Utmost for His Highest. 384p. 1997. lthr. 9.97 (*1-57748-142-9*) Barbour Pub.

Chambers, Oswald & Black, Glenn D. Still Higher for His Highest: Now with NIV Text. 192p. 1989. 14.99 (*0-310-23600-2*) Zondervan.

Chambers, Oswald & Reimann, James, eds. My Utmost for His Highest: Updated Edition in Today's Language. (Believer's Life System Ser.). 1997. ring bd. 14.99 (*0-8024-2786-3*) Moody.

Chambers, Oswald, jt. auth. see Couchman, Judith.

Chambers, P. L. The Attic Nights of Aulus Gellius: An Intermediate Reader-Grammar Review. 4th ed. (Latin Alive & Well Ser.). (LAT., Illus.). 88p. (C). 1996. 16.95 (*0-9628450-3-5*) P L Chambers.

— Latin Alive & Well: An Introductory Text. 6th ed. (LAT., Illus.). 292p. (C). 1997. reprint ed. 28.95 (*0-9628450-0-0*) P L Chambers.

Chambers, P. L., et al, eds. Biological Monitoring of Exposure & the Response at the Subcellular Level of Toxic Substances. (Illus.). xiii, 463p. 1989. 182.00 (*0-387-50336-6*) Spr-Verlag.

— Mechanisms & Models in Toxicology. (Archives of Toxicology Ser.: Supp. 11). (Illus.). viii, 365p. 1987. pap. 134.60 (*0-387-17614-4*) Spr-Verlag.

— Recent Developments in Toxicology: Trends, Methods & Problems: Proceedings of the European Society of Toxicology Meeting Held in Leipzig, September 12-14, 1990. (Archives of Toxicology Ser.: Suppl. 14). (Illus.). 320p. 1991. 158.00 (*0-387-51422-8*) Spr-Verlag.

— The Target Organ & the Toxic Process. (Archives of Toxicology Ser.: Suppl. 12). (Illus.). 465p. 1988. 182.00 (*0-387-18512-7*) Spr-Verlag.

— Toxicology in the Use, Misuse, & Abuse of Food, Drugs & Chemicals. (Archives of Toxicology Ser.: Suppl. 6). (Illus.). 380p. 1983. pap. 85.00 (*0-387-12392-X*) Spr-Verlag.

Chambers, P. L., et al. Disease, Metabolism & Reproduction in the Toxic Response to Drugs & Other Chemicals: Proceedings of the European Society of Toxicology Meeting Held in Rome, March 28-30, 1983. (Archives of Toxicology Ser.: Suppl. 7). (Illus.). 400p. 1984. 111.00 (*0-387-12452-7*) Spr-Verlag.

Chambers, Pam & Martin, Ron. Public Speaking Made Easy. 1997. 27.95 (*0-9650527-3-7*) Success Dynamic.

Chambers, Pam, ed. see Winters, Donna.

Chambers, Pamela. Cupid's Mistress. 1999. pap. 7.95 (*0-533-12982-6*) Vantage.

Chambers, Pamela Q. Family Recipe. 304p. (Orig.). 1995. mass mkt. 4.99 (*0-515-11589-4*, Jove) Berkley Pub.

Chambers, Pamela Q., ed. Unlikely Duet. LC 97-77934. (Great Lakes Romances Ser.: Pt. 1). 216p. 1998. pap. 9.95 (*0-923048-86-3*, Grt Lakes Romances) Bigwater Pub.

Chambers, Pamela Q., ed. see Winters, Donna.

Chambers, Pamela Quint. Bride Quilt. 352p. 1999. mass mkt. 5.99 (*0-8217-6214-1*) Kensgtn Pub Corp.

***Chambers, Patricia & Graham, Thomas.** The Directory of Historic House Museums. (American Association for State & Local History Book Ser.). 500p. 1999. pap. 79.95 (*0-7425-0344-5*) Rowman.

Chambers, Paul. Life on Mars: The Complete Story. LC 99-198130. 1999. 22.95 (*0-7137-2747-0*, Pub. by Blandford Pr) Sterling.

— Paranormal People: The Famous, the Infamous & the Supernatural. LC 98-170908. (Illus.). 232p. 1998. pap. 14.95 (*0-7137-2712-8*) Sterling.

***Chambers, Paul.** Sex & the Paranormal. LC 99-495099. 192p. 1999. pap. text 14.95 (*0-7137-2763-2*) Strlng Pub CA.

Chambers, Peter. Always Take the Big Ones. large type ed. (Linford Mystery Library). 320p. 1996. pap. 16.99 (*0-7089-7938-6*) Ulverscroft.

***Chambers, Peter.** The Bad Die Young. 192p. 1998. 19.50 (*0-7540-8515-5*, Black Dagger) Chivers N Amer.

— The Bad Die Young. large type ed. 312p. 1999. pap. 18.99 (*0-7089-5587-8*, Linford) Ulverscroft.

— The Blonde Wore Black. 21.95 (*0-7540-8539-2*, Black Dagger) Chivers N Amer.

— The Blonde Wore Black. large type ed. 312p. 1999. pap. 18.99 (*0-7089-5558-4*, Linford) Ulverscroft.

Chambers, Peter. Bomb Scare - Flight 147. large type ed. (Linford Mystery Library). 320p. 1997. pap. 16.99 (*0-7089-5021-3*) Ulverscroft.

— The Day of the Big Dollar. large type ed. (Linford Mystery Library). 288p. 1994. pap. 16.99 (*0-7089-7481-3*, Linford) Ulverscroft.

— The Day the Thames Caught Fire. large type ed. (Linford Mystery Library). 576p. 1992. pap. 16.99 (*0-7089-7270-5*) Ulverscroft.

— The Deader They Fall. large type ed. (Linford Mystery Library). 304p. 1994. pap. 16.99 (*0-7089-7560-7*) Ulverscroft.

— Down-Beat Kill. large type ed. (Linford Mystery Library). 368p. 1994. pap. 16.99 (*0-7089-7485-6*, Linford) Ulverscroft.

— Dragons Can Be Dangerous. large type ed. (Dales Large Print Ser.). 288p. 1996. pap. 18.99 (*1-85389-656-X*, Dales) Ulverscroft.

— Female - Handle with Care. large type ed. (Linford Mystery Library). 1995. pap. 16.99 (*0-7089-7804-5*, Linford) Ulverscroft.

— The Highly Explosive Case. large type ed. (Linford Mystery Library). 1995. pap. 16.99 (*0-7089-7801-0*, Linford) Ulverscroft.

— Hot Money Caper. large type ed. (Linford Mystery Large Print Ser.). 288p. 1998. pap. 17.99 (*0-7089-5263-1*, Linford) Ulverscroft.

— Jail Bait. large type ed. (Lythway Ser.). 208p. 1991. 21.95 (*0-7451-1251-X*, G K Hall Lrg Type) Mac Lib Ref.

— The Lady Who Never Was. large type ed. (Linford Mystery Large Print Ser.). 1995. pap. 16.99 (*0-7089-7809-6*, Linford) Ulverscroft.

— Lady, You're Killing Me. large type ed. (Linford Mystery Library). 304p. 1994. pap. 16.99 (*0-7089-7568-2*) Ulverscroft.

— A Miniature Murder Mystery. large type ed. (Dales Large Print Ser.). 240p. 1996. pap. 18.99 (*1-85389-655-1*, Dales) Ulverscroft.

— The Moving Picture Writes. large type ed. (Linford Mystery Library). 304p. 1996. pap. 16.99 (*0-7089-7976-9*) Ulverscroft.

— Murder Is Its Own Reward. large type ed. (Linford Mystery Library). 240p. 1995. pap. 16.99 (*0-7089-7797-9*, Linford) Ulverscroft.

— No Peace for the Wicked. large type ed. (Linford Mystery Library). 384p. 1998. pap. 17.99 (*0-7089-5220-8*, Linford) Ulverscroft.

— Somebody Has to Lose. large type ed. (Dales Mystery Ser.). 211p. 1992. pap. 18.99 (*1-85389-307-2*) Ulverscroft.

— Speak Ill of the Dead. large type ed. (Linford Mystery Library). 368p. 1993. pap. 16.99 (*0-7089-7385-X*, Linford) Ulverscroft.

— They Call It Murder. large type ed. (Linford Mystery Library). 288p. 1993. pap. 16.99 (*0-7089-7389-2*, Linford) Ulverscroft.

— The Vanishing Holes Murders. large type ed. (Linford Mystery Library). 304p. 1996. pap. 16.99 (*0-7089-7942-4*, Linford) Ulverscroft.

Chambers, Peter, jt. auth. see Rockwood, Alyn.

Chambers, Peter A. Dames Can Be Deadly. large type ed. 291p. 1993. pap. 18.99 (*1-85389-427-3*, Dales) Ulverscroft.

C

Chambers, Q., jt. auth. see Hatsumi, Masaaki.

Chambers, Quintin T., jt. auth. see Hatsumi, Masaaki.

Chambers, R. California Mortgage Loan Brokering & Lending. LC 98-2511. 558p. (C). 1998. 56.00 (*0-13-375007-8*, Prentice Hall) P-H.

— Popular Rhymes of Scotland. 1972. 59.95 (*0-8490-0879-4*) Gordon Pr.

Chambers, R. C. & Trippel, E. L., eds. Early Life History & Recruitment in Fish Populations. (Fish & Fisheries Ser.). (Illus.). 632p. 1997. write for info. (*0-412-64190-9*) Kluwer Academic.

Chambers, R. D., ed. Organofluorine Chemistry: Fluorinated Alkenes & Reactive Intermediates. (Topics in Current Chemistry Ser.: Vol. 192). (Illus.). 260p. 1997. 139.00 (*3-540-63171-2*) Spr-Verlag.

— Organofluorine Chemistry: Techniques & Synthons. (Topics in Current Chemistry Ser.: Vol. 193). (Illus.). 265p. 1997. 139.00 (*3-540-63170-4*) Spr-Verlag.

Chambers, R. J. Foundations of Accounting. 216p. 1995. pap. 80.00 (*0-949823-18-X*, Pub. by Deakin Univ) St Mut.

Chambers, R. J., ed. An Accounting Thesaurus: 500 Years of Accounting. LC 95-18243. 1100p. 1995. 123.00 (*0-08-042573-9*, Pergamon Pr) Elsevier.

***Chambers, R. J. & Dean, G. W.** Logic, Law & Ethics. LC 00-26480. (Chambers on Accounting Ser.). 2000. write for info. (*0-8153-3786-8*) Garland.

Chambers, R. W. The King in Yellow. 2nd ed. (Classic Fantasy Ser.). 253p. 1999. reprint ed. pap. 9.99 (*0-946626-51-0*) Dedalus.

— On the Continuity of English Prose. (EETS, OS Ser.: Vol. 191A). 1974. reprint ed. 20.00 (*0-8115-3379-4*) Periodicals Srv.

Chambers, R. W., ed. On the Continuity of English Prose from Alfred to More & His School: (An Extract from the Introduction to OS 186) (EETS Original Ser.: No. 191). 1963. reprint ed. 20.00 (*0-19-722556-X*, Pub. by EETS) Boydell & Brewer.

Chambers, R. W. & Seton, W. W., eds. A Fifteenth-Century Courtesy Book & Two Fifteenth-Century Franciscan Rules. (EETS Original Ser.: Vol. 148). 1963. reprint ed. 20.00 (*0-19-722148-3*, Pub. by EETS) Boydell & Brewer.

Chambers, R. W., jt. ed. see Hitchcock, Elsie V.

Chambers, Rae D., jt. auth. see Arnold, Harrison H.

Chambers, Raymond J. Accounting, Evaluation & Economic Behavior. LC 66-13944. 1975. reprint ed. text 35.00 (*0-914348-15-9*) Scholars Bk.

Chambers, Raymond W. Jacobean Shakespeare & Measure for Measure, Vol. 21. LC 73-109641. (Oxford Paperbacks Ser.). 58 p. 1977. 15.95 (*0-8369-5250-2*) Ayer.

— Man's Unconquerable Mind. LC 67-30811. (Studies in Poetry: No. 38). (Illus.). 1969. reprint ed. lib. bdg. 75.00 (*0-8383-0711-6*) M S G Haskell Hse.

— Place of Saint Thomas More in English Literature & History. LC 65-15870. (English Biography Ser.: No. 31). 1969. reprint ed. lib. bdg. 75.00 (*0-8383-0523-7*) M S G Haskell Hse.

— Ruskin & Others on Byron. LC 78-100737. (English Literature Ser.: No. 33). 1970. reprint ed. pap. 39.95 (*0-8383-0012-X*) M S G Haskell Hse.

— Widsith, A Study in Old English Heroic Legend. (BCL1-PR English Literature Ser.). 263p. 1992. reprint ed. lib. bdg. 79.00 (*0-7812-7166-5*) Rprt Serv.

Chambers, Richard E., ed. Plastics Composites for the 21st Century Construction: Proceedings of a Session. LC 93-32978. 80p. 1993. 17.00 (*0-87262-989-9*) Am Soc Civil Eng.

Chambers, Richard E., jt. auth. see Lewis, Robert C.

Chambers, Richard L. & Kut, Gunay, eds. Contemporary Turkish Short Stories: An Intermediate Reader. LC 76-21045. (Middle Eastern Languages & Linguistics Ser.: No. 3). 1977. 20.00 (*0-88297-013-5*) Bibliotheca.

Chambers, Richard L., ed. see Conference on the Beginnings of Modernization in t.

Chambers, Richard L., jt. ed. see Yarus, Jeffrey M.

Chambers, Rick. Anything But Free. LC 93-472. (Open Door Bks.). 1993. pap. 3.95 (*1-56212-033-6*) CRC Pubns.

— Casey's Grudge. LC 95-33211. (Open Door Bks.). 1995. pap. 3.95 (*1-56212-131-6*) CRC Pubns.

— Something to Hide. LC 95-16421. (Open Door Bks.). 1995. pap. 3.95 (*1-56212-103-0*) CRC Pubns.

Chambers, Rob. Alaska, the Last of the Land & the First. 116p. (YA). (gr. 4-12). 1988. pap., student ed., wbk. ed. 7.95 (*1-878051-25-3*) Circumpolar Pr.

— Alaska, the Last of the Land & the First. (Illus.). 182p. (YA). (gr. 4-12). 1988. pap., teacher ed. 15.95 (*1-878051-05-9*) Circumpolar Pr.

Chambers, Rob. Alaska, the Last of the Land & the First. (Teaching Alaska Ser.: Vol. 4). (Illus.). 160p. 1988. pap. text 15.95 (*1-878051-07-5*, CP019) Circumpolar Pr.

Chambers, Robert. A Biographical Dictionary of Eminent Scotsmen, 3 vols. rev. ed. (Illus.). 1731p. 1971. reprint ed. lib. bdg. 480.00 (*0-945345-44-5*) G Olms Pubs.

— Challenging the Professions: Frontiers for Rural Development. (Illus.). 180p. 1993. pap. 9.95 (*1-85339-194-8*, Pub. by Intermed Tech); text 38.00 (*1-85339-208-1*, Pub. by Intermed Tech) Stylus Pub VA.

— A Course of Lectures on the English Law: Delivered at the University of Oxford, 1767-1773, Vol. 2. Curley, Thomas M., ed. LC 84-40493. 461p. reprint ed. pap. 143.00 (*0-608-09849-3*, 206923700002) Bks Demand.

— Managing Rural Development: Ideas & Experience from East Africa. LC 85-23717. 216p. 1985. pap. 67.00 (*0-7837-2365-2*, 204004800006) Bks Demand.

— Managing Rural Development: Ideas & Experience from East Africa. 216p. 1974. write for info. (*91-7106-075-8*, Pub. by Nordic Africa) Transaction Pubs.

— Resulting Trusts. LC 96-54803. 290p. 1997. text 85.00 (*0-19-876444-8*) OUP.

— Rural Development: Putting the Last First. 256p. 1995. pap. 25.67 (*0-582-64443-7*) Addison-Wesley.

— The Scottish Ballads. LC 77-144549. reprint ed. 44.50 (*0-404-08628-4*) AMS Pr.

— Vestiges of the Natural History of Creation & Other Evolutionary Writings. LC 93-48415. 312p. 1994. pap. text 19.95 (*0-226-10073-1*) U Ch Pr.

— Vestiges of the Natural History of Creation & Other Evolutionary Writings. LC 93-48415. 304p. 1994. lib. bdg. 45.00 (*0-226-10072-3*) U Ch Pr.

— Whose Reality Counts? Putting the First Last. (Illus.). 297p. (Orig.). 1997. pap. 9.95 (*1-85339-386-X*, Pub. by Intermed Tech) Stylus Pub VA.

Chambers, Robert, ed. Scottish Songs, 2 vols. in 1. LC 70-144547. reprint ed. 76.50 (*0-404-08626-8*) AMS Pr.

— The Songs of Scotland Prior to Burns. LC 73-144548. reprint ed. 57.50 (*0-404-08627-6*) AMS Pr.

Chambers, Robert, et al, eds. Seasonal Dimensions to Rural Poverty. LC 81-2838. 276p. 1981. text 50.00 (*0-86598-057-8*, R3835) Rowman.

Chambers, Robert & Chambers, Edward L. Explorations into the Nature of the Living Cell. LC 61-8845. 376p. reprint ed. pap. 116.60 (*0-7837-4477-3*, 204418500001) Bks Demand.

Chambers, Robert & Coffin, Tristram P., intros. The Book of Days: A Miscellany of Popular Antiquities, 2 vols., Set. LC 89-63013. (Illus.). 1990. reprint ed. lib. bdg. 140.00 (*1-55888-848-9*) Omnigraphics Inc.

Chambers, Robert, et al. Farmer First. 240p. 1989. pap. 9.95 (*1-85339-007-0*, Pub. by Intermed Tech) Stylus Pub VA.

Chambers, Robert, ed. see Pacey, Arnold & Thrupp, Lori A.

Chambers, Robert G. Applied Production Analysis: A Dual Approach. 352p. 1988. pap. text 36.95 (*0-521-31427-5*) Cambridge U Pr.

***Chambers, Robert G. & Quiggin, John.** Uncertainty, Production, Choice & Agency: The State-Contingent Approach. LC 99-52880. (Illus.). 384p. (C). 2000. write for info. (*0-521-62244-1*); pap. write for info. (*0-521-78523-5*) Cambridge U Pr.

Chambers, Robert R. Political Theory & Societal Ethics. LC 91-20513. 165p. 1992. 26.95 (*0-87975-696-9*) Prometheus Bks.

***Chambers, Robert S.** The God of War: When I Rode with N. B. Forrest, The Letters of Henry Wylie. (Journal of Confederate History Book Ser.: Vol. 22). 288p. 2000. pap. 16.95 (*1-889332-30-5*, Pub. by So Herit Pr) Alexander Dist.

Chambers, Robert S. The God of War: When I Rode with N. B. Forrest/The Letters of Henry Wylie. (Illus.). vii, 293p. 1996. pap. 11.95 (*0-9654279-0-0*) King Phllip OH.

Chambers, Robert W. Better Man. LC 78-157773. (Short Story Index Reprint Ser.). (Illus.). 1977. reprint ed. 22.95 (*0-8369-3885-2*) Ayer.

— The Fighting Chance. (BCL1-PS American Literature Ser.). 499p. 1992. reprint ed. lib. bdg. 99.00 (*0-7812-6684-X*) Rprt Serv.

— The Gay Rebellion. 1975. 28.95 (*0-405-06281-8*) Ayer.

— The Gay Rebellion. LC 74-15953. (Science Fiction Ser.). (Illus.). 299p. 1975. reprint ed. 17.00 (*0-685-51337-8*) Ayer.

— Haunts of Men. LC 78-103503. (Short Story Index Reprint Ser.). 1977. 21.95 (*0-8369-3245-5*) Ayer.

— The King in Yellow. LC 72-75775. (Short Story Index Reprint Ser.). 1977. 28.95 (*0-8369-3000-2*) Ayer.

— The King in Yellow. 254p. 1992. reprint ed. lib. bdg. 31.95 (*0-89966-943-3*) Buccaneer Bks.

— Maker of Moons. LC 75-98565. (Short Story Index Reprint Ser.). 1977. 24.95 (*0-8369-3139-4*) Ayer.

— Mystery of Choice. LC 73-94710. (Short Story Index Reprint Ser.). 1977. 20.95 (*0-8369-3089-4*) Ayer.

***Chambers, Robert W.** Out of the Dark Vol. I: Origins. Lamb, Hugh, ed. xii, 170p. 1998. 38.50 (*1-899562-41-9*) Ash-Tree.

— Out of the Dark Vol. II: Diversions. Lamb, Hugh, ed. xiv, 206p. 1999. 39.50 (*1-899562-74-5*) Ash-Tree.

Chambers, Robert W. The Slayer of Souls. Reginald, R. & Melville, Douglas, eds. LC 77-84207. (Lost Race & Adult Fantasy Ser.). 1978. reprint ed. lib. bdg. 29.95 (*0-405-10963-6*) Ayer.

— Yellow Sign & Other Stories. 660p. 1998. pap. 19.95 (*1-56882-126-3*) Chaosium.

— Young Man in a Hurry & Other Short Stories. LC 71-103504. (Short Story Index Reprint Ser.). 1977. 21.95 (*0-8369-3246-3*) Ayer.

Chambers, Ron. Three Really Nasty Plays. unabridged ed. LC 97-22595. 224p. 1997. pap. 14.95 (*0-88734-928-5*, Pub. by Red Deer) Empire Pub Srvs.

Chambers, Rosalind, ed. see Wootton, Barbara.

Chambers, Rosemary. The Bily Book: (Because I Love You) (Illus.). 92p. 1998. pap. 9.95 (*1-58446-000-8*) Temple Pubg.

Chambers, Ross. Facing It: AIDS Diaries & the Death of the Author. LC 98-9005. (Illus.). 160p. 1998. text 32.50 (*0-472-10958-8*, 10958) U of Mich Pr.

***Chambers, Ross.** Facing It: AIDS Diaries & the Death of the Author. (Illus.). 160p. (C). 2000. pap. 16.95 (*0-472-08748-7*, 08748) U of Mich Pr.

Chambers, Ross. Loiterature. LC 98-33653. (Stages Ser.). 312p. 1999. text 70.00 (*0-8032-1467-7*, Bison Books); pap. text 25.00 (*0-8032-6392-9*, Bison Books) U of Nebr Pr.

— Meaning & Meaningfulness: Studies in the Analysis & Interpretation of Texts. LC 79-50280. (French Forum Monographs: No. 15). 197p. (Orig.). 1979. pap. 12.95 (*0-917058-14-3*) French Forum.

— Room for Maneuver: Reading (the) Oppositional (in) Narrative. 312p. 1991. pap. text 17.95 (*0-226-10076-6*) U Ch Pr.

— Room for Maneuver: Reading (the) Oppositional (in) Narrative. 312p. 1996. lib. bdg. 48.00 (*0-226-10075-8*) U Ch Pr.

— Story & Situation: Narrative Seduction & the Power of Fiction. LC 83-14787. (Theory & History of Literature Ser.: No. 12). 279p. (C). 1984. pap. 18.95 (*0-8166-1298-6*) U of Minn Pr.

— The Writing of Melancholy: Modes of Opposition in Early French Modernism. Trouille, Mary, tr. LC 92-27590. 256p. (C). 1993. 32.95 (*0-226-10070-7*) U Ch Pr.

Chambers, Ross, ed. Discours et Pouvoir. LC 81-50963. (Michigan Romance Studies: Vol. 2). 262p. 1982. pap. 15.00 (*0-939730-01-4*) Mich Romance.

Chambers, S. Allen, Jr. Lynchburg, an Architectural History. LC 81-3000. (Illus.). xiv, 576p. 1981. text 39.50 (*0-8139-0882-5*) U Pr of Va.

— Poplar Forest & Thomas Jefferson. LC 93-90066. (Illus.). 256p. 1998. reprint ed. 39.95 (*0-9667169-0-6*, Corp Poplar Forest) T J Poplar Forest.

Chambers, S. Allen & National Park Foundational Staff. National Landmarks, America's Treasures: The National Park Foundation's Complete Guide to National Historic Landmarks. LC 99-31114. 560p. 1999. pap. 29.95 (*0-471-19764-5*) Wiley.

Chambers, S. E., jt. ed. see Neilson, James P.

Chambers, S. M., jt. ed. see Cairney, J. W.

***Chambers, Sally.** Duck. (J). 1999. 6.95 (*1-86233-030-1*) Levinson Bks.

— Penguin. (J). 1999. 6.95 (*1-86233-020-4*) Levinson Bks.

— Pig. (J). 1999. 6.95 (*1-86233-025-5*) Levinson Bks.

Chambers, Sally. Tarquin's Shell. (Illus.). 16p. (J). 1998. 8.95 (*0-7641-5073-1*) Barron.

***Chambers, Sally.** Tortoise. (J). 1999. 6.95 (*1-86233-015-8*) Levinson Bks.

Chambers, Sally, jt. auth. see Burns, Kate.

Chambers, Sarah. From Subjects to Citizens: Honor, Culture & Politics in Arequipa, Peru, 1780-1854. LC 98-37144. 1999. pap. 19.95 (*0-271-01902-6*) Pa St U Pr.

***Chambers, Sarah.** From Subjects to Citizens: Honor, Culture & Politics in Arequipa, Peru, 1780-1854. LC 98-37144. 1999. 55.00 (*0-271-01901-8*) Pa St U Pr.

***Chambers, Shirley.** Kabalistic Healing. 2000. pap. 11.95 (*0-658-00644-4*) NTC Contemp Pub Co.

Chambers, Simone. Reasonable Democracy: Jurgen Habermas & the Politics of Discourse. 256p. 1996. pap. text 17.95 (*0-8014-8330-1*) Cornell U Pr.

— Reasonable Democracy: Jurgen Habermas & the Politics of Discourse. LC 95-45577. 256p. (C). 1996. text 45.00 (*0-8014-2668-5*) Cornell U Pr.

***Chambers, Simone & Costain, Anne N., eds.** Deliberation, Democracy & the Media. 288p. 2000. 69.00 (*0-8476-9810-6*); pap. 24.95 (*0-8476-9811-4*) Rowman.

Chambers, Steven D. Political Leaders & Military Figures of the Second World War: A Bibliography. LC 95-47697. (Illus.). 464p. 1996. text 101.95 (*1-85521-646-9*, Pub. by Dartmth Pub) Ashgate Pub Co.

Chambers, Sunshine F. Foulke: Allied Families: Some of the Descendants of Andreas Volck-Foulke & Mathias Lupfer. (Illus.). 188p. 1997. reprint ed. pap. 29.00 (*0-8328-8632-7*); reprint ed. lib. bdg. 39.00 (*0-8328-8631-9*) Higginson Bk Co.

Chambers, Susan K., ed. see Coleman, Terry S.

Chambers, Susan S., jt. auth. see Stevens, Barbara.

Chambers, Sydney & Myall, Carolynne. Women & the Values of American Librarianship. LC 93-38311. vi, 86p. 1993. pap. 10.00 (*0-86663-205-0*) Ide Hse.

Chambers, Theresa. Forbidden. Kemnitz, Myrna, ed. (Illus.). 348p. (YA). (gr. 7 up). 1995. pap. 9.99 (*0-88092-291-5*, 2915) Royal Fireworks.

Chambers, Tod. Fiction of Bioethics. LC 98-43178. 1999. pap. 22.99 (*0-415-91989-4*) Routledge.

Chambers, Veronica. Amistad Rising: A Story of Freedom. Bowen, Shelly & Johnston, Allyn M., eds. LC 97-27987. (Illus.). 40p. (J). (gr. 3-6). 1998. 16.00 (*0-15-201803-4*) Harcourt.

— Amistad Rising: A Story of Freedom. (J). 1998. 24.26 (*0-8172-5510-9*) Raintree Steck-V.

— Double Dutch. Date not set. pap. 8.99 (*0-7868-1363-6*, Pub. by Hypm Ppbks) Little.

— Double Dutch. 2000. 18.99 (*0-7868-0512-9*, Pub. by Hypm Ppbks) Little.

— The Harlem Renaissance. LC 97-20585. (African-American Achievers Ser.). 128p. (YA). (gr. 5 up). 1997. lib. bdg. 19.95 (*0-7910-2597-7*) Chelsea Hse.

— Harlem Renaissance. LC 97-20585. (African-American Achievers Ser.). 128p. (YA). (gr. 5 up). 1997. pap. 8.95 (*0-7910-2598-5*) Chelsea Hse.

— Mama's Girl. 208p. 1997. pap. 12.00 (*1-57322-599-1*, Riverhd Trade) Berkley Pub.

— Marisol & Magdalena: The Sound of Our Sisterhood. 141p. (YA). (gr. 5-8). 1998. 14.95 (*0-7868-0437-8*, Pub. by Hyperion); lib. bdg. 15.49 (*0-7868-2385-2*, Pub. by Hyperion) Little.

— Marisol y Magdalena: The Sound of Our Sisterhood. 128p. (J). 1998. pap. 5.95 (*0-7868-1304-0*, Pub. by Hyperion) Time Warner.

Chambers, Vickie. In the Silence of the Hills. Taylor, LaVonne, ed. (Illus.). (YA). (gr. 9-12). write for info. (*0-9627735-1-4*) Excllnc Entrps.

Chambers, W. A. & McRae, W. A. Clinical Scenarios in Pain. (Greenwich Medical Media Ser.). 140p. 2000. pap. 34.95 (*1-900151-70-7*) OUP.

Chambers, W. Walker & Wilkie, John R. A Short History of the German Language. 1970. pap. 12.95 (*0-416-18220-8*, NO. 2130) Routledge.

Chambers, Whittaker. Ghosts on the Roof: Selected Essays. Teachout, Terry, ed. LC 95-49142. 361p. 1996. pap. text 24.95 (*1-56000-835-0*) Transaction Pubs.

— Witness. 1976. 42.95 (*0-8488-0958-0*) Amereon Ltd.

Chambers, Whittaker & Buckley, William F. Odyssey of a Friend: Letters to William F. Buckley Jr. rev. ed. Buckley, William F., Jr., ed. & notes by. LC 87-23252. 312p. 1987. pap. 9.95 (*0-89526-788-8*); lib. bdg. 17.95 (*0-89526-567-2*) Regnery Pub.

Chambers, Whittaker & Fox, John. Witness. (Illus.). 808p. 1978. pap. 17.95 (*0-89526-789-6*, Pub. by Regnery Pub) Natl Bk Netwk.

Chambers, Whittaker, jt. auth. see De Toledano, Ralph.

Chambers, Whittaker, tr. see Weirauch, Anna E.

Chambers, Whittaker, tr. see Werfel, Franz.

Chambers, Wicke & Asher, Spring. TV/PR: How to Promote Yourself, Your Product, Your Service or Your Organization on Television. LC 85-73428. 1986. 14.95 (*0-9615565-9-5*) Chase Comns.

Chambers, Wicke, jt. auth. see Asher, Spring.

Chambers, William. Atlas of Lake Champlain, 1799-1780. LC 84-51173. (Illus.). 112p. 1984. 49.50 (*0-911853-04-9*); pap. 29.50 (*0-685-10084-7*) Vermont Herit Pr.

— Atlas of Lake Champlain, 1799-1780. limited ed. LC 84-51173. (Illus.). 112p. 1984. 200.00 (*0-911853-05-7*) Vermont Herit Pr.

— Designs of Chinese Buildings, Furniture, Dresses, Machines & Utensils. LC 68-17156. (Illus.). 1972. reprint ed. 35.95 (*0-405-08348-3*, Pub. by Blom Pubns) Ayer.

— An Explanatory Discourse, by Tan Chet-Qua, of Quang-Chew-fu, Gent, FRSS, MRAAP (from a Dissertation on Oriental Gerdening...the Second Edition, with Additions) LC 92-24906. (Augustan Reprints Ser.: No. 191). 1978. reprint ed. 14.50 (*0-404-70191-4*) AMS Pr.

— A Treatise on Civil Architecture. 3rd ed. LC 68-17154. (Illus.). 1972. reprint ed. 42.95 (*0-405-08349-1*, Pub. by Blom Pubns) Ayer.

Chambers, William & Pilowsky, Daniel J., eds. Hallucinations in Children. LC 86-10945. (Clinical Insights Ser.). 140p. reprint ed. pap. 43.40 (*0-8357-7836-3*, 203621000002) Bks Demand.

Chambers, William D. Chambers History: Trails of the Centuries. (Illus.). 198p. 1997. reprint ed. pap. 31.00 (*0-8328-7902-9*); reprint ed. lib. bdg. 41.00 (*0-8328-7901-0*) Higginson Bk Co.

***Chambers, William H. & Ortaldo, John R., eds.** Society for Natural Immunity, 5th Annual Meeting: 17th International Natural Killer Cell Workshop, Warrenton, VA., October 17-21, 1998: Abstracts. (Natural Immunity Ser.: Vol. 16, Nos. 2 & 3 (1998)). (Illus.). 80p. 1999. pap. 25.25 (*3-8055-6857-6*) S Karger.

Chambers, William N., ed. see Washington University, St. Louis, Dept. of Politic.

Chamblas-Ploton, Mic, jt. auth. see Babelon, Jean-Pierre.

Chambless, Dianne L. & Goldstein, Alan J., eds. Agoraphobia: Multiple Perspectives on Theory & Treatment. LC 82-7087. (Wiley Series on Personality Processes). 239p. reprint ed. pap. 74.10 (*0-7837-2391-1*, 204007600006) Bks Demand.

Chamblis, Darden, Jr. Artificial Intelligence & Turbo C. 1989. pap. 39.95 (*1-55623-277-2*, Irwn Prfssnl) McGraw-Hill Prof.

***Chambliss.** Power, Politics & Crime. 2000. pap. 18.95 (*0-8133-3487-X*, Pub. by Westview) HarpC.

Chambliss, Carlson. U. S. Paper Money Guide & Handbook. 512p. 1999. 35.00 (*0-931960-59-2*) BNR Pr.

Chambliss, Catherine H. Group Involvement Training: A Step-by-Step Program to Help Chronic Mentally Ill Patients. 160p. 1993. pap. text 24.95 (*0-934986-65-7*) New Harbinger.

***Chambliss, Catherine H.** Psychotherapy & Managed Care: Reconciling Research & Reality. LC 98-56528. 368p. (C). 1999. 34.50 (*0-205-27950-3*) Allyn.

Chambliss, D. D., et al, eds. Magnetic Ultrathin Films - Multilayers & Surfaces, 1997: Materials Research Society Symposium Proceedings, Vol. 475. LC 97-39818. 630p. 1997. text 75.00 (*1-55899-379-7*) Materials Res.

Chambliss, Daniel F. Beyond Caring: Hospitals, Nurses, & the Social Organization of Ethics. 192p. 1996. pap. text 17.00 (*0-226-10102-9*) U Ch Pr.

— Beyond Caring: Morality & Organization in Hospital Nursing. (Morality & Society Ser.). 1996. lib. bdg. 48.00 (*0-226-10071-5*) U Ch Pr.

Chambliss, J. J. Imagination & Reason in Plato, Aristotle, Vico, Rousseau & Keats: An Essay on the Philosophy of Experience. 82p. 1974. pap. text 53.50 (*90-247-1598-9*, Pub. by M Nijhoff) Kluwer Academic.

— The Influence of Plato & Aristotle on John Dewey's Philosophy. LC 89-13776. (Studies in Education: Vol. 10). 134p. 1990. lib. bdg. 69.95 (*0-88946-948-2*) E Mellen.

Chambliss, J. J., ed. Philosophy of Education: An Encyclopedia. LC 96-18393. 736p. 1996. text 100.00 (*0-8153-1177-X*, H1671) Garland.

Chambliss, Jac. Columns Left: A Chattanooga Legacy. LC 93-42556. 1993. write for info. (*0-916078-34-5*) Iris Pr.

Chambliss, Marilyn J. & Calfee, Robert C. Textbooks for Learning: Nurturing Children's Minds. LC 97-51454. 288p. 1998. 59.95 (*1-55786-411-X*); pap. 29.95 (*1-55786-412-8*) Blackwell Pubs.

Chambliss, Maxie, jt. auth. see Cole, Joanna.

Chambliss, Maxie, jt. auth. see Shelf, Angela.

Chambliss, Rollin. Social Thought: From Hammurabi to Comte. LC 54-10267. 469p. 1982. reprint ed. pap. text 19.95 (*0-8290-0147-6*) Irvington.

Chambliss, William J. Chiaraijima Village: Land Tenure, Taxation, & Local Trade, 1818-1884. fac. ed. LC 64-8756. (Association for Asian Studies, Monographs & Papers: No. 19). 173p. 1965. pap. 53.70 (*0-7837-7676-4*, 204742900007) Bks Demand.

— On the Take: From Petty Crooks to Presidents. 2nd ed. LC 77-15213. 320p. 1988. 31.95 (*0-253-34244-9*); pap. 14.95 (*0-253-20298-1*, MB-298) Ind U Pr.

— Power, Politics & Crime. LC 99-32625. (Crime & Society Ser.). 224p. 1999. 25.00 (*0-8133-3486-1*, Pub. by Westview) HarpC.

Chambliss, William J. & Zatz, Marjorie S., eds. Making Law: The State, the Law, & Structural Contradictions. LC 93-16103. 464p. 1993. 41.95 (*0-253-31338-4*); pap. 19.95 (*0-253-20834-3*) Ind U Pr.

Chambliss, William J., jt. auth. see Appelbaum, Richard P.

Chambon, Adrienne S., et al. Reading Foucault for Social Work. LC 98-30255. 292p. 1999. 49.50 (*0-231-10716-1*); pap. 21.50 (*0-231-10717-X*) Col U Pr.

Chambon, Alain, jt. auth. see Humbert, Jean-Baptiste.

Chambon, R., et al, eds. Localisation & Bifurcation Theory for Soils & Rocks: Proceedings of the 3rd Workshop, Grenoble, France, 6-9 September 1993. (Illus.). 288p. (C). 1994. text 116.00 (*90-5410-511-9*, Pub. by A A Balkema) Ashgate Pub Co.

Chambonnieres, Jacques C. Oeuvres Completes. Brunold, Paul & Tessier, Andre, eds. Restout, Denise, tr. (Illus.). 170p. 1965. reprint ed. lib. bdg. 75.00 (*0-8450-1001-8*) Broude.

Chambonnieres, Jacques C. De, see De Chambonnieres, Jacques.

Chambost, Edouard. Bank Accounts: A World Guide to Confidentiality. fac. ed. Walton, Peter & Thompson, Margaret, trs. LC 82-17532. 334p. 1983. reprint ed. pap. 103.60 (*0-608-00960-1*, 206180800011) Bks Demand.

Chambre, Michele. Instrument Flight Training with Microsoft Flight Simulator 98. LC 97-29193. 288p. 1997. pap. text 29.99 incl. cd-rom (*1-57231-628-4*) Microsoft.

Chambre Syndical Du Petrole et Du Gaz Naturel Staf. Dictionnaire de la Prospection Sismique: French - English, English - French. (ENG & FRE.). 328p. 1987. pap. write for info. (*0-7859-0498-0*, 2710805278) Fr & Eur.

Chambre Syndical Du Petrole et Du Gaz Staff. Dictionary of Seismic Prospecting: English & French. (ENG & FRE.). 328p. 1987. 175.00 (*0-8288-2289-1*, F1790) Fr & Eur.

— Dictionary of Seismic Prospecting: English-French - French-English. (ENG & FRE.). lib. bdg. 195.00 (*0-8288-9088-9*, F1790) Fr & Eur.

Chambrun, Adolphe De, see De Chambrun, Adolphe.

Chambrun, Clara. Shakespeare: A Portrait Restored. LC 77-109642. (Select Bibliographies Reprint Ser.). 1977. 31.95 (*0-8369-5251-0*) Ayer.

Chambrun, Clara L. De, see De Chambrun, Clara L.

Chambrun, Rene De, see De Chambrun, Rene.

Chameau, Jean-Lou A., ed. see National Science Foundation Staff, et al.

Chameides, Leon & Hazinski, Mary Fran, eds. Instructor's Manual for Pediatric Basic Life Support. LC 99-175398. 64p. 1997. pap. text, teacher ed. write for info. (*0-87493-621-7*) Am Heart.

Chameides, Leon, ed. see American Academy of Pediatrics Staff & American Heart Association Staff.

Chameides, William L. & Perdue, E. M. Biogeochemical Cycles: A Computer-Interactive Study of Earth System Science & Global Change. LC 96-38035. (Computer-Based Earth System Science Ser.). (Illus.). 240p. (C). 1997. text 62.95 (*0-19-509279-1*) OUP.

Chamelin, Neil C. Criminal Law for Police Officers. 7th ed. LC 99-31596. 320p. 1999. 78.00 (*0-13-085233-3*) P-H.

Chamelin, Neil C., jt. auth. see Swanson, Charles R., Jr.

Chamerlain, Geoffrey V., jt. ed. see De Swiet, Michael.

Chamerlat, Christian A. De, see De Chamerlat, Christian A.

Chamerovzow, L. A., ed. see Brown, John.

Chametsky, Jules. Jewish American Literature. (C). pap. text. write for info. (*0-393-97533-9*) Norton.

Chametzky, Jules. Our Decentralized Literature: Cultural Mediations in Selected Jewish & Southern Writers. LC 86-1259. 168p. 1986. pap. text 15.95 (*0-87023-540-0*) U of Mass Pr.

***Chametzky, Jules, et al, eds.** Jewish American Literature: A Norton Anthology. 1100p. 2000. 39.95 (*0-393-04809-8*) Norton.

Chametzky, Jules & Kaplan, Sidney, eds. Black & White in American Culture: An Anthology from "The Massachusetts Review" LC 74-76045. (Illus.). 496p. 1969. 40.00 (*0-87023-046-8*) U of Mass Pr.

Chametzky, Jules, ed. see Baldwin, James & University of Massachusetts Staff.

Chametzky, Jules, ed. & intro. see Cahan, Abraham.

***Chametzky, Robert A.** Phrase Structure: From GB to Minimalism. (Generative Syntax Ser.). 176p. 2000. 64.95 (*0-631-20158-0*); pap. 29.95 (*0-631-20159-9*) Blackwell Pubs.

Chametzky, Robert A. A Theory of Phrase Markers & the Extended Base. LC 95-26184. (SUNY Series in Linguistics). 206p. (C). 1996. text 54.50 (*0-7914-2971-7*); pap. text 17.95 (*0-7914-2972-5*) State U NY Pr.

Chamfort. Mustapha et Zeangir. Davies, ed. (Exeter French Texts Ser.: Vol. 83). (FRE.). 99p. Date not set. pap. text 19.95 (*0-85989-377-4*, Pub. by Univ Exeter Pr) Northwestern U Pr.

Chamfort, Sebastien R. De, see De Chamfort, Sebastien R.

Chami, Joseph G. Days of Tragedy/Wrath: Lebanon Nineteen Seventy-Five to Nineteen Eighty-Two, 2 vols., Set. Incl. Vol. 1. Days of Tragedy: Lebanon Nineteen Seventy-Five to Nineteen Seventy-Six. (Illus.). 400p. (C). 1980. 84.95 (*0-88738-036-0*); Vol. II. Days of Wrath: Lebanon Nineteen Seventy-Seven to Nineteen Eighty-Two. (Illus.). 400p. 1983. 84.95 (*0-88738-037-9*); (Illus.). 400p. 1983. 125.00 (*0-88738-038-7*) Transaction Pubs.

Chamich, Michael. History of Armenia, 2 Vols., Vol. I. 414p. 1990. 35.00 (*0-941567-08-7*) J C & A L Fawcett.

— History of Armenia, 2 Vols., Vol. II. 556p. 1990. 35.00 (*0-685-74217-2*) J C & A L Fawcett.

Chamier, John. Safety & Seamanship. (Illus.). 1979. 3.75 (*0-229-11501-2*) S&S Trade.

Chaminade, Cecile. Three Piano Works. Incl. Etude Symphonique, Opus 28. LC 79-1501. 1979. Six Concert Etudes, Opus 35. LC 79-1501. 1979. Sonata in C Minor, Opus 21. LC 79-1501. 1979. LC 79-1501. (Women Composers Ser.: No. 2). 1979. reprint ed. 27.50 (*0-306-79551-5*) Da Capo.

Chamis, Alice Y. Vocabulary Control & Search Strategies in Online Searching, 27. LC 90-25224. (New Directions in Information Management Ser.: No. 27). 136p. 1991. 47.95 (*0-313-25490-7*, CVY/, Greenwood Pr) Greenwood.

Chamis, C. C., ed. Test Methods & Design Allowables for Fibrous Composites, Vol. 2. LC 88-38493. (Special Technical Publication Ser.: No. STP 1003). (Illus.). 300p. 1989. text 54.00 (*0-8031-1196-7*, STP1003) ASTM.

— Test Methods & Design Allowables for Fibrous Composites - STP 734. 429p. 1981. 44.00 (*0-8031-0700-5*, STP734) ASTM.

Chamish, Barry. Traitors & Carpetbaggers in the Promised Land: A Journal of Israel's Betrayal. LC 98-190485. (Illus.). 190p. 1997. pap. 12.95 (*1-57558-017-9*) Hearthstone OK.

Chamisso, Adelbert Von. Peter Schlemihl. Bowring, John, tr. LC 92-26945. (GERM Ser.). (Illus.). xxxi, 122p. 1993. reprint ed. 39.95 (*1-879751-32-1*) Camden Hse.

— Peter Schlemihl's Wundersame Geschichte. unabridged ed. (World Classic Literature Ser.). (GER.). pap. 7.95 (*3-89507-020-3*, Pub. by Bookking Intl) Distribks Inc.

— Werke, 3 vols., Set. LC 75-41053. (BCL Ser.: No. II). 1976. reprint ed. 72.50 (*0-404-14850-6*) AMS Pr.

Chamisso, Adelbert Von, see Von Chamisso, Adelbert.

Chamizo, Antonio. Quimica Terrestre. (Ciencia para Todos Ser.). (SPA.). pap. 6.99 (*968-16-3439-X*, Pub. by Fondo) Continental Bk.

Chamizo, Jose A. Quimica con Nosotros. (SPA.). 1994. pap. text. write for info. (*0-201-62566-0*) Addison-Wesley.

Chamizo, Luis. El Miajon de los Castuos (Rapsodias Extremenas) Viudas, Camarasa A., ed. (Nueva Austral Ser.: Vol. 244). (SPA.). 1991. pap. text 24.95 (*84-239-7244-5*) Elliots Bks.

Chamlee, Kenneth. Absolute Faith. (Chapbook Ser.: Vol. 2). 36p. 1999. pap. 5.00 (*0-9659832-2-6*) ByLine Pr.

Chamlee, Paula. High Plains Farm. (Illus.). 176p. 1996. 70.00 (*0-9605646-8-3*) Lodima.

— High Plains Farm. limited ed. LC 96-75804. (Illus.). 176p. 1996. 200.00 (*0-9605646-9-1*) Lodima.

Chamlee, Paula, photos by. San Francisco: Twenty Corner Markets & One in the Middle of the Block. LC 98-229722. (Illus.). 32p. 1997. 50.00 (*1-888899-00-X*) Lodima.

Chamlee, Paula & Jussim, Estelle. Natural Connections: Photographs by Paula Chamlee. (Illus.). 1994. 200.00 (*0-9605646-7-5*) Lodima.

Chamlee, Roy Z., Jr. Lincoln's Assassins: A Complete Account of Their Capture, Trial, & Punishment. LC 89-42708. (Illus.). 634p. 1990. lib. bdg. 60.00 (*0-89950-420-5*) McFarland & Co.

Chamlee-Wright, Emily, jt. auth. see Lavoie, Don.

Chamley, H. Clay Sedimentology. (Illus.). 615p. 1989. 103.95 (*0-387-50889-9*, 2783) Spr-Verlag.

— Sedimentology. (Illus.). 288p. 1990. 42.95 (*0-387-52376-6*) Spr-Verlag.

Chamling, D. R. India & the United Nations. 248p. 1978. 13.95 (*0-318-37243-6*) Asia Bk Corp.

Chammah, Albert M., jt. auth. see Rapoport, Anatol.

***Chammah, Sergio, tr.** El Sutra en Cuarenta y dos Secciones: El Sutra las Ocho Comprensiones de los Grandes Seres. (SPA., Illus.). xi, 111p. 2000. pap. write for info. (*0-88139-750-4*, La Sociedad para la) Buddhist Text.

Chamness, Stefani O. The Answer to Every Question Is in the Bible. deluxe ed. write for info. (*0-9631276-0-8*) Church Liv God.

— Turn from Games & Lies to the Truth & from the Power of Satan unto God Acts 26: 18. deluxe ed. write for info. (*0-9631276-1-6*) Church Liv God.

***Chamness, William Bethea.** The China Berry Tree. (Illus.). 188p. 1999. pap. write for info. (*0-9673652-0-1*) W Henry Pubg.

Chamoiseau, Patrick. Childhood. Volk, Carol, tr. from FRE. LC 98-27493. 1999. text 40.00 (*0-8032-1487-1*) U of Nebr Pr.

— Childhood. Volk, Carol, tr. from FRE. LC 98-27493. 128p. 1999. pap. 15.00 (*0-8032-6382-1*, Bison Books) U of Nebr Pr.

— Chronicle of the Seven Sorrows. LC 99-18845. 256p. 1999. 25.00 (*0-8032-1495-2*) U of Nebr Pr.

— Chroniques De Sept Miseres Suivi De Paroles De Djobeurs. (FRE.). 279p. 1988. pap. 11.95 (*0-7859-2097-8*, 2070380629) Fr & Eur.

— Creole Folktales. Coverdale, Linda, tr. from FRE. LC 94-21475. 113p. 1995. 16.95 (*1-56584-185-9*, Pub. by New Press NY) Norton.

— Creole Folktales. 1997. pap. 10.00 (*1-56584-396-7*, Pub. by New Press NY) Norton.

— School Days. Coverdale, Linda, tr. LC 96-24210. ix, 146p. 1997. pap. 13.00 (*0-8032-6376-7*); text 40.00 (*0-8032-1477-4*) U of Nebr Pr.

— Seven Dreams of Elmira: A Tale of Martinique. Polizzotti, Mark, tr. from FRE. LC 98-54295. 80p. 1999. pap. 20.00 (*1-58195-002-0*, Pub. by Zoland Bks) Consort Bk Sales.

— Solibo Magnificent. (FRE.). 243p. 1991. pap. 10.95 (*0-7859-2166-4*, 2070383911) Fr & Eur.

— Solibo Magnificent. Rejouis, Rose-Myriam & Vinokurov, Val, trs. LC 97-18185. 1998. 23.00 (*0-679-43236-1*) Pantheon.

— Solibo Magnificent. 1999. pap. 12.00 (*0-679-75176-9*) Vin Bks.

— Texaco. 401p. 1998. pap. 14.00 (*0-679-75175-0*) Vin Bks.

Chamoli, S. P. Rafting down the Mystic Brahmaputra. 1992. 30.00 (*0-7069-6632-5*, Pub. by Vikas) S Asia.

Chamorro, Damaso Chicharro, see Machado, Manuel Y.

Chamorro, Grace, tr. see De Osso, Henry.

Chamorro, Grace, tr. see Rodriguez, Gloria & Casado, Silvia.

Chamot & Gonzales. Intercom 2000, Vol. 2. 3rd ed. (Global ESL/ELT Ser.). (J). 1990. mass mkt., teacher ed. 21.95 (*0-8384-1809-0*) Heinle & Heinle.

Chamot, et al. Building Bridges, Level 1. (YA). (gr. 8-12). 1991. teacher ed. 19.95 (*0-8384-2227-6*) Heinle & Heinle.

— Building Bridges, Level 1. (YA). (gr. 8-12). 1991. mass mkt. 17.95 (*0-8384-2224-1*) Heinle & Heinle.

— Building Bridges, Level 1. 108p. (J). 1991. mass mkt. 17.95 (*0-8384-1844-9*) Heinle & Heinle.

— Building Bridges, Level 1. (YA). (gr. 8-12). 1991. audio 17.95 (*0-8384-2230-6*) Heinle & Heinle.

— Building Bridges, Level 2. 138p. (J). 1991. mass mkt. 17.95 (*0-8384-1845-7*) Heinle & Heinle.

— Building Bridges, Level 2. (J). 1991. audio 17.95 (*0-8384-2231-4*) Heinle & Heinle.

— Building Bridges, Level 2. (YA). (gr. 8-12). 1991. teacher ed. 19.95 (*0-8384-2228-4*); mass mkt. 17.95 (*0-8384-2225-X*) Heinle & Heinle.

— Building Bridges, Level 3. 122p. (J). 1992. mass mkt. 17.95 (*0-8384-1846-5*) Heinle & Heinle.

— Building Bridges, Level 3. (J). 1992. audio 17.95 (*0-8384-2232-2*) Heinle & Heinle.

— Building Bridges, Level 3. (YA). (gr. 8-12). 1992. teacher ed. 19.95 (*0-8384-2229-2*) Heinle & Heinle.

— Building Bridges, Level 3. (YA). (gr. 8-12). 1992. mass mkt. 17.95 (*0-8384-2226-8*) Heinle & Heinle.

— Intercom 2000, Bk. 1. 3rd ed. 186p. (YA). (gr. 8-12). 1990. mass mkt. 7.25 (*0-8384-1800-7*) Heinle & Heinle.

— Intercom 2000, Bk. 1. 3rd ed. 186p. (J). 1990. mass mkt., student ed. 9.95 (*0-8384-1801-5*) Heinle & Heinle.

— Intercom 2000, Bk. 1. 3rd ed. 186p. (J). 1990. mass mkt. 38.95 (*0-8384-2164-4*) Heinle & Heinle.

— Intercom 2000, Bk. 1. 3rd ed. 186p. (YA). (gr. 8-12). 1990. audio 60.95 (*0-8384-1803-1*) Heinle & Heinle.

— Intercom 2000, Bk. 1. 3rd annot. ed. 186p. (YA). (gr. 8-12). 1990. teacher ed. 21.95 (*0-8384-1802-3*) Heinle & Heinle.

— Intercom 2000, Bk. 2. 1990. student ed. 5.25 (*0-685-45555-6*) Heinle & Heinle.

— Intercom 2000, Bk. 2. 3rd ed. 186p. (YA). (gr. 8-12). 1990. mass mkt. 15.95 (*0-8384-1807-4*) Heinle & Heinle.

— Intercom 2000, Bk. 2. 3rd ed. (J). 1996. audio 71.95 (*0-8384-1810-4*) Heinle & Heinle.

— Intercom 2000, Bk. 2. 3rd annot. ed. (J). 1990. mass mkt., teacher ed. 9.95 (*0-8384-1808-2*) Heinle & Heinle.

— Intercom 2000, Bk. 3. 3rd ed. 186p. (J). 1990. mass mkt. 13.00 (*0-8384-1813-9*) Heinle & Heinle.

— Intercom 2000, Bk. 3. 3rd ed. (J). 1991. mass mkt. 38.95 (*0-8384-2165-2*); mass mkt., student ed. 9.95 (*0-8384-1814-7*) Heinle & Heinle.

— Intercom 2000, Bk. 3. 3rd annot. ed. (J). 1991. mass mkt., teacher ed. 21.95 (*0-8384-1815-5*) Heinle & Heinle.

— Intercom 2000, Bk. 4. 3rd ed. 186p. (J). 1990. mass mkt. 13.00 (*0-8384-1819-8*) Heinle & Heinle.

— Intercom 2000, Bk. 4. 3rd ed. (J). 1991. mass mkt., student ed. 9.95 (*0-8384-1820-1*); audio 60.95 (*0-8384-1822-8*) Heinle & Heinle.

— Intercom 2000, Bk. 4. 3rd annot. ed. (J). 1991. mass mkt., teacher ed. 21.95 (*0-8384-1821-X*) Heinle & Heinle.

— Perspectives, 2000: Intermediate English, Level 2. 3rd ed. 182p. (J). 1991. mass mkt. 15.00 (*0-8384-2006-0*) Heinle & Heinle.

— Perspectives, 2000: Intermediate English, Level 2. 3rd ed. (J). 1991. mass mkt., student ed. 9.95 (*0-8384-2008-7*) Heinle & Heinle.

— Perspectives, 2000: Intermediate English, Level 2. 3rd ed. (J). 1991. audio 60.95 (*0-8384-2007-9*) Heinle & Heinle.

— Perspectives, 2000: Intermediate English, Level 2. 3rd annot. ed. (J). 1991. mass mkt., teacher ed. 21.95 (*0-8384-2053-2*) Heinle & Heinle.

Chamot, A. E., tr. see Chekhov, Anton.

Chamot, Anna. Calla Handbook. (Illus.). 352p. 1993. pap. text 39.70 (*0-201-53963-2*) Addison-Wesley.

Chamot, Anna U. Learning Strategies Hdbk. LC 99-13597. 1999. 36.00 (*0-201-38548-1*) Addison-Wesley.

Chamot, Anna U. & O'Malley, J. Michael. Mathematics: Language Development Through Content, Bk. A. (ESOL Secondary Supplements Ser.). (Illus.). 96p. 1988. pap. text 16.57 (*0-201-12931-0*); pap. text, teacher ed. 14.50 (*0-201-12935-3*) Addison-Wesley.

Chamot, Anna U., jt. auth. see O'Malley, J. Michael.

Chamouard, P. A., jt. ed. see Boudard, Alain.

Chamoux, Jean-Pierre, ed. Deregulating the Regulators? Communications Policies for the 90's. (European Communication Policy Research Ser.). 200p. (gr. 12). 1991. 60.00 (*90-5199-055-3*, Pub. by IOS Pr) IOS Press.

***Chamow, Steven M. & Ashkenazi, Avi, eds.** Antibody Fusion Proteins. LC 98-36471. 312p. 1999. 104.95 (*0-471-18358-X*) Wiley.

Champ. Teachers Manual to Accompany Model Economies with Money. 120p. 1993. pap. text 24.95 (*0-471-00615-7*) Wiley.

Champ, B. R., et al, eds. Fumigation & Controlled Atmosphere Storage of Grain. 301p. (C). 1990. pap. 159.00 (*1-86320-018-5*) St Mut.

— Fungi & Mycotoxins in Stored Products. 270p. (Orig.). (C). 1991. pap. 150.00 (*1-86320-040-1*) St Mut.

Champ, B. R. & Highley, E., eds. Bulk Handling & Storage of Grain in the Humid Tropics. 296p. (Orig.). 1987. pap. 126.00 (*0-949511-65-X*) St Mut.

Champ, B. R., et al. Postharvest Handling of Tropical Fruits. 500p. 1994. pap. 240.00 (*1-86320-101-7*, Pub. by ACIAR) St Mut.

Champ, Bruce & Freeman, Scott. Modeling Monetary Economies. LC 93-9879. 272p. 1993. text 81.95 (*0-471-57948-3*) Wiley.

Champ, Claire, jt. ed. see Landry, Pierre B.

Champ, Jack & Burgess, Colin. The Diggers of Colditz. LC 97-159144. (Illus.). 204p. 1997. pap. 16.95 (*0-86417-839-5*, Pub. by Kangaroo Pr) Seven Hills Bk.

Champ, M. A., jt. ed. see Ardus, D. A.

Champ, Michael A. Global Marine Pollution Bibliography: Ocean Dumping of Municipal & Industrial Wastes. LC 82-18060. 424p. 1982. 115.00 (*0-306-65205-6*, Kluwer Plenum) Kluwer Academic.

Champ, Minnie, jt. auth. see Pitts, Alice.

Champa, Kermit S. Masterpiece Studies: Manet, Zola, Van Gogh, & Monet. LC 93-3547. (Illus.). 160p. (C) 1994. 32.50 (*0-271-01088-6*) Pa St U Pr.

— Mondrian Studies. LC 85-980. (Illus.). xviii, 150p. 1985. 35.00 (*0-226-10078-2*) U Ch Pr.

— The Rise of Landscape Painting in France: Corot to Monet. (Illus.). 232p. 1992. pap. 29.95 (*0-8109-2520-6*, Pub. by Abrams) Time Warner.

— Studies in Early Impressionism. LC 84-81040. (Illus.). 106p. 1985. reprint ed. lib. bdg. 75.00 (*0-87817-299-8*) Hacker.

Champa, Kermit S., ed. Over Here: Modernism, the First Exile, 1914-1919. LC 89-50243. (Illus.). 225p. 1989. pap. 20.00 (*0-933519-17-6*) D W Bell Gallery.

Champa, Kermit S., et al. Monet & Bazille: A Collaboration. LC 98-31450. (Illus.). 108p. 1999. 24.95 (*0-8109-6384-1*, Pub. by Abrams) Time Warner.

Champaailler, ed. see Bossuet, Jacques-Benigne.

Champagne, Anne, ed. A Nature Guide to Ontario. 2nd rev. ed. (Illus.). 320p. (Orig.). 1992. pap. 19.95 (*0-8020-6802-2*); text 45.00 (*0-8020-2755-5*) U of Toronto Pr.

Champagne, Anne, jt. ed. see MacIsaac, Ron.

Champagne, Anthony. Sam Rayburn: A Bio-Bibliography, 4. LC 88-21341. (Bio-Bibliographies in Law & Political Science Ser.: No. 4). 161p. 1988. lib. bdg. 47.95 (*0-313-25864-3*, CSR/, Greenwood Pr) Greenwood.

— Texas Politics: A Reader. 2nd ed. LC 97-42845. 1998. pap. text. write for info. (*0-393-95878-7*) Norton

Champagne, Anthony, ed. see Haydel, Judith.

Champagne, Audrey B. Teaching for Workplace Success. 22p. 1986. 3.00 (*0-318-22211-6*, OC113) Ctr Educ Trng Employ.

Champagne, Audrey B., ed. see National Forum for School Science Staff.

Champagne, Champ. The Real Chord Changes & Substitutions - Christmas Favorites. 112p. 1992. per. 14.95 (*0-7935-1666-8*, 00240005) H Leonard.

***Champagne, David W.** A Complete Trainer's Guide for Your Usual Needs Levels: An Inventory, Vol. I. Olmstead, Phyllis M., ed. & illus. by. v, 120p. 1999. pap. 135.00 incl. cd-rom (*0-9667696-3-5*) ROC EdTech Pubg.

Champagne, David W. The Intelligent Professor's Guide to Teaching. (Illus.). iii, 203p. (C). Date not set. pap. text 39.95 (*0-9667696-1-9*) ROC EdTech Pubg.

***Champagne, David W.** Your Usual Needs Levels: An Inventory: Self-Help Tutorial. Olmstead, Phyllis M., ed. & illus. by. 40p. 1999. pap. 44.00 incl. cd-rom (*0-9667696-4-3*) ROC EdTech Pubg.

Champagne, David W. & Goldman, Richard M. Handbook for Managing Individualized Learning in the Classroom. LC 75-14101. 214p. 1975. pap. 34.95 (*0-87778-081-1*) Educ Tech Pubns.

Champagne, David W. & Hogan, R. C. Interpersonal & Consultant Supervision Skills: A Clinical Model. 3rd ed. xv, 351p. (C). 1995. pap. text 39.95 (*0-9667696-2-7*) ROC EdTech Pubg.

Champagne, David W., jt. auth. see McQuade, Finlay.

Champagne, Dominic. Playing Bare. Tepperman, Shelley, tr. 112p. 1993. pap. 11.95 (*0-88922-335-1*, Pub. by Talonbks) Genl Dist Srvs.

Champagne, Duane. Native America: Portrait of a People. (Illus.). 786p. 1994. 18.95 (*0-8103-9452-9*, 089204) Visible Ink Pr.

— Social Order & Political Change: Constitutional Governments among the Cherokee, the Choctaw, the Chickasaw, & the Creek. LC 91-27600. 328p. 1992. reprint ed. pap. 30.00 (*0-608-03978-0*, 206470700010) Bks Demand.

Champagne, Duane, ed. Chronology of Native North American History: From Pre-Columbian Times to the Present. LC 94-18455. 574p. (C). 1994. 65.00 (*0-8103-9195-3*) Gale.

***Champagne, Duane, ed.** Contemporary Native American Cultural Issues. (Contemporary Native American Communities Ser.: Vol. 2). 320p. 1998. 65.00 (*0-7619-9058-5*) AltaMira Pr.

Champagne, Duane, ed. Contemporary Native American Cultural Issues. (Contemporary Native American Communities Ser.: Vol. 2). 328p. 1999. pap. 24.95 (*0-7619-9059-3*) AltaMira Pr.

— Reference Library of Native North America, 4 vols. 1920p. 1993. 179.00 (*0-8103-8865-0*, 101507) Gale.

***Champagne, Duane & Salvatierra, Delia.** Distinguished Native American Political & Tribal Leaders. (Illus.). 344p. 2000. boxed set 69.95 (*1-57356-354-4*) Oryx Pr.

Champagne, Duane, jt. ed. see Rose, Cynthia.

Champagne, Frank. Cancel April 15th! The Plan for Painless Taxation. Champagne, Pamela, ed. LC 93-61764. 150p. (Orig.). 1994. pap. 10.95 (*0-9632698-3-6*) Veda Vangarde.

Champagne, Gloria F. Poems by Gloria Champagne. 3rd rev. ed. (Illus.). 26p. (Orig.). 1996. pap. 12.00 (*0-9655506-0-5*) Champagne Falcon Pub.

Champagne, Jane. Painting the Ontario Landscape: A Practical Guide to Working in Watercolour on Location. (Illus.). 192p. (Orig.). 1991. pap. 19.95 (*0-8020-6761-1*) U of Toronto Pr.

***Champagne, Jean.** Magic of the Senses: A Guide for Personal Enrichment. (Illus.). 100p. 1999. pap. 11.95 (*0-7414-0311-0*) Buy Books.

Champagne, John. The Blue Lady's Hands. 60p. 1988. 12.95 (*0-8184-0478-7*) Carol Pub Group.

— The Ethics of Marginality. LC 94-33607. 1995. pap. 19.95 (*0-8166-2533-6*); text 49.95 (*0-8166-2532-8*) U of Minn Pr.

— When the Parrot Boy Sings. 1990. pap. 8.95 (*0-8216-2009-6*, Univ Books) Carol Pub Group.

Champagne, Karen, ed. see Hicks, Greta.

Champagne, Lenora. French Theatre Experiment Since 1968. LC 84-60. (Theater & Dramatic Studies: No. 18). (Illus.). 193p. 1984. reprint ed. pap. 59.90 (*0-8357-1538-8*, 207053800001) Bks Demand.

Champagne, Lenora, ed. Out from Under: Texts by Women Performance Artists. LC 90-11257. 224p. 1990. reprint ed. pap. 12.95 (*1-55936-009-7*) Theatre Comm.

Champagne, Maurice. The Mysterious Valley. Bucko, Bill, tr. from FRE. (Illus.). 256p. (J). 1994. pap. 19.95 (*0-9626854-9-6*) Atlantean Pr.

— The Mysterious Valley. Bucko, Bill, tr. from FRE. LC 94-78488. (Illus.). 256p. (J). (gr. 3 up). 1994. 29.95 (*0-9626854-6-1*) Atlantean Pr.

Champagne, Pamela, ed. see Champagne, Frank.

Champagne, Paul J. & McAfee, R. Bruce. Motivating Strategies for Performance & Productivity: A Guide to Human Resource Development. LC 88-18261. 233p. 1989. 65.00 (*0-89930-312-9*, CEG/, Quorum Bks) Greenwood.

Champagne, Paul J., jt. auth. see McAfee, R. Bruce.

Champagne, Paul J., jt. auth. see McAffee, R. Bruce.

Champagne, R. Beyond the Structuralist Myth of Ecriture. 1977. 51.55 (*90-279-3166-6*) Mouton.

Champagne, Roland A. Claude Levi-Strauss. (World Authors Ser.: No. 792). 144p. 1987. 28.95 (*0-8057-6646-4*, Twyne) Mac Lib Ref.

— French Structuralism. (Twayne's World Authors Ser.: No. 818). 184p. 1990. 25.95 (*0-8057-8262-1*) Macmillan.

— Georges Bataille. LC 98-21555. 140p. 1998. 32.00 (*0-8057-7821-7*, Twyne) Mac Lib Ref.

— Jacques Derrida. (Twayne's World Authors Ser.). 160p. 1994. 32.00 (*0-8057-4310-3*, Twyne) Mac Lib Ref.

— Literary History in the Wake of Roland Barthes: Re-Defining the Myths of Reading. LC 83-50516. 158p. 1984. pap. 13.00 (*0-917786-36-X*) Summa Pubns.

Champagne, Rosana. The Politics of Survivorship. 248p. (C). 1998. pap. text 16.50 (*0-8147-1543-5*) NYU Pr.

C

An Asterisk (*) at the beginning of an entry indicates that the title is appearing for the first time.

Champagne, Rosaria. The Politics of Survivorship: Incest, Women's Literature, & Feminist Theory. 248p. (C). 1996. text 50.00 (*0-8147-1542-7*) NYU Pr.

Champagne, Rosemary. My Detour on Life's Highway: A Survivor's Story of Stem Cell Transplant. (Illus.). 80p. 1999. pap. 7.95 (*0-9650315-7-8*) Glacier Publng.

Champagne, Ruth. Friendly Math (TM) Activity Book for Addition. (Illus.). 52p. (Orig.). (J). (gr. k-2). 2000. pap. write for info. (*1-929245-02-5*) Friendly Math.

— Friendly Math (TM) Activity Book for Multiplication. (Illus.). 52p. (Orig.). (J). (gr. 3-5). 1999. pap. write for info. (*1-929245-01-7*) Friendly Math.

— Friendly Math (TM) Shape & Pattern Puzzles. (Illus.). 108p. (Orig.). (J). (gr. k up). 1999. pap. write for info. (*1-929245-00-9*) Friendly Math.

Champaign County Historical Archives Staff. Combined 1893, 1913 & 1929 Atlases of Champaign County, Illinois. 3rd rev. ed. Schlipf, Frederick A. et al, eds. LC 97-13235. (Champaign County Historical Archives Historical Publications Ser.: Vol. 12). (Illus.). 1997. reprint ed. 45.00 (*0-9609646-8-1*) Urbana Free Lib.

Champakalakemi, R. Trade, Ideology & Urbanization: South India 300 BC to AD 1300. (Illus.). 498p. 1998. text 42.00 (*0-19-563870-0*) OUP.

Champakalakshmi, R. & Gopal, S., eds. Tradition, Dissent & Ideology: Essays in Honour of Romila Thapar. (Illus.). 364p. 1996. text 35.00 (*0-19-563867-0*) OUP.

Champanier, jt. auth. see Stewart.

Champanier, Paul, jt. auth. see Stewart, Linda.

***Champarnaud, J.-M., et al, eds.** Automata Implementation: Third International Workshop on Implementing Automata, WIA'98, Rouen, France, September 17-19, 1998, Revised Papers. LC 99-49679. (Lecture Notes in Computer Science Ser.: Vol. 1660). x, 245p. 1999. pap. 52.00 (*3-540-66652-4*) Spr-Verlag.

Champaud, Jacques. Mom: Terroir Bassa (Cameroun) (Atlas Des Structures Agraires Au Sud Du Sahara: No. 9). (Illus.). 1973. pap. 36.95 (*90-279-7223-0*) Mouton.

Champault, Dominique. Arabian Moons: Passages in Time Through Yemen. (Illus.). 160p. 1988. text 45.00 (*0-7103-0318-1*) Routledge.

Champault, G. & Bourgeon, A., eds. HIV & Surgery. (Monographs of the French Surgical Association). (Illus.). 1994. 69.00 (*0-387-59607-0*) Spr-Verlag.

Champe, Flavia W. Innocents on Broadway. (Illus.). 272p. 1987. pap. 9.95 (*0-939644-24-X*) J & L Lee.

Champe, Gertrud G., ed. To Set Before the King: Katharina Schratt's Festive Recipes. Arno, Paula V. & Szathmary, Louis, trs. LC 95-45507. (Iowa Szathmary Culinary Arts Ser.). (Illus.). 236p. (C). 1996. text 24.95 (*0-87745-535-X*) U of Iowa Pr.

Champe, Gertrud G., tr. see Draley, Daniel, ed.

Champe, Pamela C. & Harvey, Richard A. Lippincott's Illustrated Reviews: Biochemistry. LC 65-9665. 441p. 1987. text 25.95 (*0-397-50801-8*, Lippnctt) Lppncott W & W.

— Lippincott's Illustrated Reviews: Biochemistry. 2nd ed. (Illus.). 440p. 1994. pap. text 29.95 (*0-397-51091-8*) Lppncott W & W.

Champe, Pamela C. & Harvey, Richard A. Lippincott's Illustrated Reviews Biochemistry. 3rd ed. 420p. pap. text. write for info. (*0-7817-2265-9*) Lppncott W & W.

Champeau, Donna. Great Ideas for Teaching Health. 160p. (C). 1997. pap. text, teacher ed. 17.00 (*0-205-19909-7*) P-H.

Champeaux, Dennis. Object Oriented System Development. 560p. 1993. 59.95 (*0-201-56355-X*) Addison-Wesley.

Champelli, Lisa & Rosenbaum, Howard. Neal-Schuman WebMaster: Policies, Templates & Icons for Library WebPages; Training Modules for Library Staff & Patrons. LC 97-16026. 182p. 1997. 190.00 incl. cd-rom (*1-55570-307-0*) Neal-Schuman.

Champeney, D. C. A Handbook of Fourier Theorems. (Illus.). 198p. 1987. text 69.95 (*0-521-26503-7*) Cambridge U Pr.

— A Handbook of Fourier Theorems. (Illus.). 198p. 1989. pap. text 28.95 (*0-521-36688-7*) Cambridge U Pr.

Champeon, Steven & Fox, David S. Building Dynamic HTML GUIs. LC QA76.9.U83C46 1999. 744p. 1999. pap. 39.99 (*0-7645-3267-7*) IDG Bks.

Champernowne, David G. Uncertainty & Estimation in Economics. LC 73-76889. (Mathematical Economics Texts Ser.). 1969. write for info. (*0-05-002006-4*) Olvr & Boyd UK.

Champernowne, David G., jt. auth. see Cowell, F. A.

Champernowne, Irene. A Memoir of Toni Wolff. 1980. pap. 7.00 (*0-317-13545-7*) C G Jung Frisco.

***Champeteir, Joel.** The Dragons Eye. 304p. 2000. pap. 13.95 (*0-312-87252-6*) Tor Bks.

Champfleury, J. F. Bibliographie Ceramique Depuis Le XVIe Siecle. xv, 352p. 1981. reprint ed. lib. bdg. 95.00 (*3-487-07058-8*) G Olms Pubs.

Champie, Clark. Cacti & Succulents of El Paso. (Illus.). 100p. 1974. pap. text 10.00 (*0-318-23616-8*) Abbey Garden.

Champigneulle, Alexis, jt. ed. see Dabrowski, Konrad.

Champigneulle, Bernard. Rodin. (Illus.). 288p. 1997. pap. 14.95 (*0-500-20296-6*) Thames Hudson.

— Rodin. LC 85-51233. (World of Art Ser.). (Illus.). 288p. 1999. reprint ed. pap. 16.95 (*0-500-20061-0*, Pub. by Thames Hudson) Norton.

Champigny, Robert. Humanism & Human Racism: A Critical Study of Essays by Sartre & Camus. LC 77-189701. (De Proprietatibus Litterarum, Ser. Practica: No. 41). 82p. (Orig.). 1973. pap. text 20.00 (*90-279-2373-6*) Mouton.

— Ontology of the Narrative. (De Proprietatibus Litterarum, Ser. Minor: No. 12). 1972. pap. text 22.35 (*90-279-2366-3*) Mouton.

Champigny, Robert. Sense, Antisense, Nonsense. LC 83-26007. (University of Florida Humanities Monographs: No. 57). 128p. 1986. pap. 19.95 (*0-8130-0791-7*) U Press Fla.

Champigny, Robert. What Will Have Happened: A Philosophical & Technical Essay on Mystery Stories. LC 77-74446. 183p. 1977. 18.95 (*0-253-36515-5*) Boulevard.

— What Will Have Happened: A Philosophical & Technical Essay on Mystery Stories. LC 77-74446. 191p. reprint ed. pap. 59.30 (*0-608-18624-4*, 205602800044) Bks Demand.

Champine, Rosa B. My Jobs in Italy. Lane, Barry, ed. (Opening Doors Ser.: No. 1). (Illus.). 32p. (Orig.). 1989. pap. 4.00 (*1-877829-02-1*) Homegrown Bks.

***Champion.** Corrections in the U. S. 2nd ed. 1998. pap. text. write for info. (*0-13-375577-0*) P-H.

Champion, A. G. Changing Places: Britain's Demographic, Economic & Social Complexion. LC 87-148942. 144p. 1987. write for info. (*0-7131-6498-0*) St Martin.

Champion, A. G., ed. Counterurbanization: The Changing Pace & Nature of Population Deconcentration. LC 91-14826. (Illus.). 288p. (Orig.). 1991. pap. 24.95 (*0-7131-6573-1*, A3674, Pub. by E A) Routldge.

Champion, A. G. & Townsend, A. R. Contemporary Britain: A Geographical Perspective. 192p. 16.95 (*0-7131-6580-4*, A2871, Pub. by E A) Routldge.

Champion, Alan. Pilgrim's Progress: Boston. (C). 1989. text 35.00 (*0-902662-40-6*, Pub. by R K Pubns); pap. text 21.00 (*0-902662-41-4*, Pub. by R K Pubns) St Mut.

Champion, B. R., ed. see Rayner, David.

Champion, Brett. America's Guide to Fraud Prevention. (Illus.). 178p. (Orig.). 1998. pap. 17.95 (*1-56072-333-5*, Nova Kroshka Bks) Nova Sci Pubs.

Champion, David. Celebrity Trouble: A Bomber Hanson Mystery. LC 97-30601. 200p. 1997. 20.00 (*1-888310-97-9*) A A Knoll Pubs.

— The Mountain Massacres: A Bomber Hanson Mystery. LC 95-9702. 161p. 1995. 14.95 (*0-9627297-4-4*) A A Knoll Pubs.

— Nobody Roots for Goliath: A Bomber Hanson Mystery. LC 96-3399. 319p. 1996. 22.95 (*1-888310-44-8*) A A Knoll Pubs.

— Phantom Virus: A Bomber Hanson Mystery. LC 98-48992. 275p. 1999. 23.00 (*1-888310-93-6*) A A Knoll Pubs.

— The Snatch. LC 93-81067. 266p. 1994. 19.95 (*0-9627297-2-8*) A A Knoll Pubs.

***Champion, David.** Too Rich & Too Thin. (Bomber Hanson Mystery Ser.: Vol. 5). 2000. 22.00 (*1-888310-50-2*) A A Knoll Pubs.

Champion, Dean J. Corrections in the United States: A Contemporary Perspective. 2nd ed. LC 97-26177. 700p. 1997. 72.00 (*0-13-293937-1*) P-H.

***Champion, Dean J.** Corrections in the United States: Contemporary Perspective. 3rd ed. 768p. 2000. pap. 69.33 (*0-13-086761-6*, Prentice Hall) P-H.

Champion, Dean J. Criminal Justice in the United States. 2nd ed. LC 97-21722. (Illus.). 450p. (C). 1998. pap. text 63.95 (*0-8304-1485-1*) Thomson Learn.

— Felony Probation: Problems & Prospects. LC 88-9744. 185p. 1988. 57.95 (*0-275-92993-0*, C2993, Praeger Pubs) Greenwood.

— The Juvenile Justice System: Delinquency, Processing & the Law. 2nd ed. LC 97-37318. 594p. 1997. 77.00 (*0-13-603408-X*) P-H.

***Champion, Dean J.** The Juvenile Justice System: Delinquency, Processing & the Law. 3rd ed. LC 00-20678. 656p. 2000. pap. 64.67 (*0-13-016639-1*) P-H.

Champion, Dean J. Measuring Offender Risk: A Criminal Justice Sourcebook. LC 93-1651. 352p. 1993. lib. bdg. 79.50 (*0-313-28593-4*, Greenwood Pr) Greenwood.

— Probation & Parole in the United States. 496p. (C). 1990. text 51.80 (*0-675-20997-8*, Merrill Coll) P-H.

— Probation, Parole, & Community Corrections. 3rd ed. LC 98-14535. 512p. (C). 1998. 79.67 (*0-13-693368-8*) P-H.

***Champion, Dean J.** Research Methods for Criminal Justice & Criminology. 2nd ed. 752p. 1999. 68.00 (*0-13-013904-1*) P-H.

Champion, Dean J. The Roxbury Dictionary of Criminal Justice: Key Terms & Major Court Cases. LC 96-8392. 350p. (C). 1997. pap. text. write for info. (*0-935732-84-5*) Roxbury Pub Co.

***Champion, Dean J.** The Roxbury Dictionary of Criminal Justice: Key Terms & Major Court Cases. 2nd rev. ed. 350p. (C). 2001. pap. text. write for info. (*1-891487-59-0*) Roxbury Pub Co.

Champion, Dean J., ed. Dictionary of American Criminal Justice: Key Terms & Major Supreme Court Cases. 355p. 1998. lib. bdg. 45.00 (*1-57958-073-4*) Fitzroy Dearborn.

— The U. S. Sentencing Guidelines: Implications for Criminal Justice. LC 89-16092. 301p. 1989. 55.00 (*0-275-93324-5*, C3324, Praeger Pubs) Greenwood.

Champion, Dean J. & Mays, G. Larry. Transferring Juveniles to Criminal Courts: Trends & Implications for Criminal Justice. LC 90-40798. 208p. 1991. 55.00 (*0-275-93534-5*, C3534, Praeger Pubs) Greenwood.

Champion, Dean J. & Rush, George E. Policing in the Community. LC 96-28494. 483p. 1996. 90.00 (*0-13-681248-1*) P-H.

Champion, Dean J., jt. auth. see Black, James A.

Champion, Edward R. Finite Element Analysis in Manufacturing Engineering: A PC-Based Approach. 310p. 1992. 62.00 (*0-07-010510-3*) McGraw.

Champion, Edward R., Jr. Numerical Methods for Engineering Applications. LC 93-1189. (Mechanical Engineering Ser.: Vol. 84). (Illus.). 464p. 1993. text 189.00 (*0-8247-9135-5*) Dekker.

Champion, Edward R. & Ensminger. Finite Element Analysis with Personal Computers. (Mechanical Engineering Ser.: Vol. 64). (Illus.). 360p. 1988. text 135.00 (*0-8247-7981-9*) Dekker.

Champion, Ernest A. Mr. Baldwin, I Presume: James Baldwin - Chinua Achebe: A Meeting of the Minds. 176p. (C). 1995. pap. text 28.50 (*0-7618-0043-3*) U Pr of Amer.

— Mr. Baldwin, I Presume: James Baldwin - Chinua Achebe: A Meeting of the Minds. 176p. (C). 1995. lib. bdg. 47.00 (*0-7618-0042-5*) U Pr of Amer.

Champion, George. Music, Myth & Consciousness. 112p. (C). 1994. pap. text, per. 21.95 (*0-8403-9893-X*) Kendall-Hunt.

Champion, George, jt. auth. see Wessels, Allison.

Champion, Ivan F. Across New Guinea from the Fly to the Sepik. LC 75-32804. (Illus.). 1976. reprint ed. 41.50 (*0-404-14108-0*) AMS Pr.

Champion, Joe E. Explanation of Observed Nuclear Events Associated with Cold Fusion & Similar Low Energy Nuclear Reactions. Briggs, Roger C., ed. (Illus.). 92p. 1994. spiral bd. 39.95 (*1-884928-52-8*) Discov Pubng.

— Producing Precious Metals at Home: A. - Q.E.D. (Alchemy - Which Was to Be Proved) Briggs, Roger C., ed. LC 94-70366. (Illus.). 410p. 1994. 69.95 (*1-884928-32-3*) Discov Pubng.

— Rhodium from Black Sands. Briggs, Roger C., ed. (Illus.). 30p. 1993. spiral bd. 19.95 (*1-884928-11-0*) Discov Pubng.

Champion, Joe E. & Thompson, Michael R. Gold Without Minerals. Briggs, Roger C., ed. 72p. 1994. spiral bd. 29.95 (*1-884928-41-2*) Discov Pubng.

Champion, John M. & James, John J. Critical Incidents in Management. 6th ed. 352p. (C). 1988. text 34.95 (*0-256-06825-9*, Irwn McGrw-H) McGrw-H Hghr Educ.

Champion, Joyce. Emily & Alice. LC 92-13575. (Illus.). 32p. 1996. pap. 5.00 (*0-15-201347-4*) Harcourt.

— Emily & Alice Again. LC 93-5004. (Illus.). 32p. (J). (gr. k-4). 1995. 14.00 (*0-15-200439-4*, Gulliver Bks) Harcourt.

***Champion, Joyce & Stevenson, Supcie.** Emily & Alice Baby-Sit Burton. LC 99-6187. (J). 2000. write for info. (*0-15-202184-1*) Harcourt.

Champion, Judith, ed. see Boeding, Conrad.

Champion, K. S., jt. auth. see Schmidtke, G.

Champion, Larry S. The Essential Shakespeare: An Annotated Bibliography of Major Modern Studies. (Reference Books - Literature). 463p. (C). 1986. 70.00 (*0-8161-8731-2*, Hall Reference) Macmillan.

— The Essential Shakespeare: An Annotated Bibliography of Major Modern Studies. 2nd ed. (G. K. Hall Reference Ser.). 200p. 1993. 70.00 (*0-8161-7332-X*, G K Hall & Co) Mac Lib Ref.

— Evolution of Shakespeare's Comedy: A Study in Dramatic Perspective. LC 73-105370. 241p. 1973. pap. 15.00 (*0-674-27141-6*) HUP.

— The Noise of Threatening Drum: Dramatic Strategy & Political Ideology in Shakespeare & the English Chronicle Plays. LC 89-40380. 176p. 1990. 32.50 (*0-87413-387-4*) U Delaware Pr.

— Thomas Dekker & the Traditions of English Drama. 2nd ed. (American University Studies: English Language & Literature: Ser. IV, Vol. 27). X, 198p. (C). 1987. text 32.00 (*0-8204-0214-1*) P Lang Pubng.

Champion, Larry S., ed. Quick Springs of Sense: Studies in the Eighteenth Century. LC 72-86783. 262p. reprint ed. pap. 81.30 (*0-608-15802-X*, 203106500073) Bks Demand.

***Champion, Laurie, ed.** American Women Writers, 1900-1945: A Bio-Bibliographical Critical Sourcebook. LC 00-22336. 432p. 2000. lib. bdg. 95.00 (*0-313-30943-4*, GR0943, Greenwood Pr) Greenwood.

Champion, Laurie, ed. The Critical Response to Eudora Welty's Fiction, 12. LC 93-43709. (Critical Responses in Arts & Letters Ser.: No. 12). 392p. 1994. lib. bdg. 55.00 (*0-313-28596-9*, Greenwood Pr) Greenwood.

— The Critical Response to Mark Twain's Huckleberry Finn, 1. LC 91-25255. (Critical Responses in Arts & Letters Ser.: No. 1). 272p. 1991. lib. bdg. 59.95 (*0-313-27575-0*, CCX, Greenwood Pr) Greenwood.

Champion, Laurie, jt. ed. see Glasrud, Bruce A.

Champion, Laurie, jt. ed. see Hill, Billy Bob.

***Champion, Lorna A.** Adult Psychological Problems: An Introduction. 2000. pap. text 29.95 (*0-86377-642-6*) Psychol Pr.

Champion, Lorna A., jt. ed. see Power, Michael J.

***Champion, Lynn & Scott- Kemmis, Judy.** The Colour of Sex. 184p. 2000. per. 11.00 (*0-684-87203-X*) S&S Trade.

Champion, M., ed. IUTAM Symposium on Combustion in Supersonic Flows: Proceedings of the IUTAM Symposium Held in Poitiers, France, 2-6 Oct. 1995. LC 96-45569. (Fluid Mechanics & Its Applications Ser.). 432p. (C). 1996. text 217.50 (*0-7923-4313-1*) Kluwer Academic.

Champion, Malcolm C. & Orr, William C., eds. Evolving Concepts in Gastrointestinal Motility. LC 96-13281. 1996. 95.00 (*0-86542-944-8*) Blackwell Sci.

***Champion, Miles.** Facture. 30p. 1999. pap. 8.00 (*0-935724-98-2*, Pub. by Figures) SPD-Small Pr Dist.

— Three Bell Zero. 72p. 2000. pap. 10.95 (*0-937804-82-7*, Pub. by Segue NYC) SPD-Small Pr Dist.

Champion, Miles, et al. Sleight of Foot. 1996. pap. 10.00 (*1-874400-10-5*, Pub. by Reality St Edits) SPD-Small Pr Dist.

Champion, Neil. D. H. Lawrence. LC 89-28276. (Life & Works Ser.). 1991. write for info. (*0-86593-017-1*) Rourke Corp.

***Champion, Neil.** James Watt. LC 00-24353. (J). 2000. lib. bdg. write for info. (*1-57572-371-9*) Heinemann Lib.

Champion, Neil. Portugal. (Modern Industrial World Ser.). (Illus.). 48p. (J). (gr. 6-8). 1995. lib. bdg. 24.26 (*1-56847-435-0*) Raintree Steck-V.

— Spain. (Modern Industrial World Ser.). (Illus.). 48p. (J). (gr. 6-8). 1996. lib. bdg. 24.26 (*1-56847-434-2*) Raintree Steck-V.

***Champion, Neil & Babbage, Charles.** Charles Babbage. LC 00-23384. (Groundbreakers Ser.). 2000. lib. bdg. write for info. (*1-57572-367-0*) Heinemann Lib.

***Champion, Nigel & Hurst, Gregg Andrew.** The Aerobics Instructor's Handbook. 136p. 2000. per. 15.00 (*0-684-87209-9*) S&S Trade.

Champion, Nigel, jt. auth. see Egger, Gary.

Champion, Pierre. Louis the Eleventh. Whale, Winifred S., tr. LC 73-109617. (Select Bibliographies Reprint Ser.). 1977. 26.95 (*0-8369-5226-X*) Ayer.

Champion, R. H., et al. Textbook of Dermatology. 6th ed. LC 97-51464. (Illus.). 3160p. 1998. 695.00 (*0-632-03796-2*) Blackwell Sci.

Champion, Robert H., et al, eds. Textbook of Dermatology, 4 vols. 5th ed. (Illus.). 3160p. 1992. cd-rom 295.00 (*0-86542-234-6*) Blackwell Sci.

Champion, Robert H. & Pye, Richard J., eds. Recent Advances in Dermatology, No. 8. 8th ed. (Illus.). 248p. 1990. text 59.00 (*0-443-04168-7*) Church.

— Recent Advances in Dermatology 9. (Illus.). 226p. 1992. text 69.95 (*0-443-04451-1*) Church.

Champion, Robert H., et al. Textbook of Dermatology, 4 vols., Set. 5th ed. (Illus.). 3452p. 1991. 595.00 (*0-632-02396-1*) Blackwell Sci.

Champion, Ron. Build Your Own Sports Car for As Little As L250. (Illus.). 160p. 1998. 29.95 (*0-85429-976-9*) Haynes Manuals.

***Champion, Ron.** Build Your Own Sports Car for As Little As 250 Pounds & Race It! 2nd ed. (Illus.). 192p. 2000. 32.95 (*1-85960-636-9*, 130707AE, Pub. by Haynes Manuals) Motorbooks Intl.

Champion, S. Disco Biscuits. 1997. mass mkt. 13.95 (*0-340-68265-5*, Pub. by Hodder & Stought Ltd) Trafalgar.

— Disco 2000. mass mkt. 15.95 (*0-340-70771-2*, Pub. by Hodder & Stought Ltd) Trafalgar.

Champion, Sara. Archeology: Dictionary of Terms & Techniques: Archeologia; Dizionario di Termini e Techniche. (ITA.). 224p. 1983. 39.95 (*0-8288-1200-4*, F31850) Fr & Eur.

— A Dictionary of Terms & Techniques in Archaeology. LC 80-66774. 144p. reprint ed. pap. 44.70 (*0-608-12110-X*, 202514700042) Bks Demand.

Champion, Steven R. The Great Taiwan Bubble: The Rise & Fall of Asia's Most Volatile Emerging Market. LC 97-45902. (Illus.). 240p. 1998. pap. 29.95 (*1-881896-18-8*) Pacific View Pr.

Champion, Stewart. Access Scaffolding. 272p. 1996. write for info. (*0-582-25436-1*) Addison-Wesley.

Champion, Tim. Centre & Periphery: Comparative Studies in Archaeology. LC 95-11342. (One World Archaeology Ser.: No. 11). (Illus.). 264p. (C). 1995. pap. 39.99 (*0-415-12253-8*, C0588) Routledge.

Champion, Tim, ed. see Erick, Miriam.

Champion, Timothy C. Nationalism & Archaeology in Europe. Diaz-Andreu, Margarita, ed. (C). 1996. pap. 75.00 (*0-8133-3051-3*, Pub. by Westview) HarpC.

Champion, Timothy C. & Collis, J. R., eds. The Iron Age in Britain & Ireland: Recent Trends. LC 96-218614. (Recent Trends Ser.: No. 4). 161p. 1996. pap. 22.50 (*0-906090-51-2*, Pub. by Sheffield Acad) CUP Services.

Champion, Timothy C., et al. Prehistoric Europe. 1984. text 125.00 (*0-12-167550-5*); pap. text 55.00 (*0-12-167552-1*) Acad Pr.

Champion, Tony, ed. Population Matters: The Local Dimension. LC 93-10934. 189p. 1993. pap. 33.00 (*1-85396-201-5*, Pub. by P Chapman) Taylor & Francis.

Champion, Tony & Fielding, Tony, eds. Migration Processes & Patterns Vol. 1: Research Progress & Prospects. LC 91-34230. 272p. 1993. 140.00 (*0-471-94504-8*) Wiley.

Champion, Tony, et al. The New Regional Map of Europe. 70p. 1996. pap. text 102.50 (*0-08-042906-8*, Pergamon Pr) Elsevier.

Champion, Tony, et al. The Population of Britain in the 1990s: A Social & Economics Atlas. (Illus.). 164p. (C). 1996. text 49.95 (*0-19-874174-X*); pap. text 26.00 (*0-19-874175-8*) OUP.

Champion, Vickie. Change Your Relationship with Food. Schmidt, Lori, ed. viii, 88p. (Orig.). 1998. pap. 9.00 (*0-9660185-9-1*) Feed the Heart.

Champion, Walter T., Jr. Fundamentals of Sports Law. annuals rev. ed. LC 89-63831. (Entertainment & Communication Law Ser.). 1990. suppl. ed. 125.00 (*0-685-59805-5*) West Group.

Champion, Walter T. Sports Law in a Nutshell. (Nutshell Ser.). 325p. 1993. pap. 21.00 (*0-314-01642-2*) West Pub.

Champlain, Jack J. Auditing Information Systems: A Comprehensive Reference Guide. LC 98-13133. 440p. 1998. 74.95 (*0-471-16890-4*) Wiley.

***Champlain Publishing Staff.** Time Passages: Commemorative Yearbooks 1999. (Illus.). 2000. pap. 15.95 (*1-894455-63-0*) Stewart Hse.

Champlain, Samuel De. The Voyages & Explorations of Samuel De Champlain, Sixteen Four to Sixteen Sixteen, 2 vols. LC 72-2825. (American Explorers Ser.). (Illus.). 1973. reprint ed. 79.50 (*0-404-54905-5*) AMS Pr.

Champlain, Samuel De, see De Champlain, Samuel.

Champlin. Flying Eagle. large type ed. LC 98-31492. 1999. 30.00 (*0-7838-0435-0*, G K Hall Lrg Type) Mac Lib Ref.

— Fundamentals of Intervention. 2000. pap. text. write for info. (*0-7216-5181-X*, W B Saunders Co) Harcrt Hlth Sci Grp.

***Champlin.** Structure & Function of the Human Auditory System. 2002. pap. 44.00 (*0-7693-0170-3*, Pub. by Singular Publishing) Thomson Learn.

Champlin. Swift Thunder. LC 98-2609. 1998. 18.95 (*0-7862-1160-1*) Thorndike Pr.

C

An Asterisk (*) at the beginning of an entry indicates that the title is appearing for the first time.

Champlin, Allen R., Sr., jt. auth. see Ross, Ellena.

Champlin, Allen R., Sr., ed. see Pidgie, Sere W.

Champlin, Charles. Back There Where the Past Was: A Small-Town Boyhood. LC 88-38643. (New York State Bks.). (Illus.). 224p. 1989. 29.95 (*0-8156-0235-9*) Syracuse U Pr.

***Champlin, Charles.** Back There Where the Past Was: A Small-Town Boyhood. 232p. 1999. pap. text 19.95 (*0-8156-0612-5*) Syracuse U Pr.

Champlin, Charles. George Lucas: The Creative Impulse: Lucasfilm's First Twenty Years. rev. ed. LC 97-7634. (Illus.). 232p. 1997. 39.95 (*0-8109-3580-5*, Pub. by Abrams) Time Warner.

— Hollywood's Revolutionary Decade: Charles Champlin Reviews the Movies of the 1970s. LC 97-34608. 176p. 1998. pap. 14.95 (*1-880284-26-X*) J Daniel.

— John Frankenheimer: A Conversation. 241p. 1994. pap. 24.95 (*1-880756-09-9*) Riverwood Pr.

— The Movies Grow up, 1940-1980. rev. ed. LC 80-29388. (Illus.). 296p. 1981. reprint ed. pap. 16.95 (*0-8040-0364-5*) Swallow.

— Woody Allen at Work: The Photographs of Brian Hamill. LC 94-48322. (Illus.). 192p. 1995. 39.95 (*0-8109-1957-5*, Pub. by Abrams) Time Warner.

Champlin, Charles, jt. auth. see Champlin, Joseph M.

Champlin, Charles, ed. see Doherty, William E.

Champlin, Connie. Storytelling with Puppets. 2nd ed. LC 97-24810. 264p. 1997. 35.00 (*0-8389-0709-1*) ALA.

Champlin, Connie, jt. auth. see Champlin, John.

Champlin, Dale. Down by the Bay Big Book: Black & White Nellie Edge I Can Read & Sing Big Book. (J). (ps-2). 1988. pap. text 20.00 (*0-922053-02-2*) N Edge Res.

— The Wheels on the Bus Big Book: Black & White Nellie Edge I Can Read & Sing Big Book. (J). (ps-2). 1988. pap. text 20.00 (*0-922053-15-4*) N Edge Res.

Champlin, DeeAnn. Eddie E & the Eggs. (Little Lyrics Short Vowel Collection: Vol. 2). (Illus.). (J). (gr. k-2). Date not set. pap. 12.00 (*1-893429-26-1*) Little Lyrics.

— Five Funny A's. (Little Lyrics Short Vowel Collection: Vol. 1). (Illus.). (J). (gr. k-2). 1998. pap. 12.00 (*1-893429-25-3*) Little Lyrics.

— Incredible I. (Little Lyrics Short Vowel Collection: Vol. 3). (Illus.). (J). (gr. k-2). 1998. pap. 12.00 (*1-893429-27-X*) Little Lyrics.

— The Land of U. (Little Lyrics Short Vowel Collection: Vol. 5). (Illus.). (J). (gr. k-2). 1998. pap. 12.00 (*1-893429-29-6*) Little Lyrics.

— Let's Do the Vowel Sounds. (Little Lyrics Short Vowel Collection: Vol. 6). (Illus.). 11p. (J). (gr. k-2). 1998. pap. 12.00 (*1-893429-30-X*) Little Lyrics.

— Oliver O & the Olives. (Little Lyrics Short Vowel Collection: Vol. 4). (Illus.). (J). (gr. k-2). 1998. pap. 12.00 (*1-893429-28-8*) Little Lyrics.

Champlin, Edward. Final Judgments: Duty & Emotion in Roman Wills, 200 B.C.-A.D. 250. LC 90-38795. 206p. 1991. 45.00 (*0-520-07103-4*, Pub. by U CA Pr) Cal Prin Full Svc.

— Fronto & Antonine Rome. LC 79-28136. 185p. 1980. 25.95 (*0-674-32668-7*) HUP.

Champlin, Elizabeth M. Jiffy Journal. (Illus.). 100p. 1997. pap. 11.00 (*0-9661911-0-2*) Jiffy Journal.

Champlin, Jeffrey H. The Bank Customer's Guide to Safe & Smart Investing: Maximizing the Power of Your Savings Using: Annuities, Tax-Free Bonds, Government Bonds, Retirement Accounts, Certificates of Deposit, Stocks, Bonds, Successful Investment Strategies, Getting Started Tips...& More. 275p. 1995. text 17.00 (*0-7863-0403-0*, Irwn Prfssnl) McGraw-Hill Prof.

Champlin, John & Champlin, Connie. Books, Puppets & the Mentally Retarded Student. (Illus.). 162p. (Orig.). (J). 1981. pap. 19.95 (*0-938594-00-1*) Spec Lit Pr.

Champlin, John, ed. see Keefe, Betty.

Champlin, John, ed. see McGowan, Tom & McGowan, Meredith.

Champlin, John, Jr., ed. see Perkins, Charles C.

Champlin, Joseph. Father Champlin on Contemporary Issues: The Ten Commandments & Today's Catholics. LC 97-71700. (Illus.). 96p. (Orig.). 1997. pap. 3.95 (*0-7648-0123-6*) Liguori Pubns.

***Champlin, Joseph.** The Mystery & Meaning of the Mass. LC 98-43977. (Illus.). 126p. 1999. pap. 9.95 (*0-8245-1782-2*) Crossroad NY.

Champlin, Joseph. Pastoral Care: A Parish Planning Workbook. (Follow Me! Ser.). 1998. pap. 9.95 (*1-881307-15-8*, B7158) Natl Pastoral LC.

***Champlin, Joseph M.** Communion of the Sick. 1999. pap. 2.95 (*0-89942-082-6*) Catholic Bk Pub.

Champlin, Joseph M. From the Heart: Personalizing Your Wedding Homily with Your Own Hopes & Expectations. LC 97-35413. 48p. 1998. pap. 2.95 (*0-87793-647-1*) Ave Maria.

— An Important Office of Immense Love: A Handbook for Eucharistic Ministers. LC 80-80085. 152p. (Orig.). 1980. pap. 7.95 (*0-8091-2287-1*) Paulist Pr.

— Juntos Para Toda la Vida. LC 93-80593. (SPA.). 96p. 1994. pap. 3.95 (*0-89243-593-3*) Liguori Pubns.

— The Lord Is Present. 1973. pap. 7.95 (*0-87193-175-3*) Dimension Bks.

***Champlin, Joseph M.** The Marginal Catholic: Challenge, Don't Crush. rev. ed. LC 00-33153. (Orig.). 2000. write for info. (*0-8189-0882-3*) Alba.

Champlin, Joseph M. El Rito del Matrimonio. (SPA.). 94p. 1996. pap. 39.95 (*0-89243-936-X*) Liguori Pubns.

— Sharing Gifts: A Spirituality of Time, Talent, & Treasure. 40p. (Orig.). 1991. pap. 2.95 (*0-8146-2054-X*) Liturgical Pr.

— Sharing Treasure, Time, & Talent: A Parish Manual for Sacrificial Giving or Tithing. LC 82-16178. 88p. (Orig.). 1982. pap. 9.95 (*0-8146-1277-6*) Liturgical Pr.

— The Stations of the Cross with Pope John Paul II. (Illus.). 40p. (Orig.). 1994. pap. 2.95 (*0-89243-679-4*) Liguori Pubns.

— Through Death to Life: Preparing to Celebrate the Funeral Mass. rev. ed. LC 86-71916. 128p. 1990. pap. 3.50 (*0-87793-347-2*) Ave Maria.

— Through the Catechism with Fr. Champlin: A Question-&-Answer Guide. LC 95-82113. 80p. (Orig.). 1996. pap. 3.95 (*0-89243-907-6*) Liguori Pubns.

— Together for Life. alternate rev. ed. LC 97-155002. (Illus.). 96p. 1970. pap. 3.25 (*0-87793-616-1*) Ave Maria.

— Together for Life: Special Edition for Marriage Outside Mass. alternate rev. ed. LC 97-155007. (Illus.). 96p. 1972. pap. 3.25 (*0-87793-617-X*) Ave Maria.

— El Via Crucis: Con el Papa Juan Pablo II. (SPA.). 40p. (Orig.). 1997. pap. 2.95 (*0-89243-876-2*) Liguori Pubns.

— What It Means to Be Catholic. (Illus.). 64p. 1986. pap. 4.95 (*0-86716-245-7*, B2457) St Anthony Mess Pr.

— Why Go to Confession? Questions & Answers about Sacramental Reconciliation. rev. ed. 32p. 1996. pap. 1.95 (*0-86716-263-5*, B2635) St Anthony Mess Pr.

Champlin, Joseph M. & Champlin, Charles. The Visionary Leader: How Anyone Can Learn to Lead Better. 224p. (Orig.). 1993. pap. 14.95 (*0-8245-1235-9*) Crossroad NY.

Champlin, Joseph M. & Taylor, Susan C. A Thoughtful Word, a Healing Touch: A Guide for Visiting the Sick. 40p. (Orig.). 1995. pap. 2.95 (*0-89622-637-9*) Twenty-Third.

Champlin, Joseph M., et al. With Hearts Light As Feathers: The First Reconciliation of Children. 112p. (Orig.). 1995. pap. 7.95 (*0-8245-1471-8*) Crossroad NY.

Champlin, Malcolm & Goldsberry, Steven. Luzon. 448p. 1997. boxed set 22.95 (*1-56647-185-0*) Mutual Pub HI.

— Luzon: A Novel. 448p. 1997. pap. 15.95 (*1-56647-190-7*) Mutual Pub HI.

Champlin, Margaret D. Raphael Pumpelly: Gentleman Geologist of the Gilded Age. LC 93-4778. (History of American Science & Technology Ser.). (Illus.). 288p. reprint ed. pap. 89.30 (*0-608-09218-5*, 205272200005) Bks Demand.

Champlin, Richard E., ed. Bone Marrow Transplantation. (Cancer Treatment & Research Ser.). (C). 1990. text 215.50 (*0-7923-0612-0*) Kluwer Academic.

Champlin, Richard L. Trees of Newport: On the Estates of the Preservation Society of Newport County. (Illus.). 94p. 1976. pap. 4.00 (*0-917012-24-0*) Preserv Soc Newport.

Champlin, Sally, et al. Promoting Teen Health: Linking Schools, Health Organizations, & Community. LC 97-45473. 304p. 1998. write for info. (*0-7619-0275-9*); pap. write for info. (*0-7619-0276-7*) Sage.

Champlin, T. S. Reflexive Paradoxes. 224p. 1988. lib. bdg. 59.95 (*0-415-00083-1*) Routledge.

Champlin, Tim. Colt Lightning. large type ed. LC 94-32529. 242p. 1995. 17.95 (*0-7862-0029-4*) Thorndike Pr.

— Dakota Gold. 1996. 17.50 (*0-7451-4677-5*, Gunsmoke) Chivers N Amer.

— Dakota Gold. large type ed. LC 94-5129. 329p. 1996. lib. bdg. 18.95 (*0-7862-0199-1*) Thorndike Pr.

— Deadly Season. LC 97-27717. (Five-Star Western Ser.). 256p. 1997. lib. bdg. 17.95 (*0-7862-0783-3*) Five Star.

— Deadly Season. large type ed. LC 98-30793. 1999. 30.00 (*0-7862-0777-9*) Thorndike Pr.

— King of the Highbinders. large type ed. LC 96-36485. 251p. 1997. 18.95 (*0-7862-0898-8*) Thorndike Pr.

— The Last Campaign. large type ed. LC 95-40637. (Five Stars Western Ser.). 1996. 16.95 (*0-7862-0566-0*) Five Star.

— Lincoln's Ransom. LC 99-19835. 250p. 1999. 30.00 (*0-7862-1574-7*) Thorndike Pr.

— Lincoln's Ransom. large type ed. LC 00-24242. (G. K. Hall Western Ser.). 275p. 2000. 24.95 (*0-7838-0313-3*, G K Hall Lrg Type) Mac Lib Ref.

— Staghorn. 1998. 17.50 (*0-7540-8019-6*, Gunsmoke) Chivers N Amer.

— Summer of the Sioux. large type ed. LC 93-35695. 315p. 1993. lib. bdg. 15.95 (*0-7862-0028-6*) Thorndike Pr.

— The Survivor. large type ed. LC 97-24018. 1997. 22.95 (*0-7838-1672-3*, G K Hall Lrg Type) Mac Lib Ref.

— The Survivor: A Western Story. LC 96-6304. 1996. 16.95 (*0-7862-0661-6*) Five Star.

***Champlin, Tim.** Swift Thunder. 240p. 2000. pap. 4.50 (*0-8439-4758-6*, Leisure Bks) Dorchester Pub Co.

— Swift Thunder: A Western Story. LC 99-12621. 1999. 20.95 (*0-7862-1172-5*) Thorndike Pr.

Champlin, Tim. Tombstone Conspiracy. LC 99-35659. (Westerns Ser.). 1999. 19.95 (*0-7862-0998-4*, Five Star MI) Mac Lib Ref.

***Champlin, Tim.** The Tombstone Conspiracy: A Western Story. LC 00-34372. 2000. write for info. (*0-7862-1037-0*) Thorndike Pr.

— Wayfaring Strangers. 307p. 2000. 30.00 (*0-7862-2104-6*, Five Star MI) Mac Lib Ref.

***Champman, Kristen.** The Way Home. 225p. 1999. 12.95 (*0-9665767-0-5*) Third Tree.

Champness, John. Lancashire. (Country Guide Ser.: No. 28). (Illus.). 64p. pap. 8.50 (*0-85263-984-8*, Pub. by Shire Pubns) Parkwest Pubns.

Champness, Thomas. Carmel's Hero: The Life & Times of Elijah. unabridged ed. 69p. 1994. reprint ed. pap. 5.99 (*0-88019-322-0*) Schmul Pub Co.

— The Young Preacher's Guide to Success. 1993. reprint ed. pap. 8.99 (*0-88019-308-5*) Schmul Pub Co.

Champness, W. To Cariboo & Back in 1862. 106p. 1972. 18.95 (*0-87770-109-1*) Ye Galleon.

Champness, Wendy, jt. auth. see Snyder, Larry.

Champney, Freeman. Art & Glory: The Story of Elbert Hubbard. LC 83-14863. (Illus.). 260p. reprint ed. pap. 80.60 (*0-7837-0498-4*, 204082200018) Bks Demand.

Champney, Leonard. Introduction to Quantitative Political Science. LC 94-5006. 294p. (C). 1997. pap. text 62.00 (*0-06-501032-9*) Addson-Wesley Educ.

***Champneys, A. R., et al, eds.** Localization & Solitary Waves in Solid Mechanics. (Advanced Series in Nonlinear Dynamics). 320p. 1999. 56.00 (*981-02-3915-7*) World Scientific Pub.

Champoux. Essentials of Organizational Behavior. LC 99-23260. (SWC-Management Ser.). 456p. 1999. pap. 47.95 (*0-324-01335-3*) Thomson Learn.

— Organizational Behavior. 2nd ed. Date not set. pap. 58.00 (*0-324-00605-5*) Sth-Wstrn College.

***Champoux.** Using Film in Management. (SWC-General Business Ser.). 2000. pap. 24.95 (*0-324-05359-2*) Sth-Wstrn College.

— Using Film in Organizational Behavior. 2000. pap. 24.95 (*0-324-04856-4*) Sth-Wstrn College.

***Champoux, G. John, ed.** The Secret of the Christian Way: A Contemplative Ascent Through the Writings of Jean Borella. (C). 2001. pap. text 19.95 (*0-7914-4844-4*) State U NY Pr.

— The Secret of the Christian Way: A Contemplative Ascent Through the Writings of Jean Borella. (C). 2001. text 59.50 (*0-7914-4843-6*) State U NY Pr.

Champoux, John, tr. see Borella, Jean.

Champoux, Joseph E. Organizational Behavior: Individuals, Groups, & Processes. Horan, ed. LC 95-16979. 668p. (C). 1996. mass mkt. 95.95 (*0-314-06242-4*) West Pub.

Champoux, Peter. Gaia Matrix: Arkhom & the Geometries of Destiny in the North American Landscape. (Illus.). 264p. 1999. pap. 25.00 (*0-9672328-0-5*) Franklin Media.

Champs, Flavia W. The Matachines Dance of the Upper Rio Grande: History, Music, & Choreography. LC 82-10892. 121p. 1983. reprint ed. pap. 37.60 (*0-608-01409-5*, 206217200002) Bks Demand.

Champsaur, Paul & Milleron, Jean-Claude. Advanced Exercises in Microeconomics. Bonin, John P. & Bonin, Helene, trs. from FRE. (Illus.). 288p. 1983. 50.95 (*0-674-00525-2*) HUP.

Champsaur, Paul, et al. Essays in Honor of Edmond Malinvaud, 3 vols., Vol. 3. 1990. 32.50 (*0-262-03160-4*) MIT Pr.

Champy, J. Reingeniera de la Direccion. (SPA.). 273p. 1996. 29.50 (*84-7978-259-5*, Pub. by Ediciones Diaz) IBD Ltd.

Champy, James. Reengineering Management: The Mandate for New Leadership. 212p. 1998. pap. text 13.00 (*0-7881-5349-8*) DIANE Pub.

— Reengineering Management: The Mandate for New Leadership. 212p. 1998. text 25.00 (*0-7881-5709-4*) DIANE Pub.

— Reengineering Management: The Mandate for New Leadership. 256p. 1995. pap. 13.00 (*0-88730-796-5*, HarpBusn) HarpInfo.

Champy, James & Nohria, Nitin. The Arc of Ambition: Defining the Leadership Journey. 254p. 2000. 26.00 (*0-7382-0103-0*, Pub. by Perseus Pubng) HarpC.

Champy, James & Nohria, Nitin, eds. Fast Forward: The Best Ideas on Managing Business Change. (Harvard Business Review Book Ser.). 320p. (C). 1996. 24.95 (*0-87584-673-4*) Harvard Busn.

Champy, James, jt. auth. see Hammer, Michael.

Champy, M., jt. ed. see Hildebrand, H. F.

Chamson, Andre. Le Chiffre De Nos Jours. (FRE.). 1973. pap. 10.95 (*0-7859-2204-0*, 207036433X) Fr & Eur.

— La Neige et la Fleur. (FRE.). 448p. 1974. pap. 10.95 (*0-7859-2205-9*, 207036531X) Fr & Eur.

Chamuris, George P. The Non-Stipitate Stereoid Fungi in the Northeastern United States & Adjacent Canada: Mycologia Memoir. (Mycologia Memoir Ser.: No. 14). (Illus.). 247p. 1988. 58.00 (*3-443-76004-X*, Pub. by Gebruder Borntraeger) Balogh.

Chan. Beyond the Developmental State: East Asia's Political Economies Reconsidered. LC 97-17804. 256p. 1998. text 65.00 (*0-312-17739-9*) St Martin.

— Facilities. (SWC-Marketing). 2000. 94.95 (*0-538-88670-6*) S-W Pub.

— Facility Location & Land Use. (GC - Principles of Management Ser.). 1996. pap. 69.00 (*0-7895-0091-4*) Course Tech.

— Managing the People's Money. (Public Administration Ser.). 1997. text 49.95 (*0-534-25356-3*) Wadsworth Pub.

— Sports Injuries of the Hand & Upper Extremity. 1995. text 109.00 (*0-443-07780-0*) Harcourt.

Chan & Prosen. Practice Test Psychiatry. 11th ed. 1998. pap. 19.95 (*0-8385-0360-8*) Appleton & Lange.

Chan, Brian, et al. West Coast Fly Fisher. limited ed. (Illus.). 152p. 1998. write for info. (*0-88839-448-9*) Hancock House.

***Chan, Adrian.** Chinese Marxism. 256p. 2001. 74.95 (*0-8264-5033-4*) Continuum.

Chan, Alan. FX Kit for Lightwave. (Illus.). 310p. (Orig.). 1996. pap. 34.95 (*0-9655313-2-5*) Lghtspeed.

— Photoreal FX. (Illus.). 292p. (Orig.). 1996. pap. 44.95 (*0-9655313-0-9*) Lghtspeed.

— Power FX 5.0 Addendum. 174p. (Orig.). 1996. pap. 24.95 (*0-9655313-1-7*) Lghtspeed.

Chan, Alan K. Two Visions of the Way: A Study of the Wang Pi & the Ho-shang Kung Commentaries on the Lao-Tzu. LC 89-78198. (SUNY Series in Chinese Philosophy & Culture). 314p. (C). 1991. text 64.50 (*0-7914-0455-2*); pap. text 21.95 (*0-7914-0456-0*) State U NY Pr.

Chan, Andrew K., jt. auth. see Goswami, Jaideva C.

Chan, Anita. China's Workers under Assault. (Asia & the Pacific Ser.). 232p. 2000. 55.00 (*0-7656-0357-8*, East Gate Bk) M E Sharpe.

***Chan, Anita, et al, eds.** Transforming Asian Socialism: China & Vietnam Compared. 256p. 1999. pap. 22.95 (*0-8476-9847-5*); text 55.00 (*0-8476-9846-7*) Rowman.

Chan, Anita, et al. Chen Village under Mao & Deng: The Recent History of a Peasant Community in Mao's China. enl. rev. ed. LC 92-14342. 1992. pap. 18.95 (*0-520-08109-9*, Pub. by U CA Pr) Cal Prin Full Svc.

Chan, Anita, ed. see Guokai, Liu.

Chan, Anja A. Women & Sexual Harassment: A Guide to the Legal Protections of Title VII & the Hostile Environment Claim. LC 92-44322. 110p. 1994. pap. 9.95 (*1-56023-040-1*, Harrington Park) Haworth Pr.

— Women & Sexual Harassment: A Guide to the Legal Protections of Title VII & the Hostile Environment Claim. LC 92-44322. 110p. 1994. lib. bdg. 29.95 (*1-56024-408-9*) Haworth Pr.

Chan, Anna, compiled by. A Research Bibliography of California's Chinese Americans. 47p. 1991. pap. text 20.00 (*1-883638-17-8*) Rose Inst.

Chan, Anthony. Hmong Textile Designs. (Illus.). 42p. 1990. pap. 6.95 (*0-88045-113-0*) Stemmer Hse.

***Chan, Anthony B.** Li Ka-Shing: Hong Kong's Elusive Billionaire. 251p. 2000. reprint ed. text 25.00 (*0-7881-6855-X*) DIANE Pub.

Chan, Anthony H. Environmental Stress Testing. (C). 1997. pap. 42.95 (*0-201-69585-5*) Addison-Wesley.

Chan, Barbara, tr. see Galtrucco, Gianluca.

Chan, Bing-Cho. The Authorship of the Dream of the Red Chamber Based on a Computerized Statistical Study of Its Vocabulary. LC 87-114997. xix, 92p. 1986. write for info. (*962-04-0474-2*) Joint Pub.

Chan, Brian, jt. auth. see Morris, Skip.

Chan, Brian M. Flyfishing Strategies for Stillwaters. 60p. 1993. spiral bd. 14.95 (*1-878175-57-2*) F Amato Pubns.

Chan, C. L., et al, eds. Transport Phenomena in Nonconventional Manufacturing & Materials Processing. LC 93-73717. 149p. 1993. pap. 47.50 (*0-7918-1004-6*) ASME.

Chan, C. L., et al. Orchids of Borneo Vol. 1: Introduction & a Selection of Species. (Illus.). xviii, 322p. 1994. 60.00 (*967-99947-3-2*, Pub. by Royal Botnic Grdns) Balogh.

Chan, Carlyle. MEPC USMLE Step 3 Review. (C). 1996. pap. text 34.95 (*0-8385-6339-2*, A6339-4, Apple Lange Med) McGraw.

Chan, Carlyle, et al. MEPC: Psychiatry. 10th ed. 250p. (C). 1997. pap. text 21.95 (*0-8385-5780-5*, A5780-0, Apple Lange Med) McGraw.

Chan, Carlyle H. Appleton & Lange's Review for the USMLE Step 2. 3rd rev. ed. LC 99-54040. (Illus.). 361p. (C). 1999. pap. 39.95 (*0-8385-0341-1*, A-0341-6, Apple Lange Med) McGraw.

Chan, Cecilia L. & Rhind, Nancy, eds. Social Work Intervention in Health Care: The Hong Kong Scene. LC 98-107747. 414p. (Orig.). 1997. pap. 48.50 (*962-209-419-8*, Pub. by HK Univ Pr) Coronet Bks.

Chan, Cecilia Lai-wan, jt. ed. see Fielding, Richard.

Chan, Charis. China. 5th ed. (Odyssey Passport Ser.). (Illus.). 350p. 1999. pap. 19.95 (*962-217-604-6*) Norton.

Chan, Charis. China. 6th ed. pap. 19.95 (*962-217-655-0*) China Guides.

Chan, Charis. China: The Middle Kingdom. 3rd ed. (China Guides Ser.). (Illus.). 308p. 1995. pap. 16.95 (*0-8442-9985-5*, Passprt Bks) NTC Contemp Pub Co.

Chan, Chi-Ming. Polymer Surface Modification & Characterization. LC 93-37465. 295p. 1993. 99.50 (*1-56990-158-9*) Hanser-Gardner.

***Chan, Ching-Yao.** Fundamentals of Crash Sensing in Automotive Air Bag Systems. LC 99-45839. 2000. write for info. (*0-7680-0499-3*) Soc Auto Engineers.

Chan Chiu Ming. Book of Changes: An Interpretation for the Modern Age. (Illus.). 232p. 1996. pap. 14.95 (*981-3068-29-9*, Pub. by Asiapac) China Bks.

Chan, Clifford. Dr. Clifford Chan's Book of Singapore Discus. (TS Ser.). (Illus.). 160p. 1991. text 35.95 (*0-86622-171-9*, TS-170) TFH Pubns.

Chan, D. S. A Pharmacist's Guide to Providing Veterinary Prescription Services. 2nd rev. ed. (Illus.). 256p. (C). 2000. pap. 45.99 (*0-9663353-1-7*) Gratefuldeb.

***Chan, D. S.** A Pharmacist's Guide to Schools Offering Nontraditional Doctor of Pharmacy Degrees. 144p. (C). 2000. pap. 24.99 (*0-9663353-2-5*) Gratefuldeb.

Chan, D. S. Veterinary Pharmacy Handbook: An Easy-to-Use Guide to Expanding & Improving Your Community Pharmacy Practice. 195p. (C). 1997. pap. text 32.99 (*0-9663353-0-9*) Gratefuldeb.

Chan, Daniel W., ed. Immunoassay Automation: A Practical Guide. (Illus.). 367p. 1992. pap. 58.00 (*0-12-167632-3*) Acad Pr.

— Immunoassay Automation: An Updated Guide to Systems. LC 95-30894. (Illus.). 312p. (C). 1995. 34.95 (*0-12-167640-4*) Acad Pr.

Chan, David, jt. auth. see Schmitt, Neal.

Chan, David W. Helping Students with Learning Difficulties. 220p. 1998. pap. 37.50 (*962-201-818-1*, Pub. by Chinese Univ) U of Mich Pr.

Chan, Dorothy, jt. auth. see Subramaniam, N.

Chan, Edward D. Bedside Critical Care Manual. LC 97-31328. 1997. 19.95 (*1-56053-216-5*) Hanley & Belfus.

Chan, Elise D. Jefferson County. (Images of America Ser.). 1999. pap. 16.99 (*0-7524-0953-0*) Arcadia Publng.

Chan, Elizabeth. Tropical Plants. (Nature Guides Ser.). (Illus.). 64p. 1998. 9.95 (*962-593-168-6*, Periplus Eds) Tuttle Pubng.

Chan, Fran. Java 2 Media Development. 1200p. 1999. pap. text 49.99 (*0-672-31706-0*) Macmillan.

Chan, Gary M., ed. Lactation: The Breast-Feeding Manual for Health Professionals. LC 96-38181. 192p. 1996. pap. 40.00 (*0-944496-48-2*) Precept Pr.

Chan, Gerald. China & International Organizations: Participation in Non-Governmental Organizations since 1971. (Illus.). 234p. 1989. text 39.95 (*0-19-582738-4*) OUP.

C

An Asterisk (*) at the beginning of an entry indicates that the title is appearing for the first time.

***Chan, Gerald.** Chinese Perspectives on International Relations: A Framework for Analysis. LC 98-40018. xvii, 201 p. 1999. write for info. (*0-333-73418-1*, Pub. by S1 & J) Trafalgar.

Chan, Gerald. International Studies in China: An Annotated Bibliography. LC 98-27351. 1998. 49.00 (*1-56072-588-5*) Nova Sci Pubs.

Chan, Gillian. Glory Days & Other Stories. 118p. (J). 1994. pap. 4.95 (*1-55074-319-8*) Kids Can Pr.

Chan, Gillian. Glory Days & Other Stories. unabridged ed. (Illus.). 128p. (J). (gr. 6-10). 1997. 16.95 (*1-55074-381-3*, Pub. by Kids Can Pr) Genl Dist Srvs.

Chan, Gillian. Golden Girl & Other Stories. 120p. (J). 1994. pap. 4.95 (*1-55074-219-1*) Kids Can Pr.

Chan, Gillian. Golden Girl & Other Stories. unabridged ed. 128p. (J). (gr. 6-10). 1997. 14.95 (*1-55074-385-6*, Pub. by Kids Can Pr) Genl Dist Srvs.

Chan, H. C., et al. Exact Analysis of Structures with Periodicity Using U-Transformation. 340p. 1998. 56.00 (*981-02-3642-5*) World Scientific Pub.

Chan, H. L. Cutaneous Clues to Systemic Diseases. (Illus.). 138p. 1986. 33.50 (*9971-69-101-9*, Pub. by Sngapore Univ Pr) Coronet Bks.

Chan, H. M. & Tsou, S. T. Some Elementary Gauge Theory Concepts. (Lecture Notes in Physics Ser.). 164p. 1993. text 40.00 (*981-02-1080-9*); pap. text 23.00 (*981-02-1081-7*) World Scientific Pub.

***Chan, Harvey.** The Child's Story. LC 99-46446. (J). 2000. per. 17.00 (*0-689-83482-9*) S&S Childrens.

Chan, Harvey T., Jr., ed. Handbook of Tropical Foods. LC 83-5119. (Food Science Ser.: Vol. 9). 651p. 1983. reprint ed. pap. 200.00 (*0-608-04614-0*, 206538300003) Bks Demand.

Chan, Helena H. An Introduction to the Singapore Legal System. vii, 140p. 1986. pap. 22.00 (*9971-70-054-9*, MICHIE) LEXIS Pub.

— The Legal System of Singapore. LC 96-945765. xxiv, 194p. 1995. pap. write for info. (*0-409-99789-7*, MICHIE) LEXIS Pub.

Chan, Heng Chee. A Sensation of Independence: Singapore's David Marshall. (Illus.). 1985. pap. 26.00 (*0-19-582607-8*) OUP.

Chan-Herur, K. C. Communicating with Customers Around the World: A Practical Guide to Effective Cross-Cultural Business Communication. LC 94-94276. (Global Business Ser.). 134p. 1994. pap. 12.95 (*1-885269-18-8*) AuMonde Intl.

Chan-hie Kim, tr. see Baird, John B.

***Chan, Hok-lam.** China & the Mongols: History & Legend under the Yuan & Ming. LC 98-53880. (Variorum Collected Studies: No. CS647). 352p. 1999. text 106.95 (*0-86078-762-1*) Ashgate Pub Co.

Chan, Hok-Lam, jt. auth. see Franke, Herbert.

Chan, Hon S., jt. auth. see Wong, Hoi-kowk.

Chan, Jackie. I Am Jackie Chan. 1999. mass mkt. 6.99 (*0-345-42913-3*) Ballantine Pub Grp.

— I Am Jackie Chan: My Life in Action. LC 98-25605. 336p. 1998. 35.00 (*0-345-41503-5*) Ballantine Pub Grp.

***Chan, James.** Spare Room Tycoon: Succeeding Independently: The 70 Lessons of Sane Self-Employment. 256p. 2000. 22.00 (*1-85788-247-4*, Pub. by Nicholas Brealey) Natl Bk Netwk.

Chan, James C. & Gill, John R., Jr., eds. Kidney Electrolyte Disorders. LC 89-17460. (Illus.). 640p. reprint ed. pap. 198.40 (*0-7837-6262-3*, 204597400010) Bks Demand.

Chan, James C., jt. ed. see Alon, Uri.

Chan, James L., ed. Research in Governmental & Nonprofit Accounting, Vol. 10. Date not set. 78.50 (*0-7623-0169-4*) Jai Pr.

Chan, James L., et al, eds. Research in Governmental & Nonprofit Accounting, Vol. 1. 347p. 1985. 78.50 (*0-89232-517-8*) Jai Pr.

— Research in Governmental & Nonprofit Accounting, Vol. 2. 273p. 1986. 78.50 (*0-89232-628-X*) Jai Pr.

— Research in Governmental & Nonprofit Accounting, 2 vols., Vol. 3. 1987. 157.00 (*0-89232-699-9*) Jai Pr.

— Research in Governmental & Nonprofit Accounting, Vol. 3, Pt. A. 206p. 1987. 78.50 (*0-89232-785-5*) Jai Pr.

— Research in Governmental & Nonprofit Accounting, Vol. 3, Pt. B. 280p. 1987. 78.50 (*0-89232-786-3*) Jai Pr.

— Research in Governmental & Nonprofit Accounting, Vol. 4. 260p. 1988. 78.50 (*0-89232-787-1*) Jai Pr.

— Research in Governmental & Nonprofit Accounting, Vol. 5. 310p. 1989. 78.50 (*0-89232-975-0*) Jai Pr.

— Research in Governmental & Nonprofit Accounting, Vol. 6. 262p. 1990. 78.50 (*1-55938-119-1*) Jai Pr.

— Research in Governmental & Nonprofit Accounting, Vol. 7. 240p. 1992. 78.50 (*1-55938-418-2*) Jai Pr.

— Research in Governmental & Nonprofit Accounting, Vol. 8. 348p. 1994. 78.50 (*1-55938-544-8*) Jai Pr.

— Research in Governmental & Nonprofit Accounting, Vol. 9. 1996. 78.50 (*1-55938-055-1*) Jai Pr.

Chan, James L. & Jones, Rowan H., eds. Governmental Accounting & Auditing International Comparisons. (Croom Helm International Accounting Ser.). 240p. 1988. lib. bdg. 59.50 (*0-415-01268-6*) Routledge.

Chan, Janet. Doing Less Time: Penal Reform in Crisis. (Institute of Criminology Monographs: No. 2). xiv, 222p. 1992. pap. 40.00 (*0-86758-566-8*) Gaunt.

Chan, Janis F. Getting Help. (On Your Own Ser.). (Illus.). 64p. (YA). (gr. 7 up). 1982. pap. text 3.95 (*0-915510-61-8*) Globe Fearon.

— Inventing Ourselves Again: Women Face Middle Age. Columbus, Marge, ed. 200p. 1996. pap. 14.95 (*0-9638327-1-9*) Sibyl Pubns.

Chan, Janis F. & Lutovich, Diane. Grammar for Grownups: A Self-Paced Training Program. 240p. 1993. pap. 45.00 (*0-9637455-1-4*) Adv Comm Designs.

— Writing Performance Documentation: A Self-Paced Training Program. 111p. 1994. pap. 32.00 (*0-9637455-3-0*) Adv Comm Designs.

Chan, Janis F., jt. auth. see Lutovich, Diane.

Chan, Janis F., jt. auth. see Mukai, Linda P.

Chan, Jeffrey P., et al, eds. The Big Aiiieeeee! An Anthology of Chinese-American & Japanese-American Literature. (Illus.). 650p. (Orig.). 1991. pap. 15.95 (*0-452-01076-4*, Mer) NAL.

Chan, Jennifer L. One Small Girl. LC 92-35423. (Illus.). 32p. (J). (gr. k-2). 1993. 12.95 (*1-879965-05-4*) Polychrome Pub.

— Why Does a B Look Like a D? LC 93-45793. (J). Date not set. write for info. (*1-879965-06-2*) Polychrome Pub.

***Chan, Johannes M. M., et al.** Hong Kong's Constitutional Debate: Conflict over Interpretation. 496p. 2000. pap. 33.50 (*962-209-509-7*, Pub. by HK Univ Pr) Coronet Bks.

Chan, Julia L., ed. Libraries & Information Centres in Hong Kong. LC 97-146164. (Libraries Publications: No. 7). 554p. (Orig.). 1996. pap. 97.50 (*962-209-409-0*, Pub. by HK Univ Pr) Coronet Bks.

Chan, Juliana C., et al. Manual for Management of Diabetes Mellitus. Date not set. pap. 23.95 (*962-201-757-6*, Pub. by Chinese Univ) U of Mich Pr.

Chan, K. L. & Cheng, K. S., eds. Proceedings of the 21st Century Chinese Astronomy Conference Dedicated to Professor C. C. Lin. 600p. 1997. text 86.00 (*981-02-3226-8*) World Scientific Pub.

Chan, K. Y. & Liu, M. C. Five Decades As a Mathematician & Educator: On the 80th Birthday of Professor Yung-Chow Wong. LC 96-162279. 440p. 1995. text 74.00 (*981-02-2343-9*) World Scientific Pub.

Chan, Kai-Ming, et al. Principles & Practices of Isokinetics in Sports Medicine & Rehabilitation. (Illus.). 232p. 1996. write for info. (*962-356-016-8*) Lppncott W & W.

— Principles & Practices of Isokinetics in Sports Medicine & Rehabilitation. (CHI., Illus.). 500p. 1997. write for info. (*962-356-027-3*) Lppncott W & W.

Chan, Kam W. Social Construction of Gender Inequality in the Housing System: Housing Experience of Women in Hong Kong. LC 97-74511. (Illus.). 356p. 1997. text 69.95 (*1-84014-163-8*, Pub. by Ashgate Pub) Ashgate Pub Co.

Chan, Karence K., jt. auth. see Pathria, Mini Nutan.

Chan, Kelly. Digest: A Primer for the International GIS Standards. LC 98-5981. (Mapping Sciences Ser.). 144p. 1998. boxed set 49.95 (*1-56670-241-0*, L1241) Lewis Pubs.

***Chan, Kelvin & Cheung, Lily.** Interactions Between Chinese Herbal Medicinal Products & Orthodox Drugs. 166p. 1999. text 60.00 (*90-5702-413-6*, Harwood Acad Pubs) Gordon & Breach.

***Chan, Kit.** Noodles Quick & Easy. 96p. 1999. pap. 12.95 (*0-7548-0554-9*) Anness Pub.

Chan, Kit. Quick After-Work Chinese Cookbook. 137p. 1999. 21.00 (*0-7499-1797-0*, Pub. by Piatkus Bks) London Brdge.

Chan, Kwai-Cheung. Defense Spending & Employment: Information Limitations Impede Thorough Assessments. (Illus.). 65p. (C). 1998. pap. text 20.00 (*0-7881-7343-X*) DIANE Pub.

— Operation Desert Storm: Evaluation of the Air Campaign. (Illus.). 235p. (C). 1998. pap. text 40.00 (*0-7881-4769-2*) DIANE Pub.

Chan, Kwai S., ed. Cleavage Fracture: Proceedings, Symposium on Cleavage Fracture, Indianapolis, IN, 1997. LC 97-73309. (Illus.). 383p. 1997. 144.00 (*0-87339-381-3*, TA460) Minerals Metals.

Chan, Kwing L., et al, eds. 1997 Pacific Rim Conference on Stellar Astrophysics. LC 98-70636. (Conference Series Proceedings: Vol. 138). 426p. 1998. 52.00 (*1-886733-58-9*) Astron Soc Pacific.

Chan, Kwok Bun, jt. ed. see Tong, Chee Kiong.

Chan, Laurence, jt. auth. see Owyong.

Chan, Leo T. The Discourse on Foxes & Ghosts: Ji Yun & Eighteenth-Century Literati Storytelling. (Chinese University Press Staff). (Illus.). (C). write for info. (*962-201-749-5*, Pub. by Chinese Univ) U of Mich Pr.

Chan, Leo T. The Discourse on Foxes & Ghosts: Ji Yun & Eighteenth-Century Literati Storytelling. LC 97-41698. 300p. 1998. text 36.00 (*0-8248-2051-7*) UH Pr.

Chan, Linda S., et al. Maternal & Child Health on the U. S.-Mexico Border. (Special Project Reports). 296p. 1988. pap. 10.00 (*0-89940-687-4*) LBJ Sch Pub Aff.

Chan, Lock L. Wet-Strength Resins & Their Application: A Project of the Papermaking Additives Committee of TAPPI's Paper & Board Manufacture Division. LC 94-33119. (Illus.). 1994. 73.00 (*0-89852-060-6*, 0102B059) TAPPI.

Chan, Lois M. Cataloging & Classification: An Introduction. 2nd ed. LC 93-22606. 544p. (C). 1994. 61.88 (*0-07-010506-5*) McGraw.

— Guide to the Library of Congress Classification. 5th ed. LC 99-15279. (Library & Information Science Text Ser.). 550p. 1999. 65.00 (*1-56308-499-6*); pap. 55.00 (*1-56308-500-3*) Libs Unl.

— Library of Congress Subject Headings: Principles & Application. LC 95-2664. xi, 541p. 1995. pap. text 45.00 (*1-56308-191-1*) Libs Unl.

— Library of Congress Subject Headings: Principles & Application. 3rd ed. LC 95-2664. xi, 541p. 1995. lib. bdg. 55.00 (*1-56308-195-4*) Libs Unl.

Chan, Lois M. & Mitchell, Joan S., eds. Dewey Decimal Classification: Edition 21 & International Perspectives. LC 96-48761. 98p. 1996. pap. 20.00 (*0-910608-56-3*) OCLC Forest Pr.

Chan, Lois M. & Pollard, Richard. Thesauri Used in Online Databases: An Analytical Guide. LC 88-10985. 284p. 1988. lib. bdg. 65.00 (*0-313-25788-4*, CTI/, Greenwood Pr) Greenwood.

Chan, Lois M., et al. Dewey Decimal Classification: A Practical Guide. 2nd rev. ed. LC 96-16307. 246p. 1996. 40.00 (*0-910608-55-5*) OCLC Forest Pr.

Chan, Luke. 101 Lessons of Tao. (Illus.). 150p. (Orig.). 1995. pap. 12.95 (*0-9637341-2-1*) Benefactor.

— 101 Miracles of Natural Healing. 144p. (Orig.). 1995. pap. 14.95 (*0-9637341-4-8*) Benefactor.

— Secrets to the Tai Chi Circle: Journey to Enlightenment. (Illus.). 144p. (Orig.). 1993. pap. 10.00 (*0-9637341-0-5*) Benefactor.

Chan, M. K. Integrated Systematic Nephrology. rev. ed. 344p. (C). 1989. pap. text 37.50 (*962-209-180-6*, Pub. by HK Univ Pr) Coronet Bks.

Chan Man Fong, C. F., et al. Advanced Mathematics for Applied & Pure Sciences. 904p. 1997. text 98.00 (*90-5699-607-X*) Gordon & Breach.

Chan, Man-Kwun, et al. Proceedings of a Workshop on Tree Resources & the Environment Held in Phy Wiang Watershed, Khon Kaen, Thailand. 1994. pap. 25.00 (*0-85954-384-6*, Pub. by Nat Res Inst) St Mut.

Chan, Margie. The Eye 'n' Hand, Bk. 1B. 1990. pap. text 8.50 (*0-9615006-7-0*) Gim-Ho.

— The Eye 'N' Hand: For Violin. (C.A.V.E. Concepts & Patterns Exploration Ser.: Bk. 1B). 1991. student ed. 7.95 (*0-685-37660-5*) Gim-Ho.

— The Eye 'N' Hand Bk. 1: For Violin. (C.A.V.E. Concepts & Vocabulary Exploration Ser.). (Orig.). 1987. pap. text 4.95 (*0-9615006-6-2*) Gim-Ho.

— The Eye 'N' Hand Book One: For Violin. (J). (gr. 2). 1988. write for info. (*0-318-62778-7*) Gim-Ho.

— Finger Fiddling Fun: Book for Violin. (C.A.V.E. Concepts & Patterns Exploration Ser.: Bk. 1A). 16p. (Orig.). 1990. pap. 4.95 (*0-9615006-3-8*) Gim-Ho.

— Finger Fiddling Fun for Violin, Bk. 1. 1990. 9.95 (*0-317-90986-X*) Gim-Ho.

— Finger Fiddling Fun for Violin, Bk. 2. 1990. 9.95 (*0-317-90987-8*) Gim-Ho.

— Music Concepts & Vocabulary for Violin. rev. ed. (C.A.V.E. Concepts & Vocabulary Exploration Ser.: Bk. 2). 48p. 1988. reprint ed. student ed., spiral bd. 8.95 (*0-9615006-8-9*); reprint ed. student ed., ring bd. 7.95 (*0-9615006-2-X*) Gim-Ho.

— Music Concepts & Vocabulary for Violin. rev. ed. (C.A.V.E. Concepts & Vocabulary Exploration Ser.: Bk. 1). 61p. 1988. student ed., spiral bd. 8.95 (*0-9615006-5-4*); student ed., ring bd. 8.95 (*0-9615006-9-7*) Gim-Ho.

— Music Concepts & Vocabulary for Violin, Bk. 1. (C.A.V.E. Concepts & Vocabulary Exploration Ser.). 41p. (J). (gr. 2 up). 1984. student ed. 4.95 (*0-9615006-0-3*) Gim-Ho.

— Music Concepts & Vocabulary for Violin, Bk. 2. (C.A.V.E. Concepts & Vocabulary Exploration Ser.). 48p. (J). (gr. 2 up). 1985. student ed. 4.95 (*0-9615006-1-1*) Gim-Ho.

***Chan, Mark L. Y.** Christology from Within & Ahead: Hermeneutics, Contingency & the Quest for Transcontextual Criteria in Christology. LC 00-37924. (Biblical Interpretation Ser.). 2000. write for info. (*90-04-11844-6*) Brill Academic Pubs.

Chan, Markorie A., et al. Deltaic & Shelf Deposits in the Cretaceous Blackhawk Formation & Mancos Shale, Grand County, Utah. (Miscellaneous Publication Ser.: Vol. 91-6). (Illus.). 83p. 1991. pap. 9.00 (*1-55791-315-3*, MP-91-6) Utah Geological Survey.

Chan, Marsha. Phrase by Phrase: Pronunciation & Listening in American English. (Illus.). 176p. (C). 1987. pap. text 27.93 (*0-13-665852-0*) P-H.

Chan, Mary. Life into Story: The Courtship of Elizabeth Wiseman. LC 97-50361. (Women & Gender in Early Modern England, 1500-1750 Ser.). 164p. 1998. text 61.95 (*1-84014-212-X*, Pub. by Ashgate Pub) Ashgate Pub Co.

— Music in the Theatre of Ben Jonson. (Illus.). 400p. 1980. text 89.00 (*0-19-812632-8*) OUP.

***Chan, Mary.** The Reluctant Warrior: A Journey Through My Baby's Heart Transplant. 256p. 2000. pap. 14.95 (*1-893162-18-4*) Erica Hse.

Chan, Mary & North, Roger. Life of the Lord Keeper North by Roger North. LC 95-2968. (Studies in British History: Vol. 41). (Illus.). 644p. 1995. text 129.95 (*0-7734-8972-X*) E Mellen.

Ch'an Master Yung Chia. The Song of Enlightenment. Buddhist Text Translation Society Staff, tr. from CHI. (Illus.). 85p. (Orig.). 1983. pap. 5.00 (*0-88139-100-X*) Buddhist Text.

Chan, Mei-Mei, ed. see Huegel, Tony.

Chan, Melissa. Getting Your Man. 160p. 1993. pap. 10.95 (*1-875559-08-6*, Pub. by SpiniFex Pr) LPC InBook.

— Too Rich. 108p. 1993. pap. 10.95 (*1-875559-02-7*, Pub. by SpiniFex Pr) LPC InBook.

Chan Meng Khoong. Reengineering in Action: The Quest for World-Class Excellence. LC 98-42982. 1999. 75.00 (*1-86094-139-7*, Pub. by Imperial College) World Scientific Pub.

Chan, Michelle. Anatomy of a Deal: A Handbook on International Project Finance. (Illus.). 91p. (Orig.). 1996. pap. 10.00 (*0-913890-85-5*) Friends of Earth.

***Chan, Mimi.** All the King's Women. 200p. 2000. 16.50 (*962-209-515-1*, Pub. by HK Univ Pr) Intl Spec Bk.

Chan, Mimi & Harris, Roy, eds. Asian Voices in English. 224p. 1991. 47.50 (*962-209-282-9*, Pub. by HK Univ Pr) Coronet Bks.

Chan, Ming K., ed. The Challenge of Hong Kong's Reintegration with China. 241p. (Orig.). 1997. pap. 42.50 (*962-209-441-4*, Pub. by HK Univ Pr) Coronet Bks.

— Precarious Balance: Hong Kong Between China & Britain, 1842-1992. 248p. 1994. pap. 52.50 (*962-209-333-7*, Pub. by HK Univ Pr) Intl Spec Bk.

— Precarious Balance: Hong Kong Between China & Britain, 1842-1992. LC 93-32290. (Hong Kong Becoming China: the Transition to 1997 Ser.). 235p. (gr. 13). 1994. 81.95 (*1-56324-380-6*, East Gate Bk); pap. 36.95 (*1-56324-381-4*, East Gate Bk) M E Sharpe.

Chan, Ming K. & Clark, David J., eds. The Hong Kong Basic Law: Blueprint for Stability & Prosperity under Chinese Sovereignty? LC 91-10299. (Hong Kong Becoming China: The Transition to 1997). 328p. (C). (gr. 13). 1991. text 79.95 (*0-87332-835-3*, East Gate Bk) M E Sharpe.

Chan, Ming K. & Dirlik, Arif. Schools into Fields & Factories: Anarchists, the Guomindang, & the National Labor University in Shanghai, 1927-1932. LC 91-7379. 351p. 1991. text 54.95 (*0-8223-1154-2*) Duke.

Chan, Ming K. & Postiglione, Gerard A., eds. The Hong Kong Reader: Passage to Chinese Sovereignty. LC 96-10816. 236p. (C). (gr. 13). 1996. pap. text 21.95 (*1-56324-870-0*, East Gate Bk) M E Sharpe.

Chan-Muehlbauer, Charlene & Gunnink, Douglas. An Agriculture That Makes Sense: Profitability of Four Sustainable Farms in Minnesota. (Illus.). 43p. (Orig.). (C). 1995. pap. text 25.00 (*0-7881-2348-3*) DIANE Pub.

Chan Nhu & Thich Nu. Chu Kinh Thuong Tung. LC 94-72617. (VIE.). 420p. 1995. text. write for info. (*0-9645062-0-3*) CCN Buddhist.

Chan-Olmsted, Sylvia, jt. ed. see Albarran, Alan.

Chan Onn, Fong. New Economic Dynamo. 270p. (C). 1987. pap. text 24.95 (*0-86861-802-0*) Routledge.

Chan, P. Choi-Ping, jt. ed. see Weilemans, W.

Chan, Pak K. & Mourad, Samiha. Digital System Design with Field Programmable Gate Arrays. LC 93-37839. 256p. 1994. text 62.00 (*0-13-319021-8*) Prntice Hall Bks.

Chan-Palay, Victoria E., ed. Second International Conference on Frontal Lobe Degeneration of Non-Alzheimer Type, Lund, Sweden, September 1992. (Journal: Dementia: Vol. 4, No. 3-4, 1993). (Illus.). 116p. 1993. pap. 45.25 (*3-8055-5824-4*) S Karger.

Chan, Patrick. Developing Professional Java Applets. 560p. 1996. pap. text 49.99 incl. cd-rom (*1-57521-083-5*) Sams.

***Chan, Patrick.** Enterprise Web Production. (C). 2000. text. write for info. (*0-201-65782-1*) Addison-Wesley.

Chan, Patrick. Java Almanac. 976p. (C). 1998. pap. text 18.95 (*0-201-37967-8*) Addison-Wesley.

— The Java Class Libraries Vol. 2: H-Z, Vol. 2. 2nd ed. LC 97-33423. 1712p. (C). 1997. 54.95 (*0-201-31003-1*) Addison-Wesley.

***Chan, Patrick.** The Java Developers Almanac: Enterprise Edition. 1104p. 2000. pap. 19.95 (*0-201-70042-5*) Addison-Wesley.

— Java Developers Almanac: 1999 Edition. 2nd ed. LC 98-43581. (Java Ser.). 880p. (C). 1998. pap. text 19.95 (*0-201-43298-6*) Addison-Wesley.

— Java Developers Almanac 2000. 3rd ed. 1204p. 2000. pap. 19.95 (*0-201-43299-4*) Addison-Wesley.

— Programming Pearls. 2nd ed. LC 99-46520. 256p. (C). 1999. pap. text 24.95 (*0-201-65788-0*) Addison-Wesley.

— Real-time UML: Developing Efficient Objects for Embedded Systems. 2nd ed. LC 99-44872. 368p. (C). 1999. pap. 39.95 (*0-201-65784-8*) Addison-Wesley.

— UML Distilled: Applying the Standard Object Modeling Language. 2nd ed. LC 99-33476. 224p. (C). 1999. pap. 29.95 (*0-201-65783-X*) Addison-Wesley.

***Chan, Patrick & Egremont, Carlton.** Mr. Bunny's Internet Startup Game. 12p. 1999. pap. 12.95 (*0-201-65781-3*) Pearson Custom.

Chan, Patrick & Lee, Rosanna. The Java Class Libraries: An Annotated Reference. (Java Ser.). 1996. 48.37 (*0-614-20264-7*) Addison-Wesley.

***Chan, Patrick & Lee, Rosanna.** The Java Class Libraries Poster. 5th ed. 2000. pap. 9.95 (*0-201-43297-8*) Prntice Hall Bks.

Chan, Patrick, et al. Java Class Libraries: 1.2 Supplement. 2nd ed. LC 97-33423. (Java Class Libraries). 1200p. 1999. pap. text 34.95 (*0-201-48552-4*) Addison-Wesley.

— The Java Class Libraries Vol. 1: A-G, Vol. 1. 2nd ed. LC 97-33423. 2080p. (C). 1998. 55.95 (*0-201-31002-3*) Addison-Wesley.

***Chan, Paul D.** Current Clinical Strategies CD-ROM Collection: 2002 Edition: Current Clinical Strategies, 17 vols. rev. ed. (Current Clinical Strategies Ser.). 1700p. 2000. pap. 49.95 incl. cd-rom (*1-881528-91-X*) Current Clin Strat.

— Family Medicine: 2000 Edition. rev. ed. (Current Clinical Strategies Ser.). 1999. pap. 46.95 incl. cd-rom (*1-881528-80-4*) Current Clin Strat.

Chan, Paul D. Family Medicine, Year 2000 Edition: Curent Clinical Strategies. rev. ed. (Current Clinical Strategies Ser.). 300p. 1999. pap. 26.95 (*1-881528-79-0*) Current Clin Strat.

***Chan, Paul D.** History & Physical Examination: 2001-2002 Edition. rev. ed. (Current Clinical Strategies Ser.). 89p. 1999. pap. 28.95 incl. cd-rom (*1-881528-82-0*) Current Clin Strat.

Chan, Paul D. History & Physical Examination, 2001 Edition: Current Clinical Strategies. rev. ed. (Current Clinical Strategies Ser.). 100p. 1999. pap. 9.95 (*1-881528-81-2*) Current Clin Strat.

— Medicine, 2001 Edition: Current Clinical Strategies. rev. ed. (Current Clinical Strategies Ser.). 100p. 1999. pap. 12.95 (*1-881528-83-9*) Current Clin Strat.

— Outpatient & Primary Care Medicine, 2001 Edition: Current Clinical Strategies. rev. ed. 195p. 1999. pap. 12.95 (*1-881528-89-8*) Current Clin Strat.

— Pediatrics, Year 2000 Edition: Current Clinical Strategies. rev. ed. (Current Clinical Strategies Ser.). 100p. 1999. pap. 12.95 (*1-881528-85-5*) Current Clin Strat.

***Chan, Paul D.** Practice Parameters in Medicine & Primary Care: 1999-2000 Edition. rev. ed. (Current Clinical Strategies Ser.). 235p. 1999. pap. 36.95 incl. cd-rom (*1-881528-64-2*) Current Clin Strat.

Chan, Paul D. Practice Parameters in Medicine & Primary Care, 1999-2000 Edition: Current Clinical Strategies. rev. ed. (Current Clinical Strategies Ser.). 88p. 1998. pap. 18.95 (*1-881528-35-9*) Current Clin Strat.

Chan, Paul D., ed. Gynecology & Obstetrics, 1999-2000 Edition: Current Clinical Strategies. rev. ed. (Current Clinical Strategies Ser.). 98p. 1998. pap. 12.95 (*1-881528-69-3*) Current Clin Strat.

***Chan, Paul D. & Gennrich, Jane.** Pediatrics: 2000 Edition. rev. ed. (Current Clinical Strategies Ser.). 104p. 2000. pap. 28.95 incl. cd-rom (*1-881528-86-3*) Current Clin Strat.

***Chan, Paul D. & Safani, Michael.** Outpatient Medicine: 2001 Edition. rev. ed. (Current Clinical Strategies Ser.). 110p. 2000. pap. 28.95 incl. cd-rom (*1-881528-90-1*) Current Clin Strat.

Chan, Paul D. & Safani, Michael. Outpatient Medicine, 1997: Current Clinical Strategies. 110p. 1997. pap. 12.75 (*1-881528-29-4*) Current Clin Strat.

***Chan, Paul D. & Winkle, Christopher R.** Gynecology & Obstetrics: 1999-2000 Edition. rev. ed. (Current Clinical Strategies Ser.). 149p. 1999. pap. 30.95 incl. cd-rom (*1-881528-70-7*) Current Clin Strat.

***Chan, Paul D., et al.** Medicine: 2001 Edition. rev. ed. (Current Clinical Strategies Ser.). 100p. 1999. pap. 28.95 incl. cd-rom (*1-881528-84-7*) Current Clin Strat.

Chan, Paul D., et al. Pediatrics, 1997 Edition: Current Clinical Strategies. (Current Clinical Strategies Medical Bks Ser.). 104p. 1997. pap. 12.75 (*1-881528-24-3*) Current Clin Strat.

Chan, Paul D., jt. auth. see Safani, Michael.

Chan, Pedro. Acupuncture, Electropuncture Anaesthesia. 1972. pap. 4.95 (*0-87505-149-9*) Borden.

— Acupuncture Is & Is Not. (Illus.). 1974. pap. 0.95 (*0-914322-01-X*) Chans Corp.

— Chinese Diet Cookbook. 91p. 10.00 (*0-317-31560-9*) Chans Corp.

— Ear Acupressure. LC 76-40734. (Illus.). 1977. pap. text 6.95 (*0-685-81897-7*) Chans Corp.

— Electro-Acupuncture: Its Clinical Applications in Therapy. (Illus.). 1974. 15.00 (*0-914322-06-0*); pap. 8.50 (*0-914322-05-2*) Chans Corp.

— Finger Acupressure. 1985. mass mkt. 5.99 (*0-345-32953-8*) Ballantine Pub Grp.

— Finger Acupressure. 92p. 3.95 (*0-317-31555-2*) Chans Corp.

— How to Free Yourself from Pain. 128p. 4.95 (*0-317-31553-6*) Chans Corp.

Chan, Peter. Better Vegetable Gardens the Chinese Way: Peter Chan's Raised Bed System. Griffith, Roger, ed. LC 84-73330. (Illus.). 104p. 1985. pap. 9.95 (*0-88266-388-7*) Storey Bks.

— Bonsai: Blow up Edition. 1989. 19.98 (*1-55521-383-9*) Bk Sales Inc.

— Bonsai: The Art of Growing & Keeping Miniature Trees. 176p. 1987. 12.98 (*0-89009-946-4*) Bk Sales Inc.

— Peter Chan's Magical Landscape: Transforming Any Small Space into a Place of Beauty. Steege, Gwen, ed. LC 86-45975. (Illus.). 128p. 1988. pap. 10.95 (*0-88266-455-7*, Garden Way Pub) Storey Bks.

— Peter Chan's Magical Landscape: Transforming Any Small Space into a Place of Beauty. Steege, Gwen, ed. LC 86-45975. (Illus.). 128p. 1988. 21.95 (*0-88266-454-9*, Garden Way Pub) Storey Bks.

— Population & Health Policy in the Peoples Republic of China. 150p. 1978. pap. 12.00 (*0-686-76148-0*) Neo Pr.

Chan, Philip, jt. ed. see Kargupta, Hillol.

Chan Poi. Fatal Flute & Stick Forms. LC 84-52680. (Illus.). 160p. (Orig.). 1985. pap. 12.95 (*0-86568-059-0*, 215) Unique Pubns.

Chan, Raymond. Welfare in Newly-Industrialized Society: The Construction of the Welfare State in Hong Kong. 336p. 1996. text 77.95 (*1-85972-464-7*, Pub. by Avebry) Ashgate Pub Co.

***Chan, Raymond K. & Abdullah, Moha A.** Foreign Labor in Asia. LC 99-41872. 208p. 1999. 59.00 (*1-56072-714-4*) Nova Sci Pubs.

Chan, Richard. Used Cars: How to Buy One. 3rd rev. ed. 250p. 1997. pap. 9.95 (*0-9612322-6-9*) Bk Express.

Chan, Roger C. K., et al, eds. China's Regional Economic Development. 460p. 1996. pap. 36.00 (*962-441-530-7*, Pub. by Chinese Univ of Hong Kong) St Mut.

Chan, Roman P. Chichen Itza: Ciudad de los Brujos del Agua (The City of the Water Wizards) (SPA., Illus.). 158p. 1980. pap. 8.99 (*968-16-0289-7*, Pub. by Fondo) Continental Bk.

— El Lenguaje de las Piedras. (SPA.). pap. 11.99 (*968-16-3990-1*, Pub. by Fondo) Continental Bk.

— Quetzalcoatl: Serpiente Emplumada (Plumed Serpent) (SPA., Illus.). 75p. 1992. reprint ed. pap. 8.99 (*968-16-0820-8*, Pub. by Fondo) Continental Bk.

Chan, S., et al. EDI Control: Management & Audit Issues. 1995. 33.00 (*0-87051-166-1*) Am Inst CPA.

Chan, S., jt. auth. see Austin, R. H.

Chan, S. H., ed. Transport Phenomena in Combustion: Proceedings of the Eighth International Symposium on Transport Phenomena in Combustion (ISTP-VIII) Held in San Francisco, California, July 16-20, 1995, 2 vols., Set. LC 96-14300. 1700p. 1996. text 299.00 (*1-56032-456-2*, Pub. by Tay Francis Ltd) Taylor & Francis.

Chan, S. H., jt. ed. see Smith, A. M.

Chan, S. L. & Teng, J. G. ICASS 96 International Conference on Advances in Steel Structures: ICASS '96, 2 vols. LC 96-35284. 1296p. 1996. 231.00 (*0-08-042830-4*, Pergamon Pr) Elsevier.

Chan, Sandra J., jt. auth. see Temple, Diana Hastings.

Chan, Shau W. Concise English-Chinese Dictionary. rev. ed. xviii, 390p. 1955. reprint ed. pap. 12.95 (*0-8047-0384-1*) Stanford U Pr.

— A Concise English-Chinese Dictionary with Romanized Standard Pronunciation. 2nd ed. LC PL1455.C42. 436p. 1955. reprint ed. pap. 30.00 (*0-608-00249-6*, 206076400006) Bks Demand.

— Elementary Chinese. 2nd ed. xxx, 508p. 1959. 39.50 (*0-8047-0413-9*) Stanford U Pr.

Chan, Shirley S. & Debrunner, Peter G., eds. Frontiers in Science: International Symposium on the Occasion of the 65th Birthday of Professor Hans Frauenfelder - Proceedings of the International Symposium on Frontiers in Science, University of Illinois at Urbana-Champaign, May 1987. (AIP Conference Proceedings Ser.: No. 180). (Illus.). 370p. 1989. 65.00 (*0-88318-380-3*) Am Inst Physics.

Chan, Silas. A Biographical Sketch of G. Campbell Morgan. (CHI.). 1984. pap. write for info. (*0-941598-21-7*) Living Spring Pubns.

Chan, Silas, tr. see Allen, R.

Chan, Silas, tr. see Forster, Roger & Marston, Paul.

Chan, Silas, tr. see Morgan, G. Campbell.

Chan, Silas, tr. see Ramm, Bernard L.

Chan, Silas, tr. see Stott, John R.

Chan, Simon. Spiritual Theology: A Systematic Study of the Christian Life. LC 98-11316. 304p. 1998. pap. 19.99 (*0-8308-1542-2*, 1542) InterVarsity.

***Chan, Siu L. & Chui, Pui T.** Non-Linear Static & Cyclic Analysis of Steel Frames with Semi-Rigid Connections. LC 99-46371. 350p. 2000. 152.50 (*0-08-042998-X*) Elsevier.

Chan, Stephen. Crimson Rain. Schultz, Patricia, ed. LC 91-34988. (Poetry Ser.: Vol. 18). 72p. 1991. pap. 12.95 (*0-7734-9658-0*) E Mellen.

— Kaunda & Southern Africa. 224p. 1992. text 69.50 (*1-85043-490-5*, Pub. by I B T) St Martin.

— Social Development in Africa Today: Some Radical Proposals. Alner, Jonathan, ed. LC 91-37447. 136p. 1992. lib. bdg. 69.95 (*0-7734-9637-8*) E Mellen.

— Twelve Years of Commonwealth Diplomatic History: Commonwealth Summit Meetings, 1979-1991. LC 91-6856. 168p. 1992. lib. bdg. 79.95 (*0-7734-9498-7*) E Mellen.

Chan, Stephen & Vencancio, Moisbes. War & Peace in Mozambique. LC 98-20956. xvii, 207 p. 1998. write for info. (*0-333-68135-5*) St Martin.

Chan, Stephen & Weiner, Jarrod. Twentieth Century International History: A Reader. 352p. 1998. pap. 19.95 (*1-86064-302-7*, Pub. by I B T); text 59.50 (*1-86064-301-9*) I B T.

Chan, Stephen & Wiener, Jarrod, eds. Theorising in International Relations: Contemporary Theorists & Their Critics. LC 97-25258. 176p. 1997. text 79.95 (*0-7734-8640-2*) E Mellen.

Chan, Stephen & Williams, Andrew J., eds. Renegade States: The Evolution of Revolutionary Foreign Policy. LC 94-12636. 1994. text 27.95 (*0-7190-3170-2*, Pub. by Manchester Univ Pr) St Martin.

Chan, Steve. East Asian Dynamism: Growth, Order & Security in the Pacific Region. 2nd ed. (Dilemmas in World Politics Ser.). 184p. (C). 1993. pap. text 22.00 (*0-8133-1713-4*, Pub. by Westview) HarpC.

— Foreign Direct Investment in Changing Global Political Economy. LC 94-22532. (International Political Economy Ser.). 270p. 1995. text 59.95 (*0-312-12378-7*) St Martin.

***Chan, Steve.** Sanctions as Economic Statecraft: Theory & Practice. 2000. text 75.00 (*0-312-23197-0*) St Martin.

Chan, Steve & Mintz, Alex, eds. Defense, Welfare & Growth: Perspectives & Evidence. 320p. 1992. 49.95 (*0-04-032402-8*, A8188) Routledge.

Chan, Steve, jt. ed. see Clark, Cal.

Chan, Steve, jt. ed. see Sylvan, Donald A.

Chan, Sucheng. The Asian Americans: An Interpretive History. (Twayne's Immigrant Heritage of America Ser.). 240p. (C). 1991. 33.00 (*0-8057-8426-8*, Twyne); pap. 20.00 (*0-8057-8437-3*, Twyne) Mac Lib Ref.

— Asian Californians. Hundley, Norris, Jr. & Schutz, John A., eds. (Golden State Ser.). 246p. 1991. 12.00 (*0-929651-00-6*) MTL.

— Entry Denied: Exclusion & the Chinese Community in America, 1882-1943. (Asian American History & Culture Ser.). 320p. 1991. 49.95 (*0-87722-798-5*) Temple U Pr.

Chan, Sucheng, ed. Hmong Means Free: Life in Laos & America. LC 93-11650. (Asian American History & Culture Ser.). (Illus.). 288p. 1994. 69.95 (*1-56639-162-8*); pap. 19.95 (*1-55639-163-3*) Temple U Pr.

— Income & Status Differences Between White & Minority Americans: A Persistent Inequality. LC 89-12659. (Studies in Sociology: Vol. 3). 376p. 1990. lib. bdg. 99.95 (*0-88946-635-1*) E Mellen.

— Social & Gender Boundaries in the United States: Studies of Asian, Black, Mexican, & Native Americans. (Studies in Sociology: Vol. 1). 357p. 1989. write for info. (*0-88946-631-9*) E Mellen.

Chan, Sucheng, et al, eds. People of Color in the American West. LC 93-78444. 584p. (C). 1994. pap. text 25.56 (*0-669-27913-7*) HM Trade Div.

Chan, Sucheng & Olin, Spencer C. Major Problems in California History. 512p. (C). 1996. pap. text 29.16 (*0-669-27588-3*) HM Trade Div.

Chan, Sucheng, jt. ed. see Wong, K. Scott.

Chan, Susan D., ed. see Baker, William K., Jr. & Guerrero, Diana L.

Chan, Susan D., jt. ed. see Clark, Bruce.

Chan, Susan D., jt. ed. see Houts, Lee.

Chan, Susan D., jt. ed. see Rogers, Rachel Watkins.

Chan, Susan D., jt. ed. see Spencer, Susan Bunn.

Chan, Sylvia, jt. auth. see Lam, Pun-Lee.

Chan, T., jt. auth. see Shi, Zhong-Ci.

Chan, T. F., et al, eds. Proceedings of the Third International Symposium on Domain Decomposition Methods for Partial Differential Equations. LC 90-34097. (Proceedings in Applied Mathematics Ser.: No. 43). xx, 491p. 1990. pap. 62.00 (*0-89871-253-X*) Soc Indus-Appl Math.

Chan, T. S. Distribution Channel Strategy for Export Marketing: The Case of Hong Kong Firms. Farmer, Richard N., ed. LC 83-18158. (Research for Business Decisions Ser.: No. 67). 140p. reprint ed. 43.40 (*0-8357-1494-2*, 207036800088) Bks Demand.

Chan, Tak-Hang, jt. auth. see Li, Chao-Jun.

Chan, Terrence. UNIX System Programming Using C++ LC 96-30559. 624p. (C). 1996. pap. text 49.99 (*0-13-331562-2*) P-H.

Chan, Thomas V., jt. auth. see Burns Knight, Margy.

Chan-Toon. Nature & Value of Jurisprudence. 2nd enl. ed. xxiv, 187p. 1982. reprint ed. 35.00 (*0-8377-0436-7*, Rothman) W S Hein.

Chan, Tsang-Sing, ed. Consumer Behavior in Asia: Issues & Marketing Practice. LC 99-29172. (Journal of International Consumer Marketing Ser.: Vol. 11, No. 1). 122p. (C). 1999. 49.95 (*0-7890-0691-X*, Intl Busn Pr) Haworth Pr.

Chan, Ts'ao. The Dream of the Red Chamber. LC 58-13296. 352p. 1958. pap. 13.95 (*0-385-09379-9*, Anchor NY) Doubleday.

— Dream of the Red Chamber. 1998. lib. bdg. 22.95 (*1-56723-060-1*) Yestermorrow.

— The Dream of the Red Chamber. McHugh, Florence & McHugh, Isabel, trs. from GER. LC 75-8833. (Illus.). 604p. 1975. reprint ed. lib. bdg. 37.50 (*0-8371-8113-5*, TSDR, Greenwood Pr) Greenwood.

— La Reve dans la Pavillon Rouge, Vol. 1. (Pleiade Ser.). (FRE.). 1981. 110.00 (*0-8288-3450-4*, F78880) Fr & Eur.

— La Reve dans la Pavillon Rouge, Vol. 2. (Pleiade Ser.). (FRE.). 1981. 110.00 (*0-7859-0641-X*, F79562) Fr & Eur.

— Story of the Stone Vol. 1: The Golden Days. Hawkes, David, tr. LC 74-165360. (Classics Ser.). 544p. 1973. pap. 19.99 (*0-14-044293-6*, Penguin Classics) Viking Penguin.

— Story of the Stone Vol. 2: The Crab-Flower Club. Hawkes, David, tr. (Classics Ser.). 606p. 1977. pap. 13.95 (*0-14-044326-6*, Penguin Classics) Viking Penguin.

— Story of the Stone Vol. 3: The Warning Voice. Hawkes, David, tr. 640p. 1981. pap. 12.95 (*0-14-044370-3*, Penguin Classics) Viking Penguin.

— Story of the Stone Vol. 4: The Debt of Tears. Gao, E., ed. Minford, John, tr. 400p. 1982. pap. 13.95 (*0-14-044371-1*) Viking Penguin.

— Story of the Stone Vol. 5: The Dreamer Awakes. Gao, E., ed. Minford, John, tr. from CHI. 384p. 1986. pap. 13.95 (*0-14-044372-X*, Penguin Classics) Viking Penguin.

— The Story of the Stone (The Dream of the Red Chamber) Vol. 3: The Warning Voice. Hawkes, David, tr. LC 78-20279. (Chinese Literature in Translation Ser.). 640p. 1981. 35.00 (*0-253-19263-3*) Ind U Pr.

— The Story of the Stone (The Dream of the Red Chamber) Vol. 5: The Dreamer Wakes. Gao E, ed. Minford, John, tr. LC 78-20279. (Chinese Literature in Translation Ser.). 384p. 1987. 35.00 (*0-253-19265-X*) Ind U Pr.

Chan, Ts'ao & E, Gao. A Dream of Red Mansions. abr. ed. Xinqu, Huang, tr. from CHI. LC 94-70302. 340p. 1995. pap. 14.95 (*0-8351-2529-7*) China Bks.

Chan, Ts'ao & Kao, Ngo. A Dream of Red Mansions: An Abridged Version. abr. ed. Yang, Hsien-yi & Yang, Gladys, trs. from CHI. 503p. (C). 1996. pap. 18.95 (*0-88727-178-2*) Cheng & Tsui.

***Chan, Tse T.** Understanding Microwave Heating Cavities. LC 00-29992. (Illus.). 356p. 2000. 95.00 (*1-58053-094-X*) Artech Hse.

Chan, Vincent S., jt. auth. see Prater, Ronald.

Chan, W. Source Book in Chinese Philosophy. 874p. 1963. pap. text 22.95 (*0-691-01964-9*, Pub. by Princeton U Pr) Cal Prin Full Svc.

Chan, W., et al, eds. Miscellaneous Foods: Supplement to McCance & Widdowson's "The Composition of Foods" 5th ed. 193p. 1994. pap. 63.00 (*0-85186-360-4*, R6360) CRC Pr.

Chan, W., ed. see Takakusu, J.

***Chan, W. C. & White, Peter D., eds.** FMOC Solid Phase Peptide Synthesis: A Practical Approach. LC 99-41250. (The Practical Approach Ser.: Vol. 222). (Illus.). 368p. 2000. pap. text 55.00 (*0-19-963724-5*) OUP.

***Chan, Wah Chun.** Performance Analysis of Telecommunications & Local Area Network. LC 99-47410. (International Series in Engineering & Computer Science). 1999. write for info. (*0-7923-7701-X*) Kluwer Academic.

Chan, Wai-Chan, ed. Management Consulting, 1994: A Harvard Business School Career Guide. 1993. pap. text 20.00 (*0-07-103433-1*) McGraw.

Chan, Wayiee, jt. ed. see Rennert, Owen M.

Chan, Wellington K. The Making of Hong Kong Society: The Studies of Class Formation in Early Hong Kong. (Illus.). 272p. 1991. 65.00 (*0-19-827320-7*) OUP.

— Merchants, Mandarins, & Modern Enterprise in Late Ch'ing China. LC 76-30743. (East Asian Monographs: No. 79). 300p. 1977. 24.00 (*0-674-56915-6*) HUP.

Chan, Wen S., et al, eds. ASME Aerospace & Materials Division: Proceedings, International Mechanical Engineering Congress & Exposition, 1996, Atlanta, Georgia. LC 96-78673. (AD Ser.: Vol. 51). 513p. 1996. pap. text 96.00 (*0-7918-1531-5*) ASME Pr.

***Chan, Weng C. & White, Peter D., eds.** FMOC Solid Phase Peptide Synthesis: A Practical Approach. LC 99-41250. (The Practical Approach Ser.: No. 222). (Illus.). 376p. 2000. text 110.00 (*0-19-963725-3*) OUP.

Chan, Wilbert, jt. auth. see Gmelch, Walter H.

Chan, Wing-tsit. Chinese Philosophy, 1949-1963: An Annotated Bibliography of Mainland China Publications. LC 65-20582. 304p. reprint ed. pap. 94.30 (*0-608-15409-1*, 202958100061) Bks Demand.

— Chu Hsi: New Studies. LC 89-4799. 592p. 1989. text 42.00 (*0-8248-1201-8*) UH Pr.

Chan, Wing-Tsit. Historical Charts of Chinese Philosophy. 6.95 (*0-88710-028-7*) Yale Far Eastern Pubns.

— An Outline & Annotated Bibliography of Chinese Philosophy. 1961. 14.95 (*0-88710-055-4*) Yale Far Eastern Pubns.

— The Way of Lao Tzu. 296p. (C). 1963. pap. text 14.40 (*0-02-320700-0*, Macmillan Coll) P-H.

Chan, Wing-tsit, ed. Chu Hsi & Neo-Confucianism. LC 85-24532. (Illus.). 656p. 1986. text 38.00 (*0-8248-0961-0*) UH Pr.

Chan, Wing-Tsit, tr. from CHI. Neo-Confucian Terms Explained: The Pei-hsi Tzu-i. LC 86-5427. (Neo-Confucian Studies). 288p. 1986. text 57.50 (*0-231-06384-9*) Col U Pr.

— Reflections on Things at Hand: The Neo-Confucian Anthology. LC 65-22548. (Records of Civilization: Sources & Studies). 441p. 1967. text 81.00 (*0-231-02819-9*) Col U Pr.

Chan Wing Tsit, ed. see Takakusu, Junjiro.

Chan, Wing-Tsit, tr. see Wang, Pi.

Chan, Winnie S., jt. auth. see Liheng, Carol.

Chan, Y. C. Dr. Chan's Cancer Healing Vol. 10: Cancer Prevention & Self-Healing. Yu, R. S., ed. & photos by by. LC 97-75491. (Illus.). 1997. 39.00 (*0-9658744-2-7*) ACOM.

Chan, Y. C. & Doraisingham, S. Current Topics in Medical Virology: Proceedings of the First Asia-Pacific Congress. 456p. 1989. text 130.00 (*9971-5-0806-0*) World Scientific Pub.

Chan, Y. S., et al, eds. Cardiovascular Sciences: Recent Advances. (Journal Ser.: Vol. 4, No. 3, 1995). (Illus.). 90p. 1995. pap. 31.50 (*3-8055-6264-0*) S Karger.

Chan, Y. T. Wavelet Basics. 144p. (C). 1994. text 89.50 (*0-7923-9536-0*) Kluwer Academic.

Chan, Y. T., ed. Underwater Acoustic Data Processing. (C). 1989. text 320.50 (*0-7923-0127-7*) Kluwer Academic.

Chan, Yupo, ed. Facility Location & Land Use: The Urban-Rural Dilemma. LC 86-25926. 48p. 1986. pap. 13.00 (*0-87262-574-5*) Am Soc Civil Eng.

Chana Faiga Brander. A Blick of Tzurik. (Illus.). 126p. (Orig.). (J). (gr. 4). 1990. pap. text 9.50 (*0-9629684-0-4*) K K Aharon.

Chana, Leonard F. The Way to Make Perfect Mountains: Native American Legends of Sacred Mountains. LC 96-40531. Orig. Title: A God on Every Mountain Top. 64p. 1997. pap. 9.95 (*0-938317-26-1*) Cinco Puntos.

Chana Radcliffe, Sara. The Delicate Balance: Love & Authority in Torah Parenting. 292p. 1989. 19.95 (*0-944070-22-1*) Targum Pr.

Chana, Richard A. The Consumer Handbook to an Educated Home Purchase: A Complete Self-Analysis Guide for Locating the Home, Community, & Mortgage Plan Best-Suited for You. (Illus.). 414p. (Orig.). 1994. pap. 39.95 (*0-9640247-3-X*); pap. text 39.95 (*0-9640247-4-8*) Consumer Housing.

Chanady, Amaryll, ed. Latin American Identity & Constructions of Difference. LC 93-25437. (Hispanic Issues Ser.: Vol. 10). 304p. 1994. pap. 19.95 (*0-8166-2409-7*); text 44.95 (*0-8166-2408-9*) U of Minn Pr.

Chanaiwa, David. Zimbabwe Controversy: A Case of Colonial Historiography. (Foreign & Comparative Studies Program, Eastern Africa Ser.: No. 8). 142p. 1973. pap. 3.00 (*0-915984-05-9*) Syracuse U Foreign Comp.

Chanan, Gabriel & European Foundation for the Improvement of Living & Working Conditions Staff. Active Citizenship & Community Involvement: Getting ro the Roots: A Discussion Paper LC 98-196000. vii, 43 p. 1997. write for info. (*92-828-2028-9*, Pub. by Comm Europ Commun) Bernan Associates.

Chanan, Gabriel, ed. see Taylor, Marilyn & Presley, Frances.

Chanan, Michael. The Dream That Kicks: The Prehistory & Early Years of Cinema in Britain. 2nd ed. LC 95-14953. 312p. (C). 1995. pap. 25.99 (*0-415-11750-X*) Routledge.

— From Handel to Hendrix: The Composer in the Public Sphere. 1999. 30.00 (*1-85984-706-4*, Pub. by Verso) Norton.

— Repeated Takes: A Short History of Recording & Its Effects on Music. LC 95-188226. 224p. (C). 1995. pap. 20.00 (*1-85984-012-4*, C0532, Pub. by Verso) Norton.

— Repeated Takes: A Short History of Recording & Its Effects on Music. LC 95-188226. 224p. (C). 1995. 65.00 (*1-85984-917-2*, C0531, Pub. by Verso) Norton.

Chanan, Michael, ed. see Desnoes, Edmundo.

Chanana, Dev R., tr. see Filliozat, J.

Chanana, Karuna, jt. ed. see Krishnaraj, Maithreyi.

Chanarin, Israel, ed. Laboratory Haematology. (Illus.). 464p. 1989. text 59.95 (*0-443-03343-9*) Church.

Chanaud, R. Sound Conditioning Manual. 1992. text. write for info. (*0-442-00631-4*, VNR) Wiley.

Chance. Applied Behavior Analysis. LC 97-25987. (Psychology Ser.). 485p. 1997. pap. 60.95 (*0-534-33936-0*) Brooks-Cole.

— An Introduction to Derivatives. 3rd ed. LC 94-69150. (C). 1994. 78.50 (*0-03-003588-0*, Pub. by Harcourt Coll Pubs) Harcourt.

— Introduction to Derivatives. 3rd ed. (C). 1997. pap. text 81.00 (*0-15-517753-2*) Harcourt Coll Pubs.

— An Introduction to Derivatives. 4th ed. LC 97-67526. (C). 1997. text 87.00 (*0-03-024483-8*, Pub. by Harcourt Coll Pubs) Harcourt.

— The Inupiat & Arctic Alaska. (C). 1990. pap. text 23.50 (*0-03-032419-X*) Harcourt Coll Pubs.

— Rereading the Bible: An Introduction to the Biblical Story. LC 99-21603. 438p. 1999. pap. text 37.80 (*0-13-674276-9*) P-H.

Chance, B. Photon Migration in Tissues. LC 90-7293. (Illus.). 206p. 1990. 79.50 (*0-306-43522-5*, Kluwer Plenum) Kluwer Academic.

Chance, B., et al, eds. Synchrotron Radiation in the Biosciences. LC 93-33962. (Illus.). 816p. (C). 1994. text 155.00 (*0-19-853986-X*) OUP.

Chance, B., Jr., jt. auth. see McDonald, Eugene T.

Chance, Beth L., jt. auth. see Rossman, Allan J.

***Chance, Brenda K. & Smith, Cynthia E.** The Cost of Being Jesus' Disciple: The End-Times Childrens Curriculum, Vol. 1. (Illus.). 55p. (J). (gr. k-6). 2000. ring bd. 40.00 (*0-9700603-0-0*, Pub. by End Times Child Curr) Radiant Life Lighthse.

***Chance, Britton, et al, eds.** Optical Tomography & Spectroscopy of Tissue III. 720p. 1999. pap. text 153.00 (*0-8194-3067-6*) SPIE.

Chance, Britton & Alfano, Robert R., eds. Optical Tomography & Spectroscopy of Tissue Vol. 2979: Theory, Instrumentation Model, & Human Studies II. LC 98-122045. 878p. 1997. 149.00 (*0-8194-2390-4*) SPIE.

Chance, Britton, jt. ed. see Emerit, Ingrid.

Chance, Clifford. Cross Border Aircraft Leasing. 2nd ed. 312p. 1995. pap. 425.00 (*1-85044-839-6*) LLP.

— Doing Business in the United Kingdom, 3 vols., Set. 1985. ring bd. 730.00 (*0-8205-1134-X*) Bender.

— Employee Share Ownership Plans (ESOPs) in the U. K. 2nd ed. 220p. 1992. boxed set 147.00 (*0-406-00538-9*, UK, MICHIE) LEXIS Pub.

— Environmental Law Guide. 104p. 1991. pap. 200.00 (*1-85044-415-3*) LLP.

— Insurance in the EEC: A Lloyd's of London Press Industry Report. 2nd ed. 204p. 1991. pap. 165.00 (*1-85044-405-6*) LLP.

— Insurance in the EEC: The European Community's Programme for a New Regime. (Industry Report Ser.). 1990. 270.00 (*1-85044-288-6*) LLP.

— Insurance Regulation in Europe. (Lloyd's List Practical Guide Ser.). 322p. 1993. 80.00 (*1-85044-580-X*) LLP.

— Project Finance. 117p. 1995. reprint ed. pap. 138.00 (*1-873446-45-4*, Pub. by IFR Pub) Am Educ Systs.

Chance, Don M. Essays in Derivatives. (Illus.). 1999. pap. 42.00 (*1-883249-46-5*) F J Fabozzi.

— An Introduction to Derivatives. 3rd ed. 272p. (C). 1995. pap. text, teacher ed. 245.50 (*0-03-007523-8*) Harcourt Coll Pubs.

— Introduction to Derivatives. 4th ed. 1997. 87.50 (*0-03-022283-4*, Pub. by Harcourt Coll Pubs) Harcourt.

Chance, Don M., et al, eds. Advances in Futures & Options Research, Vol. 1, Pt. A: Options. 245p. 1986. 78.50 (*0-89232-665-4*) Jai Pr.

— Advances in Futures & Options Research, Vol. 1, Pts. A & B. 1986. 157.00 (*0-89232-667-0*) Jai Pr.

— Advances in Futures & Options Research, Vol. 2. 319p. 1987. 78.50 (*0-89232-829-0*) Jai Pr.

— Advances in Futures & Options Research, Vol. 3. 408p. 1989. 78.50 (*0-89232-926-2*) Jai Pr.

— Advances in Futures & Options Research, Vol. 4. 295p. 1991. 78.50 (*1-55938-060-8*) Jai Pr.

***Chance, Don M. & Association for Investment Management and Research.** Derivatives in Portfolio Management: Proceedings of the AIMR Seminar "Using Derivatives in Managing Portfolios", November 13-14, 1997, Chicago, Illinois. LC 99-208081. (Illus.). 1998. write for info. (*0-935015-22-1*) Inst Charter Finan Analysts.

Chance, Don M. & Trippi, Robert R., eds. Advances in Futures & Options Research, Vol. 5. 336p. 1992. 78.50 (*1-55938-281-3*) Jai Pr.

— Advances in Futures & Options Research, Vol. 6. 422p. 1993. 78.75 (*1-55938-492-1*) Jai Pr.

— Advances in Futures & Options Research, Vol. 7. 335p. 1994. 78.75 (*1-55938-748-3*) Jai Pr.

— Advances in Futures & Options Research, Vol. 8. 1996. 78.75 (*1-55938-852-8*) Jai Pr.

— Advances in Futures & Options Research Vol. 1, Pt. B: Futures. 170p. 1986. 78.50 (*0-89232-666-2*) Jai Pr.

Chance, Edward, ed. Creating the Quality School. 530p. 1995. pap. text 45.00 (*1-891859-16-1*) Atwood Pub LLC.

Chance, Edward W. Visionary Leadership in Schools: Successful Strategies for Developing & Implementing an Educational Vision. (Illus.). 136p. 1992. pap. 20.95 (*0-398-06049-5*); text 31.95 (*0-398-05784-2*) C C Thomas.

Chance, Edward W., ed. Creating the Quality School. LC 95-3244. 526p. 1995. 45.00 (*0-912150-36-X*) Atwood Pub LLC.

Chance, Hugh E., jt. auth. see Braun, Eunice.

***Chance, Ian.** Kaltja Now. 2000. pap. 24.95 (*1-86254-486-7*, Pub. by Wakefield Pr) BHB Intl.

Chance, J. Bradley. Jerusalem, the Temple, & the New Age in Luke-Acts. LC 88-6850. xii, 168p. (C). 1988. text 24.95 (*0-86554-301-1*, H265) Mercer Univ Pr.

Chance, Jane. Christine de Pizan's Letter of Othea to Hector. (Library of Medieval Women). 176p. 1997. 19.95 (*0-85991-440-2*, DS Brewer) Boydell & Brewer.

— The Lord of the Rings: The Mythology of Power. (Twayne's Masterwork Studies). 140p. 1992. 23.95 (*0-8057-9441-7*, Twyne) Mac Lib Ref.

— The Lord of the Rings: The Mythology of Power. (Twayne's Masterwork Studies: Vol. 99). 140p. 1992. pap. 18.00 (*0-8057-8571-X*, Twyne) Mac Lib Ref.

— Medieval Mythography: From Roman North Africa to the School of Chartres, A.D. 433-1177 A.D. (Illus.). 720p. (C). 1994. 85.00 (*0-8130-1256-2*) U Press Fla.

— The Mythographic Chaucer: The Fabulation of Sexual Politics. LC 94-10265. 1994. pap. 19.95 (*0-8166-2277-9*) U of Minn Pr.

— Woman As Hero in Old English Literature. LC 85-17288. (Illus.). 175p. reprint ed. pap. 54.30 (*0-608-06981-7*, 206718900009) Bks Demand.

Chance, Jane, ed. The Assembly of Gods: Le Assemble de Dyeus, or Banquet of Gods & Goddesses, with the Discourse of Reason & Sensuality. (Teams). viii, 155p. (C). pap. 14.00 (*1-58044-022-3*) Medieval Inst.

Chance, Jane, ed. Gender & Text in the Later Middle Ages. LC 95-47596. 352p. (C). 1996. 59.95 (*0-8130-1391-7*) U Press Fla.

— The Mythographic Art: Classical Fable & the Rise of the Vernacular in Early France & England. 350p. 1990. 49.95 (*0-8130-0974-X*); pap. 19.95 (*0-8130-0984-7*) U Press Fla.

Chance, Jane, jt. ed. see Miller, Miriam Y.

Chance, Jeremy. Principles of the Alexander Technique. (Illus.). 160p. 1999. 11.00 (*0-7225-3705-0*) Thorsons PA.

Chance, John K. Conquest of the Sierra: Spaniards & Indians in Colonial Oaxaca. LC 89-40213. (Illus.). 240p. 1989. 42.95 (*0-8061-2222-6*) U of Okla Pr.

— Indice del Archivo del Juzgado de Villa Alta, Oaxaca, Epoca Colonial. (Vanderbilt University Publications in Anthropology: No. 21). 125p. 1978. pap. 5.25 (*0-935462-10-4*) VUPA.

***Chance, John N.** The Dead Tale-Tellers. large type ed. 224p. 1999. pap. 18.99 (*0-7089-5479-0*, Linford) Ulverscroft.

— The Guilty Witnesses. large type ed. 240p. pap. 18.99 (*0-7089-5455-3*) Ulverscroft.

Chance, John N. Involvement in Austria. large type ed. LC 97-94861. (Nightingale Ser.). 192p. 1998. pap. 18.95 (*0-7838-8406-0*, G K Hall & Co) Mac Lib Ref.

Chance, John N. The Man with Two Heads. large type ed. 240p. pap. 18.99 (*0-7089-5420-0*) Ulverscroft.

— The Murder Makers. large type ed. 240p. 1999. pap. 18.99 (*0-7089-5502-9*, Linford) Ulverscroft.

Chance, John N. The Offshore Conspiracy. large type ed. 224p. 1996. pap. 18.99 (*1-85389-589-X*, Dales) Ulverscroft.

— The Shadow in Pursuit. large type ed. LC 94-12703. 182p. 1994. lib. bdg. 16.95 (*0-8161-7422-9*, G K Hall Lrg Type) Mac Lib Ref.

***Chance, John Newton.** The Bad Circle. large type ed. LC 98-33776. 163p. 1999. write for info. (*0-7540-3548-4*) Chivers N Amer.

Chance, John Newton. The Bad Circle. large type ed. LC 98-33776. 1999. 30.00 (*0-7838-0361-3*, G K Hall Lrg Type) Mac Lib Ref.

***Chance, John Newton.** Dead Man's Shoes. large type ed. 256p. 1999. pap. 18.99 (*0-7089-5532-0*, Linford) Ulverscroft.

— The Double Death. large type ed. 320p. 1999. pap. 20.99 (*1-85389-922-4*, Dales) Ulverscroft.

— Looking for Samson. large type ed. 216p. 2000. pap. 18.99 (*0-7089-5652-1*, Linford) Ulverscroft.

— Madman's Will. large type ed. 240p. 1999. pap. 18.99 (*0-7089-5605-X*, Linford) Ulverscroft.

— The Monstrous Regiment. 240p. 2000. 18.99 (*0-7089-5737-4*) Ulverscroft.

— The Smiling Cadaver. large type ed. 232p. 1999. pap. 18.99 (*0-7089-5599-1*, Linford) Ulverscroft.

Chance, Joseph E. The Second Texas Infantry: From Shiloh to Vicksburg. (Illus.). 140p. 1984. pap. 16.95 (*1-57168-021-7*) Sunbelt Media.

Chance, Joseph E., ed. see Curtis, Samual R.

Chance, Joseph E., ed. & anno. see Doubleday, Abner.

Chance, Karen. Parallax. 1988. pap. 30.00 (*0-932526-17-9*) Nexus Pr.

***Chance, Kenneth Byrd.** Confessions of a Closed Male: A Story of Spiritual Awakening. 2000. pap. 12.95 (*1-928927-00-9*) Rojaketaka.

Chance, Linda H. Formless in Form: Kenko, Tsurezuregusa & the Rhetoric of Japanese Fragmentary Prose. LC 96-46175. 368p. 1997. 49.50 (*0-8047-3001-6*) Stanford U Pr.

Chance, Lucinda, ed. Professional Development Schools: Combining School Improvement & Teacher Preparation. LC 97-34895. (NEA School Restructuring Ser.). 1997. pap. write for info. (*0-8106-1869-9*, NEA Prof Lib) NEA.

Chance, Luther. Gun Rage. large type ed. 224p. 1998. pap. 17.99 (*0-7089-5376-X*, Linford) Ulverscroft.

***Chance, Mckeen.** First Class Feature Writing: Readings in Literary Journals. (Mass Communication Ser.). 2000. 29.00 (*0-534-52947-X*) Wadsworth Pub.

Chance, Megan. Fall from Grace. 1997. mass mkt. 5.99 (*0-614-20510-7*, Harp PBks) HarpC.

— The Gentleman Caller. 432p. 1998. mass mkt. 6.99 (*0-06-108704-1*, Harp PBks) HarpC.

***Chance, Megan.** The Gentleman Caller. large type ed. LC 99-22153. (Large Print Book Ser.). 1999. write for info. (*1-56895-729-7*) Wheeler Pub.

Chance, Megan. A Season in Eden. 352p. 1999. mass mkt. 5.99 (*0-06-108705-X*) HarpC.

***Chance, Megan.** A Season in Eden. large type ed. LC 00-21930. (Americana Series). 427p. 2000. 29.95 (*0-7862-2477-0*) Thorndike Pr.

Chance, Megan. The Way Home. 464p. 1997. mass mkt. 5.99 (*0-06-108491-3*, Harp PBks) HarpC.

— Way Home. large type ed. LC 98-13540. (Basic Ser.). 1998. 26.95 (*0-7862-1448-1*) Thorndike Pr.

Chance, Michael R. & Larsen, Ray R., eds. The Social Structure of Attention. LC 76-15675. (Illus.). 349p. reprint ed. pap. 108.20 (*0-608-30584-7*, 201780100008) Bks Demand.

Chance, Michael R. & Omark, Donald R., eds. Social Fabrics of the Mind. 360p. 1989. text 79.95 (*0-86377-097-5*) L Erlbaum Assocs.

Chance, Norman A. China's Urban Villagers: Changing Life in a Beijing Suburb. 2nd ed. Spindler, Louise S., ed. (Case Studies in Cultural Anthropology). (Illus.). 248p. (Orig.). (C). 1991. pap. text 23.50 (*0-03-031333-3*) Harcourt Coll Pubs.

— An Introduction to Derivatives. 4th ed. (C). 1997. pap. text, teacher ed. 40.00 (*0-03-024494-3*) Harcourt Coll Pubs.

— The Inupiat & Arctic Alaska: An Ethnography of Development. (Case Studies in Cultural Anthropology). xxx, 241p. (C). 1990. pap. text 13.50 (*0-03-029882-2*) Harcourt Coll Pubs.

Chance, Paul. The Best of Psychology Today. 268p. (C). 1990. pap. 29.06 (*0-07-557138-2*); pap. text. write for info. (*0-07-010509-X*) McGraw.

— Learning & Behavior. (C). 1979. mass mkt. 17.75 (*0-534-00700-7*) Brooks-Cole.

— Learning & Behavior. 2nd ed. 330p. (C). 1987. mass mkt. 46.00 (*0-534-08508-3*) Brooks-Cole.

— Learning & Behavior. 3rd ed. LC 93-2435. 1993. pap. 46.50 (*0-534-17394-2*) Brooks-Cole.

— Learning & Behavior. 3rd ed. 1993. pap., teacher ed. write for info. (*0-534-17395-0*) Brooks-Cole.

— Learning & Behavior. 3rd ed. 1995. student ed. write for info. (*0-534-33848-8*) Brooks-Cole.

— Learning & Behavior. 4th ed. LC 98-22400. (Psychology Ser.). 1998. pap. 66.95 (*0-534-34691-X*) Brooks-Cole.

— Learning Through Play. (Pediatric Round Table Ser.: No. 3). 60p. (Orig.). 1979. pap. 10.00 (*0-931562-02-3*) J & J Consumer Prods.

— Thinking in the Classroom: A Survey of Programs. 165p. (Orig.). 1986. pap. text 16.95 (*0-8077-2794-6*) Tchrs Coll.

Chance, R. R., jt. ed. see Bloor, D. M.

Chance, R. R., jt. ed. see Bredas, J. L.

Chance, Sue. Stoneflowers. LC 94-94172. 400p. 1994. 22.95 (*0-9638398-4-5*) Bonne Chance.

— Stronger Than Death: When Suicide Touches Your Life. 163p. 1997. reprint ed. lib. bdg. 30.00 (*0-7351-0019-5*) Replica Bks.

— Stronger Than Death: When Suicide Touches Your Life--a Mother's Story. 192p. 1994. mass mkt. 4.99 (*0-380-72110-4*, Avon Bks) Morrow Avon.

— A Voice of My Own: A Verbal Box of Chocolates. LC 93-91044. 260p. 1993. 19.95 (*0-9638398-0-2*) Bonne Chance.

Chance, Suzanne. Dig Me Up. 176p. (Orig.). (YA). 1992. pap. 3.50 (*0-380-76917-4*, Avon Bks) Morrow Avon.

Chance, Thomas H. Plato's Euthydemus: Analysis of What Is & Is Not Philosophy. (C). 1992. 55.00 (*0-520-07754-7*, Pub. by U CA Pr) Cal Prin Full Svc.

Chance, Victoria, jt. auth. see Parsons, Philip.

Chancellor. Illustrated Handbook of the Bach Flower Remedies. (Illus.). 251p. 1996. pap. write for info. (*0-85207-002-0*, Pub. by C W Daniel) Natl Bk Netwk.

***Chancellor, Alexander.** Some Times in America: And Life in a Year at the New Yorker. LC 99-488487. 288p. 1999. write for info. (*0-7475-4337-2*, Pub. by Blmsbury Pub) AMACOM.

— Some Times in America: And Life in a Year at the New Yorker. 320p. 2000. 25.00 (*0-7867-0710-0*) Carroll & Graf.

Chancellor, Ann L. Costumes, Creatures, & Characters. (Illus.). 36p. 1980. 2.00 (*0-9603146-2-8*) MA Convent Fandom.

***Chancellor, Deborah.** Holiday! Celebration Days Around the World. (Dorling Kindersley Readers). (Illus.). (J). (gr. 1-3). 1999. 12.95 (*0-7894-5710-5*, D K Ink) DK Pub Inc.

— Holiday! Celebration Days Around the World. (Dorling Kindersley Readers). (Illus.). (J). (gr. 1-3). 2000. pap. 3.95 (*0-7894-5711-3*, D K Ink) DK Pub Inc.

— Tiger Tales & Big Cat Stories. LC 99-44158. (Eyewitness Readers). (Illus.). 48p. (J). (gr. 2-3). 2000. 12.95 (*0-7894-5424-6*, D K Ink); pap. 3.95 (*0-7894-5423-8*, D K Ink) DK Pub Inc.

— Traveling on Land. (Launch Pad Library). (Illus.). 32p. (J). (gr. k-4). 1997. 11.95 (*0-915741-80-6*) C D Stampley Ent.

Chancellor, Deborah. Viajes por Tierra. (Biblioteca de Descubrimientos).Tr. of Traveling on Land. (SPA., Illus.). (J). (gr. 3-6). 1997. 11.95 (*0-915741-87-3*, SY7074) C D Stampley Ent.

***Chancellor, Debra.** Come Aboard Noah's Ark. LC 99-209684. (Illus.). (J). (ps). 1999. bds. 6.95 (*0-8294-1379-0*) Loyola Pr.

Chancellor, E. Beresford, ed. see Defoe, Daniel.

***Chancellor, Edward.** Devil Take the Hindmost: A History of Financial Speculation. 400p. 2000. pap. 13.95 (*0-452-28180-6*) NAL.

***Chancellor, James D.** Life in the Family: An Oral History of the Children of God. LC 00-22544. 296p. 2000. 29.95 (*0-8156-0645-1*) Syracuse U Pr.

Chancellor, John & Mears, Walter R. The New News Business: A Guide to Writing & Reporting. 194p. 1999. reprint ed. pap. text 12.00 (*0-7881-6221-7*) DIANE Pub.

Chancellor, Michael B. & Blaivas, Gerry, eds. Atlas of Urodynamics. (Illus.). 336p. 1996. 95.00 (*0-683-01640-7*) Lppncott W & W.

Chancellor, Michael B & Blaivas, Jerry G. Practical Neuro-Urology: Genitourinary Complications in Neurologic Disease. LC 95-2117. 390p. 1995. text 95.00 (*0-7506-9556-0*, Focal) Buttrwrth-Heinemann.

Chancellor, Philip. The Illustrated Handbook of the Bach Flower Remedies. 14th ed. (Illus.). 256p. pap. 26.95 (*0-8464-4239-6*) Beekman Pubs.

Chancellor, Phillip. Handbook on the Bach Flower Remedies. LC 79-93435. 252p. (Orig.). 1980. pap. 11.95 (*0-87983-196-0*, 31960K, Keats Publng) NTC Contemp Pub Co.

Chancellor, Robin, tr. see Dutourd, Jean.

Chancellor, T. C. & Thresh, J. M. Epidemiology & Management of Rice Tungro Disease. 108p. 1997. pap. 60.00 (*0-85954-433-8*, Pub. by Nat Res Inst) St Mut.

Chancellor, Victoria. Across the Rainbow. 368p. (Orig.). 1997. mass mkt. 5.50 (*0-505-52236-5*, Love Spell) Dorchester Pub Co.

***Chancellor, Victoria.** The Bachelor Project. (American Romance Ser.: Vol. 844). 2000. mass mkt. 4.25 (*0-373-16844-6*, 1-16844-2) Harlequin Bks.

Chancellor, Victoria. Bitterroot. 400p. (Orig.). 1996. mass mkt. 5.50 (*0-505-52087-7*, Love Spell) Dorchester Pub Co.

— A Cry at Midnight. 368p. 1999. mass mkt. 5.50 (*0-505-52300-0*) Dorchester Pub Co.

— Forever & a Day. 400p. (Orig.). 1995. mass mkt. 5.50 (*0-505-52063-X*) Dorchester Pub Co.

Chancer, Joni & Rester-Zodrow, Gina. Moon Journals: Writing, Art & Inquiry Through Focused Nature Study. LC 96-50400. 211p. 1997. pap. text 32.50 (*0-435-07221-8*, 07221) Heinemann.

Chancer, Lynn S. Reconcilable Differences: Confronting Beauty, Pornography, & the Future of Feminism. LC 97-38670. 330p. 1998. 50.00 (*0-520-20285-6*, Pub. by U CA Pr); pap. 18.95 (*0-520-20923-0*, Pub. by U CA Pr) Cal Prin Full Svc.

— Sadomasochism in Everyday Life: The Dynamics of Power & Powerlessness. LC 91-32362. 240p. 1992. pap. 16.95 (*0-8135-1808-3*); text 40.00 (*0-8135-1807-5*) Rutgers U Pr.

Chances, Ellen. Andrei Bitov: The Ecology of Inspiration. LC 92-33565. (Cambridge Studies in Russian Literature). (Illus.). 350p. (C). 1993. text 74.95 (*0-521-41897-6*) Cambridge U Pr.

Chancey, C. C. & O'Brien, M. C. The Jahn-Teller Effect in C60 & Other Icosahedral Complexes. LC 97-9078. (Illus.). 225p. 1997. text 55.00 (*0-691-04445-7*, Pub. by Princeton U Pr) Cal Prin Full Svc.

***Chancey, Jennie E. & Forstchen, William R.** Hot Shots: An Oral History of Combat Pilots of the Korean War. (Illus.). 256p. 2000. 25.00 (*0-688-16455-2*, Wm Morrow) Morrow Avon.

Chancey, Stacy. Sugar Gliders, a Pocket Full of Fun. (Illus.). 48p. (Orig.). (J). 1996. reprint ed. pap. 16.95 (*0-9655629-0-5*) Bear Tree.

Chancey, Tina & Neely, Patricia A. A Guide to Funding Early Music. MacCracken, Thomas G., ed. (Early Music America Information Resource Ser.). 16p. (Orig.). 1994. pap. 5.00 (*1-878206-06-0*) Early Music.

Chanchreek, K. L., ed. The Gulf War - A Global Crisis: Causes & Future Effects. 331p. 1991. 29.00 (*0-685-62627-X*, Pub. by H K Pubs & Dist) Nataraj Bks.

Chanchreek, K. L., et al, eds. Dr. B. R. Ambedkar, 1891-1991: Patriot, Philosopher, Statesman, Vol. IV. 391p. 1993. 39.00 (*81-7249-020-8*) Nataraj Bks.

— Dr. B. R. Ambedkar, 1891-1991 Vols. 1-3: Patriot, Philosopher, Statesman, Set. 1992. 99.00 (*81-85318-45-X*) Nataraj Bks.

Chanchreek, K. L. & Prasad, Saroj. President Dr. Shankar Dayal Sharma: Patriot, Scholar, Statesman. 231p. 1992. 25.00 (*81-7249-014-3*, Pub. by H K Pubs & Dist) Nataraj Bks.

Chanchreek, K. L. & Prasad, Saroj, eds. Crisis in India. 396p. 1993. 36.00 (*81-7249-021-6*, Pub. by H K Pubs & Dist) Nataraj Bks.

Chancogne, David, jt. auth. see Austin, Mark.

Chancy, Myriam J. Searching for Safe Spaces: Afro-Caribbean Women Writers in Exile. LC 96-46236. 272p. (C). 1997. 59.95 (*1-56639-539-9*) Temple U Pr.

— Searching for Safe Spaces: Afro-Caribbean Women Writers in Exile. LC 96-46236. 272p. (C). 1997. pap. 19.95 (*1-56639-540-2*) Temple U Pr.

Chancy, Myriam J. A. Framing Silence: Revolutionary Novels by Haitian Women. LC 96-2697. 224p. (C). 1997. text 48.00 (*0-8135-2339-7*); pap. text 17.95 (*0-8135-2340-0*) Rutgers U Pr.

Chand, Attar. Asian Security: The Great Debate. 318p. 1987. 34.95 (*0-318-37224-X*) Asia Bk Corp.

— Disarmament, Detente & World Peace: A Bibliography with Selected Abstracts, 1916-1981. 167p. 1982. 24.95 (*0-940500-49-3*, Pub. by Sterling) Asia Bk Corp.

— Global Nuclear Politics: A Survey, 1945-83. 303p. 1983. 42.95 (*0-318-37241-X*) Asia Bk Corp.

— Industrial Safety, Environmental Pollution, Health Hazards & Nuclear Accidents: A Global Survey. 1989. 68.50 (*81-7099-128-5*, Pub. by Mittal Pubs Dist) S Asia.

— Muslims & the Third World Politics. (C). 1993. 24.00 (*81-7041-625-6*, Pub. by Anmol) S Asia.

— Non-Aligned Nations: Arms Race & Disarmaments. 375p. 1983. 36.95 (*0-940500-11-6*) Asia Bk Corp.

— Non-Aligned Nations: Challenges of the '80s. 312p. 1983. 34.95 (*0-317-12336-X*, Pub. by Select Bk Serv) Asia Bk Corp.

— Pakistan: In Search of Modernization. (C). 1992. 48.00 (*81-7041-559-4*, Pub. by Anmol) S Asia.

— Pakistan Party-Politics Pressure Groups & Minorities. (C). 1991. 25.00 (*81-7169-145-5*, Pub. by Commonwealth) S Asia.

— Politics of Human Rights & Civil Liberties. 377p. 1985. 32.95 (*0-317-39866-0*) Asia Bk Corp.

— Poverty & Underdevelopment: New Challenges - A Global Survey. 512p. 1988. 46.00 (*81-212-0148-9*, Pub. by Gian Publng Hse) S Asia.

— Prime Minister H. D. Deve Gowda: The Gain & the Pain: A Biographical Study. (C). 1997. 60.00 (*81-212-0558-1*, Pub. by Gian Publng Hse) S Asia.

An Asterisk (*) at the beginning of an entry indicates that the title is appearing for the first time.

— Rajiv Gandhi: His Mind & Ideology. (C). 1991. 34.00 (*81-212-0397-X*, Pub. by Gian Publng Hse) S Asia.

— Terrorism: Political Violence & Security of Nations. 1988. 67.50 (*81-212-0199-3*, Pub. by Gian Publng Hse) S Asia.

***Chand, Candy.** Under God's Wings: Miraculous True Stories of Christian Faith & Hope. 240p. 2000. pap. 9.95 (*1-58062-428-6*) Adams Media.

Chand, D. Development Through Non-Governmental Organizations in Nepal. (C). 1991. 108.00 (*0-7855-0176-2*); text 100.00 (*0-7855-0134-7*) St Mut.

Chand, Devi. Atharvaveda. (C). 1995. 48.00 (*81-215-0172-5*, Pub. by M Manoharial) Coronet Bks.

— Yajurveda. (C). 1994. 30.00 (*81-215-0294-2*, Pub. by M Manoharial) Coronet Bks.

Chand, Diwaker. Development Through Non-Governmental Organizations in Nepal. 1991. pap. 60.00 (*0-7855-7377-1*, Pub. by Ratna Pustak Bhandar) St Mut.

Chand, Donald R. A Modular Approach to MS-DOS. 80p. (C). 1991. text 15.25 (*0-697-13337-0*, Irwn McGrw-H) McGrw-H Hghr Educ.

— A Modular Approach to MS-DOS 6.2. 96p. (C). 1995. text 15.00 (*0-697-22187-3*) Bus & Educ Tech.

Chand, Khazan. Indian Sexology. 1972. text 22.00 (*0-685-14078-4*) Coronet Bks.

Chand, Ramesh, ed. Agricultural Diversification & Development of Mountain Regions: With Special Reference to Himachal Pradesh. 416p. 1997. pap. 350.00 (*81-7533-049-X*, Pub. by Print Hse) St Mut.

***Chand, Ranga.** Best of the Best Mutual Funds: 2000 Edition. 240p. (Orig.). 1999. pap. 15.95 (*0-7737-6077-6*, Pub. by Stoddart Publ) Genl Dist Srvs.

Chand, Ranga. Ranga Chand's World of Mutual Funds. 384p. 1998. 15.95 (*0-7737-5908-5*) Stoddart Publ.

Chand, S. M. National Leaders on Communalism. 1985. 24.95 (*0-318-36589-8*) Asia Bk Corp.

***Chand, Samuel R., et al.** Failure: The Womb of Success. LC 98-88759. 146p. 1999. 10.00 (*1-57921-168-2*, Pub. by WinePress Pub) BookWorld.

***Chand, Vikram K.** Mexico's Political Awakening. (From the Helen Kellogg Institute for International Ser.). 270p. 2000. pap. 20.00 (*0-268-03459-1*, Pub. by U of Notre Dame Pr); lib. bdg. 40.00 (*0-268-03458-3*, Pub. by U of Notre Dame Pr) Chicago Distribution Ctr.

Chanda & Roy. Plastics Technology Handbook. 3rd ed. LC 98-9729. (Illus.). 1214p. 1998. text 250.00 (*0-8247-0066-X*) Dekker.

Chanda, Anuradha. Public Administration & Public Opinion in Bengal (1854-1885) 187p. 1986. 17.50 (*0-8364-2002-0*, Pub. by KP Bagchi) S Asia.

***Chanda, Ashok & Kabra, Chilpa.** Human Resource Strategy: Architecture for Change LC 99-37983. 1999. write for info. (*0-7619-9386-X*) Sage.

Chanda, Jacqueline. African Arts & Cultures. LC 92-73930. (Arts & Cultures Ser.). (Illus.). 152p. (J). (gr. 5-9). 1994. 25.95 (*0-87192-249-5*) Davis Mass.

— Discovering African Art. LC 96-83459. (Illus.). 88p. (YA). (gr. 9-12). 1996. pap. 15.55 (*0-87192-306-8*) Davis Mass.

Chanda, Linda J. XPress It! A Step-by-Step Guide to Quark Express 3.0. 352p. (C). 1992. text 33.25 (*0-697-14003-2*) Bus & Educ Tech.

Chanda, Linda J. & Mahoney, Patrick. Introducing Photoshop. 288p. (C). 1995. per. write for info. (*0-697-25596-4*) Bus & Educ Tech.

Chanda, Mrinal K. History of English Press in Bengal, 1780-1857. 1987. 28.50 (*81-7074-015-0*, Pub. by KP Bagchi) S Asia.

Chanda, Ram P. & Majumdar, Jatindra K. Raja Rammohun Roy: Letters & Documents. 1987. reprint ed. 72.50 (*81-7041-067-3*, Pub. by Anmol) S Asia.

***Chanda, S. N.** Saints in Indian Folklore: Tales of Saints Known in Various Parts of India LC 98-908718. xvi, 168p. 1998. write for info. (*81-220-0523-3*, Pub. by Konark Pubs Pvt Ltd) S Asia.

Chanda, Sunirmal, ed. Current Perspectives in Palynological Research. (Illus.). 440p. 1991. 70.00 (*1-55528-247-4*, Pub. by Today Tomorrow) Scholarly Pubns.

Chandak, Purshottam, jt. auth. see Chandak, Ramesh.

Chandak, Ramesh. High Performance Visual Basic 6 Object-Oriented Programming. LC 98-38266. (High Performance Ser.). 388p. 1998. pap. 49.99 (*1-57610-255-6*) Coriolis Grp.

— Special Edition Using Dynamic HTML. 600p. 1997. 39.99 (*0-7897-1154-0*) Que.

***Chandak, Ramesh & Chandak, Purshottam.** Advanced PowerBuilder 7 Techniques. LC 99-36712. 896p. 1999. pap. 59.99 incl. cd-rom (*0-471-35451-1*) Wiley.

Chandak, Ramesh, jt. auth. see Lalani, Suleiman S.

***Chandan, J. S.** Management Theory & Practice. 1999. pap. 14.00 (*0-7069-9030-7*, Pub. by Vikas) S Asia.

Chandansingh, R. A. The Economic Value of CAD Systems in Structural Design & Construction: A Modelling Approach. 168p. 1995. pap. 57.50 (*90-407-1102-X*, Pub. by Delft U Pr) Coronet Bks.

Chandauij, Natthapatra. Monk's Fans: A Unique Religious Art Form. (Illus.). 312p. 1996. 65.00 (*974-8225-13-5*, Pub. by River Books) Weatherhill.

Chandavarkar, Rajnarayan. Imperial Power & Popular Politics: Class, Resistance & the State in India, c. 1850-1950. LC 97-8911. 288p. (C). 1998. pap. 24.95 (*0-521-59692-0*); text 64.95 (*0-521-59234-8*) Cambridge U Pr.

— The Origins of Industrial Capitalism in India: Business Strategies & the Working Classes in Bombay, 1900-1940. (Cambridge South Asian Studies: No. 51). (Illus.). 489p. (C). 1994. text 74.95 (*0-521-41496-2*) Cambridge U Pr.

Chandavij, Natthapatra. Thai Puppets & Khon Masks. LC 98-837130. (Illus.). 160p. 1997. 39.95 (*974-8225-23-2*, Pub. by River Books) Weatherhill.

***Chande.** Betrayal of Indian Democracy. 1999. 38.50 (*81-7156-792-4*, Pub. by Atlantic Pubs) S Asia.

Chande, Abdin N. Islam, Ulamaa & Community Development in Tanzania: A Case Study of Religious Currents in East Africa. LC 97-5235. 308p. (Orig.). 1997. 69.95 (*1-57292-017-3*); pap. 49.95 (*1-57292-016-5*) Austin & Winfield.

Chande, Tushar S. Beyond Technical Analysis: How to Develop & Implement a Winning Trading System. LC 96-34436. 288p. 1996. 79.95 (*0-471-16188-8*) Wiley.

Chande, Tushar S. & Kroll, Stanley. The New Technical Trader: Boost Your Profit by Plugging into the Latest Indicators. (Finance Editions Ser.). 224p. 1994. 64.95 (*0-471-59780-5*) Wiley.

Chandebois, R. Histogenesis & Morphogenesis in Planarian Regeneration. Wolsky, A., ed. (Monographs in Developmental Biology: Vol. 11). (Illus.). 200p. 1976. 78.50 (*3-8055-2285-1*) S Karger.

Chandebois, Rosine & Faber, J., eds. Automation in Animal Development. (Monographs in Developmental Biology: Vol. 16). (Illus.). xii, 204p. 1983. 143.50 (*3-8055-3666-6*) S Karger.

Chandel, A. S. Planning in Library Resource Sharing. 237p. (C). 1986. 175.00 (*81-85009-24-4*, Pub. by Print Hse) St Mut.

Chandel, Bhuvan & Sharma, K. L., eds. Philosophy of Daya Krishna. 1996. 32.00 (*81-85636-20-6*, Pub. by M Manoharial) S Asia.

Chandel, Bhuvan, et al. Cultural Traditions & the Idea of Secularization. LC 98-909497. 138p. 1998. pap. write for info. (*81-215-0876-2*, Pub. by M Manoharial) Coronet Bks.

Chandel, L. S. Early Medieval State: Study of Delhi Sultans. 1989. 20.00 (*81-7169-011-4*, Pub. by Commonwealth) S Asia.

Chandel, M. F. Social Force in Politics: Study of U. P. 1990. 17.50 (*81-7099-193-5*, Pub. by Mittal Pubs Dist) S Asia.

Chandel, M. P. Democratic Transformation of a Social Class. (C). 1991. text 12.50 (*81-7099-314-8*, Pub. by Mittal Pubs Dist) S Asia.

— Demographic Transformation of a Social Class. (C). 1991. 12.00 (*0-8364-2665-7*, Pub. by Mittal Pubs Dist) S Asia.

***Chander, ed.** Encyclopaedia of Contemporary Indian Politics, 3 vols. 1999. 210.00 (*81-261-0314-0*, Pub. by Anmol) S Asia.

***Chander, Ernest R., ed.** Trishul to Trinity: K. N. Nambudripad & I. LC 99-64523. 1999. pap. 19.95 (*1-57736-157-1*) Providence Hse.

Chander, Jagdish & Pradhan, Narindar S., eds. Studies in American Literature: Essays in Honour of William Mulder. 1977. 9.50 (*0-19-560784-8*) OUP.

***Chander, Keshav.** The IMG's Guide to Mastering the USMLE & Residency. LC 99-54041. 352p. 2000. 29.95 (*0-07-134724-0*) McGraw-Hill HPD.

Chander, R. Tantric Yoga Techniques. (Illus.). 173p. 1979. 12.95 (*0-318-36401-8*) Asia Bk Corp.

Chander, Subhash, et al, eds. Advances in Coal & Mineral Processing Using Flotation: Proceedings of an Engineering Foundation Conference, Palm Coast, Florida, December 3-8, 1989. fac. ed. LC 89-63388. (Illus.). 384p. 1989. reprint ed. pap. 119.10 (*0-7837-7854-6*, 204761300007) Bks Demand.

Chandernagor, Francoise. L' Enfant des Lumieres, Vol. I. large type ed. 1996. pap. 25.99 (*2-84011-139-X*) Ulverscroft.

— L' Enfant des Lumieres, Vol. II. large type ed. 1996. pap. 25.99 (*2-84011-140-3*) Ulverscroft.

Chandes, Herve, ed. see Miyake, Issey.

Chandhani. Yoga for Children. (C). 1997. 14.00 (*81-86112-22-7*, Pub. by UBS Pubs Dist) S Asia.

Chandhoke, Neera. Beyond Secularism: The Rights of Religious Minorities. 396p. 2000. text 29.95 (*0-19-564950-8*) OUP.

— State & Civil Society: Explorations in Political Theory. 1995. 26.00 (*0-8039-9246-7*) Sage.

Chandhoke, Neera, ed. Understanding the Post-Colonial World: Theory & Method. LC 95-900006. (C). 1995. write for info. (*81-207-1718-X*) Sterling Pubs.

Chandhoke, S. K. Habitation & Environment: Interactions, Inter-Relations & Adjustments. (C). 1994. 27.00 (*81-241-0181-7*, Pub. by Har-Anand Pubns) S Asia.

Chandik, Zoe, jt. auth. see Corelli, Toni.

Chandlee, Robin & Sautter, Sara. Loan Closing: A Workbook on Executing the Documeents & Transferring the Funds. Askerooth, Gary & Fisher, Kathryn, eds. (Training Institute Community Revitalization Ser.). 80p. (Orig.). 1993. pap., student ed. 10.00 (*1-884356-02-8*) Neighborhd Reinvest.

— Loan Origination: A Workbook on Gathering & Verifying the Information. Askerooth, Gary & Fisher, Kathryn, eds. (Training Institute Community Revitalization Ser.). 60p. (Orig.). 1993. pap., student ed. 10.00 (*1-884356-00-1*) Neighborhd Reinvest.

Chandlee, Robin & Tetrault, Al. How to Be Your Own Developer: Making the Development Decision. Askerooth, Gary & Fisher, Kathryn, eds. (Neighborhood Reinvestment Training Institute Community Revitalization Ser.). 51p. 1994. 10.00 (*0-88435-603-5*) Neighborhd Reinvest.

Chandlee, Robin, et al. Loan Underwriting: A Workbook on Analyzing & Committing to Lend. Askerooth, Gary & Fisher, Kathryn, eds. (Training Institute Community Revitalization Ser.). 64p. (Orig.). 1993. pap., student ed. 10.00 (*1-884356-01-X*) Neighborhd Reinvest.

***Chandler.** A+ Certification DOS/Windows Exam Prep. 400p. 1999. pap. 29.99 (*0-7645-4571-X*) IDG Bks.

Chandler. Accounting Control Systems. (SWC-Accounting). 2000. pap. 56.00 (*0-324-02094-5*) Thomson Learn.

— Alternative Energy Sources. 1996. write for info. (*0-8050-5265-8*) H Holt & Co.

— Guardians of Wildlife. 1996. write for info. (*0-8050-5266-6*) H Holt & Co.

— Kids Who Make a Difference. 1996. write for info. (*0-8050-5267-4*) H Holt & Co.

— Macmillan Encyclopedia of Military History, Vol. 2. 1996. 100.00 (*0-02-897105-1*) Macmillan.

— Natural Foods & Products. 1996. write for info. (*0-8050-5268-2*) H Holt & Co.

— Paths to Learning. 1999. 30.00 (*0-02-905305-6*) S&S Trade.

— Podos: External Diseases. 1993. 99.00 (*1-56375-101-1*) Gower-Mosby.

— Recycling. 1996. write for info. (*0-8050-5270-4*) H Holt & Co.

— Tropical Flowers Coloring Book. (Illus.). (J). pap. 2.95 (*0-486-24206-4*) Dover.

Chandler, ed. Macmillan Encyclopedia of Military History, Vol. 1. 1996. 50.00 (*0-02-897106-X*) Mac Lib Ref.

— Macmillan Encyclopedia of Military History, Vol. 2. 1996. 50.00 (*0-02-897107-8*) Mac Lib Ref.

Chandler & Childs. Feeling Fine. Date not set. pap. text. write for info. (*0-582-20633-2*, Pub. by Addison-Wesley) Longman.

Chandler, A. Winter's Tale. mass mkt. 6.95 (*0-7472-5424-9*, Pub. by Headline Bk Pub) Trafalgar.

Chandler, A. B., ed. see McDonald, T. F.

Chandler, A. Bertram & Hoffman, Lee. Up to the Sky in Ships - In & Out of Quandry. Hitchcock, Charles J., ed. LC 82-60702. 172p. 1982. 13.00 (*0-915368-16-1*) New Eng SF Assoc.

Chandler, A. M., ed. see Briggs, T.

Chandler, A. M., jt. ed. see Briggs, T.

Chandler, Adrian, jt. auth. see Brown, Ian.

Chandler, Albert M., jt. auth. see Briggs, Thomas.

Chandler, Albert R. Beauty & Human Nature: Elements of Psychological Aesthetics. LC 75-3110. reprint ed. 26.00 (*0-404-59106-X*) AMS Pr.

Chandler, Albert R. & Barnhart, Edward N. Bibliography of Psychological & Experimental Aesthetics, Eighteen Sixty-Four to Nineteen Thirty-Seven. LC 75-3111. reprint ed. 64.50 (*0-404-59107-8*) AMS Pr.

Chandler, Alfred D., Jr. Henry Varnum Poor: Business Editor, Analyst, & Reformer. Bruchey, Stuart, ed. LC 80-1297. (Railroads Ser.). 1981. reprint ed. lib. bdg. 38.95 (*0-405-13767-2*) Ayer.

— Scale & Scope: The Dynamics of Industrial Capitalism. (Illus.). 800p. 1990. text 49.95 (*0-674-78994-6*) HUP.

Chandler, Alfred D. Scale & Scope: The Dynamics of Industrial Capitalism. LC 94-132234. 784p. (C) 1994. pap. text 24.95 (*0-674-78995-4*) HUP.

Chandler, Alfred D., Jr. Strategy & Structure: Chapters in the History of the American Industrial Enterprise. 463p. 1969. pap. text 20.00 (*0-262-53009-0*) MIT Pr.

— The Visible Hand: The Managerial Revolution in American Business. 624p. 1977. 54.00 (*0-674-94051-2*) Belknap Pr.

— The Visible Hand: The Managerial Revolution in American Business. 624p. 1980. pap. text 16.95 (*0-674-94052-0*) Belknap Pr.

Chandler, Alfred D., Jr., ed. The Application of Modern Systematic Management: An Original Anthology. LC 79-7522. (History of Management Thought & Practice Ser.). (Illus.). 1980. lib. bdg. 19.95 (*0-405-12307-8*) Ayer.

— History of Management Thought & Practice, 32 bks., Set. (Illus.). 1980. lib. bdg. 1182.00 (*0-405-12306-X*) Ayer.

— Management of Tomorrow. LC 79-7558. (History of Management Thought & Practice Ser.). 1980. reprint ed. lib. bdg. 33.95 (*0-405-12344-2*) Ayer.

— Management Thought in Great Britain: An Original Anthology. LC 79-7523. (History of Management Thought & Practice Ser.). 1980. lib. bdg. 28.95 (*0-405-12308-6*) Ayer.

— Managerial Innovation at General Motors: An Original Anthology. LC 79-7524. (History of Management Thought & Practice Ser.). 1980. lib. bdg. 18.95 (*0-405-12309-4*) Ayer.

— The Papers of Dwight David Eisenhower: The War Years, 5 Vols, Set. LC 65-27672. (Illus.). 1970. 175.00 (*0-8018-1078-7*) Johns Hopkins.

— Pioneers in Modern Factory Management: An Original Anthology. LC 79-7526. (History of Management Thought & Practice Ser.). 1980. lib. bdg. 21.95 (*0-405-12310-8*) Ayer.

— Precursors of Modern Management: An Original Anthology. LC 79-7527. (History of Management Thought & Practice Ser.). 1980. lib. bdg. 31.95 (*0-405-12311-6*) Ayer.

— The Railroads: Pioneers in Modern Management, an Original Anthology. LC 79-7528. (History of Management Thought & Practice Ser.). 1980. lib. bdg. 27.95 (*0-405-12312-4*) Ayer.

Chandler, Alfred D., Jr., et al, eds. Big Business & the Wealth of Nations. (Illus.). 608p. (C). 1997. text 64.95 (*0-521-48123-6*) Cambridge U Pr.

***Chandler, Alfred D., Jr., et al, eds.** Big Business & the Wealth of Nations. 608p. 1999. pap. 24.95 (*0-521-66347-4*) Cambridge U Pr.

Chandler, Alfred D., Jr., et al, eds. The Dynamic Firm: The Role of Technology, Strategy, Organization, & Regions. LC 98-202432. (Illus.). 488p. 1998. text 65.00 (*0-19-829052-7*) OUP.

Chandler, Alfred D., et al, eds. The Dynamic Firm: The Role of Technology, Strategy Organization, & Regions. (Illus.). 488p. 1999. pap. text 29.95 (*0-19-829664-5*) OUP.

Chandler, Alfred D., Jr. & Bruchey, Stuart, eds. Giant Enterprise: Ford, General Motors & the Automobile Industry. LC 80-18483. (Multinational Corporations Ser.). 1980. reprint ed. lib. bdg. 31.95 (*0-405-13349-9*) Ayer.

— The Railroads: The Nation's First Big Business Sources & Readings. LC 80-1298. (Railroads Ser.). 1981. reprint ed. lib. bdg. 23.95 (*0-405-13768-0*) Ayer.

Chandler, Alfred D., Jr. & Daems, Herman, eds. Managerial Hierarchies: Comparative Perspectives on the Rise of the Modern Industrial Enterprise. (Studies in Business History: No. 32). (Illus.). 246p. 1980. 24.95 (*0-674-54740-3*) HUP.

— Managerial Hierarchies: Comparative Perspectives on the Rise of the Modern Industrial Enterprise. (Studies in Business History: No. 32). (Illus.). 246p. 1983. pap. 9.95 (*0-674-54741-1*) HUP.

Chandler, Alfred D., Jr. & Urwick, Lyndall F., eds. The Golden Book of Management: A Historical Record of the Life & Work of Seventy Pioneers. LC 79-7557. (History of Management Thought & Practice Ser.). (Illus.). 1980. reprint ed. lib. bdg. 26.95 (*0-405-12343-4*) Ayer.

Chandler, Alfred D., et al. Management: Past & Present: A Casebook on the History of American Business. 1995. mass mkt. 102.95 (*0-538-85412-X*) S-W Pub.

Chandler, Alfred D., ed. see Arnold, Horace L., Jr.

Chandler, Alfred D., ed. see Austin, Bertram, Jr. & Lloyd, W. Francis.

Chandler, Alfred D., ed. see Berriman, A. E., Jr., et al.

Chandler, Alfred D., ed. see Cadbury, Edward, Jr.

Chandler, Alfred D., ed. see Carlson, Sune, Jr.

Chandler, Alfred D., ed. see Carney, Edward M., Jr., et al.

Chandler, Alfred D., ed. see Casson, Herbert N., Jr.

Chandler, Alfred D., ed. see Church, Alexander H., Jr.

Chandler, Alfred D., ed. see Davis, Ralph C., Jr.

Chandler, Alfred D., ed. see Devinat, Paul, Jr.

Chandler, Alfred D., ed. see Diemer, Hugo, Jr.

Chandler, Alfred D., ed. see Elbourne, Edward T., Jr.

Chandler, Alfred D., ed. see Emerson, Harrington, Jr.

Chandler, Alfred D., ed. see Kirkman, Marshall M., Jr.

Chandler, Alfred D., ed. see Laurence, Edward, Jr.

Chandler, Alfred D., ed. see Lee, John H., Jr.

Chandler, Alfred D., jt. ed. see Lee, John H., Jr.

Chandler, Alfred D., ed. see McKinsey, James O., Jr.

Chandler, Alfred D., ed. see Rowntree, B. Seebohm, Jr.

Chandler, Alfred D., ed. see Schell, Erwin H., Jr.

Chandler, Alfred D., ed. see Sheldon, Oliver, Jr.

Chandler, Alfred D., ed. see Tead, Ordway, Jr. & Metcalfe, Henry C.

***Chandler, Alfred Dupont.** A Nation Transformed by Information: How It Has Shaped the United States from Colonial Times to the Present. LC 99-49438. 368p. 2000. 35.00 (*0-19-512701-3*) OUP.

Chandler, Alfred N. Land Titles Origins. Bruchey, Stuart, ed. LC 78-56712. (Management of Public Lands in the U. S. Ser.). 1979. reprint ed. lib. bdg. 41.95 (*0-405-11324-2*) Ayer.

Chandler, Alice. A Dream of Order: The Medieval Ideal in Nineteenth-Century English Literature. LC 69-10413. 290p. reprint ed. pap. 89.90 (*0-608-13963-7*, 202501600040) Bks Demand.

Chandler, Alton H., ed. see Howell, Ann C.

Chandler, Anankha K. Therapist in a Box: Emotional Healing, 3 vols. 208p. 1999. pap. 24.95 incl. audio (*1-883955-10-6*) Penmarin Bks.

Chandler, Andrea. Institutions of Isolation: Border Controls in the Soviet Union & Its Successor States, 1917-1993. LC 00-503165. 224p. 1998. text 49.95 (*0-7735-1717-0*, Pub. by McG-Queens Univ Pr) CUP Services.

***Chandler, Andrew.** Terrible Alternative: Christian Martyrdom in the Twentieth Century. 220p. 2000. pap. 16.95 (*0-8264-4844-5*) Continuum.

Chandler, Andrew, ed. Brethren in Adversity: Bishop George Bell, the Church of England & the Crisis of German Protestantism, 1933-1939. (Church of England Record Society Ser.: No. 4). (Illus.). 200p. 1997. 75.00 (*0-85115-692-4*, Boydell Pr) Boydell & Brewer.

— Moral Imperative: New Essays on the Ethics of Resistance in National Socialist Germany, 1933-1945. LC 98-18430. 124p. (C). 1998. pap. 65.00 (*0-8133-3466-7*, Pub. by Westview) HarpC.

Chandler, Andrew & Harvey, Anthony, eds. The Terrible Alternative: Christian Martyrdom in the Twentieth Century. LC 98-220790. 256p. 1998. pap. 24.95 (*0-304-70287-0*) Continuum.

Chandler, Andrian & Holland, James. Information: Protection, Ownership & Rights, 1993. (Blackstone's Employment Law Library). 1993. pap. 38.00 (*1-85431-210-3*, Pub. by Blackstone Pr) Gaunt.

Chandler, Ann. Black Women: A Salute to Black Inventors. rev. ed. Ivery, Evelyn L., ed. (Black Inventors Activity Bks.). (Illus.). 24p. (J). (gr. 3-7). 1992. reprint ed. pap. text 1.50 (*1-877804-06-1*) Chandler White.

Chandler, Arline. Road Work: The Ultimate RVing Adventure. Copperman, Rena, ed. LC 97-90438. (Illus.). 284p. (Orig.). 1997. pap. 15.95 (*0-9657975-0-3*) Flying Horse.

***Chandler, Arline.** Road Work Vol. II: The Adventure Continues. (Illus.). 276p. 2000. pap. 15.95 (*0-9657975-2-X*) Flying Horse.

Chandler, Arline. When Heads & Hearts Collide: My Personal Journey in Parenting My Parents. (Illus.). 186p. 1998. pap. 12.00 (*0-9657975-1-1*) Flying Horse.

Chandler, Arthur. The Biography of San Francisco State University. (Illus.). 120p. 1986. 29.95 (*0-938530-34-8*); pap. 19.95 (*0-938530-33-X*) Lexikos.

Chandler, Arthur B. Old Tales of San Francisco. 2nd ed. 304p. (C). 1996. pap. text, per. 28.95 (*0-8403-4385-X*) Kendall-Hunt.

Chandler, B. & Magnus, Wilhelm. History of Combinatorial Group Theory: A Case Study of the History of Ideas. (Studies in the History of Mathematics & Physical Sciences: Vol. 9). (Illus.). 234p. 1982. 142.95 (*0-387-90749-1*) Spr-Verlag.

Chandler, B., jt. auth. see Baumslag, C. B.

Chandler, B., ed. see Magnus, Wilhelm.
Chandler, Beverly. Investing with the Hedge Fund Giants: Profit Whether Markets Rise or Fall. 256p. 1998. 35.00 (0-273-63243-4, Pub. by F T P-H) Natl Bk Netwk.
Chandler, Bill. Twenty-Five Things You Can Do to Feel Better Right Now. 156p. 1993. pap. 10.95 (0-9639167-0-X) Andante Pubng.
Chandler, Billie E., jt. auth. see Chandler, David S.
Chandler, Billy J. The Feitosas & the Sertao dos Inhamuns: The History of a Family & a Community in Northeast Brazil, 1700-1930. LC 74-178988. (Latin American Monographs: Ser. 2, No. 10). 191p. reprint ed. pap. 59.30 (0-7837-4977-5, 204464300004) Bks Demand.
— King of the Mountain: The Life & Death of Giuliano the Bandit. (Illus.). 273p. 1988. 27.50 (0-87580-140-4) N Ill U Pr.
Chandler, Bruce, ed. see Hoke, Donald R.
Chandler, Bruce, ed. see Pingree, David E.
Chandler, Bruce, ed. see Randall, Anthony G.
Chandler, Bruce, ed. see Webster, Roderick S. & Webster, Marjorie K.
Chandler, C. H. Chandler: Descendants of Roger Chandler. 152p. 1991. reprint ed. pap. 24.50 (0-8328-2112-8) Higginson Bk Co.
— Water Quality Surveys on the Niagara River - 1974 LC 83-221977. (Report Ser.). (ENG & FRE.). v, 9 p. 1977. (0-662-01447-2) Can7 Govern Pub.
Chandler, Carla E., jt. auth. see Cole, Gloria H.
***Chandler, Cathy A.** Our Lady of the New Age: The Visions of Mary & God's Test. 111p. 1999. pap. write for info. (0-9675588-0-8) C Chandler.
Chandler, Charles D. & Lahm, Frank P. How Our Army Grew Wings. Kohn, Richard H., ed. LC 78-22377. (American Military Experience Ser.). (Illus.). 1980. reprint ed. lib. bdg. 30.95 (0-405-11854-6) Ayer.
Chandler, Charles H. The History of New Ipswich, New Hampshire. 782p. 1994. reprint ed. lib. bdg. 77.50 (0-8328-3625-7) Higginson Bk Co.
***Chandler, Charles Henry.** The History of New Ipswich New Hampshire, 1735-1914: With Genealogical Records of the Principal Families. (Illus.). 818p. 1999. reprint ed. pap. 52.50 (0-7884-1292-2, C307) Heritage Bk.
Chandler, Charles L., et al. Philadelphia: Port of History, 1609-1837. (Illus.). 82p. 1976. pap. 2.00 (0-913346-02-0) Indep Seaport.
Chandler, Charlotte. I, Fellini. 419p. 1998. pap. text 22.00 (0-7881-5908-9) DIANE Pub.
— I, Fellini. 1995. 25.00 (0-614-15427-8) Random.
Chandler, Chris & Rockstroh, Phil. Protection. (Illus.). 96p. 1997. pap. 10.00 (0-916620-30-1) Portals Pr.
Chandler, Clare. Carnival. LC 97-27021. (Festivals Ser.). (Illus.). 32p. (J). (gr. 3-6). 1998. lib. bdg. 20.90 (0-7613-0373-1) Millbrook Pr.
***Chandler, Clare.** Harvest Celebrations. LC 97-32872. (Festivals Ser.). (Illus.). 32p. (J). (gr. 2-4). 1998. lib. bdg. 20.90 (0-7613-0964-0) Millbrook Pr.
Chandler, Clare. Little Green Fingers: A Kid's Guide to Growing Things. (Illus.). 28p. (J). (gr. 1-4). 5.95 (1-55110-258-7) Whitecap Bks.
***Chandler, Cliff.** The Paragons. 250p. 2000. pap. 14.95 (1-893196-03-8) Brittney Pr.
Chandler, D., jt. auth. see Houlette, Forrest.
Chandler, D. S., jt. auth. see Burkholder, Mark A.
Chandler, Daniel R. Toward Universal Religion: Voices of American & Indian Spirituality, 43. LC 95-33968. (Contributions to the Study of Religion Ser.). 280p. 1996. 69.50 (0-313-29484-4, Greenwood Pr) Greenwood.
Chandler, Darlene K. The Annuity Handbook: A Guide to Nonqualified Annuities. LC 95-69132. 224p. (Orig.). 1994. pap. 29.95 (0-87218-134-0) Natl Underwriter.
Chandler, David. The Art of Warfare in the Age of Marlborough. (Illus.). 320p. 1995. 29.95 (1-885119-14-3) Sarpedon.
Chandler, David. The Art of Warfare in the Age of Marlborough. 334p. 1997. 80.00 (0-946771-42-1, Pub. by Spellmnt Pubs) St Mut.
Chandler, David. Austerlitz, 1805. (Campaign Ser.: No. 2). (Illus.). 96p. 1990. pap. 14.95 (0-85045-957-5, 9501, Pub. by Osprey) Stackpole.
— Bosnia: Faking Democracy after Dayton. LC 98-42752. 256p. 1999. 59.95 (0-7453-1408-2, Pub. by Pluto GBR) Stylus Pub VA.
***Chandler, David.** Bosnia: Faking Democracy after Dayton. 256p. 1999. pap. 22.50 (0-7453-1403-1, Pub. by Pluto GBR) Stylus Pub VA.
— Brother Number One: A Political Biography of Pol Pot. 2nd rev. ed. LC DS554.83.P65C43 1999. 264p. 1999. pap. text 16.00 (0-8133-3510-8, Pub. by Westview) HarpC.
Chandler, David. Chronicles of World War II. 1997. 19.99 (1-85833-763-1, Pub. by CLib Bks) Whitecap Bks.
— Dictionary of the Napoleonic Wars. 1999. pap. text 12.99 (1-84022-203-4) Wrdsworth Edits.
— Exploring the Night Sky with Binoculars. 2nd rev. ed. (Illus.). 48p. (Orig.). 1995. pap. 7.95 (0-9613207-1-0) D Chandler.
— Facing the Cambodian Past: Selected Essays, 1971-1994. 340p. 1998. pap. text 17.50 (974-7100-64-9) U of Wash Pr.
***Chandler, David.** The Great Battlefields of Europe. (Wordsworth Military Library). 1998. pap. 12.99 (1-85326-694-9, 266949) Wrdsworth Edits.
Chandler, David. A History of Cambodia. 2nd ed. LC 95-46701. (C). 1996. pap. 30.00 (0-8133-2862-4, Pub. by Westview) HarpC.
— A History of Cambodia. 3rd ed. LC 99-58181. (Illus.). 324p. 2000. pap. text 26.00 (0-8133-3511-6) Westview.
— Jena, 1806. (Campaign Ser.: No. 20). (Illus.). 96p. pap. 14.95 (1-85532-285-4, 9519, Pub. by Osprey) Stackpole.
— The Killing Fields. (Illus.). 124p. 1996. 75.00 (0-944092-39-X) Twin Palms Pub.
— Marlborough As Military Commander. (Illus.). 408p. 1996. 35.00 (1-885119-30-5) Sarpedon.
Chandler, David. Marlborough As Military Commander. 408p. 1997. 100.00 (0-946771-12-X, Pub. by Spellmnt Pubs) St Mut.
— Napoleon. 2000. reprint ed. pap. 19.95 (0-85052-750-3, Pub. by Pen & Sword) Combined Pub.
Chandler, David. On the Napoleonic Wars. LC 98-49191. (Greenhill Military Paperbacks Ser.). 1999. pap. text 19.95 (1-85367-349-8) Greenhill Bks.
— Running a Perfect Web Site with UNIX. 2nd ed. LC 96-68043. 560p. 1996. pap. text 49.99 incl. cd-rom (0-7897-0745-4) Que.
— Running a Perfect Web Site with Windows NT. LC 96-67568. 720p. 1996. pap. text 49.99 incl. cd-rom (0-7897-0763-2) Que.
***Chandler, David.** Sedgemoor 1685: From Monmouth's Invasion to the Bloddy Assizes. 240p. 1999. pap. 60.00 (1-86227-046-5, Pub. by Spellmnt Pubs) St Mut.
— Voices from S-21: Terror & History in Pol Pot's Secret Prison. LC 99-13924. 300p. 1999. pap. 17.95 (0-520-22247-4, Pub. by U CA Pr) Cal Prin Full Svc.
Chandler, David. Waterloo: The Hundred Days. 224p. 1998. pap. 21.95 (1-85532-716-3, Pub. by Osprey) Stackpole.
***Chandler, David, ed.** Blenheim Preparation: Collected Essays on the Armies of William III & Marborough. 224p. 2000. 80.00 (1-873376-95-2, Pub. by Spellmnt Pubs) St Mut.
Chandler, David, et al, eds. Boxer: An Anthology of Writings on Boxing & the Visual Arts. LC 96-75615. (Illus.). 144p. 1996. pap. text 20.00 (0-262-53143-7) MIT Pr.
Chandler, David & Beckett, Ian F., eds. The Oxford History of the British Army. LC 96-13051. (Illus.). 492p. 1997. pap. 16.95 (0-19-285333-3) OUP.
— The Oxford Illustrated History of the British Army. (Illustrated Histories Ser.). (Illus.). 510p. 1994. 49.95 (0-19-869178-5) OUP.
Chandler, David, jt. auth. see Mabbett, Ian.
Chandler, David G. Atlas of Military Strategy. 1985. 29.95 (0-02-905750-7) Free Pr.
— Atlas of Military Strategy: The Art, Theory, & Practice of War 1618-1878. (Illus.). 216p. 1997. 39.95 (1-85409-383-5, Pub. by Arms & Armour) Sterling.
— Atlas of Military Strategy: The Art, Theory & Practice of War, 1618-1878. (Illus.). 1999. pap. 24.95 (1-85409-493-9) Arms & Armour.
— Battles & Battlescenes of World War Two. 192p. 1989. 19.95 (0-02-897175-2) Macmillan.
— The Campaigns of Napoleon: The Mind & Method of History's Greatest Soldier. 1182p. 1973. 85.00 (0-02-523660-1) Macmillan.
— Introduction to Modern Statistical Mechanics. (Illus.). 288p. 1987. pap. text 39.95 (0-19-504277-8) OUP.
— The Military Maxims of Napoleon. LC 88-21781. 256p. 1988. 19.95 (0-02-897171-X) Macmillan.
— On the Napoleonic Wars: Collected Essays. LC 93-32339. 240p. 1994. 34.95 (1-85367-158-4) Stackpole.
Chandler, David G., ed. Great Battles of the British Army: As Commemorated in the Sandhurst Companies. LC 90-22637. (Illus.). 288p. reprint ed. pap. 89.30 (0-7837-6862-1, 204669100003) Bks Demand.
Chandler, David G. & Wu, David. Introduction to Modern Statistical Mechanics. 96p. (C). 1988. pap. text, student ed. 15.95 (0-19-505889-5) OUP.
Chandler, David G., ed. see Bonaparte, Napoleon.
Chandler, David L. Health & Slavery in Colonial Colombia. Bruchey, Stuart, ed. LC 80-2799. (Dissertations in European Economic History Ser.). (Illus.). 1981. lib. bdg. 34.95 (0-405-13983-7) Ayer.
— Juan Jose de Aycinena: Idealista Conservador de la Guatemala del Siglo XIX. LC 89-60300. (Monograph Ser.: No. 4). (SPA.). 304p. 1989. pap. 16.50 (0-910443-06-8) Plumsock Meso Studies.
Chandler, David P. Brother Number One: A Political Biography of Pol Pot. LC 92-19229. 272p. 1992. pap. 75.00 (0-8133-0927-1, Pub. by Westview) HarpC.
— The Tragedy of Cambodian History: Politics, War, & Revolution Since 1945. (Illus.). 416p. 1993. pap. 20.00 (0-300-05752-0) Yale U Pr.
— Voices from S-21: Terror & History in Pol Pot's Secret Prison. LC 99-13924. 300p. 2000. 48.00 (0-520-22005-6, Pub. by U CA Pr) Cal Prin Full Svc.
Chandler, David P., et al, eds. Pol Pot Plans the Future: Confidential Leadership Documents from Democratic Kampuchea, 1976-1977. Kiernan, Ben et al, trs. (Monographs: No. 33). xviii, 346p. 1989. pap. 20.00 (0-938692-35-6) Yale U SE Asia.
Chandler, David P. & Kiernan, Ben, eds. Revolution & Its Aftermath in Kampuchea: Eight Essays. LC 83-50326. (Monographs: No. 25). 319p. 1983. pap. 14.00 (0-938692-05-4) Yale U SE Asia.
Chandler, David S. & Chandler, Billie E. Sky Atlas for Small Telescopes & Binoculars: The Beginners Guide to Successful Deep Sky Observing. (Illus.). 24p. (Orig.). 1996. pap. 12.95 (0-9613207-2-9) D Chandler.
***Chandler, David S. & Chandler, Billie E.** Sky Atlas for Small Telescopes & Binoculars: The Beginner's Guide to Successful Deep Sky Observing. (Illus.). 24p. 2000. pap. 12.95 (1-891938-06-1) D Chandler.
Chandler, Deborah. Learning to Warp. (Illus.). 56p. 1995. pap. 7.00 (1-883010-04-7) Interweave.
— Learning to Weave. rev. ed. LC 94-22905. (Illus.). 232p. 1995. spiral bd. 21.95 (1-883010-03-9) Interweave.
Chandler, Dewitt S. Social Assistance & Bureaucratic Politics: The Montepios of Colonial Mexico, 1767-1821. LC 91-20369. 247p. reprint ed. pap. 76.60 (0-608-07287-7, 206751500009) Bks Demand.
Chandler, Donna. Just House Manners. 1999. 9.95 (1-57860-066-9) Guild Pr IN.
Chandler, E., jt. auth. see Redfern, Darren.
Chandler, E. A., ed. Canine Medicine & Therapeutics. 3rd ed. (Illus.). 896p. 1990. pap. 72.95 (0-86542-824-7) Blackwell Sci.
Chandler, E. A., et al, eds. Feline Medicine & Therapeutics. (Illus.). 718p. pap. 69.95 (0-632-04133-1) Blackwell Sci.
Chandler, E. A., et al. Feline Medicine & Therapeutics. 2nd ed. (Illus.). 720p. 1994. 96.95 (0-632-03361-4) Blackwell Sci.
Chandler, E. J. Ancient Sagadahoc: A Narrative History. LC 96-71025. (Illus.). 1997. write for info. (0-89754-133-2) Dan River Pr.
Chandler, E. Ted & Bloomfield, Robert L. The Foremost Physician, the Farseeing Physician. LC 83-82069. 1983. 14.00 (0-9612242-0-7) Harbinger Med Pr NC.
Chandler, Edna W. Women in Prison. LC 72-88765. 7.95 (0-672-51702-7, Bobbs) Macmillan.
Chandler, Elizabeth. At First Sight. (Love Stories Ser.: V). (YA). (gr. 7-12). 1998. mass mkt. 3.99 (0-553-49254-3) BDD Bks Young Read.
— Hot Summer Nights. (Love Stories Ser.). 192p. (YA). (gr. 7-12). 1996. mass mkt. 3.99 (0-553-56671-7) Bantam.
— Hot Summer Nights. (Young Adult Ser.). 192p. (YA). (gr. 7 up). 1996. mass mkt. 3.99 (0-614-16412-5) Bantam.
— I Do. (Love Stories Ser.). 208p. (YA). (gr. 7-12). 1999. mass mkt. 3.99 (0-553-49275-6) BDD Bks Young Read.
— Kissed by an Angel: Power of Love. (YA). (gr. 7 up). 1995. mass mkt. 4.50 (0-671-89146-4, Archway) PB.
— Kissed by an Angel Collectors Edition: The Power of Love Soulmates. (J). (gr. 7 up). 1998. per. 6.99 (0-671-02346-2, Archway) PB.
***Chandler, Elizabeth.** Legacy of Lies, Dark Secrets, Vol. 1. 176p. 2000. 4.99 (0-7434-0028-3, Archway) PB.
Chandler, Elizabeth. Love Happens. (Love Stories Super Edition Ser.: No. 5). 208p. (Orig.). (YA). (gr. 7 up). 1997. mass mkt. 4.50 (0-553-49217-9) BDD Bks Young Read.
— Soulmates No. 3: Kissed by an Angel. (YA). (gr. 7 up). 1995. mass mkt. 3.99 (0-671-89147-2) PB.
— The Velveteen Rabbit. (Illus.). 16p. (J). (ps-3). 1998. 3.99 (0-689-81804-1) S&S Childrens.
Chandler, Elizabeth & Donahue, Joanne. Mini Quilt Celebrations. (Illus.). 28p. (Orig.). 1995. pap. 15.95 (0-9636371-4-2) Lizanne Pub.
— Quality Quilting Quarters. (Illus.). 240p. (Orig.). 1995. pap. 9.95 (0-9636371-3-4) Lizanne Pub.
— Quilting Designs from Grandma's Attic. (Illus.). 62p. (Orig.). 1994. pap. 8.95 (0-9636371-2-6) Lizanne Pub.
Chandler, Elizabeth L. A Study of the Sources of the Tales & Romances Written by Nathaniel Hawthorne Before 1853. (BCL1-PS American Literature Ser.). 64p. 1992. reprint ed. lib. bdg. 59.00 (0-7812-6723-4) Rprt Serv.
Chandler, Elizabeth M. Poetical Works of Elizabeth Margaret Chandler. LC 71-83930. (Black Heritage Library Collection). 1977. 27.95 (0-8369-8534-6) Ayer.
Chandler, F. M., compiled by. Cuyahoga County: Index to the Administration Dockets of the Probate Courts of Cuyahoga Co., Showing Estates Administered...from March 5, 1811 to Dec. 1, 1896. (Illus.). 192p. 1997. reprint ed. pap. 22.50 (0-8328-6309-2) Higginson Bk Co.
Chandler, F. W. Romances of Roguery: The Picaresque Novel in Spain. 1977. lib. bdg. 59.95 (0-8490-2540-0) Gordon Pr.
Chandler, Fiona. Ancient World. (World History Ser.). (Illus.). 96p. 1999. 29.95 (0-7460-2760-5, Usborne) EDC.
— Ancient World. (World History Ser.). 1999. 29.95 (1-58086-192-X) EDC.
***Chandler, Fiona, et al.** Prehistoric World. (World History Ser.). (Illus.). 96p. (YA). (gr. 3 up). 2000. 21.95 (0-7460-2758-3, Usborne) EDC.
Chandler, Frances G. Fundamentals of Business Communication. LC 94-24777. 704p. (C). 1994. text 33.75 (0-256-10699-1, Irwn McGrw-H) McGrw-H Hghr Educ.
Chandler, Frances G & Stoddard, Ted D. Fundamentals of Business Communication. (C). 1995. text 42.95 (0-256-19047-X, Irwn McGrw-H) McGrw-H Hghr Educ.
Chandler, Francis W., et al. Color Atlas & Textbook of the Histopathology of Mycotic Diseases. (Illus.). 333p. (C). (gr. 13). 1980. 129.00 (0-8151-1637-3, 09846) Mosby Inc.
Chandler, G. Chandler Family, Descendants of William & Annis Chandler Who Settled in Roxbury, Mass., 1637. (Illus.). 1323p. 1989. reprint ed. pap. 157.00 (0-8328-0387-1); reprint ed. lib. bdg. 167.00 (0-8328-0386-3) Higginson Bk Co.
Chandler, Gary. Environmental Causes. LC 97-22266. (Celebrity Activists Ser.). 64p. (YA). (gr. 5 up). 1997. 20.40 (0-8050-5232-1) TFC Bks NY.
Chandler, Gary, jt. auth. see Graham, Kevin.
***Chandler, Gary L.** An Invitation to Physical Education. (Fastback Ser.: No. 452). 50p. 1999. pap. 3.00 (0-87367-652-1, FB# 452) Phi Delta Kappa.
Chandler, George, jt. auth. see Saunders, W. L.
Chandler, George F., et al. The Policeman's Art: As Taught in the New York State School for Police. LC 70-156009. reprint ed. 32.50 (0-404-09172-5) AMS Pr.
Chandler, Gil. Getting Ready for a Career in Food Service. (Illus.). 48p. (J). (gr. 3-7). 1995. lib. bdg. 19.00 (0-516-35291-1) Childrens.
— The Green Berets. (Illus.). 48p. (J). (gr. 3-7). 1995. lib. bdg. 19.00 (0-516-35283-0) Childrens.
— Jeeps. (Cruisin' Ser.). (Illus.). 48p. (J). (gr. 3-6). 1995. 19.00 (0-516-35255-5) Childrens.
— Roller Coasters. (Cruisin' Ser.). (Illus.). 48p. (J). (gr. 3-6). 1995. 19.00 (0-516-35221-0) Childrens.
— Tractors. (Cruisin' Ser.). (Illus.). 48p. (J). (gr. 3-6). 1995. 19.00 (0-516-35254-7) Childrens.
Chandler, Gregory T., jt. ed. see Marra, James C.
Chandler, H., ed. Heat Treater's Guide: Practices & Procedures for Irons & Steels. 2nd ed. LC 94-73645. (Illus.). 600p. 1995. 229.00 (0-87170-520-6, 6400) ASM.
— Heat Treaters Guide: Practices & Procedures for Nonferrous Alloys. 669p. 1996. 229.00 (0-87170-565-6, 6325) ASM.
Chandler, H. W. A Practical Introduction to Greek Accentuation. 2nd rev. ed. (College Classical Ser.). xxxiii, 292p. (C). 1983. reprint ed. lib. bdg. 35.00 (0-89241-112-0) Caratzas.
Chandler, Harry. Metallurgy for the Non-Metallurgist. LC 98-4664. (Illus.). 284p. 1998. 146.00 (0-87170-652-0, 06169G) ASM.
***Chandler, Harry, ed.** Hardness Testing. 2nd ed. LC 99-46704. 200p. 1999. 115.00 (0-87170-640-7, 06823G) ASM.
Chandler, Harry E., ed. Technical Writer's Handbook. 418p. 1983. 20.00 (0-87170-151-0, 6028) ASM.
Chandler, Hildy & Chandler, Michael. Abiding in the Vine. 250p. 1993. pap. 10.99 (0-9635424-4-3) Gatehse Minist.
Chandler, Hildy H., jt. auth. see Chandler, Michael D.
***Chandler, J. A.** Comparative Public Administration. LC 00-20051. 2000. pap. write for info. (0-415-18458-4) Routledge.
Chandler, J. A. Local Government Today. 2nd ed. LC 95-26493. 280p. (C). 1996. text 19.95 (0-7190-4735-8, Pub. by Manchester Univ Pr) St Martin.
— Public Policy for Local Government. 224p. 1988. 65.00 (0-7099-3455-6, Pub. by C Helm) Routldge.
— X-Ray Microanalysis in the Electron Microscope. (Practical Methods in Electron Microscopy Ser.: Vol. 5, Pt. II). xxii,548p. 1981. pap. 45.50 (0-7204-0607-2, North Holland) Elsevier.
Chandler, J. A., ed. The Citizen's Charter. 190p. 1996. text 79.95 (1-85521-703-1, Pub. by Dartmth Pub) Ashgate Pub Co.
— Local Government in Liberal Democracies: An Introductory Survey. LC 92-13197. 240p. 1992. pap. 17.95 (0-415-08875-5) Routledge.
— Local Government in Liberal Democracies: An X International Survey. 240p. 1986. 47.50 (0-7099-3476-9, Pub. by C Helm) Routldge.
Chandler, J. A. & Lawless, Paul. Local Authorities & the Creation of Employment. 300p. 1985. text 77.95 (0-566-00765-7) Ashgate Pub Co.
Chandler, J. M., et al. Bibliography & Cross-Reference of Weed-Crop Interference & Corp Losses Due to Weeds. 142p. 1987. pap. 12.00 (0-911733-09-4) Weed Sci Soc.
Chandler, J. O., ed. Tabbner's Nursing Care: Theory & Practice. 3rd ed. (Illus.). 782p. 1998. pap. write for info. (0-443-05434-7) Church.
Chandler, James. Best Rated Jobs, Careers & Businesses That Can Change Your Life. 88p. (Orig.). 1996. pap. 19.97 (1-881760-01-4, BRJCB97) VistaTron.
— England in 1819: The Politics of Literary Culture & the Case of Romantic Historicism. LC 97-24564. 576p. 1998. 35.00 (0-226-10108-8) U Ch Pr.
***Chandler, James.** England in 1819: The Politics of Literary Culture & the Case of Romantic Historicism. 584p. 1999. pap. text 21.00 (0-226-10109-6) U Ch Pr.
Chandler, James, et al, eds. Questions of Evidence: Proof, Practice, & Persuasion Across the Disciplines. 528p. 1994. pap. text 19.95 (0-226-10083-9); lib. bdg. 45.00 (0-226-10082-0) U Ch Pr.
Chandler, James F. Jesus Is the Key: Poetry for the Soul. 128p. 1999. pap. 12.95 (1-892896-73-7) Buy Books.
Chandler, James K. Wordsworth's Second Nature: A Study of the Poetry & Politics. LC 84-5979. 326p. 1984. pap. text 17.95 (0-226-10081-2) U Ch Pr.
Chandler, Janet C. Time for Love: Assisted Living Viewed by One of the Very Old. LC 95-43611. (Illus.). 120p. (Orig.). 1996. pap. 9.00 (0-918949-91-2) Martz.
— Why Flowers Bloom. LC 93-39967. (Illus.). 128p. 1994. 12.00 (0-918949-38-6); pap. 8.00 (0-918949-37-8) Martz.
***Chandler, Jerry L. R. & Vijver, Gertrudis van de.** Closure: Emergent Organizations & Their Dynamics. LC 00-25698. (Annals of the New York Academy of Science Ser.). 2000. write for info. (1-57331-249-5) NY Acad Sci.
Chandler, Jim & Bearden, Brian. It's the Customer's Right to Say "No" The Professional's Guide to Sales Training. (Illus.). 100p. (Orig.). 1996. pap. 14.95 (0-9638525-8-2) Bearden.
Chandler, Jimmy D. Unto a Perfect Man. 150p. 1999. pap. 10.00 (0-7392-0068-2, PO2907) Morris Pubng.
Chandler, Joan. Women Without Husbands: An Exploration of the Margins of Marriage. LC 90-26212. 200p. 1991. text 35.00 (0-312-06107-2) St Martin.
Chandler, Joan M. Television & National Sport: The U. S. & Britain. (Sport & Society Ser.). 264p. 1988. text 27.50 (0-252-01516-9) U of Ill Pr.
— Television & National Sport: The U. S. & Britain. fac. ed. LC 87-35709. (Sport & Society Ser.). 259p. 1988. pap. 80.30 (0-7837-7612-8, 204736400007) Bks Demand.
***Chandler, John.** A Country House Christmas. 1999. 17.95 (0-7509-1820-9, Pub. by Sutton Publng) Intl Pubs Mktg.
Chandler, John. The Foundations of Education. unabridged ed. 204p. (C). 1998. pap. text 25.00 (1-893260-02-X) Harrison Pubg.
— John Leland's Itinerary: Travels in Tudor England. (Illus.). 640p. 1998. pap. 39.95 (0-7509-1751-2, Pub. by Sutton Pub Ltd) Intl Pubs Mktg.
Chandler, John. Salisbury: History & Guide. (History & Guide Ser.). 128p. 1992. pap. 13.95 (0-7509-0188-8, Pub. by Sutton Pub Ltd) Intl Pubs Mktg.

Chandler, John. Swindon: History & Guide. (History & Guide Ser.). (Illus.). 128p. 1992. pap. 13.95 (*0-7509-0190-X*, Pub. by Sutton Pub Ltd) Intl Pubs Mktg.
— Travels Through Stuart Britain The Adventures of John Taylor, the Water Poet. 1999. 36.95 (*0-7509-1944-2*) A Sutton.
Chandler, John, compiled by. Thomas Hardy's Christmas. (Illus.). 128p. 1997. pap. 17.95 (*0-7509-1434-3*, Pub. by Sutton Pub Ltd) Intl Pubs Mktg.
Chandler, Jon. Spanish Peaks: A Novel of Frontier Colorado, 1. 1999. pap. text 15.95 (*0-9662696-0-8*) Rodgers & Nelsen.
Chandler, Joseph E. The Colonial House. (Illus.). 350p. 1996. pap. 25.00 (*0-87556-830-0*) Saifer.
Chandler, K. A. & Bayliss, D. A. Corrosion Protection of Steel Structures. 428p. 1985. mass mkt. 166.95 (*0-85334-362-4*) Elsevier.
Chandler, K. A., jt. auth. see Bayliss, D. A.
Chandler, Karen, jt. auth. see Watstein, Sarah B.
Chandler, Kate, ed. see Chandler, Roy F.
Chandler, Katherine R. & Chandler, Roy F. Morgan's Park. (Illus.). 300p. (YA). 1997. lib. bdg. 35.00 (*1-885633-10-6*) Iron Brigade.
Chandler, Kathryn A., et al. Students' Reports of School Crime: 1989 & 1995. (Illus.). 52p. 1998. pap. text 20.00 (*0-7881-7312-X*) DIANE Pub.
Chandler, Kelly & Mapleton Teacher-Research Group Staff. Spelling Inquiry: How One Elementary School Caught the Mnemonic Plague. LC 99-10748. 176p. 1999. pap. 16.00 (*1-57110-303-1*) Stenhse Pubs.
Chandler, Kelly, jt. auth. see Power, Brenda.
***Chandler, Kurt.** Shaving Lessons: A Memoir of Father & Son. LC 99-87657. 256p. 2000. 22.95 (*0-8118-2360-1*) Chronicle Bks.
Chandler, Lana J. Invitation to DOS-JCL for Application Programmers. (Illus.). 120p. 1985. pap. text 13.50 (*0-89433-271-6*) Petrocelli.
— Invitation to DOS-Library Services for Application Programmers. (Illus.). 175p. 1988. pap. 19.95 (*0-89433-290-2*, NO. 8230) Petrocelli.
— Invitation to DOS-VSAM for Application. (Illus.). 160p. (Orig.). 1988. pap. text 16.95 (*0-89433-319-4*) Petrocelli.
Chandler, Lauryn. The Drifter's Gift. (Romance Ser.: No. 1268). 1997. per. 3.25 (*0-373-19268-1*, 1-19268-1) Harlequin Bks.
— Her Very Own Husband. (Romance Ser.). 1996. per. 3.25 (*0-373-19148-0*, 1-19148-5) Silhouette.
— Just Say I Do. (Romance Ser.: No. 1236). 1997. per. 3.25 (*0-373-19236-3*, 1-19236-8) Silhouette.
— Mr. Wright. (Romance Ser.). 1993. pap. 2.69 (*0-373-08936-8*, 5-08936-2) Silhouette.
— Mr. Wright. large type ed. LC 93-31004. 269p. 1994. lib. bdg. 14.95 (*0-7862-0125-8*) Thorndike Pr.
— Oh, Baby! (Silhouette Romance Ser.). 1994. per. 2.75 (*0-373-19033-6*, 1-19033-9) Harlequin Bks.
— Romantics Anonymous: Under the Mistletoe. (Romance Ser.). 1993. per. 2.75 (*0-373-08981-3*, 5-08981-8) Silhouette.
Chandler, Lester. Inflation in the United States 1940-1948. (FDR & the Era of the New Deal Ser.). 1976. reprint ed. lib. bdg. 39.50 (*0-306-70804-3*) Da Capo.
Chandler, Lester V. Benjamin Strong: Central Banker. Wilkins, Mira, ed. LC 78-3903. (International Finance Ser.). 1979. reprint ed. lib. bdg. 46.95 (*0-405-11208-4*) Ayer.
Chandler, Linda. Elementary Chemistry: Problems Guide. 96p. (C). 1993. pap. text 11.95 (*0-8403-8390-8*) Kendall-Hunt.
— Winning Strategies for Capital Formation: Secrets of Funding Start-Ups & Emerging Growth Firms Without Losing Control of Your Idea, Project or Company. 216p. 1996. pap. 32.50 (*0-7863-0892-3*, Irwn Prfssnl) McGraw-Hill Prof.
Chandler, Linda C. It's Just a K. I. S. S. Away: A Woman's Guide to Winning the Money Game. 320p. 1993. pap. 15.95 (*0-9639400-0-7*) Lrning Two-Thousand.
Chandler, Lizzie G. & Apple, Wynolia C. More than Food, Clothing, & Shelter: Stories of Lizzie Grey & Minnie Chandler. LC 98-91716. xxvi, 179 p. 1998. pap. 13.95 (*0-9666073-0-9*) Moon Lodge.
Chandler, Louis A. Assessing Stress in Children. LC 85-12188. 240p. 1985. 55.00 (*0-275-90072-X*, C0072, Praeger Pubs) Greenwood.
Chandler, Louis A. & Johnson, Virginia J. Using Projective Techniques with Children: A Guide to Clinical Assessment. (Illus.). 140p. 1991. pap. 21.95 (*0-398-06051-7*) C C Thomas.
— Using Projective Techniques with Children: A Guide to Clinical Assessment. (Illus.). 140p. (C). 1991. text 34.95 (*0-398-05726-5*) C C Thomas.
Chandler, Lynette S. & Lane, Shelly J., eds. Children with Prenatal Drug Exposure. LC 96-19136. (Physical & Occupational Therapy in Pediatrics Monographs: Vol. 16, Nos. 1/2). 199p. (C). 1996. 39.95 (*1-56024-837-8*) Haworth Pr.
— Children with Prenatal Drug Exposure. LC 96-19136. (Physical & Occupational Therapy in Pediatrics Monographs: Vol. 16, Nos. 1/2). 199p. (C). 1997. pap. 19.95 (*0-7890-0221-3*) Haworth Pr.
Chandler, M. Tournament Chess, Vol. 1. Miles, A. J., ed. 128p. 1981. pap. 21.95 (*0-08-026888-9*, Pergamon Pr) Elsevier.
Chandler, M., ed. Tournament Chess, Vol. 2. (Illus.). 128p. 1982. pap. 21.95 (*0-08-026891-9*, Pergamon Pr) Elsevier.
— Tournament Chess, Vol. 12. 215p. 1984. pap. 21.95 (*0-08-029758-7*, Pergamon Pr) Elsevier.
— Tournament Chess, Vol. 14. 178p. 1984. pap. 32.00 (*0-08-029760-9*, Pergamon Pr) Elsevier.
— Tournament Chess, Vol. 15. 188p. 1985. pap. 32.00 (*0-08-029761-7*, Pergamon Pr) Elsevier.
— Tournament Chess, Vol. 16. (Illus.). 176p. 1985. pap. 32.00 (*0-08-029762-5*, Pub. by PPL) Elsevier.
Chandler, M. & Miles, A. J., eds. Tournament Chess. (Tournament Chess Ser.: Vol. 5). 176p. 1982. pap. 21.95 (*0-08-029720-X*) Elsevier.
— Tournament Chess, Vol. 3. (Illus.). 170p. 1982. pap. 21.95 (*0-08-026892-7*, Pergamon Pr) Elsevier.
— Tournament Chess, Vol. 4. 150p. 1982. pap. 21.95 (*0-08-026893-5*, Pergamon Pr) Elsevier.
— Tournament Chess, Vol. 7. (Illus.). 143p. 1983. pap. 21.95 (*0-08-029736-6*, Pergamon Pr) Elsevier.
— Tournament Chess, Vol. 8. (Illus.). 200p. 1983. pap. 21.95 (*0-08-029737-4*, Pergamon Pr) Elsevier.
— Tournament Chess, Vol. 9. (Illus.). 176p. 1983. pap. 21.95 (*0-08-029742-0*, 62, Pergamon Pr) Elsevier.
— Tournament Chess, Vol. 10. 166p. 1983. pap. 21.95 (*0-08-029743-9*, Pergamon Pr) Elsevier.
Chandler, M., ed. see Varnusz, Egon.
Chandler, M. J., ed. see Holliday, St. G.
Chandler, Margaret K. Management Rights & Union Interests. LC 78-6226. (Illus.). 329p. 1978. reprint ed. lib. bdg. 89.50 (*0-313-20495-0*, CHMA, Greenwood Pr) Greenwood.
Chandler, Margaret K., jt. auth. see Sayles, Leonard R.
Chandler, Marilyn R. Dwelling in the Text: Houses in American Fiction. (Illus.). 326p. 1991. 45.00 (*0-520-07363-0*, Pub. by U CA Pr) Cal Prin Full Svc.
Chandler, Marsha A., jt. ed. see Atkinson, Michael M.
Chandler, Marthe A., jt. ed. see Jelen, Ted G.
Chandler, Mary. Pasta Math Problem Solving for "Alice in Pastaland" 40 Activities to Connect Math & Literature. 1997. pap., teacher ed. 12.95 (*1-57091-154-1*) Charlesbridge Pub.
Chandler, Melbourne C. Of Gary Owen & Glory: The History of the Seventh U. S. Calvary. 1976. 40.95 (*0-8488-0959-9*) Amereon Ltd.
Chandler, Michael. The Life & Work of John Mason Neale. 241p. 1995. pap. 17.95 (*0-85244-305-6*, 944, Pub. by Gra1cewing) Morehouse Pub.
— Stepfathering. limited ed. 31p. 1986. pap. 7.95 (*0-944754-11-2*) Pudding Hse Pubns.
Chandler, Michael & Chapman, David, eds. Criteria for Competence: Controversies in the Conceptualization & Assessment of Children's Abilities. 296p. (C). 1991. text 59.95 (*0-8058-0606-7*) L Erlbaum Assocs.
Chandler, Michael, jt. auth. see Chandler, Hildy.
Chandler, Michael, jt. auth. see Scotland, Nigel.
Chandler, Michael D. & Chandler, Hildy H. How to Stay Married in a Divorce Minded World. LC 96-124161. 28p. 1994. pap. 4.99 (*1-885423-00-4*) New Life Minist.
Chandler, Mittie O. Urban Homesteading: Programs & Policies, 9. LC 88-15481. 164p. 1988. 47.95 (*0-313-26338-8*, Greenwood Pr) Greenwood.
Chandler, Mitzi. Gentle Reminders for Co-Dependents: Daily Affirmations. 375p. 1989. pap. 6.95 (*1-55874-020-1*) Health Comm.
— I See Something Grand. LC 94-75653. 32p. (J). 1995. pap. 8.95 (*0-938216-50-3*) GCA.
Chandler, Murray. The Complete C3 Sicilian. LC 96-78754. (New American Batsford Chess Library). 240p. (Orig.). 1997. pap. 22.50 (*1-879479-50-8*) ICE WA.
***Chandler, Murray.** How to Beat Your Dad at Chess. 1998. 14.95 (*1-901983-05-6*) Gambit.
Chandler, Norman A. & Chandler, Roy F. Death from Afar: Marine Corps Sniping, Vol. I. (Illus.). 222p. 1992. 59.95 (*1-885633-00-9*) Iron Brigade.
— Death from Afar: Marine Corps Sniping, Vol. II. (Illus.). 213p. 1993. 59.95 (*1-885633-01-7*) Iron Brigade.
— Death from Afar: Marine Corps Sniping, Vol. V. (Illus.). 300p. 1999. 59.95 (*1-885633-11-4*) Iron Brigade.
— Death from Afar: The History of USMC Sniping, Vol. IV. (Illus.). 235p. 1996. 59.95 (*1-885633-04-1*) Iron Brigade.
— Death from Afar Vol. III: The History of USMC Sniping. (Illus.). 260p. 1994. 59.95 (*1-885633-02-5*) Iron Brigade.
Chandler, Norman A., jt. auth. see Chandler, Roy F.
Chandler, P. G. Some Methods of Teaching in Six Representative Teachers' Colleges of the United States. LC 77-176634. (Columbia University. Teachers College. Contributions to Education Ser.: No. 425). reprint ed. 37.50 (*0-404-55425-3*) AMS Pr.
Chandler, Patricia. At Her Captain's Command. (American Romance Ser.). 1993. per. 3.50 (*0-373-16497-1*, 1-16497-9) Harlequin Bks.
— Deception Bay. (Superromance Ser.: No. 489). 1992. mass mkt. 3.29 (*0-373-70489-5*, 1-70489-5) Harlequin Bks.
— Mooncaller. (Superromance Ser.). 1994. mass mkt. 3.50 (*0-373-70582-4*, 1-70582-1) Harlequin Bks.
— A Timeless Christmas. (American Romance Ser.). 1994. per. 3.50 (*0-373-16564-1*, 1-16564-6) Harlequin Bks.
Chandler, Patricia M., ed. see McDonough, Connie.
Chandler, Paul-Gordon. God's Global Mosaic: What We Can Learn from Christians Around the World. LC 99-53606. 144p. 2000. pap. 9.99 (*0-8308-2251-8*) InterVarsity.
Chandler, Pauline. Ecology. (Hands-On Minds-On Science Ser.). (Illus.). 96p. 1994. pap., teacher ed. 11.95 (*1-55734-633-X*) Tchr Create Mat.
Chandler, Peleg W. American Criminal Trials, 2 Vols, Set. LC 77-109618. (Select Bibliographies Reprint Ser.). 1977. 66.95 (*0-8369-5227-8*) Ayer.
— American Criminal Trials, 2 vols., Set. LC 71-113576. reprint ed. 87.50 (*0-404-01445-3*) AMS Pr.
Chandler, Peter, ed. see Academy of Marketing Science Staff.
Chandler, Phyllis & Burney, Joan R. Sharing the Faith with Your Child: From Birth to Age Six. LC 84-80854. 96p. 1984. pap. 3.95 (*0-89243-205-5*) Liguori Pubns.
Chandler, Phyllis A. A Place for Me: Including Children with Special Needs in Early Care & Education Settings. LC 94-65096. (Illus.). 96p. 1994. pap. text 6.00 (*0-935989-59-5*, 237) Natl Assn Child Ed.
Chandler, R. M., jt. auth. see Bichart, K. J.
Chandler, Rachel. The Most Important Lessons in Life. 1998. 10.95 (*1-86204-421-X*, Pub. by Element MA) Penguin Putnam.
— The Most Important Lessons in Life: Letters to a Young Girl. LC 98-24918. (Illus.). 128p. 1998. 10.95 (*1-86204-420-1*, Pub. by Element MA) Penguin Putnam.
Chandler, Ralph C. A Centennial History of the American Administrative State. 917p. 1987. write for info. (*0-318-61270-4*) Macmillan.
— The Constitutional Law Dictionary: Covering the 1987-1996 Terms of the Supreme Court. 280p. 1998. lib. bdg., suppl. ed. 65.00 (*0-87436-925-8*) ABC-CLIO.
— The Constitutional Law Dictionary: Covering the 1991-1994 Terms of the Supreme Court, Vol. 1, Suppl. 3. LC 84-12320. 189p. 1995. lib. bdg. 65.00 (*0-87436-758-1*) ABC-CLIO.
Chandler, Ralph C. & Plano, Jack C. The Public Administration Dictionary. 2nd ed. LC 87-32045. (Clio Dictionaries in Political Science Ser.). 430p. 1988. pap. text 24.75 (*0-87436-499-X*) ABC-CLIO.
— The Public Administration Dictionary. 2nd ed. LC 87-32045. (Clio Dictionaries in Political Science Ser.). 430p. 1988. lib. bdg. 51.50 (*0-87436-498-1*) ABC-CLIO.
Chandler, Ralph C., et al. Constitutional Law Deskbook. LC 87-80244. 1991. write for info. (*0-317-03370-7*) West Group.
— Constitutional Law Deskbook. 2nd ed. LC 93-77162. 1993. 112.50 (*0-317-01499-4*) West Group.
Chandler, Randy, jt. auth. see Winter-Damon, T.
Chandler, Raymond. Adieu, Ma Jolie. (FRE.). 301p. 1988. pap. 11.95 (*0-7859-2102-8*, 2070380793) Fr & Eur.
— The Big Sleep. 1992. pap. 9.00 (*0-394-23906-7*) Vin Bks.
— The Big Sleep. 288p. 1995. reprint ed. 35.00 (*1-883402-16-6*) S&S Trade.
— The Big Sleep. LC 87-40472. (Crime Ser.). 1988. reprint ed. pap. 11.00 (*0-394-75828-5*) Vin Bks.
— The Big Sleep: A Film Adaptation Directed by Howard Hawks. Garrett, George et al, eds. LC 71-135273. (Film Scripts Ser.). 1989. reprint ed. pap. 19.95 (*0-89197-677-9*) Irvington.
— The Big Sleep & Farewell, My Lovely. 546p. 1995. 17.95 (*0-679-60140-6*) Random.
— The Blue Dahlia: A Screenplay. Date not set. lib. bdg. 21.95 (*0-8488-0960-2*) Amereon Ltd.
— Charades Pour Ecroules. (FRE.). 253p. 1991. pap. 10.95 (*0-7859-2170-2*, 2070384098) Fr & Eur.
— La Dame Du Lac. (FRE.). 258p. 1988. pap. 10.95 (*0-7859-2088-9*, 2070379434) Fr & Eur.
— Fais Pas Ta Rosiere! (FRE.). 284p. 1987. pap. 11.95 (*0-7859-2058-7*, 2070377997) Fr & Eur.
— Farewell My Lovely. 704p. 1991. Not sold separately (*0-614-32015-1*) Random Hse Value.
— Farewell, My Lovely. 1992. pap. 10.00 (*0-679-74090-2*) Random.
— Farewell, My Lovely. 1992. pap. 10.00 (*0-394-23907-5*) Vin Bks.
— Farewell, My Lovely. large type ed. LC 93-46414. 419p. 1994. reprint ed. lib. bdg. 21.95 (*0-7862-0174-6*) Thorndike Pr.
— Farewell, My Lovely. LC 87-40473. (Crime Ser.). 1988. reprint ed. pap. 11.00 (*0-394-75827-7*) Vin Bks.
— Four Complete Philip Marlowe Novels. 1986. 8.98 (*0-685-43727-2*, 618117) Random Hse Value.
— La Grande Fenetre. (FRE.). 276p. 1989. pap. 10.95 (*0-7859-2236-9*, 207038103X) Fr & Eur.
— Le Grande Sommeil. (FRE.). 252p. 1987. pap. 10.95 (*0-7859-2071-4*, 2070378659) Fr & Eur.
— The High Window. 704p. 1991. Not sold separately (*0-614-32016-X*) Random Hse Value.
— High Window. 1992. pap. 10.00 (*0-394-23908-3*) Vin Bks.
— The High Window. large type ed. LC 93-49646. 320p. 1994. 21.95 (*0-7862-0176-2*) Thorndike Pr.
— High Window. large type ed. 23.95 (*1-85695-367-X*, Pub. by ISIS Lrg Prnt) Transaction Pubs.
— The High Window. LC 87-40474. (Crime Ser.). 1988. reprint ed. pap. 11.00 (*0-394-75826-9*) Vin Bks.
— Le Jade du Mandarin. (FRE.). 247p. 1989. pap. 10.95 (*0-7859-2119-2*, 2070381455) Fr & Eur.
— The Lady in the Lake. Date not set. lib. bdg. 20.95 (*0-8488-2136-X*) Amereon Ltd.
— The Lady in the Lake. 704p. 1991. Not sold separately (*0-614-32017-8*) Random Hse Value.
— The Lady in the Lake. LC 87-40475. (Crime Ser.). 288p. 1988. pap. 11.00 (*0-394-75825-0*) Vin Bks.
— Lady in the Lake. 1992. pap. 10.00 (*0-679-74088-0*) Random.
— Lady in the Lake. 288p. 1994. 35.00 (*1-883402-94-8*) S&S Trade.
— Lady in the Lake. 1992. pap. 10.00 (*0-394-23909-1*) Vin Bks.
— The Lady in the Lake. large type ed. 23.95 (*1-85695-362-9*, Pub. by ISIS Lrg Prnt) Transaction Pubs.
— The Lady in the Lake. large type ed. LC 93-49683. (Cloak & Dagger Ser.). 347p. 1994. lib. bdg. 20.95 (*0-7862-0175-4*) Thorndike Pr.
— Later Novels & Other Writings: The Lady in the Lake; The Little Sister; The Long Goodbye; Playback: Double Indemnity; Essays & Letters. McShane, Frank, ed. 1076p. 1995. 35.00 (*1-883011-08-6*, Pub. by Library of America) Penguin Putnam.
— The Little Sister. 256p. 1994. 35.00 (*1-883402-79-4*) S&S Trade.
— The Little Sister. LC 87-45918. (Crime Ser.). 352p. 1988. pap. 10.00 (*0-394-75767-X*) Vin Bks.
— The Long Goodbye. 1992. pap. 10.00 (*0-679-74087-2*) Random.
— The Long Goodbye. LC 87-45920. (Crime Ser.). 384p. 1988. pap. 12.00 (*0-394-75768-8*) Vin Bks.
— The Long Goodbye. 1992. pap. 10.00 (*0-394-23910-5*) Vin Bks.
— Other Side of Raymond Chandler. 23.95 (*0-88411-421-X*) Amereon Ltd.
***Chandler, Raymond.** Philip Marlowe. (Illus.). 397p. 1999. per. 16.00 (*0-671-03890-7*) PB.
Chandler, Raymond. Pick up on Noon Street. 200p. 1993. reprint ed. lib. bdg. 16.95 (*1-56849-008-9*) Buccaneer Bks.
— Playback. LC 87-45920. (Crime Ser.). 240p. 1988. pap. 10.00 (*0-394-75766-1*) Vin Bks.
— Raymond Chandler Speaking. Gardiner, Dorothy & Sorley Walker, Kathrine, eds. LC 96-34571. (Illus.). 275p. 1997. 13.95 (*0-520-20835-8*, Pub. by U CA Pr) Cal Prin Full Svc.
— Raymond Chandler Speaking. Gardiner, Dorothy & Sorley, Kathrine, eds. LC 76-146855. (Select Bibliographies Reprint Ser.). 1977. reprint ed. 23.95 (*0-8369-5622-2*) Ayer.
— The Simple Art of Murder. LC 87-45923. (Crime Ser.). 288p. 1988. pap. 12.00 (*0-394-75765-3*) Vin Bks.
— Stories & Early Novels: Pulp Stories; The Big Sleep; Farewell, My Lovely; The High Window. McShane, Frank, ed. LC 94-43705. 1199p. 1995. 35.00 (*1-883011-07-8*, Pub. by Library of America) Penguin Putnam.
— Sur un Air de Navaja. (FRE.). 256p. 1987. pap. 10.95 (*0-7859-2067-6*, 2070378497) Fr & Eur.
— Trouble Is My Business. 1992. pap. 9.00 (*0-679-74086-4*) Random.
— Trouble Is My Business. LC 87-45924. (Crime Ser.). 1988. pap. 10.00 (*0-394-75764-5*) Vin Bks.
— Trouble Is My Business. 1992. pap. 9.00 (*0-394-23911-3*) Vin Bks.
— Un Tueur sous la Pluie. (FRE.). 245p. 1988. pap. 10.95 (*0-7859-2082-X*, 2070379108) Fr & Eur.
Chandler, Raymond & Parker, Robert B. Poodle Springs. 1990. mass mkt. 5.99 (*0-425-12343-X*) Berkley Pub.
— Poodle Springs. large type ed. 303p. 1990. reprint ed. lib. bdg. 11.95 (*0-89621-977-1*) Thorndike Pr.
Chandler, Raymond, et al. Fallen Angels: Six Noir Tales Told for Television. LC 93-22888. 312p. 1993. pap. 14.00 (*0-8021-3383-5*, Grove) Grove-Atltic.
Chandler, Richard. Reisen in Griechenland (Travels in Greece, Deutscsh) xvi, 432p. 1985. reprint ed. 70.00 (*3-487-05741-7*) G Olms Pubs.
— Reisen in Kleinasien (Travels in Asia Minor, Deutsch) (GER.). xx, 396p. 1976. reprint ed. write for info. (*3-487-05997-5*) G Olms Pubs.
Chandler, Richard E. Hausdorff Compactifications. LC 76-46693. (Lecture Notes in Pure & Applied Mathematics Ser.: No. 23). 160p. reprint ed. pap. 49.60 (*0-7837-0835-1*, 204114900019) Bks Demand.
Chandler, Richard E. & Schwartz, Kessel. A New History of Spanish Literature. rev. ed. LC 91-2667. 479p. 1991. text 67.50 (*0-8071-1699-8*) La State U Pr.
Chandler, Richard E., tr. see Montero de Pedro, Jose.
Chandler, Richard F. Aircraft Crashworthiness. 400p. 1995. 79.00 (*1-56091-597-8*, PT-50) Soc Auto Engineers.
Chandler, Robert, ed. Portable Platanov: The Centenary of His Birth. (Glas Ser.: Vol. 20). (Illus.). 200p. 2000. pap. 14.95 (*1-56663-272-2*, Pub. by I R Dee) Natl Bk Netwk.
Chandler, Robert, tr. see Platonov, Andrei.
Chandler, Robert, tr. see Schweitzer, Viktoria.
Chandler, Robert J. San Francisco Clearing House Certificates: Last of California's Private Money. 32p. (Orig.). 1986. pap. text 3.95 (*0-932151-01-9*) Gypsyfoot Ent.
Chandler, Robert W. The New Face of War: Weapons of Mass Destruction & the Revitalization of America's Transoceanic Military Strategy. LC 97-68443. (Trilogy on Weapons of Mass Destruction & 21st Century Warfare: Vol. 3). 480p. 1998. 33.00 (*0-9650770-2-0*) AMCODA Pr.
— Tomorrow's War, Today's Decisions: Iraqi Weapons of Mass Destruction & the Implications of WMD-Armed Adversaries for Future U. S. Military Strategy. LC 96-84124. (Trilogy on Weapons of Mass Destruction & 21st Century Warfare: Vol. 1). 243p. 1996. pap. 17.95 (*0-9650770-0-4*) AMCODA Pr.
Chandler, Roger A. Fentress Bradburn Architects. LC 95-45336. (Illus.). 224p. 1996. 50.00 (*1-55835-146-9*) AIA Press.
Chandler, Roy, jt. auth. see Marriott, Neil.
Chandler, Roy A. & Edwards, John. British Audit Practice 1884-1900: A Case Law Perspective. LC 93-39273. (New Works in Accounting History). 232p. 1994. text 20.00 (*0-8153-1720-4*) Garland.
Chandler, Roy A. & Edwards, John, eds. Recurring Issues in Auditing: Professional Debate, 1875-1900. LC 93-29294. (New Works in Accounting History). 384p. 1994. text 25.00 (*0-8153-1719-0*) Garland.
***Chandler, Roy F.** Sniper One: USMC Snipers in Action. Chandler, Kate, ed. 350p. 1999. 39.95 (*1-885633-17-3*) Iron Brigade.
Chandler, Roy F. & Chandler, Norman A. Carlos Hathcock: White Feather - USMC Scout Sniper. large type ed. (Illus.). 275p. 1997. lib. bdg. 59.95 (*1-885633-09-2*) Iron Brigade.
Chandler, Roy F., jt. auth. see Chandler, Katherine R.
Chandler, Roy F., jt. auth. see Chandler, Norman A.
Chandler, Russel. Last Olympics. 376p. 1996. 22.95 (*0-9646872-2-4*) Wessex House.
Chandler, Russell. Feeding the Flock: Restaurants & Churches You'd Stand in Line For. LC 97-78132. 150p. 1998. pap. 14.95 (*1-56699-196-X*, AL187) Alban Inst.

C

An Asterisk (*) at the beginning of an entry indicates that the title is appearing for the first time.

— La Nueva Era. Chavez, Moises, tr. from ENG.Tr. of Understanding the New Age. (SPA.). 288p. 1992. pap. 10.50 (*0-311-05045-X*) Casa Bautista.
— Racing Toward Two Thousand One: The Forces Shaping America's Religious Future. LC 91-50588. 272p. 1992. 18.00 (*0-685-55367-1*) Harper SF.
Chandler, S., jt. auth. see Bostock, L.
Chandler, S., jt. ed. see Bostock, L.
Chandler, Seth. History of the Town of Shirley, Mass., from Its Earliest Settlement to 1882. (Illus.). 744p. 1989. reprint ed. lib. bdg. 74.50 (*0-8328-0912-8*, MA0099) Higginson Bk Co.
Chandler, Shirley K., jt. auth. see Czerlinsky, Thomas.
Chandler, Stacy. Happily Ever After. LC 93-86925. 208p. 1993. per. 10.00 (*0-9639185-0-8*) Speculators.
Chandler, Stanley B. & Molinaro, Julius A., eds. The World of Dante: Six Studies in Language & Thought. LC 66-7811. 143p. reprint ed. pap. 44.40 (*0-608-10717-4*, 202046600018) Bks Demand.
Chandler, Stephan. Quips, for 3 Recorders (ATB) (Contemporary Consort Ser.: No. 30). 15p. 1995. pap. text 7.00 (*1-56571-122-X*) PRB Prods.
***Chandler, Steve.** 50 Ways to Create Great Relationships: How to Stop Taking & Start Giving. 192p. 2000. 18.99 (*1-56414-510-7*) Career Pr Inc.
Chandler, Steve. 100 Ways to Motivate Yourself. 192p. 1996. 16.99 (*1-56414-249-3*) Career Pr Inc.
— Reinventing Yourself: How to Become the Person You've Always Wanted to Be. LC 98-21996. 192p. 1998. 18.99 (*1-56414-391-0*) Career Pr Inc.
***Chandler, Steve.** 17 Lies That Are Holding You Back & the Truth That Will Set You Free: Find Your Soul's True Purpose. 208p. 2000. 22.95 (*1-58063-130-4*) Renaissance.
Chandler, Steven D. Radioactive Waste Control & Controversy: The History of Radioactive Waste Regulation in the U. K. (Environmental Technology Ser.: Vol. 3). 220p. 1997. text 49.00 (*90-5699-065-9*); pap. text 18.00 (*90-5699-066-7*) Gordon & Breach.
Chandler, Susan M. Competing Realities: Issues in Mental Health Advocacy. LC 89-22815. 208p. 1990. 55.00 (*0-275-93356-3*, C3356, Greenwood Pr) Greenwood.
***Chandler, Ted.** A+ Certification Core Module Ace It! (Ace It Ser.). 360p. 1999. pap. 29.99 (*0-7645-3302-9*) IDG Bks.
Chandler, Ted, jt. auth. see Bloomfield, Robert.
Chandler, Ted, jt. auth. see Bloomfield, Robert L.
Chandler, Tertius. Four Thousand Years of Urban Growth: A Historical Census. LC 86-31122. 676p. 1987. lib. bdg. 129.95 (*0-88946-207-0*) E Mellen.
— Godly Kings & Early Ethics. rev. ed. (Illus.). 220p. 1981. 24.00 (*0-9603872-4-2*) Gutenberg.
— Remote Kingdoms. rev. ed. (Illus.). 111p. 1981. pap. 14.00 (*0-9603872-5-0*) Gutenberg.
— The Tax We Need. 2nd rev. ed. 103p. 1980. pap. 6.00 (*0-9603872-3-4*) Gutenberg.
***Chandler, Timothy.** Going Berserk. 100p. 1999. 26.95 (*1-929409-06-0*) Blade Pubg.
Chandler, Timothy J., jt. ed. see Nauright, John.
***Chandler, Timothy J. L. & Nauright, John, eds.** Making the Rugby World: Race, Gender, Commerce. LC 99-27732. (Sport in the Global Society Ser.: No. 10). 256p. 1999. 59.50 (*0-7146-4853-1*); pap. 24.50 (*0-7146-4411-0*) F Cass Pubs.
Chandler, Tom. The Sound the Moon Makes As It Watches. (Illus.). 68p. (Orig.). 1988. 6.00 (*0-318-64091-0*) Poets Pr.
— Wingbones: Poems. LC 96-53131. 1997. write for info. (*0-930095-08-1*) Signal Bks.
***Chandler, Tomasita M. & Heinzerling, Barbara M., eds.** Children & Adolescents in the Market Place: Twenty-Five Years of Academic Research. 1999. 145.00 (*0-87650-383-0*) Pierian.
Chandler, Tracey, jt. auth. see Taylor, Joelle.
Chandler-Vaccaro, Kimberly, jt. auth. see Kriegel, Lorraine P.
Chandler, Vicki, jt. auth. see Ulrich, Kathy.
Chandler, Vishwa & Craven, Roy C., eds. Painters of the Pahari Schools. LC 98-902737. 1998. 59.00 (*81-85026-41-6*) Art Media Resources.
Chandler, W. U., jt. auth. see Gibbons, John H.
Chandler, Walker. The Evangeline Manuscript. 1998. 24.95 (*0-9661246-1-8*) Pike Publ.
Chandler, Wallace L. Advanced Shallow Water Treasure Hunting with the Fisher 1280-X Aquanaut Metal Detector. 64p. 1991. 6.00 (*1-883170-01-X*) FRL.
***Chandler, Walter M.** The Trial of Jesus: From a Lawyer's Standpoint, 2 vols. xxxxvi, 772p. 1999. reprint ed. 155.00 (*1-56169-573-4*) Gaunt.
Chandler, Walter M. The Trial of Jesus from a Lawyer's Standpoint, 2 vols., Set. LC 83-82312. 1983. reprint ed. 155.00 (*0-89941-294-7*, 302980) W S Hein.
Chandler, Wayne B. Ancient Future. 230p. (C). 1999. pap. 18.95 (*1-57478-001-8*) Black Classic.
Chandler-Wilde, S. N., jt. auth. see Falconer, R. A.
Chandler, William F., jt. auth. see Rubin, Jonathan M.
Chandler, William J. The Science of History: A Cybernetic Approach. (Studies in Cybernetics: Vol. 7). x, 153p. 1984. text 135.00 (*2-88124-012-7*) Gordon & Breach.
Chandler, William M., jt. ed. see Bakvis, Herman.
Chandler, William U. Banishing Tobacco. LC 85-52313. (Worldwatch Papers). 1986. pap. 5.00 (*0-916468-68-2*) Worldwatch Inst.
— The Changing Role of the Market in National Economies. LC 86-50992. (Worldwatch Papers). 60p. (Orig.). 1986. pap. 5.00 (*0-916468-73-9*) Worldwatch Inst.
***Chandler, William U.** Energy & Environmental Policies in the Transition Economies: Between Cold War & Global Warming. LC 00-39880. 256p. 2000. pap. 34.00 (*0-8133-3812-3*) Westview.
Chandler, William U. Energy Productivity: Key to Environmental Protection & Economic Progress. (Worldwatch Papers). 1985. pap. 5.00 (*0-916468-63-1*) Worldwatch Inst.
— Improving World Health: A Least-cost Strategy. LC 84-51598. (Worldwatch Papers). 1984. pap. 5.00 (*0-916468-59-3*) Worldwatch Inst.
— Investing in Children. LC 85-51252. (Worldwatch Papers). 1985. pap. 5.00 (*0-916468-64-X*) Worldwatch Inst.
— Materials Recycling: The Virtue of Necessity. 1983. pap. write for info. (*0-916468-55-0*) Worldwatch Inst.
Chandler, William U., ed. Carbon Emissions Control Strategies: Case Studies in International Cooperation. LC 90-19136. (Illus.). 281p. 1990. reprint ed. pap. 87.20 (*0-608-04185-8*, 206492000011) Bks Demand.
***Chandler-Willis, Lynn.** Unholy Covenant: A True Story of Murder in North Carolina. LC 00-8522. 2000. 17.95 (*1-886039-41-0*) Addicus Bks.
***Chandler, Wilma M., ed.** The Ultimate Scene Study Series Vol. 1: 101 Short Scenes for Groups. 480p. 2000. pap. 19.95 (*1-57525-222-8*) Smith & Kraus.
— The Ultimate Scene Study Series Vol. 4: 104 Short Scenes for 4 Actors. 480p. 2000. pap. 19.95 (*1-57525-221-X*) Smith & Kraus.
***Chandler, Wilma Marcus, ed.** The Ultimate Scene Study Series Vol. 3: 103 Short Scenes for 3 Actors. 480p. 2000. pap. 19.95 (*1-57525-220-1*) Smith & Kraus.
Chandler, Yvonne J. Neal-Schuman Guide to Finding Legal & Regulatory Information on the Internet. LC 97-27285. 400p. 1997. 135.00 (*1-55570-306-2*) Neal-Schuman.
Chandmal, Asit. One Thousand Suns: Krishnamurti at Eighty-Five, & the Last Walk. (Illus.). 128p. 1995. 60.00 (*0-89381-631-0*) Aperture.
Chandna, R. C. Spatial Dimensions of Scheduled Castes in India. (C). 1989. 22.50 (*81-7076-020-8*, Pub. by Intellect Pub Hse) S Asia.
***Chandniwala, K. M.** Recent Advances in Plant Diseases, 5 vols. 1375p. 1998. pap. 1750.00 (*81-7488-163-8*, Pub. by Print Hse) St Mut.
Chandniwala, K. M. Recent Advances in Plant Pathology, 6 vols., Vols. 1-6. 1734p. 1995. pap. 1150.00 (*81-7488-150-6*, Pub. by Print Hse) St Mut.
Chandoha, Walter. The Literary Gardener. LC 97-28061. (Illus.). 125p. 1997. 19.50 (*1-57223-083-5*, 0835) Willow Creek Pr.
Chandola, Anoop. Contactics: The Daily Drama of Human Contact. 152p. (Orig.). (C). 1992. pap. 24.50 (*0-8191-8773-9*); lib. bdg. 47.50 (*0-8191-8772-0*) U Pr of Amer.
— Folk Drumming in the Himalayas: A Linguistic Approach to Music. LC 76-23549. (Illus.). 1977. 32.50 (*0-404-15403-4*) AMS Pr.
— Mystic & Love Poetry of Medieval Hindi with Introductions, Texts, Grammar, Notes, Translations & Glossary. 147p. 1982. 12.50 (*0-88065-236-5*, Pub. by Today Tomorrow) Scholarly Pubns.
— Situation to Sentence: An Evolutionary Method for Descriptive Linguistics. LC 78-7125. 1979. 32.50 (*0-404-16038-7*) AMS Pr.
— A Systematic Translation of Hindi-Urdu into English. LC 79-127886. 365p. 1970. pap. 25.95 (*0-8165-0289-7*) U of Ariz Pr.
— The Way to True Worship: A Popular Story of Hinduism. 152p. (Orig.). (C). 1990. pap. text 21.00 (*0-8191-8048-3*); lib. bdg. 44.00 (*0-8191-8047-5*) U Pr of Amer.
Chandola, L. M. Women in the Unorganized Sector. 202p. 1993. 30.00 (*0-685-60067-X*, Pub. by Radiant Pubs) S Asia.
— Women in the Unorganized Sector. LC 95-902025. (C). 1995. 14.00 (*81-7027-195-9*, Pub. by Radiant Pubs) S Asia.
Chandonnet, Ann. Alaska's Arts, Crafts & Collectibles. Chandonnet, Fernand L., ed. LC 98-92499. (Illus.). 215p. 1998. pap. 20.55 (*0-9662999-0-6*) Chandonnet.
— The Birthday Party. (Illus.). 36p. (J). 1995. pap. 11.95 (*0-9632596-3-6*) McRoy & Blackburn.
— Canoeing in the Rain. (Illus.). pap. 10.00 (*0-932191-10-X*) Mr Cogito Pr.
— Chief Stephen's Parky: One Year in the Life of an Athapascan Girl. Gilliland, Hap, ed. (Indian Culture Ser.). (Illus.). 89p. (Orig.). (J). (gr. 4-12). 1989. pap. 5.95 (*0-89992-119-1*) Coun India Ed.
— Chief Stephen's Parky: One Year in the Life of an Athapascan Girl. Gilliland, Hap, ed. (Indian Culture Ser.). 72p. (Orig.). (J). (gr. 4-12). 1989. lib. bdg. 10.95 (*0-89992-319-4*) Coun India Ed.
Chandonnet, Ann. On the Trail of Eklutna. 76p. 1979. pap. text 10.00 (*1-878100-87-4*) Todd Commns.
Chandonnet, Ann F. Auras Tendrils. 72p. 1985. 7.95 (*0-920806-45-7*, Pub. by Penumbra Pr) U of Toronto Pr.
— Canoeing in the Rain: Poems for My Aleut-Athabascan Son. (Illus.). 38p. (Orig.). 1990. pap. 10.00 (*0-9622738-2-1*) M Bliss.
— Canoeing in the Rain: Poems for My Aleut-Athabascan Son. (Poetry Chapbook Ser.). (Illus.). 40p. (Orig.). 1990. pap. 10.00 (*0-317-99720-3*) Mr Cogito Pr.
Chandonnet, Fernand L., ed. see Chandonnet, Ann.
Chandor, Anthony. Diccionario de Informatica. (SPA.). 480p. 1989. pap. 125.00 (*0-7859-5730-8*, 8420652350) Fr & Eur.
Chandor, Anthony, et al. Computers Dictionary: Dizionario di Informatica. (ENG & ITA.). 354p. 1982. 95.00 (*0-8288-0903-8*, M8975) Fr & Eur.
Chandos, Fay. Sister Sylvan. large type ed. 352p. 1988. 27.99 (*0-7089-1796-8*) Ulverscroft.
Chandos Herald. Life of the Black Prince. LC 74-178519. reprint ed. 57.50 (*0-404-56532-8*) AMS Pr.
***Chandra.** Essays on Indian Nationalism. 2nd ed. 1999. 25.00 (*81-241-0439-5*, Pub. by Har-Anand Pubns) S Asia.
— Karanda-Vyuha-Sutra: Or the Supernal Virtues of Avalokitesvara. 1999. 88.00 (*81-86471-89-8*, Pub. by Kanishka) S Asia.
Chandra. Proceedings of the International Conference on Parallel Processing, 23rd Vol. 3: Algebra/Applications. 336p. 1994. 69.95 (*0-8493-2495-5*) CRC Pr.
Chandra & Comora. George Washington's Teeth. text. write for info. (*0-374-32534-0*) FS&G.
Chandra, A. Elsevier's Dictionary of Edible Mushrooms: Botanical & Common Names in Various Languages of the World. 260p. 1989. 195.00 (*0-8288-9204-0*) Fr & Eur.
Chandra, Abhijit & Mukherjee, Subrata. Boundary Element Methods in Manufacturing. LC 95-49816. (Oxford Engineering Science Ser.: No. 47). (Illus.). 528p. 1997. text 110.00 (*0-19-507921-3*) OUP.
Chandra, Aindrila, ed. Elsevier's Dictionary of Edible Mushrooms: Botanical & Common Names in Various Languages of the World. 300p. 1989. 128.50 (*0-444-88388-6*) Elsevier.
Chandra, Aindrila, jt. auth. see Purkayastha, R. P.
Chandra, Anil. The Amazing Miracles: A Treasury of Stories. 142p. 1998. pap. 75.00 (*81-7522-066-X*, Pub. by Print Hse) St Mut.
— The Amazing Miracles: A Treasury of Stories. 142p. 1998. pap. 70.00 (*81-7533-066-X*, Pub. by Print Hse) St Mut.
— Plump Woman: A Treasury of Stories. 1998. 20.00 (*81-241-0368-2*) Har-Anand Pubns.
Chandra, Anjani. Health Aspects of Pregnancy & Childbirth, United States, 1982-88. LC 95-32301. (Vital & Health Statistics Ser.: Series 23, No. 18). 1995. write for info. (*0-8406-0509-9*) Natl Ctr Health Stats.
***Chandra, Anjani.** Surgical Sterilization in the United States: Prevalence & Characteristics, 1965-1995. 37p. 1998. pap. 3.25 (*0-16-049627-6*) USGPO.
Chandra, Ashoka, et al, eds. Technical Manpower Profile, 1995: India & the States. (Illus.). vi, 597p. 1998. 40.00 (*81-86562-49-4*, Pub. by Manak Pubns Pvt Ltd) Nataraj Bks.
Chandra, Atul, et al, eds. Arid Fruit Research. 350p. 1993. pap. 75.00 (*81-7233-026-X*, Pub. by Scientific Pubs) St Mut.
Chandra, Atul, et al. Datepalm Research in Thar Desert. (C). 1992. pap. 30.00 (*81-7233-018-9*, Pub. by Scientific Pubs) St Mut.
Chandra Banerjee, Anil. New History of Modern India, 1707-1947. (C). 1992. reprint ed. 15.00 (*81-7074-122-X*, Pub. by KP Bagchi) S Asia.
Chandra, Bipaan. Ideology & Politics in Modern India. (C). 1994. text 32.00 (*81-241-0199-X*, Pub. by Har-Anand Pubns) S Asia.
Chandra, Bipan. Indian National Movement: The Long-Term Dynamics. 101p. 1988. text 18.95 (*0-7069-4036-9*, Pub. by Vikas) S Asia.
Chandra, D. K. Mystery of Art. (C). 1995. 16.00 (*81-208-1190-9*, Pub. by Motilal Bnarsidass) S Asia.
***Chandra, Debendra.** Janina System of Education. 134p. 1999. pap. 100.00 (*81-208-1576-9*, Pub. by Motilal Bnarsidass) St Mut.
Chandra, Deborah. A Is for Amos. LC 98-17465. (Illus.). 32p. (J). (ps-1). 1999. text 16.00 (*0-374-30001-1*) FS&G.
— Balloons: And Other Poems. 48p. (J). (gr. 4-7). 1993. pap. 3.95 (*0-374-40492-5*) FS&G.
— Balloons & Other Poems. (J). 1993. 9.15 (*0-606-05749-8*, Pub. by Turtleback) Demco.
— Miss Mabel's Table. LC 93-9137. (Illus.). 32p. (J). (ps-3). 1994. 14.95 (*0-15-276712-6*, Harcourt Child Bks) Harcourt.
— Rich Lizard: And Other Poems. 48p. (J). (gr. 4-7). 1993. 14.00 (*0-374-36274-2*) FS&G.
Chandra, Durgesh & Srinivasan, R. P. Energy Scope. 1990. 24.00 (*81-7003-107-9*, Pub. by S Asia Pubs) S Asia.
Chandra, G., ed. The Handbook of Environmental Chemistry Vol. 3-H: Organosilicon Materials. (Illus.). 230p. 1997. 129.00 (*3-540-62604-2*) Spr-Verlag.
Chandra, G. S. Sari of the Gods. LC 97-43200. 237p. 1998. pap. 13.95 (*1-56689-071-3*) Coffee Hse.
***Chandra, G. S. Sharat.** Family of Mirrors: Poems. 84p. 2000. reprint ed. pap. 12.95 (*1-886157-27-8*) BkMk.
Chandra, Girish & Gupta, Virendra K. Ichneumonologia Orientalis, Pt. VII The Tribes Lissonotini & Banchini (Hym - Icheumonidae) (Oriental Insects Monographs: No. 7). 1977. 55.00 (*1-877711-06-3*) Assoc Pubs FL.
Chandra, Govind. Life & Thought of Sankaracarya. (C). 1994. 22.50 (*81-208-1104-6*, Pub. by M Manoharial) S Asia.
Chandra, Harish. Collected Papers. Varadarajan, V. S., ed. (Illus.). 2400p. 1983. 436.95 (*0-387-90782-3*) Spr-Verlag.
Chandra, Harish, jt. ed. see Saxena, Manju.
Chandra, I. Lokesh. Tibetan-Sanskrit Dictionary: Supplementary Volume. (Sata-Pitaka Series Indo-Asian Literature: Vol. 369). (C). 1992. 54.00 (*81-85689-11-3*, Pub. by Aditya Prakashan) S Asia.
Chandra, J. & Flaherty, Joseph E., eds. Computational Aspects of Penetration Mechanics. (Lecture Notes in Engineering Ser.: Vol. 3). 221p. 1983. pap. 30.00 (*0-387-12634-1*) Spr-Verlag.
Chandra, J. P. Verdict on Janata. 212p. 1979. 14.95 (*0-318-36630-4*) Asia Bk Corp.
Chandra, Jagdish & Srivastav, Ram, eds. Constitutive Models of Deformation. LC 87-60608. (Proceedings in Applied Mathematics Ser.: No. 28). (Illus.). x, 182p. 1987. text 40.75 (*0-89871-217-3*) Soc Indus-Appl Math.
Chandra, Jagdish, jt. ed. see Varadan, Vasundara V.
Chandra, Jai S. Woman & Child: A Paradigm for Rural Development. (C). 1993. 22.00 (*81-7033-210-9*, Pub. by Rawat Pubns) S Asia.
Chandra, Jeffrey & Kakabadse, Andrew, eds. Privatisation & the National Health Service: The Scope for Collaboration. LC 85-16857. 120p. 1985. text 72.95 (*0-566-00813-0*, Pub. by Dartmth Pub) Ashgate Pub Co.
Chandra, K. Ravi. Entrepreneurial Success: A Psychological Study. 160p. 1991. text 22.50 (*0-685-54369-2*) Apt Bks.
Chandra, K. Suman, jt. auth. see Prasad, R. R.
Chandra, L. Tibetan-Sanskrit Dictionary. 1987. 250.00 (*0-8288-1761-8*, M14101) Fr & Eur.
Chandra, Lakshmi. Katherine Anne Porter: Fiction As History. (C). 1992. text 16.00 (*81-7031-304-X*, Pub. by Arnold Pubs) S Asia.
Chandra, Lokesh. Buddhist Iconography: Compact Edition. (C). 1991. 98.50 (*81-85179-71-9*, Pub. by Aditya Prakashan) S Asia.
— Cultural Horizons of India. (C). 1995. 105.00 (*81-85689-44-X*, Pub. by Aditya Prakashan) S Asia.
— Cultural Horizons of India, Vol. 1. (C). 1990. 94.00 (*81-85179-52-2*, Pub. by Aditya Prakashan) S Asia.
— Cultural Horizons of India, Vol. 5. (C). 1997. 110.00 (*81-86471-12-X*, Pub. by Aditya Prakashan) S Asia.
— Cultural Horizons of India Vol. 3: Studies in Tantra & Buddhism, Art & Archaeology, Language & Literature. (C). 1993. text 84.00 (*81-85689-25-3*, Pub. by Aditya Prakashan) S Asia.
— Cultural Horizons of India, Vol. II: Studies in Tantra & Buddhism, Art & Archaeology, Language & Literature. (Sata-Pitaka Ser.: Vol. 366). (C). 1992. 78.00 (*81-85689-00-8*, Pub. by Aditya Prakashan) S Asia.
— Sarva Tathagata-Tattva Sangraha. (C). 1987. 50.00 (*81-208-0273-X*, Pub. by Motilal Bnarsidass) S Asia.
— The Thousand Armed Avalokitesvara. (C). 1988. 80.00 (*81-7017-247-0*, Pub. by Abhinav) S Asia.
Chandra, Lokesh, ed. The Art & Culture of South-East Asia. (C). 1991. 88.00 (*81-85179-73-5*, Pub. by Indian Council Cultural Relations) S Asia.
Chandra, Lokesh, jt. auth. see Raghuvira, R.
Chandra, Lokesha, jt. auth. see Vira, Raghu.
Chandra, Lokish. Iconography of the Thousand Buddhas. (C). 1996. 120.00 (*81-86471-08-1*, Pub. by Aditya Prakashan) S Asia.
Chandra, Madan P. Dowry & Position of Women of India. 211p. 1986. 34.95 (*81-210-0047-5*) Asia Bk Corp.
Chandra, Mala, jt. auth. see Chandra, Satish.
Chandra, Nirmal K. The Retarded Economies: Foreign Domination & Class Relations in India & Other Emerging Nations. 398p. (C). 1989. 42.50 (*0-19-562274-X*) OUP.
Chandra, Prabir K. & Cal-Vidal, Jose. Caking Phenomena in Powdered Foods. (Food Engineering & Manufacturing Ser.). 1999. 99.95 (*0-8493-7904-0*) CRC Pr.
Chandra, Prabir K. & Singh, R. Paul. Applied Numerical Methods for Food & Agricultural Engineers. 512p. 1994. boxed set 141.95 (*0-8493-2454-8*, 2454) CRC Pr.
***Chandra, Prakash.** Lahore Declaration & Nuclear Issues. LC 99-938603. 1999. 52.50 (*81-7169-571-X*, Pub. by Commonwealth) S Asia.
Chandra, Prakash. Modern Indian Political Thought: Chandra, Prakash. 1998. pap. 9.00 (*81-259-0527-8*, Pub. by Vikas) S Asia.
Chandra, Prakash, ed. New Experimental Modalities in the Control of Neoplasia. LC 86-22709. (NATO ASI Series A, Life Sciences: Vol. 102). 414p. 1986. 95.00 (*0-306-42464-9*, Plenum Trade) Perseus Pubng.
Chandra, Pramod. On the Study of Indian Art. (Illus.). 152p. (C). 1983. 31.50 (*0-674-63762-3*) HUP.
— The Sculpture of India, 3000 B. C.-A. D. 1300. (Illus.). 224p. 1985. 84.50 (*0-674-79590-3*) HUP.
Chandra, Pratap. The Hindu Mind. 152p. 1977. 10.95 (*0-318-37177-4*) Asia Bk Corp.
Chandra, R., jt. ed. see Srivastava, Rajesh K.
Chandra, R. K., ed. Critical Reviews in Tropical Medicine, Vol. 1. LC 82-15129. 412p. 1982. 95.00 (*0-306-40959-3*, Plenum Trade) Perseus Pubng.
— Critical Reviews in Tropical Medicine, Vol. 2. LC 82-15129. 290p. 1984. 85.00 (*0-306-41561-5*, Plenum Trade) Perseus Pubng.
— Progress in Food & Nutrition Science. (Illus.). 198p. 1984. pap. 92.00 (*0-08-030928-3*, Pergamon Pr) Elsevier.
Chandra, Rai G. Indian Symbolism: Symbols As Sources of Our Customs & Beliefs. (Illus.). 150p. (C). 1996. reprint ed. 47.50 (*81-215-0081-8*, Pub. by M Manoharial) Coronet Bks.
Chandra, Rajesh. Industrialization & Development in the Third World. LC 91-30175. (Illus.). 128p. (C). 1992. pap. 17.99 (*0-415-01380-1*, A5987) Routledge.
Chandra, Ram. Complete Works of Ram Chandra, Vol. I. 400p. 1989. 15.00 (*0-945242-08-5*) Shri Ram Chandra.
— Complete Works of Ram Chandra, Vol. II. 400p. 1991. 15.00 (*0-945242-09-3*) Shri Ram Chandra.
— Complete Works of Ram Chandra, Vol. 3. 478p. 1997. 22.00 (*0-945242-10-7*) Shri Ram Chandra.
— Reality at Dawn. (RUS.). 50p. 1990. 5.00 (*0-945242-16-6*) Shri Ram Chandra.
— Road to Freedom: Revealing Sidelights. 362p. 1980. 29.95 (*0-685-05885-9*) Asia Bk Corp.
Chandra, Ram & Rajagopalachari, Parthasarathi. Letters of the Master, Vol. 3. Rathod, Rajendrasinh N., ed. 448p. 1996. 20.00 (*0-945242-30-1*) Shri Ram Chandra.
Chandra, Ramaprasad. The Indo-Aryan Races - A Study of the Origin of Indo-Aryan. 274p. 1978. 24.95 (*0-318-36982-6*) Asia Bk Corp.
Chandra, Ramesh. Highlanders of North Western Himalayas. (Tribal Studies of India Series T: No. 153). (C). 1992. 48.50 (*81-210-0278-8*, Pub. by Inter-India Pubns) S Asia.
— Introductory Physics of Nuclear Medicine. 2nd ed. LC 81-17149. 250p. reprint ed. pap. 77.50 (*0-608-17757-1*, 205650400069) Bks Demand.

An Asterisk (*) at the beginning of an entry indicates that the title is appearing for the first time.

— Introductory Physics of Nuclear Medicine. 4th ed. (Illus.). 221p. 1992. text 32.95 (*0-8121-1442-6*) Lppncott W & W.
— Nuclear Medicine Physics: The Basics. 5th ed. LC 97-15681. (Illus.). 240p. 1998. pap. 39.00 (*0-683-30092-X*) Lppncott W & W.
Chandra, Ranjit. 100Healthy in 100 Days. 2000. 25.00 (*0-06-019245-3*) HarpC.
Chandra, Ranjit K., ed. Trace Elements in Nutrition of Children. LC 85-10649. (Nestle Nutrition Workshop Ser.: Vol. 8). 320p. 1985. reprint ed. pap. 99.20 (*0-608-00441-3*, 206115600007) Bks Demand.
— Trace Elements in Nutrition of Children, Vol. II. LC 90-9012. (Nestle Nutrition Workshop Ser.: Vol. 23). (Illus.). 248p. 1991. reprint ed. pap. 76.90 (*0-608-07266-4*, 206749400009) Bks Demand.
Chandra, S. & Bergado, D. T. Environmental Geotechnics & Problematic Soils & Rocks: Proceedings of a Symposium, Bangkok, December 1985. Balasubramaniam, A. S. et al, eds. 576p. (C). 1987. text 207.00 (*90-6191-785-9*, Pub. by A A Balkema) Ashgate Pub Co.
Chandra, Sangita. Spicy Fat Free Cooking Secrets: Over 125 Flavorful Recipes to Help. LC 96-51111. 256p. 1997. pap. 15.00 (*0-7615-0547-4*) Prima Pub.
Chandra, Satish. Historiography, Religion, & State in Medieval India. 1996. 28.00 (*0-614-25269-5*, Pub. by Har-Anand Pubns) S Asia.
— Historiography, Religion, & State in Medieval India. (C). 1996. 28.00 (*81-241-0035-7*, Pub. by Har-Anand Pubns) S Asia.
— International Documents on Human Rights. (C). 1990. 175.00 (*0-89771-319-2*) St Mut.
— Medieval India from Sultanat to the Mughals: Delhi Sultanat, 1206-1526. (C). 1997. 40.00 (*81-241-0522-7*, Pub. by Har-Anand Pubns) S Asia.
— Mughal Religious Policies: Rajputs & the Deccan. (C). 1994. 22.00 (*0-7069-8392-0*, Pub. by Vikas) S Asia.
— Polymers in Concrete: An Introduction. 224p. 1994. boxed set 173.95 (*0-8493-4815-3*, TA443) CRC Pr.
Chandra, Satish, ed. Essays in Medieval Indian Economic History. (Indian History Congress Golden Jubilee Year Publication Ser.: Vol. 3). 1988. 28.50 (*81-215-0085-0*, Pub. by M Manoharial) Coronet Bks.
— The Indian Ocean: Explorations in History, Commerce, & Politics. 348p. (C). 1987. text 28.00 (*0-8039-9534-2*) Sage.
— Waste Materials Used in Concrete Manufacturing. LC 96-12577. 500p. 1996. 129.00 (*0-8155-1393-3*) Noyes.
Chandra, Satish, et al, eds. The Indian Ocean & Its Islands: Strategic, Scientific, & Historical Perspectives. LC 92-32628. 1993. 32.00 (*0-8039-9455-9*) Sage.
Chandra, Satish & Chandra, Mala. Privatisation of Public Enterprises: A Constitutional Anatomy. LC 97-914133. xx, 138 p. 1997. write for info. (*81-7100-988-3*) Deep & Deep Pubns.
Chandra, Shanta K. Development of Women's Entrepreneurship in India. (C). 1991. 14.00 (*81-7099-302-4*, Pub. by Mittal Pubs Dist) S Asia.
— Family Planning Programme in India. 1987. 24.00 (*81-7099-023-8*, Pub. by Mittal Pubs Dist) S Asia.
Chandra, Shanta K. & Lakshmiswaramma, M. Working Women & Infant Care. (C). 1991. 12.50 (*81-7099-303-2*, Pub. by Mittal Pubs Dist) S Asia.
Chandra, Sharad. Albert Camus & Indian Thought. 1990. text 25.00 (*0-685-35401-6*, Pub. by Natl Pub House) Advent Bks Div.
Chandra, Sharat. Population Pattern & Social Change in India. (C). 1992. 42.00 (*81-85613-34-6*, Pub. by Chugh Pubns) S Asia.
Chandra, Siddharth, jt. auth. see Kammen, Douglas.
Chandra, Smita. From Bengal to Punjab: The Cuisines of India. (Illus.). 172p. 1991. pap. 12.95 (*0-89594-509-6*) Crossing Pr.
***Chandra, Smita.** Indian Grill: The Art of Tandoori Cooking at Home. LC TX724.5.I4C374 1999. 176p. 1999. 24.00 (*0-88001-687-6*) HarpC.
***Chandra, Snehlata.** Marginal Communities & Social Development LC 98-901715. vi, 329 p. 1998. write for info. (*81-7391-245-9*) S Asia.
Chandra, Subhas & Kaur, Surjit. A Nomenclatural Guide to R. H. Beddome's Ferns of South India & Ferns of British India. x, 140p. 1987. 15.00 (*1-55528-076-5*, Pub. by Today Tomorrow) Scholarly Pubns.
Chandra, Sudhir. Enslaved Daughters: Colonialism, Law & Women's Rights. LC 98-902978. 264p. (C). 1998. text 29.95 (*0-19-564213-9*) OUP.
— The Oppressive Present: Literature & Social Consciousness in Colonial India. 204p. 1994. reprint ed. pap. 7.95 (*0-19-563503-5*) OUP.
Chandra, Suresh. Photoelectrochemical Solar Cells. (Electrocomponent Science Monographs: Vol. 5). xiv, 270p. 1985. text 195.00 (*2-88124-014-3*) Gordon & Breach.
Chandra, T., ed. Thermomechanical Processing of Steels & Other Materials: Proceedings, International Conference on Thermomechanical Processing of Steels & Other Materials THERMEC'97, U Wollongong, Australia, 1997, 2 vols. LC 97-71556. (Illus.). 2397p. 1998. pap. 234.00 (*0-87339-377-5*, TA464) Minerals Metals.
Chandra, T., ed. see International Conference on Recrystallization in M.
Chandra Tripathy, Prabhat. Crime Against Working Women. 1998. 36.00 (*81-7024-989-9*) Ashish Pub Hse.
Chandra, Victor A. Podiatry: Index of Modern Information. LC 88-48010. 150p. 1989. 47.50 (*1-55914-054-2*); pap. 44.50 (*1-55914-055-0*) ABBE Pubs Assn.
Chandra, Vikram. Love & Longing in Bombay. 288p. 1998. pap. 13.00 (*0-316-13677-8*) Little.
— Love & Longing in Bombay. 1998. pap. 13.00 (*0-316-18970-7*, Back Bay) Little.
— Red Earth & Pouring Rain. LC 94-48841. 1995. write for info. (*0-316-13266-7*) Little.
— Red Earth & Pouring Rain. 560p. 1997. pap. 14.95 (*0-316-13293-4*) Little.
***Chandra, Vikram.** Red Earth & Pouring Rain. 1998. pap. 14.95 (*0-316-18971-5*, Back Bay) Little.
Chandra, Vipan. Imperialism, Resistance, & Reform in Late Nineteenth-Century Korea: Enlightenment & the Independence Club. LC 87-83157. (Korea Research Monographs: No. 13). 240p. (Orig.). 1988. pap. 17.00 (*0-912966-99-8*) IEAS.
Chandrakasan, Anantha P. & Brodersen, Robert. Low-Power CMOS Design. LC 97-38651. 644p. 1998. 99.95 (*0-7803-3429-9*, PC 5703) Inst Electrical.
Chandrakasan, Anantha P. & Broderson, Robert W. Low Power Digital CMOS Design. LC 95-16761. 424p. (C). 1995. text 115.00 (*0-7923-9576-X*) Kluwer Academic.
***Chandrakasan, Anantha P., et al.** Design of High-Performance Microprocessor Circuits. LC 00-36977. (Illus.). 2000. pap. write for info. (*0-7803-6001-X*) IEEE Standards.
Chandrakasan, Anantha P., ed. see Brodersen, Robert W.
Chandrakumar, N. & Subramanian, S. Modern Techniques in High Resoultion FT-NMR. (Illus.). 400p. 1986. 175.00 (*0-387-96327-8*) Spr-Verlag.
Chandramohan, Balasubramanyam. A Study in Trans-Ethnicity in Modern South Africa: The Writings of Alex La Guma (1925-1985) LC 92-30300. 292p. 1993. text 89.95 (*0-7734-9186-4*) E Mellen.
Chandramouli, K. Kashi: City Luminous. LC 95-903869. (C). 1995. pap. 15.00 (*81-7167-236-1*, Pub. by Rupa) S Asia.
Chandramouli, M. S., jt. auth. see Millar, Roderick.
Chandran, K. B. Cardiovascular Biomechanics. (Biomedical Engineering Ser.). (Illus.). 300p. (C). 1992. text 80.00 (*0-8147-1471-4*) NYU Pr.
Chandran, K. B., et al, eds. Proceedings of the Bioengineering Conference, Sunriver, Oregon, 1997. LC 93-71951. 609p. 1997. pap. 120.00 (*0-7918-1805-5*) ASME.
Chandran, R. S., et al, eds. Fluid Power Systems & Technology. LC 95-81261. (1995 ASME International Mechanical Engineering Congress & Exposition Ser.: FPST-Vol. 2). 168p. 1995. 72.00 (*0-7918-1729-6*, H01011) ASME.
Chandran, Ram S. & Nair, Satish S., eds. Fluid Power Systems & Technology, 1997: Proceedings, ASME International Mechanical Engineering Congress & Exposition, Dallas, TX, 1997. (FPST - DSC Ser.: Vols. 4 & 63). 223p. 1997. pap. 100.00 (*0-7918-1836-5*, TJ843) ASME Pr.
Chandran, Ram S., jt. auth. see Nair, Satish S.
Chandras, Kan V. Handbook on Counseling Adolescents, Adults & Older Persons. 72p. 1995. pap. text 10.00 (*0-9649212-0-0*) K V Chandras.
Chandrasekar, Rajkumari, ed. Women's Resource & National Development: A Perspective. (C). 1992. 14.00 (*81-85006-29-6*, Pub. by Gaurav Pub House) S Asia.
Chandrasekar, V. Hotel Management. (Hospitality, Travel & Tourism Ser.). 1996. text 49.95 (*0-442-00915-1*, VNR) Wiley.
Chandrasekar, V., jt. auth. see Bringi, V. N.
Chandrasekaran, B. & Simon, Herbert, eds. Reasoning with Diagrammatic Representations: Papers from the 1992 Spring Symposium. (Technical Reports). (Illus.). 240p. 1994. spiral bd. 25.00 (*0-929280-63-6*) AAAI Pr.
Chandrasekaran, B., jt. auth. see Brown, David.
***Chandrasekaran, C.** The Life & Works of a Demographer: An Autobiography. LC 99-938314. (Illus.). 1999. write for info. (*0-07-463065-2*) McGrw-H Hghr Educ.
Chandrasekaran, P. Educational Planning Management. (C). 1994. write for info. (*81-207-1607-8*) Sterling Pubs.
Chandrasekhar, Aruna. Oliver & the Oil Spill. Thatch, Nancy R., ed. LC 91-3340. (Books for Students by Students). (Illus.). 26p. (J). (gr. k-4). 1991. lib. bdg. 15.95 (*0-933849-33-8*) Landmark Edns.
Chandrasekhar, B. S. Why Things Are the Way They Are. LC 96-52937. (Illus.). 264p. (C). 1997. pap. 25.95 (*0-521-45660-6*) Cambridge U Pr.
***Chandrasekhar, Prasanna.** Conducting Polymers, Fundamentals & Applications: A Practical Approach LC 99-37935. 1999. write for info. (*0-7923-8564-0*) Kluwer Academic.
Chandrasekhar, Rajkumari, ed. Women's Resource & National Development. 144p. (C). 1992. 22.50 (*81-207-1386-9*) Apt Bks.
Chandrasekhar, S. Dimensions of Socio-Political Change in Mysore, 1918-1940. 1985. 32.00 (*0-8364-1471-3*, Pub. by Ashish Pub Hse) S Asia.
— Ellipsoidal Figures of Equilibrium. (Illus.). 264p. 1987. reprint ed. pap. 8.95 (*0-486-65258-0*) Dover.
— Hydrodynamic & Hydromagnetic Stability. (Illus.). 704p. (C). 1981. reprint ed. pap. 14.95 (*0-486-64071-X*) Dover.
— Liquid Crystals. 2nd ed. (Illus.). 476p. (C). 1993. text 145.00 (*0-521-41747-3*); pap. text 49.95 (*0-521-42741-X*) Cambridge U Pr.
— Math Theory Hole. (Illus.). 672p. 1993. pap. text 60.00 (*0-19-852050-6*) OUP.
— The Mathematical Theory of Black Holes. (Oxford Classic Texts in the Physical Sciences Ser.). 668p. 1998. pap. text 29.95 (*0-19-850370-9*) OUP.
— Newton's Principia for the Common Reader. (Illus.). 616p. 1995. text 145.00 (*0-19-851744-0*) OUP.
— Norman Dorlaug's Green Revolution & Indias Population Problem. 1997. pap. 7.50 (*1-890456-00-4*) Popl Rev Bks.
— Plasma Physics. LC 60-7234. (Midway Reprint Ser.). (Illus.). x, 218p. 1978. reprint ed. pap. text 15.00 (*0-226-10085-5*) U Ch Pr.
— The Population of Mauritius. (C). 1990. 20.00 (*81-85182-31-0*, Pub. by Indus Pub) S Asia.
— The Population of Mauritius: Fact, Problem & Policy. 95p. 1990. 20.00 (*0-9609080-5-6*) Popl Rev Bks.
— Selected Papers: The Non-Radial Oscillations of Stars in General Relativity & Other Writings, Vol. 7. LC 96-17573. 275p. 1997. pap. text 45.00 (*0-226-10104-5*); lib. bdg. 99.00 (*0-226-10103-7*) U Ch Pr.
— Selected Papers, Vol. 1: Stellar Structure & Stellar Atmospheres. LC 88-26110. 536p. 1989. pap. text 36.00 (*0-226-10090-1*) U Ch Pr.
— Selected Papers, Vol. 1: Stellar Structure & Stellar Atmospheres. LC 88-26110. 531p. 1989. lib. bdg. 90.00 (*0-226-10089-8*) U Ch Pr.
— Selected Papers, Vol. 2: Radiative Transfer & Negative Ion of Hydrogen. LC 88-26111. (Illus.). 640p. 1989. pap. text 36.00 (*0-226-10093-6*) U Ch Pr.
— Selected Papers, Vol. 2: Radiative Transfer & Negative Ion of Hydrogen. LC 88-26111. Vol. 2. (Illus.). 640p. 1989. lib. bdg. 90.00 (*0-226-10092-8*) U Ch Pr.
— Selected Papers, Vol. 3: Stochastic, Statistical, & Hydromagnetic Problems in Physics & Astronomy. LC 89-4883. (Illus.). 656p. 1989. reprint ed. pap. text 36.00 (*0-226-10095-2*) U Ch Pr.
— Selected Papers, Vol. 3: Stochastic, Statistical, & Hydromagnetic Problems in Physics & Astronomy. LC 89-4883. (Illus.). 656p. 1990. reprint ed. lib. bdg. 96.00 (*0-226-10094-4*) U Ch Pr.
— Selected Papers, Vol. 4: Plasma Physics, Hydrodynamic & Hydromagnetic Stability, & Applications of the Tensor-Virial Theorem. 600p. 1989. pap. text 36.00 (*0-226-10097-9*) U Ch Pr.
— Selected Papers, Vol. 4: Plasma Physics, Hydrodynamic & Hydromagnetic Stability, & Applications of the Tensor-Virial Theorem. 600p. 1990. lib. bdg. 96.00 (*0-226-10096-0*) U Ch Pr.
— Selected Papers, Vol. 5: Relativistic Astrophysics. LC 89-20400. (Illus.). 608p. 1990. pap. text 36.00 (*0-226-10099-5*); lib. bdg. 96.00 (*0-226-10098-7*) U Ch Pr.
— Selected Papers, Vol. 6: The Mathematical Theory of Black Holes & of Colliding Plane Waves. LC 90-11149. (Illus.). 768p. 1991. pap. text 42.00 (*0-226-10101-0*); lib. bdg. 96.00 (*0-226-10100-2*) U Ch Pr.
— Third World Development Experience - Tanzania. (C). 1990. 13.00 (*81-7035-092-1*, Pub. by Daya Pub Hse) S Asia.
— Truth & Beauty: Aesthetics & Motivations in Science. LC 87-13792. (Illus.). 180p. 1990. pap. text 16.95 (*0-226-10087-1*) U Ch Pr.
— Truth & Beauty: Aesthetics & Motivations in Science. (Illus.). 208p. 1996. 28.95 (*0-226-10086-3*) U Ch Pr.
Chandrasekhar, S., ed. From India to America: A Brief History of Immigration, Admission & Assimilation. LC 82-60824. 111p. 1982. 25.00 (*0-9609080-0-5*); pap. 15.00 (*0-685-07372-6*) Popl Rev Bks.
— From India to Australia. 160p. (Orig.). 1992. pap. 15.00 (*0-9609080-7-2*); lib. bdg. 30.00 (*0-9609080-6-4*) Popl Rev Bks.
— From India to Canada. 4th ed. 217p. 1997. reprint ed. 25.00 (*0-9609080-1-3*); reprint ed. pap. 15.00 (*0-9609080-2-1*) Popl Rev Bks.
— From India to Mauritius: A Brief History of Immigration & the Indo-Mauvitian Community. 214p. (Orig.). 1988. 25.00 (*0-9609080-3-X*); pap. 12,00 (*0-9609080-4-8*) Popl Rev Bks.
— Second Asia Pacific Physics Conference: Proceedings, Bangalore, India, January 13-17, 1986, 2 vols., Set. 1232p. 1987. text 156.00 (*9971-5-0268-2*) World Scientific Pub.
Chandrasekhar, S., ed. see International Conference on Liquid Crystals (6th:.
Chandrasekhar, Subrahmanyan. Ellipsoidal Figures of Equilibrium. LC 69-15441. (Mrs. Hepsa Ely Silliman Memorial Lectures). 264p. reprint ed. pap. 81.90 (*0-8357-8708-7*, 203369200087) Bks Demand.
— An Introduction to the Study of Stellar Structure. 509p. (C). 1958. pap. 13.95 (*0-486-60413-6*) Dover.
— Radiative Transfer. (Illus.). 393p. (C). 1960. pap. 12.95 (*0-486-60590-6*) Dover.
Chandrasekhar, Subrahmanyan & Hull, Morton D., eds. Classical General Relativity. LC 92-32901. (Oxford Science Publications). (Illus.). 118p. (C). 1993. text 49.95 (*0-19-853980-0*) OUP.
Chandrasekharaiah, D. S. & Debnath, Lokenath. Continuum Mechanics. LC 93-41278. (Illus.). 595p. (C). 1994. text 78.00 (*0-12-167880-6*) Acad Pr.
Chandrasekharan, K. Arithmetical Functions. LC 72-102384. (Grundlehren der Mathematischen Wissenschaften Ser.: Vol. 167). (Illus.). 1970. 82.95 (*0-387-05114-7*) Spr-Verlag.
— Classical Fourier Transforms. (Universitext Ser.). 172p. 1989. 39.95 (*0-387-50248-3*) Spr-Verlag.
— Elliptic Functions. (Grundlehren der Mathematischen Wissenschaften Ser.: Vol. 281). (Illus.). 190p. 1985. 135.95 (*0-387-15295-4*) Spr-Verlag.
— Introduction to Analytic Number Theory. LC 68-21990. (Grundlehren der Mathematischen Wissenschaften Ser.: Vol. 148). (Illus.). 1969. 54.95 (*0-387-04141-9*) Spr-Verlag.
Chandrasekharan, K., ed. Hermann Weyl, 1885-1985. 136p. 1986. 63.95 (*0-387-16843-5*) Spr-Verlag.
Chandrasekharan, K., jt. auth. see Bochner, S.
Chandrasekharan, P. C. Robust Control of Linear Dynamical Systems. (Illus.). 384p. 1996. text 89.00 (*0-12-167885-7*) Acad Pr.
Chandrashekar, S. Colonialism, Conflict, & Nationalism: South India 1857-1947. LC 95-901197. (C). 1995. 29.00 (*81-7328-040-1*, Pub. by M Manoharial) S Asia.
Chandrasoma & Taylor. Concise Pathology. 3rd ed. (Illus.). 990p. (C). 1997. pap. text 43.95 (*0-8385-1499-5*, A-1499-1, Apple Lange Med) McGraw.
Chandrasoma, Para. Gastrointestinal Pathology. LC 98-25826. (C). 1998. boxed set 215.00 (*0-8385-3093-1*, Apple Lange Med) McGraw.
Chandrasoma, Parakrama & Taylor, Clive R. Pathology Notes. (Illus.). 636p. (C). 1992. pap. text 27.95 (*0-8385-5164-5*, A5164-7, Apple Lange Med) McGraw.
Chandrkaew, Chinda. Nibbana - The Ultimate Truth of Buddhism. 254p. 1982. 12.95 (*0-318-36661-4*) Asia Bk Corp.
Chandru, V. & Vinay, V., eds. Foundations of Software Technology & Theoretical Computer Science Vol. XI: Proceedings, 16th Conference, Hyderabad, India, December 18-20, 1996. (Lecture Notes in Computer Science Ser.: Vol. 1180). 387p. 1996. pap. 62.00 (*3-540-62034-6*) Spr-Verlag.
Chandrupatla. Optimization Concepts & Applications in Engineering. LC 98-44441. 432p. 1998. 105.00 (*0-13-031279-7*) P-H.
Chandrupatla, Tirupathi R. & Belegundu, Ashok D. An Introduction to Finite Elements in Engineering. 2nd ed. LC 96-14924. 461p. (C). 1996. text 105.00 incl. disk (*0-13-207036-7*) P-H.
Chandu, Jack F. The Pendulum Book. (Illus.). 80p. pap. 20.95 (*0-8464-4268-X*) Beekman Pubs.
— The Pendulum Book. 187p. 1990. pap. 13.85 (*0-85207-222-8*, Pub. by C W Daniel) Natl Bk Netwk.
Chandy, K. Mani & Taylor, Stephen. Introduction to Parallel Programming. (Computer Science-Math Ser.). 228p. (C). 1991. 35.00 (*0-86720-208-4*) Jones & Bartlett.
Chandy, K. Mani & Yeh, Raymond T., eds. Current Trends in Programming Methodology: Software Modeling, Vol. 3. (Illus.). 1978. 41.67 (*0-13-195727-9*) P-H.
Chandy, P. R. & Garrison, Sharon. Directory of General & International Business Journals. 293p. (Orig.). 1993. pap. 24.95 (*0-87563-435-4*) Stipes.
Chane, Ken & Poy, Glenn. Entrepreneur or Employee? Should You Get Out or Stay in Your Current Job? (Illus.). 304p. 1997. 23.95 (*1-890147-04-4*) Vanalden Pr.
Chaneles, Sol. Older Offenders: Current Trends. LC 88-13805. (Journal of Offender Counseling, Services & Rehabilitation: Vol. 13, No. 2). (Illus.). 248p. 1989. text 49.95 (*0-86656-806-9*) Haworth Pr.
Chaneles, Sol, ed. Counseling Juvenile Offenders in Institutional Settings. (Journal of Offender Counseling, Services & Rehabilitation: Vol. 6, No. 3). 85p. 1983. pap. text 14.95 (*0-86656-170-6*) Haworth Pr.
— Current Trends in Correctional Education: Theory & Practice. LC 83-18542. (Journal of Offender Counseling, Services & Rehabilitation: Vol. 7, Nos. 3-4). 117p. 1983. text 39.95 (*0-86656-268-0*) Haworth Pr.
— Gender Issues, Sex Offenses & Criminal Justice: Current Trends. LC 84-15830. (Journal of Offender Counseling, Services & Rehabilitation: Vol. 9, Nos. 1 & 2). 170p. 1984. text 39.95 (*0-86656-357-1*) Haworth Pr.
— Prisons & Prisoners: Historical Documents. LC 85-17736. (Journal of Offender Counseling, Services & Rehabilitation: Vol. 10, Nos. 1-2). 218p. 1985. text 6.95 (*0-86656-464-0*); pap. text 24.95 (*0-86656-486-1*) Haworth Pr.
— Strategies of Intervention with Public Offenders. LC 82-15383. (Journal of Offender Counseling, Services & Rehabilitation: Vol. 6, Nos. 1-2). 137p. 1982. pap. text 19.95 (*0-86656-171-4*) Haworth Pr.
Chaneles, Sol & Pallone, Nathaniel J., eds. The Clinical Treatment of the Criminal Offender in Outpatient Mental Health Settings: The New & Emerging Perspectives. LC 90-4008. (Journal of Offender Counseling, Services & Rehabilitation: Vol. 15, No. 1). 175p. 1990. text 39.95 (*0-86656-982-0*) Haworth Pr.
Chanell, Jim & Greenaway, Theresa. Beetles. LC 98-34074. (Minipets Ser.). (Illus.). 32p. 1999. lib. bdg. 22.83 (*0-8172-5586-9*) Raintree Steck-V.
***Chanell, Jim & Greenaway, Theresa.** Slugs & Snails. LC 98-34070. (Minipets Ser.). (Illus.). 32p. (J). (gr. 1-5). 1999. 22.83 (*0-8172-5587-7*) Raintree Steck-V.
Chanell, Jim & Greenaway, Theresa. Worms. LC 98-34075. (Minipets Ser.). (Illus.). 32p. (J). 1999. lib. bdg. 22.83 (*0-8172-5588-5*) Raintree Steck-V.
Chanenon, Stanley A. Prairie Crossings: Illinois' Exciting Rail Junctions in the 1990s. LC 98-93264. (Illus.). 500p. 1998. 55.00 (*0-9631811-2-2*); pap. 45.00 (*0-9631811-3-0*) S A Changnon.
Chanera. I AM Adorations & Affirmations (Pocket Version) LC 91-20332. (Saint Germain Ser.: Vol. 5, Pt. 1). (Illus.). 95p. 1937. pap. 8.00 (*1-878891-25-1*) St Germain Press Inc.
***Chanes, Jerome.** Anti-semitism: A Reference Handbook. 2002. lib. bdg. 45.00 (*1-57607-209-6*) ABC-CLIO.
Chanes, Jerome. A Portrait of the American Jewish Community. Linzer, Norman J. & Schnall, David A., eds. LC 97-38800. 240p. 1998. 59.95 (*0-275-96022-6*, Praeger Pubs) Greenwood.
Chanes, Jerome A. Antisemitism in America Today: Outspoken Experts Explode the Myths. LC 96-39812. 486p. 1997. pap. 18.95 (*0-8065-1858-8*, Citadel Pr) Carol Pub Group.
Chanes, Jerome A., ed. Antisemitism in America Today: Outspoken Experts Explode the Myths. 320p. 1995. 21.95 (*1-55972-290-8*, Birch Ln Pr) Carol Pub Group.
***Chaneski, John.** Super Party Games. LC 99-39731. 1999. pap. 7.95 (*0-8069-1817-9*) Sterling.
— Super Party Games: Fun & Original Ideas for 10 or More. LC 99-39731. 1999. 16.95 (*0-8069-5915-0*) Sterling.
Chaney. Investigating Food in History. 1992. pap. 6.95 (*0-7078-0149-4*, Pub. by Natl Trust) Trafalgar.
Chaney, jt. ed. see Demars.

C

Chaney, Alfred. Computer Recycling for Education: How to Plan, Start-Up, Implement & Operate a Successful Computer Recycling, Re-Engineering, & Refurbishing Training Program. Kando, Anita & Burr, Merrilee, eds. LC 97-91552. (Illus.). 350p. (Orig.). 1998. pap. 199.95 (*0-9658664-0-8*) Comp Recycl.

Chaney, Bev, jt. auth. see Lopez, Ken.

Chaney, Bradford, et al. Programs at Higher Education Institutions for Disadvantaged Precollege Students. (Illus.). 97p. (C). 1998. reprint ed. pap. text 20.00 (*0-7881-3929-0*) DIANE Pub.

Chaney, Bradford W. Which Things Belong to Caesar? 87p. (Orig.). 1986. pap. 4.95 (*0-9615151-0-4*) Anatello.

Chaney, Bradford W., et al. School Library Media Centers, 1993-94. LC 98-196938. (Statistical Analysis Report Ser.). (Illus.). 246p. 1998. 21.00 (*0-16-049696-9*) USGPO.

Chaney, Casey. Pardon My Dust . . . I'm Remodeling: Build Your Character, Experience Your Self-Esteem. Haqq, Lisa & Moffett, Berdell, eds. 128p. (Orig.). (C). 1990. pap. text 8.95 (*0-9626403-0-1*) Mocha Pub.

— Ready, Willing & Terrified: A Coward's Guide to Risk-Taking. Moffett, Berdell & Rhiannon, Thea, eds. (Illus.). 144p. (Orig.). (YA). 1991. pap. 10.95 (*0-9626403-1-X*) Mocha Pub.

Chaney, Charles L. Birth of Missions in America. LC 75-26500. 352p. 1976. pap. 8.95 (*0-87808-146-1*) William Carey Lib.

Chaney, Darrah. Drawing Pictures with One Line. (Hi Map Ser.: No. 21). pap. text 11.99 (*0-614-05306-4*, HM 5621) COMAP Inc.

Chaney, David. Lifestyles. LC 96-3282. 208p. (C). 1996. 65.00 (*0-415-11718-6*); pap. 16.95 (*0-415-11719-4*) Routledge.

Chaney, David, ed. Sustainable Agriculture in California: Proceedings of a Research Symposium, Sacramento, California, March 15-16, 1990. 256p. (Orig.). 1991. pap. text 2.00 (*1-879906-02-3*, 3348) ANR Pubns CA.

Chaney, David C. The Cultural Turn: Scene-Setting Essays on Contemporary Cultural Theory. LC 93-46091. 256p. (C). (gr. 13). 1994. pap. 22.99 (*0-415-10298-7*, B4088) Routledge.

Chaney, Earlyne. The Eyes Have It: A Self-Help Manual for Better Vision. LC 86-23438. (Illus.). 176p. 1987. reprint ed. pap. 9.95 (*0-87728-621-3*) Weiser.

Chaney, Earlyne C. Forever Young. LC 90-84224. 178p. 1990. pap. 12.95 (*0-918936-22-5*) Astara.

— Initiation in the Great Pyramid. LC 87-71524. 227p. (Orig.). 1987. pap. 14.95 (*0-918936-21-7*) Astara.

— Lost Empire of the Gods. LC 93-72762. 224p. 1993. per. 15.95 (*0-918936-29-2*) Astara.

— Lost Secrets of the Mystery Schools: Coming of the Gods. 218p. 1991. per. 15.95 (*0-918936-24-1*) Astara.

— The Madonna & the Coming Light. LC 93-70271. 174p. (Orig.). 1993. pap. text 15.95 (*0-918936-27-6*) Astara.

— Remembering: Autobiography of a Mystic. LC 74-81047. 372p. 1987. pap. 11.95 (*0-89031-018-1*) Astara.

— Secret Wisdom of the Great Initiates. LC 92-74029. 169p. 1993. per. 15.95 (*0-918936-25-X*) Astara.

— Secrets from Mt. Shasta. 70p. 1953. pap. 9.95 (*0-918936-10-1*) Astara.

— Shining Moments of a Mystic. LC 76-24187. 78p. 1976. pap. 3.95 (*0-918936-19-5*) Astara.

— Wisdom from the Angels & the Forces of Light. LC 98-71940. 1998. per. 15.95 (*0-918936-33-0*) Astara.

— The You Book: A Treasury of Health & Healing. LC 90-84838. 328p. 1991. per. 16.95 (*0-918936-23-3*) Astara.

Chaney, Edward. The Evolution of the Grand Tour: Anglo-Italian Cultural Relations since the Renaissance. LC 98-5404. (Illus.). 432p. (C). 1998. text 59.50 (*0-7146-4577-X*, Pub. by F Cass Pubs) Intl Spec Bk.

***Chaney, Edward.** The Evolution of the Grand Tour: Anglo-Italian Cultural Relations since the Renaissance. rev. ed. (Illus.). 432p. 2000. pap. 29.50 (*0-7146-4474-9*, Pub. by F Cass Pubs) Intl Spec Bk.

Chaney, Edward, jt. ed. see Bold, John.

Chaney, Elsa. Supermadre, la Mujer Dentro de la Politica. (SPA.). pap. 8.99 (*968-16-1312-0*, Pub. by Fondo) Continental Bk.

Chaney, Elsa M. & Castro, Mary G., eds. Muchachas No More: Household Workers in Latin America & the Caribbean. (Women in the Political Economy Ser.). 498p. 1988. 39.95 (*0-87722-571-0*) Temple U Pr.

— Muchachas No More: Household Workers in Latin America & the Caribbean. (Women in the Political Economy Ser.). 498p. 1991. pap. 24.95 (*0-87722-835-3*) Temple U Pr.

Chaney, Elsa M., jt. auth. see Bunster, Ximena B.

Chaney, Elsa M., jt. ed. see Sutton, Constance R.

Chaney, Helen W. Dying to Meet God. (Illus.). 1998. 18.95 (*1-878208-77-2*) Guild Pr IN.

Chaney, J. D. Tito's Whore. 1999. pap. 13.50 (*0-88739-184-2*) Creat Arts Bk.

Chaney, J. F., et al, eds. Thermophysical Properties Research Literature Retrieval Guide 1900-1980, Vol. 1: Elements. LC 81-15776. 804p. 1982. 175.00 (*0-306-67221-9*, Kluwer Plenum) Kluwer Academic.

— Thermophysical Properties Research Literature Retrieval Guide 1900-1980, Vol. 2: Inorganic Compounds. LC 81-15776. 1094p. 1982. 235.00 (*0-306-67222-7*, Kluwer Plenum) Kluwer Academic.

— Thermophysical Properties Research Literature Retrieval Guide 1900-1980, Vol. 3: Organic Compounds & Polymeric Materials. LC 81-15776. 630p. 1982. 150.00 (*0-306-67223-5*, Kluwer Plenum) Kluwer Academic.

— Thermophysical Properties Research Literature Retrieval Guide 1900-1980, Vol. 4: Alloys, Intermetallic Compounds & Ceramics. LC 81-15776. 736p. 1982. 160.00 (*0-306-67224-3*, Kluwer Plenum) Kluwer Academic.

— Thermophysical Properties Research Literature Retrieval Guide 1900-1980, Vol. 5: Oxide Mixtures & Minerals. LC 81-15776. 414p. 1982. 115.00 (*0-306-67225-1*, Kluwer Plenum) Kluwer Academic.

— Thermophysical Properties Research Literature Retrieval Guide 1900-1980, Vol. 6: Mixtures & Solutions. LC 81-155776. 498p. 1982. 125.00 (*0-306-67226-X*, Kluwer Plenum) Kluwer Academic.

— Thermophysical Properties Research Literature Retrieval Guide 1900-1980, Vol. 7: Coatings, Systems, Composites, Foods, Animal & Vegetable Products. LC 81-15776. 642p. 1982. 150.00 (*0-306-67227-8*, Kluwer Plenum) Kluwer Academic.

— Thermophysical Properties Research Literature Retrieval Guide 1900-1980, Vol. 7: Coatings, Systems, Composites, Foods, Animal & Vegetable Products, 7 vols., Set. LC 81-15776. 642p. 1982. 850.00 (*0-685-42429-4*, Kluwer Plenum) Kluwer Academic.

Chaney, J. R. Aleksandr Pushkin: Poet for the People. LC 91-14669. (Biography & History Ser.). 112p. (YA). (gr. 5 up). 1991. lib. bdg. 23.93 (*0-8225-4911-5*, Lerner Publctns) Lerner Pub.

Chaney, James M. William the Baptist. 140p. (C). 1994. reprint ed. pap. text 8.95 (*1-884416-04-7*) A Press.

Chaney, Jean, ed. see Kaufer, Steven C. & Mattman, Jurg W.

Chaney, John, jt. auth. see Macaulay, Ruth Marris.

Chaney, Lillian H. & Martin, Jeanette S. Intercultural Business Communciation. 2nd ed. LC 99-21946. (Illus.). 277p. 1999. pap. text 36.40 (*0-13-013700-6*) P-H.

Chaney, Lillian H. & Martin, Jeannette S. Intercultural Business Communication. LC 94-17297. 352p. 1994. pap. text 45.00 (*0-13-038753-3*) P-H.

Chaney, Lillian H., jt. auth. see Simon, Judith C.

Chaney, Lilliana H., jt. auth. see Simon, Judith C.

Chaney, Linda, ed. see Norris, Miles.

***Chaney, Mairi.** The Unofficial Beanie Baby Internet Guide. 40p. 1999. pap. 10.00 (*1-883573-36-X*, Lightning Rod) Pride & Imprints.

Chaney, Margaret K. Red World/Green World: The Hidden Polarities of Nature. Whalen, E., ed. (Illus.). 144p. (Orig.). 1997. pap. 7.95 (*0-9643261-3-2*) Veritas AZ.

Chaney, Matt. Legend in Missouri. Stanard, John R., ed. LC 97-206848. 160p. 1997. 14.95 (*0-9639316-2-8*) Four Walls.

***Chaney, Matt.** Legend in Missouri. 160p. 2000. (*0-9639316-3-6*) Four Walls.

Chaney, Matt. My Name Is Mister Ryan. LC 94-173383. (Greatness in People Ser.). (Illus.). 450p. (Orig.). 1994. 27.95 (*0-9639316-0-1*); pap. 15.95 (*0-9639316-1-X*) Four Walls.

Chaney, Michael. White Pine on the Saco River: An Oral History of River Driving in Southern Maine. Ives, Edward D. & MacDougall, Pauleena M., eds. (Northeast Folklore Ser.: Vol. XXIX). (Illus.). 88p. 1993. pap. 15.00 (*0-943197-21-X*) ME Folklife Ctr.

Chaney, Michael, jt. auth. see MacDougall, Alan F.

Chaney, Michael P., jt. auth. see Linzee, Jill.

Chaney, Norman. Six Images of Human Nature. 175p. (C). 1994. pap. text 12.50 (*1-57074-232-4*) Greyden Pr.

Chaney, Oto P. Zhukov. rev. ed. LC 95-26307. (Illus.). 560p. 1996. 39.95 (*0-8061-2807-0*) U of Okla Pr.

Chaney, Pete, jt. auth. see Stoller, Lee.

Chaney, R. C. & Fang, Hsai-Yang, eds. Marine Geotechnology & Nearshore-Offshore Structures. LC 86-22200. (Special Technical Publication Ser.: No. 923). (Illus.). 380p. 1986. text 48.00 (*0-8031-0490-1*, STP923) ASTM.

Chaney, Regina. Anything for a Dream: Original Manuscript. LC 90-63437. 157p. (C). 1991. text 17.95 (*0-9628246-0-7*) Morgan Randolph & Assocs.

Chaney, Rick L. Regional Emigration & Remittances in Developing Countries: The Portuguese Experience. LC 85-19382. 270p. 1986. 59.95 (*0-275-92018-6*, C2018, Praeger Pubs) Greenwood.

***Chaney, Robert.** The Mystic Mantra: Om Mani Padme Aum. LC 99-72963. 112p. 1999. pap. 12.95 (*0-918936-34-9*) Astara.

Chaney, Robert, jt. auth. see Telepchak, Michael J.

Chaney, Robert G. Akashic Records: Past Lives & New Directions. LC 95-83812. 92p. (Orig.). 1995. 9.95 (*0-918936-31-4*) Astara.

— The Essenes & Their Ancient Mysteries. (Library of Mystical Classics). 48p. 1993. per. 6.95 (*0-918936-14-4*) Astara.

— The Inner Way. LC 75-32234. 150p. 1987. pap. 9.95 (*0-918936-00-4*) Astara.

— Mediums & the Development of Mediumship. 215p. 1977. 19.95 (*0-8369-2761-3*) Ayer.

— Mysticism: The Journey Within. LC 79-52959. 192p. 1979. pap. 13.95 (*0-918936-06-3*) Astara.

— Occult Hypnotism. (Adventures in Esoteric Learning Ser.). 46p. 1958. pap. 4.95 (*0-918936-15-2*) Astara.

— The Power of Your Own Medicine. LC 95-75540. 192p. 1995. pap. 15.95 (*0-918936-30-6*) Astara.

— Reincarnation: Cycle of Opportunity. LC 84-72387. (Adventures in Esoteric Learning Ser.). (Illus.). 56p. 1984. pap. 4.95 (*0-918936-13-6*) Astara.

— Ten Steps to Self-Fulfillment. LC 93-70705. 256p. 1993. pap. 15.95 (*0-918936-28-4*) Astara.

— Think on New Levels. (Adventures in Esoteric Learning Ser.). 56p. 1963. pap. 4.95 (*0-918936-16-0*) Astara.

— Unfolding the Third Eye. (Adventures in Esoteric Learning Ser.). 48p. 1970. pap. 4.95 (*0-918936-18-7*) Astara.

— Visits to the Manger: Enlightening Parables of Spiritual Wonder. LC 96-83970. 140p. 1996. pap. 9.95 (*0-918936-32-2*) Astara.

Chaney, Ronald C. & Demars, Kenneth R., eds. Strength Testing of Marine Sediments: Laboratory & In-Situ STP 883. LC 85-15838. (Illus.). 557p. 1985. text 69.00 (*0-8031-0431-6*, STP883) ASTM.

Chaney, Ronald C., jt. ed. see Demars, Kenneth R.

Chaney, Ronda, jt. auth. see Bottom, Lori.

Chaney, Rose & Berghan, Connie. Northern Lites: Contemporary Cooking with a Twist. (Illus.). 132p. 1998. 39.95 (*0-9662467-0-5*) Northern Lites.

Chaney, Rose D., ed. see Wright, Michelle D.

Chaney, Sky & Fisher, Pam, eds. The Discovery Book: A Helpful Guide for the World Written by Children with Disabilities. rev. ed. (Illus.). 100p. (J). (gr. 3-10). 1989. pap. 7.95 (*0-9616891-1-0*) UCPANB.

Chaney, Steve. The Puppet in the Big Black Box. (Illus.). 32p. (J). (gr. k-3). 1989. write for info. (*0-318-65294-3*) Stiff Lip.

Chaney, Victor. The Bernstein Projections: A Metaphysical Comedy. LC 90-92086. 256p. (Orig.). 1991. pap. 5.95 (*0-9628586-0-9*) V Chaney.

Chaney, Warren H. Y2K: A World in Crisis? Brasington, Leann et al, eds. LC 99-63385. (Illus.). 224p. (Orig.). 1999. pap. 14.95 (*0-943629-39-X*, Pub. by Swan Pub) Herveys Bklink.

Chaney, William F. Duty Most Sublime: The Life of Robert E. Lee As Told Through the "Carter Letters" LC 96-77584. (Illus.). 208p. 1996. 25.00 (*0-9653685-0-5*) Eighteen-Sixty-One.

Chanez, P., et al, eds. From Genetics to Quality of Life - The Optimal Treatment & Management of Asthma: Proceedings of the XVth World Congress of Asthmology - Montpellier, France, April 24-27, 1996. (Illus.). 240p. 1996. text 58.00 (*0-88937-169-5*) Hogrefe & Huber Pubs.

Chang. Chemistry. 6th ed. 539p. 1997. 34.38 (*0-07-011961-9*) McGraw.

— Chemistry. 7th ed. 2001. student ed. 22.00 (*0-07-231801-5*) McGraw.

— Chemistry: Study Guide Pkg. 6th ed. 1997. 81.25 (*0-07-561200-3*) McGraw.

— Chemistry Answers to Even-Numbered Problems. 5th ed. 1993. 3.75 (*0-07-011106-5*) McGraw.

— Chemistry Study Guide. 6th ed. 496p. 1997. pap., student ed. 33.13 (*0-07-068501-0*) McGraw.

— Clinical Application of Mechanical Ventilation - IML. 2nd abr. rev. ed. 160p. 1996. teacher ed. 14.95 (*0-8273-8287-1*) Delmar.

— Clinical Application of Mechanical Ventilation Workbook. abr. rev. ed. 224p. (C). 1996. pap. 20.25 (*0-8273-8285-5*) Delmar.

***Chang.** Clinical Applications of Mechanical Ventilation. 2nd ed. (C). 2000. pap. 18.00 (*0-7668-1377-0*) Delmar.

Chang. Essen. Chemistry & Cyberchem. Ma. 1997. 72.74 (*0-07-561240-2*) McGraw.

Chang. Microwave Solid State Circuits & Applications Solutions Management. 107p. 1994. pap. 27.50 (*0-471-07412-8*) Wiley.

Chang. PK CHEM/CS BUILD V5.1. 6th ed. 1997. 82.75 (*0-07-561201-1*) McGraw.

— Respiratory Care Calculations. 2nd ed. LC 98-43498. (Allied Health Ser.). 352p. (C). 1998. text 34.95 (*0-7668-0517-4*) Delmar.

— Vertical Cavity Surface Emitting Layer Arrays. text. write for info. (*0-471-30469-7*) Wiley.

Chang & Hudson, eds. Methods & Models for Predicting Fatigue Crack Growth under Random Loading - STP 748. 140p. 1981. 16.50 (*0-8031-0715-3*, STP748) ASTM.

***Chang & Scott.** Basic Interviewing Skills: For Practitioners. (Social Work Ser.). 1999. pap., wbk. ed. 31.95 (*0-8304-1530-0*) Wadsworth Pub.

Chang, jt. auth. see Webby.

Chang, Maria L. Early Themes: Life Cycles Butterflies, Chicks, Frogs & More!, 1. 48p. 1999. pap. 9.95 (*0-590-68572-4*) Scholastic Inc.

Chang, A. I. The Tao of Architecture. 80p. 1981. pap. text 9.95 (*0-691-00330-0*, Pub. by Princeton U Pr) Cal Prin Full Svc.

***Chang, Agnes S., et al.** Growing up in Singapore: Research Perspectives on Adolescents. LC 99-914656. xvii, 254p. 1999. write for info. (*981-4024-15-5*) P-H.

Chang, Ai-Ling. The Rice Sprout Song: A Novel of Modern China. LC 97-37527. 182p. 1998. 40.00 (*0-520-21437-4*, Pub. by U CA Pr) Cal Prin Full Svc.

— The Rice Sprout Song: A Novel of Modern China. LC 97-37527. 182p. 1998. pap. 15.95 (*0-520-21088-3*, Pub. by U CA Pr) Cal Prin Full Svc.

— The Rouge of the North. LC 97-37526. 185p. 1998. 40.00 (*0-520-21438-2*, Pub. by U CA Pr) Cal Prin Full Svc.

— The Rouge of the North. LC 97-37526. 185p. 1998. pap. 15.95 (*0-520-21087-5*, Pub. by U CA Pr) Cal Prin Full Svc.

Chang, Alfred E. & Shu, Suyu, eds. Immunotherapy of Cancer with Sensitized T Lymphocytes. (Medical Intelligence Unit Ser.). 118p. 1994. 99.00 (*1-57059-049-4*, LN9049) Landes Bioscience.

***Chang, Alice & Spruill, Karen.** A Survivor's Guide to Breast Cancer. LC 99-75281. (Illus.). 168p. 2000. pap. 13.95 (*1-57224-185-3*, Pub. by New Harbinger) Publishers Group.

Chang, Alsa. The Immigrant Experience: Stories of Success & Failure. 1999. pap. 10.00 (*0-9659141-2-7*) United Pros.

— Living & Working in New York: An Introduction to the City for the New Comers. 1998. pap. 10.00 (*0-9659141-1-9*) United Pros.

Chang, Amy. Glossary of Commercial & Business Legal Terms in English-Chinese-Japanese. 794p. 1996. 198.00 (*0-9645081-0-9*) Musheng Intl Pub.

Chang, Amy & Jackson, Mary E., eds. Managing Resource Sharing in the Electronic Age. LC 96-135. (Studies in Library & Information Science: Vol. 4). 125p. 1996. 39.50 (*0-404-64004-4*) AMS Pr.

Chang, Anthony C., et al. Pediatric Cardiac Intensive Care. LC 97-39558. (Illus.). 512p. 1998. 89.00 (*0-683-01508-7*) Lppncott W & W.

Chang, Arnold. Painting in the People's Republic of China: The Politics of Style. (Special Studies on China & East Asia). 1980. 19.00 (*0-89158-676-8*) Westview.

***Chang, Ben.** Oracle XML Handbook. 2000. pap. 59.99 (*0-07-212489-X*) Osborne-McGraw.

Chang, Bethel. Light into Dawn - Randy's Miracle. Turner, Jack, ed. Chang, Catherine, tr. from CHI. Orig. Title: Child of Oriental Face. 200p. 1999. pap. 5.95 (*0-9669393-0-1*) Mimosa.

Chang, Briankle G. Deconstructing Communication: Representation, Subject, & Economies of Exchange. 1996. pap. 22.95 (*0-8166-2645-6*); text 57.95 (*0-8166-2644-8*) U of Minn Pr.

Chang, C. Chinese Cooking at Home. 1996. 14.50 (*4-07-972418-7*) Shufu No.

— Chinese Menu Cookbook. (Illus.). 114p. 1996. 31.95 (*4-07-974794-2*) Shufu No.

Chang, C., et al. Q & A Law of Evidence: Blackstone's Law Questions & Answers. 208p. 1996. pap. 22.00 (*1-85431-496-3*, Pub. by Blackstone Pr) Gaunt.

Chang, C. C. & Keisler, H. Jerome. Model Theory. 3rd enl. ed. (Studies in Logic & the Foundations of Mathematics: No. 73). xvi,650p. 1990. 169.50 (*0-444-88054-2*, North Holland) Elsevier.

Chang, C. C., ed. see Catholic University of America, Washington, D. C.

Chang, C. I. & Sun, C. T., eds. Structural Integrity in Aging Aircraft: Proceedings of the ASME International Mechanical Engineering Congress & Exposition, 1995, San Francisco, CA. LC 95-81256. (1995 ASME International Mechanical Engineering Congress & Exposition Ser.: AD-Vol. 47). 332p. 1995. 96.00 (*0-7918-1724-5*, H01006) ASME.

Chang, C. M., ed. see ASME-ASLE Lubrication Conference Staff.

Chang, C. P., jt. auth. see Kyle, W. J.

Chang, C. P., jt. ed. see Sham, Patrick.

Chang, C. S. & Ju, J. W., eds. Homogenization & Constitutive Modeling for Heterogeneous Materials. LC 93-71580. (AMD Ser.: Vol. 166). 97p. 1993. pap. 35.00 (*0-7918-1145-X*, G00789) ASME.

Chang, C. Y. Computing Electric Filters with a PC. 2nd ed. John, Harold F., ed. (Illus.). 220p. (Orig.). 1994. pap. text 19.95 (*0-9607806-8-8*) Li Kung Shaw.

Chang, C. Y. & Kai, Francis. Gas High-Speed Devices: Physics, Technology & Circuit Applications. LC 92-20705. 612p. 1994. 125.00 (*0-471-85641-X*) Wiley.

Chang, C. Y. & Sze, S. M. ULSI Devices. LC 99-29979. 736p. 2000. 89.95 (*0-471-24067-2*) Wiley.

Chang, C. Y. & Sze, Simon M. ULSI Technology. (Illus.). 726p. (C). 1996. 106.56 (*0-07-063062-3*) McGraw.

Chang, Carsun. The Development of Neo-Confucian Thought, Vol. 1. 1957. pap. 16.95 (*0-8084-0105-X*) NCUP.

Chang, Catherine, tr. see Chang, Bethel.

Chang, Cecilia S., ed. The Republic of China on Taiwan, 1949-1988. 229p. 1991. write for info. (*0-933423-03-9*) St Johns U Asian Studies.

Chang, Chan-Sup & Chang, Nahn-Joo. The Korean Management System: Cultural, Political, Economic Foundations. LC 93-27710. 224p. 1994. 67.95 (*0-89930-858-9*, Quorum Bks) Greenwood.

Chang, Chao-Hsi, ed. see Symposium on Heavy Flavor & Electroweak Theory Sta.

Chang, Charles S. English-Chinese Dictionary of Real Estate Key Words. (CHI & ENG.). 172p. (C). 1992. pap. text 20.00 (*0-9634393-0-8*) Xin-Ichi Pub.

***Chang, Cheng-Shang.** Performance Guarantees in Communication Networks. LC 99-49543. (Telecommunication Networks & Computer Systems Ser.). 410p. 1999. 99.95 (*1-85233-226-3*, Pub. by Spr-Verlag) Spr-Verlag.

Chang, Chia-Lin. An Assessment of Chinese Thinking on Trade Liberalization. LC 97-6075. (Hoover Essays Ser.: No. 18). 1997. pap. text 5.00 (*0-8179-3812-5*) Hoover Inst Pr.

Chang, Chia-ning. And God Speaks to Muhammad. LC 96-90213. 212p. 1998. 17.95 (*0-533-11955-3*) Vantage.

— Gems of the Bible. LC 96-90215. (Orig.). 1998. pap. 7.95 (*0-533-11953-7*) Vantage.

— A Sheep's Song: A Writer's Reminiscences of Japan & the World. LC 98-49027. 508p. 1998. 50.00 (*0-520-20138-8*, Pub. by U CA Pr) Cal Prin Full Svc.

— Unpredictable Circumstances. LC 97-91436. 1998. pap. 8.95 (*0-533-12672-X*) Vantage.

Chang, Chia-ning, ed. My Life with Janacek: The Memoirs of Zdenka Janackova. (Illus.). 304p. 1998. 33.95 (*0-571-17540-6*) Faber & Faber.

Chang, Chia-ning, tr. see Tarkovsky, Andrei.

Chang, Chia-ning, tr. & anno. see Shuichi, Kato.

Chang, Chin-Cheng. Unified Approach to Uniqueness, Expansion & Approximation Problems. 120p. 1994. text 36.00 (*981-02-1805-2*) World Scientific Pub.

Chang, Chin-Liang. Fuzzy-Logic-Based Programming. 250p. 1997. text 31.00 (*981-02-3070-2*) World Scientific Pub.

— Introduction to Artificial Intelligence Techniques. LC 85-60670. 182p. (Orig.). 1985. pap. 18.00 (*0-9614742-0-3*) JMA Pr.

Chang, Ching S., et al, eds. Mechanics of Deformation & Flow of Particulate Materials: Proceedings of a Symposium. LC 97-13759. 472p. 1997. 44.00 (*0-7844-0251-5*) Am Soc Civil Eng.

Chang, Ching S., jt. ed. see Misra, Anil.

An Asterisk (*) at the beginning of an entry indicates that the title is appearing for the first time.

Chang, Chuang. Politics of Hong Kongs Reversi. LC 96-52814. 274p. 1999. pap. 24.95 (*0-312-22633-0*) St Martin.

Chang Chun Institute of Geography Staff & Chinese Academy of Sciences Staff. Deep-Water Traction Current Deposits: A Study of Internal Tides, Internal Waves, Contour Currents & Their Deposits. (Chinese Science Studies). 100p. 1998. 79.95 (*7-03-006704-5*) Intl Scholars.

Chang, Chun-shu & Chang, Shelley H. Crisis & Transformation in Seventeenth-Century China: Society, Culture, & Modernity in Li Yu's World. 472p. (C). 1998. pap. text 27.95 (*0-472-08528-X*, 08528) U of Mich Pr.

— Redefining History: Ghosts, Spirits, & Human Society in P'u Sung-ling's World, 1640-1715. LC 97-43501. (Illus.). 384p. (C). 1998. text 59.50 (*0-472-10822-0*, 10822) U of Mich Pr.

Chang Chung-Ching. Shang Han Lun: Wellspring of Chinese Medicine. 1994. pap. 14.95 (*0-941942-02-3*) Orient Heal Arts.

Chang, Chung-Fu. The Anglo-Japanese Alliance. LC 78-64282. (Johns Hopkins University. Studies in the Social Sciences. Thirtieth Ser. 1912: 12). reprint ed. 37.50 (*0-404-61382-9*) AMS Pr.

Chang, Chung-Li, ed. see Michael, Franz.

Chang, Cindy. The Seventh Sister. LC 92-43179. (Legends of the World Ser.). (Illus.). 32p. (J). (gr. 2-5). 1996. pap. 4.95 (*0-8167-3412-7*) Troll Communs.

— The Seventh Sister. LC 92-43179. (Legends of the World Ser.). (Illus.). 32p. (J). (gr. 2-5). 1997. lib. bdg. 18.60 (*0-8167-3411-9*) Troll Communs.

Chang, Cindy. Seventh Sister: A Chinese Legend. (Legends of the World Ser.). 1994. 9.70 (*0-606-06731-0*, Pub. by Turtleback) Demco.

Chang, Cindy & Sawyer, Scott. Golf: Words from the Green. LC 96-164849. (Illus.). 16p. 1995. 4.95 (*0-8362-0051-9*) Andrews & McMeel.

Chang, Clarence D. Hydrocarbons from Methanol. LC 83-1906. (Chemical Industries Ser.: Vol. 10). (Illus.). 141p. reprint ed. pap. 43.80 (*0-608-08917-6*, 206955200005) Bks Demand.

Chang, Claudia & Koster, Harold A., eds. Pastoralists at the Periphery: Herders in a Capitalist World. 262p. 1994. 47.00 (*0-8165-1430-5*) U of Ariz Pr.

Chang, Constance D. Chinese Cooking. (Quick & Easy Ser.). (Illus.). 32p. (Orig.). 1969. pap. 5.95 (*4-07-973719-X*, Pub. by Shufunomoto Co Ltd) Tuttle Pubng.

***Chang, Curtis.** Engaging Unbelief: A Captivating Strategy from Augustine & Aquinas. 180p. 2000. pap. 11.99 (*0-8308-2266-6*) InterVarsity.

Chang, Cyril F., et al. Economics & Nursing: Critical Professional Issues. (Illus.). 600p. (C). 2000. text 49.95 (*0-8036-0465-3*) Davis Co.

Chang, D. D. & Huang, S. S., eds. Plasma Space Sciences Symposium: Proceedings. 386p. 1966. pap. 88.00 (*0-677-00645-4*) Gordon & Breach.

Chang, Dae H., ed. Crime & Delinquency. LC 77-24066. 179p. 1977. pap. text 24.95 (*0-87073-398-2*) Transaction Pubs.

Chang, Dae H. & Janeksela, Galan M., eds. Juvenile Delinquency & Juvenile Justice: Comparative & International Perspectives. 300p. (Orig.). (C). 1999. pap. write for info. (*0-89386-042-5*) Acorn NC.

Chang, Dae H. & Palmiotto, Michael J. Introduction to Criminal Justice: Theory & Practice. rev. ed. xviii, 432p. (C). 1997. pap. text 34.95 (*0-9659545-0-1*) MidCont Acad.

Chang, Dae H., jt. auth. see Fagin, James.

Chang, Daniel T. Client-Server Data Access with Java & XML. LC 98-4731. 640p. 1998. pap. 49.99 incl. cd-rom (*0-471-24577-1*) Wiley.

Chang, David, tr. see Morgan, G. Campbell.

Chang, David W. China under Deng Xiaoping: Political & Economic Reform. 1990. 45.00 (*0-333-45129-5*, Pub. by Macmillan) St Martin.

— Clinical Application of Mechanical Ventilation. abr. rev. ed. LC 96-8592. (Respiratory Care Ser.). 592p. (C). 1996. mass mkt. 56.95 (*0-8273-7320-1*) Delmar.

— Clinical Application of Mechanical Ventilation. 2nd ed. (C). 2000. pap. 38.00 (*0-7668-1375-4*) Delmar.

— Resipiratory Care Calculations. LC 93-38719. 276p. (C). 1994. mass mkt. 33.25 (*0-8273-6148-3*) Delmar.

— Zhou Enlai & Deng Xiaping in the Chinese Leadership Succession Crisis. LC 83-16863. 410p. (Orig.). (C). 1984. pap. text 31.00 (*0-8191-3587-9*) U Pr of Amer.

Chang, David W. & Corn, Fred. Workbook for Respiratory Disease: A Case Study Approach to Patient Care. 2nd ed. (Illus.). 233p. (C). 1997. pap. text, wbk. ed. 21.95 (*0-8036-0156-5*) Davis Co.

Chang, David W. & Glover, Susan M. Introduction to Medical Terminology: Workbook. LC 94-6427. 1994. pap., wbk. ed. 21.95 (*0-683-16193-8*) Lppncott W & W.

***Chang, David W., et al.** The Multiskilled Respiratory Therapist: A Competency-Based Program. 3rd ed. (Illus.). 224p. (C). 2000. pap. text 29.95 (*0-8036-0380-0*) Davis Co.

Chang, Davisson K. American Business in China. (Orig.). 1995. pap. 85.00 (*0-9644322-8-5*) Caravel.

— American Business in China, 1998-1999. (Illus.). 300p. 1998. pap. 93.00 (*0-9644322-9-3*) Caravel.

***Chang, Davisson K.** American Business in China, 2000-2001. 3rd rev. ed. 286p. 2000. pap. 99.00 (*0-9644322-2-6*) Caravel.

Chang, Davisson K. Chinese Business in America. (CHI & ENG., Illus.). 220p. (Orig.). 1997. pap. 58.00 (*0-9644322-1-8*) Caravel.

— Chinese Business in America, 1999-2000. (Illus.). 300p. 1999. pap. 68.00 (*0-9644322-6-9*) Caravel.

Chang, Diana. Earth, Water, Light: Landscape Poems Celebrating the East End of Long Island. 21p. (Orig.). (C). 1991. pap. 5.00 (*1-878173-03-0*) Birnham Wood.

— The Frontiers of Love. LC 93-35512. 246p. 1993. pap. 14.95 (*0-295-97326-9*) U of Wash Pr.

— Saying Yes. Barkan, Stanley H., ed. Huang, Parker P., tr. (Review Women Writers Chapbook Ser.: No. 10). (CHI & ENG.). 48p. 1991. 15.00 (*0-89304-445-8*); 15.00 (*0-89304-447-4*); pap. 5.00 (*0-89304-446-6*); pap. 5.00 (*0-89304-448-2*) Cross-Cultrl NY.

— What Matisse Is After. (Poetry Ser.). (Illus.). 60p. (Orig.). (C). 1985. pap. 4.00 (*0-936556-12-9*) Contact Two.

Chang, Diana, jt. auth. see Barkan, Stanley H.

Chang, Diana, ed. see Huang, Parker P.

Chang, Diana M. The Days of Yore. 1997. pap. write for info. (*1-57553-558-0*) Watermrk Pr.

Chang, Donald C., et al, eds. Structure & Function of Excitable Cells. 516p. 1983. 120.00 (*0-306-41338-8*, Plenum Trade) Perseus Pubng.

Chang, Edward & Diaz-Veizades, Jeannette. Ethnic Peace in the American City: Building Community in Los Angeles & Beyond. LC 99-6222. 200p. 1999. text 55.00 (*0-8147-1583-4*) NYU Pr.

***Chang, Edward C.** Optimism & Pessimism: Implications for Theory, Research & Practice. LC 00-31310. 2000. write for info. (*1-55798-691-6*) Am Philos.

***Chang, Edward C., tr.** Knocking at the Gate of Life. 2000. 24.95 (*1-57145-662-7*, Laurel Glen Pub) Advantage Pubs.

Chang, Edward C., jt. auth. see Cho, Ta-Hung.

Chang, Edward T. Ethnic Peace in the American City: Building Community in Los Angeles & Beyond. LC 99-6222. 1999. pap. text 19.50 (*0-8147-1584-2*) NYU Pr.

Chang, Edward T. & Leong, Russell, eds. Los Angeles Struggles Toward Multiethnic Community: Asian American, African American & Latino Perspectives. LC 94-32758. (Illus.). 192p. 1994. pap. 12.95 (*0-295-97375-7*) U of Wash Pr.

Chang, Edward T., jt. ed. see Yu, Eui-Young.

***Chang, Emily, ed.** An Introduction to the Internet for Investors. (Illus.). 101p. 1999. pap. write for info. (*1-891706-03-9*) Knowldge Systs.

Chang, Evan, jt. auth. see Feldman, Larry.

Chang, Florence C. Believe It or Not: An Anthology of Ancient Tales Retold. LC 80-68258. (Chinese Can Be Fun Bks.: Level 5). (Illus.). 80p. (J). (gr. 10-12). 1980. pap., student ed. 7.50 (*0-936620-02-1*) Ginkgo Hut.

— China Is Farther Than the Sun? A Beginning Chinese-English Reader. LC 80-68256. (Chinese Can Be Fun Bks.: Level 2). (Illus.). 51p. (J). (gr. 3-4). 1980. pap., student ed. 6.00 (*0-936620-00-5*) Ginkgo Hut.

— Maomao & Mimi. LC 81-80784. (Chinese Can Be Fun Bks.: Level 3). (Illus.). 80p. (Orig.). (J). (gr. 5-6). 1981. pap. 5.00 (*0-936620-05-6*) Ginkgo Hut.

— Puppy's Tail. LC 81-82176. (Chinese Can Be Fun Bks.: Level 1). (Illus.). 72p. (Orig.). (J). (gr. 1-2). 1981. pap. 4.50 (*0-936620-06-4*) Ginkgo Hut.

— With Sound & Color: An Intermediate Chinese-English Reader. LC 80-68257. (Chinese Can Be Fun Bks.: Level 4). (Illus.). 71p. (Orig.). (J). (gr. 7-9). 1980. pap., wbk. ed. 7.00 (*0-936620-01-3*) Ginkgo Hut.

Chang, Fu-Kao, ed. Structural Health Monitoring: Current Status & Perspectives. LC 97-61700. 800p. 1997. 164.95 (*1-56676-605-2*) Technomic.

***Chang, Fu-Kuo, ed.** Structural Health Monitoring, 2000. LC 99-66093. 1088p. 1999. text 189.95 (*1-56676-881-0*) Technomic.

Chang, Garma C. Buddhist Teaching of Totality. LC 70-136965. 1971. 32.50 (*0-271-01142-4*) Pa St U Pr.

— Buddhist Teaching of Totality. LC 70-136965. 1974. pap. 17.95 (*0-271-01179-3*) Pa St U Pr.

— Teachings of Tibetan Yoga. 128p. 1974. reprint ed. pap. 3.45 (*0-8065-0460-9*, Citadel Pr) Carol Pub Group.

Chang, Garma C., tr. from TIB. Teachings of Tibetan Yoga: An Introduction to the Spiritual, Mental, & Physical Exercises of the Tibetan Religion. annot. ed. 128p. 1993. pap. 9.95 (*0-8065-1453-1*, Citadel Pr) Carol Pub Group.

Chang, Garma C. C., ed. A Treasury of Mahayana Sutras: Selections from the Maharatnakuta Sutra. Buddhist Association of the United States, tr. from CHI. LC 82-42776. (Institute for Advanced Study of World Religions Ser.). 512p. (C). 1983. 49.50 (*0-271-00341-3*) Pa St U Pr.

Chang, Gengzhe & Sederberg, Thomas. Over & Over Again. LC 97-74344. (New Mathematical Library). (Illus.). 325p. 1997. pap. text 31.50 (*0-88385-641-7*) Math Assn.

Chang, Ginger. Guide to Vancouver's Chinese Restaurants. (Illus.). 136p. (Orig.). 1985. pap. 3.99 (*0-88839-995-2*) Hancock House.

Chang, Glen, jt. auth. see Barrow, David.

Chang, Gordon H. Friends & Enemies: The United States, China, & the Soviet Union, 1948-1972. LC 89-21865. (Modern America Ser.). (Illus.). 416p. 1990. 47.50 (*0-8047-1565-3*); pap. 17.95 (*0-8047-1957-8*) Stanford U Pr.

— Morning Glory, Evening Shadow: Yamato Ichihashi & His Internment Writings, 1942-1945. (Asian America Ser.). 1999. pap. text 24.95 (*0-8047-3653-7*) Stanford U Pr.

Chang, Gordon H., ed. Morning Glory, Evening Shadow: Yamato Ichihashi & His Internment Writings, 1942-1945. LC 96-7339. 1996. 45.00 (*0-8047-2733-3*) Stanford U Pr.

Chang, Grace. Called to the Hard Places: Biography - Missionary Pioneer China, Indonesia. 1990. pap. 5.95 (*0-87508-093-6*) Chr Lit.

***Chang, Grace.** Disposable Domestics: Immigrant Women Workers in the Global Economy. LC 99-462383. 250p. 2000. 40.00 (*0-89608-618-6*, Pub. by South End Pr); pap. 18.00 (*0-89608-617-8*, Pub. by South End Pr) Consort Bk Sales.

Chang, Grace. Introduction to Civil Procedure in Malaysia & Singapore. x, 165p. 1991. pap. 30.00 (*0-409-99605-X*, MICHIE) LEXIS Pub.

— Introduction to Civil Procedure in Malaysia & Singapore. 3rd ed. 166p. 1994. pap. text. write for info. (*0-409-99686-6*, MICHIE) LEXIS Pub.

Chang, H. C., ed. Chinese Literature: Tales of the Supernatural, Vol. 3. LC 81-174030. (Chinese Literature in Translation Ser.). 169p. 1984. text 42.00 (*0-231-05794-6*) Col U Pr.

Chang, H. K. Respiratory Physiology: An Analytical Approach. Paiva, Manuel, ed. (Lung Biology in Health & Disease Ser.: Vol. 40). (Illus.). 896p. 1988. text 275.00 (*0-8247-7855-3*) Dekker.

Chang, H. K., jt. ed. see Effros, Richard M.

Chang, H. M. & But, P. P-H., eds. Pharmacology & Applications of Chinese Materia Medica, Vol. 1. 780p. 1986. text 114.00 (*9971-5-0121-X*) World Scientific Pub.

— Pharmacology & Applications of Chinese Materia Medica, Vol. 2. Wang, L. L. & Yeung, S. C., trs. 556p. 1987. text 99.00 (*9971-5-0167-8*) World Scientific Pub.

Chang, Ha-Joon & Rowthorn, Robert, eds. The Role of the State in Economic Change. (WIDER Studies in Development Economics). (Illus.). 316p. 1996. text 85.00 (*0-19-828984-7*) OUP.

Chang, Hao. Liang Ch'i-Ch'ao & Intellectual Transition in China, 1890-1907. LC 75-162635. (Harvard East Asian Ser.: No. 64). 355p. reprint ed. pap. 110.10 (*0-7837-2233-8*, 205732300004) Bks Demand.

Chang-Hasnain, Connie J., ed. Advances in Vertical Cavity Surface Emitting Lasers. LC 97-65507. (Trends in Optics & Photonics Ser.: Vol. 15). (Illus.). 253p. 1997. pap. 55.00 (*1-55752-500-5*) Optical Soc.

Chang, Hasok, ed. see Ahn, Seung-Joon.

Chang, Hedy N. Newcomer Programs: Innovative Efforts to Meet the Educational Challenges of Immigrant Students. 59p. 1990. pap. 15.00 (*1-887039-04-X*) Calif Tomorrow.

Chang, Hedy N. & Sakai, Laura. Affirming Children's Roots: Cultural & Linguistic Diversity in Early Care & Education. 101p. 1993. pap. 17.00 (*1-887039-03-2*) Calif Tomorrow.

Chang, Hedy N., et al. Drawing Strength from Diversity: Effective Services for Children, Youth & Families. 125p. 1994. pap. 21.00 (*1-887039-10-4*) Calif Tomorrow.

— Fighting Fragmentation: Collaborative Efforts to Serve Children & Families in California's Counties. 58p. 1991. pap. 12.00 (*1-887039-06-6*) Calif Tomorrow.

— Looking in Looking Out: Redefining Child Care & Early Education in a Diverse Society. Dowell, Carol, ed. (Illus.). 240p. (C). 1996. pap. 27.00 (*1-887039-12-0*) Calif Tomorrow.

Chang, Heewon. American High School Adolescent Life & Ethos: An Ethnography. 170p. 1992. 75.00 (*1-85000-865-5*, Falmer Pr) Taylor & Francis.

Chang, Heidi. Elaine & the Flying Frog. large type ed. (Orig.). 1995. 17.50 (*0-614-09574-3*, L-34785-00) Am Printing Hse.

Chang, Henry. A Top-Down Constraint-Driven Design Methodology for Analog Integrated Circuits. LC 96-41792. 384p. (C). 1996. text 126.50 (*0-7923-9794-0*) Kluwer Academic.

Chang, Hong-Mo. In Quest for a Better China. (CHI.). 230p. 1993. pap. text 9.00 (*1-879771-11-X*) Global Pub NJ.

Chang, Hou-Min, jt. auth. see Kirk, T. Kent.

Chang, Howard H. Fluvial Processes in River Engineering. LC 92-6326. (Illus.). 446p. (C). 1998. 63.50 (*1-57524-086-6*) Krieger.

— Fluvial Processes in River Engineering. LC 92-6326. 446p. (C). 1992. reprint ed. lib. bdg. 63.50 (*0-89464-737-7*) Krieger.

Chang, Hsien-Liang. Half of Man is Woman LC 89-213621. xvi, 252 p. 1988. write for info. (*0-670-81821-6*) Viking Penguin.

Chang Hsin-Chang. Allegory & Courtesy in Spenser. LC 75-30924. (English Literature Ser.: No. 33). 1975. lib. bdg. 75.00 (*0-8383-2100-3*) M S G Haskell Hse.

Chang, Hsin-Pao. Commissioner Lin & the Opium War. LC 64-21786. (Harvard East Asian Ser.: No. 18). 337p. 1964. reprint ed. pap. 104.50 (*0-7837-2232-X*, 205732200004) Bks Demand.

Chang, Hsu-Hsin & Gordon, Leonard H. Bibliography of Sun Yat-Sen in China's Republican Revolution, 1885-1925. 2nd ed. LC 97-42755. 1997. write for info. (*0-7618-0973-2*) U Pr of Amer.

Chang, Hyesun. Goethes Morphologie und Kafkas Denken: Kafkas Konzept der Asthetischen Moderne. 255p. 1998. 45.95 (*3-631-34060-5*) P Lang Pubng.

Chang, I-Ting. The Interpretation of Treaties by Judicial Tribunals. LC 68-58557. (Columbia University. Studies in the Social Sciences: No. 389). reprint ed. 20.00 (*0-404-51389-1*) AMS Pr.

Chang, Ike Y., et al. Use of Public-Private Partnerships to Meet Future Army Needs. LC 98-37972. 86p. 1998. pap. 15.00 (*0-8330-2655-0*, MR-997-A) Rand Corp.

Chang, Ina. Separate Battle: Women & the Civil War. (Young Readers' History of the Civil War Ser.). 1996. 12.19 (*0-606-09841-0*, Pub. by Turtleback) Demco.

Chang, Innie, tr. see Yeh, Jia-Tzu, et al.

***Chang, Iris.** The Rape of Nanking, Set. unabridged ed. 1998. 44.95 incl. audio (*0-7861-1258-1*, 2166) Blckstn Audio.

Chang, Iris. The Rape of Nanking: The Forgotten Holocaust of World War II. LC 97-24137. (Illus.). 290p. 1997. 25.00 (*0-465-06835-9*, Pub. by Basic) HarpC.

— The Rape of Nanking: The Forgotten Holocaust of World War II. LC 97-24137. (Illus.). 336/24p. 1998. pap. 14.95 (*0-14-027744-7*) Viking Penguin.

— Thread of the Silkworm. 480p. 1996. pap. 16.00 (*0-465-00678-7*) HarpC.

Chang, J. B., ed. International Journal of Angiology. No. 547. 1994. 129.00 (*0-614-32077-1*) Spr-Verlag.

— Part-Through Crack Fatigue Life Prediction-STP 687. 226p. 1979. 26.25 (*0-8031-0532-0*, STP687) ASTM.

Chang, J. C., et al, eds. ASME Aerospace Division: Proceedings, International Mechanical Engineering Congress & Exposition, 1996, Atlanta, Georgia. LC 96-78679. (AD Ser.: Vol. 52). 816p. 1996. pap. text 200.00 (*0-7918-1537-4*) ASME Pr.

Chang, Jaw-ling J., jt. ed. see Chiu, Hungdah.

Chang, Jeffrey, et al. Business Owners Retirement Plan Survival Guide. (Illus.). 80p. (Orig.). 1996. pap. 19.95 (*0-9654433-0-2*) Foord & Ebersole.

Chang, Jen-Chi, tr. see Fromer, Margaret & Keyes, Sharrel.

Chang, Jen-Shih, et al, eds. Handbook of Electrostatic Processes. (Illus.). 768p. 1995. text 225.00 (*0-8247-9254-8*) Dekker.

Chang, Jiin-Ju, et al. Biophotons. LC 98-7317. 414p. 1998. write for info. (*0-7923-5082-0*) Kluwer Academic.

Chang, Joanne. U. S. - China Normalization: An Evaluation of Foreign Policy. (World Affairs Ser.: Vol. 22, Bk. 4). (Orig.). 1986. pap. 9.95 (*0-87940-083-8*) Monograph Series.

Chang, John B., ed. Modern Vascular Surgery, Vol. 5. LC 92-2307. 520p. 1992. 189.00 (*0-387-97864-X*); write for info. (*3-540-97864-X*) Spr-Verlag.

— Modern Vascular Surgery, Vol. 6. 1994. write for info. (*0-387-94187-8*) Spr-Verlag.

Chang, John B., et al, eds. Textbook of Angiology. LC 98-17068. (Illus.). 1304p. 1998. 250.00 (*0-387-98449-6*) Spr-Verlag.

Chang, John K., jt. auth. see Chang, Sonia.

Chang, Jolan. The Tao of Love & Sex: The Ancient Chinese Way to Ecstasy. 136p. 1991. pap. 16.95 (*0-14-019338-3*, Arkana) Viking Penguin.

***Chang, Jui-Ming & Pedram, Massoud.** Power Optimization & Synthesis at Behavioral & System Levels Using Formal Methods LC 99-31819. 1999. write for info. (*0-7923-8560-8*) Kluwer Academic.

Chang, Juliana, ed. Quiet Fire: Asian American Poetry, 1892-1970. LC 96-78961. 164p. 1996. pap. 19.95 (*1-889876-02-X*) Asian Am Writers.

Chang, Jung. Wild Swans: Three Daughters of China. LC 92-19078. (Illus.). 524p. 1992. reprint ed. pap. 16.95 (*0-385-42547-3*, Anchor NY) Doubleday.

Chang, K. C. Art, Myth, & Ritual: The Path to Political Authority in Ancient China. (Illus.). 160p. (C). 1983. 32.00 (*0-674-04807-5*) HUP.

— Art, Myth & Ritual: The Path to Political Authority in Ancient China. (Illus.). 160p. 1988. reprint ed. pap. 13.95 (*0-674-04808-3*) HUP.

— Digital Design & Modeling with VHDL & Synthesis. LC 96-45231. 368p. 1997. 55.00 (*0-8186-7716-3*) IEEE Comp Soc.

— Digital Systems Design with VHDL & Synthesis. LC 99-24750. (Illus.). 1999. 55.00 (*0-7695-0023-4*) IEEE Comp Soc.

— Early Chinese Civilization: Anthropological Perspectives. (Harvard-Yenching Institute Monographs: No. 23). (Illus.). 251p. 1976. 19.95 (*0-674-21999-6*) HUP.

— Infinite Dimensional Morse Theory. x, 312p. 1992. 76.50 (*0-8176-3451-7*) Birkhauser.

Chang, K. C., et al. Nonlinear Analysis & Microlocal Analysis: Proceedings of the International Conference at the Nankai Institute of Mathematics. (Nankai Series in Pure, Applied Mathematics & Theoretical Physics). 400p. 1992. text 78.00 (*981-02-0913-4*) World Scientific Pub.

Chang, K. C., jt. auth. see Li Xueqin.

Chang, K. C., jt. ed. see Ambrosetti, Antonio.

Chang, K. M., et al, eds. Advanced Technologies for Superalloys Affordability. (Illus.). 316p. 80.00 (*0-87339-457-7*) Minerals Metals.

Chang, K. W. & Howes, F. A. Nonlinear Singular Perturbation Phenomena: Theory & Applications. (Applied Mathematical Sciences Ser.: Vol. 56). (Illus.). viii, 180p. 1984. 58.95 (*0-387-96066-X*) Spr-Verlag.

Chang, Kai. Handbook of Microwave & Optical Components, 4 vols. 2675p. 1991. 764.00 (*0-471-50283-9*) Wiley.

— Handbook of Microwave & Optical Components Vol. 1: Microwave Passive & Antenna Components, 4 vols., Vol. 1, Microwave Passive and Antenna Components. LC 88-27835. 928p. 1989. 295.00 (*0-471-61366-5*) Wiley.

— Handbook of Microwave & Optical Components Vol. 2: Microwave Solid-State Components, 4 vols., Vol. 2, Microwave Solid-State Components. LC 89-29222. 656p. 1990. 185.00 (*0-471-84365-2*) Wiley.

— Handbook of Microwave & Optical Components Vol. 3: Optical Components, 4 vols. 640p. 1990. 225.00 (*0-471-61367-3*) Wiley.

— Handbook of Microwave & Optical Components Vol. 4: Fiber & Elecrto-Optical Components, 4 vols., Vol. 4, Fiber and Electro-Optical Components. LC 90-12108. 496p. 1991. 185.00 (*0-471-61365-7*) Wiley.

— Microwave & Optical Technology Letters. 1988. pap. 120.00 (*0-471-60578-6*) Wiley.

— Microwave Ring Circuits & Antennas. LC 95-38581. (Series in Microwave & Optical Engineering). 296p. 1996. 125.00 (*0-471-13109-1*) Wiley.

— Microwave Solid-State Circuits & Applications. (Series in Microwave & Optical Engineering). 456p. 1994. 120.00 (*0-471-54044-7*) Wiley.

***Chang, Kai.** RF Microwave Wireless Systems. LC 99-89122. 352p. 2000. text 79.95 (*0-471-35199-7*) Wiley.

Chang, Kai, ed. Handbook of Microwave & Optical Components: Microwave Passive & Antenna Components, Vol. 1, Microwave Passive and Antenna Components. LC 88-27834. 907p. 1997. pap. 69.95 (*0-471-18442-X*) Wiley.

Chang, Kai, jt. auth. see Navarro, Julio A.

C

Chang, Kai-Ming, et al. Controversies in Orthopaedic Sports Medicine. 500p. 1997. write for info. (962-356-025-7) Lppncott W & W.

Chang, Kang-I S. The Late-Ming Poet Chen Tzu-Lung: Crises of Love & Loyalism. LC 90-12485. (Illus.). 203p. 1991. reprint ed. pap. 63.00 (0-608-07883-2, 205999000010) Bks Demand.

Chang, Kang-I Sung, et al. Women Writers of Traditional China: An Anthology of Poetry & Criticism. LC 99-19030. 1999. 29.95 (0-8047-3231-0) Stanford U Pr.

Chang, Kang-I Sung, jt. auth. see Widmer, Ellen.

Chang, Kee, ed. see Huang.

Chang, Keqian & Li, Dejie. Electromagnetic Theory for Microwaves & Optoelectronics. LC 98-8675. 1998. write for info. (3-540-63178-X) Spr-Verlag.

Chang, Kevin O. & Chen, Wayne. Reggae Routes: The Story of Jamaican Music. LC 98-164555. (Illus.). 250p. 1997. pap. 19.95 (1-56639-629-8) Temple U Pr.

Chang Kia-ngau, pseud. China's Struggle for Railroad Development. LC 74-34331. (China in the 20th Century Ser.). (Illus.). vii, 340p. 1975. reprint ed. lib. bdg. 39.50 (0-306-70689-X) Da Capo.

Chang, Kou, jt. auth. see Pinkel, Sheila.

Chang Kuo-t'ao. The Rise of the Chinese Communist Party, 1928-1938: Volume Two of the Autobiography of Chang Kuo-t'ao. LC 76-141997. viii, 628p. 1971. 40.00 (0-7006-0088-4) U Pr of KS.

Chang, Kwang-Chih. Fengpitou, Tapenkeng & the Prehistory of Taiwan. LC 69-11698. (Publications in Anthropology: No. 73). 1969. pap. 15.00 (0-913516-06-6) Yale U Anthro.

Chang, L. L., et al, eds. Non-Silicates. (Rock-Forming Minerals Ser.: No. 5B). (Illus.). 392p. 1997. 125.00 (1-897799-90-X, Pub. by Geol Soc Pub Hse) AAPG.

Chang, L. L., et al. Resonant Tunneling in Semiconductors: Physics & Applications. (NATO ASI Ser.: Vol. 277). (Illus.). 552p. (C). 1992. text 145.00 (0-306-44048-2, Kluwer Plenum) Kluwer Academic.

Chang, L. W. Heavy Metals. 73p. 1989. text 101.00 (2-88124-409-2) Gordon & Breach.

Chang, L. W., jt. auth. see Fan, A.

Chang, Lan Samantha. Hunger. LC 98-13547. 160p. 1998. 22.00 (0-393-04664-8) Norton.

***Chang, Lan Samantha.** Hunger. 192p. 2000. pap. 12.95 (0-14-028848-1) Viking Penguin.

Chang, Laura. Kaleidoscope: A Bit of East, a Bit of West. (Orig.). 1997. per. 7.95 (0-9655482-2-8) TLC Global.

Chang, Laurence & Kornbluh, Peter, eds. Cuban Missile Crisis, 1962: A National Security Archive Documents Reader. LC 92-53734. (Illus.). 448p. 1992. 25.00 (1-56584-019-4, Pub. by New Press NY) Norton.

— Cuban Missile Crisis, 1962: A National Security Archive Documents Reader. rev. ed. (National Security Archive Documents Reader Ser.). (Illus.). 429p. 1998. pap. 19.95 (1-56584-474-2, Pub. by New Press NY) Norton.

Chang, Laurence, ed. see National Security Archive Staff & Chadwyck-Healey Staff.

Chang, Leo & Feng, Yu. The Four Political Treatises of the Yellow Emperor: Original Mawangdui Texts with Complete English Translations & an Introduction. LC 97-48960. (Monographs of the Society for Asian & Comparative Philosophy: Vol. 15). 248p. 1998. pap. text 20.00 (0-8248-2008-8) UH Pr.

Chang, Leon L. & Miller, Peter. Four Thousand Years of Chinese Calligraphy. LC 89-32236. (Illus.). 463p. 1990. 55.00 (0-226-10111-8) U Ch Pr.

Chang, Leonard. Dispatches from the Cold. LC 99-173220. 282p. 1998. 23.95 (0-930773-49-7) Black Heron Pr.

— The Fruit 'n Food. LC 99-173813. 227p. (Orig.). 1996. 21.95 (0-930773-45-4) Black Heron Pr.

Chang, Leroy L. & Ploog, Klaus, eds. Molecular Beam Epitaxy & Heterostructures. 1984. text 321.50 (90-247-3118-6) Kluwer Academic.

***Chang, Leslie.** Beyond the Narrow Gate: The Journey of Four Chinese Women from the Middle Kingdom to Middle America. 2000. pap. 13.95 (0-452-27761-2, Plume) Dutton Plume.

Chang, Leslie. Beyond the Narrow Gate: The Journey of Four Chinese Women from the Middle Kingdom to Middle America. LC 98-33267. 320p. 1999. 24.95 (0-525-94257-2) NAL.

Chang, Louis W. Principles of Neurotoxicology, No. 26. LC 94-7435. (Neurological Disease & Therapy Ser.: Vol. 26). (Illus.). 824p. 1994. text 245.00 (0-8247-8836-2) Dekker.

Chang, Louis W., et al, eds. Toxicology of Metals, Vol. 1. LC 95-42586. 1232p. 1996. lib. bdg. 139.00 (0-87371-803-8, L803) Lewis Pubs.

Chang, Louis W. & Dyer, Robert A., eds. Handbook of Neurotoxicology, Vol. 2. (Neurological Disease & Therapy Ser.: Vol. 36). (Illus.). 1136p. 1995. text 215.00 (0-8247-8873-7) Dekker.

Chang, Louis W. & Slikker, William. Approaches & Methods in Neurotoxicology. 1994. text 149.00 (981-02-1798-6) World Scientific Pub.

Chang, Louis W. & Slikker, William, eds. Neurotoxicology: Approaches & Methods. (Illus.). 851p. 1995. text 149.95 (0-12-168055-X) Acad Pr.

Chang, Louis W., ed. see Fan, Hong Y.

Chang, Louis W., jt. ed. see Slikker, William.

Chang, Lucia S. & Most, Kenneth S. The Perceived Usefulness of Financial Statements for Investors' Decisions. LC 84-25788. (Illus.). 141p. 1985. reprint ed. pap. 43.80 (0-608-04477-6, 206522200001) Bks Demand.

Chang, Luh-Maan. Preparing for Construction in the 21st Century. LC 91-24956. 816p. 1991. pap. text 9.00 (0-87262-801-9) Am Soc Civil Eng.

Chang, Lung-Hsi. Mighty Opposites: From Dichotomies to Differences in the Comparative Study of China. LC 98-26223. 248 p. 1999. write for info. (0-8047-3259-0) Stanford U Pr.

Chang, Lynn. Costumes for Your Cat. LC 94-43166. (Illus.). 48p. 1995. 6.95 (0-8118-1029-1) Chronicle Bks.

***Chang, Lynn.** Disguises for Your Dog. (Illus.). 48p. 2000. pap. 9.95 (0-312-26277-9, St Martin Griffin) St Martin.

— Look at Me! Animals: My Own Photo Book. (Illus.). 20p. (J). 2000. 6.95 (0-8118-2255-9) Chronicle Bks.

— Look at Me! Vehicles: My Own Photo Book. (Illus.). 20p. (YA). 2000. 6.95 (0-8118-2278-8) Chronicle Bks.

Chang, M. Quick & Easy Science. 48p. (J). (gr. 1-3). 1997. pap. 8.95 (0-590-96375-9) Scholastic Inc.

Chang, M., et al. Chracteristics of a Humid Climate: Nacogdoches, Texas. (Illus.). 211p. (C). 1996. 25.95 (0-938361-20-1) Austin Univ Forestry.

Chang, M., ed. see Lotocki, Borys.

Chang, M., ed. see Moshinsky, George.

Chang, M. F. Current Trends in Hetero Junction Bipolar Devices. (Current Topics in Electronics & Systems Ser.). 200p. 1996. text 61.00 (981-02-2097-9) World Scientific Pub.

Chang, M. K. & Lih, K. W., eds. Algebra, Analysis & Geometry. 272p. (C). 1989. text 77.00 (9971-5-0898-2) World Scientific Pub.

Chang, Margaret & Chang, Raymond. The Cricket Warrior. LC 93-35395. (Illus.). 32p. (J). (gr. k-4). 1994. pap. 14.95 (0-689-50605-8) Atheneum Yung Read.

Chang, Margaret & Chang, Raymond. Da Wei's Treasure: A Chinese Tale. LC 97-26848. (Illus.). 32p. (J). (gr. k-4). 1999. 16.00 (0-689-81835-1) S&S Childrens.

— In the Eye of War. LC 89-38027. 208p. (J). (gr. 4-7). 1990. 14.95 (0-689-50503-5) McElderry Bks.

Chang, Margaret S. The Beggar's Magic: A Chinese Tale. LC 96-20865. (Illus.). 32p. (J). (gr. k-4). 1997. per. 16.00 (0-689-81340-6) McElderry Bks.

Chang, Margaret S., jt. auth. see Chang, Raymond.

Chang, Maria H. The Chinese Blue Shirt Society: Fascism & Developmental Nationalism. LC 85-80730. (China Research Monographs: No. 30). 144p. 1985. pap. 15.00 (0-912966-81-5) IEAS.

— The Labors of Sisyphus: The Economic Development of Communist China. LC 97-19298. 310p. 1997. 39.95 (1-56000-330-8) Transaction Pubs.

***Chang, Maria H.** The Labors of Sisyphus: The Economic Development of Communist China. 259p. 1999. pap. 24.95 (0-7658-0661-4) Transaction Pubs.

Chang, Maria H., jt. auth. see Gregor, A. James.

Chang Meemann, ed. Early Vertebrates & Related Problems of Evolutionary Biology: Papers from the Symposium on Early Vertebrates & Related Problems of Evolutionary Biology Held in Beijing on September 12-26, 1987. 514p. 1996. 49.00 (7-03-002440-0, Pub. by Sci Pr) Lubrecht & Cramer.

Chang-Ming Charlie Ma. Kilovoltage X-Ray Dosimetry for Radiotherapy. LC 98-89979. (AAPM Proceedings Ser.: No. 11). 309p. 1998. text 90.00 (1-888340-16-9) AAPM.

Chang, Mingteh. Laboratory Notes, Forest Hydrology. (Illus.). 203p. 1982. student ed. 10.00 (0-938361-03-1) Austin Univ Forestry.

Chang, Monica. Story of the Chinese Zodiac: El Zodiaco Chino. Zeller, Beatriz, tr. from CHI. (ENG & SPA., Illus.). 32p. (J). (gr. 2-4). 1994. 16.95 (957-32-2143-8) Pan Asian Pubns.

Chang, Monica & Liu, Lesley. The Mouse Bride: La Novia Raton. Zeller, Beatriz, tr. from CHI. (ENG & SPA., Illus.). 32p. (J). (gr. 2-4). 1994. 16.95 (957-32-2150-0) Pan Asian Pubns.

Chang, Nahn-Joo, jt. auth. see Chang, Chan-Sup.

Chang, NaiKang. Let Us All Sleep, Nature's Way. (Illus.). (Orig.). 1989. pap. 12.95 (0-9622374-0-X) Jupiter Pub.

Chang, Naikang. Let's All Sleep, Nature's Way, Vol. 1. (Illus.). (Orig.). 1989. pap. write for info. (0-318-64861-X) Jupiter Pub.

Chang, Namgui & Kim, Yong C. Active Korean. LC 95-76494. (Illus.). 439p. 1996. text 32.95 (1-56591-059-1, Pub. by Hollym Bks) Weatherhill.

Chang, Namgui, jt. auth. see Kim, Yong-Chol.

Chang, Ning, jt. ed. see Rao, A. R.

Chang, Ning S., jt. ed. see Tobin, Kenneth W.

Chang, Ning-San. Image Analysis & Image Database Management. Stone, Harold S., ed. LC 81-10406. (Computer Science: No. 9). (Illus.). 158p. 1981. reprint ed. pap. 49.00 (0-8357-1217-6, 207005200063) Bks Demand.

Chang, Norma. My Students' Favorite Chinese Recipes. (Illus.). 200p. (Orig.). 1987. pap. 9.75 (0-9618759-0-9) Travelling Gourmet.

— Wokking Your Way to Low Fat Cooking. Wong, Amy, ed. & illus. by. LC 93-60859. 208p. (Orig.). 1994. pap. 12.50 (0-9618759-1-7) Travelling Gourmet.

Chang, Ok Y., tr. see Moo-Sook, Hahn.

Chang, Pang-Mei N. Bound Feet & Western Dress: A Memoir. (Illus.). 288p. 1997. pap. 13.95 (0-385-47964-6, Anchor NY) Doubleday.

Chang, Pao-min. Sino-Vietnamese Territorial Dispute, 118. LC 85-19445. (Washington Papers: No. 118). 127p. 1985. 45.00 (0-275-90022-3, C0022, Praeger Pubs); pap. 12.95 (0-275-91456-9, B1456, Praeger Pubs) Greenwood.

Chang, Parris H. Elite Conflict in the Post-Mao China. rev. ed. (Occasional Papers-Reprints Series in Contemporary Asian Studies: No. 2-1983 (55)). 48p. 1983. pap. text 2.50 (0-942182-54-5) U MD Law.

Chang, Parris H. & Lasater, Martin L., eds. If China Crosses the Taiwan Strait: The International Response. LC 92-32649. (Illus.). 200p. 1993. pap. text 24.50 (0-8191-8850-6) U Pr of Amer.

— If China Crosses the Taiwan Strait: The International Response. LC 92-32649. (Illus.). 208p. 1993. lib. bdg. 51.50 (0-8191-8849-2) U Pr of Amer.

Chang, Patricia L., ed. Somatic Gene Therapy. LC 94-17728. 320p. 1994. boxed set 104.95 (0-8493-2440-8) CRC Pr.

Chang, Paul. Cancer Treatment Research. Aisner, Joseph, ed. (Developments in Oncology Ser.: Vol. 2). (Illus.). xvi, 272p. 1980. text 131.50 (90-247-2358-2) Kluwer Academic.

Chang, Paul, tr. see Parker, J. I.

Chang, Paul K. Recent Development in Flow Separation. LC 83-72431. (Illus.). 300p. 1983. write for info. (0-9612410-6-3) P K Chang.

Chang, Peter, ed. Readings in Black Aged. 212p. 1977. 32.50 (0-8422-0556-X) Irvington.

Chang, Peter, et al. Hanyu for Beginning Students. rev. ed. (Hanyu Ser.). (CHI.). 181p. (YA). 1995. pap. text 21.95 (0-88727-221-5); pap. text, teacher ed. 29.95 (0-88727-228-2) Cheng & Tsui.

— Hanyu for Beginning Students: Character Writing Book. rev. ed. (Hanyu Ser.). (CHI., Illus.). 44p. (YA). 1995. pap. text 5.95 (0-88727-213-4) Cheng & Tsui.

— Hanyu for Beginning Students: Practice Book. rev. ed. (Hanyu Ser.). (CHI., Illus.). 94p. (YA). 1995. pap. text 14.95 (0-88727-230-4) Cheng & Tsui.

— Hanyu for Intermediate Students Stage 1. (Hanyu Ser.). (CHI., Illus.). 133p. (YA). 1995. pap. text, teacher ed. 32.00 (0-88727-218-5) Cheng & Tsui.

— Hanyu for Intermediate Students Stage 1. rev. ed. (Hanyu Ser.). (CHI., Illus.). 213p. (YA). 1995. pap. text, student ed. 29.95 (0-88727-217-7) Cheng & Tsui.

— Hanyu for Intermediate Students Stage 1: Character Writing Book. rev. ed. (Hanyu Ser.). (CHI., Illus.). 60p. (YA). 1995. pap. text 7.50 (0-88727-215-0) Cheng & Tsui.

— Hanyu for Intermediate Students Stage 1: Practice Book. rev. ed. (Hanyu Ser.). (CHI., Illus.). 132p. (YA). 1995. pap. text 19.95 (0-88727-216-9) Cheng & Tsui.

— Hanyu for Intermediate Students Stage 2: Character Writing Book. rev. ed. (Hanyu Ser.). (CHI., Illus.). 68p. (YA). 1995. pap. text 7.50 (0-88727-220-7) Cheng & Tsui.

— Hanyu for Intermediate Students Stage 2: Student Book. rev. ed. (Hanyu Ser.). (CHI., Illus.). 218p. (YA). 1995. pap. text, student ed. 29.95 (0-88727-219-3) Cheng & Tsui.

— Hanyu for Intermediate Students Stage 3: Students Book. rev. ed. (Hanyu Ser.). (CHI., Illus.). (YA). 1996. pap. text 34.95 (0-88727-235-5) Cheng & Tsui.

Chang, Peter, et al. Hanyu for Senior Students Stage 4. rev. ed. student ed. 34.95 (0-88727-294-0) Cheng & Tsui.

— Hanyu for Senior Students Stage 4. rev. ed. 1999. write for info. (0-88727-325-4) Cheng & Tsui.

— Hanyu For Senior Students Stage 4. rev. ed. 2000. teacher ed. write for info. (0-88727-295-9) Cheng & Tsui.

— Hanyu 3. rev. ed. 1999. student ed. 34.95 (0-88727-335-1) Cheng & Tsui.

— Hanyu 3. rev. ed. 1999. write for info. (0-88727-337-8); teacher ed. write for info. (0-88727-339-4) Cheng & Tsui.

Chang, Peter, et al. Hanyu 3: Practice Book. rev. ed. (Hanyu Ser.). (CHI.). (YA). pap. text 17.95 (0-88727-238-X) Cheng & Tsui.

— Hanyu 3: Teacher's Book. rev. ed. (Hanyu Ser.). (CHI.). pap. text 36.95 (0-88727-237-1) Cheng & Tsui.

Chang Po-tuan. Understanding Reality: A Taoist Alchemical Classic. Cleary, Thomas, tr. LC 87-25539. 176p. 1987. pap. text 17.00 (0-8248-1139-9) UH Pr.

Chang-Po Yang. Egypt in the Global Economy: Strategic Choices for Savings, Investments, & Long-Term Growth. LC 97-31580. (Middle East & North Africa Economic Studies). 120p. 1998. pap. 22.00 (0-8213-4066-2, 14066) World Bank.

Chang, R. Jeffrey, ed. Polycystic Ovary Syndrome: Proceedings of the Symposium, Sponsored by Serono Symposia U S A, Inc., Held in Boston, Massachusetts, May 18-21, 1995. LC 96-11919. 392p. 1996. 135.00 (0-387-94741-8) Spr-Verlag.

Chang, R. K. & Barber, P. W. Optical Effects Associated with Small Particles. (Advanced Series in Applied Physics: Vol. 1). 360p. (C). 1988. pap. 51.00 (9971-5-0462-6); text 109.00 (9971-5-0412-X) World Scientific Pub.

Chang, R. P., jt. auth. see Rhee, S. C.

Chang, R. P., jt. auth. see Rhee, S. G.

Chang, R. P., jt. ed. see Ghon, Rhee S.

Chang, R. P. H., et al, eds. Proceedings of the Second International Conference on Electronic Materials: Materials Research Society Conference Proceedings, Vol. ICEM-2. 664p. 1991. text 17.50 (1-55899-092-5) Materials Res.

Chang, R. P. H. & Abeles, B., eds. Plasma Synthesis & Etching of Electronic Materials, Vol. 38. LC 85-3085. 1985. text 17.50 (0-931837-03-0) Materials Res.

Chang, Raymond. Chemistry. (C). 1991. pap. text, teacher ed. 28.12 (0-07-042449-7) McGraw.

— Chemistry. 5th ed. (C). 1994. pap. text, teacher ed. 28.12 (0-07-011007-7) McGraw.

— Chemistry: MicroGuide, Macintosh. 5th ed. (C). 1994. 19.50 (0-07-832113-1) McGraw.

— Essential Chemistry. LC 95-41428. (C). 1995. text 55.25 (0-07-011207-X) McGraw.

***Chang, Raymond.** Essential Chemistry. 2nd ed. LC 99-29970. 1999. pap. text 65.00 (0-07-290500-X) McGraw.

— Essential Chemistry: A Core Text for General Chemistry 2nd ed. LC 99-29970. 1999. write for info. (0-07-116940-7) McGraw.

Chang, Raymond. Essential Chemistry: Problem Solving Workbook. (C). 1996. pap., wbk. ed. 25.31 (0-07-011637-7) McGraw.

***Chang, Raymond.** Essential Chemistry: Solutions Manual. 2nd ed. 560p. (C). 2000. pap. 33.75 (0-07-290520-4) McGrw-H Hghr Educ.

Chang, Raymond. Physical Chemistry for the Chemical & Biological Sciences. 3rd ed. LC 99-55696. (Illus.). 960p. (C). 2000. text 86.50 (1-891389-06-8, 1-891389-06-8) Univ Sci Bks.

Chang, Raymond & Chang, Margaret S. Speaking of Chinese. (Illus.). 1983. pap. 11.95 (0-393-30061-7) Norton.

Chang, Raymond & Mills, Jerry L. Chemistry. 5th ed. (C). 1993. pap. text, student ed. 22.00 (0-07-011004-2) McGraw.

Chang, Raymond & Watkins, Kenneth W. Chemistry. 5th ed. (C). 1994. pap. text, student ed. 22.50 (0-07-011005-0) McGraw.

Chang, Raymond, et al. Chemistry. 6th ed. LC 97-16758. (C). 1997. text 74.74 (0-07-011644-X) McGraw.

Chang, Raymond, jt. auth. see Chang, Margaret.

Chang, Richard. Read Chinese, Bk. 2. enl. ed. 1983. audio 8.95 (0-88710-067-8) Yale Far Eastern Pubns.

Chang, Richard. Read Chinese, Bk. 2. expanded ed. 1983. 15.95 (0-88710-066-X) Yale Far Eastern Pubns.

— Ten Tools for Quality. LC 94-70860. (AMI How-to Ser.). 117p. (Orig.). 1994. per. 12.95 (1-884926-24-X, QUALI) Amer Media.

Chang, Richard, jt. auth. see Wang, Fred.

Chang, Richard, Associates, Inc. Staff. Meetings That Work! A Practical Guide to Shorter & More Productive Meetings. LC 93-77939. (Quality Improvement Ser.). 100p. 1993. pap. 12.95 (1-883553-18-0) R Chang Assocs.

Chang, Richard C., jt. auth. see Smith, Frank C., Jr.

Chang, Richard F., ed. Modern Chinese Poetry. 1973. 13.95 (0-88710-049-X) Yale Far Eastern Pubns.

— Under the Eaves of Shanghai: Shanghai Wuyansya, an Annotated Chinese Play. 1974. 13.95 (0-88710-122-4) Yale Far Eastern Pubns.

Chang, Richard F., retold by. Chinese Mythical Stories. (CHI.). (Orig.). 1990. pap. text 12.95 (0-88710-164-X) Yale Far Eastern Pubns.

Chang, Richard F., jt. auth. see Li, Tien-yi.

Chang, Richard K. & Campillo, Anthony J., eds. Optical Processes in Microcavities. LC 95-46571. (Advanced Series in Applied Physics: Vol. 3). 400p. 1996. text 78.00 (981-02-2344-7) World Scientific Pub.

Chang, Richard K. & Furtak, Thomas E., eds. Surface Enhanced Raman Scattering. LC 81-22739. 450p. (C). 1982. 95.00 (0-306-40907-0, Plenum Trade) Perseus Pubng.

Chang, Richard T. Historians & Meiji Statesmen. LC 78-631066. (University of Florida Monographs: Social Sciences: No. 41). 118p. reprint ed. pap. 36.60 (0-7837-4974-0, 204464000004) Bks Demand.

— The Justice of the Western Consular Courts in Nineteenth Century Japan, 10. LC 83-12573. (Contributions in Intercultural & Comparative Studies: No. 10). (Illus.). 183p. 1984. 52.95 (0-313-24103-1, CJW/, Greenwood Pr) Greenwood.

Chang, Richard Y. Building a Dynamic Team: A Practical Guide to Maximizing Team Performance. LC 93-74772. (High Performance Team Ser.). Orig. Title: Effectiveness Through Team Building. (Illus.). 120p. 1994. pap. 14.95 (0-7879-5091-2) R Chang Assocs.

— Capitalizing on Workplace Diversity: A Practical Guide to Organizational Success Through Diversity. (Workplace Diversity Ser.). (Illus.). 120p. 1995. pap. 14.95 (0-7879-5102-1) R Chang Assocs.

Chang, Richard Y. Continuous Improvement Tools Vol. 2: A Practical Guide to Achieve Quality Results. (Illus.). 1994. pap. 14.95 (1-883553-01-6) R Chang Assocs.

Chang, Richard Y. Continuous Process Improvement: A Practical Guide to Improving Processes for Measurable Results. (Quality Improvement Ser.). 120p. 1994. pap. 12.95 (1-883553-06-7) R Chang Assocs.

— Creating High-Impact Training: A Practical Guide to Successful Training Outcomes. (High Impact Training Ser.). (Illus.). 120p. 1994. pap. 14.95 (0-7879-5098-X) R Chang Assocs.

Chang, Richard Y. Improving Through Benchmarking: A Practical Guide to Achieving Peak Process Performance. (Quality Improvement Ser.). 1993. pap. 14.95 (1-883553-08-3) R Chang Assocs.

Chang, Richard Y. Mastering Change Management: A Practical Guide for Turning Obstacles into Opportunities. LC 93-74767. (Management Skills Ser.). Orig. Title: Managing in a Changing Environment. (Illus.). 108p. 1994. pap. 14.95 (0-7879-5088-2) R Chang Assocs.

Chang, Richard Y. Mastering Change Management: A Practical Guide for Turning Obstacles Into Opportunities. (Management Skills Ser.). 1994. pap. 14.95 (1-883553-54-7) R Chang Assocs.

Chang, Richard Y. Measuring Organizational Improvement Impact: A Practical Guide to Measuring Tracking Against the Right Targets. 1996. pap. 14.95 (0-7879-5101-3) Jossey-Bass.

Chang, Richard Y. Meetings That Work. 1994. pap. 12.95 (0-7879-5079-3) Jossey-Bass.

Chang, Richard Y. The Passion Play: A Step-by-Step Guide to Discovering, Developing & Living Your Passion. LC 99-6392. 320p. 1999. 25.00 (0-7879-4813-6) Jossey-Bass.

— Process Reengineering in Action: A Practical Guide to Achieving Breakthrough Results. (Quality Improvement Ser.). (Illus.). 120p. 1995. pap. 14.95 (0-7879-5096-3) R Chang Assocs.

Chang, Richard Y. Satisfying Internal Customers First! A Practical Guide to Improving Internal & External... 1991. pap. 14.95 (1-883553-04-0) R Chang Assocs.

***Chang, Richard Y.** Success Through Teamwork: A Practical Guide to Interpersonal Team Dynamics. (High Performance Team Ser.). Orig. Title: Managing Team Dynamics. 101p. 1999. pap. 14.95 (0-7879-5111-0) Jossey-Bass.

An Asterisk (*) at the beginning of an entry indicates that the title is appearing for the first time.

Chang, Richard Y. Success Through Teamwork: A Practical Guide to Interpersonal Team Dynamics. LC 93-74770. (High Performance Team Ser.). Orig. Title: Managing Team Dynamics. (Illus.). 101p. 1994. pap. 12.95 (*1-883553-25-3*) R Chang Assocs.

Chang, Richard Y. & Curtin, Mark J. Succeeding As a Self-Managed Team: A Practical Guide to Operating As a Self-Managed Work Team. LC 93-91040. (Quality Improvement Ser.). 104p. 1994. pap. 12.95 (*1-883553-20-2*) R Chang Assocs.

Chang, Richard Y. & Kelly, P. Keith. Communicating in a Diverse Workplace. (Practical Guidebks.). 14.95 (*0-7879-5103-X*, Pfffr & Co) Jossey-Bass.

Chang, Richard Y. & Kelly, P. Keith. Improving Through Benchmarking: A Practical Guide to Achieving Peak Process Performance. LC 93-91035. (Quality Improvement Ser.). 120p. 1993. pap. 14.95 (*0-7879-5084-X*) R Chang Assocs.

Chang, Richard Y. & Kelly, P. Keith. Measuring the Impact of Training. (Practical Guidebks.). 14.95 (*0-7879-5094-7*, Pfffr & Co) Jossey-Bass.

— Re-Creating Teams During Transition. 2nd ed. (Practical Guidebks.). 14.95 (*0-7879-5095-5*, Pfffr & Co) Jossey-Bass.

Chang, Richard Y. & Kelly, P. Keith. Satisfying Internal Customers First! A Practical Guide to Improving Internal & External Customer Satisfaction. (Quality Improvement Ser.). (Illus.). 120p. 1994. pap. 14.95 (*0-7879-5082-3*) R Chang Assocs.

Chang, Richard Y. & Kelly, P. Keith. Step-by-Step Problem Solving. (Practical Guidebks.). 14.95 (*0-7879-5078-5*, Pfffr & Co) Jossey-Bass.

Chang, Richard Y. & Kelly, P. Keith. Step-by-Step Problem Solving: A Practical Guide to Ensure Problems Get (& Stay) Solved. (Qualtiy Improvement Ser.). 100p. 1994. pap. 12.95 (*1-883553-11-3*) R Chang Assocs.

Chang, Richard Y. & Kelly, P. Keith. Successful Staffing in a Diverse Workplace. 14.95 (*0-7879-5104-8*, Pfffr & Co) Jossey-Bass.

***Chang, Richard Y. & Morgan, Mark W.** Performance Scorecards: Measuring the Right Things in the Real World. LC 99-50888. 2000. 28.00 (*0-7879-5272-9*) Jossey-Bass.

Chang, Richard Y. & Niedzwiecki, Matthew E. Continuous Improvement Tools: A Practical Guide to Achieve Quality Results, Vol. 1. LC 93-77938. (Quality Improvement Ser.). 100p. 1993. pap. 14.95 (*0-7879-5080-7*) R Chang Assocs.

— Continuous Improvement Tools Vol. 2: A Practical Guide to Achieve Quality Results, Vol. 2. (Quality Improvement Ser.). 120p. 1994. pap. 14.95 (*0-7879-5081-5*) R Chang Assocs.

Chang, Robert, tr. see Rookmaaker, H. R.

Chang, Robert C., ed. see Sheu, Bing J. & Choi, Joongho.

***Chang, Robert S.** Disoriented: Asian Americans, Law & the Nation State. LC 98-58131. 180p. 1999. text 34.00 (*0-8147-1521-4*) NYU Pr.

Chang, Robert S. Preventive Health Care. LC 80-24183. 1981. 35.00 (*0-8161-2165-6*) Mac Lib Ref.

Chang-Rodriguez. Latinoamerica. 2nd ed. (C). 1991. mass mkt. 37.95 (*0-8384-3540-8*) Heinle & Heinle.

***Chang-Rodriguez & Filer, M.** Voces De Hispanoamerica. 3rd ed. (SPA.). (C). 2002. pap. 46.00 (*0-8384-1653-5*) Heinle & Heinle.

Chang, Rodriguez R. & Filer, Malva. Voces de Hispanoamerica: Antologia Literaria. (C). 1996. pap. 37.25 (*0-8384-1603-9*) Heinle & Heinle.

Chang-Rodriguez, Raquel. Hidden Messages: Representation & Resistance in Andean Colonial Drama. LC 98-47707. (Illus.). 144p. 1999. 32.50 (*0-8387-5421-X*) Bucknell U Pr.

Chang-Rodriguez, Raquel & Filer, Malva E. Voces de Hispanoamerica. 2nd ed. (College Spanish Ser.). (SPA.). (C). 1996. mass mkt. 66.95 (*0-8384-5186-1*) Heinle & Heinle.

Chang-Rodriguez, Raquel & Yates, Donald A., eds. Homage to Irving A. Leonard: Essays on Hispanic Art, History, & Literature. LC 77-72628. (Illus.). 231p. reprint ed. pap. 71.70 (*0-608-11317-4*, 205037300068) Bks Demand.

Chang-Rodriquez, E., jt. auth. see Juilland, Alphonse.

Chang-Rodrmguez, Eugenio, et al. Latinoamirica: Su Civilizacisn y Su Cultura. 3rd ed. 466p. pap. 46.95 (*0-8384-0325-5*, Pub. by Heinle & Heinle) Thomson Learn.

Chang, Rouland W., et al. Rehabilitation of Persons with Rheumatoid Arthritis. 300p. 1996. 66.00 (*0-8342-0679-X*, 20679) Aspen Pub.

Chang, Ruth, ed. Incommensurability, Incomparability, & Practical Reason. LC 97-19161. (Illus.). 384p. 1998. 57.50 (*0-674-44755-7*); pap. 24.95 (*0-674-44756-5*) HUP.

Chang, S. Chinese-English Dictionary of Physical Terms. (ENG & GER.). 405p. 1969. pap. 175.00 (*0-8288-9089-7*, M15363) Fr & Eur.

Chang, S. H., jt. auth. see Pincus, Alexis G.

Chang, S. J. Introduction to Quantum Field Theory. (Lecture Notes in Physics Ser.: Vol. 29). 396p. 1990. text 78.00 (*9971-5-0627-0*); pap. text 41.00 (*9971-5-0681-5*) World Scientific Pub.

Chang, S. J., ed. Natural Hazard Phenomena & Mitigation. 135p. 1996. pap. text 70.00 (*0-7918-1777-6*, TS283) ASME Pr.

— Technologies in Reactor Safety, Fluid-Structure Interaction, Sloshing & Natural Hazards Engineering: Proceedings, ASME/JSME Joint Pressure Vessels & Piping Conference (1998, San Diego, CA) LC 98-73174. 366. 317p. 1998. pap. 140.00 (*0-7918-1862-4*) ASME.

Chang, S. K. Visual Languages. (Management & Information Systems Ser.). (Illus.). 470p. (C). 1987. 120.00 (*0-306-42350-2*, Plenum Trade) Perseus Pubng.

Chang, S. K. Visual Languages & Visual Programming. (Management & Information Systems Ser.). (Illus.). 352p. (C). 1990. 95.00 (*0-306-43428-8*, Plenum Trade) Perseus Pubng.

Chang, S. K., et al, eds. Symbolic Projection for Image Information Retrieval & Spatial Reasoning. (Signal Processing & Its Applications Ser.). (Illus.). 336p. 1996. text 59.95 (*0-12-168030-4*) Acad Pr.

***Chang, S. K., et al.** Advances in Distributed Multimedia Systems. (Series on Software Engineering & Knowledge Engineering: Vol. 9). 300p. 1999. 56.00 (*981-02-3560-7*) World Scientific Pub.

Chang, S. K., et al. Intelligent Image Database Systems. LC 97-102567. (Series on Software Engineering & Knowledge). 300p. 1996. text 68.00 (*981-02-2390-0*) World Scientific Pub.

Chang, S. L. Multiple Diffraction of X-Rays in Crystals. (Solid-State Sciences Ser.: Vol. 50). (Illus.). 320p. 1984. 108.95 (*0-387-12955-3*) Spr-Verlag.

Chang, Sam, ed. see Halim, Jacob.

Chang, Sandra. Sheedeva. (Eros Graphic Novel Ser.: Vol. 28). pap. 16.95 (*1-56097-236-X*) Fantagraph Bks.

Chang, Semoon. Modern Economics. 600p. 1990. teacher ed. write for info. (*0-318-66386-4*, H22650); student ed. 18.00 (*0-685-29840-X*, H22676); write for info. (*0-318-66387-2*, H22668) P-H.

— Practitioner's Guide to Managerial Economics. 2nd ed. LC 94-28353. 1994. pap. 24.50 (*0-8191-9652-5*) U Pr of Amer.

Chang, Shelley H., jt. auth. see Chang, Chun-shu.

Chang, Sheng-Yen. Dharma Drum: The Life & Heart of Ch'an Practice. LC 95-83637. 308p. 1996. pap. 15.00 (*0-9609854-8-4*) Dharma Drum Pubs.

— Faith in Mind: A Guide to Ch'an Practice. Zinn, Karen, ed. LC 88-70292. 131p. 1989. pap. 12.00 (*0-9609854-2-5*) Dharma Drum Pubs.

— Getting the Buddha Mind. LC 82-73979. 227p. (Orig.). 1982. pap. 12.00 (*0-9609854-0-9*) Dharma Drum Pubs.

— Infinite Mirror. LC 90-81014. 123p. 1991. pap. 12.00 (*0-9609854-4-1*) Dharma Drum Pubs.

— The Sword of Wisdom. LC 90-84026. 237p. 1991. pap. 12.00 (*0-9609854-5-X*) Dharma Drum Pubs.

— Zen Wisdom: Knowing & Doing. LC 93-70852. 372p. 1993. pap. 15.00 (*0-9609854-6-8*) Dharma Drum Pubs.

Chang, Sheng-Yen, tr. The Poetry of Enlightenment: Poems of Ancient Ch'an Masters. LC 90-84326. 103p. (Orig.). 1989. pap. 12.00 (*0-9609854-1-7*) Dharma Drum Pubs.

Chang, Shi-Kuo, ed. Languages for Automation. LC 85-17032. (Management & Information Systems Ser.). 532p. 1985. 120.00 (*0-306-42031-7*, Plenum Trade) Perseus Pubng.

— Management & Office Information Systems. LC 83-26875. (Management & Information Systems Ser.). 492p. 1984. 110.00 (*0-306-41447-3*, Plenum Trade) Perseus Pubng.

***Chang, Shi-Kuo, ed.** Proceedings of the International Conference on Chinese Language Computing. (Illus.). 288p. 2000. pap. 65.00 (*1-891706-04-7*) Knowldge Systs.

— Proceedings of the 12th International Conference on Software Engineering & Knowledge Engineering. (Illus.). 376p. 2000. pap. 65.00 (*1-891706-05-5*) Knowldge Systs.

Chang Shiang-hua. Chinese Woman in Iowa: Poems by Shiang-hua Chang. Doran, Valerie C., tr. from CHI. 135p. 1992. 12.95 (*0-88727-176-6*) Cheng & Tsui.

Chang, Shih-Chia & Pang, Stella W., eds. Micromachining & Microfabrication Process Technology III, Vol. 3223. LC 98-122577. 320p. 1997. 80.00 (*0-8194-2655-5*) SPIE.

Chang, Shih-Chia, jt. ed. see Pang, Stella W.

Chang, Shihfu. Video on Demand Systems: Technology, Interoperability & Trials. LC 97-17632. 1997. text 82.50 (*0-7923-9949-8*) Kluwer Academic.

Chang, Shu-Kuang, et al. Measuring the Cost of Protection in China. LC 97-20114. 1998. pap. 15.95 (*0-88132-247-4*) Inst Intl Eco.

China was steeped in the concepts & ideology of a planned economy for 30 years until reforms began in 1978. Although the country is now well on its way to becoming a market economy, its trading system remains shackled by its centrally planned past. Measuring the Costs of Protection in China analyzes some of the costs of trade protection & corresponding benefits of liberalization for 25 highly protected sectors in China. The book begins with a description of the development of China's trade administration system, sketching the obstacles to & prospects for further liberalization. The authors analyze the structure of Chinese trade protection & present their estimates of its static costs. They then offer an in-depth analysis of the country's trade regime & of the administrative barriers to rationalization & liberalization. The final chapter present the authors' recommendations for improving China's trade system. They conclude that the short-term costs of trade liberalization for goods examined in the study will be substantial in terms of lost domestic output & lost jobs. The long-term benefits, however, would provide some 35 billion worth of consumer benefits. Five appendices provide greater technical detail on the modeling & methodology applied in this study, as well as a brief description of some peculiarities of the Chinese trade regime-including copious levels of smuggling & monopolistic market structures. *Publisher Paid Annotation.*

Chang, Shu-Ting, et al, eds. Culture Collection & Breeding of Edible Mushrooms. LC 92-16952. 329p. 1993. text 82.00 (*2-88124-561-7*) Gordon & Breach.

Chang, Shuhua. Communications & China's National Integration: An Analysis of People's Daily & Central Daily News on the China Reunification Issue. (Occasional Papers-Reprints Series in Contemporary Asian Studies: No. 5). 120p. (Orig.). (C). 1986. pap. text 8.00 (*0-942182-79-0*) Occasional Papers.

Chang, Shung-Huei, jt. ed. see Pincus, Alexis G.

Chang, Sidney H. & Gordon, Leonard H., eds. Bibliography of Sun Yat-Sen in China's Republican Revolution, 1885-1925. 2nd ed. LC 97-42755. 584p. 1998. 74.00 (*0-7618-1180-X*) U Pr of Amer.

Chang, Sidney H. & Myers, Ramon H., eds. The Storm Clouds Clear over China: The Memoir of Ch'en Li-fu, 1900-1993. LC 93-23214. (Publication Ser.: Vol. 419). (Illus.). 360p. 1993. pap. text 24.95 (*0-8179-9272-3*) Hoover Inst Pr.

Chang, Sonia & Chang, John K. Echocardiography, Techniques & Interpretation. 2nd ed. LC 81-2200. (Illus.). 376p. 1981. reprint ed. pap. 116.60 (*0-8357-7932-7*, 205696600002) Bks Demand.

Chang-sop, Son, et al. A Respite & Other Korean Short Stories. Korean National Commission for UNESCO, ed. Chong-un, Kim et al, trs. from KOR. (Modern Korean Short Stories Ser.: No. 6). vii, 169p. 1983. 20.00 (*0-89209-207-6*) Pace Grp Intl.

Chang, Stephen. The Complete Book of Acupuncture. LC 75-28762. (Illus.). 264p. 1995. pap. 12.95 (*0-89087-124-8*) Celestial Arts.

Chang, Stephen T. Complete System of Self-Healing: Internal Exercises. LC 86-1859. (Illus.). 224p. 1986. 21.95 (*0-942196-06-6*) Tao Pub.

— The Great Tao. (Illus.). 464p. 1985. 28.95 (*0-942196-01-5*) Tao Pub.

— The Integral Management of Tao: Complete Achievement. (Illus.). 270p. 1988. 29.95 (*0-942196-08-2*) Tao Pub.

— The Tao of Balanced Diet: Secrets of a Thin & Healthy Body. LC 86-897. (Illus.). 200p. 1987. 18.95 (*0-942196-05-8*) Tao Pub.

— The Tao of Sexology: The Book of Infinite Wisdom. Orig. Title: Tao of Sexology. (Illus.). 224p. 1986. 22.95 (*0-942196-03-1*) Tao Pub.

Chang, Suk-jin. Korean. LC 96-3780. (London Oriental & African Language Library: Vol. 4). xviii, 252p. 1996. lib. bdg. 69.00 (*1-55619-728-4*) J Benjamins Pubng Co.

Chang, Sung-sheng Y. Modernism & the Nativist Resistance: Contemporary Chinese Fiction from Taiwan. LC 92-41437. 256p. 1993. text 49.95 (*0-8223-1328-6*); pap. text 18.95 (*0-8223-1348-0*) Duke.

Chang, Sung-sheng Y., jt. ed. see Carver, Ann C.

Chang, T. M., ed. Blood Substitutes - Principles, Methods, Products & Clinical Trials Vol. 2: A Karger Landes Systems Publication. (Illus.). xviii, 236p. 1998. 98.00 (*3-8055-6633-6*) S Karger.

Chang, T. M., et al. Distance Learning: On the Design of an Open University. 1982. lib. bdg. 73.50 (*0-89838-096-0*) Kluwer Academic.

Chang, T. M., jt. ed. see Bonomini, V.

Chang, T. N. Many-Body Theory of Atomic Structure & Photoionization. 500p. 1993. text 143.00 (*981-02-0876-6*) World Scientific Pub.

Chang, T. S., ed. Ion Acceleration in the Magnetosphere & Ionosphere. (Geophysical Monograph Ser.: Vol. 38). (Illus.). 350p. 1986. 42.00 (*0-87590-063-1*) Am Geophysical.

Chang, T. S. & Leung, Peter C., eds. Principles, Techniques & Applications in Microsurgery. 400p. 1986. text 130.00 (*9971-978-08-3*); pap. text 49.00 (*9971-978-09-1*) World Scientific Pub.

Chang, T. Y. & Freeman, Dale A., eds. Intracellular Cholesterol Trafficking. LC 98-45016. 294p. 1998. text 150.00 (*0-7923-8365-6*, QP752) Kluwer Academic.

Chang, T. Y., ed. see ASME-CSME Pressure Vessel & Piping Conference Staf.

***Chang, Ta-chun.** Wild Kids: Two Novels about Growing Up. Berry, Michael, tr. from CHI. LC 99-88264. 2000. 22.95 (*0-231-12096-6*) Col U Pr.

Chang, Tara L. The Friendly Beasts. LC 98-138018. 1997. 14.95 (*1-57008-328-2*) Bookcraft Inc.

Chang, Thelma. I Can Never Forget: Men of the 100th - 442nd. LC 91-90350. (Illus.). 208p. 34.95 (*0-9630228-0-6*) Sigi Prods.

Chang, Thomas M. Blood Substitutes: Principles, Methods, Products & Clinical Trials: Tissue Engineering. LC 97-36010. (Illus.). xiv, 142p. 1997. text 98.00 (*3-8055-6584-4*) S Karger.

— Blood Substitutes & Oxygen Carriers. (Illus.). 896p. 1992. text 235.00 (*0-8247-8810-9*) Dekker.

Chang, Thomas M. S. & Geyer, Robert P. Red Blood Cell Substitutes. 736p. 1988. text 175.00 (*0-8247-8027-2*) Dekker.

Chang, Tien-Chien & Wysk, Richard A. Computer-Aided Manufacturing. 2nd ed. LC 97-25852. 748p. (C). 1997. 100.00 (*0-13-754524-X*) P-H.

***Chang, Tony H., compiled by.** China During the Cultural Revolution, 1966-1976: A Selected Bibliography of English Language Works, Vol. 3. LC 98-44393. (Bibliographies & Indexes in Asian Studies Ser.: Vol. 3). 216p. 1999. lib. bdg. 65.00 (*0-313-30905-1*) Greenwood.

Chang, Tsan-Kuo. The Press & China Policy: The Illusion of Sino-American Relations, 1950-1984. LC 92-38944. (Communication & Information Science Ser.). 288p. 1993. pap. 39.50 (*1-56750-014-5*); text 73.25 (*0-89391-887-3*) Ablx Pub.

Chang, Tse Chun. Cyclical Movements in the Balance of Payments. LC 85-12539. (Illus.). 224p. 1985. reprint ed. lib. bdg. 69.50 (*0-313-24947-4*, CHCM, Greenwood Pr) Greenwood.

Chang, Tsong-How, jt. auth. see Devor, Richard E.

Chang Tsong-zung, tr. Beautiful China: Yu Yuntian Photo Exhibition. 2nd ed. (Illus.). 25p. 1997. pap. 21.00 (*0-9640498-0-5*) Asian Art Coord.

***Chang, Unyoung E.** Grants for Scholarships: A Resource Guide to Scholarship Funds for Education Institutions. 493p. 1998. 102.00 (*1-56925-104-5*) Aspen Pub.

Chang, Valerie N. I Just Lost Myself: Psychological Abuse of Women in Marriage. LC 95-30660. 184p. 1996. 49.95 (*0-275-95209-6*, Praeger Pubs) Greenwood.

Chang, W. S., et al, eds. Heat Pipes & Thermosyphons. (HTD Ser.: Vol. 221). 76p. 1992. 27.50 (*0-7918-1064-X*, G00708) ASME.

***Chang, W. S., et al.** Statistics & Finance: An Interface. LC 00-35100. 380p. 2000. 88.00 (*1-86094-237-7*) World Scientific Pub.

Chang, Wei, jt. auth. see Lew, Kim.

Chang-Wells, Gen Ling, jt. auth. see Wells, Gordon.

Chang, Wenkuang & Goldberg, Jeffrey. Lu Hong, Art & Life. (Illus.). 83p. (Orig.). 1989. pap. write for info. (*0-318-65508-X*) Segal Fine Art.

Chang, William. Handbook for Internal Auditors, 2 vols. 1985. ring bd. 340.00 (*0-8205-1390-3*) Bender.

Chang, Winston, ed. Imperfect Competition in International Trade. 288p. (C). 1995. lib. bdg. 120.50 (*0-7923-9546-8*) Kluwer Academic.

Chang, Won H. Mass Media in China: The History & the Future. LC 88-34694. (Illus.). 320p. 1989. reprint ed. pap. 99.20 (*0-608-00149-X*, 206093000006) Bks Demand.

Chang, Wynne, tr. see Wei Chuan Publishing Staff.

Chang, Y. WINQSB: Decision Support Software for MS/OM. 471p. Date not set. pap. text. write for info. (*0-471-24812-6*) Wiley.

Chang, Y. & Wang, S., eds. Advances in Extrusion Technology: Aquaculture/Animal Feeds & Foods. LC 98-88325. 355p. 1998. text 99.95 (*1-56676-717-2*) Technomic.

Chang, Y. A., ed. Thermodynamics of Alloy Formation. (Illus.). 310p. 1997. 86.00 (*0-87339-355-4*, 3554) Minerals Metals.

Chang, Y. A., ed. see Metallurgical Society of AIME Staff.

Chang, Y. Austin & Ahmad, Nazeer. Thermodynamic Data on Metal Carbonates & Related Oxides. LC 82-62692. (Technology of Metallurgy Ser.: No. 4). 241p. reprint ed. pap. 74.80 (*0-8357-2522-7*, 205240200013) Bks Demand.

Chang, Y. C., jt. auth. see Davis, K. M.

***Chang, Y. May.** Error Analysis & Calibration Uncertainty of Capacitance Standards at NIST. 110p. 2000. pap. 10.00 (*0-16-059063-9*) USGPO.

— NIST Calibration Service for Capacitance Standards at Low Frequencies. 83p. 1998. pap. 7.00 (*0-16-060876-7*) USGPO.

Chang, Y. N. Dragon's Tale. pap. 14.95 (*1-57532-142-4*) Press-Tige Pub.

— Revitalizing America's Business. 256p. 1994. boxed set 29.95 (*0-8403-9258-3*) Kendall-Hunt.

Chang, Y. S., et al. Making Quality Work: A Leadership Guide for the Results-Driven Manager. LC 92-53330. 320p. 1993. 25.00 (*0-88730-582-2*, HarpBusn) HarpInfo.

Chang, Y. W., tr. see Pan-Ling, Chen.

Chang, Yih-Long. QSB II Plus: Quantitative Business Systems. 240p. (C). 1988. write for info. (*0-318-63665-4*) P-H.

Chang, Yoon D. & Su, David H. A Study of Traffic Control & Congestion Control in Broadband ISDN. (Illus.). 175p. (Orig.). (C). 1994. pap. text 40.00 (*0-7881-0525-6*) DIANE Pub.

Chang, Yu-Chuan. Wang Shou-Jen As a Statesman. LC 75-32330. (Studies in Chinese History & Civilization). 517p. 1975. reprint ed. lib. bdg. 69.50 (*0-313-26958-0*, U6958, Greenwood Pr) Greenwood.

Chang, Yu-Kon, tr. see Hsia, Ching-Lin.

Chang, Zhang, ed. Chinese Clay Art: The Zhang Style Painted Figurines. 82p. 1989. pap. 16.95 (*7-80005-075-0*, Pub. by New World Pr) China Bks.

Chang, Zhong Y. & Sansen, Willy M. Low-Noise Wide-Band Amplifiers in Bipolar & CMOS Technologies. (International Series in Engineering & Computer Science, VLSI, Computer Architecture, & Digital Screen Processing). 224p. (C). 1990. text 110.00 (*0-7923-9096-2*) Kluwer Academic.

Changa, Ras. Illegal Truth. LC 90-86302. (Illus.). 93p. 1991. pap. 12.00 (*0-913441-11-2*) Hse of Nehesi.

Changar, Jerilynn & Harrison, Annette. Storytelling Activities Kit: Ready-To-Use Techniques. 316p. (J). 1992. pap. 37.95 incl. audio (*0-87628-869-7*) Ctr Appl Res.

Changching, Cao & Seymour, James, eds. Tibet Through Dissent Chinese Eyes: Essays on Self-Determination. LC 97-26807. 164p. (gr. 13). 1997. text 54.95 (*1-56324-922-7*, East Gate Bk) M E Sharpe.

Changchub, Gyalwa & Nyingpo, Namkhai. Lady of the Lotus-Born: The Life & Enlightenment of Yeshe Tsogyal. LC 98-6838. 176p. 1998. 29.95 (*1-57062-384-8*, Pub. by Shambhala Pubns) Random.

Change Institute, University of Maryland Staff. Frontiers in Librarianship: Proceedings of Change Institute, 1969, 2. Wasserman, Paul, ed. LC 78-149958. (Contributions in Librarianship & Information Science Ser.: No. 2). 440p. (C). 1972. 65.00 (*0-8371-5823-0*, WPC/) Greenwood.

Change, Jessie T., jt. ed. see Moser, Michael J.

Changer, S., ed. see Symposium on Emerging Process Technologies for a C.

C

Changeux, J. P., et al, eds. Molecular Basis of Nerve Activity: Proceedings of the International Symposium in Memory of David Nachmansohn (1899-1983) Berlin, West Germany, October 11-13, 1984. (Illus.). xxiv, 784p. 1985. 200.00 (3-11-010345-1) De Gruyter.

Changeux, Jean Pierre. Conversations on Mind, Matter & Mathematics. 272p. 1995. pap. 14.95 (0-691-00405-6, Pub. by Princeton U Pr) Cal Prin Full Svc.

Changeux, Jean-Pierre. Neuronal Man: The Biology of the Mind. Garey, Laurence, tr. LC 97-209028. 368p. 1983. pap. text 16.95 (0-691-02666-1, Pub. by Princeton U Pr) Cal Prin Full Svc.

Changeux, Jean-Pierre & Chavaillon, Jean, eds. Origins of the Human Brain. (Fyssen Foundation Symposium Ser.). (Illus.). 334p. 1996. reprint ed. pap. text 40.00 (0-19-852390-4) OUP.

***Changeux, Jean-Pierre & Ricoeur, Paul.** What Makes Us Think? A Neuroscientist & a Philosopher Argue about Ethics, Human Nature & the Brain. LC 00-24827. 2000. 29.95 (0-691-00940-6, Pub. by Princeton U Pr) Cal Prin Full Svc.

Changgen, Yu, jt. auth. see Barnouin, Barbara.

Changhua Sun Rich, et al. The Political Economy of International Environmental Cooperation. Richards, Alan, ed. (Policy Papers Ser.: Vol. 29). 99p. (Orig.). (C). 1997. pap. 3.50 (0-934637-45-8) U of CA Inst Global.

Changing Times Education Service Staff, et al. Career Directions: Textbook. 29.95 (0-8219-0661-5) EMC-Paradigm.

— Career Directions: Workbook. 7.95 (0-8219-0663-1) EMC-Paradigm.

— Career Directions: Workbook teacher's edition. 18.95 (0-8219-0664-X) EMC-Paradigm.

— Carreer Directions: Teacher's annotated edition. 39.00 (0-8219-0662-3) EMC-Paradigm.

***Changizi, Mandana S.** The Plain Blue Caterpillar. LC 99-58817. (Illus.). 16p. (J). (ps-5). 2000. pap. 9.95 (0-9637240-9-6) Biograph Pub.

Changjiang, Ruan. Illustrated Chinese Furniture Through the Ages. (CHI & ENG., Illus.). 319p. 1992. pap. 22.00 (957-638-089-8, ATB503, Pub. by SMC Pub) Antique Collect.

Changlong, Y., jt. ed. see Mianyu, Q.

Changnon, Stanley A. America's Rural Hub: Railroading in Central Illinois in the Late Twentieth Century. LC 91-66477. (Illus.). 216p. 1991. pap. 39.95 (1-878044-04-4) Mayhaven Pub.

— The Triangle: Busy Railroading in Southern Illinois. 104p. 1992. 25.00 (0-9631811-0-6) S A Changnon.

***Changnon, Stanley A., ed.** El Nino, 1997-1998: The Climate Event of the Century. LC 99-35619. (Illus.). 232p. 2000. pap. text 29.95 (0-19-513552-0) OUP.

— El Nino, 1997-1998: The Climate Event of the Century. LC 99-35619. (Illus.). 232p. 2000. text 60.00 (0-19-513551-2) OUP.

Changnon, Stanley Alcide. Railroad Bridges in the Heartland. (Illus.). 217p. 1997. pap. text 30.00 (0-9631811-1-4) S A Changnon.

Changon, Stanley A., ed. Metromex: A Review & Summary. (Meteorological Monograph: Vol. 18, No. 40). (Illus.). 181p. 1981. 40.00 (0-933876-52-1) Am Meteorological.

Chanillo, Sagun & Muckenhoupt, Benjamin. Weak Type Estimates for Cesaro Sums of Jacobi Polynomial Series. LC 92-38214. (Memoirs of the American Mathematical Society Ser.: No. 487). 90p. 1993. pap. 29.00 (0-8218-2548-8, MEMO/102/487) Am Math.

Chanin. Legal Research, No. 2, Chap. 2. 1989. 23.50 (0-316-13635-2, Aspen Law & Bus) Aspen Pub.

— Legal Research, No. 7, Ch. 5. 1992. 30.00 (0-316-13653-0, Aspen Law & Bus) Aspen Pub.

— Legal Research, No. 7, Ch. 7. 1992. 27.00 (0-316-13654-9, Aspen Law & Bus) Aspen Pub.

— Legal Research, No. 7, Ch. 8. 1992. 17.00 (0-316-13655-7, Aspen Law & Bus) Aspen Pub.

— Legal Research, No. 8, Ch. 9. 1993. 35.00 (0-316-13657-3, Aspen Law & Bus) Aspen Pub.

— Legal Research, No. 8, Ch. 10. 1993. 35.00 (0-316-13658-1, Aspen Law & Bus) Aspen Pub.

— Legal Research, No. 9, Ch. 12. 1994. 35.00 (0-316-13623-9, Aspen Law & Bus) Aspen Pub.

— Legal Research, No. 9, Ch. 13. 1994. 35.00 (0-316-13624-7, Aspen Law & Bus) Aspen Pub.

— Specialize Legal Research. Set. 964p. 1989. ring bd. 145.00 (0-316-13633-6, Aspen Law & Bus) Aspen Pub.

Chanin, Abraham S. The Flames of Freedom. LC 89-8889. 174p. (Orig.). (C). 1990. pap. text 19.00 (0-8191-7571-4) U Pr of Amer.

***Chanin, D.** Code Manual for MACCS2: Preprocessor Codes COMIDA2, FGRDCF, IDCF2. 98p. 1998. per. 8.00 (0-16-062925-X) USGPO.

— Code Manual for MACCS2: User's Guide. 335p. 1998. per. 26.00 (0-16-062924-1) USGPO.

Chanin, Eileen. Collecting Art: Masterpieces, Markets & Money. (Illus.). xi, 162p. 1990. pap. text 25.00 (976-8097-00-0) Gordon & Breach.

Chanin, Eileen & Miller, Steven. The Art & Life of Weaver Hawkins. (Illus.). 144p. 1995. text 50.00 (976-8097-67-1) Gordon & Breach.

Chanin, Leah F. Legal Research, No. 10, Chapter 1. 1995. 30.00 (0-316-13617-4, Aspen Law & Bus) Aspen Pub.

— Legal Research, No. 10, Chapter 3. 1995. 30.00 (0-316-13661-1, Aspen Law & Bus) Aspen Pub.

— Legal Research, No. 10, Chapter 4. 1995. 30.00 (0-316-13619-0, Aspen Law & Bus) Aspen Pub.

Chanin, Leah F., ed. Specialized Legal Research. LC 86-80068. 432p. 1987. 145.00 (0-316-13625-5, Aspen Law & Bus) Aspen Pub.

Chanin, Leah F., et al. Legal Research in the District of Columbia, Maryland & Virginia. LC 94-16191. 420p. 1995. 45.00 (0-89941-884-8, 308140) W S Hein.

***Chanin, Leah F., et al.** Legal Research in the District of Columbia, Maryland & Virginia. 2nd ed. LC 00-26782. 452p. 2000. ring bd. 65.00 (1-57588-532-8, 323530) W S Hein.

Chanin, Marie-Lise, ed. The Role of the Stratosphere in Global Change. LC 93-4662. (NATO ASI Series I: Global Environmental Change: Vol. 8). (Illus.). 560p. 1993. 307.95 (0-387-56843-3) Spr-Verlag.

Chanin, Michael. The Chief's Blanket. LC 97-7809. (Illus.). 32p. (J). (ps-5). 1998. 14.95 (0-915811-78-2, Starseed) H J Kramer Inc.

— Grandfather Four Winds & Rising Moon. LC 93-2689. (Illus.). 32p. (J). (ps-4). 1994. 14.95 (0-915811-47-2, Starseed) H J Kramer Inc.

Chanin, Paul. Otters. (Illus.). 128p. text 19.95 (0-905483-90-1, Pub. by Whittet Bks) Diamond Farm Bk.

Chanin, Robert H., jt. auth. see Wollett, Donald H.

Chanko, Pamela. Baby Animals Learn. LC 98-18816. (Science Emergent Readers Ser.). (J). 1998. pap. 2.50 (0-590-76157-9) Scholastic Inc.

— The Beak Book. LC 98-18825. (Science Emergent Readers Ser.). (J). 1998. pap. 2.50 (0-590-76969-3) Scholastic Inc.

***Chanko, Pamela.** Scientists. LC 98-45008. (J). 1998. pap. 10.01 (0-439-04601-7) Scholastic Inc.

Chanko, Pamela. Sea Creatures LC 98-23222. (Science Emergent Readers Ser.). 1998. 2.50 (0-590-63880-7) Scholastic Inc.

— Weather. LC 97-37377. (Science Emergent Readers Ser.). (J). (gr. 3-4). 1997. pap. 2.50 (0-590-10730-5) Scholastic Inc.

Chanko, Pamela & Canizares, Susan. Monkeys. LC 97-34203. (Science Emergent Readers Ser.). (J). 1997. pap. 2.50 (0-590-76964-2) Scholastic Inc.

Chanko, Pamela & Moreton, Daniel. Who Beats the Heat? LC 98-8011. (Science Emergent Readers Ser.). (J). 1998. 3.25 (0-590-63873-4) Scholastic Inc.

Chanko, Pamela, jt. auth. see Berger, Samantha.

Chanko, Pamela, jt. auth. see Canizares, Susan.

Chanko, Pamela, jt. auth. see Chessen, Betsey.

Chanko, Pamela, jt. auth. see Moreton, Daniel.

Chankong, V., jt. ed. see Haimes, Yacov Y.

Chankvetadze, Bezhan. Capillary Electrophoresis in Chiral Analysis. LC 97-3771. 572p. 1997. 270.00 (0-471-97415-3) Wiley.

Chanler, Julie. His Messengers Went Forth. LC 77-148209. (Biography Index Reprint Ser.). (Illus.). 1977. 16.95 (0-8369-8056-5) Ayer.

Chanler, Margaret. Memory Makes Music: American Autobiography. 171p. 1995. lib. bdg. 69.00 (0-7812-8475-9) Rprt Serv.

Chanler, William A. Through Jungle & Desert, Travels in E. Africa. 1896. 59.00 (0-403-00438-1) Scholarly.

Chanlett, Emil T. Environmental Protection. 2nd ed. (Environmental Engineering Ser.). (C). 1979. text 82.50 (0-07-010531-6) McGraw.

***Channa, S., ed.** International Encyclopedia of Anthropology, 12 vols. 1998. 985.00 (81-7020-726-6, Pub. by Cosmo Pubn) S Asia.

Channa, V. C. Caste: Identity & Continuity. 180p. 1979. 15.95 (0-318-36808-0) Asia Bk Corp.

Channan, O. N. The Role of the Court Interpreter. (C). 1982. pap. 60.00 (0-7219-0920-5, Pub. by Scientific) St Mut.

Channel Four, Nashville Staff. Bill Hall's Land & Lakes Cookbook. LC 93-73580. (Illus.). 1993. spiral bd. 12.95 (0-87197-391-X) Favorite Recipes.

Channell, Carolyn E. & Crurius, Timothy W. The Aims of Argument Instructor's Manual. 82p. (Orig.). (C). 1994. pap. text, teacher ed. write for info. (1-55934-115-7, 1115) Mayfield Pub.

— The Aims of Argument Instructor's Manual. 82p. (Orig.). 1997. pap. text. write for info. (0-7674-0028-3, 1115) Mayfield Pub.

Channell, Carolyn E., jt. auth. see Crusius, Timothy W.

Channell, J. G., jt. auth. see Opdyke, N. D.

Channell, Joanna. Del Vague Language. Sinclair, John & Carter, Ronald, eds. (Illus.). 248p. 1994. pap. text 19.95 (0-19-437186-7) OUP.

Channell, L. S. History of Compton County & Sketches of the Eastern Townships: District of St. Francis & Sherbrooke County. (Illus.). 304p. 1998. reprint ed. pap. 37.95 (1-58211-072-7, 097631) Quintin Pub RI.

Channell, Paul J., ed. see AIP Conference Staff.

Channels, Noreen L. Social Science Methods in the Legal Process. LC 84-11527. (Illus.). 286p. 1985. 69.00 (0-86598-013-6) Rowman.

Channen, Don. Tallis Ends & Other Tales. 184p. (J). 1992. pap. 9.95 (965-229-053-X, Pub. by Gefen Pub Hse) Gefen Bks.

Channen, Don. Uh! Oh! Hanukkah. (Uh! Oh! Hidden Objects Ser.: Vol. 1). 32p. (J). (gr. 3-7). 1993. 12.95 (0-943706-15-7) Pitspopany.

Channer, Colin. Waiting in Vain. 1999. pap. 12.00 (0-345-42552-9) Ballantine Pub Grp.

— Waiting in Vain. 1999. mass mkt. 0.00 (0-345-43012-3) Ballantine Pub Grp.

Channer, Nick, jt. auth. see Hancock, David.

Channer, Pat, et al. Help! We Need to Organize the Education Program: A Handbook for Education Committees & Congregations. unabridged ed. Dobson, David, ed. LC 99-165111. 48p. 1998. pap. 7.95 (1-57895-051-1) Curriculm Presbytrn KY.

Channing, jt. auth. see Ridley.

Channing, Alan H., jt. auth. see Kovner, Anthony R.

Channing, C. P., jt. auth. see Fujii, T.

Channing, Edward. A History of the United States. LC 92-32019. 362p. (C). 1993. pap. text 34.50 (0-8191-8915-4); lib. bdg. 62.50 (0-8191-8914-6) U Pr of Amer.

— The Jeffersonian System, 1801-1811. (BCL1 - U. S. History Ser.). 299p. 1992. reprint ed. lib. bdg. 79.00 (0-7812-6142-2) Rprt Serv.

— The Narragansett Planters: A Study of Causes. 23p. 1997. reprint ed. pap. 5.00 (0-8328-6471-4) Higginson Bk Co.

Channing, Edward & Coolidge, Archibald C. The Barrington-Bernard Correspondence, & Illustrative Matter, 1760-1770. LC 75-109612. (Era of the American Revolution Ser.). 1970. reprint ed. lib. bdg. 39.50 (0-306-71909-6) Da Capo.

Channing, Edward T. & Downey, Charlotte. Lectures Read to the Seniors in Harvard College. LC 96-53859. (Scholars' Facsimiles & Reprints Ser.). 336p. 1997. 60.00 (0-8201-1502-9) Schol Facsimiles.

Channing, John, jt. auth. see Ridley, John R.

Channing, Mark. White Python: Adventure & Mystery in Tibet. Reginald, R. & Melville, Douglas, eds. LC 77-84208. (Lost Race & Adult Fantasy Ser.). 1978. reprint ed. lib. bdg. 29.95 (0-405-10964-4) Ayer.

Channing, Steven A. The Encyclopedia of Kentucky: A Reference Guide to the Bluegrass State. (Encyclopedia of the United States Ser.). (Illus.). 500p. 1985. reprint ed. lib. bdg. 79.00 (0-403-09981-1) Somerset Pub.

Channing, Susan R., jt. auth. see Howe, Catherine.

Channing, William E. The Abolitionist. (Works of William Ellery Channing II). 1990. reprint ed. lib. bdg. 79.00 (0-685-27698-8) Rprt Serv.

— Collected Poems, 1817-1901. Harding, Walter, ed. LC 67-21749. 1056p. 1967. 100.00 (0-8201-1009-4) Schol Facsimiles.

— Collected Works. (Works of William Ellery Channing II). 1990. reprint ed. lib. bdg. 79.00 (0-7812-2474-8) Rprt Serv.

Channing, William E., II. Conversations in Rome Between an Artist, a Catholic & a Critic. (Works of William Ellery Channing II). 1990. reprint ed. lib. bdg. 79.00 (0-7812-2269-9) Rprt Serv.

Channing, William E. Discourses on War. LC 71-137531. (Peace Movement in America Ser.). lxi, 229p. 1972. reprint ed. lib. bdg. 33.95 (0-89198-059-8) Ozer.

— The Duty of the Free States. (Works of William Ellery Channing II). 1990. reprint ed. lib. bdg. 79.00 (0-685-27695-3) Rprt Serv.

Channing, William E., II. Eliot. (Works of William Ellery Channing II). 1990. reprint ed. lib. bdg. 79.00 (0-7812-2266-4) Rprt Serv.

Channing, William E. Emancipation. LC 75-82181. (Anti-Slavery Crusade in America Ser.). 1970. reprint ed. 11.95 (0-405-00619-5) Ayer.

— Emancipation. (Works of William Ellery Channing II). 1990. reprint ed. lib. bdg. 79.00 (0-685-27697-X) Rprt Serv.

Channing, William E., II. John Brown & the Heros of Harper's Ferry. (Works of William Ellery Channing II). 1990. reprint ed. lib. bdg. 79.00 (0-7812-2267-2) Rprt Serv.

Channing, William E. Miscellanies. (Works of William Ellery Channing II). 1990. reprint ed. lib. bdg. 79.00 (0-685-27700-3) Rprt Serv.

Channing, William E., II. Near Home. (Works of William Ellery Channing II). 1990. reprint ed. lib. bdg. 79.00 (0-7812-2264-8) Rprt Serv.

Channing, William E. The Perfect Life. (Works of William Ellery Channing II). 1990. reprint ed. lib. bdg. 79.00 (0-685-27694-5) Rprt Serv.

— Poems. LC 72-4955. (Romantic Tradition in American Literature Ser.). 162p. 1972. reprint ed. 23.95 (0-405-04627-8) Ayer.

Channing, William E., II. Poems. (Works of William Ellery Channing II). 1990. reprint ed. lib. bdg. 79.00 (0-7812-2261-3) Rprt Serv.

— Poems of 65 Years. Sanborn, F. B., ed. LC 72-4956. (Romantic Tradition in American Literature Ser.). 232p. 1979. reprint ed. 28.95 (0-405-04628-6) Ayer.

— Poems of 65 Years. (Works of William Ellery Channing II). 1990. reprint ed. lib. bdg. 79.00 (0-7812-2268-0) Rprt Serv.

— Poems-2nd Series. (Works of William Ellery Channing II). 1990. reprint ed. lib. bdg. 79.00 (0-7812-2262-1) Rprt Serv.

Channing, William E. Remarks on American Literature. (Works of William Ellery Channing II). 1990. reprint ed. lib. bdg. 79.00 (0-685-27614-7) Rprt Serv.

— Remarks on the Character & Writings of John Milton. 3rd ed. LC 72-966. reprint ed. 34.50 (0-404-01448-8) AMS Pr.

— Self-Culture. LC 74-89163. (Essay Index Reprint Ser.). 1977. reprint ed. 13.95 (0-405-01401-5) Ayer.

— Slavery. LC 71-82180. (Anti-Slavery Crusade in America Ser.). 1970. reprint ed. 24.95 (0-405-00620-9) Ayer.

— Slavery. (Works of William Ellery Channing II). 1990. reprint ed. lib. bdg. 79.00 (0-685-27699-6) Rprt Serv.

— Thoreau, Poet-Naturalist. enl. ed. Sanborn, Franklin B., ed. LC 65-27095. (Illus.). 1966. reprint ed. 32.00 (0-8196-0173-X) Biblo.

Channing, William E., II. Thoreau, Poet-Naturalist. (Works of William Ellery Channing II). 1990. reprint ed. lib. bdg. 79.00 (0-685-27613-9) Rprt Serv.

— The Wanderer: A Colloquial Poems. (Works of William Ellery Channing II). 1990. reprint ed. lib. bdg. 79.00 (0-7812-2265-6) Rprt Serv.

— The Woodman & Other Poems. (Works of William Ellery Channing II). 1990. reprint ed. lib. bdg. 79.00 (0-7812-2263-X) Rprt Serv.

— The Works of William Ellery Channing II. 1990. reprint ed. lib. bdg. 63.00 (0-685-27685-6) Rprt Serv.

Channon. The Russian & Soviet Peasantry, 1880-1991. 1999. pap. text. write for info. (0-582-09807-6, Pub. by Addison-Wesley) Longman.

Channon, C., et al. Banking Through the Looking Glass. (C). 1989. 40.00 (0-85297-202-4, Pub. by Chartered Bank) St Mut.

Channon, Derek F. Bank Strategic Management & Marketing. LC 85-20182. 256p. 1986. 140.00 (0-471-90383-3) Wiley.

Channon, Derek F., ed. The Blackwell Encyclopedic Dictionary of Strategic Management. LC 96-30369. (Blackwell Encyclopedia of Management Ser.). (Illus.). 256p. 1997. 110.00 (1-55786-966-9) Blackwell Pubs.

— The Blackwell Encyclopedic Dictionary of Strategic Management. 352p. 1999. reprint ed. pap. 29.95 (0-631-21078-4) Blackwell Pubs.

Channon, John. Politics, Society & Stalinism in the U. S. S. R. LC 97-40880. (Studies in Russian & East European History & Society). 208p. 1998. text 65.00 (0-312-21126-0) St Martin.

Channon, Robert I. The Cold Steel Third: Third Airborne Ranger Company Korean War (1950-1951) LC 93-79557. (Illus.). 832p. 1993. lib. bdg. 39.95 (1-881851-02-8) Genealogy Pub.

Chano, Fagir. The Secrets of a Fagir: Fagir Chano's Philosophy of Transcendental Unknowingness. Lane, David C., ed. (Jewels of India Ser.). 62p. 1992. pap. 3.00 (1-56543-003-4) Mt SA Coll Philos.

Chanock, Martin. Law, Custom & Social Order: The Colonial Experience in Malawi & Zambia. LC 98-19148. (Social History of Africa Ser.). 1998. pap. 22.50 (0-325-00016-6) Heinemann.

Chanock, Robert, et al, eds. Vaccines 88, New Chemical & Genetic Approaches to Vaccination: Prevention of Aids & Other Viral, Bacterial & Parasitic Diseases. LC 87-13175. (Vaccines Ser.). (Illus.). 460p. 1987. pap. text 95.00 (0-87969-310-X) Cold Spring Harbor.

Chanock, Robert M., et al, eds. Vaccines, '87: Modern Approaches to New Vaccines: Prevention of AIDS & Other Viral, Bacterial, & Parasitic Diseases. (Illus.). 461p. (C). 1987. pap. 95.00 (0-87969-302-9) Cold Spring Harbor.

— Vaccines, '95: Molecular Approaches to the Control of Infectious Diseases. LC 93-2729. (Illus.). 441p. (Orig.). 1995. pap. text 100.00 (0-87969-467-X) Cold Spring Harbor.

— Vaccines, '91: Modern Approaches to New Vaccines Including Prevention of AIDS. (Illus.). 425p. 1991. pap. text 85.00 (0-87969-367-3) Cold Spring Harbor.

Chanock, Robert M. & Lerner, Richard A., eds. Modern Approaches to Vaccines: Molecular & Chemical Basis of Virus Virulence & Immunogenicity. LC 83-73176. 485p. reprint ed. pap. 150.40 (0-7837-5839-1, 204555800006) Bks Demand.

Chanoff, David & Van Toai, Doan. Vietnam: A Portrait of Its People at War. 240p. 1996. pap. 18.95 (0-614-19280-3) St Martin.

Chanoff, David, jt. auth. see Diem, Bui.

Chanoff, David, jt. auth. see Elders, M. Joycelyn.

Chanoff, David, jt. auth. see Good, Kenneth.

Chanon, Art, jt. auth. see Vernin, G.

Chanon, M., jt. ed. see Fox, M. A.

Chanon, Michel, ed. Homogeneous Photocatalysis. LC 96-25955. (Series in Photoscience & Photoengineering: Vol. 2). 426p. 1997. 250.00 (0-471-96753-X) Wiley.

Chanon, Michel, et al, eds. Paramagnetic Ogranometallic Species in Activation-Selectivity: Catalysis. (C). 1988. text 292.50 (0-7923-0032-7) Kluwer Academic.

Chanover, Alice, jt. auth. see Chanover, Hyman.

Chanover, Hyman. Haggadah for the School. (Illus.). 1964. pap. 2.25 (0-8381-0175-5) USCJE.

Chanover, Hyman, adapted by. Service for the High Holy Days Adapted for Youth. LC 72-2058. 192p. (J). (gr. 8 up). 1972. pap. 6.95 (0-87441-123-8) Behrman.

Chanover, Hyman & Chanover, Alice. Pesah Is Coming. (Holiday Series of Picture Storybooks). (Illus.). (J). (gr. k-2). 1956. 5.95 (0-8381-0713-3, 10-713) USCJE.

— Pesah Is Here. (Holiday Series of Picture Storybooks). (Illus.). (J). (gr. k-2). 1956. 5.95 (0-8381-0714-1) USCJE.

Chanover, Hyman & Zusman, Evelyn. A Book of Prayer for Junior Congregations: Sabbath & Festivals. (ENG & HEB.). 256p. (J). (gr. 4-7). 4.50 (0-8381-0174-7, 10-174) USCJE.

Chanra, B. Nationalism & Colonialism in Modern India. 395p. 1979. 19.95 (0-318-36595-2) Asia Bk Corp.

Chansky, Art. Dean's Domain: The Inside Story of Dean Smith & His College Basketball Empire. LC 99-60101. (Illus.). 240p. 1999. 22.00 (1-56352-540-2) Longstreet.

***Chansky, Tamar E.** Freeing Your Child from Obsessive-Compulsive Disorder: A Powerful, Practical Program for Parents of Children & Adolescents. LC 99-85974. 2000. 23.00 (0-8129-3116-5, Times Bks) Crown Pub Group.

Chansler, Robert J. Efficient Use of Systems with Many Processors. LC 86-6962. (Computer Science: Computer Architecture & Design Ser.: No. 6). 138p. reprint ed. pap. 42.80 (0-8357-1749-6, 207042800088) Bks Demand.

Chanson. Hydraulics of Open Channel Flow. 544p. 1999. pap. 79.95 (0-470-36103-4) Wiley.

Chanson de Roland, La, see La Chanson de Roland.

Chanson, H. Hydraulic Design of Stepped Cascades, Channels, Weirs, & Spillways. 292p. 1994. 96.50 (0-08-041918-6, Pergamon Pr) Elsevier.

Chanson, H., ed. Air Bubble Entertainment in Free-Surface Turbulent Shear Flows. (Illus.). 400p. 1996. text 129.95 (0-12-168110-6) Acad Pr.

Chanson, Hubert. Air Bubble Entrainment in Free-Surface Turbulent Flows: Experimental Investigations. 368p. 1995. write for info. (0-86776-611-5) U of Queensland.

— Flow Characteristics of Undular Hydraulic Jumps Comparison with Near-Critical Flows. 202p. 1995. write for info. (0-86776-612-3) U of Queensland.

An Asterisk (*) at the beginning of an entry indicates that the title is appearing for the first time.

— Some Hydraulic Aspects During Overflow Above Inflatable Flexible Membrance Dam. 60p. 1996. write for info. (*0-86776-644-1*) U of Queensland.

Chanson, Hubert & Brattberg, Tim. Experimental Investigations of Air Bubble Entrainment in Developing Shear Layers. 309p. 1997. write for info. (*0-86776-748-0*) U of Queensland.

Chant. Darwin to Einstein: Historical Studies on Science & Belief. 1980. pap. text. write for info. (*0-582-49157-6*, Pub. by Addison-Wesley) Longman.

***Chant.** Warfare & the Third Reich: The Rise & Fall of Hitler's Armed Forces. (Illus.). 1998. pap. 16.95 (*1-84065-002-8*, Pub. by Salamander) Combined Pub.

Chant. Women of a Lesser Cost: Female Labour, Foreign Exchange, & Philippine Development. LC 94-45270. (C). pap. 35.95 (*0-7453-0945-3*) Pluto GBR.

Chant, et al. Women of a Lesser Cost: Female Labour, Foreign Exchange, & Philippine Development. LC 94-45270. (C). 107.95 (*0-7453-0946-1*, Pub. by Pluto GBR) Stylus Pub VA.

Chant, Anthony D. The Stem Doctor. (C). 1989. 45.00 (*0-89771-933-6*, Pub. by A Chant) St Mut.

Chant, Anthony D. & D'Sa, Aires A. Emergency Vascular Surgery. LC 97-152687. (Illus.). 294p. text 150.00 (*0-340-56170-X*, Pub. by E A) Routldge.

Chant, Barry. Straight Talk about Sex. 176p. 1978. mass mkt. 5.99 (*0-88368-078-5*) Whitaker Hse.

Chant, Ben & Morgan, Melissa. How to Start a Service Business. (Twenty-First Century Entrepreneur Ser.: Bk. 2). 256p. (Orig.). 1994. pap. 12.50 (*0-380-77077-6*, Avon Bks) Morrow Avon.

Chant, C. World's Greatest Aircraft. 1996. 19.98 (*0-7858-0602-4*) Bk Sales Inc.

***Chant, Chris.** German Warplanes of WWII. 160p. 1999. 80.00 (*1-86227-049-X*, Pub. by Spellmnt Pubs) St Mut.

Chant, Chris. High Tech Planes. 1992. 17.98 (*1-55521-804-0*) Bk Sales Inc.

***Chant, Christopher.** Aircraft Protorypes: Aerospace Technology, from the Light Fighter to the B2 Stealth Bomber. (Illus.). 128p. 2000. 25.00 (*0-7881-9365-1*) DIANE Pub.

Chant, Christopher. Civil Aircraft. LC 99-30414. (World's Greatest Aircraft Ser.). (Illus.). 64p. 1999. 21.95 (*0-7910-5421-7*) Chelsea Hse.

— Compendium of Armaments & Military Hardware. 1987. 99.00 (*0-7102-0720-4*, Routledge Thoemms) Routledge.

— Early Fighters. LC 99-30765. (World's Greatest Aircraft Ser.). (Illus.). 64p. 1999. 21.95 (*0-7910-5418-7*) Chelsea Hse.

— The Encyclopedia of Codenames of World War Two. 400p. 1987. 59.50 (*0-7102-0718-2*, 07182, Routledge Thoemms) Routledge.

***Chant, Christopher.** Golden Age of Steam. (Illus.). 112p. 2000. 12.99 (*0-517-16164-8*) Random Hse Value.

Chant, Christopher. Handbook of British Regiments. 304p. 1988. text 57.50 (*0-415-00241-9*) Routledge.

— An Illustrated Data Guide to Battle Tanks of World War II. (Illustrated Data Guides Ser.). (Illus.). 80p. (YA). (gr. 5 up). Date not set. lib. bdg. 16.95 (*1-85501-856-X*, Pub. by Tiger Bks Intl) Chelsea Hse.

— An Illustrated Data Guide to Bombers of World War II. (Illustrated Data Guides Ser.). (Illus.). 80p. (YA). (gr. 5 up). Date not set. lib. bdg. 16.95 (*1-85501-858-6*, Pub. by Tiger Bks Intl) Chelsea Hse.

— An Illustrated Data Guide to Fighters in World War II. (Illustrated Data Guides Ser.). (Illus.). 80p. (YA). (gr. 5 up). Date not set. lib. bdg. 16.95 (*1-85501-859-4*, Pub. by Tiger Bks Intl) Chelsea Hse.

— An Illustrated Data Guide to Maritime Attack Aircraft of World War II. (Illustrated Data Guides Ser.). (Illus.). 80p. (YA). (gr. 5 up). lib. bdg. 16.95 (*1-85501-860-8*, Pub. by Tiger Bks Intl) Chelsea Hse.

— An Illustrated Data Guide to Modern Aircraft Carriers. (Illustrated Data Guides Ser.). (Illus.). 80p. (YA). (gr. 5 up). lib. bdg. 16.95 (*1-85501-863-2*, Pub. by Tiger Bks Intl) Chelsea Hse.

— An Illustrated Data Guide to Modern Artillery. (Illustrated Data Guides Ser.). (Illus.). 80p. (YA). (gr. 5 up). lib. bdg. 16.95 (*1-85501-861-6*, Pub. by Tiger Bks Intl) Chelsea Hse.

— An Illustrated Data Guide to Modern Fast Attack Craft. (Illustrated Data Guides Ser.). (Illus.). 80p. (YA). (gr. 5 up). lib. bdg. 16.95 (*1-85501-862-4*, Pub. by Tiger Bks Intl) Chelsea Hse.

— An Illustrated Data Guide to Modern Reconnaissance Aircraft. (Illustrated Data Guides Ser.). (Illus.). 80p. (YA). (gr. 5 up). lib. bdg. 16.95 (*1-85501-864-0*, Pub. by Tiger Bks Intl) Chelsea Hse.

— An Illustrated Data Guide to Submarines of World War II. (Illustrated Data Guides Ser.). (Illus.). 80p. (YA). (gr. 5 up). lib. bdg. 16.95 (*1-85501-865-9*, Pub. by Tiger Bks Intl) Chelsea Hse.

— Illustrated History of Small Arms: From Flintlocks to the Latest Specialised Weapons of Today. (Illus.). 144p. 1997. reprint ed. text 25.00 (*0-7881-5160-6*) DIANE Pub.

***Chant, Christopher.** Jane's Pocket Guide: Fighters of WWII. 144p. 2000. 15.00 (*0-00-472206-X*) HarpC.

Chant, Christopher. Military Aircraft. LC 99-30416. (World's Greatest Aircraft Ser.). (Illus.). 64p. 1999. 21.95 (*0-7910-5420-9*) Chelsea Hse.

— Operation Overlord: Gold & Juno Beaches. (Order of Battle Ser.). (Illus.). 32p. 1994. pap. 10.95 (*1-898994-01-3*) Stackpole.

— Operation Overlord: Sword Beach & the British 6th Airborne Division. (Order of Battle Ser.). (Illus.). 32p. 1994. pap. 10.95 (*1-898994-00-5*) Stackpole.

— Role of the Fighters & Bombers. LC 99-30764. (World's Greatest Aircraft Ser.). (Illus.). 64p. 1999. 21.95 (*0-7910-5419-5*) Chelsea Hse.

— Specialized Aircraft. LC 99-30415. (World's Greatest Aircraft Ser.). (Illus.). 64p. (YA). (gr. 5 up). 1999. 21.95 (*0-7910-5422-5*) Chelsea Hse.

— Top Gun. 1992. 19.98 (*1-55521-814-8*) Bk Sales Inc.

— World Encyclopedia of the Fighting Tank: An International History of the Armoured Fighting Machine. (Illus.). 384p. 1994. 49.95 (*1-85260-114-0*, Pub. by J H Haynes & Co) Motorbooks Intl.

Chant, Colin. Pre-Industrial Cities Reader. LC 98-26901. (Cities & Technology Ser.). 1999. write for info. (*0-415-20077-6*); pap. write for info. (*0-415-20078-4*) Routledge.

Chant, Colin & Goodman, David. The European Cities & Technology Reader: Industrial to Post-Industrial City. LC 98-38748. (Cities & Technology Ser.). 1999. write for info. (*0-415-20081-4*); pap. write for info. (*0-415-20082-2*) Routledge.

Chant, S., jt. auth. see Ward, P.

Chant, Sylvia. Gender & Migration in Developing Countries. 224p. 1993. 160.00 (*0-471-94506-4*) Wiley.

Chant, Sylvia, jt. auth. see Brydon, Lynne.

Chant, Sylvia H. & McIlwaine, Cathy, eds. Three Generations, Two Genders, One World: Women & Men in a Changing Century. LC 98-19782. 224p. 1998. text 59.95 (*1-85649-603-1*, Pub. by Zed Books); text 22.50 (*1-85649-604-X*, Pub. by Zed Books) St Martin.

Chantal, Jean-Francois. Monoclonal Antibodies in Immunoscintigraphy. (Illus.). 440p. 1989. boxed set 259.00 (*0-8493-4716-5*, RC78) CRC Pr.

Chantal, Sister. French Word Games & Puzzles. (FRE.). 64p. 1995. pap. 1.50 (*0-486-28481-6*) Dover.

Chantanachat, S. & Bold, Harold C. Phycological Studies Vol. 2: Some Algae from Arid Soils. (University Texas Publication: No. 6218). (Illus.). 74p. 1975. reprint ed. pap. 37.40 (*3-87429-097-2*, 007821, Pub. by Koeltz Sci Bks) Lubrecht & Cramer.

Chanter, Barrie & Swallow, Peter. Building Maintenance Management. LC 95-47345. 336p. 1996. text 69.95 (*0-632-03419-X*) Blackwell Sci.

Chanter, Tina. The Ethics of Eros: Irigaray's Re-Writing of the Philosophers. 368p. (C). 1994. pap. 20.99 (*0-415-90523-0*, A6690) Routledge.

— The Ethics of Eros: Irigaray's Re-Writing of the Philosophers. 368p. (C). (gr. 13). 1994. 70.00 (*0-415-90522-2*, A6686) Routledge.

Chanterelle Translations Staff, tr. see Rankl, Wolfgang & Effing, Wolfgang.

Chanthunya, Charles L. & Murinde, Victor. Trade Regime & Economic Growth. LC 97-76946. (Illus.). 266p. 1998. text 69.95 (*1-85628-624-X*, Pub. by Ashgate Pub) Ashgate Pub Co.

Chantikian, Kosrof. The Future Overthrown. LC 93-9279. 2000. write for info. (*0-916426-13-0*); pap. write for info. (*0-916426-14-9*) KOSMOS.

— Prophecies & Transformations. LC 75-35012. 88p. (Orig.). 1978. pap. 12.95 (*0-916426-01-7*) KOSMOS.

Chantikian, Kosrof, ed. Octavio Paz: Homage to the Poet. LC 80-82167. 248p. (C). 1981. 25.95 (*0-916426-03-3*); pap. 15.95 (*0-916426-04-1*) KOSMOS.

Chantikian, Kosrof, ed. see Alberti, Rafael.

Chantiles, Vilma L. The Food of Greece: Cooking, Folkways & Travel in the Mainland & Islands of Greece. LC 92-19548. (Illus.). 384p. 1992. pap. 15.00 (*0-671-75096-8*, Fireside) S&S Trade Pap.

— My Village by the Sea: Folktales of Greece. (Illus.). 120p. (Orig.). 1993. pap. text 10.00 (*0-918618-58-4*) Pella Pub.

Chantilis, Peter. Do Right Rules. LC 99-27850. 1998. pap. 12.95 (*0-8281-1288-6*) Forb Custom Pub.

Chantler, Clyde. The Ghana Story. 216p. 1971. 22.00 (*0-8464-0452-4*) Beekman Pubs.

Chantler, Nicolas. Profile of a Computer Hacker. Schwartau, Winn, ed. (Illus.). 400p. (Orig.). 1997. pap. 24.95 (*0-9628700-2-1*) Inter Pact Pr.

Chantler, Paul & Harris, Sim. Local Radio Journalism. LC 97-179363. (Illus.). 144p. 1992. 26.95 (*0-240-51308-8*, Focal) Buttrwrth-Heinemann.

— Local Radio Journalism. 2nd ed. 192p. 1997. pap. 32.95 (*0-240-51422-X*, Focal) Buttrwrth-Heinemann.

Chantler, Phil. Swifts: A Guide to the Swifts & Treeswifts of the World. 2nd ed. (Illus.). 240p. 1999. 40.00 (*0-300-07936-2*) Yale U Pr.

Chantraine, P. Etymological Dictionary of the Greek Language: Dictionnaire Etymologique de la Langue Greque, 4 Vols. (FRE & GER.). 1983. 395.00 (*0-8288-1058-3*, M6693) Fr & Eur.

Chantre, Jean-Claude. Les Considerations Religieuses et Esthetiques D'un "Sturmer und Dranger" (European University Studies: German Language & Literature: Ser. 1, Vol. 507). (FRE.). 650p. 1982. 38.00 (*3-261-04989-8*) P Lang Pubng.

Chantry, Art, ed. Instant Litter: Concert Posters from Seattle Punk Culture. LC 85-14492. (Illus.). 112p. (Orig.). 1985. pap. 10.00 (*0-941104-15-X*) Real Comet.

Chantry, Art, jt. auth. see Lasky, Julie.

Chantry, Chantry J. Senales de los Apostoles: Observaciones Sobre el Pentecostalismo Antiguo Y Moderno. Zamora, Jorge E., tr. from ENG. (SPA.). 157p. 1990. pap. 4.99 (*0-85151-573-8*) Banner of Truth.

Chantry, George W. Long-Wave Optics, Vol. 1. 1984. text 162.00 (*0-12-168101-7*) Acad Pr.

Chantry, M., ed. Scholia in Aristophanem III 4b: Scholia in Thesmophoriazusas; Ranas; Ecclesiazusas et Plutum. (GRE & LAT.). xxx, 318p. 1996. lib. bdg. 157.00 (*90-6980-084-5*, Pub. by Egbert Forsten) Hodlder & Stoughton.

— Scholia in Thesmophoriazusas: Ranasi Ecclesiazusas et Plutum. (Scholia in Aristophanem III 4a in Plutum Ser.). (GEC & LAT.). xxx, 202p. 1994. lib. bdg. 127.00 (*90-6980-055-1*, Pub. by Egbert Forsten) Hodlder & Stoughton.

Chantry, Nyla. The Price. LC 98-91402. 1998. pap. 13.95 (*0-533-12662-2*) Vantage.

Chantry, Walter. Fatherhood of God. pap. 0.06 (*0-87377-123-0*) GAM Pubns.

— I Heard What You Said. pap. 0.06 (*0-87377-124-9*) GAM Pubns.

Chantry, Walter J. Call the Sabbath a Delight. 112p. (Orig.). 1991. pap. 5.99 (*0-85151-588-6*) Banner of Truth.

— El Evangelio de Hoy: Autentico o Sintetico.Tr. of Today's Gospel: Authentic or Synthetic. 107p. 1995. pap. 4.50 (*0-85151-717-X*) Banner of Truth.

— God's Righteous Kingdom. 151p. (Orig.). 1980. pap. 7.99 (*0-85151-310-7*) Banner of Truth.

— Praises for the King of Kings. 114p. (Orig.). 1991. pap. 5.99 (*0-85151-587-8*) Banner of Truth.

— Shadow of the Cross: Studies in Self-Denial. 79p. (Orig.). 1981. pap. 4.99 (*0-85151-331-X*) Banner of Truth.

— Signs of the Apostles. 1979. pap. 7.99 (*0-85151-175-9*) Banner of Truth.

— Today's Gospel. 1980. pap. 5.99 (*0-85151-027-2*) Banner of Truth.

Chanturia, T. A., jt. auth. see Kiguradze, I. T.

Chantz, N. E. Just Pick a Murricane? (Language & Literature Ser.: Vol. 3). 1969. pap. 4.50 (*0-902675-11-7*) Oleander Pr.

Chanute, Octave. Progress in Flying Machines. unabridged ed. LC 97-38658. (Illus.). 320p. 1998. reprint ed. pap. 10.95 (*0-486-29981-3*) Dover.

***Chany, Kalman A.** Paying for College, 2001. 2000. pap. 18.00 (*0-375-76156-X*) Random.

Chanzit, Gwen F. Herbert Boyer & Modernist Design in America. (Illus.). 272p. 1987. 89.98 (*0-7734-2004-5*) E Mellen.

Chanzit, Gwen Finkel. The Herbert Bayer Collection & Archive. Chambers, Marlene, ed. LC 88-70744. (Illus.). 256p. 1988. pap. 24.95 (*0-295-96697-1*) Denver Art Mus.

Chao, Alexander W. Physics of Collective Beam Instabilities in High Energy Accelerators. LC 92-39599. (Beam Physics & Accelerator Technology Ser.). 384p. 1993. 110.00 (*0-471-55184-8*) Wiley.

Chao, Alexander W., ed. Advanced Beam Dynamics Workshop on Effects of Errors in Accelerators, Their Diagnosis & Correction: AIP Conference Proceedings, No. 255. LC 92-52842. (AIP Conference Proceedings Ser.). (Illus.). 440p. 1992. 95.00 (*1-56396-006-0*) Am Inst Physics.

Chao, Alexander W. & Tigner, Maury, eds. Handbook of Accelerator Physics & Engineering: A Compilation of Formulae & Data. LC 99-13549. 500p. 1998. 78.00 (*981-02-3500-3*) World Scientific Pub.

Chao, Allen C. Civil Engineering: CE1 - Hydraulic & Sanitary Engineering. (Professional Engineering Exam Review Ser.). (Illus.). 179p. (Orig.). (C). 1983. pap. text 16.00 (*1-56049-050-0*) NCSU CE IES.

Chao, Arnold, jt. ed. see Wei, Lin.

Chao, C. Out of the Tiger's Mouth. Date not set. pap. 6.99 (*1-871676-59-2*, Pub. by Christian Focus) Spring Arbor Dist.

Chao, C. S. A Guide to Bamboos Grown in Britain. 47p. 1989. pap. 15.00 (*0-947643-17-6*, Pub. by Royal Botnic Grdns) Balogh.

***Chao, Cedric C.** Creating Your Discovery Plan - Action Guide, Fall 1999. Compton, Linda A., ed. 92p. 1999. ring bd. 58.00 (*0-7626-0358-5*, CP-11027) Cont Ed Bar-CA.

***Chao, Chan.** Burma: Something Went Wrong. (Illus.). 128p. 2000. 50.00 (*3-923922-87-6*) Nazraeli Press.

Chao, Der-Lin, jt. auth. see Chou, Chi-P'ing.

Chao-Hsiu Chen. Body Feng Shui: The Ancient Chinese Science of Body Reading. (Illus.). 176p. 1999. pap. 14.95 (*0-89281-769-0*) Inner Tradit.

Chao, Hung-Po & Huntington, Hillar G. Designing Competitive Electricity Markets. LC 98-36769. (International Series in Operations Research & Management Science). 1998. pap. write for info. (*0-7923-8283-8*) Kluwer Academic.

***Chao, Hung-Po & Huntington, Hillard G.** Designing Competitive Electricity Markets. LC 98-36769. (International Series in Operations Research & Management Science). 30p. 1998. 89.95 (*0-7923-8282-X*) Kluwer Academic.

Chao, John & Weakland, John. Secret Techniques of Wing Chun Kung Fu Vol. I: Sil Lim Tao. 372p. 1996. 18.95 (*0-901764-35-3*, 93324) P H Crompton.

— Secret Techniques of Wing Chun Kung Fu Vol. 3: Bil Jee. 136p. 1998. 19.95 (*0-901764-62-0*, 93326) P H Crompton.

Chao, John, jt. auth. see Chao, K. T.

Chao, K. C. & Robinson, Robert, eds. Equations of State in Engineering & Research. LC 79-23696. (Advances in Chemistry Ser.: No. 182). 1979. 65.95 (*0-8412-0500-0*) Am Chemical.

Chao, K. C. & Robinson, Robert L., Jr., eds. Equations of State: Theories & Applications. LC 86-1109. (ACS Symposium Ser.: No. 300). (Illus.). x, 592p. 1986. 94.95 (*0-8412-0958-8*) Am Chemical.

— Equations of State: Theories & Applications. LC 86-1109. (ACS Symposium Ser.: Vol. 300). 608p. 1986. reprint ed. pap. 188.50 (*0-608-03846-6*, 206429300008) Bks Demand.

Chao, K. T., et al, eds. Heavy Flavour Physics. 468p. 1989. text 102.00 (*9971-5-0809-5*) World Scientific Pub.

Chao, K. T. & Chao, John. Secret Techniques of Wing Chun Kung Fu Vol. 2: Chum Kil. 448p. 1996. 18.95 (*0-901764-49-3*, 93325) P H Crompton.

Chao, Kang. Agricultural Production in Communist China, 1949-1965. LC 70-121766. 373p. 1970. reprint ed. pap. 115.70 (*0-608-01906-2*, 206255800003) Bks Demand.

— Capital Formation in Mainland China, 1952-1965. LC 72-85526. (Michigan Studies on China). 192p. reprint ed. pap. 59.60 (*0-608-18496-9*, 203150200075) Bks Demand.

— The Development of Cotton Textile Production in China. (East Asian Monographs: No. 74). 418p. 1977. 30.00 (*0-674-20021-7*) HUP.

— The Economic Development of Manchuria: The Rise of a Frontier Economy. LC 83-7455. (Michigan Monographs in Chinese Studies: No. 43). 127p. (Orig.). 1983. pap. text 15.00 (*0-89264-043-X*) Ctr Chinese Studies.

— Man & Land in Chinese History: An Economic Analysis. LC 84-51715. 288p. 1986. 42.50 (*0-8047-1271-9*) Stanford U Pr.

Chao, Ko-Pao. English Dictionary of Thousand Roots: A Dictionary Compiled in "a.b.c.(e)" System. LC 96-97149. vi, 320p. (Orig.). 1997. pap. text 24.95 (*0-9656030-0-8*) Ko-Pao Chao.

Chao Kuo-Chun. Agrarian Policy of the Chinese Communist Party, Nineteen Twenty-One to Nineteen Fifty-Nine. LC 77-14587. 1978. reprint ed. lib. bdg. 65.00 (*0-8371-9861-5*, CHAP, Greenwood Pr) Greenwood.

— Economic Planning & Organization in Mainland China: A Documentary Study, 1949-1957, 2 Vols, 1. LC 59-4569. (East Asian Monographs: No. 7). 299p. 1959. pap. 20.00 (*0-674-22900-2*) HUP.

— Economic Planning & Organization in Mainland China: A Documentary Study, 1949-1957, 2 Vols, Vol. 2. LC 59-4569. (East Asian Monographs: No. 7). 196p. 1960. pap. 20.00 (*0-674-22901-0*) HUP.

Chao, Kwang-Chu & Greenkorn, R. A. Thermodynamics of Fluids: An Introduction to Equilibrium Theory. LC 75-13121. (Chemical Processing & Engineering Ser.: No. 4). (Illus.). 569p. reprint ed. pap. 176.40 (*0-7837-0968-4*, 204127300019) Bks Demand.

Chao, Lien. Beyond Silence: Chinese Canadian Literature in English. LC 98-151423. 205p. 1997. pap. 19.95 (*0-920661-69-6*, Pub. by TSAR Pubns) LPC InBook.

***Chao, Lien.** Maples & the Stream. 136p. 1999. 14.95 (*0-920661-83-1*) TSAR Pubns.

— Maples & the Stream: A Narrative Poem. 125p. 1999. pap. 14.95 (*0-920661-81-5*, Pub. by TSAR Pubns) SPD-Small Pr Dist.

Chao, Linda & Myers, Ramon H. Democracy's New Leaders in the Republic of China on Taiwan. LC 96-51765. (Hoover Essays Ser.: No. 17). 1996. pap. 5.00 (*0-8179-3802-8*) Hoover Inst Pr.

— The First Chinese Democracy: Political Life in the Republic of China on Taiwan. LC 97-18847. (Illus.). 392p. 1997. text 45.00 (*0-8018-5650-7*) Johns Hopkins.

Chao, Loran Y., tr. see Cockman, Nelda.

Chao, Lorna, tr. see Meyer, F. B.

Chao, Lorna, tr. see Morgan, G. Campbell.

Chao, Lorna Y., tr. see Clark, Robert.

Chao, Lorna Y., tr. see Dunn, Ronald.

Chao, Lorna Y., tr. see Flynn, Leslie B.

Chao, Lorna Y., tr. see Long, James.

Chao, Lorna Y., tr. see Morgan, G. Campbell.

Chao, Lorna Y., tr. see S. P. Publications Editors.

Chao, Lorna Y., tr. see Sanders, J. Oswald.

Chao, Lorna Y., tr. see Shelly, Bruce L.

Chao, Mei-Po. The Yellow Bell: A Brief Sketch of the History of Chinese Music. 1974. lib. bdg. 250.00 (*0-87968-135-7*) Krishna Pr.

Chao, Nelson J. Graft vs Host-Disease. 2nd ed. LC 98-53442. (Medical Intelligence Unit Ser.). 204p. 1999. 99.00 (*1-57059-534-8*) Landes Bioscience.

Chao, Patricia. Monkey King: A Novel. 320p. 1998. pap. 13.00 (*0-06-092893-X*) HarpC.

Chao, Paul. Chinese Kinship. 220p. 1983. 45.00 (*0-7103-0020-4*, 00204) Routledge.

— Women under Communism: Family in Russia & China. LC 77-89932. 231p. 1977. pap. text 25.95 (*0-930390-00-8*); lib. bdg. 38.95 (*0-930390-01-6*) Gen Hall.

Chao Pu-Wei. Autobiography of a Chinese Woman, Buwei Yang Chao. Chao Yuen-Ren, tr. LC 72-100225. 327p. 1970. reprint ed. lib. bdg. 38.50 (*0-8371-3712-8*, CHCW, Greenwood Pr) Greenwood.

Chao, Samuel, tr. see Sanders, J. Oswald.

Chao, Samuel H. Practical Missiology: The Life & Mission Methods of John L. Nevius, 1829-1893. LC 93-37649. (American University Studies: Vol. 151). 1994. write for info. (*0-8204-2355-6*) P Lang Pubng.

***Chao, Sheau-Yueh J.** In Search of Your Asian Roots: Genealogical Resources of Chinese Surnames. 323p. 2000. pap. 29.95 (*0-8063-4946-8*, Pub. by Clearfield Co) ACCESS Pubs Network.

— Internet Resources & Services for International Real Estate Information. 304p. 2001. text, boxed set 49.95 (*1-57356-373-0*) Oryx Pr.

Chao, Sheau-Yueh J., compiled by. The Japanese Automobile Industry: An Annotated Bibliography, 15. LC 93-35797. (Bibliographies & Indexes in Economics & Economic History Ser.: No. 15). 216p. 1994. lib. bdg. 75.00 (*0-313-28678-7*, Greenwood Pr) Greenwood.

***Chao, Shiyan, ed.** Ghana: Gender Analysis & Policymaking for Development. LC 99-15987. (Discussion Paper Ser.: No. 403). 84p. 1999. pap. 22.00 (*0-8213-4530-3*, 14530) World Bank.

Chao, Tien-Hsin, jt. ed. see Casasent, David P.

Chao, W. Q. & Shen, P. N. International Symposium on Medium Energy: ISMEP' 1994. xiii, 445 p. 1995. text 118.00 (*981-02-2089-8*) World Scientific Pub.

***Chao, Xiuli.** Operations Scheduling with Applications in Manufacturing & Services. 1998. 83.75 (*0-07-561963-6*) McGraw.

— Queueing Networks: Customers, Signals & Product form Solutions. LC 99-26511. 458p. 1999. 135.00 (*0-471-98309-8*) Wiley.

Chao, Xiuli, jt. auth. see Pinedo, Michael.

C

Chao, Y. S., et al, eds. Biomechanics of the Hand. 204p. (C). 1989. text 70.00 (*9971-5-0103-1*); pap. text 30.00 (*9971-5-0104-X*) World Scientific Pub.

Chao-yu, Yang. The Pawnshop in China. Whelan, T.S., ed. LC 79-120430. (Michigan Abstracts of Chinese & Japanese Works on Chinese History: No. 6). 1979. pap. 15.00 (*0-89264-906-2*) Ctr Chinese Studies.

Chao, Yuen R. Mandarin Primer: An Intensive Course in Spoken Chinese. LC 48-8224. 344p. 1948. reprint ed. pap. 106.70 (*0-7837-2234-6*, 205732400004) Bks Demand.

Chao, Yuen R. & Yuen Ren Chao. Sayable Chinese, 3 vols., Set. (Spoken Language Ser.). 1985. audio 230.00 (*0-87950-336-X*) Spoken Lang Serv.

Chao Yuen-Ren & Yang, Lien-Sheng. Concise Dictionary of Spoken Chinese. LC 47-5464. (Harvard-Yenching Institute Publications). 330p. 1947. 22.50 (*0-674-15800-8*) HUP.

Chao Yuen-Ren, tr. see Chao Pu-Wei.

Chaohao, Gu, ed. Soliton Theory & Its Applications. LC 95-34798. 1995. 135.00 (*0-387-57112-4*) Spr-Verlag.

Chaohao, Gu, et al, eds. Nonlinear Physics. (Research Reports in Physics). (Illus.). 315p. 1990. 71.95 (*0-387-52389-8*) Spr-Verlag.

Chaoman, D. J., jt. ed. see Round, F. E.

Chaon, Dan. Fitting Ends & Other Stories. LC 95-23447. 250p. (C). 1995. pap. 14.95 (*0-8101-5022-0*, TriQuart); text 35.00 (*0-8101-5021-2*, TriQuart) Northwestern U Pr.

Chaos. Chaos Thompson. (Trading Advantage Ser.). 300p. 2000. text 69.95 (*0-471-99865-6*) Wiley.

Chaosium Inc. Publishing Staff. Encyclopedia Cthulhiana. 2nd ed. (Call of Cthulhu Fiction Ser.). (Illus.). 448p. 1998. pap. 14.95 (*1-56882-119-0*) Chaosium.

Chaosium Inc. Staff. Book of Eibon. 1998. pap. text 12.95 (*1-56882-129-8*) Chaosium.

— Character Dossiers. (Nephilyum Roleplaying Game Ser.). (Illus.). 32p. 1995. pap. 8.95 (*1-56882-044-5*, 3105) Chaosium.

Chaosium, Inc. Staff. Other Nations, 1. 1998. pap. text 12.95 (*1-56882-128-X*) Chaosium.

— Tales of Innsmouth. 1998. pap. text 13.95 (*1-56882-127-1*) Chaosium.

Chaosium Publishing Staff. Bermuda Triangle. 1997. pap. text 16.95 (*1-56882-122-0*) Chaosium.

Chaot, Ernest, et al. Teachers & Television. 256p. 1987. text 49.50 (*0-7099-4819-0*, Pub. by C Helm) Routldge.

Chaote, Harris S. The Yaquis: A Celebration. LC 96-60761. (Illus.). 102p. 1997. pap. 17.95 (*0-9639519-7-1*) Whitewing Pr.

Chaouat, Gerard, ed. Immunology of Pregnancy. 288p. 1992. lib. bdg. 169.00 (*0-8493-8868-6*, RG557) CRC Pr.

— Immunology of the Fetus. 336p. 1989. lib. bdg. 208.00 (*0-8493-4568-5*, RG613) CRC Pr.

Chaouki, J., et al. Non-Invasive Monitoring of Multiphase Flows. LC 96-43594. 608p. 1996. 273.00 (*0-444-82521-5*) Elsevier.

Chapa, Jorge & Cardenas, Gilberto. The Economy of the Urban Ethnic Enclave. (Policy Research Project Ser.: No. 97). 156p. 1992. pap. 12.50 (*0-89940-705-6*) LBJ Sch Pub Aff.

Chapa, Jorge & Eaton, David J. Colonia Housing & Infrastructure Vol. 1: Current Characteristics, Future Needs. (Policy Research Project Report Ser.). 130p. 1997. pap. 15.00 (*0-89940-734-X*) LBJ Sch Pub Aff.

— Colonia Housing & Infrastructure Vol. 2: Water & Wastewater Infrastructure. (Policy Research Project Report Ser.). 214p. 1997. pap. 17.00 (*0-89940-735-8*) LBJ Sch Pub Aff.

— Colonia Housing & Infrastructure Vol. 3: Regulatory Issues & Policy Analysis. (Policy Research Project Report Ser.). 145p. 1997. pap. 15.00 (*0-89940-736-6*) LBJ Sch Pub Aff.

Chapa, Juan B. Texas & Northeastern Mexico, 1630-1690. Brierley, Ned F., tr. LC 96-25202. (Illus.). 248p. 1997. 24.95 (*0-292-71188-3*) U of Tex Pr.

Chapanis, Alfred R. E. Research Techniques in Human Engineering. LC 59-10765. 328p. reprint ed. pap. 101.70 (*0-608-11565-7*, 200227600012) Bks Demand.

Chapanis, Alphonse. The Chapanis Chronicles: 50 Years of Human Factors Research, Education & Design. LC 99-72642. (Illus.). 256p. 1999. 34.00 (*0-9636178-9-3*) Aegean Pub.

— Human Factors in Systems Engineering. LC 95-46163. (Wiley Series in Systems Engineering). (Illus.). 352p. 1996. 74.95 (*0-471-13782-0*, Wiley-Interscience) Wiley.

Chapanis, Alphonse, ed. see North Atlantic Treaty Organization, Advisory Group.

Chaparian, jt. auth. see Cockerman.

Chaparro, John E. Pirates Island. 170p. 2000. pap. 11.95 (*1-891929-32-1*) Four Seasons.

Chapchal, G. Reconstruction Surgery & Traumatology, Vol. 14. (Illus.). 200p. 1974. 85.25 (*3-8055-1563-4*) S Karger.

Chapchal, G., ed. Fractures in Children. (Reconstruction Surgery & Traumatology Ser.: Vol. 17). (Illus.). x, 182p. 1979. 68.75 (*3-8055-3013-7*) S Karger.

— Reconstruction Surgery & Traumatology, Vol. 12. 1971. 85.25 (*3-8055-1183-3*) S Karger.

— Reconstruction Surgery & Traumatology, Vol. 15. 1976. 42.75 (*3-8055-2250-9*) S Karger.

— Reconstruction Surgery & Traumatology, Vol. 16. (Illus.). 1977. 50.50 (*3-8055-2696-2*) S Karger.

— Reconstruction Surgery & Traumatology Vol. 13: Operative Treatment of Cerebral Palsy. (Illus.). 1972. 85.25 (*3-8055-1385-2*) S Karger.

Chapdelaine, Perry A., Sr. The Laughing Terran. 176p. 1977. 7.50 (*0-7091-5892-0*) AC Projects.

— Spork of the Ayor. 208p. 1978. 7.50 (*0-7091-6528-5*) AC Projects.

Chapdelaine, Perry A., Sr., ed. see Campbell, John W., Jr.

Chapdelaine, Perry A., Sr., ed. see Campbell, John W., Jr., et al.

Chapel. Directory of Public Golf Courses in New York State. 1993. pap. 9.95 (*0-9624738-6-3*) Six Lakes Arts.

Chapel, Hal J. & Clark, Richard G. Revelation Revealed. rev. ed. Danielpour, Debbie, ed. (Orig.). 1987. pap. 45.00 (*0-941019-66-7*) Paradigm Hlth Care.

Chapel, Helen M. & Haeney, Mansel. Essentials of Clinical Immunology. 3rd ed. (Essentials Ser.). (Illus.). 352p. 1993. pap. 49.95 (*0-632-03366-5*) Blackwell Sci.

Chapel, Helen M., et al. Essential Clinical Immunology. 4th ed. LC 98-40975. (Illus.). 1999. pap. 49.95 (*0-632-04972-3*) Blackwell Sci.

Chapel Hill Service League Staff. Nothin' Finer. (Illus.). 254p. 1993. spiral bd. 15.95 (*0-9633052-0-4*) CH Srv Leag.

Chapel of the Air Ministries, Inc. Staff. The Church You've Always Longed For: What You Can Do to Make It Happen. Oliver, Marian & Vander Vorst, Mitchell, eds. (Nineteen Ninety-Seven 50-Day Spiritual Adventure Ser.). (Illus.). 80p. (Orig.). 1996. pap., wbk. ed. 6.00 (*1-57849-000-6*) Chapel of Air.

Chapel of the Air Ministries, Inc. Staff. La Iglesia Que Simepre Has Deseador: Como Alcanzarla. Ramirez, Eduardo & Ramirez, Elvira, trs. (Nineteen Ninety-Seven 50-Day Spiritual Adventure Ser.). (ENG & SPA.). 80p. (Orig.). 1996. pap., wbk. ed. 6.00 (*1-57849-027-8*) Chapel of Air.

— Que Hacer Cuand No Sabes Que Hacer: Confiando en Cristo en Medio de la Confusion. Ramirez, Eduardo & Ramirez, Elvira, trs. (Nineteen Ninety-Six 50-Day Spiritual Adventure Ser.). (ENG & SPA.). 80p. (Orig.). 1995. pap., wbk. ed. 6.00 (*1-879050-83-8*) Chapel of Air.

— What to Do When You Don't Know What to Do: Trusting Christ When Life Gets Confusing. Oliver, Marian & Vander Vorst, Mitchell, eds. (Nineteen Ninety-Six 50-Day Spiritual Adventure Ser.). (Illus.). 80p. (Orig.). 1995. pap., wbk. ed. 6.00 (*1-879050-70-6*) Chapel of Air.

Chapel of the Air Ministries Staff. Atrevase a Sonar De Nuevo: Manual Del Adulto. Berglund, Anna et al, trs. (1994 50-Day Spiritual Adventure Ser.). (Illus.). 64p. (Orig.). 1994. pap. text, student ed. 4.99 (*1-879050-44-7*) Chapel of Air.

— Daring to Dream Again: Breaking Through Barriers That Hold Us Back. (1994 50-Day Spiritual Adventure Ser.). (Illus.). 64p. (Orig.). 1993. pap. text 4.99 (*1-879050-14-5*) Chapel of Air.

— Daring to Dream Again: Breaking Through Barriers That Hold Us Back, Church Leader's Manual. (1994 50-Day Spiritual Adventure Ser.). (Illus.). 188p. 1993. ring bd. 49.99 (*1-879050-19-6*) Chapel of Air.

— Facing down Our Fears: Finding Courage When Anxiety Grips the Heart. (1995 50-Day Spiritual Adventure Ser.). (Illus.). 80p. (Orig.). 1994. pap. text, student ed. 4.95 (*1-879050-47-1*) Chapel of Air.

— Facing down Our Fears: Finding Courage When Anxiety Grips the Heart Church Leader's Manual. (1995 50-Day Spiritual Adventure Ser.). (Illus.). 350p. 1994. ring bd. 39.99 (*1-879050-56-0*) Chapel of Air.

— Facing Down Our Fears: Small Group Starter Kit. (Illus.). 1994. 45.95 incl. vdisk (*1-879050-63-3*) Chapel of Air.

— The Family God Wants Us to Be: Your Rx for Healthier Church Relationships. (1992 50-Day Spiritual Adventure Ser.). (Illus.). 48p. (Orig.). 1991. pap. text, student ed. 4.95 (*1-879050-03-X*) Chapel of Air.

— Survival Skills for Changing Times: Purposeful Christian Living in the '90s. (1993 50-Day Spiritual Adventure Ser.). (Illus.). 48p. (Orig.). 1992. pap. text, student ed. 4.99 (*1-879050-07-2*) Chapel of Air.

— Survival Skills for Changing Times: Purposeful Christian Living in the '90s Leader's Manual. (1993 50-Day Spiritual Adventure Ser.). (Illus.). 90p. 1992. ring bd. 39.99 (*1-879050-12-9*) Chapel of Air.

— We Will Glorify: Personal Worship Journal. (1994 4-Week Worship Celebration Ser.). (Illus.). 64p. (Orig.). 1994. pap. text, student ed. 4.99 (*1-879050-45-5*) Chapel of Air.

— What to Do When You Don't Know What to Do: Braille Adult Journal. (Nineteen Ninety-Six 50-Day Spiritual Adventure Ser.). (Orig.). 1996. pap. 12.00 (*1-879050-96-X*) Chapel of Air.

Chapel of the Air Staff. 50 Days to Welcome Christ to Our Church: Adult Journal for the 50-Day Adventure Series. (1991 50-Day Spiritual Adventure Ser.). (Illus.). 48p. (Orig.). 1990. pap. text, student ed. 3.95 (*1-879050-00-5*) Chapel of Air.

Chapel, Paul A. Geophysique Appliquee: Dictionnaire et Plan D'Etude. (FRE.). 432p. 1980. 165.00 (*0-7859-7825-9*, 2225677492) Fr & Eur.

— Handbook of Exploration Geophysics: An Encyclopedic & an Algorithm Source Book. (C). 1991. 64.00 (*81-204-0652-4*, Pub. by Oxford IBH) S Asia.

— Handbook of Exploration Geophysics: An Encyclopedic & an Algorythm Sourcebook. (Illus.). 427p. (C). 1992. text 162.00 (*90-5410-206-3*, Pub. by A A Balkema) Ashgate Pub Co.

Chapela, Ignacio H., jt. ed. see Palm, Mary E.

Chapell, Bryan. Christ-Centered Preaching: Redeeming the Expository Sermon. LC 93-46468. 376p. 1994. 27.99 (*0-8010-2586-9*) Baker Bks.

— Each for the Other: Marriage as It's Meant to Be. LC 98-42906. 208p. 2000. pap. 9.99 (*0-8010-5833-3*) Baker Bks.

— The Wonder of It All: Rediscovering the Treasures of Your Faith. LC 98-53804. 300p. 1999. pap. 14.99 (*1-58134-061-3*) Crossway Bks.

Chapell, Bryan, jt. auth. see Hughes, R. Kent.

Chapell, Howard I. Yacht Designing & Planning: For Yachtsmen, Students, & Amateurs. (Illus.). 375p. 1995. 35.00 (*0-393-03756-8*) Norton.

***Chapelle.** Ground - Water Microbiology & Geochemistry. 2nd ed. 525p. 2000. 99.00 (*0-471-34852-X*) Wiley.

Chapelle, Carol, jt. ed. see Douglas, Dan.

Chapelle, Daniel. Nietzsche & Psychoanalysis. LC 92-35535. 258p. (C). 1993. text 21.50 (*0-7914-1527-9*) State U NY Pr.

Chapelle, David La, see La Chapelle, David.

Chapelle, Francis H. Ground - Water Microbiology & Geochemistry. LC 92-5589. 448p. 1993. 125.00 (*0-471-52951-6*) Wiley.

— The Hidden Sea: Ground Water, Springs, & Wells. LC 97-5640. (Illus.). 256p. 1997. pap. 20.00 (*0-945005-26-1*) Geoscience Pr.

Chapelle, Howard. The History of the American Sailing Navy. (Illus.). 560p. 1998. reprint ed. 14.95 (*1-56852-222-3*, Konecky & Konecky) W S Konecky Assocs.

Chapelle, Howard I. The American Fishing Schooners, 1825-1935: The History of the Commercial Fishing Schooner, Its Development in Design, Function, & Construction. (Illus.). 690p. 1995. 45.00 (*0-393-03755-X*) Norton.

— American Small Sailing Craft. (Illus.). 1951. 40.00 (*0-393-03143-8*) Norton.

— The Baltimore Clipper. 204p. Date not set. 20.95 (*0-8488-2235-8*) Amereon Ltd.

— The Baltimore Clipper: Its Origin & Development. (Illus.). 240p. 1988. pap. 9.95 (*0-486-25765-7*) Dover.

— Boatbuilding: A Complete Handbook of Wooden Boat Construction. 1994. 39.95 (*0-393-03554-9*) Norton.

— Chesapeake Bay Crabbing Skiffs. (Illus.). 1979. pap. 5.00 (*0-614-04337-9*) Ches Bay Mus.

— Yacht Designing & Planning. 1996. text 35.00 (*0-07-011679-2*) McGraw.

Chapelle, Howard I. & Polland, Leon D. The Constellation Question. LC 77-609565. (Smithsonian Studies in History & Technology: No. 5). (Illus.). 169p. reprint ed. pap. 52.40 (*0-608-30103-5*, 200420400042) Bks Demand.

Chapelle, Pierre & Vemier, Gerrit, eds. Proceedings of the International Conference on Noise Control Engineering Held August 24-26, 1993, in Leuven, Belgium Vols. 1-3, 3 vols., Set. (Inter-Noise Ser.). cxx, 1896p. 150.00 (*90-5204-024-9*) Noise Control.

Chapelle, Suzanne E. & Phillips, Glenn O. African-American Leaders of Maryland: A Portrait Gallery. 2000. pap. text 17.50 (*0-938420-69-0*) MD Hist.

Chapelle, Suzanne E., et al. Maryland: A History of Its People. LC 85-19888. (Illus.). 352p. (gr. 9-12). 1986. text 24.95 (*0-8018-3005-2*) Johns Hopkins.

Chapelle, Tony, jt. auth. see Smith, Rita W.

Chapellier, Dominique. Well Logging in Hydrogeology. (Illus.). (C). 1992. text 97.00 (*90-5410-207-1*, Pub. by A A Balkema) Ashgate Pub Co.

Chapepanov, S. K., jt. ed. see Bobrov, E. G.

Chapeville, F. & Haenni, A. O., eds. Chemical Recognition in Biology. (Molecular Biology, Biochemistry & Biophysics Ser.: Vol. 32). (Illus.). 430p. 1980. 90.95 (*0-387-10205-1*) Spr-Verlag.

Chapey, Geraldine. Developing Speaking Skill. 200p. 1988. pap. text 22.50 (*0-07-010545-6*) McGraw.

— Developing Speaking Skill. 200p. 1988. audio 69.45 (*0-07-087528-6*) McGraw.

— Developing Speaking Skill. 200p. 1989. VHS 99.99 (*0-07-087088-8*) McGraw.

— Ready for School: How Parents Can Prepare Children for School Success. (Illus.). 164p. (Orig.). 1986. pap. text 9.25 (*0-8191-5317-6*) U Pr of Amer.

Chapey, Roberta, ed. Language Intervention Strategies in Adult Aphasia. 3rd ed. LC 92-48908. (Illus.). 6481994p. 1993. 58.00 (*0-683-01513-3*) Lppncott W & W.

Chapian, Marie. Am I the Only One Here with Faded Genes? LC 87-11611. (Teen Devotionals Ser.). (Illus.). 176p. (YA). (gr. 9-12). 1987. pap. 7.99 (*0-87123-945-0*) Bethany Hse.

— Discovering Joy. (Heart for God Ser.: Vol. 4). 210p. (Orig.). 1990. text 11.99 (*1-55661-122-6*) Bethany Hse.

— Feeling Small . . . Walking Tall. 176p. (Orig.). (YA). (gr. 8 up). 1989. pap. 7.99 (*1-55661-029-7*) Bethany Hse.

— His Gifts to Me. LC 88-21119. (Heart for God Ser.). 28p. (Orig.). 1988. text 12.99 (*1-55661-038-6*) Bethany Hse.

— His Thoughts Toward Me. LC 87-20854. (Heart for God Ser.). 192p. (Orig.). 1987. text 12.99 (*0-87123-962-0*) Bethany Hse.

— Making His Heart Glad. (Heart for God Ser.: VOl. 3). (Illus.). 176p. 1989. text 11.99 (*1-55661-083-1*) Bethany Hse.

— Mothers & Daughters. LC 88-4199. 224p. (Orig.). 1988. pap. 9.99 (*1-55661-007-6*) Bethany Hse.

— Of Whom the World Was Not Worthy. LC 78-769. 1980. pap. text 9.99 (*0-87123-250-2*) Bethany Hse.

— The Secret Place of Strength. (Heart for God Ser.: Bk. 5). 176p. (Orig.). 1991. text 11.99 (*1-55661-219-2*) Bethany Hse.

Chapian, Marie, intro. Of Whom the World Was Not Worthy. LC 78-769. (Illus.). 256p. 1978. pap. 9.99 (*0-87123-417-3*) Bethany Hse.

Chapian, Marie & Coyle, Neva. Free to Be Thin No. 1: Getting Started. LC 79-15656. (Neva Coyle Study Guides Ser.). (Illus.). 64p. 1979. pap., student ed. 4.99 (*0-87123-163-8*) Bethany Hse.

Chapian, Marie, jt. auth. see Backus.

Chapian, Marie, jt. auth. see Backus, William.

Chapian, Marie, jt. auth. see Coyle, Neva.

Chapin. Elementary Social Studies: A Practical Guide. 4th ed. LC 98-34505. 352p. (C). 1998. pap. 56.00 (*0-8013-3061-0*) Longman.

— 365 Bible Promises for People. LC 98-208781. 1998. pap. 5.99 (*0-8423-7022-6*) Tyndale Hse.

Chapin, jt. auth. see Hotchkiss.

Chapin, A. Lyman. 365 Promesas Biblicas para Personas Ocupadas. (SPA.). 6.99 (*0-7899-0329-6*, 497554) Editorial Unilit.

Chapin, A. Lyman, jt. auth. see Piscitello, David M.

Chapin, Alice. 400 Creative Ways to Say I Love You. 2nd ed. 96p. 1984. 4.99 (*0-8423-0919-5*) Tyndale Hse.

— 400 More Creative Ways to Say I Love You. LC 96-218129. 221p. 1996. mass mkt. 4.99 (*0-8423-0912-8*) Tyndale Hse.

— Hello Baby. 48p. 1999. pap. 7.95 (*1-901881-59-8*, Pub. by Element MA) Penguin Putnam.

— A Simple Christmas. rev. ed. LC 98-24547. Orig. Title: Great Christmas Ideas. (Illus.). 256p. 1998. pap. 14.99 (*0-8361-9102-1*) Herald Pr.

— 365 Bible Promises for Busy People. LC 92-18468. 205p. 1992. mass mkt. 4.99 (*0-8423-7048-X*) Tyndale Hse.

— 365 Bible Promises for Hurting People: Verses & Thoughts for a Few Minutes Each Day. 240p. 1996. mass mkt. 4.99 (*0-8423-7049-8*) Tyndale Hse.

Chapin, Alice & Henry, Ernest. We're Having a New Baby: A Welcome Baby Kit for the Whole Family Including Flannel Book, Poetry Book, 6 Color-In Card Photo-Frames, Packet of Children's Crayons & a Baby Measuring Chart. (Illus.). 96p. (J). (ps-1). 1998. pap. 19.95 (*1-901881-60-1*, Pub. by Element MA) Penguin Putnam.

Chapin, Alice Z. Gifts of Love: Crafts & Presents That Embody the Spirit of Giving. LC 97-10152. (Illus.). 208p. 1997. pap. 11.95 (*0-385-49042-9*) Doubleday.

***Chapin, Alice Z.** Nine Months & Counting: Bible Promises & Bright Ideas for Pregnancy & After. LC 99-26601. 1999. pap. text 8.99 (*0-8423-7363-2*) Tyndale Hse.

Chapin, Alice Z. Reaching Back. LC 96-32033. 160p. 1997. pap. 14.99 (*1-55870-454-X*, Betrwy Bks) F & W Pubns Inc.

Chapin, Anna A. The Heart of Music: The Story of the Violin. LC 77-169753. (Select Bibliographies Reprint Ser.). 1977. reprint ed. 23.95 (*0-8369-5973-6*) Ayer.

Chapin, Bradley. American Law of Treason: Revolutionary & Early National Origins. LC 64-11053. (Publications in History). 182p. 1964. 25.00 (*0-295-73705-0*, UWPH) U of Wash Pr.

— Early America. LC 83-8276. 302p. 1984. lib. bdg. 29.95 (*0-89198-129-2*) Ozer.

Chapin, Bruce. The Hardest Challenge: Surviving the Death of a Spouse. 501p. (Orig.). 1990. pap. 6.50 (*0-9613704-2-4*) Tchrs Insurance.

Chapin, C. E., et al, eds. Field Guide to Selected Cauldrons & Mining Districts of the Datil-Mogollon Volcanic Field, New Mexico. (Special Publications: No. 7). (Illus.). 149p. 1978. pap. 10.00 (*1-58546-006-0*) NMex Geol Soc.

Chapin, C. E. & Callender, J. F., eds. Socorro Region, Vol. II. (Guidebook Ser.: No. 34). (Illus.). 344p. 1983. 40.00 (*1-58546-068-0*); pap. 15.00 (*1-58546-069-9*) NMex Geol Soc.

Chapin Carpenter, Mary. Dreamland: A Lullaby. LC 95-16576. (Illus.). 40p. (J). (ps-2). 1996. 13.95 (*0-06-025402-5*) HarpC Child Bks.

— Halley Came to Jackson. LC 97-34354. (Illus.). 40p. (J). (ps-3). 1998. 15.95 (*0-06-025400-9*) HarpC.

Chapin, Charles E. Charles E. Chapin's Story. (American Biography Ser.). 334p. 1991. reprint ed. lib. bdg. 79.00 (*0-7812-8063-X*) Rprt Serv.

Chapin, Charles E. & Elston, Wolfgang E., eds. Ash-Flow Tuffs. LC 79-53022. (Geological Society of America Ser.: Vol. 180). (Illus.). 220p. 1979. reprint ed. pap. 68.20 (*0-608-07720-8*, 206780800010) Bks Demand.

Chapin, Charles V. Providence Births, 1871 to 1880, Inclusive Vol. IX: Alphabetical Index of the Births, Marriages & Deaths. 545p. 1995. reprint ed. lib. bdg. 57.00 (*0-8328-4722-4*) Higginson Bk Co.

— A Report on State Public Health Work, Based on a Survey of State Boards of Health. Rosenkrantz, Barbara G., ed. LC 76-25657. (Public Health in America Ser.). (Illus.). 1977. reprint ed. lib. bdg. 23.95 (*0-405-09807-3*) Ayer.

Chapin, Donald H. & Gramling, Robert W. The Accounting Profession: Appendixes to Major Issues: Progress & Concerns. (Illus.). 174p. (C). 1996. pap. text 35.00 (*0-7881-3599-6*) DIANE Pub.

— The Accounting Profession: Major Issues: Progress & Concerns. (Illus.). 139p. (Orig.). (C). 1996. pap. text 35.00 (*0-7881-3598-8*) DIANE Pub.

Chapin, Edwin H. Humanity in the City. LC 73-11901. (Metropolitan America Ser.). 254p. 1974. reprint ed. 21.95 (*0-405-05389-4*) Ayer.

Chapin, Emerson. Japan: A Reader's Guide. 17p. 1987. pap. 3.25 (*0-317-65714-3*) Japan Soc.

Chapin, F. Stuart. Education & the Mores. LC 68-56649. (Columbia University. Studies in the Social Sciences: No. 110). reprint ed. 32.50 (*0-404-51110-4*) AMS Pr.

Chapin, F. Stuart, Jr. Human Activity Patterns in the City: Things People Do in Time & in Space. LC 74-5364. (Wiley Urban Research Ser.). 306p. reprint ed. 94.90 (*0-8357-9908-5*, 201517500092) Bks Demand.

Chapin, F. Stuart, III, et al, eds. Arctic Ecosystems in a Changing Climate: An Ecophysiological Perspective. (Physiological Ecology Ser.). (Illus.). 269p. 1991. text 90.00 (*0-12-168250-1*) Acad Pr.

Chapin, F. Stuart, Jr. & Kaiser, Edward J. Hypothetical City Exercise: Workbook to Accompany Urban Land Use Planning. 3rd ed. 144p. 1979. pap. 9.95 (*0-252-00791-3*) U of Ill Pr.

— Urban Land Use Planning. 3rd ed. LC 64-18666. (Illus.). 672p. 1986. pap. 22.50 (*0-252-01257-7*) U of Ill Pr.

Chapin, F. Stuart, III & Korner, Christian, eds. Arctic & Alpine Biodiversity: Patterns, Causes & Ecosystem Consequences. (Ecological Studies: Vol. 113). (Illus.). 300p. 1995. 157.95 (*0-387-57948-6*) Spr-Verlag.

C

Chaplin, Susan. I Can Sing My ABC's. LC 86-22890. (Illus.). 56p. (J). (ps-1). 1986. 9.95 (*0-930323-19-X*, Pub. by K Green Pubns) Gallaudet Univ Pr.

Chapline, Claudia. Calle Aldama: Poems & Drawings from San Miguel de Allende, Mexico. Loarca, Carlos, tr. (ENG & SPA., Illus.). 80p. (Orig.). 1996. pap., per. 28.00 (*0-9653569-1-4*) C Chapline.

Chapman. Achieving Job Satisfaction. LC 93-72981. (Fifty-Minute Ser.). (Illus.). 90p. (Orig.). 1994. pap. 10.95 (*1-56052-257-7*) Crisp Pubns.

— Aids to Radiological Differential Diagnosis. 3rd ed. 1995. pap. text 32.00 (*0-7020-1895-3*, W B Saunders Co) Harcrt Hlth Sci Grp.

— Assumptions: An Anthropology Perspective. (C). 1998. pap. text 28.00 (*0-15-502842-1*) Harcourt Coll Pubs.

— British at War, Cineman, State & Propaganda, 1939-1945. 308p. 1998. text 45.00 (*1-86064-158-X*, Pub. by I B T) St Martin.

***Chapman.** Circuit Analysis & Problem Solving Using Matlab. (Electrical Engineering Ser.). (C). 2001. text 20.00 (*0-534-37963-X*) Brooks-Cole.

Chapman. Color Atlas of Veterinary Forensic Medicine. (Illus.). 116p. 1993. 65.00 (*0-8151-1618-7*) Mosby Inc.

— Electronic Machinery Fund. 2nd ed. 1991. student ed. 34.68 (*0-07-010915-X*) McGraw.

— English Grammar & Exercises, Bk. 1. Date not set. pap. text. write for info. (*0-582-52066-5*, Pub. by Addison-Wesley) Longman.

— English Grammar & Exercises, Bk. 2. Date not set. pap. text. write for info. (*0-582-52067-3*, Pub. by Addison-Wesley) Longman.

— FORTRAN 90 for Engineers & Scientists. (C). 1997. text. write for info. (*0-673-99836-3*) Addison-Wesley.

***Chapman.** Goalkeeper's History of Britain. 2000. 35.00 (*1-84115-009-6*, Pub. by Fourth Estate) Trafalgar.

Chapman. Heat Transfer. 5th ed. (C). 2001. 74.00 (*0-02-321495-3*, Macmillan Coll) P-H.

— Look at Life from a Deer Stand. 1996. pap. text 9.98 (*0-9653274-0-X*) S&A Family.

— Medical & Dental Associates. 3rd ed. 304p. (C). 1997. mass mkt. 40.95 (*0-8273-7560-3*) Delmar.

— Physics for Geologists. LC 94-32051. 192p. 1994. 65.00 (*1-85728-259-0*, Pub. by UCL Pr Ltd); pap. 24.95 (*1-85728-260-4*, Pub. by UCL Pr Ltd) Taylor & Francis.

Chapman. Practical Organic Mass Spectrometry. text. write for info. (*0-471-48981-6*); pap. text. write for info. (*0-471-48982-4*) Wiley.

Chapman. Royalty Only Glance Toward Shakespeare. 1991. write for info. (*0-316-13716-2*) Little.

— Student Guide on Your Attitude Is Showing. 9th ed. 1998. pap. text 20.25 (*0-13-955618-4*) P-H.

— Your Attitude Is Showing: A Primer of Human Relations - Self Paced Guide. 7th ed. 96p. (C). 1992. pap. text 14.80 (*0-02-321512-7*, Macmillan Coll) P-H.

Chapman, ed. Creating Neighbourhoods & Places in the Built Environment. (Built Environment Series of Textbooks). (Illus.). 264p. (Orig.). (C). 1996. pap. 32.99 (*0-419-20930-1*, E & FN Spon) Routledge.

— Environmental Economics: Theory Application & Policy. LC 99-39382. 415p. (C). 1999. 85.00 (*0-321-01435-9*) Addson-Wesley Educ.

Chapman & Badasch. Language of Introductory Health Care. 3rd ed. (C). 1993. pap., wbk. ed. 11.80 (*0-89303-853-9*) P-H.

Chapman & Dear. Contemporary Authors. (New Revision Ser.: Vol. 61). 450p. 1997. 140.00 (*0-7876-2003-3*, GML00198-111440) Visible Ink Pr.

— Contemporary Authors. (New Revision Ser.: Vol. 62). 450p. 1998. 140.00 (*0-7876-2005-X*, GML00198-111442) Visible Ink Pr.

Chapman, et al. Illinois Objections at Trial. 190p. 1992. pap. text 39.50 (*0-327-03908-6*, 81121-10, MICHIE) LEXIS Pub.

— Illinois Objections at Trial, 2 vols. 1995. pap. text 39.50 (*0-562-57321-6*, 82770-10, MICHIE) LEXIS Pub.

— Warbirds Worldwide Directory: An International Survey of the World's Warbird Population. 3rd ed. (Illus.). 700p. 1996. pap. 44.95 (*1-870601-46-7*, Pub. by Warbirds Worldwide) Motorbooks Intl.

Chapman, jt. auth. see Bassette.

Chapman, Dena. Christianity, an Overview. 101p. 1985. pap. write for info. (*1-893310-01-9*) Science of Understand.

— Christianity, an Overview. 2nd ed. 118p. 1998. reprint ed. pap. write for info. (*1-893310-05-1*) Science of Understand.

— Judaism, an Overview. 85p. 1985. pap. write for info. (*1-893310-00-0*) Science of Understand.

— Judaism, an Overview. 2nd ed. 89p. 1998. reprint ed. pap. write for info. (*1-893310-04-3*) Science of Understand.

Chapman, Edmund H. Cleveland, Village to Metropolis: A Case Study of Problems of Urban Development in Nineteenth-Century America. LC 98-43835. (Werner D. Mueller Reprint Ser.). 1998. reprint ed. write for info. (*0-911704-29-9*) Western Res.

Chapman & Hall Staff. Advanced Technical Ceramics Directory & Databook. 239.00 (*0-412-80310-0*) Chapman & Hall.

— Advances in Hardware Design & Verification. text 133.00 (*0-412-81330-0*) Chapman & Hall.

— Alkaline Rocks & Carbonatites of the World. text 189.50 (*0-412-62900-3*) Chapman & Hall.

— Architectures for Enterprise Integration. text 117.00 (*0-412-73140-1*) Chapman & Hall.

— ATM Networks Performance Modelling & Evaluation. text 150.50 (*0-412-80970-2*) Chapman & Hall.

— Cellular Manufacturing Systems Design, Planning & Control. text 104.50 (*0-412-55710-X*) Chapman & Hall.

— Comms & Multimedia Security, 003. text 124.00 (*0-412-81770-5*) Chapman & Hall.

— Computer Applications in Production & Engineering. text 203.50 (*0-412-82110-9*) Chapman & Hall.

— Computing Systems for Global Telecommunications. text 150.50 (*0-412-82540-6*) Chapman & Hall.

— Condition Monitoring of Mechanical & Hydraulic Plants: A Concise Introduction. text 95.50 (*0-412-70780-2*) Chapman & Hall.

— Constrained Optimization in the Calculus of Variations. text 117.00 (*0-412-74230-6*) Chapman & Hall.

— Control Processes in Fish Physiology. (C). text 168.00 (*0-7099-2246-9*, Pub. by C Helm) Routldge.

— Decisions About Re-engineering Briefingson issues & Options. text 58.50 (*0-412-72300-X*) Chapman & Hall.

— Designing for Quality an Introduction to the Best of Taguchi & Western Methods. text 95.50 (*0-412-40020-0*) Chapman & Hall.

— Diffusion & Adoption of Information Technology. text 138.00 (*0-412-75600-5*) Chapman & Hall.

— Distributed Applications & Interoperable Systems. text 133.00 (*0-412-82340-3*) Chapman & Hall.

— Ecology & Conservation of Amphibians. text 74.50 (*0-412-62410-9*) Chapman & Hall.

— Ecology of Reproduction in Wild & Domestic Mammals. text 210.50 (*0-416-49650-4*) Chapman & Hall.

— Ecology of World Vegetation. pap. text 63.50 (*0-412-44300-7*) Chapman & Hall.

— Electrical Methods in Geophysical Exploration of Deep. text 138.00 (*0-412-73710-8*) Chapman & Hall.

— Electronic Design Automation Frameworks. text 159.50 (*0-412-71010-2*) Chapman & Hall.

— Encyclopedia of European & Asian Regional Geology. text 309.50 (*0-412-74040-0*) Chapman & Hall.

— Engineering with Fibre Polymer Laminates. 74.50 (*0-412-49620-8*) Chapman & Hall.

— Ethical Global Information Society Culture & Democracy Revisited. LC 99-177088. 1997. text 141.50 (*0-412-82960-6*) Chapman & Hall.

— Ethics of Computing Codes. text 117.00 (*0-412-72620-3*) Chapman & Hall.

— Fluvial Geomorphology of Great Britain. text 212.50 (*0-412-78930-2*) Chapman & Hall.

— Formal Description Techniques & Protocol Specification. text 175.00 (*0-412-82060-9*) Chapman & Hall.

— Formal Descriptions Techniques, 003. text 189.50 (*0-412-73270-X*) Chapman & Hall.

— Functional Biology of Free Living Protozoa. (C). text 63.50 (*0-7099-1678-7*, Pub. by C Helm) Routldge.

— Geological Methods in Mineral Exploration & Mining. text 79.50 (*0-412-80010-1*) Chapman & Hall.

— Handbook of Composites. 2nd ed. text 177.00 (*0-412-54020-7*) Chapman & Hall.

— Hardware Description Languages & Their Applications Specification, Modelling, Verification & Synthesis. text 133.00 (*0-412-78810-1*) Chapman & Hall.

— Honeycomb Technology Materials, Design, Manufacturing, Applications & Testing. text 132.50 (*0-412-54050-9*) Chapman & Hall.

— Human-Computer Interaction: Interact '97. text 203.50 (*0-412-80950-8*) Chapman & Hall.

— Implementing Systems for Supporting Management Decisions Concepts, Methods & Experiences. text 147.00 (*0-412-75540-8*) Chapman & Hall.

— Information Security: The Next Decade. text 189.50 (*0-412-64020-1*) Chapman & Hall.

— Information Systems & Technology in the International Office. text 159.50 (*0-412-79790-9*) Chapman & Hall.

— Information Systems Security Facing the Information Society of the 21st Century. text 180.50 (*0-412-78120-4*) Chapman & Hall.

— Integrity & Internal Control in Information Systems Increasing: The Confidence in Information Systems, 001. text 133.00 (*0-412-82600-3*) Chapman & Hall.

— Intelligent Networks & Intelligence in Networks. text 159.50 (*0-412-82950-9*) Chapman & Hall.

— Intelligent Systems for Manufacturing Multi-Agent Systems & Virtual Organizations. 632p. text 210.00 (*0-412-84670-5*) Chapman & Hall.

— Introduction to Classical Real Analysis. text 125.50 (*0-412-74210-1*) Chapman & Hall.

— Introduction to Quality Control. text 210.50 (*0-412-43540-3*) Chapman & Hall.

— Isotopes in the Earth Sciences. (C). text 329.00 (*0-412-53710-9*) Chapman & Hall.

— Making Customer Satisfaction Happen. pap. text 48.00 (*0-412-78630-3*) Chapman & Hall.

— Management of Technology Perception & Opportunities. text 95.50 (*0-412-64370-7*) Chapman & Hall.

— Manufacturing Excellence in Global Markets. LC 97-131163. 1997. text 180.50 (*0-412-80520-0*) Chapman & Hall.

— Metal Metabolism in Aquatic Environments. text 140.00 (*0-412-80370-4*) Chapman & Hall.

— Method Engineering Principles of Method Construction & Tool Support. text 159.50 (*0-412-79750-X*) Chapman & Hall.

— Mosquito Ecology Field Sampling Methods. 2nd ed. (C). text 286.50 (*0-412-54080-0*) Chapman & Hall.

— Open Distributed Processing & Distributed Platforms. text 124.00 (*0-412-81230-4*) Chapman & Hall.

— Optical Network Design & Modelling, 001. text 124.00 (*0-412-84260-2*) Chapman & Hall.

— Particle Size Measurement Surface Area & Pore Size Determination. 5th ed. text 117.00 (*0-412-75330-8*) Chapman & Hall.

— Performance of Information & Communication Systems. text 168.00 (*0-412-83730-7*) Chapman & Hall.

— Physics of Glassy Polymers. 2nd ed. text 159.50 (*0-412-62460-5*) Chapman & Hall.

— Polymer Latices Science & Technology: Applications Latices. 2nd ed. text 248.00 (*0-412-62890-2*) Chapman & Hall.

— Population Genetics. (C). text 69.00 (*0-416-03160-9*) Chapman & Hall.

— Princs of Freelectron Lasers. text 189.50 (*0-412-72540-1*) Chapman & Hall.

— Probabilistic Risk Assessment of Engineering Systems. text 97.50 (*0-412-80570-7*) Chapman & Hall.

— Programming Concepts & Methods: Procomet 98. text 239.00 (*0-412-83760-9*) Chapman & Hall.

— Quasioptical Systems. text 124.00 (*0-412-83940-7*) Chapman & Hall.

— Re-engineering for Sustainable Industrial Production. text 175.00 (*0-412-79950-2*) Chapman & Hall.

— Sealing of Boreholes & Underground Excavations in Rock. text 168.00 (*0-412-57300-8*) Chapman & Hall.

— Software Engineering for Parallel & Distributed Systems. text 147.00 (*0-412-75740-0*) Chapman & Hall.

— Step Change Total Quality Achieving World Class Business Performance. 2nd ed. text 95.50 (*0-412-64270-0*) Chapman & Hall.

— Strain Gage Users Handbook. text 210.50 (*0-412-53720-6*) Chapman & Hall.

— Structural Adhesive Joints in Engineering. 2nd ed. text 150.50 (*0-412-70920-1*) Chapman & Hall.

— Structural Adhesives Directory & Databook. text 210.50 (*0-412-71470-1*) Chapman & Hall.

— Structure & Properties of Oriented Polymers. 2nd ed. text 168.00 (*0-412-60880-4*) Chapman & Hall.

— Systems Implementation 2000. text 133.00 (*0-412-83530-4*) Chapman & Hall.

— Testing of Communicating Systems, 010. text 150.50 (*0-412-81730-6*) Chapman & Hall.

— Testing of Communicating Systems, 011. text 159.00 (*0-412-84430-3*) Chapman & Hall.

— Total Quality Management Proceedings of the First World Congress. text 180.50 (*0-412-64380-4*) Chapman & Hall.

— Toyota Production Systems. 3rd ed. text 97.50 (*0-412-83930-X*) Chapman & Hall.

— Tropical Rain Forest: A Wilder Perspective. LC 97-69618. 1998. text 122.00 (*0-412-81510-9*) Chapman & Hall.

— Ultrasonic Measurements & Technologies. text 83.00 (*0-412-63850-9*) Chapman & Hall.

Chapman & Hall Staff, ed. Applied Data Communications & Networks. 38.00 (*0-412-75430-4*) Chapman & Bkman.

— Communications & Multimedia Security. text 159.50 (*0-412-79780-1*) Chapman & Hall.

— Information Networks & Data Communication V: Proceedings of the IFIP TC6 International Conference, Funchal, Madeira Island, Portugal, 18-21 April 1994. text 159.50 (*0-412-75750-8*) Chapman & Hall.

Chapman, A., jt. auth. see Moore, Patrick.

Chapman, A. B., ed. General & Quantitative Genetics. (World Animal Science Ser.: Vol. A4). 408p. 1985. 230.50 (*0-444-42203-X*) Elsevier.

Chapman, A. H. & Chapman-Santana, Miriam. The Handbook of Problem-Oriented Psychotherapy: A Guide for Psychologists, Social Workers, Psychiatrists & Other Mental Health Professionals. LC 95-52522. 232p. 1997. 40.00 (*1-56821-682-3*) Aronson.

Chapman, A. R. Functional Diversity of Plants in the Sea & on Land. 256p. (C). 1986. 42.50 (*0-86720-064-2*) Jones & Bartlett.

Chapman, A. R., et al. Fourteenth International Seaweed Symposium. LC 93-3975. (Developments in Hydrobiology Ser.: Vol. 85). 1993. text 492.00 (*0-7923-2309-2*) Kluwer Academic.

Chapman, A. R., tr. see Birkholz, Heinz.

Chapman, Abraham, ed. Black Voices: An Anthology of Afro-American Literature. 1968. mass mkt. 7.99 (*0-451-62660-5*, Ment) NAL.

Chapman, Al. Santos of Spanish New Mexico Coloring Book: A Workbook. (J). 1982. pap. 4.95 (*0-86534-238-5*) Sunstone Pr.

Chapman, Al & Chapman, Trinka. 21 Carvings for the Day after Christmas. LC 95-2552. (Books for Woodworkers). (Illus.). 64p. (Orig.). 1995. pap. 12.95 (*0-88740-730-7*) Schiffer.

Chapman, Al & Learning the Art of Pyrography. Pyrography: Burning Images on Wood, Paper & Leather. LC 94-43169. (Books for Woodworkers). (Illus.). 64p. (Orig.). 1995. pap. 12.95 (*0-88740-729-3*) Schiffer.

Chapman, Alan & Marshall, Mary, eds. Dementia: New Skills for Social Workers. LC 93-38449. (Case Studies for Practice Ser.: No. 5). 160p. 1994. pap. 24.95 (*1-85302-142-3*) Taylor & Francis.

Chapman, Alexandra. Turn Right at the Fountain: Fifty-Three Walking Tours Through Europe's Most Enchanting Cities. rev. ed. 1995. pap. 15.95 (*0-8050-2356-9*) H Holt & Co.

Chapman, Alfred F. The Royal Arch Companion Adapted to the Work & Lectures of Royal Arch Masonry. 104p. 1997. reprint ed. pap. 16.95 (*0-7661-0072-3*) Kessinger Pub.

***Chapman, Alison.** The Afterlife of Christina Rossetti. LC 00-26190. 2000. write for info. (*0-312-23461-9*) St Martin.

Chapman, Allan. Astronomical Instruments & Their Users: Tycho Brahe to William Lassell. LC 96-15909. (Collected Studies: No. CS530). (Illus.). 320p. 1996. 109.95 (*0-86078-584-X*, Pub. by Variorum) Ashgate Pub Co.

— The Victorian Amateur Astronomer: Independent Astronomical Research in Britain 1820-1920. LC 95-48037. (Wiley-Praxis Series in Astronomy & Astrophysics). 448p. 1998. 98.00 (*0-471-96257-0*) Wiley.

Chapman, Anne. A Great Balancing Act: Equitable Education for Girls & Boys. 1997. pap. 30.00 (*0-934338-89-2*) NAIS.

— Making Sense. 1994. pap. 15.00 (*0-87447-470-1*) College Bd.

— Masters of Animals: Oral Traditions of the Tolupan Indians, Honduras. (Library of Anthropology). 312p. 1992. pap. text 26.00 (*2-88124-565-X*) Gordon & Breach.

— Masters of Animals: Oral Traditions of the Tolupan Indians, Honduras, Vol. 10. LC 92-11055. (Library of Anthropology). 312p. 1992. text 58.00 (*2-88124-560-9*) Gordon & Breach.

***Chapman, Annie.** Putting Anger in its Place: A Woman's Guide to Getting Emotions Under Control. 176p. 2000. pap. 8.99 (*0-7369-0442-5*) Harvest Hse.

Chapman, Annie. Running on Empty & Looking for the Next Exit: How Smart Women Learn to Cope with Everyday Life. LC 95-39285. 176p. (Orig.). 1995. pap. 8.99 (*1-55661-587-6*) Bethany Hse.

Chapman, Annie & Rank, Maureen. Smart Women Keep It Simple. 192p. (Orig.). 1992. pap. 9.99 (*1-55661-236-2*) Bethany Hse.

Chapman, Antony & Foot, Hugh, eds. Humor & Laughter: Theory, Research, & Applications. 360p. (C). 1996. pap. text 24.95 (*1-56000-837-7*) Transaction Pubs.

Chapman, Antony J., et al, eds. Pedestrian Accidents. LC HE0336.P43P4. 366p. reprint ed. pap. 113.50 (*0-8357-3104-9*, 203936000012) Bks Demand.

Chapman, Antony J. & Foot, Hugh C. It's a Funny Thing Humour: The International Conference on Humor & Laughter. LC 76-53731. 400p. 1977. 235.00 (*0-08-021376-6*, Pub. by Pergamon Repr) Franklin.

Chapman, Antony J. & Foot, Hugh C., eds. Humour & Laughter: Theory, Research & Applications. LC 75-37870. 358p. reprint ed. pap. 111.00 (*0-608-17616-8*, 203046800069) Bks Demand.

Chapman, Antony J., jt. auth. see Sheehy, Noel.

Chapman, Antony J., jt. auth. see Spurgeon, Peter.

Chapman, Antony J., jt. ed. see McGhee, Paul E.

Chapman, Antony J., jt. ed. see Sheehy, Noel.

Chapman, Arlene B. & Guay-Woodford, Lisa M. The Family & ADPKD: A Guide for Children & Parents. (Illus.). viii, 40p. (Orig.). (YA). (gr. 5-12). 1997. pap. 15.00 (*0-9614567-5-2*) PKR Foundation.

Chapman, Arlene B., jt. auth. see Guay-Woodford, Lisa M.

Chapman, Art. Art Chapman's "For the Health of It" A Lighter Look at Low-Fat Cooking. 122p. (Orig.). 1995. pap., spiral bd. 13.95 (*0-9650588-0-8*, 2000) Ft Wrth Star Telgrm.

Chapman, Arthur G. & Wray, Robert D. Christmas Trees for Pleasure & Profit. rev. ed. 220p. 1984. pap. text 18.95 (*0-8135-1074-0*) Rutgers U Pr.

Chapman, Audrey. Entitled to Good Loving. 256p. 1995. 22.50 (*0-8050-2459-X*) H Holt & Co.

— Unprecedented Choices: Religious Ethics at the Frontiers of Genetic Science. LC 99-22222. 1999. pap. 22.00 (*0-8006-3181-1*, Fortress Pr) Augsburg Fortress.

Chapman, Audrey, ed. Health Care & Information Ethics: Protecting Fundamental Human Rights. LC 97-772. 480p. (Orig.). 1997. pap. 29.95 (*1-55612-922-X*, LL1922) Sheed & Ward WI.

Chapman, Audrey B. Getting Good Loving: How Black Men & Women Can Make Love Work. 240p. 1996. pap. 11.00 (*0-345-40245-6*) Ballantine Pub Grp.

Chapman, Audrey R., ed. Health Care Reform: A Human Rights Approach. LC 94-2311. 326p. 1994. pap. 14.95 (*0-87840-555-0*) Georgetown U Pr.

— Health Care Reform: A Human Rights Approach. LC 94-2311. 326p. 1994. 37.50 (*0-87840-554-2*) Georgetown U Pr.

Chapman, B. R., jt. ed. see Martin, R. E.

Chapman, Barbara. Beatrice Darbyshire. 35.00 (*0-85564-316-1*, Pub. by Univ of West Aust Pr) Intl Spec Bk.

Chapman, Barbara, tr. see De Beaumont, Gustave.

Chapman, Barbara, tr. see De Beaumont, Gustave A.

Chapman, Ben, ed. see Harper, Steve.

Chapman, Ben, ed. see Hynson, Leon O.

Chapman, Benita, jt. auth. see Babeckis, James.

Chapman, Benjamin & Shogren, Gary S. A Card Guide to New Testament Greek. 2p. (C). 1995. 3.50 (*1-887070-01-X*) Stylus Publ.

— Greek New Testament Insert. LC 94-74634. 64p. 1995. pap. text 4.95 (*1-887070-02-8*) Stylus Publ.

Chapman, Berlin B. Federal Management & Disposition of the Lands of Oklahoma Territory, 1866-1907. Bruchey, Stuart, ed. LC 78-56717. (Management of Public Lands in the U. S. Ser.). (Illus.). 1979. lib. bdg. 31.95 (*0-405-11325-0*) Ayer.

Chapman, Beryl M. Homeopathic Treatment for Birds. 68p. (Orig.). pap. 11.95 (*0-8464-4231-0*) Beekman Pubs.

— Homeopathic Treatment for Birds. 129p. (Orig.). 1991. pap. 7.95 (*0-85207-235-X*, Pub. by C W Daniel) Natl Bk Netwk.

Chapman, Betsy & Bookman, Barbara. A Closet Full of Clothes & Something to Wear. 2nd ed. (Illus.). 40p. (Orig.). 1987. reprint ed. pap. 4.95 (*0-9613544-8-8*) Chapman & Bkman.

Chapman, Betty & Berry, Garvin. Two Minute Histories of Houston. (Illus.). 120p. 1996. pap. 9.95 (*0-9650400-2-X*) Houston Busin Jrnl.

Chapman, Betty T. Historic Houston: An Illustrated History. Elliott, Margie C., ed. (Illus.). 208p. 1997. 49.95 (*0-9654999-1-X*) Hist Pub Network.

Chapman, Blanche A. Wills & Administrations of Isle of Wight County, Virginia, 1647-1800: With an Improved Index. 370p. 1999. reprint ed. pap. 32.50 (*0-8063-0647-5*, 955, Pub. by Clearfield Co) ACCESS Pubs Network.

An Asterisk (*) at the beginning of an entry indicates that the title is appearing for the first time.

— Wills & Administrations of Southampton County, Virginia, 1749-1800. LC 80-68126. 208p. 1998. reprint ed. pap. 21.50 (*0-8063-0907-5*) Clearfield Co.

Chapman, Blanche A., compiled by. Isle of Wight County Marriages, 1628-1800. 137p. 1997. reprint ed. pap. 19.50 (*0-8328-6934-1*) Higginson Bk Co.

Chapman, Blanche Adams. Marriages of Isle of Wight County, Virginia, 1628-1800. 124p. 1999. reprint ed. pap. 16.50 (*0-8063-0710-2*, 950, Pub. by Clearfield Co) ACCESS Pubs Network.

Chapman, Brian. Glow Discharge Processes: Sputtering & Plasma Etching. LC 80-17047. 432p. 1980. 137.50 (*0-471-07828-X*) Wiley.

Chapman Brothers. Portrait & Biographical Album of Henry County, IL. (Illus.). 834p. 1993. reprint ed. lib. bdg. 85.00 (*0-8328-3081-X*) Higginson Bk Co.

— Portrait & Biographical Album of Rock Island Co, IL. (Illus.). 818p. 1993. reprint ed. lib. bdg. 82.50 (*0-8328-3082-8*) Higginson Bk Co.

Chapman, Bruce. In Praise of Politicians. Date not set. 19.95 (*0-465-03227-3*); pap. 15.00 (*0-465-03279-6*) Basic.

Chapman, Bruce, jt. auth. see Bayles, Michael D.

Chapman, Bruce, jt. auth. see Hamer, John.

***Chapman, C. J.** High Speed Flow. LC 99-37544. (Cambridge Texts in Applied Mathematics Ser.: No. 23). (Illus.). 350p. (C). 2000. 74.95 (*0-521-66169-2*) Cambridge U Pr.

— High Speed Flow. LC 99-37544. (Cambridge Texts in Applied Mathematics Ser.: No. 23). (Illus.). 350p. (C). 2000. pap. 29.95 (*0-521-66647-3*) Cambridge U Pr.

Chapman, C. Keeler & Traister, John. Architectural Layout & Design Graphics. (Illus.). 512p. 1997. text 59.95 (*0-07-011998-8*) McGraw.

Chapman, C. Keeler & Traister, John. Architectural Layout & Design Graphics. (Illus.). 512p. 1997. pap. text 36.95 (*0-07-011997-X*) McGraw.

Chapman, C. Keeler, jt. auth. see Traister, John.

Chapman, C. P. & Morrison, D., eds. Cosmic Catastrophes. (Illus.). 310p. (C). 1989. 22.95 (*0-306-43163-7*, Plenum Trade) Perseus Pubng.

Chapman, C. Richard, ed. see Bristol-Myers Squibb Symposium on Pain Research St.

Chapman, C. S., jt. auth. see Gandy, A.

Chapman, C. S., ed. see Blake, Philip.

Chapman, Carl. Who Am I among So Many? An Autobiography Plus Special Articles: The Biggest Exception in the Bible, Paul's Thorn in the Flesh, & Not Discerning the Lord's Body. LC 88-92635. 132p. (Orig.). (YA). (gr. 9-12). 1989. pap. 4.99 (*0-9621529-0-0*) C Chapman.

Chapman, Carl B. & Reinmiller, Elinor C. The Physiology of Physical Stress: A Selective Bibliography, 1500-1964. LC 74-15565. 376p. 1974. 49.95 (*0-674-66670-4*) HUP.

Chapman, Carl H. Indians & Archaeology of Missouri. rev. ed. LC 83-3596. (Illus.). 176p. (C). 1983. pap. 15.95 (*0-8262-0401-5*) U of Mo Pr.

Chapman, Carl H., et al. Archaeology in the 70's -- Mitigating the Impact, Vol. 35, No. 1-2. Bray, Robert T., ed. (Missouri Archaeologist Ser.). (Illus.). 71p. (Orig.). 1973. pap. 1.00 (*0-943414-51-2*) MO Arch Soc.

— A Brief & Incomplete History of the Archaeology of the Kansas City Vicinity, Vol. 42. (Missouri Archaeologist Ser.). (Illus.). 108p. 1981. pap. 5.00 (*0-943414-59-8*) MO Arch Soc.

— Investigation & Comparison of Two Fortified Mississippi Tradition Archaeological Sites in Southeastern Missouri: A Preliminary Compilation, Vol.38. Bray, Robert T., ed. (Missouri Archaeologist Ser.). (Illus.). 346p. 1977. pap. 7.50 (*0-943414-55-5*) MO Arch Soc.

— A Report of Progress: Archaeological Research by the University of Missouri (1955-1956) (Special Publications: No. 1). (Illus.). 57p. 1957. pap. 3.00 (*0-943414-61-X*) MO Arch Soc.

Chapman, Carl H., ed. see Adams, Lee M.

Chapman, Carl H., ed. see Adams, Robert M.

Chapman, Carl H., ed. see Healan, Dan M.

Chapman, Carl H., ed. see Hopgood, James F.

Chapman, Carl H., ed. see Perino, Gregory.

Chapman, Carl H., ed. see Shippee, J. M.

Chapman, Carl H., ed. see Stubbs, Francis L.

Chapman, Carl H., ed. see Wedel, Mildred M.

Chapman, Carleton A. Geology of Acadia National Park. LC 73-107079. (Illus.). 1970. 12.95 (*0-87638-012-7*); pap. 7.95 (*0-85699-010-8*) Chatham Pr.

Chapman, Carleton B. Dartmouth Medical School: The First One Hundred Seventy-Five Years. LC 72-89557. 120p. reprint ed. pap. 37.20 (*0-608-14821-0*, 202563400045) Bks Demand.

— Order Out of Chaos: John Shaw Billings & America's Coming of Age. (Illus.). xvl, 420p. 1994. 28.95 (*0-88135-187-3*, Countway Lib Med) Watson Pub Intl.

Chapman, Carol. Barney Bipple's Magic Dandelions. (Picture Puffin Ser.). (Illus.). (J). 1992. 11.19 (*0-606-01680-5*, Pub. by Turtleback) Demco.

— Your Guide to Planning the Wedding Day. 160p. (Orig.). 1993. pap. 13.95 (*0-572-01874-6*, Pub. by W Foulsham) Trans-Atl Phila.

— Your Wedding Planner. 160p. (Orig.). 1993. pap. 11.95 (*0-572-01761-8*, Pub. by W Foulsham) Trans-Atl Phila.

Chapman, Carole. How to Get a Professional Perm at Home: The Hair Perming Manual. (Illus.). 31p. (Orig.). 1995. pap. 3.50 (*0-9642291-0-2*, 560 298) Haircraft Pubns.

— Organising Your Second Marriage. 160p. (Orig.). 1994. pap. 11.95 (*0-572-01987-4*, Pub. by W Foulsham) Trans-Atl Phila.

Chapman, Carolyn. Basic Chemistry for Biology. 224p. (C). 1995. text 15.50 (*0-697-24121-1*, WCB McGr Hill) McGrw-H Hghr Educ.

— Basic Chemistry for Biology. 2nd ed. LC 99-160430. 312p. 1998. pap. 18.75 (*0-697-36087-3*) McGraw.

— If the Shoe Fits: How to Develop Multiple Intelligences in the Classroom. LC 93-79952. (Illus.). 256p. (Orig.). 1993. pap. text 33.95 (*0-932935-64-8*) SkyLght.

— McNeill - Beginning in Belfast: Descendants of Sampson Stuart McNeill. (Illus.). 82p. 1995. lib. bdg. 29.50 (*0-8328-4579-5*) Higginson Bk Co.

Chapman, Carolyn & Freeman, Lynn. Multiple Intelligences Centers & Projects. LC 96-75264. (Illus.). 192p. (Orig.). 1996. pap. 30.95 (*1-57517-015-9*, 1449) SkyLght.

***Chapman, Carolyn & King, Rita M.** Test Success in the Brain-Compatible Classroom. (Illus.). 244p. 2000. pap. 39.00 (*1-56976-117-5*, 1109) Zephyr Pr AZ.

Chapman, Carolyn H., ed. Becoming a Superintendent. LC 96-23190. 260p. 1996. pap. text 43.00 (*0-13-398173-8*) P-H.

Chapman, Catherine. Step Spirit: The Twelve Steps As a Spiritual Program. LC 92-19817. 112p. 1992. pap. 5.95 (*0-8091-3340-7*) Paulist Pr.

***Chapman, Charles.** Drop-2 Concept for Guitar. 88p. 2000. pap. 14.95 (*0-7866-4483-4*, 98181) Mel Bay.

Chapman, Charles, ed. see Claire, Elizabeth.

Chapman, Charles, ed. see Olshtain, Elite, et al.

Chapman, Charles, ed. see Villicana, Solveig.

Chapman, Charles E. The Founding of Spanish California, the Northwestward Expansion of New Spain, 1687-1783. (BCL1 - United States Local History Ser.). 485p. 1991. reprint ed. lib. bdg. 99.00 (*0-7812-6338-7*) Rprt Serv.

— History of California: The Spanish Period. 1988. reprint ed. lib. bdg. 69.00 (*0-7812-0413-5*) Rprt Serv.

— History of California: The Spanish Period. LC 74-144942. (Illus.). 1971. reprint ed. 79.00 (*0-403-03600-3*) Scholarly.

— A History of the Cuban Republic: A Study in Hispanic American Politics. 1976. lib. bdg. 59.95 (*0-8490-1993-1*) Gordon Pr.

Chapman, Charles Edward, ed. Diary of Fray Narciso Duran Vol. 2:5: Expedition on the Sacramento & San Joaquin Rivers in 1817. (University of California, Publications of the Academy of Pacific Coast History Ser.: Vol. 2:5). 21p. 1911. pap. text 2.50 (*1-55567-664-2*) Coyote Press.

Chapman, Charles F., jt. auth. see Rothenberg, Mikel A.

Chapman, Charles T. The Message of the Book of Revelation. 152p. (Orig.). 1994. pap. 11.95 (*0-8146-2111-2*) Liturgical Pr.

Chapman, Charles W. & Hoffman, Thomas E. Product Liability Law in Illinois. 142p. 1994. text 75.00 (*0-910095-00-0*) Law Bulletin.

Chapman, Charles W., et al. Illinois Objections at Trial. LC 92-26561. 190p. 1992. pap. 39.50 (*1-56257-321-7*, MICHIE) LEXIS Pub.

Chapman, Charlotte G. Milocca: A Sicilian Village. rev. ed. (Illus.). 256p. (C). 1971. text 32.95 (*0-87073-764-3*) Transaction Pubs.

Chapman, Cheryl. Pass the Fritters, Critters. LC 91-45055. (Illus.). 40p. (J). (ps-k). 1993. lib. bdg. 16.00 (*0-02-717975-3*, Four Winds Pr) S&S Childrens.

Chapman, Chris. Hilarious Skits for Youth Ministry. McMahan, Candace, ed. LC 97-41641. 80p. (YA). 1998. per. 14.99 (*0-7644-2033-X*) Group Pub.

***Chapman, Chris.** Hilarious Skits for Youth Ministry 2. 1999. pap. 14.99 (*0-7644-2185-9*) Group Pub.

Chapman, Chris B. Project Risk Management: Processes, Techniques & Insights. LC 96-30345. 344p. 1996. 79.95 (*0-471-95804-2*) Wiley.

Chapman, Christine. Dante Alighieri: Divine Comedy, Divine Spirituality. LC 98-46449. (Spiritual Legacy Ser.). 118p. (Orig.). 1999. pap. 16.95 (*0-8245-1604-4*) Crossroad NY.

— In Love Abiding: Responding to the Dying & Bereaved. 1996. pap. text 5.95 (*0-8245-1633-8*) Crossroad NY.

Chapman, Clodagh. The Echoes Answer. large type ed. (General Ser.). 496p. 1993. 27.99 (*0-7089-2818-8*) Ulverscroft.

— The Night Before Dark. large type ed. 1989. 27.99 (*0-7089-2187-6*) Ulverscroft.

***Chapman, Colin.** How the Stock Markets Work. 1998. pap. 19.95 (*0-7126-7970-7*, Pub. by Random) Trafalgar.

Chapman, Colin. How the Stock Markets Work: A Guide to the International Markets. 208p. 1992. 19.95 (*0-7126-6021-6*, Pub. by CEN3) Trafalgar.

***Chapman, Colin.** Islam & the West: Conflict, Co-Existence of Conversion? 198p. 1998. reprint ed. pap. 20.00 (*0-85364-781-X*, Pub. by Paternoster Pub) OM Literature.

Chapman, Colin. Tracing Your British Ancestors. 108p. 1996. reprint ed. pap. 15.00 (*0-8063-1503-2*) Genealog Pub.

***Chapman, Colin R.** Pre-1841 Censuses & Population Listings in the British Isles. 5th ed. LC 99-71501. 84p. 1999. pap. 15.00 (*0-8063-1613-6*) Genealog Pub.

Chapman, Con. The Year of the Gerbil: How the Yankees Won (And the Red Sox Lost) the Greatest Penant Race Ever. 280p. 1998. 24.95 (*1-58244-008-5*) Rutledge Bks.

Chapman, Conrad W. & Bassham, Ben L. Ten Months in the "Orphan Brigade" Conrade Wise Chapman's Civil War Memoir. LC 98-45870. (Illus.). 96p. 1999. pap. 9.50 (*0-87338-638-8*) Kent St U Pr.

Chapman, Craig S. More Terrible Than Victory: North Carolina's Bloody Bethel Regiment, 1861-1865. LC 97-27207. (Illus.). 368p. 1998. 25.95 (*1-57488-129-9*) Brasseys.

***Chapman, Craig S.** More Terrible Than Victory: North Carolina's Bloody Bethel Regiment, 1861-1865. (Illus.). 288p. 1999. pap. 16.95 (*1-57488-219-8*) Brasseys.

Chapman, D. Biological Membranes, Vol. 4. 1982. text 199.00 (*0-12-168545-4*) Acad Pr.

Chapman, D., ed. Water Quality Assessments: Guide to the use of Biota Sediments & Water Inenvironmental Monitoring. 2nd ed. 648p. (C). (gr. 13). 1996. 115.00 (*0-419-21590-5*); pap. 39.99 (*0-419-21600-6*) Routledge.

Chapman, D. & Haris, P. I., eds. New Biomedical Materials. LC 97-76731. 209p. 1998. 86.00 (*90-5199-365-X*, 365-X) IOS Press.

Chapman, D. Brent & Zwicky, Elizabeth. Building Internet Firewalls. Russell, Deborah, ed. LC 96-133474. (Illus.). 1995. pap. 34.95 (*1-56592-124-0*) Thomson Learn.

Chapman, D. G. & Gallucci, V. F., eds. Quantitative Population Dynamics. (Statistical Ecology Ser.). 290p. 1981. 30.00 (*0-89974-010-3*) Intl Co-Op.

Chapman, D. J., jt. auth. see Round, F. E.

Chapman, D. J., jt. ed. see Round, F. E.

Chapman, D. L. The Science Behind Personal Power. 169p. 1999. pap. 15.00 (*1-893310-06-X*) Science of Understand.

Chapman, D. L. You Were Born to Be Rich. 118p. 1991. pap. write for info. (*1-893310-02-7*) Science of Understand.

Chapman, D. L., jt. auth. see DeMaleissye-Melun, Judith.

Chapman, D. T. & El-Sharrawi, A. H., eds. Statistical Methods for the Assessment of Point Source Pollution: Proceedings of a Workshop on Statistical Methods for the Assessment of Point Source Polution, Held in Burlington, Ontario, Canada, September 12-14, 1988. (C). 1990. text 207.50 (*0-7923-0619-8*) Kluwer Academic.

Chapman, Daurelle, et al. Reflections: The Workers, the Gospel & the Nameless House Sect. 716p. (Orig.). 1994. pap. 10.45 (*0-9639419-1-7*) Res Info Servs.

Chapman, David. Can Civil Wars Be Avoided? Electoral & Constitutional Models for Ethnically Divided Countries. 151p. (C). 1991. pap. 50.00 (*0-948826-26-6*, Pub. by Inst Social Invent) St Mut.

— DWI - Texas Cases & Forms Annotated. 676p. 1993. ring bd. 150.00 (*1-878337-34-3*) Knowles Pub Inc.

— Natural Hazards. (Meridian Australian Geographical Perspectives Ser.). (Illus.). 192p. (C). 1995. pap. text 19.95 (*0-19-553564-2*) OUP.

— Vision, Instruction & Action. (Artificial Intelligence - Bobrow, Brady & Davis Ser.). (Illus.). 310p. 1991. 42.00 (*0-262-03181-7*) MIT Pr.

Chapman, David, ed. Adonis: The Male Physique Pin-Up 1870-1940. (Editions Aubrey Walter Ser.). (Illus.). 108p. 1997. reprint ed. pap. 30.00 (*0-85449-250-X*, Pub. by Gay Mens Pr) LPC InBook.

Chapman, David & Cowdell, Theo. New Public Sector Marketing. 336p. 1998. pap. 62.50 (*0-273-62347-8*, Pub. by Pitman Pub) Trans-Atl Phila.

Chapman, David, jt. auth. see Bissell, Chris.

Chapman, David, jt. ed. see Chandler, Michael.

***Chapman, David Ian.** The R. Austin Freeman Bibliography. 2000. pap. 10.00 (*1-55246-282-X*) Battered Silicon.

Chapman, David J. Biological Membranes: Trigger Processes in Cell Biology, Vol. 5. (Biological Membranes Ser.). 1985. text 199.00 (*0-12-168546-2*) Acad Pr.

***Chapman, David J.** Chasing Life's Shadows: Memoirs of a Roving Radiologist. LC 99-224235. (Illus.). 1998. write for info. (*0-7541-0353-6*, Pub. by Minerva Pr) Unity Dist.

Chapman, David J., et al, eds. Progress in Membrane Biotechnology. (Advances in Life Sciences Ser.). 352p. 1991. 110.00 (*0-8176-2666-2*) Birkhauser.

Chapman, David J. & Bertoli, E., eds. Biomembrane & Receptor Mechanisms. (FIDIA Research Ser.). 400p. 1987. 170.00 (*0-387-96484-3*) Spr-Verlag.

Chapman, David L. Sandow the Magnificent: Eugen Sandow & the Beginnings of Bodybuilding. LC 93-15736. (Illus.). 264p. 1994. 26.95 (*0-252-02033-2*) U of Ill Pr.

Chapman, David S., jt. auth. see Visser, John.

Chapman, David T., jt. auth. see Patry, Gilles G.

Chapman, David W. & Carrier, Carol A., eds. Improving Educational Quality: A Global Perspective, 35. LC 89-37317. (Contributions to the Study of Education Ser.: No. 35). 331p. 1990. 59.95 (*0-313-26623-9*, CIU/, Greenwood Pr) Greenwood.

Chapman, David W. & Mahlck, Lars O., eds. From Data to Action: Information Systems in Educational Planning. 274p. 1993. 89.95 (*0-08-041941-0*, Prgamon Press) Buttrwrth-Heinemann.

— From Data to Action: Information Systems in Educational Planning. LC 93-245433. (Illus.). 273p. reprint ed. pap. 84.70 (*0-608-07415-2*, 206764200009) Bks Demand.

Chapman, David W. & Waller, Preston L. The Power of Writing. LC 93-21676. 366p. (C). 1993. pap. text 35.95 (*1-55934-138-6*, 1138) Mayfield Pub.

— The Power of Writing. (C). 1994. pap. text, teacher ed. write for info. (*1-55934-139-4*, 1139) Mayfield Pub.

— The Power of Writing with Additional Readings. LC 94-32374. 568p. (C). 1994. pap. text 37.95 (*1-55934-453-9*, 1453) Mayfield Pub.

Chapman, David W., et al. From Planning to Action: Government Initiatives for Improving School Level Practice. LC 97-221387. 250p. 1997. 63.00 (*0-08-043079-1*, Pergamon Pr) Elsevier.

— Hazardous Wastes & the Consumer Connection: A Guide for Educators & Citizens Concerned with the Role of Consumers in the Generation of Hazardous Wastes. 36p. (Orig.). 1984. pap. write for info. (*0-318-57831-X*) Sci Citizens.

Chapman, David W., jt. auth. see Waller, Preston L.

Chapman, David W., jt. auth. see Windham, Douglas M.

***Chapman, Davis.** Creating Secure Applications with Visual Basic. 600p. 2000. 34.99 (*0-672-31836-9*) Sams.

Chapman, Davis. Sams Teach Yourself Visual C++ 6 in 21 Days. LC 98-84508. (Teach Yourself Ser.). 800p. 1998. pap. 34.99 (*0-672-31240-9*) Sams.

— Teach Yourself Visual C++ 6 in 21 Days: Professional Reference Edition. LC 98-86199. (Teach Yourself . . . in 21 Days Ser.). 1999. 49.99 (*0-672-31404-5*) Sams.

***Chapman, Davis.** Teach Yourself Visual C++ 6 in 21 Days, 2 vols. (Teach Yourself... in 21 Days Ser.). 1998. pap. text 49.99 (*0-672-31403-7*) Sams.

— Web Development with Visual BASIC 5. LC 97-65017. 937p. 1997. pap. 49.99 (*0-7897-0811-6*) Que.

Chapman, Dawna, ed. see Chapman, Neil.

Chapman, Dean. Growl of the Tiger. LC 94-60920. 272p. 1994. 24.95 (*1-56311-159-4*) Turner Pub KY.

— Karenni: The Forgotten War of a Nation Under Siege. 128p. 1999. 45.00 (*1-899235-96-5*, Pub. by Dewi Lewis) Dist Art Pubs.

— Where Was I When Time Went By? LC 98-29483. 160p. 1998. pap. 16.95 (*0-9649776-4-8*) Plesnt Hill.

Chapman, Dean W. The Orphan Gospel. (Biblical Seminar Ser.: No. 16). 235p. (C). 1993. pap. 28.50 (*1-85075-346-6*, Pub. by Sheffield Acad) CUP Services.

Chapman, Deborah, ed. Water Quality Assessments: A Guide to the Use of Biota, Sediments & Water in Environmental Monitoring. (Illus.). 586p. 1992. mass mkt. 102.95 (*0-412-44840-8*, A7504) Chapman & Hall.

Chapman, Dennis & Jones, Malcolm. Micelles, Monolayers, & Biomembranes. (Illus.). 264p. 1994. pap. 79.95 (*0-471-30596-0*) Wiley.

— Michelles, Monolayers & Biomembranes. 264p. 1994. 169.95 (*0-471-56139-8*) Wiley.

Chapman, Dennis, jt. ed. see Mantsch, Henry H.

Chapman, Derek. Stalin: Man of Steel. 1988. pap. text 11.64 (*0-582-85749-X*, 75156) Longman.

Chapman, Dick. The Bungee Cord Bible: According to Dick Chapman. LC 98-124932. (Illus.). 96p. 1997. pap. 7.00 (*0-9655087-1-4*) Chapman Ent.

— When 'CCO Was Cookin' Book. LC 97-170094. (Illus.). 210p. (Orig.). 1996. pap. 14.95 (*0-9655087-0-6*) Chapman Ent.

Chapman, Don W. Second Opinion. LC 99-208565. 148p. 1998. 19.95 (*1-57168-920-6*, Nortex Pr) Sunbelt Media.

Chapman, Doris. Good Personnel Practice in Small & Medium Sized Operations. (Financial Times Management Briefings Ser.). 1997. pap. 94.50 (*0-273-63179-9*, Pub. by F T P-H) Trans-Atl Phila.

Chapman, Dorothy. My Body Is Where I Live. (Drug Free Ser.). (J). (gr. k-4). 1989. text 18.95 (*0-88671-297-1*, 5102) Am Guidance.

Chapman, Dorothy H., compiled by. Index to Poetry by Black American Women, 15. LC 86-14936. (Bibliographies & Indexes in Afro-American & African Studies: No. 15). 447p. 1986. lib. bdg. 85.00 (*0-313-25152-5*, CWP/, Greenwood Pr) Greenwood.

Chapman, Duane. Energy Resources & Energy Corporations. LC 82-74022. 368p. 1983. text 39.95 (*0-8014-1305-2*) Cornell U Pr.

Chapman, Dudley H. Molting Time for Antitrust: Market Realities, Economic Fallacies, & European Innovations. LC 90-45199. 272p. 1991. 65.00 (*0-275-93478-0*, C3478, Praeger Pubs) Greenwood.

Chapman, E. Be True to Your Future: Achieve Career Success & Personal Fulfillment. Crisp, Michael, ed. LC 87-73559. (Illus.). 215p. 1988. pap. 15.95 (*0-931961-47-5*) Crisp Pubns.

— Career Discovery: Be True to Your Future. rev. ed. Crisp, Michael, ed. LC 85-72809. (Fifty-Minute Ser.). (Illus.). 73p. (Orig.). (C). 1988. pap. 10.95 (*0-931961-07-6*) Crisp Pubns.

— The College Experience: Your First Thirty Days on Campus. Hicks, Tony, ed. LC 89-82052. (Fifty-Minute Ser.). 89p. (C). 1990. pap. 10.95 (*1-56052-007-8*) Crisp Pubns.

Chapman, E. A., jt. ed. see Lynden, Frederick C.

Chapman, Edgar L. The Magic Labyrinth of Philip Jose Farmer. LC 81-21603. (Milford Series: Popular Writers of Today: Popular Writers of Today: Vol. 38). 96p. 1984. pap. 15.00 (*0-89370-258-7*) Millefleurs.

— The Road to Castle Mount: The Science Fiction of Robert Silverberg, 82. LC 99-17840. (Contributions to the Study of Science Fiction & Fantasy: Vol. 82). 224p. 1999. 59.95 (*0-313-26145-8*, Bergin & Garvey) Greenwood.

***Chapman, Edward.** Heroes of Might & Magic III: The Restoration of Erathia. LC 97-76447. (Illus.). 361p. 1999. pap. 19.99 (*0-7615-1247-0*) Prima Pub.

Chapman, Edward. Take No Prisoners: The Official Strategy Guide. LC 97-69337. 264p. 1997. per. 19.99 (*0-7615-1201-2*) Prima Pub.

Chapman, Edward A., Jr. Exhibit Marketing: A Success Guide for Managers. 2nd ed. LC 95-23276. 407p. 1995. 29.95 (*0-07-011232-0*) McGraw.

Chapman, Edward A., et al. Library Systems Analysis Guidelines. LC 75-109391. 242p. reprint ed. pap. 75.10 (*0-608-11298-4*, 201305500085) Bks Demand.

Chapman, Edward M. Chapmans: The Chapmans of Old Saybrook, Connecticut, a Family Chronicle. (Illus.). 74p. 1997. reprint ed. pap. 15.00 (*0-8328-7916-9*); reprint ed. lib. bdg. 25.00 (*0-8328-7915-0*) Higginson Bk Co.

— English Literature in Account with Religion. 1977. lib. bdg. 59.95 (*0-8490-1775-0*) Gordon Pr.

— New England Village Life. 232p. 1972. 18.95 (*0-405-18115-9*) Ayer.

Chapman, Edwood N. Comfort Zones: Looseleaf Edition. 2nd ed. Crisp, Michael G., ed. LC 88-7248. (Illus.). 320p. 1985. pap. 15.95 (*1-56052-026-4*) Crisp Pubns.

Chapman, Elizabeth. First Orchard. 68p. 1999. pap. 11.00 (*0-944920-33-0*) Bellowing Ark Pr.

Chapman, Elizabeth, jt. ed. see Lynden, Frederick C.

C

***Chapman, Elizabeth A. & Lynden, Frederick C., eds.** Advances in Librarianship. (Advances in Librarianship Ser.: Vol. 24). 225p. 2000. 89.95 (*0-12-024624-4*) Acad Pr.

Chapman, Ellwood. Podstawowe Wiadomosci o Sprzedawaniu: Podrecznik dla Osob Pragnacych Rozwinac Umiejetnosc Sprzedawania. Grycz, Czeslaw J. & Salski, Andrzej, eds. Filipczak, Agata, tr. from ENG. (POL., Illus.). iv, 74p. (Orig.). (C). 1991. pap. 7.95 (*1-56513-001-4*) W Poniecki Charit.

Chapman, Elwood & Haynes, Marion. Comfort Zones: Planning Your Future. 4th rev. ed. (Professional Ser.). 350p. 1997. pap. 14.95 (*1-56052-457-X*) Crisp Pubns.

Chapman, Elwood & Maddux, Robert. Your First 30 Days: Getting Started in a New Job. 2nd rev. ed. LC 97-67424. (50 Minute Ser.). (Illus.). 120p. 1997. pap. 10.95 (*1-56052-453-7*) Crisp Pubns.

Chapman, Elwood N. Attitude! Your Most Priceless Possession. (Orig.). 1988. 6.95 (*0-318-33264-7*, 117) Am Bartenders.

— Attitude! Your Most Priceless Possession. 3rd ed. Crisp, Michael, ed. LC 94-69534. (Fifty-Minute Ser.). (Illus.). 86p. (Orig.). 1987. pap., wbk. ed. 10.95 (*1-56052-317-4*) Crisp Pubns.

— Comfort Zones: Planning Your Future. 3rd ed. Crisp, Michael, ed. LC 92-20417. (Illus.). 337p. 1993. pap. 15.95 (*1-56052-162-7*) Crisp Pubns.

— Enhance Your Destiny: Dare to Build a Second Life. Crisp, Michael G., ed. LC 90-85865. (Illus.). 151p. (Orig.). 1991. 14.95 (*1-56052-100-7*) Crisp Pubns.

— Human Relations in a Small Business. Manber, Beverly, ed. LC 92-54351. (Small Business & Entrepreneurship Ser.). 225p. (Orig.). 1996. pap. 15.95 (*1-56052-185-6*) Crisp Pubns.

— I Got the Job! rev. ed. Crisp, Michael G., ed. LC 91-77077. (Fifty-Minute Ser.). 90p. (Orig.). 1992. pap. 10.95 (*1-56052-121-X*) Crisp Pubns.

— Life Care: The Inside Story. Armfield, Follin, ed. LC 94-70615. 136p. 1994. pap. 12.95 (*1-56052-290-9*) Crisp Pubns.

— Life Is an Attitude! Crisp, Michael G., ed. LC 91-44382. 171p. (Orig.). 1992. pap. 12.95 (*1-56052-138-4*) Crisp Pubns.

— The New Supervisor: A Guide for the Newly Promoted. 3rd rev. ed. Crisp, Michael G., ed. LC 91-77082. (Fifty-Minute Ser.). Orig. Title: Fifty-Minute Supervisor. (Illus.). 68p. 1992. pap. 10.95 (*1-56052-120-1*) Crisp Pubns.

— Plan B: Converting Change into Career Opportunity. rev. ed. Crisp, Michael, ed. LC 92-54603. (Fifty-Minute Ser.). 103p. 1993. reprint ed. pap. 10.95 (*1-56052-195-3*) Crisp Pubns.

— Rate Your Skills As a Manager: A Crisp Assessment Profile. Crisp, Michael G., ed. LC 90-85866. (Fifty-Minute Ser.). (Illus.). 104p. (Orig.). 1991. pap. 10.95 (*1-56052-101-5*) Crisp Pubns.

— Sales Training Basics: A Primer for Those New to Selling. 3rd rev. ed. Crisp, Michael G., ed. LC 91-77081. (Fifty-Minute Ser.). (Illus.). 68p. (Orig.). 1992. pap. 10.95 (*1-56052-119-8*) Crisp Pubns.

— Supervising Part-Time Employees: A Guide to Better Productivity. Armfield, Follin, ed. LC 93-72501. (Illus.). 85p. (Orig.). 1994. pap. 10.95 (*1-56052-243-7*) Crisp Pubns.

— Twelve Steps to Self-Improvement. Crisp, Michael G., ed. LC 90-85867. (Fifty-Minute Ser.). (Illus.). 107p. (Orig.). 1991. pap. 10.95 (*1-56052-102-3*) Crisp Pubns.

— The Unfinished Business of Living: Helping Aging Parents Help Themselves. Crisp, Michael G., ed. LC 86-71572. (Illus.). 232p. (Orig.). 1987. pap. 15.95 (*0-931961-19-X*) Crisp Pubns.

— Up Your Attitude! Changing the Way You Look at Life. rev. ed. LC 93-13315. 200p. 1993. pap. 12.95 (*1-56052-234-8*) Crisp Pubns.

Chapman, Elwood N. & Goodwin, Cliff. Supervisor's Survival Kit: Your First Step into Management. 8th ed. LC 98-18403. 275p. (C). 1998. pap. text 43.00 (*0-13-676644-7*) P-H.

Chapman, Elwood N. & Heim, Pat. Learning to Lead: An Action Plan for Success. Crisp, Michael G., ed. LC 90-80571. (Fifty-Minute Ser.). (Illus.). 74p. (Orig.). 1990. pap. 10.95 (*1-56052-043-4*) Crisp Pubns.

Chapman, Elwood N. & Knowdell, Richard L. Personal Counseling: A Practical Guie That Teaches Basic Counseling Skills. 3rd ed. LC 92-54366. (Fifty-Minute Ser.). 94p. 1993. pap. 10.95 (*1-56052-184-8*) Crisp Pubns.

Chapman, Elwood N. & O'Neil, Sharon L. Your Attitude Is Showing: A Primer of Human Relations. 9th ed. LC 98-7522. (Illus.). 237p. (C). 1998. pap. text 30.40 (*0-13-954793-2*) P-H.

Chapman, Elwood N. & O'Neil, Sharon Lund. Leadership: 10 Steps Every Manager Needs to Know. 3rd ed. LC 99-14824. (Illus.). 180p. (C). 1999. pap. text 28.60 (*0-13-010019-6*) P-H.

Chapman, Emalee. Chicken. Wertz, Laurie, ed. LC 92-27836. (Williams-Sonoma Kitchen Library). (Illus.). 108p. 1993. lib. bdg. write for info. (*0-7835-0226-5*) Time-Life.

— Chicken. Wertz, Laurie, ed. LC 92-27836. (Williams-Sonoma Kitchen Library). (Illus.). 108p. (J). (gr. 11). 1999. 18.95 (*0-7835-0225-7*) Time-Life.

— Vegetables. Wertz, Laurie, ed. LC 93-17991. (Williams-Sonoma Kitchen Library). (Illus.). 108p. 1993. lib. bdg. write for info. (*0-7835-0255-9*) Time-Life.

— Vegetables. Wertz, Laurie, ed. LC 93-17991. (Williams-Sonoma Kitchen Library). (Illus.). 108p. (J). (gr. 11). 1999. 18.95 (*0-7835-0254-0*) Time-Life.

Chapman, Eric G. Aquatic Beetles (Insecta - Coleoptera) of Northeastern Ohio. LC 97-76267. (Miscellaneous Contributions Ser.: Vol. 4). (Illus.). 117p. 1998. pap. text 15.00 (*0-86727-127-2*) Ohio Bio Survey.

Chapman, Ernest L. Angel Board. (Illus.). 12p. 1996. 39.95 (*0-9654166-0-7*) Angel Alliance.

Chapman, Ernest T., jt. auth. see Wanklyn, J. Alfred.

Chapman, Eugenia & Major, Jill C. Clean Your House & Everything in It. rev. ed. 160p. 1991. pap. 13.00 (*0-399-51658-1*, Perigee Bks) Berkley Pub.

— Find Your House & Everything in It: An Organization Guide for the Forgetful. 110p. 1997. pap. 10.00 (*1-56684-255-7*) Evans Bk Dist.

Chapman, F., ed. see France, Anatole, pseud.

Chapman, F. Spencer. Lhasa the Holy City. LC 75-37875. (Select Bibliographies Reprint Ser.). 1977. reprint ed. 35.95 (*0-8369-6712-7*) Ayer.

Chapman, F. W. The Buckingham Family, or the Descendants of Thomas Buckingham of Milford, CT. (Illus.). 384p. 1989. reprint ed. pap. 57.50 (*0-8328-0339-1*); reprint ed. lib. bdg. 65.50 (*0-8328-0338-3*) Higginson Bk Co.

— Bulkeley Family: Or, The Descendants of Rev. Peter Bulkeley Who Settled at Concord, MA in 1636. (Illus.). 289p. 1989. reprint ed. pap. 43.50 (*0-8328-0343-X*); reprint ed. lib. bdg. 53.50 (*0-8328-0342-1*) Higginson Bk Co.

— Chapman Family, or the Descendants of Robert Chapman, One of the First Settlers of Saybrook, Conn. With Genealogical Notes of William of New London, Edward of Windor, John of Stonington, & Rev. Benjamin of Stonington (All Connecticut) (Illus.). 414p. 1989. reprint ed. pap. 52.00 (*0-8328-0391-X*); reprint ed. lib. bdg. 62.00 (*0-8328-0390-1*) Higginson Bk Co.

— The Coit Family: or the Descendants of John Coit, at Salem, Mass., in 1638, at Gloucester in 1644, & at New London, Connecticut, in 1650. (Illus.). 341p. 1993. reprint ed. pap. 54.00 (*0-8328-1363-X*); reprint ed. lib. bdg. 64.00 (*0-8328-1362-1*) Higginson Bk Co.

— Pratt Family: or the Descendants of Lt. William Pratt One of the First Settlers of Hartford & Saybrook; with Genealogical Notes of John of Hartford, Peter of Lyme, & John Pratt. (Illus.). 421p. 1989. reprint ed. pap. 63.00 (*0-8328-0985-3*); reprint ed. lib. bdg. 71.00 (*0-8328-0984-5*) Higginson Bk Co.

— Trowbridge Family: Or, The Descendants of Thomas Trowbridge, One of the First Settlers of New Haven, Connecticut. (Illus.). 461p. 1989. reprint ed. pap. 69.00 (*0-8328-1181-5*); reprint ed. lib. bdg. 77.00 (*0-8328-1180-7*) Higginson Bk Co.

***Chapman, Fern Schumer.** Motherland: A Daughter's Journey to Reclaim the Past. LC 99-23796. 190p. 2000. 23.95 (*0-670-88105-8*, Viking) Viking Penguin.

Chapman, Ferne C. Soup 'R Sandwich Sampler. 64p. (Orig.). 1990. pap. 7.50 (*1-880222-02-7*) Red Apple Pub.

— Town & Country Creative Breads: A Healthy Tradition for Todays Family. Schlosser, Karl, ed. (Illus.). 160p. 1993. spiral bd. 12.95 (*0-9637312-9-7*) Jac-Lynn Ent.

Chapman, Frances W. The Great Pyramid of Ghizeh from the Aspect of Symbolism & Religion. (Illus.). 258p. 1997. reprint ed. pap. 19.95 (*0-7661-0083-9*) Kessinger Pub.

Chapman, Frank E., Jr., jt. ed. see Berlowitz, Marvin J.

Chapman, Frank M. Essays in South American Ornithogeography: Original Anthology. Sterling, Keir B., ed. LC 77-81087. (Biologists & Their World Ser.). (Illus.). 1978. lib. bdg. 65.95 (*0-405-10663-7*) Ayer.

Chapman, Frederic, tr. see France, Anatole, pseud.

Chapman, G. Los Cinco Lenguajes del Amor.Tr. of Five Love Languages. (SPA.). 188p. (J). 1996. 8.99 (*1-56063-680-7*, 495659) Editorial Unilit.

Chapman, G., tr. see Hesoid.

Chapman, G. A., ed. Solar & Middle Atmosphere Variability: Proceedings of Symposium 12 & Workshop VIII of the COSPAR 27th Plenary Meeting Held in Espoo, Finland, 18-29 July, 1988. (Advances in Space Research Ser.: Vol. 8/7). (Illus.). 218p. 1989. pap. 83.00 (*0-08-036889-1*, Pergamon Pr) Elsevier.

Chapman, G. Clarke. Facing the Nuclear Heresy: A Call to Reformation. fac. ed. LC 85-31417. 288p. 1986. pap. 89.30 (*0-7837-7342-0*, 204729500007) Bks Demand.

Chapman, G. O. Ferry: The Ferry's of Staffordville, Ct. & Their New England Ancestry. 47p. 1995. reprint ed. pap. 10.00 (*0-8328-4782-8*); reprint ed. lib. bdg. 20.00 (*0-8328-4781-X*) Higginson Bk Co.

Chapman, G. P. The Biology of Grasses. LC 97-112606. 288p. 1996. text 90.00 (*0-85199-111-4*) OUP.

— Reproductive Versatility in the Grasses. 310p. (C). 1990. text 100.00 (*0-521-38060-X*) Cambridge U Pr.

Chapman, G. P., ed. Desertified Grasslands: Their Biology & Management. (Linnean Society of London Symposium Ser.: No. 13). (Illus.). 376p. 1992. text 105.00 (*0-12-168570-5*) Acad Pr.

***Chapman, G. P., et al, eds.** Urban Growth & Development in Asia Vol. II: Living in the Cities. 524p. 1999. text 96.95 (*0-7546-1039-X*, Pub. by Inst Materials) Ashgate Pub Co.

Chapman, G. P. & Tarawall, S. A., eds. Systems for Cytogenetic Analysis in Vicia Faba L. (Advances in Agricultural Biotechnology Ser.). 1984. text 151.50 (*90-247-3089-9*) Kluwer Academic.

Chapman, Gary. Building Relationships: A Discipleship Guide for Married Couples. 64p. 1995. pap. text 7.95 (*0-8054-9855-9*, LifeWy Press) LifeWay Christian.

Chapman, Gary. Computers in Battle: Will They Work? Bellin, David, ed. 1987. 14.95 (*0-15-121232-5*) Harcourt.

— The Five Love Languages: Gift Edition. 1996. 19.99 (*1-881273-62-8*) Northfield Pub.

— The Five Love Languages: Gift Edition. gif. ed. 1997. 19.99 (*0-8024-7362-8*) Northfield Pub.

— The Five Love Languages: How to Express Heartfelt Commitment to Your Mate. 1995. pap. 11.99 (*1-881273-15-6*) Northfield Pub.

***Chapman, Gary.** Five Love Languages of Children: Parent Activity Guide. 80p. 1998. pap. text 7.95 (*0-7673-3898-7*, LifeWy Press) LifeWay Christian.

— Five Love Languages of Teenagers. 2000. 16.97 (*1-881273-83-0*) Northfield Pub.

Chapman, Gary. Five Signs of a Functional Family. 256p. 1997. 19.99 (*1-881273-63-6*) Moody.

— Five Signs of a Loving Family. LC 98-204579. 243p. 1998. pap. 11.99 (*1-881273-92-X*) Northfield Pub.

— Hope for the Separated: Wounded Marriages Can Be Healed. expanded rev. ed. LC 97-164242. pap. 10.99 (*0-8024-3636-6*, 167) Moody.

— Loving Solutions: Overcoming Barriers in Your Marriage. LC 98-196852. 214p. 1998. 19.99 (*1-881273-25-3*) Moody.

— Loving Solutions: Overcoming Barriers in Your Marriage. 214p. 1999. pap. 11.99 (*1-881273-91-1*) Northfield Pub.

— The Other Side of Love: Handling Anger in a Godly Way. 183p. 1999. pap. 11.99 (*0-8024-6777-6*) Moody.

— Toward a Growing Marriage. LC 97-202101. pap. 11.99 (*0-8024-8787-4*, 302) Moody.

***Chapman, Gary.** Your Gift of Love: Selections from the Five Love Languages. 2000. 12.99 (*1-881273-32-6*) Northfield Pub.

Chapman, Gary & Campbell, Ross. The Five Love Languages of Children. LC 97-200258. 224p. 1997. pap. 11.99 (*1-881273-65-2*) Northfield Pub.

***Chapman, Gary & Campbell, Ross.** Los Cinco Lenguajes de Amor de los Ninos. (SPA.). 2000. pap. 8.99 (*0-7899-0508-6*) Spanish Hse Distributors.

Chapman, Gary & Hassler, Betty. Communication & Intimacy: Covenant Marriage Couple's Guide. 132p. 1992. pap. text 6.95 (*0-7673-2678-4*, LifeWy Press) LifeWay Christian.

Chapman, Gary, jt. auth. see Campbell, Ross.

Chapman, Geoffrey. Lectionary, 3 vols. 3500p. 1985. write for info. (*0-318-59520-6*) Harper SF.

***Chapman, Geoffrey.** St. Francis of Assisi: The Impact of His Vision & Friendships. 289p. 1999. 24.95 (*0-225-66736-3*) Harper SF.

Chapman, Geoffrey P., ed. The Bamboos. LC 97-21752. (Symposium of the Linnean Society of London Ser.: No. 19). (Illus.). 312p. 1997. text 110.00 (*0-12-168555-1*) Morgan Kaufmann.

Chapman, George. All Fools. fac. ed. Manley, Frank, ed. LC 68-10664. (Regents Renaissance Drama Ser.). 123p. 1994. pap. 38.20 (*0-7837-7336-6*, 204728900007) Bks Demand.

— Bussy d'Ambois. Brooke, Nicholas, ed. (Revels Plays Ser.). 169p. 1988. reprint ed. 40.00 (*0-7190-1505-7*, Pub. by Manchester Univ Pr) St Martin.

— Bussy D'Ambois. Lordi, Robert J., ed. LC 64-11358. (Regents Renaissance Drama Ser.). 160p. 1964. reprint ed. pap. 49.60 (*0-608-02370-1*, 206301200004) Bks Demand.

— The Gentleman Usher. Smith, John H., ed. LC 69-12399. (Regents Renaissance Drama Ser.). 183p. 1970. reprint ed. pap. 56.80 (*0-608-02369-8*, 206301100004) Bks Demand.

Chapman, George. Plays & Poems. 416p. pap. 19.95 (*0-14-043636-7*, Pub. by Pnguin Bks Ltd) Trafalgar.

Chapman, George. A Treatise on Education: 1790 Edition. (Classics in Education Ser.). 298p. 1996. reprint ed. 80.00 (*1-85506-275-5*) Bks Intl VA.

— The Widow's Tears. fac. ed. Smeak, Ethel M., ed. LC 65-24305. 145p. 1966. pap. 45.00 (*0-7837-7335-8*, 204728800007) Bks Demand.

— The Widow's Tears. Yamada, Akihiro, ed. LC 75-325526. (Revels Plays Ser.). 238p. 1975. reprint ed. pap. 73.80 (*0-608-06034-8*, 206636500008) Bks Demand.

Chapman, George, et al. Eastward Ho. Van Fossen, Richard W., ed. LC 79-83851. (Revels Plays Ser.). 256p. reprint ed. pap. 79.40 (*0-7837-0050-4*, 204029700016) Bks Demand.

Chapman, George, jt. auth. see Marlowe, Christopher.

Chapman, George, tr. see Nicoll, Allardyce, ed.

Chapman, George T., ed. see Turner, William.

Chapman, Gerald. Teaching Young Playwrights. Barnett, Lisa, ed. LC 90-44760. 129p. (Orig.). (C). 1990. pap. 15.95 (*0-435-08212-4*, 08212) Heinemann.

Chapman, Gerard. The Gentleman Burglar: And Other Favorites of Historian Gerard Chapman. 32p. 1994. pap. 5.00 (*0-941583-21-X*) Attic Rev Pr.

Chapman, Giles. Cars That Time Forgot. LC 98-3262. 1998. 12.98 (*1-57145-144-7*, Thunder Bay) Advantage Pubs.

— Hot Rod Record Breakers. 1992. 9.98 (*1-55521-775-3*) Bk Sales Inc.

— World's Fastest Cars. 1990. 12.98 (*1-55521-670-6*) Bk Sales Inc.

Chapman, Gillean. Making Books: A Step-by-Step Guide to Your Own Publishing. 1992. pap. 4.95 (*0-395-94619-0*) HM.

***Chapman, Gillian.** Aztec Crafts from the Past. LC 99-42373. (Illus.). 40p. (YA). (gr. 4-7). 2000. pap. 9.95 (*0-688-17748-4*) Morrow Avon.

Chapman, Gillian. The Aztecs. LC 97-29171. (Crafts from the Past Ser.). (Illus.). 32p. (J). (gr. 4-8). 1998. 21.36 (*1-57572-555-X*) Heinemann Lib.

***Chapman, Gillian.** Egyptian Crafts from the Past. LC 99-42814. (Illus.). 40p. (YA). (gr. 4-7). 2000. pap. 9.95 (*0-688-17746-8*, Wm Morrow) Morrow Avon.

Chapman, Gillian. The Egyptians. LC 97-29172. (Crafts from the Past Ser.). 37p. (J). (gr. 4-8). 1998. 24.22 (*1-57572-556-8*) Heinemann.

— Exploring Time. LC 94-44671. (Illus.). 32p. (J). (gr. 1-4). 1995. pap. 7.95 (*1-56294-683-8*) Millbrook Pr.

— The Greeks. LC 98-15668. (Crafts from the Past Ser.). (J). 1998. 19.92 (*1-57572-733-1*) Heinemann Lib.

— The Romans. LC 98-15666. (Crafts from the Past Ser.). (J). 1998. 19.92 (*1-57572-734-X*) Heinemann Lib.

— Spring. LC 97-17159. (Seasonal Crafts Ser.). (Illus.). 32p. (J). (gr. 1-4). 1998. 22.11 (*0-8172-4872-2*) Raintree Steck-V.

— Summer. LC 97-17160. (Seasonal Crafts Ser.). (Illus.). 32p. (J). (gr. 1-4). 1997. lib. bdg. 22.83 (*0-8172-4873-0*) Raintree Steck-V.

Chapman, Gillian & Robson, Pam. Art from Fabric. (Salvaged Ser.). (Illus.). 32p. (J). (gr. 1-6). 1995. lib. bdg. 21.40 (*1-56847-381-8*) Raintree Steck-V.

— Art from Packaging: With Projects Using Cardboard, Plastics, Foil, & Tape. LC 96-8363. (Salvaged! Ser.). (Illus.). 32p. (J). (gr. 1-6). 1997. lib. bdg. 21.40 (*0-8172-4550-2*) Raintree Steck-V.

— Art from Paper. (Salvaged Ser.). (Illus.). 32p. (J). (gr. 1-6). 1995. lib. bdg. 21.40 (*1-56847-380-X*) Raintree Steck-V.

— Art from Rocks & Shells. (Salvaged! Ser.). (Illus.). 32p. (J). (gr. 1-6). 1995. lib. bdg. 21.40 (*1-56847-382-6*) Raintree Steck-V.

— Art from Sand & Earth: With Projects Using Clay, Plaster, & Natural Fibres. LC 96-8360. (Salvaged! Ser.). (Illus.). 32p. (J). (gr. 1-6). 1997. lib. bdg. 21.40 (*0-8172-4551-0*) Raintree Steck-V.

— Art from Wood. (Salvaged! Ser.). (Illus.). 32p. (J). (gr. 1-6). 1995. lib. bdg. 21.40 (*1-56847-383-4*) Raintree Steck-V.

— Exploring Time. LC 94-44671. (Illus.). 32p. (J). (gr. 1-4). 1995. lib. bdg. 19.90 (*1-56294-559-9*) Millbrook Pr.

— Making Books: A Step-by-Step Guide to Your Own Publishing. (Illus.). 32p. (J). (gr. 3-6). 1992. 13.45 (*1-56294-169-0*); pap. 6.95 (*1-56294-840-7*); lib. bdg. 19.90 (*1-56294-154-2*) Millbrook Pr.

— Making Shaped Books. LC 94-44661. (Illus.). 32p. (J). (gr. k-3). 1995. lib. bdg. 19.90 (*1-56294-560-2*) Millbrook Pr.

— Making Shaped Books. LC 94-44661. (Illus.). 32p. (J). (gr. k-3). 1996. pap. 7.95 (*0-7613-0139-9*) Millbrook Pr.

— Maps & Mazes: A First Guide to Mapmaking. LC 93-1234. (Illus.). 32p. (J). (gr. 2-4). 1993. pap. 6.95 (*1-56294-715-X*) Millbrook Pr.

Chapman, Glenn H., jt. ed. see Liss, Jeffrey G.

Chapman, Glenn P. Live in the Beautiful Islands of Hawaii. LC 92-81419. 84p. 1992. pap. 15.00 (*0-9632989-0-9*) Opport Hawaii.

Chapman, Grace O. Crouch Family of Stafford, Connecticut, & Some Other Descendant of William Crouch of Charlestown, Massachusetts, 1654. (Illus.). 36p. 1997. reprint ed. pap. 7.50 (*0-8328-8158-9*); reprint ed. lib. bdg. 17.50 (*0-8328-8157-0*) Higginson Bk Co.

— Eager Family. (Illus.). 91p. 1997. reprint ed. pap. 18.00 (*0-8328-8400-6*); reprint ed. lib. bdg. 28.00 (*0-8328-8399-9*) Higginson Bk Co.

— Ellithorpe: Ellithorpes of Killingly (Thompson Parish) & Stafford, Connecticut. (Illus.). 47p. 1997. reprint ed. pap. 9.00 (*0-8328-8472-3*); reprint ed. lib. bdg. 19.00 (*0-8328-8471-5*) Higginson Bk Co.

— Glazier Family, Mainly of Willington & Stafford, Tolland County, Connecticut. 54p. 1997. reprint ed. pap. 11.00 (*0-8328-8755-2*); reprint ed. lib. bdg. 21.00 (*0-8328-8754-4*) Higginson Bk Co.

Chapman, Graham. Environmentalism & the Mass Media: The North South Divide. LC 96-32316. (Global Environmental Change Ser.). (Illus.). 352p. (C). 1997. 100.00 (*0-415-15504-5*); pap. 29.99 (*0-415-15505-3*) Routledge.

— The Fairly Incomplete & Rather Badly Illustrated Monty Python Songbook. (Illus.). 96p. 1995. pap. 14.00 (*0-06-095116-8*, Perennial) HarperTrade.

***Chapman, Graham.** Ojril: The Completely Incomplete Graham Chapman. (Illus.). 2000. pap. 19.95 (*1-57488-270-8*) Brasseys.

***Chapman, Graham & Yoakum, Jim.** Ojril: The Completely Incomplete Graham Chapman. 2000. pap. write for info. (*0-7134-8605-8*, Pub. by B T B) Bks Intl VA.

Chapman, Graham P., ed. Timescales of Environmental Change. (Illus.). 288p. (C). 1996. 85.00 (*0-415-13252-5*); pap. 27.99 (*0-415-13253-3*) Routledge.

***Chapman, Graham P., et al, eds.** Urban Growth & Development in Asia Vol. 1: Making the Cities. (SOAS Studies in Development Geography). 498p. 1999. text 83.95 (*1-84014-964-7*, Pub. by Ashgate Pub) Ashgate Pub Co.

Chapman, Graham P. & Baker, Kathleen M., eds. The Changing Geography of Africa & the Middle East. LC 92-44795. (Illus.). 272p. (C). 1992. pap. 25.99 (*0-415-05710-8*, A7317) Routledge.

— The Changing Geography of Asia. LC 91-44801. (Illus.). 272p. (C). 1992. pap. 25.99 (*0-415-05708-6*, A7310) Routledge.

Chapman, Graham P. & Thompson, Michael. The Quest for Sustainable Development in the Ganges Basin. (Global Development & the Environment Ser.). 192p. 1995. 95.00 (*0-7201-2191-4*) Continuum.

***Chapman, Gretchen B. & Sonnenberg, Frank A., eds.** Decision Making in Health Care: Theory, Psychology & Applications. (Cambridge Series on Judgment & Decision Making). (Illus.). 400p. 2000. 59.95 (*0-521-64159-4*) Cambridge U Pr.

Chapman, Gretel. Mosan Art: An Annotated Bibliography. 1988. 65.00 (*0-8161-8329-5*, Hall Reference) Macmillan.

Chapman, H. Perry. Rembrandt's Self-Portraits: A Study in Seventeenth-Century Identity. (Illus.). 328p. 1990. reprint ed. pap. text 35.00 (*0-691-00296-7*, Pub. by Princeton U Pr) Cal Prin Full Svc.

Chapman, H. Perry, et al. Jan Steen: Painter & Storyteller. Jansen, Guido, ed. LC 96-4544. (Illus.). 1996. write for info. (*0-89468-223-7*) Natl Gallery Art.

Chapman, H. Perry, et al. Jan Steen: Painter & Storyteller. (Illus.). 1996. 60.00 (*0-300-06793-3*) Yale U Pr.

Chapman, Hank, Jr. How to Smelt Your Gold & Silver. (Illus.). 111p. 1997. per. 29.95 (0-9662678-0-X) Mineral Recovery.

Chapman, Harmon M. Sensations & Phenomenology. LC 66-22443. 173p. reprint ed. pap. 53.70 (0-608-30639-8, 205004300059) Bks Demand.

Chapman, Harold C., ed. Biological Control of Mosquitoes. (Illus.). (Orig.). 1985. pap. 10.00 (0-9606210-2-4) Am Mosquito.

Chapman, Helen E. Paul Brewster & Son. LC 79-85681. (American Fiction Reprint Ser.). 1977. 19.95 (0-8369-7010-1) Ayer.

Chapman, Herb & Chapman, Muncy. Wiregrass Country. LC 98-24079. 370p. 1998. 16.95 (1-56164-164-2); pap. 9.95 (1-56164-156-1) Pineapple Pr.

Chapman, Herrick. State Capitalism & Working-Class Radicalism in the French Aircraft Industry. LC 90-10790. (Illus.). 480p. 1990. pap. 18.95 (0-520-07125-5, Pub. by U CA Pr) Cal Prin Full Svc.

Chapman, Herrick, jt. ed. see Andrews, George R.

Chapman, Hester W. Anne Boleyn. LC 74-159472. 244 p. 1974. write for info. (0-224-00955-9) Jonathan Cape.

— Last Tudor King. large type ed. (Shadows of the Crown Ser.). 558p. 1974. 27.99 (0-85456-637-6) Ulverscroft.

— Mary II, Queen of England. LC 75-17197. 279p. 1976. reprint ed. lib. bdg. 59.75 (0-8371-8302-2, CHMQ, Greenwood Pr) Greenwood.

Chapman, Hillary. Geoffrey Wales. Brett, Simon, ed. (Illus.). 153p. 1998. pap. 24.95 (1-884718-55-8) Oak Knoll.

Chapman, Hugo, et al. Padua in the 1450s: Marco Zoppo & His Contemporaries. LC 98-183279. 80p. 1998. write for info. (0-7141-2616-0) British Mus Pr.

Chapman, I. D., et al, eds. New Drugs for Asthma Therapy Vol. 34: Agents & Actions Supplement. ix, 548p. 1991. 149.00 (0-8176-2505-4) Birkhauser.

Chapman, J. A Genealogy, Edward Chapman of Ipswich, Massachusettes, 1642-1678 & His Descendants. (Illus.). 147p. 1993. reprint ed. pap. 22.00 (0-8328-1333-8); reprint ed. lib. bdg. 32.00 (0-8328-1332-X) Higginson Bk Co.

— Maxims of Ali. 1991. pap. 4.50 (1-56744-131-9) Kazi Pubns.

Chapman, J. & Fitts, J. H. Lane Genealogy, 3 vols. in 1, Vols. I, II & III. (Illus.). 1034p. reprint ed. pap. 144.00 (0-8328-0750-8); reprint ed. lib. bdg. 152.00 (0-8328-0749-4) Higginson Bk Co.

Chapman, J. B. Dr. Schuessler's Biochemistry. 300p. 1996. spiral bd. 23.50 (0-7873-0163-9) Hlth Research.

Chapman, J. B. & Perry, Edward L. The Biochemic Handbook. Orig. Title: Biochemic Theory & Practice. 1976. pap. 1.50 (0-89378-051-0) Formur Intl.

Chapman, J. Carol, ed. see Montaigne, Michel de.

Chapman, J. D. Geography & Energy: Commercial Energy Systems & National Policies. 1989. pap. 25.95 (0-582-30085-1, Pub. by Addison-Wesley) Longman.

Chapman, J. Harley. Jung's Three Theories of Religious Experience. LC 87-20465. (Studies in the Psychology of Religion: Vol. 3). 200p. 1988. lib. bdg. 79.95 (0-88946-245-3) E Mellen.

Chapman, J. Harley & Frankenberry, Nancy, eds. Interpreting Neville. LC 98-35152. 352p. (C). 1999. text 65.50 (0-7914-4195-4); pap. text 21.95 (0-7914-4196-2) State U NY Pr.

Chapman, J. M. & Ayrey, G. The Use of Radioactive Isotopes in the Life Sciences. (Illus.). (C). 1981. pap. text 24.95 (0-04-570012-5) Routledge.

Chapman, J. N. & Craven, A. J., eds. Quantitative Electron Microscopy. (Scottish Universities Summer School in Physics, a NATO Advanced Study Institute Ser.: No. 25). (Illus.). 446p. 1983. 189.00 (0-905945-08-5) IOP Pub.

Chapman, J. R. Practical Organic Mass Spectrometry: A Guide for Chemical & Biochemical Analysis. LC 93-9129. 352p. 1995. pap. 74.95 (0-471-95831-X) Wiley.

Chapman, Jack. Negotiating Your Salary: How to Make $1000 a Minute. LC 96-225201. Orig. Title: How to Make 1000 Dollars a Minute Negotiating Your Salaries & Raises. 130p. (Orig.). 1996. pap. 11.95 (0-89815-890-7) Ten Speed Pr.

Chapman, Jake. Dinos & Jake Chapman: Unholy Libel. Dent-Brocklehurst, Mollie, ed. (Illus.). 153p. (YA). 1997. pap. 50.00 (1-880154-14-5) Gagosian Gallery.

***Chapman, James.** Daughter! I Forbid Your Recurring Dream! LC 99-96866. 217p. 2000. pap. 8.00 (1-879193-07-8) Fugue State.

Chapman, James. Glass: Pray the Electrons Back to Sand. LC 93-73510. 244p. (Orig.). 1994. pap. 9.50 (1-879193-02-7) Fugue State.

— In Candyland It's Cool to Feed on Your Friends. LC 96-83214. (Illus.). 190p. (Orig.). (C). 1997. pap. text 8.00 (1-879193-05-1) Fugue State.

***Chapman, James.** License to Thrill: A Cultural History of the James Bond Films. LC 99-50011. 2000. 27.95 (0-231-12048-6) Col U Pr.

Chapman, James. Our Plague: A Film from New York. LC 92-73394. 302p. (Orig.). (C). 1993. pap. 10.00 (1-879193-00-0) Fugue State.

— The Walls Collide As You Expand, Dwarf Maple. LC 92-75669. 92p. (Orig.). (C). 1993. pap. 6.00 (1-879193-01-9) Fugue State.

Chapman, James V. & Sgalambro, A., eds. Basic Concepts in Doppler Echocardiography. (Developments in Cardiovascular Medicine Ser.). 1987. text 184.00 (0-89838-888-0) Kluwer Academic.

Chapman, James V. & Sutherland, George R., eds. The Noninvasive Evaluation of Hemodynamcis in Congenital Heart Disease: Doppler Ultrasound Applications in the Adult & Pediatric Patient with Congenital Heart Disease. (Developments in Cardiovascular Medicine Ser.). (C). 1990. text 268.50 (0-7923-0836-0) Kluwer Academic.

***Chapman, James W., Jr., et al.** Success in Reading Recovery Depends on the Development of Phonological Processing Skills. (Illus.). 54p. (C). 2000. pap. text 20.00 (0-7567-0000-0) DIANE Pub.

Chapman, Jan. Art of Rhinoceros Horn Carving in China. 1999. 160.00 (0-903432-57-9) CMW Ltd.

Chapman, Jane. Old MacDonald Had a Farm: Level Two, Yellow. LC 98-88076. (Reading Together Ser.). (J). 1999. pap. write for info. (0-7636-0854-8) Candlewick Pr.

Chapman, Jane R., ed. Economic Independence for Women: The Foundation for Equal Rights. LC 75-11129. (Sage Yearbooks in Women's Policy Studies: No. 1). (Illus.). 285p. reprint ed. pap. 88.40 (0-8357-8483-5, 203475000091) Bks Demand.

Chapman, Jane R. & Gates, Margaret, eds. The Victimization of Women. LC 77-93701. (Sage Yearbooks in Women's Policy Studies: No. 3). 282p. 1978. reprint ed. pap. 87.50 (0-608-01516-4, 205956000002) Bks Demand.

***Chapman, Janice.** Hello Out There...! 64p. 1999. pap. 9.95 (1-56315-200-2) SterlingHse.

Chapman, Jean. The Red Pavilion. large type ed. (Magna Large Print Ser.). 540p. 1996. 27.99 (0-7505-0876-0, Pub. by Mgna Lrg Print) Ulverscroft.

— Savage Legacy. large type ed. 512p. 1988. 27.99 (0-7089-1893-X) Ulverscroft.

— The Soldier's Girl. large type ed. (Magna Large Print Ser.). 480p. 1998. 29.99 (0-7505-1189-3, Pub. by Mgna Lrg Print) Ulverscroft.

— The Someday Dog. LC 72-353257. 66p. 1968. write for info. (0-207-94963-8, Pub. by Angus & Roberts) HarpC.

— The Unreasoning Earth. large type ed. 384p. 1986. 27.99 (0-7089-1553-1) Ulverscroft.

— A World Apart. large type ed. (Dales Large Print Ser.). 1995. pap. 18.99 (1-85389-518-0, Dales) Ulverscroft.

Chapman, Jean, ed. see McDonald, Lucile.

Chapman, Jean, ed. see Mossinger, Rosemarie.

Chapman, Jean, ed. see Richards, Bradley W.

Chapman, Jeanne, ed. see Traubel, Horace.

Chapman, Jefferson. Tellico Archaeology: 12,000 Years of Native American History. rev. ed. LC 94-18737. (Illus.). 164p. (C). 1995. pap. text 16.95 (0-87049-871-1) U of Tenn Pr.

Chapman, Jeffery H., et al, eds. Contemporary Authors New Revision Series & Contemporary Authors Cumulative Index: A Bio-Bibliographical Guide to Current Writers in Fiction, General Non-Fiction, Poetry, Journalism, Drama, Motion Pictures, Television, & Other Fields. (Contemporary Authors Ser.: Vol. 51). 500p. 1996. text 150.00 (0-8103-9343-3) Gale.

Chapman, Jeffery H. & Dear, Pamela S., eds. Contemporary Authors New Revision Series: A Bio-Bibliographical Guide to Current Writers in Fiction, General Non-Fiction, Poetry, Journalism, Drama, Motion Pictures, Television, & Other Fields, Vol. 52. 500p. 1996. text 150.00 (0-7876-0123-3) Gale.

Chapman, Jeffery H. & Jorgenson, John D., eds. Contemporary Authors New Revision Series: A Bio-Bibliographical Guide to Current Writers in Fiction, General Non-Fiction, Poetry, Journalism, Drama, Motion Pictures, Television, & Other Fields, Vol. 58. 500p. 1997. text 150.00 (0-7876-1199-9, 00156316) Gale.

Chapman, Jeffery H. & Jorgenson, John D., eds. Contemporary Authors New Revision Series & Contemporary Authors Cumulative Index: A Bio-Bibliographical Guide to Current Writers in Fiction, General Non-Fiction, Poetry, Journalism, Drama, Motion Pictures, Television, & Other Fields, Vol. 57. (Contemporary Authors Ser.). 450p. 1997. 129.00 (0-7876-1198-0) Gale.

— Contemporary Authors New Revision Series & Contemporary Authors Cumulative Index: A Bio-Bibliographical Guide to Current Writers in Fiction, General Non-Fiction, Poetry, Journalism, Drama, Motion Pictures, Television, & Other Fields, Vol. 59. (Contemporary Authors Ser.). 450p. 1997. 129.00 (0-7876-1201-4) Gale.

Chapman, Jeffrey I., ed. Long-Term Financial Planning: Creative Strategies for Local Government. LC 87-2613. (Practical Management Ser.). 188p. (Orig.). 1987. pap. 23.95 (0-87326-076-7) Intl City-Cnty Mgt.

Chapman, Jennifer. Politics, Feminism & the Reformation of Gender. LC 92-9372. 368p. (C). (gr. 13). 1992. 110.00 (0-415-01698-3, A7694) Routledge.

Chapman, Jenny. Interviewing & Counselling. Macfarlane, Julie, ed. (Legal Skills Ser.). 143p. 1994. pap. 22.00 (1-874241-44-9, Pub. by Cavendish Pubng) Gaunt.

Chapman, Jeremy, jt. auth. see Allen, Richard D.

Chapman, Jeremy R., et al, eds. Organ & Tissue Donation for Transplantation. LC 97-25104. (An Arnold Publication). (Illus.). 488p. 1997. text 115.00 (0-340-61394-7) OUP.

Chapman, Jerome, jt. auth. see Blodgett, Terrell.

Chapman, Jessica, et al, eds. The Future Utilization of Schmidt Telescopes. (ASP Conference Series Proceedings: Vol. 84). 592p. 1995. 34.00 (1-886733-05-8) Astron Soc Pacific.

Chapman, Jim, jt. auth. see Butrum, Ray.

Chapman, John. The Brides of March. 1963. pap. 5.25 (0-8222-0154-2) Dramatists Play.

— Camp on the Yukon: American Autobiography. 214p. 1995. lib. bdg. 79.00 (0-7812-8477-5) Rprt Serv.

***Chapman, John.** Fragmentation in Archaeology. LC 99-38919. 288p. 2000. write for info. (0-415-15803-6) Routledge.

— Looks Good to Me. Breithoff, Connie, ed. 180p. 1999. pap. 23.95 (0-9675838-0-2) Chappys Inc.

Chapman, John. St. Benedict & the Sixth Century. LC 79-109719. 239p. 1971. reprint ed. lib. bdg. 59.50 (0-8371-4209-1, CHSB, Greenwood Pr) Greenwood.

— Tell It to Sweeney: The Informal History of the New York Daily News. LC 77-8991. (Illus.). 288p. 1977. reprint ed. lib. bdg. 65.00 (0-8371-9724-4, CHTS, Greenwood Pr) Greenwood.

— Welcome to English, Nos. 1-3. (gr. 3-6). 1978. teacher ed. 7.50 (0-88345-355-X) Prentice ESL.

— Welcome to English: Let's Begin. (Welcome to English Ser.). (Illus.). 48p. (J). (gr. 1 up). 1980. teacher ed. 4.50 (0-88345-423-8, 18493); pap. 3.25 (0-88345-422-X, 18480) Prentice ESL.

— Welcome to English: Let's Begin, Nos. 4-5. (Welcome to English Ser.). (Illus.). 48p. (J). (gr. 1 up). 1980. teacher ed. 7.50 (0-88345-368-1, 18499) Prentice ESL.

Chapman, John, ed. Burns Mantle Best Plays of Nineteen Forty-Nine to Nineteen Fifty. LC 75-19860. (Best Plays Series). 1978. 30.95 (0-405-09177-X) Ayer.

Chapman, John & Chapman, Monica. Lonely Planet Bushwalking in Australia: Walking Guide. 3rd ed. (Illus.). 360p. (Orig.). 1997. pap. 17.95 (0-86442-391-8) Lonely Planet.

— Lonely Planet Tasmania. (Illus.). 304p. 1996. pap. 14.95 (0-86442-384-5) Lonely Planet.

Chapman, John, et al. The Changing Face of Dalmatia: Archaeological & Ecological Studies in a Mediterranean Landscape. LC 95-51207. (Reports of the Research Committee of the Society of Antiquaries of London: No. 54). (Illus.). 288p. (C). 1996. 170.00 (0-7185-0048-2) Bks Intl VA.

Chapman, John, jt. auth. see Cooney, Ray.

Chapman, John, ed. see Claire, Elizabeth & Haynes, Judith L.

Chapman, John, jt. ed. see Dolukhanov, Pavel.

Chapman, John A. History of Edgefield County, South Carolina: From the Earliest Settlements to 1897. 532p. 1997. reprint ed. pap. 40.00 (0-8063-4696-5) Clearfield Co.

Chapman, John A. Papers on Shelley, Wordsworth & Others. LC 67-23191. (Essay Index Reprint Ser.). 1977. 29.95 (0-8369-0288-2) Ayer.

Chapman, John A. & O'Neall, John B. The Annals of Newberry (South Carolina) (Illus.). 823p. 1995. reprint ed. pap. 55.00 (0-8063-7992-8, 4330) Clearfield Co.

Chapman, John A., jt. auth. see O'Neall, John B.

Chapman, John B. Horace & His Poetry. LC 70-120975. (Poetry & Life Ser.). reprint ed. 16.00 (0-404-52505-9) AMS Pr.

Chapman, John D., et al, eds. Oxford Regional Economic Atlases: The United States & Canada. 2nd ed. (Illus.). 176p. 1975. pap. text 25.00 (0-19-894308-3) OUP.

Chapman, John F., jt. ed. see Bursk, Edward C.

Chapman, John H. Facing Death: Stories of Spiritual Response to Serious Illness. LC 97-77690. 112p. 1998. pap. 8.95 (0-87946-177-2, 270) ACTA Pubns.

Chapman, John J. The Collected Works of John Jay Chapman, 12 vols. Bernstein, Melvin H., ed. (Illus.). 4350p. 1970. 295.00 (0-87730-003-8) M & S Pr.

— Emerson & Other Essays. LC 75-108126. 1970. reprint ed. 36.50 (0-404-00619-1) AMS Pr.

— Glance Toward Shakespeare. LC 70-109643. (Select Bibliographies Reprint Ser.). 1977. 17.95 (0-8369-5252-9) Ayer.

— Greek Genius, & Other Essays. LC 67-23192. (Essay Index Reprint Ser.). 1977. 18.95 (0-8369-0289-0) Ayer.

— Learning & Other Essays. LC 68-16918. (Essay Index Reprint Ser.). 1977. 19.95 (0-8369-0290-4) Ayer.

— Letters & Religion. 1988. reprint ed. lib. bdg. 59.00 (0-7812-0052-0) Rprt Serv.

— Letters & Religion. 1977. reprint ed. 45.00 (0-403-07361-8) Scholarly.

— Memories & Milestones. LC 70-152161. (Essay Index Reprint Ser.). 1977. 20.95 (0-8369-2183-6) Ayer.

— William Lloyd Garrison. (American Newspapermen 1790-1933 Ser.). 1974. reprint ed. text 29.95 (0-8464-0027-8) Beekman Pubs.

Chapman, John Jay. Unbought Spirit: A John Jay Chapman Reader. LC 98-8929. 176p. 1998. text 39.95 (0-252-02417-6) U of Ill Pr.

— Unbought Spirit: A John Jay Chapman Reader. LC 98-8929. (Illus.). 176p. 1998. text 17.95 (0-252-06724-X) U of Ill Pr.

Chapman, John M. & Shay, Robert P., eds. The Consumer Finance Industry: Its Costs & Regulations. LC 67-21693. (Illus.). 203p. reprint ed. pap. 63.00 (0-608-30022-5, 201532300093) Bks Demand.

Chapman, John M. & Westerfield, Ray B. Branch Banking: Its Historical & Theoretical Position in America & Abroad. Bruchey, Stuart, ed. LC 80-1140. (Rise of Commercial Banking Ser.). 1981. reprint ed. lib. bdg. 42.95 (0-405-13640-4) Ayer.

Chapman, John M., et al. Commercial Banks & Consumer Installment Credit. (Financial Research Program II: Studies in Consumer Installment Financing: No. 3). 342p. 1940. reprint ed. 89.00 (0-87014-462-6) Natl Bur Econ Res.

***Chapman, John R., ed.** Mass Spectrometry of Proteins & Peptides. LC 99-41621. (Methods in Molecular Biology Ser.: Vol. 146). 539p. 2000. 125.00 (0-89603-609-X) Humana.

Chapman, John R., ed. Protein & Peptide Analysis by Mass Spectrometry. (Methods in Molecular Biology Ser.: Vol. 61). 360p. 1996. 79.50 (0-89603-345-7) Humana.

Chapman, John S. Byron & the Honourable Augusta Leigh. LC 74-29714. 306p. reprint ed. pap. 94.90 (0-608-14187-9, 202198700024) Bks Demand.

Chapman, John W. Rousseau: Totalitarian or Liberal? LC 68-54260. (Columbia University. Studies in the Social Sciences: No. 589). reprint ed. 20.00 (0-404-51589-4) AMS Pr.

— Ten'a Texts & Tales from Anvik, Alaska . . . with Vocabulary by Pliny Earle Goddard. LC 73-3541. (American Ethnological Society Publications: No. 6). reprint ed. 37.50 (0-404-58156-0) AMS Pr.

Chapman, John W., ed. Compensatory Justice. (Nomos Ser.: Vol. 33). 352p. (C). 1991. text 45.00 (0-8147-1453-6) NYU Pr.

— The Western University on Trial. LC 82-20120. 256p. (C). 1983. 45.00 (0-520-04940-3, Pub. by U CA Pr) Cal Prin Full Svc.

Chapman, John W. & Galston, William A., eds. Virtue: Nomos XXXIV. LC 92-17749. (American Society of Legal & Political Philosophy Ser.: Vol. 34). 416p. (C). 1992. text 45.00 (0-8147-1484-6) NYU Pr.

— Virtue: Nomos XXXIV. LC 92-17749. (American Society of Legal & Political Philosophy Ser.: Vol. 34). 416p. (C). 1993. pap. text 17.50 (0-8147-1499-4) NYU Pr.

Chapman, John W. & Pennock, J. Roland, eds. Markets & Justice. (Nomos Ser.: Vol. 31). 384p. (C). 1989. text 45.00 (0-8147-1421-8) NYU Pr.

Chapman, John W. & Shapiro, Ian, eds. Democratic Community: Nomos XXXV. LC 92-40158. (Nomos Ser.: Vol. 35). 451p. (C). 1993. text 45.00 (0-8147-1497-8) NYU Pr.

— Democratic Community: Nomos XXXV. 451p. (C). 1995. pap. text 17.50 (0-8147-1507-9) NYU Pr.

Chapman, John W. & Wertheimer, Alan, eds. Majorities & Minorities. (Nomos Ser.: Vol. 32). (C). 1990. text 45.00 (0-8147-1433-1) NYU Pr.

Chapman, John W., jt. ed. see Pennock, J. Roland.

Chapman, Johnathan & Rowbottom, Frederick. Relative Category Theory & Geometric Morphisms: A Logical Approach. (Oxford Logic Guides Ser.: No. 16). (Illus.). 280p. 1992. 79.00 (0-19-853434-5) OUP.

Chapman, Joseph A. & Feldhamer, George A., eds. Wild Mammals of North America: Biology, Management, & Economics. LC 81-8209. 1184p. 1982. text 110.00 (0-8018-2353-6) Johns Hopkins.

Chapman, Joseph A. & Flux, John E., eds. Rabbits, Hares & Pikas: Status Survey & Conservation Plan. (Illus.). 168p. (Orig.). 1991. pap. 27.00 (2-8317-0019-1, Pub. by IUCN) Island Pr.

Chapman, Joyce. If I Had 3 Wishes the Only One Would Be...the Workbook. Misiroglu, Gina, ed. 224p. (Orig.). 1995. pap., wbk. ed. 12.95 (0-87877-225-1, 1-800-932-4809) Newcastle Pub.

— If I Had 3 Wishes, the Only One Would Be...Your Personalized Plan for Discovering Your Goals. Misiroglu, Gina, ed. 208p. (Orig.). 1995. pap. 14.95 (0-87877-199-9, 1-800-932-4809) Newcastle Pub.

Chapman, Joyce. Journaling for Joy: Writing Your Way to Personal Growth & Freedom. 1991. pap. 14.95 (0-87877-163-8) Newcastle Pub.

Chapman, Joyce. Journaling for Joy - The Workbook: Writing Your Way to Personal Growth & Freedom. 1995. pap. 12.95 (0-87877-226-X) Newcastle Pub.

— Live Your Dream: Discover & Achieve Your Life Purpose. 190p. 1990. pap. 14.95 (0-87877-149-2) Newcastle Pub.

— Live Your Dream Workbook: Discover & Live the Life of Your Dreams. 224p. 1994. pap. 12.95 (0-87877-195-6) Newcastle Pub.

Chapman, Joyce, ed. see Lebra, Joyce C.

Chapman, Judith, jt. ed. see Evers, Colin.

Chapman, Judith D., ed. Improving the Quality of Australian Schools. (C). 1990. 85.00 (0-86431-086-2, Pub. by Aust Council Educ Res) St Mut.

Chapman, Judith D. & Dunstan, Jeffrey. Democracy & Bureaucracy: Tensions in the Provision of Public Education. 240p. 1990. 89.95 (1-85000-790-X, Falmer Pr); pap. 39.95 (1-85000-791-8, Falmer Pr) Taylor & Francis.

Chapman, Judith G., jt. ed. see Ferrari, Joseph R.

Chapman, K. Military Air Transport Operations. (Air Power: Aircraft, Weapons Systems & Technology Ser.: No. 6). (Illus.). 226p. 1989. 40.00 (0-08-034749-5, Pub. by Brasseys); 25.00 (0-08-036255-9, Pub. by Brasseys) Brasseys.

Chapman, K. R. Northeastern Accelerator Personnel: Proceedings of the 21st Symposium. 484p. (C). 1988. text 108.00 (9971-5-0525-8) World Scientific Pub.

Chapman, Karla J. AZ Gecko's Arizona Adventure. LC 96-166625. (Illus.). 12p. (J). (ps-3). 1995. 13.95 (0-9648791-0-7) Chapco Pubng.

— AZ Gecko's Monsoon Adventure. (Illus.). 12p. (J). (ps-3). 1996. lib. bdg. 13.95 (0-9648791-1-5) Chapco Pubng.

Chapman, Kate & Stewart, Dorothy. Adobe Notes. (Illus.). 44p. 1977. pap. 4.50 (0-941270-10-6) Ancient City Pr.

Chapman, Ken. Chance Givers & Risk Takers: A People-Sense Guide to Leadership. (Illus.). 135p. 1994. pap. 10.00 (0-9642714-1-9) K Chapman.

— Chance Givers & Risk Takers: A People-Sense Guide to Leadership. 2nd ed. 136p. 1996. pap. 10.00 (0-614-13065-4) K Chapman.

Chapman, Kennet. Rules of Green. 1996. 50.00 (1-57243-201-2) Triumph Bks.

Chapman, Kenneth C. Tarjei Vesaas. LC 78-110715. (Twayne's World Authors Ser.). 1970. lib. bdg. 20.95 (0-8057-2948-8) Irvington.

Chapman, Kenneth G. Rules of the Green: A History of the Rules of Golf. (Illus.). 240p. 1997. reprint ed. 34.95 (1-57243-173-3) Triumph Bks.

Chapman, Kenneth G., tr. see Thordarson, Thorbergur.

Chapman, Kenneth M. Pueblo Pottery Designs. LC 94-41764. (Pictorial Archive Ser.). 208p. 1995. 9.95 (0-486-28476-X) Dover.

***Chapman, Kim A., et al.** Valley of Grass: Tallgrass Prairie & Parkland of the Red River Valley. LC 98-19433. (Illus.). 129p. 1998. pap. 14.95 (0-87839-127-4) North Star.

Chapman, Kim W. The Magic Hat. 2nd ed. LC 76-20842. (Illus.). 46p. (J). (gr. k up). 1976. 5.00 (0-914996-10-X) Lollipop Power.

C

An Asterisk (*) at the beginning of an entry indicates that the title is appearing for the first time.

Chapman, Kirsten, jt. auth. see Sirak, Babette.
Chapman, Kirsten, ed. see Burton, Sarah K.
Chapman, Kymn. Prayer Bubbles. 140p. (Orig.). 1997. pap. 10.00 (*0-9660043-0-2*) K Chapman Ent.
Chapman, L., jt. auth. see Warren, W.
Chapman, Laura H. Adventures in Art, Bk. 1. (Discover Art Ser.). (J). (gr. 1-6). 1998. text 26.00 (*0-87192-251-7*); teacher ed., spiral bd. 45.00 (*0-87192-323-8*) Davis Mass.
— Adventures in Art, Bk. 2. (Discover Art Ser.). (J). (gr. 1-6). 1998. text 26.00 (*0-87192-252-5*); teacher ed., spiral bd. 45.00 (*0-87192-324-6*) Davis Mass.
— Adventures in Art, Bk. 3. (Discover Art Ser.). (J). (gr. 1-6). 1998. text 26.00 (*0-87192-253-3*); spiral bd. 45.00 (*0-87192-325-4*) Davis Mass.
— Adventures in Art, Bk. 4. (Discover Art Ser.). (J). (gr. 1-6). 1998. text 26.00 (*0-87192-254-1*); teacher ed., spiral bd. 45.00 (*0-87192-326-2*) Davis Mass.
— Adventures in Art, Bk. 5. (Discover Art Ser.). (J). (gr. 1-6). 1998. text 26.00 (*0-87192-255-X*); spiral bd. 45.00 (*0-87192-327-0*) Davis Mass.
— Adventures in Art, Bk. 6. (Discover Art Ser.). (J). (gr. 1-6). 1998. text 26.00 (*0-87192-256-8*); teacher ed., spiral bd. 45.00 (*0-87192-328-9*) Davis Mass.
— Art: Images & Ideas. (Discover Art Ser.). 1992. text, teacher ed. 56.00 (*0-87192-271-1*) Davis Mass.
— Art: Images & Ideas. (Discover Art Ser.). (Illus.). (YA). (gr. 8 up). 1992. text 39.00 (*0-87192-231-2*) Davis Mass.
— Instant Art, Instant Culture: The Unspoken Policy for American Schools. 204p. (C). 1982. text 16.95 (*0-8077-2722-9*) Tchrs Coll.
— Patricia Renick: Triceracopter. Meyer, Ruth K., ed. (Illus.). pap. 6.50 (*0-917562-06-2*) Contemp Arts.
— Teaching Art, Complete Kit 1-3. (J). (gr. 1-3). 1989. 140.90 (*0-87192-200-2*) Davis Mass.
— Teaching Art, Complete Kit 4-6. (J). (gr. 4-6). 1989. 140.90 (*0-87192-199-5*) Davis Mass.
— A World of Images. (Illus.). (YA). (gr. 7 up). 1992. text 39.00 (*0-87192-230-4*) Davis Mass.
— A World of Images. (Illus.). 1994. text, teacher ed. 56.00 (*0-87192-270-3*) Davis Mass.
Chapman, Lee, jt. auth. see Elya, Susan Middleton.
Chapman, Leigh. Church Memorial Brasses & Brass Rubbing. (Album Ser.: No. 206). (Illus.). 32p. (C). 1989. pap. 6.25 (*0-85263-905-8*, Pub. by Shire Pubns) Parkwest Pubns.
Chapman, Linda L. AvatarA. LC 98-98507. 325p. 1998. 25.00 (*0-7388-0095-3*); pap. 15.00 (*0-7388-0096-1*) Xlibris Corp.
Chapman, Lisbeth W. Get Media Smart! Build Your Reputation, Referrals & Revenues with Media Marketing. 60p. 1997. pap. write for info. incl. audio, VHS (*0-9658693-0-X*) Ink & Air.
— Get Media Smart! Create News Coverage That Builds Business. 60p. 1997. pap. write for info. (*0-9658693-1-8*) Ink & Air.
***Chapman, Lisbeth W., et al.** How to Market Financial Advisory Services, Vol. 1. 1999. ring bd. 99.00 (*0-7646-0753-7*) Prctnrs Pub Co.
Chapman, Lolin K. The Growth of British Education & Its Records. 76p. pap. 12.95 (*1-873686-01-3*) Lochin.
Chapman, Loren J., et al, eds. Progress in Experimental Personality & Psychopathology Research, Vol. 16. 304p. 1992. 49.95 (*0-8261-6091-3*) Springer Pub.
Chapman, Loring F. Pain & Suffering, 4 vols., Vols. 4, 4a, 4b & 4c. (Courtroom Medicine Ser.). 1967. ring bd. 830.00 (*0-8205-1242-7*) Bender.
Chapman, Loring F. & Dunlap, Edward A. Eye, 2 vols., Vols. 14 & 14A. (Courtroom Medicine Ser.). 1981. ring bd. 435.00 (*0-8205-1214-1*) Bender.
Chapman, Loring F. & Evans, John W. Head & Brain: Volumes 8, 8a & 8b, 3 vols., Set. (Courtroom Medicine Ser.). 1972. ring bd. 710.00 (*0-8205-1251-6*) Bender.
Chapman, Louise, et al. The Traveler's Psalm: A 40-Day Spiritual Journey. 96p. 1993. pap. 6.99 (*0-8341-1513-1*) Beacon Hill.
Chapman, Luisa W. The United American Healthcare Corporation Collection. LC 93-61338. (Illus.). 84p. 1994. pap. 24.95 (*0-8143-2532-7*) Wayne St U Pr.
Chapman, Lyn'elle. Through the Years I Have Seen . . . The Collected Works of Lyn'elle Patrice Chapman. 115p. 1998. pap. 12.00 (*0-9664237-0-4*) L Cheatum.
Chapman, Lynne F. Cathedrals. LC 98-20957. (Designing the Future Ser.). (Illus.). 32p. (J). (gr. 4 up). 1999. lib. bdg. 21.30 (*0-88682-505-9*, Creat Educ) Creative Co.
— Egyptian Pyramids. LC 98-30295. (Designing the Future Ser.). (Illus.). 40p. (YA). (gr. 4 up). 1999. lib. bdg. 21.30 (*0-88682-717-5*, Creat Educ) Creative Co.
— Jane Austen. (Illus.). 56p. (YA). (gr. 6 up). 1999. lib. bdg. 16.95 (*0-88682-740-X*, Creat Educ) Creative Co.
***Chapman, Lynne F.** Leo Tolstoy. LC 93-10629. (Notebooks Ser.). (J). 1999. spiral bd. 23.95 (*1-56846-156-9*, Creative Eds) Creative Co.
Chapman, M., jt. auth. see Rees, K.
Chapman, M., jt. auth. see Wickendon, Tony.
Chapman, M. G., et al, eds. The Embryo: Normal & Abnormal Development & Growth. (Illus.). 280p. 1991. 124.00 (*0-387-19630-7*) Spr-Verlag.
Chapman, M. G., jt. auth. see Underwood, A. J.
Chapman, M. G., jt. ed. see Underwood, A. J.
Chapman, M. J. Commercial & Consumer Arbitration: Statutes & Rules. 783p. 1997. 120.00 (*1-85431-587-0*, Pub. by Blackstone Pr) Gaunt.
Chapman, Mabel H. At Great Price: The Story of Tamsen Donner. 156p. (Orig.). 1992. pap. 5.95 (*0-9634580-0-0*) M Chapman Pub.
Chapman, Malcolm, ed. Social & Biological Aspects of Ethnicity. LC 93-22091. (Biosocial Society Ser.: No. 4). (Illus.). 144p. 1993. text 45.00 (*0-19-852280-0*) OUP.
Chapman, Malcolm K. The Gaelic Vision in Scottish Culture. LC 79-303360. 264p. reprint ed. pap. 81.90 (*0-7837-1035-6*, 204134600020) Bks Demand.
Chapman, Margaret. McCall's Creates: A Country Home. LC 97-33084. 1998. write for info. (*1-56799-621-3*, Friedman-Fairfax) M Friedman Pub Grp Inc.
***Chapman, Margaret.** Symphony for a Surgeon. large type ed. 288p. 2000. pap. 20.99 (*1-85389-978-X*, Dales) Ulverscroft.
Chapman, Margaret L., et al. Mitsubishi Motors in Illinois: Global Strategies, Local Impacts. LC 94-46195. 152p. 1995. 57.95 (*0-89930-972-0*, Quorum Bks) Greenwood.
Chapman, Maria W., compiled by. Songs of the Free. LC 71-170693. (Black Heritage Library Collection). 1977. reprint ed. 20.95 (*0-8369-8883-3*) Ayer.
Chapman, Mary & Hendler, Glenn. Sentimental Men: Masculinity & the Politics of Affect in American Culture. LC 99-21585. 304p. 1999. pap. 19.95 (*0-520-21622-9*, Pub. by U CA Pr) Cal Prin Full Svc.
Chapman, Mary & Hendler, Glenn, eds. Sentimental Men: Masculinity & the Politics of Affect in American Culture. LC 99-21585. 304p. 1999. 50.00 (*0-520-21621-0*, Pub. by U CA Pr) Cal Prin Full Svc.
Chapman, Mary, ed. see Brown, Charles Brockden.
***Chapman, Matthew.** The Fast Tract & Personal Injury Claims. 80p. 1999. 30.00 (*1-85811-226-5*, Pub. by CLT Prof) Gaunt.
***Chapman, Merrill R.** The Aegis Product Positioning Workbook. (Illus.). 50p. 1999. pap., wbk. ed. 24.95 (*0-9672008-1-4*) Aegis Resources.
— The Product Marketing Handbook for Software. 3rd ed. Ostrow, Gail, ed. (Illus.). 424p. 1999. pap. 59.95 (*0-9672008-0-6*) Aegis Resources.
Chapman, Michael. I Remember, I Remember, Chaplin in Brick Lane LC 96-218315. 164p. 1996. pap. write for info. (*1-85756-272-0*, Pub. by Janus Pubng) Paul & Co Pubs.
Chapman, Michael. Southern African Literatures. (Literature in English Ser.). 560p. (C). 1996. pap. text 36.56 (*0-582-05307-2*, Pub. by Addison-Wesley) Longman.
Chapman, Michael, ed. The Drum Decade. 256p. 1990. pap. 27.00 (*0-86980-694-7*, Pub. by Univ Natal Pr) Intl Spec Bk.
Chapman, Michael, jt. auth. see Campbell, Alexander.
Chapman, Michael, ed. see Pringle, Thomas.
Chapman, Michael J., et al. Signal Processing in Electronic Communications: For Engineers & Mathematicians. 300p. 1997. pap. 35.00 (*1-898563-30-6*, Pub. by Horwood Pub) Paul & Co Pubs.
Chapman, Michael W. & Madison, Michael, eds. Operative Orthopaedics, 4 vols., 1. 2nd ed. LC 92-49608. 1993. 395.00 (*0-397-51304-6*) Lppncott W & W.
— Operative Orthopaedics, 4 vols., 2. 2nd ed. LC 92-49608. 1993. write for info. (*0-397-51305-4*) Lppncott W & W.
— Operative Orthopaedics, 4 vols., 3. 2nd ed. LC 92-49608. 1993. write for info. (*0-397-51306-2*) Lppncott W & W.
— Operative Orthopaedics, 4 vols., 4. 2nd ed. LC 92-49608. 1993. write for info. (*0-397-51307-0*) Lppncott W & W.
— Operative Orthopaedics, 4 vols., Set. 2nd ed. LC 92-49608. 3,876p. 1993. text 399.00 (*0-397-51075-6*) Lppncott W & W.
Chapman, Michael W., et al. Chapman's Orthopaedic Surgery. 3rd ed. text 425.00 (*0-7817-1487-7*) Lppncott W & W.
Chapman, Mike. Encyclopedia of American Wrestling. LC 89-2701. (Illus.). 541p. 1990. reprint ed. pap. 167.80 (*0-608-07080-7*, 206730900009) Bks Demand.
— Fighting Back: The Inspirational Story of Bob Steenlage. (Illus.). 110p. (Orig.). 1993. pap. 9.95 (*0-9637064-0-3*) Fighting Back.
***Chapman, Mike.** Gotch: An American Hero. 279p. 1999. pap. 19.95 (*0-9676080-0-7*) Culture House.
Chapman, Mike. Introduction to Housing: Practice & Policy. text 84.00 (*0-471-98523-6*); pap. text 34.00 (*0-471-98524-4*) Wiley.
Chapman, Mike, jt. auth. see Zebas, Carole J.
Chapman, Mim, et al. Recorder Teaching: A Classroom Approach: A Practical Step-by-Step Guide. (Recorder & Flute "Let's Sing & Play" Ser.). (Illus.). 178p. 1987. lib. bdg. 23.95 (*0-913500-25-9*, L-6TE) Peg Hoenack MusicWorks.
Chapman, Monica, jt. auth. see Chapman, John.
Chapman, Morris. Wedding Collection: Twenty-Six Basic Wedding Ceremonies for Pastors. 1991. 22.99 (*0-8054-2004-5*, 4220-04) Broadman.
Chapman, Muncy, jt. auth. see Chapman, Herb.
Chapman, Myriam, tr. Double Vision: Artists Face to Face. LC 95-49895. (Illus.). (J). 1996. 12.95 (*0-8120-6584-0*) Barron.
Chapman, N. F. & Grandjean, Christian. The Construction Industry & the European Community. (Illus.). 296p. 1991. pap. 54.95 (*0-632-03121-2*) Blackwell Sci.
***Chapman, Nancy Kapp.** Doggie Dreams. LC 99-27373. (Illus.). 32p. (J). 2000. 15.99 (*0-399-23443-8*, G P Putnam) Peng Put Young Read.
***Chapman, Neil.** Santa Clara Portraits: A Proud Tradition. Chapman, Dawna & Sharp, Tamara, eds. (Illus.). 120p. 1999. 58.00 (*0-9673850-0-8*) Avanyu Passage.
Chapman, Neil A., et al. The Geological Disposal of Nuclear Waste. LC 86-15970. 292p. 1987. 315.00 (*0-471-91249-2*) Wiley.
Chapman, Neil A., jt. ed. see Come, B.
***Chapman, Nigel.** Digital Multimedia. 400p. 2000. pap. text 49.99 (*0-471-98386-1*) Wiley.
Chapman, Nigel. The Late Night Guide to C++ LC 96-28089. 376p. 1996. pap. 59.99 (*0-471-95071-8*) Wiley.
— Perl: The Programmer's Companion. 292p. 1997. pap. 44.95 (*0-471-97563-X*) Wiley.
Chapman, Norma. Deer. (Illus.). text 19.95 (*0-905483-88-X*, Pub. by Whittet Bks) Diamond Farm Bk.
Chapman, Norman B. Advances in Linear Free Energy Relationships. Shorter, J., ed. LC 78-161305. 498p. reprint ed. pap. 154.40 (*0-608-05489-5*, 206595800006) Bks Demand.
— Automotive Electricity & Electronics. LC 99-14936. (Automotive Technology Ser.). 564p. 1999. mass mkt. 47.95 (*0-8273-8479-3*) Delmar.
***Chapman, O. J. V.** RR-Prodigal, a Model for Estimating the Probabilities of Defects in Reactor Pressure Vessel Welds. 149p. 1998. per. 13.00 (*0-16-062965-9*) USGPO.
Chapman, Odie V. They Rest Quietly: Cemetery Records of Tucker County, West Virginia. 2nd rev. ed. LC 85-152021. 192p. 1985. pap. 39.95 (*0-87012-592-3*) McClain.

Chapman, Odie Velta Nestor. They Rest Quietly: Cemetery Records of Barbour County, West Virginia. 300p. 1999. pap. 39.95 (*0-87012-599-0*) McClain. Ceetery records of Barbour County up to 1995 182 cemeteries listed.** ***Publisher Paid Annotation.

— They Rest Quietly: Cemetery Records of Randolph County. 556p. 1996. 85.00 (*0-87012-559-1*) McClain.
Chapman, Orville L., ed. Organic Photochemistry, Vol. 2. LC 66-11283. 244p. reprint ed. pap. 75.70 (*0-608-09947-3*, 202782500002) Bks Demand.
Chapman, P. 1998 Good Curry. mass mkt. 13.95 (*0-340-68032-6*, Pub. by Hodder & Stought Ltd) Trafalgar.
— Pat Chapman's Balti Bible. text 50.00 (*0-340-72858-2*, Pub. by Hodder & Stought Ltd) Trafalgar.
— Thai Restaurant. pap. text 19.95 (*0-340-68036-9*, Pub. by Hodder & Stought Ltd) Trafalgar.
Chapman, P. H. Concepts in Pediatric Neurosurgery. (Concepts in Pediatric Neurosurgery Ser.: Vol. 6). (Illus.). xii, 244p. 1985. 151.50 (*3-8055-4136-8*) S Karger.
Chapman, P. T. History of Johnson County Illinois. (Illus.). 502p. 1997. reprint ed. lib. bdg. 52.50 (*0-8328-7079-X*) Higginson Bk Co.
Chapman, Pat. Balti Curry Cookbook. 1998. pap. text 7.95 (*0-7499-1669-9*, Pub. by Piatkus Bks) London Brdge.
— The Curry Club Book of Indian Cuisine: The Best 250 Recipes. (Illus.). 288p. 1995. 27.00 (*1-55958-566-8*) Prima Pub.
Chapman, Pat. Curry Club Book of Indian Cuisine: The Best 250 Recipes. 288p. Date not set. pap., per. 15.00 (*0-7615-0649-7*) Prima Pub.
Chapman, Pat. Curry Club Indian Cookbook Kit. 192p. 1997. text 19.95 (*0-7499-1692-3*, Pub. by Piatkus Bks) London Brdge.
— Homestyle Indian Cooking. LC 98-26029. (Homestyle Cooking Ser.). Orig. Title: Favorite Restaurant Curries. (Illus.). 176p. 1998. pap. 16.95 (*0-89594-923-7*) Crossing Pr.
— Homestyle Middle Eastern Cooking. LC 97-11510. (Homestyle Cooking Ser.). (Illus.). 192p. 1997. pap. 16.95 (*0-89594-860-5*) Crossing Pr.
— Meatless Indian Cooking from the Curry Club: Over 150 Delicious Dishes. LC 94-39442. (Illus.). 192p. 1995. pap. 26.95 (*1-55958-690-7*) Prima Pub.
— Quick After-Work Curries. LC 96-23135. (Quick After-Work Ser.). (Illus.). 128p. (Orig.). 1996. reprint ed. pap. 12.95 (*1-55561-108-7*) Fisher Bks.
— Quick & Easy Curries. LC 97-74405. (Illus.). 136p. 1997. pap. 9.95 (*0-563-37119-6*, BBC-Parkwest) Parkwest Pubns.
***Chapman, Pat.** Tandoori Curry Cookbook. (Illus.). 176p. 1998. pap. text 10.95 (*0-7499-1741-5*) London Brdge.
Chapman, Pat. Tandoori Curry Cookbook. 1998. pap. text 7.95 (*0-7499-1742-3*, Pub. by Piatkus Bks) London Brdge.
— Taste of the Raj: A Celebration of Anglo-Indian Cookery. (Illus.). 208p. 1998. text 29.95 (*0-340-68035-0*, Pub. by Hodder & Stought Ltd) Trafalgar.
Chapman, Paul. Trouble on Board: The Plight of International Seafarers. 208p. 1992. text 37.50 (*0-87546-180-8*, ILR Press); pap. text 16.95 (*0-87546-181-6*, ILR Press) Cornell U Pr.
Chapman, Paul, jt. ed. see Buxton, Tony.
Chapman, Paul H. Columbus, the Man. (Illus.). 100p. 1992. 13.95 (*1-880820-04-8*) ISAC Pr.
— Discovering Columbus. 240p. 1992. 19.95 (*1-880820-02-1*) ISAC Pr.
Chapman, Paul W. Smart Sensors. LC 95-36234. 1995. 48.00 (*1-55617-575-2*) ISA.
Chapman, Pauline. Madame Tussaud in England: Career Woman Extraordinary. 1992. 30.00 (*1-870948-79-3*, Pub. by Quiller Pr) St Mut.
Chapman, Peter, ed. see Boyes, G. T.
Chapman, Phil. Electricity. (Young Scientist Ser.). 32p. (J). (gr. 4-8). 1976. pap. 6.95 (*0-86020-078-7*, Usborne); lib. bdg. 14.95 (*0-88110-006-4*, Usborne) EDC.
Chapman, Polly & Lloyd, Siobhan, eds. Women & Access in Rural Areas: What Makes the Difference? What Difference Does It Make? 108p. 1996. text 58.95 (*1-85972-291-1*, Pub. by Avebry) Ashgate Pub Co.
Chapman Publishing Co. Staff, ed. Portrait & Biographical Record of Orange County, NY. (Illus.). 1573p. (Orig.). 1995. pap. text 64.00 (*0-7884-0133-5*) Heritage Bk.
Chapman, R. E. Geology & Water: An Introduction to Fluid Mechanics for Geologists. 1981. text 154.50 (*90-247-2455-4*) Kluwer Academic.
Chapman, R. F. The Insects: Structure & Function. 4th expanded rev. ed. LC 97-35219. (Illus.). 800p. (C). 1998. 130.00 (*0-521-57048-4*); pap. 54.95 (*0-521-57890-6*) Cambridge U Pr.
Chapman, R. F., et al, eds. Perspectives in Chemoreception & Behavior. (Proceedings in Life Sciences Ser.). (Illus.). 125p. 1986. 141.00 (*0-387-96374-X*) Spr-Verlag.
Chapman, R. F. & Joern, Anthony. Biology of Grasshoppers. LC 89-22666. 563p. 1990. 190.00 (*0-471-60901-3*) Wiley.
Chapman, R. L. Lunch Box. (Illus.). 104p. 1997. pap. 10.00 (*0-8059-4168-1*) Dorrance.
Chapman, R. W., et al. Primary Sclerosing Cholangitis. Manns, M. P., ed. 144p. 1998. 108.00 (*0-7923-8745-7*) Kluwer Academic.
Chapman, R. W., ed. see Austen, Jane.
Chapman, R. W., ed. see Boswell, James.
Chapman, R. W., ed. see Courtney, William P. & Smith, David N.
Chapman, R. W., ed. & intro. see Johnson, Samuel.
Chapman, Ralph J. Setting Agendas & Defining Problems: The Wesley Vale Pulp Mill Proposal, Vol. 2. 1992. pap. 53.00 (*0-7300-2018-5*, PTSSSO, Pub. by Deakin Univ) St Mut.
Chapman, Randall G. Brandmaps: The Competitive Marketing Strategy Game. 4th ed. LC 96-27803. 196p. 1996. pap. text 59.00 (*0-13-597451-8*) P-H.
— Brands: A Marketing Game. 2nd ed. LC 95-5515. 112p. (C). 1995. pap. text 49.00 (*0-13-371667-8*) P-H.
Chapman, Randall G. & Jackson, Rex. College Choices of Academically Able Students: The Influence of No-Need Financial Aid & Other Factors. (Research Monographs: No. 10). 118p. (Orig.). 1987. pap. 12.95 (*0-87447-279-2*) College Bd.
Chapman, Randy. Java Reference Package. 40p. 1996. pap. text 7.00 (*0-916151-96-4*) Specialized Sys.
Chapman, Raymond. Forms of Speech in Victorian Fiction: Studies in 18th & 19th Century Literature. LC 93-5699. (C). 1994. text 56.50 (*0-582-08746-5*) Longman.
— The Habit of Prayer. LC 99-24149. 96p. 1999. pap. 7.95 (*0-8192-1813-8*, 6123) Morehouse Pub.
***Chapman, Raymond.** A Pastoral Prayer Book: Occasional Prayers for Times of Change, Concern & Celebration. LC 99-34672. 128p. 2000. 18.95 (*0-8192-1822-7*) Morehouse Pub.
Chapman, Raymond. Stations of the Nativity: Meditations from Advent to Candlemas. (Illus.). 112p. 1999. pap. 7.95 (*0-8192-1804-9*, 6098) Morehouse Pub.
— Stations of the Resurrection: Meditations on the Fourteen Resurrection Appearances. LC 98-49528. 96p. 1999. pap. 7.95 (*0-8192-1788-3*) Morehouse Pub.
Chapman, Richard. The Complete Guitarist: The All-Visual Approach to Learning the Guitar. LC 92-56490. (Illus.). 192p. 1994. pap. 19.95 (*1-56458-711-8*) DK Pub Inc.
***Chapman, Richard.** Guitar. (Illus.). 240p. 2000. write for info. (*0-7894-5963-9*, Pub. by DK Pub Inc) Pub Resources Inc.
Chapman, Richard & Loeser, John D., eds. Issues in Pain Measurement. LC 88-42528. (Advances in Pain Research & Therapy Ser.: Vol. 12). (Illus.). 590p. 1989. reprint ed. pap. 182.90 (*0-608-07187-0*, 206741200009) Bks Demand.
Chapman, Richard A. The Treasury & Public Policy Making. LC 97-7500. 240p. (C). 1995. 75.00 (*0-415-09639-1*) Routledge.
Chapman, Richard A. & Hunt, Michael. Open Government: A Study of the Prospects of Open Government Within the Limitations of the British Political System. LC 87-9176. 194 p. 1987. write for info. (*0-7099-3484-X*) C Helm.
Chapman, Richard M. You & Your Home. 1984. pap. 50.00 (*0-7219-0990-6*, Pub. by Scientific) St Mut.
Chapman, Richard M., jt. auth. see Broaker, Frank.
Chapman, Richard M., jt. auth. see Grissom, Fred E., Jr.
Chapman, Rick, ed. see Baba, Meher.
Chapman, Robert. Practical Methods for Your Year 2000 Problem: The Lowest Cost Solution. LC 97-37378. 236p. 1998. pap. 55.00 incl. cd-rom (*1-884777-52-X*) Manning Pubns.
— Selling the '60s: The Pirates & Pop Music Radio. 256p. 1992. 39.95 (*0-04-445881-9*, A8204) Routledge.
***Chapman, Robert.** Woodturning: A Fresh Approach. (Illus.). 2000. pap. 17.95 (*1-86108-119-7*) Guild Master.
Chapman, Robert & Coxe, Louis O. Billy Budd. (Mermaid Dramabook Ser.). 90p. 1962. pap. 9.00 (*0-8090-1204-9*) Hill & Wang.
Chapman, Robert B. OS/2 2.3 Presentation Manager Programming for COBOL Programmers. rev. ed. LC 96-134078. 504p. 1993. pap. 39.95 incl. disk (*0-471-56140-1*) Wiley.
Chapman, Robert B., et al. Insourcing after the Outsourcing: Mis Survival Guide. LC 97-22507. 224p. 1997. 39.95 (*0-8144-0386-7*) AMACOM.
Chapman, Robert D., jt. auth. see Brandt, John C.
Chapman, Robert E. & Marshall, Harold E., eds. User's Guide to AHP-Expert for ASTM Building Evaluation. (Manual (MNL) Ser.: Vol. 29). (Illus.). 41p. 1998. pap. 495.00 (*0-8031-2077-X*, MNL29) ASTM.
***Chapman, Robert E. & Rennison, Roderick.** An Approach for Measuring Reductions in Delivery Time: Baseline Measures of the Constructing Industry Practices for the National Construction Goals. (Illus.). 191p. (C). 1999. pap. text 30.00 (*0-7881-8422-9*) DIANE Pub.
***Chapman, Robert F.** Thought Power: Think Better, Feel Better, Act Better: An Emotional Health Program for Children, Adolescents, Teachers & Parents. 2nd ed. LC 99-74075. 130p. (gr. 5 up). 1999. pap. 18.95 (*0-9644000-4-9*) Cypress Trail Pr.
Chapman, Robert F. Thought Power: Think Better, Feel Better, Act Better: An Emotional Health Program for Children, Adolescents, Teachers & Parents. 110p. (Orig.). (YA). (gr. 5 up). 1994. teacher ed. 19.95 (*0-9644000-6-5*) Cypress Trail Pr.

An Asterisk (*) at the beginning of an entry indicates that the title is appearing for the first time.

Chapman, Robert L. American Slang. 528p. 1987. pap. 14.00 (*0-06-273172-6*) HarpC.
— American Slang. LC 87-45028. 528p. 1995. reprint ed. mass mkt. 5.99 (*0-06-109284-3*, Harp PBks) HarpC.
— American Slang (Abridged) 2nd Edition. 2nd abr. ed. LC 98-22757. 592p. 1998. pap. 15.00 (*0-06-273293-5*, Harper Ref) HarpC.
— Concise Roget's International Thesaurus, 5Th Ed. 5th ed. 1994. 10.09 (*0-606-06902-X*, Pub. by Turtleback) Demco.
Chapman, Robert L., ed. Roget A to Z: The Classic Thesaurus in Dictionary Form. 768p. 1994. 17.00 (*0-06-270058-8*, Harper Ref) HarpC.
— Roget A to Z: The Classic Thesaurus in Dictionary Form. 768p. 1995. pap. 13.00 (*0-06-272059-7*, Harper Ref) HarpC.
— Roget International Thesaurus: 5E Indexed. 5th ed. LC 92-7615. 1168p. 1992. 21.00 (*0-06-270014-6*, Harper Ref) HarpC.
— Roget International Thesaurus: 5E Plain. 5th ed. LC 92-7615. 1168p. 1992. 19.95 (*0-06-270046-4*, Harper Ref) HarpC.
— Roget Intl Thesaurus. 5th ed. LC 92-7615. 1328p. 1993. pap. 15.00 (*0-06-272037-6*, Harper Ref) HarpC.
Chapman, Robert L., ed. The Concise Roget's International Thesaurus 5e. 5th. ed. 800p. 1994. mass mkt. 5.99 (*0-06-100709-9*, Harp PBks) HarpC.
Chapman, Robert L. & Goldstein, Ardath A., eds. Arts Festival Planning Guide. iv, 112p. 1975. pap. 3.00 (*0-86526-131-8*) NC Archives.
Chapman, Robert L., et al. Dictionary of American Slang, Third Edition: Completely Revised & Updated. 3rd ed. LC 97-2771. 640p. 1998. 42.00 (*0-06-270107-X*) HarpC.
Chapman, Robert M. The Machine That Could: PNGV, a Government-Industry Partnership. LC 98-217140. (Illus.). 94p. 1998. pap. 15.00 (*0-8330-2657-7*, MR-1011-DOC) Rand Corp.
Chapman, Robert W. Johnsonian & Other Essays & Reviews. 1988. reprint ed. lib. bdg. 59.00 (*0-7812-0125-X*) Rprt Serv.
— Johnsonian & Other Essays & Reviews. LC 78-158502. reprint ed. 49.00 (*0-403-01297-X*) Scholarly.
— Portrait of a Scholar, & Other Essays Written in Macedonia, 1916-1918. LC 68-29197. (Essay Index Reprint Ser.). 1977. reprint ed. 18.95 (*0-8369-0291-2*) Ayer.
***Chapman, Robin.** The Way In. Kaiser, Mifanwy, ed. LC 99-71412. 88p. (C). 1999. pap. 12.00 (*1-893670-08-2*) T Bach.
Chapman, Robin S. The Interpretation of Deviant Sentences in English. LC 73-87531. (Janua Linguarum, Ser. Minor: No. 189). (Illus.). 95p. 1974. pap. text 53.10 (*90-279-3112-7*) Mouton.
— Learning to Talk. 69p. (Orig.). 1991. pap. 7.50 (*1-878660-12-8*) Fireweed WI.
Chapman, Robin T. Encounters with Wales. 207p. 1995. pap. 17.95 (*0-8464-4648-0*) Beekman Pubs.
Chapman, Roger. Butterworths Family Law Journal. ring bd. write for info. (*0-409-78999-2*, NZ, MICHIE) LEXIS Pub.
Chapman, Roger, jt. auth. see Hogan, Thomas.
Chapman, Roger, jt. auth. see Landon, Robbins H.
Chapman, Rosemary, jt. ed. see Hewitt, Nicholas.
Chapman, Roy. Walk Around the Downs. 64p. 1987. pap. 45.00 (*0-905392-00-0*) St Mut.
Chapman, Royal N. Animal Ecology: Special Reference to Insects. Egerton, Frank N., 3rd, ed. LC 77-74208. (History of Ecology Ser.). 1978. reprint ed. lib. bdg. 40.95 (*0-405-10379-4*) Ayer.
Chapman, S. & Lindzen, Richard S. Atmospheric Tides: Thermal & Gravitational. x, 200p. 1970. text 252.00 (*0-677-61810-7*) Gordon & Breach.
— Atmospheric Tides: Thermal & Gravitational. 200p. 1969. text 140.00 (*90-277-0113-X*) Kluwer Academic.
Chapman, S. & Lupton, Deborah, eds. The Fight for Public Health: Principles & Practice of Media Advocacy. 270p. (Orig.). 1994. pap. text 48.00 (*0-7279-0049-8*, Pub. by BMJ Pub) Login Brothers Bk Co.
Chapman, S. D., ed. The Textile Industry, 4 vols. 1800p. 1997. text 625.00 (*1-86064-057-5*, Pub. by Textile Inst) St Mut.
Chapman, Sally. Cyberkiss. (Worldwide Library Mysteries: No. 242). 1997. per. 4.99 (*0-373-26242-6*, 1-26242-7, Wrldwide Lib) Harlequin Bks.
— Hardwired. (WWL Mystery Ser.: Vol. 288). 1998. per. 4.99 (*0-373-26288-4*, 1-26288-0, Wrldwide Lib) Harlequin Bks.
— Hardwired. LC 96-53872. 1997. text 22.95 (*0-312-15542-5*) St Martin.
— Love Bytes. (WWL Mystery Ser.). 1996. per. 4.99 (*0-373-26197-7*, 1-26197-3, Wrldwide Lib) Harlequin Bks.
Chapman, Sally P. Whistled Like a Bird: The Untold Story of Dorothy Putnam, George Putnam & Amelia Earhart. LC 97-9456. 268p. 1997. 22.00 (*0-446-52055-1*, Pub. by Warner Bks) Little.
Chapman, Samuel D. History of Tama County: Its Cities, Towns & Villages, with Early Reminiscences, Personal Incidents & Anecdotes, & a Complete Business Directory of the County. (Illus.). 296p. 1997. reprint ed. lib. bdg. 37.00 (*0-8328-6706-3*) Higginson Bk Co.
Chapman, Samuel G. Murdered on Duty: The Killing of Police Officers in America. 2nd ed. LC 97-30462. (Illus.). 218p. 1997. text 47.95 (*0-398-06820-8*) C C Thomas.
— Murdered on Duty: The Killing of Police Officers in America. 2nd ed. LC 97-30462. (Illus.). 218p. 1998. pap. text 32.95 (*0-398-06821-6*) C C Thomas.
— Police Dogs in North America. 254p. 1990. pap. 35.95 (*0-398-06053-3*) C C Thomas.
— Police Dogs in North America. 254p. (C). 1990. text 51.95 (*0-398-05693-5*) C C Thomas.
Chapman, Sandy C., ed. see Mason, Donald B.
Chapman-Santana, Miriam, jt. auth. see Chapman, A. H.
***Chapman, Sara S. & Colby, Ursula S.** One Nation Indivisible. (C). 2001. pap. text. write for info. (*0-7914-4838-X*) State U NY Pr.
— One Nation Indivisible. (C). 2001. text. write for info. (*0-7914-4837-1*) State U NY Pr.
***Chapman, Sarah K.** A Circus Girl's Cookbook: Balanced Recipes. 3rd ed. (Illus.). viii, 137p. 1998. pap. 10.00 (*0-9611172-1-4*) Circus Bufoon.
Chapman, Serle. Of Earth & Elders: Visions & Voices from Native America. LC 98-73454. (Illus.). 218p. 1999. pap. 24.95 (*0-9528607-4-0*) Mountain Pr.
— The Trail of Many Spirits: Paws - Wings - Hooves - Moccasins. LC 96-85673. (Illus.). 62p. 1998. pap. 13.95 (*0-9528607-1-6*) Bear Print.
Chapman, Siobhan. Accent in Context. 168p. 1998. pap. 27.95 (*3-906759-44-X*) P Lang Pubng.
— Accent in Context: The Ontological Status & Communicative Effects of Utterance Accent in English. LC 97-50079. 168p. (C). 1998. pap. text 27.95 (*0-8204-3425-6*) P Lang Pubng.
***Chapman, Siobhan.** Philosophy for Linguists: An Introductory Textbook. LC 99-462292. 2000. pap. write for info. (*0-415-20659-6*) Routledge.
Chapman, Spencer & Grandjean, C. The Construction Industry & the European Community. 281p. 1991. 42.00 (*0-614-16820-1*, BSP212) Am Soc Civil Eng.
Chapman, Stanley. The Rise of Merchant Banking. (Illus.). 240p. (C). 1984. text 42.95 (*0-04-332094-5*) Routledge.
— Sansculotte. LC 98-83087. 288p. 2000. pap. 15.95 (*0-88739-238-5*) Creat Arts Bk.
Chapman, Stanley D. The Early Factory Masters: The Transition of the Factory in the Midlands Textile Industry. (Modern Revivals in Economic & Social History Ser.). 256p. 1993. 61.95 (*0-7512-0078-6*, Pub. by Gregg Revivals) Ashgate Pub Co.
— The Rise of Merchant Banking. (Modern Revivals in Economic & Social History Ser.). 235p. 1992. 63.95 (*0-7512-0077-8*, Pub. by Gregg Revivals) Ashgate Pub Co.
***Chapman, Stepan.** Dossier. LC 99-63267. 176p. 2000. pap. 13.95 (*0-88739-280-6*) Creat Arts Bk.
Chapman, Stepan. The Troika. 250p. 1997. pap. 14.99 (*1-890464-02-3*) Ministry of Whimsy.
Chapman, Stephen & Nakielny, Richard, eds. A Guide to Radiological Procedures. 3rd ed. (Illus.). 448p. 1993. pap. text 33.00 (*0-7020-1678-0*, Pub. by W B Saunders) Saunders.
Chapman, Stephen, jt. auth. see Kenney, Anne R.
Chapman, Stephen, jt. ed. see Penton, Rhona.
Chapman, Stephen J. Digital Signal Processing with Labview. (C). 2002. pap. 95.00 (*0-201-36178-7*, Prentice Hall) P-H.
— Electric Machinery Fundamentals. 2nd ed. (C). 1991. text 71.25 (*0-07-010914-1*) McGraw.
— Electric Machinery Fundamentals. 3rd ed. LC 98-6407. (Series in Electrical & Computer Engineering). 1998. 90.75 (*0-07-011950-3*) McGraw.
— FORTRAN 90 & 95 for Scientists & Engineers. LC 97-15699. 888p. 1997. pap. 66.88 (*0-07-011938-4*) McGraw.
— Introduction to FORTRAN. LC 97-23252. 576p. 1997. pap. 37.81 (*0-07-011969-4*) McGraw.
***Chapman, Stephen J.** Introduction to Java for Engineers & Scientists. LC 99-17739. 344p. 1999. pap. 29.20 (*0-13-919416-9*) P-H.
— Java for Engineers. LC 99-17733. (Illus.). 571p. 1999. pap. 68.00 (*0-13-919523-8*) P-H.
Chapman, Stephen J. Matlab 5.0 Programming for Engineers. LC 99-54392. (Electrical Engineering Ser.). 444p. (C). 1999. 61.95 (*0-534-95151-1*) PWS Pubs.
Chapman, Stephen K., jt. ed. see Welch, Alan J.
Chapman, Stephen N., jt. auth. see Arnold, J. R. Tony.
Chapman, Stephen R. Environmental Law & Policy. LC 97-30111. 258p. 1997. 61.00 (*0-13-848706-5*) P-H.
Chapman, Steve. Essential Pediatric Radiology. (Illus.). 360p. 1999. text. write for info. (*0-7020-2150-4*, Pub. by W B Saunders) Saunders.
— Full Draw. 1998. pap. text 10.98 (*0-9653274-1-8*) S&A Family.
— A Look at Life from a Deer Stand: Hunting for the Meaning of Life. LC 97-42832. 130p. 1998. pap. 8.99 (*1-56507-864-0*) Harvest Hse.
***Chapman, Steve.** Married Lovers, Married Friends. 160p. 1999. pap. 9.99 (*0-7642-2226-0*) Bethany Hse.
Chapman, Steve. Outdoor Insights: What a Dad Can Teach a Child in God's Great Outdoors. LC 98-45820. 156p. 1999. pap. 8.99 (*0-7369-0059-4*) Harvest Hse.
***Chapman, Steve.** What a Hunter Brings Home. 144p. 2001. pap. 8.99 (*0-7369-0441-7*) Harvest Hse.
***Chapman, Steven Curtis.** Speechless: Living in Awe of God's Disruptive Grace. 2000. pap. 12.99 (*0-310-23582-0*) Zondervan.
Chapman, Steven Curtis. 20 Favorites of Steven Curtis Chapman. 144p. 1997. per. 14.95 (*0-7935-7663-6*) H Leonard.
Chapman, Steven Curtis & Smith, Scotty. Speechless: Living in Awe of God's Disruptive Grace. LC 99-25244. 224p. 2000. 15.99 (*0-310-22584-1*) Zondervan.
Chapman, Steven K. & Reid, Graeme A., eds. Flavoprotein Protocols. LC 99-11444. (Methods in Molecular Biology Ser.: Vol. 131). (Illus.). 258p. 1999. 79.50 (*0-89603-734-7*) Humana.
Chapman, Suzanne E. Historic Floral & Animal Designs for Embroiderers & Craftsmen. LC 77-75740. (Pictorial Archive Ser.). (Illus.). 80p. 1977. pap. 6.95 (*0-486-23526-2*) Dover.
— Historic Floral & Animal Designs for Embroiderers & Craftsmen. 1990. 16.50 (*0-8446-5564-3*) Peter Smith.
Chapman, Suzanne E., ed. Early American Design Motifs. LC 73-86040. (Illus.). 160p. 1974. reprint ed. pap. 8.95 (*0-486-22985-8*) Dover.
Chapman, Sydney J. The Lancaster Cotton Industry: A Study in Economic Development. LC 68-55503. (Reprints of Economic Classics Ser.). vii, 309p. 1973. reprint ed. 45.00 (*0-678-00896-5*) Kelley.
Chapman, T. Time: A Philosophical Analysis. 178p. 1982. text 99.50 (*90-277-1465-7*, D Reidel) Kluwer Academic.
Chapman, T. A. Controlled Simple Homotopy Theory & Applications. (Lecture Notes in Mathematics Ser.: Vol. 1009). 94p. 1983. 29.95 (*0-387-12338-5*) Spr-Verlag.
— Lectures on Hilbert Cube Manifolds. LC 76-48316. (CBMS Regional Conference Series in Mathematics: No. 28). 131p. 1977. reprint ed. pap. 19.00 (*0-8218-1678-0*, CBMS/28) Am Math.
Chapman, Ted. One: The Official Strategy Guide. LC 97-75577. 96p. 1998. per. 12.99 (*0-7615-1365-5*) Prima Pub.
— Politika: The Official Strategy Guide. LC 97-76450. 192p. 1997. per. 19.99 (*0-7615-1349-3*) Prima Pub.
Chapman, Teresa L. The Gift of God Is . . . 66p. (Orig.). 1995. pap. write for info. (*1-57502-017-3*, P00396) Morris Pubng.
Chapman, Thomas, ed. see Blanks, D. R.
Chapman, Thomas A. Approximation Results in Topological Manifolds. LC 81-12791. (Memoirs of the American Mathematical Society Ser.: No. 34/251). 64p. 1981. pap. 16.00 (*0-8218-2251-9*, MEMO/34/251) Am Math.
Chapman, Thomas J. The Valley of the Conemaugh, Pa. (Illus.). 202p. 1997. reprint ed. lib. bdg. 29.00 (*0-8328-6376-9*) Higginson Bk Co.
Chapman, Thomas W., ed. A Practical Handbook for Ministry: From the Writings of Wayne E. Oates. LC 92-2317. 624p. 1993. text 39.95 (*0-664-21975-6*) Westminster John Knox.
Chapman, Tim. The Congress of Vienna: Origins, Processes, & Results. LC 98-11040. (Illus.). 120p. (C). 1998. 50.00 (*0-415-17993-9*); pap. 14.99 (*0-415-17994-7*) Routledge.
Chapman, Tobias. In Defense of Mystical Ideas: Support for Mystic Beliefs from a Purely Theoretical Viewpoint. LC 88-32655. (Problems in Contemporary Philosophy Ser.: Vol. 12). 120p. 1989. lib. bdg. 59.95 (*0-88946-340-9*) E Mellen.
Chapman, Tom. Aunt Zona's Web: Life of Arizona Hughes, a Pioneer Teacher. rev. ed. (Illus.). 1979. 5.00 (*0-686-27735-X*) Puddingstone.
Chapman, Tom & Johnson, Alan. Growing Old & Needing Care. 384p. 1995. 91.95 (*1-85972-102-8*, Pub. by Avebry) Ashgate Pub Co.
***Chapman, Tony.** Architecture 1998. 2000. pap. 10.00 (*1-899858-91-1*, Pub. by Ellipsis) Norton.
— Architecture 1999. 2000. pap. 10.00 (*1-84166-045-0*, Pub. by Ellipsis) Norton.
Chapman, Tony. Ideal Homes? Social Change & Domestic Life. LC 98-54119. 1999. write for info. (*0-415-17121-0*); pap. write for info. (*0-415-17122-9*) Routledge.
Chapman, Trevor. Understanding Novell NetWare: A Practical Guide for Users & Network Managers. (Illus.). 256p. 1995. text 36.95 (*1-85032-236-8*) ITCP.
Chapman, Trinka, jt. auth. see Chapman, Al.
Chapman, Valentie J. Salt Marshes & Salt Deserts of the World. 2nd ed. 1974. 125.00 (*3-7682-0927-X*) Lubrecht & Cramer.
Chapman, Valentine J. Coastal Vegetation. 2nd ed. 1976. 139.00 (*0-08-020896-7*, Pub. by Pergamon Repr) Franklin.
— The Marine Algae of New Zealand, Vol. 3. Incl. Pt. 1. Bangiophycidae & Florideophycidate. 1970. 24.00 (*3-7682-0591-6*); Pt. 2. Florideophycidae: Rhodymeniales. Dromgoole, F. I. 1970. 20.00 (*3-7682-0592-4*); (Illus.). 1970. write for info. (*0-318-54143-2*) Lubrecht & Cramer.
Chapman, Valentine J., ed. The Marine Algae of New Zealand Pt. 4: Section 3 Rhodophyceae: Florideophycidae: Gigartinales. (Illus.). 510p. 1979. pap. text 64.00 (*3-7682-0594-0*) Lubrecht & Cramer.
— Wet Coastal Ecosystems. LC 77-342. (Ecosystems of the World Ser.: Vol. 1). xii,428p. 1977. 186.00 (*0-444-41560-2*) Elsevier.
Chapman, Valentine J. & Parkinson, P. G. The Marine Algae of New Zealand: Section 3 Rhodophyceae. (Florideophycidae: Cryptonemiales Ser.: Pt. 3). (Illus.). 278p. 1974. pap. text 32.00 (*3-7682-0593-2*) Lubrecht & Cramer.
Chapman, Valerie & Read, Peter, eds. Terrible Hard Biscuits: A Reader in Aboriginal History. 304p. 1997. pap. 29.95 (*1-86373-964-5*, Pub. by Allen & Unwin Pty) Paul & Co Pubs.
Chapman, Valerie A., jt. auth. see Chapman, William K.
***Chapman, Vera.** The Enchantresses. 223p. 1998. text 27.00 (*0-575-06524-9*, Pub. by V Gollancz) Trafalgar.
Chapman, Vera. The Enchantresses. 1999. pap. 8.95 (*0-575-60325-9*, Pub. by V Gollancz) Trafalgar.
— The Notorious Abbess. Zahorski, Ken, ed. LC 93-15629. 239p. 1997. 22.50 (*0-89733-387-X*) Academy Chi Pubs.
— Notorious Abbess. 1998. pap. text 12.95 (*0-89733-447-7*) Academy Chi Pubs.
— The Three Damosels LC 97-176139. 383 p. 1996. write for info. (*0-575-06340-8*) V Gollancz.
Chapman, Victoria & Lindroth, David. Latin American History on File. LC 95-30231. (Illus.). 288p. (YA). (gr. 6-12). 1996. ring bd. 165.00 (*0-8160-3068-5*) Facts on File.
Chapman, W. William Shakespeare & Robert Greene: The Evidence. LC 73-18209. (Studies in Shakespeare: No. 24). 1974. lib. bdg. 75.00 (*0-8383-1731-6*) M S G Haskell Hse.
Chapman, Wayne K. & Manson, Janet M., eds. Women in the Milieu of Leonard & Virginia Woolf: Peace, Politics, & Education. LC 97-32405. 300p. (C). 1998. 64.00 (*0-944473-37-7*) Pace Univ Pr.
— Women in the Milieu of Leonard & Virginia Woolf: Peace, Politics & Education. LC 97-32405. 279p. (C). 1998. pap. 46.50 (*0-944473-38-5*) Pace Univ Pr.
Chapman, William E. History & Theology in the Book of Order: Blood on Every Page: Leader's Guide. LC 99-21216. 1999. 19.95 (*1-57153-016-9*, Witherspoon Pr) Curriculm Presbytrn KY.
Chapman, William K. Orchids of the Northeast: A Field Guide. LC 96-5733. (Illus.). 200p. (C). 1996. pap. 17.95 (*0-8156-0342-8*, CHONP); text 39.95 (*0-8156-2697-5*, CHON) Syracuse U Pr.
— Wildflowers of New York in Color. LC 97-29901. (Illus.). 1998. 59.95 (*0-8156-2746-7*) Syracuse U Pr.
Chapman, William K. & Aprill, Dennis. Mammals of the Adirondacks: A Field Guide. 160p. 1991. pap. 13.95 (*0-932052-61-4*) North Country.
Chapman, William K. & Chapman, Valerie A. Wildflowers of New York in Color. LC 97-29901. (Illus.). 1998. pap. 24.95 (*0-8156-0470-X*) Syracuse U Pr.
Chapman, William L. Engineering Modeling & Design. 400p. 1992. boxed set 99.95 (*0-8493-8011-1*, TA168) CRC Pr.
— Wysiwyg: A Survival Manual for the Straight White American Male. 300p. 1992. pap. 24.95 (*1-880361-01-9*) Premier Pubns.
Chapman, William P. From "Unstretched in Baluchistan" & Other Poems. LC 96-36048. 60p. 1996. pap. 14.95 (*0-7734-2754-6*, Mellen Poetry Pr) E Mellen.
Chapman, Willie. Booster McKeester & Other Expendables. 1995. pap. write for info. (*1-885353-02-2*) Global Press.
Chapnick, Howard. David & Peter Turnley: In Times of War & Peace. LC 97-169336. (Illus.). 231p. 1997. 60.00 (*0-7892-0299-9*) Abbeville Pr.
— Truth Needs No Ally: Inside Photojournalism. LC 94-6737. (Illus.). 384p. (C). 1994. pap. 24.95 (*0-8262-0955-6*) U of Mo Pr.
— Truth Needs No Ally: Inside Photojournalism. LC 94-6737. (Illus.). 384p. 1994. 49.95 (*0-8262-0954-8*) U of Mo Pr.
Chapon, C., et al, eds. Small Particles & Inorganic Clusters. (Illus.). xii, 612p. 1989. 159.95 (*0-387-51390-6*) Spr-Verlag.
Chapon, Francois. Rouault's Illustrated Books: Catalogue Raisonne. (Illus.). 1993. 125.00 (*1-55660-246-4*) A Wofsy Fine Arts.
Chapon, Francois & Rouault, Isabelle. Rouault's Complete Graphic Work, 2 Vols., Vol. 1. (ENG & FRE., Illus.). 340p. 1978. 1500.00 (*0-915346-86-9*) A Wofsy Fine Arts.
Chapone, Hester & Gisborne, Thomas. Letters on the Improvement of the Mind, 1773: An Enquiry into the Duties of the Female Sex, 1797. LC 96-33667. (Female Education in the Age of Enlightenment Ser.: No. 2). 1996. write for info. (*1-85196-276-X*, Pub. by Pickering & Chatto) Ashgate Pub Co.
Chaponton, Anne-Marie. Tim Tidies Up. (Child's World Library). (Illus.). 32p. (J). (gr. k-5). 1992. lib. bdg. 18.50 (*0-89565-750-3*) Childs World.
Chapot, Frank. Winning with Frank Chapot. (Illus.). 180p. 1992. 27.95 (*0-914327-45-3*) Breakthrgh NY.
Chapot, Victor. The Roman World. 444p. reprint ed. 25.00 (*0-8196-0367-8*) Biblo.
Chapouton, Anne-Marie. Downy, Pistachio & Fanny. (I Love to Read Collection). (Illus.). 48p. (J). (ps-3). 1992. lib. bdg. 12.79 (*0-89565-808-9*) Childs World.
— If Sophie . . . (Child's World Library). (Illus.). 32p. (J). (gr. k-5). 1992. lib. bdg. 18.50 (*0-89565-760-0*) Childs World.
— Krustnkrum! (Child's World Library). (Illus.). 32p. (J). (gr. k-5). 1992. lib. bdg. 18.50 (*0-89565-744-9*) Childs World.
Chapp, Belena, et al. Through These Eyes: The Photographs of P. H. Polk. LC 97-61606. (Illus.). 64p. 1998. pap. 20.00 (*1-887421-03-3*) Univ Gall U of DE.
Chapp, Belena S., ed. see Botar, Oliver, et al.
Chapp, Belena S., ed. see Matus, Todd.
Chapp, Larry S. The God Who Speaks: Hans Urs von Balthasar's Theology of Revelation. LC 96-44893. (Distinguished Research Ser.). 250p. 1996. pap. 49.95 (*1-57309-110-3*) Intl Scholars.
— The God Who Speaks: Hans Urs von Balthasar's Theology of Revelation. LC 96-44893. (Distinguished Research Ser.). 250p. 1997. 69.95 (*1-57309-111-1*) Intl Scholars.
***Chappa, Deborah R.** Words for When There Are No Words: Writing a Memorable Condolence Note. (Illus.). 70p. (YA). (gr. 7 up). 1999. pap. 9.95 (*0-7414-0112-6*) Buy Books.
Chappat, Djenane. Diccionario de la Limpieza. (SPA.). 234p. 1970. pap. 6.95 (*0-8288-6496-9*, S-12249) Fr & Eur.
Chappe, D'Auteroche. Journey into Siberia, Made by Order of the King of France. LC 77-115518. (Russia Observed Ser.). 1970. reprint ed. 26.95 (*0-405-03074-6*) Ayer.
Chappe, Eli. Winning Government Contracts: A Complete 27 Step Guide for Small Businesses. LC 83-22954. 266p. 1984. reprint ed. 69.95 (*0-13-960998-9*, Busn) P-H.
Chappel, Allen H. Selected Poetry & Prose of Helga Novak. LC 88-28686. (American University Studies: Germanic Languages & Literature: Ser. I, Vol. 79). 208p. (C). 1989. text 34.95 (*0-8204-1042-X*) P Lang Pubng.
Chappel, Bernice M. Bittersweet Trail: An American Saga of the 1800's. LC 84-80978. (Illus.). 480p. 1985. 12.95 (*0-9606400-1-0*); pap. 9.95 (*0-9606400-2-0*) Great Lakes Bks.
— Blowing in the Wind. LC 89-40634. (Illus.). 350p. (Orig.). 1990. pap. 11.95 (*0-923568-06-9*) Wilderness Adventure Bks.

C

— Frontier Footsteps: A Sequel to Blowing in the Wind. LC 92-39966. 380p. 1992. 11.95 (*0-923568-27-1*) Wilderness Adventure Bks.

— In the Palm of the Mitten: A Memory Book of the Early 1900's. LC 81-82290. (Illus.). 300p. (Orig.). 1981. pap. 7.95 (*0-9606400-0-2*) Great Lakes Bks.

— Lure of the Arctic. Klein, Marjorie N., tr. LC 86-50153. (Illus.). 267p. (Orig.). 1986. pap. 8.95 (*0-9611596-2-6*) Wilderness Adventure Bks.

— Reap the Whirlwind. LC 87-50674. 408p. (Orig.). 1987. pap. 10.95 (*0-9611596-8-5*) Wilderness Adventure Bks.

Chappel, Julie, tr. from ENM. The Prose of Alexander of Robert Thornton: The Middle English Text with a Modern English Translation. LC 90-24425. (American University Studies: English Language & Literature: Ser. IV, Vol. 131). 291p. (C). 1992. text 49.95 (*0-8204-1508-1*) P Lang Pubng.

Chappel, Michael, jt. auth. see Haythornthwaite, Philip J.

Chappelear, Claude S. Health Subject Matter in Natural Sciences. LC 78-176637. (Columbia University. Teachers College. Contributions to Education Ser.: No. 341). reprint ed. 37.50 (*0-404-55341-9*) AMS Pr.

Chappelear, George W. Barret Vol. III: Families of Virginia - Barret. (Illus.). 208p. 1997. reprint ed. pap. 31.00 (*0-8328-7383-7*); reprint ed. lib. bdg. 41.00 (*0-8328-7382-9*) Higginson Bk Co.

— Chappelear Family of Virginia & Connecting Lines. (Illus.). 122p. 1993. reprint ed. pap. 23.00 (*0-8328-3658-3*); reprint ed. lib. bdg. 33.00 (*0-8328-3657-5*) Higginson Bk Co.

Chappelear, Kei & Hawley, W. M. Mon-The Japanese Family Crest. (Illus.). 120p. 1994. pap. 35.00 (*0-910704-93-7*) Hawley.

Chappell. Arsenic Exposure & Health. 1994. lib. bdg. 97.50 (*0-905927-49-4*) CRC Pr.

Chappell, jt. auth. see Montgomery, Rex.

Chappell, Arthur B. Regular Confession: An Exercise in Sacramental Spirituality. LC 91-44337. (American University Studies: Theology & Religion: Ser. VII, Vol. 130). 202p. (C). 1992. text 40.95 (*0-8204-1813-7*) P Lang Pubng.

Chappell, Arvel A. The Double (You) "W" Book: The You You Know & the You You Have Yet to Discover. Chappell, Bobbie D., ed. (Illus.). 156p. 1997. pap. 19.95 (*0-9662162-0-2*) Aldor Prodns.

Chappell, Bobbie D., ed. see Chappell, Arvel A.

Chappell, C. & Read, W. L. Business Communications. 216p. (Orig.). (C). 1984. 90.00 (*0-7855-5689-3*, Pub. by Inst Pur & Supply) St Mut.

Chappell, Charles. Detective Dupin Reads William Faulkner: Solutions to Six Yoknapatawpha Mysteries. LC 97-15671. 412p. 1997. 74.95 (*1-57309-166-9*); pap. 54.95 (*1-57309-165-0*) Intl Scholars.

Chappell, Clovis G. Preaching on the Words of Jesus. (Chappell Sermon Library). 712p. 1997. pap. 29.99 (*0-8010-5750-7*) Baker Bks.

Chappell, D. Understanding JCT Standard Building Contracts. 5th ed. LC 98-193927. viii, 118p. 1998. 25.99 (*0-419-23440-3*, E & FN Spon) Routledge.

Chappell, D. & Egger, Sandra, eds. Australian Violence: Contemporary Perspectives II. LC 96-204336. 436p. 1995. pap. 50.00 (*0-642-20298-2*, Pub. by Aust Inst Criminology) Advent Bks Div.

Chappell, D. & Wilson, P. The Australian Criminal Justice System. 2nd ed. 546p. 1977. pap. write for info. (*0-409-43472-8*, MICHIE) LEXIS Pub.

— The Australian Criminal Justice System: The Mid 1990s. 90th ed. LC 94-158022. 1993. 78.00 (*0-409-30583-9*, AT, MICHIE) LEXIS Pub.

— Australian Policing - Contemporary Issues. 2nd ed. LC 97-188606. 256p. 1996. pap. write for info. (*0-409-31104-9*, MICHIE) LEXIS Pub.

Chappell, David. Contractual Correspondence for Architects & Project Managers. 3rd ed. LC 95-47344. 272p. 1996. text 59.95 (*0-632-04002-5*) Blackwell Sci.

— Report Writing for Architects. 3rd rev. ed. LC 96-5630. 180p. 1996. text 49.95 (*0-632-04001-7*) Blackwell Sci.

— Standard Letters in Architectural Practice. 2nd ed. 320p. 1994. 59.95 (*0-632-03451-3*, Pub. by Blckwll Scitfc UK) Blackwell Sci.

— Understanding ActiveX & OLE: A Guide for Managers & Developers. (Strategic Technologies Ser.). 352p. 22.95 (*1-57231-216-5*) Microsoft.

***Chappell, David.** Understanding JCT Standard Building Contracts. 6th ed. LC 00-33893. (Illus.). 2000. write for info. (*0-415-23107-8*, E & FN Spon) Routledge.

Chappell, David. Understanding Microsoft Windows 2000 Distributed Services. 250p. 2000. pap. 29.99 (*1-57231-687-X*) Microsoft.

Chappell, David & Powell-Smith, Vincent. The JCT Design & Build Contract. 2nd ed. LC 99-30890. 1999. write for info. (*0-632-04899-9*) Blackwell Sci.

— The JCT Design & Build Form. LC 93-9147. 1993. 85.00 (*0-632-02081-4*) Blackwell Sci.

***Chappell, David & Powell-Smith, Vincent.** The JCT Intermediate Form of Contract. 2nd ed. LC 99-89277. 2000. pap. write for info. (*0-632-03965-5*) Blackwell Sci.

Chappell, David & Powell-Smith, Vincent. JCT Minor Works Form of Contract. 2nd ed. LC 98-52409. 1999. pap. write for info. (*0-632-03967-1*) Blackwell Sci.

— Powell-Smith & Sims' Building Contract Claims. 3rd ed. LC 97-33481. 1998. 99.95 (*0-632-03646-X*) Blackwell Sci.

Chappell, David & Willis, Christopher. The Architect in Practice. 7th ed. (Illus.). 331p. 1992. pap. 44.95 (*0-632-02267-1*) Blackwell Sci.

***Chappell, David & Willis, J. Andrew.** The Architect in Practice. 8th ed. LC 00-29785. 2000. pap. write for info. (*0-632-04913-8*) Blackwell Sci.

Chappell, David, jt. auth. see Greenstreet, Bob.

Chappell, David A. Double Ghosts: Oceanian Voyagers on Euroamerican Ships. LC 96-48629. (Sources & Studies in World History). (C). (gr. 13). 1997. text 72.95 (*1-56324-998-7*) M E Sharpe.

— Double Ghosts: Oceanian Voyagers on Euroamerican Ships. LC 96-48629. (Sources & Studies in World History). (gr. 13). 1997. pap. text 32.95 (*1-56324-999-5*) M E Sharpe.

Chappell, David L. Inside Agitators: White Southerners in the Civil Rights Movement. LC 93-43128. 303p. (C). 1994. 42.00 (*0-8018-4685-4*) Johns Hopkins.

— Inside Agitators: White Southerners in the Civil Rights Movement. 336p. (C). 1996. reprint ed. pap. text 16.95 (*0-8018-5234-X*) Johns Hopkins.

Chappell, David M. Understanding JCT Standard Building Contracts. 2nd ed. 112p. 1991. pap. 27.95 (*0-419-17320-X*, E & FN Spon) Routledge.

— Understanding JCT Standard Building Contracts. 3rd ed. LC 93-12123. (Builder's Bookshelf Ser.). 1993. mass mkt. 29.95 (*0-419-18430-9*, E & FN Spon) Routledge.

Chappell, David M., jt. auth. see Trimble, J. Harvey.

***Chappell, David W., ed.** Buddhist Peacework: Creating Cultures of Peace. LC 99-51657. 256p. 2000. pap. 14.95 (*0-86171-167-X*) Wisdom MA.

Chappell, Delores. Dee's Original Thoughts. 56p. 1998. pap. 8.00 (*0-8059-4413-3*) Dorrance.

***Chappell, Duncan & Di Martino, Vittorio.** Violence at Work. 180p. 2000. pap. 20.00 (*92-2-110840-6*, Pub. by Intl Labour Off) Balogh.

Chappell, Duncan & Di Martino, Vittorio. Violence at Work. LC 99-514748. 165p. 1998. pap. 31.00 (*92-2-110335-8*, Pub. by Statnry Office) Balogh.

Chappell, Duncan & Wilson, Paul. Australian Policing: Contemporary Issues. 224p. (C). 1989. pap. 58.00 (*0-409-49489-5*, AT, MICHIE) LEXIS Pub.

Chappell, E. B. Studies in the Life of John Wesley. 1991. reprint ed. pap. 12.99 (*0-88019-284-4*) Schmul Pub Co.

Chappell, F. P. & Shoard, John. Handy-Book of the Law of Copyright: Comprising Literary, Dramatic & Musical Copyright, & Copyright in Engravings, Sculpture & Works of Art; With an Appendix Containing the Statutes, Convention with France, & Forms under 25 & 26 Vict. c. 68. x, 159p. 1990. reprint ed. 27.50 (*0-8377-2016-8*, Rothman) W S Hein.

Chappell, Fred. Bloodfire: A Poem. LC 78-13578. 56p. 1978. text 15.95 (*0-8071-0451-5*) La State U Pr.

— Brighten the Corner Where You Are. 1990. pap. 10.95 (*0-312-05057-7*) St Martin.

— C: Poems. LC 92-28214. xiii, 64p. 1993. pap. 8.95 (*0-8071-1785-4*) La State U Pr.

— Earthsleep: A Poem. LC 80-13622. 64p. 1980. pap. 6.95 (*0-8071-0698-4*) La State U Pr.

***Chappell, Fred.** Family Gathering: Poems. 72p. 2000. pap. 22.50 (*0-8071-2625-X*); pap. 14.95 (*0-8071-2626-8*) La State U Pr.

Chappell, Fred. Farewell, I'm Bound to Leave You. 228p. 1996. 21.00 (*0-614-20643-X*, Picador USA) St Martin.

— Farewell, I'm Bound to Leave You. 2nd ed. 240p. 1997. pap. 12.00 (*0-312-16834-9*, Picador USA) St Martin.

— First & Last Words. LC 88-22041. 64p. 1989. pap. 8.95 (*0-8071-1487-1*) La State U Pr.

— The Fred Chappell Reader. LC 90-36877. 1990. pap. 14.95 (*0-312-05092-5*) St Martin.

— The Gaudy Place. LC 72-91834. (Voices of the South Ser.). 192p. 1994. reprint ed. pap. 14.95 (*0-8071-1934-2*) La State U Pr.

— I Am One of You Forever. LC 87-2933. 184p. 1987. pap. 12.95 (*0-8071-1410-3*) La State U Pr.

— The Inkling. LC 98-24403. (Voices of the South Ser.). 168p. 1998. pap. 12.95 (*0-8071-2317-X*) La State U Pr.

— It is Time, Lord. LC 96-19218. (Voices of the South Ser.). 183p. 1996. pap. 10.95 (*0-8071-2119-3*) La State U Pr.

***Chappell, Fred.** Look Back All the Green Valley. LC 99-27227. 288p. 1999. text 24.00 (*0-312-24215-8*, Picador USA) St Martin.

— Look Back All the Green Valley. LC 99-27227. 288p. 2000. pap. 13.00 (*0-312-24310-3*, Picador USA) St Martin.

Chappell, Fred. Midquest: A Poem. LC 81-8474. 208p. 1981. pap. 16.95 (*0-8071-1580-0*) La State U Pr.

— Moments of Light. LC 80-81219. 166p. 1980. 12.95 (*0-917990-05-6*, New South) C & M Online.

— More Shapes Than One. 208p. 1992. pap. 8.95 (*0-312-08265-7*) St Martin.

— Plow Naked: Selected Writings on Poetry. LC 93-23791. (Poets on Poetry Ser.). 160p. (C). 1993. pap. 13.95 (*0-472-06542-4*, 06542) U of Mich Pr.

— River: A Poem. LC 73-91773. 64p. 2000. reprint ed. pap. 12.95 (*0-8071-0094-3*) La State U Pr.

— Source: Poems. LC 85-13315. 57p. 1985. pap. 11.95 (*0-8071-1277-1*) La State U Pr.

— Spring Garden: New & Selected Poems. LC 95-22425. 157p. (C). 1995. pap. 16.95 (*0-8071-1949-0*); text 24.95 (*0-8071-1948-2*) La State U Pr.

— A Way of Happening: Observations of Contemporary Poetry. LC 97-33375. 320p. 1998. text 24.00 (*0-312-18033-0*) St Martin.

— Wind Mountain: A Poem. LC 79-12332. 45p. 1979. pap. 6.95 (*0-8071-0567-8*); text 15.95 (*0-8071-0566-X*) La State U Pr.

— The World Between the Eyes: Poems. LC 73-152706. 60p. 1971. pap. 7.95 (*0-8071-1593-2*) La State U Pr.

Chappell, Fred, ed. Editor's Choice IV: Essays from the U. S. Small Press, 1978-1997. (Contemporary Anthology Ser.: Vols. 9 & 13). (Illus.). 336p. Date not set. 22.00 (*0-930370-46-5*); pap. 16.00 (*0-930370-47-3*) Spirit That Moves.

— Editor's Choice IV: Essays from the U. S. Small Press, Signed A-Z. limited ed. (Contemporary Anthology Ser.: Vol. 9). (Illus.). 336p. Date not set. 40.00 (*0-930370-48-1*) Spirit That Moves.

Chappell, Fred, et al. A New Pleiade: Selected Poems. LC 98-24404. 232p. 1998. pap. 18.95 (*0-8071-2330-7*); text 39.95 (*0-8071-2329-3*) La State U Pr.

Chappell, Geoff. DOS Internals. 768p. 1994. pap. 39.95 incl. disk (*0-201-60835-9*) Addison-Wesley.

Chappell, Gerald E., jt. auth. see Chappell, Richard G.

Chappell, Gordon W., jt. auth. see Brinkley, M. Kent.

***Chappell, Helen.** The Chesapeake Book of the Dead: Tombstones, Epitaphs, Histories, Reflections, & Oddments of the Region. LC 98-36625. (Illus.). 160p. 1999. 24.95 (*0-8018-6041-5*) Johns Hopkins.

Chappell, Helen. Ghost of a Chance. (Sam & Hollis Mystery: No. 3). 256p. 1998. mass mkt. 5.99 (*0-440-22567-1*) Doubleday.

— Ghost of a Chance. LC 98-50925. (Beeler Large Print Mystery Ser.). 1999. write for info. (*1-57490-202-4*) T T Beeler.

— Giving Up the Ghost: A Sam & Hollis Mystery. 256p. 1999. mass mkt. 5.99 (*0-440-22575-2*) Dell.

— Oysterback Spoken Here. LC 98-16063. (Illus.). 208p. 1998. pap. 14.95 (*1-891521-01-2*) Woodholme Hse.

— The Oysterback Tales. LC 93-37407. 1994. 19.95 (*0-8018-4815-6*) Johns Hopkins.

— Slow Dancing with the Angel of Death. 1996. mass mkt. 5.50 (*0-449-14983-8*, GM) Fawcett.

Chappell, Hilary & McGregor, William, eds. The Grammar of Inalienability: A Typological Perspective on Body Part Terms & the Part-Whole Relation. LC 95-37989. (Empirical Approaches to Language Typology Ser.: No. 14). xiii, 931p. (C). 1995. lib. bdg. 306.15 (*3-11-012804-7*) Mouton.

Chappell, James. The Potter's Complete Book of Clay & Glazes: A Comprehensive Guide to Formulating, Mixing, Applying, & Firing Clay Bodies & Glazes. (Illus.). 400p. 1991. 50.00 (*0-8230-4203-0*) Watsn-Guptill.

Chappell, James A. Little Johnny Raindrop. LC 88-2173. (Illus.). 32p. (J). (ps-3). 1988. 12.95 (*0-938349-28-7*) State House Pr.

Chappell, John. Before the Bomb: How America Approached the End of the Pacific War. (Illus.). 256p. 1997. text 27.50 (*0-8131-1987-1*) U Pr of Ky.

Chappell, John. Further Letters of Mrs. Gaskell. text. write for info. (*0-7190-5415-X*, Pub. by Manchester Univ Pr) St Martin.

Chappell, John R. Laugh & Cry Your Way to Freedom: Changed into His Image Through Inner Healing. 126p. 1999. pap. 8.99 (*1-884369-97-9*, Serenity Bks) McDougal Pubng.

Chappell, Jon. Blues Rock Riffs for Guitar. 32p. 1995. pap., pap. text 17.95 incl. audio compact disk (*0-89524-933-2*, Pub. by Cherry Lane); pap., pap. text 12.95 incl. audio (*0-89524-932-4*, Pub. by Cherry Lane) H Leonard.

Chappell, Jon. Cruising Beyond Desolation Sound. rev. ed. (Illus.). 211p. 1987. pap. 24.95 (*0-9692825-0-8*) Gordon Soules Bk.

Chappell, Jon. Essential Scales & Modes with Cassette. 24p. (Orig.). (YA). 1995. pap. 14.95 (*0-89524-865-4*, 02503470, Pub. by Cherry Lane) H Leonard.

— Essential Scales & Modes with CD. 24p. (Orig.). (YA). 1995. pap. 17.95 (*0-89524-846-8*, Pub. by Cherry Lane) H Leonard.

— Gig Survival Guide: A Complete Resource for the Performing Guitarist. 32p. 1999. pap. 5.95 (*1-57560-162-1*, Pub. by Cherry Lane) H Leonard.

Chappell, Jon. Great Blues Rock Riffs. 1995. 12.95 incl. audio (*0-614-01246-5*); 14.95 incl. audio (*0-614-01247-3*) Cherry Lane.

— Great Country Riffs, Vol. 1. 1994. pap. 14.95 (*0-89524-794-1*) Cherry Lane.

Chappell, Jon. Great Country Riffs, Vol. 1. 1994. pap. 12.95 (*0-89524-795-X*, Pub. by Cherry Lane) H Leonard.

Chappell, Jon. Great Country Riffs, Vol. 2. 1994. pap. 14.95 (*0-89524-797-6*) Cherry Lane.

Chappell, Jon. Great Country Riffs, Vol. 2. 1994. pap. 12.95 (*0-89524-796-8*) Cherry Lane.

Chappell, Jon. Heavy Metal Guitar Method, Bk. 1. pap. 7.95 (*0-89524-658-9*) Cherry Lane.

— Heavy Metal Guitar Method, Bk. 2. pap. 7.95 (*0-89524-701-1*) Cherry Lane.

— Heavy Metal Guitar Method: Chords. pap. 5.95 (*0-89524-661-9*) Cherry Lane.

— Heavy Metal Guitar Method: Modes. pap. 5.95 (*0-89524-662-7*) Cherry Lane.

— Heavy Metal Guitar Method: Primer. pap. 5.95 (*0-89524-659-7*) Cherry Lane.

— Heavy Metal Guitar Method: Songbook to Primer & Book One. pap. 7.95 (*0-89524-660-0*, Pub. by Cherry Lane) H Leonard.

— Recording Guitarist: The Essential Reference Guide for Home & Studio. 200p. 1999. per. 19.95 (*0-7935-8704-2*) H Leonard.

Chappell, Jon, ed. Guns n' Roses: Just the Riffs. 29p. (YA). pap. 9.95 (*0-89524-937-5*, 02506321, Pub. by Cherry Lane) H Leonard.

— Guns n' Roses - Appetite for Destruction: Drum Edition. (Illus.). 72p. (Orig.). 1990. pap. text 18.95 (*0-89524-556-6*) Cherry Lane.

— Heavy Metal Guitar Method: Songbook 2A. pap. 7.95 (*0-89524-695-3*) Cherry Lane.

— Heavy Metal Guitar Method: Songbook 2B. pap. 7.95 (*0-89524-696-1*, Pub. by Cherry Lane) H Leonard.

— Heavy Metal Guitar Method: Songbook 2D. pap. 7.95 (*0-89524-698-8*, Pub. by Cherry Lane) H Leonard.

— Heavy Metal Mixed Bag: Drum Edition. (Illus.). 96p. (Orig.). 1990. pap. text 16.95 (*0-89524-469-1*) Cherry Lane.

— Metallica - Master of Puppets: Drum Edition. (Illus.). 70p. (Orig.). 1990. pap. text 18.95 (*0-89524-562-0*, Pub. by Cherry Lane) H Leonard.

— Richard Marx - In Person. pap. 9.95 (*0-89524-499-3*) Cherry Lane.

— Slash - Twenty-Five Great Solos. 54p. (Orig.). pap. 14.95 (*0-89524-888-3*, 02506317, Pub. by Cherry Lane) H Leonard.

Chappell, Jon & Gorenberg, Steve, eds. Slayer - Just the Riffs. 31p. reprint ed. pap. 9.95 (*0-614-04266-6*) Cherry Lane.

Chappell, Jon & Jacobson, Jeff, eds. Steve Morse - High Tension Wires: Guitar - Vocal. (Illus.). 86p. (Orig.). 1990. pap. text 17.95 (*0-89524-523-X*) Cherry Lane.

Chappell, Jon & Phillips, Mark, eds. Blues Saraceno - Never Look Back: Guitar - Vocal. (Illus.). 92p. (Orig.). 1990. pap. text 19.95 (*0-89524-454-3*) Cherry Lane.

Chappell, Jon, jt. auth. see Phillips, Mark.

Chappell, Larry W. George Will. LC 96-38640. 1997. 32.00 (*0-8057-4001-5*, Twyne) Mac Lib Ref.

***Chappell, Laura.** Introduction to Network Analysis. (Illus.). 131p. 1999. pap. 59.95 (*1-893939-00-6*) podbooks.

Chappell, Laura, ed. ACRC (Advanced Cisco Router Configuration) LC 98-85494. 1998. 60.00 (*1-57870-074-4*) Cisco Press.

***Chappell, Laura & Cisco Systems, Inc. Staff.** CRC (Introduction Cisco Router Configuration) LC 98-85495. 900p. 1998. 60.00 (*1-57870-076-0*) Cisco Press.

***Chappell, Laura A.** Laura Chappell Presents: Packet-Level Protocols: DHCP Workbook. (Illus.). 100p. (YA). 2000. wbk. ed. 150.00 (*1-893939-34-0*) podbooks.

— Laura Chappell Presents Vol. 101: Introduction to Network Analysis: Workbook. (Illus.). 100p. 2000. wbk. ed. 150.00 (*1-893939-29-4*) podbooks.

— Laura Chappell Presents Vol. 103: Introduction to Cyber Crime Workbook. (Illus.). 150p. (YA). 2000. wbk. ed. 150.00 (*1-893939-31-6*) podbooks.

— Laura Chappell Presents Vol. 104: Introduction to Network Design & Data Flows Workbook. 100p. (YA). 2000. wbk. ed. 150.00 (*1-893939-32-4*) podbooks.

— Laura Chappell Presents Vol. 201: Packet-Level Protocols: IPv4 Workbook. 100p. (YA). 2000. wbk. ed. 150.00 (*1-893939-33-2*) podbooks.

— Laura Chappell Presents Packet-Level Protocols Vol. 203: ICMP Workbook. (Illus.). 100p. 2000. wbk. ed. 150.00 (*1-893939-30-8*) podbooks.

Chappell, Laura A. NVL's Guide to LAN/WAN Analysis: IPX/SPX. LC 97-77228. 912p. 1998. pap. 59.99 (*0-7645-4508-6*) IDG Bks.

***Chappell, Laura A.** TCP/IP Analysis & Troubleshooting. (Illus.). 1999. pap. 59.95 (*1-893939-01-4*) podbooks.

Chappell, Laura A., jt. auth. see GOUGH, CLARE.

Chappell, Laverne, jt. auth. see Longtime, Sonny.

Chappell, Linda R. Coaching Cheerleading Successfully. LC 96-3038. (Illus.). 216p. (Orig.). 1996. pap. 19.95 (*0-87322-942-8*, PCHA0942) Human Kinetics.

Chappell, Michael, jt. auth. see Haythornthwaite, Philip J.

Chappell, Mike. Army Commandos 1940-1945. (Elite Ser.: No. 64). (Illus.). 64p. 1996. pap. 12.95 (*1-85532-579-9*, Pub. by Ospry) Stackpole.

— The British Army in the 1980s. (Elite Ser.: No. 14). (Illus.). 64p. pap. 12.95 (*0-85045-796-3*, 9413, Pub. by Ospry) Stackpole.

— British Battle Insignia Vol. 1: 1914-18. (Men-at-Arms Ser.: No. 182). (Illus.). 48p. pap. 11.95 (*0-85045-727-0*, 9114, Pub. by Ospry) Stackpole.

— British Battle Insignia Vol. 2: 1939-45. (Men-at-Arms Ser.: No. 187). (Illus.). 48p. pap. 11.95 (*0-85045-739-4*, 9119, Pub. by Ospry) Stackpole.

— British Cavalry Equipments,1800-1941. (Men-at-Arms Ser.: No. 138). (Illus.). 48p. pap. 11.95 (*0-85045-479-4*, 9070, Pub. by Ospry) Stackpole.

***Chappell, Mike.** British Infantry Equipments 1908-2000. rev. ed. (Men at Arms Ser.: Vol. 108). (Illus.). 2000. pap. 12.95 (*1-85532-839-9*) Ospry.

Chappell, Mike. British Infantry Equipments 1808-1908. (Men-at-Arms Ser.: No. 107). (Illus.). 48p. pap. 11.95 (*0-85045-374-7*, 9040, Pub. by Ospry) Stackpole.

— British Infantry Equipments 1908-80. (Men-at-Arms Ser.: No. 108). (Illus.). 48p. pap. 11.95 (*0-85045-375-5*, 9041, Pub. by Ospry) Stackpole.

— The Canadian Army at War. (Men-at-Arms Ser.: No. 164). (Illus.). 48p. pap. 11.95 (*0-85045-600-2*, 9096, Pub. by Ospry) Stackpole.

— The Ghurkas. (Elite Ser.). (Illus.). 64p. 1993. pap. 12.95 (*1-85532-357-5*, 9464, Pub. by Ospry) Stackpole.

— The Guards 1914-1945. (Elite Ser.). (Illus.). 64p. 1995. pap. 12.95 (*1-85532-546-2*, Pub. by Ospry) Stackpole.

***Chappell, Mike.** King's German Legion 1803-1812. (Men at Arms Ser.: Vol. 338). (Illus.). 2000. pap. 12.95 (*1-85532-996-4*) Ospry.

— King's German Legion 1812-1816. (Men at Arms Ser.: Vol. 339). (Illus.). 48p. 2000. pap. 12.95 (*1-85532-997-2*) Ospry.

Chappell, Mike. Redcaps British Military Police. 1997. 12.95 (*1-85532-670-1*, Pub. by Ospry) Stackpole.

— Scottish Infantry Units in the World Wars. (Elite Ser.). (Illus.). 64p. 1995. pap. 12.95 (*1-85532-469-5*, Pub. by Ospry) Stackpole.

Chappell, Mike, jt. auth. see Knight, Paul.

Chappell, Mike, jt. auth. see Windrow, Martin.

***Chappell, Mollie.** A Letter from Lydia. large type ed. 320p. 1999. pap. 20.99 (*1-85389-868-6*) Ulverscroft.

Chappell, Nancy A. The Cousins Discover Healing Energy: Sharing Reike with Children. Raven, Kay, ed. (Illus.). 58p. (Orig.). (J). (gr. 2-5). 1996. pap. text 9.95 (*1-57108-012-0*) Lancashire Intl.

Chappell, P. E. Chappell, Dickie, & Other Kindred Families of Virginia. rev. ed. (Illus.). 384p. 1989. reprint ed. pap. 59.00 (*0-8328-0393-6*); reprint ed. lib. bdg. 69.00 (*0-8328-0392-8*) Higginson Bk Co.

An Asterisk (*) at the beginning of an entry indicates that the title is appearing for the first time.

C

— Eloge d'une Soupconnee. (Poesie Ser.). (FRE.). pap. 11.95 (*2-07-032531-8*) Schoenhof.

— Fureur et Mystere. (FRE.). 1966. pap. 10.95 (*0-8288-3820-8*, F93230) Fr & Eur.

— Fureur et Mystere. (Poesie Ser.). (FRE.). 264p. 1949. 9.95 (*2-07-030065-X*) Schoenhof.

— L' Inclemence Lointaine. (Illus.). 30.00 (*0-686-54157-X*) Fr & Eur.

— Le Marteau Sans Maitre: Avec: Le Moulin Premier (1927-1935) 128p. 12.50 (*0-686-54158-8*) Fr & Eur.

— Les Matinaux. (Poesie Ser.). (FRE.). 156p. 1950. 11.95 (*2-07-030066-8*) Schoenhof.

— Les Matinaux, Parole en Archipel. (FRE.). 1969. pap. 10.95 (*0-8288-3821-6*, F93260) Fr & Eur.

— Le Nu Perdu & Retour Amont, Dans la Pluie Giboyeuse, le Chien de Coeur, l'Effroi la Joie, Contres une Maison Seche. (Poesie Ser.). (FRE.). 143p. 1971. pap. 9.95 (*2-07-032178-9*) Schoenhof.

— Le Nu Perdu et Autres Poemes, 1964-1975. (FRE.). 1978. pap. 10.95 (*0-8288-3822-4*, F83180) Fr & Eur.

— La Nuit Talismanique. (FRE.). 1983. pap. 16.95 (*0-7859-3403-0*) Fr & Eur.

Char, Rene. Oeuvres Completes. (Pleiade Ser.). (FRE.). 1983. 110.00 (*0-8288-3457-1*, F15070) Fr & Eur.

Char, Rene. La Parole en Archipel. (FRE.). 160p. 1986. 11.95 (*0-7859-1158-8*, 2070708098) Fr & Eur.

— Poemes et Prose Choisis. 320p. 1957. 7.95 (*0-8288-9090-0*) Fr & Eur.

— Recherche de la Base et du Sommet. (FRE.). 1977. pap. 10.95 (*0-8288-3823-2*) Fr & Eur.

— Recherche de la Base et du Sommet. (Poesie Ser.). (FRE.). 192p. 1977. pap. 7.95 (*2-07-031918-0*) Schoenhof.

— Retour Amont. (FRE.). 96p. 1966. 11.95 (*0-7859-1104-9*, 2070213773) Fr & Eur.

— Se Rencontrer Paysage avec Joseph Sema. 20p. 1974. 8.95 (*0-686-54170-7*) Fr & Eur.

— Selected Poems of Rene Char. Caws, Mary A. & Jolas, Tina, trs. from FRE. LC 92-6351. 160p. 1992. 19.95 (*0-8112-1191-6*, Pub. by New Directions); pap. 10.95 (*0-8112-1192-4*, NDP734, Pub. by New Directions) Norton.

— Sur la Poesie. 35p. 1974. 8.95 (*0-7859-0687-8*, F93360) Fr & Eur.

Char, Rene & Eluard, Paul. Deux Poemes. (Illus.). 15p. 1960. 15.00 (*0-686-54154-5*) Fr & Eur.

Char, Rene & Feld, Charles. Picasso, Dessins. 256p. 1969. 65.00 (*0-7859-0686-X*, F93300) Fr & Eur.

Char, S. V. Hinduism & Islam in India: Caste, Religion, & Society from Antiquity to Early Modern Times. LC 97-26839. 270p. (C). 1997. text 39.95 (*1-55876-150-0*) Wiener Pubs Inc.

— Hinduism & Islam in India: Caste, Religion & Society from Antiquity to Early Modern Times. LC 97-26839. 270p. (C). 1997. pap. text 18.95 (*1-55876-151-9*) Wiener Pubs Inc.

***Chara, Paul.** Art of Virtue. LC 99-66105. (Illus.). 96p. 1999. pap. 19.95 (*1-57921-189-5*, Pub. by WinePress Pub) BookWorld.

Charach, Ron. Someone Else's Memoirs. LC 94-159055. 96p. 1994. pap. 14.95 (*1-55082-105-9*, Pub. by Quarry Pr) LPC InBook.

Charach, Ron, ed. The Naked Physician. 184p. 1990. pap. 14.95 (*0-919627-77-3*, Pub. by Quarry Pr) LPC InBook.

Charachon, R. & Garcia-Ibanez, E., eds. Long-Term Results & Indications in Otology & Otoneurosurgery. LC 91-30815. (Illus.). 596p. 1991. lib. bdg. 171.50 (*90-6299-070-3*, Pub. by Kugler) Kugler Pubns.

Characklis, William G. & Marshall, Kevin C. Biofilms. LC 89-5681. (Environmental & Applied Microbiology Ser.). 816p. 1990. 299.95 (*0-471-82663-4*) Wiley.

Characklis, William G. & Wildrer, P. A., eds. Structure & Function of Biofilms. (Dahlem Workshop Reports - Life Sciences). 404p. 1989. 325.00 (*0-471-92480-6*) Wiley.

Character & Extent of the American Audience for Ar. The American Audience for Art: Proceedings of the Symposium, Wiggin Gallery, Boston Public Library, 1969 & 1970. 1972. 5.00 (*0-89073-027-X*, 102) Boston Public Lib.

Character Education Institute Staff. Character Education Curriculum: Kindergarten, K-9. Mulkey, Young J., ed. (Illus.). (J). (ps-k). 1990. 140.00 (*0-913413-00-3*) Char Ed Inst.

— Character Education Curriculum: Kindergarten, K-9, Level C: Character for Citizenship. Mulkey, Young J., ed. (Illus.). 1995. 125.00 (*0-913413-11-9*) Char Ed Inst.

— Character Education Curriculum: Kindergarten, K-9, Level D: Character for Citizenship. Mulkey, Young J., ed. (Illus.). 1997. 125.00 (*0-913413-12-7*) Char Ed Inst.

— Character Education Curriculum: Kindergarten, K-9, Level A: Character for Citizenship. Mulkey, Young J., ed. (Illus.). 1996. 125.00 (*0-913413-15-1*) Char Ed Inst.

— Character Education Curriculum: Kindergarten, K-9, Level B: Character for Citizenship. Mulkey, Young J., ed. (Illus.). 1997. 125.00 (*0-913413-10-0*) Char Ed Inst.

— Character Education Curriculum: Kindergarten, K-9, Level E: Character for Citizenship. Mulkey, Young J., ed. (Illus.). 1995. 125.00 (*0-913413-13-5*) Char Ed Inst.

— Character Education Curriculum: Kindergarten, K-9, Vol. F: Building Winners. Mulkey, Young J., ed. (Illus.). 1996. 125.00 (*0-913413-16-X*) Char Ed Inst.

Charak, S. D. & Billawaria, Anita. Pahari Styles of Indian Murals. LC 98-915504. 1998. 115.00 (*81-7017-356-6*, Pub. by Abhinav Pubns) S Asia.

Charak, Stephen. Pet Stories for Children of All Ages. (Illus.). 48p. (Orig.). 1991. pap. 5.95 (*0-9627201-1-9*) Patcha Pubng.

***Charak, Sukhdev S.** Jammu Ragamala Paintings. LC 98-906107. 1998. 64.00 (*81-7017-355-8*, Pub. by Abhinav Pubns) S Asia.

Charak, T., jt. auth. see Chhabra, S.

Charaka. Charaka Samhita, 4 vols., Set. Sharma, Ram K. & Dash, Vaidya B., trs. from SAN. 619p. 1983. text 170.00 (*0-89744-050-1*) Auromere.

Charalabidis, Alexander. The Book of IRC: The Ultimate Guide to Internet Relay Chat. LC 99-10403. 347p. 1999. pap. 24.95 (*1-886411-29-8*) No Starch Pr.

Charalambous, George. Food Flavors: Generation, Analysis & Process Influence. (Developments in Food Science Ser.: No. 37). 2280p. 1995. 491.50 (*0-444-82013-2*) Elsevier.

— Handbook of Food & Beverage Stability: Chemical, Biochemical & Microbiological Aspects. (Academic Press Handbook Ser.). 1986. text 153.00 (*0-12-169070-9*) Acad Pr.

— Off-Flavors in Foods & Beverages. (Developments in Food Science Ser.: Vol. 28). xiv,750p. 1992. 332.00 (*0-444-88558-7*) Elsevier.

— Spices, Herbs & Edible Fungi. LC 93-40928. (Developments in Food Science Ser.: Vol. 34). 780p. 1994. 316.50 (*0-444-81761-1*) Elsevier.

Charalambous, George, ed. Food Science & Human Nutrition. LC 92-9175. (Developments in Food Science Ser.: Vol. 29). xxiv,822p. 1992. 363.00 (*0-444-88834-9*) Elsevier.

— Shelf Life Studies of Foods & Beverages: Chemical, Biological, & Physical Aspects. LC 93-34767. (Developments in Food Science Ser.: No. 33). (Illus.). 1224p. 1993. 396.00 (*0-444-89459-4*) Elsevier.

Charalambous, George & Katz, Ira, eds. Phenolic, Sulfur, & Nitrogen Compounds in Food Flavors. LC 76-16544. (ACS Symposium Ser.: Vol. 26). 223p. 1976. reprint ed. pap. 69.20 (*0-608-03554-8*, 206427300008) Bks Demand.

Charalambous, George, jt. auth. see Wetzel, David L.

Charan, R., jt. auth. see Tichy, N.

Charan, Ram. Boards That Work: How Corporate Boards Create Competitive Advantage. LC 97-45422. 240p. 1997. mass mkt. 27.00 (*0-7879-1060-0*) Jossey-Bass.

— Every Business is A Growth Business. 352p. 2000. pap. 16.00 (*0-8129-3305-2*) Random Hse Lrg Prnt.

***Charan, Ram.** What the CEO Knows That You Don't: The Little Book of Big Business. 2001. 17.95 (*0-609-60839-8*) Crown Pub Group.

***Charan, Ram, et al.** Leadership Pipeline: How to Build the Leadership Powered Company. 224p. 2000. 28.50 (*0-7879-5172-2*) Jossey-Bass.

Charan, Ram, jt. auth. see Tichy, Noel M.

Charap, John M. Geometry of Constrained Dynamical Systems. (Publications of the Newton Institute: No. 3). 349p. (C). 1995. text 49.95 (*0-521-48271-2*) Cambridge U Pr.

— Physics 2000. (Bowerdean Briefings Ser.). (Illus.). 144p. 1997. pap. text 14.95 (*0-906097-79-7*, Pub. by Bowerdean Pub) Capital VA.

Charap, Joshua, jt. auth. see Webster, Leila M.

Charash, Leon I., et al, eds. Muscular Dystrophy & Allied Diseases: Impact on Patients, Family & Staff. LC 86-82709. (Current Thanatology Ser.). 90p. 1988. pap. 15.95 (*0-930194-38-1*) Ctr Thanatology.

— Realities in Coping with Progressive Neuromuscular Diseases. LC 87-71168. 228p. (C). 1987. text 34.95 (*0-914783-20-3*) Charles.

Charash, Leon I., et al. Muscular Dystrophy & Other Neuromuscular Diseases: Psychosocial Issues. (Loss, Grief & Care Ser.: Vol. 4 Nos. 3 & 4). (Illus.). 270p. 1991. text 49.95 (*1-56024-077-6*) Haworth Pr.

Charash, Ruth A. ErgoAnalyzer. 90p. 1990. text 49.00 (*1-879803-01-1*) Charash.

— ErgoAnalyzer: Handbook. 84p. 1990. pap. 22.00 (*1-879803-02-X*) Charash.

— ErgoFit: Fitting Your Job to You. 83p. 1990. 16.00 (*1-879803-00-3*) Charash.

— ErgoProducts. 112p. 1988. 79.00 (*1-879803-03-8*) Charash.

— ErgoSpecs. 120p. 1989. 89.00 (*1-879803-04-6*) Charash.

Charash, Ruth A., et al. Ergo Training: An Ergonomics Trainer Program. Kolodji, Brenda et al, eds. 50p. 1990. 500.00 incl. sl. (*1-879803-05-4*) Charash.

Charbeneau, James A. Shouts & Whispers: Stories from the Southern Chesapeake Bay. LC 96-43891. (Illus.). 175p. (Orig.). 1997. pap. 12.95 (*1-883911-11-7*) Brandylane.

***Charbeneau, Randall J.** Groundwater Hydraulics & Pollutant Transport. LC 99-38307. (Illus.). 593p. 1999. 105.00 (*0-13-975616-7*) P-H.

Charbeneau, Randall J., ed. Groundwater Management: Proceedings of the International Smposium, San Antonio, Texas, August 14-16, 1995. LC 95-34318. 432p. 1995. 49.00 (*0-7844-0107-1*) Am Soc Civil Eng.

Charbeneau, Randall J., et al, eds. Groundwater Remediation. LC 92-53524. (Water Quality Management Library: Vol. 8). 290p. 1992. text 99.95 (*0-87762-943-9*) Technomic.

Charbeneau, Randall J. & Popkin, Barney P., eds. Regional & State Water Resources Planning & Management: Proceedings of a Symposium Held in San Antonio, Texas. LC 84-73194. (American Water Resources Association Technical Publication Ser.: No. TPS-83-1). 374p. reprint ed. pap. 116.00 (*0-8357-7927-0*, 203635300002) Bks Demand.

Charbern. I Am I Am, & So Are You. 150p. 1998. mass mkt. 11.95 (*0-9666785-0-8*) Charbern Pub.

Charbon, Marie H. Historical & Theoretical Works to 1800: Vol 1 of the Hague Municipal Museum Catalog of the Music Library. LC 76-84485. (Music Ser.). 1925. 35.00 (*0-306-77221-3*) Da Capo.

Charboneau, Milton, compiled by. First Landowners, Livingston County, Michigan. LC 86-7239. (Illus.). xii, 185p. 1986. 15.00 (*0-9616142-1-8*) Livingston County.

Charboneau, Milton, photos by. Greenwood & Mount Olivet Cemeteries Fowlerville, Michigan-Transcribed Records. LC 85-19832. (Illus.). 395p. 1985. 20.00 (*0-318-19881-9*) Livingston County.

Charboneau, Milton, jt. ed. see King, Kernie.

Charbonneau, Andre. Fortifications of Ile Aux Noix: Portrait of the Defensive Strategy on the Upper Richelieu Border in the 18th & 19th Centuries. (Illus.). 382p. (Orig.). 1994. pap. 63.65 (*0-660-15194-4*, Pub. by Canadian Govt Pub) Accents Pubns.

Charbonneau, Andre & Drolet-Dube, Doris. A Register of Deceased Persons at Sea & on Grosse Ile in 1847. 2nd ed. LC 97-221209. 720p. 1997. pap. 16.95 (*0-660-16877-4*, Pub. by Canadian Govt Pub) Accents Pubns.

Charbonneau, Andre & Sevigny, Andre. Grosse Ile, 1847: A Record of Daily Events. 2nd ed. LC 97-221074. (Illus.). 344p. 1997. pap. 29.95 (*0-660-16878-2*, Pub. by Canadian Govt Pub) Accents Pubns.

Charbonneau, Christine, jt. auth. see Marino, Emiliano.

***Charbonneau, Eileen.** The Connor Emerald. Williams, Lori, ed. 170p. 1999. pap. 9.99 (*1-58365-753-3*, Timeless Romance) BT Pub.

— The Ghosts of Stony Clove. (Woods Family Saga Ser.). (J). 1995. 9.09 (*0-606-11385-1*, Pub. by Turtleback) Demco.

Charbonneau, Eileen. The Ghosts of Stony Clove. (Illus.). 160p. (YA). (gr. 5 up). 1995. reprint ed. 3.99 (*0-8125-5186-9*, Pub. by Tor Bks) St Martin.

— Honor to the Hills. LC 95-30027. 192p. (J). (gr. 7). 1996. 18.95 (*0-312-86094-3*, Pub. by Tor Bks) St Martin.

— Honor to the Hills. (FRE.). (J). (gr. 7). 1997. mass mkt. 3.99 (*0-8125-5187-7*, Pub. by Tor Bks) St Martin.

Charbonneau, Eileen. Honor to the Hills, 3. (Woods Family Saga Ser.). 1997. 9.09 (*0-606-11477-7*, Pub. by Turtleback) Demco.

Charbonneau, Eileen. In the Time of the Wolves. 192p. 1994. mass mkt. 3.99 (*0-8125-3361-5*, Pub. by Tor Bks) St Martin.

— In the Time of the Wolves. (J). 1994. 9.09 (*0-606-11506-4*, Pub. by Turtleback) Demco.

— Rachel Lemoyne. 320p. 1999. mass mkt. 5.99 (*0-8125-7114-2*, Pub. by Forge NYC) St Martin.

— Rachel Lemoyne. LC 98-5556. 320p. 1998. text 22.95 (*0-312-86448-5*) St Martin.

— The Randolph Legacy. 1998. mass mkt. 6.50 (*0-8125-4467-6*, Pub. by Forge NYC) St Martin.

— Waltzing in Ragtime. 416p. 1997. mass mkt. 6.99 (*0-8125-4468-4*, Pub. by Forge NYC) St Martin.

— Waltzing in Ragtime. LC 96-3148. 480p. 1996. 26.95 (*0-312-86180-X*) St Martin.

Charbonneau, Gerard & Seguin, Hubert. Workbook in Everyday French, 2 bks. rev. ed. 213p. (YA). (gr. 9-11). 1971. teacher ed. 2.95 (*0-685-38985-5*, 18131) Prentice ESL.

— Workbook in Everyday French, 2 bks., Bk. 2. rev. ed. 213p. (gr. 9-11). 1971. pap. text 5.45 (*0-88345-168-9*, 17480) Prentice ESL.

Charbonneau, Hubert, et al. The First French Canadians: Pioneers in the St. Lawrence Valley. Colozzo, Paola, tr. from FRE. LC 92-53879.Tr. of Naissance d'une Population. 1993. 39.50 (*0-87413-454-4*) U Delaware Pr.

Charbonneau, James. Even More Scary Stories for Stormy Nights. LC 97-4983. 96p. (J). 1997. pap. 5.95 (*1-56565-608-3*) NTC Contemp Pub Co.

Charbonneau-Lassay, Louis. Bestiary of Christ. abr. ed. Dooling, D. M., tr. from FRE. (Illus.). 467p. 1991. 29.95 (*0-930407-18-0*) Parabola Bks.

Charbonneau, Louis. The Ice: A Novel of Antarctica. large type ed. LC 91-14389. 531p. 1991. reprint ed. lib. bdg. 21.95 (*1-56054-177-6*) Thorndike Pr.

— The Ice: A Novel of Antarctica. 320p. 1993. reprint ed. mass mkt. 5.50 (*0-671-74714-2*) PB.

— The Magnificent Siberian. large type ed. (Ulverscroft Large Print Ser.). 592p. 1997. 27.99 (*0-7089-3787-X*) Ulverscroft.

***Charbonneau, Louis.** Spirit Warrior. 1999. write for info. (*1-55611-547-4*, Pub. by D I Fine) Penguin Putnam.

Charbonneau, Louis. White Harvest. large type ed. 576p. 31.50 (*0-7089-3681-4*) Ulverscroft.

Charbonneau, Manon. Hidden Rods/Hidden Numbers. 78p. (J). (gr. 1-8). 1975. pap. text 7.50 (*0-914040-13-8*) Cuisenaire.

Charbonneau, Manon P. & Reider, Barbara E. The Integrated Elementary Classroom: A Developmental Model for the Twenty-First Century. LC 94-33078. 256p. 1994. pap. text 37.00 (*0-205-15462-X*) Allyn.

Charbonneau, Rene, jt. ed. see Rigault, Andre.

Charbonneaux, Nelly. Dictionnaire des Charades. 1994p. 1994. pap. 14.95 (*0-7859-7629-9*); 14.95 (*0-614-00408-X*) Fr & Eur.

Charbonnel, Nanine, ed. Le Don de la Parole: Melanges Offerts a Daniel Hameline pour Son Soixante-Cinquieme Anniversaire. (Exploration Ser.). (FRE., Illus.). 161p. 1997. 27.95 (*3-906757-95-1*, Pub. by P Lang) P Lang Pubng.

***Charbonnel, Olivier.** Don't Do That! An Interactive Book. (Illus.). 12p. (J). (ps-6). 1999. 9.95 (*1-58260-007-4*, Pub. by Infnty Plus One) Assoc Pubs Grp.

— Whose Shoes Are These? (Illus.). 2000. 6.95 (*1-902413-39-3*) Van Der Meer.

Charbonnet, Carl. American Fables for the Politically Incorrect. (Illus.). 192p. 1995. 18.00 (*0-9648786-0-7*) Am de Tocqueville.

Charbonnet, Gabrielle. Adventure in Walt Disney World. LC 98-84830. (Disney Girls Ser.). 128p. (J). (gr. 2-5). 1999. pap. 3.95 (*0-7868-4271-7*, Pub. by Disney Pr) Time Warner.

— And Sleepy Makes Seven. (Disney Girls Ser.). 96p. (J). (gr. 2-5). 1998. pap. 3.95 (*0-7868-4158-3*, Pub. by Disney Pr) Time Warner.

— Attack of the Beast. (Disney Girls Ser.). 96p. (J). (gr. 2-5). 1998. pap. 3.95 (*0-7868-4160-5*, Pub. by Disney Pr) Time Warner.

— Balancing Act. (American Gold Gymnasts Ser.: No. 2). 144p. (J). (gr. 3-7). 1996. pap. 3.50 (*0-553-48296-3*, Skylark BDD) BDD Bks Young Read.

— Balancing Act. (American Gold Gymnasts Ser.). 1996. 8.60 (*0-606-08989-6*, Pub. by Turtleback) Demco.

— Beauty's Revenge. (Disney Girls Ser.). 96p. (J). (gr. 2-5). 1999. pap. text 3.99 (*0-7868-4272-5*, Pub. by Hyperion) Time Warner.

— Bully Coach. (American Gold Gymnasts Ser.). 1996. 8.60 (*0-606-08991-8*, Pub. by Turtleback) Demco.

— Cinderella's Castle. (Disney Girls Ser.). 96p. (J). (gr. 2-5). 1998. pap. 3.95 (*0-7868-4165-6*, Pub. by Disney Pr) Time Warner.

— Competition Fever. (American Gold Gymnasts Ser.: No. 1). 144p. (J). (gr. 3-7). 1996. pap. 3.50 (*0-553-48295-5*, Skylark BDD) BDD Bks Young Read.

— Competition Fever. (American Gold Gymnasts Ser.). 1996. 8.60 (*0-606-08988-8*, Pub. by Turtleback) Demco.

***Charbonnet, Gabrielle.** Disney Girls #7: Adventure at Walt Disney World Book Club Special Sales Edition. 1999. pap. 3.99 (*0-7868-4390-X*, Pub. by Disney Pr) Time Warner.

— Divine Miss Ariel. LC 99-60220. (Disney Girls Ser.). 96p. (J). (gr. 2-5). 2000. pap. text 3.99 (*0-7868-4276-8*, Pub. by Disney Pr) Time Warner.

Charbonnet, Gabrielle. A Fish Out of Water. LC PZ7.C37355Fi 1998. (Disney Girls Ser.). 96p. (J). (gr. 2-5). 1998. pap. 3.95 (*0-7868-4159-1*, Pub. by Disney Pr) Time Warner.

***Charbonnet, Gabrielle.** Good-Bye, Jasmine? LC 98-88405. (Disney Girls Ser.). 128p. (J). (gr. 2-5). 1999. pap. text 3.99 (*0-7868-4273-3*, Pub. by Hyperion) Time Warner.

Charbonnet, Gabrielle. The Gum Race. (Disney Girls Ser.). (J). (gr. 2-5). 1999. pap. text 3.99 (*0-7868-4275-X*, Pub. by Disney Pr) Time Warner.

— Hercules I Made Herc a Hero: By Phil. (J). 1997. pap. 3.50 (*0-7868-4195-8*, Pub. by Disney Pr) Little.

— Home at Last. (Princess Ser.: No. 3). 128p. (J). (gr. 3-7). 1995. pap. 3.50 (*0-590-22289-9*) Scholastic Inc.

— Home at Last. (Princess Ser.). 1995. 8.60 (*0-606-07658-1*, Pub. by Turtleback) Demco.

— The Lion King: Just Can't Wait to Be King. (Disney Chapters Ser.). (Illus.). 64p. (J). (gr. 2-4). 1998. pap. 3.95 (*0-7868-4178-8*, Pub. by Disney Pr) Time Warner.

— Molly's Heart. (Princess Ser.: No. 1). 128p. (J). (gr. 3-7). 1995. pap. 3.50 (*0-590-22287-2*) Scholastic Inc.

— Molly's Heart. (Princess Ser.). (J). 1995. 8.60 (*0-606-07878-9*, Pub. by Turtleback) Demco.

— Once upon a Time with Mary-Kate & Ashley: A Disney Princess Story & Activity Collection. LC 97-80386. (Illus.). 96p. (J). (gr. k-4). 1998. 16.95 (*0-7868-3189-8*, Pub. by Disney Pr) Time Warner.

— 101 Dalmatians: Escape from De Ville Mansion. (J). 1996. pap. write for info. (*0-7868-4148-6*) Disney Pr.

— One of Us. LC 97-80295. (Disney Girls Ser.). 96p. (J). (gr. 2-5). 1998. pap. 3.95 (*0-7868-4156-7*, Pub. by Disney Pr) Time Warner.

— One Pet Too Many. LC 98-84793. (Disney Girls Ser.). (J). (gr. 2-5). 1998. pap. 3.95 (*0-7868-4166-4*, Pub. by Disney Pr) Time Warner.

— Princess of Power. (Disney Girls Ser.). (J). (gr. 2-5). 1999. pap. text 3.99 (*0-7868-4274-1*, Pub. by Disney Pr) Time Warner.

— A Room in the Attic. (Princess Ser.: No. 2). 128p. (J). (gr. 3-7). 1995. pap. 3.50 (*0-590-22288-0*) Scholastic Inc.

— A Room in the Attic. (Princess Ser.). (J). 1995. 8.60 (*0-606-08083-X*, Pub. by Turtleback) Demco.

— Snakes Are Nothing to Sneeze At. (Illus.). 80p. (J). (gr. 2-4). 1995. 13.95 (*0-8050-1373-3*, Bks Young Read); pap. 4.95 (*0-8050-1842-5*, Bks Young Read) H Holt & Co.

— Split Decision. (American Gold Gymnasts Ser.: No. 3). 144p. (J). (gr. 4-7). 1996. pap. 3.50 (*0-553-48298-X*, Skylark BDD) BDD Bks Young Read.

— Split Decision. (American Gold Gymnasts Ser.). 1996. 8.60 (*0-606-08990-X*, Pub. by Turtleback) Demco.

— Tutu Much Ballet. (Illus.). 80p. (J). (gr. 2-4). 1995. pap. 5.95 (*0-8050-4643-7*) H Holt & Co.

Charbonnet, Gabrielle, et al. Once upon a Time with Mary-Kate & Ashley: A Disney Princess Story & Activity Collection. LC 97-80386. 96p. (J). (gr. k-4). 1999. pap. 9.99 (*0-7868-4343-8*, Pub. by Hyperion) Time Warner.

Charbonnet, Varela G. Ballet for Charlotte. 89p. (J). 1995. 14.95 (*0-8050-3063-8*) H Holt & Co.

Charbot, N. Dictionary des Patois du Dauphine. (FRE.). 457p. 1973. reprint ed. 195.00 (*0-320-00898-3*) Fr & Eur.

Charcot, Jean M. Clinical Lectures on Senile & Chronic Diseases. Kastenbaum, Robert J., ed. Tuke, William S., tr. LC 78-22189. (Aging & Old Age Ser.). 1979. reprint ed. lib. bdg. 25.95 (*0-405-11807-4*) Ayer.

— Oeuvres Completes de J. M. Charcot, 9 vols., Set. LC 70-169463. reprint ed. write for info. (*0-404-10000-7*) AMS Pr.

Charcot, Jean-Martin. Charcot, the Clinician: The Tuesday Lessons. Goetz, Christopher G., tr. (Illus.). 224p. 1987. text 75.00 (*0-88167-315-3*) Lppncott W & W.

Chard. Health & Safety for Nurses. 250p. 1993. pap. 41.50 (*1-56593-142-4*, 0454) Singular Publishing.

Chard. Pleasure & Guilt Grand Tour. 1999. pap. 24.95 (*0-7190-4805-2*) St Martin.

***Chard.** Pleasure & Guilt Grand Tour. LC 99-52388. 1999. text 79.95 (*0-7190-4804-4*) St Martin.

Chard, Chester S. Northeast Asia in Prehistory. LC 73-2040. (Illus.). 231p. reprint ed. pap. 71.70 (*0-8357-6236-X*, 203428000089) Bks Demand.

Chard, Chloe & Langdon, Helen, eds. Transports: Travel, Pleasure & Imaginative Geography, 1600-1830. LC 96-28226. (Studies in British Art: Vol. 3). 296p. 1996. 52.00 (*0-300-06382-2*) Yale U Pr.

An Asterisk (*) at the beginning of an entry indicates that the title is appearing for the first time.

Chard Dacey, Florence. The Necklace. LC 87-63131. (Illus.). 64p. (Orig.). 1988. pap. text 5.95 (*0-935697-03-9*) Midwest Villages.

Chard, Daniel. Landscape Illusion: A Spatial Approach to Painting. (Illus.). 144p. 1993. pap. 18.95 (*0-8230-2594-2*) Watsn-Guptill.

***Chard, David & Bos, Candace, eds.** Moving From Research to Practice: Professional Development to Promote Effective Teaching of Early Reading. A Special Issue of Learning Disabilitites Research & Practice. 88p. 1999. pap. 20.00 (*0-8058-9778-X*) L Erlbaum Assocs.

Chard, Jack, jt. auth. see Isleib, Charles R.

Chard, Judy. Appointment with Danger. large type ed. (Linford Romance Library). 1991. pap. 16.99 (*0-7089-7115-6*) Ulverscroft.

***Chard, Judy.** Betrayed. 256p. 2000. 18.99 (*0-7089-5696-3*) Ulverscroft.

Chard, Judy. Enchantment. large type ed. (Linford Romance Library). 1991. pap. 16.99 (*0-7089-7060-5*) Ulverscroft.

— Encounter in Spain. (Rainbow Romances Ser.). 160p. 1994. 14.95 (*0-7090-5406-8*, 918) Parkwest Pubns.

— Person Unknown. large type ed. (Linford Mystery Library). 1989. pap. 16.99 (*0-7089-6776-0*, Linford) Ulverscroft.

— To Be So Loved. large type ed. (Linford Romance Library). 1991. pap. 16.99 (*0-7089-7047-8*) Ulverscroft.

Chard, Lynn P., ed. Advising the Older Client. LC 90-85065. 600p. 1990. ring bd. 110.00 (*0-685-39003-9*, 90-035) U MI Law CLE.

— Advising the Older Client. LC 90-85065. 600p. 1991. suppl. ed. 60.00 (*0-685-58919-6*) U MI Law CLE.

— Advising the Older Client. LC 90-85065. 600p. 1992. suppl. ed. 55.00 (*0-685-58920-X*) U MI Law CLE.

Chard, Lynn P. & Headly, Anna, eds. Michigan Probate Sourcebook, 3 vols. 2nd ed. LC 91-71293. 1300p. 1991. ring bd., suppl. ed. 145.00 (*0-685-54242-4*, 91-004) U MI Law CLE.

— Michigan Probate Sourcebook, 3 vols. 2nd ed. LC 91-71293. 1300p. 1992. suppl. ed. 70.00 (*0-685-58917-X*, 92-003) U MI Law CLE.

— Michigan Probate Sourcebook, 3 vols. 2nd ed. LC 91-71293. 1300p. 1993. suppl. ed. 75.00 (*0-685-58918-8*, 93-006) U MI Law CLE.

Chard, Philip S. The Healing Earth: Nature's Medicine for the Troubled Soul, 1. 144p. 1999. pap. text 10.95 (*1-55971-672-X*) NorthSound Music.

Chard, Sylvia C., jt. auth. see Katz, Lilian.

Chard, Sylvia C., jt. auth. see Katz, Lilian G.

Chard, T. & Grudzinskas, J. Gedes, eds. The Uterus. (Cambridge Reviews in Human Reproduction Ser.). (Illus.). 399p. (C). 1995. pap. text 47.95 (*0-521-42453-4*) Cambridge U Pr.

Chard, T., jt. ed. see Landon, J.

Chard, Tim. Basic Sciences for Obstetrics & Gynecology - MCQs. 2nd ed. LC 97-46471. v, 123p. 1998. pap. 29.95 (*3-540-76206-X*) Spr-Verlag.

— Computing for Clinician. 2nd ed. 192p. 1995. pap. text 19.95 (*0-340-62527-9*, Pub. by E A) OUP.

— Computing for Clinicians. LC 92-2228. 1992. write for info. (*0-387-19721-4*) Spr-Verlag.

— Laboratory Techniques in Biochemistry & Molecular Biology, Vol. 6. Incl. Pt. 2. Introduction to Radioimmunoassay & Related Techniques. 1983. 72.25 1978. write for info. (*0-318-51833-3*, North Holland) Elsevier.

Chard, Tim, et al, eds. Spontaneous Abortion: Diagnosis & Treatment. (Illus.). xiv, 231p. 1992. 174.00 (*0-387-19712-5*) Spr-Verlag.

Chard, Tim, rev. An Introduction to Radioimmunoassay & Related Techniques. 5th ed. 328p. 1995. pap. text 79.50 (*0-444-82119-8*) Elsevier.

— An Introduction to Radioimmunoassay & Related Techniques. 5th ed. (Laboratory Techniques in Biochemistry & Molecular Biology Ser.: 6/II). 328p. 1995. 177.50 (*0-444-82118-X*) Elsevier.

Chard, Tim & Lilford, Richard J. Basic Sciences for Obstetrics & Gynecology. 2nd ed. (Illus.). 200p. 1986. pap. 33.00 (*0-387-16214-3*) Spr-Verlag.

— Basic Sciences for Obstetrics & Gynecology. 3rd ed. (Illus.). 216p. 1990. pap. text 33.00 (*0-387-19591-2*) Spr-Verlag.

— Basic Sciences in Obstetrics & Gynecology. 4th ed. LC 94-47954. 1996. 39.50 (*3-540-19903-9*) Spr-Verlag.

— Basic Sciences in Obstetrics & Gynecology. 4th ed. LC 94-47954. 1996. 39.50 (*0-387-19903-9*) Spr-Verlag.

— Mrcogo, Pt. 1. 1987. pap. 29.50 (*0-387-19501-7*) Spr-Verlag.

— Mrcogo, Pt. 1. 2nd ed. LC 92-13661. (Brainscan MCQs Ser.). 136p. 1992. 26.95 (*0-387-19767-2*) Spr-Verlag.

Chardaire-Riviere, Catherine & Worthington, Paul F., eds. Advances in Core Evaluation III: Reservoir Management. 512p. 1993. text 154.00 (*2-88124-904-3*) Gordon & Breach.

— Advances in Core Evaluation III: Reservoir Management, 3 vols., Set. 1564p. 1993. text 387.00 (*2-88124-923-X*) Gordon & Breach.

Chardans, J. L. & Vega, Vincente. Diccionario Ilustrado de Trucos. deluxe ed. (SPA.). 700p. 1970. 24.75 (*84-252-0206-X*) Fr & Eur.

Chardenal, Valerie, tr. see Lundstrom, Lowell.

Chardiet, Bernice. The Best Teacher in the World. (Hello, Reader! Ser.). 1996. 8.70 (*0-606-09070-3*, Pub. by Turtleback) Demco.

Chardiet, Bernice. A Book of Colors. (Monkey Pop-Ups Ser.). (Illus.). (J). 1996. 6.95 (*0-614-15774-9*, Cartwheel) Scholastic Inc.

— A Book of Opposites. (Monkey Pop-Ups Ser.). (Illus.). (J). 1996. 6.95 (*0-614-15775-7*, Cartwheel) Scholastic Inc.

— The Easter Ribbit. (Illus.). 32p. (J). (ps-3). 1998. pap. 2.99 (*0-590-10072-6*) Scholastic Inc.

— The Easter Ribbit. (Read with Me Ser.). (J). 1998. 8.19 (*0-606-13350-X*) Turtleback.

— Monkey Pop-Ups: A Book of Colors. (Illus.). 8p. (J). (ps-k). 1996. 6.95 (*0-590-54315-6*, Cartwheel) Scholastic Inc.

— Monkey Pop-Ups: A Book of Opposites. (Illus.). 8p. (J). (ps-k). 1996. 6.95 (*0-590-54314-8*, Cartwheel) Scholastic Inc.

— Rapunzel. 32p. (J). (ps-2). 1990. pap. 2.99 (*0-590-42281-2*) Scholastic Inc.

Chardiet, Bernice & Brenner, Barbara. Where's That Spider? LC 98-24746. (Hide & Seek Science Ser.). (Illus.). (J). 1999. 20.01 (*0-590-12818-3*) Scholastic Inc.

Chardiet, Bernice & Maccarone, Grace. The Best Teacher in the World. LC 95-23546. (Hello Reader! Ser.: Level 3). (Illus.). 32p. (J). (ps-3). 1996. reel tape 3.50 (*0-590-68158-3*, Cartwheel) Scholastic Inc.

— The Best Teacher in the World. (School Friends Ser.). (Illus.). 32p. (J). (ps-2). 1991. reprint ed. pap. 2.50 (*0-590-43307-5*) Scholastic Inc.

— Bunny Runs Away. (J). (ps-3). 1992. pap. 2.50 (*0-590-44932-X*) Scholastic Inc.

— Martin & the Teacher's Pet. (School Friends Ser.: No. 5). (Illus.). 48p. (J). (ps-3). 1992. pap. text 2.50 (*0-590-44931-1*) Scholastic Inc.

— Merry Christmas, What's Your Name. (Illus.). (J). (ps-3). 1990. 11.95 (*0-590-44334-8*, Scholastic Hardcover) Scholastic Inc.

— Merry Christmas, What's Your Name School Friends. (Illus.). 32p. (J). (ps-2). 1991. pap. text 2.50 (*0-590-43306-7*) Scholastic Inc.

— We Scream for Ice Cream. LC 98-22715. (Hello Reader! Ser.). (J). 1998. write for info. (*0-590-63395-3*) Scholastic Inc.

Chardiet, Bernice, et al. The Best Teacher in the World. (Hello Reader! (Je Peux Lire!) Ser.). (FRE., Illus.). 32p. (J). 1996. pap. 5.99 (*0-590-16029-X*) Scholastic Inc.

Chardiet, Bernice, jt. auth. see Brenner, Barbara.

Chardiet, Bernice, jt. auth. see Brenner, Barbara A.

Chardiet, Jon. The Magic Fish Rap. 32p. (J). (gr. k-3). 1993. pap. 5.95 incl. audio (*0-590-66152-3*) Scholastic Inc.

— Parker Penguin & the Winter Games. LC 98-27869. (Read with Me Paperback Ser.). (Illus.). 32p. (J). (gr. k-2). 1999. 3.25 (*0-590-14925-3*) Scholastic Inc.

— Parker Penguin, Big Brother Blues. LC 98-34154. (Read with Me Paperback Ser.). (Illus.). (J). 1998. write for info. (*0-590-14924-5*) Scholastic Inc.

Chardin, Jean. A Journey to Persia: Jean Chardin's Portrait of a Seventeenth-Century Empire. Ferrier, R. W., ed. (Illus.). 256p. 1996. text 39.50 (*1-85043-564-2*, Pub. by I B T) St Martin.

Chardin, John. Sir John Chardin's Travels in Persia. LC 76-181928. (BCL Ser.: No. I). reprint ed. 44.50 (*0-404-01449-6*) AMS Pr.

— Travels in Persia, 1673-1677. (Illus.). 336p. 1988. reprint ed. pap. 9.95 (*0-486-25636-7*) Dover.

Chardon, F. A. Chardon's Journal at Fort Clark, 1834-1839. Abel, Annie H., ed. & intro. by. Swagerty, William R., intro. LC 96-29657. (Illus.). lxix, 458p. 1997. pap. 20.00 (*0-8032-6375-9*, Bison Books) U of Nebr Pr.

Chardonne, Jacques. Eva Ou le Journal Interrompu. (FRE.). 1984. pap. 10.95 (*0-7859-1982-1*, 2070375196) Fr & Eur.

Charef, Mehdi. Le Au Harem d'Archi Ahmed. (FRE.). 184p. 1988. pap. 10.95 (*0-7859-2093-5*, 2070380416) Fr & Eur.

— Le Au Harem d'Archi Ahmed. (Folio Ser.: No. 1958). (FRE.). 184p. 1988. pap. 8.95 (*2-07-038041-6*) Schoenhof.

— Le Harki De Meriem. (FRE.). 211p. 1991. pap. 10.95 (*0-7859-2176-1*, 2070384225) Fr & Eur.

Charemza, Wojciech W., jt. ed. see Davis, Christopher.

Charernbhak, Wichit. Chicago School Architects & Their Critics. Foster, Stephen, ed. LC 83-24299. (Architecture & Urban Design Ser.: No. 1). 228p. reprint ed. pap. 70.70 (*0-8357-1537-X*, 207033000078) Bks Demand.

Charest-Papagno, Noella. Cosmetology Specialties for the Bedridden Patient. Bart, Stuart & Rosenberg, Dale, eds. LC 95-78324. (Illus.). 90p. 1996. per. 12.95 (*0-9604610-6-X*) JJ Pub FL.

— Handbook of Desairology for Cosmetologists Servicing Funeral Homes. 5th rev. ed. LC 95-20866. (Illus.). 90p. 1996. per. 16.95 (*0-9604610-7-8*) JJ Pub FL.

***Charest-Papagno, Noella.** HIV/AIDS Handbook for Personal Service Providers. large type ed. LC 97-93938. (Illus.). 58p. 1999. spiral bd. 8.95 (*0-9604610-9-4*, JJPLB) JJ Pub FL.

— Methods in Personal Care of the Bedridden Patient... Hair, Skin & Nails. large type ed. LC 97-93160. (Illus.). 48p. 1999. spiral bd. 10.95 (*0-9604610-8-6*, JJPLB) JJ Pub FL.

Charest, Remy, tr. see Lepage, Robert.

Charet, F. X. Spiritualism & the Foundations of C. G. Jung's Psychology. LC 91-23521. 329p. (C). 1993. pap. text 21.95 (*0-7914-1094-3*) State U NY Pr.

— Spiritualism & the Foundations of C. G. Jung's Psychology. LC 91-23521. 329p. (C). 1993. text 64.50 (*0-7914-1093-5*) State U NY Pr.

Charette, Beverly. The Story of Chanukah for Children. (Illus.). 24p. (J). (ps-3). 1981. pap. 3.95 (*0-8249-8020-4*, Ideals Child) Hambleton-Hill.

— The Story of Christmas for Children. LC 89-11048. (Illus.). 24p. (J). (ps-2). 1989. pap. 3.95 (*0-8249-8254-1*, Ideals Child) Hambleton-Hill.

— The Story of Easter for Children. (Illus.). 24p. (Orig.). (J). (ps-3). 1988. pap. 3.95 (*0-8249-8183-9*, Ideals Child) Hambleton-Hill.

***Charette, Blaine.** Restoring Presence: The Spirit in Matthew's Gospel. (Journal of Pentecostal Theology Supplement Ser.: No. 18). 160p. 2000. pap. 13.95 (*1-84127-059-8*, Pub. by Sheffield Acad) CUP Services.

Charette, Blaine, et al. The Theme of Recompense in Matthew's Gospel. (JSNT Supplement Ser.: No. 79). 184p. 1992. 57.50 (*1-85075-385-7*, Pub. by Sheffield Acad) CUP Services.

Charette, Jane, jt. auth. see Gale, Danielle.

Charette, Jean J. An Introduction to the Theory of Molecular Structure. LC 66-22648. 200p. reprint ed. pap. 62.00 (*0-608-30857-9*, 200724900063) Bks Demand.

Charette, Monik. Conditions on Phonological Government. (Cambridge Studies in Linguistics: No. 58). 246p. (C). 1991. text 64.95 (*0-521-39246-2*) Cambridge U Pr.

Charette, Normand. Queens. Gaboriau, Linda, tr. from FRE. LC 99-176483. 1998. pap. text 10.95 (*0-88922-403-X*) Talon Pr.

Charette, Rick & Bean, Laurie. A Little Peace & Quiet. (Illus.). 8p. (J). (gr. k-4). 1994. pap. 9.98 incl. audio (*1-884210-06-6*, PPC-006) Energeia Pub.

Charette, Rick. Alligator in the Elevator. LC 97-76200. 1998. write for info. (*1-884210-23-6*) Pine Pt Record.

Charette, Robert N. Risk Management. 320p. 1989. text. write for info. (*0-07-010719-X*) McGraw.

Charfoos, Lawrence & Christensen, David. Personal Injury Practice Tech & Technology. LC 85-82276. 1986. 98.00 (*0-685-59918-3*) West Group.

Chargaff, Erwin. Heraclitean Fire: Sketches from a Life before Nature. LC 77-95216. 252p. 1978. 14.00 (*0-87470-029-9*) Rockefeller.

Chari, M. V. & Silvester, P. P., eds. Finite Elements in Electrical & Magnetic Field Problems. LC 79-1037. (Wiley Series in Numerical Methods in Engineering). (Illus.). 231p. reprint ed. pap. 71.70 (*0-8357-5556-8*, 203518600093) Bks Demand.

Chari, P. R. India Towards Millennium LC 98-906534. 273p. 1998. write for info. (*81-7304-268-3*) Manohar.

— Indo-Pak Nuclear Standoff: Role of the U. S. LC 95-903276. (C). 1995. 30.00 (*81-7304-110-5*, Pub. by Manohar) S Asia.

***Chari, P. R.** Perspectives on National Security in South Asia: In Search of a New Paradigm. 1999. 44.00 (*81-7304-325-6*, Pub. by Manohar) S Asia.

Chari, P. R., et al, eds. Nuclear Non-Proliferation in India & Pakistan: South Asian Perspectives. LC 96-904933. 1996. 29.00 (*81-7304-153-9*, Pub. by Manohar) S Asia.

Chari, Ravi. Rypins' Intensive Reviews: Surgery. LC 96-18898. 338p. 1996. pap. text 19.95 (*0-397-51551-0*) Lppncott W & W.

Chari, Srinivasa M. Fundamentals of Vasistadvaita Vedanta: A Study Based on Vedanta Desika's Tattva-Mukta-Kalapa. (C). 1988. 34.00 (*81-208-0266-7*, Pub. by Motilal Bnarsidass) S Asia.

— Vaisnavism: Its Philosophy, Theology, & Religious Discipline. LC 93-910757. (C). 1994. 32.00 (*81-208-1098-8*, Pub. by M Manoharial) S Asia.

Chari, V. K. Sanskrit Criticism. LC 89-27965. 317p. 1990. reprint ed. pap. 90.40 (*0-608-04376-1*, 2065157) Bks Demand.

— Whitman in the Light of Vedantic Mysticism: An Interpretation. LC 64-19853. 192p. reprint ed. pap. 59.60 (*0-7837-1899-3*, 204210300001) Bks Demand.

Chari, Vyjayanthi & Pressley, Andrew N. A Guide to Quantum Groups. (Illus.). 667p. (C). 1995. pap. text 44.95 (*0-521-55884-0*) Cambridge U Pr.

Chari, Vyjayanthi, et al. Modular Interfaces: Modular Lie Algebras, Quantum Groups & Lie Superalgebras. LC 96-47629. (AMS-IP Studies in Advanced Mathematics: Vol. 4). 160p. 1997. pap. 35.00 (*0-8218-0748-X*, AMSIP/4) Am Math.

Charifson, Paul S. Practical Application of Computer-Aided Drug Design. LC 97-20897. (Illus.). 564p. 1997. text 150.00 (*0-8247-9885-6*) Dekker.

Charig, A. J., et al. Theodontia. (Encyclopedia of Paleoherpetology Ser.: Pt. 13). (Illus.). 137p. 1976. lib. bdg. 120.00 (*3-437-30184-5*) Lubrecht & Cramer.

Charig, Alan. New Look at the Dinosaurs. 1985. 29.95 (*0-87196-139-3*) Facts on File.

Charing, A. Lutuing Pilipino. (Illus.). 170p. 1976. 8.95 (*0-318-36297-X*) Asia Bk Corp.

Chariot. Noah's Animals Two by Two: Bag of Noah's Animals. 8p. (J). (ps). 1993. 8.99 (*0-7814-0124-0*) Chariot Victor.

Chariot Books Staff. Please. LC 50-6526. (Talking with God Ser.). 22p. (J). (ps). 1993. bds. 3.29 (*0-7814-0107-0*, Chariot Bks) Chariot Victor.

— Sorry. LC 50-6524. (Talking with God Ser.). 22p. (J). (ps). 1993. bds. 3.29 (*0-7814-0105-4*, Chariot Bks) Chariot Victor.

— Thank You. LC 50-6525. (Talking with God Ser.). 22p. (J). (ps). 1993. bds. 3.29 (*0-7814-0106-2*, Chariot Bks) Chariot Victor.

Chariot, Elaine, tr. see Ange, Daniel.

Chariot Family Products Staff. Angels, God's Special Messengers: Pencil Fun Book. 16p. (J). 1992. pap. text 0.83 (*0-7814-0009-0*) Chariot Victor.

Chariot Family Staff. God Cares for Me. (J). (gr. 2 up). 1994. 2.29 (*0-7814-1538-1*) Chariot Victor.

— God Is Always with Us. (J). (gr. 1 up). 1994. 2.29 (*0-7814-1540-3*) Chariot Victor.

— God Made Everything. (J). (gr. 1 up). 1994. 2.29 (*0-7814-1539-X*) Chariot Victor.

— The Kid-Builder Bible: New Life Version. LC 94-11889. 384p. (J). (gr. 4-7). 1994. 16.99 (*0-7814-0075-9*, Chariot Bks) Chariot Victor.

— My Jesus Pocketbook of a Very Special Birthday. 32p. (J). 1986. pap. text 7.90 (*1-55513-131-X*) Chariot Victor.

— You Too Can Know Jesus. 1992. pap. text 9.90 (*0-7814-0920-9*) Chariot Victor.

Chariot Staff. Christmas Pop-up Counting Book. 10p. (J). (ps). 1993. 9.99 (*0-7814-0127-5*, Chariot Bks) Chariot Victor.

Chariot Victor Publishing Staff. Bible Treasury, 1 vol. LC 99-204121. 1999. 12.99 (*0-7459-4084-6*) Lion USA.

— Blessings on You: God's Care & Protection. 1998. 4.99 (*0-7459-3792-6*) Chariot Victor.

— Don't Forget I Love You. 1998. 4.99 (*0-7459-3790-X*) Chariot Victor.

***Chariot Victor Publishing Staff.** Four in One Toddler Book. 2000. 12.99 (*0-7814-3423-8*) Chariot Victor.

Chariot Victor Publishing Staff. God Be With You: Thoughts & Prayers Until We Meet Again. 1998. 4.99 (*0-7459-3789-6*) Chariot Victor.

— God's Greatest Day. (J). (gr. k-4). 1986. 7.90 (*1-55513-013-5*) Chariot Victor.

***Chariot Victor Publishing Staff.** Moses. (Shadowbox Bks.). (J). 2000. write for info. (*0-7814-3421-1*) Chariot Victor.

Chariot Victor Publishing Staff. Moses Leads His People. (J). 1999. pap. text 3.99 (*0-7814-3328-2*) Chariot Victor.

***Chariot Victor Publishing Staff.** New Testament Activity Bible. 2000. pap. text 12.99 (*0-7814-3318-5*) Chariot Victor.

— Noah. (Shadowbox Bks.). (J). 2000. write for info. (*0-7814-3422-X*) Chariot Victor.

— Old Testament Activity Bible. 2000. pap. text 12.99 (*0-7814-3317-7*) Chariot Victor.

Chariot Victor Publishing Staff. Thinking of You: Celebrating Friendship. 1998. 4.99 (*0-7459-3791-8*) Chariot Victor.

— Wise Men Follow the Star, 1. 1993. pap. text 8.90 (*0-7814-0135-6*) Chariot Victor.

Chariot Victor Publishing Staff, ed. People Jesus Helped. 1992. pap. 1.99 (*0-7814-0888-1*) Chariot Victor.

Chariot Victor Publishing Staff, ed. Solomon, the Wise King. (Pocket Bible Stories Bks.). 1995. pap. 4.90 (*0-7814-0219-0*, Chariot Bks) Chariot Victor.

Charischak, Ihor. Creating Dynamic Stories with Logo Writer. Lipkin, Barbara, ed. (Illus.). 90p. (C). 1988. pap. text 19.95 (*0-685-24432-6*) Dynamic Classroom.

Charish, Chandra B. Sacred City of Anuradhapura. (Illus.). 132p. 1986. reprint ed. 26.00 (*0-8364-1746-1*, Pub. by Abhinav) S Asia.

CharismaLife Publishing Staff. Iglesia Para Ninos: Guardando la Ley de Dios en Nuestros Corazons.Tr. of Church for Children: Guarding the Law of God in our Hearts. 160p. (J). (gr. 1-6). 1998. 129.95 (*1-57405-444-9*) CharismaLife Pub.

Charite, Raymond C. La, see La Charite, Raymond C., ed.

Charite, Virginia A. La, see La Charite, Virginia A.

Chariton, Igumen. The Art of Prayer: An Orthodox Anthology. 288p. 1997. pap. 17.95 (*0-571-19165-7*) Faber & Faber.

Chariton, Wallace O. Exploring the Alamo Legends. (Regional Bks.). (Illus.). 288p. 1989. pap. 12.95 (*1-55622-255-6*, Rep of TX Pr) Wordware Pub.

— The Great Texas Airship Mystery. LC 90-12932. (Regional Bks.). (Illus.). 272p. 1990. pap. 16.95 (*1-55622-140-1*, Rep of TX Pr) Wordware Pub.

— Rainy Days in Texas Funbook. LC 89-70622. (Regional Juvenile Ser.). 160p. (J). (ps up). 1990. pap. 7.95 (*1-55622-130-4*, Rep of TX Pr) Wordware Pub.

— Texas Highway Humor. (Regional Bks.). (Illus.). 144p. (Orig.). 1991. pap. 10.95 (*1-55622-176-2*, Rep of TX Pr) Wordware Pub.

— Texas Wit & Wisdom. (Regional Bks.). (Illus.). 252p. 1989. pap. 9.95 (*1-55622-257-2*, Rep of TX Pr) Wordware Pub.

— That Cat Won't Flush. LC 90-23139. (Illus.). 288p. (Orig.). 1990. pap. 12.95 (*1-55622-175-4*, Rep of TX Pr) Wordware Pub.

— This Dog'll Hunt. (Regional Bks.). (Illus.). 300p. (Orig.). 1989. pap. 12.95 (*1-55622-125-8*, Rep of TX Pr) Wordware Pub.

— This Dog'll Really Hunt: An Informative & Entertaining Dictionary. 1999. pap. 17.95 (*1-55622-653-5*) Wordware Pub.

***Chariton, Wallace O.** This Dog'll Really Hunt: An Informative & Entertaining Texas Dictionary. LC 98-48971. 1998. 12.95 (*1-55622-676-4*) Wordware Pub.

Chariton, Wallace O., et al. Unsolved Texas Mysteries. (Illus.). 272p. 1990. pap. 12.95 (*1-55622-256-4*); boxed set 16.95 (*1-55622-136-3*) Wordware Pub.

Charitos, Minas, jt. auth. see Livadeas, Themistocles.

Charity, Arthur. Doing Public Journalism. LC 95-34661. (Communication Ser.). (Illus.). 187p. 1995. pap. text 20.00 (*1-57230-030-2*, 0030); lib. bdg. 40.00 (*1-57230-028-0*, 0028) Guilford Pubns.

— Doing Public Journalism: A Teacher's Guide. LC 95-34661. (Communication Ser.). 1995. pap. text, teacher ed. write for info. (*1-57230-079-5*, 0079) Guilford Pubns.

Charity, Blackstock. Bitter Conquest. 21.95 (*0-88411-068-0*) Amereon Ltd.

— A House Possessed. 21.95 (*0-89224-077-6*, Queens House) Amereon Ltd.

Charity, James R. History of the Sir James Reckitt Charity. (C). 1990. 46.00 (*0-7855-5097-6*, Pub. by W Sessions) St Mut.

Charity, Kate. John Bellows of Gloucester (1831-1902) 1999. pap. 23.00 (*1-85072-132-7*, Pub. by W Sessions) St Mut.

Charity League of Charlotte Staff. Carolina Sunshine Then & Now. 1998. 18.95 (*0-9652020-0-3*) Charity Leag.

Charity Organisation Society Staff. The Epileptic & Crippled Child & Adult. Phillips, William R. & Rosenberg, Janet, eds. LC 79-6899. (Physically Handicapped in Society Ser.). 1980. reprint ed. lib. bdg. 19.95 (*0-405-13109-7*) Ayer.

Charity Publications Staff. God Loves Me Too. (Wheeling Willie Ser.). 1997. 6.95 (*1-887886-02-8*); pap. text 2.95 (*1-887886-03-6*) Charity Publns.

C

An Asterisk (*) at the beginning of an entry indicates that the title is appearing for the first time.

Charity, Tom. The Right Stuff. (Modern Classics Ser.). (Illus.). 80p. 1998. pap. 9.95 (0-85170-624-X, Pub. by British Film Inst) Ind U Pr.

Chark, K. S., ed. see Dhir, K. K., et al.

Charke, Charlotte C. Narrative of the Life of Mrs. Charlotte Charke. LC 70-81365. (Illus.). 316p. 1969. reprint ed. 50.00 (0-8201-1065-5) Schol Facsimiles.

Charkham, Jonathan. Keeping Good Company: A Study of Corporate Governance in Five Countries. (Illus.). 389p. 1999. pap. 19.95 (0-19-828987-1) OUP.

Charkham, Jonathan & Simpson, Anne. Fair Shares: The Future of Shareholder Power & Responsibility. LC 99-27049. 284p. 1999. text 39.95 (0-19-829214-7) OUP.

Charkins, Hope. Children with Facial Difference: A Parents' Guide. (Illus.). 365p. 1996. pap. 16.95 (0-933149-61-1) Woodbine House.

***Charla, Leonard F.** Never Cooked before Gotta Cook Now! A Total Guide for The Beginning Cook, 1. LC 98-93626. 1999. pap. text 15.95 (0-9664732-0-5) Countinghse Pr.

Charland, Judith A. Wine Making Judy's Way. (Illus.). 80p. 1998. pap. 9.95 (1-889668-09-5) S & D.

Charland, Thomas C. Cost & Schedule Control Techniques Handbook. (Illus.). 104p. (C). 1999. spiral bd. 79.95 (0-9610754-0-6) Manage Co In.

Charland, Thomas C., ed. Project Management-Advanced Techniques Handbook. rev. ed. (Illus.). 403p. (C). 1999. spiral bd. 59.95 (0-9610754-3-0) Manage Co In.

— Project/Contract Management Techniques Handbook. rev. ed. (Illus.). 143p. (C). 2000. spiral bd. 29.95 (0-9610754-2-2) Manage Co In.

— Proposal Writing & Costing Techniques Handbook. rev. ed. (Illus.). 118p. (C). 1998. spiral bd. 29.95 (0-9610754-1-4) Manage Co In.

Charland, William. Complete Idiot's Guide to Changing Careers. LC 97-80968. 352p. 1997. 17.95 (0-02-861977-3) Macmillan Gen Ref.

***Charland, William A.** Life-Work: A Career Guide for Idealists. 2nd ed. LC 99-51412. 1999. 15.00 (0-944350-45-3) Friends United.

Charlap, L. S. Bieberbach Groups & Flat Manifolds. (Universitext Ser.). 255p. 1986. 79.95 (0-387-96395-2) Spr-Verlag.

Charle, Christophe. A Social History of France in the 19th Century. Jefferies, Matthew, tr. 313p. 1994. pap. 19.50 (0-85496-913-6, Pub. by Berg Pubs) NYU Pr.

— A Social History of France in the 19th Century. Kochan, Miriam, tr. 313p. 1994. 60.00 (0-85496-906-3, Pub. by Berg Pubs) NYU Pr.

Charle, Suzanne. Bali Island of Grace: A Complete Guide. (Illus.). 232p. 1992. pap. 15.95 (0-8442-9693-7, 96937, Passprt Bks) NTC Contemp Pub Co.

Charlebois, Lucile C. Understanding Camilo Jose Cela. LC 96-51296. 180p. 1998. text 29.95 (1-57003-151-7) U of SC Pr.

Charlebois, Peter. The Life of Louis Riel. (Illus.). 256p. 1978. text 24.95 (0-919601-12-X, Pub. by NC Ltd) U of Toronto Pr.

— Sternwheelers & Sidewheelers: The Romance of Steamdriven Paddleboats in Canada. (Illus.). 144p. 1997. 21.95 (0-919600-73-5, Pub. by NC Ltd) U of Toronto Pr.

Charlebois, Robert L., ed. Organization of the Bacterial Genome. LC 99-32407. (Illus.). 378p. 1999. 79.95 (1-55581-151-5) ASM Pr.

Charlemagne. Evolution of the Immune System. 1992. 95.00 (0-8493-8885-6, CRC Reprint) Franklin.

— The Merry Pilgrimage: How Charlemagne Went on a Pilgrimage to Jerusalem in Order to See Whether Hugo of Constantinople Was a Handsomer Man Than He. Sherwood, Merriam, tr. LC 78-63455. (Illus.). reprint ed. 29.50 (0-404-16377-7) AMS Pr.

Charles. The Cocktail Bar: A Collection of Four Hundred Recipes. Carlos, ed. (Illus.). 120p. (Orig.). 1977. pap. 11.95 (0-572-00995-X, Pub. by W Foulsham) Trans-Atl Phila.

— Defendant. 1985. 15.95 (0-02-918240-9) Free Pr.

— Feminism, the State & Social Policy. LC 99-29988. 1999. text 49.95 (0-312-22675-6) St Martin.

***Charles.** Lords of the Harvest. 2000. pap. 27.00 (0-7382-0291-6, Pub. by Perseus Pubng) HarpC.

Charles. Mass Catering. (WHO Regional Publications, European Ser.: No. 15). 70p. 1983. pap. text 13.00 (92-890-1106-8) World Health.

— Reclaiming Personal Authority. 1998. 23.00 (0-02-917305-1) Free Pr.

— Sport Karate. pap. write for info. (0-901764-63-9, 93224, Pub. by P H Crompton) Midpt Trade.

Charles, jt. auth. see Hubbard, C. E.

Charles, A., et al. Fisheries Socioeconomics in the Developing World: Regional Assessments & Annotated Bibliography. 174p. 1994. pap. write for info. (0-88936-716-7) IDRC Bks.

Charles, Alan. The Isle of Wight Coastal Path. (C). 1988. pap. 29.00 (0-946328-13-7, Pub. by Thornhill Pr) St Mut.

Charles, Amy M., ed. see Herbert, George.

Charles, Anna, jt. auth. see Pharrams, Doris.

Charles, Anthony T., ed. see Mathias, Jack A., et al.

Charles, Arthur H., Jr. How to Learn a Foreign Language. LC 93-29573. (Speak Out! Write On! Ser.). (Illus.). 96p. (YA). (gr. 7-12). 1994. lib. bdg. 24.00 (0-531-11098-2) Watts.

Charles, Asselin, tr. see Firmin, Antenor.

Charles, Barbara F. & Taylor, J. R. Dream of Santa: Haddon Sundblom's Vision. 84p. 1992. pap. 20.00 (0-9634907-0-2) Staples & Charles.

Charles, Barbara F., et al. Dream of Santa: Haddon Sundblom's Advertising Paintings for Christmas, 1931-1964. (Illus.). 84p. (J). 1997. 12.99 (0-517-18655-1) Random Hse Value.

Charles Ben Sedira Belkacem. Dictionnaire Franco-Arabe de la Langue Parlee en Algerie.Tr. of French-Arabic Dictionary of Spoken Algerian Arabic. (ARA & FRE.). 756p. 1980. 75.00 (0-8288-1587-9, F5080) Fr & Eur.

Charles, Bertram L. Whitehall Street. LC 97-90705. 1998. pap. 10.95 (0-533-12462-X) Vantage.

Charles, C. Why Is Everone So Cranky? 256p. 2000. pap. 12.95 (0-7868-8443-6, Pub. by Hypm Ppbks) Little.

Charles C. Chapman & Company Staff. History of Knox County: Together with Sketches of the Cities, Villages & Townships & Biographical Sketches. (Illus.). 718p. 1995. reprint ed. lib. bdg. 75.00 (0-8328-5001-2) Higginson Bk Co.

Charles, C. Leslie. The Customer Service Companion: The Essential Handbook for Those Who Serve Others. LC 96-90171. 208p. (Orig.). 1996. pap. 10.95 (0-9644621-1-7) Yes Pr MI.

— The Customer Service Companion Study Guide: A Self-Directed Seminar. 88p. (Orig.). 1996. pap. 6.95 (0-9644621-2-5) Yes Pr MI.

— Rule #One: If You Don't Take Care of the Customer . . . Somebody Else Will. (Power of One Ser.: Vol. 5). (Illus.). 48p. 1997. pap. 5.95 (1-880461-44-7) Successories Inc.

— Stick to It! The Power of Positive Persistence. rev. ed. LC 95-60861. 120p. 1995. pap. 11.95 (0-9644621-0-9) Yes Pr MI.

— Why Is Everyone So Cranky? The Ten Trends That Are Making Us Angry & How We Can Find Peace of Mind Instead. LC 99-22118. 400p. 1999. 22.95 (0-7868-6525-3, Pub. by Hyperion) Time Warner.

Charles, C. Leslie & Clarke-Epstein, Chris. The Instant Trainer: Quick Tips on How to Teach Others What You Know. LC 97-37422. (Illus.). 288p. 1997. 29.95 (0-07-011965-1) McGraw.

Charles, C. M. Elementary Classroom Management: A Handbook for Excellence in Teaching. LC 82-13973. (Illus.). 452p. (C). 1983. pap. text 25.95 (0-582-28349-3, 71384) Longman.

— Introduction to Educational Research. 3rd ed. LC 97-15011. 416p. (C). 1997. 77.00 (0-8013-1872-6) Addison-Wesley.

— Teacher's Petit Piaget. LC 74-83219. 1974. pap. 5.99 (0-8224-6780-1) Fearon Teacher Aids.

Charles, C. M. & Senter, Gail W. Elementary Classroom Management: A Handbook for Excellence in Teaching. 2nd rev. ed. LC 94-3648. 298p. (C). 1994. pap. 48.00 (0-8013-1474-7) Longman.

***Charles, C. M., et al.** Building Classroom Discipline. 6th ed. LC 97-49873. 336p. (C). 1998. pap. 46.00 (0-8013-3004-1) Addison-Wesley.

Charles, Carol. Synergistic Teaching & Discipline. LC 99-34542. 184p. (C). 1999. pap. 25.00 (0-321-04912-8) Addson-Wesley Educ.

Charles, Carol A., et al, eds. Preparing India for the Global Information Infrastructure: Engineering the Global Information Highway. (GIIC - International Communications Report Ser.). 91p. (C). 1997. pap. 20.00 (0-89206-375-0) CSIS.

Charles, Carol A., et al. Globalizing Electronic Commerce: Report on the International Forum on Electronic Commerce, Beijing, China, 20-21 March 1996. LC 96-30846. 1996. pap. 23.95 (0-89206-340-8) CSIS.

Charles, Carol Ann. Building the Global Information Economy: A Roadmap from the Global Information Infrastructure Commission. LC 98-33184. 90p. (C). 1998. pap. text 21.95 (0-89206-377-7) CSIS.

Charles, Cheryl L. Science & Society: Knowing, Teaching, Learning. Samples, Bob, ed. LC 78-70847. (National Council for the Social Studies Bulletin: No. 57). 96p. reprint ed. pap. 30.00 (0-608-14608-0, 202319000032) Bks Demand.

Charles, Chuck D. Something's Out There! 100p. (J). (gr. 2-6). 1996. 16.95 (0-9638639-3-2) Nimrod Hse.

Charles, Chuck D., ed. see Liles, Glennis S.

Charles, Chuck D., ed. see Lowe, Jimmy.

Charles, Chuck D., ed. see Stuart, Jesse H.

Charles, Clement & Skygazer, Clement. Christmas Unwrapped. 2nd ed. Watkins, Shelley, ed. 176p. 1997. pap. 12.95 (0-9668724-0-1, CS102198) Skyruner Pubns.

Charles County Nursing & Rehabilitation Center Staff, ed. see Zimmerman, L. E., et al.

Charles, Craig. Exploring Door County. LC 98-33271. (Illus.). 1999. pap. text 16.95 (1-55971-681-9, NorthWord Pr) Creat Pub Intl.

***Charles, Craig.** Log: A Dwarfer's Guide to Everything. 128p. 1998. pap. 13.95 (0-14-026862-6, Pub. by Pnguin Bks Ltd) Trafalgar.

— No Other Blue: His First Collection of Poetry. 64p. pap. 11.95 (0-14-058797-7, Pub. by Pnguin Bks Ltd) Trafalgar.

Charles, Curtis B. & Brown, Karen M. Multimedia Marketing for Design Firms. LC 96-13838. 222p. 1996. pap. 59.95 (0-471-14609-9) Wiley.

Charles, Curtis B., jt. auth. see Brown, Karen M.

Charles, D. & Wathes, C., eds. Livestock Housing: Environmental & Climatic Aspects. LC 95-106794. 448p. 1994. text 120.00 (0-85198-774-5) OUP.

Charles, D. F., ed. Acidic Deposition & Aquatic Ecosystems: Regional Case Studies. (Illus.). 688p. 1991. 159.00 (0-387-97316-8) Spr-Verlag.

Charles, Daniel. Nuclear Planning in NATO: Pitfalls of First Use. LC 86-17233. 200p. 1986. text 29.95 (0-88730-137-1, HarpBusn) HarpInfo.

***Charles, David.** Aristotle on Meaning & Essence. (Oxford Aristotle Studies). 376p. 2000. text 55.00 (0-19-825070-3) OUP.

Charles, David & Finland, Maxwell, eds. Obstetric & Perinatal Infections. LC 79-170731. (Illus.). 668p. reprint ed. 200.00 (0-8357-9412-1, 201453000093) Bks Demand.

Charles, David & Howells, Jeremy. Technology Transfer in Europe. (Illus.). 256p. 1992. text 54.00 (1-85293-160-4) St Martin.

Charles, David & Lennon, Kethleen, eds. Reduction, Explanation, & Realism. (Illus.). 486p. 1992. pap. text 39.95 (0-19-875131-1) OUP.

Charles, David, et al. Technology & Competition in the International Telecommunications Industry. 200p. 1992. 54.00 (0-86187-993-7) St Martin.

Charles, David, jt. ed. see Frede, Michael.

Charles-Dominique, Pierre. Ecology & Behavior of Nocturnal Primates. Martin, R. D., tr. LC 77-1227. (Illus.). 277p. 1977. text 64.50 (0-231-04362-7) Col U Pr.

Charles, Donald. Men in the Bible: Examples to Live by. 1999. pap. text 14.99 (1-56322-067-9) Hensley Pub.

Charles, Douglas K., et al, eds. The Archaic & Woodland Cemeteries at the Elizabeth Site in the Lower Illinois Valley. LC 88-14982. (Kampsville Archeological Center Research Ser.: No. 7). (Illus.). 340p. (Orig.). 1988. pap. 15.95 (0-942118-27-8) Ctr Amer Arche.

Charles, E. Some Dickens Women. 1972. 59.95 (0-8490-1076-4) Gordon Pr.

Charles E. Tuttle Company Incorporated Staff. Deluxe Origami. (Illus.). 64p. 1996. boxed set 18.95 (0-8048-3085-1) Tuttle Pubng.

Charles, Edna K. Christina Rossetti: Critical Perspectives, 1862-1982. LC 84-40392. (Illus.). 192p. 1985. 32.50 (0-941664-06-6) Susquehanna U Pr.

Charles-Edwards, D. A., et al. Modelling Plant Growth & Development. 1987. pap. text 46.00 (0-12-169362-7) Acad Pr.

***Charles-Edwards, T. M.** Early Christian Ireland. LC 99-54974. (Illus.). 600p. (C). 2000. write for info. (0-521-36395-0) Cambridge U Pr.

Charles-Edwards, T. M. Early Irish & Welsh Kinship. LC 92-17934. (Illus.). 616p. 1993. text 95.00 (0-19-820103-6, Clarendon Pr) OUP.

Charles, Elizabeth. Chronicles of the Schonberg-Cotta Family, 2 vols., 1 bk. LC 79-8251. reprint ed. 44.50 (0-404-61818-9) AMS Pr.

Charles, Ernest, jt. auth. see Brooks, C. Harry.

Charles, Eugene. The Paradox: A Conversation of Life. 82p. (Orig.). 1995. pap. 9.95 (0-9644217-0-4) Charles Semin.

Charles, Eugenia. A Future for Small States. 1997. pap. 22.50 (0-85092-511-8, Pub. by Comm Sec) Stylus Pub VA.

Charles F. Kettering Foundation & Harwood Group. Strategies for Civil Investing: Foundations & Community-building : a Kettering Foundation Report. LC 97-154667. 1997. write for info. (0-923993-03-7) Kettering Found.

***Charles, Faustin.** The Selfish Crocodile. LC 98-51888. (Illus.). 32p. (J). (gr. k-2). 1999. 14.95 (1-888444-56-8) Little Tiger.

Charles, Geoffrey S. Staffordshire Figures. LC 97-71295. (Illus.). 80p. 1997. 12.95 (0-8212-2461-1, Pub. by Bulfinch Pr) Little.

Charles, Gerald T., Jr. LAN Blueprints: Engineering It Right. LC 96-44414. (Illus.). 224p. 1997. pap., pap. text 44.95 incl. disk (0-07-011769-1) McGraw.

Charles, Glyn. Keelboat & Sportboat Racing: Winning Through Understanding. (Illus.). 94p. 1998. pap. 18.95 (1-898660-37-9) Motorbooks Intl.

Charles, Gordon. A Boy, a Bike & Buster: Fishing & Hunting in Michigan's Good Old Days. LC 94-61375. (Illus.). 169p. 1995. pap. 12.95 (0-9642948-0-X) Traverse Outdoor.

Charles, H. Robert. Last Man Out. Roberts, Melissa, ed. (Illus.). 394p. 1988. 16.95 (0-89015-647-6) Sunbelt Media.

***Charles, Hampton.** Advantage Miss Seeton. large type ed. LC 99-46180. (Thorndike Mystery Ser.). 1999. 26.95 (0-7862-2242-5) Thorndike Pr.

Charles, Harry. Make a Deal with the IRS: 1997 Edition. rev. ed. (Illus.). 148p. (Orig.). 1996. pap. 12.95 (0-9645776-1-5) Cairo Busn Pr.

Charles, Harry N., II. Air. 65p. (Orig.). 1996. pap. write for info. (0-614-23288-0) Digi Print.

Charles, Henriette. Sell Out. large type ed. 1991. 27.99 (0-7089-2426-3) Ulverscroft.

Charles, Henry. China & the Chinese, 2 vols., Set. 1977. reprint ed. 40.00 (0-89986-378-7) Oriental Bk Store.

Charles, Herman. 1906 Souvenir of the City of Riverside by the Riverside Fire Department. LC 87-61990. (Illus.). 128p. 1987. reprint ed. pap. 10.00 (0-935661-16-6) Riverside Mus Pr.

***Charles, Homer N.** La Biz: Louisiana Business Magazine. Bridgewater, Earl Edward, ed. (Illus.). 2000. pap. 2.00 (1-928772-07-2) Keepsafe.

Charles Ives Centennial Festival Conference Staff. An Ives Celebration: Proceedings of the Charles Ives Centennial Festival Conference, New York, New Haven, 1974. Hitchcock, H. Wiley & Perlis, Vivian, eds. LC 77-7987. 294p. reprint ed. pap. 91.20 (0-608-14876-8, 202591800047) Bks Demand.

Charles, J. Good Vibrations. mass mkt. 6.95 (0-7472-4185-6) Headline Bk Pub.

— Sweet Vibrations. mass mkt. 6.95 (0-7472-4634-3, Pub. by Headline Bk Pub) Trafalgar.

— Ultimate Vibrations. 1997. mass mkt. 6.95 (0-7472-5449-4, Pub. by Headline Bk Pub) Trafalgar.

Charles, J. A. Selection & Use of Engine Materials. 328p. (C). 1984. 49.95 (0-408-00997-7) Buttrwrth-Heinemann.

Charles, J. A. & Smith, G. C., eds. Advances in Physical Metallurgy: A Collection of Invited Papers Presented to Mark the 70th Birthday Year of Professor Sir Alan Cottrell. 218p. 1990. 50.00 (0-901462-85-3, Pub. by Inst Materials) Ashgate Pub Co.

Charles, J. A., et al. Selection & Use of Engineering Materials. 3rd ed. LC 97-203970. (Illus.). 352p. 1997. pap. text 49.95 (0-7506-3277-1, TA403) Buttrwrth-Heinemann.

Charles, J. Daryl. Virtue Amidst Vice: The Catalog of Virtues in 2 Peter 1. LC 98-111125. (JSNTS Ser.: Vol. 150). 194p. 1998. 57.50 (1-85075-686-4, Pub. by Sheffield Acad) CUP Services.

Charles, J. Daryl, jt. auth. see Waltner, Erland.

Charles, Jean C. The Missing Boy & the Escapee, Pt. 2. LC 83-70229. 50p. 1984. pap. 3.50 (0-9610796-8-1) Adelphi Pr.

Charles, Jeffrey. Astrophotography for Amateurs. (Practical Astronomy Ser.). (Illus.). xvii, 297p. 2000. pap. 34.95 (1-85233-023-6) Spr-Verlag.

Charles, Jeffrey A. Service Clubs in American Society: Rotary, Kiwanis, & Lions. LC 93-9803. (Illus.). 240p. 1993. text 32.50 (0-252-02015-4) U of Ill Pr.

Charles, Jerde & Kottel, Randall A. Laboratory Experiences General Biology 2nd rev. ed. 270p. (C). 1990. text 39.40 (0-536-57841-9) Pearson Custom.

***Charles, Jill, ed.** Directory of Theatre Training Programs, 1999-2001. 7th ed. 264p. 1999. reprint ed. pap. text 28.95 (0-933919-45-X) Theatre Directories.

Charles, Jill, ed. Regional Theatre Directory, 1998-99. 173p. 1998. pap. 18.95 (0-933919-39-5) Theatre Directories.

— Regional Theatre Directory, 1999-00. 173p. 1999. pap. 18.95 (0-933919-44-1) Theatre Directories.

***Charles, Jill, ed.** Regional Theatre Directory, 2000-01. 175p. 2000. pap. text 19.95 (0-933919-47-6) Theatre Directories.

Charles, Jill, ed. Summer Theatre Directory, 1999. annuals 150p. 1998. pap. 17.95 (0-933919-43-3) Theatre Directories.

***Charles, Jill, ed.** Summer Theatre Directory, 2000. 148p. 1999. pap. 17.95 (0-933919-46-8) Theatre Directories.

Charles, Jill & Bloom, Tom. Actor's Picture - Resume Book. 2nd rev. ed. 108p. 1998. pap. 16.95 (0-933919-41-7) Theatre Directories.

Charles, Joan. Elizabeth City County, Virginia Wills, 1733-1799. 219p. (Orig.). 1995. pap. 19.00 (0-7884-0328-1) Heritage Bk.

Charles, Joan, ed. see Sydney, Russell.

Charles, Joe M. Barry Irwin, Playwright. 55p. (Orig.). 1996. pap. 6.00 (0-88734-516-6) Players Pr.

***Charles, John.** The Hong Kong Filmography, 1977-1997: A Complete Reference to 1,100 Films Produced by British Hong Kong Studios. (Illus.). 397p. 2000. 75.00 (0-7864-0842-1) McFarland & Co.

Charles, John D. Endowed from on High: Understanding the Symbols of the Endowment. 112p. 1997. pap. 9.98 (0-88290-614-3, 1951) Horizon Utah.

Charles, John M. Contemporary Kinesiology: An Introduction to the Study of Human Movement in Higher Education. (Illus.). 196p. (C). 1994. pap. text 23.95 (0-89582-275-X) Wadsworth Pub.

Charles, Julius. The Ballad of Dorothy Parker. (Illus.). Date not set. write for info. (1-930112-10-6) inchanted.

— Future Love Paradise. Date not set. write for info. (1-930112-40-8) inchanted.

— The Last Psalm. Date not set. write for info. (1-930112-50-5) inchanted.

***Charles, Kackie.** Windows 2000 Routing & Remote Access Services. 400p. 2000. pap. 34.99 (0-7357-0951-3) Macmillan Tech.

Charles, Kate. Appointed to Die. 352p. 1995. mass mkt. 5.99 (0-446-40361-X, Pub. by Warner Bks) Little.

— A Dead Man Out of Mind. 288p. 1996. mass mkt. 5.99 (0-446-40432-2, Pub. by Warner Bks) Little.

— A Drink of Deadly Wine. 336p. 1992. 17.95 (0-89296-501-0) Mysterious Pr.

— Evil Angels among Them. 352p. 1997. mass mkt. 6.50 (0-446-40521-3, Mysterious Paperbk) Warner Bks.

— Hunter's Kiss. 432p. 1995. mass mkt. 4.99 (0-8217-0139-8, Zebra Kensgtn) Kensgtn Pub Corp.

— The Snares of Death. 368p. 1993. 18.95 (0-89296-498-7) Mysterious Pr.

— The Snares of Death. LC 92-50899. 352p. 1994. mass mkt. 5.50 (0-446-40195-1, Pub. by Warner Bks) Little.

Charles, Kirk. Amazing Card Tricks. LC 92-5482. (Umbrella Bks.). (Illus.). 32p. (J). (gr. 2-6). 1993. lib. bdg. 21.36 (0-89565-965-4) Childs World.

— Amazing Coin Tricks. LC 93-29259. (Umbrella Bks.). (Illus.). 24p. (J). (gr. 2-6). 1995. lib. bdg. 21.36 (1-56766-084-3) Childs World.

— Amazing Science Tricks. LC 92-9012. (Umbrella Bks.). (Illus.). 32p. (J). (gr. 2-6). 1993. lib. bdg. 21.36 (0-89565-964-6) Childs World.

— Complete Guide to Restaurant & Walk-Around Magic. (Illus.). 248p. 1998. 30.00 (0-945296-23-1) Hermetic Pr.

Charles, Leslie C. & Clarke-Epstein, Chris. The Instant Trainer: Quick Tips on How to Teach Others What You Know. LC 97-37422. (Illus.). 276p. 1997. pap. 17.95 (0-07-011958-9) McGraw.

Charles, Lindsey & Duffin, Lorna, eds. Women & Work in Pre-Industrial Britain. LC 85-14950. (Oxford Women's Ser.). 212p. 1986. pap. 15.95 (0-7099-0856-3, Pub. by C Helm) Routldge.

Charles, Lisa. Dawn of a Dream. large type ed. (Linford Romance Library). 304p. 1993. pap. 16.99 (0-7089-7463-5) Ulverscroft.

— Tender Deception. large type ed. (Linford Romance Library). 272p. 1992. pap. 16.99 (0-7089-7203-9, Linford) Ulverscroft.

Charles, M. E., jt. ed. see McGrath, H. G.

Charles M. Salter Associates, Inc. Staff, ed. Acoustics: Architecture, Engineering, the Environment. LC 97-62505. (Illus.). 344p. 1998. 75.00 (0-9651144-6-5, Pub. by W K Stout) RAM Publications.

Charles, Maggi. The Other Side of the Mirror. 1993. mass mkt. 3.39 (0-373-09795-6, 5-09795-1) Silhouette.

An Asterisk (*) at the beginning of an entry indicates that the title is appearing for the first time.

Charles, Master. The Bliss of Freedom: A Contemporary Mystic's Enlightening Journey. LC BL73.C38A3. 249p. 1997. 22.95 (*1-884068-14-6*) Synch Found.

Charles, Master. The Bliss of Freedom: A Contemporary Mystic's Enlightening Journey. LC 96-36541. (Illus.). 272p. 1997. pap. 14.95 (*0-9650958-2-7*) Synch Found.

Charles, Melvin. The Rallying Point. Lockett, Hazel, ed. LC 93-74944. (Illus.). 206p. (Orig.). (YA). 1994. pap. 14.95 (*0-9638672-1-0*) Bryant & Dillon.

Charles, Michael, ed. see Bacon, Roger.

Charles, Michael T. & Kim, John C., eds. Crisis Management: A Casebook. (Illus.). 310p. 1988. pap. 40.95 (*0-398-06054-1*) C C Thomas.

— Crisis Management: A Casebook. (Illus.). 310p. (C). 1988. text 58.95 (*0-398-05408-8*) C C Thomas.

Charles, N. N. What Am I? Looking Through Shapes at Apples & Grapes. (Illus.). 32p. (J). (ps-3). 1994. 14.95 (*0-590-47891-5*, Blue Sky Press) Scholastic Inc.

Charles, Nancy Linehan. Othello or Tracking the Green-Eyed Monster. 48p. Date not set. pap. 5.60 (*1-58342-027-4*, O63) Dramatic Pub.

***Charles, Nancy U.** MacBeth: A Kid's Cautionary Tale Concerning Greed, Power, Mayhem & Other Current Events. 52p. 1999. pap. 5.50 (*0-87129-948-8*, MB8) Dramatic Pub.

Charles, Nicholas. "Is That a Fact?" (Illus.). 142p. (YA). (gr. 5 up). 1999. pap. 12.95 (*0-9667954-1-5*) Blue Heron Corp.

— Visitation of the County of Huntingdon, Under the Authority of William Camden. Ellis, Henry, ed. LC 17-1223. (Camden Society, London. Publications, First Ser.: No. 43). reprint ed. 39.00 (*0-404-50143-5*) AMS Pr.

Charles, Nickie. Gender Divisions & Social Change. LC 93-15077. 320p. (C). 1993. lib. bdg. 65.00 (*0-389-21007-2*) B&N Imports.

***Charles, Nickie.** Through a Glass Brightly: The Fall & Rise of an Alcoholic. 194p. 1999. 28.95 (*1-86105-222-7*) Robson.

Charles, Nickie & Hintjens, Helen M., eds. Gender, Ethnicity & Political Ideologies. LC 97-14242. 208p. (C). 1997. pap. 25.99 (*0-415-14821-9*) Routledge.

Charles, Nickie, jt. ed. see Hughes-Freeland, Felicia.

Charles, Norma. Darlene's Shadow. 114p. (J). (gr. 5-7). 1991. pap. 5.95 (*0-7736-7295-8*) Stoddart Publ.

Charles, Norma M. Runaway. 192p. (J). (gr. 5-9). 1999. pap. 5.95 (*1-55050-143-7*, Pub. by Coteau) Genl Dist Srvs.

Charles, Patricia, jt. ed. see Allen, June.

***Charles, Paul.** The Ballad of Sean & Wilko. (Inspector Christy Kennedy Mystery Ser.: No. 4). 2000. 31.00 (*1-899344-58-6*, Pub. by Do-Not Pr); pap. 15.95 (*1-899344-57-8*, Pub. by Do-Not Pr) Dufour.

Charles, Paul. Fountain of Sorrow. LC 99-197337. 230p. 1999. pap. 14.95 (*1-899344-39-X*, Pub. by Do-Not Pr) Dufour.

— I Love the Sound of Breaking Glass: An Inspector Christy Kennedy Mystery. LC 97-178425. (Bloodlines Ser.). 232p. 1997. pap. 14.95 (*1-899344-16-0*, Pub. by Do-Not Pr) Dufour.

— Last Boat to Camden Town: An Inspector Christy Kennedy Mystery. 168p. 1998. 34.95 (*1-899344-29-2*, Pub. by Do-Not Pr) Dufour.

— Last Boat to Camden Town: An Inspector Christy Kennedy Mystery. 168p. 1998. pap. 15.95 (*1-899344-30-6*, Pub. by Do-Not Pr) Dufour.

Charles, Pavel. Open Quantum Systems & Feynman Integrals. 376p. 1984. text 206.50 (*90-277-1678-1*) Kluwer Academic.

Charles, Philip, jt. auth. see Seward, Frederick.

Charles Press Publishers Staff. The Charles Press Handbook of Current Medical Abbreviations. 5th ed. LC 97-12402. 472p. 1997. pap. text 16.95 (*0-914783-81-5*) Charles.

Charles, R. Book of Enoch. 1988. pap. text 13.95 (*0-687-85080-0*, 850800) Abingdon.

— Fireball. 1999. pap. write for info. (*0-670-80481-9*) Viking Penguin.

Charles, R., et al. Problem-Solving Experiences in Mathematics. 2nd ed. (Grade 1 BLMs Ser.). (J). 1995. pap. write for info. (*0-201-49361-6*) Addison-Wesley.

— Problem-Solving Experiences in Mathematics, Grade 2. Anderson, Cathy & Apple, Mali, eds. (Problem-Solving Experiences in Mathematics Ser.). (Illus.). 224p. (Orig.). 1995. pap., teacher ed. 23.95 (*0-201-49405-1*) Supplementary Div.

— Problem-Solving Experiences in Mathematics, Grade 2. 2nd ed. Anderson, Cathy & Apple, Mali, eds. (Problem-Solving Experiences in Mathematics Ser.). (Illus.). (Orig.). 1995. pap., student ed. write for info. (*0-201-49362-4*) Addison-Wesley.

— Problem-Solving Experiences in Mathematics, Grade 2, BLM. 2nd ed. Anderson, Cathy & Apple, Mali, eds. (Problem-Solving Experiences in Mathematics Ser.). (Illus.). (Orig.). (J). 1995. 9.75 (*0-201-49363-2*) Supplementary Div.

— Problem-Solving Experiences in Mathematics, Kindergarten. Anderson, Cathy & Apple, Mali, eds. (Problem-Solving Experiences in Mathematics Ser.). (Illus.). 200p. (Orig.). 1995. pap., teacher ed. 23.95 (*0-201-49085-4*) Supplementary Div.

— Problem-Solving Experiences in Mathematics, Kindergarten, BLM. Anderson, Cathy & Apple, Mali, eds. (Problem-Solving Experiences in Mathematics Ser.). (Illus.). (Orig.). (J). (gr. k). 1995. write for info. (*0-201-49086-2*) Addison-Wesley.

Charles, R., ed. see Thomas, Edith.

Charles, R. H. The Book of Enoch: One Enoch. 329p. 1997. reprint ed. pap. 17.50 (*0-7873-0164-7*) Hlth Research.

— The Book of Enoch: Together with a Reprint of the Greek Fragments (1912) 441p. 1996. reprint ed. pap. 29.95 (*1-56459-523-4*) Kessinger Pub.

— Book of the Secrets of Enoch. 1996. lib. bdg. 250.95 (*0-8490-5932-1*) Gordon Pr.

***Charles, R. H.** Book of the Secrets of Enoch. 142p. 1999. pap. 30.00 (*1-57074-440-8*) Greyden Pr.

— Eschatology: A Critical History of the Doctrine of a Future Life in Israel, in Judaism & in Christianity. 494p. 1999. pap. 35.00 (*1-57910-221-2*) Wipf & Stock.

Charles, R. H. Lectures on the Apocalypse. (British Academy, London, Schweich Lectures on Biblical Archaeology Series, 1930). 1969. reprint ed. pap. 25.00 (*0-8115-1261-4*) Periodicals Srv.

— Revelation, 2 vols., Vol. 1. Plummer, Alfred D. & Briggs, Charles A., eds. LC 21-5413. (International Critical Commentary Ser.). 568p. 1920. 39.95 (*0-567-05038-6*, Pub. by T & T Clark) Bks Intl VA.

— Revelation, 2 vols., Vol. 2. Plummer, Alfred D. & Briggs, Charles A., eds. LC 21-5413. (International Critical Commentary Ser.). 506p. 1998. 39.95 (*0-567-05039-4*, Pub. by T & T Clark) Bks Intl VA.

— Studies in the Apocalypse. 199p. 1997. pap. 18.00 (*0-9653517-9-3*) Wipf & Stock.

Charles, R. H., ed. Book of Jubilees: The Little Genesis. 1988. reprint ed. lib. bdg. 59.00 (*0-7812-0101-2*) Rprt Serv.

— The Book of Jubilees: The Little Genesis. 1984. reprint ed. 59.00 (*0-403-08996-4*, Regency) Scholarly.

— The Ethiopic Version of the Book of Enoch. LC 79-8595. reprint ed. 37.50 (*0-404-18448-0*) AMS Pr.

Charles, Rachel. Food for Healing. 1996. 9.99 (*0-7493-2411-2*) Buttrwrth-Heinemann.

— Mind, Body & Immunity. 1996. pap. 9.99 (*0-7493-2416-3*) Buttrwrth-Heinemann.

Charles, Randall. Charles Problem Solving Experiences in Mathematics: Grade 1. 2nd ed. 1996. write for info. (*0-201-49360-8*) Addison-Wesley.

Charles, Randall, et al. Mathematics for Elementary School Teachers. Guardino, Karen, ed. LC 97-7647. 914p. (C). 1997. 92.00 (*0-201-53979-9*) Addison-Wesley.

— Problem-Solving Experiences in Mathematics, Grade 1. 1994. pap. 29.95 (*0-201-49404-3*) Addison-Wesley.

Charles, Randall I. & Silver, Edward A., eds. The Teaching & Assessing of Mathematical Problem Solving. (Research Agenda for Mathematics Education Ser.: Vol. 3). 296p. 1989. text 59.95 (*0-8058-0355-6*) L Erlbaum Assocs.

***Charles, Raphael M.** The Dark Tides. LC 99-93679. 1999. pap. 10.95 (*0-533-13118-9*) Vantage.

Charles, Ray & Ritz, David. Brother Ray: Ray Charles' Own Story. rev. ed. (Illus.). 370p. 1992. reprint ed. pap. 14.95 (*0-306-80482-4*) Da Capo.

Charles, Richard, jt. ed. see Stevens, Sharon.

Charles River International Symposium on Laborator. Animal Models: Assessing the Scope of Their Use in Biomedical Research, Proceedings of the Sixth Charles River International Symposium on Laboratory Animals, Held in Kyoto, Japan, October 8-9, 1985. Kawamata, Junichi & Melby, Edward C., Jr., eds. LC 86-27718. (Progress in Clinical & Biological Research Ser.: No. 229). 400p. reprint ed. pap. 124.00 (*0-7837-2821-2*, 205765100006) Bks Demand.

Charles, Robert. Arctic Assignment. large type ed. (Linford Mystery Large Print Ser.). 368p. 1998. pap. 17.99 (*0-7089-5264-X*, Linford) Ulverscroft.

— The Arms of the Mantis. large type ed. (Linford Mystery Library). 384p. 1996. pap. 16.99 (*0-7089-7930-0*) Ulverscroft.

— Assassins for Peace. large type ed. (Linford Mystery Large Print Ser.). 368p. 1998. pap. 17.99 (*0-7089-5297-6*, Linford) Ulverscroft.

***Charles, Robert.** The Big Fish. large type ed. 352p. 1999. pap. 18.99 (*0-7089-5533-9*, Linford) Ulverscroft.

Charles, Robert. A Clash of Hawks. large type ed. (Linford Mystery Library). 368p. 1995. pap. 16.99 (*0-7089-7798-7*, Linford) Ulverscroft.

— Dark Vendetta. large type ed. (Linford Mystery Library). 448p. 1997. pap. 16.99 (*0-7089-5161-9*) Ulverscroft.

***Charles, Robert.** Falcoln S.A.S. Blood River. large type ed. 296p. 1999. pap. 18.99 (*0-7089-5559-2*, Linford) Ulverscroft.

— Falcon SAS: Firestrike. large type ed. 304p. 1999. pap. 18.99 (*0-7089-5592-4*, Linford) Ulverscroft.

Charles, Robert. The Flight of the Raven. large type ed. (Linford Mystery Library). 1996. pap. 16.99 (*0-7089-7856-8*, Linford) Ulverscroft.

— The Fourth Shadow. large type ed. (Linford Mystery Library). 416p. 1997. pap. 16.99 (*0-7089-5064-7*, Linford) Ulverscroft.

— The Hour of the Wolf. large type ed. (Linford Mystery Library). 1995. pap. 16.99 (*0-7089-7802-9*, Linford) Ulverscroft.

— A Lance for the Devil. large type ed. (Linford Mystery Library). 352p. 1997. pap. 16.99 (*0-7089-7990-4*, Linford) Ulverscroft.

— Mission of Murder. large type ed. (Linford Mystery Library). 416p. 1998. pap. 17.99 (*0-7089-5221-6*, Linford) Ulverscroft.

— Nothing to Lose. large type ed. (Linford Mystery Library). 416p. 1998. pap. 17.99 (*0-7089-5208-9*, Linford) Ulverscroft.

***Charles, Robert.** Persons Reported. 472p. 2000. 18.99 (*0-7089-5738-2*) Ulverscroft.

Charles, Robert. The Prey of the Falcon. large type ed. (Linford Mystery Library). 368p. 1996. pap. 16.99 (*0-7089-7872-X*, Linford) Ulverscroft.

— The Scream of a Dove. large type ed. (Linford Mystery Library). 368p. 1996. pap. 16.99 (*0-7089-7864-9*, Linford) Ulverscroft.

***Charles, Robert.** Sea Vengeance. large type ed. 352p. 1999. pap. 18.99 (*0-7089-5503-7*, Linford) Ulverscroft.

Charles, Robert. The Snarl of the Lynx. large type ed. (Linford Mystery Library). 368p. 1996. pap. 16.99 (*0-7089-7943-2*, Linford) Ulverscroft.

— Stamboul Intrigue. large type ed. (Linford Mystery Library). 400p. 1997. pap. 16.99 (*0-7089-5059-0*, Linford) Ulverscroft.

— Strikefast. large type ed. (Linford Mystery Large Print Ser.). 384p. 1998. pap. 17.99 (*0-7089-5286-0*, Linford) Ulverscroft.

— The Sun Virgin. large type ed. (Linford Mystery Library). 400p. 1997. pap. 16.99 (*0-7089-5024-8*, Linford) Ulverscroft.

Charles, Robert. This Side of Hell. large type ed. 400p. pap. 18.99 (*0-7089-5456-1*) Ulverscroft.

— Three Days to Live. large type ed. 368p. 1999. pap. 18.99 (*0-7089-5480-4*, Linford) Ulverscroft.

Charles, Robert. The Venom of the Cobra. large type ed. (Linford Mystery Library). 368p. 1996. pap. 16.99 (*0-7089-7906-8*, Linford) Ulverscroft.

Charles, Robert H. A Critical History of the Doctrine of a Future Life, in Israel, in Judaism, & in Christianity. LC 79-8600. reprint ed. 38.50 (*0-404-18455-3*) AMS Pr.

***Charles, Roby.** Spiritual Anatomy. LC 99-94969. 2000. pap. write for info. (*0-533-13245-2*) Vantage.

Charles, Rod, ed. Towards Democracy & Citizenship - Social Studies Education. (C). 1988. 45.00 (*0-7300-0561-5*, Pub. by Deakin Univ) St Mut.

Charles, Rod, ed. see Hovin, Carol.

Charles, Rod, ed. see Weldon, James.

Charles, Rodney. Every Day a Miracle Happens: A Collection of Miracles from Around the World. Pasco, Elizabeth, ed. LC 94-92141. (Illus.). 600p. (Orig.). 1995. pap. 17.95 (*0-9638502-0-2*) Sunstar Pubng.

— Every Day a Miracle Happens: 365 Miracles for Every Day of the Year. LC 97-65716. (Illus.). 600p. 1998. 24.95 (*1-887472-37-1*) Sunstar Pubng.

— Everyday a Miracle Happens Vol. 1: 365 Miracles for Everyday of the Year. rev. ed. (Illus.). 530p. 1998. pap. 19.95 (*1-887472-52-5*) Sunstar Pubng.

Charles, Rodney & Badhwar, Nandini. The Land of Love, Art & Genius. LC 97-65717. (Illus.). 180p. 1999. 49.00 (*1-887472-26-6*) Sunstar Pubng.

Charles, Rodney & Jordan, Anna. Lighter Than Air: Stories of Unaided Human Flight. Pasco, Elizabeth, ed. LC 95-68466. 250p. (Orig.). 1996. pap. text 14.95 (*0-9638502-7-X*) Sunstar Pubng.

Charles, Rodney, jt. auth. see Fregger, Brad.

Charles, Rodney, ed. see Allen, Harold.

Charles, Rodney, ed. see Allen, Harold W.

Charles, Rodney, ed. see Chai, Julie.

Charles, Rodney, ed. see Clute, Sylvia.

Charles, Rodney, ed. see De Herrera, Nancy C.

Charles, Rodney, ed. see Frank, Diane.

Charles, Rodney, ed. see Friedman, Gil.

Charles, Rodney, ed. see Gallo, Anna M.

Charles, Rodney, ed. see Herman, Ronna.

Charles, Rodney, ed. see Kohl, Chrystelle.

Charles, Rodney, ed. see Le Rouzic, Pierre.

Charles, Rodney, ed. see Mayhew, Ed & Mayhew, Mary.

Charles, Rodney, ed. see Mayhew, Mary.

Charles, Rodney, ed. see Murphy, Andy & Murphy, Teri.

Charles, Rodney, ed. see Norsic, Donald.

Charles, Rodney, ed. see Pop, Calin.

Charles, Rodney, ed. see Raymondo, Chris.

Charles, Rodney, ed. see Rei, Shakura.

Charles, Rodney, ed. see Saraswati, Sunyata & Avinasha, Bodhi.

Charles, Rodney, ed. see Sarath, E. Noah.

Charles, Rodney, ed. see Sims, Darla.

Charles, Rodney, ed. see Sylvest, Vernon M.

Charles, Rodney, ed. see Tarabilda, Ed & Grimes, Doug.

Charles, Rodney, ed. see Wells, Sherry.

Charles, Rodney, ed. see Yellin, Jerry.

Charles, Roland & Igus, Toyomi, eds. Life in a Day of Black L. A. The Way We See It: L. A.'s Black Photographers Present a New Perspective on Their City. (Special Publications: Vol. 8). (Illus.). 148p. 1992. 43.00 (*0-934934-38-X*); pap. 28.95 (*0-934934-39-8*) CAAS Pubns.

Charles, Ron. Bahamas Guide. 2nd ed. 248p. 1999. pap. text 13.95 (*1-892975-08-4*) Open Rd Pub.

***Charles, Ron.** Bermuda Guide. 3rd ed. 280p. 1999. pap. 14.95 (*1-892975-09-2*) Open Rd Pub.

Charles, Ron. Holland Guide. 2nd ed. 416p. 1998. pap. text 16.95 (*1-883323-80-0*) Open Rd Pub.

— Portugal Guide. 2nd ed. 552p. 1997. pap. text 16.95 (*1-883323-52-5*) Open Rd Pub.

— Spain Guide. 2nd ed. 592p. (Orig.). 1998. pap. 18.95 (*1-883323-84-3*) Open Rd Pub.

Charles, Ronal D. Street Walkin' (Illus.). 120p. (Orig.). 1986. pap. 9.95 (*1-55630-020-4*) Brentwood Comm.

***Charles, Ruth A.** Immigrant Women's Lives. LC 99-41881. (Studies in the History of American Labor). 1999. write for info. (*0-8153-3388-9*) Garland.

Charles, S. Women in the Word: Examines the Lives of 64 Women of the Bible. LC 84-72958. 250p. 1984. mass mkt. 5.99 (*0-88270-579-2*) Bridge-Logos.

Charles, Samantha. 101 Ways to Get at Your Ex. LC 97-180654. 96p. 1996. 5.99 (*0-7860-0286-7*, Pinnacle Kensgtn) Kensgtn Pub Corp.

Charles, Sara C. & Kennedy, Eugene. Defendant: A Psychiatrist on Trial for Medical Malpractice. 236p. 1985. 35.00 (*0-02-905910-0*) Free Pr.

— Defendant: A Psychiatrist on Trial for Medical Malpractice. LC 86-40147. 232p. 1986. pap. 7.95 (*0-394-74663-5*) Vin Bks.

Charles, Sara C., jt. auth. see Kennedy, Eugene.

Charles Scribners & Sons Staff, ed. Biographical Dictionary of Mathematicians, 4 vols., Set. 2200p. 1991. 250.00 (*0-684-19282-9*, Scribners Ref) Mac Lib Ref.

— Stories by Foreign Authors, Vols. 1 & 2. (C). 1988. pap. text 10.95 (*0-8290-2143-4*) Irvington.

— Stories by Foreign Authors, Vols. 9 & 10. (C). 1988. reprint ed. pap. text 10.95 (*0-8290-2147-7*) Irvington.

Charles, Searle F. Minister of Relief: Harry Hopkins & the Depression. LC 74-2585. (Illus.). 286p. 1974. reprint ed. lib. bdg. 35.00 (*0-8371-7407-4*, CHMR, Greenwood Pr) Greenwood.

Charles, Simon. Cruising Guide to Cuba. 2nd ed. 344p. 1997. pap. 24.95 (*0-944428-36-3*) Cruising Guide.

Charles, St. Narcotics Menace. 1952. 5.95 (*0-87505-229-0*) Borden.

Charles, Sylvia. Couples in the Bible: Examples to Live By. 160p. 1998. pap. 14.99 (*1-56322-062-8*) Hensley Pub.

— Women in the Bible: Examples to Live By. 329p. 1988. pap. 18.99 (*1-56322-021-0*) Hensley Pub.

Charles, T., jt. ed. see Littek, W.

***Charles, Tessa.** Seeds of Redemption. 345p. 1999. pap. 17.99 (*0-9531396-0-3*) Honest to Goodness.

Charles, Theresa. Castle Kelpiesloch. large type ed. 309p. 1989. 27.99 (*0-7089-1925-1*) Ulverscroft.

— A Girl Called Evelyn. large type ed. 448p. 1987. 27.99 (*0-7089-1594-9*) Ulverscroft.

— How Much You Mean to Me. large type ed. 320p. 1987. 27.99 (*0-7089-1570-1*) Ulverscroft.

— The Kinder Love. large type ed. (Romance Ser.). 416p. 1992. 27.99 (*0-7089-2636-3*) Ulverscroft.

— The Man for Me. large type ed. 464p. 1986. 27.99 (*0-7089-1500-0*) Ulverscroft.

— My True Love. large type ed. 304p. 1988. 27.99 (*0-7089-1770-4*) Ulverscroft.

— No Through Road. large type ed. 448p. 1986. 27.99 (*0-7089-1539-6*) Ulverscroft.

— Nurse Alice in Love. large type ed. 1990. 27.99 (*0-7089-2281-3*) Ulverscroft.

— One Who Remembers. large type ed. 352p. 1988. 27.99 (*0-7089-1862-X*) Ulverscroft.

— Patient in Love. large type ed. 368p. 1988. 27.99 (*0-7089-1817-4*) Ulverscroft.

— Proud Citadel. large type ed. 336p. 1987. 27.99 (*0-7089-1697-X*) Ulverscroft.

— Therefore Must Be Loved. large type ed. 320p. 1987. 27.99 (*0-7089-1723-2*) Ulverscroft.

— The Ultimate Surrender. large type ed. 1991. 27.99 (*0-7089-2385-2*) Ulverscroft.

Charles, Thomas. Thomas Charles' Spiritual Counsels. 477p. 1993. reprint ed. text 25.99 (*0-85151-656-4*) Banner of Truth.

Charles, Veronika M. The Crane Girl. unabridged ed. (Illus.). 32p. (J). (ps up). 1997. pap. write for info. (*0-7737-5718-X*) STDK.

— Hey! What's That Sound? unabridged ed. LC 99-172851. (Illus.). 32p. (J). (ps-3). 1994. 12.95 (*0-7737-2841-4*) STDK.

— Hey! What's That Sound? unabridged ed. LC 99-172851. (Illus.). 32p. (J). (ps-3). 1996. pap. 5.95 (*0-7737-5702-3*) STDK.

— Necklace of Stars. unabridged ed. (Illus.). 32p. (J). (gr. k-4). 1997. 17.95 (*0-7737-2967-4*) STDK.

***Charles, Veronika M.** Stretch, Swallow & Stare. large type ed. (Illus.). 32p. (J). (gr. k-3). 1999. 16.95 (*0-7737-3098-2*) Genl Dist Srvs.

Charles, Vic. Hostile Environment: A Novel of Prison Life. Smith, James C., Jr., ed. LC 94-48712. 160p. (Orig.). 1995. pap. 16.95 (*0-86534-230-X*) Sunstone Pr.

— Karate. (Skills of the Game Ser.). (Illus.). 96p. 1990. pap. 19.95 (*1-85223-224-2*, Pub. by Crolwood) Trafalgar.

Charles, Victoria. Salvador Dali. (Great Painters Ser.). (Illus.). 176p. 1999. 40.00 (*1-85995-373-5*) Parkstone Pr.

— Van Gogh. (Great Painters Ser.). 160p. 1997. 40.00 (*1-85995-391-3*) Parkstone Pr.

Charles, Victoria S. Rembrandt: Etchings & Engravings. (Temporis Ser.). (Illus.). 198p. 1997. 55.00 (*1-85995-311-5*) Parkstone Pr.

Charles, Victorin. Diccionario Atomico. (SPA.). 296p. 49.95 (*0-7859-0719-X*, S-33057) Fr & Eur.

Charlesbridge Publication Staff. Xanadu: The Imaginary Place. 1999. pap. text 6.95 (*0-9651722-3-6*) Shakti for Chldrn.

***Charlesbridge Publication Staff.** Xanadu: The Imaginary Place. (Illus.). (J). 1999. 15.95 (*0-9651722-2-8*) Shakti for Chldrn.

Charlesthom, jt. auth. see Raper, K. B.

Charleston Area Medical Center Foundation Staff. Don't Eat This Book. LC 92-31744. 1992. write for info. (*0-87197-352-9*) Favorite Recipes.

Charleston, Gordon. Armstrong Lands on the Moon. LC 93-32918. (Great Twentieth Century Expeditions Ser.). (Illus.). 32p. (J). (gr. 4 up). 1950. lib. bdg. 20.00 (*0-87518-530-4*, Dillon Silver Burdett) Silver Burdett Pr.

— Peary Reaches the North Pole. LC 92-44500. (Great Twentieth Century Expeditions Ser.). (Illus.). 32p. (J). (gr. 5 up). 1993. lib. bdg. 13.95 (*0-87518-535-5*, Dillon Silver Burdett) Silver Burdett Pr.

Charleston Mercury Staff, jt. auth. see New York Times Staff.

Charleston-Pinola, Cindy & Jordan, Harold. Veterans Administration Program for Disabled Veterans: An Overview. 1986. pap. 2.50 (*0-685-23193-3*, 40,900) NCLS Inc.

Charleston, Robert J. Masterpieces of Glass: A World History from the Corning Museum of Glass. (Illus.). 240p. 1993. pap. 29.95 (*0-8109-2557-5*, Pub. by Abrams) Time Warner.

Charleston, Robert J., et al, eds. The Glass Circle 4. 108p. (Orig.). 1983. 65.00 (*0-946095-02-7*, Pub. by Gresham Bks) St Mut.

C

— The Glass Circle 1. 64p. 1983. 40.00 (*0-85362-148-9*, Pub. by Gresham Bks) St Mut.
— The Glass Circle 2. 84p. 1983. 40.00 (*0-9502121-2-1*, Pub. by Gresham Bks) St Mut.
Charleston, Robert J., et al. The Glass Circle 3. Evans, Wendy & Polak, Ada, eds. 96p. 1983. 45.00 (*0-905418-23-9*, Pub. by Gresham Bks) St Mut.
Charleston Symphony Orchestra. Music, Menus & Magnolias. 320p. 1996. 17.95 (*0-9648219-1-5*, Pub. by CSOL) Wimmer Bks.
Charleston Symphony Orchestra League Staff. Music Menus & Magnolias: Charleston Shares Its Culture & Cuisine. LC 95-70790. (Illus.). 350p. 1996. reprint ed. 17.95 (*0-9648219-0-7*) CSOL.
Charlesworth. Math & Science for Young Children. (Early Childhood Education Ser.). 1990. pap. 35.00 (*0-8273-3402-8*, VNR) Wiley.
— Math & Science for Young Children. (Early Childhood Education Ser.). 1995. pap., teacher ed. 12.00 (*0-8273-5870-9*, VNR) Wiley.
***Charlesworth.** Math for Young Children. 4th ed. LC 99-17401. (Early Childhood Education Ser.). 400p. (C). 1999. pap. 46.95 (*0-7668-0233-7*) Delmar.
Charlesworth. Understanding Child Development. 4th ed. (Early Childhood Education Ser.). 96p. (C). 1996. teacher ed. 18.95 (*0-8273-7334-1*) Delmar.
— Understanding Child Development. 5th ed. LC 99-49326. (Early Childhood Education Ser.). (Illus.). 644p. (C). 1999. pap. 63.95 (*0-7668-0338-4*) Delmar.
Charlesworth, Andrew, et al. An Atlas of Industrial Protest in Britain, 1750-1990. LC 95-42143. 240p. 1996. text 59.95 (*0-312-15889-0*) St Martin.
Charlesworth, Andrew, jt. auth. see Randall, Adrian.
Charlesworth, Brian. Evolution in Age-Structured Populations. 2nd ed. LC 93-26151. (Cambridge Studies in Mathematical Biology: No. 1). (Illus.). 320p. (C). 1994. pap. text 33.95 (*0-521-45967-2*) Cambridge U Pr.
Charlesworth, Bruce, jt. auth. see Hagen, Charles.
Charlesworth, C. Mercantile Law. (C). 1984. 70.00 (*0-7855-4078-4*, Pub. by Witherby & Co) St Mut.
Charlesworth, Charles, ed. see Miles, Barry.
Charlesworth, Chris. Sex, Drugs & Rock 'n Roll. (Illus.). 192p. pap. 19.95 (*0-7119-3445-2*, BO 10146) Omnibus NY.
— The Who. (Complete Guides to the Music Of...Ser.). (Illus.). 136p. (Orig.). pap. 8.95 (*0-7119-4306-0*, OP 47740, Pub. by Omnibus Press) Omnibus NY.
***Charlesworth, David.** Furniture-Making Techniques. 128p. 1999. pap. text 17.95 (*1-86108-125-1*) Guild Master.
Charlesworth, Edward A. Stress Management: A Comprehensive Guide to Wellness. 1985. mass mkt. 6.99 (*0-345-32734-9*) Ballantine Pub Grp.
Charlesworth, Ernest N. Cutaneous Allergy. LC 96-47622. (Illus.). 400p. 1996. text 150.00 (*0-86542-370-9*) Blackwell Sci.
Charlesworth, Geoffrey B. A Gardener Obsessed: Observations, Reflections & Advice for Other Dedicated Gardeners. LC 94-15375. 256p. 1994. 24.95 (*1-56792-002-0*) Godine.
Charlesworth, George. A History of British Motorways. 284p. 1984. 40.00 (*0-7277-0159-2*, Pub. by T Telford) RCH.
Charlesworth, James. The Beloved Disciple. LC 95-549. 512p. (C). 1995. 30.00 (*1-56338-135-4*) Sigler Pr.
Charlesworth, James, ed. Dead Sea Scrolls Vol. 4: Angelic Liturgy, Prayers, & Psalms. (Princeton Theological Seminary Dead Sea Scrolls Project Ser.). 1997. 99.00 (*0-664-22060-6*) Westminster John Knox.
Charlesworth, James C. America's Changing Role As a World Leader. Lambert, Richard D., ed. LC 76-85466. (Annals Ser.: 384). 1969. 28.00 (*0-87761-118-1*); pap. 18.00 (*0-87761-117-3*) Am Acad Pol Soc Sci.
Charlesworth, James C., ed. Changing American People: Are We Deteriorating or Improving? LC 68-27641. (Annals of the American Academy of Political & Social Science Ser.: No. 378). 1968. 28.00 (*0-87761-109-2*); pap. 18.00 (*0-87761-108-4*) Am Acad Pol Soc Sci.
— Design for Political Science: Scope, Objectives, & Methods. LC 74-117766. (Essay Index Reprint Ser.). 1977. 21.95 (*0-8369-1789-8*) Ayer.
Charlesworth, James C. & Lambert, Richard D., eds. New American Posture Toward Asia. LC 72-120283. (Annals of the American Academy of Political & Social Science Ser.: No. 390). 1970. 28.00 (*0-685-00183-0*); pap. 18.00 (*0-87761-127-0*) Am Acad Pol Soc Sci.
Charlesworth, James H. Assessing the Uniqueness of Qumran Theology. 1999. 39.95 (*0-941037-59-2*) D & F Scott.
— Authentic Apocrypha: False & Genuine Christian Apocrypha. LC 97-53301. (Dead Sea Scrolls & Christian Origins Library). xii, 69p. 1998. pap. 8.95 (*0-941037-63-0*, BIBAL Press) D & F Scott.
— Biblical Inspiration for Qumran Theology. 1998. 39.95 (*0-941037-57-6*) D & F Scott.
— Critical Reflections on the Odes of Solomon Vol. 1: Literary Setting, Textual Studies, Gnosticism, The Dead Sea Scrolls & the Gospel of John. (JSPS Ser.: Vol. 22). 302p. 1998. 85.00 (*1-85075-660-0*, Pub. by Sheffield Acad) CUP Services.
— The Dead Sea Scrolls, Vol. 4B. Newsom, Carol A., ed. 1998. 99.00 (*0-664-22126-2*) Westminster John Knox.
— Destruction of Jerusalem. 1998. pap. 8.95 (*0-941037-62-2*, BIBAL Press) D & F Scott.
— The Hebrew Bible & Qumran LC 98-40247. (The Bible & the Dead Sea Scrolls Ser.). 1998. 39.95 (*0-941037-56-8*, BIBAL Press) D & F Scott.
— How Barisat Bellowed Vol. 3: Folklore, Humor & Iconography in the Jewish Apocalypses. LC 98-3081. (Dead Sea Scrolls & Christian Origins Library). xiii, 60 p. 1998. pap. 8.95 (*0-941037-64-9*, BIBAL Press) D & F Scott.
— Jesus & the Dead Sea Scrolls. 416p. 1995. pap. 22.95 (*0-385-47844-5*) Doubleday.
— John & the Dead Sea Scrolls. (Christian Origins Library). 256p. (Orig.). 1990. pap. 16.95 (*0-8245-1001-1*) Crossroad NY.
***Charlesworth, James H.** The Millennium Guide for Pilgrims to the Holy Land. LC 00-8353. 2000. 16.95 (*0-941037-93-2*, BIBAL Press) D & F Scott.
— The Old Testament Pseudepigrapha & the New Testament: Prolegomena for the Study of Christian Origins. LC 98-39834. 192p. 1998. pap. 17.00 (*1-56338-257-1*) TPI PA.
Charlesworth, James H. Qumran Questions. LC 96-156600. (Biblical Seminar Ser.: No. 36). 210p. 1995. pap. 23.75 (*1-85075-770-4*, Pub. by Sheffield Acad) CUP Services.
Charlesworth, James H., ed. The Dead Sea Scrolls Vol. 2: Damascus Document, War Scroll, & Related Documents. (Princeton Theological Seminary Dead Sea Scrolls Project Ser.: Vol. 2). 300p. 1996. 99.00 (*0-664-22037-1*) Westminster John Knox.
— The Dead Sea Scrolls, Vol. 1: Rules of the Community & Related Documents. (Princeton Theological Seminary Dead Sea Scrolls Project Ser.). 300p. 1994. text 99.00 (*0-664-21994-2*) Westminster John Knox.
— Jews & Christians: Rethinking Our Relationships. (Illus.). 272p. 1990. 19.95 (*0-8245-1012-7*) Crossroad NY.
— The Messiah: Developments in Earliest Judaism & Christianity. LC 91-36381. 608p. 1992. 53.00 (*0-8006-2563-3*, 1-2563, Fortress Pr) Augsburg Fortress.
— Old Testament Pseudepigrapha, 2 vols., Set. 1056p. 1986. boxed set 80.00 (*0-385-19491-9*) Doubleday.
— Old Testament Pseudepigrapha Vol. I: Apocalyptic Literature & Testaments, Vol. 1. LC 80-2443. 1056p. 1983. 49.95 (*0-385-09630-5*) Doubleday.
— Old Testament Pseudepigrapha Vol. II: Expansions of the Old Testament & Legends, Wisdom & Philosophical Literature, Prayers, Psalms & Odes, Fragments of Lost Judeo-Hellenistic Words, Vol. 2. 1056p. 1985. 49.95 (*0-385-18813-7*) Doubleday.
Charlesworth, James H., et al, eds. The Lord's Prayer & Other Prayer Texts from the Greco-Roman Era. LC 94-31. 304p. (Orig.). (C). 1994. 25.00 (*1-56338-080-3*) TPI PA.
***Charlesworth, James H., et al, eds.** Qumran-Messianism: Studies on the Messianic Expectations in the Dead Sea Scrolls. 248p. 1998. 152.50 (*3-16-146968-2*, Pub. by JCB Mohr) Coronet Bks.
Charlesworth, James H. & American Schools of Oriental Research Staff. Caves of Enlightenment: Proceedings of the ASOR Dead Sea Scrolls Jubilee Symposium, 1947-1997. LC 98-25408. 1998. pap. 14.95 (*0-941037-68-1*, BIBAL Press) D & F Scott.
Charlesworth, James H. & Evans, Craig A., eds. The Pseudepigrapha & Early Biblical Interpretation. (Journal for the Study of the Pseudepigrapha Supplement Ser.: No. 14). 319p. 1993. 60.00 (*1-85075-443-8*, Pub. by Sheffield Acad) CUP Services.
Charlesworth, James H. & Johns, Loren L., eds. Hillel & Jesus: Comparisons of Two Major Religious Leaders. LC 97-202136. 518p. 1997. 50.00 (*0-8006-2564-1*, 1-2564, Fortress Pr) Augsburg Fortress.
Charlesworth, James H. & Weaver, Walter P. The Old & New Testaments: Their Relationship & the Intertestamental Literature. LC 93-31235. (Faith & Scholarship Colloquies Ser.). 160p. 1993. pap. 14.00 (*1-56338-062-5*) TPI PA.
***Charlesworth, James H. & Weaver, Walter P., eds.** The Dead Sea Scrolls & Christian Faith: In Celebration of the Jubilee Year of the Discovery of Qumran Cave. LC 98-9269. 96p. 1998. pap. 12.00 (*1-56338-232-6*) TPI PA.
Charlesworth, James H. & Weaver, Walter P., eds. Images of Jesus Today. LC 94-993. (Faith & Scholarship Colloquies Ser.). 144p. (Orig.). (C). 1994. pap. 14.00 (*1-56338-082-X*) TPI PA.
***Charlesworth, James H. & Weaver, Walter P., eds.** Jesus Two Thousand Years Later. LC 99-53669. 128p. 2000. pap. 14.00 (*1-56338-303-9*, Pub. by TPI PA) Morehouse Pub.
Charlesworth, James H. & Weaver, Walter P., eds. What Has Archaeology to Do with Faith? LC 92-5202. (Faith & Scholarship Colloquies Ser.). 128p. 1992. pap. 14.00 (*1-56338-038-2*) TPI PA.
Charlesworth, James H., et al. Graphic Concordance to the Dead Sea Scrolls: The Princeton Theological Seminary Dead Sea Scrolls Project. 560p. 1992. text 175.00 (*0-664-21969-1*) Westminster John Knox.
Charlesworth, James H., jt. ed. see Collins, John J.
Charlesworth, James H., jt. ed. see Weaver, Walter P.
***Charlesworth, Kate.** Plastics: Collecting & Conserving. Quye, Anita & Williamson, Colin, eds. (Illus.). 128p. 1999. pap. 19.95 (*1-901663-12-4*, Pub. by Natl Mus Scotland) A Schwartz & Co.
Charlesworth, Kay, tr. see Di Terlizzi, Maurizio.
Charlesworth-Lind. Math & Science for Young Children. 3rd ed. (Early Childhood Education Ser.). 592p. (C). 1998. pap. text 58.95 (*0-8273-8635-4*) Delmar.
Charlesworth, Liza. African-Americans. 128p. (J). 1997. pap. 14.95 (*0-590-53546-3*) Scholastic Inc.
***Charlesworth, Liza.** Word Family Wheels: 32 Easy-to-Make Manipulative Wheels That Help Kids Master Key. (Turn to Learn Ser.). (Illus.). 80p. (J). (gr. k-2). 2000. pap. 17.99 (*0-590-64376-2*) Scholastic Inc.
Charlesworth, Liza & Sachatello-Sawyer, Bonniee. Dinosaurs. (Illus.). (J). 1995. pap. 11.95 (*0-590-49412-0*) Scholastic Inc.
Charlesworth, M. J., et al, eds. Ancestor Spirits. 92p. (C). 1991. 59.00 (*0-7855-6750-X*, Pub. by Deakin Univ) St Mut.
Charlesworth, M. J., tr. St. Anselm's Proslogion. LC 78-63300. 1979. reprint ed. pap. text 13.00 (*0-268-01697-6*) U of Notre Dame Pr.
Charlesworth, M. J., et al. Ancestor Spirits: Aspects of Australian Aboriginal Life & Spirituality. 92p. 1991. pap. 60.00 (*0-948823-14-3*, Pub. by Deakin Univ) St Mut.
— Ancestor Spirits: Aspects of Australian Aboriginal Life & Spirituality. 90p. 1995. pap. 40.00 (*0-949823-14-7*, Pub. by Deakin Univ) St Mut.
Charlesworth, M. P. Trade Routes & Commerce of the Roman Empire. 320p. 1986. pap. 25.00 (*0-89005-444-4*) Ares.
Charlesworth, Martin P. Five Men: Character Studies from the Roman Empire. LC 67-30202. (Essay Index Reprint Ser.). 1977. reprint ed. 22.95 (*0-8369-0292-0*) Ayer.
— The Roman Empire. LC 86-29443. (Oxford Paperbacks University Ser.). (Illus.). 158p. 1987. reprint ed. lib. bdg. 59.50 (*0-313-25669-1*, CHAR, Greenwood Pr) Greenwood.
Charlesworth, Martin P., tr. see Parvan, Vasile.
Charlesworth, Max. La Bioetica en una Sociedad Liberal.Tr. of Bioethics in a Liberal Society. (SPA.). 220p. (C). 1996. pap. 15.95 (*0-521-55596-5*) Cambridge U Pr.
Charlesworth, Max. Religious Inventions: Four Essays. LC 96-37027. 169p. (C). 1997. text 54.95 (*0-521-59076-0*); pap. text 18.95 (*0-521-59927-X*) Cambridge U Pr.
Charlesworth, Max, ed. Religious Business: Essays on Australian Aboriginal Spirituality. LC 98-4099. (Illus.). 224p. (C). 1998. text 64.95 (*0-521-63347-8*); pap. text 22.95 (*0-521-63352-4*) Cambridge U Pr.
Charlesworth, Max, et al, eds. Religion in Aboriginal Australia: An Anthology. LC 83-23437. (Illus.). 458p. (C). 1984. pap. text 19.95 (*0-7022-2008-6*) Intl Spec Bk.
Charlesworth, Max, et al. Life among the Scientists: An Anthropological Study of an Australian Scientific Community. 304p. 1995. pap. 60.00 (*0-949823-27-9*, Pub. by Deakin Univ) St Mut.
— Medical Ethics. 2nd ed. Campbell, Alastair, ed. LC 97-163622. 238p. 1997. text 45.00 (*0-19-558350-7*) OUP.
***Charlesworth, Michelle.** Public Information Officer. (Illus.). 112p. (C). 1999. pap. write for info. (*0-87939-170-7*) IFSTA.
Charlesworth, Rosalind. Experiences in Math for Young Children. 2nd ed. 1991. pap., teacher ed. 8.50 (*0-8273-4632-8*) Delmar.
Charlesworth, Rosalind. Experiences in Math for Young Children. 3rd ed. LC 95-10957. 400p. (C). 1995. pap. 33.25 (*0-8273-7226-4*) Delmar.
Charlesworth, Rosalind. Experiments in Math for Young Children. 3rd ed. (Early Childhood Education Ser.). 1996. teacher ed. 14.95 (*0-8273-7227-2*) Delmar.
— Math & Science for Young Children. 2nd ed. LC 94-34419. (Illus.). 559p. (C). 1995. pap. 37.50 (*0-8273-5869-5*) Delmar.
— Math & Science for Young Children: Instructor's Guide. 1990. pap., teacher ed. 10.00 (*0-8273-3403-6*) Delmar.
— Understanding Child Development. 3rd ed. (Orig.). 1992. pap. 40.00 (*0-8273-4891-6*) Delmar.
— Understanding Child Development: For Adults Who Work with Young Children. 4th ed. LC 95-16990. 616p. (C). 1995. pap. 40.50 (*0-8273-7332-5*) Delmar.
— Understanding Child Development: Instructor's Guide & Test Bank. 3rd ed. 1992. pap. 14.95 (*0-8273-4892-4*) Delmar.
Charlesworth, Rosalind & Radeloff, Deanna J. Experiences in Math for Young Children. LC 77-80039. (C). 1978. pap. 20.75 (*0-8273-1660-7*) Delmar.
***Charlesworth, Simon J.** A Phenomenology of Working Class Experience. (Cambridge Cultural Social Studies). 324p. (C). 2000. text 64.95 (*0-521-65066-6*); pap. text 24.95 (*0-521-65915-9*) Cambridge U Pr.
Charlesworth, Stephanie, et al. Lawyers, Social Workers & Families. xv, 255p. 1990. pap. 43.00 (*1-86287-030-6*, Pub. by Federation Pr) Gaunt.
Charlesworthy, Max, ed. Science, Non-Science & Pseudo-Science. (C). 1982. 35.00 (*0-949823-05-8*, Pub. by Deakin Univ) St Mut.
Charlet, David A. Atlas of Nevada Conifers: A Phytogeographic Reference. LC 95-9493. (Illus.). 336p. (Orig.). 1996. pap. text 35.00 (*0-87417-265-9*) U of Nev Pr.
Charlet, James D., et al. North Carolina: Our People, Places, & Past. (Illus.). 320p. (J). (gr. 4 up). 1987. lib. bdg. 22.95 (*0-89089-319-5*) Carolina Acad Pr.
— North Carolina: Our People, Places, & Past Student Workbook. (Illus.). 300p. (YA). 1988. student ed. 49.95 (*0-935911-13-8*) Cornucop Pub.
Charlet, Laurence D. & Brewer, Gary J., eds. Biological Control of Native Indigenous Insect Pests: Challenges, Constraints & Potential. (Proceedings, Thomas Say Publications in Entomology Ser.). 122p. 1999. pap. 35.00 (*0-938522-83-3*) Entomol Soc.
***Charlet, Nicholas.** Yves Klein. 2000. 50.00 (*2-84576-017-5*) Vilo Intl.
Charleton, H. B., ed. see Marlowe, Christopher.
Charleton, James H. Biblical Theology & the Qumran Community. 1999. 39.95 (*0-941037-58-4*) D & F Scott.
Charleton, James H., et al, eds. Framers of the Constitution. rev. ed. LC 86-8413. (Illus.). 260p. 1986. pap. 8.95 (*0-911333-84-3*, 200045) National Archives & Recs.
Charleton, James H., jt. auth. see Ferris, Robert G.
Charleton, Mary. Self-Directed Learning in Counsellor Training. Dryden, Windy, ed. LC 96-500. (Counselor Trainer & Supervisor Ser.). (Illus.). 128p. 1996. pap. 27.50 (*0-304-32943-6*); text 79.50 (*0-304-32941-X*) Continuum.
Charleton, Peter. Criminal Law Cases & Materials. 1992. pap. text 88.00 (*1-85475-169-7*, IE, MICHIE) LEXIS Pub.
Charleton, Walter. The Ephesian Matron: (From the Ephesian & Cimmerian Matrons, Two Notable Examples of the Power of Love & Wit) LC 92-545. (Augustan Reprints Ser.: Nos. 172-173). 1975. reprint ed. 21.50 (*0-404-70172-8*, BD436) AMS Pr.
— The Immorality of the Human Soul, Demonstrated by the Light of Nature: In Two Dialogues. LC 83-46043. (Scientific Awakening in the Restoration Ser.: No. 2). (Illus.). 224p. 1985. reprint ed. 87.50 (*0-404-63302-1*) AMS Pr.
Charleux, B., jt. ed. see Roovers, J.
Charlevoix, Pierre. Charlevoix's Louisiana/77: Selections from the History & the Journal. O'Neill, Charles E., ed. LC 77-3343. (Louisiana Bicentennial Reprint Ser.). (Illus.). xliv, 257p. 1992. reprint ed. 40.00 (*0-8071-0250-4*, CCHARL) Claitors.
Charley & Fowke. What They Don't Tell You about Art. (Illus.). (J). mass mkt. 8.95 (*0-340-71330-5*, Pub. by Hodder & Stought Ltd) Trafalgar.
Charley, Aunt, pseud. The Raindrop Children, Vol. 1. (Children of the Elements Ser.). (Illus.). 24p. (J). (gr. 1-2). 1991. pap. 5.95 (*1-880945-00-2*) Animated Elements.
Charley, Catherine. China. LC 94-15613. (Country Fact Files Ser.). 1995. lib. bdg. 24.26 (*0-8114-2789-7*) Raintree Steck-V.
— China. LC 98-20038. (Country Fact Files Ser.). (J). 1998. write for info. (*0-8172-5410-2*) Raintree Steck-V.
Charley, Helen G. Food Science. 3rd ed. (Illus.). 574p. (C). 1994. teacher ed. write for info. (*0-318-72456-1*) Macmillan.
— Foods: A Scientific Approach. 3rd ed. LC 97-22861. (Illus.). 582p. (C). 1997. 77.00 (*0-02-321951-3*, Macmillan Coll) P-H.
Charley, Kathy. The Integrity of Childhood. (Illus.). 60p. 1997. pap. 7.95 (*0-942323-25-4*) N Amer Heritage Pr.
Charlez, Philippe, ed. Mechanics of Porous Media: Lecture Notes of the Mechanics of Porous Media Summer School June 1995. Keramsi, Deborah, tr. from FRE. LC 99-227327. (Illus.). 320p. (C). 1995. text 126.00 (*90-5410-628-X*, Pub. by A A Balkema) Ashgate Pub Co.
Charlez, Philippe A. Rock Mechanics Vol. 1: Theoretical Fundamentals. (Illus.). 360p. (C). 1991. 150.00 (*2-7108-0585-5*, 9ET12) Gulf Pub.
Charlick-Paley, Tanya, jt. auth. see Sokolsky, Richard.
Charlick, Robert B. Animation Rurale Revisited: Participatory Techniques for Improving Agriculture & Social Services in 5 Francophone Nations. (Special Series on Animation Rurale: No. 1). 243p. (Orig.). (C). 1984. pap. text 10.00 (*0-86731-041-3*) Cornell CIS RDC.
— Niger: Personal Rule & Survival in the Sahel. (Profiles - Nations of Contemporary Africa Ser.). 189p. 1991. pap. 58.50 (*0-89158-968-6*) Westview.
Charlick, Robert B., et al. Animation Rurale & Rural Development: The Experience of Upper Volta. (Special Series on Animation Rurale: No. 3). 133p. (Orig.). (C). 1982. pap. text 6.65 (*0-86731-043-X*) Cornell CIS RDC.
Charlick, Tanya H., ed. see Huck, Daniel F. & Sauber, Kirk A.
Charlie, Teddy, jt. auth. see Krauss, Michael.
Charlier, B. Le, see Le Charlier, B., ed.
Charlier, Jean-Michel, et al, eds. Tensors & the Clifford Algebra: Applications to the Physics of Bosons & Fermions. (Pure & Applied Mathematics Ser.: Vol. 163). (Illus.). 344p. 1992. text 175.00 (*0-8247-8666-1*) Dekker.
Charlier, R. H. & Meyer, C. P. Coastal Erosion: Response & Management. LC 97-22225. (Lecture Notes in Earth Sciences Ser.: Vol. 70). (Illus.). 360p. 1997. pap. 99.95 (*3-540-60022-1*) Spr-Verlag.
Charlier, Roger H. Harnessing Ocean Energies: Tapping Ocean Energies to Produce Inexhaustible, Pollution-Free Electricity. (Illus.). 1977. reprint ed. 7.00 (*0-686-21178-2*) Maple Mont.
— Non-Living Ocean Resources. 1979. reprint ed. pap. 7.00 (*0-686-27713-9*) Maple Mont.
Charlier, Roger H. & Justus, J. R. Ocean Energies: Resources for the Future. LC 92-32795. (Elsevier Oceanography Ser.: No. 56). 554p. 1992. 268.00 (*0-444-88248-0*) Elsevier.
Charlip, Remy. Arm in Arm: A Collection of Connections, Endless Tales, Reiterations, & Other Echolalia. LC 96-44370. (Illus.). 48p. (J). (gr. 2). 1997. 15.95 (*1-883672-50-3*) Tricycle Pr.
— First Remy Charlip Reader. Nelson, Lisa M. & Smith, Nancy S., eds. (Illus.). 56p. (Orig.). 1986. pap. 8.00 (*0-937645-01-X*) Contact Edit.
— Fortunately. 1993. 11.19 (*0-606-02644-4*, Pub. by Turtleback) Demco.
— Fortunately. LC 92-22794. (Illus.). 48p. (J). (ps-3). 1993. reprint ed. mass mkt. 5.99 (*0-689-71660-5*) Aladdin.
— Fortunately. LC 80-36956. (Illus.). 48p. (J). (ps-3). 1984. reprint ed. lib. bdg. 14.95 (*0-02-718100-6*, Four Winds Pr) S&S Childrens.
— I Love You. (Illus.). 32p. (J). (ps-1). 1999. 4.95 (*0-590-02315-2*, Pub. by Scholastic Inc) Penguin Putnam.
— Peanut Butter Party: Including the History, Uses & Future of Peanut Butter. LC 98-43378. (Illus.). (J). (gr. 1-5). 1999. 14.95 (*1-883672-69-4*) Tricycle Pr.
— Sleepytime Rhyme. LC 98-41040. (Illus.). 32p. (J). (ps). 1999. 15.95 (*0-688-16271-1*, Grenwillow Bks); 15.89 (*0-688-16272-X*, Grenwillow Bks) HarpC Child Bks.
***Charlip, Remy.** Why I Will Never Ever Ever Ever Have Enough Time to Read This Book. LC 99-52825. (Illus.). 40p. (J). (gr. 1 up). 2000. 14.95 (*1-58246-018-3*) Tricycle Pr.
Charlip, Remy & Miller, Mary B. Handtalk: An ABC of Finger Spelling & Sign Language. LC 85-3667. (Illus.). 48p. (J). (ps up). 1984. reprint ed. text 15.95 (*0-02-718130-8*, Mac Bks Young Read) S&S Childrens.

C

An Asterisk (*) at the beginning of an entry indicates that the title is appearing for the first time.

— Handtalk Birthday: A Number & Story Book in Sign Language. LC 86-22755. (Illus.). 48p. (J). (ps up). 1987. text 15.95 (*0-02-718080-8*, Four Winds Pr) S&S Childrens.

Charlip, Remy & Moore, Lilian. Hooray for Me! (Illus.). 1995. 14.95 (*0-15-200230-8*) Harcourt.

— Hooray for Me! LC 96-2449. (Illus.). 40p. (J). (ps up). 1996. 14.95 (*1-883672-43-0*) Tricycle Pr.

Charlip, Remy & Supree, Burton. Mother Mother I Feel Sick Send for the Doctor Quick Quick Quick. (Illus.). (J). 1993. reprint ed. pap. 14.95 (*1-56849-172-7*) Buccaneer Bks.

***Charlish, Anne.** Arthritis & Rheumatism. LC 99-16028. (Alternative Answers to Ser.). 2000. 22.95 (*0-7621-0247-0*, Pub. by RD Assn) Penguin Putnam.

— Divorce. LC 98-6038. (Talking Points Ser.). (Illus.). 64p. (J). (gr. 5-9). 1999. lib. bdg. 27.12 (*0-8172-5310-6*) Raintree Steck-V.

Charlish, Anne. Your Natural Pregnancy: A Guide to Complementary Therapies. LC 95-83567. (Illus.). 160p. (Orig.). 1996. pap. 16.95 (*1-56975-059-9*) Ulysses Pr.

Charlot, Jean. Art from the Mayans to Disney. LC 78-99623. (Essay Index Reprint Ser.). 1977. 12.95 (*0-8369-1399-X*) Ayer.

— The Mexican Mural Renaissance, 1920-1925. LC 62-8238. (Illus.). 386p. reprint ed. pap. 119.70 (*0-608-18585-X*, 200538400054) Bks Demand.

Charlot, John. The Hawaiian Poetry of Religion & Politics: Some Religio-Political Concepts in Postcontact Literature. (Polynesian Studies: No. 5). 94p. (C). 1985. pap. text 8.00 (*0-939154-38-2*) Inst Polynesian.

— The Kamapua'a Literature: The Classical Traditions of the Hawaiian Pig God As a Body of Literature. LC 87-2724. (Institute for Polynesian Studies Monographs: No. 6). 176p. 1987. pap. text 10.00 (*0-939154-47-1*) Inst Polynesian.

Charlotte. Cooking with Class. 1982. 16.95 (*0-9615616-0-2*) Charlotte Latin Schls Inc.

— Cooking with Class. 1992. 16.95 (*0-9615616-1-0*) Charlotte Latin Schls Inc.

Charlotte, jt. auth. see Dickinson, Mary.

Charlotte, Elisabeth. A Woman's Life in the Court of the Sun King: Letters of Liselotte von der Pfalz. Forster, Elborg, tr. (Illus.). 287p. 1997. reprint ed. pap. 16.95 (*0-8018-5635-3*) Johns Hopkins.

Charlotte Observer Staff, ed. Dale Earnhardt: Rear View Mirror. 250p. 1998. 29.95 (*1-58261-020-7*) Sprts Pubng.

Charlotte, Susan, et al, eds. Creativity: Conversations with 28 Who Excel. (Illus.). 412p. 1993. 24.95 (*1-879094-11-8*) Momentum Bks.

— Creativity in Film: Conversations with 14 Who Excel. (Projected Ser.). (Illus.). 189p. (Orig.). 1993. pap. 14.95 (*1-879094-28-2*) Momentum Bks.

Charlsen, David, ed. Family Violence & Religion: An Interfaith Resource Guide. LC 95-19940. (Family Violence Prevention Ser.). 308p. 1995. 29.95 (*1-884244-10-6*) Volcano Pr.

Charlson, Robert J. & Heintzenberg, J., eds. Aerosol Forcing of Climate: Report of the Dahlem Workshop on Aerosol Forcing of Climate, Berlin 1994, April 24-29. LC 95-14231. (Environmental Sciences Research Reports: Vol. 17). 432p. 1995. 245.00 (*0-471-95693-7*) Wiley.

Charlton. Crosscurrents: Contemporary Political Issues. 2nd ed. 1994. 12.25 (*0-17-604234-2*) Thomson Learn.

***Charlton.** Jack Charlton -The Autobiography. 2000. 29.95 (*1-85225-256-1*, Pub. by Transworld Publishers Ltd) Trafalgar.

— Michel Sedaine (1719-1797) 78.95 (*1-84014-677-X*) Ashgate Pub Co.

Charlton, Kenneth. Women, Religion & Education in Early Modern England. LC 98-33130. 1999. text. write for info. (*0-415-18148-8*) Routledge.

Charlton, Ann. Baby down Under. (Australians Ser.). 1999. per. 4.50 (*0-373-82580-3*) Harlequin Bks.

— Hot November (Dangerous Liaisons) LC 96-507. 189p. 1995. per. 3.25 (*0-373-11777-9*) Harlequin Bks.

— Married to the Man. (Presents Ser.: No. 1892). 1997. per. 3.50 (*0-373-11892-9*, 1-11892-6) Harlequin Bks.

— Married to the Man. large type ed. (Mills & Boon Large Print Ser.). 288p. 1997. 23.99 (*0-263-14923-4*) Ulverscroft.

— Ransomed Heart. large type ed. (Magna Large Print Ser.). 267p. 1996. 27.99 (*0-7505-1054-4*, Pub. by Mgna Lrg Print) Ulverscroft.

— Steamy December. LC 96-311. 186p. 1995. per. 3.25 (*0-373-11782-5*, 1-11782-9) Harlequin Bks.

— Steamy December. large type ed. (Harlequin Romance Ser.). 1996. 20.95 (*0-263-14506-9*) Thorndike Pr.

Charlton, Anna E., jt. auth. see Francione, Gary L.

Charlton, Annie, jt. auth. see Churchill, Jane.

Charlton, Brian. Angel & the Bear: The Cosmic York Hotel Affair. 48p. 1979. pap. 5.50 (*0-919626-13-0*, Pub. by Brick Bks) Genl Dist Srvs.

Charlton, C., et al. Arms Law. (Rolemaster Standard System Ser.). (Illus.). 140p. 1994. pap. 16.00 (*1-55806-214-9*, 5520) Iron Crown Ent Inc.

Charlton, C., jt. auth. see Leng, P.

Charlton, Chris. Euro: Impact & Reality: Business Risks & Practical Responses to the Challenge of the Euro. 1998. 29.95 (*0-273-63877-7*) F T P-H.

***Charlton, Coleman, et al.** Rolemaster Fantasy Role Playing. (Illus.). 256p. (YA). (gr. 7 up). 1999. text 30.00 (*1-55806-550-4*, 5800) Iron Crown Ent Inc.

— 10,000,000 Ways to Die. (Rolemaster Standard System Ser.). (Illus.). 112p. (YA). (gr. 7 up). 1999. pap. 16.00 (*1-55806-374-9*, 5705) Iron Crown Ent Inc.

Charlton, D. G., ed. France: Companion to French Studies. 2nd ed. (Illus.). 1983. pap. 22.50 (*0-685-30072-2*, NO. 3832) Routledge.

***Charlton, David.** French Opera, 1730-1830: Meaning & Media. LC 99-41953. (Variorum Collected Studies Ser.: Vol. CS 634). 328p. 2000. text 92.95 (*0-86078-782-6*, Pub. by Ashgate Pub) Ashgate Pub Co.

Charlton, David, ed. see Mehul, Etienne-Nicolas.

Charlton, Edwin A. New Hampshire As It Is. (Illus.). 623p. 1997. reprint ed. pap. 41.00 (*0-7884-0633-7*, C306) Heritage Bk.

Charlton, Ellen M., et al, eds. Women, the State, & Development. LC 88-8531. 248p. (Orig.). (C). 1989. text 74.50 (*0-7914-0064-6*); pap. text 24.95 (*0-7914-0065-4*) State U NY Pr.

Charlton, Eric Mark, jt. auth. see Lindner, Klaus.

Charlton, George. City of Dog. 64p. 1995. pap. 14.95 (*1-85224-266-3*, Pub. by Bloodaxe Bks) Dufour.

— Nightshift Workers. LC 88-51785. 64p. (Orig.). 1989. pap. 11.95 (*1-85224-070-9*, Pub. by Bloodaxe Bks) Dufour.

Charlton, H. B. The Dark Comedies of Shakespeare. 1973. 59.95 (*0-87968-996-X*) Gordon Pr.

Charlton, Henry B. Dark Comedies of Shakespeare. LC 74-100728. (Studies in Shakespeare: No. 24). 1970. reprint ed. lib. bdg. 59.00 (*0-8383-0340-4*) M S G Haskell Hse.

— Shakespeare's Comedies: The Consummation. 1972. 59.95 (*0-8490-1041-1*) Gordon Pr.

— Shakespeare's Comedies: The Consummation. LC 71-100738. (Studies in Shakespeare: No. 24). 1970. reprint ed. lib. bdg. 59.00 (*0-8383-0339-0*) M S G Haskell Hse.

Charlton, Henry M., ed. The Oxford Reviews in Reproductive Biology, Vol. 16. (Illus.). 344p. 1994. text 89.00 (*0-19-262426-1*) OUP.

— Oxford Reviews of Reproductive Biology, Vol. 17. (Illus.). 302p. 1995. text 125.00 (*0-19-262629-9*) OUP.

Charlton, Hilda. Divine Mother Speaks. Golden Quest Staff, ed. (Illus.). 48p. (Orig.). 1993. pap. 5.50 (*0-927383-18-7*) Golden Quest.

— Hell-Bent for Heaven: The Autobiography of Hilda Charlton. Golden Quest Staff, ed. (Golden Quest Ser.: Vol. 5). (Illus.). 200p. (Orig.). 1991. pap. 9.95 (*0-927383-15-2*) Golden Quest.

— Master Hilarion. Golden Quest Staff, ed. (Golden Quest Ser.: Vol. 1). (Illus.). 104p. (Orig.). 1990. pap. text 7.95 (*0-927383-02-0*) Golden Quest.

— The New Sun. Golden Quest Staff, ed. (Golden Quest Ser.: Vol. 4). (Illus.). 160p. (Orig.). 1989. pap. text 8.95 (*0-927383-01-2*) Golden Quest.

— Pioneers of the Soul: The Last Teachings of Hilda Charlton. Golden Quest Staff, ed. (Golden Quest Ser.: Vol. 6). (Illus.). 204p. (Orig.). 1992. pap. 11.95 (*0-927383-12-8*) Golden Quest.

— Saints Alive. Golden Quest Staff, ed. (Golden Quest Ser.: Vol. 3). (Illus.). 304p. (Orig.). 1989. pap. 12.95 (*0-927383-00-4*) Golden Quest.

— Skanda. Golden Quest Staff, ed. (Golden Quest Ser.: Vol. 2). (Illus.). 126p. (Orig.). 1992. pap. 7.95 (*0-927383-03-9*) Golden Quest.

***Charlton, J. Richard.** Investing the Billionaire's Way: The Genius of Patience. 232p. 2000. pap. 26.95 (*0-7737-3239-X*) Stoddart Publ.

***Charlton, Jack.** Jack Charlton: The Autobiography. 2000. pap. 10.95 (*0-552-14519-X*, Pub. by Transworld Publishers Ltd) Trafalgar.

Charlton, Jack & Francis, Tony. Salmon Run. (Illus.). 95p. 1993. pap. 19.95 (*0-09-177264-8*, Pub. by S Paul) Trafalgar.

Charlton, James. Ho Ho Ho. 1999. pap. 9.00 (*0-14-015738-7*) Viking Penguin.

— Military Quotation Book. 1990. text 14.95 (*0-312-04350-3*) St Martin.

— Sportsayings. 1999. pap. 4.95 (*0-14-006936-4*, Viking) Viking Penguin.

— The Writer's Quotation Book: A Literary Companion. 3rd ed. 1991. 14.95 (*0-916366-66-9*, Pub. by Pushcart Pr) Norton.

Charlton, James, ed. The Executive's Quotation Book: A Treasury of Wise, Witty, Cynical, & Engaging Observations about the World of Business, Law, Finance, & Politics. 2nd rev. ed. LC 93-7991. 144p. 1993. text 12.95 (*0-312-09283-0*) St Martin.

— Fighting Words: Writers Lambast Other Writers--From Aristotle to Anne Rice. LC 94-1988. 160p. 1994. 12.95 (*1-56512-073-6*) Algonquin Bks.

— A Little Learning Is a Dangerous Thing: Six Hundred Wise & Witty Observations for Students, Teachers & Other Survivors of Higher Education. (Illus.). 128p. 1994. text 14.95 (*0-312-11021-9*) St Martin.

— A Little Learning Is a Dangerous Thing: 600 Wise & Witty Observations for Students, Teachers & Other Survivors of Higher Education. 116p. 1998. text 13.00 (*0-7881-5976-3*) DIANE Pub.

— The Writer's Quotation Book: A Literary Companion. 4th rev. ed. LC 97-14167. 184p. 1997. 16.95 (*0-571-19920-8*) Faber & Faber.

Charlton, James & Gilson, Barbara, eds. Christmas Treasury of Yuletide Stories & Poems. 416p. 1992. 8.98 (*0-88365-801-1*) Galahad Bks.

***Charlton, James I.** Nothing about Us Without Us: Disability Oppression & Empowerment. 213p. 2000. pap. 16.95 (*0-520-22481-7*, Pub. by U CA Pr) Cal Prin Full Svc.

Charlton, James I. Nothing about Us, Without Us: The Dialectics of Disability Oppression & Empowerment. LC 97-1661. 247p. 1998. 27.50 (*0-520-20795-5*, Pub. by U CA Pr) Cal Prin Full Svc.

Charlton, Jim, jt. auth. see Binswanger, Barbara.

Charlton, John. The Chartists: The First National Workers' Movement. LC 96-34396. (Socialist History of Britain Ser.). 120p. 1997. 40.00 (*0-7453-1182-2*, Pub. by Pluto GBR); pap. 14.95 (*0-7453-1183-0*, Pub. by Pluto GBR) Stylus Pub VA.

Charlton, John & Murphy, Mike, eds. Health of Adult Britain, 1841-1994 - Office for National Statistics: (Office for National Statistics 12) LC 98-130206. 1997. 90.00 (*0-11-691695-8*, HM16958, Pub. by Stanry Office) Bernan Associates.

— Health of Adults Britain, 1841-1994 Office for Nations: (Office for National Statistics 13) LC 98-130206. 1998. 90.00 (*0-11-691696-6*, HM16966, Pub. by Stanry Office) Bernan Associates.

Charlton, Judie F. & Weinstein, George W., eds. Ophthalmic Surgery Complications: Prevention & Management. LC 94-26149. (Illus.). 524p. 1995. reprint ed. pap. 162.50 (*0-608-07252-4*, 206747900009) Bks Demand.

Charlton, K. M., jt. ed. see Campbell, J. B.

Charlton, Katherine. Rock Music Styles: A History. 3rd ed. LC 96-79450. 304p. 1997. pap. 40.94 (*0-697-34055-4*) McGraw.

Charlton, Laird. Webster's New World Thesaurus. rev. ed. 1988. 16.00 (*0-13-947151-0*, Webstrs New) Macmillan Gen Ref.

Charlton, Linda, ed. see Fielding Worldwide Inc. Staff.

***Charlton, Marian E.** Life on the Causal Plane: A Glimpse of Heaven. Walker, Adam, ed. 231p. 1998. pap. 12.00 (*0-9668638-0-1*, 98-001, Pub. by Kazmar Ent) DeVorss.

Charlton, Mark W. The Making of Canadian Food Aid Policy. 256p. (Orig.). 1992. 65.00 (*0-7735-0937-2*, Pub. by McG-Queens Univ Pr); pap. 27.95 (*0-7735-0938-0*, Pub. by McG-Queens Univ Pr) CUP Services.

Charlton, Michael. The Eagle & the Small Birds: Crisis in the Soviet Empire: From Yalta to Solidarity. LC 84-16360. (Illus.). 1985. 14.95 (*0-226-10154-1*) U Ch Pr.

— The Eagle & the Small Birds: Crisis in the Soviet Empire: From Yalta to Solidarity. LC 84-16360. (Illus.). 192p. (C). 1987. pap. 8.95 (*0-226-10156-8*, R857) U Ch Pr.

— Footsteps from the Finland Station: Five Landmarks in the Collapse of Communism. 198p. (C). 1992. 34.35 (*1-56000-019-8*) Transaction Pubs.

— From Deterrence to Defense: The Inside Story of Strategic Policy. LC 87-8583. 164p. 1987. pap. 16.00 (*0-674-32347-5*) HUP.

***Charlton, Michael & Humberson, John Watkin.** Positron Physics. (Cambridge Monographs on Atomic, Molecular, & Chemical Physics: Vol. 11). (Illus.). 464p. 2000. write for info. (*0-521-41550-0*) Cambridge U Pr.

Charlton, Michael & Moncrieff, Anthony. Many Reasons Why: The American Involvement in Vietnam. 250p. 1997. reprint ed. pap. text 10.00 (*0-7881-5173-8*) DIANE Pub.

Charlton, Nancy L. Derek's Dog Days. LC 95-1846. (Illus.). 40p. (J). (ps-3). 1996. 14.00 (*0-15-223219-2*) Harcourt.

Charlton, Peter. World War II: South Queensland. iv, 59p. (C). 1991. pap. 39.00 (*0-86439-132-3*, Pub. by Boolarong Pubns) St Mut.

Charlton, Randolph S. Treating Sexual Disorders. LC 96-8762. (Jossey-Bass Library of Current Clinical Technique). 1996. 29.95 (*0-7879-0311-6*) Jossey-Bass.

Charlton, Richard. Invest & Grow Rich! Five Universal Principles for Unlimited Wealth Creation. LC 98-221667. 208p. 1998. pap. text 14.99 (*0-919292-04-6*, Pub. by McLeod Pub) Genl Dist Srvs.

Charlton, Robert E. Yellowstone Fishing Guide. (Illus.). 51p. (Orig.). 1982. pap. 4.50 (*0-943390-00-1*) Tri-County.

— Yellowstone Fishing Guide. 3rd rev. ed. (Illus.). 168p. (Orig.). 1995. pap. 17.95 (*1-885719-00-0*) Lost River Pr.

Charlton, Robert M. Better Blackjack. (Illus.). 36p. (Orig.). 1986. 4.95 (*0-9617552-0-2*, TXU247597) Charlton Hi Tech.

Charlton, Robert W., jt. auth. see Bothwell, Thomas H.

Charlton, Roger & Mucklow, J. C. Therapeutic Dilemmas for the MRCGP. LC 97-45691. 176p. 1998. pap. text 35.00 (*0-7506-2918-5*) Buttrwrth-Heinemann.

Charlton, Ruth & Dewdney, Micheline. The Mediator's Handbook. 200p. 1996. pap. 50.00 (*0-455-21361-5*, Pub. by LawBk Co) Gaunt.

Charlton, Samuel G., jt. ed. see O'Brien, Thomas G.

Charlton, Sue E. Comparing Asian Politics: India, China & Japan. LC 97-21721. (C). 1997. pap. 37.00 (*0-8133-8585-7*, Pub. by Westview) HarpC.

Charlton, Sue M., ed. see Mathiot, Elizabeth M.

***Charlton, T. J.** If I Had a Million. LC 00-190675. 108p. 2000. 25.00 (*0-7388-1601-9*); pap. 18.00 (*0-7388-1602-7*) Xlibris Corp.

Charlton, Thomas H., jt. auth. see Nichols, Deborah L.

Charlton, Thomas H., jt. ed. see Nichols, Deborah L.

Charlton, Tony & David, Kenneth, eds. Managing Misbehaviour in Schools. 2nd ed. LC 93-458. 240p. (C). 1993. pap. 25.99 (*0-415-09287-6*, B2424) Routledge.

Charlton, Tony, jt. ed. see Jones, Kevin.

Charlton, W., ed. Physics, Bks. 1 & 2. (Clarendon Aristotle Ser.). 184p. 1984. pap. text 29.95 (*0-19-872026-2*) OUP.

Charlton, William, tr. see Philoponus, John.

Charlton, William T. Croquet: Complete Guide to History, Strategy, Rules & Records. LC 76-56089. 1977. 9.95 (*0-916844-01-3*); pap. 5.95 (*0-916844-00-5*) Turtle Pr.

Charlwood, B., jt. auth. see Patterson, R. L. S.

Charlwood, Barry V., et al, eds. Methods in Plant Biochemistry Vol. 7: Terpenoids. (Illus.). 565p. 1991. text 104.00 (*0-12-461017-X*) Acad Pr.

Charlwood, Barry V. & Rhodes, M. J., eds. Secondary Products from Plant Tissue Culture. (Proceedings of the Phytochemical Society of Europe Ser.: No. 30). (Illus.). 304p. 1990. text 98.00 (*0-19-857717-6*) OUP.

Charlwood, Barry V., jt. ed. see Bell, E. A.

Charlwood, Don. Wrecks & Reputations. 192p. 1988. pap. 30.00 (*0-7855-2670-6*, Pub. by Deakin Univ) St Mut.

Charman, Andrew. Food & Farming. (Fact Finders Ser.). 1996. pap. 8.95 (*0-563-35541-7*, BBC-Parkwest) Parkwest Pubns.

— I Wonder Why Trees Have Leaves: And Other Questions about Plants. LC 97-189. (I Wonder Why Ser.). (Illus.). 32p. (J). (gr. 4-8). 1997. 9.95 (*0-7534-5094-1*, Kingfisher) LKC.

— Plants: A BBC Fact Finder Book. (Illus.). 48p. 1996. pap. text 8.95 (*0-563-35538-7*, BBC-Parkwest) Parkwest Pubns.

— Trees. (Fact Finders Ser.). (Illus.). 48p. (J). (gr. 2 up). 1993. pap. 8.95 (*0-563-35017-2*, BBC-Parkwest) Parkwest Pubns.

Charman, Andrew, et al. Factfinders: The Living World. (Fact Finders Ser.). (J). 23.95 (*0-563-37620-1*, BBC-Parkwest) Parkwest Pubns.

Charman, Andrew, ed. see Pellant, Chris.

Charman, Andy. The Dodo Is Dead & Other Questions about Extinct & Endangered Animals. LC 96-182. (I Wonder Why Ser.). (Illus.). 32p. (J). (ps-3). 1996. 11.95 (*0-7534-5014-3*) LKC.

Charman, Daniel J. & Warner, Barry G. Peatland Systems & Environmental Change. 2000. pap. text 49.95 (*0-471-96990-7*) Wiley.

Charman, Janet. End of the Dry. 64p. 1995. pap. 12.95 (*1-86940-124-7*, Pub. by Auckland Univ) Paul & Co Pubs.

***Charman, Janet.** Rapunzel, Rapunzel. 64p. 1999. pap. 14.95 (*1-86940-208-1*, Pub. by Auckland Univ) Paul & Co Pubs.

***Charman, Peter & Murphy, Brian, eds.** Soils: Their Properties & Management. 2nd ed. 384p. 2000. pap. text 45.00 (*0-19-550994-3*) OUP.

Charman, Robert. At Risk: Can the Doctor Patient Relationship Survive in the High Tech World. (Orig.). 1992. pap. 10.95 (*0-87233-094-X*) Bauhan.

***Charman, Robert A.** Complementary Therapies for Physical Therapists: A Theoretical & Clinical Exploration. (Illus.). 320p. 2000. pap. 52.50 (*0-7506-4079-0*) Buttrwrth-Heinemann.

***Charman, Terry.** Swastika: Hitler & the Nazis 1919-1939. 160p. 2000. 100.00 (*1-86227-029-5*, Pub. by Spellmnt Pubs) St Mut.

Charman, William N. Lymphatic Transport of Drugs. 352p. 1992. lib. bdg. 159.00 (*0-8493-6394-2*, RM301) CRC Pr.

— Visual Optics & Instrumentation. 1991. 137.00 (*0-8493-7501-0*) CRC Pr.

Charmant, Anne De, see De Charmant, Anne.

Charmatz, Jan P. & Daggett, Harriet S., eds. Comparative Studies in Community Property Law. LC 77-1740. ix, 190p. 1977. reprint ed. lib. bdg. 69.50 (*0-8371-9523-3*, CHCST, Greenwood Pr) Greenwood.

Charmaz, Kathleen & Paterniti, Debora A., eds. Health, Illness, & Healing: Society, Social Context, & Self : An Anthology. (Illus.). 600p. (C). 1999. pap. text. write for info. (*0-935732-98-5*) Roxbury Pub Co.

Charmaz, Kathleen C. Good Days, Bad Days: The Self in Chronic Illness & Time. LC 90-28864. 311p. 1993. pap. 16.00 (*0-8135-1967-5*) Rutgers U Pr.

— The Social Reality of Death: Death in Contemporary America. (Sociology Ser.). 1980. text 13.50 (*0-201-01033-X*) Addison-Wesley.

Charmaz, Kathleen C., et al. The Unknown Country: Death in Australia, Britain, & the U. S. A. LC 96-34794. 268p. 1997. text 59.95 (*0-312-16545-5*) St Martin.

Charmaz, Kathleen C., jt. ed. see Gubrium, Jaber F.

Charme, Rita M. Du, see Du Charme, Rita M.

Charme, Stuart Z. Vulgarity & Authenticity: Dimensions of Otherness in the World of Jean-Paul Sartre. LC 90-23296. 272p. (C). 1993. pap. 17.95 (*0-87023-868-X*); lib. bdg. 35.00 (*0-87023-740-3*) U of Mass Pr.

Charmet, J. C., et al, eds. Disorder & Fracture. LC 90-45733. (NATO ASI Ser.). (Illus.). 316p. (C). 1990. pap. text 59.00 (*0-306-43576-4*, Kluwer Plenum) Kluwer Academic.

— Disorder & Fracture. (NATO ASI Series B, Physics: Vol. 235). (Illus.). 316p. (C). 1990. 132.00 (*0-306-43688-4*, Plenum Trade) Perseus Pubng.

Charmet, R. Utrillo: Paris. (Rhythm & Color One Ser.). 1970. 9.95 (*0-8288-9510-4*) Fr & Eur.

***Charming, Cheryl.** Miss Charming's Book of Bar Amusements. (Illus.). 144p. 2000. pap. 12.00 (*0-609-80508-8*, CBK029000, Three Riv Pr) Crown Pub Group.

Charmley, John. Chamberlain & the Lost Peace. (Illus.). 272p. 1990. 27.95 (*0-929587-33-2*, Pub. by I R Dee) Natl Bk Netwk.

— Chamberlain & the Lost Peace LC 90-118662. xiv, 257 p. 1989. 15.00 (*0-340-50853-1*) Trafalgar.

— Churchill: The End of Glory: A Political Biography. 752p. 1994. pap. 17.95 (*0-15-600144-6*) Harcourt.

— Churchill's Grand Alliance: The Anglo-American Special Relationship. (Illus.). 443p. 1996. pap. 18.00 (*0-15-600470-4*) Harcourt.

— A History of Conservative Politics. LC 96-5584. 256p. 1996. text 39.95 (*0-312-16126-3*) St Martin.

Charms, George De, see De Charms, George.

Charms, R. De, see De Charms, R.

Charnace, Guy. A Star of Song: The Life of Christina Nilsson. LC 80-2264. 1981. reprint ed. 27.50 (*0-404-18817-6*) AMS Pr.

Charnas. Furies. 2000. pap. 13.95 (*0-312-86606-2*) St Martin.

Charnas, Suzy M. Dorothea Dreams. LC 85-19987. 308p. 1986. 25.00 (*0-89366-146-5*) Ultramarine Pub.

— The Furies. 416p. 1995. mass mkt. 5.99 (*0-8125-4819-1*, Pub. by Tor Bks) St Martin.

— The Kingdom of Kevin Malone. LC 92-40720. 224p. (J). 1993. 16.95 (*0-15-200756-3*, Harcourt Child Bks) Harcourt.

Charnas, Suzy M. The Kingdom of Kevin Malone. LC 92-40720. 272p. (J). (gr. 7). 1997. pap. 6.00 (*0-15-201191-9*) Harcourt.

C

Charnas, Suzy M. The Slave & the Free: Contains Walk to the End of the World & Motherlines. 2nd ed. LC 99-19838. 1999. pap. 12.95 (*0-312-86912-6*, Pub. by Tor Bks) St Martin.

— The Vampire Tapestry. 300p. 1993. pap. 13.95 (*0-945953-05-4*) Living Batch Bks.

Charnay, Desire. The Ancient Cities of the New World: Being Voyages & Explorations in Mexico & Central America from 1857 to 1882. Gonina, J. & Conant, Helen S., trs. from FRE. LC 72-5004. (Antiquities of the New World Ser.: Vol. 10). (Illus.). reprint ed. 97.50 (*0-404-57310-X*) AMS Pr.

Charneco Babilonia, Efrain & Llabres De Charneco, Amalia. Metodologia para la Ensenanza de las Artes Industriales y la Educacion Vocacional Industrial. LC 76-3715. 191p. (Orig.). 1976. pap. text 5.00 (*0-8477-2722-X*) U of PR Pr.

Charnee, David. Fangs! (Truly Ghouly Bks.). (Illus.). (J). (gr. 3-7). 1997. pap. 2.99 (*0-614-28939-4*) Random Bks Yng Read.

Charnell, Shirley L. Creating Encaustics. LC 87-70834. (Illus.). 76p. (Orig.). (C). 1987. pap. 16.00 (*0-9618514-0-6*) Artistree Studio.

***Charnell, Shirley L.** Creating Encaustics, Book II: New & Old Explorations of Encaustics. (Illus.). 80p. 1999. ring bd. 36.00 (*0-9618514-1-4*) Artistree Studio.

Charner, Ivan. Off Their Rockers: Participation in Education by Retired Workers. 13p. 1990. 3.00 (*0-86510-065-9*) Natl Inst Work.

— St. Lucie County's Performanced Based Diploma Program Case Study Report. (Cross Case Report & Case Studies). 50p. 1995. text, teacher ed. 20.00 (*0-614-24536-2*); pap. text, teacher ed. 10.00 (*0-614-24537-0*) Natl Inst Work.

Charner, Ivan. Study of School-to-Work Initiatives. 123p. 1996. pap. 11.00 (*0-16-048864-8*) USGPO.

Charner, Ivan & Fox, Shirley. Improving Workplace Literacy Through Community Collaboration: Leader's Guide. 72p. 1988. 12.50 (*0-89492-098-7*) Natl Inst Work.

— Improving Workplace Literacy Through Community Collaboration: Student Workbook. 42p. 1988. 6.00 (*0-89492-097-9*); 45.00 (*0-685-58977-3*) Natl Inst Work.

Charner, Ivan & Fraser, Bryna S. Different Strokes for Different Folks: Access & Barriers to Adult Education & Training. 118p. 1986. 10.00 (*0-86510-054-3*) Natl Inst Work.

— Fast Food Jobs. 144p. 1984. 20.00 (*0-86510-005-5*) Natl Inst Work.

— Youth & Work: What We Know; What We Don't Know; What We Need to Know. 82p. 1987. 10.00 (*0-86510-058-6*) Natl Inst Work.

Charner, Ivan & Hubbard, Susan. Roy High School Case Study Report. (Cross Case Report & Case Studies). 50p. 1995. text, teacher ed. 20.00 (*0-614-24532-X*); pap. text, teacher ed. 10.00 (*0-614-24533-8*) Natl Inst Work.

— Shawnee High School Aviation Magnet Case Study Report. (Cross Case Report & Case Studies). 50p. 1995. text, teacher ed. 20.00 (*0-614-24538-9*); pap. text, teacher ed. 10.00 (*0-614-24539-7*) Natl Inst Work.

Charner, Ivan & Schlossberg, Nancy K. Options & Opportunities: Overcoming Barriers to Worklife Education & Training. 33p. 1989. 7.50 (*0-86510-066-7*) Natl Inst Work.

Charner, Ivan, et al. Union Retirees: Enriching Their Lives, Enhancing Their Contribution, 2 vols. 500p. 1990. 37.50 (*0-86510-061-6*); write for info. (*0-318-68441-1*) Natl Inst Work.

— Union Retirees: Enriching Their Lives, Enhancing Their Contribution, 2 vols., Vol. II. 250p. 1990. 20.00 (*0-89492-096-0*) Natl Inst Work.

— Union Retirees - Enriching Their Lives, Enhancing Their Contribution: Executive Summary. 66p. 1990. 3.50 (*0-89492-094-4*) Natl Inst Work.

Charner, Ivan, jt. auth. see Fraser, Bryna S.

Charner, Ivan, jt. auth. see Zeldin, Shepherd.

Charner, Kathleen, ed. see Claycomb, Patty.

Charner, Kathleen, ed. see Dowell, Ruth I.

Charner, Kathleen, ed. see Gilbert, LaBritta.

Charner, Kathleen, ed. see Miller, Karen.

Charner, Kathleen, ed. see Raines, Shirley C. & Canady, Robert J.

Charner, Kathy, ed. Everything for Fall: An Early Childhood Curriculum Activity Book. LC 97-21503. (Illus.). 272p. 1997. pap. 24.95 (*0-87659-185-3*) Gryphon Hse.

— Everything for Spring: An Early Childhood Curriculum Activity Book. LC 97-21463. (Illus.). 272p. 1997. pap. 24.95 (*0-87659-187-X*) Gryphon Hse.

— Everything for Winter: An Early Childhood Curriculum Activity Book. LC 97-21455. (Illus.). 272p. 1997. pap. 24.95 (*0-87659-186-1*) Gryphon Hse.

— The Giant Encyclopedia of Circle Time & Group Activities for Children 3 to 6: Over 600 Favorite Circle Time Activities Created by Teachers for Teachers. LC 96-9098. (Illus.). 510p. (Orig.). 1996. pap. 29.95 (*0-87659-181-0*) Gryphon Hse.

— The Giant Encyclopedia of Science Activities. LC 98-22366. 502p. 1998. pap. 29.95 (*0-87659-193-4*) Gryphon Hse.

— The Giant Encyclopedia of Theme Activities for Children 2 to 5: Over 600 Favorite Activities Written by Teachers for Teachers. (Illus.). 510p. 1993. pap. text 29.95 (*0-87659-166-7*) Gryphon Hse.

Charner, Kathy, ed. see Williams, Robert, et al.

Charnes. Making Miss Right. (C). 1999. write for info. (*0-415-06009-5*); pap. write for info. (*0-415-06010-9*) Routledge.

Charnes, Abraham & Cooper, W. W. Management Models & Industrial Applications of Linear Programming, Vol. 2. LC 61-14807. (Illus.). 414p. reprint ed. 128.40 (*0-8357-9928-X*, 201195000080) Bks Demand.

Charnes, Abraham & Cooper, William W., eds. Creative & Innovative Management: Essays in Honor of George Kozmetsky. LC 84-2814. (Institute for Constructive Capitalism Ser.). 304p. 1984. text 35.00 (*0-88410-994-1*, HarpBusn) HarpInfo.

Charnes, Abraham, et al. Data Envelopment Analysis: Theory, Methodology & Application. LC 94-22053. 528p. (C). 1995. lib. bdg. 150.00 (*0-7923-9479-8*) Kluwer Academic.

— Data Envelopment Analysis: Theory, Methodology & Application. LC 94-22053. 528p. (C). 1995. pap. text 66.00 (*0-7923-9480-1*) Kluwer Academic.

Charnes, Linda. Notorious Identity: Materializing the Subject in Shakespeare. 232p. (Orig.). (C). 1995. pap. text 19.95 (*0-674-62781-4*) HUP.

— Notorius Identity: Materializing the Subject in Shakespeare. LC 93-9755. 256p. 1993. text 44.50 (*0-674-62780-6*) HUP.

Charness, Ann L. Stroke & Head Injury: A Guide to Functional Outcomes in Physical Therapy - Rehabilitation Institute of Chicago Procedure Manual. (Illus.). 330p. (C). 1986. 70.00 (*0-87189-226-X*) Aspen Pub.

***Charness, Ann L. & RIC Staff.** Stroke & Head Injury: A Guide to Functional Outcomes in Physical Therapy - Rehabilitation Institute of Chicago Procedure Manual. 2nd ed. 2000. 65.00 (*0-8342-1802-X*) Aspen Pub.

Charness, Neil, ed. Aging & Human Performance. LC 85-725. (Wiley Series on Studies in Human Performance). (Illus.). 416p. 1985. reprint ed. pap. 129.00 (*0-7837-9501-7*, 206025100005) Bks Demand.

***Charness, Neil, et al.** Communication, Technology & Aging: Opportunities & Challenges for the Future. LC 00-30139. 2001. pap. write for info. (*0-8261-1372-9*) Springer Pub.

Charney, ed. see Charney, Maurice.

Charney, Ann. Defiance in Their Eyes: True Stories from the Margins. 160p. (Orig.). 1995. pap. 16.95 (*1-55065-068-8*, Pub. by Vehicule Pr) Genl Dist Srvs.

— Dobryd. LC 95-8923. 172p. 1996. pap. 22.00 (*1-877946-66-4*) Permanent Pr.

Charney, Craig. Public Opinion in Kazakhstan: 1996. LC 96-41936. (Illus.). ii, 134p. 1997. pap. text 15.00 (*1-879720-20-5*) Intl Fndt Elect.

Charney, Cy. The Manager's Tool Kit: Practical Tips for Tackling 100 On-the-Job Problems. LC 94-41742. 224p. 1995. pap. 17.95 (*0-8144-7881-6*) AMACOM.

Charney, Cy & Conway, Kathy. The Trainers Tool Kit. LC 97-23134. 208p. 1997. pap. 18.95 (*0-8144-7944-8*) AMACOM.

Charney, Cyril. Time to Market: Reducing Product Lead Time. LC 90-72145. (Illus.). 260p. 1991. 12.95 (*0-87263-396-9*) SME.

Charney, Davida, jt. ed. see Secor, Marie.

Charney, Dennis S. Neurobiology of Mental Illness. LC 98-27421. (Illus.). 984p. 1999. text 150.00 (*0-19-511265-2*) OUP.

Charney, Evan, ed. see National Research Council Staff & Institute of Medicine Staff.

Charney, Hanna. The Detective Novel of Manners: Hedonism, Morality, & the Life of Reason. LC 79-17634. 160p. 1981. 27.50 (*0-8386-3004-9*) Fairleigh Dickinson.

Charney, Hannah K., ed. see Taupin, Rene.

Charney, Israel W., ed. The Widening Circle of Genocide. (Genocide: A Critical Bibliographic Review Ser.: Vol. 3). 430p. (C). 1994. 49.95 (*1-56000-172-0*) Transaction Pubs.

Charney, Jean O. A Grammar of Comanche. LC 93-30300. (Studies in the Anthropology of North American Indians). x, 273p. 1994. text 50.00 (*0-8032-1461-8*) U of Nebr Pr.

Charney, Jonathan I., ed. International Maritime Boundaries, Pts. I & II. 2172p. (C). 1993. lib. bdg. 903.50 (*0-7923-1187-6*) Kluwer Academic.

Charney, Jonathan I., et al, eds. Politics, Values, & Functions: International Law in the 21st Century: Essays in Honor of Professor Louis Henkin. LC 97-46629. 488p. 1998. 134.00 (*90-411-0514-X*) Kluwer Law Intl.

Charney, Jonathan I. & Alexander, Lewis M., eds. International Maritime Boundaries, Vol. III. (Illus.). 500p. 1998. 154.00 (*90-411-0345-7*) Kluwer Law Intl.

Charney, Jordan, jt. auth. see Gans, Sharon.

Charney, Leo. Empty Moments: Cinema, Modernity, & Drift. LC 97-41661. 1998. write for info. (*0-8223-2076-2*); pap. 16.95 (*0-8223-2090-8*) Duke.

Charney, Leo & Schwartz, Vanessa R., eds. Cinema & the Invention of Modern Life. LC 95-10821. (Illus.). 409p. 1996. 55.00 (*0-520-20111-6*, Pub. by U CA Pr); pap. 22.50 (*0-520-20112-4*, Pub. by U CA Pr) Cal Prin Full Svc.

Charney, Mark. Barry Hannah. (Twayne's United States Authors Ser.). 115p. (C). 1991. 22.95 (*0-8057-7633-8*, Twyne) Mac Lib Ref.

Charney, Maurice. All of Shakespeare. 1993. pap. 19.00 (*0-231-06863-8*) Col U Pr.

— All of Shakespeare. LC 93-6660. (C). 1993. 52.50 (*0-231-06862-X*) Col U Pr.

— Comedy High & Low: An Introduction to the Experience of Comedy. (Illus.). 203p. 1988. pap. 25.50 (*0-8204-0538-8*) P Lang Pubng.

— Hamlet's Fictions. 200p. 1988. text 35.00 (*0-415-00703-8*) Routledge.

— How to Read Shakespeare. XI, 118p. 1992. pap. 29.95 (*0-8204-1667-3*) P Lang Pubng.

— Sexual Fiction. 192p. (C). 1990. per. 39.95 (*0-8403-6323-0*, 40632301) Kendall-Hunt.

— Shakespeare on Love & Lust. LC 99-21631. 256p. 1999. 27.95 (*0-231-10428-6*) Col U Pr.

***Charney, Maurice.** Shakespeare on Love & Lust. LC 99-21631. 2000. 17.50 (*0-231-10429-4*) Col U Pr.

Charney, Maurice. Titus Andronicus. Barnet, Sylvan & Charney, eds. 1986. mass mkt. 3.95 (*0-451-52034-3*, Sig Classics) NAL.

Charney, Maurice, ed. Bad Shakespeare: Revaluations of the Shakespeare Canon. LC 87-45773. 216p. 1988. 35.00 (*0-8386-3310-2*) Fairleigh Dickinson.

Charney, Maurice & Reppen, Joseph, eds. Psychoanalytic Approaches to Literature & Film. LC 85-45931. 312p. 1987. 45.00 (*0-8386-3276-9*) Fairleigh Dickinson.

Charney, Maurice, jt. ed. see Reppen, Joseph.

Charney, Maurice, ed. see Shakespeare, William.

Charney, Melvin, ed. Parables & Other Allegories: The Work of Melvin Charney, 1975-1990. (CCA Ser.). (Illus.). 216p. 1991. pap. text 34.95 (*0-262-53110-0*) MIT Pr.

***Charney, Mitchell A. & Maple, Mary A.** Private Adoption in Kentucky. 3rd ed. (Illus.). 222p. 1998. pap. 44.00 (*1-58757-024-6*, FM031) Univ of KY.

Charney, Pamela. Coronary Artery Disease in Women: What All Physicians Need to Know. LC 98-28030. (Women's Health Ser.). (Illus.). 632p. 1999. pap. 43.00 (*0-943126-68-1*) Amer Coll Phys.

Charney, Reginald B. C++ Cheetah. 230p. (C). 1999. pap. 32.00 (*0-13-323783-4*) P-H.

Charney, Ruth, et al, eds. Geometric Group Theory: Proceedings of a Special Research Quarter at the Ohio State University, Spring 1992. LC 95-12932. (Ohio State University Mathematical Research Institute Publications: Vol. 3). x, 186p. (C). 1995. lib. bdg. 64.95 (*3-11-014743-2*) De Gruyter.

Charney, Ruth S. Habits of Goodness: Case Studies in the Social Curriculum. LC 97-65056. (Illus.). 240p. (Orig.). 1997. pap. 18.50 (*0-9618636-5-X*) NE Found Child.

— Teaching Children to Care: Management in the Responsive Classroom. LC 91-68573. (Illus.). 304p. (Orig.). 1992. pap. 23.50 (*0-9618636-1-7*) NE Found Child.

Charney, Ruth S., et al. A Notebook for Teachers: Making Changes in the Elementary Curriculum. rev. ed. LC 87-126317. (Illus.). 78p. 1993. pap. 19.95 (*0-9618636-0-9*) NE Found Child.

Charney, Steve. Let's Sing about Silly People. LC 92-24713. (Singalongs Ser.). (Illus.). 32p. (J). (gr. k-2). 1992. pap. text 4.95 (*0-8167-2979-4*) Troll Communs.

***Charney, Steve & Goldbeck, David.** The ABC's of Fruits & Vegetables: Delicious Alphabet Poems. (Illus.). 56p. (J). (ps-4). 2000. 19.95 (*1-886101-07-8*, Pub. by Ceres Pr) Bookpeople.

Charney, William. Handbook of Modern Hospital Safety. LC 98-37222. 11p. 1999. 125.00 (*1-56670-256-9*) Lewis Pubs.

Charney, William, ed. Essentials of Modern Hospital Safety, Vol. 3. 512p. 1994. lib. bdg. 85.00 (*1-56670-083-3*, L1083) Lewis Pubs.

***Charney, William & Fragala, Guy.** An Health Care Worker Injury Epidemiology. LC 98-36748. 248p. 1998. boxed set 74.95 (*0-8493-3382-2*) CRC Pr.

Charney, William & Schirmer, Joseph. Essentials of Modern Hospital Safety. (Illus.). 384p. 1990. boxed set 95.00 (*0-87371-198-X*, RA969) Lewis Pubs.

— Essentials of Modern Hospital Safety, Vol. 2. 2nd ed. (Illus.). 368p. 1993. boxed set 104.95 (*0-87371-584-5*, L584) Lewis Pubs.

Charniak, Eugene. Introduction to Artificial Intelligence. (World Student Ser.). (C). 1985. pap. text. write for info. (*0-201-11946-3*) Addison-Wesley.

— Statistical Language Learning. LC 93-28080. (Language, Speech & Communication Ser.). 190p. 1994. 30.00 (*0-262-03216-3*, Bradford Bks) MIT Pr.

— Statistical Language Learning. (Language, Speech, Computation & Communication Program Ser.). (Illus.). 192p. 1996. pap. text 15.00 (*0-262-53141-0*, Bradford Bks) MIT Pr.

Charniak, Eugene, et al, eds. Artificial Intelligence Programming. 2nd ed. 552p. (C). 1987. text 49.95 (*0-89859-609-2*) L Erlbaum Assocs.

Charnigo. From Sources to Citation, Infonautics Howework. (C). 1996. 22.00 (*0-673-78907-1*) Addison-Wesley.

Charnigo, Richard. From Sources to Citation: A Concise Guide to the Research Paper. LC 95-4156. (Illus.). 128p. (C). 1997. pap. text 15.73 (*0-673-99691-3*) Addson-Wesley Educ.

Charnizon, Marlene, ed. see Reiniger, Anne, et al.

Charnley. Short Cases in Surgery. (Illus.). 290p. 2001. text. write for info. (*0-7020-2061-3*) Harcourt.

Charnley, B. The Summer of '89. 132p. 1991. 34.95 (*0-9516022-1-7*, Pub. by Maclean Pr) Dufour.

Charnley, Bob. The Western Isles: A Postcard Tour, Barra to North Uist. (Illus.). 98p. pap. 19.95 (*0-9516022-3-3*, Pub. by Maclean Pr) Dufour.

Charnley, D. Intelligent Autonomous Vehicles. (IFAC Postprint Ser.). 540p. 1993. 122.00 (*0-08-042223-3*, Pergamon Pr) Elsevier.

Charnley, D., ed. Intelligent Autonomous Vehicles. 552p. 1993. pap. 88.00 (*0-685-68777-5*, Pergamon Pr) Elsevier.

Charnley, Gail, ed. Framework for Environmental Health Risk Management/Risk Assessment & Risk Management in Regulatory Decision-Making: Final Report, 2 vols. (Illus.). 277p. (C). 1998. pap. text 50.00 (*0-7881-2775-6*) DIANE Pub.

Charnley, Herbert W., Jr. The Value of the Propodeal Orifice & the Phallic Capsule in Vespid Taxonomy (Hymenoptera, Vespidae) LC 79-301936. (Bulletin of the Buffalo Society of Natural Sciences Ser.: Vol. 26). (Illus.). 79p. (Orig.). (C). 1973. pap. 3.00 (*0-944032-33-8*) Buffalo SNS.

Charnley, J. Low Friction Arthroplasty of the Hip: Theory & Practice. (Illus.). 1978. 176.00 (*0-387-08893-8*) Spr-Verlag.

Charnley, Jean. An American Social Worker in Italy. LC 61-7941. 331p. reprint ed. pap. 102.70 (*0-8357-5399-9*, 205584800039) Bks Demand.

Charnley, John. Acrylic Cement in Orthopaedic Surgery. LC 73-153779. 139p. reprint ed. pap. 43.10 (*0-8357-3378-5*, 203962400013) Bks Demand.

Charnley, Joy. Pierre Bayle: Reader of Travel Literature. LC 98-19237. 202p. (C). 1998. pap. text 40.95 (*0-8204-3434-5*) P Lang Pubng.

Charnley, Joy, et al, eds. 25 Years of Emancipation? Women in Switzerland, 1971-1996. (Illus.). 201p. (C). 1998. text 28.95 (*0-8204-3428-0*) P Lang Pubng.

Charnley, Joy & Pender, Malcolm. 25 Years of Emancipation? Women in Switzerland 1971-1996. Wilkin, Andrew, ed. (Illus.). 201p. 1998. write for info. (*3-906759-65-2*) P Lang Pubng.

***Charnley, Joy & Pender, Malcolm, eds.** Images of Switzerland: Challenges from the Margins. (Occasional Papers in Swiss Studies Ser.: Vol. 1). 128p. 1999. 22.95 (*0-8204-4231-3*) P Lang Pubng.

— Switzerland & War. (Occasional Papers in Swiss Studies Ser.: Vol. 2). 129p. 2000. pap. 21.95 (*0-8204-4641-6*) P Lang Pubng.

***Charnley, Judith.** The Sheep Keeper's Veterinary Handbook. 1999. 35.00 (*1-86126-235-3*, Pub. by Crolwood) Trafalgar.

Charnoc. Christ Crucified. 1996. pap. 9.99 (*1-85792-076-7*, Pub. by Christian Focus) Spring Arbor Dist.

Charnock, jt. auth. see Lewis.

Charnock, Andrew, jt. auth. see Van Ooijen, Els.

***Charnock, Ian.** Elementary Cases of Sherlock Holmes. 1999. pap. text 14.95 (*0-947533-97-4*) Breese Bks.

— Watsons Last Case. 2000. pap. 14.95 (*0-947533-92-3*, Pub. by Breese Bks) Midpt Trade.

Charnock, Stephen. The Existence & Attributes of God. 1152p. (gr. 10). 1996. reprint ed. 39.99 (*0-8010-1112-4*) Baker Bks.

— Knowledge of God. 383p. 1989. reprint ed. 27.99 (*0-85151-448-0*) Banner of Truth.

— The New Birth: The Complete Works of Stephen Charnock, B.D., Vol. 3. 534p. 1986. reprint ed. 32.99 (*0-85151-500-2*) Banner of Truth.

— Truth & Life Vol. 5: The Works of Stephen Charnock. 565p. 1997. reprint ed. 26.99 (*0-85151-724-2*) Banner of Truth.

Charnon-Deutsch, Lou. Fictions of the Feminine in the Nineteenth-Century Spanish Press. LC 98-43335. (Studies in Romance Literatures). (Illus.). 1426p. 2000. 48.50 (*0-271-01913-1*) Pa St U Pr.

— Narratives of Desire: 19th-Century Spanish Fiction by Women. LC 93-17102. (Studies in Romance Literatures). (Illus.). 224p. (C). 1994. 32.50 (*0-271-01007-X*) Pa St U Pr.

— The Nineteenth-Century Spanish Story: Textual Strategies of a Genre in Transition. (Monografias A Ser.: No. 116). 176p. 1985. 58.00 (*0-7293-0213-X*, Pub. by Tamesis Bks Ltd) Boydell & Brewer.

Charnon-Deutsch, Lou & Labanyi, Jo, eds. Culture & Gender in Nineteenth-Century Spain. (Oxford Hispanic Ser.). (Illus.). 292p. 1996. text 65.00 (*0-19-815886-6*) OUP.

Charnov, Bruce, jt. auth. see Montana, Patrick.

Charnov, Bruce H., jt. auth. see Montana, Patrick J.

Charnov, Bruce H., jt. ed. see Payne, Stephen L.

Charnov, Eric L. Life History Invariants: Some Explorations of Symmetry in Evolutionary Ecology. (Oxford Series in Ecology & Evolution). (Illus.). 184p. (C). 1993. text 45.00 (*0-19-854072-8*, 7608); pap. text 35.00 (*0-19-854071-X*) OUP.

— The Theory of Sex Allocation. LC 82-47586. (Monographs in Population Biology: Vol. 18). 367p. 1982. reprint ed. pap. 113.80 (*0-608-03384-7*, 206399200008) Bks Demand.

Charns, Alexander. Cloak & Gavel: FBI Wiretaps, Bugs, Informers, & the Supreme Court. (Illus.). 240p. (C). 1992. 24.95 (*0-252-01871-0*) U of Ill Pr.

Charns, Martin P. & Tewksbury, Laura J. Collaborative Management in Health Care: Implementing the Integrative Organization. LC 92-26467. (Health-Management Ser.). 341p. 1992. text 41.95 (*1-55542-483-X*) Jossey-Bass.

Charnwood, Godfrey R. Abraham Lincoln. LC 83-45730. reprint ed. 49.50 (*0-404-20056-7*) AMS Pr.

Charnwood, Lord. Abraham Lincoln. unabridged ed. LC 97-33377. (Illus.). 482p. 1998. reprint ed. pap. 13.95 (*0-486-29959-7*) Dover.

— Abraham Lincoln: A Biography. 352p. 1998. pap. 14.95 (*1-56833-067-7*) Madison Bks UPA.

— Abraham Lincoln: A Biography. 352p. 1996. reprint ed. 24.95 (*1-56833-066-9*) Madison Bks UPA.

Charny, Israel W. Existential - Dialectical Marital Therapy: Breaking the Secret Code of Marriage. LC 91-43195. (Frontiers in Couples & Family Therapy Ser.: No. 5). 352p. 1992. text 39.95 (*0-87630-636-9*) Brunner-Mazel.

***Charny, Israel W., ed.** Encyclopedia of Genocide, 2 vols. LC 99-52695. 718p. 1999. lib. bdg. 175.00 (*0-87436-928-2*) ABC-CLIO.

Charny, Israel W., ed. Genocide: A Critical Bibliographic Review, Vol. 2. 432p. 1991. 65.00 (*0-8160-2642-4*) Facts on File.

— Holding on to Humanity: The Message of Holocaust Survivors. (Shamai Davidson Papers). 256p. (C). 1995. pap. text 18.50 (*0-8147-1513-3*) NYU Pr.

Charny, Joel & Spragens, John, Jr. Obstacles to Recovery in Vietnam & Kampuchea. (Impact Audit Ser.: No. 3). 150p. (C). 1984. pap. 5.00 (*0-910281-02-5*) Oxfam Am.

Charo, Arthur. Continental Air Defense: A Neglected Dimension of Strategic Defense. (Occasional Papers: No. 7). (Illus.). 164p. (C). 1990. pap. text 21.00 (*0-8191-7782-2*); lib. bdg. 40.00 (*0-8191-7781-4*) U Pr of Amer.

Charoenngam, Chotchai, jt. auth. see Popescu, Calin M.

Charola, A. Alena. Death of a Moai: Easter Island Statues: Their Nature, Deterioration & Conservation. Lee, Georgia, ed. (Easter Island Ser.). (Illus.). 50p. 1997. pap. 15.00 (*1-880636-11-5*) Easter Isl Fnd.

Charon. Meaning of Sociology. 6th ed. LC 98-33680. 376p. 1998. pap. text 32.20 (*0-13-906066-9*) P-H.

***Charon.** Twelve Questions. 4th ed. (Sociology Ser.). 2000. pap. 18.00 (*0-534-57051-8*) Wadsworth Pub.

Charon, Chaim, ed. see DeWitt, Gary, et al.

Charon, Cyril & Samra, Nicholas. The History of the Melkite Patriarchates: Alexandria, Antioch, Jerusalem, from the Sixth Century Monophysite Schism until the Present (1910) LC 98-21655. 1998. pap. write for info. (*1-892278-01-4*) Eastern Chrst Pubns.

Charon, Donna & Sommers, Jo A. Great Careers for People Interested in Travel & Tourism, Vol. 5. 3rd ed. LC 95-62267. (Career Connections Ser.: Series 3). 48p. 1995. text 23.00 (*0-7876-0862-9*, UXL) Gale.

Charon, Jean. The Unknown Spirit: The Unity of Matter & Spirit in Space & Time. 1991. pap. 12.95 (*0-904575-18-7*) Sigo Pr.

Charon, Joel M. The Meaning of Sociology. 6th ed. LC 98-20626. 229p. 1998. pap. text 30.80 (*0-13-798042-6*) P-H.

— The Questions: A Sociological Perspective. 3rd ed. LC 97-21806. (Sociology Ser.). (C). 1997. 28.95 (*0-534-52569-5*) Wadsworth Pub.

Charon, Joel M. Symbolic Interactionism. 6th ed. LC 97-30940. 245p. (C). 1997. pap. text 30.20 (*0-13-671694-6*) P-H.

Charon, Joel M. Ten Questions: A Sociological Perspective. 254p. (C). 1991. mass mkt. 12.75 (*0-534-16050-6*) Wadsworth Pub.

Charon, Kurt. The Ultimate Fantasy Football Notebook. 200p. 1993. 19.95 (*0-9637224-0-9*) Turn The Pg.

Charon, Rita, jt. auth. see Demarest, Robert J.

Charosh, Mannis. The Ellipse. LC 73-132293. (Young Math Ser.). (Illus.). (J). (gr. 1-4). 1971. 9.89 (*0-690-01120-2*) HarpC Child Bks.

— Number Ideas Through Pictures. LC 73-4370. (Young Math Ser.). (Illus.). 40p. (J). (gr. 1-5). 1974. lib. bdg. 12.89 (*0-690-00156-8*) HarpC Child Bks.

— Straight Lines, Parallel Lines, Perpendicular Lines. LC 76-106569. (Young Math Ser.). (Illus.). (J). (gr. 1-4). 1970. 7.95 (*0-690-77992-5*) HarpC Child Bks.

Charosh, Paul. Berliner Gramophone Records: American Issues, 1892-1900, 60. LC 95-6268. (Discographies Ser.: Vol. 60). 336p. 1995. lib. bdg. 82.95 (*0-313-29217-5*, Greenwood Pr) Greenwood.

Charosh, Paul & Fremont, Robert. Song Hits from the Turn of the Century. LC 74-20444. 296p. 1975. pap. 8.95 (*0-486-23158-5*) Dover.

Charpa, Ulrich. Methodologie der Wissenschaft und Literaturwissenschaftliche Praxis. (Philosophische Texte und Studien: Vol. 6). (GER.). 152p. 1983. write for info. (*3-487-07432-X*) G Olms Pubs.

Charpak, A., jt. auth. see Balzac, Honore de.

Charpak, Georges. Research on Particle Detectors. (Twentieth Century Physics Ser.). 450p. 1995. text 99.00 (*981-02-1902-4*); pap. text 61.00 (*981-02-1903-2*) World Scientific Pub.

Charpentier. How to Read the New Testament: Facilitator's Guide. (Adult Christian Formation Program Ser.). pap. 5.95 (*0-8245-7001-4*) Crossroad NY.

— How to Read the Old Testament: Facilitator's Guide. (Adult Christian Formation Program Ser.). pap. 5.95 (*0-8245-7003-0*) Crossroad NY.

Charpentier, Aristide-Christian. The Violin of Passing Time. (J). (gr. 1-7). 1972. 6.00 (*0-87602-217-4*) Anchorage.

Charpentier, Bonnie A. & Sevenants, Michael R., eds. Supercritical Fluid Extraction & Chromatography: Techniques & Applications. LC 88-3466. (ACS Symposium Ser.: Vol. 366). 264p. 1988. reprint ed. pap. 81.90 (*0-608-03888-1*, 206433500008) Bks Demand.

***Charpentier, Cliff.** Charpentier's 1998 Fantasy Football. 120p. (J). 1998. pap. text 12.95 (*0-8225-9947-3*) Lerner Pub.

Charpentier, Cliff. Charpentier's 1998 Fantasy Football Digest. 1998. pap. 129.50 (*0-8225-9948-1*) Lerner Pub.

— Cliff Charpentier's 1997 Fantasy Football Digest. 14th ed. (J). 1997. pap. text 9.95 (*0-8225-9964-3*); pap. text 9.95 (*0-8225-9969-4*) Lerner Pub.

— Fantasy Football Digest, 1999. 1999. pap. text 14.95 (*0-8225-9949-X*) Lerner Pub.

***Charpentier, Cliff.** Fantasy Football Digest 2000. (Illus.). (YA). 2000. pap. 14.95 (*0-8225-9945-7*) Lerner Pub.

Charpentier, Cliff, jt. auth. see Lerner, Adam.

Charpentier, Etienne. How to Read the Bible. 256p. 1993. 9.99 (*0-517-05590-2*) Random Hse Value.

— How to Read the New Testament. LC 82-13028. (How-to Ser.: Vol. 1). (Illus.). 128p. 1982. pap. 14.95 (*0-8245-0541-7*, Pub. by Crossroad NY) Natl Bk Netwk.

— How to Read the Old Testament. LC 82-12728. (Adult Christian Formation Program Ser.: Vol. 1). (Illus.). 128p. 1982. pap. 14.95 (*0-8245-0540-9*, Pub. by Crossroad NY) Natl Bk Netwk.

Charpentier, J. Coleridge: The Sublime Somnambulist. LC 74-130259. (Studies in Coleridge: No. 7). 1970. reprint ed. lib. bdg. 75.00 (*0-8383-1163-6*) M S G Haskell Hse.

Charpentier, Marc-Antoine. Marc-Antoine Charpentier: Nine Settings of the "Litanies de la Vierge" Rayl, David C., ed. (Recent Researches in Music of the Baroque Era Ser.: Vol. RRB72). (Illus.). xx, 242p. 1994. pap. 80.00 (*0-89579-302-4*) A-R Eds.

— Marc-Antoine Charpentier: Vocal Chamber Music. Preston, Robert, ed. (Recent Researches in Music of the Baroque Era Ser.: Vol. RRB48). (Illus.). xxi, 98p. 1986. pap. 40.00 (*0-89579-202-8*) A-R Eds.

Charpentier, Marc-Antoine, jt. auth. see Moliere.

Charpentreau, Jacque. Dictionnaire des Poetes. (FRE.). 432p. 1983. 34.95 (*0-7859-7716-3*, 2070510190) Fr & Eur.

Charpentreau, Jacque & Borchers, E. Livre de Tous les Jours. (Gallimard - Decouverte Cadet Ser.: No. 14). (FRE.). (J). (gr. 4-9). 1980. 17.95 (*2-07-039514-6*) Schoenhof.

Charpentreau, Jacque & Jean, G. Dictionnaire des Poetes et de la Poesie. (Folio - Junior Ser.). (FRE.). 427p. (J). (gr. 5-10). 1983. 27.95 (*2-07-051019-0*) Schoenhof.

Charpin, P., jt. ed. see Camion, P.

Charpy, Elisabeth, jt. auth. see Roux, Marie-Genevieve.

Charques, Richard. The Twilight of Imperial Russia. (Illus.). 258p. 1974. pap. text 20.95 (*0-19-519787-9*) OUP.

Charques, Richard D. Contemporary Literature & Social Revolution. LC 68-2035. (Studies in Comparative Literature: No. 35). 1969. reprint ed. lib. bdg. 75.00 (*0-8383-0654-3*) M S G Haskell Hse.

Charr, Easurk E. The Golden Mountain: The Autobiography of a Korean Immigrant, 1895-1960. 2nd ed. Patterson, Wayne, ed. & intro. by. (Asian American Experience Ser.). (Illus.). 360p. (C). 1995. 14.95 (*0-252-06513-1*); text 34.95 (*0-252-02217-3*) U of Ill Pr.

Charra, Pierre-Jean. Microsoft Excel 1.5 Teaching Guide. 106p. 1989. ring bd. 495.00 incl. disk (*0-929533-11-9*) Tutorland.

— Teach Yourself Excel PC. 224p. 1989. ring bd. 89.95 incl. disk (*0-929533-07-0*) Tutorland.

— Teach Yourself Microsoft Excel 1.5. 171p. 1989. ring bd. 79.95 incl. disk (*0-929533-09-7*) Tutorland.

— Teach Yourself Microsoft Word 4 for IBM PC, PS - Compatibles. EDIDACOM Staff, tr. from FRE. 252p. 1988. ring bd. 89.95 incl. disk (*0-317-90949-5*) Tutorland.

Charra, Pierre-Jean & Meys, Marie-Jose. Teach Yourself dBASE III Plus. EDIDACOM Staff, tr. from FRE. 171p. ring bd. 69.95 incl. disk (*0-317-90950-9*) Tutorland.

Charran, R. & Maharaj, B. Va de Cuento. (Illus.). 1977. pap. text 10.40 (*0-582-76616-8*, 74839) Longman.

Charre, Alain, et al. Dan Graham. 128p. 1995. pap. 23.50 (*2-906571-42-3*) Dist Art Pubs.

Charrell, P. J. & Jaakkola, H., eds. Modelling & Knowledge Basis IX. (Frontiers in Artificial Intelligence & Applications Ser.: Vol. 45). 1998. 98.00 (*90-5199-396-X*, Pub. by IOS Pr) IOS Press.

***Charrett, Sheldon.** Identity, Privacy, & Personal Freedom: Big Brother v. the New Resistance. 240p. 1999. pap. 40.00 (*1-58160-042-9*) Paladin Pr.

Charrett, Sheldon. The Modern Identity Changer: How to Create & Use a New Identity for Privacy & Personal Freedom. LC 98-119248. (Illus.). 152p. 1997. pap. 20.00 (*0-87364-946-X*) Paladin Pr.

Charrier, Jean-Michel. Polymeric Materials & Processing: Plastics, Elastomers & Composites. 655p. (C). 1991. 59.95 (*1-56990-010-8*) Hanser-Gardner.

Charrier, Larry. Alaskan Holiday. 200p. 1998. pap. 9.95 (*0-9640637-2-7*) Great Wave AK.

Charriere, Doris. Beyond the Forbidden Sea. (Illus.). 369p. 1987. pap. 9.95 (*0-9620717-0-6*) Chalet Pub Co.

— Cataclysm. 250p. (Orig.). 1998. pap. 9.95 (*0-9620717-1-4*) Chalet Pub Co.

— Tamar the Tender Twig. (Illus.). 256p. (Orig.). (J). 1997. pap. 9.95 (*0-9620717-3-0*) Chalet Pub Co.

Charriere, Henri. Papillon. 1994. pap. 12.95 (*84-01-49084-7*) Plaza.

— Papillon: D Level. text 8.95 (*0-88436-997-8*) EMC-Paradigm.

Charriere, Isabella A. De, see De Charriere, Isabella A.

Charriere, Isabelle De. Letters of Mistress Henley Published by Her Friend. Stewart, Philip & Vache, Jean, trs. from FRE. LC 93-26862. (MLA Texts & Translations Ser.: No. 1b). xxix, 42p. (Orig.). 1993. pap. 3.95 (*0-87352-776-3*, P001P) Modern Lang.

— Lettres de Mistriss Henley Publiees par son Amie. Stewart, Philip, ed. LC 93-26864. (MLA Texts & Translations Ser.: No. 1a). (FRE.). xxx, 45p. (Orig.). 1993. pap. 3.95 (*0-87352-775-5*, Q001P) Modern Lang.

Charrom, Ray, jt. auth. see Stewart, Janet.

***Charron, Andy.** Desks: Outstanding Projects from America's Best Craftsmen. (Illus.). 2000. pap. 24.95 (*1-56158-348-0*) Taunton.

Charron, Andy. Spray Finishing. LC 96-33748. (Illus.). 176p. 1996. pap. 19.95 (*1-56158-114-3*, 70239) Taunton.

— Water-Based Finishes. LC 98-6988. (Illus.). 176p. 1998. pap. 19.95 (*1-56158-236-0*, 70363) Taunton.

Charron, Donna C., ed. & intro. see Kirzner, Israel M., et al.

Charron, Francois. After 10,000 Years, Desire. Whitman, Bruce & Farley-Chevrier, Francis, trs. from FRE. LC 95-190432. 88p. 1995. pap. 12.00 (*1-55022-224-4*, Pub. by ECW) Genl Dist Srvs.

Charron, Helene & Stephenson, Marian. Fundamentals of Psychiatric Nursing: A Basic Needs Nursing Approach. 328p. (C). 1996. pap. text 71.95 (*0-7872-2441-3*, 41244101) Kendall-Hunt.

Charron, Jacqueline. Dictionnaire Raisonne des Mots Croises. (FRE.). 1977. 39.95 (*0-7859-8593-X*, 0775905410) Fr & Eur.

Charron, Jean. Wisdom. LC 78-12595. (Illus.). 1979. reprint ed. lib. bdg. 65.00 (*0-313-21064-0*, CHWO, Greenwood Pr) Greenwood.

Charron, Katherine Mellen, ed. see Singleton, William Henry.

Charron, Pierre. Of Wisdome, 3 bks. LC 79-171739. (English Experience Ser.: No. 315). 1971. reprint ed. 127.00 (*90-221-0315-3*) Walter J Johnson.

Charron, Sylvie, tr. see Sand, George.

Charrow, Veda R., et al. Clear & Effective Legal Writing. 2nd ed. 384p. 1995. teacher ed. write for info. (*0-316-13781-2*, 37812) Aspen Law.

— Clear & Effective Legal Writing. 2nd ed. 384p. 1995. pap. text 28.95 (*0-316-13754-5*, Aspen Law & Bus) Aspen Pub.

Charry, Elias & Segal, Abraham. The Eternal People. (Illus.). 448p. (J). (gr. 9-11). 7.50 (*0-8381-0206-9*, 10-206) USCJE.

Charry, Ellen T. By the Renewing of Your Minds: The Pastoral Function of Christian Doctrine. 280p. 1999. pap. 16.95 (*0-19-513486-9*) OUP.

Charry, Ellen T., ed. Inquiring after God: Classic & Contemporary Readings. LC 99-32755. (Readings in Modern Theology Ser.). 400p. 1999. 62.95 (*0-631-20543-8*); pap. 29.95 (*0-631-20544-6*) Blackwell Pubs.

***Charry, Eric S.** Mande Music. 1999. pap. text 39.00 (*0-226-10162-2*); lib. bdg. 89.00 (*0-226-10161-4*) U Ch Pr.

Charry, Jonathan M., ed. Air Ions: Physical & Biological Aspects. 240p. 1987. 125.00 (*0-8493-6535-X*, QP82, CRC Reprint) Franklin.

Charsha. Neonatal Emergency, No. 1. 1997. text, wbk. ed. 16.95 (*0-8151-2377-9*) Mosby Inc.

— Neonatal Emergency, No. 2. 1997. text, wbk. ed. 16.95 (*0-8151-2378-7*) Mosby Inc.

— Neonatal Emergency, No. 3. 1997. text, wbk. ed. 16.95 (*0-8151-2380-9*) Mosby Inc.

— Neonatal Infectious Diseases, No. 2. 1997. text, wbk. ed. 16.95 (*0-8151-2368-X*) Mosby Inc.

Charsley, S. R. & Karanth, G. K. Challenging Untouchability: Dalit Initiative Experience from Karnataka. LC 98-24650. (Cultural Subordination & the Dalit Challenge Ser.). 1998. 45.00 (*0-7619-9263-4*) Sage.

— Challenging Untouchability: Dalit Initiative Experience from Karnataka. LC 98-24650. (Cultural Subordination & the Dalit Challenge Ser.). 1998. pap. 45.00 (*0-7619-9264-2*) Sage.

Charsley, Simon R. Wedding Cakes & Cultural History. LC 91-24278. (Illus.). 176p. (Orig.). (C). 1992. pap. 22.99 (*0-415-02649-0*, A6791) Routledge.

***Chart, David.** Heirs to Merlin: The Stonehedge Tribunal. Kasab, John, ed. (Ars Magica Ser.). (Illus.). 176p. 1999. pap. 22.95 (*1-887801-79-0*, Atlas Games) Trident MN.

Chart, David, jt. ed. see Kasab, John.

Chart, Henrik, ed. Methods in Practical Laboratory Bacteriology. LC 94-1321. 176p. 1994. spiral bd. 83.95 (*0-8493-8692-6*, 8692) CRC Pr.

Chartain, Bob. Paul McCarthy. (Illus.). 128p. 1999. pap. text 29.95 (*88-8158-210-4*, Pub. by Charta) Dist Art Pubs.

***Charter, Anne Goddard.** Cowboys Don't Walk: A Tale of Two. 1998. pap. 15.95 (*0-9666476-0-2*) Westrn Org.

Charter Institute of Bankers Staff. The CIB Directory of Corporate Banking in the U. K., 1997. 1998. pap. 560.00 (*0-85297-431-0*, Pub. by Chartered Bank) St Mut.

Charter, Roger. Frenchness in the History of the Book: From the History of Publishing to the History of Reading. (James Russell Wiggins Lecture in the History of the Book Ser.: Vol. 5). 42p. 1988. pap. 8.95 (*0-944026-01-X*) Am Antiquarian.

Chartered Institute of Arbitrators (Great Britain). The Commercial Way to Justice: The 1996 International Conference of the Chartered Institute of Arbitrators. Beresford Hartwell, Geoffrey M. et al, eds. LC 97-30709. 332p. 1998. 114.00 (*90-411-0478-X*) Kluwer Law Intl.

Chartered Institute of Bankers Staff. Documentary Credit Specialist Manual. 1998. pap. 240.00 (*0-85297-397-7*, Pub. by Chartered Bank) St Mut.

— Finance of International Trade: Practitioner's Edition. 400p. 1998. pap. 70.00 (*0-85297-531-7*, Pub. by Chartered Bank) St Mut.

— Trade Finance: A Complete Guide to Documentary Credits. 400p. 1998. pap. 465.00 (*0-85297-488-4*, Pub. by Chartered Bank) St Mut.

Chartered Institute of Patent Agents Staff. European Patents Handbook, 4 vols. 1979. 980.00 (*0-8205-2060-8*) Bender.

Charteris, Evan. John Sargent. LC 71-174842. (Illus.). 320p. 1972. reprint ed. 30.95 (*0-405-08350-5*, Pub. by Blom Pubns) Ayer.

— The Life & Letters of Sir Edmund Gosse. LC 72-2097. (English Literature Ser.: No. 33). 1972. reprint ed. lib. bdg. 75.00 (*0-8383-1456-2*) M S G Haskell Hse.

Charteris, Henry, jt. auth. see Robertson, George.

Charteris, Hugo. The Tide Is Right. LC 90-14062. (Illus.). x, 145p. 1991. 19.95 (*0-916583-71-6*) Dalkey Arch.

— The Tide Is Right. (Illus.). 145p. 1992. reprint ed. pap. 9.95 (*0-916583-78-3*) Dalkey Arch.

Charteris, Leslie. Angels of Doom. 1994. reprint ed. lib. bdg. 32.95 (*1-56849-263-4*) Buccaneer Bks.

— Arrest the Saint. 1993. reprint ed. lib. bdg. 21.95 (*1-56849-129-8*) Buccaneer Bks.

— The Avenging Saint. 20.95 (*0-88411-267-5*) Amereon Ltd.

— Daredevil. (Saint Ser.). 1976. reprint ed. lib. bdg. 25.95 (*0-89190-383-6*, Rivercity Pr) Amereon Ltd.

— The First Saint Omnibus. LC 90-80771. 642p. 1990. reprint ed. pap. 10.95 (*1-55882-060-4*) Intl Polygonics.

— Follow the Saint. 202p. 1976. reprint ed. lib. bdg. 21.95 (*0-89190-382-8*, Rivercity Pr) Amereon Ltd.

— Getaway. 1975. reprint ed. lib. bdg. 24.95 (*0-89190-388-7*, Rivercity Pr) Amereon Ltd.

— Getaway. 1994. reprint ed. lib. bdg. 29.95 (*1-56849-262-6*) Buccaneer Bks.

— Getaway. LC 90-84280. 250p. 1990. reprint ed. pap. 5.95 (*1-55882-084-1*) Intl Polygonics.

— Holy Terror. LC 72-106261. (Short Story Index Reprint Ser.). 1977. 20.95 (*0-8369-3298-6*) Ayer.

— Knight Templar. 262p. 1989. reprint ed. pap. 5.95 (*1-55882-010-8*, Lib Crime Classics) Intl Polygonics.

— The Last Hero. LC 88-82345. 312p. 1988. reprint ed. pap. 4.95 (*0-930330-96-X*, Lib Crime Classics) Intl Polygonics.

— The Saint Abroad. 1993. reprint ed. lib. bdg. 21.95 (*1-56849-130-1*) Buccaneer Bks.

— The Saint & the Templar Treasure. 20.95 (*0-88411-266-7*) Amereon Ltd.

— The Saint Goes West. 18.95 (*0-89190-391-7*) Amereon Ltd.

— The Saint in Europe. 1975. reprint ed. lib. bdg. 20.95 (*0-89190-387-9*, Rivercity Pr) Amereon Ltd.

— The Saint in Miami. large type ed. 454p. 1973. 27.99 (*0-85456-223-0*) Ulverscroft.

— The Saint in New York. LC 88-82346. 229p. 1988. reprint ed. pap. 4.95 (*0-930330-97-8*, Lib Crime Classics) Intl Polygonics.

— Saint Intervenes. 1976. 23.95 (*0-89190-384-4*) Amereon Ltd.

— The Saint Meets His Match. 21.95 (*0-89190-343-7*) Amereon Ltd.

— The Saint on Guard. 1975. reprint ed. lib. bdg. 22.95 (*0-89190-386-0*, Rivercity Pr) Amereon Ltd.

— The Saint Overboard. Date not set. reprint ed. lib. bdg. 24.95 (*0-614-25287-3*, Am Repr) Amereon Ltd.

— The Saint Overboard. 1993. reprint ed. lib. bdg. 20.95 (*1-56849-131-X*) Buccaneer Bks.

— Saint Sees It Through. 1976. 23.95 (*0-89190-389-5*) Amereon Ltd.

— The Saint Steps In. 1976. reprint ed. lib. bdg. 21.95 (*0-89190-385-2*, Rivercity Pr) Amereon Ltd.

— The Saint vs. Scotland Yard. 21.95 (*0-89190-390-9*) Amereon Ltd.

— The Saint vs. Scotland Yard. 1993. reprint ed. lib. bdg. 17.95 (*1-56849-132-8*) Buccaneer Bks.

— The Saint's Sporting Chance. 22.95 (*0-89190-344-5*) Amereon Ltd.

Charteris, Richard. Giovanni Gabrielli: A Thematic Catalogue of His Works. (Thematic Catalogues Ser.: No. 20). 597p. 1996. 64.00 (*0-945193-66-1*) Pendragon NY.

Charteris, Richard & Gumpeltzhaimer, Adam. Adam Gumpelzhaimer's Little-Known Score-Books in Berlin & Krakbow. LC 97-122501. xii, 156 p. 1996. write for info. (*0-377-51240-0*) Friendship Pr.

Charteris, Richard, ed. see Bach, Johann Sebastian.

Charteris, Richard, ed. see Bassano, Giovanni.

Charteris, Richard, ed. see Coprario, John.

Charteris, Richard, ed. see Gabrieli, Giovanni.

Charteris, Richard, ed. see Hassler, Hans L.

Charteris, Richard, ed. see Hingeston, John.

Charteris, Richard, ed. see Monteverdi, Claudio.

Charters. American Story & Its Writer. 1999. pap. text 46.95 (*0-312-19176-6*) St Martin.

***Charters.** Literature & Its Writers. 2nd ed. 2000. pap. text. write for info. (*0-312-20979-7*) St Martin.

Charters. The Story & Its Writer. 5th ed. LC 98-85190. xxviii, 1748p. 1998. pap. 46.95 (*0-312-17158-7*); pap. text, teacher ed. 5.00 (*0-312-19421-8*) St Martin.

***Charters.** Story & its Writer High School. 5th ed. 1999. pap. text 46.95 (*0-312-25104-1*) St Martin.

Charters. Story & Writing: Research Paper. 4th ed. 1998. pap. text 31.00 (*0-312-20092-7*) St Martin.

Charters, Alexander N. Accessibility of Resources for Educators of Adults. (MS Ser.: No. 9). 1977. 3.50 (*0-686-63885-9*, MSS 9) Syracuse U Cont Ed.

— Adult Education Activity of Selected International Organizations. 1971. 5.00 (*0-87060-076-1*, WPT 4) Syracuse U Cont Ed.

— Adult Education Master's Theses & Doctoral Dissertations on Microfilm in Syracuse University Libraries. 1977. pap. 5.00 (*0-685-87565-2*, MSS 17) Syracuse U Cont Ed.

— Adult Education Sound & Video Recordings E. S. Bird Library. 1982. 8.00 (*0-87060-031-1*, MSS 23) Syracuse U Cont Ed.

— Aids to Access: Resources for Educators of Adults. (MS Ser.). 1978. 4.25 (*0-686-52208-7*, MSS 1) Syracuse U Cont Ed.

— Continuing Education for Educators of Adults: The Roles of Research. (MS Ser.). 1977. 4.00 (*0-686-52213-3*, MSS 6) Syracuse U Cont Ed.

— Dessarollo Professional de Educadores de Adultos. 1977. 4.00 (*0-87060-077-X*, MSS 3) Syracuse U Cont Ed.

— Hill & the Valley: The Story of University College at Syracuse University Through 1964. LC 77-18954. (Occasional Papers: No. 27). 1972. pap. text 2.25 (*0-87060-050-8*, OCP 27) Syracuse U Cont Ed.

— The International Handbook of Resources for the Educators of Adults. 1977. 20.00 (*0-685-87564-4*, MSS 18) Syracuse U Cont Ed.

— Professional Development of Educators of Adults. (MS Ser.). (SPA.). 1977. 3.50 (*0-686-52209-5*, MSS 2) Syracuse U Cont Ed.

— Publications in Continuing Education. (MS Ser.: No. 12). 1980. 4.50 (*0-686-64687-8*, MSS 12) Syracuse U Cont Ed.

— Real Estate Tax Exemption for Continuing Education. LC 76-189508. (Occasional Papers: No. 26). 1972. pap. 2.00 (*0-87060-049-4*, OCP 26) Syracuse U Cont Ed.

— Report on the 1969 Galaxy Conference of Adult Education Organizations. (Landmark Ser.: No. 1). 1971. pap. text 2.00 (*0-87060-005-2*, LNH 1) Syracuse U Cont Ed.

— Toward the Educative Society. LC 74-149023. (Notes & Essays Ser.: No. 67). 1971. pap. 2.50 (*0-87060-039-7*, NES 67) Syracuse U Cont Ed.

Charters, Alexander N., compiled by. Abstracts of Theses & Dissertations in Adult Education, Syracuse University. 1979. 4.50 (*0-686-65496-X*, MSS 11) Syracuse U Cont Ed.

— Adult & Continuing Education Collections: A Descriptive List of Manuscript Holdings in Syracuse University Libraries. 1977. 5.00 (*0-686-50189-6*, MSS 16) Syracuse U Cont Ed.

— Audio Tapes: E. S. Bird Library. 1976. 3.75 (*0-686-63886-7*, MSS 22) Syracuse U Cont Ed.

— Omnibus Series: E. S. Byrd Library. 1976. 4.65 (*0-686-50190-X*, MSS 24) Syracuse U Cont Ed.

— The Paul Hoy Helms Library in Liberal Adult Education. 1973. 4.55 (*0-686-50191-8*, MSS 20) Syracuse U Cont Ed.

Charters, Alexander N., ed. Publications in Continuing Education. 1983. 8.00 (*0-87060-038-9*, MSS 26) Syracuse U Cont Ed.

Charters, Alexander N. & Goodman, Edward. Acquisition List Pamphlet File. rev. ed. (E. S. Bird Library). 1983. 8.00 (*0-87060-073-7*, MSS 13) Syracuse U Cont Ed.

Charters, Alexander N. & Gschwender, Edward. Adult Education Periodicals & Newsletters in Bird Library. 1983. 8.00 (*0-87060-037-0*, MSS 29) Syracuse U Cont Ed.

Charters, Alexander N. & Hilton, R. Who We Are: What Some Educators Say About Their Characteristics, Competencies & Roles. (MS Ser.). 1977. 5.00 (*0-686-52212-5*, MSS 5) Syracuse U Cont Ed.

Charters, Alexander N. & Holmwood, D. Periodicals, Newsletters & Indexes in E. S. Bird Library & Clearinghouse of Resources for Educators of Adults. (MS Ser.: No. 8). 1978. 3.50 (*0-686-63883-2*, MSS 8) Syracuse U Cont Ed.

Charters, Alexander N. & Holmwood, Donald. Professional Development for Educators of Adults: A Bibliography. 1977. 8.00 (*0-87060-078-8*, CRE 3) Syracuse U Cont Ed.

Charters, Alexander N. & Rivera, William M., eds. International Seminar on Publications in Continuing Education. LC 76-39028. (Notes & Essays Ser.: No. 72). 112p. (Orig.). 1972. pap. 3.00 (*0-87060-048-6*, NES 72) Syracuse U Cont Ed.

Charters, Alexander N., et al. Comparing Adult Education Worldwide. LC 80-8911. (Jossey-Bass Series in Higher Education). 296p. reprint ed. pap. 91.80 (*0-8357-4936-3*, 203786600009) Bks Demand.

Charters, Ann. Kerouac: A Biography. LC 75-306152. x, 403 p. 1974. 3.95 (*0-233-96516-5*) Andre Deutsch.

— Kerouac: A Biography. (Illus.). 416p. 1994. pap. 15.95 (*0-312-11347-1*) St Martin.

— Major Writers of Short Fiction: Stories & Commentaries. LC 92-52525. 1461p. (C). 1993. pap. text 46.95 (*0-312-07944-3*) St Martin.

— Major Writers of Short Fiction: Stories & Commentaries - Instructor's Manual. 1993. teacher ed. 6.66 (*0-312-08369-6*) St Martin.

— Story: Turn. 2000. pap. text 32.40 (*0-312-13757-5*) St Martin.

— The Story & Its Writer. 4th ed. 1994. pap. text, teacher ed. 5.00 (*0-312-10340-9*) St Martin.

Charters, Ann. The Story & Its Writer: An Introduction to Short Fiction. 4th ed. 926p. 1994. pap. text 33.95 (*0-312-11170-3*) St Martin.

Charters, Ann, ed. The Beats, 2 vols. (Dictionary of Literary Biography Ser.: Vol. 16). 721p. 1983. text 296.00 (*0-8103-1148-8*) Gale.

Charters, Ann, ed. Jack Kerouac: Selected Letters, 1940-1956. 656p. 1996. pap. 16.95 (*0-14-023444-6*, Viking) Viking Penguin.

— The Portable Beat Reader. 608p. 1992. reprint ed. pap. 15.95 (*0-14-015102-8*, Penguin Bks) Viking Penguin.

— The Portable Jack Kerouac. 656p. 1996. pap. 15.95 (*0-14-017819-8*, Viking) Viking Penguin.

***Charters, Ann, ed.** Jack Kerouac: Selected Letters, 1957-1969. 656p. 2000. pap. 17.00 (*0-14-029615-8*) Penguin Putnam.

Charters, Ann & Charters, Samuel. Resources for Teaching "Literature & Its Writers" 2151p. 1997. pap. text, teacher ed. 13.33 (*0-312-13804-0*) St Martin.

Charters, Ann, ed. see Olson, Charles.

Charters, Ann, ed. & intro. see Kerouac, Jack.

Charters, David. Charters on Charting: How to Improve Your Stockmarket Decision-Making. 1998. pap. text 19.95 (*0-7134-8389-X*, Pub. by B T B) Branford.

Charters, David, ed. Democratic Responses to International Terrorism. 374p. 1991. 49.50 (*0-941320-66-9*) Transnatl Pubs.

Charters, David A. The Deadly Sin of Terrorism: Its Effect on Democracy & Civil Liberty in Six Countries, 340. LC 93-31604. (Series Contributions in Political Science: Vol. 340). 264p. 1994. 59.95 (*0-313-28964-6*, Greenwood Pr) Greenwood.

Charters, David A., et al, eds. Intelligence Analysis & Assessment: The Producer/Policy-Maker Relationship in a Changing World. (Studies in Intelligence). 240p. (C). 1996. 47.50 (*0-7146-4709-8*, Pub. by F Cass Pubs); pap. 24.50 (*0-7146-4249-5*, Pub. by F Cass Pubs) Intl Spec Bk.

— Military History & the Military Profession. LC 92-9114. 264p. 1992. 55.00 (*0-275-94072-1*, C4072, Praeger Pubs) Greenwood.

Charters, J. N. Brampton Railway. 96p. (C). 1985. 39.00 (*0-85361-099-1*) St Mut.

Charters, Jill & Gately, Anne. Drama Anytime. 88p. (Orig.). (C). (gr. 1). 1987. pap. text 16.00 (*0-909955-64-6*, 00591) Heinemann.

Charters, Lowell. Thunderheart. 1992. mass mkt. 4.50 (*0-380-76881-X*, Avon Bks) Morrow Avon.

Charters, Margaret. Consumer Education Programming in Continuing Education. LC 72-13366. (Occasional Papers: No. 34). 36p. (Orig.). 1973. pap. 2.00 (*0-87060-057-5*, OCP 34) Syracuse U Cont Ed.

***Charters, Sam.** Blues Faces: A Portrait of the Blues. (Imago Mundi Ser.). (Illus.). 160p. 2000. 40.00 (*1-56792-116-7*) Godine.

***Charters, Samuel.** The Day Is So Long & the Wages So Small: Music on a Summer Island. LC 98-46735. 160p. 1999. pap. 14.95 (*0-7145-3056-5*, Pub. by M Boyars Pubs) LPC InBook.

Charters, Samuel, jt. auth. see Charters, Ann.

Charters, Samuel B. The Country Blues. LC 75-14114. (Roots of Jazz Ser.). (Illus.). 288p. 1975. reprint ed. pap. 12.95 (*0-306-80014-4*); reprint ed. lib. bdg. 29.50 (*0-306-70678-4*) Da Capo.

— Elvis Presley Calls His Mother after the Ed Sullivan Show. LC 92-2573. 128p. 1992. pap. 10.95 (*0-918273-98-6*) Coffee Hse.

— From a Swedish Notebook. 1973. 5.00 (*0-685-36814-9*); pap. 2.50 (*0-685-36815-7*) Oyez.

— Jelly Roll Morton's Last Night at the Jungle Inn. pap. 11.95 (*0-7145-2897-8*) M Boyars Pubs.

— Of Those Who Died. 1980. pap. 3.00 (*0-317-17645-5*) Oyez.

— Robert Johnson. (Illus.). 88p. 1973. pap. 14.95 (*0-8256-0059-6*, OK62745, Oak) Music Sales.

— The Roots of the Blues: An African Search. (Illus.). 151p. 1991. reprint ed. pap. 10.95 (*0-306-80445-X*, Pub. by Da Capo) HarpC.

— Some Poems - Poets. 1971. 5.95 (*0-685-04674-5*); pap. 2.95 (*0-685-04675-3*) Oyez.

Charters, Samuel B. & Kunstadt, Leonard. Jazz: A History of the New York Scene. (Roots of Jazz Ser.). (Illus.). 390p. 1981. reprint ed. pap. 13.95 (*0-306-80225-2*) Da Capo.

Charters, SamuelB. The Blues Makers. (Quality Paperbacks Ser.). (Illus.). 416p. (Orig.). 1991. pap. 16.95 (*0-306-80438-7*) Da Capo.

— In Lagos, Ereko Street, Nine p.m. 1976. 1.50 (*0-685-79011-8*) Oyez.

— The Legacy of the Blues: Art & Lives of Twelve Great Bluesmen. LC 76-51809. (Roots of Jazz Ser.). (Illus.). 1977. 25.00 (*0-306-70847-7*); pap. 9.95 (*0-306-80054-3*) Da Capo.

Charters, W. W. Curriculum Construction. LC 74-165713. (American Education, Ser. No. 2). 1979. reprint ed. 33.95 (*0-405-03702-3*) Ayer.

— Motion Pictures & Youth: A Summary. LC 73-124025. (Literature of Cinema Ser.: Payne Fund Studies of Motion Pictures & Social Values). reprint ed. 11.95 (*0-405-01642-5*) Ayer.

Charters, W. W., Jr. On Understanding Variables & Hypotheses in Scientific Research. LC 91-77518. viii, 44p. 1992. pap. 5.95 (*0-86552-115-8*) U of Oreg ERIC.

Chartier, Alain. Belle Dame sans Mercy. 127p. 1949. 19.95 (*0-8288-7476-X*) Fr & Eur.

— Familiar Dialogue of the Friend & the Fellow: A Translation of Alain Chartier's Dialogus Familiaris Amici et Sodalis. Blayney, Margaret S., ed. (OS 295 Ser.: No. 295). 80p. 1989. 38.00 (*0-19-722297-8*) OUP.

— Fifteenth Century Translations of Alain Chartier's Le Traite de l'Esperance & Le Quadrilogue Invectif Vol. I: Text, Vol. I, Text. Blayney, Margaret S., ed. (OS 270 Ser.: No. 270). 268p. (C). 1974. 21.95 (*0-19-722272-2*) OUP.

— Fifteenth Century Translations of Alain Chartier's Le Traite de l'Esperance & Le Quadriloque Invectif: Introduction, Notes & Glossary, Vol. II. Blayney, Margaret S., ed. (OS 281 Ser.: No. 281). (Illus.). 268p. 1980. 26.50 (*0-19-722283-8*) OUP.

Chartier, Allen T., jt. auth. see Fisher, Chris.

***Chartier, Armand.** The Franco-Americans of New England: A History. rev. ed. Quintal, Claire, ed. (Illus.). 537p. 1999. pap. 19.95 (*1-880261-05-7*) FI Assump Coll.

Chartier, Armand B. Barbey D'Aurevilly. LC 77-8024. (Twayne's World Authors Ser.). 182p. (C). 1977. lib. bdg. 20.95 (*0-8057-6305-8*) Irvington.

Chartier, Bonnie. A Birder's Guide to Churchill. 3rd rev. ed. Baicich, Paul J., ed. LC 93-74273. (ABA-Lane Birdfinding Guide Ser.). (Illus.). 132p. (Orig.). 1994. pap., spiral bd. 17.95 (*1-878788-07-8*, 490) Amer Birding Assn.

***Chartier, Duane R., et al, eds.** Scientific Detection of Fakery in Art II. 1999. pap. text 50.00 (*0-8194-3444-2*) SPIE.

Chartier, Genevieve. The Diplomatic Pouch. (Illus.). 184p. 1995. pap. 11.95 (*0-9634891-3-5*) La Presse des Mich.

— La Fille des Michettes. (FRE.). 242p. 1992. pap. 15.95 (*0-9634891-0-0*) La Presse des Mich.

Chartier, George E. Full House: The Definitive Guide for Successfully Promoting School & Community Theater. LC 92-71038. (Illus.). 232p. (Orig.). 1992. pap. 24.95 (*1-881237-00-1*) Dramatic Concepts.

Chartier, Jack W. The Art of Whistling. (Illus.). 40p. (J). (gr. 1 up). 1993. lib. bdg. 4.95 (*0-9636343-1-3*) Jamar Pub House.

***Chartier, JoAnn & Enss, Chris.** With Great Hope. LC 99-54899. 2000. pap. 10.95 (*1-56044-888-1*) Falcon Pub Inc.

Chartier-Kastler, C., jt. auth. see Quang, Pham T.

Chartier, Normand. Gertie's Not Alone. LC 96-179998. (Illus.). 40p. (J). (ps-3). 1996. 8.99 (*0-88070-920-0*, Gold n Honey) Zondervan.

— Jingle Bells. (Chubby Board Bks.). (Illus.). 16p. (J). (ps-k). 1989. 3.95 (*0-671-68269-5*) Litle Simon.

Chartier, Normand, jt. auth. see Singer, Marilyn.

Chartier, P., et al, eds. Biomass for Energy, Environment, Agriculture & Industry: Proceedings of the 8th European Community Conference, Held in Vienna, October 1994. 2850p. 1995. 482.50 (*0-08-042135-0*, Pergamon Pr) Elsevier.

Chartier, Philippe & Palz, Wolfgang, eds. Energy from Biomass. x, 220p. 1981. text 94.00 (*90-277-1348-0*) Kluwer Academic.

Chartier, Philippe, et al. Biomass for Energy & the Environment: Proceedings of the 9th European Bioenergy Conference, Copenhagen, Denmark, 24-27 June 1996, 3 vols. LC 96-38026. 2294p. 1996. 423.00 (*0-08-042849-5*, Pergamon Pr) Elsevier.

Chartier, Pierre. Les Faux Monnayeurs de Gide. (FRE.). 253p. 1991. pap. 14.95 (*0-7859-2161-3*, 2070383490) Fr & Eur.

Chartier, Roger. Cultural History: Between Practices & Representations. Cochrane, Lydia G., tr. from FRE. LC 88-3823. 230p. 1988. text 39.95 (*0-8014-2223-X*) Cornell U Pr.

— The Cultural Origins of the French Revolution. Baker, Keith M. & Kaplan, Steven L., eds. Cochrane, Lydia G., tr. LC 90-24404. (Bicentennial Reflections on the French Revolution Ser.). 240p. (C). 1991. text 46.95 (*0-8223-0981-5*); pap. text 16.95 (*0-8223-0993-9*) Duke.

— The Cultural Uses of Print in Early Modern France. LC 87-45515. (Illus.). 367p. reprint ed. pap. 113.80 (*0-608-09108-1*, 206974000005) Bks Demand.

— Forms & Meanings: Texts, Performances & Audiences from Codex to Computer. LC 95-16701. (New Cultural Studies). 144p. 1995. 29.95 (*0-8122-3302-6*); pap. 12.95 (*0-8122-1546-X*) U of Pa Pr.

— On the Edge of the Cliff: History, Language, & Practices. Cochrane, Lydia G., tr. LC 96-18980. (Parallax). 288p. 1996. text 45.00 (*0-8018-5435-0*); pap. text 16.95 (*0-8018-5436-9*) Johns Hopkins.

— The Order of Books: Readers, Authors & Libraries in Europe Between the 14th & 18th Centuries. LC 93-84986. xii, 126p. 1994. 45.00 (*0-8047-2266-8*) Stanford U Pr.

— The Order of Books: Readers, Authors & Libraries in Europe Between the 14th & 18th Centuries. LC 93-84986. xii, 126p. 1994. pap. 12.95 (*0-8047-2267-6*) Stanford U Pr.

Chartier, Roger, et al, eds. A History of Private Life Vol. 3: Passions of the Renaissance. Goldhammer, Arthur, tr. from FRE. LC 86-18286. (Illus.). 645p. 1989. 39.95 (*0-674-39977-3*) Belknap Pr.

Chartier, Roger, et al. Correspondence: Models of Letter-Writing from the Middle Ages to the Nineteenth Century. LC 97-1567. 162p. 1997. text 35.00 (*0-691-01696-8*, Pub. by Princeton U Pr) Cal Prin Full Svc.

Chartier, Roger, ed. see Boureau, Alain, et al.

Chartier, Roger, jt. ed. see Cavallo, Guglielmo.

Chartism & Chartists. Joneg. 1975. 25.00 (*0-685-04735-0*) St Martin.

Chartists, jt. auth. see Chartism.

Chartkoff, Joseph L. Test Excavations at the May Site (CA-SIS-57) in Seiad Valley, Northwestern, California. (Archives of California Prehistory Ser.: Vol. 17). (Illus.). 86p. (Orig.). (C). 1988. pap. text 9.69 (*1-55567-051-2*) Coyote Press.

Chartkoff, Joseph L. & Chartkoff, Kerry K. The Archaeology of California. LC 82-60182. (Illus.). 480p. 1984. pap. 24.95 (*0-8047-1483-5*) Stanford U Pr.

Chartkoff, Kerry K., jt. auth. see Chartkoff, Joseph L.

***Chartock.** Educational Foundations. LC 99-25024. 344p. 1999. pap. text 36.00 (*0-13-660176-6*) P-H.

Chartock, Alan S. Me & Mario Cuomo: Conversations in Candor. LC 95-706. 304p. 1995. pap. 14.00 (*1-56980-056-1*) Barricade Bks.

Chartock, Roselle K., jt. ed. see Spencer, Jack.

Charton, Barbara. The Facts on File Dictionary of Marine Science. (Illus.). 336p. 1988. 29.95 (*0-8160-1031-5*) Facts on File.

— The Facts on File Dictionary of Marine Science. (Illus.). 336p. 1990. pap. 15.95 (*0-8160-2369-7*) Facts on File.

Charton, Marvin, ed. Advances in Quantitative Structure-Property Relationships, Vol. 2. Date not set. 109.50 (*0-7623-0067-1*) Jai Pr.

Chartove, Alex. Patent Law Developments in the Federal Circuit, 1996. 300p. 1996. pap. 81.25 (*0-614-17117-2*, G1-1027) PLI.

Chartrain, Nathalie, tr. see Styple, William B., ed.

Chartrand, Claude. The Art of Fly Tying. (Illus.). 206p. 1996. pap. 24.95 (*1-55209-07-4*) Firefly Bks Ltd.

Chartrand, Gary. Introductory Graph Theory. (Popular Science Ser.). 320p. 1984. reprint ed. pap. 8.95 (*0-486-24775-9*) Dover.

Chartrand, Gary & Lesniak, Linda. Graphs & Diagraphs. 2nd ed. LC 86-1519. 359p. (C). (gr. 13). 1986. ring bd. 94.95 (*0-534-06324-1*, Chap & Hall CRC) CRC Pr.

Chartrand, Gary & Oellerman, Ortrud R. Applied & Algorithmic Graph Theory. (International Series in Pure & Applied Mathematics). 432p. (C). 1992. 78.75 (*0-07-557101-3*) McGraw.

Chartrand, M. Collins Wildlife Trust Guide: Night Sky. 512p. 1999. pap. 26.95 (*0-00-220014-7*, Pub. by HarpC) Trafalgar.

Chartrand, Mark R., III. The Audubon Society Field Guide to the Night Sky. LC 91-52708. (Audubon Field Guide Ser.). (Illus.). 714p. 1991. 19.00 (*0-679-40852-5*) Knopf.

Chartrand, Mark R. Exploring Space. (Golden Guide Ser.). 1991. 11.05 (*0-606-11306-1*, Pub. by Turtleback) Demco.

— Planets. (Golden Guide Ser.). 1990. 11.05 (*0-606-11755-5*, Pub. by Turtleback) Demco.

Chartrand, Mark R. Skyguide, a Field Guide to the Heavens. (Golden Field Guide Ser.). 1982. 19.05 (*0-606-11849-7*, Pub. by Turtleback) Demco.

***Chartrand, Micheline & Desputeaux, Helene.** Caillou Knows How. (Illus.). 4p. (J). 1998. bds. 4.49 (*1-58048-033-0*) Sandvik Pub.

— Caillou's Room. (Illus.). (J). 1998. bds. 4.49 (*1-58048-034-9*) Sandvik Pub.

Chartrand, P., ed. see Bacon, F.

Chartrand, P., ed. see Fortin, A.

Chartrand, R. The French Army in the American War of Independence. (Men-at-Arms Ser.: No. 244). (Illus.). 48p. pap. 11.95 (*1-85532-167-X*, 9204, Pub. by Osprey) Stackpole.

Chartrand, Rene. British Infantry Equipments 1808-1908, 107. 1999. pap. text 12.95 (*1-85532-838-0*) Osprey.

— British Troops in the West Indies 1792-1815. (Illus.). 48p. 1996. pap. 12.95 (*1-85532-600-0*, Pub. by Osprey) Stackpole.

— Canadian Campaigns, 1860-70. (Men-at-Arms Ser.: No. 249). (Illus.). 48p. pap. 11.95 (*1-85532-226-9*, 9220, Pub. by Osprey) Stackpole.

— Canadian Military Heritage Vol. 1: 1000-1754. (Illus.). 240p. 1997. 50.00 (*2-920718-49-5*, Pub. by A4rt Global) Howell Pr VA.

Chartrand, Rene. Canadian Military Heritage Vol. 1: 1000-1754. 240p. 1997. 200.00 (*1-86227-014-7*, Pub. by Spellmnt Pubs) St Mut.

— Canadian Military Heritage Vol. 2: Napoleonic Wars 1755-1871. 240p. 1997. 200.00 (*1-86227-015-5*, Pub. by Spellmnt Pubs) St Mut.

Chartrand, Rene. Canadian Military Heritage Vol. 2: 1755-1871. (Illus.). 240p. 1997. 50.00 (*2-920718-50-9*, Pub. by A4rt Global) Howell Pr VA.

***Chartrand, Rene.** Emigre & Foreign Troops in British Service 1803-15. (Men at Arms Ser.: Vol. 335). (Illus.). 2000. pap. 12.95 (*1-85532-859-3*) Ospry.

Chartrand, Rene. Emigre Troops in British Service: 1792-1803. (Men at Arms Ser.: Vol. 328). (Illus.). 48p. 1999. pap. 12.95 (*1-85532-766-X*, Pub. by Osprey) Stackpole.

— Louis XV's Army Vol. 2: French Infantry. (Men-at-Arms Ser.: Vol. 302). (Illus.). 48p. pap. 12.95 (*1-85532-602-7*, Pub. by Osprey); pap. 12.95 (*1-85532-625-6*, Pub. by Osprey) Stackpole.

— Louis XIV's Army. (Men-at-Arms Ser.: No. 203). (Illus.). 48p. 1988. pap. 11.95 (*0-85045-850-1*, 9136, Pub. by Osprey) Stackpole.

— The Mexican Adventure, 1861-67. (Men-at-Arms Ser.: No. 272). (Illus.). 48p. 1994. pap. 11.95 (*1-85532-430-X*, 9244, Pub. by Osprey) Stackpole.

— Napoleonic Wars: Napoleon's Army. (Brassey's History of Uniforms Ser.). (Illus.). 144p. 1996. 31.95 (*1-85753-183-3*, Pub. by Brasseys) Brasseys.

— Napoleonic Wars: Napoleon's Army. (Illus.). 144p. 1998. pap. text 21.95 (*1-85753-220-1*, Pub. by Brasseys) Brasseys.

— Napoleon's Overseas Army. (Men-at-Arms Ser.: No. 211). (Illus.). 48p. pap. 11.95 (*0-85045-900-1*, 9144, Pub. by Osprey) Stackpole.

— Napoleon's Sea-Soldiers. (Men-at-Arms Ser.: No. 227). (Illus.). 48p. pap. 11.95 (*0-85045-998-2*, 9185, Pub. by Osprey) Stackpole.

— Quebec, 1759. (Order of Battle Ser.: Vol. 3). (Illus.). 96p. 1999. pap. 19.95 (*1-85532-847-X*, Pub. by Osprey) Stackpole.

— Spanish Army of the Napoleonic Wars 1808-1812, Vol. 332. 1999. pap. text 12.95 (*1-85532-765-1*) Greenhill Bks.

— Spanish Army of the Napoleonic Wars 1812-1815, 334. 1999. pap. text 12.95 (*1-85532-764-3*) Ospry.

Chartrand, Rene & Leliepvre, Eugene. Louis XV's Army Vol. 5: Colonial & Naval Troops. (Men-at-Arms Ser.: No. 313). (Illus.). 48p. 1998. pap. 12.95 (*1-85532-709-0*, Pub. by Osprey) Stackpole.

Chartrand, Rene & Lellepvre, Eugene. Louis XV's Army Vol. 3: Foreign Infantry. (Men-at-Arms Ser.: Vol. 304). (Illus.). 48p. 1997. pap. 12.95 (*1-85532-623-X*, Pub. by Osprey) Stackpole.

— Louis XV's Army Vol. 4: Specialist & Light Troops. (Men-at-Arms Ser.: Vol. 308). (Illus.). 48p. 1997. pap. 12.95 (*1-85532-624-8*, Pub. by Osprey) Stackpole.

Chartrand, Robert L., ed. Critical Issues in the Information Age. LC 91-8790. (Illus.). 352p. 1991. 47.50 (*0-8108-2402-7*) Scarecrow.

Chartrand, Sabra, jt. auth. see Jett, Joseph.

Chartrand, Sabra, jt. auth. see Schiavo, Mary.

Chartwell. Illustrated Reference Manual: Hands & Faces. 1990. 22.98 (*1-55521-506-8*) Bk Sales Inc.

— Illustrator's Reference Manual: Children. 1990. 22.98 (*1-55521-565-3*) Bk Sales Inc.

— Illustrator's Reference Manual: Nudes. 1990. 22.98 (*1-55521-507-6*) Bk Sales Inc.

Charubel. The Degrees of the Zodiac Symbolised. 2nd ed. 136p. 1996. pap. 15.00 (*0-7873-0165-5*) Hlth Research.

Charubhun, S. Dictionary English - Thai. (ENG & THA.). 691p. 1991. reprint ed. lib. bdg. 59.95 (*0-8288-2623-4*, F55520) Fr & Eur.

Charuchandra Guha. Modern Anglo Bengali Dictionary with Scientific & Technical Terms, 2 vols. (BEN & ENG.). 2528p. 1919. 95.00 (*0-7859-9829-2*) Fr & Eur.

***Charuhas, Chris.** In-House Web Publishing: How to Build & Maintain Effective Web Sites Using Your... Burke, Kate & Mull, Meghan, eds. (Illus.). 130p. 2000. pap. 36.00 (*0-9702795-0-7*) Topografik.

Charuhas, Mary S. Algebra. 4th ed. (Essential Mathematics for Life Ser.: No. 6). 1995. pap. text 7.95 (*0-02-802612-8*) Glencoe.

— Decimals & Fractions. 4th ed. (Essential Mathematics for Life Ser.: No. 2). 1995. pap. text 7.95 (*0-02-802609-8*) Glencoe.

— Geometry. 4th ed. (Essential Mathematics for Life Ser.: No. 5). 1995. pap. text 7.95 (*0-02-802613-6*) Glencoe.

— Graphs, Measures & Statistics. 4th ed. (Essential Mathematics for Life Ser.: No. 4). 1995. pap. text 7.95 (*0-02-802611-X*) Glencoe.

— Percents & Proportions. 4th ed. (Essential Mathematics for Life Ser.: No. 3). 1995. pap. text 7.95 (*0-02-802610-1*) Glencoe.

— Problem Solving. (Essential Mathematics for Life Ser.: No. 8). 1995. pap. text 7.95 (*0-02-802614-4*) Glencoe.

An Asterisk (*) at the beginning of an entry indicates that the title is appearing for the first time.

— Review of Whole Numbers Through Algebra. (Essential Mathematics for Life Ser.: No. 7). 1995. pap. text 7.95 (*0-02-802615-2*) Glencoe.

— Whole Numbers. 4th ed. (Essential Mathematics for Life Ser.: No. 1). 1995. pap. text 7.95 (*0-02-802608-X*) Glencoe.

Charukov, Georgi. Bulgarian Monasteries: Monuments of History, Culture & Art. 382p. 1981. 149.00 (*0-569-08507-1*) St Mut.

***Charupakorn, Joe.** Chords: Over 40,000 Chords. 208p. 1999. otabind 14.95 (*1-57560-198-2*, Pub. by Cherry Lane) H Leonard.

— Scales. 224p. 2000. otabind 14.95 (*1-57560-245-8*, Pub. by Cherry Lane) H Leonard.

Charushin, Victor. Alekhine's Block: The Tactician's Handbook. 96p. 1997. pap. 11.95 (*1-886846-06-5*) Pickard & Son.

— Combination Cross: The Tactician's Handbook. 96p. 1997. pap. 11.95 (*1-886846-08-1*) Pickard & Son.

— Lasker's Combination Vol. 4: The Tacticions Handbook. 112p. 1998. pap. 15.95 (*1-886846-13-8*) Pickard & Son.

— Mitrofanovs Deflection. 1998. pap. 13.50 (*1-886846-12-X*) Pickard & Son.

Charvat, J., et al. Review of the Nature & Uses of Examinations in Medical Education. (Public Health Papers: No. 36). 74p. 1968. pap. text 7.00 (*92-4-130036-1*, 1110036) World Health.

Charvat, Jan M. Managing Operations in the Chemical Industry by Aggregate Quality. (European University Studies: Economics & Management: Ser. 5, Vol. 1086). (Illus.). 123p. 1990. pap. 22.00 (*3-261-04213-3*) P Lang Pubng.

Charvat, William. Literary Publishing in America, 1790-1850. LC 92-2663. 104p. (C). 1993. reprint ed. pap. 10.95 (*0-87023-801-9*) U of Mass Pr.

— Origins of American Critical Thought, 1810-1835. (BCL1-PS American Literature Ser.). 218p. 1993. reprint ed. lib. bdg. 79.00 (*0-7812-6564-9*) Rprt Serv.

— The Profession of Authorship in America, 1800-1870. 368p. 1992. text 57.50 (*0-231-07076-4*); pap. text 20.00 (*0-231-07077-2*) Col U Pr.

Charvat, William, ed. see Hawthorne, Nathaniel.

Charvet, John. The Idea of an Ethical Community. LC 95-6969. 280p. 1995. text 37.50 (*0-8014-3155-7*) Cornell U Pr.

— The Social Problems in the Philosophy of Rousseau. LC 73-88311. (Cambridge Studies in the History & Theory of Politics). 158p. reprint ed. pap. 45.10 (*0-608-12261-0*, 2024436) Bks Demand.

Charvet, Shelle. Words That Change Minds: Mastering the Language of Influence. 2nd ed. LC 97-70788. 240p. 1997. per. 14.95 (*0-7872-3479-6*) Kendall-Hunt.

***Charvier-Berman, Evelyne & Cummings, Anne C.** A L'Aventure: An Introduction to French Language & Francophone Cultures. 288p. 1998. pap., wbk. ed. 45.95 (*0-471-16586-7*) Wiley.

— Student Tape to Accompany a L'Aventure: An Introdoction to French Language & Francophone Cultures & Workbook & Laboratory Manual to Accompany a L'Aventure. 487p. 1997. 115.90 incl. audio (*0-471-19719-X*) Wiley.

Charvier-Berman, Evelyne, jt. auth. see Cummings, Anne C.

Charvolin, J., et al, eds. Liquids at Interfaces: Proceedings of the Les Houches Summer School, Course XLVIII, May-June, 1988. (Houches Summer School Proceedings Ser.: Vol. 48). xxxvi, 644p. 1990. 256.50 (*0-444-88450-5*, North Holland) Elsevier.

Charvosset, H. & Nickel-Pepin-Donat, B., eds. Advanced Methodologies in Coal Characterization. (Coal Science & Technology Ser.: No. 15). xxii,442p. 1990. 281.50 (*0-444-88695-8*) Elsevier.

Chary, M. Srinivas. The Eagle & the Peacock: U.S. Foreign Policy Toward India since Independence, 345. LC 93-44511. (Contributions in Political Science Ser.: No. 345). 208p. 1995. 62.95 (*0-313-27602-1*, Greenwood Pr) Greenwood.

***Charyn, Jerome.** The Black Swan: A Memoir. LC 00-25192. (Illus.). 192p. 2000. 21.95 (*0-312-20877-4*, Thomas Dunne) St Martin.

Charyn, Jerome. El Bronx. 1998. mass mkt. write for info. (*0-446-40538-8*, Mysterious Paperbk) Warner Bks.

— El Bronx. large type ed. LC 97-6332. (Cloak & Dagger Ser.). 292p. 1997. 23.95 (*0-7862-1092-3*) Thorndike Pr.

— Captain Kidd. LC 99-21747. 208p. 1999. text 20.95 (*0-312-20506-6*) St Martin.

— Citizen Sidel. LC 98-16360. 224p. 1999. 23.00 (*0-89296-605-X*, Pub. by Mysterious Pr) Little.

— Death of a Tango King. LC 97-33913. 216p. 1998. 21.95 (*0-8147-1575-3*) NYU Pr.

— Elsinore. 256p. 1992. mass mkt. 4.99 (*0-446-40111-0*, Pub. by Warner Bks) Little.

— Margot in Badtown. Bharucha, Fershid, ed. Irwin, Mary, tr. from FRE. (Illus.). 48p. 1991. reprint ed. 14.95 (*1-879450-61-5*) Kitchen Sink.

— Maria's Girls. 288p. 1993. mass mkt. 5.50 (*0-446-40046-7*, Pub. by Warner Bks) Little.

— Marilyn la Dingue.Tr. of Marilyn the Wild. (FRE.). 246p. 1988. pap. 10.95 (*0-7859-2106-0*, 2070380920) Fr & Eur.

— Metropolis: New York As Myth, Marketplace, & Magical Land. 304p. 1987. pap. 8.95 (*0-380-70401-3*, Avon Bks) Morrow Avon.

— Montezuma's Man. 288p. 1993. 18.95 (*0-89296-461-8*) Mysterious Pr.

— Montezuma's Man. 272p. 1994. mass mkt. 5.99 (*0-446-40047-5*, Pub. by Warner Bks) Little.

— Movieland: Hollywood & the Great American Dream Culture. LC 96-22128. (Illus.). 304p. (C). 1996. pap. text 18.50 (*0-8147-1550-8*) NYU Pr.

— The Seventh Babe. LC 95-50635. 352p. (C). 1996. pap. 16.95 (*0-87805-882-6*) U Pr of Miss.

— The Tar Baby. LC 94-25163. (Illus.). 243p. 1995. pap. 10.95 (*1-56478-078-3*) Dalkey Arch.

— Zyeux-Bleus. (FRE.). 253p. 1989. pap. 10.95 (*0-7859-2111-7*, 2070381137) Fr & Eur.

Charyn, Jerome, ed. The Crime Lover's Casebook. 400p. 1996. mass mkt. 5.99 (*0-451-18679-6*, Sig) NAL.

Chas, Cherokee. Y2K & You & Yours. 50p. 1999. 9.95 (*0-9670685-0-9*) H & H Ltd.

Chasan, Alice, ed. Attacks on the Press in 1997: A Worldwide Survey. (Attacks on the Press Ser.). (Illus.). 443p. 1998. pap. 30.00 (*0-944823-17-3*) Comm to Protect Jrnlists.

Chasan, Alice, ed. see Bilello, Suzanne, et al.

Chasan, Alice, ed. see Simon, Joel & Kerina, Kakuna.

Chasan, D. J. Water Link: A History of Puget Sound As a Resource. LC 81-11457. (Puget Sound Bks.). (Illus.). 192p. 1981. pap. 9.95 (*0-295-95782-4*) U of Wash Pr.

Chasan, Daniel J. On the Air: The King Broadcasting Story. (Illus.). 256p. Date not set. 22.95 (*0-9615580-6-7*); pap. 14.95 (*0-9615580-7-5*) Island Pubs WA.

— Speaker of the House: The Political Career & Times of John L. O'Brien. (Illus.). 208p. 1989. 19.95 (*0-295-96848-6*) U of Wash Pr.

Chasan, Daniel J., jt. auth. see Strickland, Richard.

***Chasan, Neil. Total Conditioning for Golfers: The Swing Reaction System Biochemical Golf Fitness Program. LC 00-190521. (Illus.). 146p. 2000. pap. 24.95 (*0-9679331-0-2*) Sports Reaction.**

Total Conditioning for Golfers is the definitive work on golf specific fitness on the market today. Based on the award winning video (The Swing Reaction System, 1996), the book represents a significant update to the original exercises presented in the video. New exercises are introduced & the original exercises are updated & explained with careful instructions, making it an easy read. A clear scientific basis for the model is offered allowing the reader to really understand the various exercises. Further, in this book, there is much, much more offered to help the golfer prepare to play. Over 200 clear photographs illustrate: - The biomechanics of the golf swing - The Swing Reaction System exercises - Pre game warm up routine - Swing Reaction exercises for Natural Golf - Daily stretching routine & more. Total Conditioning for Golfers also offers a very practical approach to the mental side of the game, as well as a sensible approach to nutrition for golfers. A new fitness tool, The Golf Gizmo is introduced with several specific illustrated exercises. Finally, there are pages of additional total body conditioning exercises in the appendix for players who wish to take their exercise program beyond golf. *Publisher Paid Annotation.*

Chasdi, Eleanor H., ed. Culture & Human Development: The Selected Papers of John Whiting. LC 92-38907. (Publications of the Society for Psychological Anthropology: No. 6). (Illus.). 372p. (C). 1994. text 74.95 (*0-521-43515-3*) Cambridge U Pr.

Chasdi, Richard J. Serenade of Suffering: A Portrait of Middle East Terrorism, 1968-1993. LC 98-52753. 304p. 1999. 45.00 (*0-7391-0057-2*) Lxngtn Bks.

Chase. Cpsm Prod & Ops Mgmt Sel Cpt. 8th ed. 1998. pap. text 41.25 (*0-07-229422-1*) McGraw.

— Developing Perspectives in College Literacy. 2nd ed. (C). 1997. 36.93 (*0-673-38155-2*) Addson-Wesley Educ.

***Chase.** General Statistics. 4th ed. 1999. pap. text, teacher ed. 59.95 (*0-471-28312-6*) Wiley.

— General Statistics. 4th ed. 70p. 1999. pap. 27.95 (*0-471-28311-8*) Wiley.

— General Statistics 4th ed. 1999. text 89.95 incl. audio compact disk (*0-471-35963-7*) Wiley.

— General Statistics with Minitab Set. 769p. 1996. text 122.45 (*0-471-17532-3*) Wiley.

— Guide to Office 2000: Troubleshooting & Problem Solving. (Programming Language Ser.). (C). 2000. text 48.95 (*0-619-01519-5*) Course Tech.

Chase. Prod. Oper. Manag. 8th ed. 1997. 89.06 (*0-07-561278-X*) McGraw.

— Prod. Oper. Manag. 8th ed. 240p. 1998. pap. 30.00 (*0-07-292737-2*) McGraw.

***Chase.** Production Operation Management. 9th ed. 2000. pap. text 23.50 (*0-07-239279-7*) McGraw.

Chase, ed. Testbank Modern Labor Economy. 5th ed. 1997. pap. text 11.00 (*0-673-55514-3*) P-H.

Chase & Krantz. International Relations Between Wars. 1990. pap. text. write for info. (*0-582-86840-8*, Pub. by Addison-Wesley) Longman.

Chase, A. R. Compendium of Ornamental Foliage Plant Diseases. LC 87-70833. (Disease Compendium Ser.). (Illus.). 120p. (Orig.). 1987. pap. text 42.00 (*0-89054-077-2*) Am Phytopathol Soc.

— Foliage Plant Diseases: Diagnosis & Control. (Illus.). 168p. 1997. 79.00 (*0-89054-179-5*) Am Phytopathol Soc.

Chase, A. R. & Broschat, T. K., eds. Diseases & Disorders of Ornamental Palms. LC 91-70724. (Illus.). 64p. 1991. 42.00 (*0-89054-119-1*) Am Phytopathol Soc.

Chase, A. R., et al. Diseases of Annuals & Perennials; A Ball Guide: Identification & Control. LC 95-11629. (Illus.). 208p. 1995. pap. text 59.95 (*1-883052-08-4*, B025) Ball Pub.

Chase, A. R., jt. auth. see Daughtrey, Margery.

Chase, Agnes. First Book of Grasses: The Structure of Grasses Explained for Beginners. 3rd ed. LC 76-48919. (Smithsonian Publication Ser.: No. 4351). (Illus.). 149p. reprint ed. pap. 46.20 (*0-608-17454-8*, 202992000067) Bks Demand.

Chase, Agnes, ed. see Smithsonian Institution, Washington, D. C. Staff.

Chase, Aleka. The Beginning of Difficulty. High, John & Garcia, Malcolm, eds. LC 89-83408. (Five Fingers Book Ser.: No. 1). 60p. (Orig.). 1989. pap. 5.00 (*0-9618409-3-5*) Five Fingers.

Chase, Aleka, et al, eds. Mapping Codes: A Collection of New Writing from Moscow to San Francisco. (Review Ser.: No. 8/9). 286p. (Orig.). 1990. pap. 9.00 (*0-9618409-8-6*) Five Fingers.

— Vanishing Points: Spirituality & the Avant-Garde. (Review Ser.: No. 10). (Illus.). 300p. (Orig.). 1991. pap. 9.00 (*0-9618409-5-1*) Five Fingers.

Chase, Alex. Technology in the 20th Century. (In the 20th Century Ser.). (Illus.). 184p. (YA). (gr. 7 up). 1997. pap. 9.95 (*0-912517-25-5*) Bluewood Bks.

Chase, Alston. In a Dark Wood: The Fight over Forest & the New Tyranny of Ecology. 479p. 1995. 29.95 (*0-395-60837-6*, Pub. by Ticknor & Fields) HM.

***Chase, Alston.** In a Dark Wood: The Fight over Forests & the Rising Tyranny of Ecology. 545p. 2000. pap. 21.95 (*0-7658-0752-1*) Transaction Pubs.

Chase, Alston. Playing God in Yellowstone: The Destruction of America's First National Park. (Illus.). 480p. 1987. pap. 16.00 (*0-15-672036-1*, Harvest Bks) Harcourt.

Chase, Alston H. & Phillips, Henry, Jr. New Introduction to Greek. 3rd enl. rev. ed. LC 61-13748. (Illus.). 235p. 1961. 29.00 (*0-674-61600-6*) HUP.

Chase, Alston H. & Phillips, Henry, Jr., eds. New Greek Reader. LC 54-12234. (Illus.). 480p. (gr. 10 up). reprint ed. 148.80 (*0-8357-9169-6*, 201672800005) Bks Demand.

Chase, Alyssa. Jomo & Mata. LC 93-25206. (Key Concepts in Personal Development Ser.). (Illus.). 32p. (J). (gr. k-4). 1993. teacher ed. 79.95 incl. VHS (*1-55942-054-5*, 9375) Marsh Media.

— Jomo & Mata. LC 93-25206. (Key Concepts in Personal Development Ser.). (Illus.). 32p. (J). (gr. 1-4). 1993. 16.95 (*1-55942-051-0*, 7656) Marsh Media.

— Tessa on Her Own. (Key Concepts in Personal Development Ser.). (Illus.). 32p. (J). (gr. 1-4). 1994. 16.95 (*1-55942-064-2*, 7659) Marsh Media.

Chase, Andrew. The Asian Bistro Cookbook. (Illus.). 192p. (Orig.). 1997. pap. 17.95 (*1-896503-21-7*, Pub. by R Rose Inc) Firefly Bks Ltd.

Chase, Anna, jt. auth. see Ford, Judy.

Chase, Anthony. Law & History: The Evolution of the American Legal System. LC 96-54048. 1997. 25.00 (*1-56584-367-3*, Pub. by New Press NY) Norton.

— Law & History: The Evolution of the American Legal System. 219p. 1999. pap. 15.95 (*1-56584-516-1*, Pub. by New Press NY) Norton.

Chase, Arlen F., jt. ed. see Chase, Diane Z.

Chase, Audrie A., ed. see Harmon, Ada D.

Chase, Barbara, compiled by. The Life & Times of William S. Kelly: His Descendants & Related Families. LC 96-6967. 1996. write for info. (*0-87152-497-X*) Reprint.

Chase, Billy & Grimaldi, Lenny. Chased: Alone, Black & Undercover. LC 93-84522. 1993. 22.95 (*0-88282-077-X*) New Horizon NJ.

Chase Brass & Copper Co. Evaluation of Clears for Protection of Copper-Base Alloys. 131p. 1966 19.60 (*0-317-34523-0*, 16) Intl Copper.

Chase, C. B. Sherwood Anderson. LC 72-3565. (Studies in Fiction: No. 34). 1972. reprint ed. lib. bdg. 75.00 (*0-8383-1543-7*) M S G Haskell Hse.

***Chase, C. David.** Wiesenberger's Investment Performance Digest 1999: Performance & Rankings of the World's Major Investments, 1960-1999. (Illus.). 412p. 1999. 28.95 (*0-944822-11-8*) Wiesenberger.

Chase, Carl A. Introduction to Nautical Science. 1991. 24.95 (*0-393-02850-X*) Norton.

Chase, Carol, jt. auth. see Chase, Deborah.

Chase, Carole F. Suncatcher: A Study of Madeleine L'Engle & Her Writing. 2nd rev. ed. LC 98-36232. 224p. 1998. pap. 15.95 (*1-880913-31-3*) Innisfree Pr.

— Suncatcher: A Study of Madeleine L'Engle & Her Writing. 2nd rev. ed. LC 98-36232. 224p. 1998. 25.95 (*1-880913-32-1*) Innisfree Pr.

Chase, Carole F., jt. auth. see L'Engle, Madeleine.

Chase, Carroll & Cabeen, Richard M. The First Hundred Years of United States Territorial Postmarks Seventeen Eighty-Seven to Eighteen Eighty-Seven. LC 79-67393. 341p. 1980. reprint ed. lib. bdg. 40.00 (*0-88000-112-7*) Quarterman.

Chase, Charles E., jt. auth. see Metropolitan Dade County, Historic Preservation Di.

Chase, Charles M. & Chase, Jacqueline E. Tips from the Trenches: America's Best Teachers Describe Effective Classroom Methods. LC 93-60578. 180p. 1997. pap. text 24.95 (*1-56676-054-2*) Scarecrow.

Chase, Charlie. Little Book Poems & Other Things from the Connecticut Store. 24p. 1996. pap. text 5.00 (*1-887012-02-8*) Hanovr Pr.

Chase, Chris, jt. auth. see King, Alan.

Chase, Christopher, jt. auth. see Abboud, Hisham.

Chase, Christopher H., et al, eds. Developmental Dyslexia: Neural, Cognitive, & Genetic Mechanisms. LC 96-10323. 1996. pap. 38.00 (*0-912752-39-4*) York Pr.

Chase, Cleveland B. The Young Voltaire. LC 79-160962. (Select Bibliographies Reprint Ser.). 1977. reprint ed. 24.95 (*0-8369-5830-6*) Ayer.

Chase, Clifford. The Hurry-Up Song: A Memoir of Losing My Brother. LC 99-15553. (Living Out). (Illus.). 220p. 2000. reprint ed. pap. 18.95 (*0-299-16624-4*) U of Wis Pr.

— Queer 13: Lesbian & Gay Writers Recall Seventh Grade. 288p. 1999. pap. 14.00 (*0-688-17161-3*, Wm Morrow) Morrow Avon.

Chase, Clifford, ed. Queer 13: Lesbian & Gay Writers Recall Seventh Grade. LC 98-17147. 288p. 1999. 24.00 (*0-688-15811-0*, Wm Morrow) Morrow Avon.

Chase, Clint. Essentials of Measurement for Educators. LC 98-25259. 432p. (C). 1998. pap. text 59.00 (*0-8013-1372-4*) Addison-Wesley.

Chase, Clinton I. Measurement for Educational Evaluation. 2nd ed. LC 77-79456. (Illus.). 1978. teacher ed. write for info. (*0-201-01006-2*); student ed. write for info. (*0-201-01029-1*) Addison-Wesley.

Chase, Clinton I., jt. auth. see Jacobs, Lucy C.

Chase, Colin. Dating of Beowulf. rev. ed. LC 97-179838. (Toronto Old English Studies). 220p. 1997. reprint ed. pap. text 19.95 (*0-8020-7879-6*) U of Toronto Pr.

Chase, Colin, ed. The Dating of Beowulf. (Old English Ser.). 1981. text 45.00 (*0-8020-5576-1*) U of Toronto Pr.

— The Dating of Beowulf. LC 82-102433. (Toronto Old English Ser.: No. 6). 229p. reprint ed. pap. 71.00 (*0-608-16746-0*, 205612800050) Bks Demand.

— Two Alcuin Letter-Books. (LAT.). viii, 84p. pap. text 7.43 (*0-88844-454-0*) Brill Academic Pubs.

Chase, Craig L., ed. Biomass Energy: A Glossary of Terms. (Illus.). 61p. 1998. pap. text 20.00 (*0-7881-7256-5*) DIANE Pub.

Chase, Cynthia. Decomposing Figures: Rhetorical Readings in the Romantic Tradition. LC 85-45868. 248p. reprint ed. pap. 76.90 (*0-608-05932-3*, 206626800008) Bks Demand.

— Romanticism. (C). 1992. text 57.50 (*0-582-05000-6*) Addison-Wesley.

— Romanticism Longman Crit. (C). 1993. pap. text 28.13 (*0-582-04799-4*, Pub. by Addison-Wesley) Longman.

Chase, Cynthia, intro. Romanticism. LC 92-14309. (Critical Readers Ser.). 272p. (C). 1992. pap. text 18.25 (*0-685-72519-7*, 79348) Longman.

Chase, D., et al. The History of the Church Family. Arnold, J. N., et al. 144p. 1993. reprint ed. pap. 21.00 (*0-8328-1347-8*); reprint ed. lib. bdg. 31.00 (*0-8328-1346-X*) Higginson Bk Co.

Chase, D. B. & Rabolt, J. F., eds. Fourier Transform Raman Spectroscopy: From Concept to Experiment. (Illus.). 274p. 1994. text 78.00 (*0-12-169430-5*) Acad Pr.

Chase, D. P., tr. from GRE. The Ethics of Aristotle. 357p. 1986. reprint ed. pap. 28.95 (*0-935005-83-8*) Lincoln-Rembrandt.

Chase, D. P., tr. see Aristotle.

Chase, David. A Peasant of West Brattleboro. 192p. (Orig.). 1987. pap. 9.95 (*0-9618750-0-3*) Elm Corners Pr.

Chase, David J., jt. auth. see Seng, Phil T.

Chase, Deborah. Fruit Acids for Fabulous Skin. 1996. mass mkt. 5.99 (*0-312-95769-6*) St Martin.

— The New Medically Based No-Nonsense Beauty Book. 416p. 1990. reprint ed. pap. 8.95 (*0-380-71203-2*, Avon Bks) Morrow Avon.

***Chase, Deborah.** Terms of Adornment: The Ultimate Guide to Accessories. LC 98-12710. (Illus.). 256p. 2000. pap. 15.00 (*0-06-273729-5*, HarpRes) HarpInfo.

Chase, Deborah. Terms of Adornment: The Ultimate Guide to Accessories: Everything You Need to Know about Buying, Collecting, Wearing & Caring for Them. LC 98-12710. (Illus.). 256p. 1999. 22.00 (*0-06-273454-7*) HarpC.

Chase, Deborah & Chase, Carol. Every Bride Is Beautiful: The Complete Guide to Wedding Beauty from Head to Toe. LC 98-30163. (Illus.). 208p. 1999. 25.00 (*0-688-15426-3*, Wm Morrow) Morrow Avon.

Chase, Debra. Child Crying Rock: The Blood Remembers. LC 98-56001. 396p. 1999. pap. 16.95 (*1-893652-05-X*, Writers Club Pr) iUniversecom.

***Chase, Diana.** Surf's Up. 1999. 12.95 (*1-86368-250-3*, Pub. by Fremantle Arts) Intl Spec Bk.

Chase, Diana. Timeslip. 165p. 1997. pap. 10.95 (*1-86368-187-6*, Pub. by Fremantle Arts) Intl Spec Bk.

Chase, Diane Z. & Chase, Arlen F., eds. Mesoamerican Elites: An Archaeological Assessment. LC 91-40064. (Illus.). 375p. 1994. reprint ed. pap. 18.95 (*0-8061-2666-3*) U of Okla Pr.

Chase Doane, Doris. The Versatility of Astrology. LC 98-200283. 208p. 1997. pap. 22.00 (*0-86690-480-8*, D3696-014) Am Fed Astrologers.

Chase, Don M. He Opened the West. LC 97-12160. (Illus.). 40p. 1986. reprint ed. pap. 3.00 (*0-9612094-1-0*) J Smith Soc.

Chase-Dunn, Christopher. Global Formation: Structures of the World Economy. 2nd ed. LC 98-8613. 500p. 1998. reprint ed. 65.00 (*0-8476-9101-2*) Rowman.

***Chase-Dunn, Christopher.** Global Formation: Structures of the World Economy. 2nd ed. LC 98-8613. 500p. 1998. reprint ed. pap. 26.95 (*0-8476-9102-0*) Rowman.

Chase-Dunn, Christopher, jt. auth. see Boswell, Terry.

Chase-Dunn, Christopher K., ed. The Historical Evolution of the International Political Economy, 2 vols. LC 94-47403. (Library of International Political Economy: Vol. 9). 1184p. 1995. 415.00 (*1-85278-985-9*) E Elgar.

— Socialist States in the World-System. LC 82-10725. (Sage Focus Editions Ser.: No. 58). (Illus.). 304p. reprint ed. pap. 94.30 (*0-8357-8484-3*, 203475200091) Bks Demand.

C

Chase-Dunn, Christopher K. & Hall, Thomas D. Rise & Demise: Comparing World Systems. LC 96-52141. (New Perspectives in Sociology Ser.). 336p. (C). 1997. pap. text 30.00 (*0-8133-1006-7*, Pub. by Westview) HarpC.

Chase-Dunn, Christopher K. & Mann, Kelly M. The Wintu & Their Neighbors: A Very Small World-System in Northern California. LC 97-45386. (Illus.). 310p. 1998. 35.00 (*0-8165-1800-9*) U of Ariz Pr.

Chase-Dunn, Christopher K., jt. auth. see Bornschier, Volker.

Chase, Edith N. The New Baby Calf. (Illus.). 32p. (J). (ps-3). 1991. pap. 4.99 (*0-590-44776-9*) Scholastic Inc.

— Twigs from My Tree. LC 83-22408. (Illus.). 79p. (Orig.). 1984. pap. 8.95 (*0-87233-074-5*) Bauhan.

Chase, Edith N. & Lefebvre, Yolaine. Model Clause Library. 32p. 55.00 (*0-614-05184-3*, MCL11943.0M) ASFE.

Chase, Edward T., ed. see Geus, Averill D.

Chase, Elaine R. Calculated Risk. large type ed. LC 98-31819. 1999. 30.00 (*0-7862-1737-5*, G K Hall Lrg Type) Mac Lib Ref.

***Chase, Elaine Raco.** Video Vixen. large type ed. LC 00-21591. (Thorndike Romance Ser.). 2000. 25.95 (*0-7862-2490-8*) Thorndike Pr.

Chase, Elaine Raco & Wingate, Anne. Amateur Detectives: A Writer's Guide to How Private Citizens Solve Criminal Cases. (Howdunit Ser.). 240p. 1996. pap. 16.99 (*0-89879-725-X*, Wrtrs Digest Bks) F & W Pubns Inc.

Chase, Elise, compiled by. Healing Faith: An Annotated Bibliography of Christian Self-Help Books, 3. LC 85-929. (Bibliographies & Indexes in Religious Studies: No. 3). 199p. 1985. lib. bdg. 55.00 (*0-313-24014-0*, DHF/, Greenwood Pr) Greenwood.

Chase, Emily. Dinner Menus With Wine. Jacobs, Marjorie K. & Bannerman, Elizabeth, eds. (Wine Cookbook Ser.). (Illus.). 128p. 1983. pap. 9.95 (*0-932664-30-X*) Wine Appreciation.

— Three of a Kind. (J). 1985. pap. 1.95 (*0-590-33706-8*) Scholastic Inc.

— Wine Cookbook of Dinner Menus. (Illus.). 1978. 6.95 (*0-932664-04-0*) Wine Appreciation.

— With Friends Like That. (Girls of Canby Hall Ser.: No. 11). 192p. (Orig.). (J). (gr. 7 up). 1985. pap. 2.25 (*0-590-40869-0*) Scholastic Inc.

Chase, Emma L., ed. see Chivers, Thomas Holley.

Chase, Ezra B. Teachings of Patriots & Statesmen: Or, the 'Founders of the Republic' on Slavery. LC 72-83941. (Black Heritage Library Collection). 1977. 24.95 (*0-8369-8535-4*) Ayer.

Chase, Fannie S. Wiscasset in Pownalborough: A History of the Shire Town & Salent Historical Features of the Territory Between the Sheepscot & Kennebee Rivers. (Illus.). 640p. 1990. reprint ed. lib. bdg. 64.50 (*0-8328-1643-4*) Higginson Bk Co.

Chase, Francis S. Education Faces New Demands. LC 56-12940. (Horace Mann Lecture Sers). 57p. reprint ed. 30.00 (*0-8357-9754-6*, 201787400010) Bks Demand.

Chase, Franklin H. Syracuse & Its Environs: A History, 3 vols. in 2. (Illus.). 3385p. 1997. reprint ed. lib. bdg. 140.00 (*0-8328-6256-8*) Higginson Bk Co.

Chase, Fred, ed. see Jones, Frances.

Chase, Frederic H. Lemuel Shaw, Chief Justice of the Supreme Court of Massachusetts, 1830-1860. 1977. 17.95 (*0-8369-7104-3*, 7938) Ayer.

Chase, Frederic H., Jr., tr. see St. John of Damascus.

Chase, G. Anderson. Auxiliary Sail Vessel Operations: For the Aspiring Professional Sailor. LC 97-4133. (Illus.). 320p. 1997. text 35.00 (*0-87033-493-X*) Cornell Maritime.

Chase, G. B. The Lowndes of South Carolina, an Historical & Genealogical Memoir. (Illus.). 81p. 1990. reprint ed. pap. 16.00 (*0-8328-1497-0*); reprint ed. lib. bdg. 24.00 (*0-8328-1496-2*) Higginson Bk Co.

Chase, G. H. The Shield Devices of the Greeks in Art & Literature. (Illus.). 90p. 1979. reprint ed. pap. 12.50 (*0-89005-260-3*) Ares.

Chase, Gail. The Eye & the Eyebrow: A History of Kas, Turkey & Castellorizo, Greece. 64p. (Orig.). (C). 1988. pap. 6.50 (*0-9619339-9-2*) G Chase.

Chase, Gary A., jt. auth. see Murphy, Edmond A.

Chase, George W. History of Haverhill. (Illus.). xx, 663p. 1993. reprint ed. lib. bdg. 68.50 (*0-8328-3146-8*) Higginson Bk Co.

— The History of Haverhill, Massachusetts. LC 83-61980. (Illus.). 700p. 1997. reprint ed. 59.50 (*0-89725-314-0*, 1230) Picton Pr.

— The History of Haverhill (Massachusetts) From Its First Settlement, in 1640, to the Year 1860. (Illus.). 683p. 1996. reprint ed. pap. 55.00 (*0-8063-4619-1*, 9178) Clearfield Co.

Chase, Georgiana P. Stratton's Islands of Saco Bay: An Interwoven History, 1605-1993. LC 93-78914. (Illus.). 126p. 1994. pap. 16.98 (*0-9637490-1-3*) Mendocino Lith.

***Chase, Gerald B.** The Earth Between. 256p. 2000. pap. 10.99 (*1-58169-046-0*, Third Stry Window) Genesis Comm Inc.

Chase, Gilbert. America's Music: From the Pilgrims to the Present. 3rd fac. rev. ed. LC 86-30795. (Music in American Life Ser.). (Illus.). 742p. 1994. pap. 200.00 (*0-7837-7613-6*, 204736500007) Bks Demand.

— America's Music: From the Pilgrims to the Present. 3rd rev. ed. 744p. 1992. pap. text 24.95 (*0-252-06275-2*) U of Ill Pr.

— Guide to the Music of Latin America. 2nd enl. rev. ed. LC 70-18910. (BCL Ser.: No. II). reprint ed. 62.50 (*0-404-08306-4*) AMS Pr.

Chase, Gordon & Reveal, Betsy. How to Manage in the Public Sector. 150p. (C). 1983. pap. 30.94 (*0-07-554853-4*) McGraw.

Chase, Grafton D. & Rabinowitz, Joseph L. Principles of Radioisotope Methodology. 3rd ed. LC 66-19903. (C). 1967. text. write for info. (*0-8087-0308-0*) Pearson Custom.

***Chase, H. Peter.** A Book for Coloring & Learning about Diabetes. 4th ed. Reece, Regina, ed. Orig. Title: A Coloring Book about Diabetes. (SPA., Illus.). 102p. (YA). (gr. 9 up). 2000. pap. 5.00 (*0-9675398-1-1*) Chldrn Diabte.

Chase, Harold S. Hope Ranch: A Rambling Record. rev. ed. Miller, Nancy, ed. (Illus.). 152p. 1994. reprint ed. text 22.50 (*0-929702-04-2*); reprint ed. pap. text 15.00 (*0-929702-05-0*) Mission Creek.

Chase, Harold W. Federal Judges: The Appointing Process. LC 72-189381. 256p. reprint ed. pap. 79.40 (*0-608-16071-7*, 203321100084) Bks Demand.

Chase, Harold W., jt. auth. see Ducat, Craig R.

Chase, Harold W., ed. see Corwin, Edward S.

Chase, Harry E. Eden in Winter. LC 78-71941. 1978. write for info. (*0-9601662-2-X*) C Schneider.

— Gold I Have Given Away. LC 82-62610. 1982. write for info. (*0-9601662-3-8*) C Schneider.

Chase, Helen W. Jethro Coffin House Chronology, 1686-1986. (Illus.). xiv, 163p. 1986. pap. text 15.00 (*0-9607340-7-4*) Nantucket Hist Assn.

Chase, Heman. Beginning at Williams Monument. LC 81-3605. (Illus.). 72p. 1981. pap. 8.95 (*0-87233-060-5*) Bauhan.

Chase, Henry. In Their Footsteps. 608p. 1995. write for info. (*0-8050-3246-0*) H Holt & Co.

— In Their Footsteps: The American Visions Guide to African-American Historical Sites. (Illus.). 608p. 1995. pap. 16.95 (*0-8050-2089-6*) H Holt & Co.

Chase, Henry & Sanbourn, Charles W. North & South: A Statistical View of the Conditions of the Free & Slave States. LC 75-116280. 191p. 1972. reprint ed. 13.00 (*0-403-00437-3*) Scholarly.

Chase, Holly. Turkish Tapestry: A Traveller's Portrait of Turkey. LC 92-74019. 300p. (Orig.). 1992. pap. 12.95 (*1-882443-00-4*) Bosphorus Bks.

Chase, J. Munsell. The Riddle of the Sphinx: A Key to the Mysteries & a Synthesis of Philosophy. 1991. lib. bdg. 79.95 (*0-8490-4999-7*) Gordon Pr.

— The Riddle of the Sphinx: A Key to the Mysteries & a Synthesis of Philosophy. 87p. 1996. reprint ed. spiral bd. 10.00 (*0-7873-0166-3*) Hlth Research.

— The Riddle of the Sphinx (1915) 86p. 1996. reprint ed. pap. 8.95 (*1-56459-934-5*) Kessinger Pub.

Chase, J. Smeaton. California Desert Trails. 1992. reprint ed. lib. bdg. 75.00 (*0-7812-5012-9*) Rprt Serv.

— Our Araby: Palm Springs & the Garden of the Sun. LC 87-18318. (Illus.). 86p. 1987. reprint ed. 9.95 (*0-9618724-0-3*) Palm Springs CA.

Chase, Jacqueline E., jt. auth. see Chase, Charles M.

Chase, James H. Le Fin Mot de l'Histoire. (FRE.). 1991. pap. 13.95 (*0-7859-2175-3*, 2070384209) Fr & Eur.

Chase, Jane. Kid-Tastic Birthday Parties: The Complete Party Planner for Today's Kids. LC 95-2014. (Illus.). 144p. (Orig.). 1995. pap. 11.95 (*0-918420-24-5*) Brighton Pubns.

Chase, Jean H. Georgie of Assateague: An Assateague Island Story. unabridged ed. Chase, Laurence I., ed. (Illus.). 48p. Date not set. 10.95 (*0-9641394-0-5*) Seachase Bks.

***Chase, Jefferson S.** Inciting Laughter: The Development of "Jewish Humor" in 19th Century German Culture. LC 99-58591. (European Cultures Ser.). 1999. write for info. (*3-11-016299-7*) De Gruyter.

Chase, Jefferson S., tr. see Mann, Thomas.

Chase, Jerry. Cinderella Wore Combat Boots. 1979. pap. 3.25 (*0-8222-0213-1*) Dramatists Play.

Chase, Jim. Backpacker Magazine's Guide to the Appalachian Trail. LC 88-28258. (Illus.). 256p. (Orig.). 1989. pap. 14.95 (*0-8117-2237-6*) Stackpole.

Chase, Joan. Bonneville Blue: Stories. 226p. 1991. 19.95 (*0-374-11539-7*) FS&G.

— During the Reign of the Queen of Persia. LC 96-216265. 1996. pap. 11.00 (*0-345-41046-7*) Ballantine Pub Grp.

— The Evening Wolves. 356p. 1989. text 18.95 (*0-374-15003-6*) FS&G.

Chase, Joan B. Retrolental Fibroplasia & Autistic Symptomatology: An Investigation into Some Relationships among Neonatal Environmental, Developmental & Affective Variables in Blind Prematures. LC 72-155922. (American Foundation for the Blind Research Ser.: No. 24). 237p. reprint ed. pap. 73.50 (*0-7837-0137-3*, 204042600016) Bks Demand.

Chase, JoAnne, jt. auth. see Moon, Constance.

Chase, John. Exterior Decoration: Hollywood's Inside-Out Houses. Gebhard, David, ed. LC 82-9268. (California Architecture & Architects Ser.: No. 2). (Illus.). 128p. 1982. pap. 24.50 (*0-912158-88-3*) Hennessey.

***Chase, John.** Glitter Stucco & Dumpster Diving. (Illus.). 1999. 45.00 (*1-85984-701-3*, Pub. by Verso) Norton.

Chase, John. Glitter, Stucco, & Dumpster Diving: Reflections on Building Production in the Vernacular City. 288p. 2000. 25.00 (*1-85984-807-9*, Pub. by Verso) Norton.

Chase, John, jt. auth. see Anderton, Frances.

Chase, John C. History of Chester, New Hampshire, Including Auburn: Supplement to History of Old Chester (1869) (Illus.). 535p. 1988. reprint ed. lib. bdg. 55.00 (*0-8328-0046-5*, NH0005) Higginson Bk Co.

Chase, John C. & Chamberlain, George W. Seven Generations of the Descendants of Aquila & Thomas Chase. LC 83-60849. (Illus.). 650p. 1998. reprint ed. 49.50 (*0-89725-038-9*, 1260) Picton Pr.

Chase, Jon. The Fight for Newton Corner: A Story of Neighborhood Development. LC 87-71133. (Illus.). 80p. (Orig.). (C). 1987. pap. 14.95 (*0-9618643-0-3*) Jon Chase.

Chase, Julianne. Inside Passage Walking Tours: Exploring Major Ports of Call in Southeast Alaska. (Illus.). 152p. 1998. pap. 14.95 (*1-57061-132-7*) Sasquatch Bks.

Chase, Karen. Eros & Psyche: The Representation of Personality in Charlotte Bronte, Charles Dickens, & George Eliot. 213p. 1984. pap. 11.95 (*0-416-36520-5*, NO. 4015) Routledge.

— George Eliot: "Middlemarch" (Landmarks of World Literature Ser.). (Illus.). 117p. (C). 1991. text 34.95 (*0-521-35021-2*); pap. text 11.95 (*0-521-35915-5*) Cambridge U Pr.

***Chase, Karen.** Kazimierz Square. LC 00-29502. 2000. pap. write for info. (*0-9678856-0-4*) Cavankerry.

Chase, Karen. Paddy Paws & Friends Presents Christmas. (Illus.). 60p. Date not set. pap. 9.95 (*1-57377-052-3*, 01988402248) Easl Pubns.

***Chase, Karen & Levenson, Michael H.** The Spectacle of Intimacy: A Public Life for the Victorian Family. LC 99-58479. (Illus.). 248p. 2000. text 39.50 (*0-691-00668-7*, Pub. by Princeton U Pr) Cal Prin Full Svc.

Chase, Kate. The Irq Book. LC 99-14544. 324p. (Orig.). 1999. pap. text 29.99 (*0-07-134698-8*) McGraw.

***Chase, Kate.** Sending & Receiving Instant Messages with ICQ. (Illus.). 128p. 2000. pap. 8.99 (*0-7645-8632-7*, CPG Pr) IDG Bks.

***Chase, Katherin.** Indian Painters of the Southwest: The Deep Remembering. (Indian Artists Convocation Ser.). (Illus.). 100p. 2000. pap. 30.00 (*0-933452-66-7*) Schol Am Res.

Chase, L., jt. ed. see Miller, B. E.

Chase-Lansdale, P. Lindsay & Brooks-Gunn, Jeanne, eds. Escape from Poverty: What Makes a Difference for Children? (Illus.). 352p. 1997. pap. text 24.95 (*0-521-62985-3*) Cambridge U Pr.

Chase-Lansdale, P. Lindsay & Gunn, Jeanne B., eds. Escape from Poverty: What Makes a Difference for Children? (Illus.). 341p. (C). 1996. text 59.95 (*0-521-44521-3*) Cambridge U Pr.

Chase, Larry. Essential Business m/OL. LC 98-13040. (Internet World Ser.). 320p. 1998. pap. text 29.99 (*0-471-25722-2*) Wiley.

Chase, Laurence I., ed. see Chase, Jean H.

Chase, Leah. The Dooky Chase Cookbook. LC 89-48272. (Illus.). 224p. 1990. 21.00 (*0-88289-661-X*) Pelican.

— Down Home Healthy: Family Recipes of Black American Chefs. 44p. (Orig.). 1994. pap. 4.75 (*0-16-045166-3*) USGPO.

Chase, Leah & Rivers, Johnny. Down Home Healthy: Family Recipes of Black American Chefs. (Illus.). 44p. (Orig.). (C). 1995. pap. text 20.00 (*0-7881-2063-8*) DIANE Pub.

Chase, Leslie R. & Landers, Robert, eds. Artificial Intelligence: Reality or Fantasy? 1984. 59.95 (*0-942774-19-1*) Info Indus.

Chase, Lewis N. Poe & His Poetry. LC 72-120973. (Poetry & Life Ser.). reprint ed. 16.00 (*0-404-52506-7*) AMS Pr.

— Poe & His Poetry. LC 75-38649. (Studies in Poe: No. 23). 1976. reprint ed. lib. bdg. 75.00 (*0-8383-2112-7*) M S G Haskell Hse.

Chase, Linda & Cerwinske, Laura. In Your Own Style: The Air of Creating Wonderful Rooms. LC 94-60035. (Illus.). 192p. 1999. pap. 24.95 (*0-500-28164-5*, Pub. by Thames Hudson) Norton.

Chase, Linda & St. George, Joyce. Perfect Cover. LC 93-14213. 352p. (J). 1994. 19.45 (*0-7868-6001-4*, Pub. by Hyperion) Time Warner.

Chase, Linda, et al. Perfect Cover. 320p. 1997. per. 6.99 (*0-671-52296-5*) PB.

Chase, Linda, jt. auth. see Cerwinske, Laura.

Chase, Linda, jt. ed. see Chase, Robert.

Chase, Loretta. Captives of the Night. 416p. (Orig.). 1994. mass mkt. 4.99 (*0-380-76648-5*, Avon Bks) Morrow Avon.

— The Devil's Delilah. 228p. 1989. 19.95 (*0-8027-1058-1*) Walker & Co.

— The English Witch. 192p. 1989. pap. 2.95 (*0-380-70660-1*, Avon Bks) Morrow Avon.

— The English Witch. large type ed. LC 90-11099. 317p. 1990. reprint ed. lib. bdg. 18.95 (*1-56054-046-X*) Thorndike Pr.

— Isabella. 176p. 1989. pap. 2.95 (*0-380-70597-4*, Avon Bks) Morrow Avon.

— Isabella. large type ed. LC 90-10983. 257p. 1990. reprint ed. lib. bdg. 19.95 (*1-56054-010-9*) Thorndike Pr.

Chase, Loretta. Knaves' Wager. 228p. 1990. 19.95 (*0-8027-1114-6*) Walker & Co.

Chase, Loretta. Knaves' Wager. large type ed. LC 90-47662. 350p. 1991. reprint ed. lib. bdg. 18.95 (*1-56054-085-0*) Thorndike Pr.

***Chase, Loretta.** The Last Hellion. LC 99-26433. 1999. 26.95 (*0-7862-1989-0*) Five Star.

Chase, Loretta. The Last Hellion. 304p. 1998. mass mkt. 5.99 (*0-380-77617-0*, Avon Bks) Morrow Avon.

— The Lion's Daughter. 384p. (Orig.). 1992. mass mkt. 5.99 (*0-380-76647-7*, Avon Bks) Morrow Avon.

***Chase, Loretta.** Lord of Scoundrels. LC 99-45472. 1999. 26.95 (*0-7862-2252-2*) Mac Lib Ref.

Chase, Loretta. Lord of Scoundrels. 384p. 1995. mass mkt. 6.50 (*0-380-77616-2*, Avon Bks) Morrow Avon.

— The Sandalwood Princess. 240p. 1991. mass mkt. 3.99 (*0-380-71455-8*, Avon Bks) Morrow Avon.

Chase, Loretta. The Sandalwood Princess. 224p. 1991. 18.95 (*0-8027-1128-6*) Walker & Co.

— Viscount Vagabond. 240p. 1990. mass mkt. 2.95 (*0-380-70836-1*, Avon Bks) Morrow Avon.

Chase, Loretta. Viscount Vagabond. 192p. 1988. 18.95 (*0-8027-1046-8*) Walker & Co.

***Chase, Loretta L.** Captives of the Night. LC 99-89599. 2000. write for info. (*0-7862-2368-5*) Mac Lib Ref.

Chase, Lucien B. English Serfdom & American Slavery: Or, Ourselves As Others See Us. LC 77-83929. (Black Heritage Library Collection). 1977. 16.95 (*0-8369-8536-2*) Ayer.

Chase, M. W. & National Institute of Standards & Technology Staff. NIST-JANAF Thermochemical Tables, 2 vols. 4th ed. LC 98-86732. (Journal of Physical & Chemical Reference Data Ser.). xi, 1951p. 1998. write for info. (*1-56396-820-7*) Am Inst Physics.

***Chase, Malcolm.** Early Trade Unionism: Fraternity, Skill & the Politics of Labour. LC 99-41555. (Studies in Labour History). 286p. (C). 2000. text 79.95 (*1-85928-243-1*) Ashgate Pub Co.

Chase, Malcolm. The People's Farm: English Radical Agrarianism, 1775-1840. 232p. 1988. 59.00 (*0-19-820105-2*) OUP.

Chase, Malcolm, ed. The Life & Literary Pursuits of Allen Davenport: With a Further Selection of the Author's Work. LC 94-5838. 1994. 69.95 (*1-85928-068-4*, Pub. by Scolar Pr) Ashgate Pub Co.

Chase, Malcolm & Dyck, Ian, eds. Living & Learning: Essays in Honour of J. F. C. Harrison. 288p. 1996. 86.95 (*1-85928-110-9*, Pub. by Scolar Pr) Ashgate Pub Co.

Chase, Malcolm W., Jr. NIST JANAF Thermochemical Tables, 2 vols. 4th ed. LC 98-86732. 1952p. 1998. 195.00 (*1-56396-831-2*) Am Inst Physics.

Chase, Mark, ed. The Pictorial Encyclopedia of Oncidium. LC 98-131602. (Illus.). 152p. 185.00 (*0-9661344-0-0*) ZAI Pubns.

Chase, Mark E. Collectible Drinking Glasses: Identification & Values. 160p. 1995. pap. 17.95 (*0-89145-670-8*, 4561) Collector Bks.

Chase, Mark W. A Monograph of Leochilus (Orchidaceae) Anderson, Christiane, ed. LC 86-22258. (Systematic Botany Monographs: Vol. 14). (Illus.). 97p. (Orig.). 1986. pap. 12.00 (*0-912861-14-2*) Am Soc Plant.

— Thesaurus Woolwardiae Vol. 3: Oncidium Alliance. 1993. pap. 60.00 (*0-915279-16-9*, TW3) Miss Botan.

— Thesaurus Woolwardiae Orchids of the Marquis of Lothian Pt. 3: Oncidium Alliance. Cribb, Phillip J. & Luer, Carlyle A., eds. (Thesaurus Woolwardiae Ser.). (Illus.). 64p. 1993. pap. 60.00 (*0-614-03697-6*) Miss Botan.

Chase, Marlene J. & Waldron, John D. A Seed in the Wind: The Story of Commissioner George Scott Railton & the Work of the Salvation Army in St. Louis, Missouri. 1995. pap. 9.95 (*0-9648347-0-7*) Salvtn Army.

Chase, Mary. Bernardine. 1954. pap. 5.25 (*0-8222-0105-4*) Dramatists Play.

— Cocktails with Mimi. 1974. pap. 5.25 (*0-8222-0226-3*) Dramatists Play.

— The Dog Sitters. 1963. pap. 5.25 (*0-8222-0321-9*) Dramatists Play.

— Loretta Mason Potts. (J). (gr. 4-8). 1990. 23.25 (*0-8446-6428-6*) Peter Smith.

— Mickey. 1969. pap. 5.25 (*0-8222-0752-4*) Dramatists Play.

— Midgie Purvis. 1963. pap. 5.25 (*0-8222-0754-0*) Dramatists Play.

— Mrs. McThing. 1954. pap. 5.25 (*0-8222-0787-7*) Dramatists Play.

— The Prize Play. 1961. pap. 3.25 (*0-8222-0918-7*) Dramatists Play.

— The Terrible Tattoo Parlor. 1981. pap. 3.25 (*0-8222-1123-8*) Dramatists Play.

Chase, Mary Coyle. Harvey. 1951. pap. 5.25 (*0-8222-0500-9*) Dramatists Play.

Chase, Mary E. A Goodly Fellowship. LC 83-45731. reprint ed. 29.50 (*0-404-20057-5*) AMS Pr.

— A Goodly Fellowship. (American Biography Ser.). 305p. 1991. reprint ed. lib. bdg. 79.00 (*0-7812-8064-8*) Rprt Serv.

— A Goodly Heritage. (American Biography Ser.). 298p. 1991. reprint ed. lib. bdg. 69.00 (*0-7812-8065-6*) Rprt Serv.

— The Lovely Ambition. 1960. 5.95 (*0-393-08477-9*) Norton.

— Thomas Hardy from Serial to Novel. (BCL1-PR English Literature Ser.). 210p. 1992. reprint ed. lib. bdg. 79.00 (*0-7812-7550-4*) Rprt Serv.

Chase, Mary E. & Macgregor, Margaret E., eds. Writing of Informal Essays. LC 79-93326. (Essay Index Reprint Ser.). 1977. 29.95 (*0-8369-1556-9*) Ayer.

Chase, Mary Earle, jt. auth. see Wesley-Hosford, Zia.

***Chase, Maureen & Trupp, Sandy.** Office E-Mails That Really Click. (Illus.). 150p. 2000. pap. 12.95 (*1-890154-18-0*) Aegis Pub Grp.

Chase, Michael, tr. see Hadot, Pierre.

Chase, Milton. Electric Power: An Industry at a Crossroads. LC 88-2392. 185p. 1988. 57.95 (*0-275-92927-2*, C2927, Praeger Pubs) Greenwood.

Chase, Nancy, jt. ed. see Flynn, Barbara.

Chase, Nancy D. Burdened Children: Theory, Research & Treatment Of Parentification. LC 99-6009. 1999. write for info. (*0-7619-0764-5*) Sage.

***Chase, Nancy D., ed.** Burdened Children: Theory, Research, & Treatment of Parentification. LC 99-6009. 199p. 1999. 46.00 (*0-7619-0763-7*) Sage.

Chase, Nancy D., jt. auth. see Robinson, Bryan E.

Chase, Naomi F., jt. auth. see Agee, Jon.

Chase, Niann Emerson, jt. auth. see Gabriel of Sedona.

Chase, Oscar G. Weinstein, Korn & Miller CPLR Manual. 2nd ed. 1980. ring bd. 200.00 (*0-8205-1802-6*) Bender.

Chase, Oscar G. & Barker, Robert A. Civil Litigation in New York. 3rd ed. LC 96-35869. (Cases & Materials Ser.). 1996. 60.00 (*0-8205-2750-5*) Bender.

***Chase, Owen.** The Shipwreck of the Whaleship Essex. rev. ed. LC 99-24889. 144p. 1999. pap. 12.95 (*1-55821-878-5*) Lyons Pr.

Chase, Owen, et al. Narratives of the Wreck of the Whale-Ship Essex. 96p. 1989. pap. 5.95 (*0-486-26121-2*) Dover.

C

An Asterisk (*) at the beginning of an entry indicates that the title is appearing for the first time.

Chase, Pamela L. & Pawlik, Jonathan. The Newcastle Guide to Healing with Crystals: Balancing the Human Energy Field for Physical & Spiritual Well-Being. 171p. 1988. pap. 10.95 (*0-87877-134-4*) Newcastle Pub.

Chase, Pamela L. & Pawlik, Jonathan. The Newcastle Guide to Healing with Gemstones. (Illus.). 260p. (Orig.). 1989. pap. 12.95 (*0-87877-140-9*) Newcastle Pub.

— Trees for Healing: Harmonizing with Nature for Personal Growth & Planetary Balance. 256p. (Orig.). 1991. pap. 12.95 (*0-87877-157-3*) Newcastle Pub.

Chase, Patrick J. Seek, Strike, Destroy: The History of the 894th Tank Destroyer Battalion in World War II. LC 95-75464. (Illus.). 240p. 1995. 35.00 (*0-9645659-0-0*) P J Chase.

Chase, Paul. The Soldier, the Athlete, the Farmer. Stevens, Andrell, ed. 1992. write for info. (*0-9628168-1-7*) Keys Freedom.

— VM/CMS: A User's Guide. LC 88-26069. 466p. 1989. pap. 51.95 (*0-471-50170-0*) Wiley.

Chase, Penelle & Doan, Jane. Choosing to Learn: Student Ownership & Responsibility in the Classroom. LC 96-28534. 1996. pap. text 21.00 (*0-435-07223-4*) Heinemann.

— Full Circle: A New Look at Multiage Education. LC 94-2168. 184p. 1994. pap. text 22.00 (*0-435-08814-9*, 08814) Heinemann.

***Chase, Philander D., et al, eds.** The Papers of George Washington, Vol. 9. Vol. 9. 672p. 2000. 62.50 (*0-8139-1922-3*) U Pr of Va.

***Chase, Philander D. & Grizzard, Frank E., Jr., eds.** The Papers of George Washington. (Revolutionary War Ser.: Vol. 10). 768p. 2000. 67.50 (*0-8139-1901-0*) U Pr of Va.

Chase, Philander D. & Grizzard, Frank E., Jr., eds. The Papers of George Washington: 13 August - 20 October 1776. (Revolutionary War Ser.: Vol. 6). 680p. (C). text 47.50 (*0-8139-1538-4*) U Pr of Va.

Chase, Philander D., jt. ed. see Twohig, Dorothy.

Chase, Philander D., ed. see Washington, George.

Chase, Philip N., jt. ed. see Hayes, Linda J.

Chase, Ray E., tr. see Rocker, Rudolf.

Chase, Renee W. CAD for Fashion Design. LC 96-1694. 174p. 1996. pap. text 63.00 (*0-13-373242-8*) P-H.

Chase-Riboud, Barbara. Sally Hemings. 416p. 1980. mass mkt. 4.95 (*0-380-48686-5*, Avon Bks) Morrow Avon.

— Sally Hemings. LC 99-36363. 368p. 1999. pap. 14.95 (*0-312-24704-4*) St Martin.

— Sally Hemings. 416p. 1994. reprint ed. pap. 12.00 (*0-345-38971-9*) Ballantine Pub Grp.

— Sally Hemings. 300p. 1992. reprint ed. lib. bdg. 37.95 (*0-89966-915-8*) Buccaneer Bks.

— Valide: A Novel of the Harem. 432p. 1988. mass mkt. 4.95 (*0-380-70443-9*, Avon Bks) Morrow Avon.

Chase, Richard. American Folk Tales & Songs. 1971. pap. 5.95 (*0-486-22692-1*) Dover.

— American Folk Tales & Songs. (Illus.). 1990. 20.00 (*0-8446-0057-1*) Peter Smith.

— The American Novel & Its Tradition. LC 78-3457. 280p. 1978. reprint ed. 50.00 (*0-87752-209-X*) Gordian.

— The American Novel & Its Tradition. LC 79-3702. 288p. 1980. reprint ed. pap. 15.95 (*0-8018-2303-X*) Johns Hopkins.

— Grandfather Tales, 001. (Illus.). 240p. (J). (gr. 4-6). 1973. 18.00 (*0-395-06692-1*) HM.

— Grandfather Tales. 256p. (J). (gr. 4-7). 1990. pap. 7.95 (*0-395-56150-7*) HM.

— Grandfather Tales: American-English Folk Tales. (J). 1976. 13.05 (*0-606-04683-6*, Pub. by Turtleback) Demco.

— Jack Tales, 001. (Illus.). 202p. (J). (gr. 4-6). 1943. 16.00 (*0-395-06694-8*) HM.

— Jack Tales. 50th anniversary ed. LC 94-217671. 224p. (J). (gr. 4-7). 1993. pap. 5.95 (*0-395-66951-0*) HM.

— Singing Games & Playparty Games. (Illus.). 63p. (J). (gr. 1-4). 1967. pap. 3.95 (*0-486-21785-X*) Dover.

— Singing Games & Playparty Games. (Illus.). (J). (gr. 4-8). 1990. 18.75 (*0-8446-4721-7*) Peter Smith.

Chase, Richard, ed. Old Songs & Singing Games. LC 72-85499. (Illus.). 64p. 1972. reprint ed. pap. 2.95 (*0-486-22879-7*) Dover.

Chase, Richard & Aquilano, Nicholas. Production & Operations Management. 8th ed. LC 97-36919. 880p. (C). 1997. text 65.50 (*0-256-22556-7*, Irwn McGrw-H) McGrw-H Hghr Educ.

Chase, Richard, jt. auth. see Corliss, Ralph.

Chase, Richard, ed. see Crane, Stephen.

Chase, Richard, ed. see Harris, Joel Chandler.

Chase, Richard B. Gestion de la Produccion. (SPA.). 1104p. (C). 1994. pap. text. write for info. (*0-201-60110-9*) Addison-Wesley.

Chase, Richard B. & Aquilano, Nicholas J. Production & Operations Management: Manufacturing Services. 7th ed. LC 94-31409. 896p. (C). 1994. text 73.75 (*0-256-14023-5*, Irwn McGrw-H) McGrw-H Hghr Educ.

***Chase, Richard B., et al.** Operations Management for Competitive Advantage. 9th ed. LC 00-38321. 2001. write for info. (*0-07-232315-9*) McGraw.

Chase, Richard B., et al. Production & Operations Management: Manufacturing & Services. 8th ed. LC 97-36919. 1997. write for info. (*0-256-26921-1*, Irwn Prfssnl) McGraw-Hill Prof.

— Production & Operations Management (Prosim W/350 Package) 7th ed. (C). 1996. pap., text 85.75 incl. disk (*0-256-21563-4*, Irwn McGrw-H) McGrw-H Hghr Educ.

— Production & Operations Management Study Guide. 7th ed. 254p. (C). 1995. text, student ed. 30.00 (*0-256-18752-5*, Irwn McGrw-H) McGrw-H Hghr Educ.

Chase, Richard B., jt. auth. see Aquilano, Nicholas.

Chase, Richard V. The Democratic Vista. LC 72-12325. 180p. 1973. reprint ed. lib. bdg. 59.50 (*0-8371-6732-9*, CHDV, Greenwood Pr) Greenwood.

— Emily Dickinson. LC 70-136058. (Illus.). 328p. 1971. reprint ed. lib. bdg. 59.50 (*0-8371-5208-9*, CHD, Greenwood Pr) Greenwood.

***Chase, Robert.** Pivotal States. (C). 2000. pap. text 12.50 (*0-393-97583-5*) Norton.

Chase, Robert & Chase, Linda, eds. Presbyterian Patchwork. 128p. (Orig.). 1989. text 39.95 (*0-9622902-0-3*); pap. text 19.95 (*0-9622902-1-1*) CCM Inc.

Chase, Robert A. The Bassett Atlas of Human Anatomy. 112p. (C). 1989. 38.40 (*0-8053-0118-6*) Benjamin-Cummings.

Chase, Robert A. Bassett Atlas of Human Anatomy & Student Notebook. 1996. 49.00 (*0-8053-1029-0*) Benjamin-Cummings.

Chase, Robert O., et al. Spanish for Health Care Workers: Communication & Culture. LC 97-34802. (Yale Language Ser.). (SPA., Illus.). 272p. 1998. 20.00 (*0-300-07077-2*) Yale U Pr.

Chase, Robert S., et al, eds. The Pivotal States: A New Framework for U. S. Policy in the Developing World. LC 98-29490. 448p. 1998. 35.00 (*0-393-04675-3*) Norton.

Chase, Roland F., jt. auth. see Alperin, Howard J.

Chase, S. U., et al. Galois Theory & Cohomology of Commutative Rings. LC 52-42839. (Memoirs Ser.: No. 1/52). 79p. 1978. reprint ed. pap. 16.00 (*0-8218-1252-1*, MEMO/1/52) Am Math.

Chase, Salmon P. Diary & Correspondence of Salmon P. Chase. (American Biography Ser.). 527p. 1991. reprint ed. lib. bdg. 99.00 (*0-7812-8066-4*) Rprt Serv.

— Reclamation of Fugitives from Service. LC 77-138334. (Black Heritage Library Collection). 1977. 15.95 (*0-8369-8726-8*) Ayer.

Chase, Salmon P., et al. The Salmon P. Chase Papers. LC 88-23408. (Research Collections in American Politics Ser.). 43p. 1987. write for info. (*0-89093-519-X*) U Pubns Amer.

Chase, Sam, ed. see Putnam, Jeff.

Chase, Sam, ed. see Stegner, Lynn.

Chase, Samuel. Trial of Samuel Chase, an Associate Justice of the Supreme Court Impeached by the House of Representatives, 2 vols. LC 69-11324. (Law, Politics & History Ser.). 1970. reprint ed. lib. bdg. 79.50 (*0-306-71181-8*) Da Capo.

Chase, Samuel B., Jr., ed. Problems in Public Expenditure Analysis: Papers Presented at a Conference of Experts: Sept. 15-16 1966. LC 67-30589. (Brookings Institution Studies of Government Finance). 283p. reprint ed. pap. 87.80 (*0-608-12160-6*, 202536900043) Bks Demand.

Chase, Sara B. Painting Historic Interiors. 14p. 1992. pap. 1.00 (*0-16-061649-2*) USGPO.

Chase, Sarah L. Cold-Weather Cooking. LC 90-50359. (Illus.). 432p. 1990. 22.95 (*0-89480-844-3*, 1844); pap. 15.95 (*0-89480-752-8*, 1752) Workman Pub.

— The Nantucket Open-House Cookbook. LC 86-40598. (Illus.). 336p. 1987. pap. 14.95 (*0-89480-465-0*, 1465) Workman Pub.

— Pedaling Through Burgundy Cookbook. LC 95-32829. (Illus.). 208p. 1995. pap. 14.95 (*1-56305-359-4*, 3359) Workman Pub.

— Pedaling Through Provence Cookbook. LC 95-32831. (Illus.). 256p. 1995. pap. 14.95 (*0-7611-0233-7*, 10233) Workman Pub.

***Chase, Sarah L.** Sarah Leah Chase's Year Around Cookbook. LC 00-27319. (Illus.). 2000. write for info. (*1-57912-131-4*) Blck Dog & Leventhal.

Chase, Scott B. Why Are There No Tall Grandma's? A Guide to Assist You in Researching Your Family History. LC 90-4741. (Illus.). 1990. pap. 12.95 (*1-55787-072-1*, SR01001) Hrt of the Lakes.

Chase, Shirley A., et al. Courseware Evaluation: Form & Guide for Vocational & Technical Education. 24p. 1984. 2.50 (*0-318-22068-7*, SN44) Ctr Educ Trng Employ.

Chase, Shoddy. What Kind of Woman Is This? Unique Insights into Proverbs 31. Crittenden, Delores, ed. 185p. 2000. pap. 9.95 (*0-9628168-0-9*, 920-010, Pub. by Keys Freedom) BookWorld.

Chase, Simon, jt. auth. see Bati, Anwer.

Chase, Stephen U., et al. Galois Theory & Cohomology of Cummutative Rings. LC 52-42839. (American Mathematical Society Ser.: No. 52). 85p. 1965. pap. 30.00 (*0-608-05167-5*, 205258800001) Bks Demand.

Chase, Steve, ed. Defending the Earth: A Dialogue Between Murray Bookchin & Dave Foreman. 148p. (C). 1991. 25.00 (*0-89608-383-7*) South End Pr.

***Chase, Steve & Society of Photo-optical Instrumentation Engineers.** Nondestructive Evaluation of Bridges & Highways III: 3-5 March 1999, Newport Beach, California. LC 99-226076. (Illus.). 294p. 1999. 72.00 (*0-8194-3057-9*) SPIE.

Chase, Steven. Angelic Wisdom: The Cherubim & the Grace of Contemplation in Richard of St. Victor. LC 94-47439. (Studies in Spirituality & Theology: Vol. 2). (C). 1996. text 32.95 (*0-268-00644-X*) U of Notre Dame Pr.

Chase, Steven B., ed. Nondestructive Evaluation of Bridges & Highways, Vol. 2946. 340p. 1996. 66.00 (*0-8194-2350-5*) SPIE.

Chase, Stuart. The Economy of Abundance. LC 79-37876. (Select Bibliographies Reprint Ser.). 1977. reprint ed. 23.95 (*0-8369-6713-5*) Ayer.

— Government in Business. LC 71-136849. 296p. 1973. reprint ed. lib. bdg. 35.00 (*0-8371-5283-6*, CHGB, Greenwood Pr) Greenwood.

— The Most Probable World. LC 81-2307. 239p. 1981. reprint ed. lib. bdg. 65.00 (*0-313-22971-6*, CHMP, Greenwood Pr) Greenwood.

— Rich Land, Poor Land. LC 70-92612. (Illus.). reprint ed. 57.50 (*0-404-01478-X*) AMS Pr.

— Some Things Worth Knowing. LC 76-90622. (Essay Index Reprint Ser.). 1977. 23.95 (*0-8369-1557-7*) Ayer.

— The Tyranny of Words. LC 38-27108. 420p. 1959. pap. 7.95 (*0-15-692394-7*, Harvest Bks) Harcourt.

Chase, Stuart & Brunner, Edmund de S. The Proper Study of Mankind. rev. ed. LC 78-87. 327p. 1978. reprint ed. lib. bdg. 35.00 (*0-313-20261-3*, CHPS, Greenwood Pr) Greenwood.

Chase, Stuart, ed. see American Trade Union Delegation to the Soviet Unio.

Chase, Susan E. Ambiguous Empowerment: The Work Narratives of Women School Superintendents. LC 94-16897. 288p. (C). 1995. lib. bdg. 45.00 (*0-87023-949-X*) U of Mass Pr.

— Ambiguous Empowerment: The Work Narratives of Women School Superintendents. LC 94-16897. 288p. (C). 1995. pap. 18.95 (*0-87023-950-3*) U of Mass Pr.

***Chase, Susan E. & Rogers, Mary F.** Mothers & Children: Feminist Analyses & Personal Narratives. LC 00-39032. 384p. (C). 2001. text 55.00 (*0-8135-2875-5*); pap. text 25.00 (*0-8135-2876-3*) Rutgers U Pr.

***Chase, Suzi F.** Recommended Bed & Breakfasts Mid-Atlantic States. 2nd ed. LC 99-43808. (Illus.). 360p. 1999. pap. text 16.95 (*0-7627-0551-5*) Globe Pequot.

Chase, Suzi Forbes. The Hamptons Book: A Complete Guide, with Special Chapters on the North Shore & Shelter Island. 3rd rev. ed. LC 98-33695. (Great Destinations Ser.). (Illus.). 352p. 1998. pap. 17.95 (*1-58157-002-3*, Pub. by Berkshire Hse) Natl Bk Netwk.

***Chase, Suzi Forbes.** New Red Lion Inn Cookbook. rev. ed. LC 99-87036. (Illus.). 224p. 2000. pap. 23.95 (*1-58157-012-0*, Pub. by Berkshire Hse) Natl Bk Netwk.

***Chase, Taylor, pseud.** Heart of Deception. 496p. 1999. mass mkt. 5.99 (*0-06-101289-0*) HarpC.

Chase, Teresa, jt. auth. see Lanig, Indira S.

Chase, Theodore, ed. Markers: The Journal of the Association for Gravestone Studies, No. 7. LC 81-642903. (Illus.). 281p. (Orig.). (C). 1990. pap. text 13.00 (*1-878381-00-8*) Assn Gravestone Studies.

— Markers: The Journal of the Association for Gravestone Studies, No. 9. LC 81-642903. (Markers Ser.). (Illus.). 288p. (Orig.). 1992. pap. 16.00 (*1-878381-02-4*) Assn Gravestone Studies.

— Markers No. 6: The Journal of the Association for Gravestone Studies. LC 81-642903. (Illus.). 245p. (Orig.). (C). 1989. 25.00 (*0-8191-7316-9*); pap. 13.00 (*0-8191-7317-7*) U Pr of Amer.

Chase, Theodore & Gabel, Laurel K. Gravestone Chronicles: Some Eighteenth-Century New England Carvers & Their Work, Vol. I. LC 97-193793. 262p. 1990. 20.00 (*0-88082-024-1*, S2-62350H) New Eng Hist.

— Gravestone Chronicles II: More Eighteenth-Century New England Carvers & an Exploration of Gravestone Heraldica. LC 97-7020. 1997. 20.00 (*0-88082-059-4*) New Eng Hist.

Chase, Theodore, jt. ed. see Feistritzer, W. P.

Chase, Thomas. The English Religious Lexis. LC 87-31377. (Texts & Studies in Religion: Vol. 37). 516p. 1988. lib. bdg. 119.95 (*0-88946-826-5*) E Mellen.

Chase, Thomas C. Am I? Am I Not? An Alcoholic. LC 98-30619. 96p. 1999. pap. 9.95 (*1-56474-292-X*) Fithian Pr.

Chase, Thomas N., et al, eds. Tourette Syndrome: Genetics, Neurobiology, & Treatment. LC RC0375.T645. (Advances in Neurology Ser.: No. 58). 396p. 1992. reprint ed. pap. 122.80 (*0-608-05824-6*, 205978900007) Bks Demand.

Chase, Thomas N., jt. ed. see Friedhoff, Arnold J.

Chase, Thornton. In Galilee. (Illus.). 98p. 1985. reprint ed. 14.95 (*0-933770-38-3*) Kalimat.

Chase, Tommy B. Invitation to Guam: Everything You Need to Know about Guam, Its People, & Culture. rev. ed. LC 90-61193. (Illus.). 192p. (Orig.). (C). 1992. pap. 10.00 (*0-9623530-0-0*) Lets Go Travel.

Chase, Truddi. When Rabbit Howls. 1990. mass mkt. 6.99 (*0-515-10329-2*, Jove) Berkley Pub.

Chase, Valerie J., jt. ed. see Reti, Irene.

***Chase, Victoria & Knappman, Edward W.** Best Educational Internet Sites for English & Literature Students LC 98-84284. (Sofwest Press Internet Site Ser.). viii, 158 p. 1998. write for info. (*1-57163-902-0*) Sofsource.

***Chase, Victoria, et al.** Best Educational Internet Sites for Science & Math Students. LC 98-84196. (Sofwest Press Internet Site Ser.). 160p. 1998. write for info. (*1-57163-901-2*) Sofsource.

Chase, W. General Statistics: Minitab Manual. 2nd ed. 185p. 1992. pap. 28.95 (*0-471-55759-5*) Wiley.

Chase, W. Howard. Issue Management: Origins of the Future. LC 83-83079. (Illus.). 170p. 1984. 24.95 (*0-913869-01-5*) Issue Action Pubns.

Chase, W. Parker & Goldberger, Paul. New York, 1932: The Wonder City. (Illus.). 304p. 1983. 18.95 (*0-9608788-3-1*) NY Bound.

Chase, Warren. The Life-Line of the Lone One. LC 72-2950. reprint ed. 49.50 (*0-404-10715-X*) AMS Pr.

— The Life-Line of the Lone One. (American Biography Ser.). 310p. 1991. reprint ed. lib. bdg. 79.00 (*0-7812-8067-2*) Rprt Serv.

Chase, Warren & Bown, Fred. General Statistical. 4th ed. LC 99-31329. 617p. 1999. text 90.95 (*0-471-28310-X*) Wiley.

Chase, Wes. ISO 9001 Quality System Self-Study Guide Vol. W: Worksheets. 44p. 1995. pap., student ed. 5.95 (*1-888398-96-5*) WJC Designs.

Chase, Wes, jt. auth. see Chase, Wesley J., Jr.

Chase, Wesley J. ISO 9001 Quality System Self-Study Guide, 5 vols., Set. rev. ed. (Illus.). 702p. 1995. pap. 140.00 (*1-888398-90-6*) WJC Designs.

— ISO 9001 Quality System Self-Study Guide Vol. I: 0001-0301 (4.1-4.3) rev. ed. (Illus.). 144p. 1995. pap. 29.95 (*1-888398-91-4*) WJC Designs.

— ISO 9001 Quality System Self-Study Guide Vol. II: 0401-0701 (4.4-4.7) rev. ed. (Illus.). 128p. 1995. pap. 29.95 (*1-888398-92-2*) WJC Designs.

— ISO 9001 Quality System Self-Study Guide Vol. III: 0801-1301 (4.8-4.13) rev. ed. (Illus.). 168p. 1995. pap. 29.95 (*1-888398-93-0*) WJC Designs.

— ISO 9001 Quality System Self-Study Guide Vol. IV: 1401-1701 (4.14-4.17) rev. ed. (Illus.). 134p. 1995. pap. 29.95 (*1-888398-94-9*) WJC Designs.

— ISO 9001 Quality System Self-Study Guide Vol. V: 1801-2001 (4.18-4.20) rev. ed. (Illus.). 128p. 1995. pap. 29.95 (*1-888398-95-7*) WJC Designs.

Chase, Wesley J., Jr. & Chase, Wes. The Excellent Journey to ISO 9000 Quality Systems. (Illus.). 64p. (Orig.). 1995. pap. 19.95 (*1-888398-89-2*) WJC Designs.

Chase, William C. The American Law School & the Rise of Administrative Government. LC 81-69816. 192p. 1982. reprint ed. pap. 59.60 (*0-608-01911-9*, 206256300003) Bks Demand.

Chase, William J. Workers, Society, & the Soviet State: Labor & Life in Moscow, 1918-1929. LC 85-28823. (Working Class in European History Ser.). 368p. 1987. text 34.95 (*0-252-01319-0*); pap. text 14.95 (*0-252-06129-2*) U of Ill Pr.

Chase, Wilton P. Management of System Engineering. LC 83-18746. 256p. 1985. reprint ed. text 30.50 (*0-89874-682-5*) Krieger.

***Chasek, Ruth.** Essential Gardening for Teens. (High Interest Bks.). (Illus.). (YA). 2000. 19.00 (*0-516-23356-4*) Childrens.

— Essential Gardening for Teens. (High Interest Bks.). (Illus.). 48p. (J). (gr. 4-7). 2000. pap. 6.95 (*0-516-23556-7*) Childrens.

— Essential Gardening for Teens. LC 99-44797. (Outdoor Life Ser.). (Illus.). (YA). 2000. pap. write for info. (*0-531-17644-4*) Watts.

— Rocks & Minerals. (High Interest Bks.). (Illus.). (J). 2000. 19.00 (*0-516-23333-5*) Childrens.

— Rocks & Minerals. LC 00-24279. (High Interest Bks.). (Illus.). 48p. (J). (gr. 4-7). 2000. pap. 6.95 (*0-516-23533-8*) Childrens.

Chasemore, Richard, jt. auth. see Harvey, Ian.

Chasen, Chyrelle D., jt. auth. see Stubbs, Kenneth Ray.

Chasen, Estelle. Chavas Story. 1997. 13.95 (*0-87306-826-2*) Feldheim.

Chasen, Jerry S., jt. auth. see Norwick, Kenneth P.

Chasen, S. H. & Dow, J. W. The Guide for the Evaluation & Implementation of Cad-Cam Systems. 2nd ed. (Illus.). 461p. 1983. text 250.00 (*0-938800-01-9*) Cad Cam.

Chasey, William C. Pan Am 103: The Lockerbie Coverup. (Illus.). 372p. (Orig.). 1995. pap. 17.95 (*0-9640104-1-0*) Bridger Hse.

Chasidah, Yishai. Encyclopedia of Biblical Personalities: Ishei HaTanach. LC 94-21191. 1994. 54.99 (*0-89906-025-0*) Mesorah Pubns.

Chasin. Digital Hearing Aid Handbook. 2000. pap. 49.95 (*1-56593-978-6*, C3969) Thomson Learn.

Chasin, Alexandra. Selling Out: Gay & Lesbian Movement Goes to Market. LC 99-43339. (Illus.). 384p. 2000. text 27.95 (*0-312-21449-9*) St Martin.

Chasin, Barbara, jt. auth. see Franke, Richard.

Chasin, Barbara H. Casualties of Capitalism: Violence & Inequality in the United States. LC 95-41550. (Cornerstone Bks.). 1996. 26.00 (*0-85345-913-4*) Monthly Rev.

— Casualties of Capitalism: Violence & Inequality in the United States. LC 95-41550. (Cornerstone Bks.). 1996. pap. 13.00 (*0-85345-914-2*) Monthly Rev.

— Inequality & Violence in the United States: Casualties of Capitalism. LC 97-7901. 192p. 1997. 49.95 (*0-391-04046-4*); pap. 15.00 (*0-391-04047-2*) Humanities.

— Inequality & Violence in the United States: Casualties of Capitalism. LC 98-52851. (Illus.). 229p. 1999. 49.95 (*1-57392-443-1*, Humanity Bks); pap. 18.95 (*1-57392-446-6*, Humanity Bks) Prometheus Bks.

Chasin, Barbara H. & Chasin, Gerald. Power & Ideology: A Marxist Approach to Political Sociology. LC 73-82376. 272p. 1974. reprint ed. pap. 84.40 (*0-608-05344-9*, 206504900012) Bks Demand.

Chasin, Barbara H., jt. ed. see Franke, Richard W.

Chasin, Barbara M., jt. auth. see Chasin, Gerald.

Chasin, Barbara M., jt. auth. see Franke, Richard W.

Chasin, David G., jt. ed. see Bode, Loren E.

Chasin, Gerald & Chasin, Barbara M. Power & Ideology: A Marxist Approach to Political Sociology. 312p. 1974. pap. 11.95 (*0-87073-277-3*) Schenkman Bks Inc.

Chasin, Gerald, jt. auth. see Chasin, Barbara H.

Chasin, Helen. Coming Close & Other Poems. LC 75-21576. (Yale Series of Younger Poets: No. 63). reprint ed. 18.00 (*0-404-53863-0*) AMS Pr.

Chasin, Helen, ed. see Baishi, Qi.

Chasin, Mark, ed. Methods in Cyclic Nucleotide Research. LC 72-89528. (Methods in Molecular Biology Ser.: No. 3). 331p. reprint ed. pap. 102.70 (*0-7837-0782-7*, 204109600019) Bks Demand.

Chasin, Mark & Langer. Biodegradable Polymers As Drug Delivery Systems. (Drugs & the Pharmaceutical Sciences Ser.: Vol. 45). (Illus.). 368p. 1990. text 155.00 (*0-8247-8344-1*) Dekker.

Chasin, Marshall. Musicians & the Prevention of Hearing Loss. (Illus.). 204p. (Orig.). 1996. pap. 45.00 (*1-56593-626-4*, 1298) Thomson Learn.

Chasin, Marshall, ed. CIC Handbook. LC 97-11451. (Illus.). 240p. (Orig.). 1997. pap. 39.95 (*1-56593-829-1*, 1596) Thomson Learn.

Chasin, Noah, ed. see Ponce de Leon, Carolina & Andreus, Alejanoro.

Chasin, Noah, ed. see Ponce de Leon, Carolina & Torruella Leval, Susana.

C

***Chasin, Rachel.** Cut, Paste & Write a School Story. Rogers, Kathy, ed. (Illus.). 32p. 2000. pap., wbk. ed. 4.95 (*1-56472-184-1*); teacher ed. 4.95 Edupress Inc.

— Cut, Paste & Write a Seasonal Story. Rogers, Kathy, ed. (Illus.). 32p. 2000. teacher ed. 4.95 (*1-56472-181-7*) Edupress Inc.

— Cut, Paste & Write an Alphabet Story. Rogers, Kathy, ed. 32p. 2000. teacher ed. 4.95 (*1-56472-183-3*) Edupress Inc.

— Cut, Paste & Write an Animal Story. Rogers, Kathy, ed. (Illus.). 32p. 2000. teacher ed. 4.95 (*1-56472-182-5*) Edupress Inc.

Chasin, Richard, et al, eds. One Couple, Four Realities: Multiple Perspectives on Couple Therapy. LC 90-3037. 420p. 1990. lib. bdg. 45.00 (*0-89862-437-1*) Guilford Pubns.

— One Couple, Four Realities: Multiple Perspectives on Couple Therapy. LC 90-3037. 420p. 1992. reprint ed. pap. text 25.00 (*0-89862-029-5*) Guilford Pubns.

Chasis, David A. Plastic Piping Systems. 2nd ed. (Illus.). 172p. 1988. 32.95 (*0-8311-1181-X*) Indus Pr.

Chasis, Herbert. Three Worlds of Medicine: Stories of Hope & Courage. Egan, Roger E., Sr., ed. (Illus.). 160p. (Orig.). 1994. pap. 21.95 (*0-9632687-4-0*) PenRose Pub.

Chasis, Herbert & Goldring, William, eds. Homer William Smith, Sc. D. His Scientific & Literary Achievements. LC 65-10765. 308p. reprint ed. pap. 95.50 (*0-8357-9478-4*, 201028900068) Bks Demand.

Chasis, Sarah, jt. auth. see Kyle, Amy D.

***Chaska, Norma L.** The Nursing Profession: Tomorrow & Beyond. LC 00-9517. 2000. write for info. (*0-7619-1943-0*) Sage.

Chaskalson, Matthew, jt. auth. see Spitz, Richard.

Chaskalson, Matthew, et al, eds. Constitutional Law of South Africa. LC 96-218716. 1996. ring bd. 97.50 (*0-7021-3561-5*, Pub. by Juta & Co) Gaunt.

Chaskin, David. Freddy's Revenge. New Line Cinema Staff, ed. LC 92-501. (Nightmare on Elm Street Ser.). 1992. lib. bdg. 13.95 (*1-56239-157-7*) ABDO Pub Co.

Chasler, Charles N. Atlas of Roentgenology Anatomy of the Newborn & Infant Skull. LC 76-96981. (Illus.). 228p. 1972. 25.00 (*0-87527-028-X*) Green.

Chasman, Deborah, ed. see Cintron, Ralph.

Chasman, Deborah, ed. see Felman, Jyl Lynn.

Chasman, Deborah, ed. see Gornick, Vivian.

Chasman, Deborah, ed. see Price, Richard.

Chasman, Deborah, ed. see Sanchez, Sonia.

Chasman, Herbert, jt. auth. see White, Edwin H.

Chasnoff, Ira J., ed. Drug Use in Pregnancy: Mother & Child. 1986. text 124.00 (*0-85200-949-6*) Kluwer Academic.

— Drugs, Alcohol, Pregnancy & Parenting. (C). 1988. text 95.50 (*0-7462-0095-1*) Kluwer Academic.

Chasnoff, Ira J. & Consumer Guide Editors. Your Child: A Medical Guide: The Illustrated Medical & Health Adviser LC 95-200659. (Illus.). 384p. 1994. write for info. (*0-7853-0951-9*) Pubns Intl Ltd.

Chasnoff, Ira J., et al. Understanding the Drug-Exposed Child: Approaches to Behavior & Learning. LC 98-70479. 216p. (Orig.). 1998. pap. 29.95 (*1-879176-29-7*) Imprint Pubns.

Practical research-based strategies to help children reach their full potential. Designed for teachers, parents, physicians, psychologists - anyone who works with children. This book is based on longitudinal research of prenatally exposed children, some of whom may display a wide array of behavioral, learning & emotional problems. Through a clear, practical approach, it presents behavioral management techniques that can help prevent problems in the classroom as well as manage specific problem situations. Chapters include: Research Basis of Intervention Strategies; Managing Behavior: The Effective Classroom; & Toward One on One: Individual Behavior Interventions. The methods presented are appropriate to any learning situation, at school or at home, & for any child, not only the prenatally exposed child. An indispensable resource for anyone who works with children & an exceptionally useful text for educators & parents. "There is no child who cannot learn." This book is based on a commitment to that conviction. Paper, ISBN 1-879176-29-7, US $29.95, 214 pp., index, June 1998. Order from Imprint Publications, Inc., 230 East Ohio St., Suite 300, Chicago, IL 60611. 312-337-9268, FAX: 312-337-9622, e-mail: imppub@aol.com, add $5.00 for single copy shipping; credit cards accepted. www.imprint-chicago.com
Publisher Paid Annotation.

Chasnoff, Ira J., jt. auth. see Consumer Guide Editors.

Chasnoff, Robert & Muniz, Peter. Consultation: A Training Program. 18p. 1980. pap. text 4.50 (*0-943300-02-9*) LABS.

— Managing Human Resources: A Practical Guide. 63p. (C). 1981. pap. text 9.25 (*0-943300-00-2*) LABS.

Chasnoff, Robert, jt. auth. see Muniz, Peter.

Chason, Anne B. Alphabet Belonging to Christ. 198p. (J). 1995. pap. 17.95 (*0-9649034-0-7*) ABC Orig.

Chass, Vikentia. The Visiting Angels. 16p. (J). (gr. k-6). 1999. pap. 8.00 (*0-8059-4713-2*) Dorrance.

Chassaguet-Smirgel, Janine, et al. Female Sexuality: New Psychoanalytic Views. 228p. 1989. reprint ed. pap. text 29.00 (*0-946439-14-1*, Pub. by H Karnac Bks Ltd) Other Pr LLC.

Chassaigne, P. Lexique de l'Histoire et Civilisation Brittanique. (FRE.). 1998. 45.00 (*0-320-00147-4*) Fr & Eur.

Chassaing, Ralph. Digital Signal Processing with C & the TMS320C30. LC 92-10635. (Topics in Digital Signal Processing Ser.). 432p. 1992. 145.00 incl. disk (*0-471-55780-3*); pap. 89.95 incl. disk (*0-471-57777-4*) Wiley.

Chassaing, Ralph & Horning, Darrell. Digital Signal Processing with the TMS320C25. LC 89-34031. (Topics in Digital Signal Processing Ser.). 480p. 1990. 129.00 (*0-471-51066-1*) Wiley.

Chassaing, Rulph. Digital Signal Processing: Laboratory Experiments Using the TMS320C31 DSK. LC 98-7866. (Topics in Digital Signal Processing Ser.). 328p. 1998. 74.95 (*0-471-29362-8*) Wiley.

Chassan, J. B. Research Design in Clinical Psychology & Psychiatry. 496p. 1982. text 22.50 (*0-8290-1009-2*) Irvington.

Chassant, Louis-Alphonse. Dictionnaire des Abreviations Latines et Francaises Usitees Dans les Inscriptions Lapidaires et Metalliques, le Manuscrits et les Chartes Du Moyen Age. xlviii, 172p. 1970. reprint ed. 50.00 (*3-487-05406-X*) G Olms Pubs.

— Dictionnaire des Devises Heraldiques: Avec Supplement. (FRE.). 1624p. 165.00 (*0-7859-8402-X*, 3487071827) Fr & Eur.

Chassant, Louis-Alphonse & Delbarre, P. J. Dictionnaire de Sigillographie Pratique. (FRE.). vi, 264p. 1987. reprint ed. 55.00 (*3-487-07942-9*) G Olms Pubs.

Chassant, Louis-Alphonse & Tausin, Henri. Dictionnaire Des Devises Historiques et Heraldiques - Supplement Au Dictionnaire Des Devises Historiques et Heraldiques, 3 vols. in 1. (FRE.). xlviii, 1624p. 1980. reprint ed. 290.00 incl. 3.5 hd (*3-487-07180-0*) G Olms Pubs.

Chassany, Jean-Philippe. Dictionnaire de Meteorologie Populaire. rev. ed. (FRE.). 410p. 1989. pap. 185.00 (*0-7859-4812-0*) Fr & Eur.

Chassard, Jean & Weil, Gonthier. Dictionnaire des Oeuvres et des Themes de la Litterature Allemande.Tr. of Dictionary of Works & Themes in German Literature. (FRE.). 1973. pap. 19.95 (*0-8288-6264-8*, M-6631) Fr & Eur.

Chassbe, Charles. The Nabis & Their Period. LC 73-412171. 136p. 1969. write for info. (*0-85331-074-2*) Lund Humphries.

Chasseaud, L. F., jt. ed. see Bridges, James W.

Chasseguet-Smirgel, J. Sexuality & Mind: The Role of the Father & the Mother in the Psyche. 182p. 1988. pap. 27.50 (*0-946439-75-3*, Pub. by H Karnac Bks Ltd) Other Pr LLC.

***Chassell, Robert J.** Programming in Emacs Lisp: An Introduction, Edition 1.05. 273p. 1999. per. 20.00 (*1-882114-42-6*) Free Software.

***Chassell, Robert J. & Stallman, Richard M.** Texinfo: The GNU Documentation Format. 270p. 1999. per. 25.00 (*1-882114-67-1*) Free Software.

Chassignet, Eric P., et al. Ocean Modeling & Parameterization. LC 98-34113. (NATO ASI Ser.). 1998. write for info. (*0-7923-5228-9*) Kluwer Academic.

Chassin, Charles L. Les Elections et les Cahiers de Paris en 1789, 4 vols., Set. LC 76-38039. reprint ed. 540.00 (*0-404-52590-3*) AMS Pr.

— Les Volontaires Nationaux Pendant la Revolution, 3 vols. LC 70-38040. reprint ed. 405.00 (*0-404-52600-4*) AMS Pr.

Chassin, J. L. Operative Strategy in General Surgery, Vol. 2. (Illus.). 655p. 1984. 109.00 (*0-387-90984-2*) Spr-Verlag.

— Operative Strategy in General Surgery: An Expositive Atlas. 2nd ed. (Illus.). 1055p. 1997. reprint ed. 170.00 (*0-387-97968-9*) Spr-Verlag.

Chassler, Joseph, jt. auth. see Bellamy, Peter.

***Chassman, Gary.** In the Spirit of Martin. 2002. write for info. (*0-688-17508-2*, Wm Morrow) Morrow Avon.

Chassman, Gary & Danforth, Randi. The United States: A Culinary Discovery. (Culinaria Ser.). (Illus.). 640p. 1998. 39.95 (*3-8290-0259-9*, 520178) Konemann.

Chassman, Milton. Quicken 5, IBM PC: Quick Reference Guide. 1993. pap. 12.00 (*1-56243-094-7*, QB-17) DDC Pub.

— Quicken for Windows. 1993. pap. 12.00 (*1-56243-103-X*, C-18) DDC Pub.

Chastagner, Gary A., ed. Christmas Tree Diseases, Insects, & Disorders in the Pacific Northwest: Identification & Management. (Illus.). 156p. 1998. pap. text 50.00 (*0-7881-7334-0*) DIANE Pub.

Chastain & Guntermann. Imaginate! Managing Conversations in Spanish. 2nd ed. (C). 1991. pap. 35.95 (*0-8384-2360-4*) Heinle & Heinle.

***Chastain & Guntermann.** Imaginate with cd. 3rd ed. (SPA.). (C). 2001. pap. 40.00 (*0-8384-1645-4*) Heinle & Heinle.

Chastain, C. B. & Ganjam, V. K. Clinical Endocrinology of Companion Animals. LC 85-18159. 580p. reprint ed. pap. 179.80 (*0-7837-2985-5*, 205746800006) Bks Demand.

Chastain, Clark E. Corporate Asset Management: A Guide for Financial & Accounting Professionals. LC 87-2493. 368p. 1987. 79.50 (*0-89930-237-8*, CGU/, Quorum Bks) Greenwood.

Chastain, Clay. Tilting at Windmills: The Clay Chastain Story. 172p. 1998. pap. 14.95 (*1-890622-38-9*) Leathers Pub.

Chastain, Dayne. Follow the Signs: A Treasure Hunter's Handbook. (Illus.). 296p. 1997. pap. 19.95 (*0-9660797-0-1*) Tiwinke Pub.

Chastain, Frances. Animals of Ancient China. (Illus.). 34p. (J). (ps-2). 1986. text 5.95 (*0-8351-1790-1*) China Bks.

Chastain, Garvin & Landrum, R. Eric, eds. Protecting Human Subjects: Departmental Subject Pools & Institutional Review Boards. LC 99-22348. 228p. 1999. pap. 29.95 (*1-55798-575-8*, 431-617A) Am Psychol.

Chastain, Gerald, Jr., jt. auth. see Kamm, Karlyn.

Chastain, Jane. I'd Speak Out on the Issues If I Only Knew What to Say. LC 87-20507. 300p. 1987. pap. 9.99 (*0-8307-1185-6*, 5418968, Regal Bks) Gospel Lght.

Chastain, Jill, ed. see Moulder, John F., et al.

Chastain, Joel W., ed. see AEC Technical Information Center Staff.

***Chastain, John P., ed.** Fourth International Dairy Housing Conference: Proceedings: January 1998, St. Louis, Missouri. LC 97-77950. (Illus.). 388p. 1998. pap. 55.75 (*0-929355-89-X*, P0198) Am Soc Ag Eng.

Chastain, Kenneth. Developing Second - Language Skills: Theory to Practice. 3rd ed. 438p. (C). 1988. pap. text 16.00 (*0-15-517619-6*) Harcourt Coll Pubs.

— Imaginate! 2nd ed. (College Spanish Ser.). (C). 1991. mass mkt., teacher ed. 21.95 (*0-8384-2223-3*) Heinle & Heinle.

— Spanish Grammar in Review. LC 94-137654. (SPA., Illus.). 352p. 1994. pap. 16.95 (*0-8442-7670-7*, 76707, Natl Textbk Co) NTC Contemp Pub Co.

Chastain, Kenneth & Guntermann. Imaginate! Managing Conversations in Spanish. (C). 1987. 28.95 (*0-8384-1495-8*); 16.95 (*0-8384-1488-5*) Heinle & Heinle.

Chastain, Larry. Fundamentals of Industrial Mechanics. LC 99-28945. (Illus.). 293p. (C). 1999. 72.00 (*0-13-506981-5*, Macmillan Coll) P-H.

***Chastain, Sandra.** Baring It All: (Sweet Talkin' Guys) (Temptation Ser.: No. 768). 2000. per. 3.99 (*0-373-25868-2*, 1-25868-0, Harlequin) Harlequin Bks.

Chastain, Sandra. Jasmine & Silk. 1993. mass mkt. 3.99 (*0-373-28756-9*, 1-28756-4) Harlequin Bks.

***Chastain, Sandra.** The Outlaw Bride. 2000. mass mkt. 5.99 (*0-553-58047-7*) Bantam.

Chastain, Sandra. The Runaway Bride. 304p. 1999. mass mkt. 5.99 (*0-553-57584-8*) Bantam.

— Shotgun Groom. 336p. 1998. mass mkt. 5.99 (*0-553-57583-X*, Fanfare) Bantam.

— Summer of the Soldiers. 416p. 1993. mass mkt. 4.99 (*1-55817-676-4*, Pinncle Kensgtn) Kensgtn Pub Corp.

— Sweetwater. 352p. 1990. mass mkt. 4.95 (*0-446-35881-9*, Pub. by Warner Bks) Little.

***Chastain, Sandra, et al.** Sweet Tea & Jesus Shoes. 190p. 2000. pap. 14.95 (*0-9673035-0-8*, M-2000) BelleBks.

Chastain Sowa, Helen. Louise Moillon Seventeenth Century Still-Life Artist. LC 98-73394. (Illus.). vii, 96p. (C). 1998. 29.95 (*0-9666424-0-6*) Chateau Pubg.

***Chastain, Stephen D.** Iron Melting Cupola Furnaces for the Small Foundry, Vol. I. (Illus.). 128p. 2000. 19.95 (*0-9702203-0-8*) S D Chastain.

Chastain, Thomas. Perry Mason in the Case of the Burning Bequest. 224p. 1991. mass mkt. 3.99 (*0-380-71318-7*, Avon Bks) Morrow Avon.

— Perry Mason in the Case of Too Many Murders. 256p. 1990. pap. 3.95 (*0-380-70787-X*, Avon Bks) Morrow Avon.

— Perry Mason in the Case of Too Many Murders. large type ed. LC 90-10732. 322p. 1990. 19.95 (*0-89621-974-7*) Thorndike Pr.

— The Prosecutor. large type ed. LC 92-44635. (General Ser.). 293p. 1993. reprint ed. lib. bdg. 17.95 (*1-56054-656-5*) Thorndike Pr.

Chasteen. Accounting: Income Taxes. 2nd ed. 1998. 6.00 (*0-07-229777-8*) McGraw.

— Accounting: Leases. 2nd ed. 1998. 6.50 (*0-07-229778-6*) McGraw.

— Accounting Pensions. 2nd ed. 1998. 7.50 (*0-07-229776-X*) McGraw.

— Inter. Accounting. 6th ed. 440p. 1997. pap. 28.13 (*0-07-011959-7*) McGraw.

— Inter. Accounting Word, Vol. 1. 6th ed. 416p. 1998. pap. 35.00 (*0-07-292924-3*) McGraw.

— Intermediate Accounting. 5th ed. 1994. teacher ed. 32.50 (*0-07-011090-5*) McGraw.

— Intermediate Accounting: Check Figures. 5th ed. 1994. 32.50 (*0-07-011091-3*) McGraw.

— Intermediate Accounts & Update Supplement. 5th ed. 1996. 72.25 (*0-07-913295-2*) McGraw.

***Chasteen.** Principles of Accounting. 2nd ed. 1999. pap. text 7.78 (*0-07-010954-0*); pap. text, wbk. ed. 7.78 (*0-07-010955-9*) McGraw.

Chasteen, Edgar R. Runner. LC 79-53673. (Illus.). 177p. 1980. 12.95 (*0-934864-00-4*) Amity Bks MO.

***Chasteen, John.** Born in Blood & Fire: A Concise History of Latin America. 320p. 2000. 26.95 (*0-393-05048-3*) Norton.

***Chasteen, John C.** Born in Blood & Fire: A Concise History of Latin America. LC 00-41868. 2000. pap. write for info. (*0-393-97613-0*, Norton Paperbks) Norton.

Chasteen, John C. Heroes on Horseback: A Life & Times of the Last Gaucho Caudillos. LC 94-18720. (Dialogos Ser.). (Illus.). 241p. (C). 1995. pap. 19.95 (*0-8263-1598-4*) U of NM Pr.

Chasteen, John C. & Tulchin, Joseph S., eds. Problems in Modern Latin American History: A Reader. LC 93-17715. (Latin American Silhouettes Ser.). 348p. (C). 1993. text 45.00 (*0-8420-2327-5*, SR Bks) Scholarly Res Inc.

Chasteen, John C., ed. & tr. see Halperin Donghi, Tulio.

Chasteen, John C., tr. see Vianna, Hermano.

Chasteen, Joseph E., jt. auth. see Miyasaki-Ching, Cara M.

Chasteen, Lanny G., et al. Intermediate Accounting. 5th ed. LC 94-13722. 6p. (C). 1994. text 73.74 (*0-07-011087-5*) McGraw.

— Intermediate Accounting. 6th ed. LC 97-39530. 1328p. 1997. 94.06 (*0-07-011901-5*) McGraw.

— Intermediate Accounting, Vol. 2. 448p. (C). 1984. 8.00 (*0-685-07261-4*) McGraw.

— Intermediate Accounting Chapters 11-21: Working Papers. 5th ed. 1994. pap. text, wbk. ed. 26.00 (*0-07-011195-2*) McGraw.

Chasteen, N. Dennis, ed. Vanadium in Biological Systems: Physiology & Biochemistry. (C). 1990. text 166.50 (*0-7923-0733-X*) Kluwer Academic.

Chasteen, Thomas G., ed. Qualitative & Instrumental Analysis of Environmental Significant Elements. 140p. 1993. pap. 50.95 (*0-471-58649-8*) Wiley.

Chastel, A. Atelier du Peintre: Dictionnaire des Termes Techniques. (FRE.). 1998. 35.00 (*0-320-00399-X*) Fr & Eur.

Chastel, Andre. A Chronicle of Italian Renaissance Painting. Murray, Linda & Murray, Peter, trs. LC 83-73211. (Illus.). 256p. 1984. text 135.00 (*0-8014-1524-1*) Cornell U Pr.

— French Art: Prehistory to the Middle Ages. (Illus.). 336p. 75.00 (*2-08-013566-X*, Pub. by Flammarion) Abbeville Pr.

— French Art: The Ancien Regime 1620-1775. (Illus.). 336p. 1996. 75.00 (*2-08-013617-8*, Pub. by Flammarion) Abbeville Pr.

— French Art Vol. 2: The Renaissance, 1430-1620. Dusinberre, Deke, tr. LC 97-123672. (Illus.). 336p. 1995. 75.00 (*2-08-013583-X*, Pub. by Flammarion) Abbeville Pr.

— The Sack of Rome, 1527. Archer, Beth, tr. LC 82-47587. (Illus.). 430p. 1982. text 75.00 (*0-691-09947-2*, Pub. by Princeton U Pr) Cal Prin Full Svc.

Chastellux, Francois J. An Essay on Public Happiness: Investigating the State of Human Nature, under Each of Its Particular Appearances, Through the Several Periods of History. 2 vols., Set. LC 67-29497. (Reprints of Economic Classics Ser.). 1969. reprint ed. 125.00 (*0-678-00557-5*) Kelley.

Chastellux, Francois J. De, see De Chastellux, Francois J.

Chastin, Thomas, jt. auth. see Adler, Bill, Jr.

Chaston. Lois Lowry. LC 97-8271. 1997. 32.00 (*0-8057-4034-1*, Twyne) Mac Lib Ref.

Chaston, Ian. Customer-Focused Marketing. LC 92-26506. (Marketing for Professionals Ser.). 1992. write for info. (*0-07-707698-2*) McGraw.

Chaston, Ian, jt. auth. see Badger, Beryl.

Chaston, James F., Jr., jt. auth. see Darling, George K.

Chaston, Peter R. Hurricanes! (Illus.). 182p. (Orig.). (C). 1996. pap. 29.00 (*0-9645172-2-1*) Chaston Scient.

— Terror from the Skies! (Illus.). 136p. (Orig.). (C). 1995. pap. 29.00 (*0-9645172-1-3*) Chaston Scient.

— Thunderstorms, Tornadoes & Hail! unabridged ed. LC 98-94957. (Illus.). 224p. 1999. pap. 29.00 (*0-9645172-6-4*) Chaston Scient.

— Weather Maps: How to Read & Interpret All the Basic Weather Charts. 2nd unabridged ed. (Illus.). 230p. (Orig.). 1997. pap., per. 29.00 (*0-9645172-4-8*) Chaston Scient.

Chaston, Peter R., jt. auth. see Balsama, Joseph J.

Chaston, Peter R., jt. auth. see Moore, James T.

Chasuk, Tom. The Bean Gourmet Presents the Canned Bean Cookbook. LC 91-158335. 48p. 1993. pap. 5.95 (*0-9637249-0-8*) T Chasuk.

Chaszar, Edward. The International Problem of National Minorities. 3rd rev. ed. (Illus.). 180p. (C). 22.00 (*1-882785-02-9*) Matthias Corvinus.

Chatalian, George. Epistemology & Skepticism: An Enquiry into the Nature of Epistemology. LC 90-38855. (Journal of the History of Philosophy Monograph Ser.). 96p. (Orig.). (C). 1991. pap. 17.95 (*0-8093-1672-2*) S Ill U Pr.

Chatani, Masahiro. Origamic Architecture: Tour of Nara, Ancient Capital of Japan. 82p. 1993. pap. 39.95 (*4-395-27043-3*, Pub. by Shokokusha) Bks Nippan.

— Origamic Architecture Goes Modern: Building Masterpieces. (Illus.). 96p. 1991. pap. 39.95 (*4-395-27040-9*, Pub. by Shokokusha) Bks Nippan.

— Paper Magic: Pop-Up Paper Craft. (Illus.). 92p. 1988. pap. 15.00 (*0-87040-757-0*) Japan Pubns USA.

— Pop-Up Gift Cards. LC 88-80140. (Illus.). 92p. (Orig.). 1988. pap. 15.00 (*0-87040-768-6*) Japan Pubns USA.

— Pop-up Greeting Cards: A Creative Personal Touch for Every Occasion. (Illus.). 96p. (Orig.). 1986. pap. 15.00 (*0-87040-733-3*) Japan Pubns USA.

— Pop-Up Origamic Architecture. (Illus.). 87p. (Orig.). 1985. pap. 15.00 (*0-87040-656-6*) Japan Pubns USA.

Chatani, Masahiro, ed. Origamic Architecture Around the World. 2nd ed. (Illus.). 66p. 1989. pap. 29.95 (*4-395-27017-4*, Pub. by Shokokusha) Bks Nippan.

Chatani, Masahiro & Nakawa, Keiko, eds. A Paradise of Origamic Architecture. 2nd ed. (Illus.). 76p. 1989. pap. 34.95 (*4-395-27018-2*, Pub. by Shokokusha) Bks Nippan.

Chatani, Masahiro & Nakazawa, Keiko. Great American Buildings: Origami Cutouts of Everybody's Favorite Landmarks. (Illus.). 52p. (Orig.). 1991. pap. 15.95 (*4-7700-1538-0*) Kodansha.

— Pop-Up Geometric Origami. (Illus.). 86p. 1994. pap. 15.00 (*0-87040-943-3*) Japan Pubns USA.

Chateau, B. & Lapillone, B. Energy Demand: Facts & Trends. (Topics in Energy Ser.). (Illus.). 280p. 1982. 68.95 (*0-387-81675-5*) Spr-Verlag.

Chateau Elan Staff. A Taste of Chateau Elan, Vol. 1. LC 95-61994. 224p. 1995. 21.95 (*0-9649347-0-1*) Chateau Elan.

Chateau, Jean. Los Grandes Pedagogos. (SPA.). 340p. 1999. pap. 7.99 (*968-16-0468-7*, Pub. by Fondo) Continental Bk.

Chateaubriand, Francois-Rene de. Atala. Letessier, Fernand, ed. (Class. Garnier Ser.). pap. 10.95 (*0-8288-9344-6*, F58479) Fr & Eur.
— Atala. unabridged ed. (FRE.). pap. 5.95 (*2-87714-169-1*, Pub. by Bookking Intl) Distribks Inc.
— Atala, Rene, Les Aventures du Dernier Abencerage. (Folio Ser.: No. 1017). (FRE.). (Orig.). pap. 8.95 (*2-07-037017-8*) Schoenhof.
— Itineraire de Paris a Jerusalem. 366p. reprint ed. write for info. (*0-318-71328-4*) G Olms Pubs.
— Lettres Inedites et Manuscripts: Bulletins de la Societe Chateaubriand, Vol. 15. (FRE., Illus.). 96p. 1972. pap. 79.95 (*0-7859-5362-0*) Fr & Eur.
— Maximes et Pensees. 8.95 (*0-686-54369-6*) Fr & Eur.
— Memoires d'Outre-Tombe, 3 vols., Set. (FRE.). 256p. 1980. 13.95 (*0-7859-1182-0*, 2259005403) Fr & Eur.
— Memoires D'Outre-Tombe, Tombe 2. (Pleiade Ser.). (FRE.). 1496p. 1951. pap. 73.95 (*2-07-010128-2*) Schoenhof.
— Memoires D'Outre-Tombe, Tome 1. (Pleiade Ser.). (FRE.). 1232p. 1951. pap. 74.95 (*2-07-010127-4*) Schoenhof.

Chateaubriand, Francois-Rene de. Oeuvres Romanesques et Voyages, 2 vols., 1. deluxe ed. Regard, Maurice, ed. (Pleiade Ser.). 74.95 (*2-07-010129-0*) Schoenhof.
— Oeuvres Romanesques et Voyages, 2 vols., 2. deluxe ed. Regard, Maurice, ed. (Pleiade Ser.). 76.95 (*2-07-010130-4*) Schoenhof.
— Oeuvres Romanesques et Voyages, Vol. 1. deluxe ed. Regard, Maurice, ed. (FRE.). 1504p. 1969. 110.00 (*0-7859-3748-X*, 2070101290) Fr & Eur.
— Oeuvres Romanesques et Voyages, Vol. 2. Regard, Maurice, ed. (FRE.). 1824p. 1969. lib. bdg. 125.00 (*0-7859-3749-8*, 2070101304) Fr & Eur.

Chateaubriand, Francois-Rene de & Giraud, Victor. Amour et Vieillesse: Avec: Etude sur Chateaubriand Romanesque et Amoreaux. 43p. 1922. 50.00 (*0-686-54359-9*) Fr & Eur.

Chateaubriand, Francois-Rene de & Guyard, Marius Francois. Vie de Rance. (Folio Ser.: No. 1769). (FRE.). 7.95 (*2-07-037769-5*) Schoenhof.

Chateaubriand, Francois-Rene de & Roy, Claude. Memoires. 576p. 1964. 8.95 (*0-686-54370-X*) Fr & Eur.

Chateaubriand, Francois-Rene de, et al. Les Aventures Du Dernier Abencerage. (FRE.). 306p. 1978. pap. 13.95 (*0-7859-1537-0*, 2070370178) Fr & Eur.
— Correspondance Generale: 1789-1807, Vol. 1. (FRE.). 682p. 1977. 89.95 (*0-7859-1141-3*, 2070291154) Fr & Eur.

Chateaubriand, Francois-Rene De, see De Chateaubriand, Francois-Rene.

Chateauneuf, Francois. Dialogue sur la Musique des Anciens. fac. ed. (Monuments of Music & Music Literature in Facsimile Ser., Series II: Vol. 38). (FRE.). 1966. lib. bdg. 35.00 (*0-8450-2238-5*) Broude.

Chateauraynaud, P. Dictionnaire de L'Urbanisme. (FRE.). 1998. 180.00 (*0-320-00166-0*) Fr & Eur.

Chateauvert, Melinda M. Marching Together: Women of the Brotherhood of Sleeping Car Porters. LC 97-4579. (Working Class in American History Ser.). 320p. 1997. text 46.95 (*0-252-02340-4*); pap. text 17.95 (*0-252-06636-7*) U of Ill Pr.

Chatel, Eiko & Tanegashima, Kaori. Elementary Japanese. 2nd ed. 144p. (C). 1996. pap. text, per., wbk. ed. 16.95 (*0-7872-3316-1*, 41331601) Kendall-Hunt.

Chatel, M., et al, eds. Brain Oncology. (Developments in Oncology Ser.). (C). 1987. text 345.50 (*0-89838-954-2*) Kluwer Academic.

***Chatelain, Bonnie.** . . . And the Fat Came Back. LC 99-196364. ix, 271 p. 1998. write for info. (*1-56684-346-4*) Evans Bk Dist.

Chatelain, Heli, tr. Folk-Tales of Angola. LC 09-697. (AFS Memoirs Ser.: Vol. 1). 1969. reprint ed. 32.00 (*0-527-01053-7*) Periodicals Srv.

Chatelain, Maurice. Our Cosmic Ancestors. rev. ed. Donovan, Marlene, ed. (Illus.). 226p. 1988. reprint ed. pap. 9.95 (*0-929686-00-4*) Temple Golden Pubns.

Chatelaine & Levine. Good Me, Bad Me, Not Me: Harry Stack Sullivan: An Introduction to His Thought. 96p. (C). 1992. pap. text 14.95 (*0-8403-7720-7*) Kendall-Hunt.

Chatelant, Charles. Vocabulaire de Base Allemand-Francais. (FRE & GER.). 211p. 1984. pap. 20.95 (*0-7859-4848-1*) Fr & Eur.

Chatelet, Francois. Dictionnaire des Oeuvres Politiques. 3rd ed. (FRE.). 1360p. 1995. 225.00 (*0-7859-9933-7*) Fr & Eur.

Chatelet, Francois, et al. Dictionnaire des Oeuvres Politiques. 2nd ed. (FRE.). 1168p. 1989. 175.00 (*0-8288-7648-7*) Fr & Eur.

Chatelet, Gabrielle E. Institutions Physiques Adressees a Mr. Son Fils. (Christian Wolff, Gedammelte Werke, Materialien und Dokumente Ser.: No. 28). xi, 542p. 1988. reprint ed. 135.00 (*3-487-07984-4*) G Olms Pubs.

***Chatelet, Gilles.** Figuring Space: Philosophy, Mathematics & Physics. LC 99-38092. (Science & Philosophy Ser.). 224p. 1999. 138.00 (*0-7923-5880-5*) Kluwer Academic.

Chatelet, Noelle. A Contre-Sens. (FRE.). 214p. 1990. pap. 11.95 (*0-7859-2151-6*, 2070382966) Fr & Eur.
— Histoires des Bouches. (FRE.). 192p. 1988. pap. 10.95 (*0-685-66711-1*, 2070379035) Fr & Eur.

Chatelier, P. R., jt. auth. see Seidel, R. J.

Chatelier, Paul R., jt. ed. see Seidel, Robert J.

Chatelin, Francois & Ahues, Mario. Eigenvalues of Matrices. LC 93-3430. (Pure & Applied Mathematics: A Wiley-Interscience Series of Texts, Monographs & Tracts). 400p. 1993. 225.00 (*0-471-93538-7*) Wiley.

Chatelin, Francoise. Spectral Approximation of Linear Operators. (Computer Science & Applied Mathematics Ser.). 1983. text 124.00 (*0-12-170620-6*) Acad Pr.

Chatelin, Francoise C. & Fraysse, Valerie. Lectures on Finite Precision Computations. LC 95-45140. (Software, Environments & Tools Ser.: No. 1). xvi, 235p. 1996. pap. 47.50 (*0-89871-358-7*, SE01) Soc Indus-Appl Math.

***Chatelin, Raymond.** City-Smart Guidebook: Vancouver. (Illus.). 272p. 2000. pap. 15.95 (*1-56261-482-7*, City Smart) Avalon Travel.

Chatelin, Raymond. Guide to Western Canada: Featuring Canada's World-Class Cities. 5th ed. LC 97-49599. (Illus.). 352p. 1998. pap. 17.95 (*0-7627-0182-X*) Globe Pequot.

Chatellard, Isabelle. City Mouse & Country Mouse: A Classic Fairy Tale. LC 98-36159. (Little Pebbles Ser.). 32p. (J). (ps-1). 1999. 6.95 (*0-7892-0513-0*, Abbeville Kids) Abbeville Pr.

Chatellier, Louis. The Religion of the Poor: Rural Missions in Europe & the Formation of Modern Catholicism, c. 1500-1800. Pearce, Brian, tr. (Illus.). 260p. (C). 1997. text 59.95 (*0-521-56201-5*) Cambridge U Pr.

***Chatenever, Robert.** Understanding Electricity & Wiring Diagrams for HVAC/R. LC 99-18026. (Illus.). 311p. 1999. 65.00 (*0-13-517897-5*) P-H.

Chatenoud, Lucienne. Monoclonal Antibodies in Transplantation. LC 95-24139. (Medical Intelligence Unit Ser.). 181p. 1995. 89.00 (*1-57059-269-1*) Landes Bioscience.

Chater, A. G., tr. see Ibsen, Henrik.

Chater, A. G., tr. see Nansen, Fridtjof.

Chater, A. G., tr. see Undset, Sigrid.

Chater, A. G., tr. see Valentin, Hugo.

Chater, Arthur G., tr. see Nansen, Fridtjof.

Chater, Arthur G., tr. see Undset, Sigrid.

Chater, James M. Luca Marenzio & the Italian Madrigal, 1577-1593, 2 vols., 1. LC 81-13095. (Studies in British Musicology). 273p. reprint ed. pap. 84.70 (*0-8357-1255-9*, 207025900001) Bks Demand.
— Luca Marenzio & the Italian Madrigal, 1577-1593, 2 vols., 2. LC 81-13095. (Studies in British Musicology). 243p. reprint ed. pap. 75.40 (*0-8357-1256-7*, 207025900002) Bks Demand.

Chater, K. W. A. & Somerville, H. J., eds. The Oil Industry & Microbial Ecosystems: Proceedings of a Meeting Organized by the Institute of Petroleum & Held at the University of Warwick, England, September, 1977. LC 80-462468. (Illus.). 260p. reprint ed. pap. 80.60 (*0-8357-3088-3*, 203934500012) Bks Demand.

Chater, Kathy. Production Research. LC 97-151437. 160p. 1998. pap. 29.95 (*0-240-51466-1*, Focal) Buttrwrth-Heinemann.

Chater, Keith F., jt. ed. see Hopwood, David A.

Chater, N., jt. ed. see Oaksford, M.

Chater, Robin. The National Childcare Directory. (C). 1990. 300.00 (*1-872838-01-4*, Pub. by IPM Hse) St Mut.

Chater, Shirley. Understanding Research in Nursing. (Offset Publications: No. 14). 1975. pap. text 3.60 (*92-4-170014-9*, 1120014) World Health.

Chater, Shirley, jt. ed. see Stern, Phyllis N.

Chaterjee. International Engineering & Construction Contracts. 272p. 1999. pap. 74.00 (*0-419-21670-7*) Thomson Learn.

Chaterjee, A. K., et al. Cement & Concrete Science & Technology, Vol. 1, Pt. II. (Progress in Cement & Concrete Ser.). (Illus.). 525p. 1992. text 125.00 (*81-85522-01-4*, Pub. by ABI Books) Humanities.

Chaterjee, K. & Sutton, G., eds. Clinical Cardiology: An Illustrated Text. 2nd ed. (Illus.). 440p. 1999. text 98.50 (*0-412-78310-X*, Pub. by E A) OUP.

Chaterjee, Pratap, jt. auth. see Finger, Matthias.

Chaterjee, Rajeswari. Advanced Microware Engineering: Special Advanced Topics. 1988. text 62.95 (*0-470-21244-6*) P-H.

Chateu, Kathy & Miller, Paula. Celebrating Catholic Rites & Rituals in Religion Class. 80p. (J). 1998. pap. 9.95 (*0-89622-939-4*) Twenty-Third.

Chatfield, Averil B. Fundamentals of High Accuracy Inertial Navigation. 300p. 1997. 99.95 (*1-56347-243-0*) AIAA.

Chatfield, C., ed. see Sprent, P.

***Chatfield, Carl S. & Johnson, Tim.** Microsoft Project 2000 Step by Step. 2000. pap. 29.99 incl. cd-rom (*0-7356-0920-9*) Microsoft.

Chatfield, Carl S., jt. auth. see Johns, Timothy.

Chatfield, Charles. The American Peace Movement: Ideals & Activism. (Social Movements Past & Present Ser.). 226p. 1992. pap. 33.00 (*0-8057-3851-7*, Twyne) Mac Lib Ref.

Chatfield, Charles & Ilukhina, Ruzanna, eds. Peace-Mir: An Anthology of Historic Alternatives to War. (Studies on Peace & Conflict Resolution). 386p. 1994. text 49.50 (*0-8156-2601-0*) Syracuse U Pr.

Chatfield, Charles & Van Den Dungen, Peter, eds. Peace Movements & Political Cultures. LC 88-1902. 320p. 1988. text 41.00 (*0-87049-576-3*) U of Tenn Pr.

Chatfield, Charles, jt. auth. see DeBenedetti, Charles.

Chatfield, Cheryl A. The Trust Factor: The Art of Doing Business. LC 97-21295. 160p. (Orig.). 1997. pap. 16.95 (*0-86534-264-4*) Sunstone Pr.

Chatfield, Chris. The Analysis of Time Series: An Introduction. 5th ed. 1998. 39.95 (*0-412-71640-2*) Thomson Learn.

Chatfield, Christopher. Analysis Time Series ED4, 1 vol. 4th ed. 288p. (gr. 13). 1989. ring bd. 34.95 (*0-412-31820-2*, Chap & Hall CRC) CRC Pr.
— Problem Solving: A Statistician's Guide. 300p. 1989. 79.95 (*0-412-28670-X*) Chapman & Hall.
— Statistics for Technology: A Course in Applied Statistics. 3rd ed. 384p. (C). (gr. 13). 1983. lib. bdg. 34.95 (*0-412-25340-2*, NO. 6845) Chapman & Hall.

Chatfield, Christopher & Collins, A. J. Introduction to Multivariate Analysis. 248p. (C). (gr. 13). 1981. per. 41.95 (*0-412-16040-4*, NO.6696, Chap & Hal CRC) CRC Pr.

Chatfield, Donald F. Dinner with Jesus: And Other Left-Handed Story-Sermons. 112p. 1988. pap. 8.99 (*0-310-52021-5*, 12825P) Zondervan.

Chatfield, Douglas, jt. auth. see Lawlis, G. Frank.

Chatfield, Gary R. No Vacancy! Apartment Manager's Guide to Full Occupancy. xii, 50p. 1999. pap. 10.95 (*0-9672105-0-X*) WordsNumbers.

Chatfield, Hale. Episodes: A Post-Midcentury Album. (Illus.). 206p. (Orig.). 1993. pap. 10.00 (*0-9628478-2-8*) North Star OH.
— North Star: A Novella. (Illus.). 76p. (Orig.). 1992. pap. 6.00 (*0-9628478-1-X*) North Star OH.
— Possesions. (Cleveland Poets Ser.: No. 36). 34p. (Orig.). 1984. pap. 4.00 (*0-914946-39-0*) Cleveland St Univ Poetry Ctr.
— The Sotto Voce Massacres. (Orig.). 1990. pap. 8.00 (*0-9628478-0-1*) North Star OH.
— Vox. (Illus.). 62p. (Orig.). 1995. pap. 13.00 (*0-9628478-5-2*) North Star OH.

Chatfield, Hale, ed. see Tinsley, William C., et al

Chatfield, June. Reptiles: A Unique First Visual Reference. (Look Inside Ser.). (Illus.). 20p. (J). (gr. 4-6). 1995. 10.99 (*0-89577-801-7*) Rdrs Digest.

Chatfield, Kimball. Medicine from the Mountains: Medicinal Plants of the Sierra Nevada. LC 97-92169. (Illus.). 219p. 1997. pap. 17.95 (*0-9658001-0-5*) Range Light.

Chatfield, Michael & Brief, Richard P., eds. The English View of Accountants Duties & Responsibilities: 1881-1902. LC 77-87312. (Development of Contemporary Accounting Thought Ser.). 1978. lib. bdg. 24.95 (*0-405-10925-3*) Ayer.

Chatfield, Michael & Nielson, Denis P. Cost Accounting. 1172p. (C). 1983. teacher ed. write for info. (*0-15-514142-2*); student ed. write for info. (*0-318-56981-7*) Harcourt Coll Pubs.

Chatfield, Michael & Vangermeersch, Richard, eds. The History of Accounting: An Encyclopedia. LC 95-20710. (Reference Library of the Humanities Ser.: Vol 1573). 680p. 1996. text 100.00 (*0-8153-0809-4*) Garland.

Chatfield, Sandra, ed. see Harris, Henry A.

Chatfield, Steve, et al. Animaly ABC. LC 99-191926. (Illus.). iii, 42p. (J). (ps-6). 1998. pap. 19.95 (*0-9663505-0-2*) Bubba Bear.

Chatfield-Taylor, Joan. The San Francisco Opera: Celebrating the First Seventy-Five Years. LC 97-5085. 1997. 50.00 (*0-8118-1368-1*) Chronicle Bks.

Chatgilialoglu, Chryssostomos & Snieckus, Victor, eds. Chemical Synthesis: Gnosis to Prognosis. (NATO ASI Ser.: Series E, Vol. 320). 1996. text 327.50 (*0-7923-4041-8*) Kluwer Academic.

Chatha, G. S., jt. auth. see Bir, S. S.

Chatham, Anne B. Tidewater Families of the New World & Their Westward Migrations: Case Studies in Southern States Research. Clifford, Karen, ed. & illus. by. 1312p. Date not set. 109.95 (*1-881825-13-2*) Hist Pubns TX.

Chatham-Baker, Odette. Baby Lore: Ceremonies, Myths & Traditions to Celebrate a Baby's Birth. (Illus.). 160p. 1992. text 22.95 (*0-02-550665-X*) Macmillan.

Chatham, Bernie. Time Out for Cooking. (Illus.). 320p. 1997. pap. 19.95 (*0-9654406-1-3*) Time Out Cooking.

Chatham, Glenda. Time Pieces. 68p. 1998. pap. 8.00 (*1-57502-766-6*, P02116) Morris Pubng.

Chatham, Hugh H., Jr., jt. auth. see McClain, Dan.

Chatham, James O. Sundays down South: A Pastor's Stories. LC 99-24148. (Folklife in the South Ser.). 224p. 1999. 25.00 (*1-57806-175-X*) U Pr of Miss.
— Sundays down South: A Pastor's Stories LC 99-24148. (Folklife in the South Ser.). 1999. write for info. (*1-57806-176-8*) U Pr of Miss.

Chatham, Joe. Eternal Security Obtained after Completing a Faithful Course. 1978. pap. 1.50 (*0-934942-05-6*) White Wing Pub.

Chatham, John C., et al, eds. The Heart in Diabetes. (Developments in Cardiovascular Medicine Ser.: Vol. 185). 272p. (C). 1996. text 140.50 (*0-7923-4052-3*) Kluwer Academic.

Chatham, Judy McCart. A Whirlwind's Breath: A Memoir of Healing & Faith at Indiana's Riley Hospital. LC 98-72784. 88 p. 1998. 18.95 (*1-57860-088-X*) Guild Pr IN.

Chatham, Larry. Smith's Canyon. large type ed. (Dales Large Print Ser.). 224p. 1996. pap. 18.99 (*1-85389-654-3*, Dales) Ulverscroft.

***Chatham, Robina & Patching, Keith.** How the IT Manager Gets Streetwise. 256p. 2000. pap. 47.95 (*0-7506-4792-2*, Digital DEC) Buttrwrth-Heinemann.

Chatham, Romara D. Fasting: A Biblical Historical Study. 2nd ed. LC 85-73212. 184p. 1999. pap. 9.99 (*0-88270-769-8*, Bridge) Bridge-Logos.

Chatham, Russell. The Angler's Coast. 2nd ed. LC 88-63678. (Illus.). 184p. 1991. 34.95 (*0-944439-12-8*) Clark City Pr.

Chatham, Russell, ed. & illus. see McGuane, Thomas, et al.

Chathan, James R. Dissertations in Hispanic Languages & Literatures: An Index of Dissertations Completed in the United States & Canada, 2 vols., Vol. 1: 1876-1966. LC 70-80093. 134p. 1970. reprint ed. pap. 41.60 (*0-608-03957-8*, 204549100001) Bks Demand.
— Dissertations in Hispanic Languages & Literatures: An Index of Dissertations Completed in the United States & Canada, 2 vols., Vol. 2: 1967-1977. LC 70-80093. 174p. 1981. reprint ed. pap. 54.00 (*0-608-03958-6*, 204549100002) Bks Demand.

Chathasaigh, Maire Ni, ed. see Woods, Sylvia.

***Chaticleer Press Incorporation.** Audubon Guide to Southwest. 5th ed. 1999. 19.95 (*0-676-59253-8*) Knopf.

Chatila, R. & Hirzinger, Gerhard, eds. Experimental Robotics II: The Second International Symposium, Toulouse, France, June 25-27, 1991. (Lecture Notes in Control & Information Sciences: Vol. 190). 575p. 1993. 111.95 (*0-387-19851-2*) Spr-Verlag.

Chatillon, Jean. D'Isidore de Seville a Saint Thomas d'Aquin: Etudes d'Histoire et de Theologie. (Collected Studies: No. CS225). (FRE.). 379p. (C). 1985. reprint ed. text 119.95 (*0-86078-173-9*, Pub. by Variorum) Ashgate Pub Co.

Chatillon, Walther Von, see Von Chatillon, Walther.

Chatman, Elfreda A. The Information World of Retired Women, 29. LC 92-8679. (New Directions in Information Management Ser.: No. 29). 168p. 1992. 45.00 (*0-313-25492-3*, CIW/, Greenwood Pr) Greenwood.

Chatman, Seymour. Coming to Terms: The Rhetoric of Narrative in Fiction & Film. LC 90-55119. (Illus.). 272p. 1990. pap. text 16.95 (*0-8014-9736-1*) Cornell U Pr.

Chatman, Seymour, jt. ed. see Van Peer, Willie.

Chatman, Seymour B. Antonioni, or, the Surface of the World. LC 85-1025. 384p. 1996. pap. 19.95 (*0-520-05341-9*, Pub. by U CA Pr) Cal Prin Full Svc.
— Coming to Terms: The Rhetoric of Narrative in Fiction & Film. LC 90-55119. (Illus.). 272p. 1990. text 42.50 (*0-8014-2485-2*) Cornell U Pr.
— The Later Style of Henry James. LC 86-15043. (Language & Style Ser.). 135p. 1986. reprint ed. lib. bdg. 55.00 (*0-313-25218-1*, CHLA, Greenwood Pr) Greenwood.
— Reading Narrative Fiction. 638p. (Orig.). (C). 1992. pap. text 23.60 (*0-02-322111-9*, Macmillan Coll) P-H.
— Story & Discourse: Narrative Structure in Fiction & Film. 288p. 1978. pap. text 15.95 (*0-8014-9186-X*) Cornell U Pr.

Chatman, Seymour B., et al, eds. A Semiotic Landscape (Panorama Semiotique) (Approaches to Semiotics Ser.: No. 29). (FRE.). 1979. text 192.35 (*90-279-7928-6*) Mouton.

Chatman, Seymour B. & Fink, Guido, eds. L' Avventura. (Films in Print Ser.). (Illus.). 192p. (Orig.). (C). 1988. text 35.00 (*0-8135-1334-0*); pap. text 17.00 (*0-8135-1335-9*) Rutgers U Pr.

Chatman, Urella, ed. see Lynch, L. Riddick.

Chaton, Roland. Recipes for Success: A Guide to Advanced Cuisine. LC 87-22380. 1988. pap. 35.95 (*0-8273-3027-8*) Delmar.

Chatopadhyay, Subhash C. Subhas Chandra Bose: Man, Mission, Means. (C). 1989. 19.50 (*0-8364-2482-4*, Pub. by Minerva) S Asia.

Chatrand, Rene & Embleton, Gerry. British Army in North America, 1793-1815. (Men-at-Arms Ser.). (Illus.). 48p. 1999. pap. 12.95 (*1-85532-741-4*, Pub. by Ospry) Stackpole.
— Spanish Army of the Napoleonic Wars (1), 1793-1808. (Men-at-Arms Ser.). (Illus.). 48p. 1999. pap. 12.95 (*1-85532-763-5*, Pub. by Ospry) Stackpole.

Chatrath, K. J. S., et al. Education for Human Rights & Democracy. LC 99-931771. 177 p. 1998. write for info. (*81-85952-58-2*) Indian Inst.

***Chatrath, Paul & Rahim, Omar.** The MRCS Examination: MCQS & EMQS. LC 99-35373. 1999. write for info. (*0-632-05402-6*, Pub. by Blckwell Science) Iowa St U Pr.

Chatt, Amares & Katz, Seymour. Hair Analysis: Applications in the Biomedical & Environmental Sciences. LC 88-33812. 134p. 1989. 45.00 (*0-89573-310-2*, Wiley-VCH) Wiley.

Chattapadhyay, Swapan, et al, eds. Nonlinear & Collective Phenomena in Beam Physics-1998 WKSP: International Committee on Future Accelerators. LC 99-61288. (Conference Proceedings Ser.). (Illus.). 366p. 1999. 110.00 (*1-56396-862-2*) Am Inst Physics.

Chattapadhyaya. Muhammad, the Prophet of Islam. 1981. 1.50 (*1-56744-152-1*) Kazi Pubns.

Chattell, Alf. Creating Value in the Digital Era: Achieving Success Through Insight, Imagination & Innovation. LC 98-18071. 272p. 1998. text 35.00 (*0-8147-1580-X*) NYU Pr.
— Managing for the Future: An Ecology of Tomorrow's Organization. LC 94-43720. 1995. text 55.00 (*0-312-12431-7*) St Martin.

Chatten, Leslie G. Pharmaceutical Chemistry: Theory & Application, Vol. 1. LC 66-11286. 520p. 1966. pap. 161.20 (*0-608-08301-1*, 205506300001) Bks Demand.

Chatten, Leslie G., ed. Pharmaceutical Chemistry: Instrumental Techniques, Vol. 2. LC 66-11286. 789p. 1969. pap. 200.00 (*0-608-08302-X*, 205506300002) Bks Demand.

Chattergy, Rahul. Spicey Circuits: Elements of Computer-Aided Circuit Analysis. 256p. 1992. boxed set 78.95 (*0-8493-7173-2*, QA) CRC Pr.

Chatterjee, jt. auth. see Robbins, Stephens P.

Chatterjee, A., et al. A New Conformal Absorbing Boundary Condition for Finite Element Meshes & Parallelization of FEMATS. fac. ed. LC QC0020.7. (University of Michigan Report: No. 031155-1-T). 72p. 1993. pap. 30.00 (*0-7837-7694-2*, 204745100007) Bks Demand.

Chatterjee, A., jt. auth. see Varma, M. N.

Chatterjee, A. K., ed. see Abdulov, M. V.

Chatterjee, A. N. Sri Krsna Caitanya: A Historical Study of Gaudiya Vaisnavism. 1985. 22.00 (*0-8364-1321-0*, Pub. by Assoc Bks IA) S Asia.

***Chatterjee, Amal.** Across the Lake. 1998. pap. 17.95 (*1-86159-053-9*, Pub. by Orion Pubng Grp) Trafalgar.
— Across the Lakes. 246p. 1998. pap. 27.00 (*1-86159-052-0*, Pub. by Orion Pubng Grp) Trafalgar.

Chatterjee, Amal. Across the Lakes. LC 98-905444. 246 p. 1998. write for info. (*0-14-027706-4*) Viking Penguin.

C

An Asterisk (*) at the beginning of an entry indicates that the title is appearing for the first time.

Chatterjee, Amit. Beyond the Blast Furnace. LC 93-13331. 272p. 1993. lib. bdg. 210.00 (*0-8493-6676-3*, TN706) CRC Pr.

Chatterjee, Arindam. Investigation of Finite Element-ABC Methods for Electromagnetic Field Simulation. fac. ed. LC QC0665.S3. (University of Michigan Report: No. RL906). 156p. 1994. pap. 48.40 (*0-7837-7696-9*, 204745300007) Bks Demand.

Chatterjee, Arun, et al, eds. Goods Transportation in Urban Areas. 176p. 1989. 5.00 (*0-87262-691-1*) Am Soc Civil Eng.

Chatterjee, Arun & Hendrickson, Chris, eds. Innovative Strategies to Improve Urban Transportation Performance: Proceedings of a Specialty Conference Sponsored by the Urban Transportation Division. 328p. 1985. 6.00 (*0-87262-435-8*) Am Soc Civil Eng.

Chatterjee, Arun K. & Vidaver, Anne K., eds. Advances in Plant Pathology, Vol. 4. (Serial Publication Ser.). 1986. text 104.00 (*0-12-033704-5*) Acad Pr.

Chatterjee, Ashok K. The Yogacara Idealism. (C). 1987. reprint ed. 12.75 (*81-208-0315-9*, Pub. by Motilal Bnarsidass) S Asia.

Chatterjee, Asim K. A Comprehensive History of Jainism. 1978. 20.00 (*0-8364-0225-1*) S Asia.

— Comprehensive History of Jainism, 1000 AD to 1600 AD, Vol. II. 1984. 28.50 (*0-8364-1123-4*, Pub. by Mukhopadhyaya) S Asia.

Chatterjee, B. K. Theory & Design of Concrete Shells. (C). 1988. 44.00 (*81-204-0316-9*, Pub. by Oxford IBH) S Asia.

Chatterjee, B. N. & Das, P. K. Forage Crop Production. (C). 1989. 21.50 (*81-204-0398-3*, Pub. by Oxford IBH) S Asia.

Chatterjee, B. P. Short Text Book of Surgery, Vol. II. (C). 1989. 170.00 (*0-89771-365-6*, Pub. by Current Dist); 170.00 (*0-89771-364-8*, Pub. by Current Dist) St Mut.

— Surgical Diagnosis & Methods of Examination. (C). 1989. 150.00 (*0-89771-366-4*, Pub. by Current Dist) St Mut.

Chatterjee, Bankim C. Kamalakanta: A Collection of Satirical Essays & Reflections. (C). 1992. pap. 7.50 (*81-7167-082-2*, Pub. by Rupa) S Asia.

Chatterjee, Bankimchandra. Rajmohan's Wife. LC 97-904062. (C). 1996. pap. 9.50 (*81-7530-009-4*, Pub. by Ravi Dayal) S Asia.

Chatterjee, Bhabatosh. Rabindranath Tagore & Modern Sensibility. LC 96-902103. 196p. (C). 1996. text 22.00 (*0-19-563796-8*) OUP.

Chatterjee, Bijan R. Indian Cultural Influences in Cambodia. LC 77-87486. reprint ed. 28.00 (*0-404-16799-3*) AMS Pr.

Chatterjee, Biswadeb. Tax Performance in Indian States: A Comparative Study. LC 97-913871. (Illus.). xvi, 319p. 1997. 25.00 (*81-7099-672-4*, Pub. by Mittal Pubs Dist) Nataraj Bks.

Chatterjee, Biswajit, et al. Regional Dimensions of the Indian Economy. LC 99-933672. xv, 332 p. 1998. write for info. (*81-7023-871-4*) Allied Pubs.

Chatterjee, C. Human Physiology, 2 vols. (C). 1987. 100.00 (*0-7855-4649-9*, Pub. by Current Dist) St Mut.

Chatterjee, C., jt. auth. see Sengupta, S.

Chatterjee, Charles. Legal Aspects of Transnational Marketing & Sales Contracts. 141p. 1996. pap. 40.00 (*1-85941-035-9*, Pub. by Cavendish Pubng) Gaunt.

Chatterjee, Choitali. Celebrating Women: International Women's Day in the Soviet Union, 1917-1939. Cuffel, Victoria, ed. (MacArthur Scholar Series, Occasional Paper). 54p. (Orig.). 1991. pap. 1.85 (*1-881157-02-4*) In Ctr Global.

Chatterjee, Debashis. Leading Consciously: A Pilgrimage Toward Self-Mastery. LC 98-154520. 256p. 1998. pap. text 18.95 (*0-7506-9864-0*) Buttrwrth-Heinemann.

Chatterjee, Debjani. Albino Gecko. 100p. 1999. 12.95 (*3-7052-0161-1*, Pub. by Poetry Salzburg) Intl Spec Bk.

— Monkey God & Other Hindu Tales. (Orig.). (C). 1993. 5.00 (*81-7167-146-2*, Pub. by Rupa) S Asia.

Chatterjee, Gautam. Sacred Hindu Symbols. LC 95-910437. (C). 1996. 28.00 (*81-7017-320-5*, Pub. by Abhinav) S Asia.

Chatterjee, Gautam, jt. ed. see Sengupta, Syamalendu.

Chatterjee, Gayatri. Awara. 1992. 10.00 (*81-224-0421-9*) S Asia.

***Chatterjee, Indrani.** Gender, Slavery & Law in Colonial India. LC 99-932758. 300p. 1999. write for info. (*0-19-564181-7*) OUP.

Chatterjee, Jatindra M. Panchadasigita: Gita-Texts Re-Arranged into Fifteen Chapters According to the Principles of Karma, Bhakti & Jnana Yogas with English Translations & Notes. LC 98-902472. 1998. 36.00 (*81-215-0773-1*, Pub. by M Manoharial) Coronet Bks.

Chatterjee, Kumkum. Merchants, Politics & Society in Early Modern India: Bihar, 1733-1820. (Brill's Indological Library: No. 10). (Illus.). 305p. 1996. 94.50 (*90-04-10303-1*) Brill Academic Pubs.

Chatterjee, Lata & Nijkamp, Peter. Urban Problems & Economic Development. (NATO Advanced Study, Behavioral & Social Sciences Ser.: No. 6). 359p. 1981. lib. bdg. 112.50 (*90-286-2661-1*) Kluwer Academic.

Chatterjee, Margaret. The Concept of Spirituality. (C). 1989. 12.50 (*0-8364-2733-5*, Pub. by Allied Pubs) S Asia.

— Gandhi's Religious Thought. LC 83-5841. 208p. 1986. pap. 14.00 (*0-268-01011-0*) U of Notre Dame Pr.

— The Language of Philosophy. 152p. 1981. text 94.00 (*90-247-2372-8*) Kluwer Academic.

— The Religious Spectrum. (Studies in an Indian Context). 196p. 1984. 24.95 (*0-317-39860-1*, Pub. by Allied Pubs) Asia Bk Corp.

— Studies in Modern Jewish & Hindu Thought. LC 96-43150. 192p. 1997. text 59.95 (*0-312-16594-3*) St Martin.

Chatterjee, Margaret, ed. The Philosophy of Nikunja Vihari Banerjee. 1990. 23.00 (*0-685-37829-2*, Pub. by M Manoharial) S Asia.

Chatterjee, Meera. Implementing Health Policy. 324p. (C). 1988. 34.00 (*81-85054-36-3*, Pub. by Manohar) S Asia.

Chatterjee, Meera, jt. auth. see Measham, Anthony R.

Chatterjee, Mitali. Education in Ancient India: From Literary Sources of the Gupta Age. LC 99-931097. xii, 303 p. 1999. 22.00 (*81-246-0113-5*, Pub. by D K Printwrld) Nataraj Bks.

Chatterjee, Molly S., ed. Biochemical Monitoring of the Fetus. LC 93-1477. 1993. 40.00 (*0-387-97892-5*) Spr-Verlag.

Chatterjee, N. D. Applied Mineralogical Thermodynamics Selected Topics. (Illus.). 328p. 1990. 76.95 (*0-387-53215-3*) Spr-Verlag.

Chatterjee, Nandini. Irrigated Agriculture: Case Study of West Bengal. (C). 1995. 24.00 (*0-614-13264-9*, Pub. by Rawat Pubns) S Asia.

Chatterjee, P. K., ed. Absorbency. (Textile Science & Technology Ser.: Vol. 7). xiv, 334p. 1985. 220.50 (*0-444-42377-X*) Elsevier.

Chatterjee, P. K. & Wetherall, P. J. Winding Engine Calculations for the Mining. 1982. 39.95 (*0-419-12650-3*, NO. 6693, E & FN Spon) Routledge.

Chatterjee, Partha. Bengal, Nineteen Twenty to Forty-Seven: The Land Question. 1985. 18.50 (*0-8364-1305-9*, Pub. by KP Bagchi) S Asia.

— The Nation & Its Fragments: Colonial & Postcolonial Histories. LC 93-15536. (Studies in Culture - Power - History). 264p. 1994. text 55.00 (*0-691-03305-6*, Pub. by Princeton U Pr); pap. text 17.95 (*0-691-01943-6*, Pub. by Princeton U Pr) Cal Prin Full Svc.

— Nationalist Thought & the Colonial World: A Derivative Discourse. 190p. (C). 1993. pap. 16.95 (*0-8166-2311-2*) U of Minn Pr.

***Chatterjee, Partha.** The Partha Chatterjee Omnibus: Nationalist Thought & the Colonial World, the Nation & Its Fragments, A Possible India. 802p. 2000. text 29.95 (*0-19-565156-1*) OUP.

Chatterjee, Partha. A Possible India: Essays in Political Criticism. 316p. 1999. pap. text 11.95 (*0-19-564766-1*) OUP.

— The Present History of West Bengal: Essays in Political Criticism. LC 96-912037. (Illus.). 238p. 1997. text 26.00 (*0-19-563945-6*) OUP.

***Chatterjee, Partha.** Present History of West Bengal: Essays in Political Criticism. (Illus.). 240p. 1999. pap. 10.95 (*0-19-564767-X*) OUP.

***Chatterjee, Partha, ed.** State & Politics in India. (Oxford in India Readings: Themes in Indian History Ser.). (Illus.). 588p. 2000. pap. text 14.95 (*0-19-564765-3*) OUP.

Chatterjee, Partha, ed. Texts of Power: Emerging Disciplines in Colonial Bengal. (C). 1996. 28.00 (*81-85604-16-9*, Pub. by Manohar) S Asia.

— Texts of Power: Emerging Disciplines in Colonial Bengal. 232p. 1995. pap. 22.95 (*0-8166-2687-1*); text 57.95 (*0-8166-2686-3*) U of Minn Pr.

— Wages of Freedom: Fifty Years of the Indian Nation-State. LC 98-903535. 338p. 1998. text 32.00 (*0-19-564524-3*) OUP.

Chatterjee, Partha & Pandey, Gyanendra, eds. Subaltern Studies: Writings on South Asian History & Society, Vol. VII. (Oxford India Paperbacks Ser.). 282p. 1994. reprint ed. pap. text 10.95 (*0-19-563362-8*) OUP.

Chatterjee, Pranab. Approaches to the Welfare State. 311p. (Orig.). (C). 1996. pap. 34.95 (*0-87101-262-6*, 2626) Natl Assn Soc Wkrs.

***Chatterjee, Pranab.** Repackaging of the Welfare State. LC 98-43521. 200p. 1999. 32.95 (*0-87101-304-5*) Natl Assn Soc Wkrs.

Chatterjee, Pranab. The Transferability of Social Technology: Explorations in the Knowledge Structures of the Helping Professions & Their Transfer. LC 89-12648. (Studies in Health & Human Services: Vol. 16). 244p. 1990. lib. bdg. 89.95 (*0-88946-141-4*) E Mellen.

Chatterjee, Pranab & Abramovitz, Albert J., eds. Structure of Nonprofit Management: A Casebook. LC 93-2206. 296p. (Orig.). (C). 1993. pap. text 34.00 (*0-8191-9148-5*); lib. bdg. 59.50 (*0-8191-9147-7*) U Pr of Amer.

Chatterjee, R. Elements of Microwave Engineering. (Electrical & Electronic Engineering Ser.). 1986. text 62.95 (*0-470-20311-0*) P-H.

Chatterjee, R. N. & Sanchez, L., eds. Genome Analysis in Eukaryotes: Developmental & Evolutionary Aspects. 260p. 1998. 135.00 (*3-540-63524-6*) Spr-Verlag.

Chatterjee, Ranjit. Aspect & Meaning in Slavic & Indic. LC 88-7602. (Current Issues in Linguistic Theory Ser.: Vol. 51). xxiii, 137p. (C). 1989. 47.00 (*90-272-3545-7*) J Benjamins Pubng Co.

Chatterjee, Ratnabali. From the Karkhana to the Studio: Changing Social Roles of Patron & Artist in Bengal. 1990. 62.00 (*81-85016-28-3*, Pub. by Bks & Bks) S Asia.

***Chatterjee, S., et al, eds.** Languages & Compilers for Parallel Computing: 11th International Workshop, LCPC'98, Chapel Hill, NC, USA, August 7-9, 1999, Proceedings. (Lecture Notes in Computer Science Ser.: Vol. 1656). xi, 384p. 1999. pap. 62.00 (*3-540-66426-2*) Spr-Verlag.

Chatterjee, S. K. Emergence of a Dynamic Economy. xii, 209p. 1986. 19.00 (*81-7045-000-4*, Pub. by Assoc Pub Hse) Nataraj Bks.

— Legal Aspects of International Drug Control. 612p. 1981. 117.00 (*90-286-2091-5*) Kluwer Academic.

— Legal Aspects of International Drug Control. 612p. 1981. lib. bdg. 286.50 (*90-247-2556-9*) Kluwer Academic.

Chatterjee, S. P. Junior College Geography, Vol. 1. (Illus.). 268p. 1977. pap. text 8.95 (*0-86125-446-5*) Apt Bks.

— Junior College Geography, Vol. II. (Illus.). 132p. 1983. reprint ed. pap. 10.00 (*0-86131-090-X*) Apt Bks.

Chatterjee, Samprit & Hadi, Ali S. Sensitivity Analysis in Linear Regression. LC 87-28580. (Probability & Mathematical Statistics Ser.). 315p. 1988. 139.95 (*0-471-82216-7*) Wiley.

Chatterjee, Samprit & Price, Bertram. Regression Analysis by Example. 2nd ed. LC 91-11046. (Probability & Mathematical Statistics: Applied Probability & Statistics Section Ser.). 304p. 1991. 94.95 (*0-471-88479-0*) Wiley.

Chatterjee, Samprit, et al. A Casebook for a First Course in Statistics & Data Analysis. 328p. 1994. pap. 33.95 (*0-471-11030-2*) Wiley.

***Chatterjee, Samprit, et al.** Regression Analysis by Example. 3rd ed. 384p. (C). 1999. text 79.95 (*0-471-31946-5*, Wiley-Interscience) Wiley.

Chatterjee, Sandeep. Quick & Easy Indian Vegetarian Cookery. (Illus.). 136p. 1993. pap. 9.95 (*0-563-36325-8*, BBC-Parkwest) Parkwest Pubns.

— The Spice Trail: One Hundred Hot Dishes from India to Indonesia. LC 95-12649. (Illus.). 144p. (Orig.). 1995. pap. 15.95 (*0-89815-781-1*) Ten Speed Pr.

***Chatterjee, Sangit.** Cosmic Go: A Guide to Four Stone Handicap Games. 1999. pap. write for info. (*4-906574-69-6*) Kiseido Pubng Co.

Chatterjee, Sankar. The Rise of Birds: 225 Million Years of Evolution. LC 97-9474. (Illus.). 312p. 1997. 39.95 (*0-8018-5615-9*) Johns Hopkins.

Chatterjee, Sankar & Hotton, Nicholas, III. New Concepts in Global Tectonics. 480p. 1992. 65.00 (*0-89672-269-4*) Tex Tech Univ Pr.

Chatterjee, Sarajit K. The Scheduled Castes in India, 4 vols. LC 96-906267. (Illus.). 3000p. (C). 1996. 199.00 (*81-212-0511-5*, Pub. by Gyan Publishing Hse) Nataraj Bks.

Chatterjee, Saratchandra & Samaj, Palli. The Homecoming. (C). 1989. 10.00 (*0-8364-2458-1*, Pub. by Rupa) S Asia.

Chatterjee, Sayan. A Bureaucrat's Yarns. (C). 1994. text 15.00 (*81-241-0228-7*, Pub. by Har-Anand Pubns) S Asia.

Chatterjee, Sayan, jt. auth. see Kosnik, Rita D.

***Chatterjee, Shibashis.** Nuclear Non-Proliferation & the Problem of Threshold States. LC 99-936951. 1999. 17.50 (*81-85195-89-7*, Pub. by Minerva Assocs) S Asia.

Chatterjee, Sivranjan. Governor's Role in the Indian Constitution. (C). 1992. 27.50 (*81-7099-325-3*, Pub. by Mittal Pubs Dist) S Asia.

Chatterjee, Subir K. Anorectal Malformations: A Surgeon's Experience. LC 93-5318. (Illus.). 228p. 1993. text 48.95 (*0-19-262453-9*) OUP.

***Chatterjee, Suhas.** Indian Civilization & Culture. 544p. 1998. pap. 300.00 (*81-7533-083-X*, Pub. by Print Hse) St Mut.

Chatterjee, Suhas. Making of Mizoram: Role of Laldenga, 2 vols. 445p. (C). 1994. pap. 325.00 (*81-85880-38-7*, Pub. by Print Hse) St Mut.

Chatterjee, Syamal. Legal Aspects of Drug Control & Treatment of Drug-Dependent Persons Within the European Community. (European Community Law Ser.). 240p. (C). 1995. text 85.00 (*0-485-70008-5*, Pub. by Athlone Pr) Humanities.

Chatterjee, U. K. & Bose, S. K. Basic Degradation of Metals: Basic Mechanisms & Methods of Prevention. (Mechanical Engineering Ser.). (Illus.). 340p. Date not set. text. write for info. (*0-8247-9920-8*) Dekker.

Chatterjes, Suhas. Makinig of Mizoram: Role of Laldenga, 2 vols. LC 95-901189. 445p. 1995. pap. 138.00 (*81-85880-72-7*, Pub. by Print Hse) St Mut.

Chatterji. Health Care Management Policy. 78.95 (*1-85972-606-2*) Ashgate Pub Co.

Chatterji, et al. Conflict Management of Water Resources. 65.95 (*1-84014-860-8*) Ashgate Pub Co.

Chatterji, Bankim C. Anandamath: A Novel. (C). 1991. 14.00 (*81-7094-091-5*, Pub. by Vision) S Asia.

Chatterji, Basudev. Trade, Tariffs & Empire: Lancashire & British Policy in India, 1919-1939. 500p. 1992. 49.95 (*0-19-562815-2*) OUP.

Chatterji, Basudev, ed. Towards Freedom 1938: Documents on the Movement for Independence in India, 3 vols. (Illus.). 4,000p. 2000. text 460.00 (*0-19-564449-2*) OUP.

Chatterji, J. C. Kashmir Shaivaism. LC 85-30365. (SUNY Series in Cultural Perspectives). 175p. (C). 1986. reprint ed. pap. text 14.95 (*0-88706-180-X*) State U NY Pr.

— Kashmir Shaivaism. LC 85-30365. (SUNY Series in Cultural Perspectives). 175p. (C). 1986. reprint ed. text 42.50 (*0-88706-179-6*) State U NY Pr.

Chatterji, Jagadish C. The Wisdom of the Vedas. LC 92-50142. 151p. 1992. pap. 12.00 (*0-8356-0684-8*, Quest) Theos Pub Hse.

Chatterji, Joya. Bengal Divided: Hindu Communalism & Partition, 1932-1947. (Cambridge South Asian Studies: No. 57). (Illus.). 323p. (C). 1995. text 69.95 (*0-521-41128-9*) Cambridge U Pr.

Chatterji, Jyotsna. Religions & the Status of Women. 1990. 17.50 (*81-85024-67-7*, Pub. by Uppal Pub Hse) S Asia.

Chatterji, Jyotsna, ed. Customary Laws & Women in Manipur. LC 96-900939. (C). 1996. 18.00 (*81-85565-69-4*, Pub. by Uppal Pub Hse) S Asia.

Chatterji, Manas. Health Care Cost-Containment Policy: An Econometric Study. 1983. lib. bdg. 169.00 (*0-89838-119-3*) Kluwer Academic.

— Management & Regional Science for Economic Development. 1982. lib. bdg. 119.00 (*0-89838-108-8*) Kluwer Academic.

Chatterji, Manas, ed. Analytical Techniques in Conflict Management. 400p. 1992. 69.95 (*1-85521-221-8*, Pub. by Dartmth Pub) Ashgate Pub Co.

— Energy & Environment in the Developing Countries. LC 80-42143. (Illus.). 369p. reprint ed. pap. 114.40 (*0-608-17892-6*, 205667600080) Bks Demand.

— Regional Science: Perspectives for the Future. 464p. 1997. text 79.95 (*0-312-15930-7*) St Martin.

Chatterji, Manas, et al, eds. Arms Spending, Development & Security. xxix, 431p. 1996. 40.00 (*81-7024-691-1*, Pub. by Ashish Pub Hse) Nataraj Bks.

— The Economics of International Security: Essays in Honour of Jan Tinbergen. LC 93-34313. 1994. text 69.95 (*0-312-12018-4*) St Martin.

Chatterji, Manas & Forcey, Linda R., eds. Disarmament, Economic Conversion, & Management of Peace. LC 91-39901. 352p. 1992. 75.00 (*0-275-93540-X*, C3540, Praeger Pubs) Greenwood.

Chatterji, Manas, et al. Environment & Health in Developing Countries. 1998. 74.00 (*81-7024-991-0*, Pub. by Ashish Pub Hse) S Asia.

Chatterji, Mohini M., tr. see Samkaracarya, Sri.

Chatterji, P. C. Broadcasting in India. 2nd ed. 228p. 1992. 29.95 (*0-8039-9107-X*) Sage.

— Secular Values for Secular India. LC 95-905622. (C). 1995. 40.00 (*81-7304-004-4*, Pub. by Manohar) S Asia.

Chatterji, Rakhahari. Working Class & the Nationalist Movement in India: The Critical Years. 1985. 14.50 (*0-685-10918-6*, Pub. by S Asia Pubs) S Asia.

Chatterji, Rakhahari, ed. Religion, Politics, & Communism: The South Asian Experience. (C). 1994. 17.00 (*81-7003-174-5*, Pub. by S Asia Pubs) S Asia.

Chatterji, Ruchira. The Behaviour of Industrial Prices in India. 240p. 1989. 32.50 (*0-19-562207-3*) OUP.

Chatterji, S. D., ed. Proceedings of the International Congress of Mathematicians 1994, August 3-11, Zurich, Switzerland, 2 vols. LC 95-43141. 717p. 1995. 275.00 (*3-7643-5153-5*) Birkhauser.

— Proceedings of the International Congress of Mathematicians 1994, August 3-11, Zurich, Switzerland. LC 95-43141. 1995. 275.00 (*0-8176-5153-5*) Birkhauser.

Chatterji, Shoma A. The Indian Woman's Search for an Identity. 250p. 1988. text 27.50 (*0-7069-3854-2*, Pub. by Vikas) S Asia.

Chatterji, Shoma A. Indian Women's Search for an Identity. 2nd rev. ed. 1997. reprint ed. 29.50 (*0-7069-9888-X*, Pub. by Vikas) S Asia.

Chatterji, Shoma A., ed. Indian Women in Perspective. (C). 1993. 34.00 (*81-202-0332-1*, Pub. by Ajanta) S Asia.

Chatterji, Subrhendu & Hedges, Paul. Corporate Financial Restructurings. 450p. 1998. pap. 260.00 (*0-85297-487-6*, Pub. by Chartered Bank) St Mut.

Chatterji, Suniti K. The Origin & Development of the Bengali Language. 1993. reprint ed. 29.00 (*81-7167-117-9*, Pub. by Rupa) S Asia.

***Chatterley, L. Matthew.** Wend Your Way: A Guide to Sites along the Iowa Mormon Trail Guide. (Illus.). 120p. 2000. pap. 12.95 (*0-8138-0482-5*) Iowa St U Pr.

Chatters, A. W. & Hajarnavis, C. R. An Introductory Course in Commutative Algebra. (Illus.). 152p. 1998. text 75.00 (*0-19-853423-X*); pap. text 35.00 (*0-19-850144-7*) OUP.

Chatters, Linda M., ed. see Jackson, James S.

Chatterton, B. D., jt. ed. see Stelck, C. R.

Chatterton, Betty J. Grandma's Down-Home Recipes. LC 77-85849. (Illus.). 1978. 11.95 (*0-930574-02-8*); pap. 9.95 (*0-930574-01-X*) Chatterton Pr.

— Grandma's Down-Home Recipes. 2nd rev. ed. (Illus.). 79p. 1996. spiral bd. 9.95 (*0-930574-03-6*, 3) Chatterton Pr.

Chatterton, Brian, jt. auth. see Chatterton, Lynne.

Chatterton, Brigadier G. Wings of Pegasus. (Airborne Ser.: No. 14). (Illus.). 282p. 1982. reprint ed. 29.95 (*0-89839-060-5*) Battery Pr.

Chatterton, Clifford E. Bail - Law & Practice. 280p. 1986. pap. 84.00 (*0-406-10180-9*, UK, MICHIE) LEXIS Pub.

Chatterton, Clifford E. & Brown, Philip K. Committals for Trial to the Crown Court: The Law & Practice. 305p. (C). 1988. 95.00 (*1-85190-058-6*, Pub. by Fourmat Pub) St Mut.

Chatterton, David A. Pensions Law & Practice. xxiv, 180p. 1998. pap. 72.00 (*1-85941-340-4*, Pub. by Cavendish Pubng) Gaunt.

— Wills. 2nd ed. (Practice Notes Ser.). 90p. 1990. pap. write for info. (*0-85121-697-8*, Pub. by Cavendish Pubng) Gaunt.

— Wills. 3rd ed. (Cavendish Practice Notes Ser.). 1996. pap. 32.00 (*1-85941-296-3*, Pub. by Cavendish Pubng) Gaunt.

— Wills, Executorship & Tax Planning. (C). 1990. 150.00 (*1-85431-085-2*, Pub. by Blackstone Pr) St Mut.

Chatterton, E. Keble. English Seamen & the Colonization of America. LC 74-37332. (Select Bibliographies Reprint Ser.). (Illus.). 1977. reprint ed. 29.95 (*0-8369-6679-1*) Ayer.

— King's Cutters & Smugglers, 1700-1855. LC 79-173106. (Illus.). 436p. 1972. reprint ed. 24.95 (*0-405-08351-3*, Pub. by Blom Pubns) Ayer.

— Q-Ships & Their Story. LC 79-6105. (Navies & Men Ser.). (Illus.). 1980. reprint ed. lib. bdg. 31.95 (*0-405-13034-1*) Ayer.

— Sailing Ships & Their Story. LC 68-54240. (Illus.). 1968. reprint ed. 25.00 (*0-87266-004-4*) Argosy.

Chatterton-Hill, Georges. Philosophy of Nietzsche: An Exposition & Appreciation. LC 70-152409. (Studies in German Literature: No. 13). 1971. reprint ed. lib. bdg. 75.00 (*0-8383-1232-2*) M S G Haskell Hse.

— The Sociological Value of Christianity. LC 83-45605. reprint ed. 36.00 (*0-404-19873-2*) AMS Pr.

Chatterton, Howard A. A Pocket Guide to Maryland's Chesapeake Bay. (Illus.). 48p. (Orig.). 1984. pap. 5.95 (*0-933852-46-0*) Nautical & Aviation.

— Volunteer Training Drills: A Year of Weekly Drills to Help You: Know the Area, Get There Safely, Make the Rescue, Extinguish the Fire, Care for the Injured. LC 98-21540. 1998. pap. 32.50 (*0-912212-68-3*) Fire Eng.

An Asterisk (*) at the beginning of an entry indicates that the title is appearing for the first time.

Chatterton, Howard A. & Chatterton, Margaret. Making & Managing Money. 125p. 1994. 34.95 (*0-912212-32-2*) Fire Eng.

Chatterton, Leigh A. & Clack, Mary E., eds. Serial Connections: People, Information, & Communication. LC 86-32021. (Serials Librarian Ser.: Vol. 11, Nos. 3-4). 200p. 1987. text 5.95 (*0-86656-654-6*) Haworth Pr.

— The Serials Information Chain: Discussion, Debate & Dialog. LC 87-31063. (Serials Librarian Ser.: Vol. 13, Nos. 2-3). (Illus.). 174p. 1988. text 39.95 (*0-86656-744-5*) Haworth Pr.

— Serials Information from Publisher to User: Practice, Programs & Progress Proceedings of the North American Serials Interest Group. LC 88-32871. (Serials Librarian Ser.: Vol. 15, Nos. 3-4). (Illus.). 187p. 1989. text 5.95 (*0-86656-894-8*) Haworth Pr.

Chatterton, Louise. American Heritage: History of the United States for Young People. (First Love Ser.). 186p. (YA). (gr. 7 up). 1997. pap. 32.95 (*0-671-53392-4*) S&S Trade.

Chatterton, Lynne & Chatterton, Brian. Sustainable Dryland Farming: Combining Farmer Innovation & Medic Pasture in a Mediterranean Climate. (Illus.). 355p. (C). 1996. text 100.00 (*0-521-33141-2*) Cambridge U Pr.

Chatterton, M., jt. ed. see Nevill, A. M.

Chatterton, M. D. Immortality of Man from the Standpoint of Reason (1904) 188p. 1998. reprint ed. pap. 17.95 (*0-7661-0523-7*) Kessinger Pub.

Chatterton, Margaret, jt. auth. see Chatterton, Howard A.

***Chatterton, Mark & Carter, Gary.** Blowin' Free: Thirty Years of Wishbone Ash. (Illus.). 2000. pap. 18.95 (*0-946719-33-0*, Pub. by SAF Pub) Interlink Pub.

Chatterton, Martin. Nutty Footy Book. (Illus.). (J). 1995. pap. 7.95 (*0-14-037057-9*, Pub. by Pnguin Bks Ltd) Trafalgar.

— Nutty World of Animals. (Illus.). 96p. (J). pap. 7.95 (*0-14-038988-1*, Pub. by Pnguin Bks Ltd) Trafalgar.

Chatterton, Martin. Silly Circus! Puzzles, Jokes, & Things to Make & Do. (Illus.). 32p. (J). (ps up). 1994. pap. 2.99 (*1-56402-405-9*) Candlewick Pr.

Chatterton, Martin. Utterly Nutty History of Footy. (Illus.). 96p. (J). pap. 7.50 (*0-14-038465-0*, Pub. by Pnguin Bks Ltd) Trafalgar.

— Utterly Nutty World of Sports. (Illus.). 96p. (J). pap. 7.95 (*0-14-038986-5*, Pub. by Pnguin Bks Ltd) Trafalgar.

Chatterton, Martin, jt. auth. see Beal, George.

Chatterton, N. J., ed. see Suzuki, Michio.

Chatterton, Paul A. & Houlden, Michael A. EMC: Electromagnetic Theory to Practical Design. LC 91-28311. 310p. 1992. 235.00 (*0-471-92878-X*) Wiley.

Chatterton, Pauline. Scandinavian Knitting Designs. LC 76-27879. (Encore Editions Ser.). (Illus.). 272p. 1982. 5.95 (*0-684-16538-4*) S&S Trade.

Chatterton, Thomas. Poetical Works of Thomas Chatterton, 2 vols. Skeat, Walter W., ed. LC 68-59008. (BCL Ser.: No. I). reprint ed. 125.00 (*0-404-01484-4*) AMS Pr.

— The Poetical Works of Thomas Chatterton, 2 vols. (BCL1-PR English Literature Ser.). 1992. reprint ed. lib. bdg. 150.00 (*0-7812-7330-7*) Rprt Serv.

— The Rowley Poems. 1977. 20.95 (*0-8369-7105-1*, 7939) Ayer.

— The Rowley Poems. (BCL1-PR English Literature Ser.). 333p. 1992. reprint ed. lib. bdg. 89.00 (*0-7812-7331-5*) Rprt Serv.

— The Rowley Poems, 1794. LC 90-39171. (Revolution & Romanticism Ser.). 374p. 1990. reprint ed. 55.00 (*1-85477-040-3*) Continuum.

— Thomas Chatterton (1752-1770) Selected Poems. Lindop, Greves, ed. 1979. pap. 7.95 (*0-902145-54-1*) Carcanet Pr.

— Works of Thomas Chatterton, 3 vols. Southey, Robert & Cottle, Joseph, eds. LC 71-80892. 1968. reprint ed. 230.00 (*0-404-01540-9*) AMS Pr.

Chattin-McNichols, John. The Montessori Controversy. 224p. (C). 1991. mass mkt. 26.25 (*0-8273-4517-8*) Delmar.

Chattington, Jenny. The Ancient Greeks. (British Museum Activity Bks.). (Illus.). 16p. (J). (gr. 2 up). 1995. pap. 5.95 (*0-500-27788-5*, Pub. by Thames Hudson) Norton.

Chattman, Gerald B. An Education in Murder. LC 98-89888. 365p. 1999. 25.00 (*0-7388-0323-5*); pap. 15.00 (*0-7388-0324-3*) Xlibris Corp.

***Chattman, Lauren.** Cool Kitchen: No Oven, No Stove, No Sweat! LC 99-53484. 176p. 2000. pap. 9.95 (*0-688-17903-7*, Wm Morrow) Morrow Avon.

Chattman, Lauren. Cool Kitchen: No Oven, No Stove, No Sweat! 125 Delicious, No-Work Recipes For Summertime Or Anytime. Glikman, Naomi, ed. LC 97-25661. (Illus.). 288p. 1998. 22.00 (*0-688-15513-8*, Wm Morrow) Morrow Avon.

***Chattman, Lauren.** Instant Gratification: No-Hassel Desserts in Just about No Time. LC 99-53370. 240p. 2000. 22.00 (*0-688-16910-4*, Wm Morrow) Morrow Avon.

Chattman, Lauren. Just Add Water: The Ideal Cookbook for Anyone Who Can Boil a Pot of Water! Hoenig, Pam, ed. LC 98-8295. 272p. 1999. 22.00 (*0-688-16188-X*, Wm Morrow) Morrow Avon.

Chatto, Beth. Beth Chatto's Green Tapestry: Perennial Plants for Your Garden. 2nd ed. (Illus.). 1999. 27.50 (*0-00-414064-8*, Pub. by HarpC) Trafalgar.

***Chatto, Beth.** Chatto's Gravel Garden: Drought-Resistant Planting Throughout the Year. (Illus.). 2000. 35.00 (*0-670-89260-2*, Viking) Viking Penguin.

Chatto, Beth. The Damp Garden. rev. ed. LC 96-12834. (Illus.). 352p. 1996. 32.95 (*0-89831-048-2*) Sagapr.

— The Dry Garden. rev. ed. (Illus.). 200p. 1996. 29.95 (*0-89831-047-4*) Sagapr.

Chatto, Beth & Fischer, Thomas. Beth Chatto's Garden Notebook. LC 96-41954. 1997. 34.95 (*0-89831-049-0*) Sagapr.

Chatto, Beth & Lloyd, Christopher. Dear Friend & Gardener. 254p. 1997. 22.95 (*0-7112-1227-9*, Pub. by F Lincoln) Trafalgar.

***Chatto, James.** The Man Who Ate Toronto: Memoirs of a Food Critic. 360p. 2000. pap. 18.95 (*1-55199-050-4*) MW&R.

Chatto, James & Martin, W. L. A Kitchen in Corfu. LC 87-38323. 199p. (C). 1988. 18.95 (*0-941533-17-4*, NAB) I R Dee.

Chatton, Barbara. Using Poetry Across the Curriculum: A Whole Language Approach. LC 93-1428. 240p. 1993. pap. 28.50 (*0-89774-715-1*) Oryx Pr.

***Chatton, Barbara & Collins, Lynne D.** Blurring the Edges: Integrated Curriculum Through Writing & Children's Literature. LC 98-50477. 144p. 1999. pap. text 19.00 (*0-325-00144-8*) Heinemann.

Chatton, Edouard. Peridiniens Parasites: Morphologie, Reproduction, Ethologie. (Archives de Zoologie Experimentale et Generale Ser.: Vol. 59, 1920). 475p. 1975. reprint ed. 168.30 (*3-87429-100-6*, 002582, Pub. by Koeltz Sci Bks) Lubrecht & Cramer.

Chatton, Moira, jt. auth. see Gill, James O.

Chatton, Walter. Reportatio et Lectura Super Sententias: Collatio ad Librum Primum et Prologus. Wey, Joseph C., ed. (ENG & LAT.). viii, 424p. pap. text 43.43 (*0-88844-090-1*) Brill Academic Pubs.

Chattopadhaya, B. C. Rural Development-Planning in India. 1979. text 52.50 (*0-685-14097-0*) Coronet Bks.

Chattopadhaya, Kamaladevi. Indian Women's Battle for Freedom. 134p. 1983. 14.95 (*0-318-37065-4*) Asia Bk Corp.

— Inner Recesses Outer Spaces: Memoirs. 410p. 1986. 49.95 (*81-7013-038-7*) Asia Bk Corp.

Chattopadhayay-Dutt, Purnima. Loops & Roots: The Conflict Between Official & Traditional Family Planning in India. LC 94-905654. (Illus.). xxxv, 655p. (C). 1995. 69.00 (*81-7024-659-8*, Pub. by Ashish Pub Hse) Nataraj Bks.

Chattopadhya, A. Why Have I Accepted Islam? 1992. pap. 2.00 (*0-933511-92-2*) Kazi Pubns.

Chattopadhyay, Alaka, ed. see Das, Sarat C.

Chattopadhyay, Arun K. & Mittal, K. L. Surfactants in Solution, No. 64. LC 96-23963. (Surfactant Science Ser.: Vol. 64). (Illus.). 440p. 1996. text 190.00 (*0-8247-9792-2*) Dekker.

Chattopadhyay, Ashok K. & Zentner, Mark R. Aerospace & Aircraft Coatings. (Illus.). 32p. 1990. pap. 30.00 (*0-934010-08-0*) Fed Soc Coat Tech.

Chattopadhyay, Boudhayan. Food Insecurity & the Social Environment. (Food Systems & the Human Environment in Eastern India Ser.: Vol. I). (C). 1991. text 42.00 (*81-7074-087-8*, Pub. by KP Bagchi) S Asia.

— Food Insecurity, Climate Variability & Community. (Food Systems & the Human Environment in Eastern India Ser.: Vol. II). (C). 1993. text 42.00 (*81-7707-412-1*, Pub. by KP Bagchi) S Asia.

Chattopadhyay, Brajadulal. Aspects of Rural Settlements & Rural Society in Early Medieval India. (C). 1990. 19.00 (*81-7074-055-X*, Pub. by KP Bagchi) S Asia.

Chattopadhyay, C. An Advanced Course in Practical Physics. (C). 1989. 70.00 (*0-89771-404-0*, Pub. by Current Dist) St Mut.

Chattopadhyay, C. & Rakshit, R. Electricity & Magnetism (with Electro-Magnetic Theory & Special Theory of Relativity) (C). 1989. 90.00 (*0-89771-400-8*, Pub. by Current Dist) St Mut.

Chattopadhyay, C., et al. T. B. of Advanced Practical Physics. (C). 1989. 45.00 (*0-89771-405-9*, Pub. by Current Dist) St Mut.

***Chattopadhyay, Collette, et al.** Shifting Perceptions: Contemporary LA Visions. Snow, Hilary K., ed. (Illus.). 96p. 2000. pap. 20.00 (*1-877921-18-1*) Pacific Asia.

Chattopadhyay, D., et al. Foundations of Electronics. 2nd ed. (C). 1988. pap. 10.00 (*81-224-0071-X*) S Asia.

Chattopadhyay, D. P., et al, eds. Phenomenology & Indian Philosophy. (C). 1992. 30.00 (*81-208-0770-7*, Pub. by Motilal Bnarsidass) S Asia.

Chattopadhyay, Debiprasad. History of Science & Technology in Ancient India, Vol. V, No. 2: Formation of the Theoretical Fundamentals of Natural Science. (C). 1991. 72.50 (*0-8364-2646-0*, Pub. by Firma KLM) S Asia.

— Knowledge & Intervention: A Study in Society & Consciousness. 1986. 35.00 (*0-8364-1544-2*) S Asia.

Chattopadhyay, Debiprasad, ed. Taranatha's History of Buddhism in India. 1990. reprint ed. 29.50 (*81-208-0696-4*, Pub. by Motilal Bnarsidass) S Asia.

Chattopadhyay, Debiprasad, ed. see Thibaut, G.

Chattopadhyay, Dilip K. Dynamics of Social Change in Bengal. (C). 1990. text 62.50 (*81-85094-32-2*, Pub. by Punthi Pus) S Asia.

Chattopadhyay, Kamaladevi. Carpets & Floor Coverings of India. (Illus.). 71p. 1985. 34.95 (*0-318-36261-9*) Asia Bk Corp.

— The Glory of Indian Handicrafts. (Illus.). 205p. 1985. 18.95 (*0-318-36268-6*) Asia Bk Corp.

— Handicrafts of India. (Illus.). 225p. 1985. 34.95 (*0-318-36262-7*) Asia Bk Corp.

— Handicrafts of India. (C). 1995. reprint ed. 84.00 (*81-224-0797-8*, Pub. by New Era Pub) S Asia.

— India's Craft Tradition. (Illus.). 83p. 1980. 9.95 (*0-318-36264-3*) Asia Bk Corp.

Chattopadhyay, Kanti, tr. see Chattopadhyay, Rampada.

Chattopadhyay, Kunal. Economic Impact of Tourism Development: An Indian Experience LC 94-906186. xv, 240 p. 1995. write for info. (*81-7391-047-2*) Kaniska Pubs Dist.

Chattopadhyay, Manabendu, et al, eds. Planning & Economic Policy in India: Evaluation & Lessons for the Future. 220p. 1996. 32.00 (*0-8039-9280-7*) Sage.

Chattopadhyay, Manju. Petition to Agitation: Bengal, 1857-1885. 1986. 22.00 (*0-8364-1621-X*, Pub. by KP Bagchi) S Asia.

Chattopadhyay, Marabendu. Conditions of Labour in Indian Agriculture. 1985. 17.50 (*0-8364-1399-7*, Pub. by KP Bagchi) S Asia.

Chattopadhyay, P. Boiler Operation Engineering: Questions & Answers. LC 95-5964. 640p. 1995. 69.00 (*0-07-460296-9*) McGraw.

Chattopadhyay, Paresh. The Marxian Concept of Capital & the Soviet Experience: Essay in the Critique of Political Economy. LC 93-37881. (Praeger Series in Political Economy). 208p. 1994. 59.95 (*0-275-94530-8*, Praeger Pubs) Greenwood.

***Chattopadhyay, Parthasarthy.** Boiler Operations Questions & Answers. 2nd ed. 640p. 2000. 79.95 (*0-07-135675-4*) McGraw-Hill Prof.

Chattopadhyay, Rampada. A Vaisnava Interpretation of the Brahmasutras: Vedanta & Theism. Chattopadhyay, Kanti, tr. from BEN. LC 91-47654. (Indian Thought Ser.: Vol. 3). xxvi, 299p. 1992. 112.00 (*90-04-09570-5*) Brill Academic Pubs.

Chattopadhyay, S., ed. Impedance Beyond Cutoff: A Special Issue of the Journal Particle Accelerators. ii, 210p. 1990. pap. text 742.00 (*2-88124-425-4*) Gordon & Breach.

Chattopadhyay, S. B. Principles & Procedures of Plant Protection. 3rd rev. ed. (C). 1991. 18.00 (*81-204-0013-5*, Pub. by Oxford IBH) S Asia.

Chattopadhyay, Santi N. The Universal Man: Tagore's Vision of the Religion of Humanity. (C). 1987. 27.50 (*81-85169-16-0*, Pub. by Naya Prokash) S Asia.

Chattopadhyay, Siddheswar. Theatre in Ancient India. (C). 1993. 16.00 (*81-7304-016-8*, Pub. by Manohar) S Asia.

Chattopadhyay, Srikumar, et al. Sustainable Development: Issues & Case Studies. LC 98-909087. 307p. 1998. write for info. (*81-7022-694-5*) Concept.

Chattopadhyay, Swapan, et al, eds. Advanced Accelerator Concepts Vol. 398: 7th Workshop, Held Lake Tahoe, California, 1996. LC 97-72788. (Illus.). 992p. 1997. 220.00 incl. cd-rom (*1-56396-697-2*, AIP Pr) Spr-Verlag.

— Nonlinear & Collective Phenomena in Beam Physics: Proceedings of the 12th Advanced ICFA Beam Dynamics Workshop Held in Arcidosso, Italy, 1996. LC 97-72970. (Illus.). 448p. 1997. 115.00 (*1-56396-668-9*, CP 395, AIP Pr) Spr-Verlag.

Chattopadhyay, Swapan, ed. see Conference on Nonlinear Dynamics in Particle Accel, et al.

Chattopadhyay, Tapan. Lepchas & Their Heritage. 1990. 24.00 (*81-7018-571-8*, Pub. by BR Pub) S Asia.

Chattopadhyaya, Alaka. Atisa & Tibet. (C). 1996. reprint ed. 32.00 (*81-208-0928-9*, Pub. by Motilal Bnarsidass) S Asia.

Chattopadhyaya, B. D. The Making of Early Medieval India. 284p. 1994. 24.00 (*0-19-563415-2*) OUP.

Chattopadhyaya, Basudeb, et al, eds. Dissent & Consensus: Social Protest in Pre-Industrial Societies. (C). 1989. 31.50 (*81-7074-043-6*, Pub. by KP Bagchi) S Asia.

Chattopadhyaya, Brajadulal. The Making of Early Medieval India. (Illus.). 282p. 1997. reprint ed. pap. text 15.95 (*0-19-564076-4*) OUP.

— Representing the Other? Sanskrit Sources & the Muslims; Eighth to Fourteenth Century LC 98-909931. 129 p. 1998. write for info. (*81-7304-252-7*, Pub. by Manohar) S Asia.

Chattopadhyaya, Brajadulal, ed. Essays in Ancient Indian Economic History. (Indian History Congress Golden Jubilee Year Publication Ser.: Vol. 2). 1988. 32.00 (*81-215-0084-2*, Pub. by M Manoharial) Coronet Bks.

Chattopadhyaya, D. P. Interdisciplinary Studies in Science Technology Philosophy & Culture. 1996. 34.50 (*81-215-0720-0*, Pub. by M Manoharial) Coronet Bks.

— Sociology, Ideology & Utopia: Socio-Political Philosophy of East & West. LC 97-14142. (Philosophy of History & Culture Ser.: Vol. 18). 248p. 1997. text 89.50 (*90-04-10807-6*) Brill Academic Pubs.

Chattopadhyaya, D. P. & Kumar, Ravinder, eds. Mathematics, Astronomy & Biology in Indian Tradition: Some Conceptual Preliminaries. LC 95-905857. (C). 1995. 14.00 (*81-215-0688-3*, Pub. by M Manoharial) S Asia.

— Science Philosophy & Culture, Vol. 2. LC 96-900936. (C). 1997. 72.50 (*81-215-0785-5*, Pub. by M Manoharial) Coronet Bks.

Chattopadhyaya, D. P., jt. ed. see Gupta, Chhanda.

Chattopadhyaya, Debiprasad. Anthropology & Historiography of Science. LC 89-26582. (Series in Continental Thought : Vol. 16). 299p. 1990. text 36.95 (*0-8214-0952-2*) Ohio U Pr.

— History of Science & Technology in Ancient India: Astronomy Science & Society. (C). 1996. 26.00 (*0-614-18148-8*, Pub. by Firma KLM) S Asia.

— History of Science & Technology in Ancient India: The Beginnings. 556p. 57.50 (*0-8364-1935-9*) S Asia.

— Knowledge, Freedom & Language: An Interwoven Fabric of Man, Time & World. (C). 1989. 58.50 (*81-208-0630-1*, Pub. by Motilal Bnarsidass) S Asia.

— Sri Aurobindo & Karl Marx: Integral Sociology & Dialectical Sociology. 2nd ed. (C). 1988. 38.50 (*81-208-0388-4*, Pub. by Motilal Bnarsidass) S Asia.

Chattopadhyaya, Debiprasad, ed. Carvaka - Lokayata: Anthology of Source Materials & Some Recent Studies. (C). 1994. text 24.00 (*81-85636-11-7*, Pub. by M Manoharial) S Asia.

— Indian Studies: Past & Present, 1959-1960, Vol 1. 1960. 50.00 (*0-88065-031-1*) Scholarly Pubns.

— Indian Studies: Past & Present, 1960-1961, Vol. 2. 723p. 1961. 50.00 (*0-88065-032-X*) Scholarly Pubns.

— Indian Studies: Past & Present, 1962-1963, Vol. 4. 508p. 1963. 80.00 (*0-88065-034-6*) Scholarly Pubns.

— Indian Studies: Past & Present, 1963-1964, Vol. 5. 376p. 1964. 80.00 (*0-88065-035-4*) Scholarly Pubns.

— Indian Studies: Past & Present, 1964-1965, Vol. 6. 466p. 1965. 80.00 (*0-88065-036-2*) Scholarly Pubns.

— Indian Studies: Past & Present, 1965-1966, Vol. 7. 454p. 1966. 80.00 (*0-88065-037-0*) Scholarly Pubns.

— Indian Studies: Past & Present, 1967-1968, Vol. 9. 398p. 1968. 60.00 (*0-88065-039-7*) Scholarly Pubns.

— Indian Studies: Past & Present, 1968-1969, Vol. 10. 383p. 1969. 60.00 (*0-88065-040-0*) Scholarly Pubns.

— Indian Studies: Past & Present, 1969-1970, Vol. 11. 430p. 1970. 50.00 (*0-88065-041-9*) Scholarly Pubns.

— Select Bibliography of Journal Articles on Philosophy Religion, Science & Related Aspects of Indian Culture. (C). 1989. 8.00 (*0-685-30851-0*, Pub. by M Manoharial) S Asia.

— Studies in the History of Indian Philosophy, 3 vols., Set. 1990. 82.00 (*81-7074-063-0*, Pub. by KP Bagchi) S Asia.

Chattopadhyaya, Debiprasad, et al, eds. Phenomenology & Indian Philosophy. LC 90-42910. 376p. 1992. text 54.50 (*0-7914-0662-8*) State U NY Pr.

Chattopadhyaya, Debiprasad & Kumar, Ravinder, eds. Science, Philosophy, & Culture: Historical Perspective. LC 95-905859. (C). 1995. 20.00 (*81-215-0686-7*, Pub. by M Manoharial) Coronet Bks.

— Science Philosophy & Culture: Multi-Disciplinary Explorations, Pt. 1. LC 96-900936. (C). 1996. 67.50 (*81-215-0718-9*, Pub. by M Manoharial) Coronet Bks.

Chattopadhyaya, Debiprasad & Singh, Ravinder, eds. Some Aspects of India's Philosophical & Scientific Heritage. LC 95-905860. (C). 1995. 20.00 (*81-215-0687-5*, Pub. by M Manoharial) Coronet Bks.

Chattopadhyaya, Debiprasad, et al. Language, Logic & Science in India: Some Conceptual & Historical Perspectives, No. 4. Kumar, Ravinder, ed. LC 95-905858. (PHISPC Monographs: Ser. 4). 100p. (C). 1995. 21.00 (*81-215-0689-1*, Pub. by M Manoharial) Coronet Bks.

Chattopadhyaya, Debiprasad, ed. see Dasgupta, Surendranath.

Chattopadhyaya, Debiprasad, jt. ed. see Kirkland, Frank M.

Chattopadhyaya, Debiprasad, jt. ed. see Parthasarasthi, G.

Chattopadhyaya, Debiprsasad, ed. Indian Studies: Past & Present, 1966-1967, Vol. 8. 401p. 1967. 60.00 (*0-88065-038-9*) Scholarly Pubns.

Chattopadhyaya, H. P. Ethnic Unrest in Modern Sri Lanka: An Account of Tamil-Sinhalese Race Relations. LC 96-902080. 196p. 1994. pap. 125.00 (*81-85880-52-2*, Pub. by Print Hse) St Mut.

Chattopadhyaya, Haraprasad. From Marsh to Township East of Calcutta. (C). 1990. 14.50 (*81-7074-073-8*, Pub. by KP Bagchi) S Asia.

— Internal Migration in India: A Cast Study of Bengal. 551p. (C). 1987. 48.50 (*81-7074-008-8*, Pub. by KP Bagchi) S Asia.

Chattopadhyaya, Kamaladevi. Indian Woman's Battle. 1983. 10.00 (*0-8364-0948-5*, Pub. by Abhinav) S Asia.

— Tribalism in India. 302p. 1978. 19.95 (*0-318-36985-0*) Asia Bk Corp.

***Chattopadhyaya, Rajgopal.** Swami Vivekananda in India: A Corrective Biography. 440p. 1999. pap. 475.00 (*81-208-1586-6*, Pub. by Motilal Bnarsidass) St Mut.

Chattopadhyaya, S. Evolution of Hindu Sects. 1970. text 22.00 (*0-685-13840-2*) Coronet Bks.

Chattopadhyaya, Sudhakar. Reflections of Tantras. 106p. 1979. 11.95 (*0-318-36386-0*) Asia Bk Corp.

— Reflections on the Tantras. (C). 1990. 14.00 (*81-208-0691-3*, Pub. by Motilal Bnarsidass) S Asia.

Chattot, J. J., ed. see Jiang, Bo N.

Chattot, J. J., ed. see Liseikin, V. D.

Chattot, J. J., ed. see Wilkins, M. L.

Chattpadhyaya, D. P., ed. Indian Studies: Past & Present, 1961-1962, Vol. 3. 658p. 1962. 80.00 (*0-88065-033-8*) Scholarly Pubns.

Chatty, Dawn. Mobile Pastoralists: Development Planning & Social Change in Oman. (Illus.). 256p. 1996. pap. 19.50 (*0-231-10549-5*) Col U Pr.

Chatty, Dawn, ed. Organizing Women: Formal & Informal Women's Groups in the Middle East. LC 97-204030. 1997. 55.00 (*1-85973-910-5*, Pub. by Berg Pubs); pap. 19.50 (*1-85973-915-6*, Pub. by Berg Pubs) NYU Pr.

***Chatu, Sukhdev, et al.** Hands-On Guide to Clinical Pharmacology. 176p. 2000. pap. 19.95 (*0-632-05518-9*) Blackwell Sci.

Chaturbhuj, ed. see Tayler, William.

Chaturshreni, Ved V. Indo-U. S. Relations. 388p. 1980. 26.00 (*0-940500-08-6*) Asia Bk Corp.

Chaturvedi, A. Diplomatic Laws in Contemporary International Relations. 200p. 1986. 24.95 (*0-318-37233-9*) Asia Bk Corp.

Chaturvedi, A. N. Forest Mensuration. 416p. 1982. 100.00 (*0-7855-6548-5*, Pub. by Intl Bk Distr) St Mut.

— Forest Mensuration. 416p. (C). 1982. 150.00 (*0-7855-6886-7*, Pub. by Intl Bk Distr); text 200.00 (*0-7855-6593-0*, Pub. by Intl Bk Distr) St Mut.

— Forest Mensuration. 416p. 1992. 175.00 (*81-7089-005-5*, Pub. by Intl Bk Distr) St Mut.

Chaturvedi, A. N. & Khanna, L. S. Forest Mensuration. 406p. 1994. pap. 475.00 (*81-7089-203-1*, Pub. by Intl Bk Distr) St Mut.

Chaturvedi, Abha & Chaturvedi, Anil, eds. Sociology of Formal Organizations. (Oxford in India Readings in Sociology & Social & Cultural Anthropology Ser.). 410p. 1995. text 35.00 (*0-19-563609-0*) OUP.

Chaturvedi, Anil. District Administration: The Dynamics of Discord. 278p. (C). 1988. 27.50 (*0-8039-9560-1*) Sage.

Chaturvedi, Anil, jt. ed. see Chaturvedi, Abha.

C

An Asterisk (*) at the beginning of an entry indicates that the title is appearing for the first time.

***Chaturvedi, Anuradha.** Delhi: Agra & Jaipur. LC 99-88872. (Travel Guides Ser.). (Illus.). 320p. 2000. 24.95 (0-7894-5543-9) DK Pub Inc.

Chaturvedi, Divya. Administering SQL: Server 7. LC 99-35123. 608p. 1999. pap. text 44.99 incl. cd-rom (0-07-134168-4) McGraw.

Chaturvedi, Harivansh R. J. Bureaucracy & Local Community: Dynamics of Rural Deveolpment, India. 1977. 9.50 (0-88386-990-X) S Asia.

Chaturvedi, K. Bharatiya Dand Sanhita, Eighteen Sixty. (HIN.). 816p. 1982. 150.00 (0-7855-1397-3) St Mut.

Chaturvedi, K. & Pithisaria, M. K., eds. Three Taxes, Law of Wealth, Gift & Expenditure Tax, 2 vols. (C). 1989. 660.00 (0-7855-4730-4) St Mut.

Chaturvedi, Laxmi N. The Teachings of Bhagavad Gita. (Religion & Philosophy Ser.). 383p. 1991. 19.95 (81-207-1272-2) L N Chaturvedi.

Chaturvedi, M. D. Indian Penal Code, 1860. (HIN.). (C). 1993. 125.00 (81-7012-503-0, Pub. by Eastern Book) St Mut.

Chaturvedi, M. K., jt. auth. see Srivastava, H. C.

Chaturvedi, Mahendra & Bhola, Nath T. A Practical Hindi-English Dictionary. (ENG & HIN.). 700p. 1974. 16.00 (0-88386-380-4) S Asia.

Chaturvedi, Mahendra & Tiwari, B. N. A Practical Hindi-English Dictionary. 9th ed. 875p. 1987. 49.95 (0-8288-1741-3, M14105) Fr & Eur.

Chaturvedi, Pradeep. Energy Management Policy, Planning & Utilization. LC 97-913869. xiv, 178 p. 1997. write for info. (81-7022-669-4) Concept.

***Chaturvedi, Pradeep & Indian Association for the Advancement of Science Staff.** Rural Energy for Sustainable Development Technology & Environmental Issues LC 98-907062. xiv, 186 p. 1998. write for info. (81-7022-721-6) S Asia.

Chaturvedi, Prem Sagar. Technology in Vedic Literature. (C). 1993. 58.00 (81-85016-38-0, Pub. by Bks & Bks) S Asia.

Chaturvedi, S. K. Indo-Nepal Relations in Linkage Perspectives. 1990. 21.00 (81-7018-610-2, Pub. by BR Pub) S Asia.

Chaturvedi, Sanjay. Dawning of Antarctica: A Geopolitical Analysis. 1990. 74.00 (81-85330-06-9, Pub. by Usha) S Asia.

— The Polar Regions: A Political Geography. LC 95-44829. (Polar Research Ser.). 330p. 1996. 145.00 (0-471-94898-5) Wiley.

Chaturvedi, Shive K., jt. auth. see Sierakowski, Robert L.

Chaturvedi, T. N., frwd. Government Auditing. 2nd ed. (C). 1988. 27.00 (81-7024-192-8, Pub. by Ashish Pub Hse) S Asia.

Chaturvedi, T. N. & Pithisaria, V. Income Tax Law, 7 vols. (C). 1988. 1275.00 (0-7855-3525-X) St Mut.

Chaturvedi, Vinayak. Mapping Subaltern Studies & the Postcolonial. 1999. pap. text 20.00 (1-85984-214-3, Pub. by Verso) Norton.

***Chaturvedi, Vinayak.** Mapping Subaltern Studies & the Postcolonial. 1999. 60.00 (1-85984-723-4, Pub. by Verso) Norton.

Chaturverdi, D. K. & Murch, G. E., eds. Disordered Materials: Current Developments. (Materials Science Ser.: 223-224). (Illus.). 450p. 1996. text 186.00 (0-87849-737-4, Pub. by Trans T Pub) Enfield Pubs NH.

Chaturyedi, S. K. Nepal: Internal Politics & Its Constitutions. (C). 1992. 32.00 (81-210-0315-6, Pub. by Inter-India Pubns) S Asia.

***Chatwal, G. R.** Encyclopaedia of Environmental Soil & Marine Pollution, 2 vols. 650p. 1998. pap. 750.00 (81-7488-434-3, Pub. by Print Hse) St Mut.

***Chatwal, G. R., et al, eds.** Encyclopaedia of World Great Scientists, 8 vols. 3032p. 1998. pap. 2500.00 (81-7041-650-7, Pub. by Print Hse) St Mut.

Chatwal, G. R., et al, eds. Environmental Land & Marine Pollution & Their Control. 1989. 60.00 (81-7041-208-0, Pub. by Anmol) S Asia.

Chatwick, Charley G., et al. Ceiling Framing. Harrington, Louis G., ed. (Basic Carpentry Skills Ser.). (Illus.). 12p. 1990. teacher ed. 5.00 (0-89606-319-4, 702TK); pap. text 7.00 (0-89606-272-4, 702) Am Assn Voc Materials.

Chatwin, Bruce. Anatomy of Restlessness: Selected Writings 1969-1989. 1996. 23.95 (0-614-96858-5, Viking) Viking Penguin.

— Anatomy of Restlessness: Selected Writings 1969-1989. LC 96-3003. ix, 205p. 1997. pap. 12.95 (0-14-025698-9) Viking Penguin.

— In Patagonia. 1988. pap. 13.95 (0-14-011291-X, Penguin Bks) Viking Penguin.

— On the Black Hill. LC 83-7575. 256p. 1984. pap. 12.95 (0-14-006896-1, Penguin Bks) Viking Penguin.

— Songlines. 1987. 10.95 (0-224-02452-3) Random.

— The Songlines. 304p. 1988. pap. 13.95 (0-14-009429-6, Penguin Bks) Viking Penguin.

— Utz. 160p. 1989. pap. 11.95 (0-14-011576-5, Penguin Bks) Viking Penguin.

— Utz. large type ed. 130p. 1990. 17.95 (1-85089-328-4, Pub. by ISIS Lrg Prnt) Transaction Pubs.

— The Viceroy of Ouidah. 1988. pap. 11.95 (0-14-011290-1, Penguin Bks) Viking Penguin.

— What am I Doing Here? 384p. 1990. pap. 13.95 (0-14-011577-3, Penguin Bks) Viking Penguin.

— What Am I Doing Here? large type ed. 450p. 1990. 24.95 (1-85089-400-0) ISIS Lrg Prnt.

Chatwin, Terrence D., ed. see Metallurgical Society of AIME Staff.

***Chatzky, Jean.** Talking Money: Everything You Need to Know about Your Finances & Your Future. 304p. 2001. 24.95 (0-446-52570-7) Warner Bks.

Chatzky, Jean Sherman. The Rich & Famous Money Book: Investment Strategies of Leading Celebrities. LC 97-22835. 224p. 1997. 19.95 (0-471-18540-X) Wiley.

— The Rich & Famous Money Book: Investment Strategies of Leading Celebrities. 210p. 1999. pap. 14.95 (0-471-32707-7) Wiley.

Chau, Fook S. & Lim, C. T., eds. International Conference on Experimental Mechanics Vol. 2921: Advances & Applications. LC 96-70749. 724p. 1997. 124.00 (0-8194-2323-8) SPIE.

Chau, A. S. & Afghan, B. K. Analysis of Pesticides in Water: Analysis Nitrogen-Containing Pesticides, Vol. III, Vol. III. 264p. 1982. 148.00 (0-8493-5212-6, TP248, CRC Reprint) Franklin.

Chau, Alfred S. & Afghan, B. K., eds. Analysis of Pesticides in Water: Analysis Chlorine & Phosphorus-Containing Pesticides, Vol. II, Vol. II. 256p. 1982. 143.00 (0-8493-5211-8, TP248, CRC Reprint) Franklin.

Chau, Alfred S., jt. ed. see Afghan, B. K.

Chau, Bhiksu Thich. The Chinese Madhyama Agama & the Pali Majjhima Nikaya. (C). 1991. 23.50 (81-208-0794-4, Pub. by Motilal Bnarsidass) S Asia.

Chau, F. S., jt. auth. see Sirohi, R. S.

Chau, Heng, jt. auth. see Sure, Heng.

Chau, Kenneth L., ed. Ethnicity & Biculturalism: Emerging Perspectives of Social Group Work. (Social Work with Groups Ser.). 136p. 1991. text 39.95 (1-56024-094-6); pap. text 16.95 (1-56024-095-4) Haworth Pr.

***Chau, Kevin & Dimitrijev, Sima, eds.** Device & Process Technologies for MEMS & Microelectronics. 1999. pap. text 92.00 (0-8194-3493-0) SPIE.

Chau, Kevin & French, Patrick J., eds. Micromachined Devices & Components III, Vol. 3224. LC 98-122098. 392p. 1997. 80.00 (0-8194-2656-3) SPIE.

Chau, Kevin & Roop, Ray M., eds. Micromachined Devices & Components II, Vol. 2882. 350p. 1996. 66.00 (0-8194-2280-0) SPIE.

Chau, Kevin, jt. ed. see French, Patrick J.

Chau, Ling-Lie & Nahm, W., eds. Differential Geometric Methods in Theoretical Physics: Physics & Geometry. (NATO ASI Ser.: Vol. 245). (Illus.). 846p. (C). text 210.00 (0-306-43807-0, Kluwer Plenum) Kluwer Academic.

Chau, Monica, et al, contrib. by. CEPA Journal: Uncommon Traits: Relocating Asia Exhibition Journal. (Illus.). 16p. 1997. pap. write for info. (0-939784-24-6) CEPA Gall.

Chau, Monica, et al. The Subject of Rape. (Illus.). 80p. (Orig.). 1993. pap. 12.95 (0-87427-089-8) Whitney Mus.

Chau Phan Thien. Vietnamese Communism: A Research Bibliography. LC 75-16961. 359p. 1975. lib. bdg. 85.00 (0-8371-7950-5, CVC/, Greenwood Pr) Greenwood.

Chau, S. Y., ed. see Afghan, B. K.

Chau, Ta N., jt. auth. see Carron, Gabriel.

Chau, Wai-Shing. The Letter & the Spirit: A History of Interpretation from Origen to Luther, Vol. 167. LC 93-32451. (American University Studies: Series VII). VIII, 250p. (C). 1995. text 48.95 (0-8204-2328-9) P Lang Pubng.

Chaube, A., jt. auth. see Chaube, S. P.

Chaube, H. S., ed. Plant Disease Management: Principles & Practice. 304p. 1991. lib. bdg. 228.00 (0-8493-5758-6, SB562) CRC Pr.

Chaube, S. P. Educational Philosophies in India. (C). 1993. 32.00 (0-7069-7402-6, Pub. by Vikas) S Asia.

Chaube, S. P. & Chaube, A. Education in Ancient & Medieval India: A Survey of the Main Features & a Critical Evaluation of Major Trends. LC 98-915793. 1999. 32.00 (81-259-0434-4, Pub. by Vikas); pap. 14.00 (81-259-0435-2, Pub. by Vikas) S Asia.

Chaubey, N. P., jt. ed. see Rangarao, B. V.

Chaucer, Geoffrey. The Book of Troilus & Criseyde. (BCL1-PR English Literature Ser.). 572p. 1992. reprint ed. lib. bdg. 129.00 (0-7812-7169-X) Rprt Serv.

***Chaucer, Geoffrey.** Canterbury Quintet: The General Prologue & Four Tales: A Reader-Friendly Edition. Murphy, Michael, ed. 224p. (C). 2000. pap. 11.95 (1-893385-02-7) Little Leaf.

Chaucer, Geoffrey. The Canterbury Tales. Hieatt, A. Kent & Hieatt, Constance B., eds. LC 98-146197. (Bantam Classics Ser.). 448p. (gr. 9-12). 1982. mass mkt. 4.95 (0-553-21082-3, Bantam Classics) Bantam.

***Chaucer, Geoffrey.** The Canterbury Tales. vii, 528p. 1998. pap. 22.95 (0-9665678-6-2) Buy Books.

Chaucer, Geoffrey. The Canterbury Tales. 1992. 20.00 (0-679-41322-7) Everymns Lib.

— The Canterbury Tales. Ecker, Ronald L. & Crook, Eugene J., trs. LC 93-77730. 592p. (C). 1993. pap. text 17.95 (0-9636512-3-4) Hodge & Braddock.

— The Canterbury Tales. LC 86-21045. (Illus.). 96p. (YA). (gr. 5 up). 1988. 20.00 (0-688-06201-6) Lothrop.

— The Canterbury Tales. Halverson, John, ed. LC 79-153880. (Library of Literature: No. 27). 1971. pap. text 12.19 (0-672-61006-X, Bobbs) Macmillan.

— The Canterbury Tales. 658p. 1994. 18.50 (0-679-60125-2) Modern Lib NY.

— The Canterbury Tales. McCaughrean, Geraldine, ed. (Illus.). 128p. (YA). 1999. pap. 12.95 (0-19-274181-0) OUP.

Chaucer, Geoffrey. The Canterbury Tales. Lumiansky, R. M., tr. (Illus.). 383p. 1981. mass mkt. 5.50 (0-671-72769-9, WSP) PB.

Chaucer, Geoffrey. The Canterbury Tales. (Illus.). 128p. (YA). (gr. 5 up). 1997. pap. 3.99 (0-14-038053-1) Penguin Putnam.

— The Canterbury Tales. (Penguin Classics). 1986. 13.05 (0-606-00447-5, Pub. by Turtleback) Demco.

— The Canterbury Tales. Baker, Donald C., ed. LC 81-40286. (Variorum Edition of the Works of Geoffrey Chaucer, The Canterbury Tales Ser.: Vol. II, Pt. 3). 304p. 1983. 49.95 (0-8061-1785-0) U of Okla Pr.

— The Canterbury Tales. Coghill, Nevill, tr. 528p. (C). 2000. pap. 8.95 (0-14-044022-4) Viking Penguin.

— The Canterbury Tales. Wright, David, tr. 1965. pap. 10.00 (0-394-70293-X) Vin Bks.

Chaucer, Geoffrey. The Canterbury Tales. (Poetry Library). 640p. 1997. pap. 7.95 (1-85326-436-9, 4369WW, Pub. by Wrdsworth Edits) NTC Contemp Pub Co.

Chaucer, Geoffrey. Canterbury Tales. 1992. 20.00 (0-679-40989-0) Everymns Lib.

— The Canterbury Tales. Werthamer, Cynthia C., ed. (Barron's Book Notes Ser.). (C). 1984. pap. 3.95 (0-8120-3406-6) Barron.

— The Canterbury Tales. large type ed. 1997. pap. 19.95 (1-55701-209-1) BNI Pubns.

— The Canterbury Tales. Wright, David, tr. & intro. by. (Oxford World's Classics Ser.). 510p. 1998. reprint ed. pap. 6.95 (0-19-283360-X) OUP.

— Canterbury Tales, 2 vols. rev. ed. Lee, Sophia, ed. LC 71-162886. (Illus.). reprint ed. 90.00 (0-404-54550-5) AMS Pr.

— The Canterbury Tales. rev. ed. Cawley, A. C., ed. & intro. by. 632p. 1991. pap. 5.95 (0-460-87027-0, Everyman's Classic Lib) Tuttle Pubng.

— The Canterbury Tales. 2nd ed. Hopper, Vincent F., tr. 1977. pap. 11.95 (0-8120-0039-0) Barron.

— The Canterbury Tales: A Facsimile & Transcription of the Hengwrt Manuscript with Variants from the Ellesmere Manuscript. Ruggiers, Paul G., ed. LC 77-18611. (Illus.). 1078p. 1979. 185.00 (0-8061-1416-9) U of Okla Pr.

— The Canterbury Tales: A Selection. Howard, Donald R. & Dean, James M., eds. 1988. mass mkt. 4.95 (0-451-52400-4, CE1514, Sig Classics) NAL.

— The Canterbury Tales: Fifteenth-Century Continuations & Additions. Bowers, John M., ed. LC 92-22583. 1992. pap. 9.00 (1-879288-23-0) Medieval Inst.

Chaucer, Geoffrey. The Canterbury Tales: Illustrated Prologue. 1996. pap. 13.50 (0-614-20447-X) Antique Collect.

Chaucer, Geoffrey. The Canterbury Tales: Illustrated Prologue. Alexander, Michael, ed. (Illus.). 64p. 1996. pap. 13.50 (1-85759-113-5, Pub. by P Wilson) Scala Books.

— The Canterbury Tales: Nine Tales & the General Prologue. Kolve, V. A. & Olson, Glending, eds. (Critical Editions Ser.). 400p. (Orig.). (C). 1989. pap. text 12.50 (0-393-95245-2) Norton.

— The Canterbury Tales: The First Fragment. 320p. 1996. pap. 8.95 (0-14-043409-7, Viking) Viking Penguin.

— The Canterbury Tales: The General Prologue & Twelve Major Tales in Modern Spelling. Murphy, Michael, ed. 414p. (C). 1991. lib. bdg. 67.00 (0-8191-8148-X) U Pr of Amer.

— The Canterbury Tales: The New Ellesmere Chaucer Monochromatic Facsimile. Woodward, Daniel & Stevens, Martin, eds. (Illus.). 484p. 1997. 275.00 (0-87328-162-4) Huntington Lib.

— The Canterbury Tales of Chaucer, 5 vols. Tyrwhitt, Thomas, ed. LC 74-39160. reprint ed. 385.00 (0-404-01550-6) AMS Pr.

— Chanticleer & the Fox. LC 58-10449. (Illus.). 44p. (J). (gr. 4-7). 1958. 16.95 (0-690-18561-8) HarpC Child Bks.

— Chanticleer & the Fox. LC 58-10449. (Illus.). 44p. (J). (ps-3). 1961. lib. bdg. 16.89 (0-690-18562-6) HarpC Child Bks.

— Chanticleer & the Fox. LC 58-10449. (Illus.). 40p. (J). (ps-3). 1982. mass mkt. 3.95 (0-690-04318-X) HarpC Child Bks.

— Chanticleer & the Fox. LC 58-10449. (Trophy Picture Bk.). (Illus.). 44p. (J). (ps-3). 1982. reprint ed. pap. 6.95 (0-06-443087-1, HarpTrophy) HarpC Child Bks.

— Chaucer. (J). (gr. 1-9). 1992. pap. 3.95 (0-88388-017-2) Bellerophon Bks.

— Chaucer's "Boece" & the Medieval Tradition of Boethius. Minnis, Alastair J., ed. (Chaucer Studies: Vol. XVIII). 213p. (C). 1993. 75.00 (0-85991-368-6) Boydell & Brewer.

Chaucer, Geoffrey. Chaucer's Pardoner's Tale. (York Notes Ser.). Date not set. pap. text. write for info. (0-582-78140-X, Pub. by Addison-Wesley) Longman.

Chaucer, Geoffrey. Chaucers Poetry. 2nd ed. Donaldson, E. T., ed. & selected by by. 1167p. (C). 1998. 73.00 (0-673-15667-2) Addson-Wesley Educ.

— The Clerk's Prologue & Tale. Winny, J., ed. (Selected Tales from Chaucer Ser.). 122p. 1966. pap. text 10.95 (0-521-04632-7) Cambridge U Pr.

— Cliffs Chaucer's Prologue: Complete Study Edition. 101p. 1966. pap. 6.95 (0-8220-1406-8, Cliff) IDG Bks.

— Cliffs Chaucer's Wife of Bath, Complete Study Edition. 101p. 1966. pap. 6.95 (0-8220-1409-2, Cliff) IDG Bks.

— Comp Poetry /Prose Chaucer. 2nd ed. Fisher, John H., ed. LC 88-29400. 1000p. (C). 1989. text 81.00 (0-03-028612-3, Pub. by Harcourt Coll Pubs) Harcourt.

— Cuentos de Canterbury. 1998. pap. text 12.95 (84-08-01726-8) Planeta.

— Facsimile Series of the Works of Geoffrey Chaucer Vol. I: MS Tanner 346, Bodleian Library, Oxford. LC 81-1364. 329p. 1981. 125.00 (0-937664-50-2) Pilgrim Bks OK.

— Facsimile Series of the Works of Geoffrey Chaucer Vol. II: MS Bodley 368, Bodleian Library, Oxford. LC 82-356. 487p. 1982. 125.00 (0-937664-51-0) Pilgrim Bks OK.

— Facsimile Series of the Works of Geoffrey Chaucer Vol. III: Troilus & Criseyde, St. John's College, Cambridge, MS L. 1. LC 83-13079. 300p. 1983. 130.00 (0-937664-52-9) Pilgrim Bks OK.

— Facsimile Series of the Works of Geoffrey Chaucer Vol. V: Manuscript Trinity R. 3.19, Trinity College, Cambridge. Ruggiers, Paul G., ed. (Illus.). 550p. 1988. 140.00 (0-937664-77-4) Pilgrim Bks OK.

— Facsimile Series of the Works of Geoffrey Chaucer Vol. VI: MS Pepys 2006, Magdalene College, Cambridge. 427p. 1985. 144.00 (0-937664-69-3) Pilgrim Bks OK.

— The Floure & the Leafe; the Assembly of Ladies; the Isle of Ladies. Pearsall, Derek, ed. (TEAMS Middle English Text Ser.). 1990. pap. 7.00 (0-918720-43-5) Medieval Inst.

— The Franklin's Prologue & Tale from the Canterbury Tales. 2nd ed. Spearing, A. C., ed. LC 93-33752. (Selected Tales from Chaucer Ser.). (Illus.). 152p. (C). 1994. pap. text 10.95 (0-521-46694-6) Cambridge U Pr.

— The Franklin's Tale. 2nd ed. Hodgson, Phyllis, ed. 160p. (C). 1973. pap. 12.50 (0-485-61007-8, Pub. by Athlone Pr) Humanities.

— The Friar's, Summoner's & Pardoner's Tales. Havely, Nick R., ed. LC 75-19090. (London Medieval & Renaissance Ser.). 164p. (C). 1976. 16.50 (0-8419-0220-8); pap. 9.95 (0-8419-0224-0) Holmes & Meier.

— The General Prologue. LC 93-34265. (Variorum Edition of the Works of Geoffrey Chaucer, The Canterbury Tales Ser.: Pts. 1A-1B). 1993. 115.00 (0-8061-2552-7) U of Okla Pr.

— The General Prologue, the Canon's Yeoman's Prologue & Tale. Schmidt, A. V., ed. LC 75-17975. (London Medieval & Renaissance Ser.). 175p. (C). 1976. 17.95 (0-8419-0219-4) Holmes & Meier.

— The General Prologue, the Canon's Yeoman's Prologue & Tale. Schmidt, A. V., ed. LC 75-17975. (London Medieval & Renaissance Ser.). 175p. (C). 1976. pap. 9.95 (0-8419-0223-2) Holmes & Meier.

— The General Prologue to the Canterbury Tales. Winny, J., ed. (Selected Tales from Chaucer Ser.). 144p. 1965. pap. text 10.95 (0-521-04629-7) Cambridge U Pr.

— The General Prologue to the Canterbury Tales. 3rd ed. Hodgson, Phyllis, ed. 220p. (C). 1969. pap. 8.95 (0-485-61006-X, Pub. by Athlone Pr) Humanities.

— Geoffrey Chaucer: The Canterbury Tales: The General Prologue & Twelve Major Tales in Modern Spelling. Murphy, Michael, ed. 414p. (Orig.). (C). 1991. pap. 29.00 (0-8191-8149-8) U Pr of Amer.

— Italian Tales from the Age of Shakespeare. rev. ed. Benson, Pamela & Mills, Maldwyn, eds. (Everyman Paperback Classics Ser.). 320p. (Orig.). (C). 1995. pap. 12.50 (0-460-87551-5, Everyman's Classic Lib) Tuttle Pubng.

— The Knight's Tale, from the Canterbury Tales. 2nd ed. Spearing, A. C., ed. LC 94-44398. 254p. 1996. pap. text 15.95 (0-521-49912-7) Cambridge U Pr.

— The Legend of Good Women. Cowen, Janet & Kane, George, eds. (Medieval Texts & Studies: No. 16). 360p. 1995. 95.00 (0-937191-34-5) Mich St U Pr.

— Love Visions. Stone, Brian, tr. (Classics Ser.). 272p. 1983. pap. 11.95 (0-14-044408-4, Penguin Classics) Viking Penguin.

— The Manciple's Tale. Baker, Donald C., ed. LC 83-14734. (Variorum Edition of the Works of Geoffrey Chaucer, The Canterbury Tales Ser.: Vol. II, Pt. 10). (Illus.). 176p. 1984. 49.95 (0-8061-1872-5) U of Okla Pr.

— The Merchant's Prologue & Tale. Hussey, Maurice, ed. (Selected Tales from Chaucer Ser.). 116p. 1966. pap. text 10.95 (0-521-04631-9) Cambridge U Pr.

— The Miller's Prologue & Tale. Winny, J., ed. LC 76-132283. (Selected Tales from Chaucer Ser.). 108p. 1971. pap. text 10.95 (0-521-08033-9) Cambridge U Pr.

— The Minor Poems, Pt. 1. David, Alfred & Pace, George B., eds. LC 80-5943. (Variorum Edition of the Works of Geoffrey Chaucer, The Canterbury Tales Ser.: Vol. V). 200p. 1982. 49.95 (0-8061-1629-3) U of Okla Pr.

— Monarch Quick & Easy Notes: "Canterbury Tales" by Chaucer. write for info. (0-318-58791-2) S&S Trade.

— The New Ellesmere Chaucer Facsimile: The Canterbury Tales. Woodward, Daniel & Stevens, Martin, eds. (Illus.). 1995. write for info. (0-87328-151-9) Huntington Lib.

— The Nun's Priest's Prologue & Tale. Hussey, Maurice, ed. & intro. by. (Selected Tales from Chaucer Ser.). 104p. 1966. pap. text 10.95 (0-521-04626-2) Cambridge U Pr.

— The Nun's Priest's Tale. Pearsall, Derek, ed. LC 83-5760. (Variorum Edition of the Works of Geoffrey Chaucer, The Canterbury Tales Ser.: Vol. II, Pt. 9). 300p. 1984. 49.95 (0-8061-1779-6) U of Okla Pr.

— Pardoner's Prologue. (Longman Critical Essays Ser.). Date not set. pap. text. write for info. (0-582-06049-4, Pub. by Addison-Wesley) Longman.

— The Pardoner's Prologue & Tale from the Canterbury Tales. 2nd ed. Winny, J., ed. (Selected Tales from Chaucer Ser.). 111p. (C). 1994. pap. text 10.95 (0-521-46818-3) Cambridge U Pr.

Chaucer, Geoffrey. The Physician's Tale. Corsa, Helen S., ed. LC 79-33146. (Variorum Edition of the Works of Geoffrey Chaucer, The Canterbury Tales Ser.: Vol. 2, Pt. 17). (Illus.). 208p. 1987. 49.95 (0-8061-2038-X) U of Okla Pr.

Chaucer, Geoffrey. The Pierpont Morgan Library Manuscript M.817: A Facsimile. Ruggiers, Paul G., ed. (Illus.). 265p. 1987. 125.00 (0-937664-74-X) Pilgrim Bks OK.

— The Poetical Works of Geoffrey Chaucer, 6 vols. Nicolas, Harris & Morris, Richard, eds. LC 72-971. reprint ed. 495.00 (0-404-01560-3) AMS Pr.

— The Portable Chaucer. rev. ed. Morrison, Theodore, ed. LC 75-2224. (Portable Library: No. 81). 800p. 1977. pap. 15.95 (0-14-015081-1, Penguin Bks) Viking Penguin.

— The Prioress' Prologue & Tale. Winny, J., ed. LC 74-19531. (Selected Tales from Chaucer Ser.). 64p. 1975. pap. text 10.95 (0-521-20744-4) Cambridge U Pr.

— The Prioress's Tale. Boyd, Beverly, ed. LC 86-25064. (Variorum Edition of the Works of Geoffrey Chaucer, The Canterbury Tales Ser.: Vol. II, Pt. 20). (Illus.). 224p. 1987. 49.95 (0-8061-2045-2) U of Okla Pr.

— The Reeve's Prologue & Tale. Spearing, A. C. et al, eds. LC 78-19695. (Selected Tales from Chaucer Ser.). 136p. 1979. pap. text 10.95 (0-521-22211-7) Cambridge U Pr.

C

An Asterisk (*) at the beginning of an entry indicates that the title is appearing for the first time.

Chaucer, Geoffrey. The Riverside Chaucer, 3 vols. 3rd ed. Benson, Larry D., ed. LC 86-81304. (C). 1986. text 63.96 (*0-395-29031-7*) HM.

Chaucer, Geoffrey. Romancing the Goddess: Three Middle English Romances about Women. Osborn, Marijane, ed. & tr. by. LC 97-4702. (ENG & ENM.). 288p. 1997. pap. text 19.95 (*0-252-06655-3*) U of Ill Pr.

— Romancing the Goddess: Three Middle English Romances about Women. Osborn, Marijane, ed. & tr. by. LC 97-4702. (ENG & ENM.). 288p. 1997. text 46.95 (*0-252-02350-1*) U of Ill Pr.

Chaucer, Geoffrey. Selected Canterbury Tales. LC 94-35008. (Thrift Editions Ser.). 128p. (Orig.). 1994. pap. text 1.00 (*0-486-28241-4*) Dover.

Chaucer, Geoffrey. The Squire's Tale. Baker, Donald C., ed. LC 89-24928. (Variorum Edition of the Works of Geoffrey Chaucer, The Canterbury Tales Ser.: Vol. II, Pt. 12). (Illus.). 304p. 1990. 49.95 (*0-8061-2154-8*) U of Okla Pr.

— The Summoner's Tale. variorum ed. Plummer, John F., 3rd, ed. LC 94-38951. (Chaucer Variorium Ser.: Vol. 2, Pt. 7). (Illus.). 270p. 1995. 49.95 (*0-8061-2744-9*, 2744) U of Okla Pr.

***Chaucer, Geoffrey.** The Three Tales about Marriage. 128p. 1998. pap. text 3.50 (*0-460-87870-0*, Everyman's Classic Lib) Tuttle Pubng.

Chaucer, Geoffrey. Troilus & Criseyde. Coghill, Nevill, tr. (Classics Ser.). 336p. 1971. pap. 9.95 (*0-14-044239-1*, Penguin Classics) Viking Penguin.

— Troilus & Criseyde: A New Translation. Windeatt, Barry, tr. (Oxford World's Classics Ser.). 256p. 1998. pap. 8.95 (*0-19-283290-5*) OUP.

— The Wife of Bath. Beidler, Peter G., ed. (Case Studies in Contemporary Criticism). 304p. 1996. text 39.95 (*0-312-15859-9*) St Martin.

— The Wife of Bath. Beidler, Peter G., ed. 306p. 1995. pap. text 9.95 (*0-312-11128-2*) St Martin.

— The Wife of Bath's Prologue & Tale & the Clerk's Prologue & Tale from the Canterbury Tales. Cigman, Gloria, ed. LC 75-17976. (London Medieval & Renaissance Ser.). 94p. (C). 1976. 17.95 (*0-8419-0225-9*) Holmes & Meier.

— The Wife of Bath's Prologue & Tale from the Canterbury Tales. 2nd ed. Winny, J., ed. (Selected Tales from Chaucer Ser.). (Illus.). 144p. (C). 1995. pap. text 10.95 (*0-521-46689-X*) Cambridge U Pr.

— Works of Geoffrey Chaucer. Pollard, Alfred W., ed. LC 73-399393. (Select Bibliographies Reprint Ser.). 1977. reprint ed. 36.95 (*0-8369-9903-7*) Ayer.

— Works of Geoffrey Chaucer & Others: Being a Reproduction in Facsimile of the First Collected Edition 1532, from the Copy in the British Museum. (BCL1-PR English Literature Ser.). 793p. 1992. reprint ed. lib. bdg. 109.00 (*0-7812-7168-1*) Rprt Serv.

— The Works of Geoffrey Chaucer & 'The Kingis Quair' A Facsimile of Bodlein Library, Oxford, MS Arch. Selden. B. 24. fac. ed. Boffey, Julia & Edwards, A. S., eds. LC 95-32704. 572p. (C). 1997. 710.00 (*0-85991-476-3*) Boydell & Brewer.

Chaucer, Geoffrey & Bredon, Simon. The Equatorie of the Planetis. LC 55-1173. (Illus.). 232p. reprint ed. pap. 66.20 (*0-608-30524-3*, 2050724) Bks Demand.

***Chaucer, Geoffrey & De Lorris, Guillaume.** The Romaunt of the Rose & Le Roman de la Rose. LC 98-37724. (Variorum Edition of the Works of Geoffrey Chaucer, The Canterbury Tales Ser.). 368p. 1999. 75.00 (*0-8061-3147-0*) U of Okla Pr.

Chaucer, Geoffrey & Donohoe, James J. Chaucer's Lesser Poems Complete in Presentday English. LC 74-84878. 275p. 1974. write for info. (*0-936875-02-X*) Loras Coll Pr.

— Chaucer's Troilus & Cressida: Five Books in Presentday English. LC 75-29910. 201p. 1975. write for info. (*0-936875-01-1*) Loras Coll Pr.

Chaucer, Geoffrey, et al. Chaucer's Dream Poetry. LC 96-54627. 272p. (C). 1997. pap. 35.00 (*0-582-04011-6*) Longman.

— Chaucer's Dream Poetry. LC 96-54627. (C). 1998. 76.88 (*0-582-04012-4*) Longman.

***Chaucer, Geoffrey, et al.** Troilus & Criseyde. LC 99-87754. 2000. write for info. (*0-87013-536-8*) Mich St U Pr.

Chaucer, Geoffrey, jt. auth. see Center for Learning Network Staff.

Chaucer, Geoffrey, jt. auth. see Hatton, Thomas J.

Chaucer, Geoffrey, tr. see Boethius, Anicius Manlius Severinus.

Chaudburi, Haridas. Integral Yoga. 160p. 1990. pap. text 13.95 (*0-85-46021-5*) Routledge.

Chaudet-Miranda, Mrs., jt. ed. see Brebbia, Carlos A.

Chaudhari, A. B. A Comprehensive, Eco-Botanical Survey of Monocotyledons, Pt. V. 71p. 1985. pap. 25.00 (*81-7089-077-2*, Pub. by Intl Bk Distr) St Mut.

— A Comprehensive Ecological Botanical Survey of the Grasses (Gramineae) & Sedges (Cyperaceae), Pt. IV. 66p. 1985. pap. 25.00 (*81-7089-076-4*, Pub. by Intl Bk Distr) St Mut.

— A Comprehensive Survey of Epiphytes, Pt. II. 1985. pap. 25.00 (*81-7089-074-8*, Pub. by Intl Bk Distr) St Mut.

— A Comprehensive Survey of Tropical & Mangrove Forests of Sundarbans & Andaman, Pt. 1. (C). 1985. text 110.00 (*0-89771-583-7*, Pub. by Intl Bk Distr) St Mut.

— Environment & Resource of Tropical & Temperate Forests of India. 299p. 1985. 125.00 (*81-7089-073-X*, Pub. by Intl Bk Distr) St Mut.

— Environmental & Resources of Tropical & Temperate Forests of India. 299p. 1985. pap. 275.00 (*81-7089-025-X*, Pub. by Intl Bk Distr) St Mut.

— Lianas, Climber & Shrubby Climbers, Pt. III. 89p. (C). 1985. pap. 40.00 (*81-7089-075-6*, Pub. by Intl Bk Distr) St Mut.

Chaudhari, Raghuveer, ed. see Shah, Kirit N.

Chaudhary. Time Measure & Compositional Types in Indian Music. Ramanathan, Hema, tr. (C). 1997. 49.00 (*81-86471-02-2*, Pub. by Aditya Prakashan) S Asia.

Chaudhary, Angraj. Comparative Aesthetics: East & West. xvi, 296p. 1991. 27.00 (*0-685-62636-9*, Pub. by Eastern Bk Linkers) Nataraj Bks.

— Essays on Buddhism & Pali Literature. LC 94-902190. iv, 221p. (C). 1994. 20.00 (*81-85133-68-9*, Pub. by Eastern Bk Linkers) Nataraj Bks.

Chaudhary, B. R. & Agrawal, S. B., eds. Cytology, Genetics & Molecular Biology of Algae. (Illus.). 439p. 1996. 145.00 (*90-5103-126-2*, Pub. by SPB Acad Pub) Balogh.

Chaudhary, M. R. Industrial Morale & Productivity. (C). 1990. text 32.00 (*81-7100-261-7*, Pub. by Deep & Deep Pubns) S Asia.

***Chaudhary, Muhammad Azam.** Justice in Practice: A Legal Ethnography of a Pakistani Punjabi Village. 258p. 1999. text 23.95 (*0-19-579063-4*) OUP.

Chaudhary, Neelam. Socio-Economic History of Mughal India. 1987. 26.00 (*0-8364-2314-3*) S Asia.

Chaudhary, P. K., jt. auth. see Singh, Chhatrapati.

Chaudhary, Pratima, jt. auth. see Chaudhary, S. N.

Chaudhary, S. N. Employment of Women: With Special Reference to Embroidery Work. (C). 1994. 14.00 (*81-7100-612-4*, Pub. by Deep & Deep Pubns) S Asia.

Chaudhary, S. N. & Chaudhary, Pratima. National Development & Women. 192p. (C). 1992. 18.95 (*0-7069-5956-6*, Pub. by Vikas) S Asia.

Chaudhary, Valmiki. President & the Indian Constitution. 379p. 1985. 32.95 (*0-318-36598-7*) Asia Bk Corp.

Chaudhri, A. B. Santals, Religion & Rituals. (C). 1987. 26.50 (*81-7024-085-9*, Pub. by Ashish Pub Hse) S Asia.

***Chaudhri, Akmal & Zicari, Roberto.** Succeeding with Object Databases: A Practical Look at Today's Implementations with Java & XML. 416p. 2000. 59.99 (*0-471-38384-8*) Wiley.

Chaudhri, Anna, jt. auth. see Davidson, Hilda Ellis.

Chaudhri, D. P., jt. ed. see Lea, David A.

Chaudhri, V. K., jt. auth. see Bagchi, T. P.

***Chaudhri, Vinay & Fikes, Richard, eds.** Question Answering Systems: Papers from the AAAI Fall Symposium. (Illus.). 119p. 1999. spiral bd. 25.00 (*1-57735-104-5*) AAAI Pr.

Chaudhry, Abdus Sattar, jt. ed. see Ashoor, Mohammad Saleh Jamil.

Chaudhry, G. Rasul. Biological Degradation & Bioremediation of Toxic Chemicals. LC 93-25453. (Illus.). 520p. 1995. 69.95 (*0-931146-27-5*, Dioscorides) Timber.

Chaudhry, Kiren A. The Price of Wealth: Economics & Institutions in the Middle East. LC 97-1536. (Cornell Studies in Political Economy). 344p. 1996. text 45.00 (*0-8014-3164-6*); pap. text 19.95 (*0-8014-8430-8*) Cornell U Pr.

Chaudhry, M. Hanif & Mays, Larry W., eds. Computer Modeling of Free-Surface & Pressurized Flows: Proceedings of NATO Advanced Study Institute. LC 94-21770. (NATO ASI Ser.: Series E, Applied Sciences: Vol. 274). 1994. text 420.50 (*0-7923-2946-5*) Kluwer Academic.

Chaudhry, M. Hanif & Yevjevich, V. Closed-Conduit Flow. LC 81-51337. 1981. 45.00 (*0-918334-41-1*) WRP.

Chaudhry, M. Hanif, ed. see Applied Mechanics, Bioengineering & Fluids Enginee.

***Chaudhry, Minakshi.** Exploring Pangi Himalaya: A World Beyond Civilization. LC 98-907464. 326p. 1998. write for info. (*81-7387-084-5*, Pub. by Indus Pub) S Asia.

Chaudhry, Muhammad S. Women's Rights in Islam. 204p. 1991. 19.95 (*1-56744-419-9*) Kazi Pubns.

Chaudhry, Saida. Call to Prophethood. (Illus.). (J). (gr. 2-5). pap. 4.00 (*0-89259-046-7*) Am Trust Pubns.

— We Are Muslim Children. (J). (gr. 4). 1993. pap. 4.00 (*0-89259-126-9*) Am Trust Pubns.

Chaudhuri & Mukerjee, Rahul. Randomized Response: Theory & Techniques. (Statistics: Textbooks & Monographs: Vol. 85). (Illus.). 192p. 1987. text 125.00 (*0-8247-7785-9*) Dekker.

Chaudhuri, jt. auth. see Gupta, Das.

Chaudhuri, A. & Stenger, H. Survey Sampling: Theory & Methods. (Statistics Ser.: Vol. 130). (Illus.). 384p. 1992. text 185.00 (*0-8247-8689-0*, 8689-0) Dekker.

Chaudhuri, A. B. Environment & Ecology of Herb Shrub Flora. (C). 1991. 56.00 (*81-7024-415-3*, Pub. by Ashish Pub Hse) S Asia.

— Forest Plants of Eastern India. xii, 649p. 1993. 59.00 (*81-7024-537-0*, Pub. by Ashish Pub Hse) Nataraj Bks.

— Himalayan Ecology & Environment. (Illus.). xiv, 596p. 1992. 39.95 (*1-881338-29-0*) Nataraj Bks.

— Lianas, Climber & Shrubby Climbers, Pt. III. 1985. 90.00 (*0-7855-3076-2*, Pub. by Intl Bk Distr) St Mut.

— Plant, Wildlife & Man: A Conservation Scenario of Bay Islands & the Himalayas. (C). 1992. 42.00 (*81-7024-464-1*, Pub. by Ashish Pub Hse) S Asia.

— State Formation among Tribals: A Quest for Santal Identity. (C). 1993. 20.00 (*81-212-0422-4*, Pub. by Gian Publng Hse) S Asia.

— Tree & the Environment: An Indian Scenario. (Illus.). xvii, 602p. 1993. 59.00 (*81-7024-562-1*, Pub. by Ashish Pub Hse) Nataraj Bks.

Chaudhuri, Adhip. The Mexican Debt Crisis, 1982. (Pew Case Studies in International Affairs). 50p. (C). 1993. pap. text 3.50 (*1-56927-204-2*) Geo U Inst Dplmcy.

Chaudhuri, Amit. Freedom Song: Three Novels. LC 98-35260. 480p. 1999. 24.00 (*0-375-40427-9*) Knopf.

***Chaudhuri, Amit.** Freedom Song: Three Novels. LC 98-35260. 448p. 2000. pap. 14.00 (*0-375-70400-0*) Knopf.

— A New World: A Novel. 224p. 2000. 23.00 (*0-375-41093-7*) Knopf.

Chaudhuri, B. K. Industrial Finance. 1985. 85.00 (*0-7855-0739-6*, Pub. by Current Dist) St Mut.

Chaudhuri, Buddhadeb, ed. Tribal Development in India No. 2: Problems & Prospects. rev. ed. (C). 1990. 74.00 (*81-210-0254-0*, Pub. by Inter-India Pubns) S Asia.

Chaudhuri, C. Concise Medical Physiology. (C). 1988. 140.00 (*0-7855-6120-X*, Pub. by Current Dist) St Mut.

Chaudhuri, Debu, ed. Indian Music & Ustad Mushtaq Ali Khan. (C). 1994. 22.00 (*81-241-0091-8*, Pub. by Har-Anand Pubns) S Asia.

Chaudhuri, Duddhadeb, ed. Tribal Transformation in India Vol. I: Economy & Agrarian Issues. (C). 1992. 58.00 (*81-210-0272-9*, Pub. by Inter-India Pubns) S Asia.

— Tribal Transformation in India Vol. II: Socio-Economic & Ecological Development. (C). 1992. 40.00 (*0-8364-2822-6*, Pub. by Inter-India Pubns) S Asia.

— Tribal Transformation in India Vol. III: Ethnopolitics & Identity Crisis. (C). 1992. 60.00 (*0-8364-2823-4*, Pub. by Inter-India Pubns) S Asia.

— Tribal Transformation in India Vol. IV: Education & Literacy Programmes. (C). 1992. 34.00 (*81-210-0275-3*, Pub. by Inter-India Pubns) S Asia.

Chaudhuri, Haridas. The Essence of Spiritual Philosophy. Somers, Dionne, ed. 253p. 1990. pap. 12.95 (*1-85274-074-4*, Pub. by Aqrn Pr) Harper SF.

***Chaudhuri, J.** The Principles of the Law of Sedition: With an Appendix Giving the Law in India as It Was & as Amended. vii, 48p. 1999. reprint ed. 35.00 (*1-56169-547-5*) Gaunt.

Chaudhuri, J. Gan. A Political History of Tripura. 1986. 27.95 (*0-318-36961-3*) Asia Bk Corp.

Chaudhuri, Jayasri R. Migration & Remittances: Inter-Urban & Rural-Urban Linkages. LC 92-34738. (Illus.). 328p. 1993. 38.95 (*0-8039-9458-3*) Sage.

Chaudhuri, Joyotpaul. Founding America: The Political Legacy of Rights, Religion, Commerce, & Diversity. 80p. (C). 1992. pap. text 12.95 (*0-8403-7310-4*) Kendall-Hunt.

Chaudhuri, Joyotpaul, ed. India's Beleaguered Federalism: The Pluralist Challenge. (Monograph Ser.: No. 27). 1992. 10.00 (*0-939252-24-4*) ASU Ctr Asian.

Chaudhuri, Joyotpaul, jt. auth. see Haya-atke/Hiyutke, Jean.

Chaudhuri, K. N. Asia Before Europe: Economy & Civilisation of the Indian Ocean from the Rise of Islam to 1750. (Illus.). 495p. (C). 1991. pap. text 32.95 (*0-521-31681-2*) Cambridge U Pr.

— Trade & Civilisation in the Indian Ocean: An Economic History from the Rise of Islam to 1750. (Illus.). 288p. 1985. pap. text 27.95 (*0-521-28542-9*) Cambridge U Pr.

Chaudhuri, Kalyan. Legal Theory: A Text Book of Jurisprudence & Comparative Law. (C). 1989. 40.00 (*0-89771-457-1*, Pub. by Current Dist) St Mut.

— Public International Law. (C). 1989. 25.00 (*0-89771-459-8*, Pub. by Current Dist) St Mut.

Chaudhuri, Maitrayee. Indian's Women's Movement: Reform & Revival. 250p. (C). 1993. 28.00 (*81-7027-163-0*, Pub. by Radiant Pubs) S Asia.

Chaudhuri, Narayan. That Compassionate Touch of Ma Anadamayee. vii, 171p. 1986. reprint ed. 12.50 (*81-208-0204-7*, Pub. by Motilal Bnarsidass) S Asia.

Chaudhuri, Nirad C. The Autobiography of an Unknown Indian. 1989. pap. 16.30 (*0-201-15576-1*) Addison-Wesley.

— Hinduism: A Religion to Live By. 352p. 1997. pap. 15.95 (*0-19-564013-6*) OUP.

— Three Horsemen of the New Apocalypse. LC 97-906440. 144p. 1998. text 15.95 (*0-19-564189-2*) OUP.

Chaudhuri, Nirad C. Three Horsemen of the New Apocalypse. 145p. 1999. pap. 8.95 (*0-19-564857-9*) OUP.

Chaudhuri, Nirad C. Thy Hand, Great Anarch! India Nineteen Twenty-One to Nineteen Fifty-Two. 1008p. 1988. 28.95 (*0-201-15577-X*) Addison-Wesley.

— Thy Hand, Great Anarch! India, 1921-1952. 1989. pap. 19.18 (*0-201-19606-9*) Addison-Wesley.

Chaudhuri, Nupur & Strobel, Margaret, eds. Western Women & Imperialism: Complicity & Resistance. LC 91-809. (Illus.). 288p. 1992. text 39.95 (*0-253-31341-4*); pap. text 15.95 (*0-253-20705-3*, MB-705) Ind U Pr.

Chaudhuri, Nupur, jt. ed. see Boris, Eileen.

Chaudhuri, Nupur, jt. ed. see Pierson, Ruth R.

Chaudhuri, P. Pal. Additive Cellular Automata Vol. 1: Theory & Applications. LC 96-45234. 368p. 1997. 55.00 (*0-8186-7717-1*) IEEE Standards.

Chaudhuri, Pramit. Economic Theory of Growth. LC 89-15628. (Illus.). 189p. 1989. reprint ed. pap. 58.60 (*0-608-00091-4*, 206085600006) Bks Demand.

Chaudhuri, Pramit, ed. Readings in Indian Agricultural Development. LC 72-191003. 192p. reprint ed. pap. 59.60 (*0-608-14747-8*, 202332400032) Bks Demand.

Chaudhuri, S. Depth Recovery from Defocused Images. LC 98-45797. 1999. 39.95 (*0-387-98635-9*) Spr-Verlag.

Chaudhuri, Sambhu, jt. auth. see Clauer, Norbert.

Chaudhuri, Sambhu, jt. ed. see Clauer, Norbert.

Chaudhuri, Sukanta. Renaissance Pastoral & Its English Developments. 500p. 1989. 98.00 (*0-19-811736-1*) OUP.

Chaudhuri, Sukanta. Translation & Understanding. 98p. 1999. text 18.95 (*0-19-564877-3*) OUP.

Chaudhuri, Sukanta, ed. An Anthology of Elizabethan Poetry. 180p. 1993. pap. text 8.95 (*0-19-563204-4*) OUP.

— Calcutta: The Living City, Vol. I: The Past. (Illus.). 232p. (C). 1991. 75.00 (*0-19-562585-4*) OUP.

— Calcutta: The Living City, Vol I; The Past: Vol. II: The Present & Future, 2 vols., Set. (Illus.). 676p. 1995. pap. 45.00 (*0-19-563698-8*) OUP.

— Calcutta: The Living City, Vol. II: The Present & the Future. (Illus.). 400p. 1991. 75.00 (*0-19-562586-2*) OUP.

— Renaissance Essays for Kitty Scoular Datta. (Illus.). 300p. 1995. 27.00 (*0-19-563702-X*) OUP.

Chaudhuri, Sukanta, jt. auth. see Das, Jibanananda.

Chaudhuri, Sukanta, ed. see Tagore, Rabindranath.

Chaudhuri, Sukanta, tr. see Ray, Sukumar.

Chaudhuri, Una. No Man's Stage: A Semiotic Study of Jean Genet's Major Plays. Brockett, Oscar G., ed. LC 85-28886. (Theater & Dramatic Studies: No. 34). 162p. reprint ed. 50.30 (*0-8357-1731-3*, 207046800095) Bks Demand.

— Staging Place: The Geography of Modern Drama. 256p. (C). 1997. pap. text 18.95 (*0-472-06589-0*, 06589) U of Mich Pr.

Chaudhuri, Una & Fuchs, Elinor, eds. Theater & Landscape: Scenes of the Twentieth Century. (Illus.). (C). text. write for info. (*0-472-09720-2*); pap. text. write for info. (*0-472-06720-6*) U of Mich Pr.

Chaudhury, B. D., jt. auth. see Singh, R. K.

Chaudhury, P. C. Best Loved Folk Tales of India. (C). 1995. reprint ed. pap. write for info. (*81-207-1660-4*) Sterling Pubs.

Chaudhury, Pratima. Women's Education in India, Myth & Reality. (C). 1995. 23.00 (*81-241-0310-0*, Pub. by Har-Anand Pubns) S Asia.

Chaudhury, R. R. Herbal Medicine for Human Health. (WHO Regional Publications: No. 20). ix, 87p. 1992. pap. text 8.00 (*92-9022-162-3*, 1560020) World Health.

Chaudhury, Ray. Living on the Edge Essays on the Chittagong Hill Tracts. 1997. pap. 43.00 (*0-7855-7428-X*, Pub. by Ratna Pustak Bhandar) St Mut.

Chaudhury, Subrata R. The Rule of Law in a State of Emergency. (C). 1989. 980.00 (*0-7855-4808-4*) St Mut.

Chaudhury, Sukant K. Myopic Development & Cultural Lens. (C). 1992. 19.00 (*81-210-0309-1*, Pub. by Inter-India Pubns) S Asia.

Chaudhury, Sukomal. Analytical Study of the Abhidharmakosa. 1983. 18.00 (*0-8364-1017-3*, Pub. by Mukhopadhyaya) S Asia.

***Chaudhury, Sushil.** Prelude to Empire: Plassey Revolution of 1757. 2000. 27.50 (*81-7304-301-9*, Pub. by Manohar) S Asia.

Chaudhury, Sushil & Morineau, Michel, eds. Merchants, Companies & Trade: Europe & Asia in The Early Modern Era. LC 98-38433. (Studies in Modern Capitalism). (Illus.). 400p. (C). 1999. text 69.95 (*0-521-56367-4*) Cambridge U Pr.

Chaudouet-Miranda, A., jt. ed. see Brebbia, Carlos A.

Chaudron, Chris & Childs, Caro. Face Painting. (How to Make Ser.). (Illus.). 32p. (J). (gr. 3-7). 1993. lib. bdg. 14.95 (*0-88110-649-6*, Usborne) EDC.

Chaudron, Chris, et al. Face Painting. (How to Make Ser.). (Illus.). 32p. (J). (gr. 3-7). 1993. pap. 6.95 (*0-7460-1445-7*, Usborne) EDC.

Chaudron, Craig. Second Language Classrooms: Research on Teaching & Learning. (Cambridge Applied Linguistics Ser.). (Illus.). 240p. 1988. pap. text 22.95 (*0-521-33980-4*) Cambridge U Pr.

Chaudron, Laurent, jt. ed. see Tessier, Catherine.

Chaudry. Color Atlas of Paediatric. 2001. text 37.00 (*0-7234-2436-5*) Wolfe Pubng AZ.

Chaudry, Nina, jt. auth. see Larner, Mary.

Chaudry, Shahid A., et al, eds. Civil Service Reform in Latin America & the Caribbean: Proceedings of a Conference. LC 94-35275. (Technical Papers: Vol. 259). 294p. 1994. pap. 22.00 (*0-8213-3041-1*) World Bank.

Chauez, Angelico. La Conquistadora: The Autobiography of an Ancient Statue. rev. ed. LC 81-14473. 96p. 1984. pap. 6.95 (*0-86534-041-2*) Sunstone Pr.

Chauhan, C. P. Higher Education in India: Achievements, Failures & Strategies. 1990. 32.00 (*81-7024-302-5*, Pub. by Ashish Pub Hse) S Asia.

Chauhan, H. G. The Novels of Dorothy M. Richardson: Streams of Consciousness & Beyond. 1991. text 25.00 (*81-85151-37-7*, Pub. by Harman Pub Hse) Advent Bks Div.

Chauhan, I. S. & Bais, V. S. Social Structure & Rural Development. (C). 1995. 22.00 (*0-614-13261-4*, Pub. by Rawat Pubns) S Asia.

Chauhan, L. S. Leadership & Social Cleavages: Political Processes among the Indians in Fiji. (C). 1988. 26.00 (*81-7033-047-5*, Pub. by Rawat Pubns) S Asia.

Chauhan, Poonam S. Lengthening Shadows: Status of Women in India. LC 96-904811. (Illus.). 237p. 1996. 29.00 (*81-86562-01-X*, Pub. by Manak Pubns Pvt Ltd) Nataraj Bks.

Chauhan, R. S. Society & State Building in Nepal. 1989. 65.00 (*0-7855-0297-1*, Pub. by Ratna Pustak Bhandar) St Mut.

— Society & State Building in Nepal. 163p. (C). 1989. 225.00 (*0-89771-092-4*, Pub. by Ratna Pustak Bhandar) St Mut.

Chauhan, Ramesh K. Punjab & the Nationality Question in India. LC 95-905851. (C). 1995. 26.00 (*81-7100-717-1*, Pub. by Deep & Deep Pubns) S Asia.

Chauhan, S. K., ed. Current Trends in Life Sciences. (Current Trends in Life Sciences Ser.: Vol. 9). xvii, 392p. 1982. 39.00 (*0-88065-230-6*) Scholarly Pubns.

Chauhan, Sandeep. Demand for New International Economic Order. 203p. 1997. pap. 175.00 (*81-7533-027-9*, Pub. by Print Hse) St Mut.

Chauhan, Subhadra K. Scattered Debris: Bikhare Moti. (C). 1994. text 14.00 (*81-7001-102-7*, Pub. by Chanakya) S Asia.

Chauhan, T. S. Agricultural Geography: A Study of Rajasthan State. 342p. (C). 1988. 300.00 (*0-7855-2291-3*, Pub. by Scientific) St Mut.

Chauley, G. C. Early Buddhist Art in India: 300 B. C. to 300 A. D. LC 98-902049. xiii, 104 p. 1998. write for info. (*81-7574-006-X*) S Asia.

Chauls. Alice in Wonderland: Vocal Score. 200p. 1991. otabind 35.00 (*0-7935-0412-0*, 50488951) H Leonard.

Chauls, Robert, jt. auth. see Robinett, Joseph.

Chauls, Robert, jt. auth. see Robinette, Joseph.

C

An Asterisk (*) at the beginning of an entry indicates that the title is appearing for the first time.

Chaum, David & Price, W. L., eds. Advances in Cryptology - Eurocrypt '87. (Lecture Notes in Computer Science Ser.: Vol. 304). vii, 314p. 1988. pap. 35.00 (*0-387-19102-X*) Spr-Verlag.

Chaumerliac, N., jt. auth. see Gryning, S. E.

Chaumeton, Herve. Pilze Mitteleuropas. Juelich, Ute, tr. from FRE. (GER., Illus.). 484p. 1987. lib. bdg. 50.00 (*0-318-33439-9*) Lubrecht & Cramer.

Chaumette, Pierre G., jt. auth. see De Loos, Onesime-Henri.

Chaumont, Eric, jt. auth. see Al-Sayh Abu Ishaq Ibrahim Al-Sirazi.

Chaumont Guitry, Guy de. Lettres d'Indochine. LC 79-179177. (South & Southeast Asia Studies). reprint ed. 37.50 (*0-404-54807-5*) AMS Pr.

Chauncey, George. Making of a Modern Gay World, 1935-1975. 448p. Date not set. pap. write for info. (*0-465-04303-8*) Basic.

— Making of a Modern Gay World, 1935-1975. 448p. 1998. 25.00 (*0-465-04302-X*, Pub. by Basic) HarpC.

Chauncey, Helen. American-Vietnamese Negotiations: May 1977-October 1978. (Pew Case Studies in International Affairs). 50p. (C). 1988. pap. text 3.50 (*1-56927-446-0*) Geo U Inst Dplmcy.

Chauncey, Helen R. Schoolhouse Politicians: Locality & State During the Chinese Republic. LC 92-28367. 378p. 1992. text 33.50 (*0-8248-1415-0*) UH Pr.

Chauncey, Marlin R. The Educational & Occupational Preferences of College Seniors: Their Significance for College Achievement. LC 75-176639. (Columbia University. Teachers College. Contributions to Education Ser.: No. 533). reprint ed. 37.50 (*0-404-55533-0*) AMS Pr.

Chauncy, Charles. Mystery Hid from All Ages & Generations. LC 70-83414. (Religion in America, Ser. 1). 1980. reprint ed. 25.95 (*0-405-00235-1*) Ayer.

Chaundler, Thomas. Liber Apologeticus de Omni Statu Humanae Naturae (1460) Shoukri, Doris E., ed. No. 5. 1974. write for info. (*0-318-59382-3*) Renaiss Soc Amer.

Chaundy, Theodore W., et al. The Printing of Mathematics: Aids for Authors & Editions & Rules for Compositors & Readers at the University Press, Oxford. LC Z 0250.6.M3C. 119p. reprint ed. pap. 36.90 (*0-608-11126-0*, 205189600013) Bks Demand.

C

Chauprade, Aymeric. Eternal Casablanca. (Illus.). 96p. 1999. 24.95 (*2-911589-46-7*, Pub. by Editions dIndochine) BHB Intl.

Chauprade, Aymeric & Thual, Francois. Dictionnaire du Geopolitique. (FRE.). 1998. 95.00 (*0-320-00381-7*) Fr & Eur.

Chaurasia, B. P. Women's Status in India: (Policies & Programmes) (C). 1992. 36.00 (*81-85613-59-1*, Pub. by Chugh Pubns) S Asia.

Chauser, Geoffrey & Donohoe, James J. Chaucer's Canterbury Tales Complete in Presentday English. LC 79-90384. 626p. 1979. write for info. (*0-936875-03-8*) Loras Coll Pr.

Chausse, Sylvie. The Egg & I. (Illus.). (J). (gr. 1-2). 1997. 15.95 (*0-382-39728-2*); pap. 5.95 (*0-382-39729-0*) Silver Burdett Pr.

— The Thirty-Six Cats of Marie Tatin. (Illus.). 32p. (J). (gr. 2). 1996. pap. 5.95 (*0-382-39283-3*, Silver Pr NJ) Silver Burdett Pr.

— The Thirty-Six Cats of Marie Tatin. (Illus.). 32p. (J). (gr. 1-3). 1996. lib. bdg. 13.95 (*0-382-39282-5*, Silver Pr NJ) Silver Burdett Pr.

Chausse, Sylvie, ed. The Egg & I. LC 95-36014. (Illus.). 32p. (J). (gr. 2-3). 1997. pap. 5.95 (*0-382-39286-8*, Silver Pr NJ) Silver Burdett Pr.

Chaussinand-Nogaret, Guy. The French Nobility in the Eighteenth Century: From Feudalism to Enlightenment. Doyle, William, tr. 203p. 1985. pap. text 19.95 (*0-521-27590-3*) Cambridge U Pr.

— Une Histoire des Elites, 1700-1848. (Recueil De Textes Presentes et Commentes Par le Savoir Historique Ser.: No. 6). 1975. pap. 28.00 (*90-279-7872-7*) Mouton.

***Chausson, Ernest.** Concerto in D for Piano, Violin & String Quartet, Op. 21, in Full Score. 1999. pap. text 11.95 (*0-486-40632-6*) Dover.

Chausson, Ernest. Selected Songs for Voice & Piano. 128p. 1998. pap. 12.95 (*0-486-40415-3*) Dover.

Chaussonnet, Valerie. Crossroads Alaska: Native Cultures of Alaska & Siberia. LC 65-804. (Illus.). 112p. 1995. pap. 24.95 (*1-56098-661-1*) Smithsonian.

Chaussonnet, Valerie, jt. ed. see Fitzhugh, William W.

Chaussy, Christian, ed. Extracorporeal Shock Wave Lithotripsy. 2nd enl. rev. ed. (Illus.). viii, 156p. 1986. 71.50 (*3-8055-4360-3*) S Karger.

Chautard, Jean-Baptiste. The Soul of the Apostolate. 1977. reprint ed. pap. 10.00 (*0-89555-031-8*) TAN Bks Pubs.

Chautauqua Co. Heritage Association Staff, compiled by. History of Chautauqua County, Vol. II. (Illus.). 260p. 1992. 57.50 (*0-88107-191-9*) Curtis Media.

Chautauqua History Company Staff. Centennial History of Chautauqua County, New York, Vol. I. (Illus.). 698p. 1993. reprint ed. lib. bdg. 69.00 (*0-8328-2913-7*) Higginson Bk Co.

— Centennial History of Chautauqua County, New York, Vol. II. (Illus.). 1173p. 1993. reprint ed. lib. bdg. 109.00 (*0-8328-2914-5*) Higginson Bk Co.

Chautems, Alain. Revision Taxonomique et Possibilities d'Hybridations de Nemathanthus Schrader (Gesneriaceae) Genre Endemique de la Fores Cotiere Bresilienne. (Dissertationes Botanicae Ser.: Band 112). (FRE., Illus.). 226p. 1988. pap. 53.00 (*3-443-64024-9*, Pub. by Gebruder Borntraeger) Balogh.

***Chauveau, Michel.** Egypt in the Age of Cleopatra: History & Society under the Ptolemies. Lorton, David, tr. from FRE. LC DT61.C4613 2000. 2000. pap. 17.95 (*0-8014-8576-2*) Cornell U Pr.

Chauveinc, Marc & Bisbrouck, Marie-Francoise, eds. Intelligent Library Buildings: Proceedings of the 10th Seminar of the ILFA Section on Library Buildings & Equipment. (IFLA Publications: 88). viii, 294p. 1999. write for info. (*3-598-21810-9*) K G Saur Verlag.

Chauvel, Alain & Lefebvre, Gilles. Petrochemical Processes, Tech. & Economic Characteristics: Synthesis-Gas Derivative & Major Hydrocarbons. (Illus.). 432p. (C). 1989. 680.00 (*2-7108-0562-6*, Pub. by Edits Technip) Enfield Pubs NH.

— Petrochemical Processes, Tech. & Economic Characteristics Vol. 2: Major Oxygenated, Chlorinated & Nitrated Derivatives. (Illus.). 424p. (C). 1989. 660.00 (*2-7108-0563-4*, Pub. by Edits Technip) Enfield Pubs NH.

Chauvel, Daniel, jt. auth. see Despres, Charles.

Chauvel, Patrick, et al, eds. Frontal Lobe Seizures & Epilepsies. (Advances in Neurology Ser.: Vol. 57). 768p. 1992. text 103.00 (*0-88167-827-9*) Lppncott W & W.

— Frontal Lobe Seizures & Epilepsies. Ed. 57. (Advances in Neurology Ser.: Vol. 57). (Illus.). 768p. reprint ed. pap. 200.00 (*0-608-09752-7*, 206992500007) Bks Demand.

Chauvet, Gilbert A. Theoretical Systems in Biology: Hierarchial & Functional Integration, 3 vols. Malkani, K., tr. from FRE. LC 95-30324. (Studies in Neurosciences: No. 13). 1800p. 1995. 390.00 (*0-08-041995-X*, Pergamon Pr) Elsevier.

***Chauvet, J. P., et al, eds.** Annuaire European 1997 (European Yearbook 1997), Vol. XLV. 1257p. 1999. text 351.00 (*90-411-1309-6*) Kluwer Law Intl.

Chauvet, Jean-Marie, et al. Dawn of Art, the Chauvet Cave: The Oldest Known Paintings in the World. Bahn, Paul G., tr. from FRE. LC 95-47571. (Illus.). 135p. 1996. 39.95 (*0-8109-3232-6*, Pub. by Abrams) Time Warner.

Chauvet, Louis M. & Tomka, Miklos. Illness & Healing. 150p. 1998. pap. 15.00 (*1-57075-191-9*) Orbis Bks.

Chauvet, Louis-Marie. Symbol & Sacrament: A Sacramental Reinterpretation of Christian Existence. 592p. (Orig.). 1994. 49.95 (*0-8146-6124-6*, Pueblo Bks) Liturgical Pr.

Chauvet, Louis-Marie & Lumbala, Francois K., eds. Liturgy & the Body. 150p. (Orig.). 1995. pap. 15.00 (*0-88344-884-X*) Orbis Bks.

Chauvette, Roger. A Pilgrim Adrift in the Dunes. 121p. 1998. pap. 12.95 (*0-9666275-0-4*, 1-0001) Vital Links.

Chauvicourt, J. & Chauvicourt, S. Fanorona: The National Game of Madagascar. Fox, Leonard, tr. from FRE. (Illus.). ix, 44p. 1984. pap. 3.75 (*0-932329-00-4*) Intl Fanorona.

Chauvicourt, S., jt. auth. see Chauvicourt, J.

Chauville, C. Dictionnaire Jeune Cinema Francais. (FRE.). 1998. 69.95 (*0-320-00258-6*) Fr & Eur.

Chauvin, jt. auth. see Buchanan.

Chauvin, Brigitte, et al. Trees: Workshop in Versailles, June 14-16, 1995. LC 96-39024. (Progress in Probability Ser.). 1996. write for info. (*0-8176-5453-4*) Birkhauser.

— Trees: Workshop in Versailles, June 14-16, 1995. LC 96-39024. (Progress in Probability Ser.). 168p. 1996. 78.00 (*3-7643-5453-4*) Birkhauser.

Chauvin, Jane C., jt. auth. see Karnes, Frances A.

Chauvin, Lilyan. Hollywood Scams & Survival Tactics. Lamothe, Irene, ed. (Illus.). 284p. (YA). 1993. pap. 19.95 (*1-883109-01-9*) LCJ Prods.

Chauvin, Remy. Ethology-the Biological Study of Animal Behavior. Diamanti, Joyce, tr. from FRE. LC 76-46818. 245p. (Orig.). 1977. 37.50 (*0-8236-1770-X*) Intl Univs Pr.

Chauvin, William & Apperson, Carl. Bassin' in New England: A Practical Guide to Productive Black Bass Angling in the Six State Region. LC 85-2800. (Illus.). 175p. (Orig.). 1985. 15.95 (*0-89621-089-8*); pap. 7.95 (*0-89621-090-1*) Nrth Country Pr.

Chauvin, Yves & Rumelhart, David E., eds. Back-Propagation: Theory, Architecture, & Applications. (Developments in Connectionist Theory Ser.). 568p. 1995. pap. 49.95 (*0-8058-1259-8*); text 125.00 (*0-8058-1258-X*) L Erlbaum Assocs.

Chavaillon, Jean, jt. ed. see Berthelet, Arlette.

Chavaillon, Jean, jt. ed. see Changeux, Jean-Pierre.

Chavalas, M. W., ed. Emar: The History, Religion, & Culture of a Syrian Town in the Late Bronze Age. LC 96-11389. 1996. 30.00 (*1-883053-18-8*) CDL Pr.

Chavalas, Mark W. & Hayes, John L., eds. New Horizons in the Study of Ancient Syria. LC 92-42733. (Bibliotheca Mesopotamica Ser.: Vol. 25). 1992. 41.00 (*0-89003-324-2*); pap. 31.00 (*0-89003-323-4*) Undena Pubns.

Chavan, Sunanda P. The Fair Voice - A Study of Indian Women Poets in English. 137p. 1986. 12.95 (*0-318-36921-4*) Asia Bk Corp.

Chavan, V. P. The Konkani Proverbs. (C). 1995. 10.00 (*81-206-0664-7*, Pub. by Asian Educ Servs) S Asia.

— Vaishnavism of the Gowd Saraswat Brahmins & a Few Konkani Folklore Tales. (C). 1991. reprint ed. 11.00 (*0-8364-2647-9*, Pub. by Asian Educ Servs) S Asia.

Chavana, Herminia B. Biographies of Noble Hispanics. (Illus.). 200p. 1996. write for info. (*1-57579-048-3*) Pine Hill Pr.

Chavance, R., jt. auth. see Baty, G.

***Chavanne, J.** The Literature of the Polar Regions. xvi, 336p. 1999. reprint ed. 60.00 (*1-57898-141-7*) Martino Pubng.

Chavannes, Albert. Future Commonwealth, or What Samuel Balcom Saw in Socioland. LC 71-154433. (Utopian Literature Ser.). 1976. reprint ed. 17.95 (*0-405-03516-0*) Ayer.

Chavannes-Mazel, Claudine A. & Smith, Margaret M., eds. Medieval Manuscripts of the Latin Classics: Production & Use. (Proceedings of the Seminar in the History of the Book to 1500 Ser.: Vol. 3). (Illus.). 256p. 1996. 105.00 (*0-9626372-4-6*) Anderson-Lovelace Pubs.

Chavarria, Andres S. & Cuartas, A. Diccionario de Incorrecciones, Particularidades, Curiosidades del Lenguaje. 5th ed. (SPA.). 520p. 1992. pap. 29.95 (*0-7859-3687-4*, S12185) Fr & Eur.

***Chavarria-Chairez, Becky.** Las Tortillas de Magda. Castilla, Julia Mercedes, tr. (SPA., Illus.). 32p. (ps-3). 2000. 14.95 (*1-55885-286-7*) Arte Publico.

***Chavarria, Daniel.** Aquel Ano En Madrid. 1999. pap. text 18.95 (*968-406-801-8*) F Planeta.

Chavarria, Joaquim. The Art of Mosaics: A Guide to the History, Materials, Equipment & Techniques. 160p. 1999. pap. 29.95 (*0-8230-5864-6*) Watsn-Guptill.

— The Big Book of Ceramics: A Guide to the History, Materials, Equipment & Techniques of Hand-Building, Throwing, Molding, Kiln-Firing, & Glazing Pottery & Other Ceramic Objects. LC 94-11057. (Illus.). 192p. 1994. pap. 35.00 (*0-8230-0508-9*) Watsn-Guptill.

***Chavarria, Joaquim.** Ceramic Class: Hand Building Techniques. (Illus.). 64p. 1999. text 14.95 (*0-8230-0591-7*) Watsn-Guptill.

— Ceramics Class: Glazing Techniques. (Illus.). 64p. 1999. text 14.95 (*0-8230-0592-5*) Watsn-Guptill.

— Ceramics Class: Throwing Techniques. 64p. 1999. text 14.95 (*0-8230-0593-3*) Watsn-Guptill.

— Decorating Techniques: Ceramics Class. (Illus.). 64p. 2000. write for info. (*0-8230-0594-1*) Watsn-Guptill.

— Molding Techniques: Ceramics Class. (Illus.). 64p. 2000. write for info. (*0-8230-0595-X*) Watsn-Guptill.

Chavarria, Zulma, ed. see Graham, Warren, et al.

Chavas, Jean-Paul, jt. auth. see Helmberger, Peter G.

Chavasse, Antoine, ed. Le Sacramentaire dans le Groupe Dit "Gelasiens du VIIIe Siecle", 2 Vols. (FRE.). 1985. pap. text 274.00 (*90-247-3173-9*) Kluwer Academic.

Chavchavadze, N. V. & Nodia, Ghia, eds. National Identity As an Issue of Knowledge & Morality: Georgian Philosophical Studies I. LC 93-11929. (Cultural Heritage & Contemporary Change Series IVA: Vol. 7). 110p. 1994. 45.00 (*1-56518-052-6*); pap. 17.50 (*1-56518-053-4*) Coun Res Values.

Chavda, Mahesh. The Hidden Power of Prayer & Fasting. 1998. pap. 10.99 (*0-7684-2017-2*) Destiny Image.

Chavda, Mahesh Bonnie. Watch of the Lord. LC 99-32779. 1999. pap. text 12.99 (*0-88419-562-7*) Creation House.

Chave, Anna C. Mark Rothko: Subjects in Abstraction. (Illus.). 224p. (C). 1991. reprint ed. pap. 30.00 (*0-300-04961-7*) Yale U Pr.

Chave, Anna C., jt. auth. see Barilleaux, Rene P.

Chave, E. H. & Malahoff, Alexander. In Deeper Waters: Photographic Studies of Hawaiian Deep-Sea Habitats & Life-Forms. LC 97-46936. (Illus.). 160p. 1998. pap. 19.95 (*0-8248-2003-7*); text 36.00 (*0-8248-1946-2*) UH Pr.

Chave, Edith H., jt. auth. see Hobson, Edmund.

Chave, Leonard. Forty Years On: The Wynkn de Worde Society, 1957-1997. 55p. 40.00 (*1-871224-14-4*) J Taylor.

Chaveau, Jean-Pierre, ed. Anthologie de la Poesie Francaise du XVIIe Siecle. (Poesie Ser.). (FRE.). 501p. 1987. pap. 17.95 (*2-07-032437-0*) Schoenhof.

Chavel, Pierre H., et al, eds. Optics in Computing '98, Vol. 3490. LC 98-234083. 616p. 1998. 107.00 (*0-8194-2949-X*) SPIE.

Chavel, Charles B. Between Man & His Fellow Man. 64p. 1980. pap. 3.50 (*0-88328-030-2*) Shilo Pub Hse.

— The Book of Redemption. 72p. 1978. pap. 3.95 (*0-88328-027-2*) Shilo Pub Hse.

— Encyclopedia of Torah Thoughts. Orig. Title: Rabeinu Bachya Ben Asher "Kad Hakemach". 734p. 1980. 25.50 (*0-88328-016-7*) Shilo Pub Hse.

— Prayer at the Ruins of Jerusalem. 32p. 1978. pap. 2.50 (*0-88328-031-0*) Shilo Pub Hse.

— Ramban (Nachmanides) Commentary on the Torah, 5 vols. 2575p. 1971. 115.00 (*0-686-86743-2*) Shilo Pub Hse.

— Ramban (Nachmanides) Commentary on the Torah, Vol. I: Book of Genesis. 640p. 1971. 23.00 (*0-88328-006-X*) Shilo Pub Hse.

— Ramban (Nachmanides) Commentary on the Torah, 5 vols., Vol. II: Book of Exodus. 656p. 1971. 23.00 (*0-88328-007-8*) Shilo Pub Hse.

— Ramban (Nachmanides) Commentary on the Torah, 5 vols., Vol. III: Book of Leviticus. 512p. 1972. 23.00 (*0-88328-008-6*) Shilo Pub Hse.

— Ramban (Nachmanides) Commentary on the Torah, 5 vols., Vol. IV: Book of Numbers. 416p. 1974. 23.00 (*0-88328-009-4*) Shilo Pub Hse.

— Ramban (Nachmanides) Commentary on the Torah, 5 vols., Vol. V: Book of Deuteronomy. 448p. 1975. 23.00 (*0-88328-010-8*) Shilo Pub Hse.

— Ramban (Nachmanides) Writings & Discourses, 2 vols., Set. 768p. 1978. boxed set 48.00 (*0-88328-013-2*) Shilo Pub Hse.

— Thought for Rosh Hashonoh. 64p. 1980. pap. 3.50 (*0-88328-029-9*) Shilo Pub Hse.

— Thought for Yom Kippur. 64p. 1980. pap. 3.50 (*0-88328-028-0*) Shilo Pub Hse.

Chavel, Charles B., tr. The Commandments of Maimonides, 2 vols. (HEB.). 305p. 1967. pap. 29.95 (*1-871055-20-2*) Soncino Pr.

— The Disputation at Barcelona. 48p. 1983. pap. 3.50 (*0-88328-025-6*) Shilo Pub Hse.

— The Gate of Reward. 144p. 1983. pap. 4.95 (*0-88328-024-8*) Shilo Pub Hse.

— The Law of the Eternal Is Perfect. 128p. 1983. pap. 4.95 (*0-88328-023-X*) Shilo Pub Hse.

Chavel, Isaac. Eigenvalues in Riemannian Geometry: Monograph. (Pure & Applied Mathematics Ser.). 1984. text 124.00 (*0-12-170640-0*) Acad Pr.

— Riemannian Geometry: A Modern Introduction. (Tracts in Mathematics Ser.: No. 108). 400p. (C). 1995. pap. text 28.95 (*0-521-48578-9*) Cambridge U Pr.

— Riemannian Symmetric Spaces of Rank One. LC 72-76060. (Lecture Notes in Pure & Applied Mathematics Ser.: Vol. 5). 93p. reprint ed. pap. 30.00 (*0-608-17018-6*, 202711400054) Bks Demand.

Chavel, Isaac & Farkas, H. M., eds. Differential Geometry & Complex Analysis. (Illus.). 225p. 1984. 115.95 (*0-387-13543-X*) Spr-Verlag.

Chavel, P., jt. ed. see Lalanne, P.

Chavel, P., jt. ed. see Wherrett, Brian S.

Chavent, G., et al, eds. Inverse Problems of Wave Propagation & Diffraction: Proceedings of the Conference Held at Aix-les-Bains, France, September 23-27, 1996, Vol. 486. LC 97-20854. (Lecture Notes in Physics Ser.: No. 486). xv, 379p. 1997. 79.00 (*3-540-62865-7*) Spr-Verlag.

Chavent, Guy, et al, eds. Inverse Problems in Wave Propagation. LC 97-998. (IMA Volumes in Mathematics & Its Applications Ser.: Vol. 90). (Illus.). 514p. 1997. 69.95 (*0-387-94976-3*) Spr-Verlag.

Chavers-Wright, Madrue. The Guarantee: P. W. Chavers; Banker, Entrepreneur, Philanthropist in Chicago's Black Belt of the Twenties. Messmer, Sara E., ed. LC 85-51854. (Illus.). 432p. (Orig.). (C). 1985. pap. 14.95 (*0-931505-02-X*) Wright-Armstead.

— The Guarantee: P. W. Chavers, Banker, Entrepreneur, Philanthropist, in Chicago's Black Belt of the Twenties. 2nd ed. Messmer, Sara E., ed. LC 86-51447. (Illus.). 448p. 1987. reprint ed. 27.95 (*0-931505-05-4*); reprint ed. pap. 16.95 (*0-931505-04-6*) Wright-Armstead.

Chaves, A. S., et al, eds. Semiconductor Physics: Proceedings of the 4th Brazilian School. 472p. (C). 1990. text 147.00 (*9971-5-0968-7*) World Scientific Pub.

Chaves, Alvaro & Puerta, Mauricio. Vivienda Precolombina e Indigena Actual en Tierradentro. (SPA., Illus.). 284p. 1988. pap. 8.50 (*1-877812-33-1*, BR031) UPLAAP.

Chaves, Antonia, jt. auth. see Craig, D.

Chaves, John F., jt. ed. see Spanos, Nicholas P.

Chaves, Jonathan. Singing of the Source: Nature & God in the Poetry of the Chinese Painter Wu Li. LC 93-3878. (SHAPS Library of Translations). (Illus.). 288p. (C). 1992. text 42.00 (*0-8248-1485-1*) UH Pr.

Chaves, Jonathan, ed. from CHI. The Columbia Book of Later Chinese Poetry: Yuan, Ming, & Ch'ing Dynasties (1279-1911) LC 86-2302. (Illus.). 520p. 1988. pap. text 24.50 (*0-231-06149-8*) Col U Pr.

Chaves, Jonathan, tr. see Hung-tao, Yuan.

Chaves, Jonathan, tr. see Konishi, Jin I., et al.

Chaves, Jonathan, jt. tr. see Thomas, Rimer J.

Chaves, Jonathan, tr. & comment see Addiss, Stephen.

Chaves, Jonathan, tr. & intro. see Yuan Hung-Tao.

Chaves, Mark. Ordaining Women: Culture & Conflict in Religious Organizations. LC 97-12518. (Illus.). 240p. 1997. 31.00 (*0-674-64145-0*) HUP.

— Ordaining Women: Culture & Conflict in Religious Organizations. 249p. 1999. pap. text 16.95 (*0-674-64146-9*) HUP.

Chaves, Mark & Miller, Sharon L., eds. Financing American Religion. LC 98-25448. 220p. (C). 1998. 59.00 (*0-7619-9036-4*); pap. 24.95 (*0-7619-9037-2*) AltaMira Pr.

***Chavez.** Mexican War: A Brief History with Documents. 2002. pap. text. write for info. (*0-312-24921-7*) St Martin.

Chavez. My Conversation Book, Bk. 1. (My English Book Ser.). 1987. pap. text 8.10 (*0-673-19181-8*) Addison-Wesley.

— My Conversation Book, Bk. 2. (My English Book Ser.). 1997. pap. text 8.10 (*0-673-19182-6*) Addison-Wesley.

— My Conversation Book, Bk. 3. (My English Book Ser.). 96p. 1997. pap. text 8.11 (*0-673-19183-4*) Addison-Wesley.

— My Conversation Book, Bk. 4. (My English Book Ser.). 1987. pap. text 8.10 (*0-673-19184-2*) Addison-Wesley.

— My Pre Reading Book. (My English Book Ser.). 88p. 1997. pap. text 8.10 (*0-673-19400-0*) Addison-Wesley.

— My Reading Book. (My English Book Ser.). 88p. 1997. pap. text 8.11 (*0-673-19186-9*) Addison-Wesley.

— My Spelling Book. (My English Book Ser.). 88p. 1997. pap. text 8.11 (*0-673-19187-7*) Addison-Wesley.

Chavez & Hojel. My Conversation, Bk. 2. (C). 1997. pap. text, teacher ed. 20.19 (*0-673-19192-3*) Addson-Wesley Educ.

— My Conversation, Bk. 3. (C). 1997. text, teacher ed. 15.14 (*0-673-19193-1*) Addson-Wesley Educ.

Chavez, Andres, et al. What It Is, What It Was: Black Film Explosion of the '70s in Words & Pictures. LC 98-20517. (Illus.). 224p. (J). 1998. pap. 19.45 (*0-7868-8377-4*, Pub. by Hyperion) Time Warner.

Chavez, Angelico. Coronado's Friars: The Franciscans in the Coronado Expedition. (Monograph Ser.). (Illus.). 1968. 20.00 (*0-88382-058-7*) AAFH.

— From an Altar Screen, el Retablo: Tales from New Mexico. LC 72-85690. (Short Story Index Reprint Ser.). 1977. 15.95 (*0-8369-3031-2*) Ayer.

Chavez, Angelico, ed. The Oroz Codex: or Relation of the Description of the Holy Gospel Province in New Spain, & the Lives of the Founders & Other Note-Worthy Men of Said Province Composed by Fray Pedro Oroz, 1584-1586. (Documentary Ser.). 1972. 35.00 (*0-88382-011-0*) AAFH.

***Chavez Ballejos, Gilberto & Witt, Shirley H.** El Indio Jesus: A Novel. LC 99-88182. (American Indian Literature & Critical Studies: Vol. 35). (SPA.). 272p. 2000. 24.95 (*0-8061-3230-2*) U of Okla Pr.

Chavez, C. Cuartro Estudios: Four Studies. 1992. pap. 14.95 (*0-7935-1992-6*) H Leonard.

— Vocalizacion Aguda: Coloratura Vocalise for Flute & Piano. 1992. pap. 9.95 (*0-7935-1993-4*) H Leonard.

An Asterisk (*) at the beginning of an entry indicates that the title is appearing for the first time.

Chavez, Carlos. Musical Thought. LC 60-15236. (Charles Norton Lectures: 1958-1959). (Illus.). 134p. reprint ed. pap. 41.60 (*0-608-11019-1*, 200641600059) Bks Demand.

— Three Pieces for Guitar. Stang, Aaron, ed. 12p. (Orig.). (C). 1985. pap. text 5.00 (*0-7692-1325-1*, 88984) Wrner Bros.

— Toward a New Music: Music & Electricity. Weinstock, Herbert, tr. from SPA. LC 74-28308. (Music Reprint Ser.). (Illus.). 180p. 1975. reprint ed. lib. bdg. 29.50 (*0-306-70719-5*) Da Capo.

Chavez-Davalos, Laura, tr. see Scruggs, Sandy.

Chavez, Deborah. Fallen Feather: A Spiritual Odyssey. LC 98-141347. v, 184p. 1998. pap. 11.00 (*0-9645173-7-X*) Four Dir Pub.

Chavez, Deborah J., ed. Proceedings of the Second Symposium on Social Aspects & Recreation Research. (Illus.). 186p. (C). 1997. reprint ed. pap. text 40.00 (*0-7881-3768-9*) DIANE Pub.

Chavez, Denise. Face of an Angel. 480p. 1995. reprint ed. mass mkt. 13.95 (*0-446-67185-1*, Pub. by Warner Bks) Little.

— The Last of the Menu Girls. LC 84-72304. 192p. (C). 1986. reprint ed. pap. 11.95 (*0-934770-46-8*) Arte Publico.

***Chavez, Denise.** Loving Pedro Infante. 272p. 2001. 24.00 (*0-374-19411-4*) FS&G.

Chavez, Denise & Feyder, Linda, eds. Shattering the Myth: Plays by Latina Women. LC 91-40997. 256p. 1992. pap. 16.95 (*1-55885-041-4*, Pub. by Arte Publico) Empire Pub Srvs.

Chavez, Fray A. But Time & Chance: The Biography of Padre Martinez of Taos. LC 81-27. 176p. 1981. 35.00 (*0-913270-96-2*) Sunstone Pr.

— The Lady from Toledo: An Historical Novel in Santa Fe. abr. ed. (Illus.). 200p. (Orig.). 1993. reprint ed. pap. 9.95 (*0-941108-03-1*) Friends Palace Pr.

— My Penitente Land: Reflections on Spanish New Mexico. 272p. 1993. pap. 14.95 (*0-89013-255-0*) Museum NM Pr.

— New Mexico Roots Ltd, 11 vols., Set. 2308p. 1982. lib. bdg. 120.00 (*0-913630-06-3*) UNM Gen Lib.

— Origins of New Mexico Families: A Genealogy of the Spanish Colonial Period. 442p. 1992. pap. 45.00 (*0-89013-239-9*) Museum NM Pr.

Chavez, Fray A., tr. see Velez de Escalante, Silvestre.

Chavez, Fray A., tr. see Warner, Ted J., ed.

***Chavez, Fray Angelico.** Cantares: Canticles & Poems of Youth. 192p. 2000. pap. 12.95 (*1-55885-311-1*) Arte Publico.

Chavez, Gloria, ed. see Martinez-Zanca, Minerva.

Chavez, J. The Lost Land: The Chicano Image of the Southwest. LC 84-11950. 214p. 1984. pap. 13.95 (*0-8263-0750-7*) U of NM Pr.

Chavez, Jerry R. Haunted House Halloween Handbook. LC 97-23721. (Illus.). 148p. 1997. pap. 25.00 (*0-7864-0375-6*) McFarland & Co.

Chavez, Jim, Sr., ed. see Young, John L.

Chavez, John R. Eastside Landmark: A History of the East Los Angeles Community Union, 1968-1993. LC 97-49167. 336p. 1998. 49.50 (*0-8047-3333-3*) Stanford U Pr.

Chavez, Leo R. SHADOWED LIVES. 2nd ed. LC 97-70723. 240p. (C). 1997. pap. text 23.50 (*0-15-508089-X*) Harcourt Coll Pubs.

Chavez, Linda. From Sugar Daddies to Uncle Sam. 224p. 1997. 24.00 (*0-465-08903-8*, Pub. by Basic) HarpC.

— From Sugar Daddies to Uncle Sam. 224p. 1998. pap. write for info. (*0-465-08904-6*) Basic.

— Out of the Barrio: Toward a New Politics of Hispanic Assimilation. LC 91-70060. 224p. 1992. pap. 13.50 (*0-465-05431-5*, Pub. by Basic) HarpC.

Chavez, Lisa D. Destruction Bay. 61p. 1999. pap. 8.95 (*0-931122-92-9*) West End.

Chavez, Lydia. The Color Blind: The Campaign to End Affirmative Action. LC 97-13397. 305p. 1998. 40.00 (*0-520-20687-8*, Pub. by U CA Pr) Cal Prin Full Svc.

Chavez, lydia. The Color Blind: The Campaign to End Affirmative Action. LC 97-13397. 320p. 1998. pap. 17.95 (*0-520-21344-0*, Pub. by U CA Pr) Cal Prin Full Svc.

***Chavez Metoyer, Cynthia.** Women & the State in Post-Sandinista Nicaragua. LC 99-34284. (Women & Change in the Developing World Ser.). 154p. 1999. lib. bdg. 40.00 (*1-55587-751-6*) L Rienner.

Chavez, Moises. Diccionario de Hebreo Biblico: A Dictionary of Hebrew. (SPA.). 864p. 1992. 51.99 (*0-311-42094-X*) Casa Bautista.

— Hebreo Biblico Juego de Dos Tomos: Biblical Hebrew, 2 vols. (SPA.). 1989. reprint ed. pap. 29.99 (*0-311-42071-0*, Edit Mundo) Casa Bautista.

Chavez, Moises, tr. see Chandler, Russell.

Chavez, Moises, tr. see Ladd, George E.

***Chavez, Monika.** Gender in the Language Classroom. LC 00-32885. 2000. write for info. (*0-07-236749-0*) McGraw.

***Chavez, Nick.** Perfect Hair Everyday. (Illus.). 2000. 27.50 (*1-928998-36-4*) Q V C Pubg.

Chavez, Patricio, et al. Counter Colon-Ialismo. 96p. 1991. 15.00 (*0-9631354-0-6*) C C De La Raza.

Chavez Ramirez, Juan A., jt. auth. see Guzman, Gabino M.

Chavez, Randy L., jt. auth. see Simon, Charlie B.

Chavez, Rudolfo C. Multicultural Education in the Everyday: A Renaissance for the Recommitted. 1995. 18.00 (*0-89333-138-4*) AACTE.

Chavez, Rudolfo C. & O'Donnell, James, eds. Speaking the Unpleasant: The Politics of (Non)Engagement in the Multicultural Education Terrain. LC 97-45208. (Social Context of Education Ser.). 354p. (C). 1998. text 68.50 (*0-7914-3757-4*); pap. text 22.95 (*0-7914-3758-2*) State U NY Pr.

Chavez, Rudolfo C., jt. ed. see Padilla, Raymond V.

***Chavez-Silverman, Susana & Hernandez, Librada, eds.** Reading & Writing the Ambiente: Queer Sexualities in Latino, Latin American & Spanish Culture. 2000. 69.95 (*0-299-16780-1*); pap. 24.95 (*0-299-16784-4*) U of Wis Pr.

Chavez-Silverman, Susana, jt. ed. see Aparicio, Francis R.

Chavez, Thomas. Quest for Quivira: Spanish Explorers on the Great Plains, 1540-1821. McNamee, Gregory et al, eds. LC 91-67395. (Illus.). 58p. (Orig.). 1992. pap. 5.95 (*1-877856-05-3*) SW Pks Mnmts.

Chavez, Thomas E. An Illustrated History of New Mexico. (Illus.). 272p. 1996. reprint ed. pap. text 22.50 (*0-87081-389-7*) Univ Pr Colo.

Chavez-Vasquez, Gloria. Akum, the Magic of Dreams. LC 96-60241. (ENG & SPA., Illus.). 224p. (Orig.). (J). 1996. pap. 14.95 (*0-9650774-1-1*) White Owl Edits.

— Opus Americanus. (ENG & SPA., Illus.). 192p. 1993. pap. 12.95 (*0-9650774-0-3*) White Owl Edits.

***Chavez, Virgilio.** People, Places & Reflections: A Journey with United Nations. 200p. 2000. pap. 16.00 (*0-8059-4824-4*) Dorrance.

Chavez, Vivian, tr. see Lehman, Yvette K.

Chaviano, Diana. El Hombre, la Hembra y el Hambre. (SPA.). 312p. 1997. 24.95 (*84-08-02530-9*) Planeta Editorial.

Chavich, Cinda. Wild West Cookbook. (Illus.). 192p. 1998. pap. 17.95 (*1-896503-65-9*) Firefly Bks Ltd.

Chavich, Naji & Issa, Jihad. Toward an Environmental Policy in Lebanon. Talhawk, Ajij, tr. (ARA., Illus.). 62p. 1997. pap. write for info. (*1-886604-12-6*) Lebanese Ctr.

Chavigny. Clinical Epidemiology for Nurses. 1993. text. write for info. (*0-397-54657-2*) Lppncott W & W.

Chavin, Melanie. The Lost Chord: Reaching the Person with Dementia Through the Power of Music. 95p. (Orig.). 1991. pap. text 17.95 (*1-879633-08-6*) Eldersong.

Chavin, Remy & Muckenstrum-Chavin, Bernadette. Behavioral Complexities. LC 79-20944. xiv, 257p. 1980. 37.50 (*0-8236-0495-0*, BN#00495) Intl Univs Pr.

Chavira, Juan A., jt. auth. see Trotter, Robert T., 2nd.

Chavis, Geri G., ed. Family: Stories from the Interior. LC 87-80024. (Short Fiction Ser.). 432p. (Orig.). 1987. pap. 14.95 (*0-915308-93-2*) Graywolf.

Chavis, Lisa. The Natural Pharmacist Guide to Antioxidants. 1999. pap. 9.99 (*0-7615-1561-5*) Prima Pub.

Chavis, William M. Designs/Lines. unabridged ed. (Illus.). 71p. 1995. pap. 8.00 (*0-940713-10-1*) Broadside Pr.

Chavkin, Allan. The Chippewa Landscape of Louise Erdrich. LC 98-58015. 176p. 1999. pap. text 16.95 (*0-8173-0955-1*) U of Ala Pr.

Chavkin, Allan, ed. English Romanticism & Modern Fiction: A Collection of Critical Essays. LC 91-3404. (Studies in Modern Literature: No. 21). 210p. 1993. 37.50 (*0-404-61591-0*) AMS Pr.

Chavkin, Allan, ed. see Erdrich, Louise.

Chavkin, Allan R. The Chippewa Landscape of Louise Erdrich. LC 98-58015. 176p. 1999. 34.95 (*0-8173-0942-X*) U of Ala Pr.

Chavkin, Nancy F. The Use of Research in Social Work Practice: A Case Example from School Social Work. LC 93-19111. 168p. 1993. 62.95 (*0-275-94648-7*, C4648, Praeger Pubs) Greenwood.

Chavkin, Nancy F., ed. Families & Schools in a Pluralistic Society. LC 91-42020. (SUNY Series, Family Systems & the Life Cycle). 268p. (C). 1993. text 74.50 (*0-7914-1227-X*); pap. text 24.95 (*0-7914-1228-8*) State U NY Pr.

Chavkin, Nancy F., ed. see Erdrich, Louise.

Chavkin, Wendy, ed. Double Exposure: Women's Health Hazards on the Job & at Home. LC 83-42525. (New Feminist Library). 288p. 1984. 26.00 (*0-85345-632-1*, Pub. by Monthly Rev); pap. 15.00 (*0-85345-633-X*, Pub. by Monthly Rev) NYU Pr.

Chavy, Paul. Dictionnaire des Traducteurs et de la Litterature Traduite en Ancien et Moyen Francais 842-1600. (FRE.). 1545p. 1988. 495.00 (*0-7859-7712-0*, 2051008590) Fr & Eur.

Chawaf, Chantal. Mother Love, Mother Earth. Nagem, Monique F., tr. from FRE. LC 90-3034. (Library of World Literature in Translation: Vol. 20). 150p. 1992. text 15.00 (*0-8240-4399-5*) Garland.

— Redemption. Nagem, Monique F., tr. from FRE. LC 92-511. 97p. 1992. 19.95 (*1-56478-003-1*) Dalkey Arch.

Chawan, D. D. Environment & Adaptive Biology of Plants. 1995. pap. 135.00 (*81-7233-099-5*, Pub. by Scientific Pubs) St Mut.

Chawan, D. D., ed. Environment & Adaptive Biology of Plants. 260p. 1994. pap. 200.00 (*81-7233-098-7*, Pub. by Scientific Pubs) St Mut.

Chawdhri, L. R. Secrets of Astrology: Based on Hindu Astrology. (Illus.). viii, 191p. 1989. text 27.95 (*81-207-0986-1*) Apt Bks.

— Secrets of Astrology: Based on Hindu Astrology. (C). 1994. write for info. (*81-207-1065-7*) Sterling Pubs.

— Secrets of Occult Sciences. (C). 1993. pap. write for info. (*81-207-1067-3*) Sterling Pubs.

***Chawdhry, P. K., et al, eds.** Advances in Concurrent Engineering: CE99. LC 99-66157. 511p. 1999. pap. text 110.95 (*1-56676-790-3*) Technomic.

Chawla. Ophthalmology. 354p. 1999. pap. text 37.50 (*0-7506-3963-6*) Buttrwrth-Heinemann.

Chawla-Duggan, Rita & Pole, Christopher J. Reshaping Education in the 1990s: Perspectives on Primary Schooling. LC 96-18406. 208p. 1996. 79.95 (*0-7507-0526-4*, Falmer Pr); pap. 29.95 (*0-7507-0527-2*, Falmer Pr) Taylor & Francis.

Chawla-Duggan, Rita, jt. ed. see Pole, Christopher J.

***Chawla, H. S.** Introduction to Plant Biotechnology. LC 00-38797. (Illus.). 384p. 2000. text 38.50 (*1-57808-130-0*) Science Pubs.

Chawla, Hector B. Retinal Detachment: The Essentials of Management. 3rd ed. LC 98-28063. 144p. 1998. pap. text 70.00 (*0-7506-3980-6*) Buttrwrth-Heinemann.

***Chawla, Hector Bryson.** Instant Ophthalmology. (Illus.). 288p. 2000. pap. text 77.00 (*0-7506-4461-3*) Buttrwrth-Heinemann.

Chawla, Hector Bryson. Ophthalmology: A Symptom-Based Approach. 3rd ed. LC 99-19071. 215p. 1999. pap. text 40.00 (*0-7506-3979-2*) Buttrwrth-Heinemann.

Chawla, Jyotsna. The Rgvedic Deities & Their Iconic Forms. 1988. 49.50 (*81-215-0082-6*, Pub. by M Manoharial) Coronet Bks.

Chawla, K. K. Composite Materials. (Materials Research & Engineering Ser.). (Illus.). 300p. 1993. 69.95 (*0-387-96478-9*) Spr-Verlag.

— Fibrous Materials. (Solid State Science Ser.). (Illus.). 310p. (C). 1998. text 85.00 (*0-521-57079-4*) Cambridge U Pr.

Chawla, Krishan. Social Cost-Benefit Analysis: An Introduction to Financial & Economic Appraisal of Projects. 1987. 24.00 (*81-7099-022-X*, Pub. by Mittal Pubs Dist) S Asia.

Chawla, Krishan K., jt. auth. see Meyers, Marc A.

Chawla, Krishnan K. Composite Materials: Science & Engineering. 2nd ed. LC 97-43749. (Materials Research & Engineering Ser.). 1998. 69.00 (*0-387-98409-7*) Spr-Verlag.

Chawla, Louise. In the First Country of Places: Nature, Poetry, & Childhood Memory. LC 93-41811. (SUNY Series in Environmental & Architectural Phenomenology). 234p. (C). 1994. text 59.50 (*0-7914-2073-6*); pap. text 19.95 (*0-7914-2074-4*) State U NY Pr.

Chawla, Navin. Mother Teresa: The Authorized Biography. LC 97-45124. (Illus.). 256p. 1996. pap. 24.95 (*1-85230-911-3*, Pub. by Element MA) Penguin Putnam.

— Mother Teresa: The Authorized Biography. LC 97-45124. (Illus.). 256p. 1998. pap. 16.95 (*1-86204-222-5*, Pub. by Element MA) Penguin Putnam.

Chawla, Navin, jt. auth. see Rai, Raghu.

Chawla, Sanjay, jt. auth. see Shekhar, Shashi.

Chawla, Sarita & Renesch, John, eds. Learning Organizations: Developing Cultures for Tomorrow's Workplace. (Illus.). 575p. 1995. 35.00 (*1-56327-110-9*) Productivity Inc.

Chawla, Sohan L. & Gupta, R. K. Materials Selection for Corrosion Control. LC 93-38047. 508p. 1993. 153.00 (*0-87170-474-9*, 6189) ASM.

Chawla, T. C., ed. Annual Review of Numerical Fluid Mechanics & Heat Transfer, Vol. 1. 454p. 1987. 280.00 (*0-89116-455-3*) Hemisp Pub.

Chawla, T. C., jt. ed. see Tien, Chang L.

***Chawla, Yogesh.** Atlas on Crack. 55p. 1999. pap. write for info. (*1-930254-03-2*) Premiere Gen.

***Chawla, Yogesh, et al.** Attack of the 50 Ft. Poets. 71p. 1999. pap. write for info. (*1-930254-00-8*) Premiere Gen.

Chawner, Allan & Kavanagh, Paul. Soundings. (C) 1990. 65.00 (*0-7316-4447-6*, Pub. by Pascoe Pub) St Mut.

Chay, Allan & Smith, Judith. Legal Interviewing in Practice. 402p. 1996. pap. 49.00 (*0-455-21413-1*, Pub. by LawBk Co) Gaunt.

Chay, Hongusk, ed. Culture & International Relations. LC 89-16191. 308p. 1990. 59.95 (*0-275-93018-1*, C3018, Praeger Pubs) Greenwood.

Chay, Jongsuk. Diplomacy of Asymmetry: Korean-American Relations to 1910. LC 89-20502. 256p. 1990. reprint ed. pap. 79.40 (*0-608-04375-3*, 206515600001) Bks Demand.

Chayanov, A. Journey of My Brother Alexsey to the Land of Peasant Utopia. 2nd ed. Poliak, Gregory, ed. Polochina, V., tr. (RUS., Illus.). (Orig.). 1982. pap. 8.50 (*0-940294-00-1*) Silver Age Pub.

Chayanov, Alexander V. The Theory of Peasant Economy. LC 85-40758. 400p. 1986. reprint ed. 35.00 (*0-299-10570-9*); reprint ed. pap. text 19.95 (*0-299-10574-1*) U of Wis Pr.

Chayat, Roko S., ed. Subtle Sound: The Zen Teachings of Maurine Stuart. 120p. (Orig.). 1996. pap. 10.00 (*0-318-14561-8*) Shambhala Pubns.

Chayat, Roko S., ed. see Stuart, Maurine.

Chayat, Sherry. Life Lessons: The Art of Jerome Witkin. LC 93-38713. (Illus.). 160p. 1994. 39.95 (*0-8156-2617-7*) Syracuse U Pr.

Chayat, Shlomit, et al. Israeli Hebrew for Speakers of English, Bk. 3. 190p. 1971. pap. text 22.00 (*0-943443-03-2*) Duben Bks.

Chayat, Sylvia, ed. see Wachtel, Joseph H.

Chayefsky, Paddy. The Collected Works of Paddy Chayefsky. deluxe ed. 1994. pap., boxed set 59.80 (*1-55783-195-5*) Applause Theatre Bk Pubs.

— The Collected Works of Paddy Chayefsky: Screenplays I. LC 94-24706. 344p. 1994. pap. 16.95 (*1-55783-193-9*) Applause Theatre Bk Pubs.

— The Collected Works of Paddy Chayefsky: Screenplays II. LC 94-24706. 344p. 1994. pap. 16.95 (*1-55783-194-7*) Applause Theatre Bk Pubs.

— The Collected Works of Paddy Chayefsky: Stage Plays. 448p. 1994. pap. 12.95 (*1-55783-192-0*) Applause Theatre Bk Pubs.

— The Collected Works of Paddy Chayefsky: The Television Plays. LC 94-185845. 288p. 1994. pap. 12.95 (*1-55783-191-2*) Applause Theatre Bk Pubs.

— Gideon. 1962. pap. 5.25 (*0-8222-0442-8*) Dramatists Play.

Chayefsky, Terry. Acting in Prime Time: The Mature Person's Guide to Breaking into Show Business. LC 96-27003. 128p. 1996. pap. 15.95 (*0-435-07011-8*, 07011) Heinemann.

Chayen, Joseph & Bitensky, Lucille. Practical Histochemistry. LC 90-19606. 336p. 1991. 240.00 (*0-471-92931-X*, Wiley-Interscience) Wiley.

Chayen, Joseph & Bitensky, Lucille, eds. Cytochemical Bioassays: Techniques & Clinical Applications. LC 83-17661. (Basic & Clinical Endocrinology Ser.: No. 3). 437p. 1983. reprint ed. pap. 135.50 (*0-608-01278-5*, 206202600001) Bks Demand.

— Investigative Microtechniques in Medicine & Biology, Vol. 1. LC 84-1720. (Illus.). 404p. reprint ed. pap. 125.30 (*0-7837-3370-4*, 204332800001) Bks Demand.

Chayen, Joseph, et al. Practical Histochemistry. LC 72-8596. 285p. reprint ed. pap. 88.40 (*0-608-18840-9*, 203049500069) Bks Demand.

Chayes, Abram & Chayes, Antonia H. The New Sovereignty: Compliance with International Regulatory Agreements. LC 95-21960. (Illus.). 368p. (C). 1996. text 56.00 (*0-674-61782-7*) HUP.

— The New Sovereignty: Compliance with International Regulatory Agreements. 432p. 1998. pap. 22.95 (*0-674-61783-5*) HUP.

Chayes, Abram & Chayes, Antonia H., eds. Preventing Conflict in the Post-Communist World: Mobilizing International & Regional Organizations. 605p. 1996. pap. 24.95 (*0-8157-1385-1*) Brookings.

Chayes, Abram, et al. Satellite Broadcasting. (Royal Institute of International Affairs Ser.). 1973. 17.95 (*0-19-214994-6*) OUP.

Chayes, Abram, jt. auth. see Chayes, Antonia H.

Chayes, Antonia H. & Chayes, Abram. Planning for Intervention: International Cooperation in Conflict Management. LC 99-11646. 200p. 1999. 65.00 (*90-411-0643-X*) Kluwer Law Intl.

***Chayes, Antonia H. & Chayes, Abram.** Planning for Intervention: International Cooperation in Conflict Management. LC 99-11646. ix, 224p. 1999. pap. 65.00 (*90-411-9242-5*) Kluwer Law Intl.

Chayes, Antonia H., jt. auth. see Chayes, Abram.

Chayes, Antonia H., jt. ed. see Chayes, Abram.

Chayes, Antonia Handlert. Peace Operations: Developing an American Strategy. 188p. 1995. per. 6.00 (*0-16-051681-1*) USGPO.

Chayes, Felix. Ratio Correlation: A Manual for Students of Petrology & Geochemistry. LC 71-146110. 108p. 1971. pap. text 5.50 (*0-226-10220-3*) U Ch Pr.

Chayet, Stephanie, jt. auth. see Lubro, Camille.

Chaykin, Howard. American Flagg! Southern Comfort, No. 8. deluxe limited ed. Gold, Mike, ed. (Illus.). 96p. 1988. 35.95 (*0-936211-06-7*) Graphitti Designs.

— American Flagg!, No. 10: Hard Times. limited ed. Gold, Mike, ed. (Illus.). 96p. (Orig.). 1988. 35.95 (*0-936211-08-3*) Graphitti Designs.

— American Flagg!, No. 17: State of the Union. deluxe limited ed. Gold, Mike, ed. (Illus.). 96p. 1989. 35.95 (*0-936211-15-6*) Graphitti Designs.

— Batman: Dark Allegiances. O'Neil, Dennis, ed. (Illus.). 64p. 1995. pap. 5.95 (*1-56389-233-2*) DC Comics.

— Batman: Thrillkiller. (Illus.). 128p. 1998. pap. text 12.95 (*1-56389-424-6*, Pub. by DC Comics) Time Warner.

— Ironwolf: Fires of the Revolution. Helfer, Andrew, ed. (Illus.). 104p. 1993. pap. 14.95 (*1-56389-065-8*, Pub. by DC Comics) Time Warner.

***Chaykin, Howard.** Son of Superman. (Illus.). 96p. (YA). 1999. 24.95 (*1-56389-595-1*, Pub. by DC Comics) Time Warner.

Chaykin, Howard & Moore, J. F. Batman & Houdini: The Devil's Workshop. O'Neil, Dennis, ed. (Illus.). 64p. 1993. pap. 5.95 (*1-56389-113-1*) DC Comics.

***Chaykin, Howard & Tischman, David.** Son of Superman. (Illus.). 96p. 2000. pap. 14.95 (*1-56389-596-X*, Pub. by DC Comics) Time Warner.

Chaykin, Howard, jt. auth. see Goodwin, Archie.

Chayoun, Yehudah. When Moshiach Comes: Halachic & Aggadic Perspectives. Rapoport, Yaakov M. & Grossman, Mushe, trs. from HEB. 288p. 1994. 15.95 (*1-56871-065-8*) Targum Pr.

***Chayray.** Schaum's Outline of Japanese Grammar. 256p. 2000. 15.95 (*0-07-134220-6*, Schaums Outlne) McGraw-Hill Prof.

Chayton, H. J., ed. see Ferrero, Guglielmo.

Chayton, H. J., tr. see Ferrero, Guglielmo.

Chaytor, Henry J. History of Aragon & Catalonia. LC 73-92610. (BCL Ser.: No. II). (Illus.). 1969. reprint ed. 39.50 (*0-404-01479-8*) AMS Pr.

Chazalviel, J. N. Coulomb Screeing by Mobile Charges: Applications to Materials Science, Chemistry, & Biology. LC 98-37163. 320p. 1999. 69.50 (*0-8176-3950-0*) Birkhauser.

***Chazan.** Profiles of Play the Process. 2000. 40.00 (*0-465-09540-2*, Pub. by Basic) HarpC.

Chazan, Barry. Contemporary Approaches to Moral Education: An Analysis of Alternative Theories. 176p. (C). 1985. pap. text 16.95 (*0-8077-2765-2*) Tchrs Coll.

Chazan, Barry I. & Soltis, Jonas F., eds. Moral Education. LC 72-89127. 204p. reprint ed. pap. 63.30 (*0-8357-9603-5*, 201776400008) Bks Demand.

***Chazan, Daniel.** Beyond Formulas in High School Algebra. LC 99-53646. (Series on School Reform). 216p. 2000. text 16.95 (*0-8077-3919-7*) Tchrs Coll.

Chazan, Daniel, jt. ed. see Lehrer, Richard.

C

Chazan, M., et al. Helping Socially Withdrawn & Isolated Children & Adolescents. LC 98-220794. 1998. 75.00 (*0-304-33969-5*); pap. 24.95 (*0-304-33970-9*) Continuum.

Chazan, Maurice, et al. Emotional & Behavioral Difficulties in Middle Childhood: Identification, Assessment & Intervention in School. LC 94-3569. 180p. 1994. 85.00 (*0-7507-0346-6*, Falmer Pr); pap. 29.95 (*0-7507-0347-4*, Falmer Pr) Taylor & Francis.

Chazan, Maurice, jt. ed. see Brown, Roy I.

Chazan, Naomi, et al. Politics & Society in Contemporary Africa. 3rd ed. LC 99-24154. 1999. pap. 23.50 (*1-55587-679-X*) L Rienner.

***Chazan, Naomi, et al.** Politics & Society in Contemporary Africa. 3rd ed. LC 99-24154. 1999. 59.95 (*1-55587-668-4*) L Rienner.

Chazan, Naomi H., ed. Irredentism & International Politics. LC 90-9010. 161p. 1991. lib. bdg. 37.00 (*1-55587-221-2*) L Rienner.

Chazan, Pauline. The Moral Self. LC 97-40021. 252p. (C). 1998. 75.00 (*0-415-16861-9*); pap. 24.99 (*0-415-16862-7*) Routledge.

Chazan, Robert. Barcelona & Beyond: The Disputation of 1263 & Its Afermath. LC 91-35284. (C). 1992. 50.00 (*0-520-07441-6*, Pub. by U CA Pr) Cal Prin Full Svc.

— Daggers of Faith: Thirteenth-Century Christian Missionizing & Jewish Response. 256p. (C). 1988. 55.00 (*0-520-06297-3*, Pub. by U CA Pr) Cal Prin Full Svc.

— European Jewelry & the First Crusade. LC 86-6938. 380p. (C). 1996. pap. 18.95 (*0-520-20506-5*, Pub. by U CA Pr) Cal Prin Full Svc.

***Chazan, Robert.** God, Humanity & History: The Hebrew First-Crusade Narratives. LC 99-50352. 272p. 2000. 40.00 (*0-520-22127-3*, Pub. by U CA Pr) Cal Prin Full Svc.

Chazan, Robert. In the Year 1096: The First Crusade & the Jews. LC 95-43077. 200p. 1996. 19.95 (*0-8276-0575-7*) JPS Phila.

— In the Year 1096: The First Crusade & the Jews. 200p. 1997. reprint ed. pap. 19.95 (*0-8276-0632-X*) JPS Phila.

— Medieval Jewry in Northern France: A Political & Social History. LC 73-8129. (Johns Hopkins University Studies in Historical & Political Science: 91st; 2). 252p. reprint ed. pap. 78.20 (*0-608-12096-0*, 202413200035) Bks Demand.

— Medieval Stereotypes & Modern Antisemitism. LC 96-29259. 196p. 1997. 40.00 (*0-520-20394-1*, Pub. by U CA Pr) Cal Prin Full Svc.

Chazan, Robert, et al, eds. Ki Baruch Hu: Ancient Near Eastern, Biblical & Judaic Studies in Honor of Baruch A. Levine. LC 99-11847. xxxiv, 675p. 1999. text 59.50 (*1-57506-030-2*) Eisenbrauns.

Chazan, Robert & Kozodoy, Neal, eds. Church, State & Jew in the Middle Ages. LC 78-27221. (Library of Jewish Studies). 1979. pap. text 19.95 (*0-87441-302-8*) Behrman.

Chazanof, William. Joseph Ellicott & the Holland Land Company: The Opening of Western New York. LC 76-130979. (New York State Study Ser.). 252p. reprint ed. pap. 78.20 (*0-8357-3121-9*, 203938200012) Bks Demand.

— Welch's Grape Juice: From Corporation to Co-Operative. LC 77-20849. (New York State Study Ser.). (Illus.). 424p. 1977. reprint ed. pap. 131.50 (*0-608-06979-5*, 206718700009) Bks Demand.

Chazdon, Scott. Investing in Change: Community Reinvestment. Hurley, Larry, ed. (Capitols & Communities Ser.). (Illus.). 1991. pap. text 15.00 (*1-55516-803-5*, 3906) Natl Conf State Legis.

Chazeau, Eunice De, see De Chazeau, Eunice.

Chazeau, Jean. Bibliographie Indexbee de la Faune Terrestre de Nouvelle-Calbedonie: Systbematique, Becologie Et Biogbeographie. LC 98-157158. (ENG, GER, ITA & POR.). 95 p. 1995. write for info. (*2-7099-1274-0*) LInstitut Francais.

***Chazelle, Bernard.** The Discrepancy Method: Randomness & Complexity. LC 99-58374. 448p. 2000. 59.95 (*0-521-77093-9*) Cambridge U Pr.

Chazelle, Bernard, et al, eds. Advances in Discrete & Computational Geometry. LC 98-34538. (Contemporary Mathematics Ser.: Vol. 223). 463p. 1998. pap. 99.00 (*0-8218-0674-2*) Am Math.

Chazelle, Celia M., ed. Literacy, Politics, & Artistic Innovation in the Early Medieval West: Papers Delivered at a Symposium on Early Medieval Culture, Bryn Mawr College, Bryn Mawr, PA. (Illus.). 146p. (Orig.). (C). 1992. pap. text 19.50 (*0-8191-8563-9*); lib. bdg. 41.50 (*0-8191-8562-0*) U Pr of Amer.

Chazen, Saralea, jt. auth. see Kernberg, Paulina F.

Chazin-Bennahum, Judith. Dance in the Shadow of the Guillotine. LC 88-12199. 244p. (C). 1988. text 31.95 (*0-8093-1487-8*) S Ill U Pr.

***Chazin, Daniel, ed.** Appalachian Trail Data Book 2000. 22nd ed. 86p. 1999. pap. 4.95 (*1-889386-10-3*) Appalachian Trail.

Chazin, Daniel D., ed. Appalachian Trail Guide to New York - New Jersey. 14th ed. (Illus.). 212p. 1998. pap. 19.95 (*1-889386-01-4*) Appalachian Trail.

Chazin, Daniel D., ed. see Miskowksi, Nick.

Chazon, Esther G., jt. ed. see Stone, Michael E.

***Chazonof, William.** A Legacy of Faith. LC 99-69427. 100p. 2000. 21.95 (*1-888160-00-4*) Ice Cube.

Chazot, Evelyne. French-Nepali Dictionary: Dictionnaire Francais-Nepali. (FRE & NEP.). 299p. 1986. 19.95 (*0-8288-1107-5*, M4751) Fr & Eur.

Chazotte, Cynthia, et al. The March of Dimes Substance Abuse Curriculum for Obstetricians & Gynecologists. Rosen, Rochelle K. et al, eds. LC 95-36651. 1995. write for info. (*0-86525-066-9*) March of Dimes.

Chazournes, Laurence B. De, see De Chazournes, Laurence B., ed.

Chazournes, Laurence B. De, see Salman, Salman M. A. & De Chazournes, Laurence B.

Chazournes, Laurence Boisson De, see Salman, Salman M. A. & Boisson De Chazournes, Laurence, eds.

Chazov, E. I., et al. Preventive Cardiology Vol. 2, Pt. B: Metabolism of Ischemic Myocardium, Vol. 2. Smirnov, V. N., ed. (Soviet Medical Reviews Supplement Ser.). xii, 304p. 1989. pap. text 437.00 (*3-7186-4925-X*) Gordon & Breach.

Chazov, Eugene I., ed. Cardiology Reviews: Regulation of Myocardial Contractile Function & Metabolism, Vol. 2. (Soviet Medical Reviews Ser.: Vol. 2, Pt. A). xii, 388p. 1989. pap. text 582.00 (*3-7186-4893-8*, Harwood Acad Pubs) Gordon & Breach.

Chazov, Eugene I., et al, eds. Preventive Cardiology. (Soviet Medical Reviews Supplement, Cardiology Ser.: No. 1). xviii, 680p. 1987. text 436.00 (*3-7186-0338-1*) Gordon & Breach.

Chazov, Eugene I. & Lakin, K. M. Anticoagulants & Fibrinolytics. LC 80-18003. 365p. reprint ed. pap. 113.20 (*0-8357-7610-7*, 205693300096) Bks Demand.

Chazov, Eugene I. & Oganov, Raphael G., eds. Preventive Cardiology. LC 89-15394. 320p. 1989. 45.00 (*0-8236-4293-3*) Intl Univs Pr.

Chazov, Eugene I. & Smirnov, V. N., eds. Cardiology Reviews 1: Human Atherosclerosis, Vol. 1. (Soviet Medical Reviews Ser., Section A). xviii, 406p. 1987. text 544.00 (*3-7186-0349-7*) Gordon & Breach.

— Thrombosis & Thrombolysis. LC 86-20472. (Illus.). 444p. (C). 1986. text 150.00 (*0-306-10989-1*, Kluwer Plenum) Kluwer Academic.

Chbosky, Stacy. Who Owns the Sun? LC 88-12694. (Books for Students by Students). (Illus.). 26p. (J). (gr. 3-12). 1988. lib. bdg. 15.95 (*0-933849-14-1*) Landmark Edns.

Chbosky, Stephen. The Perks of Being a Wallflower. 213p. (YA). (gr. 7-12). 1999. per. 12.00 (*0-671-02734-4*) PB.

***Chbosky, Stephen, ed.** MTV's Pieces. 176p. 2000. pap. 11.95 (*0-671-00195-7*, MTV Bks) PB.

Chciuk-Celt, Alexandra, ed. & tr. see Lesmian, Boleslaw.

Chciuk-Celt, Alexandra, tr. see Wasilewski, Marian.

CHD Staff. Trilingual Dictionary: Hindi - Kashmiri - English, 3 vols. 1992. reprint ed. 95.00 (*0-8288-8428-5*) Fr & Eur.

***Che, Cathay.** Deborah Harry. (Illus.). 272p. 2000. 27.00 (*0-88064-218-1*) Fromm Intl Pub.

Che, Chi-Ming, ed. Advances in Transition Metal Coordination Chemistry, Vol. 1. 1996. 109.50 (*1-55938-335-6*) Jai Pr.

***Che Guevara, Ernesto.** Che Guevara Speaks. 2nd ed. 188p. 2000. pap. 14.95 (*0-87348-910-1*) Pathfinder NY.

Che Guevara, Ernesto & Castro, Fidel. Socialism & the Man in Cuba. (FAR.). 81p. pap. 9.95 (*0-87348-576-9*) Pathfinder NY.

— Le Socialisme et l'Homme a Cuba (Socialism & Man in Cuba) 56p. 1989. pap. 4.00 (*0-87348-580-7*) Pathfinder NY.

— Socialismen och Manniskan pa Kuba. (SWE., Illus.). 42p. pap. 4.00 (*0-87348-537-8*) Pathfinder NY.

Che Guevara, Ernesto, et al. Che Guevara, Cuba y el Camino al Socialismo: Che Guevara, Cuba, & the Road to Socialism. (SPA.). 210p. (Orig.). (C). 1991. pap. 12.00 (*0-87348-725-7*) Pathfinder NY.

Che, M. & Bond, G. C., eds. Adsorption & Catalysis on Oxide Surfaces: Proceedings of a Symposium Brunel University Uxbridge, U. K., June 28-29, 1984. LC 85-10320. (Studies in Surface Science & Catalysis: Vol. 21). 442p. 1985. 235.75 (*0-444-42512-8*) Elsevier.

Che Man, Abu B. & Gold, David. Safety & Health in the Use of Chemicals at Work: A Training Manual. v, 78p. (Orig.). 1993. pap. 15.75 (*92-2-106470-0*) Intl Labour Office.

***Che, Sunny.** Forever Alien: A Korean Memoir, 1930-1951. LC 99-54799. (Illus.). 261p. 2000. lib. bdg. 37.50 (*0-7864-0685-2*) McFarland & Co.

Chea, Augustine S. Joy after Mourning: The Liberian Civil War. 176p. (Orig.). 1997. pap. write for info. (*1-57502-556-6*, P01615) Morris Pubng.

Cheadle, Dave. Arctic Obsession: The Victorian Race for the North Pole. (Illus.). 30p. 1993. pap. 10.00 (*0-9679622-0-X*) Cheadle.

— Family Ashes: A Novel. LC 00-190194. 2000. 25.00 (*0-7388-1591-8*); pap. 18.00 (*0-7388-1592-6*) Xlibris Corp.

Cheadle, Dave. Victorian Trade Cards: Historical Reference & Value Guide. LC 96-210207. (Illus.). 224p. 1996. pap. 19.95 (*0-89145-706-2*, 4654) Collector Bks.

***Cheadle, Halton, et al.** Current Labour Law 1999: The Authority Annual Review of Labour Law. 10th ed. 157p. 1999. pap. 36.50 (*0-7021-5124-6*, Pub. by Juta & Co) Gaunt.

Cheadle, Halton, et al. Current Labour Law, 1997. 182p. 1997. pap. 27.00 (*0-7021-4543-2*, Pub. by Juta & Co) Gaunt.

— Current Labour Law, 1993. 1993. pap. 38.00 (*0-7021-2989-5*, Pub. by Juta & Co) Gaunt.

— Current Labour Law 1996. 271p. 1996. pap. 40.00 (*0-7021-3899-1*, Pub. by Juta & Co) Gaunt.

Cheadle, J. A. A Donkey's Life: A Story for Children. LC 80-123421. iii, 88p. (Orig.). (J). (gr. 2-6). 1979. pap. 7.00 (*0-9604244-0-7*) Heahstan Pr.

Cheadle, J. R. Basic Greek Vocabulary. 1996. pap. 21.95 (*0-17-439918-9*) Focus Pub-R Pullins.

Cheadle, Mary P. Ezra Pound's Confucian Translations. LC 96-49592. 336p. (C). 1997. text 49.50 (*0-472-10754-2*, 10754) U of Mich Pr.

***Cheadle, Norman.** The Ironic Apocalypse in the Novels of Leopoldo Marechal. LC 99-86336. 192p. 2000. 60.00 (*1-85566-070-9*, Pub. by Tamesis Bks Ltd) Boydell & Brewer.

Cheadle, Rand, jt. auth. see Hill, Jim.

Cheadle, Russell F., jt. auth. see Leventhal, Ruth.

Cheah Boon Kheng. From PKI to the Comintern, 1924-1941: The Apprenticeship of the Malayan Communist Party. (Southeast Asia Program Ser.: No. 8). 147p. (Orig.). (C). 1992. pap. text 14.00 (*0-87727-125-9*) Cornell SE Asia.

— The Peasant Robbers of Kedah, 1900-1929: Historical & Folk Perceptions. (East Asian Historical Monographs). (Illus.). 168p. 1988. text 26.00 (*0-19-588882-0*) OUP.

Cheah, Jonathon. Practical Wireless Data Modem Design. LC 99-27667. (Artech House Mobile Communications Library). 427p. 1999. 97.00 (*1-58053-047-8*) Artech Hse.

Cheah, Pheng, et al, eds. Thinking Through the Body of the Law. 304p. 1996. pap. 29.95 (*1-86373-604-2*, Pub. by Allen & Unwin Pty) Paul & Co Pubs.

— Thinking Through the Body of the Law. LC 95-44549. (C). 1996. text 55.00 (*0-8147-1544-3*); pap. text 20.00 (*0-8147-1545-1*) NYU Pr.

Cheah, Pheng, et al. Cosmopolitics: Thinking & Feeling Beyond the Nation. LC 97-43051. (Cultural Politics Ser.). 1998. 54.95 (*0-8166-3067-4*); pap. 21.95 (*0-8166-3068-2*) U of Minn Pr.

***Cheairs, L. Steven.** Forces & Faces. (Illus.). 145p. 1999. pap. 15.95 (*0-7414-0207-6*) Buy Books.

— The Great Wall of Forgetfullness. LC 00-190837. 2000. 25.00 (*0-7388-1959-X*); pap. 18.00 (*0-7388-1960-3*) Xlibris Corp.

Cheal, Brian, jt. auth. see Owens, Graham W.

Cheal, David. Family & the State of Theory. 1991. text 45.00 (*0-8020-5994-5*); pap. text 18.95 (*0-8020-6928-2*) U of Toronto Pr.

— The Gift Economy. 240p. (C). 1988. lib. bdg. 57.50 (*0-415-00641-4*) Routledge.

— New Poverty: Families in Postmodern Society. LC 95-50520. 232p. 1999. pap. 22.95 (*0-275-96584-8*, Praeger Pubs) Greenwood.

— New Poverty: Families in Postmodern Society, 115. LC 95-50520. (Contributions in Sociology Ser.: No. 115). 232p. 1996. 59.95 (*0-313-29444-5*, Greenwood Pr) Greenwood.

***Cheaney, Janie.** The Playmaker. 256p. (ps up). 2000. lib. bdg. 17.99 (*0-375-90577-4*) Knopf.

— The Playmaker. 256p. (J). (ps up). 2000. 15.95 (*0-375-80577-X*, Pub. by Knopf Bks Yng Read) Random.

Cheaney, Lee & Cotter, Maury. Real People, Real Work: Parables on Leadership in the '90s. 2nd ed. (Illus.). 178p. 1991. pap. 10.00 (*0-945320-11-6*) Stat Process Contrl.

Cheang, Loh S. Business Guide to Malaysia. LC 98-140097. 250p. 1997. pap. 17.95 (*981-00-6794-1*, Pub. by Select Bks) Weatherhill.

Cheape. Tartan: Highland Habit. (Illus.). 96p. 1995. pap. 14.95 (*0-948636-70-X*, 6238, Pub. by Natl Mus Scotland) A Schwartz & Co.

Cheape, Charles W. Family Firm to Modern Multinational: Norton Company, a New England Enterprise. (Studies in Business History: No. 36). (Illus.). 448p. 1985. 25.00 (*0-674-29261-8*) HUP.

— Moving the Masses: Urban Public Transit in New York, Boston, & Philadelphia, 1880 to 1912. LC 79-15875. (Studies in Business History: No. 31). (Illus.). 291p. 1980. 18.50 (*0-674-58827-4*) HUP.

— Strictly Business: Walter Carpenter at Du Pont & General Motors. LC 94-22652. (Studies in Industry & Society: No. 6). (Illus.). 328p. 1995. text 48.50 (*0-8018-4941-1*) Johns Hopkins.

Cheape, Hugh, ed. Tools & Traditions: Studies in European Ethnology Presented to Alexander Fenton. (Illus.). 256p. 1995. 45.00 (*0-948636-53-X*, 653-X) A Schwartz & Co.

Cheape, Hugh, ed. & intro. see Campbell, John L.

Chearney, Lee A. A House Divided... A Century of Great Civil War Quotations. Ayers, Edward, ed. LC 97-225834. (Illus.). 258p. 1997. pap. 14.95 (*0-471-19264-3*) Wiley.

— Visits: Caring for an Aging Parent. LC 97-28256. 160p. 1998. pap. 10.00 (*0-609-80059-0*) Crown Pub Group.

Chearney, Lee A., ed. The Quotable Angel: A Treasury of Inspiring Quotations Spanning the Ages. LC 95-31931. 240p. 1995. 14.95 (*0-471-13148-2*) Wiley.

Cheasebro, Margaret. Puppet Scripts by the Situation. LC 88-7537. (Orig.). 1989. pap. 6.99 (*0-8054-7527-3*, 4275-27) Broadman.

Cheasley, Clifford W. Numerology. 80p. 1996. reprint ed. spiral bd. 10.50 (*0-7873-1144-8*) Hlth Research.

— What's in Your Name: The Science of Letters & Numbers. 1991. lib. bdg. 65.75 (*0-8490-4516-9*) Gordon Pr.

— What's in Your Name: The Science of Letters & Numbers. 105p. 1996. spiral bd. 11.00 (*0-7873-1228-2*) Hlth Research.

— What's in Your Name: The Science of Letters & Numbers. 105p. 1993. reprint ed. pap. 7.95 (*1-56459-402-5*) Kessinger Pub.

Cheasty, Adrienne, jt. ed. see Blejer, Mario I.

Cheater, Angela P. The Anthropology of Power: Empowerment & Disempowerment in Changing Structures. LC 98-27573. (ASA Monographs Ser.). 1999. 85.00 (*0-415-19388-5*) Routledge.

— The Anthropology of Power: Empowerment & Disempowerment in Changing Structures. LC 98-27573. (ASA Monographs Ser.). ix, 213 p. 1999. pap. 27.99 (*0-415-19389-3*) Routledge.

Cheatham, et al. Tutor: A Collaborative Approach to Literacy Instruction. 198p. 1993. pap. 12.50 (*0-930713-81-8*) Lit Vol Am.

Cheatham, Adolphus. I Guess I'll Get the Papers & Go Home: The Life of Doc Cheatham. Shipton, Alyn, ed. LC 96-1828. (Bayou Press Ser.). (Illus.). 160p. 1996. 30.00 (*0-304-33611-4*) Continuum.

Cheatham, Adophus. I Guess I'll Get the Papers & Go Home: The Life of Doc Cheatham. Shipton, Alyn, ed. LC 97-49640. 156p. 1998. pap. 17.95 (*0-304-70316-8*) Continuum.

Cheatham, Carole B. & Cheatham, Leon R. Updating Standard Cost Systems. LC 92-34376. 256p. 1993. 65.00 (*0-89930-716-7*, CUC, Quorum Bks) Greenwood.

Cheatham, Carolyn. Sleep with the Wolf--Walk with the Bear. LC 98-73876. 168p. pap. 12.95 (*0-9651232-4-3*, AC503) Ammons Communs.

Cheatham, David W., jt. auth. see Hillgren, James S.

Cheatham, George, ed. see Rowley, William D.

Cheatham, Harold E. & Stewart, James B., eds. Black Families: Interdisciplinary Perspectives. 300p. 1990. pap. 24.95 (*0-88738-812-4*) Transaction Pubs.

Cheatham, James T. The Atlantic Turkey Shoot: U-Boats off the Outer Banks in World War II. (Illus.). 1990. pap. 9.95 (*0-932705-09-X*) Gan Prodns.

— Sailing the Carolina Sounds: Historical Places & My Favorite People. (Illus.). 80p. 1992. pap. 9.95 (*0-9636714-3-X*) Gan Prodns.

***Cheatham, Jo Whatley.** Homecare - The Best! How to Get It, Give It, & Live with It: A Complete Planning & Action Guide for Care Recipients, Advocates, & Caregivers. LC 99-74180. xviii, 198p. 1999. pap. 14.95 (*0-9670880-0-3*) ProSo Pr.

Cheatham, John B., Jr., jt. auth. see Burr, Arthur H.

***Cheatham, Judy Blankenship.** Help a Child Learn to Read. 167p. 1998. 12.50 (*0-930713-97-4*) Lit Vol Am.

***Cheatham, K. Follis.** The Adventures of Elizabeth Fortune. 256p. 2000. pap. 16.95 (*0-936085-44-4*, Pub. by Blue Heron OR) Consort Bk Sales.

Cheatham, Kae. Dennis Banks: Native American Activist. LC 96-39560. (Native American Biographies Ser.). (Illus.). 112p. (YA). (gr. 6 up). 1997. lib. bdg. 20.95 (*0-89490-869-3*) Enslow Pubs.

Cheatham, Leon R., jt. auth. see Cheatham, Carole B.

Cheatham, Lillian. Shadowed Reunion. large type ed. 304p. 1984. 27.99 (*0-7089-1197-8*) Ulverscroft.

Cheatham, Melvin L. Come Walk with Me. 1993. 15.99 (*0-7852-8291-2*) Nelson.

Cheatham, Melvin L. & Cutshall, Mark. Come Walk with Me. LC 93-4069. 1993. pap. 12.99 (*0-8407-4249-5*) Nelson.

Cheatham, Melvin L. & Cutshell, Mark. Living a Life That Counts. 224p. 1995. pap. 14.99 (*0-7852-7724-2*) Nelson.

Cheatham, Mike. An Athens Diary: 1996: One Georgia City's Olympic Experience. (Orig.). 1996. pap. 11.95 (*0-9634240-1-7*) Bee Tree Bks.

— Your Friendly Neighbor: The Story of Georgia's Coca-Cola Bottling Families. LC 99-36854. (Illus.). 300p. 1999. 29.95 (*0-86554-686-X*) Mercer Univ Pr.

Cheatham, Robert W. & Merrit, Robert G., Jr. California Real Estate Forms & Commentaries. (Marxist Regimes Ser.). 730p. 1984. 85.00 (*0-317-14888-5*) Harcourt.

Cheatham, Scooter, et al. The Useful Wild Plants of Texas, the Southeastern & Southwestern United States, the Southern Plains, & Northern Mexico. LC 95-16542. 1995. 125.00 (*1-887292-01-2*) Useful Wild Plants.

Cheatham, Val R. Christmas in Oz. 1983. pap. 4.95 (*0-686-39595-6*) Eldridge Pub.

Cheatham, Wallace M., ed. Dialogues on Opera & the African-American Experience. LC 96-7914. 208p. 1997. 44.00 (*0-8108-3147-3*) Scarecrow.

Cheatheam, Charles, ed. Eternal Judgment, Bk. Seven: A Study of the Elementary Principles of Christ. (First Principles Ser.). (Orig.). 1992. student ed. 5.00 (*0-923968-07-5*) Shady Grove Ch Pubns.

— Eternal Judgment, Bk. Seven: A Study of the Elementary Principles of Christ, Set. (First Principles Ser.). (Orig.). 1992. 6.00 (*0-685-59230-8*) Shady Grove Ch Pubns.

— Resurrection Life, Bk. 6: A Study of the Elementary Principles of Christ. (First Principles Ser.). (Orig.). 1992. student ed. 5.00 (*0-923968-06-7*) Shady Grove Ch Pubns.

— Resurrection Life, Bk. 6: A Study of the Elementary Principles of Christ, Set. (First Principles Ser.). (Orig.). 1992. 6.00 (*0-685-54890-2*) Shady Grove Ch Pubns.

***Cheatum, Billye Ann & Hammond, Allison A.** Physical Activities for Improving Children's Learning & Behavior: A Guide to Sensory Motor Development. LC 99-41127. (Illus.). 360p. (C). 2000. pap. 19.95 (*0-88011-874-1*) Human Kinetics.

Cheatwood, Derral. The Human Image: Sociology & Photography. 60p. 1976. pap. 21.95 (*0-87855-637-0*) Transaction Pubs.

Cheatwood, Derral, jt. auth. see Harries, Keith D.

Cheatwood, Kiarri T-H. Bloodstorm: Five Books of Poems & Docupoems - Towards Liberation. LC 85-82524. 160p. 1986. pap., per. 10.50 (*0-916418-62-6*) Lotus.

— The Butchers' Grand Ball: Meditations on Goree Island in Photographs & Carefully Chosen Words. LC 93-84326. (Illus.). 96p. (Orig.). 1993. pap. 14.50 (*1-879289-03-2*) Native Sun Pubs.

— A Life on an April Canvas: An Afrikan Man's Story of Love, Betrayal, & Struggle. LC 91-68263. 128p. (Orig.). 1992. 22.98 (*0-9625169-8-8*); pap. 12.98 (*0-9625169-9-6*) Native Sun Pubs.

— Psalms of Redemption. LC 82-83855. 50p. 1983. per. 5.00 (*0-916418-41-3*) Lotus.

— Seeds of Consistency, Fruits of Life: An Historio-Philosophical Narrative. LC 89-63844. 556p. (Orig.). 1990. 21.95 (*0-9625169-1-0*); pap. 15.95 (*0-9625169-0-2*) Native Sun Pubs.

— Shattered Kente & A Maelstrom of Blackness: A 3-Suite of Scorched Earth Poetry & Afrikan Love Songs. LC 99-70001. 128p. 2000. 25.50 (*1-879289-08-3*); pap. 15.50 (*1-879289-09-1*) Native Sun Pubs.

— To Save the Blood of Black Babies. LC 94-68864. 184p. (Orig.). 1995. pap. 15.50 (*1-879289-05-9*) Native Sun Pubs.

— Valley of the Anointers. LC 78-70230. 73p. 1979. per. 5.00 (*0-916418-19-7*) Lotus.

Cheatwood, Kiarri T-H., ed. The Race: Matters Concerning Pan Afrikan History, Culture & Genocide. LC 90-63873. 560p. 1991. 24.98 (*0-9625169-4-5*); pap. 16.98 (*0-9625169-5-3*) Native Sun Pubs.

Cheatwood, Roy C., et al. Louisiana Courtroom Evidence. 400p. 1993. ring bd. 115.00 (*1-55943-150-4*, MICHIE) LEXIS Pub.

Cheavens, Frank. Child of the Sun: A Historical Novel Based on the Journey of Cabeza de Vaca Across North America. 194p. 1985. pap. 10.00 (*0-89540-161-4*, SB-161) Sun Pub.

Cheavens, Frank. Survivor of the Goliad, Texas Massacre. 80p. lib. bdg. 16.95 (*1-878096-34-6*, Epigram Pr) Best E TX Pubs.

Chebat, Jean. Services Management. 1997. text. write for info. (*0-201-89225-1*) Addison-Wesley.

Chebat, Jean-Charles, ed. see Academy of Marketing Science Staff.

Chebel, Malek. Symbols of Islam. LC 98-129632. (Illus.). 1997. text 40.00 (*2-84323-007-1*) St Martin.

Chebib, Farouk S. Everything Men Know about Women. 160p. 1997. pap. text 4.95 (*1-56236-980-6*, Pub. by Aspen Bks) Origin Bk Sales.

Chebli-Saadi, M., jt. auth. see Batchelor, R. E.

Chebotaev, V. P., jt. auth. see Beterov, I. M.

Chebotarev, V. P., ed. see International Astronomical Union Staff.

Chebotayev, V. P., jt. auth. see Letokhov, V. S.

***Chebran, Yves.** The Bluffer's Guide to Seduction: Bluff Your Way in Seduction. (Bluffer's Guides Ser.). 64p. 1999. pap. 5.95 (*1-902825-60-8*) Oval Bks.

Chebyshev, Pafnuti L. Theorie der Congruenzen. 2nd ed. LC 71-113123. (GER.). xvii, 366p. 1972. text 19.95 (*0-8284-0254-X*) Chelsea Pub.

Checa, Jorge. Gracian y la Imagination Arquitectonica. 28.00 (*0-916379-28-0*) Scripta.

***Checchini, Marie.** Weather-Thematic. 80p. 2000. pap. 9.95 (*1-57690-612-4*) Durkin Hayes Pub.

Checchio, Michael. A Clean, Well-Lighted Stream. LC 95-30347. 204p. 1995. 23.00 (*1-56947-045-6*) Soho Press.

***Checchio, Michael.** Sundown Legends: A Journey into the American Southwest. 256p. 2000. text 22.95 (*0-312-20593-7*) St Martin.

Checci, Mary Jane. Are You the Pet for Me? Chosing the Right Pet for Your Family. LC 99-227405. (Illus.). 289p. 1999. mass mkt. 5.99 (*0-312-96793-4*) St Martin.

Checck, William R. & Marling, Arthur E., eds. Pediatric Neurosurgery: Surgery of the Developing Nervous System. 3rd ed. LC 93-38501. (Illus.). 656p. 1994. text 230.00 (*0-7216-3767-1*, W B Saunders Co) Harcrt Hlth Sci Grp.

Chechile, Richard A., et al, eds. Environmental Decision Making: A Multidisciplinary Perspective. 1991. text 65.95 (*0-442-00659-4*, VNR) Wiley.

Checinski, Michael M. My Father's Watch: Lodz Ghetto Underground. 248p. (Orig.). 1994. pap. text 14.95 (*965-229-112-9*, Pub. by Gefen Pub Hse) Gefen Bks.

Check, Albert F., jt. auth. see Krar, Steve F.

Check-Chart Publication Staff. Automotive Electrical Systems. 3rd ed. Fennema, Roger L., ed. LC 93-47370. (C). 1997. teacher ed. 10.00 (*0-06-500760-3*) Addison-Wesley Educ.

— Fuel Systems & Emissions Controls. DuPuy, Richard K. et al, eds. LC 94-27859. (C). 1994. 37.00 (*0-673-99519-4*) HarpC.

Check, Christopher, jt. auth. see Carlson, Allan.

***Check, Laura.** Paper Plate Crafts: Creative Art Fun for 3- to 7-Year Olds. (Little Hands Ser.). (Illus.). 144p. (J). (ps-2). 2000. pap. 12.95 (*1-885593-43-0*) Williamson Pub Co.

Check, Walter, jt. auth. see Gailey, Paul.

Check, William A. AIDS. rev. ed. (Encyclopedia of Health Ser.). (Illus.). 128p. (YA). (gr. 7 up). 1998. lib. bdg. 19.95 (*0-7910-0054-0*) Chelsea Hse.

— AIDS. rev. ed. (Illus.). 128p. (YA). (gr. 7 up). 1999. lib. bdg. 19.95 (*0-7910-4885-3*) Chelsea Hse.

— Alzheimer's Disease. (Encyclopedia of Health Ser.). (Illus.). 116p. (YA). (gr. 7 up). 1989. lib. bdg. 19.95 (*0-7910-0056-7*) Chelsea Hse.

— Child Abuse. Irwin, Charles E., Jr. et al, eds. (Encyclopedia of Health Ser.). (Illus.). 128p. (YA). (gr. 7 up). 1995. pap. 8.95 (*0-7910-0509-7*) Chelsea Hse.

— Drugs of the Future. (Encyclopedia of Psychoactive Drugs Ser.: No. 2). (Illus.). 128p. (YA). (gr. 7 up). 1987. lib. bdg. 19.95 (*1-55546-208-1*) Chelsea Hse.

Checkaneck, Bob, et al. Supplier Quality Management: Foundations. Hankinson, Mari-Lynn, ed. (AT&T Quality Library). (Illus.). 111p. (Orig.). 1994. pap. 19.95 (*0-932764-43-6*) AT&T Customer Info.

Checkel, Jeffrey T. Ideas & International Change: Soviet Russian Behavior & the End of the Cold War. LC 96-18149. 208p. 1997. 30.00 (*0-300-06377-6*) Yale U Pr.

***CheckerBee Publishing Staff.** Agatha Christie: A Reader's Checklist & Reference Guide. 1999. pap. text 4.95 (*1-58598-010-2*) CheckerBee.

— Anne Rice: A Reader's Checklist & Reference Guide. 1999. pap. text 4.95 (*1-58598-032-3*) CheckerBee.

— Barbara Taylor Bradford: A Reader's Checklist & Reference Guide. 1999. pap. text 4.95 (*1-58598-007-2*) CheckerBee.

CheckerBee Publishing Staff. Boyds Bears & Friends 1999 Value Guide. (Illus.). 205p. 1999. pap. 14.95 (*1-888914-47-5*) CheckerBee.

***CheckerBee Publishing Staff.** Boyds Bears Collection Ltd. Resin 2000. 5th ed. (Illus.). 192p. 2000. pap. 15.95 (*1-888914-76-9*) CheckerBee.

— The Boyds Collection Ltd. Plush 2000. 5th ed. (Illus.). 192p. 2000. pap. 15.95 (*1-888914-75-0*) CheckerBee.

— Boyds Plush Animals 1999 Value Guide. (Illus.). 224p. 1999. pap. 14.95 (*1-888914-46-7*) CheckerBee.

— Charming Tails 1999 Value Guide. (Illus.). 128p. 1999. pap. 13.95 (*1-888914-54-8*) CheckerBee.

— Charming Tails 2000. 2nd ed. (Illus.). 128p. 2000. pap. 14.95 (*1-888914-77-7*) CheckerBee.

— Cherished Teddies 1999 Value Guide. (Illus.). 192p. 1999. pap. 13.95 (*1-888914-51-3*) CheckerBee.

— Cherished Teddies 2000. 4th ed. (Illus.). 160p. 2000. pap. 14.95 (*1-888914-78-5*) CheckerBee.

— Children's Picture Books: A Reader's Checklist & Reference Guide. 1999. pap. 4.95 (*1-58598-000-5*) CheckerBee.

— Danielle Steel: A Reader's Checklist & Reference Guide. 1999. pap. text 4.95 (*1-58598-035-8*) CheckerBee.

— Dean Koontz: A Reader's Checklist & Reference Guide. 1999. pap. text 4.95 (*1-58598-025-0*) CheckerBee.

— Department 56 Snowbabies 2000. 4th ed. (Illus.). 128p. 2000. pap. 13.95 (*1-888914-85-8*) CheckerBee.

CheckerBee Publishing Staff. Department 56 Snowbabies Value Guide. (Illus.). 128p. 1999. pap. 13.95 (*1-888914-56-4*) CheckerBee.

***CheckerBee Publishing Staff.** Department 56 Villages 2000. 5th ed. (Illus.). 208p. 2000. pap. 16.95 (*1-888914-79-3*) CheckerBee.

CheckerBee Publishing Staff. Department 56 Villages Value Guide. (Illus.). 224p. 1999. pap. 15.95 (*1-888914-48-3*) CheckerBee.

***CheckerBee Publishing Staff.** Detective Mysteries: A Reader's Checklist & Reference Guide. 1999. pap. text 4.95 (*1-58598-001-3*) CheckerBee.

— Dick Francis: A Reader's Checklist & Reference Guide. 1999. pap. text 4.95 (*1-58598-018-8*) CheckerBee.

— Digimon Collector's Value Guide. (Illus.). 128p. 2000. pap. 9.95 (*1-58598-058-7*) CheckerBee.

— Dragon Ball Z Collector's Value Guide. (Illus.). 128p. 2000. pap. 9.95 (*1-58598-059-5*) CheckerBee.

CheckerBee Publishing Staff. Dreamsicles 1999 Value Guide. (Illus.). 192p. 1999. pap. 13.95 (*1-888914-43-2*) CheckerBee.

***CheckerBee Publishing Staff.** Dreamsicles 2000. 3rd ed. (Illus.). 160p. 2000. pap. 14.95 (*1-888914-80-7*) CheckerBee.

— Elmore Leonard: A Reader's Checklist & Reference Guide. 1999. pap. text 4.95 (*1-58598-026-9*) CheckerBee.

— Fifty State Quarters Collector Kids Guide Handbook & Coin Album. (Illus.). 72p. (J). 2000. pap. 9.95 (*1-888914-95-5*) CheckerBee.

— Fifty State Quarters Collector's Value Guide Handbook & Coin Album. (Illus.). 72p. 2000. pap. 12.95 (*1-888914-94-7*) CheckerBee.

— Hallmark Keepsake Ornaments 1999 Value Guide. (Illus.). 368p. 1999. pap. write for info. (*1-888914-53-X*) CheckerBee.

— Hallmark Keepsake Ornaments 2000. 4th ed. (Illus.). 336p. 2000. pap. 19.95 (*1-888914-81-5*) CheckerBee.

— Harbour Lights 1999 Value Guide. (Illus.). 128p. 1999. pap. 13.95 (*1-888914-55-6*) CheckerBee.

— Harbour Lights 2000. 2nd ed. (Illus.). 128p. 2000. pap. 13.95 (*1-888914-82-3*) CheckerBee.

— Harmony Kingdom 2000. (Illus.). 160p. 2000. pap. 14.95 (*1-888914-83-1*) CheckerBee.

— Historical Romance: A Reader's Checklist & Reference Guide. 1999. pap. text 4.95 (*1-58598-002-1*) CheckerBee.

— James Michener: A Reader's Checklist & Reference Guide. 1999. pap. text 4.95 (*1-58598-029-3*) CheckerBee.

— James Patterson: A Reader's Checklist & Reference Guide. 1999. pap. text 4.95 (*1-58598-031-5*) CheckerBee.

— John Grisham: A Reader's Checklist & Reference Guide. 1999. pap. text 4.95 (*1-58598-020-X*) CheckerBee.

— Ken Follett: A Reader's Checklist & Reference Guide. 1999. pap. text 4.95 (*1-58598-017-X*) CheckerBee.

— Larry Mcmurty: A Reader's Checklist & Reference Guide. 1999. pap. text 4.95 (*1-58598-028-5*) CheckerBee.

— Legal Thrillers: A Reader's Checklist & Reference Guide. 1999. pap. text 4.95 (*1-58598-003-X*) CheckerBee.

— Lilian Jackson Braun: A Reader's Checklist & Reference Guide. 1999. pap. text 4.95 (*1-58598-008-0*) CheckerBee.

— Mary Higgins Clark: A Reader's Checklist & Reference Guide. 1999. pap. text 4.95 (*1-58598-012-9*) CheckerBee.

— Michael Crichton: A Reader's Checklist & Reference Guide. 1999. pap. text 4.95 (*1-58598-015-3*) CheckerBee.

— Nelson De Mille: A Reader's Checklist & Reference Guide. 1999. pap. text 4.95 (*1-58598-016-1*) CheckerBee.

— Nora Roberts: A Reader's Checklist & Reference Guide. 1999. pap. text 4.95 (*1-58598-033-1*) CheckerBee.

— Orson Scott Card: A Reader's Checklist & Reference Guide. 1999. pap. text 4.95 (*1-58598-009-9*) CheckerBee.

— Patricia Cornwell: A Reader's Checklist & Reference Guide. 1999. pap. text 4.95 (*1-58598-014-5*) CheckerBee.

— P.D. James: A Reader's Checklist & Reference Guide. 1999. pap. text 4.95 (*1-58598-022-6*) CheckerBee.

— Pokemon Collector's Value Guide. 2nd ed. 270p. 2000. pap. text 12.95 (*1-888914-88-2*) CheckerBee.

— Pokemon 2000 Collector's Value Guide. (Illus.). 250p. 1999. pap. 9.95 (*1-888914-68-8*) CheckerBee.

— Pokemon 2000 Collector's Value Guide. (Illus.). 256p. 1999. pap. 9.95 (*1-888914-67-X*) CheckerBee.

CheckerBee Publishing Staff. Precious Moments 1999 Value Guide. (Illus.). 287p. 1999. pap. 19.95 (*1-888914-44-0*) CheckerBee.

***CheckerBee Publishing Staff.** Precious Moments 2000. 3rd ed. (Illus.). 240p. 2000. pap. 19.95 (*1-888914-84-X*) CheckerBee.

— Robert Jordan: A Reader's Checklist & Reference Guide. 1999. pap. text 4.95 (*1-58598-023-4*) CheckerBee.

— Robert Ludlum: A Reader's Checklist & Reference Guide. 1999. pap. text 4.95 (*1-58598-027-7*) CheckerBee.

— Robin Cook: A Reader's Checklist & Reference Guide. 1999. pap. text 4.95 (*1-58598-013-7*) CheckerBee.

— Science Fiction: A Reader's Checklist & Reference Guide. 1999. pap. 4.95 (*1-58598-004-8*) CheckerBee.

— Sidney Sheldon: A Reader's Checklist & Reference Guide. 1999. pap. text 4.95 (*1-58598-034-X*) CheckerBee.

— Stephen King: A Reader's Checklist & Reference Guide. 1999. pap. text 4.95 (*1-58598-024-2*) CheckerBee.

— Sue Grafton: A Reader's Checklist & Reference Guide. 1999. pap. text 4.95 (*1-58598-019-6*) CheckerBee.

— Swarovski Crystal 1999 Value Guide. (Illus.). 1999. pap. 13.95 (*1-888914-52-1*) CheckerBee.

— Tom Clancy: A Reader's Checklist & Reference Guide. 1999. pap. 4.95 (*1-58598-011-0*) CheckerBee.

— Toni Morrison: A Reader's Checklist & Reference Guide. 1999. pap. text 4.95 (*1-58598-030-7*) CheckerBee.

— Tony Hillerman: A Reader's Checklist & Reference Guide. 1999. pap. text 4.95 (*1-58598-021-8*) CheckerBee.

— Ty Beanie Babies: A Personal Checklist. (Collector's Pocket Planner Ser.). (Illus.). 2000. 2.95 (*1-888914-89-0*) CheckerBee.

CheckerBee Publishing Staff. Ty Beanie Babies. (Collector's Value Guides Ser.). (Illus.). 175p. 1999. pap. 9.95 (*1-888914-49-1*) CheckerBee.

***CheckerBee Publishing Staff.** Ty Beanie Babies Spring 2000 Collector's Value Guide. 9th ed. (Illus.). 144p. 2000. pap. 9.95 (*1-888914-87-4*) CheckerBee.

— TY Beanie Babies Winter 2000 Value Guide. (Illus.). 192p. 1999. pap. 9.95 (*1-888914-62-9*) CheckerBee.

CheckerBee Publishing Staff. Ty Plush Animals 1999 Value Guide. (Illus.). 240p. 1999. pap. 14.95 (*1-888914-50-5*) CheckerBee.

***CheckerBee Publishing Staff.** Ty Plush 2000. 3rd ed. (Illus.). 160p. 2000. pap. 14.95 (*1-888914-86-6*) CheckerBee.

— V.C. Andrews: A Reader's Checklist & Reference Guide. 1999. pap. text 4.95 (*1-58598-006-4*) CheckerBee.

— Young Adult: A Reader's Checklist & Reference Guide. 1999. pap. 4.95 (*1-58598-005-6*) CheckerBee.

Checkers. 1994 Tax Savings Book: Checkers, Simon & Rosner Certified Public Accountants. 1994. pap. 6.95 (*1-878667-04-1*) H & S Media.

Checket-Hanks, B. A., ed. see Manz, Kenneth W.

Checketts, Darby. Customer Astonishment Handbook: The Total Service Commitment. (Illus.). 150p. 1998. pap. 17.50 (*0-9618170-7-0*, CAHB) Corner Pro-Dev Pr.

Checketts, Darby V. Baseball, Bouillabaisse & the Best of Class: How to Increase Your Personal Power, Energize Your Team & Astonish Your Customers. LC 91-73363. (Illus.). 287p. (Orig.). 1992. pap. 14.95 (*0-9618170-1-1*) Corner Pro-Dev Pr.

— How to Survive the Workplace Revolution: 2050. (Illus.). 40p. (Orig.). 1994. pap., student ed. 9.95 (*0-9618170-5-4*) Corner Pro-Dev Pr.

— Twenty-Nine Questions That Will Energize Your Team & Positively Astonish Your Customers. (Illus.). 40p. (Orig.). 1993. pap., student ed. 9.95 (*0-9618170-4-6*) Corner Pro-Dev Pr.

Checketts, Guiliana, jt. auth. see Freeth, Mariolina.

***Checkland, David.** Teen Pregnancy & Parenting: Social & Ethical Issues. 2000. pap. text 18.95 (*0-8020-8070-7*) U of Toronto Pr.

Checkland, O. & Lamb, M. Health Care As Social History: The Glasgow Case. (Illus.). 308p. 1982. 105.00 (*0-08-028444-2*, R130, Pergamon Pr) Elsevier.

Checkland, Olive. Isabella Bird & a Woman's Right. 256p. 1990. pap. 51.00 (*1-898218-33-1*) St Mut.

Checkland, Olive, ed. Japanese Whiskey, Scotch Blend: The Story of Masataka Taketsuru, His Scottish Wife & the Japanese Whiskey Industry. 160p. 1994. pap. 30.00 (*1-84017-003-4*) St Mut.

Checkland, Olive, et al, eds. Pacific Banking, 1859-1959: East Meets West. LC 94-27000. 1994. text 75.00 (*0-312-12386-8*) St Martin.

Checkland, Olive & Checkland, Sydney G. Industry & Ethos: Scotland, Eighteen Thirty-Two to Nineteen Fourteen. 224p. 1989. pap. 20.00 (*0-7486-0102-3*, Pub. by Edinburgh U Pr) Col U Pr.

***Checkland, Peter B.** Soft Systems Methodology in Action. LC 99-36690. 418p. 1999. pap. 45.00 (*0-471-98505-4*) Wiley.

Checkland, Peter B. Systems Thinking, Systems Practice. LC 80-41381. 344p. 1981. 151.95 (*0-471-27911-0*) Wiley.

***Checkland, Peter B.** Systems Thinking, Systems Practice: Includes a 30-Year Retrospective. LC 99-37608. 416p. 1999. pap. 39.95 (*0-471-98606-2*) Wiley.

Checkland, Peter B. & Holwell, Sue. Information, Systems & Information Systems: Making Sense of the Field. LC 97-34187. 278p. 1997. 129.95 (*0-471-95820-4*) Wiley.

Checkland, Sydney G. British Public Policy, 1776-1939: An Economic & Social Perspective. LC 82-9552. 440p. 1985. pap. text 27.95 (*0-521-27086-3*) Cambridge U Pr.

— The Elgins, 1766-1917: A Tale of Aristocrats, Proconsuls & Their Wives. (Illus.). 304p. 1988. text 50.00 (*0-08-036395-4*, Pub. by Aberdeen U Pr) Macmillan.

— Voices Across the Water: An Anglo-Canadian Boyhood. (Illus.). 154p. 1990. pap. 19.95 (*0-08-037972-9*, Pub. by Aberdeen U Pr) Macmillan.

Checkland, Sydney G., jt. auth. see Checkland, Olive.

Checkland, Sydney G., jt. auth. see Slaven, A.

Checkland, Sydney G., jt. ed. see Slaven, A.

***Checkley, Keith.** Cash Is Still King. 225p. 2000. 55.00 (*0-8144-0559-2*) AMACOM.

Checkley, Keith. Cash Is Still King. 212p. 1999. pap. 100.00 (*0-85297-505-8*, Pub. by Chartered Bank) St Mut.

***Checkley, Keith.** Cash is Still King: The Survival Guide to Cash Flow Management. 225p. 1999. 55.00 (*1-888998-77-6*) Glenlake Pub.

Checkley, Keith. Finance for Farming: A Guide for the Lending Banker. 1985. 85.00 (*0-85297-063-3*, Pub. by Chartered Bank) St Mut.

— Lending. 214p. 1999. pap. 130.00 (*0-85297-474-4*, Pub. by Chartered Bank) St Mut.

***Checkley, Keith.** Problem Loans: A Banker's Guide. 200p. 1999. pap. text 200.00 (*1-85564-748-6*, Pub. by Euromoney) Am Educ Systs.

Checkley, Keith, ed. Finance for Farming. 150p. 1990. pap. 125.00 (*0-85297-297-0*, Pub. by Chartered Bank) St Mut.

Checkley, Keith & Jury, Timothy. Advanced Credit Analysis. 1996. 250.00 (*1-85564-517-3*, Pub. by Euromoney) Am Educ Systs.

Checkley, P. Economics. 1985. 75.00 (*0-946796-02-5*) St Mut.

— Investment. 1986. 75.00 (*0-7855-1830-4*) St Mut.

— Monetary Economics. 1986. 100.00 (*0-946796-00-9*) St Mut.

Checkley, Stuart. The Management of Depression. LC 97-6410. (Illus.). 1998. 165.00 (*0-86542-987-1*) Blackwell Sci.

Checkover, V., jt. auth. see Averbakh, Yuri.

Checkoway, Allan. Disability Income Insurance. 248p. 1995. pap. 25.95 (*0-7931-1548-5*, 54260202) Dearborn.

Checkoway, B. & Patton, C. V., eds. The Metropolitan Midwest: Policy Problems & Prospects for Change. (Illus.). 320p. 1985. text 29.95 (*0-252-01114-7*) U of Ill Pr.

Checkoway, Harvey, et al. Research Methods in Occupational Epidemiology. (Monographs in Epidemiology & Biostatistics: No. 13). (Illus.). 368p. 1989. text 52.50 (*0-19-505224-2*) OUP.

Checkoway, Julie. Little Sister. 1999. pap. 9.95 (*0-14-017654-3*) Viking Penguin.

Checkoway, Julie, ed. Creating Fiction: Instructions & Insights from Teachers of the Associated Writing Programs. LC 98-54596. 304p. 1999. 18.99 (*1-884910-40-8*, 48041, Story Press) F & W Pubns Inc.

Chedd, Graham, et al, eds. The Malpractice Suit: A Survival Guide for Physicians & their Families. 123p. 1989. 295.00 incl. VHS (*0-9624044-0-3*) Eidetics.

Cheddie, Harry, jt. auth. see Gruhn, Paul.

***Chedekel, David & O'Connell, Karen.** The Blended Family Sourcebook: A Guide to Negotiating Change. 2000. pap. 16.95 (*0-7373-0387-5*, Pub. by Lowell Hse) NTC Contemp Pub Co.

***Chedgzoy, Kate.** Shakespeare, Feminism & Gender. LC 00-42066. (Contemporary Critical Essays Ser.). (YA). 2000. write for info. (*0-312-23742-1*) St Martin.

Chedgzoy, Kate, et al. Voicing Women: Gender & Sexuality in Early Modern Writing. LC 97-15999. 208p. 1998. pap. text 19.95 (*0-8207-0300-1*) Duquesne.

Chedid, Andree. L' Autre. (FRE.). 1991. pap. 10.95 (*0-7859-3280-1*, 2277227307) Fr & Eur.

— La Cite Fertile. (FRE.). 1992. pap. 10.95 (*0-7859-3289-5*, 2277233196) Fr & Eur.

— L' Enfant Multiple. (FRE.). 1991. pap. 10.95 (*0-7859-3283-6*, 2277229709) Fr & Eur.

— From Sleep Unbound. Spencer, Sharon & Knapp, Bettina L., trs. from FRE. LC 82-22459. xvi, 141p. 1983. pap. 14.95 (*0-8040-0837-X*) Swallow.

— Fugitive Suns: Selected Poems. Goodhart, Lynne & Wagner, Jon, trs. (Green Integer Bks.: No. 37). 192p. 1999. pap. 11.95 (*1-892295-25-3*, Pub. by Green Integer) SPD-Small Pr Dist.

— Les Marches de Sable. (FRE.). 1990. pap. 10.95 (*0-7859-3281-X*, 2277228869) Fr & Eur.

— The Multiple Child. Radke, Judith, tr. from FRE. 144p. (Orig.). 1995. pap. 12.95 (*1-56279-079-X*) Mercury Hse Inc.

— Nefertiti et la Reve de Akhnaton. (FRE.). 1988. pap. 12.95 (*0-7859-2994-0*) Fr & Eur.

— The Prose & Poetry of Andree Chedid: Selected Poems, Short Stories, & Essays. Linkhorn, Renee, ed. & tr. by. from FRE. LC 90-70298. (Illus.). 214p. 1990. lib. bdg. 24.95 (*0-917786-78-5*) Summa Pubns.

— The Return to Beirut. Schwartss, Ros, tr. from FRE. Orig. Title: Maison sans racines. 176p. (Orig.). 1990. pap. 10.95 (*1-85242-149-5*) Serpents Tail.

— The Show-Man. Londre, Felicia H., tr. from FRE. 120p. (Orig.). 1984. pap. text 8.95 (*0-913745-07-3*) Ubu Repertory.

— Le Sixieme Jour. (FRE.). 1989. pap. 10.95 (*0-7859-3278-X*, 2277225290) Fr & Eur.

— The Sixth Day. 176p. 1992. pap. 9.95 (*1-85242-111-8*) Serpents Tail.

— Le Sommeil Delivre. (FRE.). 1989. pap. 10.95 (*0-7859-3437-5*) Fr & Eur.

— Le Survivant. (FRE.). 1992. pap. 10.95 (*0-7859-3285-2*, 2277231711) Fr & Eur.

Chedid, L., ed. Immunostimulation. (Illus.). 236p. 1980. 36.00 (*0-387-10354-6*) Spr-Verlag.

Chedin, Alain, ed. Microwave Remote Sensing of the Earth System. LC 89-1335. (Illus.). 173p. 1989. 50.00 (*0-937194-17-4*) A Deepak Pub.

Chedin, Alain, et al, eds. High Spectral Resolution Infrared Remote Sensing for Earth's Weather & Climate Studies. LC 93-4816. (NATO ASI Series I: Global Environmental Change: Vol. 9). 1993. 262.95 (*0-387-54582-4*) Spr-Verlag.

An Asterisk (*) at the beginning of an entry indicates that the title is appearing for the first time.

Chedin, Alain, et al. High Spectral Resolution: Infrared Remote Sensing for Earth's Weather & Climate Studies. (NATO ASI Series I: Global Environmental Change: Vol. 9). (Illus.). 510p. 1993. write for info. (*3-540-54582-4*) Spr-Verlag.

Chedmail, P., et al, eds. Integrated Design & Manufacturing in Mechanical Engineering: Proceedings of the 1st IDMME Conference Held in Nantes, France, 15-17 April 1996. LC 97-30198. 545p. 1997. text 264.50 (*0-7923-4739-0*) Kluwer Academic.

Chedqzoy, Kate. Shakespeare's Queer Children: Appropriation in Contemporary Culture. 224p. 1996. text 27.95 (*0-7190-4658-0*, Pub. by Manchester Univ Pr) St Martin.

Chedzoy, Alan. A Scandalous Woman: The Story of Caroline Norton. 320p. 1995. pap. write for info. (*0-7490-0166-6*) Allison & Busby.

Chedzoy, Olaf B. & Ford, Sandra E. Programming by Case Studies: An Algol Primer. LC 76-490790. (Introductory Monographs in Mathematics). vi, 90 p. 1969. write for info. (*0-333-10146-4*) Macmillan.

Chedzoy, Sue. Physical Education: For Teachers & Coordinators & Key Stages 1 & 2. LC 96-219386. 112p. 1996. pap. 24.95 (*1-85346-410-4*, Pub. by David Fulton) Taylor & Francis.

Chedzoy, Sue, jt. auth. see Knight, Elizabeth.

Chee, Anthony N. Anatomy & Physiology: A Dynamic Approach. 4th ed. (Illus.). 344p. 1991. pap. text 33.95 (*0-89641-198-2*) American Pr.

Chee-Beng, Tan, jt. ed. see Wu, David Y.

Chee, Cheng-Khee. The Watercolor World of Cheng-Khee Chee. Tan, Sylvia, ed. & tr. by. (CHI & ENG., Illus.). viii, 200p. 1997. 65.00 (*0-9655807-0-9*) Chee Studio.

***Chee, Choung Il.** Korean Perspectives on Ocean Law Issues for the 21st Century. LC 99-50377. (Nijhoff Law Specials Ser.). 1999. 75.00 (*90-411-1301-0*) Kluwer Law Intl.

Chee, Harold W. & Harris, Rod. Global Marketing Strategy. 800p. 2000. pap. write for info. (*0-273-62348-6*) F T P H.

Chee Kai Chua & Kah Fai Leong. Rapid Prototyping: Principles & Applictions in Manufacturing. LC 96-36533. 300p. 1998. pap. 65.95 (*0-471-19004-7*) Wiley.

Chee, Siew N. Developmental Challenge in Malaysia. LC 69-10443. (Papers in International Studies: No. 3). 26p. reprint ed. pap. 30.00 (*0-608-30144-2*, 200437700051) Bks Demand.

Chee, Tham S. A Study of the Evolution of the Malay Language: Social Change & Cognitive Development. 182p. (Orig.). 1990. pap. 29.50 (*9971-69-136-1*, Pub. by Sngapore Univ Pr) Coronet Bks.

Chee, Tham S., ed. Essays on Literature & Society in Southeast Asia: Political & Sociological Perspectives. 372p. 1981. 47.50 (*9971-69-035-7*, Pub. by Sngapore Univ Pr) Coronet Bks.

Chee, Won K. Rapid-Sequence Review of Anesthesiology: With Time-Limited Pressure. LC 96-50977. 168p. 1997. pap. text 40.00 (*0-7506-9933-7*) Buttrwrth-Heinemann.

Chee, Yeon Kyung, jt. auth. see Levkoff, Sue.

***Cheek.** Mao Zedong & China's Revolutions. 2001. pap. text. write for info. (*0-312-25626-4*) St Martin.

Cheek, jt. auth. see Collins1.

Cheek, Aimee L., jt. auth. see Cheek, William.

Cheek, Bill. Scanner Modification Handbook, Vol. 2. (Illus.). 220p. (Orig.). 1991. pap. 18.95 (*0-939780-14-3*) CRB Res.

— Scanner Modification Handbook: Upgrade Your Scanner. (Illus.). 160p. (Orig.). 1990. pap. 18.95 (*0-939780-11-9*) CRB Res.

— The Ultimate Scanner: Cheek 3. LC 95-75846. (Illus.). 244p. (Orig.). 1995. pap. 29.95 (*1-56866-058-8*) Index Pub Grp.

Cheek, Cris & Jones, Sianed. Songs from Navigation. 72p. 1997. 25.00 incl. audio compact disk (*1-874400-09-1*) Reality St Edits.

Cheek, David B. Clinical Hypnotherapy: The Application of Ideometer Technicians. 2nd ed. 320p. write for info. (*0-205-18595-9*) Allyn.

— Hypnosis: The Application of Ideomotor Techniques. enl. rev. ed. LC 93-29853. 336p. 1993. 74.00 (*0-205-15595-2*, Longwood Div) Allyn.

Cheek, David B., jt. auth. see Rossi, Ernest L.

Cheek, Dennis W. Thinking Constructively about Science, Technology, & Society Education. LC 91-9607. (SUNY Series in Curriculum Issues & Inquiries). (Illus.). 262p. (C). 1992. text 21.50 (*0-7914-0939-2*) State U NY Pr.

Cheek, Donald B., ed. Human Growth: Body Composition, Cell Growth, Energy & Intelligence. LC 67-25087. (Illus.). 811p. reprint ed. 180.00 (*0-8357-9405-9*, 2014531) Bks Demand.

Cheek, Earl H., Jr., et al. Reading for Success in Elementary Schools. LC 95-83801. 512p. (C). 1996. text. write for info. (*0-697-27926-X*) Brown & Benchmark.

Cheek, Earl H., Jr., jt. auth. see Rickards, Debbie.

Cheek, G. Manufacturing Processes: Woods. 1975. 7.20 (*0-13-555656-2*); pap. text 10.16 (*0-13-555649-X*) P-H.

***Cheek, Jimmy G., et al.** Effective Oral Communication. 2nd ed. LC 99-71741. x, 330p. 2000. pap. text 42.95 (*0-8134-3166-2*) Interstate.

Cheek, John C. & Lesce, Tony. Plainclothes & Off-Duty Officer Survival: A Guide to Survival for Plainclothes Officers, Undercover Officers, & Off-Duty Police Officers. (Illus.). 202p. 1988. pap. 26.95 (*0-398-06055-X*) C C Thomas.

— Plainclothes & Off-Duty Officer Survival: A Guide to Survival for Plainclothes Officers, Undercover Officers, & Off-Duty Police Officers. (Illus.). 202p. (C). 1988. text 38.95 (*0-398-05528-9*) C C Thomas.

***Cheek, Joseph, et al.** Integrating Your Networks with Caldera Openlinux 2.3. 500p. 2000. pap. 49.99 (*0-7615-2301-4*) Prima Pub.

***Cheek, Larry & Saarinen, Eero.** Eero Saarinen: Architect, Sculptor, Visionary. LC 99-179681. 1998. pap. 1.95 (*0-931056-16-0*) Jefferson Natl.

***Cheek, Lawrence.** Fodor's Sunbelt Leisure Guide. 5th ed. (Illus.). 1999. pap. 19.95 (*0-679-00432-7*) Fodors Travel.

Cheek, Lawrence. Santa Fe. rev. ed. LC 95-2933. (Compass American Guides Ser.). (Illus.). 304p. 1995. pap. 18.95 (*1-878867-75-X*) Fodors Travel.

Cheek, Lawrence W. A. D. 1250: Ancient Peoples of the Southwest. LC 93-910480. (Illus.). 176p. 1995. 49.95 (*0-916179-45-1*) Ariz Hwy.

— Arizona. 2nd ed. Parr, Barry, ed. (Discover America Ser.). (Illus.). 268p. 1993. pap. 16.95 (*0-685-66621-2*, Compass Amrcn) Fodors Travel.

— David Muench's Arizona: Cherish the Land, Walk in Beauty. 2nd ed. LC 97-71453. (Illus.). 144p. 2000. 47.95 (*0-916179-66-4*) Ariz Hwy.

***Cheek, Lawrence W.** Nature's Extremes: Eight Seasons Shape a Southwester Land. LC 00-100903. (Illus.). 160p. 2000. 34.95 (*1-893860-08-6*) Ariz Hwy.

Cheek, Lawrence W. Photographing Arizona: Practical Techniques to Improve Your Pictures. 96p. 1992. pap. 12.95 (*0-916179-36-2*) Ariz Hwy.

***Cheek, Lawrence W.** Sedona Calling: A Guide to Red Rock Country. LC 98-87498. (Illus.). 1998. pap. 12.95 (*0-916179-81-8*) Ariz Hwy.

Cheek, Lawrence W. Utah. 4th ed. LC 97-42991. (Compass American Guides Ser.). 352p. 1998. pap. 18.95 (*0-679-00030-5*, Compass Amrcn) Fodors Travel.

Cheek, Lawrence W. Voices in the Desert: Writings & Photographs. (Wilderness Experience Ser.). (Illus.). 100p. 1995. 30.00 (*1-887656-27-8*) Tehabi Bks.

Cheek, Lawrence W., ed. Voices in the Desert: Writings & Photographs. LC 95-12539. (Wilderness Experience Ser.). (Illus.). 108p. 1995. pap. 19.95 (*0-15-600225-6*, Harvest Bks) Harcourt.

Cheek, Linda G. Ancestors & Descendants of Smiths. 400p. 1987. 32.00 (*0-89308-622-3*, BFH 29) Southern Hist Pr.

Cheek, Logan M. Zero-Base Budgeting Comes of Age: What It Is & What It Takes to Make It Work. LC 77-4362. 328p. reprint ed. pap. 101.70 (*0-608-12714-0*, 202352600033) Bks Demand.

Cheek, Logan M., jt. auth. see Austin, L. Allan.

Cheek, M., jt. auth. see Cable, S.

***Cheek, Martin.** Moon Handbooks: Silicon Valley: Including San Jose, Sunnyvale, Palo Alto & South Valley. (Illus.). 250p. 2000. pap. 15.95 (*1-56691-196-6*, Moon Handbks) Avalon Travel.

Cheek, Martin. Mosaics: Design Sourcebook. LC 97-80886. (Design Sourcebooks Ser.). (Illus.). 128p. 1998. 24.95 (*1-57076-111-6*, Trafalgar Sq Pub) Trafalgar.

— The Weekend Crafter - Mosaics: Inspirational Ideas & Practical Projects to Make in a Weekend. LC 97-28544. (Weekend Crafter Ser.). Orig. Title: Mosaics in a Weekend. 80p. 1998. pap. 14.95 (*1-57990-003-8*, Pub. by Lark Books) Random.

Cheek, Matthew. Digital UNIX System Administrator's Guide. 1998. pap. text 39.95 (*1-55558-199-4*) DEC.

Cheek, Mavis. Dog Days. large type ed. 1991. 11.50 (*0-7089-8594-7*) Ulverscroft.

Cheek-Milby, Kathleen. A Legislature Comes of Age: Hong Kong's Search for Influence & Indentity. 334p. 1995. text 55.00 (*0-19-585955-3*) OUP.

Cheek, Pauline B. Appalachian Scrapbook: An A-B-C of Growing up in the Mountains. (Illus.). 166p. (J). (gr. 1-8). 1995. reprint ed. pap. 14.95 (*1-57072-018-5*) Overmountain Pr.

Cheek, Philip. History of the Sauk County Riflemen. 240p. 1985. reprint ed. 26.50 (*0-942211-42-1*) Olde Soldier Bks.

***Cheek, Richard.** Land of the Commonwealth: A Portrait of the Conserved Landscapes of Massachusetts. (Illus.). 2000. 40.00 (*1-55849-265-8*) U of Mass Pr.

Cheek, Richard, et al, photos by. The Chapel: Duke University. (Illus.). 96p. 1986. 30.00 (*0-917585-01-1*) Gothic.

Cheek, Robert. Florida Communications Guide. 420p. 1995. pap. 29.95 (*0-939430-17-7*) Scanner Master.

Cheek, Roland. Dance on the Wild Side. Elman, Robert, ed. LC 98-91129. (Illus.). 352p. 1999. pap. 19.95 (*0-918981-05-0*) Skyline Pub.

— Learning to Talk Bear: So Bears Can Listen. LC 96-71778. (Illus.). 304p. (Orig.). 1997. pap. 19.95 (*0-918981-02-6*) Skyline Pub.

— Montana's Bob Marshall Wilderness. (Illus.). 80p. 1982. 15.95 (*0-918981-00-X*); pap. 10.95 (*0-918981-01-8*) Skyline Pub.

***Cheek, Roland.** My Best Work Is Done at the Office. Elman, Robert, ed. Donavan, Laura, tr. LC 99-76467. 320p. 2000. pap. 19.95 (*0-918981-06-9*) Skyline Pub.

Cheek, Roland. Phantom Ghost of Harriet Lou: And Other Elk Stories. Elman, Robert, ed. Donavan, Laura, tr. LC 98-201551. (Illus.). 352p. 1998. pap. 19.95 (*0-918981-04-2*) Skyline Pub.

Cheek, Timothy. Propaganda & Culture in Mao's China: Deng Tuo & the Intelligentsia. LC 97-7811. (Studies on Conemporary China). (Illus.). 406p. 1998. text 85.00 (*0-19-829066-7*) OUP.

Cheek, Timothy & Saich, Tony, eds. New Perspectives on State Socialism in China. LC 97-5272. 422p. (C). (gr. 13). 1997. text 74.95 (*0-7656-0041-2*, East Gate Bk) M E Sharpe.

— New Perspectives on State Socialism in China. LC 97-5272. (Illus.). 422p. (C). 1997. pap. text 27.95 (*0-7656-0042-0*, East Gate Bk) M E Sharpe.

Cheek, Timothy, jt. ed. see Hamrin, Carol L.

Cheek, Timothy, jt. ed. see Lindau, Juan D.

Cheek, Timothy, ed. see Qing, Dai.

Cheek, Timothy, ed. see Zhongmei, Yang.

Cheek, William & Cheek, Aimee L. John Mercer Langston & the Fight for Black Freedom, 1829-1865. (Blacks in the New World Ser.). 502p. 1996. pap. text 21.95 (*0-252-06591-3*) U of Ill Pr.

Cheek, William R. Atlas of Pediatric Neurosurgery. Zorab, Richard, ed. 192p. 1996. text 165.00 (*0-7216-5138-0*, W B Saunders Co) Harcrt Hlth Sci Grp.

Cheeke, Peter R. Applied Animal Nutrition: Feeds & Feeding. 2nd ed. LC 98-18894. 525p. (C). 1998. 100.00 (*0-13-779331-6*) P-H.

— Contemporary Issues in Animal Agriculture. 2nd ed. LC 98-71815. Orig. Title: Impacts of Lifestock Production. 256p. 1998. pap. 49.95 (*0-8134-3150-6*, 3150) Interstate.

— Natural Toxicants in Feeds, Forages, & Poisonous Plants. LC 97-937. 496p. 1997. pap. 58.75 (*0-8134-3128-X*) Interstate.

— Rabbit Feeding & Nutrition. (Animal Feeding & Nutrition Ser.). 376p. 1987. text 94.00 (*0-12-170605-2*) Acad Pr.

— Toxicants of Plant Origin, 4 Vols. 288p. 1989. lib. bdg. 239.00 (*0-8493-6991-6*, SF757) CRC Pr.

— Toxicants of Plant Origin, 4 Vols., Vol. I. 336p. 1989. lib. bdg. 249.00 (*0-8493-6990-8*, SF757) CRC Pr.

— Toxicants of Plant Origin, 4 Vols., Vol. III. 288p. 1989. lib. bdg. 229.00 (*0-8493-6992-4*) CRC Pr.

— Toxicants of Plant Origin, 4 Vols., Vol. IV. 240p. 1989. lib. bdg. 210.00 (*0-8493-6993-2*, SF757) CRC Pr.

Cheeks, Rudy. How to Be a Rhode Island Politician. (Illus.). 128p. Date not set. pap. 10.95 (*1-58066-005-3*, Covered Brdge Pr) Douglas Charles Ltd.

Cheely, W. W., jt. auth. see Rabun, H. P.

Cheema, G. Shabbir. Urban Shelter & Services: Public Policies & Management Approaches. LC 87-6982. 230p. 1987. 59.95 (*0-275-92653-2*, C2653, Praeger Pubs) Greenwood.

Cheema, G. Shabbir, ed. Corruption & Good Governance. 138p. (C). 1999. reprint ed. pap. text 30.00 (*0-7881-7405-3*) DIANE Pub.

— Urban Management: Policies & Innovations in Developing Countries. LC 92-18365. 352p. 1993. 69.50 (*0-275-94085-3*, C4085, Praeger Pubs) Greenwood.

Cheema, G. Shabbir & Rondinelli, Dennis A., eds. Decentralization & Development: Policy Implementation in Developing Countries. LC 83-3051. 319p. 1983. reprint ed. pap. 98.90 (*0-608-01539-3*, 205958300002) Bks Demand.

Cheema, G. Shabbir, jt. auth. see Bamberger, Michael.

Cheen, Bruce B. & Fratrik, Mark R. Fair Market Value of Radio Stations: A Buyer's Guide. 2nd ed. 204p. 1990. 100.00 (*0-89324-081-8*) Natl Assn Broadcasters.

Cheeney, R. F. Statistical Methods in Geology: For Field & Lab Decisions. (Illus.). 192p. 1983. pap. text 24.95 (*0-04-550030-4*) Routledge.

Cheepen, Christine. The Predictability of Informal Conversation. 224p. 1992. 49.00 (*0-86187-707-1*) St Martin.

Cheepen, Christine & Monaghan, James. English Speech: A Practical Guide. 224p. 1990. text 49.00 (*0-86187-753-5*, Pub. by P P Pubs) Cassell & Continuum.

— Spoken English: A Practical Guide. 224p. 1992. pap. text 14.95 (*0-86187-754-3*, Pub. by P P Pubs) Cassell & Continuum.

— Spoken English: A Practical Guide. 240p. 1990. text 49.00 (*0-685-61124-8*) St Martin.

Cheer, A. Y. & Van Dam, C. P., eds. Fluid Dynamics in Biology: (Proceedings of an AMS-IMS-SIAM 1991 Joint Research Conference Held July 6-12, 1991 at the University of Washington, Seattle with Support from the National Science Foundation & NASA Headquarters) LC 92-26926. (Contemporary Mathematics Ser.: Vol. 141). 586p. 1993. pap. 73.00 (*0-8218-5148-9*, CONM/141) Am Math.

Cheers, Brian. Welfare Bushed. LC 98-72806. 7p. 1998. text 67.95 (*1-84014-535-8*, Pub. by Ashgate Pub) Ashgate Pub Co.

***Cheesbrough, Monica.** District Laboratory Practice in Tropical Countries. (Illus.). 460p. (C). 1999. pap. 64.95 (*0-521-66547-7*) Cambridge U Pr.

Cheese, A. Parallel Execution of Parlog. Goos, G. & Hartmanis, J., eds. LC 92-16603. (Lecture Notes in Computer Science Ser.: Vol. 586). x, 184p. 1992. 36.95 (*0-387-55382-7*) Spr-Verlag.

Cheese, Bernard, jt. illus. see Harris, Frank.

Cheese Factory Restaurant Chiefs Staff. Vegetarian International Cuisine: An Essential Cookbook. LC 97-13995. (Illus.). 212p. 1997. pap. 16.95 (*0-9655965-1-6*) Palmer Pubns Inc.

Cheesebrough, Dean L., jt. auth. see Fredericks, Anthony D.

Cheeseman, jt. auth. see Garvey.

Cheeseman, Chris, jt. auth. see Neal, Ernest G.

Cheeseman, Graeme & Bruce, Robert, eds. Discourses of Danger & Dread Frontiers: Australian Defense & Security Thinking after the Cold War. 317p. 1997. pap. 24.95 (*1-86373-975-0*, Pub. by Allen & Unwin Pty) Paul & Co Pubs.

***Cheeseman, Harry.** Business Law: Ethical, International & E-Commerce Environment. 4th ed. 1232p. 2000. 102.67 (*0-13-087913-4*, Prentice Hall) P-H.

Cheeseman, Henry R. Business Law: The Legal, Ethical & International Environment. 2nd ed. LC 94-29244. 1328p. 1994. text 105.00 (*0-13-309758-7*) P-H.

— Business Law: The Legal, Ethical, & International Environment. 3rd ed. LC 97-16598. 991p. 1997. 105.00 (*0-13-597972-2*) P-H.

— Contemporary Business Law. 2nd ed. LC 96-25783. 1996. text 87.00 (*0-13-532078-X*) P-H.

***Cheeseman, Henry R.** Contemporary Business Law. 3rd ed. LC 99-12571. 1010p. 1999. text 100.00 incl. cd-rom, audio compact disk (*0-13-084051-3*) P-H.

Cheeseman, Henry R. Essentials of Contemporary Business Law. LC 98-21985. 865p. 1998. pap. text 73.00 incl. audio compact disk (*0-13-080400-2*) P-H.

— International Business. (GN - International Business Ser.). 2002. mass mkt. 55.95 (*0-538-86093-6*) S-W Pub.

— International Business Law. (LA - Business Law Ser.). 2002. mass mkt. 62.95 (*0-538-86092-8*) S-W Pub.

***Cheeseman, Henry R.** Legal & Regulatory Environment: Contemporary Perspectives in Business. 2nd ed. LC 99-24455. (Illus.). 692p. 1999. text 94.00 incl. cd-rom, audio compact disk (*0-13-012954-2*) P-H.

***Cheeseman, John.** Saying Grace. 136p. 2000. pap. 7.99 (*0-85151-772-2*) Banner of Truth.

Cheeseman, K. H., jt. ed. see Slater, T. F.

Cheeseman, Lawrence, jt. auth. see Bielefield, Arlene.

Cheeseman, Lawrence, jt. auth. see Bielefield, Arlene C.

Cheeseman, Linda. Educational Crossword Puzzles in Health. 60p. (YA). (gr. 9-12). 1990. pap. text 4.90 (*0-921369-06-9*) J C George Ent.

Cheeseman, P. & Oldford, R. W., eds. Selecting Models from Data: AI & Statistics IV. (Lecture Notes in Statistics Ser.: Vol. 89). xvii, 485p. 1994. 65.95 (*0-387-94281-5*) Spr-Verlag.

Cheeseright, Paul & Oktemgil, Mehmet. Doing Business with Turkey. 1999. pap. text 65.00 (*0-7494-2954-2*, Pub. by Kogan Page Ltd) LPC InBook.

***Cheesley, David.** Bristol Transport. (Transport Ser.). 1999. pap. 18.99 (*0-7524-1083-0*) Arcadia Publng.

Cheesman, jt. auth. see Palmer.

***Cheesman, Clive & Williams, Jonathan T.** Rebels, Pretenders && Imposters. LC 00-40437. 2000. write for info. (*0-312-23866-5*) St Martin.

Cheesman, David. Landlord Power & Rural Indebtedness in Colonial Sind. (SOAS London Studies on South Asia: No. 11). 288p. (C). 1996. text 48.00 (*0-7007-0470-1*, Pub. by Curzon Pr Ltd) UH Pr.

Cheesman, G. L. Auxilia of the Roman Imperial Army. 190p. 1975. pap. 15.00 (*0-89005-096-1*) Ares.

Cheesman, Les. Dial Survey of Company Car Schemes 1995-96. Molloy, Ciaran, ed. 160p. 1995. pap. 210.00 (*1-86012-028-8*, Pub. by Tolley Pubng) St Mut.

Cheesman, Millie Foster. Pioneer Recipes & Remedies: Enriched with Poetry : A Sesquicentennial Collection. LC 98-222646. xxiv, 402 p. 1997. write for info. (*0-9658406-0-3*) Daughters Utah.

Cheesman, Paul R. Ancient American Indians: Their Origins, Civilizations & Old World Connections. 288p. 1991. 18.98 (*0-88290-416-7*) Horizon Utah.

— Ancient Writing on Metal Plates: Archaeological Findings Support Mormon Claims. LC 85-80542. 93p. 1985. 11.98 (*0-88290-303-9*, 1002) Horizon Utah.

Cheesman, Paul R., ed. The Book of Mormon: The Keystone Scripture. (Symposium Ser.: Vol. 1). 1988. 10.95 (*0-88494-637-1*) Bookcraft Inc.

— Scriptures for the Modern World. (Monograph Ser.: Vol. 11). 1984. 7.95 (*0-88494-538-3*) Bookcraft Inc.

Cheesman, Peter, jt. auth. see Carter, Frank.

Cheesman, R. E. Lake Tana & the Blue Nile: Abyssinian Quest. (Illus.). 400p. 1967. reprint ed. 47.50 (*0-7146-1641-9*, BHA-01641, Pub. by F Cass Pubs) Intl Spec Bk.

Cheesman, Tom. The Shocking Ballad Picture Show: German Popular Literature & Cultural History. LC 94-10059. 256p. 1994. 46.00 (*0-85496-893-8*) Berg Pubs.

Cheesman, Tom & Rieuwerts, Sigrid, eds. Ballads into Books: The Legacies of Francis James Child. 2nd rev. ed. LC 99-171073. 283p. 1998. pap. 53.95 (*0-8204-4218-6*) P Lang Pubng.

— Ballads into Books: The Legacies of Francis James Child: Selected Papers from the 26th International Ballad Conference (SIEF Ballad Commission), Swansea, Wales, 19-24 July, 1996. LC 97-21870. 283p. 1997. 60.95 (*0-8204-3404-3*, Pub. by P Lang) P Lang Pubng.

— Ballads into Books: The Legacies of Francis James Child, Selected Papers from the 26th International Ballad Conference (SIEF Ballad Commission), Swansea, Wales, 19-24 July 1996. LC 97-21870. 283p. 1997. 60.95 (*3-906757-34-X*, Pub. by P Lang) P Lang Pubng.

Cheetham, A. K. & Day, Peter. Solid-State Chemistry: Techniques. (Illus.). 416p. 1990. pap. text 50.00 (*0-19-855286-6*) OUP.

Cheetham, A. K. & Day, Peter, eds. Solid State Chemistry Vol. 2: Compounds. (Illus.). 318p. 1992. text 95.00 (*0-19-855166-5*) OUP.

Cheetham, Alan H. Late Eocene Zoogeography of the Eastern Gulf Coast Region. LC 63-23109. (Geological Society of America, Memoir Ser.: No. 91). 129p. reprint ed. pap. 40.00 (*0-608-15639-6*, 203179500077) Bks Demand.

Cheetham, Anthony. The Life & Times of Richard III. Fraser, Antonia, ed. (Kings & Queens of England Ser.). (Illus.). 224p. 1992. 24.95 (*1-55859-447-7*) Abbeville Pr.

— Richard III. (Illus.). 224p. 1998. pap. 18.95 (*1-56649-038-3*) Welcome Rain.

Cheetham, D. W., compiled by. Dealing with Vandalism: A Guide to the Control of Vandalism. 226p. 1994. 15.00 (*0-7277-1977-7*) Am Soc Civil Eng.

Cheetham, Eric. Fundamentals of Mainstream Buddhism. (Tuttle Library of Enlightenment). 224p. (Orig.). 1994. pap. 16.95 (*0-8048-3008-8*) Tuttle Pubng.

Cheetham, Erika, ed. The Final Prophecies of Nostradamus. 448p. (Orig.). 1989. pap. 12.95 (*0-399-51516-X*, Perigee Bks) Berkley Pub.

Cheetham, Erika, jt. auth. see Nostradamus.

***Cheetham, J. Keith.** On the Trail of Mary Queen of Scots. (On the Trail of... Ser.). (Illus.). 224p. 1999. pap. 14.95 (*0-946487-50-2*, Pub. by Luath Pr Ltd) Midpt Trade.

— On the Trail of the Pilgrim Fathers. 192p. 2000. pap. 14.95 (*0-946487-83-9*, Pub. by Luath Pr Ltd) Midpt Trade.

C

Cheetham, Janet H., ed. Immigration Practice & Procedure under the North American Free Trade Agreement. LC 95-142429. 275p. 1995. 57.00 (*1-878677-82-9*, 54.70) Amer Immi Law Assn.

Cheetham, John. The Life of Thomas Paine. LC 89-10446. 368p. 1989. 50.00 (*0-8201-1439-1*) Schol Facsimiles.

Cheetham, Juliet, ed. Social Work & Ethnicity. 1982. 45.00 (*0-7855-0578-4*, Pub. by Natl Inst Soc Work) St Mut.

Cheetham, Juliet & Kazi, Mansoor, eds. The Working of Social Work. LC 98-150930. 200p. 1997. pap. 26.95 (*1-85302-498-8*, Pub. by Jessica Kingsley) Taylor & Francis.

Cheetham, Juliet, et al. Evaluating Social Work Effectiveness. 192p. 1992. pap. 35.95 (*0-335-19005-7*) OpUniv Pr.

Cheetham, Mark. Alex Colville: The Observer Observed. (Illus.). 160p. 1994. pap. 9.95 (*1-55022-206-6*, Pub. by ECW) LPC InBook.

Cheetham, Mark A. Alex Colville: The Observer Observed. large type ed. (Illus.). 185p. 1995. pap. 15.95 (*1-55022-240-6*, Pub. by ECW) Genl Dist Srvs.

— The Rhetoric of Purity: Essentialist Theory & the Advent of Abstract Painting. (Cambridge Studies in New Art History & Criticism). (Illus.). 216p. (C). 1994. pap. text 19.95 (*0-521-47759-X*) Cambridge U Pr.

Cheetham, Mark A., et al, eds. The Subjects of Art History. LC 97-38628. (Illus.). 336p. (C). 1998. 75.00 (*0-521-45490-5*); pap. text 22.95 (*0-521-45572-3*) Cambridge U Pr.

Cheetham, Mark A. & Hutcheon, Linda. Remembering Postmodernism: Trends in Recent Canadian Art. (Illus.). 160p. 1991. pap. text 26.00 (*0-19-540817-9*) OUP.

Cheetham, Nicolas. Mediaeval Greece. LC 80-13559. 351p. reprint ed. pap. 108.90 (*0-7837-2500-0*, 208021000003) Bks Demand.

Cheetham, Paul, ed. see Austen, Jane.

Cheetham, Paul, ed. see Shakespeare, William.

Cheetham, Tom, jt. auth. see Hewitt, Christopher.

Cheever, et al. School Administrator's Guide to Computers in Education. 1985. pap. text. write for info. (*0-318-59749-7*) Addison-Wesley.

***Cheever, Benjamin.** Famous after Death. 224p. 2000. pap. 13.95 (*1-58234-087-0*) Bloomsbury Pubg.

Cheever, Benjamin. Famous after Death. LC 98-29645. 256p. 1999. 23.00 (*0-609-60005-2*, Crown) Crown Pub Group.

***Cheever, Benjamin.** Famous after Death. large type ed. LC 99-46309. 1999. 26.95 (*0-7862-2254-9*) Thorndike Pr.

Cheever, Benjamin. The Partisan. large type ed. LC 94-14546. (Americana: the Making of the Cities Ser.). 445p. 1994. lib. bdg. 21.95 (*0-7862-0253-X*) Thorndike Pr.

Cheever, David. Daytrips Hawaii: 50 One-Day Adventures by Car, Boat, Bus & Plane. (Illus.). 288p. 1999. pap. 16.95 (*0-8038-9401-5*, Pub. by Hastings) Midpt Trade.

— Daytrips San Francisco & Northern California: 50 One Day & Overnight Adventures. (Daytrips Ser.). 352p. 1999. pap. 16.95 (*0-8038-9441-4*, Pub. by Hastings) Midpt Trade.

Cheever, George B. The American Common-Place Book of Poetry. LC 74-15734. (Popular Culture in America Ser.). 406p. 1975. reprint ed. 35.95 (*0-405-06369-5*) Ayer.

— God Against Slavery. LC 76-78995. (Black Heritage Library Collection). 1977. 28.95 (*0-8369-8537-0*) Ayer.

— God Against Slavery & the Freedom & Duty of the Pulpit to Rebuke It, As a Sin Against God. LC 79-82182. (Anti-Slavery Crusade in America Ser.). 1970. reprint ed. 28.95 (*0-405-00621-7*) Ayer.

— Punishment by Death: Its Authority & Expediency. (Capital Punishment Ser.). reprint ed. 37.50 (*0-404-62409-X*) AMS Pr.

Cheever, Henry T. The Whale & Its Captors: or The Whaleman's Adventures. enl. ed. 315p. 1991. 24.95 (*0-87770-487-2*) Ye Galleon.

Cheever, John. The Best of John Cheever. 1999. pap. write for info. (*0-671-03291-7*) S&S Trade.

— Bullet Park. LC 91-55304. (Vintage International Ser.). 256p. 1992. pap. 13.00 (*0-679-73787-1*) Vin Bks.

— Bullet Park. large type ed. LC 93-35696. 1993. lib. bdg. 21.95 (*0-7862-0082-0*) Thorndike Pr.

— Falconer. LC 91-55303. (Vintage International Ser.). 224p. 1992. pap. 12.00 (*0-679-73786-3*) Vin Bks.

— The Journals of John Cheever. LC 91-52728. 399p. 1991. 25.00 (*0-394-57274-2*) Knopf.

***Cheever, John.** Listening for God. (Listening for God Ser.). 2000. pap. 11.99 (*0-8066-3962-8*) Augsburg Fortress.

— Listening for God: Leader Edition. (Listening for God Ser.). 2000. pap. 3.99 (*0-8066-3963-6*) Augsburg Fortress.

Cheever, John. Oh, What a Paradise It Seems. LC 91-55305. (Vintage International Ser.). 112p. 1992. pap. 10.00 (*0-679-73785-5*) Vin Bks.

— Some People, Places & Things That Will Not Appear in My Next Novel. LC 79-116947. (Short Story Index Reprint Ser.). 1977. 18.95 (*0-8369-3449-0*) Ayer.

— The Stories of John Cheever. 704p. 1985. mass mkt. 7.99 (*0-345-33567-8*) Ballantine Pub Grp.

— The Stories of John Cheever. LC 78-106. 1978. 40.00 (*0-394-50087-3*) Knopf.

***Cheever, John.** The Stories of John Cheever. (International Rediscovery Ser.). 704p. 2000. pap. 16.00 (*0-375-72442-7*) Vin Bks.

Cheever, John. Thirteen Uncollected Stories. Dennis, Franklin, ed. 240p. 1994. 19.95 (*0-89733-405-1*) Academy Chi Pubs.

***Cheever, John.** The Wapshot Chronicle. LC 98-48264. 1999. 26.95 (*0-7838-8488-5*) Macmillan Gen Ref.

Cheever, John. The Wapshot Chronicle. LC 91-58072. 1992. pap. 13.00 (*0-679-73899-1*) Random.

— The Wapshot Scandal. LC 91-58073. 1992. pap. 14.00 (*0-679-73900-9*) Vin Bks.

— The Way Some People Live. 1994. lib. bdg. 24.95 (*1-56849-389-4*) Buccaneer Bks.

Cheever, Kay. Up a Tree. (Illus.). 55p. (Orig.). 1995. pap. write for info. (*1-57579-005-X*) Pine Hill Pr.

Cheever, Mary. The Changing Landscape: A History of Briarcliff Manor - Scarborough. LC 90-45613. (Illus.). 256p. 1990. 35.00 (*0-914659-49-9*) Phoenix Pub.

Cheever, Raymond C., ed. Accent on Living Reprint Series, No. 1. 26p. 1975. pap. text 1.95 (*0-915708-01-9*) Cheever Pub.

Cheever, Raymond C. & Elmer, Charles D., eds. Bowel Management: A Manual of Ideas & Techniques. 32p. 1975. pap. 3.50 (*0-915708-02-7*, #1420) Cheever Pub.

Cheever, Raymond C. & Garee, Betty, eds. An Accessible Home of Your Own. LC 90-80563. (Illus.). 52p. 1990. reprint ed. pap. 5.95 (*0-915708-29-9*) Cheever Pub.

— A Place to Live. LC 90-80564. (Illus.). 64p. (Orig.). 1990. pap. 4.95 (*0-915708-30-2*) Cheever Pub.

Cheever, Raymond C., jt. auth. see Garee, Betty.

Cheever, Raymond C., ed. see Gregory, Martha F.

Cheever, Susan. Home Before Dark: A Biographical Memoir of John Cheever by His Daughter. 244p. 1999. per. 14.00 (*0-671-02850-2*) S&S Trade.

— Note Found in a Bottle: My Life as a Drinker. 208p. 2000. per. 12.95 (*0-671-04073-1*, WSP) PB.

— Note Found in a Bottle: My Life as a Drinker. LC 98-26463. 192p. 1999. 22.50 (*0-684-80432-8*) S&S Trade.

— Treetops: A Family Memoir. 244p. 1999. pap. 14.00 (*0-671-02851-0*) S&S Trade.

Chef, R., ed. Real Time Ultrasound in Perinatal Medicine. (Contributions to Gynecology & Obstetrics Ser.: Vol. 6). (Illus.). 1979. pap. 68.75 (*3-8055-2976-7*) S Karger.

Chefdor, Monique, et al, eds. Modernism: Challenges & Perspectives. LC 84-21932. (Illus.). 360p. 1986. text 29.95 (*0-252-01207-0*) U of Ill Pr.

Chefdor, Monique, ed. & tr. see Cendrars, Blaise.

Chefetz, Paul K., jt. ed. see Namazi, Kevan H.

Chefetz, Sheila. Antiques for the Table: A Complete Guide to Dining Room Accessories for Collecting & Entertaining. LC 92-50728. (Illus.). 240p. 1993. 37.95 (*0-670-84057-2*, Viking Studio) Studio Bks.

— Modern Antiques for the Table: A Guide to Tabletop Accessories, 1890-1940. LC 98-216542. (Illus.). 240p. 1998. 39.95 (*0-670-87515-5*) Viking Penguin.

***Cheff, Adelle.** A Help to Each Other: Memories. (Illus.). 124p. 1999. pap. 12.95 (*0-912299-81-9*) Stoneydale Pr Pub.

Cheff, Bud. Indian Trails & Grizzly Tales. 1994. pap. text 14.95 (*0-912299-54-1*) Stoneydale Pr Pub.

Cheff, Bud, Sr. Indian Trails & Grizzly Tales. (Illus.). 232p. 1993. 19.95 (*0-912299-53-3*) Stoneydale Pr Pub.

— The Woodsman & His Hatchet: Eighty Years on Back Country Survival. 1996. pap. 12.95 (*0-912299-62-2*) Stoneydale Pr Pub.

Cheffers, John, ed. see Sullivan, Eileen.

Cheffins, Brian R. Company Law: Theory, Structure & Operation. 778p. 1997. text 95.00 (*0-19-825973-5*) OUP.

Cheffins, Brian R. Company Law: Theory, Structure & Operation. 778p. 1997. pap. text 49.00 (*0-19-876469-3*) OUP.

***Cheffins, Richard.** Parliamentary Constituencies & Their Registers since 1832. 247p. 1998. pap. 62.00 (*0-7123-0844-X*) L Erlbaum Assocs.

Cheffo, Joseph. He Came on a Horse. LC 97-180170. 48p. 1997. pap. write for info. (*1-57579-059-9*) Pine Hill Pr.

Chef's of Enola Prudhomme's Cajun Cafe & Staff. Enola Prudhomme's Cajun Cafe: Enola Prudhomme & Staff. Goldsworthy, Sharon et al, eds. (Illus.). 1997. 17.95 (*0-9658651-0-X*) Chef Enola Prudhomme.

***Chegwidden, R. W., ed.** The Carbonic Anhydrases: New Horizons. (Experientia Supplementa Ser.: Vol. 90). (Illus.). 350p. 2000. 155.00 (*3-7643-5670-7*, Pub. by Birkhauser) Spr-Verlag.

Chehabi, H. E. Iranian Politics & Religious Modernism: The Liberation Movement of Iran under the Shah & Khomeini. LC 89-46180. (Illus.). 358p. reprint ed. pap. 111.00 (*0-608-08083-7*, 206904200002) Bks Demand.

Chehabi, H. E., ed. Politics, Society & Democracy: Juan J. Linz - Untranslated Writings & Complete Annotated Bibliography, Vol. 2. (C). 2000. pap. 44.00 (*0-8133-8547-4*) Westview.

Chehabi, H. E. & Linz, Juan J., eds. Sultanistic Regimes. LC 97-41153. 264p. 1998. text 48.00 (*0-8018-5693-0*); pap. text 16.95 (*0-8018-5694-9*) Johns Hopkins.

Chehak, Gail, jt. auth. see Halliday, Jan.

Chehak, Susan T. Smithereens. 1996. pap. 10.00 (*0-614-97794-0*, WSP) PB.

— Smithereens: A Novel. 320p. 1996. pap. 10.00 (*0-671-56779-9*) S&S Trade.

Chehrazi, Shahla S., ed. Psychosocial Issues in Day Care. LC 90-561. 292p. 1990. text 14.95 (*0-88048-310-5*, 8310) Am Psychiatric.

Cheich, Jhoong S., ed. Hypertension in Kidney Disease. (Developments in Nephrology Ser.). 1986. text 218.00 (*0-89838-797-3*) Kluwer Academic.

Cheich, Jhoong S., et al. Manual of Clinical Nephrology. Stenzel, Kurt H. & Rubin, Albert L., eds. 470p. 1981. text 180.50 (*90-247-2397-3*) Kluwer Academic.

Cheifetz, Nance. A Sense of Delight: Living Ordinary Life in an Extraordinary Way. LC 99-165732. (Illus.). 216p. 1998. pap. 15.00 (*0-9662896-3-3*) Ruby Shoes.

Cheilik, Michael. Ancient History: From Its Beginnings to the Fall of Rome. LC 90-56012. (HarperCollins College Outline Ser.). (Illus.). 256p. (Orig.). 1991. pap. 15.00 (*0-06-467119-4*, Harper Ref) HarpC.

Cheim, John & Rowley, Alexandra, eds. Paul Strand: Rebecca. (Illus.). 48p. (Orig.). 1996. pap. 35.00 (*0-944680-48-8*) R Miller Gal.

Cheim, John, ed. see Geldzahler, Henry.

Cheim, John, ed. see Greene, Robert & Saltz, Jerry.

Cheim, John, ed. see Kozloff, Max.

Cheim, John, ed. see Krasner, Lee & Howard, Richard.

Chein, Edmund. Control the Aging Process Through Age Reversal. Harding, Trina & Angelastro, Lynda, eds. LC 97-68535. 208p. 1997. pap. 20.00 (*0-9662442-0-6*, WorldLink) WorldLink Med.

Chein, Libby. My Parsha Bereishis Learn & Play Book, Vol. I. (Illus.). 150p. (Orig.). (J). pap., student ed. 9.95 (*1-884535-93-3*) Empire Press.

Chein, Michel, jt. ed. see Mugnier, Marie-Laure.

Chein, Orin. Moufang Loops of Small Order. LC 77-25155. (Memoirs Ser.: No. 13/197). 131p. 1978. pap. 22.00 (*0-8218-2197-0*, MEMO/13/197) Am Math.

Chein, S., et al, eds. Clinical Hemorheology. 1987. lib. bdg. 184.00 (*0-89838-807-4*) Kluwer Academic.

Cheiro. Cheiro's Language of the Hand. 202p. 1998. reprint ed. pap. 18.50 (*0-7873-0167-1*) Hlth Research.

— Cheiro's Language of the Hand (1897) 226p. 1996. reprint ed. pap. 17.50 (*1-56459-849-7*) Kessinger Pub.

— Cheiro's World Predictions. 240p. 1981. pap. 22.00 (*0-89540-088-X*, SB-088) Sun Pub.

— Language of the Hand Palmistry. 1999. 7.99 (*0-517-18930-5*) Random Hse Value.

— When Were You Born? 122p. 1996. pap. 10.00 (*0-89540-233-5*, SB-233, Sun Bks) Sun Pub.

Cheisura, Giorgio. Light Without Motion. 1989. pap. 15.00 (*0-937669-33-4*) Owl Creek Pr.

Cheisura, Giorgio. Light Without Motion. 1989. 22.00 (*0-937669-34-2*) Owl Creek Pr.

Cheit, Ross E. Setting Safety Standards: Regulation in the Public & Private Sectors. LC 89-20339. (Illus.). 320p. 1990. 50.00 (*0-520-06733-9*, Pub. by U CA Pr) Cal Prin Full Svc.

Cheitlin, Melvin D. Clinical Cardiology. 7th ed. (C). 1999. pap. text 43.95 (*0-8385-1385-9*) Appleton & Lange.

Cheitlin, Melvin D. & Sokolow, Maurice. Clinical Cardiology. 6th ed. 741p. (C). 1996. pap. text 54.95 (*0-8385-1093-0*, A1093-2, Apple Lange Med) McGraw.

***Chejnacki, Stanislas.** Churches of Lake Tana Architecture & Religious Painting in Ethiopia. 2000. 60.00 (*88-8118-529-6*) Skira IT.

Chejne, Anwar G. Ibn Hazm. 340p. 1996. 29.50 (*0-614-21708-3*, 477); pap. 15.95 (*0-614-21707-5*, 477) Kazi Pubns.

— Muslim Spain, Its History & Culture. LC 73-87254. (Illus.). 587p. reprint ed. pap. 182.00 (*0-608-15949-2*, 203321200084) Bks Demand.

Chek, ed. Automotive Steering, Suspension & Wheel Alignment. 2nd ed. (C). 1997. text. write for info. (*0-673-98104-5*) Addison-Wesley.

— Engine Repair & Rebuilding. 3rd ed. (C). 1997. text. write for info. (*0-673-98101-0*) Addison-Wesley.

Chek-Chart Staff. Advanced Engine Performance Specialist Test Level 1. 160p. 1998. pap. 29.95 (*0-02-862658-3*) Macmillan.

— Auto Mechanics Refresher Course. (C). student ed. 42.00 (*0-88098-078-8*, H M Gousha) Prntice Hall Bks.

— Automatic Transmission, 2 vols. 2nd ed. (C). 1989. student ed. 53.00 (*0-06-454012-X*, H M Gousha) Prntice Hall Bks.

— Automotive Brake System. 2nd ed. (C). 1996. pap. text, teacher ed. 9.00 (*0-06-500762-X*) Addison-Wesley Educ.

— Automotive Preview, 1985. (Illus.). 16p. (C). 1984. pap. text 2.25 (*0-88098-025-7*, H M Gousha) Prntice Hall Bks.

— Brakes: For ASE Test A5. (Chek-Chart's ASE Study Guides Ser.). 96p. 1998. pap. 19.95 (*0-02-862663-X*) Macmillan.

— Car & Light Truck Diesel Engine Service Manual. (Automotive Service Ser.). 128p. 1983. pap. text 9.95 (*0-88098-016-8*, H M Gousha); 3.50 (*0-88098-046-X*, H M Gousha) Prntice Hall Bks.

— Car Care Guide, 1985. Fennema, Roger L., ed. (Illus.). 432p. 1985. pap., student ed. 39.75 (*0-88098-058-3*, H M Gousha) Prntice Hall Bks.

— Car Service Manual. rev. ed. Fenneman, Roger L. & Phelps, Jennifer, eds. (Apprentice Mechanics Ser.). (Illus.). 144p. 1984. pap., student ed. 9.15 (*0-88098-051-6*, H M Gousha); student ed. 3.45 (*0-317-18170-X*, H M Gousha) Prntice Hall Bks.

***Chek-Chart Staff.** CHEK-CHART ASE Study Guide A1 for Engine Repair. 104p. 1998. pap. text 19.99 (*1-57932-092-9*) Chek-Chart.

— CHEK-CHART ASE Study Guide for A8, Engine Performance. 104p. 1998. pap. text 19.99 (*1-57932-099-6*) Chek-Chart.

— CHEK-CHART ASE Study Guide for A5, Brakes. 104p. 1998. pap. text 19.99 (*1-57932-096-1*) Chek-Chart.

— CHEK-CHART ASE Study Guide for A4, Suspension & Steering. 104p. 1998. pap. text 19.99 (*1-57932-095-3*) Chek-Chart.

— CHEK-CHART ASE Study Guide for A7, Heat & Air Conditioning. 104p. 1998. pap. text 19.99 (*1-57932-098-8*) Chek-Chart.

— CHEK-CHART ASE Study Guide for A6, Electrical & Electronic Systems. 104p. 1998. pap. text 19.99 (*1-57932-097-X*) Chek-Chart.

— CHEK-CHART ASE Study Guide for A3, Manual Drive Trains & Axles. 104p. 1998. pap. text 19.99 (*1-57932-094-5*) Chek-Chart.

— CHEK-CHART ASE Study Guide for A2, Automatic Transmission & Transaxles. 104p. 1998. pap. text 19.99 (*1-57932-093-7*) Chek-Chart.

— CHEK-CHART ASE Study Guide for L1, Advanced Engine Performance Test. 104p. 1999. pap. text 29.99 (*1-57932-364-2*) Chek-Chart.

— CHEK-CHART Automatic Tranmission Fluid Service Guide. 248p. 2000. pap. text 99.99 (*1-57932-385-5*) Chek-Chart.

— CHEK-CHART Brake Specifications Guide. 140p. 2000. pap. text 19.99 (*1-57932-382-0*) Chek-Chart.

— CHEK-CHART Car Care Guide. 576p. 1999. pap. text 74.99 (*1-57932-377-4*) Chek-Chart.

— CHEK-CHART Car Service Manual. 140p. 1999. pap. text 24.99 (*1-57932-323-5*) Chek-Chart.

— CHEK-CHART Classic Lubrication Guide. 48p. 1999. pap. text 29.99 (*1-57932-261-1*) Chek-Chart.

— CHEK-CHART Engine Performance & Tune Up Specifications Guide. 352p. 2000. pap. text 59.99 (*1-57932-263-8*) Chek-Chart.

— CHEK-CHART Farm Tractor Lubrication Guide. 328p. 2000. pap. text 59.99 (*1-57932-388-X*) Chek-Chart.

— CHEK-CHART Gearbox Fluid Service Guide. 194p. 2000. pap. text 99.99 (*1-57932-384-7*) Chek-Chart.

— CHEK-CHART Lubrication Recommendations Guide. 64p. 2000. pap. text 19.99 (*1-57932-386-3*) Chek-Chart.

— CHEK-CHART Quick Lubrication Guide. 384p. 2000. pap. text 119.99 (*1-57932-383-9*) Chek-Chart.

— CHEK-CHART Tire Fitment Guide. 104p. 2000. pap. text 19.99 (*1-57932-379-0*) Chek-Chart.

— CHEK-CHART Wheel Alignment Specifications. 104p. 2000. pap. text 19.99 (*1-57932-387-1*) Chek-Chart.

Chek-Chart Staff. Complete Automotive Service Library. (Automotive Service Ser.). (Illus.). 665p. 1983. pap. text 52.55 (*0-88098-053-2*, H M Gousha) Prntice Hall Bks.

— Electrical & Electronic Systems: For ASE Test A6. (Chek-Chart's ASE Study Guides Ser.). 144p. 1998. pap. 19.95 (*0-02-862664-8*) Macmillan.

— Engine Performance: For ASE Test A8. (Chek-Chart's ASE Study Guides Ser.). 144p. 1998. pap. 19.95 (*0-02-862666-4*) Macmillan.

— Fuel Systems & Emission Controls, 2 vols., Set. 2nd ed. 1988. 52.00 (*0-06-454016-2*, H M Gousha) Prntice Hall Bks.

— Heating & Air Conditioning: For ASE Test A7. 96p. 1998. pap. 19.95 (*0-02-862665-6*) Macmillan.

— Manual Drive Trains & Axles: For ASE Test A3. (Chek-Chart's ASE Study Guides Ser.). 112p. 1998. pap. 19.95 (*0-02-862661-3*) Macmillan.

— Master Lubrication Handbook, 1985. (Illus.). 1000p. student ed. 90.00 (*0-88098-059-1*, H M Gousha); suppl. ed. 85.45 (*0-88098-075-3*, H M Gousha) Prntice Hall Bks.

— Suspension & Steering: For ASE Test A4. (Chek-Chart's ASE Study Guides Ser.). 112p. 1998. pap. 19.95 (*0-02-862662-1*) Macmillan.

— Truck Lubrication Guide, 1987. rev. ed. Fenneman, Roger L., ed. (Illus.). 96p. 1987. student ed. 35.80 (*0-88098-091-5*, H M Gousha) Prntice Hall Bks.

— Tune-Up Service. 3rd ed. 1976. pap. 7.20 (*0-672-21449-0*, Bobbs) Macmillan.

Chek-Chart Staff, ed. Automotive Brake Systems, 2 vols., Set. 250p. (C). 1990. 53.00 (*0-06-454010-3*, H M Gousha) Prntice Hall Bks.

— Automotive Electrical & Electronic Systems. 2nd ed. 300p. (C). 1990. 54.50 (*0-06-454014-6*, H M Gousha) Prntice Hall Bks.

Chek-Chart Staff & Clark, George T. Engine Performance Diagnosis & Tune-Up. 3rd rev. ed. LC 96-8650. (Illus.). 878p. 1997. pap. 49.00 (*0-673-98102-9*) Chek-Chart.

Chek, Paul. Awesome Abs! The Gut-Busting Solution for Men & Women. (Illus.). 47p. 1996. pap. 9.95 (*1-55210-002-2*, Pub. by MuscleMag Intl) BookWorld.

Chekaluk, Eugene & Llewellyn, Keith R., eds. The Role of Eye Movements in Perceptual Processes. LC 92-13138. (Advances in Psychology Ser.: Vol. 88). 348p. 1992. 157.00 (*0-444-89005-X*, North Holland) Elsevier.

Cheke, Dudley. Josephine & Emilie: Stars of the Bel Canto. 1994. 59.95 (*1-897766-08-4*, Pub. by Jon Carpenter) Paul & Co Pubs.

Cheke, Marcus. Carlota Joaquina, Queen of Portugal. LC 70-94266. (Select Bibliographies Reprint Ser.). 1977. 21.95 (*0-8369-5040-2*) Ayer.

— Dictator of Portugal: A Life of the Marquis of Pombal, 1699-1782. LC 74-94267. (Select Bibliographies Reprint Ser.). 1977. 26.95 (*0-8369-5041-0*) Ayer.

Chekhov, Anton. The Anniversary. Landes, William-Alan, ed. Ponomarov, Sergius, tr. LC 92-53530. 17p. (Orig.). 1992. pap. 5.00 (*0-88734-334-1*) Players Pr.

— Anton Chekhov: Four Plays - Seagull, Uncle Vanya, Three Sisters & Cherry Orchard. Magarshack, David, tr. (Mermaid Dramabook Ser.). 244p. 1969. pap. 8.95 (*0-8090-0743-6*) Hill & Wang.

— Anton Chekhov: Literary & Theatrical Reminiscences. Koteliansky, Samuel S., tr. LC 65-16231. 1927. 20.00 (*0-685-06946-X*, Pub. by Blom Pubns) Ayer.

***Chekhov, Anton.** Anton Chekhov: Longer Stories from the Last Decade, 2000 Edition. LC 99-45466. 640p. 2000. 24.95 (*0-679-60663-7*) Modern Lib NY.

Chekhov, Anton. Anton Chekhov, Selected Stories. (Classics Library). 208p. 1998. pap. 3.95 (*1-85326-288-9*, 2889WW, Pub. by Wrdsworth Edits) NTC Contemp Pub Co.

— Anton Chekhov's Letters on the Short Story, the Drama, & Other Literary Topics. Friedland, Louis S., ed. LC 64-14695. 1972. 29.95 (*0-405-08352-1*, Pub. by Blom Pubns) Ayer.

— Anton Chekhov's Life & Thought: Selected Letters & Commentary. Karlinsky, Simon, ed. Heim, Michael H., tr. from RUS. LC 96-41240. 494p. 1997. pap. 19.95 (*0-8101-1460-7*) Northwestern U Pr.

— Anton Chekhov's Plays. Bristow, Eugene K., ed. (Critical Editions Ser.). (C). 1977. pap. text 14.75 (*0-393-09163-5*) Norton.

— Anton Chekhov's Short Stories. Matlaw, Ralph E., ed. Garnett, Constance et al, trs. LC 78-17052. (Critical Editions Ser.). 369p. (C). 1979. pap. text 11.25 (*0-393-09002-7*) Norton.

— The Bear. Landes, William-Alan, ed. Ponomarov, Sergius, tr. from RUS. LC 90-52700. (Chekhov Collection). (Illus.). 1991. pap. 5.00 (*0-88734-317-1*) Players Pr.

C

An Asterisk (*) at the beginning of an entry indicates that the title is appearing for the first time.

— The Bear. adapted ed. 12p. 1967. 11.95 (*0-19-338442-6*) OUP.

— Best Known Works, Vol. 1. LC 72-5899. (Short Story Index Reprint Ser.). 1977. reprint ed. 36.95 (*0-8369-4198-5*) Ayer.

— Best Plays. Young, Stark, tr. LC 56-8837. 1966. pap. 3.95 (*0-685-06607-X*) Modern Lib NY.

— The Bishop & Other Stories. Garnett, Constance, tr. from RUS. LC 85-10285. (Tales of Anton Chekhov Ser.: Vol. 7). 302p. 1985. reprint ed. pap. 9.95 (*0-88001-054-1*) HarpC.

— The Black Monk, Set. unabridged ed. Setlok, Richard, ed. & reader by. (Commuter's Library). 1993. 16.95 incl. audio (*1-883049-03-2*, 390222, Pub. by Sound Room) Lndmrk Audiobks.

Chekhov, Anton. The Black Monk: Library Edition. unabridged ed. 1993. lib. bdg. 18.95 incl. audio (*1-883049-22-9*) Sound Room.

Chekhov, Anton. The Black Monk & Other Stories. Long, R. E., tr. LC 79-121527. (Short Story Index Reprint Ser.). 1977. 19.95 (*0-8369-3483-0*) Ayer.

— The Brute & Other Farces. 1985. 14.95 (*0-87910-224-1*) Applause Theatre Bk Pubs.

— The Brute & Other Farces: Seven Short Plays. Bentley, Eric & Hoffman, Theodore, trs. from RUS. 96p. 1987. reprint ed. 19.95 (*1-55783-003-7*); reprint ed. pap. 7.95 (*1-55783-004-5*) Applause Theatre Bk Pubs.

— Chekhov: Plays. Frayn, Michael, tr. (Methuen World Dramatists Ser.). 382p. (C). 1988. pap. 11.95 (*0-413-18160-X*, A0332, Methuen Drama) Methn.

Chekhov, Anton. Chekhov: Selected Stories. 1960. mass mkt. 5.95 (*0-451-52511-6*, Sig Classics) NAL.

Chekhov, Anton. Chekhov: The Cherry Orchard. Hitchcock, Donald R., ed. (Bristol Russian Texts Ser.). (RUS.). 129p. (C). 1992. reprint ed. pap. 18.95 (*1-85399-256-9*, Pub. by Brist Class Pr) Focus Pub-R Pullins.

— Chekhov: The Major Plays. annot. ed. Van Itallie, Jean-Claude, tr. from RUS. LC 94-27070. 320p. 1994. pap. 7.95 (*1-55783-162-9*) Applause Theatre Bk Pubs.

— Chekhov Vol. 1: Four Plays. Rocamora, Carol, tr. from RUS. LC 96-36228. (Translation Ser.). 320p. (Orig.). 1996. pap. 19.95 (*1-57525-065-9*) Smith & Kraus.

— Chekhov for the Stage: The Sea Gull; Uncle Vanya; The Three Sisters; The Cherry Orchard. Ehre, Milton, tr. from RUS. & intro. by. 250p. (Orig.). 1992. 43.95 (*0-8101-1023-7*); pap. 15.95 (*0-8101-1048-2*) Northwestern U Pr.

— Chekhov Omnibus. 256p. 1994. 12.50 (*0-460-87472-1*, Everyman's Classic Lib) Tuttle Pubng.

— Chekhov, the Major Plays: Ivanov, Sea Gull, Uncle Vanya, Three Sisters, Cherry Orchard. Dunnigan, Ann, tr. 1968. mass mkt. 5.95 (*0-451-52270-2*, Sig Classics) NAL.

— Chekhov Translations. Schmidt, Paul, tr. 1998. pap. 5.25 (*0-8222-1645-0*) Dramatists Play.

— Chekhov's Early Plays: Ivanov, Platanov, the Wood Demon. LC 99-38692. (Great Translations Ser.). 320p. 1999. pap. 19.95 (*1-57525-152-3*) Smith & Kraus.

— Chekhov's Major Plays: Ivanov, The Seagull, Uncle Vanya, The Three Sisters, & The Cherry Orchard. Kramer, Karl & Booker, Margaret, trs. LC 96-43305. 334p. 1996. pap. 32.50 (*0-7618-0564-8*) U Pr of Amer.

— Chekhov's Three Sisters: Critical Study. 2nd rev. ed. Davidson, J., ed. (Russian Texts Ser.). (RUS.). 128p. (C). 1997. pap. text 18.95 (*1-85399-520-7*, Pub. by Brist Class Pr) Focus Pub-R Pullins.

— Chekhov's Vaudevilles. Rocamora, Carol, tr. LC 97-42181. 320p. 1997. pap. 24.95 (*1-57525-127-2*) Smith & Kraus.

— The Cherry Orchard. Woolland, Brian, ed. (Literature Ser.). 128p. (C). 1996. pap. 11.95 (*0-521-57670-9*) Cambridge U Pr.

— The Cherry Orchard. 64p. 1991. pap. 1.00 (*0-486-26682-6*) Dover.

— The Cherry Orchard. Lavrova, Elisaveta, tr. 71p. 1980. pap. 5.50 (*0-87129-283-1*, C87) Dramatic Pub.

— The Cherry Orchard. LC 86-45246. 112p. 1987. pap. 11.00 (*0-8021-3002-X*, Grove) Grove-Atltic.

— The Cherry Orchard. LC 95-11908. (Plays for Performance Ser.). 85p. 1995. pap. 7.95 (*1-56663-085-1*, Pub. by I R Dee); lib. bdg. 15.95 (*1-56663-086-X*, Pub. by I R Dee) Natl Bk Netwk.

— The Cherry Orchard. Frayn, Michael, tr. from RUS. 67p. (C). 1978. pap. write for info. (*0-413-39340-2*, A0048, Methuen Drama) Methn.

Chekhov, Anton. The Cherry Orchard. 55p. (YA). 1996. pap. 7.00 (*0-88734-289-2*) Players Pr.

Chekhov, Anton. The Cherry Orchard. Gill, Peter, tr. (Oberon Bks.). 72p. 1997. 16.95 (*1-870259-75-0*) Theatre Comm.

— The Cherry Orchard. Mulrine, Stephen, tr. 96p. 1999. pap. 6.95 (*1-85459-412-5*, Pub. by Theatre Comm) Consort Bk Sales.

***Chekhov, Anton.** The Cherry Orchard. 1998. lib. bdg. 19.95 (*1-56723-028-8*) Yestermorrow.

Chekhov, Anton. The Cherry Orchard: A Comedy in Four Acts. 3rd rev. ed. 1995. pap. 5.25 (*0-8222-1450-4*) Dramatists Play.

— The Comic Stories. Pitcher, Harvey, tr. from RUS. LC 98-49198. 224p. 1999. pap. 14.95 (*1-56663-242-0*, Pub. by I R Dee); text 26.00 (*1-56663-241-2*, Pub. by I R Dee) Natl Bk Netwk.

— The Cook's Wedding & Other Stories. Garnett, Constance, tr. from RUS. (Tales of Anton Chekhov Ser.: Vol. 12). 320p. 1986. reprint ed. pap. 9.50 (*0-88001-059-2*) HarpC.

— The Crooked Mirror: And Other Stories. 240p. 1995. pap. 11.00 (*0-8217-5031-3*, Zebra Kensgtn) Kensgtn Pub Corp.

— The Duel & Other Stories. Wilks, Ronald, tr. & intro. by. 240p. 1984. pap. 9.95 (*0-14-044415-7*, Penguin Classics) Viking Penguin.

— Early Short Stories: 1883-1888. Foote, Shelby, ed. Garnett, Constance, tr. LC 98-20049. 642p. 1999. 21.95 (*0-679-60317-4*) Modern Lib NY.

— Early Stories. 208p. 1999. pap. 6.95 (*0-19-283756-7*) OUP.

***Chekhov, Anton.** The Essential Tales of Chekhov. LC 00-28149. 368p. 2000. pap. 14.00 (*0-06-095656-9*, Ecco Press) HarperTrade.

Chekhov, Anton. The Essential Tales Of Chekhov. Ford, Richard, ed. Garnett, Constance, tr. LC 98-8436. 368p. 1998. 27.50 (*0-88001-607-8*) HarpC.

— Fiancee & Other Stories. Wilks, Ronald, tr. & intro. by. 240p. 1986. pap. 6.95 (*0-14-044470-X*, Penguin Classics) Viking Penguin.

***Chekhov, Anton.** Five Comic One-Act Plays. LC 99-31504. (Thrift Editions Ser.: No. 18b). 96p. 1999. pap. 1.50 (*0-486-40887-6*) Dover.

Chekhov, Anton. Five Great Short Stories. 96p. 1990. pap. 1.00 (*0-486-26463-7*) Dover.

***Chekhov, Anton.** Five Great Short Stories. 1998. lib. bdg. 19.95 (*1-56723-029-6*) Yestermorrow.

Chekhov, Anton. Five Plays: Ivanov, The Seagull, Uncle Vanya, Three Sisters, & The Cherry Orchard. Hingley, Ronald, tr. from RUS. & intro. by. LC 98-215863. (Oxford World's Classics Ser.). 326p. 1998. pap. 7.95 (*0-19-283412-6*) OUP.

— Forty Stories. Payne, Robert, tr. LC 90-50473. 704p. 1991. pap. 14.00 (*0-679-73375-2*) Vin Bks.

— Grasshopper & Other Stories. Chamot, A. E., tr. from RUS. LC 72-37538. (Short Story Index Reprint Ser.). 1977. reprint ed. 18.95 (*0-8369-4097-0*) Ayer.

— The Horse-Stealers & Others Stories. Garnett, Constance, tr. from RUS. (Tales of Anton Chekhov Ser.: Vol. 10). 312p. 1986. reprint ed. pap. 9.95 (*0-88001-057-6*) HarpC.

— The Island: A Journey to Sakhalin. Terpak, Luba & Terpak, Michael, trs. from RUS. LC 76-56795. (Illus.). 374p. 1977. reprint ed. lib. bdg. 38.50 (*0-8371-9430-X*, CHTI, Greenwood Pr) Greenwood.

— Ivanov. Schmidt, Paul, tr. LC 99-224317. 1998. pap. 5.25 (*0-8222-1646-9*) Dramatists Play.

— Kashtanka. LC 94-39549. (Illus.). 40p. (J). (gr. 3 up). 1995. 16.00 (*0-15-200539-0*, Gulliver Bks) Harcourt.

— The Kentucky Marriage Proposal. adapted ed. 1973. pap. 3.25 (*0-8222-0608-0*) Dramatists Play.

Chekhov, Anton. The Kiss, Set. unabridged ed. (Anton Chekhov Ser.). 1993. 16.95 incl. audio (*1-883049-05-9*, 390213, Pub. by Sound Room) Lndmrk Audiobks.

— The Kiss: Library Edition. unabridged ed. 1993. lib. bdg. 18.95 incl. audio (*1-883049-24-5*) Sound Room.

Chekhov, Anton. The Kiss & Other Stories. Wilks, Ronald, tr. & intro. by. 224p. 1982. pap. 6.95 (*0-14-044336-3*, Penguin Classics) Viking Penguin.

— The Kiss, & Other Stories. Long, R. E., tr. LC 76-37539. (Short Story Index Reprint Ser.). 1977. reprint ed. 25.95 (*0-8369-4098-9*) Ayer.

— Lady with Lapdog & Other Stories. Magarshack, David, tr. (Classics Ser.). 288p. (Orig.). 1964. pap. 13.99 (*0-14-044143-3*, Penguin Classics) Viking Penguin.

— The Lady with the Dog & Other Stories. Garnett, Constance, tr. from RUS. LC 84-6121. (Tales of Anton Chekhov Ser.: Vol. 3). 300p. 1984. reprint ed. pap. 13.00 (*0-88001-050-9*) HarpC.

— The Lady with the Dog & Other Stories: Russian Reader with Explanatory Notes & Cassette. 252p. 1991. pap. text 12.95 (*0-8285-4900-1*) Firebird NY.

— Later Short Stories: 1888-1903. Foote, Shelby, ed. Garnett, Constance, tr. LC 98-20048. 628p. 1999. 21.95 (*0-679-60316-6*) Modern Lib NY.

— Letters of Anton Chehov to Olga Knipper. Garnett, Constance, tr. LC 65-16232. 415p. 1972. 26.95 (*0-405-08354-8*, Pub. by Blom Pubns) Ayer.

— Letters on the Short Story. 1973. 59.95 (*0-8490-0513-2*) Gordon Pr.

— The Life & Letters of Anton Chekhov. Koteliansky, Samuel S. & Tomlinson, Phillip, trs. LC 65-16230. (Illus.). 1972. 29.95 (*0-405-08355-6*, Pub. by Blom Pubns) Ayer.

— Love & Other Stories. Garnett, Constance, tr. from RUS. (Tales of Anton Chekhov Ser.: Vol. 13). 351p. 1987. reprint ed. pap. 9.50 (*0-88001-060-6*) HarpC.

— The Marriage Proposal. Landes, William-Alan, ed. Ponomarov, Sergius, tr. from RUS. LC 90-53061. (Players Press Chekhov Collection). (Illus.). 20p. 1990. pap. 5.00 (*0-88734-318-X*) Players Pr.

— Monologues from Chekhov. Cartwright, Mason W., tr. from RUS. & intro. by. LC 95-25799. 64p. (Orig.). 1987. pap. 8.95 (*0-940669-03-X*, D-18) Dramaline Pubns.

— My Life & Other Stories. Koteliansky, Samuel S. & Cannan, Gilbert, trs. LC 77-169544. (Short Story Index Reprint Ser.). 1977. reprint ed. 18.95 (*0-8369-4005-9*) Ayer.

— Nine Humorous Tales. LC 76-106262. (Short Story Index Reprint Ser.). 1918. 7.50 (*0-8369-3299-4*) Ayer.

— Oeuvres: Theatre Complet-Recits (1882-1886), Vol. 1. 1560p. 41.50 (*0-686-56579-7*) Fr & Eur.

— Oeuvres Vol. 1: Theatre. (Pleiade Ser.). (FRE.). 1970. lib. bdg. 105.00 (*0-8288-3544-6*, M5194) Fr & Eur.

— Oeuvres Vol. 2: Recits de 1887-1892. (Pleiade Ser.). (FRE.). 1970. lib. bdg. 95.00 (*0-8288-3545-4*, M5195) Fr & Eur.

— Oeuvres Vol. 3: Recits de 1892-1903. (Pleiade Ser.). (FRE.). 1971. lib. bdg. 95.00 (*0-8288-3546-2*, F19130) Fr & Eur.

— Orchards: 7 Adaptations of Chekhov. 1987. pap. 6.95 (*0-88145-055-3*) Broadway Play.

— The Oxford Chekhov. Hingley, Ronald, ed. Incl. Vol. 1. Short Plays. 222p. 1968. 65.00 (*0-19-211349-6*); Vol. 8. Stories, 1895-1897. Hingley, Ronald, tr. 340p. 1965. text 65.00 (*0-19-211340-2*); write for info. (*0-318-54870-4*) OUP.

Chekhov, Anton. The Party: Library Edition. unabridged ed. 1993. lib. bdg. 18.95 incl. audio (*1-883049-23-7*) Sound Room.

Chekhov, Anton. The Party & Other Stories. 1976. 23.95 (*0-8488-0747-2*) Amereon Ltd.

— The Party & Other Stories. Garnett, Constance, tr. from RUS. LC 84-6122. (Tales of Anton Chekhov Ser.: Vol. 4). 340p. 1984. reprint ed. pap. 9.50 (*0-88001-051-7*) HarpC.

— Peasants & Other Stories. Garnett, Constance, tr. from RUS. LC 99-14551. 480p. 1999. reprint ed. pap. 14.95 (*0-940322-14-5*, Pub. by NY Rev Bks) Midpt Trade.

— Perepiska A. P. Chekhova, 2 vols. Collet's Holdings, Ltd. Staff, ed. 448p. 1984. 110.00 (*0-7855-0900-3*) St Mut.

— Platonov: A Play in 4 Acts. Magarshack, David, tr. from RUS. 195p. 1964. 17.95 (*0-910278-93-8*) Boulevard.

— Plays by A. P. Chekhov: Russian Reader with Explanatory Notes. 238p. 1989. pap. text 7.95 (*0-8285-4904-4*) Firebird NY.

— The Plays of Anton Chekhov. 24.95 (*0-89190-432-8*) Amereon Ltd.

— The Plays of Anton Chekhov. Schmidt, Paul, tr. 400p. 1998. pap. 14.00 (*0-06-092875-1*) HarpC.

***Chekhov, Anton.** The Plays of Anton Chekhov. 1999. 25.25 (*0-8446-6987-3*) Peter Smith.

Chekhov, Anton. The Plays of Anton Chekhov. Schmidt, Paul, tr. LC 96-42456. 400p. 1997. 30.00 (*0-06-018705-0*) HarpC.

— The Portable Chekhov. Yarmolinsky, Avrahm, ed. (Portable Library: No. 35). 640p. 1977. pap. 15.95 (*0-14-015035-8*, Penguin Bks) Viking Penguin.

***Chekhov, Anton.** The Princess & Other Stories. Hingley, Ronald, tr. (Oxford World's Classics Ser.). 272p. 1999. pap. 7.95 (*0-19-283788-5*) OUP.

Chekhov, Anton. Rothschild's Fiddle & Other Stories. 1976. 22.95 (*0-8488-0182-2*) Amereon Ltd.

— Rothschild's Fiddle & Other Stories. LC 72-121528. (Short Story Index Reprint Ser.). 1977. 18.95 (*0-8369-3484-9*) Ayer.

***Chekhov, Anton.** The Russian Master & Other Stories. Hingley, Ronald, tr. (Oxford World's Classics Ser.). 256p. 2000. pap. 7.95 (*0-19-283687-0*) OUP.

Chekhov, Anton. Russian Silhouettes. Fell, Marian, tr. LC 72-142260. (Short Story Index Reprint Ser.). 1977. 23.95 (*0-8369-3744-9*) Ayer.

— The Schoolmaster & Other Stories. Garnett, Constance, tr. from RUS. (Tales of Anton Chekhov Ser.: Vol. 11). 302p. 1986. reprint ed. pap. 9.50 (*0-88001-058-4*) HarpC.

— The Schoolmistress & Other Stories. Garnett, Constance, tr. from RUS. (Tales of Anton Chekhov Ser.: Vol. 9). 305p. 1986. reprint ed. pap. 9.95 (*0-88001-056-8*) HarpC.

— The Sea Gull. unabridged ed. LC 99-12248. 64p. 1999. pap. text 1.50 (*0-486-40656-3*) Dover.

— The Seagull. Eisemann, Fred & Murphy, Oliver F., trs. pap. 5.95 (*0-8283-1454-3*) Branden Bks.

— The Seagull. Heim, Michael H., tr. from RUS. 1992. pap. 5.50 (*0-87129-123-1*, S85) Dramatic Pub.

— The Seagull. (Plays for Performance Ser.). 89p. 1992. pap. 7.95 (*0-929587-88-X*, Pub. by I R Dee); lib. bdg. 15.95 (*0-929587-89-8*, Pub. by I R Dee) Natl Bk Netwk.

— The Seagull. Frayn, Michael, tr. from RUS. (Methuen Theatre Classics Ser.). 67p. (C). 1988. pap. write for info. (*0-413-42140-6*, A0258, Methuen Drama) Methn.

— The Seagull. Mulrine, Stephen, tr. (Nick Hern Books, Drama Classics). 96p. 1997. pap. 6.95 (*1-85459-193-2*, Pub. by N Hern Bks) Theatre Comm.

— The Seagull. Gems, Pam, tr. 96p. 1998. pap. 14.95 (*1-85459-261-0*, Pub. by N Hern Bks) Theatre Comm.

— The Seagull. Landes, William-Alan, ed. & intro. by. 50p. 1996. pap. 7.00 (*0-88734-299-X*) Players Pr.

— The Seagull. French, David, tr. from RUS. 112p. 1993. pap. 11.95 (*0-88922-324-6*, Pub. by Talonbks) Genl Dist Srvs.

***Chekhov, Anton.** Seagull. 100p. 2000. pap. 12.95 (*1-84002-150-0*) Theatre Comm.

Chekhov, Anton. The Seagull: Chaika. Saunders, Nicholas & Dwyer, Frank, trs. LC 94-7990. (Great Translations for Actors Ser.). 112p. 1994. pap. 11.95 (*1-880399-53-9*) Smith & Kraus.

— The Seagull, Uncle Vanya . . . unabridged ed. (World Classic Literature Ser.). (RUS.). pap. 6.95 (*2-87714-265-5*, Pub. by Bookking Intl) Distribks Inc.

— The Shooting Party: A Novel. LC 86-14605. 220p. (C). 1987. reprint ed. pap. 8.95 (*0-226-10241-6*) U Ch Pr.

— Short Stories. 464p. Date not set. 29.95 (*0-8488-2575-6*) Amereon Ltd.

— Short Stories. unabridged ed. (World Classic Literature Ser.). (RUS.). pap. 8.95 (*2-87714-277-9*, Pub. by Bookking Intl) Distribks Inc.

— Sinner from Toledo & Other Stories. Hinchliffe, Arnold, tr. LC 70-147269. 168p. 1975. 24.50 (*0-8386-7890-4*) Fairleigh Dickinson.

— The Steppe & Other Stories. Kaye, Adeline L., tr. LC 70-106263. (Short Story Index Reprint Ser.). 1977. 18.95 (*0-8369-3300-1*) Ayer.

— The Steppe & Other Stories. 400p. 1991. 17.00 (*0-679-40546-1*) Everymns Lib.

— The Steppe & Other Stories. Hingley, Ronald, tr. & intro. by. (Oxford World's Classics Ser.). 272p. 1998. pap. 6.95 (*0-19-283698-6*) OUP.

— Stories of Anton Chekhov. unabridged ed. 140p. 1997. reprint ed. pap. 14.95 (*1-57002-044-2*) Univ Publng Hse.

— Stories of Men. Rpss, Paula P., tr. LC 96-38096. 372p. 1997. pap. 14.95 (*1-57392-135-1*) Prometheus Bks.

— Stories of Women. Ross, Paula P., tr. from RUS. LC 94-6501. 308p. 1994. pap. 16.95 (*0-87975-901-1*) Prometheus Bks.

— Stories of Women. Ross, Paula P., tr. from RUS. LC 94-6501. 308p. (C). 1994. 29.95 (*0-87975-893-7*) Prometheus Bks.

— Tales of Chekhov, 13 vols., Vol. 1. Garnett, Constance, tr. from RUS. 1984. pap. 9.50 (*0-88001-038-X*) HarpC.

— Tales of Chekhov, 13 vols., Vol. 2. Garnett, Constance, tr. from RUS. 1984. pap. 9.95 (*0-88001-039-8*) HarpC.

— The Three Sisters. Nelson, R., ed. 1991. pap. 6.95 (*0-88145-098-7*) Broadway Play.

Chekhov, Anton. The Three Sisters. 55p. 1996. pap. 7.00 (*0-88734-705-3*) Players Pr.

Chekhov, Anton. The Three Sisters. adapted ed. Wilson, Lanford, tr. from RUS. 1984. pap. 5.25 (*0-8222-1144-0*) Dramatists Play.

— The Three Sisters. LC 93-10454. (Thrift Editions Ser.). 64p. 1993. reprint ed. pap. 1.00 (*0-486-27544-2*) Dover.

— The Three Sisters. 64p. 1999. reprint ed. pap. 6.95 (*1-57002-101-5*) Univ Publng Hse.

— The Three Sisters: A Drama in Four Acts. rev. ed. LC 95-177466. 1995. pap. 5.25 (*0-8222-1451-2*) Dramatists Play.

— The Three Sisters: A Play. LC 91-12802. 128p. 1991. reprint ed. pap. 12.00 (*0-8021-3276-6*, Grove) Grove-Atltic.

— The Three Sisters: Tri Sestry. Wilson, Lanford, tr. from RUS. LC 94-19394. (Great Translations for Actors Ser.). Orig. Title: Tri Sestra. 128p. pap. 11.95 (*1-880399-28-8*) Smith & Kraus.

— The Three Sisters: Tri Sewiry. Schmidt, Paul, tr. from RUS. LC 92-11369. (TCG Translations Ser.). Orig. Title: Tri Sestra. 112p. 1992. 21.95 (*1-55936-056-9*); pap. 8.95 (*1-55936-055-0*) Theatre Comm.

— Twelve Plays. Hingley, Ronald, ed. (Oxford World's Classics Ser.). 400p. 2000. pap. 7.95 (*0-19-283674-9*) OUP.

— Uncle Vanya. LC 98-5424. 64p. 1998. pap. 1.50 (*0-486-40159-6*) Dover.

— Uncle Vanya. Gems, Pam, tr. 80p. 1998. pap. 13.95 (*1-85459-176-2*, Pub. by N Hern Bks) Theatre Comm.

— Uncle Vanya. write for info. (*0-318-56842-X*) OUP.

Chekhov, Anton. Uncle Vanya. 55p. 1996. pap. 7.00 (*0-88734-707-X*) Players Pr.

— Uncle Vanya. 1999. pap. 7.95 (*1-85459-430-3*, Pub. by Theatre Comm) Consort Bk Sales.

Chekhov, Anton. Uncle Vanya. (Classics Ser.). write for info. (*0-318-55068-7*) Viking Penguin.

— Uncle Vanya. LC 88-21455. 96p. 1989. reprint ed. pap. 10.00 (*0-8021-3151-4*, Grove) Grove-Atltic.

— Uncle Vanya: Scenes from Country Life in Four Acts. LC 75-75974. (Minnesota Drama Editions Ser.: 5). 92p. reprint ed. pap. 30.00 (*0-608-13279-9*, 205584900039) Bks Demand.

***Chekhov, Anton.** The Undiscovered Chekhov: Forty-Three New Stories. rev. ed. Constantine, Peter, tr. 224p. 2000. pap. 16.95 (*1-58322-026-7*) Seven Stories.

Chekhov, Anton. The Undiscovered Chekhov: Thirty-Eight New Stories. Constantine, Peter, tr. from RUS. LC 98-34461. 224p. 1998. 24.00 (*1-888363-76-2*) Seven Stories.

— Vishnevi Saad: The Cherry Orchard. (RUS.). 175p. 1946. 29.95 (*0-8236-0720-8*) Intl Univs Pr.

— Ward Number Six & Other Stories. Hingley, Ronald, tr. & intro. by. (Oxford World's Classics Ser.). 272p. 1999. pap. 6.95 (*0-19-283733-8*) OUP.

— Ward Six & Other Stories. 1976. 19.95 (*0-8488-1267-0*) Amereon Ltd.

***Chekhov, Anton.** Ward Six & Other Stories. large type ed. LC 99-462348. 500p. 2000. 34.95 (*1-56000-495-9*) Transaction Pubs.

Chekhov, Anton. Ward Six & Other Stories. 384p. 1986. reprint ed. lib. bdg. 18.95 (*0-89966-523-3*) Buccaneer Bks.

— The Wedding. Landes, William-Alan, ed. Ponomarov, Sergius, tr. 55p. (Orig.). 1996. pap. 5.00 (*0-88734-358-9*) Players Pr.

— The Wife & Other Stories. Garnett, Constance, tr. from RUS. (Tales of Anton Chekhov Ser.: Vol. 5). 200p. 1985. reprint ed. pap. 8.50 (*0-88001-052-5*) HarpC.

— Wild Honey. Frayn, Michael, tr. 104p. (C). 1988. pap. write for info. (*0-413-55160-1*, A0318, Methuen Drama) Methn.

— The Witch & Other Stories. Garnett, Constance, tr. from RUS. (Tales of Anton Chekhov Ser.: Vol. 6). 200p. 1985. reprint ed. pap. 8.50 (*0-88001-053-3*) HarpC.

— The Wood Demon: Leshii. Saunders, Nicholas & Dwyer, Frank, trs. LC 93-21865. (Great Translations for Actors Ser.). 128p. 1993. pap. 11.95 (*1-880399-30-X*) Smith & Kraus.

Chekhov, Anton & Dunai. The Parasol. (Illus.). 96p. (Orig.). 1987. pap. text 5.95 (*0-318-22831-9*) Polyglot VA.

Chekhov, Anton & Suvorin, Alexei. Tatyana Repina: Two Translated Texts. Racin, John, ed. & tr. by. LC 98-40995. (Illus.). 286p. 1999. lib. bdg. 45.00 (*0-7864-0575-9*) McFarland & Co.

Chekhov, Anton, et al. Motley Tales & a Play. deluxe ed. LC 97-40220. (New York Public Library Collector's Edition Ser.). 432p. 1998. 18.50 (*0-385-48730-4*) Doubleday.

***Chekhov, Anton, et al.** Stories. LC 00-37894. 2000. pap. 11.95 (*0-553-38100-8*) Broadway BDD.

Chekhov, Anton, jt. auth. see Caywood, Paul.

Chekhov, Anton, jt. auth. see Koteliansky, Samuel S.

Chekhov, Michael. Lessons for the Professional Actor. Hurst, D. Deirdre, ed. 1985. pap. 14.95 (*0-933826-80-X*) PAJ Pubns.

— Michael Chekhov: On Theatre & the Art of Acting, 4 vols. Powers, Mala, ed. (Acting Ser.). 48p. 1992. 39.95 incl. audio (*1-55783-117-3*) Applause Theatre Bk Pubs.

An Asterisk (*) at the beginning of an entry indicates that the title is appearing for the first time.

— To the Director & Playwright. LC 77-8158. (Illus.). 329p. 1977. reprint ed. lib. bdg. 35.00 (*0-8371-9615-9*, CHTD, Greenwood Pr) Greenwood.

Chekivay, Sam, ed. see Greek Children Staff.

Chekki, Dan A. Religion & Social System of the Virasaiva Community, 8. LC 96-29950. (Contributions to the Study of Anthropology: Vol. 8). 168p. 1997. 57.95 (*0-313-30251-0*, Greenwood Pr) Greenwood.

— Research in Community Sociology Vol. 8: American Community Issues & Patterns of Development, Vol. 8. 1998. 73.25 (*0-7623-0477-4*) Jai Pr.

Chekki, Danesh A. American Sociological Hegemony: Transnational Explorations. 184p. (C). 1987. pap. text 20.50 (*0-8191-6612-X*); lib. bdg. 45.00 (*0-8191-6611-1*) U Pr of Amer.

— Sociology of Contemporary India. 216p. 1978. 18.95 (*0-318-36865-X*) Asia Bk Corp.

— Sociology of Contemporary India. 1978. 12.50 (*0-8364-0245-6*) S Asia.

Chekki, Danesh A., ed. Research in Community Sociology, Vol. 1: Contemporary Community: Change & Challenge. 231p. 1990. 73.25 (*1-55938-074-8*) Jai Pr.

— Research in Community Sociology, Vol. 3: The Ethnic Quest for Comm.: Searching for. 250p. 1993. 73.25 (*1-55938-360-7*) Jai Pr.

Chekrezi, Constantine A. Albania, Past & Present. LC 75-135798. (Eastern Europe Collection). 1971. reprint ed. 18.95 (*0-405-02740-0*) Ayer.

Chekwas, Sam. Ogbanje: Son of the Gods. Appia, Tracy, ed. (ENG & GRE.). 140p. 1994. 18.95 (*1-885778-01-5*); pap. 10.95 (*1-885778-00-7*) Seaburn.

— 100 Steps Necessary for Survival in America: (For People of Color) (Survival Ser.). 112p. 1998. pap. 4.95 (*1-885778-46-5*) Seaburn.

— 100 Steps Necessary for Survival in America: (For the Immigrant) (Survival Ser.). 112p. 1998. pap. 4.95 (*1-885778-47-3*) Seaburn.

Chekwas, Sam & Soccolich, R. M. Mischievious Acts & Repercussions. 176p. 1998. pap. 13.00 (*1-885778-45-7*) Seaburn.

Chekwas, Sam, jt. auth. see Mason, Tyra.

Chekwas, Sam, ed. see Amaru, Tuppacc, III.

Chekwas, Sam, ed. see Horattas, Chrystom G.

Chekwas, Sam, ed. see Soccolich, R. M.

Chela-Flores, Julian, et al, eds. Chemical Evolution: Self-Organization of the Macromolecules of Life. LC 95-19705. (Illus.). 352p. 1995. 64.00 (*0-937194-32-8*) A Deepak Pub.

Chela-Flores, Julian, ed. see Ponnamperuma, Cyril N., et al.

Chela-Flores, Julian, jt. ed. see Ponnamperuma, Cyril.

***Chelack, Stephen.** Oracle & SQL Server Integration. (Illus.). 400p. 2001. pap. text 39.99 (*0-7645-4699-6*) IDG Bks.

Chelaflores, Julian & Raulin, F. Exobiology: Matter, Energy, & Information in the Origin & Evolution of Life in the Universe: Proceedings of the Fifth Trieste Conference on Chemical Evolution: An Abdus Salam Memorial, Trieste, Italy, 22-26 September, 1997. LC 98-28195. 1998. 173.00 (*0-7923-5172-X*) Kluwer Academic.

Chelak, Alexander. Jenny with Pigtails. LC 96-98851. 106p. (Orig.). (YA). 1996. pap. 7.95 (*1-57502-147-1*) Morris Pubng.

Chelazzi, G. & Vannini, M., eds. Behavioral Adaptation to Intertidal Life. LC 88-17956. (NATO ASI Series A, Life Sciences: Vol. 151). (Illus.). 534p. 1988. 125.00 (*0-306-42930-6*, Plenum Trade) Perseus Pubng.

Chelazzidini, Giulietta, et al. Sienese Painting. LC 98-4128. (Illus.). 440p. 1998. 95.00 (*0-8109-4184-8*, Pub. by Abrams) Time Warner.

Cheldelin, Larry V. Your Baby's Secret World: Four Phases for Effective Parenting (A Professional & Practical Guide) Brown, J., ed. (Illus.). 1983. pap. 11.95 (*0-8283-1850-6*) Branden Bks.

Chelekis, George. The Action Guide to Government Grants, Loans, & Giveaways. LC 92-38818. 512p. (Orig.). 1993. pap. 24.95 (*0-399-51792-8*, Perigee Bks) Berkley Pub.

Cheles. Neo-Fascism in Europe. 1991. text. write for info. (*0-582-03950-9*, Pub. by Addison-Wesley) Longman.

Cheles, Luciano. The Studiolo of Urbino: An Iconographic Investigation. LC 85-25984. (Illus.). 195p. 1986. 60.00 (*0-271-00423-1*) Pa St U Pr.

Cheles, Luciano, et al, eds. The Far Right in Europe. 2nd rev. ed. LC 94-33068. 416p. (C). 1996. pap. text 29.06 (*0-582-23881-1*, 76980, Pub. by Addison-Wesley) Longman.

***Cheles, Luciano & Sponza, Lucio.** The Art of Persuasion: Political Communication in Italy from 1945 to the 1900s. LC 99-43346. 1999. pap. write for info. (*0-7190-4170-8*, Pub. by Manchester Univ Pr) St Martin.

— The Art of Persuasion: Political Communication in Italy from 1945 to the 1900s. LC 99-43346. 2000. text. write for info. (*0-7190-4169-4*) St Martin.

Chelette, Iona M., et al. California Grandeur & Genre: From the Collection of James L. Coran & Walter A. Nelson-Rees. LC 91-28616. (Illus.). 108p. 1992. pap. 29.95 (*0-295-97189-4*) U of Wash Pr.

Chelf, Carl P. Controversies in Social Welfare Policy: Government & the Pursuit of Happiness. (Controversial Issues In Public Policy Ser.: Vol. 3). (Illus.). 200p. (C). 1992. 42.00 (*0-8039-4042-4*); pap. 18.95 (*0-8039-4043-2*) Sage.

Chelf, Vicki R. Arrowhead Mills Cookbook: Healthy Homestyle Cooking from the Heartland. LC 93-17146. (Illus.). 278p. pap. 14.95 (*0-89529-546-6*, Avery) Penguin Putnam.

— Cooking with the Right Side of the Brain: Creative Vegetarian Cooking. LC 89-17807. (Illus.). 283p. pap. 16.95 (*0-89529-431-1*, Avery) Penguin Putnam.

Cheli, Rodolfo, ed. Gastric Protection. LC 88-11638. 312p. 1988. reprint ed. pap. 96.80 (*0-608-00311-5*, 206102800007) Bks Demand.

Chelias, Jane, ed. see Murphy, Dallas.

***Chelikowsky, J. R., et al, eds.** The Optical Properties of Materials Vol. 579: Materials Research Society Symposium Proceedings. 2000. text 86.00 (*1-55899-487-4*) Materials Res.

Chelikowsky, J. R. & Franciosi, A., eds. Electronic Materials: A New Era in Materials Science. (Solid-State Sciences Ser.: Vol. 95). (Illus.). xiv, 341p. 1991. 96.95 (*0-387-53445-8*) Spr-Verlag.

Chelikowsky, J. R., jt. auth. see Cohen, M. L.

Chelikowsky, James R. & Louie, Steven G., eds. Quantum Theory of Real Materials. LC 95-45353. (International Series in Engineering & Computer Science, Natural Language Processing & Machine Translation: No. 348). 568p. (C). 1996. text 236.00 (*0-7923-9666-9*) Kluwer Academic.

***Chelimsky, Eleanor, ed.** Reproductive & Developmental Toxicants: Regulatory Actions Provide Uncertain Protection. (Illus.). 116p. (C). 2000. reprint ed. pap. text 25.00 (*0-7881-8626-4*) DIANE Pub.

Chelimsky, Eleanor, intro. Program Evaluation: Patterns & Directions. (Illus.). 316p. 1985. pap. text 14.95 (*0-936678-08-9*) Am Soc Pub Admin.

Chelimsky, Eleanor & Shadish, William R., eds. Evaluation for the 21st Century: A Resource Book. LC 96-25373. 540p. 1997. 79.95 (*0-7619-0610-X*); pap. 35.00 (*0-7619-0611-8*) Sage.

Chelius, Carl R. & Frentz, Henry J., eds. Basic Meteorology Exercise Manual. 3rd ed. 240p. 1996. spiral bd. 24.95 (*0-8403-6742-2*) Kendall-Hunt.

Chelius, James & Dworkin, James R., eds. Reflections on the Transformation of Industrial Relations. LC 89-48376. (Institute of Management & Labor Relations Ser.: No. 1). (Illus.). 233p. 1990. 35.00 (*0-8108-2259-8*) Scarecrow.

Chelius, James R., ed. Current Issues in Workers' Compensation. LC 86-9267. 372p. (C). 1986. text 25.00 (*0-88099-037-6*); pap. text 15.00 (*0-88099-036-8*) W E Upjohn.

Chelius, James R. & Muscovitch, Edward. Toward a Safer Workplace: Reform & Deregulation of Workers' Compensation. Ciffolillo, Kathryn, ed. LC 96-34775. (Pioneer Paper Ser.: No. 11). 220p. (Orig.). 1996. pap. 15.00 (*0-929930-16-9*) Pioneer Inst.

Chelius, Jane, ed. see Adams, George.

Chelius, Jane, ed. see Adams, James R. & Frantz, Douglas.

Chelius, Jane, ed. see Adcock, Thomas.

Chelius, Jane, ed. see Alexis, Kim.

Chelius, Jane, ed. see Bard, Margaret.

Chelius, Jane, ed. see Barrymore, Drew & Gold, Todd.

Chelius, Jane, ed. see Campbell, Robert.

Chelius, Jane, jt. ed. see Campbell, Robert.

Chelius, Jane, ed. see Carlson, P. M.

Chelius, Jane, ed. see Carpenter, Scott.

Chelius, Jane, ed. see Dibdin, Michael.

Chelius, Jane, ed. see Fallon, Ann C.

Chelius, Jane, ed. see Farrell, Gillian B.

Chelius, Jane, ed. see Feldmeyer, Dean.

Chelius, Jane, ed. see Fliegel, Richard.

Chelius, Jane, ed. see Fyfield, Frances.

Chelius, Jane, ed. see Gunning, Sally.

Chelius, Jane, ed. see Healy, Jeremiah.

Chelius, Jane, ed. see Hegarty, Frances.

Chelius, Jane, ed. see Hegerty, Frances.

Chelius, Jane, ed. see Knight, Kathryn L.

Chelius, Jane, ed. see Kraft, Gabrielle.

Chelius, Jane, ed. see Lileks, James.

Chelius, Jane, ed. see Llewellyn, Sam.

Chelius, Jane, ed. see McCafferty, Taylor.

Chelius, Jane, ed. see McGrady, Sean.

Chelius, Jane, ed. see Mosley, Walter.

Chelius, Jane, ed. see Neel, Janet.

Chelius, Jane, ed. see Presents, Elizabeth P.

Chelius, Jane, ed. see Shankman, Sarah.

Chelius, Jane, ed. see Stacey, Susannah.

Chelius, Jane, ed. see Sussman, Susan.

Chelius, Jane, ed. see Washburn, Stan.

Chelius, Terry. Death in the San Juans. LC 98-90614. 2000. pap. 18.95 (*0-533-12864-1*) Vantage.

Chelkowski, J., ed. Cereal Grain: Mycotoxins, Fungi & Quality in Drying & Storage. (Developments in Food Science Ser.: Vol. 26). xxii,610p. 1991. 290.00 (*0-444-88554-4*) Elsevier.

Chelkowski, Peter J. & Dabashi, Hamid. Staging a Revolution: The Art of Persuasion in the Islamic Republic of Iran. LC 99-20633. 1999. text 75.00 (*0-8147-1597-4*) NYU Pr.

Chelkowski, Peter J. & Pranger, Robert J., eds. Ideology & Power in the Middle East: Studies in Honor of George Lenczowski. LC 87-30371. xii, 530p. (C). 1988. text 74.95 (*0-8223-0781-2*); pap. text 23.95 (*0-8223-0788-X*) Duke.

Chell. Entrepreneurial Behavior, Vol. 1. (ITBP Textbooks Ser.). 2000. pap. 19.99 (*1-86152-318-1*) Thomson Learn.

Chell, Elizabeth, et al. The Entrepreneurial Personality: Concepts, Cases & Categories. (Small Business Ser.). 192p. (C). (gr. 13). 1991. pap. 71.95 (*0-415-03872-3*, A6186) Thomson Learn.

Chelladurai, Packianathan. Human Resource Management in Sport & Recreation. LC 98-37051. (Illus.). 312p. 1999. text 39.00 (*0-87322-973-8*, BCHE0973) Human Kinetics.

Chelland, Patrick. One for the Gipper. rev. ed. DiMarco, Tony, ed. (Illus.). 256p. 1996. pap. 16.95 (*1-886571-01-5*) Arrowhead Classics.

Chellaney, Brahma. Stopping the Indian Bomb: A Study of U. S. Policy. 240p. (C). 1998. pap. 49.95 (*0-8133-2329-0*) Westview.

Chellappa, M. Laparoscopic Cholecystectomy. 1994. text 38.00 (*981-02-1094-9*) World Scientific Pub.

Chellappa, R., jt. auth. see Zhou, Y. T.

Chellappa, Rama. Digital Image Processing. 2nd ed. LC 91-33360. (Illus.). 816p. (C). 1992. 64.00 (*0-8186-2362-4*, 2362) IEEE Comp Soc.

Chellappa, Rama & Jain, Anil, eds. Markov Random Fields: Theory & Applications. (Illus.). 581p. 1993. text 88.00 (*0-12-170608-7*) Acad Pr.

Chellaraj, Gnanaraj, et al. Trends in Health Status, Services, & Finance: The Transition in Central & Eastern Europe, Statistical Annex, Vol. II. LC 96-40968. (Technical Papers: No. 348). 152p. 1997. pap. 22.00 (*0-8213-3828-5*, 13828) World Bank.

Chellen, Sydney S. Information Technology for the Caring Professions: A User's Handbook. LC 94-18463. 1995. pap. 29.95 (*0-304-33164-3*) Continuum.

— Information Technology for the Caring Professions: A User's Handbook. LC 94-18463. 1996. 90.00 (*0-304-33162-7*) Continuum.

***Chelleri, Fortunato.** Fortunato Chelleri: Keyboard Music. Vavoulis, Vassilis, ed. (Recent Researches in the Music of the Baroque Era Ser.: Vol. B101). (Illus.). 2000. pap. 45.00 (*0-89579-457-8*) A-R Eds.

Chellew, Robert E. Journeyman Electrician's Exam Workbook Based on the 1996 NEC. LC 96-208608. (Illus.). 132p. 1995. 24.96 (*0-8269-1708-9*) Am Technical.

Chelliah, Raja J. Towards Sustainable Growth: Essays in Fiscal & Financial Sector Reforms in India. LC 97-119029. (Illus.). 236p. 1996. text 24.00 (*0-19-563946-4*) OUP.

Chelliah, Shobhana L. A Grammar of Meithei. LC 97-8086. (Grammar Library: Vol. 17). 504p. 1997. lib. bdg. 199.00 (*3-11-014321-6*) Mouton.

Chelliah, Shobhana L. & De Reuse, Willem J., eds. Papers from the Fifth Annual Meeting of the Southeast Asian Linguistics Society, 1995. (Illus.). xxi, 333p. (C). 1998. pap. 24.95 (*1-881044-17-3*) ASU Prog SE Asian.

***Chellis, James.** MCSE: Accelerated Windows 2000 Exam Notes. 2000. pap. 29.99 (*0-7821-2770-3*) Sybex.

— MCSE: Accelerated Windows 2000 Study Guide. 2000. 69.99 (*0-7821-2760-6*) Sybex.

— MCSE: Windows 2000 Core Requirements Exam Notes, 3 vols. 2000. pap. 79.96 (*0-7821-2764-9*) Sybex.

— MCSE: Windows 2000 Professional Study Guide. (Illus.). 2000. pap. 49.99 (*0-7821-2751-7*) Sybex.

— MCSE: Windows 2000 Server Study Guide. (Illus.). 2000. pap. 49.99 (*0-7821-2752-5*) Sybex.

— MCSE: Windows 2000 Upgrade Study Guide. 2000. 49.99 (*0-7821-2768-1*) Sybex.

Chellis, James. MCSE Proxy Server 2 Study Guide. LC 97-80847. 672p. 1998. pap. text 49.99 (*0-7821-2194-2*) Sybex.

***Chellis, James.** Networking Essentials Study Guide. 3rd ed. (MCSE Exam Preparation Guide Ser.). 688p. 1999. pap., student ed. 49.99 (*0-7821-2695-2*) Sybex.

Chellis, James. Novell Certified Internet Professional. 1664p. 1997. student ed. 99.99 (*0-7821-2035-0*) Sybex.

***Chellis, James.** NT Server 4 Study Guide. 3rd ed. (MCSE Exam Preparation Guide Ser.). (Illus.). 816p. 1999. pap., student ed. 49.99 (*0-7821-2696-0*) Sybex.

— NT Workstation 4 Study Guide. 3rd ed. (MCSE Exam Preparation Guide Ser.). (Illus.). 768p. 1999. pap., student ed. 49.90 (*0-7821-2698-7*) Sybex.

— Windows 2000 Professional. (MCSE Exam Notes Ser.). (Illus.). 2000. pap. text 24.99 (*0-7821-2753-3*, Network Pr) Sybex.

— Windows 2000 Server. (MCSE Exam Notes Ser.). (Illus.). 352p. 2000. pap. text 24.99 (*0-7821-2754-1*, Network Pr) Sybex.

Chellis, James, et al. Networking Essentials Study Guide: Exam 70-058 With CDROM. 2nd ed. (MCSE Ser.). (Illus.). 683p. 1998. student ed. 54.99 (*0-7821-2220-5*) Sybex.

***Chellis, James, et al.** Windows 2000 Core Requirements. (MCSE Ser.). (Illus.). 2000. pap. text 149.96 (*0-7821-2763-0*, Network Pr) Sybex.

Chellis, James, jt. auth. see Easlick, Richard L.

Chellis, James, jt. auth. see Lammle, Todd.

Chellis, James, jt. auth. see Moncur, Michael.

***Chellman, Chester E. & Spielberg, Franklin.** Traditional Neighborhood Development Street Design Guidelines. LC 99-58903. (Illus.). 44p. 1999. pap. text 35.00 (*0-935403-34-5*, RP-027A) Inst Trans Eng.

Chellus, Jane, ed. see Perry, Michael R.

***Chelly, Jacques E., ed.** Peripheral Nerve Blocks: A Color Atlas. LC 99-11892. 1999. 95.00 (*0-7817-1626-8*) Lppncott W & W.

Chelmsford Historical Society Staff. Chelmsford. (Images of America Ser.). 1997. pap. 16.99 (*0-7524-0580-2*) Arcadia Publng.

Chelnik, Peter. Wildflower Serenade: Selected Poems. LC 98-186669. 161 p. 1997. write for info. (*0-9642708-9-7*) P Chelnik.

Chelsea, David. Perspective! For Cartoonists & Illustrators. LC 97-28757. (Illus.). 176p. 1997. pap. 19.95 (*0-8230-0567-4*) Watsn-Guptill.

— Welcome to the Zone. Amara, Philip, ed. (Illus.). 96p. 1994. pap. 9.95 (*0-87816-312-3*) Kitchen Sink.

Chelsea House Publishing Staff. Albania: Major World Nations. LC 99-15680. (Major World Nations Ser.). (Illus.). 144p. (YA). (gr. 5 up). 1999. 19.95 (*0-7910-4754-7*) Chelsea Hse.

— American Adventure. 1998. 127.60 (*0-7910-5049-1*) Chelsea Hse.

— American Kennel Club Boxed Set. 1999. 239.40 (*0-7910-5469-1*) Chelsea Hse.

***Chelsea House Publishing Staff.** American Statesmen, 6 vols. (American Statesmen Ser.). 1998. 240.32 (*0-7910-4549-8*) Chelsea Hse.

Chelsea House Publishing Staff. Botticelli. (World's Greatest Artists Ser.). 1997. 17.95 (*1-85813-801-9*) Chelsea Hse.

***Chelsea House Publishing Staff.** Central & East Africa. (Exploration of Africa Ser.). (Illus.). 144p. (gr. 8-12). 2000. 29.95 (*0-7910-5743-7*) Chelsea Hse.

Chelsea House Publishing Staff. Cezanne. (World's Greatest Artists Ser.). 1997. 17.95 (*1-85813-933-3*) Chelsea Hse.

***Chelsea House Publishing Staff.** Colonial Leaders. (Illus.). 1999. 169.50 (*0-7910-5340-7*); pap. 89.50 (*0-7910-5694-5*) Chelsea Hse.

— Congo & Angola Regions. (Exploration of Africa Ser.). (Illus.). 144p. (gr. 7-12). 1999. 29.95 (*0-7910-5742-9*) Chelsea Hse.

Chelsea House Publishing Staff. Dali. (World's Greatest Artists Ser.). 80p. (YA). (gr. 7 up). 1997. 17.95 (*1-85813-656-3*) Chelsea Hse.

— Dinosaurs. (Concise Collection). (Illus.). 48p. (J). (gr. 3 up). 1997. 15.95 (*1-85627-767-4*) Chelsea Hse.

***Chelsea House Publishing Staff.** Early Pioneers. LC 99-39209. (World's Railroads Ser.). (Illus.). 64p. 1999. 21.95 (*0-7910-5559-0*) Chelsea Hse.

— Egypt. (Exploration of Africa Ser.). (Illus.). 144p. 2000. 29.95 (*0-7910-5744-5*) Chelsea Hse.

— Exploration of Ethiopia: Emerging Nations. (Exploration of Africa Ser.). (Illus.). 144p. (gr. 8-12). 2000. 29.95 (*0-7910-5745-3*) Chelsea Hse.

— Exploration of North Africa: Emerging Nations. (Exploration of Africa Ser.). (Illus.). 144p. (gr. 8-12). 2000. 29.95 (*0-7910-5746-1*) Chelsea Hse.

— Exploration of Southeast Africa: Emerging Nations. (Exploration of Africa Ser.). (Illus.). 144p. (gr. 8-12). 2000. 29.95 (*0-7910-5747-X*) Chelsea Hse.

— Exploration of Sudan: Emerging Nations. (Exploration of Africa Ser.). (Illus.). 144p. 2000. 29.95 (*0-7910-5453-5*) Chelsea Hse.

— Exploration of West Africa: Emerging Nations. (Exploration of Africa Ser.). (Illus.). 144p. (gr. 8-12). 2000. 29.95 (*0-7910-5748-8*) Chelsea Hse.

Chelsea House Publishing Staff. Fables & Their Morals, 4. 64p. 1999. 17.49 (*0-7910-5214-1*) Chelsea Hse.

— Fables & Their Morals: The Fighting Roosters & the Eagle to the Lion in Love, 2. LC 98-36355. 64p. 1999. 17.49 (*0-7910-5212-5*) Chelsea Hse.

— Fables & Their Morals: The Lion & the Mouse to the Redbreast & the Sparrow, 3. (Illus.). 64p. 1999. 17.49 (*0-7910-5213-3*) Chelsea Hse.

— Fables & Their Morals Set. 1999. 69.95 (*0-7910-5210-9*) Chelsea Hse.

***Chelsea House Publishing Staff.** Famous Trains of the 20th Century. LC 99-57682. (Illus.). 64p. 1999. 21.95 (*0-7910-5563-9*) Chelsea Hse.

Chelsea House Publishing Staff. Female Firsts in Their Fields, 8 vols. 1999. 135.60 (*0-7910-5138-2*) Chelsea Hse.

— Ferdinand & Isabella: Monarchs. 1996. 14.95 (*0-7910-2507-1*) Chelsea Hse.

— Ferdinand Magellan. 1996. 14.95 (*0-7910-2510-1*) Chelsea Hse.

— Fighters of World War II. (Concise Collection). (Illus.). 48p. (J). (gr. 3 up). 1997. 15.95 (*1-85627-777-1*) Chelsea Hse.

— Fish: Keeping & Breeding Them in Captivity, 9 vols. 1998. 161.55 (*0-7910-5086-6*) Chelsea Hse.

***Chelsea House Publishing Staff.** Freight by Rail. (Illus.). 64p. 1999. 21.95 (*0-7910-5562-0*) Chelsea Hse.

Chelsea House Publishing Staff. Freshwater Fish. (Concise Collection). (Illus.). 48p. (J). (gr. 3 up). 1997. 15.95 (*1-85627-797-6*) Chelsea Hse.

— Galaxy of the Superstars. 1998. 101.70 (*0-7910-5147-1*) Chelsea Hse.

— George Washington Carver: Devout Scientist. (Heroes of the Faith Ser.). 208p. (YA). (gr. 5 up). 1999. lib. bdg. 17.95 (*0-7910-5040-8*) Chelsea Hse.

***Chelsea House Publishing Staff.** Georgia O'Keefe. 1999. 15.40 (*0-606-16414-6*) Turtleback.

Chelsea House Publishing Staff. Geronimo. 1996. 14.95 (*0-7910-2295-1*) Chelsea Hse.

— Hernan Cortes: Explorer. 1996. 14.95 (*0-7910-2505-5*) Chelsea Hse.

— Heroes of the Faith. 1998. 179.50 (*0-7910-5050-5*) Chelsea Hse.

***Chelsea House Publishing Staff.** High Speed Trains. LC 99-88743. (World's Railroads Ser.). (Illus.). 64p. 1999. 21.95 (*0-7910-5565-5*) Chelsea Hse.

Chelsea House Publishing Staff. Horses. (Concise Collection). (Illus.). 48p. (J). (gr. 3 up). 1997. 15.95 (*1-85627-772-0*) Chelsea Hse.

— How Our Muscles Work. LC 94-28304. (Invisible World Ser.). (Illus.). 32p. (J). (gr. 4 up). 1995. lib. bdg. 15.95 (*0-7910-3150-0*) Chelsea Hse.

— I Still Miss Him. (Heartbeats Ser.). 112p. (YA). (gr. 7 up). 1995. pap. 5.95 (*0-7910-3016-4*) Chelsea Hse.

— Jackie Joyner-Kersee: Track & Field Star. 1996. 14.95 (*0-7910-4202-2*) Chelsea Hse.

— Julio Cesar Chavez: Boxing Champion. 1996. 14.95 (*0-7910-2503-9*) Chelsea Hse.

— Keats: Truth & Imagination. (Illustrated Poetry Anthology Ser.). (Illus.). 96p. (YA). (gr. 7 up). 1997. 17.95 (*1-86019-276-9*) Chelsea Hse.

— Klee. (World's Greatest Artists Ser.). (Illus.). 80p. (YA). (gr. 7 up). 1997. 17.95 (*0-7525-1195-5*) Chelsea Hse.

***Chelsea House Publishing Staff.** Latinos in the Limelight, 8 vols. 2000. 143.60 (*0-7910-6096-9*) Chelsea Hse.

Chelsea House Publishing Staff. Lautrec. (World's Greatest Artists Ser.). 1997. 17.95 (*1-85813-948-1*) Chelsea Hse.

C

An Asterisk (*) at the beginning of an entry indicates that the title is appearing for the first time.

Chelsea House Publishing Staff. Los Cinco Sentidos En El Mundo Animal, 5 vols. (SPA.). 1997. 79.75 (*0-7910-4000-3*) Chelsea Hse.

Chelsea House Publishing Staff. Male Sports Stars. 1998. 83.74 (*0-7910-4592-7*) Chelsea Hse.

— Manet. (World's Greatest Artists Ser.). 1997. 17.95 (*1-85813-908-2*) Chelsea Hse.

— Marine Aquarium. (Fish Ser.). (Illus.). 64p. (YA). (gr. 3 up). 1999. lib. bdg. 17.95 (*0-7910-5092-0*) Chelsea Hse.

— Military Badges & Insignia. (Concise Collection). 48p. (J). (gr. 3 up). 1997. 15.95 (*1-85627-792-5*) Chelsea Hse.

— Modern Sports Cars. (Concise Collection). (Illus.). 48p. (J). (gr. 3 up). 1997. 15.95 (*1-85627-733-X*) Chelsea Hse.

— Morocco: Major World Nations. (Major World Nations Ser.). (Illus.). 144p. 1999. 19.95 (*0-7910-5389-X*) Chelsea Hse.

— Native America Medicine: Indians of North America. LC 97-11427. (Indians of North America Ser.). 120p. (YA). (gr. 5 up). 1997. pap. 9.95 (*0-7910-4464-5*) Chelsea Hse.

— The New England Indians. LC 96-41644. (Illus.). 144p. (YA). (gr. 5 up). 1999. 19.95 (*0-7910-4525-0*) Chelsea Hse.

***Chelsea House Publishing Staff.** Passenger Trains. LC 99-51667. (Illus.). 64p. 1999. 21.95 (*0-7910-5561-2*) Chelsea Hse.

Chelsea House Publishing Staff. People & Customs of the World. 1998. 79.80 (*0-7910-5137-4*) Chelsea Hse.

— Picasso. (World's Greatest Artists Ser.). 1997. 17.95 (*1-85813-606-7*) Chelsea Hse.

— Planets & Stars. (Concise Collection). 48p. (J). (gr. 3 up). 1997. 15.95 (*1-85627-738-0*) Chelsea Hse.

— Plantas del Desierto. (SPA., Illus.). 32p. (YA). (gr. 3 up). 1996. lib. bdg. 15.95 (*0-7910-4018-6*) Chelsea Hse.

— Plantos Debajo del Mar. (SPA., Illus.). 32p. (YA). (gr. 3 up). 1996. lib. bdg. 15.95 (*0-7910-4022-4*) Chelsea Hse.

— Prowrestling Stars Boxed Set. 1999. 287.20 (*0-7910-5440-3*) Chelsea Hse.

***Chelsea House Publishing Staff.** Railway Locomotives. LC 99-42726. (World's Railroads Ser.). (Illus.). 64p. 1999. 21.95 (*0-7910-5560-4*) Chelsea Hse.

— Rapid Transit Systems. LC 99-58700. (World's Railroads Ser.). (Illus.). 64p. (YA). (gr. 5 up). 1999. 21.95 (*0-7910-5564-7*) Chelsea Hse.

Chelsea House Publishing Staff. Rembrandt. (World's Greatest Artists Ser.). 1997. 17.95 (*1-85813-918-X*) Chelsea Hse.

— Reptile & Amphibian, 9 vols. 1998. 161.55 (*0-7910-5076-9*) Chelsea Hse.

— Robert Burns: The Scottish Bard. (Illustrated Poetry Anthology Ser.). 96p. (YA). (gr. 7 up). 1997. 17.95 (*1-86019-286-6*) Chelsea Hse.

— Smart Woman's Guides, 7 vols. (Smart Woman's Guides Ser.). 1998. 128.32 (*0-7910-4504-8*) Chelsea Hse.

— Steam Trains. (Concise Collection). (Illus.). 48p. (J). (gr. 3 up). 1997. 15.95 (*1-85627-743-7*) Chelsea Hse.

— Superstars of Women's Basketball. LC 96-34781. (Female Sports Stars Ser.). 64p. (J). (gr. 3 up). 1997. lib. bdg. 15.95 (*0-7910-4389-4*) Chelsea Hse.

— Switzerland: Major World Nations. (Illus.). 144p. 1999. 19.95 (*0-7910-5399-7*) Chelsea Hse.

— El Tacto. (SPA., Illus.). 32p. (YA). (gr. 3 up). 1996. 15.95 (*0-7910-4009-7*) Chelsea Hse.

— Tanks. (Concise Collection). (Illus.). 48p. (YA). (gr. 3 up). 1997. 15.95 (*1-85627-748-8*) Chelsea Hse.

— Tarantulas & Scorpions. LC 98-214374. (Basic Domestic Reptile & Amphibian Library). (Illus.). 64p. (YA). (gr. 3 up). 1999. lib. bdg. 17.95 (*0-7910-5081-5*) Chelsea Hse.

— Topgun. (Concise Collection). (Illus.). 48p. (J). (gr. 3 up). 1997. 15.95 (*1-85627-787-9*) Chelsea Hse.

***Chelsea House Publishing Staff.** Untold History of the Civil War. (Illus.). 1999. 215.40 (*0-7910-5439-X*) Chelsea Hse.

— La Vida Empieza en el Mar. Sanchez, Isidro, ed. (SPA., Illus.). 32p. (YA). (gr. 3 up). 1996. lib. bdg. 15.95 (*0-7910-4027-5*) Chelsea Hse.

Chelsea House Publishing Staff. La Vista. (SPA., Illus.). 32p. (YA). (gr. 3 up). 1996. 15.95 (*0-7910-4003-8*) Chelsea Hse.

— W. B. Yeats: Romantic Visionary. (Illustrated Poetry Anthology Ser.). (Illus.). 96p. (YA). (gr. 7 up). 1997. 17.95 (*1-86019-291-2*) Chelsea Hse.

— Whitney Houston: Singer/Actress. LC 97-21869. (Junior Black Americans of Achievement Ser.). (Illus.). 76p. (J). (gr. 3-6). 1997. lib. bdg. 15.95 (*0-7910-4565-X*) Chelsea Hse.

— William Hastie. (Black Americans of Achievement Ser.). 1996. 18.95 (*1-55546-589-7*) Chelsea Hse.

— William Shakespeare: Love Sonnets. (Illustrated Poetry Anthology Ser.). (Illus.). 96p. (J). (gr. 7). 1997. 17.95 (*1-86019-296-3*) Chelsea Hse.

***Chelsea House Publishing Staff.** Wonders of the World Set. 2000. 67.80 (*1-56706-051-9*) Chelsea Hse.

— World in the Time Of... Set. 2000. 143.60 (*0-7910-6036-5*) Chelsea Hse.

Chelsea House Publishing Staff, ed. Native Son. 1998. pap. text 4.95 (*0-7910-4139-5*) Chelsea Hse.

Chelsea House Publishing Staff & Llamas, Andrew. El Gusto. (Los Cinco Sentidos del Mundo Animal Ser.). (SPA., Illus.). 32p. (YA). (gr. 3 up). 1996. 15.95 (*0-7910-4007-0*) Chelsea Hse.

— El Oido. (SPA., Illus.). 32p. (YA). (gr. 3 up). 1996. lib. bdg. 15.95 (*0-7910-4001-1*) Chelsea Hse.

— El Olfato. (SPA., Illus.). 32p. (YA). (gr. 3 up). 1996. 15.95 (*0-7910-4005-4*) Chelsea Hse.

Chelsea House Publishing Staff & Marvis, B. Las Aves Conquistan el Aire. Sanchez, Isidro, ed. (Incredible Mundo de las Plantas Ser.). (SPA., Illus.). 32p. (YA). (gr. 3 up). 1996. lib. bdg. 15.95 (*0-7910-4036-4*) Chelsea Hse.

— Las Grandes Planicies. (SPA., Illus.). 32p. (YA). (gr. 3 up). 1996. lib. bdg. 15.95 (*0-7910-4013-5*) Chelsea Hse.

— Los Reptiles Primitivos. (SPA., Illus.). 32p. (YA). (gr. 3 up). 1996. lib. bdg. 15.95 (*0-7910-4034-8*) Chelsea Hse.

Chelsea House Publishing Staff & Mavis, B. Plantas de los Bosques. (SPA., Illus.). 32p. (YA). (gr. 3 up). 1996. lib. bdg. 15.95 (*0-7910-4020-8*) Chelsea Hse.

Chelsea House Publishing Staff, et al. Las Junglas Misteriosas. (SPA., Illus.). 32p. (YA). (gr. 3 up). 1996. lib. bdg. 15.95 (*0-7910-4015-1*) Chelsea Hse.

Chelsea House Publishing Staff, et al. Los Mamiferos Dominan la Tierra. (SPA., Illus.). 32p. (YA). (gr. 3 up). 1996. lib. bdg. 15.95 (*0-7910-4038-0*) Chelsea Hse.

— Los Primeros Anfibios. Sanchez, Isidro, ed. (SPA., Illus.). 32p. (YA). (gr. 3 up). 1996. lib. bdg. 15.95 (*0-7910-4031-3*) Chelsea Hse.

— La Vegetacion de los Rios, Lagos y Pantanos. (SPA., Illus.). 32p. (YA). (gr. 3 up). 1996. lib. bdg. 15.95 (*0-7910-4024-0*) Chelsea Hse.

Chelsea House Publishing Staff, jt. auth. see Campbell, Jim.

Chelsea House Publishing Staff, jt. auth. see James, Brant.

Chelsea House Publishing Staff, jt. auth. see Macht, Norman.

Chelsea House Publishing Staff, jt. auth. see Muskat, Carrie.

Chelton, C. F., ed. Manual of Recommended Practice for Combustible Gas Indicators & Portable Direct-Reading Hydrocarbon Detectors. 2nd ed. 61p. (C). 1993. pap. 28.00 (*0-932627-48-X*, 158SI93) Am Indus Hygiene.

Chelton, David, ed. see McKeague, Patrick.

Chelton, Mary K. Excellence in Library Services to Young Adults: The Nation's Top Programs. LC 94-15407. xiv, 76 p. 1994. pap. text 22.00 (*0-8389-3440-4*) ALA.

Chelton, Mary K. & Broderick, Dorothy M., eds. VOYA Reader Two. LC 97-43610. 272p. 1998. pap. 24.50 (*0-8108-3460-X*) Scarecrow.

Chelton, Mary K. & Rosinia, James M. Bare Bones: Young Adult Services Tips for Public Library Generalists. 73p. 1993. 17.00 (*0-8389-7665-4*) ALA.

Chelton, Mary K. & Young Adult Library Services Association Staff. Excellence in Library Services to Young Adults: The Nation's Top Programs. 2nd ed. LC 97-16917. 120p. 1997. 22.00 (*0-8389-3474-9*) ALA.

***Chelton, Mary K. & Young Adult Library Services Association Staff.** Excellence in Library Services to Young Adults: The Nation's Top Programs. 3rd ed. LC 00-27741. (YA). 2000. write for info. (*0-8389-0786-5*) ALA.

Chelune, Gordon J., et al. Self-Disclosure: Origins, Patterns & Implications of Openness in Interpersonal Relationships. LC 79-88766. (Jossey-Bass Social & Behavioral Science Ser.). 416p. reprint ed. pap. 129.00 (*0-8357-4972-X*, 203790500009) Bks Demand.

Chelvam, Reginald T. Einstein Was Wrong: The Scroll Theory of Cosmology & of Matter. LC 82-71689. (Illus.). 268p. (Orig.). (C). 1982. pap. text 19.95 (*0-943796-00-8*) Penso Pubns.

Chem Ed Res Staff. Chemistry. 1994. teacher ed., lab manual ed. 90.62 (*0-8151-6541-2*) Mosby Inc.

Chem-Intell Staff. Chem-Facts: PVC. (C). 1992. 920.00 (*0-7855-0063-4*, Pub. by Chem Intell Srvs) St Mut.

Chem Systems International, Ltd. Staff. Reducing Pollution from Selected Energy Transformation Sources. 230p. 1976. lib. bdg. 73.00 (*0-86010-036-7*) G & T Inc.

ChemADVISOR, Inc. Staff. Regulated Chemicals Directory, 1995. 1988p. 1995. 425.00 (*0-471-28724-5*, VNR) Wiley.

ChemADVISOR, Inc. Staff, compiled by. Regulated Chemicals Directory, 1995. (Environmental Engineering Ser.). 2000p. 1995. text 345.95 (*0-442-02124-0*, VNR) Wiley.

Chemama, Roland. Larousse Dictionnaire de Psychanalyse. (FRE.). 307p. 1993. pap. 29.95 (*0-7859-7686-8*, 2037202229) Fr & Eur.

Chemelynski, Carol C. Opportunities in Food Service Careers. 2nd ed. (Opportunities In . . . Ser.). (Illus.). 160p. pap. 12.95 (*0-8442-8175-1*, 297OIFS, VGM Career) NTC Contemp Pub Co.

— Opportunities in Food Service Careers. 2nd ed. (Opportunities in...Ser.). (Illus.). 160p. 1992. 14.95 (*0-8442-8174-3*, VGM Career) NTC Contemp Pub Co.

Chemelynski, Carol Caprioni. Opportunities in Food Service Careers. LC 99-38250. (Opportunities in... Ser.). 160p. 1999. 14.95 (*0-8442-3330-7*); pap. 11.95 (*0-8442-3407-9*) NTC Contemp Pub Co.

Chemerins. Federal Jurisdictions. LC 93-80780. 960p. 1994. 31.95 (*0-316-13775-8*, Aspen Law & Bus) Aspen Pub.

Chemerinsky, Erwin. Constitutional Law: Principles & Policies. LC 96-79676. 1000p. 1997. pap. text 36.95 (*1-56706-532-5*, 65325) Panel Pubs.

— Federal Jurisdiction. 900p. 1989. 35.00 (*0-316-13759-6*, Aspen Law & Bus) Aspen Pub.

— Federal Jurisdiction. 3rd ed. LC 98-49917. 1040p. 1999. pap. text 38.95 (*0-7355-0037-1*) Panel Pubs.

— Interpreting the Constitution. LC 87-2484. 209p. 1987. 55.00 (*0-275-92674-5*, C2674, Praeger Pubs) Greenwood.

Chemerka, William R. The Alamo Almanac & Book of Lists. LC 97-2623. (Illus.). 160p. 1997. pap. 16.95 (*1-57168-150-7*, 150-7, Eakin Pr) Sunbelt Media.

***Chemerka, William R.** The Davy Crockett Almanac & Book of Lists. LC 99-35289. 2000. write for info. (*1-57168-319-4*, Eakin Pr) Sunbelt Media.

Chemers, jt. auth. see Altman.

Chemers, Martin M. An Integrative Theory of Leadership. LC 97-893. 300p. 1997. 49.95 (*0-8058-2678-5*); pap. 24.50 (*0-8058-2679-3*) L Erlbaum Assocs.

Chemers, Martin M., et al, eds. Diversity in Organizations: New Perspectives for a Changing Workplace. LC 95-8231. (Claremont Symposium on Applied Social Psychology Ser.: Vol. 8). 252p. (C). 1995. 45.00 (*0-8039-5548-0*); pap. 22.50 (*0-8039-5549-9*) Sage.

Chemers, Martin M. & Ayman, Roya, eds. Leadership Theory & Research: Perspectives & Directions. (Illus.). 347p. 1992. text 59.95 (*0-12-170609-5*) Acad Pr.

Chemers, Martin M., jt. auth. see Altman, Irwin.

Chemiakin, Mihail. Illiustratsii K Proizvedeniiam Vladimira Vysotskogo. (RUS., Illus.). 50p. 1988. pap. 25.00 (*0-89830-127-0*) Russica Pubs.

— Petersburg & Paris Period, 2 vols. Incl. Vol. II. Transformation: New York Period. 286p. 1986. (Illus.). 504p. 1986. Set boxed set 250.00 (*0-317-56275-4*, Pub. by Mosaic Pr) Empire Pub Srvs.

Chemical Congress of North America Staff. Molecular & Biomolecular Electronics: Developed from a Symposium Sponsored by the Division of Biochemical Technology of the American Chemical Society at the 4th Annual Chemical Congress of North America (202nd National Meeting of the American Chemical Society), New York, NY, 8/25-8/30, 1991. Birge, Robert R., ed. LC 94-28455. (Advances in Chemistry Ser.: No. 240). (Illus.). 608p. 1994. text 149.00 (*0-8412-2698-9*, Pub. by Am Chemical) OUP.

Chemical Engineering Magazine Editors & McNaughton, Kenneth J., eds. The Chemical Engineering Guide to Heat Transfer: Plant Principles, Vol. 1. 368p. 1986. 79.95 (*0-89116-465-0*) Hemisp Pub.

Chemical Engineering Progress Staff & Chopay, Nicholas P., eds. Fluid Movers. 2nd ed. LC 94-10483. 320p. 1994. 55.00 (*0-07-011159-6*) McGraw.

Chemical Gas & Oil Terminals Staff, ed. Marine Terminal Survey Guidelines. 1995. 125.00 (*1-85609-062-0*, Pub. by Witherby & Co) St Mut.

Chemical Heritage Foundation Staff. Introducing the Chemical Sciences. LC 97-46771. 1998. pap. 7.50 (*0-941901-18-1*) Chem Heritage Fnd.

Chemical Industry Institute of Toxicology Staff, et al, eds. Nasal Toxicity & Dosimetry of Inhaled Xenibiotics: Implications for Human Health. LC 94-29943. 450p. 1995. 125.00 (*1-56032-366-3*) Taylor & Francis.

Chemical Intelligence Services Staff. Chem-Facts: European Review. (C). 1990. 525.00 (*1-871798-08-6*, Pub. by Chem Intell Srvs) St Mut.

— Chem-Facts: Styrenics. (C). 1990. 525.00 (*1-871798-07-8*, Pub. by Chem Intell Srvs) St Mut.

— Chem-Facts: United Kingdom. (C). 1990. 525.00 (*1-871798-06-X*, Pub. by Chem Intell Srvs) St Mut.

Chemical Intelligence Services Staff, ed. Chem-Facts: Belgium (1990) (C). 1990. 525.00 (*1-871798-03-5*, Pub. by Chem Intell Srvs) St Mut.

— Chem-Facts: Ethylene & Propylene. (C). 1990. 525.00 (*1-871798-05-1*, Pub. by Chem Intell Srvs) St Mut.

— Chem-Facts: France. (C). 1990. 525.00 (*1-871798-04-3*, Pub. by Chem Intell Srvs) St Mut.

— Chem-Facts: Netherlands. (C). 1990. 525.00 (*1-871798-02-7*, Pub. by Chem Intell Srvs) St Mut.

***Chemical Packaging Committee.** Shippers Guide to Loading & Securement of Packaged Matereials & Dangerous Goods in Intermodal Equipment: Highway, Rail & Water. xiii, 112p. (C). 1999. pap. 50.00 (*1-930268-14-9*) Packaging Prof.

Chemical Society (Great Britain) Staff, jt. auth. see University of Exeter Staff.

Chemical Technician Curriculum Project Staff. Chemical Technology Handbook: Guidebook for Industrial Chemical Technologists & Technicians. Pecsok, Robert L. et al. eds. LC 75-22497. 225p. 1975. reprint ed. pap. 69.80 (*0-608-03842-3*, 206428900008) Bks Demand.

Chemie, B. G., ed. Potential Health Hazards of Existing Chemicals. LC 90-10020. (Toxicological Evaluations Ser.: Vol. 1). (Illus.). 368p. 1990. 62.95 (*0-387-52577-7*) Spr-Verlag.

— Toxicological Evaluations Vol. 2: Potential Health Hazards of Existing Chemicals. LC 90-10020. (Illus.). 224p. 1991. 64.95 (*0-387-53435-0*) Spr-Verlag.

— Toxicological Evaluations Vol. 3: Potential Health Hazards of Existing Chemicals. LC 90-10020. (Illus.). 192p. 1991. 54.95 (*0-387-54331-7*) Spr-Verlag.

— Toxicological Evaluations Vol. 5: Potential Health Hazards of Existing Chemicals. vii, 193p. 1993. 62.95 (*0-387-56138-2*) Spr-Verlag.

— Toxicological Evaluations Vol. 9: Potential Health Hazards of Existing Chemicals. (Illus.). 171p. 1995. 53.95 (*3-540-59148-6*) Spr-Verlag.

Chemie, B. G. & Heidelberg, eds. Toxicological Evaluations Vol. 8: Potential Health Hazards of Existing Chemicals. 300p. 1994. 62.95 (*0-387-58287-8*) Spr-Verlag.

***Chemillier-Gendreau, Monique.** Sovereignty over the Paracel & Spratly Island. LC 00-37547. 2000. write for info. (*90-411-1381-9*) Kluwer Law Intl.

Chemin, J. English-French Vocabulary of Architectural Materials Terminology. (ENG & FRE.). 308p. 1992. pap. 42.50 (*0-7859-8841-6*) Fr & Eur.

— English-French Vocabulary of Architectural Materials Terminology. 308p. 1992. pap. 44.50 (*2-85608-049-9*, Pub. by La Maison Du Dict) IBD Ltd.

Chemin, Jean-Yves. Perfect Incompressible Fluids. Gallagher, Isabelle & Iftimie, Dragos, trs. LC 98-35385. (Oxford Lecture Series in Mathematics & Its Applications: No. 14). 198p. 1998. text 68.00 (*0-19-850397-0*) OUP.

Cheminais, J., et al. Fundamentals of Public Personnel Management. 287p. 1998. pap. 39.95 (*0-7021-4379-0*) Intl Spec Bk.

— Provision & Maintenance of Public Personnel. LC 99-215250. 192p. 1998. pap. 39.95 (*0-7021-4380-4*) Intl Spec Bk.

— Public Management & Administration for Effective Governance. 1998. pap. 39.95 (*0-7021-4421-5*) Intl Spec Bk.

Chemins de fer China Staff. Dictionnaire Francais - Chinois du Chemin de Fer. (CHI & FRE.). 1140p. 1991. 95.00 (*0-8288-9528-7*) Fr & Eur.

Chemistry An. Diels Alder. 1995. text. write for info. (*0-13-524588-5*) Allyn.

Chemitz, Martin. Ministry, Word, & Sacraments: An Enchiridion. Poellot, Luther, tr. 1981. pap. 23.00 (*0-570-03295-4*, 15-2730) Concordia.

Chemla, M., et al, eds. Molten Salt Chemistry & Technology. 814p. 1992. text 266.00 (*0-87849-600-9*, Pub. by Trans T Pub) Enfield Pubs NH.

Chemnitz, Martin. Examination of the Council of Trent, Pt. I. Kramer, Fred, tr. from LAT. LC 79-143693. 706p. 1971. 37.00 (*0-570-03213-X*, 15-2113) Concordia.

— Examination of the Council of Trent, Pt. II. Kramer, Fred, tr. 824p. 1979. 37.00 (*0-570-03272-5*, 15-2717) Concordia.

— Examination of the Council of Trent, Pt. III. Kramer, Fred, tr. 1979. 37.00 (*0-570-04229-1*, 15-2188) Concordia.

— Examination of the Council of Trent, Pt. IV. Kramer, Fred, tr. 1979. 37.00 (*0-570-04230-5*, 15-2189) Concordia.

— Examination of the Council of Trent, 4 Vols., Set. Kramer, Fred, tr. 1979. 119.99 (*0-570-04232-1*, 15-2191) Concordia.

— Justification: The Chief Article of Christian Doctrine. Preus, J. A., tr. 200p. 1986. 25.00 (*0-570-04227-5*, 15-2186) Concordia.

***Chemnitz, Martin.** The Lord's Prayer. Williams, George, ed. & tr. by. LC 99-53101. 128p. 2000. 19.99 (*0-570-04283-6*) Concordia.

Chemnitz, Martin. The Lord's Supper. Preus, J. A., tr. 296p. 1979. 26.00 (*0-570-03275-X*, 15-2720) Concordia.

— Two Natures in Christ. Preus, J. A., tr. LC 74-115465. Orig. Title: De Duabus Naturis in Christo. 608p. 1970. 32.00 (*0-570-03210-5*, 15-2109) Concordia.

Chemofsky, Barbara & Gage, Diane. Changing Your Child's Behavior by Changing Yours: Effective Solutions for Common Parenting Problems. LC 95-24089. 224p. (Orig.). 1996. pap. 14.00 (*0-517-88463-1*) Crown Pub Group.

Chemsak, John A. Illustrated Revision of the Cerambycidae of North America Vol. I: Parandrinae, Spondylidinae, Aseminae Prioninae. (Illus.). (C). 1996. 138.60 (*1-885850-02-6*) Wolfsgarden.

Chemsak, John A. & Linsley, E. Gorton. Checklist of the Beetles of North & Central America & the West Indies Vol. 7: The Longhorned Beetles. 138p. 1982. pap. 18.00 (*0-937548-04-9*) Sandhill Crane.

Chemsak, John A., jt. auth. see Linsley, E. Gordon.

Chemsak, John A., jt. auth. see Linsley, E. Gorton.

Chemsak, John A., jt. auth. see Linsley, Earle G.

Chen. Analogue Digital Control. 624p. (C). 1995. pap. text, teacher ed. 27.95 (*0-03-097056-3*) OUP.

— Asian Management Systems: Chinese, Japanese & Korean Styles Of Business. 1995. pap. text 19.99 (*1-86152-500-1*) Thomson Learn.

— Linear System Theory & Design. 2nd ed. 688p. 1995. pap., student ed. 26.00 (*0-19-511595-3*) OUP.

— One-Dimensional Digital Signal Processing. (Electrical Engineering & Electronics Ser.: Vol. 9). (Illus.). 464p. 1979. text 69.75 (*0-8247-6877-9*) Dekker.

— Structural Engineering Handbook on CD-ROM. 1559p. 1998. 129.00 incl. cd-rom (*0-8493-9759-6*) CRC Pr.

— Structural Steel Design. (C). 1994. text 46.00 (*0-03-005153-3*) Harcourt Coll Pubs.

Chen & Chin-Mai. Parliamentary Opinion of Delegated Legislation. LC 70-76628. (Columbia University. Studies in the Social Sciences: No. 394). reprint ed. 20.00 (*0-404-51394-8*) AMS Pr.

***Chen, et al.** Proceedings of the 14th World Congress of IFAC, 18 vols. LC 99-51730. 1999. pap. 1967.50 (*0-08-043247-6*, Pergamon Pr) Elsevier.

Chen, jt. auth. see Blocher.

Chen, jt. auth. see Klein.

***Chen, In Chin.** Das Institut der Vertretung im Verwaltungsverfahren zwischen Verwaltungseffizienz und Rechtsschutzauftrag. 2000. 45.95 (*3-631-35474-6*) P Lang Pubng.

Chen, A. & Chen, B., contrib. by. The Art of War: A Treatise on Chinese Military Science. 2nd ed. 78p. Date not set. reprint ed. 6.95 (*0-89346-921-1*) Heian Intl.

Chen, A. B. & Sher, A. Semiconductor Alloys: Physics & Materials Engineering. (Microdevices: Physics & Fabrication Technologies Ser.). (Illus.). 364p. (C). 1995. text 95.00 (*0-306-45052-6*, Kluwer Plenum) Kluwer Academic.

***Chen, AI-Yen.** Reflective Spin: Case Studies of Teachers in Higher Education Transforming Action. 386p. 1999. 62.00 (*981-02-4185-2*); pap. 38.00 (*981-02-4186-0*) World Scientific Pub.

Chen, Albert H., jt. ed. see Wesley-Smith, Peter.

Chen, Andrew. Research in Finance, Vol. 16. 360p. 1998. 78.50 (*0-7623-0328-X*) Jai Pr.

Chen, Andrew H., ed. Research in Finance, Vol. 7. 1988. 78.50 (*0-89232-796-0*) Jai Pr.

— Research in Finance, Vol. 15. 360p. 1997. 78.50 (*0-7623-0259-3*) Jai Pr.

Chen, Andrew H., et al, eds. Research in Finance, Vol. 1. 310p. 1979. 78.50 (*0-89232-043-5*) Jai Pr.

— Research in Finance, Vol. 2. 237p. 1980. 78.50 (*0-89232-130-X*) Jai Pr.

— Research in Finance, Vol. 3. 184p. 1981. 78.50 (*0-89232-218-7*) Jai Pr.

— Research in Finance, Vol. 4. 215p. 1983. 78.50 (*0-89232-279-9*) Jai Pr.

— Research in Finance, Vol. 5. 261p. 1985. 78.50 (*0-89232-587-9*) Jai Pr.

C

An Asterisk (*) at the beginning of an entry indicates that the title is appearing for the first time.

— Research in Finance, Vol. 6. 277p. 1986. 78.50 (*0-89232-650-6*) Jai Pr.

— Research in Finance, Vol. 8. 270p. 1990. 78.50 (*0-89232-969-6*) Jai Pr.

— Research in Finance, Vol. 9. 248p. 1991. 78.50 (*1-55938-339-9*) Jai Pr.

— Research in Finance, Vol. 10. 260p. 1993. 78.50 (*1-55938-424-7*) Jai Pr.

— Research in Finance, Vol. 11. 226p. 1994. 78.50 (*1-55938-651-7*) Jai Pr.

— Research in Finance, Vol. 12. 1995. 78.50 (*1-55938-781-5*) Jai Pr.

— Research in Finance, Vol. 13. 1996. 78.50 (*1-55938-578-2*) Jai Pr.

— Research in Finance: Supplement Management under Government Intervention, No. 1: Management under Government Intervention. 301p. 1984. suppl. ed. 78.50 (*0-89232-427-9*) Jai Pr.

Chen, Andrew H. & Kensinger, John W. Innovations in Equity Financing. LC 91-7811. 208p. 1991. 52.95 (*0-89930-478-8*, CIA, Quorum Bks) Greenwood.

Chen, Andrie T. & Leidersdorf, Craig B., eds. Arctic Coastal Processes & Slope Protection Design. (Symposium Proceedings Ser.). 256p. 1988. 26.00 (*0-87262-639-3*) Am Soc Civil Eng.

Chen, Anna, et al. Through the Storm of an Affair: Collected True Stories. 286p. 1994. pap. 10.95 (*1-885216-01-7*) Evan Formosan.

Chen, Arbee L., ed. Cooperative Information Systems: Proceedings of the 2nd IFCIS International Conference on Cooperative Information Systems, Kiawah Island, South Carolina, 1997. LC 97-71762. 264p. 1997. pap. 115.00 (*0-8186-7946-8*) IEEE Comp Soc.

Chen, B., jt. contrib. by see Chen, A.

Chen, Baizhu, et al, eds. Financial Market Reform in China: Progress, Problems, & Prospects. LC 99-42078. (Political Economy of Global Interdependence Ser.). 350p. (C). 1999. 69.00 (*0-8133-3619-8*) Westview.

Chen, Bang-yen. Geometry of Submanifolds. LC 73-78558. (Pure & Applied Mathematics Ser.: Vol. 22). 320p. reprint ed. pap. 99.20 (*0-608-16548-4*, 202780300054) Bks Demand.

Chen, Bang-Yen. Total Mean Curvature & Submanifolds of Finite Type. (Pure Mathematics Ser.: Vol. 1). 352p. 1984. text 54.00 (*9971-966-02-6*); pap. text 28.00 (*9971-966-03-4*) World Scientific Pub.

Chen, Ben M. H - Control & Its Applications. Thoma, M., ed. LC 98-6586. (Lecture Notes in Control & Information Sciences: Vol. 235). (Illus.). 356p. 1998. pap. 92.00 (*1-85233-026-0*) Spr-Verlag.

***Chen, Ben M.** Robust & H-Infinity Control. Dickinson, B. W. et al, eds. (Consensus & Controversy Ser.). xii, 452p. 2000. 89.95 (*1-85233-255-7*) Spr-Verlag.

Chen, Bonnie. Through the Path of Grace: An Extraordinary Journey for an Ordinary Woman. 291p. 1994. pap. 10.95 (*0-9631789-7-0*) Evan Formosan.

Chen, C. C. & Koh, K. M. Principles & Techniques in Combinatorics. 312p. 1992. text 44.00 (*981-02-1114-7*); pap. text 21.00 (*981-02-1139-2*) World Scientific Pub.

Chen, C. E., ed. see Liu, T. S. & Li, K.

Chen, C. H. Computer Engineering Handbook. 688p. 1992. 100.00 (*0-07-010924-9*) McGraw.

Chen, C. H., ed. Applied Time Series Analysis: Proceedings of the IEEE International Workshop, Beijing, 9 August 1988. 212p. (C). 1989. text 70.00 (*9971-5-0712-9*) World Scientific Pub.

— Digital Waveform Processing & Recognition. 224p. 1982. 125.00 (*0-8493-5777-2*, TK5102, CRC Reprint) Franklin.

— Expert Systems & Pattern Analysis: Proceedings. 136p. (C). 1987. text 74.00 (*9971-5-0475-8*) World Scientific Pub.

— Neural Networks for Pattern Recognition & Their Applications. 200p. (C). 1994. text 59.00 (*981-02-0766-2*) World Scientific Pub.

— Pattern Recognition & Signal Processing, No. 29. (NATO Advanced Study Institute Ser.). 666p. 1978. text 162.50 (*90-286-0978-4*) Kluwer Academic.

— Signal Processing & Pattern Recognition in Nondestructive Evaluation of Materials. (NATO Asi Series F: Vol. 44). viii, 344p. 1988. 100.95 (*0-387-19100-3*) Spr-Verlag.

Chen, C. H., et al, eds. Handbook of Pattern Recognition & Computer Vision. 2nd ed. LC 98-51616. 1019p. 1997. text 124.00 (*981-02-3071-0*) World Scientific Pub.

Chen, C. H., et al. Handbook of Pattern Recognition & Computer Vision. 996p. 1993. text 86.00 (*981-02-2276-9*) World Scientific Pub.

— Handbook on Pattern Recognition & Computer Vision. 996p. 1993. text 184.00 (*981-02-1136-8*) World Scientific Pub.

***Chen, C. J.** Finite Analytic Method in Flows & Heat Transfer. LC 00-37721. (Illus.). 2000. pap. write for info. (*1-56032-898-3*) Taylor & Francis.

Chen, C. K., et al, eds. Silicon-on-Insulator & Buried Metals in Semiconductors. (Symposium Proceedings Ser.: Vol. 107). 1988. text 17.50 (*0-931837-75-8*) Materials Res.

Chen, C. N. Signal Processing Handbook. (Electrical Engineering & Electronics Ser.: Vol. 51). (Illus.). 840p. 1988. text 235.00 (*0-8247-7956-8*) Dekker.

Chen, C. N. & Hoult, D. I. Biomedical Magnetic Resonance Technology. (Medical Science Ser.). (Illus.). 362p. 1989. 163.00 (*0-85274-118-9*) IOP Pub.

Chen, C. S. Essays on Taiwan. 1995. reprint ed. 35.00 (*957-638-284-X*) Oriental Bk Store.

Chen, C. S., et al, eds. Boundary Element Technology XIII: Proceedings of the International Conference. (Boundary Elements Ser.: Vol. 2). 708p. 1999. 344.00 (*1-85312-688-8*, 6888, Pub. by WIT Pr) Computational Mech MA.

Chen, C. S., jt. ed. see Golberg, M. A.

Chen, C. T. Development of New NLO Crystals in the Borate Series. LC 91-41424. (Laser Science & Technology Ser.: Vol. 15). 75p. 1993. pap. text 53.00 (*3-7186-5351-6*) Gordon & Breach.

Chen, C. Y., ed. Science & Technology in Chinese Civilization: Proceedings of the Workshop held at the University of California, San Diego, California, September 1985. 372p. 1987. text 89.00 (*9971-5-0192-9*) World Scientific Pub.

Chen, C. Y., et al, eds. Two-Tone Set-Bells of Marquis Yi: Hubei Provincial Museum, Wuhan, China - University of California, San Diego, U. S. A., August 1988. 500p. (C). 1994. text 130.00 (*981-02-0740-9*) World Scientific Pub.

Chen, C. Y. & Berra, P. Bruce, eds. Proceedings of the International Conference on Parallel Processing, 1993, Vol. I: Architecture. 376p. 1993. lib. bdg. 79.95 (*0-8493-8984-4*, QA) CRC Pr.

Chen, Chang W. & Zhang, Ya-Qin. Visual Information Representation, Communication & Image Processing. LC 99-26366. (Optical Engineering Ser.). (Illus.). 576p. 1999. text 195.00 (*0-8247-1928-X*) Dekker.

Chen, Changgui, jt. auth. see Zweig, David.

Chen, Chao-Hsiu. The Bamboo Oracle: Confucian Wisdom for Every Day. LC 98-86147. (Illus.). 144p. 1998. pap. 26.95 (*1-885203-67-5*) Jrny Editions.

***Chen, Chao-Hsiu.** Beauty Feng Shui: Chinese Techniques for Unveiling Your Inner Beauty. (Illus.). 160p. 2001. pap. 14.95 (*0-89281-852-2*) Inner Tradit.

***Chen, Chaomei.** Information Visualization & Virtual Environments. LC 99-12444. 250p. 1999. 95.00 (*1-85233-136-4*) Spr-Verlag.

Chen, Charlie C., ed. Experimental Verification of Process Models: Proceedings of a Symposium Held at the 1981 Metals Congress, Cincinnati, Ohio, 21-23 September 1981 - Sponsored by the Process Modeling Activity of the ASM Mechanical Working & Forming Division. LC 83-70638. (ASM Conference Proceedings Ser.). 400p. reprint ed. pap. 124.00 (*0-608-16828-9*, 202703800053) Bks Demand.

***Chen, Chauncey.** Dynamic ChiKung. LC 99-64079. (Illus.). 128p. 1999. pap. 19.95 (*1-56167-553-9*, Five Star Spec Ed) Am Literary Pr.

Chen, Chen. Come Watch the Sun Go Home: A Memoir of Upheaval & Revolution in China. LC 99-30405. 336p. 1999. pap. 13.95 (*1-56924-680-7*, Pub. by Marlowe & Co) Publishers Group.

Chen, Chen & King, Ted. Come Watch the Sun Go Home: A Memoir of Upheaval & Revolution in China. LC 98-5342. 336p. 1999. 22.95 (*1-56924-742-0*, Pub. by Marlowe & Co) Publishers Group.

Chen, Cheng-lung, ed. Debris-Flow Hazards Mitigation: Mechanics, Prediction, Assessment: Proceedings of First International Conference. LC 97-24995. 840p. 1997. 64.00 (*0-7844-0268-X*) Am Soc Civil Eng.

Chen Chi. Heaven & Water. deluxe ed. LC 83-71448. (Illus.). 80p. 1983. 60.00 (*0-9604652-2-7*) Chen Chi Studio.

Chen Chi-lu. Material Culture of the Formosan Aborigines. (Illus.). 422p. 1986. reprint ed. 65.00 (*0-89986-362-0*) Oriental Bk Store.

Chen, Chi-Lu. People & Culture. 160p. 1987. 22.00 (*0-89986-370-1*) Oriental Bk Store.

Chen, Chi-Tsong. Analog & Digital Control System Design: Transfer-Function, State-Space, & Algebraic Methods. (Illus.). 88p. (C). 1995. pap. text, student ed. write for info. (*0-03-094071-0*) OUP.

— Analog & Digital Control System Design: Transfer-Function, State-Space & Algebraic Methods. (Illus.). 624p. (C). 1993. text 89.95 (*0-03-094070-2*) OUP.

***Chen, Chi-Tsong.** Digital Signal Processing: Spectral Computation & Filter Design. (The/Oxford Series in Electrical & Computer Engineering). (Illus.). 528p. (C). 2000. text 99.95 (*0-19-513638-1*) OUP.

Chen, Chi-Tsong. Linear System Theory & Design. 662p. (C). 1984. student ed. write for info. (*0-03-071691-8*) SCP.

— Linear System Theory & Design. 3rd ed. (The Oxford Series in Electrical & Computer Engineering). (Illus.). 352p. 1998. text 88.00 (*0-19-511777-8*) OUP.

— System & Signal Analysis. 576p. (C). 1989. teacher ed. write for info. (*0-03-027918-6*) SCP.

— System & Signal Analysis. 2nd ed. (Illus.). 88p. (C). 1994. pap. text, student ed. write for info. (*0-03-008089-4*) OUP.

— System & Signal Analysis. 2nd ed. (The/Oxford Series in Electrical & Computer Engineering). (Illus.). 736p. 1994. text 82.00 (*0-19-510722-5*) OUP.

Chen, Chia-jui, et al. Systematics of Epilobium (Onagraceae) in China. Anderson, Christiane, ed. (Systematic Botany Monographs: Vol. 34). (Illus.). 209p. 1992. pap. 25.00 (*0-912861-34-7*) Am Soc Plant.

Chen, Chih-Wen. Magnetism & Metallurgy of Soft Magnetic Materials. (Illus.). 592p. 1986. reprint ed. pap. 16.95 (*0-486-64997-0*) Dover.

***Chen, Chin T. & Clough, Anne V., eds.** Physiology & Function from Multidimensional Images. 524p. 1999. pap. text 103.00 (*0-8194-3132-X*) SPIE.

Chen, Ching-Chih. HyperSource on Multimedia-HyperMedia Technologies. 237p. 1989. pap. 14.00 (*0-8389-7371-X*) ALA.

— HyperSource on Optical Technologies. 275p. 1989. pap. 15.00 (*0-8389-7359-0*) ALA.

— Library Management Without Bias. Stueart, Robert D., ed. LC 80-82482. (Foundations in Library & Information Science: Vol. 13). 225p. 1981. 78.50 (*0-89232-163-6*) Jai Pr.

— MicroUse Directory: Software. 440p. (Orig.). 1984. pap. 99.50 (*0-931555-01-9*) MicroUse Info.

— Scientific & Technical Information Sources. 2nd ed. 861p. 1987. 90.00 (*0-262-03120-5*) MIT Pr.

Chen, Ching-Chih, ed. Planning Global Information Infrastructure. 548p. 1995. pap. text 39.50 (*1-56750-200-8*, Z674) Ablx Pub.

Chen, Ching-Jen, et al, eds. Flow Modeling & Turbulence Measurements VI: Proceedings of the 6th International Symposium, Tallahassee, Florida, USA, 8-10 September 1996. (Illus.). 932p. (C). 1996. 175.00 (*90-5410-826-6*, Pub. by A A Balkema) Ashgate Pub Co.

Chen, Ching-Jen & Jaw, Shenq-Yuh. Fundamentals of Turbulence Modeling. LC 97-18161. (Combustion: an International Ser.). 192p. 1996. text 65.00 (*1-56032-405-8*) Taylor & Francis.

Chen-Ch'Ing Li. Practical Newspaper Readings. rev. ed. (CHI., Illus.). 279p. 1989. 26.95 (*0-318-42726-5*) Yale Far Eastern Pubns.

Chen-Ch'Ing Li & Te-Ming Yeh. Practical Business Conversations. (CHI.). 225p. (Orig.). 1992. pap. text 18.95 (*0-88710-172-0*) Yale Far Eastern Pubns.

Chen-ch'ing Li, ed. see Chin-ming Ch'ian, et al.

Chen-ch'ing Li, ed. see Ching-yi Li, et al.

Chen, Chiou-sen D. Serials Management: A Practical Guide. LC 95-17986. (Frontiers of Access to Library Materials: 3). 186p. (Orig.). 1995. pap. 38.00 (*0-8389-0658-3*, 0658-3-2045) ALA.

Chen, Christian. Michtams of David. (CHI.). 128p. 1997. pap. 14.00 (*0-9661121-3-X*) Liv Word.

— Night unto Night: The Night Scenes in the Bible. (Illus.). 118p. 1997. pap. 12.00 (*0-9661121-0-5*) Liv Word.

— Samson's Riddle. (CHI., Illus.). 68p. 1997. pap. 10.00 (*0-9661121-2-1*) Liv Word.

— Yoked with Christ: An Outline of the Book of Jonah. (CHI., Illus.). 144p. 1997. pap. 14.00 (*0-9661121-1-3*) Liv Word.

Chen, Christian & Wong, K. H. On the Top of Pisgah - A Bird's Eye View of the Bible: A Glimpse into the Old Testament. (CHI.). 440p. 1998. pap. 30.00 (*0-9661121-4-8*) Liv Word.

— On the Top of Pisgah - A Bird's Eye View of the Bible Vol. 2: A Glimpse into the New Testament. (CHI.). 336p. 1998. pap. 28.00 (*0-9661121-5-6*) Liv Word.

Chen, Christopher. Recent Advantages in the Management of Infertility. 368p. 1989. 50.00 (*0-07-099144-8*) McGraw.

Chen, Chuangtian, ed. Electro-Optic & Second Harmonic Generation Materials, Devices & Application II. LC 99-161874. (Proceedings of SPIE Ser.: Vol. 3556). 248p. 1998. 80.00 (*0-8194-3017-X*) SPIE.

Chen, Chuanmiao M. & Shih, Tsimin M. Finite Element Methods for Integrodifferential Equations. LC 97-18449. (Series on Applied Mathematics). 300p. 1998. 48.00 (*981-02-3263-2*) World Scientific Pub.

Chen, Chung-Hwan. Sophia: The Science Aristotle Sought. (Studien und Materialien Zur Geschichte der Philosophie Ser.: Vol. 2). xiv, 827p. 1976. 160.00 (*3-487-05834-0*) G Olms Pubs.

Chen, Clarence, et al, eds. Chinese Americans in Loss & Separation: Social, Medical & Psychiatric Perspectives. LC 92-74036. 110p. 1996. pap. 16.95 (*0-930194-48-9*) Ctr Thanatology.

Chen, Constance M. The Sex Side of Life: Mary Ware Dennett's Pioneering Battle for Birth Control & Sex Education. (Illus.). 368p. 1996. 25.00 (*1-56584-132-8*, Pub. by New Press NY) Norton.

— Sex Side of Life Mary Ware Dennett's Pioneering Battle for Birth Control & Sex Education. 1997. pap. 15.00 (*1-56584-133-6*, Pub. by New Press NY) Norton.

Chen, D. L. World Consumption Economics. 300p. 1999. 68.00 (*981-02-3847-9*) World Scientific Pub.

Chen, Da. Colors of the Mountain. 320p. 2000. 25.00 (*0-375-50288-2*) Random.

***Chen, Da.** Colors of the Mountain. 2001. reprint ed. pap. 13.00 (*0-385-72060-2*, Anchor NY) Doubleday.

Chen, Daniel, tr. see Howard, Grant.

Chen, Daniel, tr. see Wiersbe, Warren W.

Chen, David L., tr. see Hummel, Charles E.

Ch'en, David Y. Lu Hsun: Complete Poems - A Translation with Introduction & Annotation. LC 88-70039. (Monograph Ser.: No. 22). 275p. (Orig.). 1988. pap. 10.00 (*0-939252-19-8*) ASU Ctr Asian.

Chen, Debby, jt. auth. see Kraus, Robert.

Chen, Deborah, ed. Essential Elements in Early Intervention: Visual Impairment & Multiple Disabilities. LC 99-41221. 400p. 1998. pap. 34.95 (*0-89128-305-6*) Am Foun Blind.

Chen, Diexian. The Money Demon. Hanan, Patrick, tr. from CHI. LC 98-33911. 344p. (C). 1999. text 42.00 (*0-8248-2096-7*); pap. text 19.95 (*0-8248-2103-3*) UH Pr.

Chen, Duxiu. Chen Duxiu's Last Articles & Letters, 1937-1942. Benton, Gregor, tr. from CHI. LC 98-23410. (Chinese Worlds Ser.). 288p. 1998. text 45.00 (*0-8248-2112-2*) UH Pr.

Chen, E., et al, eds. Calorimetry in High Energy Physics: Proceedings of the 7th International Conference Tucson, Arizona, U. S. A. 9-14 November, 1997. 600p. 1998. 58.00 (*981-02-3400-7*) World Scientific Pub.

— Tantalum. LC 96-79464. (Illus.). 493p. 1996. 140.00 (*0-87339-330-9*, 3309) Minerals Metals.

Chen, E. J. & Pantano, Garlo G., eds. Interfaces in Composites Vol. 170: Materials Research Society Symposium Proceedings. 361p. 1990. text 17.50 (*1-55899-058-5*) Materials Res.

Chen, E. P. & Luk, V. K., eds. Advances in Numerical Simulation Techniques for Penetration & Perforation of Solids. LC 93-73261. 201p. pap. 55.00 (*0-7918-1025-9*) ASME.

Chen, Eachou. Cross-Sectional Anatomy of Acupoints. Flower, Andrew, tr. LC 94-27579. 1995. text 51.95 (*0-443-04974-2*) Church.

Chen, Edward & Kwan, C. H., eds. Asia's Borderless Economy: The Emergence of Sub-Regional Zones. (Illus.). 216p. 1998. 69.95 (*1-86448-449-7*, Pub. by Allen & Unwin Pty); pap. 35.00 (*1-86373-664-6*, Pub. by Allen & Unwin Pty) Paul & Co Pubs.

Chen, Edward K. Transnational Corporations & Legal Issues. LC 93-15974. (United Nations Library on Transnational Corporations: Vol. 19). 1994. write for info. (*0-415-08549-7*) Routledge.

Chen, Edward K., ed. Corporate Links & Foreign Direct Investment in Asia & the Pacific. 320p. (C). 1996. pap. text 40.00 (*0-8133-8973-9*, Pub. by Westview) HarpC.

Chen, Edward S., jt. ed. see Crowson, Andrew.

Chen, Edwin. Deadly Scholarship: The True Story of Gang Lu & Mass Murder in America's Heartland. LC 94-19041. (Illus.). 288p. 1994. 19.95 (*1-55972-241-X*, Birch Ln Pr) Carol Pub Group.

Chen, Ellen. La Mesa China. (SPA., Illus.). 138p. 1988. write for info. (*0-9650407-9-8*) Chanyii.

Chen, Ellen M. Tao Te Ching: A New Translation with Commentary. 274p. 1989. pap. 12.95 (*1-55778-238-5*) Paragon Hse.

Chen, Evan. Praise Favorite I: For Worship. 150p. 1991. pap. 5.75 (*0-9631789-0-3*) Evan Formosan.

Chen, F. F. Introduction to Plasma Physics & Controlled Fusion Vol. 1: Plasma & Physics. 2nd ed. (Illus.). 438p. (C). 1984. text 37.50 (*0-306-41332-9*, Kluwer Plenum) Kluwer Academic.

Chen, F. H. Foundation of Expansive Soils. 2nd rev. ed. (Developments in Geotechnical Engineering Ser.: No. 54). xxii,464p. 1988. 172.50 (*0-444-43036-9*) Elsevier.

***Chen, F. H.** Soil Engineering: Testing, Design & Remediation LC 99-23653. 304p. 1999. boxed set 89.95 (*0-8493-2294-4*) CRC Pr.

Chen, Fei & Schuurmann, Gerrit, eds. Quantitative Structure - Activity Relationships in Environmental Sciences Vol. VII: Proceedings of QSAR 96, 24-28 June 1996, Elsinore, Denmark. LC 97-30982. (SETAC Technical Publications Ser.). (Illus.). 1997. 98.00 (*1-880611-23-6*, SETAC Pr) SETAC.

***Chen, Fen.** Regular Polygons I: Applying New Theory of Trisection to Construct a Regular Heptagon for Centuries in the History of Mathematics. (New Discoveries in the Euclidean Geometry Ser.). (Illus.). 170p. 1999. pap. 20.00 (*0-9671511-1-2*, 990002) Intl Sch Math & Sci.

***Chen, Fen-Ling.** Working Women & State Policies in Taiwan: A Study in Political Economy. LC 00-27827. 2000. write for info. (*0-312-23462-7*) St Martin.

Chen, Feng. Economic Transition & Political Legitimacy in Post-Mao China: Ideology & Reform. LC 95-8783. 246p. (C). 1995. text 49.50 (*0-7914-2657-2*); pap. text 16.95 (*0-7914-2658-0*) State U NY Pr.

Chen, Fu H., tr. see Torrey, R. A.

Chen, G. Approximate Kalman Filtering. (Approximations & Decomposition Ser.). 300p. 1993. text 81.00 (*981-02-1359-X*) World Scientific Pub.

***Chen, G.** Controlling Chaos & Bifurcations in Engineering Systems. LC 99-16242. 672p. 1999. boxed set 89.95 (*0-8493-0579-9*) CRC Pr.

Chen, G., jt. auth. see Chui, C.

Chen, G., jt. auth. see Chui, Charles K.

Chen, G. R., et al. Linear Stochastic Control Systems. LC 95-10426. 400p. 1995. boxed set 99.95 (*0-8493-8075-8*, 8075) CRC Pr.

Chen, George P., jt. auth. see Copper, John Franklin.

Chen, Gerald H., jt. auth. see Rockefeller, R. D.

Chen, Gong. A New Concept of Self-Defense. LC 98-148285. 144p. (C). 1998. per. 38.95 (*0-7872-4350-7*, 41435001) Kendall-Hunt.

Chen, Goong. Vibration & Damping in Distributed Systems, Set. 1993. write for info. (*0-8493-7153-8*) CRC Pr.

Chen, Goong, et al, eds. Distributed Parameter Control Systems: Trends & Applications. (Lecture Notes in Pure & Applied Mathematics Ser.: Vol. 128). (Illus.). 544p. 1990. pap. text 199.00 (*0-8247-8444-8*) Dekker.

Chen, Goong & Zhou, Jianxin. Boundary Element Methods. (Computational Mathematics & Applications Ser.). (Illus.). 646p. 1992. text 116.00 (*0-12-170940-X*) Acad Pr.

— Vibration & Damping in Distributed Systems, I. LC 93-19888. 464p. 1993. lib. bdg. 110.00 (*0-8493-7161-9*) CRC Pr.

— Vibration & Damping in Distributed Systems, II. LC 93-19888. 400p. 1993. lib. bdg. 99.50 (*0-8493-7162-7*, TA355) CRC Pr.

***Chen, Graham.** Integrated Telecommunications Management Solutions. LC 99-47335. (IEEE Series on Network Management). 1999. 69.95 (*0-7803-5353-6*) Inst Electrical.

***Chen, Guanrong.** Introduction to Fuzzy Control Systems. 2000. 89.95 (*0-8493-1658-8*) CRC Pr.

Chen, Guanrong, jt. auth. see Chui, Charles K.

Chen, Guanrong, jt. auth. see DeFigueiredo, Rui J.

Chen, Gui-Qiang, et al, eds. Nonlinear Partial Differential Equations: A Volume in Honor of Xiaqi Ding. 460p. 1999. 86.00 (*981-02-3664-6*) World Scientific Pub.

Chen, Guo Bang. Cryogenics & Refrigeration: Proceedings of the International Conference on Cryogenics & Refrigeration. 1998. pap. text 168.00 (*7-80003-414-3*) World Scientific Pub.

Chen, Guo-Ming. Foundations of Intercultural Communication. LC 97-18261. 340p. 1997. pap. text 50.00 (*0-205-17529-5*) Allyn.

Chen, Guo-Ming & Starosta, William J. Foundations of Intercultural Communication. 112p. (C). 1997. pap. text, teacher ed. write for info. (*0-205-28016-1*, T8016-2) Allyn.

***Chen, Guo-Ming & Starosta, William J., eds.** Communication & Global Society. LC 99-48693. 328p. (C). 2000. pap. text 31.95 (*0-8204-4865-6*) P Lang Pubng.

C

An Asterisk (*) at the beginning of an entry indicates that the title is appearing for the first time.

Chen, Guobang & Flynn, Thomas M., eds. Cryogenics & Refrigeration: Proceedings of International Conference. (International Academic Publishers Ser.). 394p. 1989. 115.00 (*0-08-037534-0*, 1107; 1712; 1708, Pub. by IAP) Elsevier.

Chen Guoda. Tectonics of China. (International Academic Publishers Ser.). (Illus.). 266p. 1989. 81.00 (*0-08-037033-0*, Pergamon Pr) Elsevier.

Chen, Guoqing. Fuzzy Logic in Data Modeling: Semantics, Constraints, & Database Design. LC 98-29391. (Chinese Studies in Information Science). 1998. 115.00 (*0-7923-8253-6*) Kluwer Academic.

***Chen, Guoqing, et al, eds.** Fuzzy Logic & Soft Computing. LC 99-44508. 1999. text 129.95 (*0-7923-8650-7*) Kluwer Academic.

Chen, H. & Guo, L. Identification & Stochastic Adaptive Control. (Systems & Control: Foundations & Applications Ser.). xi, 435p. 1991. 99.00 (*0-8176-3597-1*) Birkhauser.

***Chen, H. F., et al, eds.** Discrete Event Systems, Stochastic Systems, Fuzzy & Neural Systems I. 486p. 1999. pap. 126.00 (*0-08-043221-2*) Elsevier.

— Fuzzy & Neural Systems, Control in Agricultural Processes, Vol. II. 526p. 1999. pap. 126.00 (*0-08-043222-0*) Elsevier.

— Modeling, Identification, Signal Processing, Adaptive Control Vol. H, Pt. 2. 510p. 1999. pap. 126.00 (*0-08-043220-4*) Elsevier.

***Chen, H. F. & Wahlberg, B., eds.** Modeling, Identification, Signal Processing I, Vol. H. 480p. 1999. pap. 126.00 (*0-08-043219-0*) Elsevier.

***Chen, H. K.** Dynamic Travel Choice Models: A Variational Inequality Approach. LC 98-50977. (Illus.). 320p. 1998. 99.00 (*3-540-64953-0*) Spr-Verlag.

Chen, H. S. Space Remote Sensing System: An Introduction. 1985. text 133.00 (*0-12-170880-2*) Acad Pr.

Chen, Han-Fu, ed. Identification & System Parameter Estimation 1988: Proceedings of the 8th IFAC-IFORS Symposium, Beijing, People's Republic of China, August 27-31, 1988, 2 vols., Set. LC 88-36926. (IFAC Proceedings Ser.: 8908). (Illus.). 1434p. 1989. 577.00 (*0-08-035739-3*, Pergamon Pr) Elsevier.

***Chen, Han-Fu, et al, eds.** Plenary Volume. 268p. 1999. pap. 126.00 (*0-08-042756-1*, Pergamon Pr) Elsevier.

Chen, Harold. Medical Genetics Handbook. (Illus.). 396p. 1988. pap. 52.50 (*0-87527-371-8*) Green.

Chen, Harold, jt. ed. see Gall, G. A.

Chen, He-Sheng, jt. auth. see Zheng, Zhi-Peng.

Chen, Helen. Helen Chen's Chinese Home Cooking. 1996. pap. 16.00 (*0-688-14609-0*, Hearst) Hearst Commns.

Chen, Helen. Peking Cuisine. (Illus.). 40p. pap. 2.95 (*0-297-82278-0*, Pub. by Weidenfeld & Nicolson) Trafalgar.

Chen, Herbert, et al. Manual of Common Bedside Surgical Procedures. LC 95-4786. (Illus.). 400p. 1996. spiral bd. 25.95 (*0-683-01549-4*) Lppncott W & W.

***Chen, Herbert, et al.** Manual of Common Bedside Surgical Procedures. 2nd ed. LC 99-40830. 2000. write for info. (*0-683-30792-4*) Lppncott W & W.

Chen-Ho, Wang. Rose, Rose, I Love You. Goldblatt, Howard, tr. from CHI. LC 97-33519. (Modern Literature from Taiwan Ser.). 192p. 1998. 24.50 (*0-231-11202-5*) Col U Pr.

***Chen-Ho, Wang.** Rose, Rose, I Love You: A Novel. 2000. reprint ed. pap. 14.95 (*0-231-11203-3*) Col U Pr.

Chen, Hollis C. Theory of Electromagnetic Waves. (Illus.). 467p. (C). 1992. reprint ed. text 107.00 (*1-878907-58-1*) TechBooks.

***Chen, Hongyi.** Institutional Transition of China's Township & Village Enterprises: Market Liberalization, Conceptual Form Innovation & Privatization. (Studies on the Economic Reform of China). 292p. 2000. text 74.95 (*0-7546-1050-0*, Pub. by Ashgate Pub) Ashgate Pub Co.

Chen, Hsi. Remote Sensing Calibration Systems: An Introduction. LC 96-29865. 250p. 1997. 64.00 (*0-937194-38-7*) A Deepak Pub.

Ch'En Hsi-Ju, et al. Twenty Papers on Statistics & Probability. LC 61-9803. (Selected Translations in Mathematical Statistics & Probability Ser.: Vol. 12). 312p. 1973. 62.00 (*0-8218-1462-1*, STAPRO/12) Am Math.

Chen-Hsia Wang. Small Cookbook - Very! Very! Vegetarian! LC 96-102476. (CHI & ENG.). 80p. 1994. pap. 7.95 (*0-941676-51-X*) Wei-Chuan Pub.

Chen, Hsiang-shui. Chinatown No More: Taiwan Immigrants in Contemporary New York. LC 91-55547. (Anthropology of Contemporary Issues Ser.). (Illus.). 296p. 1992. text 45.00 (*0-8014-2697-9*); pap. text 17.95 (*0-8014-9989-5*) Cornell U Pr.

Chen, Hsuan Chih & Tzeng, Ovid J., eds. Language Processing Chinese. LC 92-15112. (Advances in Psychology Ser.: Vol. 90). xii,394p. 1992. 164.50 (*0-444-89139-0*, North Holland) Elsevier.

Chen, Hsuan-Shan. The Comparative Coachability of Certain Types of Intelligence Tests. (Columbia University. Teachers College. Contributions to Education Ser.: No. 338). reprint ed. 32.50 (*0-404-55338-9*) AMS Pr.

***Chen, Hsueh-Hsia.** Creative Chinese Oven Cooking: The New Trend. (Illus.). 104p. 1999. pap. 15.95 (*0-941676-78-1*) Wei-Chuan Pub.

Chen, Hsueh-Hsia, jt. auth. see Lee, Mu-Tsun.

Chen-hua. In Search of the Dharma: Memoirs of a Modern Chinese Buddhist Pilgrim. Yu, Chun-fang, ed. Mair, Denis C., tr. LC 90-27564. (Series in Buddhist Studies). (Illus.). 292p. (C). 1992. pap. text 19.95 (*0-7914-0846-9*) State U NY Pr.

Chen-hua. In Search of the Dharma: Memoirs of a Modern Chinese Buddhist Pilgrim. Yu, Chun-Fang, ed. Mair, Denis C., tr. LC 90-27564. (SUNY Series in Buddhist Studies). (Illus.). 292p. (C). 1992. text 59.50 (*0-7914-0845-0*) State U NY Pr.

Chen, Huan-Chang. The Economic Principles of Confucius & His School, 2 vols, Set. 1973. lib. bdg. 600.00 (*0-87968-080-6*) Krishna Pr.

Chen, Huey-tsyh. Theory Driven Evaluations. 336p. (C). 1990. pap. 25.00 (*0-8039-5899-4*); text 52.00 (*0-8039-3532-3*) Sage.

Chen, Huey-tsyh & Rossi, Peter H., eds. Using Theory to Improve Program & Policy Evaluations. 290. LC 91-27813. (Contributions in Political Science Ser.: No. 290). 288p. 1992. 75.00 (*0-313-28346-X*, CTV/, Greenwood Pr) Greenwood.

Chen, Huimin. Inversion of Revolutoinary Ideals: A Study of the Tragic Essence of Georg Buchner's 'Dantons Tod', Ernst Toller's 'Masse Mensch' & Bertolt Brecht's 'Die Massnahme' LC 96-45509. (Studies on the Themes & Motifs in Literature: Vol. 33). 113p. (C). 1998. 36.95 (*0-8204-3718-2*) P Lang Pubng.

Chen, Ih-Chin, et al, eds. Microelectronic Device & Multilevel Interconnection Technology II, Vol. 2875. 400p. 1996. 76.00 (*0-8194-2273-8*) SPIE.

Chen, J. & Patton, Ron. Robust Model-based Fault Diagnosis for Dynamic Systems LC 98-45861. (International Series On Asian Studies in Computer & Information Science). 19p. 1999. write for info. (*0-7923-8411-3*) Kluwer Academic.

Chen, J. C., et al, eds. Developments in Fluidization & Fluid-Particle Systems. LC 96-158298. 180p. 1995. 35.00 (*0-8169-0688-2*, S-308) Am Inst Chem Eng.

Chen, J. C., ed. see National Heat Transfer Conference Staff.

Chen, J. L., jt. ed. see Vafai, K.

Chen, J. Q. Group Representation Theory for Physicists. 564p. 1989. text 90.00 (*9971-5-0105-8*); pap. text 48.00 (*9971-5-0099-X*) World Scientific Pub.

Chen, J. Q., et al. Tables of the SU(mn) SU(m) x SU(n) Coefficients of Fractional Parentage. 456p. 1991. text 74.00 (*981-02-0113-3*) World Scientific Pub.

Chen, Jack. Inside the Cultural Revolution. LC 76-376844. xxvi, 483 p. 1976. 7.00 (*0-85969-071-7*) Intl Pubs Mktg.

Chen, Jai-er, et al. Development & Applications of Free Electron Lasers. (China Center of Advanced Science & Technology (World Laboratory) Symposium - Workshop Proceedings Ser.: Vol. 12). 176p. 1997. text 72.00 (*90-5699-502-2*, Harwood Acad Pubs) Gordon & Breach.

Chen, James. Essentials of Cardiac Imaging. 2nd ed. LC 97-19921. (Illus.). 400p. 1997. text 132.50 (*0-316-13784-7*) Lppncott W & W.

— The Passing of the Torch. LC 88-63263. 92p. (Orig.). 1988. pap. 9.95 (*0-940232-31-6*) Seedsowers.

Chen, James C. & Chou, Chung-Chi. Cane Sugar Handbook: A Manual for Cane Sugar Manufacturers & Their Chemists. 2nd ed. LC 92-39597. 1120p. 1993. 350.00 (*0-471-53037-9*) Wiley.

Chen, Janey. Practical English-Chinese Pronouncing Dictionary. LC 78-77122. (CHI & ENG.). 602p. 1992. pap. 19.95 (*0-8048-1877-0*) Tuttle Pubng.

— A Practical English-Chinese Pronouncing Dictionary. (CHI & ENG.). 601p. 1980. 39.95 (*0-8288-1605-0*, M9545) Fr & Eur.

Chen, Jason, jt. auth. see Hinton, David W.

Chen, Jau-Fei. Nutritional Immunology. Stewart, Taig D. et al, eds. Date not set. pap. 9.95 (*0-9651025-0-5*) Bright Ideas Pr.

Chen, Jen-Gwo & Mital, Anil, eds. Advances in Industrial Engineering Applications & Practice, Vol. I. (Illus.). (Orig.). 1996. pap. text 69.99 (*0-9654599-1-8*) Intl Jrnl Indust.

Chen, Jennifer & Seattle Art Museum Staff. Bottles of Delight: The Thal Collection of Chinese Snuff Bottles. LC 98-10907. 1998. pap. 19.95 (*0-932216-49-8*) Seattle Art.

Chen, Jenny, ed. see Chen, Nolan.

Ch'en, Jerome. The Highlanders of Central China: A History, 1895-1937. LC 90-9156. (Socialism & Social Movements Ser.). 326p. (gr. 13). 1993. text 70.95 (*0-87332-729-2*, East Gate Bk) M E Sharpe.

— Yuan Shih-k'ai. 2nd ed. LC 76-153815. xii, 258p. 1972. 39.50 (*0-8047-0789-8*) Stanford U Pr.

Chen Jian. China's Road to the Korean War: The Making of the Sino-American Confrontation. (Illus.). 352p. 1995. 46.50 (*0-231-10024-8*) Col U Pr.

— China's Road to the Korean War: The Making of the Sino-American Confrontation. (U. S. & Pacific Asia Ser.). (Illus.). 368p. 1996. pap. 18.50 (*0-231-10025-6*) Col U Pr.

***Chen, Jian, ed.** Technology of Object-Oriented Languages & Systems: Proceedings Conference Nanjing, P. R. China 1999. LC 99-62630. 493p. 1999. 135.00 (*0-7695-0393-4*) IEEE Comp Soc.

***Chen, Jian Jiang.** Lord of the Cranes: A Chinese Tale. LC 99-57811. 36p. (J). (gr. k-3). 2000. lib. bdg. 15.88 (*0-7358-1193-8*, Pub. by North-South Bks NYC) Chronicle Bks.

Chen, Jiande Z. & McCallum, Richard W., eds. Electrogastrography: Principles & Applications. LC 94-9177. (Illus.). 448p. 1994. text 90.00 (*0-7817-0213-5*) Lppncott W & W.

— Electrogastrography: Principles & Applications. LC 94-9177. (Illus.). 447p. reprint ed. pap. 138.60 (*0-608-09761-6*, 206993400007) Bks Demand.

Chen, Jianfu. From Administrative Authorisation to Private Law: A Comparative Perspective of the Developing Civil Law in the People's Republic of China. LC 94-40158. 352p. (C). 1994. lib. bdg. 123.50 (*0-7923-3200-8*, Pub. by M Nijhoff) Kluwer Academic.

***Chen, Jiang Hong.** The Legend of the Kite: A Story of China. LC 99-28855. Orig. Title: La Legende du Cerf-Volant. (Illus.). 32p. (J). (gr. k-3). 1999. pap. 5.95 (*1-56899-811-2*) Soundprints.

— The Legend of the Kite: A Story of China. LC 99-28855. Orig. Title: La Legende du Cerf-Volant. (Illus.). 32p. (J). (ps-3). 1999. 15.95 (*1-56899-810-4*) Soundprints.

Chen, Jiang Hong. The Legend of the Kite: A Story of China - Includes Doll. Orig. Title: La Legende du Cerf-Volant. (Illus.). 32p. (J). (gr. k-3). 1999. pap. 16.95 (*1-56899-814-7*) Soundprints.

Chen, Jianming, jt. auth. see Yang, Chi-Wan.

Chen, Jianping, jt. auth. see Sorensen, Henrik V.

Chen, Jie & Deng, Peng. China since the Cultural Revolution: From Totalitarianism to Authoritarianism. LC 94-28006. 144p. 1994. 55.00 (*0-275-94647-9*, Praeger Pubs) Greenwood.

Chen, Jie & Gu, Guoxiang. Control Oriented System Identification: An H Approach. 440p. 2000. text 84.95 (*0-471-32048-X*) Wiley.

***Chen, Jie & Gupta, A. K.** Parametrical Statistical Change Point Analysis. 192p. 2000. 59.95 (*0-8176-4169-6*) Birkhauser.

Chen, Jie-Qi, ed. Project Zero Framework Vol. II: Project Spectrum - Learning Activities Guide. LC 98-30414. 264p. 1998. pap. text 18.95 (*0-8077-3767-4*) Tchrs Coll.

Chen, Jin-Quan & Wang, Pei-Ning. Tables of Clebsch-Gordan, Racah, & Subduction Coefficients of SU(n) Groups. 240p. 1987. text 114.00 (*9971-5-0072-8*); pap. text 64.00 (*9971-5-0073-6*) World Scientific Pub.

Chen, Jinosong. Greener Mountain at Younger Age. (CHI.). 151p. 1997. pap. 10.00 (*1-890474-03-7*) Nrth Amer Chinese Wrters.

Chen Jo-hsi. Execution of Mayor Yin & Other Stories from the Great Proletarian Cultural Revolution. (Chinese Literature in Translation Series) Ing, Nancy & Goldblatt, Howard, trs. LC 78-1956. (Chinese Literature in Translation Ser.). 248p. 1979. pap. 12.95 (*0-253-20231-0*, MB-231) Ind U Pr.

Chen, Jo-Shui. Liu Tsung-yuan & Intellectual Change in T'ang China, 773-819. (Studies in Chinese History, Literature & Institutions). (Illus.). 235p. (C). 1992. text 80.00 (*0-521-41964-6*) Cambridge U Pr.

Chen, John. Architecture in Pen & Ink. 1994. 42.95 (*0-07-011079-4*) McGraw.

Chen, John & Cooper, Tim. Architectural Perspective Grids: An Easy Method of Three Dimensional Design & Perspective Construction. 160p. 1995. 44.95 incl. disk (*0-07-011133-2*) McGraw.

Chen, John C., et al, eds. Convective Flow Boiling. 304p. 1996. text 95.00 (*1-56032-507-0*) Taylor & Francis.

Chen, John C. & Bishop, A. A., eds. Liquid-Metal Heat Transfer & Fluid Dynamics: Presented at the Annual Winter Meeting of ASME, New York,N. Y., November 30, 1970. LC 76-141816. 185p. 1970. reprint ed. pap. 57.40 (*0-608-10921-5*, 201689300005) Bks Demand.

Chen, John C., jt. auth. see Arastoopour, Hamid.

Chen, John H., ed. see De Lafayette, J. Maximillien.

Chen, John H., ed. see De LaFayette, Jean M.

Chen, John H., ed. see De Lafayette, Jean M.

Chen, John H., ed. see De LaFayette, Jean M.

***Chen, John-ren.** Foreign Direct Investment. 2000. text 69.95 (*0-312-23404-X*) St Martin.

***Chen, John-ren, ed.** Economic Effects of Globalization. 198p. 1998. text 59.95 (*1-84014-822-5*) Ashgate Pub Co.

Chen, John S. Architecture in Color Drawings. (Illus.). 219p. 1996. 49.95 (*0-07-011405-6*) McGraw.

Chen, Julian. Introduction to Scanning Tunneling Microscopy. LC 92-40047. (Oxford Series in Optical & Imaging Sciences: Vol. 4). (Illus.). 472p. 1993. 90.00 (*0-19-507150-6*) OUP.

Chen, Junshi, et al. Diet, Lifestyle, & Mortality in China: A Study of the Characteristics of 65 Chinese Counties. Campbell, T. Colin et al, eds. LC 89-38882. (Illus.). 920p. 1990. text 185.00 (*0-8014-2453-4*) Cornell U Pr.

Chen, K. & Uppal, Jogindar S. India & China. LC 71-142355. 1971. 22.95 (*0-02-905420-6*) Free Pr.

Chen, K. C. Anatomy of Financial Management. LC 96-92604. 99p. (C). 1996. pap. text 10.00 (*0-9654264-0-8*) Premier CA.

— Wireless Local Area Networks. 300p. (C). 2001. 61.00 (*0-13-173494-6*) P-H.

Chen, K. H., tr. see Hyles, Jack.

Chen, K. Y. & Liu, A. Y., eds. Hypusyne Formation on Eukaryotic Initiation Factor 5A: Biochemistry & Function. (Biological Signals Ser.: Vol. 6, No. 3, 1997). (Illus.). 76p. 1997. pap. 31.50 (*3-8055-6575-5*) S Karger.

***Chen, Kan.** ITS Handbook: Recommendations from the World Road Association [PIARC]. LC 99-36662. (ITS Library). (Illus.). 434p. 1999. 89.00 (*1-58053-103-2*) Artech Hse.

Chen, Kan, ed. Urban Dynamics: Expansions & Reflections. 1971. 10.00 (*0-911302-18-2*) San Francisco Pr.

Chen, Kan, jt. ed. see Dluhy, Milan J.

Canadian Waste Management Conference Staff. Proceedings, 8th Canadian Waste Management Conference: September 3-5, 1986, Sheraton Hotel, Halifax E. LC 99-36662. (ITS Library). (Illus.). 434p. 1999. 89.00 (*1-58053-103-2*) Artech Hse.

Chen, Kan, ed. Urban Dynamics: Expansions & Reflections. 1971. 10.00 (*0-911302-18-2*) San Francisco Pr.

Chen, Kan, jt. ed. see Dluhy, Milan J.

Chen, Kao. Energy Effective Industrial Illuminating Systems. LC 94-14242. 180p. 1994. 74.00 (*0-88173-168-4*) Fairmont Pr.

— Energy Management in Illuminating Systems. LC 99-20866. 176p. 1999. boxed set 69.95 (*0-8493-2628-1*) CRC Pr.

— Industrial Power Distribution & Illuminating Systems. (Electrical Engineering & Electronics Ser.: Vol. 65). (Illus.). 488p. 1990. text 165.00 (*0-8247-8237-2*) Dekker.

Chen, Ke, et al. Mathematical Explorations with MATLAB. LC 99-19617. (Illus.). 320p. (C). 1999. text 64.95 (*0-521-63078-9*); pap. text 24.95 (*0-521-63920-4*) Cambridge U Pr.

Ch'en, Kenneth. Buddhism in China: A Historical Survey. (Studies in History of Religion: Vol. 1). 576p. 1974. pap. text 24.95 (*0-691-00015-8*, Pub. by Princeton U Pr) Cal Prin Full Svc.

Chen, Kenneth Kuan Sh-Eng. Buddhism Lt. of Asia. 1977. pap. 12.95 (*0-8120-0272-5*) Barron.

***Chen, Kerstin.** Lord of the Cranes: A Chinese Tale. James, J. Alison, tr. 36p. 2000. 15.95 (*0-7358-1192-X*) North-South Bks NYC.

Chen, Kevin. Political Alienation & Voting Turnout in the United States, 1960-1988. LC 92-20375. 272p. 1992. text 89.95 (*0-7734-9833-8*) E Mellen.

Chen, King C. China's War with Vietnam, 1979: Issues, Decisions, & Implications. (Publication Ser.: No. 357). 234p. 1987. 31.95 (*0-8179-8571-9*); pap. 18.95 (*0-8179-8572-7*) Hoover Inst Pr.

— Vietnam & China, 1938-1954. LC 78-83684. 452p. reprint ed. pap. 140.20 (*0-8357-3433-1*, 203969000013) Bks Demand.

Chen, King C., ed. China & the Three Worlds: A Foreign Policy Reader. LC 78-51973. 396p. reprint ed. pap. 122.80 (*0-8357-2584-7*, 204028900015) Bks Demand.

Chen, Kitty. Eating Chicken Feet. 1995. 5.50 (*0-87129-469-9*, E32) Dramatic Pub.

Chen, Kuan-Hsing & Ang, Ien. Trajectories: Inter-Asia Cultural Studies. LC 98-10389. (Culture & Communication in Asia Ser.). 416p. (C). 1998. 85.00 (*0-415-15279-8*); pap. 25.99 (*0-415-15324-7*) Routledge.

Chen, Kuan-Hsing, jt. ed. see Morley, David.

Chen, L., ed. Waves & Instabilities in Plasmas. 188p. (C). 1987. text 70.00 (*9971-5-0389-1*); pap. text 37.00 (*9971-5-0390-5*) World Scientific Pub.

Chen, L. C., et al. AIDS & Women's Reproductive Health. (Reproductive Biology Ser.). (Illus.). 216p. (C). 1992. text 79.50 (*0-306-44200-0*, Kluwer Plenum) Kluwer Academic.

Chen, L. Q. & Fultz, Brent, eds. Mathematics of Microstructure Evolution. (Illus.). 380p. 1996. 50.00 (*0-87339-351-1*, 3511) Minerals Metals.

Chen, L. T., ed. see Yat-sen Sun.

Chen, Lai N. Images of Southeast Asia in Children's Literature. 122p. (Orig.). 1981. pap. 22.50 (*9971-69-042-X*, Pub. by Sngapore Univ Pr) Coronet Bks.

Chen, Lansun, et al, eds. Advanced Topics in Biomathematics: Proceedings of the International Conference on Mathematical Biology. 340p. 1998. 78.00 (*981-02-3518-6*) World Scientific Pub.

Chen Lee Ling. The Six Year Self-Discovery & Personal Fortune Diary: Spiritual Growth, Enlightenment, Fresh Beginnings, New Relationships, Home & Family & Happiness & Longevity. deluxe ed. (Illus.). 158p. 1997. vinyl bd. 22.00 (*1-886197-06-7*) Joy Books.

Chen, Lin. Interest Rate Dynamics, Derivatives Pricing, & Risk Management. LC 96-12924. (Lecture Notes in Economics & Mathematical Systems Ser.: Vol. 435). (Illus.). 149p. 1997. pap. 52.00 (*3-540-60814-1*) Spr-Verlag.

Chen, Lincoln C., et al, eds. Advancing Health in Developing Countries: The Role of Social Research. LC 91-26133. 248p. 1992. 49.95 (*0-86569-034-0*, T034, Auburn Hse) Greenwood.

— Health & Social Change in International Perspective. LC 93-1755. (Series on Population & International Health). (Illus.). 420p. 1994. pap. text 17.95 (*0-674-38562-4*) HUP.

— Women's Health in India: Risk & Vulnerability. (Illus.). 332p. 1996. text 24.95 (*0-19-563620-1*) OUP.

Chen, Lincoln C. & Scrimshaw, Nevin S., eds. Diarrhea & Malnutrition: Interactions, Mechanisms, & Interventions. LC 82-18894. 334p. 1983. 85.00 (*0-306-41046-X*, Plenum Trade) Perseus Pubng.

Chen, Linda H. Nutritional Aspects of Aging, 2 vols., Vol. 1. LC 85-9720. 336p. 1986. 171.00 (*0-8493-5737-3*, QP86, CRC Reprint) Franklin.

— Nutritional Aspects of Aging, 2 vols., Vol. II. LC 85-9720. 288p. 1986. 144.00 (*0-8493-5738-1*, QP86, CRC Reprint) Franklin.

Chen, Linda H., tr. see Wei-Chuan Cultural-Education Staff.

Chen, Liu F. The Confucian Way: A New & Systematic Study of the Four Books. Liu, Shih S., tr. 620p. 1986. pap. 9.95 (*0-7103-0250-9*); text 47.50 (*0-7103-0171-5*) Routledge.

Chen, Liwei, et al, eds. Information Technology: Advancement, Productivity & International Cooperation: Proceedings of the Third Pan Pacific Computer Conference, Beijing, China, 16-19 August 1989, 2 vols., Set. LC 89-19755. (International Academic Publishers Ser.). 1650p. 1990. 355.00 (*0-08-037889-7*, 1302; 1305; 130, Pub. by IAP) Elsevier.

Chen, Long-Qing, et al, eds. Mathematics of Microstructure Evolution: Proceedings of a Symposium on Mathematics of Microstructure Evolution, Cleveland, OH, 1995. LC 96-78157. (Proceedings in Applied Mathematics Ser.: No. 90). (Illus.). x, 391p. 1996. pap. 53.50 (*0-89871-386-2*, PR90) Soc Indus-Appl Math.

Chen, Loris. Where Are the Gardens in the Garden State? Brown, Jeffrey L. & Schnarr, W. A., eds. 86p. (J). (gr. 6-9). 1998. pap. text 12.00 (*0-928630-04-8*) Global Learning.

An Asterisk (*) at the beginning of an entry indicates that the title is appearing for the first time.

Chen, Louis H., et al, eds. Probability Theory: Proceedings of the 1989 Singapore Probability Conference Held at the National University of Singapore, June 8-16, 1989. LC 92-14169. xiv, 208p. (C). 1992. lib. bdg. 103.95 (*3-11-012233-2*) De Gruyter.

Chen, Lung-Chu. An Introduction to Contemporary International Law: A Policy-Oriented Perspective. LC 88-28318. 480p. (C). 1989. 57.50 (*0-300-03910-7*); pap. 27.00 (*0-300-03911-5*) Yale U Pr.

***Chen, Lung-Chu.** An Introduction to Contemporary International Law: A Policy-Oriented Perspective. 2nd ed. LC 00-36815. 448p. 2000. 60.00 (*0-300-08454-4*); pap. 30.00 (*0-300-08477-3*) Yale U Pr.

Chen, Lydia. Easy Chinese Phrase Book & Dictionary. LC 97-42418. (ENG & CHI., Illus.). 224p. 1990. pap. 12.95 (*0-8442-8526-9*, 85269, Natl Textbk Co) NTC Contemp Pub Co.

Chen, Lydia & Bian, Ying. The Pocket Interpreter: Chinese. (Illus.). 216p. 1988. pap. 7.95 (*0-8351-2320-0*) China Bks.

Chen, Lydia, jt. auth. see Echo Books Staff.

Chen, M., et al, eds. High Performance Computing for Computer Graphics & Visualiszation: Proceedings of the International Workshop on High Performance Computing for Computer Graphics & Visualisation, Swansea, 3-4 July 1995. LC 95-46456. 289p. 1995. pap. 99.00 (*3-540-76016-4*) Spr-Verlag.

Chen, M., et al, eds. Phase Transformation Kinetics in Thin Films Vol. 230: Materials Research Society Symposium Proceedings. 365p. 1992. text 30.00 (*1-55899-124-7*) Materials Res.

— Volume Graphics. LC 99-56902. (Illus.). 465p. 2000. 119.00 (*1-85233-192-5*) Spr-Verlag.

Chen, M., jt. auth. see Mott, K.

Chen, M. F. From Markov Chains to Non-Equilibrium Particle Systems. 450p. (C). 1992. text 74.00 (*981-02-0639-9*) World Scientific Pub.

Chen, M. W. The Subauroral Inonsphere, Plasmasphere, Ring Current & Inner Magnetosphere System. (Advances in Space Research Ser.: Vol. 20). 224p. 1997. pap. 108.00 (*0-08-043299-9*, Pergamon Pr) Elsevier.

Chen, Mao. Between Tradition & Change: The Hermeneutics of May Fourth Literature. LC 96-35242. 176p. 1996. lib. bdg. 34.50 (*0-7618-0576-1*) U Pr of Amer.

Chen, Marcia T., jt. auth. see Olsen, Laurie.

Chen, Martha A. Coping with Seasonality & Drought. 258p. (C). 1991. text 29.95 (*0-8039-9689-6*) Sage.

***Chen, Martha A.** Perpetual Mourning: Widowhood in Rural India. 416p. 2000. pap. 24.95 (*0-19-564885-4*) OUP.

Chen, Martha A. A Quiet Revolution: Women in Transition in Rural Bangladesh. 256p. 1983. pap. 17.95 (*0-87073-453-9*) Schenkman Bks Inc.

— Widows in India: Social Neglect & Public Action. LC 98-11272. 1998. 49.95 (*0-7619-9248-0*); pap. write for info. (*0-7619-9249-9*) Sage.

***Chen, Martha A., ed.** Windows in India: Social Neglect & Public Action. 1998. 18.00 (*81-7036-703-4*, Pub. by Sage Pubns IND) S Asia.

***Chen, Matthew Y.** Tone Sandhi: Patterns Across Chinese Dialects. LC 99-44921. (Cambridge Studies in Linguistics). (Illus.). 450p. 2000. write for info. (*0-521-65272-3*) Cambridge U Pr.

Chen Meilan, pref. Six Contemporary Chinese Women Writers, Vol. IV. 374p. 1995. pap. 8.95 (*0-8351-3175-0*) China Bks.

Chen, Michael Y., et al. Basic Radiology. LC 95-19434. (Illus.). 496p. 1996. pap. 45.00 (*0-07-011148-0*) McGraw-Hill HPD.

Chen, Milton. The Smart Parent's Guide to Kids' TV. LC 94-20570. (Illus.). 224p. (Orig.). 1994. pap. 8.95 (*0-912333-47-2*) BB&T Inc.

Chen, Milton & Paisley, William J., eds. Children & Microcomputers: Research on the Newest Medium. LC 85-1789. (Sage Focus Editions Ser.: No. 70). (Illus.). 320p. reprint ed. pap. 99.20 (*0-8357-8485-1*, 203475300091) Bks Demand.

Chen, Min. Asian Management Systems: Chinese, Japanese & Korean Styles of Business. LC 94-17741. (Thunderbird/Routledge Series in International Management). 320p. (C). 1995. mass mkt. 23.95 (*0-415-11651-1*, C0088) Routledge.

— Asian Management Systems: Chinese, Japanese & Korean Styles of Business. LC 94-17741. (Thunderbird/ Routledge Series in International Management). 336p. (C). (gr. 13). 1996. pap. 88.95 (*0-415-11650-3*, C0087) Thomson Learn.

— Managing International Technology Transfer. LC 95-31021. (Thunderbird/Routledge Series in International Management). 256p. 1996. pap. 60.00 (*0-415-13323-8*) Thomson Learn.

Chen, Ming & Chen, Wah. Sassparilla's New Shoes. LC 98-49701. (Illus.). 40p. (J). 1999. 19.95 (*1-880664-26-7*) E M Pr.

***Chen, Ming-Hui, et al.** Monte Carlo Methods in Bayesian Computation. Bickel, P. et al, eds. LC 99-46366. (Series in Statistics). (Illus.). 400p. 2000. 79.95 (*0-387-98935-8*) Spr-Verlag.

Chen, Ming Li. Top of the Table, Top of the World: An Autobiography. LC 98-945744. xvi, 167p. 1998. write for info. (*0-13-960097-3*) P-H.

Chen, Moxun, et al. Atlas of Cross Sectional Anatomy of Human 14 Meridians & Acupoints. (Illus.). 346p. 1996. pap. text 52.00 (*1-880132-21-4*) Sci Pr NY.

Chen, N. Y. Normal-State Properties & Laser Distribution of Semiconductor Thin Films. 140p. 1995. pap. 57.50 (*90-407-1087-2*, Pub. by Delft U Pr) Coronet Bks.

Chen, N. Y., et al. Molecular Transport & Reaction in Zeolites: Design & Application of Shape Selective Catalysis. 328p. 1994. 159.00 (*0-471-18548-5*) Wiley.

Chen, N. Y., et al. Molecular Transport & Reaction in Zeolites: Design & Application of Shape Selective Catalysts. LC 94-2231. 1994. 95.00 (*0-89573-765-5*, Wiley-VCH) Wiley.

— Shape Selective Catalysis in Industrial Applications. 2nd expanded rev. ed. LC 96-15466. (Chemical Industries Ser.: Vol. 65). (Illus.). 304p. 1996. text 155.00 (*0-8247-9737-X*) Dekker.

— Shape Selective Catalysts in Industrial Applications. LC 88-32354. (Chemical Industries Ser.: Vol. 36). (Illus.). 319p. reprint ed. pap. 98.90 (*0-608-08918-4*, 206955300005) Bks Demand.

Chen, Ni, jt. ed. see Culbertson, Hugh M.

Chen, Ningxin. An Investigation of Globoidal Wormgear Drives. (Technical Papers: Vol. 96FTM12). (Illus.). 15p. 1996. pap. text 30.00 (*1-55589-679-0*) AGMA.

Chen, Nolan. Darius Discovers Derivatives: An Introduction to Calculus for Kids. LC 95-92093. (Illus.). 40p. (Orig.). (J). (gr. 5-8). 1995. 4.95 (*0-9645233-0-2*) Nolan Learn.

— Darius Discovers Forces. Chen, Jenny, ed. (Darius Discovers Ser.). (Illus.). 56p. (Orig.). (J). (gr. 5-8). 1996. pap. 9.95 (*0-9645233-1-0*) Nolan Learn.

— Darius Discovers Power. Chen, Jenny, ed. (Darius Discovers Ser.). (Illus.). 56p. (Orig.). (J). (gr. 5-8). 1996. pap. 9.95 (*0-9645233-3-7*) Nolan Learn.

Chen, P. C., jt. auth. see Phoon, Wai-On.

***Chen, P. P., et al, eds.** Advances in Conceptual Modeling: ER'99 Workshops on Evolution & Change in Data Management, Reverse Engineering in Information Systems & the World Wide Web & Conceptual Modelling, Paris, France, November 15-18, 1999, Proceedings. LC 99-49678. (Lecture Notes in Computer Science Ser.: Vol. 1727). xiii, 389p. 1999. pap. 69.00 (*3-540-66653-2*) Spr-Verlag.

Chen, P. S. Biochemical Aspects of Insect Development. (Monographs in Developmental Biology: Vol. 3). (Illus.). 1971. 62.75 (*3-8055-1265-1*) S Karger.

Chen, P. S., jt. auth. see Chen, T. S.

Chen, Pah I., jt. auth. see Holbrook, Edward L.

Chen, Patrick. Intimacy with the Beloved. 1999. 17.99 (*0-88419-590-2*) Creation House.

Ch'en, Paul H. The Formation of the Early Meiji Legal Order: The Japanese Code of 1871 & Its Chinese Foundation. (London Oriental Ser.: No. 35). 1982. 36.00 (*0-19-713601-X*) OUP.

Chen, Paul L., jt. auth. see Raun, R.Roger.

Chen Peiji, jt. ed. see Zhou Zhiyi.

***Chen, Peter P., et al.** Conceptual Modeling: Current Issues & Future Directions. Goos, G. et al, eds. LC 99-30930. (Lecture Notes in Computer Science Ser.: Vol. 1565). xxiii, 309p. 1999. pap. 56.00 (*3-540-65926-9*) Spr-Verlag.

Chen, Peter S., jt. auth. see Chen, Thomas S.

Chen, Peter S., jt. auth. see Kuo, Eddie C.

Chen, Philip T., et al, eds. Optical Systems Contamination & Degradation, Vol. 3427. 1998. 89.00 (*0-8194-2882-5*) SPIE.

***Chen, Pi T. & Gu, Zu-Han, eds.** Rough Surface Scattering & Contamination. 1999. pap. text 92.00 (*0-8194-3270-9*) SPIE.

Chen, Ping. Modern Chinese: History & Sociolinguistics. LC 98-38449. (Illus.). 250p. (C). 1999. text 59.95 (*0-521-64197-7*); pap. text 21.95 (*0-521-64572-7*) Cambridge U Pr.

Chen, Pisin. Quantum Aspects of Beam Physics. 1998. 84.00 (*981-02-3551-8*) World Scientific Pub.

***Chen, Pisin & Wong, Cheuk-Yin, eds.** Recent Advances & Cross-Century Outlooks in Physics: Interplay Between Theory & Experiment. 700p. 2000. 86.00 (*981-02-4256-5*) World Scientific Pub.

Chen, Q. M., et al. Future Databases Ninety-Two: Proceedings of the 2nd Far-East Workshop on Future Database Systems. (Advanced Database Research & Development Ser.). 432p. 1992. text 95.00 (*981-02-1040-X*) World Scientific Pub.

Chen, Qi-Jia. Love's Tour. 110p. 1996. pap. text 5.00 (*0-614-13434-X*) New Wrld Poetry.

Chen, R. Early Chinese Work in Natural Science: A Re-Examination of the Physics of Motion, Acoustics Astronomy & Scientific Thoughts. 224p. 1996. pap. 47.50 (*962-209-385-X*, Pub. by HK Univ Pr) Coronet Bks.

Chen, R. & McKeever, S. W. Theory of Thermoluminescence & Related Phenomena. 300p. 1997. text 54.00 (*981-02-2295-5*) World Scientific Pub.

Chen, R. S. Wu Guanzhong on Life & Art: Selected Works of Wu Guanzhong. 380p. 1992. pap. text 13.00 (*1-879771-00-4*) Global Pub NJ.

Chen Ran. Zai Jinsho Zhong. (CHI.). pap. 9.95 (*7-80005-258-3*, Pub. by China Intl Bk) Distribks Inc.

Chen, Ray T., et al, eds. Integrated Optoelectronics, Vol. 2891. 322p. 1996. 85.00 (*0-8194-2292-4*) SPIE.

Chen, Ray T. & Bristow, Julian P., eds. Optoelectronic Interconnects V, Vol. 3288. 298p. 1998. 69.00 (*0-8194-2727-6*) SPIE.

Chen, Ray T. & Guilfoyle, Peter S., eds. Optoelectronic Interconnects & Packaging IV, Vol. 3005. LC 97-175324. 370p. 1997. 89.00 (*0-8194-2416-1*) SPIE.

— Optoelectronic Interconnects & Packaging, 1996: Proceedings of a Conference Held 30-31 January 1996, San Jose, California. LC 95-49833. (Critical Reviews of Optical Science & Technology Ser.: Vol. CR62). 1996. pap. 80.00 (*0-8194-2017-4*) SPIE.

Chen, Ray T. & Lome, Louis S., eds. Wavelength Division Multiplexing: Conference on Wavelength Division Multiplexing. LC 98-33418. (Critical Reviews of Optical Science & Technology Ser.: Vol. CR71). 266p. 1999. 50.00 (*0-8194-3104-4*) SPIE.

Chen, Ray T., et al. Design & Manufacturing of WDM Devices: 4-5 November 1997, Dallas, Texas. LC 99-165370. (Proceedings Ser.). 230 p. 1998. 59.00 (*0-8194-2667-9*) SPIE.

— Optoelectronic Interconnects III: 8-9 February, 1995, San Jose, California LC 94-69345. (Proceedings Ser.). viii, 366p. 1995. pap. write for info. (*0-8194-1747-5*) SPIE.

Chen, Ray T., jt. ed. see DeBusk, Damon K.

Chen, Ray T., jt. ed. see Zhou, Bingkun.

Chen, Raymond F. & Edelhoch, Harold, eds. Biochemical Fluorescence Vol. 2: Concepts. LC 74-31689. 603p. 1976. reprint ed. pap. 187.00 (*0-7837-8325-6*, 204911200002) Bks Demand.

Chen, Ren-Raw. Understanding & Managing Interest Rate Risks. LC 96-9289. (Series in Mathematical Finance). 200p. 1996. write for info. (*981-02-2751-5*) World Scientific Pub.

Chen, Robert, tr. see Wang, Jesse Y.

Chen, Robert S. A Comparative Study of Chinese & Western Cyclic Myths. LC 91-21217. (Asian Thought & Culture Ser.: Vol. 8). 216p. (C). 1992. text 47.95 (*0-8204-1675-4*) P Lang Pubng.

Chen, Robert S., et al. Social Science Research & Climate Change. 1983. text 151.50 (*90-277-1490-8*) Kluwer Academic.

Chen, Ruth, tr. see White, John.

Chen, Ruth T., tr. see Demarest, Bruce A.

Chen, Ruth T., tr. see Meyer, F. B.

Chen, Ruth T., tr. see Nee, Watchman.

Chen, Ruth T., tr. see Spurgeon, Charles H.

Chen, Ruth T., tr. see Strauss, Richard L.

Chen, S. H. & Rajagopalan, R., eds. Micellar Solutions & Microemulsions. (Illus.). 304p. 1990. 144.00 (*0-387-97106-8*) Spr-Verlag.

Chen, S. J. & Hwang, C. L. Fuzzy Multiple Attribute Decision Making: Methods & Applications. Beckmann, Martin J. & Krelle, W., eds. (Lecture Notes in Economics & Mathematical Systems Ser.: Vol. 375). (Illus.). xii, 536p. 1992. pap. 78.00 (*0-387-54998-6*) Spr-Verlag.

Chen, S. P. & Anderson, Mary P., eds. Modeling of Composites, Processing & Properties: A Collection of Papers from the 1996 TMS Annual Meeting & Exhibition in Anaheim, California, February 4-8, 1996. (Illus.). 77p. 1996. pap. 54.00 (*0-87339-321-X*, 321X) Minerals Metals.

Chen, S. P. & Yong, J. M. Control Theory, Stochastic Analysis & Applications: Proceedings of Symposium on Sys. Sciences & Control Theory. 300p. 1992. text 95.00 (*981-02-0942-8*) World Scientific Pub.

Chen, S. S., ed. Flow-Induced Vibration of Circular Cylindrical Structures. 600p. 1987. 215.00 (*0-89116-602-5*) Hemisp Pub.

— Image Understanding in Unstructured Environment. 216p. (C). 1988. text 59.00 (*9971-5-0477-4*); pap. text 36.00 (*9971-5-0478-2*) World Scientific Pub.

Chen, S. S., jt. ed. see Chu, B. T.

Chen, Samuel S. The Theory & Practice of International Organization. 2nd ed. 133p. 1974. text 32.75 (*0-8422-5139-1*); pap. text 12.75 (*0-8422-0362-1*) Irvington.

Chen, San-Ching, jt. auth. see Levine, Marilyn A.

Chen, Sarah Wei-ming, tr. see Lao She.

***Chen, Shane.** Installing, Configuring & Customizing Linux Suse 6.1. 2000. pap. 39.99 (*0-7615-2308-1*) Prima Pub.

Chen, Shao-Kwan. System of Taxation in China in the Tsing Dynasty, 1644-1911. LC 79-120215. (Columbia University. Studies in the Social Sciences: No. 143). 1970. reprint ed. 39.50 (*0-404-51143-0*) AMS Pr.

Chen, Sheying. Measurement & Analysis in Psychosocial Research: The Failing & Saving of Theory. 336p. 1997. text 83.95 (*1-85972-571-6*, Pub. by Avebry) Ashgate Pub Co.

— Social Policy of the Economic State & Community Care in Chinese Culture: Aging, Family, Urban Change & the Socialist Welfare Pluralism. 352p. 1996. 82.95 (*1-85972-294-6*, Pub. by Avebry) Ashgate Pub Co.

Chen, Shing-Ling, ed. see Couch, Carl J.

Chen, Shoei-Sheng, ed. see National Congress on Pressure Vessels & Piping Staff.

Chen, Shou-jung. Elementary Chinese. 2nd ed. LC 59-10639. (CHI & ENG.). 538p. 1959. reprint ed. pap. 30.00 (*0-608-04328-1*, 206510800012) Bks Demand.

Chen, Shou-liang. Chinese Bamboos. (CHI & LAT.). 1988. 156.00 (*0-7855-2847-4*, Pub. by Wanhai Books) St Mut.

***Chen, Shu-Ching, et al.** Semantic Models for Multimedia Database Searching & Browsing. LC 00-41596. (International Series on Advances in Database Systems). 2000. write for info. (*0-7923-7888-1*) Kluwer Academic.

Chen, Sidong. Pretest & Review for Acupuncture Examination. Jones, Elizabeth, ed. (Illus.). 275p. (C). 1995. pap. text 109.00 (*0-9645339-0-1*) Dr Chens.

***Chen, Simon K. & Dong, Mike.** China's Engine Industry. LC 99-26178. 158p. 2000. 99.00 (*0-7680-0394-6*, RR-001) Soc Auto Engineers.

Chen Singchi, et al, eds. Bibliography of Chinese Systematic Botany (1949-1990) 810p. 1996. 98.00 (*7-5359-1164-1*, Pub. by Sci Pr) Lubrecht & Cramer.

Chen, Son-Nan & Lee, Cheng-Few, eds. Advances in Investment Analysis & Portfolio Management, Vol. 1. 293p. 1991. 78.50 (*1-55938-135-3*) Jai Pr.

— Advances in Investment Analysis & Portfolio Management, Vol. 2. 237p. 1994. 78.50 (*1-55938-592-8*) Jai Pr.

— Advances in Investment Analysis & Portfolio Management, Vol. 3. 301p. 1995. 78.50 (*1-55938-765-3*) Jai Pr.

Chen, Sophie, jt. auth. see Wang, Xuhui.

***Chen, Sow-Hsin.** Interaction of Photons & Neutrons with Matter: An Introduction. 2nd ed. 2000. 78.00 (*981-02-4214-X*) World Scientific Pub.

Chen, Sow-Hsin, et al, eds. Structure & Dynamics of Strongly Interacting Colloids & Supramolecular Aggregates in Solution: Proceedings of the NATO Advanced Study Institute, Acquafredda di Maratea, Italy, June 11-21, 1991. LC 92-8532. (NATO Advanced Science Institutes Series C: Mathematical & Physical Sciences). 872p. (C). 1992. text 396.50 (*0-7923-1729-7*) Kluwer Academic.

Chen, Sow-Hsin & Kotlarchyk, Michael. Interaction of Radiation with Matter & Applications. 500p. 1997. text 78.00 (*981-02-2026-X*) World Scientific Pub.

Chen, Stephen S. Missouri in the Federal System. 3rd ed. 240p. (Orig.). (C). 1986. pap. text 26.00 (*0-8191-5498-9*) U Pr of Amer.

Chen, Steve, jt. auth. see Demster, Stanley J.

Chen, Steven. The Apple Programmer's Challenge. (Illus.). 240p. (Orig.). 1987. pap. 14.95 (*0-8306-2827-4*, 2827) McGraw-Hill Prof.

— The IBM Programmer's Challenge. (Illus.). 240p. (Orig.). 1987. pap. 14.95 (*0-8306-2807-X*, 2807) McGraw-Hill Prof.

Chen, Steven S. Windows 95: A Programmer's Casebook. LC 94-40098. 1994. pap. 39.95 incl. cd-rom (*1-55851-411-2*, M&T Bks) IDG Bks.

Chen, Su-Shing & Caulfield, John H., eds. Adaptive Computing: Mathematics, Electronics & Optics. LC 94-2409. (Critical Reviews of Optical Science & Technology Ser.). 1994. 30.00 (*0-8194-1551-0*, CR55); pap. 30.00 (*0-8194-1550-2*) SPIE.

Chen, Su-Shing, jt. ed. see Caulfield, H. John.

Chen, SuShing, jt. ed. see Kak, Avinash C.

Chen, T. P. Aquaculture Practices in Taiwan. 1978. 100.00 (*0-7855-6910-3*) St Mut.

Chen, T. S. & Chen, P. S. The History of Gastroenterology: Essays on Its Development & Accomplishments. (History of Medicine Ser.). (Illus.). 328p. 1995. 88.00 (*1-85070-365-5*) Prthnon Pub.

Chen, T. S. & Chu, T. Y., eds. Fundamentals of Mixed Convection. (HTD Ser.: Vol. 213). 88p. 1992. 30.00 (*0-7918-1053-4*, G00697) ASME.

Chen, T. T. Fault Diagnosis & Fault Tolerance: A Systematic Approach to Special Topics. (Illus.). xii, 197p. 1992. 58.95 (*0-387-54962-5*) Spr-Verlag.

Chen, Ta-Chuan, jt. auth. see Nichols, Paul L.

Chen, Ta-tuan. Chinese Primer Vols. 1-3: Gr. Version, 3 vols., Set. 608p. 1994. pap. text 47.50 (*0-691-03696-9*, Pub. by Princeton U Pr) Cal Prin Full Svc.

— Chinese Primer Vols. 1-3: Pinyin Version, 3 vols., Set. 144p. 1994. pap. text 47.50 (*0-691-03695-0*, Pub. by Princeton U Pr) Cal Prin Full Svc.

Chen, Ta-tuan, et al. Chinese Primer: Character Text. LC 93-45904. 608p. 1994. reprint ed. pap. text 15.50 (*0-691-03694-2*, Pub. by Princeton U Pr) Cal Prin Full Svc.

Ch'en, Ta-Tuan, et al. Chinese Primer: GR Edition, 3 vols., Set. LC 89-2218. 590p. (C). 1989. pap. text 42.00 (*0-674-12476-6*) HUP.

— Chinese Primer: Pinyin Edition, 3 vols. LC 89-2218. 590p. (C). 1989. 37.50 (*0-685-28017-9*); 10.50 (*0-685-28018-7*) HUP.

— Chinese Primer: Pinyin Edition, 3 vols., Set. LC 89-2218. 608p. (C). 1989. pap. text 42.00 (*0-674-12475-8*) HUP.

***Chen, Terry Yuan-Fang.** Selected Papers on Photoelasticity LC 99-39204. (Milestone Ser.). 1999. pap. 72.00 (*0-8194-3482-5*) SPIE.

Chen, Thomas M. & Liu, Stephen S. ATM Switching Systems. LC 94-44500. (McGraw-Hill Series on Computer Communications). 261p. 1995. 83.00 (*0-89006-682-5*) Artech Hse.

Chen, Thomas P., jt. auth. see Wuu-Long Lin.

Chen, Thomas S. & Chen, Peter S. Understanding the Liver: A History, 14. LC 83-22631. (Contributions in Medical History Ser.: No. 14). (Illus.). 293p. 1984. 75.00 (*0-313-23472-8*, CLV/, Greenwood Pr) Greenwood.

Chen, Thomas T., et al. The Global Guide to the World of CBT Authoring. (Illus.). 198p. (Orig.). 1993. pap. text 19.95 (*0-9642591-0-9*) Global Informat.

Chen, Tongwen & Francis, Bruce A. Optimal Sampled-Data Control Systems. LC 95-6882. (Communications & Control Engineering Ser.). (Illus.). 374p. 1996. 89.95 (*3-540-19949-7*) Spr-Verlag.

Chen, Tony H., jt. ed. see Li, Paul H.

Chen, Tower. Contextual Reality: A New Approach to Study Mathematics & Physics Paradoxes. 90p. (C). 1993. text. write for info. (*0-9630276-1-1*) Jern Charng.

— Statistics Lab No. 123: Using Electronic Spreadsheet. 60p. (C). 1993. student ed. write for info. (*0-9630276-5-4*) Jern Charng.

Chen, Tsing-Chang & Wiin-Nielsen, Aksel C. Fundamentals of Atmospheric Energetics. LC 92-24612. (Illus.). 400p. (C). 1993. text 71.95 (*0-19-507127-1*) OUP.

Chen, Tsuhan, jt. ed. see Puri, Atul.

Chen, Tzu-Yu, et al. The Development of Controlled Hydrodynamic Techniques for Corrosion Testing. LC TA0462.C43. (MTI Publication: No. 23). (Illus.). 196p. reprint ed. pap. 60.80 (*0-8357-4635-6*, 203756400008) Bks Demand.

Chen, Vicky S., et al. Guides to Clinical Aspiration Biopsy: Head & Neck. 2nd ed. LC 95-22621. (Guides to Clinical Aspiration Biopsy Ser.). (Illus.). 432p. 1996. 98.50 (*0-89640-286-X*) Igaku-Shoin.

***Chen, Victor.** The Age of Illusion: Some Writings & a Memoir. 430p. 1999. 30.00 (*0-9673828-0-7*) My Own Pubg Co.

Chen, Vincent & Montgomery, John. Hacker's Guide to Visual Basics 4.0. LC 96-19354. 704p. (C). 1996. pap. 44.95 (*0-201-87042-8*) Addison-Wesley.

Chen, Vincent, jt. auth. see Leonhard, Woody.

Chen, Violet W., tr. see Graham, Billy.

C

Chen, Virginia, compiled by. The Economic Conditions of East & Southeast Asia: A Bibliography of English-Language Material, 1965 to 1977. LC 78-57762. 788p. 1978. lib. bdg. 185.00 (0-313-20565-5, CEC/, Greenwood Pr) Greenwood.

Chen, Vivia. Ethan Allen Home Design Book. 2001. 30.00 (0-609-60156-3) C Potter.

Chen, W. F. Advanced Analysis: Steel Frames Theory. Toma, S., ed. 400p. 1993. boxed set 136.95 (0-8493-8281-5) CRC Pr.

— Stability Design of Steel Frames. Lui, E. M, ed. 400p. 1991. boxed set 120.95 (0-8493-8606-3, TA) CRC Pr.

Chen, W. K. Linear Networks & Systems: Algorithm & CPT-Aided Implementations. 2nd ed. (Advanced Series in Electrical & Computer Engineering: Vol. 3). 900p. 1990. text 61.00 (9971-5-0684-X) World Scientific Pub.

Chen, W. T., jt. ed. see Engel, P. A.

Chen, Wah, jt. auth. see Chen, Ming.

Chen, Wai-Fah. Handbook of Structural Engineering. LC 97-148. 1600p. 1997. boxed set 149.95 (0-8493-2674-5, 2674) CRC Pr.

Chen, Wai-Fah, ed. The Civil Engineering Handbook. 2640p. 1995. boxed set 139.95 (0-8493-8953-4, 8953C2W) CRC Pr.

— Connection Flexibility & Steel Frames. 122p. 1985. 19.00 (0-87262-482-X) Am Soc Civil Eng.

Chen, Wai-Fah & Baladi, G. Y. Soil Plasticity: Theory & Implementation. (Developments in Geotechnical Engineering Ser.: No. 38). xii,234p. 1985. 155.00 (0-444-42455-5) Elsevier.

Chen, Wai-Fah & Duan, Lian. Bridge Engineering Handbook. LC 99-33175. 2000p. 1999. boxed set 139.95 (0-8493-7434-0) CRC Pr.

Chen, Wai-Fah & Kim, Seung-Eock. LRFD Steel Design Using Advanced Analysis. LC 96-36957. (New Directions in Civil Engineering Ser.). 464p. 1997. boxed set 84.95 (0-8493-7432-4) CRC Pr.

Chen, Wai-Fah & Lewis, A. D., eds. Recent Advances in Engineering Mechanics & Their Impact on Civil Engineering Practice, 2 Vols. 1378p. 1983. pap. 15.00 (0-87262-358-0) Am Soc Civil Eng.

Chen, Wai-Fah & Liu, X. L. Limit Analysis in Soil Mechanics. (Developments in Geotechnical Engineering Ser.: No. 52). xiv,478p. 1990. 226.50 (0-444-43042-3) Elsevier.

Chen, Wai-Fah & Lui, E. M. Structural Stability: Theory & Implementation. LC 86-19931. 534p. 1987. 56.75 (0-444-01119-6) P-H.

— Structural Stability: Theory & Implementation. LC 93-16335. (C). 1987. text 64.60 (0-13-500539-6) P-H.

Chen, Wai-Fah & Mizuno, E. Nonlinear Analysis in Soil Mechanics: Theory & Implementation. (Developments in Geotechnical Engineering Ser.: No. 53). 672p. 1990. 245.50 (0-444-43043-1) Elsevier.

Chen, Wai-Fah & Mosallan, K. H. Concrete Buildings: Analysis for Safe Construction. 232p. 1991. boxed set 131.95 (0-8493-4213-9, TA683) CRC Pr.

Chen, Wai-Fah & Saleeb, Atef F. Constitutive Equations for Engineering Materials, 2 vols. LC 94-9081. (Studies in Applied Mechanics: Vol. 37A-B). 1096p. 1994. 364.50 (0-444-88408-4) Elsevier.

Chen, Wai-Fah & Sohal, I. Plastic Design & Second-Order Analysis of Steel Frames. LC 94-11614. 1994. 109.95 (0-387-94314-5) Spr-Verlag.

Chen, Wai-Fah & Ting, E. C., eds. Fracture in Concrete. LC 80-69656. 114p. 1980. pap. 13.00 (0-87262-259-2) Am Soc Civil Eng.

Chen, Wai-Fah & Toma, Shouji, eds. Analysis & Software of Cylindrical Members. (New Directions in Civil Engineering Ser.). 320p. 1995. lib. bdg. 119.95 incl. disk (0-8493-8282-3, 8282) CRC Pr.

Chen, Wai-Fah & Zhang, H. Structural Plasticity: Theory, Problems & CAE Software. (Illus.). x, 250p. 1990. 64.95 (0-387-96789-3) Spr-Verlag.

Chen, Wai-Fah, et al. Stability Design of Semi-Rigid Frames. LC 95-10783. 488p. 1995. 110.00 (0-471-07670-8); text. write for info. (0-471-15214-5) Wiley.

Chen, Wai-Fah, ed. see Marek, Pavel, et al.

Chen, Wai-Fah, ed. see Vigneswaran, Saravanamuthu & Visvanathan, C.

Chen, Wai-Fah, jt. ed. see White, Donald W.

Chen Wai-Kai. Active Network Analysis: Advanced Series in Electrical & Computer Engineering, Vol. 2. 660p. (C). 1991. pap. text 61.00 (9971-5-0913-X) World Scientific Pub.

— Active Network Analysis - Problems & Solution. (Electrical & Computer Engineering Ser.). 1993. text 28.00 (981-02-1404-9) World Scientific Pub.

— Active Network Analysis - Problems & Solutions. (Electrical & Computer Engineering Ser.). 308p. 1993. pap. text 36.00 (981-02-1336-0) World Scientific Pub.

Chen, Wai Kai. Broadband Matching: Theory & Implementations. 350p. 1993. pap. text 40.00 (981-02-1453-7) World Scientific Pub.

— Graph Theory & Its Engineering Applications. LC 97-159597. (Advanced Series in Electrical & Computer). 500p. 1997. text 67.00 (981-02-1859-1) World Scientific Pub.

— Linear Networks & Systems: Algorithm & CPT-Aided Implementations, 1. 2nd ed. (Advanced Series in Electrical & Computer Engineering: Vol. 3). 700p. 1990. pap. text 36.00 (9971-5-0998-9) World Scientific Pub.

— Linear Networks & Systems: Algorithms. 500p. 1994. pap. text 48.00 (981-02-1454-5) World Scientific Pub.

Chen Wai-Kai. Passive & Active Filters: Theory & Implementation. LC 85-9497. 528p. 1986. text 109.95 (0-471-82352-X) Wiley.

— Theory & Design of Broadband Matching Networks. 360p. 1976. 211.00 (0-08-019702-7, Pub. by Pergamon Repr) Franklin.

— The VLSI Handbook. LC 99-47682. (Electrical Engineering Handbook Ser.). 1788p. 1999. boxed set 129.95 (0-8493-8593-8) CRC Pr.

Chen, Wai Kai, ed. Broadband Matching: Theory & Implementation. 744p. (C). 1988. text 97.00 (9971-5-0219-4) World Scientific Pub.

Chen Wai-Kai, ed. The Circuits & Filters Handbook. LC 95-7037. (Electrical Engineering Handbook Ser.). 2896p. 1995. boxed set 159.95 (0-8493-8341-2, 8341C2W) CRC Pr.

Chen, Wai Kai, jt. auth. see Zhu, Y. S.

***Chen, Wai-Kai.** Mathematics for Linear Circuits & Filters. LC 99-43798. 263p. 1999. boxed set 59.95 (0-8493-0052-5) CRC Pr.

Chen, Wai-Kai. Structural Engineering Handbook: CRCnetBASE. 1999th ed. 1998. pap. 129.00 (0-8493-9579-8) CRC Pr.

Chen, Walter Y. DSL: Simulation Techniques & Standards Development for Digital Subscriber Lines. LC 96-80469. 400p. 1998. 54.99 (1-57870-017-5) Macmillan Tech.

Chen Wan Heng & Xiaoxiang, Li. Wisdom in Chinese Proverbs. (CHI & ENG., Illus.). 112p. 1996. pap. 9.95 (981-3068-27-2, Pub. by Asiapac) China Bks.

***Chen, Wang.** The Tao of Peace: Lessons from Ancient China on the Dynamics of Conflict. Sawyer, Ralph, tr. from CHI. LC 99-36591. 240p. 2000. 22.50 (1-57062-511-5, Pub. by Shambhala Pubns) Random.

Chen, Wang-Chuan. Chinese Herb Cooking for Health. Wolhardt, Connie, tr. from CHI. (ENG & CHI., Illus.). 128p. 1997. pap. 23.95 (0-941676-70-6) Wei-Chuan Pub.

Chen, Wayne, jt. auth. see Chang, Kevin O.

Chen, Wei, jt. auth. see Lee, Kai F.

Chen, Wei, tr. see Chou, Kung-tu & Zhou, Gong-du.

Chen Wei-Ming. T'ai Chi Ch'uan Ta Wen: Questions & Answers on T'a Chi Ch'uan. Pang Jeng Lo, Benjamin & Smith, Robert, trs. from CHI. 64p. (Orig.). 1985. pap. 7.95 (0-938190-67-9) North Atlantic.

Chen Weiji. A History of the Science & Technology of Textile of Ancient China. 412p. 1991. text 93.45 (1-880132-02-8) Sci Pr NY.

Chen, Weixing. The Political Economy of Rural Development in China, 1978-1999. LC 99-15397. 192p. 1999. 55.00 (0-275-96687-9) Greenwood.

Chen, Weiying. Active X Programming Unleashed. LC 96-68938. 1000p. 1996. pap. text 39.99 incl. cd-rom (1-57521-154-8) Sams.

— ActiveX Programming Unleashed. 1996. 49.99 incl. cd-rom (0-614-20292-2, SamsNet Software) MCP SW Interactive.

Chen, Weiying & Berry, Wayne. Windows NT Registry Guide. LC 96-29753. 288p. (C). 1997. pap. 34.95 (0-201-69473-5) Addison-Wesley.

Chen, William. Tai Chi Ch'uan: The Gentle Workout for Mind & Body. LC 95-17865. (Illus.). 128p. 1995. pap. 10.95 (0-8069-1366-5) Sterling.

Chen, William C. Body Mechanics of Tai Chi Chuan. 176p. (Orig.). 1994. reprint ed. pap. text. write for info. (0-9644084-0-6) W C C Chen.

Chen, William P. Asian Blepharoplasty: A Surgical Atlas. LC 94-27419. (Illus.). 200p. 1995. text 130.00 (0-7506-9496-3) Buttrwrth-Heinemann.

Chen, William S., jt. auth. see Balakrishnan, N.

Chen, William T. & Read, David T., eds. Application of Fracture Mechanics in Electronic Packaging: Proceedings, ASME International Mechanical Engineering Congress & Exposition, Dallas, TX, 1997. LC 97-76706. (AMD - EEP Ser.: Vols. 222 & 20). 193p. 1997. pap. 90.00 (0-7918-1827-6, TA492) ASME Pr.

Chen, William W., jt. auth. see Balakrishnan, N.

Chen, William Y., ed. Annals of Combinatorics, 4 issues. 1997. 195.00 (0-614-30187-4, 798) Spr-Verlag.

— Functional Disorders of the Digestive Tract. LC 81-40854. (Illus.). 366p. 1983. reprint ed. pap. 113.50 (0-7837-9552-1, 206030100005) Bks Demand.

***Chen, Willie Y. W.** The Comprehensive Guide to Ophthalmology Review. 750p. (C). 2000. pap. text 55.00 (1-55642-479-5) SLACK Inc.

— The Pocket Guide to Ophthalmology Review. 144p. (C). 2000. pap. text 29.00 (1-55642-478-7) SLACK Inc.

Chen-Wishart, Mindy. Chen-Wishart: Contract. (Butterworths Core Text Ser.). 1997. pap. write for info. (0-406-03311-0, MC1, MICHIE) LEXIS Pub.

— Unconscionable Bargains. 184p. 1989. pap. 27.00 (0-409-78881-3, NZ, MICHIE) LEXIS Pub.

***Chen, Xiang.** Instrumental Traditions & Theories of Light: The Uses of Instruments in the Optical Revolution. LC 00-30182. (Science & Philosophy Ser.). 2000. write for info. (0-7923-6349-3) Kluwer Academic.

***Chen, Xiangli, et al, eds.** High-Power Lasers in Manufacturing. 2000. pap. text 136.00 (0-8194-3486-8) SPIE.

Chen, Xiao-Ming. Limit Theorems for Functionals of Ergodic Markov Chains with General State Space LC 99-19209. (Memoirs of the Society Ser.). 1999. write for info. (0-8218-1060-X) Am Math.

Chen, Xiaomei. Occidentalism: A Theory of Counter-Discourse in Post-Mao China. LC 93-44883. (Illus.). 256p. 1995. text 45.00 (0-19-508579-5) OUP.

Chen, Xionghao & Bushnell, Michael L. Efficient Branch & Bound Search with Application to Computer-Aided Design. LC 95-45502. (Frontiers in Electronic Testing Ser.). 160p. (C). 1995. text 104.00 (0-7923-9673-1) Kluwer Academic.

Chen, Xue-Jun, et al, eds. Multiphase Flow & Heat Transfer Second International Symposium, 2 vols., Set. 1500p. 1990. 405.00 (1-56032-050-8) Hemisp Pub.

Chen, Xuemin, jt. auth. see Reed, Irving S.

Chen, Xuezhao. Surviving the Storm: A Memoir. Kinkley, Jeffrey C., ed. Hua, Ti & Greene, Caroline, trs. LC 92-1300. (Foremothers Legacies Ser.). 176p. (gr. 13). 1995. pap. 21.95 (1-56324-553-1, East Gate Bk) M E Sharpe.

Chen, Y. & Avnimelech, Y., eds. The Role of Organic Matter in Modern Agriculture. (Developments in Plant & Soil Sciences Ser.). 1986. text 192.00 (90-247-3360-X) Kluwer Academic.

Chen, Y. & Hadar, Y., eds. Iron Nutrition & Interactions in Plants. (Developments in Plant & Soil Sciences Ser.). (C). 1991. text 292.50 (0-7923-1095-0) Kluwer Academic.

Chen, Y. & Leung, A. Y. Bifurcation & Chaos in Engineering. (Illus.). xii, 452p. 1998. 129.00 (3-540-76242-6) Spr-Verlag.

Chen, Y. P., tr. see Little, Paul E.

Chen, Y. T., jt. auth. see Cook, Alan.

Chen-Ya Tien. Chinese Military Theory: Ancient & Modern. 320p. 1992. 29.95 (0-88962-423-2); pap. 18.95 (0-88962-422-4) Mosaic.

— The Mass Militia System & Chinese Modernization. 180p. 1994. pap. 14.95 (0-88962-162-4) Mosaic.

Chen, Ya-Zhe & Wu, Lan-Cheng. Second Order Elliptic Equations & Elliptic Systems. Hu, Bei, tr. LC 97-46794. (Translations of Mathematical Monographs: No. 174). 246p. 1998. 99.00 (0-8218-0970-9, MMONO/174) Am Math.

***Chen, Yangquan & Wen, Changyun.** Iterative Learning Control: Convergence, Robustness & Applications. LC 99-40879. (Lecture Notes in Control & Information Sciences Ser.: Vol. 248). (Illus.). xii, 204p. 1999. pap. 69.80 (1-85233-190-9, Pub. by Spr-Verlag) Spr-Verlag.

Chen, Yearniing K. Tai-Chi Ch'uan: Its Effects & Practical Application. 3rd ed. (Illus.). 192p. 1996. reprint ed. pap. 9.95 (0-87877-043-7) Newcastle Pub.

Chen, Yen-Lin. Tai-Chi Ch'uan: Its Effects & Practical Application. LC 80-19810. vi, 184p. 1993. reprint ed. pap. 23.00 (0-89370-995-6) Millefleurs.

Chen, Yeshen, jt. auth. see Lee, Paul S.

Chen, Yi-Xin. 3rd International Conference on Thin Film Physics & Applications, Vol. 3175. Zhou, Shixun et al, eds. LC 98-184978. 498p. 1998. 89.00 (0-8194-2673-3) SPIE.

Chen, Ying. Ingratitude. Volk, Carol, tr. from FRE. LC 98-71376. 160p. 1998. text 20.00 (0-374-17554-3) FS&G.

***Chen, Ying & Volk, Carol.** Ingratitude. LC 99-20035. 154p. 1999. pap. 13.95 (0-520-22013-7, Pub. by U CA Pr) Cal Prin Full Svc.

***Chen, Yong.** Chinese San Francisco, 1850-1943: A Trans-Pacific Community. LC 99-55529. (Asian America Ser.). 424p. 2000. 45.00 (0-8047-3605-7) Stanford U Pr.

Chen Yong, et al. The Great Tangshan Earthquake of 1976. LC 88-5916. (Illus.). 162p. 1988. text 65.00 (0-08-034875-0, Pergamon Pr) Elsevier.

***Chen, Yu hui.** Absolutes Nichts und rhythmisches Sein. 1999. 35.95 (3-631-35559-9) P Lang Pubng.

Chen, Yu-shih. Images & Ideas in Chinese Classical Prose: Studies of Four Masters. LC 87-26720. 256p. 1988. 39.50 (0-8047-1409-6) Stanford U Pr.

Chen, Yuan-Tsun. The Dragon's Village. 1981. pap. 13.95 (0-14-005811-7, Penguin Bks) Viking Penguin.

Chen, Yud-Ren, et al, eds. Pathogen Detection & Remediation for Safe Eating, Vol. 3544. (Proceedings of SPIE Ser.: Vol. 3545). 646p. 1999. 59.00 (0-8194-3006-4) SPIE.

Chen, Yung-Ping & De Vos, Robert C. Choices & Constraints: Economic Decisionmaking. 2nd ed. LC 94-70026. 207p. (C). 1994. pap. text 41.00 (0-89463-065-2) Am Inst FCPCU.

Chen, Z. Y. & Chai, T. Y. Low Cost Automation 1998. LC 99-39975. (IFAC Proceedings Ser.). 1999. pap. 75.50 (0-08-043027-9, Pub. by Elsevier) Elsevier.

***Chen, Ze-lin.** Chinese Herbal Medicine: Comprehensive Guide. 1999. pap. text 9.99 (0-7858-1076-5) Bk Sales Inc.

Chen, Zhaoguang. A Family Massage Manual. Zhao, Yong, tr. from CHI. (Illus.). 149p. (Orig.). 1992. pap. 6.95 (0-8351-2571-8) China Bks.

***Chen, Zhen-Yu & Siegler, Robert S., eds.** Across the Great Divide: Bridging the Gap Between Understanding of Toddlers' & Other Children's Thinking. (Monographs of the Society for Research in Children Development). 200p. 2000. pap. 32.95 (0-631-22153-0) Blackwell Pubs.

Chen, Zhen-Yu, jt. ed. see Gu, Yan.

***Chen, Zhengxin.** Computational Intelligence for Decision Support. LC 99-49863. (International Series on Computational Intelligence). 380p. 1999. boxed set 89.95 (0-8493-1799-1) CRC Pr.

***Chen, Zhiqun.** A Programmer's Guide to Java Smart Cards. 352p. 2000. pap. 39.95 (0-201-70329-7) Addison-Wesley.

Chen, Zhongying. Computational Mathematics: Proceedings of the Guangzhou International Symposium. LC 98-38673. (Lecture Notes in Pure & Applied Mathematics Ser.). (Illus.). 608p. 1998. pap. text 175.00 (0-8247-1946-8) Dekker.

Chenail, Jan, jt. auth. see Chenail, Ronald J.

Chenail, Ronald J. & Chenail, Jan. New Careers for Therapists. 224p. (C). 1999. 27.00 (0-393-70241-3) Norton.

Chenail, Ronald U., jt. ed. see Morris, G. H.

Chenault, S. L. Computers. 4th ed. 1995. pap. text, teacher ed. write for info. (0-13-366675-1) Allyn.

Chenciner. Daghestan: Tradition & Survival. LC 97-5245. 320p. 1997. text 49.95 (0-312-17380-6) St Martin.

Chendra, Anidrila, jt. auth. see Purkayastha, R. P.

Chene, Adele & Chervin, Michael. Popular Education in Quebec: Strengthening Social Movements. 1991. 13.95 (0-88379-051-3) A A A C E.

Chene, Henri. Paradox pour windows, Mode d'Emploi. 250p. 1993. pap. 32.95 (0-7859-5643-3, 2736110781) Fr & Eur.

Chenel, Laura. American Country Cheese. 1990. pap. 12.45 (0-201-52337-X) Addison-Wesley.

— Chevre! the Goat Cheese Cookbook. (Orig.). 1990. pap. 9.57 (0-201-52383-3) Addison-Wesley.

Chenel, Laura & Siegfried, Linda. American Country Cheese: Cooking with America's Speciality & Farmstead Cheeses. 1989. 18.22 (0-201-19662-X) Addison-Wesley.

— Chevre! the Goat Cheese Cookbook. LC 83-62381. (Illus.). 119p. (Orig.). 1983. pap. 9.95 (0-914015-00-1) Aris Bks.

Chenery & Clark. Interindustry Economics. 368p. 1993. 69.95 (0-7512-0156-1) Ashgate Pub Co.

Chenery, H. J., ed. see Murdoch, B. E.

Chenery, Hollis B. Studies in Developmental Planning. LC 70-143227. (Economic Studies: No. 136). 436p. 1971. 30.00 (0-674-84725-3) HUP.

Chenery, Hollis B., et al, eds. Handbook of Development Economics, Vols. IIIA&IIIB. Incl. Vol. 9. Handbook of Development Economics Vol. IIIa. (Illus.). 768p. 1995. 110.00 (0-444-82301-8); Vol. 9. Handbook of Development Economics Vol. IIIb. 608p. 1995. 110.00 (0-444-82302-6); 155.00 (0-444-88481-5) Elsevier.

Chenery, Hollis B. & Srinivasan, T. N., eds. Handbook of Development Ecomomics, Vol. 1. (Handbooks in Economics Ser.: No. 1). 872p. 1988. 110.00 (0-444-70337-3, North Holland) Elsevier.

— Handbook of Development Economics, 2 vols. 954p. 1989. 110.00 (0-444-70338-1) Elsevier.

Chenery, Richard. Old Coast Guard Stations Vol. I: Virginia: Popes Island to False Cape. LC 98-184652. (Illus.). viii, 94p. 1998. pap. 19.95 (0-9665204-0-8) Station Bks.

Chenery, William L. Industry & Human Welfare. Stein, Leon, ed. LC 77-70487. 1977. reprint ed. lib. bdg. 23.95 (0-405-10159-7) Ayer.

Chenery, William L. & Merrit, Ella A., eds. Standards of Child Welfare: A Report of the Children's Bureau Conferences, May & June, 1919. LC 74-1672. (Children & Youth Ser.: Vol. 6). 464p. 1974. reprint ed. 36.95 (0-405-05952-3) Ayer.

Chenetier, Marc. Beyond Suspicion: New American Fiction since 1960. Houlding, Elizabeth A., tr. LC 95-38105. (Penn Studies in Contemporary American Fiction). 336p. 1996. text 38.95 (0-8122-3059-0) U of Pa Pr.

Chenevert, Martin E., et al. HP-41CV Applied Drilling Engineering Manual. LC 82-20983. (Illus.). 151p. reprint ed. pap. 46.90 (0-608-04546-2, 206528800001) Bks Demand.

Chenevert, Melodie. Mosby's Tour Guide to Nursing School: A Student's Road Survival Guide. 3rd ed. LC 94-32030. (Illus.). 216p. (C). (gr. 13). 1994. pap. text 21.95 (0-8151-1539-3, 24868) Mosby Inc.

Chenevert, Melodie. Pass NCLEX-RN Survival Guide. 1994. write for info. (0-8151-1535-0) Mosby Inc.

Chenevert, Melodie. Professional-Nurse Handbook. 3rd ed. (Illus.). 192p. (C). (gr. 13). 1996. pap. text 22.00 (0-8151-1215-7, 29588) Mosby Inc.

— Stat: Special Techniques in Assertiveness Training for Women in the Health Professions. 4th rev. ed. LC 93-26505. Orig. Title: STAT Special Techniques in Assertiveness Training for Women in the Health Professions. (Illus.). 168p. (C). (gr. 13). 1993. pap. text 20.95 (0-8016-7233-3, 07233) Mosby Inc.

Chenevert, Melodie & Bramhall, Martha. Pass NCLEX-LPN Survival Kit. 1994. write for info. (0-8151-7881-6) Mosby Inc.

***Cheneviere, Alain.** Central America: The Lands of the Rainbow. (Illus.). 2000. 50.00 (2-7191-0454-X) La Manufacture.

Cheneviere, Alain. Maud in France. Davidson, Lisa, tr. LC 95-30976. (My Future Ser.). (J). 1996. lib. bdg. 22.60 (0-8225-2828-2, Lerner Publctns) Lerner Pub.

Cheneviere, Alan. Syria. (Illus.). 192p. 1996. 65.00 (0-905743-98-9, Pub. by Stacey Intl) Intl Bk Ctr.

***Cheney.** Early Modern Englishwoman Part. 2, Vol. 7. LC 99-55418. 2000. 51.95 (1-84014-220-0) Ashgate Pub Co.

Cheney. Math & Computing. 4th ed. LC 98-49447. (Mathematics). 671p. 1999. pap. 88.95 (0-534-35184-0) Brooks-Cole.

— Numerical Math & Computing. 3rd ed. (Mathematics Ser.). 1994. mass mkt., teacher ed. write for info. (0-534-20113-X) Brooks-Cole.

— Systems in Transition. (DC - Introduction to Computing Ser.). 1997. pap. 57.95 (0-7895-0193-7) Course Tech.

Cheney & Austin. Circle Time Activities. (Illus.). 112p. (J). (ps-1). 1998. pap., teacher ed. 14.95 (1-55799-664-4, 739) Evan-Moor Edu Pubs.

— Holiday Fun. (Illus.). 112p. (J). (ps-1). 1998. pap., teacher ed. 14.95 (1-55799-667-9, 742) Evan-Moor Edu Pubs.

Cheney, et al. From Farm to Table. (Illus.). 48p. (J). (gr. 1-3). 1996. pap., teacher ed. 9.95 (1-55799-565-6, 551) Evan-Moor Edu Pubs.

Cheney, Alan, jt. auth. see Buzzotta, V. R.

Cheney, Anne. The Burg & Other Poems. LC 98-13708. 128p. 1998. pap. 24.95 (0-7734-2831-3, Mellen Poetry Pr) E Mellen.

— The Life & Letters of Jesse Hill Ford, Southern Writer: With Annotations & Commentary. annot. ed. LC 95-20588. (Studies in American Literature: Vol. 19). (Illus.). 580p. 1996. 119.95 (0-7734-8876-6) E Mellen.

— Lorraine Hansberry. (United States Authors Ser.: No. 430). 184p. 1984. 32.00 (0-8057-7365-7, Twyne) Mac Lib Ref.

Cheney, Anne, ed. Dead Snakes, Cats, & the IRS: Poetry of Rock & Rebellion. LC 95-51018. (Illus.). 120p. 1995. 19.95 (0-7734-2757-0, Mellen Poetry Pr) E Mellen.

Cheney, Anne, ed. see Gillespie, Theresa.

An Asterisk (*) at the beginning of an entry indicates that the title is appearing for the first time.

Cheney, Brainard. This Is Adam. 1958. 12.95 (*0-8392-1116-3*) Astor-Honor.

Cheney, C. R. English Bishops' Chanceries, 1100-1250. 192p. 1998. pap. 24.95 (*0-7190-5438-9*, Pub. by Manchester Univ Pr) St Martin.

***Cheney, C. R. & Jones, Michael, eds.** A Handbook of Dates: For Students of British History. rev. ed. LC 99-27383. (Royal Historical Society Guides & Handbks.: No. 20). (Illus.). 264p. (C). 2000. 54.95 (*0-521-77095-5*); pap. 20.95 (*0-521-77845-X*) Cambridge U Pr.

Cheney, Charles C. The Marenos: Tradition & Transition in Huave Community Organization. (Vanderbilt University Publications in Anthropology: No. 15). (Illus.). 1976. pap. 3.10 (*0-935462-04-X*) VUPA.

Cheney, Christopher R. The English Church & Its Laws, 12th-14th Centuries. (Collected Studies: No. CS160). 348p. (C). 1982. reprint ed. text 117.95 (*0-86078-108-9*, Pub. by Variorum) Ashgate Pub Co.

— Episcopal Visitation of Monasteries in the Thirteenth Century. 2nd rev. ed. xxxi, 192p. 1983. lib. bdg. 35.00 (*0-87991-638-9*) Porcupine Pr.

Cheney, Christopher R., et al, eds. English Episcopal Acta. 2 vols., Set. (English Episcopal Acta II & III British Academy Ser.). (Illus.). 758p. 1991. reprint ed. pap. text 65.00 (*0-19-726104-3*) OUP.

Cheney-Coker, Syl. The Blood in the Desert's Eyes. (African Writers Ser.). (Illus.). 112p. (Orig.). (C). 1990. pap. 7.95 (*0-435-90574-0*, 90574) Heinemann.

— The Graveyard Also Has Teeth. (African Writers Ser.). 128p. (Orig.). (C). 1980. pap. 9.95 (*0-435-90221-0*, 90221) Heinemann.

Cheney-Coker, Syl. The Last Harmattan of Alusine Dunbar. (African Writers Ser.). 398p. (Orig.). (C). 1990. pap. 9.95 (*0-435-90572-4*, 90572) Heinemann.

Cheney, Cora. Vermont: The State with the Storybook Past. rev. ed. LC 86-60341. (Illus.). 288p. (J). (gr. 5-9). 1996. pap. 22.95 (*1-881535-21-5*) New Eng Pr VT.

Cheney Cowles Memorial Museum of the Eastern Washi. Cornhusk Bags of the Plateau Indians. LC 76-9025. 32p. 1976. lib. bdg. 36.00 (*0-226-68987-5*) U Ch Pr.

Cheney, Daniel P. & Mumford, Thomas F., Jr. Shellfish & Seaweed Harvests on Puget Sound. LC 85-17913. (Illus.). 180p. 1984. pap. 8.95 (*0-295-95990-8*) U of Wash Pr.

Cheney, Darwin, ed. Ethical Issues in Research. 258p. 1993. 39.00 (*1-55572-016-1*) Univ Pub Group.

Cheney, David M. Son of Minos. LC 64-25838. (J). (gr. 7). 1970. 22.00 (*0-8196-0142-X*) Biblo.

Cheney, Deborah, jt. auth. see Leech, Mark.

Cheney, Donna B. Thoughts on Being Human. LC 83-82480. (Illus.). 160p. (C). 1984. 5.50 (*0-87527-332-7*) Green.

Cheney, Dorothy L. & Seyfarth, Robert M. How Monkeys See the World: Inside the Mind of Another Species. LC 90-30295. (Illus.). x, 388p. 1992. pap. 16.95 (*0-226-10246-7*) U Ch Pr.

— How Monkeys See the World: Inside the Mind of Another Species. LC 90-30295. (Illus.). 389p. 1994. 24.95 (*0-226-10245-9*) U Ch Pr.

Cheney, E. W. Multivariate Approximation Theory: Selected Topics. LC 86-61533. (CBMS-NSF Regional Conference Series in Applied Mathematics: No. 51). (Illus.). vi, 68p. 1986. pap. text 22.50 (*0-89871-207-6*) Soc Indus-Appl Math.

Cheney, E. W. & Light, Will. Second Course in Approximation Theory. LC 99-26162. (Mathematics Ser.). 359p. 1999. pap. 87.95 (*0-534-36224-9*) Brooks-Cole.

Cheney, E. W., jt. auth. see Light, W. A.

Cheney, Ednah D. Louisa May Alcott. 1998. 39.95 (*0-7910-4535-8*) Chelsea Hse.

Cheney, Emily. She Can Read: Feminist Reading Strategies for Biblical Narrative. LC 96-24734. 192p. (Orig.). 1996. pap. 18.00 (*1-56338-167-2*) TPI PA.

Cheney, Frances Neel, jt. auth. see Sweetland, James H.

Cheney, Frank & Sammarco, Anthony M. Trolleys under the Hub. (Images of America Ser.). 1999. pap. 16.99 (*0-7524-0907-7*) Arcadia Publng.

***Cheney, Frank & Sammarco, Anthony Mitchell.** When Boston Rode the El: Massachusetts. LC 00-104042. (Images of America Ser.). (Illus.). 128p. 2000. pap. 18.99 (*0-7385-0462-9*) Arcadia Publng.

Cheney, Fred D. Nickel Rate Color Photography Vol. 3: The Railfan Perspective. LC 95-79970. (Illus.). 127p. 1997. 49.95 (*1-878887-71-8*) Morning NJ.

Cheney, Fred D. & Sweetland, David R. Southern Railway in Color. LC 92-63038. (Illus.). 128p. 1993. 49.95 (*1-878887-14-9*) Morning NJ.

Cheney, Gay. Basic Concepts in Modern Dance. 3rd ed. LC 88-60951. (Illus.). 128p. 1989. pap. 13.95 (*0-916622-76-2*) Princeton Bk Co.

***Cheney, George.** Values at Work: Employee Participation Meets Market Pressure at Mondragon. LC 99-37026. 2000. 35.00 (*0-8014-3325-8*) Cornell U Pr.

Cheney, Georgeann & Meronek, Theodora. Superior Catholics: Memories of a Parochial Education. LC 96-72270. (Illus.). 150p. (Orig.). 1997. pap. 15.95 (*1-886028-23-0*) Savage Pr.

Cheney, Glenn. Journey to Chernobyl: Encounters in a Radioactive Zone. 200p. 1999. pap. 15.95 (*0-89733-481-7*) Academy Chi Pubs.

Cheney, Glenn A. Journey to Chernobyl: Encounters in a Radioactive Zone. (Illus.). 165p. 1995. 20.00 (*0-89733-418-3*) Academy Chi Pubs.

— Life in Caves. 158p. (Orig.). (YA). (gr. 9-12). 1995. pap. 9.99 (*0-88092-127-7*) Royal Fireworks.

— Nuclear Proliferation. LC 98-4526. (Impact Bks.). 144 p. (J). 1999. 24.00 (*0-531-11431-7*) Watts.

— Teens with Physical Disabilities: Real-Life Stories of Meeting the Challenge. LC 94-3603. (Issues in Focus Ser.). (Illus.). 112p. (YA). (gr. 6 up). 1995. lib. bdg. 20.95 (*0-89490-625-9*) Enslow Pubs.

Cheney, Jean E., jt. auth. see Cheney, Robert S.

Cheney, Jonathan D., ed. Land Policy & Boom-Bust Real Estate Markets. 32p. 1994. pap. 14.00 (*1-55844-126-3*) Lincoln Inst Land.

***Cheney, Joyce.** Aprons. (Illus.). 2000. 17.95 (*0-7624-0694-1*) Running Pr.

Cheney, Joyce, ed. Lesbian Land. (Illus.). 200p. 1985. pap. 15.00 (*0-9615605-0-9*) Word Weavers.

Cheney, Karen. How to Start a Successful Home Business. (Money America's Financial Advisor Ser.). 1997. mass mkt. 87.92 (*0-446-16482-8*) Warner Bks.

Cheney, Karen & Alderman, Lesley. How to Start a Successful Home Business. LC 97-8920. 224p. 1997. mass mkt. 10.99 (*0-446-67316-1*, Pub. by Warner Bks) Little.

Cheney, Kimberly B. Labor & Employment in Vermont: Guide to Employment Laws, Regulations & Practices. 375p. 1994. pap. 65.00 (*0-88063-789-7*, 82712-10, MICHIE) LEXIS Pub.

Cheney, Liana. Botticelli's Neoplatonic Images. LC 93-20743. (Scripta Humanistica Ser.). 1993. 49.50 (*1-882528-03-4*) Scripta.

Cheney, Liana De Girolami, see De Girolami Cheney, Liana, ed.

Cheney, Lianna D., ed. Readings in Italian Mannerism. LC 96-48734. (American University Studies XX: Vol. 24). (Illus.). XXXIII, 348p. (C). 1997. text 55.95 (*0-8204-2483-8*) P Lang Pubng.

Cheney, Lynne & Cheney, Richard. Kings of the Hill: How 9 Powerful Men Changed the Course of American History. (Illus.). 240p. 1996. pap. 12.00 (*0-684-82340-3*, Touchstone) S&S Trade Pap.

Cheney, Lynne V. Academic Freedom. 30p. 1992. pap. text 3.00 (*1-878802-13-5*) J M Ashbrook Ctr Pub Affairs.

— Telling the Truth: Why Our Schools, Culture & Country Have Stopped Making Sense & What We Can Do About It. 256p. 1995. 23.00 (*0-684-81101-4*) Simon & Schuster.

Cheney, Mack L. Facial Surgery: Plastic & Reconstructive. LC 96-39122. (Illus.). 1040p. 1997. 199.99 (*0-683-01615-6*) Lppncott W & W.

Cheney, Margaret. Tesla. 416p. 1998. pap. 12.95 (*0-385-33382-X*) Doubleday.

— Tesla: Man Out of Time. Date not set. lib. bdg. 24.95 (*0-8488-2137-8*) Amereon Ltd.

Cheney, Marth C. Reading Comprehension: A Workbook for Ages 6-8. (Gifted & Talented Ser.). (Illus.). 64p. (J). (gr. 1-3). 1996. pap., wbk. ed. 4.95 (*1-56565-506-0*, 05060W, Pub. by Lowell Hse Juvenile) NTC Contemp Pub Co.

Cheney, Martha. Alphabet Workbook: A Workbook for Preschoolers. (Gifted & Talented Ser.). (Illus.). 312p. (J). (ps-k). 1998. pap., wbk. ed. 5.95 (*1-56565-839-6*, 08396W, Pub. by Lowell Hse Juvenile) NTC Contemp Pub Co.

— Animal Almanac: A Reference Book. LC 98-75623. (Gifted & Talented Ser.). (Illus.). 80p. (J). (gr. 1-3). 1999. pap. 6.95 (*0-7373-0052-3*) Lowell Hse Juvenile.

***Cheney, Martha.** Animals Workbook for Preschoolers. (Gifted & Talented Ser.). (Illus.). 48p. (J). (ps-k). 1999. pap., wbk. ed. 5.95 (*0-7373-0137-6*) Lowell Hse.

Cheney, Martha. Colors Workbook: For Preschoolers. (Gifted & Talented Ser.). (Illus.). 48p. (J). (ps-k). 1999. pap., wbk. ed. 5.95 (*0-7373-0202-X*, Pub. by Lowell Hse) NTC Contemp Pub Co.

— Counting Workbook: A Workbook for Preschoolers. (Gifted & Talented Ser.). (Illus.). 48p. (J). (ps-k). 1998. pap., wbk. ed. 5.95 (*1-56565-841-8*, 08418W, Pub. by Lowell Hse Juvenile) NTC Contemp Pub Co.

***Cheney, Martha.** Daily Summer Activities, Moving from Third to Fourth Grade. Evans, Marilyn, ed. (Daily Summer Activities Ser.). (Illus.). 160p. 2000. pap. 14.95 (*1-55799-768-3*, 1030) Evan-Moor Edu Pubs.

Cheney, Martha. Dinosaurs: A Science Workbook. Gorman, Linda & Siebert, Joanna, eds. (Gifted & Talented Ser.). (Illus.). 64p. (J). (gr. 1-2). 1999. pap., wbk. ed. 5.95 (*0-7373-0054-X*) Lowell Hse Juvenile.

— Gifted & Talented Word Workbook for Preschoolers. (Gifted & Talented Ser.). (Illus.). 48p. (J). (ps-k). 1999. pap. 5.95 (*1-56565-670-9*, 06709W, Pub. by Lowell Hse Juvenile) NTC Contemp Pub Co.

***Cheney, Martha.** Language Arts Puzzles & Games: A Workbook for Ages 6-8. (Gifted & Talented Ser.). (Illus.). 64p. (J). (gr. 1-3). 2000. pap., wbk. ed. 4.95 (*0-7373-0372-7*, 03727W, Pub. by Lowell Hse) NTC Contemp Pub Co.

Cheney, Martha. Math, Bk. II. (Gifted & Talented Ser.). (Illus.). 64p. (J). (gr. 1-3). 1998. pap. 4.95 (*1-56565-666-0*, 06660W, Pub. by Lowell Hse Juvenile) NTC Contemp Pub Co.

— Math Puzzles & Games: A Workbook for Ages 6-8. (Gifted & Talented Ser.). (Illus.). 64p. (J). 1998. pap. 4.95 (*1-56565-835-3*, 08353W, Pub. by Lowell Hse Juvenile) NTC Contemp Pub Co.

— Phonics Puzzles & Games: A Workbook for Ages 6-8. (Gifted & Talented Ser.). 64p. (J). (gr. 1-3). 1997. pap., wbk. ed. 4.95 (*1-56565-750-0*, 07500W, Pub. by Lowell Hse Juvenile) NTC Contemp Pub Co.

— Puzzles & Games for Critical & Creative Thinking. (Gifted & Talented Ser.). (Illus.). 80p. (J). (gr. 1-3). 1994. pap. 4.95 (*1-56565-139-1*, 01391W, Pub. by Lowell Hse) NTC Contemp Pub Co.

— Read Newspapers & Magazines. (Real-Life Reading Activities Ser.). (Illus.). 64p. (J). (gr. 4-6). 1996. pap., teacher ed. 7.95 (*1-55799-594-X*, 571) Evan-Moor Edu Pubs.

— Reading Puzzles & Games: A Workbook for Ages 6-8. (Gifted & Talented Ser.). (Illus.). 64p. (J). 1998. pap., wbk. ed. 4.95 (*1-56565-837-X*, 08379W, Pub. by Lowell Hse Juvenile) NTC Contemp Pub Co.

— Reading Reference Materials. (Real-Life Reading Activities Ser.). (Illus.). 64p. (J). (gr. 4-6). 1996. pap., teacher ed. 7.95 (*1-55799-593-1*, 570) Evan-Moor Edu Pubs.

***Cheney, Martha.** Things That Go Workbook: For Preschoolers. (Gifted & Talented Ser.). (Illus.) 48p. (J). (ps-k). 2000. pap., wbk. ed. 5.95 (*0-7373-0340-9*, 03409W, Pub. by Lowell Hse Juvenile) NTC Contemp Pub Co.

Cheney, Martha C. Gifted & Talented Math, Bk. 2. (Gifted & Talented Ser.). 64p. (J). (ps-1). 1995. pap. 4.95 (*1-56565-291-6*, 02916W, Pub. by Lowell Hse) NTC Contemp Pub Co.

— Gifted & Talented Math Puzzles & Games: A Workbook for Ages 4-6. (Gifted & Talented Ser.). (Illus.). 64p. (J). (ps). 1996. pap., wbk. ed. 4.95 (*1-56565-500-1*, 05001W, Pub. by Lowell Hse Juvenile) NTC Contemp Pub Co.

— Gifted & Talented Reading, Bk. 2. (Gifted & Talented Ser.). 64p. (J). 1995. pap. 4.95 (*1-56565-289-4*, 02894W, Pub. by Lowell Hse) NTC Contemp Pub Co.

— Gifted & Talented Reading Puzzles & Games: A Workbook for Ages 4-6. (Gifted & Talented Ser.). (Illus.). 64p. (J). (ps-1). 1996. pap., wbk. ed. 4.95 (*1-56565-502-8*, 05028W, Pub. by Lowell Hse Juvenile) NTC Contemp Pub Co.

— Monster Math Workbook, Bk. 2. 64p. (J). 1995. pap., wbk. ed. 4.95 (*1-56565-309-2*, 03092W, Pub. by Lowell Hse) NTC Contemp Pub Co.

— Phonics. (Gifted & Talented Ser.). (Illus.). 64p. (J). (ps-3). 1996. pap., wbk. ed. 4.95 (*1-56565-365-3*, 03653W, Pub. by Lowell Hse Juvenile); pap., wbk. ed. 4.95 (*1-56565-366-1*, 03661W, Pub. by Lowell Hse Juvenile) NTC Contemp Pub Co.

— Phonics Puzzles & Games. (Gifted & Talented Ser.). 64p. (J). Date not set. pap. 4.95 (*1-56565-568-0*, 05580W, Pub. by Lowell Hse Juvenile) NTC Contemp Pub Co.

— Puzzles & Games for Reading & Math, Bk. 2. (Gifted & Talented Ser.: Vol. 2). (Illus.). 64p. (Orig.). (J). (ps-3). 1996. pap. text, wbk. ed. 4.95 (*1-56565-374-2*, 03742W, Pub. by Lowell Hse Juvenile) NTC Contemp Pub Co.

Cheney, Martha C., jt. auth. see Cheney, Sheldon W.

Cheney, Martha C., jt. auth. see Cron, Mary.

Cheney, Mary A. Life & Letters of Horace Bushnell. LC 74-83415. (Religion in America, Ser. 1). 1975. reprint ed. 25.95 (*0-405-00236-X*) Ayer.

Cheney, Mary G. Roger, Bishop of Worcester, 1164-1179: An English Bishop of the Age of Becket. (Oxford Historical Monographs). (Illus.). 1981. 63.00 (*0-19-821879-6*) OUP.

Cheney, Michael. Dust, Wind & Agony: Character, Speech & Genre in Job. (Coniectanea Biblica Old Testament Ser.: No. 36). 323p. (Orig.). 1994. pap. 62.50 (*91-22-01603-1*) Coronet Bks.

Cheney, P. & Sullivan, A. Grassfires: Fuel, Weather & Fire Behavior. (Illus.). 144p. 1997. pap. 24.95 (*0-643-06324-2*, Pub. by CSIRO) Accents Pubns.

Cheney, Patricia. The Land & People of Zimbabwe. LC 89-36244. (Portraits of the Nations Ser.). (Illus.). 256p. (J). (gr. 6 up). 1990. 15.95 (*0-397-32392-1*) HarpC Child Bks.

Cheney, Patrick. Marlowe's Counterfeit Profession: Ovid, Spenser, Counter-Nationhood. LC 98-146977. 368p. 1997. text 60.00 (*0-8020-0971-9*) U of Toronto Pr.

— Spenser's Famous Flight: A Renaissance Idea of a Literary Career. 352p. 1993. text 60.00 (*0-8020-2934-5*) U of Toronto Pr.

***Cheney, Patrick G. & Prescott, Anne Lake.** Approaches to Teaching Shorter Elizabethan Poetry. LC 00-25804. (Approaches to Teaching World Literature Ser.: Vol. 65). 331p. 2000. pap. 18.00 (*0-87352-754-2*) Modern Lang.

***Cheney, Patrick G. & Prescott, Anne Lake, eds.** Approaches to Teaching Shorter Elizabethan Poetry. (Approaches to Teaching World Literature Ser.: Vol. 65). 331p. 2000. 37.50 (*0-87352-753-4*) Modern Lang.

Cheney, Patrick G. & Silberman, Lauren. Worldmaking Spenser: Explorations in the Early Modern Age. LC 99-13690. (Studies in the English Renaissance). 288p. (C). 1999. 39.95 (*0-8131-2126-4*) U Pr of Ky.

Cheney, Ray E. Equipment Specifications for High Schools, Their Use & Improvement: A New Aproach. LC 73-176641. (Columbia University. Teachers College. Contributions to Education Ser.: No. 612). reprint ed. 37.50 (*0-404-55612-4*) AMS Pr.

Cheney, Richard, jt. auth. see Cheney, Lynne.

Cheney, Robert & Zea, Philip M. New England Clocks & Their Makers. LC 92-27611. 1992. pap. 34.95 (*0-913387-03-7*) Old Sturbridge.

Cheney, Robert A. Computer-Aided Acquisition & Logistic Support. 316p. 1989. 40.00 (*0-9624643-0-9*) EMCA.

Cheney, Robert B. Basketball: Sixty-Five Programmed Principles. (Educational-Athletic Principles Ser.). (Illus.). 84p. (Orig.). (C). 1972. pap. 1.35 (*0-912934-02-6*) Bear.

Cheney, Robert B., ed. see Naismith, James.

Cheney, Robert S. & Cheney, Jean E. Coping: Survival in a Computerized Society. 1984. pap. text 19.95 (*0-89433-232-5*) Petrocelli.

***Cheney, Roberta & Erskine, Clyde.** Music, Saddles & Flapjacks: Dudes at the OTO Ranch. (Illus.). 302p. 2000. reprint ed. pap. 16.00 (*0-87842-422-9*) Mountain Pr.

Cheney, Roberta C. Names of the Face of Montana. LC 83-15401. 320p. (Orig.). 1983. pap. 12.00 (*0-87842-150-5*) Mountain Pr.

— A Sioux Wintercount: 131 Years of Dakota History, 1796-1926. rev. ed. LC 98-21072. Orig. Title: The Big Missouri Winter Count. (Illus.). 64p. 1998. pap. 8.95 (*0-87961-249-5*) Naturegraph.

Cheney, Roberta C., jt. auth. see Cheney, Truman M.

Cheney, Roland. Si'wren of the Patriarchs. 309p. mass mkt. 5.99 (*1-55197-619-6*) Picasso Publ.

Cheney, Roland J., jt. auth. see Hedge-Cheney, Jacquelyn.

Cheney, Sally. Tapestry. (Historical Ser.). 1993. per. 3.99 (*0-373-28792-5*, 1-28792-9) Harlequin Bks.

— Thief in the Night. (Historical Ser.: No. 711). 1992. per. 3.99 (*0-373-28712-7*, 1-28712-7) Harlequin Bks.

— The Wager. (Historical Ser.). 1996. per. 4.99 (*0-373-28934-0*, 1-28934-7) Harlequin Bks.

Cheney, Sheldon W. Men Who Have Walked with God: Being the Story of Mysticism Through the Ages Told in the Biographies of Representative Seers & Saints with Excerpts from Their Writings & Sayings. 415p. 1992. reprint ed. pap. 27.50 (*1-56459-268-5*) Kessinger Pub.

— The New Movement in the Theatre. LC 70-88532. 1972. 24.95 (*0-405-08356-4*, Pub. by Blom Pubns) Ayer.

— The New Movement in the Theatre. LC 70-95089. 303p. 1971. reprint ed. lib. bdg. 59.75 (*0-8371-3081-6*, CHNT, Greenwood Pr) Greenwood.

— New World Architecture. LC 72-100513. (BCL Ser.: No. II). (Illus.). reprint ed. 55.00 (*0-404-01487-9*) AMS Pr.

— Stage Decoration. LC 66-29421. (Illus.). 1972. reprint ed. 23.95 (*0-405-08357-2*, Pub. by Blom Pubns) Ayer.

Cheney, Sheldon W. & Cheney, Martha C. Art & the Machine: An Account of Industrial Design in 20th-Century America. (Twentieth Century: Landmarks in Design Ser.: Vol. 1). (Illus.). 307p. 1992. reprint ed. 49.95 (*0-926494-00-7*) Acanthus Pr.

Cheney, Sheldon W., ed. see Duncan, Isadora.

Cheney, Susan J. Stir Crazy! LC 97-33125. (Illus.). 192p. 1998. pap. 12.95 (*0-8092-3001-1*, 300110, Contemporary Bks) NTC Contemp Pub Co.

***Cheney, Theodore A. R.** Writing Creative Nonfiction: Fiction Techniques for Crafting Great Nonfiction. rev. ed. 160p. 2001. pap. 11.95 (*1-58008-229-7*) Ten Speed Pr.

Cheney, Thomas E., ed. Mormon Songs from the Rocky Mountains: A Compilation of Mormon Folksong. LC 68-63018. (Publications of the American Folklore Society, Bibliographical & Special Ser.: No. 53). 239p. reprint ed. pap. 74.10 (*0-7837-5531-7*, 204530400005) Bks Demand.

Cheney, Timothy D. Who Makes the Law? LC 97-41066. 109p. 1997. pap. text 19.60 (*0-13-493081-9*) P-H.

***Cheney, Tracey & Eden, Connie.** The Pitiful Gardener's Handbook: Successful Gardening, in Spite of Yourself. unabridged ed. LC 99-25415. (Illus.). 176p. 1999. pap. 12.95 (*1-881409-23-6*) Jhnstn Assocs.

Cheney, Truman M. & Cheney, Roberta C. So Long, Cowboys of the Open Range. LC 90-91858. (Illus.). 143p. (Orig.). 1990. pap. 9.95 (*1-56044-048-1*) Falcon Pub Inc.

Cheney, Victor T. The American Focus on Rape Series Vol. 2: A Brief History of Castration. Peterson, Alan H., tr. (Illus.). 212p. (Orig.). (C). 1996. pap. text 25.00 (*1-877858-76-5*, ABHOC) Amer Focus Pub.

Cheney, Victor T., jt. auth. see Peterson, Alan H.

Cheney, Walter J., et al. The Second Fifty Years: A Reference Manual for Senior Citizens. large type ed. (Illus.). 448p. (Orig.). 1992. pap. 21.95 (*1-55778-531-7*) Paragon Hse.

— The Second Fifty Years: A Reference Manual for Senior Citizens. (Illus.). 445p. (Orig.). reprint ed. pap. 21.95 (*0-9641660-0-3*) Writers Consort.

Cheney, Ward. Introduction to Approximation Theory. 2nd ed. LC 81-6208. x, 260p. (C). 1991. text 19.95 (*0-8284-0317-1*) Chelsea Pub.

Cheney, Ward & Kincaid, David. Numerical Math & Computing. 2nd ed. LC 84-27420. (Math). 512p. (C). 1985. mass mkt. 59.50 (*0-534-04356-9*) Brooks-Cole.

— Numerical Mathematics & Computing. 3rd ed. LC 93-43850. 1994. mass mkt. 67.50 (*0-534-20112-1*) Brooks-Cole.

Cheney, Ward, jt. auth. see Kincaid, David.

Cheney, Ward, jt. auth. see Kincaid, David R.

Cheney, William A. Can We Be Sure of Mortality? A Lawyer's Brief (1910) 205p. 1998. reprint ed. pap. 17.95 (*0-7661-0480-X*) Kessinger Pub.

Cheney, William R., jt. auth. see Logan, Albert B.

Chenfeld, Mimi B. Creative Experiences for Young Children. 2nd ed. LC 93-80876. 320p. (C). 1994. pap. text 57.50 (*0-15-501280-0*) Harcourt.

— Teaching in the Key of Life. LC 93-85701. (Illus.). 84p. (Orig.). 1993. pap. text 5.00 (*0-935989-57-9*, 315) Natl Assn Child Ed.

Cheng. Basic Documents International. 1997. lib. bdg. 392.00 (*90-411-0725-8*) Kluwer Law Intl.

— Business & Law. 5th ed. Date not set. pap. text, teacher ed. write for info. (*0-314-71586-X*) West Pub.

— Cheng Field & Wave Electromagnetics. 2nd ed. 720p. (C). 1989. pap. text 30.33 (*0-201-52820-7*) Addison-Wesley.

— Mastering AutoCAD: Native Solids. LC 97-30211. (General Engineering Ser.). 272p. (C). 1997. 43.95 (*0-534-95108-2*) PWS Pubs.

— Mastering Autosurf 3.0. LC 97-29789. (General Engineering Ser.). 240p. (C). 1997. mass mkt. 43.95 (*0-534-95085-X*) PWS Pubs.

***Cheng.** Mastering Mechanical Desktop. LC 99-35674. (General Engineering Ser.). 1999. pap. text 63.95 (*0-534-95760-9*) PWS Pubs.

Cheng. Mastering Mechanical Desktop: Parametric. LC 97-29788. (General Engineering Ser.). 304p. (C). 1997. 43.95 (*0-534-95109-0*) PWS Pubs.

— On Lao Tzu. (Philosophy Ser.). 1999. pap. text 13.95 (*0-534-57609-5*) Brooks-Cole.

— Surface Modeling Using Autosurf. LC 96-25870. (General Engineering Ser.). 200p. (C). 1996. 22.00 (*0-534-95694-7*) PWS Pubs.

Cheng & Smith. Tai Chi. 29.95 (*0-685-22124-5*) Wehman.

C

Cheng, et al. Management of Communication Disorders in Multicultural. 448p. 1994. pap. 39.95 (*0-8016-6818-2*) Mosby Inc.

Cheng, A. H. & Yang, C. Y., eds. Computational Stochastic Mechanics. 688p. 1993. 305.00 (*1-85312-250-5*) Computational Mech MA.

Cheng, A. H. & Yang, C. Y., eds. Computational Stochastic Mechanics. 1993. 256.00 (*1-85861-023-0*) Elsevier.

***Cheng, A. H. D.** Multilayered Aquifer Systems: Fundamentals & Applications. LC 00-31596. (Civil & Environmental Engineering Ser.). (Illus.). 2000. write for info. (*0-8247-9875-9*) Dekker.

Cheng, Alethea. Design & Feminism: Revisioning Spaces, Places, & Everyday Things. Rothschild, Joan, ed. LC 98-45275. (Illus.). 256p. (C). 1999. pap. 25.00 (*0-8135-2667-1*); text 50.00 (*0-8135-2666-3*) Rutgers U Pr.

***Cheng, Andrea.** Grandfather Counts. 2000. 15.95 (*1-58430-010-8*) Lee & Low Bks.

Cheng, Andrea. Let's Make a Present! Easy to Make Gifts for Friends & Relatives of Any Age. (Projects for Parents Ser.). (Illus.). 128p. (J). (gr. k-5). 1991. pap. 9.95 (*1-878767-16-X*) Murdoch Bks.

***Cheng, Anne Anlin.** The Melancholy of Race: Psychoanalysis, Assimilation & Hidden Grief. (Race & American Culture Ser.). (Illus.). 320p. 2001. 29.95 (*0-19-513403-6*) OUP.

Cheng, Bin. General Principles of Law As Applied by International Courts & Tribunals. 541p. (C). 1987. 180.00 (*0-949009-06-7*, Pub. by Grotius Pubns Ltd) St Mut.

— Studies in International Space Law. (Illus.). 866p. 1998. text 125.00 (*0-19-825730-9*) OUP.

Cheng, C. H. Information Processing for Remote Sensing. 1999. 110.00 (*981-02-3737-5*) World Scientific Pub.

Cheng, C. H., jt. ed. see Paillet, Frederick.

Cheng, C. P., jt. auth. see Yannakoudakis, E. J.

Cheng, C. S. Agnes, jt. auth. see Manes, Rene P.

Cheng, Charles L., et al. Goods & Services Tax - The Law & Practice, 2 vols., Issue 0. 1946p. 1995. ring bd. write for info. (*0-409-99773-0*, MICHIE) LEXIS Pub.

Cheng, Chi-Lun & Van Ness, John W. Statistical Regression with Measurement Error. LC 99-230993. (Kendall's Library of Statistics: No. 6). (Illus.). 280p. 1999. text 55.00 (*0-340-61461-7*, Pub. by E A) OUP.

C

Cheng, Chia-Jui. Basic Documents on International Trade Law. LC 85-8804. 1986. lib. bdg. 292.00 (*90-247-3168-2*) Kluwer Academic.

— Basic Documents on International Trade Law. rev. ed. (C). 1990. lib. bdg. 290.50 (*1-85333-359-X*) Kluwer Academic.

— The Use of Air & Outer Space Cooperation & Competition: Proceedings of the International Conference on Air & Outer Space at the Service of World Peace & Prosperity, Held in Beijing from 21-23 August 1995. LC 98-6566. 1998. 148.50 (*90-411-0597-2*) Kluwer Law Intl.

Cheng, Chia-Jui, ed. Clive M. Schmithoff's Select Essays on International Trade Law. (C). 1988. lib. bdg. 347.00 (*90-247-3702-8*) Kluwer Academic.

Cheng, Chia-Jui, et al, eds. The Highways of Air & Outer Space over Asia. LC 92-26612. 364p. (C). 1992. lib. bdg. 131.00 (*0-7923-1946-X*) Kluwer Academic.

Cheng, Chia-Jui & Liu, Lawrence S., eds. International Harmonization of Competition Laws. LC 94-44294. 1995. lib. bdg. 166.00 (*0-7923-3279-2*) Kluwer Academic.

Cheng, Chia-Jui, jt. ed. see Norton, J. J.

Cheng, Chin-Chuan. A Synchronic Phonology of Mandarin Chinese. LC 72-88180. (Monographs on Linguistic Analysis: No. 4). 81p. (Orig.). 1973. pap. text 32.35 (*90-279-2407-4*) Mouton.

***Cheng, Ch'ing-wen.** Three-Legged Horse. LC 98-22603. (Modern Literature from Taiwan Ser.). 240p. 1999. 22.95 (*0-231-11386-2*) Col U Pr.

***Cheng, Christina M.** Macau - A Cultural Janus. 232p. 1999. pap. (*962-209-486-4*) HK Univ Pr.

Cheng, Christopher C. Air Mobility: The Development of a Doctrine. LC 93-5853. 264p. 1994. 65.00 (*0-275-94721-1*, Praeger Pubs) Greenwood.

***Cheng, Christopher C.** One Child. LC 99-38380. (Illus.). 32p. (J). (gr. 3-6). 1999. 14.95 (*1-56656-330-5*) Interlink Pub.

Cheng, Chu-yuan. The Demand & Supply of Primary Energy in Mainland China. (Mainland China Economic Ser.: No. 3). (Illus.). 186p. 1985. pap. text 30.00 (*0-295-96206-2*) U of Wash Pr.

***Cheng, Chun-Kuang, et al.** Interconnect Analysis & Synthesis, Vol. 1. LC 99-21918. 262p. 1999. 69.95 (*0-471-29366-0*) Wiley.

Cheng, Chung-ying. New Dimensions of Confucian & Neo-Confucian Philosophy. LC 89-19655. (SUNY Series in Philosophy). 619p. (C). 1991. text 29.50 (*0-7914-0283-5*) State U NY Pr.

Cheng, Chung-ying. Tai Chen's Inquiry into Goodness: A Translation of the Yuan Shan, with an Introductory Essay. LC 70-113573. 184p. reprint ed. pap. 57.10 (*0-7837-3984-2*, 204381400011) Bks Demand.

Cheng, Chung-Ying, jt. ed. see Hsiung, James C.

Cheng, Civi, jt. auth. see Young, Russell.

Cheng, Cliff, ed. Masculinities in Organizations. LC 96-10041. (Research on Men & Masculinities Ser.: Vol. 9). 288p. 1996. 58.00 (*0-7619-0223-6*); pap. 26.00 (*0-7619-0224-4*) Sage.

Cheng, David K. Field & Wave Electromagnetics. 640p. 1983. text 48.50 (*0-201-01239-1*) Addison-Wesley.

— Field & Wave Electromagnetics. 2nd ed. (Electrical Engineering Ser.). (Illus.). 71p. (C). 1989. 100.00 (*0-201-12819-5*) Addison-Wesley.

— Fundamentals of Engineering Electromagnetics. (Illus.). 495p. (C). 1992. 100.00 (*0-201-56611-7*) Addison-Wesley.

Cheng, Davy C., jt. auth. see David, Tirone E.

Cheng, Eva. The Elder Chinese. LC 77-83484. (Elder Minority Ser.). 56p. 1978. 9.50 (*0-916304-35-3*) SDSU Press.

Cheng, F. T., tr. from CHI. The Chinese Supreme Court Decisions: Relating to General Principles of Civil Law, Obligations & Commercial Law. LC 76-11421. 229p. 1976. reprint ed. lib. bdg. 62.50 (*0-313-26967-X*, U6967, Greenwood Pr) Greenwood.

— Judgments of the High Prize Court of the Republic of China. vi, 146p. 1983. reprint ed. 36.00 (*0-8377-0449-9*, Rothman) W S Hein.

Cheng, F. Y. & Sheu, M. S., eds. Urban Disaster Mitigation: The Role of Engineering & Technology. LC 95-12167. 340p. 1995. 141.00 (*0-08-041920-8*, Pergamon Pr) Elsevier.

Cheng, Fa-Hwa. Statics & Strength of Materials. 2nd ed. 1995. 50.06 (*0-02-803067-2*); write for info. (*0-02-803068-0*) Glencoe.

Cheng Few, Lee. Final Analysis Planning. LC 84-317. (C). 1985. teacher ed. 80.00 (*0-201-04476-5*) Addison-Wesley.

— Financial Analysis & Planning: Theory & Application. LC 84-317. (C). 1985. pap. text 35.16 (*0-201-04475-7*) Addison-Wesley.

Cheng, Francois. Empty & Full: The Language of Chinese Painting. Kohn, Michael H., tr. LC 94-9541. (Illus.). 192p. 1994. pap. 15.00 (*0-87773-956-0*, Pub. by Shambhala Pubns) Random.

— The River Below. Orig. Title: Le dit de Tiamyi. 400p. 2000. 24.95 (*1-56649-100-2*) Welcome Rain.

Cheng, Franklin Y., ed. Analysis & Computation: Proceedings of the Eleventh Computation Conference - Formerly Electronic Computation Conference. LC 94-7104. 400p. 1994. 6.00 (*0-87262-974-0*) Am Soc Civil Eng.

— Analysis & Computation: Proceedings of the Twelfth Congress Held in Conjunction with Structures Congress XIV - Chicago, Illinois, April 15-18, 1996. LC 96-11789. 536p. 1996. pap. 64.00 (*0-7844-0163-2*) Am Soc Civil Eng.

— Recent Developments in Structural Optimization. (Sessions Proceedings Ser.). 108p. 1986. 5.00 (*0-87262-557-5*) Am Soc Civil Eng.

— Stability under Seismic Loading. (Sessions Proceedings Ser.). 80p. 1986. 3.00 (*0-87262-556-7*) Am Soc Civil Eng.

***Cheng, Franklin Y. & Gu, Yuanxian.** Computational Mechanics in Structural Engineering: Recent Developments. LC 98-51822. 392p. 1999. 172.50 (*0-08-043008-2*) Elsevier.

Cheng, Franklin Y. & Wang, Y. Y. Post-Earthquake Rehabilitation & Reconstruction. LC 96-26972. 484p. 1996. 131.50 (*0-08-042825-8*, Pergamon Pr) Elsevier.

Cheng, Franklin Y. & Zizhi, Fu, eds. Recent Developments & Future Trends of Computational Mechanics in Structural Engineering. LC 92-13306. xiii, 466 p. 1992. mass mkt. 276.50 (*1-85166-867-5*) Elsevier.

Cheng, Franklin Y., jt. ed. see Frangopol, Dan M.

***Cheng, Fu-Ding.** Dream-House. 2000. 16.95 (*1-57174-186-0*) Hampton Roads Pub Co.

Cheng, Grace, ed. Guide to Hong Kong Medical, Health & Welfare Libraries & Information Resources. 256p. (Orig.). 1996. pap. 67.50 (*962-209-410-4*, Pub. by HK Univ Pr) Coronet Bks.

Cheng, Grace, jt. auth. see Storey, Colin.

Cheng, H. H., ed. Pesticides in the Soil Environment: Processes, Impacts, & Modeling. (Book Ser.: No. 2). 554p. 1990. 36.00 (*0-89118-791-X*) Soil Sci Soc Am.

Cheng, H. L. Nagarjuna's Twelve Gate Treatise. 165p. 1982. text 121.50 (*90-277-1380-4*, D Reidel) Kluwer Academic.

*** Cheng, H. N., et al, eds.** Application of Polymers in Foods Macromolecular Symposia, Vol. 140. 270p. 1999. 120.00 (*3-527-29808-8*, Wiley-VCH) Wiley.

Cheng, H. S., ed. see American Society of Mechanical Engineers Staff.

***Cheng, Hai-Yang.** Particle Physics Phenomenology: Proceedings of IV International Workshop Taiepi, Roc 18 - 21 Jun. 350p. 1999. 78.00 (*981-02-3817-7*) World Scientific Pub.

Cheng, Hang-Sheng, ed. Monetary Policy in Pacific Basin Countries. (C). 1988. lib. bdg. 120.00 (*0-89838-290-4*) Kluwer Academic.

Cheng, Haw. Sixth Grade Was a Nightmare, & Seventh Is Worse: A 12-Year Old Speaks Out. Thurman, Joann M., ed. (Illus.). 128p. (J). (gr. 3-9). Date not set. 11.95 (*0-89896-335-4*) Larksdale.

— Sixth Grade Was a Nightmare, & Seventh Is Worse: A 12-Year Old Speaks Out. Thurman, Joann M., ed. (Illus.). 128p. (J). (gr. 3-9). 1996. pap. 7.95 (*0-89896-336-2*) Larksdale.

Cheng, Henry, jt. auth. see Bishop, Errett.

Cheng, Herbert S., jt. ed. see Kennedy, Francis E.

Cheng, Hsueh-li. Exploring Zen. 2nd ed. Fu, Charles W., ed. (Asian Thought & Culture Ser.: Vol. 2). XI, 236p. 1996. pap. 29.95 (*0-8204-3653-4*) P Lang Pubng.

Cheng, Hsueh-li, ed. New Essays in Chinese Philosophy. LC 95-21520. (Asian Thought & Culture Ser.: Vol. 28). XIII, 256p. (C). 1997. text 48.95 (*0-8204-2875-2*) P Lang Pubng.

Cheng Huikun. Basics of Long-Style Boxing. 179p. 1996. pap. 8.95 (*7-119-01538-9*, Pub. by Foreign Lang) China Bks.

Cheng Imm Tan. Liberation of Asians. LC 98-183050. 1993. pap. 3.00 (*0-913937-82-7*) Rational Isl.

Cheng, J. Chester, tr. Documents of Dissent: Chinese Political Thought since Mao. (Publication Ser.: No. 230). 120p. (Orig.). 1980. pap. 7.95 (*0-8179-7302-8*) Hoover Inst Pr.

Cheng, Jaiho, tr. Tales from Within the Clouds: Nakhi Stories of China. LC 96-47892. (Illus.). 64p. (J). (gr. 4-7). 1997. 13.50 (*0-8248-1820-2*, Kolowalu Bk) UH Pr.

Cheng, James C. Chinese Sources for the Taiping Rebellion, 1850-1864. LC 63-4982. 199p. reprint ed. pap. 61.70 (*0-7837-0117-9*, 204039400016) Bks Demand.

Cheng, Jan-Jan, tr. see Breslin, Dee.

Cheng, Jing, jt. auth. see Mitchelson, Keith R.

Cheng, Jonathan S. C., ed. Geosynthetic Soil-Reinforcement Testing Procedures. 250p. 1993. 49.00 (*0-614-16829-5*, ASTM12) Am Soc Civil Eng.

Cheng, Joseph & Peterson, Richard. Advances in International Comparative Management, Vol. 12. 1999. 73.25 (*0-7623-0174-0*) Jai Pr.

Cheng, Joseph, jt. ed. see Leung, Beatrice.

Cheng, Joseph L., et al, eds. Advances in International Comparative Management, Vol. 11. 288p. 1996. 73.25 (*0-7623-0007-8*) Jai Pr.

Cheng, Joseph T., jt. ed. see Koehn, Peter.

Cheng, Joseph Y. Hong Kong: In Search of a Future. 1984. pap. 17.95 (*0-19-583747-9*) OUP.

Cheng, Joseph Y., ed. China in the Post-Deng Era. LC 98-165603. 700p. 1998. pap. text 37.50 (*962-201-792-4*, Pub. by Chinese Univ) U of Mich Pr.

— China Review, 1998. 500p. (C). Date not set. 65.00 (*962-201-800-9*, Pub. by Chinese Univ) U of Mich Pr.

— The Other Hong Kong Report 1997. 1997. pap. 32.50 (*962-201-778-9*, Pub. by Chinese Univ) U of Mich Pr.

Cheng, Joseph Y. & Lo, Sonny S., eds. From Colony to Special Administrative Region: Hong Kong's Challenges Ahead. LC 96-118902. 600p. (Orig.). (C). 1997. pap. text 39.50 (*962-201-671-5*, Pub. by Chinese Univ) U of Mich Pr.

Cheng, Joseph Y., jt. ed. see MacPherson, Stewart.

Cheng, Joseph Y. S., jt. ed. see Kwok, Joseph.

Cheng, Josephine & Malaika, Susan, eds. Web Gateway Tools: Connecting IBM & Lotus Applications to the Web. LC 96-29922. 442p. 1997. pap. 34.95 (*0-471-17555-2*) Wiley.

Cheng, K. C. & Seki. Freezing & Melting Heat Transfer in Engineering. 1991. 120.00 (*0-89116-985-7*) Hemisp Pub.

Cheng, K. E. & Ohta, T., eds. Feature Interactions in Telecommunications III. LC 95-7902. 223p. (YA). (gr. 12). 1995. 97.00 (*90-5199-238-6*, 238-6) IOS Press.

Cheng, K. L., et al, eds. Handbook of Organic Analytical Reagents. 544p. 1982. lib. bdg. 123.00 (*0-8493-0771-6*, QD77) CRC Pr.

— Handbook of Organic Analytical Reagents. 2nd ed. 624p. 1992. boxed set 241.95 (*0-8493-4287-2*) CRC Pr.

Cheng, K. M., jt. ed. see Wong, K. C.

Cheng, K. S., jt. ed. see Chan, K. L.

Cheng, Kai N. & Leong, Yu K., eds. Group Theory: Proceedings of the Singapore Group Theory Conference Held at the National University of Singapore, June 8-19, 1987. xviii, 586p. (C). 1989. lib. bdg. 119.95 (*3-11-011366-X*) De Gruyter.

Cheng-Kui, Zeng, jt. ed. see Di, Zhou.

Cheng, Kwang-Ting & Agrawal, Vishwani D. Unified Methods for VLSI Simulation & Test Generation. (C). 1989. text 72.50 (*0-7923-9025-3*) Kluwer Academic.

Cheng, Kwang-Ting, jt. auth. see Krstic, Angela.

Cheng, Kwant-Ting, jt. auth. see Huang, Shi-Yu.

Cheng, L. K., jt. auth. see Tang, C. L.

Cheng, L. M. Food Machinery: For the Production of Cereal Foods, Snack Foods & Confectionary. 312p. 1992. 153.00 (*1-85573-269-6*) Am Educ Systs.

Cheng, Li-Rong L. Assessing Asian Language Performance: Guidelines for Evaluating Limited-English Proficient Students. 222p. 1991. pap. text 29.95 (*0-614-04586-X*) Acad Comm.

— Integrating Language & Learning for Inclusion: An Asian - Pacific Focus. (Culture, Rehabilitation, & Education Ser.). (Illus.). 256p. (Orig.). (C). 1995. pap. 45.00 (*1-56593-451-2*, 1068) Thomson Learn.

Cheng, Li-Rong L., jt. ed. see Butler, Katharine.

Cheng, Li-Rong L., jt. ed. see Pang, Valerie O.

Cheng, Lilly, et al. Myth or Reality: Adaptive Strategies of Asian Americans in California. LC 92-38080. 212p. 1992. pap. 27.95 (*0-7507-0073-4*, Falmer Pr) Taylor & Francis.

Cheng, Lisa L. On the Typology of Wh-Questions. rev. ed. LC 97-12243. (Outstanding Dissertations in Linguistics Ser.). 220p. 1997. text 51.00 (*0-8153-2887-7*) Garland.

Cheng, Lucie, et al. Linking Our Lives: Chinese American Women of Los Angeles. LC 84-72431. (Illus.). xvii, 122p. (Orig.). (C). 1993. pap. 10.95 (*0-930377-00-1*) Chinese Hist CA.

Cheng, M. D., jt. ed. see Wu, W. T.

Cheng, M. T., et al, eds. Harmonic Analysis: Proceedings of the Special Program at the Nankai Institute of Mathematics, Tianjin, the People's Republic of China, March-July 1988. (Lecture Notes in Mathematics Ser.: Vol. 1494). ix, 226p. 1991. pap. 39.00 (*0-387-54901-3*) Spr-Verlag.

Cheng Man-Ch'ing. Master Cheng's Thirteen Chapters on T'ai-Chi Ch'uan. 12th ed. Wile, Douglas, tr. from CHI. (Illus.). 102p. (Orig.). 1985. pap. 8.95 (*0-912059-00-1*) Sweet Ch I Pr.

Cheng, Man-Ch'ing & Smith, Robert W. T'ai-Chi: The Supreme Ultimate Exercise for Health, Sport, & Self-Defense. LC 67-23009. (Illus.). 112p. 1967. 29.95 (*0-8048-0560-1*) Tuttle Pubng.

Cheng, Mignonette Y., et al. Watercolors of Italy. LC 96-164318. 86p. 1996. text 39.50 (*0-472-10738-0*, 10738) U of Mich Pr.

Cheng, Minde, et al, eds. Harmonic Analysis in China. LC 95-17464. (Mathematics & Its Applications Ser.: Vol. 327). 320p. (C). 1995. text 163.00 (*0-7923-3566-X*) Kluwer Academic.

Cheng, Nien. Life & Death in Shanghai. ix, 547p. 1987. pap. 24.95 (*0-394-55548-1*) Random.

— Life & Death in Shanghai. (Illus.). 560p. 1988. pap. 14.95 (*0-14-010870-X*, Penguin Bks) Viking Penguin.

Cheng, P. C., et al, eds. Multidimensional Microscopy. LC 93-5146. (Illus.). 408p. 1993. 71.95 (*0-387-94118-5*) Spr-Verlag.

Cheng, P. C. & Jan, G. X-Ray Microscopy. (Illus.). 430p. 1987. 129.95 (*0-387-18148-2*) Spr-Verlag.

***Cheng-Pang, G.** Mongolia, 6 vols. , Set. LC 98-31897. (Cultures of the World Ser.). (Illus.). 128p. (YA). (gr. 5 up). 1999. lib. bdg. 35.64 (*0-7614-0954-8*) Marshall Cavendish.

Cheng, Pang G., jt. auth. see Barias, Bob.

***Cheng, Pang Guek.** Grenada. (Cultures of the World Ser.). (Illus.). (J). 2000. 35.64 (*0-7614-1160-7*, Benchmark NY) Marshall Cavendish.

— Kazakhstan. (Cultures of the World Ser.). (Illus.). (J). 2001. 35.64 (*0-7614-1193-3*, Benchmark NY) Marshall Cavendish.

Cheng, Pei-kai, et al, eds. The Search for Modern China: A Documentary Collection. LC 98-44315. 1999. pap. text. write for info. (*0-393-97372-7*) Norton.

Cheng, Peter. Problems for Management Accounting I. (C). 1993. student ed. 10.00 (*1-881592-37-5*) Hayden-McNeil.

Cheng, Peter P. Chronology of the People's Republic of China, 1970-1979. LC 84-20231. 629p. 1984. 60.50 (*0-8108-1751-9*) Scarecrow.

Cheng, Philip C. Accounting & Finance in Mass Transit. LC 80-70920. (Illus.). 336p. 1982. text 80.00 (*0-86598-035-7*) Rowman.

— Financial Management in the Shipping Industry. LC 79-15869. (Illus.). 378p. 1979. reprint ed. pap. 117.20 (*0-7837-9065-1*, 204981400003) Bks Demand.

— Steamship Accounting. LC 70-80637. (Illus.). 192p. 1969. reprint ed. pap. 59.60 (*0-7837-9071-6*, 204982000003) Bks Demand.

Cheng, Philippe, photos by. Forever & a Day. (Illus.). 1999. 49.95 (*3-908161-74-6*) Abbeville Pr.

Cheng Qingtai, ed. Latin-Chinese-English Names of Fishes. (CHI, ENG & LAT.). 296p. 1996. 12.00 (*7-03-000454-X*, Pub. by Sci Pr) Lubrecht & Cramer.

Cheng, R. Design Load Tables for Laterally Loaded Masonry Panels Pts. 1 & 2: Guide to British Standard 5628. (Illus.). 54p. 1996. 48.00 (*0-7277-2526-2*) Am Soc Civil Eng.

Cheng, Ralph T., jt. ed. see Spaudling, Malcolm L.

Cheng, Richard. Design of Concrete Structures for Retaining Aqueous Liquids: Design Tables to BS 8007. LC 96-229974. 64p. 1996. 48.00 (*0-7277-2517-3*) Am Soc Civil Eng.

Cheng, Ron. Mastering AutoCAD Release 13. LC 97-28667. 352p. (C). 1997. mass mkt. 53.95 (*0-534-95506-1*) Brooks-Cole.

Cheng, Runwei, jt. auth. see Gen, Mitsuo.

Cheng, S., et al, eds. Recent Developments in Geometry. LC 89-18039. (Contemporary Mathematics Ser.: Vol. 101). 338p. 1989. pap. 46.00 (*0-8218-5107-1*, CONM/101) Am Math.

Cheng, S. C. Jonathan, ed. Geosynthetic Soil Reinforcement Testing Procedures, STP 1190. LC 93-8893. (Special Technical Publication Ser.: Vol. 1190). (Illus.). 248p. 1993. text 49.00 (*0-8031-1885-6*, STP1190) ASTM.

Cheng, S. S. MOS Digital Electronics. 224p. (C). 1987. text 54.00 (*9971-5-0372-7*) World Scientific Pub.

Cheng, Sally, jt. auth. see Feuerwerke, Albert.

Cheng-Sen Li, ed. see Li Wenyan & Lu Dadao.

Cheng, Seymour C. Schemes for the Federation of the British Empire. LC 68-59048. (Columbia University. Studies in the Social Sciences: No. 335). reprint ed. 32.50 (*0-404-51335-2*) AMS Pr.

Cheng, Shujan, tr. see Yun, Hsing.

***Cheng, Sonia.** Myths & Civilization of the Ancient Chinese. (Myths & Civilization Ser.). (Illus.). 48p. (J). (gr. 3-7). 2000. 16.95 (*0-87226-592-7*, 65927B, P Bedrick Books) NTC Contemp Pub Co.

Cheng, Stephen C. The Tao of Voice: A New East-West Approach to Transforming the Singing & Speaking Voice. 208p. 1991. pap. 14.95 (*0-89281-260-5*, Destiny Bks) Inner Tradit.

***Cheng, Sui Sun, et al, eds.** New Developments in Difference Equations & Applications: Proceedings of the Third International Conference on Difference Equations. 380p. 1999. text 120.00 (*90-5699-669-X*) Gordon & Breach.

Cheng, T., jt. ed. see Seymour, Raymond B.

Cheng, T. C. Introduction to Just-in-Time Manufacturing. 1992. 49.95 (*0-442-31698-4*) Chapman & Hall.

Cheng, Ta-Pei & Li, Ling-Fong. Gauge Theory of Elementary Particle Physics. (Illus.). 546p. 1988. pap. text 52.95 (*0-19-851961-3*) OUP.

***Cheng, Ta-Pei & Li, Ling-Fong.** Gauge Theory of Elementary Particle Physics: Problems & Solutions. LC 99-56412. (Illus.). 352p. 2000. pap. text 45.00 (*0-19-850621-X*) OUP.

Cheng, Tai, jt. ed. see Seymour, Raymond B.

Cheng, Te-k'un. The World of the Chinese: A Struggle for Human Unity. (Illus.). 251p. 1980. 33.50 (*962-201-207-8*, Pub. by Chinese Univ) Coronet Bks.

Cheng, Thomas C., ed. Parasitic & Related Diseases: Basic Mechanisms, Manifestations, & Control. LC 85-24447. (Comparative Pathobiology Ser.: Vol. 8). 176p. 1986. 65.00 (*0-306-42119-4*, Plenum Trade) Perseus Pubng.

Cheng, Thomas C., ed. Pathogens of Invertebrates: Application in Biological Control & Transmission Mechanisms. (Comparative Pathobiology Ser.: Vol. 7). 286p. 1984. 79.50 (*0-306-41700-6*, Plenum Trade) Perseus Pubng.

Cheng, Thomas C., jt. auth. see Bogitsch, Burt J.

Cheng, Thomas C., jt. ed. see Perkins, Frank O.

Cheng, Thomas S. General Parasitology. 2nd ed. (C). 1986. text 104.00 (*0-12-170755-5*) Acad Pr.

An Asterisk (*) at the beginning of an entry indicates that the title is appearing for the first time.

Cheng Tsohsin, contrib. by. Birds of the World: Latin, Chinese & English Names. (CHI, ENG & LAT.). 470p. 1996. 14.80 (*7-03-001389-1*, Pub. by Sci Pr) Lubrecht & Cramer.

Cheng Tsohsin, ed. A Complete Checklist of Species & Subspecies of the Chinese Birds. 318p. 1996. 29.90 (*7-03-004227-1*, Pub. by Sci Pr) Lubrecht & Cramer.

Cheng, Tun-jen & Haggard, Stephan. Newly Industrializing Asia in Transition: Policy Reform & American Response. LC 87-80821. (Policy Papers in International Affairs: No. 31). (Illus.). x, 106p. (C). 1987. pap. text 8.50 (*0-87725-531-8*) U of Cal IAS.

Cheng, Tun-jen, et al. Inherited Rivalry: Conflicts Across the Taiwan Straits. 1995. pap. text 25.00 (*1-55587-551-3*) L Rienner.

Cheng, Tun-jen, jt. ed. see Tien, Hung-mao.

Cheng-Tzu, Chiu, ed. see Hsueh-Hsia, Chen.

Cheng, Vincent J. Shakespeare & Joyce: A Study of Finnegans Wake. LC 82-42781. 256p. (C). 1984. 32.50 (*0-271-00342-1*) Pa St U Pr.

Cheng, Vincent J., et al, eds. Joycean Cultures/Culturing Joyces. LC 97-40258. (Illus.). 296p. 1998. 39.50 (*0-87413-636-9*) U Delaware Pr.

Cheng, Vincent J., tr. see Corneille, Pierre.

Cheng, Wei, jt. auth. see Lew, Kim.

***Cheng, Wilson C. H. & Sajeev, A. S. M., eds.** Parallel & Real-Time Systems: Proceedings of the 6th Australasian Conference on Parallel & Real-Time Systems, Melbourne, Australia, 29 November-1 December 1999. LC 99-49592. 450p. 1999. 69.95 (*981-4021-59-8*) Spr-Verlag.

Cheng, Wu-Hsun & Kung, Harold H., eds. Methanol Production & Use. LC 94-14916. (Chemical Industries Ser.: Vol. 57). (Illus.). 344p. 1994. text 160.00 (*0-8247-9223-8*) Dekker.

Cheng, XiaoDong. S-Adenosylmethionine-Dependent Methyltransferases: Structures & Functions. 400p. 1999. 78.00 (*981-02-3870-3*) World Scientific Pub.

Cheng, XiaoGuang. Assessment of Human Vertebral Strength: Relationships to Bone Mass & Trabecular Microstructure in Vitro. (Acta Biomedica Lovaniensia Ser.: Vol. 147). (Illus.). 154p. 1997. pap. 49.50 (*90-6186-806-8*, Pub. by Leuven Univ) Coronet Bks.

Cheng, Xue-Min, jt. auth. see Corey, Elias James.

Cheng, Y. K. & Yuan, J. X., eds. Recent Advances in Soft Soil Engineering: Proceedings of the International Conference on Soft Soil Engineering. 952p. 1996. 70.00 (*7-03-003953-X*, Pub. by Sci Pr) Lubrecht & Cramer.

***Cheng, Y. W.** Constitutive Behavior Modeling of Steels Under Hot-Rolling Conditions. 111p. 1999. pap. 9.50 (*0-16-056993-1*) USGPO.

***Cheng, Yi-Kan.** Electrothermal Analysis of VLSI Systems. LC 00-30175. 2000. write for info. (*0-7923-7861-X*) Kluwer Academic.

Cheng, Yin-Cheong. School Effectiveness & School-Based Management: A Mechanism for Development. LC 96-18260. 256p. 1996. 79.95 (*0-7507-0457-8*, Falmer Pr); pap. 29.95 (*0-7507-0458-6*, Falmer Pr) Taylor & Francis.

Cheng, Ying-Wan. Postal Communication in China & Its Modernization, 1860-1896. LC 70-120316. (East Asian Monographs: No. 34). (Illus.). 162p. 1970. pap. 20.00 (*0-674-69320-5*) HUP.

Cheng Yu-K'Uei. Foreign Trade & Industrial Development of China: An Historical & Integrated Analysis Through 1948. LC 77-26190. (Illus.). 278p. 1978. reprint ed. lib. bdg. 65.00 (*0-313-20062-9*, CHFO, Greenwood Pr) Greenwood.

Cheng, Yuan-Jung. Heralds of the Postmodern: Madness & Fiction in Conrad, Woolf & Lessing. LC 96-24033. (Studies in Literary Criticism & Theory: Vol. 4). xiii, 120p. (C). 1999. text 38.95 (*0-8204-3376-4*) P Lang Pubng.

***Cheng, Yuhua & Hu, Chenming.** MOSFET Modeling & BSIM 3 User's Guide. LC 99-37157. 1999. write for info. (*0-7923-8575-6*) Kluwer Academic.

Cheng, Yung-Chi, et al, eds. The Development of Target-Oriented Anticancer Drugs. LC 83-15968. (Progress in Cancer Research & Therapy Ser.: No. 28). (Illus.). 262p. 1983. reprint ed. pap. 81.30 (*0-7837-9515-7*, 206026400005) Bks Demand.

Chengappa, M. M., jt. auth. see Carter, G. R.

***Chengappa, Raj.** Weapons of Peace: Secret Story of India's Quest to Be a Nuclear Power. 2000. 34.00 (*81-7223-330-2*, Pub. by CE25) S Asia.

Chengcai, L., jt. ed. see Yubin, L.

Chengelis, Angelique, et al. Amazing Blue: History of the 1997 Michigan Football Champion Season. gif. ed. (Illus.). 200p. 1998. 49.95 incl. VHS (*0-9654671-3-9*) C T C Sports.

— A Legacy of Champions: The Story of the Men Who Built University of Michigan Football. (Illus.). 224p. 1996. 29.95 (*0-9654671-0-4*) C T C Sports.

Chengelis, Christopher P., jt. auth. see Gad, Shayne C.

Chengelis, Christopher P., jt. ed. see Gad, A.

Chengfa, Chang. Geology & Tectonics of Qinghai-Xizang Plateau. (Illus.). 161p. 1996. 95.00 (*90-6764-225-8*, Pub. by VSP) Coronet Bks.

Chenghui, Liu, jt. auth. see Huayou, Zhu.

Chengjun, Zhang & Jianye, Liu. An Illustrated History of China's War of Resistance Against Japan. (Illus.). 142p. 1995. pap. 19.95 (*7-119-01739-X*, Pub. by Foreign Lang) China Bks.

Chengli, Li. Romance of the Three Kingdoms, Vol. 1. 1995. 9.95 (*981-3029-62-5*, Pub. by Asiapac) China Bks.

— Romance of the Three Kingdoms, Vol. 2. 1995. 9.95 (*981-3029-63-3*, Pub. by Asiapac) China Bks.

— Romance of the Three Kingdoms, Vol. 3. 1995. 9.95 (*981-3029-64-1*, Pub. by Asiapac) China Bks.

— Romance of the Three Kingdoms, Vol. 4. 1995. 9.95 (*981-3029-65-X*, Pub. by Asiapac) China Bks.

— Romance of the Three Kingdoms, Vol. 5. 1995. 9.95 (*981-3029-66-8*, Pub. by Asiapac) China Bks.

— Romance of the Three Kingdoms, Vol. 6. 1995. 9.95 (*981-3029-67-6*, Pub. by Asiapac) China Bks.

— Romance of the Three Kingdoms, Vol. 7. 1995. 9.95 (*981-3029-68-4*, Pub. by Asiapac) China Bks.

— Romance of the Three Kingdoms, Vol. 8. 1995. 9.95 (*981-3029-69-2*, Pub. by Asiapac) China Bks.

— Romance of the Three Kingdoms, Vol. 9. 1995. 9.95 (*981-3029-70-6*, Pub. by Asiapac) China Bks.

— Romance of the Three Kingdoms, Vol. 10. 1995. 9.95 (*981-3029-71-4*, Pub. by Asiapac) China Bks.

Chengnan, Sun, ed. Chinese Bodywork: A Complete Manual of Chinese Theapeutic Massage. Qiliang, Wang, tr. LC 93-85293. (Illus.). 320p. 1993. pap. text 50.00 (*1-881896-23-4*) Pacific View Pr.

Chengnan, Sun, ed. Chinese Bodywork: A Complete Manual of Chinese Therapeutic Massage. Qiliang, Wang, tr. LC 93-85293. (Illus.). 320p. 1993. text 50.00 (*1-881896-06-4*) Pacific View Pr.

Chengnian Huang, tr. see Wenfu Li.

Chengru, Zhu, jt. auth. see Xin, Yang.

Chengsen, Li & Jinzhong, Cui, eds. Atlas of Fossil Plant Anatomy in China. (Illus.). 144p. 1996. 87.50 (*90-6764-229-0*, Pub. by VSP) Coronet Bks.

Chengxiang, Li & Ling, Yang, eds. International Conference on Experimental Mechanics: Proceedings, Beijing, China, October 7-10, 1985. 1100p. 1986. text 201.00 (*9971-5-0094-9*) World Scientific Pub.

Chenhall, Robert G. & Vance, David. Museum Collections & Today's Computers. LC 88-3091. 177p. 1988. lib. bdg. 49.95 (*0-313-25339-0*, CCM/, Greenwood Pr) Greenwood.

Chenier. Jean Calas. Cook, ed. (Exeter French Texts Ser.: Vol. 64). (FRE.). 105p. Date not set. pap. text 19.95 (*0-85989-268-9*, Pub. by Univ Exeter Pr) Northwestern U Pr.

Chenier, Andre. Oeuvres Completes. Walter, Laurent, ed. (FRE.). 1120p. 1940. lib. bdg. 105.00 (*0-7859-3750-1*, 2070101320) Fr & Eur.

— Oeuvres Completes. deluxe ed. (Pleiade Ser.). (FRE.). 67.95 (*2-07-010132-0*) Schoenhof.

Chenier, Clifton. Clifton Chenier - King of Zydeco. Dahl, Gary, tr. 36p. 1997. 9.95 incl. audio compact disk (*0-7866-1780-2*) Mel Bay.

— Clifton Chenier-King of Zydeco. 36p. 1997. pap. 9.95 (*0-7866-2838-3*, 96616) Mel Bay.

Chenier, Norman J. Chenier Math Method: A Practical Math Dictionary & Workbook-Textbook. (Illus.). 268p. (YA). (gr. 9 up). 1989. text 24.95 (*0-9626061-0-3*) Chenier Educ Enter.

Chenier, Philip J. Survey of Industrial Chemistry. LC 86-7813. 432p. 1986. text 52.00 (*0-471-01077-4*) Krieger.

— Survey of Industrial Chemistry. 440p. (C). 1990. reprint ed. lib. bdg. 55.25 (*0-89464-504-8*) Krieger.

— Survey of Industrial Chemistry. 2nd rev. ed. 544p. 1992. 84.50 (*0-471-18798-4*) Wiley.

Chenier, Philip J. Survey of Industrial Chemistry. 2nd rev. ed. LC 92-19693. (Illus.). xv, 528p. 1992. 55.00 (*1-56081-082-3*, Wiley-VCH) Wiley.

Chenieux-Gendron, Jacqueline. Surrealism. Folkenflik, Vivian, tr. from FRE. (European Perspectives Ser.). 224p. 1990. text 57.50 (*0-231-06810-7*) Col U Pr.

— Surrealism. 1994. pap. 19.50 (*0-231-06811-5*) Col U Pr.

Chenille. Teaching Hippopotomi to Fly Songbook. LC 97-75032. (Illus.). 84p. (J). (ps-3). 1998. spiral bd. 17.98 (*0-9659936-9-8*, CTR03) Cantoo Recs.

Chenko, Rybal, et al. Deep Injection Disposal of Liquid Radioactive Waste in Russia. LC 98-25116. 206p. 1998. 79.95 (*1-57477-064-0*) Battelle.

Chenn, Lynn P. Burns: Therapy & Psychology with Subject Analysis & Research Bibliography. rev. ed. 149p. 1997. 47.50 (*0-7883-1626-5*); pap. 44.50 (*0-7883-1627-3*) ABBE Pubs Assn.

— Seat Belts: Index of Modern Information. LC 88-47990. 150p. 1990. 47.50 (*1-55914-056-9*); pap. 44.50 (*1-55914-057-7*) ABBE Pubs Assn.

Chennaiah, E., jt. ed. see Pullaiah, T.

Chennakesavan, Sarasvati. Concepts of Indian Philosophy. 258p. 1976. 12.95 (*0-318-37016-6*) Asia Bk Corp.

— Concepts of Mind in Indian Philosophy. 1980. 14.00 (*0-8364-0638-9*) S Asia.

Chennault, Claire L. Way of a Fighter. 1991. 35.00 (*0-685-41106-0*) Beachcomber Bks.

— Way of a Fighter: Memoirs. (History - United States Ser.). 375p. 1993. reprint ed. lib. bdg. 89.00 (*0-7812-4813-2*) Rprt Serv.

Chennault, Max, et al. Up Sun. Goodman, Charles & Little, Wallace H., eds. (American Heroes Ser.). 142p. 1990. pap. 9.95 (*0-916693-14-7*) Castle Bks.

Chennault, Steve, ed. Re'lize Whut Ahm Talkin' Bout? LC 97-145298. 196p. (C). 1996. pap. text 22.20 (*0-536-59852-5*) Pearson Custom.

Chennells, P., ed. Explaining Adoption to Your Adopted Child. (C). 1989. 39.00 (*0-903534-71-1*, Pub. by Brit Ag for Adopt & Fost) St Mut.

Chennells, P. & Hammond, C. Adopting a Child: A Guide for People Interested in Adoption. (C). 1989. 60.00 (*0-903534-91-6*, Pub. by Brit Ag for Adopt & Fost) St Mut.

Chennells, Prue & Hammond, Christ. Adopting a Child: A Guide for People Interested in Adoption. 104p. 1998. pap. 33.00 (*1-873868-54-5*, Pub. by BAAF) St Mut.

Chennells, Prue & Morrison, Marjorie. About Adoption. 96p. 1998. pap. 33.00 (*1-873868-55-3*, Pub. by BAAF) St Mut.

Chenneviere, Alain. Aru in the Solomon Islands. Davidson, Lisa, tr. LC 95-31073. (My Future Ser.). (J). 1996. lib. bdg. 22.60 (*0-8225-2827-4*, Lerner Publctns) Lerner Pub.

— Pak in Indonesia. Davidson, Lisa, tr. LC 95-31072. (My Future Ser.). 1996. lib. bdg. 22.60 (*0-8225-2826-6*, Lerner Publctns) Lerner Pub.

— Ramachandra in India. Davidson, Lisa, tr. LC 95-30981. (My Future Ser.). 1996. lib. bdg. 22.60 (*0-8225-2825-8*, Lerner Publctns) Lerner Pub.

Chenot, Jean-Loup, et al, eds. Numiform 92: Numerical Methods in Industrial Forming Processes. (Illus.). 928p. (C). 1992. text 188.00 (*90-5410-087-7*, Pub. by A A Balkema) Ashgate Pub Co.

Chenot, Jean-Loup & O'Nate, E., eds. Modelling of Metal Forming Processes. (C). 1988. text 201.00 (*90-247-3748-6*) Kluwer Academic.

Chenot, Jean-Loup, jt. auth. see Wagoner, Robert.

***Chenoune, Farid.** Beneath It All: A Century of French Lingerie. (Illus.). 200p. 2000. 65.00 (*0-8478-2204-4*, Pub. by Rizzoli Intl) St Martin.

Chenoune, Farid. Brioni. 1998. 18.95 (*0-7893-0248-9*, Pub. by Universe) St Martin.

— Jean-Paul Gaultier. 1998. 18.95 (*0-7893-0120-2*, Pub. by Universe) St Martin.

Chenoweth, Avery. Wingtips. LC 98-19492. 143p. 1999. 22.50 (*0-8018-6023-7*) Johns Hopkins.

***Chenoweth, Bruce.** Changing Your Mind about Smoking: A Guide for People Who Want to Become Non-Smokers Without Ever Having to Quit. 152p. 2000. 9.95 (*0-9679798-0-3*); ring bd. 6.95 (*0-9679798-1-1*) AB Co.

Chenoweth, C. C., jt. auth. see Raymond, E. T.

Chenoweth, Candace A. & Napier, A. Kam. Shuffleboard Pilots: The History of the Women's Air Raid Defense in Hawaii, 1941-1945. (Illus.). 88p. (Orig.). 1991 pap. 8.95 (*0-9631388-0-4*) AZ Mem Mus.

Chenoweth, Candace A., ed. see Matthews, Jack.

Chenoweth, Carla, jt. auth. see Synowiec, Bertie Ryan.

Chenoweth, D., jt. ed. see Henderson, L. W.

Chenoweth, David H. Worksite Health Promotion. LC 97-39341. (Illus.). 200p. (C). 1998. 34.00 (*0-88011-542-4*, BCHE0542) Human Kinetics.

Chenoweth, Harry H., jt. auth. see Jensen, Alfred E.

Chenoweth, James. Oddity Odyssey: A Journey Through New England's Colorful Past. LC 96-3713. (Illus.). 88p. 1995. pap. 9.95 (*0-8050-3671-7*) H Holt & Co.

Chenoweth, James M., ed. see American Society of Mechanical Engineers Staff.

Chenoweth, James M., ed. see National Heat Transfer Conference Staff.

Chenoweth, Jim & Kushner, Bill. From Tee to Green to Hollywood: Golfing with the Stars. (Illus.). 256p. 1998. pap. 16.95 (*1-885758-13-8*) Quality Sports.

Chenoweth, Mary E. The Civil Reserve Air Fleet & Operation Desert Shield/Desert Storm. LC 93-28795. 1994. pap. text 13.00 (*0-8330-1437-4*, MR-298-AF) Rand Corp.

Chenoweth, Mary E. & Abell, John B. Contractual Component Repair Policy: A Key to Improving Depot Responsiveness. LC 94-42951. 61p. (Orig.). 1995. pap. text 13.00 (*0-8330-1607-5*, MR-440-AF) Rand Corp.

Chenoweth, Maynard B., ed. Modern Inhalation Anesthetics. LC 76-156998. (Handbook of Experimental Pharmacology Ser.: Vol. 30). (Illus.). 1972. 175.00 (*0-387-05135-X*) Spr-Verlag.

— Synthetic Membranes. (MMI Press Symposium Ser.: Vol. 5). viii, 288p. 1986. text 267.00 (*3-7186-0327-5*) Gordon & Breach.

Chenowith, William L. The Geology & Production History of the Uranium Deposits in the White Canyon Mining District, San Juan County, Utah. (Miscellaneous Publication Ser.: Vol. 93-3). (Illus.). 26p. 1993. pap. 6.00 (*1-55791-322-6*, MP-93-3) Utah Geological Survey.

Chenoy, A. M., jt. auth. see Mustafa, S.

Chentalinski. Arrested Voices. 1996. 25.00 (*0-02-905425-7*) Free Pr.

Chentsov, A. G. Asymptotic Attainability. LC 96-36624. (Mathematics & Its Applications Ser.). 336p. (C). 1996. text 176.50 (*0-7923-4302-6*) Kluwer Academic.

— Finitely Additive Measures & Relaxations of Extremal Problems. (Monographs in Contemporary Mathematics). (Illus.). 241p. (C). 1996. 114.00 (*0-306-11038-5*, Kluwer Plenum) Kluwer Academic.

***Chenu, Greg.** Fishing Muddy Water. LC 00-131385. 88p. 2000. pap. 10.00 (*0-9679510-0-3*) Three Jacks Pr.

Chenu, M. D. Nature, Man, & Society in the 12th Century: Essays on New Theological Perspectives in the Latin West. Taylor, Jerome & Little, Lester K., eds. & trs. by. LC 68-15574. (Midway Reprint Ser.). xxii, 362p. 1983. pap. text 21.95 (*0-226-10256-4*) U Ch Pr.

— Nature, Man & Society in the 12th Century. 37th ed. (Medieval Academy Reprints for Teaching Ser.). 384p. 1997. reprint ed. pap. text 16.95 (*0-8020-7175-9*) U of Toronto Pr.

Cheo. Handbook of Molecular Lasers. (Optical Engineering Ser.: Vol. 14). (Illus.). 680p. 1987. text 260.00 (*0-8247-7651-8*) Dekker.

Cheo. Handbook of Solid-State Lasers. (Optical Engineering Ser.: Vol. 18). (Illus.). 640p. 1988. text 240.00 (*0-8247-7857-X*) Dekker.

Cheo Chao Teng & Hsueh-Hsia, Chen. Low-Cholesterol Chinese Cuisine. (CHI & ENG.). 124p. 1990. pap. 19.95 (*0-941676-22-6*) Wei-Chuan Pub.

Cheon, Samuel. The Exodus Story in the Wisdom of Solomon: A Study in Biblical Interpretation. (JSP Supplement Ser.: No. 23). 176p. 1997. 52.50 (*1-85075-670-8*, Pub. by Sheffield Acad) CUP Services.

Cheon, Tong. Recent Development of Nuclear Study Using Electron & Photon Beams. 250p. 1995. text 71.00 (*981-3049-04-9*) World Scientific Pub.

Cheong, Fah-chun, jt. auth. see New Riders Development Group Staff.

Cheong, Fiona. The Scent of the Gods. 256p. 1993 pap. 8.95 (*0-393-31012-4*) Norton.

Cheong, In T. The Valleys. (Illus.). 50p. (Orig.). 1989. write for info. (*0-318-65965-4*) Cheong Co.

Cheong, Sung-Hwa. The Politics of Anti-Japanese Sentiment in Korea: Japanese-South Korean Relations under American Occupation, 1945-1952, 24. LC 90-47325. (Contributions to the Study of World History Ser.: No. 24). 208p. 1991. 55.00 (*0-313-27410-X*, CJK/, Greenwood Pr) Greenwood.

Cheong, Un-Bok. Korean for the Business Traveler. 2nd ed. LC 93-34045. (Foreign Language Business Dictionaries Ser.). (KOR & ENG.). 600p. 1994. pap. 11.95 (*0-8120-1772-2*) Barron.

Cheong, Yeong-Han, jt. auth. see Siracusa, Joseph M.

Chepaitis, B. A. The Fear of God. 1999. mass mkt. 5.99 (*0-441-00622-1*) Ace Bks.

— The Fear Principle. 1998. mass mkt. 5.99 (*0-441-00497-0*) Ace Bks.

***Chepaitis, B. A.** Learning Fear. 2000. mass mkt. 5.99 (*0-441-00696-5*) Ace Bks.

***Chepaitis, Barbara.** Feeding Christine. LC 99-55210. 256p. 2000. 23.95 (*0-553-80165-1*, Spectra) Bantam.

Chepaitis, Barbara, jt. auth. see North, Stephen M.

Chepesiuk, Magdalena, jt. auth. see Chepesiuk, Ron.

Chepesiuk, Ron. Hard Target: The U. S. War Against International Drug Trafficking, 1982-1997. (Illus.). 363p. 1998. lib. bdg. 49.95 (*0-7864-0507-4*) McFarland & Co.

***Chepesiuk, Ron.** The Scotch-Irish: From the North of Ireland to the Making of America. LC 99-55348. 182p. 2000. boxed set 24.95 (*0-7864-0614-3*) McFarland & Co.

Chepesiuk, Ron. Sixties Radicals, Then & Now: Candid Conversations with Those Who Shaped the Era. LC 94-37664. (Illus.). 334p. 1995. lib. bdg. 42.50 (*0-89950-778-6*) McFarland & Co.

— The War on Drugs: An International Encyclopedia. LC 99-54389. 360p. 1999. lib. bdg. 75.00 (*0-87436-985-1*) ABC-CLIO.

***Chepesiuk, Ron & Chepesiuk, Magdalena.** Winthrop University, South Carolina. (College History Ser.). 128p. (YA). 2000. pap. 19.99 (*0-7385-0550-1*) Arcadia Publng.

***Chepesiuk, Ron & Price, Gina White.** Palmetto Women, South Carolina. (Images of America Ser.). (Illus.). 128p. 1999. pap. 18.99 (*0-7385-0035-6*) Arcadia Publng.

***Chepesiuk, Ron, et al.** Along the Catawba River, South Carolina. (Images of America Ser.). (Illus.). 128p. 1999. pap. 18.99 (*0-7385-0291-X*) Arcadia Publng.

Chepesiuk, Ron, et al. Raising Hell: Straight Talk with Investigative Journalists. LC 97-18934. 191p. 1997. pap. 28.50 (*0-7864-0356-X*) McFarland & Co.

Chepesiuk, Ron, jt. ed. see Lee, J. Edward.

Chepesiuk, Ronald & Shankman, Arnold M., compiled by. American Indian Archival Material: A Guide to Holdings in the Southeast. LC 82-15447. 325p. 1982. lib. bdg. 69.50 (*0-313-23731-X*, CAI/, Greenwood Pr) Greenwood.

Chepko-Sade, Diane B. & Halpin, Zuleyma T., eds. Mammalian Dispersal Patterns: The Effect of Social Structure on Population Genetics. LC 87-6026. (Illus.). 352p. (Orig.). 1987. pap. text 22.95 (*0-226-10268-8*) U Ch Pr.

— Mammalian Dispersal Patterns: The Effect of Social Structure on Population Genetics. LC 87-6026. (Illus.). 360p. (Orig.). 1996. lib. bdg. 66.00 (*0-226-10266-1*) U Ch Pr.

Chepko, Steveda F. & Arnold, Ree K. Guidelines for Physical Education Programs: Standards, Objectives, & Assessments for Grades K-12. LC 00-551332. 287p. 1999. pap. text 29.50 (*0-205-28326-8*) Allyn.

Cheplick, G. P., ed. Population Biology of Grasses. LC 97-26257. (Illus.). 412p. (C). 1998. text 90.00 (*0-521-57205-3*) Cambridge U Pr.

Cheppelle. Diversity in Action. LC 99-164449. 448p. (C). 1998. pap. text 22.20 (*0-536-01175-3*) Pearson Custom.

***Chepponis, James.** Jubilation Mass. (Illus.). 1999. 15.95 (*5-550-72300-X*); pap. 10.95 (*5-550-72302-6*); pap. 5.00 (*5-550-72306-9*) Nairi.

Cheqey, Dick. U. S. Defense: The Way Forward. 1997. pap. text 9.95 (*0-8447-4017-9*) Am Enterprise.

Cher & Coplon, Jeff. The First Time. (Illus.). 270p. 1998. 25.00 (*0-684-80900-1*) Simon & Schuster.

Cher, jt. auth. see Coplon, Jeff.

Cheramie, David, tr. see Conrad, Glenn R., ed.

Cheraskin, Emanuel. Health & Happiness: Simple, Safe & Sound Systems & Solutions. LC 88-62803. 250p. (Orig.). 1989. pap. 14.95 (*0-942333-05-5*) Bio-Comns Pr.

— The Vitamin C Controversy: Questions & Answers. LC 87-71003. (Illus.). 221p. (Orig.). 1988. pap. 12.95 (*0-942333-01-2*) Bio-Comns Pr.

Cheraskin, Emanuel, et al. Psychodietetics: Food As the Key to Emotional Health. LC 86-43196. 228p. 1987. pap. 7.95 (*0-8128-6266-X*, Scrbrough Hse) Madison Bks UPA.

Cherault, Inez B., jt. auth. see Kelley, Maria L.

Cherayil, Joseph D., ed. Transfer RNAs & Other Soluble RNAs. 184p. 1990. lib. bdg. 159.00 (*0-8493-5744-6*, QP623) CRC Pr.

Cherbit, G. Fractals: Non-Integral Dimensions & Applications. LC 90-12468. 266p. 1991. 220.00 (*0-471-92798-8*) Wiley.

Cherbo, Joni M. & Peters, Monnie. American Participation in Opera & Musical Theater: Research Division Report. LC 95-32894. (National Endowment for the Arts Research Division Report Ser.: No. 32). 104p. 1996. pap. 10.95 (*0-929765-38-9*) Seven Locks Pr.

Cherbo, Joni M., jt. ed. see Zolberg, Vera L.

***Cherbo, Joni Maya & Wyszomirski, Margaret Jane, eds.** The Public Life of the Arts in America. LC 99-42390. (Public Life of the Arts Ser.). 288p. 2000. text 55.00 (*0-8135-2767-8*) Rutgers U Pr.

C

— The Public Life of the Arts in America. LC 99-42390. (Public Life of the Arts Ser.). (Illus.). 288p. (C). 2000. pap. text 27.00 (*0-8135-2768-6*) Rutgers U Pr.

Cherches, Peter. Between a Dream & a Cup of Coffee. LC 87-42544. 48p. 1987. pap. 4.00 (*0-87376-054-9*) Red Dust.

Cherchi, Paolo. Andreas & the Ambiguity of Courtly Love. (Italian Studies). 200p. 1994. text 50.00 (*0-8020-0577-2*) U of Toronto Pr.

***Cherchi, Paolo.** The Griffith Project: Films Produced in January - June 1909, Vol. 2. 188p. 1999. 75.00 (*0-85170-749-1*) Ind U Pr.

Cherchneff, I. & Millar, T. J. Dust & Molecules in Evolved Stars. LC 98-9815. 1998. 173.00 (*0-7923-5009-X*) Kluwer Academic.

Cherdron, Harald, jt. auth. see Braun, Dietrich.

Cherdyntsev, Viktor. Abundance of Chemical Elements. LC 61-11892. 314p. reprint ed. pap. 97.40 (*0-8357-5025-6*, 202408700035) Bks Demand.

Chere, Lewis M. The Diplomacy of the Sino-French War (1883-85) Global Complications of an Undeclared War, Vol. III. LC 87-72449. (West & the Wider World Ser.: Vol. 3). 270p. 1987. 35.85 (*0-940121-06-9*) Cross Cultural Pubns.
This study of a war that was footnote to the history of European imperialism but a clear turning point in the growth of modern China, abounds with insights valuable to students of European expansion, Chinese nationalism & intercultural communications. For scholars of modern China's relations with the West, this study is essential. Well written, it clearly set out & defines many areas heretofore unexamined.
Publisher Paid Annotation.

C

Chereb, David. Night Dreams. LC 86-90369. (Illus.). 65p. (Orig.). 1986. pap. 8.95 (*0-937001-05-8*) Merz Prod.

Cherednichenko, V. G. Inverse Logarithmic Potential Problems. (Inverse & Ill-Posed Problems Ser.). 256p. 1996. 157.50 (*90-6764-202-9*, Pub. by VSP) Coronet Bks.

Cherednichok, V. T., jt. auth. see Kuchuk-Yatsenko, S. I.

Cherednik, Ivan. Basic Methods of Soliton Theory. LC 96-633. 264p. 1996. write for info. (*981-02-2643-8*) World Scientific Pub.

Cherednik, Ross & Eidson, Ken. Mandolin Classics. 68p. 1986. pap. 9.95 (*0-87166-943-9*, 94043) Mel Bay.

Cherednik, Ross, jt. auth. see Eidson, Ken.

Cherednychenko, V. Anatomy of Treason. 278p. 1984. 40.00 (*0-7855-0935-6*) St Mut.

Cherel, Albert O. Duits Zonder Moeite. 24.95 (*0-685-11150-4*); audio 125.00 (*0-685-01704-4*) Fr & Eur.

— Englisch Ohne Muhe Heure. 24.95 (*0-685-11163-6*); audio 125.00 (*0-685-42121-X*) Fr & Eur.

— Francuski Bez Muke. (Assimil Textbks.). 24.95 (*0-685-11203-9*); audio 125.00 (*0-685-01717-6*) Fr & Eur.

— Franzoesisch Ohne Muhe Heure. 29.95 (*0-685-11205-5*); audio 125.00 (*0-685-01719-2*) Fr & Eur.

— French with Case. 24.95 (*0-685-11209-8*) Fr & Eur.

— French with Case, Set 3. audio 125.00 (*0-685-01721-4*) Fr & Eur.

— German With Case. 24.95 (*0-685-11213-6*); audio 125.00 (*0-685-01722-2*) Fr & Eur.

— Le Grec Sans Peine. (FRE & GRE.). 24.95 (*0-685-11224-1*) Fr & Eur.

— Le Grec Sans Peine, Set. audio 125.00 (*0-685-01723-0*) Fr & Eur.

— Het Nieuive Engels Zonder Moeite. 24.95 (*0-685-11162-8*) Fr & Eur.

— Het Nieuive Engels Zonder Moeite, Set. audio 125.00 (*0-685-01707-9*) Fr & Eur.

— Het Nieuve Frans Zonder Moeite. 24.95 (*0-685-11204-7*) Fr & Eur.

— Het Nieuve Frans Zonder Moeite., Set. audio 125.00 (*0-685-01718-4*) Fr & Eur.

— Het Nieuve Spaans Zonder Moeite. 24.95 (*0-685-11570-4*) Fr & Eur.

— Het Nieuve Spaans Zonder Moeite., Set. audio 125.00 (*0-685-01764-8*) Fr & Eur.

— Italiaans Zonder Moeite. 24.95 (*0-685-11262-4*) Fr & Eur.

— Italiaans Zonder Moeite, Set. audio 125.00 (*0-685-01735-4*) Fr & Eur.

— Italian Without Toil. 24.95 (*0-685-11263-2*) Fr & Eur.

— Italian Without Toil, Set. audio 125.00 (*0-685-01736-2*) Fr & Eur.

— Latin Sans Peine. 24.95 (*0-685-11288-8*); audio 125.00 (*0-685-01739-7*) Fr & Eur.

— Neerlandais Sans Peine. 24.95 (*0-685-11415-5*); audio 125.00 (*0-685-01741-9*) Fr & Eur.

— Nemacki Bez Muke. 24.95 (*0-685-11417-1*); audio 125.00 (*0-685-01742-7*) Fr & Eur.

— Niederlandisch Ohne Muhe. 24.95 (*0-685-11422-8*); audio 125.00 (*0-685-01743-5*) Fr & Eur.

— Le Nouveau Allemand sans Pier. 24.95 (*0-685-10990-9*); audio. write for info. (*0-318-51925-9*) Fr & Eur.

— Le Nouveau Anglais Sans Peine. 24.95 (*0-685-11001-X*) Fr & Eur.

— Le Nouveau Anglais Sans Peine, Set. audio 125.00 (*0-685-11003-6*) Fr & Eur.

— Le Nouveau Italien Sans Peine. 24.95 (*0-685-11264-0*); audio 125.00 (*0-685-01737-0*) Fr & Eur.

— Nouvell Espagnol Sans Peine. 24.95 (*0-685-11166-0*); audio 125.00 (*0-685-01711-7*) Fr & Eur.

— Novo Frances Sem Custo. 24.95 (*0-685-11200-4*); audio 125.00 (*0-685-01714-1*) Fr & Eur.

— Novo Ingles Sem Custo. 24.95 (*0-685-11249-7*); audio 125.00 (*0-685-01732-X*) Fr & Eur.

— Il Nuevo Ingles Sin Esfuerzo. 24.95 (*0-685-11250-0*); audio 125.00 (*0-685-01733-8*) Fr & Eur.

— Il Nuovo Francese senza Sforzo. 24.95 (*0-685-11202-0*); audio 125.00 (*0-685-01716-8*) Fr & Eur.

— Il Nuovo Inglese senza Sforzo. 24.95 (*0-685-11251-9*); audio 125.00 (*0-685-01734-6*) Fr & Eur.

— Il Nuovo Tedesco senza Sforzo. 24.95 (*0-685-11582-8*); audio 125.00 (*0-685-01770-2*) Fr & Eur.

— Portugais Sans Peine. 24.95 (*0-685-11505-4*); audio 125.00 (*0-685-01760-5*) Fr & Eur.

— Portugiesisch Ohne Muhe. 24.95 (*0-685-11507-0*); audio 125.00 (*0-685-01761-3*) Fr & Eur.

— Russe sans Peine. 24.95 (*0-685-11550-X*); audio 125.00 (*0-685-01763-X*) Fr & Eur.

— Spagnolo Senza Sforzo. 24.95 (*0-685-11571-2*); audio 125.00 (*0-685-01765-6*) Fr & Eur.

— Spanish Ohne Muhe Heure. 24.95 (*0-685-11573-9*); audio 125.00 (*0-685-01766-4*) Fr & Eur.

— Spanish WithCase. 24.95 (*0-685-11574-7*); audio 125.00 (*0-685-01767-2*) Fr & Eur.

Cherel, Jean L. El Nuevo Frances Sin Esfuerzo. (FRE & SPA.). 1983. 28.95 (*0-685-11201-2*) Fr & Eur.

— El Nuevo Frances Sin Esfuerzo, 4 cass., Set. (FRE & SPA.). 1983. audio 125.00 (*0-7859-5546-1*, 2700501039) Fr & Eur.

Cherel, Jean L., jt. auth. see Bulger, Anthony.

Cheremensky, A. & Fomin, V. Operator Approach to Linear Control Systems. (Mathematics & Its Applications Ser.: Vol. 345). 416p. (C). 1996. text 217.50 (*0-7923-3765-4*) Kluwer Academic.

Cheremeteff, Maria. Pak: Readings in Art History. 346p. (C). 1998. pap. text 60.95 (*0-7872-4437-6*, 41443701) Kendall-Hunt.

Cheremetieff, Alexander, tr. see Thaisia.

Cheremisinoff, Paul N. & Morresi, Angelo C. Energy from Solid Wastes. LC 76-1799. (Pollution Engineering & Technology Ser.: Vol. 1). (Illus.). 515p. reprint ed. pap. 159.70 (*0-608-08919-2*, 206955400005) Bks Demand.

Cheremisinoff, Nicholas P. Applied Fluid Flow Measurement: Fundamentals & Technology. (Biomedical Engineering Instrumentation Ser.: Vol. 1). (Illus.). 216p. 1979. text 135.00 (*0-8247-6871-X*) Dekker.

— Biotechnology for Waste & Wastewater Treatment. LC 96-45255. (Illus.). 233p. 1997. 109.00 (*0-8155-1409-3*) Noyes.

***Cheremisinoff, Nicholas P.** Chemical Engineer's Condensed Encyclopedia of Process Equipment. LC 99-29947. 1999. 125.00 (*0-88415-144-1*) Gulf Pub.

— Concise Polymer Encyclopedia. 169th ed. 800p. 2000. 125.00 (*0-7506-7210-2*) Buttrwrth-Heinemann.

Cheremisinoff, Nicholas P. Electrotechnology: Industrial & Environmental Applications. LC 96-28820. 178p. 1996. 98.00 (*0-8155-1402-6*) Noyes.

— Encyclopedia of Fluid Mechanics. LC 85-9742. (Flow Phenomena & Measurement Ser.: Vol. 2). (Illus.). 1519p. pap. 200.00 (*0-608-05059-8*, 206528400002) Bks Demand.

— Encyclopedia of Fluid Mechanics. LC 85-9742. (Flow Phenomena & Measurement Ser.: Vol. 3). (Illus.). 1550p. pap. 200.00 (*0-608-05060-1*, 206528400003) Bks Demand.

— Encyclopedia of Fluid Mechanics. LC 85-9742. (Solids & Gas-Solids Flows Ser.: Vol. 7). (Illus.). 1199p. pap. 200.00 (*0-608-05057-1*, 206528400007) Bks Demand.

— Encyclopedia of Fluid Mechanics. LC 85-9742. (Solids & Gas-Solids Flows Ser.: Vol. 4). 1431p. 1986. pap. 200.00 (*0-608-05054-7*, 206528400004) Bks Demand.

— Encyclopedia of Fluid Mechanics. LC 85-9742. (Flow Phenomena & Measurement Ser.: Vol. 1). (Illus.). 1535p. 1986. pap. 200.00 (*0-608-05058-X*, 206528400001) Bks Demand.

— Encyclopedia of Fluid Mechanics. LC 85-9742. (Solids & Gas-Solids Flows Ser.: Vol. 5). (Illus.). 1500p. 1986. pap. 200.00 (*0-608-05055-5*, 206528400005) Bks Demand.

— Encyclopedia of Fluid Mechanics. LC 85-9742. (Solids & Gas-Solids Flows Ser.: Vol. 6). (Illus.). 1517p. 1986. pap. 200.00 (*0-608-05056-3*, 206528400006) Bks Demand.

— Encyclopedia of Fluid Mechanics. LC 85-9742. (Polymer Flow Engineering Ser.: Vol. 9). (Illus.). 767p. 1990. pap. 200.00 (*0-608-05061-X*, 206528400009) Bks Demand.

— Engineer's Guide to Fluid Flow. (Illus.). 300p. 1989. 39.95 (*0-925760-30-7*) SciTech Pubs.

— Flow Measurement for Engineers & Scientists. (Chemical Industries Ser.: Vol. 32). (Illus.). 408p. 1987. text 210.00 (*0-8247-7831-6*) Dekker.

— Groundwater Remediation & Treatment Technologies. LC 98-22341. (Illus.). xi, 395p. 1998. 129.00 (*0-8155-1411-5*) Noyes.

***Cheremisinoff, Nicholas P.** Handbook of Chemical Processing Equipment. 512p. 2000. 99.00 (*0-7506-7126-2*, Newnes) Buttrwrth-Heinemann.

Cheremisinoff, Nicholas P. Handbook of Emergency Response & Toxic Chemical Releases: A Guide to Compliance. LC 94-31268. (Illus.). 315p. 1995. 98.00 (*0-8155-1365-8*) Noyes.

***Cheremisinoff, Nicholas P.** Handbook of Hazardous Chemical Properties. 433p. 1999. 95.00 (*0-7506-7209-9*, Newnes) Buttrwrth-Heinemann.

Cheremisinoff, Nicholas P. Handbook of Heat & Mass Transfer Vol. 3: Catalysis, Kinetics & Reactor Engineering. LC 84-25338. 1484p. 1990. reprint ed. pap. 200.00 (*0-608-01339-0*, 206208300003) Bks Demand.

— Handbook of Industrial Toxicology & Hazardous Materials. LC 98-55662. (Illus.). 928p. 1999. text 225.00 (*0-8247-1935-2*) Dekker.

— Handbook of Polymer Science & Technology, Vol. 1: Synthesis & Properties. (Illus.). 798p. 1989. text 275.00 (*0-8247-8173-2*) Dekker.

— Handbook of Polymer Science & Technology, Vol. 2: Performance Properties of Plastics & Elastomers. (Illus.). 758p. 1989. text 275.00 (*0-8247-8174-0*) Dekker.

— Handbook of Polymer Science & Technology, Vol. 3: Applications & Processing Operations. (Illus.). 680p. 1989. text 275.00 (*0-8247-8004-3*) Dekker.

— Handbook of Polymer Science & Technology, Vol. 4: Composites & Specialty Applications. (Illus.). 760p. 1989. text 275.00 (*0-8247-8021-3*) Dekker.

— Hazardous Chemicals in the Polymer Industry, No. 14. LC 94-22884. (Environmental Science & Pollution Control Ser.: Vol. 14). (Illus.). 648p. 1994. text 210.00 (*0-8247-9273-4*) Dekker.

— Health & Toxicology. LC 96-40506. (Advances in Environmental Control Technology Ser.: Vol. 12). 650p. 1997. 125.00 (*0-88415-386-X*, 5386) Gulf Pub.

— Heat Transfer Pocket Handbook. fac. ed. LC 84-654. (Illus.). 252p. 1984. pap. 78.20 (*0-7837-8351-5*, 204914100010) Bks Demand.

— Intro to Polymer, 001. 288p. 1992. boxed set 139.00 (*0-8493-4402-6*, TA455) CRC Pr.

— Materials Selection Deskbook. LC 96-10911. 191p. 1996. 79.00 (*0-8155-1400-X*) Noyes.

— Pocket Handbook for Solid-Liquid Separations. LC 84-8970. (Illus.). 160p. 1984. reprint ed. pap. 49.60 (*0-608-07939-1*, 206791200012) Bks Demand.

— Pollution Prevention Software Systems Handbook. LC 96-36451. 398p. 1996. 98.00 (*0-8155-1405-0*) Noyes.

— Polymer Characterization: Laboratory Techniques & Analysis. LC 96-10962. 251p. 1996. 98.00 (*0-8155-1403-4*) Noyes.

— Polymer Mixing & Extrusion Technology. (Plastics Engineering Ser.). (Illus.). 456p. 1987. text 185.00 (*0-8247-7793-X*) Dekker.

— Practical Statistics for Engineers & Scientists. LC 86-72352. 224p. 1986. 29.95 (*0-87762-505-0*) Technomic.

— Pressure Safety Design Practices for Refinery & Chemical Operations. LC 97-46603. (Illus.). 384p. 1998. 145.00 (*0-8155-1414-X*) Noyes.

— Process Level Instrumentation & Control. LC 80-21922. (Engineering Measurements & Instrumentation Ser.: No. 2). 264p. reprint ed. pap. 81.90 (*0-7837-0920-X*, 204122500019) Bks Demand.

— Product Design & Testing of Polymeric Materials. (Illus.). 576p. 1990. text 199.00 (*0-8247-8261-5*) Dekker.

— Transportation of Hazardous Materials: A Guide to Compliance. LC 94-3866. (Illus.). 262p. 1994. 89.00 (*0-8155-1350-X*) Noyes.

Cheremisinoff, Nicholas P., ed. Advanced Polymer Processing Operations. LC 97-51237. (Illus.). 287p. 1998. 109.00 (*0-8155-1426-3*) Noyes.

— Elastomer Technology Handbook. 1120p. 1993. boxed set 246.95 (*0-8493-4401-8*, TA455) CRC Pr.

— Encyclopedia of Fluid Mechanics Supplement 1: Applied Mathematics in Fluid Dynamics, Including Comprehensive Index. (Illus.). 750p. 1993. 139.00 (*0-87201-547-5*, 1547) Gulf Pub.

— Encyclopedia of Fluid Mechanics Supplement 2: Advances in Multiphase Flow. 650p. 1993. 139.00 (*0-88415-098-4*) Gulf Pub.

— Encyclopedia of Fluid Mechanics Vol. 10: Surface & Groundwater Flow Phenomena. LC 85-9742. (Illus.). 736p. 1990. reprint ed. pap. 180.00 (*0-608-04542-X*, 2065284) Bks Demand.

— Handbook of Applied Polymer Processing Technology. (Plastics Engineering Ser.: Vol. 31). (Illus.). 808p. 1996. text 225.00 (*0-8247-9679-9*) Dekker.

Cheremisinoff, Nicholas P., ed. Handbook of Ceramics & Composites: Mechanical Properties & Specialty Applications, Vol. 2. (Illus.). 528p. 1991. text 255.00 (*0-8247-8006-X*) Dekker.

— Handbook of Ceramics & Composites, Vol. 1: Synthesis & Properties. (Illus.). 664p. 1990. text 255.00 (*0-8247-8005-1*) Dekker.

Cheremisinoff, Nicholas P., ed. Handbook of Engineering Polymeric Materials. LC 97-20896. (Illus.). 888p. 1997. text 250.00 (*0-8247-9799-X*) Dekker.

— Handbook of Heat & Mass Transfer, Vol. 1 - 1986. LC 84-25338. (Illus.). 1470p. 1986. reprint ed. pap. 200.00 (*0-608-04455-5*, 206208300001) Bks Demand.

— Handbook of Heat & Mass Transfer, Vol. 2 - 1986. LC 84-25338. (Illus.). 1534p. 1986. reprint ed. pap. 200.00 (*0-608-04456-3*, 206208300002) Bks Demand.

— Handbook of Heat & Mass Transfer Vol. 4: Advances in Reactor Design & Combustion Science. LC 84-25338. 1224p. 1990. reprint ed. pap. 200.00 (*0-608-01340-4*, 206208300004) Bks Demand.

— Mixed-Flow Hydrodynamics, Vol. 1. (Advances in Engineering Fluid Mechanics Ser.: Vol. 11). (Illus.). 914p. 1996. 155.00 (*0-88415-256-1*, 5256) Gulf Pub.

— Noise Control in Industry: A Practical Guide. LC 96-12580. 190p. 1996. 89.00 (*0-8155-1399-2*) Noyes.

— Waste Minimization & Recycling. LC 92-12009. (Encyclopedia of Environmental Control Technology Ser.: Vol. 5). 1992. 155.00 (*0-87201-258-1*) Gulf Pub.

Cheremisinoff, Nicholas P. & Abid, M., eds. Multiphase Reactor & Polymerization System Hydrodynamics. LC 95-51777. (Advances in Engineering Fluid Mechanics Ser.: Vol. 12). (Illus.). 656p. 1996. 145.00 (*0-88415-497-1*, 5497) Gulf Pub.

Cheremisinoff, Nicholas P. & Azbel, David S. Liquid Filtration for Process & Pollution Control. (Illus.). 530p. (C). 1989. pap. text 39.95 (*0-925760-00-5*) SciTech Pubs.

Cheremisinoff, Nicholas P. & Cheremisinoff, Paul N. Cooling Towers: Selection, Design & Practice. (Illus.). 272p. 1989. reprint ed. pap. text 39.95 (*0-925760-02-1*) SciTech Pubs.

— Engineering Mathematics & Statistics Pocket Handbook. LC 89-50812. 210p. 1989. pap. 14.95 (*0-87762-621-9*) Technomic.

— Fiberglass Reinforced Plastics: Manufacturing Techniques & Applications. LC 95-23436. (Illus.). 258p. 1995. 98.00 (*0-8155-1389-5*) Noyes.

— Hazardous Materials & Waste Management: A Guide for the Professional Hazards Manager. LC 94-38698. (Illus.). 265p. 1995. 98.00 (*0-8155-1372-0*) Noyes.

— Hydrodynamics of Gas-Solids Fluidization. LC 83-18555. 880p. 1984. reprint ed. pap. 200.00 (*0-608-01579-2*, 206199900001) Bks Demand.

— Pumps-Compressors-Fans Pocket Handbook. LC 88-51422. 160p. 1988. 19.95 (*0-87762-623-5*) Technomic.

Cheremisinoff, Nicholas P. & Cheremisinoff, Paul N., eds. Handbook of Advanced Materials Testing. LC 94-33625. (Engineering Materials Ser.: Vol. 9). (Illus.). 1040p. 1994. text 225.00 (*0-8247-9196-7*) Dekker.

Cheremisinoff, Nicholas P. & Graffia, Madelyn. Handbook of Pollution & Hazardous Materials Compliance: A Sourcebook for Environmental Managers. LC 95-49401. (Environmental Science & Pollution Control Ser.: No. 17). (Illus.). 520p. 1996. text 199.00 (*0-8247-9704-3*) Dekker.

— Safety Management Practices for Hazardous Materials. LC 95-37548. (Illus.). 368p. 1995. text 155.00 (*0-8247-9687-X*) Dekker.

Cheremisinoff, Nicholas P. & Graffia, Madelyn L. Environmental & Health & Safety Management: A Guide to Compliance. LC 95-24875. (Illus.). 502p. 1995. 129.00 (*0-8155-1390-9*) Noyes.

Cheremisinoff, Nicholas P. & King, John A., eds. Toxic Properties of Pesticides. (Environmental Science & Pollution Ser.: Vol. 12). (Illus.). 344p. 1994. text 170.00 (*0-8247-9253-X*) Dekker.

Cheremisinoff, Nicholas P. & Neglia, J. P. Handbook of Chemical Hygiene Practices. Date not set. write for info. (*0-8247-9938-0*) Dekker.

Cheremisinoff, Nicholas P., et al. Biomass: Applications, Technology & Production, Vol. 5. (Energy, Power, & Enviroment Ser.: Vol. 1). (Illus.). 232p. 1980. text 150.00 (*0-8247-6933-3*) Dekker.

— Dangerous Properties of Industrial & Consumer Chemicals. LC 94-14912. (Illus.). 816p. 1994. text 220.00 (*0-8247-9183-5*) Dekker.

Cheremisinoff, Nicholas P., jt. auth. see Cheremisinoff, Paul N.

Cheremisinoff, Nicholas P., jt. auth. see Davletshina, Tatyana A.

Cheremisinoff, Nicholas P., ed. see National Association of Safety & Health Profession.

Cheremisinoff, Paul & Young, Richard, eds. Air Pollution Control & Design Handbook, Pt. 1. (Pollution Engineering & Technology Ser.: Vol. 2). (Illus.). 624p. 1977. text 225.00 (*0-8247-6444-7*) Dekker.

Cheremisinoff, Paul N. Calculating & Reporting Toxic Chemical: Releases for Pollution Control. 540p. 1989. 59.95 (*0-925760-07-2*) SciTech Pubs.

— Ecological Issues & Environmental Impact Assessment. (Advances in Environmental Control Technology Ser.). 768p. 1997. 145.00 (*0-88415-237-5*, 5237) Gulf Pub.

— Emerging Electrotechnology: Industrial - Environmental - Applications & Potentials. (Illus.). 290p. 1990. text 34.95 (*0-925760-12-9*) SciTech Pubs.

— Handbook of Polymer Processing Technology. 1994. write for info. (*0-8493-8968-2*) CRC Pr.

— Handbook of Water & Wastewater Treatment Technology. LC 94-33927. (Illus.). 840p. 1994. text 215.00 (*0-8247-9277-7*) Dekker.

— Hazardous Materials Manager's Desk Book on Regulation. (Illus.). 236p. 1986. 19.95 (*0-317-46852-9*, Pollution Eng) Cahners Busn Des Plaines.

— Solids/Liquids Separation. LC 95-60053. (Process Engineering Handbook Ser.). (Illus.). 400p. 1995. pap. 29.95 (*1-56676-246-4*, 762464) Technomic.

— Underground Storage Tanks Handbook. (Illus.). 400p. 1991. text 59.95 (*0-925760-56-0*) SciTech Pubs.

— Waste Minimization & Cost Reduction for the Process Industries. (Illus.). 331p. 1995. 89.00 (*0-8155-1388-7*) Noyes.

Cheremisinoff, Paul N., ed. Air Pollution Control & Design for Industry. LC 93-18115. (Illus.). 608p. 1993. text 199.00 (*0-8247-9057-X*) Dekker.

— Containment of Hazardous Wastes. (Encyclopedia of Environmental Control Technology Ser.: Vol. 4). 776p. 1990. 155.00 (*0-87201-251-4*, 1251) Gulf Pub.

— Encyclopedia of Environmental Control Technology: Air Polution Technology. (Encyclopedia of Environmental Control Technology Ser.: Vol. 2). (Illus.). 1066p. 1989. 155.00 (*0-87201-245-X*) Gulf Pub.

— Encyclopedia of Fluid Mechanics Supplement 3: Advances in Flow Dynamics. 506p. 1994. 139.00 (*0-88415-125-5*) Gulf Pub.

— Geotechnical Applications, Leak Detection, Treatment Options. (Encyclopedia of Environmental Control Technology Ser.: Vol. 9). (Illus.). 1138p. 1995. 155.00 (*0-87201-327-8*, 1327) Gulf Pub.

— Hazardous Waste Containment & Treatment. LC 90-2820. (Encyclopedia of Environmental Control Technology Ser.: Vol. 4). (Illus.). 776p. 1990. reprint ed. pap. 200.00 (*0-608-07947-2*, 206792000012) Bks Demand.

— Storage Tanks, Vol. 1. LC 95-51188. (Adavnces in Environmental Control Technology Ser.: Vol. 10). (Illus.). 304p. 1996. 89.00 (*0-87201-332-4*, No. 1332) Gulf Pub.

An Asterisk (*) at the beginning of an entry indicates that the title is appearing for the first time.

— Thermal Treatment of Hazardous Wastes. (Encyclopedia of Environmental Control Technology Ser.: Vol. 1). (Illus.). 828p. 1989. 155.00 (*0-87201-241-7*) Gulf Pub.

— Wastewater Treatment Technology. (Encyclopedia of Environmental Control Technology Ser.: Vol. 3). 684p. 1989. 155.00 (*0-87201-247-6*) Gulf Pub.

— Work Area Hazards. (Encyclopedia of Environmental Control Technology Ser.: Vol. 8). (Illus.). 804p. 1995. 155.00 (*0-87201-304-9*, 1304) Gulf Pub.

Cheremisinoff, Paul N., et al, eds. Civil Engineering Practice, 5 vols., Set. Incl. Vol. 2. Hydraulics-Mechanics. LC 87-50629. 850p. 1988. 49.95 (*0-87762-546-8*); Vol. 3. Geotechnical-Ocean Engineering. LC 87-50629. 850p. 1988. 49.95 (*0-87762-554-9*); Vol. 4. Surveying-Construction-Transportation-Energy-Economics & Government-Computers. LC 87-50629. 700p. 1987. 49.95 (*0-87762-537-9*); Vol. 5. Water Resources-Environmental. LC 87-50629. 832p. 1988. 49.95 (*0-87762-540-9*); LC 87-50629. write for info. (*0-87762-966-8*) Technomic.

Cheremisinoff, Paul N. & Cheremisinoff, Nicholas P. Process Engineering Data Book. LC 94-61845. (Process Engineering Handbook Ser.). 360p. 1995. pap. text 29.95 (*1-56676-224-3*) Technomic.

— Professional Environmental Auditors' Guidebook. LC 93-31337. (Illus.). 257p. 1993. 98.00 (*0-8155-1335-6*) Noyes.

Cheremisinoff, Paul N. & Ferrante, Louise M. Waste Reduction for Pollution Prevention. LC 92-6801. 1992. text. write for info. (*0-7506-0601-0*) Buttrwrth-Heinemann.

Cheremisinoff, Paul N. & Ferrante, Louise M., eds. Biotechnology - Current Progress, Vol. 1. 366p. 1991. 74.95 (*0-87762-776-2*) Technomic.

Cheremisinoff, Paul N. & Morresi, Angelo C. Benzene, Basic & Hazardous Properties. LC 79-17512. (Pollution Engineering & Technology Ser.: Vol. 9). (Illus.). 260p. reprint ed. pap. 80.60 (*0-608-08920-6*, 206955500005) Bks Demand.

Cheremisinoff, Paul N. & Trattner, Richard B. Fundamentals of Disinfection for Pollution Control. (Illus.). 172p. 1990. text 39.95 (*0-925760-08-0*) SciTech Pubs.

Cheremisinoff, Paul N. & Young, Richard A., eds. Air Pollution Control & Design Handbook, Pt. 2. LC 76-588. (Pollution Engineering & Technology Ser.: No. 2). (Illus.). 423p. reprint ed. pap. 131.20 (*0-7837-3418-2*, 205246400002) Bks Demand.

Cheremisinoff, Paul N., et al. Introduction to Biotechnology for Waste-Wastewater Treatment. (Illus.). 275p. 1990. 34.95 (*0-925760-13-7*) SciTech Pubs.

Cheremisinoff, Paul N., jt. auth. see Cheremisinoff, Nicholas P.

Cheremisinoff, Paul N., jt. auth. see Ruiz, M. A.

Cheremisinoff, Paul N., jt. auth. see Teresinski, Michael F.

Cheremisinoff, Paul N., jt. ed. see Cheremisinoff, Nicholas P.

Cheremisinoff, Paul N., jt. ed. see Dickinson, William C.

Cheremisnoff, Nicholas P. Liquid Filtration. 2nd ed. 512p. 1998. text 75.00 (*0-7506-7047-9*) Buttrwrth-Heinemann.

Cheren, Mark E., ed. Learning Management: Emerging Directions for Learning to Learn in the Workplace. 57p. 1987. 6.00 (*0-318-35270-2*, IN 320) Ctr Educ Trng Employ.

***Cheren, Mel.** My Life & the Paradise Garage: Keep on Dancin' (Illus.). 495p. 2000. 24.95 (*0-9678994-0-0*) TWENTY-FOUR HRS.

Cheren, Stanley, ed. Psychosomatic Medicine: Theory, Physiology, & Practice. (Stress & Health Ser.: No. 1-2). 1000p. 1989. 62.50 (*0-8236-5725-6*, BN#05725); 75.00 (*0-8236-5726-4*, BN#05726) Intl Univs Pr.

Cherenault, Tracy & Weaver, Jeffrey C. Eighteenth & Twentieth Battalions of Heavy Artillery. (Virginia Regimental Histories Ser.). (Illus.). 128p. 1995. 19.95 (*1-56190-085-0*) H E Howard.

Cherenkov, P. A., ed. Undulator Radiation & Free-Electron Lasers. 190p. 1995. pap. 93.00 (*1-898326-13-4*, Pub. by CISP) Balogh.

Cherep-Spriridovich, Count. The Secret World Government: Or, the Hidden Hand of the Unrevealed in History. 1977. lib. bdg. 250.00 (*0-8490-2586-9*) Gordon Pr.

Cherepakhov, M. S. Rystari Dukha. 78p. 1983. 25.00 (*0-7855-2927-6*) St Mut.

Cherepanov, A. I. Cerambycidae of Northern Asia, Vol. 3: Lamiinae, Pt. 3. LC 89-9836. (Illus.). xiv, 395p. 1991. 149.50 (*90-04-09308-7*) Brill Academic Pubs.

— Cerambycidae of Northern Asia, Vol. 3 Pt. 2: Lamiinae. LC 89-9836. (Illus.). xi, 308p. 1991. 134.00 (*90-04-09307-9*) Brill Academic Pubs.

— Cerambycidae of Northern Asia, Vol. 3, Pt. 1 Vol. 3, Pt. 1: Lamiinae. LC 89-9836. (Illus.). xiii, 300p. 1991. 89.50 (*90-04-09306-0*) Brill Academic Pubs.

Cherepanov, G. P., jt. auth. see Annin, B. D.

Cherepanov, Genady P., ed. Fracture: A Topical Encyclopedia of Current Knowledge. LC 95-48219. (Illus.). 892p. 1998. 179.50 (*0-89464-924-8*) Krieger.

Cherepanov, Gennadi I. Methods of Fracture Mechanics: Solid Matter Physics. LC 96-52467. (Solid Mechanics & Its Applications Ser.). 1997. text 164.00 (*0-7923-4408-1*) Kluwer Academic.

Cherepashchuk, A. M. & Khruzina, T. S. Highly Evolved Close Binary Stars: Catalogue. 368p. 1996. text 60.00 (*90-5699-012-8*) Gordon & Breach.

— Highly Evolved Close Binary Stars: Finding Chart. 256p. 1996. text 48.00 (*90-5699-014-4*) Gordon & Breach.

Cherepashchuk, A. M., et al. Highly Evolved Close Binary Stars, 2 pts., Vol. 3. Incl. Highly Evolved Close Binary Stars: Catalogue. Shugarov, S. Yu. 368p. 1996. pap. text 21.00 (*90-5699-013-6*); Vol. 2. Finding Charts. Shugarov, S. Yu. 256p. 1996. pap. text 18.00 (*90-5699-015-2*); 1996. Set pap. text 58.00 (*90-5699-011-X*) Gordon & Breach.

Cherepin, V. T. Secondary Ion Mass Spectroscopy of Solid Surfaces. viii, 138p. 1987. lib. bdg. 102.00 (*90-6764-078-6*, Pub. by VSP) Coronet Bks.

Cheresh, David A. & Mecham, Robert P., eds. Integrins: Molecular & Biological Responses to the Extracellular Matrix. LC 94-10457. (Biology of Extracellular Matrix Ser.). (Illus.). 278p. 1994. text 100.00 (*0-12-171160-9*) Acad Pr.

Cheret, Jules & Broido, Lucy. The Posters of Jules Cheret. (Illus.). 128p. (Orig.). 1980. pap. 10.95 (*0-486-24010-X*) Dover.

— The Posters of Jules Cheret: Forty Six Full-Color Plates & an Illustrated Catalogue Raisonne. 2nd enl. rev. ed. (Illus.). 144p. (Orig.). 1992. pap. 17.95 (*0-486-26966-3*) Dover.

Cheret, Roger. Detonation of Condensed Explosives. LC 92-16118. 1992. write for info. (*0-387-53616-7*) Spr-Verlag.

— Detonation of Condensed Explosives. Graham, R. A., ed. (High Pressure Shock Compression of Condensed Matter Ser.). (Illus.). 496p. 1992. 198.95 (*0-387-97898-4*) Spr-Verlag.

***Cherewatenko, Vern.** The Diabetes Cure: A Natural Plan That Can Slow, Stop, Even Cure Type 2 Diabetes. 288p. 2000. pap. 13.00 (*0-06-109725-X*, Cliff Street) HarperTrade.

Cherewatenko, Vern & Perry, Paul. The Diabetes Cure: A Medical Approach That Can Slow, Stop, Even Cure Type 2 Diabetes. LC 98-43193. 288p. 1999. 25.00 (*0-06-019210-0*, Cliff Street) HarperTrade.

***Cherewatenko, Vern S.** Diabetes Cure: A Natural Plan that can Slow, Stop, Even Cure Type 2 DiseasesCherewatenko,&Dr. Ver, Set. 1999. audio 18.00 (*0-694-52114-0*) HarperAudio.

Cherewatuk, Karen & Wiethaus, Ulrike, eds. Dear Sister: Medieval Women & the Epistolary Genre. (Middle Ages Ser.). 232p. (Orig.). (C). 1993. text 39.95 (*0-8122-3170-8*); pap. text 15.95 (*0-8122-1437-4*) U of Pa Pr.

Cherf, William J., ed. From Alpha to Omega: Studies in Honor of George J. Szemler. (Illus.). vii, 265p. (Orig.). (C). 1993. pap. text 27.50 (*0-89005-529-7*) Ares.

Cherfas, J. J., et al, eds. Round Table Discussion on Bioscience Society. (Schering Foundation Workshop Ser.: Vol. 2). 96p. 1991. 54.95 (*0-387-55032-1*) Spr-Verlag.

Cherian. Management Information Systems. 446p. 1998. pap. text 32.00 (*0-536-01457-4*) Pearson Custom.

Cherian, Anne, ed. see Eiseman, Fred B. & Eiseman, Margaret.

Cherian, George M., ed. see Ballatori, N.

Cherian, Joy. Our Relay Race: A Compilation of Selected Articles & Speeches. LC 96-41458. 192p. 1996. lib. bdg. 36.50 (*0-7618-0531-1*) U Pr of Amer.

Cherici, Peter, jt. auth. see Culligan, Matthew J.

Cherico, Daniel J. & Margolis, Otto S. Thanatology Course Outlines, Vol. 2. 1979. 18.95 (*0-405-12514-3*) Ayer.

Cherico, Daniel J., jt. auth. see Margolis, Otto S.

***Cherie, Carter-Scott.** If Love Is a Game, These Are the Rules: Ten Rules for Finding Love & Creating Long-Lasting Authentic Relationships. 1999. mass mkt. 7.50 (*0-7679-0479-6*) Broadway BDD.

— Naturally Slim Without Dieting. 2000. 12.95 (*0-385-40528-6*, Pub. by Transworld Publishers Ltd) Trafalgar.

— Negaholics: How to Overcome Negativity & Turn Your Life Around. 272p. 1999. pap. 12.00 (*0-345-43899-X*) Wellspring.

***Cheriet, Mohamed & Yang, Yee H., eds.** Vision Interface. (Series in Machine Perception & Artificial Intelligence). 200p. 1999. 56.00 (*981-02-4109-7*) World Scientific Pub.

Cherim, Michael S. The Green Methods Manual: The Original Bio-Control Primer. 4th ed. LC 96-94578. (Illus.). 238p. 1998. pap. 9.95 (*0-9648682-0-2*, EGMM4) Green Spot.

Cherim, Stanley M., jt. auth. see Masterton, William L.

Cherin, David Alex & Huba, George J., eds. AIDS Capitation. LC 98-33964. (Home Health Care Services Quarterly Ser.: Vol. 17, No. 1). 115p. 1998. pap. 54.95 (*0-7890-0654-5*, Hawrth Medical) Haworth Pr.

Cherington, Charles R. The Regulation of Railroad Abandonments. Bruchey, Stuart, ed. LC 80-1299. (Railroads Ser.). (Illus.). 1981. reprint ed. lib. bdg. 27.95 (*0-405-13769-9*) Ayer.

Cherington, Paul T. Advertising As a Business Force: A Compilation of Experience Records. LC 75-39238. (Getting & Spending: The Consumer's Dilemma Ser.). (Illus.). 1976. reprint ed. 26.50 (*0-405-08015-8*) Ayer.

Cheripko, Jan. Get Ready to Play Tee Ball. LC 98-73074. (Illus.). 32p. (J). (ps-1). 1999. pap. 7.95 (*1-56397-716-8*) Boyds Mills Pr.

— Imitate the Tiger. LC 95-77785. 224p. (YA). (gr. 8 up). 1996. 14.95 (*1-56397-514-9*) Boyds Mills Pr.

— Imitate the Tiger. LC 95-77785. 224p. (YA). (gr. 7 up). 1998. pap. 8.95 (*1-56397-705-2*) Boyds Mills Pr.

— Voices of the River: Adventures on the Delaware. LC 93-71611. (Illus.). 48p. (J). (gr. 7 up). 1996. pap. 9.95 (*1-56397-622-6*) Boyds Mills Pr.

— Voices of the River, Adventures on the Delaware. LC 93-71611. 1996. 14.15 (*0-606-10354-6*, Pub. by Turtleback) Demco.

Cheris, Elaine. Fencing: Steps to Success. 2nd rev. ed. (Illus.). 168p. 1999. pap. 16.95 (*0-87322-972-X*, PCHE0972) Human Kinetics.

Cherkaev, A. Topics in the Mathematical Modelling of Composite Materials. LC 97-180. (Progress in Nonlinear Differential Equations & Their Applications Ser.). 300p. 1997. write for info. (*3-7643-3662-5*) Birkhauser.

— Variational Methods for Structural Optimization. LC 99-52755. (Interdisciplinary Applied Mathematics Ser.). (Illus.). 560p. 2000. 79.95 (*0-387-98462-3*) Spr-Verlag.

Cherkaev, Andrej & Kohn, Robert V., eds. Topics in the Mathematical Modelling of Composite Materials. LC 97-180. (Progress in Nonlinear Differential Equations & Their Applications Ser.). 300p. 1997. 120.00 (*0-8176-3662-5*) Birkhauser.

***Cherkas, Michael & Hancock, Larry.** The Silent Invasion, Vols. 1 & 2. 1999. pap. 16.95 (*1-56163-240-6*) NBM.

Cherkas, Michael & Hancock, Larry. Suburban Nightmares Vol. 2: Childhood Secrets. (Illus.). 64p. 1996. pap. 11.95 (*1-56163-166-3*) NBM.

Cherkas, Michael & Sabljic, John. The New Frontier. LC 96-121366. 112p. 1994. pap. 12.95 (*1-56163-101-9*) NBM.

Cherkas, Michael, et al. Science Experiments. 112p. 1990. pap. 10.95 (*0-918348-80-3*, Comics Lit) NBM.

Cherkas, Michael, jt. auth. see Hancock, Larry.

Cherkasky, Lisa & Comet, Renee. The Artful Pie: Unforgettable Recipes for Creative Cooks. (Illus.). 160p. 1993. pap. 17.95 (*1-57630-022-6*, Chapters Bks) HM.

Cherkassky, Vladimier S., et al, eds. From Statistics to Neural Networks: Theory & Pattern Recognition Applications. LC 94-34254. (NATO ASI Series F: Computer & Systems Science: Vol. 136). 1994. write for info. (*3-540-58199-5*) Spr-Verlag.

Cherkassky, Vladimier S. & Mulier, Filip. Learning from Data: Concepts, Theory & Methods. LC 97-43019. (Adaptive & Learning Systems for Signal Processing, Communications & Control Ser.). 464p. 1998. 79.95 (*0-471-15493-8*, Wiley-Interscience) Wiley.

Cherkassky, Vladimier S., et al. From Statistics to Neural Networks: Theory & Pattern Recognition Applications, 136. (Computer & Systems Sciences Ser.). 408p. 1996. 98.50 (*0-387-58199-5*) Spr-Verlag.

Cherken, Harry S. Ladner on Conveyancing in Pennsylvania, 2 vols. 4th rev. ed. LC 79-53058. 1999. ring bd. 195.00 (*1-887024-34-4*) Bisel Co.

Cherkerzian, Diane. Christmas Fun: Holiday Crafts & Treats. LC 92-75840. (Illus.). 32p. (J). (ps-5). 1994. pap. 4.95 (*1-56397-277-8*) Boyds Mills Pr.

— Easter Fun. LC 92-71270. (Illus.). 32p. (J). (ps-3). 1993. pap. 3.95 (*1-56397-164-X*) Boyds Mills Pr.

— Indoor Sunshine: Great Things to Make & Do on Rainy Days. LC 92-73628. (Illus.). 32p. (J). (gr. 2-7). 1993. pap. 3.95 (*1-56397-163-1*) Boyds Mills Pr.

— Outdoor Fun: Great Things to Make & Do on Sunny Days. LC 92-74583. (Illus.). 32p. (J). (gr. 2-7). 1993. pap. 3.95 (*1-56397-162-3*) Boyds Mills Pr.

— Recyclables Fun: Creative Craft Ideas. LC 94-71024. (Illus.). 48p. (J). (ps-2). 1995. pap. 4.95 (*1-56397-275-1*) Boyds Mills Pr.

Cherkes-Julkowski, M. & Gertner, N. Spontaneous Cognitive Processes in Handicapped Children. (Disorders of Human Learning, Behavior, & Communication Ser.). (Illus.). 175p. 1988. 80.95 (*0-387-96801-6*) Spr-Verlag.

Cherkinian, Ann S., ed. see Kochakian, Garabed D.

Cherkis, Lawrence D., et al. Collier Real Estate Transactions & the Bankruptcy Code. LC 84-70341. 1984. ring bd. 230.00 (*0-8205-2034-9*) Bender.

Cherkovski, Neeli. Animal. 103p. (Orig.). 1996. pap. 8.95 (*1-880766-13-2*) Pantograph Pr.

— Bukowski: A Life. LC 97-10989. (Illus.). 354p. 1997. pap. 18.00 (*1-883642-29-9*) Steerforth Pr.

— Elegy for Bob Kaufman. LC 96-47699. 112p. (Orig.). 1996. pap. 11.95 (*0-941543-13-7*) Sun Dog Pr.

— Elegy for Bob Kaufman. deluxe ed. LC 96-47699. 112p. (Orig.). 1996. pap. 19.95 (*0-941543-14-5*) Sun Dog Pr.

— The Waters Re-Born. 1975. pap. 2.50 (*0-88031-017-0*) Invisible-Red Hill.

— Whitman's Wild Children: Portraits of Twelve Poets. 2nd ed. 300p. 1999. pap. 18.00 (*1-883642-86-8*) Steerforth Pr.

***Cherlain, Anne.** Insight Pocket Guide San Francisco with Map. 5th rev. ed. (Illus.). 95p. 2000. pap. 12.95 (*1-58573-017-3*, Insight Guides) Langenscheidt.

Cherland, Meredith Rogers. Private Practices: Girls Reading Fiction & Constructing Identity. LC 94-14194. (Critical Perspectives of Literacy & Education Ser.). 240p. 1994. 85.00 (*0-7484-0225-X*, Pub. by Tay Francis Ltd); pap. 29.95 (*0-7484-0226-8*, Pub. by Tay Francis Ltd) Taylor & Francis.

Cherlin. Public & Private Families. 2nd ed. 416p. 2000. pap. 31.25 (*0-07-231992-5*) McGraw.

Cherlin, Andrew J. Marriage, Divorce, Remarriage. LC 81-2901. (Social Trends in the United States Ser.). (Illus.). 158p. (C). 1981. 28.50 (*0-674-55080-5*) HUP.

— Marriage, Divorce, Remarriage. enl. rev. ed. (Illus.). 244p. 1992. pap. 16.95 (*0-674-55082-X*) HUP.

— Public & Private Families: A Reader. LC 97-1314. 384p. 1997. pap. 33.13 (*0-07-011929-5*) McGraw.

— Public & Private Families: An Introduction. LC 95-8973. 530p. (C). 1995. 57.19 (*0-07-010632-0*) McGraw.

— Public & Private Families: An Introduction. 2nd ed. LC 98-18511. 1998. 56.38 (*0-07-011987-2*) McGraw.

Cherlin, Andrew J., ed. The Changing American Family & Public Policy. 263p. 1988. lib. bdg. 43.50 (*0-87766-422-6*) U Pr of Amer.

— The Changing American Family & Public Policy. 263p. 1988. pap. text 23.50 (*0-87766-421-8*) U Pr of Amer.

Cherlin, Andrew J. & Celebuski, Carin. Are Jewish Families Different? 12p. 1982. pap. 1.00 (*0-686-91970-X*) Am Jewish Comm.

Cherlin, Andrew J. & Furstenberg, Frank F., Jr. The New American Grandparent: A Place in the Family, a Life Apart. (Illus.). 278p. 1992. pap. 16.95 (*0-674-60838-0*) HUP.

Cherlin, Andrew J., jt. auth. see Furstenberg, Frank F., Jr.

Cherlin, Gregory L. The Classification of Countable Homogeneous Directed Graphs & Countable Homogeneous N-Tournaments. LC 97-31683. (Memoirs of the American Mathematical Society Ser.). 161p. 1998. pap. 47.00 (*0-8218-0836-2*) Am Math.

Cherlin, Michael, jt. ed. see Atlas, Rafael.

Cherlow, Jay R. Recreation Fees: Demonstration Fee Program Successful in Raising Revenues but Could Be Improved. (Illus.). 116p. (C). 1999. text 25.00 (*0-7881-7735-4*) DIANE Pub.

Cherm, S. S., ed. Seminar on Nonlinear Partial, & Differential Equations. (Mathematical Sciences Research Institute Publications: Vol. 2). (Illus.). 373p. 1984. 65.95 (*0-387-96079-1*) Spr-Verlag.

Chermak, jt. auth. see Head.

Chermak, A. Czech-English - English-Czech Dictionary: Large Edition. (CZE & ENG.). 43.95 (*0-87557-012-7*) Saphrograph.

Chermak, Gail D. & Musiek, Frank E. Central Auditory Processing Disorders: New Perspectives. LC 97-4466. 392p. 1997. pap. 55.00 (*1-56593-697-3*, 1354) Thomson Learn.

***Chermayeff, Catherine.** Fashion Photography Now. LC 99-53247. (Illus.). 160p. 2000. pap. 29.95 (*0-8109-2712-8*, Pub. by Abrams) Time Warner.

Chermayeff, Ivan. Fishy Facts. LC 93-31091. (Illus.). 32p. (J). (ps-1). 1994. 10.95 (*0-15-228175-4*, Gulliver Bks) Harcourt.

— Furry Facts. LC 93-30147. (Illus.). 32p. (J). (ps-1). 1994. 10.95 (*0-15-230425-8*, Gulliver Bks) Harcourt.

— Tomato & Other Colors. (J). (ps-3). 1981. 13.55 (*0-13-924753-X*) P-H.

Chermayeff, Ivan, et al. Scaly Facts. LC 94-2958. (Illus.). 32p. (J). (ps-1). 1995. 11.00 (*0-15-200109-3*, Gulliver Bks) Harcourt.

***Chermayeff, Ivan, et al.** Trademarks Designed by Chermayeff & Geismar. (Illus.). 288p. 2000. 40.00 (*1-56898-256-9*) Princeton Arch.

Chermayeff, Ivan, jt. auth. see Richardson, Nan F.

Chermesh, Ran. A State Within a State: Industrial Relations in Israel, 1965-1987, 43. LC 92-9264. (Contributions in Labor Studies: No. 43). 320p. 1993. 59.95 (*0-313-28547-0*, CWT, Greenwood Pr) Greenwood.

Chermet, Jacques. Atlas of Phlebography of the Lower Limbs. 256p. 1982. text 226.00 (*90-247-2525-9*) Kluwer Academic.

Chern. Ophthalmology Review Manual. 560p. pap. text 69.95 (*0-683-30364-3*) Lppncott W & W.

Chern, Chiing-Chen. Set Theory of the Continuum. Just, Winifrid et al, eds. LC 92-28316. (Mathematical Sciences Research Institute Publications: Vol. 26). ix, 416p. 1992. 79.95 (*0-387-97874-7*) Spr-Verlag.

Chern, J., jt. auth. see Helfferich, F. G.

Chern, Kenneth C. & Wright, Kenneth W. Review of Ophthalmology. LC 96-20671. (Illus.). 600p. 1997. write for info. (*0-683-18239-0*) Lppncott W & W.

Chern, S. S., et al. Lectures on Differential Geometry. LC 98-22031. 250p. 1998. 38.00 (*981-02-3494-5*) World Scientific Pub.

Chern, S. S., ed. see Bridson, M. & Haefliger, A.

Chern, S. S., ed. see Grimmett, G.

Chern, S. S., ed. see Neukirch, J.

Chern, S. S., ed. see Rockafellar, R. Tyrrell & Wets, Roger J.

Chern, Shiing-Shen. Complex Manifolds Without Potential Theory. (Universitexts Ser.). 1995. 42.95 (*0-387-90422-0*) Spr-Verlag.

— Differential Geometry. (Series on University Mathematics: Vol. 1). 1998. pap. text 26.00 (*981-02-2647-0*) World Scientific Pub.

— Geometric Analysis & Computer Graphics: Proceedings of a Workshop Held May 23-25, 1988. Concus, P. et al, eds. (Mathematical Sciences Research Institute Publications: Vol. 17). (Illus.). 216p. 1990. 65.95 (*0-387-97402-4*) Spr-Verlag.

— Selected Papers. (Illus.). 1978. 89.95 (*0-387-90339-9*) Spr-Verlag.

— Selected Papers, Vol. II. (Illus.). 465p. 1989. 84.95 (*0-387-96816-4*) Spr-Verlag.

— Selected Papers, Vol. III. (Illus.). 520p. 1989. 89.95 (*0-387-96817-2*) Spr-Verlag.

— Selected Papers, Vol. IV. (Illus.). 385p. 1989. 84.95 (*0-387-96820-2*) Spr-Verlag.

Chern, Shiing-Shen, ed. Partial Differential Equations, Proceedings, Tianjin, 1986. (Lecture Notes in Mathematics Ser.: Vol. 1306). vi, 294p. 1988. 44.95 (*0-387-19097-X*) Spr-Verlag.

— Studies in Global Differential Geometry. (MAA Studies in Mathematics: Vol. 27). 320p. 1989. text 8.00 (*0-88385-129-6*, MAS-27) Math Assn.

Chern, Shiing-Shen, et al, eds. Entire Functions & Related Parts of Analysis. LC 68-10458. (Proceedings of Symposia in Pure Mathematics Ser.: Vol. 11). 554p. 1987. reprint ed. pap. 52.00 (*0-8218-1411-7*, PSPUM/11) Am Math.

— Logic from Computer Science: Proceedings of a Workshop Held November 13-17, 1989. (Mathematical Sciences Research Institute Publications: Vol. 21). (Illus.). 624p. 1991. 89.95 (*0-387-97667-1*) Spr-Verlag.

— Physics & Mathematics of Anyons: Proceedings of the TCSUH Workshop, Houston, Texas, 1-2 February 1991. 340p. (C). 1991. pap. 32.00 (*981-02-0722-0*); text 118.00 (*981-02-0650-X*) World Scientific Pub.

Chern, Shiing-Shen & Smale, S. Global Analysis, Pt. I. LC 70-95271. (Proceedings of Symposium in Pure Mathematics Ser.: Vol. 14). 367p. 1992. reprint ed. pap. 55.00 (*0-8218-1414-1*, PSPUM/14) Am Math.

Chern, Shiing-Shen & Smale, S., eds. Global Analysis, Pt. III. LC 70-95271. (Proceedings of Symposia in Pure Mathematics Ser.: Vol. 16). 250p. 1970. reprint ed. pap. 45.00 (*0-8218-1416-8*, PSPUM/16) Am Math.

C

Chern, Shiing-Shen & Smale, Stephen, eds. Global Analysis, Pt. 2. LC 70-95271. (Proceedings of Symposia in Pure Mathematics Ser.: No. 15). 313p. 1970. reprint ed. pap. 97.10 (*0-608-02656-5*, 205255100002) Bks Demand.

Chern, Shiing-Shen, jt. ed. see Cecil, Thomas E.

Chern, Shiing-Shen, ed. see Pure Mathematics Symposium Staff.

Chern, Shiing-Shen, ed. see Symposium in Pure Mathematics - Berkeley - 1968.

*__Chern, Wen S., et al.__ Food Security in Asia: Economics & Policies. LC 00-37675. (Academia Studies in Asian Economies). 2000. write for info. (*1-84064-441-9*) E Elgar.

Chernaik, Judith. Love's Children. 1992. 20.00 (*0-685-55206-3*) Knopf.

Chernaik, Warren. Sexual Freedom in Restoration Literature. 280p. (C). 1995. text 59.95 (*0-521-46497-8*) Cambridge U Pr.

Chernaik, Warren L. & Dzelzainis, Martin. Marvell & Liberty. LC 98-55451. 1999. text 59.95 (*0-312-22171-1*) St Martin.

*__Chernaik, Warren L., et al.__ The Art of Detective Fiction. LC 99-46987. 2000. text 59.95 (*0-312-22989-5*) St Martin.

Chernatony, Leslie De, see De Chernatony, Leslie.

Chernayakhovskaya, leonora, ed. see Berkin, Ephim.

*__Cherne, Barbara.__ Bella Donna: A Renaissance Mystery Novel. 160p. 2001. pap. write for info. (*1-56474-362-4*) Fithian Pr.

Cherne, Leo. U. S. Intelligence Requirements for the Late 1980s. 1986. write for info. (*0-935067-10-8*) Nathan Hale Inst.

Chernecky, Cynthia C. Cancer, Diagnostics, & Chemotherapy: A Reference Manual. 1991. pap. text 34.00 (*0-7216-3187-8*, W B Saunders Co) Harcrt Hlth Sci Grp.

Chernecky, Cynthia C. & Berger, Barbara J. Advanced & Critical Care Oncology Nursing: Managing Primary Complications. Cullen, Barbara N., ed. LC 97-7109. 624p. 1997. pap. text 39.95 (*0-7216-6860-7*, W B Saunders Co) Harcrt Hlth Sci Grp.

— Laboratory Tests & Diagnostic Procedures. 2nd ed. Cullen, Barbara N., ed. LC 96-43069. (Illus.). 1180p. 1996. pap. text 28.00 (*0-7216-6793-7*, W B Saunders Co) Harcrt Hlth Sci Grp.

Chernega, Janet B. Emergency Guide for Dental Auxiliaries. LC 86-24303. 198p. (C). 1986. pap. 29.95 (*0-8273-2335-2*) Delmar.

*__Chernega, Janet B.__ Emergency Guide for Dental Auxiliaries. 2000. pap. 33.71 (*0-7668-1887-X*) Delmar.

— Emergency Guide for Dental Auxiliaries. 2nd ed. LC 93-41955. 179p. (C). 1994. pap. 46.95 (*0-8273-4109-1*) Delmar.

Chernela, Janet. The Wanano Indians of the Brazilian Amazon: A Sense of Space. (Illus.). 207p. (Orig.). 1996. pap. 16.95 (*0-292-71186-7*) U of Tex Pr.

Chernenko, Konstantin U. Human Rights in Soviet Society. LC 81-6948. 152p. reprint ed. pap. 47.20 (*0-608-17700-8*, 203004000067) Bks Demand.

— The Soviets Want Peace: Chernenko, Gromyko, Gorbachev, Tikhonov, Ustinov, Ponomarev. LC 85-5219. 143p. reprint ed. pap. 44.40 (*0-608-17699-0*, 203003900067) Bks Demand.

Chernenkoff, Russell A. & Bonnen, John J., eds. Recent Developments in Fatigue Technology. (Progress in Technology Ser.). 528p. 1997. pap. 89.00 (*0-7680-0037-8*) Soc Auto Engineers.

Cherner, Anne. The Surveyor's Hand. LC 81-70100. 80p. (Orig.). 1981. pap. 10.00 (*0-9607302-0-6*) Compton Pr.

Cherner, Linda L. The Universal Healthcare Almanac: Quarterly Updates. 480p. 1989. ring bd. 195.00 (*0-9645024-0-2*) Silver Cherner.

Cherness, Claudia. Leroy, the Lizard Coloring Book. (ENG, FRE & SPA.). 24p. (J). (ps-2). 1993. pap. 3.95 (*0-943864-66-6*) Davenport.

Chernetsov, A. V. Carved Staves of the Fifteenth Century. 80p. (C). 1987. 30.00 (*0-7855-3128-9*) St Mut.

Chernetsov, Valeriu & Moszynska, W. Prehistory of Western Siberia. LC 73-79092. (Arctic Institute of North America-Anthropology of the North; Translation from Russian Sources Ser.: No. 9). (Illus.). 407p. reprint ed. pap. 126.20 (*0-7837-1174-3*, 204170200022) Bks Demand.

Chernev, Irving. Capablanca's Best Chess Endings: 60 Complete Games. (Illus.). 299p. (C). 1982. pap. 7.95 (*0-486-24249-8*) Dover.

— Combinations: The Heart of Chess. (Illus.). 245p. 1967. pap. 6.95 (*0-486-21744-2*) Dover.

— The Most Instructive Games of Chess Ever Played: Sixty-Two Masterpieces of Chess Strategy. unabridged ed. LC 92-25679. (Illus.). 81p. 1992. reprint ed. pap. text 7.95 (*0-486-27302-4*) Dover.

— Practical Chess Endings. LC 69-15362. (Illus.). 318p. 1969. reprint ed. pap. 8.95 (*0-486-22208-X*) Dover.

— Twelve Great Chess Players & Their Best Games. LC 95-5916. (Illus.). 256p. 1995. pap. text 11.95 (*0-486-28674-6*) Dover.

Chernev, Irving & Harkness, Kenneth. Invitation to Chess. 224p. 1985. pap. 10.00 (*0-671-21270-2*, Fireside) S&S Trade Pap.

*__Chernewski, Anita.__ How-to-Make Three Corrugated Pinhole Cameras: Wide-Angle, Normal, Telephoto. (Illus.). 16p. 1999. 15.00 (*0-9679147-0-1*) Pinhole Format.

Cherney, Alison. Capitation & Risk Sharing: A Guidebook for Physicians & Alternate Site Providers. LC 95-36379. 300p. (C). 1995. text 60.00 (*1-55738-643-9*, Irwn Prfssnl) McGraw-Hill Prof.

— How to Create a Homecare Marketing Plan. 1999. text 295.00 (*0-7863-0561-4*, Irwn Prfssnl) McGraw-Hill Prof.

Cherney, D. J. R., jt. ed. see Cherney, Jerome H.

Cherney, Ila. My Haggadah. (Illus.). 66p. (J). (gr. 4-7). 1985. pap. text 4.95 (*0-87441-483-0*) Behrman.

Cherney, Jerome H. & Cherney, D. J. R., eds. Grass for Dairy Cattle. LC 98-22773. (CABI Publishing Ser.). (Illus.). 418p. 1999. text 110.00 (*0-85199-288-9*) OUP.

Cherney, Kenneth A. Prayer: Bible Study Kit-HWML. 1998. 37.99 (*0-8100-0765-7*, 22N0965) Northwest Pub.

Cherney, Leora R., et al, eds. Clinical Management of Dysphagia in Adults & Children. 2nd ed. 246p. 1993. 65.00 (*0-8342-0376-6*, 20376) Aspen Pub.

Cherney, Leora R., et al. Analyzing Discourse in Communicatively Impaired Adults. LC 98-18602. (Rehabilitation Institute of Chicago Publication Ser.). 251p. 1998. 54.00 (*0-8342-0632-3*) Aspen Pub.

Cherng, John G. CADKey Companion. LC 95-13811. (Graphics Ser.). 728p. (C). 1995. text 27.95 (*0-256-17142-4*, Irwn McGrw-H) McGrw-H Hghr Educ.

Cherniack, H. D. & Schneider, Jerry B. A New Approach to the Delineation of Hospital Service Areas. (Discussion Papers: No. 16). 1967. pap. 10.00 (*1-55869-077-8*) Regional Sci Res Inst.

Cherniack, Louis, jt. auth. see Cherniack, Reuben M.

Cherniack, Martin. The Hawk's Nest Incident: America's Worst Industrial Disaster. LC 86-7088. 224p. (C). 1989. reprint ed. pap. 18.00 (*0-300-04485-2*) Yale U Pr.

Cherniack, Neil S. & Widdicombe, John G., eds. Handbook of Physiology: Section 3, The Respiratory System, Vol. II, Pts. 1 & 2: Control of Breathing. (American Physiological Society Book). (Illus.). 972p. 1988. text 245.00 (*0-19-520668-1*) OUP.

Cherniack, Neil S., et al. Rehabilitation of the Patient with Respiratory Disease. LC 99-10475. (Illus.). 1100p. 1999. 155.00 (*0-07-011649-0*) McGraw-Hill HPD.

Cherniack, Neil S., jt. ed. see Nochomovitz, Michael L.

Cherniack, Neil S., jt. ed. see Takishima, T.

Cherniack, Reuben M. Pulmonary Function Testing. 2nd ed. 1992. pap. text 34.50 (*0-7216-4014-1*, W B Saunders Co) Harcrt Hlth Sci Grp.

— Review of Pulmonary & Critical Care Medicine. 281p. 1996. pap. 25.95 (*1-55009-027-5*) DEKR.

Cherniack, Reuben M., ed. Lung Disease: State-of-the-Art, 1984-1986. (Lung Disease: State-of-the-Art Ser.). (Illus.). 224p. 1987. 20.50 (*0-915116-05-7*, 9807) Am Lung Assn.

— Lung Disease: State of the Art, 1986-1987. (State of the Art Ser.). (Illus.). 202p. 1988. write for info. (*0-915116-06-5*, 9801) Am Lung Assn.

— Lung Disease: State of the Art, 1987-1988. (Illus.). 224p. 1989. 35.00 (*0-915116-07-3*, 9622) Am Lung Assn.

— Lung Disease: State of the Art, 1988-1989. (State of the Art Ser.). (Illus.). 230p. 1990. 50.00 (*0-915116-08-1*, 9620) Am Lung Assn.

Cherniack, Reuben M. & Cherniack, Louis. Respiration in Health & Disease. 3rd ed. (Illus.). 480p. 1983. text 57.00 (*0-7216-2527-4*, W B Saunders Co) Harcrt Hlth Sci Grp.

Cherniak, Betty, ed. see Foroutan, Iraj M.

Cherniak, Christopher. Minimal Rationality. 176p. 1990. reprint ed. pap. text 14.50 (*0-262-53087-2*, Bradford Bks) MIT Pr.

Cherniak, Neil S., jt. ed. see Nochomovitz, Michael L.

Cherniak, Samuel, tr. see Hyppolite, Jean.

Cherniakhovskaia, L. English-Russian Phrasebook. 252p. (C). 1989. 50.00 (*0-569-09126-8*, Pub. by Collets) St Mut.

Cherniavskaia, T. N. Artistic Culture of the U. S. S. R. 356p. (C). 1984. 125.00 (*0-7855-5064-X*, Pub. by Collets) St Mut.

Cherniavsky, Eva. That Pale Mother Rising: Sentimental Discourses & the Imitation of Motherhood in Nineteenth-Century America. LC 94-13186. 176p. 1995. 25.00 (*0-253-31343-0*); pap. 10.95 (*0-253-20934-X*) Ind U Pr.

Cherniavsky, John C., jt. auth. see Wallace, Dolores R.

Cherniavsky, O. F., jt. auth. see Gokhfeld, D. A.

*__Chernick.__ Bootstrap Methods: A Practitioner's Guide. LC 99-21924. 272p. 1999. 74.95 (*0-471-34912-7*) Wiley.

Chernick, Michael, ed. Essential Papers on Talmud. LC 94-17490. (Essential Papers on Jewish Studies). 484p. (C). 1994. pap. text 27.50 (*0-8147-1505-2*) NYU Pr.

— Essential Papers on Talmud. LC 94-17490. (Essential Papers on Jewish Studies). 580p. (C). 1994. text 75.00 (*0-8147-1496-X*) NYU Pr.

Chernick, Richard. Private Judging: Privatizing Civil Justice. LC 99-165594. 60 p. 1997. pap. write for info. (*0-937299-55-3*) Natl Legal Ctr Pub Interest.

Chernick, Sidney E. The Commonwealth Caribbean: The Integration Experience. LC 77-17246. (World Bank Country Economic Report). 537p. reprint ed. pap. 166.50 (*0-7837-4212-6*, 204304000012) Bks Demand.

Chernick, Victor & Boat, Thomas F. Kendig's Disorders of the Respiratory Tract in Children. 6th ed. Fletcher, Judy, ed. LC 96-42343. (Illus.). 1104p. 1997. text 205.00 (*0-7216-6541-1*, W B Saunders Co) Harcrt Hlth Sci Grp.

Chernicoff. Essentials of Geology Windows. 1997. 109.20 (*1-57259-475-6*) W H Freeman.

Chernicoff, Stanley. Geology: An Introduction to Physical Geology. LC 98-72010. 1998. text 51.27 (*0-395-92351-4*) HM.

— Geology: An Introduction to Physical Geology. (Illus.). 672p. 1995. write for info. (*0-87901-882-8*) Worth.

— Geology, 1995. 593p. 1994. text 50.60 (*0-87901-451-2*) Worth.

— Geology, 1995. 672p. 1994. pap. text 42.60 (*1-57259-017-3*) Worth.

Chernicoff, Stanley & Fox, Chip. Essentials of Geology. LC 96-60596. 416p. 1996. pap. text 35.00 (*1-57259-109-9*) Worth.

Chernicoff, Stanley, jt. auth. see Shellenberger, W. Carl.

Chernigovski, A. A., ed. Application of Directional Blasting in Mining & Civil Engineering. 2nd enl. rev. ed. 340p. (C). 1986. 168.00 (*90-6191-573-2*, Pub. by A A Balkema) Ashgate Pub Co.

Chernik, Barbara E. Introduction to Library Services. rev. ed. (Library Science Text Ser.). (Illus.). xi, 230p. 1992. pap. text 27.50 (*1-56308-053-2*) Libs Unl.

Chernikov, A. A., et al. Mathematical Physics Reviews: Weak Chaos & Structures, Vol. 8. Novikov, S. P. & Sinai, Ya G., eds. (Soviet Scientific Reviews Ser.: Vol. 8, Pt. 2). ii, 94p. 1989. pap. text 59.00 (*3-7186-4865-2*) Gordon & Breach.

Chernikowski, Stephanie, photos by. Dream Baby Dream: Images from the Blank Generation. (Illus.). 121p. 1996. 40.00 (*1-880985-40-3*); pap. 25.00 (*1-880985-27-6*) Two Thirteen Sixty-one.

Chernin, Albert D., jt. ed. see Friedman, Murray.

Chernin, Alex. The Pirc Defense. 176p. 1997. pap. 17.95 (*1-880673-16-9*) Hays Pub.

*__Chernin, Ariel.__ Fanfare: Dave Matthews Band. (Illus.). 2000. pap. 15.95 (*1-55022-417-4*) ECW.

Chernin, David A., ed. see Eustachi, Bartolomeo, et al.

Chernin, Jack. Basic Parasitology. (Modules in Life Sciences Ser.). 1999. pap. text 24.95 (*0-7484-0817-7*) Taylor & Francis.

Chernin, Kim. Crossing the Border: An Erotic Journey. LC 93-22131. 352p. 1994. 0.22 (*0-449-90522-5*, Columbine) Fawcett.

*__Chernin, Kim.__ A Different Kind of Listening: My Psychoanalysis & Its Shadow. 215p. 1999. reprint ed. pap. text 12.00 (*0-7881-6241-1*) DIANE Pub.

Chernin, Kim. The Hungry Self: Women, Eating & Identity. 240p. 1994. reprint ed. pap. 13.00 (*0-06-092504-3*, Perennial) HarperTrade.

— In My Father's Garden: A Daughter's Search for a Spiritual Life. 196p. 1996. 17.95 (*1-56512-100-7*, 72100) Algonquin Bks.

— In My Mother's House: A Daughter's Story. LC 93-41852. 352p. 1994. reprint ed. pap. 14.00 (*0-06-092506-X*, Perennial) HarperTrade.

— My Life As a Boy: A Woman's Story. LC 96-53978. 196p. 1997. 16.95 (*1-56512-163-5*, 72163) Algonquin Bks.

— The Obsession: Reflections on the Tyranny of Slenderness. LC 93-40213. 224p. 1994. reprint ed. pap. 13.00 (*0-06-092505-1*, Perennial) HarperTrade.

— Reinventing Eve: Modern Woman in Search of Herself. 2nd ed. LC 93-40772. 224p. 1994. reprint ed. pap. 13.00 (*0-06-092503-5*, Perennial) HarperTrade.

— Woman Who Gave Birth to Her Mother: Tales of Transformation In Womens Lives. 240p. 1999. pap. 13.95 (*0-14-028466-4*, PuffinBks) Peng Put Young Read.

— The Woman Who Gave Birth to Her Mother: Tales of Women in Transformation. LC 98-11417. 224p. 1998. 23.95 (*0-670-88096-5*) Viking Penguin.

*__Chernin, Kim & Stendhal, Renate.__ Cecilia Bartoli: The Passion of Song. (Illus.). 252p. 2000. reprint ed. pap. 24.95 (*0-7043-4623-0*, Pub. by Womens Press) Trafalgar.

Chernington, David. Rearing Responsible Children. 2nd rev. ed. LC 97-45344. 232p. 1997. pap. 11.95 (*0-8425-2354-5*, Friends of the Library) Brigham.

Cherniske, Stephen. Caffeine Blues: Wake up to the Hidden Dangers of America's #1 Drug. LC 98-24372. 464p. 1998. mass mkt. 12.99 (*0-446-67391-9*, Pub. by Warner Bks) Little.

Cherniske, Stephen A. The DHEA Breakthrough. 1997. pap. 12.00 (*0-345-41391-1*) Ballantine Pub Grp.

— The DHEA Breakthrough. 1998. mass mkt. 6.99 (*0-345-42646-0*) Ballantine Pub Grp.

Cherniss, Cary. Beyond Burnout: How Teachers, Nurses, Therapists, & Lawyers Recover from Stress & Disillusionment. LC 95-3601. 240p. (gr. 13). 1995. pap. 18.99 (*0-415-91206-7*) Routledge.

— Beyond Burnout: How Teachers, Nurses, Therapists, & Lawyers Recover from Stress & Disillusionment. LC 95-3601. 248p. (C). (gr. 13). 1995. 65.00 (*0-415-91205-9*) Routledge.

— Professional Burnout in Human Services Organizations. LC 80-12136. 318p. 1980. 37.95 (*0-275-90462-8*, C0462, Praeger Pubs) Greenwood.

— Staff Burnout: Job Stress in the Human Services. LC 80-19408. (Sage Studies in Community Mental Health: No. 2). 199p. reprint ed. pap. 61.70 (*0-8357-8486-X*, 203475400091) Bks Demand.

Cherniss, Cary, jt. ed. see Fishman, Daniel B.

Cherniss, Harold, tr. Plutarch, Moralia Vol. XIII, PT. 2: Stoic Essays: Loeb No. 470. 21.25 (*0-674-99517-1*) HUP.

— Plutarch, Moralia Vol. XIII, Pt. 1: Platonic Essays. 392p. 1957. text 18.95 (*0-674-99470-1*) HUP.

Cherniss, Michael D. Boethian Apocalypse: Studies in Middle English Vision Poetry. 330p. 1986. 29.95 (*0-937664-71-5*) Pilgrim Bks OK.

— Ingeld & Christ: Heroic Conceptions & Values in Old English Christian Poetry. (Studies in English Literature: No. 74). 267p. 1972. text 56.95 (*90-279-2335-3*) Mouton.

Chernoff. International Herald Tribune: In the News: Mastering Reading & Language Skills with the Newspaper. (Illus.). 1995. pap., teacher ed. 15.46 (*0-8442-0795-0*) NTC Contemp Pub Co.

Chernoff, jt. ed. see Gorth.

*__Chernoff, Barry.__ Aquatic Ecosystems Upper Rio Orthon Basin. 2000. pap. text 20.00 (*1-881173-30-5*) U Ch Pr.

Chernoff, Daniel P. Federal Circuit Patent Case Digests, 2 vols. LC 90-44464. (IP Ser.). 1990. ring bd. 220.00 (*0-87632-753-6*) West Group.

Chernoff, Dona, ed. see Davis, Michaela A.

Chernoff, Dona, ed. see Iovine, Vicki.

Chernoff, Dona, ed. see Mercer, Judy.

Chernoff, Dona, ed. see Trimboli, Joseph & McAlary, Mike.

Chernoff, Fred. After Bipolarity: The Vanishing Threat, Theories of Cooperation & the Future of the Atlantic Alliance. 320p. 1995. text 52.50 (*0-472-10550-7*, 10550) U of Mich Pr.

Chernoff, Goldie. Easy Costumes You Don't Have to Sew. (J). (gr. 1-5). 1977. 7.95 (*0-590-07491-1*) Scholastic Inc.

Chernoff, Goldie T. Easy Costumes You Don't Have to Sew. LC 76-46428. (Illus.). 48p. (J). (gr. 1-3). 1984. lib. bdg. 13.95 (*0-02-718230-4*, Four Winds Pr) S&S Childrens.

Chernoff, Herman. Sequential Analysis & Optimal Design. (CBMS-NSF Regional Conference Series in Applied Mathematics: No. 8). (Illus.). v, 119p. 1972. reprint ed. pap. text 25.50 (*0-89871-006-5*) Soc Indus-Appl Math.

Chernoff, Herman & Moses, Lincoln E. Elementary Decision Theory. 364p. 1987. reprint ed. pap. 10.95 (*0-486-65218-1*) Dover.

Chernoff, Johanna. Born a Jew...Die a Jew: The Story of Martin Chernoff - a Pioneer in Messianic Judaism. 256p. 1996. pap. 12.99 (*1-884369-39-1*, EBED Pubns) McDougal Pubng.

Chernoff, John & Chernoff, John M. African Rhythm & African Sensibility. LC 79-189. xviii, 262p. 1981. lib. bdg. 18.00 incl. audio (*0-226-10346-3*) U Ch Pr.

Chernoff, John M. African Rhythm & African Sensibility: Aesthetics & Social Action in African Musical Idioms. LC 79-189. xviii, 280p. 1981. pap. 13.95 (*0-226-10345-5*) U Ch Pr.

Chernoff, John M., jt. auth. see Chernoff, John.

Chernoff, Ken, jt. auth. see Fischer, Roger A.

Chernoff, Maxine. American Heaven. LC 96-3143. 256p. (C). 1996. 21.95 (*1-56689-041-1*) Coffee Hse.

— A Boy in Winter. LC 99-20430. 256p. 1999. 23.00 (*0-609-60522-4*, Crown) Crown.

— Japan. 48p. (Orig.). 1987. pap. 6.00 (*0-939691-01-9*) Avenue B.

— Leap Year Day: New & Selected Poems. 144p. 1998. pap. 9.95 (*1-893032-07-8*) Jensen Daniels.

— New Faces of 1952. LC 84-25214. 57p. (Orig.). 1985. pap. 6.00 (*0-87886-124-6*, Greenfld Rev Pr) Greenfld Rev Lit.

— Utopia TV Store. LC 79-14606. 1979. pap. 3.00 (*0-916328-13-9*) Yellow Pr.

Chernoff, Maxine, jt. auth. see Tiersky, Ethel.

Chernoff, Michael, et al, eds. The Validity Issue: What Should Teacher Certification Tests Measure? 152p. (C). 1987. text 29.95 (*0-89859-947-4*) L Erlbaum Assocs.

Chernoff, Paul A., et al, eds. Massachusetts Superior Court Civil Forms: Includes Forms on Disk. LC 96-80042. 782p. 1997. ring bd. 95.00 incl. disk (*1-57589-051-8*, 97-05.13-BK) Mass CLE.

— Massachusetts Superior Court Civil Practice Manual. LC 96-80041. 616p. 1997. ring bd. 95.00 (*1-57589-050-X*, 97-05.12-BK) Mass CLE.

Chernoff, Paul R. Product Formulas, Nonlinear Semigroups, & Addition of Unbounded Operators. LC 73-22235. (American Mathematical Society Ser.: No. 140). 128p. 1974. pap. 39.70 (*0-608-05170-5*, 205259100001) Bks Demand.

— Product Formulas, Nonlinear Semigroups & Addition of Unbounded Operators. LC 73-22235. (Memoirs Ser.: No. 1/140). 121p. 1974. pap. 18.00 (*0-8218-1840-6*, MEMO/1/140) Am Math.

Chernoff, Ronnie. Geriatric Nutrition: The Health Professional's Handbook. LC 91-17210. 522p. 1991. 74.00 (*0-8342-0228-X*) Aspen Pub.

— Geriatric Nutrition: The Health Professional's Handbook. 2nd ed. LC 99-14492. 518p. 1999. 65.00 (*0-8342-1082-7*, 10827) Aspen Pub.

Chernoff-Rosen, Diane & Levinson, Lisa. The Grownup's Guide to Living with Kids in Manhattan. LC 98-91399. 1998. pap. 18.95 (0-9663392-0-7) Res Mktg Grp.

If children were born with an instruction manual, parents would sigh in relief. Raising children is an awesome task, especially in New York City with its virtually limitless goods, services & actvities. This guide to the special pleasures & challenges of raising children in Manhattan covers the city as a community resource & provides the information that every parent needs. The book educates parents by guiding them through the school application process, choosing doctors & caregivers, handling birthday parties, networking with other parents, dealing with emergencies, scheduling activities & play date etiquette. Also included are detailed listings of over 275 retail establishments specializing in children's goods & over 450 actvities for children (classes, cultural activities & "boredom busters). Business & services are not rated or reviewed, but are presented in an objective, easy to use, format. *Publisher Paid Annotation.*

— The Grownup's Guide to Visiting New York City with Kids. 300p. 2000. pap. write for info. (*0-9663392-1-5*) Res Mktg Grp.

*__Chernoff/Silver Associate Staff, ed.__ Columbia: Gem of the South. (American Enterprise Ser.). (Illus.). 240p. 2000. 49.95 (*1-885352-77-8*) Community Comm.

Chernofsky, Charles B. & DeNoyelles, Griffith, Jr. Step-by-Step Legal Forms & Agreements. 446p. 1992. pap. 19.95 (*0-929543-10-6*) Round Lake Pub.

Chernofsky, Ellen. The Traveling Jewish in America: The Complete Guide for Business & Pleasure. 3rd ed. 1991. pap. 11.95 (*0-9617104-2-X*) Wandering You Pr.

C

An Asterisk (*) at the beginning of an entry indicates that the title is appearing for the first time.

C

Cherry, Deborah. Painting Women: Victorian Women Artists. LC 92-36713. (Illus.). 240p. (C). (gr. 13). 1993. pap. 25.99 (*0-415-06053-2*, B0717) Routledge.

Cherry, Denise. Step by Step Children's Guide to Dog Training. (Illus.). 64p. (J). 1993. pap. 5.95 (*0-86622-518-8*, SK044) TFH Pubns.

Cherry, Don. Grapes Les Raisins de Vi. (FRE.). 2000. mass mkt. 4.50 (*0-380-68163-3*, 68163, Avon Bks) Morrow Avon.

Cherry, Don & Fischler, Stan. Grapes: A Vintage View of Hockey. 288p. 1983. mass mkt. 5.99 (*0-380-65177-7*, 65177, Avon Bks) Morrow Avon.

Cherry, Don T. Total Facility Control. (Illus.). 432p. 1986. 54.95 (*0-409-95149-8*) Buttrwrth-Heinemann.

Cherry, E., ed. Complete Index to Optical Engineering Journal: 1962-1984, Vols. 1-23. 192p. 1995. 50.00 (*0-89252-587-8*, 552) SPIE.

Cherry, Edith. Programming for Design: From Theory to Practice. LC 98-15978. 352p. 1998. 54.95 (*0-471-19645-2*) Wiley.

Cherry, Florence. Parent Adolescent Communication. Calvert, Trudie, ed. 76p. 1996. ring bd. 10.50 (*1-57753-088-8*, 321HDFS54) Corn Coop Ext.

Cherry, Frances. Legs & Bizou. (Illus.). 36p. (J). (ps-8). 1986. 7.95 (*0-920806-60-0*, Pub. by Penumbra Pr) U of Toronto Pr.

Cherry, Frances E. The Stubborn Particulars of Social Psychology: Essays on the Research Process. LC 94-10637. (Critical Psychology Ser.). 144p. (C). (gr. 13). 1994. text 49.95 (*0-415-06666-2*, A7782) Routledge.

— The Stubborn Particulars of Social Psychology: Essays on the Research Process. LC 94-10637. (Critical Psychology Ser.). 172p. (C). 1995. pap. 24.99 (*0-415-06667-0*, A7786) Routledge.

Cherry, Frank, jt. auth. see James, John W.

Cherry-Garrard, Apsley. The Worst Journey in the World. (Adventure Library: Vol. 13). (Illus.). 1998. reprint ed. lib. bdg. 35.00 (*1-885283-12-1*) Advent Library.

— The Worst Journey in the World. 2nd ed. LC 96-54510. 656p. 1997. pap. 16.95 (*0-7867-0437-3*) Carroll & Graf.

— The Worst Journey in the World: Antarctic, 1910-1913. (Illus.). 660p. 1994. 34.00 (*0-330-33585-5*, Pub. by Picador) Trans-Atl Phila.

C

Cherry, George L. Convention Parliament, 1689: A Biographical Study of Its Members. LC 65-24394. 218p. 1966. text 32.00 (*0-8290-0163-8*) Irvington.

Cherry, George W. Software Construction with Object-Oriented Pictures: Specifying Reactive & Interactive Systems. LC 89-51266. (Illus.). 156p. (C). 1989. pap. text 28.95 (*0-9625003-0-5*) Thought-Tools.

Cherry, Gordon E. Birmingham: A Study in Geography, History, & Planning. LC 93-46899. (Belhaven World Cities Ser.). 268p. 1994. 100.00 (*0-471-94900-0*) Wiley.

***Cherry, Gordon E.** Holford: Study in Architecture Planning & Civic Design. 8. 304p. (C). (gr. 13). 1998. text 80.00 (*0-7201-1786-0*) Continuum.

Cherry, Gordon E. Town Planning in Britain since 1900: The Rise & Fall of the Planning Ideal. LC 96-8104. (Making Contemporary Britain Ser.). 224p. 1996. 66.95 (*0-631-19993-4*); pap. 25.95 (*0-631-19994-2*) Blackwell Pubs.

Cherry-Henderson, Tammy, jt. auth. see Ellis, Cathy.

Cherry, J. H., ed. Environmental Stress in Plants. (NATO ASI Series G: Vol. 19). (Illus.). 369p. 1989. 181.95 (*0-387-18559-3*) Spr-Verlag.

Cherry, Jack D. Two-Cylinder Collector's Series, Vol. 3. (Illus.). 148p. 1995. 24.95 (*1-887446-00-1*) Two-Cylinder.

Cherry, Jack D., ed. The John Deere Model B Tractor Production Register. 615p. 1998. 44.95 (*1-887446-05-2*) Two-Cylinder.

— Production Register: The John Deere Model "G" Tractor. 190p. (Orig.). 1997. pap. 16.95 (*1-887446-03-6*) Two-Cylinder.

Cherry, Jack D., ed. see Brown, Theo.

***Cherry, James.** Loco for Lizards. LC 00-37972. (Illus.). 2000. pap. 7.95 (*0-87358-763-4*) Northland AZ.

Cherry, James D., jt. auth. see Feigin, Ralph D.

***Cherry, Janet T.** Cps Examination Review for Office Systems & Administration. 4th ed. 2000. pap., student ed., suppl. ed. 40.00 (*0-13-030030-6*) P-H.

Cherry, Jeanne. Tennis Antiques & Collectibles. (Illus.). 208p. (Orig.). 1995. pap. 39.95 (*0-9646571-0-4*) Amaryllis CA.

Cherry, Joanna. Self Initiations: A Manual for Spiritual Breakthrough. LC 98-8127. 1998. write for info. (*0-9664892-7-6*) AMI Pubg.

— Self Initiations: A Manual for Spiritual Breakthrough. 280p. 1999. pap. 14.95 (*0-9658545-3-1*, Pub. by Little Whte Buffalo) New Leaf Dist.

Cherry, Joe H. Molecular Biology of Plants: A Text Manual. LC 72-13090. (Molecular Biology Ser.). 204p. 1973. text 64.00 (*0-231-03642-6*) Col U Pr.

Cherry, Joe H., ed. Biochemical & Cellular Mechanisms of Stress Tolerance in Plants. LC 94-21155. (NATO ASI Ser.: Series H, Cell Biology: Vol. 86). 1994. 287.95 (*0-387-58215-0*) Spr-Verlag.

Cherry, John. Goldsmiths. (Medieval Craftsmen Ser.). (Illus.). 72p. 1992. pap. text 19.95 (*0-8020-7711-0*) U of Toronto Pr.

Cherry, John, et al, compiled by. Guidelines for the Assessment of General Damages in Personal Injury Cases. 4th ed. LC 99-199815. 57p. 1998. pap. 38.00 (*1-85431-756-3*) Gaunt.

Cherry, John, et al. Guidelines for the Assessment of General Damages in Personal Injury Cases. 3rd ed. 51p. 1996. pap. 36.00 (*1-85431-577-3*, Pub. by Blackstone Pr) Gaunt.

Cherry, John A., jt. auth. see Freeze, R. Allan.

Cherry, John P., ed. Food Protein Deterioration: Mechanisms & Functionality. LC 82-20739. (ACS Symposium Ser.: No. 206). 445p. 1982. lib. bdg. 54.95 (*0-8412-0751-8*) Am Chemical.

— Food Protein Deterioration: Mechanisms & Functionality. LC 82-20739. (ACS Symposium Ser.: No. 206). (Illus.). 456p. 1982. reprint ed. pap. 141.40 (*0-608-03224-7*, 206374300007) Bks Demand.

— Protein Functionality in Foods. LC 81-97. (ACS Symposium Ser.: No. 147). 1981. 49.95 (*0-8412-0605-8*) Am Chemical.

— Protein Functionality in Foods: Based on a Symposium. LC 81-97. (ACS Symposium Ser.: Vol. 147). 343p. 1981. reprint ed. pap. 106.40 (*0-608-03033-3*, 206348600007) Bks Demand.

Cherry, John P. & Barford, Robert A., eds. Methods for Protein Analysis. 272p. 1989. 75.00 (*0-935315-19-5*) Am Oil Chemists.

Cherry, John R., III. Ear, Nose & Throat Surgery. Scott, Sir Walter, ed. LC 97-167502. (Medico-Legal Practitioner Ser.). 582p. 1997. 80.00 (*1-85941-210-6*, Pub. by Cavendish Pubng) Gaunt.

Cherry, K., jt. auth. see Sinha, P. G.

Cherry, Kelly. Augusta Played. LC 97-49987. (Voices of the South Ser.). 320p. 1998. pap. 14.95 (*0-8071-2279-3*) La State U Pr.

— Benjamin John. Bixby, Robert, ed. 36p. 1993. pap. 6.00 (*1-882983-01-7*) March Street Pr.

— Death & Transfiguration. LC 97-14754. 64p. 1997. pap. 11.95 (*0-8071-2212-2*); text 19.95 (*0-8071-2211-4*) La State U Pr.

— Exiled Heart: A Meditative Autobiography. LC 90-13332. 268p. 1991. 24.95 (*0-8071-1620-3*) La State U Pr.

— Lessons from Our Living Past. (J). 1995. pap., teacher ed. 14.95 (*0-87441-086-X*) Behrman.

— Lovers & Agnostics. LC 94-68940. (Classic Contemporaries Ser.). 88p. 1995. reprint ed. pap. 12.95 (*0-88748-208-2*) Carnegie-Mellon.

— Natural Theology, Poems. LC 87-12479. 64p. (C). 1988. pap. 7.95 (*0-8071-1431-6*) La State U Pr.

— The Society of Friends: Stories. LC 99-15516. 208p. 1999. pap. 17.95 (*0-8262-1243-3*) U of Mo Pr.

— Time Out of Mind. Bixby, Robert, ed. LC 98-164989. 21p. 1993. pap. 6.00 (*1-882983-08-4*) March Street Pr.

— Writing the World. 160p. 1995. 22.50 (*0-8262-0992-0*) U of Mo Pr.

Cherry, Kenneth F. Asbestos Engineering, Management & Control. (Illus.). 280p. 1988. lib. bdg. 95.00 (*0-87371-127-0*, L127) Lewis Pubs.

Cherry, Kenneth F., jt. auth. see Null, Roberta L.

Cherry, Kittredge. Womansword: What Japanese Words Say about Women. (Illus.). 160p. 1992. pap. 8.00 (*4-7700-1655-7*) Kodansha.

Cherry, Kittredge & Sherwood, Zalmon, eds. Equal Rites: Lesbian & Gay Worship, Ceremonies & Celebrations. LC 94-3516. 192p. 1995. pap. 16.00 (*0-664-25535-3*) Westminster John Knox.

***Cherry Lane Music Company Staff.** The Best of Steve Morse: Cherry Lane Music. 1998. pap. 19.95 (*1-57560-115-X*, Pub. by Cherry Lane) H Leonard.

— Broadway Melodies of Yesterday & Today. 1998. pap. 12.95 (*1-57560-091-9*, Pub. by Cherry Lane) H Leonard.

— Civil War. 88p. 2000. pap. 17.95 (*1-57560-353-5*) Cherry Lane.

— Fundamental Bonnie Raitt. 1998. pap. 17.95 (*1-57560-117-6*, Pub. by Cherry Lane) H Leonard.

— Gold & Glory: The Road to El Dorado. 56p. 2000. pap. 14.95 (*1-57560-365-9*) Cherry Lane.

— John Denver: Best of Piano Solo. 1998. pap. 10.95 (*1-57560-104-4*, Pub. by Cherry Lane) H Leonard.

— Leslie Bricusse Book of Love Songs: Cherry Lane Music. 1998. otabind 19.95 (*1-57560-101-X*, Pub. by Cherry Lane) H Leonard.

Cherry Lane Music Company Staff. On Broadway. 1998. pap. 14.95 (*1-57560-090-0*, Pub. by Cherry Lane) H Leonard.

***Cherry Lane Music Company Staff.** Pokemon 2 B. A. Master: E-Z Play Songbook. (Pokemon Ser.). (Illus.). 64p. (J). 2000. otabind 12.95 (*1-57560-289-X*, Pub. by Cherry Lane) H Leonard.

Cherry Lane Music Staff. Barbra Streisand: Higher Ground. 1998. pap. 17.95 (*1-57560-103-6*, Pub. by Cherry Lane) H Leonard.

— Jekyll & Hyde Vocal Selections - Broadway Edition. 112p. 1997. pap. 17.95 (*1-57560-071-4*, HL02502211, Pub. by Cherry Lane) H Leonard.

— John Tesh: Grand Passion. 1998. pap. 15.95 (*1-57560-118-4*, Pub. by Cherry Lane) H Leonard.

— Magic of Music. 1999. pap. text 19.95 (*1-57560-106-0*, Pub. by Cherry Lane) H Leonard.

— Prince of Egypt. 1999. pap. text 14.95 (*1-57560-156-7*, Pub. by Cherry Lane); pap. text 16.95 (*1-57560-155-9*, Pub. by Cherry Lane) H Leonard.

***Cherry Lane Music Staff, contrib. by.** Pop/Rock Love Songs. 88p. 1999. otabind 10.95 (*1-57560-297-0*, Pub. by Cherry Lane) H Leonard.

***Cherry Lane Music Staff, ed.** Pokemon Recorder Fun. (Illus.). (J). 2000. pap. 9.95 (*1-57560-324-1*, Pub. by Cherry Lane) H Leonard.

Cherry, Lina V. Cherry: Ancestry of My Three Children, Lewis W. Cherry, George Denison Cherry, Carolyn Vandegrift Cherry McDonnell. Cox, John, Jr., ed. (Illus.). 704p. 1997. reprint ed. pap. 109.00 (*0-8328-7920-7*); reprint ed. lib. bdg. 119.00 (*0-8328-7919-3*) Higginson Bk Co.

Cherry, Lohr A., jt. ed. see Pankow, James F.

Cherry, Lynne. Archie, Follow Me. 1999. pap. 4.99 (*0-14-055492-0*) NAL.

— The Armadillo from Amarillo. LC 93-11185. (Illus.). 40p. (J). (ps-4). 1994. 16.00 (*0-15-200359-2*, Gulliver Bks) Harcourt.

— The Armadillo from Amarillo. LC 93-11185. (Illus.). 40p. (J). 1999. pap. 6.00 (*0-15-201955-3*) Harcourt.

— The Dragon & the Unicorn. LC 92-30321. (Gulliver Green Book Ser.). (Illus.). 40p. (J). (gr. 1-5). 1995. 16.00 (*0-15-224193-0*, Gulliver Bks) Harcourt.

— The Dragon & the Unicorn. 1998. 12.20 (*0-606-13347-X*, Pub. by Turtleback) Demco.

— Flute's Journey: The Life of a Wood Thrush. LC 96-17024. (Illus.). 40p. (J). 1997. 15.00 (*0-15-292853-7*) Harcourt.

— El Gran Capoquero: Un Cuento de la Selva Amazonica. Ada, Alma Flor, tr. LC 93-36401.Tr. of Great Kapok Tree. (SPA., Illus.). 40p. (J). (ps-3). 1994. pap. 6.00 (*0-15-232320-1*) Harcourt.

Cherry, Lynne. El Gran Capoquero: Un Cuento De La Selva Amazonica. Ada, Alma Flor, tr. (J). 1994. 11.20 (*0-606-06357-9*, Pub. by Turtleback) Demco.

Cherry, Lynne. The Great Kapok Tree. LC 89-2208. (Illus.). 40p. (J). (ps-3). 1998. pap. 23.95 (*0-15-201818-2*) Harcourt.

— The Great Kapok Tree. (J). 1998. pap. 7.95 (*1-57690-084-3*) Tchr Create Mat.

— The Great Kapok Tree: A Tale of the Amazon Rain Forest. LC 89-2208. (Gulliver Green Book Ser.). (Illus.). 33p. (J). (ps-3). 1990. 16.00 (*0-15-200520-X*, Gulliver Bks) Harcourt.

***Cherry, Lynne.** The Great Kapok Tree: A Tale of the Amazon Rain Forest. (Illus.). 40p. (J). (ps-3). 2000. pap. 7.00 (*0-15-202614-2*, Voyager Bks) Harcourt.

— Making a Difference in the World. (Meet the Author Ser.). (Illus.). 32p. (YA). (gr. 7-10). 2000. 14.95 (*1-57274-373-5*) R Owen Pubs.

Cherry, Lynne. A River Ran Wild: An Environmental History. (J). (gr. 4). 1995. 9.00 (*0-395-73240-9*) HM.

— A River Ran Wild: An Environmental History. LC 91-12892. (Gulliver Green Book Ser.). (Illus.). 40p. (J). (gr. 1-5). 1992. 16.00 (*0-15-200542-0*, Gulliver Bks) Harcourt.

— A River Ran Wild: An Environmental History. 1998. 14.20 (*0-606-13093-4*, Pub. by Turtleback) Demco.

— A River Ran Wild: An Environmental History. large type ed. 54p. (J). (gr. 4). 13.50 (*0-614-20617-0*, L-38211-00 APHB) Am Printing Hse.

Cherry, M. L., et al, eds. Solar Neutrinos & Neutrino Astronomy. LC 84-63143. (AIP Conference Proceeding Ser.: No. 126). 320p. 1985. lib. bdg. 44.25 (*0-88318-325-0*) Am Inst Physics.

Cherry, Marjorie. Diversification. 72p. (Orig.). 1992. pap. 10.95 (*0-9637041-0-9*) Louis IX Pr.

— Josephine. (Illus.). 96p. (Orig.). (YA). (gr. 6 up). 1995. pap. 9.50 (*0-936015-52-7*) Pocahontas Pr.

Cherry, Mark J. Persons & Their Bodies: Rights, Responsibilities, Relationships. LC 99-25030. (Philosophy & Medicine Ser.). 1999. write for info. (*0-7923-5701-9*) Kluwer Academic.

Cherry, Marlin O. & Hart, Billy J. Zoology Laboratory Workbook. 266p. (C). 1997. spiral bd. 30.95 (*0-7872-3245-9*) Kendall-Hunt.

Cherry, Marlin O. & Schumacher, Barbara J. Experiences in Botany: Laboratory Workbook. 208p. (C). 1995. spiral bd. 20.95 (*0-8403-9114-5*) Kendall-Hunt.

Cherry, N. & Ogden, T., eds. Inhaled Particles VIII: Proceedings of an International Symposium on Inhaled Particles Organised by the British Occupational Hygiene Society, August 26-30, 1996. 744p. 1997. 249.00 (*0-08-042740-5*, Pergamon Pr) Elsevier.

Cherry, Nancy. Deposition. 26p. 1995. pap. 4.00 (*1-887853-00-6*) Radiolarian.

— The Field. 39p. 1995. pap. 8.00 (*1-887853-01-4*) Radiolarian.

Cherry, Philip J., jt. auth. see Clark, Edwin H.

Cherry, R. C., ed. see American Society of Mechanical Engineers Staff.

Cherry, R. J., jt. ed. see Quinn, P. J.

Cherry, R. L. Words under Construction. LC 89-4813. 298p. (Orig.). 1989. pap. text 14.95 (*0-8165-1040-7*) U of Ariz Pr.

Cherry, R. L., ed. see National Society of Fund Raising Executives Staff.

Cherry, R. L., ed. see Saxton, Dean, et al.

Cherry, Randall, tr. see Francastel, Pierre.

Cherry, Randall, tr. see Vaneigem, Raoul.

Cherry, Raymond. Leathercrafting: Procedures & Projects. LC 79-83885. (Illus.). 1979. pap. 15.18 (*0-02-672700-5*) Glencoe.

Cherry, Reginald. The Bible Cure. LC RA776.5.C4715 1999. 176p. 1999. pap. 9.95 (*0-06-251615-9*, Pub. by Harper SF) HarpC.

— The Bible Cure. large type ed. LC 99-38231. 240p. 2000. reprint ed. pap. 14.95 (*0-8027-2750-6*) Walker & Co.

— The Bible Cure: A Renowned Physician Uncovers the Bible's Hidden Health Secrets. LC 98-15698. 240p. 1999. 16.99 (*0-88419-535-X*) Dake Pub.

— The Doctor & the Word. 1998. pap. 11.99 (*0-88419-513-9*) Creation House.

Cherry, Reginald. Healing Prayer. Date not set. 17.00 (*0-06-251618-3*) HarpC.

Cherry, Reginald. Healing Prayer: God's Divine Intervention in Medicine, Faith, & Prayer. LC 99-39351. 187p. 1999. 19.99 (*0-7852-6940-1*) Nelson.

***Cherry, Reginald.** Healing Prayer: God's Divine Intervention in Medicine, Faith & Prayer. 208p. 2000. pap. 12.99 (*0-7852-6751-4*) Nelson.

***Cherry, Reginald B.** God's Pathway to Healing: Herbs That Heal. (Illus.). 1999. pap. 6.99 (*1-57778-135-X*) Albury Pub.

Cherry, Reginald B. God's Pathway to Healing on Menopause. (God's Pathway to Healing Ser.: Vol. 1). 120p. 1999. pap. text 5.99 (*1-57778-118-X*) Albury Pub.

***Cherry, Reginald B.** Healing Prayer. (EZ Lesson Plan Ser.). 1999. pap., student ed. 7.99 (*0-7852-9667-0*) Tommy Nelson.

— El Remedio Biblico. (SPA., Illus.). 1998. pap. 9.99 (*0-88419-556-2*) Casa Creacion.

Cherry, Richard A. Intermediate Emergency Care Exam Review. LC 95-33565. 96p. 1995. pap. text 31.20 (*0-8359-4978-8*) P-H.

— Intermediate Emergency Care Exam Review. LC 95-33565. 1996. write for info. (*0-614-09445-3*) P-H.

Cherry, Richard J., ed. New Techniques of Optical Microscopy & Microspectroscopy. 1991. 105.00 (*0-8493-7117-1*, QH) CRC Pr.

***Cherry, Robert & Rodgers, William, eds.** Tight-Labor Markets & Black Employment. 320p. 2000. 34.95 (*0-87154-197-1*) Russell Sage.

Cherry, Robert D. Macroeconomics. LC 79-3130. (Economics Ser.). 1980. text. write for info. (*0-201-00911-0*) Addison-Wesley.

Cherry, Sheldon H. Understanding Pregnancy & Childbirth. LC 72-89700. 1973. 8.95 (*0-672-51614-4*, Bobbs) Macmillan.

— Understanding Pregnancy & Childbirth. rev. ed. LC 82-17800. 272p. 1983. write for info. (*0-672-52758-8*) Macmillan.

— Understanding Pregnancy & Childbirth. 3rd rev. ed. (Illus.). 288p. 1992. pap. 11.95 (*0-02-030981-3*) Macmillan.

Cherry, Sheldon H. & Runowicz, Carolyn. The Menopause Book: A Guide to Health & Well-Being for Women After Forty. (Illus.). 320p. 1994. 20.00 (*0-02-524758-1*) Macmillan.

Cherry, Sheldon H. & Runowicz, Carolyn D. The Menopause Book: A Guide to Health & Well-Being for Women. LC 95-2054. 272p. 1995. 11.95 (*0-02-860416-4*) Macmillan.

***Cherry, Sheldon H. & Runowicz, Carolyn D.** The Menopause Book: A Guide to Health & Well-Being for Women. (Illus.). 252p. 2000. reprint ed. pap. text 12.00 (*0-7881-9012-1*) DIANE Pub.

Cherry, Sheldon H., et al. Complications of Pregnancy: Medical, Surgical, Gynecologic, Psychosocial & Perinatal. 4th ed. (Illus.). 1352p. 1991. 155.00 (*0-683-01672-5*) Lppncott W & W.

Cherry, Steven. Medical Services & the Hospital in Britain, 1860-1939. (New Studies in Economic & Social History: No. 28). 100p. (C). 1996. text 34.95 (*0-521-57126-X*) Cambridge U Pr.

— Medical Services & the Hospital in Britain, 1860-1939. (New Studies in Economic & Social History: No. 28). 200p. (C). 1996. pap. text 10.95 (*0-521-57784-5*) Cambridge U Pr.

Cherry, Tammy, jt. auth. see Ellis, Cathy.

Cherry, Veronica. By Hook or by Crook: A Tale of Adventure Surviving Child Abuse. 152p. 1998. pap. 13.00 (*0-8059-4451-6*) Dorrance.

Cherry, W., jt. auth. see Lang, Serge A.

Cherry, Winky. Mi Primer Libro de Costura: Hand Sewing - Level 1. Alas, Rosy A., tr. (My First Sewing Book Ser.). (SPA., Illus.). 40p. (J). (gr. k-6). 1994. pap. 12.95 (*0-935278-37-0*) Palmer-Pletsch.

— My First Doll Book Level 3: Hand Sewing. Palmer, Pati & Wisner, Linda, eds. LC 94-66067. (My First Sewing Book Ser.). (Illus.). 40p. (Orig.). (J). (gr. k-5). 1994. pap. 12.95 (*0-935278-36-2*) Palmer-Pletsch.

— My First Embroidery Book Level 2: A Name Sampler. Palmer, Pati, ed. (My First Sewing Book Ser.). (Illus.). 40p. (J). (ps-6). 1995. pap. 12.95 (*0-935278-31-1*) Palmer-Pletsch.

— My First Machine Sewing Book Level 4: Straight Stitching. Black, Lynette R. et al, eds. (My First Sewing Book Ser.). (Illus.). 40p. (Orig.). (J). (gr. k-6). 1994. pap. 12.95 (*0-935278-40-0*) Palmer-Pletsch.

— My First Patchwork Book: Hand & Machine Sewing. (My First Sewing Book Ser.). (Illus.). 40p. (J). (gr. 1-6). 1997. pap. 12.95 (*0-935278-48-6*) Palmer-Pletsch.

— My First Quilt Book: Machine Sewing. (My First Sewing Book Ser.). (Illus.). 40p. (J). (gr. k-6). 1997. pap. 12.95 (*0-935278-49-4*) Palmer-Pletsch.

— My First Sewing Book Level 1: Hand Sewing. (My First Sewing Book Ser.). Orig. Title: Is That Sew?. (Illus.). 40p. (J). (ps-6). 1994. pap. 12.95 (*0-935278-29-X*) Palmer-Pletsch.

— Teach Children to Sew: Video & Manual. (Illus.). 112p. 1995. pap. 29.95 incl. VHS (*0-935278-33-8*) Palmer-Pletsch.

— The Winky Cherry System of Teaching Young Children to Sew: How to Teach - A Script for Classes - How to Start a Teaching Business. Palmer, Pati, ed. & intro. by. (My First Sewing Book Ser.). (Illus.). 112p. (Orig.). 1994. pap. 24.95 (*0-935278-34-6*) Palmer-Pletsch.

***Cherryh, C. J.** Chanur Saga. 672p. 2000. mass mkt. 7.99 (*0-88677-930-8*, Pub. by DAW Bks) Penguin Putnam.

Cherryh, C. J. Chanur's Homecoming. (Chanur Ser.: Bk. 4). 320p. 1986. 18.00 (*0-932096-42-5*) Phantasia Pr.

— Chanur's Legacy. (Chanur Ser.: Bk. 5). 1993. mass mkt. 6.99 (*0-88677-559-0*, Pub. by DAW Bks) Penguin Putnam.

— Chanur's Venture. (Chanur Ser.: Bk. 2). 320p. 1987. pap. 3.95 (*0-88677-293-1*, Pub. by DAW Bks) Penguin Putnam.

— Chanur's Venture. (Chanur Ser.: Bk. 2). 1984. 17.00 (*0-932096-31-X*) Phantasia Pr.

— Cloud's Rider. 464p. 1997. mass mkt. 5.99 (*0-446-60424-0*, Pub. by Warner Bks); mass mkt. 161.73 (*0-446-16383-X*) Warner Bks.

— Cuckoo's Egg. 320p. 1985. mass mkt. 5.99 (*0-88677-371-7*, Pub. by DAW Bks) Penguin Putnam.

— Cuckoo's Egg. 1985. 17.00 (*0-932096-34-4*) Phantasia Pr.

Cherryh, C. J. Cyteen. 696p. 1995. reprint ed. mass mkt. 14.99 (*0-446-67127-4*, Pub. by Warner Bks) Little.

An Asterisk (*) at the beginning of an entry indicates that the title is appearing for the first time.

Cherryh, C. J. Cyteen Pt. 1: The Betrayal. 368p. 1989. mass mkt. 5.50 (*0-445-20452-4*, Pub. by Warner Bks) Little.

***Cherryh, C. J.** Devil to the Belt. 2000. reprint ed. pap. 13.95 (*0-446-67653-5*, Aspect) Warner Bks.

Cherryh, C. J. Downbelow Station. 432p. 1981. mass mkt. 6.99 (*0-88677-431-4*, Pub. by DAW Bks) Penguin Putnam.

— The Dreaming Tree: The Dreamstone - The Tree of Swords & Jewels. 464p. 1997. mass mkt. 6.99 (*0-88677-782-8*, Pub. by DAW Bks) Penguin Putnam.

— Exile's Gate. (Morgaine Ser.: Bk. 4). 416p. 1988. mass mkt. 5.50 (*0-88677-254-0*, Pub. by DAW Bks) Penguin Putnam.

— The Faded Sun Pt. 1: Kesrith. 256p. 1978. mass mkt. 4.50 (*0-88677-449-7*, Pub. by DAW Bks) Penguin Putnam.

— The Faded Sun Pt. 2: Shon'jir. 256p. 1979. mass mkt. 4.50 (*0-88677-448-9*, Pub. by DAW Bks) Penguin Putnam.

— The Faded Sun Pt. 3: Kutath. 256p. (Orig.). 1980. mass mkt. 4.50 (*0-88677-133-1*, Pub. by DAW Bks) Penguin Putnam.

— The Faded Sun Trilogy. 784p. 1999. mass mkt. 6.99 (*0-88677-869-7*, Pub. by DAW Bks) Penguin Putnam.

— Finity's End. 576p. 1998. mass mkt. 6.50 (*0-446-60560-3*, Pub. by Warner Bks) Little.

— Fires of Azeroth. (Morgaine Ser.: Bk. 3). 240p. 1979. pap. 4.50 (*0-88677-323-7*, Pub. by DAW Bks) Penguin Putnam.

— Foreigner. (Foreigner Trilogy: Bk. 1). 432p. 1994. mass mkt. 6.99 (*0-88677-637-6*, Pub. by DAW Bks) Penguin Putnam.

— Fortress in the Eye of Time. 1995. 22.00 (*0-06-105195-0*) HarpC.

— Fortress in the Eye of Time. 784p. 1996. mass mkt. 6.99 (*0-06-105689-8*, HarperPrism) HarpC.

***Cherryh, C. J.** Fortress of Dragons. LC 00-25811. 432p. 2000. 25.00 (*0-06-105055-5*) Morrow Avon.

Cherryh, C. J. Fortress of Eagles. (Illus.). 496p. 1999. mass mkt. 5.99 (*0-06-105710-X*) HarpC.

— Fortress of Owls. LC 98-39207. 416p. 1999. 24.00 (*0-06-105054-7*, HarperPrism) HarpC.

***Cherryh, C. J.** Fortress of Owls. 560p. 2000. mass mkt. 6.99 (*0-06-102008-7*, HarperPrism) HarpC.

Cherryh, C. J. Forty Thousand in Gehenna. 1984. mass mkt. 6.99 (*0-88677-429-2*, Pub. by DAW Bks) Penguin Putnam.

— Forty Thousand in Gehenna. 1983. 17.00 (*0-685-14033-4*) Phantasia Pr.

— Gate of Ivrel. (Morgaine Ser.: Bk. 1). 192p. 1976. pap. 4.50 (*0-88677-321-0*, UE2321, Pub. by DAW Bks) Penguin Putnam.

Cherryh, C. J. The Hanan Rebellion. 7.99 (*0-88677-902-2*, Pub. by DAW Bks) Penguin Putnam.

Cherryh, C. J. Heavy Time. 336p. 1992. reprint ed. mass mkt. 4.99 (*0-446-36223-9*, Pub. by Warner Bks) Little.

— Hellburner. 400p. 1993. reprint ed. mass mkt. 5.50 (*0-446-36451-7*, Pub. by Warner Bks) Little.

— Hunter of Worlds. 256p. 1987. pap. 5.99 (*0-88677-217-6*, Pub. by DAW Bks) Penguin Putnam.

— Inheritor. (Foreigner Trilogy: Bk. 3). 432p. 1996. 21.95 (*0-88677-689-9*, Pub. by DAW Bks) Penguin Putnam.

— Inheritor. (Foreigner Trilogy: Bk. 3). 512p. 1997. pap. 6.99 (*0-88677-728-3*, Pub. by DAW Bks) Penguin Putnam.

— Invader. (Foreigner Trilogy: Bk. 2). 464p. 1996. mass mkt. 6.99 (*0-88677-687-2*, Pub. by DAW Bks) Penguin Putnam.

— The Kif Strike Back. (Chanur Ser.: Bk. 3). 304p. 1991. mass mkt. 5.99 (*0-88677-184-6*, Pub. by DAW Bks) Penguin Putnam.

— The Kif Strike Back. (Chanur Ser.: Bk. 3). 1985. 17.00 (*0-932096-35-2*) Phantasia Pr.

— Lois & Clark: A Superman Novel. 288p. 1997. per. 12.00 (*0-7615-1169-5*) Prima Pub.

— Merchanter's Luck. 208p. 1982. pap. 5.99 (*0-88677-139-0*, Pub. by DAW Bks) Penguin Putnam.

***Cherryh, C. J.** The Morgaine Saga: Gate of Ivrel, Well of Shiuan, Fires of Azeroth. (Morgaine Ser.). 2000. mass mkt. 7.99 (*0-88677-877-8*, Pub. by DAW Bks) Penguin Putnam.

Cherryh, C. J. The Paladin. 400p. (Orig.). 1988. mass mkt. 4.99 (*0-671-65417-9*) Baen Bks.

— Port Eternity. 192p. 1987. pap. 5.99 (*0-88677-206-0*, Pub. by DAW Bks) Penguin Putnam.

— Precursor. 416p. 1999. 23.95 (*0-88677-836-0*, Pub. by DAW Bks) Penguin Putnam.

***Cherryh, C. J.** Precursor. 2000. mass mkt. 6.99 (*0-88677-910-3*, Pub. by DAW Bks) Penguin Putnam.

Cherryh, C. J. The Pride of Chanur. (Chanur Ser.: Bk. 1). 224p. 1982. mass mkt. 5.99 (*0-88677-292-3*, Pub. by DAW Bks) Penguin Putnam.

— The Pride of Chanur. rev. ed. (Chanur Ser.: Bk. 1). 225p. 1987. 17.00 (*0-932096-45-X*) Phantasia Pr.

— Rider at the Gate. 496p. 1996. mass mkt. 6.50 (*0-446-60345-7*, Pub. by Warner Bks) Little.

— Rusalka. 352p. 1990. mass mkt. 5.99 (*0-345-36934-3*, Del Rey) Ballantine Pub Grp.

— Serpent's Reach. 288p. 1980. mass mkt. 5.99 (*0-88677-088-2*, Pub. by DAW Bks) Penguin Putnam.

— Tripoint. 400p. 1995. reprint ed. mass mkt. 5.99 (*0-446-60202-7*, Pub. by Warner Bks) Little.

— Visible Light. 230p. 1986. 17.00 (*0-932096-40-9*) Phantasia Pr.

***Cherryh, C. J.** Voyager in Night. large type ed. LC 00-36983. 245p. 2000. pap. 25.95 (*0-7838-9068-0*, G K Hall & Co) Mac Lib Ref.

Cherryh, C. J. Well of Shiuan. (Morgaine Ser.: Bk. 2). 256p. 1978. mass mkt. 4.50 (*0-88677-322-9*, Pub. by DAW Bks) Penguin Putnam.

Cherryh, C. J. & Fish, Leslie. A Dirge for Sabis. (Sword of Knowledge Ser.: Bk. I). 400p. 1991. per. 4.95 (*0-671-72067-8*) Baen Bks.

Cherryh, C. J. & Lackey, Mercedes. Reap the Whirlwind. (Sword of Knowledge Ser.: Bk. III). 288p. (Orig.). 1989. per. 4.99 (*0-671-69846-X*) Baen Bks.

Cherryh, C. J., et al. The Sword of Knowledge: A Dirge for Sabis - Wizard Spawn - Reap the Whirlwind. LC 94-24611. (Sword of Knowledge Ser.). 816p. 1995. pap. 15.00 (*0-671-87645-7*) Baen Bks.

Cherryholmes, Cleo H. Power & Criticism: Poststructural Investigations in Education. (Advances in Contemporary Educational Thought Ser.). 240p. 1988. pap. 18.95 (*0-8077-3107-2*) Tchrs Coll.

— Reading Pragmatism. LC 99-12634. 168p. 1999. pap. 24.95 (*0-8077-3846-8*); text 52.00 (*0-8077-3847-6*) Tchrs Coll.

— Understanding the United States. (McGraw-Hill Social Studies). (Illus.). (gr. 5). 1979. text 26.76 (*0-07-011985-6*) McGraw.

Cherryholmes, Cleo H. & Manson, G. Investigating Societies. (Illus.). (J). (gr. 6). 1979. text 28.04 (*0-07-011986-4*) McGraw.

— Studying Cultures. (Illus.). (J). (gr. 4). 1979. text 24.64 (*0-07-011984-8*) McGraw.

Cherryholmes, J. Edward & Demouchette, Roy. The Meanest Man on Death Row: A Life of Crime - From Black Ghetto to Drugs to Murder to Execution. 256p. Date not set. pap. 19.95 (*0-89896-322-2*) Larksdale.

Cherryholmes, J. Edward, jt. auth. see Brennan, Howard.

Chershnia, Valery. Svoe Vremia - One's Own Time. LC 96-8479. (RUS.). 106p. (Orig.). 1996. pap. 9.00 (*1-55779-079-5*) Hermitage Pubs.

Cherspanov, Sergey. The International Chicken. 100p. pap. 8.95 (*1-883274-00-1*) Watt Pub.

Chertkoff, Jerome & Kushigian, Russell H. Don't Panic: The Psychology of Emergency Egress & Ingress. LC 98-47812. 160p. 1999. 55.00 (*0-275-96268-7*, Praeger Pubs) Greenwood.

Chertoff, Mordecai S., jt. ed. see Alexander, Yona.

Chertoff, Mordecai S., jt. ed. see Curtis, Michael.

Chertoff, Mordecai S., tr. see Aleichem, Sholem.

Chertoff, Mordechai, ed. Zionism: A Basic Reader. 1976. 1.00 (*0-685-82601-5*) Herzl Pr.

Chertok, et al. Teaching American History: With Art Master. (Illus.). 80p. 1998. pap. 18.95 (*0-590-96402-X*, 893238Q) Scholastic Inc.

Chertok, Bobbi, et al. Meet the Masterpieces: Learning about Ancient Civilizations Through Art. 1994. pap. 18.95 (*0-590-49505-4*) Scholastic Inc.

— Month-by-Month Masterpieces: Exploration of 10 Great Works with Step-by-Step Art Projects. 1996. pap. text 18.95 (*0-590-25101-5*) Scholastic Inc.

Chertok, Haim. Israeli Preoccupations: Dualities of a Confessional Citizen. LC 93-45638. ix, 210p. 1994. 25.00 (*0-8232-1546-6*); pap. 16.95 (*0-8232-1547-4*) Fordham.

— Stealing Home: Israel Bound & Rebound. LC 87-80546. (Illus.). 295p. 1988. pap. 15.95 (*0-8232-1306-4*) Fordham.

— Stealing Home: Israel Bound & Rebound. LC 87-80546. (Illus.). 295p. (C). 1988. 22.50 (*0-8232-1188-6*) Fordham.

— We Are All Close: Conversations with Israel Writers. LC 89-80058. (Illus.). 265p. 1989. pap. 19.95 (*0-8232-1223-8*) Fordham.

Chertok, Jeffers. Social Interest & Categorical Structure: Conceptions of History & Social Change. LC 89-13612. (American University Studies: Anthropology & Science: Ser. XI, Vol. 44). (Illus.). XI, 185p. (C). 1990. text 43.95 (*0-8204-1128-0*) P Lang Pubng.

Chertok, Leon & Stengers, Isabelle. A Critique of Psychoanalytic Reason: Hypnosis as a Scientific Problem from Lavoisier to Lacan. Evans, Martha N., tr. from FRE. LC 91-22388. 356p. (C). 1992. 42.50 (*0-8047-1950-0*) Stanford U Pr.

Chertok, Leon, ed. see International Congress of Psychosomatic Obstetrics.

Chertov, O. G., et al. Modern Approaches in Forest Ecosystem Modelling. LC 99-12155. (European Forest Institute Research Report Ser.). 130p. 1999. 59.00 (*90-04-11415-7*) Brill Academic Pubs.

Chertow, Doris S., ed. Agenda for Comparative Studies in Adult Education. 1972. 3.00 (*0-87060-052-4*, OCP 29) Syracuse U Cont Ed.

Chertow, Doris S., jt. auth. see Whipple, J.

Chertow, Doris S., jt. ed. see Reagen, Michael V.

Chertow, Ken. Wrestling: A Commitment to Excellence. 156p. 1994. pap. text 9.95 (*0-944183-15-8*) PRC Pub.

Chertow, Marian. Thinking Ecologically: An Agenda for the Next Generation Project. LC 97-14996. 256p. 1998. pap. 16.00 (*0-300-07303-8*) Yale U Pr.

Chertow, Marian R. Thinking Ecologically: An Agenda for the Next Generation Project. LC 97-14996. 256p. 1998. 35.00 (*0-300-07301-1*) Yale U Pr.

Cheru, Fantu. Silent Revolution in Africa: Debt, Development & Democracy. LC 89-22579. 160p. (C). 1990. pap. 19.95 (*0-86232-891-8*, Pub. by St Martin) St Martin.

— Silent Revolution in Africa: Debt, Development & Democracy. LC 89-22579. 160p. (C). 1989. text 49.95 (*0-86232-890-X*, Pub. by Zed Books) St Martin.

Cherub. Kids Worship Adventure Songbook. 1997. pap. 4.95 (*3-512-60057-3*) Vineyard Music.

Cherubim, Archimandrite & Sederholm, Clement. Elder Anthony of Optina. LC 94-65658. (Optima Elder Ser.: Vol. 2). (Illus.). 269p. 1994. pap. 10.00 (*0-938635-51-4*) St Herman Pr.

Cherubim, Dieter, ed. Sprachwandel: Reader Zur diachronischen Sprachwissenschaft. (Grundlagen der Kommunikation Ser.). x, 362p. (C). 1975. pap. 27.70 (*3-11-004330-0*) De Gruyter.

Cherubim, Dieter, et al, eds. Sprache und Burgerliche Lebenswelt: Beitrage des 2. Bad Homburger Kolloquiums zur Deutschen und Europaischen Sprachgeschichte im 19. Jahrhundert. 496p. 1998. 175.00 (*3-11-014495-6*) De Gruyter.

Cherubini, Isabella, tr. see Roncaglia, Alessandro.

***Cherubini, Laura.** Vettor Pisani: Virginia Art Theatrum. 1999. pap. text 32.00 (*88-8158-209-0*) Charta

Cherubini, R. & Dalpiaz, P. Problems of Fundamental Modern Physics. Minetti, B., ed. 608p. (C). 1990. text 161.00 (*981-02-0085-4*) World Scientific Pub.

Cherubini, R., et al. Problems of Fundamental Modern Physics II: Proceedings of the 5th Winter School on Hadronic Physics, Folgaria, Italy, February 5-10, 1990. 544p. (C). 1991. text 137.00 (*981-02-0295-4*) World Scientific Pub.

Cherukuri, Rao, jt. auth. see Onvural, Raid O.

Cherulnik, Paul D. Applications of Environment-Behavior Research: Case Studies & Analysis. (Cambridge Series in Envirinment & Behavior: No. 9). 358p. (C). 1993. text 64.95 (*0-521-33189-7*) Cambridge U Pr.

— Applications of Environment-Behavior Research: Case Studies & Analysis. LC 93-2760. (Cambridge Series in Environment & Behavior: No. 9). (Illus.). 358p. (C). 1993. pap. text 25.95 (*0-521-33770-4*) Cambridge U Pr.

Chervel, ed. see Saint-Simon.

***Chervenak, F. A. & Kurjak, A., eds.** Fetal Medicine: The Clinical Care of the Fetus As a Patient. LC 99-26995. (Illus.). 402p. 1999. 85.00 (*1-85070-072-9*) Prthnon Pub.

Chervenak, Frank A., jt. auth. see Kurjak, A.

Chervenak, Frank A., et al, eds. Ultrasound & the Fetal Brain. LC 95-23988. (Progress in Obstetric & Gynecological Sonography Ser.). (Illus.). 254p. 1995. text 78.00 (*1-85070-612-3*) Prthnon Pub.

— Ultrasound in Obstetrics & Gynecology, Vol. 2. (Illus.). 1919p. 1993. text 241.00 (*0-316-13865-7*) Lppncott W & W.

Chervenak, Frank A. & Kurjak, Asim, eds. Current Perspectives on the Fetus As a Patient. LC 96-17371. (Illus.). 666p. 1996. 128.00 (*1-85070-742-1*) Prthnon Pub.

Chervenak, Frank A., et al. Anomalies of the Fetal Head, Neck & Neural Axis: Ultrasound Diagnosis & Management. (Illus.). 192p. 1988. text 98.00 (*0-7216-1957-6*, W B Saunders Co) Harcrt Hlth Sci Grp.

Chervenak, Frank A., jt. auth. see McCullough, Laurence B.

Chervenak, Frank A., jt. ed. see Kurjak, Asim.

Chervenak, Frank A., jt. ed. see Levi, Salvator.

Chervin, Michael, jt. auth. see Chene, Adele.

Chervin, Rhonda D. En Route to Eternity. 160p. 1995. pap. 11.95 (*0-939409-02-X*) Miriam Press.

— Feminine, Free & Faithful. rev. ed. 160p. 1995. pap. 9.95 (*0-940535-83-1*, UP184) Franciscan U Pr.

— Hungry for Heaven: The Story of Charles Rich, Contemplative. LC 93-373. 85p. 1993. pap. 9.95 (*0-932506-98-4*) St Bedes Pubns.

— Living in Love: About Christian Ethics. LC 88-18485. 136p. (C). 1989. pap. 6.95 (*0-8198-4452-7*) Pauline Bks.

— Treasury of Women Saints. 400p. (Orig.). 1991. pap. 12.99 (*0-89283-707-1*, Charis) Servant.

— Victory over Death. LC 85-8213. 63p. (Orig.). 1985. pap. 7.95 (*0-932506-43-7*) St Bedes Pubns.

Chervin, Rhonda D., ed. The Holy Dybbuk: Letters of Charles Rich, Contemplative 1960-1982. LC 87-16663. 143p. (Orig.). 1988. pap. 11.95 (*0-932506-50-X*) St Bedes Pubns.

— Letters for Eternity: Collected from the Correspondence of Charles Rich with Ronda Chervin 1985-1993. LC 94-14778. 112p. (Orig.). 1994. pap., pap. text 11.95 (*1-879007-11-8*) St Bedes Pubns.

Chervin, Rhonda D. & Janis, Lois A. Voyage to Insight. 116p. (C). 1994. pap., teacher ed. 13.95 (*1-887582-02-9*) Chiaro Oscuro Pr.

Chervin, Rhonda D. & Neill, Mary. Great Saints, Great Friends. LC 89-28931. 154p. (Orig.). 1990. pap. 7.95 (*0-8189-0574-3*) Alba.

Chervin, Rhonda D. & Spotts, Eileen. Becoming a Woman of God: Your Fifteen Week Guided Journal. 125p. 1995. pap. 11.45 (*1-887582-04-5*) Chiaro Oscuro Pr.

Chervin, Ronda. Holding Hands with God. LC 97-67056. 1997. pap. text 7.95 (*0-87973-577-5*) Our Sunday Visitor.

Chervin, Ronda. Spiritual Friendship: Darkness & Light. LC 92-9890. 88p. (Orig.). 1992. pap. 4.95 (*0-8198-6892-2*) Pauline Bks.

Chervin, Ronda. Widow's Walk: Encouragement, Comfort & Wisdom from the Widow-Saints. LC 98-6585. 160p. 1998. pap. 9.95 (*0-87973-951-7*) Our Sunday Visitor.

Chervin, Ronda, ed. Bread from Heaven. (Illus.). xii, 195p. 1994. reprint ed. pap. 10.00 (*1-892875-80-2*, 3101, Remnant Israel) New Hope Publicatns.

Chervin, Stan, ed. Short Pieces from the New Dramatists. 92p. (Orig.). 1985. pap. 6.95 (*0-88145-029-4*) Broadway Play.

Chervokas, John V. Pinstripe Prayers: Or How to Talk to God While Pursuing Mammon. 48p. (Orig.). 1984. 2.95 (*0-86683-874-0*, 7457) Harper SF.

Chervonenkis, O., jt. auth. see Lyusternik, L.

Chervyakov, A. Ostankino Palace Museum: A Guide. (Illus.). 144p. (C). 1985. 40.00 (*0-7855-5191-3*, Pub. by Collets) St Mut.

Cherwitz, Richard A., ed. Rhetoric & Philosophy. 336p. (C). 1990. text 49.95 (*0-8058-0413-7*) L Erlbaum Assocs.

Cheryan, Munir. Ultrafiltration & Microfiltration Handbook. LC 97-62251. 545p. 1997. 110.95 (*1-56676-598-6*) Technomic.

— Ultrafiltration Handbook. LC 86-50330. 369p. 1986. 74.95 (*0-87762-456-9*) Technomic.

Chery. The Menopause Book. 320p. 1993. 20.00 (*0-685-70477-7*) Macmillan.

Chesal, Robert E., tr. see De Costa, Denise.

Chesanow, Neil. Where Do I Live? LC 95-8463. (Illus.). 48p. (J). (gr. k-4). 1995. pap. 5.95 (*0-8120-9241-4*) Barron.

— Where Do I Live? (J). 1995. 11.15 (*0-606-13910-9*, Pub. by Turtleback) Demco.

Chesapeake Research Consortium Staff, ed. Background Papers on Chesapeake Bay in Research & Related Matters. 1982. pap. 2.00 (*0-943676-14-2*) MD Sea Grant Col.

Chesbro. Chesbro, Vol. 2. 1996. 20.00 (*1-883402-68-9*) S&S Trade.

***Chesbro, E. Michael.** Security Officer's Resource Guide. 2nd rev. ed. 2000. 18.00 (*1-928987-61-3*) Intl Fdtn Protect.

Chesbro, George C. Bleeding In the Eye of a Brainstorm: A Mongo Mystery. 224p. 1995. 21.00 (*1-883402-67-0*) S&S Trade.

— Bleeding In the Eye of a Brainstorm: A Mongo Mystery. LC 95-17732. 224p. 1995. 21.00 (*0-684-81495-1*) Simon & Schuster.

— Bone. 1990. mass mkt. 4.95 (*0-445-40876-6*, Pub. by Warner Bks) Little.

Chesbro, George C. Chant. 1986. pap. write for info. (*1-930253-05-2*) Apache Beach.

— Chant: Code of Blood. 1987. pap. write for info. (*1-930253-04-4*) Apache Beach.

— Chant: Silent Killer. 1986. pap. write for info. (*1-930253-06-0*) Apache Beach.

Chesbro, George C. The Fear in Yesterday's Rings. 224p. 1992. mass mkt. 4.99 (*0-446-40102-1*, Pub. by Warner Bks) Little.

— In the House of Secret Enemies. 240p. 1992. mass mkt. 4.99 (*0-446-40043-2*, Pub. by Warner Bks) Little.

— An Incident at Bloodtide. LC 92-50270. 208p. 1993. 18.95 (*0-89296-464-2*) Mysterious Pr.

— An Incident at Bloodtide. 256p. 1994. mass mkt. 5.50 (*0-446-40054-8*, Pub. by Warner Bks) Little.

— Jungle of Steel & Stone. 208p. 1987. 16.45 (*0-89296-204-6*, Pub. by Mysterious Pr) Little.

— Jungle of Steel & Stone. 1988. mass mkt. 3.95 (*0-445-40522-8*, Pub. by Warner Bks) Little.

Chesbro, George C. King's Gambit. 1976. pap. write for info. (*1-930253-07-9*) Apache Beach.

Chesbro, George C. Second Horseman Out of Eden. 256p. 1990. reprint ed. mass mkt. 4.95 (*0-445-40862-6*, Pub. by Warner Bks) Little.

***Chesbro, George C.** Turn Loose the Dragons. 1999. pap. write for info. (*1-930253-02-8*) Apache Beach.

Chesbro, Michael. Security Officers Resource Guide. 90p. 1995. spiral bd. 15.00 (*1-928987-60-5*) Intl Fdtn Protect.

***Chesbro, Michael E.** Privacy for Sale: How Big Brother & Others Are Selling Your Private Secrets for Profit. 184p. 1999. pap. 20.00 (*1-58160-033-X*) Paladin Pr.

Chescheir, Martha W., jt. auth. see Comarow, Donna D.

Chesebro, Doreen, jt. auth. see Badasch, Shirley A.

Chesebro, Doreen S., jt. auth. see Badasch.

Chesebro, Doreen S., jt. auth. see Badasch, Shirley A.

Chesebro, James W., ed. Extensions of the Burkeian System. LC 92-31644. (Studies in Rhetoric & Communication). 376p. (C). 1993. text 39.95 (*0-8173-0674-9*) U of Ala Pr.

Chesebro, James W. & Bertelsen, Dale A. Analyzing Media: Communication Technologies as Symbolic & Cognitive Systems. LC 96-29009. (Revisioning Rhetoric Ser.). 228p. 1996. lib. bdg. 40.00 (*1-57230-154-6*) Guilford Pubns.

— Analyzing Media: Communication Technologies as Symbolic & Cognitive Systems. (Studies in Rhetoric). 228p. 1998. pap. text 22.00 (*1-57230-419-7*) Guilford Pubns.

Chesebro, James W. & Bonsall, Donald G. Computer-Mediated Communication: Human Relationships in a Computerized World. LC 89-32991. (Studies in Rhetoric & Communication). 292p. 1989. pap. 90.60 (*0-608-05124-1*, 206568300005) Bks Demand.

Chesebrough, David B. Clergy Dissent in the Old South, 1830-1865. LC 96-7669. 176p. (C). 1996. 29.95 (*0-8093-2080-0*) S Ill U Pr.

— Frederick Douglass: Oratory from Slavery, 26. LC 97-33138. (Great American Orators Ser.: Vol. 26). 200p. 1998. lib. bdg. 59.95 (*0-313-30287-1*, Greenwood Pr) Greenwood.

— No Sorrow Like Our Sorrow: Northern Protestant Ministers & the Assassination of Lincoln. LC 93-31508. (Illus.). 224p. 1994. 24.00 (*0-87338-491-1*) Kent St U Pr.

***Chesebrough, David B.** Phillips Brooks: Pulpit Eloquence. 2000. lib. bdg. write for info. (*0-313-31374-1*) Greenwood.

— Theodore Parker: Orator of Superior Ideas, 29. LC 98-47760. (Great American Orators Ser.: Vol. 29). 168p. 1999. lib. bdg. 65.00 (*0-313-30873-X*) Greenwood.

Chesely, Mary. Miss Purdy's Problem. Weinberger, Jane, ed. LC 93-61195. (Illus.). 48p. (J). (ps-4). 1994. pap. 7.95 (*0-932433-75-8*) Windswept Hse.

Chesham, Henry. The Angry Atoll. large type ed. (Dales Large Print Ser.). 276p. 1996. pap. 18.99 (*1-85389-675-6*, Dales) Ulverscroft.

— Saboteurs from the Sea. large type ed. (Linford Mystery Library). 368p. 1996. pap. 16.99 (*0-7089-7931-9*) Ulverscroft.

C

An Asterisk (*) at the beginning of an entry indicates that the title is appearing for the first time.

— A Tide of Chariots. large type ed. (Linford Mystery Library). 384p. 1996. pap. 16.99 (0-7089-7934-3) Ulverscroft.

— Torpedo Tide. large type ed. (Dales Large Print Ser.). 304p. 1996. pap. 18.99 (1-85389-676-4, Dales) Ulverscroft.

Chesham, Sallie. The Brengle Treasury: A Samuel Logran Brengle Treasury. 1988. 12.95 (0-86544-049-2) Salv Army Suppl South.

— Catalogue Roses. 150p. 1987. 7.95 (0-86544-042-5) Salv Army Suppl South.

— Wind Chimes. 1983. 7.95 (0-86544-021-2) Salv Army Suppl South.

Chesher, Andrew & Harrison, Robert. Vehicle Operating Costs Vol. 4: Evidence from Developing Countries. LC 87-22178. (Highway Design & Maintenance Standards Ser.). 352p. (Orig.). 1988. pap. text 27.95 (0-8018-3588-7, 43588) Johns Hopkins.

Chesher, James E. & Machan, Tibor R. The Business of Commerce: Examining an Honorable Profession. LC 98-47216. (Publication Ser.: Vol. 454). 310p. 1999. pap. 19.95 (0-8179-9622-2) Hoover Inst Pr.

Chesher, Michael & Kaura, R. Electronic Commerce & Business Communications. LC 98-11200. (Practitioner Ser.). (Illus.). xii, 276p. 1998. pap. 59.95 (3-540-19930-6) Spr-Verlag.

Chesher, R. Donna. The End: Closing Lines of over 3,000 Theatrically-Released American Films. LC 91-43699. 240p. 1992. lib. bdg. 37.50 (0-89950-652-6) McFarland & Co.

— The End: Over 3,000 Closing Lines from Hollywood's Most Memorable Movies. 240p. 1996. pap. 12.95 (0-8065-1725-5, Citadel Pr) Carol Pub Group.

***Cheshier, David, et al.** Public Speaking: From Ideas to Action. 190p. (C). 1998. spiral bd. 33.95 (0-7872-4696-4) Kendall-Hunt.

Cheshier, Stephen R. Studying Engineering Technology: A Blueprint for Success. (Illus.). 250p. (C). 1998. pap. text 22.95 (0-9646969-3-2) Discover CA.

Cheshik, S., jt. auth. see Barinsky, I.

***Cheshire.** Lo Esencial en Aparato Digesti. (C). 1998. text 14.09 (84-8174-365-8) Mosby Inc.

Cheshire, et al. The Law of Contract. 12th ed. 768p. 1991. 90.00 (0-409-90625-5, MICHIE) LEXIS Pub.

Cheshire, Barbara W. The Best Dissertation is a Finished Dissertation. 122p. (C). 1992. pap. 9.95 (0-89420-289-8, 343810) Natl Book.

Cheshire, Carolyn, jt. auth. see Diamond, Nikki.

Cheshire, Charles, jt. auth. see DK Publishing Staff.

Cheshire, Chloe. A Gypsy at Almack's. 1994. mass mkt. write for info. (0-312-95178-7) St Martin.

Cheshire, D. F. Music Hall in Britain. LC 74-2581. (Illus.). 112p. 1974. 26.50 (0-8386-1563-5) Fairleigh Dickinson.

Cheshire, Ellen, jt. auth. see Ashbrook, John M.

Cheshire, Gifford Paul. Black List. large type ed. 1998. 18.95 (1-57490-159-1, Sagebrush LP West) T T Beeler.

— Edge of the Desert. large type ed. LC 96-53966. (Sagebrush Large Print Westerns Ser.). 1997. lib. bdg. 17.95 (1-57490-054-4) T T Beeler.

— Wenatchie Bend. large type ed. LC 96-8317. (Sagebrush Large Print Westerns Ser.). 272p. 1996. lib. bdg. 17.95 (1-57490-018-8) T T Beeler.

***Cheshire, Gifford Paul.** Ambush at Bedrock. large type ed. LC 99-30782. 1999. write for info. (1-57490-197-4, Sagebrush LP West) T T Beeler.

Cheshire, Gifford Paul. Renegade River: Western Stories. Pronzini, Bill, ed. LC 97-38420. 1998. 18.95 (0-7862-0992-5) Thorndike Pr.

— Renegade River: Western Stories. large type ed. LC 98-43046. 1999. 18.95 (0-7862-1031-1) Mac Lib Ref.

— Stronghold. 1998. 17.50 (0-7540-8027-7, Gunsmoke) Chivers N Amer.

— Stronghold. large type ed. LC 98-7916. 1998. 21.95 (0-7838-0293-5, G K Hall Lrg Type) Mac Lib Ref.

***Cheshire, Gifford Paul.** The Sudden Guns. LC 00-31958. 2000. write for info. (0-7838-9092-3, G K Hall & Co) Mac Lib Ref.

***Cheshire, Greer.** Bryce, the Desert's Hoodoo Heart. (Illus.). 2000. pap. 9.95 (1-58071-019-0, Wish You Were Here) Panorama Intl.

Cheshire, Jenny. Variation in an English Dialect: A Sociolinguistic Study. LC 82-4189. (Cambridge Studies in Linguistics: No. 37). 152p. reprint ed. pap. 43.40 (0-608-15703-1, 2031630) Bks Demand.

Cheshire, Jenny, et al, eds. Dialect & Education: Some European Perspectives. 270p. 1989. 99.00 (1-85359-036-3, Pub. by Multilingual Matters); pap. 44.95 (1-85359-035-5, Pub. by Multilingual Matters) Taylor & Francis.

Cheshire, Jenny & Stein, Dieter. Tamimg the Vernacular. LC 97-8801. 1998. pap. text 23.02 (0-582-29809-1) Longman.

Cheshire, Jenny & Trudgill, Peter, eds. The Sociolinguistics Reader: Gender & Discourse, Vol. 2. LC 97-20091. (Arnold Linguistics Readers). (Illus.). 416p. 1998. text 85.00 (0-340-69182-4); pap. text 19.95 (0-340-69999-X) OUP.

Cheshire, Jenny, jt. ed. see Trudgill, Peter.

Cheshire, Julie A., ed. see Mobility International U. S. A. Staff.

Cheshire, Julie A., ed. see Mobility International U. S. A. Staff & Natl Clearinghouse on Disability & Exch. Staff.

Cheshire, Leonard. Where Is God in All This? 230p. (C). 1996. pap. 39.95 (0-85439-380-3, Pub. by St Paul Pubns) St Mut.

***Cheshire, Nancy R. & Kenney, Martha L.** Everything for A to Y: The Zest Is up to You! Older Adult Activities for Every Day of the Year. LC 98-88293. (Illus.). 1999. pap. 39.95 (1-892132-00-1, ATY106) Venture Pub PA.

Cheshire, Neil & Thomae, Helmut, eds. Self, Symptoms, & Psychotherapy. LC 86-32565. (Wiley Series on Methods in Psychotherapy). (Illus.). 316p. 1987. reprint ed. pap. 98.00 (0-608-05261-2, 206579900001) Bks Demand.

Cheshire, Neil M. The Nature of Psychodynamic Interpretation. LC 75-1391. 241p. reprint ed. pap. 74.80 (0-608-14532-7, 202479800038) Bks Demand.

Cheshire, Neil M., tr. see Erasmus, Desiderius.

Cheshire, P. C. & Mills, E. S. Handbook of Regional & Urban Economics, Vol. III. (Handbooks in Economics Ser.: III). 800p. 1999. 125.00 (0-444-82138-4, North Holland) Elsevier.

Cheshire, Paul & Evans, Alan, eds. Urban & Regional Economics. (International Library of Critical Writings in Economics: No. 14). 416p. 1991. text 215.00 (1-85278-181-5) E Elgar.

Cheshire, Paul C. & Gordon, Ian R., eds. Territorial Competition in an Integrating Europe. 336p. 1995. 82.95 (1-85972-112-5, Pub. by Avebry) Ashgate Pub Co.

Cheshire, Paul C. & Hay, Dennis G. Urban Problems in Western Europe: An Economic Analysis. 256p. 1989. text 70.00 (0-04-445010-9) Routledge.

Cheshire, Paul C., jt. auth. see Bowers, J. K.

Chesin, Amir S., et al. Separate & Unequal: The Inside Story of Israeli Rule in East Jerusalem. LC 98-53991. (Illus.). 288p. 1999. 27.95 (0-674-80136-9) HUP.

Chesire, John. Waterboy. 140p. (Orig.). 1996. pap. 3.95 (1-57502-179-X, PO803) Morris Pubng.

Chesire, Leone, et al. Computing Diagrams for the Tetrachoric Correlation Coefficient. 58p. 1968. pap. text 5.00 (0-317-11974-5) Psychometric.

Cheskin, Jonathan, ed. see Verdi, Giuseppe.

Cheskin, Lawrence J. Losing Weight for Good: Developing Your Personal Plan of Action. LC 96-31948. 264p. 1997. 24.95 (0-8018-5499-7) Johns Hopkins.

Cheskin, Suellen, tr. see Meyer, Jean.

Chesky, Sheldon R., et al. Playing It Safe: Milady's Guide to Decontamination, Sterilization, & Personal Protection. LC 93-36024. (Career Development Ser.). 1993. pap. 15.75 (1-56253-179-4) Thomson Learn.

Chesla, Elizabeth L. Improve Your Writing for Work. Gish, Jim, ed. LC 97-21549. (Basics Made Easy Ser.). 192p. (Orig.). 1997. pap. 13.95 (1-57685-061-7) LrningExprss.

— Pre-GED Interpreting Literature & the Arts. LC 97-67680. (GED Test Ser.). 192p. 1998. pap. 10.95 (0-87891-797-7) Res & Educ.

— Read Better & Remember More. Gish, Jim, ed. LC 97-24256. (Basics Made Easy Ser.). 192p. (Orig.). 1997. pap. 13.95 (1-57685-060-9) LrningExprss.

— Reading Comprehension Success 20 Minutes a Day. 2nd ed. LC 98-12958. (Skill Builders Ser.). 1998. pap. 16.00 (1-57685-126-5) LrningExprss.

— Reasoning Skills Success in 20 Minutes a Day. LC 98-35662. (Skill Builders Ser.). 1998. pap. 16.00 (1-57685-116-8) LrningExprss.

***Chesla, Elizabeth L.** Write Better Essays in Just 20 Minutes a Day: Your Guide to Great Grades & Top Test Scores. (Illus.). 208p. 2000. pap. text 13.95 (1-57685-309-8) LrningExprss.

***Chesla, Elizabeth L.** Improve Your Writing for Work: Write It Right & Get Your Point Across. 2nd ed. 2000. pap. 14.95 (1-57685-337-3) LrningExprss.

— Read Better, Remember More: 20 Simple Steps to Becoming a Smart Reader, 1. 2nd ed. 2000. pap. 14.95 (1-57685-336-5) LrningExprss.

Chesla, Elizabeth L. Reading Skills for College Students. LC 97-43621. (Learning Express Basic Skills for College Students Ser.). 177p. (C). 1997. pap. text 20.40 (0-13-080258-1) P-H.

Chesla, Elizabeth L. & Learning Express Staff. Critical Thinking & Logic Skill. LC 98-26091. 171p. 1998. pap. text 20.40 (0-13-082838-6) P-H.

Chesla, Erik. Successful Teamwork. LC 99-11367. 224p. 1999. pap. 14.95 (1-57685-204-0) LrningExprss.

Chesla, Liz. Practical Solutions for Everyday Work Problems. LC 99-11368. 224p. 1999. pap. 14.95 (1-57685-203-2) LrningExprss.

Chesler, Bernice. Bed & Breakfast in New England: Connecticut, Maine, Massachusetts, New Hampshire, Rhode Island. 6th ed. LC 98-224174. (Bed & Breakfast Ser.). 1998. pap. 17.95 (0-8118-1971-X) Chronicle Bks.

— Bernice Chesler's B & B in the Mid-Atlantic States: Delaware, Maryland, New Jersey, New York, North Carolina, Pennsylvania, Virginia, Washington D. C., West Virginia. 5th rev. ed. LC 97-7643. 480p. 1997. pap. 17.95 (0-8118-1281-2) Chronicle Bks.

***Chesler, Bernice.** Bernice Chesler's Bed & Breakfast in New England, 2000: Connecticut, Maine, Massachusetts, New Hampshire, Rhode Island, Vermont. 7th rev. expanded ed. (Illus.). 536p. 2000. pap. 17.95 (0-8118-2389-X) Chronicle Bks.

Chesler, Elliot. Clinical Cardiology. 5th ed. (Illus.). 416p. 1992. 139.00 (0-387-97712-0) Spr-Verlag.

Chesler, Elliot, ed. Clinical Cardiology in the Elderly. 2nd ed. LC 98-42493. (Illus.). 840p. 1999. 165.00 (0-87993-421-2) Futura Pub.

Chesler, Evan R. The Russian Jewry Reader. 1976. 18.95 (0-8488-0694-8) Amereon Ltd.

Chesler, Mark A. & Chesney, Barbara K. Cancer & Self-Help: Bridging the Troubled Waters of Childhood Illness. LC 95-18996. 410p. 1995. 54.00 (0-299-14820-3); pap. 19.95 (0-299-14824-6) U of Wis Pr.

Chesler, Mark A., et al. Social Science in Court: Mobilizing Experts in the School Desegregation Cases. LC 88-6088. 296p. 1988. text 45.00 (0-299-11620-4); pap. text 18.95 (0-299-11624-7) U of Wis Pr.

Chesler, Phyllis. Letters to a Young Feminist. LC 97-42846. 176p. 1998. 18.00 (1-56858-093-2) FWEW.

***Chesler, Phyllis.** Letters to a Young Feminist. (Women's Studies). 176p. 1999. pap. 11.00 (1-56858-151-3) FWEW.

Chesler, Phyllis. Patriarchy: Notes of an Expert Witness. LC 94-21995. 150p. (Orig.). 1994. pap. 12.95 (1-56751-038-8); lib. bdg. 29.95 (1-56751-039-6) Common Courage.

— With Child: A Diary of Motherhood. 2nd ed. LC 97-38939. 304p. 1998. reprint ed. pap. 15.95 (1-56858-095-9) FWEW.

— Woman & Child: The Legacy of Baby M. 256p. 16.95 (0-318-37102-2, Times Bks) Crown Pub Group.

— Woman's Inhumanity to Woman. 2000. write for info. (0-688-17189-3, Wm Morrow) Morrow Avon.

— Women & Madness. (Illus.). 400p. 1989. pap. 12.00 (0-15-698295-1) Harcourt.

— Women & Madness. 3rd ed. LC 97-41573. (Illus.). 400p. 1997. reprint ed. pap. 15.00 (1-56858-096-7) FWEW.

Chesler, Phyllis, et al, eds. Feminist Foremothers in Women's Studies, Psychology & Mental Health. (Women & Therapy Ser.: Vol. 17, Nos. 1, 2, 3, & 4). 575p. 1995. pap. 29.95 (1-56023-078-9, Harrington Park) Haworth Pr.

— Feminist Foremothers in Women's Studies, Psychology & Mental Health. (Women & Therapy Ser.: Vol. 17, Nos. 1, 2, 3, & 4). 575p. 1996. 69.95 (1-56024-767-3) Haworth Pr.

Chesler, Phyllis, jt. auth. see Ortiz, David.

Chesler, Phyllis, jt. auth. see Ramis, Magali G.

Chesler, Vicki, ed. & intro. see New York Cooperator Staff.

Chesley, Alan B. Cabooses of the New Haven & New York Central Railroads. (Plan & Photo Ser.: No. 1). 48p. 1989. pap. 14.95 (0-934088-04-7) NJ Intl Inc.

Chesley, Donald. Black Vendetta. 224p. (Orig.). 1988. mass mkt. 2.95 (0-87067-327-0) Holloway.

Chesley, Ed, tr. see Aldridge, Carrie.

Chesley, Robert. Hard Plays - Stiff Parts: The Homoerotic Plays of Robert Chesley. LC 90-81936. (Illus.). 160p. (Orig.). 1990. pap. 9.95 (0-9624751-1-4) Alamo Sq Pr.

— Stray Dog Story: An Adventure in Ten Scenes. LC 84-776. (Gay Play Script Ser.). (Illus.). 97p. 1984. pap. 7.95 (0-935672-11-7) T n T Class.

Cheslik-DeMeyer, Steven, jt. auth. see Byrd, James D.

Chesman, Andrea. Favorite Pickles & Relishes. 1985. pap. 2.95 (0-88266-334-8, Storey Pub) Storey Bks.

— Salad Suppers. 1999. pap. 14.00 (0-395-97180-2) HM.

Chesman, Andrea. Pickles & Relishes: One Hundred Fifty Recipes - Apples to Zucchini. 2nd rev. ed. Lloyd, Louise & Foster, Kim, eds. LC 91-10887. (Illus.). 152p. 1991. pap. 12.95 (0-88266-744-0, Garden Way Pub) Storey Bks.

— Pickles & Relishes: One Hundred Fifty Recipes, Apples to Zucchini. LC 83-1460. (Illus.). 160p. (Orig.). 1983. pap. 6.95 (0-88266-321-6, Garden Way Pub) Storey Bks.

— Salad Suppers. 1998. 25.50 (0-8446-6938-5) Peter Smith.

— Salsas! LC 85-17114. (Illus.). 146p. (Orig.). 1985. pap. 8.95 (0-89594-178-3) Crossing Pr.

— Simply Healthful Pasta Salads: Delicious New Low-Fat Recipes. LC 92-39973. (Simply Healthful Ser.). (Illus.). 96p. (Orig.). 1993. pap. 9.95 (1-881527-06-9, Chapters Bks) HM.

— Simply Healthful Skillet Suppers: Delicious New Low-Fat Recipes. LC 93-45014. (Simply Healthful Ser.). (Illus.). 96p. (Orig.). 1994. pap. 9.95 (1-881527-33-6, Chapters Bks) HM.

— Summer in a Jar: Making Pickles, Jams & More. Williamson, Susan, ed. LC 85-6543. (Illus.). 160p. 1985. pap. 8.95 (0-913589-14-4) Williamson Pub Co.

— Sun-Dried Tomatoes! LC 97-24473. (Speciality Cookbook Ser.). (Illus.). 144p. (Orig.). 1997. pap. 6.95 (0-89594-900-8) Crossing Pr.

— 366 delicious Ways to Cook Rice, Beans & Grains. LC 97-24289. 1998. pap. 16.95 (0-452-27654-3, Plume) Dutton Plume.

— The Vegetarian Grill: 200 Recipes for Inspired Flame-Kissed Meals. LC 98-11527. (Illus.). 368p. 1998. 29.95 (1-55832-126-8); pap. 14.95 (1-55832-127-6) Harvard Common Pr.

***Chesman, Andrea & Rankin, Dorothy.** Noodle Fusion: Asian Pasta Dishes for Western Palates. LC 99-33920. 224p. 2000. pap. 16.95 (0-89594-956-3) Crossing Pr.

Chesman, Andrea, jt. auth. see Perry, Susan K.

Chesman, Andrea, ed. see Garden Way Publishing Editors.

Chesman, Andrea, ed. see Haedrich, Ken.

Chesman, Andrea, ed. see Shelton, Jay W.

Chesmond, C. J. Basic Control System Technology. (gr. 13). 1991. pap. text 51.95 (0-442-30386-6) Chapman & Hall.

***Chesnais, Francois, et al.** European Integration & Global Corporate Strategies. LC 99-46624. (Studies in International Business & the World Economy Ser.). 304p. 2000. 100.00 (0-415-21278-2) Routledge.

Chesnais, Jean-Claude. The Demographic Transition: Stages, Patterns, & Economic Implications. Kraeger, Philip, tr. (Illus.). 646p. 1993. text 125.00 (0-19-828659-7) OUP.

Chesnaye Des Bois. Lettre a Mme la Comtesse. Adams, ed. 48p. Date not set. pap. text 19.95 (0-85989-159-3, Pub. by Univ Exeter Pr) Northwestern U Pr.

Chesne, John De Beau, see De Beau Chesne, John.

Chesneau, Charles, see D'Angers, Julien E., pseud.

Chesneau, Howard L. & Dorris, Michele M., eds. Distillate Fuel: Contamination, Storage & Handling, STP 1005. LC 88-23587. (Special Technical Publication (STP) Ser.). (Illus.). 200p. 1988. pap. text 34.00 (0-8031-1186-X, STP1005) ASTM.

Chesneau, Roger. Aircraft Carriers of the World: 1914 to the Present. (Illus.). 256p. 1984. 48.95 (0-87021-902-2) Naval Inst Pr.

— Hunter: Hawker Hunter F Mk6-T. (Aeroguide Ser.: No. 9). 1985. pap. 5.50 (0-918805-08-2) Pac Aero Pr.

— Hunter Squadrons of the Royal Air Force & Fleet Air Arm. 1985. pap. 3.00 (0-918805-18-X) Pac Aero Pr.

— Sea King: Westland Sea King HAR Mk3. (Aeroguide Ser.: No. 10). 1985. pap. 5.50 (0-918805-09-0) Pac Aero Pr.

— Victor: Handley Page Victor K Mk2. (Aeroguide Ser.: No. 11). 1985. pap. 5.95 (0-918805-10-4) Pac Aero Pr.

Chesneau, Roger & Rimell, Raymond L. Canberra: EE Canberra B Mk 2-T Mk 4. (Aeroguide Ser.: No. 7). 1984. pap. 5.50 (0-918805-06-6) Pac Aero Pr.

— Hawk: British Aerospace Hawk T Mk1. (Aeroguide Ser.: No. 1). 1984. pap. 5.50 (0-918805-00-7) Pac Aero Pr.

— Jaguar: Specat Jaquar Mk1. (Aeroguide Ser.: No. 2). 1984. pap. 5.50 (0-918805-01-5) Pac Aero Pr.

— Lightning: BAC Lightning F Mk3-Mk6. (Aeroguide Ser.: No. 8). 1984. pap. 5.50 (0-918805-07-4) Pac Aero Pr.

— Sea Harrier: BAe Sea Harrier, FRS Mk1. (Aeroguide Ser.: No. 3). 1984. pap. 6.00 (0-918805-02-3) Pac Aero Pr.

Chesner, Anna. Dramatherapy with People with Learning Disabilities. 200p. 1994. pap. 29.50 (1-85302-208-X) Taylor & Francis.

Chesney, Alan M. The Johns Hopkins Hospital & the Johns Hopkins University School of Medicine Vol. 2: A Chronicle: 1893-1905. 499p. 1958. 55.00 (0-8018-0113-3) Johns Hopkins.

— The Johns Hopkins Hospital & the Johns Hopkins University School of Medicine Vol. 3: A Chronicle: 1905-1914. 350p. 1963. 45.00 (0-8018-0114-1) Johns Hopkins.

Chesney, Barbara K., jt. auth. see Chesler, Mark A.

Chesney, Charles C. Waterloo Lectures. LC 97-19005. (Napoleonic Library). 1997. write for info. (1-85367-288-2) Stackpole.

Chesney, D. Noreen, jt. auth. see Chesney, Pauline J.

Chesney, Helena C., jt. auth. see Foster, John W.

Chesney, Helena C. G., jt. auth. see Foster, John Wilson.

Chesney, James D. & Feinstein, Otto. Building Civic Literacy: A Practical Guide. LC 96-23083. 120p. (C). 1996. pap. text, student ed. 22.00 (0-13-309741-2) P-H.

Chesney, Lee & Miyamoto, Wayne. Lee Chesney: Twenty-Five Years of Printmaking. LC 78-13555. 96p. reprint ed. pap. 30.00 (0-7837-4914-7, 204457900004) Bks Demand.

***Chesney-Lind, Meda.** Bad Girls. (Criminal Justice Ser.). 2001. 25.00 (0-534-53371-X) Wadsworth Pub.

Chesney-Lind, Meda. The Female Offender: Girls, Women & Crime. LC 96-45845. (Women in the Criminal Justice System Ser.: Vol. 2). 222p. (C). 1997. 46.00 (0-8039-5099-3, 50993); pap. 21.95 (0-8039-5100-0, 51000) Sage.

***Chesney-Lind, Meda & Hagedorn, John M., eds.** Female Gangs in America: Essays on Girls, Gangs & Gender. LC 98-53160. 364p. 1999. 35.00 (0-941702-48-0); pap. 19.95 (0-941702-47-2) Lake View Pr.

Chesney-Lind, Meda & Shelden, Randall G. Girls, Delinquency & Juvenile Justice. 288p. (C). 1991. mass mkt. 22.95 (0-534-16980-5) Wadsworth Pub.

Chesney-Lind, Meda & Sheldon, Randall G. Girls, Delinquency & Juvenile Justice. 2nd ed. LC 97-7428. (Criminal Justice Ser.). 275p. (C). 1997. 29.95 (0-534-26478-6) Wadsworth Pub.

Chesney, Margaret A., ed. see Rosenstein, Alan H.

Chesney, Marion. Back in Society. (Poor Relation Ser.: Vol. 6). 160p. 1994. 18.95 (0-312-10932-6) St Martin.

— Back in Society. (Poor Relation Ser.: Vol. 6). 1995. mass mkt. 4.50 (0-312-95338-0, Pub. by Tor Bks) St Martin.

— Belinda Goes to Bath. large type ed. (Travelling Matchmaker Ser.: Vol. 2). 232p. 1992. pap. 14.95 (0-8161-5375-2, G K Hall Lrg Type) Mac Lib Ref.

— The Chocolate Debutante. 1995. mass mkt. 4.50 (0-449-22259-4, Crest) Fawcett.

***Chesney, Marion.** The Chocolate Debutante. large type ed. 224p. 2000. write for info. (0-7089-4190-7) Ulverscroft.

Chesney, Marion. Deborah Goes to Dover. large type ed. LC 92-46713. (Travelling Matchmaker Ser.: Vol. 5). 254p. 1993. lib. bdg. 15.95 (0-8161-5545-3, G K Hall Lrg Type) Mac Lib Ref.

— The Dreadful Debutante. LC 98-32201. 1999. 20.95 (0-7838-8502-4, G K Hall & Co) Mac Lib Ref.

***Chesney, Marion.** The Dreadful Debutante. large type ed. LC 98-32201. 199 p. 1999. write for info. (0-7540-3631-6) Chivers N Amer.

Chesney, Marion. Emily Goes to Exeter. large type ed. (Travelling Matchmaker Ser.: Vol. 1). 245p. 1992. pap. 14.95 (0-8161-5157-1, G K Hall Lrg Type) Mac Lib Ref.

— Finessing Clarissa. large type ed. (School for Manners Ser.: Vol. 4). 243p. 1991. lib. bdg. 14.95 (0-8161-5013-3, G K Hall Lrg Type) Mac Lib Ref.

— The Folly. large type ed. LC 97-30901. (Daughters of Mannerling Ser.: Vol. 4). 255p. 1998. lib. bdg. 19.95 (0-7838-8288-2, G K Hall Lrg Type) Mac Lib Ref.

— The Ghost & Lady Alice. 1994. reprint ed. lib. bdg. 20.00 (0-7278-4697-3) Severn Hse.

— The Glitter & the Gold. LC 99-18823. 1999. 20.95 (0-7838-8597-0, G K Hall & Co) Mac Lib Ref.

— A Governess of Distinction. LC 98-53067. (Orig.). 1999. pap. text 22.95 (0-7838-8519-9) Thorndike Pr.

***Chesney, Marion.** The Highland Countess. large type ed. LC 99-37951. 221p. 1999. pap. 23.95 (0-7838-8740-X) Macmillan.

— The Homecoming. large type ed. LC 00-21758. (Daughters of Mannerling Ser.). 240p. 2000. pap. 21.95 (0-7838-8982-8, G K Hall Lrg Type) Mac Lib Ref.

Chesney, Marion. The Intrigue. (Daughters of Mannerling Ser.: Vol. 2). 1996. mass mkt. 4.50 (0-449-22420-1) Fawcett.

— Lady Anne's Deception. large type ed. (Magna Romance Ser.). 220p. 1992. 27.99 (0-7505-0153-7) Ulverscroft.

— Lady Lucy's Lover. 160p. 1992. reprint ed. 18.00 (0-7278-4356-7) Severn Hse.

— The Loves of Lord Granton. 1997. mass mkt. 4.50 (0-449-22260-8, Crest) Fawcett.

An Asterisk (*) at the beginning of an entry indicates that the title is appearing for the first time.

— The Loves of Lord Granton. large type ed. LC 97-30533. (ROMC-Hall Ser.). 206p. 1997. lib. bdg. 25.95 (*0-7838-8301-3*, G K Hall Lrg Type) Mac Lib Ref.

***Chesney, Marion.** The Marquis Takes a Bride. large type ed. LC 99-44278. (Romance Ser.). 1999. 27.95 (*0-7838-8777-9*, G K Hall & Co) Mac Lib Ref.

Chesney, Marion. A Marriage of Inconvenience. 184p. 1996. 22.00 (*0-7278-5121-7*) Severn Hse.

— A Marriage of Inconvenience. large type ed. LC 98-7843. (Romance Ser.). 197 p. 1998. pap. write for info. (*0-7540-3415-1*) Chivers N Amer.

— Marrying Harriet. large type ed. (School for Manners Ser.: Vol. 6). 252p. 1992. pap. 15.95 (*0-8161-5158-X*, G K Hall Lrg Type) Mac Lib Ref.

— Miss Tonks Turns to Crime. large type ed. LC 93-29303. (Poor Relation Ser.: Vol. 2). 251p. 1994. lib. bdg. 17.95 (*0-8161-5898-3*, G K Hall Lrg Type) Mac Lib Ref.

— Penelope Goes to Portsmouth. large type ed. LC 92-17128. (Travelling Matchmaker Ser.: Vol.). 247p. 1992. pap. 14.95 (*0-8161-5547-X*, G K Hall Lrg Type) Mac Lib Ref.

— Pretty Polly. large type ed. LC 97-43616. 204p. 1998. 21.95 (*0-7838-8389-7*, G K Hall & Co) Mac Lib Ref.

— Rainbird's Revenge. large type ed. (House for the Season Ser.: Vol. 6). 248p. 1990. pap. 14.95 (*0-8161-4705-1*, G K Hall Lrg Type) Mac Lib Ref.

— Regency Gold: A Novel. LC 97-22563. (Five Star Romances Ser.). 214p. 1997. lib. bdg. 21.95 (*0-7862-1186-5*) Five Star.

— The Romance. large type ed. LC 97-32594. (Daughters of Mannerling Ser.: Vol. 5). 238p. 1998. pap. 19.95 (*0-7838-8385-4*, G K Hall & Co) Mac Lib Ref.

***Chesney, Marion.** The Savage Marquess. large type ed. LC 99-46551. (G. K. Hall Paperback Ser.). 1999. pap. 23.95 (*0-7838-8809-0*, G K Hall Lrg Type) Mac Lib Ref.

Chesney, Marion. The Scandalous Lady Wright. large type ed. LC 98-19076. 1998. 21.95 (*0-7838-0287-0*, G K Hall Lrg Type) Mac Lib Ref.

— Silken Bonds. 208p. 1998. 24.00 (*0-7278-2201-2*) Severn Hse.

— Sir Philip's Folly. large type ed. LC 94-17132. (Poor Relation Ser.: Vol. 4). 223p. 1994. lib. bdg. 17.95 (*0-8161-7414-8*, G K Hall Lrg Type) Mac Lib Ref.

— The Viscount's Revenge. large type ed. 287p. 1992. 27.99 (*0-7505-0157-X*) Ulverscroft.

— The Viscount's Revenge. 1991. reprint ed. 18.00 (*0-7278-4184-X*) Severn Hse.

— Yvonne Goes to York. large type ed. LC 93-8878. (Travelling Matchmaker Ser.: Vol. 6). 264p. 1993. lib. bdg. 15.95 (*0-8161-5834-7*, G K Hall Lrg Type) Mac Lib Ref.

Chesney, Marion, see Beaton, M. C., pseud.

Chesney, Marion, see Tremaine, Jennie, pseud.

Chesney, P. Joan, jt. auth. see Bergdoll, Merlin S.

Chesney, Pauline J. & Chesney, D. Noreen. Chesney's Care of the Patient in Diagnostic Radiography. 7th ed. LC 94-30883. (Illus.). 416p. 1995. 34.95 (*0-632-03762-8*) Blackwell Sci.

Chesney, Rose J. Judgement. 1986. 35.00 (*0-946270-25-2*, Pub. by Pentland Pr) St Mut.

Chesney, W. D. You Are Sentenced to Life. 118p. 1996. reprint ed. spiral bd. 14.00 (*0-7873-0168-X*) Hlth Research.

— Zone Therapy Is Scientific: Subjectively & Objectively. 9p. 1996. reprint ed. spiral bd. 8.00 (*0-7873-0169-8*) Hlth Research.

Chesneylind & Maker, Janet. Girls, Delinquency & Juvenile Justice. 4th ed. LC 96-8557. (Developmental Study/Study Skills Ser.: Bk. 1). 1996. 28.00 (*0-534-26472-7*) Wadsworth Pub.

Chesni, Yves. Dialectical Realism: Towards a Philosophy of Growth. rev. ed. Zenk, Joseph, tr. 191p. 1987. text 37.50 (*0-931095-00-X*) Live Oak.

— Studies on the Development of Consciousness. Zenk, Joseph, tr. 153p. 1994. text 37.50 (*0-931095-02-6*) Live Oak.

Chesnic, Carrie, et al. Teacher of the Heart: A Self Health Journey. LC 97-72310. (Illus.). 230p. 1997. pap. 24.00 (*1-887747-08-7*) Legendary Pub.

***Chesnoff, Richard.** Pack of Thieves. 2001. reprint ed. pap. 14.00 (*0-385-72064-5*, Anchor NY) Doubleday.

Chesnoff, Richard Z. Pack of Thieves: How Hitler & Europe Plundered the Jews & Committed the Greatest Theft in History. LC 99-33257. 320p. 1999. 27.50 (*0-385-48763-0*) Doubleday.

***Chesnokov, Sergei S., et al, eds.** Nonlinear Optical Phenomena & Coherent Optics in Information Technologies. 484p. 1999. pap. text 103.00 (*0-8194-3207-5*) SPIE.

Chesnut, D. B. Finite Groups & Quantum Theory. LC 81-19351. 270p. 1982. reprint ed. lib. bdg. 30.50 (*0-89874-468-7*) Krieger.

Chesnut, Glenn F. The First Christian Histories: Eusebius, Socrates, Sozomen, Theodoret, & Evagrius. rev. ed. LC 85-28515. xiv, 296p. 1986. pap. text 19.95 (*0-86554-203-1*, MUP\P022) Mercer Univ Pr.

— Images of Christ: An Introduction to Christology. 160p. (Orig.). 1984. 8.95 (*0-86683-875-9*, 7918) Harper SF.

Chesnut, Mark. The Gay Vacation Guide: The Best Trips & How to Plan Them. LC 97-3235. xxiv, 214p. 1997. pap. 14.95 (*0-8065-1882-0*, Citadel Pr) Carol Pub Group.

Chesnut, Mary Boykin Miller. A Diary from Dixie. Williams, Ben A., ed. 600p. 1980. pap. text 18.50 (*0-674-20291-0*) HUP.

— A Diary from Dixie. Martin, Isabella & Avary, Myrta L., eds. (Illus.). 1990. 28.75 (*0-8446-1109-3*) Peter Smith.

— Diary from Dixie. (History - United States Ser.). 423p. 1992. reprint ed. lib. bdg. 99.00 (*0-7812-6183-X*) Rprt Serv.

Chesnut, R. Andrew. Born Again in Brazil: The Pentecostal Boom & the Pathogens of Poverty. LC 97-9191. (Illus.). 224p. (C). 1997. text 50.00 (*0-8135-2405-9*); pap. text 19.95 (*0-8135-2406-7*) Rutgers U Pr.

Chesnut, Thomas J., jt. auth. see Ciccone, Kathleen R.

Chesnutt, Anna. Destined. 140p. (Orig.). 1997. pap. 12.95 (*1-57502-364-4*, P01078) Morris Pubng.

Chesnutt, Charles Waddell. The Adventures of Shirley Holmes: The Case of the Burning Building & the Case of the Ruby Ring. LC 98-29782. (Adventures of Shirley Holmes Ser.). 112p. (J). (gr. 3-7). 1999. pap. 3.99 (*0-440-41500-4*) BDD Bks Young Read.

— Collected Stories of Charles W. Chesnutt. Date not set. lib. bdg. 24.95 (*0-8488-1660-9*) Amereon Ltd.

— Colonel's Dream. LC 73-83928. (Black Heritage Library Collection). 1977. 28.95 (*0-8369-8538-9*) Ayer.

— Colonel's Dream. LC 77-100261. 294p. 1970. reprint ed. lib. bdg. 35.00 (*0-8371-2857-9*, CCD) Greenwood.

— The Colonel's Dream. LC 68-57517. (Muckrakers Ser.). reprint ed. lib. bdg. 16.00 (*0-8398-0257-9*) Irvington.

— Conjure Woman. 256p. 1969. pap. text 14.95 (*0-472-06156-9*, 06156, Ann Arbor Bks) U of Mich Pr.

***Chesnutt, Charles Waddell.** Conjure Woman. (Penguin Classics Ser.). 304p. 2000. pap. 10.95 (*0-14-118502-3*) Viking Penguin.

Chesnutt, Charles Waddell. The Conjure Woman. 1988. reprint ed. lib. bdg. 59.00 (*0-7812-0047-4*) Rprt Serv.

— The Conjure Woman. reprint ed. 45.00 (*0-403-07386-3*) Scholarly.

— The Conjure Woman & Other Conjure Tales. LC 93-4215. 216p. 1993. pap. 13.95 (*0-8223-1387-1*); text 39.95 (*0-8223-1378-2*) Duke.

— The House Behind Cedars. (X Press Black Classics Ser.). 185p. 1996. pap. 9.95 (*1-874509-26-3*, Pub. by X Pr) LPC InBook.

***Chesnutt, Charles Waddell.** The House Behind the Cedars. LC 99-88134. 2000. pap. 11.95 (*0-8203-2194-X*) U of Ga Pr.

Chesnutt, Charles Waddell. The House Behind the Cedars. Gibson, Donald, ed. & intro. by. LC 98-143616. 304p. 1993. pap. 12.95 (*0-14-018685-9*, Penguin Classics) Viking Penguin.

— The House Behind the Cedars. large type ed. LC 99-30028. 440p. 1999. 27.95 (*1-56000-494-0*) Transaction Pubs.

— The Journals of Charles W. Chesnutt. Brodhead, Richard H., ed. LC 93-10872. (Illus.). 200p. 1993. pap. 15.95 (*0-8223-1424-X*); text 49.95 (*0-8223-1379-0*) Duke.

— Mandy Oxendine: A Novel. Hackenberry, Charles, ed. LC 93-553. 112p. 1994. 11.95 (*0-252-06347-3*); text 27.50 (*0-252-02051-0*) U of Ill Pr.

— The Marrow of Tradition. 1976. 25.95 (*0-8488-0962-9*) Amereon Ltd.

— The Marrow of Tradition. LC 70-83927. (Black Heritage Library Collection). 1977. 16.95 (*0-8369-8539-7*) Ayer.

— The Marrow of Tradition. Sundquist, Eric J., ed. & intro. by. LC 92-31334. (Twentieth-Century Classics Ser.). 128p. 1993. pap. 13.95 (*0-14-018686-7*, Penguin Classics) Viking Penguin.

— The Marrow of Tradition. large type ed. LC 99-14583. 450p. 1999. 27.95 (*1-56000-493-2*) Transaction Pubs.

— The Marrow of Tradition. LC 72-1564. reprint ed. 42.50 (*0-404-00014-2*) AMS Pr.

— The Marrow of Tradition. 2nd ed. (Illus.). 352p. 1969. pap. text 14.95 (*0-472-06147-X*, 06147) U of Mich Pr.

— The Marrow of Tradition: American Negro. LC 69-18585. (His History & Literature Ser.: No. 2). 1968. reprint ed. 16.95 (*0-405-01855-X*) Ayer.

— Paul Marchand: Free Man of Color. LC 98-24049. 144p. 1998. 20.00 (*1-57806-055-9*) U Pr of Miss.

— Tales of Conjure & the Color Line: 10 Stories. LC 98-35058. 128p. 1998. pap. 1.50 (*0-486-40426-9*) Dover.

— Tradition. (X Press Black Classics Ser.). 231p. 1996. pap. 9.95 (*1-874509-12-3*, Pub. by X Pr) LPC InBook.

— Wife of His Youth & Other Stories. (Illus.). 336p. (C). 1968. reprint ed. pap. text 14.95 (*0-472-06134-8*, 06134, Ann Arbor Bks) U of Mich Pr.

Chesnutt, Charles Waddell & McWilliams, Dean. Paul Marchand, F. M. C. LC 98-26423. 1998. 35.00 (*0-691-05993-4*, Pub. by Princeton U Pr) Cal Prin Full Svc.

— Paul Marchand, F. M. C. LC 98-26423. 1999. pap. 14.95 (*0-691-05994-2*, Pub. by Princeton U Pr) Cal Prin Full Svc.

— The Quarry. LC 98-26422. 1998. 35.00 (*0-691-05995-0*, Pub. by Princeton U Pr) Cal Prin Full Svc.

— The Quarry. LC 98-26422. 1999. pap. 14.95 (*0-691-05996-9*, Pub. by Princeton U Pr) Cal Prin Full Svc.

Chesnutt, Charles Waddell, et al. Charles W. Chesnutt: Essays & Speeches. LC 98-30654. 1999. 60.00 (*0-8047-3549-2*) Stanford U Pr.

Chesnutt, David R. & Taylor, C. James, eds. The Papers of Henry Laurens, Vol. XV. 768p. 49.95 (*1-57003-307-2*) U of SC Pr.

Chesnutt, David R., ed. see Laurens, Henry.

Chesnutt, J. C., ed. see Metallurgical Society of AIME Staff.

Chesnutt, Randall D. From Death to Life: Conversion in Joseph & Aseneth. (Journal for the Study of the Pseudepigrapha Supplement Ser.: No. 16). 308p. 1995. 85.00 (*1-85075-516-7*, Pub. by Sheffield Acad) CUP Services.

Chesny, George T. & Munro, Hector H. The Battle of Dorking & When William Came. (Oxford Popular Fiction Ser.). 208p. 1997. pap. 9.95 (*0-19-283285-9*) OUP.

Cheson, Bruce D., ed. Chronic Lymphocytic Leukemia: Scientific Advances & Clinical Development. LC 92-49857. (Basic & Clinical Oncology Ser.: Vol. 1). (Illus.). 440p. 1992. text 145.00 (*0-8247-8736-6*) Dekker.

Cheson, Bruce D., et al. Nucleoside Analogs in Cancer Therapy. LC 97-11276. (Basic & Clinical Oncology Ser.). (Illus.). 488p. 1997. text 175.00 (*0-8247-9850-3*) Dekker.

Chess, Caron. Winning the Right to Know: A Handbook for Toxics Activists. 100p. 1983. 8.95 (*0-89788-073-0*) CPA Washington.

Chess, David M. Programming in IBM PC DOS Pascal. (Illus.). 240p. 1986. 27.95 (*0-13-730292-4*) P-H.

***Chess, James M.** How to Refinance America: Spreading Capitalism into the 21st Century. (Illus.). 265p. 1999. pap. 19.95 (*0-9675399-0-0*) Okay.

Chess, Paul & Gronvold, Frits. Corrosion Investigation: A Guide to Half Cell Mapping. LC 96-225216. 40p. 1996. 48.00 (*0-7277-2504-1*) Am Soc Civil Eng.

Chess, Paul M., ed. Cathodic Protection of Steel in Concrete. LC 98-172304. (Illus.). 208p. (C). (gr. 13). 1998. 110.00 (*0-419-23010-6*, D5576, E & FN Spon) Routledge.

***Chess, Stella.** Goodness of Fit: Clinical Applications from Infancy Through Adult Life. LC 98-43420. 229p. 1999. 34.95 (*0-87630-893-0*) Brunner-Mazel.

Chess, Stella, et al, eds. Annual Progress in Child Psychiatry & Child Development, 1986. LC 68-23452. 704p. 1986. text 66.95 (*0-87630-437-4*) Brunner-Mazel.

— Annual Progress in Child Psychiatry & Child Development, 1987. LC 68-23452. 650p. 1987. text 66.95 (*0-87630-476-5*) Brunner-Mazel.

— Annual Progress in Child Psychiatry & Child Development, 1988. LC 68-23452. 704p. 1988. text 66.95 (*0-87630-538-9*) Brunner-Mazel.

Chess, Stella & Hassibi, Mahin. Principles & Practice of Child Psychiatry. 2nd ed. (Illus.). 550p. (C). 1986. text 78.00 (*0-306-42167-4*, Kluwer Plenum) Kluwer Academic.

Chess, Stella & Hertzig, Margaret E., eds. Annual Progress in Child Psychiatry & Child Development, 1989. LC 68-23452. 576p. 1989. text 52.95 (*0-87630-569-9*) Brunner-Mazel.

— Annual Progress in Child Psychiatry & Child Development, 1990. LC 68-23452. (Illus.). 624p. 1990. text 66.95 (*0-87630-602-4*) Brunner-Mazel.

— Annual Progress in Child Psychiatry & Child Development, 1991. LC 68-23452. 656p. 1991. text 66.95 (*0-87630-651-2*) Brunner-Mazel.

Chess, Stella & Thomas, Alexander. Origins & Evolution of Behavior Disorders: From Infancy to Adult Life. LC 87-7582. 344p. 1987. pap. 19.50 (*0-674-64477-8*) HUP.

— Temperament: Theory & Practice. LC 96-28525. (Basic Principles into Practice Ser.: Vol. 12). 224p. 1996. pap. 24.95 (*0-87630-835-3*) Brunner-Mazel.

— Temperament in Clinical Practice. LC 85-17733. 315p. 1995. pap. text 24.00 (*0-89862-813-X*, 2813) Guilford Pubns.

— Temperament in Clinical Practice. LC 85-17733. 333p. reprint ed. pap. 103.30 (*0-7837-3880-3*, 204372800010) Bks Demand.

Chess, Stella & Thomas, Alexander, eds. Annual Progress in Child Psychiatry & Child Development, Vols. 1-12. Incl. Vol. 6. LC 68-23452. 1973. text 66.95 (*0-87630-080-8*); Vol. 10. LC 68-23452. 1977. text 66.95 (*0-87630-155-3*); Vol. 11. LC 68-23452. 1978. text 66.95 (*0-87630-180-4*); Vol. 12. LC 68-23452. 1979. text 66.95 (*0-87630-216-9*); LC 68-23452. (Illus.). Set text 66.95 (*0-318-51243-2*) Brunner-Mazel.

— Annual Progress in Child Psychiatry & Child Development, 1980. LC 68-23452. 624p. 1980. text 66.95 (*0-87630-248-7*) Brunner-Mazel.

— Annual Progress in Child Psychiatry & Child Development, 1983. LC 68-23452. 562p. 1983. text 66.95 (*0-87630-343-2*) Brunner-Mazel.

— Annual Progress in Child Psychiatry & Child Development, 1984. LC 68-23452. 514p. 1984. text 66.95 (*0-87630-375-0*) Brunner-Mazel.

— Annual Progress in Child Psychiatry & Child Development, 1985. LC 68-23452. 664p. 1985. text 66.95 (*0-87630-402-1*) Brunner-Mazel.

Chess, Susanne, ed. see Evans, Bob.

Chess, Victoria. The Bullies Halloween Party. (J). 1990. write for info. (*0-316-13866-5*) Little.

Chess, Victoria. Ghosts! Ghostly Tales from Folklore. (I Can Read Bks.). 64p. (J). (gr. 1-3). 1993. pap. 3.95 (*0-06-444170-9*, HarpTrophy) HarpC Child Bks.

Chessa, Antonio G. Conditional Simulation of Spatial Stochastic Models for Reservoir Heterogeneity. (Illus.). 174p. (Orig.). 1995. pap. 59.50 (*90-407-1123-2*, Pub. by Delft U Pr) Coronet Bks.

Chesse, Ralph. The Marionette Actor. 114p. (Orig.). (C). 1987. text 43.00 (*0-8026-0011-5*); pap. text 22.50 (*0-8026-0012-3*) Univ Pub Assocs.

Chesselet, Marie-Francoise, ed. In Situ Hybridization Histochemistry. 208p. 1990. lib. bdg. 139.00 (*0-8493-6912-6*, QP620) CRC Pr.

***Chesselet, Marie-Francoise, ed.** Molecular Mechanisms of Neurodegenerative Diseases. (Contemporary Clinical Neuroscience Ser.). (Illus.). 411p. 2000. 125.00 (*0-89603-804-1*) Humana.

Chessell & Edwards. Do Frogs Wear Jeans? 1985. pap. text. write for info. (*0-582-66767-4*, Pub. by Addison-Wesley) Longman.

Chessell, G. S. J. Photo DX, 4 vols., 3. (C). (gr. 13). 1985. 16.00 (*0-8151-1655-1*, 09050) Mosby Inc.

— Photo DX, 4 vols., 4. (C). (gr. 13). 1985. 16.00 (*0-8151-1656-X*, 09052) Mosby Inc.

Chessen, Betsey & Cahanko, Pamela. Animal Homes. LC 97-29186. (Science Emergent Readers Ser.). (Illus.). (J). 1997. pap. 2.50 (*0-590-76166-8*) Scholastic Inc.

Chessen, Betsey. Pet Care. LC 98-35284. (Learning Center Emergent Readers Ser.). 1998. pap. 2.50 (*0-439-04589-4*) Scholastic Inc.

— Rainforest. LC 97-34211. (Science Emergent Readers Ser.). (J). 1997. pap. 2.50 (*0-590-76960-X*) Scholastic Inc.

— Sharks. LC 98-8012. (Science Emergent Readers Ser.). (J). 1998. 3.25 (*0-590-63881-5*) Scholastic Inc.

— The Things Birds Eat! LC 98-18824. (Science Emergent Readers Ser.). (J). 1998. pap. 3.25 (*0-590-76965-0*) Scholastic Inc.

Chessen, Betsey & Berger, Samantha. Hello. LC 98-54253. 1998. 2.50 (*0-439-04560-6*) Scholastic Inc.

Chessen, Betsey & Chanko, Pamela. Buildings. LC 98-34076. 1998. pap. 3.25 (*0-439-04584-3*) Scholastic Inc.

— Counting Penguins. LC 97-34208. (Science Emergent Readers Ser.). (J). 1997. pap. 2.50 (*0-590-76154-4*) Scholastic Inc.

— Crafts. LC 98-53337. (Social Studies Emergent Readers Ser.). 1999. 2.50 (*0-439-04568-1*) Scholastic Inc.

— A Dolphin Is Not a Fish. LC 98-23223. (Science Emergent Readers Ser.). (J). 1998. pap. 3.25 (*0-05-906388-2*) Scholastic Inc.

— A Dolphin Is Not a Fish. LC 98-23223. (Science Emergent Readers Ser.). 1998. 2.50 (*0-590-63882-3*) Scholastic Inc.

— Jane Goodall & Her Chimpanzees. LC 98-53335. (Social Studies Emergent Readers Ser.). (J). 1999. 2.50 (*0-439-04576-2*) Scholastic Inc.

— Orange Juice. LC 97-34206. (Science Emergent Readers Ser.). (Illus.). (J). (ps-3). 1997. pap. 2.50 (*0-590-14999-7*) Scholastic Inc.

— Thank You! LC 98-54177. (Social Studies Emergent Readers Ser.). 1998. 2.50 (*0-439-04558-4*) Scholastic Inc.

***Chessen, Betsey & Chanko, Pamela.** What's in a Park? LC 98-35585. (Learning Center Emergent Readers Ser.). 1998. pap. write for info. (*0-439-04582-7*) Scholastic Inc.

Chessen, Betsey & Moreton, Daniel. Where Do Birds Live? LC 98-23988. (Science Emergent Readers Ser.). (J). 1998. pap. 2.50 (*0-590-76967-7*) Scholastic Inc.

Chessen, Betsey, jt. auth. see Berger, Samantha.

Chessen, Betsey, jt. auth. see Canizares, Susan.

Chessen, Betsey, jt. auth. see Reid, Mary.

Chessen, Sherri. The Gorp's Gift. (Illus.). 28p. (J). 1996. 14.95 (*0-9642160-0-0*) Roundtop Pr.

Chesser, Barbara J., jt. auth. see Meyer, Paul J.

Chesser, Beverly. Day by Day with Your Health Coach. LC 93-86324. 192p. 1994. pap. 10.95 (*0-89221-247-0*) New Leaf.

Chesser, Beverly & Cox, Gale. Easy Low-Fat Cooking. LC 92-60941. 224p. (Orig.). 1992. pap. 11.95 (*0-89221-226-8*) New Leaf.

Chesser, Grayson & Badger, Curtis J. Making Decoys: The Century-Old Way. LC 88-16085. (Illus.). 176p. 1989. 29.95 (*0-8117-0986-8*) Stackpole.

Chesser, Jerald W. The Art & Science of Culinary Preparation: A Culinarian's Manual. Fernald, Stephen C. & Jacoby, William B., eds. LC 91-76371. (Illus.). 586p. (C). 1992. text 35.00 (*0-9631023-1-1*) ACF Educ Inst.

Chesser, Margaret, jt. auth. see Krusch, Barry.

Chesshyre, Hubert & Ailes, Adrian. Heralds of Today: Biographical List of Officers of College of Arms. 72p. 1987. pap. 16.95 (*0-905715-31-4*, Pub. by Smyth) Dufour.

Chesshyre, Robert. Cost of Living. 1990. pap. 37.95 (*0-89381-439-3*) Aperture.

Chessick, Richard. Emotional Illness & Creativity: A Psychoanalytic & Phenomenologic Study. LC 99-22630. 445p. 1999. 59.95 (*0-8236-1665-7*, No. 01665) Intl Univs Pr.

***Chessick, Richard.** Psychoanalytic Clinical Practice. 300p. 2000. 30.00 (*1-85343-479-5*, Pub. by Free Assoc Bks) Intl Spec Bk.

Chessick, Richard D. Dialogue Concerning Contemporary Psychodynamic Therapy. LC 95-32111. 200p. 1997. pap. 30.00 (*1-56821-371-9*) Aronson.

— How Psychotherapy Heals. LC 77-91953. 1987. reprint ed. 45.00 (*0-87668-821-0*) Aronson.

— Intensive Psychotherapy of the Borderline Patient. LC 76-22867. 303p. 1977. 50.00 (*0-87668-254-9*) Aronson.

— The Psychology of the Self & the Treatment of Narcissism. LC 85-15621. 366p. 1985. 45.00 (*0-87668-745-1*) Aronson.

— The Psychology of the Self & the Treatment of Narcissism. LC 85-15621. 384p. 1993. reprint ed. pap. 50.00 (*0-87668-171-2*) Aronson.

— Technique & Practice of Intensive Psychotherapy. LC 84-45011. 392p. 1983. 60.00 (*0-87668-657-9*) Aronson.

— The Technique & Practice of Listening in Intensive Psychotherapy. LC 89-104. 296p. 1989. 50.00 (*0-87668-862-8*) Aronson.

— The Technique & Practice of Listening in Intensive Psychotherapy. LC 89-104. 296p. 1992. reprint ed. pap. 50.00 (*0-87668-300-6*) Aronson.

— What Constitutes the Patient in Psychotherapy? Alternative Approaches to Understanding Humans. LC 91-41341. 248p. 1993. 45.00 (*0-87668-549-1*) Aronson.

— Why Psychotherapists Fail. LC 84-45108. 203p. 1983. 40.00 (*0-87668-700-1*) Aronson.

Chessid, Ilona. Thresholds of Desire: Authority & Transgression in the Rougon-Macquart. LC 92-30423. (Reading Plus Ser.: Vol. 12). VII, 146p. (C). 1993. text 45.95 (*0-8204-2037-9*) P Lang Pubng.

Chessier, Mike. Passing in Constantsa (1996 Epilogue Included) And Other Tales of Eastern Europe in Change. (Illus.). 116p. (Orig.). 1996. pap., spiral bd. 9.95 (*0-614-30235-8*) M Chessin.

C

An Asterisk (*) at the beginning of an entry indicates that the title is appearing for the first time.

Chessin, Meyer. Antiviral Proteins in Higher Plants. 190p. 1994. lib. bdg. 149.00 (*0-8493-6989-4*) CRC Pr.

Chessin, Mike. Passing in Contantsa: And Other Tales of Eastern Europe in Change. 84p. 1991. pap. 8.95 (*0-9632512-0-1*) M Chessin.

Chessler, Karen E. & Carmen, Christopher U. Office Relocating Planner. (Illus.). 57p. 1998. 29.95 (*1-928742-00-9*) Vision Pubns IN.

— Office Relocation Planner. 2nd ed. 57p. 1999. 29.95 (*1-928742-01-7*) Vision Pubns IN.

Chessman, Andrea, ed. see Jamison, Cheryl A. & Jamison, Bill.

Chessman, Caryl. Cell 2455, Death Row. 1995. reprint ed. lib. bdg. 24.95 (*1-56849-599-4*) Buccaneer Bks.

Chessman, G. Wallace. Governor Theodore Roosevelt: The Albany Apprenticeship, 1898-1900. LC 65-13838. 344p. reprint ed. pap. 106.70 (*0-7837-2235-4*, 205732500004) Bks Demand.

— Theodore Roosevelt & the Politics of Power. 214p. (C). 1994. reprint ed. pap. text 11.50 (*0-88133-795-1*) Waveland Pr.

Chessman, Harriet, ed. see Stein, Gertrude.

Chessman, Harriet S. Ohio Angels. LC 98-34208. 144p. 1999. 22.00 (*1-57962-020-5*); pap. 16.00 (*1-57962-071-X*) Permanent Pr.

— The Public Is Invited to Dance: Representation, the Body, & Dialogue in Gertrude Stein. 264p. 1989. 35.00 (*0-8047-1484-3*) Stanford U Pr.

Chessman, Harriet S., ed. Literary Angels. 288p. 1994. pap. 10.00 (*0-449-90774-0*) Fawcett.

Chessmen, Louise. On the Trail of Scotland's Past. LC 99-189859. (Illus.). 64p. 1998. pap. 6.95 (*1-901663-05-1*, Pub. by Natl Mus Scotland) A Schwartz & Co.

Chesson, Andrew, jt. ed. see Wallace, R. John.

Chesson, Frederick W. New Haven from the Collection of Charles Rufus Harte. (Images of America Ser.). 1995. pap. 16.99 (*0-7524-0212-9*) Arcadia Publng.

— Secret Wires: Codes & Telegraphers of the Civil War. (Illus.). 2000. write for info. (*1-883522-16-1*, Rockbridge) Howell Pr VA.

— Waterbury. (Images of America Ser.). 128p. 1996. pap. 16.99 (*0-7524-0421-0*) Arcadia Publng.

Chesson, Jean, jt. auth. see Keyes, Dale L.

Chesson, Rosemary & Chisholm, Douglas, eds. Child Psychiatric Units: At the Crossroads. LC 95-36660. 278p. 1995. 29.95 (*1-85302-329-9*, Pub. by Jessica Kingsley) Taylor & Francis.

Chessum. From Immigrants to Ethnic Minority. 61.95 (*0-7546-1019-5*) Ashgate Pub Co.

Chestang, Leon, jt. ed. see Cafferty, Pastora S.

Chestek, James H., jt. auth. see Cox, Donald W.

Chester. Spring Fever. mass mkt. 6.95 (*0-7472-5423-0*, Pub. by Headline Bk Pub) Trafalgar.

Chester, A. N., jt. auth. see Martellucci, S.

Chester, Alden. Legal & Judicial History of New York, 3 vols., Set. LC 83-82570. 1983. reprint ed. 140.00 (*0-89941-297-1*, 303000) W S Hein.

Chester, Alfred. Head of a Sad Angel: Stories 1953-1966. Field, Edward, ed. LC 90-817. 382p. 1990. 25.00 (*0-87685-804-3*); pap. 15.00 (*0-87685-803-5*) Black Sparrow.

— Looking for Genet: Literary Essays & Reviews. Field, Edward, ed. LC 92-11477. 260p. (Orig.). 1992. 25.00 (*0-87685-873-6*); pap. 12.50 (*0-87685-872-8*) Black Sparrow.

Chester, Allan G., ed. see Latimer, Hugh.

Chester, Alvin P. A Sailors Odyssey Vol. 1: At Peace & War, 1935-1945. Feinberg, Barbara et al, eds. LC 91-172665. (Illus.). 289p. 1991. 19.95 (*0-9631239-0-4*) Odysseus Bks.

Chester, Andrew. Divine Revelation & Divine Titles in the Pentateuchal Targumim. (Texte und Studien zum Antiken Judentum: No. 14). 432p. 1986. 84.50 (*3-16-145113-9*, Pub. by JCB Mohr) Coronet Bks.

Chester, Ann E. My Journey in the House of Prayer. (Illus.). (Orig.). 1991. pap. 8.95 (*0-9628739-0-X*) Sstrs Srvnts.

Chester, Arthur N., et al, eds. Laser Science & Technology. LC 88-25582. (Ettore Majorana International Science Series, Life Sciences: Vol. 35). (Illus.). 466p. 1988. 125.00 (*0-306-43033-9*, Plenum Trade) Perseus Pubng.

— Laser Systems for Photobiology & Photomedicine. (NATO ASI Ser.: Vol. 252). (Illus.). 320p. (C). 1991. text 132.00 (*0-306-43886-0*, Kluwer Plenum) Kluwer Academic.

Chester, Arthur N., et al. Optical Fiber Sensors. (C). 1987. text 278.50 (*90-247-3518-1*) Kluwer Academic.

Chester, Arthur N., jt. ed. see Martellucci, S.

Chester, Carole. Jobs in Shops & Stores. 96p. (Orig.). 1990. pap. 17.95 (*0-8464-1404-X*) Beekman Pubs.

— San Francisco. (Essential Guides Ser.). (Illus.). 128p. 1994. pap. 7.95 (*0-8442-8931-0*, 89248, Passprt Bks) NTC Contemp Pub Co.

— Working in Public Relations: How to Gain the Skills & Opportunities for a Career in Public Relations. 144p. 1998. pap. 21.95 (*1-85703-253-5*, Pub. by How To Bks) Trans-Atl Phila.

Chester, D. N. & Bowring, Nona. Questions in Parliament. LC 74-9164. 335p. 1974. reprint ed. lib. bdg. 69.50 (*0-8371-7614-X*, CHQP, Greenwood Pr) Greenwood.

Chester, Daniel Norman, et al. Policy & Politics: Essays in Honour of Norman Chester. LC 78-318575. 214 p. 1978. write for info. (*0-333-23561-4*) Macmillan.

Chester, David. Volcanoes & Society. LC 93-1620. (Illus.). 288p. 1993. pap. text 25.00 (*0-340-51761-1*, A9530, Pub. by E A) Routldge.

Chester, David K. Mount Etna: The Anatomy of a Volcano. (C). text 189.50 (*0-412-23890-X*) Chapman & Hall.

Chester, David T., jt. auth. see Feistritzer, C. Emily.

Chester, David T., ed. see Feistritzer, C. Emily.

Chester, Deborah. The Crimson Claw. (Lucasfilm's Alien Chronicles Ser.: Bk. II). 352p. 1998. pap. 5.99 (*0-441-00565-9*) Ace Bks.

***Chester, Deborah.** Golden One. (Lucasfilm's Alien Chronicles). 1998. mass mkt. 5.99 (*0-441-00561-6*) ACE.

Chester, Deborah. A Love So Wild. large type ed. 473p. 1982. 27.99 (*0-7089-0764-4*) Ulverscroft.

— Lucasfilm's Alien Chronicles: The Golden One. (Lucasfilm Alien Chronicles Bk.: No. I). 1997. mass mkt. 5.99 (*1-57297-278-5*) Blvd Books.

— Lucasfilm's Alien Chronicles Book Bk. III: The Crystal Eye. 1999. mass mkt. 6.99 (*0-441-00635-3*) Ace Bks.

— Reign of Shadows. 1996. mass mkt. 5.99 (*0-441-00340-0*) Ace Bks.

— The Ruby Throne: Realm of Light. 400p. 1997. mass mkt. 6.99 (*0-441-00480-6*) Ace Bks.

— Shadow War. 400p. 1997. mass mkt. 6.99 (*0-441-00400-8*) Ace Bks.

***Chester, Deborah.** The Sword, the Ring & the Chalice: The Ring. 2000. mass mkt. 9.99 (*0-441-00757-0*) Ace Bks.

— The Sword, the Ring & the Chalice: The Sword. 2000. mass mkt. 6.99 (*0-441-00702-3*) Ace Bks.

Chester, Donald. Inheritance, Wealth, & Society. LC 81-48082. 247p. 1982. reprint ed. pap. 76.60 (*0-608-01054-5*, 205936200001) Bks Demand.

Chester, Edward W. The Scope & Variety of U. S. Diplomatic History Vol. II: Readings since 1900. 384p. (C). 1989. pap. text. write for info. (*0-318-65459-8*) P-H.

— United States Oil Policy & Diplomacy: A Twentieth Century Overview, 52. LC 82-9379. (Contributions in Economics & Economic History Ser.: No. 52). (Illus.). 399p. 1983. 55.00 (*0-313-23174-5*, CUO/, Greenwood Pr) Greenwood.

***Chester, Edward W. & Ellis, William H.** Wildflowers of Land Between the Lakes, Kentucky & Tennessee. 2nd ed. (Illus.). 220p. 2000. pap. text 8.00 (*1-880617-08-0*) APSU Ctr Fld Bio.

Chester, Edward W. & Ellis, William H. Wildflowers of the Land Between the Lakes, Kentucky & Tennessee. LC 95-74974. (Illus.). 180p. (Orig.). (C). 1995. pap. text 10.00 (*1-880617-04-8*) APSU Ctr Fld Bio.

Chester, Edward W. & Wallace, Betty J. Fort Donelson National Military Battlefield: A Botanical & Historical Perspective. LC 97-66338. (Illus.). 228p. (Orig.). (C). 1997. pap. 10.00 (*1-880617-07-2*) APSU Ctr Fld Bio.

Chester, Edward W., et al. Atlas of Tennessee Vascular Plants Vol. 1: Pteriodophytes, Gymnosperms, Angiosperms: Monocots. LC 93-72167. (Illus.). 120p. (Orig.). 1993. pap. 7.00 (*1-880617-02-1*) APSU Ctr Fld Bio.

— Atlas of Tennessee Vascular Plants Vol. 2: Dicots. (Miscellaneous Publications: No. 13). (Illus.). 240p. (C). 1997. pap. text 8.00 (*1-880617-06-4*) APSU Ctr Fld Bio.

Chester, England Diocese Staff. Child-Marriages, Divorces, & Ratifications Etc. 1561-66. Furnivall, F. J., ed. (EETS, OS Ser.: No. 108). 1972. reprint ed. 55.00 (*0-527-00112-0*) Periodicals Srv.

***Chester, Eric.** Lead Now or Step Aside: The Ultimate Handbook for Student Leaders. 1999. pap. 16.95 (*0-9651447-4-7*) ChesPress.

Chester, Eric. Preteen Power: A Treasury of Solid Gold Advice for Those Just Entering Their Teens. 193p. (YA). (gr. 6 up). 1997. pap. text 11.95 (*0-9651447-3-9*) ChesPress.

— Teen Empower: A Treasury of Solid Gold Advice for Today's Teens. 193p. (YA). (gr. 6 up). 1997. pap. text 11.95 (*0-9651447-2-0*) ChesPress.

— Teen Power: A Treasury of Solid Gold Advice for Today's Teens. 193p. (YA). (gr. 6 up). 1997. pap. text 11.95 (*0-9651447-0-4*) ChesPress.

— Teen Power Too: More Solid Gold Advice for Teens. 193p. (YA). (gr. 6 up). 1997. pap. 11.95 (*0-9651447-1-2*) ChesPress.

Chester, Eric T. Covert Network: Progressives, the International Rescue Committee, & the CIA. LC 95-3037. (Illus.). 276p. (C). (gr. 13). 1995. 77.95 (*1-56324-550-7*); pap. 39.95 (*1-56324-551-5*) M E Sharpe.

— Socialists & the Ballot Box: An Historical Analysis. LC 85-6475. 192p. 1985. 49.95 (*0-275-90073-8*, C0073, Praeger Pubs) Greenwood.

Chester, Gail, ed. Feminism & Censorship, Vol. 1. 288p. (Orig.). (C). 1989. pap. 9.95 (*1-85327-023-7*, Pub. by Prism Pr) Assoc Pubs Grp.

Chester, Gail A. Modern Medical Assisting. Williams, Adrianne, ed. LC 97-30097. (Illus.). 768p. (C). 1998. pap. text 52.00 (*0-7216-4997-1*, W B Saunders Co) Harcrt Hlth Sci Grp.

— Modern Medical Assisting. (C). 1998. pap. text, student ed. 16.95 (*0-7216-4998-X*, W B Saunders Co) Harcrt Hlth Sci Grp.

Chester, Gary. The New Breed: Drum. 48p. 1986. pap. 9.95 (*0-88188-749-8*, 06631619) H Leonard.

Chester, Gary & Adams, Chris. The New Breed II: The Sequel - Independence, Inspiration, Innovation. (Illus.). 96p. (C). 1990. pap. 14.95 (*0-7935-0004-4*, 00660125) H Leonard.

Chester, George R. The Jingo. Reginald, R. & Melville, Douglas, eds. LC 77-84210. (Lost Race & Adult Fantasy Ser.). (Illus.). 1978. reprint ed. lib. bdg. 39.95 (*0-405-10965-2*) Ayer.

Chester, Isabelle, ed. Listen to Women for a Change. (Illus.). 65p. 1986. pap. 3.00 (*0-686-30399-7*) WILPF.

***Chester, James Wesley.** The African American Ethnicity. (Illus.). 269p. 2000. pap. 15.99 (*0-9674456-0-4*) IAANH.

Chester, John C., Sr. "From Foggy Bottom to Capitol Hill" Exploits of a G. I., Diplomat & Congressional Aide. (Illus.). 2000. pap. 20.00 (*0-9653949-1-3*, Arlington Hall Pr) Assn Diplomatic Studies.

Chester, Jonathan. A for Antarctica. (Illus.). 32p. (J). (ps up). 1998. pap. text 7.95 (*1-883672-73-2*) Tricycle Pr.

Chester, Jonathan. Penguins: A Postcard Book. 107.40 (*0-89087-798-X*) Celestial Arts.

Chester, Jonathan. Penguins: 23 Postcards. (Illus.). 48p. 1996. pap. 8.95 (*0-89087-764-5*) Celestial Arts.

***Chester, Jonathan.** Splash! A Penguin Counting Book. (Illus.). 24p. (J). (ps-k). 2000. pap. 5.95 (*1-58246-042-6*) Tricycle Pr.

Chester, Jonathan. Trekking & Climbing in the Himalaya. (Illus.). 224p. 1989. pap. 24.95 (*0-938567-17-9*) Mountaineers.

— The World of the Penguin. LC 96-17675. (Illus.). 128p. 1996. 27.50 (*0-87156-900-0*, Pub. by Sierra) Random.

Chester, Jonathan, jt. auth. see Melville, Kirsty.

Chester-Jones, I. & Henderson, I. W., eds. General, Comparative & Clinical Endocrinology of the Adrenal Cortex, 3 vols., Vol. 3. 1981. 247.00 (*0-318-59010-7*) Acad Pr.

Chester-Jones, I., et al. Fundamentals of Comparative Vertebrate Endocrinology. LC 86-22703. (Illus.). 682p. (C). 1987. text 145.00 (*0-306-42314-6*, Kluwer Plenum) Kluwer Academic.

Chester, K. Starr, tr. see Vavilov, N. I.

Chester, Kate. Dead & Buried. (Hear No Evil Ser.). 1996. 9.09 (*0-606-10208-6*, Pub. by Turtleback) Demco.

— Death in the Afternoon. (Hear No Evil Ser.). (J). 1996. 9.09 (*0-606-09398-2*, Pub. by Turtleback) Demco.

— Hear No Evil, No. 4. (J). 1996. pap. 3.99 (*0-590-67329-7*) Scholastic Inc.

— Hear No Evil #5. (J). 1997. mass mkt. 3.99 (*0-590-87991-X*) Scholastic Inc.

— Missing. (Hear No Evil Ser.: No. 2). 1996. mass mkt. 3.99 (*0-590-67327-0*) Scholastic Inc.

— Missing! (Hear No Evil Ser.). (J). 1996. 9.09 (*0-606-09399-0*, Pub. by Turtleback) Demco.

— Playing with Fire. (Hear No Evil Ser.). (J). (gr. 6-10). 1997. pap. 3.99 (*0-614-29021-X*) Scholastic Inc.

Chester, Kate. Playing with Fire, 6. (Hear No Evil Ser.). 1997. 9.09 (*0-606-11449-1*, Pub. by Turtleback) Demco.

Chester, Kate. Playing with Fire, Vol. 6. (Hear No Evil Ser.). 1997. mass mkt. 3.99 (*0-590-87992-8*, Point) Scholastic Inc.

— Sudden Death. (Hear No Evil Ser.). (J). (gr. 6-10). 1997. 3.99 (*0-614-29020-1*) Scholastic Inc.

Chester, Kate. Sudden Death. (Hear No Evil Ser.). 1997. 9.09 (*0-606-10838-6*, Pub. by Turtleback) Demco.

Chester, Kate. A Time of Fear. (Hear No Evil Ser.: No. 3). (YA). 1996. mass mkt. 3.99 (*0-590-67328-9*) Scholastic Inc.

— A Time of Fear. (Hear No Evil Ser.). 1996. 9.09 (*0-606-10207-8*, Pub. by Turtleback) Demco.

Chester, Keith. East European Narrow Gauge. LC 94-27118. 104p. 1994. pap. 22.90 (*1-873150-04-0*) Taylor & Francis.

Chester, L. Course of Pleasure. mass mkt. 6.95 (*0-7472-5422-2*, Pub. by Headline Bk Pub) Trafalgar.

— Liaison Driven by Desire. 1998. mass mkt. 6.95 (*0-7472-5760-4*, Pub. by Headline Bk Pub) Trafalgar.

— Liaison True Colours. 1997. mass mkt. 6.95 (*0-7472-5629-2*, Pub. by Headline Bk Pub) Trafalgar.

— Portrait in Blue. mass mkt. 6.95 (*0-7472-5283-1*, Pub. by Headline Bk Pub) Trafalgar.

— Vermilion Gates. mass mkt. 6.95 (*0-7472-5210-6*, Pub. by Headline Bk Pub) Trafalgar.

Chester, Laura. Bitches Ride Alone. LC 91-31699. 204p. (Orig.). 1991. pap. 12.00 (*0-87685-847-7*) Black Sparrow.

— Bitches Ride Alone. LC 91-31699. 204p. (Orig.). 1991. 25.00 (*0-87685-848-5*) Black Sparrow.

— Bitches Ride Alone, signed ed. deluxe ed. LC 91-31699. 204p. (Orig.). 1991. 35.00 (*0-87685-849-3*) Black Sparrow.

— Free Rein. (Poetry Ser.). 72p. (Orig.). 1988. pap. 7.00 (*0-930901-54-1*) Burning Deck.

— Free Rein. deluxe ed. (Poetry Ser.). 72p. (Orig.). 1988. pap. 15.00 (*0-930901-55-X*) Burning Deck.

***Chester, Laura.** Holy Personal: Looking for Small Private Places of Worship. LC 00-38288. (Illus.). 2000. 29.95 (*0-253-33804-2*) Ind U Pr.

Chester, Laura. In the Zone: New & Selected Writing. LC 88-7530. 236p. (Orig.). (C). 1988. 20.00 (*0-87685-748-9*) Black Sparrow.

— In the Zone: New & Selected Writing. LC 88-7530. 236p. (Orig.). (C). 1988. pap. 12.50 (*0-87685-747-0*) Black Sparrow.

— In the Zone: New & Selected Writing, signed ed. deluxe limited ed. LC 88-7530. 236p. (Orig.). (C). 1988. 30.00 (*0-87685-749-7*) Black Sparrow.

— Lupus Novice: Toward Self-Healing. 2nd rev. expanded ed. LC 99-11490. 224p. 1999. pap. 13.95 (*1-58177-020-0*, P2083, Pub. by Barrytown Ltd) Consort Bk Sales.

— Lupus Novice: Towards Self Healing. Quasha, George, ed. LC 87-9758. 192p. (C). 1987. 16.95 (*0-88268-037-4*) Station Hill Pr.

— My Pleasure. 1980. pap. 10.00 (*0-935724-03-6*) Figures.

— Proud & Ashamed. 1977. 5.00 (*0-87922-128-3*) Christophers Bks.

— The Stone Baby. LC 89-39003. 228p. (Orig.). 1989. 20.00 (*0-87685-776-4*); pap. 12.50 (*0-87685-775-6*) Black Sparrow.

— Watermark. 1978. pap. 10.00 (*0-935724-81-8*) Figures.

— Watermark. deluxe ed. 1978. 15.00 (*0-935724-56-7*) Figures.

Chester, Laura, intro. Deep Down: The New Sensual Writing by Women. 348p. 1989. pap. 12.95 (*0-571-12968-4*) Faber & Faber.

Chester, Laura, jt. auth. see Phelan, J. R.

Chester, Lewis, jt. auth. see Phelan, James R.

Chester, Lucinda. The Challenge. pap. 6.95 (*0-7472-5282-3*, Pub. by Headline Bk Pub) Trafalgar.

Chester, Marcella. Cherry Love. LC 96-76218. 180p. (Orig.). 1996. pap. 11.95 (*1-888675-50-0*) Wlking Brdge.

Chester, Mark I. Diary of a Thought Criminal. LC 96-70238. 64p. 1996. 45.00 (*0-9627616-1-3*); pap. 30.00 (*0-9627616-2-1*) RFD Pr.

Chester, Marvin. Primer of Quantum Mechanics. rev. ed. LC 91-44779. 328p. (C). 1992. reprint ed. 54.50 (*0-89464-701-6*) Krieger.

Chester, Myrvin, jt. auth. see Moreton, Robert.

Chester, Newell, ed. see Bishop, Judson W.

Chester, Newell L., ed. A Drummer Boy's Diary. 160p. 1995. reprint ed. pap. 14.95 (*0-87839-095-2*) North Star.

Chester, Newell L., ed. see Bircher, William.

Chester, Nia L., jt. ed. see Grossman, Hildreth Y.

Chester, Pamela & Forrester, Sibelan. Engendering Slavic Literatures. 272p. 1996. 44.95 (*0-253-33016-5*); pap. text 19.95 (*0-253-21042-9*) Ind U Pr.

Chester, Penfield. Sisters on a Journey: Portraits of American Midwives. LC 97-7711. (Illus.). 288p. (C). 1997. pap. 19.95 (*0-8135-2408-3*); text 50.00 (*0-8135-2407-5*) Rutgers U Pr.

Chester, Peter. Killing Comes Easy. large type ed. (Linford Mystery Library). 336p. 1998. pap. 17.99 (*0-7089-5222-4*) Ulverscroft.

— Murder Forestalled. large type ed. (Linford Mystery Library). 352p. 1992. pap. 16.99 (*0-7089-7265-9*, Linford) Ulverscroft.

— The Pay-Grab Murders. large type ed. 264p. 1989. 23.95 (*0-7451-0985-3*, G K Hall Lrg Type) Mac Lib Ref.

— The Traitors. large type ed. (Linford Mystery Library). 288p. 1989. pap. 16.99 (*0-7089-6737-X*, Linford) Ulverscroft.

Chester, Quentin, jt. auth. see McGregor, Alasdair.

Chester, R. Marine Geochemistry. 416p. 1989. pap. text 59.95 (*0-04-551109-8*) Routledge.

Chester, R., ed. Divorce in Europe. 1977. pap. text 78.50 (*90-207-0652-7*) Kluwer Academic.

Chester, R. J. Hypnotism in the East & West: Twenty Hypnotic Methods. 1977. pap. 9.00 (*0-900860-98-7*, Pub. by Octagon Pr) ISHK.

Chester, R. O., jt. auth. see Hooper, J. W.

Chester, Robert. Workers & Farmers Governments since the Second World War. 39p. pap. 6.00 (*0-87348-723-0*) Pathfinder NY.

Chester, Robert, jt. auth. see Atwood, Joan.

Chester, Roberta. Light Years. Hunting, Constance, ed. 96p. 1983. pap. 5.95 (*0-913006-29-7*) Puckerbrush.

Chester, Ronald & Epstein, Cynthia F., frwds. Unequal Access: Women Lawyers in a Changing America. LC 84-9355. 143p. (C). 1984. 49.95 (*0-89789-052-3*, Bergin & Garvey) Greenwood.

Chester, Roy. Marine Geochemistry. 2nd ed. LC 99-17623. (Illus.). 1999. 175.00 (*0-632-05432-8*) Blackwell Sci.

Chester, Samuel B. Anomalies of the English Law. 287p. 1980. reprint ed. 35.00 (*0-8377-0426-X*, Rothman) W S Hein.

***Chester, Samuel Beach.** Anomalies of the English Law. 287p. 2000. reprint ed. 88.00 (*1-56169-594-7*) Gaunt.

Chester, Samuel H. Pioneer Days in Arkansas. Sperry, Phillip A. & Goss, Joe R., eds. (Illus.). 76p. 1993. reprint ed. 23.95 (*1-56869-024-X*); reprint ed. pap. 13.95 (*1-56869-025-8*) Oldbuck Pr.

Chester, Sharon, et al. Marquesas Islands - Mave Mai. (Illus.). 114p. 1998. pap. 20.00 (*0-9638511-8-7*) Wander Albatross.

Chester, Sharon R. The Birds of Chile: Illustrated in Color. (Illus.). 44p. 1995. pap. text 16.00 (*0-9638511-1-X*) Wander Albatross.

Chester, Sharon R., jt. auth. see Araya, Braulio.

Chester, Thomas. Mastering Excel for Windows 95. 3rd ed. LC 95-70847. 1040p. 1995. 29.99 (*0-7821-1785-6*) Sybex.

Chester, Thomas & Alden, Richard H. Excel 97. 4th ed. LC 96-70738. 1056p. 1996. pap. text 34.99 (*0-7821-1921-2*) Sybex.

Chester, Thomas & Martin, Mindy. Mastering Excel 2000: Premium Edition. LC 99-60015. (Mastering Ser.). 1328p. 1999. pap. 39.99 (*0-7821-2317-1*) Sybex.

Chester, Thomas M. Thomas Morris Chester, Black Civil War Correspondent: His Dispatches from the Virginia Front. (Quality Paperbacks Ser.). (Illus.). 375p. 1991. reprint ed. pap. 13.95 (*0-306-80453-0*) Da Capo.

Chester, Tom L., jt. auth. see Parcher, Jon F.

Chester, W. Mechanics. (Illus.). 1980. text 50.00 (*0-04-510058-6*) Routledge.

Chesterfield, Lord. Lord Chesterfield's Letters. Roberts, David, ed. LC 99-181683. 480p. 1998. pap. 13.95 (*0-19-283715-X*) OUP.

Chesterfield, Philip Dormer Stanhope. Characters by Lord Chesterfield Contrasted with Characters of the Same Great Personages by Other Respectable Writers: And Four Additional Characters from the Letters of Philip Dormer Stanhope, Earl of Chesterfield, Ed. Lord Mahon, Vol. 2. Mahon, Lord, ed. LC 92-22685. (Augustan Reprints Ser.: Nos. 259-260). 1990. reprint ed. 21.50 (*0-404-70259-7*) AMS Pr.

Chesterfield, Trevor, jt. auth. see McGlew, Jackie.

Chesterman. First Amendment Down Under. 78.95 (*1-84014-052-6*) Ashgate Pub Co.

Chesterman, Andrew. Contrastive Functional Analysis. LC 97-50498. (Pragmatics & Beyond NS Ser.: Vol. 47). viii, 230p. 1998. lib. bdg. 59.00 (*1-55619-809-4*) J Benjamins Pubng Co.

An Asterisk (*) at the beginning of an entry indicates that the title is appearing for the first time.

— Memes of Translation: The Spread of Ideas in Translation Theory. LC 97-16461. (Benjamins Translation Library: Vol. 22). vii, 219p. 1997. lib. bdg. 69.00 (*1-55619-706-3*) J Benjamins Pubng Co.

— On Definiteness: A Study with Special Reference to English & Finnish. (Cambridge Studies in Linguistics: No. 56). (Illus.). 228p. (C). 1991. text 69.95 (*0-521-39194-6*) Cambridge U Pr.

Chesterman, Andrew, jt. auth. see Karlsson, Fred.

Chesterman, Andrew, jt. ed. see Karlsson, Fred.

Chesterman, Charles W., contrib. by. Familiar Rocks & Minerals of North America. (Illus.). 192p. 1988. pap. 9.00 (*0-394-75794-7*) Knopf.

Chesterman, Charles W., jt. auth. see Audubon Society Staff.

Chesterman, John. Poverty Law & Social Change: The Story of the Fitzroy Legal Service. LC 96-230377. (Illus.). 296p. 1997. pap. 24.95 (*0-522-84739-0*, Pub. by Melbourne Univ Pr) Paul & Co Pubs.

Chesterman, John & Galligan, Brian. Citizens Without Rights: Aborigines & Australian Citizenship. LC 97-17467. (Illus.). 288p. (C). 1998. text 64.95 (*0-521-59230-5*); pap. text 24.95 (*0-521-59751-X*) Cambridge U Pr.

Chesterman, Michael, jt. auth. see Moffatt, Graham.

Chesterman, Simon & Rhoden, Clare. Studying Law at University: Everything You Need to Know. 144p. 1998. pap. 14.95 (*1-86448-803-4*, Pub. by Allen & Unwin Pty) Paul & Co Pubs.

Chesters, Graham, ed. see Baudelaire, Charles.

Chesters, Kathy. The Horse Owner's Stable Handbook. (Illus.). 160p. 1997. 39.95 (*1-86126-012-1*, Pub. by Cro1wood) Trafalgar.

Chesterton, jt. auth. see Christie, Agatha.

Chesterton, G. K. All I Survey. LC 67-26723. (Essay Index Reprint Ser.). 1977. 23.95 (*0-8369-0293-9*) Ayer.

— All Is Grist: A Book of Essays. LC 67-22058. (Essay Index Reprint Ser.). 1977. 19.95 (*0-8369-0294-7*) Ayer.

— All Is Grist: A Book of Essays. 1988. reprint ed. lib. bdg. 59.00 (*0-7812-0143-8*) Rprt Serv.

— All Things Considered. LC 70-84060. 1969. 16.95 (*0-8023-1225-X*) Dufour.

— All Things Considered. LC 74-156629. (Essay Index Reprint Ser.). 1977. reprint ed. 21.95 (*0-8369-2275-1*) Ayer.

— The Annotated Innocence of Father Brown. LC 97-20612. (Illus.). 280p. 1998. pap. 9.95 (*0-486-29859-0*) Dover.

— Appreciations & Criticism of the Works of Charles Dickens. LC 68-766. (Studies in Fiction: No. 34). (C). 1969. reprint ed. lib. bdg. 75.00 (*0-8383-0524-5*) M S G Haskell Hse.

— As I Was Saying. LC 67-22085. (Essay Index Reprint Ser.). 1977. 19.95 (*0-8369-0295-5*) Ayer.

— The Ball & the Cross. unabridged ed. LC 95-11742. xiii, 178p. 1995. reprint ed. pap. text 6.95 (*0-486-28805-6*) Dover.

— The Ballad of the White Horse. Sheridan, Bernadette, ed. & intro. by. LC 94-194375. (Illus.). 278p. (Orig.). 1993. 22.95 (*0-8187-0183-8*) Harlo Press.

— The Ballad of the White Horse. Sheridan, Bernadette, ed. (Illus.). 154p. (Orig.). 1950. pap. text 12.95 (*0-910334-21-8*) Neumann Pr.

— The Ballad of the White Horse. (BCL1-PR English Literature Ser.). 295p. (Orig.). 1992. reprint ed. lib. bdg. 79.00 (*0-7812-7496-6*) Rprt Serv.

— The Best of Father Brown. Keating, H. R. F., ed. 310p. 1993. pap. 7.95 (*0-460-87395-4*, Everyman's Classic Lib) Tuttle Pubng.

— The Book of Father Brown. reprint ed. lib. bdg. 19.95 (*0-89190-576-6*, Rivercity Pr) Amereon Ltd.

— The Book of Father Brown. 1990. reprint ed. lib. bdg. 16.95 (*0-89968-494-7*) Buccaneer Bks.

— Brave New Family: Men & Women, Children, Sex, Divorce, Marriage, & the Family. De Silva, Alvaro, ed. LC 90-82989. 279p. (Orig.). 1990. pap. text 12.95 (*0-89870-314-X*) Ignatius Pr.

— Charles Dickens: A Critical Study. (BCLI-PR English Literature Ser.). 300p. 1992. reprint ed. lib. bdg. 79.00 (*0-7812-7511-3*) Rprt Serv.

— Chaucer. LC 69-13856. 285p. 1970. reprint ed. lib. bdg. 59.75 (*0-8371-2237-6*, CHCH, Greenwood Pr) Greenwood.

— The Club of Queer Trades. 1976. 18.95 (*1-56723-030-X*) Yestermorrow.

— Club of Queer Trades. 1976. 21.95 (*0-8488-0793-6*) Amereon Ltd.

— Club of Queer Trades. (Classics Library). 1998. pap. 3.95 (*1-85326-260-9*, 2609WW) NTC Contemp Pub Co.

— The Club of Queer Trades. (Mystery Classics Ser.). (Illus.). 128p. 1988. reprint ed. pap. 6.95 (*0-486-25534-4*) Dover.

— Collected Works: Illustrated London News, 1926-1928, Vol. XXXIV. Clipper, Lawrence, ed. LC 85-81511. 669p. (Orig.). 1991. 39.95 (*0-89870-293-3*); pap. 24.95 (*0-89870-294-1*) Ignatius Pr.

— Collected Works of G. K. Chesterton. Clipper, Lawrence, ed. LC 85-81511. 650p. 1992. 39.95 (*0-89870-366-2*) Ignatius Pr.

— Collected Works of G. K. Chesterton, Vol. XXXV. Clipper, Lawrence, ed. LC 85-81511. 650p. 1992. pap. 24.95 (*0-89870-367-0*) Ignatius Pr.

— Collected Works of G. K. Chesterton Vol. I: Heretics, Orthodoxy, Blatchford Controversies. LC 85-81511. 397p. 1986. 29.95 (*0-89870-077-9*); pap. 16.95 (*0-89870-079-5*) Ignatius Pr.

— Collected Works of G. K. Chesterton Vol. II: The Everlasting Man, St. Francis of Assisi, St. Thomas Aquinas, Vol. II. Marlin, George & Azar, Rutler, eds. LC 85-81511. 553p. 1986. 39.95 (*0-89870-116-3*); pap. 19.95 (*0-89870-117-1*) Ignatius Pr.

— Collected Works of G. K. Chesterton Vol. III: The Catholic Church & Conversion; Where All Roads Lead; The Well & the Shallows & Others. Marlin, George, ed. LC 85-81511. 579p. (Orig.). 1990. text 39.95 (*0-89870-310-7*); pap. text 24.95 (*0-89870-311-5*) Ignatius Pr.

— Collected Works of G. K. Chesterton Vol. V: Outline of Sanity, Etc. Marlin, George et al, eds. LC 85-81511. 663p. 1987. 39.95 (*0-89870-171-6*); pap. 24.95 (*0-89870-170-8*) Ignatius Pr.

— Collected Works of G. K. Chesterton Vol. VI: The Club of Queer Trades; The Man Who Was Thursday; The Ball & the Cross. Marlin, George, ed. LC 85-81511. (Illus.). 636p. (Orig.). 1991. 39.95 (*0-89870-364-6*); pap. 24.95 (*0-89870-365-4*) Ignatius Pr.

— Collected Works of G. K. Chesterton Vol. XI: Collected Plays & Chesterton on Shaw. Conlon, Dennis J., ed. LC 85-81511. (Illus.). 611p. 1989. 39.95 (*0-89870-231-3*); pap. 24.95 (*0-89870-237-2*) Ignatius Pr.

— Collected Works of G. K. Chesterton Vol. XIV: Short Stories, Fairy Tales, Mystery Stories. LC 85-81511. (Illus.). 808p. 1992. 39.95 (*0-89870-400-6*); pap. 29.95 (*0-89870-401-4*) Ignatius Pr.

— Collected Works of G. K. Chesterton Vol. XVI: The Autobiography, Vol. XVI. Marlin, George, ed. LC 85-81511. Vol. 16. (Illus.). 341p. 1988. 29.95 (*0-89870-200-3*) Ignatius Pr.

— Collected Works of G. K. Chesterton Vol. XVI: The Autobiography, Vol. XVI. Marlin, George, ed. LC 85-81511. (Illus.). 341p. 1988. pap. 16.95 (*0-89870-199-6*) Ignatius Pr.

— Collected Works of G. K. Chesterton Vol. XVIII: Robert Louis Stevenson, Chaucer, Leo Tolstoy, Thomas Carlyle. LC 85-81511. 375p. 1991. 29.95 (*0-89870-373-5*); pap. 19.95 (*0-89870-374-3*) Ignatius Pr.

— Collected Works of G. K. Chesterton Vol. XXI: What I Saw in America, The Resurrection of Rome, Sidelights. Marlin, George, ed. LC 85-81511. 667p. (Orig.). 1990. 34.95 (*0-89870-271-2*); pap. 24.95 (*0-89870-272-0*) Ignatius Pr.

— Collected Works of G. K. Chesterton Vol. XXVII: The Illustrated London News, 1905-1907. Clipper, Lawrence, ed. LC 85-81511. 623p. 1986. 39.95 (*0-89870-118-X*); pap. 24.95 (*0-89870-119-8*) Ignatius Pr.

— Collected Works of G. K. Chesterton Vol. XXVIII: The Illustrated London News, 1908-1910. Clipper, Lawrence, ed. LC 85-81511. 669p. 1987. 39.95 (*0-89870-137-6*); pap. 24.95 (*0-89870-138-4*) Ignatius Pr.

— Collected Works of G. K. Chesterton Vol. XXIX: The Illustrated London News, 1911-1913. LC 85-81511. 617p. (Orig.). 1988. pap. 39.95 (*0-89870-173-2*); pap. 24.95 (*0-89870-172-4*) Ignatius Pr.

— Collected Works of G. K. Chesterton Vol. XXX: Illustrated London News, 1914-1916. Clipper, Lawrence, ed. LC 85-81511. 579p. 1988. 39.95 (*0-89870-198-8*); pap. text 24.95 (*0-89870-197-X*) Ignatius Pr.

— Collected Works of G. K. Chesterton Vol. XXXI: Illustrated London News, 1917-1919. Clipper, Lawrence, ed. LC 85-81511. (Illus.). 597p. (Orig.). 1989. 39.95 (*0-89870-232-1*); pap. 24.95 (*0-89870-238-0*) Ignatius Pr.

— Collected Works of G. K. Chesterton Vol. XXXII: Illustrated London News, 1920-1922. Clipper, Lawrence, ed. LC 85-81511. 609p. (Orig.). 1989. text 39.95 (*0-89870-245-3*); pap. text 24.95 (*0-89870-244-5*) Ignatius Pr.

— Collected Works of G. K. Chesterton Vol. XXXIII: The Illustrated London News, 1923-1925. Clipper, Lawrence, ed. LC 85-81511. 699p. (Orig.). 1990. text 39.95 (*0-89870-273-9*); pap. text 24.95 (*0-89870-274-7*) Ignatius Pr.

— The Collected Works of G. K. Chesterton, Volume XV: Chesterton on Dickens. LC 85-81511. 573p. 1989. 39.95 (*0-89870-257-7*); pap. text 24.95 (*0-89870-258-5*) Ignatius Pr.

— Come to Think of It. LC 73-142614. (Essay Index Reprint Ser.). 1977. 20.95 (*0-8369-2042-2*) Ayer.

— The Complete Father Brown. 1987. pap. 16.95 (*0-14-009766-X*, Penguin Bks) Viking Penguin.

— Defendant. LC 70-177955. (Essay Index Reprint Ser.). 1977. reprint ed. 15.95 (*0-8369-2841-5*) Ayer.

— Do We Agree: A Debate. LC 65-15899. (Studies in Irish Literature: No. 16). 1969. reprint ed. lib. bdg. 49.00 (*0-8383-0525-3*) M S G Haskell Hse.

— The End of the Armistice. LC 78-117767. (Essay Index Reprint Ser.). 1977. 19.95 (*0-8369-1644-1*) Ayer.

***Chesterton, G. K.** Eugenics & Other Evils: An Argument Against the Scientifically Organized State. Perry, Michael W., ed. (Illus.). 160p. (C). 2000. pap. 12.95 (*1-58742-002-3*) Inkling Bks.

Chesterton, G. K. The Everlasting Man. LC 92-75662. 276p. 1993. pap. 12.95 (*0-89870-444-8*) Ignatius Pr.

— The Everlasting Man. LC 72-11233. 372p. 1974. reprint ed. lib. bdg. 69.50 (*0-8371-6636-5*, CEVM, Greenwood Pr) Greenwood.

— Father Brown: A Selection. LC 94-17038. (World's Classics Ser.). 582p. 1995. pap. write for info. (*0-19-282309-4*) OUP.

— Father Brown: Selected Stories. (Classics Library). 1998. pap. 3.95 (*1-85326-003-7*, 0037WW, Pub. by Wrdsworth Edits) NTC Contemp Pub Co.

— Father Brown of the Church of Rome: Selected Mystery Stories. LC 96-83638. 270p. 1996. 17.95 (*0-89870-590-8*) Ignatius Pr.

— Favorite Father Brown Stories. LC 92-36570. (Thrift Editions Ser.). (Illus.). 96p. 1993. reprint ed. pap. 1.00 (*0-486-27545-0*) Dover.

— Five Types: A Book of Essays. LC 79-86741. (Essay Index Reprint Ser.). 1977. 15.95 (*0-8369-1125-3*) Ayer.

— Four Faultless Felons. (Illus.). 224p. 1989. pap. 6.95 (*0-486-25852-1*) Dover.

— G. K. C. As M. C. Being a Collection of Thirty-Seven Introductions. LC 77-23193. (Essay Index Reprint Ser.). 1977. 18.95 (*0-8369-0297-1*) Ayer.

— G. K. Chesterton: (A Collection of Poems) Thompson, Edward, ed. (Augustan Books of Modern Poetry Ser.). 36p. 1998. reprint ed. 10.00 (*0-89904-738-6*, Silhouette Imprints); reprint ed. pap. 5.00 (*0-89904-739-4*, Silhouette Imprints) Crumb Elbow Pub.

— Generally Speaking. LC 68-14898. (Essay Index Reprint Ser.). 1977. 21.95 (*0-8369-0296-3*) Ayer.

— Heretics. LC 75-128220. (Essay Index Reprint Ser.). 1977. 39.65 (*0-8369-1869-X*) Ayer.

***Chesterton, G. K.** Heretics/Orthodoxy, Vol. 10. (Royal Classics Ser.: Vol. 10). 320p. 2000. 9.97 (*0-7852-4261-9*) W1CL.

Chesterton, G. K. The Incredulity of Father Brown. 20.95 (*0-89190-339-9*) Amereon Ltd.

— The Innocence of Father Brown. 22.95 (*0-89190-338-0*) Amereon Ltd.

— Lunacy & Letters. Collins, Dorothy, ed. LC 72-4607. (Essay Index Reprint Ser.). 1977. reprint ed. 18.95 (*0-8369-2937-3*) Ayer.

***Chesterton, G. K.** Man Who Knew to Much, Tales of the Long Bow, The Return of Don Quixote, Vol. 8. 1999. pap. text 29.95 (*0-89870-675-0*) Ignatius Pr.

Chesterton, G. K. Man Who Knew Too Much. 1976. 20.95 (*0-8488-0350-7*) Amereon Ltd.

— The Man Who Was Chesterton. LC 79-128221. (Essay Index Reprint Ser.). 1977. 46.95 (*0-8369-1908-4*) Ayer.

— The Man Who Was Thursday. (Classics Ser.). 192p. 1990. pap. 12.99 (*0-14-018388-4*, Penguin Classics) Viking Penguin.

— The Man Who Was Thursday. (Classics Library). 184p. 1998. pap. 3.95 (*1-85326-236-6*, 2366WW, Pub. by Wrdsworth Edits) NTC Contemp Pub Co.

— The Man Who Was Thursday. large type ed. LC 98-52504. 288p. 1999. 24.95 (*1-56000-492-4*) Transaction Pubs.

— The Man Who Was Thursday. reprint ed. lib. bdg. 20.95 (*0-89190-577-4*, Rivercity Pr) Amereon Ltd.

— The Man Who Was Thursday. 1990. reprint ed. lib. bdg. 16.95 (*0-89968-495-5*) Buccaneer Bks.

— The Man Who Was Thursday. (Illus.). 128p. 1986. reprint ed. pap. 3.95 (*0-486-25121-7*) Dover.

***Chesterton, G. K.** Manalive. LC 00-31388. 2000. pap. write for info. (*0-486-41405-1*) Dover.

Chesterton, G. K. A Miscellany of Men. LC 73-93624. (Essay Index Reprint Ser.). 1977. 23.95 (*0-8369-1281-0*) Ayer.

— A Miscellany of Men. LC 74-84061. (G. K. Chesterton Reprint Ser). 1969. 22.95 (*0-8023-1224-1*) Dufour.

— A Miscellany of Men. 1988. reprint ed. lib. bdg. 49.00 (*0-7812-0168-3*) Rprt Serv.

— Napoleon of Notting Hill. (Classics Library). 1998. pap. 3.95 (*1-85326-280-3*, 2803WW, Pub. by Wrdsworth Edits) NTC Contemp Pub Co.

— The Napoleon of Notting Hill. (Illus.). 160p. 1991. pap. 5.95 (*0-486-26551-X*) Dover.

— The New Jerusalem. 1976. lib. bdg. 59.95 (*0-8490-2339-4*) Gordon Pr.

— Le Nomme Jeudi. (FRE.). 248p. 1979. pap. 10.95 (*0-7859-1790-X*, 2070366057) Fr & Eur.

— Orthodoxy. 160p. Date not set. 160.00 (*0-8488-2648-5*) Amereon Ltd.

— Orthodoxy. 160p. 1991. pap. 9.95 (*0-385-01536-4*, Image Bks) Doubleday.

— Orthodoxy. LC 95-75659. 168p. 1995. pap. 10.95 (*0-89870-552-5*) Ignatius Pr.

— Orthodoxy. LC 94-18847. (Wheaton Literary Ser.). 188p. 1994. 14.99 (*0-87788-630-X*, H Shaw Pubs) Waterbrook Pr.

— Paradoxes of Mister Pond. xiii, 126p. 1990. pap. 5.95 (*0-486-26185-9*) Dover.

— The Paradoxes of Mr. Pond. 1998. lib. bdg. 15.95 (*1-56723-031-8*) Yestermorrow.

— Platitudes Undone. LC 96-78010. 92p. 1997. 14.95 (*0-89870-628-9*) Ignatius Pr.

— La Sagesse du Pere Brown. (FRE.). 247p. 1985. pap. 10.95 (*0-7859-2014-5*, 2070376567) Fr & Eur.

— St. Francis of Assisi. LC 57-1230. 160p. 1987. pap. 11.95 (*0-385-02900-4*, Image Bks) Doubleday.

— St. Thomas Aquinas. 192p. 1974. pap. 10.95 (*0-385-09002-1*, Image Bks) Doubleday.

— The Secret of Father Brown. 20.95 (*0-89190-337-2*) Amereon Ltd.

— Sidelights of New London & Newer New York. 1988. reprint ed. lib. bdg. 49.00 (*0-7812-0466-6*) Rprt Serv.

— Sidelights of New London & Newer York, & Other Essays. LC 68-8447. (Essay Index Reprint Ser.). 261p. 1977. reprint ed. 18.95 (*0-8369-0298-X*) Ayer.

— Sidelights on New London & Newer York, & Other Essays. 1981. reprint ed. lib. bdg. 29.00 (*0-403-00551-5*) Scholarly.

— Tennyson. 1977. reprint ed. 17.00 (*0-403-07393-6*) Scholarly.

— Thirteen Detectives. Date not set. lib. bdg. 23.95 (*0-8488-1658-7*) Amereon Ltd.

— Thomas Carlyle. LC 73-9601. (Studies in Thos. Carlyle: No. 53). 1973. reprint ed. lib. bdg. 75.00 (*0-8383-1705-7*) M S G Haskell Hse.

— Twelve Types. LC 75-30017. reprint ed. 32.50 (*0-404-14022-X*) AMS Pr.

— Utopia of Usurers, & Other Essays. LC 67-26724. (Essay Index Reprint Ser.). 1977. 18.95 (*0-8369-0299-8*) Ayer.

— Varied Types. LC 68-16919. (Essay Index Reprint Ser.). 1977. 19.95 (*0-8369-0300-5*) Ayer.

— What's Wrong with the World. LC 93-80844. 205p. 1994. pap. 12.95 (*0-89870-489-8*) Ignatius Pr.

— What's Wrong with the World. 224p. 1992. reprint ed. pap. 10.95 (*0-89385-037-3*) Sugden.

— The Wisdom of Father Brown. 21.95 (*0-89190-336-4*) Amereon Ltd.

Chesterton, G. K. & Schall, James V. The Collected Works of G. K. Chesterton Vol. IV: What's Wrong with the World, Superstition of Divorce, Etc. LC 85-81511. 443p. 1987. 39.95 (*0-89870-146-5*); pap. 24.95 (*0-89870-147-3*) Ignatius Pr.

Chesterton, G. K., et al. Twelve Modern Apostles & Their Creeds. LC 68-16982. (Essay Index Reprint Ser.). 1977. 19.95 (*0-8369-0955-0*) Ayer.

***Chestney, Linda J.** Bicycling Southern New Hampshire: Discover 48 Rides for Novice to Expert. 2nd rev. ed. LC 99-86479. Orig. Title: Cycling the Backroads of Southern New Hampshire. 224p. 2000. pap. 17.95 (*0-9637077-5-2*, Pub. by Nicolin Flds) A C Hood.

Chestney, Linda J. Cycling the Backroads of Southern New Hampshire 30 Scenic Tours. LC 93-32173. 192p. 1994. pap. 12.95 (*0-9637077-0-1*) Nicolin Flds.

— Mountain Biking New Hampshire's State Parks & Forests. LC 95-50711. (Illus.). 176p. (Orig.). 1996. pap. 14.95 (*0-9637077-3-6*) Nicolin Flds.

Chestney, P. L. When the Animals Left. (Illus.). 52p. (J). (gr. 1-6). 1994. pap. 12.95 (*1-883533-00-7*) PL&R Chestney.

Chestnut, Arthur B. Put . . . Shoes on His Feet. 240p. 1989. pap. 6.95 (*0-88144-137-6*) Christian Pub.

Chestnut, Bill. Bridgeton: In & Around the Old County Town. (Images of America Ser.). 1999. pap. 16.99 (*0-7524-0467-9*) Arcadia Publng.

Chestnut, Charles W. To Be an Author: Letters of Charles W. Chestnut, 1889-1905. McElrath, Joseph R., Jr. & Lietz, Robert C., 3rd, eds. 1997. 24.95 (*0-614-27817-1*) Princeton U Pr.

Chestnut, D. R. & Ettensohn, F. R. Bulletins of American Paleontology Vol. 95: Hombergian (Chesterian) Echinoderm Paleontology & Paleoecology, South-Central Kentucky, Vol. 330. 102p. 1988. 30.00 (*0-87710-411-5*) Paleo Res.

***Chestnut, David H.** Obstetric Anesthesia: Principles & Practice. 2nd ed. LC 99-25600. (Illus.). 1056p. (C). 1999. text. write for info. (*0-323-00383-4*) Mosby Inc.

Chestnut, Faye, ed. see Isaac, Mia.

Chestnut, H., et al. International Conflict Resolution Using System Engineering (SWIIS) (IFAC Workshop Ser.: Vol. 9001). 162p. 1990. 104.00 (*0-08-037529-4*, Pergamon Pr) Elsevier.

Chestnut, Harold. Systems Engineering Methods. LC 67-17336. (Wiley Series on Systems Engineering & Analysis). 404p. reprint ed. pap. 125.30 (*0-608-30317-8*, 205160100097) Bks Demand.

— Systems Engineering Tools. LC 65-19484. (Wiley Series on Systems Engineering & Analysis). (Illus.). 664p. reprint ed. pap. 200.00 (*0-608-30316-X*, 205515800008) Bks Demand.

***Chestnut, J. L., Jr. & Cass, Julia.** Black in Selma: The Uncommon Life of J. L. Chestnut, Jr.: Politics & Power in a Small American City. (Illus.). 432p. 1999. pap. 15.00 (*0-374-52688-5*) FS&G.

Chestnut, Lauraline G., jt. auth. see Rowe, Robert D.

Chestnut, Mary A. High-Risk Newborn Home Care Manual. LC 97-25844. 320p. 1997. pap. text 36.95 (*0-397-55477-X*) Lppncott W & W.

— High-Risk Perinatal Home Care Manual. 320p. 1997. pap. text 36.95 (*0-397-55478-8*) Lppncott W & W.

— Maternal-Newborn Home Care Manual. LC 97-25845. 320p. 1997. pap. text 36.95 (*0-397-55474-5*) Lppncott W & W.

Chestnut, Mary Ann. Lippincott's Home Care Manual Package. 1997. pap. text 127.00 (*0-7817-1622-5*) Lppncott W & W.

— Maternal-Child Home Health Aide Training Manual. LC 97-25842. 208p. 1997. pap. text 36.95 (*0-7817-1204-1*) Lppncott W & W.

— Pediatric Home Care Manual. LC 97-25843. 208p. 1997. pap. text 36.95 (*0-7817-1203-3*) Lppncott W & W.

Chestnut, Mary B. A Diary from Dixie. (Illus.). 480p. 1997. 9.99 (*0-517-18266-1*) Random.

Chestnut, Mary B., jt. ed. see Woodward, C. Vann.

***Chestnut, Randall M., ed.** Rehabilitation for Traumatic Brain Injury. 176p. (C). 1999. pap. text 35.00 (*0-7881-8376-1*) DIANE Pub.

Chestnut, Renate, tr. see Babyak, Jolene.

***Chestnut, Robert A.** Transforming the Mainline Church. (Illus.). 186p. 2000. pap. 19.95 (*0-664-50101-X*, Pub. by Geneva Press) Presbyterian Pub.

Chestnut, V. K. Thirty Poisonous Plants of North America. (Illus.). 33p. 1998. reprint ed. pap. 10.00 (*0-8466-6051-2*, S-51) Shoreys Bkstore.

Chestnutt, David R. South Carolina's Expansion into Colonial Georgia, 1720-1765. (Outstanding Studies in Early American History). 251p. 1989. reprint ed. 15.00 (*0-8240-6175-6*) Garland.

Chestnutt, I. G. & Gibson, J. Churchill's Pocketbook of Clinical Dentistry. LC 97-6335. 1997. pap. text 29.95 (*0-443-05375-8*) Church.

Chestnutt, Mary & Dewar, Thomas. Office & Bedside Procedures: Clinical Manual. (Illus.). 483p. (C). 1996. pap. text 29.95 (*0-8385-1095-7*, A1095-7, Apple Lange Med) McGraw.

Chesto, Elizabeth E., jt. auth. see Chesto, Kathleen O.

Chesto, Kathleen O. Family-Centered Intergenerational Religious Education: Director's Guide, Director's guide. 108p. 1996. pap. 8.95 (*1-55612-186-5*, LL1186) Sheed & Ward WI.

— Family-Centered Intergenerational Religious Education: Introductory Segment: Creation. 108p. 1996. pap., teacher ed. 12.95 (*1-55612-189-X*, LL1189) Sheed & Ward WI.

— Family-Centered Intergenerational Religious Education: Introductory Segment: Creation: Home Hand-Outs, Pak of 8 sets. 108p. 1996. 12.95 (*1-55612-190-3*, LL1190) Sheed & Ward WI.

C

— Family-Centered Intergenerational Religious Education Year 1: God Speaks. 108p. 1996. pap., teacher ed. 29.95 (*1-55612-191-1*, LL1191) Sheed & Ward WI.

— Family-Centered Intergenerational Religious Education Year 1: God Speaks: Home Hand-Outs. 1996. pap. 8.95 (*1-55612-192-X*, LL1192) Sheed & Ward WI.

— Family-Centered Intergenerational Religious Education Year 2: We Respond in Sign & Symbol. 1996. pap., teacher ed. 29.95 (*1-55612-193-8*, LL1193) Sheed & Ward WI.

— Family-Centered Intergenerational Religious Education Year 2: We Respond in Sign & Symbol: Home Hand-Outs. 1996. pap. 8.95 (*1-55612-194-6*, LL1194) Sheed & Ward WI.

— Family-Centered Intergenerational Religious Education Year 3: Salvation History. 1996. pap., teacher ed. 29.95 (*1-55612-316-7*, LL1316) Sheed & Ward WI.

— Family-Centered Intergenerational Religious Education Year 3: Salvation History: Home Hand-Outs. 1996. pap. 8.95 (*1-55612-317-5*, LL1317) Sheed & Ward WI.

— Family-Centered Intergenerational Religious Education Year 4: The Creed. 1996. pap., teacher ed. 29.95 (*1-55612-318-3*, LL1318) Sheed & Ward WI.

— Family-Centered Intergenerational Religious Education Year 4: The Creed: Home Hand-Outs. 1996. pap. 8.95 (*1-55612-319-1*, LL1319) Sheed & Ward WI.

— Family Prayer for Family Times: Traditions, Celebrations & Rituals. LC 95-78537. 144p. (Orig.). 1995. pap. 9.95 (*0-89622-668-9*) Twenty-Third.

— Raising Kids Who Care: About Themselves, about Their World, about Each Other. 112p. (Orig.). 1996. pap. 14.95 (*1-55612-921-1*, LL1921-1) Sheed & Ward WI.

— Risking Hope: Fragile Faith in the Healing Process. expanded ed. LC 89-64498. (Illus.). 128p. (C). 1996. pap. 8.95 (*1-55612-322-1*, LL1322) Sheed & Ward WI.

— Rituals & Icebreakers: Practical Tools for Forming Community. 110p. (Orig.). 1995. pap. 8.95 (*1-55612-757-X*) Sheed & Ward WI.

— Why Are the Dandelions Weeds? LC 98-75393. 160p. 1999. pap. 7.95 (*0-7648-0406-5*) Liguori Pubns.

— Why Are the Dandelions Weeds? Stories for Growing Faith. 160p. (Orig.). 1995. pap. 8.95 (*1-55612-610-7*, LL1610) Sheed & Ward WI.

Chesto, Kathleen O. & Chesto, Elizabeth E. Children's Scripture Puzzles: Reproducible Activities & Family Discussion for Sundays Through the Year. (Cycle C Ser.). (Illus.). 64p. (Orig.). 1991. pap. 39.95 (*1-55612-471-6*) Sheed & Ward WI.

— Children's Scripture Puzzles: Reproducible Activities & Family Discussion for Sundays Through the Year. (Illus.). 64p. (Orig.). 1992. pap. 39.95 (*1-55612-571-2*, LL1571) Sheed & Ward WI.

— Children's Scripture Puzzles: Reproducible Activities & Family Discussion for Sundays Through the Year. (Illus.). 64p. (Orig.). (J). (gr. k-8). 1993. pap. 39.95 (*1-55612-619-0*) Sheed & Ward WI.

***Chesto, Kathleen O'Connell.** Becoming Community. LC 99-71459. (F. I. R. E. Ser.). 144p. 1999. pap. 19.95 (*0-7648-0474-X*, Liguori Lifespan) Liguori Pubns.

— For the Director. LC 99-71460. (F. I. R. E. Ser.). 104p. 1999. pap. 19.95 (*0-7648-0473-1*, Liguori Lifespan) Liguori Pubns.

— The Living Community. LC 99-71458. (F. I. R. E. Ser.). 144p. 1999. pap. 19.95 (*0-7648-0475-8*, Liguori Lifespan) Liguori Pubns.

— Risking Hope: Fragile Faith in the Healing Process. LC 98-75661. 128p. 1999. pap. 7.95 (*0-7648-0451-0*, Liguori Lifespan) Liguori Pubns.

Chesto, Kathleen O'Connell, jt. auth. see O'Connell, Katie C.

Chestochowski, Ben. Gridiron Greats: Century of Polish Americans in College Football. (Illus.). 200p. 1996. 24.95 (*0-7818-0449-3*) Hippocrene Bks.

Cheston, F. C. Cheston: The New Jersey Chestons. (Illus.). 45p. 1997. reprint ed. pap. 9.00 (*0-8328-7922-3*); reprint ed. lib. bdg. 19.00 (*0-8328-7921-5*) Higginson Bk Co.

Cheston, Richard. Understanding Dementia: The Man with the Worried Eyes. LC 99-42883. 1998. pap. text 26.95 (*1-85302-479-1*) Taylor & Francis.

Cheston, Richard, jt. auth. see Dyckman, Lawrence J.

Cheston, Richard, jt. auth. see Robertson, Robert E.

Cheston, Sharon. Making Effective Referrals. 1991. text 29.95 (*0-89876-170-0*) Gardner Pr.

Cheston, Sharon E. As You & the Abused Person Journey Together. LC 94-30804. (Illumination Bks.). 80p. 1994. pap. 3.95 (*0-8091-3513-2*) Paulist Pr.

Cheston, Sharon E. & Wicks, Robert J., eds. Essentials for Chaplains. LC 93-26013. 144p. (Orig.). 1993. pap. 9.95 (*0-8091-3420-9*) Paulist Pr.

Cheswick, William & Bellovin, Steven M. Firewalls & Internet Security: Repelling the Wily Hacker. 320p. (C). 1994. pap. text 36.95 (*0-201-63357-4*) Addison-Wesley.

Cheswick, William R. Firewalls & Internet Security: Repelling the Wiley Hacker. 2nd ed. 384p. 2001. pap. 36.95 (*0-201-63466-X*) Addison-Wesley.

Chesworth, Jennifer, ed. The Ecology of Health: Issues & Alternatives. (Illus.). 288p. 1996. 52.00 (*0-8039-7302-0*); pap. 24.00 (*0-8039-7303-9*) Sage.

Chesworth, Michael. Colors. LC 98-67335. (Touch & Feel Concepts Ser.). 14p. (J). (ps). 1999. 6.95 (*0-7613-0979-9*, Copper Beech Bks) Millbrook Pr.

Chesworth, Michael. This is the Story of Archibald Frisby: Who Was as Crazy for Science as Any Kid Could Be. LC 93-35477. 1994. 11.15 (*0-606-09011-8*, Pub. by Turtleback) Demco.

Chesworth, Michael D. Archibald Frisby. LC 93-35477. 32p. (J). (ps-3). 1994. 16.00 (*0-374-30392-4*) FS&G.

— Archibald Frisby. LC 93-35477. 32p. (J). (ps-3). 1996. pap. 5.95 (*0-374-40436-4*) FS&G.

— Build a Book with Rubber Stamps. (Build a Book Ser.). (Illus.). 24p. (J). (gr. 4-6). 1995. boxed set 17.95 (*0-89577-830-0*) Rdrs Digest.

— Monsters on the Loose. LC 96-205412. (Illus.). 32p. (Orig.). (J). (ps-3). 1996. pap. 2.95 (*0-8167-4122-0*, Whistlstop) Troll Communs.

— Rainy Day Dream. 32p. (J). (ps-3). 1992. 14.00 (*0-374-36177-0*) FS&G.

Chesworth, Michael D. Cookin' with the Lion: A Pinch of Blue, a Pinch of White. unabridged ed. LC 88-61553. 304p. 1988. 19.95 (*0-9620696-0-4*) Penn St Alumni.

Chesworth, N. Food Hygiene Auditing. 198p. 1996. 100.00 (*0-8342-1680-9*) Aspen Pub.

Chesworth, Niki. The Emu Fact Book: Making Sense of Emu & What It Means For You. 1999. pap. 19.95 (*0-7494-2815-5*); pap. text 19.95 (*0-7494-2404-4*) Kogan Page Ltd.

Chesworth, W., jt. auth. see Martini, I. P.

Chet, Ilan. Biotechnology in Plant Disease Control. LC 92-32197. (Ecological & Applied Microbiology Ser.). 390p. 1993. 199.95 (*0-471-56084-7*, Wiley-Interscience) Wiley.

Chet, Ilan. Innovative Approaches to Plant Disease Control. 9th ed. LC 86-15829. (Environmental & Applied Microbiology Ser.). 372p. 1987. 225.00 (*0-471-80962-4*) Wiley.

Cheta. Preventing Diabetes. LC 99-14783. 198p. 1999. 64.95 (*0-471-99914-8*) Wiley.

Chetal, C. Indraprastha Sports Complex. (C). 1982. 75.00 (*81-7136-001-7*, Pub. by Periodical Expert) St Mut.

Chetan, Anand & Brueton, Diana. The Sacred Yew: Rediscovering the Ancient Tree of Life Through the Work of Allen Meredith. 256p. 1995. pap. 12.95 (*0-14-019476-2*, Arkana) Viking Penguin.

Chetanananda, Swami. Choose to Be Happy: The Craft & the Art of Living Beyond Anxiety. LC 96-28213. vii, 312p. 1996. pap. 14.95 (*0-915801-48-5*) Rudra Pr.

— Dynamic Stillness: The Practice of Trika Yoga, Pt. I. Barnes, Linda L., ed. xxiii,263p. 1990. 26.95 (*0-915801-29-9*) Rudra Pr.

— Dynamic Stillness: The Practice of Trika Yoga, Pt. I. Barnes, Linda L., ed. LC 90-62101. Vol. 1. xxiii, 263p. 1990. pap. 15.95 (*0-915801-19-1*) Rudra Pr.

— Dynamic Stillness Pt. 2: The Fulfillment of Trika Yoga. LC 90-62101. xx, 358p. 1991. 29.95 (*0-915801-28-0*) Rudra Pr.

— Dynamic Stillness Pt. 2: The Fulfillment of Trika Yoga, Pt. 2. LC 90-62101. xx, 358p. 1991. pap. 18.95 (*0-915801-27-2*) Rudra Pr.

— God Lived with Them: Life Stories of Sixteen Monastic Disciples of Sri Ramakrishna. LC 97-3157. (Illus.). 655p. 1997. 25.95 (*0-916356-79-5*) Vedanta Soc St Louis.

— Open Heart, Open Mind: Practical Lessons in Loving Your Life. 2nd ed. LC 97-35518. xiv, 208p. 1998. pap. 14.95 (*0-915801-80-9*) Rudra Pr.

— The Open Moment: Reflections on the Spiritual Life. LC 95-19822. xi, 90p. 1995. 16.00 (*0-915801-52-3*) Rudra Pr.

— Songs from the Center of the Well. rev. ed. LC 93-15561. 76p. 1985. pap. 7.95 (*0-915801-03-5*) Rudra Pr.

— Spiritual Cannibalism. 3rd ed. LC 90-20059. ix, 182p. 1987. pap. 14.95 (*0-915801-07-8*) Rudra Pr.

— Swami Adbhutananda: Teachings & Reminiscences. LC 80-50962. (Illus.). 175p. 1980. pap. 6.95 (*0-916356-59-0*) Vedanta Soc St Louis.

***Chetanananda, Swami.** There Is No Other. LC 99-56811. xi, 269p. 2000. 14.95 (*0-915801-88-4*) Rudra Pr.

Chetanananda, Swami. They Lived with God: Life Stories of Some Devotees of Sri Ramakrishna. LC 88-5775. (Illus.). 434p. 1989. 17.95 (*0-916356-61-2*) Vedanta Soc St Louis.

— Vivekananda: East Meets West, a Pictorial Biography. LC 94-45710. (Illus.). 175p. 1996. 35.00 (*0-916356-78-7*) Vedanta Soc St Louis.

— Will I Be the Hero of My Own Life? Barnes, Linda L., ed. LC 95-23272. xv, 183p. 1995. pap. 14.95 (*0-915801-38-8*) Rudra Pr.

Chetanananda, Swami, ed. Ramakrishna As We Saw Him. LC 90-32015. (Illus.). 495p. 1990. 22.95 (*0-916356-64-7*); pap. 12.95 (*0-916356-65-5*) Vedanta Soc St Louis.

— Spiritual Treasures: Letters of Swami Turiyananda. LC 92-15574. (Illus.). 288p. 1992. 11.50 (*0-916356-77-9*) Vedanta Soc St Louis.

Chetanananda, Swami, tr. from BEN. A Guide to Spiritual Life: Spiritual Teachings of Swami Brahmananda. LC 87-34048. (Illus.). 191p. 1988. 8.50 (*0-916356-60-4*) Vedanta Soc St Louis.

Chetanananda, Swami, jt. auth. see Hatengdi, M. U.

Chetanananda, Swami, ed. & intro. see Vivekananda, Swami.

Chetanananda, Swami, tr. see Dattareya.

Chetave, N. G. Theoretical Mechanics. 700p. 1990. 53.95 (*0-387-51379-5*) Spr-Verlag.

Chetelat, Dona, ed. see Chetelat, Larree.

Chetelat, Larree. Cruise Mate: The How, Why, When & Where to Cruise. large type ed. Chetelat, Dona, ed. LC 97-91947. (Illus.). 172p. 1997. pap. 12.95 (*0-9658398-1-8*) Pony Pub.

***Chetelat, Larree.** Cruise Mate... And the Voyage Continues: The How, Why, When & Where to Cruise. 2nd rev. ed. Chetelat, Dona & Taylor, Edith, eds. LC 99-94783. Orig. Title: Cruise Mate. (Illus.). 250p. 1999. pap. 12.75 (*0-9658398-2-6*) Pony Pub.

Chetglov, Ivan, jt. auth. see Debord, Guy.

Chetham. Before Deluge. 1999. text. write for info. (*0-312-21417-0*) St Martin.

Chetham, Charles S. Modern Painting, Drawing & Sculpture: Collected by Louise & Joseph Pulitzer, Jr., Vol. III. (Catalog of the Emily & Joseph Pulitzer, Jr. Collection). (Illus.). 233p. 1971. pap. 4.95 (*0-916724-35-2*) Harvard Art Mus.

Chetham, Charles S., et al, eds. A Guide to the Collections, Smith College Museum of Art. LC 86-64015. 312p. 1986. pap. 15.00 (*0-87391-039-7*) Smith Coll Mus Art.

Chethik, Morton. Techniques of Child Therapy: Psychodynamic Strategies. LC 88-24384. 276p. 1989. lib. bdg. 33.95 (*0-89862-745-1*) Guilford Pubns.

***Chethik, Morton.** Techniques of Child Therapy: Psychodynamic Strategies. 2nd ed. 314p. 2000. lib. bdg. 35.00 (*1-57230-528-2*, C0528) Guilford Pubns.

***Chethik, Neil.** Fatherloss. (Illus.). 288p. 2001. pap. 13.95 (*0-7868-8449-5*, Pub. by Disney Pr) Time Warner.

— Fatherloss. 288p. 2000. 24.95 (*0-7868-6532-6*, Pub. by Hyperion) Time Warner.

Chetin, Helen & Kurz, Anita. The Lady of the Strawberries. 89p. (J). (gr. 3-6). 1982. pap. 3.95 (*0-7725-9013-3*) Stoddart Publ.

Chetkovich, Carol. Real Heat: Gender & Race in the Urban Fire Service. 304p. (C). 1997. text 50.00 (*0-8135-2409-1*); pap. text 18.95 (*0-8135-2410-5*) Rutgers U Pr.

Chetkovich, Dane. Danger at Rocky River: A Memorable Misadventure. (BrainLink Ser.: Vol. 4). (Illus.). iv, 38p. (gr. k-8). 1993. pap. write for info. (*1-888997-02-8*) Baylor Coll Med.

— Danger at Rocky River: A Memorable Misadventure. rev. ed. (BrainLink Ser.: Vol. 4). (Illus.). iv, 38p. (gr. k-8). 1997. pap. write for info. (*1-888997-20-6*) Baylor Coll Med.

Chetkovich, Kathryn. Friendly Fire. LC 98-24438. (John Simmons Short Fiction Award Ser.). 132p. 1998. pap. 15.95 (*0-87745-643-7*) U of Iowa Pr.

Chetkow-Yanoov, Benjamin. Celebrating Diversity: Coexisting in a Multicultural Society. LC 98-41559. (Illus.). 126p. 1999. lib. bdg. 39.95 (*0-7890-0437-2*) Haworth Pr.

Chetkow-Yanoov, Benyamin. Social Work Approaches to Conflict Resolution: Making Fighting Obsolete, Incl. instr's. manual. LC 96-13118. 174p. (C). 1996. 39.95 (*0-7890-6035-3*); pap. 19.95 (*0-7890-0185-3*) Haworth Pr.

— Social Work Practice: A Systems Approach. LC 91-18004. 158p. 1992. pap. 19.95 (*1-56024-176-4*) Haworth Pr.

— Social Work Practice: A Systems Approach. LC 91-18004. (Illus.). 172p. 1992. lib. bdg. 39.95 (*1-56024-175-6*) Haworth Pr.

— Social Work Practice: A Systems Approach. 2nd ed. LC 97-20082. (Illus.). 171p. 1997. 39.95 (*0-7890-0137-3*); pap. 19.95 (*0-7890-0246-9*) Haworth Pr.

Chetkowski, Emily. Amasa Walker's Splendid Garment. (Illus.). 40p. (J). (gr. 3-6). 1996. 14.95 (*0-929537-03-3*); pap. 9.95 (*0-929537-02-5*) Herit Pub Inc.

— Mabel Takes a Sail. (Illus.). 64p. (J). (gr. k-4). 1999. pap. text 10.50 (*1-880158-26-4*) J N Townsend.

— Mabel Takes the Ferry. McIntire, Donald, ed. LC 95-199886. (Illus.). 32p. (Orig.). (J). (ps-4). 1995. pap. text 7.95 (*0-929537-01-7*) Herit Pub Inc.

Chettiar, Lakshmanan. Folklore of Tamilnadu. 208p. 1980. 8.95 (*0-318-36321-6*) Asia Bk Corp.

Chettle, Henry. Hoffman. LC 78-133645. (Tudor Facsimile Texts. Old English Plays Ser.: No. 138). reprint ed. 59.50 (*0-404-53438-4*) AMS Pr.

Chettle, Henry, et al. Patient Grissil. LC 78-133653. (Tudor Facsimile Texts. Old English Plays Ser.: No. 101). reprint ed. 59.50 (*0-404-53401-5*) AMS Pr.

Chettle, Henry, jt. auth. see Day, John.

Chettle, Henry, jt. auth. see Munday, Anthony.

Chetty, K. M. Sarvodaya & Freedom: A Gandhian Appraisal. (C). 1991. 24.00 (*81-7141-135-5*) S Asia.

Chetverikov, D. & Kropatsch, W. G., eds. Computer Analysis of Images & Patterns: Fifth International Conference, CAIP '93 Budapest, Hungary, September 13-15, 1993 Proceedings. (Lecture Notes in Computer Science Ser.: Vol. 719). 857p. 1993. 117.95 (*0-387-57233-3*) Spr-Verlag.

Chetverikov, S. S. S. S. Chetverikov's "On Certain Aspects of the Evolutionary Process from the Standpoint of Modern Genetics" (1926) Mellon, Charles D., ed. Barker, Malina, tr. from RUS. LC 97-73089. 100p. 1997. pap. 14.95 (*0-9653362-6-3*) Genetics Heritage.

Chetverikov, Sergius. Elder Ambrose of Optina. LC 96-68651. (Optina Elder Ser.). (RUS., Illus.). 472p. 1997. pap. 17.00 (*0-938635-60-3*) St Herman Pr.

Chetwin, Grace. Beauty & the Beast. (Illus.). 71p. (J). 1998. text 25.00 (*0-9649349-5-7*, Rivet Bks) Feral Press.

— Beauty & the Beast. (Illus.). 71p. (J). 1998. pap. text 14.50 (*0-9649349-6-5*, Rivet Bks) Feral Press.

— Briony's ABC of Abominable Children. (Illus.). 56p. (J). 1998. text 19.95 (*0-9649349-3-0*, Rivet Bks); pap. text 11.75 (*0-9649349-4-9*, Rivet Bks) Feral Press.

***Chetwin, Grace.** The Burning Tower. 281p. 2000. pap. 25.00 (*1-930094-05-1*, Rivet Bks) Feral Press.

Chetwin, Grace. The Crystal Stair: From Tales of Gom in the Legends of Ulm. LC 87-27395. 240p. (YA). (gr. 5 up). 1988. lib. bdg. 14.95 (*0-02-718311-4*, Bradbury S&S) S&S Childrens.

***Chetwin, Grace.** The Crystal Stair Bk. III: Tales of Gom in the Legends of Ulm. (Illus.). 201p. 1999. pap. 25.00 (*1-930094-02-7*, Rivet Bks) Feral Press.

— Deathwindow. 1999. 25.00 (*1-930094-04-3*, Rivet Bks) Feral Press.

Chetwin, Grace. Everychild & the Twelve Days of Christmas. (Illus.). 50p. (J). (gr. k-4). 1997. pap. text 12.75 (*0-9649349-8-1*, Rivet Bks); lib. bdg. 24.99 (*0-9649349-2-2*, Rivet Bks) Feral Press.

— Gerrad's Quest. (Ulm Ser.). (Illus.). 151p. (J). 1998. pap. 12.75 (*0-9649349-7-3*, Rivet Bks) Feral Press.

***Chetwin, Grace.** Gom on Windy Mountain: From Tales of Gom in the Legends of Ulm. (Illus.). 196p. 1999. pap. 20.00 (*1-930094-00-0*, Rivet Bks) Feral Press.

— On All Hallows' Eve. (Illus.). 127p. (J). (ps-3). 1999. pap. 20.00 (*0-9649349-9-X*, Rivet Bks) Feral Press.

— The Orborgon Vol. 2: The Last Legacy Tetralogy. (Illus.). 334p. 1999. pap. 25.00 (*1-930094-03-5*, Rivet Bks) Feral Press.

— The Riddle & the Rune: From Tales of Gom in the Legends of Ulm. (Illus.). 1999. pap. 25.00 (*1-930094-01-9*, Rivet Bks) Feral Press.

Chetwin, Grace. Rufus. (Illus.). 32p. (J). (ps-k). 1996. boxed set 15.95 incl. audio (*0-9649349-0-6*) Feral Press.

***Chetwin, Grace.** The Starstone. (Tales of Gom in the Legends of Ulm Ser.: Vol. 4). (Illus.). 221p. 2000. pap. 25.00 (*1-930094-06-X*, Rivet Bks) Feral Press.

Chetwynd. Discrete Mathematics. (Plastics Ser.). 1996. pap. 15.00 (*0-340-61047-6*, VNR) Wiley.

Chetwynd, Amanda, jt. auth. see Burn, Bob.

Chetwynd, D. G., jt. auth. see Smith, S. T.

Chetwynd-Hayes, Ronald. Shocks. 59p. 1996. pap. 14.95 (*0-9524153-2-1*, Pub. by BFS) Firebird Dist.

Chety, Sida. Research on Thailand in the Philippines: An Annotated Bibliography of Theses, Dissertations, & Investigation Papers. LC 77-152541. (Cornell University, Southeast Asia Program, Data Paper Ser.: No. 107). 100p. reprint ed. pap. 31.00 (*0-608-14221-2*, 202184900023) Bks Demand.

Cheung. Exploring Multivariable Calculus with Maple to Accompany Multivariarble Calculus. 228p. 1995. pap. text 33.95 (*0-471-13753-7*) Wiley.

— McCallum/Multivariable Calculus: Exploring Multivariable Calculus with Mathematica. 234p. 1996. pap. text, suppl. ed. 28.95 (*0-471-13754-5*) Wiley.

Cheung. Modern Digital System Design. (West Engineering Ser.). 1990. pap. 78.75 (*0-534-93872-8*); pap., student ed. 8.75 (*0-534-93871-X*) PWS Pubs.

Cheung, Alex T. Idol Food in Corinth: Jewish Background & Pauline Legacy. (JSNTS Ser.: 176). 368p. 1999. 85.00 (*1-85075-904-9*, Pub. by Sheffield Acad) CUP Services.

Cheung, Anthony B., ed. see Huque, Ahmed S.

Cheung, Anthony B., jt. ed. see Lee, Jane C.

***Cheung, Chi-Keung.** Getting Started with Mathematica. LC 98-173821. 200p. 1998. pap. 24.95 (*0-471-24050-8*) Wiley.

Cheung, Chi-Keung. Multivariable Calculus with Maple V. 392p. 1993. pap. 34.95 (*0-471-59835-6*) Wiley.

***Cheung, Chi-Keung, et al.** Getting Started with Maple: (For Release 3, 4, & 5) LC 98-173818. 192p. 1998. pap. 24.95 (*0-471-25249-2*) Wiley.

Cheung, Chiu-yee. Nietzsche in China, 1904-1992: An Annotated Bibliography. (Faculty of Asian Studies Monographs: Vol. 19). 185p. 1997. pap. text 25.00 (*0-7315-1438-6*, Pub. by Aust Nat Univ) UH Pr.

***Cheung, Dominic.** Drifting. 60p. 2000. pap. 9.95 (*1-892295-71-7*) Green Integer.

Cheung, Dominic, ed. The Isle Full of Noises: Modern Chinese Poetry from Taiwan. LC 86-13614. 272p. 1986. text 52.50 (*0-231-06402-0*) Col U Pr.

***Cheung, Dona, et al.** Protecting the Privacy of Student Records: Guidelines for Education Agencies. 143p. (C). 1999. reprint ed. pap. text 25.00 (*0-7881-8129-7*) DIANE Pub.

Cheung, Euphine, jt. auth. see Guo, Tony.

Cheung, F. B. Critical Heat Flux (CHF) Phenomenon on a Downward Facing Curved Surface. 171p. 1997. per. 17.00 (*0-16-062847-4*) USGPO.

— Critical Heat Flux Phenomenon on a Downward Facing Curved Surface: Effects of Thermal Insulation. 93p. 1998. per. 11.00 (*0-16-062956-X*) USGPO.

Cheung, F. B., et al, eds. Proceedings of the 1995 National Heat Transfer Conference: August 6-9, 1995, Portland, Oregon, Vol. 1. 128p. 1995. 76.00 (*0-7918-1715-6*, H00997) ASME.

Cheung, F. B. & McAssey, E. V., eds. Natural Circulation Phenomena in Nuclear Reactor Systems: Proceedings: International Mechanical Engineering Congress & Exposition (1994: Chicago, IL) LC 94-78960. (HTD Ser.: Vol. 281). 67p. 1995. pap. 40.00 (*0-7918-1386-X*, G00881) ASME Pr.

Cheung, F. B. & Peterson, P. F., eds. Thermal Hydraulics of Advanced & Special Purpose Reactors. (HTD Ser.: Vol. 209). 128p. 1992. 37.50 (*0-7918-0799-1*, G00693) ASME.

***Cheung, Fanny M., et al, comments.** A Bibliography of Gender Studies in Hong Kong: 1991-1997. 101p. 1998. pap. 27.00 (*962-441-541-2*, Pub. by Chinese Univ of Hong Kong) St Mut.

Cheung, Fanny M., ed. Engendering Hong Kong Society: A Gender Perspective of Women's Status. LC 97-218979. 1997. pap. text 29.95 (*962-201-736-3*, Pub. by Chinese Univ) U of Mich Pr.

Cheung, Frederick H. & Lai, Ming-Chiu, eds. Politics & Religion in Ancient & Medieval Europe & China. (Illus.). 210p. (C). pap. text 30.00 (*962-201-850-5*, Pub. by Chinese Univ) U of Mich Pr.

Cheung, Gordon. Market Liberalism: American Foreign Policy Toward China. LC 98-18320. 328p. 1998. text 34.95 (*1-56000-378-2*) Transaction Pubs.

***Cheung, Gordon.** The Political Economy of Japan. 1999. write for info. (*981-210-109-8*, Pub. by Times Academic) Intl Spec Bk.

Cheung, H. W. & Butler, J. N., eds. Heavy Quarks at Fixed Target. (Conference Proceedings Ser.: Vol. 459). (Illus.). 544p. 1999. (*1-56396-864-9*) Am Inst Physics.

Cheung, Hung-nin S., et al. A Practical Chinese Grammar. 550p. 1997. pap. text 39.50 (*962-201-595-6*, Pub. by Chinese Univ) U of Mich Pr.

Cheung, J. S. & Ong, L. S. Pressure Vessel & Piping Technology. 528p. 1993. text 121.00 (*981-02-1435-9*) World Scientific Pub.

Cheung, Jackqueline T. & Tang, Kwong-Leung. Models of Workplace Training: Lessons from the Employees Retraining Scheme in Hong Kong. LC 97-29034. (Studies in Business: Vol. 9). 152p. 1997. text 69.95 (*0-7734-8544-9*) E Mellen.

***Cheung, Juanita.** Drink in London. 1999. pap. 12.95 (*1-899858-76-8*, Pub. by Ellipsis) Norton.

Cheung, Kevin C., ed. Twenty-First Century Timber Engineering: Proceedings of the ASCE Convention in Dallas, Texas, October 24-28, 1993. LC 93-35386. 56p. 1993. 15.00 (*0-87262-985-6*) Am Soc Civil Eng.

***Cheung, Kin P.** Plasma Charging Damage. LC 99-34071. 1999. write for info. (*1-85233-144-5*, Pub. by Spr-Verlag) Spr-Verlag.

Cheung, King-Kog, ed. Words Matter: Conversations with Asian American Writers. LC 99-36654. (Intersections Ser.). 408p. 2000. 58.00 (*0-8248-2134-3*); pap. 27.95 (*0-8248-2216-1*) UH Pr.

Cheung, King-Kok. Articulate Silences: Hisaye Yamamoto, Maxine Hong Kingston, Joy Kogawa. LC 92-46452. (Reading Women Writing Ser.). (Illus.). 216p. 1993. pap. text 15.95 (*0-8014-8147-3*) Cornell U Pr.

Cheung, King-Kok, ed. An Interethnic Companion to Asian American Literature. (Illus.). 430p. (C). 1996. pap. text 22.95 (*0-521-44790-9*) Cambridge U Pr.

— An Interethnic Companion to Asian American Literature. (Illus.). 281p. (C). 1997. text 64.95 (*0-521-44312-1*) Cambridge U Pr.

Cheung, King-Kok & Yogi, Stan, eds. Asian American Literature: An Annotated Bibliography. LC 88-5355. x, 276p. 1988. pap. 19.75 (*0-87352-961-8*, B202P); lib. bdg. 37.50 (*0-87352-960-X*, B202C) Modern Lang.

Cheung, King-Kok, jt. ed. see Yamamoto, Hosaye.

Cheung, Kwan P. A Collection of Waves. (CHI.). 144p. 1998. pap. 10.00 (*1-890474-11-8*, 012) Nrth Amer Chinese Wrters.

Cheung, Lilian W. & Richmond, Julius B., eds. Child Health, Nutrition, & Physical Activity. LC 94-43674. (Illus.). 392p. 1995. text 39.00 (*0-87322-774-3*, BCHE0774) Human Kinetics.

***Cheung, Lilian W., et al.** Eat Well & Keep Moving: An Interdisciplinary Curriculum for Teaching Nutrition. (Illus.). 408p. 2000. pap. write for info. (*0-7360-3096-4*) Human Kinetics.

Cheung, Lily, jt. auth. see Chan, Kelvin.

Cheung, M. S. Finite Strip Analysis of Bridges. 368p. (C). (gr. 13). 1996. 145.00 (*0-419-19150-X*) Chapman & Hall.

Cheung, Martha, tr. & intro. see Liu, Sola C.

Cheung, Martha P., ed. Hong Kong Collage: Contemporary Stories & Writings. 264p. 1998. pap. 19.95 (*0-19-587483-8*) OUP.

Cheung, Martha P. & Lai, Jane, eds. An Oxford Anthology of Contemporary Chinese Drama. LC 97-5298. (Illus.). 900p. 1997. text 105.00 (*0-19-586880-3*) OUP.

Cheung, Michael T. & Yeung, David W. Pricing Foreign Exchange Options: Incorporating Purchasing Power Parity. 96p. 1992. pap. 22.50 (*962-209-322-1*, Pub. by HK Univ Pr) Coronet Bks.

Cheung, N. W., et al, eds. Ion Beam Processing of Advanced Electronic Materials Vol. 147: Materials Research Society Symposium Proceedings. 402p. 1989. text 17.50 (*1-55899-020-8*) Materials Res.

Cheung, Oona. Protecting the Privacy of Student Records: Guidelines for Education Agencies. 151p. 1997. pap. 14.00 (*0-16-049118-5*) USGPO.

Cheung, Oswald, jt. ed. see Matthews, Clifford N.

Cheung, P. H., jt. auth. see Leung, K. T.

Cheung, Peter T., et al, eds. Provincial Strategies of Economic Reform in Post-Mao China: Leadership, Politics & Implementation. LC 97-32756. (Studies on Contemporary China). 472p. (C). (gr. 13). 1998. pap. text 38.95 (*0-7656-0147-8*, East Gate Bk) M E Sharpe.

Cheung, Peter T. Y., et al, eds. Provincial Strategies of Economic Reform in Post-Mao China: Leadership, Politics & Implementation. LC 97-32756. (Studies on Contemporary China). 472p. (C). (gr. 13). 1998. text 76.95 (*0-7656-0146-X*, East Gate Bk) M E Sharpe.

Cheung, R., et al, eds. Advanced Metallization & Interconnect Systems for ULSI Applications in 1997 Vol. V-13: Proceedings Materials Research Society Symposium. 765p. 1998. text 72.00 (*1-55899-412-2*) Materials Res.

***Cheung, Sidney C. H., ed.** On the South China Track: Perspectives on Anthropological Research & Teaching. 279p. 1998. pap. 27.00 (*962-441-540-4*, Pub. by Chinese Univ of Hong Kong) St Mut.

Cheung, Stephen. Refining Fire. Ching, Billy S., tr. (CHI.). 154p. 1993. pap. 8.00 (*1-882840-02-X*) Comm Christian.

Cheung, Stephen Y. & Sze, Stephen M., eds. The Other Hong Kong Report, 1995. (Hong Kong Ser.). 486p. (C). 1997. pap. text 34.50 (*962-201-681-2*, Pub. by Chinese Univ) U of Mich Pr.

Cheung, Steven N. Deng Xiaoping's Great Transformation & the Economic Future of China. (New Ser.: Nol. 15). 1997. pap. 15.00 (*0-86682-102-3*) Ctr Intl Relations.

— The Myth of Social Cost. LC 80-26083. (Cato Papers: No. 16). 74p. 1980. reprint ed. pap. 1.00 (*0-932790-21-6*) Cato Inst.

— Theory of Share Tenancy. LC 70-80862. 1969. lib. bdg. 17.00 (*0-226-10358-7*) U Ch Pr.

Cheung, T. Y., et al. Database Reengineering & Interoperability. (Illus.). 364p. (C). 1996. 95.00 (*0-306-45288-X*, Plenum Trade) Perseus Pubng.

Cheung, Theresa. Androgen Disorders in Women: The Most Neglected Hormone Problem. LC 99-26580. (Illus.). 208p. 1999. 23.95 (*0-89793-260-9*); pap. 13.95 (*0-89793-259-5*) Hunter Hse.

— A Break in Your Cycle: The Medical & Emotional Causes & Effects of Amenorrhea. LC 98-230252. 144p. 1998. pap. 14.95 (*1-56561-164-0*) Wiley.

Cheung, V. K. & Tham, L. G. Finite Strip Method. LC 97-24697. (New Directions in Civil Engineering Ser.). 416p. 1997. boxed set 94.95 (*0-8493-7430-8*) CRC Pr.

Cheung, William. Advanced Wing Chun. Lee, Mike, ed. LC 87-43325. (Illus.). 256p. (Orig.). 1988. pap. 19.95 (*0-89750-118-7*, 457) Ohara Pubns.

— How to Develop Chi Power. Lee, Mike, ed. LC 86-63060. (Chinese Arts Ser.: 450). 192p. 1986. pap. 12.95 (*0-89750-110-1*, 450) Ohara Pubns.

— Kung Fu Dragon Pole. Lee, Mike, ed. LC 86-42769. (Weapons Ser.). (Illus.). 128p. (YA). 1986. reprint ed. pap. 12.95 (*0-89750-107-1*, 447) Ohara Pubns.

— Wing Chun Bil Jee: The Deadly Art of Thrusting Fingers. LC 83-50021. (Illus.). 160p. (Orig.). 1983. pap. 10.95 (*0-86568-045-0*, 214) Unique Pubns.

Cheung, William & Wong, Ted. Wing Chun - Jeet Kune Do, Vol. 1. Lee, Mike, ed. LC 90-63463. (Illus.). 192p. 1990. pap. 14.95 (*0-89750-124-1*, 464) Ohara Pubns.

Cheung, Y. K. Finite Element Implementation. 1996. pap. text 65.00 (*0-632-03937-X*) Blackwell Sci.

Cheung, Y. K., et al, eds. Computational Mechanics: Proceedings of the Asian Pacific Conference on, Hong Kong, 11-13 December 1991, 2 vols., Set. (Illus.). 1700p. (C). 1991. text 252.00 (*90-5410-029-X*, Pub. by A A Balkema) Ashgate Pub Co.

Cheung, Y. K. & Leung, A. Y. Finite Element Methods in Dynamics. (C). 1992. text 179.50 (*0-7923-1313-5*) Kluwer Academic.

Cheung, Y. K., jt. ed. see Lee, J. H.

Cheung, Yuet-Wah. Missionary Medicine in China: A Study of Two Canadian Protestant Missions in China Before 1937. LC 88-173. (Illus.). 192p. (C). 1988. lib. bdg. 38.00 (*0-8191-6901-3*) U Pr of Amer.

Cheur, Dan L. Generational Legacy: Breaking a Curse - Starting a Blessing. 50p. 1994. student ed. 4.95 (*0-9642286-1-0*) Family Survival.

Cheuse, Alan. The Grandmother's Club. LC 94-28813. 348p. 1994. reprint ed. pap. 10.95 (*0-87074-374-0*) SMU Press.

— The Light Possessed: A Novel. LC 98-12774. 336p. 1998. reprint ed. pap. 12.95 (*0-87074-430-5*) SMU Press.

— Lost & Old Rivers: Stories. LC 98-25210. 224p. 1998. 19.95 (*0-87074-432-1*) SMU Press.

— The Tennessee Waltz & Other Stories. LC 92-53615. 160p. 1992. reprint ed. pap. 10.95 (*0-87074-340-6*) SMU Press.

Cheuse, Alan, ed. see Malamud, Bernard.

Cheutharassery, T. H. History of the Indigenous Indians. LC 98-908549. viii, 165p. 1998. 22.00 (*81-7024-959-7*, Pub. by Ashish Pub Hse) S Asia.

Cheval, Richie. Shark Attack! (J). 1995. pap. 4.99 (*0-553-54228-1*) BDD Bks Young Read.

Chevaldin, L. E. Jargons de la Farce de Pathelin. (FRE.). 515p. 1903. 9.95 (*0-8288-7429-8*) Fr & Eur.

Chevalier, ed. see Pascal, Blaise.

Chevalier, A. J. On the Client's Path: A Manual for the Practice of Solution-Focused Therapy. LC 95-69483. 176p. 1995. 49.95 (*1-57224-021-0*) New Harbinger.

— On the Counselor's Path: A Guide to Teaching Brief Solution-Focused Therapy. 92p. (Orig.). 1996. pap. 24.95 (*1-57224-048-2*) New Harbinger.

Chevalier, A.J. Shudda, Cudda, Wudda: Affirmations to Cope with Self-Doubt. 380p. 1996. pap. 8.95 (*1-55874-387-1*) Health Comm.

— What If. . . Daily Thoughts for Those Who Worry Too Much. 380p. 1995. pap. 8.95 (*1-55874-342-1*, 3421) Health Comm.

Chevalier, C. Ulysse. Repertoire des Sources Historiques du Moyen Age: Bio-Bibliographie, 2 vols. 2nd ed. 1907. 500.00 (*0-527-16700-2*) Periodicals Srv.

Chevalier, Charles. Nouvelles Instructions Sur L'usage De Daguerreotype et Melanges Photographiques, 2 vols. Bunnell, Peter C. & Sobieszek, Robert A., eds. LC 76-23036. (Sources of Modern Photography Ser.). (Illus.). 1979. reprint ed. lib. bdg. 15.95 (*0-405-09599-6*) Ayer.

Chevalier, Cyr U. Repertoire des Sources Historiques du Moyen Age: Topo Bibliographie, 1894-1903, 2 vols. (FRE.). 1974. 420.00 (*0-527-16710-X*) Periodicals Srv.

Chevalier, Elizabeth. Drivin' Woman. 1994. lib. bdg. 24.95 (*1-56849-427-0*) Buccaneer Bks.

***Chevalier, Francois.** Legendary Yachts. LC 99-88024. 200p. (J). 2000. 55.00 (*0-7892-0637-4*, Abbeville Kids) Abbeville Pr.

Chevalier, Francoise & Segalla, Michael, eds. Organizational Behaviour & Change in Europe: Case Studies. LC 96-190442. (Contemporary European Management Ser.: Vol. 2). 320p. 1996. 85.00 (*0-8039-7909-6*); pap. 29.95 (*0-8039-7910-X*) Sage.

Chevalier, Haakon, tr. see Fanon, Frantz.

Chevalier, Haakon, tr. & frwd. see Dali, Salvador.

Chevalier, Haakon M., tr. see Dali, Salvador.

Chevalier, Haakon M., tr. see Malraux, Andre.

Chevalier, J. Cando Medical et Pharmaceutique. 4th ed. 1016p. 1984. 99.95 (*0-8288-1796-0*, M6069) Fr & Eur.

— Precis de Terminologie Medicale. 4th ed. 280p. 1983. 35.00 (*0-8288-1795-2*, M6070) Fr & Eur.

Chevalier, J. & Gheerbrant, Alain. Dictionary of Symbols: Dictionnaire des Symboles. 2nd ed. (ENG & FRE.). 1060p. 1982. pap. 45.00 (*0-8288-0751-5*, M6068) Fr & Eur.

Chevalier, Jacques. Henri Bergson. LC 78-107797. (Select Bibliographies Reprint Ser.). (Illus.). 1977. 28.95 (*0-8369-5179-4*) Ayer.

Chevalier, Jacques M. A Postmodern Revelation: Signs of Astrology & the Apocalypse. LC 97-180034. (Illus.). 416p. 1997. pap. text 22.95 (*0-8020-7976-8*) U of Toronto Pr.

— A Postmodern Revelation: Signs of Astrology & the Apocalypse. LC 97-180034. (Illus.). 415p. 1997. text 60.00 (*0-8020-4172-8*, BS2825) U of Toronto Pr.

— Semiotics, Romanticism & the Scriptures. (Approaches to Semiotics Ser.: No. 88). viii, 368p. (C). 1990. lib. bdg. 121.55 (*0-89925-619-8*) Mouton.

Chevalier, Jacquie, jt. auth. see Chevalier, Wil.

Chevalier, Jean. Diccionario de los Simbolos. 3rd ed. (SPA.). 1108p. 1991. 175.00 (*0-7859-5826-6*, 8425415144) Fr & Eur.

— Dictionnaire des Symboles. (FRE.). 842p. 1994. 150.00 (*0-7859-9932-9*) Fr & Eur.

Chevalier, Jean & Gheerbrant, Alain. Dictionary of Symbols. 1200p. 1996. pap. 19.95 (*0-14-051254-3*) Viking Penguin.

Chevalier, Jean C., ed. see Zwanenburg, Wiecher.

Chevalier, Jean-Claude. Larousse Grammaire du Francais Contemporain. (FRE.). 494p. 1964. 34.95 (*0-7859-7082-7*, 2038000441) Fr & Eur.

Chevalier, Jean-Marie. The New Oil Stakes. Rock, Ian, tr. from FRE. 187p. (C). 1973. 22.95 (*0-8464-1182-2*) Beekman Pubs.

Chevalier, Joan, et al. Biodiversity, Science, & the Human Prospect. (Illus.). 30p. 1997. pap. write for info. (*1-930465-01-7*) Ctr Biodiv & Conserv.

Chevalier, Louis. Laboring Classes & Dangerous Classes: In Paris During the First Half of the 19th Century. Jellinek, Frank, tr. from FRE. 512p. 2000. reprint ed. pap. 17.95 (*0-86527-425-8*) Fertig.

— Laboring Classes & Dangerous Classes in Paris During the First Half of the 19th Century. Jellinek, Frank, tr. from FRE. 544p. 1973. 45.00 (*0-86527-114-3*) Fertig.

Chevalier, Michael. Society, Manners & Politics in the United States: Letters on North America. Ward, John W., ed. Bradford, T. G., tr. 1990. 16.50 (*0-8446-1111-5*) Peter Smith.

Chevalier, Michel. On the Probable Fall in the Value of Gold: The Commercial & Social Consequences Which May Ensue, & the Measures Which It Invites. 211p. 1968. reprint ed. lib. bdg. 69.50 (*0-8371-0045-3*, CHPF, Greenwood Pr) Greenwood.

— Society, Manners & Politics in the United States: Being a Series of Letters on North America. LC 66-21661. iv, 467p. 1966. reprint ed. 12.50 (*0-678-00195-2*) Kelley.

Chevalier, Noel, ed. see Garrick, David & Colman, George.

Chevalier, Paul. So You Want to Be a Snowbird. Ciano, Jim, ed. 180p. (Orig.). 1997. pap. 14.95 (*1-888672-16-1*) J Ciano Pubng.

Chevalier-Skolinikoff, Suzanne. The Ontogeny of Communication in the Stumptail Macaque. (Contributions to Primatology Ser.: Vol. 2). (Illus.). 174p. 1974. 64.50 (*3-8055-1647-9*) S Karger.

Chevalier, Steven A. The Children's Hospital Killer. LC 92-17538. 1991. pap. 14.95 (*0-87949-298-8*) Ashley Bks.

Chevalier, Susan M., ed. see Cook, Harry T.

Chevalier, T. Le, see Arriagada, R. & Le Chevalier, T., eds.

***Chevalier, Tracy.** Girl with a Pearl Earring. LC 99-32493. 240p. 2000. 21.95 (*0-525-94527-X*, Dutt) Dutton Plume.

— Girl with a Pearl Earring. large type ed. LC 99-86686. 2000. 25.95 (*1-56895-850-1*) Wheeler Pub.

— Girl with a Pearl Earring. 2001. reprint ed. pap. 12.00 (*0-452-28215-2*, Plume) Dutton Plume.

Chevalier, Tracy, ed. Contemporary Poets. 5th ed. 1179p. 1991. 145.00 (*1-55862-035-4*, 200030-M99019) St James Pr.

— Contemporary World Writers. 2nd ed. 686p. 1993. 140.00 (*1-55862-200-4*) St James Pr.

— Encyclopedia of the Essay. LC 98-121007. 1000p. 1997. lib. bdg. 140.00 (*1-884964-30-3*) Fitzroy Dearborn.

— Twentieth-Century Children's Writers. 3rd ed. 1288p. 1989. 132.00 (*0-912289-95-3*, 200015-M99019) St James Pr.

Chevalier, Wil & Chevalier, Jacquie. The Agony & Ecstasy of Intimacy. 164p. 1997. pap. text. write for info. (*0-9659780-0-1*, 71-4-5888068) Lifebranch Inst.

Chevalley, Abel. The Modern English Novel. LC 72-3283. (Studies in Fiction: No. 34). 1972. reprint ed. lib. bdg. 75.00 (*0-8383-1530-5*) M S G Haskell Hse.

Chevalley, C., ed. Methode et Philosophie en Physique Fondamentale Aujourd'Hui. 104p. 1984. pap. 19.75 (*0-08-031846-0*, Pergamon Pr) Elsevier.

Chevalley, Claude C. Introduction to the Theory of Algebraic Functions of One Variable. LC 51-4717. (Mathematical Surveys & Monographs: No. 6). 188p. 1957. reprint ed. pap. 36.00 (*0-8218-1506-7*, SURV/6) Am Math.

— Theory of Lie Groups. (Mathematical Ser.: Vol. 8). 232p. 1946. text 69.50 (*0-691-08052-6*, Pub. by Princeton U Pr) Cal Prin Full Svc.

***Chevalley, Claude C.** Theory of Lie Groups. (Landmarks in Mathematics Ser.). 217p. 2000. pap. text 19.95 (*0-691-04990-4*) Princeton U Pr.

Chevalley, Claude C., et al, eds. The Algebraic Theory of Spinors & Clifford Algebras: Collected Works of Claud Chevalley, Vol. 2. LC 96-7951. 214p. 1996. 59.95 (*0-387-57063-2*) Spr-Verlag.

***Chevallier, Andrew.** Encyclopedia of Herbal Medicine. (Illus.). 336p. 2000. 40.00 (*0-7894-6783-6*) DK Pub Inc.

Chevallier, Andrew. The Encyclopedia of Medicinal Plants. 1996. 39.95 (*0-614-20664-2*) DK Pub Inc.

— The Encyclopedia of Medicinal Plants: A Practical Reference Guide to More Than 550 Herbs, Oils, & Medicinal Plants. LC 96-15192. (Illus.). 336p. 1996. pap. 39.95 (*0-7894-1067-2*) DK Pub Inc.

***Chevallier, Andrew.** St. John's Wort: The Natural Anti-Depressant & More. (Illus.). 144p. 2000. pap. 9.95 (*1-55643-331-X*) North Atlantic.

***Chevallier, Florence.** Charmed. (Illus.). 96p. 1999. 49.95 (*3-929078-81-3*, Kehayoff) te Neues.

***Chevallier, Franpcois-Xavier.** Greenspan's Taming of the Wave, or Golden Age Revisited. LC 00-40459. 2000. write for info. (*0-312-23859-2*) St Martin.

Chevallier, P., et al. L' Enseignement Francais de la Revolution a Nos Jours: Publications De L'universite Des Sciences Sociales De Grenoble-Collection Du Centre De Recherche D'histoire Economique, Sociale et Instututionnelle, 2 tomes. Incl. Tome II. Documents. 1971. pap. 38.60 (*90-279-6932-9*); (Serie I). Set pap. 21.25 (*0-685-03430-5*) Mouton.

Chevanne, Reine. Fontane et l'Histoire: Presences et Survivances, 2 vols. (Publications Universitaires Europeennes Ser.: Series 1, Vol. 1528). (FRE.). ii, 834p. 1995. 78.95 (*3-906754-20-0*, Pub. by P Lang) P Lang Pubng.

Chevannes, Barry. Rastafari: Roots & Ideology. LC 94-18608. (Utopianism & Communitarianism Ser.). 416p. 1994. pap. 17.95 (*0-8156-0296-0*) Syracuse U Pr.

Chevannes, Barry, ed. Rastafari & Other African-Caribbean Worldviews. LC 97-464. 304p. (C). 1997. text 48.00 (*0-8135-2411-3*); pap. text 18.00 (*0-8135-2412-1*) Rutgers U Pr.

Chevassu, Francois. Dictionnaire Anglais-Francais de Medias et de Multimedia. (ENG & FRE.). 3654p. 1995. 39.95 (*0-7859-9753-9*) Fr & Eur.

Chevat, Edith, et al. Girls: An Anthology. 340p. 1997. pap. 14.00 (*1-887369-05-8*) Global Cty Pr.

Chevat, Richie. Allegra's Window No. 4: No Blue Food! (Illus.). 24p. (J). (ps-1). 1996. 3.25 (*0-689-80401-6*) Aladdin.

— Big Stink & Five Other Mysteries. (Ghostwriter Ser.). 1995. 8.60 (*0-606-07575-5*, Pub. by Turtleback) Demco.

— Funny & Fabulous Story Prompts: 50 Reproducible Story Starters that Get Kids Writing & Loving, 1 vol. (Illus.). 64p. (J). 1999. pap. text 9.95 (*0-590-96732-0*) Scholastic Inc.

— The Marble Book & the Marbles. LC 96-604. (Illus.). 192p. (J). (ps-7). 1996. pap. 9.95 (*0-7611-0449-6*, 10449) Workman Pub.

— The Sinister Six: You Are Spider-Man. (Spider-Man Ser.: No. 1). 144p. (YA). 1996. per. 3.99 (*0-671-00319-4*) PB.

— You are Spider-Man Vs. the Incredible Hulk, Vol. 2. (Illus.). (J). 1997. pap. 4.99 (*0-671-00797-1*, Archway) PB.

C

Chevchuc, Carol L. In God's Immortal Season: Poetic Thoughts & Reflections. McFarland, Randy, ed. (Illus.). 100p. (Orig.). 1995. pap. write for info. (*0-9645955-0-8*) Sutton-Keig Pubns.

Chevedden, John & Kowalke, Ron. Standard Catalog of Oldsmobile, 1897-1997. (Illus.). 304p. (Orig.). 1997. pap. 21.95 (*0-87341-484-5*, OLDS) Krause Pubns.

Chevedden, Paul E. The Photographic Heritage of the Middle East: An Exhibition of Early Photographs of Egypt, Palestine, Syria, Turkey, Greece, & Iran, 1849-1893. (Occasional Papers on the Near East: Vol. 1, Fascicle 3). (Illus.). 40p. (Orig.). 1981. pap. text 9.00 (*0-89003-096-0*) Undena Pubns.

Chevedden, Paul E., et al. Iberia & the Mediterranean World of the Middle Ages Vol. II: Essays in Honor of Robert I. Burns, S. J. (Medieval Mediterranean Ser.: No. 8). xl, 464p. 1996. 178.50 (*90-04-10573-5*) Brill Academic Pubs.

Chevedden, P.E., jt. auth. see Burns, R.I.

Chevelier, Pierre. Subterranean Climbers: Twelve Years in the World's Deepest Chasm. Hatt, E. M., tr. LC 75-34044. (Illus.). 223p. 1975. reprint ed. pap. 6.95 (*0-914264-15-X*) Cave Bks MO.

Cheverie, Joan F., ed. Government Information Collections in the Networked Environment: New Issues & Models. LC 98-47470. 120p. 1998. 39.95 (*0-7890-0680-4*, Haworth Info Pr) Haworth Pr.

Chevers, Margo. Stop the Bad Service. 64p. 1994. per. 9.95 (*0-8403-9449-7*) Kendall-Hunt.

— What Do You Want to Be When You Grow Up? A Creative Approach to Choosing Your Life's Goals. (Illus.). 95p. (Orig.). 1993. pap. 14.95 (*0-9636202-0-7*) Grand Pub.

***Cheverton, Peter.** Key Account Management: The Route to Key Supplier Status. (Illus.). 2000. pap. text 27.95 (*0-7494-3098-2*) Kogan Page Ltd.

Cheverton, Richard E. A Fine Madness: An American Family Faces Life's Cruelest Test. LC 99-90457. 1999. 21.00 (*0-9668226-0-9*) Waypoint Bks.

***Cheverton, Richard E.** The Last Story. 272p. 2000. pap. 18.00 (*0-7388-2068-7*) Xlibris Corp.

— The Maverick Way: Profiting from the Power of the Corporate Misfit. (Illus.). 288p. 2000. 22.95 (*0-9668226-1-7*, Maverick Way) Waypoint Bks.

Chevigny, Bell G. The Woman & the Myth: Margaret Fuller's Life & Writings. rev. ed. LC 93-27933. 608p. 1993. reprint ed. text 50.00 (*1-55553-182-2*); reprint ed. pap. text 20.00 (*1-55553-181-4*) NE U Pr.

***Chevigny, Bell G., ed.** Doing Time: Twenty-Five Years of Prison Writing from PEN. LC 98-51940. 384p. 1999. 26.95 (*1-55970-478-0*, Pub. by Arcade Pub Inc) Time Warner.

— Doing Time: Twenty-Five Years of Prison Writing from PEN. 2000. pap. 15.95 (*1-55970-514-0*, Pub. by Arcade Pub Inc) Time Warner.

Chevigny, Hector. Lost Empire: The Life of Nikolai Rezanov. LC 58-11484. 368p. 1965. pap. 9.95 (*0-8323-0345-3*) Binford Mort.

— My Eyes Have a Cold Nose: American Autobiography. 273p. 1995. lib. bdg. 79.00 (*0-7812-8478-3*) Rprt Serv.

— Russian America: The Great Alaskan Venture, 1741-1867. LC 65-12027. 288p. 1998. reprint ed. pap. 12.95 (*0-8323-0320-8*) Binford Mort.

Chevigny, Paul. Edge of the Knife: Police Violence in the Americas. LC 95-70651. 320p. 1995. 25.00 (*1-56584-183-2*, Pub. by New Press NY) Norton.

— Edge of the Knife: Police Violence in the Americas. 1997. pap. 14.00 (*1-56584-180-4*, Pub. by New Press NY) Norton.

— More Speech: Dialogue Rights & Modern Liberty. LC 87-10075. (C). 1987. 32.95 (*0-87722-514-1*) Temple U Pr.

Chevillard, Eric. The Crab Nebula. Stump, Jordan & Hardin, Eleanor, trs. LC 96-19972. ix, 128p. 1997. pap. 12.00 (*0-8032-6370-8*, Bison Books) U of Nebr Pr.

***Chevillard, Eric.** On the Ceiling. Stump, Jordan, tr. 96p. 2000. 45.00 (*0-8032-1504-5*); pap. 15.00 (*0-8032-6396-1*, Bison Books) U of Nebr Pr.

Chevillard, Eric, et al. The Crab Nebula. Stump, Jordan & Hardin, Eleanor, trs. LC 96-19972. ix, 128p. 1997. text 40.00 (*0-8032-1475-8*) U of Nebr Pr.

Cheville, Norman. Introduction to Veterinary Pathology. 2nd ed. LC 99-22664. (Illus.). 352p. 1999. text 74.95 (*0-8138-2496-6*) Iowa St U Pr.

***Cheville, Julie.** Splintered Learning, Splintered Lives: Student Athletes in the Court & in the Classroom. 2000. pap. text. write for info. (*0-86709-499-0*, Pub. by Boynton Cook Pubs) Heinemann.

Cheville, Norman F. Ultrastructural Pathology: An Introduction to Interpretation. LC 93-37657. (Illus.). 954p. (C). 1994. text 199.95 (*0-8138-2398-6*) Iowa St U Pr.

Chevillot, Frederique. La Reouverture du Texte. LC 91-77569. (Stanford French & Italian Studies: Vol. 74). (FRE.). 128p. 1993. pap. 56.50 (*0-915838-90-7*) Anma Libri.

Cheviot, Andrew. Proverbs, Proverbial Expressions & Popular Rhymes of Scotland. 1972. 59.95 (*0-8490-0911-1*) Gordon Pr.

Chevlowe, Susan. Common Man, Mythic Vision: The Paintings of Ben Shahn. LC 98-24384. (Illus.). 208p. 1998. 45.00 (*0-691-00406-4*, Pub. by Princeton U Pr); pap. 21.95 (*0-691-00407-2*, Pub. by Princeton U Pr) Cal Prin Full Svc.

***Chevlowe, Susan, ed.** Paris in New York: French Jewish Artists in Private Collections. LC 00-131238. (Illus.). 64p. 2000. pap. 19.95 (*0-87334-079-5*) Jewish Mus NY.

Chevlowe, Susan, jt. ed. see Kleeblatt, Norman L.

Chevray, Rene & Mathieu, Jean. Topics in Fluid Mechanics. LC 92-10886. (Illus.). 336p. (C). 1993. text 155.00 (*0-521-41082-7*); pap. text 54.95 (*0-521-42272-8*) Cambridge U Pr.

Chevreau, Guy. Share the Fire. LC 97-215138. 182p. pap. 10.99 (*1-56043-688-3*, Revival Pr) Destiny Image.

Chevrel, J. P., ed. Hernia & Surgery of the Abdominal Wall. 2nd ed. Goldstein, E. & Marston, N., trs. from FRE. LC 97-41300. xxvii, 340p. 1998. 150.00 (*3-540-62749-9*) Spr-Verlag.

— Surgery of the Abdominal Wall. Goldstein, E., tr. from FRE. (Illus.). 290p. 1986. 238.00 (*0-387-12640-6*) Spr-Verlag.

Chevremont, Evaristo Ribera, see Ribera Chevremont, Evaristo.

Chevreuil, L. Proofs of the Spirit World (1920) 300p. 1998. reprint ed. pap. 24.95 (*0-7661-0510-5*) Kessinger Pub.

Chevreul, M. E. Principles of Harmony & Contrast of Colors & Their Applications to the Arts. LC 87-60121. 256p. 1987. 49.50 (*0-88740-090-6*) Schiffer.

Chevrier, Jean-Francois. John Coplans: A Self Portrait, 1984-1997. 168p. 1997. 29.95 (*1-881616-86-X*) Dist Art Pubs.

Chevrier, Jean-Francois, jt. auth. see Hers, Francois.

Chevrillon, Claire. Code Name Christine Clouet: A Woman in the French Resistance. Stott, Jane K., tr. from FRE. LC 94-33349. (Illus.). 208p. 1995. pap. 15.95 (*0-89096-629-X*) Tex A&M Univ Pr.

Chevrot, Georges. The Prodigal Son. 56p. 1999. pap. 2.95 (*0-906138-48-5*) Scepter Pubs.

Chevry-Saintil, Florie N. Marcus Garvey - Makis Gave. (Illus.). 21p. (J). (gr. 1-6). 1996. pap. text 9.95 (*0-912469-32-3*) Majority Pr.

***Chevys Inc. Staff.** The Chevys & Rio Bravo Fresh Mex Cookbook. LC 99-86936. (Illus.). 134p. 2000. 14.95 (*1-58008-191-6*) Ten Speed Pr.

Chew, Alex L. A Primer on Adlerian Psychology: Behavior Management Techniques for Children at Home & in School. Brand, Nancy, ed. (Illus.). 1997. pap. 16.95 (*0-89334-271-8*, Humanics Pub); lib. bdg. 26.95 (*0-89334-272-6*) Humanics Ltd.

Chew, Alexander L. The Lollipop Test Manual: A Diagnostic Screening Test for School Readiness. rev. ed. 32p. (J). (ps-k). 1989. pap., student ed. 15.95 (*0-89334-101-0*) Humanics Ltd.

Chew, Benjamin. Sketch of the Politics, Relations & Statistics of the Western World. LC 77-128427. reprint ed. 55.00 (*0-404-01489-5*) AMS Pr.

Chew, C. Y. Butterworths' Student Companions - Finance Security & Banking. 144p. 1995. pap. write for info. (*0-409-30318-6*, MICHIE) LEXIS Pub.

Chew, Charles R., ed. Computers in the English Classroom: Promises & Pitfalls. 148p. 1984. pap. text 7.00 (*0-930348-11-7*) NY St Eng Coun.

— English Programs for Gifted Students. 77p. 1985. pap. text 7.00 (*0-930348-12-5*) NY St Eng Coun.

— Reflections by Teachers Who Write. 250p. 1987. pap. text 7.00 (*0-930348-14-1*) NY St Eng Coun.

Chew, Charles R., et al, eds. Reader Response in the Classroom. 119p. 1986. pap. text 7.00 (*0-930348-13-3*) NY St Eng Coun.

Chew, Charles R. & Schlawin, Sheila A., eds. Written Composition: Process, Product, Program. 165p. 1983. pap. text 7.00 (*0-930348-09-5*) NY St Eng Coun.

Chew, Daniel. Chinese Pioneers on the Sarawak Frontier, 1841-1941. (South-East Asian Historical Monographs). (Illus.). 302p. 1990. 32.00 (*0-19-588915-0*) OUP.

Chew, David C. Civil Service Pay in South Asia. International Labour Office Staff, ed. v, 149p. (Orig.). 1992. pap. 20.25 (*92-2-107759-4*) Intl Labour Office.

— Government Wage Policy Formulation in Developing Countries: Seven Country Studies. (Labour-Management Relations Ser.: No. 73). viii, 128p. (Orig.). 1989. pap. 15.75 (*92-2-106504-9*) Intl Labour Office.

***Chew, Dennis J. & DiBartola, Stephen P.** Interpretation of Canine & Feline Urinalysis. (Illus.). 84p. 2000. write for info. (*0-9678005-2-8*) Gloyd Grp Inc.

Chew, Dennis J. & DiBartola, Stephen P. Manual of Small Animal Nephrology & Urology. LC 86-17134. 350p. (Orig.). reprint ed. pap. 108.50 (*0-7837-1373-8*, 204152200021) Bks Demand.

Chew, Donald, ed. Discussing the Revolution in Corporate Finance: The Stern Stewart Roundtables. 480p. 1997. pap. 35.95 (*0-631-20822-4*) Blackwell Pubs.

— Studies in International Corporate Finance & Governance Systems: A Comparison of the U. S., Japan, & Europe. LC 96-34701. (Illus.). 384p. (C). 1997. text 34.95 (*0-19-510795-0*) OUP.

Chew, Donald H., Jr. New Corporate Finance. 2nd ed. LC 98-10511. 768p. 1998. pap. 43.44 (*0-07-011675-X*) McGraw.

Chew, Donald H. The New Corporate Finance: Where Theory Meets Practice. (C). 1992. text 34.00 (*0-07-011046-8*) McGraw.

Chew, Donald H., Jr., ed. Six Roundtable Discussions of Corporate Finance with Joel Stern. LC 86-12382. 345p. 1986. 59.95 (*0-89930-162-2*, SFV/, Quorum Bks) Greenwood.

Chew, Donald H., jt. ed. see Stern, Joel M.

Chew, Earl, ed. see Badillo, Tony.

Chew, Felix S. Musculoskeletal Imaging: A Teaching File. LC 99-15483. (Illus.). 644p. 1998. write for info. (*0-683-30175-6*) Lppncott W & W.

— Skeletal Radiology: The Bare Bones. LC 89-14846. 276p. reprint ed. pap. 85.60 (*0-608-07239-7*, 206746400009) Bks Demand.

Chew, Felix S. M. Skeletal Radiology: The Bare Bones. 2nd ed. LC 96-28914. (Illus.). 336p. 1996. 89.00 (*0-683-01680-6*) Lppncott W & W.

Chew, Felix S. M., et al. Radiology: MGH Clinical Review. Rosenthal, Daniel I. et al, eds. LC 93-20747. (Illus.). 464p. 1994. pap. text 58.00 (*0-7216-4609-3*, W B Saunders Co) Harcrt Hlth Sci Grp.

Chew, Frederick. Java-C++ Cross Reference Handbook. LC 97-29164. 480p. (C). 1997. pap. text 39.95 (*0-13-848318-3*) P-H.

Chew, Helena M. The English Ecclesiastical Tenants-in-Chief & Knight Service, Especially in the Thirteenth & Fourteenth Centuries. LC 80-2310. reprint ed. 37.50 (*0-404-18558-4*) AMS Pr.

Chew, J. C. & Bawkoff, S. G., eds. Interfacial Transport Phenomena. (Bound Conference Volumes in Heat Transfer Ser.: Vol. 23). 109p. 1983. pap. text 24.00 (*0-317-02628-3*, H00269) ASME.

Chew, Jane C. Human Factors in Computing Systems: Empowering People. (C). 1990. pap. text 39.95 (*0-201-50932-6*) Addison-Wesley.

Chew, Joe & Corey, Jim. Storms above the Desert: Atmospheric Research in New Mexico, 1935-1985. LC 87-6020. (Illus.). 179p. 1987. reprint ed. pap. 55.50 (*0-608-04144-0*, 206487700011) Bks Demand.

Chew, Joella. Awakening Sacred Dance Through Spirituals & Scripture. 1987. pap. 3.00 (*0-941500-48-9*) Sharing Co.

Chew, Jonathan, jt. auth. see Marsland, Tim.

Chew, Judy. Women Survivors of Childhood Sexual Abuse: Healing Through Group Work - Beyond Survival. LC 97-7517. (Illus.). 160p. 1997. 39.95 (*0-7890-0110-1*); pap. 14.95 (*0-7890-0284-1*) Haworth Pr.

Chew, Kenneth K. & Wilson, Anthony. Victorian Science & Engineering: Portrayed in the Illustrated London News. (Illus.). 160p. 1993. pap. 22.95 (*0-7509-0326-0*, Pub. by Sutton Pub Ltd) Intl Pubs Mktg.

Chew, Lilian. Managing Derivative Risk. (Frontiers in Finance Ser.). 332p. 1996. 99.00 (*0-471-95622-8*) Wiley.

Chew, M. Y., et al. Building Facades: A Guide to Common Defects in Tropical Climates. LC 99-163544. 80p. 1998. 24.00 (*981-02-3417-1*) World Scientific Pub.

Chew, Pat K. Directors' & Officers' Liability. 380p. 1993. ring bd. 125.00 (*0-614-17135-0*, B1-1343) PLI.

Chew, Paul A. Penn's Promise: Still Life Painting in Pennsylvania, 1795-1930. LC 89-50637. 112p. (Orig.). 1988. 10.00 (*0-931241-20-0*) Westmoreland.

— Playthings, Selected Toys from the Collection of the Westmoreland Museum of Art. (Illus.). 36p. (Orig.). 1994. pap. text 9.95 (*0-931241-26-X*) Westmoreland.

— A Sampler of American Folk Art from Pennsylvania Collections. LC 89-50234. (Illus.). 100p. (Orig.). 1989. pap. 8.00 (*0-931241-22-7*) Westmoreland.

— Southwestern Pennsylvania Painters, 1800-1945: Collection of Westmoreland Museum of Art. LC 89-50233. (Illus.). 136p. (Orig.). 1989. pap. 14.95 (*0-931241-21-9*) Westmoreland.

Chew, Paul A. & Burke, Russell E. George Hetzel & the Scalp Level Tradition. LC 93-61902. (Illus.). 196p. (Orig.). 1994. 34.95 (*0-931241-24-3*); pap. 24.95 (*0-931241-25-1*) Westmoreland.

Chew, Phyllis G. The Chinese Religion & the Baha'i Faith. 256p. (Orig.). 1993. pap. 13.25 (*0-85398-358-5*) G Ronald Pub.

Chew, Phyllis G. & Kramer-Dahl, Anneliese, eds. Reading Culture: Textual Practices in Singapore. LC 98-474040. 248p. 1999. pap. 29.00 (*981-210-131-4*, Pub. by Times Academic) Intl Spec Bk.

Chew, Robert Z. & Pavoni, David. Golf in Hollywood: Where the Stars Come Out to Play. LC 98-25484. (Illus.). 144p. 1998. 35.00 (*1-883318-08-4*) Angel City Pr.

Chew, Rosalind, jt. auth. see Chew Soon Beng.

Chew, Rosalind, jt. ed. see Chew Soon Beng.

Chew, Ruth. Last Chance for Magic. (J). (gr. 4-7). 1996. pap. text 2.99 (*0-590-60210-1*) Scholastic Inc.

— Magic of the Black Mirror. 128p. (J). (gr. 4-7). 1990. pap. 2.99 (*0-590-43186-2*) Scholastic Inc.

— Witch's Cat. 128p. (J). (gr. 4-7). 1994. pap. 2.95 (*0-590-48341-2*) Scholastic Inc.

— Witch's Cat. 1994. 8.05 (*0-606-06887-2*, Pub. by Turtleback) Demco.

Chew, S. H. & Zheng, Q. Integral Global Optimization. (Lecture Notes in Economics & Mathematical Systems Ser.: Vol. 298). 179p. 1988. 32.00 (*0-387-18772-3*) Spr-Verlag.

Chew, S. L., ed. Post-Transcriptional Processing & the Endocrine System. LC 99-19309. (Frontiers of Hormone Research Ser.: Vol. 25). (Illus.). x, 146p. 1999. 147.00 (*3-8055-6849-5*) S Karger.

***Chew, Sally.** A Fatal Lie: A True Story of a Betrayal & Murder in the New South. 1999. mass mkt. 6.50 (*0-312-97014-5*, St Martins Paperbacks) St Martin.

Chew, Samuel C. Byron in England: His Fame & After-Fame. (BCL1-PR English Literature Ser.). 415p. 1992. reprint ed. lib. bdg. 99.00 (*0-7812-7475-3*) Rprt Serv.

— Byron in England: His Fame & After-Fame. LC 79-115233. (Illus.). 420p. 1972. reprint ed. 9.00 (*0-403-00475-6*) Scholarly.

— Dramas of Lord Byron: A Critical Study. 1988. reprint ed. lib. bdg. 69.00 (*0-7812-0476-3*) Rprt Serv.

— Dramas of Lord Byron: A Critical Study. LC 70-131665. 1970. reprint ed. 8.00 (*0-403-00552-3*) Scholarly.

— The Dramas of Lord Byron, a Critical Study. (BCL1-PR English Literature Ser.). 181p. 1992. reprint ed. lib. bdg. 69.00 (*0-7812-7476-1*) Rprt Serv.

— Swinburne. (BCL1-PR English Literature Ser.). 335p. 1992. reprint ed. lib. bdg. 89.00 (*0-7812-7677-2*) Rprt Serv.

— Thomas Hardy, Poet & Novelist. (BCL1-PR English Literature Ser.). 196p. 1992. reprint ed. lib. bdg. 69.00 (*0-7812-7551-2*) Rprt Serv.

***Chew, Shirley & Stead, Alistair, eds.** Translating Life: Studies in Transpositional Aesthetics. (English Texts & Studies: Vol. 33). 352p. 1999. 49.95 (*0-85323-674-7*, Pub. by Liverpool Univ Pr); pap. 24.95 (*0-85323-684-4*, Pub. by Liverpool Univ Pr) Intl Spec Bk.

Chew, Shirley, ed. see Clough, Arthur H.

Chew, Sing C. Logs for Capital: The Timber Industry & Capitalist Enterprise in the 19th Century, 138. LC 92-3033. (Contributions in Economics & Economic History Ser.: No. 138). 208p. 1992. 55.00 (*0-313-28497-0*, CLJ/, Greenwood Pr) Greenwood.

Chew, Sing C. & Denemark, Robert A., eds. The Underdevelopment of Development: For Andre Gunder Frank & Beyond. 427p. 1996. 58.00 (*0-8039-7260-1*); pap. 27.95 (*0-8039-7261-X*) Sage.

Chew, Sock F. Ethnicity & Nationality in Singapore. LC 86-33177. (Monographs in International Studies, Southeast Asia Ser.: No. 78). 252p. reprint ed. pap. 78.20 (*0-7837-6479-0*, 204648400001) Bks Demand.

Chew Soon Beng. Small Firms in Singapore. (Illus.). 264p. 1988. pap. 24.95 (*0-19-588883-9*) OUP.

Chew Soon Beng & Chew, Rosalind. Employment Driven Industrial Relations Regimes: The Singapore Experience. LC 95-76032. 288p. 1995. 72.95 (*1-85972-103-6*, Pub. by Avebry) Ashgate Pub Co.

Chew Soon Beng & Chew, Rosalind, eds. Industrial Relations in Singapore Industry. LC 95-41366. 1995. write for info. (*0-201-88906-4*) Addison-Wesley.

***Chew, Stephen, et al.** Laparoscopic Techniques & Advanced Endoscopic Suturing. (Illus.). 300p. 2000. 152.50 (*9971-69-234-1*, Pub. by Sngapore Univ Pr) Coronet Bks.

Chew, Teresa, jt. auth. see Jue, Daniel N.

Chew, V. Collins. Underfoot: A Geologic Guide to the Appalachian Trail. 2nd ed. LC 93-4652. (Illus.). 270p. 1993. pap. 12.95 (*0-917953-59-2*) Appalachian Trail.

Chew, Weng Cho. Waves & Fields in Inhomogeneous Media. LC 94-32641. (Electromagnetic Waves Ser.). 632p. 1994. 79.95 (*0-7803-1116-7*) Inst Electrical.

***Chew, Willa C.** The Maithunian Trilogy. LC 97-91123. 1999. 22.95 (*0-533-12564-2*) Vantage.

Chew, William L., III, ed. Images of America: Through the European Looking Glass. (Illus.). 225p. 1997. pap. 26.50 (*90-5487-159-8*, Pub. by VUB Univ Pr) Paul & Co Pubs.

Chew Yen Fook, jt. auth. see Davison, G. W.

Chew, Yen Fook, jt. auth. see Webster, Michael.

Chewning, Alpheus J. The Approaching Storm: U-Boats off the Virginia Coast During World War II. Pruett, Robert H., ed. LC 93-42262. (Illus.). 192p. (Orig.). 1994. pap. 18.95 (*0-9627635-9-4*) Brandylane.

Chewning, Paul, jt. auth. see Webb, Charles.

Chewning, Paul B., jt. ed. see Unkefer, Jane M.

Chewning, Phyllis J., jt. auth. see Chewning, Ronald J.

Chewning, Randy. You Can Name 100 Dinosaurs! And Other Prehistoric Animals. LC 93-85688. (Illus.). 14p. (J). (ps). 1994. bds. 8.95 (*0-590-47913-X*, Cartwheel) Scholastic Inc.

Chewning, Randy. You Can Name 100 Cars, Trains, Boats, & Planes! (You Can Name 100 . . . Ser.). 14p. (J). (ps). 1998. bds. 8.95 (*0-590-96200-0*) Scholastic Inc.

Chewning, Richard C. Business Through the Eyes of Faith. 288p. 1990. pap. 13.00 (*0-06-061350-5*, Pub. by Harper SF) HarpC.

Chewning, Ronald J. Becoming Money Wise. 160p. pap. 12.99 (*0-570-04998-9*, 12-3347) Concordia.

***Chewning, Ronald J. & Chewning, Phyllis J.** Life at Its Best: Living Wisely in an Unwise World. Looker, Lori, ed. (Illus.). 180p. 1999. pap. 13.99 (*0-9673463-0-4*) Stwardshp Adv Pubns.

***Cheydleur, John R.** Called to Counsel: Counseling Skills Handbook. LC 99-51873. 1999. write for info. (*0-8423-3243-X*) Tyndale Hse.

Cheydleur, John R. How to Find & Be Yourself: Your Personality Portrait. (Illus.). 203p. (Orig.). (C). 1988. pap. 9.95 (*0-922693-00-5*) Living Pubns.

Cheyenne, Nur. Tests of Being. LC 98-123380. (Illus.). 159p. (Orig.). 1996. pap. 15.95 (*1-56072-329-7*, Nova Kroshka Bks) Nova Sci Pubs.

Cheyenne, Patty. Children of the River: A Study Guide. Friedland, J. & Kessler, R., eds. (Novel-Ties Ser.). (J). (gr. 6-8). 1998. pap. text, student ed. 15.95 (*0-7675-0298-1*) Lrn Links.

— The Golden Goblet: A Study Guide. Friedland, J. & Kessler, R., eds. (Novel-Ties Ser.). (J). (gr. 5-7). 1998. pap. text, student ed. 15.95 (*0-7675-0301-5*) Lrn Links.

— Zlata's Diary: A Study Guide. Friedland, J. & Kessler, R., eds. (Novel-Ties Ser.). (J). (gr. 5-7). 1998. pap. text, student ed. 15.95 (*0-7675-0321-X*) Lrn Links.

Cheyette, Bryan. Between "Race" & Culture: Representations of "the Jew" in English & American Literature. LC 96-12895. (Jewish History & Culture Ser.). (C). 1996. text. write for info. (*0-8047-2635-3*) Stanford U Pr.

— Between "Race" & Culture: Representations of the Jew in English & American Literature. 1996. pap. text 16.95 (*0-8047-2853-4*) Stanford U Pr.

— Constructions of "the Jew" in English Literature & Society: Racial Representations, 1875-1945. 317p. (C). 1996. pap. text 20.95 (*0-521-55877-8*) Cambridge U Pr.

Cheyette, Bryan, ed. Contemporary Jewish Writing in Britian & Ireland. LC 97-24412. (Jewish Writing in the Contemporary World Ser.). 336p. 1998. pap. 18.95 (*0-8032-6388-0*, Bison Books); text 55.00 (*0-8032-1479-0*, Bison Books) U of Nebr Pr.

Cheyette, Bryan & Marcus, Laura, eds. Modernity, Culture, & 'the Jew' (Contraversions Ser.). 320p. 1998. 55.00 (*0-8047-3069-5*); pap. 18.95 (*0-8047-3070-9*) Stanford U Pr.

Cheyette, Bryan, ed. see Wells, H. G.

Cheyette, Fredric L., ed. see Beaune, Colette.

Cheyfitz, Eric. The Poetics of Imperialism: Translation & Colonization from the Tempest to Tarzan. LC 96-45596. (Illus.). 272p. 1997. pap. 17.50 (*0-8122-1609-1*) U of Pa Pr.

— The Trans-parent: Sexual Politics in the Language of Emerson. LC 80-25750. 206p. reprint ed. pap. 63.90 (*0-8357-6606-3*, 203525100094) Bks Demand.

Cheyne, A. C. The Practical & the Pious: Essays on Thomas Chalmers (1780-1847) (C). 1988. text 75.00 (*0-7152-0582-X*) St Mut.

***Cheyne, A. C.** Studies in Scottish Church History. (Illus.). 352p. 1999. 49.95 (*0-567-08644-5*, Pub. by T & T Clark) Bks Intl VA.

Cheyne, A. C. The Transforming of the Kirk: Victorian Scotland's Religious Revolution. 244p. (C). 1988. pap. text 30.00 (*0-7152-0545-5*) St Mut.

Cheyne, Ann. The Legal Secretary's Guide. 272p. (C). 1991. 46.00 (*1-85431-116-6*, Pub. by Blackstone Pr) Gaunt.

— The Legal Secretary's Guide. 2nd ed. 278p. 1996. pap. 48.00 (*1-85431-548-X*, Pub. by Blackstone Pr) Gaunt.

***Cheyne, Ann.** The Legal Secretary's Guide. 3rd ed. 363p. 1999. pap. 48.00 (*1-85431-897-7*, Pub. by Blackstone Pr) Gaunt.

Cheyne, Charles H. An Elementary Treatise in the Planetary Theory. Cohen, I. Bernard, ed. LC 80-2117. (Development of Science Ser.). (Illus.). 1981. lib. bdg. 15.00 (*0-686-73597-8*) Ayer.

— An Elementary Treatise on the Planetary Theory. 1981. 18.95 (*0-405-13837-7*) Ayer.

Cheyne, Christine, et al. Social Policy in Aotearoa New Zealand: A Critical Introduction. (Illus.). 288p. 1997. pap. text 55.00 (*0-19-558334-5*) OUP.

Cheyne, George. The English Malady. LC 76-49853. (History of Psychology Ser.). 304p. 1976. reprint ed. 50.00 (*0-8201-1281-X*) Schol Facsimiles.

— An Essay of Health & Long Life. Kastenbaum, Robert J., ed. LC 78-22191. (Aging & Old Age Ser.). 1979. reprint ed. lib. bdg. 23.95 (*0-405-11808-2*) Ayer.

Cheyne, George J. A Bibliographical Study of the Writings of Joaquin Costa (1846-1911) (Monagrafias A Ser.: Vol. XXIV). (Illus.). 189p. (Orig.). (C). 1972. pap. 40.00 (*0-900411-36-8*, Pub. by Tamesis Bks Ltd) Boydell & Brewer.

Cheyne, John. Incarnational Agents: A Guide to Developmental Ministry. Hansen, Susan, ed. 272p. 1996. pap. text 10.95 (*1-56309-168-2*, N963117, New Hope) Womans Mission Union.

Cheyne, T. K. & Black, J. S., eds. Encyclopedia Biblica, 4 vols. 1977. lib. bdg. 425.95 (*0-8490-1764-5*) Gordon Pr.

Cheynet, B. Thermodynamic Properties of Inorganic Materials: A Literature Database Covering the Period 1970-1987, 2 pts. (Physical Sciences Data Ser.: Vol. 38). xvi,2402p. 1989. 1165.00 (*0-444-88036-4*) Elsevier.

***Cheyney, Arnold B.** Athletes of Purpose. (Illus.). 1999. pap. 12.95 (*0-673-58667-7*, GoodYrBooks) Addson-Wesley Educ.

Cheyney, Arnold B. GeoChallenge: 180 Daily Geography Brainteasers for Kids! Budding Genius, Level 1, Ages 8-10. (Illus.). 192p. (Orig.). (J). (gr. 3-5). 1995. pap. 9.95 (*0-673-36230-2*, GoodYrBooks) Addson-Wesley Educ.

— GeoChallenge: 180 Daily Geography Brainteasers for Kids! Genius, Level 2, Ages 9-11. (Illus.). 192p. (Orig.). (J). (gr. 4-6). 1995. pap. 9.95 (*0-673-36231-0*, GoodYrBooks) Addson-Wesley Educ.

— GeoChallenge: 180 Daily Geography Brainteasers for Kids! Super Genius, Level 3, Ages 10 Up. (Illus.). 192p. (Orig.). (YA). (gr. 5 up). 1995. pap. 9.95 (*0-673-36232-9*, GoodYrBooks) Addson-Wesley Educ.

***Cheyney, Arnold B.** History Challenge, Level 1: 180 Brainteasers about the United States & the World. 1999. pap. text 10.95 (*0-673-36381-3*) Addson-Wesley Educ.

 An Asterisk (*) at the beginning of an entry indicates that the title is appearing for the first time.

Cheyney, Arnold B. People of Purpose: 80 People Who Have Made a Difference. LC 98-181588. (Illus.). 192p. 1998. pap. 12.95 (*0-673-36371-6*, GoodYrBooks) Addson-Wesley Educ.
— The Poetry Corner: Grades 4-6. (Illus.). 128p. (Orig.). 1982. pap. 12.95 (*0-673-16461-6*, GoodYrBooks) Addson-Wesley Educ.
— Teaching Reading Skills Through the Newspaper. 2nd ed. LC 84-10884. (IRA Reading Aids Ser.). 58p. reprint ed. pap. 30.00 (*0-8357-2639-8*, 204012700014) Bks Demand.
Cheyney, Arnold B. & Capone, Donald. The Map Corner. (Illus.). 128p. (Orig.). 1983. pap. 12.95 (*0-673-16615-5*, GoodYrBooks) Addson-Wesley Educ.
Cheyney, Arnold B., jt. auth. see Cheyney, Jeanne.
Cheyney, Edward P. Anti-Rent Agitation in the State of New York, 1839-1846. 64p. 1993. reprint ed. lib. bdg. 69.00 (*0-7812-5170-2*) Rprt Serv.
— History of the University of Pennsylvania: 1740-1940. Metzger, Walter P., ed. LC 76-55192. (Academic Profession Ser.). 1977. reprint ed. lib. bdg. 39.95 (*0-405-10020-5*) Ayer.
— Introduction to the Industrial & Social History of England. rev. ed. LC 79-92609. (BCL Ser.: No. I). (Illus.). reprint ed. 32.50 (*0-404-01524-7*) AMS Pr.
— Law in History, & Other Essays. 1977. lib. bdg. 59.95 (*0-8490-2134-0*) Gordon Pr.
— Social Changes in England in the Sixteenth-Century As Reflected in Contemporary Literature. LC 76-168055. (Illus.). reprint ed. 36.50 (*0-404-01523-9*) AMS Pr.
Cheyney, Jeanne. Captive's Promise. 224p. (Orig.). 1988. pap. 5.95 (*0-310-47561-9*, 15608P) Zondervan.
— Conviction of Charlotte Gray, No. 26. (Serenade Saga Ser.). 1985. pap. 2.50 (*0-310-47182-6*, 15565P) Zondervan.
— More Bulletin Boards for Every Month. (Illus.). 128p. 1998. pap. text 11.95 (*0-673-36385-6*) Addson-Wesley Educ.
— Presidential Puzzlers. 1998. pap. text 12.95 (*0-673-58654-5*) Addson-Wesley.
Cheyney, Jeanne & Cheyney, Arnold B. Bulletin Boards for Every Month. (Illus.). 112p. (Orig.). (J). (gr. k-3). 1990. pap. 9.95 (*0-673-38828-X*, GoodYrBooks) Addson-Wesley Educ.
— The Continents: Puzzles for Learning World Geography. (Illus.). 184p. (J). (gr. 4-6). 1994. pap. 11.95 (*0-673-36072-5*, GoodYrBooks) Addson-Wesley Educ.
— Finger Plays for Home & School, P-1. 48p. (Orig.). 1989. pap. 7.95 (*0-673-38454-3*, GoodYrBooks) Addson-Wesley Educ.
— States of Wonder: Puzzles for Learning State Facts. (Illus.). 128p. (Orig.). (J). (gr. 4-6). 1991. pap. 9.95 (*0-673-46352-4*, GoodYrBooks) Addson-Wesley Educ.
Cheyney, Jeanne, et al. Ageless Love Vol. 1: The Conviction of Charlotte Grey; Summer Snow; To Dwell in the Land, Vol. 1. 450p. 1996. 19.99 (*0-310-20955-2*) Zondervan.
Cheze, B., jt. ed. see Stout, B. A.
Chezet, Jean-Paul de, tr. see Larbaud, Valery.
Chhabra, B. C. Findings in Indian Archaeology. (C). 1991. text 78.00 (*81-85067-76-7*, Pub. by Sundeep Prak) S Asia.
Chhabra, B. C., et al. Reappraising Gupta History for S. R. Goyal. (C). 1992. 34.00 (*81-85179-78-6*, Pub. by Aditya Prakashan) S Asia.
Chhabra, K. M. Assam Challenge. 1993. text 22.50 (*81-220-0273-0*, Pub. by Konark Pubs) Advent Bks Div.
Chhabra, R. Soil Salinity & Water Quality. (Illus.). 300p. (C). 1996. text 84.00 (*90-5410-727-8*, Pub. by A A Balkema) Ashgate Pub Co.
Chhabra, R. P. Bubbles, Drops & Particles in Non-Newtonian Fluids. 432p. 1992. lib. bdg. 224.95 (*0-8493-6718-2*, QC189) CRC Pr.
Chhabra, R. P., jt. auth. see De Kee, D.
Chhabra, Raj & Richardson, J. F. Non-Newtonian Flow. LC 99-36996. (Illus.). 436p. 2000. text 66.95 (*0-7506-3770-6*) Buttrwrth-Heinemann.
Chhabra, Rami & Petterson, Willy. Liv Och Lek i Indien. 92p. 1980. write for info. (*91-7106-168-1*, Pub. by Nordic Africa) Transaction Pubs.
Chhabra, S. & Charak, T. Jammu & Kashmir: Aspects of Socio-Political History. 100p. 1986. 175.00 (*0-7855-1816-9*, Pub. by Archives Pubs) St Mut.
Chhachhi, Amrita. Confronting State, Capital, & Patriarchy: Women Organizing in the Process of Industrialization. 318p. 1996. text 69.95 (*0-312-12980-7*) St Martin.
Chhangani, V. Inter-State Relation in Ancient India. 1986. 150.00 (*0-7855-1815-0*, Pub. by Archives Pubs) St Mut.
Chhatrapate, A. C. The Vanaspati Industry: A Historical Review. 1986. 27.50 (*0-8364-1601-5*, Pub. by Popular Prakashan) S Asia.
Chhatwal, G. R. Encyclopaedia of Biotechnology, 3 vols., Set. 1110p. (C). 1993. pap. 175.00 (*81-7041-723-6*, Pub. by Anmol) S Asia.
— Encyclopaedia of Environmental Air Pollution, 3 vols. 1997. 1250.00 (*81-7488-438-6*, Pub. by Print Hse) St Mut.
— Encyclopaedia of Environmental Analysis, 3 vols. 1997. 1250.00 (*81-7488-437-8*, Pub. by Print Hse) St Mut.
— Encyclopaedia of Environmental Waste Pollution, 2 vols. 1997. 750.00 (*81-7488-439-4*, Pub. by Print Hse) St Mut.
— Encyclopaedia of Environmental Water Pollution, 3 vols. 1996. 1250.00 (*81-7488-435-1*, Pub. by Print Hse) St Mut.
— Environmental Analysis. 1989. 42.00 (*81-7041-229-3*, Pub. by Anmol) S Asia.
— History of Biology, 2 vols. (Encyclopaedic History of Science & Technology Ser.). 574p. 1995. pap. 72.00 (*81-7488-130-1*, Pub. by Anmol) S Asia.
— History of Mathematics & Computer Science. (Encyclopaedic History of Science & Technology Ser.). 636p. 1995. pap. 140.00 (*81-7488-132-8*, Pub. by Print Hse) St Mut.
Chhatwal, G. R., et al, eds. Environmental Noise Pollution & Its Control. 1989. 52.00 (*81-7041-137-8*, Pub. by Anmol) S Asia.
Chhatwal, G. S., et al, eds. Environmental Radiation & Thermal Pollution & Their Control. 1989. 40.00 (*81-7041-201-3*, Pub. by Anmol) S Asia.
***Chhem, Rethy & Cardinal, Etienne, eds.** Guidelines & Gamuts in Musculoskeletal Ultrasound. LC 98-21528. 390p. 1998. 115.00 (*0-471-19755-6*, Wiley-Liss) Wiley.
Chhetru, et al. Facts about Nepalese Economy. 1997. pap. 21.00 (*0-7855-7402-6*, Pub. by Ratna Pustak Bhandar) St Mut.
Chhibber, Ajay, et al, eds. Reviving Private Investment in Developing Countries. LC 92-12342. (Contributions to Economic Analysis Ser.: Vol. 208). x,246p. 1992. 122.50 (*0-444-89395-4*, North Holland) Elsevier.
Chhibber, Ajay & Fischer, Stanley, eds. Economic Reform in Sub-Saharan Africa. 348p. 1992. pap. 33.00 (*0-8213-2063-7*, 12063) World Bank.
Chhibber, Harbans L. The Physiography of Burma. LC 72-179178. (Illus.). reprint ed. 39.50 (*0-404-54808-3*) AMS Pr.
Chhibber, Pradeep K. Democracy Without Associations: Transformation of the Party System & Social Cleavages in India. LC 98-25511. (Interests, Identities, & Institutions in Comparative Politics Ser.). 304p. 1999. text 49.50 (*0-472-10962-6*, 10962) U of Mich Pr.
Chhikara, Raj S. & Folks, J. Leroy. The Inverse Gaussian Distribution: Theory, Methodology & Applications. (Statistics: Textbooks & Monographs: Vol. 95). (Illus.). 232p. 1988. text 137.50 (*0-8247-7997-5*) Dekker.
Chhodzin, Sherab, tr. see Hesse, Hermann.
Chi, ed. see Harris, Bernard, et al.
Chi, Hsin Y. Artist & Attic: A Study of Poetic Space in Nineteenth-Century Women's Writing. 178p. 1998. 39.00 (*0-7618-1288-1*); pap. 24.50 (*0-7618-1289-X*) U Pr of Amer.
Ch'i-ch'ao, Liang & Shih, Hu. Two Self-Portraits: Liang Chi'i-ch'ao & Hu Shih. Yu-ning, Li & Wycoff, William A., trs. from CHI. (C). 1992. 30.00 (*0-9622934-0-7*) Outer Sky.
Chi, Ch'ao-ting. Key Economic Areas in Chinese History: As Revealed in the Development of Public Works for Water Control. LC 70-104612. (Reprints of Economic Classics Ser.). (Illus.). xxii, 168p. 1970. reprint ed. 35.00 (*0-678-00594-X*) Kelley.
Chi, Chen. Chen Chi Watercolors, Drawings, Sketches. LC 81-101747. (Illus.). 108p. 1980. 30.00 (*0-9604652-0-0*) Chen Chi Studio.
Chi Chen. Chen Chi Watercolors, Drawings, Sketches: Deluxe Edition. deluxe ed. (Illus.). 108p. 1980. ring bd. 100.00 (*0-9604652-1-9*) Chen Chi Studio.
— Heart & Chance: Chen Chi Watercolor Paintings. (Illus.). 44p. 1993. 50.00 (*0-9604652-3-5*) Chen Chi Studio.
Chi, Cheryl, ed. see Chi, Tsu-Tsair.
Chi, Emily. A Can of Jasmine. 32p. Date not set. 3.95 (*1-879934-27-2*) St Andrews NC.
Chi Fulin, jt. ed. see Gao, Shangquan.
Ch'i, Hsi-Kheng, et al. Toward a Global Community of Scholars: The Special Partnership Between the Carnegie Foundation for the Advancement of Teaching & China's National Center for Education Development Research, 1988-1997. LC 96-36012. (Illus.). 80p. (Orig.). 1997. pap. 13.00 (*0-931050-61-8*) Carnegie Fnd Advan Teach.
Ch'i, Hsi-sheng. Politics of Disillusionment: The Chinese Communist Party under Deng Xiaoping, 1978-1989. LC 90-20867. (Studies on Contemporary China). 352p. (C). (gr. 13). 1991. pap. text 35.95 (*0-87332-690-3*, East Gate Bk) M E Sharpe.
— Warlord Politics in China, 1916-1928. LC 75-7482. xiv, 282p. 1976. 42.50 (*0-8047-0894-0*) Stanford U Pr.
Chi, Hsiaojung S., jt. auth. see Kubler, Cornelius C.
Chi, Hsing. Folk Customs at Traditional Chinese Festivities. LC 89-147544. v, 125 p. 1988. write for info. (*7-119-00451-4*) Foreign Lang.
Chi, Hyeong-Eun. Philipp Jakob Spener und Seine Pia Desideria: Die Weiterfuhrung der Reformvorschlage der Pia Desideria in Seinem Spateren Schrifttum. (Europaische Hochschulschriften Ser.: Reihe 23, Bd. 562). (GER., Illus.). 208p. 1997. 42.95 (*3-631-49393-2*) P Lang Pubng.
Chi, Joseph. Computer Aided Design of Scientific & Engineering Systems. 268p. 1984. pap. text 24.95 (*0-930945-01-8*) HCP Systems.
Chi-Lin, Liu, ed. Diet Therapy in Traditional Chinese Medicine. LC 94-44954. 1995. pap. text 48.00 (*0-443-04967-X*) Church.
***Chi, Lu.** The Art of Writing: Lu Chi's Wen Fu. Hamill, Sam, tr. 75p. 2000. pap. 14.95 (*1-57131-412-1*) Milkweed Ed.
Chi, M. T., ed. Trends in Memory Development Research. (Contributions to Human Development Ser.: Vol. 9). (Illus.). xii, 128p. 1983. pap. 42.75 (*3-8055-3661-5*) S Karger.
Chi, Madeleine. China Diplomacy, Nineteen Fourteen to Nineteen Eighteen. LC 77-82302. (East Asian Monographs: No. 31). 213p. 1970. pap. 20.00 (*0-674-11825-1*) HUP.
Chi, Marilyn Mei-Ying, jt. ed. see Park, Clara C.
Chi, Meng, jt. auth. see Boulding, Kenneth E.
Chi, Michelene T., et al, eds. The Nature of Expertise. 464p. 1988. pap. 49.95 (*0-8058-0404-8*) L Erlbaum Assocs.
***Chi, Pang-yuan & Wang, David Der-wei, eds.** Chinese Literature in the Second Half of a Modern Century: A Critical Survey. LC 99-58462. 344p. 2000. 39.95 (*0-253-33710-0*) Ind U Pr.
CHI Research/Computer Horizons Inc. Staff, jt. auth. see Venture Economics Inc. Staff.
Chi, Robert T., et al. Information Systems Management Handbook. 544p. (C). 1998. text 69.95 (*0-13-913989-3*) P-H.
Chi, Sien & Lee, Tien-Pei. Current Research on Optical Materials, Devices & Systems in Taiwan. LC 98-228275. (Selected Topics in Electronics & Systems Ser.: Vol. 12). 200p. 1998. 32.00 (*981-02-3297-7*) World Scientific Pub.
Chi Sun Rhee. Under the Aruban Sun. LC 96-69279. (Illus.). 208p. 1996. 19.95 (*1-884570-51-8*) Research Triangle.
Chi, T. Do, jt. auth. see Meaden, G.
Chi-Tai, Chuang, jt. ed. see Chung-Chun, Yang.
Chi-Tang Ho, et al, eds. Flavor Technology: Physical Chemistry, Modification, & Process. LC 95-37875. (ACS Symposium Ser.: No. 610). (Illus.). 28Cp. 1995. text 75.00 (*0-8412-3326-8*, Pub. by Am Chemical) OUP.
— Food Phytochemicals for Cancer Prevention II: Teas, Spices & Herbs. LC 93-33774. (ACS Symposium Ser.: Vol. 547). 368p. 1994. text 98.00 (*0-8412-2769-1*, Pub. by Am Chemical) OUP.
Chi Tien. Granular Filtration of Aerosols & Hydrosols. (Illus.). 384p. 1989. text 110.00 (*0-409-90043-5*) Buttrwrth-Heinemann.
***Chi, Tsu-Tsair.** Dr. Chi's Herbal Formulas. Chi, Cheryl et al, eds. 215p. 2000. pap. 25.00 (*0-9657847-7-0*) Chis Enterprise.
Chi, Tsu-Tsair. Dr. Chi's Method of Fingernail & Tongue Diagnosis Vol. I. unabridged ed. Chi's Enterprise Staff, ed. (Illus.). 201p. 1997. pap. 39.95 (*0-9657847-9-7*) Chis Enterprise.
Chi, Wen-Shun. Ideological Conflicts in Modern China: Democracy & Authoritarianism. 430p. (C). 1992. pap. 24.95 (*1-56000-608-0*) Transaction Pubs.
Chi Wen-Shun. Readings in Chinese Communist Ideology: A Manual for Students of the Chinese Language. LC 67-11201. 452p. reprint ed. pap. 140.20 (*0-608-17467-X*, 202994900066) Bks Demand.
Chi Wen-Shun, ed. Chinese-English Dictionary of Contemporary Usage. (CHI & ENG.). 1977. 65.00 (*0-520-02655-1*, Pub. by U CA Pr) Cal Prin Full Svc.
Chi-Wing Ho, Daniel, jt. auth. see Wai-Chung Lai, Lawrence.
Chi-won, Kim. Words of Farewell: Stories by Korean Women Writers. Fulton, Ju-Chan & Fulton, Bruce, trs. from KOR. LC 89-10860. (Women in Translation Ser.). 274p. (Orig.). 1989. pap. 12.95 (*0-931188-76-8*) Seal Pr WA.
Chi, Y. & You, J. H. Molecular Clouds & Star Formation: Proceedings of the 7th Guo-Shoujing Summer School on Astrophysics. 330p. 1995. text 104.00 (*981-02-1871-0*) World Scientific Pub.
Chia. The Multi-Orgasmic Couple. 2001. pap. 16.00 (*0-06-251614-0*) HarpC.
Chia-Ao, see Chang Kia-ngau, pseud.
Chia, B. L. Clinical Electrocardiography. 150p. 1999. pap. text 25.00 (*981-02-3762-6*) World Scientific Pub.
— Clinical Electrocardiography. 3rd ed. 150p. 1999. 58.00 (*981-02-3761-8*) World Scientific Pub.
Chia, E. Henry, ed. see Metallurgical Society of AIME Staff.
Chia-Erh, Chen, et al, eds. Free Electron Laser: Beijing Free Electron Laser Seminar. 480p. (C). 1985. text 109.00 (*9971-5-0783-8*) World Scientific Pub.
Chia, Fu-Shiang, ed. see Harrison, Frederick W.
Chia, I., jt. auth. see Svarverud, Rune.
Chia Kee Seng, jt. auth. see Jeyaratnam, J.
Chia, L. S. Singapore's Urban Coastal Area: Strategies for Management. LC 97-945824. (ICLARM Technical Reports: No. 31). 99p. 1992. per. write for info. (*971-8709-17-7*, Pub. by ICLARM) Intl Spec Bk.
Chia, M. Tai Chi Chi Kung I. 1996. 14.95 (*0-935621-12-1*) Heal Tao Bks.
Chia, Mabel, ed. see Caballero, Juan.
Chia, Maneewan, jt. auth. see Chia, Mantak.
Chia, Mannewan, jt. auth. see Chia, Mantak.
Chia, Mantak. Awaken Healing Energy Through the Tao Mantak Chia. 205p. 1983. pap. 14.00 (*0-943358-07-8*) Aurora Press.
— Chi Self-Massage: The Tao of Rejuvenation. LC 85-82051. (Illus.). 175p. (Orig.). 1986. pap. 10.95 (*0-935621-01-6*) Heal Tao Bks.
— Fusion of the Five Elements. 1996. 9.95 incl. audio (*0-935621-14-8*) Heal Tao Bks.
— Iron Shirt Chi Kung I. LC 85-52427. (Illus.). 320p. (Orig.). 1986. pap. 14.95 (*0-935621-02-4*) Heal Tao Bks.
***Chia, Mantak.** Tao Yin: Excercises for Revitalization, Health & Longevity. Holden, Lee & Huntington, Dennis, eds. (Illus.). 198p. 1999. pap. 18.95 (*0-9671718-1-4*) IHT Pubns.
Chia, Mantak. Taoist Secrets of Love: Cultivating Male Sexual Energy. 300p. 1984. pap. 16.95 (*0-943358-19-1*) Aurora Press.
— Taoist Ways to Transform Stress into Vitality: The Inner Smile - Six Healing Sounds. LC 85-81656. (Illus.). 146p. (Orig.). 1986. pap. 10.95 (*0-935621-00-8*) Heal Tao Bks.
***Chia, Mantak.** World Link Meditation: Healing Yourself & Others. large type ed. Huntington, Dennis, ed. (Illus.). 30p. 1999. pap. 6.95 (*0-9671718-0-6*) IHT Pubns.
Chia, Mantak & Arava, Douglas A. The Multi-Orgasmic Man: Sexual Secrets Every Man Should Know. 1997. pap. 13.00 (*0-614-27644-6*) Harper SF.
Chia, Mantak & Arava, Douglas Abrams. The Multi-Orgasmic Man: Sexual Secrets Every Man Should Know. LC 95-51976. (Illus.). 256p. 1997. pap. 15.00 (*0-06-251336-2*, Pub. by Harper SF) HarpC.
Chia, Mantak & Chia, Maneewan. Awaken Healing Light of the Tao: The Microcosmic Orbit Meditation. (Illus.). 594p. (Orig.). 1993. pap. 16.95 (*0-935621-46-6*) Heal Tao Bks.
— Chi Nei Tsang: Internal Organ Chi Message. (Illus.). 448p. 1991. pap. 16.95 (*0-935621-35-0*) Heal Tao Bks.
— Fusion of the Five Elements I: Basic & Advanced Meditations for Transforming Negative Emotions. (Illus.). 193p. 1991. pap. 12.95 (*0-935621-18-0*) Heal Tao Bks.
— Healing Love Through the Tao: Cultivating Female Sexual Energy. LC 86-81049. (Illus.). 328p. (Orig.). 1986. 22.50 (*0-935621-04-0*); pap. 14.95 (*0-935621-05-9*) Heal Tao Bks.
Chia, Mantak & Chia, Mannewan. Bone Marrow Nei Kung: Iron Shirt Chi Kung III. (Healing Tao Bks.). 288p. 1989. pap. 14.95 (*0-935621-17-2*) Tuttle Pubng.
Chia, Mantak & Le, Juan. The Inner Structure of Tai Chi. LC 95-82138. 1996. pap. 14.95 (*0-935621-50-4*) Heal Tao Bks.
Chia, Mantak, et al. The Multi-Orgasmic Couple: Sexual Secrets Every Couple Should Know. 176p. 2000. 24.00 (*0-06-251613-2*) HarpC.
Chia, Robert K. Organizational Analysis As Deconstructive Practice. LC 96-18620. (Studies in Organization: Vol. 77). xiv, 245p. (C). 1996. text 59.95 (*3-11-014559-6*) De Gruyter.
Chia, Robert K., ed. In the Realm of Organization: Essays for Robert Cooper. 256p. 1996. pap. 23.95 (*0-415-12700-9*) Routledge.
— In the Realm of Organization: Essays for Robert Cooper. LC 97-43300. 256p. (C). 1998. 85.00 (*0-415-12699-1*) Routledge.
***Chia, Roland.** Revelation & Theology: The Knowledge of God in Balthasar & Barth. LC 99-56828. 273p. (C). 1999. pap. 42.95 (*0-8204-4607-6*) P Lang Pubng.
Chia, S. P., et al. Asia-Pacific Physics Conference: Proceedings of the Fifth Conference. 2 vols. 1404p. 1994. text 213.00 (*981-02-1741-2*) World Scientific Pub.
Chia-yee, Teng, jt. auth. see DeFrancis, John.
Chia-yee, Yung Teng, jt. auth. see Williams, Jack F.
Chiabi, Emmanuel. The Making of Modern Cameroon: A History of Substate Nationalism & Disparate Union, 1914-1961. LC 97-33470. 304p. (C) 1997. 42.50 (*0-7618-0896-5*) U Pr of Amer.
Chiabo, Maria, ed. Ammianus Marcellinus - Index Verborum Ammiani Marcellini, 2 vols. (Alpha-Omega, Reihe A Ser.: Bd. XLIV). (GER.). xii, 903p. 1983. 240.00 (*3-487-07353-6*) G Olms Pubs.
Chiabo, Maria & Roberti, L., eds. Hyginus - Index Verborum Hygini de Astronomia. vi, 159p. 1990. 55.00 (*0-318-71151-6*) G Olms Pubs.
Chiabotta, William. Employee Assistance Programs: How to Make Them Work for You. 302p. 1987. ring bd. 67.96 (*1-55645-519-4*, 519) Busn Legal Reports.
Chiabrera, A., et al, eds. Interactions Between Electromagnetic Fields & Cells. LC 85-16788. (NATO ASI Series A, Life Sciences: Vol. 97). 654p. 1985. 125.00 (*0-306-42083-X*, Plenum Trade) Perseus Pubng.
Chiacchio, Pasquale & Chiaverini, Stefano. Complex Robotic Systems. LC 98-16078. (Lecture Notes in Control & Information Sciences: Vol. 233). 1998. pap. 59.00 (*3-540-76265-5*) Spr-Verlag.
Chiacos, Elias, ed. Mountain Drive: Santa Barbaras Pioneer Bohemian Community. (Illus.). 133p. (Orig.). 1995. pap. 12.95 (*1-885375-00-X*, Shore Line Pr) Pacific Books.
Chiaferi. Developing Fieldwork Skills: Guide for Human Services Counseling. 2nd ed. (Counseling Ser.). 2001. pap. 27.00 (*0-534-36759-3*) Brooks-Cole.
Chiaferi, Rosemary. Developing Fieldwork Skills. LC 96-33371. (Counseling Ser.). 1996. pap. 37.95 (*0-534-34654-5*) Wadsworth Pub.
Chiagouris, Larry, jt. ed. see Kahle, Lynn R.
Chial, Debra M. M Is for Minnesota. LC 93-34643. (Illus.). 32p. (J). 1994. 12.95 (*0-89658-234-5*) Voyageur Pr.
— St. Croix Valley. (Illus.). 48p. (Orig.). 1993. pap. 3.95 (*0-89658-183-7*) Voyageur Pr.
Chiam, Madelaine, jt. ed. see Alston, Philip.
Chiampo, Luigi. Gould Chiampo Encyclopedia of Medicine: Il Gould Chiampo Dizionario Enciclopedico di Medicina Inglese-Italiano: Italiano-Inglese. (ENG & ITA.). 2304p. 1988. lib. bdg. 295.00 (*0-8288-3359-1*, F39060) Fr & Eur.
Chiancone, Aldo, ed. see International Institute of Public Finance Congress.
Chianelli, Chris, ed. see Gierke, C. David.
Chianelli, Russell, jt. auth. see Occelli, MArio.
***Chiang, Alpha C.** Elements of Dynamic Optimization. 327p. (C). 1999. 57.95 (*1-57766-096-X*) Waveland Pr.
Chiang, Alpha C. Fundamental Methods of Mathematical Economics. 3rd ed. (C). 1984. pap. text, teacher ed. 50.00 (*0-07-010814-5*) McGraw.
— Fundamentals Methods of Mathematical Economics. 3rd ed. 800p. (C). 1984. 87.81 (*0-07-010813-7*) McGraw.
Chiang, Alpha C., et al, eds. Semiconductor-on-Insulator & Thin Film Transistor Technology, Vol. 53. (Materials Research Society Symposium Proceedings Ser.). 1986. text 17.50 (*0-931837-18-9*) Materials Res.
***Chiang, C. H.** Kinematics & Design of Planar Mechanisms. LC 00-39066. (Illus.). (C). 2000. text. write for info. (*1-57524-154-4*) Krieger.
Chiang, C. Nora & Hawks, Richard L., eds. Research Findings on Smoking of Abused Substances. (Illus.). 178p. (Orig.). (C). 1994. pap. text 30.00 (*0-7881-0372-5*) DIANE Pub.
Chiang, Chin L. Introduction to Stochastic Processes & Their Applications. LC 74-14821. 544p. 1980. 64.50 (*0-88275-200-6*) Krieger.
Chiang, Chin Long. Life Table & Its Applications. LC 82-20331. 336p. (C). 1983. 46.50 (*0-89874-570-5*) Krieger.
***Chiang, Chun-Hung.** Kinematics of Spherical Mechanisms. (Illus.). (C). 2000. reprint ed. text. write for info. (*1-57524-155-2*) Krieger.

C

Chiang, Dean. The Yearning. (Illus.). 96p. (C). pap. 10.95 (*0-943151-11-2*) Slave Labor Bks.

***Chiang, Doug.** Star Wars: Episode I: The Phantom Menace Portfolio, 20 vols. (Star Wars Ser.). 1999. 55.00 (*0-8118-2580-9*); 500.00 (*0-8118-2581-7*) Chronicle Bks.

Chiang, Gregory. Language of the Dragon: A Classical Chinese Reader, Vol. 1. 385p. 1998. pap. 28.95 (*0-88727-298-3*) Cheng & Tsui.

***Chiang, Gregory.** Language of the Dragon Vol. 2: A Classical Chinese Reader. 400p. 1999. pap. 29.95 (*0-88727-318-1*) Cheng & Tsui.

— Language of the Dragon Vol. 3: A Classical Chinese Reader. 200p. 1999. pap. 49.95 (*0-88727-319-X*) Cheng & Tsui.

Chiang, Gregory K., jt. ed. see Seybolt, Peter J.

Chiang, H. C. & Zheng, L. S., eds. Medium Energy Physics: Proceedings of the International Symposium. 684p. (C). 1988. text 125.00 (*9971-5-0403-0*) World Scientific Pub.

Chiang, Hai Hung. Electrical & Electronic Instrumentation. LC 83-21742. (Wiley-Interscience Publications). 602p. reprint ed. pap. 186.70 (*0-7837-2392-X*, 204007700006) Bks Demand.

Chiang, Jack. Images of Kingston. rev. ed. (Illus.). 144p. 1990. 40.00 (*0-919627-93-5*, Pub. by Quarry Pr) LPC InBook.

Chiang Kai-Shek. China's Destiny. LC 76-24849. 260p. 1976. reprint ed. lib. bdg. 32.50 (*0-306-70821-3*) Da Capo.

— China's Destiny. Chung-Hui, Wang, tr. from CHI. LC 84-22503. 260p. 1985. reprint ed. lib. bdg. 65.00 (*0-313-24676-9*, CHCD, Greenwood Pr) Greenwood.

— Resistance & Reconstruction. LC 71-111819. (Essay Index Reprint Ser.). 1977. 26.95 (*0-8369-1597-6*) Ayer.

Chiang, Kuei. A Translation of the Chinese Novel Chung-Yang (Rival Suns) by Chiang Kuei (1908-1980) Ross, Timothy A., tr. from CHI. LC 98-31939. (Chinese Studies: Vol. 8). 740p. 1999. text 139.95 (*0-7734-8188-5*) E Mellen.

Chiang, Long Y., et al, eds. Advanced Organic Solid State Materials Vol. 173: Materials Research Society Symposium Proceedings. 706p. 1990. text 17.50 (*1-55899-061-5*) Materials Res.

— Electrical, Optical, & Magnetic Properties of Organic Solid State Materials. (Symposium Proceedings Ser.: Vol. 247). 899p. 1992. text 64.00 (*1-55899-141-7*) Materials Res.

Chiang, Nancy S., jt. auth. see Wolf, Carolyn E.

Chiang, Steve T., jt. auth. see Hoffman, Klaus A.

Chiang, Steve T., jt. auth. see Hoffmann, Klaus A.

Chiang, W. Walter, jt. auth. see Qasim, Sayed R.

Chiang, Weiling & Lee, Jonathan, eds. Fuzzy Theory & Applications: Proceedings of the International Joint Conference of CFSA/IFIS/SOFT '95: Taipei, Taiwan, 7-9 December 1995. 600p. 1995. 128.00 (*981-02-2485-0*) World Scientific Pub.

Chiang, William W. We Two Know the Script; We have Become Good Friends: Linguistic & Social Aspects of The Women's Script Literacy in Southern Hunan, China. (Illus.). 336p. (Orig.). (C). Date not set. lib. bdg. 59.50 (*0-7618-0013-1*) U Pr of Amer.

— We Two Know the Script; We have Become Good Friends: Linguistic & Social Aspects of The Women's Script Literacy in Southern Hunan, China. (Illus.). 336p. (Orig.). (C). 1995. pap. text 38.50 (*0-7618-0014-X*) U Pr of Amer.

Chiang, Win-Shin S. Louisiana Legal Research. 2nd ed. 260p. 1990. boxed set 60.00 (*0-409-25172-0*, MICHIE) LEXIS Pub.

Chiang, Win-Shin S. & Dickson, Lance E., eds. Legal Bibliography Index (1985) 273p. 1986. 35.00 (*0-317-01337-8*) LSU Law Center.

— Legal Bibliography Index, 1986. 278p. 1987. 40.00 (*0-318-32983-2*) LSU Law Center.

Chiang Yee. Chinese Calligraphy: An Introduction to Its Aesthetic & Technique. 3rd ed. LC 72-75400. (Illus.). 270p. 1973. pap. 19.50 (*0-674-12226-7*) HUP.

— The Silent Traveller in San Francisco. (Illus.). 1964. 12.50 (*0-393-08422-1*) Norton.

Chiang, Yet-Ming, et al. Physical Ceramics: Principles for Ceramics Science & Engineering. LC 95-32997. (MIT Series in Materials Science & Engineering). 544p. 1996. text 103.95 (*0-471-59873-9*) Wiley.

***Chiang, Yung-chen.** Social Engineering & the Social Sciences in China, 1919-1949. LC 99-56830. (Cambridge Modern China Ser.). (Illus.). 304p. 2000. 59.95 (*0-521-77014-9*) Cambridge U Pr.

Chianis, Sotirios. Folk Songs of Mantneia, Greece. LC 65-65513. (University of California Publications, Folklore Studies: No. 15). (Illus.). 183p. reprint ed. pap. 56.80 (*0-608-10915-0*, 201135600079) Bks Demand.

Chianni, Marco, et al. Pitti Palace: Guide to the Collections & Complete Catalogue of the Palatine Gallery. (Illus.). 128p. 1992. 21.95 (*0-8161-0606-1*, G K Hall & Co) Mac Lib Ref.

Chiantia, Barbara. Christmas: A Time for Family: With Christmas Classics CD. LC 99-181932. (BookNotes Ser.). 56p. 1998. 13.99 incl. cd-rom (*0-88088-403-7*) Peter Pauper.

— The Road to Friendship. (Pocket Gift Editions Ser.). 64p. 1999. 4.95 (*0-88088-102-X*) Peter Pauper.

Chiantini, Luca, jt. ed. see Orecchia, Ferruccio.

***Chiao, Karen L. & O'Brien, Mariellen B.** Spies' Wives. LC 99-68402. 304p. 2000. pap. 17.25 (*0-88739-321-7*) Creat Arts Bk.

***Chiao, Paul, et al, eds.** Pancreatic Cancer Methods & Protocols. 375p. 2000. 99.50 (*0-89603-628-6*) Humana.

Chiao, Raymond Y., ed. Amazing Light: A Volume Dedicated to Charles Hard Townes on His 80th Birthday. 700p. 1996. 69.95 (*0-7803-1181-7*, PC5658) Inst Electrical.

— Amazing Light: A Volume Dedicated to Charles Hard Townes on His 80th Birthday. LC 95-449220. 712p. 1996. 69.00 (*0-387-94658-6*) Spr-Verlag.

Chiao, T. T. & Schuster, D. M., eds. Failure Modes in Composites III. LC 76-23498. 326p. reprint ed. pap. 101.10 (*0-608-30444-1*, 201265000083) Bks Demand.

Chiao Wan-Hsuan. Devolution in Great Britain. LC 76-78010. (Columbia University. Studies in the Social Sciences: No. 272). reprint ed. 32.50 (*0-404-51272-0*) AMS Pr.

Chiappa, Joseph A. & Forish, Joseph J. VD Book: For People Who Care about Themselves & Others. LC 76-17596. (Illus.). 145p. 1977. pap. 6.95 (*0-8290-0287-1*) Irvington.

Chiappa, Keith H. Evoked Potentials in Clinical Medicine. 3rd ed. LC 96-47700. 720p. 1997. text 79.00 (*0-397-51659-2*) Lppncott W & W.

Chiappe, Luis & Dingus, Lowell. The Tiniest Giants. LC 98-28886. 48p. (J). 1999. 17.95 (*0-385-32642-4*) BDD Bks Young Read.

Chiappe, Luis, tr. see MacPhee, Ross.

Chiappetta. Student Learning Tools. 2nd ed. 1997. pap., student ed. 24.69 (*0-256-25577-6*) McGraw.

Chiappetta, Barbara & Larson, Kermit D. Fundamental Accounting Principles: Student Learning Tools. 14th ed. 304p. (C). 1996. text 22.50 (*0-256-20748-8*, Irwn McGrw-H) McGrw-H Hghr Educ.

— Fundamental Accounting Principles: With Tutorial Software Windows 3.5 Diskette. 14th ed. (C). 1996. text, pap. text 89.25 incl. 3.5 hd (*0-256-24425-1*, Irwn McGrw-H) McGrw-H Hghr Educ.

Chiappetta, Eugene L. & Collette, Alfred T. Science Instruction in the Middle & Secondary Schools. 4th ed. LC 97-14717. 417p. (C). 1997. pap. text 72.00 (*0-13-651118-X*) P-H.

Chiappetta, Joe. Silly Daddy: A Death in the Family. unabridged ed. (Illus.). 96p. 1999. pap. 8.00 (*0-9644323-1-5*) J Chiappetta.

— Silly Daddy: The Long Goodbye. (Silly Daddy Ser.). (Illus.). 98p. (Orig.). (YA). 1994. pap. text 7.95 (*0-9644323-0-7*) J Chiappetta.

Chiappone, Anthony, jt. auth. see Derwald, Richard.

Chiappone, Mark, jt. auth. see Sullivan, Kathleen M.

Chiapuris, John P. The Ait Ayash of the High Molouuya Plain: Rural Social Organization in Morocco. (Anthropological Papers Ser.: No. 69). 1980. pap. 3.00 (*0-932206-83-2*) U Mich Mus Anthro.

Chiapusso, Jan. Bach's World. LC 79-20813. (Illus.). 338p. 1980. reprint ed. lib. bdg. 79.50 (*0-313-22139-1*, CHBW, Greenwood Pr) Greenwood.

Chiara. I Giovedi della Signora Giulia: B Level. text 8.95 (*0-88436-292-2*) EMC-Paradigm.

Chiara, A. Di, see Di Chiara, A.

Chiara, M. L., ed. Italian Studies in the Philosophy of Science. Fawcett, Carolyn, tr. (Boston Studies in the Philosophy of Science: No. 47). 525p. 1980. pap. text 102.50 (*90-277-1073-2*, D Reidel); lib. bdg. 182.50 (*90-277-0735-9*, D Reidel) Kluwer Academic.

Chiara, Maria L., jt. ed. see Bicchieri, Cristina.

Chiara, Maria L. Dalla, see Corsi, Giovanna.

Chiara, Maria L. Dalla, see Dalla Chiara, Maria L., ed.

***Chiara, Peter A.** Ashes, Glory, Spirit: Daily Mediations for Lent, Easter Season & Pentecost. 128p. 1999. pap. 7.95 (*0-88489-619-6*) St Marys.

Chiara, Piero. Las Aventuras de Pierino en el Mercado de Luino (The Adventures of Pierino in the Luino Market) Morabito, Fabio, tr. (SPA., Illus.). (J). (gr. 5-6). 1993. pap. 5.99 (*968-16-4036-5*, Pub. by Fondo) Continental Bk.

Chiara, Robert Di, see Di Chiara, Robert.

Chiaramonte. Food Allergy: A Practical Approach to Diagnosis & Management. Schneider, Arlene et al, eds. (Clinical Pediatrics Ser.: Vol. 5). (Illus.). 504p. 1988. text 185.00 (*0-8247-7652-6*) Dekker.

Chiaramonte, Mark. Las Vegas & Laughlin. 147p. 1999. 6.95 (*1-56413-460-1*) Auto Club.

Chiaranda, M. & Giron, G. P. High-Frequency Jet Ventilation: Experimental & Clinical Studies. 182p. 1985. text 30.00 (*1-57235-045-8*) Piccin Nuova.

Chiarappa, Luigi & Chiarappa, Nicla. Two Immigrants from Italy: A Lively Tale of a Wanderful Life. (Illus.). 352p. 1999. pap. 24.95 (*0-9665594-0-1*) GG Press.

Chiarappa, Nicla, jt. auth. see Chiarappa, Luigi.

Chiarella, C. Elements of a Non-Linear Theory of Economic Dynamics. (C). (gr. 13). 1997. mass mkt. 78.00 (*0-412-38760-3*) Chapman & Hall.

***Chiarella, C., et al.** Disequilibrium, Growth & Labor Market Dynamics: Macro Perspectives. x, 480p. 2000. (*3-540-64909-3*) Spr-Verlag.

***Chiarella, Carl & Flaschel, Peter.** The Dynamics of Keynesian Monetary Growth: Macro Foundations. LC 99-47714. (Illus.). 433p. 2000. 90.00 (*0-521-64351-1*) Cambridge U Pr.

Chiarella, Gail. Yokibics . . . A Mindbody Workbook for Everyday Living. Aron, Leah, ed. (Illus.). 120p. 1992. student ed. 19.95 (*0-9635563-1-2*) Yokibics.

Chiarella, Tom. Writing Dialogue. LC 97-36717. 176p. 1998. pap. 14.99 (*1-884910-32-7*, Story Press) F & W Pubns Inc.

Chiarelli, Brunetto. Man Between Past & Future. (Mankind Quarterly Monographs: No. 7). 132p. 1996. pap. 16.50 (*0-941694-50-X*) Inst Study Man.

Chiarelli, Brunetto, et al, eds. Comparative Karyology of Primates. (World Anthropology Ser.). text 44.00 (*90-279-7840-9*) Mouton.

— Comparative Karyology of Primates. (World Anthropology Ser.). (Illus.). xiv, 336p. 1979. 50.80 (*90-279-7850-6*) Mouton.

Chiarelli, Brunetto, et al. The Atlas of World Cultures. LC 96-52309. (Illus.). 64p. (YA). (gr. 5-9). 1999. 19.95 (*0-87226-499-8*, 64998B, P Bedrick Books) NTC Contemp Pub Co.

Chiarelli, Carl. Firemania: The Turbulent Saga of a New York City Firefighter. (Illus.). 305p. 1996. 23.95 (*1-56072-312-2*, Nova Kroshka Bks) Nova Sci Pubs.

Chiarelli, Pauline E. Womens Waterworks: Curing Incontinence. (Health Bks.). 64p. 1995. pap. 8.95 (*0-9640719-0-8*) Khera Pubns.

Chiarello, Christine, jt. auth. see Beeman, Mark.

Chiarello, Gail D. Bhandra Dance: Poems, Nineteen Sixty-Seven to Nineteen Seventy. 1970. pap. 2.00 (*0-685-04665-6*) Oyez.

Chiarello, Mark, ed. see DC Comics Staff.

Chiarello, Michael & Wisner, Penelope. Flavored Vinegars: 50 Recipes for Cooking with Infused Vinegars. LC 95-21547. (Illus.). 96p. 1996. pap. 12.95 (*0-8118-0872-6*) Chronicle Bks.

— The Tra Vigne Cookbook: Seasons in the California Wine Country. LC 98-32289. (Illus.). 208p. 1999. 35.00 (*0-8118-1986-8*) Chronicle Bks.

Chiarello, Michael & Wisner, Penny. Flavored Oils: Recipes for Cooking with Infused Oils. LC 94-27961. (Illus.). 96p. 1995. pap. 12.95 (*0-8118-0898-X*) Chronicle Bks.

Chiarelott, Leigh. Lessons on Teaching. 3rd ed. LC 97-74037. (C). 1997. pap. text 33.50 (*0-15-505470-8*, Pub. by Harcourt Coll Pubs) Harcourt.

Chiarenza, Frank & Slater, James. The Milk Glass Book. LC 98-29623. 208p. 1998. 49.95 (*0-7643-0661-8*) Schiffer.

Chiarenza, Marguerite M. The Divine Comedy: Tracing God's Art. (Masterwork Studies). 144p. 1989. 29.00 (*0-8057-7985-X*, MWS 25, Twyne) Mac Lib Ref.

— The Divine Comedy: Tracing God's Art. (Twayne's Masterwork Studies: No. 25). 152p. 1989. pap. 18.00 (*0-8057-8034-3*, Twyne) Mac Lib Ref.

Chiari, Joseph. Art & Knowledge. LC 76-57236. 132p. 1977. 35.00 (*0-87752-208-1*) Gordian.

— Christopher Columbus: A Play. LC 78-23741. 79p. 1979. 20.00 (*0-87752-216-2*) Gordian.

— Contemporary French Poetry. LC 68-20289. (Essay Index Reprint Ser.). 1977. 18.95 (*0-8369-0301-3*) Ayer.

— Contemporary French Theatre: The Flight from Naturalism. LC 76-128187. 255p. (C). 1970. reprint ed. 45.00 (*0-87752-126-3*) Gordian.

— Landmarks of Contemporary Drama. LC 76-148616. 233p. (C). 1971. reprint ed. 45.00 (*0-87752-144-1*) Gordian.

— The Necessity of Being. LC 73-3338. 168p. 1973. 45.00 (*0-87752-167-0*) Gordian.

— Poetic Drama of Paul Claudel. LC 71-90365. (C). 1969. reprint ed. 50.00 (*0-87752-018-6*) Gordian.

— Realism & Imagination. LC 74-131248. 218p. (C). 1970. reprint ed. 50.00 (*0-87752-019-4*) Gordian.

— Reflections on Life & Death. LC 77-4054. 141p. 1977. 35.00 (*0-87752-212-X*) Gordian.

— Religion & Modern Society. 215p. 1964. 69.50 (*0-614-00168-4*) Elliots Bks.

— Symbolisme from Poe to Mallarme: The Growth of a Myth. LC 76-114096. 208p. (C). 1970. reprint ed. 50.00 (*0-87752-020-8*) Gordian.

— T. S. Eliot: Poet & Dramatist. LC 79-158. 167p. 1979. reprint ed. 50.00 (*0-87752-218-9*) Gordian.

— Twentieth Century French Thought: From Bergson to Levi-Strauss. LC 75-1574. 210p. 1975. 50.00 (*0-87752-185-9*) Gordian.

Chiari, Joseph, ed. Harrap Anthology of French Poetry. LC 70-131247. 515p. 1970. reprint ed. 75.00 (*0-87752-017-8*) Gordian.

Chiari, Joseph & MacDiarmid, Hugh. Collected Poems. LC 77-26826. 200p. 1978. 45.00 (*0-87752-213-8*) Gordian.

Chiariglione, L., jt. ed. see Niomiya, Y.

Chiarihi, Arupa. The Ancestors Are Calling down the Rainbow. 50p. 1997. pap. 12.00 (*1-887694-09-9*) C Mautz Pubng.

Chiarini, Arupa. Waiting for Captain Ha Ha. 24p. (Orig.). (J). 1997. pap. 4.00 (*0-87440-038-4*) Bakers Plays.

Chiarini, Francoise Pouncey, tr. see Paolucci, Antonio.

Chiarito, Marian D. Alamance County, North Carolina 1850 Census with Ancestors & Descendants of Selected Families. 240p. 1987. 25.00 (*0-945503-12-1*) Clarkton Pr.

— Census of Halifax County, Virginia, 1850. 270p. 1982. 16.00 (*0-945503-00-8*) Clarkton Pr.

— Deed Book One, Halifax County, Virginia, 1752-1759. 64p. 1985. 10.00 (*0-945503-09-1*) Clarkton Pr.

— Deed Book Seven, Halifax County, VA, 1767-1770. 60p. 1990. 12.00 (*0-945503-18-0*) Clarkton Pr.

— Deed Books Two, Three, Four, Five & Six, Halifax County, Virginia, 1759-1767. 225p. 1986. 30.00 (*0-945503-10-5*) Clarkton Pr.

— Entry Record Book (Land Entries in Present Virginia Counties of Halifax, Pittsylvania, Henry, Franklin, & Patrick) 1737-1770. 432p. 1984. 50.00 (*0-945503-06-7*) Clarkton Pr.

— Entry Record Book (Land Entries in Present Virginia Counties of Pittsylvania, Henry, Franklin, & Patrick) 1770-1796. 138p. 1988. 25.00 (*0-945503-13-X*) Clarkton Pr.

— List of Voters for Elections of Burgesses, 1764-1769, Halifax County, Virginia. 44p. 1986. 6.00 (*0-945503-11-3*) Clarkton Pr.

— Old Survey Bk. 1: 1746-1782, Pittsylvania County, Virginia. 400p. 1988. 35.00 (*0-945503-15-6*) Clarkton Pr.

— Old Survey Book 2, 1797-1829, Pittsylvania County, Virginia. 102p. 1988. 12.00 (*0-945503-16-4*) Clarkton Pr.

— Plea Book 1, Halifax County, Virginia, 1752-1755. 146p. (Orig.). 1988. per. 25.00 (*0-945503-14-8*) Clarkton Pr.

— Vestry Book of Antrim Parish, Halifax County, Virginia, 1752-1817. 160p. 1983. 25.00 (*0-945503-07-5*) Clarkton Pr.

— Will Book One, Halifax County, Virginia, 1773-1783. 136p. 1984. 18.00 (*0-945503-04-0*) Clarkton Pr.

— Will Book Zero, Halifax County, Virginia, 1752-1773. 88p. 1982. 15.00 (*0-945503-02-4*) Clarkton Pr.

Chiarito, Marian D. & Prendergast, James H. Marriages of Halifax County, Virginia, 1801-1830. 183p. 1985. 25.00 (*0-945503-08-3*) Clarkton Pr.

— Will Book Two, Halifax County, Virginia, 1783-1792. 136p. 1989. 22.00 (*0-945503-17-2*) Clarkton Pr.

Chiarito, Robert, tr. see Sanchez, Elba R.

Chiarliiglione, L., et al, eds. Signal Processing of HDTV, V: Proceedings of the International Workshop on HDTV '93, Ottawa, Canada, October 26-28, 1993. LC 94-29287. 868p. 1994. 292.00 (*0-444-81844-8*) Elsevier.

Chiarmonte, Paula. Women Artists in the U. S. Guide on the Fine & Decorative Arts, 1750-1986. (Reference Ser.). 1080p. 1990. 75.00 (*0-8161-8917-X*, Hall Reference) Macmillan.

Chiaro. S/G CONCISE AMER&PEO VL2, Vol. 2. (C). 1995. pap. text, student ed. 17.81 (*0-673-99234-9*) Addson-Wesley Educ.

— S/G CONCISE HIS AMER&VL1, Vol. 1. (C). 1995. pap. text, student ed. 17.81 (*0-673-99233-0*) Addson-Wesley Educ.

Chiaro, Delia. The Language of Jokes: Analyzing Verbal Play. LC 91-33616. (Interface Ser.). 144p. (Orig.). (C). 1992. pap. 22.99 (*0-415-03090-0*, A6777) Routledge.

Chiaro, Mario D. Etruscan Ghiaccio Forte. (Illus.). 78p. 1976. pap. 10.00 (*0-942006-41-0*) U of CA Art.

— Greek Art: An Exhibition Selected from Private Collections in Southern California. (Illus.). 44p. 1966. pap. 3.00 (*0-942006-44-5*) U of CA Art.

— Re-Exhumed Etruscan Bronzes. (Illus.). 55p. 1981. pap. 6.00 (*0-942006-51-8*) U of CA Art.

Chiaro, Mario D., jt. auth. see Gebhard, David.

Chiaroscuro, Nick. The Home Workshop Spy: Spookware for the Serious Hobbyist. LC 97-198136. (Illus.). 104p. 1997. pap. 25.00 (*0-87364-922-2*) Paladin Pr.

Chiarotti, G. F., ed. Landolt-Bornstein Vol. 24: Physics of Solid Surfaces. xii, 516p. 1996. 2007.00 (*3-540-56750-X*) Spr-Verlag.

— Physics of Solid Surfaces. 370p. 1993. 1105.95 (*0-387-56069-6*) Spr-Verlag.

Chiarotti, G. F., et al, eds. Physics of Solid Surfaces: Electronic & Vibrational Properties. 270p. 1994. 1919.95 (*0-387-56070-X*) Spr-Verlag.

Chiarugi, Vincenzo. On Insanity & Its Classification. Mora, George, ed. & tr. by. LC 86-17746. 1987. 35.00 (*0-88135-084-2*) Watson Pub Intl.

Chiasson, Annette. Africa by Journey. (Illus.). 310p. (gr. 6-9). 1999. pap. 23.95 (*0-9672602-0-5*) Chia Pr.

Chiasson, Jean-Louis, jt. ed. see Srivastava, Ashok K.

Chiasson, Joan, ed. see Cowdrey, Mike.

Chiasson, Lloyd, Jr., ed. The Press on Trial: Crimes & Trials As Media Events. LC 96-53030. (Contributions to the Study of Media & Communications Ser.). 248p. 1997. pap. 23.95 (*0-275-95936-8*, Praeger Pubs) Greenwood.

— The Press on Trial: Crimes & Trials As Media Events, 51. LC 96-53030. (Contributions to the Study of Mass Media & Communications Ser.: Vol. 51). 248p. 1997. 59.95 (*0-313-30022-4*, Greenwood Pr) Greenwood.

Chiasson, Lloyd, jt. auth. see Frair, John.

Chiasson, Lloyd E., Jr., ed. The Press in Times of Crisis. LC 95-2903. 272p. 1995. pap. 24.95 (*0-275-95340-8*, Praeger Pubs) Greenwood.

— The Press in Times of Crisis: An Historical Analysis, 48. LC 95-2903. (Contributions to the Study of Mass Media & Communications Ser.: No. 48). 272p. 1995. 65.00 (*0-313-29364-3*, Greenwood Pr) Greenwood.

Chiasson, Robert B. Laboratory Anatomy of the Pigeon. 3rd ed. (Laboratory Anatomy Ser.). 116p. (C). 1984. text. write for info. (*0-697-04927-2*, WCB McGr Hill) McGrw-H Hghr Educ.

— Laboratory Anatomy of the White Rat. 5th ed. 144p. (C). 1987. text. write for info. (*0-697-05132-3*, WCB McGr Hill) McGrw-H Hghr Educ.

Chiasson, Robert B. & Booth, Ernest. Laboratory Anatomy of the Cat. 8th ed. 160p. (C). 1988. text. write for info. (*0-697-04934-5*, WCB McGr Hill) McGrw-H Hghr Educ.

Chiasson, Robert B. & Radke, William J. Lab Anatomy of the Mink. 3rd ed. LC 97-70108. 96p. (C). 1997. spiral bd. write for info. (*0-697-04793-8*, WCB McGr Hill) McGrw-H Hghr Educ.

— Lab Anatomy of the Vertebrates. 240p. (C). 1992. text. write for info. (*0-697-10160-6*, WCB McGr Hill) McGrw-H Hghr Educ.

— Laboratory Anatomy of the Cat. 208p. (C). 1995. text 29.00 (*0-697-24926-3*, WCB McGr Hill) McGrw-H Hghr Educ.

— Laboratory Anatomy of the Perch. 4th ed. 112p. (C). 1991. text. write for info. (*0-697-04939-6*, WCB McGr Hill) McGrw-H Hghr Educ.

Chiasson, Robert B. & Underhill, Raymond A. Laboratory Anatomy of the Frog & Toad. 6th ed. 80p. (C). 1993. text 23.50 (*0-697-12313-8*, WCB McGr Hill) McGrw-H Hghr Educ.

Chiasson, Robert B., jt. auth. see Ashley, Laurence M.

Chiasson, Robert B., jt. auth. see McLaughlin, Charles A.

Chiasson, Robert B., jt. auth. see Odlaug, Theron O.

Chiat, Marilyn. America's Religious Architecture: Sacred Places for Every Community. LC 97-7457. (Illus.). 465p. 1997. pap. 34.95 (*0-471-14502-5*) Wiley.

Chiat, Marilyn Segal & Reyerson, Kathryn. The Medieval Mediterranean: Cross-Cultural Contacts LC 88-28150. (Medieval Studies at Minnesota). xvii, 133 p. 1988. 22.95 (0-87839-049-9) North Star.

***Chiat, Shula.** Understanding Children with Language Problems. (Approaches to Linguistics Ser.). (Illus.). 301p. (C). 2000. text 54.95 (0-521-57386-6); pap. text 19.95 (0-521-57474-9) Cambridge U Pr.

Chiat, Shula, et al, eds. Language Disorders in Children & Adults: Psycholinguistic Approaches to Therapy. 280p. 1997. 65.00 (1-56593-878-X, 1720) Singular Publishing.

Chiatante, Donato, jt. auth. see Bryant, J. A.

Chiauzzi, Emil. Preventing Relapse in Addictions. (Practitioner Guidebook Ser.). 176p. (C). 1991. pap. text 41.00 (0-205-14303-2, H4303, Longwood Div) Allyn.

Chiauzzi, Emil. Relapse Risk Survey. 1994. pap. 12.50 (1-55691-112-2, 122) Learning Pubns.

Chiauzzi, Emil & Liljegren, Steven K. Staying Straight: A Relapse Prevention Workbook for Young People. 1991. pap. 11.50 (1-55691-069-X, 69x) Learning Pubns.

Chiauzzi, Emil, et al. Substance Abuse: Principles, Strategies & Protocols Designed. 2nd rev. ed. (Time Effective Treatment Ser.). (Illus.). 200p. 1998. 39.95 (0-9670049-0-X) Innovative Train.

Chiavaroli, Neville, tr. see Mews, Constant J.

Chiaventone, Frederick J. A Road We Do Not Know: A Novel of Custer at the Little Bighorn. LC 96-26015. 288p. 1996. 23.50 (0-684-83056-6) S&S Trade.

— A Road We Do Not Know: A Novel of Custer at the Little Bighorn. LC 97-37578. (Illus.). 333p. 1998. pap. write for info. (0-8263-1885-1) Univ of New Mexico Schl.

Chiaverina, Christopher, jt. auth. see Rossing, Thomas D.

Chiaverini, Evelyn & Roberts, Rozella. Your Youth Can Be Restored: The Truth about Aging. 2nd rev. ed. Holms, Bruce S., ed. 318p. 1994. pap. text 12.95 (0-9633452-1-4) Roxanne Unltd.

***Chiaverini, Jennifer.** The Quilter's Apprentice: A Novel. LC 99-89443. 271p. 2000. pap. 10.95 (0-452-28172-5, Plume) Dutton Plume.

Chiaverini, Jennifer. The Quilter's Apprentice: A Novel. LC 98-31179. 271p. 1999. 16.50 (0-684-84972-0) S&S Trade.

***Chiaverini, Jennifer.** Round Robin: An Elm Creek Quilts Novel. LC 99-45743. 304p. 2000. 20.00 (0-684-86892-X) Simon & Schuster.

Chiaverini, Stefano, jt. auth. see Chiacchio, Pasquale.

Chiavetta, Janet M., et al. Eat, Drink & Be Healthy: A Guide to Healthful Eating & Weight Control. LC 92-60883. (Illus.). xvi, 424p. 1993. 24.95 (0-9633991-0-1) Piedmont NC.

Chiazzari, Susy. The Healing Home: Creating the Perfect Place to Live with Color, Aroma, Light & Other Natural Elements. LC 97-61179. (Illus.). 120p. (J). 1998. 24.95 (1-57076-104-3, Trafalgar Sq Pub) Trafalgar.

Chiazzari, Suzy. The Complete Book of Color: Using Color for Lifestyle, Health & Well-Being. LC 98-23425. (Illus.). 256p. 1998. pap. 21.95 (1-86204-259-4, Pub. by Element MA) Penguin Putnam.

***Chiazzari, Suzy.** Flower Readings: Discover Your True Self with Flowers Through the Ancient Art of Flower Psychometry. 2000. pap. 29.95 (0-85207-338-0, Pub. by C W Daniel) Natl Bk Netwk.

— The Healing Home: Creating the Perfect Place to Live with Color, Aroma, Light & Other Natural Resources. (Illus.). 128p. 2000. reprint ed. pap. 17.95 (1-57076-160-4) Trafalgar.

Chiazzari, Suzy. Nutritional Healing with Color: Includes Diets & Recipes for Optimum Health. LC 98-52358. (Illus.). 208p. 1999. pap. 16.95 (1-86204-393-0, Pub. by Element MA) Penguin Putnam.

Chiba, Masaji. Asian Indigenous Law. 250p. 1987. text 97.50 (0-7103-0113-8, 01138) Routledge.

Chiba, Reiko. Hiroshige's Tokaido in Prints & Poetry. LC 57-11672. (Illus.). 70p. 1957. 19.95 (0-8048-0246-7) Tuttle Pubng.

— Japanese Screens in Miniature: Six Masterpieces from the Momoyama Period. LC 60-9285. 1960. boxed set 28.95 (0-8048-0317-X) Tuttle Pubng.

— Painted Fans of Japan: 15 Noh Drama Masterpieces. LC 62-20775. (Illus.). 42p. 1962. 29.95 (0-8048-0468-0) Tuttle Pubng.

— Sesshu's Long Scroll: A Zen Landscape Journey. LC 54-14085. (Illus.). 1959. 19.95 (0-8048-0677-2) Tuttle Pubng.

Chiba, Reiko, ed. Down the Emperor's Road with Hiroshige. LC 65-18959. (Illus.). 72p. 1965. 19.95 (0-8048-0143-6) Tuttle Pubng.

— Japanese Fortune Calendar. LC 54-14085. (Illus.). 39p. 1965. 17.95 (0-8048-0300-5) Tuttle Pubng.

Chiba, Shunzo. Viral Gastroenteritis. LC 96-29701. (Archives of Virology: Supplement Ser.). 1996. write for info. (3-211-82875-3) Spr-Verlag.

Chiba, Shunzo, et al, eds. Viral Gastroenteritis, Vol. VII. LC 96-29701. (Archives of Virology Ser.: Supplement 12, 1996). (Illus.). 311p. 1997. 198.00 (3-211-82947-4) Spr-Verlag.

Chibaudo, Gerard, jt. ed. see Christofides, Constantinos.

***Chibbaro, Anthony.** South Carolina's Lowcountry. (Images of America Ser.). (Illus.). 128p. 1999. pap. 18.99 (0-7385-0210-3) Arcadia Publng.

Chibbaro, Mat. Model Railroading in Small Spaces. LC 97-225323. (Illus.). 96p. (Orig.). 1997. pap. 16.95 (0-89024-295-X, 12176, Kalmbach Books) Kalmbach.

Chibbaro, Tony. South Carolina Tokens. Schenkman, David E., ed. LC 90-71295. (Illus.). 262p. 1991. text 49.95 (0-918492-09-2) TAMS.

Chibber, M. L. Military Leadership to Prevent Military Coup. 1987. 26.00 (0-8364-2211-2, Pub. by Lancer India) S Asia.

***Chibber, M. L.** Pakistan's Criminal Folly in Kashmir: The Drama of Accession & Rescue of Ladakh. LC 98-901168. (Illus.). 247p. 1998. 30.00 (81-7049-095-2, Pub. by Manas Pubns) S Asia.

Chibber, M. L. Sai Baba's Mahavakya on Leadership. LC 95-77760. (Illus.). 232p. (Orig.). 1995. pap. 12.00 (0-9629835-4-3) Leela Pr.

Chibbett, David G., tr. see Doppo, Kunikida.

Chibbett, David G., tr. see Kato, Shuichi.

Chibi, Andrew A. Henry VIII's Conservative Scholar: Bishop John Stokesley & the Divorce, Royal Supremacy & Doctrinal Reform. 204p. (C). 1997. text 33.95 (0-8204-3403-5) P Lang Pubng.

Chibisova, O. I., et al. English-Russian Biological Dictionary. 5th rev. ed. (ENG & RUS.). 736p. (C). 1993. 35.00 (0-8285-5020-4) Firebird NY.

***Chibnall.** Debate On The Norman Conquest. 1999. text 79.95 (0-7190-4912-1) St Martin.

Chibnall, Albert C. Protein Metabolism in the Plant. 1939. pap. 39.50 (0-685-69796-7) Elliots Bks.

Chibnall, Majorie. Charters & Custumals of the Abbey of Holy Trinity, Caen. (Records of Social & Economic History Ser.: Vol. V). (Illus.). 1982. 37.50 (0-19-726009-8) OUP.

Chibnall, Majorie, jt. auth. see Vitalis, Orderic.

Chibnall, Marjorie. The Empress Matilda: Queen Consort, Queen Mother & Lady of the English. (Illus.). xii, 228p. 1993. pap. text 27.95 (0-631-19028-7) Blackwell Pubs.

***Chibnall, Marjorie.** The Normans. 2001. 26.95 (0-631-18671-9) Blackwell Pubs.

Chibnall, Marjorie. Select Documents of the English Lands of the Abbey of Bec. (Camden Third Ser.). 63.00 (0-86193-073-8) David Brown.

— The World of Orderic Vitalis: Norman Monks & Norman Knights. LC 96-3456. (Illus.). 264p. 1996. pap. 29.95 (0-85115-621-5, Boydell Pr) Boydell & Brewer.

Chibnall, Marjorie, ed. Anglo-Norman Studies XII Proceedings of the Battle Conference, 1989. (Illus.). 264p. 1990. 75.00 (0-85115-257-0) Boydell & Brewer.

— Anglo-Norman Studies XIII Proceedings of the Battle Conference, 1990. (Illus.). 296p. (C). 1991. 75.00 (0-85115-286-4) Boydell & Brewer.

— Anglo-Norman Studies XIV Proceedings of the Battle Conference, 1991. (Illus.). 350p. (C). 1992. 75.00 (0-85115-316-X) Boydell & Brewer.

— Anglo-Norman Studies XV Proceedings of the Battle Conference, 1992. (Illus.). 327p. 1993. 75.00 (0-85115-336-4) Boydell & Brewer.

— Anglo-Norman Studies XVI Proceedings of the Battle Conference, 1993. (Illus.). 301p. (C). 1994. 75.00 (0-85115-366-6) Boydell & Brewer.

— The Historia Pontificalis of John of Salisbury. 160p. 1986. text 65.00 (0-19-822275-0) OUP.

Chibnall, Marjorie, ed. The Ecclesiastical History of Orderic Vitalis, Vol. 2, Bks. 3 & 4. (Oxford Medieval Texts Ser.). (Illus.). 452p. 1991. pap. text 35.00 (0-19-820220-2) OUP.

Chibnall, Marjorie, ed. see Mortimer, Richard.

Chibnall, Marjorie, ed. see Vitalis, Orderic.

Chibnall, Marjorie, jt. ed. see Watkiss, Leslie.

Chibnall, Marjorie, ed. & tr. see Vitalis, Orderic.

Chibnall, Steve. British Crime Cinema. LC 98-49739. 1999. pap. write for info. (0-415-16870-8); text. write for info. (0-415-16869-4) Routledge.

Chibnik, Michael. Risky Rivers: The Economics & Politics of Floodplain Farming in Amazonia. (Arizona Studies in Human Ecology). (Illus.). 267p. 1994. 27.95 (0-8165-1482-8) U of Ariz Pr.

***Chibois, Jacques & Baussan, Olivier.** The Book of Olive Oil. (Illus.). 160p. 2000. text 35.00 (2-08-013676-3, Pub. by Flammarion) Abbeville Pr.

***Chibuko, Patrick Chukwudezie.** Igbo Christian Rite of Marriage: A Proposed Rite for Study & Celebration. LC 99-38485. (Studies in the Intercultural History of Christianity: Vol. 119). xxii, 183p. (C). 1999. pap. 35.95 (0-8204-4368-9) P Lang Pubng.

— IGBO Christian Rite of Marriage: A Proposed Rite for Study & Celebration. (Studies in the Intercultural History of Christianity). XXII, 183p. 1999. pap. 35.95 (3-631-35303-0) P Lang Pubng.

— Paschal Mystery of Christ: Foundation for Liturgical Inculturation in Africa. (Studies in the Intercultural History of Christianity). XVI, 197p. 1999. pap. 35.95 (3-631-35560-2) P Lang Pubng.

— Paschal Mystery of Christ: Foundation for Liturgical Inculturation in Africa. LC 99-49816. (Studies in the Intercultural History of Christianity: Vol. 120). xvi, 197p. (C). 1999. pap. 35.95 (0-8204-4703-X) P Lang Pubng.

Chica, Jimmy J. La Novela Ecuatoriana Contemporanea de 1970-1985, Vol. 14. (Wor(l)ds of Change Ser.). (SPA.). X, 193p. (C). 1996. text 45.95 (0-8204-2698-9) P Lang Pubng.

Chicadee Magazine Editors, jt. auth. see Owl Magazine Editors.

Chicadee Magazine Editors, jt. auth. see Penrose, Gordon.

Chicago Bears Staff. Chicago Bears. CWC Sports Inc., ed. (NFL Team Yearbooks Ser.). (J). (gr. 1-12). 1998. pap. 9.99 (1-891613-03-0) Everett Sports.

Chicago Board of Trade, Education & Marketing Depa. Grains: Production, Processing, Marketing. rev. ed. Catania, Patrick J., ed. 174p. 1992. pap. text 12.00 (0-917456-02-5) Chicago Bd Trade.

Chicago Board of Trade Staff. Commodity Trading Manual. LC 99-461895. (Illus.). 410p. 1999. 55.00 (0-8144-0511-8) AMACOM.

— Commodity Trading Manual. 1997. 55.00 (1-888998-14-8) Glenlake Pub.

Chicago Board of Trade Staff, ed. Chicago Board of Trade Commodity Trading Manual. 9th ed. 325p. 1997. lib. bdg. 55.00 (1-57958-002-5) Fitzroy Dearborn.

Chicago Civil Service Commission. Chicago Police Investigations: Three Reports. LC 76-154567. (Police in America Ser.). 1971. reprint ed. 13.95 (0-405-03365-6) Ayer.

Chicago Commission on Race Relations Editors. Negro in Chicago: A Study of Race Relations & a Race Riot. LC 68-28990. (American Negro: His History & Literature. Series 1). 1978. reprint ed. 23.95 (0-405-01807-X) Ayer.

Chicago Community Trust Staff. Reports Comprising the Survey of the Cook County Jail. LC 73-3818. (Criminal Justice in America Ser.). (Illus.). 230 p. 1974. reprint ed. 26.95 (0-405-06139-0) Arno Press.

Chicago Council on Foreign Relations Staff. American Public Opinion & U. S. Foreign Policy, 1982. 2nd ed. LC 84-81558. 1984. write for info. (0-89138-896-6) ICPSR.

Chicago Dietetic Association Staff. Manual of Clinical Dietetics. 5th ed. LC 96-36492. 868p. 1996. 70.00 (0-88091-153-0) Am Dietetic Assn.

Chicago Dietetic Association Staff & South Surburban Dietetic Association Staff. Manual of Clinical Dietetics. 4th ed. LC 92-49557. 1992. ring bd. 62.00 (0-88091-108-5, 0127A) Am Dietetic Assn.

Chicago Editorial Staff. Chicago Guide to Preparing Electronic Manuscripts. 156p. 1987. 30.00 (0-226-10392-7); pap. 11.95 (0-226-10393-5) U Ch Pr.

— The Chicago Manual of Style. 13th enl. rev. ed. LC 82-2832. 752p. (C). 1982. 37.00 (0-226-10390-0) U Ch Pr.

— The Chicago Manual of Style: Indexes. 13th ed. 52p. (C). 1982. pap. text 5.95 (0-226-10391-9) U Ch Pr.

— The Chicago Manual of Style: The Essential Guide for Writers, Editors & Publishers. 14th ed. LC 92-37475. 933p. 1993. 40.00 (0-226-10389-7) U Ch Pr.

— Indexes: A Chapter from The Chicago Manual of Style. 14th ed. 64p. 1993. pap. text 6.00 (0-226-10388-9) U Ch Pr.

Chicago Editorial Staff, ed. The University of Chicago Spanish Dictionary. 4th ed. (ENG & SPA., Illus.). viii, 484p. (C). 1987. 23.95 (0-226-10400-1); pap. 9.00 (0-226-10402-8) U Ch Pr.

Chicago Historical Society Staff & Darling, Sharon S. Decorative & Architectural Arts in Chicago, 1871-1933. LC 81-16253. (Chicago Visual Library: No. 39). (Illus.). 336p. 1982. lib. bdg. 78.00 (0-226-68884-4) U Ch Pr.

Chicago Inst. for Psychoanalysis Staff, ed. The Annual of Psychoanalysis, Vol. 19. 280p. 1991. text 32.50 (0-88163-094-2) Analytic Pr.

Chicago Institute for Psychanalysis Staff, ed. see Fleming, Joan & Benedek, Therese.

Chicago Institute for Psychoanalysis Staff. The Annual of Psychoanalysis, Vol. I. LC 72-91376. 395p. (C). 1973. 70.00 (0-8236-0361-X) Intl Univs Pr.

— Annual of Psychoanalysis, Vol. XIV. LC 72-91376. 375p. (C). 1987. 70.00 (0-8236-0374-1) Intl Univs Pr.

Chicago Institute for Psychoanalysis Staff, ed. Annual of Psychoanalysis, Vol. IX. 1981. 70.00 (0-8236-0370-9) Intl Univs Pr.

— Annual of Psychoanalysis, Vol. X. 1982. 70.00 (0-8236-0371-7) Intl Univs Pr.

— Annual of Psychoanalysis, Vol. XV. (Chicago Institute for Psychoanalysis Ser.). 1987. 70.00 (0-8236-0375-X, BN00375) Intl Univs Pr.

— Annual of Psychoanalysis, Vol. 17. 376p. 1989. text 36.00 (0-88163-092-6) Analytic Pr.

— The Annual of Psychoanalysis, Vol. 20. 336p. 1992. 34.50 (0-88163-133-7) Analytic Pr.

— Annual of Psychoanalysis, 1974, Vol. II. LC 72-91376. (Illus.). x, 420p. (C). 1975. 70.00 (0-8236-0362-8) Intl Univs Pr.

— Annual of Psychoanalysis, 1975, Vol. III. LC 72-91376. viii, 441p. (C). 1976. 70.00 (0-8236-0363-6) Intl Univs Pr.

— Annual of Psychoanalysis, 1976, Vol. IV. LC 72-91376. (Illus.). xi, 508p. (C). 1977. 70.00 (0-8236-0364-4) Intl Univs Pr.

— Annual of Psychoanalysis, 1977, Vol. V. LC 72-91376. (Illus.). ix, 443p. (C). 1978. 70.00 (0-8236-0366-0) Intl Univs Pr.

— Annual of Psychoanalysis, 1978, Vol. VI. LC 72-91376. (Illus.). x, 489p. (C). 1979. 70.00 (0-8236-0367-9) Intl Univs Pr.

— Annual of Psychoanalysis, 1979, Vol. VII. LC 72-91376. (Illus.). x, 416p. (C). 1980. 70.00 (0-8236-0368-7) Intl Univs Pr.

— Annual of Psychoanalysis, 1980, Vol. VIII. LC 72-91376. (Illus.). xiii, 359p. (C). 1981. 70.00 (0-8236-0369-5) Intl Univs Pr.

— Annual of Psychoanalysis, 1983, Vol. XI. LC 72-91376. xii, 365p. (C). 1984. 70.00 (0-8236-0372-5) Intl Univs Pr.

— Annual of Psychoanalysis, 1985, Vol. XII-XIII. LC 72-91376. 452p. 1985. 70.00 (0-8236-0373-3, 00373) Intl Univs Pr.

Chicago Institute for Psychoanalysis Staff, ed. see Alexander, Franz.

Chicago Institute for Psychoanalysis Staff, ed. see Novey, Samuel.

Chicago Institute of Psychoanalysis Staff, ed. Annual of Psychoanalysis, Vol. XVI. 391p. 1988. 70.00 (0-8236-0376-8) Intl Univs Pr.

— The Annual of Psychoanalysis, Vol. 18. (Annual Ser.). 272p. 1990. text 29.95 (0-88163-093-4) Analytic Pr.

Chicago Jewish News Staff. The Guide: The Who's What's & Where's of Jewish Chicago. Aaron, Joe & Winer, Todd, eds. (Illus.). 56p. (Orig.). 1995. 4.00 (0-9648427-0-X) Chicago Jewish.

Chicago, Judy. Through the Flower: My Struggle As a Woman Artist. LC 93-19313. (Illus.). 248p. 1993. pap. 14.95 (0-14-023122-6, Penguin Bks) Viking Penguin.

Chicago, Judy & Lucie-Smith, Edward. Women & Art: Contested Territory. (Illus.). 192p. 1999. 35.00 (0-8230-5852-2) Watsn-Guptill.

Chicago, Judy, jt. auth. see Lucie-Smith, Edward.

Chicago, South Shore & South Bend Railroad Staff, et al. Moonlight in Duneland: The Illustrated Story of the Chicago South Shore & South Bend Railroad. Cohen, Ronald D. & McShane, Stephen G., eds. LC 98-16812. (Illus.). 160p. 1998. 39.95 (0-253-33418-7) Ind U Pr.

***Chicago Sun-Times Staff.** Chicago Sports Century. Lazenby, Roland, ed. (Illus.). 192p. 2000. 29.95 (1-58382-060-4) Sports Pub.

***Chicago Sun-Times Staff, ed.** 20th Century Chicago: 100 Years, 100 Voices. (Illus.). 216p. 1999. 29.95 (1-58261-239-0, Pub. by Sprts Pubng) Partners-West.

Chicago Tribune Staff. Century of Tribune Editorials. LC 72-93327. (Essay Index Reprint Ser.). 1977. 19.95 (0-8369-1558-5) Ayer.

— Chicago Tribune Chicagoland Map, 1983-1984. 1983. reprint ed. 195.00 (0-686-40853-5) Chicago Trib.

— Chicago's Schools: 'Worst in America' (Illus.). 208p. (Orig.). 1988. pap. write for info. (0-9621267-0-5) Chicago Trib.

— Crossroads, U. S. A. Discovering American Culture & Language with the Daily Newspaper. (Illus.). pap., teacher ed. 15.46 (0-8442-0449-8) NTC Contemp Pub Co.

— Crossroads, U. S. A. Discovering American Culture & Language with the Daily Newspaper. (Illus.). 176p. 1998. pap., teacher ed., student ed. 67.98 incl. audio (0-8442-0451-X) NTC Contemp Pub Co.

— Tribune Sesquicentenial. LC 96-51735. 1996. write for info. (0-8092-3155-7) NTC Contemp Pub Co.

Chicago University, Graduate Library School Staff. Education for Librarianship. LC 71-117776. (Essay Index Reprint Ser.). 1977. 23.95 (0-8369-1701-4) Ayer.

— Operations Research: Implications for Libraries: The 35th Annual Conference of the Graduate Library School, August 2-4, 1971. Swanson, Don R. & Bookstein, Abraham, eds. LC 73-185760. (University of Chicago Studies in Library Science). 166p. reprint ed. pap. 51.50 (0-608-16376-7, 202674700051) Bks Demand.

— The Public Library: Circumstances & Prospects: Proceedings of the Thirty-Ninth Conference of the Graduate Library School, April 10-11, 1978. Rayward, W. Boyd, ed. LC 78-19604. 168p. reprint ed. pap. 52.10 (0-608-16501-8, 202673900051) Bks Demand.

— The Role of Libraries in the Growth of Knowledge: Proceedings of the 40th Conference of the Graduate Library School, May 18-19, 1978. Swanson, Don R., ed. LC 79-5467. (University of Chicago Studies in Library Science). 142p. reprint ed. pap. 44.10 (0-608-16373-2, 202674600051) Bks Demand.

Chicago University Staff. English Studies, 5 vols. reprint ed. 127.50 (0-404-50260-1) AMS Pr.

— Germanic Studies, 3 vols. reprint ed. 54.00 (0-404-50270-9) AMS Pr.

— Linguistic Studies in Germanic, 5 vols., Set. reprint ed. 105.00 (0-404-50280-6) AMS Pr.

— The People Shall Judge: Readings in the Formation of American Policy, Vol. 2. LC 49-3028. 945p. reprint ed. pap. 200.00 (0-608-16365-1, 202674400002) Bks Demand.

Chicago Urban League Staff, et al. Metro Chicago Political Atlas, 1994. LC 94-24833. (Illus.). 102p. (Orig.). 1994. pap. 20.00 (0-938943-07-3) U IL Spgfld Pub Affrs.

— Metro Chicago Political Atlas, 97-98. (Illus.). 166p. 1997. pap. 19.95 (0-938943-13-8) U IL Spgfld Pub Affrs.

Chicago Zoological Society Staff, ed. Animal Families. (Brookfield Zoo Connections Ser.). (Orig.). (J). (gr. k-2). 1986. pap. text 30.00 (0-913934-04-6) Chicago Zoo.

— Brookfield Zoo Connections: A Program to Enhance Classroom Studies. (Orig.). (J). (gr. k-8). 1986. pap. text 30.00 (0-913934-03-8) Chicago Zoo.

— Creature Features. (Brookfield Zoo Connections Ser.). (Orig.). (J). (gr. 2-3). 1986. pap. text 30.00 (0-913934-05-4) Chicago Zoo.

— Desert Communities. (Brookfield Zoo Connections Ser.). (Orig.). (J). (gr. 4-6). 1986. pap. text 30.00 (0-913934-06-2) Chicago Zoo.

Chicharro Chamorro, Antonio, ed. see Alonso, Damaso.

Chicharro Chamorro, Damaso, ed. see Machado, Manuel Y.

Chiche, Gerard & Pinault, Alain. Esthetics of Anterior Fixed Prosthodontics. LC 93-25776. (Illus.). 204p. 1994. text 98.00 (0-86715-258-3) Quint Pub Co.

Chichester, A. Lee, jt. auth. see Matthews, Billie P.

Chichester, A. Lee, ed. see Moore, Jack S.

Chichester, Brent. Forty-Five, Bks. I & II. 760p. 1997. pap. 35.00 (0-8059-4134-7) Dorrance.

Chichester, C. O., ed. see International Nutritional Anemia Consulative Group, et al.

Chichester Clark, Emma. I Love You, Blue Kangaroo! LC 98-16342. 32p. (J). (ps-3). 1999. 15.95 (0-385-32638-6, DD Bks Yng Read) BDD Bks Young Read.

Chichester Clark, Emma, jt. auth. see Cecil, Laura.

Chichester-Clark, Emma, jt. auth. see McCaughrean, Geraldine.

Chichester, D. G. Daredevil: Fall of the Kingpin. (Illus.). 1993. pap. 12.95 (0-87135-965-0) Marvel Entrprs.

— Daredevil & Batman: An Eye for an Eye. 1997. pap. 5.99 (0-7851-0552-2) Marvel Entrprs.

— Stress Blaster. LC 96-27694. (Illus.). 176p. 1997. pap. 14.95 (0-87596-358-7) St Martin.

Chichester, D. G. & Wright, Greg. The Suit Countdown Digest. (The Suit Digest Ser.). (Illus.). 80p. 1997. per. 3.99 (0-671-01173-1) PB.

C

Chichester, D. G., et al. Invasion The Suit 1 Digest. (J). 1997. per. 3.99 (*0-671-01166-9*) PB.

***Chichester, Francis.** Gipsy Moth Circles the World. (Sailor's Classics). (Illus.). 288p. 2000. 19.95 (*0-07-136449-8*) McGraw.

Chichester, Francis B. London Man. 1988. mass mkt. 8.95 (*0-446-38740-1*, Pub. by Warner Bks) Little.

— London Woman. 1988. mass mkt. 8.95 (*0-446-38742-8*, Pub. by Warner Bks) Little.

— Ride on the Wind. Gilbert, James B., ed. LC 79-7236. (Flight: Its First Seventy-Five Years Ser.). (Illus.). 1980. reprint ed. lib. bdg. 26.95 (*0-405-12152-0*) Ayer.

Chichester, Michael & Wilkinson, J. A. British Defence: A Blueprint for Reform. 224p. 1987. 38.00 (*0-08-034745-2*, Pergamon Pr) Elsevier.

Chichester, Ross. Walking Backwards. (Illus.). 80p. 1998. pap. 8.00 (*0-8059-4326-9*) Dorrance.

Chichester, Teddi L. Shelley's Mirrors of Love: Narcissism, Sacrifice & Sorority. LC 98-6222. (Series in Psychoanalysis & Culture). 320p. (C). 1998. pap. text 21.95 (*0-7914-3978-X*) State U NY Pr.

— Shelley's Mirrors of Love: Narcissism, Sacrifice & Sorority. LC 98-6222. (Series in Psychoanalysis & Culture). 320p. (C). 1998. text 65.50 (*0-7914-3977-1*) State U NY Pr.

Chichetto, James. Stones: A Litany. (Illus.). 20p. 1980. pap. 4.00 (*0-939622-06-8*) Four Zoas Night Ltd.

Chichetto, James W. Homage to Father Edward Sorin, C. S. C. 2nd rev. ed. LC 98-7759. 54p. 1998. pap. 11.95 (*0-9618657-4-1*) CT Poetry Rev Pr.

— Homage to Father Edward Sorin, C.S.C. 54p. (Orig.). (C). 1992. 20.95 (*0-9618657-2-5*); pap. 8.95 (*0-9618657-3-3*) CT Poetry Rev Pr.

— Victims. LC 87-70891. 52p. (Orig.). (C). 1987. 5.95 (*0-9618657-0-9*); pap. 3.95 (*0-9618657-1-7*) CT Poetry Rev Pr.

***Chichetto, James Wm.** Dream of Norumbega, Bk. 1. (Illus.). 55p. 2000. 25.00 (*0-9618657-5-X*); pap. 11.95 (*0-9618657-6-8*) CT Poetry Rev Pr.

Chichibu, Shigefusa F., jt. auth. see Nakamura, Shuji.

***Chichikov, Pavel.** Lion Sun: Poems by Pavel Chichikov. LC 99-90616. (Illus.). 96p. 1999. pap. 12.95 (*0-9671901-0-X*) Grey Owl.

Chichilnisky, Fraciela, et al, eds. Sustainability: Dynamics & Uncertainty. LC 97-23951. (Economics, Energy & Environment Ser.: No. 9). 348p. 1998. 112.00 (*0-7923-4698-X*) Kluwer Academic.

Chichilnisky, Graciela. Topology & Markets. LC 98-44414. (Fields Institute Communications Ser.). 110p. 1999. 39.00 (*0-8218-1071-5*) Am Math.

Chichilnisky, Graciela, ed. Markets, Information & Uncertainty: Essays in Economic Theory in Honor of Kenneth Arrow. LC 97-25548. (Illus.). 424p. (C). 1998. text 69.95 (*0-521-55355-5*) Cambridge U Pr.

Chichilnisky, Graciela, ed. Mathematical Economics, 3 vols. LC 98-15017. (International Library of Critical Writings in Economics Ser.: Vol. 93). 1644p. 1998. 590.00 (*1-85898-260-X*) E Elgar.

***Chichilnisky, Graciela & Heal, G. M.** Environmental Markets: Equity & Efficiency. LC 99-40305. (Economics for a Sustainable Earth Ser.). 1999. pap. write for info. (*0-231-11589-X*) Col U Pr.

Chichilnisky, Graciela & Heal, Geoffrey. The Evolving International Economy. (Illus.). 176p. 1987. text 64.95 (*0-521-26716-1*) Cambridge U Pr.

Chichilnisky, Graciela, jt. auth. see Heal, Geoffrey.

***Chichin, Eileen R., et al.** End-of-Life Ethics & the Nursing Assistant: And Accompanying Workbook 1309-7. (Illus.). 168p. 2000. text. write for info. (*0-8261-1307-9*) Springer Pub.

Chichinadze, A. V., ed. Polymers in Friction Assemblies of Machines & Devices: A Handbook. xii, 280p. 1984. 68.50 (*0-89864-010-5*) Allerton Pr.

***Chichoni, Oscar.** Mekanika. 80p. 2000. pap. 18.95 (*1-56163-256-2*) NBM.

***Chicilo, Dawn M.** Pinky Swear: The Gift of a Lifetime. Korpi, Sid, ed. LC 00-91460. 150p. 2000. 16.95 (*0-9678920-0-7*, PS-3858) TreeHouse Pubng Co.

Chicione, David L., jt. ed. see Walzer, Norman L.

Chick, Edson M., tr. see Kohlmeier, Michael.

Chick, Jack T. The Big Betrayal. (Illus.). 64p. (Orig.). 1993. pap. 2.95 (*0-937958-08-5*) Chick Pubns.

— Cortinas de Humo. (SPA., Illus.). 96p. (Orig.). 1984. pap. 3.95 (*0-937958-20-4*) Chick Pubns.

— King of Kings. (Illus.). 64p. (Orig.). 1980. pap. 2.95 (*0-937958-07-7*) Chick Pubns.

— The Last Call. (Illus.). 64p. 1963. pap. 3.50 (*0-937958-06-9*) Chick Pubns.

— The Next Step. (Illus.). 64p. 1978. pap. 3.50 (*0-937958-04-2*) Chick Pubns.

— O Proximo Passo: Para Cristaos em Crescimento. (POR., Illus.). 64p. 1997. pap. 3.50 (*0-937958-54-9*) Chick Pubns.

— El Proximo Paso. (SPA., Illus.). 64p. 1983. pap. 3.50 (*0-937958-15-8*) Chick Pubns.

— Rey de Reyes: La Biblia en Cuadros. (SPA., Illus.). 64p. (Orig.). (YA). (gr. 7-12). 1989. pap. 2.95 (*0-937958-37-9*) Chick Pubns.

— Smokescreens. (Illus.). 93p. 1982. pap. 3.95 (*0-937958-14-X*) Chick Pubns.

— La Ultima Llamada. (SPA., Illus.). 64p. 1972. pap. 3.50 (*0-937958-02-6*) Chick Pubns.

Chick, Jean M. Form As Expression: A Study of the Lyric Poetry Written Between 1910 & 1915 by Lasker-Schueler, Stramm, Stadler, Benn, & Heym. (Studie in Modern German Literature: Vol. 10). VIII, 210p. (C). 1988. text 33.50 (*0-8204-0441-1*) P Lang Pubng.

Chick, Martin. Industrial Policy in Britain, 1945-1951: Economic Planning, Nationalisation & the Labour Governments. LC 97-10272. 240p. (C). 1997. text 59.95 (*0-521-48291-7*) Cambridge U Pr.

***Chick, Sandra.** Cheap Street. (Livewire Ser.). 1999. pap. 11.95 (*0-7043-4949-3*, Pub. by Womens Press) Trafalgar.

— Don't Look Back. (Livewire Ser.). (J). 1999. pap. 11.95 (*0-7043-4958-2*, Pub. by Womens Press) Trafalgar.

Chick, Sandra. I Never Told Her I Loved Her. (Livewire Ser.). 128p. (Orig.). (J). (gr. 6-9). 1998. pap. 8.95 (*0-7043-4947-7*, Pub. by Womens Press) Trafalgar.

— On the Rocks. (Livewire Ser.). 148p. (YA). (gr. 7-11). 1997. pap. 7.95 (*0-7043-4938-8*, Pub. by Womens Press) Trafalgar.

— Push Me, Pull Me. (Livewire Ser.). 128p. (J). (gr. 6-9). pap. 5.95 (*0-7043-4901-9*, Pub. by Womens Press) Trafalgar.

Chick, Victoria. Macroeconomics after Keynes: A Reconsideration of the General Theory. 356p. 1983. 32.50 (*0-262-03095-0*); pap. text 22.50 (*0-262-53045-7*) MIT Pr.

Chick, Victoria, jt. ed. see Arestis, Philip.

Chick, William L., jt. ed. see Lanza, Robert P.

Chicka, C. & Chimpa, Anthony C. Diabetic's Jet Ejectors: Diabetic Gun for Personal Insulin Injection. LC 88-92324. (Illus.). 78p. (Orig.). 1989. pap. 9.95 (*0-922958-03-3*) H W Parker.

***Chickadee & Owl Editors.** The Anti-Boredom Book: 133 Completely Unboring Things to Do! 128p. (J). (gr. k-4). 2000. 22.95 (*1-894379-00-4*, Pub. by GDPB) Firefly Bks Ltd.

Chickadee Magazine Editors. Play & Learn: Puzzles & Fun. (Illus.). 64p. (J). (gr. k-4). 1999. pap. 8.95 (*1-895688-92-2*, Pub. by Owl Bks) Firefly Bks Ltd.

— Science Fun: Hands-On Science with Dr. Zed. (Illus.). 80p. (J). (ps-3). 1998. pap. 12.95 (*1-895688-74-4*) Firefly Bks Ltd.

— Science Fun: Hands-On Science with Dr. Zed. (Illus.). 80p. (J). (ps-3). 1998. 19.95 (*1-895688-73-6*, Pub. by Owl Bks) Firefly Bks Ltd.

Chickadel, Charles & Straughn, Greg. Building a Profitable Business: The Proven Step-by-Step Guide to Starting & Running Your Own Business. 2nd ed. LC 93-45484. 320p. 1994. pap. 17.95 (*1-55850-272-6*) Adams Media.

Chickalusion, Maxim & Chickalusion, Nellie. Tubughna Elnena (The Tyonek People's Country) 24p. 1979. pap. 3.00 (*0-933769-95-4*) Alaska Native.

Chickalusion, Nellie, jt. auth. see Chickalusion, Maxim.

Chickanagappa, L. L., jt. ed. see Ramiah, B. K.

Chicken, J. C. Strategy & Priority. (ITBP Textbooks Ser.). 224p. 1999. pap. 19.99 (*1-86152-484-6*) Thomson Learn.

Chicken, John C. Hazard Control Policy in Britain. LC 75-12900. 204p. 1975. 92.00 (*0-08-019739-6*, Pub. by Pergamon Repr) Franklin.

— Managing Risks & Decisions in Major Projects. 224p. 1994. mass mkt. 68.95 (*0-412-58730-0*) Chapman & Hall.

— Nuclear Power Hazard Control Policy. LC 80-40992. (Illus.). 300p. 1982. 126.00 (*0-08-023254-X*, Pub. by Pergamon Repr) Franklin.

— Risk Management Handbook. 554p. 1996. mass mkt. 75.00 (*0-412-62750-7*) Chapman & Hall.

Chicken, John C. & Hayns, Michael R. The Risk Ranking Technique in Decision Making. 136p. 1989. 44.50 (*0-08-037212-0*, Pergamon Pr) Elsevier.

Chickering, A. Lawrence. Beyond Left & Right: Breaking the Political Stalemate. LC 92-47007. 256p. 1993. 24.95 (*1-55815-209-1*) ICS Pr.

Chickering, A. Lawrence & Salahdine, Mohamed, eds. The Silent Revolution: The Informal Sector in Five Asian & Near Eastern Countries. 245p. 1991. 29.95 (*1-55815-163-X*); pap. 19.95 (*1-55815-162-1*); 6.95 (*1-55815-177-X*) ICS Pr.

Chickering, A. Lawrence, jt. ed. see Taylor, Flagg.

Chickering, Arthur W. Commuting Versus Resident Students: Overcoming the Educational Inequities of Living off Campus. LC 74-6737. (Jossey-Bass Higher Education Ser.). 168p. reprint ed. pap. 52.10 (*0-608-17905-1*, 205220000058) Bks Demand.

— Education & Identity. fac. ed. LC 70-75938. (Jossey-Bass Series in Higher Education). 383p. 1969. reprint ed. pap. 118.80 (*0-7837-8047-8*, 204780000008) Bks Demand.

Chickering, Arthur W. & Gamson, Zelda F., eds. Applying the Seven Principles for Good Practice in Undergraduate Education. LC 85-644763. (New Directions for Teaching & Learning Ser.: No. TL 47). 1991. pap. 22.00 (*1-55542-781-2*) Jossey-Bass.

Chickering, Arthur W. & Reisser, Linda. Education & Identity. 2nd ed. LC 93-5392. (Higher Education Ser.). 556p. 1993. text 38.95 (*1-55542-591-7*) Jossey-Bass.

Chickering, Arthur W. & Schlossberg, Nancy K. Getting the Most Out of College. LC 94-18263. 384p. 1994. pap. 21.33 (*0-205-16291-6*) Allyn.

— Getting the Most Out of College: Examination Copy. 320p. (C). 1994. pap. text. write for info. (*0-205-16946-5*, H6946-1) Allyn.

Chickering, Arthur W., et al. Developing the College Curriculum: A Handbook for Faculty & Administrators. Quehl, Gary H. & Gee, Marguerite, eds. LC 77-90328. 1977. pap. text 10.00 (*0-937012-04-1*) Coun Indep Colleges.

Chickering, Bill & Nuckols, Cardwell C. Healing an Angry Heart: Finding Solace in a Hostile World. LC 98-3079. 200p. 1997. pap. 10.95 (*1-55874-517-3*) Health Comm.

***Chickering, Helen L.** Momma Chick's Recipes: A Collection of Favorite Recipes. 2nd ed. Hobson, Timothy J., ed. 105p. 1999. 14.95 (*1-893822-01-X*) Hobsons.

Chickering, Howell & Seiler, Thomas H., eds. The Study of Chivalry: Resources & Approaches. 1988. pap. 19.95 (*0-918720-94-X*); boxed set 39.95 (*0-918720-93-1*) Medieval Inst.

Chickering, Howell D., Jr., ed. Beowulf: A Dual Language Edition. LC 75-21250. (Anchor Literary Library). 432p. 1977. pap. 14.95 (*0-385-06213-3*, Anchor NY) Doubleday.

Chickering, K., ed. Pipeline Engineering Symposium. 96p. 1983. pap. text 24.00 (*0-317-02640-2*, I00157) ASME.

Chickering, Lawrence, ed. Readings in Public Policy. 338p. (Orig.). 1984. pap. 19.95 (*0-917616-66-9*) ICS Pr.

Chickering, Robert B. How to Register Copyrights & Protect Them. 1981. 12.95 (*0-684-16705-0*, Scribners Ref) Mac Lib Ref.

Chickering, Robert B. & Hartman, Susan. How to Copyright & Protect Your Creations. 216p. 1987. pap. 13.95 (*0-684-18878-3*, Scribners Ref) Mac Lib Ref.

Chickering, Roger. Imperial Germany & a World Without War: The Peace Movement & German Society, 1892-1914. fac. ed. LC 75-2983. 502p. 1975. reprint ed. pap. 155.70 (*0-7837-8164-4*, 204786900008) Bks Demand.

— Imperial Germany & the Great War, 1914-1918. (New Approaches to European History Ser.: No. 13). (Illus.). 248p. (C). 1998. text 54.95 (*0-521-56148-5*); pap. text 16.95 (*0-521-56754-8*) Cambridge U Pr.

— Karl Lamprecht: A German Academic Life (1856-1915) LC 92-9140. (Studies in Central European Histories). 512p. (C). 1993. text 65.00 (*0-391-03766-8*) Humanities.

Chickering, Roger, ed. Imperial Germany: A Historiographical Companion. LC 95-36431. 552p. 1996. lib. bdg. 105.00 (*0-313-27641-2*, Greenwood Pr) Greenwood.

***Chickering, Roger & Forster, Stig, eds.** Great War, Total War: Combat & Mobilization on the Western Front, 1914-1918. LC D530.G68 1999. (Publications of the German Historical Institute, Washington, D. C.). (Illus.). 584p. (C). 2000. 54.95 (*0-521-77352-0*) Cambridge U Pr.

Chickering, Roger, ed. see Thiebault, John.

Chickering, Roger, ed. see Wallace, Peter G.

Chickerneo, Nancy Barrett. Portraits of Spirituality in Recovery: The Use of Art in Recovery from Co-Dependency and-or Chemical Dependency. LC 92-42194. (Illus.). 254p. 1993. text 54.95 (*0-398-05845-8*) C C Thomas.

— Portraits of Spirituality in Recovery: The Use of Art in Recovery from Co-Dependency and/or Chemical Dependency. LC 92-42194. (Illus.). 254p. 1993. pap. 37.95 (*0-398-06056-8*) C C Thomas.

Chickey, Angela, jt. auth. see Kahre, Kathy.

Chicklas, Claudia, jt. auth. see Bacon, Warren.

***Chicko, Joe & Chicko, Terri.** The Itsy Bitsy Spider. large type ed. (Getting Ready to Read with Mother Goose). 8p. (J). (gr. k). 1999. 39.00 (*0-8215-6956-2*) Sadlier.

— The Itsy Bitsy Spider. large type ed. (Getting Ready to Read with Mother Goose). 8p. (J). (gr. k). 1999. 18.89 (*0-8215-6962-7*) Sadlier.

Chicko, Joe & Chicko, Terri. Space. (At Your Fingertips Ser.). (J). 1998. 6.95 (*0-7681-0075-5*, McClanahan Book) Learn Horizon.

Chicko, Terri, jt. illus. see Chicko, Joe.

Chiclana, Angel, ed. & tr. see Aretino, Pietro.

Chico Area Writers. This Little Bit of Earth: Fiction & Poetry by Chico Area Writers. 104p. 1997. pap. 12.00 (*0-9656222-0-7*) Valley Oaks.

Chicoine, David L. & Walzer, Norman L., eds. Financing Local Infrastructure in Nonmetropolitan Areas. LC 86-20543. 264p. 1986. 55.00 (*0-275-92375-4*, C2375, Praeger Pubs) Greenwood.

Chicoine, Francine. Caresse de Porc-Epic: Suivi de, Lettres: Reflexions sur l'Urgence de l'Essentiel. LC 96-941267. (FRE.). 154p. 1996. 19.95 (*2-89466-005-7*) Edns Roseau.

Chicoine, Stephen. A Liberian Family. LC 96-16739. (Journey Between Two Worlds Ser.). (J). 1997. lib. bdg. 22.60 (*0-8225-3411-8*, Lerner Publctns) Lerner Pub.

— A Liberian Family. (Illus.). 56p. (gr. 3-6). 1997. pap. 8.95 (*0-8225-9758-6*) Lerner Pub.

— A Tibetan Family. LC 97-12645. (Journey Between Two Worlds Ser.). (J). 1998. lib. bdg. 22.60 (*0-8225-3408-8*, Lerner Publctns) Lerner Pub.

Chicoine, Stephen D., jt. auth. see Ayer, Eleanor H.

Chicola, Nancy A. & English, Eleanor B. Discovering World Geography with Books Kids Love. LC 98-49150. (Learning with Books Kids Love Ser.). (Illus.). 176p. 1999. pap. 17.95 (*1-55591-965-0*) Fulcrum Pub.

Chicone, Carmen Charles. A Course of Ordinary Differential Equations with Applications. LC 99-26376. (Texts in Applied Mathematics Ser.). 552p. 1999. 59.95 (*0-387-98535-2*) Spr-Verlag.

***Chicone, Carmen Charles & Latushkin, Yuri.** Evolution Semigroups in Dynamical Systems & Differential Equations. LC 99-23729. (Mathematical Surveys & Monographs Ser.: Vol. 70). 361p. 1999. 109.00 (*0-8218-1185-1*) Am Math.

Chicone, Jerry, Jr. & Burnette, Brenda E. Florida Citrus Crate Labels: An Illustrated History. 102p. 1996. text 39.50 (*0-9649282-0-5*) Burnette & Assocs.

***Chicora Foundation Staff & South Carolina State Museum Staff.** Curricula Materials for the First South Carolinians: The Life & Times of Native Peoples in the Palmetto State. LC 99-57234. (Illus.). 2000. 20.00 (*1-58317-052-9*) Chicora Found.

Chicorel, Marietta S. Chicorel Abstracts to Reading & Learning Disabilities, 1976 Annual. (Chicorel Index Ser.: Vol. 19). 384p. 1976. text 125.00 (*0-934598-15-0*) Am Lib Pub Co.

— Chicorel Index to Abstracting & Indexing, 2 vols., Set. 2nd ed. (Chicorel Index Ser.: Vols. 11 & 11A). 1978. text 250.00 (*0-934598-20-7*) Am Lib Pub Co.

Chicorel, Marietta S., ed. Chicorel Abstracts to Reading & Learning Disabilities: 1977 Annual. (Chicorel Index Ser.: Vol. 19). 1977. text 125.00 (*0-934598-17-7*) Am Lib Pub Co.

— Chicorel Abstracts to Reading & Learning Disabilities, Periodicals, 1980 Annual. (Chicorel Index Ser.: Vol. 19). 380p. 1982. 125.00 (*0-934598-80-0*) Am Lib Pub Co.

— Chicorel Bibliography to Books on Music & Musicians. LC 74-161012. (Chicorel Index Ser.: Vol. 10). 500p. 1974. 125.00 (*0-934598-18-5*) Am Lib Pub Co.

— Chicorel Bibliography to the Performing Arts. LC 73-155102. (Chicorel Index Ser.: Vol. 3A). 498p. reprint ed. pap. 154.40 (*0-7837-3086-1*, 205760500003) Bks Demand.

— Chicorel Index to Biographies, Vol. 15. LC 74-175082. (Chicorel Index Ser.: Vol. 15 & 15a). 475p. reprint ed. pap. 147.30 (*0-7837-3105-1*, 205761300001) Bks Demand.

— Chicorel Index to Biographies, Vol. 15A: LC 74-175082. (Chicorel Index Ser.: Vol. 15 & 15a). 426p. reprint ed. pap. 132.10 (*0-7837-3106-X*, 205761300002) Bks Demand.

— Chicorel Index to Environment & Ecology, Vol. 16. LC 75-306805. (Chicorel Index Ser.: Vol. 16 & 16A). 392p. reprint ed. pap. 121.60 (*0-7837-3107-8*, 205761400001) Bks Demand.

— Chicorel Index to Environment & Ecology, Vol. 16A. LC 75-306805. (Chicorel Index Ser.: Vol. 16 & 16A). 355p. reprint ed. pap. 110.10 (*0-7837-3108-6*, 205761400002) Bks Demand.

— Chicorel Index to Film Literature, Vol. 22. LC 75-22340. (Chicorel Index Ser.: Vol. 22 & 22A). 454p. reprint ed. pap. 140.80 (*0-7837-3114-0*, 205761800001) Bks Demand.

— Chicorel Index to Film Literature, Vol. 22A. LC 75-22340. (Chicorel Index Ser.: Vol. 22 & 22A). 467p. reprint ed. pap. 144.80 (*0-7837-3115-9*, 205761800002) Bks Demand.

— Chicorel Index to Learning Disorders, 2 vols., 18. LC 75-9713. (Chicorel Index Ser.: Vols. 18 & 18A). 1000p. 1975. lib. bdg. write for info. (*0-934598-30-4*) Am Lib Pub Co.

— Chicorel Index to Learning Disorders, 2 vols., 18A. LC 75-9713. (Chicorel Index Ser.: Vols. 18 & 18A). 1000p. 1975. lib. bdg. write for info. (*0-934598-31-2*) Am Lib Pub Co.

— Chicorel Index to Learning Disorders, 2 vols., Set. LC 75-9713. (Chicorel Index Ser.: Vols. 18 & 18A). 1000p. 1975. 250.00 (*0-934598-32-0*) Am Lib Pub Co.

— Chicorel Index to Literary Criticism in Books: U. S. A., Canada. LC 79-116354. (Chicorel Index Ser.: Vol. 23). 350p. reprint ed. pap. 108.50 (*0-7837-3116-7*, 205761900001) Bks Demand.

— Chicorel Index to Mental Health Book Reviews, 1974 Annual. (Chicorel Index Ser.: Vol. 26). 322p. 1982. text 125.00 (*0-934598-81-9*) Am Lib Pub Co.

— Chicorel Index to Mental Health Book Reviews, 1975 Annual. (Chicorel Index Ser.: Vol. 26). 287p. 1982. 125.00 (*0-934598-82-7*) Am Lib Pub Co.

— Chicorel Index to Mental Health Book Reviews, 1980-84, 3 vols. (Chicorel Index Ser.: Vol. 26). 1986. text 375.00 (*0-934598-93-2*) Am Lib Pub Co.

— Chicorel Index to Parapsychology & Occult. (Chicorel Index Ser.: Vol. 24). 1978. text 125.00 (*0-934598-33-9*) Am Lib Pub Co.

— Chicorel Index to Poetry & Poets: Literature, Vol. 20. LC 75-40039. (Chicorel Index Ser.: Vol. 20 & 20A). 472p. reprint ed. pap. 146.40 (*0-7837-3111-6*, 205761600001) Bks Demand.

— Chicorel Index to Poetry & Poets: Literature, Vol. 20A. LC 75-40039. (Chicorel Index Ser.: Vol. 20 & 20A). 555p. reprint ed. pap. 172.10 (*0-7837-3112-4*, 205761600002) Bks Demand.

— Chicorel Index to Poetry in Anthologies & Collections: Retrospective, Vol. 6. LC 75-9587. (Chicorel Index Ser.: Vols. 6, 6A, 6B & 6C). 461p. reprint ed. pap. 143.00 (*0-7837-3091-8*, 205760700001) Bks Demand.

— Chicorel Index to Poetry in Anthologies & Collections: Retrospective, Vol. 6A. LC 75-9587. (Chicorel Index Ser.: Vols. 6, 6A, 6B & 6C). 465p. reprint ed. pap. 144.20 (*0-7837-3092-6*, 205760700002) Bks Demand.

— Chicorel Index to Poetry in Anthologies & Collections: Retrospective, Vol. 6B. LC 75-9587. (Chicorel Index Ser.: Vols. 6, 6A, 6B & 6C). 456p. reprint ed. pap. 141.40 (*0-7837-3093-4*, 205760700003) Bks Demand.

— Chicorel Index to Poetry in Anthologies & Collections: Retrospective, Vol. 6C. LC 75-9587. (Chicorel Index Ser.: Vols. 6, 6A, 6B & 6C). 483p. reprint ed. pap. 149.80 (*0-7837-3094-2*, 205760700004) Bks Demand.

— Chicorel Index to Poetry in Anthologies & Collections in Print, Vol. 5. LC 74-195254. (Chicorel Index Ser.: Vols. 5, 5A, 5B & 5C). 450p. reprint ed. pap. 139.50 (*0-7837-3087-X*, 205760600001) Bks Demand.

— Chicorel Index to Poetry in Anthologies & Collections in Print, Vol. 5A. LC 74-195254. (Chicorel Index Ser.: Vols. 5, 5A, 5B & 5C). 455p. reprint ed. pap. 141.10 (*0-7837-3088-8*, 205760600002) Bks Demand.

— Chicorel Index to Poetry in Anthologies & Collections in Print, Vol. 5B. LC 74-195254. (Chicorel Index Ser.: Vols. 5, 5A, 5B & 5C). 355p. reprint ed. pap. 110.10 (*0-7837-3089-6*, 205760600003) Bks Demand.

— Chicorel Index to Poetry in Anthologies & Collections in Print, Vol. 5C. LC 74-195254. (Chicorel Index Ser.: Vols. 5, 5A, 5B & 5C). 452p. reprint ed. pap. 140.20 (*0-7837-3090-X*, 205760600004) Bks Demand.

— Chicorel Index to Poetry in Anthologies, 1975-1977, 2 vols., Set. 2nd ed. (Chicorel Index Ser.: Vols. 5 & 5A). 1979. text 250.00 (*0-934598-13-4*) Am Lib Pub Co.

— Chicorel Index to Poetry in Collections on Discs & Tapes. LC 71-106198. (Chicorel Index Ser.: Vol. 4). 443p. 1972. text 125.00 (*0-934598-48-7*) Am Lib Pub Co.

An Asterisk (*) at the beginning of an entry indicates that the title is appearing for the first time.

— Chicorel Index to Reading & Learning Disabilities: An Annotated Guide, 1976. (Chicorel Index Ser.: Vol. 14A). 1976. text 125.00 (*0-934598-49-5*) Am Lib Pub Co.

— Chicorel Index to Reading & Learning Disabilities: Books, 1977 Annual. LC 76-14381. (Chicorel Index Ser.: Vol. 14A). 1977. text 125.00 (*0-934598-50-9*) Am Lib Pub Co.

— Chicorel Index to Reading Disabilities: An Annotated Guide. (Chicorel Index Ser.: Vol. 14). 500p. 1974. 125.00 (*0-934598-51-7*) Am Lib Pub Co.

— Chicorel Index to Short Stories: 1977 Edition, 2 vols., Set. 2nd ed. (Chicorel Index Ser.: Vols. 12 & 12A). 1977. text 250.00 (*0-934598-05-3*) Am Lib Pub Co.

— Chicorel Index to Short Stories in Anthologies & Collections, Vol. 12. LC 75-330087. (Chicorel Index Ser.: Vol. 12, 12A, 12B, & 12C). 391p. reprint ed. pap. 121.30 (*0-7837-3098-5*, 205761100001) Bks Demand.

— Chicorel Index to Short Stories in Anthologies & Collections, Vol. 12A. LC 75-330087. (Chicorel Index Ser.: Vol. 12, 12A, 12B, & 12C). 428p. reprint ed. pap. 132.70 (*0-7837-3099-3*, 205761100002) Bks Demand.

— Chicorel Index to Short Stories in Anthologies & Collections, Vol. 12B. LC 75-330087. (Chicorel Index Ser.: Vol. 12, 12A, 12B, & 12C). 566p. reprint ed. pap. 175.50 (*0-7837-3100-0*, 205761100003) Bks Demand.

— Chicorel Index to Short Stories in Anthologies & Collections, Vol. 12C. LC 75-330087. (Chicorel Index Ser.: Vol. 12, 12A, 12B, & 12C). 539p. reprint ed. pap. 167.10 (*0-7837-3101-9*, 205761100004) Bks Demand.

— Chicorel Index to the Crafts, Vol. 13: Needlework: Crocheting to Tie-Dyeing. LC 74-195924. (Chicorel Index Ser.: Vol. 13, 13A & 13C). 428p. reprint ed. pap. 132.70 (*0-7837-3102-7*, 205761200001) Bks Demand.

— Chicorel Index to the Crafts, Vol. 13A: Glass, Enamel, Metal. LC 74-195924. (Chicorel Index Ser.: Vol. 13, 13A & 13C). 507p. reprint ed. pap. 157.20 (*0-7837-3103-5*, 205761200002) Bks Demand.

— Chicorel Index to the Crafts, Vol. 13C: Education, Recreation, Therapy. LC 74-195924. (Chicorel Index Ser.: Vol. 13, 13A & 13C). 500p. reprint ed. pap. 155.00 (*0-7837-3104-3*, 205761200004) Bks Demand.

— Chicorel Index to the Crafts: Ceramics, Leather, Wood. (Chicorel Index Ser.: Vol. 13B). 1977. text 125.00 (*0-934598-58-4*) Am Lib Pub Co.

— Chicorel Index to the Spoken Arts on Discs, Tapes, & Cassettes. LC 71-106198. (Chicorel Index Ser.: Vol. 7B). 476p. reprint ed. pap. 147.60 (*0-7837-3095-0*, 205760800007) Bks Demand.

— Chicorel Index to Urban Planning & Environmental Design, Vol. 17. LC 75-30637. (Chicorel Index Ser.: Vol. 17 & 17A). 526p. reprint ed. pap. 163.10 (*0-7837-3109-4*, 205761500001) Bks Demand.

— Chicorel Index to Urban Planning & Environmental Design, Vol. 17A. LC 75-30637. (Chicorel Index Ser.: Vol. 17 & 17A). 527p. reprint ed. pap. 163.40 (*0-7837-3110-8*, 205761500002) Bks Demand.

— Chicorel Index to Video Tapes & Cassettes. (Chicorel Index Ser.: Vol. 27). 1978. text 125.00 (*0-934598-66-5*) Am Lib Pub Co.

— Chicorel Theater Index to Drama Literature. LC 75-14467. (Chicorel Index Ser.: Vol. 21). 474p. reprint ed. pap. 147.00 (*0-7837-3113-2*, 205761700001) Bks Demand.

— Chicorel Theater Index to Plays for Young People in Periodicals, Anthologies, & Collections. LC 74-173632. (Chicorel Index Ser.: Vol. 9). 492p. reprint ed. pap. 152.60 (*0-7837-3097-7*, 205761000009) Bks Demand.

— Chicorel Theater Index to Plays in Anthologies & Collections: 1970-1976. LC 76-54172. (Chicorel Index Ser.: Vol. 25). 1976. text 125.00 (*0-934598-68-1*) Am Lib Pub Co.

— Chicorel Theater Index to Plays in Collections, Anthologies, Periodicals, & Discs in England. LC 73-174046. (Chicorel Index Ser.: Vol. 3). 476p. reprint ed. pap. 147.60 (*0-7837-3085-3*, 205760400003) Bks Demand.

— Chicorel Theater Index to Plays in Periodicals. LC 73-174118. (Chicorel Index Ser.: Vol. 8). 500p. reprint ed. pap. 155.00 (*0-7837-3096-9*, 205760900008) Bks Demand.

— Chicorel Theatre Index to Plays in Anthologies, Periodicals, Disc & Tapes, Vol. 1. LC 71-106198. (Chicorel Index Ser.: Vols. 1 & 2). 591p. 1970. reprint ed. pap. 183.30 (*0-7837-3083-7*, 205760300001) Bks Demand.

— Chicorel Theatre Index to Plays in Anthologies, Periodicals, Disc & Tapes, Vol. 2. LC 71-106198. (Chicorel Index Ser.: Vols. 1 & 2). 520p. reprint ed. pap. 161.20 (*0-7837-3084-5*, 205760300002) Bks Demand.

Chicorel, Marietta S., ed. Chicorel Index to the Spoken Arts on Discs, Tapes, & Cassettes. (Chicorel Index Ser.: Vol. 7). 500p. 1973. text 125.00 (*0-934598-62-2*) Am Lib Pub Co.

Chida, Tomohei & Davies, Peter N. The Japanese Shipping & Shipbuilding Industries: A History of Their Modern Growth. LC 89-18524. 220p. (C). 1990. text 65.00 (*0-485-11271-X*, Pub. by Athlone Pr) Humanities.

Chidambaram, M. Nonlinear Process Control. 140p. 1995. 54.95 (*0-470-23552-7*) Wiley.

Chidambaram, R., jt. auth. see Kamat, R. V.

Chidester. Patterns of Transcendence. (Adaptable Courseware-Softside Ser.). Date not set. mass mkt. 28.00 (*0-534-56587-5*) Wadsworth Pub.

— Patterns of Transcendence: Religion, Death & Dying. 2nd ed. (Religion Ser.). 2000. mass mkt. 27.50 (*0-534-50607-0*) Wadsworth Pub.

***Chidester.** Peoples History of Religion. 2000. 28.00 (*0-06-061451-X*); pap. 18.00 (*0-06-061452-8*) HarpC.

Chidester, Ann. The Long Year. LC 74-26097. (Labor Movement in Fiction & Non-Fiction Ser.). reprint ed. 49.50 (*0-404-58411-X*) AMS Pr.

Chidester, Ardis, ed. see Katzakian, Norma.

***Chidester, David.** Christianity: A Global History. 480p. 2000. 28.00 (*0-06-251708-2*) Harper SF.

Chidester, David. Salvation & Suicide: An Interpretation of Jim Jones, the Peoples Temple, & Jonestown. LC 87-45015. (Religion in North America Ser.). (Illus.). 208p. 1991. reprint ed. pap. 6.95 (*0-253-20690-1*, MB-690) Ind U Pr.

— Savage Systems: Colonialism & Comparative Religion in Southern Africa. 352p. 1996. pap. 59.95 (*1-919713-01-8*, U Pr W Africa) Intl Scholars.

— Savage Systems: Colonialism & Comparative Religion in Southern Africa. LC 96-12909. (Studies in Religion & Culture). 352p. 1996. 49.50 (*0-8139-1664-X*); pap. text 19.50 (*0-8139-1667-4*) U Pr of Va.

— Word & Light: Seeing, Hearing, & Religious Discourse. 184p. 1992. text 29.95 (*0-252-01863-X*) U of Ill Pr.

Chidester, David & Linenthal, Edward T., eds. American Sacred Space. LC 95-3986. (Religion in North America Ser.). (Illus.). 320p. 1995. 39.95 (*0-253-32915-9*); pap. 18.95 (*0-253-21006-2*) Ind U Pr.

Chidester, David, et al. African Traditional Religion in South Africa: An Annotated Bibliography, 42. LC 97-6414. (Bibliographies & Indexes in Religious Studies: Vol. 42). 480p. 1997. lib. bdg. 79.50 (*0-313-30474-2*, Greenwood Pr) Greenwood.

— Christianity in South Africa: An Annotated Bibliography, 43. LC 97-9393. (Bibliographies & Indexes in Religious Studies: Vol. 43). 504p. 1997. lib. bdg. 105.00 (*0-313-30473-4*, Greenwood Pr) Greenwood.

— Islam, Hinduism & Judaism in South Africa: An Annotated Bibliography, 44. LC 97-2732. (Bibliographies & Indexes in Religious Studies: Vol. 44). 312p. 1997. lib. bdg. 77.95 (*0-313-30472-6*, Greenwood Pr) Greenwood.

Chidester, Jane E. & Macko, John L. Budget Yes! 21st Century Solutions for Taking Control of Your Money Now. LC 97-90123. (Illus.). 224p. 1998. pap. 19.95 (*0-9655198-3-X*) Tulip Tree Pr.

Chideya, Farai. The Color of Our Future: Our Multiracial Future. LC 98-48033. 288p. 1999. 23.00 (*0-688-16530-3*, Wm Morrow) Morrow Avon.

***Chideya, Farai.** The Color of Our Future: Race in the 21st Century. 288p. 2000. reprint ed. pap. 12.00 (*0-688-17580-5*) Morrow Avon.

Chideya, Farai. Don't Believe the Hype: Fighting Cultural Misinformation about African Americans. 256p. (Orig.). 1995. pap. 13.00 (*0-452-27096-0*, Plume) Dutton Plume.

Chidgey, Catherine. In a Fishbone Church. LC 98-196905. 272p. 2000. pap. 19.95 (*0-86473-335-6*, Pub. by Victoria Univ Pr) Paul & Co Pubs.

Chidgey, Peter, jt. auth. see Bevan, Simon.

Chidley, John. Discovering Book Collecting. 1989. pap. 25.00 (*0-85263-588-5*, Pub. by Shire Pubns) St Mut.

— Discovering Book Collecting. (Discovering Ser.: Vol. 267). 120p. 1999. pap. text 12.50 (*0-7478-0387-0*, Pub. by Shire Pubns) Parkwest Pubns.

Chidsey, A. D., Jr. A Frontier Village: Pre-Revolutionary Easton. 2nd ed. (Publications of the Northampton County Historical & Genealogical Society: No. 3). (Illus.). 272p. 1966. reprint ed. 30.00 (*1-877701-14-9*) NCH&GS.

Chidsey, A. D., Jr., et al. The Old County Court House & Other Northampton County History: Papers on the Court House, the Easton Flag, & the Early Easton Settlers. 24p. (Orig.). 1964. pap. text 5.00 (*1-877701-03-3*) NCH&GS.

Chidsey, Larry, ed. see Worth, D. Earl.

Chidsey, Thomas C., Jr. & Laine, Michael D. Summary of Oil & Gas Drilling in Utah, 1989. LC QE169.A322. (Circular Ser.: Vol. 83). (Illus.). 31p. 1991. pap. 5.00 (*1-55791-288-2*, C-83) Utah Geological Survey.

Chidsey, Thomas C., Jr., et al. Oil & Gas Drilling in Utah, 1990. (Circular of the Utah Geological Survey Ser.: Vol. 86). (Illus.). 30p. (Orig.). 1994. pap. 5.00 (*1-55791-291-2*, C86) Utah Geological Survey.

Chidvilasananda, Gurumayi. Courage & Contentment: A Collection of Talks on Spiritual Life. LC 99-23685. 1999. pap. write for info. (*0-911307-77-X*, Pub. by SYDA Found) Words Distrib.

***Chidvilasananda, Gurumayi.** The Frogs & Their Monster. (Illus.). 32p. 2000. reprint ed. 14.00 (*0-911307-91-5*, 205200, Pub. by SYDA Found) Words Distrib.

Chidvilasananda, Gurumayi. Kindle My Heart. 1991. 19.95 (*0-13-516121-5*) P-H.

***Chidvilasananda, Gurumayi.** Pulsation of Love. 2nd ed. 2001. pap. write for info. (*0-911307-88-5*, Pub. by SYDA Found) Words Distrib.

Chidvilasananda, Gurumayi. Remembrance. LC 98-18494. 104p. 1998. pap. 12.95 (*0-911307-63-X*) SYDA Found.

— Smile, Smile, Smile! LC 98-42386. 106p. 1998. pap. write for info. (*0-911307-69-9*, Pub. by SYDA Found) Words Distrib.

Chidvilasananda, Gurumayi, tr. see Swami Muktananda.

Chidvilasananda, Gurumayi, tr. & intro. see Muktananda, Swami.

Chidvilasananda, Swami. Enthusiasm. LC 97-3130. 240p. (Orig.). 1997. pap. 13.95 (*0-911307-52-4*) SYDA Found.

— Inner Treasures. LC 95-41464. 128p. 1995. pap. 12.95 (*0-911307-41-9*) SYDA Found.

— Kindle My Heart. 2nd rev. ed. LC 96-392. 1996. pap. 14.95 (*0-911307-30-3*) SYDA Found.

— The Magic of the Heart: Reflections on Divine Love. LC 96-70628. 256p. (Orig.). 1996. pap. 12.95 (*0-911307-43-5*) SYDA Found.

— My Lord Loves a Pure Heart: The Yoga of Divine Virtues. LC 94-14948. 192p. (Orig.). 1994. pap. 12.95 (*0-911307-29-X*) SYDA Found.

— The Yoga of Discipline. LC 96-19254. 264p. (Orig.). 1996. pap. 13.95 (*0-911307-44-3*) SYDA Found.

Chidvilasananda, Swami, jt. contrib. by see Muktananda, Swami.

Chidvilasananda, Swami, tr. see Muktananda, Swami.

***Chidwick, Ann D.** New Beginnings: A Remarriage Preparation Program Manual: Facilitators Guide. 110p. 1999. ring bd. 50.00 (*0-9697856-0-7*) Manticore Bks.

— New Beginnings: A Remarriage Preparation Program Workbook. spiral bd., wbk. ed. 50.00 (*0-9697856-1-5*, Pub. by A D Chidwick) Manticore Pubs.

Chief Buffalo Child & Long, Sylvester. Long Lance. LC 95-18985. 320p. 1995. lib. bdg. 45.00 (*0-87805-829-X*) U Pr of Miss.

Chief FAMA Aina Adewale Staff. Odidere Orunmila: A Quarterly Newspaper of the Orisas. (YOR.). 7p. (Orig.). 1997. pap. text 2.50 (*0-9644247-4-6*) ILE Orunmila.

Chief Joseph. That All People May Be One People, Send Rain to Wash the Face of the Earth. LC 94-77351. (Illus.). 60p. (Orig.). 1995. pap. 12.95 (*0-945519-15-X*) Mountn Meadw Pr.

Chief Lelooska. Spirit of the Cedar People. LC 98-3522. 40p. (J). (gr. 1-6). 1998. 24.95 (*0-7894-2571-8*, D K Ink) DK Pub Inc.

Chief Little Summer & Warm Night Rain. His Only Begotten Son: H.O.B.S. (Illus.). 108p. (Orig.). 1993. pap. 9.95 (*1-880440-05-9*) Piqua Pr.

— The Misfit. (Illus.). 300p. (YA). (gr. 8-12). 1991. 14.95 (*1-880440-03-2*) Piqua Pr.

— The Monitor. (Illus.). 445p. (Orig.). 1993. 19.45 (*1-880440-06-7*) Piqua Pr.

— Reflections on a Rainy April Day. (Illus.). 23p. (J). (gr. 1-5). 1991. 8.95 (*1-880440-02-4*) Piqua Pr.

— The Teachings for the Fourth Density Aquarian, Vol. 1. (Illus.). 320p. (Orig.). 1991. 17.95 (*1-880440-01-6*) Piqua Pr.

— The Teachings for the Fourth Density Aquarian, 4 vols., Vols. 1 thru 4. unabridged ed. (Illus.). (Orig.). 1991. pap. 11.95 incl. audio compact disk (*1-880440-00-8*) Piqua Pr.

— The Teachings for the Fourth Density Aquarian Vol. 2: The Teachings. (Illus.). 440p. (Orig.). 1992. 18.95 (*1-880440-04-0*) Piqua Pr.

Chief Little Summer, ed. & intro. see Tekonsha.

***Chief Seattle.** Speech of Chief Seattle. (Little Books of Wisdom). 24p. 2000. 9.95 (*1-55709-456-X*) Applewood.

Chieger, Bob, ed. see Cottone, Vince.

Chieger, Bob, ed. & intro. see Baker, Kim & Baker, Sunny.

Chieger, M. Husband & Wife in Israeli Law. 296p. 1985. 35.00 (*965-09-0113-2*, 73819, Pub. by R Mass Ltd) Lambda Pubs.

Chiego, W. J., intro. Oberlin Alumni Collect: Modern & Contemporary Art. (Illus.). 1989. pap. 20.00 (*0-942946-04-9*) Ober Coll Allen.

Chiego, William J. Carl Rice Embrey: A Retrospective. LC 97-71115. (Illus.). 84p. 1997. pap. 24.95 (*0-916677-37-0*) U of Tex Pr.

— Reginald Rowe: A Retrospective, 1963-1995. (Illus.). 76p. 1996. pap. 24.95 (*0-916677-36-2*) U of Tex Pr.

Chiego, William J., et al. Sir David Wilkie of Scotland (1785-1841) LC 86-63234. (Illus.). xix, 370p. 1987. pap. 24.95 (*0-88259-953-4*) NCMA.

Chieh-Ju, Chen. Chiang Kai-Shek's Secret Past: The Memoir of His Second Wife, Chen Chieh-Ju. LC 93-21728. 312p. (C). 1994. pap. 30.00 (*0-8133-1825-4*, Pub. by Westview) HarpC.

Chiel, Arthur A., ed. Perspectives on Jews & Judaism: Essays in Honor of Wolfe Kelman. 25.00 (*0-87068-683-6*) Ktav.

Chiel, Deborah. Sabrina (Movie Tie-in) 1996. mass mkt. 5.99 (*0-671-53751-2*) PB.

— School Ties. Peters, Sally, ed. 224p. (Orig.). 1992. mass mkt. 4.50 (*0-671-77715-7*) PB.

— The War. 224p. (Orig.). 1994. mass mkt. 4.99 (*0-515-11447-2*, Jove) Berkley Pub.

Chiel, Deborah, jt. auth. see Dickens, Charles.

Chiel, Kinneret. Complete Book of Hanukah. (Illus.). (J). (gr. 6-8). pap. 6.95 (*0-87068-367-5*) Ktav.

Chiel, Samuel. Discovering Life's Meaning. 20.00 (*0-88125-362-6*) Ktav.

— Overcoming Life's Challenges. LC 94-10837. 1994. 20.00 (*0-88125-240-9*) Ktav.

***Chiel, Samuel & Dreher, Henry.** For Thou Art with Me: The Healing Power of Psalms. 244p. 2000. 21.95 (*1-57954-176-3*, Daybrk) Rodale Pr Inc.

Chielens, Edward E., ed. American Literary Magazines: The Eighteenth & Nineteenth Centuries. LC 85-24793. (Historical Guides to the World's Periodicals & Newspapers Ser.). 519p. 1986. lib. bdg. 75.00 (*0-313-23985-1*, CHA/, Greenwood Pr) Greenwood.

Chielens, Edward E., ed. American Literary Magazines: The Twentieth Century. LC 91-30603. (Historical Guides to the World's Periodicals & Newspapers Ser.). 488p. 1992. lib. bdg. 105.00 (*0-313-23986-X*, CHT/, Greenwood Pr) Greenwood.

Chiellini, Emo & Giusti, P., eds. Polymers in Medicine I: Biomedical & Pharmacological Applications. 425p. 1983. 105.00 (*0-306-41360-4*, Plenum Trade) Perseus Pubng.

Chiellini, Emo, et al. Structure & Transport Properties. 500p. 1997. text 162.00 (*981-02-1894-X*) World Scientific Pub.

Chiellini, Emo, jt. ed. see Ottenbrite, Raphael M.

Chiellino, Gino. Fremde: A Discourse on the Foreign. Von Flotow, Luise, tr. from GER. LC 93-81343. (Essay Ser.: No. 23). 60p. 1995. pap. 8.00 (*1-55071-020-6*) Guernica Editions.

Chiem, C. Y., et al, eds. Impact Loading & Dynamic Behaviour of Materials, 2 vols., Set. (Illus.). 1100p. 1988. lib. bdg. 142.00 (*0-685-21713-2*, Pub. by DGM Metallurgy Info) IR Pubns.

— Impact Loading & Dynamic Behaviour of Materials, Vol. 1. (Illus.). 1100p. 1988. lib. bdg. write for info. (*3-88355-125-2*, Pub. by DGM Metallurgy Info) IR Pubns.

— Impact Loading & Dynamic Behaviour of Materials, Vol. 2. (Illus.). 1100p. 1988. lib. bdg. write for info. (*3-88355-126-0*, Pub. by DGM Metallurgy Info) IR Pubns.

Chiem, David P., jt. auth. see Caswell, Brian.

Chien, Andris G. Mummies Old & New - Their Health, Disease & Research Investigations: Index of New Information. 150p. 1998. 47.50 (*0-7883-2038-6*); pap. 44.50 (*0-7883-2039-4*) ABBE Pubs Assn.

Chien, Chao C. Introduction to the Microcomputer & Its Applications. 2nd ed. LC 90-167137. xii, 138p. 1990. write for info. (*0-256-08477-7*, Irwn McGrw-H) McGrw-H Hghr Educ.

Chien, Chao C. Introductions to the Microcomputer & Its Applications. 2nd ed. (Illus.). 531p. (C). 1990. spiral bd. 34.95 incl. disk (*0-256-08258-8*, 14-2402-02, Irwn McGrw-H) McGrw-H Hghr Educ.

Chien, Cheng. Sun-Face Buddha: The Teachings of Ma-Tsu & the Hung-Chou School of Chan. LC 92-28980. 170p. 1992. pap. 48.50 (*0-608-04960-3*, 2065539) Bks Demand.

Ch'ien, Chung-Shu. Fortress Besieged. Kelly, Jeanne & Mao, Nathan K., trs. from CHI. LC 78-24846. (Chinese Literature in Translation Ser.). 409p. reprint ed. pap. 116.60 (*0-608-17404-1*, 2056416) Bks Demand.

Chien, Chung-Shu. Limited Views: Essays on Ideas & Letters. Egan, Ronald C., tr. from CHI. LC 97-37383. (Harvard-Yenching Institute Monograph Ser.). 1998. 45.00 (*0-674-53411-5*) HUP.

Chien, David. About 85 Years Ago: Photo Postcards from America, 1907-1920. (Illus.). 132p. 1997. 22.95 (*1-57098-150-7*) Roberts Rinehart.

Ch'ien, Edward T. Chiao Hung & the Restructuring of Neo-Confucianism in the Late Ming. (Neo-Confucian Studies). 328p. 1986. text 57.50 (*0-231-06022-X*) Col U Pr.

Chien, Frederick F. The Opening of Korea: A Study of Chinese Diplomacy, 1876-1885. LC 67-30793. 381p. reprint ed. pap. 118.20 (*0-608-30666-5*, 201021000068) Bks Demand.

— Opportunity & Challenge. Mica, Daniel A. & Emerson, J. Terry, eds. 1995. 29.95 (*0-614-10452-1*) AZ Hist Foun.

***Chien, Gao, et al, eds.** Moss Flora of China Vol. 1: Sphagnaceae Through Leucobryaceae. (Moss Flora of China Ser.). (Illus.). viii, 288p. 1999. 75.00 (*0-915279-68-1*) Miss Botan.

— Moss Flora of China Vol. 2: Fissidentaceae Through Ptychomitriaceae. (Illus.). 2000. 75.00 (*0-915279-89-4*) Miss Botan.

Chien, Helen H., tr. see Hsieh, Fucheng.

Chien, Kenneth R. Molecular Basis of Cardiovascular Disease: A Companion to Braunwald's Heart Disease. Zorab, Richard, ed. LC 98-34730. (Illus.). 592p. (C). 1998. text 135.00 (*0-7216-6401-6*, W B Saunders Co) Harcrt Hlth Sci Grp.

Chien, Lisa, tr. see Tomasi, Lucia T. & Blakely, Julia.

Chien, Ning & Wan, Zhaohui. Mechanics of Sediment Transport. LC 98-44496. 936p. 1998. 149.00 (*0-7844-0400-3*) Am Soc Civil Eng.

Chien, Po-Tsan. Concise History of China. 1976. lib. bdg. 59.95 (*0-8490-1661-4*) Gordon Pr.

Chien, S. H. & Hammond, L. L. Agronomic Evaluation of Partially Acidulated Phosphate Rocks in the Tropics: IFDC's Experience. Roth, E. N., ed. LC 88-32883. (Papers: No. P-7). (Illus.). 10p. (Orig.). 1988. pap. text 4.00 (*0-88090-070-9*) Intl Fertilizer.

Chien, Shu, ed. Molecular Biology in Physiology. LC 87-42838. (Illus.). 179p. 1989. reprint ed. pap. 55.50 (*0-608-05785-1*, 205975000007) Bks Demand.

— Vascular Endothelium in Health & Disease. LC 88-26583. (Advances in Experimental Medicine & Biology Ser.: Vol. 242). (Illus.). 246p. 1988. 75.00 (*0-306-43034-7*, Plenum Trade) Perseus Pubng.

Chien, Shu, jt. ed. see Liu, C. Y.

Chien, Shui-Sheng, et al. Fiber Optic Components & Optical Communication: 4-5 November, 1996, Beijing, China. LC 96-69642. (Proceedings Ser.). xi, 588p. 1996. pap. 102.00 (*0-8194-2294-0*) SPIE.

Chien, Ssu-ma. The Grand Scribe's Records Vol. 1: The Basic Annals of Pre-Han China. Nienhauser, William H., Jr., ed. LC 94-18408. 1995. 37.50 (*0-253-34021-7*) Ind U Pr.

Ch'ien, T'ao. Selected Poems of T'ao Ch'ien. Hinton, David, tr. & intro. by. LC 93-1635. 96p. (Orig.). 1993. pap. 11.00 (*1-55659-056-3*) Copper Canyon.

Ch'ien, Tuan-sheng. The Government & Politics of China. LC 50-8563. 545p. reprint ed. pap. 169.00 (*0-608-30950-8*, 200600500055) Bks Demand.

Chien Weizang. Advances in Applied Mathematics & Mechanics in China, Vol. 2. (International Academic Publishers Ser.). (Illus.). 350p. 1990. 86.00 (*0-08-036975-8*, Pergamon Pr) Elsevier.

Chien Weizang & Fu Zizhi, eds. Advances in Applied Mathematics & Mechanics in China, Vol. 3. (International Academic Publishers Ser.). 250p. 1991. 50.00 (*0-08-037943-5*, Pub. by IAP) Elsevier.

Chien, Y. T. Interactive Pattern Recognition. (Electrical Engineering & Electronics Ser.: Vol. 3). (Illus.). 320p. 1978. text 150.00 (*0-8247-6631-8*) Dekker.

Chien, Yie W. Novel Drug Delivery Systems. 2nd enl. rev. ed. (Drugs & the Pharmaceutical Sciences Ser.: Vol. 50). (Illus.). 816p. 1991. text 225.00 (*0-8247-8520-7*) Dekker.

— Transdermal Controlled Systemic Medications. (Drugs & the Pharmaceutical Sciences Ser.: Vol. 31). (Illus.). 464p. 1987. text 189.00 (*0-8247-7760-3*) Dekker.

Chien, Yie W., et al. Nasal Systemic Drug Delivery. (Drugs & the Pharmaceutical Sciences Ser.: Vol. 39). (Illus.). 320p. 1989. text 167.50 (*0-8247-8093-0*) Dekker.

Chien, Yie W., jt. auth. see Wang, Y. John.

C

Chien, Yu-wen. The Taiping Revolutionary Movement. Suddard, Adrienne, ed. LC 72-91299. 633p. reprint ed. pap. 196.30 (0-8357-8340-5, 203377000087) Bks Demand.

Chienl, Szuma. Selections from Records of the Historian. Hsien-yi, Yang & Yang, Gladys, trs. 59p. 1979. pap. 12.95 (962-07-1054-1, Pub. by Commercial Pr) Cheng & Tsui.

Chier, Ruth. Danger: Alcohol. LC 96-14333. (Drug Awareness Library). (Illus.). 24p. (J). (gr. k-4). 1996. lib. bdg. 15.93 (0-8239-2339-8, PowerKids) Rosen Group.

— Danger: Cocaine. LC 96-7862. (Drug Awareness Library: Set 2). (Illus.). 24p. (J). (gr. k-4). 1996. lib. bdg. 15.93 (0-8239-2337-1, PowerKids) Rosen Group.

— Danger: Crack. LC 96-7861. (Drug Awareness Library). (Illus.). 24p. (J). (gr. k-4). 1996. lib. bdg. 15.93 (0-8239-2338-X, PowerKids) Rosen Group.

— Danger: Inhalants. LC 96-14645. (Drug Awareness Library). (Illus.). 24p. (J). (gr. k-4). 1996. lib. bdg. 15.93 (0-8239-2340-1, PowerKids) Rosen Group.

— Danger: Marijuana. LC 95-50791. (Drug Awareness Library). (Illus.). 24p. (J). (gr. k-4). 1996. lib. bdg. 15.93 (0-8239-2335-5, PowerKids) Rosen Group.

— Danger: Tobacco. LC 95-50797. (Drug Awareness Library). (Illus.). 24p. (J). (gr. k-4). 1996. lib. bdg. 15.93 (0-8239-2336-3, PowerKids) Rosen Group.

Chiera, Edward. Inscriptions from Adab. 1996. lib. bdg. 4.00 (0-226-49645-7) U Ch Pr.

Chiera, Edward. Lists of Personal Names from the Temple School of Nippur: Lists of Sumerian Personal Names. LC 17-5006. (University of Pennsylvania, the University Museum, Publications of the Babylonian Section: Vol. 11, No. 3). 136p. pap. 42.20 (0-608-13635-2, 205202700027) Bks Demand.

— They Wrote on Clay: The Babylonian Tablets Speak Today. Cameron, George G., ed. LC 38-27631. (Illus.). 251p. 1956. pap. text 13.95 (0-226-10425-7, P2) U Ch Pr.

Chierchia, Gennaro. Dynamics of Meaning: Anaphora, Presupposition, & the Theory of Grammar. LC 94-42522. 286p. 1995. lib. bdg. 75.00 (0-226-10434-6) U Ch Pr.

Chierchia, Gennaro, et al, eds. Properties, Types & Meaning: Foundational Issues. 264p. (C). 1988. lib. bdg. 122.00 (1-55608-067-0, Pub. by Kluwer Academic) Kluwer Academic.

Chierchia, Gennaro & McConnell-Ginet, Sally. Meaning & Grammar: An Introduction to Semantics. 2nd ed. LC 99-20030. (Illus.). 522p. 2000. 75.00 (0-262-03269-4); pap. 32.50 (0-262-53164-X) MIT Pr.

Chierchia, Gennaro, et al. Properties, Types & Meaning: Foundational Issues. 578p. (C). 1988. lib. bdg. 129.00 (1-55608-088-3, Pub. by Kluwer Academic) Kluwer Academic.

— Properties, Types & Meaning: Foundational Issues, Vol. I. 578p. (C). 1988. pap. text 47.50 (1-55608-089-1, Pub. by Kluwer Academic) Kluwer Academic.

— Properties, Types & Meaning, Vol. II: Semantic Issues. 314p. (C). 1988. lib. bdg. 130.00 (1-55608-069-7, Pub. by Kluwer Academic) Kluwer Academic.

Chierci, F. Dictionnaire de la Guitare. Lefferts, Michael, ed. (FRE.). 124p. (Orig.). (C). 1997. pap. text 40.95 (0-7692-1311-1, 01010353) Wrner Bros.

Chierichetti, David. Edith Head. Date not set. 37.50 (0-06-019428-6) HarpC.

— Mitchell Leisen, Hollywood Director. expanded rev. ed. 1995. pap. text 19.95 (0-929330-04-8) Photoventures Co.

— Mitchell Leisen, Hollywood Director. rev. ed. 1994. pap. 19.95 (1-880756-07-2) Riverwood Pr.

Chierici, G. L. Principles of Petroleum Reservoir Engineering, No. 2. Westaway, Peter J., tr. LC 93-26019. 388p. 1994. 126.95 (0-387-56742-9) Spr-Verlag.

Chierici, Gian Luigi. Principles of Petroleum Reservoir Engineering, Vol. 1. Westaway, Peter J., tr. from ITA. LC 93-26019.Tr. of Principi di Ingegneria dei Giacimenti Petroliferi. 1994. 126.95 (0-387-56037-8) Spr-Verlag.

Chiesa, C., jt. ed. see Ravagnan, G.

Chiesa, Giulietto & Northrop, Douglas T. Transition to Democracy: Political Change in the Soviet Union, 1987-1991. LC 92-56901. (Nelson A. Rockefeller Series in Social Science & Public Policy). (Illus.). 322p. 1993. pap. 25.00 (0-87451-615-3); text 50.00 (0-87451-614-5) U Pr of New Eng.

Chiesa, Marian. High Doses of Wisdom Low Doses of Advice: A Collection of Essays about Doing the Right Thing. 166p. 2000. pap. 12.95 (0-9669146-4-3, Pub. by Ind Psychology Pr) ACCESS Pubs Network.

Chiesa, Mecca. Radical Behaviorism: The Philosophy & the Science. LC 93-73792. 241p. (C). pap. 19.95 (0-9623311-4-7) Authors Coop.

Chiesi, Antonio M. & Martinelli, Alberto. Recent Social Trends in Italy, 1960-1995. 512p. 75.00 (0-7735-1842-8) McG-Queens Univ Pr.

Chieu, Mach, jt. auth. see Guillaume, Gerard.

Chife, Aloy. The Political Economy of Post-Cold War Africa. LC 97-2366. (Studies in African Economic & Social Development: Vol. 9). 264p. 1997. pap. 89.95 (0-7734-8683-6) E Mellen.

Chifflet, Jean-Loup. Victoria & Her Times. LC 96-28394. (W5 Who, What, Where, When, & Why Ser.). (Illus.). 96p. 1996. 19.95 (0-8050-5084-1) H Holt & Co.

***Chiffolo, Anthony.** Padre Pio: In My Own Words. (Illus.). 128p. 2000. 13.95 (0-7648-0657-2) Liguori Pubns.

***Chiffolo, Anthony F.** Be Mindful of Us: Prayers to the Saints. 320p. 2000. pap. 14.95 (0-7648-0380-8) Liguori Pubns.

Chiffolo, Anthony F., compiled by. At Prayer with the Saints. LC 97-32385. 240p. (Orig.). 1998. pap. 11.00 (0-7648-0173-2) Liguori Pubns.

***Chiffolo, Anthony F., ed.** Pope John Paul XXIII: In My Own Words. LC 99-26792. 128p. 1999. 13.95 (0-7648-0498-7) Liguori Pubns.

Chiffolo, Anthony F., ed. & compiled by see John Paul, II, pseud.

Chiflet. Victoria & Her Times Index. 1996. write for info. (0-8050-5285-2) H Holt & Co.

Chiflet, Jean-Loup. Ciel Ma Femme! Sky My Wife! Dictionnaire de l'Anglais Courant. (ENG & FRE.). 126p. 1991. pap. 12.95 (0-7859-7626-4, 2020125528) Fr & Eur.

— Dictionnaire des Mots qui n'Existent Pas. (FRE.). 168p. 1992. pap. 36.95 (0-7859-7864-X, 2258035724) Fr & Eur.

— Sky My Kid! Dictionnaire de l'Anglais Branche. (FRE.). 153p. 1993. pap. 12.95 (0-7859-7628-0, 2020159945) Fr & Eur.

Chiganos, William S. Preparing to Serve As a God Parent. 1986. pap. 1.95 (0-937032-44-1) Light&Life Pub Co MN.

***Chigara, Ben.** Legitimacy Deficit in Custom: Towards a Deconstructionist Theory. LC 00-42041. 2000. write for info. (0-7546-2077-8, Pub. by Ashgate Pub) Ashgate Pub Co.

Chigas, George, ed. Cambodia's Lament: A Selection of Cambodian Writing. LC 91-62374. 112p. 1991. pap. 7.00 (0-9630295-0-9) Mealea Pubns.

Chigas, George, ed. from CAM. Resolute Heart: Selected Writing from Lowell's Cambodian Community. LC 94-94026. 112p. 1994. pap. 7.00 (0-9630295-1-7) Mealea Pubns.

Chigier. Progress in Energy & Combustion Science, 3 vols., Vol. 3. 1978. pap. 22.00 (0-08-022706-6, Pergamon Pr) Elsevier.

Chigier, Norman A. Energy, Combustion & Environment. (Illus.). 689p. (C). 1981. text 86.25 (0-07-010766-1) McGraw.

— Progress in Energy & Combustion Science, Vol. 4. 224p. 1980. 140.00 (0-08-024257-X, Pergamon Pr) Elsevier.

Chigier, Norman A., ed. Combustion Measurements. (Combustion: An International Ser.). 512p. 1991. 142.00 (1-56032-028-1) Hemisp Pub.

— Progress in Energy & Combustion Science, Vol. 6. (Illus.). 388p. 1981. 145.00 (0-08-027153-7, Pergamon Pr) Elsevier.

— Progress in Energy & Combustion Science, Vol. 6, Pt. 2. 102p. 1980. pap. 30.00 (0-08-026059-4, Pergamon Pr) Elsevier.

— Progress in Energy & Combustion Science, Vol. 7. (Illus.). 316p. 1982. 160.00 (0-08-029124-4, Pergamon Pr) Elsevier.

— Progress in Energy & Combustion Science, Vol. 8. 354p. 1983. 160.00 (0-08-031041-9, Pergamon Pr) Elsevier.

— Progress in Energy & Combustion Science, Vol. 9. (Illus.). 378p. 1984. 160.00 (0-08-031727-8, Pergamon Pr) Elsevier.

— Progress in Energy & Combustion Science, Vol. 10. (Illus.). 478p. 1986. 162.00 (0-08-033677-9, B110, Pub. by PPL) Elsevier.

Chigier, Norman A. & Stern, Edward A., eds. Collective Phenomena & the Applications of Physics to Other Fields of Science. 491p. 1976. pap. text 25.00 (0-916088-01-4) Brain Res.

Chigier, Norman A., jt. auth. see Chiu, H. H.

Chigier, Norman A., jt. ed. see Chiu, H. H.

Chignard, Michel. Cytokines & Adhesion Molecules in Lung Inflammation. LC 96-43703. (Annals of the New York Academy of Sciences Ser.). 1996. pap. 95.00 (0-89766-980-0) NY Acad Sci.

— Cytokines & Adhesion Molecules in Lung Inflammation. LC 96-43703. (Annals of the New York Academy of Sciences Ser.: Vol. 796). 297p. 1996. 95.00 (0-89766-979-7) NY Acad Sci.

Chignard, Michel, et al, eds. Cells & Cytokines in Lung Inflammation. LC 94-18939. (Annals Ser.: Vol. 725). 1994. pap. 110.00 (0-89766-856-1) NY Acad Sci.

Chignell, A. H. Retinal Detachment Surgery. (Illus.). 1980. 45.00 (0-387-09475-X) Spr-Verlag.

Chignell, A. H., jt. auth. see Wong, D.

Chignell, Marc, jt. auth. see Parsaye, Kamran.

Chignell, Mark, jt. auth. see Parsaye, Kamran.

Chignell, Meg. The Universal Jesus. 1999. pap. 21.00 (1-85072-067-3, Pub. by W Sessions) St Mut.

Chignell, Philip. From Our Home Correspondent. (C). 1989. text 35.00 (0-948929-21-9) St Mut.

Chigogidze, A. Inverse Spectra. LC 96-1173. (North-Holland Mathematical Library: Vol. 53). 432p. 1996. 143.50 (0-444-82225-9, North Holland) Elsevier.

Chigriniv, Vladimir G., jt. auth. see Blinov, Lev M.

Chigrinov, Vladimir G. Liquid Crystal Devices: Physics & Applications. LC 99-10564. 380p. 1999. 99.00 (0-89006-898-4) Artech Hse.

Chigrinov, Vladimir G., jt. auth. see Blinov, Lev M.

Chigwada-Bailey, Ruth. Black Women's Experiences of Criminal Justice: A Discourse on Disadvantage. LC 98-102995. 144p. 1997. write for info. (1-872870-54-6) Waterside Pr.

Chigwell, Meg. John on Jesus. 180p. 1999. pap. 21.00 (1-85072-141-6, Pub. by W Sessions) St Mut.

Chih, Hwang N. Fiberoptic Guided Tracheal Intubation: A Practical Approach. LC 94-43119. (Illus.). 155p. 1995. pap. text 19.95 (0-07-113379-8) McGraw-Hill HPD.

***Chih, Hwang N. & Chih, Nian, eds.** Anaesthesia: A Practical Handbook. (Illus.). 236p. 1998. text 42.50 (0-19-588422-1) OUP.

Chih, Nian, jt. ed. see Chih, Hwang N.

Chih-p'ing Chou & Wang, Xuedong. Newspaper Readings: The U. S. A. in the People's Daily. 255p. 1993. pap. text 24.50 (0-691-00070-0, Pub. by Princeton U Pr) Cal Prin Full Svc.

Chih-p'ing Chou, et al. Advanced Reader of Modern Chinese: China's Own Critics, 2 vols., Set. 357p. 1993. pap. text 42.50 (0-691-00069-7, Pub. by Princeton U Pr) Cal Prin Full Svc.

Chih, Yu-Ju. A Primer of Newspaper Chinese. rev. ed. 1982. 14.95 (0-88710-056-2) Yale Far Eastern Pubns.

Chih, Yu-Ju. A Primer of Newspaper Chinese. rev. ed. 1982. audio 8.95 (0-88710-057-0) Yale Far Eastern Pubns.

Chihabi, jt. auth. see Khatib, Ahmed.

***Chihal, H. Jane & London, Steve.** Menopause: Clinical Concepts. 3rd rev. ed. (Illus.). 235p. 1999. pap. 17.95 (0-917634-03-9) EMIS.

Chihal, Jane & Brinker, Nancy. 1000 Questions about Women's Health. 504p. 1997. pap. 16.99 (1-56530-264-8) Summit TX.

Chihara, Charles S. Constructibility & Mathematical Existence. (Illus.). 298p. 1991. reprint ed. pap. text 29.95 (0-19-823975-0) OUP.

— The Worlds of Possibility: Modal Realism & the Semantics of Modal Logic. LC 98-6633. (Illus.). 354p. 1998. text 59.00 (0-19-823767-7) OUP.

Chihara, Daigoro. Hindu-Buddhist Architecture in Southeast Asia. LC 96-19498. (Studies in Asian Art & Archaeology). xxiv, 437p. 1996. 182.50 (90-04-10512-3) Brill Academic Pubs.

Chihara, H. & Nakamura, N. Nuclear Quadrupole Resonance Spectroscopy Data: Supplement. (Numerical Data & Functional Relationships in Science & Technology Ser.: Vol. 39). viii, 424p. 1997. 1869.00 (3-540-62428-7) Spr-Verlag.

Chihara, H., ed. see International Conference on Thermal Analysis Staff.

Chihara, K. & Nakamura, Norio. Lanolt-Boernstein Numerical Data & Functional Relationships in Science & Technology: Solid State Physics; Nuclear Quadrupole Resonance Spectroscopy Data, Group III; Vol. 31; Subvol. B. Hellwege, A. M. & Hellwege, K., eds. 360p. 1993. 1072.95 (0-387-55147-6) Spr-Verlag.

Chihara, K., jt. ed. see Kitabatake, A.

Chihara, T. S. An Introduction to Orthogonal Polynomials, Vol. 13. (Mathematics & Its Applications Ser.: Vol. 12). xii, 250p. 1978. text 322.00 (0-677-04150-0) Gordon & Breach.

Chihaya, Masataka, tr. see Goldstein, Donald M. & Dillon, Katherine V., eds.

Chih'chi, Liu. Shih-t'ung (Comprehensive Historiography) Hardy, Grant, tr. 1999. pap. 17.00 (1-883058-49-X, Consort Bilingual) Global Pubns.

Chihiro, O., et al, eds. World Society for Stereotatic & Functional Neurosurgy, 10th Meeting, Maebashi, Japan, 1989: Journal: Stereotactic & Functional Neurosurgery, Vols. 54 & 55, 1990. (Illus.). xiv, 564p. 1990. pap. 327.00 (3-8055-5337-4) S Karger.

Chihuly, Dale. Atlantis Chihuly. (Illus.). 104p. 1999. 35.00 (1-57684-010-7) Portland Pr.

***Chihuly, Dale.** Chihulu Jerusalem 2000. (Illus.). 240p. 2000. 50.00 (1-57684-014-X, Pub. by Portland Pr) Partners-West.

— Chihuly's Pendletons... And Their Influence on His Work. (Illus.). 256p. 2000. 65.00 (1-57684-015-8, Pub. by Portland Pr) U of Ariz Pr.

Chihuly, Dale. Dale Chihuly: Bellagio. (Illus.). 72p. 1999. 30.00 (1-57684-009-3) Portland Pr.

Chihuly, Dale. Chihuly Over Venice: Nuutajarvi, Finland Part I, June 1995. 28p. 75.00 (0-9608382-9-5) Portland Pr.

Chihuly, Dale, et al. Chihuly: The George R. Stroemple Collection. LC 97-36096. 1997. write for info. (1-883124-06-9) Portland Art Mus.

***Chihuly, Dale, et al.** Chihuly Projects. (Illus.). 364p. 2000. 75.00 (0-8109-6708-1, Pub. by Abrams) Time Warner.

Chihuly, Dale, jt. auth. see Jenkins, Speight.

Chijiiwa, Hideaki. Color Harmony: A Guide to Creative Color Combinations. rev. ed. Mandel, Geoffrey, ed. NaKamura, Kaiko, tr. from JPN. (Illus.). 160p. 1987. reprint ed. pap. 15.95 (0-935603-06-9, 7310) Rockport Pubs.

Chijioke. Begining History of Ancient Africa. Date not set. pap. text. write for info. (0-582-59501-0, Pub. by Addison-Wesley) Longman.

Chijioke, F. A. Ancient Africa. LC 75-80850. (Illus.). 48p. (J). (gr. 5-8). 1969. pap. 6.95 (0-8419-0013-2, Africana) Holmes & Meier.

Chik, Claire A., jt. auth. see He, Liyi.

Chik Hon Man & Ng Lam Sim Yuk, eds. Chinese-English Dictionary: Cantonese in Yale Romanization, Mandarin in Pinyin. (CHI & ENG.). 521p. (Orig.). 1989. pap. 42.50 (962-7141-14-3) Coronet Bks.

Chikamatsu, X. & Keene, Donald. Four Major Plays of Chikamatsu. LC 98-148374. 220p. 1997. pap. 17.50 (0-231-11101-0) Col U Pr.

Chikan, Atilla. Inventory Models. 418p. (C). 1990. 575.00 (0-89771-839-9, Pub. by Collets) St Mut.

Chikan, Atilla, ed. Progress in Decision, Utility & Risk Theory. (C). 1991. lib. bdg. 194.00 (0-7923-1211-2) Kluwer Academic.

Chikan, Attila. Progress in Inventory Research: A Selection of Papers Presented at the Fourth International Syumposium on Inventories, Budapest, August 25-19, 1986. 446p. (C). 1989. 125.00 (963-05-4900-X, Pub. by Akade Kiado) St Mut.

Chikan, Attila, ed. Inventory Models. (C). 1991. lib. bdg. 336.00 (0-7923-0494-2) Kluwer Academic.

Chikan, Attila, jt. ed. see Beracs, Jozsef.

Chikane, Frank. Beyond the Barricades: South Africa in the 1980s. (Illus.). 144p. (Orig.). 1989. pap. 37.95 (0-89381-375-3) Aperture.

— No Life of My Own: An Autobiography. LC 89-2906. 158p. reprint ed. pap. 49.00 (0-7837-5504-X, 204527400005) Bks Demand.

Chikane, Frank, jt. ed. see Alberts, Louw.

Chikashige, Masumi. Alchemy & Other Chemical Achievements of the Ancient Orient. LC 79-8602. reprint ed. 27.50 (0-404-18456-1) AMS Pr.

Chikawa, J., et al, eds. Defects & Properties of Semiconductors: Defect Engineering. 1987. text 256.00 (90-277-2352-4) Kluwer Academic.

Chikazumi, Soshin. Physics of Ferromagnetism. 2nd ed. Graham, C. D., tr. LC 96-27148. (The International Series of Monographs on Physics: No. 94). (Illus.). 668p. 1997. text 225.00 (0-19-851776-9) OUP.

Chikeka, Charles O. Africa & the European Economic Community, 1957-1992. LC 93-905. 236p. 1993. 89.95 (0-7734-9259-3) E Mellen.

— Britain, France, & the New African States: A Study in Post-Independence Relationships. LC 89-13073. (Studies in African Economic & Social Development: Vol. 3). 256p. 1989. lib. bdg. 89.95 (0-88946-516-9) E Mellen.

— Decolonization Process in Africa During the Post-War Era, 1960-1990. LC 98-10050. (African Studies: Vol. 45). 314p. 1998. text 99.95 (0-7734-8471-X) E Mellen.

— Decolonization Process in Africa During the Post-war Era, 1960-1990. LC 98-10050. (African Studies). vii, 314p. 1998. write for info. (0-88946-175-9) E Mellen.

Chikere, Chidi. The Adventures of Alfalfa. LC 99-72745. (Illus.). 100p. 1999. pap. text 10.95 (1-58521-000-5) Bks Black Chldn.

Chikileva, Tatiana, ed. see Marx, Karl & Engels, Friedrich.

***Chikishev, Andrey Y., et al, eds.** Laser Spectroscopy & Optical Diagnostics. 386p. 1999. pap. text 84.00 (0-8194-3206-7) SPIE.

Chikota, Richard A., ed. see Journal of Urban Law Editors.

Chikrii, A. Conflict-Controlled Processes. LC 97-8154. 403p. 1997. text 227.50 (0-7923-4522-3) Kluwer Academic.

Chiland, Colette & Yound, J. Gerald. Why Children Reject School: Views from Seven Countries. (International Association for Child & Adolescent Psychiatry & Allied Prefessions Yearbook Ser.: Vol. 10). 256p. (C). 1990. 40.00 (0-300-04828-9) Yale U Pr.

Chilcoat, Beth & Chilcoat, David. A Taste of Columbus II. (Illus.). 128p. (Orig.). 1982. pap. 8.95 (0-9608710-1-2) Corban Prods.

Chilcoat, David, jt. auth. see Chilcoat, Beth.

Chilcoat, George. Popular Culture As Method: An Approach to Social Studies Instruction. 2nd ed. 288p. (C). 1995. pap. text, per. 30.95 (0-8403-9725-9) Kendall-Hunt.

Chilcoat, George W., jt. auth. see Tunnell, Michael O.

***Chilcoat, Richard A., pref.** Strategic Assessment, 1999: Priorities for a Turbulent World. (Illus.). 314p. (C). 2000. pap. text 45.00 (0-7567-0017-5) DIANE Pub.

Chilcote, Brian. A Sure Thing. (Inter Acta Ser.). (Illus.). 6p. (C). 1994. teacher ed., ring bd. 1.25 (0-9629245-2-0, 741-002t, Inter Acta); student ed., ring bd. 3.25 (0-9629245-1-2, 741-002s, Inter Acta) WSN Pr.

Chilcote, Kathy & Mulkey, Kent. Get Real: Emotional Authenticity. (Inter Acta Ser.). (Illus.). 6p. (C). 1994. teacher ed., ring bd. 1.25 (1-885702-21-3, 741-018t, Inter Acta); student ed., ring bd. 3.25 (1-885702-20-5, 741-018s, Inter Acta) WSN Pr.

Chilcote, Paul W. John Wesley & the Women Preachers of Early Methodism. LC 91-24598. (American Theological Library Association Monograph: No. 25). (Illus.). 389p. 1991. 50.00 (0-8108-2414-0) Scarecrow.

— She Offered Them Christ: The Legacy of Women Preachers in Early Methodism. LC 92-31400. 176p. (Orig.). 1993. pap. 11.95 (0-687-38345-5) Abingdon.

***Chilcote, R.** Comparative Political Economy. LC 99-88513. 336p. 2000. text 65.00 (0-8133-1018-0) Westview.

Chilcote, Ronald H. Comparative Inquiry in Politics & Political Economy: Theories & Issues. LC 99-34286. 288p. 2000. text 60.00 (0-8133-8151-7) HarpC.

— Comparative Inquiry in Politics & Political Economy: Theories & Issues. LC 99-34286. 288p. 1999. pap. text 22.00 (0-8133-8152-5) Westview.

— The Political Economy of Imperialism: Critical Appraisals. LC 99-12023. (Recent Economic Thought Ser.). 1999. write for info. (0-7923-8470-9) Kluwer Academic.

— Power & Ruling Classes in Northeast Brazil: Juazeiro & Petrolina in Transition. (Cambridge Latin American Studies: No. 69). (Illus.). 400p. (C). 1990. text 89.95 (0-521-37384-0) Cambridge U Pr.

***Chilcote, Ronald H.** Theories of Comparative Political Economy: New Paradigms. LC 99-88513. 336p. 2000. pap. text 28.00 (0-8133-1019-9) Westview.

Chilcote, Ronald H. Theories of Comparative Politics: The Search for a Paradigm. LC 80-19762. 480p. (Orig.). (C). 1982. pap. text 24.90 (0-89158-971-6) Westview.

— Theories of Comparative Politics: The Search for a Paradigm Reconsidered. 2nd ed. 440p. (C). 1994. pap. text 32.00 (0-8133-1017-2, Pub. by Westview) HarpC.

***Chilcote, Ronald H., ed.** Imperialism: Theoretical Directions. 340p. 2000. pap. 24.95 (1-57392-821-6, Humanity Bks) Prometheus Bks.

Chilcote, Ronald H. & Johnson, Dale L., eds. Theories of Development: Mode of Production or Dependency? LC 82-19141. (Class, State & Development Ser.: No. 2). 256p. 1983. reprint ed. pap. 79.40 (0-608-01509-1, 205955300001) Bks Demand.

Chilcote, Ronald H., et al. Transitions from Dictatorship to Democracy: Comparative Studies of Spain, Portugal, & Greece. (Illus.). 270p. (C). 1990. text 75.00 (0-8448-1675-2, Crane Russak) Taylor & Francis.

Chilcott, Tim. A Publisher & His Circle: The Life & Work of John Taylor, Keats's Publisher. LC 72-194396. xi, 247p. 1972. write for info. (0-7100-7198-1, Routledge Thoemms) Routledge.

***Child.** Rangeland Ecology & Management. 2nd ed. 2000. 69.00 (0-8133-3801-8, Pub. by Westview) HarpC.

Child, jt. auth. see Hoiby, L.

Child, jt. auth. see Mohrig, Jerry R.

An Asterisk (*) at the beginning of an entry indicates that the title is appearing for the first time.

Child, J. A. The Lymphoproliferative Disorders: Handbook of Investigation, Diagnosis & Management. (Illus.). 420p. 1999. text 59.95 (*0-412-58030-6*, Pub. by E A) OUP.

Child & Family Agency of Ct. Staff. Charted Courses. LC 95-60895. 1995. 16.95 (*0-87197-431-2*) Favorite Recipes.

Child & Sport Conference (1984, Urbino, Italy) Staff. Young Athletes Biological, Psychological & Educational Perspectives. Malina, Robert M., ed. LC 87-22539. 311p. reprint ed. pap. 96.50 (*0-608-20826-4*, 207192500003) Bks Demand.

Child, A. The Cloud Song. (Foundations Ser.). 15p. (J). (gr. 1). 1992. pap. text 4.50 (*1-56843-073-6*) EMG Networks.

— The Cloud Song: Big Book. (Foundations Ser.). 15p. (J). (gr. 1). 1992. pap. text 23.00 (*1-56843-023-X*) EMG Networks.

— My Best Friend & Me. (Foundations Ser.). 19p. (J). (gr. 1). 1992. pap. text 4.50 (*1-56843-072-8*) EMG Networks.

— My Best Friend & Me: Big Book. (Foundations Ser.). 19p. (J). (gr. 1). 1992. pap. text 23.00 (*1-56843-022-1*) EMG Networks.

— Show Me a Face. (Foundations Ser.). 14p. (J). (ps). 1992. pap. text 23.00 (*1-56843-006-X*); pap. text 4.50 (*1-56843-056-6*) EMG Networks.

— What Would It Be? (Foundations Ser.). 13p. (J). (gr. k). 1992. pap. text 4.50 (*1-56843-061-2*) EMG Networks.

— What Would It Be? Big Book. (Foundations Ser.). 13p. (J). (gr. k). 1992. pap. text 23.00 (*1-56843-011-6*) EMG Networks.

— Yabba Dabba Dinosaur. (Foundations Ser.). 23p. (J). (gr. k). 1992. pap. text 23.00 (*1-56843-009-4*); pap. text 4.50 (*1-56843-059-0*) EMG Networks.

Child, Abigail. From Solids. (Segue Bks.). 30p. (Orig.). 1983. pap. text 5.00 (*0-937804-12-6*) Segue NYC.

— Mob. LC 94-67492. 96p. 1994. 9.50 (*1-882022-21-1*) O Bks.

— A Motive for Mayhem. 96p. (Orig.). 1989. pap. 8.50 (*0-937013-26-9*) Potes Poets.

— Scatter Matrix. 1996. pap. 9.95 (*0-937804-63-0*) Segue NYC.

Child, Alice B. & Child, Irvin L. Religion & Magic in the Life of Traditional Peoples. 272p. 1992. pap. text 31.33 (*0-13-012451-6*) P-H.

Child, Arthur H. Interpretation: A General Theory. LC 65-64890. (University of California Publications in Social Welfare: Vol. 36). 150p. reprint ed. pap. 46.50 (*0-608-11081-7*, 202117900022) Bks Demand.

Child, Barbara. Drafting Legal Documents: Materials & Problems. 2nd ed. (University Casebook Ser.). 425p. (C). 1992. pap. 31.50 (*0-314-00325-8*) West Pub.

— Drafting Legal Documents: Principles & Practices, Teacher's Manual to Accompany. 2nd ed. (American Casebook Ser.). 333p. (C). 1992. pap. text. write for info. (*0-314-01085-8*) West Pub.

Child, Brenda J. Boarding School Seasons: American Indian Families, 1900-1940. (North American Indian Prose Award Ser.). 154p. 2000. pap. 14.95 (*0-8032-6405-4*, Bison Books) U of Nebr Pr.

Child, C. Allan. Deep-Sea Pycnogonida from the Temperate West Coast of the U. S. fac. ed. LC 94-15498. (Smithsonian Contributions to Zoology Ser.: No. 556). 27p. 1994. reprint ed. pap. 30.00 (*0-7837-8261-6*, 204904200009) Bks Demand.

— Pycnogonida of the Western Pacific Islands Vol. 10: Collections from the Aleutians & Other Bering Sea Islands, Alaska. LC 94-28013. (Smithsonian Contributions to Zoology Ser.: Vol. 569). 34p. 1995. reprint ed. pap. 30.00 (*0-608-00506-1*, 206132600008) Bks Demand.

Child, C. Allan, jt. auth. see Nakamura, Koichiro.

Child, Camilla, jt. auth. see Hills, Dione.

Child, Charles M. Senescence & Rejuvenescence. Kastenbaum, Robert J., ed. LC 78-22192. (Aging & Old Age Ser.). (Illus.). 1979. reprint ed. lib. bdg. 37.95 (*0-405-11809-0*) Ayer.

Child, Charles M., et al. Unconscious, a Symposium. LC 67-22125. (Essay Index Reprint Ser.). 1977. 19.95 (*0-8369-0957-7*) Ayer.

Child, Clarence G., intro. Ralph Roister Doister. (BCL1-PR English Literature Ser.). 175p. 1992. reprint ed. lib. bdg. 69.00 (*0-7812-7313-7*) Rprt Serv.

Child, Clifton J. German-Americans in Politics, 1914-1917. LC 70-129394. (American Immigration Collection. Series 2). (Illus.). 1970. reprint ed. 15.95 (*0-405-00549-0*) Ayer.

Child, David L. Despotism of Freedom: Or, Tyranny & Cruelty of American Republican Slavemasters. LC 76-149865. (Black Heritage Library Collection). 1977. 15.95 (*0-8369-8747-0*) Ayer.

Child, Dennis. The Essentials of Factor Analysis. 2nd ed. 112p. 1991. pap. text 31.95 (*0-304-32331-4*) Continuum.

— Psychology & the Teacher. 5th ed. (Education Ser.). 416p. 1993. pap. 39.95 (*0-304-32649-6*) Continuum.

Child, Douglas. Calculus. (C). 1997. text. write for info. (*0-201-59948-1*) Addison-Wesley.

— Calculus, Vol. 1. alternate ed. (C). 1997. text. write for info. (*0-201-59330-0*) Addison-Wesley.

— Calculus: Preliminary Edition, Vol. 2. (C). 1997. text. write for info. (*0-201-59331-9*) Addison-Wesley.

— Calculus T/L. (Mathematics Ser.). 1993. 29.95 (*0-534-17344-6*) Brooks-Cole.

— Calculus T/L. (Mathematics Ser.). 1993. mass mkt. 20.75 (*0-534-17343-8*) Brooks-Cole.

Child Education Committee of the National Spiritua, compiled by. Magnified Be Thy Name: Prayers & Thoughts for Children from the Baha'i Holy Writings. 64p. (J). 1983. 7.50 (*0-900125-35-7*) Bahai.

Child, Elias. Genealogy of the Child, Childs & Childe Families of the Past & Present in the United States & the Canadas, from 1630 to 1881. (Illus.). 856p. 1989. reprint ed. pap. 128.00 (*0-8328-0397-9*); reprint ed. lib. bdg. 136.00 (*0-8328-0396-0*) Higginson Bk Co.

Child, Elizabeth. Eco-Educators Guide. Berg, Julie, ed. LC 93-28029. (Target Earth Ser.). 1993. pap. 15.98 (*1-56239-428-2*) ABDO Pub Co.

— Eco-Educators Guide. Berg, Julie, ed. LC 93-28029. (Target Earth Ser.). 128p. (J). (ps-7). 1993. ring bd. 14.96 (*1-56239-193-3*) ABDO Pub Co.

Child, Francis J., ed. "Lord Randal" & Other British Ballads. (Thrift Editions Ser.). (Illus.). 64p. (Orig.). 1996. pap. text 1.00 (*0-486-28987-7*) Dover.

Child, Frank C. Theory & Practice of Exchange in Germany. Wilkins, Mira, ed. LC 78-3904. (International Finance Ser.). 1979. reprint ed. lib. bdg. 25.95 (*0-405-11209-2*) Ayer.

Child, Frank S. Fairfield Ancient & Modern, 1639-1909: Brief Account, Historic & Descriptive, of a Famous Connecticut Town. 73p. 1997. reprint ed. pap. 15.00 (*0-8328-5643-6*) Higginson Bk Co.

— An Old New England Town, Sketches of Life, Scenery, Character (Fairfield, Connecticut) (Illus.). 230p. 1994. reprint ed. lib. bdg. 29.50 (*0-8328-4263-X*) Higginson Bk Co.

Child, Gloria. Precalculus Learning Activites. (C). 1997. pap. text. write for info. (*0-201-54852-6*) Addison-Wesley.

Child, Graham. World Mirrors. (Illus.). 400p. 1990. 95.00 (*0-85667-355-2*, Pub. by P Wilson) Scala Books.

Child, Greg. Climbing: The Complete Reference. LC 94-33254. (Illus.). 272p. 1995. 40.00 (*0-8160-2692-0*) Facts on File.

— Mixed Emotions. 1994. 24.75 (*0-8446-6745-5*) Peter Smith.

— Mixed Emotions: Mountaineering Writings of Greg Child. 272p. 1993. pap. 14.95 (*0-89886-363-5*) Mountaineers.

— Postcards from the Ledge: Collected Mountaineering Writings of Greg Child. LC 98-21175. (Illus.). 224p. 1998. 22.95 (*0-89886-584-0*) Mountaineers.

***Child, Greg.** Postcards from the Ledge: Collected Mountaineering Writings of Greg Child. (Illus.). 224p. 2000. reprint ed. pap. 16.95 (*0-89886-753-3*) Mountaineers.

Child, Greg. Thin Air: Encounters in the Himalayas. 2nd ed. LC 98-20400. (Illus.). 192p. 1998. pap. 16.95 (*0-89886-588-3*) Mountaineers.

Child, Greg, compiled by. Climbing: The Complete Reference. (Illus.). 272p. 1997. pap. 19.95 (*0-8160-3653-5*) Facts on File.

Child, Hamilton, compiled by. Gazetteer & Business Directory of Bennington County for 1880-81. (Illus.). 500p. 1996. reprint ed. lib. bdg. 53.00 (*0-8328-5124-8*) Higginson Bk Co.

— Gazetteer of Cheshire County, 1736-1885. With Town Histories & Directories, Biographical Sketches. (Illus.). 832p. 1997. reprint ed. lib. bdg. 85.00 (*0-8328-5982-6*) Higginson Bk Co.

Child, Hamilton, ed. Geographical Gazetteer of Jefferson County, NY. (Illus.). 1247p. 1993. reprint ed. lib. bdg. 119.00 (*0-8328-3193-X*) Higginson Bk Co.

Child, Harold, ed. see Hudson, Derek.

Child, Harold H. Thomas Hardy. LC 72-3631. (Studies in Thomas Hardy: No. 14). 1972. reprint ed. lib. bdg. 75.00 (*0-8383-1584-4*) M S G Haskell Hse.

Child Health Volunteers Staff, ed. see Pittsburg Community Staff.

Child, Heather. Calligraphy Today: Twentieth-Century Tradition & Practice. (Illus.). 128p. 1988. bds. 22.95 (*0-8008-1206-9*) Taplinger.

Child, Heather, ed. The Calligrapher's Handbook. 2nd ed. (Illus.). 272p. 1986. pap. 15.95 (*0-8008-1198-4*) Taplinger.

Child, Heather, et al. More Than Fine Writing: The Life & Calligraphy of Irene Wellington. LC 86-62197. (Illus.). 140p. 1999. 35.00 (*0-87951-269-5*, Pub. by Overlook Pr) Penguin Putnam.

Child, Heather, ed. see Johnston, Edward.

Child, Irvin L., jt. auth. see Child, Alice B.

Child, Irvin L., jt. auth. see Whiting, John W.

Child, J. A. Aids to Clinical Haematology. 2nd ed. (Illus.). 194p. (Orig.). 1992. pap. text 17.95 (*0-443-04192-X*) Church.

Child, J. Douglas. Calculus T - L II. rev. ed. 1993. pap. text 45.00 incl. disk (*0-534-17341-1*) Brooks-Cole.

— Calculus T/l (single User W /maple) (Math). (C). 1990. pap. text 58.50 incl. disk (*0-534-11815-1*) Brooks-Cole.

Child, J. M. Geometrical Lectures of Isaac Barrow (1916) 234p. 1998. reprint ed. pap. 17.95 (*0-7661-0719-1*) Kessinger Pub.

Child, Jack. Antarctica & South American Geopolitics: Frozen Lebensraum. LC 87-29948. 245p. 1988. 59.95 (*0-275-92886-1*, C2886, Praeger Pubs) Greenwood.

— The Central American Peace Process, 1983-1991: Sheathing Swords, Building Confidence. LC 92-10645. 200p. 1992. lib. bdg. 37.00 (*1-55587-343-X*) L Rienner.

— Geopolitics & Conflict in South America: Quarrels among Neighbors. LC 84-18326. 208p. 1985. 65.00 (*0-275-90074-6*, C0074, Praeger Pubs) Greenwood.

— Introduction to Spanish Translation. 236p. (Orig.). (C). 1992. pap. text 26.50 (*0-8191-8589-2*) U Pr of Amer.

Child, Jack, ed. Conflict in Central America: Approaches to Peace & Security. 208p. 1986. 27.50 (*1-85065-015-2*) Intl Peace.

— Regional Cooperation for Development & the Peaceful Settlement of Disputes in Latin America. No. 26. 1987. write for info. (*0-318-61801-X*) Intl Peace.

Child, Jack, ed. Introduction to Latin American Literature: A Bilingual Anthology. LC 94-26826. 1994. pap. 29.50 (*0-8191-9694-0*) U Pr of Amer.

Child, Jack, jt. ed. see Kelly, Philip.

Child, James E. History of Waseca County: From Its First Settlement in 1854 to the Close of Year 1904: A Record of Fifty Years, the Story of the Pioneers. (Illus.). 848p. 1997. reprint ed. lib. bdg. 87.50 (*0-8328-6817-5*) Higginson Bk Co.

— Nuclear War: The Moral Dimension. (Studies in Social Philosophy & Policy: No. 6). 150p. (Orig.). 1986. 16.95 (*0-912051-09-4*); pap. 8.95 (*0-912051-10-8*) Soc Phil Pol.

Child, James E., ed. Nuclear War: The Moral Dimension. 160p. (Orig.). 1985. pap. 18.95 (*0-912051-05-1*) Transaction Pubs.

Child, James E., jt. auth. see Scherer, Donald.

Child, James W. Nuclear War: The Moral Dimension. 224p. (Orig.). 1986. 39.95 (*0-912051-04-3*) Transaction Pubs.

Child, John. Management in China: Owning in the Age of Reform. (Illus.). 352p. 1996. pap. text 22.95 (*0-521-57466-8*) Cambridge U Pr.

— Management in China During the Age of Reform. (Cambridge Studies in Management: No. 23). (Illus.). 352p. (C). 1994. text 64.95 (*0-521-42005-9*) Cambridge U Pr.

— Organization: A Guide to Problems & Practice. 316p. (C). 1984. pap. 70.00 (*0-06-318275-0*, Pub. by P Chapman) St Mut.

— Photographic Lighting. 148p. 2000. pap. text 29.95 (*0-240-51549-8*, Focal) Buttrwrth-Heinemann.

— The Rise of Islam. LC 94-37633. (Biographical History Ser.). (Illus.). 64p. (YA). (gr. 5 up). Date not set. 17.95 (*0-87226-116-6*, 61166B, P Bedrick Books) NTC Contemp Pub Co.

— Studio Photography. LC 00-501693. (Illus.). 174p. 2000. pap. text 29.95 (*0-240-51550-1*, Focal) Buttrwrth-Heinemann.

— Unequal Alliance: The Inter-American Military System, Nineteen Thirty-Eight to Nineteen Seventy-Nine. LC 79-28707. (Replica Edition Ser.). 254p. 1980. text 39.00 (*0-89158-677-6*) Westview.

Child, John & Bate, Paul, eds. Organization of Innovation: East-West Perspectives. (Studies in Organization: No. 11). 238p. (C). 1987. lib. bdg. 84.65 (*3-11-010700-7*) De Gruyter.

Child, John & Faulkner, David. Strategies of Cooperation: Managing Alliances, Networks & Joint. LC 98-20620. (Illus.). 392p. 1998. pap. text 24.95 (*0-19-877485-0*) OUP.

— Strategies of Cooperation: Managing Alliances, Networks & Joint. (Illus.). 386p. 1998. text 85.00 (*0-19-877484-2*) OUP.

Child, John & Lu, Yuan, eds. Management Issues in China: International Enterprises. LC 95-15788. 240p. (C). 1995. pap. 18.99 (*0-415-13004-2*) Thomson Learn.

— Management Issues in China: International Enterprises. LC 95-15788. 240p. (C). (gr. 13). 1995. pap. 69.95 (*0-415-13003-4*) Thomson Learn.

Child, John, et al. The Crusades. LC 95-44426. (Biographical History Ser.). (Illus.). 64p. (YA). (gr. 5 up). 1996. 17.95 (*0-87226-119-0*, 61190B, P Bedrick Books) NTC Contemp Pub Co.

— Societal Change Between Market & Organization. (Public Policy & Social Welfare Ser.: Vol. 11). 228p. 1993. 41.95 (*1-85628-517-0*, Pub. by Avebry) Ashgate Pub Co.

Child, John, jt. auth. see Allison, K. W.

Child, John S., jt. auth. see Perloff, Joseph K.

Child, Julia. Cooking at Home with the Master Chefs. LC 93-20241. 1993. pap. 17.95 (*0-679-74829-6*) Knopf.

***Child, Julia.** The French Chef Cookbook. LC 98-96078. 480p. 1998. pap. 14.00 (*0-345-42542-1*) Ballantine Pub Grp.

Child, Julia. From Julia Child's Kitchen. LC 99-20209. 1999. 13.99 (*0-517-20712-5*) Random.

— In Julia's Kitchen with Master Chefs. LC 94-39380. 1995. 35.00 (*0-679-43896-3*) Knopf.

***Child, Julia.** James Beard's Pasta. 2000. 16.95 (*0-7624-0612-7*) Running Pr.

— Julia & Jacques: Cooking at Home. 1999. 40.00 (*0-676-54089-9*, Pub. by Knopf) Random House.

Child, Julia. Julia's Breakfasts, Lunches & Suppers. LC 98-38186. (Illus.). 128p. 1999. 19.95 (*0-375-40339-6*) Knopf.

— Julia's Casual Dinners: Seven Glorious Menus for Informal Occasions. LC 98-38188. (Illus.). 112p. 1999. 19.95 (*0-375-40337-X*) Random.

***Child, Julia.** Julia's Kitchen Wisdom: Lessons from a Lifetime of Cooking. (Illus.). 176p. 2000. 19.95 (*0-375-41151-8*) Knopf.

Child, Julia. The Way to Cook. LC 88-45832. (Illus.). 544p. 1989. 65.00 (*0-394-53264-3*) Knopf.

— The Way to Cook. (Illus.). 1993. pap. 35.00 (*0-679-74765-6*) Knopf.

Child, Julia & Yntema, E. S. Julia's Menus for Special Occasions. LC 98-6374. (Illus.). 1998. 18.00 (*0-375-40338-8*) Knopf.

Child, Julia, et al. Julia & Jacques: Cooking at Home. LC 98-32418. 416p. 1999. 40.00 (*0-375-40431-7*) Knopf.

— Mastering the Art of French Cooking, 2 vols., 1. rev. ed. (Illus.). 1983. pap. 30.00 (*0-394-72178-0*) Knopf.

— Mastering the Art of French Cooking, 2 vols., 1. rev. ed. (Illus.). 1983. 50.00 (*0-394-53399-2*) Knopf.

— Mastering the Art of French Cooking, 2 vols., 2. rev. ed. (Illus.). 1983. pap. 30.00 (*0-394-72177-2*) Knopf.

— Mastering the Art of French Cooking, 2 vols., Vol. 2. rev. ed. (Illus.). 1970. 50.00 (*0-394-40152-2*) Knopf.

Child, L. Maria, ed. see Brent, Linda, pseud.

Child Language Program. Children's Language Program: I Have Money. 1980. pap. text 13.64 (*0-201-23873-X*) Addison-Wesley.

— Children's Language Program: I Like Vegetables. 1987. pap. text 13.64 (*0-201-23871-3*) Addison-Wesley.

— Children's Language Program: I'm a Spider. 1987. pap. text 13.64 (*0-201-23870-5*) Addison-Wesley.

***Child, Lauren.** Beware of the Storybook Wolves. LC 00-30167. (Illus.). 2001. write for info. (*0-439-20500-X*, A A Levine) Scholastic Inc.

— Clarice Bean, Guess Who's Babysitting? LC 00-37963. (Illus.). (J). 2001. write for info. (*0-7636-1373-8*) Candlewick Pr.

Child, Lauren. Clarice Bean, That's Me. LC 99-10713. (Illus.). 32p. (J). (ps-2). 1999. text 16.99 (*0-7636-0961-7*) Candlewick Pr.

— I Want a Pet. LC 98-7228. (Illus.). 24p. (J). (ps-3). 1999. 13.95 (*1-883672-82-1*) Tricycle Pr.

Child, Lee. Die Trying. LC 97-39763. 384p. 1998. 23.95 (*0-399-14379-3*, G P Putnam) Peng Put Young Read.

— Die Trying. 434p. 1999. reprint ed. mass mkt. 6.99 (*0-515-12502-4*, Jove) Berkley Pub.

— Killing Floor. 419p. 1998. mass mkt. 6.99 (*0-515-12344-7*, Jove) Berkley Pub.

***Child, Lee.** Running Blind: A Jack Reacher Novel. LC 99-59196. 352p. 2000. 18.95 (*0-399-14623-7*) Putnam Pub Group.

— Tripwire. 432p. 2000. mass mkt. 7.50 (*0-515-12863-5*, Jove) Berkley Pub.

Child, Lee. Tripwire. LC 98-42578. 343p. 1999. 23.95 (*0-399-14467-6*, G P Putnam) Peng Put Young Read.

Child, Lee H., et al. Close to Home: Revelations & Reminiscences by North Carolina Authors. LC 96-20229. (Illus.). 1996. 19.95 (*0-89587-154-8*) Blair.

Child, Lincoln, jt. auth. see Preston, Douglas J.

Child, Lydia M. Hobomok & Other Writings on Indians. Karcher, Carolyn L., ed. (American Women Writers Ser.). 350p. (C). 1986. pap. text 15.00 (*0-8135-1164-X*) Rutgers U Pr.

— Letters from New York. Mills, Bruce, ed. LC 98-19480. 304p. 1999. 45.00 (*0-8203-2038-2*); pap. 19.95 (*0-8203-2077-3*) U of Ga Pr.

Child, Lydia Maria. The American Frugal Housewife. 140p. 1999. pap. text 6.95 (*0-486-40840-X*) Dover.

— The American Frugal Housewife. (Illus.). 130p. 1971. 7.00 (*0-88215-022-7*) Friends Ohio St U Lib.

— The American Frugal Housewife. 132p. 1985. reprint ed. 9.95 (*0-918222-98-2*, Pub. by Applewood) Consort Bk Sales.

— An Appeal in Favor of That Class of Americans Called Africans. Karcher, Carolyn L., ed. & intro. by. LC 95-21667. 272p. (C). 1996. 40.00 (*1-55849-006-X*); pap. 17.95 (*1-55849-007-8*) U of Mass Pr.

— Appeal in Favor of That Class of Americans Called Africans. LC 68-28988. (American Negro: His History & Literature. Series 1). 1969. reprint ed. 25.95 (*0-405-01808-8*) Ayer.

— The Family Nurse: Companion of the Frugal Housewife. LC 97-84. 288p. 1997. reprint ed. 12.95 (*1-55709-461-6*) Applewood.

— Freedmen's Book. LC 68-28989. (American Negro: His History & Literature. Series 1). (Illus.). 1974. reprint ed. 16.95 (*0-405-01809-6*) Ayer.

Child, Lydia Maria. Girls Own Book. LC 92-10815. 288p. (J). (gr. 3-12). 1991. reprint ed. pap. 12.95 (*1-55709-134-X*) Applewood.

Child, Lydia Maria. Hobomok & Other Writings on Indians. Karcher, Carolyn L., ed. 350p. (C). 1986. text 40.00 (*0-8135-1163-1*) Rutgers U Pr.

— Letters from New York. 3rd ed. LC 79-137726. (American Fiction Reprint Ser.). 1977. 21.95 (*0-8369-7025-X*) Ayer.

— Letters of Lydia Maria Child. LC 72-82183. (Anti-Slavery Crusade in America Ser.). 1970. reprint ed. 15.95 (*0-405-00622-5*) Ayer.

— Letters of Lydia Maria Child. LC 73-92740. 280p. 1969. reprint ed. lib. bdg. 52.50 (*0-8371-2189-2*, CHL&) Greenwood.

— The Mother's Book. LC 92-17577. 169p. 1989. 12.95 (*1-55709-124-2*) Applewood.

— The Mother's Book. LC 73-169377. (Family in America Ser.). 184p. 1976. reprint ed. 15.95 (*0-405-03854-2*) Ayer.

— Over the River & Through the Wood. LC 96-2012. (Illus.). 32p. (J). (ps-3). 1995. 15.95 (*0-8050-3825-6*, B Martin BYR) H Holt & Co.

— Over the River & Through the Wood. 32p. (J). (gr. k-3). 1999. 6.95 (*0-8050-6311-0*) H Holt & Co.

— Over the River & Through the Wood. ALC Staff, ed. LC 88-4712. (Illus.). 32p. (J). (ps up). 1992. mass mkt. 4.95 (*0-688-11839-9*, Wm Morrow) Morrow Avon.

— Over the River & Through the Wood. LC 93-16614. (Illus.). 32p. (J). (gr. k-3). 1993. lib. bdg. 14.88 (*1-55858-211-8*, Pub. by North-South Bks NYC) Chronicle Bks.

— Over the River & Through the Wood. LC 93-16614. (Illus.). 32p. (J). (gr. k-3). 1998. pap. 6.95 (*1-55858-959-7*, Pub. by North-South Bks NYC) Chronicle Bks.

— Over the River & Through the Wood. (Reading Rainbow Bks.). (J). 1992. 9.15 (*0-606-01367-9*, Pub. by Turtleback) Demco.

— Over the River & Through the Wood. (Blue Ribbon Bks.). (Illus.). 32p. (J). (gr. k-3). 1987. reprint ed. pap. 3.95 (*0-590-41190-X*, Blue Ribbon Bks) Scholastic Inc.

Child, Lydia Maria. Over the River & Through the Wood: Big Book Edition. Cohn, Amy, ed. LC 88-4712. (Illus.). 32p. (J). (ps-3). 1992. pap. 18.95 (*0-688-13632-X*, Wm Morrow) Morrow Avon.

Child, Lydia Maria. Philothea: A Romance. LC 72-85682. (American Fiction Reprint Ser.). Orig. Title: Philothea: A Grecian Romance. 1977. 19.95 (*0-8369-7011-X*) Ayer.

— Right Way the Safe Way, Proved by Emancipation in the British West Indies, & Elsewhere. LC 76-82184. (Anti-Slavery Crusade in America Ser.). 1970. reprint ed. 20.95 (*0-405-00623-3*) Ayer.

An Asterisk (*) at the beginning of an entry indicates that the title is appearing for the first time.

— A Romance of the Republic. LC 76-83926. (Black Heritage Library Collection). 1977. 24.95 (*0-8369-8540-0*) Ayer.

— A Romance of the Republic. Nelson, Dana D., ed. & intro. by. LC 97-10443. 464p. 1997. pap. 19.95 (*0-8131-0928-0*) U Pr of Ky.

***Child, Lydia Maria, contrib. by.** The American Frugal Housewife. 130p. 1999. reprint ed. 9.95 (*0-939218-22-4*) Chapman Billies.

Child, Lydia Maria & Greenleaf, John Whittier. Letters of Lydia Maria Child. LC 73-165169. reprint ed. 37.50 (*0-404-00141-6*) AMS Pr.

Child, Lydia Maria, jt. auth. see Karcher, Carolyn L.

Child, Lydia Maria, ed. see Jacobs, Harriet B.

Child, M. S. Molecular Collison Theory. unabridged ed. LC 96-38426. 310p. 1996. reprint ed. pap. text 9.95 (*0-486-69437-2*) Dover.

— Semiclassical Mechanics with Molecular Applications. (International Series of Monographs on Chemistry: No. 25). (Illus.). 432p. 1991. 105.00 (*0-19-855654-3*) OUP.

Child, M. S., ed. Molecular Rydberg Dynamics. 240p. 1998. 38.00 (*1-86094-094-3*, Pub. by Imperial College) World Scientific Pub.

Child, M. S., ed. see NATO Advanced Study Institute Staff.

Child Magazine Staff. Eating. LC 98-220780. 1997. per. 5.99 (*0-671-88041-1*) PB.

— Sleep, Tantrums & Goodbyes. 1996. pap. write for info. (*0-614-98087-9*, Pocket Books) PB.

Child, Margaret. Directory of Information Sources on Scientific Research Related to the Preservation of Sound Recordings, Still & Moving Images, & Magnetic Tape. 16p. 1993. pap. 10.00 (*1-887334-27-0*) Coun Lib & Info.

Child, Mark. Discovering Church Architecture. (Handbook Ser.: No. 214). (Illus.). 64p. 1996. pap. 8.50 (*0-85263-328-9*, Pub. by Shire Pubns) Parkwest Pubns.

— Discovering Churchyards. 1989. pap. 25.00 (*0-85263-603-2*, Pub. by Shire Pubns) St Mut.

— Wiltshire. (Country Guide Ser.: No. 5). 160p. 1993. pap. 12.50 (*0-7478-0273-4*, Pub. by Shire Pubns) Parkwest Pubns.

C

***Child, Mary.** Gifts of Love & Kindness. LC 00-190308. 72p. 2000. 2.95 (*1-57579-185-4*) Pine Hill Pr.

Child, Maureen. Colonel Daddy. 1999. per. 3.75 (*0-373-76211-9*, 1-76211-1) Silhouette.

***Child, Maureen.** Daddy Salute. (Desire Ser.). 2000. mass mkt. 3.99 (*0-373-76275-5*) Silhouette.

— Un Detalle Muy Importante.Tr. of A Very Important Detail. (ENG & SPA.). 2000. per. 3.50 (*0-373-35321-9*) Harlequin Bks.

— Un Falso Novio. (Deseo Ser.: Bk. 207).Tr. of False Boyfriend. (SPA.). 156p. 2000. per. 3.50 (*0-373-35337-5*, 1-35337-4) Harlequin Bks.

Child, Maureen. Have Bride, Need Groom. (Desire Ser.). 1997. per. 3.50 (*0-373-76059-0*, 1-76059-4) Silhouette.

***Child, Maureen.** The Last Santini Virgin. (Desire Ser.). 2000. mass mkt. 3.99 (*0-373-76312-3*, 1-76312-7) Silhouette.

Child, Maureen. The Littlest Marine. (Desire Ser.). 1998. per. 3.75 (*0-373-76167-8*, 1-76167-5) Silhouette.

***Child, Maureen.** Marine under the Mistletoe: Bachelor Battalion. (Desire Ser.). 1999. mass mkt. 3.75 (*0-373-76258-5*) Silhouette.

— Marooned with a Marine. (Desire Ser.: Bk. 1325). 2000. mass mkt. 3.99 (*0-373-76325-5*, 1-76325-9) Silhouette.

Child, Maureen. Maternity Bride. 1998. per. 3.75 (*0-373-76138-4*, 1-76138-6) Silhouette.

— Mom in Waiting. (Desire Ser.: No. 1234). 1999. per. 3.75 (*0-373-76234-8*, 1-76234-3) Silhouette.

***Child, Maureen.** The Next Santini Bride. (Desire Ser.: Vol. 1317). 2000. mass mkt. 3.99 (*0-373-76317-4*, 1-76317-6) Harlequin Bks.

Child, Maureen. No Huyas de Mi: Maternity Bride. (Deseo Ser.: No. 137).Tr. of Don't Run Away from Me. 1999. mass mkt. 3.50 (*0-373-35267-0*, 1-35267-3) Harlequin Bks.

— The Non-Commissioned Baby: The Bachelor Battalion. (Desire Ser.: No. 1174). 1998. per. 3.75 (*0-373-76174-0*, 1-76174-1) Harlequin Bks.

— The Oldest Living Married Virgin: The Bachelor Battalion. 1998. per. 3.75 (*0-373-76180-5*, 1-76180-8) Silhouette.

— Un Pere de Circonstance. (Rouge Passion Ser.). 1999. mass mkt. 3.50 (*0-373-37512-3*, 1-37512-0) Harlequin Bks.

— Un Regalo en la Puerta.Tr. of The Door Gift. (SPA.). 1999. per. 3.50 (*0-373-35285-9*, 1-35285-5) Harlequin Bks.

***Child, Maureen.** Run Wild My Heart. large type ed. 384p. 1999. 31.99 (*0-7089-4084-6*) Ulverscroft.

Child, Maureen. The Surprise Christmas Bride. (Desire Ser.: No. 1112). 1997. per. 3.50 (*0-373-76112-0*, 1-76112-1) Harlequin Bks.

— Toda una Vida (All Life Long) (Deseo Ser.). (SPA.). 1998. per. 3.50 (*0-373-35227-1*, 1-35227-7) Harlequin Bks.

Child, Nellise. If I Come Home. LC 74-29041. (Labor Movement in Fiction & Non-Fiction Ser.). reprint ed. 28.75 (*0-404-58522-1*) AMS Pr.

Child, Nicole L. Disaster Preparedness Manual for Day Care Centers. (Illus.). 1994. pap. text 25.00 (*0-9632988-0-1*) Normandy Herit.

Child, Peter. Craftsman Woodturner. (Illus.). 256p. 1998. pap. text 17.95 (*1-86108-075-1*) Guild Master.

Child, R. Dennis, et al. Arid & Semiarid Rangelands: Guidelines for Development. Jones, R. Katherine, ed. (Illus.). 291p. 1987. per. 13.50 (*0-933595-08-5*) Winrock Intl.

Child Study Association of America Staff, ed. Our Children Today: A Guide to Their Needs from Infancy Through Adolescence. LC 72-4512. (Essay Index Reprint Ser.). 1977. reprint ed. 23.95 (*0-8369-2938-1*) Ayer.

Child Study Children's Book Committee. Friends Are Like That! Stories to Read to Yourself. LC 78-22513. (Illus.). (J). (gr. 3-6). 1979. 12.95 (*0-690-03979-4*); lib. bdg. 12.89 (*0-690-03980-8*) HarpC Child Bks.

Child, V. Gene & Youngmann, Gene. Shaggy Dogs Have Punny Tales. 192p. 1992. pap. 7.95 (*0-9633899-1-2*) Vaden Bks.

***Child Welfare League of America Staff.** Child Abuse & Neglect: A Look at the States. (CWLA Stat Bks.). (Illus.). 1999. pap. 32.95 (*0-87868-771-8*, CWLA Pr) Child Welfare.

Child Welfare League of America Staff. Children's Legislative Agenda, 1998: Budget Updates & Issue Briefs. 192p. 1998. pap. 9.95 (*0-87868-731-9*, 7319, CWLA Pr) Child Welfare.

— Crack & Other Addictions: Old Realities & New Challenges for Child Welfare. 255p. 1990. pap. 14.95 (*0-87868-409-3*) Child Welfare.

— CWLA Board Self-Assessment Checklist. rev. ed. 1996. pap. 8.95 (*0-87868-503-0*, 5030) Child Welfare.

— CWLA Standards for Adoption Service. rev. ed. LC 78-73022. 115p. 1988. pap. 14.50 (*0-87868-365-8*, 0173) Child Welfare.

— CWLA Standards for Health Care Services for Children in Out-of-Home Care. 58p. 1988. pap. 14.50 (*0-87868-378-X*, 3780) Child Welfare.

— CWLA Standards for In-Home Aide Services for Children & Their Families. LC 59-12714. 45p. 1989. pap. 14.50 (*0-87868-386-0*) Child Welfare.

— CWLA Standards for Independent-Living Services. 1989. pap. 14.50 (*0-87868-379-8*) Child Welfare.

— CWLA Standards for Organization & Administration for All Child Welfare Services. 122p. 1984. pap. 14.50 (*0-87868-222-8*) Child Welfare.

— CWLA Standards for Services to Strengthen & Preserve Families with Children. 1989. pap. 14.50 (*0-87868-385-2*) Child Welfare.

— CWLA Standards of Excellence for Child Day Care Services. 1991. pap. 14.50 (*0-87868-463-8*) Child Welfare.

— CWLA Standards of Excellence for Family Foster Care. 1995. pap. 14.50 (*0-87868-464-6*) Child Welfare.

— CWLA Standards of Excellence for Residential Group Care Services. 1991. pap. 14.50 (*0-87868-462-X*, 4620) Child Welfare.

— CWLA Standards of Excellence for Services for Abused or Neglected Children & Their Families. Orig. Title: CWLA Standards for Services for Abused & Neglected Children & Their Families. 1998. pap. 16.50 (*0-87868-712-2*, 7122, CWLA Pr) Child Welfare.

— CWLA Standards of Excellence for Services for Adolescent Pregnancy Prevention, Pregnant Adolescents, & Young Parents. rev. ed. Orig. Title: CWLA Standards for Pregnant Adolescents & Young Parents. 1998. pap. 16.50 (*0-87868-689-4*) Child Welfare.

— CWLA Standards of Excellence for the Management & Governance of Child Welfare Organizations. 152p. 1996. pap. 16.50 (*0-87868-651-7*) Child Welfare.

— Homelessness: The Impact on Child Welfare in the '90s. 1991. pap. 6.95 (*0-87868-494-8*) Child Welfare.

— Maternal Deprivation. LC 61-18462. 76p. reprint ed. pap. 30.00 (*0-608-11297-6*, 200366800038) Bks Demand.

— Serving Children with HIV Infection in Child Day Care: A Guide for Center-Based & Family Day Care Providers. 48p. 1991. pap. 11.95 (*0-87868-439-5*) Child Welfare.

— Serving Gay & Lesbian Youths: The Role of Child Welfare Agencies. 1991. pap. 6.95 (*0-87868-495-6*) Child Welfare.

***Child Welfare League of America Staff.** Washington Workbook for Child Advocates: 106th Congress, 1999. 190p. 1999. spiral bd. 12.95 (*0-87868-755-6*) Child Welfare.

Child Welfare League of America Staff, jt. auth. see Battistelli, Ellen S.

Child Welfare League of America Staff, jt. auth. see Gritter, James L.

Child Welfare League of America Staff, jt. auth. see Hoyle, Sally G.

Child Welfare League of America Staff, jt. auth. see McNamara, Robert P.

Child, Wiliam. Learning from the Book of Nature. (Illus.). 200p. 1996. pap. 6.85 (*0-7399-0147-8*, 2307) Rod & Staff.

Child, William. Causality, Interpretation, & the Mind. (Oxford Philosophical Monographs). 244p. 1996. pap. text 17.95 (*0-19-823625-5*) OUP.

— A History of the Fifth Regiment New Hampshire Volunteers in the American Civil War 1861-1865. unabridged ed. LC 96-44049. (Illus.). xviii, 568p. (C). 1996. reprint ed. 40.95 (*1-889881-01-5*) Old Bks Pub.

Child, William H. History of the Town of Cornish New Hampshire with Genealogical Record, 1763-1910. 2 vols. in 1. LC 75-28084. (Illus.). 879p. 1975. reprint ed. 25.00 (*0-87152-213-6*) Reprint.

— History of the Town of Cornish, with Genealogical Record, 1763-1910. 855p. 1997. reprint ed. lib. bdg. 94.50 (*0-8328-5984-2*) Higginson Bk Co.

Child, William S. Legal Revolution of 1902. LC 75-154434. (Utopian Literature Ser.). 1976. reprint ed. 26.95 (*0-405-03517-9*) Ayer.

Childe, Henry L. Everyman's Guide to Concrete Work. LC 71-487900. 170p. reprint ed. pap. 52.70 (*0-608-13168-7*, 202523800043) Bks Demand.

Childe, V. Los Origenes de la Civilizacion. (Breviarios Ser.). (SPA.). pap. 8.99 (*968-16-0178-5*, Pub. by Fondo) Continental Bk.

Childe, V. Gordon. The Bronze Age. (Irvington Reprint Series in Anthropology). (C). 1991. reprint ed. pap. text 1.00 (*0-8290-2604-5*, A-32) Irvington.

— Prehistoric Migrations in Europe. 1976. lib. bdg. 69.95 (*0-8490-2467-6*) Gordon Pr.

Childe, Vere G. The Bronze Age. LC 63-18050. 1930. pap. 23.00 (*0-8196-0123-3*) Biblo.

— Prehistoric Communities of the British Isles. LC 72-82207. (Illus.). 1980. reprint ed. 29.95 (*0-405-08358-0*, Pub. by Blom Pubns) Ayer.

Childe, Vere G., et al. Skara Brae: A Pictish Village in Orkney. LC 77-86427. reprint ed. 24.50 (*0-404-16633-4*) AMS Pr.

Childerhose, Buffy. Pacific Salmon. pap. text 27.75 (*0-88894-342-3*) Sierra.

Childers. The Air War in Europe. 1999. pap. 13.95 (*0-8050-5753-6*, Owl) H Holt & Co.

— Designers of Time. 49.95 (*0-8478-2192-7*, Pub. by Rizzoli Intl) St Martin.

— Haute Jewelry. 49.95 (*0-8478-2190-0*, Pub. by Rizzoli Intl) St Martin.

Childers, Barbara & Wheeler, Eugenie G. Sexual Challenges: Navigating Your Course Through Troubled Waters to Loving Relationships. LC 96-7507. 160p. 1996. pap. 11.95 (*0-934793-58-1*) Pathfinder CA.

***Childers, Caroline.** Masters of the Millennium. (Illus.). 244p. 2000. 50.00 (*0-8478-2276-1*) Rizzoli Intl.

— Rainbow of Jewelry. (Illus.). 264p. 2000. 50.00 (*0-8478-2277-X*) Rizzoli Intl.

— Watches International: The Original Annual of the World's Finest Watches 2000. (Illus.). 400p. 2000. pap. 30.00 (*0-8478-2309-1*) Rizzoli Intl.

Childers, Darin G. Environmental Economics: Profiting From Waste Minimization. LC 97-52223. 1998. 92.00 (*1-57278-124-6*) Water Environ.

Childers, Donald G. Probability & Random Processes Using MATLAB: With Applications to Discrete & Continuous Time Systems. LC 96-35875. 448p. (C). 1996. text 61.00 (*0-256-13361-1*, Irwn Prfssnl) McGraw-Hill Prof.

***Childers, Donald G.** Speech Processing & Synthesis Toolboxes. LC 99-38270. 496p. 1999. text 91.95 (*0-471-34959-3*) Wiley.

Childers, Dorothy. Preparing for Grief. 80p. (Orig.). 1994. pap. 13.95 (*0-9640973-0-3*) D Childers.

Childers, Doug, jt. auth. see Millman, Dan.

Childers, Doug, jt. auth. see Sun-Childers, Jaia.

Childers, Douglas, jt. auth. see Sun-Childers, Jaia.

Childers, Erskine. In the Ranks of the C. I. V. 272p. 1997. 80.00 (*1-86227-053-8*, Pub. by Spellmnt Pubs) St Mut.

Childers, Erskine. The Riddle of the Sands. 284p. 1976. pap. 5.95 (*0-486-23280-8*) Dover.

— The Riddle of the Sands. LC 99-29902. (Thrift Editions Ser.). 304p. 1999. pap. text 2.00 (*0-486-40879-5*) Dover.

— The Riddle of the Sands. Sweetman, Jack, ed. LC 90-45843. (Classics of Naval Literature Ser.). 320p. 1991. 32.95 (*0-87021-601-5*) Naval Inst Pr.

***Childers, Erskine.** The Riddle of the Sands. (Classics Ser.). 336p. 2000. pap. 7.95 (*0-14-118165-6*, Penguin Classics) Viking Penguin.

Childers, Erskine. The Riddle of the Sands. (Classics Library). pap. 3.95 (*1-85326-038-X*, 038XWW, Pub. by Wrdsworth Edits) NTC Contemp Pub Co.

— The Riddle of the Sands. large type ed. (Large Print Ser.). 543p. 1992. reprint ed. lib. bdg. 24.00 (*0-939495-38-4*) North Bks.

— The Riddle of the Sands. 1976. reprint ed. lib. bdg. 24.95 (*0-89190-240-6*, Rivercity Pr) Amereon Ltd.

— The Riddle of the Sands. 310p. 1990. reprint ed. lib. bdg. 23.95 (*0-89966-743-0*) Buccaneer Bks.

— The Riddle of the Sands. 420p. 1998. reprint ed. lib. bdg. 24.00 (*1-58287-008-X*) North Bks.

— The Riddle of the Sands. LC 98-230186. (Illus.). 270p. 1998. reprint ed. 14.95 (*1-57409-015-1*) Sheridan.

— The Riddle of the Sands: A Record of Secret Service. Trotter, David & Snaith, Anna, eds. (Oxford World's Classics Ser.). (Illus.). 300p. 1998. pap. 7.95 (*0-19-283347-2*) OUP.

Childers, Evelyn. Kiss a Mule, Cure a Cold: Omens, Signs & Sayings. (Illus.). (Orig.). 1988. pap. 6.95 (*0-934601-44-5*) Peachtree Pubs.

Childers-Gandy, Mildred. Have You Been to Fifty-Six, No. 1. (Journey Ser.). (Illus.). 166p. 1994. pap. text 6.00 (*0-9642549-0-5*) Childbrant.

Childers, Greer. Be a Loser. 1999. pap. 14.00 (*0-8129-3141-6*, Times Bks) Crown Pub Group.

***Childers, Hugh.** Romantic Trials of Three Centuries. xvii, 303p. 1999. reprint ed. 95.00 (*1-56169-566-1*) Gaunt.

Childers, J. Wesley. Motif-Index of the Cuentos of Juan Timoneda. Dorson, Richard M., ed. LC 80-791. (Folklore of the World Ser.). 1981. reprint ed. lib. bdg. 17.95 (*0-405-13330-8*) Ayer.

Childers, James S. War Eagles. Gray, James A., ed. 369p. reprint ed. 24.00 (*0-941624-71-4*) Eagle Publ.

Childers, Jana. Performing the Word: Preaching As Theater. LC 98-28390. 192p. 1998. pap. 16.00 (*0-687-07423-1*) Abingdon.

Childers, Jana L. & Rose, Lucy A., compiled by. The Abingdon Women's Preaching Annual: Year A. pap. 16.95 (*0-687-05709-4*) Abingdon.

Childers, Jana L. & Rose, Lucy A., eds. The Abingdon Women's Preaching Annual: Series I, Year C. 168p. 1997. pap. 16.95 (*0-687-05848-1*) Abingdon.

***Childers, Jana L. & Rose, Lucy A., eds.** The Abingdon Women's Preaching Annual: Series 1, Year A. 160p. 1998. pap. 16.95 (*0-687-06732-4*) Abingdon.

Childers, Jana L. & Rose, Lucy A., eds. The Abingdon Women's Preaching Annual Vol. 1: Series I, Year B. 192p. 1996. pap. 16.95 (*0-687-00224-9*) Abingdon.

— The Abingdon Women's Preaching Annual 1997 Vol. 1: Series I, Year B. 1996. disk 29.95 (*0-687-01896-X*); disk 29.95 (*0-687-01895-1*) Abingdon.

Childers, John V., Jr. Million Heirs. LC 98-28110. 200p. 1998. 20.00 (*0-910019-76-2*) Lghthse Pub Gp.

***Childers, John V., Jr.** The Secret Millionaire Asset Security System. (Illus.). xviii, 296p. 1999. 29.95 (*1-929755-00-7*); pap. 19.95 (*1-929755-01-5*) Profit Pub Grp.

Childers, John V., Jr. The Secret Millionaire Guide to Nevada Corporations, 3 vols., Set. LC 98-15610. 316p. 1998. text 29.95 (*0-910019-57-6*) Lghthse Pub Gp.

Childers, Joseph & Hentzi, Gary, eds. The Columbia Dictionary of Modern Literary & Cultural Criticism. LC 94-42535. 362p. 1995. 57.50 (*0-231-07242-2*); pap. 23.00 (*0-231-07243-0*) Col U Pr.

Childers, Joseph W. Novel Possibilities: Fiction & the Formation of Early Victorian Culture. 240p. 1995. text 32.95 (*0-8122-3324-7*) U of Pa Pr.

***Childers, Leta N.** The Best Laid Plans. 1999. 6.50 incl. audio (*1-58495-025-0*) DiskUs Publishing.

— Chasing Butterflies & Finding Rainbows. (J). (gr. k-3). 1999. 6.50 incl. audio (*1-58495-023-4*) DiskUs Publishing.

— On the Road to Love. 1999. 6.50 incl. audio (*1-58495-026-9*) DiskUs Publishing.

— The Window to Summer. (J). 1999. 6.50 incl. audio (*1-58495-024-2*) DiskUs Publishing.

***Childers, Martin K.** Botulinum Toxic Type A in Pain Management. (Illus.). 136p. 2000. pap. text 24.95 (*0-9663422-2-4*, Pub. by Acad Info Systs) Demos Medical.

Childers, Max. Alpha Omega. 324p. 1993. 18.95 (*0-941711-21-8*) Wyrick & Co.

— The Congregation of the Dead. 282p. 1996. 21.95 (*0-941711-32-3*) Wyrick & Co.

— Things Undone. 279p. 1990. 16.95 (*0-941711-10-2*) Wyrick & Co.

Childers, N. F., jt. ed. see Eck, Paul.

Childers, N. Tracy, jt. auth. see Kelly, John J.

Childers, Norman F. Modern Fruit Science. rev. ed. 1995. 59.00 (*0-938378-10-4*) N F Childers.

Childers, Norman F., ed. Childers' Diet to Stop Arthritis: Nightshades, Aging & Ill Health. 5th rev. ed. (Illus.). 246p. 1995. pap. 18.00 (*0-938378-05-8*) N F Childers.

— The Strawberry: Cultivars to Marketing. (Illus.). 400p. 1981. 15.00 (*0-317-03715-3*) N F Childers.

Childers, Norman F., et al, eds. Nutrition of Fruit Crops: Tropical, Sub-Tropical, Temperate: Tree & Small Fruits. 2nd ed. LC 66-63534. (Illus.). 904p. 1966. reprint ed. pap. 200.00 (*0-608-04329-X*, 206510900012) Bks Demand.

Childers, Norman F. & Sherman, Wayne B., eds. The Peach-World Cultivars to Marketing. 1000p. 1998. 35.00 (*0-938378-03-1*) N F Childers.

Childers, Norman F., jt. ed. see Eck, Paul.

Childers, Norman F., ed. see National Strawberry Conference Staff.

Childers, Norman F., jt. ed. see Van der Zwet, Tom.

Childers, Peggy, jt. illus. see Crofts, Trudy.

Childers, Peter, jt. auth. see Schank, Roger C.

Childers, Richard, jt. auth. see Jones, Edwin.

Childers, Richard L., jt. auth. see Jones, Edwin R.

Childers, Roberta, ed. California Water Resources Directory: A Guide to Organizations & Information Resources. 2nd ed. LC 90-1636. (California Information Guides Ser.). 120p. (Orig.). 1991. pap. 25.00 (*0-912102-93-4*) Cal Inst Public.

***Childers, Sonya Kate.** Slice of Pie. 1999. pap. 11.95 (*0-9672664-1-6*) LazerBks.

Childers, Terry L., ed. see American Marketing Association Staff.

Childers, Thomas. Information & Referral: Public Libraries. LC 83-21492. (Libraries & Information Science). 356p. (Orig.). (C). 1984. text 73.25 (*0-89391-147-X*) Ablx Pub.

— Measures of Interlibrary Reference: A Manual. 120p. 1991. pap. text 22.50 (*0-929722-50-7*) CA State Library Fndtn.

— The Nazi Voter: The Social Foundations of Fascism in Germany, 1919-1933. LC 83-5924. xvi, 367p. 1986. reprint ed. pap. 18.95 (*0-8078-4147-1*) U of NC Pr.

— Of War & Memory. 1998. write for info. (*0-201-87044-4*) Addison-Wesley.

— We'll Meet Again: The Air War in Europe, 1939-1945. (Illus.). 496p. 1998. 27.50 (*0-8050-5752-8*) H Holt & Co.

— Wings of Morning. 288p. 1996. pap. 15.00 (*0-201-40722-1*) Addison-Wesley.

Childers, Thomas & Caplan, Jane, eds. Reevaluating the Third Reich. LC 91-37761. (Europe Past & Present Ser.). 286p. 1993. 39.95 (*0-8419-1178-9*); pap. 19.95 (*0-8419-1228-9*) Holmes & Meier.

Childers, Thomas A. & Van House, Nancy A. What's Good: Describing Your Public Library's Effectiveness. LC 93-3683. (Illus.). 94p. (Orig.). 1993. pap. text 25.00 (*0-8389-0617-6*) ALA.

Childers, Thomas A., jt. auth. see Van House, Nancy A.

Childhelp Staff. Celebrity Cookbook. 1992. 12.00 (*0-9636711-0-3*) WA Area Chapter.

Childish, Billy. Big Hart & Balls. LC 96-139668. 99p. 1994. 24.95 (*1-871894-91-3*, Pub. by Hangman Bks) AK Pr Dist.

— Child's Death Letter: Selected Lyrics. (Illus.). 76p. (Orig.). 1987. pap. 10.95 (*1-871894-36-0*, Pub. by Hangman Bks) AK Pr Dist.

— Companions in a Death Boat. (Illus.). 44p. (Orig.). 1987. pap. 8.95 (*1-871894-10-7*, Pub. by Hangman Bks) AK Pr Dist.

— Day with a Hart Like a Dog. (Illus.). 65p. (Orig.). 1994. pap. 13.95 (*1-871894-81-6*, Pub. by Hangman Bks) AK Pr Dist.

— The Hart Rises. 105p. (Orig.). 1992. pap. 13.95 (*1-871894-51-4*, Pub. by Hangman Bks) AK Pr Dist.

— Like a God I Love All Things. 71p. (Orig.). 1991. pap. 12.95 (*1-871894-46-8*, Pub. by Hangman Bks) AK Pr Dist.

***Childish, Billy.** My Fault. 2001. pap. 15.95 (*1-899598-18-9*) Codex.

Childish, Billy. My Fault: The Saga of Chatham Jack. 354p. (Orig.). 1997. pap. 16.95 (*1-899598-06-5*, Pub. by Codex) AK Pr Dist.

— Notebooks of a Naked Youth. LC 98-9601. 244p. pap. 14.00 (*0-941543-21-8*) Sun Dog Pr.

— Notebooks of a Naked Youth. deluxe ed. LC 98-9601. 192p. 1998. 35.00 (*0-941543-22-6*) Sun Dog Pr.

— Poems of Laughter & Violence: Selected Poems, 1981-1986. 204p. (Orig.). 1992. pap. 18.95 (*1-871894-76-X*, Pub. by Hangman Bks) AK Pr Dist.

— Poems to Break the Harts of Impossible Princesses. (Illus.). 69p. (Orig.). 1994. pap. 13.95 (*1-871894-86-7*, Pub. by Hangman Bks) AK Pr Dist.

— 17Hendrix Was Not The Only Musician. 1999. pap. text 17.50 (*1-899866-17-5*) Slab-O-Concrete Pubns.

Childoe, Doclaw. The HeartMath Solution: The Institute of HeartMath's Revolutionary Program for Engaging the Power of theHeart's Intelligence. LC 98-55300. 304p. 2000. pap. 14.00 (*0-06-251606-X*, Pub. by Harper SF) HarpC.

***Childre, Doc.** Heartmath Solution: The Institute of HeartMath's Revolutionary Program for Engaging the Power of theHeart's IntelligenceMartin,&Howard, Set. 1999. audio 18.00 (*0-694-52175-2*) HarperAudio.

Childre, Doc Lew. Cut-Thru: How to Care Without Becoming a Victim. LC 95-26111. 144p. 1996. pap. 11.95 (*1-879052-33-4*) Planetary Pubns.

— Freeze-Frame: One Minute Stress Management. 2nd rev. ed. Cryer, Bruce, ed. LC 98-33558. Orig. Title: Freeze-Frame: Fast Action Stress Relief (A Scientifically Proven Technique). 160p. 1998. pap. 11.95 (*1-879052-42-3*) Planetary Pubns.

— The How to Book of Teen Self Discovery: Helping Teens Find Balance, Security & Esteem. 2nd ed. LC 92-24296. (Illus.). 120p. (J). (ps-12). 1992. pap. 11.95 (*1-879052-36-9*) Planetary Pubns.

— Self Empowerment: The Heart Approach to Stress Management: Common Sense Strategies. Rozman, Deborah A. & Cryer, Bruce, eds. LC 91-38576. 141p. (Orig.). 1992. pap. 13.95 (*1-879052-34-2*) Planetary Pubns.

— Teaching Children to Love: Eighty Games & Fun Activities for Raising Balanced Children in Unbalanced Times. Paddison, Sara H., ed. LC 96-12013. 154p. 1996. pap. text 16.95 (*1-879052-26-1*) Planetary Pubns.

***Childre, Doc Lew & Cryer.** From Chaos to Coherence: Advancing Emotional & Organizational Intelligence. 255p. 2000. pap. 16.00 (*1-879052-46-6*, 363-033, Pub. by Planetary Pubns) BookWorld.

Childre, Doc Lew & Cryer, Bruce. From Chaos to Coherence: Advancing Individual & Organizational Intelligence Through Inner Quality Management. LC 98-29911. 248p. 1998. pap. text 18.95 (*0-7506-7007-X*) Buttrwrth-Heinemann.

Childre, Doc Lew & Martin, Howard. The HeartMath Solution: The Institute of HartMath's Revolutionary Program for Engaging the Power of theHeart's Intelligence. LC 98-55300. 304p. 1999. 24.00 (*0-06-251605-1*, Pub. by Harper SF) HarpC.

Childre, Doc Lew & Paddison, Sara. HeartMath Discovery Program Level One: Daily Readings & Self-Discovery Exercises for Creating a More Rewarding Life. Martin, Howard, ed. LC 98-5774. 408p. 1998. pap. 29.95 (*1-879052-28-8*) Planetary Pubns.

***Childree, Betty, ed.** The Heritage of Dale County, Alabama. (Heritage of Alabama Ser.: Vol. 23). 320p. 2001. 50.00 (*1-891647-45-8*) Herit Pub Consult.

Children & Youth Program Staff. State Legislature Summary, 1986: Children & Youth Issues. Robison, Susan D., ed. 138p. (Orig.). 1986. pap. 15.00 (*1-55516-619-9*) US HHS.

Children at Sunrise Ranch. Songs for the Joy of Living. 50p. (J). (gr. 1-10). 1985. ring bd. 11.95 (*0-932869-01-7*) Emissaries.

Children in Scotland (Organization), jt. auth. see Tisdall, E. Kay M.

Children of America Staff. The 11th Commandment: Wisdom from Our Children. Jewish Lights Publishing Staff, ed. LC 95-38956. (Illus.). 48p. (J). (ps-3). 1996. 16.95 (*1-879045-46-X*) Jewish Lights.

Children of Burlingame School District Staff & Children of Hillsborough School District Staff. Something New Is Building. (Illus.). vii, 83p. (Orig.). (J). (gr. 2-8). 1997. pap. 7.00 (*1-891165-03-8*) Sera Pub.

Children of Hillsborough School District Staff, jt. auth. see Children of Burlingame School District Staff.

Children's Aid Society Staff. Children's Aid Society Annual Reports, Nos. 1[00ad]10, February, LC 72-137191. (Poverty U. S. A. Historical Record Ser.). 1975. reprint ed. 51.95 (*0-405-03135-1*) Ayer.

Children's Allowance Conference Staff. Children's Allowance & the Economic Welfare of Children: Proccedings of the Children's Allowance Conference, 1967. Burns, Eveline M., ed. LC 74-1695. (Children & Youth Ser.). 208p. 1974. reprint ed. 23.95 (*0-405-05971-X*) Ayer.

Children's Book Council Staff, ed. Books Remembered: Nurturing the Budding Writer. 120p. 1997. pap. 25.00 (*0-933633-04-1*) Child Bk Coun.

— Children's Books: Awards & Prizes. 497p. 1996. 60.00 (*0-933633-03-3*) Child Bk Coun.

Childrens Books Staff. Sports: Speed Skating. (True Bks.). (Illus.). 48p. (J). (gr. 2-4). 1997. pap. 6.95 (*0-516-26206-8*) Childrens.

Children's Bureau of Southern California Staff. Family Assessment Form: A Practice-Based Approach to Assessing Family Functioning. LC 97-13456. 1997. pap. 14.95 (*0-87868-688-6*, CWLA Pr) Child Welfare.

Children's Creative Response to Conflict Program S, ed. The Friendly Classroom for a Small Planet: A Handbook on Creative Approaches to Living & Problem Solving for Children. rev. ed. (Illus.). 134p. 1988. pap. 15.95 (*0-86571-129-1*) New Soc Pubs.

Children's Defense Fund Staff. The Adolescent & Young Adult Fact Book. 164p. (Orig.). 1991. pap. 12.95 (*0-938008-83-8*) Childrens Defense.

— An Advocate's Guide to the Media. 24p. (Orig.). 1990. pap. 4.95 (*0-938008-75-7*) Childrens Defense.

— An Advocate's Guide to the Summer Food Service Program. 36p. 1994. pap. 4.95 (*1-881985-07-5*) Childrens Defense.

— An Advocate's Guide to Using Data. 20p. (Orig.). 1990. pap. 5.95 (*0-938008-80-3*) Childrens Defense.

— Building a National Immunization System: A Guide to Immunization Services & Resources. 136p. 1994. pap. 9.95 (*1-881985-06-7*) Childrens Defense.

***Children's Defense Fund Staff.** The State of America's Children. 2000. pap. 18.00 (*0-8070-4213-7*) Beacon Pr.

Children's Defense Fund Staff. The State of America's Children Yearbook, 1996. 110p. (Orig.). 1996. pap. 14.95 (*1-881985-11-3*) Childrens Defense.

— The State of America's Children Yearbook, 1999: A Report from the Children's Defense Fund. (Illus.). 188p. 1999. pap. 18.00 (*0-8070-4199-8*) Beacon Pr.

— The State of America's Children, Yearbook 1998: A Report from the Children's Defense Fund. LC 97-39587. (Illus.). 128p. 1998. pap. 16.00 (*0-8070-4147-5*) Beacon Pr.

— The State of America's Children Yearbook, 1995. 144p. 1995. pap. 14.95 (*1-881985-10-5*) Childrens Defense.

— Wasting America's Future: The Children's Defense Fund Report on the Costs of Child Poverty. 192p. 1994. pap. 18.00 (*0-8070-4107-6*) Beacon Pr.

— Your Family's Rights under the New Fair Housing Law. 26p. (Orig.). 1989. pap. 4.75 (*0-938008-74-9*) Childrens Defense.

Children's Defense Fund Staff & Northeastern University Center for Labor Market St. Vanishing Dreams: The Economic Plight of America's Young Families. 40p. 1992. pap. text 6.50 (*0-938008-93-5*) Childrens Defense.

Children's Defense Fund Staff, ed. see Hughes, Dana.

Children's Foundation Staff. Caring for Infants & Toddlers with Disabilities in Family Child Care: Annotated Resource Directory. 44p. 1995. pap. text 8.00 (*1-884093-06-X*) Chldrns Fnd.

Children's Health Care Inc. Staff. Childhood Constipation & Soiling: A Practical Guide for Parents & Children. 75p. 1995. pap. text. write for info. (*0-9644972-0-4*) Chldrns Hosps.

Children's Hospital at Yale New-Haven Staff. Now I Know Better: Kids Tell Kids about Safety. (Illus.). 96p. (J). (gr. 4 up). 1996. pap. 7.95 (*0-7613-0149-6*); lib. bdg. 21.90 (*0-7613-0109-7*) Millbrook Pr.

Children's Hospital of Los Angeles Staff. Skills & Knowledge for AIDS & Pregnancy Prevention. 1995. 45.00 (*1-56071-503-0*) ETR Assocs.

***Children's Hospital of Philadelphia Staff, et al.** The Children's Hospital of Philadelphia Book of Pregnancy & Child Care. Pasquariello, Patrick S., ed. LC 98-39009. 636p. 1999. pap. 19.95 (*0-471-32012-9*) Wiley.

***Children's Hospital Staff.** Childrens Hospital Great Parenting. 2000. pap. 35.00 (*0-7382-0241-X*, Pub. by Perseus Pubng) HarpC.

Children's Language Program Staff. Children's Language Program: Blackline Masters for Experience Stories & Language Units. 1980. pap. text 37.45 (*0-201-12360-6*) Addison-Wesley.

Children's Literature Association Staff. Touchstones, Reflections on the Best in Children's Literature Vol. 1: Children's Novels. Nodelman, Perry, ed. 315p. 1985. 26.50 (*0-8108-2561-9*) Scarecrow.

— Touchstones, Reflections on the Best in Children's Literature Vol. 3: Picture Books. Nodelman, Perry, ed. 191p. 1989. 26.50 (*0-8108-2563-5*) Scarecrow.

— Touchstones, Reflections on the Best of Children's Literature, 3 vols. Nodelman, Perry, ed. 1989. 63.00 (*0-8108-2564-3*) Scarecrow.

— Touchstones, Reflections on the Best of Children's Literature Vol. 2: Fairy Tales, Fables, Myths, Legends, & Poetry. Nodelman, Perry, ed. 236p. 1987. 26.50 (*0-8108-2562-7*) Scarecrow.

Childrens Marketplace Staff. Get Busy Izzy: 1996 Olympic Games Activity Book. (J). 1995. pap., per. 3.95 (*0-87197-443-6*) Favorite Recipes.

Children's Museum of Oak Ridge, Tennessee Staff, ed. Ridges & Valleys: A Mini-Encyclopedia of Anderson County, TN. 3rd ed. (Illus.). 126p. (Orig.). (J). (gr. 5-12). 1990. pap. 5.50 (*0-9606832-5-9*) Chldrns Mus.

Children's Museum Staff. Original Shirley Temple Dolls in Full Color. 81st ed. (Illus.). 32p. (J). (gr. 2 up). 1988. pap. 4.95 (*0-486-25461-5*) Dover.

Children's National Medical Center Staff. Children's National Medical Center A to Z Guide to Your Child's Behavior. 384p. (Orig.). 1993. pap. 14.95 (*0-399-51796-0*, Perigee Bks) Berkley Pub.

Children's Place Staff. Children's Place: At the Heart of Recovery. (Illus.). 64p. 1998. pap. 12.95 (*1-888358-22-X*) Acid Test Prodns.

Childrens Press Incoporated, Staff. Greg Maddux: Pitching Ace. (J). (gr. 3-4). 1995. pap. text 4.50 (*0-516-44395-X*) Childrens.

Childrens Press Staff. Animals-Lib. (Illus.). (J). 1996. write for info. (*0-516-29975-1*) Childrens.

Childrens Press Staff. E-Mail. (True Bks.). (J). 1997. pap. 6.95 (*0-516-26168-1*) Childrens.

— Earth Science & Ecology: Classroom Theme Set. (Rookie Read-About Science Ser.). 1998. pap. 43.11 (*0-516-29987-5*) Childrens.

— Galaxy. (J). 1998. lib. bdg. 56.00 (*0-516-29712-0*) Childrens.

— The Internet for Kids. (New True Books Ser.). (J). 1997. pap. 6.95 (*0-516-26170-3*) Childrens.

— Louisiana. (From Sea to Shining Sea Ser.). (Illus.). 64p. (J). 1995. pap. 7.95 (*0-516-43818-2*) Childrens.

— Set-Amer The Beautiful Spr 99. 1999. 320.00 (*0-516-21642-2*) Childrens.

— South Dakota-Sea to Shining Sea. (From Sea to Shining Sea Ser.). (Illus.). 64p. (J). (gr. 3-5). 1995. pap. 7.95 (*0-516-43841-7*) Childrens.

— Space: Black Holes. (True Bks.). 48p. (J). (gr. 2-4). 1997. pap. 6.95 (*0-516-26162-2*) Childrens.

— Space: Comets & Meteor Showers. (True Bks.). (J). (gr. 3-5). 1997. pap. 6.95 (*0-516-26166-5*) Childrens.

— Space: Galaxies. (True Bks.). (J). (gr. 3-5). 1997. pap. 6.95 (*0-516-26169-X*) Childrens.

— Space: Stars. (True Bks.). (Illus.). 48p. (J). (gr. 2-4). 1997. pap. 6.95 (*0-516-26177-0*) Childrens.

— Space: The Solar System. (True Bks.). (Illus.). 48p. (J). (gr. 2-4). 1997. pap. 6.95 (*0-516-26175-4*) Childrens.

— Sports: Bobsledding & the Luge. (True Bks.). (J). (gr. 3-5). 1997. pap. 6.95 (*0-516-26203-3*) Childrens.

— Sports: Figure Skating. (New True Books Ser.). (Illus.). 48p. (J). (gr. 2-4). 1997. pap. 6.95 (*0-516-26204-1*) Childrens.

— Sports: Skiing. (True Bks.). (J). (gr. 3-5). 1997. pap. 6.95 (*0-516-26205-X*) Childrens.

— Sports: The Winter Olympics. (True Bks.). (Illus.). 48p. (J). (gr. 2-4). 1997. pap. 6.95 (*0-516-26207-6*) Childrens.

***Childrens Press Staff.** Thirteen Colonies. LC 99-53533. (Cornerstones to Freedom Ser.). (J). (gr. 4-7). 2000. 20.00 (*0-516-21603-1*) Childrens.

Childrens Press Staff. Transporation: Blimps. (True Bks.). (J). 1997. pap. 6.95 (*0-516-26163-0*) Childrens.

— Transporation: Helicopters. (True Bks.). (J). 1997. pap. 6.95 (*0-516-26171-1*) Childrens.

— Transporation: Trains. (True Bks.). 1997. pap. 6.95 (*0-516-26178-9*) Childrens.

— True Books Sports. (J). 1999. 105.00 (*0-516-20871-3*) Childrens.

— Weather & Seasons. (Rookie Read-About Science Ser.). 1998. pap. 23.22 (*0-516-29990-5*) Childrens.

— The World Wide Web. (True Books). (J). 1999. pap. 6.95 (*0-516-26181-9*) Childrens.

Childrens Press Staff, ed. Farm Animals. (Rookie Read-About Science Ser.). 1998. pap. 29.85 (*0-516-29983-2*) Childrens.

— Insects, Spiders, & Worms. (Rookie Read-About Science Ser.). 1998. pap. 19.90 (*0-516-29985-9*) Childrens.

— Wild Animals. (Rookie Read-About Science Ser.). 1998. pap. 33.17 (*0-516-29982-4*) Childrens.

Children's Rights Project Staff. Unaccompanied Children Retained by the U. S. Immigration & Naturalization Service (INS) Slipping Through the Cracks. LC 97-71373. 120p. (Orig.). 1997. pap. 10.00 (*1-56432-209-2*) Hum Rts Watch.

Childrens Rights Project Staff, jt. auth. see Human Rights Watch/Asia Staff.

Childrens Rights Project Staff, jt. auth. see Human Rights Watch/Helsinki Staff.

Children's Television Workshop Staff. Anywhere I Am Is Here... Anywhere I'm Not Is There: The Eternal Wisdoms of Sesame Street. (Illus.). 176p. 2000. pap. 14.95 (*0-7868-8334-0*, Pub. by Hyprn Ppbks) Little.

Children's Television Workshop Staff, jt. auth. see Jim Henson Company Staff.

Children's Theatre Company (Minneapolis, Minn.) St, jt. auth. see Mason, Timothy.

Children's TV Workshop Staff, ed. see Mathieu, Joseph.

Children's Writers' Workshop Staff. Shivers In Your Nightshirt: Eerie Stories To Read In Bed. (Illus.). 106p. (J). 1991. pap. 6.95 (*0-920852-94-7*) Nimbus Publ.

Childres, Caroline, ed. Great Jewelry of the Word. (Illus.). 200p. 1998. pap. 49.95 (*0-8478-2092-0*, Pub. by Rizzoli Intl) St Martin.

Childres, Robert & Johnson. Equity, Restitution & Damages. 2nd ed. 1974. text 31.50 (*0-88277-498-0*) Foundation Pr.

Childres, Robert & Johnson, William F., Jr. Equity, Restitution & Damages. (University Casebook Ser.). 100p. 1974. pap. text. write for info. (*0-88277-437-9*) Foundation Pr.

Childres Television Workshop Staff. Parents' Guide To Feeding Your Kids Right. 1989. 19.95 (*0-13-649922-8*) P-H.

— Parents' Guide To Raising Kids Who Love To Learn. 1989. 19.95 (*0-13-650094-3*) P-H.

Childress, Alice. A Hero Ain't Nothin' but a Sandwich. LC 73-82035. 128p. (J). (gr. 5-9). 1973. pap. 15.95 (*0-698-20278-3*, Coward) Putnam Pub Group.

— A Hero Ain't Nothin but a Sandwich. 128p. (YA). (gr. 7 up). 1977. mass mkt. 4.50 (*0-380-00132-2*, Avon Bks) Morrow Avon.

— Hero Ain't Nothin' But a Sandwich. 1973. 9.60 (*0-606-03528-1*, Pub. by Turtleback) Demco.

***Childress, Alice.** Hero Ain't Nothin' but a Sandwich. 128p. (gr. 7-12). 1999. pap. 4.99 (*0-698-11854-5*) Putnam Pub Group.

Childress, Alice. Like One of the Family: Conversations from a Domestic's Life. LC 85-73367. (Black Women Writers Ser.). 237p. 1986. reprint ed. pap. 15.00 (*0-8070-0903-2*) Beacon Pr.

— Mojo & String. 1971. pap. 5.25 (*0-8222-0768-0*) Dramatists Play.

— Rainbow Jordan. LC 81-596. 128p. (gr. 7-12) 1982. mass mkt. 3.99 (*0-380-58974-5*, Avon Bks) Morrow Avon.

— Rainbow Jordan. (YA). 1998. 18.75 (*0-8446-6966-0*) Peter Smith.

Childress, Alice. Rainbow Jordan. 1981. 9.60 (*0-606-00560-9*, Pub. by Turtleback) Demco.

Childress, Alice. Those Other People. LC 88-10309. 144p. (YA). (gr. 8 up). 1989. 14.95 (*0-399-21510-7*, G P Putnam) Peng Put Young Read.

— Wine in the Wilderness. 1969. pap. 3.25 (*0-8222-1261-7*) Dramatists Play.

Childress, Barry L., ed. Psychoanalytic Approaches to the Very Troubled Child: Therapeutic Practice Innovations in Residential & Educational Settings. LC 89-11010. (Residential Treatment for Children & Youth Ser.: Vol. 6, No. 4). 88p. 1989. text 39.95 (*0-86656-928-6*) Haworth Pr.

Childress, Barry L., jt. ed. see Sanders, Jacquelyn S.

Childress, Celia W. Persuasive Delivery in the Courtroom. Harrison, David B., ed. LC 95-78204. 600p. 1995. text. write for info. (*0-7620-0026-0*) West Group.

Childress, David, jt. auth. see Thomas, Kenn.

Childress, David Hatcher. Ancient Micronesia. (Lost Cities of the Pacific Ser.). 1997. pap. 16.95 (*0-932813-49-6*) Adventures Unltd.

— Ancient Tonga & the Lost City of Mu'a: Including Samoa, Fiji, & Rarotonga. (Lost Cities of the Pacific Ser.). 218p. 1996. pap. 15.95 (*0-932813-36-4*) Adventures Unltd.

— Anti-Gravity & the Unified Field. (New Science Ser.). 250p. 1990. pap. 14.95 (*0-932813-10-0*) Adventures Unltd.

— Anti-Gravity Handbook. (New Science Ser.). 230p. 1993. pap. 14.95 (*0-932813-20-8*) Adventures Unltd.

***Childress, David Hatcher.** Extraterrestrial Archaeology. rev. ed. 320p. 2000. 19.95 (*0-932813-77-1*, Pub. by Adventures Unltd) SCB Distributors.

— A Hitchhiker's Guide to Armageddon. 320p. 2000. pap. 16.95 (*0-932813-84-4*, Pub. by Adventures Unltd) SCB Distributors.

Childress, David Hatcher. Lost Cities & Ancient Mysteries of Africa & Arabia. (Lost Cities Ser.: Bk. 4). (Illus.). 400p. (Orig.). 1987. pap. 14.95 (*0-932813-06-2*) Adventures Unltd.

— Lost Cities & Ancient Mysteries of South America. (Lost Cities Ser.: Bk. 3). (Illus.). 400p. (Orig.). 1986. pap. 14.95 (*0-932813-02-X*) Adventures Unltd.

— Lost Cities of Ancient Lemuria & the Pacific. (Lost Cities Ser.). (Illus.). 400p. (Orig.). 1987. pap. 14.95 (*0-932813-04-6*) Adventures Unltd.

— Lost Cities of Atlantis, Ancient Europe & the Mediterranean. (Lost Cities Ser.). 488p. 1995. pap. 16.95 (*0-932813-25-9*) Adventures Unltd.

— Lost Cities of China, Central Asia & India. 2nd rev. ed. (Lost Cities Ser.). (Illus.). 400p. 1987. pap. 14.95 (*0-932813-07-0*) Adventures Unltd.

— Lost Cities of North & Central America. (Lost Cities Ser.). (Illus.). 400p. (Orig.). 1992. pap. 14.95 (*0-932813-09-7*) Adventures Unltd.

***Childress, David Hatcher.** Technology of the Gods: The Incredible Sciences of the Ancients. (Illus.). 320p. 1999. pap. text 16.95 (*0-932813-73-9*) Advent Unltd.

Childress, David Hatcher. Vimana Aircraft of Ancient India & Atlantis. (New Science Ser.). (Illus.). 334p. 1991. pap. 15.95 (*0-932813-12-7*) Adventures Unltd.

Childress, David Hatcher, ed. Anti-Gravity & the World Grid. (New Science Ser.). (Illus.). 280p. (Orig.). 1986. pap. 14.95 (*0-932813-03-8*) Adventures Unltd.

— The Time Travel Handbook: A Manual of Practical Teleportation & Time Travel. 316p. 1999. pap. 16.95 (*0-932813-68-2*) Adventures Unltd.

Childress, David Hatcher, ed. The Free Energy Device Handbook. (New Science Ser.). (Illus.). 320p. (Orig.). 1994. pap. 16.95 (*0-932813-24-0*) Adventures Unltd.

Childress, David Hatcher & Shaver, Richard. Lost Continents & the Hollow Earth: I Remember Lemuria & the Shaver Mystery. (Illus.). 280p. 1998. pap. 16.95 (*0-932813-63-1*) Adventures Unltd.

Childress, David Hatcher, jt. auth. see Tesla, Nikola.

Childress, David Hatcher, jt. auth. see Vesco, Renato.

Childress, David Hatcher, ed. see Tesla, Nikola.

***Childress, Diana.** Chaucer's England. (Illus.). 136p. (YA). (gr. 9 up). 2000. 25.00 (*0-208-02489-1*, Linnet Bks) Shoe String.

Childress, Harvey A. Back to the Bible. 1958. pap. 4.15 (*0-89137-569-4*) Quality Pubns.

— Expanding Outlines of the New Testament Books. 1959. 8.55 (*0-89137-536-8*) Quality Pubns.

— The Lord's Own Church. 1980. pap. 2.25 (*0-88027-086-1*) Firm Foun Pub.

— My Triumphant Life. 1978. pap. 2.25 (*0-88027-087-X*) Firm Foun Pub.

— My Wonderful Salvation. 1978. pap. 1.75 (*0-88027-088-8*) Firm Foun Pub.

***Childress, Herb.** Landscapes of Betrayal, Landscapes of Joy: Curtisville in the Lives of its Teenagers. LC 99-87617. (C). 2000. text 49.50 (*0-7914-4577-1*) State U NY Pr.

— Landscapes of Betrayal, Landscapes of Joy: Curtisville in the Lives of Its Teenagers. LC 99-87617. 2000. pap. 16.95 (*0-7914-4578-X*) State U NY Pr.

Childress, J. J., ed. Hydrothermal Vents: A Case Study of the Biology & Chemistry of a Deep-Sea Hydrothermal Vent of the Galapagos Rift. (Deep-Sea Research Ser.: No. 35). (Illus.). 180p. 1989. pap. 45.00 (*0-08-037232-5*, Pergamon Pr) Elsevier.

Childress, James F. Civil Disobedience & Political Obligation: A Study in Christian Social Ethics. LC 75-158137. (Yale Publications in Religion Ser.: No. 16). 266p. reprint ed. pap. 82.50 (*0-608-30072-1*, 202198800024) Bks Demand.

— Moral Responsibility in Conflicts: Essays on Nonviolence, War, & Conscience. LC 82-15197. xvi, 224p. (C). 1982. text 35.00 (*0-8071-1019-1*) La State U Pr.

C

— Practical Reasoning in Bioethics. LC 96-25001. (Medical Ethics Ser.). 1997. 39.95 (*0-253-33218-4*) Ind U Pr.

Childress, James F. Who Should Decide? Paternalism in Health Care. 264p. 1985. pap. text 19.95 (*0-19-503976-9*) OUP.

Childress, James F. & Macquarrie, John, eds. The Westminster Dictionary of Christian Ethics. rev. ed. LC 85-22539. 704p. 1986. 39.95 (*0-664-20940-8*) Westminster John Knox.

Childress, James F., jt. auth. see Beauchamp, Thomas L.

Childress, James F., jt. ed. see Cahill, Lisa S.

Childress, John R. Building a Winning Culture. 1998. pap. text 18.00 (*0-9648466-3-2*) Leadrship Pr.

***Childress, John R.** A Time for Leadership: Global Perspectives from an Accelerated European Market Place. 208p. 2000. 25.00 (*0-9648466-8-3*, Pub. by Leadrship Pr) Gulf Pub.

Childress, John R. & Senn, Larry E. In the Eye of the Storm: Re-Engineering Corporate Culture. 236p. 1995. 25.00 (*0-9648466-0-8*); pap. 18.00 (*0-9648466-1-6*) Leadrship Pr.

Childress, John R., jt. auth. see Senn, Larry E.

Childress, Lynda M. Cruising Guide to Narragansett Bay, & the South Coast of Massachusetts. 416p. 1995. 34.95 (*0-07-016304-9*) Intl Marine.

Childress, Mark. Crazy in Alabama. 1999. mass mkt. 6.99 (*0-345-43247-9*) Ballantine Pub Grp.

***Childress, Mark.** Crazy in Alabama. abr. ed. 1999. audio 18.00 (*0-694-52235-X*) HarperAudio.

Childress, Mark. Crazy in Alabama. 384p. 1994. reprint ed. pap. 12.00 (*0-345-38924-7*) Ballantine Pub Grp.

— Gone for Good. 1999. pap. 12.95 (*0-345-41453-5*) Ballantine Pub Grp.

— Gone for Good. LC 97-49171. 368p. 1998. 25.00 (*0-375-40021-4*) Random.

— Henry Bobbity Is Missing: And It Is All Billy Bobbity's Fault. (Illus.). 32p. (J). 1996. 12.95 (*1-881548-90-2*) Crane Hill AL.

— Tender. 576p. 1998. pap. 12.95 (*0-345-41903-0*) Ballantine Pub Grp.

— V Is for Victor. LC 97-93512. 304p. 1998. pap. 12.00 (*0-345-42005-5*) Ballantine Pub Grp.

— A World Made of Fire. LC 97-93513. 304p. 1998. pap. 12.00 (*0-345-41904-9*) Ballantine Pub Grp.

Childress, Michael T. The Effectiveness of U. S. Training Efforts in Internal Defense & Development: The Cases of El Salvador & Honduras. 123p. (Orig.). 1995. pap. text 13.00 (*0-8330-1462-5*, MR-250-USDP) Rand Corp.

— A System Description of the Marijuana Trade. LC 93-26051. 1994. pap. 13.00 (*0-8330-1430-7*, MR-235-A/DPRC) Rand Corp.

Childress, Michael T. & McCarthy, Paul A. The Implications for the U. S. Army of Demographic Patterns in the Less Developed World. LC 93-21666. 1993. pap. text 6.00 (*0-8330-1411-0*, MR-256-A) Rand Corp.

Childress, Nancy & Jones, John W., eds. Arithmetic Geometry, Vol. 174. LC 94-22801. 220p. 1994. 48.00 (*0-8218-5174-8*, CONM/174C) Am Math.

Childress, Rennie. Race & the Production of Modern American Nationalism. Cain, William & Reynolds, Scott-Childress, eds. LC 98-39893. (Wellesley Studies in Critical Theory, Literary History & Culture: No. 18). 406p. 1998. text 65.00 (*0-8153-2016-7*) Garland.

Childress, Reynolds, ed. Museums in the Social & Economic Life of a City. 80p. 1996. pap. 10.00 (*0-931201-30-6*) Am Assn Mus.

Childress, Rhonda, jt. auth. see Granowsky, Alvin.

Childress, Richard E. Aluminum in Health & Disease: Index of New Information with Authors, Subjects, Research Categories & References. 150p. 1996. 47.50 (*0-7883-1178-6*); pap. 44.50 (*0-7883-1179-4*) ABBE Pubs Assn.

Childress, Robert L. Fundamentals of Finite Mathematics. (Illus.). 1976. 27.95 (*0-685-03862-9*) P-H.

Childress, Robert L., et al. Mathematics for Managerial Decisions. 2nd ed. 704p. (C). 1989. text 66.80 (*0-13-563024-X*) P-H.

Childress, S., jt. auth. see Ghil, M.

Childress, Stephen, ed. Some Mathematical Questions in Biology. LC 77-25086. (Lectures on Mathematics in the Life Sciences: Vol. 14). 214p. 1981. pap. 33.00 (*0-8218-1164-9*, LLSCI/14) Am Math.

Childress, Stephen & Gilbert, A. D. Stretch, Twist, Fold: The Fast Dynamo, Vol. XI. Beiglbock, W. et al, eds. LC 95-38008. (Lecture Notes in Physics Ser.: No. M37). 410p. 1995. 69.95 (*3-540-60258-5*) Spr-Verlag.

Childress, Steven A. & Davis, Martha S. Federal Standards of Review, 2 vols. 2nd ed. 1570p. 1993. suppl. ed. 47.50 (*0-685-74394-2*, MICHIE) LEXIS Pub.

— Federal Standards of Review, 2 vols. 2nd ed. 1570p. 1994. 195.00 (*0-88063-781-1*, 80464-10, MICHIE) LEXIS Pub.

— Federal Standards of Review, 1998 Cumulative Supplement. 250p. 1998. pap. write for info. (*0-327-00591-2*, 8046714) LEXIS Pub.

Childress, Steven Alan & Davis, Martha S. Federal Standards of Review, 2 Vols. 3rd ed. 210.00 (*0-327-10221-7*) LEXIS Pub.

Childress, Valerie. Winning Friends for the School Library: A PR Handbook. LC 93-37828. (Professional Growth Ser.). 205p. 1993. student ed., ring bd. 29.95 (*0-938865-24-2*) Linworth Pub.

Childress, William. Burning the Year-Lobo: Poems 1962-1975. LC 86-81734. 1986. 15.00 (*0-9607958-4-7*); pap. 10.00 (*0-9607958-5-5*) Essai Seay Pubns.

— Out of the Ozarks. LC 87-4609. 200p. 1987. 11.95 (*0-8093-1365-0*) S Ill U Pr.

Childrey, Don. Uwharrie Lakes Region Trail Guide. (Illus.). 302p. 1998. pap. 18.95 (*0-9643698-3-4*) Earthbnd Spts.

***Childs.** All Goalies Are Crazy. (J). 2000. pap. 6.95 (*0-440-86350-3*, Pub. by Transworld Publishers Ltd) Trafalgar.

— Big Break. 2000. pap. 6.95 (*0-552-52966-4*, Pub. by Transworld Publishers Ltd) Trafalgar.

— Big Day. 2000. pap. 6.95 (*0-552-52581-2*, Pub. by Transworld Publishers Ltd) Trafalgar.

— Big Football Collection Omnibus. 2000. pap. 8.95 (*0-552-54297-0*, Pub. by Transworld Publishers Ltd) Trafalgar.

— Big Football Feast. 2000. pap. 7.95 (*0-552-54596-1*, Pub. by Transworld Publishers Ltd) Trafalgar.

— Big Kick. 2000. pap. 6.95 (*0-552-52663-0*, Pub. by Transworld Publishers Ltd) Trafalgar.

— Big Match. 2000. pap. 6.95 (*0-552-52451-4*, Pub. by Transworld Publishers Ltd) Trafalgar.

— Big Prize. (J). 2000. pap. 6.95 (*0-552-52823-4*, Pub. by Transworld Publishers Ltd) Trafalgar.

— Big Star. (J). 2000. pap. 6.95 (*0-552-52825-0*, Pub. by Transworld Publishers Ltd) Trafalgar.

— Football Daft. 2000. pap. 6.95 (*0-440-86353-8*, Pub. by Transworld Publishers Ltd) Trafalgar.

— Football Flukes. 2000. pap. 6.95 (*0-440-86359-7*, Pub. by Transworld Publishers Ltd) Trafalgar.

Childs. Parking Spaces. LC 98-48077. 289p. 1999. 59.95 (*0-07-012107-9*) McGraw.

***Childs.** Sanford on Tour. (J). 2000. pap. 6.95 (*0-440-86320-1*, Pub. by Transworld Publishers Ltd) Trafalgar.

— Soccer Mad. (J). 2000. pap. 6.95 (*0-440-86344-9*, Pub. by Transworld Publishers Ltd) Trafalgar.

Childs, et al. 80286 System Guide. 1985. 24.95 (*0-13-246810-7*) P-H.

Childs, jt. auth. see Chandler.

Childs, Alan W. & Melton, Gary B., eds. Rural Psychology. 458p. 1983. 75.00 (*0-306-41045-1*, Plenum Trade) Perseus Pubng.

Childs, Alexandria, ed. see Monsell, Mary E.

Childs, Ann, ed. see Leisure Arts Staff.

Childs, Ann, ed. see Oxmoor House Staff.

***Childs, Anne Van Wagner, ed.** Christmas Gifts of Good Taste. (Illus.). 128p. 2000. reprint ed. 20.00 (*0-7881-9310-4*) DIANE Pub.

Childs, Anne Van Wagner, ed. see Leisure Arts Staff.

Childs, Arney R. & Sproat, John G., eds. Rice Planter & Sportsman: The Recollections of J. Motte Alston, 1821-1909. LC 99-33521. (Southern Classics Ser.). 160p. 1999. pap. 14.95 (*1-57003-316-1*) U of SC Pr.

Childs, B. J. & Ptacnik, Donald J. Emergency Ambulance Driving. (Illus.). 288p. 1985. pap. text 20.50 (*0-89303-427-4*) P-H.

Childs, Barton. Genetic Medicine: A Logic of Disease. LC 99-12783. 376p. 1999. 55.00 (*0-8018-6130-6*) Johns Hopkins.

Childs, Barton, et al, eds. Codes for Boundary-Value Problems in Ordinary Differential Equations. (Lecture Notes in Computer Science Ser.: Vol. 76). 388p. 1979. 32.00 (*0-387-09554-3*) Spr-Verlag.

Childs, Barton, jt. ed. see Scriver, Charles R.

Childs, Barton, jt. ed. see Simopoulos, Artemis P.

Childs, Brevard S. Biblical Theology of the Old & New Testaments: Theological Reflection on the Christian Bible. LC 92-30612. 768p. 1993. 47.00 (*0-8006-2675-3*, 1-2675, Fortress Pr) Augsburg Fortress.

— The Book of Exodus: A Critical, Theological Commentary. LC 73-23120. (Old Testament Library). 686p. 1974. 34.00 (*0-664-20985-8*) Westminster John Knox.

— Introduction to the Old Testament As Scripture. LC 78-14665. 688p. 1979. 45.00 (*0-8006-0532-2*, 1-532) Augsburg Fortress.

***Childs, Brevard S.** Isaiah: A Commentary. (Old Testament Library). 928p. 2000. 55.95 (*0-664-22143-2*) Westminster John Knox.

Childs, Brevard S. The New Testament As Canon: An Introduction. LC 94-9101. 608p. (C). 1992. reprint ed. pap. 25.00 (*1-56338-089-7*) TPI PA.

— Old Testament Theology in a Canonical Context. LC 85-45503. 272p. 1986. pap. 21.00 (*0-8006-2772-5*, 1-2772, Fortress Pr) Augsburg Fortress.

Childs, Brian H. Short-Term Pastoral Counseling. 1990. pap. 12.95 (*0-687-38432-X*) Abingdon.

Childs, Brian H. & Waanders, David W., eds. The Treasure of Earthen Vessels: Explorations in Theological Anthropology. LC 94-524. 256p. (Orig.). 1994. pap. 22.95 (*0-664-25493-4*) Westminster John Knox.

Childs, Caro, jt. auth. see Chaudron, Chris.

Childs, Caro, jt. auth. see Watt, Fiona.

***Childs, Christopher.** The Spirit's Terrain: Creativity, Activism & Transformation. LC 97-23335. 176p. 1998. 22.00 (*0-8070-2006-0*) Beacon Pr.

***Childs, Craig.** Colorado. 160p. 2000. pap. 29.95 (*1-57061-253-6*) Sasquatch Bks.

— Colorado. 160p. 2000. 40.00 (*1-57061-252-8*) Sasquatch Bks.

Childs, Craig. Crossing Paths: Uncommon Encounters with Animals in the Wild. LC 97-22152. 256p. (Orig.). 1997. pap. 14.95 (*1-57061-101-7*) Sasquatch Bks.

***Childs, Craig.** Grand Canyon: Time below the Rim. 2nd ed. (Illus.). 2000. 48.95 (*0-916179-78-8*) Ariz Hwy.

— Secret Knowledge of Water: Discovering the Essence of the American Desert. LC 99-57283. 304p. 2000. 23.95 (*1-57061-159-9*) Sasquatch Bks.

***Childs, Craig & Banks, Leo W.** Grand Canyon Stories: Then & Now. LC 99-60041. 1999. pap. text 10.95 (*0-916179-79-6*) Ariz Hwy.

Childs, Dara. Turbomachinery Rotordynamics: Phenomena, Modeling, & Analysis. LC 92-35452. 496p. 1993. 150.00 (*0-471-53840-X*) Wiley.

Childs, David. Britain Since 1939: Progress & Decline. LC 94-28906. 294p. 1995. text 55.00 (*0-312-12399-X*) St Martin.

— Britain since 1945. 3rd ed. 400p. (C). 1994. pap. 19.95 (*0-415-02976-7*, A6942) Routledge.

— Britain Since 1945: A Political History. 4th ed. LC 97-13199. 312p. (C). 1997. 75.00 (*0-415-16459-1*); pap. 24.99 (*0-415-16460-5*) Routledge.

— The GDR: Moscow's German Ally. 2nd ed. 384p. 1988. pap. text 17.95 (*0-04-445095-8*) Routledge.

***Childs, David.** Two Red Flags: European Social Democracy & Soviet Communism since 1945. LC 99-40178. 208p. (C). 2000. text. write for info. (*0-415-22195-1*) Routledge.

— Two Red Flags: European Social Democracy & Soviet Communism Since 1945. LC 99-40178. 208p. 2000. pap. 18.99 (*0-415-17181-4*) Routledge.

Childs, David, ed. Honecker's Germany. (Illus.). 200p. (C). 1985. text 49.95 (*0-04-354031-7*) Routledge.

Childs, David & Popplewell, Richard. The Stasi: The East German Intelligence & Security Service, 1917-89. LC 96-35553. 253p. (C). 1996. text 45.00 (*0-8147-1551-6*) NYU Pr.

Childs, David J. A Peripheral Weapon? The Production & Employment of British Tanks in the First World War, 173. LC 98-47130. (Contributions in Military Studies Ser.: No. 173). 232p. 1999. 57.95 (*0-313-30832-2*, GM0832, Greenwood Pr) Greenwood.

Childs, Elizabeth C., ed. Suspended License: Censorship & the Visual Arts. LC 97-16469. (Samuel & Althea Stroum Book Ser.). (Illus.). 413p. 1997. pap. 25.00 (*0-295-97627-6*) U of Wash Pr.

Childs, Elizabeth C., jt. auth. see Powell, Kirsten H.

Childs, Elsie. A Thankful Heart. large type ed. (Ulverscroft Large Print Ser.). (Illus.). 336p. 1997. 27.99 (*0-7089-3875-2*) Ulverscroft.

***Childs, Faye.** Going Off. 224p. 2000. text 23.95 (*0-312-24541-6*) St Martin.

Childs, Frances W. French Refugee Life in the United States, 1790-1800: An American Chapter of the French Revolution. LC 78-15085. (Perspectives in American History Ser.: No. 47). (Illus.). xvii, 229p. 1978. reprint ed. lib. bdg. 37.50 (*0-87991-371-1*) Porcupine Pr.

Childs, Frank H. Where & How to Find the Law. LC 85-60261. (Legal Bibliographic & Research Reprint Ser.: Vol. 4). vi, 119p. 1985. reprint ed. lib. bdg. 37.50 (*0-89941-397-8*, 303640) W S Hein.

***Childs, Frank Hall.** Principles of the Law of Personal Property: Chattels & Choses Including Sales of Goods, Sales on Execution, Chattel Mortgages, Gifts, Lost Property, Insurance, Patents, Copyrights, Trade Marks, Limitations of Actions, Etc. xv, 607p. 2000. reprint ed. 156.00 (*1-56169-585-8*) Gaunt.

Childs, Fred & Childs, Monica. Church Leadership Essentials Vol. 1: Rediscovering & Restoring Biblical Leadership Paradigms to the Body of Christ. 2nd ed. 236p. 1999. pap. 14.95 (*0-7392-0209-X*, PO3225) F & M Childs.

***Childs, Fred & Childs, Monica.** Church Leadership Essentials Vol. II: Rediscovering & Restoring Biblical Leadership Paradigms to the Body of Christ. 240p. 1999. pap. write for info. (*0-7392-0482-3*, PO3870) F & M Childs.

Childs, Geoffrey S. The Golden Thread. (Illus.). 207p. 1986. 7.95 (*0-910557-15-2*) Acad New Church.

***Childs, Geoffrey S.** Stone Palaces: Tales of Vertical Imagination. LC 00-8895. 256p. 2000. 22.95 (*0-89886-732-0*) Mountaineers.

***Childs, Gilbert.** Balancing Your Temperament. 124p. 1999. pap. 16.95 (*1-85584-067-7*, Pub. by R Steiner Pr) Anthroposophic.

— The Realities of Prayer. 112p. 1994. pap. 14.95 (*1-85584-015-4*, Pub. by R Steiner Pr) Anthroposophic.

Childs, Gilbert. Rudolf Steiner: His Life & Work, an Illustrated Biography. (Rudolf Steiner's Ideas in Practice Ser.). (Illus.). 111p. (Orig.). 1994. pap. 9.95 (*0-88010-391-4*) Anthroposophic.

— Steiner Education in Theory & Practice. pap. 29.50 (*0-86315-131-0*, 1529, Pub. by Floris Bks) Anthroposophic.

***Childs, Gilbert.** Truth, Beauty & Goodness: Steiner Waldorf Education as a Demand of Our Time, An Esoteric Study. 160p. 1999. pap. 11.95 (*1-902636-05-8*, Pub. by Temple Lodge) Anthroposophic.

— Understand Your Temperament: A Guide to the Four Temperaments. 146p. 1995. pap. 12.95 (*1-85584-025-1*, Pub. by R Steiner Pr) Anthroposophic.

Childs, Gilbert. Your Reincarnating Child. 1996. pap. text 14.95 (*1-85584-037-5*, Pub. by R Steiner Pr) Anthroposophic.

Childs, Gilbert & Childs, Sylvia. The Journey Continues: Finding a New Relationship to Death. LC 99-187181. 112p. 1998. pap. 14.95 (*1-85584-086-3*, 3050, Pub. by R Steiner Pr) Anthroposophic.

Childs, Gladwyn M. Umbundu Kinship & Character: Being a Description of Social Structure & Individual Development of the Ovimbundu of Angola, with Observations Concerning the Bearing on the Enterprise of Christian Missions of Certain Phases of the Life & Culture Described. LC 50-2385. 264p. reprint ed. pap. 81.90 (*0-8357-3227-4*, 205712200011) Bks Demand.

Childs-Gowell, Elaine. Good Grief Rituals: Tools for Healing. LC 92-27479. 112p. 1992. pap. 8.95 (*0-88268-118-4*) Station Hill Pr.

Childs, Harwood L. Labor & Capital in National Politics. LC 73-19137. (Politics & People Ser.). (Illus.). 290p. 1974. reprint ed. 23.95 (*0-405-05862-4*) Ayer.

Childs, Harwood L., ed. Propaganda & Dictatorship: A Collection of Papers. LC 72-4659. (International Propaganda & Communications Ser.). 153p. 1972. reprint ed. 13.95 (*0-405-04742-8*) Ayer.

Childs, Harwood L., tr. from GER. The Nazi Primer: Offical Handbook for Schooling the Hitler Youth. LC 71-180391. reprint ed. 27.50 (*0-404-56107-1*) AMS Pr.

Childs, Harwood L. & Whitton, John B., eds. Propaganda by Short Wave. LC 72-4660. (International Propaganda & Communications Ser.). (Illus.). 365p. 1972. reprint ed. 26.95 (*0-405-04743-6*) Ayer.

Childs, Henry C. Connecticut's Litchfield County: A Photographic Narrative. LC 93-83683. (Illus.). 118p. 1993. 39.95 (*0-9638486-0-7*) Connecticut Bk.

Childs, J. F., ed. see International Organization of Citrus Virologists C.

***Childs, J. Rives.** General Solution of the ADFGVX Cipher System. (Cryptographic Series: c-88). x, 245p. 2000. pap. 36.80 (*0-89412-284-3*) Aegean Park Pr.

Childs, Jack L. & Glenn, Warner. Tracking the Fields of the Borderlands. (Illus.). 78p. 1990. spiral bd. 16.50 (*0-9651159-1-7*) Printing Corner.

Childs, James J. Numerical Control Part Programming. LC 73-9766. (Illus.). 354p. 1973. 26.95 (*0-8311-1099-6*) Indus Pr.

Childs, James M., Jr. Ethics in Business: Faith at Work. 144p. 1995. pap. 15.00 (*0-8006-2908-6*, 1-2908) Augsburg Fortress.

— Faith, Formation & Decision: Ethics in the Community of Promise. LC 91-24867. 160p. (Orig.). 1991. pap. 16.00 (*0-8006-2500-5*, 1-2500, Fortress Pr) Augsburg Fortress.

***Childs, James M., Jr.** Greed: Economics & Ethics in Conflict. LC 99-59243. 2000. pap. 15.00 (*0-8006-3230-3*, Fortress Pr) Augsburg Fortress.

Childs, James R. Reliques of the Rives. (Illus.). 750p. 1994. pap. text 45.00 (*0-7884-0091-6*) Heritage Bk.

***Childs, James S., Jr.** Preaching Justice: The Ethical Vocation of Word & Sacrament Ministry. LC 99-87137. 2000. pap. 13.00 (*1-56338-313-6*) TPI PA.

Childs, Joan E. The Myth of the Maiden: On Being a Woman. 250p. (Orig.). 1995. pap. 9.95 (*1-55874-315-4*, 3154) Health Comm.

Childs, John. Making Music Special: Practical Ways to Create Music. LC 96-214420. 176p. 1996. pap. text 24.95 (*1-85346-417-1*, Pub. by David Fulton) Taylor & Francis.

— The Military Use of Land: A History of the Defense Estate. 302p. 1998. pap. 45.95 (*3-906757-66-8*) P Lang Pubng.

— The Military Use of Land: A History of the Defense Estate. LC 97-32733. 302p. (C). 1998. pap. 45.95 (*0-8204-3410-8*) P Lang Pubng.

Childs, John B. Leadership, Conflict, & Cooperation in Afro-American Social Thought. 224p. 1993. pap. 19.95 (*1-56639-085-0*) Temple U Pr.

Childs, John L. Education & Morals: An Experimentalist Philosophy of Education. LC 72-165734. (American Education, Ser, No. 2). 1978. reprint ed. 21.95 (*0-405-03603-5*) Ayer.

— Education & the Philosophy of Experimentalism. LC 76-165735. (American Education, Ser, No. 2). 1978. reprint ed. 20.95 (*0-405-03604-3*) Ayer.

Childs, John S. Modernist Form: Pound's Style in the Early Cantos. LC 85-62781. 192p. 1986. 36.50 (*0-941664-15-5*) Susquehanna U Pr.

Childs, Joy. Dorothy. large type ed. 1991. 27.99 (*0-7089-2550-2*) Ulverscroft.

Childs, Karin A. The Temple of Wisdom. 200p. (YA). (gr. 7-12). 1997. pap. 5.95 (*0-9659164-0-5*) Fountain Publ.

Childs, Karin A., ed. see Brock, Bryn J.

Childs, Kenneth M., Jr., ed. Ports, 1989. LC 89-6760. 750p. 1989. pap. text 76.00 (*0-87262-703-9*, 703) Am Soc Civil Eng.

***Childs, L.** Taming Wild Extensions: Hopf Algebras & Local Galois Module Theory. (Mathematical Surveys & Monographs Ser.). 215p. 2000. 54.00 (*0-8218-2131-8*) Am Math.

***Childs, L. N.** A Concrete Introduction to Higher Algebra. 2nd ed. (Undergraduate Texts in Mathematics Ser.). 536p. 2000. pap. 39.95 (*0-387-98999-4*) Spr-Verlag.

Childs, Laura. Nimble with Numbers. 160p. (ps-3). 1999. pap. text 15.95 (*1-57232-983-1*) Seymour Pubns.

Childs, Leigh. Nimble with Numbers. 160p. (J). 1997. pap. text 14.95 (*1-57232-439-2*) Seymour Pubns.

— Nimble with Numbers. 1998. pap. text 14.95 (*1-57232-986-6*) Seymour Pubns.

— Nimble with Numbers. 160p. 1999. pap. text 15.95 (*1-57232-985-8*) Seymour Pubns.

— Nimble with Numbers. 1999. pap. text 15.95 (*1-57232-984-X*) Seymour Pubns.

Childs, Leigh & Adams, Nancy. Math Sponges. 112p. 1997. pap. text 8.95 (*0-86651-248-9*) Seymour Pubns.

Childs, Leigh & Choate, Laura. Nimble with Numbers. Brill, Patricia et al, eds. (Practice Bookshelf Ser.). (Illus.). 162p. (J). (gr. 3-4). 1997. pap. text 14.95 (*1-57232-842-8*, 21850) Seymour Pubns.

Childs, Leigh, jt. auth. see Adams, Nancy.

***Childs, Lewis.** Ladysmith. 1998. pap. text 16.95 (*0-85052-611-6*, Pub. by Leo Cooper) Trans-Atl Phila.

Childs, Lewis. Ladysmith: The Siege. 1999. pap. 16.95 (*0-85052-653-1*, Pub. by Leo Cooper) Combined Pub.

Childs, Lindsay N. A Concrete Introduction to Higher Algebra. LC 78-21870. (Undergraduate Texts in Mathematics Ser.). (Illus.). 340p. 1993. 49.00 (*0-387-90333-X*) Spr-Verlag.

Childs, Lindsay N., et al. Hopf Algebras, Polynomial Formal Groups & Raynaud Orders. LC 98-34748. (Memoirs of the American Mathematical Society Ser.: Vol. 136, No. 651). 118p. 1998. pap. 41.00 (*0-8218-1077-4*) Am Math.

Childs, Madge, tr. see Holtzapfel, Walter.

Childs, Margaret H. Rethinking Sorrow: Revelatory Tales of Late Medieval Japan. LC 89-25394. (Michigan Monographs in Japanese Studies: No. 6). xiv, 182p. 1991. 27.95 (*0-939512-42-4*) U MI Japan.

An Asterisk (*) at the beginning of an entry indicates that the title is appearing for the first time.

— Rethinking Sorrow: Revelatory Tales of Late Medieval Japan. LC 89-25394. (Michigan Monographs in Japanese Studies: No. 6). xiv, 182p. 1996. pap. 14.95 (0-939512-74-2) U MI Japan.
Childs, Margery P. New Life Naturally: The Home Guide to Harmonious Health. 152p. 1995. pap. 9.95 (1-885857-14-4) Four Wnds Pubng.
Childs, Marilyn C. & Wallen, Rick M. Training Your Colt to Ride & Drive: A Complete Guide for Pleasure or Show. rev. ed. LC 93-28286. 1993. 19.95 (0-943955-83-1, Trafalgar Sq Pub) Trafalgar.
Childs, Mark. The Perverted Adult Survey Game. 160p. 1991. per. 7.95 (0-8187-0145-5) Harlo Press.
Childs, Marquis. The Farmer Takes a Hand: The Electric Power Revolution in Rural America. LC 73-19736. (FDR & the Era of the New Deal Ser.). (Illus.). 256p. 1974. reprint ed. lib. bdg. 35.00 (0-306-70478-1) Da Capo.
Childs, Marquis & Engel, Paul. This Is Iowa. Andrews, Clarence A., ed. LC 82-61137. (Illus.). 320p. 1982. lib. bdg. 14.95 (0-934582-04-1) Midwest Heritage.
Childs, Marquis W. Sweden: The Middle Way on Trial. LC 79-24714. (Illus.). 197p. reprint ed. pap. 61.10 (0-8357-3743-8, 203646900003) Bks Demand.
— Yesterday, Today & Tomorrow: The Farmer Takes a Hand. rev. ed. LC 52-5629. 178p. 1980. reprint ed. pap. 2.25 (0-686-28113-6) Natl Rural.
Childs, Marquis W. & Reston, James, eds. Walter Lippmann & His Times. 246p. 1977. 18.95 (0-8369-0106-1) Ayer.
Childs, Martha & Westfall, Virginia. A Childs Family. 79p. 1992. pap. 10.00 (1-883166-01-2) Frst Edition.
Childs, Marti & Marsh, Jeffery L. Echoes of the Sixties. LC 99-49826. (Illus.). 352p. 1999. pap. 19.95 (0-8230-8316-0) Watsn-Guptill.
Childs, Michael, et al, eds. The Evolution of Socialism (L'Evolution du Socialisme) (Journal of History & Politics (Revue d'Histoire et de Politique) Ser.: Vol. 10). (ENG & FRE.). 160p. 1993. 49.95 (0-7734-9323-9) E Mellen.
Childs, Michael J. Labour's Apprentices: Working-Class Lads in Late Victorian & Edwardian England. 248p. 1992. 65.00 (0-7735-0915-1, Pub. by McG-Queens Univ Pr) CUP Services.
— Labour's Apprentices: Working-Class Lads in Late Victorian & Edwardian England. 248p. 1994. pap. 19.95 (0-7735-1289-6, Pub. by McG-Queens Univ Pr) CUP Services.
Childs, Mimi P., ed. The Summer House Sampler: A Collection of Memories & Recipes of Wynnton Elementary School. 264p. 1992. 14.95 (0-9634091-0-7) Summer Hse Pr.
Childs, Monica, jt. auth. see Childs, Fred.
Childs, Nick. Flashpoints, 6 bks., Set II, Reading Level 8. (Illus.). 560p. (J). (gr. 7 up). 1988. 83.70 (0-685-58795-9) Rourke Corp.
— Flashpoints, 5 bks., Set II, Reading Level 8. (Illus.). 560p. (YA). (gr. 7 up). 1988. lib. bdg. 119.65 (0-86592-513-5) Rourke Enter.
Childs, Nicky & Walwin, Jeni, eds. A Split Second of Paradise: Live Art, Installation & Performance. LC 98-222998. (Illus.). 192p. 1998. text 50.00 (1-85489-098-0); pap. text 17.50 (1-85489-099-9) NYU Pr.
***Childs, Peter.** Encyclopedia of Contemporary British Culture. LC 98-32205. 648p. 1999. text 140.00 (0-415-14726-3) Routledge.
— Modernism. LC 99-86582. 200p. 2000. pap. write for info. (0-415-19648-5) Routledge.
— Modernism. LC 99-86582. (New Critical Idiom Ser.). 200p. 2000. 50.00 (0-415-19647-7) Routledge.
— Post-Colonial Theory & English Literature: A Reader. 2000. pap. 27.00 (0-7486-1068-5, Pub. by Edinburgh U Pr) Col U Pr.
Childs, Peter. Twentieth Century in Poetry. LC 98-7836. 208p. (C). 1999. 75.00 (0-415-17100-8) Routledge.
Childs, Peter, et al. Introduction to Post-Colonial Theory. 224p. 1997. pap. 29.00 (0-13-232919-0) P-H.
Childs, Peter, jt. auth. see Storry, Mike.
Childs, Peter O. Musings of a Modern Mystic. LC 95-92015. 160p. (Orig.). 1995. pap. text 12.50 (0-9644830-0-9) Dos Plumas Pub.
***Childs, Peter R.** Mechanical Design: A Rotary Component Approach. LC 98-50988. 240p. 1998. pap. 59.95 (0-470-32740-5) Wiley.
Childs, Phyllis. Color Me. 35p. (J). (ps). 1985. student ed. 2.95 (0-931749-03-4) PJC Lrng Mtrls.
— The Language Ladder, Bk. I. (Illus.). 76p. (J). (ps). 1985. student ed. 6.50 (0-931749-01-8) PJC Lrng Mtrls.
— The Language Ladder, Bk. 2. 54p. (J). (ps). 1987. pap., student ed. 5.95 (0-317-60748-0) PJC Lrng Mtrls.
— Speak Up. 78p. (J). (ps). 1985. student ed. 6.50 (0-931749-00-X) PJC Lrng Mtrls.
Childs, Phyllis, et al. First Book of Numbers. 55p. (J). (ps). 1985. student ed. 4.95 (0-931749-02-6) PJC Lrng Mtrls.
— I've Got Something for You to Do...& It's Fun! (J). (ps). 1986. student ed. 2.25 (0-931749-04-2) PJC Lrng Mtrls.
***Childs Play Inc. Staff.** Cyfri'r Plant. 1999. 9.99 (0-85953-483-9) Childs Play.
— Hyd A Lled. 1999. 9.99 (0-85953-482-0) Childs Play.
— Mae'n Braf Allan. 1999. pap. text 2.99 (0-85953-652-1) Childs Play.
— Pawb Yn Coginio! 1999. pap. text 2.99 (0-85953-651-3) Childs Play.
— Seirff Y Swltan. 1999. pap. text 3.99 (0-85953-690-4) Childs Play.
Child's Play Staff. Elderly People: Who Cares about Them. (J). 1996. lib. bdg. 11.95 (0-85953-869-9) Childs Play.
Childs Play Staff. Fruit Salad Game: Compare & Count, Match & Measure. (J). 1998. pap. 14.99 (0-85953-019-1) Childs Play.
Child's Play Staff. Law & Order: Who Cares about Them. (J). 1996. lib. bdg. 11.95 (0-85953-879-6) Childs Play.
Childs Play Staff. Plush Toy-Scaredy Kittens. 1995. 24.99 (0-85953-410-3) Childs Play.
Child's Play Staff. Race & Colour: Who Cares about Them. (J). 1996. lib. bdg. 11.95 (0-85953-874-5) Childs Play.
— Special People: Who Cares about Them. (J). 1996. lib. bdg. 11.95 (0-85953-884-2) Childs Play.
***Childs, Rob.** Big Chance. 2000. pap. 6.95 (0-552-52824-2, Pub. by Transworld Publishers Ltd) Trafalgar.
— Big Freeze. 2000. pap. 5.95 (0-552-52967-2, Pub. by Transworld Publishers Ltd) Trafalgar.
— The Big Game. 2000. pap. 6.95 (0-552-52804-8, Pub. by Transworld Publishers Ltd) Trafalgar.
Childs, S. Terry & De Maret, Pierre. Memory: Luba Art & the Making of History. Roberts, Mary N. & Roberts, Allen F., eds. LC 93-80699. (Illus.). 256p. 1996. pap. write for info. (0-945802-14-5) Museum African.
Childs, Sharon G. & Baird-Holmes, Sue. Guidelines for Orthopaedic Nursing: Adult Trauma. (Illus.). 40p. 1998. pap. 25.00 (1-892665-01-8) Natl Assn Ortho Nurse.
***Childs, Sharon G., et al.** The Upper Extremity: Traumatic Injuries & Conditions. vi, 114p. 1999. pap. 55.00 (1-892665-02-6) Natl Assn Ortho Nurse.
Childs, Stacy J. Laser-Assisted Transurethral Resection of the Prostate. LC 93-25355. (Illus.). 96p. 1993. 25.00 (0-683-01540-0) Lppncott W & W.
Childs, Sylvia, jt. auth. see Childs, Gilbert.
Childs, Timothy W. Italo-Turkish Diplomacy & the War over Libya 1911-1912. (Social, Economic & Political Studies of the Middle East: Vol. 42). (Illus.). xviii, 271p. 1990. 100.00 (90-04-09025-8) Brill Academic Pubs.
Childs, W. H. Physical Constants. 9th ed. 1972. pap. 7.95 (0-412-21050-9, NO. 6057) Chapman & Hall.
Childs, W. V. & Fuchigami, T., eds. Electrochemistry in the Preparation of Fluorine & Its Compounds. LC 97-211289. (Proceedings Ser.: Vol. 97-15). 222p. 1997. 46.00 (1-56677-142-0) Electrochem Soc.
Childs, William M. American Donated Books Abroad: A Guide to Distributing Organizations. 67p. (Orig.). 1989. pap. 5.95 (1-877965-00-6) AIBDC.
Childs, William M. & McNeil, Donald E., eds. American Books Abroad: Toward a National Policy. LC 85-17540. 309p. 1986. 35.00 (0-916882-05-5) Heldref Pubns.
Childs, William R. Trucking & the Public Interest: The Emergence of Federal Regulation, 1914-1940. LC 85-5315. 269p. 1985. pap. 83.40 (0-608-05191-8, 206572800001) Bks Demand.
Chiles, Caroline & Putman, Charles E. Pulmonary & Cardiac Imaging. LC 97-722. (Lung Biology in Health & Disease Ser.: Vol. 103). (Illus.). 680p. 1997. text 215.00 (0-8247-9743-4) Dekker.
Chiles, Chester L. Beyond Belief: The Weltanschauung of a Born-Again Heretic. LC 91-60978. 1992. 18.95 (0-87212-249-2) Libra.
Chiles, H. C. When Trouble Comes. LC 97-8992. 80p. 1997. reprint ed. 12.95 (1-57736-038-9) Providence Hse.
Chiles, Hampton. The American Indian: Bronze Sculpture by Griffin. (Illus.). 1997. pap. 35.00 (0-9661568-0-3) H Chiles.
***Chiles, James.** Master of Diaster. 2000. 27.00 (0-06-662081-3); pap. 16.00 (0-06-662082-1) HarpC.
Chiles, Jean-Paul & Delfiner, Pierre. Geostatistics: Modeling Spatial Uncertainty. LC 98-3599. (Probability & Statistics Ser.). 695p. 1999. 125.00 (0-471-08315-1) Wiley.
Chiles, L. William, jt. auth. see Knitter, Harry.
Chiles, Nick, jt. auth. see Millner, Denene.
Chiles, Paul N. The Puerto Rican Press Reaction to the United States, 1888-1898. LC 74-14225. (Puerto Rican Experience Ser.). 124p. 1975. reprint ed. 13.95 (0-405-06215-X) Ayer.
Chiles, Rhea, ed. see Gephardt, Dennis & Bullard, Lacy.
Chiles, Robert E. Theological Transition in American Methodism, 1790-1935. LC 83-16666. 238p. 1983. reprint ed. pap. text 22.00 (0-8191-3551-8) U Pr of Amer.
Chiles, Robert E., ed. see Wesley, John.
Chiles, V. & Jenkinson, D., eds. Laser Metrology & Machine Performance IV. LC 99-63949. (Lamdamap Ser.: Vol. 4). 500p. 1999. 245.00 (1-85312-661-6, 6616, Pub. by WIT Pr) Computational Mech MA.
Chiles, Vic, et al. Principles of Engineering Manufacturing. 3rd ed. 637p. 1996. pap. text 59.95 (0-470-23558-6) Halsted Pr.
Chiles, Webb. A Single Wave: Stories of Storms & Survival. LC 99-10828. (Illus.). 224p. 1999. 22.95 (1-57409-072-0) Sheridan.
Chiligarian, G. V., jt. ed. see Wolf, K. H.
Chilingar, George V., et al. Oil & Gas Production from Carbonate Rocks. LC 70-153417. 108p. 1972. write for info. (0-444-00099-2) Elsevier.
***Chilingar, George V., et al.** Strategies for Oil & Gas Exploration. LC 99-11043. 323p. 1999. 75.00 (0-88415-949-3) Gulf Pub.
Chilingarian, G. V., et al, eds. Carbonate Reservoir Characterization: A Geologic-Engineering Analysis. (Developments in Petroleum Science Ser: 44). 1010p. 1996. 345.00 (0-444-82103-1) Elsevier.
— Surface Operations in Petroleum Production, Vol. II. (Developments in Petroleum Science Ser.: No. 19B). xx,562p. 1989. 270.50 (0-444-42677-9) Elsevier.
Chilingarian, G. V., et al. Carbonate Reservoir Characterization: A Geologic-Engineering Analysis, Pt. I. (Developments in Petroleum Science Ser.: Vol. 30). xviii,640p. 1992. 260.50 (0-444-88849-7) Elsevier.
Chilingarian, G. V., jt. auth. see Rahman, S. S.
Chilingarian, G. V., jt. auth. see Wolf, K. H.
Chilingarian, G. V., jt. ed. see Yen, T. F.
Chilingarian, George V., jt. ed. see Eremenko, N. A.
Chilingerian, Jon A., ed. see Institute of Medicine Staff.
Chilkovsky, Nadia. American Bandstand Dances in Labanotation. (Illus.). 24p. 1969. pap. text 9.95 (0-932582-68-0) Dance Notation.
— Short Modern Dances in Labanotation. (Illus.). 35p. 1957. pap. text 10.00 (0-932582-67-2, Pub. by Dance Notation) Princeton Bk Co.
— Three R's for Dancing, Vol. II. 32p. 1956. pap. text 9.95 (0-932582-61-3) Dance Notation.
— Three R's for Dancing, Vol. III. (Illus.). 32p. 1961. pap. text 9.95 (0-932582-62-1) Dance Notation.
Chill, Abraham. The Minhagim: The Customs & Ceremonies of Judaism, Their Origins & Rationale. 6th ed. LC 78-62153. (Illus.). 339p. 1980. 24.95 (0-87203-076-8); pap. 17.50 (0-87203-077-6) Hermon.
— The Sidrot. 102p. 1992. 12.95 (965-229-012-2, Pub. by Gefen Pub Hse) Gefen Bks.
Chill, Abraham, tr. & intro. see Abrabanel, Isaac.
Chill, Paul & Brooks, Hollace P. Jones vs. Kids R'Ours. 80p. 1995. pap. 22.95 (1-55681-458-5) Natl Inst Trial Ad.
Chilla, R., ed. Sialadenosis & Sialadenitis. (Advances in OtoRhinoLaryngology Ser.: Vol. 26). (Illus.). viii, 252p. 1981. 137.50 (3-8055-1669-X) S Karger.
Chilletti, Barb, ed. see Smith, Brian S.
***Chillicothe Historical Society Staff.** Around Chillicothe, Illinois. (Images of America Ser.). (Illus.). 128p. 2000. pap. 18.99 (0-7385-0725-3) Arcadia Publng.
Chillicothe Historical Society Staff. The History of Chillicothe, Illinois, Vol. 3. 3rd unabridged ed. (Illus.). 254p. 1995. pap. write for info. (1-889849-03-0) Riverbeach Pub.
***Chillida, Eduardo.** Chillida: 1948-1998. (Illus.). 374p. 2000. 54.95 (84-8003-112-3) Dist Art Pubs.
— Eduardo Chillida: Opus P. III: Catalogo Completo de la Obra Grafica. (SPA.). 1999. 150.00 (3-931876-03-9) Koelen OHG.
***Chillington, Carol Rutter.** Documents of the Rose Playhouse. 2nd ed. 1999. pap. 29.95 (0-7190-5801-5, Pub. by Manchester Univ Pr) St Martin.
Chillingworth, D., tr. see Demazure, Michel.
Chillingworth, William. Works of William Chillingworth, 3 vols. reprint ed. lib. bdg. 255.00 (0-404-01570-0) AMS Pr.
Chilly Collective Staff, ed. Breaking Anonymity: The Chilly Climate for Women Faculty. x, 390p. (C). 1995. pap. 24.95 (0-88920-245-1) W Laurier U Pr.
Chilman, Anne M. & Thomas, Margaret, eds. Understanding Nursing Care. 3rd ed. LC 85-24653. (Illus.). 681p. (Orig.). 1987. pap. text 43.00 (0-443-03040-5) Church.
Chilman, Catherine S., et al, eds. Chronic Illness & Disability. LC 89-104935. (Families in Trouble Ser.: No. 2). (Illus.). 288p. 1988. reprint ed. pap. 89.30 (0-608-01099-5, 205940800001) Bks Demand.
— Employment & Economic Problems. LC 89-134584. (Families in Trouble Ser.: No. 1). (Illus.). 269p. 1988. reprint ed. pap. 83.40 (0-608-01128-2, 205942200001) Bks Demand.
— Variant Family Forms. LC 89-111125. (Families in Trouble Ser.: Vol. 5). 336p. 1988. reprint ed. pap. 104.20 (0-608-01713-2, 206236800003) Bks Demand.
***Chilo, V.** Life Threatening Emergencies in Dentistry. (Illus.). 188p. 1999. text 40.00 (88-299-0264-9, Pub. by Piccin Nuova) Gordon & Breach.
Chilo, V., et al. Life Threatening Emergencies in Dentistry. 188p. 1988. text 40.00 (1-57235-015-6) Piccin Nuova.
Chilsen, Liz & Rampton, Sheldon. Friends in Deed: The Story of U. S. - Nicaragua Sister Cities. LC 88-17161. (Illus.). 180p. (Orig.). 1988. pap. 25.00 (0-9620731-0-5) WCCN.
***Chilson, Adam.** Rifts Deceptions Web. Marciniszyn, Alex et al, eds. (Rifts Novel Ser.: Vol. 2). 416p. (YA). (gr. 12 up). 1999. pap. 7.95 (1-57457-029-3) Palladium Bks.
— Rifts Sonic Boom. Marciniszyn, Alex et al, eds. (Rifts Novel Ser.). (Illus.). 416p. (YA). (gr. 8 up). 1999. pap. 7.95 (1-57457-026-9, 301) Palladium Bks.
***Chilson, Dave.** Dave Chilson's Fisherman's Journal. (Illus.). 80p. 2000. pap. 11.95 (0-9700693-1-6) D Chilson.
Chilson, Herman, jt. auth. see Johnson, Norma.
Chilson, Kathleen, ed. see Bourdon, David, et al.
Chilson, Kathleen G., ed. see Perlman, Meg & Dean, Kevin.
Chilson, Kathleen G., ed. see Sheppard, Ileen.
Chilson, Kathryn E., ed. see Jarrell, Howard R.
Chilson, Peter. Riding the Demon: On the Road in West Africa. LC 98-23609. 216p. 1999. 24.95 (0-8203-2036-6) U of Ga Pr.
Chilson, Richard W. All Will Be Well: Based on the Classic Spirituality of Julian of Norwich. LC 95-77233. (Thirty Days with a Great Spiritual Teacher Ser.). 216p. 1995. pap. 7.95 (0-87793-563-7) Ave Maria.
— Catholic Christianity: A Guide to the Way, the Truth, & the Life. LC 87-7028. 576p. 1987. pap. 14.95 (0-8091-2878-0) Paulist Pr.
***Chilson, Richard W.** Evangelization Homily Hints: A Resource for Catholic Preachers. LC 99-58997. 208p. 2000. pap. 16.95 (0-8091-3932-4) Paulist Pr.
Chilson, Richard W. Faith of Catholics: An Introduction. rev. ed. LC 72-81229. 320p. 1975. pap. 4.95 (0-8091-1873-4) Paulist Pr.
— God Awaits You: Based on the Classic Spirituality of Meister Eckhart. LC 95-80888. (Thirty Days with a Great Spiritual Teacher Ser.). 216p. (Orig.). 1996. pap. 6.95 (0-87793-572-6) Ave Maria.
— You Shall Not Want: A Spiritual Journey Based on the Psalms. LC 95-80889. (Thirty Days with a Great Spiritual Teacher Ser.). 216p. (Orig.). 1996. pap. 7.95 (0-87793-571-8) Ave Maria.
Chilson, Rob. Black As Blood. 1998. per. 5.99 (0-671-87883-2) S&S Trade.
Chilson, Robert. Men Like Rats. 224p. (Orig.). 1989. mass mkt. 3.95 (0-445-20763-9, Pub. by Warner Bks) Little.
— Rounded with Sleep. 1990. mass mkt. 3.95 (0-445-21026-5, Pub. by Warner Bks) Little.
Chilson, Steve. Fumbling in a Greasy Till. Lammers, Laura, ed. 44p. 1998. pap. 14.99 (1-893231-03-8) Poet Born.
Chilstrom, E. Corinne. Andrew, You Died too Soon: A Family Experience of Grieving & Living Again. LC 93-28083. 144p. 1993. pap. 9.99 (0-8066-2684-4, 9-2684) Augsburg Fortress.
Chilstrom, Ken, ed. & frwd. see Wright Stuff Pilots & Engineers Staff.
***Chiltern Society Staff.** Goring & Mapledurham. 1999. pap. 2.95 (0-7478-0404-4) Shire Pubns.
Chiltern Society Staff. Hughenden Valley & Great Missenden. 1999. write for info. (0-7478-0252-1) Shire Pubns.
Chiltick, William, tr. see Nurbakhsh, Javad.
***Chilton.** Acura 1994-98. (C). 2000. pap. 22.95 (0-8019-9094-7) Thomson Learn.
— Auto Service Manual: Domestic Cars 1997-2001. (C). 2000. pap. 45.00 (0-8019-9306-7) NP-Chilton.
— B & S 4-Stroke Horizon Crankshaft from 1950. (C). 1998. pap. 24.95 (0-9637661-0-4) Thomson Learn.
— B & S 4 Stroke Overhead Valve from 1988. (C). 1998. pap. 24.95 (0-9637661-2-0) Thomson Learn.
— Bonding/Murcury. 1999. 211.95 (0-7668-7524-5) Delmar.
— The Complete Trailer Manual. (Porter Manuals Ser.). (C). 1998. pap. 26.25 (1-899238-21-2, Pub. by Porter Pub) Nichols Pub.
— Easy Car Care/Quaker State. (C). 1994. pap. 17.25 (0-8019-8619-2) Thomson Learn.
— Faces & Forces. (C). 1982. text. write for info. (0-8019-7287-6) Thomson Learn.
— Ford Mercury Villager/Nissan Quest 1997-2000. (C). 2000. pap. 22.95 (0-8019-9324-5) NP-Chilton.
— Ford Probe 1989-1998. (C). 2000. pap. 17.25 (0-8019-8965-5) Thomson Learn.
— General Motors-Metro/Spirit 1985-99. (Illus.). 352p. (C). 2000. pap. 17.25 (0-8019-8958-2) NP-Chilton.
— General Motors-Prizm/Nova 1985-98. (C). 2000. pap. 17.25 (0-8019-8962-0) Thomson Learn.
— GM Bonneville/Eighty Eight/LeSabre 86-99. LC 98-74835. (C). 1999. pap. 22.95 (0-8019-8963-9) Thomson Learn.
— GM Deville/Fleetwood/Eldorado/Seville 1990-98. (C). 2000. pap. 22.95 (0-8019-9104-8) Thomson Learn.
— GM Lumina/Silhouette/Trans/Ventura 1990-00. (C). 2000. pap. 22.95 (0-8019-9109-9) Thomson Learn.
— GM Malibu/Cutlass 1997-2000. (C). 2000. pap. 22.95 (0-8019-9320-2) NP-Chilton.
— Groundwater in the Urban Environment. 356p. 1999. pap. 30.00 (90-5809-120-1) Ashgate Pub Co.
Chilton. Groundwater in the Urban Environment. 416p. 1997. text. write for info. (0-419-21830-0, E & FN Spon) Routledge.
***Chilton.** Groundwater in the Urban Environment, Vol. 1. LC 99-496406. 700p. 1998. 78.00 (90-5410-923-8) Ashgate Pub Co.
— Honda Accord/Prelude 1996-99. (C). 2000. pap. 22.95 (0-8019-9118-8) Thomson Learn.
— Honda Civic/Del Sol 1996-99. (C). 2000. pap. 22.95 (0-8019-9116-1) Thomson Learn.
— Import Car: Auto Service Manual 1997-2001. (C). 2000. pap. 45.00 (0-8019-9307-5) NP-Chilton.
— Isuzu Cars & Trucks: 1981-1991. (C). 2000. pap. 17.25 (0-8019-9120-X) Thomson Learn.
— Johnson/Evinrude Outboards 1995-2000. (C). 2000. pap. 34.95 (0-89330-052-7) NP-Chilton.
— Labor Guide Manual 1982-2001. (C). 2000. pap. 93.75 (0-8019-9337-7) NP-Chilton.
Chilton. Language & the Nuclear Arms Debate. (C). 1985. text. write for info. (0-86187-524-9) St Martin.
***Chilton.** Mercruiser Stern Drives 1992-2000. (C). 2000. pap. 34.95 (0-89330-053-5) NP-Chilton.
Chilton. Nuclear Pharmacy. 2nd ed. 244p. 1998. text 45.00 (0-397-55400-1) Lppncott W & W.
— Space Grid Structures. LC 99-43760. 180p. 2000. text 69.95 (0-7506-3275-5) Buttrwrth-Heinemann.
***Chilton.** Toyota Camry/Avalon 1997-2000. (C). 2000. pap. 22.95 (0-8019-9326-1) NP-Chilton.
— Truck/Van/Suv Service Manual: Domestic/Import 1997-2001. (C). 2000. pap. 45.00 (0-8019-9308-3) NP-Chilton.
— Vw Golf/Jetta/Cabriolet 1990- 1999. (C). 2000. pap. 22.95 (0-8019-9322-9) NP-Chilton.
Chilton, jt. auth. see Collins, Gary.
Chilton, Arthur B., et al. Engineering Compendium on Radiation Shielding, Vols. 1 & 3. Blizard, E. P. et al, eds. Incl. Shielding Fundamentals & Methods. LC 68-19816. (Illus.). xii, 537p. 1968. 343.95 (0-387-04080-3); LC 68-19816. (Illus.). write for info. (0-318-55784-3) Spr-Verlag.
***Chilton Automotive Editorial Staff.** Absolute Beginners: Step-by-Step Service Guide. (Porter Manuals Ser.). (C). 1998. pap. 26.25 (1-899238-05-0, Pub. by Porter Pub) Nichols Pub.
Chilton Automotive Editorial Staff. Acura 1986-93. (Illus.). 880p. (C). 1994. pap. 22.95 (0-8019-8426-2) Thomson Learn.
— Air Conditioning & Heating Manual, 1991-93. 2304p. 1993. text 97.00 (0-8019-8444-0) Nichols Pub.
— Air Conditioning Repair Manual, 1992-95, Vol. 1. 1536p. 1995. text 97.00 (0-8019-8693-1) Nichols Pub.
— AMC, 1975-1987: Coupes, Sedans & Wagons. (New Total Car Care Ser.). 456p. (C). 1997. pap. text 22.95 (0-8019-9075-0) Thomson Learn.
— Auto Detailing. (New Total Service Ser.). (C). 1992. pap. text 22.95 (0-8019-8394-0) Thomson Learn.

C

***Chilton Automotive Editorial Staff.** Auto-Electrics: DIY Service Manual. (Porter Manuals Ser.). (C). 1998. pap. text 26.25 (1-899238-18-2, Pub. by Porter Pub) Nichols Pub.

Chilton Automotive Editorial Staff. Auto Repair Manual, 1992-96. annuals (Illus.). 1648p. 1995. 28.95 (0-8019-7916-1) Nichols Pub.

— Auto Repair Manual, 1990-94. 1632p. 1993. text 28.95 (0-8019-7912-9) Nichols Pub.

— Auto Repair Manual 1991-95. 1648p. 1994. text 28.95 (0-8019-7915-3) Nichols Pub.

— Auto Repair Manual, 1994-1998. (C). 1998. 59.95 (0-8019-7922-6) Thomson Learn.

— Auto Service Manual. 2496p. 1994. text 100.00 (0-8019-8569-2) Nichols Pub.

— Auto Service Manual 1987-91. (SPA.). 1344p. 1992. 47.00 (0-8019-8326-6) Nichols Pub.

— Auto Service Manual 1989-93. 2304p. 1992. text 95.00 (0-8019-8290-1) Nichols Pub.

— Auto Service Manual, 1990-94. 2304p. 1993. text 100.00 (0-8019-8470-X) Nichols Pub.

— Automatic Transmissions & Transaxles: Diagnosis & Repair. (New Total Service Ser.). (C). 1999. pap. text 22.95 (0-8019-8944-2) Thomson Learn.

— BMW 1970-1988 Repair & Tune-up Guide. LC 88-43185. (Illus.). 480p. (C). 1989. pap. text 16.95 (0-8019-7941-2) Thomson Learn.

— BMW 1970-88. (Total Car Care Ser.). 720p. (C). 1996. pap. 22.95 (0-8019-8789-X) Thomson Learn.

— BMW-318/325/M3, 1989-1998. (Chilton's Total Car Care Ser.). (C). 2000. pap. text 22.95 (0-8019-9096-3) Thomson Learn.

— BMW, 318/325/M3/525/M5 1989-93. (Total Car Care Ser.). (Illus.). 544p. (C). 1994. pap. 22.95 (0-8019-8427-0) Thomson Learn.

— Brake System: Diagnosis & Repair. (New Total Service Ser.). 300p. (C). 1998. pap. text 22.95 (0-8019-8945-0) Thomson Learn.

***Chilton Automotive Editorial Staff.** Brakes, 1990-2000. (Illus.). 650p. (C). 2000. pap. 34.95 (0-8019-9312-1) NP-Chilton.

Chilton Automotive Editorial Staff. Buick-Olds Pontiac, 1975-90 Repair & Tune-up Guide. (Illus.). 464p. (C). 1990. pap. text 16.95 (0-8019-8039-9) Thomson Learn.

— Cadillac FWD, 1990-93. (Total Car Care Ser.). (Illus.). 720p. (C). 1994. pap. 22.95 (0-8019-8420-3) Thomson Learn.

— Cadillac 1967-89 Repair & Tune-up Guide. LC 88-43187. (Illus.). 512p. (C). 1989. pap. text 16.95 (0-8019-7943-9) Thomson Learn.

— Camaro: 1967-1981. LC 78-7168. (Illus.). 368p. (C). 1981. pap. 17.95 (0-8019-7045-8) Thomson Learn.

***Chilton Automotive Editorial Staff.** Caravan: Owner's Manual & Service Guide. (Porter Manuals Ser.). (Illus.). 128p. (C). 1998. pap. 24.95 (1-899238-04-2, Pub. by Porter Pub) Nichols Pub.

Chilton Automotive Editorial Staff. Cascade Emission Control Application Guide, 1966-1994. 672p. 1994. pap. 35.00 (0-8019-8550-1) Nichols Pub.

— Cascade Emission Control Application Guide, 1966-1995. 912p. 1995. pap. 45.00 (0-8019-8692-3) Nichols Pub.

— Cavalier - Skyhawk - Cimarron - Frenza - Sunbird 82-92. (Chilton's Total Car Care). (Illus.). 371p. (C). 1992. pap. 16.95 (0-8019-8366-5) Thomson Learn.

— Chassis Electronic Service Manual, European Cars, 1990-93. 1696p. 1993. text 97.00 (0-8019-8468-8) Nichols Pub.

— Chassis Electronics Service Manual, Asian Cars & Trucks, A-M, 1991-93. 1776p. 1993. text 97.00 (0-8019-8449-1) Nichols Pub.

— Chassis Electronics Service Manual, Asian Cars & Trucks, N-Z, 1991-93. 2016p. 1993. text 97.00 (0-8019-8450-5) Nichols Pub.

— Chassis Electronics Service Manual, Chrysler, 1991-93. 2112p. 1993. pap. text 97.00 (0-8019-8440-8) Nichols Pub.

— Chassis Electronics Service Manual, Ford, 1991-93. 1376p. 1993. text 97.00 (0-8019-8439-4) Nichols Pub.

— Chassis Electronics, 1991-93 General Motors. 2304p. 1992. 97.00 (0-8019-8289-8) Nichols Pub.

— Chevrolet Astro - GMC Safari, 1985-90. (Illus.). 624p. 1990. pap. 22.95 (0-8019-8056-9) Nichols Pub.

— Chevrolet Camaro, 1967-81. 496p. (C). 1997. pap. 22.95 (0-8019-9058-0) Thomson Learn.

— Chevrolet Corsica-Beretta, 1988-92. rev. ed. 392p. (C). 1992. pap. 16.95 (0-8019-8300-2) Thomson Learn.

— Chevrolet Corvette, 1963-83. 488p. (C). 1997. pap. 22.95 (0-8019-9071-8) Thomson Learn.

— Chevrolet Engine Overhaul. (Total Service Ser.). 232p. (C). 1996. pap. 22.95 (0-8019-8794-6) Thomson Learn.

— Chevy - GMC Vans, 1987-90. 368p. 1991. pap. 16.95 (0-8019-8216-2) Nichols Pub.

— Chevy Astro - GMC Safari, 1985-90. 448p. (C). 1991. pap. 16.95 (0-8019-8217-0) Thomson Learn.

— Chevy Camaro, 1982-92. rev. ed. 408p. (C). 1992. pap. 16.95 (0-8019-8306-1) Thomson Learn.

— Chevy Lumina, Pontiac Grand Prix, Olds Cutlass Supreme, Buick Regal 1988-92. rev. ed. 320p. (C). 1992. pap. 17.95 (0-8019-8304-5) Thomson Learn.

— Chevy Two & Nova, 1962 to 1979. LC 78-20253. (Chilton's Repair & Tune-up Guides Ser.). (Illus.). 296p. (C). 1979. pap. 17.95 (0-8019-6841-0, 6841) Thomson Learn.

— Chilton Chrysler Concord, Intrepid, LHS, New Yorker & Vision, 1993-1996. (Illus.). 536p. (C). 1997. pap. text 22.95 (0-8019-8817-9) Thomson Learn.

— Chilton Chrysler, Dodge & Plymouth Full-Size Trucks, 1989-1996. rev. ed. (Illus.). 744p. (C). 1999. pap. text 22.95 (0-8019-8847-0) Thomson Learn.

— Chilton Chrysler-Dodge-Plymouth 81-88. 704p. 1989. pap. 25.95 (0-8019-8029-1) Nichols Pub.

— Chilton Ford Aerostar, 1985-1996. rev. ed. (Illus.). 664p. (C). 1996. pap. text 22.95 (0-8019-8824-1) Thomson Learn.

— Chilton Ford Full-Size Trucks, 1987-1996. rev. ed. (Total Car Care Ser.). (Illus.). 848p. (C). 1997. pap. text 22.95 (0-8019-8828-4) Thomson Learn.

— Chilton Ford Mustang, 1989-1993. rev. ed. (Illus.). 616p. (C). 1996. pap. text 22.95 (0-8019-8815-2) Thomson Learn.

— Chilton General Motors Chevrolet S10, GMAC S15 Pick-Ups, 1982-1993. rev. ed. (Illus.). 960p. (C). 1999. pap. text 22.95 (0-8019-8844-6) Thomson Learn.

— Chilton General Motors Chevy & GMC Full-Size Trucks, 1988-96. rev. ed. (Illus.). 808p. 1996. pap. text 22.95 (0-8019-8798-9) Nichols Pub.

— Chilton Guide to Fuel Injection, Ford-Chrys-Jeep-1988-90. 672p. 1989. pap. 19.95 (0-8019-8024-0) Nichols Pub.

— Chilton Lumina, Monte Carlo, Grand Prix, Cutlass & Supreme Regal, 1988-1996. rev. ed. (Illus.). 720p. (C). 1996. pap. text 22.95 (0-8019-8800-4) Thomson Learn.

— Chilton Nissan Sentra & Pulsar, 1982-1996. rev. ed. (Illus.). 736p. (C). 1997. pap. text 22.95 (0-8019-8816-0) Thomson Learn.

— Chilton's Air Conditioning & Heating Service Manual 1986-88. LC 88-43177. (Motor Age Professional Mechanics Edition Ser.). (Illus.). 1488p. 1989. text 97.00 (0-8019-7963-3) Nichols Pub.

***Chilton Automotive Editorial Staff.** Chilton's Auto Repair Manual: 1996-2000, Shop Ed. (C). 1999. 79.95 (0-8019-9300-8, Pub. by NP-Chilton) Natl Bk Netwk.

Chilton Automotive Editorial Staff. Chilton's Auto Repair Manual (CARM) 1980-87. LC 76-648878. (Illus.). 1344p. (C). 1987. 34.95 (0-8019-7670-7) Thomson Learn.

— Chilton's Auto Repair Manual, 1940-1953. LC 54-17274. (Collector's Edition Manual Ser.). (Illus.). 752p. (C). 1971. reprint ed. 34.95 (0-8019-5631-5) Thomson Learn.

— Chilton's Auto Repair Manual, 1954-1963. LC 54-17274. 1141p. reprint ed. pap. 200.00 (0-608-17215-4, 202702100053) Bks Demand.

— Chilton's Auto Repair Manual, 1964-1971. LC 54-17274. (Collector's Edition Manual Ser.). (Illus.). 1536p. (C). 1974. 34.95 (0-8019-5974-8) Thomson Learn.

— Chilton's Auto Repair Manual, 1964-1971. LC 54-17274. 1542p. reprint ed. pap. 200.00 (0-608-18707-0, 202702200053) Bks Demand.

— Chilton's Auto Repair Manual, 1982-1989. LC 76-648878. (Illus.). 1536p. (C). 1989. 30.00 (0-8019-7835-1) Thomson Learn.

— Chilton's Auto Repair Manual 1987-1991. (SPA.). 1344p. (C). 1992. 39.95 (0-8019-8138-7) Thomson Learn.

— Chilton's Auto Repair Manual, 1993-1997. (Illus.). 2064p. (C). 1996. 39.95 (0-8019-7919-6) Thomson Learn.

— Chilton's Auto Service Manual: 1987-1991 Domestic Cars, Motor-Age Professional Mechanic's Edition. 2112p. 1990. text 95.00 (0-8019-8074-7) Nichols Pub.

— Chilton's Auto Service Manual, 1983-1987. LC 82-72944. 1856p. 1987. pap. 97.00 (0-8019-7690-1) Nichols Pub.

— Chilton's Auto Service Manual, 1985-1989: Motor Age Professional Mechanic's Edition. LC 82-72944. (Illus.). 1856p. 1988. text 95.00 (0-8019-7854-8) Nichols Pub.

— Chilton's Auto Service Manual, 1986-1990: Motor-Age Professional Mechanic's Edition. LC 82-72944. (Illus.). 1920p. 1989. text 95.00 (0-8019-7955-2) Nichols Pub.

— Chilton's Automatic Transmission Repair Manual, 1984-1988: Import Cars & Trucks: Motor-Age Professional Mechanic's Edition. LC 88-43196. (Illus.). 1920p. 1989. text 97.00 (0-8019-7960-9) Nichols Pub.

— Chilton's Automatic Transmission Service Manual, 1980-1984. LC 83-45327. 1472p. 1984. pap. 97.00 (0-8019-7390-2) Nichols Pub.

— Chilton's Automatic Transmission Service Manual, 1984-1988: Domestic Cars & Trucks. LC 88-43180. (Motor Age Professional Mechanics Edition Ser.). (Illus.). 1920p. 1989. pap. text 97.00 (0-8019-7959-5) Nichols Pub.

— Chilton's Buick Century & Regal, 1975-1987. LC 87-47943. 368p. (Orig.). (C). 1988. pap. 17.95 (0-8019-7823-8) Thomson Learn.

— Chilton's Chassis Electronic & Power Accessory Service Manual 1982-86: Motor-Age Professional Mechanic's Edition. LC 85-43611. 1536p. 1986. 97.00 (0-8019-7726-6) Nichols Pub.

— Chilton's Chassis Electronics & Power Accessories Service Manual 1987-89: Motor-Age Professional Mechanic's Edition. LC 87-47920. (Illus.). 1536p. 1988. text 97.00 (0-8019-7857-2) Nichols Pub.

— Chilton's Chevette & Pontiac T1000 1976-1988. LC 87-47930. (Illus.). 304p. (Orig.). (C). 1989. pap. 17.95 (0-8019-7845-9) Thomson Learn.

— Chilton's Chevrolet-GMC Pick-Ups & Suburban 1970-87. LC 87-47947. 480p. (Orig.). (C). 1988. pap. 17.95 (0-8019-7828-9) Thomson Learn.

— Chilton's Chevrolet Mid-Size 1964-88. LC 87-47938. 488p. (Orig.). (C). 1988. pap. 16.95 (0-8019-7824-6) Thomson Learn.

— Chilton's Chevrolet Repair Manual 1980-1987. LC 86-47792. (Update Ser.). (Illus.). 640p. 1987. pap. 19.95 (0-8019-7772-X) Nichols Pub.

— Chilton's Corvette 1963-83. LC 85-47981. 320p. (Orig.). (C). 1986. pap. 17.95 (0-8019-7681-2) Thomson Learn.

— Chilton's Datsun-Nissan, Maxima-Datsun 200SX 510, 610, 710, 810 1973-1989. LC 87-47922. (Illus.). 488p. (Orig.). (C). 1989. pap. 17.95 (0-8019-7852-1) Thomson Learn.

— Chilton's Datsun-Nissan Z & ZX 1970-1988. LC 87-47924. (Illus.). 384p. (Orig.). (C). 1989. pap. 16.95 (0-8019-7851-3) Thomson Learn.

— Chilton's Dodge-Plymouth Trucks 1967-1988. LC 87-47931. (Illus.). 672p. (Orig.). (C). 1989. pap. 16.95 (0-8019-7844-0) Thomson Learn.

— Chilton's Dodge, 1968-1977. LC 77-71635. (Chilton's Repair & Tune-up Guides Ser.). (Illus.). 280p. 1977. pap. 17.95 (0-8019-6554-3) Nichols Pub.

— Chilton's Firebird, 1982-90 Repair & Tuneup Guide. rev. ed. 400p. 1990. pap. 16.95 (0-8019-8060-7) Nichols Pub.

— Chilton's for Barracuda & Challenger 1965-1972. LC 72-7036. (Illus.). 232p. 1972. pap. 17.95 (0-8019-5807-5) Nichols Pub.

— Chilton's Ford Pickups, 1965-1986. LC 85-47964. 416p. (Orig.). (C). 1986. pap. 16.95 (0-8019-7662-6) Thomson Learn.

— Chilton's Ford Vans, 1961-1988. LC 87-47934. 672p. (C). 1988. pap. 17.95 (0-8019-7841-6) Thomson Learn.

— Chilton's Granada-Monarch, 1975-1982. LC 82-72933. 264p. 1983. pap. 17.95 (0-8019-7311-2) Nichols Pub.

— Chilton's Guide to Air Conditioning Service & Repair, 1982-1985. LC 84-45472. (Illus.). 560p. (Orig.). (C). 1985. pap. 22.98 (0-8019-7580-8) Thomson Learn.

— Chilton's Guide to Automatic Transmission Repair, 1984-1989 Import Cars & Trucks. 800p. (C). 1990. pap. 25.95 (0-8019-8053-4) Thomson Learn.

— Chilton's Guide to Brakes, Steering & Suspension,1980-87: Domestic & Import Cars & Trucks. LC 87-47939. (Illus.). 592p. (Orig.). (C). 1988. pap. 19.95 (0-8019-7819-X) Thomson Learn.

— Chilton's Guide to Electronic Engine Controls & Fuel Injection 1984-88: Import Cars & Trucks. (Illus.). 704p. (Orig.). 1988. pap. 19.95 (0-8019-7818-1) Nichols Pub.

— Chilton's Guide to Electronic Engine Controls, 1984-1988. 704p. 1987. pap. 22.95 (0-8019-7768-1) Nichols Pub.

— Chilton's Guide to Fuel Injection & Carburetors, 1978-1985. LC 83-45323. 416p. 1985. pap. 22.95 (0-8019-7488-7) Nichols Pub.

— Chilton's Honda, 1973-1988. LC 87-47936. 464p. (Orig.). (C). 1989. pap. 16.95 (0-8019-7840-8) Thomson Learn.

— Chilton's Import Car Repair Manual: 1980-87. LC 80-68280. (Illus.). 1488p. (C). 1987. 34.95 (0-8019-7672-3) Thomson Learn.

***Chilton Automotive Editorial Staff.** Chilton's Import Car Repair Manual 1996-2000. LC 87-658187. (Illus.). 1500p. (C). 1999. 79.95 (0-8019-9301-6, Pub. by NP-Chilton) Natl Bk Netwk.

Chilton Automotive Editorial Staff. Chilton's Import Car Repair Manual, 1993-1997. (Illus.). 2080p. (C). 1996. 39.95 (0-8019-7920-X) Thomson Learn.

— Chilton's Labor Guide Manual: 1981-2000. (C). 1999. 169.00 (0-8019-9303-2, Pub. by NP-Chilton) Natl Bk Netwk.

— Chilton's Mercedes-Benz, 1959-1970. LC 70-131236. (Illus.). 288p. 1970. pap. 17.95 (0-8019-6065-7) Nichols Pub.

— Chilton's Minor Auto Body Repair Manual. LC 88-43167. (Illus.). 368p. (C). 1989. pap. 22.95 (0-8019-7898-X) Thomson Learn.

— Chilton's Mustang No. II: 1974-1978, Repair & Tune-up Guide. LC 78-22143. (Repair & Tune-up Guides Ser.). (Illus.). 292p. (C). 1979. pap. 16.95 (0-8019-6812-7) Thomson Learn.

— Chilton's Mustang & Cougar, 1965-1973. LC 83-70992. 240p. (Orig.). (C). 1983. pap. 17.95 (0-8019-7405-4) Thomson Learn.

— Chilton's Mustang-Capri-Merkur, 1979-1988. LC 87-47944. 416p. (Orig.). (C). 1989. pap. 16.95 (0-8019-7825-4) Thomson Learn.

— Chilton's Nissan Sentra, Datsun 1200 & B210, 1973-1988. LC 87-47925. (Illus.). 320p. (C). 1989. pap. 17.95 (0-8019-7850-5) Thomson Learn.

— Chilton's Nissan Stanza-Datsun F-10, 310, 1976-1988. LC 87-47921. (Illus.). 360p. (C). 1989. pap. 17.95 (0-8019-7853-X) Thomson Learn.

— Chilton's Pontiac Mid-Size, 1974-1983. LC 82-72928. 336p. (C). 1983. pap. 17.95 (0-8019-7346-5) Thomson Learn.

— Chilton's Porsche 924 & 928, 1977-1981. LC 87-70328. (Illus.). 232p. 1981. pap. 17.95 (0-8019-7048-2) Nichols Pub.

— Chilton's Repair & Tune-Up Guide: Toyota 2. LC 73-3442. iv, 219p. 1973. write for info. (0-8019-5812-1) NP-Chilton.

— Chilton's Repair & Tune-up Guide - Chevrolet, 1968 to 1983: Bel Air, Biscayne, Brookwood, Caprice. 1983. pap. text. write for info. (0-8019-7313-9) Nichols Pub.

Chilton Automotive Editorial Staff. Chilton's Repair & Tune-up Guide for BSA Thru 1972. (Illus.). 176p. (C). 1973. pap. 6.95 (0-8019-6048-7) Thomson Learn.

— Chilton's Repair & Tune-up Guide for Bultaco, Montesa, & Ossa 1963-1972. (Illus.). (C). 1974. pap. 8.95 (0-8019-5888-1) Thomson Learn.

— Chilton's Repair & Tune-up Guide for Honda 350-360 Twins, 1968-1975. (Illus.). (C). 1975. pap. 6.95 (0-8019-6038-X) Thomson Learn.

Chilton Automotive Editorial Staff. Chilton's Repair & Tune-up Guide, Toyota Land Cruiser. LC 74-32156. iv, 151 p. 1974. 8.95 (0-8019-6275-7) NP-Chilton.

Chilton Automotive Editorial Staff. Chilton's Repair & Tune-Up Guide, Toyota 2. 2nd ed. LC 75-15749. iv, 245p. 1975. write for info. (0-8019-6260-9) NP-Chilton.

Chilton Automotive Editorial Staff. Chilton's Repair & Tune-up, Saab 99: All Models, 1969-1975. LC 75-40448. 232p. reprint ed. pap. 72.00 (0-608-17212-X, 202702000053) Bks Demand.

— Chilton's Saab 900: 1979-1985. LC 84-45477. 176p. (Orig.). (C). 1985. pap. 17.95 (0-8019-7572-7) Thomson Learn.

— Chilton's Spanish Auto Repair Manual 1976-1983. LC 76-648878. (SPA.). 1336p. (C). 1984. 39.95 (0-8019-7476-3) Thomson Learn.

— Chilton's Subaru 1970-1988. LC 87-47945. 446p. (Orig.). (C). 1988. pap. 17.95 (0-8019-7826-2) Thomson Learn.

— Chilton's Toyota Celica-Supra, 1971-1987: Repair & Tune-Up Guide. LC 86-47784. 384p. (C). 1987. pap. 17.95 (0-8019-7763-0) Thomson Learn.

— Chilton's Toyota Corolla - Tercel - Mr2, 1984-90 Rtug. 504p. (C). 1991. pap. 17.95 (0-8019-8061-5) Thomson Learn.

— Chilton's Toyota Corolla, Carina, Tercel, Starlet, 1970-1987. LC 86-47788. 320p. (C). 1987. pap. 16.95 (0-8019-7767-3) Thomson Learn.

— Chilton's Toyota Cressida, Van 1983-1990 Rtug. 488p. (C). 1991. pap. 17.95 (0-8019-8068-2) Thomson Learn.

— Chilton's Toyota Trucks 1970-1988. LC 87-47950. 560p. (Orig.). (C). 1988. pap. 16.95 (0-8019-7831-9) Thomson Learn.

— Chilton's Truck & Van Repair Manual: 1979-86. LC 78-52225. (Illus.). 1440p. (C). 1986. 34.95 (0-8019-7655-3) Thomson Learn.

— Chilton's Truck & Van Repair Manual, 1986-1990. (Illus.). 1536p. (C). 1990. text 34.95 (0-8019-7902-1) Thomson Learn.

— Chilton's Truck & Van Repair Manual, 1993-1997. (Illus.). 2096p. (C). 1996. 39.95 (0-8019-7921-8) Thomson Learn.

— Chilton's Truck & Van Repair Manual 1996-2000. (Chilton's Truck & Van Repair Manual Ser.). (C). 1999. 79.95 (0-8019-9302-4, Pub. by NP-Chilton) Natl Bk Netwk.

— Chilton's Truck & Van Service Repair Manual, 1992-1996. annuals (Illus.). 1408p. 28.95 (0-8019-7918-8) Nichols Pub.

— Chilton's Vacuum Diagram Manual 1980-1986: Domestic Cars & Trucks. LC 87-47941. (Illus.). 480p. (Orig.). 1988. pap. text 22.95 (0-8019-7821-1) Nichols Pub.

— Chilton's Volkswagon, 1949-1971. LC 74-154691. (Illus.). 232p. (C). 1972. reprint ed. pap. 17.95 (0-8019-5796-6) Thomson Learn.

— Chrysler: Ram 50/D50/Arrow, 1979-93. (Total Car Care Ser.). 550p. (C). 1998. pap. 22.95 (0-8019-9089-0) Thomson Learn.

— Chrysler Caravan - Voyager, 1984-95. (Total Car Care Ser.). 640p. (C). 1996. pap. 22.95 (0-8019-8796-2) Thomson Learn.

— Chrysler-Caravan/Voyager/Town & Country 1996-99. (C). 1999. pap. text 22.95 (0-8019-9115-3) Thomson Learn.

— Chrysler-Cirrus/Stratus/Sebring/Avenger/Breeze, 1994-1998. (Chilton's Total Car Care Ser.). (C). 1998. pap. text 22.95 (0-8019-9090-4) Thomson Learn.

— Chrysler Colt/Vista 1990-93. (Total Car Care Ser.). (Illus.). 816p. (C). 1993. pap. 22.95 (0-8019-8418-1) Thomson Learn.

— Chrysler Compact, 1987-95. 448p. pap. 16.95 (0-8019-8678-8) Nichols Pub.

— Chrysler Front Wheel Drive Cars: 4 Cylinder 1981-95. (Total Car Care Ser.). 784p. (C). 1997. pap. 22.95 (0-8019-8673-7) Thomson Learn.

— Chrysler Front Wheel Drive Cars, 6 Cylinder, 1981-1995. LC 96-84182. (Illus.). 816p. (C). 1996. pap. 22.95 (0-8019-8672-9) Thomson Learn.

***Chilton Automotive Editorial Staff.** Chrysler-Full Size Trucks 1997-00. (Illus.). 2000. pap. 22.95 (0-8019-9325-3) NP-Chilton.

Chilton Automotive Editorial Staff. Chrysler Full-Size Trucks 1967-1988. LC 94-69445. (Illus.). 608p. (C). 1995. pap. 22.95 (0-8019-8662-1) Thomson Learn.

— Chrysler-Full Size Vans: 1989-98 Covers All U. S. & Canadian Models of Dodge B150, 250, 350, Ram. (Total Car Care Ser.). (C). 1998. pap. text 22.95 (0-8019-8966-3) Thomson Learn.

— Chrysler LWD, 81-92. 432p. (C). 1993. pap. 16.95 (0-8019-8367-3) Thomson Learn.

— Chrysler Mid-Size, 1981-95. 448p. pap. 16.95 (0-8019-8677-X) Nichols Pub.

— Chrysler-Neon, 1995-98: Covers All U. S. & Canadian Models of Dodge & Plymouth Neon. (Total Car Care Ser.). (C). 1998. pap. text 22.95 (0-8019-8971-X) Thomson Learn.

— Chrysler Omni - Horizon - Rampage, 1978-1989. (Total Car Care Ser.). 384p. (C). 1996. pap. 22.95 (0-8019-8787-3) Thomson Learn.

— Chrysler, 1967-1988: Full Size Vans. (Total Car Care Ser.). 688p. (C). 1997. pap. text 22.95 (0-8019-9063-7) Thomson Learn.

— Chrysler, 1976-1980: Aspen & Volare. (New Total Car Care Ser.). 384p. (C). 1997. pap. text 22.95 (0-8019-9082-3) Thomson Learn.

***Chilton Automotive Editorial Staff.** Classic Bike 1940-On: Step-by-Step Service Guide. (Porter Manuals Ser.). (C). 1998. pap. text 26.25 (1-899238-08-5, Pub. by Porter Pub) Nichols Pub.

Chilton Automotive Editorial Staff. Colt-Challenger-Conquest-Vista, 1971-88: Repair & Tune-Up Guide. LC 88-43184. (Illus.). 336p. (C). 1989. pap. text 17.95 (0-8019-7940-4) Thomson Learn.

***Chilton Automotive Editorial Staff.** The Complete Motor Caravan Manual. (Porter Manuals Ser.). (Illus.). 128p. (C). 1998. pap. 24.95 (1-899238-20-4, Pub. by Porter Pub) Nichols Pub.

Chilton Automotive Editorial Staff. Component Locator Manual 1991-93. 736p. 1994. pap. 62.00 (0-8019-8545-5) Nichols Pub.

— Gm-Corsica/Beretta 1988-1996. (Total Car Care Ser.). 550p. (C). 1998. pap. 22.95 (0-8019-8825-X) Thomson Learn.

— Datsun - Nissan Z & ZX 1970-88. LC 96-83966. (Total Car Care Ser.). 536p. (C). 1999. pap. 22.95 (0-8019-8846-2) Thomson Learn.

An Asterisk (*) at the beginning of an entry indicates that the title is appearing for the first time.

***Chilton Automotive Editorial Staff.** Diesel Engines Fault Finding & Diagnostic Manual. (Porter Manuals Ser.). (C). 1998. pap. text 26.25 (*1-899238-26-3*, Pub. by Porter Pub) Nichols Pub.

Chilton Automotive Editorial Staff. Dodge Caravan - Plymouth Voyager 1984-94. 450p. pap. 16.95 (*0-8019-8563-3*) Nichols Pub.

— Dodge Caravan - Plymouth Voyager 1984-94. (Illus.). 576p. 1994. pap. 21.95 (*0-8019-8561-7*) Nichols Pub.

— Dodge Colt/Challenger/Conquest/Vista 1971-89. 566p. (C). 1997. pap. 22.95 (*0-8019-9062-9*) Thomson Learn.

— Domestic & Import Labor Guide, 1982-96. 1800p. text 147.00 (*0-8019-8724-5*) Nichols Pub.

— Domestic Auto Service Manual, 1992-96. 2504p. text 100.00 (*0-8019-8726-1*) Nichols Pub.

— Domestic Labor Guide & Parts Manual, 1992-96. 1632p. text 97.00 (*0-8019-8727-X*) Nichols Pub.

— Domestic Wiring Diagram Manual 1992. 1560p. 1994. pap. 97.00 (*0-8019-8546-3*) Nichols Pub.

— Domestic Wiring, 1991. 1344p. 1993. pap. 97.00 (*0-8019-8442-4*) Nichols Pub.

— Driveability Manual Asian A. M., 1992-94, Vol. A-M. 2304p. 1995. text 112.00 (*0-8019-8551-X*) Nichols Pub.

— Driveability Manual Asian, 1992-94, European. 2304p. text 112.00 (*0-8019-8553-6*) Nichols Pub.

— Driveability Manual Asian, 1992-94, Vol. N-Z. 2304p. 1995. text 112.00 (*0-8019-8552-8*) Nichols Pub.

— Driveability Manual Chrysler 1992-94. 1856p. 1994. text 112.00 (*0-8019-8543-9*) Nichols Pub.

— Driveability Manual Ford 1992-94. 1984p. 1994. text 112.00 (*0-8019-8542-0*) Nichols Pub.

— Easy Car Care. 3rd ed. 672p. 1990. pap. 22.95 (*0-8019-8042-9*) Nichols Pub.

— Easy Car Care. 4th rev. ed. (Illus.). 472p. (C). 1998. pap. 22.95 (*0-8019-8852-7*) Thomson Learn.

— EEC-GM - Saturn Driveability 1992-94. 600p. 1994. pap. write for info. (*0-8019-8597-8*) Nichols Pub.

***Chilton Automotive Editorial Staff.** Electric Cooling Fans, Accessory Drive Belts & Water Pumps, 1990-2000. (Illus.). 356p. 2000. pap. 34.95 (*0-8019-9309-1*) NP-Chilton.

Chilton Automotive Editorial Staff. Engine Code Manual. (Total Service Ser.). 416p. (C). 1999. pap. 22.95 (*0-8019-8851-9*) Thomson Learn.

— Fiat Cinquecento 1993-98. (Porter Manuals Ser.). (Illus.). 128p. (C). 1998. pap. 24.95 (*1-899238-28-X*, Pub. by Porter Pub) Nichols Pub.

— Fiat Panda 1981-94. (Porter Manuals Ser.). (Illus.). 128p. (C). 1998. pap. 24.95 (*1-899238-22-0*, Pub. by Porter Pub) Nichols Pub.

— Fiat Tipo & Tempra 1988-96. (Porter Manuals Ser.). (Illus.). 128p. (C). 1998. pap. 24.95 (*1-899238-24-7*, Pub. by Porter Pub) Nichols Pub.

— Fiat Uno 1983-96. (Porter Manuals Ser.). (Illus.). 128p. (C). 1998. pap. 24.95 (*1-899238-23-9*, Pub. by Porter Pub) Nichols Pub.

— Firebird, 1982-1992. (Total Car Care Ser.). 550p. (C). 1998. pap. 22.95 (*0-8019-9100-5*) Thomson Learn.

— Firebird, 1967 to 1981. LC 80-70326. (Illus.). 368p. (C). 1981. pap. 17.95 (*0-8019-7046-6*) Thomson Learn.

— Ford: Aspire, 1995-98. (Total Car Care Ser.). 550p. (C). 1998. pap. 22.95 (*0-8019-8972-8*) Thomson Learn.

***Chilton Automotive Editorial Staff.** Ford-Aerostar 1986-97. (Total Car Care Ser.). (C). 2000. pap. 17.25 (*0-8019-9132-3*) NP-Chilton.

Chilton Automotive Editorial Staff. Ford Bronco II - Explorer - Ranger, 1983-94. (Total Car Care Ser.). (Illus.). 900p. 1994. pap. 22.95 (*0-8019-8555-2*) Nichols Pub.

***Chilton Automotive Editorial Staff.** Ford-Coupes & Sedans 1989-2000. (Total Car Care Repair Manual Ser.). (C). 2000. pap. text 22.95 (*0-8019-9314-8*) NP-Chilton.

Chilton Automotive Editorial Staff. Ford Engine Overhaul. (Total Service Ser.). 272p. (C). 1996. pap. 22.95 (*0-8019-8793-8*) Thomson Learn.

— Ford Escort - Mercury Lynx, 1981-95. 448p. pap. 16.95 (*0-8019-8685-0*) Nichols Pub.

— Ford Escort & Orion 1980-94. (Porter Manuals Ser.). (Illus.). 128p. (C). 1998. pap. 24.95 (*1-899238-13-1*, Pub. by Porter Pub) Nichols Pub.

— Ford Escort-Mercury Lynx, 1981-92. LC 91-58835. 480p. (C). 1992. pap. 16.95 (*0-8019-8316-9*) Thomson Learn.

— Ford-Escort/Lynx, 1981-1990: Covers All U. S. & Canadian Models of Ford Escort, Exp, Mercury Lynx. LC 98-71365. (Chilton's Total Car Care Ser.). (C). 1999. pap. text 22.95 (*0-8019-9093-9*) Thomson Learn.

— Ford-Escort/Tracer, 1991-1998: Covers All U. S. & Canadian Modles of Ford Escort & Mercury Tracer. LC 98-71358. (Chilton's Total Car Care Ser.). (Illus.). 550p. (C). 1998. pap. text 22.95 (*0-8019-9098-X*) Thomson Learn.

***Chilton Automotive Editorial Staff.** Ford Fiesta, 1977-94. (Porter Manuals Ser.). (Illus.). 128p. (C). 1998. pap. 24.95 (*1-899238-10-7*, Pub. by Porter Pub) Nichols Pub.

Chilton Automotive Editorial Staff. Ford Full Size Vans, 1961-1988. (Total Car Care Ser.). 688p. (C). 1997. pap. text 22.95 (*0-8019-8978-7*) Thomson Learn.

— Ford Full-Size Vans, 1989-1996. rev. ed. (Total Car Care Ser.). (Illus.). 550p. (C). 1998. pap. text 22.95 (*0-8019-8848-9*) Nichols Pub.

— Ford Mercury Full Size, 1968-1988. LC 94-69447. (Illus.). 640p. (C). 1995. pap. 22.95 (*0-8019-8665-6*) Thomson Learn.

— Ford Mercury Lincoln, Mid-Size: 1971-1985. LC 84-45484. 424p. (Orig.). (C). 1985. pap. 16.95 (*0-8019-7566-2*) Thomson Learn.

— Ford Mid Size Cars 1971-1985. LC 94-69443. (Illus.). 776p. (C). 1996. pap. 22.95 (*0-8019-8667-2*) Thomson Learn.

— Ford Mustang - Mercury Capri, 1979-1988. (Illus.). 624p. (C). 1995. pap. 22.95 (*0-8019-8580-3*) Thomson Learn.

— Ford Mustang & Cougar, 1964-1973. LC 97-65891. 450p. (C). 1997. pap. 22.95 (*0-8019-9060-2*) Thomson Learn.

— Ford Mustang-Mercury Capri, 1989-92. 450p. (C). 1992. pap. 16.95 (*0-8019-8299-5*) Thomson Learn.

— Ford Mustang, 1994-1998. (Total Car Care Ser.). (Illus.). 550p. (C). 1998. pap. text 22.95 (*0-8019-8823-3*) Thomson Learn.

— Ford, 1978-1983: Fairmont & Zephyr. (New Total Service Ser.). 448p. (C). 1997. pap. text 22.95 (*0-8019-9080-7*) Thomson Learn.

— Ford Pick-Up & Bronco, 1976-86. (Total Car Care Ser.). (Illus.). 832p. (C). 1994. pap. 22.95 (*0-8019-8576-5*) Thomson Learn.

— Ford-Pick-ups/Expedition/Navigator 1997-00. (Chilton's Total Car Care). (C). 1999. pap. text 22.95 (*0-8019-9119-6*) Thomson Learn.

— Ford Probe, 1989-92. 450p. 1992. pap. 16.95 (*0-8019-8312-6*) Nichols Pub.

— Ford Ranger - Bronco II - Explorer 1983-94. 450p. pap. 16.95 (*0-8019-8557-9*) Nichols Pub.

— Ford-Ranger, Explorer & Mountaineer: 1991-1999. (C). 1999. pap. text 22.95 (*0-8019-9131-5*) Thomson Learn.

***Chilton Automotive Editorial Staff.** Ford Sierra & Sapphire, 1982-93. (Porter Manuals Ser.). (Illus.). 128p. (C). 1998. pap. 24.95 (*1-899238-15-8*, Pub. by Porter Pub) Nichols Pub.

Chilton Automotive Editorial Staff. Ford Taurus & Mercury Sable, 1986-1995. (Illus.). 816p. (C). 1995. pap. 22.95 (*0-8019-8687-7*) Thomson Learn.

— Ford Taurus-Mercury Sable, 1986-92. 368p. (C). 1992. pap. 16.95 (*0-8019-8297-9*) Thomson Learn.

— Ford-Taurus/Sable 1996-99. (Chilton's Total Car Care). (C). 1999. pap. text 22.95 (*0-8019-9117-X*) Thomson Learn.

— Ford Tempo - Mercury Topaz, 1984-95. 448p. pap. 16.95 (*0-8019-8679-6*) Nichols Pub.

— Ford Tempo & Mercury Topaz, 1984-94. LC 94-69441. (Illus.). 704p. (C). 1995. pap. 22.95 (*0-8019-8670-2*) Thomson Learn.

— Ford Tempo-Mercury Topaz, 1984-92. 328p. (C). 1992. pap. 16.95 (*0-8019-8317-7*) Thomson Learn.

— Ford-Thunderbird, Cougar, 1983-1997. (Total Car Care Ser.). 352p. (C). 2000. pap. text 17.25 (*0-8019-9133-1*) NP-Chilton.

— Ford Thunderbird-Mercury Cougar, 1983-92. 464p. (C). 1992. pap. 17.95 (*0-8019-8314-2*) Thomson Learn.

— Fuel Injection: Diagnosis & Repair. (New Total Service Ser.). 300p. (C). 1998. pap. text 22.95 (*0-8019-8946-9*) Thomson Learn.

— Fuel Injection & Drive Manual 90-92, Europe. 1056p. 1992. text 97.00 (*0-8019-8275-8*) Nichols Pub.

— Gearbox Fluid Service Location, 91. 176p. 1991. text 22.50 (*0-8019-8224-3*) Nichols Pub.

— General Motors Chevy-GMC Full Size Trucks, 1970-79. (Total Car Care Ser.). 464p. (C). 1997. pap. text 22.95 (*0-8019-8973-6*) Thomson Learn.

— General Motors Chevy-GMC Full Size Vans, 1967-1986. (Total Car Care Ser.). (Illus.). 424p. (C). 1997. pap. text 22.95 (*0-8019-8977-9*) Thomson Learn.

— General Motors Chevy-GMC Full-Size Vans, 1987-1997. rev. ed. LC 97-77878. (Total Car Care Ser.). (Illus.). 550p. (C). 1998. pap. text 22.95 (*0-8019-8819-5*) Thomson Learn.

— General Motors, 1967-1981: Firebird. (New Total Car Care Ser.). 572p. (C). 1997. pap. text 22.95 (*0-8019-9065-3*) Thomson Learn.

— General Motors, 1962-1979: Nova-Chevy II. (New Total Car Care Ser.). 400p. (C). 1997. pap. text 22.95 (*0-8019-9067-X*) Thomson Learn.

— General Motors, 1968-1978: Chevy Full Sized Cars. (New Total Car Care Ser.). 456p. (C). 1997. pap. text 22.95 (*0-8019-9078-5*) Thomson Learn.

— General Motors, 1969-82: Blazer & Jimmy. (New Total Car Care Ser.). 416p. (C). 1997. pap. text 22.95 (*0-8019-9077-7*) Thomson Learn.

— General Motors, 1974-1983: Pontiac Mid Size. (New Total Car Care Ser.). 488p. (C). 1997. pap. text 22.95 (*0-8019-9074-2*) Thomson Learn.

— General Motors, 1980-1985: Citation, Omega, Phoenix & Skylark-XII. LC 97-67985. (New Total Car Care Ser.). 416p. (C). 1997. pap. text 22.95 (*0-8019-9072-6*) Thomson Learn.

— GM Achieva-Calais--Grand Am-Skylark-Somerset, 1985-95. (Illus.). 704p. (C). 1996. pap. 22.95 (*0-8019-8688-5*) Thomson Learn.

— GM Astro/Safari 1985-1996. 752p. (C). 1997. pap. 22.95 (*0-8019-8826-8*) Thomson Learn.

— GM-Buick - Olds - Pontiac Full Size, 1975-1990. (Illus.). 560p. (C). 1994. pap. 22.95 (*0-8019-8584-6*) Thomson Learn.

— GM-Cadillac, 1967-1989. (Illus.). 600p. (C). 1994. pap. 22.95 (*0-8019-8587-0*) Thomson Learn.

— Gm-Camaro & Firebird 1993-1998. (Total Car Care Ser.). (Illus.). 550p. (C). 1998. pap. text 22.95 (*0-8019-8814-4*) Thomson Learn.

— GM-Cavalier/Sunfire 1995-00. (C). 1999. pap. text 22.95 (*0-8019-9114-5*) Thomson Learn.

— GM Celebrity - Century, 1982-95. 448p. pap. 16.95 (*0-8019-8689-3*) Nichols Pub.

***Chilton Automotive Editorial Staff.** GM-Century/Regal/ Lumina/Monte Carlo/Cutlass Supreme/Grand Prix 1997-2000. (Total Car Care Repair Manual Ser.). (C). 2000. pap. text 22.95 (*0-8019-9317-2*) NP-Chilton.

Chilton Automotive Editorial Staff. GM Chevette/1000, 1976-88. 400p. (C). 1997. pap. 22.95 (*0-8019-9069-6*) Thomson Learn.

— GM-Chevrolet - GEO Prizm, 1985-1993. 528p. (C). 1994. pap. 16.95 (*0-8019-8457-2*) Thomson Learn.

— GM-Chevrolet Caprice: 1990-1993. (Total Car Care Ser.). (Illus.). 528p. (C). 1993. pap. 22.95 (*0-8019-8421-1*) Thomson Learn.

— GM-Chevrolet Mid-Size, 1964-88. (Total Car Care Ser.). (Illus.). 608p. (C). 1994. pap. 22.95 (*0-8019-8594-3*) Thomson Learn.

— GM-Chevrolet Nova - GEO Prizm, 1985-93. (Illus.). 816p. (C). 1993. pap. 22.95 (*0-8019-8422-X*) Thomson Learn.

— GM-Chevrolet S-10 - GMC S-15 Pick-Up, 1982-89. 450p. pap. 16.95 (*0-8019-8540-4*) Nichols Pub.

— GM-Chevrolet Spectrum - GEO Storm, 1985-1993. (Illus.). 576p. (C). 1993. pap. 22.95 (*0-8019-8425-4*) Thomson Learn.

— GM-Chevrolet Spectrum, GEO Storm, 1985-1993. 450p. 1994. pap. 16.95 (*0-8019-8460-2*) Nichols Pub.

— GM-Chevy Pick-Up & Suburban, 1980-87. (Total Car Care Ser.). (Illus.). 528p. (C). 1994. pap. 22.95 (*0-8019-8577-3*) Thomson Learn.

— Gm-Electra/Park Ave/Ninety-Eight 1990-93. (Illus.). 360p. (C). 1994. pap. 22.95 (*0-8019-8430-0*) Thomson Learn.

— GM, Electronic Engine Controls Manual, 1992-94, 3 vols. 1656p. 1993. text 212.00 (*0-8019-8474-2*) Nichols Pub.

— Gm H-Body-Bonneville Olds/Lesabre 88-93. 264p. (C). 1994. pap. 16.95 (*0-8019-8458-0*) Thomson Learn.

— GM-Pontiac Firebird, 1982-94. (Total Car Care Ser.). (Illus.). 900p. 1995. pap. 22.95 (*0-8019-8534-X*) Nichols Pub.

— Gm-Regal/Century 1975-1987. (Total Car Care Ser.). 536p. (C). 1997. pap. text 22.95 (*0-8019-8981-7*) Thomson Learn.

— GM X-Body: 1980-1985. LC 84-45462. 224p. (Orig.). (C). 1985. pap. 17.95 (*0-8019-7592-1*) Thomson Learn.

— Guide to Electronic Engine Control 1978-1985, Vol. 8. LC 84-45481. 480p. (Orig.). (C). 1985. pap. 22.95 (*0-8019-7535-2*) Thomson Learn.

***Chilton Automotive Editorial Staff.** Heater Cores, 1990-2000. (Professional Ser.). (Illus.). 900p. (C). 2000. pap. 34.95 (*0-8019-9311-3*) NP-Chilton.

Chilton Automotive Editorial Staff. Heavy Duty Truck Service Manual, 1989-92. 1920p. 1993. text 97.00 (*0-8019-8443-2*) Nichols Pub.

— Honda Accord - Prelude 1984-95. 448p. pap. 16.95 (*0-8019-8691-5*) Nichols Pub.

— Honda Accord & Prelude, 1984-1995. (Illus.). 936p. (C). 1995. pap. 22.95 (*0-8019-8680-X*) Thomson Learn.

Chilton Automotive Editorial Staff. Honda Accord-Prelude, 1984-91. LC 91-58848. 400p. (C). 1992. pap. 16.95 (*0-8019-8301-0*) Thomson Learn.

Chilton Automotive Editorial Staff. Honda Accord/Civic/Prelude 1973-1983. (Total Car Care Ser.). (Illus.). 336p. (C). 1994. pap. 22.95 (*0-8019-8591-9*) Thomson Learn.

— Honda Civic, Crx & Del Sol 1984-1995. 864p. (C). 1996. pap. 22.95 (*0-8019-8683-4*) Thomson Learn.

— Honda Civic-CRX, 1984-91. 368p. (C). 1992. pap. 16.95 (*0-8019-8302-9*) Thomson Learn.

— Honda Civic-CRX 1984-95. 448p. pap. 16.95 (*0-8019-8690-7*) Nichols Pub.

***Chilton Automotive Editorial Staff.** Honda-CR-V/Odyssey 1995-2000. (Total Car Care Repair Manual Ser.). (C). 2000. pap. text 22.95 (*0-8019-9313-X*) NP-Chilton.

Chilton Automotive Editorial Staff. Hyundai: Coupes/Sedans, 1995-98. (Total Car Care Ser.). 550p. (C). 1998. pap. 22.95 (*0-8019-8953-1*) Thomson Learn.

— Hyundai, 1986-93. (Illus.). 832p. (C). 1993. pap. 22.95 (*0-8019-8412-2*) Thomson Learn.

— Hyundai, 1986-93. (Chilton's Total Car Care). (Illus.). 572p. (C). 1994. pap. 16.95 (*0-8019-8432-7*) Thomson Learn.

— Import Auto Service Manual, 1989-93. 2304p. 1993. text 97.00 (*0-8019-8448-3*) Nichols Pub.

— Import Car Repair Manual. (C). 1998. 59.95 (*0-8019-7923-4*) Thomson Learn.

— Import Labor Guide & Parts Manual, 1989-93. 1872p. 1993. text 95.00 (*0-8019-8446-7*) Nichols Pub.

— Import Labor Guide & Parts Manual, 1990-94. 1200p. 1994. text 97.00 (*0-8019-8548-X*) Nichols Pub.

— Import Service Manual, 1991-95. 2304p. text 100.00 (*0-8019-8696-6*) Nichols Pub.

— Import Wiring Diagram Manual 1992. 1536p. 1994. pap. 97.00 (*0-8019-8544-7*) Nichols Pub.

— Import Wiring, 1991. 1344p. 1993. pap. 97.00 (*0-8019-8441-6*) Nichols Pub.

— International Scout, 1967-1973. 224p. 1974. pap. 17.95 (*0-8019-5912-8*) Nichols Pub.

— Jeep CJ - Scrambler, 1971-1986. (Total Car Care Ser.). (Illus.). 504p. (C). 1994. pap. 22.95 (*0-8019-8536-6*) Thomson Learn.

— Jeep CJ, 1945-1970. (Total Car Care Ser.). 352p. (C). 1997. pap. text 22.95 (*0-8019-8976-0*) Thomson Learn.

— Jeep CJ5, CJ6, CJ7, Scrambler & Wrangler, 1988-1990. 272p. (C). 1991. pap. 16.95 (*0-8019-8221-9*) Thomson Learn.

— Jeep Wagoneer - Commando - Cherokee - Truck, 1957-1983. 552p. (C). 1997. pap. 22.95 (*0-8019-9059-9*) Thomson Learn.

— Jeep Wagoneer - Commando - Cherokee. Truck, 1957-1986. LC 86-70144. 528p. (C). 1986. pap. 17.95 (*0-8019-7720-7*) Thomson Learn.

— Jeep, Wagoneer, Comanche, Cherokee, 1984-1995. 448p. pap. 16.95 (*0-8019-8676-1*) Nichols Pub.

— Jeep Wrangler - GT, 1988-1994. 450p. pap. 16.95 (*0-8019-8600-1*) Nichols Pub.

— Labor Guide, 1981-95. 2112p. 1994. text 137.00 (*0-8019-8571-4*) Nichols Pub.

— Labor Guide, 1980-'94. 1984p. 1993. text 135.00 (*0-8019-8472-6*) Nichols Pub.

— Labor Guide, 1979-'93. 2240p. 1992. text 135.00 (*0-8019-8292-8*) Nichols Pub.

— Land Rover Discovery & Range Rover "Classic" 1970-1996. (Porter Manuals Ser.). (C). 1998. pap. text 26.25 (*1-899238-19-0*, Pub. by Porter Pub) Nichols Pub.

— Light Truck & Van Repair Manual, 1994-1998. (C). 1998. 59.95 (*0-8019-7924-2*) Thomson Learn.

— Light Truck & Van Service Manual, 1992-96. 2504p. text 100.00 (*0-8019-8725-3*) Nichols Pub.

— Mazda 323/626/929/Glc/Mx-6/Rx-7 1978-1989. 632p. (C). 1995. pap. 22.95 (*0-8019-8581-1*) Thomson Learn.

— Mazda 1978-89 Repair & Tune-Up Guide. LC 88-43189. (Illus.). 512p. (C). 1989. pap. 16.95 (*0-8019-7945-5*) Thomson Learn.

— Mazda Pick-Ups, 1972-89 Repair & Tune up Guide. LC 88-43190. (Illus.). 448p. (C). 1989. pap. 17.95 (*0-8019-7946-3*) Thomson Learn.

***Chilton Automotive Editorial Staff.** Mazda 323/Mx-3/626/Mx-6/Millenia/Protege/Probe 1990-1998. (Chilton's Total Car Care Ser.). (C). 1999. 22.95 (*0-8019-9130-7*) Thomson Learn.

— Mazda-Trucks, 1994-98. LC 98-71363. (Chilton's Total Car Care Ser.). (Illus.). 550p. (C). 1999. pap. text 22.95 (*0-8019-9097-1*) Thomson Learn.

Chilton Automotive Editorial Staff. Mazda Trucks, 1972-1986. 512p. (C). 1997. pap. 22.95 (*0-8019-9057-2*) Thomson Learn.

— Medium-Heavy Duty Truck Service Manual, 1989-92. 1216p. 1992. 77.00 (*0-8019-8282-0*) Nichols Pub.

— Mercedes Benz, 1974-1984: RTUG. LC 83-45305. 288p. (C). 1984. pap. 17.95 (*0-8019-7463-1*) Thomson Learn.

— Mercedez-Benz, 1974-1984: Coupes, Sedans & Wagons. (New Total Car Care Ser.). 450p. (C). 1998. pap. text 22.95 (*0-8019-9076-9*) Thomson Learn.

— Metro 1980-1990. (Porter Manuals Ser.). (Illus.). 128p. (C). 1998. pap. 24.95 (*1-899238-12-3*, Pub. by Porter Pub) Nichols Pub.

***Chilton Automotive Editorial Staff.** MG Midget & Austin Healey Sprite: Step-by-Step Service Guide. (Porter Manuals Ser.). (C). 1998. pap. text 26.25 (*1-899238-07-7*, Pub. by Porter Pub) Nichols Pub.

Chilton Automotive Editorial Staff. Mini & Mini Cooper 1959-95. (Porter Manuals Ser.). (Illus.). 128p. (C). 1998. pap. 24.95 (*1-899238-01-8*, Pub. by Porter Pub) Nichols Pub.

— Mitsubishi: Eclipse, 1990-98. (Total Car Care Ser.). (C). 1998. pap. 22.95 (*0-8019-8957-4*) Thomson Learn.

— Mitsubishi Cars & Trucks, 1983-89. LC 88-43191. (Illus.). 944p. 1990. pap. text 22.95 (*0-8019-7947-1*) Nichols Pub.

— Mitsubishi Eclipse, 1990-93. (Illus.). 800p. 1993. pap. 22.95 (*0-8019-8415-7*) Nichols Pub.

***Chilton Automotive Editorial Staff.** Mitsubishi-Galant/ Mirage/Diamante 1990-2000. (Total Car Care Repair Manual Ser.). (C). 2000. pap. text 22.95 (*0-8019-9315-6*) NP-Chilton.

Chilton Automotive Editorial Staff. Mitsubishi, 1985-89. 544p. (C). 1991. pap. 16.95 (*0-8019-8220-0*) Thomson Learn.

— Mitsubishi Pick-Ups & Montero 1983-1995. LC 94-69448. (Illus.). 928p. (C). 1996. pap. 22.95 (*0-8019-8666-4*) Thomson Learn.

***Chilton Automotive Editorial Staff.** Motorcycle Handbook. (New Total Service Ser.). (C). 1998. pap. text 22.95 (*0-8019-9099-8*) Thomson Learn.

Chilton Automotive Editorial Staff. Nissan: 240SX/Altima, 1993-98. (Total Car Care Ser.). 550p. (C). 1998. pap. 22.95 (*0-8019-8970-1*) Thomson Learn.

— Nissan-Infiniti Repair Manual, 1988-92. 256p. (C). 1992. pap. 19.95 (*0-8019-8322-3*) Thomson Learn.

— Nissan Maxima, 1985-92. 320p. 1992. pap. 16.95 (*0-8019-8307-X*) Nichols Pub.

— Nissan-Maxima, 1993-98: Covers All U.S. & Canadian Models of Nissan Maxima. (Total Car Care Ser.). (C). 1999. pap. text 22.95 (*0-8019-8961-2*) Thomson Learn.

— Nissan, 1973-1984: Datsun 200SX, 510, 610, 710, 810 & Maxima. (New Total Car Care Ser.). 512p. (C). 1997. pap. text 22.95 (*0-8019-9070-X*) Thomson Learn.

— Nissan, 1973-1981: Datsun 210, 310, 1200 & F10. (New Total Car Care Ser.). 450p. (C). 1997. pap. text 22.95 (*0-8019-9068-8*) Thomson Learn.

— Nissan Pick-Ups & Pathfinder, 1989-1995. (Illus.). 688p. (C). 1995. pap. 22.95 (*0-8019-8671-0*) Thomson Learn.

— Nissan Sentra, Pulsar, 1982-92. 416p. (C). 1992. pap. 16.95 (*0-8019-8309-6*) Thomson Learn.

— Nissan Stanza, 200SX, 240SX, 1982-92. 424p. 1992. pap. 16.95 (*0-8019-8308-8*) Nichols Pub.

— Gm Cutlass Rwd 1970-87. LC 94-69442. (Illus.). 472p. (C). 1996. pap. 22.95 (*0-8019-8668-0*) Thomson Learn.

— Omni-Horizon-Rampage, 1978-89: Repair & Tune-Up Guide. LC 88-43176. (Illus.). 352p. (C). 1989. pap. 16.95 (*0-8019-7934-X*) Thomson Learn.

— Peugeot 205 1983-1995. (Porter Manuals Ser.). (Illus.). 128p. (C). 1998. pap. 24.95 (*1-899238-17-4*, Pub. by Porter Pub) Nichols Pub.

— Pontiac Fiero, 1984-88. LC 88-43193. (Illus.). 344p. (C). 1989. pap. text 17.95 (*0-8019-7949-8*) Thomson Learn.

— Pontiac-Fiero, 1984-1988. 488p. (C). 1997. pap. 22.95 (*0-8019-9064-5*) Thomson Learn.

— Pontiac Firebird, 1982-94: All U.S. & Canadian Models. (Chilton's Repair & Tune-up Guides Ser.). (Illus.). 492p. (C). 1995. pap. 16.95 (*0-8019-8598-6*) Thomson Learn.

— Professional Air Conditioning & Heating Labor Guide, 1989-91. 1920p. 1991. pap. 17.00 (*0-8019-8222-7*) Nichols Pub.

— Quick Lube Guide, 1991. 304p. 1991. pap. 27.50 (*0-8019-8223-5*) Nichols Pub.

— Quick-Sew Quilts: Wallhangings & Coordinating Projects from America's Top Designers. LC 96-31936. (Illus.). 144p. 1996. pap. 24.95 (*0-8019-8891-8*) Krause Pubns.

— Ford Ranger/Bronco Ii 1983-90. LC 97-78112. (Total Car Care Ser.). 550p. (C). 1998. pap. 22.95 (*0-8019-8967-1*) Thomson Learn.

— Renault, 1975-1985: Coupes, Sedans & Wagons. (New Total Car Care Ser.). 416p. (C). 1997. pap. text 22.95 (*0-8019-9079-3*) Thomson Learn.

C

An Asterisk (*) at the beginning of an entry indicates that the title is appearing for the first time.

— Renault, 1975-85. LC 84-45489. 192p. (Orig.). (C). 1985. pap. 17.95 (0-8019-7561-1) Thomson Learn.
— Saturn: Coupes/Sedans/Wagons, 1991-98. (Total Car Care Ser.). 550p. (C). 1998. pap. 22.95 (0-8019-8956-6) Thomson Learn.
— Service Bay Handbook. 560p. 1993. pap. write for info. (0-8019-8469-6) Nichols Pub.
— Small Engine Repair 0-20hp, 1982-92. 728p. (C). 1994. pap. 19.95 (0-8019-8325-8) Thomson Learn.
***Chilton Automotive Editorial Staff.** Specification & Maintenance Intervals, 1990-2000. (Illus.). 900p. (C). 2000. pap. 34.95 (0-8019-9310-5) NP-Chilton.
Chilton Automotive Editorial Staff. Subaru Coupes/Sedans/Wagons 1985-1996. rev. ed. (Illus.). 848p. (C). 1996. pap. text 22.95 (0-8019-8797-0) Thomson Learn.
— Subaru, 1985-92. 496p. (C). 1992. pap. 16.95 (0-8019-8305-3) Thomson Learn.
— Subaru, 1970-1984. (Total Car Care Ser.). 448p. (C). 1996. pap. 22.95 (0-8019-8790-3) Thomson Learn.
— Suzuki: Samurai/Sidekick/Tracker, 1986-98. (Total Car Care Ser.). 550p. (C). 1998. pap. 22.95 (0-8019-9088-2) Thomson Learn.
***Chilton Automotive Editorial Staff.** Timing Belts, 1980-2000. (Illus.). 550p. (C). 2000. pap. 34.95 (0-8019-9305-9) NP-Chilton.
Chilton Automotive Editorial Staff. Toyota: Camry, 1983-96. (Total Car Care Ser.). (Illus.). 560p. (C). 1998. pap. 22.95 (0-8019-8955-8) Thomson Learn.
— Toyota Camry, 1983-88: Repair & Tune-Up Guide. LC 88-43175. (Illus.). 384p. (C). 1989. pap. 15.95 (0-8019-7933-1) Thomson Learn.
— Toyota Camry, 1983-1992. rev. ed. 496p. (C). 1992. pap. 16.95 (0-8019-8311-8) Thomson Learn.
— Toyota Celica, 1986-93. (Illus.). 832p. (C). 1993. pap. 22.95 (0-8019-8413-0) Thomson Learn.
***Chilton Automotive Editorial Staff.** Toyota-Celica, 1994-1998: Covers All U.S. & Canadian Models of Toyota Celica. LC 99-72521. (New Total Car Care Ser.). (Illus.). 550p. (C). 1999. pap. text 22.95 (0-8019-8959-0) Thomson Learn.
Chilton Automotive Editorial Staff. Toyota Celica-Supra (RWD), 1971-1987. (Total Car Care Ser.). (Illus.). 552p. (C). 1997. pap. text 22.95 (0-8019-8980-9) Thomson Learn.
— Toyota Corolla, 1988-1997. (New Total Car Care Ser.). 550p. (C). 1998. pap. text 22.95 (0-8019-8827-6) Thomson Learn.
— Toyota Corolla, 1970-1987. (Illus.). 480p. (C). 1995. pap. 22.95 (0-8019-8586-2) Thomson Learn.
— Toyota Corolla, 1990-93. 304p. (C). 1994. pap. 16.95 (0-8019-8434-3) Thomson Learn.
— Toyota, 1983-1990: Cressida-Van. LC 97-67984. (New Total Car Care Ser.). 608p. (C). 1997. pap. text 22.95 (0-8019-9066-1) Thomson Learn.
— Toyota, 1970-1982: Cressida, Corona, Crown & MKII. LC 97-67988. (New Total Car Care Ser.). 520p. (C). 1997. pap. text 22.95 (0-8019-9081-5) Thomson Learn.
— Toyota Pick-ups-Land Cruiser-4-Runner, 1989-1995. rev. ed. (Illus.). 920p. (C). 1996. pap. 22.95 (0-8019-8682-6) Thomson Learn.
***Chilton Automotive Editorial Staff.** Toyota-Pick-ups/Land Cruiser/4Runner 1997-2000. (Total Car Care Repair Manual Ser.). (C). 2000. pap. text 22.95 (0-8019-9316-4) NP-Chilton.
— Toyota-Previa, 1991-97: Covers All U. S. & Canadian Models of Toyota Previa. (Total Car Care Ser.). (C). 1998. pap. text 22.95 (0-8019-9091-2) Thomson Learn.
Chilton Automotive Editorial Staff. Toyota Tercel 1984-1994. LC 96-171497. 450p. (C). 1995. pap. 16.95 (0-8019-8599-4) Thomson Learn.
— Toyota Tercel 1984-94. (Total Car Care Ser.). (Illus.). 536p. (C). 1995. pap. 22.95 (0-8019-8595-1) Thomson Learn.
— Transmission Diagnostic Manual, 1988-1993. 1368p. 1993. text 97.00 (0-8019-8473-4) Nichols Pub.
— Truck & Van Service Manual, 1990-94. 2112p. 1994. pap. 97.00 (0-8019-8547-1) Nichols Pub.
***Chilton Automotive Editorial Staff.** Vauxhall Cavalier 1981-1995. (Porter Manuals Ser.). (Illus.). 128p. (C). 1998. pap. 24.95 (1-899238-11-5, Pub. by Porter Pub) Nichols Pub.
Chilton Automotive Editorial Staff. Vauxhall Nova 1983-93. (Porter Manuals Ser.). (Illus.). 128p. (C). 1998. pap. 24.95 (1-899238-16-6, Pub. by Porter Pub) Nichols Pub.
— Volkswagen - Air Cooled, 1970-81. 331p. (C). 1997. pap. 22.95 (0-8019-8975-2) Thomson Learn.
***Chilton Automotive Editorial Staff.** Volkswagen Beetle up to 1980: Step-by-Step Service Guide. (Porter Manuals Ser.). (C). 1998. pap. text 26.25 (1-899238-02-6, Pub. by Porter Pub) Nichols Pub.
— Volkswagen Golf MKL & II 1974-92. (Porter Manuals Ser.). (Illus.). 128p. (C). 1998. pap. 26.25 (1-899238-29-8, Pub. by Porter Pub) Nichols Pub.
Chilton Automotive Editorial Staff. Volkswagen, 1949-1969: Air Cooled. LC 97-67981. (New Total Car Care Ser.). 374p. (C). 1997. pap. text 22.95 (0-8019-9073-4) Thomson Learn.
— Volkswagen, 1970-81. LC 78-20249. (Chilton's Repair & Tune-up Guides Ser.). (Illus.). 304p. (C). 1979. pap. 17.95 (0-8019-6837-2) Thomson Learn.
— Volvo-Coupes/Sedans/Wagons, 1990-1998: Covers All U. S. & Canadian Models of Volvo 240, 240Dl, 240. LC 99-72522. (Chilton's Total Car Care Ser.). (C). 1999. pap. text 22.95 (0-8019-9095-5) Thomson Learn.
— Volvo, 1990-93. (Illus.). 432p. 1994. pap. 22.95 (0-8019-8428-9) Nichols Pub.
— Volvo Coupes/Sedans/Wagons 1970-1989. (Total Car Care Ser.). 520p. (C). 1996. pap. 22.95 (0-8019-8786-5) Thomson Learn.
— Volvo, 1970-89: Repair & Tune-Up Guide. LC 88-43188. (Illus.). 512p. (C). 1989. pap. text 16.95 (0-8019-7944-7) Thomson Learn.
— VW Front Wheel Drive: 1974-90 RTUG. (Illus.). 384p. (C). 1990. pap. text 16.95 (0-8019-8041-0) Thomson Learn.
— VW Front Wheel Drive, 1974-90. (Illus.). 544p. (C). 1995. pap. 22.95 (0-8019-8663-X) Thomson Learn.
— VW, Golf, Jetta, Cabriolet, Passat & Beetle, 1990-99. (Chilton's Total Car Care). (Illus.). 352p. (C). 2000. pap. text 22.95 (0-8019-9122-6) NP-Chilton.
— Ford Windstar 1995-98. (Total Car Care Ser.). 550p. (C). 1998. pap. 22.95 (0-8019-8969-8) Thomson Learn.
Chilton Automotive Editorial Staff, ed. Chilton's Auto Repair Manual 1988-1992. (Illus.). 1284p. (C). 1991. 34.95 (0-8019-7906-4) Thomson Learn.
— Spanish-Language Auto Repair Manual 1992-96. (Spanish-Language Manuals). (SPA.). (C). 1998. 39.95 (0-8019-8947-7) Thomson Learn.
— Spanish Language Import Car Repair Manual 1992-96. (Spanish-Language Manuals Ser.). (SPA.). (C). 2000. 39.95 (0-8019-8948-5) NP-Chilton.
— Spanish Language Truck & Van Repair Manual 1992-1996. (Spanish-Language Manuals Ser.). (SPA.). (C). 2000. pap. 39.95 (0-8019-8949-3) NP-Chilton.
Chilton Automotive Editorial Staff, et al. Chilton's Repair & Tune-up Guide for the Fiat. LC 74-116919. 124 p. 1970. write for info. (0-8019-5556-4) NP-Chilton.
Chilton, Bruce. A Feast of Meanings: Eucharistic Theologies from Jesus Through Johannine Circles. LC 93-36639. (Supplements to Novum Testamentum Ser.: No. 72). xi, 210p. 1994. 99.50 (90-04-09949-2) Brill Academic Pubs.
— Jesus' Baptism & Jesus' Healing: His Personal Practice of Spirituality. LC 98-39833. 144p. 1998. pap. 12.00 (1-56338-248-2) TPI PA.
— Jesus' Prayer & Jesus' Eucharist: His Personal Practice of Spirituality. LC 97-12981. 112p. 1997. pap. 11.00 (1-56338-204-0) TPI PA.
***Chilton, Bruce.** Rabbi Jesus: An Intimate Biography. 320p. 2000. 25.00 (0-385-49792-X) Doubleday.
Chilton, Bruce & Evans, Craig A. Authenticating the Words of Jesus. LC 99-165885. (New Testament Tools & Studies). xvi, 480 p. 1999. write for info. (90-04-11141-7) Brill Academic Pubs.
— The Proclamation of Jesus. LC 97-38945. (Arbeiten zur Geschichte des Antiken Judentums und des Urchristentums Ser.: No. 39). xi, 572p. 1997. 193.00 (90-04-10746-0) Brill Academic Pubs.
***Chilton, Bruce & Evans, Craig A., eds.** James the Just & Christian Origins. Vol. 98. (Illus.). Xii, 300p. 1999. text (90-04-11550-1) Brill Academic Pubs.
Chilton, Bruce & Evans, Craig A., eds. Studying the Historical Jesus: Evaluations of the State of Current Research. (New Testament Tools & Studies: Vol. 19). xvi, 612 Seconp. 1998. reprint ed. pap. 84.00 (90-04-11142-5) Brill Academic Pubs.
***Chilton, Bruce & Neusner, Jacob.** Jewish & Christian Doctrines: Classics Compared. 224p. (C). 1999. text 85.00 (0-415-17328-0) Routledge.
Chilton, Bruce, jt. auth. see Neusner, Jacob.
Chilton, Bruce D. Beginning New Testament Study. fac. ed. LC 87-5233. 206p. (Orig.). 1987. reprint ed. pap. 63.90 (0-7837-7949-6, 204770500008) Bks Demand.
— God in Strength: Jesus' Announcement of the Kingdom. (Biblical Seminar Ser.: Vol.8). 347p. 1987. 24.95 (1-85075-162-5) CUP Services.
— Pure Kingdom: Jesus' Vision of God. (Studying the Historical Jesus Ser.). 188p. (Orig.). 1996. pap. 15.00 (0-8028-4187-2) Eerdmans.
— The Temple of Jesus: His Sacrificial Program Within a Cultural History of Sacrifice. 224p. 1992. 38.50 (0-271-00824-5) Pa St U Pr.
Chilton, Bruce D. & Evans, Craig A., eds. Authenticating the Activities of Jesus. LC 99-174429. (New Testament Tools & Studies: No. 28,2). xvi, 480p. 1998. 153.00 (90-04-11302-9) Brill Academic Pubs.
— Authenticating the Words of Jesus. (New Testament Tools & Studies: No. 28,1). 496p. 1998. 153.00 (90-04-11301-0) Brill Academic Pubs.
Chilton, Bruce D. & McDonald, J. I. Jesus & the Ethics of the Kingdom. LC 88-3815. 160p. reprint ed. pap. 49.60 (0-7837-5554-6, 204532900005) Bks Demand.
***Chilton, Bruce D. & Neusner, Jacob.** Comparing Spiritualities: Formative Christianity & Judaism on Finding Life & Meeting Death. LC 99-57784. 2000. pap. 16.00 (1-56338-309-8) TPI PA.
Chilton, Bruce D. & Neusner, Jacob. Judaism in the New Testament: Practices & Beliefs. LC 94-45962. (Illus.). 224p. (C). 1995. pap. 22.99 (0-415-11844-1) Routledge.
— Judaism in the New Testament: Practices & Beliefs. LC 94-45962. (Illus.). 224p. (C). (gr. 13). 1995. 75.00 (0-415-11843-3) Routledge.
— Trading Places: The Intersecting Histories of Judaism & Christianity. LC 96-44694. 296p. (Orig.). 1996. pap. 16.95 (0-8298-1141-9) Pilgrim OH.
Chilton, Bruce D. & Neusner, Jacob, eds. Trading Places Sourcebook: Readings in the Intersecting Histories of Judaism & Christianity. LC 96-44694. 304p. (Orig.). 1997. pap. 16.95 (0-8298-1154-0) Pilgrim OH.
Chilton, Bruce D., et al. Forging a Common Future: Catholic, Judaic & Protestant Relations for a New Millenium. Neusner, Jacob, ed. LC 97-211. 128p. (Orig.). 1997. pap. 12.95 (0-8298-1170-2) Pilgrim OH.
Chilton, Bruce D., jt. auth. see Neusner, Jacob.
Chilton, Bruce D., jt. ed. see Evans, Craig A.
Chilton, Charles. Oh What a Lovely War. (Methuen Modern Plays Ser.). (Illus.). 109p. (C). 1988. pap. write for info. (0-413-30210-5, A0196, Methuen Drama) Methn.
Chilton, Charles A. The Indigo Bunting: And 365 Other Ways to Experience God in Your Life - A Daily Devotional. (Illus.). 376p. (Orig.). 1996. pap. 10.00 (1-888565-00-4) Trinity Rivrs.
Chilton, Craig. How to Get Paid $30,000 a Year to Travel* *Without Selling Anything. 3rd ed. (Illus.). 160p. 1988. pap. 24.95 (0-933638-07-8) Xanadu Ent.
— How to Get Paid $30,000 a Year to Travel* *Without Selling Anything. 4th ed. (Illus.). 192p. 1992. pap. 24.95 (0-933638-08-6) Xanadu Ent.
— How to Get Paid $30,000 a Year to Travel* *Without Selling Anything. 5th rev. ed. (Illus.). 352p. 1995. pap. 24.95 (0-933638-09-4) Xanadu Ent.
— The Pro-Choice VICTORY Handbook: Strategies for Keeping Your Abortion Rights. 208p. (Orig.). 1991. pap. 8.95 (0-9631248-0-3) Boiled Owl.
Chilton, David. La Gran Tribulacion. Howden, Paul & Zapata, Elias, trs. from ENG. (SPA.). 202p. 1991. pap. 5.95 (0-930464-40-0) Inst Christian.
— Productive Christians in an Age of Guilt Manipulators: A Biblical Response to Ronald J. Sider. 3rd ed. LC 90-44055. 439p. 1990. reprint ed. 25.00 (0-930464-38-9); reprint ed. pap. 12.50 (0-930464-04-4) Inst Christian.
— The Wealthy Barber: Everyone's Common-Sense Guide to Becoming Financially Independent. 2nd rev. ed. 208p. 1995. pap. text 12.95 (0-7615-0166-5) Prima Pub.
— The Wealthy Barber: Evryone's Commonsense Guide to Becoming Financially Independent. 3rd expanded rev. ed. LC 97-43079. 211p. 2000. pap. 14.00 (0-7615-1311-6) Prima Pub.
— The Wealthy Barber: The Common-Sense Guide to Becoming Financially Independent. 208p. 1991. 19.95 (1-55958-096-8) Prima Pub.
Chilton Designs Publishers Staff. Alice's Adventures. (C). 1992. pap. 45.00 (0-9503527-6-4, Pub. by Chilton Designs) St Mut.
— Alice's Diary. (C). 1989. pap. 50.00 (0-9503527-1-3, Pub. by Chilton Designs) St Mut.
— The Bilbury Chronicles. (C). 1992. 45.00 (0-9503527-5-6, Pub. by Chilton Designs) St Mut.
— Bilbury Grange. (C). 1992. pap. 45.00 (0-9503527-7-2, Pub. by Chilton Designs) St Mut.
***Chilton Designs Publishers Staff.** Jeep Wrangler/1987-95. (C). 1999. pap. 22.95 (0-8019-9092-0) Thomson Learn.
— Mazda Trucks 1987-1993. (C). 1999. pap. 22.95 (0-8019-8964-7) Thomson Learn.
Chilton Designs Publishers Staff. Mrs. Caldicot's Cabbage War. (C). 1992. 50.00 (0-9503527-8-0, Pub. by Chilton Designs) St Mut.
Chilton, Earl W., II. Freshwater Fishes of Texas. (Illus.). 98p. 1998. pap. 12.95 (1-885696-23-X, CHIFRP) U of Tex Pr.
***Chilton, Elizabeth S., ed.** Material Meanings: Critical Approaches to the Intepretation of Material Culture. LC 99-15804. (Illus.). 208p. 1999. 55.00 (0-87480-607-0) U of Utah Pr.
— Material Meanings: Critical Approaches to the Interpretation of Material Culture. LC 99-15804. (Illus.). 208p. 1999. pap. 25.00 (0-87480-608-9) U of Utah Pr.
Chilton, Henry M. & Witcofski, Richard L. Nuclear Pharmacy: An Introduction to the Clinical Application of Radiopharmaceuticals. LC 85-23910. (Illus.). 190p. 1986. text 35.00 (0-8121-1021-8) Lppncott W & W.
Chilton, Irma. A Glimmer of Light. (J). (gr. 4). 1992. pap. 7.95 (0-8464-4846-7) Beekman Pubs.
Chilton, J., et al, eds. Groundwater in the Urban Environment: Proceedings of the 27th IAH Congress, Nottingham, 21-27 September 1997. 2 vols. LC 99-496406. 1000p. (C). 1997. text 146.00 (90-5410-837-1, Pub. by A A Balkema) Ashgate Pub Co.
Chilton, J. Joseph. Guide to Auto Detailing. LC 92-19772. 176p. 1992. pap. 22.95 (0-8019-8196-4) Nichols Pub.
Chilton, John. Billie's Blues: The Billie Holiday Story, 1933-1959. (Quality Paperbacks Ser.). (Illus.). 272p. 1989. pap. 13.95 (0-306-80363-1) Da Capo.
***Chilton, John.** Groundwater in the Urban Environment: Selected City Profiles. LC 99-496406. (Illus.). 356p. 1999. text 79.00 (90-5410-924-6, Pub. by A A Balkema) Ashgate Pub Co.
Chilton, John. Let the Good Times Roll: The Story of Louis Jordan & His Music. 320p. (C). 1997. reprint ed. pap. 21.95 (0-472-08478-X, 08478) U of Mich Pr.
— Ride, Red, Ride: The Life of Henry "Red" Allen. LC 76-15648. (Illus.). 160p. 1999. 35.00 (0-304-70407-5) Continuum.
***Chilton, John.** Ride, Red, Ride: The Life of Henry "Red" Allen. 2000. pap. text 19.95 (0-8264-4744-9) Continuum.
Chilton, John. Sidney Bechet: The Wizard of Jazz. LC 95-43924. (Illus.). 380p. 1996. reprint ed. pap. 14.95 (0-306-80678-9) Da Capo.
— The Song of the Hawk: The Life & Recordings of Coleman Hawkins. (American Music Ser.). (Illus.). 460p. 1990. pap. 27.95 (0-472-08201-9, 08201) U of Mich Pr.
— Who's Who of British Jazz. (Cassell Jazz Ser.). 512p. 1997. 89.95 (0-304-33909-1); pap. 29.95 (0-304-33910-5) Continuum.
— Who's Who of Jazz. 4th ed. LC 84-20062. (Roots of Jazz Ser.). (Illus.). 362p. 1985. 29.50 (0-306-76271-4); pap. 13.95 (0-306-80243-0) Da Capo.
Chilton, John, jt. auth. see Jones, Max.
Chilton, Karen, jt. auth. see Lynne, Gloria.
Chilton, Kenneth. The Dynamic American Firm. Weidenbaum, Murray & Batterson, Robert, eds. LC 95-45636. 264p. (C). 1996. lib. bdg. 103.00 (0-7923-9662-6) Kluwer Academic.
Chilton, Kenneth, et al, eds. American Manufacturing in a Global Market. (C). 1989. lib. bdg. 86.00 (0-7923-9051-2) Kluwer Academic.
Chilton, Kenneth, jt. ed. see Weidenbaum, Murray.
***Chilton, Leanne.** Seizure Free: From Epilepsy to Brain Surgery, I Survived & You Can Too! 134p. 1998. pap. 12.95 (0-9663819-1-2) English Press.
Chilton, Margaret. Virgin of the Candy Scoop. 44p. (Orig.). 1998. pap. 4.95 (1-886895-11-2) Poetry Harbor.
Chilton, Pamela, et al. Odyssey of the Soul: Apocatastasis. LC 97-92477. (Illus.). 286p. 1998. pap. 15.00 (0-9659891-0-0) Quick Bk Pub.
***Chilton, Pamela, et al.** Odyssey of the Soul: When Gods Walk the Earth. 2000. pap. 12.00 (0-9659891-2-7) Quick Bk Pub.
Chilton, Paul A. Security Metaphors: Cold War Discourse from Containment to Common House. (Conflict & Consciousness: Studies in War, Peace & Social Thought: Vol. 2). 478p. (C). 1996. text 39.95 (0-8204-2178-2) P Lang Pubng.
Chilton, Paul A., et al, eds. Political Discourse in Transition in Europe 1989-1991. LC 97-44191. (Pragmatics & Beyond Ser.: No. 36). xi, 272p. 1998. lib. bdg. 69.00 (1-55619-329-7) J Benjamins Pubng Co.
Chilton, Paul A., et al. Language & Conflict: A Neglected Relationship. LC 98-22409. 65p. 1998. 49.00 (1-85359-422-9, Pub. by Multilingual Matters) Taylor & Francis.
Chilton, Paul A., tr. & intro. see Navarre, Marguerite de.
Chilton, S., ed. see Burley, S.
Chilton, Shirlene M. Ashby Funeral Home Records, Vol. 1: 1916-1928. 81p. 1986. spiral bd. 13.75 (0-945183-02-X) Saline Cnty Hist Heritage Soc.
Chilton, Stephen. Grounding Political Development. LC 90-27769. 150p. 1991. lib. bdg. 32.00 (1-55587-172-0) L Rienner.
Chiltosky, Mary U. Aunt Mary, Tell Me a Story: A Collection of Cherokee Legends & Tales. Galloway, Mary Regina Ulmer, ed. (Illus.). 82p. 1991. pap. 3.00 (0-9628630-0-9, Pub. by Cherokee Comn) Book Pub Co.
Chilver, Guy E. Cisalpine Gaul: Social & Economic History from 49 B.C. to the Death of Trajan. LC 75-7308. (Roman History Ser.). (Illus.). 1979. reprint ed. 26.95 (0-405-07190-6) Ayer.
— A Historical Commentary on Tacitus' Histories I & II. (Illus.). 1980. text 69.00 (0-19-814830-5) OUP.
Chilver, Guy E. & Townend, G. B. A Historical Commentary on Tacitus' Histories IV & V. 1985. 39.95 (0-19-814852-6) OUP.
Chilver, Peter. In the Picture Level 1. (In the Picture Ser.). (Illus.). 176p. 1985. pap., teacher ed. 14.95 (0-85950-503-0) Dufour.
— In the Picture Level 1: Consolidation Book. 136p. (C). 1985. pap. 10.95 (0-85950-501-4) Dufour.
— In the Picture Level 1: Core Book. (In the Picture Ser.). (Illus.). 176p. 1985. pap. 10.95 (0-85950-500-6) Dufour.
— In the Picture Level 1: Extension Book. (In the Picture Ser.). (Illus.). 176p. 1985. pap. 10.95 (0-85950-502-2) Dufour.
— Spotlight. 207p. (C). 1987. pap. 15.95 (0-85950-567-7) Dufour.
Chilvers, C. J. The Van Halen Encyclopedia. LC 98-96627. 320p. 1998. 19.95 (0-9667539-0-9) Malpractice Pub.
Chilvers, Donald R., et al. Litigation Support & Financial Assessment of Damages. 2nd ed. 346p. 1991. boxed set 120.00 (0-406-00259-2, UK, MICHIE) LEXIS Pub.
Chilvers, Ian. A Dictionary of Twentieth-Century Art. 688p. 1999. pap. 18.95 (0-19-280092-2) OUP.
Chilvers, Ian, ed. The Concise Oxford Dictionary of Art & Artists. 2nd ed. LC 96-22660. (Oxford Paperback Reference Ser.). 594p. 1996. pap. 13.95 (0-19-280048-5) OUP.
— A Dictionary of Twentieth-Century Art. 684p. 1998. 45.00 (0-19-211645-2) OUP.
Chilvers, Ian, et al, eds. The Oxford Dictionary of Art. (Paperback Reference Ser.). 558p. 1994. reprint ed. pap. 19.95 (0-19-280022-1) OUP.
— The Oxford Dictionary of Art. 2nd rev. ed. LC 97-200771. (Illus.). 660p. (C). 1997. 49.95 (0-19-860084-4) OUP.
Chilvers, Ian, jt. auth. see Howatson, Margaret.
Chilvers, Lloyd & Foster, Robin. The International Sugar Market: Prospects for the 1980s. LC HD9105.C54. (EIU Special Report: No. 106). 120p. reprint ed. pap. 37.20 (0-608-12022-7, 202284000030) Bks Demand.
Chim, Rath, jt. auth. see Headley, Robert K., Jr.
Chima, Christopher. How to Accumulate Wealth with Mutual Funds. LC 96-60254. 148p. (Orig.). 1996. pap. 12.00 (0-9651416-0-8) Uplift Books.
Chimaera, Shin. Japan Art of Living PC 1: The Art of Living Postcards 1. 1991. pap. 8.95 (0-8048-1699-9) Tuttle Pubng.
— Japan Art of Living PC 2: The Art of Living Postcards 2. 1991. pap. 8.95 (0-8048-1700-6) Tuttle Pubng.
Chimako, Tada. Moonstone Woman: Selected Prose & Poems. Fitzsimmons, Thomas, ed. Brady, Robert et al, trs. from JPN. (Asian Poetry in Translation Ser.: No. 11). 64p. 1990. text 20.00 (0-942668-21-9) Katydid Bks.
— Moonstone Woman: Selected Prose & Poems. Fitzsimmons, Thomas, ed. Brady, Robert et al, trs. from JPN. (Asian Poetry in Translation Ser.: No. 11). 64p. 1990. pap. 15.00 (0-942668-22-7) Katydid Bks.
Chimenes & Buckland. Pierre Bernac 1899-1979. 51.95 (1-85928-362-4) Ashgate Pub Co.
Chimenes, Myriam, jt. ed. see Buckland, Sidney.
Chiment, John J. Physical Geology. (C). 2000. pap. text. write for info. (0-8053-4424-1) Addison-Wesley.
Chimenti, D. E., jt. auth. see Thompson, D. O.
Chimenti, Dale E., ed. see Thompson, Donald O.
Chimenti, Dale E., jt. ed. see Thompson, Donald O.
Chimenti, Elisa. Tales & Legends of Morocco. Benamy, Arnon, tr. (Illus.). (J). (gr. 5 up). 1965. 10.95 (0-8392-3049-4) Astor-Honor.

C

An Asterisk (*) at the beginning of an entry indicates that the title is appearing for the first time.

Chimento, Carmen C. Beyond the Universe: The New Christian Theology. LC 97-143273. xx, 300p. 1997. pap. 14.95 (*0-9656847-0-9*) Spiritual Hse.

Chimera, Donna. WolfStar. (Illus.). 1997. 17.95 (*0-9656422-8-3*) WolfStar Pr.

Chimera, Mary A., ed. see Brennan, James A.

***Chimeric Inc. Staff.** Baby Story: Publish Your Memories in Baby's Very Own Keepsake Book! 1999. pap. 29.95 (*0-9636796-8-6*) Chimeric.

Chimeric Inc. Staff. Illustory: Write & Illustrate Your Own Book! (Illus.). 15p. (J). (gr. k-4). 19.95 (*0-9636796-0-0*, IKR) Chimeric.

***Chimeric Inc. Staff.** Pet Story: Publish Your Own Keepsake Pet Book! (Illus.). 2000. 28.95 (*0-9636796-5-1*) Chimeric.

Chimes, Thomas. Thomas Chimes: Pataphysician Redivivus, the Panel Portraits, 1973-1978, March 5-April 10, 1999 LC 99-60266. 60p. 1999. write for info. (*1-879173-40-9*) Locks Gallery.

Chimianti, Giovanni, ed. see Douglas, J. Leigh.

***Chimire, Krishna.** Forest or Farm? The Politics of Poverty & Land Hunger in Nepal. 1998. 28.50 (*81-7304-213-6*, Pub. by Manohar) S Asia.

Chimni, B. S. International Commodity Agreements: A Legal Study. Gordon-Ashworth, Fiona, ed. (Commodities Ser.). 368p. 1987. lib. bdg. 49.95 (*0-7099-5420-4*, Pub. by C Helm) Routldge.

— International Law & World Order: Critique of Contemporary Approaches. LC 92-42837. (Illus.). 292p. 1993. 38.95 (*0-8039-9471-0*) Sage.

***Chimni, B. S.** International Refugee Law. LC 99-41686. 1999. write for info. (*0-7619-9362-2*) Sage.

Chimo. Lila Says: A Novel. LC 98-15753. 128p. 1999. 20.00 (*0-684-83603-3*) S&S Trade.

Chimol, Carlos, tr. see Brown, Rosellen.

Chimombo, Moira & Roseberry, Robert L. The Power of Discourse: An Introduction to Discourse Analysis. LC 97-14162. 350p. 1997. write for info. (*0-8058-2635-1*); pap. write for info. (*0-8058-2636-X*) L Erlbaum Assocs.

Chimombo, Steve. Napolo & the Python. (African Writers Ser.). 192p. 1994. pap. 15.95 (*0-435-91199-6*) Heinemann.

Chimpa, Anthony, jt. auth. see Chimpa, C. Anthony.

Chimpa, Anthony C., jt. auth. see Chicka, C.

Chimpa, C. Anthony & Chimpa, Anthony. Women, Minority & Small Business Discrimination. LC 89-91070. 96p. (Orig.). 1989. pap. 15.95 (*0-922958-07-6*) H W Parker.

Chimporas. Chistes XXX. 1997. pap. text 6.98 (*970-643-132-2*) Selector.

Chimutengwende, Chenhamo C. South Africa: The Press & the Politics of Liberation. 208p. (C). 1978. pap. 110.00 (*0-905507-05-3*, Pub. by Barbican Bks) St Mut.

Chin. Color Atlas Human Anatomy. 2nd ed. (Illus.). (C). 1993. pap. text 24.50 (*0-03-001806-4*, Pub. by Harcourt Coll Pubs) Harcourt.

— On Call: Obstetrics & Gynecology. (C). 1998. text. write for info. (*0-8089-2076-6*, Grune & Strat) Harcrt Hlth Sci Grp.

Chin, Alvin J. Noninvasive Imaging of Congenital Heart Disease: Before & after Surgical Reconstruction. LC 93-39613. (Illus.). 400p. 1994. 128.00 (*0-87993-574-X*) Futura Pub.

Chin, Anthony & Choi, Alfred, eds. Law, Social Sciences & Public Policy: Towards a Unified Framework. LC 98-942058. 390p. 1998. 49.50 (*9971-69-205-8*, Pub. by Sngapore Univ Pr) Coronet Bks.

Chin, Anthony T. & Guan, Ng H. Economic Management & Transition Towards a Market Economy: An Asian Perpective. 500p. 1996. text 90.00 (*981-02-2049-9*) World Scientific Pub.

Chin, Art. Anything, Anytime, Anywhere: The Legacy of the Flying Tiger Line, 1945-89. 312p. (C). 1993. pap. 18.95 (*0-9637826-8-1*) Tassels & Wings.

Chin, Audrey & Peterson, Mark A. Deep Pockets, Empty Pockets: Who Wins in Cook County Jury Trials. LC 85-9517. 1985. pap. text 10.00 (*0-8330-0651-7*, R-3249-ICJ) Rand Corp.

Chin, Barry, jt. auth. see Zinns, Ken.

Chin, Beverly Ann. On Your Own: Grammar. (C). 1991. pap. text 9.15 (*0-13-634106-3*) P-H.

Chin, Brian B. Artillery at the Golden Gate: The Harbor Defenses of San Francisco in World War II. LC 94-65848. (Illus.). 170p. 1994. pap. 12.95 (*0-929521-85-4*) Pictorial Hist.

Chin, Brian B. Seacoast Cannon Coloring Book. 48p. 1996. pap. 3.95 (*1-57510-015-0*) Pictorial Hist.

Chin, Charlie. China's Bravest Girl: The Legend of Hua Mu Lan. Chu, Wang Xing, tr. LC 93-15255. (ENG & CHI., Illus.). 32p. (YA). (gr. 1 up). 1993. 14.95 (*0-89239-120-0*) Childrens Book Pr.

— China's Bravest Girl: The Legend of Mu Lan. Chu, Wang Xing, tr. (ENG & CHI.). (YA). (gr. 5-7). 1997. pap. 6.95 (*0-89239-148-0*) Childrens Book Pr.

Chin, Chen-An & Song, Pill-Soon. Reactivity Indices for Biomolecules. (Graduate Studies: No. 24). (Illus.). 176p. 1981. 33.00 (*0-89672-093-4*); pap. 20.00 (*0-89672-092-6*) Tex Tech Univ Pr.

Chin, Christine. In Service & Servitude: Foreign Female Domestic Workers & the Malaysian "Modernity" Project. LC 97-43048. (Illus.). 400p. 1998. 47.50 (*0-231-10986-5*) Col U Pr.

— In Service & Servitude: Foreign Female Domestic Workers & the Malaysian "Modernity" Project. LC 97-43048. 336p. 1998. pap. 18.50 (*0-231-10987-3*) Col U Pr.

Chin-Chuan Lee, ed. Voices of China: The Interplay of Politics & Journalism. LC 90-14003. (Guilford Communication Ser.). 353p. 1990. pap. text 21.95 (*0-89862-288-3*) Guilford Pubns.

Chin-Chuan Lee, jt. auth. see Joseph Man Chan.

Chin-Chuan Li. Media Imperialism Reconsidered: The Homogenizing of Television Culture. LC 80-16763. (People & Communication Ser.: No. 10). 277p. 1980. reprint ed. pap. 85.90 (*0-608-01177-0*, 205947500001) Bks Demand.

Chin, D. T., et al, eds. Proceedings of the Symposium on Metal Deposition & Dissolution. LC 92-74474. (Proceedings Ser.: Vol. 92-23). 342p. 1992. 43.00 (*1-56677-024-6*) Electrochem Soc.

***Chin, David.** The China Cupboard & the Coal Furnace: Poems. LC 99-55219. 108p. 2000. pap. text 19.95 (*0-7734-2796-1*) E Mellen.

Chin, David. Water-Resources Engineering. LC 99-21054. 750p. (C). 1999. 105.00 (*0-201-35091-2*, Prentice Hall) P-H.

Chin, Der-Tau, ed. see Symposium on Load Leveling & Energy Conservation i.

Chin, Duncan. Growing up on Grove Street, 1931-46: Sketches & Memories of a Chinese American Boyhood. LC 95-30681. (Illus.). 110p. (Orig.). 1995. pap. text 18.95 (*0-932319-04-1*) Capitola Bk.

Chin, Frank. Bulletproof Buddhists & Other Essays. LC 97-39399. (Intersections Ser.). 376p. 1997. pap. 29.95 (*0-8248-1959-4*) UH Pr.

— Bulletproof Buddhists & Other Essays. LC 97-39399. (Intersections Ser.). 376p. 1998. text 42.00 (*0-8248-1999-3*) UH Pr.

— Chickencoop Chinaman/Dragn: Two Plays. LC 81-985. (Illus.). 172p. 1981. pap. 14.95 (*0-295-95833-2*) U of Wash Pr.

— Chinaman Pacific & Frisco R. R. Co. LC 88-30326. 224p. (Orig.). 1988. pap. 10.95 (*0-918273-44-7*) Coffee Hse.

— Donald Duk. LC 90-29994. 176p. (Orig.). (YA). (gr. 9-12). 1991. pap. 11.95 (*0-918273-83-8*) Coffee Hse.

— Gunga Din Highway. LC 94-12597. 400p. 1994. 24.95 (*1-56689-024-1*) Coffee Hse.

— Gunga Din Highway. LC 94-12597. 400p. 1995. pap. 14.95 (*1-56689-037-3*) Coffee Hse.

Chin, Gabriel J. Immigration & Nationality Law Review, 1976-1997, 18 bks., Set. LC 92-72525. 1976. lib. bdg. 1035.00 (*0-930342-68-2*, 103280) W S Hein.

Chin, Gabriel J., ed. Affirmative Action & the Constitution, 3 vols. LC 98-29069. (Controversies in Constitutional Law Ser.). 1184p. 1998. reprint ed. 235.00 (*0-8153-2742-0*) Garland.

— New York City Police Corruption Investigation Commissions, 1894-1994, 6 vols. LC 97-70840. 1997. 325.00 (*1-57588-211-6*, 310740) W S Hein.

Chin, Gabriel J., ed. see U.S. Commission on Immigration Reform Staff.

Chin, Gilbert Y., ed. Advances in Powder Technology: Papers Presented at the 1981 ASM Materials Science Seminar Held October 10-11, 1981, in Louisville, KY. LC 82-72485. (Illus.). 358p. 1982. reprint ed. pap. 111.00 (*0-608-02652-2*, 206331200004) Bks Demand.

Chin, Gilbert Y., jt. ed. see Wessels, B. W.

Chin, H. E. Surinam: Politics, Economics & Society. (Marxist Regimes Ser.). 220p. 1987. text 49.00 (*0-86187-516-8*); text 17.50 (*0-86187-517-6*) St Martin.

Chin, Harris. Computer Data Analy. 3rd ed. 1999. write for info. (*0-07-236928-0*) McGraw.

Chin, Harry. Newspaper Advertising Sales: The Complete Guide to Job Finding, Facts, & Forecasts. Utterback, Laura, ed. LC 93-87294. 240p. 1994. pap. 19.95 (*0-9637975-0-6*) Newspaper Res.

Chin, Homer G. On Call: Obstetrics & Gynecology. Schmitt, Williams, ed. LC 96-16716. 416p. 1997. pap. text 21.95 (*0-7216-1316-0*, W B Saunders Co) Harcrt Hlth Sci Grp.

Chin, Hong-Sop, et al. Cultural Treasures of Korea, 8 vols., Set. LC 91-73742. (Illus.). 1993. lib. bdg. 775.50 (*1-56591-100-8*) Hollym Intl.

Chin-Hsiung, Hsu. The Menzies Collection of Shange Dynasty Oracle Bones Vol. I: A Catalogue. (Illus.). 300p. 37.14 (*0-88854-022-1*) Brill Academic Pubs.

— The Menzies Collection of Shange Dynasty Oracle Bones Vol. II: The Text. (Illus.). 294p. 37.14 (*0-88854-023-X*) Brill Academic Pubs.

— Oracle Bones from the White & Other Collections. (Illus.). 280p. 37.14 (*0-88854-231-3*) Brill Academic Pubs.

***Chin, James E.** Control of Communicable Diseases Manual. (Illus.). 2000. pap. 30.00 (*0-87553-242-X*) Am Pub Health.

Chin, Jean L., et al. Diversity in Psychotherapy: The Politics of Race, Ethnicity & Gender. LC 93-18240. 224p. 1993. 59.95 (*0-275-94180-9*, C4180, Praeger Pubs) Greenwood.

— Transference & Empathy in Asian American Psychotherapy: Cultural Values & Treatment Needs. LC 92-48757. 168p. 1993. 52.95 (*0-275-94493-X*, C4493, Praeger Pubs) Greenwood.

***Chin, Jean Lau.** Relationships among Asian American Women. LC 00-27411. (Psychology of Women Ser.: Vol. 5). 304p. 2000. 39.95 (*1-55798-680-0*) Am Psychol.

Chin, Justin. Bite Hard. LC 97-4716. 160p. 1997. pap. text 11.95 (*0-916397-47-5*) Manic D Pr.

— Mongrel. LC 98-37185. 160p. 1998. pap. 11.95 (*0-312-19513-3*) St Martin.

Chin, K. K. & Kumarasivam, K., eds. Industrial Water Technology: Treatment, Reuse & Recycling: Proceedings of a Conference Held in Singapore, 28-31 May 1985. (Water Science & Technology Ser.: 18). (Illus.). 178p. 1986. pap. 56.50 (*0-08-034017-2*, Pub. by PPL) Elsevier.

Chin, Katie, jt. auth. see Chin, Leeann.

Chin, Kee K., ed. see Field, Richard, et al.

Chin-Keong, Ng. Trade & Society: The Amoy Network on the China Coast, 1683-1735. 346p. 1984. 49.50 (*9971-69-068-3*, Pub. by Sngapore Univ Pr) Coronet Bks.

***Chin, Ko-Lin.** Chinatown Gangs: Extortion, Enterprise & Ethnicity. (Illus.). 256p. 2000. pap. 17.95 (*0-19-513627-6*) OUP.

Chin, Ko-Lin. Chinese Subculture & Criminality: Non-Traditional Crime Groups in America, 29. LC 89-71441. (Contributions in Criminology & Penology Ser.: No. 29). 208p. 1990. 55.00 (*0-313-27262-X*, CCK/, Greenwood Pr) Greenwood.

— Smuggled Chinese: Clandestine Immigration to the United States. LC 99-36086. (Asian American History & Culture Ser.). (Illus.). 296p. 1999. 64.50 (*1-56639-732-4*); pap. 22.95 (*1-56639-733-2*) Temple U Pr.

Chin, Kon Y. Kuala Lumpur: A Sketch Book LC 99-914491. 96 p. 1995. write for info. (*981-3018-20-8*) Arch Pr.

Chin, Kwei C. & Tarlow, Michael J. Paediatrics Revision. (Illus.). 180p. 1989. pap. text 26.00 (*0-443-03274-2*) Church.

Chin-Lee, Cynthia. A Is for Asia. LC 96-36346. (Illus.). 32p. (J). (gr. k-5). 1997. 15.95 (*0-531-30011-0*); lib. bdg. 16.99 (*0-531-33011-7*) Orchard Bks Watts.

***Chin-Lee, Cynthia.** A Is for Asia. LC 96-36346. (Illus.). 32p. (J). (gr. k-5). 1999. pap. 5.95 (*0-531-07141-3*) Orchard Bks Watts.

Chin-Lee, Cynthia. Almond Cookies & Dragon Well Tea. LC 92-21518. (Illus.). 36p. (J). (gr. k-3). 1993. 14.95 (*1-879965-03-8*) Polychrome Pub.

— It's Who You Know: The Magic of Networking in Person & on the Internet. LC 97-71613. 168p. 1998. pap. 14.95 (*1-885221-71-1*) BookPartners.

Chin-Lee, Cynthia & De la Pena, Terri. A Is for the Americas. LC 99-11720. (Illus.). 32p. (J). (gr. k-4). 1999. 15.95 (*0-531-30194-X*) Orchard Bks Watts.

Chin-Lee, Cynthia & de la Pina, Terri. A Es para decir Americas. LC 99-12357. (SPA., Illus.). 32p. (J). (gr. k-4). 1999. pap. text 6.95 (*0-531-07134-0*) Orchard Bks Watts.

Chin-Lee, Cynthia, et al. A Is for the Americas. LC 99-11720. (Illus.). 32p. (J). (gr. k-4). 1999. lib. bdg. 16.99 (*0-531-33194-6*) Orchard Bks Watts.

***Chin, Leeann & Chin, Katie.** Everyday Chinese Cooking: Quick & Delicious Recipes from the Leeann Chin Restaurants. LC 00-20900. (Illus.). 208p. 2000. 22.00 (*0-609-60586-0*) C Potter.

Chin, Lily. Mosaic Afghans: The Easy Way to Colorful Crochet. (Illus.). 144p. 1999. pap. 14.95 (*0-8487-1903-4*) Oxmoor Hse.

***Chin, Lily M.** Mosaic Magic: Afghans Made Easy. LC 99-75769. (Illus.). 144p. 1999. pap. 14.95 (*0-8487-1902-6*) Oxmoor Hse.

Chin-Lin Chen. Elements of Optoelectronics & Fiber Optics. 600p. (C). 1995. text 71.50 (*0-256-14182-7*, Irwn McGrw-H) McGrw-H Hghr Educ.

***Chin, Llewellyn P., et al.** California Real Property Sales Transactions - 12/98 Update, 2 vols. 3rd ed. Blanchette, Janis L., ed. LC 97-78051. 690p. 1998. ring bd. 89.00 (*0-7626-0280-5*, RE-32991) Cont Ed Bar-CA.

Chin, Llewellyn P., jt. auth. see Mangus, Jon L.

Chin-Mai, jt. auth. see Chen.

Chin, Marilyn. Dwarf Bamboo. LC 87-80181. (Illus.). 84p. (Orig.). 1987. pap. 8.95 (*0-912678-71-2*, Greenfld Rev Pr) Greenfld Rev Lit.

— The Phoenix Gone, the Terrace Empty: Poems. LC 93-33206. (Illus.). 104p. (Orig.). 1994. pap. 11.95 (*0-915943-87-5*) Milkweed Ed.

Chin, Mario D., et al, eds. Proceedings, 7th European Simulation Symposium, ESS, '95. (Illus.). 806p. 1995. 180.00 (*1-56555-083-8*, ESS-95) Soc Computer Sim.

Chin-ming Ch'ian, et al. Business Readings (in Chinese) Chen-ch'ing Li & Te-ming Yeh, eds. (Mandarin Training Center Ser.). (CHI.). 229p. (Orig.). 1991. pap. text 18.95 (*0-88710-171-2*) Yale Far Eastern Pubns.

Chin, N. Y. Excluding Liability in Contracts. 227p. 1985. 88.00 (*0-409-99500-2*, MICHIE) LEXIS Pub.

Chin, Nan H. Basic Buddhism: Exploring Buddhism & Zen. LC 97-25613. 256p. (Orig.). 1997. pap. 15.95 (*1-57863-020-7*) Weiser.

Chin-Ning Chu. Thick Face, Black Heart: The Warrior Philosophy for Conquering the Challenges of Business & Life. 384p. 1994. reprint ed. mass mkt. 14.99 (*0-446-67020-0*, Pub. by Warner Bks) Little.

Chin, Patricia, et al, eds. Rehabilitation Nursing Practice. (Illus.). 800p. 1997. text 38.00 (*0-07-105482-0*) McGraw-Hill HPD.

Chin, Patrick, jt. auth. see Roffel, Brian.

***Chin, Paul L.** The AAM Guide to Human Resources Policy. (Illus.). 200p. 2000. pap. 42.00 (*0-931201-66-7*) Am Assn Mus.

Chin, R. D. Feng Shui Revealed. LC 97-20867. (Illus.). 240p. 1998. 30.00 (*0-609-60294-2*) C Potter.

Chin, R. T., et al, eds. Computer Vision - ACCV '98: 3rd Asian Conference on Computer Vision, Hong Kong, China, January 8-10, 1998, Proceedings, Vol. II. (Lecture Notes in Computer Science Ser.: Vol. 1352). xxiv, 757p. 1997. pap. text 90.00 (*3-540-63931-4*) Spr-Verlag.

— Computer Vision - ACCV'98: 3rd Asian Conference on Computer Vision, Hong Kong, China, January 8-10, 1998, Proceedings, Vol. I. LC 97-48774. (Lecture Notes in Computer Science Ser.: Vol. 1351). xxiv, 761p. 1997. pap. text 90.00 (*3-540-63930-6*) Spr-Verlag.

Chin, Richard, jt. auth. see Ribner, Susan.

Chin, Richard M. The Energy Within: Qi Kung, Energetics & the Science Behind Eastern Healing Techniques. 2nd ed. (Illus.). 202p. 1998. reprint ed. pap. 13.95 (*1-56924-672-6*, Pub. by Marlowe & Co) Publishers Group.

Chin, Rockwood. Management, Industry & Trade in Cotton Textiles. 1965. 18.95 (*0-8084-0207-2*) NCUP.

Chin, Roland T., et al, eds. Image Analysis Applications & Computer Graphics: Proceedings, Third International Computer Science Conference, ICSC '95, Hong Kong, December 11-13, 1995. LC 95-47129. (Lecture Notes in Computer Science Ser.: No. 1024). 533p. 1996. pap. 81.00 (*3-540-60697-1*) Spr-Verlag.

Chin, Roland T. & Pong, Ting-Chuen. Computer Vision, ACCV '98: Proceedings of the 3rd Asian Conference on Computer Vision, Hong Kong, China, January, 1998. LC 97-48774. (Lecture Notes in Computer Science Ser.: Vol. 135). 1998. 90.00 (*0-354-06931-4*) Spr-Verlag.

Chin, S., jt. ed. see Clementi, Enrico.

Chin, S., jt. ed. see Clementi, E.

Chin, S. L. Fundamentals of Laser Optoelectronics. (Series in Optics & Photonics: Vol. 1). 376p. 1989. text 64.00 (*981-02-0072-2*); pap. text 28.00 (*981-02-0073-0*) World Scientific Pub.

— This Is Life. 172p. 1990. pap. text 7.00 (*0-9625118-2-X*) World Scientific Pub.

Chin, S. L. & Evans, D. K. Multiphonton Processes: Proceedings of the International Conference. 496p. 1994. text 109.00 (*981-02-1586-X*) World Scientific Pub.

Chin, Sara. Below the Line. LC 97-27593. 160p. 1997. pap. 9.95 (*0-87286-331-X*) City Lights.

Chin-Sheng, Chou. An Economic History of China. Kaplan, Edward H., tr. from CHI. LC 74-620032. (Program in East Asian Studies Occasional Papers Ser: No. 7). Orig. Title: Chung-Kuo Ching-Chi Shih. (Illus.). 250p. 1974. reprint ed. pap. 12.00 (*0-914584-91-X*) WWUCEAS.

Chin-shing Huang. Philosophy, Philology & Politics in Eighteenth-Century China: Li Fu & the Lu-Wang School under the Ch'ing. (Cambridge Studies in Chinese History, Literature & Institutions). 224p. (C). 1995. text 52.95 (*0-521-48225-9*) Cambridge U Pr.

Chin, Shunshin. Murder in a Peking Studio. Fogel, Joshua A., tr. LC 85-47732. (Occasional Paper Arizona State Univ., Center for Asian Studies: No. 19). 183p. (Orig.). 1986. pap. 10.00 (*0-939252-15-5*) ASU Ctr Asian.

— The Taiping Rebellion. Fogel, Joshua, tr. (East Gate Readers Ser.). 728p. 2000. text 79.95 (*0-7656-0099-4*, East Gate Bk) M E Sharpe.

***Chin, Shunshin.** The Taiping Rebellion. Fogel, Joshua, tr. from JPN. LC 99-49758. 672p. 2000. pap. 35.00 (*0-7656-0100-1*, East Gate Bk) M E Sharpe.

Chin, Soo-Young. Doing What Had to Be Done: The Life Narrative of Dora Yum Kim. LC 99-20104. (Asian American History & Culture Ser.). 272p. 1999. pap. 21.95 (*1-56639-694-8*) Temple U Pr.

— Doing What Had to Be Done: The Life Narrative of Dora Yum Kim. LC 99-20104. (Asian American History & Culture Ser.). (Illus.). 272p. 1999. 65.50 (*1-56639-693-X*) Temple U Pr.

Chin, Soo-Young, et al, eds. ReViewing Asian America: Locating Diversity. (Association for Asian American Studies: No. 6). 214p. (Orig.). 1995. pap. text 29.00 (*0-87422-118-8*) Wash St U Pr.

Chin, Soo-Young, jt. auth. see Lochmann, Christina.

Chin, Steven A. Dragon Parade: A Chinese New Year Story. Haley, Alex, ed. LC 92-18079. (Stories of America Ser.). (Illus.). 32p. (J). (gr. 2-5). 1992. lib. bdg. 22.83 (*0-8114-7215-9*) Raintree Steck-V.

— Dragon Parade: A Chinese New Year Story. Haley, Alex, ed. LC 92-18079. (Stories of America Ser.). (Illus.). 32p. (J). (gr. 4-7). 1996. pap. write for info. (*0-8114-8055-0*) Raintree Steck-V.

— The Success of Gordon H. Chong & Associates: An Architect's Success Story. (Success Ser.). (Illus.). 112p. (J). (gr. 4-7). 1996. 15.95 (*0-8027-8307-4*); lib. bdg. 16.85 (*0-8027-8308-2*) Walker & Co.

— When Justice Failed: The Fred Korematsu Story. LC 92-18086. (Stories of America Ser.). (Illus.). 105p. (J). (gr. 2-5). 1992. lib. bdg. 25.68 (*0-8114-7236-1*) Raintree Steck-V.

Chin, Steven B. & Pisoni, David B., eds. Alcohol & Speech. LC 96-33482. (Illus.). 362p. 1997. text 49.95 (*0-12-172775-0*) Morgan Kaufmann.

***Chin, Tung Pok & Chin, Winifred C.** Paper Son: One Man's Story. (Asian American History & Culture Ser.). (Illus.). 208p. 2000. 59.50 (*1-56639-800-2*); pap. 19.95 (*1-56639-801-0*) Temple U Pr.

Chin Ung-Ho. Chinese Politics in Sarawak: A Study of the Sarawak United People's Party. 352p. pap. text (*983-56-0039-2*) OUP.

***Chin, Vicente Hao, Jr., ed.** The Mahatma Letters to A. P. Sinnett: In Chronological Sequence. 600p. 1998. pap. 26.95 (*81-7059-273-9*, Pub. by Theos Pub Hse) Natl Bk Netwk.

***Chin, Walter, photos by.** Walter Chin: Selects. (Illus.). 2000. 75.00 (*3-908163-27-7*, Pub. by Edit Stemmle) Abbeville Pr.

Chin, Wanda & Danowski, Michael P. Dim Sum - How about Some? A Guide to New York's Liveliest Chinese Dining & How to Make a Day of It. LC 90-62423. (Illus.). (Orig.). 1991. pap. 8.95 (*0-9627444-0-9*) NY Niche Pr.

Chin, Wee Y. & Corlett, Richard. The City & the Forest: Plant Life in Urban Singapore. (Illus.). 194p. (Orig.). 1986. pap. 32.50 (*9971-69-103-5*, Pub. by Sngapore Univ Pr) Coronet Bks.

Chin, Wee Y., et al. Snake Bites & Their Treatment. 1991. pap. 19.95 (*9971-69-151-5*) Intl Spec Bk.

Chin, Wee Y., jt. auth. see Wei, Teo L.

Chin, William W. & Boime, Irving, eds. Glycoprotein Hormones: Structure, Synthesis & Biologic Function. (Serono Symposia, USA Ser.). (Illus.). 462p. (C). 1990. text 75.00 (*1-878601-01-6*) Serono Symposia USA.

Chin, Wilson C. Borehole Flow Modeling in Horizontal, Deviated, & Vertical Wells. 214p. 1991. 65.00 (*0-88415-034-8*) Gulf Pub.

— Formation Invasion: With Applications to Measurement-While-Drilling, Time Lapse Analysis, & Formation Damage. (Illus.). 240p. 1995. 75.00 (*0-88415-286-3*, 5286) Gulf Pub.

C

— Modern Reservoir Flow & Well Transient Analysis. LC 92-35620. (Illus.). 400p. 1993. reprint ed. pap. 124.00 (*0-608-07945-6*, 206791800012) Bks Demand.
— Wave Propagation in Petroleum Engineering: Modern Applications to Drillstring Vibrations, Measurement-While-Drilling, Swab-Surge, & Geophysics. LC 93-48179. (Illus.). 408p. 1994. pap. 126.50 (*0-608-05081-4*, 206563500005) Bks Demand.

Chin, Winifred C., jt. auth. see Chin, Tung Pok.

Chin, Wutha, jt. ed. see Koung, Leendavy.

Chin, Yee Wah. Antitrust Litigation: Strategies for Success. LC 99-170055. (Corporate Law & Practice Course Handbook Ser.). 392 p. 1998. 129.00 (*0-87224-542-X*) PLI.

Chin, Yin-lien C., et al, trs. Chinese Folktales: An Anthology. LC 96-5158. 192p. (C). (ps up). 1996. pap. 15.95 (*1-56324-800-X*, N Castle) M E Sharpe.
— The Stone Lion & Other Chinese Detective Stories: The Wisdom of Lord Bau. LC 91-46520. 200p. (YA). (gr. 8-12). 1992. 60.95 (*0-87332-634-2*, East Gate Bk); pap. 22.95 (*0-87332-635-0*, East Gate Bk) M E Sharpe.
— Traditional Chinese Folktales. LC 88-31129. (Illus.). 192p. (YA). (gr. 8-12). 1989. 41.95 (*0-87332-507-9*, East Gate Bk) M E Sharpe.

Chin, Yin-Lien C., et al. Dragons in the Flowery Land: An Introduction to Chinese History & Literature. 283p. 1985. pap. 14.95 (*0-614-16172-X*, DFLCHL) Cheng & Tsui.

***Chin, Yu & Hakim, Chris.** Handbook of Obstetrics & Gynecology in Chinese Medicine: An Integrated Approach. LC 97-76732. 1998. pap. write for info. (*0-939616-28-9*) Eastland.

***Chin, Yung & Minford, John.** The Deer & the Cauldron: A Martial Arts Novel. LC 97-36366. 596p. 2000. 35.00 (*0-19-590323-4*) OUP.

China Academy of Traditional Chinese Medicine, Institute of Acupuncture & Moxibustion Staff, compiled by. The Location of Acupoints. LC 93-242403. 276p. 1990. write for info. (*7-119-01368-8*) Foreign Lang.

China Books & Periodicals, Inc. Staff, tr. see Bochuan, He.

China Books Staff. Neue Chinesisch-Deutsche Woertbuch. (CHI & GER.). 1164p. 1985. 75.00 (*0-7859-8552-2*, 3922373054) Fr & Eur.

China Business Update Staff, ed. CBU Directory of Chinese Vehicle, Component & Parts Manufacturers 1996. 620p. (Orig.). 1996. pap. 395.00 (*0-9650671-1-4*) China Business.
— China's Automotive Policies, Laws & Regulations. 158p. (Orig.). 1996. pap. 295.00 (*0-9650671-2-2*) China Business.

China Center of Advanced Science & Technology Staff & Winick, Herman. Applications of Synchrotron Radiation: Proceedings of the CCAST World Laboratory Symposium Workshop Held at the Institute of High Energy Physics, Beijing, the People's Republic of China, May 26-June 7, 1988. LC 88-24431. (China Center of Advanced Science & Technology (World Laboratory) Symposium - Workshop Proceedings Ser.). xi, 625 p. 1988. write for info. (*2-88124-696-6*) Gordon & Breach.

China Educational Commission. Christian Education in China: A Study. LC 75-36223. reprint ed. 34.50 (*0-404-14474-8*) AMS Pr.

China Guide Series Editors. Shanghai. (Illus.). 142p. 1994. pap. 8.95 (*0-8442-9816-6*, Passprt Bks) NTC Contemp Pub Co.

China Guides Editors. All China. 2nd ed. (China Guides Series Editors). (Illus.). 144p. 1995. pap. 9.95 (*0-8442-9802-6*, Passprt Bks) NTC Contemp Pub Co.
— Hong Kong. 2nd ed. (China Guides Series Editors). 207p. 1991. pap. 9.95 (*0-8442-9803-4*, Passprt Bks) NTC Contemp Pub Co.
— The Silk Road. (China Guides Series Editors). 224p. 1994. pap. 12.95 (*0-8442-9823-9*, Passprt Bks) NTC Contemp Pub Co.
— Yangzi River. (China Guides Series Editors). 192p. 1991. pap. 10.95 (*0-8442-9805-0*, Passprt Bks) NTC Contemp Pub Co.

China Machine Pr. Staff. Business Information on Beijing. (C). 1988. 110.00 (*0-7855-3789-9*, Pub. by China Machine-Bldg) St Mut.
— China Directory of Mechanical & Electrical Enterprises. 1500p. (C). 1988. 175.00 (*0-7855-3790-2*, Pub. by China Machine-Bldg) St Mut.
— China Machinery Industries Yearbook 1988. (C). 1988. 150.00 (*0-7855-3791-0*, Pub. by China Machine-Bldg) St Mut.
— Who Publish in China? (C). 1988. 75.00 (*0-7855-3813-5*, Pub. by China Machine-Bldg) St Mut.

China National Committee for Natural Scientific Te. Terms of Astrology (English-Chinese, Chinese-English) (CHI & ENG.). 120p. 1989. 49.95 (*0-8288-7331-3*, 7030012976) Fr & Eur.
— Terms of Atmosphere Science (English-Chinese, Chinese-English) (CHI & ENG.). 70p. 1989. 29.95 (*0-8288-7332-1*, 703001510X) Fr & Eur.
— Terms of Forestry (English-Chinese, Chinese-English) (CHI & ENG.). 134p. 1989. 39.95 (*0-8288-7336-4*, 7030014952) Fr & Eur.
— Terms of Geography (English-Chinese, Chinese-English) (CHI & ENG.). 85p. 1989. 29.95 (*0-8288-7333-X*, 703001152X) Fr & Eur.
— Terms of Microbiology (English-Chinese, Chinese-English) (CHI & ENG.). 98p. 1989. 29.95 (*0-8288-7334-8*, 7030014060) Fr & Eur.
— Terms of Pedology (English-Chinese, Chinese-English) (CHI & ENG.). 103p. 1988. 39.95 (*0-8288-7335-6*, 7030007751) Fr & Eur.
— Terms of Physics (English-Chinese, Chinese-English) (CHI & ENG.). 145p. 1989. 49.95 (*0-8288-7330-5*, 7030012488) Fr & Eur.

China, People's Republic of, State Statistical Bur, compiled by. China Trade & Price Statistics in 1987. 2nd rev. ed. 254p. 1988. pap. 55.00 (*0-19-584297-9*) OUP.

***China Pictorial Staff.** Beijing & Xian: China's Great Capitals. (Illus.). 2000. 25.00 (*0-88363-159-8*) H L Levin.
— China's Splendors. (Illus.). 2000. 25.00 (*0-88363-158-X*) H L Levin.

China Poultry & Veterinary Society Staff, ed. International Symposium on Waterfowl Production: Satellite Conference for the XVIII World Poultry Congress, Beijing, China, September 1988. (International Academic Publishers Ser.). 450p. 1989. 115.00 (*0-08-036147-1*, Pergamon Pr) Elsevier.

China Sports Magazine Staff. The Wonders of Qigong: A Chinese Exercise for Fitness, Health, & Longevity. Wayfarer Publications Staff, ed. LC 85-51522. 112p. 1985. pap. 14.95 (*0-935099-07-7*) Wayfarer Pubns.

China Sports, Peking Staff. Health Exercises from China. 63p. 5.75 (*0-317-31557-9*) Chans Corp.

China State Science & Technology Commission Ser., ed. Guide to China's Science & Technology Policy: White Paper, No. 2. (International Academic Publishers Ser.). 600p. 1989. 250.00 (*0-08-036501-9*, Pergamon Pr) Elsevier.

China Statistical Information & Consultancy Servic. The 1987 Survey of Income & Expenditure of Urban Households of China. 176p. 1991. pap. text 32.95 (*0-86638-125-2*) EW Ctr HI.

***China Union Staff.** CEV Slimline NT/Psalms/Proverbs. 1999. 2.50 (*1-58516-047-4*) Am Bible.

Chinaglia, A. The Original Bassini Operation for Inguinal Hernia. (Illus.). 116p. 1988. text 44.00 (*88-299-0229-2*, Pub. by Piccin Nuova) Gordon & Breach.

Chinaglia, A. The Original Bassini Operation for Inguinal Hernia: Centenary Edition. 116p. 1988. text 40.00 (*1-57235-038-5*) Piccin Nuova.

Chinaka, B., et al. Pamphlet Literature from Onitsha. (B. E. Ser.: No. 34). 1965. 75.00 (*0-8115-2985-1*) Periodicals Srv.

Chinara, Benudhar. Education & Democracy. (Illus.). viii, 202p. 1997. 26.00 (*81-7024-906-6*, Pub. by APH Pubng) Nataraj Bks.

Chinard, Gilbert. Benjamin Franklin on the Art of Eating. LC 58-10724. (APS Ser.: No. 10). 70p. 1980. reprint ed. pap. 10.00 (*0-87169-985-0*, A010-CHG) Am Philos.
— George Washington As the French Knew Him: A Collection of Texts. (History - United States Ser.). 161p. 1993. reprint ed. lib. bdg. 69.00 (*0-7812-4830-2*) Rprt Serv.
— Houdon in America. 1979. 11.95 (*0-405-10590-8*) Ayer.
— Jefferson et les Ideologues. Mayer, J. P., ed. LC 78-67341. (European Political Thought Ser.). (FRE.). 1980. reprint ed. lib. bdg. 23.95 (*0-405-11685-3*) Ayer.
— Mondesir, Edouard de Mondesir: Avec une Introd par Gilbert Chinard. 1979. 15.95 (*0-405-10594-0*) Ayer.
— The Treaties of 1778: Proceedings of French Treaties, 1774-1792 (Louis XVI) & United States Treaties, Feb. 7, 1778. 1979. 15.95 (*0-405-10595-9*) Ayer.

Chinard, Gilbert, ed. The Treaties of 1778 & Allied Documents. LC 73-181911. (BCL Ser.: No. I). reprint ed. 24.50 (*0-404-52421-4*) AMS Pr.

Chinard, Gilbert, ed. George Washington As the French Knew Him. LC 69-13858. reprint ed. lib. bdg. 15.00 (*0-8371-1058-0*, CHGW, Greenwood Pr) Greenwood.

Chinard, Gilbert, jt. auth. see Colbert, Edouard C.

Chinard, Gilbert, jt. auth. see Durand, John.

Chinard, Gilbert, jt. auth. see Laperouse, Jean F.

Chinas, Beverly N. The Isthmus Zapotecs. 2nd ed. Klein, Chris, ed. (Case Studies in Cultural Anthropology). (Illus.). 200p. (C). 1992. pap. text 23.50 (*0-03-055057-2*) Harcourt Coll Pubs.
— La Zandunga: Of Fieldwork & Friendship in Southern Mexico. (Illus.). 178p. (C). 1993. pap. text 11.50 (*0-88133-680-7*) Waveland Pr.

Chinburg, T. The Analytic Theory of Multiplicative Galois Structure. LC 88-8134. (Memoirs Ser.: No. 77/395). 158p. 1989. pap. 21.00 (*0-8218-2458-9*, MEMO/77/395) Am Math.

Chinca, Mark. Gottfried von Strassburg: Tristan. LC 96-24762. (Landmarks of World Literature Ser.). 126p. (C). 1997. text 44.95 (*0-521-40294-8*); pap. text 14.95 (*0-521-40852-0*) Cambridge U Pr.

Chincarini, G., et al, eds. Observational Cosmology Symposium. (ASP Conference Series Proceedings: Vol. 51). 746p. 1993. 34.00 (*0-937707-70-8*) Astron Soc Pacific.

Chinchar, Gerald, jt. auth. see Huck, Gabe.

Chinchille, Madame. Stewed Screwed & Tattooed. LC 94-75673. (Illus.). 104p. (Orig.). 1997. pap. 20.00 (*0-9602600-1-3*) Isadore Pr.

Chinchilli, Vernun M., jt. auth. see Vonesh, Edward F.

Chinchinian, Harry. Beware of the Drifters. unabridged ed. LC 98-84852. (Illus.). 186p. (J). 1998. 14.95 (*1-892476-00-2*) Plum Tree.
— Holly Brown & the Dragon Dingle. LC 98-84852. (Heather & Hally Brown Ser.). (Illus.). 134p. (J). (gr. k-3). 1998. pap. 9.95 (*0-9653535-9-1*, 1883697) Plum Tree.
— Immigrant Son: An American Boyhood. LC 96-60967. (Illus.). 128p. 1996. 18.95 (*0-9653535-1-6*) Plum Tree.
— Immigrant Son Bk. 2: Refusing to Grow Up. LC 97-69993. (Illus.). 188p. 1997. 21.95 (*0-9653535-7-5*) Plum Tree.
— Immigrant Son Vol. 1: An American Boyhood. LC 96-60967. (Illus.). 128p. 1996. pap. 7.95 (*0-9653535-0-8*) Plum Tree.
— Immigrant Son Vol. II: Refusing to Grow Up. LC 97-69993. (Illus.). 188p. 1997. pap. 9.95 (*0-9653535-6-7*) Plum Tree.
— Pathologist in Peril. 1996. pap. 8.95 (*0-9653535-2-4*) Plum Tree.
— The Princess & the Beggar. LC 98-65251. (Heather & Hally Brown Ser.). (Illus.). 152p. (J). (gr. 4-9). 1998. 16.95 (*0-9653535-8-3*) Plum Tree.

Chinchore, Mangala R. Anatta - Anatmata: Analysis of Buddhist Anti-Substantialist Crusade. LC 95-903828. (C). 1995. 28.00 (*81-7030-455-5*, Pub. by Sri Satguru Pubns) S Asia.
— Santana & Santanantara. (C). 1996. 42.00 (*81-7030-493-8*, Pub. by Sri Satguru Pubns) S Asia.

Chinea, F. J. & Gonzalez, Romero, eds. Rotating Objects & Relativistic Physics: Proceedings of the El Escarial Summer School on Gravitation & General Relativity 1992. (Lecture Notes in Physics Ser.). 1993. 80.95 (*0-387-57364-X*); write for info. (*3-540-57364-X*) Spr-Verlag.

Chinelly, Cynthia. The Coralroot. 24p. 1987. pap. 5.00 (*0-942979-01-X*) Livingston U Pr.

Chinen, Allan B. In the Ever After: Fairy Tales & the Second Half of Life. LC 88-28826. 216p. (Orig.). 1989. pap. 17.95 (*0-933029-41-1*) Chiron Pubns.
— Once upon a Midlife: Classic Stories & Mythic Tales to Illuminate the Middle Years. 256p. 1993. pap. 13.95 (*0-87477-725-9*, Tarcher Putnam) Putnam Pub Group.

Chinen, Allan B., et al. Clinical Approaches to Adult Development. Commons, Michael L. et al, eds. (Illus.). 384p. 1996. pap. 39.50 (*1-56750-135-4*); text 73.25 (*1-56750-134-6*) Ablx Pub.

Chinen, Jon J. The Great Mahele: Hawaii's Land Division of 1848. LC 57-14473. 44p. (Orig.). 1978. pap. text 5.00 (*0-87022-125-6*) UH Pr.

Chinen, Joyce N., ed. Women in Hawaii: Sites, Identities, & Voices. (Social Process in Hawaii Ser.: Vol. 38). 192p. 1997. pap. text 18.00 (*0-614-31323-6*) U of HI Sociology.

Chinen, Karleen & Hiura, Arnold T., eds. From Bento to Mixed Plate: Americans of Japanese Ancestry in Multicultural Hawaii. 110p. 1997. pap. 18.95 (*1-881161-12-9*) Japanese Museum.

Chinere, David S. & McGowan, M. The Beauty of Art. large type ed. Slapper, M., ed. (Illus.). 32p. (Orig.). 1996. pap. text. write for info. (*0-614-18899-7*) Interspace Bks.

***Chinery.** Simple GPS Navigation: Sea, Air, Land. (Illus.). 89p. 2000. pap. 16.95 (*1-898660-00-X*, Pub. by Fernhurst Bks) Motorbooks Intl.

Chinery, M. Collins Field Guide: Insects of Britain & Northern Europe. 3rd ed. (Illus.). 320p. 1993. 29.95 (*0-00-219918-1*, Pub. by HarpC) Trafalgar.
— Collins Nature Guide: Garden Wildlife. 255p. 1997. pap. 14.95 (*0-00-220072-4*, Pub. by HarpC) Trafalgar.
— Collins Wildlife Trust Guide: Butterflies of Britain & Europe. (Illus.). 720p. 1998. 26.95 (*0-00-220059-7*, Pub. by HarpC) Trafalgar.

Chinery, Michael. Ant. LC 90-10947. (Life Story Ser.). (Illus.). 32p. (J). (gr. 4-6). 1997. pap. 4.95 (*0-8167-2099-1*) Troll Communs.
— Butterfly. LC 90-10942. (Life Story Ser.). (Illus.). 32p. (J). (gr. 4-6). 1997. lib. bdg. 17.25 (*0-8167-2100-9*) Troll Communs.
— Butterfly. LC 90-10942. (Life Story Ser.). (Illus.). 32p. (J). (gr. 4-6). 1997. pap. 4.95 (*0-8167-2101-7*) Troll Communs.

***Chinery, Michael.** Collins Gem Insects. (Illus.). 1999. 7.95 (*0-00-472269-8*, Pub. by HarpC) Trafalgar.

Chinery, Michael. Frog. LC 90-10962. (Life Story Ser.). (Illus.). 32p. (J). (gr. 4-6). 1991. lib. bdg. 17.25 (*0-8167-2102-5*) Troll Communs.
— Frog. LC 90-10962. (Life Story Ser.). (Illus.). 32p. (J). (gr. 4-6). 1997. pap. 4.95 (*0-8167-2103-3*) Troll Communs.
— Garden Creepy-Crawlies. (Illus.). 172p. text 19.95 (*0-905483-44-8*, Pub. by Whittet Bks) Diamond Farm Bk.

Chinery, Michael. Insects of Britain & Western Europe. (Illus.). 1987. pap. 24.95 (*0-00-219137-7*, Pub. by HarpC) Trafalgar.

Chinery, Michael. New Generation Guide to the Butterflies & Day-Flying Moths of Britain & Europe. Attenborough, David, ed. (Corrie Herring Hooks Ser.: No. 13). (Illus.). 320p. 1989. 22.95 (*0-292-75539-2*) U of Tex Pr.

***Chinery, Michael.** Partners & Parents. (Secrets of the Rainforest Ser.). (Illus.). 32p. (J). (gr. k-8). 2000. pap. 7.95 (*0-7787-0226-X*); lib. bdg. 19.96 (*0-7787-0216-2*) Crabtree Pub Co.
— People & Places. (Secrets of the Rainforest Ser.). (Illus.). 32p. (J). (gr. 3-9). 2000. pap. 7.95 (*0-7787-0230-8*); lib. bdg. 19.96 (*0-7787-0220-0*) Crabtree Pub Co.
— Plants & Plant Eaters. (Secrets of the Rainforest Ser.). (Illus.). 32p. (J). (gr. k-8). 2000. pap. 7.95 (*0-7787-0228-6*); lib. bdg. 19.96 (*0-7787-0218-9*) Crabtree Pub Co.
— Poisoners & Pretenders. (Secrets of the Rainforest Ser.). (Illus.). 32p. (J). (gr. k-8). 2000. pap. 7.95 (*0-7787-0229-4*); lib. bdg. 19.96 (*0-7787-0219-7*) Crabtree Pub Co.
— Predators & Prey. LC 00-20390. (Secrets of the Rainforest Ser.). (Illus.). 32p. (J). (gr. k-8). 2000. lib. bdg. 19.96 (*0-7787-0217-0*) Crabtree Pub Co.
— Predators & Prey. (Secrets of the Rain Forest Ser.). (Illus.). 32p. (J). (gr. 3-8). 2000. pap. 7.95 (*0-7787-0227-8*) Crabtree Pub Co.

Chinery, Michael. Questions & Answers about Seashore Animals. LC 93-29428. (Questions & Answers about Ser.). (Illus.). 40p. (J). (gr. 4-7). 1994. pap. 8.95 (*1-85697-965-2*) LKC.

***Chinery, Michael.** Resources & Conservation. (Secrets of the Rainforest Ser.). (Illus.). 32p. (J). (gr. 3-9). 2000. pap. 7.95 (*0-7787-0231-6*); lib. bdg. 19.96 (*0-7787-0221-9*) Crabtree Pub Co.

Chinery, Michael. Shark. LC 90-33361. (Life Story Ser.). (Illus.). 32p. (J). (gr. 4-6). 1997. pap. 4.95 (*0-8167-2105-X*) Troll Communs.
— Snake. LC 90-10951. (Life Story Ser.). (Illus.). 32p. (J). (gr. 4-6). 1991. pap. 4.95 (*0-8167-2107-6*) Troll Communs.
— Snake. LC 90-10951. (Life Story Ser.). (Illus.). 32p. (J). (gr. 4-6). 1997. lib. bdg. 17.25 (*0-8167-2106-8*) Troll Communs.
— Spider. LC 90-10941. (Life Story Ser.). (Illus.). 32p. (J). (gr. 4-6). 1991. pap. 4.95 (*0-8167-2109-2*) Troll Communs.
— Spiders. (Illus.). 128p. text 19.95 (*1-873580-09-6*, Pub. by Whittet Bks) Diamond Farm Bk.

Chinery, Michael, ed. The Kingfisher Illustrated Encyclopedia of Animals. LC 92-53113. (Illus.). 380p. (J). (gr. 4 up). 1992. 22.95 (*1-85697-801-X*, Kingfisher) LKC.

Chinery, Mik. Simple Electronic Navigation. 2nd ed. 64p. (C). 1990. text 59.00 (*0-906754-67-4*, Pub. by Fernhurst Bks) St Mut.

Chinese Academy of Sciences & State Planning Commi, jt. ed. see State Statistical Bureau, Institute of Statistics Staff.

Chinese Academy of Sciences, Biodiversity Committe. Advances in Biodiversity Research. (CHI & LAT.). 1996. pap. 140.00 (*0-7855-0527-X*, Pub. by Wanhai Books) St Mut.

Chinese Academy of Sciences, Institute of the Hist, jt. ed. see People's Republic of China, State Council Staff.

Chinese Academy of Sciences Staff. Science & Technlogy in China, Vol. II. (International Academic Publishers Ser.). (Illus.). 550p. 1989. 200.00 (*0-08-036386-5*, Pergamon Pr) Elsevier.

Chinese Academy of Sciences Staff, jt. auth. see Chang Chun Institute of Geography Staff.

Chinese Academy of Sciences Staff, jt. auth. see Environmental Impact Assessment Department Staff.

Chinese Academy of Sciences Staff, jt. compiled by see Institute of Geography Staff.

Chinese Academy of Sciences Staff, jt. compiled by see Team of Integrated Scientific Investigation of the.

Chinese Academy of Sciences Staff, jt. ed. see National Conditions Investigation Group Staff.

Chinese Academy of Social Science Staff, ed. Information China: The Comprehensive & Authoritative Reference Source of New China & Its Historical Background, 3 vols., Set. (World Information Ser.). (Illus.). 1700p. 1988. text 300.00 (*0-08-034764-9*, Pergamon Pr) Elsevier.

Chinese Association of Refrigeration Staff, et al, eds. Advances in Cryosurgery: Proceedings of the Seventh International Congress of Cryosurgery, Beijing, 11-14 October, 1989. LC 89-20117. (International Academic Publishers Ser.: No. 13). 626p. 1990. 180.00 (*0-08-037503-0*, Pub. by IAP) Elsevier.

Chinese Botanical Society Staff. Bibliography of Chinese Botany. (CHI & LAT.). 1955. pap. 158.00 (*0-7855-0518-0*, Pub. by Wanhai Books) St Mut.

Chinese Business Update Staff, ed. from CHI. China's Development Plan for Key Automotive Parts, 1996-2000. Orig. Title: Bufen Qiche Guanjian Lingbujian Jiuwu Guihua Shexiang. 158p. (Orig.). 1996. pap. 295.00 (*0-9650671-0-6*) China Business.

Chinese Canadian National Council's Women's Book C. Jin Guo: Voices of Chinese Canadian Women. (Illus.). 353p. pap. 17.95 (*0-88961-147-5*, Pub. by Womens Pr) LPC InBook.

Chinese-English Translation Assistance Group. Chinese-English Glossary of Astro-Science Terms. LC 86-71163. (Chinese-English Technical Glossary Ser.). 130p. (Orig.). 1986. pap. 18.75 (*0-931745-16-0*) Dunwoody Pr.

Chinese-English Translation Assistance Group, ed. Chinese-English Glossary of Linguistic Terms. LC 86-71174. (Chinese-English Technical Glossary Ser.). 130p. (Orig.). 1986. pap. 15.00 (*0-931745-21-7*) Dunwoody Pr.
— Chinese-English Glossary of Military Affairs Terms with Diagrams. LC 86-71176. (Chinese-English Technical Glossary Ser.). 200p. (Orig.). (C). 1986. pap. 17.50 (*0-931745-22-5*) Dunwoody Pr.
— Chinese-English Glossary of Names of Foreign Arms Manufacturers & Satellite Systems. LC 86-71173. (Chinese-English Technical Glossary Ser.). 35p. (Orig.). 1986. pap. 7.50 (*0-931745-23-3*) Dunwoody Pr.
— Chinese-English Glossary of Oil Well Terms. LC 86-71166. (Chinese-English Technical Glossary Ser.). 650p. (Orig.). (C). 1986. pap. 68.75 (*0-931745-24-1*) Dunwoody Pr.
— Chinese-English Glossary of Particle Physics Supplement. LC 86-71170. (Chinese-English Technical Glossary Ser.). 15p. (Orig.). (C). 1986. pap. 6.25 (*0-931745-29-2*) Dunwoody Pr.
— Chinese-English Glossary of Petrochemical Terms. LC 86-71164. (Chinese-English Technical Glossary Ser.). 110p. (Orig.). 1986. pap. 15.00 (*0-931745-26-8*) Dunwoody Pr.
— Chinese-English Glossary of Selected Posts & Telecommunications Terms. LC 86-71165. (Chinese-English Technical Glossary Ser.). 25p. (Orig.). 1986. pap. 6.25 (*0-931745-27-6*) Dunwoody Pr.
— Chinese-English Glossary of Spectrum Analysis Terms. LC 86-71175. (Chinese-English Technical Glossary Ser.). 30p. (Orig.). (C). 1986. pap. 7.50 (*0-931745-25-X*) Dunwoody Pr.
— Chinese-English Glossary of Thermal Power Terms. LC 86-71167. (Chinese-English Technical Glossary Ser.). 45p. (Orig.). 1986. pap. 10.00 (*0-931745-30-6*) Dunwoody Pr.

— Chinese-English Glossary of Naval Terms. LC 86-71172. (Chinese-English Technical Glossary Ser.). 95p. (Orig.). (C). 1986. pap. 12.50 (*0-931745-28-4*) Dunwoody Pr.

Chinese-English Translation Assistance Group Staff, ed. Chinese Dictionaries: An Extensive Bibliography of Dictionaries in Chinese & Other Languages. LC 82-923. (CHI & ENG.). 446p. 1982. lib. bdg. 115.00 (*0-313-23505-8*, MDC/) Greenwood.

— Chinese-English Glossary of Aviation Technology Terms. 205p. 1986. pap. 16.00 (*0-931745-32-2*) Dunwoody Pr.

— Chinese-English Glossary of Demographic Terms Accompanied by Chinese-English Glossary of Selected U. S. Economic & Statistical Terms. LC 86-71169. (Chinese-English Technical Glossary Ser.). 45p. (Orig.). 1986. pap. 10.00 (*0-931745-19-5*) Dunwoody Pr.

— Chinese-English Glossary of Military Terms, 3 vols., Set. 1988. pap. 100.00 (*0-931745-55-1*) Dunwoody Pr.

Chinese Heritage Center Staff, jt. auth. see Pan, Lynn.

Chinese Institute of Electronics Antenna Society S, ed. Antennas & EM Theory: Proceedings of the Second International Symposium on Antennas & EM Theory (ISAE '89), Shanghai, PRC, 29 August -1 September 1989. LC 89-19954. (International Academic Publishers Ser.). 726p. 1990. 170.00 (*0-08-037891-9*, 1105; 1704, Pub. by IAP) Elsevier.

Chinese Nuclear Society Staff, ed. Hydrometallurgy: Proceedings of 1st International Conference, Beijing, China, 12-15 October 1988. (International Academic Publishers Ser.). (Illus.). xvi, 748 p. 1989. 220.00 (*0-08-037201-5*, Pergamon Pr) Elsevier.

Chinese People's Institute of Foreign Affairs Staf. China Supports the Arab People's Struggle for National Independence: A Selection of Important Documents. LC 75-38060. reprint ed. 39.50 (*0-404-56916-1*) AMS Pr.

***Chinese School Association Staff.** Essays on Chinese Education in the United States. Zheng, Jeff Lianggen, ed. (Illus.). 178p. 2000. pap. 25.00 (*0-9674658-1-8*) PacifiCom.

Chinese Society for Measurement Staff, ed. Electromagnetic Metrology: Proceedings of the International Symposium on Electromagnetic Metrology (ISEM '89), Beijing, PRC, August 19-22, 1989. LC 89-16011. (International Academic Publishers Ser.). 500p. 1990. 145.00 (*0-08-037888-9*, 1105; 1704, Pub. by IAP) Elsevier.

Chinese Society of Corrosion & Protection Staff, ed. Corrosion & Corrosion Control for Offshore & Marine Constructions: Proceedings of the International Conference on Corrosion & Corrosion Control for the Offshore & Marine Constructions, Xiamen, PRC, 6-9 September 1988. (International Academic Publishers Ser.). (Illus.). 1000p. 1989. 150.00 (*0-08-036626-0*, , Pergamon Pr) Elsevier.

Chinese Society of Metals Staff, ed. The International Symposium on Refractories, Hangzhou, PRC, 15-19 November 1988: Proceedings. (International Academic Publishers Ser.). (Illus.). 700p. 1989. 235.00 (*0-08-036976-6*, Pergamon Pr) Elsevier.

Chinese University of Hong Kong, Department of Arc. The Living Building: Vernacular Environments of South China. 1997. pap. text 18.95 (*0-472-50064-3*, Pub. by Chinese Univ) U of Mich Pr.

Chinese University of Hong Kong Staff. Tenth International Conference on Integrated Optics & Optical Fibre Communication. 1997. pap. text 100.00 (*962-201-709-6*, Pub. by Chinese Univ) U of Mich Pr.

Chinese University Press Staff, ed. Tenth International Conference on Integrated Optics & Optical Fibre Communication, Vol. 1. (Chinese University Press Ser.). (Illus.). (C). pap. text. write for info. (*962-201-704-5*, Pub. by Chinese Univ) U of Mich Pr.

— Tenth International Conference on Integrated Optics & Optical Fibre Communication, Vol. 5. (Chinese University Press Staff). (Illus.). (C). pap. text. write for info. (*962-201-708-8*, Pub. by Chinese Univ) U of Mich Pr.

— Tenth International Conference on Integrated Optics & Optical Fibre Communication, VOL.2. (Chinese University Press Staff). (Illus.). (C). pap. text. write for info. (*962-201-705-3*, Pub. by Chinese Univ) U of Mich Pr.

— Tenth International Conference on Integrated Optics & Optical Fibre Communication, Vol.4. (Chinese University Press Staff). (Illus.). (C). pap. text. write for info. (*962-201-707-X*, Pub. by Chinese Univ) U of Mich Pr.

— Tenth International Conference on Integrated Optics & Optical Fibre Communication Vol.3. (Chinese University Press Staff). (Illus.). (C). pap. text. write for info. (*962-201-706-1*, Pub. by Chinese Univ) U of Mich Pr.

Chineworth, Mary A., ed. see Conwell, Charles A., et al.

Ching. Architecture: Architectural Graphics. 2nd ed. pap. text 63.00 (*0-471-38144-6*) Wiley.

Ching. Interior Design Illustration. 2nd rev. ed. (Architecture Ser.). (Illus.). 1999. pap. 32.95 (*0-442-02277-8*, VNR) Wiley.

***Ching, Barbara.** Wrong's What I Do Best: Hard Country Music & Contemporary Culture. LC 99-49466. 2000. write for info. (*0-19-510835-3*) OUP.

Ching, Barbara & Creed, Gerald. Knowing Your Place: Rural Identity & Cultural Hierarchy. LC 96-28866. 285p. (C). 1996. pap. 21.99 (*0-415-91545-7*) Routledge.

— Knowing Your Place: Rural Identity & Cultural Hierarchy. LC 96-28866. 285p. (C). 1996. 70.00 (*0-415-91544-9*) Routledge.

Ching, Billy S., tr. see Cheung, Stephen.

Ching, Chauncey. Simple Computing: What Computers Can Do for You. LC 84-33. (Orig.). 1984. pap. 9.95 (*0-915805-00-6*) Total Concepts.

Ching, Chauncey T., jt. auth. see Yanagida, John F.

Ching, Chee, ed. Network Organizations & Information Technology: A Special Issue of the Journal of Organizational Computing & Electronic Commerce, Vol. 7, Nos. 2 & 3. 210p. 1997. pap. 20.00 (*0-8058-9857-3*) L Erlbaum Assocs.

Ching-chih Chen. Optical Discs in Libraries: Use & Trends. 240p. 1991. 79.50 (*0-938734-49-0*) Info Today Inc.

Ching-chih Chen, ed. NIT, '90: Third International Conference on New Information Technology. 354p. (Orig.). 1990. pap. text 59.50 (*0-931555-07-8*) MicroUse Info.

Ching-Chih, Chen & Raitt, David I., eds. The First Pacific Conference on New Information Techology, Bangkok: Proceedings. 413p. 1987. pap. 45.00 (*0-931555-05-1*) MicroUse Info.

Ching-Chin Chen & Hernon, Peter, eds. Numeric Databases. LC 83-25761. 304p. 1984. 73.25 (*0-89391-247-6*) Ablx Pub.

Ching Chung Wang, ed. Molecular & Immunological Aspects of Parasitism. LC 90-27340. (AAAS Miscellaneous Publications: No. 91-01S). (Illus.). 207p. reprint ed. pap. 64.20 (*0-7837-6748-X*, 204637600011) Bks Demand.

Ching, Darlene O.S., ed. see Moore, Ralph E.

Ching, Emily, ed. see Hwa-I Publishing Co., Staff.

Ching, Emily, ed. see Wonder Kids Publications Staff.

Ching, Eugene & Ching, Nora. 201 Chinese Verbs: Compounds & Phrases for Everyday Usage. LC 77-8811. (ENG & CHI.). 1977. pap. text 14.95 (*0-8120-0674-7*) Barron.

Ching, Francis D. K. Architectural Graphics. 2nd ed. (Illus.). 192p. 1985. pap. 32.95 (*0-442-21864-8*, VNR) Wiley.

Ching, Francis D. K. Architectural Graphics. 3rd ed. (Illus.). 192p. 1996. pap. 34.95 (*0-471-28753-9*, VNR) Wiley.

Ching, Francis D. K. Architectural Graphics. 3rd rev. ed. (Architecture Ser.). (Illus.). 224p. 1996. pap. 32.95 (*0-442-02237-9*, VNR) Wiley.

Ching, Francis D. K. Architecture: Form, Space & Order. 2nd ed. 416p. 1995. pap. 34.95 (*0-471-28616-8*, VNR) Wiley.

Ching, Francis D. K. China in Transition. (Illus.). 216p. 1995. pap. text 17.95 (*962-7010-56-1*) Tuttle Pubng.

— Drawing: A Creative Process. (Illus.). 208p. 1989. pap. 34.95 (*0-471-28968-X*, VNR) Wiley.

— Drawing: A Creative Process. (Illus.). 210p. 1990. pap. 34.95 (*0-442-31818-9*, VNR) Wiley.

— Hong Kong & China: For Better or for Worse. LC 85-80364. (Illus.). 96p. 1985. pap. 6.95 (*0-87124-098-X*) Foreign Policy.

— Hong Kong & China: One Country, Two Systems? Hoepli-Phalon, Nancy L., ed. LC 96-95425. (Headline Ser.: Vol. 310). (Illus.). 64p. (Orig.). 1996. pap. text 5.95 (*0-87124-170-6*) Foreign Policy.

Ching, Francis D. K. Interior Design Illustrated. (Illus.). 318p. 1987. pap. 34.95 (*0-471-28868-3*, VNR) Wiley.

Ching, Francis D. K. Interior Design Illustrated. (Illus.). 320p. (C). 1987. pap. 32.95 (*0-442-21537-1*, VNR) Wiley.

***Ching, Francis D. K.** The Li Dynasty: Hong Kong Aristocrats. LC 99-34979. (Illus.). 296p. 1999. text 35.00 (*0-19-590904-6*) OUP.

— Sketches from Japan. 192p. 2000. text 29.95 (*0-471-36360-X*) Wiley.

— Visual Dictionary Architecture. (Architecture Ser.). 319p. 1995. 44.95 (*0-471-28451-3*, VNR) Wiley.

Ching, Francis D. K. A Visual Dictionary of Architecture. (Architecture Ser.). (Illus.). 448p. 1995. text 44.95 (*0-442-00904-6*, VNR) Wiley.

Ching, Francis D. K. A Visual Dictionary of Architecture. 319p. 1996. pap. 34.95 (*0-471-28821-7*, VNR) Wiley.

Ching, Francis D. K. A Visual Dictionary of Architecture. (Architecture Ser.). 1997. pap. 29.95 (*0-442-02462-2*, VNR) Wiley.

Ching, Francis D. K. & Adams, Cassandra. Building Construction. 2nd ed. 392p. 1991. pap. 39.95 (*0-471-28885-3*, VNR) Wiley.

— Building Construction Illustrated. 2nd enl. ed. (Illus.). 400p. 1991. pap. 32.95 (*0-442-23498-8*, VNR) Wiley.

***Ching, Francis D. K. & Adams, Cassandra.** Building Construction Illustrated. 3rd ed. LC 99-57440. (Illus.). 432p. 2000. pap. 39.95 (*0-471-35898-3*) Wiley.

Ching, Francis D. K. & Juroszek, Steven P. Design Drawing. LC 97-15928. (Architecture Ser.). (Illus.). 346p. 1997. 42.95 (*0-442-01909-2*, VNR) Wiley.

Ching, Francis D. K. & Juroszek, Steven P. Design Drawing. (Illus.). 352p. 1997. pap. 44.95 (*0-471-28654-0*, VNR) Wiley.

Ching, Francis D. K. & Miller, Dale E. Home Renovation. 350p. 1983. pap. 32.95 (*0-442-21592-4*, VNR) Wiley.

Ching, Francis D. K. & Miller, Dale E. Home Renovation. 352p. 1983. pap. 39.95 (*0-471-28869-1*, VNR) Wiley.

Ching Hai, Suma. I Have Come to Take You Home: A Collection of Quotes & Spiritual Teachings by the Supreme Master Ching Hai. Lapaire, Sophie & Miller, Pamela, eds. LC 95-9464. (VIE., Illus.). 146p. (Orig.). 1995. pap. 12.95 (*1-886544-01-8*) Suma Ching Hai Intl.

Ching, Heng, tr. see Hua, Hsuan.

Ch'ing Hua Ta Hsueh Staff. Who's Who of American Returned Students: Yu Mei T'ung Hshueh Lu, Min Kou Liu Nien. LC 84-157866. (Reprint Ser.). 215p. 1978. write for info. (*0-89644-562-3*) Chinese Materials.

Ching-Hwang, Yen. Coolies & Mandarins: China's Protection of Overseas Chinese During the Late Ch'ing Period, 1851-1911. 429p. (Orig.). 1985. pap. 47.50 (*9971-69-087-X*, Pub. by Sngapore Univ Pr) Coronet Bks.

Ching-Hwang, Yen, ed. Community & Politics: The Chinese in Colonial Singapore & Malaysia. LC 95-948069. 360p. 1995. pap. 28.50 (*981-210-062-8*, Pub. by Times Academic) Intl Spec Bk.

— Studies in Modern Overseas Chinese History. LC 95-948004. 272p. 1995. pap. 25.00 (*981-210-065-2*, Pub. by Times Academic) Intl Spec Bk.

Ching, I. Chinese Monks in India. Lahiri, Latika, tr. 160p. (C). 1995. reprint ed. 16.00 (*81-208-0062-1*, Pub. by Motilal Bnarsidass) S Asia.

Ching-I, Tu, ed. Classics & Interpretations: The Hermeneutic Traditions in Chinese Culture. LC 99-41851. 225p. 1999. 39.95 (*1-56000-431-2*) Transaction Pubs.

Ching-I Tu, ed. Tradition & Creativity: Contributions to East Asian Civilization. 192p. (Orig.). 1988. pap. 24.95 (*0-88738-738-1*) Transaction Pubs.

***Ching, Jacqueline.** Camping: Have Fun, Be Smart. (Explore the Outdoors Ser.). (Illus.). 64p. (YA). (gr. 7-12). 2000. lib. bdg. 17.95 (*0-8239-3173-0*) Rosen Group.

Ching Jen Chen, et al, eds. Turbulence Measurement & Flow Modeling. 869p. 1987. 240.00 (*0-89116-558-4*) Hemisp Pub.

Ching, Julia. The Butterfly Healing: A Life Between East & West. LC 98-18346. 1998. pap. 16.00 (*1-57075-237-0*) Orbis Bks.

— The Butterfly Healing: A Life Between East & West. LC 98-18346. 224p. 1998. 22.00 (*1-57075-208-7*) Orbis Bks.

— Chinese Religions. LC 93-2896. 300p. 1993. pap 19.50 (*0-88344-875-0*) Orbis Bks.

— Mysticism & Kingship in China: The Heart of Chinese Wisdom. LC 96-51602. (Studies in Religious Traditions: Vol. 11). 324p. (C). 1997. text 69.95 (*0-521-46293-2*); pap. text 22.95 (*0-521-46828-0*) Cambridge U Pr.

***Ching, Julia.** The Religious Thought of Chu Hsi. LC 99-19667. (Illus.). 368p. 2000. text 75.00 (*0-19-509189-2*) OUP.

Ching, Julia & Oxtoby, Willard G., eds. Discovering China: European Interpretations in the Enlightenment. LC 92-24272. (Library of the History of Ideas: Vol. 7). 243p. (C). 1992. 65.00 (*1-878822-14-4*) Univ Rochester Pr.

Ching, Julia, ed. see Huang, Tsung-hsi.

Ching-Lai Hwang, jt. auth. see Young-Jou Lai.

Ch'Ing Liang. Flower Adornment Sutra Preface. Buddhist Text Translation Society Staff, tr. from CHI. (Illus.). 198p. 1979. pap. 7.00 (*0-88139-450-5*) Buddhist Text.

— Flower Adornment Sutra Prologue, 4 vols. Buddhist Text Translation Society Staff, tr. Incl. Flower Adornment Sutra Prologue: Vol. I, The First Door. (Illus.). 230p. 1981. pap. 38.00 (*0-917512-66-9*); Flower Adornment Sutra Prologue Vol. III: The Second Door, Pt. II. (Illus.). 192p. 1983. pap. 38.00 (*0-917512-98-7*); Flower Adornment Sutra Prologue Vol. IV: The Second Door, Pt. III. 122p. 1983. pap. 38.00 (*0-88139-009-7*); 1981. Set pap. 38.00 (*0-917512-75-8*) Buddhist Text.

Ching-Liang, Gail. White Skin, Black Masks: Representation & Colonialism. 312p. (C). 1996. pap. 25.99 (*0-415-08148-3*) Routledge.

Ching, Linda. Story of the Stone. (Illus.). 138p. 1997. 40.00 (*0-9619891-5-7*) Hawaiian Goddesses.

— Story of the Stone. LC 98-26725. (Illus.). 136p. 1998. pap. 19.95 (*1-58008-027-8*); pap. text 19.95 (*1-58008-018-9*) Ten Speed Pr.

Ching, Linda & Chun, Malcolm N. Ano Lani: The Hawaiian Monarchy Years. (Illus.). 168p. 1993. 21.00 (*0-9619891-3-0*) Hawaiian Goddesses.

Ching, Linda & Shurley, Bruce. Hawaiian Goddesses. LC 87-83553. (Illus.). 125p. (C). 1988. 29.95 (*0-9619891-0-6*); pap. 22.95 (*0-9619891-1-4*) Hawaiian Goddesses.

Ching, Linda & Stephens, Robin. Powerstones. 25.00 (*0-9619891-4-9*) Hawaiian Goddesses.

Ching, Nora, jt. auth. see Ching, Eugene.

Ching, Patrick. Beautiful Birds of Hawaii Coloring Book. (Illus.). 32p. (J). (ps-2). 1992. pap. 4.95 (*1-880188-43-0*) Bess Pr.

— Endangered Animals of Hawaii Coloring Book. 32p. 1995. pap. 4.95 (*1-57306-015-1*) Bess Pr.

— Exotic Animals in Hawaii Coloring Book. (Illus.). 32p. (J). (ps-6). 1988. pap. 4.95 (*0-935848-56-8*) Bess Pr.

— The Hawaiian Monk Seal. LC 94-12429. (Illus.). 48p. (J). (gr. 4 up). 1994. 14.95 (*0-8248-1622-6*) UH Pr.

— Native Animals of Hawaii Coloring Book. (Illus.). 32p. (Orig.). (J). (ps-6). 1988. pap. 4.95 (*0-935848-55-X*) Bess Pr.

Ching, Paul, et al. Creating, Managing, & Evaluating Multidisciplinary Teams. LC 94-109638. (AAPG Continuing Education Course Note Ser.: No. 35). (Illus.). 97p. (Orig.). 1993. reprint ed. pap. 30.10 (*0-608-04227-7*, 206498400012) Bks Demand.

Ching, R. C. Icones Filicum Sinicarum, Set, Vols 1-5. (C). 1988. 600.00 (*0-7855-3254-4*) St Mut.

Ching-Shan. Diary of His Excellency Ching-Shan: Being a Chinese Account of the Boxer Trouble. Duyvendak, Jan J., tr. from CHI. LC 75-32319. (Studies in Chinese History & Civilization). 134p. 1976. reprint ed. lib. bdg. 62.50 (*0-313-27015-5*, U7015) Greenwood.

Ching, Theresa L. Efficacious Love: Its Meaning & Function in the Theology of Juan Luis Segundo. LC 89-36838. 168p. (C). 1989. lib. bdg. 41.00 (*0-8191-7561-7*) U Pr of Amer.

Ching Ti, tr. see Shen Ts'Ung-Wen.

Ching-tzu, Wu. The Scholars. Hsien-yi, Yang & Yang, Glagys, trs. from CHI. LC 92-24471. (Illus.). 448p. (C). 1993. pap. 25.00 (*0-231-08153-7*, Mrngside); text 52.50 (*0-231-08152-9*, Mrngside) Col U Pr.

Ching-Tzu, Wu. The Scholars (Rulin Waishi) Hsien-yi, Yang & Xang, Gladys, trs. 620p. 1991. 19.95 (*0-8351-2407-X*) China Bks.

Ching, W. Y., jt. auth. see Fernandez Baca, J. A.

***Ch'ing-wen, Cheng.** Three-Legged Horse. 2000. reprint ed. pap. 14.95 (*0-231-11387-0*) Col U Pr.

Ching-yi Li, et al. Practical Chinese Dialogues Two. Chen-ch'ing Li & Te-ming Yeh, eds. (Mandarin Training Center Ser.). (CHI.). 619p. (Orig.). 1991. pap. text 28.95 (*0-88710-166-6*) Yale Far Eastern Pubns.

Ching-Yuen, Loy. The Supreme Way: Inner Teachings of the Southern Mountain Tao. Carolan, Trevor & Liang, Du, trs. from CHI. LC 96-39808. 120p. (Orig.). 1997. pap. 11.95 (*1-55643-239-9*) North Atlantic.

Chingen. Miraculous Tales of the Lotus Sutra from Ancient Japan: The Dainihonkoku Hokeky Okenki of Priest Chingen. Dykstra, Yoshiko K., tr. & anno. by. LC 86-30744. 180p. 1987. reprint ed. pap. 51.30 (*0-608-00530-4*, 2061409) Bks Demand.

Chinggaltai. A Grammar of Mongol Language. rev. ed. LC 77-985065. 177p. reprint ed. pap. 54.90 (*0-608-11057-4*, 201960000013) Bks Demand.

Chinghua Tang. A Treasury of China's Wisdom: A Story Book for Everyone. 407p. 1996. pap. 14.95 (*7-119-01861-2*, Pub. by Foreign Lang) China Bks.

Chingono, Mark. The State, Violence & Development: The Political Economy of War in Mozambique, 1975-1992. (Making of Modern Africa Ser.). 303p. 1996. 77.95 (*1-85972-077-3*, Pub. by Avebry) Ashgate Pub Co.

Chingos, Peter T., jt. auth. see KPMG Peat Marwick.

Chinhengo, Austin M. Essential Jurisprudence. Bourne, Nicholas, ed. (Essential Law Ser.). 148p. 1995. pap. write for info. (*1-85941-129-0*, Pub. by Cavendish Pubng) Gaunt.

***Chini, Abdol R. & American Society of Civil Engineers Staff.** Who Provides Inspection: Report. LC 99-33479. 64p. 1999. 19.00 (*0-7844-0450-X*) Am Soc Civil Eng.

Chinian, Lin, jt. ed. see Ping Chen.

Chiniquy, Charles. Fifty Years in the "Church" of Rome. abr. ed. 366p. 1985. pap. 11.95 (*0-937958-21-2*) Chick Pubns.

— The Priest, the Woman, & the Confessional. 144p. 1979. pap. 6.95 (*0-937958-03-4*) Chick Pubns.

Chinitz, Benjamin, ed. Central City Economic Development. 212p. 1984. reprint ed. lib. bdg. 52.50 (*0-8191-4112-7*) U Pr of Amer.

— Escalating Land Values: Causes & Consequences for the Next Decade. LC 90-138987. 129p. (Orig.). 1989. reprint ed. pap. 40.00 (*0-608-02094-X*, 206274700004) Bks Demand.

Chinitz, Benjamin Ed, ed. City & Suburb. LC 76-1850. 181p. 1976. reprint ed. lib. bdg. 65.00 (*0-8371-8679-X*, CHCS, Greenwood Pr) Greenwood.

Chinitz, David P., et al. Governments & Health Systems: Implications of Differing Involvements. LC 97-45912. 646p. 1998. 175.00 (*0-471-98199-0*) Wiley.

Chinitz, Jacob, ed. see Adler, Morris.

Chinitz, Jonathan. DCE System Administration. 400p. 1995. pap. 23.95 (*1-56592-110-0*) Thomson Learn.

Chinkin. International Dispute. 203.95 (*1-84014-410-6*) Ashgate Pub Co.

Chinkin, Christine. Third Parties in International Law. LC 92-35563. (Oxford Monographs in International Law). 430p. 1993. text 69.00 (*0-19-825715-5*) OUP.

Chinkin, Christine, jt. auth. see Astor, Hilary.

Chinloy, Peter. The Cost of Doing Business: Legal & Regulatory Issues in the U. S. & Abroad. LC 89-3650. 194p. 1989. 57.95 (*0-275-93332-6*, C3332, Praeger Pubs) Greenwood.

— Labor Productivity. (Illus.). 160p. 1982. text 32.00 (*0-89011-561-3*) Abt Bks.

Chinlund, Gregory J., jt. auth. see Raiff, Angela M.

Chinmaya, P., ed. see Osho.

Chinmayananda. Discourses on Isavasya Upanishad. 150p. 1998. reprint ed. pap. 17.95 (*0-7661-0378-1*) Kessinger Pub.

Chinmoy, Sri. Astrology, the Supernatural & the Beyond. LC 74-75131. 135p. (Orig.). 1974. pap. 6.95 (*0-88497-037-X*) Aum Pubns.

— Beyond Within: A Philosophy for the Inner Life. 522p. 1985. pap. 13.95 (*0-88497-115-5*) Aum Pubns.

— Birthdays. (Illus.). 47p. 1998. pap. 4.95 (*0-9664613-0-4*, BK-9) Jharna Kala.

— A Child's Heart & a Child's Dreams: Growing up with Spiritual Wisdom, a Guide for Parents & Children. 123p. 1986. pap. text 7.95 (*0-88497-862-1*) Aum Pubns.

— Death & Reincarnation: Eternity's Voyage. LC 74-81308. (Illus.). 157p. (Orig.). 1974. pap. 8.95 (*0-88497-038-8*) Aum Pubns.

— Diana, Princess of Wales, Empress of the World. 105p. 1997. pap. 6.95 (*1-885479-07-7*) McKeever Pubng.

— Encouragement. (Illus.). 51p. 1998. pap., per. 4.95 (*0-9664613-2-0*) Jharna Kala.

— Everest Aspiration. 150p. 1997. pap. 9.95 (*0-88497-902-4*) Aum Pubns.

— Flame Waves: Questions Answered at the United Nations, Pts. 6-11. Incl. Pt. 6. 49p. 1979. 2.00 (*0-88497-325-5*); Pt. 7. 49p. 1979. 2.00 (*0-88497-326-3*); Pt. 8. 52p. 1979. 2.00 (*0-88497-327-1*); Pt. 9. 52p. 1979. 2.00 (*0-88497-451-0*); Pt. 10. 50p. 1979. 2.00 (*0-88497-452-9*); Pt. 11. 57p. 1979. 2.00 (*0-88497-453-7*); 1979. write for info. (*0-318-50952-0*) Aum Pubns.

— Garden of the Soul: Lessons on Living in Peace, Happiness & Harmony. LC 94-23026. (Illus.). 200p. (Orig.). 1994. pap. 9.95 (*1-55874-314-6*, 3146) Health Comm.

— The Garland of Nation-Souls: Complete Talks at the United Nations. 300p. (Orig.). 1995. pap. 11.95 (*1-55874-357-X*, 357X) Health Comm.

— God Is . . . Selected Writings of Sri Chinmoy. 240p. (Orig.). 1997. pap. 12.95 (*0-88497-059-0*) Aum Pubns.

— Great Indian Meals: Divinely Delicious & Supremely Nourishing, 4 pts. Incl. Pt. 1. 54p. 1979. 2.00 (*0-88497-462-6*); Pt. 2. 67p. 1979. 2.00

C

(*0-88497-463-4*); Pt. 3. 68p. 1979. 2.00 (*0-88497-464-2*); Pt. 4. 58p. 1979. 2.00 (*0-88497-465-0*); 1979. write for info. (*0-318-50953-9*) Aum Pubns.
— Harmony. (Little Books of Wisdom: Vol. 16). (Illus.). 1999. pap. 4.95 (*0-9664613-9-8*, BK-16) Jharna Kala.
— Imagine. (Little Books of Wisdom: Vol. 17). (Illus.). 1999. pap. 4.95 (*1-893161-00-5*, BK-17) Jharna Kala.
— Inner & Outer Peace. 113p. (Orig.). 1984. pap. 7.95 (*0-88497-769-2*) Aum Pubns.
*__Chinmoy, Sri.__ Inner Promise: Discovering & Fulfilling Your Unlimited Spiritual Potential. 2000. pap. 14.95 (*0-88497-131-7*) Aum Pubns.
__Chinmoy, Sri.__ Let It Be. (Little Books of Wisdom: Vol. 18). (Illus.). 1999. pap. 4.95 (*1-893161-01-3*, BK-18) Jharna Kala.
— The Master & the Disciple. LC 85-72172. 115p. (Orig.). 1985. pap. 5.95 (*0-88497-884-2*) Aum Pubns.
— Meditation: Man-Perfection in God-Satisfaction. (Illus.). 261p. (C). 1979. pap. 9.95 (*0-88497-444-8*) Aum Pubns.
— My Life's Soul-Journey: Daily Meditations for Ever-Increasing Spiritual Fulfillment. 430p. 1995. pap. text 13.95 (*0-88497-244-5*) Aum Pubns.
— On Wings of Silver Dreams. 102p. 1997. pap. 6.95 (*0-88497-991-1*) Aum Pubns.
— Opportunity. (Illus.). 50p. 1998. pap., per. 4.95 (*0-9664613-3-9*) Jharna Kala.
— Siddhartha Becomes the Buddha. 83p. 1974. pap. 6.95 (*0-88497-116-3*) Aum Pubns.
— The Silent Teaching: A Beginner's Guide to Meditation. 64p. 1997. pap. 4.95 (*0-88497-601-7*) Aum Pubns.
*__Chinmoy, Sri.__ Source of Music: Music & Mantra for Self-Realisation. 2000. pap. 8.95 (*0-88497-575-4*) Aum Pubns.
__Chinmoy, Sri.__ Sri Chinmoy Speaks, 10 pts. Incl. Pt. 1. 55p. 1977. 2.00 (*0-88497-282-8*); Pt. 2. 58p. 1977. 2.00 (*0-88497-285-2*); Pt. 3. 65p. 1977. 2.00 (*0-88497-286-0*); Pt. 4. 62p. 1977. 2.00 (*0-88497-288-7*); Pt. 5. 56p. 1977. 2.00 (*0-88497-289-5*); Pt. 6. 57p. 1977. (*0-88497-290-9*); Pt. 7. 58p. 1977. (*0-88497-294-1*); Pt. 8. 56p. 1977. (*0-88497-295-X*); Pt. 9. 51p. 1977. (*0-88497-296-8*); Pt. 10. 62p. 1977. (*0-88497-335-2*); 1977. pap. write for info. (*0-318-50955-5*) Aum Pubns.
— The Summits of God Life: Samadhi & Siddhi. LC 80-65397. 145p. 1984. reprint ed. pap. 7.95 (*0-88497-145-7*) Aum Pubns.
— Sympathy. (Little Books of Wisdom: Vol. 13). (Illus.). 52p. 1999. pap. 4.95 (*0-9664613-1-2*, BK-13) Jharna Kala.
— Three Branches of India's Life-Tree: Commentaries on the Vedas, the Upanishads, & the... 254p. 1997. pap. text 13.95 (*0-88497-113-9*) Aum Pubns.
*__Chinmoy, Sri.__ The Wisdom of Sri Chinmoy. 456p. 2000. pap. 19.95 (*1-884997-23-6*) Blue Dove Pr.
__Chinmoy, Sri.__ Yoga & Spiritual Life. rev. ed. LC 74-81309. 210p. 1974. pap. 8.95 (*0-88497-040-X*) Aum Pubns.
__Chinmoy, Sri & Canfield, Jack.__ The Wings of Joy. LC 96-32387. 1997. per. 10.00 (*0-684-82242-3*) S&S Trade.
__Chinn, Carl.__ Poverty Amidst Prosperity. 1995. text 22.95 (*0-7190-3990-8*, Pub. by Manchester Univ Pr) St Martin.
— They Worked All Their Lives: Women of the Urban Poor in England, 1880-1939. LC 87-36701. 199p. 1989. text 29.95 (*0-7190-2437-4*, Pub. by Manchester Univ Pr) St Martin.
__Chinn, Daryl N.__ Soft Parts of the Back. (University of Central Florida Contemporary Poetry Ser.). 88p. 1989. 19.95 (*0-8130-0922-7*); pap. 10.95 (*0-8130-0938-3*) U Press Fla.
__Chinn, Douglas & Chinn, Virginia.__ A Post-Trib Alternative to the Pre-Trib Rapture. LC 91-77954. 140p. 1992. pap. 9.95 (*0-944788-95-5*) IBRI.
__Chinn, Edward.__ Questions of the Heart. (Orig.). 1987. pap. 6.75 (*0-89536-877-3*, 7863) CSS OH.
__Chinn, Garry.__ Carpenter's Companion. 192p. 1995. 17.98 (*0-7858-0476-5*) Bk Sales Inc.
__Chinn, Jeff.__ Manipulating Soviet Population Resources. LC 77-11683. 163p. 1978. 34.50 (*0-8419-0345-X*) Holmes & Meier.
— Russians As the New Minority: Ethnicity & Nationalism in the Soviet Successor States. 8p. (C). 1996. pap. 27.00 (*0-8133-2248-0*, Pub. by Westview) HarpC.
__Chinn, Jeff & Kaiser, Robert.__ Russians As the New Minority: Ethnicity & Nationalism in the Soviet Successor States. 1996. pap. 79.00 (*0-8133-2249-9*, Pub. by Westview) HarpC.
__Chinn, Jennie A., ed.__ Don't Ask Me My History, Just Listen to My Music: An Exploration of Kansas Folklore. LC 92-70544. (Illus.). 64p. 1992. pap. 8.00 (*0-87726-043-5*) Kansas St Hist.
— Images of Strawberry Hill: Works by Marijana. LC 85-81315. (Illus.). 1985. pap. 8.00 (*0-87726-032-X*) Kansas St Hist.
__Chinn, Jennie A. & Magnuson, Carl R.__ Kansas Folk Arts Apprenticeship Program: Selected Portraits. LC 88-83739. (Illus.). 51p. 1989. pap. 3.50 (*0-87726-035-4*) Kansas St Hist.
__Chinn, Karen.__ Sam & the Lucky Money. LC 94-11766. (Illus.). 32p. (J). (ps-4). 1995. 15.95 (*1-880000-13-X*) Lee & Low Bks.
— Sam & the Lucky Money. 1997. 12.15 (*0-606-12804-2*, Pub. by Turtleback) Demco.
— Sam & the Lucky Money. (Illus.). 32p. (J). (gr. k-4). 1997. reprint ed. pap. 6.95 (*1-880000-53-9*) Lee & Low Bks.
__Chinn, Leiton E.__ International Student Reentry: A Select, Annotated Bibliography. LC 92-13802. 56p. 1992. 12.00 (*0-912207-60-4*) NAFSA Washington.
__Chinn, Leland J.__ Selection of Oxidants in Synthesis: Oxidation at the Carbon Atom. LC 71-134781. (Oxidation in Organic Chemistry Ser.). 203p. reprint ed. pap. 63.00 (*0-8357-3530-3*, 203452100090) Bks Demand.
__Chinn, Lisa.__ Think Home. 1987. pap. 4.95 (*0-317-04077-4*) Intl Students Inc.
*__Chinn, Lisa Espineli.__ ReEntry Guide for Short Term Mission Leaders. 2nd rev. ed. Lisech, Howard, ed. & photos by. by. (Illus.). 78p. 1998. spiral bd. 10.00 (*1-930547-14-5*) Deeper Roots.
__Chinn, Nancy.__ Spaces for Spirit: Adorning the Church. LC 98-85925. (Illus.). 72p. 1998. pap. 26.00 (*1-56854-242-9*, SPACES) Liturgy Tr Pubns.
__Chinn, Nancy & Gleeson, Harriet.__ Wisdom Searches: Seeking the Feminine Presence of God. LC 99-32540. (Illus.). 128p. 1999. 29.95 (*0-8298-1338-1*) Pilgrim OH.
__Chinn, Peggy L.__ Advances in Nursing Science Series, 5. 1996. pap. 160.00 (*0-8342-0576-9*) Aspen Pub.
— Developing Nursing Perspectives in Women's Health, Vol. 4. (Advances in Nursing Science Ser.: Vol. 1). 270p. 1994. 42.00 (*0-8342-0577-7*, 20577) Aspen Pub.
— Exemplars in Criticism, Challenge & Controversy, Vol. 3. (Advances in Nursing Science Ser.). 240p. 1994. 42.00 (*0-8342-0579-3*, 20579) Aspen Pub.
*__Chinn, Peggy L.__ Peace & Power: Building Communities for Future. 4th ed. (Illus.). 148p. (C). 1998. pap. text 22.50 (*0-7637-0944-1*) JB Pubns.
__Chinn, Peggy L.__ Peace & Power: Building Communities for the Future. 4th rev. ed. LC 95-22950. 1995. 14.95 (*0-88737-657-6*) Natl League Nurse.
__Chinn, Peggy L., ed.__ Advances in Methods of Inquiry for Nursing, Vol. 5. LC 94-4853. (Advances in Nursing Science Ser.). 204p. 1994. pap. 42.00 (*0-8342-0595-5*) Aspen Pub.
— Anthology on Caring. 352p. 1991. 32.95 (*0-88737-516-2*) Natl League Nurse.
— Developing Substance: Mid-Range Theory in Nursing, Vol. 2. LC 94-7364. (Advances in Nursing Science Ser.). 286p. 1994. 42.00 (*0-8342-0578-5*) Aspen Pub.
— Developing the Discipline: Critical Studies in Nursing & Professional Issues, Vol. 1. LC 94-4879. (Advances in Nursing Science Ser.: Vol. 4). 270p. 1994. 45.00 (*0-8342-0580-7*, 20580) Aspen Pub.
__Chinn, Peggy L. & Kramer, Maeona K.__ Theory & Nursing: Integrated Knowledge Development. 5th ed. LC 98-31652. (Illus.). 256p. 1998. pap. text 39.00 (*0-323-00317-6*) Mosby Inc.
__Chinn, Peggy L. & Watson, Jean.__ Art & Aesthetics in Nursing. 363p. 1994. 32.95 (*0-88737-609-6*, 14-2611, NLN Pr) Natl League Nurse.
__Chinn, Philip C., jt. auth. see Gollnick, Donna M.__
__Chinn, S. J. & Ashcroft, J. R.__ Mathematics for Dyslexics: A Teaching Handbook. 2nd ed. 250p. 1999. 39.95 (*1-56593-887-9*, 1738) Singular Publishing.
__Chinn, Sandra H.__ At Your Service: KMOX & Bob Hardy: Pioneers of Talk Radio. (Illus.). 200p. 1997. pap. 15.95 (*0-9631448-9-8*) VA Pub Corp.
*__Chinn, Sarah E.__ Technology & the Logic of American Racism: A Cultural History of the Body as Evidence. 2000. 74.95 (*0-8264-4729-5*); pap. text. write for info. (*0-8264-4750-3*) Continuum.
__Chinn, Stephen J. & Ashcroft, J. Richard.__ Mathematics for Dyslexics: A Teaching Handbook. 246p. 1993. 29.99 (*1-56593-250-1*, 0547) Thomson Learn.
— Mathematics for Dyslexics: A Teaching Handbook. 2nd ed. LC 98-184658. xiv, 268p. 1998. write for info. (*1-86156-043-5*) Whurr Pub.
__Chinn, Steven D.__ Associateships: A Guide for Health Care Providers. LC 95-15484. 1995. 29.95 (*0-87814-446-3*) PennWell Bks.
__Chinn, Susan, jt. auth. see Rona, Roberto J.__
__Chinn, Susan, ed. see Pendlum, David W.__
__Chinn, Virginia, jt. auth. see Chinn, Douglas.__
__Chinn, Wilberta L.__ Beginning My Spiritual Journey. (Bible Studies for New Christians: Vol. 1). (Illus.). 25p. 1997. pap. 1.99 (*0-937673-17-X*) Peacock Ent LA.
— Finding My Identity As a Woman. 87p. (Orig.). 1987. pap. 3.95 (*0-937673-03-X*) Peacock Ent LA.
— Fruit of the Spirit. (Christian Life Ser.). 52p. 1998. pap. 3.95 (*0-937673-20-X*) Peacock Ent LA.
*__Chinn, Wilberta L.__ Increasing My Faith in God: Four Lessons for Individual or Group Study. 35p. 1999. pap. 1.95 (*0-937673-23-4*) Peacock Ent LA.
__Chinn, Wilberta L.__ Life Progress Map: Faith Stages Toward Maturity. 2nd rev. ed. (Illus.). 59p. (Orig.). 1997. spiral bd. 7.95 (*0-937673-15-3*) Peacock Ent LA.
— Life Progress Map Leader's Guide: A 12-Session Curriculum to Guide Others Through Six Stages of Faith. 38p. (Orig.). 1997. spiral bd. 7.95 (*0-937673-14-5*) Peacock Ent LA.
— Man's Problem - God's Solution, Lessons from Genesis 1 to 3: Discover Course. (Illus.). 24p. 1998. pap., student ed. 1.95 (*0-937673-21-8*) Peacock Ent LA.
— Man's Problem - God's Solution, Lessons from Genesis 1 to 3: Discovery Course. (Discovery Course Ser.: Vol. 1). (Illus.). 24p. 1998. pap., teacher ed. 1.95 (*0-937673-18-8*) Peacock Ent LA.
— Personal Goal Setting for a Purposeful & Fulfilled Life. 2nd rev. ed. (Illus.). 56p. (Orig.). 1996. spiral bd. 6.95 (*0-937673-13-7*) Peacock Ent LA.
— Singles Sorting It Out. (Illus.). 335p. (Orig.). 1991. pap. 11.95 (*0-937673-08-0*) Peacock Ent LA.
*__Chinn, Wilberta L.__ Understanding My Guidebook, the Bible: Four Lessons for Individual or Group Study. 32p. 1999. pap. 1.95 (*0-937673-26-9*) Peacock Ent LA.
__Chinn, Wilberta L., ed.__ A Father's Heart As Seen in the Letters & Journals of Gregory R. Owyang. 116p. 1987. pap. 5.95 (*0-937673-04-8*) Peacock Ent LA.
— A Father's Heart As Seen in the Letters & Journals of Gregory R. Owyang. 88p. 1988. pap. 5.95 (*0-937673-05-6*) Peacock Ent LA.
__Chinn, William G. & Steenrod, N. E.__ First Concepts of Topology. LC 66-20367. (New Mathematical Library: No. 18). 160p. 1966. pap. text, suppl. ed. 17.50 (*0-88385-618-2*, NML-18) Math Assn.
*__Chinnery, Dave.__ Fly Electric. 2nd rev. ed. (Illus.). 120p. 1999. pap. 20.00 (*1-85486-198-0*, Pub. by Nexus Special Interests) Trans-Atl Phila.
__Chinnery, John, tr. see Siebert, W. & Buch, M., eds.__
__Chinnery, Philip D.__ Air Commando. 1997. mass mkt. 6.99 (*0-312-95881-1*) St Martin.
— Any Time, Any Place: Fifty Years of the U. S. A. F. Air Commando & Special Operations Forces, 1944-1994. LC 94-66597. (Illus.). 303p. 1994. 32.95 (*1-55750-037-1*) Naval Inst Pr.
*__Chinnery, Philip D.__ Boneyard Badges. (Illus.). 112p. 2000. pap. 24.95 (*1-84037-102-1*, 130514AE, Pub. by Airlife Publishing) Motorbooks Intl.
__Chinnery, Philip D.__ 50 Years of the Desert Boneyard: Davis Monthan AFB Arizona. LC 96-108699. (Illus.). 112p. 1995. pap. 24.95 (*0-7603-0187-5*) MBI Pubg.
__Chinnery, Victor.__ Oak Furniture: The British Tradition. 2nd ed. (Illus.). 620p. 1986. 99.50 (*1-85149-013-2*) Antique Collect.
__Chinni, ed.__ Military & Government Simulation, 1993. 74p. 1993. pap. 30.00 (*1-56555-053-6*, SMC93-1) Soc Computer Sim.
__Chinni, Michael J., ed.__ First Conference on Ballistics Simulation. 72p. 1990. pap. 32.00 (*0-911801-69-3*, EMC90-1) Soc Computer Sim.
*__Chinni, Michael J., ed.__ Military, Goverment & Aerospace Simulation. 188p. 1999. pap. 80.00 (*1-56555-168-0*) Soc Computer Sim.
__Chinni, Michael J., ed.__ Military, Government & Aerospace Simulation. 200p. 1994. 80.00 (*1-56555-072-2*) Soc Computer Sim.
— Military, Government & Aerospace Simulation. 191p. 1995. 100.00 (*1-56555-075-7*, SS-27-4) Soc Computer Sim.
— Military, Government & Aerospace Simulation. 270p. 1996. 80.00 (*1-56555-093-5*, SS-28-3) Soc Computer Sim.
*__Chinni, Michael J., ed.__ Military, Government & Aerospace Simulation. (Simulation Ser.: Vol. 29, No. 4). 252p. 1998. 80.00 (*1-56555-120-6*, SS-29-4) Soc Computer Sim.
— Military, Government & Aerospace Simulation. Vol. 30. 236p. 1998. 50.00 (*1-56555-143-5*) Soc Computer Sim.
__Chinni, Michael J., ed.__ Second Conference on Ballistics Simulation. 72p. 1991. pap. 32.00 (*0-911801-90-1*, EMC91-1) Soc Computer Sim.
__Chinnici & Wadkowski.__ Biology. 5th ed. 1998. pap. text, student ed. 28.00 (*0-13-081039-8*) P-H.
__Chinnici, et al.__ Life on Earth. 654p. 1997. pap. text, student ed. 26.67 (*0-13-271859-6*) P-H.
*__Chinnici, Joseph.__ Genetics: Practice Problems & Solutions. 350p. (C). 1998. pap. text, student ed. 30.60 (*0-8053-4525-6*) Benjamin-Cummings.
__Chinnici, Joseph P.__ The English Catholic Enlightenment: John Lingard & the Cisalpine Movement, 1780 to 1850. LC 79-20250. (Illus.). xiv, 262p. 1980. 24.95 (*0-915762-10-2*) Patmos Pr.
— Living Stones: The History & Structure of Catholic Spiritual Life in the United States. 282p. (Orig.). 1996. pap. 16.00 (*1-57075-092-0*) Orbis Bks.
__Chinnici, Joseph P., ed.__ Devotion to the Holy Spirit in American Catholicism. LC 85-60956. (Sources of American Spirituality Ser.: Vol. 3). 256p. 1985. 12.95 (*0-8091-0366-4*) Paulist Pr.
*__Chinnici, Joseph P. & Dries, Angelyn, eds.__ Prayer & Practice in the American Catholic Community. (American Catholic Identities Ser.). 300p. 2000. 50.00 (*1-57075-346-6*) Orbis Bks.
— Prayer & Practice in the American Catholic Community. (American Catholic Identities Ser.). (Illus.). 300p. 2000. pap. 30.00 (*1-57075-342-3*) Orbis Bks.
__Chinnici, Joseph P., et al.__ Biology. 4th ed. 1996. pap. text, student ed. 29.20 (*0-13-378027-9*) P-H.
*__Chino, Allan F. & Davis, Corinne D.__ Validate Your Pain! Exposing the Chronic Pain Cover up. LC 97-65268. 374p. 2000. pap. 19.95 (*0-9673439-2-5*) InSync Commn.
__Chino, N. & Melvin, J. L., eds.__ Functional Evaluation of Stroke Patients. (Illus.). 140p. 1996. 78.00 (*4-431-70156-7*) Spr-Verlag.
__Chino, Naoko.__ All About Particles. (Power Japanese Ser.). 128p. (Orig.). 1991. pap. 12.00 (*0-87011-954-0*) Kodansha.
— Basic Sentence Patterns: Building Strong Foundations. (Power Japanese Ser.). 144p. 1999. pap. text 12.00 (*4-7700-2336-7*) Kodansha.
*__Chino, Naoko.__ Dictionary of Basic Japanese Sentence Patterns. 2000. pap. 22.00 (*4-7700-2608-0*) Kodansha.
__Chino, Naoko, jt. auth. see Vance, Timothy J.__
__Chinodoros, Sandra, jt. ed. see Barlow, Andy.__
__Chinodya, Shimmer.__ Harvest of Thorns. (African Writers Ser.). 248p. (C). 1991. pap. 9.95 (*0-435-90582-1*, 90582) Heinemann.
__Chinosole, ed.__ Schooling/Generations in/Politics of Prison. 1997. pap. 15.95 (*0-915117-02-9*) Freedom Voices Pubns.
__Chinousky, Paul S. & Meredith, James E.__ Strategic Corporate Management for Engineering. LC 99-16338. (Illus.). 416p. (C). 2000. text 60.00 (*0-19-512467-7*) OUP.
__Chinoy, Ely S.__ Automobile Workers & the American Dream. 2nd ed. 192p. (C). 1992. pap. text 12.95 (*0-252-06263-9*) U of Ill Pr.
__Chinoy, Helen Krich.__ Broadway's Dreamers. 1999. pap. 9.95 (*0-14-011588-9*, Viking) Viking Penguin.
__Chinoy, Helen Krich., jt. auth. see Cole, Toby.__
*__Chinoy, Helen Krich & Jenkins, Linda Walsh, eds.__ Women in American Theatre. rev. ed. LC 00-37753. 500p. 2000. pap. 18.95 (*1-55936-180-8*, Pub. by Theatre Comm) Theatre Comm.
*__Chinoy, Marc Paul.__ Getting Started: An Introduction to the Strategic Planning Process. 2000. pap. write for info. (*1-930081-00-6*) Regis Group Inc.
__Chinoy, Mike.__ China Live: People Power & the Television Revolution. rev. ed. LC 98-52035. (Illus.). 420p. 1999. pap. 17.95 (*0-8476-9318-X*) Rowman.
— China Live: Two Decades in the Heart of the Dragon. (Illus.). 397p. 1999. pap. text 15.00 (*0-7881-5984-4*) DIANE Pub.
— China Live: Two Decades in the Heart of the Dragon. LC 98-52035. 420p. 1999. 69.00 (*0-8476-9317-1*) Rowman.
*__Chinoy, Mike.__ China Live: Two Decades in the Heart of the Dragon. (Illus.). 397p. 2000. reprint ed. text 24.00 (*0-7881-9124-1*) DIANE Pub.
__Chinoy, N. J., ed.__ Acute Toxicities of Organic Chemicals to Fathead Minnows (Pimephales promelas) (Advances in Agricultural Biotechnology Ser.). 1984. text 160.50 (*90-247-2908-4*) Kluwer Academic.
__Chinoy, Toni L.__ In Search of a Yatz: A Love Story. rev. ed. 329p. 1998. pap. 19.95 (*0-9668591-6-2*, Writers Club Pr) iUniversecom.
— Perfect Speed: Throw Away That Plan. 68p. 1998. pap. 11.95 (*0-9668591-5-4*, Writers Club Pr) iUniversecom.
— What to Do When It Rains: A Handbook for Leaders in Crisis. (Illus.). 201p. 1999. pap. 24.95 (*1-893652-09-2*, Writers Club Pr) iUniversecom.
__Chinski, Arthur.__ Drug & Alcohol Issues in the Workplace. Vinson, Kathleen, ed. 530p. 1992. pap. text 49.95 (*1-880940-01-9*) Inst Busn Law.
— Employee Termination: The Right to Fair Treatment. Vinson, Kathleen, ed. 564p. (Orig.). 1992. pap. text 49.95 (*1-880940-00-0*) Inst Busn Law.
__Chinula, Donald M.__ Building King's Beloved Community: Foundations for Pastoral Care & Counseling with the Oppressed. LC 97-33605. 128p. (Orig.). 1997. pap. 12.95 (*0-8298-1202-4*) Pilgrim OH.
__Chinweizu.__ Energy Crisis & Other Poems. LC 77-90075. 1978. 9.95 (*0-88357-062-9*); pap. 4.50 (*0-88357-063-7*) NOK Pubs.
— The West & the Rest of Us: White Predators, Black Slavers & the African Elite. 544p. 1978. pap. 9.95 (*0-88357-016-5*); text 21.95 (*0-88357-015-7*) NOK Pubs.
__Chinweizu, et al.__ Toward the Decolonization of African Literature, Vol. I. LC 82-23357. 320p. 1982. pap. 12.95 (*0-88258-123-6*) Howard U Pr.
__Chinwezu, Onwuchekwa, et al.__ Toward the Decolonization of African Literature: African Fiction & Poetry & Their Critics. 320p. 1998. 42.50 (*0-7103-0123-5*, Pub. by Kegan Paul Intl) Col U Pr.
__Chinyelu, Mamadou.__ Debunking the Bell Curve & Scientific Racism, Vol. 1. LC 96-94386. 104p. 1996. reprint ed. pap. 10.00 (*0-9652664-0-0*) Mstrd Seed.
— Harlem Ain't Nothin' but a Third World Country: The Colonial Status of Africans in America. 225p. 1999. pap. 15.00 (*0-9652664-3-5*, MSPO004) Mstrd Seed.
— Regeneration. 459p. 1998. pap. 25.00 (*0-9652664-2-7*, Vsn Pubng NYC) Mstrd Seed.
— Sons of the Prophets Vol. 1: Nine Inspirational Stories about African Men & Boys in the Land of Captivity. LC 95-90985. 80p. (Orig.). 1996. pap. 9.95 (*0-9652664-1-9*) Mstrd Seed.
__Chiocca, E. Antonio & Breakefield, Xandra O., eds.__ Gene Therapy for Neurological Disorders & Brain Tumors. LC 97-42613. (Contemporary Neuroscience Ser.). (Illus.). 464p. 1997. 165.00 (*0-89603-507-7*) Humana.
*__Chiocca, Olindo Romeo.__ Mobsters & Thugs: Quotes from the Underworld. (Prose Ser.: No. 50). 128p. 2000. pap. 13.00 (*1-55071-104-0*, , Pub. by Guernica Editions) Paul & Co Pubs.
__Chiocchi, Leonardo.__ Guide for American Exporters: Environmental Technologies: Europe. 2nd ed. (Illus.). 132p. (C). 1999. pap. text 35.00 (*0-7881-7773-7*) DIANE Pub.
__Chiodi, Albert M.__ The Watershed: Selected Poems. limited ed. (Illus.). 48p. 1997. pap. 9.95 (*0-9663285-0-7*, A9810010) Coyote Pr FL.
__Chiodini, R. J., et al.__ Proceedings of the Fifth International Colloquium on Paratuberculosis, September 29-October 4, 1996: A Meeting of the International Association for Paratuberculosis, Madison, Wisconsin, U. S. A. LC 97-25264. 1997. pap. write for info. (*0-9633043-3-X*) Intl Assn Paratuber.
__Chiodini, Rodrick J., compiled by.__ The History of Paratuberculosis, Johne's Disease: A Review of the Literature 1985-1992. LC 93-12657. 1993. 125.00 (*0-9633043-1-3*) Intl Assn Paratuber.
__Chiodini, Rodrick J., et al, eds.__ International Colloquium on Paratuberculosis: 4th, 1994: Cambridge, England; Proceedings of the Fourth International Colloquium on Paratuberculosis, July 17-July 21, 1994: A Meeting of the International Association for Paratuberculosis, St. John's College, Cambridge, U. K. LC 95-2324. 1994. write for info. (*0-9633043-2-1*) Intl Assn Paratuber.
__Chiodini, Rodrick J. & Kreeger, J.__ Proceedings of the Third International Colloquium on Paratuberculosis. (C). 1992. pap. text 145.00 (*0-9633043-0-5*) Intl Assn Paratuber.
__Chiodo, Joe & Peterson, Jonathan.__ The Mechanic: Graphic Novel. (Illus.). 48p. 1998. pap. 5.95 (*1-58240-024-5*) Image Comics.
__Chiodo, Peggy.__ Health Aspects of Drug Use: Health Science 336. 1998. text 17.52 (*1-56870-340-6*) RonJon Pub.

An Asterisk (*) at the beginning of an entry indicates that the title is appearing for the first time.

Chioffi, Nancy & Mead, Gretchen. Keeping the Harvest: Preserving Your Fruits, Vegetables & Herbs. rev. ed. Mason, Jill & Foster, Kim, eds. LC 90-50413. (Illus.). 216p. 1991. reprint ed. pap. 14.95 (*0-88266-650-9*) Storey Bks.

Chiogioji, Melvin H. Industrial Energy Conservation. LC 79-15191. (Energy, Power, & Environment Ser.: No. 4). 627p. reprint ed. pap. 194.40 (*0-7837-5396-9*, 204516000005) Bks Demand.

Chiogioji, Melvin H. & Oura, Eleanor N., eds. Energy Conservation in Commercial & Residential Buildings. LC 82-2539. (Energy, Power, & Environment Ser.: No. 14). 463p. 1982. reprint ed. pap. 143.60 (*0-608-01297-1*, 206204300001) Bks Demand.

Chiomenti, Lyndelle B. Parables of Jesus: The Master's Stories of Love & Grace. LC 96-46582. 1997. pap. 2.97 (*0-8163-1376-8*) Pacific Pr Pub Assn.

Chion, Michel. Audio-Vision: Sound on Screen. Gorbman, Claudia, ed. & tr. by. from FRE. LC 93-23982.Tr. of Audio-Vision. 1994. 64.50 (*0-231-07898-6*); pap. 19.50 (*0-231-07899-4*) Col U Pr.

***Chion, Michel.** Cinematic Voice. LC 98-19048. (Illus.). 183p. 1998. pap. 16.50 (*0-231-10823-0*); lib. bdg. 45.00 (*0-231-10822-2*) Col U Pr.

Chion, Michel. David Lynch. Julian, Robert, tr. (Illus.). 208p. 1995. 19.95 (*0-85170-457-3*, MB) Ind U Pr.

— The Films of Jacques Tati. Vinas, Monique et al, trs. from FRE. LC 95-75616. (Essay Ser.: No. 14). 167p. Date not set. pap. 12.00 (*0-920717-70-5*) Guernica Editions.

Chiong, Jane A. Racial Categorization of Multiracial Children in Schools. LC 97-40998. (Critical Studies in Education & Culture). 176p. 1998. 45.00 (*0-89789-499-5*, Bergin & Garvey) Greenwood.

Chiong, John. ATM Internet Working: Concepts, Protocols & Applications. LC 97-24048. (Illus.). 377p. 1997. pap. 55.00 (*0-07-011941-4*) McGraw.

Chiong, John A. SNA Interconnections: Routing SNA in Hierarchial, Peer, & High-Speed Networks. 1996. 55.00 (*0-07-011486-2*) McGraw.

Chionides, H. English-Greek Technical Lexicon. (GRE & ENG.). 356p. 1990. 95.00 (*0-320-03233-7*) Fr & Eur.

— Greek-English Technical Lexicon. (GRE & ENG.). 333p. 1990. pap. 95.00 (*0-320-03236-1*) Fr & Eur.

Chiorazzi, Michael G., ed. see American Association of Law Libraries Staff.

Chiorazzi, Nicholas, et al, eds. B-Lymphocytes & Autoimmunity, Vol. 815. LC 97-3680. 1997. 170.00 (*1-57331-076-X*) NY Acad Sci.

Chiorazzi, Nicholas & New York Academy of Sciences Staff. B Lymphocytes & Autoimmunity. LC 97-3680. (Annals of the New York Academy of Sciences Ser.). 1997. pap. 170.00 (*1-57331-077-8*) NY Acad Sci.

Chiosi, Cesare & Renzini, Alvio, eds. Spectral Evolution of Galaxies. (Astrophysics & Space Science Library). 1986. text 221.50 (*90-277-2187-4*) Kluwer Academic.

— Stellar Nucleosynthesis. 1984. text 185.50 (*90-277-1729-X*) Kluwer Academic.

Chiosi, Cesare & Stalio, R., eds. Effects of Mass Loss on Stellar Evolution. 375p. 1981. text 248.50 (*90-277-1292-1*) Kluwer Academic.

Chiosso, Giorgio. In Italy: Textbook. 13.95 (*0-8219-0480-9*) EMC-Paradigm.

— In Italy: Workbook. text 8.95 (*0-8219-0481-7*) EMC-Paradigm.

Chiou, C. L. Democratizing Oriental Despotism: China from 4 May, 1919 to 4 June, 1989 & Taiwan from 28 February 1947 to 28 June 1990. LC 95-17858. 204p. 1995. text 69.95 (*0-312-12871-1*) St Martin.

***Chiou, George C.** Ophthalmic Toxicology. 2nd ed. LC 99-31971. 500p. 1999. 135.00 (*1-56032-722-7*) Taylor & Francis.

Chiozza, Luis A. Hidden Affects in Somatic Disorders: Psychoanalytic Perspectives on Asthma, Psoriasis, Diabetes, Cerebrovascular Disease, & Other Disorders. LC 98-15126. 200p. 1998. 35.00 (*1-887841-16-4*, Psychosocial) Intl Univs Pr.

— Why Do We Fall Ill? The Story Hiding in the Body. LC 98-26756. 125p. 1999. 27.50 (*1-887841-18-0*, No. 66879, Psychosocial) Intl Univs Pr.

Chipangu, Florita. Bird Meets Fish. (Illus.). 36p. (J). 1993. pap. 2.50 (*1-878181-07-6*) Discovery Comics.

Chiparus, Demetrius, jt. auth. see Shayo, Alberto.

Chipasula, Frank. Whispers in the Wings. (African Writers Ser.). 112p. (Orig.). (C). 1991. pap. 8.95 (*0-435-91192-9*, 91192) Heinemann.

Chipasula, Frank, jt. ed. see Chipasula, Stella.

Chipasula, James C. & Miti, Katabaro. Botswana in Southern Africa: What Lies Ahead. 1989. 21.00 (*81-202-0258-9*, Pub. by Ajanta) S Asia.

Chipasula, Stella & Chipasula, Frank, eds. The Heinemann Book of African Women's Poetry. (African Writers Ser.). 256p. (Orig.). 1995. pap. 10.95 (*0-435-90680-1*, 90680) Heinemann.

***Chipchase, Lucinda.** Inpatient Orthopaedic Physiotherapy. (Illus.). 256p. 2000. pap. text 38.00 (*0-7506-4459-1*) Buttrwrth-Heinemann.

Chipev, N., jt. ed. see Golemansky, V.

***Chipkin, Dana.** Successful Court Reporting for Freelance Reporters. (Paralegal Ser.). 312p. (C). 2000. pap. text 43.95 (*0-7668-1746-6*) Delmar.

Chipkin, Kenn. Blues - Rock Guitar U. S. - U. K. Stang, Aaron, ed. 120p. (Orig.). (YA). 1995. pap. text 19.95 (*0-89724-586-5*, GF9504CD); pap. text 17.95 (*0-89724-587-3*, GF9504AT) Wrner Bros.

***Chipkin, Kenn.** Classic Rock Guitar Sourcebook: 50 Classic Rock Guitar Hits. 2000. pap. 19.95 (*0-7692-9119-8*) Wrner Bros.

Chipkin, Kenn, jt. ed. see Stang, Aaron.

Chiplin, Alfred J., Jr., ed. see National Senior Citizen Law Center Staff.

Chiplin, C. K. Roads from the Bottom: A Survival Journal for America's Black Community. LC 96-28990. 1996. 15.95 (*0-937552-73-9*) Quail Ridge.

Chipman, A. L. Chipmans of America. (Illus.). 232p. 1993. reprint ed. pap. 34.50 (*0-8328-1339-7*); reprint ed. lib. bdg. 44.50 (*0-8328-1338-9*) Higginson Bk Co.

Chipman, Bert L. Chipman Family: Genealogy of the Chipmans in America, 1631-1920. 321p. 1997. reprint ed. pap. 49.00 (*0-8328-7926-6*); reprint ed. lib. bdg. 59.00 (*0-8328-7925-8*) Higginson Bk Co.

***Chipman, Bruce.** Into America's Dream-Dump: A Postmodern Study of the Hollywood Novel. LC 99-16869. 248p. 1999. pap. 25.50 (*0-7618-1466-3*) U Pr of Amer.

***Chipman, Daniel.** Memoir of Colonel Seth Warner. large type enl. ed. 84p. 2000. 12.95 (*1-928837-30-1*) Essence of Vermont.

Chipman, Dawn, et al. Cool Women: The Reference. Nelson, Pamela, ed. (Illus.). 116p. (J). (gr. 5-12). 1998. pap. 19.95 (*0-9659754-0-1*) Girl Pr.

Chipman, Donald E. Spanish Texas, 1519-1821. LC 92-6116. (Illus.). 359p. (C). 1992. pap. 14.95 (*0-292-77659-4*) U of Tex Pr.

***Chipman, Donald E. & Joseph, Harriett D.** Notable Men & Women of Spanish Texas. LC 99-19906. (Illus.). 368p. 1999. 40.00 (*0-292-71217-0*) U of Tex Pr.

***Chipman, Donald E. & Joseph, Harriett Denise.** Notable Men & Women of Spanish Texas. LC 99-19906. 368p. 1999. pap. 17.95 (*0-292-71218-9*) U of Tex Pr.

Chipman, Doug. Flying Ultralights: Instructional Briefings. LC 95-10216. (Illus.). 102p. 1988. pap. 14.95 (*1-56027-218-X*, ASA-ULF) ASA Inc.

Chipman-Evans, Carolyn, jt. auth. see Evans, Brent.

Chipman, Jack. California Pottery. 2nd ed. LC 98-231706. (Collector's Encyclopedia Ser.). 1998. 24.95 (*1-57432-037-8*) Collector Bks.

— Colector's Guide to Bauer Pottery. LC 98-114048. (Illus.). 176p. 1997. 24.95 (*1-57432-004-1*, 4931) Collector Bks.

Chipman, Jeremy. Good Life San Francisco Guide. 1999. pap. 15.95 (*1-886776-17-2*) Good Life.

— Good Life San Francisco Nightlife Guide: The Insider's Guide to Bars & Clubs in the City. Good Life Publications Staff, ed. (Good Life Guides). (Illus.). 152p. (Orig.). 1997. pap. 9.95 (*1-886776-08-3*) Good Life.

Chipman, Jeremy, jt. auth. see Massik, Peter.

Chipman, John S. A History of Balance-of-Payments Theory. 192p. 1994. 49.95 (*0-8133-0722-8*) Westview.

— The Theory of Inter-Sectoral Money Flows & Income Formation. LC 78-64212. (Johns Hopkins University. Studies in the Social Sciences. Thirtieth Ser. 1912: 2). 160p. 1982. reprint ed. 45.00 (*0-404-61317-9*) AMS Pr.

Chipman, Jonathan. Qumran Prayer & Religious Poetry. LC 93-41774. (Studies on the Texts of the Desert of Judah: Vol. 12). xxi, 415p. 1994. 125.50 (*90-04-09658-2*) Brill Academic Pubs.

Chipman, Jonathan, ed. see Frimer, Norman E.

Chipman, Jonathan, tr. see Etkes, Immanuel.

Chipman, Jonathan, tr. see Ravitzky, Aviezer.

Chipman, Jonathan, tr. see Scholem, Gershom.

Chipman, Jonathan, tr. see Uffenheimer, Rivka S.

Chipman, Kathe, ed. Index to Personal Names: Cole's History of Rockland County. LC 86-22841. 137p. 1985. 9.45 (*0-911183-23-X*) Rockland County Hist.

Chipman, Kathe, jt. compiled by see Parry, Pamela J.

***Chipman, Mary & Baron, Andy.** Microsoft Access 2000 Developer's Guide to Microsoft SQL Server. 650p. 2000. 39.99 (*0-672-31944-6*) Sams.

Chipman, Mary, jt. auth. see Gunderloy, Mike.

***Chipman, N. P.** The Tragedy of Andersonville: The Trial of Capt. Henry Wirz. (Illus.). 532p. (C). 1999. pap. 29.95 (*1-58218-168-3*) Digital Scanning.

Chipman, Nathaniel. Principles of Government: A Treatise on Free Institutions. LC 76-99478. (American Constitutional & Legal History Ser). 1970. reprint ed. 39.50 (*0-306-71851-0*) Da Capo.

***Chipman, Nathaniel.** Principles of Government: A Treatise on Free Institutions, Including the Constitution. fac. ed. LC 99-48863. 2000. write for info. (*1-58477-046-5*) Lawbk Exchange.

Chipman, Russell A., jt. ed. see Goldstein, Dennis H.

Chipman, S. F., et al, eds. Thinking & Learning Skills Vol. 2: Research & Open Questions. 640p. 1985. text 125.00 (*0-89859-166-X*) L Erlbaum Assocs.

Chipman, Scott L. New England Vital Records form the Exeter News-Letter, 1841-1846. 294p. 1993. 30.00 (*0-89725-145-8*, 1460) Picton Pr.

— New England Vital Records from the Exeter News-Letter, 1831-1840. 288p. 1993. 30.00 (*0-89725-144-X*, 1459) Picton Pr.

— New England Vital Records from the Exeter News-Letter, 1847-1852. 344p. 1994. 30.00 (*0-89725-161-X*, 1513) Picton Pr.

Chipman, Scott L., ed. New England Vital Records from the Exeter News-Letter 1853-1858, No. 4. (New Hampshire Society of Genealogists Special Publication Ser.: No. 5). 352p. 1994. 30.00 (*0-89725-189-X*, 1579) Picton Pr.

— New England Vital Records from the Exeter News-Letter, 1859-1865. 404p. 1996. 30.00 (*0-89725-261-6*, 1743) Picton Pr.

Chipman, Susan & Meyrowitz, Alan L., eds. Foundations of Knowledge Acquisition: Cognitive Models of Complex Learning. LC 92-36720. (International Series in Engineering & Computer Science, VLSI, Computer Architecture, & Digital Screen Processing). (C). 1992. text 125.00 (*0-7923-9277-9*) Kluwer Academic.

Chipman, Susan F., et al, eds. Women & Mathematics: Balancing the Equation. 400p. (C). 1985. text 79.95 (*0-89859-369-7*) L Erlbaum Assocs.

Chipot, Michel. Progress in Partial Differential Equations: The Metz Surveys 2. LC 92-205887. 1993. lib. bdg. 59.95 (*0-582-22769-0*, Pub. by Addison-Wesley) Longman.

Chipot, Michel. Progress in Partial Differential Equations: The Metz Surveys 3. LC 92-205887. 1994. lib. bdg. 69.95 (*0-582-25380-2*, Pub. by Addison-Wesley) Longman.

Chipot, Michel. Progress in Partial Differential Equations: The Metz Surveys 4. (Pitman Research Notes in Mathematics Ser.). 1996. lib. bdg. 58.95 (*0-582-27730-2*) Longman.

— Variational Inequalities & Flow in Porous Media. (Applied Mathematical Sciences Ser.: Vol. 52). (Illus.). 120p. 1984. 54.95 (*0-387-96002-3*) Spr-Verlag.

Chipot, Michel & Paulin, J. Saint-Jean, eds. Progress in Partial Differential Equations: The Metz Surveys. LC 90-28942. (Pitman Research Notes in Mathematics Ser.: Vol. 249). 212p. 1991. reprint ed. pap. 65.80 (*0-608-03603-X*, 206442600009) Bks Demand.

Chipp, Herschel B. Theories of Modern Art: A Source Book by Artists & Critics. LC 68-12038. (California Studies in the History of Art: No. 11). 680p. reprint ed. pap. 200.00 (*0-608-17275-8*, 202958900061) Bks Demand.

Chipp, Herschel B., et al. Theories of Modern Art: A Source Book by Artists & Critics. (California Studies in the History of Art: No. XI). (Illus.). 680p. (C). 1968. pap. 19.95 (*0-520-05256-0*, Pub. by U CA Pr) Cal Prin Full Svc.

Chippa, Abdul K. The Beauty & Wisdom of the Holy Qu r'an. 128p. 1979. 8.95 (*0-318-37186-3*) Asia Bk Corp.

***Chippaux, J. P.** Les Serpents d'Afrique Occidentale et Centrale (The Snakes of Western & Central Africa) (FRE., Illus.). 280p. 1999. 45.00 (*2-7099-1439-5*, Pub. by LInstitut Francais) Balogh.

Chippaux, J. P. Les Serpents de la Guyane Francaise (The Snakes of French Guiana) (Faune Tropicale Ser.: Vol. XXVII). (ENG & FRE.). 166p. 1987. pap. 26.00 (*2-7099-0829-8*, Pub. by LInstitut Francais) Balogh.

***Chippendale, Brian.** Maggots. 2000. pap. 16.95 (*0-9700858-3-4*) Highwater Bks.

***Chippendale, Lisa.** Apollo One/Challenger. 2000. 19.95 (*0-7910-5783-6*) Chelsea Hse.

— San Francisco Earthquake of 1906. (Great Disasters Ser.). (Illus.). 128p. (YA). (gr. 5 up). 2000. write for info. (*0-7910-5270-2*) Chelsea Hse.

Chippendale Staff. Gentleman & Cabinet-Maker's Director. 3rd ed. (Illus.). 249p. pap. 14.95 (*0-486-21601-2*) Dover.

***Chipperfield, John.** Non-aqueous Solvents. LC QD544.5.C57 1999. (Illus.). 96p. 1999. pap. text 12.95 (*0-19-850259-1*) OUP.

Chippindale, Anne, tr. see Joussaume, Roger.

Chippindale, Christopher. Stonehenge Complete. rev. ed. LC 93-61371. (Illus.). 296p. 1994. pap. 24.95 (*0-500-27750-8*, Pub. by Thames Hudson) Norton.

Chippindale, Christopher & Tacon, Paul S., eds. The Archaeology of Rock-Art. LC 99-188038. (New Directions in Archaeology Ser.). 392p. (C). 1998. text 80.00 (*0-521-57256-8*); pap. text 29.95 (*0-521-57619-9*) Cambridge U Pr.

Chippindale, Christopher, tr. see Joussaume, Roger.

Chippindale, Warren & Defliese, Philip L., eds. Current Value Accounting: A Practical Guide for Business. LC 77-21422. 192p. reprint ed. pap. 59.60 (*0-608-12703-5*, 202352200033) Bks Demand.

Chipping, jt. auth. see Croser.

Chipps, Esther. Neurologic Disorders, No. 1. (Illus.). 336p. (C). (gr. 13). 1992. text 36.00 (*0-8016-1372-8*, 01372) Mosby Inc.

Chipps, Genie, jt. auth. see Jessup, Claudia.

Chipps, Genie D. & Henderson, Bill, eds. Love Stories for the Rest of Us. 500p. 1994. 29.50 (*0-916366-90-1*, Pub. by Pushcart Pr) Norton.

— Love Stories for the Rest of Us. 500p. 1995. pap. 15.00 (*0-916366-93-6*, Pub. by Pushcart Pr) Norton.

— Love Stories for the Time Being. 450p. 1987. 25.00 (*0-916366-42-1*, Pub. by Pushcart Pr) Norton.

— Love Stories for the Time Being. 450p. 1989. pap. 12.95 (*0-916366-53-7*, Pub. by Pushcart Pr) Norton.

— Love Stories for the Time Being. 459p. 1999. pap. 19.00 (*0-916366-22-7*, Pub. by Pushcart Pr) Norton.

Chiprout, Eli. Asymptotic Waveform Evaluation & Moment Matching for Interconnect Analysis. LC 93-37220. (International Series in Engineering & Computer Science, VLSI, Computer Architecture, & Digital Screen Processing). 216p. (C). 1993. text 116.50 (*0-7923-9413-5*) Kluwer Academic.

***Chips, Allen S.** Clinical Hypnotherapy: A Transpersonal Approach. (Illus.). 304p. 1999. text 27.95 (*1-929661-00-2*) EIH Pubng.

Chiquart. Chiquart's On Cookery: A Fifteenth-Century Savoyard Culinary Treatise. Scully, Terrence, ed. (American University Studies: History: Ser. IX, Vol. 22).Tr. of Du Fait de Cuisine. XLVI, 138p. (C). 1986. text 29.00 (*0-8204-0352-0*) P Lang Pubng.

Chiquoine, Walter A. & Hist, Elizabeth R. The Connectivity Management Handbook: A Guide to Using Cable Management Systems for Cable Plant & Physical Network Management. LC 95-61022. (Illus.). 388p. (Orig.). 1995. pap. 379.00 (*0-9647162-0-8*) Transport Mgmt.

Chir, B., jt. auth. see Hall-Craggs, E. C.

Chira-Chavala, T., et al. Feasibility Study of Roadway-Powered Electric Vehicle Technology: El Monte Busway Case Study (Nov. 1992) (Electric Vehicle Information Ser.: Vol. 9). (Illus.). 94p. 1996. pap. 85.00 (*0-89934-257-4*, BT036); lib. bdg. 135.00 (*0-89934-258-2*, BT936) Bus Tech Bks.

Chira, Susan. A Mother's Place: Taking the Debate about Working Mothers Beyond Guilt & Blame. LC 97-44916. 336p. 1998. 25.00 (*0-06-017327-0*) HarpC.

— A Mother's Place: Taking the Debate about Working Mothers Beyond Guilt & Blame. LC 97-44916. 336p. 1999. pap. 13.00 (*0-06-093024-1*) HarpC.

Chiranjeevi, T. Tea Economy of India. (C). 1995. 22.00 (*81-7033-243-5*, Pub. by Rawat Pubns) S Asia.

— Tea Economy of India. (C). 1994. 24.00 (*0-614-13260-6*) S Asia.

Chirapravati, Pattaratorn. Votive Tablets in Thailand: Origin, Styles, & Uses. (Images of Asia Ser.). (Illus.). 94p. (C). 1998. text 19.95 (*983-56-0025-2*) OUP.

Chiras. Biology's Web of Life: Testbank. Date not set. pap. text, teacher ed., suppl. ed. write for info. (*0-314-02050-0*) West Pub.

— Environmental Science with Infotrac. 5th ed. (Biology Ser.). 1998. 54.00 incl. cd-rom (*0-534-53882-7*) Wadsworth Pub.

Chiras, Daniel. Human Biology: Health. 2nd ed. (Life Science Ser.). 361p. 1995. pap., student ed. 24.95 (*0-314-04749-2*) Jones & Bartlett.

***Chiras, Daniel.** The Natural House: A Complete Guide to Healthy, Energy Independent, Environmental Homes. (Illus.). 400p. 2000. pap. 35.00 (*1-890132-57-8*) Chelsea Green Pub.

Chiras, Daniel D. Enviromental Science. 4th ed. (C). 1994. pap. text 8.50 (*0-8053-4231-1*) Addison-Wesley.

— Environmental Science. 5th ed. LC 97-46582. (Illus.). 550p. 1998. 54.00 (*0-534-53874-6*) Brooks-Cole.

— Environmental Science: South Module. 4th ed. (C). 1994. pap. text 8.50 (*0-8053-4230-3*) Addison-Wesley.

— Environmental Science West M. 4th ed. (C). 1994. pap. text 8.50 (*0-8053-4232-X*) Addison-Wesley.

— Human Biology. 2nd ed. (Life Science Ser.). (Illus.). 195p. (C). 1995. pap. text 18.75 (*0-314-04954-1*) Jones & Bartlett.

***Chiras, Daniel D.** Human Biology. 3rd ed. (Illus.). 64p. (C). 1999. pap. text, suppl. ed. write for info. (*0-7637-1098-9*) JB Pubns.

Chiras, Daniel D. Human Biology: Health & Environment. Westby, ed. (Life Science Ser.). 610p. (C). 1991. pap. text 46.25 (*0-314-79498-0*) Jones & Bartlett.

— Human Biology: Health & Environment. 2nd ed. LC 94-12440. (Life Science Ser.). 720p. (C). 1995. pap. 50.00 (*0-314-03921-X*) Jones & Bartlett.

— Human Biology: Health, Homeostasis & the Environment. 3rd ed. LC 98-49008. 1998. write for info. (*0-7637-0808-9*) Jones & Bartlett.

— Human Biology: Health, Test Bank. 2nd ed. (Life Science Ser.). 344p. 1995. pap., teacher ed. 10.00 (*0-314-05093-0*) Jones & Bartlett.

— Lessons from Nature: Learning to Live Sustainably on the Earth. LC 91-39156. 289p. 1992. text 40.00 (*1-55963-107-4*); pap. text 22.00 (*1-55963-106-6*) Island Pr.

— Study Skills for Science Students. Westby, ed. 86p. (C). 1994. pap. 8.50 (*0-314-03983-X*) Brooks-Cole.

***Chiras, Daniel D. & Blahnik, Jim.** Human Biology. 3rd ed. (Illus.). 352p. (C). 1999. pap. text, student ed. 22.50 (*0-7637-0960-3*) JB Pubns.

***Chiras, Daniel D. & Templin, Jay M.** TB- Human Biology. 3rd ed. (Illus.). 416p. (C). 1999. pap. text, teacher ed. 15.00 (*0-7637-0959-X*) JB Pubns.

Chiras, Daniel D., jt. auth. see Owen, Oliver S.

Chiras, Daniel D., jt. auth. see Sustainable Futures Staff.

Chiras/Causey & Causey. Environmental Action Guide. 3rd ed. (Biology Ser.). 1998. mass mkt. 5.25 (*0-534-53883-5*) Wadsworth Pub.

Chirazi, Steffan. Faith No More: The Real Story. (Illus.). 144p. 1994. pap. 12.00 (*0-685-72585-5*, Pub. by Castle Communs) Viking Penguin.

Chirban, J., ed. Science & Orthodox Life. 1993. 9.95 (*0-917651-98-7*, Pub. by Holy Cross Orthodox) BookWorld.

Chirban, John T. Healing: Orthodox Christian Perspectives in Medicine, Psychology, & Religion. LC 91-6678. 84p. (Orig.). (YA). (gr. 10-12). 1991. pap. 6.95 (*0-917651-84-7*, Pub. by Holy Cross Orthodox) BookWorld.

— Interviewing in Depth: The Interactive-Relational Approach. 200p. (C). 1996. 42.00 (*0-8039-7317-9*); pap. 18.50 (*0-8039-7318-7*) Sage.

— Personhood: Orthodox Christianity & the Connection Between Body, Mind, & Soul. LC 95-34302. 216p. 1996. 57.95 (*0-89789-463-4*, Bergin & Garvey) Greenwood.

Chirban, John T., ed. Coping with Death & Dying: An Interdisciplinary Approach. 108p. 1986. pap. text 15.00 (*0-8191-4985-3*) U Pr of Amer.

— Ethical Dilemmas: Crises in Faith & Modern Medicine. 172p. (Orig.). (C). 1994. pap. 29.50 (*0-8191-9338-0*); lib. bdg. 49.50 (*0-8191-9337-2*) U Pr of Amer.

— Health & Faith: Medical, Psychological & Religious Dimensions. 152p. (Orig.). (C). 1991. pap. text 19.50 (*0-8191-8285-0*); lib. bdg. 38.00 (*0-8191-8284-2*) U Pr of Amer.

— Marriage & the Family: New Directions, New Integrations. (Series on Medicine, Psychology & Religion). (Illus.). 94p. (Orig.). pap. 4.95 (*0-916586-63-4*) Holy Cross Orthodox.

— Thalassemia: An Interdisciplinary Approach. (Illus.). 106p. (C). 1987. lib. bdg. 35.50 (*0-8191-5675-2*) U Pr of Amer.

Chirban, John T. & Talagan, Dean. Youth & Sexuality. 52p. 1984. pap. 3.95 (*0-917653-10-6*, Pub. by Holy Cross Orthodox) BookWorld.

Chirbes, Rafael. Mimoun. (Masks Ser.). 144p. 1993. pap. 12.99 (*1-85242-220-3*) Serpents Tail.

Chirchirillo, Charles. Mixed Signals: We Went All the Way. Young, Frank, ed. LC 98-60413. 364p. 1998. 35.50 (*1-885001-12-6*) Via Press.

C

Chirco, John. JT's Conversations on True Basic: Becoming Acquainted with Basic. 292p. (C). 1998. per. 27.00 (*0-7872-5090-2*, 41509010) Kendall-Hunt.

Chirco, T. The Market for Bakery Products. 1999. 1295.00 (*0-685-08040-4*) Busn Trend.

— The Market for Intimate Apparel & Women's Hosiery. 930p. 1999. 1495.00 (*0-685-17773-4*) Busn Trend.

— The Market for Musical Instruments. 560p. 1999. 1295.00 (*0-685-08045-5*) Busn Trend.

— The Market for Watches & Clocks. 430p. 1999. 1295.00 (*0-318-00526-3*) Busn Trend.

— The U. S. Market for Writing Instruments. 360p. 1998. 1195.00 (*0-318-00529-8*) Busn Trend.

— The U. S. Processed Meat Industry. 800p. 2000. pap. 1295.00 (*0-318-00494-1*) Busn Trend.

Chircop, Aldo. Ocean Yearbook, Vol. 13. 2000. lib. bdg. 87.00 (*0-226-06616-9*) U Ch Pr.

Chircop, Gerolyma. Aegean Sea after the Cold War. LC 99-37673. 272p. 1999. text 68.00 (*0-312-22603-9*) St Martin.

Chircop, Lionel, jt. ed. see Agius, Emmanuel.

Chireau, Yvonne & Deutsch, Nathaniel, eds. Black Zion: African American Religious Encounters with Judaism. LC 99-39278. (Religion in America Ser.). (Illus.). 256p. 1999. pap. 17.95 (*0-19-511258-X*); text 49.95 (*0-19-511257-1*) OUP.

Chirelstein, Marvin A. Concepts & Case Analysis in the Law of Contracts. 2nd ed. (University Textbook Ser.). 185p. 1993. pap. text 15.95 (*1-56662-065-1*) Foundation Pr.

— Concepts & Cases Analysis in the Law of Contracts. 3rd ed. LC 98-3537. (University Casebook Ser.). 193p. 1998. pap. 13.50 (*1-56662-610-2*) Foundation Pr.

— Federal Income Taxation: A Guide to the Leading Cases & Concepts. 7th ed. (University Textbook Ser.). 384p. (C). 1994. pap. text 19.95 (*1-56662-162-3*) Foundation Pr.

***Chirelstein, Marvin A.** Federal Income Taxation: A Law Students Guide to the Leading Cases & Concepts. 8th rev. ed. LC 99-203045. (Paralegal). (C). 1999. pap. 18.00 (*1-56662-786-9*) Foundation Pr.

Chirelstein, Marvin A. Federal Income Taxation - A Guide to the Leading Cases & Concepts. 8th ed. LC 97-19214. (University Textbook Ser.). 398p. 1997. pap. text. write for info. (*1-56662-538-6*) Foundation Pr.

Chirenje, J. Mutero. Ethiopianism & Afro-Americans in Southern Africa, 1883-1916. LC 87-3199. (Illus.). 224p. 1987. text 32.50 (*0-8071-1319-0*) La State U Pr.

— A History of Northern Botswana 1850-1910. LC 74-194. (Illus.). 316p. 1976. 38.50 (*0-8386-1537-6*) Fairleigh Dickinson.

Chirgotis, William G. Encyclopedia of Architect-Designed Homes. Theuerkauf, Bruce H., ed. (Illus.). 312p. 1985. lib. bdg. 25.00 (*0-933133-00-6*) Nat Home Planning.

Chirgwin, B. H. & Plumpton, C. A. Course of Mathematics for Engineers & Scientists. LC 62-9696. (Course of Mathematics for Engineers & Scientists Ser.: Vol. 5). 1964. 99.00 (*0-08-025060-2*, Pub. by Pergamon Repr) Franklin.

— Course of Mathematics for Engineers & Scientists. 2nd ed. 1982. text 243.00 (*0-08-015970-2*, Pub. by Pergamon Repr) Franklin.

— Course of Mathematics for Engineers & Scientists, Vol. 1. rev. ed. LC 60-13894. 1961. reprint ed. 147.00 (*0-08-009373-6*, Pub. by Pergamon Repr) Franklin.

— Course of Mathematics for Engineers & Scientists Vol. 3: Theoretical Mechanics. rev. ed. LC 60-13894. 1963. 166.00 (*0-08-009376-0*, Pub. by Pergamon Repr) Franklin.

Chirgwin, B. H., et al. Elementary Electromagnetic Theory, 3 vols. Incl. Vol. 3. Maxwell's Equations & Their Consequences. 1973. text 83.00 (*0-08-017120-6*); pap. write for info. (*0-318-55159-4*, Pub. by Pergamon Repr) Franklin.

Chiri, Judith A., et al. Information Processing: Keyboarding, Formatting, & Applications Mastery, Bk. 1. large type ed. 1993. 101.00 (*0-614-09831-9*, L-31449-00) Am Printing Hse.

Chiriboga, David A. & Catron, Linda S. Divorce: Crisis, Challenge, or Relief? 328p. (C). 1992. pap. text 22.50 (*0-8147-1485-4*) NYU Pr.

Chiriboga, David A., jt. auth. see Fiske, Marjorie.

***Chirichiello, Giuseppe.** Intertemporal Macroeconomic Models Money & Rational Choices. LC 99-86836. 2000. text 75.00 (*0-312-23218-7*) St Martin.

Chirichiello, Giuseppe. Macroeconomic Models & Controversies. LC 93-44299. 1994. text 75.00 (*0-312-12097-4*) St Martin.

Chirichigno, F. Norma. Clave para Identificar los Peces Marinos del Peru. (Instituto del Mark del Peru Ser.: Vol. 44). (SPA., Illus.). 388p. 1978. reprint ed. pap. 70.00 (*3-87429-131-6*, 011269, Pub. by Koeltz Sci Bks) Lubrecht & Cramer.

Chirichigno, Gregory C. Debt Slavery in Israel & the Ancient Near East. (Journal for the Study of the Old Testament Supplement Ser.: Vol. 141). 409p. 1993. 85.00 (*1-85075-359-8*, Pub. by Sheffield Acad) CUP Services.

Chirico, Giorgio de, see De Chirico, Giorgio.

Chirico, JoAnn. Electronics. LC 95-18548. (VGM Career Portraits Ser.). (Illus.). 96p. (J). (gr. 7 up). 1995. 13.95 (*0-8442-4373-6*, 43736, Passprt Bks) NTC Contemp Pub Co.

— Opportunities in Science Technician Careers. (Opportunities In . . . Ser.). (Illus.). 160p. pap. 11.95 (*0-8442-4597-6*, 45976, Natl Textbk Co) NTC Contemp Pub Co.

— Opportunities in Science Technician Careers. (Opportunities in...Ser.). (Illus.). 160p. 1996. 14.95 (*0-8442-4596-8*, 45968, Natl Textbk Co) NTC Contemp Pub Co.

***Chirico, Patty.** The Genesis Principle: The ABC's of Throwing Disorganization, Procrastination & Humiliation Out of Your Life. (Organize Your Life Ser.). 176p. 2000. 19.95 (*1-888237-31-7*) Baxter Pr.

Chirico, Robert. Martini Madness. 32p. 1997. pap. 3.95 (*0-942320-60-3*) Am Cooking.

— Up in Smoke: A Guide to Cigar Basics. (Illus.). 32p. 1998. pap. 3.95 (*0-942320-61-1*) Am Cooking.

Chirigos, Michael A., ed. Control of Neoplasia by Modulation of the Immune System. fac. ed. LC 76-5665. (Progress in Cancer Research & Therapy Ser.: No. 2). (Illus.). 619p. pap. 191.90 (*0-7837-7206-8*, 204709300005) Bks Demand.

— Immune Modulation & Control of Neoplasia by Adjuvant Therapy. fac. ed. LC 76-5665. (Progress in Cancer Research & Therapy Ser.: No. 7). (Illus.). 519p. pap. 160.90 (*0-7837-7522-9*, 204698300005) Bks Demand.

Chirigos, Michael A., et al, eds. Mediation of Cellular Immunity in Cancer by Immune Modifiers. LC 80-5877. (Progress in Cancer Research & Therapy Ser.: No. 19). 287p. 1981. reprint ed. pap. 89.00 (*0-608-00606-8*, 206119300007) Bks Demand.

***Chirikba, Slava.** The Georgian-Abkhaz War. 288p. 1999. 72.00 (*0-7007-1166-X*, Pub. by Curzon Pr Ltd) Paul & Co Pubs.

***Chirikjian, Gregory S. & Kyatkin, Alexander B.** Engineering Applications of Noncommutative Harmonic Analysis: With Emphasis on Rotation & Motion Groups. LC 00-31236. 2000. write for info. (*0-8493-0748-1*) CRC Pr.

Chirikjian, Jack. Biotech Resource Manual. (Life Science Ser.). 216p. 1995. pap. 35.00 (*0-86720-895-3*) Jones & Bartlett.

— Biotech Resource Manual, Vol. 2. 288p. 1995. pap. 35.00 (*0-86720-896-1*) Jones & Bartlett.

Chirikov, Boris, jt. ed. see Casati, Giulio.

Chirinian, Alain. Boys' Puberty. 1991. pap. 6.95 (*0-8125-1125-5*, Pub. by Tor Bks) St Martin.

— Internet Activities for Math. (Illus.). 144p. (J). (gr. 1-3). 1998. pap., teacher ed. 14.95 (*1-57690-191-2*, TCM2191) Tchr Create Mat.

— Internet Activities for Science. Forbes, Evan D., ed. (Illus.). 144p. (J). (gr. 1-3). 1996. pap., teacher ed. 14.95 (*1-57690-409-1*, TCM2409) Tchr Create Mat.

— Internet Activities for Science. Forbes, Evan D., ed. (Illus.). 144p. (J). (gr. 3-5). 1997. pap., teacher ed. 14.95 (*1-57690-410-5*, TCM2410) Tchr Create Mat.

— Internet Activities for Science: TechKnowledgey. (Illus.). 144p. (J). (gr. 5-8). 1997. pap., teacher ed. 14.95 (*1-57690-411-3*, TCM2411) Tchr Create Mat.

— Simple Internet Activities. (Illus.). (J). pap., teacher ed. 11.95 (*1-57690-460-1*, TCM2460) Tchr Create Mat.

Chirinian, Helene. Daring Detective Challenge. (Crossword Mysteries Ser.). (Illus.). 96p. (J). 1994. pap. 3.95 (*1-56565-171-5*, 01715W, Pub. by Lowell Hse Juvenile) NTC Contemp Pub Co.

— Technology Connections for Ancient Egypt. (Technology Connections Ser.). 48p. (J). (gr. 5-8). 1997. pap. 7.95 (*1-57690-400-8*) Tchr Create Mat.

— Technology Connections for Ancient Greece. (Technology Connections Ser.). 48p. (J). (gr. 5-8). 1997. pap. 7.95 (*1-57690-401-6*) Tchr Create Mat.

— Technology Connections for Ancient Rome. (Technology Connections Ser.). 48p. (J). (gr. 5-8). 1997. pap. 7.95 (*1-57690-402-4*) Tchr Create Mat.

Chirinian, Helene & Yamamoto, Neal. Secret Spy Challenge & Other Private Eye Puzzles. (Crossword Mysteries Ser.). 64p. (J). 1997. pap. 5.95 (*1-56565-768-3*, 07683W, Pub. by Lowell Hse Juvenile) NTC Contemp Pub Co.

— Super Sleuth Challenge. (Crossword Mysteries Ser.). 96p. (J). (gr. 4-7). 1994. pap. 3.95 (*1-56565-170-7*, 01707W, Pub. by Lowell Hse Juvenile) NTC Contemp Pub Co.

Chirinian, Linda, ed. Secrets of Cooking: Armenian, Lebanese, Persian. (Cookbook Ser.). (Illus.). 264p. 1994. 29.95 (*0-9617033-0-X*) Lionhart Inc Pub.

Chirino, Alfonso. Text & Concordances of Biblioteca Nacional Manuscript 3384 Espejo de Medicina. Wasick, Cynthia M. & Ardemagni, Enrica J., eds. (Medieval Spanish Medical Texts Ser.: No. 5). 9p. 1988. 10.00 incl. fiche (*0-942260-56-2*) Hispanic Seminary.

Chirino, Alfonso, et al. The Texts & Concordances of Escorial Manuscript b.IV.34: Menor Dano de Medicina. Ardemagni, Enrica J., ed. (Medieval Spanish Medical Texts Ser.: No. 2). 11p. 1984. 10.00 incl. fiche (*0-942260-41-4*) Hispanic Seminary.

Chirka, E. M. Complex Analytic Sets. (C). 1989. text 207.50 (*0-7923-0234-6*) Kluwer Academic.

Chirka, E. M., et al. Introduction to Complex Analysis. (Encyclopaedia of Mathematical Sciences Ser.: Vol. 7). vii, 248p. 1997. pap. 49.95 (*3-540-63005-8*) Spr-Verlag.

Chirkov, A. M., et al. Emotional Stress in Monkeys. (Illus.). 187p. (C). 1995. per. 125.00 (*1-56072-239-8*) Nova Sci Pubs.

Chirlian, Paul M. Analysis & Design of Integrated Electronic Circuits. 2nd ed. 152p. 1986. pap. 106.95 (*0-471-60356-2*) Wiley.

— Digital Circuits with Microprocessor Applications. 432p. (C). 1981. text 49.95 (*0-916460-32-0*, Matrix Pubs Inc) Weber Systems.

— Signals, Systems, & Filters. LC 93-12670. 1993. text 59.95 (*0-442-01324-8*, VNR) Wiley.

— Signals, Systems, & the Computer. 615p. (C). 1986. text 64.95 (*0-938862-81-2*) Weber Systems.

Chirodea, Doru. Aletheia Raped. (Illus.). 31p. (Orig.). 1989. pap. 3.00 (*0-926935-36-4*) Runaway Spoon.

— Nonathambia. 26p. 1995. pap. 3.00 (*1-57141-014-7*) Runaway Spoon.

— On Metascrotum & Infradeaths. (Illus.). 36p. (Orig.). 1990. pap. 3.00 (*0-926935-41-0*) Runaway Spoon.

Chirol, Valentine. India. LC 72-2561. (Select Bibliographies Reprint Ser.). 1977. reprint ed. 24.95 (*0-8369-6851-4*) Ayer.

Chiroldes, Alberto H. A Diez Pasos del Paraiso. LC 96-86448. (Coleccion Caniqui). (SPA.). 214p. (Orig.). 1996. pap. 13.00 (*0-89729-812-8*) Ediciones.

Chiron, R. J., jt. auth. see Fear, Richard A.

Chironis, Nicholas P. & Sclater, Neil J., eds. Mechanisms & Mechanical Devices Sourcebook. 2nd rev. ed. LC 96-5438. (Illus.). 463p. 1996. 84.95 (*0-07-011356-4*) McGraw.

Chironna, Carlynn, ed. Adweek Agency Directory 1998. annuals 1060p. 1997. pap. 295.00 (*1-891204-06-8*) Adweek Direct.

***Chironna, Mark.** To Believe & Not Doubt. 224p. 2000. pap. 12.99 (*0-88419-731-X*) Creation House.

Chironna, Mark J. The Elisha Principle. 54p. (Orig.). 1985. pap. 3.95 (*0-938612-11-5*, Revival Pr) Destiny Image.

— The Elisha Principle. 96p. (Orig.). 1989. pap. 8.99 (*1-56043-006-0*) Destiny Image.

— Elisha Principle. (SPA.). 96p. (Orig.). 1992. pap. 8.99 (*1-56043-080-X*) Destiny Image.

— Stepping into Greatness, Vol. 1. 1999. pap. 12.99 (*0-88419-567-8*) Creation House.

— Undiscovered Christ. 112p. (Orig.). 1992. pap. 8.99 (*1-56043-085-0*) Destiny Image.

Chirot, Daniel. How Societies Change. (Sociology for a New Century Ser.). 164p. 1994. pap. 18.95 (*0-8039-9017-0*) Pine Forge.

— Modern Tyrants: The Power & Prevalence of Evil in Our Age. 400p. 1994. 29.95 (*0-02-905477-X*) Free Pr.

— Modern Tyrants: The Power & Prevalence of Evil in Our Age. LC 95-53117. 510p. (C). 1996. pap. text 19.95 (*0-691-02777-3*, Pub. by Princeton U Pr) Cal Prin Full Svc.

Chirot, Daniel, ed. The Crisis of Leninism & the Decline of the Left: The Revolutions of 1989. LC 91-11289. (Jackson School Publications in International Studies). 262p. 1991. pap. 17.50 (*0-295-97111-8*); text 35.00 (*0-295-97110-X*) U of Wash Pr.

— The Origins of Backwardness in Eastern Europe: Economics & Politics from the Middle Ages until the Early Twentieth Century. 269p. 1991. reprint ed. pap. 17.95 (*0-520-07640-0*, Pub. by U CA Pr) Cal Prin Full Svc.

Chirot, Daniel & Reid, Anthony, eds. Essential Outsiders: Chinese & Jews in the Modern Transformation of Southeast Asia & Central Europe. LC 96-6516. (Jackson School Publications in International Studies). 368p. 1997. 25.00 (*0-295-97613-6*) U of Wash Pr.

***Chirot, Dave.** Anar Key Ology. 31p. 1999. pap. 5.00 (*1-57141-051-1*) Runaway Spoon.

Chirouze, Yves & Metherell, Victoria. French-English, English-French Dictionary of Marketing. (ENG & FRE.). 307p. 1990. 79.95 (*0-8288-7294-5*, 271270312X) Fr & Eur.

Chirovsky, Nicholas L. & Mott, Vincent. Philosophical Foundations of Economic Doctrines. 3rd ed. 1981. pap. 5.95 (*0-912598-20-4*) Florham.

Chirra, Joseph. A Life of Riches: Your Own Personal Success Manual. LC 93-81278. 112p. (Orig.). 1994. pap. 13.95 (*0-9639958-7-1*) Mervilla.

Chirri, Imam Mohamad Jawad. Ameer Al-Mumineen (Leader of the Believers) 2nd ed. 600p. 15.00 (*0-317-52359-7*) Islamic Ctr.

— The Brother of the Prophet Mohammad: The Imam Ali, 2 vols., Vol. II. LC 79-127838. 400p. 1982. 15.00 (*0-942778-00-6*) Islamic Ctr.

— The Faith of Islam. 24p. pap. 3.00 (*0-317-52358-9*) Islamic Ctr.

— The Five Daily Prayers. 24p. pap. 3.00 (*0-317-52360-0*) Islamic Ctr.

— Imam Hussein, Leader of the Martyrs. 40p. pap. 3.00 (*0-317-52361-9*) Islamic Ctr.

— Inquiries about Islam. 197p. 1965. 15.95 (*0-318-37190-1*) Asia Bk Corp.

— Inquiries about Islam. 3rd ed. 200p. 7.00 (*0-317-52357-0*) Islamic Ctr.

Chirstliche. Panorama Biblico de Espiral.Tr. of Panorama of the Bible. (SPA., Illus.). 14.99 (*0-614-27096-0*, 490471) Editorial Unilit.

Chirurg, Riva. Bridge of Sorrow, Bridge of Hope. 2nd rev. ed. Fromer, Rebecca, ed. Orig. Title: Henai Hem Ba'im. (Illus.). 208p. 1994. pap. 13.95 (*0-943376-61-0*) Magnes Mus.

Chi's Enterprise Staff, ed. see Chi, Tsu-Tsair.

Chisci, G. & Morgan, Royston P., eds. Soil Erosion in the European Community--Impact of Changing Agriculture: Proceedings of a Seminar on Land Degradation Due to Hydrological Phenomena in Hilly Areas: Impact of Change of Land Use & Management, Cesena, 9-11 October 1985. 248p. (C). 1986. text 97.00 (*90-6191-657-7*, Pub. by A A Balkema) Ashgate Pub Co.

Chisenhall, Frank. The Complete Typing Business Guide: Everything You Need to Know to Start & Successfully Operate a Home Typing Business. (Illus.). 128p. (Orig.). 1990. pap. 12.95 (*0-9625133-3-4*) Supertext Pub.

Chisenhall, Fred, jt. auth. see McKee, Margaret.

Chisenhall, Jack, jt. auth. see Remus, Timothy S.

Chisenhall, Nestrud & Julian Staff. Arkansas Handbook on Environmental Laws. 2nd ed. (State Environmental Law Ser.). 221p. 1998. pap. text 85.00 (*0-86587-628-2*) Gov Insts.

Chiseri-Strater, Elizabeth. Academic Literacies: The Public & Private Discourse of University Students. LC 90-42400. (Illus.). 205p. (Orig.). (C). 1991. pap. text 26.00 (*0-86709-273-4*, 0273, Pub. by Boynton Cook Pubs) Heinemann.

***Chiseri-Strater, Elizabeth & Sunstein, Bonnie S.** Fieldworking: Reading & Writing Research. 2nd ed. 2001. pap. text. write for info. (*0-312-25825-9*) St Martin.

Chisesi, T., ed. Third Spring Meeting, New Insights in Haematology, Cini Foundation-Venice. 130p. 1997. pap. text 111.00 (*90-5702-252-4*, Harwood Acad Pubs) Gordon & Breach.

Chisholm & Courti. How to Write about Yourself. 1999. pap. text 9.95 (*0-7490-0367-7*) Allison & Busby.

Chisholm, A. A., jt. auth. see Shaw, J.

Chisholm, A. H. First Kuwait Oil Concession: Record of the Negotiations, 1911-1934. 272p. 1975. 49.50 (*0-7146-3002-0*, Pub. by F Cass Pubs) Intl Spec Bk.

Chisholm, Alan R. Towards Herodiade: A Literary Genealogy. LC 77-10255. reprint ed. 41.50 (*0-404-16310-6*) AMS Pr.

Chisholm, Alison. A Practical Poetry Coarse. 144p. 1995. pap. 9.95 (*0-7490-0114-3*) Allison & Busby.

***Chisholm, Alison, ed.** Derbyshire: Poets England - Local Life & Topography Depicted in Regional Verse. 92p. 2000. pap. 14.95 (*1-902096-45-2*, Pub. by Headland Pubns) Intl Spec Bk.

***Chisholm, Anne.** Rumer Godden: A Storyteller's Life. LC 98-46259. (Illus.). 352p. (J). 1999. 24.00 (*0-688-16944-9*, Grenwillow Bks) HarpC Child Bks.

Chisholm, Barbara, jt. auth. see Gutsche, Andrea.

Chisholm, Cathy C. Landscapes of the Heart. Basham, Beth, ed. LC 98-33953. (Illus.). 116p. 1998. 13.95 (*1-57895-063-5*) Bridge Resources.

***Chisholm, Colin.** Through Yup'ik Eyes: An Adopted Son Explores the Landscape of Family. 2000. 23.95 (*0-88240-533-0*, Alaska NW Bks) Gr Arts Ctr Pub.

Chisholm, Craig. Hawaii, the Big Island, Hiking Trails. LC 91-71624. (Illus.). 120p. 1994. pap. 12.95 (*0-9612630-4-0*) Fernglen Pr.

***Chisholm, Craig.** Hawaiian Hiking Trails: The Guide for All Islands. 9th ed. LC 98-54249. (Illus.). 152p. 1999. 18.95 (*0-9612630-8-3*) Fernglen Pr.

Chisholm, Craig. Hawaiian Hiking Trails, the Guide for All the Islands. 8th ed. LC 94-83996. (Illus.). 152p. 1994. pap. 15.95 (*0-9612630-5-9*) Fernglen Pr.

— Kauai Hiking Trails. LC 91-71623. (Illus.). 120p. 1991. pap. 12.95 (*0-9612630-3-2*) Fernglen Pr.

Chisholm, Craig. Our Earth. (Explainers Ser.). (Illus.). 24p. (J). (gr. 2-4). 1982. pap. 4.95 (*0-86020-582-7*, Usborne) EDC.

Chisholm, D. The Catechism in Examples, 5 vols., Set. 2224p. (J). (gr. 4 up). 1996. reprint ed. pap. 79.95 (*0-912141-37-9*) Roman Cath Bks.

Chisholm, Donald. Coordination Without Hierarchy: Informal Structures in Multiorganizational Systems. (C). 1989. pap. 17.95 (*0-520-08037-8*, Pub. by U CA Pr) Cal Prin Full Svc.

***Chisholm, Donald.** Waiting for Dead Men's Shoes: Origins & Development of the U. S. Navy's Officer Personnel System, 1793-1941. LC 00-33857. 2000. write for info. (*0-8047-3525-5*) Stanford U Pr.

Chisholm, Douglas, jt. ed. see Chesson, Rosemary.

Chisholm, Francis P. Introductory Lectures on General Semantics. 1971. reprint ed. 10.95 (*0-910780-05-6*) Inst Gen Seman.

Chisholm, Geoffrey D., ed. Handbook on Benign Prostatic Hyperplasia. LC 93-38114. 164p. 1994. text 50.00 (*0-7817-0148-1*) Lppncott W & W.

Chisholm, Geoffrey D., et al. Surgical Management. 2nd rev. ed. Williamson, R. C., ed. 848p. 1991. pap. text 150.00 (*0-7506-0025-X*) Buttrwrth-Heinemann.

Chisholm, Geoffrey D., jt. ed. see Pryor, J. P.

***Chisholm, Gloria.** Forgive One Another. 128p. 2000. 8.95 (*1-57856-311-9*) Waterbrook Pr.

— Love One Another: How to Let God's Heart Shine Through Your Life. LC 00-22846. 128p. 2000. pap. 8.95 (*1-57856-310-0*) Waterbrook Pr.

Chisholm, J. Biology. (Introductions Ser.). (Illus.). 48p. (J). (gr. 6-12). 1983. pap. 7.95 (*0-86020-707-2*) EDC.

— Book of Science. (Introductions Ser.). (Illus.). 48p. (J). (gr. 6 up). 1984. pap. 16.95 (*0-7460-0830-9*) EDC.

— World History Dates. (Illustrated World History Ser.). (Illus.). 128p. (J). (gr. 6 up). 1987. lib. bdg. 22.95 (*0-88110-232-6*) EDC.

— World History Dates. (Illustrated World History Ser.). (Illus.). 128p. (J). (gr. 6 up). 1987. pap. 14.95 (*0-86020-954-7*) EDC.

Chisholm, J., jt. auth. see Milard, A.

Chisholm, J. S. & Common, A. K., eds. Clifford Algebras & Their Applications in Mathematical Physics. 1986. text 261.50 (*90-277-2308-7*) Kluwer Academic.

Chisholm, James. South Pass, 1868: James Chisholm's Journal of the Wyoming Gold Rush. Homsher, Lola M., ed. & intro. by. LC 60-12692. (Illus.). vi, 246p. 1996. pap. 12.00 (*0-8032-5824-0*, Bison Books) U of Nebr Pr.

Chisholm, James. True Hearth: A Practical Guide to Traditional Householding. 130p. pap. 12.95 (*1-885972-03-2*) Runa-Raven Pr.

Chisholm, James A. True Hearth: A Guide to True Householding. (Illus.). 1993. pap. 12.95 (*1-885972-02-4*) Runa-Raven Pr.

***Chisholm, James S.** Death, Hope & Sex: Steps to an Evolutionary Ecology of Mind & Morality. LC 98-48321. (Illus.). 300p. (C). 1999. 74.95 (*0-521-59281-X*); pap. 29.95 (*0-521-59708-0*) Cambridge U Pr.

— Navajo Infancy: An Ethological Study of Child Development. LC 83-12258. (Evolutionary Foundations of Human Behavior Ser.). 279p. (C). 1983. lib. bdg. 49.95 (*0-202-01169-0*) Aldine de Gruyter.

Chisholm, James S., jt. auth. see Rushforth, Scott.

Chisholm, Jan. Roman Times. (First History Ser.). (Illus.). 24p. (J). (gr. 2-4). 1982. pap. 4.50 (*0-86020-619-X*) EDC.

An Asterisk (*) at the beginning of an entry indicates that the title is appearing for the first time.

— Roman Times. (First History Ser.). (Illus.). 24p. (J). (gr. 3-6). 1982. lib. bdg. 12.95 (*0-88110-105-2*) EDC.

Chisholm, Jane. World History Dates. 2nd rev. ed. (Illustrated World History Ser.). (Illus.). 194p. (YA). (gr. 4-7). 1998. lib. bdg. 30.95 (*1-58086-114-8*, Usborne) EDC.

— World History Dates. 2nd rev. ed. (Illustrated World History Ser.). (Illus.). 194p. (YA). (gr. 6 up). 1998. pap. 22.95 (*0-7460-2318-9*, Usborne) EDC.

Chisholm, Jane & Millard, Anne. The Usborne Book of the Ancient World. (Illus.). 288p. (YA). (gr. 6 up). 1991. lib. bdg. 32.95 (*1-58086-022-2*, Usborne) EDC.

Chisholm, Jane, jt. auth. see Treays, Rebecca.

Chisholm, Jane, ed. see Wingate, Philippa.

Chisholm, Joanna. I'm Going to Make You a Star. 154p. mass mkt. 4.99 (*1-55197-190-9*) Picasso Publ.

Chisholm, Joe, jt. auth. see Cohn, Alfred.

Chisholm, John, jt. auth. see Ellis, Norman.

Chisholm, John W., jt. auth. see Wise, Leonard A.

***Chisholm, Judith.** Voices from Paradise: How the Dead Speak to Us. 160p. 2000. pap. 19.95 (*1-897766-59-9*, Pub. by Jon Carpenter) Paul & Co Pubs.

Chisholm, Karen S. The Fat Tracker: Write It Down, Take It Off. rev. ed. (Illus.). 114p. (Orig.). 1995. pap., spiral bd. 9.95 (*0-9641444-2-5*) Soln Graphx.

***Chisholm, Lilian.** New Nurse at St. Benedict's. large type ed. (Dales Romance Ser.). 352p. 1999. pap. 20.99 (*1-85389-920-8*) Ulverscroft.

Chisholm, Louey, ed. The Golden Staircase: Poems & Verses for Children. LC 79-51973. (Granger Poetry Library). (Illus.). (J). (gr. 3-8). 1980. reprint ed. 30.00 (*0-89609-182-1*) Roth Pub Inc.

Chisholm, Lovey, ed. The Golden Staircase: Poems & Verses for Children. LC 71-37011. (Granger Index Reprint Ser.). 1977. 24.95 (*0-8369-6310-5*) Ayer.

Chisholm, Lynne, et al, eds. Childhood, Youth & Social Change: A Comparative Perspective. 250p. 1990. 85.00 (*1-85000-650-4*, Falmer Pr); pap. 39.95 (*1-85000-651-2*, Falmer Pr) Taylor & Francis.

— Growing up in Europe: Contemporary Horizons in Childhood & Youth Studies. LC 95-13599. (International Studies on Childhood & Adolescence: No. 2). vii, 314p. (C). 1995. lib. bdg. 64.95 (*3-11-014475-1*) De Gruyter.

Chisholm, M. F., et al, eds. Mechanisms of Heteroepitaxial Growth. (Materials Research Society Symposium Proceedings Ser.: Vol. 263). 513p. 1992. text 17.50 (*1-55899-158-1*) Materials Res.

Chisholm, Malcolm H., ed. Early Transition Metal Clusters with Pi-Donor Ligands. 289p. 1995. 159.00 (*0-471-18606-6*) Wiley.

Chisholm, Malcolm H., ed. Early Transition Metal Clusters with Pi-Donor Ligands. LC 95-2175. (Chemistry of Metal Clusters Ser.). (Illus.). xii, 292p. 1995. 115.00 (*1-56081-684-8*, Wiley-VCH) Wiley.

— Inorganic Chemistry: Toward the Twenty-First Century. LC 82-24505. (ACS Symposium Ser.: No. 211). 567p. 1983. lib. bdg. 65.95 (*0-8412-0763-1*) Am Chemical.

— Inorganic Chemistry: Toward the 21st Century. LC 82-24505. (ACS Symposium Ser.: No. 211). 576p. 1983. reprint ed. pap. 178.60 (*0-608-03220-4*, 206373900007) Bks Demand.

— Reactivity of Metal-Metal Bonds. LC 81-361. (ACS Symposium Ser.: No. 155). 1981. 46.95 (*0-8412-0624-4*) Am Chemical.

— Reactivity of Metal-Metal Bonds: Based on a Symposium. LC 81-361. (ACS Symposium Ser.: Vol. 155). 334p. 1981. reprint ed. pap. 103.60 (*0-608-03042-2*, 206349500007) Bks Demand.

Chisholm, Margaret & Lane, Nancy, eds. Information Technology: Design & Applications. (Professional Librarian Ser.). 330p. (C). 1991. 45.00 (*0-8161-1908-2*, Hall Reference); 30.00 (*0-8161-1909-0*, Hall Reference) Macmillan.

Chisholm, Margo & Bruce, Ray. To the Summit. LC 96-45210. (Illus.). 344p. 1998. reprint ed. pap. 12.50 (*0-380-78884-5*, Avon Bks) Morrow Avon.

— To the Summit: A Woman's Journey into the Mountains to Find Her Soul. LC 96-45210. 336p. 1997. mass mkt. 24.00 (*0-380-97359-6*, Avon Bks) Morrow Avon.

***Chisholm, Marie A. & Cooper, James, eds.** Geriatric Musculoskeletal Drug Therapy. LC 99-55307. (Journal of Geriatric Drug Therapy Ser.). 96p. 2000. pap. text 19.95 (*0-7890-0824-6*, Pharmctl Prods) Haworth Pr.

***Chisholm, Marla & Ganschow, Jackie.** Experiences in Public Speaking: An Activity Book for Fundamentals of Public Speaking. 2nd ed. 288p. (C). 1999. spiral bd. 21.95 (*0-7872-6222-6*) Kendall-Hunt.

Chisholm, Marla & Ganschow, Jackie. Experiences in Public Speaking: An Activity Book for Fundamentals of Public Speaking, Speech 1311. 228p. (C). 1996. pap. text, spiral bd. 17.95 (*0-8403-9573-6*) Kendall-Hunt.

Chisholm, Matt A. Death Trail. large type ed. (Linford Western Library). 320p. 1992. pap. 16.99 (*0-7089-7165-2*) Ulverscroft.

— McAllister: Die-Hard. large type ed. (Linford Western Library). 336p. 1985. pap. 16.99 (*0-7089-6134-7*, Linford) Ulverscroft.

— McAllister: Quarry. large type ed. (Linford Western Library). 304p. 1985. pap. 16.99 (*0-7089-6141-X*, Linford) Ulverscroft.

— McAllister & Cheyenne Death. large type ed. (Linford Western Library). 304p. 1985. pap. 16.99 (*0-7089-6138-X*, Linford) Ulverscroft.

— McAllister & the Spanish Gold. large type ed. (Linford Western Library). 320p. 1985. pap. 16.99 (*0-7089-6090-1*, Linford) Ulverscroft.

— McAllister Never Surrenders. large type ed. (Linford Western Library). 320p. 1985. pap. 16.99 (*0-7089-6094-4*, Linford) Ulverscroft.

— McAllister on the Comanche Crossing. large type ed. (Linford Western Library). 320p. 1985. pap. 16.99 (*0-7089-6086-3*, Linford) Ulverscroft.

Chisholm, Michael. The Mega-Trade Method. 1987. pap. 75.00 (*0-930233-18-2*) Windsor.

— Modern World Development: A Geographical Perspective. LC 82-11404. (Illus.). 216p. (C). 1982. text 52.00 (*0-389-20320-3*, N7160) B&N Imports.

Chisholm, Michael. Regions in Recession & Resurgance. (Illus.). 256p. (C). 1990. text 55.00 (*0-685-46014-2*) Routledge.

Chisholm, Michael. Resources for Britain's Future: A Series from the Geographical Magazine. LC 72-194332. 182 P.p. 1972. write for info. (*0-389-04612-4*) B&N Imports.

— Resources for Britain's Future: A Series from the "geographical Magazine" LC 72-186458. 183p. 1972. write for info. (*0-7153-5463-9*) D & C Pub.

***Chisholm, Michael.** Structural Reform of British Local Government: Rhetoric & Reality. LC 99-56021. 2000. text. write for info. (*0-7190-5771-X*, Pub. by St Martin) St Martin.

Chisholm, Michael. The Taurus Method. 2nd ed. 1985. pap. 75.00 (*0-930233-08-5*) Windsor.

Chisholm, Michael & Smith, David M., eds. Shared Space, Divided Space: Essays on Conflict & Territorial Organization. (Illus.). 288p. (C). 1990. pap. 29.95 (*0-04-445714-6*) Routledge.

***Chisholm, P. F.** A Famine of Horses: A Sir Robert Carey Mystery. LC 99-68774. (Missing Mystery Ser.: Vol. 14). 400p. 1999. pap. 14.95 (*1-890208-27-2*) Poisoned Pen.

Chisholm, P. F. A Famine of Horses: A Sir Robert Carey Mystery. LC 94-45095. 270p. 1995. text 20.95 (*0-8027-3252-6*) Walker & Co.

— A Famine of Horses: A Sir Robert Carey Mystery. large type ed. 447p. 1995. 27.99 (*0-7505-0838-8*, Pub. by Mgna Lrg Print) Ulverscroft.

***Chisholm, P. F.** Plague of Angels. 2000. pap. 14.95 (*1-890208-43-4*) Poisoned Pen.

— A Season of Knives: A Sir Robert Carey Mystery. LC 99-68784. (Missing Mystery Ser.: No. 18). 250p. 2000. pap. 14.95 (*1-890208-32-9*) Poisoned Pen.

Chisholm, P. F. A Season of Knives: A Sir Robert Carey Mystery. (Sir Robert Carey Mystery Ser.). 240p. 1996. 19.95 (*0-8027-3276-3*) Walker & Co.

***Chisholm, P. F.** Surfeit of Guns, Vol. 20. (Missing Mysteries Ser.: Vol. 20). 2000. pap. 14.95 (*1-890208-35-3*) Poisoned Pen.

Chisholm, P. F. A Surfeit of Guns: A Sir Robert Carey Mystery. LC 97-7080. 233p. 1997. 20.95 (*0-8027-3304-2*) Walker & Co.

Chisholm, R., jt. auth. see Nettheim, Garth.

Chisholm, Richard, ed. The Family Law Reports: Australia, 15 vols. ring bd. 665.00 (*0-00-090003-6*, MICHIE) LEXIS Pub.

Chisholm, Robert B., Jr. From Exegesis to Exposition: A Practical Guide to Using Biblical Hebrew. LC 98-43458. 304p. 1999. pap. 19.99 (*0-8010-2171-5*) Baker Bks.

Chisholm-Robinson, Sandra, jt. auth. see Robinson, George B.

Chisholm, Roderick M. The Foundations of Knowing. LC 81-19707. 225p. 1982. reprint ed. pap. 69.80 (*0-608-00834-6*, 206162500010) Bks Demand.

— The Problem of the Criterion, 1973. LC 73-75504. (Aquinas Lectures). 1973. 15.00 (*0-87462-138-0*) Marquette.

— A Realistic Theory of Categories: An Essay on Ontology. 155p. (C). 1996. text 54.95 (*0-521-55426-8*); pap. text 16.95 (*0-521-55616-3*) Cambridge U Pr.

Chisholm, Roderick M., ed. Realism & the Background of Phenomenology. vii, 308p. 1981. reprint ed. pap. text 15.00 (*0-917930-14-2*); reprint ed. lib. bdg. 30.00 (*0-917930-34-7*) Ridgeview.

Chisholm Roth Associates Staff. Foreign Exchange Training Manual (Complete) 350p. 1992. 295.00 (*1-85564-107-0*, Pub. by Euromoney) Am Educ Systs.

Chisholm, Rupert F. Developing Network Organizations: Learnings from Practice & Theory. LC 97-18089. 200p. (C). 1997. pap. 40.00 (*0-201-87444-X*, Prentice Hall) P-H.

Chisholm, Sarah R. Easter Hunt: A Hide-&-Seek Story. LC 94-72211. (Illus.). 32p. (J). (ps-3). 1994. pap. 6.99 (*0-8066-2740-9*, 9-2740, Augsburg) Augsburg Fortress.

— Harry Is Gone! A Hide-&-Seek Story. LC 94-72212. (Illus.). 32p. (J). (ps). 1994. pap. 6.99 (*0-8066-2741-7*, 9-2741, Augsburg) Augsburg Fortress.

— My Christmas Angel: A Hide & Seek Story. (Illus.). 32p. (J). (ps). 1993. pap. 6.99 (*0-8066-2601-1*, 9-2601) Augsburg Fortress.

— My Christmas Star: A Hide & Seek Story. (Illus.). 32p. (J). (ps). 1993. pap. 6.99 (*0-8066-2600-3*, 9-2600) Augsburg Fortress.

Chisholm, William, et al, eds. Interrogativity: A Colloquium on the Grammar, Typology & Pragmatics of Questions in Seven Diverse Languages, Cleveland, Ohio, October 5th, 1981 to May 3rd, 1982. (Typological Studies in Language: 4). v, 302p. 1984. 65.00 (*0-915027-02-X*); pap. 34.95 (*0-915027-03-8*) J Benjamins Pubng Co.

Chishom, J., et al. Chemistry. (Introductions Ser.). (Illus.). 48p. (J). (gr. 6 up). 1983. pap. 7.95 (*0-86020-709-9*) EDC.

Chishti, Hakim. The Traditional Healer's Handbook. 395p. 1996. pap. 16.95 (*0-614-21561-7*, 1250) Kazi Pubns.

Chishti, Hakim G. The Traditional Healer's Handbook: A Classic Guide to the Medicine of Avicenna. rev. ed. (Illus.). 385p. 1991. pap. 19.95 (*0-89281-438-1*) Inner Tradit.

Chishti, Shaykh H. Book of Sufi Healing. LC 91-14595. 205p. 1991. pap. 16.95 (*0-89281-324-5*) Inner Tradit.

Chishti, Shaykh M. Book of Sufi Healing. 190p. 1996. pap. 16.95 (*0-614-21257-X*, 114); pap. 16.95 (*0-614-21543-9*, 114) Kazi Pubns.

Chisick, Harvey. The Limits of Reform in the Enlightenment: Attitudes Toward the Education of the Lower Classes in Eighteenth-Century France. LC 80-7512. 341p. 1981. reprint ed. pap. 105.80 (*0-7837-9317-0*, 206005700004) Bks Demand.

— The Production, Distribution, & Readership of a Conservative Journal of the Early French Revolution: The Ami du Roy of the Abbe Royou. LC 91-57945. (Memoirs Ser.: Vol. 198). 233p. (C). 1992. pap. 20.00 (*0-87169-198-1*, M198-CHH) Am Philos.

Chisin, Roland, et al. MRI-CT & Pathology in Head & Neck Tumors: A Correlative Study. (Series in Radiology). (C). 1989. text 213.50 (*0-7923-0227-3*) Kluwer Academic.

Chisko, Ann M., jt. auth. see Matthews, Pamela E.

Chislers, Inc. Staff. Victorian Secrets: The South's Newest Collection of Exceptionally Fine Recipes. LC 97-68231. (Illus.). 1997. 24.95 (*0-9658316-0-4*) Chiselers.

Chislett, Anne. Another Season's Promise. 1988. pap. 5.25 (*0-8222-0053-8*) Dramatists Play.

— Flipin' in, & Then & now. 96p. (Orig.). 1998. pap. 13.95 (*0-88754-574-2*, Pub. by Theatre Comm) Consort Bk Sales.

— Quiet in the Land. 12.95 (*0-88910-270-8*, Pub. by Talonbks) Genl Dist Srvs.

— Yankee Notions. LC 93-243252. 142p. (Orig.). 1997. pap. 10.95 (*0-88754-497-5*) Theatre Comm.

Chislett, Gail. Whump! (Annikins Ser.: Vol. 12). (Illus.). (J). (ps-2). 1992. pap. 0.99 (*1-55037-253-X*, Pub. by Annick) Firefly Bks Ltd.

Chislett, Helen, jt. auth. see Walters, Dawn.

Chislett, M. S., jt. ed. see Kasper, Erich.

Chislett, W. Portugal: Investment & Growth. (Euromoney Country Guide Ser.). 185p. 1997. 170.00 (*1-85564-565-3*, Pub. by Euromoney) Am Educ Systs.

Chislett, William. Chile. (Illus.). 230p. 1993. 170.00 (*1-85564-226-3*, Pub. by Euromoney) Am Educ Systs.

— Ecuador. (Illus.). 210p. 1994. pap. 170.00 (*1-85564-260-3*, Pub. by Euromoney) Am Educ Systs.

— Finland. (Illus.). 180p. 1995. pap. 170.00 (*1-85564-437-1*, Pub. by Euromoney) Am Educ Systs.

— George Meredith: A Study & an Appraisal. LC 68-905. (Studies in Fiction: No. 34). 1969. reprint ed. lib. bdg. 58.95 (*0-8383-0526-1*) M S G Haskell Hse.

— Moderns & Near-Moderns: Essays on Henry James, Stockton, Shaw & Others. LC 67-30180. (Essay Index Reprint Ser.). 1977. 18.95 (*0-8369-0302-1*) Ayer.

— Panama: Latin America's Best Kept Secret. (Illus.). 200p. 1995. 170.00 (*1-85564-351-0*, Pub. by Euromoney) Am Educ Systs.

Chislovsky, Carol, jt. illus. see McMahon, Brad.

Chism. Handbook of Food Additives. 3rd ed. 1994. write for info. (*0-8493-0544-6*) CRC Pr.

Chism, Denise. The High-Risk Pregnancy Sourcebook. 304p. 1998. pap. 16.00 (*1-56565-858-2*, 08582W, Pub. by Lowell Hse) NTC Contemp Pub Co.

Chism, Jerry, ed. see White, Joseph A.

Chism, Keith A. Christian Education for the African American Community. LC 95-78963. 96p. 1996. pap. 12.95 (*0-88177-147-3*, DR147) Discipleship Res.

Chism, Nancy V., jt. ed. see Border, Laura L.

Chism, Nancy Van Note, see Van Note Chism, Nancy.

Chism, Stephen J. The Arkansas Gazette Obituaries Index, 1819-1879. 120p. 1990. 27.50 (*0-89308-398-4*, AR 23) Southern Hist Pr.

Chisman, James A. Industrial Cases in Simulation Modeling. LC 95-23438. (C). 1995. pap. 9.95 (*0-534-23718-5*) Wadsworth Pub.

Chismoso, Leon Manzo. Chistes y Andanza de Pepito, 1. 1997. pap. text 4.98 (*968-15-0422-4*) Ed Mex.

Chisnall, Peter M. Consumer Behaviour. 3rd ed. LC 94-31098. 1994. 34.95 (*0-07-707616-8*) McGraw.

— Marketing Research. 3rd ed. (Marketing Ser.). 312p. (C). 1986. text 30.75 (*0-07-084155-1*) McGraw.

— Marketing Research. 5th ed. LC 96-38336. 1996. pap. write for info. (*0-07-709175-2*) McGraw.

Chisnell, Mark. Rig Your Dinghy Right: A Design & Installation Guide for Racing Sailors. 1994. pap. 18.95 (*0-07-029123-3*) McGraw.

— Sails for Cruising: Trim to Perfection. (Illus.). 94p. 1998. pap. 16.95 (*1-898660-46-8*) Motorbooks Intl.

Chisolm, A. J. & English, Marianne. Alberta Hailstorms. (Meteorological Monograph: Vol. 14, No. 36). (Illus.). 98p. 1973. 23.00 (*0-933876-39-4*) Am Meteorological.

***Chisolm, Elise T.** Are We There Yet: Recollections of Life's Many. 302p. 1999. pap. 13.95 (*1-893116-10-7*) Baltimore Sun.

Chisolm, J. J., Jr., et al, eds. Diagnosis & Treatment of Lead Poisoning. 213p. 1976. text 42.50 (*0-8422-7262-3*) Irvington.

Chisolm, J. Julian. A Manual of Military Surgery: Suregeons in the Confederate States Army. (Illus.). 581p. 1997. reprint ed. 45.00 (*0-89029-068-7*) Morningside Bkshop.

Chisolm, Jane. Prehistoric Times. (Illus.). 24p. (J). (gr. 2-4). 1985. pap. text 4.50 (*0-86020-623-8*) EDC.

Chisolm, John. Obeying God Is . . . Easy. 90p. 1998. pap. 12.00 (*1-57502-982-0*, PO2683) Morris Pubng.

Chisolm, John, jt. auth. see Enoeda, K.

Chisolm, John J. A Manual of Military Surgery, for the Use of Surgeons in the Confederate States Army: With an Appendix of the Rules & Regulations of the Medical Department in the Confederate Army. LC 88-60871. (American Civil War Surgery Ser.: No. 4). 447p. 1989. reprint ed. 60.00 (*0-930405-03-X*) Norman SF.

Chisolm, Kitty & Ferguson, John. Rome: The Augustan Age: A Source Book. (Illus.). 734p. (C). 1981. pap. text 35.00 (*0-19-872109-9*) OUP.

Chisolm, Marie A. How to Prepare for the PCAt. LC 97-41979. 224p. 1998. pap. text 14.95 (*0-8120-9808-0*) Barron.

***Chisolm, Marie A. & Cooper, James W., eds.** Geriatric Musculoskeletal Drug Therapy. LC 99-55307. (Journal of Geriatric Drug Therapy Ser.). 96p. 2000. 29.95 (*0-7890-0789-4*, Pharmctl Prods) Haworth Pr.

Chisolm, Michael. Inside Alcoholism: A Handbook on Chemical Dependency. 108p. (Orig.). (C). 1988. pap. 4.95 (*0-685-22987-4*) Daylight Pubns.

Chisolm, W. G. Chisolm Genealogy; Being a Record of the Name from 1254, with Short Sketches of Allied Families. (Illus.). 101p. 1993. reprint ed. pap. 19.50 (*0-8328-1341-9*); reprint ed. lib. bdg. 29.50 (*0-8328-1340-0*) Higginson Bk Co.

Chisom, Ronald, jt. auth. see Washington, Michael.

Chissale, Beatrice. Anne Cuneo: Temoignage et Ecriture. (Publications Universitaires Europeennes Ser.: Series 13, Vol. 210). (FRE.). 437p. 1997. 55.95 (*3-906754-47-2*, Pub. by P Lang) P Lang Pubng.

Chissick, Seymour S. & Derricott, R., eds. Occupational Health & Safety Management. LC 79-41218. (Properties of Materials Safety & Environmental Factors Ser.). (Illus.). 723p. reprint ed. pap. 200.00 (*0-8357-6240-8*, 203421700089) Bks Demand.

Chissick, Seymour S., jt. ed. see Derricott, R.

Chissick, Seymour S., jt. ed. see Michaels, Leslie.

Chissick, Seymour S., jt. ed. see Price, William C.

Chissin, Chaim. A Palestine Diary. 1976. 10.00 (*0-685-82598-1*) Herzl Pr.

Chisti, Anees. Dateline Bhopal. (C). 1986. 24.95 (*0-317-66154-X*) Asia Bk Corp.

Chistman, Calvin L., ed. Lost in the Victory: Reflections of American War Orphans of World War II. LC 97-26872. (Illus.). 252p. 1998. 29.95 (*1-57441-033-4*) UNTX Pr.

Chistoph-Arnold, Johann. Lost Art of Forgiving: Stories of Healing from the Cancer of Bitterness. 149p. 1998. pap. text 13.00 (*0-87486-950-1*) Plough.

Chistyakov, V. P., et al. Probability Theory for Engineers. Balakrishnan, A. V., ed. LC 85-25939. (Translations Series in Mathematics & Engineering).Tr. of Teoriia veroiatnostei. 174p. 1987. text 30.00 (*0-911575-13-8*) Optimization Soft.

Chisum, D. S. & Cornish, W. R. World Intellectual Property Guidebooks: Germany, Austria & Switzerland. 600p. 50.00 (*0-8205-1899-9*) Juris Pubng.

Chisum, Donald S. Patent Law Digest. text 79.00 (*0-8205-4248-2*) Bender.

Chisum, Donald S. Patent Law Digest. 1991. write for info. (*0-8205-3052-2*) Bender.

— Patents, 13 vols. 1978. ring bd. 1735.00 (*0-8205-1525-6*) Bender.

Chisum, Donald S. & Sobmon, Derek. World Intellectual Property Guidebooks: United States. 650p. 50.00 (*0-8205-1886-7*) Juris Pubng.

Chisum, Donald S., et al. Principles of Patent Law. LC 98-8153. (University Casebook Ser.). 1409p. 1998. text 42.50 (*1-56662-614-5*) Foundation Pr.

— World Intellectual Property Guidebooks: Canada. 500p. 50.00 (*0-8205-1888-3*) Juris Pubng.

Chisum, Donald S., jt. auth. see Cover, Kathi.

Chiswick, Barry R. Illegal Aliens: Their Employment & Employers. LC 88-10062. 153p. 1988. text 22.00 (*0-88099-059-7*); pap. text 12.00 (*0-88099-058-9*) W E Upjohn.

— Income Inequality: Regional Analyses Within a Human Capital Framework. (Studies in Human Behavior & Social Institutions: No. 4). 228p. 1974. 59.30 (*0-87014-264-X*) Natl Bur Econ Res.

— Income Inequality: Regional Analyses Within a Human Capital Framework. LC 73-88509. (Human Behavior & Social Institutions Ser.: No. 4). 228p. reprint ed. pap. 70.70 (*0-8357-7577-1*, 205689800096) Bks Demand.

Chiswick, Barry R., ed. The Gateway: United States Immigration Issues & Policies. LC 81-8009. (AEI Symposia Ser.: No. 81I). (Illus.). 492p. reprint ed. pap. 152.60 (*0-8357-4484-1*, 203733600008) Bks Demand.

Chiswick, D., et al. Prosecution of the Mentally Disturbed: Dilemmas of Identification & Discretion. 192p. 1984. text 35.90 (*0-08-028481-7*, Pergamon Pr) Elsevier.

Chiswick, Linton. Milestones of Jazz. 1997. 14.99 (*1-85833-764-X*, Pub. by CLib Bks) Whitecap Bks.

Chiszar, David & Smith, Rozella B. Fifty Years of Herpetology Publications of Hobart M. Smith. 90p. 1982. pap. text 6.00 (*0-910914-17-6*) J Johnson.

Chit, Sadhu A., tr. see Osho.

Chitakasem, Manas, jt. tr. see Smyth, David.

Chitale, P. K. A Comparative Study of Ayurveda & Treatment by Indian Drugs. (C). 1998. 32.00 (*81-7030-555-1*, Pub. by Sri Satguru Pubns) S Asia.

Chitale, V. P. Capital Output Ratio in the Indian Economy. 120p. (C). 1986. text 15.95 (*81-7027-099-5*, Pub. by Radiant Pubs) S Asia.

Chitalwala, Y. M., jt. auth. see Rissman, Paul.

Chitayat, Gideon. Trade Union Mergers & Labor Conglomerates. LC 79-2966. (Praeger Special Studies). 225p. 1979. 59.95 (*0-275-90340-0*, C0340, Praeger Pubs) Greenwood.

Chite, Jack. A Cry from the Forest. (Orig.). 1996. pap. text 21.95 (*0-940429-16-0*) M B Glass Assocs.

Chitester, Ken. Aboard Air Force One: 200,000 Miles with a White House Aide. LC 97-12389. (Illus.). 304p. (Orig.). 1997. pap. 15.95 (*1-56474-234-2*) Fithian Pr.

Chitgopekar, Nilima. Encountering Sivaism: The Deity, the Milieu, the Entourage. LC 98-906647. xiv, 224 p. 1998. write for info. (*81-215-0792-8*, Pub. by M Manoharial) Coronet Bks.

Chitham, Edward. A Life of Anne Bronte. (Illus.). 232p. 1993. reprint ed. pap. 25.95 (*0-631-18944-0*) Blackwell Pubs.

Chitham, Edward, ed. see Bronte, Emily Jane.

Chiti, Patricia A., ed. Songs & Duets of Garcia, Malibran & Viardot: High Voice. 1997. pap. 12.95 (*0-88284-785-6*) Alfred Pub.

C

An Asterisk (*) at the beginning of an entry indicates that the title is appearing for the first time.

Chiti, Patricia A., jt. auth. see Paton, John G.

Chiti, Patricia A., jt. auth. see Paton, John J.

Chitkara, M. G. Bangladesh: Mujib to Hasina. xii, 286p. 1997. 35.00 (*81-7024-832-9*, Pub. by Ashish Pub Hse) Nataraj Bks.

— Benazir: A Profile. x, 186p. 1996. 21.00 (*81-7024-752-7*, Pub. by Ashish Pub Hse) Nataraj Bks.

— Buddhism Reincarnation & Dalai Lamas of Tibet. LC 98-901132. xxx, 236p. 1998. 40.00 (*81-7024-930-9*, Pub. by Ashish Pub Hse) S Asia.

— Bureaucracy & Social Change. (Illus.). xvii, 162p. 1994. 20.00 (*81-7024-614-8*, Pub. by Ashish Pub Hse) Nataraj Bks.

— Consumerism, Crime & Corruption. LC 98-908064. 1998. 54.00 (*81-7024-980-5*, Pub. by APH Pubng) S Asia.

— Converts Do Not Make a Nation. LC 98-908366. xxiii, 719 p. 1998. 82.00 (*81-7024-982-1*, Pub. by Ashish Pub Hse) S Asia.

— Dr. Ambadkar Towards Buddhism. LC 97-905478. xiii, 278p. (C). 1997. 36.00 (*81-7024-857-4*, Pub. by APH Pubng) Nataraj Bks.

— Encyclopedia of Ecology, Environment & Pollution, 15 vols. (Illus.). 1998. 695.00 (*81-7024-880-9*, Pub. by APH Pubng) Nataraj Bks.

— Hindutva. LC 96-905514. 303p. 1997. 32.00 (*81-7024-798-5*, Pub. by APH Pubng) Nataraj Bks.

— Human Rights: Commitment & Betrayal. LC 95-906501. xxiv, 306p. 1996. 26.00 (*81-7024-727-6*, Pub. by Ashish Pub Hse) Nataraj Bks.

— Human Rights in Pakistan. LC 96-914078. xii, 407p. (C). 1997. 55.00 (*81-7024-820-5*, Pub. by APH Pubng) Nataraj Bks.

— Indo-Pak Amity: A New Concept. LC 94-906184. xxvi, 204p. 1994. 25.00 (*81-7024-666-0*, Pub. by Ashish Pub Hse) Nataraj Bks.

— Jiy-e-Singh: G. M. Syed. xviii, 212p. 1996. 22.00 (*81-7024-768-3*, Pub. by Ashish Pub Hse) Nataraj Bks.

— Law & the Poor: A Socio-Legal Study. (C). 1991. text 22.50 (*81-7024-391-2*, Pub. by Ashish Pub Hse) S Asia.

— Mohajir's Pakistan. xii, 166p. (C). 1996. 20.00 (*81-7024-746-2*, Pub. by Ashish Pub Hse) Nataraj Bks.

— Mother Teresa. LC 98-908788. 1998. 42.00 (*81-7024-968-6*, Pub. by Ashish Pub Hse) S Asia.

— Nuclear Pakistan. LC 96-903071. xv, 332p. 1996. 35.00 (*81-7024-767-5*, Pub. by Ashish Pub Hse) Nataraj Bks.

— Tibet: A Reality. LC 94-905336. xviii, 162p. (C). 1994. 18.00 (*81-7024-639-3*, Pub. by Ashish Pub Hse) Nataraj Bks.

Chitkara, M. G. & Sharma, B. R. Indian Republic: Issues & Perspective. LC 97-905302. vi, 580p. 1997. 57.00 (*81-7024-836-1*, Pub. by APH Pubng) Nataraj Bks.

Chitkara, Mona, ed. see Elz, Ron.

Chitla, Santhosh R., et al. Effects of Air Entrainment on Portland Cement Concrete. (Illus.). 81p. (Orig.). (C). 1994. pap. text 35.00 (*0-7881-0220-6*) DIANE Pub.

Chitnis, Suma & Altbach, Philip G., eds. Higher Education Reform in India: Experience & Perspectives. LC 92-45240. (Illus.). 400p. 1993. 44.00 (*0-8039-9111-8*) Sage.

Chitra Publications Staff. Mini Classics: Baskets. Johnson, Janice P., ed. LC 95-33336. (Illus.). 20p. (Orig.). 1995. pap. 6.95 (*1-885588-05-4*) Chitra Pubns.

— Mini Classics: Flowers. Nolt, Joanne S., ed. LC 95-35542. (Illus.). 20p. (Orig.). 1995. pap. 6.95 (*1-885588-08-9*) Chitra Pubns.

— Mini Classics: Log Cabin. Nolt, Joanne S., ed. LC 95-35541. (Illus.). 20p. (Orig.). 1995. pap. 6.95 (*1-885588-06-2*) Chitra Pubns.

— Miniatures from the Heart Judges' Choice. Nolt, Joanne S., ed. LC 94-45253. (Illus.). 40p. (Orig.). 1995. pap. 9.95 (*1-885588-00-3*) Chitra Pubns.

Chitrakar, Ramesh C. Foreign Investment & Technology Transfer in Development Countries: Motivating Factors & Financial & Economic Performance in Nepal. LC 94-4296. 241p. 1994. 72.95 (*1-85628-690-8*, Pub. by Avebry) Ashgate Pub Co.

Chitre, Dilip. Anubhavamrut: The Immortal Experience of Being. 1996. 12.00 (*81-260-0002-3*) S Asia.

Chitre, Dilip, et al, eds. Tender Ironies: A Tribute to Lothar Lutze. 1994. 32.00 (*81-7304-088-5*) S Asia.

Chitre, Dilip, jt. auth. see Karandikar, Govind V.

Chitrick, Aaron, ed. see Tzedek, Menachem M.

Chitrick, Yehuda. From My Father's Shabbos Table: A Treasury of Chabad Chasidic Stories. Touger, Eliyahu, tr. 220p. 1991. 14.00 (*0-940118-64-5*) Moznaim.

Chitrik, Aharon, ed. see Keller, Yosef Y.

Chitrik, Aharon, ed. see Schneersohn, Menachem M.

Chittenden & Kiniry, Malcolm. Making Connections Across the Curriculum: Reading for Analysis. 1986. pap. text 18.50 (*0-312-50666-X*) St Martin.

Chittenden, Francis, et al, eds. Small Firms: Partnerships for Growth. 240p. 1995. text 75.00 (*1-85396-288-0*, Pub. by P Chapman) Taylor & Francis.

Chittenden, Gertrude. Experimental Study in Measuring & Modifying Assertive Behavior in Young Children. (SRCD M Ser.: Vol. 7, No. 1). 1942. pap. 25.00 (*0-527-01522-9*) Periodicals Srv.

Chittenden, Hiram Martin. The American Fur Trade of the Far West, 3 vols. 1992. reprint ed. lib. bdg. 270.00 (*0-7812-5013-7*) Rprt Serv.

— The American Fur Trade of the Far West, Vol. 1. LC 86-11227. (Illus.). xliv, 584p. 1986. reprint ed. pap. 19.95 (*0-8032-6320-1*, Bison Books) U of Nebr Pr.

— The American Fur Trade of the Far West, Vol. 2. LC 86-11227. (Illus.). xxiv, 457p. 1986. reprint ed. pap. 16.95 (*0-8032-6321-X*, Bison Books) U of Nebr Pr.

— H. M. Chittenden: A Western Epic. limited ed. Le Roy, Bruce, ed. LC 61-64226. (Illus.). 136p. 1961. 9.50 (*0-917048-17-2*) Wash St Hist Soc.

— The Yellowstone National Park. LC 64-11334. (Illus.). 246p. 1973. pap. 11.95 (*0-8061-0937-8*) U of Okla Pr.

Chittenden, Howard. From Chinese Marine to Japanese POW: My 1,364 Day Journey Through Hell. 200p. Date not set. 24.95 (*1-56311-247-7*) Turner Pub KY.

Chittenden, L. E. The Capture of Ticonderoga. LC 98-145602. 131p. 1998. pap. 14.50 (*0-7884-0802-X*, C337) Heritage Bk.

— Personal Reminiscences, 1840-1890. LC 72-37302. (Black Heritage Library Collection). 1977. reprint ed. 28.95 (*0-8369-8939-2*) Ayer.

Chittenden, Lucius E. Lucius Chittenden's Journey to "The Inside of the Earth" (Occasional Papers: No. 17). (Illus.). 87p. 1995. pap. text 7.50 (*0-944277-31-4*) U VT Ctr Rsch VT.

Chittenden, Margaret. As Years Go By (Showcase) 1995. per. 3.75 (*0-373-70666-9*) Harlequin Bks.

— Dead Beat & Deadly. LC 97-76038. 304p. 1998. 20.00 (*1-57566-314-7*, Knsington) Kensgtn Pub Corp.

— Dead Beat & Deadly, 1. (Charlie Plato Mystery Ser.). 320p. 1999. mass mkt. 5.99 (*1-57566-436-4*) Kensgtn Pub Corp.

— Dead Men Don't Dance. 320p. 1997. 18.95 (*1-57566-184-5*, Knsington) Kensgtn Pub Corp.

— Dead Men Don't Dance. 304p. 1998. pap. 5.99 (*1-57566-318-X*) Kensgtn Pub Corp.

— Don't Forget to Die. 1999. text 20.00 (*1-57566-435-6*) Kensgtn Pub Corp.

***Chittenden, Margaret.** Don't Forget to Die. 320p. 2000. mass mkt. 5.99 (*1-57566-566-2*) Kensgtn Pub Corp.

— Dying to See You. LC 99-68822. 320p. 2000. 20.00 (*1-57566-561-1*, Knsington) Kensgtn Pub Corp.

Chittenden, Margaret. Dying to Sing. 288p. 1996. 18.95 (*1-57566-052-0*, Knsington) Kensgtn Pub Corp.

— Dying to Sing. 288p. 1997. mass mkt. 5.50 (*1-57566-189-6*, Knsington) Kensgtn Pub Corp.

— How to Write Your Novel. LC 95-35730. 149p. 1995. pap. text 12.00 (*0-87116-178-8*) Writer.

— Shadow of a Doubt. (Intrigue Ser.). 1993. mass mkt. 2.99 (*0-373-22242-4*, 1-22242-1) Harlequin Bks.

— This Time Forever. (Harlequin Dreamscape Ser.: No. 1). 1990. per. 3.25 (*0-373-79001-5*) Harlequin Bks.

— The Wainwright Secret. (Intrigue Ser.: No. 183). 1992. pap. 2.89 (*0-373-22183-5*, 1-22183-7) Harlequin Bks.

— When the Spirit Is Willing. (Superromance Ser.). 1993. mass mkt. 3.50 (*0-373-70575-1*, 1-70575-5) Harlequin Bks.

Chittenden, Penelope B. Camel for a King. LC 96-5416. (Illus.). 32p. (J). (ps-3). 1996. pap. 6.95 (*0-8091-6633-X*, 6633-X) Paulist Pr.

Chittenden, Russ. Good Ole Boys Wild Game Cookbook. 1991. 14.95 (*0-89145-416-0*, 2073) Collector Bks.

— Uncle Russ's Way. 200p. 1995. 16.95 (*0-9649228-0-0*) Good Ole Boys.

Chittenden, Varick A. Vietnam Remembered: The Folk Art of Marine Veteran Michael D. Cusino. LC 95-13654. (Folk Art & Artists Ser.). (Illus.). 72p. 1995. pap. 16.95 (*0-87805-716-1*); text 32.50 (*0-87805-715-3*) U Pr of Miss.

Chittenden, William H. From Chinese Marine to Japanese POW: My 1,364 Day Journey Through Hell. LC 95-60088. 200p. 1995. 24.95 (*1-56311-174-8*) Turner Pub KY.

Chittick, Donald E. The Controversy: Roots of the Creation-Evolution Conflict. 280p. 1994. reprint ed. pap. 7.95 (*0-9640978-0-X*) Creation Compass.

Chittick, H. Neville & Rotberg, Robert I., eds. East Africa & the Orient: Cultural Syntheses in Pre-Colonial Times. LC 73-89568. 350p. 1975. 55.00 (*0-8419-0142-2*, Africana) Holmes & Meier.

Chittick, Kathryn. The Critical Reception of Charles Dickens, 1833-1841. LC 88-33644. 290p. 1989. text 50.00 (*0-8240-5620-5*, 900) Garland.

Chittick, Lee & Fox, Terry. Travelling with Percy: A South Coast Journey. LC 98-156032. x, 202p. 1997. write for info. (*0-85575-305-6*) AIB & TSIS.

Chittick, Neville. Manda: Excavation at an Island Port on the Kenya Coast. (Illus.). 258p. 1984. 45.00 (*1-872566-05-7*, Pub. by Brit Inst Estrn Africa) David Brown.

Chittick, Victor L. Thomas Chandler Haliburton, "Sam Slick" LC 24-29336. reprint ed. 42.50 (*0-404-01525-5*) AMS Pr.

Chittick, William C. Faith & Practice of Islam: Three Thirteenth-Century Sufi Texts. LC 92-6106. (SUNY Series in Islam). 322p. (C). 1992. pap. text 21.95 (*0-7914-1368-3*) State U NY Pr.

— Faith & Practice of Islam: Three Thirteenth-Century Sufi Texts. LC 92-6106. (SUNY Series in Islam). 322p. (C). 1992. text 64.50 (*0-7914-1367-5*) State U NY Pr.

— Faith & Practice of Islam: Three Thirteenth Century Sufi Texts. 306p. 1996. pap. 19.95 (*0-614-21276-6*, 282) Kazi Pubns.

— Imaginal Worlds: Ibn al-'Arabi & the Problem of Religious Diversity. LC 94-17044. (SUNY Series in Islam). 208p. 1994. pap. text 19.95 (*0-7914-2250-X*) State U NY Pr.

— Imaginal Worlds: Ibn al-'Arabi & the Problem of Religious Diversity. LC 94-17044. (SUNY Series in Islam). 208p. (C). 1994. text 59.50 (*0-7914-2249-6*) State U NY Pr.

— Imaginal Worlds: Ibn al-Arabi & the Problem of Religious Diversity. 224p. 1996. pap. 19.95 (*0-614-21287-1*, 1357) Kazi Pubns.

— The Self-Disclosure of God: Principles of Ibn al-'Arabi's Cosmology. LC 97-30521. (SUNY Series in Islam). 504p. (C). 1997. pap. text 24.95 (*0-7914-3404-4*) State U NY Pr.

— The Self-Disclosure of God: Principles of Ibn al-'Arabi's Cosmology. LC 97-30521. (SUNY Series in Islam). 504p. (C). 1998. text 74.50 (*0-7914-3403-6*) State U NY Pr.

— The Sufi Path of Knowledge: Ibn al-Arabi's Metaphysics of Imagination. 478p. 1996. pap. 24.95 (*0-614-21358-4*, 1187) Kazi Pubns.

— The Sufi Path of Knowledge: Ibn al-Arabi's Metaphysics of Imagination. LC 88-7040. 478p. (C). 1989. text 74.50 (*0-88706-884-7*); pap. text 26.95 (*0-88706-885-5*) State U NY Pr.

— The Sufi Path of Love. 435p. 1996. pap. 19.95 (*0-614-21359-2*, 1188) Kazi Pubns.

— The Sufi Path of Love: The Spiritual Teachings of Rumi. LC 82-19511. (SUNY Series in Islam). 433p. (C). 1984. pap. text 21.95 (*0-87395-724-5*) State U NY Pr.

***Chittick, William C.** Sufism: A Short Introduction. 2000. pap. 15.95 (*1-85168-211-2*, Pub. by Onewrld Pubns) Penguin Putnam.

Chittick, William C. The Vision of Islam. 370p. 1996. pap. 24.95 (*0-614-21477-7*, 1286) Kazi Pubns.

Chittick, William C., ed. from ARA. A Shi'ite Anthology. 160p. (C). 1981. text 59.50 (*0-87395-510-2*); pap. text 19.95 (*0-87395-511-0*) State U NY Pr.

Chittick, William C., et al, trs. Fakhruddin Iraqi: Divine Flashes. (Classics of Western Spirituality Ser.). 1982. pap. 19.95 (*0-8091-2372-X*) Paulist Pr.

Chittick, William C., jt. auth. see Murata, Sachiko.

Chittick, William C., tr. see Nurbakhsh, Javad.

Chittick, William C., tr. see Tabatabai, Muhammad.

Chittick, William O. & Pingel, Lee Ann. American Foreign Policy: History, Substance & Process. (Illus.). 500p. 2001. pap. text 42.95 (*1-889119-31-8*, Chatham House Pub) Seven Bridges.

Chittister, Joan. The Benedictine Way: A Novena. (Illus.). 44p. 1995. pap. 3.00 (*1-890890-00-6*) Benetvision.

— Gospel Days: Reflections for Every Day of the Year. LC 99-31687. 180p. 1999. pap. 14.00 (*1-57075-280-X*) Orbis Bks.

— In Search of Belief. LC 98-27726. 224p. 1999. pap. 15.95 (*0-7648-0337-9*, Liguori Triumph) Liguori Pubns.

***Chittister, Joan.** Life Ablaze: A Woman's Novena. deluxe ed. LC 99-51454. 80p. 2000. pap. 10.95 (*1-58051-041-8*) Sheed & Ward WI.

Chittister, Joan. Light in the Darkness. LC 97-52355. 160p. 1998. pap. 12.95 (*0-8245-1748-2*, Crsrd) Crossroad NY.

***Chittister, Joan.** Living Well: Scriptural Reflections for Every Day. 160p. 2000. pap. 14.00 (*1-57075-320-2*) Orbis Bks.

— A Passion for Life: Fragments of the Face of God. LC 99-56489. (Illus.). 132p. 2000. reprint ed. pap. 24.00 (*1-57075-318-0*) Orbis Bks.

Chittister, Joan. Songs of Joy: New Meditations on the Psalms for Every Day of the Year. LC 97-1676. 144p. (Orig.). 1997. pap. 12.95 (*0-8245-1661-3*) Crossroad NY.

Chittister, Joan D. Beyond Beijing: The Next Step for Women. 224p. (Orig.). 1996. pap. 15.95 (*1-55612-903-3*, LL1903) Sheed & Ward WI.

— The Fire in These Ashes: A Spirituality of Contemporary Religious Life. 184p. (Orig.). 1995. pap. 14.95 (*1-55612-802-9*) Sheed & Ward WI.

— Heart of Flesh: A Feminist Spirituality for Women & Men. LC 97-38367. (Illus.). 200p. 1998. pap. 20.00 (*0-8028-4282-8*) Eerdmans.

***Chittister, Joan D.** The Heart of God: A Call to Forgiveness. 60p. 2000. pap. 5.00 (*1-890890-09-X*) Benetvision.

— Illuminated Life: Monastic Wisdom for Seekers of Light. LC 99-58636. 142p. 2000. 15.00 (*1-57075-233-8*) Orbis Bks.

— Living in the Breath of the Spirit: Reflections on Prayer. 64p. 1999. pap. 5.00 (*1-890890-08-1*) Benetvision.

Chittister, Joan D. A Passion for Life: Fragments of the Face of God. LC 95-43388. (Illus.). 132p. 1996. 30.00 (*1-57075-076-9*) Orbis Bks.

— Psalm Journal, Bk. II. 112p. (Orig.). 1988. pap. 6.95 (*0-934134-45-6*) Sheed & Ward WI.

— The Psalms: Meditations for Every Day of the Year. LC 96-13864. 144p. (Orig.). 1996. pap. text 14.95 (*0-8245-1581-1*) Crossroad NY.

— The Rule of Benedict. 180p. (C). 1993. text 45.00 (*0-85439-428-1*, Pub. by St Paul Pubns) St Mut.

— The Rule of Benedict: Insights for the Ages. (Spiritual Legacy Ser.). 192p. 1992. pap. 12.95 (*0-8245-2503-5*, Pub. by Crossroad NY) Natl Bk Netwk.

***Chittister, Joan D.** The Story of Ruth: Twelve Moments in Every Woman's Life. LC 99-86148. (Illus.). 96p. 2000. 28.00 (*0-8028-4742-0*) Eerdmans.

Chittister, Joan D. There Is a Season. LC 94-38523. (Illus.). 128p. 1995. 30.00 (*1-57075-022-X*) Orbis Bks.

— Way of the Cross: Gateway to Resurrection. (Illus.). 36p. 1999. pap. 3.50 (*1-890890-07-3*) Benetvision.

— Wisdom Distilled from the Daily: Living the Rule of Saint Benedict Today. LC 90-55779. 224p. 1991. pap. 12.00 (*0-06-061399-8*, Pub. by Harper SF) HarpC.

— WomanStrength: Modern Church, Modern Women. LC 90-61956. 190p. (Orig.). (C). 1996. pap. 9.95 (*1-55612-373-6*, LL1373) Sheed & Ward WI.

— Women's Role in the Church. 20p. 1993. pap. text 2.95 (*1-55612-603-4*) Sheed & Ward WI.

Chittister, Joan D., intro. In Good Company: A Woman's Journal for Spiritual Reflection 1999. (Illus.). 344p. 1998. spiral bd. 16.95 (*0-8298-1240-7*) Pilgrim OH.

Chittle, Charles R. Industrialization & Manufactured Export Expansion in a Worker-Managed Economy. 182p. 1977. lib. bdg. 47.50 (*3-16-339671-2*) Coronet Bks.

Chittum, Thomas W. Civil War II: The Coming Breakup of America. LC 96-48938. (Illus.). 202p. (Orig.). 1997. pap. 12.95 (*0-929408-17-9*) Amer Eagle Pubns Inc.

Chitty, Andrew, jt. ed. see Bertram, Christopher.

Chitty, Arthur B. Reconstruction at Sewanee. (Illus.). 206p. 1993. pap. 15.00 (*0-9627687-6-6*) Univ South Pr.

Chitty, Arthur B. & Chitty, Elizabeth N. Sewanee Sampler. 198p. 1978. pap. 15.00 (*0-9627687-7-4*) Univ South Pr.

Chitty, Arthur B., ed. see Givens, Wendell.

Chitty, Ben, jt. auth. see Murolo, Priscilla.

Chitty, Clyde. Towards a New Educational System: The Victory of the New Right. 225p. 1989. 65.00 (*1-85000-448-X*, Falmer Pr); pap. 39.95 (*1-85000-449-8*, Falmer Pr) Taylor & Francis.

Chitty, Clyde & Dunford, John. State Schools: New Labour & the Conservative Legacy. LC 99-28050. 176p. 1999. 54.50 (*0-7130-0214-X*, Pub. by Woburn Pr) Intl Spec Bk.

***Chitty, Clyde & Dunford, John.** State Schools: New Labour & the Conservative Legacy. LC 99-28050. 176p. 1999. pap. 24.50 (*0-7130-4034-3*, Pub. by Woburn Pr) Intl Spec Bk.

Chitty, Clyde & Simon, Brian, eds. Education Answers Back: Critical Responses to Government Policy. 176p. (C). 1993. pap. 19.50 (*0-85315-781-2*, Pub. by Lawrence & Wishart) NYU Pr.

Chitty, Clyde, jt. auth. see Simon, Brian.

Chitty, Craig. Reflections of a Wounded Heart. 130p. (Orig.). 1996. pap. write for info. (*1-57502-363-6*, P01167) Morris Pubng.

Chitty, Dennis. Do Lemmings Commit Suicide? Beautiful Hypotheses & Ugly Facts. LC 95-22673. (Illus.). 288p. 1996. pap. 29.95 (*0-19-509786-6*) OUP.

— Do Lemmings Commit Suicide? Beautiful Hypotheses & Ugly Facts. LC 95-22673. (Illus.). 288p. 1996. text 65.00 (*0-19-509785-8*) OUP.

Chitty, Derwas J. The Desert a City: An Introduction to the Study of Egyptian & Palestinian Monasticism under the Christian Empire. 222p. 1977. pap. 13.95 (*0-913836-45-1*) St Vladimirs.

Chitty, Elizabeth N., jt. auth. see Chitty, Arthur B.

Chitty, Elizabeth N., ed. see Givens, Wendell.

***Chitty, Gill & Baker, David.** Managing Historic Sites & Buildings: Balancing Presentation & Preservation. LC 98-54678. 1999. write for info. (*0-415-20814-9*) Routledge.

Chitty, Gill & Baker, David. Managing Historic Sites & Buildings: Balancing Presentation & Preservation. LC 98-54678. (Issues in Heritage Management Ser.). 1999. pap. write for info. (*0-415-20815-7*) Routledge.

Chitty, Janet. The Stone's Ripple Mission. LC 98-92495. 93p. 1998. per. 9.95 (*0-9662657-0-X*) Eldorado Bks.

Chitty, Kay K. Professional Nursing: Concepts & Challenges. 2nd ed. Connor, Maura, ed. (Illus.). 576p. 1996. pap. text 32.00 (*0-7216-6882-8*, W B Saunders Co) Harcrt Hlth Sci Grp.

— Professional Nursing: Concepts & Challenges. 2nd ed. (Illus.). 575p. 1997. pap., teacher ed. write for info. (*0-7216-6883-6*, W B Saunders Co) Harcrt Hlth Sci Grp.

Chitty, Naren. Framing South Asian Transformation: An Examination of Regional Views on South Asian Cooperation. LC 94-903768. (C). 1994. 22.00 (*81-7003-184-2*, Pub. by S Asia Pubs) S Asia.

Chitty, Simon C. The Castes, Customs, Manners & Literature of the Tamils. 1988. reprint ed. 15.00 (*81-206-0409-1*, Pub. by Asian Educ Servs) S Asia.

— The Ceylon Gazetteer. (C). 1989. 48.50 (*81-7013-053-0*, Pub. by Navarang) S Asia.

Chitty, Vera R. Now, I Can Fly! Simple Words for the Complex Journey Through Life. 80p. 1998. pap. 13.95 (*0-9663459-0-8*) Chitty Ents.

Chitwood. The American Pipe Dream. (C). 1995. pap. text 26.50 (*0-15-503093-0*, Pub. by Harcourt Coll Pubs) Harcourt.

***Chitwood, Chuck.** The Trial of Job. LC 99-47441. 350p. 2000. pap. 11.99 (*0-7814-3308-8*) Chariot Victor.

Chitwood, Dale D., et al. A Community Approach to AIDS Intervention: Exploring the Miami Outreach Project for Injecting Drug Users & Other High Risk Groups, 33. LC 91-19872. (Contributions in Medical Studies: No. 33). 248p. 1991. 62.95 (*0-313-27319-7*, ICP, Greenwood Pr) Greenwood.

Chitwood, Henry C., et al. Connecticut Decoys. LC 87-61705. (Illus.). 192p. 1987. 45.00 (*0-88740-104-X*) Schiffer.

Chitwood, Linda. Common Gynecologic Disorders & Procedures. Elster, Charles, ed. 28p. (C). 1992. pap. text 19.95 (*1-878025-95-3*) Western Schls.

— Healthcare of the Mature & Older Woman. 28p. (Orig.). 1995. pap. 24.95 (*1-57801-004-7*) Western Schls.

Chitwood, Linda B. Ambulatory Patient Care. 250p. (Orig.). (C). 1994. pap. 49.95 (*1-878025-63-5*) Western Schls.

— Basic Trauma Nursing Skills. 2nd ed. 240p. (Orig.). (C). 1995. pap. 49.95 (*1-878025-66-X*) Western Schls.

— Nursing for Women's Health. LC 94-60085. (Illus.). 232p. (Orig.). (C). 1992. pap. 49.95 (*1-878025-34-1*) Western Schls.

— Nursing Skills for the Management of Head, Spinal, Chest, Abdominal & Orthopedic Trauma. Halliburton, Barbara, ed. 99p. (C). 1991. pap. text 24.95 (*1-878025-94-5*) Western Schls.

— Overview of Anesthesia for Nurses. LC 94-60203. 81p. (Orig.). (C). 1992. pap. text 19.95 (*1-878025-40-6*) Western Schls.

Chitwood, Linda B. & Swain, Diane C. Perioperative Nursing. LC 91-4737. (Notes Ser.). 128p. 1991. pap. 16.95 (*0-87434-368-2*) Springhouse Corp.

Chitwood, Martha. Southern-Style Diabetic Cooking. LC 96-47060. 116p. 1996. pap. 11.95 (*0-945448-69-4*, 00694Q, Pub. by Am Diabetes) NTC Contemp Pub Co.

Chitwood, Michael. Hitting below the Bible Belt: Blood Kin, Baptist Voodoo, Grandma's Teeth & Other Stories from the South. 145p. 1998. pap. 13.95 (*1-878086-67-7*, Pub. by Down Home NC) Blair.

— The Weave Room. LC 97-8422. (Phoenix Poets Ser.). 96p. 1998. pap. 11.00 (*0-226-10398-6*); lib. bdg. 21.00 (*0-226-10397-8*) U Ch Pr.

— Whet. 64p. (Orig.). 1995. pap. 13.00 (*0-942148-16-9*) Ohio Review.

An Asterisk (*) at the beginning of an entry indicates that the title is appearing for the first time.

Chitwood, Michale. Salt Works: Ohio Review Books. LC 92-27430. 72p. 1992. 16.95 (*0-942148-15-0*) Ohio Review.

Chitwood, Oliver P. John Tyler: Champion of the Old South. Speirs, Katherine E., ed. LC 90-84223. (Signature Ser.). (Illus.). 496p. 1990. reprint ed. 32.50 (*0-945707-02-9*) Amer Political.

Chitwood, Roy. World Class Selling: The Complete Selling Process. 274p. 1995. 24.95 (*0-9636268-3-3*) Best Sell Pub.

Chiu, Ben. Microsoft Flight Simulator 98: Inside Moves. LC 97-29194. 288p. 1997. pap. text 16.99 (*1-57231-635-7*) Microsoft.

***Chiu, Ben.** Microsoft Flight Simulator 2000: Offical Strategies & Secrets. 4th ed. 352p. 1999. pap. 19.99 (*0-7821-2634-0*) Sybex.

Chiu, Ben. Microsoft Internet Gaming Zone: Fighter Ace: Inside Moves. LC 97-29195. 256p. 16.99 (*1-57231-646-2*) Microsoft.

Chiu, Beverly D. How You Too Can Outsmart Your Food Allergies Using the Diversified Rotation Diet. 95p. (Orig.). 1988. pap. 14.95 (*0-921937-01-6*) Gordon Soules Bk.

Chiu, Catherine C. Small Family Business in Hong Kong: Accumulation & Accommodation. 160p. 1998. pap. text 42.50 (*962-201-802-5*, Pub. by Chinese Univ) U of Mich Pr.

Ch'iu, Chang-Wei. Speaker of the House of Representatives since 1896. LC 68-58558. (Columbia University. Studies in the Social Sciences: No. 297). reprint ed. 32.50 (*0-404-51297-6*) AMS Pr.

***Chiu, Christina.** Eating Disorder Survivors Tell Their Stories. 1999. pap. text 6.95 (*1-56838-259-6*) Hazelden.

Chiu, Christina. Eating Disorder Survivors Tell Their Stories. LC 98-4416. (Teen Health Library of Eating Disorder Prevention). (Illus.). 64p. (YA). (gr. 7-12). 1998. lib. bdg. 17.95 (*0-8239-2767-9*, EDSUST) Rosen Group.

— Teen Guide to Staying Sober. (Drug Abuse Prevention Library). 64p. (J). (gr. 7-12). 1998. pap. 6.95 (*1-56838-249-9*) Hazelden.

— Teen Guide to Staying Sober. LC 98-16213. (Drug Abuse Prevention Library). 64p. (YA). (gr. 7-12). 1998. 16.95 (*0-8239-2765-2*, PowerKids) Rosen Group.

Chiu-Duke, Josephine. To Rebuild the Empire: Lu Chih's Confucian Pragmatist Approach to the Mid-T'ang Predicament. LC 99-40512. (C). 2000. text 59.50 (*0-7914-4501-1*); pap. text 19.95 (*0-7914-4502-X*) State U NY Pr.

***Chiu, Edmond, et al, eds.** Cerebral Vascular Disease & Dementia. (Illus.). 241p. 2000. 65.00 (*1-85317-759-8*, Pub. by Martin Dunitz) Blackwell Sci.

Chiu, Edmond & Ames, David, eds. Functional Psychiatric Disorders of the Elderly. LC 93-33740. (Illus.). 649p. (C). 1994. text 120.00 (*0-521-43160-3*) Cambridge U Pr.

Chiu, Edmond, jt. ed. see Ames, David.

Chiu, Esther. The Lobster & the Sea. LC 97-10221. (Illus.). 32p. (J). (gr. 1-4). 1998. 14.95 (*1-879965-14-3*) Polychrome Pub.

Chiu, H., jt. auth. see Knight, G.

Chiu, H. H. & Chigier, Norman A. Mechanics & Combustion of Droplets & Sprays. 393p. 1996. 97.50 (*1-56700-051-7*) Begell Hse.

Chiu, H. H. & Chigier, Norman A., eds. Mechanics & Combustion of Droplets & Sprays. LC 95-49179. 1995. write for info. (*0-15-670051-4*) Begell Hse.

***Chiu, Hsi-Kuei, et al.** Chinese Writing. LC 00-32221. (Early China Special Monographs). 2000. write for info. (*1-55729-071-7*) IEAS.

Chiu, Hungdah. Agreements of the People's Republic of China: A Calendar of Events, 1966-1980. LC 81-8686. 329p. 1981. 80.00 (*0-275-90594-2*, C0594, Praeger Pubs) Greenwood.

— China & the Taiwan Issue. LC 79-14270. (Praeger Special Studies). 310p. 1979. 65.00 (*0-275-90341-9*, C0341, Praeger Pubs) Greenwood.

— Chinese Law & Justice: Trends over 3 Decades. (Occasional Papers-Reprints Series in Contemporary Asian Studies: No. 7-1982 (52)). 39p. (Orig.). 1982. pap. text 2.00 (*0-942182-51-0*) U MD Law.

— Chinese Yearbook of International Law & Affairs, 1983, Vol. 3. LC 82-645664. 350p. 1984. 24.00 (*0-942182-95-2*) Occasional Papers.

— Chinese Yearbook of International Law & Affairs, 1984, Vol. 4. LC 82-645664. 400p. 1985. 24.00 (*0-942182-96-0*) Occasional Papers.

— People's Republic of China & the Law of Treaties. LC 72-173411. (Studies in East Asian Law: No. 5). 196p. 1972. 24.00 (*0-674-66175-3*) HUP.

— The Taiwan Relations Act & Sino-American Relations, No. 5. 34p. 1990. 4.00 (*0-925153-11-7*, 100) Occasional Papers.

Chiu, Hungdah, ed. Chinese Yearbook of International Law & Affairs, 1981, Vol.I. (Chinese Yearbook of International Law & Affairs Ser.). 392p. 1982. reprint ed. 24.00 (*0-942182-93-6*) Occasional Papers.

— The International Law of the Sea Suppl. 1: Through Summer 1996. LC 96-50490. 228p. 1997. 50.00 (*1-85182-296-8*, Pub. by Four Cts Pr) Intl Spec Bk.

— Socialist Legalism: Reform & Continuity in Post-Mao People's Republic of China. (Occasional Papers-Reprints Series in Contemporary Asian Studies: No. 1). 35p. (Orig.). 1982. pap. text 4.00 (*0-942182-45-6*) Occasional Papers.

— Symposium on Hong Kong, 1997. (Occasional Papers-Reprints Series in Contemporary Asian Studies: No. 3-1985 (68)). 100p. (Orig.). (C). 1986. reprint ed. pap. 4.00 (*0-942182-70-7*) Occasional Papers.

Chiu, Hungdah, et al, eds. The Future of Hong Kong: Toward 1997 & Beyond. LC 86-25573. 268p. 1987. 55.00 (*0-89930-241-6*, CFH/, Quorum Bks) Greenwood.

Chiu, Hungdah & Chang, Jaw-ling J., eds. Survey of Recent Developments in China (Mainland & Taiwan), 1985-1986, No. 2. 222p. 1987. 8.00 (*0-942182-82-0*, 79) Occasional Papers.

Chiu, Hungdah & Downen, Robert, eds. Multi-System Nations & International Law, International Status of Germany, Korea & China. LC 81-85785. (Occasional Papers-Reprints Series in Contemporary Asian Studies: No. 8-1981). 203p. (Orig.). (C). 1981. pap. text 8.00 (*0-942182-44-8*) Occasional Papers.

Chiu, Hungdah & Leng, Shao-Chuan, eds. China: Seventy Years after the Hsin-Hai Revolution. 601p. 1998. pap. text 30.00 (*0-7881-5468-0*) DIANE Pub.

— China, Seventy Years after the 1911 Hsin-Hai Revolution. LC 84-7217. 611p. 1984. reprint ed. pap. 189.50 (*0-7837-8572-0*, 204938700011) Bks Demand.

Chiu, Hungdah, jt. auth. see Cohen, Jerome A.

Chiu, Hungdah, jt. ed. see Knight, Gary.

Chiu, Hungdah, jt. ed. see Leng, Shao-Chuan.

Chiu, Jen, ed. see Symposium on Polymer Characterization by Thermal M.

Chiu, Lee C., et al. Clinical Computer Tomography for the Technologist. 2nd ed. LC 94-3656. (Illus.). 224p. 1994. text 69.00 (*0-7817-0235-6*) Lppncott W & W.

— Computed Tomographic Angiography of the Mediastinum. (Illus.). 224p. (C). 1986. 57.50 (*0-87527-363-7*) Green.

Chiu, Marcus Y. L. Social Evolution of Love: A Study of Mate Selection among Psychiatrid Sufferers. LC 99-72557. 202p. 1999. 61.95 (*1-84014-940-X*, Pub. by Ashgate Pub) Ashgate Pub Co.

Chiu-Nan Lai. The Pursuit of Life. 90p. 1993. pap. 12.95 (*0-9638477-0-8*) Chiu-Nan Lai.

Chiu, Peter, tr. see Rhoton, Dale.

Chiu, Peter, tr. see Toyotome, Masumi.

Chiu, Ray C., jt. auth. see Kao, Race L.

Chiu, Shui-Chen, jt. auth. see Townes, Henry.

Chiu, Siu W. & Moore, David, eds. Patterns in Fungal Development. 238p. 1996. text 59.95 (*0-521-56047-0*) Cambridge U Pr.

Chiu, Stephen W., jt. auth. see So, Alvin Y.

***Chiu, Stephen Wing Kai & Tai Lok Lui, eds.** The Dynamics of Social Movement in Hong Kong. (Culture & Society Ser.). 327p. 2000. pap. 38.50 (*962-209-497-X*, Pub. by HK Univ Pr) Coronet Bks.

Chiu, T. N. The Port of Hong Kong: A Survey of Its Development. LC 73-88376. 158p. reprint ed. pap. 49.00 (*0-8357-2744-0*, 203985300013) Bks Demand.

Chiu, Thomas, et al. Legal Systems of the PRC. vii, 134p. 1991. pap. 27.50 (*962-359-427-5*, Pub. by Longman Far East) Gaunt.

Chiu, Thomas L. Ana & Victoria. LC 93-85382. 95p. (Orig.). 1993. pap. 12.95 (*1-884092-01-2*) R Altschuler.

— He Called Her Lilie. LC 95-81472. 1996. pap. 25.00 (*1-884092-02-0*) R Altschuler.

Chiu, Tony. Positive Match. 480p. 1998. mass mkt. 6.50 (*0-553-57546-5*) Bantam.

— Ross Perot: In His Own Words. 208p. 1992. mass mkt. 4.99 (*0-446-36456-8*) Warner Bks.

Chiu, Tony, jt. ed. see Stolley, Richard B.

Chiu, Wah, et al, eds. Structural Biology of Viruses. LC 95-26844. (Illus.). 512p. 1997. pap. text 55.00 (*0-19-511850-2*) OUP.

Chiu-Yin Kwan, ed. Membrane Abnormalities in Hypertension, 2 Vols., Vol. 2. LC 88-23605. 224p. 1989. 123.00 (*0-8493-4528-6*, RC685, CRC Reprint) Franklin.

Chiu-Yin Kwan, ed. see Kwan, C.

Chiu, Yuan-Yuan H. & Gueriguian, John L. Drug Biotechnology Regulation: Scientific Basis & Practices. (Bioprocess Technology Ser.: Vol. 13). (Illus.). 568p. 1991. text 199.00 (*0-8247-8420-0*) Dekker.

Chiucos, Thomas R. & Lerner, Richard M. Serving Children & Families Through Community-University Partnerships: Success Stories. LC 99-24717. (Outreach Scholarship Ser.). 1999. write for info. (*0-7923-8540-3*) Kluwer Academic.

Chiuderi, Claudio & Einaudi, Giorgio, eds. Plasma Astrophysics: Lectures Held at the Astrophysics School VII, Organized by the European Astrophysics Doctoral Network (EADN) in San Miniato, Italy, 3-14 October 1994. LC 96-2418. (Lecture Notes in Physics Ser.: Vol. 468). 326p. 1996. 78.00 (*3-540-61014-6*) Spr-Verlag.

***Chiueh, Chuang C. & Gilbert, Daniel L.** Reactive Oxygen Species: From Radiation to Molecular Biology: A Festschrift in Honor of Daniel L. Gilbert. LC 99-86493. (Annals of the New York Academy of Science Ser.). 2000. pap. write for info. (*1-57331-239-8*) NY Acad Sci.

Chiueh, Tzi-cker & Tescher, Andrew G., eds. Video Techniques & Software for Full-Service Networks. LC 96-69767. 198p. 1997. 66.00 (*0-8194-2317-3*) SPIE.

Chiuini, Michele & Underwood, James R. Structural Design. LC 97-52009. 720p. 1998. 79.00 (*0-471-14066-X*) Wiley.

Chiulli, Roy M. Quantitative Analysis: An Introduction. (Automation & Production Systems Ser.: Vol. 3). 592p. 1998. text 60.00 (*90-5699-629-0*, ECU86, Harwood Acad Pubs) Gordon & Breach.

Chiulli, Roy M., ed. International Launch Site Guide. (Illus.). 92p. (Orig.). 1995. pap. write for info. (*1-884989-01-2*) Aerospace CA.

Chiumello, Giuseppe & Sperling, Mark, eds. Recent Progress in Pediatric Endocrinology. LC 82-47695. (Illus.). 391p. reprint ed. pap. 121.30 (*0-7837-7130-4*, 204695900004) Bks Demand.

Chiusoli, Alessandro & Boriani, Maria L. Simon & Schuster's Guide to House Plants. (Nature Guide Ser.). (Illus.). 320p. 1987. per. 14.00 (*0-671-63131-4*) S&S Trade Pap.

Chiv, Thomas L. From the Couch to the Jungle: The Story of My Life As a Multicultural Psychiatrist. (Illus.). 180p. 1998. pap. 29.95 (*1-884092-04-7*) R Altschuler.

Chivell, Janette, jt. auth. see Henderson, Stephanie.

Chivers. Chivers Paragon Hummingbird. 1993. 8.88 (*0-8161-2063-3*, G K Hall Lrg Type) Mac Lib Ref.

Chivers, David J., et al, eds. Food Acquisition & Processing in Primates. LC 84-4876. 584p. 1984. 125.00 (*0-306-41701-4*, Plenum Trade) Perseus Pubng.

Chivers, David J. & Langer, Peter, eds. The Digestive System in Mammals: Food, Form, & Function. LC 93-32561. (Illus.). 460p. (C). 1994. text 95.00 (*0-521-44016-5*) Cambridge U Pr.

Chivers, David J., et al. The Siamang in Malaya: A Field Study of a Primate in Tropical Rain Forest. Hofer, H. & Schultz, A. H., eds. (Contributions to Primatology Ser.: Vol. 4). (Illus.). 250p. 1974. 149.75 (*3-8055-1668-1*) S Karger.

Chivers, David J., jt. ed. see Preuschoft, Holger.

Chivers, G. R. Introduction to Parliamentary Democracy. LC 74-19741. 1973. 30.00 (*0-8420-1783-6*) Scholarly Res Inc.

***Chivers, I. D.** Essential Visual C++ 6.0 Fast: An Introduction to Windows Programming using the Microsoft Foundation Class Library. LC 99-41996. (Essential Series). 214p. 1999. pap. 24.95 (*1-85233-170-4*) Spr-Verlag.

Chivers, I. D. A Practical Introduction to Standard PASCAL. (Computers & Their Applications Ser.). 276p. 1986. text 36.95 (*0-470-20359-5*) P-H.

***Chivers, I. D. & Sleighthome, Jane.** Introducing Fortran 95. LC 00-34505. 2000. write for info. (*1-85233-276-X*) Spr-Verlag.

Chivers, Ian D. & Sleightholme, Jane. Introducing Fortran 90, Vol. XVIII. LC 95-36870. 375p. 1995. 34.95 (*3-540-19940-3*) Spr-Verlag.

Chivers, Keith. The Lodon Harness Horse Parade. 1997. 49.00 (*0-85131-690-5*, Pub. by J A Allen) Trafalgar.

— The Shire Horse. 872p. 1990. 100.00 (*0-85131-245-4*, Pub. by J A Allen) Trafalgar.

Chivers, Mary D., jt. auth. see Dominick, DeWitt.

Chivers, P., jt. auth. see Bird, J. O.

Chivers Staff. City of Strangers Portway. 1991. pap. 5.00 (*0-7451-7291-1*, Pub. by Chivers N Amer) Chivers N Amer.

Chivers, Thomas H. Memoralia: or Phials of Amber Full of the Tears of Love. (Works of Thomas Holley Chivers). 1990. reprint ed. lib. bdg. 79.00 (*0-7812-2287-7*) Rprt Serv.

Chivers, Thomas Holley. Atlanta: Or the True Blessed Island of Poetry. (Works of Thomas Holley Chivers). 1990. reprint ed. lib. bdg. 79.00 (*0-7812-2289-3*) Rprt Serv.

— Birthday Song of Liberty. (Works of Thomas Holley Chivers Ser.). 1990. reprint ed. lib. bdg. 90.00 (*0-7812-2290-7*) Rprt Serv.

— The Complete Works of Thomas Holley Chivers. Vol. 1. Chase, Emma L. & Parks, Lois F., eds. LC 57-8677. 336p. reprint ed. pap. 104.20 (*0-608-12093-6*, 202412900001) Bks Demand.

— Conrad & Eudora. LC 78-18338. 1978. reprint ed. 50.00 (*0-8201-1315-8*) Schol Facsimiles.

— Conrad & Eudora: Or the Death of Alonzo. (Works of Thomas Holley Chivers Ser.). 1990. reprint ed. lib. bdg. 90.00 (*0-7812-2282-6*) Rprt Serv.

— Eonchs of Ruby: A Gift of Love. LC 72-4957. (Romantic Tradition in American Literature Ser.). 172p. 1978. reprint ed. 20.95 (*0-405-04629-4*) Ayer.

— Eonchs of Ruby: A Gift of Love. (Works of Thomas Holley Chivers Ser.). 1990. reprint ed. lib. bdg. 90.00 (*0-7812-2286-9*) Rprt Serv.

— The Lost Pleiad & Other Poems. (Works of Thomas Holley Chivers Ser.). 1990. reprint ed. lib. bdg. 79.00 (*0-7812-2284-2*) Rprt Serv.

— Nacoochee. LC 77-24233. 160p. 1977. reprint ed. 50.00 (*0-8201-1295-X*) Schol Facsimiles.

— Nacoochee: or The Beautiful Star. (Works of Thomas Holley Chivers Ser.). 1990. reprint ed. lib. bdg. 79.00 (*0-7812-2283-4*) Rprt Serv.

— Path of Sorrow (1832), Eonchs of Ruby (1851), Memoralia (1849), Virginalia (1853), Sons of Usna (1858), 5 vols. in 1. LC 79-22103. 580p. 1979. 80.00 (*0-8201-1340-9*) Schol Facsimiles.

— The Path of Sorrow: or The Lament of Youth: Or the Lament of Youth. (Works of Thomas Holley Chivers Ser.). 1990. reprint ed. lib. bdg. 79.00 (*0-7812-2281-8*) Rprt Serv.

— Search after Truth. (Works of Thomas Holley Chivers Ser.). 1990. reprint ed. lib. bdg. 79.00 (*0-7812-2285-0*) Rprt Serv.

— The Sons of Usna. (Works of Thomas Holley Chivers Ser.). 1990. reprint ed. lib. bdg. 79.00 (*0-7812-2291-5*) Rprt Serv.

— Unpublished Plays of Thomas Holley Chivers. LC 79-29747. 512p. 1980. 75.00 (*0-8201-1350-6*) Schol Facsimiles.

— Virginalia: or Songs of My Summer Nights. (Works of Thomas Holley Chivers Ser.). 1990. reprint ed. lib. bdg. 79.00 (*0-7812-2288-5*) Rprt Serv.

— Virginalia: or Songs of My Summer Nights: A Gift of Love for the Beautiful. LC 72-4958. (Romantic Tradition in American Literature Ser.). 136p. 1972. reprint ed. 18.95 (*0-405-04630-8*) Ayer.

— The Works of Thomas Chivers. 1990. reprint ed. lib. bdg. 63.00 (*0-685-27674-0*) Rprt Serv.

Chivers, Thomas Holley & Lombard, Charles M. Search after the Truth, 1848, the Lost Pleiad, 1845, & Atlanta, 1853. LC 76-18173. 144p. 1976. reprint ed. lib. bdg. 50.00 (*0-8201-1269-0*) Schol Facsimiles.

Chivers, Tristan, ed. Proceedings of the Seventh International Symposium on Inorganic Ring Systems, IRIS VII. 448p. 1995. pap. text 1095.00 (*2-88449-168-6*) Gordon & Breach.

Chivian, Eric, et al, eds. Critical Condition: Human Health & the Environment. (Illus.). 256p. 1993. pap. text 17.50 (*0-262-53118-6*) MIT Pr.

Chivukula, Upendra, et al. Supplier Quality Management: Monitoring & Improvement. Hankinson, Mari-Lynn, ed. (AT&T Quality Library). (Illus.). 139p. (Orig.). 1994. pap. 19.95 (*0-932764-48-7*) AT&T Customer Info.

***Chiwele, Dennis.** Private Sector Response to Agricultural Marketing Liberlisation in Zambia: A Case Study of Eastern Province Maize Markets. LC 99-165856. (Research Report Ser.). 90p. 1999. pap. write for info. (*91-7106-436-2*) Nordisk Afrikainstitutet.

ChiWhan Yoo. Banner: And Other Poems. Okhee Kim & McClanahan, Kay, trs. from KOR. (Illus.). 48p. 1998. pap. 19.95 (*1-879934-57-4*) St Andrews NC.

Chiyo, Uno. The Story of a Single Woman. Copeland, Rebecca, tr. from JPN. & intro. by. 132p. 1993. pap. 19.95 (*0-7206-0878-3*, Pub. by P Owen Ltd) Dufour.

Chiyokura, H., jt. ed. see Toriya, H.

Chiyokura, Hiroaki. Solid Modelling. (Illus.). 256p. (C). 1988. text 41.66 (*0-201-19245-4*) Addison-Wesley.

Chiyotani, Keizo & Hosoda, Yutaka. Advances in the Prevention of Occupational Respiratory Diseases: Proceedings of the 9th International Conference on Occupational Respiratory Diseases, Kyoto, 13-16 October, 1997. LC 98-27177. (International Congress Ser.). 1236p. 1998. 296.00 (*0-444-82791-9*) Elsevier.

Chizek, Jim. Game Warden Centurion: Game Wardens Break Trail for Future Protectors of the Outdoors, Encouraging Them to, As Ernie Swift Would Say, Float Their Own Stick. (Illus.). 200p. (Orig.). 1992. pap. 12.95 (*0-9633353-5-9*) Flambeau River.

Chizhov, Oleg, ed. Organic Synthesis: Modern Trends. 1991. 66.00 (*0-632-02014-8*) CRC Pr.

Chizmar, Richard, ed. The Best of Cemetery Dance. 800p. Date not set. 35.00 (*1-881475-24-7*) Cemetery Dance.

Chizmar, Richard & Greenberg, Martin. Screamplays. 1997. pap. write for info. (*0-614-27456-7*, Del Rey) Ballantine Pub Grp.

Chizmar, Richard, ed. see Greenberg, Martin.

Chizner, Michael A., ed. Classic Teachings in Clinical Cardiology: A Tribute to W. Proctor Harvey, 2 vols. 1996. boxed set 145.00 (*1-886128-06-5*) Laennec Pub.

***Chlamtac, Imrich & Lin, Jason Yi-Bing.** Wireless & Mobile Network Architectures. 2000. 59.99 (*0-471-39492-0*) Wiley.

Chlapowski, Dezydery. Memoirs of a Polish Lancer. Simmons, Tim, tr. (Illus.). 160p. 1992. 27.00 (*0-9626655-2-5*, Pub. by Emperors Pr) Combined Pub.

Chlapowski, Francis J. Biochemistry. 9th ed. LC 98-215436. (Basic Sciences: Pretest Self Assessment & Review Ser.). (Illus.). 1998. pap. text 18.95 (*0-07-052684-2*) McGraw-Hill HPD.

Chlebus, Bogdan & Czaja, Ludwik, eds. Fundamentals of Computation Theory: Proceedings, 11th International Symposium, FCT '97, Krakow, Poland, September 1-3, 1997, Vol. 127. LC 97-33254. (Lecture Notes in Computer Science Ser.: Vol. 1279). xi, 475p. pap. 69.00 (*3-540-63386-3*) Spr-Verlag.

Chlenov, M. A., tr. see Bessonov, M. I., et al.

Chlenov, M. A., tr. see Tarchevsky, I. A. & Marchenko, G. N.

Chlewinski, Zdzislaw. Search for Maturity: Personality, Conscience, Religion. (American University Studies VII: Vol. 198). VII, 137p. (C). 1998. text 32.95 (*0-8204-3471-X*) P Lang Pubng.

Chliwniak, Luba. Higher Education Leadership: An Analysis of the Gender Gap. Fife, Jonathan D., ed. LC 97-72902. (ASHE-ERIC Higher Education Reports: Vol. 25-4). 97p. 1997. pap. 24.00 (*1-878380-76-1*) GWU Grad Schl E&HD.

Chloe, Anne-Marie. Therapy: A Message of Love about a Survivor. (Illus.). xxv, 15p. (Orig.). 1996. pap. text 9.98 (*0-9655557-9-8*) Anne-Maries Peaceful Connect.

Chlorine Bicentennial Symposium Staff. Chlorine Bicentennial Symposium: Papers. Jeffery, Thomas C. et al, eds. LC 74-78467. (Illus.). 412p. reprint ed. pap. 127.80 (*0-8357-8072-4*, 205229200087) Bks Demand.

Chlorine Institute Staff. Properties of Chlorine in SI Units. LC 81-67483. (Illus.). 87p. 1986. pap. text 27.00 (*0-940230-02-X*) Chlorine Inst.

Chloupek, Jan, et al, eds. Reader in Czech Sociolinguistics. LC 86-17024. (Linguistic & Literary Studies in Eastern Europe: No. 23). 344p. 1987. 94.00 (*90-272-1528-6*) J Benjamins Pubng Co.

Chlu, Ben. Microsoft Combat Flight Simulator: Inside Moves. LC 98-38263. 224p. 1998. 16.99 (*1-57231-592-X*) Microsoft.

Chmaj, Betty E., ed. Multicultural America: A Resource Book for Teachers of Humanities & American Studies. LC 92-33140. (C). 1993. pap. text 37.50 (*0-8191-8917-0*); lib. bdg. 64.00 (*0-8191-8916-2*) U Pr of Amer.

Chmel, H., et al. Pulmonary Infections & Immunity. (Infectious Agents & Pathogenesis Ser.). (Illus.). 378p. (C). 1994. text 95.00 (*0-306-44609-X*, Kluwer Plenum) Kluwer Academic.

Chmela, Harriet, et al. I Am! I Can! Vol. 2: A Preschool Curriculum, Vol. II. LC 91-67110. 219p. (C). 1992. pap. 19.95 (*0-910287-10-4*) TelShare Pub Co.

Chmelar, Robin & Fitt, Sally S. Diet for Dancers: A Complete Guide to Nutrition & Weight Control. LC 94-48618. (Illus.). 164p. 1990. pap. 16.95 (*0-916622-89-4*) Princeton Bk Co.

Chmelick, Stefan. Chinese Herbal Secrets: The Key to Total Health. (Illus.). 192p. 1999. pap. text 17.95 (*0-89529-986-0*, Avery) Penguin Putnam.

Chmelynski, Carol C. Opportunities in Restaurant Careers. (Opportunities In . . . Ser.). (Illus.). 160p. pap. 12.95 (*0-8442-8664-8*, 297OIREST, VGM Career) NTC Contemp Pub Co.

— Opportunities in Restaurant Careers. LC 98-4607.

C

An Asterisk (*) at the beginning of an entry indicates that the title is appearing for the first time.

(Opportunities in...Ser.). (Illus.). 160p. 1998. 14.95 (*0-8442-2335-2*, 23352, VGM Career); pap. 11.95 (*0-8442-2336-0*, 23360, VGM Career) NTC Contemp Pub Co.

Chmelynsky, Carol C. Opportunities in Restaurant Careers. (Illus.). 160p. 1992. 14.95 (*0-8442-8662-1*, VGM Career) NTC Contemp Pub Co.

***Chmiel, David.** Golf Past 50. 2000. 16.95 (*0-7360-0211-1*) Human Kinetics.

Chmiel, Horst & Walitze, Eckehard. On the Rheology of Blood & Synovial Fluids. LC 80-40948. (Chemical Engineering Aspects of Biomedicine Research Studies: No. 1). (Illus.). 178p. reprint ed. pap. 55.20 (*0-608-18492-6*, 203149400075) Bks Demand.

Chmiel, Nik. Jobs, Technology & People. LC 97-50042. (Psychology Focus Ser.). 176p. (C). 1998. 50.00 (*0-415-15816-8*); pap. 16.99 (*0-415-15817-6*) Routledge.

Chmiel, Nik, ed. Introduction to Work & Organizational Psychology: A European Perspective. LC 99-32109. 608p. 1999. text 74.95 (*0-631-20675-2*); pap. text 39.95 (*0-631-20676-0*) Blackwell Pubs.

Chmielarz, Sharon. Different Arrangements. LC 82-61650. (Minnesota Voices Project Ser.: No. 10). (Illus.). 103p. 1982. pap. 3.00 (*0-89823-042-X*) New Rivers Pr.

— Down at Angel's. LC 93-11020. (Illus.). 32p. (J). (ps-2). 1994. 14.95 (*0-395-65993-0*) Ticknor & Flds Bks Yng Read.

Chmielewski, Edward. The Polish Question in the Russian State Duma. LC 77-100411. 196p. reprint ed. pap. 60.80 (*0-608-14260-3*, 202221300025) Bks Demand.

Chmielewski, Gary. Riddles. LC 86-17720. (Smile-a-While Ser.). (Illus.). (J). (gr. 2-3). 1986. 9.95 (*0-685-58363-5*) Rourke Corp.

— Sports Jokes. (Smile-a-While Ser.). (Illus.). (J). (gr. 2-3). 1986. lib. bdg. 9.95 (*0-685-58364-3*) Rourke Corp.

— Teacher Jokes. LC 86-17773. (Smile-a-While Ser.). (Illus.). (J). (gr. 2-3). 1986. 9.95 (*0-685-58365-1*) Rourke Corp.

— Tongue Twisters. LC 86-17701. (Smile-a-While Ser.). (Illus.). (J). (gr. 2-3). 1986. 9.95 (*0-685-58366-X*) Rourke Corp.

Chmielewski, Gena. Angel Visions & Miracles Vol. 1: Seven Sacred Steps to Creating Miracles in Your Life. 2nd rev. ed. Krier, Beth A. et al, eds. (Illus.). 200p. (Orig.). 1995. reprint ed. pap., student ed. 22.00 (*0-9647744-0-2*) Angel Visions Intl.

Chmielewski, Philip J. Bettering Our Condition: Work, Workers, & Ethics in British & German Economic Thought. LC 92-13304. (American University Studies: Philosophy: Ser. V, Vol. 137). XVIII, 299p. (C). 1993. text 49.95 (*0-8204-1851-X*) P Lang Pubng.

Chmielewski, Wendy, et al, eds. Women in Spiritual & Communitarian Societies in the United States. (Utopianism & Communitarianism Ser.). (Illus.). 320p. 1992. text 49.00 (*0-8156-2568-5*); pap. text 19.95 (*0-8156-2569-3*) Syracuse U Pr.

Chmora, Andrew, ed. see Wecker, Stephen B.

Chmykhalov, Timothy & Smith, Danny. The Last Christian: Release of the Siberian Seven. 208p. 1985. pap. 7.70 (*0-310-34021-7*, 12411P) Zondervan.

Chng Meng Kng, et al. Industrial Restructuring in Singapore: For ASEAN-Japan Investment & Trade Expansion. 126p. 1989. text 45.00 (*9971-68-134-X*, Pub. by Chopmen Singapore) Advent Bks Div.

Chnoupek, B. The Breaking of Seals. 1996. pap. text 9.00 (*0-08-037129-9*, Pergamon Pr) Elsevier.

Cho, Alfred, ed. Molecular Beam Epitaxy. LC 94-1433. (Key Papers in Applied Physics). 400p. 1994. 59.95 (*1-56396-132-6*) Spr-Verlag.

Cho, Arthur K., ed. Annual Review of Pharmacology & Toxicology, Vol. 34. LC 61-5649. (Illus.). 1994. text 47.00 (*0-8243-0434-9*) Annual Reviews.

— Annual Review of Pharmacology & Toxicology, Vol. 35. LC 61-5649. (Illus.). 650p. 1995. text 47.00 (*0-8243-0435-7*) Annual Reviews.

— Annual Review of Pharmacology & Toxicology, Vol. 38. LC 61-5649. 581p. 1998. text 60.00 (*0-8243-0438-1*) Annual Reviews.

Cho, Arthur K., et al, eds. Annual Review of Pharmacology & Toxicology, Vol. 31. LC 61-5649. 1991. text 40.00 (*0-8243-0431-4*) Annual Reviews.

— Annual Review of Pharmacology & Toxicology, Vol. 32. LC 61-5649. 1992. text 44.00 (*0-8243-0432-2*) Annual Reviews.

— Annual Review of Pharmacology & Toxicology, Vol. 33. LC 61-5649. (Illus.). 1993. text 44.00 (*0-8243-0433-0*) Annual Reviews.

— Annual Review of Pharmacology & Toxicology, Vol. 36. LC 61-5649. (Illus.). 1996. text 52.00 (*0-8243-0436-5*) Annual Reviews.

***Cho, Arthur K., et al, eds.** Annual Review of Pharmacology & Toxicology Vol. 39: 1999. LC 61-5649. 470p. 1999. 120.00 (*0-8243-0439-X*) Annual Reviews.

Cho, Arthur K. & Lindeke, B., eds. Biotransformation of Organic Nitrogen Compounds. (Progress in Basic & Clinical Pharmacology Ser.: Vol. 1). (Illus.). x, 218p. 1988. 172.25 (*3-8055-4650-5*) S Karger.

Cho, Arthur K. & Segal, David S., eds. Amphetamine & Its Analogs: Psychopharmacology, Toxicology, & Abuse. (Illus.). 503p. 1994. text 99.00 (*0-12-173375-0*) Acad Pr.

Cho, Brandon, et al. Korean Family Devotions. 1994. pap. 8.95 (*0-687-60604-7*) Abingdon.

— Korean Family Devotions. (KOR.). 112p. 1994. pap. 9.00 (*0-8358-0712-6*) Upper Room Bks.

Cho, Byung K. Korean Culture, Tourism & Language: For Everything You Need to Know about Korea. 357p. 1992. 29.00 (*0-9631874-1-4*) Chos Black Belt.

— Martial Arts Dynamic Management & Marketing Seminar Book. 450p. 1992. 99.00 (*0-9631874-0-6*) Chos Black Belt.

Cho Chikun Nine-Dan. All about Life & Death, Vol. 1. Olsen, Bruce, tr. from JPN. (Illus.). 192p. (Orig.). 1993. pap. 14.95 (*4-87187-042-1*, G42) Ishi Pr Intl.

— All about Life & Death, Vol. 2. Olsen, Bruce, tr. from JPN. (Illus.). 192p. (Orig.). 1993. pap. 14.95 (*4-87187-043-X*, G43) Ishi Pr Intl.

Cho Chikun, Nine-Dan. The Three-Three Point: Modern Opening Strategy. Dowsey, Stuart, tr. from JPN. (Illus.). 216p. (Orig.). 1991. pap. 12.95 (*4-87187-044-8*, G44) Ishi Pr Intl.

Cho, Choong Y., tr. see Miyadera, Isao.

Cho, Chun H. Measurement & Control of Liquid Level. LC 82-48156. (Independent Learning Module from the Instrument Society of America Ser.). (Illus.). 279p. 1982. reprint ed. pap. 86.50 (*0-7837-9046-5*, 204979700003) Bks Demand.

***Cho, D. H.** Experiments on Interactions Between Zirconium- Containing Melt & Water. 171p. 1998. per. 14.00 (*0-16-062960-8*) USGPO.

Cho, David Y. Como Tener Exito en la Vida.Tr. of Successful Living. (SPA.). 240p. 1995. pap. 7.99 (*0-8297-1873-7*) Vida Pubs.

— Cuarta Dimension.Tr. of Fourth Dimension. (SPA.). 160p. 1980. pap. 6.99 (*0-8297-0994-0*) Vida Pubs.

— Enseigne - Nous A Prier.Tr. of Praying with Jesus. (FRE.). 160p. 1991. mass mkt. 6.95 (*0-8297-1471-5*) Vida Pubs.

— The Fourth Dimension Vol. 1: The Key to Putting Your Faith to Work for a Successful Life. LC 79-65588. 186p. 1979. pap. 9.99 (*0-88270-380-3*) Bridge-Logos.

— Grupos Familiares Crecimiento Igelesia.Tr. of Successful Home Cell Groups. (SPA.). 208p. 1982. pap. 6.99 (*0-8297-1346-8*) Vida Pubs.

— Guia - Para el Estudio en Grupo.Tr. of Homecell Group. (SPA.). 304p. 1995. pap., student ed. 12.99 (*0-8297-1872-9*) Vida Pubs.

— The Leap of Faith. LC 84-71457. 120p. 1984. mass mkt. 4.99 (*0-88270-574-1*) Bridge-Logos.

— Mi Companero el Espiritu Santo.Tr. of Holy Spirit, My Senior Partner. (SPA.). 168p. 1992. pap. 8.99 (*0-8297-0334-9*) Vida Pubs.

— Modelos para Orar.Tr. of Patterns of Prayer. (SPA.). 112p. 1995. pap. 5.99 (*0-8297-1859-1*) Vida Pubs.

— Mucho Mas Que Numeros. Bernal, Luis L., ed. Lievano, M. Francisco, tr.Tr. of More Than Numbers. (SPA.). 208p. 1985. pap. 6.99 (*0-8297-0531-7*) Vida Pubs.

— Orando Con Jesus.Tr. of Praying with Jesus. (POR.). 116p. 1991. pap. 5.95 (*0-8297-1662-9*) Vida Pubs.

— Soluciones Para los Problemas.Tr. of Solving Life's Problems. (SPA.). 160p. 1980. pap. 6.99 (*0-8297-0999-1*) Vida Pubs.

— Solving Life's Problems. LC 80-62782. 142p. (Orig.). 1980. pap. 7.99 (*0-88270-450-8*) Bridge-Logos.

— Suffering . . . Why Me? LC 86-70741. 105p. 1987. mass mkt. 4.99 (*0-88270-601-2*) Bridge-Logos.

— Sufrir, Por Que Yo?Tr. of Suffering, Why Me?. (SPA.). 120p. 1995. pap. 5.99 (*0-8297-2034-0*) Vida Pubs.

Cho, David Y., ed. Micromechanical Systems. (DSC Ser.: Vol. 40). 380p. 1992. 67.50 (*0-7918-1099-2*, G00743) ASME.

Cho, David Y. & Hostetler, Harold. Successful Home Cell Groups. LC 81-80025. 176p. 1981. pap. 10.99 (*0-88270-513-X*) Bridge-Logos.

Cho, David Y. & Manzano, R. Whitney. The Fourth Dimension Vol. II: More Secrets for a Successful Faith Life. LC 79-65588. 183p. 1983. pap. 8.99 (*0-88270-561-X*) Bridge-Logos.

— More Than Numbers. 172p. 1983. mass mkt. 5.99 (*1-85030-000-3*) Bridge-Logos.

Cho, David Yonggi. Prayer That Brings Revival: Interceding for God to Move in Your Family, Church & Community. LC 98-44139. 204p. 1998. pap. 12.99 (*0-88419-580-5*) Creation House.

***Cho, David Yonggi.** Secretos del Crecimiento de la Iglesia. (SPA.). 2000. pap. 8.99 (*0-88113-576-3*) Caribe Betania.

Cho, Dong-Sung, jt. auth. see Mathews, John A.

Cho, Emily & Fisher, Neila. Instant Style: 500 Professional Tips for Quick Changes in Fashion, Beauty, & Attitude. LC 95-46584. (Illus.). 160p. 1996. pap. 12.00 (*0-06-273399-0*) HarpC.

— Instant Style: 500 Professional Tips on Fashion, Beauty, & Attitude. (Illus.). 147p. 1998. pap. text 10.00 (*0-7881-5288-2*) DIANE Pub.

Cho, F. L., ed. Risk Assessment Technologies & Transporation, Storage & Disposal of Radioactive Materials Proceedings, Asme/Jsme Joint Pressure Vessels & Piping Conference (1998, San Diego, Ca) LC 98-73222. (PVP Ser.: 378). 197p. 1998. pap. 84.00 (*0-7918-1874-8*) ASME.

Cho, F. L., jt. ed. see Jones, E. D.

Cho, Gene J. Anthology & Handbook for Music Analysis. 176p. (C). 1992. pap. text, per. 26.95 (*0-8403-7327-9*) Kendall-Hunt.

— Melody Harmonization at the Keyboard. 2nd ed. 96p. 1996. spiral bd. 15.95 (*0-8403-7562-X*) Kendall-Hunt.

— Theories & Practice of Harmonic Analysis. LC 92-6539. 132p. 1992. pap. 19.95 (*0-7734-9917-2*) E Mellen.

***Cho, George.** Geographical Information Systems & the Law: Mapping the Legal Frontiers. LC 98-12084. 358p. 1998. 140.00 (*0-471-94857-8*) Wiley.

Cho, George. Trade, Aid & Global Interdependence. LC 94-44561. (Introductions to Development Ser.). (Illus.). 184p. (C). 1995. pap. 16.99 (*0-415-09159-4*) Routledge.

Cho, Hee I. The Complete Black Belt Hyung. 1990. pap. 15.95 (*0-86568-143-0*) Unique Pubns.

— Complete Martial Artist, 2 vols., Vol. 1. (Illus.). 1981. 27.95 (*0-86568-033-7*, 5111) Unique Pubns.

— Complete Tae Kwon Do Hyung, 2 vols., Vol. 2. (Illus.). 205p. (Orig.). 1984. pap. 13.95 (*0-86568-055-8*, 531) Unique Pubns.

— Complete Tae Kwon Do Hyung, Vol. 3. (Orig.). 1984. pap. 13.95 (*0-86568-056-6*, 532) Unique Pubns.

— Complete Tae Kwon Do Hyung Vol. 1, Vol. 1. 1984. pap. 13.95 (*0-86568-054-X*, 530) Unique Pubns.

— Man of Contrasts. (Illus.). 224p. (Orig.). 1977. pap. 16.95 (*0-86568-039-6*, 508) Unique Pubns.

Cho, J. D. & Franzon, P. D. High Performance Design Automation for Multi-Chip Modules. LC 96-195850. (Selected Topics in Electronics & Systems Ser.: Vol. 5). 250p. 1996. text 64.00 (*981-02-2307-2*) World Scientific Pub.

Cho, John. Spam-Ku: Tranquil Reflections on Luncheon Loaf. LC 98-29749. (Illus.). 96p. 1998. pap. 7.95 (*0-06-095278-4*, Perennial) HarperTrade.

***Cho, Jun-Ku.** Infinitivkonstruktionen im Deutschen: Sprachsystem und Sprachentwicklung Seit Dem 18, Jahrhundert. (Europaische Hochschulschriften Ser.). 200p. 1999. 35.95 (*3-631-34993-9*) P Lang Pubng.

Cho, K., ed. Excitons. (Topics in Current Physics Ser.: Vol. 14). (Illus.). 1979. 49.95 (*0-387-09567-5*) Spr-Verlag.

Cho, Kang R. Multinational Banks: Their Identities & Determinants. LC 85-1123. (Research in Business Economics & Public Policy Ser.: No. 8). (Illus.). 190p. reprint ed. pap. 58.90 (*0-8357-1668-6*, 207036900088) Bks Demand.

Cho, Kwang S. Emblems in Shakespeare's Last Plays. LC 97-39862. 180p. (C). 1997. text 37.00 (*0-7618-0932-5*) U Pr of Amer.

***Cho, Kyu-Hong.** Zeit Als Abbild der Ewigkeit: Historische und Systematische Erlauterungen Zu Plotins Enneade III 7. 324p. 1999. 51.95 (*3-631-34691-3*) P Lang Pubng.

Cho, Lee-Jay, et al, eds. Economic Development in the Republic of Korea: A Policy Perspective. 700p. 1991. text 52.00 (*0-86638-131-7*) EW Ctr HI.

Cho, Lee-Jay & Hearn, Robert L., eds. Censuses of Asia & the Pacific: 1980 Round. LC 84-28662. xxiv, 380p. 1985. 8.00 (*0-86638-052-3*) EW Ctr HI.

Cho, Lee-Jay & Kim, Yoon H., eds. Economic Development in the Republic of Korea: A Policy Perspective. 750p. (C). 1990. pap. text. write for info. (*0-8133-7773-0*) Westview.

Cho, Lee-Jay & Yada, Moto, eds. Tradition & Change in the Asian Family. 664p. (C). 1994. text 48.00 (*0-86638-161-9*) EW Ctr HI.

— Tradition & Change in the Asian Family. 664p. (C). 1995. pap. text 34.95 (*0-86638-174-0*) EW Ctr HI.

Cho, Lee-Jay, et al. The Own-Children Method of Fertility Estimation. 188p. 1986. text 25.00 (*0-86638-082-5*) EW Ctr HI.

Cho, Litt D. Myong-Won, see Myong-Won Cho, Litt D.

Cho, Oh-Kon. Traditional Korean Theatre. LC 87-71272. (Studies in Korean Religions & Culture: Vol. 2). (Illus.). 364p. 1988. reprint ed. pap. 112.90 (*0-608-01783-3*, 206244100003) Bks Demand.

Cho, P. & Quintere, J. G., eds. Heat & Mass Transfer in Fire & Combustion Systems - 1992. (HTD Ser.: Vol. 223). 144p. 1992. 45.00 (*0-7918-1068-2*, G00712) ASME.

Cho, Paul Y. Orando con Cristo.Tr. of Praying with Jesus. (SPA.). 176p. 1990. pap. 6.99 (*0-8297-0389-6*) Vida Pubs.

Cho, Paul Y. & Manzano, R. Whitney. La Oracion - Clave del Avivamiento. Araujo, Juan S., tr. from ENG.Tr. of Prayer - Key to Revival. (SPA.). 128p. 1987. pap. 8.99 (*0-88113-241-1*) Caribe Betania.

***Cho, Robert W., et al, eds.** Orchestral Music in Print: 1999 Supplement. (Music in Print Ser.: Vol. 5u). 272p. 2000. lib. bdg. 95.00 (*0-88478-051-1*) Musicdata.

Cho, Robert W., et al, eds. Organ Music in Print: 1997 Supplement. LC 83-26956. (Music-in-Print Ser.: Vol. 3t). 228p. 1997. lib. bdg. 95.00 (*0-88478-043-0*) Musicdata.

— Secular Choral Music in Print: 1996 Supplement. LC 87-24749. (Music-in-Print Ser.: Vol. 2u). 165p. 1996. lib. bdg. 95.00 (*0-88478-041-4*) Musicdata.

***Cho, Robert W., et al, eds.** String Music in Print: 1998 Supplement. (Music in Print Ser.: Vol. 6t). 273p. 1998. lib. bdg. 95.00 (*0-88478-047-3*) Musicdata.

Cho, S. K. Electromagnetic Scattering. (Illus.). xvii, 389p. 1990. 98.95 (*0-387-97380-X*) Spr-Verlag.

Cho, S. M., jt. ed. see Hassan, Y. A.

Cho, Shinta. The Gas We Pass: The Story of Farts. Stinchecum, Amanda M., tr. from JPN. LC 94-14267. (Illus.). 32p. (J). (ps-k). 1994. 11.95 (*0-916291-52-9*) Kane-Miller Bk.

Cho, Sihak H. Tae Kwon Do: Secrets of Korean Karate. (Illus.). 256p. 1992. pap. 21.95 (*0-8048-1704-9*) Tuttle Pubng.

Cho, Soon Sung. The Dynamics of Korean Economic Development. LC 93-42822. 216p. 1994. pap. 25.00 (*0-88132-162-1*) Inst Intl Eco.

Cho, Sung-Woon. The Dynamics of Institutional Reform in Telecommunications: Globalization, Liberalization & Regulatory Change. rev. ed. LC 98-34176. (Studies on Industrial Productivity). (Illus.). 230p. 1998. 60.00 (*0-8153-3202-5*) Garland.

***Cho, Sungsoo & Prosky, Leon, eds.** Complex Carbohydrates in Foods. LC 98-55664. (Food Science & Technology Ser.). (Illus.). 700p. 1999. text 195.00 (*0-8247-0187-9*) Dekker.

Cho, Ta-Hung & Chang, Edward C. Knocking at the Gate of Life & Other Healing Exercises from China: The Official Handbook of the People's Republic of China. LC 97-66915. (CHI.). xvii, 202p. 1997. write for info. (*1-57087-331-3*) Prof Pr NC.

Cho, W. D. & Sohn, H. Y., eds. Value-Addition Metallurgy: Proceedings, International Symposium on Value-Addition Metallurgy, San Antonio, Texas, 1998. LC 97-75970. (Illus.). 362p. 1998. 174.00 (*0-87339-399-6*, TN609) Minerals Metals.

Cho, Y. M. Current Topics in Theoretical Physics: Proceedings of the First Pacific Winter School for Theoretical Physics. 320p. 1995. text 99.00 (*981-02-2042-1*) World Scientific Pub.

— Group Theoretical Methods in Physics: Proceedings of the 14th International Colloquium. 720p. 1986. text 159.00 (*9971-5-0060-4*) World Scientific Pub.

— Lectures on Mathematical Physics: Proceedings of the 1st Winter School on Mathematical Physics. 236p. 1989. text 74.00 (*981-02-0065-X*) World Scientific Pub.

— Physics in 2 Plus 1 Dimension: Proceedings of the Second Winter School on Mathematical Physics. 368p. 1992. text 105.00 (*981-02-1111-2*) World Scientific Pub.

Cho, Y. M., et al, eds. Current Topics in Physics: Proceedings of the Inauguration Conference of the Asia-Pacific Center for Theoretical Physics Seoul National University, Korea 4-10 June, 1996. 1000p. 1997. 118.00 (*981-02-3288-8*) World Scientific Pub.

***Cho, Yeol Je.** Differential Equations & Applications. 264p. 2000. lib. bdg. 89.00 (*1-56072-767-5*) Nova Sci Pubs.

— Fixed Point Theory & Applications. 260p. 2000. lib. bdg. 89.00 (*1-56072-766-7*) Nova Sci Pubs.

— Stochastic Analysis Applications. 125p. 2000. lib. bdg. 69.00 (*1-56072-768-3*) Nova Sci Pubs.

Cho, Yong-Doo. Financial Factors & Corporate Investment. 224p. 1996. 72.95 (*1-85972-366-7*, Pub. by Avebry) Ashgate Pub Co.

Cho, Yonggi. Apocalipsis: Visiones de Nuestra Victoria Final.Tr. of Revelation: A Vision. (SPA.). pap. 8.99 (*1-56063-530-4*, 550107) Editorial Unilit.

Cho, Yoon-Je & Kim, Joon-Kyung. Credit Policies & the Industrialization of Korea. LC 95-2870. (Discussion Paper Ser.: Vol. 286). 106p. 1995. pap. 22.00 (*0-8213-3246-5*, 13246) World Bank.

Cho, Young I. Advances in Heat Transfer: Bioengineering Heat Transfer, Vol. 22. (Illus.). 443p. 1992. text 152.00 (*0-12-020022-8*) Acad Pr.

***Cho, Young-mee.** Integrated Korean: Beginning 1. LC 00-39298. (Klear Textbooks in Language). 2000. pap. write for info. (*0-8248-2342-7*) UH Pr.

— Integrated Korean: Beginning 2. LC 00-33782. (Klear Textbooks in Korean Language). (Illus.). 2000. write for info. (*0-8248-2343-5*) UH Pr.

Cho-yun Hsu. Ancient China in Transition: An Analysis of Social Mobility, 722-222 B. C. LC 65-13110. (Illus.). viii, 240p. 1965. 37.50 (*0-8047-0223-3*); pap. 12.95 (*0-8047-0224-1*) Stanford U Pr.

Cho, Z. H., et al. Foundations of Medical Imaging. LC 92-26906. 600p. 1993. 120.00 (*0-471-54573-2*) Wiley.

Choa, G. H. The Life & Time of Sir Kai Ho Kai. rev. ed. (Illus.). 320p. (C). text 20.00 (*962-201-873-4*, Pub. by Chinese Univ) U of Mich Pr.

Choat, Kay. For the Love of Baja: Seafood Cookbook. (Illus.). 165p. 1993. pap., spiral bd. 14.95 (*0-9643442-0-3*) For the Love of Baja.

Choate, Albert G. The Core of Creation: An Investigation into the Fundamentals of Reality & the Foundation of Existence. LC 82-80727. (Illus.). 128p. 1982. pap. 7.50 (*0-943108-00-4*) Syzygy.

— Fundamental Geometrical Formulations of the Universe. (Illus.). 27p. (C). 1989. pap. text 10.00 (*0-943108-01-2*) Syzygy.

Choate, Alec & Main, Barbara Y., eds. Summerland: A Western Australian Sesquicentenary Anthology of Poetry & Prose. 242p. 4.95 (*0-85564-166-5*, Pub. by Univ of West Aust Pr) Intl Spec Bk.

Choate, Betty B. Love Poems. (Illus.). 78p. 1986. 6.95 (*0-9616352-0-7*) B B Choate.

Choate, C., jt. auth. see Liston, B.

***Choate, Chilco.** Born for the Wild Country: Big Feet & a Mouth to Match. (Illus.). 192p. 1998. pap. 17.95 (*1-895811-59-7*) Heritage Hse.

Choate, Curt. Harley-Davidson Sportsers Owners Workshop Manual. (Illus.). 1997. 23.95 (*1-56392-344-0*) Haynes Manuals.

Choate, Curt. Haynes Small Engine Repair Owners Workshop Manual. (Illus.). 1990. pap. 17.95 (*1-85010-666-5*) Haynes Manuals.

Choate, Curt & Haynes, J. H. Haynes Yamaha XZ 550 Vision V-Twins Owner Workbook Manual, No. M821: 1982. pap. 16.95 (*1-85010-761-0*) Haynes Manuals.

Choate, Curt, et al. Harley-Davidson Glides: Owner's Workshop Manual. 2nd ed. LC 89-82762. (Illus.). 216p. 1991. pap. 16.95 (*1-56392-000-X*) Haynes Manuals.

Choate, Curt, jt. auth. see Haynes, J. H.

Choate, Curt, jt. auth. see Meek, Martyn.

Choate, Ernest. The Dictionary of American Bird Names. rev. ed. LC 84-28975. 226p. 1985. pap. 10.95 (*0-87645-117-2*) Harvard Common Pr.

Choate, Ernest & Griffin, Harry. Using Television in the Primary School. LC 89-34491. 114p. reprint ed. pap. 35.40 (*0-608-20327-0*, 207158000002) Bks Demand.

Choate, Frederick S., ed. & tr. see Voronsky, Aleksandr K.

Choate, Frederick S., tr. see Joffe, Nadezhda A.

Choate, Frederick S., tr. see Rogovin, Vadim Z.

Choate, George F. Treatise on the Law of Highways. 3rd ed. Helmholz, R. H. & Reams, Bernard D., Jr., eds. LC 86-62941. (Historical Writings in Law & Jurisprudence Ser.: No. 9). xl, 625p. 1986. reprint ed. lib. bdg. 55.00 (*0-89941-524-5*, 304600) W S Hein.

Choate, Glenda J. Gold Rush Cemetery. (Illus.). (Orig.). 1989. pap. 5.00 (*0-945284-01-2*) Lynn Canal Pub.

Choate, J. E. Roll Jordan Roll: A Biography of Marshall Keeble. 2nd rev. ed. (Classics Ser.). 143p. 1998. reprint ed. pap. 9.99 (*0-89225-377-0*, G53770) Gospel Advocate.

Choate, Jane M. Cheyenne's Rainbow Warrior. LC 98-96227. 192p. 1998. 18.95 (*0-8034-9305-3*, Avalon Bks) Bouregy.

— Convincing David. LC 97-93729. 192p. 1997. 18.95 (*0-8034-9247-2*, Avalon Bks) Bouregy.

***Choate, Jane M.** Desert Paintbox. LC 99-94440. 192p. 1999. 18.95 (*0-8034-9363-0*, Avalon Bks) Bouregy.

An Asterisk (*) at the beginning of an entry indicates that the title is appearing for the first time.

Choate, Jane M. Design to Deceive. large type ed. LC 93-42209. 1994. lib. bdg. 13.95 (*0-7862-0138-X*) Thorndike Pr.

— Heartsong Lullaby. LC 97-94016. 192p. 1997. 18.95 (*0-8034-9254-5*, Avalon Bks) Bouregy.

— A Match Made in Heaven. LC 96-95282. 192p. 1997. 18.95 (*0-8034-9192-1*, Avalon Bks) Bouregy.

— Mile-High Love. LC 98-96071. 192p. 1998. 18.95 (*0-8034-9297-9*) Bouregy.

— Never Too Late for Christmas. LC 97-94271. 192p. 1997. 18.95 (*0-8034-9265-0*, Avalon Bks) Bouregy.

— Sweet Lies & Rainbow Skies. large type ed. LC 95-9787. (Nightingale Ser.). 192p. 1995. reprint ed. pap. 17.95 (*0-7838-1290-6*, G K Hall Lrg Type) Mac Lib Ref.

— Think of Me. LC 97-93468. 192p. 1997. lib. bdg. 18.95 (*0-8034-9237-5*, Avalon Bks) Bouregy.

Choate, Jerry R. Systematics & Zoogeography of Middle American Shrews of the Genus Cryptotis. (Museum Ser.: Vol. 19, No. 3). 123p. 1970. 6.25 (*0-317-04961-5*) U KS Nat Hist Mus.

Choate, Jerry R., et al. Handbook of Mammals of the South-Central States. LC 94-7369. (Illus.). 336p. 1994. text 45.00 (*0-8071-1819-2*) La State U Pr.

Choate, Jerry R., jt. auth. see Genoways, Hugh H.

Choate, Joseph H. American Addresses. LC 76-93328. (Essay Index Reprint Ser.). 1977. 26.95 (*0-8369-1400-7*) Ayer.

***Choate, Joyce S.** Successful Inclusive Teaching: Proven Ways to Detect & Correct Special Needs. 3rd ed. LC 99-40231. 478p. 1999. pap. 53.00 (*0-205-30621-7*) P-H.

Choate, Joyce S. & Rakes, Thomas A. Inclusive Instruction for Struggling Readers. (Fastback Ser.: No. 434). 61p. 1998. pap. 3.00 (*0-87367-634-3*, FB434) Phi Delta Kappa.

Choate, Joyce S., et al. Curriculum-Based Assessment & Programming. 3rd ed. LC 94-28845. 480p. 1994. 81.00 (*0-205-16174-X*) Allyn.

Choate, Joyce S., et al. Curriculum-Based Assessment & Programming. 3rd ed. (C). 1994. pap. write for info. (*0-205-16697-0*, H6697-0) Allyn.

Choate, Judith. Cooking with Yogurt: The Complete Cookbook for Indulging with the World's Healthiest Food. LC 93-33785. 224p. 1993. pap. 11.00 (*0-87113-566-3*, Atlntc Mnthly) Grove-Atltic.

— The Great American Pie Book: Recipes for the Sweet & the Savory, from Chicken Pot Pie to Peach Blueberry. (American Kitchen Classics Ser.). (Illus.). 128p. 1992. 20.00 (*0-671-73550-0*) S&S Trade.

— The Great Pie Book. 128p. 1992. 15.00 (*0-385-25308-7*) Doubleday.

— Hot Cookbook. 128p. 1992. 15.00 (*0-385-25350-8*) Doubleday.

— Meat & Potatoes. 128p. 1992. 15.00 (*0-385-25306-0*) Doubleday.

— Meat & Potatoes: Home-Cooked Favorites from Perfect Pot Roast to Chocolate Cream Pie. (American Kitchen Classics Ser.). (Illus.). 128p. 1992. 20.00 (*0-671-73548-9*) S&S Trade.

— Rediscovered Bean. write for info. (*1-85391-217-4*) Sterling.

Choate, Judith & Green, Jane. The Gift Giver's Cookbook: Delicious Foods to Make & Give. LC 94-7350. (Illus.). 144p. 1994. 11.95 (*1-56799-099-1*, Friedman-Fairfax) M Friedman Pub Grp Inc.

Choate, Judith, jt. auth. see Bergman, Abraham.

Choate, Judith, jt. auth. see Jallepalli, Raji.

Choate, Judith, jt. auth. see Palmer, Charlie.

Choate, Julian E., Jr., jt. auth. see Frantz, Joe B.

Choate, Larry L. The Mammals of the Llano Estacado. (Special Publications). (Illus.). 240p. Date not set. pap. text 19.95 (*0-9640188-6-1*) Mus TX Tech.

Choate, Laura, jt. auth. see Childs, Leigh.

Choate, Laura D. Pictograms: Graphing Pictures for a Reusable Classroom Grid. 56p. 1997. pap. text 9.95 (*0-86651-487-2*) Seymour Pubns.

Choate, Lisa A., ed. see American Councils for International Education Staff.

***Choate, Natalie B.** Life & Death Planning for Retirement Benefits: The Essential Handbook for Estate Planners. 3rd rev. ed. 572p. 1999. pap. 89.95 (*0-9649440-3-0*, Pub. by Ataxplan) BookMasters.

Choate, Pat. Hot Property. 1999. write for info. (*0-375-40212-8*) Knopf.

Choate, Pat & Walter, Susan M. Thinking Strategically: A Primer for Public Leaders. LC 84-15544. 103p. 1984. 14.95 (*0-934842-19-1*) CSPA.

Choate, R., ed. A Guide to Sources of Information on the Arts in Australia. (Guides to Australian Information Sources Ser.). 120p. 1984. pap. 14.00 (*0-08-029835-4*, Pergamon Pr) Elsevier.

Choate, Richard B. Turf Irrigation Manual: The Complete Guide to Turf & Landscape Irrigation Systems. rev. ed. LC 93-50092. Orig. Title: Turf Irrigation Manual. 1994. 49.95 (*0-9635096-0-8*) Telsco Indust.

Choate, Robert A., ed. see Tanglewood Symposium Staff.

Choate, Rufus. Works of Rufus Choate, 2 vols., Set. Brown, Samuel G., ed. LC 72-70. reprint ed. 157.50 (*0-404-01526-3*) AMS Pr.

Choate, Scott. Your Guide to Corporate Survival. Carle, Cliff, ed. (Illus.). 192p. (Orig.). 1990. pap. 4.95 (*0-918259-20-7*) CCC Pubns.

***Choay, Francoise.** The Invention of the Historic Monument. O'Connell, Lauren M., tr. (Illus.). 304p. (C). 2000. text Price not set. (*0-521-45474-3*) Cambridge U Pr.

Choay, Francoise. Modern City: Planning in the Nineteenth Century. LC 77-90408. (Planning & Cities Ser.). (Illus.). 1969. pap. 9.95 (*0-8076-0520-4*) Braziller.

— The Rule & the Model: On the Theory of Architecture & Urbanism. LC 95-38793. (Illus.). 400p. (C). 1997. 49.50 (*0-262-03226-0*) MIT Pr.

Choay, Francoise, jt. auth. see Merlin, Pierre.

Chobanian, Sarkis J., jt. auth. see Overholt, Bergein F.

Chobanian, Sarkis J., jt. ed. see Van Ness, Michael M.

Chobor, K. L., jt. ed. see Serby, M. J.

Chobotor, Vladimir A., ed. Orbital Mechanics. 2nd rev. ed. 375p. 1996. 89.95 (*1-56347-179-5*) AIAA.

Chobotov, Vladimir A. Orbital Mechanics. (Educ Ser.). 375p. 1991. 89.95 (*1-56347-007-1*, 07-1) AIAA.

— Spacecraft Attitude Dynamics & Control. (Orbit Ser.). 150p. 1991. 79.50 (*0-89464-031-3*) Krieger.

Choca. Pharmacology. 1996. write for info. (*0-7216-4579-8*, W B Saunders Co) Harcrt Hlth Sci Grp.

Choca, James P. & Van Denburg, Eric J. Interpretive Guide to the Millon Clinical Multiaxial Inventory. 2nd ed. LC 96-28271. 355p. 1996. text 49.95 (*1-55798-383-6*) Am Psychol.

— Manual for Clinical Psychology Trainees, No. 10. 3rd ed. LC 96-8894. (Basic Principles into Practice Ser.: Vol. 10). 256p. 1996. pap. text 27.95 (*0-87630-814-0*) Brunner-Mazel.

Chocano, Jose S. Spirit of the Andes. Underwood, Edna W., tr. 1977. lib. bdg. 59.95 (*0-8490-2660-1*) Gordon Pr.

Chocat, B., jt. ed. see Brelot, E.

Chochem, Corinne. Palestine Dances! Folk Dances of Palestine: Music Book Index. 63p. 1993. reprint ed. lib. bdg. 69.00 (*0-7812-9676-5*) Rprt Serv.

Chocheyras, Jacques, ed. De l'Aventure Epique a l'Aventure Romanesque: Hommage a Andre de Mandach. (FRE., Illus.). 307p. 1997. 47.95 (*3-906758-01-X*, Pub. by P Lang) P Lang Pubng.

Chochezi, V. S. & Staajabu. Bamm! 40p. 1993. pap. 5.00 (*0-9642340-1-7*) Straight Out.

— Crucial Comments & Vicious Verses. 22p. 1991. pap. 10.00 (*0-9642340-2-5*) Straight Out.

— This Queendom Come. 77p. 1994. pap. 7.00 (*0-9642340-0-9*) Straight Out.

Chochezi, V. S., jt. auth. see Staajabu.

Chochinov, Harvey M. & Breitbart, William, eds. Handbook of Psychiatry in Pallative Medicine. LC 99-11188. (Illus.). 432p. 2000. text 75.00 (*0-19-509299-6*) OUP.

Chochola, Frantisek. The Forest. (Illus.). (J). (ps). 1988. bds. 5.50 (*0-86315-073-X*, 20234, Pub. by Floris Bks) Gryphon Hse.

— On the Farm. (J). (ps). 1988. bds. 5.50 (*0-86315-051-9*, 20235, Pub. by Floris Bks) Gryphon Hse.

Chociolko, Christina, jt. auth. see Leiss, William.

Chock, Eric. Last Days Here. (Bamboo Ridge Ser.: Nos. 45-46). 88p. 1989. pap. 8.00 (*0-910043-18-3*) Bamboo Ridge Pr.

Chock, Eric, ed. Small Kid Time Hawaii. (Bamboo Ridge Ser.: No. 12). 204p. (J). (gr. k-12). 1981. pap. 8.00 (*0-910043-03-5*) Bamboo Ridge Pr.

— Talk Story: An Anthology of Hawaii's Local Writers. 1978. pap. 3.95 (*0-932136-03-6*) Petronium HI.

Chock, Eric, et al, eds. Growing up Local: An Anthology of Poetry & Prose from Hawaii. (Bamboo Ridge Ser.: Issue 72). (Illus.). 382p. 1998. text 22.00 (*0-910043-55-8*) Bamboo Ridge Pr.

— Growing up Local: An Anthology of Poetry & Prose from Hawaii. (Bamboo Ridge Ser.: Vol. 72). (Illus.). 382p. 1998. pap. 15.00 (*0-910043-53-1*) Bamboo Ridge Pr.

***Chock, Eric & Lum, Darrell, eds.** The Best of Honolulu Fiction. 352p. 1999. pap. 15.00 (*0-910043-57-4*, Pub. by Bamboo Ridge Pr) SPD-Small Pr Dist.

Chock, Eric & Lum, Darrell H., eds. Bamboo Ridge Issue 73: A Hawaii Writer's Journal. 488p. 1998. pap. 10.00 (*0-910043-56-6*) Bamboo Ridge Pr.

— Bamboo Ridge No. 69: A Hawaii Writer's Journal, Issue 69. 344p. 1996. pap. 8.00 (*0-910043-48-5*) Bamboo Ridge Pr.

***Chock, Eric & Lum, Darrell H. Y., eds.** Bamboo Ridge: Journal of Hawaii Literature & Arts, No. 75. 248p. 1999. pap. 10.00 (*0-910043-58-2*) Bamboo Ridge Pr.

Chock, Eric & Lum, Darrell H. Y., eds. The Best of Bamboo Ridge. LC 83-73232. (Bamboo Ridge Ser.: Nos. 31-32). 325p. 1986. pap. 10.00 (*0-910043-07-8*) Bamboo Ridge Pr.

Chock, Gary, et al. First Hawaiian Center Honolulu. (Design Decisions, Methods, & Procedures Ser.: Vol. 3). (Illus.). 43p. 1997. pap. 15.00 (*0-943198-59-3*, DS-3) Earthquake Eng.

Chock, P. Boon, jt. ed. see Stadtman, Earl R.

Choco, Ronalyn. My Gift to You. LC 88-71341. (Illus.). 80p. 1988. 7.95 (*0-939596-02-4*) Country Rd.

Chocolate, Debbi. Elizabeth's Wish. (NEATE Ser.: Bk. 2). (Illus.). 96p. (YA). (gr. 5 up). 1994. pap. 3.95 (*0-940975-45-9*) Just Us Bks.

— Kente Colors. LC 95-23505. (Illus.). 32p. (J). (ps-4). 1997. lib. bdg. 16.85 (*0-8027-8389-9*) Walker & Co.

— Kente Colors. LC 95-23505. (Illus.). 32p. (J). (ps-4). 1997. pap. 6.95 (*0-8027-7528-4*) Walker & Co.

— Kente Colors. LC 95-23505. (Illus.). 32p. (J). (ps-4). 1997. reprint ed. 15.95 (*0-8027-8388-0*) Walker & Co.

— On the Day I Was Born. LC 94-40994. (Illus.). 32p. (J). (gr. k-4). 1995. 12.95 (*0-590-47609-2*, Cartwheel) Scholastic Inc.

— The Piano Man. LC 97-22668. (Illus.). 32p. (J). (gr. k-3). 1998. 15.95 (*0-8027-8646-4*); lib. bdg. 16.85 (*0-8027-8647-2*) Walker & Co.

***Chocolate, Debbi.** Piano Man. 32p. (J). (gr. k-3). 2000. pap. 7.95 (*0-8027-7578-0*) Walker & Co.

Chocolate, Debbi & Hudson, Wade. Neate To the Rescue! LC 92-72004. (NEATE Ser.). (Illus.). 112p. (Orig.). (YA). (gr. 5 up). 1992. pap. 3.95 (*0-940975-42-4*) Just Us Bks.

Chocolate, Deborah M. Spider & the Sky God: An Akan Legend. LC 92-13277. (Legends of the World Ser.). (Illus.). 32p. (J). (gr. 2-5). 1997. pap. 4.95 (*0-8167-2812-7*) Troll Communs.

— Spider & the Sky God: An Akan Legend. LC 92-13277. (Legends of the World Ser.). (Illus.). 32p. (J). (gr. 2-5). 1997. lib. bdg. 18.60 (*0-8167-2811-9*) Troll Communs.

— Talk, Talk: An Ashanti Legend. LC 92-13278. (Legends of the World Ser.). (Illus.). 32p. (J). (gr. 2-5). 1997. lib. bdg. 18.60 (*0-8167-2817-8*) Troll Communs.

— Talk, Talk: An Ashanti Legend. LC 92-13278. (Legends of the World Ser.). (Illus.). 32p. (J). (gr. 2-5). 1998. pap. 4.95 (*0-8167-2818-6*) Troll Communs.

Chocolate, Deborah M. Newton. Imani in the Belly. LC 93-33803. (Illus.). 32p. (J). (gr. k-4). 1997. 14.95 (*0-8167-3466-6*) BrdgeWater.

— Imani in the Belly. LC 93-33803. (Illus.). 32p. (J). (gr. k-4). 1996. pap. 4.95 (*0-8167-3467-4*, Troll Medallion) Troll Communs.

— Imani in the Belly. LC 93-33803. 1994. 10.15 (*0-606-09459-8*, Pub. by Turtleback) Demco.

— My First Kwanzaa Book. LC 92-1200. (Illus.). 32p. (J). (ps-2). 1992. 10.95 (*0-590-45762-4*, Cartwheel) Scholastic Inc.

***Chocolate, Deborah M. Newton.** My First Kwanzaa Book. (Illus.). 32p. (J). (ps-2). 1999. mass mkt. 5.99 (*0-439-12926-5*) Scholastic Inc.

Chocolate, Deborah N. Kwanzaa. LC 89-25418. (Special Holiday Bks.). (Illus.). 32p. (J). (ps-3). 1990. pap. 4.95 (*0-516-43991-X*) Childrens.

— A Very Special Kwanzaa. LC 49-122830. (J). (gr. 5-7). 1996. pap. 2.99 (*0-590-84862-3*) Scholastic Inc.

— A Very Special Kwanzaa. 1996. 9.34 (*0-606-10353-8*) Turtleback.

Chocron, Daya S. Healing the Heart: Opening & Healing the Heart with Crystals & Gemstones. LC 88-33755. 136p. 1989. pap. 8.95 (*0-87728-694-9*) Weiser.

— Healing with Crystals & Gemstones. LC 86-4072. (Illus.). 144p. 1986. pap. 12.95 (*0-87728-646-9*) Weiser.

Chocron, Isaac E. Three Plays by Isaac Chocron. Younoszai, Barbara & Irausquin-Johnson, Rossi, trs. LC 94-17357. (Taft Memorial Fund & University of Cincinnati Studies in Latin American, Chicano, & U. S. Latino Theatre: Vol. 4). XIII, 234p. (C). 1995. 39.95 (*0-8204-2320-3*) P Lang Pubng.

***Chodak, Eric & Seltzer, Barry.** It Takes 2 Judges to Try a Cow & Other Strange Legal Twists. 173p. 2000. pap. 12.00 (*1-895856-01-9*) Pism Publg Inc.

Chodak, Szymon. The New State: Etatization of Western Societies. LC 88-18552. 355p. 1989. lib. bdg. 55.00 (*1-55587-107-0*) L Rienner.

Chodakowska, Elizbieta, tr. see Pomorski, Stanislaw.

***Chodakowski, Ann F. & Wood, Susan.** 101 Ways to Stretch Your Dollars. gif. ed. (Illus.). 64p. 2000. pap. 6.99 (*0-7369-0285-6*) Harvest Hse.

Chodat, R. & Fischer, W. La Vegetation du Paraguay: Resultats Scientifiques d'une Mission Botanique au Paraguay. 1977. reprint ed. 96.00 (*3-7682-1106-1*) Lubrecht & Cramer.

Chodera, J. Practical German-Polish Dictionary: Podreczny Slownik Niemiecko-Polski. (GER & POL.). 1023p. 1984. 39.95 (*0-8288-0482-6*, F33230) Fr & Eur.

— A Practical Polish-German Dictionary: Podreczny Slownik Polsko-Niemiecki. (GER & POL.). 1018p. 1984. 39.95 (*0-8288-0483-4*, F46690) Fr & Eur.

Chodes, John. The Story of Ted Corbitt. 1974. 12.95 (*5-415-28717-5*); pap. text 12.95 (*0-915297-17-5*) Cedarwinds.

Chodkiewicz, K. & Abel, R. Christopher. Nostradamus' Oracles. Abel, R. C., ed. (Illus.). (Orig.). 1999. pap. 7.95 (*1-55818-384-1*, Sure Fire) Holmes Pub.

Chodkiewicz, Michel. An Ocean Without Shore: Ibn Arabi, the Book, & the Law. LC 92-38413. 184p. (C). 1993. text 21.50 (*0-7914-1625-9*) State U NY Pr.

— An Ocean Without Shore: Ibn Arabi, the Quran, & the Shariah. 250p. 1996. pap. 19.95 (*0-614-21324-X*, 915) Kazi Pubns.

— The Seal of the Saints. 192p. 1996. pap. 17.95 (*0-614-21340-1*, 192) Kazi Pubns.

— The Seal of the Saints: Prophethood & Sainthood in the Doctrine of Ibn'Arabi. Sherrard, Liadain, tr. from FRE. (Golden Palm Ser.). 138p. 1995. 44.95 (*0-946621-39-X*, Pub. by Islamic Texts); pap. 21.95 (*0-946621-40-3*, Pub. by Islamic Texts) Intl Spec Bk.

— The Spiritual Writings of Amir 'Abd al-Kader. Chrestensen, James & Manning, Tom, trs. LC 94-28385. (SUNY Series in Western Esoteric Traditions). 233p. (C). 1995. text 49.50 (*0-7914-2445-6*); pap. text 16.95 (*0-7914-2446-4*) State U NY Pr.

Chodkiewicz, Michel, tr. Spiritual Writings of Amir Abd Al-Kader. 233p. 1996. pap. 16.95 (*0-614-21349-5*, 1485) Kazi Pubns.

Chodog, Tiley. Tibet: The Land & the People. Tailing, W., tr. (Illus.). 354p. 1989. pap. 9.95 (*7-80005-072-6*, Pub. by New World Pr) China Bks.

Chodoro. Mainstream Civilization to 1500. 6th ed. (C). 1994. pap. text 15.95 (*0-15-501198-7*) Harcourt Coll Pubs.

Chodorov, Edward. The Spa. 1951. pap. 5.25 (*0-8222-1063-0*) Dramatists Play.

Chodorov, Frank. Fugitive Essays: Selected Writings of Frank Chodorov. Hamilton, Charles H., ed. LC 79-28720. 430p. 1980. 14.00 (*0-913966-72-X*); pap. 6.00 (*0-913966-73-8*) Liberty Fund.

— Income Tax: The Root of All Evil. rev. ed. 1959. 12.95 (*0-8159-5809-9*) Devin.

— Out of Step: An Autobiography. 1962. 6.95 (*0-8159-6408-0*) Devin.

Chodorov, Jerome & Fields, Joseph. Anniversary Waltz. 1957. pap. 5.25 (*0-8222-0050-3*) Dramatists Play.

— Junior Miss. 1943. pap. 3.25 (*0-8222-0603-X*) Dramatists Play.

— My Sister Eileen. 1946. pap. 5.25 (*0-8222-0801-6*) Dramatists Play.

Chodorov, Jerome, jt. auth. see Fields, Joseph.

Chodorow, Joan. Dance Therapy & Depth Psychology: The Moving Imagination. (Illus.). 176p. (C). 1991. pap. 25.99 (*0-415-04113-9*, A5111) Routledge.

Chodorow, Joan, ed. see Stewart, Louis.

Chodorow, Joan, ed. & intro. see Jung, C. G.

Chodorow, Nancy Julia. Femininities, Masculinities, Sexualities: Freud & Beyond. 144p. 1994. pap. 12.50 (*0-8131-0828-4*) U Pr of Ky.

— Femininities, Masculinities, Sexualities: Freud & Beyond. LC 93-39481. (Blazer Lectures: Vol. 1990). 144p. 1994. 25.00 (*0-8131-1872-7*) U Pr of Ky.

— Feminism & Psychoanalytic Theory. 296p. (C). 1991. reprint ed. pap. 18.00 (*0-300-05116-6*) Yale U Pr.

***Chodorow, Nancy Julia.** The Power of Feelings: Personal Meaning in Psychoanalysis, Gender & Culture. (Illus.). 320p. 1999. 27.50 (*0-300-07959-1*) Yale U Pr.

Chodorow, Nancy Julia. The Reproduction of Mothering: Psychoanalysis & the Sociology of Gender. 263p. 1978. pap. 17.95 (*0-520-03892-4*, Pub. by U CA Pr) Cal Prin Full Svc.

— The Reproduction of Mothering: Psychoanalysis & the Sociology of Gender. 276p. 1999. pap. 17.95 (*0-520-22155-9*, Pub. by U CA Pr) Cal Prin Full Svc.

Chodorow, Stanley, et al. The Mainstream of Civilization, 4 vols. 5th ed. (C). 1989. trans. write for info. (*0-318-65020-7*) Harcourt Coll Pubs.

— The Mainstream of Civilization. 6th ed. (Illus.). 120p. (C). 1994. text 26.95 (*0-15-501197-9*) Harcourt.

— The Mainstream of Civilization since 1500. 6th ed. (Illus.). 650p. (C). 1994. pap. text 17.95 (*0-15-501199-5*) Harcourt Coll Pubs.

— The Mainstream of Civilization to 1715. 6th ed. (Illus.). 630p. (C). 1994. pap. text 17.95 (*0-15-501201-0*) Harcourt Coll Pubs.

Chodorow, Stanley, jt. ed. see Sweeney, James R.

Chodos, A., et al. Solitons in Nuclear & Elementary Particle Physics: Proceedings of the Lewes Workshop. 324p. 1984. 64.00 (*9971-966-89-1*) World Scientific Pub.

Chodos, Robert. The CPR: A Century of Corporate Welfare. 178p. 1973. 19.95 (*0-88862-047-0*, Pub. by J Lorimer) Formac Dist Ltd.

— Quebec: A Chronicle, 1968-1972. Auf der Maur, Nick, ed. 166p. 1972. mass mkt. 7.95 (*0-88862-025-X*, Pub. by J Lorimer) Formac Dist Ltd.

Chodos, Robert, et al. Lost in Cyberspace? Canada & the Information Revolution. LC 98-107658. 149p. 1997. 34.95 (*1-55028-519-X*, Pub. by J Lorimer); pap. 19.95 (*1-55028-518-1*, Pub. by J Lorimer) Formac Dist Ltd.

Chodos, Robert, tr. see Bellon, Bertrand & Niosi, Jorge.

Chodosh, Joshua, et al. Geriatric Assessment & the Twenty Minute Visit: Instructional Manual for Residents & Attending Physicians. 24p. 1997. 80.00 (*1-892273-02-0*) U Rchstr Med & Dntstry.

***Chodroff, Michael.** The Penn State Students' Unofficial Guide to College: A Book of Bests & Worsts of Penn State Students' Life at College. (Illus.). 160p. (C). 1999. pap. 9.95 (*0-9662801-1-3*) Arm in Arm.

Chodroff, Michael. The Rutgers Students Unofficial Guide to College: A Book of Bests & Worsts of Rutgers Students Life at College. LC 97-78206. (Illus.). 160p. (C). 1998. pap. 9.95 (*0-9662801-0-5*) Arm in Arm.

***Chodroff, Michael.** The University of Connecticut Students' Unofficial Guide to College: A Book of Bests & Worsts of UConn Students' Life at College. (Illus.). 160p. (C). 1999. pap. 9.95 (*0-9662801-4-8*) Arm in Arm.

— The University of Maryland Students' Unofficial Guide to College: A Book of Bests & Worsts of University of Maryland Students' Life at College. (Illus.). 160p. (C). 1999. pap. 9.95 (*0-9662801-2-1*) Arm in Arm.

— The University of Massachusetts Students' Life at College: A Book of Bests & Worsts of UMass Students' Life at College. (Illus.). 160p. (C). 1999. pap. 9.95 (*0-9662801-5-6*) Arm in Arm.

Chodron, Ani T., ed. see Rinpoche, H. H. Chetsang.

Chodron, Pema. Awakening Loving-Kindness. (Pocket Classics Ser.). 192p. 1996. pap. 6.95 (*1-57062-259-0*, Pub. by Shambhala Pubns) Random.

— Good Medicine. 160p. Date not set. 19.95 (*1-57062-409-7*) Shambhala Pubns.

— Start Where You Are: A Guide to Compassionate Living. LC 93-39135. 1994. pap. 12.95 (*0-87773-880-7*, Pub. by Shambhala Pubns) Random.

— When Things Fall Apart: Heart Advice for Difficult Times. 144p. 1997. 20.00 (*1-57062-160-8*, Pub. by Shambhala Pubns) Random.

— When Things Fall Apart: Heart Advice for Difficult Times. 1999. pap. 12.00 (*1-57062-344-9*, Pub. by Shambhala Pubns) Random.

— The Wisdom of No Escape: And the Path of Loving-Kindness. LC 90-53585. 128p. (Orig.). 1991. pap. 11.95 (*0-87773-632-4*, Pub. by Shambhala Pubns) Random.

***Chodron, Thubten.** Blossoms of the Dharma: Living as a Buddhist Nun. LC 99-43221. (Illus.). 204p. 2000. pap. text 16.95 (*1-55643-325-5*) North Atlantic.

Chodron, Thubten. Open Heart, Clear Mind. LC 90-41454. 224p. 1990. pap. 12.95 (*0-937938-87-4*) Snow Lion Pubns.

— Taming The Monkey Mind. 189p. 1999. pap. text 9.95 (*0-89346-893-2*) Heian Intl.

— What Color Is Your Mind? 192p. 1993. pap. 12.95 (*1-55939-015-8*) Snow Lion Pubns.

Chodron, Thubten, ed. see Geshe Jampa Tegchok.

Chodzin, Sherab & Kohn, Alexandra. The Wisdom of the Crows & Other Buddhist Tales. LC 97-30441. (Illus.). 80p. (J). (gr. 2 up). 1998. pap. 16.95 (*1-883672-68-6*) Tricycle Pr.

Chodzin, Sherab, ed. see Trungpa, Chogyam.

Chodzko, Mark, prod. Old Mother Witch. (Literature to Go Ser.). (YA). (gr. 4-9). 1989. pap., student ed. 99.00 incl. vdisk (*0-7919-2686-9*) Phoenix Films.

C

Choe Ching Young. The Rule of the Taewon'gun, 1864-1873: Restoration in Yi Korea. LC 73-183975. (East Asian Monographs: No. 45). 287p. 1972. pap. 15.00 (0-674-78030-2) HUP.

Choe, Hongkyue A., ed. see Joe, Wayne J.

Choe, Hui Son. HapKiDo: The Korean Martial Art of Self Defense. 3rd deluxe ed. (Illus.). 167p. 1998. pap. 24.95 (0-9668254-0-3) World Hap Ki Do.

***Choe, Hui Son.** Practical HapKiDo Textbook. (Illus.). 206p. 1999. pap. 29.95 (0-9668254-1-1) World Hap Ki Do.

Choe, Hyondok. Ideologie: Eine Geschichte der Entstehung des Gesellschaftskritischen Begriffs. Sandkuhler, Hans J. & Stekeler-Weithofer, Pirmin, eds. (Philosophie und Geschichte der Wissenschaften, Studien und Quellen: Bd. 37). (GER.). 297p. 1997. 57.95 (3-631-32199-6) P Lang Pubng.

Choe, Jae C. & Crespi, Bernard J., eds. The Evolution of Mating Systems in Insects & Arachnids. (Illus.). 397p. (C). 1997. text 115.00 (0-521-58029-3); pap. text 47.95 (0-521-58976-2) Cambridge U Pr.

— The Evolution of Social Behaviour in Insects & Arachnids. 160p. 1997. pap. text 18.95 (0-521-56860-9) Cambridge U Pr.

— The Evolution of Social Behaviour in Insects & Arachnids. LC 96-2861. (Illus.). 554p. (C). 1997. text 139.95 (0-521-58028-5); pap. text 49.95 (0-521-58977-0) Cambridge U Pr.

Choe, Jae-Suck. Greene & Unamuno: Two Pilgrims to La Mancha. (American University Studies: Ser. III, Vol. 36). 216p. (C). 1990. text 44.00 (0-8204-1268-6) P Lang Pubng.

Choe, Jae Y. Choe Notes: A Handbook of Pharmacology. 2nd rev. ed. LC 96-14950. (Illus.). xii, 411p. 1996. pap. 34.95 (0-940473-34-8) Wm Caxton.

Choe, Joe P. Unforgettable Trips to Motherland: China. (CHI.). 153p. 1997. pap. 10.00 (1-890474-00-2) Nrth Amer Chinese Wrters.

Choe, Minja K., jt. auth. see Retherford, Robert D.

Ch'oe, Pu. Ch'oe Pu's Diary: A Record of Drifting Across the Sea. Meskill, John, tr. LC 64-19165. (Association for Asian Studies, Monographs & Papers: No. 17). 185p. reprint ed. pap. 57.40 (0-7837-1461-0, 205536200017) Bks Demand.

***Choe-Wall, Yang-hi.** Encyclopedia of Korea. (Illus.). 1500p. 1999. 330.00 (0-7103-0658-X, Pub. by Kegan Paul Intl) Col U Pr.

Choe-Wall, Yang-hi, ed. see Lady Hong of Hyegyong Palace.

Choe, Wolhee. Toward an Aesthetic Criticism of Technology. (Worcester Polytechnic Institute Studies in Science, Technology, & Culture: Vol. 2). 218p. (C). 1989. text 39.95 (0-8204-0654-6) P Lang Pubng.

Choe, Wolhee & Fusco, Peter, trs. Day-Shine: Poems by Chong Hyon-Jong. (Cornell East Asia Ser.: Vol. 94). (Illus.). 117p. (C). 1998. 18.70 (1-885445-54-7); pap. 11.90 (1-885445-94-6) Cornell East Asia Pgm.

Choe, Wolhee, jt. tr. see Contogenis, Constantine.

***Ch'oe, Yongho, et al, eds.** Sources of Korean Tradition Vol. 2: From the Sixteenth to the Twentieth Centuries. 448p. 2000. text 49.50 (0-231-12030-3); pap. text 22.50 (0-231-12031-1) Col U Pr.

Choedon, Yeshi. China & the United Nations. 1990. 17.50 (81-7003-119-2, Pub. by S Asia Pubs) S Asia.

Choen, Shu-Poing, jt. auth. see Conference on Control of Distributed Parameter & Stochastic Systems Staff.

Choephel, Gedun, tr. see Buddha Sakyamuni.

Chofetz Chaim Staff. Let My People Go. 168p. 1993. 17.95 (1-58330-096-1) Feldheim.

— Let My People Go Haggadah. 168p. 1994. 14.95 (1-58330-095-3) Feldheim.

— Let Them Serve Me. 272p. 1995. 17.95 (1-58330-097-X) Feldheim.

— Mishnah Berurah, Vol. 5A. large type ed. 25.95 (0-87306-710-X) Feldheim.

— Mishnah Berurah, Vol. 5B. 22.95 (0-87306-712-6) Feldheim.

— Mishnah Berurah, Vol. 5B. large type ed. 28.95 (0-87306-713-4) Feldheim.

— Mishnah Berurah, Vol. 5C. 22.95 (0-87306-778-9) Feldheim.

— Mishnah Berurah, Vol. 5C. large type ed. 28.95 (0-87306-777-0) Feldheim.

— Mishnah Berurah, Vol. 6A. 22.95 (0-87306-862-9) Feldheim.

— Mishnah Berurah, Vol. 6A. large type ed. 27.95 (0-87306-861-0) Feldheim.

Chofetz Chaim Staff. Mishnah Berurah, Vol. 6B. 22.95 (0-87306-942-0) Feldheim.

— Mishnah Berurah, Vol. 6B. large type ed. 27.95 (0-87306-943-9) Feldheim.

Chofflon, Michel & Steinman, Lawrence, eds. Immunoneurology. LC 96-30167. 272p. 1996. 134.95 (3-540-61559-8) Spr-Verlag.

Choffrut, C. & Jantzen, M., eds. STACS, '91: Proceedings of the 8th Annual Symposium on Theoretical Aspects of Computer Science Hamburg, Germany, February 14-16, 1991, Vol. 480. x, 549p. 1991. 64.00 (0-387-53709-0) Spr-Verlag.

Choffrut, C. & Lengauer, Thomas, eds. STACS, '99, Vol. 415. vi, 312p. 1990. 38.00 (0-387-52282-4) Spr-Verlag.

Chogoshvili, G. S., ed. Topological Projective & Combinatorial Properties of Space. 192p. 1992. text 165.00 (1-56072-058-1) Nova Sci Pubs.

Choguill, C. L. New Communities for Urban Squatters: Lessons from the Plan That Failed in Dhaka, Bangladesh. (Urban Innovation Abroad Ser.). (Illus.). 228p. (C). 1987. 79.50 (0-306-42545-9, Plenum Trade) Perseus Pubng.

Chogyam, Ngakpa. Spectrum of Ecstasy. Antonoff, Andrea, ed. (Illus.). 336p. 1997. pap. text 21.00 (0-9653948-0-8) Aro Bks Inc.

— Wearing the Body of Vision. 296p. 1995. 20.00 (0-9653948-1-6) Aro Bks Inc.

Choh, S. J., jt. auth. see Seni, S. J.

Chohan, et al. Economics: Syllabus. 1974. pap. text 11.95 (0-89420-028-3, 112050); audio 223.15 (0-89420-142-5, 112000) Natl Book.

Choi. The Multifibre Arrangement in Theory & Practice. 153 p. (C). 1992. text 39.00 (0-86187-552-4) St Martin.

Choi & Mariotte, Edme. Gen 13 Collected Edition. 144p. pap. 12.95 (1-56389-496-3) DC Comics.

Choi & Mueller. International Accounting. 3rd ed. LC 98-41091. 478p. 1998. 96.00 (0-13-260761-1) P-H.

— Review Copy International Accounting. 3rd ed. 1998. text. write for info. (0-13-082976-5) P-H.

Choi, Hong K. & Zory, Peter S., eds. In-Plane Semiconductor Lasers Vol. 3001: From Ultraviolet to Midinfrared. LC 97-200956. 432p. 1997. 89.00 (0-8194-2412-9) SPIE.

— In-Plane Semiconductor Lasers Vol. 3284: From Ultraviolet to Mid-Infrared II. LC 98-171715. 344p. 1998. 80.00 (0-8194-2723-3) SPIE.

***Choi, Hong K. & Zory, Peter S., eds.** In-Plane Semiconductor Lasers III. 294p. 1999. pap. text 72.00 (0-8194-3098-6) SPIE.

Choi, Alfred. An Examination of Police Intervention in Domestic Disturbances in a Canadian Context. LC 97-36802. 152p. 1993. text 69.95 (0-7734-2248-X) E Mellen.

Choi, Alfred, jt. ed. see Chin, Anthony.

Choi, B. K. ARMA Model Identification. Berger, J. O. et al, eds. (Series in Statistics - Subseries: Probability & Its Applications). 216p. 1992. 59.95 (0-387-97795-3) Spr-Verlag.

— Surface Modeling for CAD - CAM. (Advances in Industrial Engineering Ser.: No. 11). xvi,390p. 1991. 180.00 (0-444-88482-3) Elsevier.

***Choi, Brandon & Lee, Jim.** Deathblow: Sinners & Saints. (Illus.). 256p. 1999. pap. text 19.95 (1-56389-547-1, Pub. by DC Comics) Time Warner.

***Choi, Brandon & Wyn, Daffyd.** Wild C. A. T. S. Trilogy. (Illus.). 72p. 1999. pap. text 7.95 (1-56389-571-4, Pub. by DC Comics) Time Warner.

***Choi, Brandon, et al.** Gen13: Starting Over. (Illus.). 192p. 1999. pap. text 14.95 (1-56389-544-7, Pub. by DC Comics) Time Warner.

***Choi, Byoung K. & Jerard, Robert B.** Sculptured Surface Machining: Theory & Applications. 612p. 1999. write for info. (0-412-78020-8, Kluwer Plenum) Kluwer Academic.

Choi, Chungmoo. Comfort Women, Vol. 5. (Positions Bks.). 1997. pap. text 12.00 (0-8223-6464-6) Duke.

Choi, Chungmoo. Comfort Women, Vol. 5. 1997. pap. text 12.00 (0-8223-6446-8) Duke.

Choi, Chungmoo, jt. ed. see Kim, Elaine H.

Choi, Frederick D. Multinational Accounting: A Research Framework for the Eighties. LC 81-16448. (Research for Business Decisions Ser.: No. 46). 240p. 1981. reprint ed. pap. 74.40 (0-8357-1267-2, 207005500063) Bks Demand.

Choi, Frederick D., ed. International Accounting & Finance Handbook. 2nd ed. LC 96-53593. 1184p. 1997. 165.00 (0-471-15281-1) Wiley.

Choi, Frederick D. S. & Mueller, Gerhard G. Globalization of Financial Accounting & Reporting. LC 92-70836. 96p. (Orig.). 1993. pap. 25.00 (0-910586-88-8, 093-97) Finan Exec.

Choi, Frederick D. S. & Mueller, Gerhard G., eds. Frontiers of International Accounting: An Anthology. LC 85-5865. (Research for Business Decisions Ser.: No. 77). (Illus.). 329p. reprint ed. pap. 102.00 (0-8357-1660-0, 207037100088) Bks Demand.

Choi, Frederick S. International Accounting Handbook: 1998 Supplement. 2nd ed. 78p. 1999. pap., suppl. ed. 60.00 (0-471-19592-8) Wiley.

Choi, H. K., et al, eds. Heteroepitaxy on Silicon: Fundamentals, Structures & Devices. (Symposium Proceedings Ser.: Vol. 116). 1988. text 17.50 (0-931837-86-3) Materials Res.

***Choi, Hae-Suk.** Spinoza und Chu Hsi: Die Absolute Natur Als der Grund des Menschlichen Seins in der Ethik Spinozas und der Neokonfuzianischen Lehre Chu Hsis. VII, 177p. 1999. 37.95 (3-631-34065-6) P Lang Pubng.

Choi, Hyaeweol. An International Scientific Community: Asian Scholars in the United States. 1995. write for info. (0-614-00956-1, Praeger Pubs) Greenwood.

Choi, Hyaeweol, jt. auth. see Altbach, Philip G.

Choi, Hye-Won. Optimizing Structure in Context: Scrambling & Information Structure. LC 99-20043. (Dissertations in Linguistics Ser.: No. 16). 256p. (C). 1999. text 59.95 (1-57586-157-7); pap. text 22.95 (1-57586-156-9) CSLI.

Choi, Inn-Chull. An Application of Item Response Theory to Language Testing. LC 91-16472. (Theoretical Studies in Second Language Acquisition: Vol. 2). XII, 196p. (C). 1992. text 41.95 (0-8204-1573-1) P Lang Pubng.

Choi, Insik. Die Taologische Frage Nach Gott: Paul Tillichs Philosophischer Gottesbegriff des "Seins-Selbst" und Sprachliche Verantwortung des Glaubens in Begegnung Mit Dem Taogedanken Laotzus. (Kontexte Ser.: Bd. 9). (GER.). XIX, 380p. 1992. 64.80 (3-631-44017-0) P Lang Pubng.

Choi, J. Jay & Doukas, John A., eds. Emerging Capital Markets: Financial & Investment Issues. LC 98-6842. 360p. 1998. 69.50 (1-56720-177-6, Quorum Bks) Greenwood.

Choi, Joongho, jt. auth. see Sheu, Bing J.

Choi, Joseph. The Active Practice of Statistics: A Text for Multimedia Learning - Instructor's Manual with Solutions. 1997. teacher ed. write for info. (0-7167-3245-9) W H Freeman.

Choi, Jung Min & Murphy, John W. The Politics & Philosophy of Political Correctness. LC 92-19834. 186p. 1992. 49.95 (0-275-94286-4, C4286, Praeger Pubs) Greenwood.

Choi, Jung Min, et al. The Politics of Culture: Race, Violence, & Democracy. LC 95-3333. 192p. 1995. 55.00 (0-275-94889-7, Praeger Pubs) Greenwood.

Choi, Jung Min, jt. auth. see Murphy, John W.

Choi, K. S., ed. Recent Developments in Turbulence Management: Proceedings of the 5th Drag Reduction in Engineering Flows Meeting. 358p. (C). 1991. lib. bdg. 153.50 (0-7923-1477-8) Kluwer Academic.

Choi, Kwang. Theories of Comparative Economic Growth. LC 83-284. (Illus.). 306p. 1983. reprint ed. pap. 94.90 (0-608-00123-6, 206088800006) Bks Demand.

***Choi, Kwang & Jensen, Bjarne, eds.** Economic Growth & International Trade. 1999. pap. text 32.95 (0-631-21811-4) Blackwell Pubs.

Choi, Myung-Keun. Changes in Korean Society, Between 1884-1910 As a Result of the Introduction of Christianity. LC 96-37006. (Asian Thought & Culture Ser.: Vol. 20). (Illus.). XX, 323p. (C). 1997. 54.95 (0-8204-2549-4) P Lang Pubng.

Choi, Nakgyoon. An Empirical Analysis of International Trade Policy. LC 96-47512. (Financial Sector of the American Economy Ser.). (Illus.). 208p. 1997. text 62.00 (0-8153-2795-1) Garland.

Choi, Namkee & Snyder, Lydia. Homeless Families with Children: A Subjective Experience of Homelessness. LC 99-15738. (Series on Social Work). (Illus.). 160p. 1999. text 31.95 (0-8261-1285-4) Springer Pub.

Choi, Noah C. & Grillo, Hermes C., eds. Thoracic Oncology. LC 79-63971. (Illus.). 384p. 1983. reprint ed. pap. 119.10 (0-608-00596-7, 206118300007) Bks Demand.

***Choi, Precilla Y. L.** Femininity & the Physically Active Woman. LC 00-30596. (Women & Psychology Ser.). 2000. pap. write for info. (0-415-16561-X) Routledge.

Choi, S. C., ed. Statistical Methods of Discrimination & Classification: Advances in Theory & Applications. (International Series in Modern Applied Mathematics & Computer Science). 135p. 1986. 39.00 (0-08-034000-8, A110,C110,D110,D130,H100, Pergamon Pr) Elsevier.

Choi, Samuel L., tr. from KOR. Christian Distress. 360p. (Orig.). 1997. pap. 10.00 (0-9655790-0-X) Young Hie Paik.

— Selected Sermons: Selected Sermons of the Martyr, Young Hie Paik. 360p. (Orig.). 1997. pap. 10.00 (0-9655790-2-6) Young Hie Paik.

Choi, Seong M. Mimesis und Historische Erfahrung: Untersuchungen Zur Mimesistheorie Walter Benjamins. (Europaische Hochschulschriften Ser.: Reihe 1, Bd. 1591). (GER.). 246p. 1996. 44.95 (3-631-31153-2) P Lang Pubng.

Choi, So-In. Selbstbewusstsein und Selbstanschauung: Eine Reflexion Ueber Einheit und Entzweiung des Subjekts in Kants "Opus Postumum" (Kantstudien Ergaenzungsheft Ser.: Vol. 130). (GER.). xii, 154p. (C). 1996. lib. bdg. 72.60 (3-11-015264-9, 120/96) De Gruyter.

Choi, Sook N. Echoes of White Giraffe. (J). 1994. pap. 4.50 (0-440-91020-X) BDD Bks Young Read.

Choi, Sook Nyui. Halmoni & the Picnic. (Illus.). 32p. (J). (ps-3). 1993. 14.95 (0-395-61626-3) HM.

Choi Sook Nyul. Echoes of the White Giraffe. 144p. (J). (gr. 4-7). 1995. pap. 4.50 (0-440-40970-5) Dell.

— Echoes of the White Giraffe. LC 92-17476. 144p. (YA). (gr. 5 up). 1993. 16.00 (0-395-64721-5) HM.

— Echoes of the White Giraffe. 1995. 9.09 (0-606-07464-3, Pub. by Turtleback) Demco.

— Echoes of the White Giraffe. large type ed. 1995. 30.00 (0-614-09573-5, L-81912-00) Am Printing Hse.

Choi, Sook-Nyul. Gathering of Pearls. LC 94-10868. 176p. (J). (gr. 7 up). 1994. 15.00 (0-395-67437-9) HM.

Choi Sook Nyul. Year of Impossible Goodbyes. 176p. (J). (gr. 4-7). 1993. pap. 4.99 (0-440-40759-1) Dell.

— Year of Impossible Goodbyes. LC 91-10502. 176p. (YA). (gr. 4-7). 1991. 16.00 (0-395-57419-6, Sandpiper) HM.

Choi, Soonja, ed. Japanese-Korean Linguistics, Vol. 3. 430p. 1993. 59.95 (1-881526-22-4); pap. 21.95 (1-881526-21-6) CSLI.

***Choi, Sung Soo.** Koreanisches Christentum in der Begegnung Mit Einheimischen Religionen: Dargestellt an der Konzeption Koreanischer Theologie Bei Byunghun Choi und Tongshik Ryu. (Beitrage zur Theologischen Urteilsbildung Ser.). 241p. 1999. 37.95 (3-631-35313-8) P Lang Pubng.

Choi, Susan M. The Foreign Student: A Novel. LC 98-11919. 336p. 1998. 23.00 (0-06-019149-X, HarperFlamingo) HarpC.

— The Foreign Student: A Novel. 336p. 1999. pap. 13.00 (0-06-092927-8, HarperFlamingo) HarpC.

Choi, Susan M., jt. ed. see Remnick, David.

***Choi, T. S.** Assessment of RELAP5/MOD3.2: Using Loft Large Break Loca Test, LP-02-6. 114p. 1998. per. 13.00 (0-16-063032-0) USGPO.

Choi, Tae-Hee, tr. see Frangipane, Francis.

Choi, Trieu T. & Isaak, Marcel. The Food of Vietnam: Authentic Recipes from the Heart of Indochina. 1997. pap. 12.95 (0-614-28097-4) Periplus.

Choi, Woonsang. Legal Regulation of Employment Relations Within International Organizations: With Special Reference to the Jurisprudence of International Administrative Tribunals & the Practice of the United Nations. 2000. text 85.00 (0-379-21397-4) Oceana.

Choi, Y. D. Practical Tae Kwon Do. 414p. 1997. write for info. (0-9658285-0-6) Martial Arts.

Choi, Yang-Do. Enzymes for Carbohydrate Engineering. Park, Kwan-Hwa & Robyt, John F., eds. LC 96-26657. (Enzymes for Carbohydrate Engineering Ser.). 224p. 1996. 145.25 (0-444-82408-1) Elsevier.

***Choi, Yangsook.** The Name Jar. LC 00-39103. (Illus.). (J). 2001. lib. bdg. write for info. (0-375-90613-4) Knopf Bks Yng Read.

Choi, Yangsook. New Cat. LC 97-15668. (Illus.). 32p. (J). (gr. k-3). 1999. 16.00 (0-374-35512-6) FS&G.

— The Sun Girl & the Moon Boy: A Korean Folk Tale. LC 96-51186. (Illus.). 32p. (J). (gr. k-3). 1997. 17.00 (0-679-88386-X, Pub. by Knopf Bks Yng Read) Random.

Choi, Yangsook, jt. illus. see Wong, Janet S.

Choi, Yeam H., ed. see Im, Julia K.

Choi, Youngrak. Dynamic Techno-Management Capability: The Case of Samsung Semiconductor Sector in Korea. 252p. 1996. 72.95 (1-85972-262-8, Pub. by Avebry) Ashgate Pub Co.

Choi, Zaeshick. Der Phanomenologische Feldbegriff Bei Aron Gurwitsch. (Europaische Hochschulschriften Ser.: Reihe 20, Bd. 519). (GER.). 293p. 1996. 57.95 (3-631-48021-0) P Lang Pubng.

Choice, Lesley. World Enough. LC 98-231547. 350p. 1999. pap. 16.95 (0-86492-246-9) Genl Dist Srvs.

Choices. Show Us The Money: The Politics & Process of Alternative Budgets. LC 99-187766. 112p. 1998. pap. 14.95 (1-894037-03-0) Arbeiter Ring.

Choices for 21st Century Education Project, ed. Coming to Terms with Power: U. S. Choices after World War II. (Choices for the 21st Century Ser.). 68p. (YA). (gr. 9-12). 1992. pap. text 12.00 (1-891306-17-0) Watson Inst Intl.

— Crisis, Conscience, & Choices: Weimar Germany & the Rise of Hitler. (Choices for the 21st Century Ser.). 88p. (YA). (gr. 9-12). 1994. pap. text 12.00 (1-891306-11-1) Watson Inst Intl.

— Global Environmental Problems: Implications for U. S. Policy. (Choices for the 21st Century Ser.). 64p. (YA). (gr. 9-12). 1992. pap. text 12.00 (1-891306-09-X) Watson Inst Intl.

— Help, Handout, or Hindrance: U. S. Support for the Developing World. (Choices for the 21st Century Ser.). 67p. (YA). (gr. 9-12). 1995. pap. text 12.00 (1-891306-16-2) Watson Inst Intl.

— In the Shadow of the Cold War: Central America U. S. Foreign Policy. (Choices for the 21st Century Ser.). 111p. (YA). (gr. 9-12). 1991. pap. 14.00 (1-891306-08-1) Watson Inst Intl.

— The Limits of Power: The United States in Vietnam. (Choices for the 21st Century Ser.). 114p. (YA). (gr. 9-12). 1993. pap. text 14.00 (1-891306-14-6) Watson Inst Intl.

— Russia's Uncertain Transition: Challenges for U. S. Policy. (Choices for the 21st Century Ser.). 76p. (YA). (gr. 9-12). 1994. pap. text 12.00 (1-891306-10-3) Watson Inst Intl.

— Shifting Sands: Balancing U. S. Interests in the Middle East. (Choices for the 21st Century Ser.). 70p. (YA). (gr. 9-12). 1998. pap. text 12.00 (1-891306-12-X) Watson Inst Intl.

Choiniere, Ray, jt. auth. see Keirsey, David West.

Choinski, John S. Experimental Cell & Molecular Biology. 176p. (C). 1992. text. write for info. (0-697-12793-1, WCB McGr Hill) McGrw-H Hghr Educ.

Choinski, John S., Jr. Experimental Cell & Molecular Biology. 2nd ed. 192p. (C). 1996. text 31.00 (0-697-15892-6, WCB McGr Hill) McGrw-H Hghr Educ.

Choisser, John, jt. auth. see Foster, John.

***Chojnacka, Monica.** Working Women in Early Modern Venice. LC 00-9273. (Studies in Historical & Political Science). 224p. 2001. 32.50 (0-8018-6485-2) Johns Hopkins.

Chojnacki, Joseph, jt. auth. see Gelberg, Susan.

***Chojnacki, Stanislaw & Gossage, Carolyn M.** Ethiopian Icons: Catalogue of the Collection of the Institute of Ethiopian Studies Addis Ababa University. 560p. 2000. 120.00 (88-8118-646-2, Pub. by Skira IT) Abbeville Pr.

Chojnacki, Stanislaw, jt. auth. see Langmuir, Elizabeth C.

***Chojnacki, Stanley.** Women & Men in Renaissance Venice. LC 99-38575. 2000. 39.95 (0-8018-6269-8) Johns Hopkins.

Chokai, M. Sherlock Holmes & the Jewel & Other Short Plays. (Sangam English Supplementary Readers Ser.). (Illus.). 169p. (J). (gr. 6). 1983. pap. 3.95 (0-86131-330-5) Apt Bks.

***Choker, Dennis.** Seal Team 6. 2001. write for info. (0-380-97804-0) Morrow Avon.

Choko, A. Cote des Vins, 1991. (FRE.). 232p. 1991. 75.00 (0-8288-7298-8, 2859170944) Fr & Eur.

Choko, Marc. Canadian War Posters. LC 95-122424. (Illus.). 192p. (Orig.). 1994. pap. 51.95 (0-929058-04-6, Pub. by Canadian Govt Pub) Accents Pubns.

Choko, S. Cote de l'Affiche de Cinema. (FRE.). 288p. 1991. 125.00 (0-8288-7229-5, 2859171215) Fr & Eur.

Chokroverty, Sudhansu. Clinical Companion to Sleep Disorders Medicine. 2nd ed. LC 99-53900. 232p. 2000. pap. text 30.00 (0-7506-9687-7) Buttrwrth-Heinemann.

— Magnetic Stimulation in Clinical Neurophysiology. 308p. 1989. text 75.00 (0-409-90151-2) Buttrwrth-Heinemann.

— The Management of Epilepsy. LC 96-16864. 414p. 1996. pap. text 49.95 (0-7506-9754-7) Buttrwrth-Heinemann.

***Chokroverty, Sudhansu.** Sleep Disorders. (100 Questions to Ask Your Doctor about Ser.). 2000. pap. 14.95 (0-86542-583-3) Blackwell Sci.

Chokroverty, Sudhansu. Sleep Disorders Medicine: Basic Science, Technical Considerations & Clinical Aspects. (Illus.). 504p. 1993. text 140.00 (0-7506-9002-X) Buttrwrth-Heinemann.

— Sleep Disorders Medicine: Basic Science, Technical Considerations & Clinical Aspects. 2nd ed. LC 98-4115. 781p. 1998. text 145.00 (0-7506-9954-X) Buttrwrth-Heinemann.

***Chokroverty, Sudhansu, et al.** Sleep & Movement Disorders. (Illus.). 400p. 2000. 135.00 (*0-7506-7200-5*) Buttrwrth-Heinemann.

Chokshi, Atul H., ed. Superplasticity in Advanced Materials: ICSAM-97. (Materials Science Forum Ser.: Vols. 243-245). (Illus.). 808p. (C). 1997. text 265.00 (*0-87849-759-5*, Pub. by Trans T Pub) Enfield Pubs NH.

Choksi, Mithan. India's Indira. 180p. 1975. 5.95 (*0-318-36631-2*) Asia Bk Corp.

Choksy. The Kodaly Method II: Folksong to Masterwork. LC 98-10892. 210p. 1998. 48.00 (*0-13-949173-2*) P-H.

— Kodaly Method 1. 3rd ed. LC 98-36152. 303p. 1998. 48.00 (*0-13-949165-1*) P-H.

Choksy, Jamsheed K. Conflict & Cooperation: Zoroastrian Subalterns & Muslim Elites in Medieval Iranian Society. LC 96-50320. 1997. 42.00 (*0-231-10684-X*); pap. write for info. (*0-231-10685-8*) Col U Pr.

Choksy, Lois. Kodaly Context. 304p. 1981. pap. text 65.00 (*0-13-516666-7*) P-H.

— Teaching Music Effectively in the Elementary School. 320p. (C). 1991. pap. text 40.60 (*0-13-892704-9*) P-H.

***Choksy, Lois.** Teaching Music in the Twenty-First Century. LC 00-31368. 432p. 2000. 48.00 (*0-13-028027-5*) P-H.

Choksy, Lois & Brummitt, David. 120 Singing Games & Dances for Elementary Schools. (Illus.). 208p. (C). 1996. pap. 61.00 (*0-13-635038-0*) P-H.

Choksy, Lois, et al. Teaching Music in Twentieth-Century. (Illus.). 400p. (C). 1985. text 48.00 (*0-13-892662-X*) P-H.

Chokya, Deepockets. The Seven Spiritual Laws of Making Big Bucks: A Practical Guide to the Self-Righteous Amassing of an Obscene Fortune. 88p. 1998. pap. 9.95 (*0-910575-07-X*, B07X) RGE Publishing.

Chol, Samuel L., tr. from KOR. Final Testimonies: Final Testimonies of the Martyr, Young Hie Paik. 335p. (Orig.). 1997. pap. 10.00 (*0-9655790-1-8*) Young Hie Paik.

***Cholak, P., et al, eds.** Computability Theory & Its Applications: Current Trends & Open Problems. 320p. 2000. 79.00 (*0-8218-1922-4*) Am Math.

Cholak, Peter. Automorphisms of the Lattice of Recursively Enumerable Sets. LC 94-35340. (Memoirs Ser.: No. 541). 151p. 1995. pap. 37.00 (*0-8218-2601-8*, MEMO/113/541) Am Math.

Cholakian, Patricia F. Rape & Writing in the "Heptameron" of Marguerite de Navarre. LC 90-19799. (Ad Feminam Ser.). 288p. (C). 1991. 36.95 (*0-8093-1708-7*) S Ill U Pr.

***Cholakian, Patricia Francis.** Women & the Politics of Self-Representation in 17th-Century France. LC 00-29910. 2000. write for info. (*0-87413-735-7*) U Delaware Pr.

Cholakian, Rouben C. The Bayeux Tapestry & the Ethos of War. LC 98-18153. 122p. 1998. 35.00 (*0-88206-090-2*) Caravan Bks.

— Deflection - Reflection in the Lyric Poetry of Charles D'Orleans. 1985. 25.00 (*0-916379-21-3*) Scripta.

Cholakian, Rouben C., ed. Complete Narratives of Francophone Caribbean Tales. LC 95-15705. (Caribbean Studies: Vol. 3). 196p. 1996. text 79.95 (*0-7734-8906-1*) E Mellen.

Cholawsky, Shalom. The Jews of Bielorussia During World War II. 320p. 1997. text 44.00 (*90-5702-193-5*, Harwood Acad Pubs) Gordon & Breach.

Cholden, Harriett, et al. The Homework Handbook. LC 98-6083. 240p. 1998. pap. 12.95 (*0-8092-2881-5*, 288150, Contemporary Bks) NTC Contemp Pub Co.

Cholden, Louis S. A Psychiatrist Works with Blindness: Selected Papers. LC 58-3610. 119p. reprint ed. pap. 36.90 (*0-7837-2757-7*, 204314000006) Bks Demand.

Choldenko, Gennifer. Moonstruck: The True Story of the Cow That Jumped over the Moon. LC 95-14846. (Illus.). 32p. (ps-3). 1999. 5.99 (*0-7868-1394-6*, Pub. by Hyperion) Time Warner.

— Moonstruck: The True Story of the Cow That Jumped over the Moon. LC 95-14846. (Illus.). 32p. (J). (ps-3). 1997. 14.95 (*0-7868-0158-1*, Pub. by Hyprn Child); lib. bdg. 14.89 (*0-7868-2130-2*, Pub. by Hyprn Child) Little.

Choldin, Harvey M. Looking for the Last Percent: The Controversy over Census Undercounts. LC 93-24224. 296p. (C). 1994. text 48.00 (*0-8135-2039-8*); pap. text 19.00 (*0-8135-2040-1*) Rutgers U Pr.

Choldin, Marianna T. A Fence Around the Empire: Russian Censorship of Western Ideas under the Tsars. LC 85-4557. (Duke Press Policy Studies). (Illus.). xii, 282p. (C). 1985. text 49.95 (*0-8223-0625-5*) Duke.

Choldin, Marianna T., ed. Access to Resources in the Eighties: Proceedings of the First International Conference of Slavic Librarians & Information Specialists. LC 82-60216. (Russica Bibliography Ser.: No. 2). (Orig.). 1982. pap. 18.00 (*0-89830-049-5*) Russica Pubs.

— Books, Libraries, & Information in Slavic & East European Studies: Proceedings of the Second International Conference of Slavic Librarians & Information Specialists. LC 85-43530. (Russica Bibliography Ser.: No. 8). 540p. (Orig.). 1986. pap. 48.00 (*0-89830-107-6*) Russica Pubs.

Choldin, Marianna T. & Friedberg, Maurice. The Red Pencil: Artists, Scholars, & Censors in the U. S. S. R. 256p. 1989. text 55.00 (*0-04-445203-9*) Routledge.

Choldin, Marianna T., tr. see Jensen, Adolf E.

Chole, Esbetu, jt. auth. see Bedrani, S.

Chole, Eshetu. Democratisation Processes in A. 1996. pap. text 9.95 (*2-86978-052-4*) Codesria.

Cholet, Henri. Progressing Cavity Pumps. LC 98-132907. 128p. 1997. pap. 160.00 (*2-7108-0724-6*, Pub. by Edits Technip) Enfield Pubs NH.

***Cholewa, Jan W. & Dlotko, Tomasz.** Global Attractors in Abstract Parabolic Problems. (London Mathematical Society Lecture Note Ser.: Vol. 278). 250p. (C). 2000. pap. text Price not set. (*0-521-79424-2*) Cambridge U Pr.

Cholewczynski, George F. Poles Apart: The First Polish Airborne at Arnhem. (Illus.). 352p. 1993. 21.95 (*0-9627613-5-4*) Sarpedon.

Cholewinski, Frank M. A Hankel Convolution Complex Inversion Theory. LC 52-42839. (Memoirs Ser.: Vol. 1/58). 67p. 1965. pap. 16.00 (*0-8218-1258-0*, MEMO/1/58) Am Math.

Cholewinski, Frank M., ed. The Finite Calculus Associated with Bessel Functions. LC 88-14597. (Contemporary Mathematics Ser.: Vol. 75). 122p. 1988. pap. 25.00 (*0-8218-5083-0*, CONM/75) Am Math.

Cholewinski, Ryszard. Migrant Workers in International Human Rights Law: Their Protection in Countries of Employment. LC 98-101421. 538p. (C). 1997. text 95.00 (*0-19-825992-1*) OUP.

Cholfin, Brian, ed. The Best of Crank. LC 98-18818. 320p. 1998. 23.95 (*0-312-86740-9*, Pub. by Tor Bks) St Martin.

***Cholfin, Brian, ed.** The Best of Crank! 320p. 2000. pap. text 14.95 (*0-312-86739-5*, Pub. by Tor Bks) St Martin.

Cholfin, Bryan. Monochrome: The Readercon Anthology. LC 95-176810. 157 p. 1990. pap. write for info. (*0-9623824-3-4*) Broken Mirrors Pr.

Cholfin, Bryan, ed. Monochrome: The Readercon Anthology. 160p. 1990. 25.00 (*0-9623824-2-6*); pap. 9.95 (*0-685-50105-1*) Broken Mirrors Pr.

Cholidis, Nadja. Mobel in Ton: Untersuchungen Zur Archaologischen und Religionsgeschichtlichen Bedeutung der Terrakottamodelle von Tischen, Stuhlen und Betten aus dem Alten Orient. (Altertumskunde des Vorderen Orients Ser.: Vol. 1). (GER., Illus.). xii, 323p. 1992. text 86.00 (*3-927120-10-3*, Pub. by UGARIT) Eisenbrauns.

Chollat-Traquet, C. Evaluating Tobacco Control Activities Experiences & Guiding Principles. LC 96-185675. 242p. 1996. pap. text 54.00 (*92-4-154490-2*, 1150436) World Health.

Chollat-Traquet, C., et al. Women & Tobacco. (Illus.). 128p. (Orig.). (C). 1994. pap. text 35.00 (*0-7881-1342-9*) DIANE Pub.

— Women & Tobacco. (CHI, ENG, FRE, RUS & SPA.). xi, 128p. (Orig.). 1992. pap. text 26.00 (*92-4-156147-5*, 1150373) World Health.

Choller Instituty (Turkmenistan SSR ylymlar akademiiasy) Staff. Desert Problems & Desertification in Central Asia: The Researches of the Desert Institute. Babaev, Agadzhan Gel'dyevich, ed. LC 99-22315. 350p. 1999. 119.00 (*3-540-65647-2*) Spr-Verlag.

Chollet, Deborah J., jt. auth. see Employee Benefit Research Institute Staff.

Chollet, G., et al, eds. Speech Processing, Recognition & Artificial Neural Networks: Proceedings of the 3rd International Summer School on Neural Nets "Eduardo R. Caianiello" LC 99-19384. (Illus.). xii, 348p. 1999. pap. 110.00 (*1-85233-094-5*) Spr-Verlag.

Chollet, Jean-Jacques. Georgius, L'Amuseur Public No. 1: Suivi des Souvenirs Inedits de Georgius. (Illus.). 184p. 1997. pap. 34.95 (*2-86808-113-4*) Intl Scholars.

Chollet, Jean-Pierre, et al, eds. Direct & Large-Eddy Simulation II II: Proceedings of the ERCOFTAC Workshop Held in Grenoboble, France, 16-19 September 1996. LC 97-26108. (ERCOFTAC Ser.: No. 5). 422p. 1997. 194.00 (*0-7923-4687-4*) Kluwer Academic.

Chollick, Jay. Resurrected. (Lost City: Poetic Broadside Ser.: Vol. 1). (Illus.). 2p. 1998. pap. 2.00 (*1-892494-12-4*) Repossessed Head.

Cholmondeley, Mary. Moth & Rust & Other Stories. LC 71-101794. (Short Story Index Reprint Ser.). 1977. 20.95 (*0-8369-3182-3*) Ayer.

— Romance of His Life, & Other Romances. LC 70-37540. (Short Story Index Reprint Ser.). 1977. reprint ed. 19.95 (*0-8369-4099-7*) Ayer.

Cholnoky, B. J. Die Oekologie der Diatomeen in Binnengewaessern. (Illus.). 1968. 120.00 (*3-7682-5421-6*) Lubrecht & Cramer.

Cholnoky, B. J., jt. ed. see Gerloff, J.

Cholodenko, Alan, ed. see Weber, Samuel.

Cholodenko, Marc. Histoire de Vivant Lanon. (FRE.). 241p. 1986. pap. 11.95 (*0-7859-2232-6*, 207037744X) Fr & Eur.

— Mordechai Schamz. Di Bernardi, Dominic, tr. from FRE. LC 88-25050. 128p. 1989. 19.95 (*0-916583-31-7*) Dalkey Arch.

***Cholodenko, Marc.** Mordechai Schamz. Di Bernardi, Dominic, tr. from FRE. LC 88-25050. 121p. 2000. pap. 10.95 (*1-56478-246-8*, Pub. by Dalkey Arch) Chicago Distribution Ctr.

Cholpanova, L., et al. Bulgarian Environmental Projects, 1992-1995. 158p. 1996. pap. 34.95 (*954-642-008-5*) Intl Scholars.

Cholst, Sheldon. Brighton Beach: Grains of Sand - Poetry of the Sea. (Illus.). 160p. 1999. pap. 20.00 (*0-931174-06-6*) Beau Rivage.

— The Gentle Rebel. (Illus.). 1991. pap. 2.00 (*0-931174-03-1*) Beau Rivage.

— Hydra: Summer Season Sixty-Two. (Illus.). 118p. (Orig.). 1978. reprint ed. pap. 9.95 (*0-931174-02-3*) Beau Rivage.

— The Only Baby: Poems & Notes on Psychiatric Theory. 72p. (Orig.). 1978. reprint ed. pap. 9.95 (*0-931174-01-5*) Beau Rivage.

— The Psychology of the Artist. LC 91-7319. 1978. pap. 9.95 (*0-931174-00-7*) Beau Rivage.

— The Psychology of the Artist. 2nd rev. ed. (Illus.). 333p. 1997. pap. 14.95 (*0-931174-05-8*) Beau Rivage.

Cholvis, F. Diccionario de Contabilidad. (SPA.). 469p. 1977. 65.00 (*0-8288-5314-2*, S33738) Fr & Eur.

Choma. Electronic Circuits. 1997. text 49.56 (*0-256-08281-2*) McGraw.

Choma, John, Jr. Electrical Networks: Theory & Analysis. 794p. (C). 1991. reprint ed. lib. bdg. 83.50 (*0-89464-553-6*) Krieger.

Chomarat, J. Erasmi Opera Omnia, Vol. V-4. 496p. 1991. 349.00 (*0-444-88747-4*, North Holland) Elsevier.

— Erasmi Opera Omnia, Vol. V-5. 430p. 1994. 285.50 (*0-444-89742-9*, North Holland) Elsevier.

Chomeau, Mary D., tr. see Duboin, Alain-Marie.

Chomei, Kamo. Hojoki: Visions of a Torn World. Moriguchi, Yasuhiko & Jenkins, David, trs. from JPN. (Illus.). 96p. (Orig.). 1996. pap. 9.95 (*1-880656-22-1*) Stone Bridge Pr.

Chomei, Kamo N. Notebook of a Ten Square Rush-mat Sized World. 1979. 10.95 (*0-85105-343-2*, Pub by Smyth) Dufour.

Chomei, Kamono. Hojoki: Ten Foot Square House. Muro, Masaru, tr. (ENG & JPN.). 127p. 1997. pap. 18.95 (*4-590-00861-0*, Pub. by Hokuseido Pr) Book East.

Chomei, Toshiko. A New Analysis of Language Learning. (American University Studies: Linguistics: Ser. XIII, Vol. 15). 190p. (C). 1989. text 32.80 (*0-8204-1105-1*) P Lang Pubng.

***Chomet, S.** Helena: Princess Reclaimed: The Life & Times of Queen Victoria's Third Daughter. LC 99-462251. (Illus.). 2000. write for info. (*1-56700-145-9*) Begell Hse.

Chomet, S., jt. auth. see Isenberg, C.

Chomet, S., tr. see Gurevich, Alexander V., et al.

Chomet, S., tr. see Koltun, M. M.

Chomet, S., tr. see Smolyakov, A. V. & Tkachenko, V. M.

Chomet, S., tr. see Sokolov, A. A. & Ternov, I. M.

Chomiak, Jerzy. Combustion: A Study in Theory, Fact & Application, Vol. 8. (Abacus Bks.). (Illus.). xviii, 464p. 1990. text 332.00 (*0-85626-453-9*); pap. text 142.00 (*0-85626-500-4*) Gordon & Breach.

***Chomiak, Joseph N. & Swanson, Matt.** Mookie: A Girl in Maximsubornia. (Illus.). 48p. (J). 2000. 17.95 (*0-9676688-0-8*) Tremiak Pubng.

Chomicki, Jan & Saake, Gunter. Logics for Databases & Information Systems, Vol. 436. LC 98-2579. (Engineering & Computer Science Ser.). 430p. 1998. 148.00 (*0-7923-8129-7*) Kluwer Academic.

Chomin, Nakae. A Discourse by Three Drunkards on Government. Tsukui, Nobuko, tr. from JPN. 138p. (Orig.). 1984. pap. 12.50 (*0-8348-0192-2*) Weatherhill.

***Chominsky, Dennis.** Director to Go. 397p. 1999. 34.99 (*0-13-013782-0*) P-H.

— Premiere to Go. 350p. 2000. pap. text 34.99 (*0-13-027739-8*, Prentice Hall) P-H.

Chommie, John C., jt. auth. see Rose, Michael D.

Chompff, A. J., ed. see ACS Symposium on Highly Cross-Linked Polymer Networks.

Chomsky, Aviva. West Indian Workers & the United Fruit Company in Costa Rica, 1870-1940. LC 95-21958. (Illus.). 312p. (C). 1996. text 42.50 (*0-8071-1979-2*) La State U Pr.

Chomsky, Aviva, jt. auth. see Lauria-Santiago, Aldo.

Chomsky, Naom. World Orders: Old & New. 29.95 (*0-7453-0919-4*); 95.95 (*0-7453-0920-8*) Pluto GBR.

Chomsky, Noam. Ano 501: La Conquista Continua. (SPA.). 444p. (C). 1993. pap. 18.00 (*0-89608-488-4*) South End Pr.

***Chomsky, Noam.** The Architecture of Language. Mukherjee, Nirmalangshu et al, eds. 128p. 2000. 12.95 (*0-19-564834-X*) OUP.

Chomsky, Noam. Aspects of the Theory of Syntax. 261p. 1969. reprint ed. pap. text 16.00 (*0-262-53007-4*) MIT Pr.

— Barriers. (Linguistic Inquiry Monographs: Vol. 13). 112p. (Orig.). (C). 1986. pap. text 12.00 (*0-262-53067-8*) MIT Pr.

***Chomsky, Noam.** Chomsky on Democracy & Education. Otero, Carlos, ed. 2001. 85.00 (*0-415-92631-9*); pap. 22.95 (*0-415-92632-7*) Routledge.

— Chomsky on MisEducation. Macedo, Donaldo P., ed. & intro. by. LC 00-35297. (Critical Perspectives Ser.). 176p. 2000. 19.95 (*0-7425-0129-9*, Pub. by Rowman) Natl Bk Netwk.

Chomsky, Noam. The Chomsky Reader. Peck, Jim, ed. LC 86-42975. 384p. 1987. pap. 18.00 (*0-394-75173-6*) Pantheon.

— The Chomsky Trilogy, 3 vols., Set. (Real Story Ser.). 333p. (Orig.). 1988. pap. 20.00 (*1-878825-07-0*) Odonian Pr.

— Class Warfare: Interviews with David Barsamian. 224p. 1996. pap. 15.00 (*1-56751-092-2*); lib. bdg. 29.95 (*1-56751-093-0*) Common Courage.

— The Cold War & the University. LC 96-25426. 320p. 1996. 25.00 (*1-56584-005-4*, Pub. by New Press NY) Norton.

— The Common Good. LC 98-36584. (Real Story Ser.). 192p. (Orig.). 1998. pap. 12.00 (*1-878825-08-9*) Odonian Pr.

— The Culture of Terrorism. LC 87-28788. 268p. (Orig.). 1988. 35.00 (*0-89608-335-7*); pap. 18.00 (*0-89608-334-9*) South End Pr.

— Culture of Terrorism. 296p. write for info. (*0-921689-29-2*); pap. write for info. (*0-921689-28-4*) Black Rose.

— Current Issues in Linguistic Theory. (Janua Linguarum, Ser. Minor: No. 38). (Orig.). 1964. pap. text 22.95 (*90-279-0700-5*) Mouton.

— Deterring Democracy. 424p. 1992. pap. 16.00 (*0-374-52349-5*) Hill & Wang.

— Deterring Democracy. 384p. (gr. 13). 1991. 30.00 (*0-86091-318-X*, A5347, Pub. by Verso) Norton.

— The Essential Chomsky: Essays on Freedom & Democracy. Pavlick, Mark, ed. 400p. Date not set. pap. 19.95 (*1-56751-144-9*) Common Courage.

— The Essential Chomsky: Essays on the Struggle for Freedom & Democracy. Pavlick, Mark, ed. 400p. Date not set. lib. bdg. 39.95 (*1-56751-145-7*) Common Courage.

***Chomsky, Noam.** Fateful Triangle: The United States, Israel & the Palestinians. rev. ed. 578p. 1999. pap. 24.99 (*1-55164-160-7*, Pub. by Black Rose) Consort Bk Sales.

Chomsky, Noam. Fateful Triangle: The United States, Israel & the Palestinians. 2nd ed. LC 98-55140. (Classics Ser.: Vol. 3). 578p. 1999. 40.00 (*0-89608-602-X*); pap. 22.00 (*0-89608-601-1*) South End Pr.

— Keeping the Rabble in Line: Interviews with David Barsamian. LC 94-13221. 256p. 1994. lib. bdg. 29.95 (*1-56751-033-7*) Common Courage.

— Keeping the Rabble in Line: Interviews with David Barsmian. LC 94-13221. 256p. 1994. pap. 16.95 (*1-56751-032-9*) Common Courage.

— Knowledge of Language. 1985. pap. 9.95 (*0-03-005552-0*) Holt R&W.

— Knowledge of Language: Its Nature, Origin, & Use. LC 85-12234. (Convergence Ser.). 314p. 1985. 55.00 (*0-275-90025-8*, C0025, Praeger Pubs) Greenwood.

— Knowledge of Language: Its Nature, Origin, & Use. LC 85-12234. (Convergence Ser.). 314p. 1986. pap. 22.95 (*0-275-91761-4*, B1761, Praeger Pubs) Greenwood.

— Language & Mind. enl. ed. 194p. (C). 1972. pap. text 31.00 (*0-15-549257-8*) Harcourt Coll Pubs.

— Language & Politics. Otero, Carlos P., ed. 779p. 1998. 57.99 (*0-921689-35-7*, Pub. by Black Rose); pap. 28.99 (*0-921689-34-9*, Pub. by Black Rose) Consort Bk Sales.

— Language & Problems of Knowledge: The Managua Lectures. 215p. 1987. pap. text 13.50 (*0-262-53070-8*) MIT Pr.

— Language & Problems of Knowledge: The Managua Lectures. 215p. 1987. 27.00 (*0-262-03133-7*) MIT Pr.

— Language & Thought. (Anshen Transdisciplinary Lectureships in Art, Science, & the Philosophy of Culture Ser.). 96p. 1995. pap. 9.95 (*1-55921-076-1*) Moyer Bell.

— Language & Thought: Anshen Transdisciplinary Lectureships in Art, Science, & the Philosophy of Culture Monograph Ser., No. 3. LC 93-36148. (Anshen Transdisciplinary Lectureships in Art, Science, & the Philosophy of Culture Ser.). 96p. 1995. 14.95 (*1-55921-074-5*) Moyer Bell.

— Latin America: From Colonization to Globalization. 1999. pap. 12.95 (*1-876175-13-3*) Ocean Pr NJ.

— Lectures on Government & Binding: The Pisa Lectures. 7th ed. (Studies in Generative Grammar: No. 9). x, 371p. 1993. pap. text 24.95 (*3-11-014131-0*) Mouton.

— Letters from Lexington: Reflections on Propaganda. LC 93-2687. 1993. pap. 10.95 (*1-56751-010-8*); lib. bdg. 29.95 (*1-56751-011-6*) Common Courage.

— The Logical Structure of Linguistic Theory. LC 84-16211. 592p. 1985. pap. text 17.50 (*0-226-10436-2*) U Ch Pr.

— Media Control: The Spectacular Achievements of Propaganda. (Open Magazine Pamphlet Ser.: No. 10). 21p. (Orig.). 1994. 4.00 (*1-884519-03-2*) Open Media.

— Media Control: The Spectacular Achievements of Propaganda. LC 96-53580. (Open Media Pamphlet Ser.: Vol. 2). 64p. (Orig.). 1997. pap. 5.95 (*1-888363-49-5*) Seven Stories.

— The Minimalist Program. (Current Studies in Linguistics). 426p. (Orig.). 1995. pap. text 24.00 (*0-262-53128-3*) MIT Pr.

— Modular Approaches to the Study of the Mind. LC 82-62962. (Distinguished Graduate Research Lectures). 118p. 1984. 15.00 (*0-916304-56-6*) SDSU Press.

— Necessary Illusions: Thought Control in Democratic Societies. LC 89-6074. 422p. 1989. 40.00 (*0-89608-367-5*); pap. 22.00 (*0-89608-366-7*) South End Pr.

***Chomsky, Noam.** A New Generation Draws the Line: Kosovo, East Timor & the Standards of the West. 160p. 2000. 22.00 (*1-85984-789-7*, Pub. by Verso) Norton.

— New Horizons in the Study of Language & Mind. 256p. 2000. 54.95 (*0-521-65147-6*); pap. 19.95 (*0-521-65822-5*) Cambridge U Pr.

— The New Military Humanism: Lessons from Kosovo. LC 99-38488. 208p. (C). 1999. 29.95 (*1-56751-177-5*); pap. 11.96 (*1-56751-176-7*, Pub. by Common Courage) LPC InBook.

Chomsky, Noam. Objectivity & Liberal Scholarship. 142p. 1997. pap. 6.00 (*0-934868-33-6*) Black & Red.

— On Language: Chomsky's Classic Works "Reflections on Language" & "Language & Responsibility", 2 vols. in 1. 512p. 1998. reprint ed. pap. 16.95 (*1-56584-475-0*, Pub. by New Press NY) Norton.

— On Power & Ideology. 146p. write for info. (*0-921689-05-5*); pap. write for info. (*0-921689-04-7*) Black Rose.

— On Power & Ideology: The Managua Lectures. LC 87-4569. 140p. (Orig.). 1987. 25.00 (*0-89608-290-3*); pap. 13.00 (*0-89608-289-X*) South End Pr.

— Perspectives on Power: Reflections on Human Nature & the Social Order. 272p. write for info. (*1-55164-049-X*); pap. write for info. (*1-55164-048-1*) Black Rose.

— Pirates & Emperors. 206p. 1996. 48.99 (*1-895431-21-2*, Pub. by Black Rose); pap. 19.99 (*1-895431-20-4*, Pub. by Black Rose) Consort Bk Sales.

— Pirates & Emperors: International Terrorism in the Real World. 175p. (Orig.). pap. 8.95 (*0-912439-06-8*) Amana Bks.

— Powers & Prospects: Reflections on Human Nature & the Social Order. 244p. 1996. 40.00 (*0-89608-536-8*); pap. 16.00 (*0-89608-535-X*) South End Pr.

— Profit over People: Neoliberalism & Global Order. LC 98-35985. 288p. 1998. pap. 15.95 (*1-888363-82-7*) Seven Stories.

— Profit over People: Neoliberalism & Global Order. LC 98-35985. 288p. 1998. 32.00 (*1-888363-89-4*) Seven Stories.

— The Prosperous Few & the Restless Many. LC 93-35814. (Real Story Ser.). 95p. (Orig.). 1994. pap. 7.00 (*1-878825-03-8*) Odonian Pr.

C

— Questions of Form & Interpretation. v, 40p. (Orig.). (C). 1975. pap. text 11.55 (*3-11-013282-6*) Mouton.

— Radical Priorities. 2nd rev. ed. Otero, Carlos P., ed. 307p. 1981. 48.99 (*0-920057-16-0*, Pub. by Black Rose); pap. 19.99 (*0-920057-17-9*, Pub. by Black Rose) Consort Bk Sales.

— Rethinking Camelot: JFK, the Vietnam War, & U. S. Political Culture. 172p. write for info. (*1-895431-73-5*); pap. write for info. (*1-895431-72-7*) Black Rose.

— Rethinking Camelot: JFK, the Vietnam War, & U. S. Political Culture. LC 93-297. 172p. 1993. 30.00 (*0-89608-459-0*); pap. 14.00 (*0-89608-458-2*) South End Pr.

— Review of Verbal Behavior by B. F. Skinner. (Irvington Reprint Series in Anthropology). (C). 1991. reprint ed. pap. text 2.90 (*0-8290-2603-7*, A-34) Irvington.

***Chomsky, Noam.** Rogue States: The Rule of Force in World Affairs. LC 99-49570. 164p. 2000. 40.00 (*0-89608-612-7*, Pub. by South End Pr); pap. 14.00 (*0-89608-611-9*, Pub. by South End Pr) Consort Bk Sales.

Chomsky, Noam. Rules & Representations. LC 79-26145. (Woodbridge Lectures Ser.: No. 11). 1982. pap. text 22.00 (*0-231-04827-0*) Col U Pr.

— Secrets, Lies & Democracy. Naiman, Arthur, ed. & compiled by by. LC 95-141339. (The Real Story Ser.). 127p. (Orig.). 1994. pap. 9.00 (*1-878825-04-6*) Odonian Pr.

— Selected Readings. Allen, J. P. & Van Buren, Paul M., eds. (Language & Language Learning Ser.). (C). 1971. text 16.95 (*0-19-437046-1*) OUP.

— Some Concepts & Consequences of the Theory of Government & Binding. (Linguistic Inquiry Monographs). 96p. 1982. pap. text 10.95 (*0-262-53042-2*) MIT Pr.

— Studies on Semantics in Generative Grammar. LC 74-189711. (Janua Linguarum, Ser. Minor: No. 107). 207p. (Orig.). 1972. pap. text 24.65 (*90-279-7964-2*) Mouton.

— Syntactic Structures. (Janua Linguarum, Series Minor: No. 4). 1978. 17.95 (*0-89925-090-4*) Mouton.

— Syntactic Structures. 12th ed. (Janua Linguarum Series Minor 4). 117p. pap. 20.00 (*90-279-3385-5*) Mouton.

— Topics in the Theory of Generative Grammar. (Janua Linguarum, Ser. Minor: No. 56). (Orig.). 1978. pap. text 15.40 (*90-279-3122-4*) Mouton.

— Turning the Tide. 330p. 36.95 (*0-920057-90-X*, Pub. by Black Rose); pap. 19.99 (*0-920057-91-8*, Pub. by Black Rose) Consort Bk Sales.

— Turning the Tide. 334p. 1996. 48.99 (*0-920057-78-0*, Pub. by Black Rose) Consort Bk Sales.

— Turning the Tide: U. S. Intervention in Central America & the Struggle for Peace. LC 85-27940. 298p. 1985. 35.00 (*0-89608-267-9*) South End Pr.

— The Umbrella of U. S. Power: The Universal Declaration of Human Rights & the Contradictions of U. S. Policy. LC 98-30157. (Open Media Pamphlet Ser.: No. 9). 80p. 1999. pap. 5.95 (*1-888363-85-1*) Seven Stories.

— What Uncle Sam Really Wants. LC 92-23824. (Real Story Ser.). 111p. (Orig.). 1998. pap. 7.00 (*1-878825-01-1*) Odonian Pr.

— World Orders: Old & New. 311p. 1996. pap. 16.95 (*0-231-10157-0*) Col U Pr.

— Year 501: The Conquest Continues. 331p. write for info. (*1-895431-63-8*); pap. write for info. (*1-895431-62-X*) Black Rose.

— Year 501: The Conquest Continues. 330p. 1993. 30.00 (*0-89608-445-0*); pap. 19.00 (*0-89608-444-2*) South End Pr.

Chomsky, Noam & Barsamian, David. Chronicles of Dissent. 416p. (Orig.). 1993. pap. 16.95 (*0-9628838-8-3*); lib. bdg. 29.95 (*0-9628838-9-1*) Common Courage.

Chomsky, Noam & Halle, Morris. The Sound Pattern of English. 487p. 1991. pap. text 26.50 (*0-262-53097-X*) MIT Pr.

Chomsky, Noam & Herman, Edward S. After the Cataclysm: Postwar Indochina & the Reconstruction of Imperial Ideology. LC 79-64138. (Political Economy of Human Rights Ser.: Vol. II). 393p. 1979. 40.00 (*0-89608-101-X*); pap. 18.00 (*0-89608-100-1*) South End Pr.

— Political Economy of Human Rights Vol. 1: The Washington Connection & Third World Fascism, Vol. 1. 441p. write for info. (*0-919618-89-8*); pap. write for info. (*0-919618-88-X*) Black Rose.

— Political Economy of Human Rights Vol. 2: After the Cataclysm: Postwar Indochina & the Reconstruction of Imperial Ideology, Vol. 2. 392p. write for info. (*0-919618-91-X*); pap. write for info. (*0-919618-90-1*) Black Rose.

— The Washington Connection & Third World Facism. LC 79-64085. (Political Economy of Human Rights Ser.: Vol. I). 441p. 1979. 40.00 (*0-89608-091-9*) South End Pr.

Chomsky, Noam & Miller, George A. Analyse Formelle Des Langues Naturelles. (Mathematiques et Sciences de l'Homme Ser.: No. 8). 1971. pap. text 27.70 (*90-279-6796-2*) Mouton.

Chomsky, Noam & Zinn, Howard. The Cold War & the University: Toward an Intellectual History of the Postwar Years. 304p. 1998. pap. 12.00 (*1-56584-397-5*, Pub. by New Press NY) Norton.

***Chomsky, Noam, et al.** Acts of Aggression: Policing Rogue States. (Open Media Pamphlet Ser.: Vol. 13). 64p. (Orig.). 1999. pap. 6.95 (*1-58322-005-4*, Pub. by Seven Stories) Publishers Group.

Chomsky, Noam, et al. Talking about a Revolution: Interviews with Noam Chomsky, Bell Hooks, Howard Zinn & Others. South End Press Collective Staff, ed. LC 98-16040. 132p. 1998. 40.00 (*0-89608-588-0*) South End Pr.

— Talking about a Revolution: Interviews with Noam Chomsky, Bell Hooks, Howard Zinn & Others. South End Press Collective Staff, ed. LC 98-16040. 132p. 1998. pap. 14.00 (*0-89608-587-2*) South End Pr.

Chomsky, Noam, jt. auth. see Herman, Edward S.

Chomycz, Bob. Fiber Optic Installations: A Practical Guide. (Illus.). 234p. (Orig.). 1996. 45.00 (*0-07-011635-0*) McGraw.

***Chomycz, Bob.** Fiber Optic Installer's Field Manual. (Illus.). 368p. 2000. pap. 49.95 (*0-07-135604-5*) McGraw.

***Chon.** Welcome to Hospitality: An Introduction. 2nd ed. LC 99-40092. 466p. (C). 1999. pap. 71.95 (*0-7668-0850-5*) Delmar.

Chon, H. Ional, et al, eds. Recent Advances & New Horizons in Zeolite Science & Technology. LC 96-22634. (Studies in Surface Science & Catalysis: Vol. 102). 484p. 1996. text 244.00 (*0-444-82499-5*) Elsevier.

Chon, K. S., ed. Practice of Graduate Research in Hospitality & Tourism. LC 99-32018. 240p. (C). 1999. 39.95 (*0-7890-0727-4*) Haworth Pr.

***Chon, K. S., ed.** Tourism in Southeast Asia: A New Direction. LC 00-22107. 202p. 2000. pap. text 34.95 (*0-7890-1122-0*); lib. bdg. 59.95 (*0-7890-0732-0*) Haworth Pr.

***Chon, K. S., et al.** Japanese Tourists: Socio-Economic, Marketing & Psychological Analysis. LC 00-36964. 2000. write for info. (*0-7890-0988-9*) Haworth Pr.

Chon, Kye-Sung, et al. Welcome to Hospitality: An Introduction. LC 93-49743. (C). 1994. 43.00 (*0-538-71246-5*) S-W Pub.

— Welcome to Hospitality: An Introduction. LC 93-49743. 1994. disk. write for info. (*0-538-71125-6*) S-W Pub.

Ch'on Sang Pyong. Back to Heaven: Selected Poems of Ch'on Sang Pyong. Anthony of Taize & Kim, Young-Moo, trs. (Cornell East Asia Ser.: Vol. 77). (Illus.). 142p. 1995. 18.70 (*1-885445-69-5*, CEAS77) Cornell East Asia Pgm.

— Back to Heaven: Selected Poems of Ch'on Sang Pyong. Anthony of Taize & Young-Moo Kim, trs. from KOR. (Cornell East Asia Ser.: Vol. 77). (Illus.). 142p. (C). 1995. pap. 11.90 (*1-885445-77-6*, 77) Cornell East Asia Pgm.

— Back to Heaven: Selected Poems of Ch'on Sang Pyong. Brother Anthony of Taize & Kim, Young-Moo, trs. from KOR. (Cornell East Asia Ser.: Vol. 77). 207p. (C). 1996. pap. 11.90 (*1-885445-75-X*) Cornell East Asia Pgm.

— Singing Like a Cricket, Hooting Like an Owl: Selected Poems by Yi Kyu-bo. O'Rourke, Kevin D., tr. from KOR. (Cornell East Asia Ser.: No. 78). 106p. (C). 1995. 18.70 (*1-885445-68-7*, 78) Cornell East Asia Pgm.

Chon, Sun & Opperman, Martin. Tourism in Developing Countries. 177p. 1997. pap. 17.99 (*0-415-13939-2*) Thomson Learn.

Chona, Ravinder & Corwin, William R., eds. Rapid Load Fracture Testing. LC 91-45387. (Special Technical Publication Ser.: No. 1130). (Illus.). 192p. 1992. text 63.00 (*0-8031-1429-X*, STP1130) ASTM.

Chona, Rawinder, ed. Fracture Mechanics: Twenty-Third Symposium 1189. (Special Technical Publication Ser.). (Illus.). 873p. 1993. text 195.00 (*0-8031-1867-8*, STP1189) ASTM.

Chonam, Lama, jt. tr. see Khandro, Sangye.

Chonchuenchob, Pradit, et al. Hanging Culture of the Green Mussel in Thailand (Mytilus Smaragdinus Chemnitz) (Illus.). 1983. pap. 2.00 (*0-89955-383-4*, Pub. by ICLARM) Intl Spec Bk.

Chong. Culture & Strategy. LC 99-44629. 2000. lib. bdg. 50.00 (*0-226-10438-9*) U Ch Pr.

— Elasticity in Engineering Mechanics. 2nd ed. LC 99-15236. 632p. 1999. 90.00 (*0-471-31614-8*) Wiley.

Chong, jt. auth. see Boresi, Arthur P.

Chong, Ada & Pena, Elena de la. Manual de Ministerios con Jovenes: Youth Ministries Manual. (SPA.). 52p. 1996. pap. 6.95 (*0-88177-190-2*, DR190) Discipleship Res.

Chong, Alan, compiled by. European & American Paintings in the Cleveland Museum of Art: A Summary Catalogue. LC 93-11560. (Illus.). 316p. 1993. pap. 39.95 (*0-940717-21-2*) Cleveland Mus Art.

***Chong, Alan & Kloek, Walter.** Still-Life Paintings from the Netherlands, 1550-1720. (Illus.). 320p. 2000. 75.00 (*90-400-9317-2*, Pub. by Waanders) U of Wash Pr.

Chong, Alan, tr. see Jiang, Wei.

Chong, Alan, tr. see Wang Xuanming.

Chong, C. T. Techniques of Admissible Recursion Theory. (Lecture Notes in Mathematics Ser.: Vol. 1106). ix, 214p. 1985. 37.95 (*0-387-13902-8*) Spr-Verlag.

Chong, C. T., et al, eds. Proceedings of the 6th Asian Logic Conference Beijing, China, 20-24 May 1996. 350p. 1998. 68.00 (*981-02-3432-5*) World Scientific Pub.

Chong, Chong K., ed. Moral Perspectives. 150p. (Orig.). 1992. pap. 34.95 (*9971-69-162-0*, Pub. by Sngapore Univ Pr) Coronet Bks.

***Chong, D. W.** Algernon Hent: My Life, Your Dimes. LC 99-90818. 1999. 25.00 (*0-7388-0512-2*); pap. 18.00 (*0-7388-0513-0*) Xlibris Corp.

Chong, Delano P., ed. Recent Advances in Density Functional Methods, Pt. 1. LC 95-45326. (Recent Advances in Computational Chemistry Ser.: Vol. 1). 400p. 1995. 86.00 (*981-02-2442-7*) World Scientific Pub.

Chong, Denise. The Concubine's Children: The Story of a Chinese Family Living on Two Sides of the Globe. (Illus.). 304p. 1996. pap. 13.95 (*0-14-025427-7*) Viking Penguin.

— The Girl in the Picture: The Story of Kim Phuc & the Photograph That Changed the Course of the Vietnam War. LC 99-53415. (Illus.). 400p. 2000. 25.95 (*0-670-88040-X*, Viking) Viking Penguin.

Chong, Dennis. Collective Action & the Civil Rights Movement. LC 90-48848. (American Politics & Political Economy Ser.). (Illus.). 276p. 1991. pap. text 18.95 (*0-226-10441-9*) U Ch Pr.

— Collective Action & the Civil Rights Movement. LC 90-48848. (American Politics & Political Economy Ser.). (Illus.). 256p. 1993. lib. bdg. 42.50 (*0-226-10440-0*) U Ch Pr.

— Culture & Strategy. LC 99-44629. 292p. 2000. pap. text 18.00 (*0-226-10439-7*) U Ch Pr.

Chong, Dianne, jt. ed. see Carriveau, Gary W.

Chong-Diaz, Guillermo. Die Salare in Nordchile - Geologie, Struktur und Geochemie. (Geotektonische Forschungen Ser.: Vol. 67). (GER.). 146p. 1984. 76.00 (*3-510-50033-4*, Pub. by E Schweizerbartsche) Balogh.

Chong, Douglas D. Ancestral Reflections: Hawaii's Early Chinese of Waipahu, an Ethnic Community Experience, 1885-1935. (Illus.). 358p. 1998. 27.95 (*0-9656220-0-2*) Tsoong Nyee.

Chong, Edwin K. & Zak, Stanislaw H. An Introduction to Optimization. LC 95-6111. (Interscience Series in Discrete Mathematics & Optimization). 424p. 1995. 79.95 (*0-471-08949-4*) Wiley.

Chong-hui, Choe. The Cry of the Harp & Other Korean Short Stories. Korean National Commission for UNESCO, ed. Poitras, Genell, tr. from KOR. (Best Korean Short Stories Ser.: No. 2). xiii, 207p. 1983. 20.00 (*0-89209-213-0*) Pace Grp Intl.

Chong Ju Choi & Kelemen, Mihaela. Cultural Competences: Co-Operative Approaches to International Business Strategy. (Illus.). 250p. 1995. text 77.95 (*1-85521-636-1*, Pub. by Dartmth Pub) Ashgate Pub Co.

***Chong-Jun, Yi.** The Prophet & Other Stories. Pickering, Julie, tr. from KOR. LC 99-232443. (Illus.). 208p. (C). 1998. 18.70 (*1-885445-61-X*); pap. 11.90 (*1-885445-01-6*) Cornell East Asia Pgm.

Chong, K. C., et al. Inputs as Related to Output in Milkfish Production in the Philippines. (ICLARM Technical Reports: No. 3). (Illus.). 82p. (Orig.). 1982. pap. 10.00 (*0-89955-421-0*, Pub. by ICLARM) Intl Spec Bk.

— Milkfish Production Dualism in the Philippines: A Multi-Disciplinary Perspective on Continous Low Yields & Constraints to Aquaculture Development. (ICLARM Technical Reports: No. 15). (Illus.). 70p. (Orig.). 1984. pap. 10.50 (*971-10-2210-9*, Pub. by ICLARM) Intl Spec Bk.

Chong, K. P. & Ward-Smith, J., eds. Mechanics of Oil Shale. 603p. 1984. 194.50 (*0-85334-273-3*) Elsevier.

Chong, K. P., jt. auth. see Boresi, Arthur P.

Chong, K. P., ed. see American Society of Civil Engineers Staff.

Chong, Ken P., et al, eds. University Programs in Computer-Aided Engineering, Design, & Manufacturing. 346p. 1989. pap. text 7.00 (*0-87262-709-8*) Am Soc Civil Eng.

Chong, Key R. Cannibalism in China. LC 90-5997. 350p. 1990. 36.00 (*0-89341-618-5*, Longwood Academic) Hollowbrook.

— Won Buddhism: A History & Theology of Korea's New Religion. LC 97-39717. (Studies in Asian Thought & Religion: Vol. 22). 168p. (Orig.). 1997. text 79.95 (*0-7734-8436-1*) E Mellen.

— Won Buddhism: A History & Theology of Korea's New Religion. 164p. (Orig.). (C). 1995. pap. text 19.95 (*0-89341-758-0*); lib. bdg. 37.50 (*0-89341-757-2*) Hollowbrook.

Chong, Kim-Chong. Moral Agoraphobia Vol. 25: The Challenge of Egoism, Vol. 25. (Revisioning Philosophy Ser.). 104p. (C). 1996. text 34.95 (*0-8204-2839-6*) P Lang Pubng.

Chong, Lu-Sheng, jt. tr. see Young, Judy D.

Chong, N. Victor. Clinical Ocular Physiology: An Introductory Text. LC 96-20041. 192p. 1997. pap. text 36.50 (*0-7506-2718-2*) Buttrwrth-Heinemann.

Chong, Ping, et al. Between Worlds: Contemporary Asian-American Plays. LC 90-10821. 272p. (Orig.). 1989. reprint ed. pap. 16.95 (*1-55936-004-6*) Theatre Comm.

Chong-Rae, Cho. Playing with Fire. Kyung-Ja, Chun, tr. from KOR. (Cornell East Asia Ser.: Vol. 85). 188p. (C). 1997. 18.70 (*1-885445-65-2*, CEAS 85); pap. 11.90 (*1-885445-85-7*, CEAS 85) Cornell East Asia Pgm.

Chong, Ronald K. Euro 1999 & Beyond: Value Creation Strategies for International Business. Jeschke, Katherine R., ed. (Illus.). 64p. 1999. pap. 24.95 (*1-888505-07-9*) NACM.

Chong, T. Mike. Functional Polyolefins. 300p. 1998. 38.00 (*1-86094-075-7*, Pub. by Imperial College) World Scientific Pub.

Chong-un, Kim & Fulton, Bruce, eds. A Ready-Made Life: Early Masters of Modern Korean Fiction. LC 98-16635. 200p. 1998. text 38.00 (*0-8248-2015-0*); pap. text 15.95 (*0-8248-2071-1*) UH Pr.

Chong-un, Kim, tr. see Chang-sop, Son, et al.

Chong-un, Kim, tr. see Hwi, Sonu & In-hun, Choe.

***Chong, Victor.** Visual Diagnosis Self-Tests on Eye Diseases. (Illus.). 2000. pap. text 19.95 (*1-873413-32-7*) Merit Pub Intl.

Chong-Wha, Chung, ed. Modern Korean Literature: An Anthology, 1908-1965. LC 94-9433. (Korean Culture Ser.). 475p. 1995. 76.50 (*0-7103-0490-0*) Routledge.

Chong-Wha, Chung, tr. from KOR. Love in Mid-Winter Night: Korean Sijo Poetry. (KOR., Illus.). 112p. 1986. 35.00 (*0-7103-0104-9*) Routledge.

Chong Yang-Mo, et al. Arts of Korea. LC 98-6404. (Illus.). 512p. 1998. 50.00 (*0-87099-850-1*) Metro Mus Art.

Chongju, So. Selected Poems of So Chongju. McCann, David R., tr. from KOR. (Modern Asian Literature Ser.). 160p. 1989. text 49.50 (*0-231-06794-1*) Col U Pr.

Chongpeepien, T., jt. ed. see McCoy, E. W.

Chongxi, Yue, jt. auth. see Foster, Steven.

Chongyi, Feng & Goodman, David S. China's Hainan Province: Economic Development & Investment Environment. LC 96-171485. (Asia Papers: No. 5). 96 p. 1995. pap. 15.95 (*1-875560-56-4*, Pub. by Univ of West Aust Pr) Intl Spec Bk.

***Chongyi, Feng & Goodman, David S., eds.** North China at War: The Social Ecology of Revolution, 1937-1945. LC 99-89422. 145p. 2000. pap. 29.95 (*0-8476-9939-0*); text 74.00 (*0-8476-9938-2*) Rowman.

Chonko, Lawrence B. Business. 4th ed. 202p. (C). 1996. text 19.80 (*0-536-59661-1*) Pearson Custom.

— Business Economy & World Affairs: Customized. 2nd ed. 810p. (C). 1995. text 42.00 (*0-536-58878-3*) S&S Trade.

— Business Economy & World Affairs: Reader. 186p. (C). 1996. pap. 18.50 (*0-536-59662-X*) Pearson Custom.

Chonko, Lawrence B. Ethical Decision Making in Marketing. LC 95-1876. (Sage Series on Business Ethics: Vol. 1). (Illus.). 328p. 1995. 39.95 (*0-8039-5545-6*); pap. 18.95 (*0-8039-5546-4*) Sage.

Chonpairot, Jarernchai, jt. auth. see Miller, Terry E.

Choo & Taylor. Introduction to Discrete Mathematics. 1994. pap. text. write for info. (*0-582-80055-2*, Pub. by Addison-Wesley) Longman.

Choo, Andrew L. Abuse of Process & Judicial Stays of Criminal Proceedings. (Oxford Monographs on Criminal Law & Justice). 240p. (C). 1994. text 49.95 (*0-19-825801-1*, 8947) OUP.

— Evidence: Text & Materials. LC 97-31550. (Longman Law Ser.). 1998. pap. text. write for info. (*0-582-08756-2*, Pub. by Addison-Wesley) Longman.

Choo, B. S. & MacGinley, T. J. Reinforced Concrete: Design Theory & Examples. 2nd ed. (Illus.). 544p. (Orig.). 1990. mass mkt. 51.95 (*0-419-13830-7*, E & FN Spon) Routledge.

Choo, Chun W. Information Management for the Intelligent Organization: The Art of Scanning the Environment. 2nd ed. LC 98-9816. (ASIS Monographs). 255p. 1998. 39.50 (*1-57387-057-9*) Info Today Inc.

— The Knowing Organization: How Organizations Use Information to Construct Meaning, Create Knowledge & Make Decisions. LC 97-9034. (Illus.). 320p. (C). 1998. pap. text 29.95 (*0-19-511012-9*) OUP.

***Choo, Chun Wei, et al.** Web Work: Information & Seeking Knowledge Work on the World Wide Web. LC 00-42031. (Information Science & Knowledge Management Ser.). 2000. write for info. (*0-7923-6460-0*) Kluwer Academic.

Choo, K. H. The Centromere. LC 97-3361. (Illus.). 318p. 1997. pap. text 41.95 (*0-19-857780-X*) OUP.

— The Centromere. LC 97-3361. (Illus.). 318p. (C). 1998. text 85.00 (*0-19-857781-8*) OUP.

Choo, Miho & O'Grady, William D. Handbook of Korean Vocabulary: A Resource for Word Recognition & Comprehension. LC 95-38076. 1996. pap. text 26.95 (*0-8248-1815-6*) UH Pr.

Choo, Miho & O'Grady, William P. Handbook of Korean Vocabulary: A Resource for Word Recognition & Comprehension. LC 95-38076. 1996. text 48.00 (*0-8248-1738-9*) UH Pr.

Choo, Myung-Gun. New Asia in Global Perspectives. LC 99-22105. 2000. text 69.95 (*0-312-22172-X*) St Martin.

Choo, Vincent K. Composite Materials. (Illus.). (C). 1988. lib. bdg. write for info. (*0-929785-01-0*) Knowen Academic.

— Fundamentals of Composite Materials. (Illus.). 313p. (C). 1990. text 69.95 (*0-929785-00-2*) Knowen Academic.

Choo, Y. S. & Van Der Vegte, G. J., eds. Tubular Structures VIII: Proceedings of the 8th International Symposium, Singapore, 26-28 August, 1998. 672p. (C). 1998. text 125.00 (*90-5809-001-9*, Pub. by A A Balkema) Ashgate Pub Co.

Choo, Y. S., jt. ed. see Shanmugam, N. E.

Chooey Low, Jeanie W. China Connection: Finding Ancestral Roots for Chinese in America. 2nd ed. LC 93-91747. (Illus.). 65p. 1996. reprint ed. pap. 11.95 (*0-9638835-1-8*) JWC Low.

Chooluck, Leon. So You Want to Produce a Picture. Rado, Ivan J., ed. (Illus.). 204p. (Orig.). (C). 1992. pap. 20.00 (*0-9633948-0-0*) I J Rado.

Choon, Ban Kah, et al, eds. Imagining Singapore. 2nd ed. 336p. 2000. pap. 35.00 (*981-210-105-5*, Pub. by Times Academic) Intl Spec Bk.

Choong-Soon Kim. Japanese Industry in the American South. LC 95-10266. 224p. (C). 1995. pap. 21.99 (*0-415-91403-5*) Routledge.

— Japanese Industry in the American South. LC 95-10266. 224p. (C). (gr. 13). 1995. 75.00 (*0-415-91402-7*) Routledge.

Choong, T. C. & Rajah, Harry. Judicial Management in Singapore. 1990. boxed set 195.00 (*0-409-99585-1*, MICHIE) LEXIS Pub.

Choongh, Satnam. Policing as Social Discipline. (Clarendon Studies in Criminology). 274p. 1998. text 69.00 (*0-19-826478-X*) OUP.

Chop, Carol Bousquet, see Bousquet Chop, Carol.

Chop, Walter & Robnett, Regula H. Gerontology for the Health Care Professional. LC 99-10900. (Illus.). 384p. (C). 1999. pap. text 21.95 (*0-8036-0398-3*) Davis Co.

Chopard, Bastine & Droz, Michel. Cellular Automata Modeling of Physical Systems. LC 97-28284. (Collection Alea-Saclay: No. 6). (Illus.). 354p. (C). 1998. text 90.00 (*0-521-46168-5*) Cambridge U Pr.

Chopay, Nicholas P., jt. ed. see Chemical Engineering Progress Staff.

Chopdar, Amresh. Fundus Fluorescein Angiography. LC 95-14151. (Illus.). 192p. 1995. text 130.00 (*0-7506-1885-X*) Buttrwrth-Heinemann.

Chope, R. P. The Dialect of Hartland, Devonshire. (English Dialect Society Publications: No. 65). 1972. reprint ed. pap. 25.00 (*0-8115-0485-9*) Periodicals Srv.

An Asterisk (*) at the beginning of an entry indicates that the title is appearing for the first time.

***Chope, Robert C.** Dancing Naked: Breaking Through the Emotional Limits That Keep You from the Job You Want. 220p. 2000. pap. 14.95 (*1-57224-184-5*) New Harbinger.

Chopel, Gedun. Tibetan Arts of Love: Sex, Orgasm & Spiritual Healing. Hopkins, Jeffrey, ed. & tr. by. 282p. 1992. pap. 14.95 (*0-937938-97-1*) Snow Lion Pubns.

Chopell, M. William. Guide to Owning a Dachshund: AKC Rank #7. (Guide to Owning Ser.). (Illus.). 64p. 1995. pap. 6.95 (*0-7938-1851-6*, RE-307) TFH Pubns.

Choper. Corporation. 4th ed. 1152p. 1995. 57.00 (*0-316-14014-7*, Aspen Law & Bus) Aspen Pub.

— Gilbert Constitutional Law. 28th ed. 1997. pap. text 19.95 (*0-15-900375-X*) Harcourt Legal.

— Gilbert Corporations. 14th ed. 1996. pap. text 19.95 (*0-15-900342-3*) Harcourt Legal.

Choper, Jesse & Sheffy, Steve H. First Amendment, Cases - Comments - Questions: 1994 Supplement. 160p. 1994. pap. text 11.50 (*0-314-04478-7*) West Pub.

Choper, Jesse & Shiffrin, Steven H. First Amendment-Cases, Comments, Questions, 1996 Supplement. 2nd ed. (American Casebook Ser.). 50p. 1996. pap. text, suppl. ed. write for info. (*0-314-20243-9*) West Pub.

Choper, Jesse, jt. auth. see Shiffrin, Steven H.

Choper, Jesse H. Judicial Review & the National Political Process: A Functional Reconsideration of the Role of the Supreme Court. LC 79-21135. 1980. lib. bdg. 42.00 (*0-226-10443-5*) U Ch Pr.

— Judicial Review & the National Political Process: A Functional Reconsideration of the Role of the Supreme Court. LC 79-21135. 494p. 1983. reprint ed. pap. text 12.95 (*0-226-10444-3*) U Ch Pr.

— Securing Religious Liberty: Principles for Judicial Interpretation of the Religion Clauses. LC 94-36239. 212p. 1995. 24.95 (*0-226-10445-1*) U Ch Pr.

***Choper, Jesse H. & American Bar Association Staff.** Supreme Court & It's Justices. 2nd ed. LC 00-44752. (Best of the Aba Journal Ser.). (Illus.). 2000. write for info. (*1-57073-760-6*) Amer Bar Assn.

***Choper, Jesse H., et al.** Cases & Materials on Corporations. 5th ed. LC 99-42241. 2000. boxed set 64.00 (*0-7355-1245-0*) Panel Pubs.

Choper, Jesse H., et al. The Supreme Court: Trends & Developments, Set, Vols. 1-5. 150.00 (*1-55917-683-0*, 811B) Natl Prac Inst.

— The Supreme Court: Trends & Developments, Vol. 4: 1981-82. 40.00 (*1-55917-681-4*, 800B) Natl Prac Inst.

— The Supreme Court: Trends & Developments, Vol. 5: 1982-83. 40.00 (*1-55917-682-2*, 810B) Natl Prac Inst.

Choper, Jesse H., jt. auth. see Sheffrin, Steven H.

Choper, Jesse H., jt. auth. see Shiffrin, Steven H.

Chopey, Nicholas P. Environmental Engineering in the Process Plant. 1992. 46.00 (*0-07-011035-2*) McGraw.

Chopey, Nicholas P. & Hicks, Tyler Gregory, eds. Handbook of Chemical Engineering Calculations. 2nd ed. LC 93-25590. 656p. 1992. 89.95 (*0-07-011021-2*) McGraw.

Chophel, Norbu. Folk Culture of Tibet. 105p. 1986. reprint ed. 7.50 (*0-8364-1676-7*, Pub. by Manohar) S Asia.

Chopich, Erika J., jt. auth. see Paul, Margaret.

Chopin. Chopin Masterpieces for Solo Piano. pap. text 8.95 (*0-486-40150-2*) Dover.

Chopin, Alonzo B. Glastenbury for Two Hundred Years (Connecticut) 252p. 1994. reprint ed. lib. bdg. 29.50 (*0-8328-4257-5*) Higginson Bk Co.

***Chopin, Frederic.** Ballades. (Music Scores Ser.). 1998. pap. 7.98 (*963-9059-43-9*) Kone Music.

Chopin, Frederic. Ballades. Paderewski, Ignacy J., ed. 72p. 1999. pap. 7.95 (*0-934009-10-4*, 410-41326) Presser Co.

— Chopin: Individual Pieces I. 1999. pap. 7.95 (*963-9059-45-5*) Kone Music.

— Chopin: Individual Pieces II. 1999. pap. 7.95 (*963-9059-46-3*) Kone Music.

— Chopin: Sonatas. 1999. pap. 7.95 (*963-9059-37-4*) Konemann.

— Chopin's Letters. 448p. 1988. reprint ed. pap. 10.95 (*0-486-25564-6*) Dover.

Chopin, Frederic. Complete Ballades, Impromptus & Sonatas: The Paderewski Edition. Bronarski, L. & Turczynski, J., eds. 240p. 1981. pap. 10.95 (*0-486-24164-5*) Dover.

Chopin, Frederic. Complete Preludes & Etudes for Solo Piano. Paderewski, Ignacy J., ed. 224p. 1980. reprint ed. pap. 8.95 (*0-486-24052-5*) Dover.

— Etudes. 130p. (Orig.). 1998. pap. text 7.98 (*963-8303-32-8*) Konemann.

— Fantasy in F Minor, Barcarolle, Berceuse & Other Works for Solo Piano. 224p. 1989. pap. 7.95 (*0-486-25950-1*) Dover.

***Chopin, Frederic.** Mazurka. (Music Scores Ser.). 1998. pap. 7.98 (*963-8303-31-X*) Kone Music.

Chopin, Frederic. Mazurkas. 160p. 1987. pap. 8.95 (*0-486-25548-4*) Dover.

— Nocturnes. Paderewski, Ignacy J., ed. 128p. 1999. pap. 11.95 (*0-934009-13-9*, 410-41329) Presser Co.

— Nocturnes & Polonaises. (Music Ser.). viii, 272p. 1985. reprint ed. pap. 10.95 (*0-486-24564-0*) Dover.

— The Piano Concertos Arranged for 2 Pianos. 208p. 1993. pap. 11.95 (*0-486-27498-5*) Dover.

— The Piano Concertos in Full Score. 176p. 1989. pap. 10.95 (*0-486-25835-1*) Dover.

***Chopin, Frederic.** Polonaises. (Music Scores Ser.). (Illus.). 1998. pap. text 7.98 (*963-8303-80-8*) Kone Music.

Chopin, Frederic. Preludes. Paderewski, Ignacy J., ed. 76p. 1999. pap. 9.95 (*0-934009-14-7*, 410-41330) Presser Co.

***Chopin, Frederic.** Preludes & Impromptus. 1998. pap. 7.98 (*963-8303-81-6*) Konemann.

Chopin, Frederic. Preludes, Opus 28. Higgins, Thomas, ed. (C). 1974. pap. text 15.50 (*0-393-09699-8*) Norton.

— Studies. Paderewski, Ignacy J., ed. 156p. 1999. pap. 13.95 (*0-934009-12-0*, 410-41328) Presser Co.

— Valses for Piano. 112p. pap. 7.95 (*963-8303-04-2*) Konemann.

— Various Preludes Transcribed for Guitar. Stang, Aaron, ed. 16p. (Orig.). (C). 1985. pap. text 4.95 (*0-7692-1334-0*, K04223) Wrner Bros.

— Waltzes. Paderewski, Ignacy J., ed. 124p. 1999. pap. 12.95 (*0-934009-11-2*, 410-41327) Presser Co.

— Waltzes & Scherzos, Vols. IX, XII, V. (Music Scores Ser.). (Illus.). 214p. 1982. reprint ed. pap. 9.95 (*0-486-24316-8*) Dover.

Chopin, Kate. The Awakening. 240p. 1995. pap. 9.00 (*1-57322-511-8*, Riverhd Trade) Berkley Pub.

— The Awakening. LC 92-52897. 1992. 15.00 (*0-679-41721-4*) Everymns Lib.

— The Awakening. 1974. 250.00 (*0-87968-395-3*) Gordon Pr.

***Chopin, Kate.** The Awakening. Knights, Pamela, ed. (Oxford World's Classic Ser.). 480p. 2000. pap. 7.95 (*0-19-282300-0*) OUP.

Chopin, Kate. The Awakening. 256p. 1998. per. 5.99 (*0-671-01547-8*, WSP) PB.

— The Awakening. LC 96-9623. (Literary Classics Ser.). 182p. 1996. pap. 6.95 (*1-57392-098-3*) Prometheus Bks.

— The Awakening. 3.95 (*0-686-85783-6*, Pub. by Quartet) Charles River Bks.

— Awakening. 192p. 1982. mass mkt. 4.50 (*0-380-00245-0*, Avon Bks) Morrow Avon.

— The Awakening. large type ed. 266p. 1995. lib. bdg. 22.00 (*0-939495-83-X*) North Bks.

— The Awakening. large type ed. LC 96-31076. (Perennial Ser.). 232p. 1996. 21.95 (*0-7838-1979-X*) Thorndike Pr.

— The Awakening. 1992. reprint ed. lib. bdg. 21.95 (*0-89968-270-7*, Lghtyr Pr) Buccaneer Bks.

— The Awakening. 128p. 1993. reprint ed. pap. text 1.00 (*0-486-27786-0*) Dover.

***Chopin, Kate.** The Awakening. 172p. 1998. reprint ed. lib. bdg. 22.00 (*1-58287-017-9*) North Bks.

Chopin, Kate. The Awakening. 1988. reprint ed. lib. bdg. 79.00 (*0-7812-1102-6*) Rprt Serv.

— The Awakening. 2nd ed. (Critical Editions Ser.). (C). 1993. pap. text 9.25 (*0-393-96057-9*) Norton.

***Chopin, Kate.** The Awakening. 2nd ed. (Norton Critical Editions Ser.). (C). 1999. pap. text 22.50 (*0-393-99009-5*) Norton.

Chopin, Kate. The Awakening & Other Stories. 1976. 24.95 (*0-8488-0457-0*) Amereon Ltd.

— The Awakening & Other Stories. Baxter, Judith, ed. (Cambridge Literature Ser.). 256p. (C). 1997. pap. 8.50 (*0-521-56766-1*) Cambridge U Pr.

— The Awakening & Other Stories. 420p. 1993. 16.50 (*0-679-42469-5*) Modern Lib NY.

— The Awakening & Other Stories. Baym, Nina, ed. 354p. (C). 1981. pap. text. write for info. (*0-318-57304-0*) Random.

— The Awakening & Other Stories. (Classics Library). 1998. pap. 3.95 (*1-85326-556-X*, 556XWW, Pub. by Wrdsworth Edits) NTC Contemp Pub Co.

— The Awakening & Selected Short Stories. 240p. 1985. mass mkt. 4.95 (*0-553-21330-X*, Bantam Classics) Bantam.

— The Awakening & Selected Short Stories. Gilbert, Sandra M., ed. 1990. 22.00 (*0-8446-6229-1*) Peter Smith.

— The Awakening & Selected Stories. Gilbert, Sandra M., ed. & intro. by. LC 80-24429. (American Library). 320p. (C). 1998. pap. 7.95 (*0-14-039022-7*) Addson-Wesley Educ.

— The Awakening & Selected Stories. Baym, Nina, ed. 354p. (C). 1981. pap. 5.00 (*0-07-554269-2*) McGraw.

— Awakening & Selected Stories of Kate Chopin. LC 75-37380. (Signet Classics). 1976. 10.05 (*0-606-03719-5*, Pub. by Turtleback) Demco.

— Bayou Folk. 1974. lib. bdg. 250.00 (*0-87968-712-6*) Gordon Pr.

***Chopin, Kate.** Bayou Folks. (Works of Kate Chopin). 2000. reprint ed. lib. bdg. 79.00 (*0-7812-1103-4*) Rprt Serv.

Chopin, Kate. Charlie, Set. unabridged ed. (Kate Chopin Ser.). 1994. 16.95 incl. audio (*1-883049-14-8*, Pub. by Sound Room) Lndmrk Audiobks.

— Charlie: Library Edition. unabridged ed. 1994. lib. bdg. 18.95 incl. audio (*1-883049-34-2*) Sound Room.

— The Collected Works of Kate Chopin, 4 vols., Set. Incl. At Fault. LC 72-78673. reprint ed. 65.00 (*0-403-04558-4*); Bayou Folk. LC 72-78673. reprint ed. 65.00 (*0-403-04559-2*); Night at Acadie. LC 72-78673. 65.00 (*0-403-04560-6*); LC 72-78673. 225.00 (*0-403-03454-X*) Somerset Pub.

— Complete Works of Kate Chopin. Seyersted, Per, ed. LC 73-80043. (Southern Literary Studies). 1032p. 1969. text 95.00 (*0-8071-0849-9*) La State U Pr.

— Desiree's Baby. unabridged ed. 1994. lib. bdg. 18.95 incl. audio (*1-883049-33-4*) Sound Room.

— Desiree's Baby, Set. unabridged ed. (Kate Chopin Ser.). 1994. 16.95 incl. audio (*1-883049-13-X*, 390227, Pub. by Sound Room) Lndmrk Audiobks.

— K CHOPIN SHORT STORIES *RE*142. Leary, L., ed. LC 70-103399. (Rinehart Editions Ser.). (C). 1970. pap. text 29.00 (*0-03-078395-X*, Pub. by Harcourt Coll Pubs) Harcourt.

— Kate Chopin, the Awakening: Complete, Authoritative Text with Biographical & Historical Contexts, Critical History, & Essays from Five Contemporary Critical Perspectives. Walker, Nancy A., ed. LC 92-72222. (Case Studies in Contemporary Criticism). 343p. (C). 1992. pap. text 11.95 (*0-312-06235-4*) St Martin.

— A Night in Acadie. 1972. 69.95 (*0-8490-0734-8*) Gordon Pr.

— A Pair of Silk Stockings & Other Stories. LC 96-20049. (Thrift Editions Ser.). 64p. 1998. reprint ed. pap. text 1.00 (*0-486-29264-9*) Dover.

— Portraits. 4.95 (*0-7043-3844-0*, Pub. by Quartet) Charles River Bks.

— A Vocation & a Voice. 1993. 23.25 (*0-8446-6708-0*) Peter Smith.

— A Vocation & a Voice: Stories. Toth, Emily, ed. & intro. by. 1991. pap. 10.95 (*0-14-039078-2*, Penguin Classics) Viking Penguin.

Chopin, Kate & Koloski, Bernard. Bayou Folk: And, A Night in Acadie. LC 98-36398. (Penguin Classics Ser.). 416p. 1999. pap. 11.95 (*0-14-043681-2*) Viking Penguin.

Chopin, Kate, jt. auth. see Toth, Emily.

***Choplin, Neil T. & Edwards, Russell P.** Visual Field Testing with the Humphrey Field Analyzer: A Text & Clinical Atlas. 2nd ed. LC 99-26556. 256p. 1999. 49.00 (*1-55642-389-6*) SLACK Inc.

Choplin, Neil T. & Edwards, Russell P. Visual Fields. LC 97-48545. (Basic Bookshelf for Eyecare Professionals Ser.). 272p. 1998. pap. 33.00 (*1-55642-363-2*) SLACK Inc.

Choplin, Robert H., ed. see MacMahon, Heber, et al.

Chopourian, Giragos. A Brief History of the Armenian Missionary Association of America. (ARM.). 25p. 1998. pap. write for info. (*1-883131-05-7*) Armenian Mission.

Chopp, Rebecca S. The Praxis of Suffering: An Interpretation of Liberation & Political Theologies. LC 86-824. 190p. (Orig.). 1986. reprint ed. pap. 58.90 (*0-608-02150-4*, 206281900003) Bks Demand.

— Saving Work: Feminist Practices of Theological Education. LC 94-36761. 160p. 1995. pap. 14.00 (*0-664-25539-6*) Westminster John Knox.

Chopp, Rebecca S. & Davaney, Sheila G., eds. Horizons in Feminist Theology: Identity, Tradition, & Norms. LC 97-26135. 256p. 1997. pap. text 21.00 (*0-8006-2996-5*, 1-2996, Fortress Pr) Augsburg Fortress.

Chopp, Rebecca S. & Taylor, Mark L., eds. Reconstructing Christian Theology. LC 94-2827. 400p. 1994. pap. 25.00 (*0-8006-2696-6*, 1-2696, Fortress Pr) Augsburg Fortress.

Choppa, Anthony J., et al. Vocational Evaluation in Private Sector Rehabilitation. 201p. (Orig.). (C). 1992. pap. 24.00 (*0-916671-96-8*) TRR.

Choppa, Karen. Bessie Pease Gutmann: Over Fifty Years of Published Art. LC 98-24607. (Illus.). 160p. 1998. 49.95 (*0-7643-0625-1*) Schiffer.

***Choppa, Karen.** Bessie Pease Gutmann, over Fifty Years of Published Art. 2nd ed. (Illus.). 160p. 1999. pap. 29.95 (*0-7643-1004-6*) Schiffer.

Choppa, Karen & Humphrey, Paul. Maud Humphrey: Her Permanent Imprint on American Illustration. LC 93-85279. (Illus.). 160p. 1993. 59.95 (*0-88740-540-1*); pap. 29.95 (*0-88740-546-0*) Schiffer.

Choppin. Evaluation in Education, ser. vol. 4. (Evaluation in Education-International). 1980. pap. 21.00 (*0-08-026076-4*, 1, Pergamon Pr) Elsevier.

Choppin, B. H. Evaluation in Education, ser. vol. 3. (Evaluation in Education-International). 1979. pap. 21.00 (*0-08-025190-0*, no. 2, Pergamon Pr) Elsevier.

— Evaluation in Education, ser. vol. 3. (Evaluation in Education-International). 1980. pap. 21.00 (*0-08-025191-9*, no. 3, Pergamon Pr) Elsevier.

— Evaluation in Education: An Experiment in Rural Primary Schools in Malaysia, Vol. 4, No. 2. (Illus.). 121p. 1980. pap. 22.00 (*0-08-027138-3*, Pergamon Pr) Elsevier.

— Evaluation in Education: Vol. 1, International Progress. Postlethwaite, T. Neville, ed. 1979. 168.00 (*0-08-023352-X*, Pub. by Pergamon Repr) Franklin.

Choppin, B. H., ed. Evaluation in Education, Vol. 4, No. 3. LC 77-81507. (Illus.). 93p. 1981. pap. 25.00 (*0-08-027134-0*, Pergamon Pr) Elsevier.

Choppin, B. H. & Postlethwaite, T. Neville, eds. Evaluation in Education, Vol. 3. (Reviews in Educational Evaluation Ser.). 250p. 1980. 68.00 (*0-08-026066-7*, Pergamon Pr) Elsevier.

— Evaluation in Education: Four Complete. (Illus.). 370p. 1981. 76.00 (*0-08-028404-3*, Pergamon Pr) Elsevier.

Choppin, G. & Ryberg, J., eds. Nuclear Chemistry: Theory & Applications. (Illus.). 1980. 294.00 (*0-08-023826-2*, Pergamon Pr) Elsevier.

Choppin, G. R., jt. auth. see Nash, K. L.

Choppin, Gregory R., et al, eds. Actinide-Lanthanide Separations: Proceedings of the International Symposium. 400p. 1985. 78.00 (*9971-978-68-7*) World Scientific Pub.

Choppin, Gregory R. & Ryberg, J., eds. Nuclear Chemistry: Theory & Applications. (Illus.). 1980. pap. 275.00 (*0-08-023823-8*, Pergamon Pr) Elsevier.

Choppin, Gregory R., et al. Radiochemistry & Nuclear Chemistry: Theory & Applications. 1994. text. write for info. (*0-08-037955-9*, Pergamon Pr) Elsevier.

— Radiochemistry & Nuclear Chemistry: Nuclear Chemistry, Theory & Applications. 2nd ed. LC 94-40183. (Illus.). 722p. 1995. pap. text 56.95 (*0-7506-2300-4*, Prgamon Press) Buttrwrth-Heinemann.

— Radiochemistry & Nuclear Chemistry: Theory & Applications. 1994. pap. text. write for info. (*0-08-037954-0*) Elsevier.

Choppin, Gregory R., jt. ed. see Carnall, William T.

Choppin, Hazel, ed. see Lynch, James R.

Choppy, C., jt. ed. see Bidoit, M.

***Chopra.** Vietnam Today & Indo-Vietnam Relations. 1999. 30.00 (*81-212-0663-4*, Pub. by Gyan Publishing Hse) S Asia.

***Chopra, A. J.** Managing the People Side of Innovation: 8 Rules for Engaging Minds & Hearts. LC 99-22634. (Illus.). 211p. 1999. 24.95 (*1-56549-098-3*) Kumarian Pr.

Chopra, A. K. Dynamics of Structures: A Primer. (Illus.). 126p. 1981. 25.00 (*0-943198-50-X*, MNO-2) Earthquake Eng.

Chopra, Ajai, et al. India: Recent Reforms & the Growth Response. (Occasional Papers: No. 134). 1995. pap. 15.00 (*1-55775-539-6*) Intl Monetary.

Chopra, Anil K. Dynamics of Structures: Theory & Applications to Earthquake Engineering. LC 94-46527. 1995. write for info. (*0-614-32228-6*) P-H.

— Dynamics of Structures: Theory & Applications to Earthquake Engineering. 729p. 1995. 105.00 (*0-13-855214-2*, Pub. by P-H) S&S Trade.

***Chopra, Anil K.** Dynamics of Structures: Theory & Applications to Earthquake Engineering. LC 00-42751. 2000. write for info. (*0-13-086973-2*) P-H.

Chopra Center for Well Being Staff. Celebrating Nourishment. 1996. 25.00 (*0-614-19360-5*) Harmony Bks.

Chopra, Chiv. The Flood & Modern Science. (Illus.). 187p. (Orig.). 2000. pap. 23.95 (*1-56072-349-1*, Nova Kroshka Bks) Nova Sci Pubs.

Chopra, Deepak. Addiction. 1997. pap. write for info. (*0-609-80077-9*) Harmony Bks.

— Ageless Body, Timeless Mind: The Quantum Alternative to Growing Old. 352p. 1994. pap. 14.00 (*0-517-88212-4*, Three Riv Pr) Crown Pub Group.

— Allergies. 1997. pap. write for info. (*0-609-80078-7*) Harmony Bks.

— Being in Love. 1996. write for info. (*0-517-59258-4*) Harmony Bks.

— Boundless Energy. 144p. 1997. pap. 12.00 (*0-609-80075-2*) Harmony Bks.

— Boundless Energy: The Complete Mind/Body Program for Overcoming Chronic Fatigue. 1997. pap. 12.00 (*0-614-27349-8*, Crown) Crown Pub Group.

— El Camino de la Abundancia: La Riqueza en Todos los Campos de la Conciencia y de la Vida.Tr. of Creating Affluence: Wealth Consicousness in the Field of All Possibilities. (SPA.). 112p. (Orig.). 1997. pap. 10.95 (*1-878424-05-X*) Amber-Allen Pub.

— The Complete Mind/Body Program for Identifying & Soothing the Source of Your Body's Reaction. 1997. pap. 12.00 (*0-614-27348-X*, Crown) Crown Pub Group.

— Creating Affluence: The A to Z Steps to a Richer Life. LC 93-27861. 120p. 1998. pap. 10.95 (*1-878424-34-3*) Amber-Allen Pub.

— Creating Affluence: Wealth Consciousness in the Field of All Possibilities. LC 93-27861. 112p. 1993. 14.00 (*1-880032-42-2*) New Wrld Lib.

— Creating Health: How to Wake up the Body's Intelligence. rev. ed. 205p. 1995. pap. 11.95 (*0-395-75515-8*) HM.

C

— Cuerpos sin Edad, Mentes sin Tiempo. 1997. pap. 15.00 (*0-609-80103-1*) Harmony Bks.

— Dancing on the Razor's Edge. 1998. write for info. (*0-609-60004-4*) Harmony Bks.

— A Deepak Chopra Companion. Nacson, Leon, ed. LC 99-13857. 1999. pap. 10.00 (*0-609-80454-5*) Crown Pub Group.

— Everyday Immortality: A Concise Course in Spiritual Transformation. LC 98-47763. 208p. 1999. 18.00 (*0-609-60484-8*) Crown Pub Group.

— Finding God. abr. ed. 1998. audio 18.00 (*0-375-40442-2*) Knopf.

— The Higher Self, Set. 1993. 17.00 incl. audio (*0-671-87028-9*) S&S Audio.

— How to Know God: The Soul's Journey into the Mystery of Mysteries. LC 99-42777. 320p. 2000. 24.00 (*0-609-60078-8*) Harmony Bks.

***Chopra, Deepak.** How to Know God: The Soul's Journey into the Mystery of Mysteries. large type ed. 2000. 24.00 (*0-375-40869-X*) Random Hse Lrg Prnt.

Chopra, Deepak. Journey Into Healing: A Step-by-Step Personal Guide Compiled from the Timeless Wisdom of Deepak Chopra, M.D. LC 94-20937. 1994. 15.00 (*0-517-79973-1*) Crown Pub Group.

— Journey into Healing: Awakening the Wisdom Within You. 1999. 16.00 (*0-609-60498-8*) Harmony.

— Magical Beginning, Enchanted Land. 2001. 23.00 (*0-517-70220-7*) Crown Pub Group.

***Chopra, Deepak.** On the Shores of Eternity: Poems from Tagore on Death & Immortality. Tagore, Rabindranath, tr. from BEN. LC 99-20930. 96p. 1999. 14.00 (*0-609-60564-X*) Harmony Bks.

Chopra, Deepak. Overcoming Addictions: The Spiritual Solution. LC 97-168267. 1997. 17.50 (*0-609-60034-6*) Harmony Bks.

— Overcoming Addictions: The Spiritual Solution. LC 97-50046. 144p. 1998. pap. 12.00 (*0-609-80195-3*) Three Rivers Pr.

— Overcoming Intestinal Disorders. 1995. pap. 11.00 (*0-517-88492-5*) Random Hse Value.

— The Path to Love: Renewing the Power of Spirit in Your Life. LC 97-133633. 1996. 24.00 (*0-517-70622-9*) Random Hse Value.

— The Path to Love: Spiritual Strategies for Healing. LC 97-50035. 352p. 1998. pap. 14.00 (*0-609-80135-X*) Crown Pub Group.

— Perfect Digestion. 144p. 1997. pap. 12.00 (*0-609-80076-0*) Harmony Bks.

— Perfect Digestion: The Key to Balanced Living. 1997. pap. 12.00 (*0-614-27346-3*, Crown) Crown Pub Group.

***Chopra, Deepak.** Perfect Health: A Practical System of Mind/Body Medicine. rev. ed. LC 00-32595. 2000. pap. write for info. (*0-609-80694-7*, Three Riv Pr) Crown Pub Group.

Chopra, Deepak. Perfect Health: Allergies. 1997. pap. 12.00 (*0-614-27347-1*, Crown) Crown Pub Group.

— Perfect Health: The Complete Mind-Body Guide. (Illus.). 336p. 1991. pap. 14.00 (*0-517-58421-2*) Harmony Bks.

— Perfect Weight: The Complete Mind-Body Program for Acheiving & Maintaining Your Ideal Weight. (Perfect Health Library). 144p. 1996. pap. 12.00 (*0-517-88458-5*) Crown Pub Group.

— La Perfecta Salud: La Guia Completa del Mente & Cuerpo. (SPA.). 448p. 1997. pap. 14.00 (*0-609-80104-X*) Harmony Bks.

— Quantum Healing: Exploring the Frontiers of Body, Mind, Medicine. 272p. 1990. pap. 14.95 (*0-553-34869-8*) Bantam.

— Restful Sleep: The Complete Mind-Body Program for Overcoming Insomnia. (Perfect Health Library). 144p. 1996. 12.00 (0-517-88457-7) Crown Pub Group.

— El Retorno de Merlin. 1998. pap. text 25.95 (84-270-2152-6) E Martinez Roca.

— The Return of Merlin. 432p. 1996. pap. 12.95 (0-449-91074-1) Fawcett.

— The Return of Merlin. large type ed. LC 95-50039. 1996. 23.95 (1-56895-288-0) Wheeler Pub.

— Return of the Rishi: A Doctor's Story of Spiritual Transformation & Ayurvedic Healing. 212p. 1991. pap. 14.00 (0-395-57420-X) HM.

— Seven Spiritual Laws. 2001. 16.95 (0-609-60079-6) Harmony Bks.

***Chopra, Deepak.** Seven Spiritual Laws, No. 2. 2001. 16.95 (0-609-60390-6, Pub. by Crown Pub Group) Random House.

Chopra, Deepak. The Seven Spiritual Laws for Parents: Guiding Your Children to Success & Fulfillment. LC 97-19609. 1997. 16.95 (0-609-60077-X) Harmony Bks.

— The Seven Spiritual Laws of Success. 2001. pap. 12.00 (0-609-80219-4) Harmony Bks.

— The Seven Spiritual Laws of Success: A Practical Guide to the Fulfillment of Your Dreams. 128p. 1995. 15.00 (1-878424-11-4) Amber-Allen Pub.

— Las Siete Leyes Espirituales Del Exito: Una Guia Practica Para la Realizacion de tus Suenos. (SPA.). 128p. 1995. pap. 10.95 (1-878424-19-X) Amber-Allen Pub.

***Chopra, Deepak.** The Soul in Love: Poems of Prayer & Ecstasy. 2001. 14.00 (0-609-60648-4) Harmony Bks.

— The Spirit of Love: 11 Spiritual Lessons for Creating the Love You Want. 1997. 16.95 (0-614-20427-5, Dutt) Dutton Plume.

— Unconditional Life: Discovering the Power to Fulfill Your Dreams. 288p. 1992. pap. 14.95 (0-553-37050-2) Bantam.

Chopra, Deepak. The Way of the Wizard: Twenty Spiritual Lessons in Creating the Life You Want. 176p. 1995. 15.95 (0-517-70434-X) Crown Pub Group.

— The Wisdom Within. 1997. pap., wbk. ed. write for info. (0-517-88816-5) Harmony Bks.

Chopra, Deepak, ed. The Love Poems of Rumi. Kia, Fereydoun, tr. LC 97-35690. 1998. 12.00 (0-609-60243-8) Harmony Bks.

***Chopra, Deepak & Greenberg, Martin.** Deepak Chopra's Lords of Light, Vol. 2. 352p. 2000. mass mkt. 6.99 (0-312-97024-2, St Martins Paperbacks) St Martin.

Chopra, Deepak & Greenberg, Martin. Lords of Light. 343p. 1999. mass mkt. 6.99 (0-312-96892-2, Thomas Dunne) St Martin.

***Chopra, Deepak & Kubler-Ross, Elizabeth.** Conscious Aging, 2. Vol. 2. 2000. 12.00 (0-7435-0537-9) S&S Trade.

Chopra, Deepak, jt. auth. see Simon, David.

Chopra, Gautama. Child of the Dawn: A Magical Journey of Awakening. 208p. 1998. pap. text 10.95 (1-878424-38-6) Amber-Allen Pub.

— Child of the Dawn: A Magical Journey of Awakening. 180p. 1998. text 16.00 (0-7881-5798-1) DIANE Pub.

***Chopra, H. S., et al, eds.** National Identity & Regional Cooperation: Experiences of European Integration & South Asian Perceptions. 1999. 48.00 (81-7304-233-0, Pub. by Manohar) S Asia.

Chopra, Ian, jt. auth. see Russell, A. D.

Chopra, J. K. Women in the Indian Parliament (A Critical Study of Their Role) (C). 1993. 44.00 (81-7099-513-2, Pub. by Mittal Pubs Dist) S Asia.

Chopra, J. McGowan, jt. auth. see McGowan, Mary P.

Chopra, Jarat. Peace-Maintenance: The Evolution of International Political Authority. LC 98-27103. xviii, 261p. 1999. write for info. (0-415-19483-0) Routledge.

Chopra, Jorat, ed. The Politics of Peace - Maintenance. LC 98-6172. 150p. 1998. pap. 14.95 (1-55587-757-5); lib. bdg. 28.50 (1-55587-756-7) L Rienner.

Chopra, Judith W. Something Worth Doing: The Sub-Arctic Voayge of Aqua Star. 1996. text 9.95 (0-07-011879-5) McGraw.

Chopra, K. Law Dictionary: English to Hindi. 444p. 1977. 60.00 (0-7855-1395-7) St Mut.

— Law Dictionary (English to Hindi) (C). 1992. 140.00 (0-89771-779-1, Pub. by Eastern Book) St Mut.

— Law Dictionary (English to Hindi) Pocket. (C). 1991. 110.00 (0-7855-5593-5) St Mut.

Chopra, Kanchan, et al. Participatory Development: People & Common Property Resources. (Illus.). 152p. (C). 1990. text 22.00 (0-8039-9631-4) Sage.

Chopra, Kanchan R. & Kadekodi, Gopal K. Operationalising Sustainable Development: Economic-Ecological Modelling for Developing Countries. LC 99-17243. (Indo-Dutch Studies on Development Alternatives). 1999. write for info. (0-7619-9330-4) Sage.

Chopra, Kasturi L. & Das, Sunhit R. Thin Film Solar Cells. (Illus.). 624p. (C). 1983. text 174.00 (0-306-41141-5, Kluwer Plenum) Kluwer Academic.

Chopra, Kasturi L. & Kaur, I. Thin Film Device Applications. LC 83-9632. (Illus.). 312p. 1983. 85.00 (0-306-41297-7, Plenum Trade) Perseus Pubng.

***Chopra, Krishan.** Su Vida Esta en Sus Manos. (SPA.). 2000. pap. 16.95 (0-553-06111-9) Bantam.

— Your Life Is in Your Hands: The Path to Lasting Health & Happiness. 131.70 (1-86204-522-4, Pub. by Element MA) Penguin Putnam.

Chopra, Krishan. Your Life Is in Your Hands: The Path to Lasting Health & Happiness. 320p. 1999. 21.95 (1-86204-500-3, Pub. by Element MA) Penguin Putnam.

Chopra, Kusum. The Emerging Growth Challenges to Indian Agriculture. 1990. 47.50 (81-7033-094-7, Pub. by Rawat Pubns) S Asia.

Chopra, L. C. & Abrol, B. K. Medicinal Plants of the Arid Zones. 96p. 1983. 11.00 (1-55528-035-8, Pub. by Today Tomorrow) Scholarly Pubns.

***Chopra, Mannica.** Frommer's India. (Illus.). 2000. pap. 21.99 (0-02-863479-9) Macmillan Gen Ref.

***Chopra, O. K.** Effects of LWR Coolant Environments on Fatigue Design Curves of Carbon & Low-Alloy Steels. 127p. 1998. per. 10.00 (0-16-062903-9) USGPO.

— Environmentally Assisted Cracking in Light- Water Reactors: Semiannual Report, July 1997-December 1997. 106p. 1998. per. 12.00 (0-16-062955-1) USGPO.

— Environmentally Assisted Cracking in Light Water Reactors: Semiannual Report, January 1996- June 1996. 94p. 1997. per. 8.50 (0-16-062845-8) USGPO.

— Environmentally Assisted Cracking in Light Water Reactors: Semiannual Report, January 1997- June 1997. 112p. 1998. per. 9.00 (0-16-062915-2) USGPO.

— Environmentally Assisted Cracking in Light Water Reactors: Semiannual Report, July 1996- December 1996. 106p. 1997. per. 9.00 (0-16-054750-4) USGPO.

Chopra, P. India's Second Liberation. 270p. 1973. 18.95 (0-7069-0259-9) Asia Bk Corp.

Chopra, P. N. The Collected Works of Sardar Vallabhbhai Patel Vol. 9: Sardar Patel & the Quit India Movement of 1942 Castigates Communists for Betrayal, May 1940-Dec. 1942. 1995. pap. 250.00 (81-220-0472-5, Pub. by Print Hse) St Mut.

— Encyclopedia of India, 30 Vols. (Illus.). (C). 1992. text 1750.00 (0-8364-2750-5) S Asia.

— Indian Gazetteers: A Manual. 170p. 1990. text 22.50 (81-220-0159-9, Pub. by Konark Pubs Pvt Ltd) Advent Bks Div.

— Ladakh. 109p. 1980. 14.95 (0-940500-14-0, Pub. by S Chand & Co) Asia Bk Corp.

— Ladakh. 120p. 1987. 35.00 (0-7855-1195-4) St Mut.

— Maulana Abul Kalam Azad: Unfulfilled Dreams. 188p. (C). 1990. 195.00 (81-85017-43-3, Pub. by Interprint) St Mut.

— Quit India Movement British Secret Documents. 440p. (C). 1990. 195.00 (81-85017-32-8, Pub. by Interprint) St Mut.

— Sikkim. 114p. 1979. 11.95 (0-940500-65-5) Asia Bk Corp.

— Social, Cultural & Political History of Tibet. 1989. 30.00 (0-8364-2599-5) S Asia.

— Society & Culture During the Mughal Age. 1987. 74.95 (0-318-36978-8) Asia Bk Corp.

Chopra, P. N., ed. Historic Judgement on Quit India Movement: Justice Wickenden's Report. 266p. 1989. text 27.95 (81-220-0113-0, Pub. by Konark Pubs Pvt Ltd) Advent Bks Div.

— India: An Encyclopaedic Survey. 1984. text 87.50 (0-685-14076-8) Coronet Bks.

— Quit India Movement Vol. 11: Role of Indian Big Business British Secret Documents. 150p. (C). 1991. 160.00 (81-85017-56-5, Pub. by Interprint) St Mut.

Chopra, P. N. & Chopra, Prabha, eds. Collected Works of Sardar Vallabhbhai Patel, Vol. V. (C). 1994. 44.00 (81-220-0392-3, Pub. by Konark Pubs) S Asia.

— The Collected Works of Sardar Vallabhbhai Patel: Volume 3: 1930-1931. 1993. 60.00 (81-220-0307-9, Pub. by Konark Pubs Pvt Ltd) Advent Bks Div.

— The Collected Works of Sardar Vallabhbhai Patel, 1932-1934, Vol. IV. (C). 1994. text 42.00 (81-220-0343-5, Pub. by Konark Pubs) S Asia.

— Encyclopedia of India, 2 vols., 1. 1988. 110.00 (0-8364-2296-1, Pub. by Agam) S Asia.

— Encyclopedia of India, 2 vols., 2. 1988. 110.00 (0-8364-2297-X, Pub. by Agam) S Asia.

Chopra, P. N., jt. auth. see Chopra, Prabha.

Chopra, P. N., ed. see Patel, Sardar V.

Chopra, Prabha. A Panorama of Indian Culture. (Illus.). 183p. 1983. 11.95 (0-318-36986-9) Asia Bk Corp.

Chopra, Prabha & Chopra, P. N. Forgotten Heroes of India's Freedom Struggle: A Who's Who. (C). 1992. 28.50 (0-8364-2773-4, Pub. by Agam Kala Prakashan) S Asia.

Chopra, Prabha, jt. ed. see Chopra, P. N.

Chopra, Pran. Future of South Asia. 174p. 1986. 19.95 (0-318-37235-5) Asia Bk Corp.

Chopra, Prem N. Lorita: A Novel. (C). 1997. pap. text. write for info. (81-207-1848-8) Sterling Pubs.

Chopra, R. Dictionary of Management. 192p. 1990. 80.00 (81-7041-134-3, Pub. by Scientific Pubs) St Mut.

Chopra, R. C. Indigenous Drugs of India. (C). 1988. 60.00 (0-7855-2256-5, Pub. by Scientific) St Mut.

Chopra, R. N. Dictionary of Library Science. 1990. 33.50 (81-7041-291-9, Pub. by Anmol) S Asia.

— Drug Addiction with Special Reference to India. 264p. 1965. 12.95 (0-318-36932-X) Asia Bk Corp.

— Food Policy in India: A Survey. 400p. (C). 1987. 48.50 (81-7076-008-9, Pub. by Intellectual) S Asia.

— Glossary of Indian Medicinal Plants. (C). 1988. 40.00 (0-7855-2287-5, Pub. by Scientific) St Mut.

— Supplement to Glossary of Indian Medicinal Plants. (C). 1988. 30.00 (0-7855-2288-3, Pub. by Scientific) St Mut.

Chopra, R. N., et al. Poisonous Plants of India. 762p. (C). 1984. 750.00 (0-7855-1984-X, Pub. by Scientific); 210.00 (0-7855-2270-0, Pub. by Scientific) St Mut.

Chopra, R. N., jt. auth. see Biswa, K.

Chopra, R. N., jt. ed. see Bhatia, Satish C.

Chopra, Rohini, ed. see Gujral, Satish.

Chopra, S. B. Dictionary of Mechanical Engineering. 1989. 33.50 (81-7041-169-6, Pub. by Anmol) S Asia.

Chopra, S. K. Brain Drain & How to Reverse It. 1986. 20.00 (0-8364-1878-6, Pub. by Lancer India) S Asia.

Chopra, S. N. India: An Area Study. 238p. 1978. 25.95 (0-318-36999-0) Asia Bk Corp.

— India & China: Perspective on the Culture of the Hans & the Hindus. 1997. 25.00 (81-259-0204-X, Pub. by Vikas) S Asia.

Chopra, S. R., ed. Early Man in North West India. 141p. 1979. 13.95 (0-318-36796-3) Asia Bk Corp.

***Chopra, Sanjiv.** The Liver Book: The Patients Guide to Diagnosis, Treatment & Recovery. 2001. 25.95 (0-7434-0584-6, PB Hardcover) PB.

Chopra, Sanjiv & May, Roger J. Pathophysiology of the Gastrointestinal System. 400p. 1989. pap. text 46.95 (0-316-13890-8) Lppncott W & W.

Chopra, Shiv. Four Five. (Illus.). 218p. (C). 1995. lib. bdg. 95.00 (1-56072-193-6) Nova Sci Pubs.

Chopra, Sudhir, jt. ed. see Joyner, Christopher C.

Chopra, Suhita. Tourism & Development in India. (C). 1991. 27.00 (81-7024-363-7, Pub. by Ashish Pub Hse) S Asia.

Chopra, Surendra. Pakistan's Thrust in the Muslim World: India As a Factor: A Study of RCD. (C). 1992. 20.00 (81-7100-408-3, Pub. by Deep & Deep Pubns) S Asia.

Chopra, U. B. Dictionary of Electrical Civil Engineering. 1989. 33.50 (81-7041-140-8, Pub. by Anmol) S Asia.

Chopra, V. D. Disarmament & Development: Their Relationship. 1988. 18.00 (81-7050-064-8, Pub. by Patriot Pubs) S Asia.

— Double Talk on Weapons of Mass Destruction & Indian Security. 1998. 29.50 (81-212-0477-1) Gyan Publishing Hse.

Chopra, V. D., ed. Afghanistan & Asian Stability. 238p. 1998. 24.00 (81-212-0585-9, Pub. by Gyan Publishing Hse) Nataraj Bks.

Chopra, V. D & Rasgotra, M., eds. Genesis of Regional Conflicts. LC 95-911174. (C). 1995. 48.00 (81-212-0502-6, Pub. by Gian Publng Hse) S Asia.

Chopra, V. D., et al. Indo-Soviet Relations: Prospects & Problems. (C). 1991. 26.00 (81-7050-129-6, Pub. by Patriot Pubs) S Asia.

— Socio-Economic Reforms in the U. S. S. R. 1990. 150.00 (0-317-99589-8, Pub. by Patriot Pubs) S Asia.

Chopra, V. D., jt. ed. see Rasgotra, M.

Chopra, V. K. Corporate Strategy & Structure in India. (C). 1990. text 24.00 (81-7100-260-9, Pub. by Deep & Deep Pubns) S Asia.

Chopra, V. L., ed. Crop Productivity & Sustainability: Shaping the Future. rev. ed. (Illus.). 1100p. (C). 1997. 195.00 (1-57808-004-5) Science Pubs.

— Plant Breeding. (C). 1988. 34.00 (81-204-0388-6, Pub. by Oxford IBH) S Asia.

Chopra, V. L., et al, eds. Agricultural Biotechnology: 2nd Asia Pacific Conference. 312p. (C). 1997. 75.00 (1-886106-78-9) Science Pubs.

Chopra, V. L. & Prakash, Shyam, eds. Oilseed Brassicas in Indian Agriculture. (Series in Agricultural Sciences). 1991. text 35.00 (0-7069-5605-2, Pub. by Vikas) S Asia.

Chopra, V. L., et al. Applied Plant Biotechnology. LC 98-56139. (Illus.). 375p. 1999. 89.00 (1-57808-033-9) Science Pubs.

Chopra, Veena. Classic One Thousand Indian Recipes. 448p. 1994. pap. 14.95 (0-572-01863-0, Pub. by W Foulsham) Trans-Atl Phila.

— Indian Vegetarian. (Quick & Easy Ser.). 192p. 1996. pap. text 13.95 (0-572-01886-X, Pub. by W Foulsham) Trans-Atl Phila.

— The Real Indian Cookery Course. rev. ed. (Illus.). 256p. (Orig.). 1997. pap. 23.50 (0-572-02270-0, Pub. by W Foulsham) Trans-Atl Phila.

***Chopra, Veena.** Veena Chopra's Real Indian Cookery. (Illus.). 256p. 2000. pap. 14.95 (0-572-02507-6) W Foulsham.

Chopra, Vikram, ed. Shakespeare: Varied Perspectives. 1996. 44.00 (81-7018-822-9, Pub. by BR Pub) S Asia.

***Chops, Chutley.** Elvis: The King on Film. (Illus.). 2000. pap. 14.95 (1-902588-08-8) Glitter Bks.

Chopyak, James. Pak: Readings in World Music. 272p. (C). 1995. pap. text 17.95 (0-7872-1338-1, 41133801) Kendall-Hunt.

Chopyck, Dan B., tr. see Skovoroda, Gregory S.

Choquet-Bruhat, Y. & DeWitt-Morette, C. Analysis, Manifolds & Physics, Set. 117.75 (0-444-82647-5) Elsevier.

Choquet-Bruhat, Y., et al. Analysis, Manifolds & Physics Pt. I: Basics. 2nd rev. ed. 650p. 1991. reprint ed. 63.50 (0-444-86017-7, North Holland) Elsevier.

Choquet-Bruhat, Yvonne & Dewitt-Morette, C. Analysis, Manifolds & Physics Pt. II: 92 Applications. 462p. 1989. 75.00 (0-444-87071-7, North Holland) Elsevier.

Choquet-Bruhat, Yvonne, jt. ed. see Anile, A. M.

Choquet, Gustav. What Is Modern Mathematics? 46p. 1963. pap. 5.00 (0-87825-250-9) Ed Solutions.

Choquet, Y. & Karade, T. M., eds. On Relativity Theory: Sir Arthur Eddington Century Symposium Vol. 2, India, 1984. 284p. 1985. 66.00 (9971-978-21-0) World Scientific Pub.

Choquette, Clifford J., jt. auth. see Ogilvie, Marilyn Bailey.

Choquette, Diane, compiled by. New Religious Movements in the United States & Canada: A Critical Assessment & Annotated Bibliography, 5. LC 85-9964. (Bibliographies & Indexes in Religious Studies: No. 5). 235p. 1985. lib. bdg. 69.50 (0-313-23772-7, CRM/) Greenwood.

Choquette, Joseph S. Vest Pocket French. LC 89-15397. (ENG & FRE.). 1986. pap. 5.95 (0-8489-5102-6) Inst Lang Study.

Choquette, Kent D., ed. Vertical-Cavity Surface-Emitting Lasers, Vol. 3003. 212p. 1997. 69.00 (0-8194-2414-5) SPIE.

***Choquette, Kent D. & Lei, Chun, eds.** Vertical-Cavity Surface-Emitting Lasers III. 216p. 1999. pap. text 72.00 (0-8194-3097-8) SPIE.

Choquette, Kent D. & Morgan, Robert A., eds. Vertical-Cabity Surface-Emitting Lasers II, Vol. 3286. LC 99-164775. 264p. 1998. 69.00 (0-8194-2725-X) SPIE.

Choquette, P. W., jt. auth. see Roehl, P. O.

Choquette, P. W., jt. ed. see James, N. P.

Choquette, Sonia. The Psychic Pathway: A Guidebook to Developing Your Intuition & Spiritual Power. LC 94-40628. 1995. pap. 18.00 (0-517-88407-0) Crown Pub Group.

***Choquette, Sonia.** True Balance: A Commonsense Guide for Renewing Your Spirit. LC 99-59793. 253p. 2000. pap. 18.00 (0-609-80398-0, Three Riv Pr) Crown Pub Group.

Choquette, Sonia. Les Vrais Desires: Appreuez 2 Creer la Vie Que Cotre Coeur Reclause. (FRE.). 1998. 22.95 (2-89466-018-9) Edns Roseau.

— The Wise Child. LC 98-38273. 1999. pap. 18.00 (0-609-80399-9) Crown Pub Group.

— Your Heart's Desire: Instructions for Creating the Life You Really Want. LC 97-220322. 1997. pap. 18.00 (0-609-80011-6, Chatham River Pr) Random Hse Value.

***Chorafas D.** Credit Derivatives & the Management of Risk. 1999. 70.00 (0-13-089260-2) P-H.

Chorafas, D. How to Understand & Use Mathematics for Derivatives: Understanding the Behaviour of Markets, Vol. 1. 230p. 1995. pap. 250.00 (1-85564-446-0, Pub. by Euromoney) Am Educ Systs.

— How to Understand & Use Mathematics for Derivatives Vol. 2: Advanced Modelling Methods. 300p. 1995. 250.00 (1-85564-447-9, Pub. by Euromoney) Am Educ Systs.

— The Money Magnets: Regulating International Finance & Analysing Money Flows. 1997. 170.00 (1-85564-551-3, Pub. by Euromoney) Am Educ Systs.

Chorafas, Dimitris N. Network Computers vs. High Performance Computers. LC 97-185528. 176p. 1997. pap. 28.95 (0-304-70029-0) Continuum.

Chorafas, Dimitris N. & Steinmann, Heinrich. The New Wave in Information Technology. (Illus.). 416p. 1996. pap. 37.95 (0-304-33608-4) Continuum.

Chorafas, Dimitris N. Agent Technology Handbook. LC 97-15385. (Computer Communications Ser.). (Illus.). 416p. 1997. pap. text 44.50 (0-07-011923-6) McGraw.

— Computer in der Medizin. (IS-Informations-Systeme Ser.). (Illus.). 127p. (C). 1973. 43.10 (3-11-004031-X) De Gruyter.

— Credit Derivatives & the Management of Risk. LC 99-23606. (Illus.). 352p. 1999. 70.00 (0-7352-0104-8) PH Pr.

— Data Communications for Distributed Information Systems. (Illus.). 300p. text 25.00 (0-89433-108-6) Petrocelli.

— Database Management Systems for Distributed Computer & Networks. (Illus.). 240p. 1983. text 27.50 (0-89433-184-1) Petrocelli.

— Electronic Document Handling: The New Communications Architectures. (Illus.). 282p. 1988. text 29.95 (0-89433-281-3) Petrocelli.

— The Engineering Database: Design, Normalization & Implementation for Successful CAD-CAM Applications. (Illus.). 241p. 1988. pap. text 47.95 (0-408-02280-9) Buttrwrth-Heinemann.

— Handbook of Data Communications. 1990. 44.95 (0-8306-9690-3) McGraw-Hill Prof.

— Handbook of Database Management & Distributed Database. (Illus.). 650p. 1988. text 49.95 (0-89433-292-9, 8244) Petrocelli.

— The Handbook of Management. 440p. 1988. 44.95 (0-89433-305-4) Petrocelli.

— Information Systems in Financial Institutions: A Guide to Strategic Planning Based on the Japanese Experience. (Illus.). 208p. (C). 1983. spiral bd. 64.00 (0-13-464669-X) P-H.

— Interactive Workstations. (Illus.). 272p. 1986. text 27.95 (0-89433-258-9, 8139) Petrocelli.

***Chorafas, Dimitris N.** Managing Credit Risk Vol. I: Analysing Rating & Pricing the Probability of Default. 2000. pap. 170.00 (1-85564-761-3, Pub. by Euromoney) Am Educ Systs.

— Managing Credit Risk Vol. II: The Lessons of Variable Failures & Imprudent Exposure. 2000. pap. 170.00 (1-85564-762-1, Pub. by Euromoney) Am Educ Systs.

Chorafas, Dimitris N. Managing Derivatives Risk: Establishing Internal Systems & Controls. 300p. 1995. text 65.00 (1-55738-778-8, Irwn Prfssnl) McGraw-Hill Prof.

— Manufacturing Databases & Computer Integrated Systems. 320p. 1993. boxed set 89.95 (0-8493-8689-6) CRC Pr.

— The Market Risk Amendment: Understanding the Marking-To-Model & Value-at-Risk. LC 97-8664. 1997. 75.00 (0-7863-1224-6, Irwn Prfssnl) McGraw-Hill Prof.

— Money: Bank of the Eighties. (Illus.). 256p. 1981. 27.50 (0-89433-182-5) Petrocelli.

— Network Computers vs. High Performance Computers. LC 97-185528. 1997. 85.00 (0-304-70028-2) Continuum.

— The New Technology of Financial Management. LC 92-1023. (Finance Editions Ser.). 304p. 1992. 55.00 (0-471-57402-3) Wiley.

***Chorafas, Dimitris N.** Reliable Financial Reporting & Internal Control: A Global Implementation Guide. 268p. 2000. 65.00 (0-471-38261-2) Wiley.

Chorafas, Dimitris N. Risk Management in Financial Institutions: Risk Management in Financial Institutions. 370p. 1990. boxed set 150.00 (0-406-16390-1, UK, MICHIE) LEXIS Pub.

— Simulation, Optimization & Expert Systems: How Technology Is Revolutionizing the Way Securities Are Underwritten, Analyzed & Traded. (Institutional Investor Publications). 450p. 1991. text 70.00 (1-55738-231-X, Irwn Prfssnl) McGraw-Hill Prof.

— Strategic Planning for Electronic Banking. 260p. 1987. boxed set 60.00 (0-88063-204-6, MICHIE); boxed set 60.00 (0-614-05971-2, MICHIE) LEXIS Pub.

An Asterisk (*) at the beginning of an entry indicates that the title is appearing for the first time.

— Telephony: Today & Tomorrow. (Illus.). 272p. 1984. 33.95 (*0-13-902700-9*) P-H.

— Treasury Operations & the Foreign Exchange Challenge: A Guide to Risk Management Strategies for the New World Markets. LC 91-35940. (Finance Editions Ser.). 304p. 1992. 49.95 (*0-471-54393-4*) Wiley.

— Understanding Volatility & Liquidity in the Financial Markets: Building a Comprehensive System of Risk Management. 220p. 1998. pap. 225.00 (*1-85564-655-2*, Pub. by Euromoney) Am Educ Systs.

***Chorafas, Dimitris N., contrib. by.** New Regulation of the Financial Industry. LC 99-50145. 2000. text 65.00 (*0-312-22899-6*) St Martin.

Chorafas, Dimitris N. & Steinman, Heinrich. Off-Balance Sheet Financial Instruments: Maximizing Profitability & Managing Risk in Financial Services. 475p. (C). 1994. text 75.00 (*1-55738-398-7*, Irwn Prfssnl) McGraw-Hill Prof.

Chorafas, Ditmitris N. & Trippi, Robert L. Chaos Theory in the Financial Markets: Applying Fractals, Fuzzy Logic, Genetic Algorithms. LC 94-158436. (Illus.). 400p. 1994. text 85.00 (*1-55738-555-6*, Irwn Prfssnl) McGraw-Hill Prof.

Chorafas, N. Dimitris. Advanced Financial Analysis Self-Study Workbook. 240p. 1994. pap. 295.00 (*1-85564-312-X*, Pub. by Euromoney) Am Educ Systs.

Chorafas, N.Dimitris & Steimnann, Heinrich. The New Wave in Information Technology. (Illus.). 416p. 1996. text 90.00 (*0-304-33607-6*) Continuum.

Chorao, Kay. Baby's Bedtime. (Illus.). 64p. (J). (ps-k). 1997. pap. 9.99 incl. audio (*0-14-095419-8*, PuffinBks) Peng Put Young Read.

— The Baby's Bedtime Book. LC 84-6067. (Illus.). 64p. (J). (ps). 1984. 16.99 (*0-525-44149-2*, Dutton Child) Peng Put Young Read.

— Baby's Lap Book. LC 89-23273. (Illus.). 64p. (J). (ps). 1990. 17.99 (*0-525-44604-4*, Dutton Child) Peng Put Young Read.

— Baby's Lap Book: A Collection of Classic Nursery Rhymes. (Picture Puffin Ser.). 64p. 1998. pap. 6.99 (*0-14-056363-6*, PuffinBks) Peng Put Young Read.

— Baby's Lap Book: An Collection of Classic Nursery Rhymes. (J). 1998. 12.19 (*0-606-13158-2*, Pub. by Turtleback) Demco.

— The Baby's Story Book. LC 84-26005. (Illus.). 64p. (J). (ps-1). 1985. 16.99 (*0-525-44200-6*, Dutton Child) Peng Put Young Read.

***Chorao, Kay.** Bay Summer. 2002. text 16.95 (*0-8050-6411-7*) St Martin.

Chorao, Kay. The Cats Kids. LC 98-3449. (Illus.). 48p. (J). (ps-3). 1998. lib. bdg. 16.95 (*0-8234-1405-1*) Holiday.

***Chorao, Kay.** Here Comes Kate. LC 00-20936. (Illus.). 48p. (J). (ps-2). 2000. 13.99 (*0-525-46443-3*, Dutton Child) Peng Put Young Read.

— Jumpety Bumpety Hop: A Parade of Animal Poems. (Illus.). (J). 2000. 12.44 (*0-606-18415-5*) Turtleback.

— Jumpety-Bumpety Hop: A Parade of Animal Poems. (Illus.). 48p. (J). (ps-1). 2000. pap. 6.99 (*0-14-056671-6*, PuffinBks) Peng Put Young Read.

Chorao, Kay. Little Farm by the Sea. LC 97-24431. (Illus.). 32p. (J). (ps-2). 1998. 15.95 (*0-8050-5053-1*) H Holt & Co.

— Number One Number Fun. LC 94-9926. (Illus.). 32p. (J). (gr. k-3). 1995. lib. bdg. 15.95 (*0-8234-1142-7*) Holiday.

Chorao, Kay. The Christmas Story. LC 96-5066. 32p. (J). (ps-3). 1996. lib. bdg. 16.95 (*0-8234-1251-2*) Holiday.

— Jumpety Bumpety Hop. (J). 1997. pap. 9.99 (*1-58048-021-7*) Sandvik Pub.

***Chorao, Kay.** Pig & Crow. LC 99-31776. 32p. (J). 1999. 15.95 (*0-8050-5863-X*) H Holt & Co.

Chorao, Kay. The Baby's Bedtime Book. 64p. (J). (ps up). 1994. pap. 5.99 (*0-14-055384-3*, PuffinBks) Peng Put Young Read.

Choraqui, Andre. A Man Alone. 284p. 1970. 39.95 (*0-87855-180-8*) Transaction Pubs.

Chorba, Ronald W., jt. auth. see Bommer, Michael R.

Chorbajian. Studies in Comparative Genocide. LC 98-38455. 304p. 1999. text 72.00 (*0-312-21933-4*) St Martin.

Chorbajian, Levon, tr. see Verluise, Pierre.

Chorda, Ramon M. Programacion Basica con Foxpro 2.5. (SPA.). (C). 1993. pap. text 32.00 (*0-201-64192-5*) Addison-Wesley.

Chorell, Walentin. Five Modern Scandinavian Plays. Friis, Erik J. et al, eds. Kundesen, Barbara et al, trs. from DAN. LC 70-126439. (Library of Scandinavian Literature). 1971. lib. bdg. 21.25 (*0-8057-3312-4*) Irvington.

Chorepenning, Charlotte. Hansel & Gretel. 64p. 1956. pap. 3.50 (*0-87129-074-X*, H58) Dramatic Pub.

Chorfas, Dimitrius N., ed. Intelligent Networks: Telecommunications Solutions for the 1990's. 380p. 1990. boxed set 84.95 (*0-8493-7401-4*, Q) CRC Pr.

Chorier, Benedicte, tr. see Levi-Strauss, Claude.

Chorin, A.J. & Majda, A. J., eds. Wave Motion: Theory, Modelling, & Computation. (Mathematical Sciences Research Institute Publications: Vol. 7). (Illus.). 350p. 1987. 65.95 (*0-387-96594-7*) Spr-Verlag.

Chorin, Alexandre. Vorticity & Turbulence. LC 93-43311. (Applied Mathematical Sciences Ser.: Vol. 103). (Illus.). 192p. 1997. 44.95 (*0-387-94197-5*) Spr-Verlag.

Chorin, Alexandre J. & Marsden, Jerrold E. A Mathematical Introduction to Fluid Mechanics. 2nd ed. (Texts in Applied Mathematics Ser.: Vol. 4). (Illus.). ix, 168p. 1990. 29.00 (*0-387-97300-1*) Spr-Verlag.

— A Mathematical Introduction to Fluid Mechanics. 3rd ed. LC 92-26645. (Texts in Applied Mathematics Ser.: Vol. 4). (Illus.). 170p. 1994. 41.95 (*0-387-97918-2*) Spr-Verlag.

***Choris, Ludwig York.** Journal des Malers Ludwig York Choris: Herausgegeben und Kommentiert von Niklaus R. Schweizer. (Illus.). 428p. 1999. 54.95 (*3-906756-63-7*, Pub. by P Lang) P Lang Pubng.

Chorley, Henry F. Modern German Music: Recollections & Criticisms, 2 vols. LC 79-110994. (Music Reprint Ser.). 1973. reprint ed. 85.00 (*0-306-71911-8*) Da Capo.

— Thirty Years' Musical Recollections, 2 vols. LC 83-7558. (Music Reprint Ser.). 1983. reprint ed. lib. bdg. 65.00 (*0-306-76216-1*) Da Capo.

— Thirty Years' Musical Recollections, 2 vols., Vol. I. 312p. 1983. reprint ed. lib. bdg. write for info. (*0-318-56917-5*) Da Capo.

— Thirty Years' Musical Recollections, 2 vols., Vol. II. 323p. 1983. reprint ed. lib. bdg. write for info. (*0-318-56918-3*) Da Capo.

Chorley, Richard J., et al. Geomorphology. (Orig.). (C). 1985. pap. text 30.00 (*0-416-32590-4*, 9361) Routledge.

Chorley, Richard J., jt. auth. see Barry, Roger B.

Chorley, Richard J., jt. auth. see Barry, Roger G.

Chorley, T. & Smart, T. Leading Cases in the Law of Banking. 5th ed. 1983. 155.00 (*0-7855-2955-1*, Pub. by Chartered Bank); pap. 60.00 (*0-421-29350-0*, Pub. by Chartered Bank) St Mut.

Chorlton, David. Country of Two Seasons. 28p. 1997. pap. 7.95 (*0-944754-42-2*) Pudding Hse Pubns.

— The Epistemological Question Mark. Bixby, Robert, ed. 24p. 1993. pap. 6.00 (*1-882983-09-2*) March Street Pr.

— Forget the Country You Came From. 44p. (Orig.). 1992. pap. 6.50 (*1-880286-11-4*) Singular Speech Pr.

— The Human Flower. (Chaplets Ser.). 8p. (Orig.). 1993. pap. 1.50 (*0-916155-22-6*) Trout Creek.

— Measuring Time. (Dog River Review Poetry Ser.: No. 8). 30p. (Orig.). 1990. pap. 4.00 (*0-916155-12-9*) Trout Creek.

Chorlton, Frank. Textbook of Dynamics. 2nd ed. LC 82-25484. (Mathematics & Its Applications Ser.). 271p. 1983. pap. text 41.95 (*0-470-27408-5*) P-H.

Chorlton, Frank, jt. auth. see O'Neil, M. E.

Chorlton, Frank, jt. auth. see O'Neill, Michael E.

Chorn, Larry, jt. ed. see Mansoori, G. Ali.

Chorne, Laudie. Following the Custer Trail of 1876. (Illus.). 200p. (C). Date not set. 34.95 (*0-9644389-6-8*); pap. 19.95 (*0-9644389-5-X*) Smoky Water Pr.

Chornet, E., jt. auth. see Overend, R. P.

Chorney, Harold & Hansen, Phillip. Toward a Humanist Political Economy. LC 92-70623. 224p. 1992. 48.99 (*1-895431-23-9*, Pub. by Black Rose); pap. text 19.99 (*1-895431-22-0*, Pub. by Black Rose) Consort Bk Sales.

Chornovil, Vyacheslav, ed. Ukrain Hearld, Issue 7, 8-9, 10. LC 88-90879. 624p. 1988. 24.50 (*0-914834-60-6*) Smoloskyp.

Chorofas. Transaction Management: Managing Complex Transactions & Sharing Distributed Databases. LC 97-28357. 305p. 1998. text 65.00 (*0-312-21018-3*) St Martin.

Choron, A. E. & Fayolle, F. J. Dictionnaire Historique des Musiciens, Artistes et Amateurs, Morts ou Vivant, 2 vols., Set. (FRE.). 965p. 1910. lib. bdg. 240.00 (*0-685-13867-4*, 05103285) G Olms Pubs.

Choron, Harry, jt. auth. see Choron, Sandra.

Choron, Rose. Family Stories: Travels Beyond the Shtetl. LC 88-38796. (Illus.). 128p. 1989. boxed set 17.50 (*0-934710-17-1*) NightinGale Res.

Choron, Rose, ed. & tr. see Stauben, Daniel.

Choron, Sandra & Choron, Harry. The Book of Lists for Kids. (Illus.). 400p. (J). (gr. 3-9). 1995. pap. 11.00 (*0-395-70815-X*) HM.

Choron, Sandra & Oskam, Bob, eds. Elvis! The Last Word: The Man, the Myth, the King - in the Words of His Subjects! (Illus.). 128p. (Orig.). 1991. pap. text 8.95 (*0-8065-1280-6*, Citadel Pr) Carol Pub Group.

Choronzey, Darryl. Secret Fish Recipes from a Canadian Fishing Guide. LC 98-87359. (Illus.). 164p. 1999. pap. 12.95 (*0-87341-726-7*, FIREC) Krause Pubns.

***Chorosinski, Eugene C.** Days Remembered. 1999. pap. write for info. (*1-58235-356-5*) Watermrk Pr.

Choroszewski, Walter. New Jersey: A Photographic Celebration. LC 96-86342. (Illus.). 152p. 1996. 35.00 (*0-933605-06-4*) Aesthetic Pr.

— New Jersey: A Photographic Journey. LC 87-72222. (Illus.). 136p. 1987. 30.00 (*0-933605-01-3*) Aesthetic Pr.

— New Jersey: A Scenic Discovery. (Scenic Discovery Ser.). (Illus.). 120p. 1984. 27.50 (*0-89909-049-4*) Foremost Pubs.

— New Jersey, Naturescapes & Detail. LC 92-70484. (Illus.). 80p. 1995. 20.00 (*0-933605-05-6*) Aesthetic Pr.

— Pennsylvania: A Photographic Celebration. (Illus.). 108p. 1997. 25.00 (*0-933605-07-2*) Aesthetic Pr.

Chorpenning, Charlotte B. The Adventures of Tom Sawyer. 91p. 1956. reprint ed. pap. 3.50 (*0-87129-046-4*, A43) Dramatic Pub.

— Alice in Wonderland. 63p. 1946. reprint ed. pap. 5.50 (*0-87129-035-9*, A48) Dramatic Pub.

— Cinderella. (J). (gr. 1-7). 1940. 6.00 (*0-87602-116-X*) Anchorage.

— Jack & the Beanstalk. (J). 1935. 6.00 (*0-87602-143-7*) Anchorage.

— Little Red Riding Hood. 47p. (J). 1946. 6.00 (*0-87602-149-6*) Anchorage.

— Rip Van Winkle. 55p. 1938. pap. 3.50 (*0-87129-050-2*, R45) Dramatic Pub.

— Rumpelstiltskin. (J). (gr. 1-7). 1944. 6.00 (*0-87602-195-X*) Anchorage.

— The Sleeping Beauty. (J). (gr. 1-7). 1947. 6.00 (*0-87602-203-4*) Anchorage.

— The Three Bears. 50p. (J). 1949. 6.00 (*0-87602-208-5*) Anchorage.

Chorpenning, Charlotte B., jt. auth. see Defoe, Daniel.

Chorpenning, Charlotte B., jt. auth. see McAlvay, Nora.

Chorpenning, Charlotte B., jt. auth. see Nicholson, Anne.

Chorpenning, Joseph F. Christophorus Blancus' Engravings for Jeronimo Gracian's Summary of the Excellencies of St. Joseph. LC 96-5972. 129p. 1996. pap. 8.95 (*0-916101-23-1*) St Joseph.

— The Holy Family in Art & Devotion. LC 96-39975. 1996. write for info. (*0-916101-25-8*) St Joseph.

Chorpenning, Joseph F., ed. Patron Saint of the New World: Spanish American Colonial Images of St. Joseph. LC 95-6648. 61p. 1992. 14.95 (*0-916101-11-8*) St Joseph.

Chorpenning, Joseph F., ed. Just Man, Husband of Mary, Guardian of Christ: An Anthology of Readings from Jeronimo Gracian's Summary of the Excellencies of St. Joseph (1597) LC 95-6641. (Illus.). 272p. 1993. 21.95 (*0-916101-14-2*) St Joseph.

Chorpenning, Joseph F. & Von Barghahn, Barbara. The Holy Family as Prototype of the Civilization of Love: Images from the Viceregal Americas. LC 96-16704. 1996. pap. write for info. (*0-916101-21-5*) St Joseph.

Chortatsis, Georgios. Plays of the Cretan Renaissance. Bancroft-Marcus, Rosemary, ed. 1150p. 2001. 125.00 (*0-19-815808-4*) OUP.

Chorus, J. M. Introduction to Dutch Law for Foreign Lawyers. 3rd ed. LC 98-46514. 1998. 150.00 (*90-411-1120-4*) Kluwer Law Intl.

Chorus, J. M., ed. see Nederlandse Vereniging voor Rechtsvergelijking Staff.

Chorzelski. Serologic Diagnosis of Celiac Diseases. 216p. 1990. 121.00 (*0-8493-5436-6*, RC862, CRC Reprint) Franklin.

Chorzempa, Rosemary A. Design Your Own Coat of Arms: An Introduction to Heraldry. (Illus.). 48p. (Orig.). 1987. pap. 3.50 (*0-486-24993-X*) Dover.

— My Family Tree Workbook: Genealogy for Beginners. (Illus.). 64p. (J). (gr. 5 up). 1982. pap. 2.95 (*0-486-24229-3*) Dover.

— Polish Roots (Korzenie Polskie) (Illus.). 262p. 2000. pap. 17.95 (*0-8063-1378-1*, 983) Genealog Pub.

Chorzempa, Rosemary A. & Helon, George W. Index to the Newsletters, Journals & Bulletins of the Polish Genealogical Society of America, 1979-1993. 96p. (Orig.). 1994. pap. 5.00 (*0-924207-01-9*) Polish Genealog.

Chosen People Ministries Staff. Al Judio Primeramente: To the Jew First. rev. ed. 272p. 1995. reprint ed. pap. 12.95 (*1-882675-05-3*) Chosen People.

— God's Man in Babylon: (The Visions & Prophecies of Daniel) 300p. (Orig.). 1994. pap. 12.95 (*1-882675-02-9*) Chosen People.

— How to Introduce Your Jewish Friends to the Messiah. rev. ed. 83p. 1991. pap. 6.95 (*1-882675-00-2*) Chosen People.

— Israel's Glorious Future: The Prophecies & Promises of God Revealed. LC 96-163791. 88p. (Orig.). 1996. pap. 7.95 (*1-882675-07-X*) Chosen People.

— A Rabbi's Vision, a Century of Proclaiming the Messiah: A History of Chosen People Ministries. 708p. (Orig.). 1994. pap. 39.00 (*1-882675-04-5*) Chosen People.

— To an Ancient People: The Autobiography of Rabbi Leopold Cohn. LC 96-136913. 83p. (Orig.). 1996. pap. 6.95 (*1-882675-06-1*) Chosen People.

Choset, Howie M., et al, eds. Mobile Robots XIII & Intelligent Transportation Systems, Vol. 3525. 478p. 1999. 89.00 (*0-8194-2986-4*) SPIE.

Choset, Howie M., jt. ed. see Gage, Douglas W.

Chossat, Pascal. Methods in Equivariant Bifurcation & Dynamical Systems: With Applications. (Advanced Series in Nonlinear Dynamics). 300p. 1999. 46.00 (*981-02-3828-2*) World Scientific Pub.

Chossat, Pascal, ed. Dynamics, Bifurcation & Symmetry, New Trends & New Tools. LC 94-20807. (NATO ASI, Series F, Computer & Systems Sciences: Vol. 437). 1994. text 225.50 (*0-7923-2958-9*) Kluwer Academic.

Chossat, Pascal & Iooss, Gerard. The Couette-Taylor Problem. LC 93-21048. (Applied Mathematical Sciences Ser.: Vol. 102). (Illus.). 233p. 1994. 59.95 (*0-387-94154-1*) Spr-Verlag.

***Chossudovsky, Michel.** The Globalization of Poverty: Impacts of IMF & World Bank Reforms. 280p. 2000. pap. 15.95 (*1-56751-200-3*, Pub. by Common Courage); lib. bdg. 29.95 (*1-56751-201-1*, Pub. by Common Courage) Login Brothers Bk Co.

Chossudovsky, Michel. The Globalization of Poverty: Impacts of IMF & World Bank Reforms. 255p. (C). 1997. text 59.95 (*1-85649-401-2*, Pub. by Zed Books); text 25.00 (*1-85649-402-0*, Pub. by Zed Books) St Martin.

Chote, Robert. Financial Crises & Asia: CEPR Conference Report No. 6. 72p. 1998. pap. 14.95 (*1-898128-36-7*, Pub. by Ctr Econ Policy Res) Brookings.

Chothia, Jean. English Drama Early Modrn. LC 95-47320. (Literature in English Ser.). 352p. (C). 1996. text 56.75 (*0-582-06738-3*, Pub. by Addison-Wesley) Longman.

Chothia, Jean. English Drama of the Early Modern Period 1890-1940: Longman Literature in English Series. (Literature in English Ser.). 352p. (C). 1996. pap. 33.53 (*0-582-06739-1*) Longman.

Chothia, Jean, ed. The New Woman & Other Emancipated Woman Plays. LC 97-31284. (Oxford World's Classics Ser.). 352p. 2001. pap. 12.95 (*0-19-282427-9*) OUP.

Chotianovsky, Olga, ed. see Kogan, Mark.

Chotikapanich, Duangkamon. Techniques for Measuring Income Inequality. 272p. 1994. 72.95 (*1-85628-653-3*) Ashgate Pub Co.

Chotikapanich, Duangkamon, jt. auth. see Griffiths, William E.

Chotiner, Barbara A. Khrushchev's Party Reform: Coalition Building & Institutional Innovation, 106. LC 83-10733. (Contributions in Political Science Ser.: No. 106). (Illus.). 313p. 1984. 65.00 (*0-313-23730-1*, CHO/) Greenwood.

Chotkowski, L. A. Chiropractic, The Greatest Hoax of The Century? 197p. 1998. pap. text 14.95 (*0-9657855-1-3*) N E Novelty.

— To Your Body: The Health Effects of Illicit Drugs & Alcohol. 1989. pap. 12.95 (*1-55691-043-6*, 436) Learning Pubns.

Chotner, Deborah. American Naive Paintings. LC 92-4780. (Collections of the National Gallery of Art Systematic Catalogue). (Illus.). 688p. (C). 1997. 170.00 (*0-521-44301-6*) OUP.

Chotner, Deborah, et al. Masterworks of American Painting & Sculpture from the Smith College Museum of Art. Muehlig, Linda, ed. LC 99-35616. (Illus.). 308p. 1999. 65.00 (*1-55595-170-8*) Hudson Hills.

Chotvacs, Donna E. I Went for a Walk. (J). (gr. 4-7). 1996. pap. text 4.95 (*0-9644076-0-4*) Calliope Pub.

— My Feet Are Big. (J). (gr. 4-7). 1996. pap. text 4.95 (*0-9644076-2-0*) Calliope Pub.

— Tracks in the Snow. (J). (gr. 4-7). 1996. pap. text 4.95 (*0-9644076-1-2*) Calliope Pub.

Chotzen, Theodor M. Recherches sur la poesie de Dafydd ab Gwilym, Barde gallois du XIVe Siecle. LC 78-72622. (Celtic Language & Literature Ser.: Goidelic & Brythonic). reprint ed. 42.50 (*0-404-17546-5*) AMS Pr.

Chotzinhof, Robin. People with Dirty Hands. 1996. pap. 20.00 (*0-02-525201-1*) Macmillan.

***Chotzinoff Grossman, Anne & Grossman Thomas, Lisa.** Lobscouse & Spotted Dog: Which It's a Gastronomic Companion to the Aubrey/Maturin Novels. 336p. 2000. reprint ed. pap. 16.95 (*0-393-32094-4*) Norton.

***Chotzinoff, Robin.** People Who Sweat: My Middle-Aged Adventures among Tree Climbers, Mall Walkers, Surfing Housewives. 2000. pap. text 13.00 (*0-15-601170-0*) Harcourt.

— People Who Sweat: Ordinary People, Extraordinary Pursuits. LC 98-42847. 224p. (C). 1999. 22.00 (*0-15-100286-X*) Harcourt.

Chotzinoff, Robin. People with Dirty Hands: The Passion for Gardening. LC 96-47267. (Harvest Book Ser.). 256p. 1996. pap. 12.00 (*0-15-600515-8*) Harcourt.

— People with Dirty Hands: The Passion for Gardening. LC 95-30585. 256p. 1996. 22.00 (*0-02-860990-5*) Macmillan Info.

Chotzinoff, Samuel. Eroica: A Novel Based on the Life of Ludwig Von Beethoven. LC 72-1021. reprint ed. 45.00 (*0-404-01529-8*) AMS Pr.

— A Lost Paradise: Early Reminiscences. LC 74-27970. (Modern Jewish Experience Ser.). 1975. reprint ed. 34.95 (*0-405-06700-3*) Ayer.

— Toscanini: An Intimate Portrait. LC 76-7576. (Music Reprint Ser.). 1976. reprint ed. lib. bdg. 27.50 (*0-306-70777-2*) Da Capo.

***Chou.** Gas Monitors. 256p. 1999. 79.95 (*0-07-135876-5*) McGraw.

— Spanish for the Eye Care Professional. (SPA.). 144p. 2000. pap. text 16.50 (*0-7506-7285-4*) Buttrwrth-Heinemann.

Chou, jt. auth. see Ramaiah, L. S.

Chou, B. Ralph & Abel, Ken. Your Complete Guide to the Solar Eclipse of May 10, 1994. 128p. 1994. pap. 6.95 (*0-944214-04-5*) ABELexpress.

Chou, C. L., jt. ed. see Chyi, L. L.

Chou, Calvin. The Hollow Line in Dating Chinese Porcelains. LC 77-87445. (Illus.). 1978. pap. 12.00 (*0-930940-00-8*) Chinese Art App.

— The Hollow Line in Dating Chinese Porcelains. limited ed. LC 77-87445. (Illus.). 1978. 20.00 (*0-930940-03-2*) Chinese Art App.

***Chou, Chi Chung.** Handbook of Sugar Refining: A Manual for Design & Operation of Sugar Refining Facilities. LC 99-42174. 750p. 2000. 250.00 (*0-471-18357-1*) Wiley.

Chou, Chi-P'ing & Chao, Der-Lin. Intermediate Reader of Modern Chinese, 2 vols., Set. 362p. 1992. pap. text 39.50 (*0-691-01529-5*, Pub. by Princeton U Pr) Cal Prin Full Svc.

Chou, Chih-Ping. China's Peril & Promise: An Advanced Reader of Modern Chinese, 2 vols. 652p. 1996. pap. text 39.50 (*0-691-02884-2*, Pub. by Princeton U Pr) Cal Prin Full Svc.

— Literature & Society: Advanced Reader of Modern Chinese. 504p. (C). 1999. pap. text 49.50 (*0-691-01044-7*, Pub. by Princeton U Pr) Cal Prin Full Svc.

— New China: Intermediate Reader of Modern Chinese. 446p. 1999. pap. text 49.50 (*0-691-01045-5*, Pub. by Princeton U Pr) Cal Prin Full Svc.

— Trip to China: Intermediate Reader of Modern Chinese, 2 vols. 460p. 1996. pap. text 39.50 (*0-691-02883-4*, Pub. by Princeton U Pr) Cal Prin Full Svc.

Chou, Chih-P'ing. Yuan Hung-Tao & the Kung-An School. (Cambridge Studies in Chinese History, Literature & Institutions). 192p. 1988. text 64.95 (*0-521-34207-4*) Cambridge U Pr.

Chou, Chih-Ping, et al. Oh, China! Elementary Reader of Modern Chinese for Advanced Beginners. LC 97-35876. 536p. 1998. pap. text 39.50 (*0-691-05878-4*, Pub. by Princeton U Pr) Cal Prin Full Svc.

Chou, Chung-Chi, jt. auth. see Chen, James C.

***Chou, Clayton.** Lake Como. 1999. pap. write for info. (*1-58235-085-X*) Watermrk Pr.

Chou, En-Lai. In Quest: Poems of Chou En-Lai. 2nd ed. Lin, Nancy T., tr. from CHI. LC 79-84647. 51p. (C). 1979. pap. 2.95 (*0-917056-41-8*) Cheng & Tsui.

Chou, Eva Shan. Reconsidering Tu Fu: Literary Greatness & Cultural Context. (Studies in Chinese History, Literature & Institutions). 251p. (C). 1995. text 44.95 (*0-521-44039-4*) Cambridge U Pr.

***Chou, Hsaio Chin.** Charting Culinary Courses: A Collection of Recipes by Yacht Chef Dirk de Cuyper. Durant, Judith, ed. 2000. 24.95 (*0-9678752-0-X*) A B Hirschfeld.

C

An Asterisk (*) at the beginning of an entry indicates that the title is appearing for the first time.

Chou, Hung-hsiang. Oracle Bone Collections in the United States. LC 74-34551. (University of California Publications, Occasional Papers: No. 10). (Illus.). 188p. reprint ed. pap. 58.30 (*0-8357-6864-3*, 203556200095) Bks Demand.

Chou, Joy, ed. see Lin, S. C., et al.

***Chou, Ju-hsi.** Art at the Close of China's Empire. (Illus.). 219p. 1999. pap. 18.00 (*1-878529-64-1*) Art Media Resources.

Chou, Ju-hsi. Journeys on Paper & Silk: The Roy & Marilyn Papp Collection of Chinese Painting. LC 98-9448. (Illus.). 176p. 1998. pap. 39.95 (*0-910407-34-7*) Phoenix Art.

***Chou, Ju-hsi & Brown, Claudia.** Chinese Painting under the Qianlong Emperor, 2 vols. (Illus.). 418p. 1999. pap. 24.00 (*1-878529-63-3*) Art Media Resources.

Chou, Ju-Hsi, jt. auth. see Brown, Claudia.

Chou, Kung-tu & Zhou, Gong-du. Fundamentals of Structural Chemistry. Chen, Wei, tr. 496p. 1993. pap. text 44.00 (*981-02-2039-1*) World Scientific Pub.

Chou, KuoTung. Oxygen Application to Chloride Leaching of Complex Sulfide Ores. (MIRL Reports: No. 77). (Illus.). 27p. (Orig.). (C). 1988. pap. 4.00 (*0-911043-04-7*) UAKF Min Ind Res Lab.

Chou, L. M. Physics & Chemistry of Lakes. 2nd ed. Lerman, Abraham et al, eds. LC 95-6098. 1995. write for info. (*3-540-57891-9*) Spr-Verlag.

Chou, L. M., et al, eds. The Third Asian Fisheries Forum. 1135p. 1994. write for info. (*971-8709-64-9*, Pub. by ICLARM) Intl Spec Bk.

— Towards an Integrated Management of Tropical Coastal Resources. (ICLARM Conference Proceedings Ser.: No. 22). 455p. 1991. write for info. (*971-10-2268-0*, Pub. by ICLARM) Intl Spec Bk.

Chou, L. M., jt. ed. see Gopalkrishnakone, P.

Chou, Li-wei, et al. International Symposium on Photoelectronic Detection & Imaging, Technology & Applications: 17-20 May 1993, Beijing, China, Proceedings ISPDI '93. LC 93-83651. (Proceedings Ser.). xii, 536 p. 1993. write for info. (*0-8194-1229-5*) SPIE.

Chou, Marilyn, et al. World Food Prospects & Agriculture Potential. LC 76-24346. 316p. 1977. 65.00 (*0-275-90258-7*, C0258, Praeger Pubs) Greenwood.

Chou, Min-chih. Hu Shih & Intellectual Choice in Modern China. (Studies on China). 320p. 1984. text 47.50 (*0-472-10039-4*, 10039) U of Mich Pr.

Chou, S. C., jt. auth. see Iyer.

Chou, Shang C., et al. Machine Proofs in Geometry: Automated Production of Readable Proofs for Geometry Theorems. LC 94-5809. (Series on Applied Mathematics: Vol. 6). 480p. 1994. text 86.00 (*981-02-1584-3*) World Scientific Pub.

Chou, Shang C., jt. ed. see Sih, G. C.

Chou, Shizhen. Chinese Written Transfer No. 135, Vol. 3: Foreign Language Publications. (CHI., Illus.). 248p. (Orig.). (C). 1995. pap. text 21.00 (*0-87415-304-2*, 135) Foreign Lang.

Chou, T. W. & Ko, F., eds. Textile Structural Composite. (Composite Materials Ser.: No. 3). xii,388p. 1989. 239.00 (*0-444-42992-1*) Elsevier.

***Chou Wah-shan.** Tongzhi: Politics of Same-Sex Eroticism in Chinese Societies. 160p. 2000. pap. 27.95 (*1-56023-154-8*); lib. bdg. 69.95 (*1-56023-153-X*) Haworth Pr.

Chou, Y. L. Statistical Analysis for Business & Economics. 856p. 1989. 48.00 (*0-444-01301-6*) P-H.

Chou, Yue-Hong. Exploring Spatial Analysis: In Geographic Information Systems. 496p. (C). 1996. pap. 55.95 (*1-56690-119-7*) Thomson Learn.

Choubey, V. D., ed. Hydro Power Development in the Himalayas: Proceedings of the International Conference, Shimla, India, 20-22 April, 1998. (Illus.). 552p. (C). 1998. text 104.00 (*90-5410-781-2*) Ashgate Pub Co.

Choucha, Nadia. Surrealism & the Occult: Shamanism, Magic, Alchemy, & the Birth of an Artistic Movement. LC 92-1329. (Illus.). 144p. 1992. pap. 12.95 (*0-89281-373-3*) Inner Tradit.

Choucri, Nazli, ed. Global Accord: Environmental Challenges & International Responses. (Global Environmental Accords Ser.). (Illus.). 586p. 1995. pap. text 29.50 (*0-262-53134-8*) MIT Pr.

— Multidisciplinary Perspectives on Population & Conflict. LC 84-2641. 240p. 1984. text 45.00 (*0-8156-2314-3*); pap. text 16.95 (*0-8156-2315-1*) Syracuse U Pr.

Choudary, Pavan. The Rx Factor: Strategic Creativity in Pharmaceutical Marketing. LC 97-18645. 1997. 26.00 (*0-8039-9378-1*); pap. write for info. (*0-8039-9379-X*) Sage.

Choudhary, A. N., jt. ed. see Bukhees, E. O.

Choudhary, Alok N. & Berra, P. Bruce, eds. Proceedings of the International Conference on Parallel Processing, 1993, Vol. II: Software. 336p. 1993. lib. bdg. 79.95 (*0-8493-8985-2*, QA) CRC Pr.

Choudhary, Alok N. & Patel, Janak H. Parallel Architectures & Parallel Algorithms for Integrated Vision Systems. (C). 1990. text 95.50 (*0-7923-9078-4*) Kluwer Academic.

Choudhary, B. The Elements of Complex Analysis. 2nd ed. 333p. 1993. text 79.95 (*0-470-22116-X*) Halsted Pr.

Choudhary, Bani R. The Story of Krishna. (Illus.). (J). (gr. 3-10). 1979. 8.00 (*0-89744-134-6*) Auromere.

— Story of Mahabharata. (Introduction to Classical Indian Lore for Children Ser.). (J). (ps up). 1988. 8.00 (*0-318-37379-3*) Auromere.

— The Story of Ramayan. (Illus.). (J). (gr. 3-10). 1979. 8.00 (*0-89744-133-8*) Auromere.

Choudhary, Gangadhar, ed. Chemical Hazards in the Workplace: Measurement & Control. LC 81-130. (ACS Symposium Ser.: No. 149). 1981. 60.95 (*0-8412-0608-2*) Am Chemical.

— Chemical Hazards in the Workplace: Measurement & Control. LC 81-130. (ACS Symposium Ser.: Vol. 149). 641p. 1981. reprint ed. pap. 198.80 (*0-608-03035-X*, 206348800007) Bks Demand.

Choudhary, J. N. Divorce in Indian Society. (C). 1988. 26.50 (*81-7044-090-4*) S Asia.

Choudhary, M. Iqbal, ed. Biological Inhibitors. (Studies in Medicinal Chemistry). 494p. 1996. text 90.00 (*3-7186-5879-8*, Harwood Acad Pubs) Gordon & Breach.

— Progress in Medicinal Chemistry, Vol. 31. (Studies in Medicinal Chemistry). 400p. 1996. text 90.00 (*3-7186-5795-3*, Harwood Acad Pubs) Gordon & Breach.

Choudhary, M. Iqbal, jt. auth. see Rahman, Attaur.

Choudhary, Muhammad I., jt. auth. see Atta-ur-Rahman.

Choudhary, Paramesh. Indian Origin of the Chinese Nation. (C). 1990. 44.00 (*81-900127-1-1*, Pub. by Naya Prokash) S Asia.

— Indian Origin of the Chinese Nation, Vol. 2. (C). 1990. 38.00 (*81-900127-0-3*, Pub. by Naya Prokash) S Asia.

Choudhary, U. K. Trade Unions Act, 1926. 2nd ed. (C). 1991. 110.00 (*0-7855-5400-9*) St Mut.

Choudhary, Valmiki, ed. Dr. Rajendra Prasad: Correspondence & Select Documents, Vol. I. 1984. 24.00 (*0-8364-1179-X*, Pub. by Allied Pubs) S Asia.

— Dr. Rajendra Prasad: Correspondence & Select Documents, Vol. II. 1985. 22.50 (*0-8364-1440-3*, Pub. by Allied Pubs) S Asia.

— Dr. Rajendra Prasad: Correspondence & Select Documents, Vol. III. 1985. 22.50 (*0-8364-1441-1*, Pub. by Allied Pubs) S Asia.

— Dr. Rajendra Prasad: Correspondence & Select Documents, Vol. IX. 1987. 27.00 (*81-7023-012-8*, Pub. by Allied Pubs) S Asia.

Choudhary, Vilmiki, ed. Dr. Rajendra Prashad: Correspondence & Select Documents, Vol. 21. (C). 1995. 30.00 (*81-7023-469-7*, Pub. by Allied Pubs) S Asia.

Choudhry, Ghulam G. Humic Substances: Structural, Photophysical, Photochemical & Free Radical Aspects & Interactions with Environmental Chemicals. (Current Topics In Environmental & Toxicological Chemistry Ser.: Vol. 7). x, 186p. 1984. text 195.00 (*0-677-06440-3*) Gordon & Breach.

Choudhry, Ghulam G. & Hutzinger, O. Mechanistic Aspects of the Thermal Formation of Halogenated Organic Compounds Including Polychlorinated Dibenzo-p-Dioxins. LC 83-1640. (Current Topics In Environmental & Toxicological Chemistry Ser.: Vol. 4). (Illus.). x, 194p. 1983. text 173.00 (*0-677-06130-7*) Gordon & Breach.

***Choudhry, Moorad.** Bond Markets Trading & Analysis. 224p. 2000. 59.95 (*0-7506-4677-2*) Buttrwrth-Heinemann.

— Gilts Market. 115p. 2001. 115.00 (*0-7506-5163-6*) Buttrwrth-Heinemann.

— Repo Market. 256p. 2001. 95.00 (*0-7506-5162-8*) Buttrwrth-Heinemann.

Choudhry, Nanda K., ed. Canada & South Asian Development: Trade & Aid. LC 91-2773. (International Studies in Sociology & Social Anthropology: No. 57). 163p. 1991. pap. 45.50 (*90-04-09416-4*) Brill Academic Pubs.

Choudhry, Nanda K. & Mansur, Salim. The Indira-Rajiv Years: The Indian Economy & Polity, 1966-1991, No. 8. (C). 1995. 36.00 (*1-895214-11-4*, Pub. by Ctre South Asian) S Asia.

Choudhry, Nanda K., jt. auth. see Gupta, Satya D.

Choudhry, Nanda K., jt. auth. see Gupta, Satyadev.

Choudhry, V. K., jt. auth. see Hawthorne, David.

Choudhuri, Arnab R. The Physics of Fluids & Plasmas: An Introduction for Astrophysicists. LC 97-31092. (Illus.). 446p. (C). 1998. text 74.95 (*0-521-55487-X*); pap. text 29.95 (*0-521-55543-4*) Cambridge U Pr.

***Choudhury, A. K. R.** Modern Concepts of Color & Appearance. (Illus.). 340p. 2000. 75.00 (*1-57808-079-7*); pap. text 49.50 (*1-57808-078-9*) Science Pubs.

Choudhury, A. K. R., jt. auth. see Basu, S. C.

Choudhury, Ashok. Vacuum Metallurgy. 248p. 1990. 87.00 (*0-87170-398-X*, 6101) ASM.

— Vacuum Metallurgy. LC 90-83642. (Illus.). 255p. 1990. reprint ed. pap. 79.10 (*0-608-02631-X*, 206328900004) Bks Demand.

Choudhury, Ashok, jt. auth. see Sinha, Biswajit.

Choudhury, Bikram & Reynolds, Bonnie J. Bikram's Beginning Yoga. LC 76-29218. (Illus.). 212p. 1978. pap. 15.95 (*0-87477-082-3*, Tarcher Putnam) Putnam Pub Group.

Choudhury, D. P. Trade & Politics in the Himalaya-Karakoram Borderlands. 1996. 18.50 (*81-250-0642-7*, Pub. by Orient Longman Ltd) S Asia.

***Choudhury, Dhriti Kanta Lahiri, ed.** The Great Indian Elephant Book. (Illus.). 488p. 2000. 19.95 (*0-19-564892-7*) OUP.

Choudhury, Dilara. Bangladesh & the South Asian International System. 380p. 1992. 35.00 (*0-933511-15-9*) Kazi Pubns.

— Constitutional Development in Bangladesh: Stresses & Strains. 250p. 1997. text 29.95 (*0-19-577507-4*) OUP.

Choudhury, G. W. Islam & the Contemporary World. 230p. 1994. pap. 10.50 (*0-934905-19-3*) Kazi Pubns.

***Choudhury, Ifte.** Water & Plumbing. LC 99-32441. (Efficient Building Design Ser.: Vol. 3). 92p. 1999. pap. text 32.20 (*0-13-080337-5*) P-H.

***Choudhury, Jamil, ed.** Cultural Cooperation in South Asia: The Search for Community. 2000. 34.00 (*81-7304-346-9*, Pub. by Manohar) S Asia.

Choudhury, K. & Zaman, Tahamina, eds. Healthcare Economics: Text, Cases, Readings. 250p. 1997. 39.95 (*1-884015-84-0*) St Lucie Pr.

Choudhury, M. H. Electromagnetism. 1989. text 149.00 (*0-470-21479-1*) P-H.

Choudhury, Masudul A. Economic Theory & Social Institutions: A Critique with Special Reference to Canada. (Illus.). 418p. (Orig.). (C). 1994. pap. text 37.50 (*0-8191-9526-X*); lib. bdg. 59.50 (*0-8191-9525-1*) U Pr of Amer.

— An Islamic Social Welfare Function. Quinlan, Hamid, ed. LC 82-74125. (Illus.). 66p. 1983. pap. 3.50 (*0-89259-041-6*) Am Trust Pubns.

— The Islamic World View: Soci-Scientific Perspectives. 180p. 1999. 110.00 (*0-7103-0656-3*, Pub. by Kegan Paul Intl) Col U Pr.

— Money in Islam: Study in Islamic Political Economy. LC 97-8285. 313p. (C). 1997. 85.00 (*0-415-16302-1*) Routledge.

Choudhury, Masudul A. Reforming the Muslim World. LC 97-29387. 1997. 110.00 (*0-7103-0575-3*, Pub. by Kegan Paul Intl) Col U Pr.

Choudhury, Masudul A. Studies in Islamic Science & Polity. LC 97-22307. 1998. text 69.95 (*0-312-17740-2*) St Martin.

— Studies in Islamic Social Sciences. LC 97-3011. 272p. 1998. text 65.00 (*0-312-17516-7*) St Martin.

— The Unicity Precept & the Socio-Scientific Order. LC 93-6688. 194p. (C). 1993. lib. bdg. 42.50 (*0-8191-9079-9*) U Pr of Amer.

Choudhury, Masudul A., ed. Alternative Perspectives in Third-World Development: The Case of Malaysia. 3rd ed. 272p. 1996. text 79.95 (*0-312-15947-1*) St Martin.

***Choudhury, Masudul Alam.** Comparative Economic Theory: Occidental & Islamic Perspectives LC 99-37132. 1999. write for info. (*0-7923-8601-9*) Kluwer Academic.

***Choudhury, Mita.** Interculturalism & Resistance in the London Theater, 1660-1800: Identity, Performance, Empire. LC 00-20140. (Studies in Eighteenth-Century Literature & Culture). (Illus.). 2000. write for info. (*0-8387-5448-1*) Bucknell U Pr.

Choudhury, P. R. Left Experiment in West Bengal. 1986. 19.00 (*0-8364-1833-6*, Pub. by Heritage IA) S Asia.

Choudhury, Pravat K., jt. auth. see Cui, Geng.

Choudhury, S. R., jt. ed. see Debnath, L.

Choudhury, Sharmila & White, Adam. Identifying Parrots. (Illus.). 80p. 1997. 7.98 (*0-7858-0868-X*) Bk Sales Inc.

Choue, Young-Seek, jt. auth. see Perez De Cuellar, Javier.

Choueiri, Youssef. Islamic Fundamentalism. 2nd ed. LC 97-9808. 192p. 1997. 75.00 (*1-85567-444-0*) Bks Intl VA.

— Islamic Fundamentalism. 2nd rev. ed. LC 97-9808. 201p. 1997. pap. 24.95 (*1-85567-445-9*) Bks Intl VA.

Choueiri, Youssef M. Arab History & the Nation State. 272p. 1989. 56.95 (*0-415-03113-3*) Routledge.

— Islamic Fundamentalism. (Twayne's Themes in Right-Wing Politics & Ideology Ser.: No. 2). 224p. (C). 1990. pap. 16.95 (*0-8057-9553-7*, Twyne) Mac Lib Ref.

Choueiri, Youssef M., ed. State & Society in Syria & Lebanon, 1919-1991. LC 93-7555. 208p. 1994. text 49.95 (*0-312-09586-4*) St Martin.

Choueke, Esmond. Aphrodisiacs: A Guide to What Really Works. LC 98-13659. 160p. 1998. pap. text 10.95 (*0-8065-1997-5*, Citadel Pr) Carol Pub Group.

Choueke, Esmond, ed. see Myles, Elizabeth & MacFarlane, Bert.

Chouemi, Moustafa & Pellat, C. H. Al-Kamil Arabic-French-English Dictionary: Al-Kamil Dictionnaire Arabe-Francais-Anglais. (ARA, ENG & FRE.). 64p. 1981. 795.00 (*0-8288-4426-7*, M9286) Fr & Eur.

Chouemi, Moustafa, jt. auth. see Blachere, Regis.

Chouffot, Martha & Whalen, Karen. Ecrivons: Strategies d'Ecriture en Francais Langue Seconde. 93p. (C). 1991. pap. text 14.20 (*0-13-235037-8*) P-H.

***Chough, Sung Kwun, et al.** Marine Geology of Korean Seas. 2nd ed. LC 00-26493. 2000. write for info. (*0-444-50438-9*) Elsevier.

***Chouglay, Naazish.** Glass Painting. (Illus.). 96p. 2000. spiral bd. 29.95 (*1-86126-227-2*, Pub. by Crolwood) Trafalgar.

Chouhan, T. S. Agricultural Geography. (C). 1987. text 150.00 (*0-7855-6900-6*, Pub. by Scientific Pubs) St Mut.

— Desertification of World & Their Control. (C). 1993. text 225.00 (*81-7233-043-X*, Pub. by Scientific Pubs) St Mut.

— Geography of Rajasthan (Hindi) (C). 1993. text 175.00 (*81-7233-047-2*, Pub. by Scientific Pubs) St Mut.

— Integrated Area Development of Indian Desert. (C). 1988. text 175.00 (*0-7855-0108-8*, Pub. by Scientific Pubs) St Mut.

— Natural & Human Resources of Rajasthan. 503p. 1993. pap. 425.00 (*81-7233-068-5*, Pub. by Scientific Pubs) St Mut.

— Natural & Human Resources of Rajasthan. 1993. pap. 240.00 (*81-7233-062-6*, Pub. by Scientific Pubs) St Mut.

— Natural & Human Resources of Rajasthan. 1996. pap. 60.00 (*81-7233-146-0*, Pub. by Scientific Pubs) St Mut.

Chouhan, T. S., ed. Integrated Area Development of Indian Desert. 339p. (C). 1988. 60.00 (*81-85147-21-3*, Pub. by Scientific) St Mut.

Chouhan, T. S. & Joshi, K. N. Readings in Remote Sensing Applications. (C). 1992. text 460.00 (*81-7233-040-5*, Pub. by Scientific Pubs) St Mut.

— Studies in Arid Land Management. 432p. 1993. pap. 105.00 (*81-7233-064-2*, Pub. by Scientific Pubs) St Mut.

Chouinard, Jean-Yves, et al. Information Theory & Applications: 4th Canadian Workshop, Lac Delage, Quebec, Canada, May 1995:Selected Papers, Vol. 113. LC 96-41743. (Lecture Notes in Computer Science Ser.). xii, 309p. 1996. 56.00 (*3-540-61748-5*) Spr-Verlag.

Chouinard, Jeffrey. Mouths of Stone: Stories of the Ancient Maya from Newly Deciphered Inscriptions & Recent Archaeological Discoveries. LC 93-73799. (Centers of Civilization Ser.). (Illus.). 260p. (C). 1995. lib. bdg. 75.00 (*0-89089-565-1*) Carolina Acad Pr.

Chouinard, Larry. Matthew. LC 97-43055. (College Press NIV Commentary Ser.). 1997. 21.99 (*0-89900-628-0*) College Pr Pub.

Chouinard, Lauren D. Get off Your Butt. LC 89-92242. (Illus.). 71p. 1989. pap. 9.95 (*0-945744-01-3*) Provideo Ent.

Chouinard, Yvon. Climbing Ice. LC 77-19137. (Illus.). 192p. 1982. pap. 24.00 (*0-87156-208-1*, Pub. by Sierra) Random.

Choukas-Bradley, Melanie & Alexander, Polly. City of Trees: The Complete Field Guide to the Trees of Washington, D. C. rev. ed. LC 86-20912. (Illus.). 394p. 1987. pap. 15.95 (*0-8018-3320-5*) Johns Hopkins.

Choukr-Allah, R., et al, eds. Halophytes & Biosaline Agriculture. LC 95-34361. (Illus.). 424p. 1995. text 175.00 (*0-8247-9664-0*) Dekker.

Choukri, Mohamed. Jean Genet in Tangier. Bowles, Paul, tr. from ARA. 96p. 1990. pap. 7.95 (*0-88001-246-3*) HarpC.

— Streetwise. LC 95-126836. 220p. 1997. 27.50 (*0-86356-093-8*, Pub. by Saqi); pap. 18.50 (*0-86356-045-8*, Pub. by Saqi) Intl Spec Bk.

Choukroun, Jean-Marc & Snow, Roberta M., eds. Planning for Human Systems: Essays in Honor of Russell L. Ackoff. LC 91-45087. (Illus.). 448p. (C). 1992. text 49.95 (*0-8122-3128-7*) U of Pa Pr.

Choulant, Johann L. Bibliotheca Medico-Historia. 279p. 1988. reprint ed. lib. bdg. 70.00 (*3-487-00014-8*) G Olms Pubs.

— Graphische Inkunabeln Fur Naturgeschichte und Medicin. xx, 168p. 1963. reprint ed. 110.00 (*0-318-71755-7*) G Olms Pubs.

Choulant, Ludwig. History & Bibliography of Anatomic Illustration. Frank, Mortimer, tr. from GER. (Illus.). 462p. 1993. reprint ed. 85.00 (*1-888262-41-9*) Martino Pubng.

***Chouliaraki, Lilie.** Discourse in Late Modernity: Rethinking Critical Discourse Analysis. 2000. pap. 25.00 (*0-7486-1082-0*, Pub. by Edinburgh U Pr) Col U Pr.

***Choun, Jane.** Round-the-World Crafts, Games & Activities: Fun Ways to Grow Mission-Minded Children: Grades 1-6. (Illus.). 2000. pap. 16.99 (*0-7644-2082-8*) Group Pub.

Choun, Robert J. & Lawson, Michael S. The Christian Educator's Handbook on Children's Ministry: Reaching & Teaching the Next Generation. 2nd rev. ed. LC 98-33621. 320p. 1998. 21.99 (*0-8010-9058-X*, The Complete Ha) Baker Bks.

Choun, Robert J., Jr., jt. auth. see Lawson, Michael S.

Choundhry, G. G., et al, contrib. by. The Natural Environment & the Biogeochemical Cycles. (Handbook of Environmental Chemistry Ser.: Vol. I, Pt. C). (Illus.). 250p. 1984. 142.95 (*0-387-13226-0*) Spr-Verlag.

Chouquet, Gustave. Histoire de la Musique Dramatique En France Depuis Ses Origines Jusqu'a Nos Jours. LC 80-2265. reprint ed. 45.00 (*0-404-18818-4*) AMS Pr.

Chouraqui, Andre N. Letter to an Arab Friend. Gugli, William V., tr. LC 72-77573. 284p. 1972. 32.50 (*0-87023-108-1*) U of Mass Pr.

— A Man in Three Worlds. Kilmer, Kenton, tr. from FRE. LC 84-15338. (Illus.). 246p. (Orig.). 1985. lib. bdg. 44.50 (*0-8191-4242-5*) U Pr of Amer.

— The People & the Faith of the Bible. Gugli, William V., tr. LC 74-21237. 224p. 1975. 30.00 (*0-87023-172-3*) U of Mass Pr.

Chousalkar, Ashok. Indian Idea of Political Resistance: Aurobindo, Tilak, Gandhi & Ambedkar. (C). 1990. 19.50 (*81-202-0296-1*, Pub. by Ajanta) S Asia.

Choutka, Jeanne, ed. see Moe, Harold R.

Choux, M., ed. Shunts & Problems in Shunts. (Monographs in Neural Sciences: Vol. 8). (Illus.). x, 230p. 1982. pap. 100.00 (*3-8055-2465-X*) S Karger.

— Sixth International Symposium on Pediatric Neuro-Oncology, Marseille, June 1993: Abstracts. (Journal: Pediatric Neurosurgery: Vol. 19, No. 6, 1993). (Illus.). 62p. 1993. pap. 48.00 (*3-8055-5883-X*) S Karger.

Choux, M., et al, eds. Paediatric Neurosurgery. (Illus.). 700p. (C). 1999. text 250.00 (*0-443-05630-7*) Church.

— Pediatric Neurosurgery. LC 98-11502. (Illus.). 700p. 1998. write for info. (*0-443-06149-1*, W B Saunders Co) Harcrt Hlth Sci Grp.

Chovan, et al. Vykladovy Slovnik Poistovnictva. (SLO.). 96p. 1996. write for info. (*80-08-01818-6*, Pub. by Slov Pegagog Naklad) IBD Ltd.

***Chovanec, Libby, et al.** MCSE IIS 4 Exam Cram. 3rd ed. LC 00-21533. (Illus.). 385p. 2000. pap. write for info. (*1-57610-678-0*) Coriolis Grp.

Chovanec, Tina, ed. see Jacobs, Ronne T.

Chovelon, Bernadette. George Sand et Solange, Mere et Fille. (Voyage Immobile Collection). (FRE., Illus.). 432p. 1995. pap. 69.95 (*2-86808-081-2*) Intl Scholars.

Chow. Applied Hydrology. 1988. student ed. 37.18 (*0-07-010811-0*) McGraw.

— Fugitive Dust. (General Engineering Ser.). 1993. text. write for info. (*0-442-00965-8*, VNR) Wiley.

— Managerial Accounting. (AB - Accounting Principles Ser.). Date not set. write for info. (*0-538-82742-4*); student ed. write for info. (*0-538-82743-2*) S-W Pub.

Chow & Liu, eds. Design & Analysis of Animal Studies in Pharmaceutical Development. LC 98-135840. (Biostatistics Ser.: Vol. 1). (Illus.). 424p. 1998. text 175.00 (*0-8247-0130-5*) Dekker.

Chow, Amy. Magnificent Seven: The Authorized Story of American Gold. (Illus.). 112p. (YA). (gr. 6 up). 1996. 19.95 (*0-553-09774-1*) Bantam.

An Asterisk (*) at the beginning of an entry indicates that the title is appearing for the first time.

Chow, Ben, et al, eds. Elliptic & Parabolic Methods in Geometry. LC 96-20163. (Illus.). 216p. (C). 1996. text 59.00 (1-56881-064-4) AK Peters.

Chow, Brian. An Evolutionary Approach to Space Launch Commercialization. LC 93-20680. 1993. pap. text 15.00 (0-8330-1400-5, MR-121-ACQ) Rand Corp.

Chow, Brian G., et al. The Proposed Fissile-Material Production Cutoff: Next Steps. LC 95-12856. 60p. 1996. pap. text 15.00 (0-8330-2359-4, MR-586-1-OSD) Rand Corp.

Chow, Ching K., ed. Cellular Antioxidant Defense Mechanisms, 3 vols., Vol. I. 224p. 1988. 134.00 (0-8493-6916-9, RB170, CRC Reprint) Franklin.

— Cellular Antioxidant Defense Mechanisms, 3 vols., Vol. II. 256p. 1988. 149.00 (0-8493-6917-7, RB170, CRC Reprint) Franklin.

— Cellular Antioxidant Defense Mechanisms, 3 vols., Vol. III. 256p. 1988. 150.00 (0-8493-6918-5, RB170, CRC Reprint) Franklin.

Chow, Ching Kuang, ed. Fatty Acids in Foods & Their Health Implications. (Food Science & Technology Ser.: Vol. 53). (Illus.). 896p. 1992. text 275.00 (0-8247-8622-X) Dekker.

Chow, Chuen-Yen, jt. auth. see Kuethe, Arnold M.

***Chow, Claire S.** Leaving Deep Water: Asian American Women at the Crossroads of Two Cultures. 302p. 1999. pap. 13.95 (0-452-28049-4, Plume) Dutton Plume.

Chow, Daniel, tr. see Ten Boom, Corrie.

Chow, David & Spangler, Richard. Kung Fu: History, Philosophy & Techniques. LC 73-14043. (Illus.). 220p. 1980. pap. 14.95 (0-86568-011-6, 103) Unique Pubns.

Chow, Effie. Miracle Healing from China . . . Qugong. LC 94-96177. 258p. 1994. pap. 15.95 (0-9636979-5-1) MediPress.

Chow, Esther N., et al, eds. Race, Class & Gender: Common Bonds, Different Voices. (Gender & Society Readers Ser.). 384p. (C). 1996. 56.00 (0-8039-7056-0); pap. 26.00 (0-8039-7057-9) Sage.

Chow, Esther N. & Berheide, Catherine W., eds. Women, the Family, & Policy: A Global Perspective. LC 93-847. (SUNY Series in Gender & Society). 293p. (C). 1994. pap. text 21.95 (0-7914-1786-7) State U NY Pr.

Chow, Gan-Moog & Gonsalves, Kenneth E., eds. Nanotechnology: Molecularly Designed Materials. LC 96-6023. (ACS Symposium Ser.: No. 622). (Illus.). 424p. 1996. text 120.00 (0-8412-3392-6, Pub. by Am Chemical) OUP.

***Chow, Gan-Moog, et al.** Nanostructured Films & Coatings: Proceedings of the NATO Advanced Research Workshop on Nanostructured Films & Coatings, Santorini, Greece, June 28-30, 1999. LC 00-29624. 2000. write for info. (0-7923-6265-9, Kluwer Acad) Kluwer Academic.

Chow, Gan-Moog, Gan-Moog & Noskova, Nina I. Nanostructured Materials: Science & Technology. LC 98-20260. (NATO ASI Series: Partnership Sub-Series 3). 457p. 1998. write for info. (0-7923-5071-5) Kluwer Academic.

Chow, Gregory C. The Chinese Economy. 320p. 1987. text 93.00 (9971-5-0466-9); pap. text 47.00 (9971-5-0467-7) World Scientific Pub.

— Dynamic Economics: Organization by the LaGrange Method. (Illus.). 248p. 1997. text 49.95 (0-19-510192-8) OUP.

— Understanding China's Economy. 250p. 1994. text 61.00 (981-02-1841-9); pap. text 33.00 (981-02-1858-3) World Scientific Pub.

Chow, Gregory C. & Corsi, Paolo, eds. Evaluating the Reliability of Macro-Economic Models. LC 81-19766. (Illus.). 323p. reprint ed. pap. 100.20 (0-608-16011-3, 203308800083) Bks Demand.

Chow, Irene. Business Strategies: An Asia-Pacific Focus. LC 96-9086. 637p. (C). 1997. pap. text 54.00 (0-13-525858-8) P-H.

***Chow, J. C. Y., ed.** Advanced Arthroscopy. (Illus.). 792p. 2000. 250.00 (0-387-98808-4) Spr-Verlag.

Chow, J. K., ed. Industrial Pollution Control. 198p. 1983. pap. text 40.00 (0-317-02626-7, I00156) ASME.

Chow, Janny, tr. see Lu, Sheng-Yen.

Chow, Janny, tr. see Sheng-Yen Lu.

Chow, Joe H. & Koktovic, Petar V., eds. Systems Control Theory for Power Systems. LC 94-44183. (IMA Volumes in Mathematics & Its Applications: Vol. 6). 1995. 83.95 (0-387-94438-9) Spr-Verlag.

Chow, Joe H., jt. auth. see Frederick, Dean K.

Chow, John, ed. see International Conference on Microcomputers in Tran.

Chow, John K. Patronage & Power: Studies on Social Networks in Corinth. (Journal for the Study of the New Testament, Supplement Ser.: No. 75). 230p. (C). 1992. 65.00 (1-85075-370-9, Pub. by Sheffield Acad) CUP Services.

Chow, Jose. Sunday, Sunday. 192p. 1998. pap. write for info. (1-896705-24-3) Sister Vis Pr.

Chow, K. L., et al. Vision: Structure & Function. 624p. (C). 1988. text 90.00 (9971-5-0365-4) World Scientific Pub.

Chow, K. W. Solitons, Bilinear Transformation & Theta Functions. LC 96-46747. 1997. write for info. (0-582-30403-2) Longman.

Chow, Kai-Wing. The Rise of Confucian Ritualism in Late Imperial China: Ethics, Classics, & Lineage Discourse. LC 93-16633. xii, 344p. (C). 1994. 45.00 (0-8047-2173-4) Stanford U Pr.

— The Rise of Confucian Ritualism in Late Imperial China: Ethics, Classics & Lineage Discourse. 1996. pap. text 19.95 (0-8047-2791-0) Stanford U Pr.

Chow, Kai-Wing, et al, eds. Constructing Nationhood in Modern East Asia: Narrative Schemes, Nostalgia, & Ambiguity of Identities. (Illus.). 416p. (C). pap. text 19.95 (0-472-06735-4, 06735) U of Mich Pr.

— Constructing Nationhood in Modern East Asia: Narrative Schemes, Nostalgia, & Ambiguity of Identities. (Illus.). 416p. (C). text 59.50 (0-472-09735-0, 09735) U of Mich Pr.

Chow, Kai-Wing, et al, eds. Imagining Boundaries: Changing Confucian Doctrines, Texts, & Hermeneutics. LC 98-38760. (SUNY Series in Chinese Philosophy & Culture). 269p. (C). 1999. pap. text 24.95 (0-7914-4198-9) State U NY Pr.

— Imagining Boundaries: Changing Confucian Doctrines, Texts, & Hermeneutics. LC 98-38760. (SUNY Series in Chinese Philosophy & Culture). (Illus.). 288p. (C). 1999. text 73.50 (0-7914-4197-0) State U NY Pr.

***Chow, Kam Thye.** Thai Yoga Massage: A Gentle Therapy for Physical Well-Being & Spiritual Energy. (Illus.). 160p. 2001. 29.95 (0-89281-937-5) Inner Tradit.

Chow, Kit & Kramer, Ione. All the Tea in China. LC 89-60878. (Illus.). 206p. (Orig.). 1990. pap. 14.95 (0-8351-2194-1) China Bks.

— A Pocket Guide to All the Tea in China. rev. ed. 175p. 1998. pap. 6.95 (0-8351-2629-3) China Bks.

Chow, L. C. & Emery, A. F., eds. Heat Transfer Measurements & Analysis. (HTD Ser.: Vol. 249). 108p. 1993. 35.00 (0-7918-1162-X, G00806) ASME.

Chow, Larry C., jt. ed. see Fan, Yiu-Kwan.

Chow, Marilyn P., et al. Handbook of Pediatric Primary Care. 2nd ed. LC 83-26038. 1304p. 1990. text 62.95 (0-8273-4224-1) Delmar.

Chow, Mayling, et al. Whole Language: Practical Ideas. (Pippin Teacher's Library Ser.). 114p. 1995. pap. text 14.50 (0-88751-032-9, 00711) Heinemann.

Chow, Ming-Chwan. Understanding SONET/SDH Vol. 1: Standards & Applications. (Illus.). 504p. 1995. text 65.00 (0-9650448-2-3) Andan Pub.

***Chow, Ming-Chwan.** Understanding Telecommunications: Systems, Networks & Applications, Vol. 1. LC 99-97227. (Illus.). 712p. 2000. 65.00 (0-9650448-3-1) Andan Pub.

— Understanding Telecommunications: Systems, Networks & Applications, Vol. 2. LC 99-97227. (Illus.). 712p. 2000. 65.00 (0-9650448-8-2) Andan Pub.

Chow, Ming-Chwan. Understanding Wireless: Digital Mobile, Cellular & PCS. LC 98-70775. (Illus.). 592p. (C). 1998. text 65.00 (0-9650448-5-8) Andan Pub.

Chow, Mo-Yuen. Methodologies of Using Neural Network & Fuzzy Logic Technologies for Motor Incipient Fault Detection. LC 97-34193. 1997. 30.00 (981-02-3265-9) World Scientific Pub.

Chow, Moses C. & Choy, Leona. Let My People Go! 180p. (Orig.). 1995. pap. 13.95 (1-882324-13-7) Ambsssdrs Christ.

Chow, Paul, ed. MIPS-X RISC Microprocessor. (C). 1989. text 126.00 (0-7923-9045-8) Kluwer Academic.

Chow, Paul, jt. auth. see Vasquez-Patterson, Anne-Rae.

Chow, Paul N., et al, eds. Adjuvants & Agrochemicals, 2 vols., Vol. I. 240p. 1989. lib. bdg. 201.00 (0-8493-6532-5, S587) CRC Pr.

— Adjuvants & Agrochemicals, 2 vols., Vol. II. 256p. 1989. lib. bdg. 201.00 (0-8493-6533-3, S587) CRC Pr.

Chow, Peter C. & Kellman, Mitchell H. Trade: The Engine of Growth in the Pacific Basin. LC 92-27965. (Illus.). 184p. 1993. text 55.00 (0-19-507895-0) OUP.

***Chow, Peter C. Y.** Weathering the Storm: Taiwan, Its Neighbors & the Asian Financial Crisis. 2000. pap. write for info. (0-8157-1399-1) Brookings.

Chow, Rey. Ethics after Idealism: Theory, Culture, Ethnicity, Reading. LC 97-21576. (Theories of Contemporary Culture Ser.). 264p. 1998. 29.95 (0-253-33363-6); pap. 14.95 (0-253-21155-7) Ind U Pr.

***Chow, Rey.** Modern Chinese Literary & Cultural Studies in the Age of Theory: Reimagining a Field. LC 00-29425. (Illus.). 328p. 2000. pap. write for info. (0-8223-2597-7) Duke.

Chow, Rey. Primitive Passions: Visuality, Sexuality, Ethnography & Contemporary Chinese Cinema. LC 94-27796. (Film & Culture Ser.). 253p. 1995. 57.50 (0-231-07682-7); pap. 19.00 (0-231-07683-5) Col U Pr.

— Woman & Chinese Modernity: The Politics of Reading Between West & East. (Theory & History of Literature Ser.: Vol. 75). 224p. 1991. pap. 16.95 (0-8166-1871-2) U of Minn Pr.

— Writing Diaspora: Tactics of Intervention in Contemporary Cultural Studies. LC 92-23064. (Arts & Politics of the Everyday Ser.). 236p. 1993. 31.50 (0-253-31366-X); pap. 11.95 (0-253-20785-1, MB-785) Ind U Pr.

***Chow, Rey, ed.** Modern Chinese Literary & Cultural Studies in the Age of Theory: Reimagining a Field. LC 00-29425. (Illus.). 328p. 2000. lib. bdg. 59.95 (0-8223-2584-5) Duke.

Chow, S. N. & Hale, Jack K. Dynamics of Infinite Dimentional Systems. (NATO Asi Series F: Vol. 37). ix, 514p. 1987. 135.95 (0-387-18374-4) Spr-Verlag.

Chow, S. Y. General Theory of Lie Algebras, 2 vols., Set. xiii, 900p. 1978. text 521.00 (0-677-03890-9) Gordon & Breach.

***Chow, Shein-Chung & Liu, Jen-Pei.** Design & Analysis of Bioavailability & Bioequivalence Studies. 2nd ed. LC 99-51464. (Biostatistics Ser.: Vol. 3). 584p. 2000. 195.00 (0-8247-7572-4) Dekker.

Chow, Shein-Chung & Liu, Jen-Pei. Design & Analysis of Bioavailability & Bioequivalence Studies, No. 133. (Statistics: Textbooks & Monographs: Vol. 133). (Illus.). 432p. 1992. text 165.00 (0-8247-8682-3) Dekker.

***Chow, Shein-Chung & Liu, Jen-Pei.** Design & Analysis of Clinical Trials. LC 97-28675. (Wiley Series in Probability & Statistics). 672p. 1998. 135.00 (0-471-13404-X, Wiley-Interscience) Wiley.

Chow, Shein-Chung & Liu, Jen-Pei, eds. Statistical Design & Analysis of Pharmaceutical Sciences: Validation, Process Controls, & Stability. No. 143. (Statistics: Textbooks & Monographs: Vol. 143). (Illus.). 580p. 1995. text 165.00 (0-8247-9336-6) Dekker.

Chow, Shein-Chung, jt. auth. see Wang, Song-Gui.

Chow, Shui-Nee & Hale, Jack K. Methods of Bifurcation Theory. (Grundlehren der Mathematischen Wissenschaften Ser.: Vol. 251). (Illus.). 512p. 1996. 97.95 (0-387-90664-9) Spr-Verlag.

Chow, Simon. The Sign of Jonah Reconsidered: A Study of Its Meaning in the Gospel Traditions. LC 96-230002. (Coniectanea Biblica New Testament Ser.: No. 27). (Illus.). 244p. (Orig.). 1995. pap. 47.50 (91-22-01695-3) Coronet Bks.

Chow, Siu L. Experimental Psychology: Rationale, Procedures & Issues. 325p. (Orig.). (C). 1987. pap. text 23.95 (0-920490-68-9) Temeron Bks.

— Research Methods in Psychology: A Primer. 320p. (Orig.). (C). 1992. pap. text 25.95 (1-55059-031-6) Temeron Bks.

— Statistical Significance: Rationale, Validity & Utility. 208p. 1996. 69.95 (0-7619-5204-7); pap. 26.95 (0-7619-5205-5) Sage.

Chow-Soon Chuang Ju. Beyond the Good Earth. LC 91-70811. (Illus.). 160p. (Orig.). 1991. pap. 10.00 (0-9611726-4-9) Art Farm Gal.

Chow, Sunny. Classic Poems of Sunny Chow. 120p. Date not set. pap. text 8.00 (1-888065-14-1) New Wrld Poetry.

Chow, T. J., jt. ed. see Tu Guangzhi.

***Chow, T. S.** Mesoscopic Physics of Complex Materials. (Graduate Texts in Contemporary Physics Ser.). (Illus.). 252p. 2000. 49.95 (0-387-95032-X) Spr-Verlag.

Chow, Tai L. Classical Mechanics. LC 94-39839. 560p. 1995. text 99.95 (0-471-04365-6) Wiley.

***Chow, Tai L.** Mathematical Physics: Mathematical Methods for Scientists & Engineers. LC 99-44592. 2000. write for info. (0-521-65227-8); write for info. (0-521-65544-7) Cambridge U Pr.

Chow Tse-Tsung. The May Fourth Movement: Intellectual Revolution in Modern China. (East Asian Monographs: Vol. No. 6). 501p. (C). 1960. pap. 21.50 (0-674-55751-4) HUP.

Chow, V. W., ed. Multimedia Technology & Applications: Proceedings of the International Conference. 600p. (C). 1998. pap. 49.00 (981-3083-16-6, Pub. by Spr-Verlag) Spr-Verlag.

Chow Ven Te. Advances in Hydroscience, Vols. 1-12. Incl. Vol. 10. 1975. lib. bdg. 120.00 (0-12-021874-7); (Serial Publication Ser.). write for info. (0-318-50189-9) Acad Pr.

Chow Ven-Te. Open-Channel Hydraulics. (Civil Engineering Ser.). 680p. (C). 1959. 113.44 (0-07-010776-9) McGraw.

Chow Ven Te, et al. Applied Hydrology. 572p. (C). 1988. 103.44 (0-07-010810-2) McGraw.

Chow, Vic, jt. auth. see Coast Community College Staff.

Chow, W. S., ed. Multimedia Information Systems in Practice. 620p. 1999. pap. 59.95 (981-4021-53-9) Spr-Verlag.

Chow, W. W., et al. Semiconductor-Laser Physics. LC 93-46745. (Illus.). xii, 497p. 1997. 54.95 (0-387-57614-2) Spr-Verlag.

Chow, We-Min. Assembly Line Design: Methodology & Applications. (Manufacturing Engineering & Materials Processing Ser.: Vol. 33). (Illus.). 448p. 1990. text 165.00 (0-8247-8322-0) Dekker.

Chow, Weng W. & Koch, S. W. Semiconductor-Laser Fundamentals: Physics of the Gain Materials. LC 99-11674. 250p. 1999. 54.95 (3-540-64166-1) Spr-Verlag.

Chow, Weng W., jt. ed. see Osinski, Marek.

Chow, Winston. Managing Hazardous Air Pollutants: State of the Art. 608p. 1993. lib. bdg. 110.00 (0-87371-866-6, L866) Lewis Pubs.

Chow, Winston, et al, eds. Clean Water - Factors That Influence Its Availablity, Quality & Its Use: International Clean Water Conference, La Jolla, California, 28-30 November 1995. LC 96-9397. (Illus.). 354p. (C). 1996. text 166.00 (0-7923-4133-3) Kluwer Academic.

Chow, Y. Modern Abstract Algebra, 2 vols., Set. 782p. 1976. text 552.00 (0-677-03880-1) Gordon & Breach.

Chow, Y. M., jt. ed. see Agarwal, Ravi P.

Chow, Y. S. & Teicher, H. Probability Theory. 2nd ed. (Texts in Statistics Ser.). 490p. 1993. 59.95 (0-387-96695-1) Spr-Verlag.

Chow, Yuan S. & Teicher, Henry. Probability Theory: Independence, Interchangeability, Martingales. 3rd ed. Casella, G. et al, eds. LC 97-9299. (Texts in Statistics Ser.). 520p. 1997. 69.95 (0-387-98228-0) Spr-Verlag.

Chow, Yuen-Chien. Distriubted Operating Systems. LC 96-48480. 550p. (C). 1997. 70.00 (0-201-49838-3) Addison-Wesley.

Chowanietz, Eric. Automobile Electronics. 320p. 1995. 45.00 (1-56091-739-3, R-166) Soc Auto Engineers.

Chowdari, B. V. Solid State Icons: Science & Technology. 1998. 166.00 (981-02-3763-4) World Scientific Pub.

— Solid State Ionics: 3rd Asian Conference. 792p. 1992. text 116.00 (981-02-1138-4) World Scientific Pub.

Chowdari, B. V. & Radhakrishna, S., eds. Materials for Solid State Batteries: Proceedings of the Regional Workshop, Nus, Singapore, June 2-6, 1985. 516p. 1986. text 113.00 (9971-5-0149-X) World Scientific Pub.

— Solid State Ionic Devices. 740p. (C). 1988. text 138.00 (9971-5-0626-2) World Scientific Pub.

Chowdari, B. V., et al. Recent Advances in Fast Ion Conducting Materials & Devices: Second Asian Conf on S S Ionics. 620p. 1990. text 127.00 (981-02-0294-6) World Scientific Pub.

Chowdbury, J. N. Tribal Culture & History of Arunachal Pradesh. (C). 1990. 26.00 (81-7035-095-6, Pub. by Daya Pub Hse) S Asia.

Chowder, Ken. Mark Twain. 1998. write for info. (0-679-45061-0) Knopf.

Chowdhary, et al. Encyclopaedia of Economic Development. 20 vols. 7293p. 1991. 4000.00 (81-7041-202-1, Pub. by Scientific Pubs) St Mut.

***Chowdhary, Savitri.** Indian Cooking. (Cookery Classics). 188p. 1999. 19.95 (0-233-99630-3, Pub. by Andre Deutsch) Trafalgar.

Chowdhary, Savitri. Indian Cooking. 172p. 1990. 6.95 (0-318-36294-5) Asia Bk Corp.

Chowdhery, H. J. Flora of Himachal Pradesh, Vols. 1 & 2. (C). 1986. text 35.00 (0-7855-7057-8, Pub. by Scientific); text 35.00 (0-7855-7058-6, Pub. by Scientific) St Mut.

Chowdhery, H. J. & Wadhwa, B. M. Flora of Himachal Pradesh, 3 vols., Set. (Flora of India Ser.: No. 2). 1984. text 75.00 (0-945345-65-8, Pub. by Mahendra Pal Singh) Lubrecht & Cramer.

Chowdhry, Babur Z., jt. auth. see Ladbury, John E.

Chowdhry, D. Paul. Women Welfare & Development: A Source Book. (Women in South Asia Ser.: No. W 013). (C). 1992. 32.00 (81-210-0284-2, Pub. by Inter-India Pubns) S Asia.

Chowdhry, Kamla, ed. see Sarabhai, Vikram A.

Chowdhry, Maya, jt. ed. see Rapi, Nina.

Chowdhry, Paul. Aging & the Aged. (C). 1992. 28.00 (81-210-0257-5, Pub. by Inter-India Pubns) S Asia.

Chowdhry, Paul D. Child Welfare - Development. 440p. 1995. pap. 150.00 (81-7043-289-8, Pub. by Print Hse) St Mut.

***Chowdhry, Prem.** Image Ideology & Identity. (Illus.). 224p. 2000. text 74.95 (0-7190-5725-6, Pub. by Manchester Univ Pr) St Martin.

— Image Ideology & Identity: The Making Of Empire Cinema. (Illus.). 224p. 2000. pap. 29.95 (0-7190-5792-2) Manchester Univ Pr.

Chowdhry, Prem. The Veiled Woman: Shifting Gender Equations in Rural Haryana, 1880-1990. (Illus.). 480p. 1994. text 29.95 (0-19-563134-X) OUP.

Chowdhurry, Subrata R., ed. The Right to Development in International Law. 432p. (C). 1992. lib. bdg. 151.50 (0-7923-1682-7) Kluwer Academic.

Chowdhury, A. M. Raza, jt. auth. see Jalaluddin, A. K.

Chowdhury, A. R. Lie Algebraic Methods in Integrable Systems. LC 96-35718. (Pitman Research Notes in Mathematics Ser.). 1997. write for info. (0-582-30267-6) Longman.

C

***Chowdhury, A. R.** LIE Algebraic Methods in Integrable Systems. (Research Notes in Mathematics Ser.). (Illus.). 1999. pap. text (0-8493-0637-X, Chap & Hall CRC) CRC Pr.

— LIE Algebraic Methods in Integrable Systems, Vol. 415. (C&H/CRC Research Notes in Mathematics Series). 368p. 1999. per. 74.95 (1-58488-037-6, Chap & Hall CRC) CRC Pr.

Chowdhury, Aditee N. Let Grassroots Speak. (C). 1989. 28.00 (81-85054-79-7, Pub. by Manohar) S Asia.

Chowdhury, Amitabha, ed. Bankers Handbook for Asia: 1988 Guide to Banks & Finance Companies in Asia Plus 22 Countries of Iran-Arab Region. 12th ed. 449p. 1987. 70.00 (962-7185-01-9) Am Overseas Bk Co.

Chowdhury, Anis & Islam, Iyanatul. Asia Pacific Economies: An Analytical Survey. LC 96-13403. 320p. (C). 1997. 100.00 (0-415-10765-2); pap. 22.95 (0-415-10766-0) Routledge.

— The Newly Industrializing Economies of East Asia. LC 93-16568. (Illus.). 304p. (C). 1993. pap. 29.99 (0-415-09749-5, B2338) Routledge.

Chowdhury, Anis & Kirkpatrick, Colin. Development Policy & Planning: An Introduction to Models & Techniques. LC 93-7404. (Illus.). 144p. (C). 1993. pap. 24.99 (0-415-09889-0) Routledge.

Chowdhury, Anis, jt. auth. see Hossain, Akhtar.

***Chowdhury, Bernie.** The Last Dive: A Father & Son's Fatal Descent into the Ocean's Depths. 304p. 2000. 25.00 (0-06-019462-6) HarpC.

***Chowdhury, D. D.** High Speed LAN Technology Handbook. 650p. 2000. 81.00 (3-540-66597-8) Spr-Verlag.

Chowdhury, Debashish. Spin Glasses & Other Frustrated Systems. 200p. 1986. text 40.00 (9971-5-0029-9) World Scientific Pub.

— Spin Glasses & Other Frustrated Systems. LC 86-28923. (Princeton Series in Physics). (Illus.). 399p. 1986. reprint ed. pap. 123.70 (0-7837-9496-7, 206024000004) Bks Demand.

***Chowdhury, Dhinam D.** High Speed Enterprise Networking. (Illus.). 2000. 75.00 (3-540-65974-9) Spr-Verlag.

Chowdhury, G. & Miles, D. K. An Empirical Model of Companies' Debt & Dividend Decisions: Evidence from Company Accounts Data. fac. ed. LC HG0152.5. (Bank of England, Discussion Papers: No. 28). (Illus.). 62p. 1987. pap. 30.00 (0-7837-7644-6, 204739700007) Bks Demand.

Chowdhury, G., et al. An Empirical Model of Company Short-Term Financial Decisions: Evidence from Company Accounts Data. LC HG2993.. (Bank of England, Discussion Papers: No. 26). 73p. 1986. reprint ed. pap. 30.00 (0-608-01360-9, 206209900002) Bks Demand.

***Chowdhury, G. G.** Introduction to Modern Information Retrieval. 448p. 1999. pap. 69.00 (1-85604-318-5, Pub. by Library Association) Bernan Associates.

Chowdhury, Hasanuzzaman. Underdevelopment State & Mode of Production in Bangladesh: A Sociological Outline. 120p. 1986. 12.50 (0-8364-1561-2, Pub. by Minerva) S Asia.

Chowdhury, Indira. The Frail Hero & Virile History: Gender & the Politics of Culture in Colonial Bengal. LC 98-903527. (School of Oriental & African Studies). 208p. 1998. text 22.95 (0-19-564429-8) OUP.

Chowdhury, J. B., jt. ed. see Kalloo, G.

Chowdhury, K. C. British History. (C). 1989. 50.00 (0-89771-443-1, Pub. by Current Dist) St Mut.
— History of Ancient India. (C). 1989. 40.00 (0-89771-444-X, Pub. by Current Dist) St Mut.
— History of Greece. (C). 1989. 40.00 (0-89771-442-3, Pub. by Current Dist) St Mut.
— History of Medieval India. (C). 1989. 35.00 (0-89771-445-8, Pub. by Current Dist) St Mut.
— History of Modern India. (C). 1989. 35.00 (0-7855-6558-2, Pub. by Current Dist) St Mut.
— The Middle Ages. (C). 1989. 35.00 (0-89771-441-5, Pub. by Current Dist) St Mut.
Chowdhury, Kowsar P. Efforts in Universalization of Primary Education & the Case of Bangladesh. (Special Studies in Comparative Education: No. 12). 72p. (Orig.). 1984. pap. text 10.00 (0-937033-02-2) Grad Schl of Educ.
Chowdhury, Mustafa. Pakistan: Its Politics & Bureaucracy. xi, 244p. 1988. text 30.00 (81-7045-025-X, Pub. by Assoc Pub Hse) Advent Bks Div.
***Chowdhury, N. & Aguirre, Alonso A., eds.** Helminths of Wildlife. (Illus.). 420p. 2000. text 118.00 (1-57808-092-4) Science Pubs.
Chowdhury, N. & Tada, I. Helminthology. 373p. 1994. 131.00 (0-387-57715-7) Spr-Verlag.
Chowdhury, Najma, jt. ed. see Nelson, Barbara J.
Chowdhury, Osman H., jt. auth. see Khandker, Shahidur K.
Chowdhury, Profulla Roy, see Roy Chowdhury, Profulla.
Chowdhury, R. N., ed. Geomechanics & Water Engineering in Environmental Management. (Illus.). 640p. (C). 1992. text 168.00 (90-5410-112-1, Pub. by A A Balkema) Ashgate Pub Co.
Chowdhury, R. N., jt. ed. see Sivakumar, M.
Chowdhury, Robin N. & Sivakumar, Siva M., eds. Environmental Management Geo-Water & Engineering Aspects: Proceedings of the International Conference on Environmental Management Geo-Water & Engineering Aspects, Wollongong - New South Wales, Australia 8-11 February, 1993. (Illus.). 838p. (C). 1993. text 188.00 (90-5410-099-0, Pub. by A A Balkema) Ashgate Pub Co.
Chowdhury, Roy. Corporate Audit Committees. (C). 1990. 100.00 (0-89771-219-6) St Mut.
Chowdhury, Roy, ed. Internal Audit Programming. (C). 1990. 70.00 (0-89771-218-8) St Mut.
— Performance Audit. (C). 1990. 80.00 (0-89771-217-X) St Mut.
Chowdhury, S. Concise Medical Physiology. (C). 1989. 190.00 (0-89771-376-1, Pub. by Current Dist) St Mut.
***Chowdhury, Subir.** Management 21C: New Visions for a New Millennium. (Illus.). 289p. 2000. 28.00 (0-273-63963-3, Pub. by F T P-H) Natl Bk Netwk.
Chowdhury, Subir & Zimmer, Ken. QS 9000 Pioneers: Registered Companies Share Their Strategies for Success. LC 96-10433. (Illus.). 288p. 1996. text 50.00 (0-7863-0865-6, H0947) ASQ Qual Pr.
Chowdhury, Sue, jt. auth. see Mears, Catherine.
Chowdry. Pathophysiology. 1993. 53.75 (0-697-09850-8) McGraw.
Chowdry, N. K., jt. auth. see Aggarwal, J. C.
Chowdry, Phyllis. Pathophysiology with Practical Applications. 576p. (C). 1992. text 64.50 (0-697-08538-4) Brown & Benchmark.
Chowla, S. Riemann Hypothesis & Hilberts Tenth Problem, Vol. 4. (Mathematics & Its Applications Ser.). xvi, 120p. 1965. text 195.00 (0-677-00140-1) Gordon & Breach.
Chown. Newstrom Organizational Behavior. 9th ed. 1992. teacher ed. 51.56 (0-07-015621-2) McGraw.
Chown, Alice A. The Stairway. rev. ed. (Illus.). 351p. 1988. pap. 14.95 (0-8020-6683-6); text 30.00 (0-8020-5769-1) U of Toronto Pr.
Chown, Jeffery. Hollywood Auteur: Francis Coppola. LC 87-3035. 236p. 1988. 59.95 (0-275-92910-8, C2910, Praeger Pubs) Greenwood.
Chown, John F. History of Money: From A.D. 800. 320p. (C). 1997. pap. 29.99 (0-415-13729-2) Routledge.
Chown, John F., ed. Origins of American Banking, 7 vols., Set. 1800p. (C). 1997. 745.00 (0-415-14450-7) Routledge.
— Tax Efficient Foreign Exchange Management. LC 89-10884. 284p. 1990. 75.00 (0-89930-541-5, DTE/, Quorum Bks) Greenwood.
Chown, Marcus. Afterglow of Creation: From the Fireball to the Discovery of Cosmic Ripples. LC 95-38781. 171p. (C). 1996. 28.50 (0-935702-40-7) Univ Sci Bks.
Chown, Marcus, jt. auth. see Gribbin, John.
Chown, Paul & Tellew, Pam. Unemployment Insurance & Disability Insurance in California: A Guide for Union Representatives. 65p. 1986. pap. text 7.00 (0-937817-04-X) CLRE UCAL Berk.
Chowning, Ann, jt. auth. see Goodale, Jane C.
Chowning, Larry S. Chesapeake Legacy: Tools & Traditions. LC 94-39899. (Illus.). 304p. 1995. pap. 29.95 (0-87033-468-9, Tidewtr Pubs) Cornell Maritime.
— Harvesting the Chesapeake: Tools & Traditions. LC 89-20600. (Illus.). 296p. 1990. pap. 29.95 (0-87033-469-7, Tidewtr Pubs) Cornell Maritime.
***Chowning, Larry S.** Soldiers at the Doorstep: Civil War Lore. LC 99-27180. (Illus.). 141p. 1999. 19.95 (0-87033-519-7, Tidewtr Pubs) Cornell Maritime.
Chowning, Margaret. Wealth & Power in Provincial Mexico: Michoacan from the Late Colony to the Revolution. LC 99-24871. 1999. 60.00 (0-8047-3428-3) Stanford U Pr.
Chows. Chinese Painting No. 1. (How to Draw & Paint Ser.). (Illus.). 32p. (Orig.). 1989. pap. 6.95 (1-56010-016-8, HT069) W Foster Pub.
Choy. Basic Grammar & Usage. 4th ed. (C). 1993. pap. text, teacher ed. 33.75 (0-15-500153-1) Harcourt Coll Pubs.
— Basic Grammar & Usage. 5th ed. (C). 1997. pap. text, teacher ed. 28.00 (0-15-503692-0) Harcourt Coll Pubs.
Choy, et al. Coming Man: 19th Century American Perceptions of the Chinese. LC 96-216802. (Illus.). 178p. 1995. pap. 24.95 (0-295-97453-2) U of Wash Pr.
***Choy, Bruce & Reible, Danny D.** Diffusion Models of Environmental Transport. LC 99-41787. 1999. write for info. (1-56670-414-6) Lewis Pubs.
Choy, Carol E., jt. auth. see Yarber, Yvonne.
Choy, Cheuk, tr. see Adams, Jay Edward.
Choy, Chong L., et al, eds. Business, Society & Development in Singapore. 128p. 1990. pap. 13.50 (981-00-2063-5, Pub. by Times Academic); boxed set 22.50 (981-00-2099-6, Pub. by Times Academic) Intl Spec Bk.
Choy, Dexter J. L., jt. auth. see Gee, Chuck Y.
Choy, F., et al. Analytical & Experimental Vibration Analysis of a Damaged Gear. (Nineteen Ninety-Four Fall Technical Meeting Ser.: Vol. 94FTM9). (Illus.). 8p. 1994. pap. text 30.00 (1-55589-644-8) AGMA.
Choy, Lee K. Japan - Between Myth & Reality. 300p. 1995. pap. text 24.00 (981-02-1865-6) World Scientific Pub.
Choy, Leona. Andrew & Emma Murrary: An Intimate Portrait of Their Marriage & Ministry. (Illus.). 287p. 2000. pap. 15.95 (1-889283-15-0) Golden Morning.
***Choy, Leona.** Andrew & Emma Murray: Intimate Portrait of Their Marriage & Ministry. 269p. 2000. pap. 11.99 (0-88965-191-4, Pub. by Horizon Books) Chr Pubns.
Choy, Leona. Are You Mad at Me, God? Jumping Illness Hurdles. 90p. 1998. pap. 9.95 (1-889283-12-6) Golden Morning.
— Celebrate This Moment: Prime Time Is Now. 374p. 1997. pap. 16.95 (1-889283-06-1) Golden Morning.
— Divine Applications. 21p. (Orig.). 1994. pap. 2.50 (1-882324-08-0) Ambssdrs Christ.
— Heaven & Nature Sing. 71p. (Orig.). 1994. pap. 5.95 (1-882324-06-4) Ambssdrs Christ.
— Hospital Gowns Don't Have Pockets: Why Me? What Now? Discovering Meaning in Physical Distress. (Illus.). 324p. 1997. pap. 16.95 (1-889283-04-5) Golden Morning.
— How to Capture & Develop Ideas for Writing. 46p. 1996. pap. 6.95 (1-889283-00-2) Golden Morning.
— Life - Stop Crowding Me. 190p. (Orig.). 1994. pap. text 8.95 (1-882324-05-6) Ambssdrs Christ.
— Living It Up: Meditations for "Seasoned Saints" 300p. 1998. pap. 16.95 (1-889283-14-2) Golden Morning.
— Powerlines: What Great Evangelicals Believed about the Holy Spirit, 1850-1930. LC 90-81459. 321p. (Orig.). (C). 1990. pap. 12.99 (0-87509-434-1) Chr Pubns.
— Release the Poet Within: How to Launch & Improve Poetry Craft & Ministry. 101p. 1996. pap. 14.95 (1-889283-02-9) Golden Morning.
— Singled Out for God's Assignment: A Widow's Valley of Learning. 234p. 1996. pap. 14.95 (1-889283-03-7) Golden Morning.
— Songs of My Pilgrimage. 84p. (Orig.). 1994. pap. 5.95 (1-882324-07-2) Ambssdrs Christ.
— Study Guide: To Accompany the Book "Singled Out for God's Assignment" 60p. 1997. pap. 5.50 (1-889283-11-8) Golden Morning.
— Touching China: Close Encounters of the Christian Kind. Troup, W. Lee, ed. (Illus.). 224p. 1993. pap. 9.95 (1-882324-00-5) Ambssdrs Christ.
— Walk the Green Valley: Travel Tips for Your Journey Through Loss. 90p. 1998. pap. 9.95 (1-889283-13-4) Golden Morning.
— The Widow's Might: Strength from the Rock. 156p. 1996. pap. 14.95 (1-889283-01-0) Golden Morning.
Choy, Leona, jt. auth. see Chow, Moses C.
Choy, Leona, jt. auth. see Choy, Ted.
Choy, Leona, jt. auth. see Murray, Andrew.
Choy, Leona, ed. see Wang, Esther C.
Choy, Penelope. Basic Grammar & Usage. 4th alternate ed. (Orig.). (C). 1997. pap. text. write for info. (0-15-502324-1) Harcourt Coll Pubs.
— Basic Grammar & Usage. 5th ed. (Orig.). (C). 1997. pap. text 24.50 (0-15-503634-3, Pub. by Harcourt Coll Pubs) Harcourt.
Choy, Penelope & McCormick, James R. Basic Grammar & Usage. 3rd ed. 291p. (Orig.). (C). 1989. pap. text 3.00 (0-15-504936-4) Harcourt Coll Pubs.
— Basic Grammar & Usage: Alternate. 3rd ed. 300p. (C). 1992. pap. text 3.00 (0-15-504938-0) Harcourt Coll Pubs.
Choy, Rita M. Read & Write Chinese: A Simplified Guide to the Chinese Characters. 1983. pap. 11.95 (0-941340-09-0) China West.
— Read & Write Chinese: A Simplified Guide to the Chinese Characters. 5th ed. (CHI.). 350p. (C). 1990. pap. 15.00 (0-941340-11-2) China West.
***Choy, Rita Mei-Wah.** Understanding Chinese: A Guide to the Usage of Chinese Characters. 2nd rev. ed. (CHI.). 577p. 2000. pap. 17.50 (0-941340-13-9) China West.
Choy, Sam. Choy of Seafood: Sam Choy's Pacific Harvest. (Illus.). 216p. 1998. pap. 29.95 (1-56647-222-9) Mutual Pub HI.
— The Choy of Seafood-Sam Choy's Pacific Harvest. 216p. 1998. 35.00 (1-56647-173-7) Mutual Pub HI.
Choy, Sam. Sam Choy's Cooking: Island Cuisine at Its Best. (Illus.). 240p. 1996. 35.00 (1-56647-312-8) Mutual Pub HI.
Choy, Sam. Sam Choy's Island Flavors. LC 98-44345. (Illus.). 288p. 1999. 26.95 (0-7868-6474-5, Pub. by Hyperion) Time Warner.
— Untitled Cookbook. (Illus.). 288p. 2001. 29.95 (0-7868-6475-3, Pub. by Hyperion) Time Warner.
Choy, Sam & Cook, Evelyn. With Sam Choy: Cooking from the Heart. (Illus.). 224p. 1995. 35.00 (1-56647-098-6) Mutual Pub HI.
— With Sam Choy: Cooking from the Heart. (Illus.). 224p. 1995. pap. 30.00 (1-56647-109-5) Mutual Pub HI.
***Choy, Sam & Cook, Lynn.** Sam Choy's Kitchen: Cooking Doesn't Get Any Easier Than This. (Illus.). 256p. 1999. 24.95 (1-56647-282-2) Mutual Pub HI.
***Choy, Sam & Francisco, Randall.** Sam Choy's Poke: Hawaii's Soul Food. (Illus.). 280p. 1999. 24.95 (1-56647-284-9) Mutual Pub HI.
***Choy, Susan P.** Choosing a Postsecondary Institution. 109p. 1998. pap. 14.00 (0-16-063678-7) USGPO.
— Graduate & First-Professional Students, National Postsecondary Student Aid Study, 1996. 24p. 1998. pap. 3.00 (0-16-049637-3) USGPO.
— How Low Income Undergraduates Financed Postsecondary Education: 1992-93. 78p. 1996. pap. 6.50 (0-16-063580-2) USGPO.
— Student Financing of Graduate & First-Professional Education, 1992-93, with an Essay on Student Borrowing. 128p. 1995. pap. 8.50 (0-16-048427-8) USGPO.
— Student Financing of Graduate & First-Professional Education, 1995-96: With Profiles of Students in Selected Degree Programs. 149p. 1998. pap. 8.50 (0-16-049525-3) USGPO.
— Teachers' Working Conditions. 30p. 1997. pap. 4.75 (0-16-048969-5) USGPO.
Choy, Susan P. & National Center for Education Statistics Staff. Public & Private Schools: How Do They Differ? LC 98-179013. (Findings from the Condition of Education Ser.). 39 p. 1997. write for info. (0-16-049221-1) USGPO.
Choy, Susan P., et al. America's Teachers: Profile of a Profession. (Illus.). 189p. (Orig.). (C). 1994. pap. text 45.00 (0-7881-0682-1) DIANE Pub.
— Early Labor Force Experiences & Debt Burden LC 98-108869. (Statistical Analysis Report/National Center for Education Statistics Ser.). xv, 119 p. 1997. pap. write for info. (0-16-049179-7) USGPO.
Choy, Susan P., jt. auth. see Cuccaro-Alamin, Stephen.
Choy, Ted & Choy, Leona. My Dreams & Visions: An Autobiography. 255p. 1997. pap. 15.95 (1-889283-09-6) Golden Morning.
***Choy, Tuck C.** Effective Medium Theory: Principles & Applications. LC 99-16239. 1999. write for info. (0-19-851891-9) OUP.
***Choy, Tuck C.** Effective Medium Theory: Principles & Applications. (The International Series of Monographs on Physics: No. 102). (Illus.). 208p. 1999. text 95.00 (0-19-851892-7) OUP.
Choy, Wai, et al. National Household Survey on Drug Abuse: Main Findings, (1993) (Illus.). 330p. (C). 1998. reprint ed. pap. text 45.00 (0-7881-4285-2) DIANE Pub.
Choy, Wayson. The Jade Peony. 240p. 1998. pap. 12.00 (0-312-18692-4) St Martin.
***Choy, Wayson.** Paper Shadows: A Memoir of a Past Lost & Found. 352p. 2000. 24.00 (0-312-26218-3, Picador USA) St Martin.
Choyce. Transcendental Anarchy Confessions of a Metaphysical Tourist. 240p. 1994. per. 11.95 (1-55082-073-7, Pub. by Quarry Pr) LPC InBook.
Choyce, Lesley. Carrie's Crowd. (First Novels Ser.). (Illus.). 64p. (J). (gr. 1-4). 1999. text 3.99 (0-88780-464-0, Pub. by Formac Publ Co) Orca Bk Pubs.
***Choyce, Lesley.** Carrie's Crowd. (First Novels). (Illus.). 64p. (J). 1998. bds. write for info. (0-88780-465-9, Pub. by J Lorimer) Formac Dist Ltd.
Choyce, Lesley. Clearcut Danger. 132p. (YA). (gr. 6 up). 1995. pap. 8.95 (0-88780-213-3) Formac Dist Ltd.
Choyce, Lesley. Clearcut Danger. 132p. (J). 1992. mass mkt. 6.95 (0-88780-338-5, Pub. by Formac Publ Co) Formac Dist Ltd.
Choyce, Lesley. Clearcut Danger. 132p. (YA). (gr. 6 up). 1995. bds. 16.95 (0-88780-214-1, Pub. by Formac Publ Co) Formac Dist Ltd.
— Dance the Rocks Ashore. LC 97-162664. 280p. 1997. pap. 14.95 (0-86492-218-3, Pub. by Goose Ln Edits) Genl Dist Srvs.
— Dark End of Dream Street. 188p. (YA). (gr. 6 up). 1995. pap. 8.95 (0-88780-296-6, Pub. by Formac Publ Co); bds. 16.95 (0-88780-297-4, Pub. by Formac Publ Co) Formac Dist Ltd.
— The End of Ice. 96p. 1985. pap. 10.95 (0-86492-054-7, Pub. by Goose Ln Edits) Genl Dist Srvs.
Choyce, Lesley. Falling Through the Cracks. 160p. (J). 1996. bds. 16.95 (0-88780-365-2, Pub. by Formac Publ Co) Formac Dist Ltd.
Choyce, Lesley. Falling Through the Cracks. 160p. (YA). (gr. 6-11). 1998. pap. 6.95 (0-88780-364-4, Pub. by Formac Publ Co) Formac Dist Ltd.
Choyce, Lesley. Go for It, Carrie. LC 96-950185. (First Novels). (Illus.). 64p. (J). 1997. bds. 4.95 (0-88780-393-8, Pub. by Formac Publ Co) Formac Dist Ltd.
Choyce, Lesley. Go for It, Carrie. LC 96-950185. (First Novels). (Illus.). 64p. (J). (gr. 1-4). 1998. mass mkt. 3.99 (0-88780-392-X, Pub. by Formac Publ Co) Formac Dist Ltd.
— Good Idea Gone Bad. 128p. (J). (gr. 6-11). 1998. pap. 6.95 (0-88780-239-7) Formac Dist Ltd.
— Good Idea Gone Bad. 128p. (YA). (gr. 6 up). 1995. bds. 16.95 (0-88780-241-9, Pub. by Formac Publ Co) Formac Dist Ltd.
— Good Idea Gone Bad. 151p. (J). (gr. 7-12). 1998. text 4.95 (0-88780-470-5, Pub. by Formac Publ Co) Formac Dist Ltd.
— Magnificent Obsessions: A Photo Novel. (Illus.). 144p. 1991. pap. 14.95 (1-55082-020-6, Pub. by Quarry Pr) LPC InBook.
***Choyce, Lesley.** Nova Scotia: Shaped by the Sea: A Living History. (Illus.). 304p. 1999. text 30.00 (0-7881-6781-2) DIANE Pub.
Choyce, Lesley. The Republic of Nothing. LC 95-170744. 363p. 1994. pap. 14.95 (0-86492-153-5, Pub. by Goose Ln Edits) Genl Dist Srvs.
***Choyce, Lesley.** Roid Rage. 112p. 1999. pap. 6.95 (1-55017-206-9) Harbour Pub Co.
Choyce, Lesley. Skateboard Shakedown. 2nd rev. ed. 124p. (J). (gr. 6-9). 1989. reprint ed. bds. 16.95 (0-88780-074-2, Pub. by Formac Publ Co) Formac Dist Ltd.
— Skateboard Shakedown. 2nd rev. ed. 124p. (J). (gr. 6-9). 1993. reprint ed. mass mkt. 6.95 (0-88780-232-X, Pub. by Formac Publ Co) Formac Dist Ltd.
— The Summer of Apartment X. 143p. 1999. 17.95 (0-86492-270-1, Pub. by Goose Ln Eds) Genl Dist Srvs.
— Trapdoor to Heaven. 224p. 1997. pap. 12.95 (1-55082-157-1, Pub. by Quarry Pr) LPC InBook.
— Wave Watch. 2nd ed. 120p. (J). (gr. 6-9). 1994. reprint ed. mass mkt. 6.95 (0-88780-300-8, Pub. by Formac Publ Co); reprint ed. bds. 16.95 (0-88780-081-5, Pub. by Formac Publ Co) Formac Dist Ltd.
— Wrong Time, Wrong Place. 116p. (YA). (gr. 6 up). 1995. pap. 8.95 (0-88780-098-X) Formac Dist Ltd.
Choyce, Lesley. Wrong Time, Wrong Place. 116p. (J). 1991. mass mkt. 6.95 (0-88780-340-7, Pub. by Formac Publ Co) Formac Dist Ltd.
Choyce, Lesley. Wrong Time, Wrong Place. 115p. (YA). (gr. 6 up). 1995. bds. 16.95 (0-88780-099-8, Pub. by Formac Publ Co) Formac Dist Ltd.
Choyin, Detong. Waking from the Dream: A Wealth of Practical Information Relating to the Buddhist Path to Enlightenment. LC 96-46041. 320p. (Orig.). 1996. pap. 18.95 (0-8048-3084-3) Tuttle Pubng.
Choyk, Wolfgang, et al, eds. Silicon Carbide: A Review of Fundamental Questions & Applications to Current Device Technology, 2 vol. set. 1168p. 1997. 195.00 (3-05-501792-7) Wiley.
Choyke, Wolfgang J., et al, eds. Silicon Carbide: A Review of Fundamental Questions & Applications to Current Device Technology , 2 vols. Set. 1168p. 1997. 175.00 (3-527-40127-X) Wiley.
Choznacka, Dagmara. Przepowiednie Nostradamasa. Polish Book Fair, Inc. Staff, ed. (Illus.). 144p. 1995. pap. 8.00 (1-885889-62-3) Home Tutor.
Chposky, James & Leonsis, Ted. Blue Magic: The People, Power & Politics Behind the IBM Personal Computer. LC 88-509. 240p. reprint ed. pap. 74.40 (0-7837-5343-8, 204508500005) Bks Demand.
Chr Etien & Raffel, Burton. Perceval: The Story of the Grail. LC 98-18938. 1999. write for info. (0-300-07585-5); pap. 16.00 (0-300-07586-3) Yale U Pr.
Chraibi, Driss. Birth at Dawn. Woollcombe, Ann, tr. from FRE. LC 86-51006. Orig. Title: Le Noussance de l'Aube. 136p. 1990. 18.00 (0-89410-576-0, Three Contnts); pap. 12.00 (0-89410-577-9, Three Contnts) L Rienner.
— Les Boucs. (FRE.). 181p. 1989. pap. 11.95 (0-7859-2122-2, 2070381609) Fr & Eur.
— The Butts. Harter, Hugh A., tr. from FRE.Tr. of Les Boucs. 123p. 1983. reprint ed. 12.00 (0-89410-324-5, Three Contnts) L Rienner.
— Civilisation, ma Mere!... (Folio Ser.: No. 1902). (FRE.). 180p. 1972. pap. 8.95 (2-07-037902-7) Schoenhof.
— La Civilisation, Ma Mere! (FRE.). 180p. 1988. pap. 10.95 (0-7859-2080-3, 2070379027) Fr & Eur.
— Une Enquete au Pays. (FRE.). 1982. pap. 14.95 (0-7859-2689-5) Fr & Eur.
— Heirs to the Past. (African Writers Ser.). 107p. (C). 1971. pap. 8.95 (0-435-90079-X, 90079) Heinemann.
— Inspector Ali. McGlashlan, Lara, tr. from FRE. 143p. 1994. 26.00 (0-89410-746-1, Three Contnts); pap. 12.95 (0-89410-747-X, Three Contnts) L Rienner.
— La Mere du Printemps, l'Oum-er-Bia. (FRE.). 1986. pap. 14.95 (0-7859-2707-7) Fr & Eur.
— Mother Comes of Age. Harter, Hugh A., tr. from FRE. LC 81-51655.Tr. of La Civilisation, Ma Mere!. 121p. 1984. reprint ed. pap. 12.00 (0-89410-323-7, Three Contnts) L Rienner.
— The Mother Spring. Harter, Hugh A., tr. from FRE. LC 83-50206. 118p. 1990. 18.00 (0-89410-401-2, Three Contnts); pap. 12.00 (0-89410-402-0, Three Contnts) L Rienner.
— Muhammad. Benabid, Nadia, tr. LC 98-5353. (Three Continents Ser.). 90p. 1998. lib. bdg. 22.00 (0-89410-858-1) L Rienner.
— Passe Simple. (FRE.). 273p. 1986. pap. 11.95 (0-7859-2031-5, 2070377288) Fr & Eur.
— Passe Simple. (Folio Ser.: No. 1728). (FRE.). 272p. 1987. pap. 10.95 (2-07-037728-8) Schoenhof.
— Succession Ouverte. (FRE.). 192p. 1979. pap. 10.95 (0-7859-1900-7, 2070371360) Fr & Eur.
Chramosta, W. M., et al, eds. The New Schoolhouse. (Illus.). 260p. 1997. 58.00 (3-211-82814-1, Pub. by Birkhauser) Princeton Arch.
***Chramosta, Walter M.** Keith Sonnier: Public Commissions, 1990-1999. 2000. pap. 12.95 (3-7757-0893-6) Gerd Hatje.
Chrastina, Paul, ed. & illus. see Jackson, George L.
Chrebet, Wayne & Carucci, Vic. Every Down, Every Distance: My Journey to the NFL. LC 99-30499. 288p. 1999. 23.95 (0-385-49630-3) Doubleday.
Chrenkova, E., et al. Hungarian-Slovak Concise Dictionary. 928p. 1992. 45.00 (963-05-6265-0, Pub. by Akade Kiado) St Mut.
Chrenkova, E., jt. auth. see Stelczer, A.
Chrest, Anthony P., et al. Parking Structures: Planning, Design, Construction, Maintenance, & Repair. (Illus.). 432p. 1989. mass mkt. 65.00 (0-442-20655-0) Chapman & Hall.
Chrestensen, James, tr. see Chodkiewicz, Michel.
Chrestionson, George. Automotive Hand Tools Explained. LC 79-730979. 1980. student ed. 7.00 (0-8064-0125-7, 430) Bergwall.

— The Limited Slip Differential Pinion Operation & Service. LC 79-731072. 1978. student ed. 7.00 (*0-8064-0121-4*, 428) Bergwall.

— Starting System Explained. LC 80-730402. (Orig.). 1979. student ed. 7.00 (*0-8064-0135-4*, 435) Bergwall.

Chreston, Pangiotes. Byzantine Fathers & Theologians. 1998. 12.00 (*1-891295-11-X*) Oakwood Pubns.

Chrestou, Panagiotes. Partakers of God. (Patriarch Athenagoras Memorial Lectures). 66p. 1984. pap. 4.95 (*0-916586-67-7*, Pub. by Holy Cross Orthodox) BookWorld.

Chretien. Lancelot: The Knight of the Cart. Raffel, Burton, tr. from FRO. LC 97-14424. 208p. 1997. 35.00 (*0-300-07120-5*) Yale U Pr.

— Perceval: or The Story of the Holy Grail. 260p. 1983. 74.00 (*0-08-026296-1*, Pergamon Pr) Elsevier.

Chretien, et al. The Pleura in Health & Disease. (Lung Biology in Health & Disease Ser.: Vol. 30). (Illus.). 906p. 1985. text 295.00 (*0-8247-7380-2*) Dekker.

Chretien, C. Douglas. Cultural Element Distribution No. XXV: Reliability of Statistical Procedures & Results. fac. ed. Kroeber, A. L. et al, eds. (University of California Publications: No. 8:5). 26p. (C). 1945. reprint ed. pap. 3.13 (*1-55567-095-4*) Coyote Press.

Chretien de Troyes. Le Chevalier au Lion. 240p. 1970. 7.95 (*0-686-54376-9*) Fr & Eur.

— Lancelot: or The Knight of the Cart. Cline, Ruth H., tr. from FRE. LC 89-20283. 272p. 1990. pap. 15.00 (*0-8203-1213-4*) U of Ga Pr.

— Perceval le Gallois ou le Conte du Graal: Avec: Mis en Francais Moderne Par Lucien Foulet. 226p. 1970. 13.50 (*0-7859-0690-8*, S31794) Fr & Eur.

Chretien de Troyes. Perceval: or The Story of the Grail. Cline, Ruth H., tr. from FRE. LC 85-8600. 280p. 1985. pap. text 15.00 (*0-8203-0812-9*) U of Ga Pr.

Chretien de Troyes. Perceval: ou le Roman du Graal: Traducion de l'Ancien Francais. (Folio Ser.: No. 537). (FRE.). 384p. 1974. pap. 8.95 (*2-07-036537-9*) Schoenhof.

— Perceval: ou le Roman du Graal Suivi de Continuations (Choix) (FRE.). 384p. 1974. pap. 10.95 (*0-7859-1775-6*, 2070365379) Fr & Eur.

— Romans de la Table Ronde . . . (FRE.). 1975. pap. 11.95 (*0-7859-1809-4*, 2070366960) Fr & Eur.

— Yvain: or The Knight with the Lion. Cline, Ruth H., tr. from FRE. LC 73-85026. 222p. 1984. pap. text 15.00 (*0-8203-0758-0*) U of Ga Pr.

Chretien de Troyes & De Boer, C. Philomena: Conte Raconte d'Apres Ovide. (FRE.). 315p. 1974. 95.00 (*0-685-73321-1*) Fr & Eur.

Chretien de Troyes & Frppier, Jean. Le Chevalier de la Charette (Lancelot) Roman Traduit en Francais Moderne. 193p. 1971. 17.95 (*0-8288-9101-X*) Fr & Eur.

Chretien de Troyes & Micha, Alexandre. Cliges. 187p. 1969. 9.95 (*0-8288-9098-6*, F26532) Fr & Eur.

— Romans: Cliges, Vol. 2. (FRE.). 256p. 1982. pap. 24.95 (*0-7859-5366-3*) Fr & Eur.

Chretien de Troyes & Potvin, Charles. Perceval le Gallois: ou Le Conte du Graal, 1866-1871, 3 vols. (FRE.). 1970. pap. 250.00 (*0-8288-9102-8*) Fr & Eur.

Chretien de Troyes & Roques, Marlo. Romans: Avec: Erec et Enide, Vol. 1. (FRE.). 288p. 1973. pap. 15.00 (*0-7859-5365-5*) Fr & Eur.

— Romans: Le Chevalier au Lion, Vol. 4. (FRE.). 266p. 1982. pap. 24.95 (*0-7859-5368-X*) Fr & Eur.

— Romans: Le Chevalier de la Charrette, Vol. 3. (FRE.). 244p. 1982. pap. 24.95 (*0-7859-5367-1*) Fr & Eur.

Chretien de Troyes & Trottin, Jean. Guillaume d'Angleterre: Traduit en Francais Moderne. (FRE.). 147p. 1978. pap. 18.95 (*0-7859-5363-9*) Fr & Eur.

Chretien de Troyes, et al. Le Chevalier au Lion (Yvain) (FRE.). 266p. 1991. pap. 24.95 (*0-7859-4638-1*) Fr & Eur.

Chretien, Heidi L. The Festival of San Giovanni: Imagery & Political Power in Renaissance Florence. LC 93-6961. (American University Studies, IX, History: Vol. 138). (Illus.). X, 172p. (C). 1994. text 47.95 (*0-8204-2143-X*) P Lang Pubng.

Chretien, Jacques & Dusser, Daniel, eds. Environmental Impact on the Airways: From Injury to Repair, No. 93. LC 96-13129. (Lung Biology in Health & Disease Ser.: Vol. 93). (Illus.). 600p. 1996. text 190.00 (*0-8247-9485-0*) Dekker.

Chretien, M. & Deser, S., eds. Brandeis University Summer Institute in Theoretical Physics: 1965 Lectures, 2 vols. Incl. Vol. 2. Particle Symmetries. xii, 692p. 1966. pap. text 779.00 (*0-677-10755-2*); 1966. write for info. (*0-318-52694-8*) Gordon & Breach.

Chretien, M. & McKerns, Kenneth W., eds. Molecular Biology of Brain & Endocrine Peptidergic Systems. (Biochemical Endocrinology Ser.). (Illus.). 388p. 1988. 110.00 (*0-306-42980-2*, Plenum Trade) Perseus Pubng.

Chretienne, Philippe, et al, eds. Scheduling Theory & Its Applications. 382p. 1995. 155.00 (*0-471-94059-3*) Wiley.

Chrichley, Janine, jt. auth. see Langham, Josephine.

Chrichton, J. D. Christian Celebration: A Three-in-One Textbook. 604p. (Orig.). (C). 1984. 14.95 (*0-225-66399-6*) Harper SF.

Chrimes, Mike. The Civil Engineering of Canals & Railways Before 1850: Studies in the History of Civil Engineering. LC 98-3723. (Studies in the History of Civil Engineering: Vol. 7). (Illus.). 371p. 1998. text 153.95 (*0-86078-756-7*, Pub. by Ashgate Pub) Ashgate Pub Co.

Chrimes, Stanley B. Henry VII. LC 99-61177. (Illus.). 400p. 1999. pap. text 18.00 (*0-300-07883-8*) Yale U Pr.

Chrimes, Stanley B., et al, eds. Fifteenth Century England, 1399-1509. 208p. 1998. pap. 17.95 (*0-7509-1540-4*, Pub. by Sutton Pub Ltd) Intl Pubs Mktg.

— Fifteenth Century England, 1399-1509: Studies in Politics & Society. (Fifteenth Century Ser.). 208p. 54.00 (*0-7509-1198-0*, Pub. by Sutton Pub Ltd) Intl Pubs Mktg.

Chrimes, Stanley B. & Fortescue, John. De Laudibus Legum Anglia. LC 85-81802. (Cambridge Studies in English Legal History). 349p. 1986. reprint ed. 85.00 (*0-912004-41-X*) Gaunt.

Chrimes, Stanley B., ed. see Broughton, Rhoda.

Chris, Cynthia & Pearl, Monica, eds. La Mujer, el SIDA y el Activismo: The Spanish Language Edition of Women, AIDS, & Activism - The ACT UP-NY Women & AIDS Book Group. 340p. 1992. 25.00 (*0-89608-455-8*); pap. 10.00 (*0-89608-454-X*) South End Pr.

Chris, Jerry. Shakespeare, Me Thinks: A Collection of Modern Plays for Oral Reading & Comprehension: Trust - Othello. 32p. (Orig.). (YA). (gr. 9-12). 1993. pap. text 5.00 (*0-88092-061-0*) Royal Fireworks.

— Shakespeare, Me Thinks - A Collection of Modern Plays for Oral Reading & Comprehension: Quicksand - Macbeth. 32p. (YA). (gr. 9-12). 1993. pap. text 5.00 (*0-88092-062-9*) Royal Fireworks.

— Shakespeare, Me Thinks - A Collection of Modern Plays for Oral Reading & Comprehension: The Choice - Romeo & Juliet. 32p. (Orig.). (YA). (gr. 9-12). 1993. pap. text 5.00 (*0-88092-059-9*) Royal Fireworks.

— Shakespeare, Me Thinks - A Collection of Modern Plays for Oral Reading & Comprehension: The Price of Silence - Julius Caesar. 32p. (Orig.). (YA). (gr. 9-12). 1993. pap. text 5.00 (*0-88092-060-2*) Royal Fireworks.

— Shakespeare, Me Thinks - A Collection of Modern Plays for Oral Reading & Comprehension: Top Priority - Hamlet. 32p. (YA). (gr. 9-12). 1993. pap. text 5.00 (*0-88092-063-7*) Royal Fireworks.

— Shakespeare, Me Thinks - A Collection of Modern Plays for Oral Reading & Comprehension, Teacher's Guide. 32p. 1993. pap., teacher ed. 5.00 (*0-88092-058-0*) Royal Fireworks.

— 60 Ways to Assure Success for Your Gifted Children. (Orig.). 1994. pap. 14.99 (*0-88092-197-8*) Royal Fireworks.

***Chris, Jerry.** 30 Ways to Bring Philosphy into Every Classroom. 153p. (YA). (gr. 7-12). 1998. pap. 15.00 (*0-88092-450-0*, 4500, Kav Bks) Royal Fireworks.

Chris Mystery Publishing Staff, ed. see Orszula, Edward.

Chris, Patrick, jt. auth. see Baister, Stephen.

Chris, Teresa, jt. auth. see Lawrence, Richard R.

***Chrisawn, Margaret Scott.** The Emperor's Friend: Marshal Jean Lannes, 191. LC 00-25679. (Contributions in Military Studies: Vol. 191). 270p. 2000. 55.00 (*0-313-31062-9*, GM1062, Greenwood Pr) Greenwood.

Chrisci, John. Mysticism: The Search for Ultimate Meaning. 78p. (C). 1986. text 32.00 (*0-8191-5609-4*); pap. text 14.50 (*0-8191-5610-8*) U Pr of Amer.

Chrisco, Carrie. Reactions to the Persian Gulf War: Editorials in the Conflict Zone. 140p. (C). 1995. lib. bdg. 29.00 (*0-7618-0082-4*) U Pr of Amer.

***Chrisey, D. B., et al, eds.** Materials Development for Direct Write Technologies: Materials Research Society Symposium Proceedings, Vol. 624. 2000. text 77.00 (*1-55899-532-3*) Materials Res.

Chrisey, Douglas B., jt. ed. see Hubler, Graham K.

Chrisfield, Debbie. Radio. LC 93-26393. (Now Hiring Ser.). (J). 1994. pap. 5.95 (*0-382-24749-3*, Crstwood Hse) Silver Burdett Pr.

***Chrisler.** Lectures on Psychology Women. 2nd ed. LC 99-29468. 1999. 25.25 (*0-07-234860-7*, McGrw-H College) McGrw-H Hghr Educ.

Chrisler. Women's Health. 2000. 53.00 (*0-07-012000-5*) McGraw.

Chrisler, Joan C., et al, eds. Lectures on the Psychology of Women. LC 95-40755. 384p. (C). 1995. pap. 34.38 (*0-07-011111-1*) McGraw.

Chrisler, Joan C. & Hemstreet, Alyce H., eds. Variations on a Theme: Diversity & the Psychology of Women. LC 94-26207. (SUNY Series, the Psychology of Women). 238p. (C). 1995. text 59.50 (*0-7914-2435-9*); pap. text 19.95 (*0-7914-2436-7*) State U NY Pr.

Chrisler, Joan C. & Howard, Doris, eds. New Directions in Feminist Psychology: Practice, Theory & Research. LC 91-5168. (Focus on Women Ser.: Vol. 13). 272p. 1992. 34.95 (*0-8261-7540-6*) Springer Pub.

Chrislip, David D. & Larson, Carl E. Collaborative Leadership: How Citizens & Civic Leaders Can Make a Difference. LC 94-10751. (Public Administration-Nonprofit Ser.). 218p. 1994. text 26.95 (*0-7879-0003-6*) Jossey-Bass.

Chrislock, C. Winston. Charles Jonas 1840-1896: Czech National Liberal, Wisconsin Bourbon Democrat. LC 91-58967. 216p. 1993. 37.50 (*0-944190-11-1*) Balch IES Pr.

Chrislock, Carl. Ethnicity Challenged: The Upper Midwest Norwegian-American Experience. Lovoll, Odd Sverre, ed. (Topical Studies: Vol. 3). (Illus.). 174p. 1981. 15.00 (*0-87732-066-7*) Norwegian-Am Hist Assn.

Chrislock, Carl H. The Progressive Era in Minnesota, 1899-1918. LC 79-178677. (Public Affairs Center Publications). (Illus.). xiii, 242p. 1971. 8.95 (*0-87351-067-4*) Minn Hist.

— Watchdog of Loyalty: The Minnesota Commission of Public Safety During World War I. LC 91-11228. (Illus.). xvi, 387p. 1991. 39.95 (*0-87351-263-4*); pap. 19.95 (*0-87351-264-2*) Minn Hist.

Chrisman, Andy, et al. The Basics of Life: Walking on the Side of Faith. LC 98-12445. (Artists Devotional Ser.). 256p. 1998. 14.99 (*1-878990-85-3*) Howard Pub LA.

Chrisman, Arthur B. Shen of the Sea. (Illus.). (J). (gr. 4-7). 1968. 16.99 (*0-525-39244-0*, Dutton Child) Peng Put Young Read.

Chrisman, Catherine. My War. 200p. (Orig.). 1989. pap. 12.00 (*1-882021-22-3*) Summer.

Chrisman, Cheryl L. Problems in Small Animal Neurology. 2nd ed. LC 90-5881. (Illus.). 526p. 1991. text 70.00 (*0-8121-1349-7*) Lppncott W & W.

Chrisman, David. Tao Chi: The Ascension of the Immortal Dragons Fantasy Martial Arts Roleplaying Game. LC 99-176456. 371p. 1998. 24.95 (*0-9660900-0-4*) Rade Corp.

Chrisman, Harry E. Lost Trails of the Cimarron. 2nd ed. LC 98-21220. (Illus.). 320p. 1998. pap. 16.95 (*0-8061-3017-2*) U of Okla Pr.

— The One Thousand & One Most Asked Questions about the American West. LC 82-6337. (Illus.). xiv, 349p. 1982. pap. 19.95 (*0-8040-0383-1*) Swallow.

Chrisman, Harry E., ed. see Hancock, Charles.

Chrisman, James J., ed. see Sharma, Pramodita & Chua, Jess H.

***Chrisman, Laura.** Rereading the Imperial Romance: British Imperialism & South African Resistance in Haggard, Schreiner, & Plaatje. (Oxford English Monographs). 2000. text 65.00 (*0-19-812299-3*) OUP.

***Chrisman, Laura & Parry, Benita, eds.** Postcolonial Theory & Criticism. (Essays & Studies). 192p. 1999. 55.00 (*0-85991-554-9*, DS Brewer) Boydell & Brewer.

Chrisman, Laura, jt. ed. see Williams, Patrick.

Chrisman, Lewis H. John Ruskin, Preacher, & Other Essays. LC 67-22086. (Essay Index Reprint Ser.). 1977. 20.95 (*0-8369-1328-0*) Ayer.

Chrisman, Miriam U. Conflicting Visions of Reform: German Lay Propaganda Pamphlets, 1519-1530. LC 95-8888. (Studies in Central European Histories). 304p. 1996. 60.00 (*0-391-03944-X*) Humanities.

Chrisman, Nicholas. Exploring Geographic Infomation Systems. LC 96-46941. 320p. 1996. pap. 61.95 (*0-471-10842-1*) Wiley.

Chrisman, Noel & Maretski, Thomas. Clinically Applied Anthropology. 1982. lib. bdg. 187.00 (*90-277-1418-5*) Kluwer Academic.

Chrisman, Randolph L. TSCA Compliance Handbook. (Environmental Compliance Handbook Ser.: Vol. 4). 1989. pap. 32.50 (*1-55840-108-3*) Exec Ent Pubns.

Chrisman, Robert. Minor Casualties. 60p. 1993. pap. 10.00 (*0-916418-82-0*) Lotus.

Chrisman, Robert, ed. & pref. see Crockett-Smith, D. L.

Chrisman, Robert, ed. & pref. see McClendon, William H.

Chrisomalis, Marion. Day's End for Gunmen. large type ed. (Linford Western Library). 240p. 1993. pap. 16.99 (*0-7089-7373-6*) Ulverscroft.

Chrisomalli-Henrich, K. & Henrich, G. S. Langenscheidts Euroworterbucher: Griechisch. 1997. pap. write for info. (*3-468-12210-1*) Langenscheidt.

Chrisoph, Peter R., intro. Calendar of N. Y. Colonial Manuscripts: Indorsed Land Papers, 1643-1803. LC 87-14830. 1090p. 1987. reprint ed. 59.50 (*0-916346-59-5*, 1363) Picton Pr.

Chrisp. Great Journeys. (Remarkable World Ser.). 48p. (J). (gr. 4-5). 1996. 24.26 (*0-8172-4537-5*) Raintree Steck-V.

Chrisp, Peter. Ancient Greece. LC 97-49404. (My World Ser.). (Illus.). 32p. (J). (gr. 2-7). 1998. write for info. (*0-7166-9406-9*) World Bk.

***Chrisp, Peter.** Ancient Greece. rev. ed. (My Word Ser.). (Illus.). (J). 2000. 9.95 (*1-58728-060-4*); pap. 5.95 (*1-58728-066-3*) Two Can Pub.

Chrisp, Peter. Ancient Rome. LC 97-1364. (My World Ser.). (Illus.). 32p. (J). (gr. 2-7). 1998. write for info. (*0-7166-9400-X*) World Bk.

— The Aztecs. LC 99-27438. (History Beneath Your Feet Ser.). 48p. 1999. lib. bdg. 25.89 (*0-8172-5753-5*) Raintree Steck-V.

— Celebraciones y Festivales. Sanz, Maria T., tr. (Biblioteca de Descubrimientos Ser.). (SPA., Illus.). 32p. (J). (gr. k-4). 1998. 11.95 (*1-58087-012-0*) C D Stampley Ent.

— Celebrations & Festivals. (Launch Pad Library). (Illus.). 32p. (J). (gr. k-4). 1998. 11.95 (*1-58087-005-8*) C D Stampley Ent.

— Factfinders: Invaders. (Fact Finders Ser.). (Illus.). (J). pap. 8.95 (*0-563-37626-0*, BBC-Parkwest) Parkwest Pubns.

— Great Journeys. (Remarkable World Ser.). (Illus.). 48p. (J). (gr. 4 up). 1996. lib. bdg. 24.26 (*1-56847-417-2*) Raintree Steck-V.

— The Incas. LC 94-4553. (Look into the Past Ser.). (Illus.). 32p. (J). 1994. lib. bdg. 22.83 (*1-56847-171-8*) Raintree Steck-V.

***Chrisp, Peter.** Look into the Past Maya. 1999. 21.35 (*0-7398-1410-9*) Raintree Steck-V.

Chrisp, Peter. Mapping the Unknown. LC 96-8344. (Remarkable World Ser.). (Illus.). 48p. (J). (gr. 3-8). 1996. lib. bdg. 24.26 (*0-8172-4535-9*) Raintree Steck-V.

— The Maya. LC 93-46604. (Look into the Past Ser.). (Illus.). 32p. (J). (gr. 4-6). 1994. 22.83 (*1-56847-170-X*) Raintree Steck-V.

— The Middle Ages. LC 97-1833. (My World Ser.). (Illus.). 32p. (J). (gr. 2-7). 1997. write for info. (*0-7166-9408-5*) World Bk.

***Chrisp, Peter.** The Middle Ages. rev. ed. (My Word Ser.). (Illus.). (J). 2000. 9.95 (*1-58728-063-9*); pap. 5.95 (*1-58728-069-8*) Two Can Pub.

Chrisp, Peter. The Normans. (Look into the Past Ser.). (Illus.). 32p. (J). (gr. 4-6). 1995. lib. bdg. 22.83 (*1-56847-174-2*) Raintree Steck-V.

— The Romans. LC 93-29441. (Journey into Civilization Ser.). (Illus.). 32p. (J). (gr. 4-7). 1994. pap. 7.95 (*0-7910-2731-7*) Chelsea Hse.

— Romans. (Journey into Civilization Ser.). (J). 1994. 13.15 (*0-606-08081-3*) Turtleback.

— Romans. LC 98-22897. (Interfact Ser.). (Illus.). 48p. (J). (gr. 2-8). 1999. spiral bd. write for info. incl. cd-rom (*0-7166-7215-4*) World Bk.

***Chrisp, Peter.** A Shakespearean Theater. LC 99-87636. (Look Inside Ser.). (Illus.). (J). 2000. 25.69 (*0-7398-2381-7*) Raintree Steck-V.

— The Soldier Through History. (Illus.). 48p. (J). (gr. 4-7). 2000. reprint ed. 16.00 (*0-7881-9447-X*) DIANE Pub.

Chrisp, Peter. Vikings. (Fact Finder Bk.). 1995. pap. 8.95 (*0-563-35259-0*, BBC-Parkwest) Parkwest Pubns.

— Vikings. LC 97-47638. (My World Ser.). (Illus.). 32p. (J). (gr. 2-7). 1998. write for info. (*0-7166-9412-3*) World Bk.

***Chrisp, Peter.** Welcome to the Globe! The Story of Shakespeare's Theater. LC 00-21931. (Dorling Kindersley Readers). (Illus.). 48p. (J). (gr. 2-4). 2000. 3.95 (*0-7894-6640-6*) DK Pub Inc.

— Welcome to the Globe! The Story of Shakespeare's Theater. LC 00-21931. (Eyewitness Readers). 48p. (gr. 2-4). 2000. 12.95 (*0-7894-6641-4*, D K Ink) DK Pub Inc.

Chrisp, Peter. The Whalers. (Remarkable World Ser.). (Illus.). 48p. (YA). (gr. 3-8). 1995. lib. bdg. 24.26 (*1-56847-421-0*) Raintree Steck-V.

— The World of the Roman Emperor. LC 99-25317. (World of...Ser.). (Illus.). 64p. (J). (gr. 5-9). 1999. 19.95 (*0-87226-296-0*, 62960B, P Bedrick Books) NTC Contemp Pub Co.

***Chrisp, Peter & Hook, Adam.** A Greek Theater. LC 99-51704. (Look Inside Ser.). (Illus.). (J). 2000. 25.69 (*0-7398-2379-5*) Raintree Steck-V.

***Chrisp, Peter & Hook, Adam.** A Roman Villa. LC 99-51705. (Look Inside Ser.). (J). 2000. 25.69 (*0-7398-2380-9*) Raintree Steck-V.

Chrisp, Peter, et al. The Romans. LC 93-29441. (Journey into Civilization Ser.). (Illus.). 32p. (J). (gr. 4-7). 1994. lib. bdg. 15.95 (*0-7910-2707-4*) Chelsea Hse.

Chrisp, Peter, jt. auth. see Burns, Peggy.

Chrispeels, Janet H. Purposeful Restructuring: Creating a Culture for Learning & Achievement in Elementary Schools. 224p. 1992. 85.00 (*0-7507-0022-X*, Falmer Pr) Taylor & Francis.

Chrispeels, Maarten J. & Sadava, David E. Plants, Genes, & Agriculture. LC 93-45677. (Life Science Ser.). 512p. (C). 1994. 61.25 (*0-86720-871-6*) Jones & Bartlett.

Chrispeels, Maarten J., jt. ed. see Shannon, Leland M.

Chriss, James J. Alvin W. Gouldner: Sociologist & Outlaw Marxist. LC 99-71888. 230p. 1999. text 65.95 (*1-84014-911-6*, Pub. by Ashgate Pub) Ashgate Pub Co.

Chriss, James J., ed. Counseling & the Therapeutic State. LC 99-19052. (Social Problems & Social Issues Ser.). 7p. 1999. pap. text 24.95 (*0-202-30624-0*); lib. bdg. 49.95 (*0-202-30623-2*) Aldine de Gruyter.

Chriss, Jim. Guardian Angel. LC 98-83089. 288p. 2000. 23.50 (*0-88739-236-9*) Creat Arts Bk.

Chriss, Michael & Brooks, Judith K. Astronomy One Hundred: A Handbook. LC 79-92143. (Illus.). 250p. (Orig.). 1980. pap. text 11.20 (*0-936064-00-5*) Perspicilli Pr.

Chriss, Michael & Hayes, G. R. An Introduction to Charts & Their Use. (C). 1987. pap. 50.00 (*0-85174-275-0*) St Mut.

Chriss, Neil A. Black-Scholes & Beyond: Option Pricing Models. LC 96-17361. 480p. 1996. 65.00 (*0-7863-1025-1*, Irwn Prfssnl) McGraw-Hill Prof.

— The Black-Scholes & Beyond Interactive Toolkit: A Step-By-Step Guide to In-Depth Option Pricing Models. LC 96-40002. 288p. 1997. pap. 65.00 (*0-7863-1026-X*, Irwn Prfssnl) McGraw-Hill Prof.

Chriss, Neil A. & Ginzburg, Victor. Representation Theory & Complex Geometry. LC 94-27574. 495p. 1997. 64.50 (*0-8176-3792-3*) Birkhauser.

Christ. Media Education Assessment Handbook & Assessing Communication. 1996. 42.00 (*0-8058-2714-5*) L Erlbaum Assocs.

Christ, B. & Cihak, R., eds. Development & Regeneration of Skeletal Muscles. (Bibliotheca Anatomica Ser.: No. 29). (Illus.). viii, 224p. 1986. 155.75 (*3-8055-4227-5*) S Karger.

Christ, Carl F. Econometrics, Macroeconomics & Economic Policy: Selected Papers of Carl F. Christ. LC 95-39640. (Economists of the Twentieth Century Ser.). (Illus.). 544p. 1996. 120.00 (*1-85898-135-2*) E Elgar.

Christ, Carl F., ed. Simultaneous Equations Estimation. 560p. 1994. 230.00 (*1-85278-661-2*) E Elgar.

Christ, Carol P. Diving Deep & Surfacing: Women Writers on Spiritual Quest. 3rd ed. 208p. (C). 1995. pap. 12.95 (*0-8070-6207-3*) Beacon Pr.

— Rebirth of the Goddess: Finding Meaning in Feminist Spirituality. LC 98-37858. (Illus.). 224p. 1998. pap. 17.99 (*0-415-92186-4*, D5980) Routledge.

Christ, Carol P. & Plaskow, Judith. Womanspirit Rising: A Feminist Reader in Religion. LC 91-58254. 320p. (Orig.). 1992. reprint ed. pap. 15.00 (*0-06-061377-7*, Pub. by Harper SF) HarpC.

Christ, Carol P., jt. ed. see Plaskow, Judith.

Christ, Carol T. Victorian & Modern Poetics. LC 83-18200. x, 178p. 1984. lib. bdg. 16.00 (*0-226-10458-3*) U Ch Pr.

— Victorian & Modern Poetics. LC 83-18200. x, 188p. 1986. pap. text 10.95 (*0-226-10459-1*) U Ch Pr.

Christ, Carol T. & Jordan, John O., eds. Victorian Literature & the Victorian Visual Imagination. LC 94-40328. 400p. 1995. pap. 24.95 (*0-520-20022-5*, Pub. by U CA Pr) Cal Prin Full Svc.

Christ, Carol T., ed. see Eliot, George, pseud.

Christ, Charles L., jt. auth. see Garrels, Robert M.

***Christ Church Cathedral Staff, ed.** Magnificooks: Recipes of Celebrations from the Choir, Congregation & Clergy. 121p. 2000. pap. 12.00 (*0-615-11221-8*) Ch Church Cath.

***Christ, Claus, ed.** Production-Integrated Environmental Protection & Waste Management in the Chemical Industry. 212p. 1999. 135.00 (*3-527-28854-6*) Wiley.

Christ, Dean, jt. auth. see Sumichrast, Michael J.

Christ, Debbie. Wildlife of the North. (Illus.). 36p. (Orig.). 1995. pap. 14.95 (*0-935133-55-0*) CKE Pubns.

Christ, Ed, jt. auth. see Krause, John.

Christ, Elwood. Struggle for the Bliss Farm of Gettysburg: "Over a Wide Hot . . . Crimson Plain" 2nd ed. (Illus.). 220p. (C). 1994. 25.00 (*0-935523-31-6*) Butternut & Blue.

Christ for the Nations Staff, ed. see Lindsay, Gordon.

***Christ, Frank, et al, eds.** Starting a Learning Assistance Center: Conversations with CRLA Members Who Have Been There & Done That. LC 99-97216. 125p. 2000. 21.95 (*0-943202-72-8*) H & H Pub.

Christ, Grace H. & Zabora, James R., eds. Cancer & the Family. 361p. 1998. 49.95 (*0-7890-6011-6*, Hawrth Medical) Haworth Pr.

Christ, Grace Hyslop. Healing Children's Grief: Surviving a Parent's Death from Cancer. LC 99-15342. (Illus.). 288p. (C). 2000. pap. 24.95 (*0-19-510591-5*); text 45.00 (*0-19-510590-7*) OUP.

Christ, J. F., jt. ed. see Hassler, R. G.

Christ, J. F., jt. ed. see Hassler, R.

Christ-Janer, Albert. American Hymns Old & New. 1980. text 87.50 (*0-231-03458-X*) Col U Pr.

— Eliel Saarinen: Finnish-American Architect & Educator. rev. ed. LC 79-832. (Illus.). 190p. 1985. pap. 17.95 (*0-226-10465-6*) U Ch Pr.

Christ, Jean-Frederic. Dictionnaire des Monogrammes, Chiffres, Lettres Initiales, Logoriphes, Rebus, etc. Sous Leguels le Plus Celebres Peintres, Graveurs et Dessinateurs ont Dessine Leurs Noms. (FRE.). 484p. 1972. 275.00 (*0-7859-8648-0*, 282660161X) Fr & Eur.

***Christ, Jesus H., pseud.** Whips & Furs. Home, Stewart, ed. & intro. by. 160p. 2000. pap. 10.95 (*1-84068-035-0*, Pub. by Creation Books) Last Gasp.

Christ, Karl. The Romans: An Introduction to Their History & Civilization. Holme, Christopher, tr. from GER. LC 83-40483. (Illus.). 275p. (C). 1984. pap. 17.95 (*0-520-05634-5*, Pub. by U CA Pr) Cal Prin Full Svc.

Christ, Linda. Social Security Disability Training Manual. 511p. 1986. 35.00 (*0-685-23190-9*, 41,875) NCLS Inc.

Christ, Linda M. Words of Comfort, Peace, & Hope for Hurting Hearts. 125p. (Orig.). 1989. pap. write for info. (*0-318-65906-9*) Lindys Lifelines.

Christ, M. Lectures on Singular Integral Operators. LC 90-20270. (CBMS Regional Conference Series in Mathematics: No. 77). 132p. 1990. pap. 28.00 (*0-8218-0728-5*, CBMS/77) Am Math.

Christ, Mark, ed. Outside the Pale: The Architecture of Fay Jones. LC 98-46529. (Illus.). 112p. 1999. pap. 18.00 (*1-55728-543-8*) U of Ark Pr.

Christ, Mark K., ed. Rugged & Sublime: The Civil War in Arkansas. LC 94-15017. (Illus.). 192p. 1994. pap. 18.00 (*1-55728-357-5*); text 25.00 (*1-55728-356-7*) U of Ark Pr.

***Christ, Mark K. & Slater, Cathy Buford.** Sentinels of History. LC 99-54979. (Illus.). 360p. 2000. pap. 25.00 (*1-55728-605-1*) U of Ark Pr.

Christ, Matthew R. The Litigious Athenian. LC 97-52752. (Ancient Society & History Ser.). 264p. 1998. 39.95 (*0-8018-5863-1*) Johns Hopkins.

***Christ, Ronald.** Woody Vasulka, the Brotherhood A Series of Six Interactive Media Constructions. 1999. pap. 30.00 (*4-7571-7000-9*) Lumen Inc.

Christ, Ronald, tr. see Eltit, Diamela.

Christ, Ronald, tr. see Jujol, Josep M.

Christ, Ronald J. Narrow Act: Borges' Art of Allusion. 240p. 1994. pap. 15.00 (*0-930829-34-4*) Lumen Inc.

— Narrow Act: Borges' Art of Allusion. LC 69-16345. (Studies in Comparative Literature, Vol. 2). 264p. reprint ed. 81.90 (*0-8357-9479-2*, 201028800068) Bks Demand.

Christ, Ronald J., jt. ed. see Dollens, Dennis.

Christ, Ronald J., tr. see Cozarinsky, Edgardo.

Christ, Ronald J., tr. see Puig, Manuel.

Christ, Ronald J., tr. see Vargas Llosa, Mario.

Christ, Steve. How to Rebuild Your Big-Block Ford. LC 82-84702. (Illus.). 160p. 1989. pap. 17.95 (*0-89586-070-8*, Price Stern) Peng Put Young Read.

Christ, Steve, jt. auth. see Neaderland, Louise O.

Christ, Wilhelm Von, see Von Christ, Wilhelm.

Christ, William B., et al. Materials & Structures of Music, Vol. 1. 3rd ed. 1980. text. write for info. (*0-318-54922-0*) P-H.

Christ, William G. Leadership in Times of Change: A Handbook for Communication & Media Administrators. LC 98-35455. 1998. pap. 39.95 (*0-8058-2911-3*) L Erlbaum Assocs.

Christ, William G., ed. Assessing Communication Education: A Handbook for Media, Speech, & Theatre Educators. (Communication Ser.). 400p. 1994. pap. 36.00 (*0-8058-1623-2*); text 89.95 (*0-8058-1622-4*) L Erlbaum Assocs.

— Assessing Media Education. LC 96-32296. (Communication Ser.). 350p. (C). 1996. text 29.95 (*0-8058-2185-6*) L Erlbaum Assocs.

— Leadership in Times of Change: A Handbook for Communication & Media Administrators. LC 98-35455. (Communication Ser.). 328p. 1998. write for info. (*0-8058-2698-X*) L Erlbaum Assocs.

Christ, William G., jt. auth. see Blanchard, Robert.

Christ, Yvan. Eglises Parisiennes: Actuelles et Disparues. (FRE., Illus.). 1947. pap. 35.00 (*0-8288-3989-1*) Fr & Eur.

***Christain, Kathy.** The Australian Cattle Dog. Anderson, Mark, ed. (Illus.). 284p. 2000. 26.95 (*0-944875-65-3*, Pub. by Doral Pub) Natl Bk Netwk.

Christakis, George, ed. see Sylligardakis, Titus M.

Christakis, Nicholas. Death Foretold. 1997. pap. 17.50 (*0-226-10471-0*) U Ch Pr.

Christakis, Nicholas. Death Foretold: Prophecy & Prognosis in Medical Care. LC 99-16442. 307p. 2000. 30.00 (*0-226-10470-2*) U Ch Pr.

Christakos, George. Random Field Models in Earth Sciences. (Illus.). 512p. 1992. text 116.00 (*0-12-174230-X*) Acad Pr.

Christakos, George, ed. Nutritional Assessment in Health Programs. LC 74-120960. 90p. 1973. 7.50 (*0-87553-116-4*, 070) Am Pub Health.

Christakos, George & Hristopulos, Dionissios T. Spatiotemporal Environmental Health Modelling: A Tractatus Stochasticus. LC 98-24443. 400p. 1998. 130.00 (*0-7923-8211-0*) Kluwer Academic.

Christal, Melodie E., jt. ed. see Russell, Alene B.

Christaller, J. G. Three Thousand Six Hundred Ghanian Proverbs (from the Asante & Fante Language) Lange, Kofi R., tr. LC 89-28424. (Studies in African Literature: Vol. 2). 323p. 1990. lib. bdg. 99.95 (*0-88946-234-8*) E Mellen.

Christaller, Thomas, et al, eds. The AI Workbench: Babylon: An Open & Portable Development Environment for Expert Systems. (Knowledge Based Systems Ser.). (Illus.). 474p. 1992. pap. text 100.00 (*0-12-174235-0*) Acad Pr.

Christan, J. W., et al, eds. Progress in Materials Science, Vol. 28. (Illus.). 450p. 1985. 170.00 (*0-08-032741-9*, Pub. by PPL) Elsevier.

Christansen, Mike. Complete Electric Blues Guitar Book. (Complete Book). 128p. 1993. spiral bd. 14.95 (*1-56222-556-1*, 94846); audio 9.98 (*1-56222-555-3*, 94846C); audio compact disk 15.98 (*0-7866-0439-5*, 94846CD) Mel Bay.

— Complete Electric Blues Guitar Book. (Complete Book). 1993. vdisk 29.95 (*0-7866-2573-2*, 94846VX) Mel Bay.

— Complete Guitar Scale Dictionary. (Complete Book). 60p. 1992. pap. 9.95 (*1-56222-417-4*, 94756) Mel Bay.

Christansen, Peder G., et al. Sidonius Apollinaris - Concordantia in Sidonii Apollinaris Epistulas. (Alpha-Omega, Reihe A Ser.: Vol. CLXVI). (GER.). 800p. 1997. write for info. (*3-487-10567-5*) G Olms Pubs.

Christe, Nathalie G., ed. Contingent Valuation, Transport Safety & the Value of Life. (Studies in Risk & Uncertainty). 208p. (C). 1995. lib. bdg. 97.00 (*0-7923-9578-6*) Kluwer Academic.

Christe, P. & Henkel, M. Introduction to Conformal Invariance & Its Applications to Critical Phenomena. LC 93-18443. (Lecture Notes in Physics Ser.: Vol. M16). 1993. 59.95 (*0-387-56504-3*) Spr-Verlag.

Christel, Linda. Mad about You Because . . . LC 97-221668. 80p. 1997. 4.95 (*0-88088-817-2*) Peter Pauper.

Christel, Mary T., jt. auth. see Kruger, Ellen L.

Christelow, Allan. Muslim Law Courts & the French Colonial State in Algeria. LC 84-42878. 334p. reprint ed. pap. 103.60 (*0-608-06368-1*, 206672900008) Bks Demand.

Christelow, Allan, ed. Thus Ruled Emir Abbas: Selected Cases from the Records of the Emir of Kano's Judicial Council. (African Historical Sources Ser.: Vol. 5). 285p. (C). 1994. 28.00 (*0-87013-309-8*) Mich St U Pr.

Christelow, Dorothy B. When Giants Converge: The Role of U. S. - Japan Direct Investment. LC 94-28479. 274p. (C). (gr. 13). 1995. text 74.95 (*1-56324-114-5*); pap. text 38.95 (*1-56324-115-3*) M E Sharpe.

Christelow, Eileen. Don't Wake up Mama! Another Five Little Monkeys Story. (Illus.). 32p. (J). (ps-3). 1992. 15.00 (*0-395-60176-2*, Clarion Bks) HM.

— Don't Wake up Mama! Another Five Little Monkeys Story. (Illus.). 32p. (J). (gr. k-3). 1996. pap. 5.95 (*0-395-76479-3*, Clarion Bks) HM.

— Don't Wake up Mama! Another Five Little Monkeys Story. 1992. 11.15 (*0-606-08728-1*, Pub. by Turtleback) Demco.

— The Five-Dog Night. LC 92-36958. (Illus.). 40p. (J). (gr. k-3). 1993. 14.95 (*0-395-62399-5*, Clarion Bks) HM.

— The Five-Dog Night. (J). (gr. k-4). 1998. pap. 6.95 (*0-395-92862-1*, Clarion Bks) HM.

— Five Little Monkeys Jumping on the Bed. (Illus.). 32p. (J). (gr. k-3). 1989. pap. 5.95 (*0-395-55701-1*, Clarion Bks) HM.

— Five Little Monkeys Jumping on the Bed. (Carry-Along Book & Cassette Favorites Ser.). (Illus.). 1p. (J). (ps-3). 1991. pap. 9.95 incl. audio (*0-395-60115-0*, 111894, Clarion Bks) HM.

— Five Little Monkeys Jumping on the Bed. LC 88-22839. (Illus.). 28p. (J). (ps). 1998. bds. 5.95 (*0-395-90023-9*, Clarion Bks) HM.

Christelow, Eileen. Five Little Monkeys Jumping on the Bed. (Illus.). 32p. (J). (gr. k-3). 1989. 15.00 (*0-89919-769-8*, Pub. by Ticknor & Fields) HM.

— Five Little Monkeys Jumping on the Bed. (Illus.). (J). 2000. 11.40 (*0-606-18041-9*) Turtleback.

Christelow, Eileen. Five Little Monkeys Sitting in a Tree. Giblin, James C., ed. (Illus.). 32p. (J). (gr. k-3). 1991. 15.00 (*0-395-54434-3*, Clarion Bks) HM.

— Five Little Monkeys Sitting in a Tree. (Illus.). 32p. (J). (ps-3). 1993. pap. 5.95 (*0-395-66413-6*, Clarion Bks) HM.

***Christelow, Eileen.** Five Little Monkeys Sitting in a Tree. (Illus.). 28p. (J). (ps-k). 1999. bds. 5.95 (*0-395-98033-X*, Clarion Bks) HM.

Christelow, Eileen. Five Little Monkeys Sitting in a Tree. (J). 1991. 11.15 (*0-606-05292-5*, Pub. by Turtleback) Demco.

***Christelow, Eileen.** Five Little Monkeys Wash the Car. LC 99-38920. (Illus.). 32p. (J). (ps-1). 2000. 15.00 (*0-395-92566-5*, Clarion Bks) HM.

Christelow, Eileen. Five Little Monkeys with Nothing to Do. LC 95-25873. (Illus.). 32p. (J). (gr. k-3). 1996. 15.00 (*0-395-75830-0*, Clarion Bks) HM.

***Christelow, Eileen.** Five Little Monkeys with Nothing to Do. (Illus.). 32p. (J). 2000. pap. 5.95 (*0-618-04032-3*, Clarion Bks) HM.

— Five Little Monkeys with Nothing to Do. (Illus.). (J). 2000. 11.40 (*0-606-18042-7*) Turtleback.

Christelow, Eileen. Five Monkeys Sitting in a Tree. (Carry-Along Book & Cassette Favorites Ser.). (Illus.). (J). (ps-1). 1995. pap. 8.95 incl. audio (*0-395-72090-7*, 111770, Clarion Bks) Ticknor & Flds Bks Yng Read.

— The Great Pig Escape. LC 93-38788. (Illus.). 32p. (J). (gr. k-3). 1994. 14.95 (*0-395-66973-1*) HM.

— The Great Pig Escape. LC 93-38788. (Illus.). 32p. (J). (ps-3). 1996. pap. 5.95 (*0-395-79724-1*) HM.

Christelow, Eileen. The Great Pig Escape. LC 93-38788. (J). 1994. 11.15 (*0-606-10203-5*, Pub. by Turtleback) Demco.

Christelow, Eileen. Jerome Camps Out. LC 97-24024. (Illus.). 32p. (J). 1998. 16.00 (*0-395-75831-9*, Clarion Bks) HM.

— Not Until Christmas, Walter! LC 96-52217. (Illus.). 40p. (J). (gr. k-3). 1997. 15.00 (*0-395-82273-4*) HM.

— The Robbery at the Diamond Dog Diner. LC 86-2682. (Illus.). 32p. (J). (ps-3). 1988. pap. 6.95 (*0-89919-722-1*, Clarion Bks) HM.

— The Robbery at the Diamond Dog Diner. LC 86-2682. (Carry-Along Book & Cassette Favorites Ser.). (J). (ps-3). 1986. pap. 9.95 incl. audio (*0-89919-894-5*, 111301) Ticknor & Flds Bks Yng Read.

— The Robbery at the Diamond Dog Diner. (J). 1986. 12.15 (*0-606-02801-3*, Pub. by Turtleback) Demco.

— What Do Authors Do? LC 94-19725. (Illus.). 32p. (J). (gr. k-3). 1995. 15.00 (*0-395-71124-X*, Clarion Bks) HM.

— What Do Authors Do? LC 94-19725. (Illus.). 32p. (J). (gr. k-3). 1997. pap. 5.95 (*0-395-86621-9*, Clarion Bks) HM.

Christelow, Eileen. What Do Authors Do? (J). 1997. 10.15 (*0-606-13895-1*, Pub. by Turtleback) Demco.

Christelow, Eileen. What Do Illustrators Do? LC 98-8297. (Illus.). 40p. (J). (ps-3). 1999. 15.00 (*0-395-90230-4*, Clarion Bks) HM.

Christen. The EMS Incident Management System: Operations for Mass Casualty & High Impact Incidents. LC 97-53270. 240p. (C). 1998. 46.00 (*0-89303-972-1*, Prentice Hall) P-H.

Christen, jt. auth. see Barnes.

Christen, Arden & Klein, Jennifer. Tobacco & Your Oral Health. LC 97-25101. (Illus.). 36p. 1997. pap. 22.00 (*0-86715-326-1*) Quint Pub Co.

Christen, Arden G. & Pronych, Peter M. Painless Parker: A Dental Renegade's Fight to Make Advertising "Ethical" (Illus.). 492p. 1995. pap. 24.95 (*1-885873-01-8*) Dental Tobacco.

Christen, Arden G., jt. auth. see Christen, Joan A.

Christen, Arden G., jt. ed. see Harris, Norman O.

Christen, Carol, jt. auth. see Bolles, Richard.

Christen, D. K., jt. auth. see Jin, Sung-Ho.

Christen, Dorothy. How to Survive Belonging to a Club. 1979. pap. 1.95 (*0-916774-02-3*) Tolvan Co.

Christen, Joan A. & Christen, Arden G. The Female Smoker: From Addiction to Recovery. LC 98-84879. 231p. 1998. pap. text 10.00 (*1-885873-02-6*) Dental Tobacco.

Christen, Kimberly A. & Gill, Sam D., eds. Clowns & Tricksters: An Encyclopedia of Tradition & Culture. LC 98-27562. (Illus.). 296p. 1998. lib. bdg. 65.00 (*0-87436-936-3*, AD-CLOWNC) ABC-CLIO.

Christen, Lesley. Drama Skills for Life: A Handbook for Secondary Teachers. 134p. 1994. pap. 13.95 (*0-435-08636-7*) Heinemann.

Christen, P., et al, eds. EJB Reviews, 1996. 280p. 1997. pap. 22.00 (*3-540-62051-6*) Spr-Verlag.

Christen, P. & Hofmann, E., eds. EJB Reviews, 1993. 244p. 1994. 23.95 (*0-387-57620-7*) Spr-Verlag.

Christen, P., jt. ed. see Korpela, T.

Christen, Robert J. King Sears: Politician & Patriot in a Decade of Revolution. 1981. 49.95 (*0-405-14077-0*) Ayer.

Christen, William L. & Murphy, Thomas. Smart Learning: A Study Skills Guide for Teens. Strother, Deborah B. & Strother, William C., eds. LC 91-48274. (Illus.). 111p. (Orig.). (YA). (gr. 6 up). 1992. pap. 10.95 (*0-9628556-5-0*) Grayson Bernard Pubs.

Christen, William L., jt. auth. see Schmelzer, Ronald V.

Christen, Y., et al, eds. Retine, Vieillissement et Transplantation, Vol. 5. 200p. 1994. 73.00 (*2-906077-42-9*) Elsevier.

— Retine, Vieillissement et Transplantation, Vol. 6. 200p. 1995. 84.00 (*2-906077-60-7*) Elsevier.

Christen, Y., et al. Effects of Ginkgo Biloba Extract (EGb 761) on the Central Nervous System: Proceedings of the International Symposium, Montreux, Switzerland, 20 April 1991. (Advances in Ginkgo Biloba Extract Research Ser.). 184p. pap. 66.00 (*2-906077-28-3*) Elsevier.

Christen, Y., jt. ed. see Mayeux, Richard.

Christen, Yves. Sex Differences: Modern Biology & the Unisex Fallacy. Davidson, Nicholas, tr. from FRE. 256p. (C). 1990. 34.95 (*0-88738-869-8*) Transaction Pubs.

Christen, Yves & Churchland, Patricia S., eds. Neurophilosophy & Alzheimer's Disease. (Research & Perspectives in Alzheimer's Disease Ser.). (Illus.). 153p. 1992. 100.00 (*0-387-54779-7*) Spr-Verlag.

Christen, Yves, jt. auth. see Gage, F.

Christen, Yves, jt. auth. see Grafman, Jordan.

Christen, Yves, jt. ed. see Gage, F.

Christen, Yves, jt. ed. see Galaburda, Albert M.

***Christena, Karol & Lynch, Mary Ann.** A Guide to Teaching Beginning Reading for Teachers & Parents. (Illus.). 256p. 1999. pap., teacher ed. 24.95 (*1-57690-598-5*, TCM 2598) Tchr Create Mat.

***Christenberry, Judy.** Amor de Compraventa (Sale & Purchase Love) (Bianca Ser.). (SPA.). 2000. mass mkt. 3.50 (*0-373-33566-0*, 1-33566-0) Harlequin Bks.

— Un Amor para Toda la Vida. (Bianca Ser.).Tr. of Love for All Life. (SPA.). 2000. mass mkt. 3.50 (*0-373-33570-9*, 1-33570-2) Harlequin Bks.

Christenberry, Judy. Baby in Her Arms: Lucky Charm Sisters. 1999. per. 3.50 (*0-373-19350-5*, Harlequin) Harlequin Bks.

***Christenberry, Judy.** Baby 2000: Deliviery Room Dads, 802. (American Romance Ser.). 1999. mass mkt. 3.99 (*0-373-16802-0*) Harlequin Bks.

— The Borrowed Groom. (Romance Ser.: Bk. 1457). 2000. mass mkt. 3.50 (*0-373-19457-9*, 1-19457-0) Silhouette.

— Cherish the Boss. (Romance Ser.). 2000. mass mkt. 3.50 (*0-373-19463-3*, 1-19463-8) Silhouette.

— Compromiso Ficticio. Vol. 224. (SPA.). 2000. per. 3.50 (*0-373-33574-1*) S&S Trade.

Christenberry, Judy. A Cowboy at Heart. (Harlequin American Romance Ser.). 248p. 1998. per. 3.99 (*0-373-16726-1*, 0-16726-2) Harlequin Bks.

— Cowboy Come Home: 4 Brides for 4 Brothers. (American Romance Ser.: Vol. 744). 1998. per. 3.99 (*0-373-16744-X*, 1-16744-4) Harlequin Bks.

— Cowboy Cupid. (American Romance Ser.). 1996. per. 3.75 (*0-373-16649-4*, 1-16649-5) Harlequin Bks.

— Cowboy Daddy. (American Romance Ser.: No. 653). 1996. per. 3.75 (*0-373-16653-2*, 1-16653-7) Harlequin Bks.

— Cowboy Groom. 1997. per. 3.75 (*0-373-16661-3*, 1-16661-0) Silhouette.

— Cowboy Santa: Christmas Is for Kids. (American Romance Ser.: No. 755). 1998. per. 3.99 (*0-373-16755-5*, 1-16755-0) Harlequin Bks.

— Cowboy Surrender. (American Romance Ser.). 1997. per. 3.75 (*0-373-16665-6*, 1-16665-1) Harlequin Bks.

— Daddy on Demand. (American Romance Ser.). 1996. per. 3.75 (*0-373-16626-5*, 1-16626-3) Harlequin Bks.

— Daddy Unknown: 4 Tots for 4 Texans. (American Romance Ser.: Bk. 781). 1999. per. 3.99 (*0-373-16781-4*, 1-16781-6) Harlequin Bks.

***Christenberry, Judy.** Une Famille Heureuse. (Horizon Ser.: No. 526). (FRE.). 1999. mass mkt. 3.99 (*0-373-39526-4*, 1-39526-8) Harlequin Bks.

Christenberry, Judy. Finding Daddy. 1994. per. 3.50 (*0-373-16555-2*, 1-16555-4) Harlequin Bks.

***Christenberry, Judy.** Great Texas Wedding Bargain. (American Romance Ser.: Vol. 817). 2000. per. 4.25 (*0-373-16817-9*) Harlequin Bks.

Christenberry, Judy. In Papa Bear's Bed. 1997. per. 3.75 (*0-373-16701-6*, 1-16701-4) Harlequin Bks.

— The Last Stubborn Cowboy: 4 Tots for 4 Texans. 1999. per. 3.99 (*0-373-16785-7*, 1-16785-7) Harlequin Bks.

— Marry Me, Kate: Lucky Charm Sisters. (Romance Ser.). 1998. per. 3.50 (*0-373-19344-0*, 1-19344-0) Silhouette.

— My Daddy the Duke. (American Romance Ser.: Vol. 735). 1998. per. 3.99 (*0-373-16735-0*, 1-16735-2) Harlequin Bks.

***Christenberry, Judy.** Never Let You Go: The Circle K Sisters. (Romance Ser.: Bk. 1453). 2000. per. 3.50 (*0-373-19453-6*, 1-19453-9) Silhouette.

Christenberry, Judy. The Nine-Month Bride: Virgin Brides. (Silhouette Romance Ser.: No. 1324). 1998. per. 3.50 (*0-373-19324-6*, 1-19324-2) Harlequin Bks.

— One Hot Daddy-to-Be? 4 Tots for 4 Texans. (American Romance Ser.: No. 773). 1999. per. 3.99 (*0-373-16773-3*, 1-16773-3) Harlequin Bks.

***Christenberry, Judy.** Patchwork Family. (American Romance Ser.). 2000. mass mkt. 4.25 (*0-373-16853-5*, 1168533) Harlequin Bks.

— Rent-a-Dad: Heart of the West. 2000. per. 4.50 (*0-373-82595-1*) Harlequin Bks.

Christenberry, Judy. A Ring for Cinderella (Lucky Charm Sisters) (Silhouette Romance Ser.: No. 1356). 1999. per. 3.50 (*0-373-19356-4*, 1-19356-4) Harlequin Bks.

***Christenberry, Judy.** Snowbound Sweetheart. (Romance Ser.: Bk. 1476). 2000. mass mkt. 3.50 (*0-373-19476-5*, 1-19476-0) Silhouette.

Christenberry, Judy. Surprise--You're a Daddy! 4 Tots for 4 Texans. (American Romance Ser.: No. 777). 1999. per. 3.99 (*0-373-16777-6*, 1-16777-4, Harlequin) Harlequin Bks.

***Christenberry, Judy.** The $10,000,000 Texas Wedding. (American Romance Ser.: Vol. 842). 2000. mass mkt. 4.25 (*0-373-16842-X*, 1-16842-6) Harlequin Bks.

Christenberry, Judy. Wanted: Christmas Mommy. LC 95-22390. 248p. 1995. per. 3.50 (*0-373-16612-5*, 1-16612-3) Harlequin Bks.

— Who's the Daddy? (Promo Ser.). 1999. per. 4.50 (*0-373-21962-8*, 1-21962-5) Harlequin Bks.

— Who's the Daddy? (New Arrival) LC 95-6865. (American Romance Ser.). 250p. 1995. per. 3.50 (*0-373-16579-X*, 1-16579-4) Harlequin Bks.

Christenberry, Judy & Gillen Thacker, Cathy. The Baby Game: Who's the Daddy?: Make Room for Baby, 2 vols. in 1. (By Request 2's Ser.). 2001. mass mkt. 4.99 (*0-373-21713-7*, 1-21713-2) Harlequin Bks.

Christenberry, Mary A. & Stevens, Barbara. Can Piaget Cook? LC 83-83224. (Illus.). 128p. 1984. lib. bdg. 25.95 (*0-89334-184-3*, 184-3) Humanics Ltd.

Christenberry, William. Southern Photographs. deluxe limited ed. (Illus.). 138p. 1985. 750.00 (*0-89381-130-0*) Aperture.

Christenberry, William, jt. auth. see Gruber, Richard J.

***Christenbury, Leila.** Making the Journey: Being & Becoming a Teacher of English Language Arts. 2nd ed. LC 99-87970. 336p. 2000. pap. text 24.00 (*0-86709-476-1*, Pub. by Boynton Cook Pubs) Heinemann.

Christenbury, Leila & Kelly, Patricia P. Questioning: A Path to Critical Thinking. 33p. 1983. pap. 5.95 (*0-8141-3804-7*) NCTE.

Christenbury, Leila, jt. auth. see Mitchell, Diana.

Christensen. Chemical Principle Experiments. 300p. 1998. pap. text 28.75 (*0-536-01665-8*) Pearson Custom.

An Asterisk (*) at the beginning of an entry indicates that the title is appearing for the first time.

***Christensen.** Developing Research Skills: Experimental Methodology. 8th ed. 2000. pap., lab manual ed. 21.00 (*0-205-32719-2*) Allyn.

Christensen. Foundations of Nursing. 3rd ed. (Illus.). 828p. 1998. pap. text 35.00 (*0-323-00160-2*) Mosby Inc.

— Inner Victory. (C). 1995. pap. text 38.36 (*0-395-77167-6*) HM.

Christensen & Stoup. Introduction to Statistics for Social Behavioral Sciences. (Psychology Ser.). 1986. 11.25 (*0-534-05611-3*) Brooks-Cole.

Christensen, A. O. Danish-English Technical Dictionary. (DAN & ENG.). 1990. 120.00 (*0-7859-8948-X*) Fr & Eur.

— Danish-English Technical Dictionary. 2nd ed. (DAN & ENG.). 471p. 1995. 110.00 (*87-11-12199-8*) IBD Ltd.

Christensen, Abigail M. Afro-American Folklore. LC 71-157364. (Black Heritage Library Collection). 1977. 10.95 (*0-8369-8802-7*) Ayer.

— Afro-American Folklore: Told Round Cabin Fires on the Sea Islands of South Carolina. LC 73-78761. (Illus.). 116p. 1969. lib. bdg. 35.00 (*0-8371-1387-3*, CHA&) Greenwood.

Christensen, Alice. American Yoga Association. 1997. pap. text 15.95 (*0-614-27345-5*) NTC Contemp Pub Co.

— The American Yoga Association Beginner's Manual. 208p. 1987. per. 16.00 (*0-671-61935-7*) S&S Trade.

— American Yoga Association Wellness Book. 1996. pap. 18.95 (*1-57566-025-3*) Kensgtn Pub Corp.

***Christensen, Alice.** American Yoga Association's Easy Does It Yoga: The Safe & Gently Way to Health & Well-Being. LC 99-39751. 192p. 1999. per. 16.00 (*0-684-84890-2*) S&S Trade.

Christensen, Alice. The American Yoga Association's New Yoga Challenge. LC 96-44651. 192p. 1997. pap. 15.95 (*0-8092-3175-1*, 317510, Contemporary Bks) NTC Contemp Pub Co.

Christensen, Alice. Easy Does It Yoga. LC 96-148239. 112p. 1995. spiral bd. 21.95 (*0-7872-1190-7*) Kendall-Hunt.

Christensen, Alice. The Light of Yoga. (Illus.). 83p. 3.95 (*0-318-14774-2*) Am Yoga Assn.

Christensen, Alice, ed. Conversations with Swami Lakshmanjoo Vol. I: Aspects of Kashmir Shaivism. (Illus.). 150p. (Orig.). 1996. pap. 16.95 (*1-887267-04-2*) Amer Yoga.

***Christensen, Alice & American Yoga Association Staff.** The American Yoga Association's Yoga for Sport. LC 99-39627. 208 p. 2000. pap. 16.95 (*0-8092-2621-9*, Contemporary Bks) NTC Contemp Pub Co.

Christensen, Alice & Grant, Stephenson. Easy Does It Yoga Trainer's Guide. 50p. 14.95 (*0-318-14773-4*) Am Yoga Assn.

Christensen, Alice & Rankin, David. Easy Does It Yoga: For Older People. (Illus.). 56p. 10.95 (*0-318-14772-6*) Am Yoga Assn.

— The Light of Yoga Society Beginner's Manual. (Illus.). 64p. 1974. pap. 7.95 (*0-671-21831-X*, Fireside) S&S Trade Pap.

— The Light of Yoga Society Beginners Manual. (Illus.). 62p. 1972. pap. 7.95 (*0-317-01148-0*) Am Yoga Assn.

Christensen, Alice, jt. auth. see American Yoga Association Staff.

Christensen, Amy, jt. auth. see Hall, Kirsten.

Christensen, Andrew & Jacobson, Neil S. Reconcilable Differences. LC 99-41183. 332p. 1999. 23.95 (*1-57230-261-5*) Guilford Pubns.

Christensen, Anne-Lise. Neuropsychological Treatment after Brain Injury. Ellis, David W., ed. (Foundations of Neuropsychology Ser.). (C). 1989. text 227.50 (*0-7923-0014-9*) Kluwer Academic.

Christensen, Anne-Lise & Uzzell, Barbara P., eds. Brain Injury & Neuropsychological Trauma & Rehabilitation: International Perspectives. (Institute for Research in Behavioral Neuroscience Ser.). 344p. 1994. pap. 36.00 (*0-8058-1448-5*) L Erlbaum Assocs.

— Brain Injury Neuropsychological Trauma & Rehabilitation: International Perspectives. (Institute for Research in Behavioral Neuroscience Ser.). 344p. 1994. text 69.95 (*0-8058-1447-7*) L Erlbaum Assocs.

— Neuropsychological Rehabilitation. (C). 1988. text 85.50 (*0-89838-374-9*) Kluwer Academic.

Christensen, Arne E., ed. The Earliest Ships: The Evolution of Boats into Ships. (Conway's History of the Ship Ser.). (Illus.). 192p. 1996. 46.95 (*1-55750-201-3*) Naval Inst Pr.

Christensen, Art W., ed. see Allen, James.

Christensen, B. R. Getting a Free Education. LC 94-61435. (Illus.). 132p. (Orig.). 1994. pap. 11.95 (*0-9643699-0-7*) Effect Living.

— Getting Your Dream Life: Career, Sex & Leisure. LC 96-83391. (Illus.). 120p. (Orig.). 1996. pap. 11.95 (*0-9643699-1-5*) Effect Living.

Christensen, B. R. & Christensen, E. S. Adding to Your Financial Portfolio. (Illus.). 89p. (YA). (gr. 9 up). 1998. pap. 12.95 (*0-9643699-5-8*) Effect Living.

***Christensen, Barbara L. & Kockrow, Elaine O.** Adult Health Nursing. 3rd ed. (Illus.). 768p. 1998. student ed. write for info. (*0-323-00153-X*) Mosby Inc.

— Foundations: Adult Health Nursing. 3rd ed. (Illus.). 828p. (C). 1998. student ed. write for info. (*0-323-00315-X*); text. write for info. (*0-323-00316-8*) Mosby Inc.

— Foundations of Nursing: Adult Health Nursing: Includes Testbank. 3rd ed. (Illus.). 828p. (C). 1998. teacher ed. write for info. (*0-323-00156-4*) Mosby Inc.

Christensen, Barbara L., et al. Adult Health Nursing. 3rd ed. (Illus.). 768p. (C). 1998. pap. text 39.00 (*0-323-00157-2*) Mosby Inc.

Christensen, Ben, adapted by. Las Aventures de Hector, I. (C). 1992. mass mkt. 21.95 (*0-8384-2550-X*) Heinle & Heinle.

— Las Aventures de Hector, II. (C). 1992. mass mkt. 21.95 (*0-8384-2551-8*) Heinle & Heinle.

Christensen, Benedicte V. The Russian Federation in Transition: External Developments. LC 94-5967. (Occasional Paper Ser.: No. 111). vii, 45p. 1994. 15.00 (*1-55775-371-7*) Intl Monetary.

— Switzerland's Role As an International Financial Center. (Occasional Paper Ser.: No. 45). 40p. 1986. pap. 7.50 (*0-939934-74-4*) Intl Monetary.

Christensen, Bent. Annelida. John, Bernard et al, eds. (Animal Cytogenetics Ser.: Vol. 2). (Illus.). iv, 81p. 1980. 44.00 (*3-443-26010-1*, Pub. by Gebruder Borntraeger) Balogh.

Christensen, Bernhard M. The Inward Pilgrimage: An Introduction to Christian Spiritual Classics. rev. ed. 192p. 1996. pap. 14.99 (*0-8066-2036-6*, 9-2036, Augsburg) Augsburg Fortress.

Christensen, Beth, jt. auth. see Harrington, Barry.

Christensen, Bev. Prince George: Rivers, Railways. 1989. 29.95 (*0-89781-266-2*, 5314) Am Historical Pr.

— Too Good to Be True: Alcan's Kemano Completion Project. LC 95-196519. (Illus.). 352p. 1995. pap. 16.95 (*0-88922-354-8*) Genl Dist Srvs.

Christensen, Bob. Satan, You're Not Stealing My Marriage. 36p. (Orig.). 1989. pap. 2.00 (*1-886045-00-3*) Covenant Marriages.

— The Seagull & the Pigeon: For the Children in Your Life. (Illus.). 42p. (Orig.). (YA). (gr. 4-12). 1991. pap. 5.95 (*1-886045-02-X*) Covenant Marriages.

— Why I Chose to Believe in My Marriage Healing. 2nd rev. ed. 76p. 1993. pap. 5.95 (*1-886045-04-6*) Covenant Marriages.

Christensen, Bob & Christensen, Lynne. Miracles along the Way. 91p. (Orig.). 1992. pap. 5.95 (*1-886045-03-8*) Covenant Marriages.

— Standing in Love: A Guide to Repairing Broken Marriages. (Illus.). 73p. (Orig.). 1990. pap. 5.95 (*1-886045-01-1*) Covenant Marriages.

Christensen, Bob & Griego, Roy. When You Say I Do God Says I Will: God's Covenant Gives Power to Say "I Won't" to Divorce. 292p. 1998. 15.00 (*1-886045-14-3*) Covenant Marriages.

***Christensen, Bobbie & Christensen, Eric S.** Building Your Financial Portfolio on $25 a Month (Or Less) 3rd rev. ed. LC 96-91018. 110p. 2000. pap. 14.95 (*0-9643699-7-4*, Pub. by Effect Living) Baker & Taylor.

— Top 50 Best Stock Investments. 110p. 2000. pap. 18.95 (*0-9643699-8-2*, Pub. by Effect Living) Baker & Taylor.

Christensen, Borge. COMAL from A to Z. (Amazing Adventures of Captain COMAL Ser.). (Illus.). 64p. 1984. pap. 6.95 (*0-928411-00-1*) COMAL Users.

Christensen, Bruce A., jt. auth. see Kavass, Igor I.

Christensen, Bryce J., intro. Day Care: Child Psychology & Adult Economics. (Family in America Research Ser.). 150p. (Orig.). (C). 1989. 15.95 (*0-9619364-3-6*); pap. 9.95 (*0-9619364-2-8*) Rockford Inst.

Christensen, Burke A. & Cooper, Ken, eds. The Best of "Strictly Speaking" Ethics Readings from the Journal of the American Society of CLU & CHFC with Study Materials for Life Insurance & Financial Services Professionals. LC 95-75460. 135p. (Orig.). (C). 1995. pap. text 9.95 (*0-943590-69-8*) Amer College.

Christensen, Burke A., jt. ed. see Graves, Edward E.

Christensen, C. Revised List of Hawaiian Pteridophyta. (BMB Ser.). 1974. reprint ed. pap. 25.00 (*0-527-02128-8*) Periodicals Srv.

— A Revision of the Pteridophyta of Samoa. (BMB Ser.). 1974. reprint ed. 25.00 (*0-527-02285-3*) Periodicals Srv.

Christensen, C. Ben, jt. auth. see Christensen, Kathee M.

Christensen, C. M. E. C. Stakman, Statesman of Science. LC 84-70114. 156p. 1984. 32.00 (*0-89054-056-X*) Am Phytopathol Soc.

Christensen, C. Roland. Education for Judgment: The Artistry of Discussion Leadership. 320p. (C). 1992. pap. 14.95 (*0-87584-365-4*) Harvard Busn.

Christensen, C. Roland, et al, eds. Education for Judgment: The Artistry of Discussion Leadership. 1991. text 29.95 (*0-07-103307-6*) McGraw.

Christensen, C. Roland & Hahsen, Abby J. Teaching & the Case Method. 1987. text 29.95 (*0-07-103221-5*) McGraw.

Christensen, Carey, jt. auth. see Leach, Joel.

Christensen, Carl. The Green Bible. LC 90-92158. 86p. (Orig.). 1990. pap. 7.95 (*0-9628113-0-0*) Johnny Pub.

— Index Filicum, Sive Enumeratio Omnium Generum Specierumque Filicum et Hydropteridum Ab Anno 1753 Ad Finem Anni 1905 Descriptorum Adjectis Synonymis Principalibus, Area Geographica... (Illus.). xiv, 744p. 1973. reprint ed. 170.00 (*3-87429-048-4*, 002596, Pub. by Koeltz Sci Bks) Lubrecht & Cramer.

Christensen, Carl C. Princes & Propaganda: Electoral Saxon Art of the Reformation. (Sixteenth Century Essays & Studies: Vol. 20). (Illus.). 149p. 1992. text 40.00 (*0-940474-21-2*, SCJP) Truman St Univ.

Christensen, Carl J., jt. auth. see Nelson, Robert.

Christensen, Carol, ed. Disability & the Dilemmas of Education & Justice. 160p. 1996. 102.95 (*0-335-19584-9*); pap. 31.95 (*0-335-19583-0*) OpUniv Pr.

Christensen, Carol, jt. auth. see Christensen, Thomas.

Christensen, Carol, jt. auth. see Christensen, Tom.

Christensen, Carol, tr. see Carpentier, Alejo.

Christensen, Carol, tr. see Celine, Louis-Ferdinand.

Christensen, Carol, tr. see Esquivel, Laura.

Christensen, Carol, tr. see Meunier, Jacques & Savarin, A. M.

Christensen, Carol, tr. see Montalban, Manuel V.

Christensen, Carol A. The American Garden City & the New Towns Movement. Foster, Stephen, ed. LC 85-20866. (Architecture & Urban Design Ser.: No. 13). 215p. 1986. reprint ed. pap. 66.70 (*0-8357-1684-8*, 207045000093) Bks Demand.

Christensen, Carol W., compiled by. Guide to Religion-Based Organizations of Attorneys. (Legal Bibliography Ser.: No. 19). 33p. 1979. 15.00 (*0-935630-01-5*) U of Tex Tarlton Law Lib.

Christensen, Chuck & Christensen, Winnie. Acts 1-12: God Moves in the Early Church. rev. ed. (Fisherman Bible Studyguide Ser.). 96p. 1979. pap. 4.99 (*0-87788-007-7*, H Shaw Pubs) Waterbrook Pr.

— James: Faith in Action. LC 75-33442. (Fisherman Bible Studyguide Ser.). 55p. 1975. pap. 4.99 (*0-87788-421-8*, H Shaw Pubs) Waterbrook Pr.

— Mark: God in Action. LC 72-88935. (Fisherman Bible Studyguide Ser.). 94p. 1972. pap. 4.99 (*0-87788-309-2*, H Shaw Pubs) Waterbrook Pr.

— Paul: Thirteenth Apostle (Acts 13-28) (Fisherman Bible Studyguide Ser.). 64p. (Orig.). 1987. pap. 4.99 (*0-87788-652-0*, H Shaw Pubs) Waterbrook Pr.

Christensen, Clark, jt. auth. see Lee, Michael.

Christensen, Clay B., et al. Vistas Hispanicas: Introduccion a la Lengua y la Cultura. 2nd ed. 1981. 2.75 (*0-685-05580-9*) HM.

***Christensen, Clayton.** The Innovator's Dilemma: When New Technologies Cause Great Firms to Fail. 224p. 2000. 16.00 (*0-06-662069-4*) HarpC.

Christensen, Clayton M. Innovation & the General Manager. LC 98-50562. (Illus.). 600p. 1999. pap. 58.44 (*0-07-365915-0*) McGraw.

— The Innovator's Dilemma: When New Technologies Cause Great Firms to Fail. LC 96-10894. (Management of Innovation & Change Ser.). (Illus.). 225p. 1997. 27.50 (*0-87584-585-1*) Harvard Busn.

Christensen, Clyde M. Edible Mushrooms. 2nd rev. ed. LC 81-161364. 138p. 1981. reprint ed. pap. 42.80 (*0-608-00788-9*, 205933700010) Bks Demand.

— The Molds & Man: An Introduction to the Fungi. 3rd ed. LC 65-17718. 292p. reprint ed. pap. 90.60 (*0-608-18632-5*, 205585000039) Bks Demand.

— Molds, Mushrooms, & Mycotoxins. LC 74-21808. 276p. 1975. reprint ed. pap. 85.60 (*0-7837-2971-5*, 205748300006) Bks Demand.

Christensen, D., ed. Yearbook for Traditional Music. Orig. Title: International Folk Music Council Journal. (ENG, FRE & GER.). 230p. 1997. 45.00 (*0-318-14547-2*) Intl Coun Trad.

Christensen, D. & Schramm, A. Reyes, eds. Working Papers of the 23rd Conference. (ENG, FRE & GER.). 163p. 1975. 7.00 (*0-318-17461-8*) Intl Coun Trad.

***Christensen, D. L.** Hebrew Bible: Bible 101-104. 2000. pap. text. write for info. (*0-941037-80-0*) D & F Scott.

Christensen, D. N., ed. Directory of Traditional Music. 100p. 1995. 10.00 (*0-317-01462-5*) Intl Coun Trad.

Christensen-Dalsgaard, Jorgen & Frandsen, Soren, eds. Advances in Helio & Asteroseismology. (C). 1987. pap. text 87.00 (*90-277-2615-9*); lib. bdg. 212.00 (*90-277-2614-0*) Kluwer Academic.

Christensen, Dan C., ed. European Historiography of Technology: Technology's Role in the Modernization Process. 242p. (Orig.). 1993. pap. 57.50 (*87-7492-910-0*, Pub. by Odense Universitets Forlag) Coronet Bks.

Christensen, Dana N. & Todahl, Jeffery. Solution-Based Casework. LC 99-22992. (Modern Applications of Social Work Ser.). 216p. 1999. lib. bdg. 47.95 (*0-202-36117-9*) Aldine de Gruyter.

— Solution-Based Casework: An Introduction to Clinical & Case Management Skills in Casework Practice. LC 99-22992. (Modern Applications of Social Work Ser.). 216p. 1999. pap. text 23.95 (*0-202-36118-7*) Aldine de Gruyter.

Christensen, Dana N., jt. auth. see Brown, Joseph H.

Christensen, Darcy. Folk Art Friends. (Illus.). 60p. 1998. pap. 10.50 (*1-56770-437-9*) S Scheewe Pubns.

Christensen, Darrel E. The Search for Concreteness - Reflections on Hegel & Whitehead: A Treatise on Self-Evidence & Critical Method in Philosophy. LC 85-63421. 516p. 1986. 50.00 (*0-941664-22-8*) Susquehanna U Pr.

***Christensen, Daryl.** Journal of a Walleye Pro. Barringer, Bernie, ed. (Illus.). 212p. 1999. pap. 16.95 (*1-885149-08-5*) Moving Mtn.

Christensen, Dave & Peterson, James A. Coaching Offensive Lineman. LC 98-85406. (Art & Science of Coaching Ser.). (Illus.). 248p. 1998. pap. 17.95 (*1-57167-208-7*) Coaches Choice.

Christensen, David, jt. auth. see Charfoos, Lawrence.

***Christensen, Dean.** The Right to Riches. 1999. pap. 11.95 (*1-55517-444-2*) CFI Dist.

***Christensen, Donald E.** Coming Home to Scottsbluff, Nebraska: The First One Hundred Years. LC 99-47950. 1999. write for info. (*1-57864-093-8*) Donning Co.

Christensen, Douglas A., jt. auth. see Durney, Carl H.

Christensen, Douglas D., jt. auth. see Contine, Tom.

Christensen, Duane. Deuteronomy. (Word Biblical Commentary Ser.: Vol. 6B). 2000. 32.99 (*0-8499-1032-3*) Word Pub.

— Word Biblical Commentary on Deuteronomy. Vol. 6A. expanded rev. ed. 592p. 1999. 32.99 (*0-7852-4220-1*) Nelson.

Christensen, Duane L. Bible 101: God's Story in Human History. 1998. pap. text 19.95 (*0-941037-42-8*, BIBAL Press) D & F Scott.

— Prophecy & War in Ancient Israel: Studies in the Oracles Against the Nations. LC 88-71437. (BIBAL Monographs: No. 3). Orig. Title: Transformations of the War Oracle in Old Testament Prophecy. 310p. 1989. reprint ed. pap. 14.95 (*0-941037-06-1*, BIBAL Press) D & F Scott.

Christensen, Duane L., ed. Experiencing the Exodus from Egypt. LC 88-2596. 95p. 1988. pap. 7.95 (*0-941037-03-7*, BIBAL Press) D & F Scott.

— A Song of Power & the Power of Song: Essays on the Book of Deuteronomy. LC 93-6413. (American Schools of Oriental Research Dissertation Ser.: No. 3). xiv, 418p. 1993. 37.95 (*0-931464-74-9*) Eisenbrauns.

Christensen, Duane L., ed. see Clements, Ronald E.

Christensen, Duane L., ed. see Lohfink, Norbert.

Christensen, Duane L., ed. see Reid, Stephen B.

Christensen, E. R., et al. Contaminated Aquatic Sediments: Proceedings of the First International Specialized Conference on Contiminated Aquatic Sediments: Historic Records, Environmental Impact & Remediation, Held in Milwaukee, WI, 14-16 June, 1993, Vol. 28/8-9. (Water Science & Technology Ser.: No. 28/8-9). 424p. 1994. pap. 193.00 (*0-08-042492-9*, Pergamon Pr) Elsevier.

Christensen, E. S., jt. auth. see Christensen, B. R.

Christensen, Elaine. I Learned Five Things. Spelius, Carol, ed. 75p. 1996. 9.95 (*0-941363-08-2*) Lake Shore Pub.

Christensen, Eli H., jt. auth. see Acosta-Belen, Edna.

Christensen, Eloise, jt. auth. see Zilly, John.

Christensen, Eric S. Building Your Financial Power. 2nd ed. 1998. pap. 12.95 (*0-9643699-6-6*) Effect Living.

Christensen, Eric S., jt. auth. see Christensen, Bobbie.

Christensen, Erwin O. Early American Woodcarving. (Illus.). 160p. 1972. pap. 5.95 (*0-486-21840-6*) Dover.

Christensen, Esther. Merry Christmas! Leih, Janet, ed. 8p. (Orig.). 1990. pap. 1.00 (*1-877649-10-4*) Tesseract SD.

Christensen, Eugenia, ed. see Miller, Fremont.

***Christensen, Evelyn.** Gaining Through Losing. 2000. pap. 10.99 (*0-7814-3441-6*) Chariot Victor.

— A Time to Pray God's Way. 254p. 1996. mass mkt. 5.99 (*0-7369-0146-9*) Harvest Hse.

Christensen, Evelyn B. Clip Clue Puzzles. Gideon, Joan, ed. (Illus.). 112p. (Orig.). (J). (gr. 5-8). 1995. pap. 10.95 (*0-86651-936-X*, 21356) Seymour Pubns.

Christensen, Everett M. Fifty-Five Magic Management Words. 96p. (Orig.). 1989. pap. 8.95 (*0-317-93515-1*) PPSD Inc.

Christensen, F. M. Pornography: The Other Side. LC 89-26543. 208p. 1990. 35.00 (*0-275-93537-X*, C3537, Greenwood Pr) Greenwood.

— Space-Like Time: Consequences of, Alternatives to, & Arguments Regarding the Theory That Time Is Like Space. 384p. 1993. text 60.00 (*0-8020-2816-0*) U of Toronto Pr.

***Christensen, Fred A. & Manuele, Fred A.** Safety Through Design: Best Practices. LC 99-30661. 1999. 69.95 (*0-87912-204-8*) Natl Safety Coun.

Christensen, G. Jay, jt. auth. see Jacobi, Ernst.

Christensen, G. S. & Soliman, S. A. Optimal Long-Term Operation of Electric Power Systems. LC 88-15268. (Mathematical Concepts & Methods in Science & Engineering Ser.: Vol. 38). (Illus.). 324p. (C). 1988. text 95.00 (*0-306-42875-X*, Kluwer Plenum) Kluwer Academic.

Christensen, G. S., et al. Optimal Control Applications in Electric Power Systems. (Mathematical Concepts & Methods in Science & Engineering Ser.: Vol. 35). (Illus.). 208p. (C). 1987. 75.00 (*0-306-42517-3*, Plenum Trade) Perseus Pubng.

— Optimal Control of Distributed Nuclear Reactors. LC 95-25531. (Mathematical Concepts & Methods in Science & Engineering Ser.: Vol. 41). (Illus.). 232p. (C). 1990. text 85.00 (*0-306-43305-2*, Kluwer Plenum) Kluwer Academic.

Christensen, Garry & Lacroix, Richard. Competitiveness & Employment: A Framework for Rural Development in Poland. LC 97-50069. (Discussion Paper Ser.: No. 383). 68p. 1997. pap. 22.00 (*0-8213-4164-2*, 14164) World Bank.

Christensen, George E. Back Trail; or An Upper Peninsula Boyhood. 143p. 1985. 26.00 (*0-933249-00-4*); pap. 7.50 (*0-933249-01-2*) Mid-Peninsula Lib.

Christensen, Gordon J. Buyer's Guide to Dentistry. 256p. (C). (gr. 13). 1994. text 56.95 (*0-8016-6776-3*, 06776) Mosby Inc.

Christensen, H., et al. Active Robot Vision: Camera Heads, Model Based Navigation & Reactive Control. 200p. 1993. text 67.00 (*981-02-1321-2*) World Scientific Pub.

Christensen, H. I. Experimental Environments for Machine Vision. (Machine Perception & Artificial Intelligence Ser.). 304p. 1994. text 86.00 (*981-02-1510-X*) World Scientific Pub.

Christensen, H. I., et al, eds. Computer Vision Systems: Proceedings of the 1st International Conference, ICVS '99 Las Palmas, Gran Canaria, Spain, January 13-15, 1999. LC 98-72621. xi, 554p. 1999. pap. 79.00 (*3-540-65459-3*) Spr-Verlag.

— Computing in Object-Oriented Parallel Environments: 2nd International Symposium, Iscope 98, Santa Fe, N. M., U. S. A., December 1998: Proceedings. LC 98-51719. (Lecture Notes in Computer Science Ser.). xi, 243p. 1998. pap. 49.00 (*3-540-65387-2*) Spr-Verlag.

***Christensen, H. I., et al, eds.** Sensor Based Intelligent Robots: International Workshop, Dagstuhl Castle, Germany, September 28-October 2, 1998: Selected Papers. LC 99-88770. (Lecture Notes in Artificial Intelligence: 1724). viii, 327p. 2000. pap. 56.00 (*3-540-66933-7*) Spr-Verlag.

Christensen, Harold T. & Johnsen, Kathryn P. Marriage & the Family. LC 71-155205. 554p. reprint ed. pap. 171.80 (*0-608-31000-X*, 201247600081) Bks Demand.

Christensen, Harriet H., jt. auth. see McGinnis, Wendy J.

***Christensen, Heather.** Real Faith, Real Life: Wake Up & Live Your Life. LC 99-34422. 48p. 1999. 7.95 (*1-57895-075-9*) Curriculum Presbytrn KY.

Christensen, Heinrich. Das Alexanderlied Walters von Chatillon. xii, 225p. 1969. reprint ed. 50.00 (*0-318-71448-5*) G Olms Pubs.

Christensen, Helen. Math Modeling. 2nd ed. 148p. (C). 1995. pap. text, per. 37.95 (*0-7872-1575-9*) Kendall-Hunt.

C

Christensen, Howard B. Introduction to Statistics. (C). 1992. pap. text, teacher ed., suppl. ed. 10.00 (*0-03-092737-4*) Harcourt Coll Pubs.
— Introduction to Statistics: A Calculus-Based Approach. 500p. (C). 1992. text 93.50 (*0-15-545965-1*) SCP.
Christensen, Ian. Answered Prayer is God's Will for You. 1997. pap. text. write for info. (*0-9748529-0-2*) Renew Am.
Christensen, Inger. Alphabet. (Orig.). 1996. pap. 15.95 (*1-85224-310-4*, Pub. by Bloodaxe Bks) Dufour.
***Christensen, Inger.** Painted Room. Newman, Denise, tr. (Illus.). 96p. 2000. pap. text 18.00 (*1-86046-593-5*) Harvill Press.
Christensen, J., jt. ed. see Kumar, D.
***Christensen, J. A.** Nichiren: Leader of Buddhist Reformation in Japan. LC 99-88875. 2000. pap. write for info. (*0-87573-086-8*) Jain Pub Co.
Christensen, J. A. Young Writer. LC 74-88375. (Illus.). xii, 364p. (YA). (gr. 8-12). 1970. text 21.95 (*0-87015-180-0*) Pacific Bks.
Christensen, J. P., jt. auth. see Barahona, Pedro.
Christensen, J. P., jt. auth. see Gordon, C.
Christensen, James. Bedside Logic in Diagnostic Gastroenterology. (Illus.). 174p. (Orig.). (C). 1987. pap. text 28.00 (*0-443-08518-8*) Church.
— Chamber Music: Notes for Players. LC 92-16712. 256p. 1992. pap. 16.95 (*0-942963-23-7*) Distinctive Pub.
Christensen, James, ed. Transfer Credit Practices of Designated Educational Institutions (1994-96) 176p. 1994. pap. 35.00 (*0-614-23455-7*, 3008) Am Assn Coll Registrars.
— Transfer Credit Practices of Designated Educational Institutions, 1998-2000. 192p. 1998. pap., per. 42.00 (*1-57858-017-X*, 3013) Am Assn Coll Registrars.
Christensen, James. The Art of James Christensen: A Journey of the Imagination. LC 94-14086. 180p. 1994. 39.95 (*0-86713-021-0*, 88072) Greenwich Wrkshop.
Christensen, James, jt. ed. see Bennett, William.
Christensen, James, ed. see International Symposium on Gastrointestinal Motili.
***Christensen, James C.** Parables. LC 99-36919. (Illus.). 72p. 1999. 19.95 (*1-57345-558-X*, Shadow Mount) Deseret Bk.
Christensen, James C. Rhymes & Reasons: An Annotated Collection of Mother Goose Rhymes. LC 96-46815. 56p. (J). (gr. k up). 1997. bds. 19.95 (*0-86713-040-7*, 88082) Greenwich Wrkshop.
Christensen, James C., et al. Voyage of the Basset. LC 96-24758. (Illus.). 168p. (J). 1996. 29.95 (*1-885183-58-5*) Artisan.
Christensen, James J. & Izatt, Reed M. Handbook of Metal Ligand Heats & Related Thermodynamic Quantities. 3rd rev. ed. LC 83-1908. 795p. reprint ed. pap. 200.00 (*0-608-08921-4*, 206955600005) Bks Demand.
Christensen, James J., et al. Handbook of Metal Ligand Heats & Related Thermodynamic Quantities. 2nd enl. rev. ed. LC 75-4480. (Center for Thermochemical Studies, Brigham Young University, Contribution: No. 66). (Illus.). 507p. reprint ed. pap. 157.20 (*0-8357-6136-3*, 203452200090) Bks Demand.
Christensen, James L. Communion Reflections & Prayers. LC 84-29361. 64p. (Orig.). 1985. pap. 5.99 (*0-8272-0446-9*) Chalice Pr.
— Contemporary Worship Services. LC 75-137445. 256p. reprint ed. 79.40 (*0-8357-9517-9*, 201144400078) Bks Demand.
Christensen, James P., et al. Rich on Any Income: The Easy Budgeting System That Fits in Your Checkbook. LC 85-22222. (Illus.). 75p. 1986. pap. 10.95 (*0-87579-009-7*, Shadow Mount) Deseret Bk.
Christensen, Janet & Levin, Betty B. Apple Orchard Cookbook. 2nd ed. LC 92-30992. (Illus.). 160p. 1992. pap. 9.95 (*0-936399-32-5*) Berkshire Hse.
***Christensen, Jens.** It & Business: A History of Scandinavian Airlines. 448p. 2000. pap. 39.95 (*87-7288-820-2*, Pub. by Aarhus Univ Pr) David Brown.
Christensen, Jens P., jt. ed. see Van Goor, Jaap N.
Christensen, Jerome. Lord Byron's Strength: Romantic Writing & Commercial Society. (Illus.). 416p. 1995. pap. text 17.95 (*0-8018-4356-1*) Johns Hopkins.
— Practicing Enlightenment: Hume & the Formation of a Literary Career. LC 95-18996. 336p. 1986. pap. 19.95 (*0-299-10754-X*) U of Wis Pr.
— Practicing Enlightenment: Hume & the Formation of a Literary Career. LC 86-40048. 299p. 1987. reprint ed. pap. 92.70 (*0-608-07000-9*, 206720800009) Bks Demand.
***Christensen, Jerome.** Romanticism at the End of History LC 99-43278. 248p. 2000. 45.00 (*0-8018-6319-8*) Johns Hopkins.
Christensen, Jo I. Needlepoint Book: 303 Stitches with Patterns & Projects. 400p. 1976. pap. 20.00 (*0-671-76662-7*, Fireside) S&S Trade Pap.
Christensen, Jo Ippolito. The Needlepoint Book: A Complete Update of the Classic Guide. expanded rev. ed. LC 98-33812. (Illus.). 448p. 1999. per. 25.00 (*0-684-83230-5*) S&S Trade Pap.
Christensen, Joe J. One Step at a Time: Building a Better Marriage, Family, & You. LC 96-16342. viii, 152p. 1996. 13.95 (*1-57345-188-6*) Deseret Bk.
— To Grow in Spirit. viii, 81p. 1989. reprint ed. pap. 6.95 (*0-87579-207-3*) Deseret Bk.
Christensen, John, jt. auth. see Lampkin, Rita L.
Christensen, John F., ed. see Feldman, W.
Christensen, Judith. Action in Teacher Education: Tenth Year Anniversary Issue. Sikula, John P., ed. 1988. 12.50 (*0-685-41073-0*) Assn Tchr Ed.
— Nursing Partnership: A Model for Nursing Practice. LC 93-12698. 272p. 1993. pap. text. write for info. (*0-443-04934-3*) Church.
Christensen, K., jt. auth. see Altman, I.
Christensen, K. K., et al, eds. Neonatal Group B Streptococcal Infections. (Antibiotics & Chemotherapy Ser.: Vol. 35). (Illus.). x, 350p. 1985. 215.00 (*3-8055-3953-3*) S Karger.
Christensen, K. Richard. Philosophy & Choice: Selected Readings from Around the World. LC 98-8246. 1998. pap. text 45.95 (*1-55934-964-6*, 1964) Mayfield Pub.
Christensen, Karen. Home Ecology: Simple & Practical Ways to Green Your Home. LC 90-38258. (Illus.). 354p. (Orig.). 1990. pap. 15.95 (*1-55591-062-9*) Fulcrum Pub.
— Worldmark Chronologies Vol. 1: Chronology of Africa. LC 99-44217. 2100p. 1997. 249.00 (*0-7876-0521-2*, 00152859) Gale.
Christensen, Karen, jt. auth. see Christensen, Roger.
Christensen, Karen, jt. auth. see Levinson, David.
Christensen, Karen, jt. ed. see Levinson, David.
Christensen, Karen S. Cities & Complexity: Intergovernmental Decision Making. LC 98-9069. (Cities & Planning Ser.). 1998. 51.00 (*0-7619-1164-2*); pap. 24.50 (*0-7619-1165-0*) Sage.
Christensen, Kate. In the Drink. LC 99-18876. 278p. 1999. 22.95 (*0-385-49450-5*) Doubleday.
***Christensen, Kate.** In the Drink. 288p. 2000. pap. 12.00 (*0-385-72021-1*, Anchor NY) Doubleday.
Christensen, Kathee M. & Christensen, C. Ben. Trilingual Education: Sign Language, Spanish, English. LC 85-70169. (ENG & SPA., Illus.). 1985. 16.25 (*0-916304-70-1*) SDSU Press.
***Christensen, Kathee M. & Delgado, Gilbert L.** Deaf Plus: A Multicultural Perspective. LC 00-22086. 2000. write for info. (*1-58121-017-5*) Dawn Sign.
Christensen, Katheren. Arkansas Military Bounty Grants War of 1812. 265p. (Orig.). 1971. pap. 25.00 (*0-929604-23-7*) Arkansas Ancestors.
Christensen, Kathleen, jt. ed. see Barker, Kathleen.
Christensen, Kathryn. Good Math Beginnings. Jones, Allan & Gorney, Janifer, eds. (Illus.). (Orig.). 1987. pap. 9.95 (*0-9607458-5-8*) Arts Pubns.
Christensen, Kathy. Let's Be Circus Animals. Linse, Barbara B., ed. (Using Themes Ser.). (Illus.). 60p. 1988. pap. text 6.95 (*0-9607458-9-0*) Arts Pubns.
— Let's Be Circus Stars. Linse, Barbara B., ed. (Using Themes Ser.). (Illus.). 57p. 1988. pap. text 6.95 (*0-685-45616-1*) Arts Pubns.
— Let's Be Circus Stars. (Illus.). 60p. 1990. 6.95 (*1-878079-13-1*) Arts Pubns.
— Let's Have a Circus. Linse, Barbara B., ed. (Using Themes Ser.). (Illus.). 70p. 1988. pap. text 6.95 (*0-685-45615-3*) Arts Pubns.
— Let's Have a Circus. (Illus.). 70p. 1990. 7.95 (*1-878079-12-3*) Arts Pubns.
Christensen, Kathy & Li, Barbara. Put on a Circus. (Illus.). 96p. (Orig.). 1991. 9.95 (*1-878079-02-6*) Arts Pubns.
Christensen, Ken. Romantic California: And the Pacific Northwest. (Romantic America Ser.). (Illus.). 272p. 1997. pap. 14.95 (*0-9640185-1-9*) Romantic Amer.
Christensen, Ken. The Romantic California Rivers. (Romantic America Ser.). (Illus.). 80p. 1996. pap. 9.95 (*0-9624978-1-5*) Romantic Amer.
***Christensen, Ken.** Romantic Pacific Northwest. (Illus.). 1999. pap. 11.95 (*0-9640185-6-X*) Premier Pubng.
Christensen, Ken. Romantic San Diego. 120p. (Orig.). 1989. pap. text 5.95 (*0-685-29966-X*) Romantic Amer.
— Romantic San Diego. 4th ed. (Romantic America Ser.). (Illus.). 144p. (Orig.). 1996. pap. 12.95 (*0-9624978-6-X*) Romantic Amer.
— Romantic Santa Barbara. (Romantic America Ser.). (Illus.). 96p. 1996. pap. 9.95 (*0-9624978-2-7*) Romantic Amer.
Christensen, Ken. Romantic Texas. (Romantic America Ser.). (Illus.). 144p. 1997. pap. 12.95 (*0-9640185-2-7*) Romantic Amer.
Christensen, Ken & Burher, Bratt. Romantic Big Bear. (Romantic America Ser.). (Illus.). 80p. 1995. pap. 8.95 (*0-9624978-8-6*) Romantic Amer.
Christensen, Ken & Burher, Brett. Romantic Julian. 2nd ed. (Romantic America Ser.). (Illus.). 80p. 1995. pap. 8.95 (*0-9624978-7-8*) Romantic Amer.
***Christensen, Kip.** Turning Pens & Pencils. 2000. pap. 17.95 (*1-86108-100-6*) Guild Master.
Christensen, Kit R. The Politics of Character Development: A Marxist Reappraisal of the Moral Life, 52. LC 93-44512. (Contributions in Philosophy Ser.: Vol. 52). 152p. 1994. 57.95 (*0-313-29213-2*, Greenwood Pr) Greenwood.
Christensen, Kit Richard. Philosophy & Choice Instructor's Manual. 1998. pap. text, teacher ed. write for info. (*0-7674-0600-1*, 0600-1) Mayfield Pub.
Christensen, Knud I. Revision of Crataegus Sect. Crataegus & Nothosect. Crataeguineae (Rosaceae-Maloideae) in the Old World. Anderson, Christiane, ed. (Systematic Botany Monographs: Vol. 35). (Illus.). 199p. 1992. pap. 25.00 (*0-912861-35-5*) Am Soc Plant.
***Christensen, Kyle D.** Herbal First Aid & Health Care: Medicine for a New Millennium. (Illus.). 250p. 2000. pap. 19.95 (*0-914955-90-X*) Lotus Pr.
Christensen, Larry. Diet-Behavior Relationships: Focus on Depression. LC 96-4665. 209p. (Orig.). 1996. pap. text 29.95 (*1-55798-325-9*, 431-7580) Am Psychol.
Christensen, Larry B. Experimental Methodology. 7th ed. LC 96-9207. 590p. 1996. 85.00 (*0-205-26365-8*) Allyn.
***Christensen, Larry B.** Experimental Methodology. 8th ed. 464p. 2000. 78.00 (*0-205-30832-5*) Allyn.
Christensen, Larry B. & Johnson, Burke. Research Methods in Education: A Multimethod Approach. LC 99-33623. 517p. (C). 1999. 77.00 (*0-205-26659-2*, Macmillan Coll) P-H.
Christensen, Larry B. & Stoup, Charles M. Introduction to Statistics for the Social & Behavioral Sciences. LC 86-2313. (Psychology Ser.). 566p. (C). 1986. mass mkt. 42.50 (*0-534-05610-5*) Brooks-Cole.
— Introduction to Statistics for the Social & Behavioral Sciences. 2nd ed. 464p. (C). 1991. mass mkt., student ed. 18.25 (*0-534-15043-8*); student ed. 20.75 (*0-534-15045-4*) Brooks-Cole.
Christensen, Larry B., jt. auth. see Crawford, Helen J.
Christensen, Lars S. Herman. Nordby, Steven, tr. 186p. 1992. pap. 12.00 (*1-877727-24-5*) White Pine.
— The Joker. Nordby, Steven, tr. 200p. 1991. pap. 10.00 (*1-877727-11-3*) White Pine.
Christensen, Lawrence O., et al, eds. Dictionary of Missouri Biography. LC 99-15518. 848p. 1999. 49.95 (*0-8262-1222-0*) U of Mo Pr.
Christensen, Lawrence O. & Kremer, Gary R. A History of Missouri Vol. IV: 1875 to 1919. 304p. 1997. spiral bd. 34.95 (*0-8262-1112-7*) U of Mo Pr.
Christensen, Leese, ed. see Martin, Sharline M.
Christensen, Lela Guymon. Spirit of Music: A Missionary Tool. 5.45 (*1-55517-093-5*) CFI Dist.
Christensen, Linda. Facts, Feelings, Family & Friends: Alcohol & Other Drug-Use Prevention Through Life Skills Development; a Curriculum for Grade K. (Illus.). 156p. (J). (gr. k). 1990. pap. text 32.95 (*0-935908-57-9*, 3047, HazeldenJohnson Inst) Hazelden.
— Facts, Feelings, Family & Friends: Alcohol & Other Drug-Use Prevention Through Life Skills Development; a Curriculum for Grade 1. (Illus.). 155p. 1990. pap. text 32.95 (*0-935908-58-7*, 3048, HazeldenJohnson Inst) Hazelden.
— Facts, Feelings, Family & Friends: Alcohol & Other Drug-Use Prevention Through Life Skills Development; a Curriculum for Grade 1, 7 vols., Set. (Illus.). 1990. 199.95 (*1-56246-173-7*, 3055, HazeldenJohnson Inst) Hazelden.
— Facts, Feelings Family, & Friends: Alcohol & Other Drug-Use Prevention Through Life Skills Development; a Curriculum for Grade 2. (Illus.). 151p. (J). (gr. 2). 1990. pap. text 32.95 (*0-935908-59-5*, 3049, HazeldenJohnson Inst) Hazelden.
— Facts, Feelings, Family & Friends: Alcohol & Other Drug-Use Prevention Through Life Skills Development; a Curriculum for Grade 3. (Illus.). 162p. (J). (gr. 3). 1990. pap. text 32.95 (*0-935908-60-9*, 3051, HazeldenJohnson Inst) Hazelden.
— Facts, Feelings, Family & Friends: Alcohol & Other Drug-Use Prevention Through Life Skills Development; a Curriculum for Grade 4. (Illus.). 168p. (J). (gr. 4). 1990. pap. text 32.95 (*0-935908-61-7*, 3052, HazeldenJohnson Inst) Hazelden.
— Facts, Feelings, Family & Friends: Alcohol & Other Drug-Use Prevention Through Life Skills Development; a Curriculum for Grade 5. (Illus.). 176p. (J). (gr. 5). 1990. pap. text 32.95 (*0-935908-62-5*, 3053, HazeldenJohnson Inst) Hazelden.
Christensen, Linda & DeVol, Philip. How to Start an Elementary Student Assistance Program. LC 93-10670. 1993. 14.95 (*0-89486-941-8*) Hazelden.
Christensen, Linda P., jt. auth. see Smith, Jackie A.
***Christensen, Lisa.** A Hiker's Guide to Art of the Canadian Rockies. 2nd ed. (Illus.). 144p. 2000. pap. 19.95 (*1-894004-39-6*) Fifth Hse Publ.
— A Hiker's Guide to the Rocky Mountain Art of Lawren Harris. (Illus.). 144p. 2000. pap. 19.95 (*1-894004-43-4*) Fifth Hse Publ.
Christensen, Loren. Far Beyond Defensive Tactics: Advanced Concepts, Techniques, Drills, & Tricks for Cops on the Street. LC 99-168662. 208p. 1998. pap. 25.00 (*0-87364-986-9*) Paladin Pr.
— Skid Row Beat: A Street Cop's Walk on the Wild Side. 200p. 1999. pap. 20.00 (*1-58160-012-7*) Paladin Pr.
Christensen, Loren & Artwohl, Alexis. Deadly Force Encounters: What Cops Need to Know to Mentally & Physically Prepare for & Survive a Gunfight. LC 98-120280. 272p. 1997. pap. 22.00 (*0-87364-935-4*) Paladin Pr.
Christensen, Loren W. Anything Goes: Practical Karate for the Streets. (Illus.). 176p. 1990. pap. 16.00 (*0-87364-568-5*) Paladin Pr.
***Christensen, Loren W.** Fighters Fact Book: Over 400 Concepts, Principles & Drills to Make You a Better Fighter. (Illus.). 304p. 2000. pap. 18.95 (*1-880336-37-5*, Pub. by Turtle CT) Weatherhill.
Christensen, Loren W. Fighting Power: How to Develop Explosive Punches, Blocks, & Grappling. LC 97-126441. (Illus.). 248p. 1996. pap. 21.00 (*0-87364-901-X*) Paladin Pr.
***Christensen, Loren W.** Gangbangers: Understanding the Deadly Minds of America's Street Gangs. (Illus.). 200p. 1999. pap. 25.00 (*1-58160-047-X*) Paladin Pr.
Christensen, Loren W. How to Live Safely in a Dangerous World: The Most Complete, Practical Guide on Self... 1996. pap. text 17.95 (*0-918751-45-4*) Act Direct.
— Missing Children. (The Family Ser.). (Illus.). 64p. (J). (gr. 7 up). 1990. lib. bdg. 17.95 (*0-86593-076-7*) Rourke Corp.
— Missing Children. (Family Ser.). (Illus.). 64p. (YA). (gr. 7 up). 1990. lib. bdg. 12.95 (*0-685-46440-7*) Rourke Corp.
— Skinhead Street Gangs. (Illus.). 240p. 1993. pap. 25.00 (*0-87364-756-4*) Paladin Pr.
— Speed Training: How to Develop Your Maximum Speed for Martial Arts. (Illus.). 256p. 1996. pap. 24.00 (*0-87364-859-5*) Paladin Pr.
— The Way Alone: Your Path to Excellence in the Martial Arts. (Illus.). 128p. 1987. pap. 15.00 (*0-87364-421-2*) Paladin Pr.
Christensen, Lowell. Beginning Farming: And What Makes a Sheep Tick. LC 95-151219. (Illus.). 144p. (Orig.). 1994. pap. 9.00 (*0-9642483-0-1*) Pinon Pubng.
— Coping with Texas & Other Staggering Feets: Humor for Texas. LC 91-33930. (Illus.). 96p. 1992. pap. 8.95 (*0-86534-169-9*) Sunstone Pr.
Christensen, Lynn H. The Nonsmoker Solution. LC 94-94331. 192p. 1994. pap. 10.95 (*0-9641059-1-8*) Crystal VA.
Christensen, Lynne, jt. auth. see Christensen, Bob.
Christensen, M. N., jt. auth. see Gilbert, C. M.
Christensen, Marge. Developing Literacy & Workplace Skills: Teaching for 21st Century Employment. LC 98-177599. 278p. 1997. ring bd. 157.00 (*1-879639-51-3*) Natl Educ Serv.
— Motivational English for At-Risk Students: A Language Arts Course That Works. LC 98-160771. 95p. (Orig.). 1992. pap. 18.95 (*1-879639-19-X*) Natl Educ Serv.
Christensen, Mark. Aloha. 1994. 21.00 (*0-671-87023-8*) S&S Trade.
— Faith in Ice Times. (Illus.). 102p. 1997. pap. text 9.95 (*0-926147-10-2*) Loonfeather.
— Wild Life: Unusual Oregon. LC 97-9948. 256p. (Orig.). 1997. pap. 18.95 (*1-57061-050-9*) Sasquatch Bks.
***Christensen, Mark G., et al.** Job Analysis of Chiropractic 2000: A Project Report, Survey Analysis & Summary of Chiropractic Practice Within the United States. 210p. 2000. pap. text 25.00 (*1-884457-04-5*) Natl Bd Chiropract.
Christensen, Matthew B. Teaching Kaleidoscope: A Course in Intermediate to Advanced Spoken Cantonese. 182p. 1996. spiral bd. 35.00 (*0-87415-311-5*, 113A) Foreign Lang.
Christensen, Matthew B. & Jian, Xiaobin. Spoken Cantonese: Performance & Acquisition. (Kaleidoscope Ser.). (Illus.). (Orig.). 1995. 135.00 incl. audio, VHS (*0-87415-268-2*, 114B) Foreign Lang.
— Spoken Cantonese: Performance & Acquisition, Vol. 2. (Kaleidoscope Ser.). (Illus.). 315p. (Orig.). 1995. pap. 35.00 (*0-87415-267-4*, 114E) Foreign Lang.
Christensen, Matthew B., et al. Spoken Cantonese: Acquisition & Presentation. (Kaleidoscope Spoken Cantonese Ser.: No. 3). (Illus.). 267p. 1995. pap. 35.00 (*0-87415-270-4*, 115E); pap. 130.00 incl. audio, VHS (*0-87415-271-2*, 115B) Foreign Lang.
— Spoken Cantonese: Acquisition & Presentation. (Kaleidoscope Spoken Cantonese Ser.: Vol. 3). (Illus.). 267p. 1995. 140.00 incl. VHS, audio compact disk (*0-87415-326-3*, 115D) Foreign Lang.
— Spoken Cantonese: Performance & Acquisition. (Kaleidoscope Spoken Cantonese Ser.: No. 2). (Illus.). 289p. (Orig.). 1995. 140.00 incl. VHS, cd-rom (*0-87415-325-5*, 114D) Foreign Lang.
— Spoken Cantonese: Presentation & Context. (Kaleidoscope Spoken Cantonese Ser.: No. 4). (Illus.). 180p. 1995. pap. 30.00 (*0-87415-273-9*, 116E); pap. 110.00 incl. audio, VHS (*0-87415-274-7*, 116B); pap. 105.00 incl. VHS, cd-rom (*0-87415-327-1*, 116D) Foreign Lang.
Christensen, Matthew B., jt. auth. see Jian, Xiaobin.
Christensen, Max L. Heroes & Saints: More Stories of People Who Made a Difference. LC 97-1588. 144p. 1997. pap. 13.00 (*0-664-25702-X*) Westminster John Knox.
— Poetry of Probably Rare Beauty. LC 98-73079. 85p. 1998. pap. 9.95 (*0-9648562-1-2*) Aspermont.
— Turning Points: Stories of People Who Made a Difference. LC 92-17831. 128p. 1993. pap. 12.00 (*0-664-25357-1*) Westminster John Knox.
Christensen, Max L., jt. auth. see Azzara, Thomas P.
Christensen, Merton, jt. ed. see Coburn, Kathleen.
***Christensen, Michael.** Equipping the Saints: Mobilizing Laity for Ministry. LC 00-29967. 176p. 2000. pap. 16.00 (*0-687-02445-5*) Abingdon.
Christensen, Michael D. Just Be Yourself. LC 97-76974. 1997. pap. 9.95 (*1-57008-343-6*) Bookcraft Inc.
Christensen, Michael J. The Samaritan's Imperative: Compassionate Ministry to People Living with AIDS. LC 90-47212. 208p. 1991. pap. 9.95 (*0-687-36790-5*) Abingdon.
Christensen, Monk D. Not of This World: The Life & Teaching of Fr Seraphim Rose. LC 93-83654. (Illus.). 1056p. 1994. pap. 29.95 (*0-938635-52-2*) St Herman Pr.
Christensen, N. Good Night, Little Kitten. (My First Reader Ser.). (Illus.). 28p. (J). (gr. k-2). 1990. pap. 3.95 (*0-516-45354-8*) Childrens.
Christensen, Nadia, tr. see Flogstad, Kjartan.
Christensen, Nadia, tr. see Larsen, Marianne.
Christensen, Nadia, tr. see Wassmo, Herbjorg.
Christensen, Nadia M., tr. see Wassmo, Herbjorg.
Christensen, Nancy. Who Am I? LC 92-36006. (Illus.). 32p. (J). 1993. pap. 3.99 (*0-590-46192-3*) Scholastic Inc.
Christensen-O'Brien, Janet. The Shattering Hero's Checkered Past. 154p. (Orig.). 1996. pap. 9.95 (*0-9658633-0-1*) Skykomish.
Christensen, Oscar C., ed. Alderian Family Counseling: A Manual for Counselor, Educator, & Psychotherapist. rev. ed. LC 93-70537. 186p. 1993. pap. text 12.95 (*0-932796-56-7*) Ed Media Corp.
Christensen, P. W. Cost Determination Is Not a Mystery. (Technical Papers: Vol. P200A). (Illus.). 12p. 1939. pap. text 30.00 (*1-55589-448-8*) AGMA.
Christensen, Paul. Minding the Underworld: Clayton Eshleman & Late Postmodernism. LC 91-2933. 250p. (C). 1991. 25.00 (*0-87685-822-1*); pap. 15.00 (*0-87685-821-3*) Black Sparrow.
Christensen, Paul T. Russia's Workers in Transition: Labor, Management & the State under Gorbachev & Yeltsin. LC 99-30604. 258p. 2000. 36.00 (*0-87580-253-2*) N Ill U Pr.
Christensen, Peder S. Strategy, Opportunity Identification & Entrepreneurship. 200p. (Orig.). 1989. pap. 40.00 (*87-980308-7-6*) Coronet Bks.
— Strategy, Opportunity Identification & Entrepreneurship: A

An Asterisk (*) at the beginning of an entry indicates that the title is appearing for the first time.

Study of the Entrepreneurial Opportunity Identification Process. 194p. (C). 1990. pap. 16.95 (*87-7288-292-1*, Pub. by Aarhus Univ Pr) David Brown.

Christensen, Per A., jt. auth. see Hansen, Jon L.

Christensen, Peter. The Decline of Iranshahr: Irrigation & Environments in the History of the Middle East 500 B. C. to A. D. 1500. (Illus.). 352p. 1994. 58.00 (*87-7289-259-5*, Pub. by Mus Tusculanum) Paul & Co Pubs.

Christensen, Peter C. Retail Wheeling: A Guide for End-Users. 2nd ed. LC 96-9920. 1996. 89.95 (*0-87814-651-2*) PennWell Bks.

— Retail Wheeling: A Guide for End-Users. 3rd ed. LC 98-34599. 1998. 89.95 (*0-87814-747-0*) PennWell Bks.

Christensen, Pia & James, Alison, eds. Research with Children: Perspectives & Practices. LC 99-39561. (Illus.). 264p. 1999. 66.00 (*0-7507-0975-8*, Pub. by Falmer Pr UK) Taylor & Francis.

***Christensen, Pia M. & James, Allison.** Research with Children. LC 99-39561. 1999. pap. 24.95 (*0-7507-0974-X*, Falmer Pr) Taylor & Francis.

Christensen, R. Computer Implementation of Entropy Minimax. LC 81-202346. (Entropy Minimax Sourcebook Ser.: Vol. 3). x, 254p. 1980. 32.95 (*0-938876-05-8*) Entropy Ltd.

— Fitting Distributions to Data, Vol. XI. (Entropy Minimax Sourcebook Ser.: Vol. 11). 340p. 1990. 34.95 (*0-938876-22-8*) Entropy Ltd.

— Foundations of Inductive Reasoning. LC 80-67726. (Entropy Minimax Sourcebook Ser.: Vol. 7). xii, 363p. 1964. 34.95 (*0-938876-00-7*) Entropy Ltd.

— General Description of Entropy Minimax. LC 81-202346. (Entropy Minimax Sourcebook Ser.: Vol. 1). 692p. 1981. text 39.50 (*0-938876-06-6*) Entropy Ltd.

— Linear Models for Multivariate, Time Series & Spatial Data. (Texts in Statistics Ser.). (Illus.). 336p. 1997. 72.95 (*0-387-97413-X*) Spr-Verlag.

— Log-Linear Models. (Texts in Statistics Ser.). (Illus.). 424p. 1994. 59.95 (*0-387-97398-2*) Spr-Verlag.

— Mathematical Analysis of Bluffing in Poker. LC 80-67727. 60p. 9.50 (*0-938876-33-3*) Entropy Ltd.

— Multivariate Statistical Modeling. LC 81-202346. (Entropy Minimax Sourcebook Ser.: Vol. 5). (Illus.). x, 724p. 1983. lib. bdg. 49.95 (*0-938876-14-7*) Entropy Ltd.

— Philosophical Origins of Entropy Minimax. LC 81-202346. (Entropy Minimax Sourcebook Ser.: Vol. 2). x, 218p. 1980. 29.95 (*0-938876-04-X*) Entropy Ltd.

— Plane Answers to Complex Questions: The Theory of Linear Models. LC 87-4978. (Texts in Statistics Ser.). (Illus.). 390p. (C). 1987. 49.95 (*0-387-96487-8*) Spr-Verlag.

— Statistical Distributions Software Sourcebook. (Entropy Minimax Sourcebook Ser.: Vol. 9). 1985. lib. bdg. 149.00 (*0-938876-20-1*) Entropy Ltd.

— Thermal Mechanical Behavior of UO2 Nuclear Fuel Vol. I: Statistical Analysis of Acoustic Emission Axial Elagation, & Crack Characteristics. xi, 240p. 1978. 34.50 (*0-938876-09-0*) Entropy Ltd.

— Thermal Mechanical Behavior of UO2 Nuclear Fuel Vol. II: Electrothermal Analysis. x, 122p. 1978. 19.50 (*0-938876-10-4*) Entropy Ltd.

— Thermal Mechanical Behavior of UO2 Nuclear Fuel Vol. III: Single Cycle Test Data Discriptions. xii, 321p. 1978. 46.50 (*0-938876-11-2*) Entropy Ltd.

— Thermal Mechanical Behavior of UO2 Nuclear Fuel Vol. IV: Multi-Cycle Test Description. xii, 329p. 1978. 49.50 (*0-938876-12-0*) Entropy Ltd.

Christensen, R., ed. Applications of Entropy Minimax. LC 81-202346. (Entropy Minimax Sourcebook Ser.: Vol. 4). xxii, 787p. 1981. 59.50 (*0-938876-07-4*) Entropy Ltd.

— Thermal Mechanical Behavior of UO2 Nuclear Fuel, 4 vols. 1978. 130.00 (*0-938876-13-9*) Entropy Ltd.

— Thermal Mechanical Behavior of UO2 Nuclear Fuel, 4 vols., Vol. I. 240p. 1978. write for info. (*0-318-51861-9*) Entropy Ltd.

— Thermal Mechanical Behavior of UO2 Nuclear Fuel, 4 vols., Vol. II. 121p. 1978. write for info. (*0-318-51862-7*) Entropy Ltd.

— Thermal Mechanical Behavior of UO2 Nuclear Fuel, 4 vols., Vol. III. 321p. 1978. write for info. (*0-318-51863-5*) Entropy Ltd.

— Thermal Mechanical Behavior of UO2 Nuclear Fuel, 4 vols., Vol. IV. 329p. 1978. write for info. (*0-318-51864-3*) Entropy Ltd.

Christensen, R., et al. Futuristic Community Development: East Central Florida Crime Impact 1974-1984. xxii, 390p. 1973. pap. 15.00 (*0-686-28750-9*, 04-80-04) Entropy Ltd.

Christensen, R. M. Mechanics of Composite Materials. 364p. (C). 1991. reprint ed. 65.95 (*0-89464-501-3*) Krieger.

***Christensen, Ray.** Ending the LDP Hegemony: Party Cooperation in Japan. LC 99-45572. 248p. 2000. text 52.00 (*0-8248-2230-7*); pap. text 27.95 (*0-8248-2295-1*) UH Pr.

Christensen, Ray. Golden Memories. 228p. 1993. 21.95 (*0-931714-52-4*, Pub. by Nodin Pr) Bookmen Inc.

Christensen, Raymond P. Efficient Use of Food Resources in the United States. LC 75-26300. (World Food Supply Ser.). (Illus.). 1976. reprint ed. 15.95 (*0-405-07772-6*) Ayer.

Christensen, Richard L. The Ecumenical Orthodoxy of Charles Augustus Briggs (1841 - 1913) LC 95-3938. 244p. 1995. text 89.95 (*0-7734-2273-0*) E Mellen.

Christensen, Robert, et al. A Review of Diagnostic Clinical Chemistry. (Illus.). 288p. 1999. pap. 29.00 (*0-07-031847-6*) McGraw-Hill HPD.

Christensen, Robert D. Duck Calls of Illinois, 1863-1963. LC 93-30766. (Illus.). 275p. 1994. 65.00 (*0-87580-183-8*) N Ill U Pr.

— Duck Calls of Illinois, 1863-1963. deluxe limited ed. LC 93-30766. (Illus.). 275p. 1994. lthr. 150.00 (*0-87580-182-X*) N Ill U Pr.

— Hematologic Problems in the Neonate. Fletcher, Judy, ed. LC 98-52044. (Illus.). 395p. 1999. text. write for info. (*0-7216-7727-4*, W B Saunders Co) Harcrt Hlth Sci Grp.

Christensen, Roger & Christensen, Karen. Christensen's Ultimate Movie, TV & Rock 'N' Roll Directory. 3rd ed. 1006p. 1988. 39.95 (*0-9608038-3-1*) Cardiff.

Christensen, Roland C. Management Succession in Small & Growing Enterprises. Bruchey, Stuart & Carosso, Vincent P., eds. LC 78-18957. (Small Business Enterprise in America Ser.). 1979. reprint ed. lib. bdg. 19.95 (*0-405-11516-4*) Ayer.

Christensen, Ronald. Belief & Behavior. LC 81-202346. (Entropy Minimax Sourcebook Ser.: Vol. 6). xii, 379p. 1982. 37.95 (*0-938876-16-3*) Entropy Ltd.

— Data Distributions. 2nd ed. (Entropy Minimax Sourcebook Ser.: Vol. 8). (Illus.). x, 364p. 1989. lib. bdg. 36.95 (*0-685-44660-3*) Entropy Ltd.

— The Death of Plato, the Aftermath. LC 84-147854. vii, 120p. 1983. lib. bdg. 8.95 (*0-938876-18-X*) Entropy Ltd.

— Log-Linear Models & Logistic Regression. 2nd ed. LC 97-12465. (Springer Texts in Statistics Ser.). 1997. 64.95 (*0-387-98247-7*) Spr-Verlag.

— Order & Time. (Entropy Minimax Sourcebook Ser.: Vol. 10). (Illus.). x, 134p. (C). 1984. lib. bdg. 19.95 (*0-938876-19-8*) Entropy Ltd.

— Plane Answers to Complex Questions: The Theory of Linear Models. 2nd ed. 452p. 1996. 57.95 (*0-387-94767-1*) Spr-Verlag.

Christensen, Roxane, jt. auth. see Furgitt, Douglas.

Christensen, S., ed. Lithium & the Kidney. (Lithium Therapy Monographs: Vol. 3). (Illus.). xii, 188p. 1990. 164.50 (*3-8055-5042-1*) S Karger.

Christensen, S. A. & Duncan, W. D. Sale of Business in Australia. 378p. 1997. 79.00 (*1-86287-273-2*, Pub. by Federation Pr) Gaunt.

Christensen, Sally H. In Retrospect. 1998. pap. write for info. (*1-57553-837-7*) Watermrk Pr.

Christensen, Sandra, ed. see Caraulia, Algene & Steiger, Linda.

Christensen, Scott, et al. Thailand: The Institutional & Political Underpinnings of Growth. LC 93-23260. (Lessons of East Asia Ser.). 46p. 1993. pap. 22.00 (*0-8213-2608-2*, 12608) World Bank.

Christensen, Scott M. & Turner, Dale R., eds. Folk Psychology & the Philosophy of Mind. 456p. 1993. pap. 59.95 (*0-8058-0931-7*) L Erlbaum Assocs.

Christensen, Scott R. Sagwitch: Shoshone Chieftain, Mormon Elder, 1822-1887. LC 99-6663. (Illus.). 227p. 1999. 36.95 (*0-87421-271-5*); pap. 19.95 (*0-87421-270-7*) Utah St U Pr.

Christensen, Soren, jt. ed. see Scott, W. Richard.

Christensen, Steven M., jt. auth. see Parker, Leonard.

Christensen, T. H. Landfilling of Waste Biogas. 864p. (C). (gr. 13). 1996. 220.00 (*0-419-19400-2*) Chapman & Hall.

Christensen, T. H., ed. Landfilling of Waste Leachate. 656p. (C). (gr. 13). 1992. text 200.00 (*0-419-16140-6*) Chapman & Bkman.

Christensen, T. H., et al, eds. Landfilling of Waste: Barriers. LC 94-211287. (Illus.). 656p. (C). 1994. 200.00 (*0-419-15990-8*, E & FN Spon) Routledge.

Christensen, Terry. Local Politics: Governing at the Grassroots. LC 94-15912. 382p. (C). 1994. pap. text 35.50 (*0-534-13332-0*) Harcourt.

Christensen, Terry, et al. Reflections of the Past: An Anthology of San Jose. Henderson, Judith, ed. LC 96-79975. (Illus.). 400p. 1997. 49.95 (*1-886483-07-8*) Heritge Media.

Christensen, Terry, jt. auth. see Gerston, Larry N.

Christensen, Thomas. Rameau & Musical Thought in the Enlightenment. LC 92-39886. (Cambridge Studies in Music Theory & Analysis: No. 4). (Illus.). 345p. (C). 1994. text 69.95 (*0-521-42040-7*) Cambridge U Pr.

Christensen, Thomas & Christensen, Carol. The U. S. Mexican War. LC 98-24576. 1998. write for info. (*0-912333-57-X*) Bay Books.

Christensen, Thomas, jt. ed. see Baker, Nancy.

Christensen, Thomas, ed. see Carroll, Lewis, pseud.

Christensen, Thomas, tr. see Carpentier, Alejo.

Christensen, Thomas, tr. see Celine, Louis-Ferdinand.

Christensen, Thomas, tr. see Esquivel, Laura.

Christensen, Thomas, tr. see Montalban, Manuel V.

Christensen, Thomas G. An African Tree of Life. LC 89-72148. (American Society of Missiology Ser.). 1990. pap. 22.00 (*0-88344-656-1*) Orbis Bks.

Christensen, Thomas H., et al, eds. Landfilling of Waste - Lining & Leachate Collection. LC 92-26269. 1993. write for info. (*1-85166-898-5*) Elsevier.

Christensen, Thomas J. Useful Adversaries: Grand Strategy, Domestic Mobilization, & Sino-American Conflict, 1947-1958. LC 96-8082. (Studies in International History & Politics). 352p. 1996. text 49.50 (*0-691-02638-6*, Pub. by Princeton U Pr) Cal Prin Full Svc.

— Useful Adversaries: Grand Strategy, Domestic Mobilization, & Sino-American Conflict, 1947-1958. LC 96-8082. (Studies in International History & Politics). 352p. 1996. pap. text 19.95 (*0-691-02637-8*, Pub. by Princeton U Pr) Cal Prin Full Svc.

Christensen, Thomas P. A History of the Danes in Iowa. Scott, Franklyn D., ed. LC 78-15212. (Scandinavians in America Ser.). 1979. reprint ed. lib. bdg. 23.95 (*0-405-11634-9*) Ayer.

Christensen, Tina. Country Celebrations. 1997. pap. 10.50 (*1-56770-378-X*) S Scheewe Pubns.

Christensen, Tom & Christensen, Carol. The U. S. Mexican War. LC 98-24576. (Illus.). 272p. 1998. pap. 24.95 (*0-912333-44-8*) BB&T Inc.

Christensen, Tom & Peters, B. Guy, eds. Structure, Culture, & Governance: A Comparison of Norway & the United States. LC 99-29374. 192p. 1999. 65.00 (*0-8476-9313-9*); pap. 22.95 (*0-8476-9314-7*) Rowman.

Christensen, Tyge. Tribophyceae (Xanthophyceae) (Seaweeds of the British Isles Ser.: Vol. 4). (Illus.). 36p. 1987. pap. 14.95 (*0-11-310004-3*, Pub. by Statnry Office) Balogh.

Christensen, V., jt. ed. see Pauly, Daniel.

Christensen, W. N., jt. auth. see King-Farlow, J.

Christensen, Warren. The National Resource Guide for the Placement of Artists: An Annotated Guide to Organizations & Publications Essential to Artists. Slean, Cheryl, ed. 249p. (Orig.). pap. 45.00 (*0-945941-04-8*) NNAP.

Christensen, Warren, ed. National Directory of Arts Internships: Millenium 7th Edition. 7th rev. ed. LC 89-659041. 443p. 1998. pap. 65.00 (*0-945941-08-0*) NNAP.

***Christensen, Wayne C. & Manuele, Fred A., eds.** Safety Through Design. 279p. 1999. 69.95 (*0-7918-0092-X*) ASME.

Christensen, William E. Glimpses of Our Past: A Pictorial History of Dodge County, Nebraska. LC 94-22575. (Illus.). 1994. write for info. (*0-89865-900-0*) Donning Co.

Christensen, William W. & Stearns, Eugene I. Microcomputers in Health Care Management: Strategies & Applications for the 1990's. 2nd ed. LC 90-271. 256p. 1990. 69.00 (*0-8342-0152-6*) Aspen Pub.

Christensen, Winnie. Spiritual Legacy: Faith for the Next Generation. 1997. pap. text 4.99 (*0-87788-612-1*, H Shaw Pubs) Waterbrook Pr.

— Women Who Achieved for God. (Fisherman Bible Studyguide Ser.). 80p. 1984. pap. text 4.99 (*0-87788-937-6*, H Shaw Pubs) Waterbrook Pr.

— Women Who Achieved for God - Chinese Edition. Wu, Jane C., tr. (CHI.). 90p. 1999. pap. 5.50 (*1-56582-004-5*) Christ Renew Min.

— Women Who Believed God. (Fisherman Bible Studyguide Ser.). 77p. 1983. pap. text 4.99 (*0-87788-936-8*, H Shaw Pubs) Waterbrook Pr.

Christensen, Winnie, jt. auth. see Christensen, Chuck.

Christenso, Evelyn. What Happens When Women Pray. 144p. pap. 9.99 (*0-89693-975-8*, 6-1975) SP Pubns.

— What Happens When Women Pray. deluxe ed. 192p. 12.99 (*1-56476-630-6*) SP Pubns.

***Christenson, Allen J.** Popol Vuh: The Mythic Sections, Tales of First Beginnings from the Ancient Kbicheb-Maya. LC 00-25329. (Ancient Texts & Mormon Studies). 2000. write for info. (*0-934893-52-7*, F A R M S) Brigham.

Christenson, Andrew L. The Last of the Great Expeditions. (Illus.). 32p. 1987. 4.95 (*0-89734-060-4*, PL58-4) Mus Northern Ariz.

Christenson, Andrew L., ed. Tracing Archaeology's Past: The Historiography of Archaeology. LC 88-27278. (Publications in Archaeology). (Illus.). 288p. (C). 1989. 36.95 (*0-8093-1523-8*) S Ill U Pr.

Christenson, Andrew L. & Parry, William J., eds. Excavations on Black Mesa, 1983: A Descriptive Report. LC 82-72189. (Center for Archaeological Investigations Research Paper Ser.: No. 46). xxiv, 719p. 1985. pap. 27.50 incl. fiche (*0-88104-024-X*) Center Archaeol.

Christenson, Andrew L., jt. auth. see Parry, William J.

Christenson, Carroll L. Economic Redevelopment in Bituminous Coal: The Special Case of Technological Advance in United States Coal Mines, 1930-1960. LC 62-8178. (Wertheim Publications in Industrial Relations). (Illus.). 334p. 1962. 20.00 (*0-674-23000-0*) HUP.

Christenson, Charles O. & Voxman, William L. Aspects of Topology. 2nd ed. LC 98-45593. 1998. 75.00 (*0-914351-07-9*); pap. 48.00 (*0-914351-08-7*) BCS Assocs.

Christenson, Charles O., ed. see Brandal, Willy.

Christenson, Christina, et al. Supervising. 336p. 1982. write for info. (*0-201-03431-X*) Addison-Wesley.

Christenson, Cornelia V. Kinsey: A Biography. LC 72-154897. (Illus.). 271p. reprint ed. pap. 84.10 (*0-608-30566-9*, 205521500011) Bks Demand.

Christenson, David M., ed. see Plautus.

Christenson, Dawn E. Veterinary Medical Terminology. Kaszczuk, Selma, ed. 320p. 1996. pap. text 29.00 (*0-7216-4859-2*, W B Saunders Co) Harcrt Hlth Sci Grp.

Christenson, Douglas. Ultrasonic Bioinstrumentation. LC 87-34066. 256p. 1988. text 111.95 (*0-471-60496-8*) Wiley.

Christenson, Duane L. Bible 101: Introduction to Biblical Studies. LC 96-38518. 264p. 1996. pap. 19.95 (*0-941037-37-1*, BIBAL Press) D & F Scott.

— Deuteronomy 1. (Biblical Commentary Ser.: Vol. 6a). 29.99 (*0-8499-0205-3*) Word Pub.

Christenson, E. Guia de Estudio para la Oracion Evangelistica.Tr. of Study Guide for Evangelism Praying. (SPA.). 51p. 1995. student ed. 2.29 (*0-7899-0078-5*, 497280) Editorial Unilit.

Christenson, Evelyn. Cambiame, Senor!Tr. of Lord, Change Me!. 224p. 1992. 8.99 (*0-88113-035-4*) Caribe Betania.

— Changing Your Life Through the Power of Prayer. 512p. 1993. 12.99 (*0-88486-081-7*) Arrowood Pr.

— Gaining Through Losing. LC 80-51630. 180p. 1981. pap. 9.99 (*0-88207-344-3*, 6-2344, Victor Bks) Chariot Victor.

— A Journey into Prayer. 204p. 1995. 9.99 (*1-56476-501-6*, 6-3501, Victor Bks) Chariot Victor.

— A Journey into Prayer. rev. ed. 208p. 1997. 12.99 (*1-56476-629-2*) Chariot Victor.

***Christenson, Evelyn.** Journey into Spiritual Growth: Devotional Selections from Evelyn Christenson. LC 99-15578. 1999. pap. 14.99 (*1-56476-765-5*) SP Pubns.

Christenson, Evelyn. Journey Through Prayer: Reading Is Fun Version. 208p. (J). 1997. 12.99 (*1-56476-710-8*, Victor Bks) Chariot Victor.

— Lord, Change Me! 2nd ed. 192p. 1993. pap. 9.99 (*1-56476-054-5*, 6-3054, Victor Bks) Chariot Victor.

— Lord, Change Me! Leader's Guide. 64p. 1993. pap., teacher ed. 6.50 (*1-56476-055-3*, 6-3055, Victor Bks) Chariot Victor.

— Que Sucede Cuando Oramos por Nuestras Familias?Tr. of What Happens When We Pray for Our Families?. (SPA.). 216p. 1995. 7.99 (*0-7899-0013-0*, 498563) Editorial Unilit.

***Christenson, Evelyn.** What God Does When Women Pray. 168p. 2000. pap. text 11.99 (*0-8499-3761-2*) J Countryman.

Christenson, Evelyn. What Happens When God Answers Prayer? LC 93-38254. 204p. (Orig.). pap. 9.99 (*1-56476-243-2*, 6-3243) SP Pubns.

— What Happens When We Pray for Our Families? LC 92-486. 204p. pap. 9.99 (*0-89693-541-8*, 6-1541) SP Pubns.

— What Happens When Women Pray. 64p. 1992. pap., teacher ed. 6.50 (*0-89693-976-6*, 6-1976, Victor Bks) Chariot Victor.

Christenson, Gary E. Quaternary Faults, Folds & Selected Volcanic Features in the Cedar City 1x2-Degree Quadrangle, Utah. (Miscellaneous Publication Ser.: Vol. 89-6). (Illus.). 29p. 1989. pap. 5.00 (*1-55791-306-4*, MP-89-6) Utah Geological Survey.

— Suggested Approaches to Geologic Hazards Ordinances in Utah. LC QE169.A322. (Circular Ser.: Vol. 79). (Illus.). 16p. 1987. pap. 3.00 (*1-55791-284-X*, C-79) Utah Geological Survey.

Christenson, Gary E., ed. The September 2, 1992, ML 5.8 St. George Earthquake, Washington County, Utah. (Circular of the Utah Geological Survey Ser.: No. 88). (Illus.). 41p. (Orig.). 1995. pap. 6.95 (*1-55791-367-6*, C-88) Utah Geological Survey.

Christenson, Gordon A., jt. auth. see Lillich, Richard B.

Christenson, James A. Zion in Our Neighborhood: The Story of Harvest Hills (1970-1995) LC 97-76078. 121p. 1998. 12.95 (*1-890622-19-2*) Leathers Pub.

Christenson, James A. & Robinson, Jerry W., eds. Community Development in America. LC 80-11046. 255p. reprint ed. pap. 79.10 (*0-608-15240-4*, 202916900059) Bks Demand.

Christenson, Jean M. The Keepers & the Caged: Heroes & Necromancers in the Prison System Today. LC 96-75380. 256p. 1996. pap. text, per. 16.95 (*0-7872-2066-3*) Kendall-Hunt.

Christenson, Kathy. Apples, Bunnies & Bears. (Illus.). 28p. 1984. pap. 5.95 (*0-9605904-8-X*) Hot off Pr.

Christenson, Larry. The Christian Family. LC 75-324692. 224p. 1970. pap. 9.99 (*0-87123-114-X*) Bethany Hse.

— The Covenant. (Trinity Bible Ser.). 152p. 1974. pap., wbk. ed. 5.99 (*0-87123-551-X*) Bethany Hse.

— The Covenant. (Trinity Bible Ser.). 96p. 1985. teacher ed. 9.99 (*0-87123-800-4*) Bethany Hse.

— La Familia Cristiana.Tr. of Christian Family. 238p. 1992. 8.99 (*0-88113-080-X*) Caribe Betania.

— The Kingdom. (Trinity Bible Ser.). 136p. 1972. pap. 5.99 (*0-87123-548-X*) Bethany Hse.

***Christenson, Larry.** Ride the River. 240p. 2000. pap. 10.99 (*0-7642-2374-7*) Bethany Hse.

— Wonderful Way Babies Are Made. rev. ed. (Backyard Ser.). (Illus.). (J). 2000. 12.99 (*0-7642-2341-0*) Bethany Hse.

Christenson, Larry. The Wonderful Way That Babies Are Made. LC 82-12813. 48p. (J). (ps up). 1982. text 12.99 (*0-87123-627-3*) Bethany Hse.

Christenson, Larry & Hendricks, Howard. El Orden de Dios para la Familia. 2nd ed. Carrodeguas, Angel, tr. from ENG.Tr. of Families Go Better. (SPA.). 80p. (C). 1989. pap. 6.99 (*0-88113-242-X*) Caribe Betania.

Christenson, Laurie. Exception to the Rule. (Orig.). 1997. pap. write for info. (*1-57553-499-1*) Watermrk Pr.

Christenson, Lynne E. Mammalian Faunal Butchering Practices at an Inland La Jollan Site (CA-SDI-6153) viii, 115p. (C). 1985. reprint ed. pap. text 13.75 (*1-55567-015-6*) Coyote Press.

Christenson, Margaret A. Aging in the Designed Environment. LC 90-4421. (Physical & Occupational Therapy in Geriatrics Ser.: Vol. 8, Nos. 3 & 4). 133p. 1990. text 39.95 (*1-56024-031-8*) Haworth Pr.

Christenson, Norman, ed. see Gagnon, William C.

Christenson, Peter G. & Roberts, Donald F. It's Not Only Rock & Roll: Popular Music in the Lives of Adolescents. LC 97-43499. (Communication Ser.). 320p. (C). 1998. text 65.00 (*1-57273-142-7*); pap. text 23.95 (*1-57273-143-5*) Hampton Pr NJ.

Christenson, Rand A. Rocky Mountain Gourmet: The Complete How-To Guide on Starting Your Own Gourmet Dining Group. (Illus.). 75p. (Orig.). 1997. pap. 12.95 (*0-9651602-0-3*) Colo Weight-Away.

Christenson, Reo M. The Brannan Plan: Farm Politics & Policy. LC 74-10728. 207p. 1974. reprint ed. lib. bdg. 59.50 (*0-8371-7650-6*, CHBP, Greenwood Pr) Greenwood.

Christenson, Ron. Political Trials: Gordian Knots in the Law. 2nd expanded rev. ed. LC 98-27092. 327p. 1998. pap. 29.95 (*0-7658-0473-5*) Transaction Pubs.

Christenson, Ronald J., ed. Political Trials in History: From Antiquity to the Present. 420p. (C). 1991. 59.95 (*0-88738-406-4*) Transaction Pubs.

Christenson, Ronald S. Political Trials: Gordian Knots in the Law. 252p. (Orig.). 1989. pap. 24.95 (*0-88738-776-4*) Transaction Pubs.

Christenson, Sandra L., jt. auth. see Ysseldyke, James E.

Christenson, Tom D., jt. auth. see Taylor, James C.

C

Christenson, Toni, et al. The Tree Book: Teaching Responsible Enviromental Education, Vol. 1. (Illus.). 78p. (Orig.). 1981. teacher ed. 6.95 (*0-686-36286-1*) Creative Curriculum.

Christer, Anthony H., et al. Stochastic Modelling in Innovative Manufacturing. LC 96-43259. (Lecture Notes in Economics & Mathematical Systems Ser.: Vol. 445). (Illus.). 361p. 1996. 78.00 (*3-540-61768-X*) Spr-Verlag.

Christesen, C. B. The Troubled Eyes of Women & Other Stories. 1990. pap. 14.95 (*0-7022-2271-2*, Pub. by Univ Queensland Pr) Intl Spec Bk.

Christeson, R. P. The Old-Time Fiddler's Repertory: Two Hundred Forty-Five Traditional Tunes, Vol. 2. 188p. 1984. 27.50 (*0-8262-0440-6*) U of Mo Pr.

Christgau, John. The Origins of the Jump Shot: Eight Men Who Shook the World of Basketball. LC 98-37508. (Illus.). xii, 220p. 1999. pap. 15.00 (*0-8032-6394-5*) U of Nebr Pr.

— Sierra Sue II: The Story of a P-51 Mustang. (Illus.). 188p. (Orig.). 1994. pap. 15.00 (*0-9640256-0-4*) Great Planes.

***Christgau, Robert.** Any Old Way You Choose It: Rock & Other Pop Music, 1967-1973. 2000. pap. 16.95 (*0-8154-1041-7*) Cooper Sq.

— Christgau's Consumer Guide: Albums of the 90's. 544p. 2000. pap. 19.95 (*0-312-24560-2*, St Martin Griffin) St Martin.

Christgau, Robert. Grown up All Wrong: 75 Great Rock & Pop Artists from Vaudeville to Techno. LC 98-25779. 448p. 1998. 29.95 (*0-674-44318-7*) HUP.

***Christgau, Robert.** Grown up All Wrong: 75 Great Rock & Pop Artists from Vaudeville to Techno. 528p. 2000. pap. 18.95 (*0-674-00382-9*) HUP.

Christgau, Robert. Rock Albums of the Seventies: A Critical Guide. (Quality Paperbacks Ser.). Orig. Title: Christgau's Record Guide: Rock Albums of the 70's. 480p. 1990. reprint ed. pap. 15.95 (*0-306-80409-3*) Da Capo.

Christhilf, Mark M. W. S. Merwin the Mythmaker. LC 85-20123. (Literary Frontiers Ser.: No. 26). 88p. 1986. pap. 9.95 (*0-8262-0478-3*) U of Mo Pr.

Christi, Patricia, ed. see Galatz, Malcolm.

Christiaans, Henri, jt. ed. see Cross, Nigel.

Christiaens, M. R. & De Wever, I., eds. Non Palpable Breast Lesions. (Surgical Oncology Ser.: No. 3). (Illus.). 126p. (Orig.). 1996. pap. 49.50 (*90-6186-734-7*, Pub. by Leuven Univ) Coronet Bks.

Christian. Art of Wondering. 7th ed. (C). 1998. text 71.00 (*0-15-505592-5*, Pub. by Harcourt Coll Pubs) Harcourt.

Christian. Can It Really Rain Frogs? Shake, Rattle & Roll ; What Makes the Grand Canyon Grand? 372p. pap. 34.95 (*0-471-29582-5*) Wiley.

Christian. Developing Client/Server Applications. 1996. text 50.00 (*0-07-011277-0*) McGraw.

— Materials Science Progression, ser. vol. 24. (Progress in Materials Science Ser.). 1980. pap. 39.00 (*0-08-026014-4*, no. 3, Pergamon Pr) Elsevier.

— Philosophy. 6th ed. (C). 1994. pap. text, teacher ed. 33.75 (*0-15-500612-6*) Harcourt Coll Pubs.

Christian & Scamehorn, John F., eds. Solubilization in Surfactant Aggregates. (Surfactant Science Ser.: 55). (Illus.). 568p. 1995. text 215.00 (*0-8247-9099-5*) Dekker.

***Christian, James W.** The Courier. LC 00-190544. 428p. 2000. 25.00 (*0-7388-1800-3*); pap. 18.00 (*0-7388-1801-1*) Xlibris Corp.

Christian & Missionary Alliance Home Department St. The Pastor's Handbook: (KJV) King James Version. 102p. 1989. 10.99 (*0-87509-118-0*, KJV) Chr Pubns.

— Pastor's Handbook: (NIV) New International Version. rev. ed. LC 88-93031. 1989. 10.99 (*0-87509-417-1*, NIV) Chr Pubns.

Christian, Abraham D. La Salle des Pieds Perdus: Drawing (Zeichung) LC 98-74406. 64p. 1999. pap. 10.00 (*1-893207-01-3*) Edgewise Pr.

***Christian, Anna.** Meet it, Greet it & Defeat It. 196p. 1999. pap. 13.95 (*1-881524-47-7*) Milligan Bks.

Christian, Anne H. The Search for Holmes, Robson, Hind, Steele & Graham Families of Cumberland & Northumberland, England. (Illus.). 184p. 1985. 12.95 (*0-9613723-0-3*) Search CA.

Christian, Barbara. Black Feminist Criticism: Perspectives on Black Women Writers. LC 84-22805. (Athene Ser.). 350p. 1985. text 50.00 (*0-08-031956-4*, Pergamon Pr); pap. text 19.95 (*0-08-031955-6*, Pergamon Pr) Elsevier.

— Black Feminist Criticism: Perspectives on Black Women Writers. LC 97-6898. (Athene Ser.). 276p. (C). 1985. pap. text 19.95 (*0-8077-6253-9*) Tchrs Coll.

— Black Women Novelists: The Development of a Tradition, 1892-1976, 52. LC 79-8953. (Contributions in Afro-American & African Studies: No. 52). 275p. 1980. 59.95 (*0-313-20750-X*, CBW/) Greenwood.

Christian Broadcasting Network Staff, ed. The Christian Counselor's Handbook. 240p. 1987. pap. 16.99 (*0-8423-0255-7*) Tyndale Hse.

Christian, C. Donald, jt. auth. see Zuspan, Frederick P.

Christian, Catherine. The Pendragon. 1984. mass mkt. 3.95 (*0-446-32342-X*, Pub. by Warner Bks) Little.

Christian, Charles. Brief Treatise on the Police of the City of New York. LC 76-112548. (Rise of Urban America Ser.). 1976. reprint ed. 17.95 (*0-405-02442-8*) Ayer.

Christian, Charles B. Understanding Revelation. (Illus.). 168p. 1996. pap. 12.95 (*0-614-97244-2*) Anchor Pub Co.

***Christian, Charles M.** Black Saga: The African American Experience: A Chronology. LC 98-45495. 624p. 1998. pap. text 20.00 (*1-58243-000-4*) Basic Civitas.

Christian, Cheryl. Donde Esta el Bebe? Fiol, Maria, tr. LC 99-70752. Orig. Title: Where's the Baby?. (SPA., Illus.). 12p. (J). 2000. bds. 5.50 (*1-887734-26-0*) Star Brght Bks.

— Donde Esta el Gatito? Fiol, Maria, tr. from ENG. LC 99-70753. Orig. Title: Where's the Kitten?. (SPA., Illus.). 12p. (J). 2000. bds. 5.50 (*1-887734-28-7*) Star Brght Bks.

— Donde Esta el Perrito? Fiol, Maria, tr. from ENG. LC 99-70754. Orig. Title: Where's the Puppy?. (SPA., Illus.). 12p. (J). 2000. bds. 5.50 (*1-887734-29-5*) Star Brght Bks.

— How Many? LC 99-70747. (Illus.). 12p. (J). 2000. bds. 4.95 (*1-887734-66-X*) Star Brght Bks.

— Matty & Patty. LC 97-25375. (Domino Readers Ser.). (Illus.). 24p. (J). (ps-1). 1998. pap. 5.95 (*1-887734-30-9*) Star Brght Bks.

— What Happens Next? large type ed. LC 96-67573. (Peek-A-Boo Ser.). (J). 1997. 3.95 (*1-887734-10-4*) Star Brght Bks.

— Where Does It Go? LC 99-70746. (Illus.). 12p. (J). 2000. bds. 4.95 (*1-887734-65-1*) Star Brght Bks.

— Where's the Baby? large type ed. LC 96-67572. (Peek-A-Boo Ser.). (J). 1997. 3.95 (*1-887734-07-4*) Star Brght Bks.

— Where's the Kitten? large type ed. LC 96-67575. (Peek-A-Boo Ser.). (J). 1997. 3.95 (*1-887734-08-2*) Star Brght Bks.

— Where's the Puppy? large type ed. (Peek-A-Boo Ser.). (J). 1997. 3.95 (*1-887734-09-0*) Star Brght Bks.

— Y Ahora, Que Pasara? Fiol, Maria, tr. from ENG. LC 99-70751. Orig. Title: What Happens Next?. (SPA., Illus.). 12p. (J). 2000. bds. 5.50 (*1-887734-27-9*) Star Brght Bks.

Christian, Cheryl, ed. What Happens Next? (Photo Flap Bks.). (Illus.). 12p. (J). (ps). 1991. 4.95 (*1-56288-131-0*) Checkerboard.

— Where's the Baby? (Illus.). 12p. (J). (ps). 1992. 4.95 (*1-56288-128-0*) Checkerboard.

— Where's the Kitten? (Photo Flap Bks.). (Illus.). 12p. (J). (ps). 1992. 4.95 (*1-56288-130-2*) Checkerboard.

— Where's the Puppy? (Photo Flap Bks.). (Illus.). 12p. (J). (ps). 1992. 4.95 (*1-56288-129-9*) Checkerboard.

Christian, Chris. The Gun Digest Book of Trap & Skeet Shooting. 3rd ed. LC 83-70143. (Illus.). 288p. 1994. pap. 17.95 (*0-87349-163-7*, TS3, DBI Bks) Krause Pubns.

— Handgun Digest. 3rd ed. LC 87-71767. (Illus.). 256p. 1995. pap. 18.95 (*0-87349-176-9*, HAN3, DBI Bks) Krause Pubns.

— How to Get Started in Christian Music. Styll, John, ed. 167p. 1986. 12.95 (*0-9616817-0-5*) Home Sweet Home.

Christian Coalition Staff. The Contract with the American Family. 176p. 1995. pap. 8.99 (*0-345-40253-7*, Moorings) Ballantine Pub Grp.

Christian Communities, Lugdumun & Vienna Staff. Epistle of the Gallican Churches, Lugdunum & Vienna. 1990. pap. 2.95 (*0-89981-123-X*) Eastern Orthodox.

Christian, D., et al. Robotech: Zentraedi Breakout. Marciniszyn, Alex et al, eds. (Robotech RPG Adventures Ser.). (Illus.). 64p. (Orig.). (YA). (gr. 8 up). 1994. pap. 9.95 (*0-916211-67-3*, 561) Palladium Bks.

Christian, David. A History of Russia, Central Asia, & Mongolia: Inner Eurasia from Prehistory to the Mongol Empire. LC 98-3677. (History of the World Ser.: Vol. I). (Illus.). 464p. 1999. 62.95 (*0-631-18321-3*); pap. 27.95 (*0-631-20814-3*) Blackwell Pubs.

— Imperial & Soviet Russia: Power, Priviledge, & the Challenge of Modernity. LC 96-50058. 472p. 1997. text 59.95 (*0-312-17351-2*) St Martin.

— Imperial & Soviet Russia: Power, Priviledge & the Challenge of Modernity. LC 96-50058. 472p. 1997. pap. 19.95 (*0-312-17352-0*) St Martin.

— Living Water: Vodka & Russian Society on the Eve of Emancipation. (Illus.). 458p. 1990. text 95.00 (*0-19-822286-6*) OUP.

Christian, Deborah. Kar Kalim. LC 97-7599. 384p. 1997. text 23.95 (*0-312-86341-1*) St Martin.

— Kar Kalim. 1998. mass mkt. 5.99 (*0-8125-7190-8*, Pub. by Tor Bks) St Martin.

— Mainline. 1997. mass mkt. 5.99 (*0-614-27808-2*); mass mkt. 5.99 (*0-8125-4908-2*, Pub. by Tor Bks) St Martin.

***Christian, Deborah.** The Seeker's Acolyte. 2001. text. write for info. (*0-312-86517-1*) St Martin.

— The Truthsayer's Apprentice. 384p. 1999. pap. 15.95 (*0-312-86516-3*, Pub. by Tor Bks); text 27.95 (*0-312-87269-0*, Pub. by Tor Bks) St Martin.

Christian, Diane. Wide-Ons. LC 81-8979. 64p. 1981. 9.00 (*0-912184-00-0*); pap. 4.00 (*0-912184-01-9*) Synergistic Pr.

Christian, Diane, jt. auth. see Jackson, Bruce.

Christian Difference Staff, ed. Christian Difference. 544p. 1999. pap. text 35.00 (*0-536-02642-4*) P-H.

Christian, Donna. Guide to Newspaper Holdings at the Center for Archival Collections. 64p. 1980. write for info. (*0-932690-03-3*) Ctr for Arch Collects.

Christian, Donna, et al. Variation & Change in Geographically Isolated Communities: Appalachian English & Ozark English. (Publications of the American Dialect Society: No. 74). 176p. 1989. pap. text 22.00 (*0-8173-0419-3*) U of Ala Pr.

Christian, Donna, jt. auth. see Wolfram, Walt.

Christian, Durnell. Rude Awakening. (Illus.). 112p. 1996. pap. 12.95 (*0-939767-25-2*) D McMillan.

***Christian, Edmund B.** Post-Colonial Detective. LC 99-43512. 2000. text 55.00 (*0-312-22831-7*) St Martin.

Christian, Edmund B. Short History of Solicitors. xiv, 255p. 1983. reprint ed. 35.00 (*0-8377-0448-0*, Rothman) W S Hein.

Christian Education Staff. Foundations: Shaping the Ministry of Christian Education in Your Congregation. LC 93-71103. 96p. 1993. pap. 11.95 (*0-88177-123-6*, DR123) Discipleship Res.

Christian, Edwin E. Joyce Cary's Creative Imagination. (American University Studies: English Language & Literature: Ser. IV, Vol. 68). X, 266p. (C). 1988. text 34.95 (*0-8204-0576-0*) P Lang Pubng.

***Christian, Eleanor & Roth-Singer, Lyzz.** Let's Make Butter. LC 00-36475. (Illus.). (J). 2000. write for info. (*0-7368-0728-4*) Capstone Pr.

— Looking at Ants. LC 00-36474. (Illus.). (J). 2000. write for info. (*0-7368-0725-X*) Capstone Pr.

Christian, Erich. LC-Filters: Design, Testing & Manufacturing. LC 82-13425. (Wiley Series on Filters). 262p. reprint ed. pap. 81.30 (*0-7837-2833-6*, 205763900006) Bks Demand.

Christian, F., et al, eds. Dependable Computing for Critical Applications 4. LC 95-3217. (Dependable Computing & Fault-Tolerant Systems Ser.: Vol. 9). 1995. 137.00 (*3-211-82649-1*) Spr-Verlag.

Christian, F. W. Vocabulary of the Mangaian Language. (BMB Ser.). 1974. reprint ed. pap. 25.00 (*0-527-02114-8*) Periodicals Srv.

***Christian Focus Publishing Staff.** Chequebook of the Bank of Faith. 378p. 2000. pap. 15.99 (*1-85792-494-0*); pap. 15.99 (*1-85792-495-9*) Christian Focus.

Christian Focus Publishing Staff. A Fistful of Heroes. 1998. pap. 9.99 (*1-85792-237-9*, Pub. by Christian Focus) Spring Arbor Dist.

***Christian Focus Publishing Staff.** God's Dreamer: The Story of Joseph. (Bible Wise Ser.). 2000. pap. 2.99 (*1-85792-343-X*) Christian Focus.

Christian Focus Publishing Staff. God's Words. 1998. pap. 12.99 (*1-85792-388-X*, Pub. by Christian Focus) Spring Arbor Dist.

***Christian Focus Publishing Staff.** Little Rich Man. 2000. 3.99 (*1-85792-345-6*) Christian Focus.

— Miracle on the Road: The Story of Paul. (Bible Wise Ser.). 2000. pap. 2.99 (*1-85792-344-8*) Christian Focus.

— On the Way, Vol. 7. (J). 2000. pap. 10.99 (*1-85792-327-8*) Christian Focus.

— Safe at Sea. 2000. pap. 3.99 (*1-85792-346-4*) Christian Focus.

— Singing Shepherd - David. 1999. 3.99 (*1-85792-463-0*) Christian Focus.

— Special Baby - Jesus. (Illus.). 10p. (ps-k). 1999. 3.99 (*1-85792-464-9*) Christian Focus.

Christian Focus Staff. Los Amigos de Jesus. (Serie Uniendo los Puntos - Dot to Dot Ser.: No. 1).Tr. of Friends of Jesus. (SPA.). 18p. (J). 1994. pap. 1.59 (*1-56063-388-3*, 494013) Editorial Unilit.

— Finding God in the Darkness. 1998. pap. 7.99 (*1-85792-121-6*, Pub. by Christian Focus) Spring Arbor Dist.

— Personas Ocupadas. (Serie Uniendo los Puntos - Dot to Dot Ser.: No. 2).Tr. of Busy People. (SPA.). 17p. (J). 1993. pap. 1.59 (*1-56063-387-5*, 494012) Editorial Unilit.

Christian Focus Staff. Shorter Catechism. 1997. pap. 1.99 (*1-85792-288-3*, Pub. by Christian Focus) Spring Arbor Dist.

Christian Focus Staff. Traveling Though the Promised Land, 1. 1998. 9.99 (*1-85792-272-7*) Christian Focus.

Christian Focus Staff, ed. The Authentic Church. 1998. pap. 12.99 (*1-85792-197-6*, Pub. by Christian Focus) Spring Arbor Dist.

— Daniel. 1998. pap. 11.99 (*1-85792-249-2*, Pub. by Christian Focus) Spring Arbor Dist.

— On the Way, Bk. 6. 1998. pap. 6.99 (*1-85792-326-X*, Pub. by Christian Focus) Spring Arbor Dist.

— Territorial Spirit & World Evangelisation. 1998. pap. 15.99 (*1-85792-399-5*, Pub. by Christian Focus) Spring Arbor Dist.

— That's Just the Way It Is. 1998. pap. 10.99 (*1-85792-331-6*, Pub. by Christian Focus) Spring Arbor Dist.

***Christian Focus U. K. Staff.** Pleasantness of a Religious Life. 1998. 6.99 (*1-85792-391-X*, Pub. by Christian Focus) Spring Arbor Dist.

Christian, Frank & Brown, Cal. Augusta National & the Masters: A Photographer's Scrapbook. (Illus.). 210p. 1996. 45.00 (*1-886947-11-2*) Sleeping Bear.

Christian, Frank, jt. auth. see Gelsanliter, Wendy.

Christian, Frederick W. Eastern Pacific Lands: Tahiti & the Marquesas Islands. LC 75-35185. (Illus.). reprint ed. 47.50 (*0-404-14212-5*) AMS Pr.

Christian, G. D. Talanta U. S. A. Honor Issue. 320p. 1989. pap. 76.50 (*0-08-037208-2*, Pergamon Pr) Elsevier.

Christian, Gabriel J. Rain on a Tin Roof. pap. 10.00 (*0-9668454-1-2*) Pond Casse.

Christian, Garna L. Black Soldiers in Jim Crow Texas, 1899-1917. LC 94-42428. (Centennial Series of the Association of Former Students: No. 57). (Illus.). 256p. 1995. 35.00 (*0-89096-637-0*) Tex A&M Univ Pr.

Christian, Gary D. Analytical Chemistry. 5th ed. LC 93-32933. 840p. 1993. text 102.95 (*0-471-59761-9*) Wiley.

— Analytical Chemistry: Solutions Manual. 5th ed. 168p. 1994. pap. 36.95 (*0-471-30978-8*) Wiley.

Christian, Gary D. & Feldman, Fredric J. Atomic Absorption Spectroscopy: Applications in Agriculture, Biology & Medicine. LC 78-23204. 512p. 1979. reprint ed. lib. bdg. 39.50 (*0-88275-797-0*) Krieger.

Christian, Gary D., jt. auth. see Hadjiioannou, T. P.

Christian, George. The World of Texas Politics. (Symposia Ser.). 170p. 1989. pap. 7.00 (*0-89940-424-3*) LBJ Sch Pub Aff.

Christian, Glynn. Edible France: A Traveller's Guide. (Illus.). 200p. 1997. pap. 15.00 (*1-56656-221-X*) Interlink Pub.

Christian, Harry. The Making of Anti-Sexist Men. LC 93-39857. (Male Orders Ser.). 224p. (C). 1994. pap. 24.99 (*0-415-09762-2*, B4219) Routledge.

***Christian Heritage Staff.** Christian Heritage of Our Nation: History Curriculum, U.S. Presidents & Their Churches. 1999. 24.95 (*0-9658616-4-3*) Christ Herit.

***Christian History Magazine Staff.** 131 Christians Everyone Should Know. 2000. pap. 14.99 (*0-8054-9040-X*) Broadman.

Christian, J. E., jt. auth. see Jocson, Antonio.

Christian, J. L., et al, eds. Environmental Effects on Advanced Composite Materials - STP 602. 102p. 1976. 10.00 (*0-8031-0333-6*, STP602) ASTM.

Christian, J. W., et al, eds. Materials Science Progress: Anniversary Vol. - Progress in Materials Science. (Illus.). 330p. 1981. 61.00 (*0-08-027147-2*, Pergamon Pr) Elsevier.

— Progress in Material Science, Vol. 24. (Illus.). 346p. 1980. 115.00 (*0-08-027107-3*, Pergamon Pr) Elsevier.

— Progress in Materials Science, Vol. 26. (Illus.). 420p. 1982. 145.00 (*0-08-029122-8*, Pergamon Pr) Elsevier.

— Progress in Materials Science, Vol. 27. (Illus.). 460p. 1983. 145.00 (*0-08-030029-4*, Pergamon Pr) Elsevier.

— Progress in Materials Science, Vol. 29. (Illus.). 394p. 1986. 156.00 (*0-08-034154-3*, Pub. by PPL) Elsevier.

Christian, J. W., et al. Progress in Materials Science, Vol. 25. 1982. 120.00 (*0-08-029096-5*, Pergamon Pr) Elsevier.

Christian, Jack. Marketing Designs for Nonprofit Organizations. 250p. 1992. 49.00 (*0-930807-38-3*, 600316) Fund Raising.

Christian, James L. Extra-Terrestrial Intelligence: The First Encounter. 1976. pap. 6.00 (*0-87980-350-9*) Wilshire.

— Philosophy: An Introduction to the Art of Wondering. 6th ed. 650p. (C). 1994. text 71.00 (*0-15-500373-9*) Harcourt Coll Pubs.

Christian, James L., ed. Extraterrestrial Intelligence: The First Encounter. LC 76-25328. (Science & the Paranormal Ser.). 303p. (C). 1976. pap. 22.95 (*0-87975-064-2*) Prometheus Bks.

Christian, Janet L. & Greger, Janet. Assess Pads Nutritn Livg. 3rd ed. (Illus.). 736p. 1991. pap. text 5.95 (*0-8053-1007-X*) Benjamin-Cummings.

— Nutrition for Living: Study Guide. 3rd ed. (Illus.). 736p. 1991. pap. text, student ed. 19.95 (*0-8053-1004-5*) Benjamin-Cummings.

— Trans Nutrition Living. 3rd ed. (Illus.). 736p. 1991. trans. 268.95 (*0-8053-1005-3*) Benjamin-Cummings.

Christian, Janus. Rebirth of Eden: The Final Sexual Culture Revolution. 110p. Date not set. 20.01 (*0-614-97217-5*) Powerhse Publng.

Christian, Jay & Heavirland, Helen. Falling for a Lie: New Age Beliefs Nearly Killed Me. Wade, Kenneth R., ed. LC 97-47666. 218p. 1998. pap. 10.99 (*0-8163-1646-5*) Pacific Pr Pub Assn.

Christian, Jeffery. Forgiveness & Reconciliation. (C). 1988. 40.00 (*0-85439-137-1*, Pub. by St Paul Pubns) St Mut.

Christian, Johan. The Miracle of the Sacred Scroll: A Novel of Hope & Inspiration. LC 97-68721. Orig. Title: The Merchant from Bethelehem. 112p. 1997. 14.95 (*0-914984-73-X*) Starburst.

Christian, Johann. Systema Piezatorum. Fabricus. fac. ed. (DAN.). 472p. 1974. reprint ed. 53.00 (*3-201-00879-6*, Pub. by Akademische Druck-und) Balogh.

— Systema Rhyngotorum. Fabricus. fac. ed. (DAN.). 346p. 1971. reprint ed. 44.00 (*3-201-00724-2*, Pub. by Akademische Druck-und) Balogh.

Christian, John. The Oxford Union Murals. LC 79-23664. (Chicago Visual Library: CVL 33). (Illus.). 84p. 1981. lib. bdg. 29.00 (*0-226-68922-0*) U Ch Pr.

Christian, John, ed. The Last Romantics: The Romantic Tradition in British Art: Burne-Jones to Stanley Spencer. (Illus.). 208p. (C). 1995. reprint ed. pap. 39.95 (*0-85331-552-3*, Pub. by Lund Humphries) Antique Collect.

Christian, John G., jt. auth. see Turner, William W.

Christian, K. A Guide to Modula-2. (Texts & Monographs in Computer Science). (Illus.). 465p. 1985. pap. 51.00 (*0-387-96242-5*) Spr-Verlag.

Christian, Kaare. The UNIX Command Reference Guide: The Top 50 UNIX Commands. LC 87-20969. 361p. 1988. pap. 32.95 (*0-471-85580-4*) Wiley.

Christian, Kaare & Raskin, Robin. The Illuminated Manuscript: Mastering Lotus' Word Processing Software. 400p. (C). 1988. pap. 21.95 (*0-685-19355-1*) P-H.

Christian, Karen. Show & Tell: Identity As Performance in U. S. Latino/A Fiction. LC 97-4875. 189p. 1997. 39.95 (*0-8263-1796-0*); pap. 19.95 (*0-8263-1831-2*) U of NM Pr.

Christian, Karon. Lottery of Love: The Romance Guide for the Next Century, an Astrological Handbook to Relationships - the Ultimate Formula for Marriage! 160p. (Orig.). 1994. pap. 14.95 (*0-9648317-3-2*) Patterson CA.

Christian, Kent, jt. ed. see Cohen, Jennifer.

Christian, Kristy L. & Merrill, Kathryn L. Moses & the Law. (Illus.). (Orig.). (J). (gr. 3 up). 1996. spiral bd. 19.95 (*0-9626535-0-0*) Infinite Discovery.

— Paul & Early Christianity Vol. I: Acts 1-9. (Illus.). 208p. (YA). (gr. 6-12). 1996. spiral bd., wbk. ed. 19.95 (*0-9626535-1-9*) Infinite Discovery.

— Paul & Early Christianity Vol. II: Acts 10-28. (Illus.). 234p. (YA). (gr. 6-12). 1996. spiral bd., wbk. ed. 19.95 (*0-9626535-2-7*) Infinite Discovery.

Christian, Lana & Makely, Sherry. Go Bananas or Get the Facts! A Student Guide to Career Hunting in Today's Changing Health Care Scene. (Illus.). 23p. (YA). 1996. pap. 5.95 (*0-9652954-1-9*) Pine Ridge Publns.

Christian, Lana, jt. auth. see Makely, Sherry.

Christian, Lana, ed. see Makely, Sherry.

Christian, Leah. Discover Turkey: Year-Round Recipes for Parts & Leftovers. 24p. (Orig.). 1988. pap. 4.00 (*0-685-25279-5*) Family Rm Pr.

Christian Life Magazine Staff. America's Great Revivals. 96p. 1970. reprint ed. mass mkt. 4.99 (*0-87123-003-8*) Bethany Hse.

Christian, Lucia. Prayers & Poems from the Leeward Side. Schrader, Richard A., Sr., ed. LC 97-91269. (Illus.). 108p. 1998. pap. write for info. (*0-9622987-7-8*) R A Schrader.

***Christian, Lue & Christian, Shannon.** Cycling Across North America: A Leisurely Route from Coast to Coast. (Cycling Resources Ser.). (Illus.). 272p. 2000. pap. 16.95 (*1-892495-24-4*, 244, Pub. by Van der Plas) Seven Hills Bk.

***Christian, M., ed.** Dirty Words: Provocative Erotica. 224p. 2001. pap. 14.95 (*1-55583-563-5*, Pub. by Alyson Pubns) Consort Bk Sales.

Christian, M., ed. Eros Ex Machina. 1998. mass mkt. 7.95 (*1-56333-593-X*, Rhinoceros) Masquerade.

***Christian, M., ed.** Guilty Pleasures. 240p. 2000. pap. 15.00 (*1-892723-02-6*) Black Books.

Christian, M., ed. Midsummer Night's Dreams: One Story, Many Tales. 1998. mass mkt. 7.95 (*1-56333-679-0*, Rhinoceros) Masquerade.

Christian, M., jt. ed. see Sheppard, Simon.

Christian, M. I., et al. Text Generation & Systemic-Functional Linguistics. 384p. 1992. text 69.00 (*0-86187-711-X*, Pub. by P P Pubs) Cassell & Continuum.

Christian, Marcus. I Am New Orleans: And Other Poems by Marcus Christian. Lewis, Rudolph & Sharif, Amin, eds. (Occasional Publications Ser.). 112p. 1999. pap. 8.95 (*1-883275-08-3*) Xavier Rev.

Christian, Margaret. Performance Enhancement - Plans for LTC Employees. 309p. 1995. student ed. 39.50 (*0-929442-24-5*, 2237pp) Prof Prntng & Pub.

***Christian, Mark A.** Multiracial Identity: an International Perspective. 2000. text 59.95 (*0-312-23219-5*) St Martin.

Christian, Mark A., tr. see Schnackenburg, Rudolf.

***Christian, Marvin, ed.** Friends of the Libraries Year 2000 Calendar. (Illus.). 113p. 1999. spiral bd. 14.95 (*0-9661647-1-7*) WSU Ofc Pub Rel.

Christian, Mary B. Bigfoot. LC 87-9024. (Mystery of...Ser.). (Illus.). 48p. (J). (gr. 5-6). 1987. lib. bdg. 12.95 (*0-89686-341-7*, Crstwood Hse) Silver Burdett Pr.

— Growin' Pains. LC 86-30246. 188p. (J). (gr. 5-12). 1987. pap. 3.95 (*0-317-63785-1*, PuffinBks) Peng Put Young Read.

— Hats Are for Watering Horses: Why the Cowboy Dressed That Way. LC 93-35748. (Illus.). 64p. (J). (gr. 2 up). 1993. reprint ed. pap. 12.95 (*0-937460-95-8*) Hendrick-Long.

— Just Once. (Sundown Fiction Collection). (Illus.). 48p. (J). (gr. 3). 1993. 3.95 (*0-88336-208-2*) New Readers.

— Just Once: Reading Level 3. (Sundown Fiction Collection). 48p. 1993. audio 9.95 (*0-88336-258-9*) New Readers.

— Sebastian (Super Sleuth) & the Bone to Pick Mystery. LC 83-5406. (Sebastian Barth Super Sleuth Mystery Ser.). (Illus.). 64p. (J). (gr. 2-5). 1983. lib. bdg. 12.00 (*0-02-718440-4*, Mac Bks Young Read) S&S Childrens.

— Sebastian (Super Sleuth) & the Copycat Crime. LC 93-7038. (Sebastian Super Sleuth Ser.). (Illus.). 64p. (J). (gr. 2-6). 1993. lib. bdg. 13.00 (*0-02-718211-8*, Mac Bks Young Read) S&S Childrens.

— Sebastian (Super Sleuth) & the Crummy Yummies Caper. large type ed. (Illus.). 1993. 17.50 (*0-614-09853-X*, L-34094-00) Am Printing Hse.

— Sebastian (Super Sleuth) & the Time Capsule Caper. LC 88-29295. (Sebastian Super Sleuth Ser.). (Illus.). 64p. (J). (gr. 2-6). 1989. lib. bdg. 10.95 (*0-02-718570-2*, Mac Bks Young Read) S&S Childrens.

Christian, Mary Blount. Fatal Fiction. LC 99-190441. (Thumbprint Mysteries Ser.). 128p. 1999. pap. 5.95 (*0-8092-0673-0*, 067300) NTC Contemp Pub Co.

— Go West, Swamp Monsters. (Puffin Easy-to-Read Ser.). (J). 1996. 8.70 (*0-606-08528-9*, Pub. by Turtleback) Demco.

— Gory Alleluia. (Thumbprint Mysteries Ser.). 128p. (J). (gr. 1). 1999. pap. 5.95 (*0-8092-0674-9*, 067490) NTC Contemp Pub Co.

***Christian, Mary Blount.** Murder on the Menu. (Thumbprint Mysteries Ser.). 128p. 1999. pap. 5.95 (*0-8092-0675-7*, 067570) NTC Contemp Pub Co.

— Swamp Monsters. 48p. (J). (gr. 1-2). pap. 3.99 (*0-8072-1355-1*) Listening Lib.

Christian, Mary Blount. The Toady & Dr. Miracle. LC 96-19214. (Illus.). 40p. 1997. pap. 3.99 (*0-689-80891-7*) S&S Bks Yung.

— The Toady & Dr. Miracle. LC 96-19214. (Illus.). 40p. (J). (gr. k-4). 1997. per. 15.00 (*0-689-80890-9*) S&S Bks Yung.

***Christian, Matthew.** Aquarium Style. (Illus.). 144p. 2000. 24.95 (*0-7641-5280-7*) Barron.

Christian-Meyer, Patricia. Catholic America: Self-Renewal Centers & Retreats. (Illus.). 281p. 1993. reprint ed. pap. 13.95 (*1-56907-005-9*) Beacon Pt Pr.

Christian, Michael. Pet Budgies. (Illus.). 48p. (Orig.). 1994. pap. 10.95 (*0-86417-589-2*, Pub. by Kangaroo Pr) Seven Hills Bk.

Christian, Michael D. Every Word the Bible Says about Love. (Every Word Topical Bible Ser.: Vol. 1). 284p. 1995. spiral bd. 24.95 (*0-9635014-1-0*) Jubilee Ridge.

Christian, N. L. & Passauer, L. K. Fiber Optic Component Design, Fabrication, Testing, Operation, Reliability & Maintainability. LC 89-30276. (Illus.). 434p. 1989. 109.00 (*0-8155-1203-1*) Noyes.

Christian, Nick. Ronin. 320p. 1999. mass mkt. 5.99 (*0-8125-2429-2*, Pub. by Forge NYC) St Martin.

Christian Parenting Staff. They Eat Dirt, Don't They? Miller, Colin, ed. LC 50-4017. (Illus.). 240p. (Orig.). 1993. pap. 6.99 (*0-7814-0144-5*, LifeJourney) Chariot Victor.

***Christian, Paul.** American Paid in Full. 122p. 1999. pap. 11.95 (*0-7414-0167-3*) Buy Books.

Christian, Paul. The History & Practice of Magic. 630p. 1994. reprint ed. pap. 39.95 (*1-56459-471-8*) Kessinger Pub.

Christian, Peggy. The Bookstore Mouse. LC 95-8454. (Illus.). 128p. (J). (gr. 3 up). 1995. 16.00 (*0-15-200203-0*, Harcourt Child Bks) Harcourt.

— Chocolate, a Glacier Grizzly. (Illus.). 32p. (J). (gr. 1-5). 1997. 12.95 (*1-882728-63-7*); 34.95 incl. audio (*1-882728-65-3*); pap. 14.95 (*1-882728-68-8*) Benefactory.

— Chocolate, a Glacier Grizzly. (J). (gr. k-3). 1997. 5.95 (*1-882728-66-1*) Benefactory.

— Chocolate, A Glacier Grizzly. (Humane Society of the United States Animal Tales Ser.). (Illus.). 32p. (J). (gr. 1-5). 34.95 incl. audio (*1-882728-64-5*); pap. 9.95 incl. audio (*1-882728-67-X*); pap. 19.95 incl. audio (*1-882728-69-6*) Benefactory.

***Christian, Peggy.** If You Find a Rock. LC 98-48938. (Illus.). 32p. (J). (gr. k-4). 2000. 16.00 (*0-15-239339-0*, Harcourt Child Bks) Harcourt.

***Christian, Peter.** Web Publishing for Genealogy. 2nd ed. 73p. 2000. pap. 10.95 (*0-8063-1630-6*) Genealog Pub.

Christian Publications Staff, compiled by. Prayer Warriors: Powerful Portraits of Men & Women on God's Front Lines. 200p. 1998. mass mkt. 5.99 (*0-87509-702-2*) Chr Pubns.

Christian, Purnell. Modern Physics: And Other Tales. 272p. 1991. 19.50 (*0-922820-16-3*) Watermark Pr.

Christian, Rebecca. Cooking the Spanish Way. LC 82-4709. (Easy Menu Ethnic Cookbooks Ser.). (Illus.). 48p. (J). (gr. 5 up). 1982. lib. bdg. 19.93 (*0-8225-0908-3*, Lerner Publctns) Lerner Pub.

Christian, Rebecca, et al. Time & Chance: An Iowa Murder Mystery. unabridged ed. 190p. 1998. pap. 10.95 (*0-9662041-1-5*) KUNI.

Christian Reformed Church Staff, contrib. by. Ecumenical Creeds & Reformed Confessions. 2nd ed. LC 87-18222. 78p. 1989. pap. text 6.75 (*0-930265-34-3*) CRC Pubns.

Christian, Reginald F., jt. auth. see Borras, F. M.

Christian, Reinar. Backhoe Loader Handbook, Advance Techniques for Operators. LC 95-43905. 1995. pap. 24.95 (*0-924659-72-6*, 1260) Hanley.

— Efflorescense in Masonry. LC 99-41860. 32p. 1998. pap. 7.95 (*0-924659-06-8*, 4535) Hanley.

Christian, Reiner. Excavator Operator Handbook. (Illus.). 1999. pap. 24.95 (*0-924659-26-2*, 1440) Hanley.

Christian, Robert, ed. see Cotten, Martha L.

Christian, Robert R. Introduction to Logic & Sets. 2nd ed. LC 65-14567. (Blaisdell Books in the Pure & Applied Sciences). 128p. reprint ed. pap. 39.70 (*0-608-30889-7*, 205512600008) Bks Demand.

Christian, Ruby B. Lord Jim's Many Marriages. 278p. (Orig.). 1995. pap. 12.00 (*0-9647882-0-9*) Bkshelf Pubns.

Christian, S. Rickly. Alive 1: Daily Devotions. rev. ed. 272p. (YA). 1995. pap. 12.99 (*0-310-49901-1*) Zondervan.

Christian, S. Rickly. Alive 2: Daily Devotions. rev. ed. 272p. (YA). 1995. pap. 12.99 (*0-310-49911-9*) Zondervan.

— Completely Alive: A Year of Daily Devotions, 2 vols. 576p. 1996. 19.99 (*0-310-20966-8*) Zondervan.

Christian, Sandy S. Instant Icebreakers. LC 96-51244. 1997. 24.95 (*1-57025-125-8*) Whole Person.

— Working with Groups on Family Issues: Structured Exercises for Exploring Divorce, Balancing Work & Family, Family Problems, Solo-Parenting, Boundaries, Intimacy, Stepfamilies. LC 96-10142. 1996. pap. 24.95 (*1-57025-124-X*) Whole Person.

Christian, Sandy S., ed. Working with Groups to Explore Food & Body Connections. LC 95-49465. (Structured Exercises in Healing Ser.). 1996. pap. 24.95 (*1-57025-105-3*) Whole Person.

Christian, Sandy S., jt. ed. see Tubesing, Nancy L.

Christian Science Monitor Editors. Man's Great Future. Canham, Erwin D., ed. LC 71-37866. (Essay Index Reprint Ser.). 1977. reprint ed. 20.95 (*0-8369-2585-8*) Ayer.

Christian Science Monitor Editors, jt. auth. see Ladies Home Journal Editors.

Christian, Scott. Exchanging Lives: Middle School Writers Online. LC 97-23713. 147p. 1997. pap. 15.95 (*0-8141-1643-4*) NCTE.

Christian, Scott, jt. ed. see Benson, Chris.

Christian, Shannon, jt. auth. see Christian, Lue.

Christian, Shirley, ed. see Evans, Judith, et al.

Christian-Smith, Linda & Kellor, Kristine. Everyday Knowledge & Uncommon Truths: Women of the Academy. LC 98-27912. (Edge: Critical Studies in Education Theory Ser.). 256p. 1998. pap. text 19.00 (*0-8133-3461-6*, Pub. by Westview) HarpC.

Christian-Smith, Linda K., ed. Texts of Desire: Essays on Fiction, Femininity & Schooling. (Critical Perspectives on Literacy & Education Ser.). 224p. 1993. 89.95 (*0-7507-0003-3*, Falmer Pr); pap. 27.95 (*0-7507-0004-1*, Falmer Pr) Taylor & Francis.

Christian-Smith, Linda K., jt. auth. see Apple, Michael W.

Christian Soldiers Staff. David. LC 97-68657. (Footsteps to Follow Ser.: No. 1). (Illus.). 32p. (J). (gr. k-4). 1997. 14.95 (*0-9657091-0-8*); pap. 9.95 (*0-9657091-1-6*) Christian Soldiers.

Christian, Spencer & Biracree, Tom. Electing Our Government. 1996. 21.95 (*0-614-96911-5*) St Martin.

Christian, Spencer & Felix, Antonia. Can It Really Rain Frogs? The World's Strangest Weather Events. LC 96-47735. (Spencer Christian's World of Wonders Ser.). 128p. (J). (gr. 3-7). 1997. pap. 12.95 (*0-471-15290-0*) Wiley.

***Christian, Spencer & Felix, Antonia.** Is There a Dinosaur in Your Backyard? The World's Most Fascinating Fossils, Rocks, & Minerals. LC 97-53177. (Spencer Christian's World of Wonders Ser.). 120p. (J). (gr. 3-7). 1998. pap. 12.95 (*0-471-19616-9*) Wiley.

Christian, Spencer & Felix, Antonia. Shake, Rattle & Roll: The World's Most Amazing Volcanoes, Earthquakes & Other Forces. LC 97-5541. (Spencer Christian's World of Wonders Ser.). 128p. (J). (gr. 6-10). 1997. pap. 12.95 (*0-471-15291-9*) Wiley.

— What Makes the Grand Canyon Grand? The World's Most Awe-Inspiring Natural Wonders. LC 97-29470. (Spencer Christian's World of Wonders Ser.). 116p. (J). (gr. 4-6). 1998. pap. 12.95 (*0-471-19617-7*) Wiley.

Christian, Stephen M. New Directions for Child Protective Services Supporting Children, Families & Communities Through Legislative Reform. LC 97-207221. 58p. 1997. 25.00 (*1-55516-754-3*, 6138) Natl Conf State Legis.

Christian, Thomas F. Conflict Management & Conflict Resolution in Corrections. LC 98-50580. 96p. 1999. pap. 19.95 (*1-56991-096-0*) Am Correctional.

***Christian, Traci M.** Dr. Laura Gets on My Nerves: An Approach to Morality Without Smugness. LC 99-73257. 99p. 1999. pap. 9.95 (*1-890622-88-5*) Leathers Pub.

Christian, U. Selberg's Zeta-, L-, & Eisensteinseries. (Lecture Notes in Mathematics Ser.: Vol. 1030). 196p. 1983. 35.95 (*0-387-12701-1*) Spr-Verlag.

Christian, Virgil L., Jr., jt. ed. see Marshall, Ray.

Christian, Virginia, et al. Three Cautionary Tales. 153p. (Orig.). 1993. pap. 14.00 (*0-9630164-3-1*) Canios Edit.

Christian, W. Asbury. Richmond, Her Past & Present. (Illus.). 618p. 1997. reprint ed. lib. bdg. 64.00 (*0-8328-6521-4*) Higginson Bk Co.

Christian, Walter P., et al, eds. Programming Effective Human Services: Strategies for Institutional Change & Client Transition. 538p. 1984. 75.00 (*0-306-41526-7*, Plenum Trade) Perseus Pubng.

Christian, Walter P., jt. auth. see Luce, Stephen C.

Christian, William. The George Grant Reader. LC 98-140169. 328p. 1997. text 60.00 (*0-8020-0973-5*); pap. text 24.95 (*0-8020-7934-2*) U of Toronto Pr.

Christian, William, ed. George Grant: A Biography. (Illus.). 495p. 1996. text 39.95 (*0-8020-5922-8*) U of Toronto Pr.

— George Grant: A Biography. (Illus.). 495p. 1996. pap. 17.95 (*0-8020-7860-5*) U of Toronto Pr.

— George Grant: Selected Letters. 300p. 1996. text 50.00 (*0-8020-0757-0*) U of Toronto Pr.

— George Grant: Selected Letters. 300p. 1996. pap. 21.95 (*0-8020-7807-9*) U of Toronto Pr.

Christian, William, jt. auth. see Grant, Irving M.

Christian, William, ed. see Innis, Harold Adams.

Christian, William, ed. & intro. see Grant, George.

Christian, William A. Divided Island: Faction & Unity on Saint Pierre. LC 69-12720. (Illus.). 228p. 1969. 34.95 (*0-674-21289-4*) HUP.

— An Interpretation of Whitehead's Metaphysics. LC 77-5619. 419p. 1977. reprint ed. lib. bdg. 41.50 (*0-8371-9638-8*, CHIW, Greenwood Pr) Greenwood.

— Lynchburg & Its People. (Illus.). 463p. 1995. reprint ed. lib. bdg. 49.00 (*0-8328-5133-7*) Higginson Bk Co.

— Marah. LC 76-39079. (Black Heritage Library Collection). 1977. reprint ed. 28.95 (*0-8369-9017-X*) Ayer.

Christian, William A., Jr. Person & God in a Spanish Valley. 244p. 1989. pap. text 16.95 (*0-691-02845-1*, Pub. by Princeton U Pr) Cal Prin Full Svc.

— Visionaries: The Spanish Republic & the Reign of Christ. LC 95-16729. (Illus.). 544p. (C). 1996. 45.00 (*0-520-20040-3*, Pub. by U CA Pr) Cal Prin Full Svc.

***Christian, William A.** Visionaries: The Spanish Republic & the Reign of Christ. LC 95-16729. (Illus.). 544p. 1999. pap. 19.95 (*0-520-21948-1*, Pub. by U CA Pr) Cal Prin Full Svc.

Christian, William A., Jr. Visions of Moving Crucifixes in Modern Spain. 232p. 1992. text 35.00 (*0-691-07387-2*, Pub. by Princeton U Pr) Cal Prin Full Svc.

Christian, William A., Jr., tr. see Apolito, Paolo.

Christian, William A., Jr., tr. see Catedra, Maria.

Christian, William C., ed. & intro. see Grant, George.

Christian, Wolff Von, see Von Christian, Wolff.

Christian, Wolfgang, et al. Waves & Optics Simulations: The Consortium for Upper-Level Physics Software. LC 95-24813. 272p. 1995. pap. 46.95 (*0-471-54887-1*) Wiley.

Christiana, Anna & Lindsey, Deborah. Anna Christiana's "Un-a-Fancii" New Orleans Cookbook. LC 99-36131. 126p. 1999. pap. 16.95 (*0-943734-38-X*) Ocean Tree Bks.

Christiana, Arama. The Children of Sierra Leone. (Books for Young Learners). (Illus.). 16p. (J). (gr. k-2). 1997. pap. text 5.00 (*1-57274-084-1*, A2730) R Owen Pubs.

Christiana, David. Drawer in a Drawer. 32p. (J). (ps-3). 1990. 13.95 (*0-374-31874-3*) FS&G.

— The First Snow. LC 95-25062. (Illus.). 32p. (J). (ps-3). 1996. 15.95 (*0-590-22855-2*, Scholastic Hardcover) Scholastic Inc.

— A Tooth Fairy's Tale. LC 93-73033. 32p. (J) (gr. k-3). 1994. 16.00 (*0-374-37677-8*) FS&G.

— A Tooth Fairy's Tale. 32p. (J). (ps-3). 1996. pap. 6.95 (*0-374-47942-9*) FS&G.

Christiana, David. The Mouse Bride. LC 94-32409. 32p. (J). (ps-2). 1995. 13.95 (*0-590-47503-7*, Scholastic Hardcover) Scholastic Inc.

Christiana, David, jt. auth. see Yolen, Jane.

Christiani, Adolph. The Principles of Expression in Pianoforte Playing. LC 74-1348. (Music Reprint Ser.). 303p. 1974. reprint ed. lib. bdg. 35.00 (*0-306-70623-7*) Da Capo.

Christiani, Leon. St. Francis of Assisi. LC 74-79802. 166p. 1975. pap. 4.95 (*0-8198-2623-5*) Pauline Bks.

Christianica Staff. Bible Birthday Book. 1982. 8.95 (*0-911346-06-6*) Christianica.

— Biblijny Rosaniec (Polish) (POL., Illus.). 1995. 8.95 (*0-911346-13-9*) Christianica.

— Biblische Rosenkranz (German) (GER., Illus.). 1988. 8.95 (*0-911346-10-4*) Christianica.

***Christianica Staff.** The Prayerpath to Jesus Through Mary: Sequel to the Scriptural Rosary. rev. ed. Orig. Title: The Christianica. (Illus.). 160p. 2000. 9.95 (*0-911346-15-5*) Christianica.

Christianica Staff. Rosaire Biblique (French) (FRE., Illus.). 1988. 8.95 (*0-911346-12-0*) Christianica.

— Rosario Biblico (Italian) 1988 Edition. (ITA., Illus.). 1988. 8.95 (*0-911346-11-2*) Christianica.

— Rosario Biblico (Portuguese) (POR., Illus.). 1995. 8.95 (*0-911346-14-7*) Christianica.

— Rosario Biblico (Spanish) (SPA., Illus.). 1980. 8.95 (*0-911346-04-X*) Christianica.

— Scriptural Rosary (English) LC 64-66463. (Illus.). 1961. 8.95 (*0-911346-01-5*) Christianica.

Christianity Today Inc., Staff. Men of Integrity. LC 99-38049. 375p. 1999. pap. 14.99 (*0-8499-3774-4*) Word Pub.

***Christianity Today Staff, contrib. by.** The Best Cartoons from Leadership Journal, Vol. 1. (Illus.). 160p. 1999. pap. 8.99 (*0-8054-1292-1*) Broadman.

Christianity Today Staff, contrib. by. The Best Cartoons from Leadership Journal, Vol. 2. (Illus.). 160p. 1999. pap. 8.99 (*0-8054-1293-X*) Broadman.

***Christianity Today Staff, contrib. by.** Leadership Cartoon Treasury, Vol. 3. (Illus.). 160p. 1999. pap. 8.99 (*0-8054-1294-8*) Broadman.

— Leadership Cartoon Treasury, Vol. 4. (Illus.). 160p. 1999. pap. 8.99 (*0-8054-1295-6*) Broadman.

Christiano, Alene, jt. auth. see Grupe, Arthur S.

Christiano, David, jt. ed. see Ginger, Ann Fagan.

***Christiano, Joseph.** The Answer is in Your Bloodtype. 2nd ed. 278p. 1999. pap. 19.95 (*0-9670125-0-3*, Pub. by Personal Nutri) ACCESS Pubs Network.

Christiano, Joseph. My Body - God's Temple: Are You Using Your Body for Jesus? LC 99-166171. 152p. 1997. write for info. (*0-9623058-2-0*) Trinity Pub & Mktg.

***Christiano, Joseph.** 7 Pillars of Health. 2000. 19.99 (*0-88419-693-3*) Creation House.

Christiano, Kevin J. Pierre Elliott Trudeau: Reason Before Passion. LC 94-194904. (Illus.). 160p. 1994. pap. 9.95 (*1-55022-188-4*, Pub. by ECW) LPC InBook.

— Pierre Elliott Trudeau: Reason Before Passion. large type ed. (Illus.). 220p. 1995. pap. 15.95 (*1-55022-241-4*, Pub. by ECW) Genl Dist Srvs.

— Religious Diversity & Social Change: American Cities, 1890-1906. (Illus.). 262p. 1988. text 75.00 (*0-521-34145-0*) Cambridge U Pr.

Christiano, Thomas. The Rule of the Many: Fundamental Issues in Democratic Theory. LC 96-8404. (Focus Ser.). 320p. (C). 1996. pap. 75.00 (*0-8133-1454-2*, Pub. by Westview); pap. 30.00 (*0-8133-1455-0*, Pub. by Westview) HarpC.

Christiano, Thomas D., jt. auth. see Cummins, Robert C.

Christians, Charles J. Aberdeen Angus Bloodlines. LC 60-63767. 140p. 1958. 5.00 (*0-911042-03-2*) NDSU Inst Reg.

Christians, Clifford E., et al. Good News: Social Ethics & the Press. LC 92-11131. 288p. (C). 1993. pap. text 29.95 (*0-19-508432-2*) OUP.

Christians, Clifford G. & Cooper, Thomas W., eds. New Media Technologies: A Special Issue of the Journal of Mass Media Ethics. 72p. 1998. pap. write for info. (*0-8058-9816-6*) L Erlbaum Assocs.

Christians, Clifford G. & Covert, Catherine L. Teaching Ethics in Journalism Education. LC 80-10426. (Teaching of Ethics Ser.). 71p. 1980. pap. 4.00 (*0-916558-08-8*) Hastings Ctr.

Christians, Clifford G. & Traber, Michael, eds. Communication Ethics & Universal Values. LC 96-51209. 384p. 1997. 59.95 (*0-7619-0584-7*); pap. 27.95 (*0-7619-0585-5*) Sage.

Christians, Clifford G. & Van Hook, Jay M., eds. Jacques Ellul: Interpretive Essays. LC 80-12342. 352p. (C). 1981. text 29.95 (*0-252-00812-X*) U of Ill Pr.

— Jacques Ellul: Interpretive Essays. fac. ed. LC 80-12342. 350p. 1994. pap. 108.50 (*0-7837-7614-4*, 204736600007) Bks Demand.

Christians, Nick. Fundamentals of Turfgrass Management. LC 97-48520. (Illus.). 290p. (C). 1998. 49.95 (*1-57504-051-4*) Sleepng Bear.

***Christians, Nick & Agnew, Michael.** The Mathematics of Turfgrass Maintenance. 3rd ed. LC 99-462014. (Illus.). 150p. 2000. text 34.95 (*1-57504-147-2*, Ann Arbor Press) Sleepng Bear.

Christians, Nick & Agnew, Michael. The Mathematics of Turfgrass Maintenance, Vol. 2. 150p. (C). 1997. pap. text 34.95 (*1-57504-059-X*, 059-X, Ann Arbor Press) Sleepng Bear.

Christianse, Yvette. Castaways. LC 99-25490. 120p. 1999. pap. 14.95 (*0-8223-2421-0*) Duke.

***Christianse, Yvette.** Castaways. LC 99-25490. 128p. 1999. 39.95 (*0-8223-2386-9*) Duke.

Christiansen. Exploring World Agriculture Activity Manual. (Agriculture Ser.). 1995. teacher ed. 10.00 (*0-8273-7003-2*); text, lab manual ed. 16.95 (*0-8273-7002-4*) Delmar.

Christiansen, et al, eds. Perspectives on Mathematics Education. 1985. pap. text 73.50 (*90-277-2118-1*) Kluwer Academic.

Christiansen, jt. auth. see Hamblin.

Christiansen, A. O. Danish-English Technical Dictionary. (DAN & ENG.). 379p. 1990. 110.00 (*0-8288-4035-0*, F101210) Fr & Eur.

Christiansen, Alfred O. Keeping the Angels Busy. 96p. 1991. pap. text 7.95 (*1-881579-00-X*) Theophilus Pr.

— No Day Repeats Itself. 108p. 1987. 12.95 (*0-9615098-4-8*) Prairie Imp.

C

***Christiansen, Alfred W. & Pilato, Louis A., eds.** International Contributions to Wood Adhesion Research. 148p. 1999. pap. 50.00 (*1-892529-04-1*) Forest Prod.

Christiansen, Alice. Yoga of the Heart: The 10 Principles of Achieving Limitless Growth, Confidence & Inner Harmony. LC 97-49103. 224p. 1998. 21.95 (*0-87596-429-X*) Rodale Pr Inc.

Christiansen, Anne B. & Quigstau, Jan F., eds. Choosing a Monetary Policy Target. (Illus.). 208p. 1997. text 32.00 (*82-00-12788-5*) Scandnavn Univ Pr.

Christiansen, Bjorn. Thus Speaks the Body: Attempts Toward a Personology from the Point of View of Respiration & Postures. LC 72-342. (Body Movement Perspectives in Research Ser.). 246p. 1980. reprint ed. 24.95 (*0-405-03141-6*) Ayer.

Christiansen, Bob. Choosing A Shelter Dog: Complete Guide to Help You Rescue & Rehome a Dog. 128p. (Orig.). 1995. pap. 9.95 (*1-884421-66-0*) Canine Lrning.

— Choosing & Caring for a Shelter Dog: A Complete Guide to Help You Rescue & Rehome a Dog. rev. ed. (Illus.). 192p. 1996. pap. 12.00 (*1-884421-55-5*) Canine Lrning.

— Save Our Strays: A Current Look at Pet Overpopulation & the Management of Orphaned Cats & Dogs. (Illus.). 104p. 1999. pap. 15.00 (*1-884421-49-0*) Canine Lrning.

Christiansen, Bob & Christiansen, Laura. Northern California Dog Owners Guide: The Starter Book. 240p. (Orig.). 1994. pap. 9.95 (*1-884421-21-0*) Canine Lrning.

— Southern California Dog Owners Guide: The Starter Book. rev. ed. LC 93-90942. 240p. 1994. pap. 9.95 (*1-884421-88-1*) Canine Lrning.

— Southern California Dog Owners Guide: Your Complete Resource for Successful Dog Ownership. 192p. (Orig.). pap. 9.95 (*1-884421-93-8*) Canine Lrning.

Christiansen, C. B. I See the Moon. (Illus.). 128p. (J). (gr. 5 up). 1994. 14.95 (*0-689-31928-2*) Atheneum Yung Read.

Christiansen, C. B. I See the Moon. (Illus.). 128p. (YA). (gr. 5 up). 1996. mass mkt. 3.99 (*0-689-80441-5*) Aladdin.

— I See the Moon. LC 94-10856. 1996. 9.09 (*0-606-09450-4*, Pub. by Turtleback) Demco.

— A Small Pleasure. LC 87-19313. 144p. (YA). (gr. 7 up). 1988. 13.95 (*0-689-31369-1*) Atheneum Yung Read.

— A Small Pleasure. 128p. (YA). (gr. 7 up). 1989. pap. 2.95 (*0-380-70699-7*, Avon Bks) Morrow Avon.

— A Snowman on Sycamore Street. (Illus.). 48p. (J). (gr. 1-3). 1996. 15.00 (*0-689-31927-4*) Atheneum Yung Read.

— Sycamore Street. LC 92-33685. (Illus.). 48p. (J). (gr. 1-3). 1993. 13.95 (*0-689-31784-0*) Atheneum Yung Read.

Christiansen, Candace. The Ice Horse. LC 92-28964. (Illus.). (J). 1993. lib. bdg. write for info. (*0-318-69675-4*, Dial Yng Read) Peng Put Young Read.

— The Mitten Tree. LC 96-53358. (Illus.). (J). (gr. 1). 1997. 16.95 (*1-55591-349-0*) Fulcrum Pub.

Christiansen, Carol & Weber, Janet. Fitness Survival Guide. 220p. (C). 1996. pap. text, per. 31.95 (*0-7872-1790-5*) Kendall-Hunt.

Christiansen, Carol D. The Experience of Circumcision in Immigrant Somali Women. 1997. 19.95 (*0-88737-727-0*, 14-7270, NLN Pr) Natl League Nurse.

Christiansen, Charles, ed. Ways of Living: Self-Care Strategies for Special Needs. 600p. (C). 1994. text 65.00 (*1-56900-008-5*) Am Occup Therapy.

Christiansen, Charles & Baum, Carolyn M. Occupational Therapy: Enabling Function & Well-Being. 2nd ed. 672p. 1997. 61.00 (*1-55642-361-6*, 33616) SLACK Inc.

— Occupational Therapy: Enabling Function & Well-Being. 2nd ed. LC 97-9050. (Illus.). 664p. 1997. pap. 54.00 (*1-55642-248-2*, 32482) SLACK Inc.

***Christiansen, Charles H., ed.** Ways of Living: Self-Care Strategies for Special Needs. 2nd ed. (Illus.). 2000. pap. write for info. (*1-56900-141-3*) Am Occup Therapy.

Christiansen, Chris. Seven Years among Prisoners of War. Winther, Ida E., tr. from DAN. (Illus.). 232p. 1994. text 34.95 (*0-8214-1069-5*) Ohio U Pr.

Christiansen, Christine & Leathem, Cecilia, eds. Pioneering New Serials Frontiers: From Petroglyphs to Cyberserials. LC 97-11234. 407p. 1997. 89.95 (*0-7890-0324-4*) Haworth Pr.

Christiansen, D., jt. auth. see Ducheyne, P.

Christiansen, Dave. The Clara Claus Cool Colorbook & Other Neat Stuff. (Illus.). 32p. (J). (gr. k-5). 1997. pap. text 4.29 (*0-9658599-1-6*) ShyBks.

Christiansen, Dennis, jt. auth. see Keiter, Les.

Christiansen, Donald. Electrical Engineer's Handbook. 4th ed. LC 96-32698. (Illus.). 2400p. 1996. 150.00 (*0-07-021077-2*) McGraw.

***Christiansen, Donald.** Electronics Engineers, 1. 3110p. 1999. 225.00 (*0-07-135534-0*) McGraw.

Christiansen, Drew. Peacemaking: Moral & Policy Challenges for a New World. 368p. 1995. pap. 19.95 (*1-55586-682-4*) US Catholic.

Christiansen, Drew & Grazer, Walter, eds. And God Saw That It Was Good: Catholic Theology & the Environment. 3p. (Orig.). (C). 1996. pap. 24.95 (*1-57455-089-6*) US Catholic.

Christiansen, Elinor. Dr. Lois, Woman Surgeon of China. LC 98-73984. (Illus.). 196p. 1999. 24.95 (*1-889385-04-2*); pap. 16.95 (*1-889385-03-4*) Alpenrose Pr.

Christiansen, Ellen J. The Covenant in Judaism & Paul: A Study of Ritual Boundaries As Identity Markers. (Arbeiten zur Geschichte des Antiken Judentums und des Urchristentums Ser.: No. 27). 300p. 1995. 109.50 (*90-04-10333-3*) Brill Academic Pubs.

Christiansen, Eric. Northern Crusades. LC 98-161230. 304p. 1998. pap. 13.95 (*0-14-026653-4*) Viking Penguin.

Christiansen, Eric, tr. Dudo of St. Quentin: History of the Normans, Translation with Introduction & Notes. LC 98-15874. 296p. 1998. 90.00 (*0-85115-552-9*, Boydell Pr) Boydell & Brewer.

Christiansen, Eric H., et al. The Geology & Geochemistry of Cenozoic Topaz Rhyolites from the Western United States. LC 86-273. (Geological Society of America Ser.: Vol. 205). (Illus.). 88p. 1986. reprint ed. pap. 30.00 (*0-608-07734-8*, 206782200010) Bks Demand.

Christiansen, Eric H., jt. auth. see Best, Myron G.

Christiansen, Eric H., jt. auth. see Hamblin, Kenneth W.

Christiansen, Eric H., jt. auth. see Hamblin, W. Kenneth.

Christiansen, Erik. The Roman Coins of Alexandria: Quantitative Studies, 2 vols., Set. 550p. (C). 1988. 47.00 (*87-7288-158-5*, Pub. by Aarhus Univ Pr) David Brown.

Christiansen, F. B. & Fenchel, T. M. Theories of Populations in Biological Communities. LC 76-49871. (Ecological Studies: Vol. 20). 1977. 39.00 (*3-540-08010-4*) Spr-Verlag.

Christiansen, Flemming & Junzou, Zhang, eds. Village, Inc: Chinese Rural Society in the 1990s. (Chinese Worlds Ser.). 288p. 1998. text 45.00 (*0-8248-2113-0*) UH Pr.

Christiansen, Flemming & Junzuo, Zhang, eds. Sea Song. LC HN740.Z9C6823 1998. (J). 1997. 8.98 (*1-57082-526-2*, Pub. by Mouse Works) Time Warner.

Christiansen, Flemming & Zhang, Junzuo. Village Inc. Chinese Rural Society in the 1990s. LC 98-130189. (Chinese Worlds Ser.). xv, 277 p. 1998. write for info. (*0-7007-0619-4*) Curzon Pr Ltd.

***Christiansen, Freddy B.** Population Genetics of Multiple Loci. LC 99-41803. (Mathematical & Computational Biology Ser.). (Illus.). 380p. 1999. 170.00 (*0-471-97979-1*) Wiley.

Christiansen, Greg, jt. auth. see Haveman, Robert H.

Christiansen, Grey, jt. auth. see Jackson, W. D.

Christiansen, Harley D. Basic Background for Test Interpretation. LC 81-7285. (Illus.). 96p. (Orig.). (C). 1981. pap. text 15.95 (*0-915456-04-4*) P Juul Pr.

— Self Relaxation: Comfort in Times of Tension. LC 81-2595. (Illus.). 96p. (Orig.). 1981. pap. 15.95 (*0-915456-02-8*) P Juul Pr.

— Testing in Counseling, Uses & Misuses. LC 81-3715. (Illus.). 96p. (Orig.). (C). 1981. pap. text 15.95 (*0-915456-03-6*) P Juul Pr.

Christiansen, Harley D. & Vergata, Marie L. Study Power: Better Study Skills-Greater Success in College. LC 75-5919. 96p. (Orig.). (C). 1975. pap. text 15.95 (*0-915456-00-1*) P Juul Pr.

Christiansen, Helen. More Goodies & Guess-Whats: A Treasured Recipe Collection. 192p. 1989. ring bd. 13.00 (*0-9621419-1-7*) H Christiansen.

Christiansen, Helen, et al, eds. Recreating Relationships: Collaboration & Educational Reform. LC 96-24411. (SUNY Series, Teacher Preparation & Development). 330p. (C). 1997. text 65.50 (*0-7914-3303-X*); pap. text 21.95 (*0-7914-3304-8*) State U NY Pr.

Christiansen, Helen, intro. Goodies & Guess-Whats: A Treasured Recipe Collection. 3rd ed. 228p. 1981. reprint ed. ring bd. 13.00 (*0-9621419-2-5*) H Christiansen.

Christiansen, Helen E. Trinkets & Treasures: A Collection of Favorite Bits of Wisdom. 130p. (Orig.). (YA). (gr. 7 up). 1984. reprint ed. pap. 8.50 (*0-9621419-0-9*) H Christiansen.

***Christiansen, J. A.** Building the Innovative Organization: Management Systems That Encourage Innovation. LC 99-59819. 2000. write for info. (*0-312-23283-7*) St Martin.

— Competitive Innovation Management: Techniques to Improve Innovation Performance. LC 99-49750. 1999. text 55.00 (*0-312-23025-7*) St Martin.

Christiansen, J. H., jt. auth. see Sestoft, Jorgen.

Christiansen, J. S. & Girard, J., eds. The Sixth HGH Symposium. (Journal Ser.: Vol. 45, Nos. 1 & 2, 1996). (Illus.). 112p. 1996. pap. 88.75 (*3-8055-6280-2*) S Karger.

***Christiansen, J. S. & Ranke, M. B., eds.** The Tenth HGH Symposium: 10th Symposium, Seville, April 1999. (Hormone Research Ser.: Vol. 51, Suppl. 3). (Illus.). iv, 180p. 1999. pap. 45.25 (*3-8055-7013-9*) S Karger.

Christiansen, J. S., jt. ed. see Girard, J.

Christiansen, Jack, ed. Hyperbolic Paraboloid Shells: State of the Art. LC 88-71659. (American Concrete Institute Publication: No. SP-110). 181p. 1988. reprint ed. pap. 56.20 (*0-608-01424-9*, 206218700002) Bks Demand.

***Christiansen, Jan.** Desert Morsels: A Journal with Encouraging Tidbits from My Journey on the Weigh down Diet. (Illus.). 160p. 2000. 17.95 (*1-892016-21-4*, Pub. by Starburst) Natl Bk Netwk.

Christiansen, Jan. More of Him, Less of Me: A Daybook of My Personal Insights, Inspirations, & Meditations on the Weigh down Diet. 384p. 1999. 17.95 (*1-892016-00-1*, Pub. by Starburst) Natl Bk Netwk.

Christiansen, Janet R. Cardiac Pacemakers & Implantable Defibrillators Vol. 3: A Workbook in 3 Volumes: Transtelephonic, Electrocardiography, & Troubleshooting: A Case Approach, 3 vols. Hayes, David L. et al, eds. (Illus.). 98p. 1997. wbk. ed. 25.00 (*0-87993-697-5*) Futura Pub.

Christiansen, Jens, et al, eds. Working Europe: Reshaping European Employment Systems. LC 98-74442. 7p. 1999. text 87.95 (*1-84014-956-6*) Ashgate Pub Co.

Christiansen, John B. & Barnartt, Sharon N. Deaf President Now! The 1988 Revolution at Gallaudet University. LC 94-41793. 270p. 1995. text 24.95 (*1-56368-035-1*) Gallaudet Univ Pr.

Christiansen, John I. Walden 3: Pop Psych & the Decline of Male Influence. 125p. pap. text 9.00 (*1-57833-115-3*) Todd Commns.

***Christiansen, Jorgen.** The History of Mind Control (From Ancient Times Until Now) (Illus.). 2000p. 1999. pap. 24.95 (*87-987537-0-3*) DBG.

Christiansen, Karl O., jt. auth. see Hurwitz, Stephan.

Christiansen, Keith. Andrea Mantegna: Padua & Mantua. LC 94-11626. (Great Fresco Cycles of the Renaissance Ser.). (Illus.). 104p. 1994. 25.00 (*0-8076-1327-4*) Braziller.

Christiansen, Keith, ed. see Metropolitan Museum of Art (New York, N. Y.) Staff.

Christiansen, Keith A., et al. Marital Property Law in Wisconsin, 3 vols. 2nd ed. 1400p. 1984. ring bd. 195.00 (*0-945574-34-7*) State Bar WI.

Christiansen, Ken. Fundamentals of Property Management. 353p. 1989. pap. 72.00 (*0-409-78778-7*, NZ, MICHIE) LEXIS Pub.

Christiansen, Kenneth & Bellinger, Peter. The Collembola of North America, North of the Rio Grande: A Taxonomic. (Illus.). 1322p. 1981. 35.00 (*0-686-34383-2*) Grinnell Coll.

— Insects of Hawaii Vol. 15: Collembola: A Manual of the Insects of the Hawaiian Islands, Including an Enumeration of the Species & Notes on Their Origin, Distribution, Hosts, Parasites, Etc. LC 48-45482. (Illus.). 453p. 1992. reprint ed. pap. 140.50 (*0-608-04396-6*, 206517700015) Bks Demand.

Christiansen, Kirsti K., jt. ed. see Hellan, Lars.

Christiansen, L. A., et al. Fresh Ink No. Three: A Collection by Ten Bay Area Poets. Rae, Leila, ed. 107p. 1992. pap. 5.00 (*1-883348-02-1*) Fresh Ink.

— Fresh Ink No. Two: A Collection by Eleven Bay Area Poets. 87p. 1991. pap. 4.00 (*1-883348-01-3*) Fresh Ink.

***Christiansen, Larry.** Critical Thinking & Effective Expression. 3rd ed. 96p. (C). 1999. per. 16.25 (*0-7872-6033-9*) Kendall-Hunt.

— Storming the Barricades. (Illus.). 160p. 2000. pap. 19.95 (*1-901983-25-0*, Pub. by Gambit) BHB Intl.

Christiansen, Larry. The U. S. Championship, 1983. (U. S. Tournament Ser.). (Illus.). 135p. (Orig.). 1984. pap. 6.50 (*0-931462-28-2*) Chess Ent.

Christiansen, Larry, et al. Alekhine's Defense as White: The Four Pawns Attack. Raingruber, Bob & Long, Robert B., eds. (Illus.). 57p. (Orig.). 1989. pap. 12.95 (*0-938650-43-2*) Thinkers Pr.

— On Top of the Chess World: The 1995 World Chess Championships. (Competitive Chess Ser.). (Illus.). 100p. (Orig.). Date not set. pap. 14.95 (*1-886040-20-6*) Hypermodern Pr.

Christiansen, Laura, jt. auth. see Christiansen, Bob.

Christiansen, Loren. Way of the Warrior: The Violent Side. 128p. 1991. 15.00 (*0-87364-627-4*) Paladin Pr.

Christiansen, M. E., ed. see European Marine Biology Symposium Staff.

Christiansen, M. N. & Lewis, Charles F., eds. Breeding Plants for Less Favorable Environments. LC 81-10346. 469p. reprint ed. pap. 145.40 (*0-7837-2367-9*, 204005300006) Bks Demand.

Christiansen, Matrona, et al. A Short Dictionary of Alaska Peninsula Sugtestun & Alaska Peninsula Alutiiq Workbook: Orthography, 1996. 2nd rev. ed. LC 97-134889. Orig. Title: A Short Dictionary of Alaska Peninsula Sugcestun & Alaska Peninsula Alutiiq. x, 66p. 1996. pap., wbk. ed. 9.00 (*1-55500-060-6*) Alaska Native.

Christiansen, Merete & Elling, Jens. European Financial Reporting: Denmark. LC 93-2627. (European Financial Reporting Ser.). 208p. (C). (gr. 13). 1993. pap. 114.95 (*0-415-06201-2*, A9709) Thomson Learn.

Christiansen, Michael. Guitar Basics: A Beginning Guitar Method Book One. 96p. 1996. pap. text, spiral bd. 12.95 (*0-8403-9644-9*) Kendall-Hunt.

— Guitar Basics Bk. 2: A Beginning Guitar Method. 80p. 1996. spiral bd. 12.95 (*0-7872-0194-4*) Kendall-Hunt.

Christiansen, Mike. Complete Blues Guitar. 88p. 1991. pap. 27.95 incl. audio compact disk (*0-7866-1396-3*, 94682CDP) Mel Bay.

Christiansen, Mike. Complete Blues Guitar Book. (Complete Book). 1991. 21.95 incl. audio (*0-7866-1090-5*, 94682P); pap. 12.95 (*1-56222-311-9*, 94682); audio 9.98 (*1-56222-323-2*, 94682); audio compact disk 15.98 (*0-7866-0440-9*, 94682CD) Mel Bay.

Christiansen, Mike. Complete Electric Blues Guitar. 128p. 1993. spiral bd. 23.95 incl. audio (*0-7866-1152-9*, 94846P) Mel Bay.

Christiansen, Mike. Complete Guitar Scale Dictionary. (Complete Book). 1996. vdisk 29.95 (*0-7866-2578-3*, 94756VX) Mel Bay.

— Complete Jazz Guitar Method. 256p. 1995. pap. 25.00 (*0-7866-0264-3*, MB95384) Mel Bay.

Christiansen, Mike. Complete Jazz Guitar Method. 256p. 1995. pap. 39.95 incl. audio compact disk (*0-7866-1307-6*, 95384CDP) Mel Bay.

— Complete Rock Guitar. 160p. 1991. pap. 23.95 incl. audio (*0-7866-1065-4*, 94560P) Mel Bay.

Christiansen, Mike. Complete Rock Guitar Book. (Complete Book). 1991. pap. 17.95 (*1-56222-181-7*, 94560); audio 9.98 (*1-56222-159-0*, 94560C); audio compact disk 15.98 (*0-7866-0441-7*, 94560CD) Mel Bay.

— Complete Rock Guitar Book. (Complete Book). 1993. vdisk 29.95 (*0-7866-2572-4*, 94560VX) Mel Bay.

— Easiest Blues Guitar Book. 32p. 1991. pap. 3.95 (*1-56222-286-4*, 94686) Mel Bay.

***Christiansen, Mike.** Guitar Scale Dictionary. (QwikGuide Ser.). 56p. 2000. pap. 5.95 (*0-7866-5222-5*, 98696) Mel Bay.

— Mel Bay's Guide to Guitar Chord Progression. 56p. 1998. pap. 8.95 (*0-7866-3528-2*, 97169) Mel Bay.

Christiansen, Mike. Rock Lead Scales for Guitar. 48p. 1996. 9.95 incl. audio compact disk (*0-7866-2684-4*, 96538BCD) Mel Bay.

— Rock Rhythms for Guitar. 56p. 1996. 9.95 incl. audio compact disk (*0-7866-2681-X*, 96535BCD) Mel Bay.

— You Can Teach Yourself Blues Guitar. 80p. 1992. pap. 9.95 (*1-56222-308-9*, 94699); audio 9.98 (*1-56222-329-1*, 94699C); audio compact disk 15.98 (*0-7866-0385-2*, 94699CD) Mel Bay.

— You Can Teach Yourself Blues Guitar. 1993. 24.95 incl. audio compact disk (*0-7866-1097-2*, 94699CDP); pap. 18.95 incl. audio (*1-56222-516-2*, 94699P) Mel Bay.

— You Can Teach Yourself Blues Guitar. 1995. VHS 29.95 (*0-7866-1397-1*, 94699VX) Mel Bay.

— You Can Teach Yourself Guitar by Ear. 1995. VHS 29.95 (*0-7866-1403-X*, 95121VX) Mel Bay.

— You Can Teach Yourself Guitar by Ear. 68p. 1997. 17.95 incl. audio compact disk (*0-7866-2866-9*, 95121BCD) Mel Bay.

Christiansen, Mike & Bay, William. Mastering the Guitar, 3 bks. 440p. 1997. 26.95 (*0-7866-2894-4*, 96716BP) Mel Bay.

Christiansen, Mike, jt. auth. see Bay, William.

Christiansen, Monty L., ed. Playground Safety: Proceedings of the 1995 International Conference. 211p. 1995. pap. 35.00 (*0-9650342-0-8*) PSU Ctr Hospitality.

Christiansen, Nancy. Deadly Deep. 352p. 1995. mass mkt. 4.50 (*0-8217-4811-4*, Pinncle Kensgtn) Kensgtn Pub Corp.

***Christiansen, Ole Comoll.** Excreta: Bodily Fluid Explored. 1999. pap. 9.95 (*1-899866-28-0*) Slab-O-Concrete Pubns.

Christiansen, P. L., et al. Future Directions of Nonlinear Dynamics in Physical & Biological Systems. (NATO ASI Ser.: Vol. 312). (Illus.). 574p. (C). 1993. text 149.50 (*0-306-44562-X*, Kluwer Plenum) Kluwer Academic.

Christiansen, P. Thorpe. A Distant Calling. LC 98-87147. (Illus.). 325p. 1998. 25.00 (*0-7388-0083-X*); pap. 15.00 (*0-7388-0084-8*) Xlibris Corp.

Christiansen, Paul & Muller, Mark. An Illustrated Guide to Iowa Prairie Plants. LC 98-47433. (Bur Oak Original Ser.). (Illus.). 252p. 1999. pap. 22.95 (*0-87745-661-5*); text 44.95 (*0-87745-660-7*) U of Iowa Pr.

Christiansen, Paul D. & Young, Michelle. Yesterday, Today & Tomorrow: Meeting the Challenge of Our Multicultural America & Beyond. LC 96-30359. 1996. 29.95 (*1-880192-18-7*) Caddo Gap Pr.

Christiansen, Peder G., ed. see Apollinaris, Sidonius.

Christiansen, Peder G., ed. see Claudianus.

Christiansen, Peter, tr. see Valat, Pierre-Marie.

Christiansen, Peter L. & Scott, A. C., eds. Davydov's Soliton Revisited: Self-Trapping of Vibrational Energy in Protein. LC 90-20930. (NATO ASI Ser.: Vol. 243). (Illus.). 534p. (C). 1990. text 174.00 (*0-306-43734-1*, Kluwer Plenum) Kluwer Academic.

***Christiansen, Peter L., et al.** Nonlinear Science at the Dawn of the 21st Century. LC 00-26993. (Lecture Notes in Physics Ser.: Vol. 542). xxvi, 458p. 2000. 98.00 (*3-540-66918-3*) Spr-Verlag.

Christiansen, R., jt. auth. see Driver, P.

Christiansen, Reidar T. The Migratory Legends: List of Types with a Systematic Catalogue of the Norwegian Variants. Dorsen, Richard M., ed. LC 77-70585. (International Folklore Ser.). 1977. reprint ed. lib. bdg. 24.95 (*0-405-10087-6*) Ayer.

Christiansen, Reidar T., ed. Folktales of Norway. Iversen, Pat S., tr. LC 64-15830. (Folktales of the World Ser.). 334p. 1968. reprint ed. pap. text 18.00 (*0-226-10510-5*, FW5) U Ch Pr.

Christiansen, Reider T. Studies in Irish & Scandinavian Folktales. Dorson, Richard M., ed. LC 80-741. (Folklore of the World Ser.). 1981. reprint ed. lib. bdg. 29.95 (*0-405-13307-3*) Ayer.

Christiansen, Robert. Electric Ballast Design for Gas Discharge Lighting. (Electrical Engineering Ser.). 1995. text 49.95 (*0-442-00948-8*, VNR) Wiley.

Christiansen, Rupert. Paris Babylon: The Story of the Paris Commune. 320p. 1996. pap. 13.95 (*0-14-012980-4*, Penguin Bks) Viking Penguin.

***Christiansen, Shelley.** The Wedding Guide for the Grownup Bride. 2000. pap. 12.95 (*0-425-17436-0*) Berkley Pub.

Christiansen, Sigurd. Chaff Before the Wind. Anderson, Isaac, tr. LC 73-22750. 319p. 1974. reprint ed. lib. bdg. 65.00 (*0-8371-7349-3*, CHCB, Greenwood Pr) Greenwood.

— Two Living & One Dead. Bjorkman, Edwin A., tr. from NOR. LC 73-22751. 288p. 1975. reprint ed. lib. bdg. 65.00 (*0-8371-7348-5*, CHTL, Greenwood Pr) Greenwood.

Christiansen, Susan & Mitchell, Kevin M. Time Travelers Guide Music History. 1996. pap. 7.50 (*0-88284-805-4*) Alfred Pub.

***Christiansen, Thomas.** Administering New Europe. 2000. text. write for info. (*0-7190-5552-0*, Pub. by Manchester Univ Pr) St Martin.

Christiansen, Thomas. EU Commission & European Governance: Institutional Analysis. (Routledge Research in European Public Policy Ser.: Vol. 4). 224p. (C). 1998. 75.00 (*0-415-15826-5*) Routledge.

Christiansen, Thomas & Jorgensen, Knud E. European Space: Exploring the Changing Nature of Borders. (Critical Perspectives Ser.). 200p. 2001. write for info. (*1-55587-260-3*) L Rienner.

Christiansen, Tom & Torkington, Nathan. Perl Cookbook. LC 99-176053. (Illus.). 794p. 1998. pap. 39.95 (*1-56592-243-3*) OReilly & Assocs.

Christiansen, Tom, et al. Programming Perl. 2nd rev. ed. (Illus.). 670p. 1996. pap. 39.95 (*1-56592-149-6*) Thomson Learn.

Christiansen, Tom, jt. auth. see Schwartz, Randal L.

Christiansen, Wayne & Kaitchuck, Ron. Investigations in Observational Astronomy. 1978. spiral bd. 24.75 (*0-88252-054-7*) Paladin Hse.

Christianson, et al. Insects & Spiders. (Illus.). 48p. (J). (ps-1). 1995. pap., teacher ed. 9.95 (*1-55799-386-6*, 536) Evan-Moor Edu Pubs.

An Asterisk (*) at the beginning of an entry indicates that the title is appearing for the first time.

***Christianson, et al.** Lobbying PACS, & Campaign Finance, 50 State Handbook. 1184p. 1998. pap. text 65.00 (*0-314-22868-3*) West Pub.

Christianson, B., et al, eds. Security Protocols: Proceedings of the 5th International Workshop, Paris, France, April 7-9, 1997, Vol. 136. LC 98-2586. (Lecture Notes in Computer Science Ser.: Vol. 1361). viii, 217p. 1998. pap. 43.00 (*3-540-64040-1*) Spr-Verlag.

***Christianson, B., et al, eds.** Security Protocols: 6th International Workshop, Cambridge, Uk, April 1998, Proceedings. LC 99-18462. (Lecture Notes in Computer Science Ser.). viii, 241p. 1999. 45.00 (*3-540-65663-4*) Spr-Verlag.

***Christianson, Bruce, et al, eds.** Security Protocols: Seventh International Workshop, Cambridge, U. K., April 19-21, 1999. LC 00-38606. (Lecture Notes in Computer Science Ser.: Vol. 1796). xii, 229p. 2000. pap. 45.00 (*3-540-67381-4*) Spr-Verlag.

Christianson, C. Bruce, ed. Soil Fertility & Fertilizer Management in Semiarid Tropical India. LC 89-24489. (Special Publications: No. SP-11). (Illus.). 160p. (Orig.). 1989. pap. text 20.00 (*0-88090-081-4*) Intl Fertilizer.

Christianson, C. Paul. Directory of London Stationers & Book Artisans, 1300-1500. LC 89-15064. 254p. 1990. 50.00 (*0-914930-11-7*) Oak Knoll.

Christianson, Cindy. Magnets. (Hands-On Minds-On Science Ser.). (Illus.). 96p. 1995. pap., teacher ed. 11.95 (*1-55734-612-7*) Tchr Create Mat.

Christianson, Dick, ed. see Hafer, Richard.

Christianson, Dick, ed. see Kalmbach Publishing Co. Staff.

Christianson, Elin B., et al. Special Libraries: A Guide for Management. 3rd ed. LC 91-33524. 98p. 1991. reprint ed. pap. 30.40 (*0-608-02392-2*, 206303300004) Bks Demand.

Christianson, Elin B., jt. auth. see Porter, Cathy A.

Christianson, Eric S. A Time to Tell: Narrative Strategies in Ecclesiastes. LC 99-169562. (JSOTS Ser.: Vol. 280). 299p. 1998. 82.00 (*1-85075-982-0*, Pub. by Sheffield Acad) CUP Services.

Christianson, Gale E. Edwin Hubble: Mariner of the Nebulae. LC 94-45995. (Illus.). 432p. 1995. 27.50 (*0-374-14660-8*) FS&G.

— Edwin Hubble: Mariner of the Nebulae. LC 96-54874. 1997. write for info. (*0-7503-0423-5*) Institute of Personal Magnetism.

— Edwin Hubble: Mariner of the Nebulae. (Illus.). xii, 428p. 1996. pap. 18.95 (*0-226-10521-0*) U Ch Pr.

***Christianson, Gale E.** Fox at the Wood's Edge: A Biography of Loren Eiseley. (Illus.). 527p. 2000. reprint ed. pap. 20.00 (*0-8032-6410-0*, Bison Books) U of Nebr Pr.

— Greenhouse: The 200-Year Story of Global Warming. 320p. 2000. pap. 13.95 (*0-14-029258-6*) Viking Penguin.

— Greenhouse: The 200-Year Story of Global Warming. LC 98-55251. (Illus.). 280p. 1999. 24.00 (*0-8027-1346-7*) Walker & Co.

Christianson, Gale E. Isaac Newton: And the Scientific Revolution. (Oxford Portraits in Science Ser.). (Illus.). 160p. (YA). (gr. 7 up). 1996. 22.00 (*0-19-509224-4*) OUP.

— Isaac Newton: And the Scientific Revolution. (Oxford Portraits in Science Ser.). (Illus.). 160p. (J). 1998. reprint ed. pap. 11.95 (*0-19-512080-9*) OUP.

— Writing Lives Is the Devil: Essays of a Biographer at Work. LC 93-22847. xvi, 229p. (C). 1993. lib. bdg. 27.50 (*0-208-02382-8*, Archon Bks) Shoe String.

Christianson, Gerald & Izbicki, Thomas M., eds. Nicholas of Cusa: In Search of God & Wisdom. LC 90-22415. (Studies in the History of Christian Thought: No. 45). xvi, 298p. 1990. 105.50 (*90-04-09362-1*) Brill Academic Pubs.

Christianson, Gerald, ed. see American Cusanus Society Staff.

Christianson, Gerald, ed. see Cranz, F. Edward.

Christianson, Helen M. Bodily Rhythmic Movements of Young Children in Relation to Rhythm in Music. LC 74-176644. (Columbia University. Teachers College. Contributions to Education Ser.: No. 736). reprint ed. 37.50 (*0-404-55736-8*) AMS Pr.

Christianson, J. Scott. Computer & Network Professional's Certification Guide. LC 98-84266. xli, 512 p. 1998. pap. text 19.99 (*0-7821-2260-4*) Sybex.

— Computer & Network Professional's Certification Guide. 2nd ed. (Certification Ser.). 656p. 1999. pap. text 19.99 (*0-7821-2545-X*) Sybex.

Christianson, J. Scott, jt. auth. see Hobbs, Vicki M.

Christianson, Jack R. As Good As I Want to Be: A Parent's Guide to Help Your Teen Succeed. 144p. 1998. pap. 12.95 (*1-883051-19-3*, Pub. by ALTI Pub) Natl Bk Netwk.

— Making the Music Decision. LC 95-77390. 1995. pap. 8.95 (*0-88494-990-7*) Bookcraft Inc.

***Christianson, John Robert.** On Tycho's Island: Tycho Brahe & His Assistants, 1570-1601. (Illus.). 464p. 2000. 34.95 (*0-521-65081-X*) Cambridge U Pr.

Christianson, Jon B., et al. Restructuring Chronic Disease Management: Best Practices & Innovations in Team-Based Treatment. LC 97-46162. 256p. 1998. 45.95 (*0-7879-4070-4*) Jossey-Bass.

Christianson, Jon B., jt. auth. see Marmor, Theodore R.

Christianson, Leslie L. & Rohrbach, Roger P. Design in Agricultural Engineering. LC 86-71552. (Illus.). 312p. (C). 1986. 41.25 (*0-916150-80-1*, M1086) Am Soc Ag Eng.

Christianson, Neil B. Two Hundred Years Astray: The Epistle to the Creationists. LC 96-92371. (Illus.). (Orig.). 1996. pap. text 12.00 (*0-9627240-1-7*) Ne-Do-Pr.

Christianson, Nick, compiled by. Dad, You're the Best! LC 98-232343. (Charming Petites Ser.). 1998. 4.95 (*0-88088-828-8*) Peter Pauper.

Christianson, Paul. Discourse on History, Law & Governance in the Public Career of John Selden, 1610-1635. 432p. 1996. text 65.00 (*0-8020-0838-0*) U of Toronto Pr.

***Christianson, Robbin C. & Allen, Jennifer Q.** Chartwell's Guide to the New Customer Care Center. Smith, L. Dennis, ed. 326p. 1999. spiral bd. 975.00 (*1-891790-22-6*) Chartwell Inc.

Christianson, Robbin C., jt. auth. see Barata, Sharyn.

***Christianson, Scott.** Balancing Justice in New York State: A Citizens' Fact Book in Criminal Justice. 48p. (Orig.). 1999. pap. write for info. (*0-938588-16-8*) LWV NYS.

— Condemned: Inside the Sing Sing Death House. LC 99-6819. (Illus.). 184p. 2000. 24.95 (*0-8147-1596-6*) NYU Pr.

— With Liberty for Some: 500 Years of Imprisonment in America. LC 98-23541. 384p. 1998. text 35.00 (*1-55553-364-7*) NE U Pr.

***Christianson, Scott.** With Liberty for Some: 500 Years of Imprisonment in America. 416p. 2000. pap. 18.95 (*1-55553-468-6*) NE U Pr.

Christianson, Stephen G. Business Law Made Simple. LC 94-41819. 208p. 1995. pap. 12.00 (*0-385-47557-8*, Made) Doubleday.

— Facts about the Congress. LC 95-53691. (Illus.). 464p. 1996. 165.00 (*0-8242-0883-8*) Wilson.

— How to Administer an Estate 1997-1998: Astep by Step Guide for Familes & Friends. 144p. 1997. pap. text 16.95 (*0-8065-1948-7*, Citadel Pr) Carol Pub Group.

— One Hundred Ways to Avoid Common Legal Pitfalls Without a Lawyer. (Illus.). 288p. 1992. pap. 12.95 (*0-8065-1330-6*, Citadel Pr) Carol Pub Group.

***Christianson, Stephen G., ed. The American Book of Days. 4th ed. LC 99-86611. (Illus.). 1200p. 2000. 105.00 (*0-8242-0954-0*) Wilson.**

A Day-By-Day Record of American Histoy from January 1 through December 31 compiled & edited by Stephen G. Christianson. For each of the366 days of the year (Including February 29) several substantial essays explore significant events of military, scientific, ethnic, or cultural significance. This completely updated & reivsed Fourth Edition nearly doubles the number of articles that were published in the Third Edition. (1978). To order: H.W.Wilson - 1-800-367-6770 (1-718-588-8400 outside U.S. & Canada); custserv@hwwilson.com, or visit www.hwwilson.com. *Publisher Paid Annotation.*

Christianson, Sven-Ake, ed. The Handbook of Emotion & Memory: Research & Theory. 432p. 1992. text 99.95 (*0-8058-0704-7*) L Erlbaum Assocs.

Christiansson, Carl. Soil-Erosion & Sedimentation in Semi-Arid Tanzania. 208p. 1981. write for info. (*91-7106-197-5*, Pub. by Nordic Africa) Transaction Pubs.

Christiavo, Aleve. Inland Empire, Palm Springs,California Retirement & Relocation Guide. large type ed. (Retirement & Relocation Guides Ser.). (Illus.). 350p. Date not set. pap. 24.95 (*1-56559-118-6*) HGI-Over Fifty.

Christidis, Les. Aves. John, Bernard et al, eds. (Animal Cytogenetics Ser.: Vol. 4: Chordata 3). (Illus.). iv, 116p. 1990. 70.00 (*3-443-26014-4*, Pub. by Gebruder Borntraeger) Balogh.

Christie. Southeast Asia. 240p. 1998. text 59.50 (*1-86064-063-X*, Pub. by I B T) St Martin.

Christie. Wilkes Wyvill & Reform. 264p. 1994. 61.95 (*0-7512-0280-0*) Ashgate Pub Co.

Christie. Word Strands 3, No. 3. (College ESL Ser.). 70p. (J). 1996. pap. 20.95 (*0-8384-5882-3*) Heinle & Heinle.

Christie, A. Managing AIDS & HIV: A Practical Guide to Achieving Best Practice. 1996. pap. 129.00 (*1-85953-075-3*, Pub. by Tech Comm) St Mut.

— Statutes on Intellectual Property. (C). 1992. 45.00 (*1-85431-186-7*, Pub. by Blackstone Pr) Gaunt.

Christie, A. M. Software Process Automation: The Technology & Its Adoption. (Illus.). 215p. 1995. 39.95 (*3-540-58414-5*) Spr-Verlag.

Christie, A. V. Nine Skies: Poems. LC 96-45773. (National Poetry Ser.). 72p. 1997. 11.95 (*0-252-06644-8*) U of Ill Pr.

Christie, Agatha. The A. B. C. Murders. (Hercule Poirot Mystery Ser.). 192p. 1999. pap. text 5.99 (*0-425-13024-X*) Berkley Pub.

— ABC Murders. (Agatha Christie Collection). 1998. mass mkt. 3.99 (*0-425-16920-0*) Berkley Pub.

— The A.B.C. Murders: A Hercule Poirot Mystery. 1991. 11.09 (*0-606-12156-0*, Pub. by Turtleback) Demco.

***Christie, Agatha.** After the Funeral. (Hercule Poirot Mysteries Ser.). 2000. mass mkt. 5.99 (*0-425-17390-9*) Berkley Pub.

Christie, Agatha. After the Funeral. 256p. 1992. mass mkt. 5.99 (*0-06-100371-9*, Harp PBks) HarpC.

— Agatha Christie, 4 vols. 1989. boxed set 14.00 (*0-671-92233-5*) PB.

— Agatha Christie, 4 vols. 1990. boxed set 15.80 (*0-671-96363-5*) S&S Trade.

— Agatha Christie: An Autobiography. 656p. 1996. reprint ed. mass mkt. 7.99 (*0-425-15260-X*) Berkley Pub.

— Agatha Christie's Detectives: Five Complete Novels. LC 95-13164. 608p. 1995. 11.98 (*0-399-14079-4*, G P Putnam) Peng Put Young Read.

— Agathie Christie. 1987. boxed set 14.00 (*0-671-91549-5*) PB.

— And Then There Were None. 208p. 1999. mass mkt. 5.99 (*0-425-12958-6*) Berkley Pub.

— And Then There Were None. 1991. 11.09 (*0-606-05717-X*, Pub. by Turtleback) Demco.

— Appointment with Death. Pliner, Jayne, ed. 224p. 1988. mass mkt. 5.99 (*0-425-10858-9*) Berkley Pub.

— Appointment with Death. 240p. 1996. 24.95 (*0-399-14136-7*, G P Putnam) Peng Put Young Read.

— Appointment with Death. 1988. 10.60 (*0-606-12169-2*, Pub. by Turtleback) Demco.

***Christie, Agatha.** At Bertram's Hotel. (Miss Marple Mysteries Ser.). 2000. mass mkt. 5.99 (*0-451-19993-6*, Sig) NAL.

Christie, Agatha. At Bertram's Hotel: A Miss Marple Mystery. 256p. 1992. mass mkt. 5.99 (*0-06-100363-8*, Harp PBks) HarpC.

— An Autobiography. 1976. 36.95 (*0-8488-0458-9*) Amereon Ltd.

— The Big Four. 224p. 1987. mass mkt. 5.99 (*0-425-09882-6*) Berkley Pub.

— Black Coffee. LC 98-21147. (Hercule Poirot Mysteries Ser.). 221p. 1998. text 22.95 (*0-312-19241-X*) St Martin.

— Black Coffee. large type ed. LC 98-49983. 1999. 26.95 (*1-56895-625-8*) Wheeler Pub.

— Black Coffee. 3rd ed. (Hercule Poirot Mysteries Ser.). 290p. 1999. mass mkt. 6.99 (*0-312-97007-2*, Minotaur) St Martin.

***Christie, Agatha.** The Body in the Library. 2000. mass mkt. 5.99 (*0-451-19987-1*, Sig) NAL.

Christie, Agatha. The Body in the Library. (Miss Marple Mysteries Ser.). 1992. 10.09 (*0-606-12195-1*, Pub. by Turtleback) Demco.

— The Body in the Library: A Miss Marple Mystery. 224p. 1992. mass mkt. 5.99 (*0-06-100364-6*, Harp PBks) HarpC.

***Christie, Agatha.** By the Pricking of My Thumbs. 224p. 2000. mass mkt. 5.99 (*0-451-20052-7*, Sig) NAL.

Christie, Agatha. By the Pricking of My Thumbs. 1992. 11.09 (*0-606-12207-9*, Pub. by Turtleback) Demco.

— By the Pricking of My Thumbs: A Tommy & Tuppence Mystery. 272p. 1992. mass mkt. 5.99 (*0-06-100335-2*, Harp PBks) HarpC.

— Cards on the Table. (Agatha Christie Collection). 1998. mass mkt. 3.99 (*0-425-16924-3*) Berkley Pub.

— Cards on the Table. 240p. 1999. mass mkt. 5.99 (*0-425-10567-9*) Berkley Pub.

— Cards on the Table. (Hercule Poirot Mystery Ser.). 1984. 11.09 (*0-606-12211-7*, Pub. by Turtleback) Demco.

— A Caribbean Mystery. 224p. 1992. mass mkt. 5.99 (*0-06-100365-4*, Harp PBks) HarpC.

***Christie, Agatha.** A Caribbean Mystery. (Miss Marple Mysteries Ser.). 2000. mass mkt. 5.99 (*0-451-19992-8*, Sig) NAL.

Christie, Agatha. A Caribbean Mystery. (Miss Marple Mysteries Ser.). 1992. 11.09 (*0-606-12212-5*, Pub. by Turtleback) Demco.

***Christie, Agatha.** Cat Among the Pigeons. (Hercule Poirot Mysteries Ser.). 2000. mass mkt. 5.99 (*0-425-17547-2*) Berkley Pub.

Christie, Agatha. Cat Among the Pigeons. 304p. 1991. mass mkt. 5.99 (*0-06-100284-4*, Harp PBks) HarpC.

— Cat Among the Pigeons. (Hercule Poirot Mystery Ser.). 1991. 10.09 (*0-606-12214-1*, Pub. by Turtleback) Demco.

***Christie, Agatha.** The Clocks. 2000. mass mkt. 5.99 (*0-425-17391-7*) Berkley Pub.

Christie, Agatha. The Clocks. 288p. 1992. mass mkt. 5.99 (*0-06-100279-8*, Harp PBks) HarpC.

— The Clocks. (Hercule Poirot Mystery Ser.). 1991. 11.09 (*0-606-12222-2*, Pub. by Turtleback) Demco.

— Crooked House. 240p. 1991. mass mkt. 5.99 (*0-06-100277-1*, Harp PBks) HarpC.

— Crooked House. 1991. 11.09 (*0-606-12231-1*, Pub. by Turtleback) Demco.

— Crooked House. large type ed. (Popular Author Ser.). 300p. 1988. lib. bdg. 19.95 (*0-8161-4463-X*, G K Hall Lrg Type) Mac Lib Ref.

— Curtain. 1976. 22.95 (*0-88411-386-8*) Amereon Ltd.

***Christie, Agatha.** Curtain. 2000. mass mkt. 5.99 (*0-425-17374-7*) Berkley Pub.

Christie, Agatha. Curtain. 240p. 1993. mass mkt. 5.99 (*0-06-100366-2*, Harp PBks) HarpC.

Christie, Agatha. Curtain. pap. 14.95 (*0-8161-4540-7*, G K Hall & Co) Mac Lib Ref.

Christie, Agatha. Curtain. 1993. 11.09 (*0-606-12235-4*, Pub. by Turtleback) Demco.

***Christie, Agatha.** Dead Man's Folly. (Hercule Poirot Mysteries Ser.). 240p. 2000. mass mkt. 5.99 (*0-425-17473-5*) Berkley Pub.

Christie, Agatha. Dead Man's Folly. 208p. 1992. mass mkt. 5.99 (*0-06-100367-0*, Harp PBks) HarpC.

— Death Comes As the End. 1992. 10.09 (*0-606-12246-X*, Pub. by Turtleback) Demco.

— Death Comes as the End: Death Comes as the End. 224p. 1995. mass mkt. 5.99 (*0-06-100368-9*, Harp PBks) HarpC.

— Death in the Air. large type ed. Orig. Title: Death in the Clouds. 1987. 16.95 (*0-7089-1738-0*) Ulverscroft.

— Death in the Clouds. 240p. 1987. pap. text 5.99 (*0-425-09914-8*) Berkley Pub.

— Death in the Clouds. (Agatha Christie Collection). 1998. mass mkt. 3.99 (*0-425-16921-9*) Berkley Pub.

— Death in the Clouds. LC 98-21328. 256p. 1998. 24.95 (*0-399-14432-3*, G P Putnam) Peng Put Young Read.

***Christie, Agatha.** Death on the Nile. 2000. mass mkt. 5.99 (*0-425-17373-9*) Berkley Pub.

Christie, Agatha. Death on the Nile. 320p. 1992. mass mkt. 5.99 (*0-06-100369-7*, Harp PBks) HarpC.

— Death on the Nile. 1992. 11.09 (*0-606-12248-6*, Pub. by Turtleback) Demco.

***Christie, Agatha.** Death on the Nile. 320p. 2000. reprint ed. 12.00 (*0-425-17441-7*) Berkley Pub.

Christie, Agatha. Death on the Nile, Set. abr. ed. 1997. audio 16.99 (*0-553-47811-7*) BDD Aud Pub.

— Destination Unknown. 224p. 1992. mass mkt. 5.99 (*0-06-100381-6*, Harp PBks) HarpC.

— Double Sin & Other Stories. 224p. 1984. pap. 5.99 (*0-425-06781-5*) Berkley Pub.

— Double Sin & Other Stories. large type ed. (Agatha Christie Ser.). 266p. 1990. lib. bdg. 19.95 (*0-8161-4541-5*, G K Hall Lrg Type) Mac Lib Ref.

— Dumb Witness. 256p. 1986. pap. text 5.99 (*0-425-09854-0*) Berkley Pub.

— Elephants Can Remember. 1992. 10.60 (*0-606-12274-5*, Pub. by Turtleback) Demco.

— Endless Night. 256p. 1992. mass mkt. 5.99 (*0-06-100334-4*, Harp PBks) HarpC.

— Endless Night. 1992. 10.09 (*0-606-12279-6*, Pub. by Turtleback) Demco.

— Endless Night. large type ed. (General Ser.). 336p. 1989. lib. bdg. 20.95 (*0-8161-4547-4*, G K Hall Lrg Type) Mac Lib Ref.

— English Country House Murders. Godfrey, Thomas, ed. 533p. 1990. mass mkt. 6.99 (*0-445-40845-6*, Pub. by Warner Bks) Little.

— Evil under the Sun. 208p. 1991. pap. text 5.99 (*0-425-12960-8*) Berkley Pub.

— Evil under the Sun. (Hercule Poirot Mystery Ser.). 1991. 10.60 (*0-606-12281-8*, Pub. by Turtleback) Demco.

— Five Little Pigs. 224p. 1985. pap. text 5.99 (*0-425-09325-5*) Berkley Pub.

— Five Little Pigs. (Agatha Christie Collection). 1998. mass mkt. 3.99 (*0-425-16923-5*) Berkley Pub.

***Christie, Agatha.** 4:50 from Paddington. (Miss Marple Mysteries Ser.). 2000. mass mkt. 5.99 (*0-451-20051-9*, Sig) NAL.

Christie, Agatha. Funerals Are Fatal. (Hercule Poirot Mystery Ser.). 1992. 11.09 (*0-606-12301-6*, Pub. by Turtleback) Demco.

Christie, Agatha. Funerals Are Fatal. large type ed. pap. 14.95 (*0-8161-4552-0*, G K Hall Lrg Type) Mac Lib Ref.

Christie, Agatha. Funerals Are Fatal. large type ed. 1992. lib. bdg. 19.95 (*0-8161-4551-2*, G K Hall Lrg Type) Mac Lib Ref.

— The Golden Ball & Other Stories. 240p. 1986. mass mkt. 5.99 (*0-425-09922-9*) Berkley Pub.

— The Golden Ball & Other Stories. 1988. 14.95 (*0-396-09296-9*, G P Putnam) Peng Put Young Read.

— Hallowe'en Party. (Agatha Christie Collection). 1998. mass mkt. 3.99 (*0-425-16922-7*) Berkley Pub.

— Hallowe'en Party. (Hercule Poirot Mystery Ser.). 1992. 10.60 (*0-606-12321-0*, Pub. by Turtleback) Demco.

— Hallowe'en Party. large type ed. 368p. 1987. 16.95 (*0-7089-1666-X*) Ulverscroft.

— The Harlequin Tea Set & Other Stories. LC 96-51140. 208p. 1997. 21.95 (*0-399-14287-8*, G P Putnam) Peng Put Young Read.

— The Harlequin Tea Set & Other Stories. 214p. 1998. reprint ed. mass mkt. 5.99 (*0-425-16515-9*) Berkley Pub.

— Hercule Poirot's Casebook: Fifty Stories. 1998. 18.95 (*0-399-15021-8*, G P Putnam) Peng Put Young Read.

— Hercule Poirot's Christmas. Orig. Title: A Holiday for Murder. 256p. 1992. mass mkt. 5.99 (*0-06-100373-5*, Harp PBks) HarpC.

— Hercule Poirot's Early Cases. 22.95 (*0-88411-388-4*) Amereon Ltd.

***Christie, Agatha.** Hickory Dickory Dock. (Hercule Poirot Mysteries Ser.). 2000. mass mkt. 5.99 (*0-425-17546-4*) Berkley Pub.

Christie, Agatha. Hickory Dickory Dock. 224p. 1992. mass mkt. 5.99 (*0-06-100372-7*, Harp PBks) HarpC.

— The Hollow. 240p. 1984. mass mkt. 5.99 (*0-425-06784-X*) Berkley Pub.

— The Hollow. 304p. 1992. 24.95 (*0-399-13727-0*, G P Putnam) Peng Put Young Read.

— The Labors of Hercules. LC 92-8415. 224p. 1993. 24.95 (*0-399-13777-7*, G P Putnam) Peng Put Young Read.

— The Labors of Hercules. 256p. 1984. reprint ed. mass mkt. 5.99 (*0-425-06785-8*) Berkley Pub.

— The Listerdale Mystery. Date not set. lib. bdg. 20.95 (*0-8488-1964-0*) Amereon Ltd.

— Lord Edgeware Dies. 1984. 10.60 (*0-606-00969-8*, Pub. by Turtleback) Demco.

— Lord Edgware Dies. 240p. 1986. mass mkt. 5.99 (*0-425-09961-X*) Berkley Pub.

— The Man in the Brown Suit. 240p. 1984. mass mkt. 5.99 (*0-425-06786-6*) Berkley Pub.

— The Man in the Brown Suit. 1984. 10.60 (*0-606-00964-7*, Pub. by Turtleback) Demco.

— The Man in the Brown Suit. 1998. lib. bdg. 19.95 (*1-56723-032-6*) Yestermorrow.

***Christie, Agatha.** The Man in the Brown Suit, Set. unabridged ed. 1999. 35.95 incl. audio (*1-55685-595-8*) Audio Bk Con.

Christie, Agatha. Miracles of Christmas. LC 97-15467. 145p. 1997. 16.99 (*0-87788-563-X*, H Shaw Pubs) Waterbrook Pr.

***Christie, Agatha.** The Mirror Crack'd. 2000. mass mkt. 5.99 (*0-451-19989-8*, Sig) NAL.

Christie, Agatha. The Mirror Crack'd from Side to Side. 240p. 1992. mass mkt. 5.99 (*0-06-100285-2*, Harp PBks) HarpC.

— Miss Marple: The Complete Short Stories. 352p. 1986. pap. 12.95 (*0-425-09486-3*) Berkley Pub.

— Mr. Parker Pyne, Detective. large type ed. 296p. 1989. lib. bdg. 19.95 (*0-8161-4563-6*, G K Hall Lrg Type) Mac Lib Ref.

— Mr. Parker Pyne, Detective. large type ed. (Agatha Christie Ser.). 296p. 1990. pap. 13.95 (*0-8161-4564-4*, G K Hall Lrg Type) Mac Lib Ref.

C

— The Mousetrap & Other Plays. 752p. 1993. mass mkt. 7.50 (*0-06-100374-3*, Harp PBks) HarpC.

***Christie, Agatha.** The Mousetrap & Other Plays. (Miss Marple Mysteries Ser.). 752p. 2000. mass mkt. 6.99 (*0-451-20114-0*, Sig) NAL.

Christie, Agatha. The Moving Finger. 208p. 1987. mass mkt. 5.99 (*0-425-10569-5*) Berkley Pub.

— The Moving Finger. 1991. 10.60 (*0-606-12432-2*, Pub. by Turtleback) Demco.

— The Moving Finger. large type ed. (General Ser.). 264p. 1989. lib. bdg. 19.95 (*0-8161-4561-X*, G K Hall Lrg Type) Mac Lib Ref.

***Christie, Agatha.** Mrs. McGinty's Dead. (Hercule Poirot Mysteries Ser.). 2000. mass mkt. 5.99 (*0-425-17545-6*) Berkley Pub.

Christie, Agatha. Mrs. McGinty's Dead. 256p. 1992. mass mkt. 5.99 (*0-06-100375-1*, Harp PBks) HarpC.

— Mrs. McGinty's Dead. (Hercule Poirot Mystery Ser.). 1992. 10.09 (*0-606-12434-9*, Pub. by Turtleback) Demco.

— Mrs. McGinty's Dead. large type ed. 320p. 1988. 17.95 (*0-7089-1771-2*) Ulverscroft.

— Murder at Hazelmoor. large type ed. 1987. 16.95 (*0-85456-203-6*) Ulverscroft.

— The Murder at the Vicarage. 240p. 1986. mass mkt. 5.99 (*0-425-09453-7*) Berkley Pub.

***Christie, Agatha.** The Murder at the Vicarage. (Miss Marple Mysteries Ser.). 224p. 2000. mass mkt. 5.99 (*0-451-20115-9*, Sig) NAL.

— The Murder at the Vicarage. 70th anniversary ed. (Miss Marple Mysteries Ser.). 2000. mass mkt. 12.00 (*0-451-19978-2*, Sig) NAL.

Christie, Agatha. The Murder at the Vicarage. Set. abr. ed. 1997. audio 16.99 (*0-553-47767-6*) BDD Aud Pub.

— Murder for Christmas. large type ed. 416p. 1987. 16.95 (*0-7089-1724-0*) Ulverscroft.

— Murder in Mesopotamia. 240p. 1987. mass mkt. 5.99 (*0-425-10363-3*) Berkley Pub.

— Murder in Mesopotamia. 1984. 11.09 (*0-606-00965-5*, Pub. by Turtleback) Demco.

— Murder in Mesopotamia. large type ed. 348p. 1992. 14.95 (*0-8161-4568-7*, G K Hall Lrg Type) Mac Lib Ref.

— Murder in the Mews. 1984. 11.09 (*0-606-00967-1*, Pub. by Turtleback) Demco.

— Murder in the Mews & Other Stories. 240p. 1987. mass mkt. 5.99 (*0-425-10435-4*) Berkley Pub.

— Murder in Three Acts. large type ed. (General Ser.). 360p. 1989. lib. bdg. 19.95 (*0-8161-4569-5*, G K Hall Lrg Type) Mac Lib Ref.

— A Murder Is Announced. 240p. 1991. mass mkt. 5.99 (*0-425-12962-4*) Berkley Pub.

— A Murder Is Announced. (Miss Marple Mysteries Ser.). 1991. 10.60 (*0-606-12436-5*, Pub. by Turtleback) Demco.

— Murder Is Easy. 224p. 1992. mass mkt. 5.99 (*0-06-100370-0*, Harp PBks) HarpC.

— Murder Is Easy. 1992. 11.09 (*0-606-12437-3*, Pub. by Turtleback) Demco.

— The Murder of Roger Ackroyd. 277p. Date not set. 23.95 (*0-8488-2236-6*) Amereon Ltd.

***Christie, Agatha.** The Murder of Roger Ackroyd. (Hercule Poirot Mysteries Ser.). 2000. mass mkt. 5.99 (*0-425-17389-5*) Berkley Pub.

Christie, Agatha. The Murder of Roger Ackroyd. LC 84-72782. 288p. 1991. mass mkt. 5.99 (*0-06-100286-0*, Harp PBks) HarpC.

— The Murder of Roger Ackroyd. (Hercule Poirot Mystery Ser.). 1991. 11.09 (*0-606-12438-1*, Pub. by Turtleback) Demco.

***Christie, Agatha.** Murder of Roger Ackroyd. (Hercule Poirot Mysteries Ser.). 2000. pap. 12.00 (*0-425-17651-7*) Berkley Pub.

Christie, Agatha. The Murder on the Links. 240p. 1984. pap. text 5.99 (*0-425-06794-7*) Berkley Pub.

— The Murder on the Links. 1984. 11.09 (*0-606-00970-1*, Pub. by Turtleback) Demco.

— The Murder on the Links. large type ed. (Agatha Christie Ser.). 323p. 1990. lib. bdg. 19.95 (*0-8161-4573-3*, G K Hall Lrg Type) Mac Lib Ref.

***Christie, Agatha.** Murder on the Orient Express. 2000. mass mkt. 5.99 (*0-425-17375-5*) Berkley Pub.

— Murder on the Orient Express. 2000. pap. text 12.00 (*0-425-17393-3*) Berkley Pub.

Christie, Agatha. Murder on the Orient Express. 256p. 1991. mass mkt. 5.99 (*0-06-100274-7*, Harp PBks) HarpC.

***Christie, Agatha.** Murder on the Orient Express. LC 99-35293. 1999. write for info. (*0-7621-0255-1*) RD Assn.

Christie, Agatha. Murder on the Orient Express. (Hercule Poirot Mystery Ser.). 1991. 11.09 (*0-606-12439-X*, Pub. by Turtleback) Demco.

Christie, Agatha. Murder on the Orient Express: Murder on the Orient Express. 1997. mass mkt. 5.99 (*0-06-105881-5*) HarpC.

Christie, Agatha. The Mysterious Affair at Styles. 22.95 (*0-88411-385-X*) Amereon Ltd.

Christie, Agatha. The Mysterious Affair at Styles. 1992. 19.95 incl. audio (*1-882071-21-2*) B&B Audio.

Christie, Agatha. The Mysterious Affair at Styles. 208p. 1991. mass mkt. 5.99 (*0-425-12961-6*) Berkley Pub.

— The Mysterious Affair at Styles. LC 97-1451. (Dover Mystery Classics Ser.). 160p. 1997. reprint ed. pap. text 2.00 (*0-486-29695-4*) Dover.

— The Mysterious Affair at Styles & the Secret Adversary: An Agatha Christie Omnibus. LC 97-4269. 464p. 1998. pap. 12.95 (*0-7867-0434-9*) Carroll & Graf.

— The Mysterious Mr. Quin. 256p. 1987. mass mkt. 5.99 (*0-425-10353-6*) Berkley Pub.

— The Mystery of the Blue Train. Date not set. lib. bdg. 20.95 (*0-8488-2138-6*) Amereon Ltd.

— The Mystery of the Blue Train. (Hercule Poirot Mystery Ser.). 224p. 1991. reprint ed. mass mkt. 5.99 (*0-425-13026-6*) Berkley Pub.

— N or M? 240p. 1986. mass mkt. 5.99 (*0-425-09845-1*) Berkley Pub.

— N or M? (Agatha Christie Collection). 1998. mass mkt. 3.99 (*0-425-16929-4*) Berkley Pub.

***Christie, Agatha.** N or M? (Tommy & Tuppence Mysteries Ser.). 224p. 2000. mass mkt. 5.99 (*0-451-20113-2*, Sig) NAL.

Christie, Agatha. Nemesis. 256p. 1992. mass mkt. 5.99 (*0-06-100326-3*, Harp PBks) HarpC.

***Christie, Agatha.** Nemesis. 2000. mass mkt. 5.99 (*0-451-20018-7*, Sig) NAL.

Christie, Agatha. Nemesis. (J). 1992. 11.34 (*0-606-12448-9*) Turtleback.

— One, Two, Buckle My Shoe. Cooper, Roger, ed. 240p. 1987. pap. text 5.50 (*0-425-10570-9*) Berkley Pub.

— One, Two, Buckle My Shoe. (Agatha Christie Collection). 1998. mass mkt. 3.99 (*0-425-16925-1*) Berkley Pub.

— One, Two, Buckle My Shoe. 1984. 11.09 (*0-606-00968-X*, Pub. by Turtleback) Demco.

— Ordeal by Innocence. 272p. 1991. mass mkt. 5.99 (*0-06-100278-X*, Harp PBks) HarpC.

— Ordeal by Innocence. 1991. 11.09 (*0-606-12463-2*, Pub. by Turtleback) Demco.

— The Pale Horse. LC 00-1941. 256p. 1992. mass mkt. 5.99 (*0-06-100377-8*, Harp PBks) HarpC.

— Pale Horse. 1992. 11.09 (*0-606-12472-1*, Pub. by Turtleback) Demco.

— The Pale Horse. large type ed. 1987. 16.95 (*0-7089-1739-9*) Ulverscroft.

— Parker Pyne Investigates. 1992. 10.60 (*0-606-12473-X*, Pub. by Turtleback) Demco.

— Partners in Crime. 240p. 1987. pap. text 5.50 (*0-425-10352-8*) Berkley Pub.

— Partners in Crime. large type ed. 1986. 15.95 (*0-7089-1540-X*) Ulverscroft.

— Passenger to Frankfurt. 23.95 (*0-88411-384-1*) Amereon Ltd.

— Passenger to Frankfurt. 288p. 1992. mass mkt. 5.99 (*0-06-100378-6*, Harp PBks) HarpC.

— The Patriotic Murders. large type ed. 312p. 1989. lib. bdg. 20.95 (*0-8161-4585-7*, G K Hall Lrg Type) Mac Lib Ref.

— Peril at End House. (Hercule Poirot Mystery Ser.). 1991. 10.60 (*0-606-12477-2*, Pub. by Turtleback) Demco.

— A Pocket Full of Pye: A Miss Marple Mystery. 192p. 1991. mass mkt. 5.99 (*0-425-13028-2*) Berkley Pub.

***Christie, Agatha.** A Pocket Full of Rye. 2000. mass mkt. 5.99 (*0-451-19986-3*, Sig) NAL.

— Poirot Investigates. (Hercule Poirot Mysteries Ser.). 256p. 2000. mass mkt. 5.99 (*0-425-17472-7*) Berkley Pub.

— Poirot Investigates. pap. 14.95 (*0-8161-4590-3*, G K Hall & Co) Mac Lib Ref.

Christie, Agatha. Poirot Investigates. large type ed. (General Ser.). 330p. 1992. lib. bdg. 19.95 (*0-8161-4589-X*, G K Hall Lrg Type) Mac Lib Ref.

— Poirot Investigates: A Hercule Poirot Mystery. 256p. 1992. mass mkt. 5.99 (*0-06-100287-9*, Harp PBks) HarpC.

— Poirot Loses a Client. large type ed. (Agatha Christie Ser.). 420p. 1992. 14.95 (*0-8161-4592-X*, G K Hall Lrg Type) Mac Lib Ref.

— Postern of Fate. 304p. 1991. mass mkt. 5.99 (*0-06-100276-3*, Harp PBks) HarpC.

***Christie, Agatha.** Postern of Fate. 224p. 2000. mass mkt. 5.99 (*0-451-20053-5*, Sig) NAL.

Christie, Agatha. Postern of Fate. (General Ser.). 1991. 10.09 (*0-606-12483-7*, Pub. by Turtleback) Demco.

— Postern of Fate. large type ed. (General Ser.). 376p. 1992. lib. bdg. 19.95 (*0-8161-4593-8*, G K Hall Lrg Type) Mac Lib Ref.

— The Regatta Mystery & Other Stories. 224p. 1986. pap. text 5.99 (*0-425-10041-3*) Berkley Pub.

— Remembered Death. large type ed. 368p. 1992. lib. bdg. 19.95 (*0-8161-4597-0*, G K Hall Lrg Type) Mac Lib Ref.

— Sad Cypress. LC 93-31257. 320p. 1994. 24.95 (*0-399-13924-9*, G P Putnam) Peng Put Young Read.

— Sad Cypress. (Hercule Poirot Mystery Ser.). 1984. 11.09 (*0-606-00971-X*, Pub. by Turtleback) Demco.

— The Secret Adversary: A Tommy & Tuppence Mystery. LC 94-122418. 240p. 1991. mass mkt. 5.99 (*0-425-13027-4*) Berkley Pub.

— The Secret of Chimneys. 224p. 1984. mass mkt. 5.99 (*0-425-06802-1*) Berkley Pub.

— The Seven Dials Mystery. 272p. 1991. mass mkt. 5.99 (*0-06-100275-5*, Harp PBks) HarpC.

— The Sittaford Mystery. 240p. 1987. pap. 4.99 (*0-425-01040-6*) Berkley Pub.

— Sleeping Murder. 22.95 (*0-88411-387-6*) Amereon Ltd.

— Sleeping Murder. 224p. 1992. mass mkt. 5.99 (*0-06-100380-8*, Harp PBks) HarpC.

***Christie, Agatha.** Sleeping Murder. (Miss Marple Mysteries Ser.). 2000. mass mkt. 5.99 (*0-451-20019-5*, Sig) NAL.

— Sleeping Murder. (Miss Marple Mysteries Ser.). 2000. pap. text 12.00 (*0-451-20099-3*) Signet.

Christie, Agatha. Sleeping Murder. 1992. 11.34 (*0-606-12521-3*) Turtleback.

— Sparkling Cyanide. 240p. 1992. mass mkt. 5.99 (*0-06-100379-4*, Harp PBks) HarpC.

— Sparkling Cyanide. 1992. 10.09 (*0-606-12526-4*, Pub. by Turtleback) Demco.

***Christie, Agatha.** Spider's Web. LC 00-40227. 240p. 2000. 23.95 (*0-312-26650-2*) St Martin.

Christie, Agatha. Star over Bethlehem & Other Stories. 1991. pap. 6.95 (*0-425-13229-3*) Berkley Pub.

— Taken at the Flood. LC 94-130926. 240p. 1984. mass mkt. 5.99 (*0-425-06803-X*) Berkley Pub.

— Taken at the Flood. (Agatha Christie Collection). 1998. mass mkt. 3.99 (*0-425-16927-8*) Berkley Pub.

— Ten Little Indians. 1984. pap. 5.50 (*0-573-61639-6*) S French Trade.

— They Came to Baghdad. 240p. 1984. pap. 5.99 (*0-425-06804-8*) Berkley Pub.

— They Came to Baghdad. 1984. 11.09 (*0-606-00960-4*, Pub. by Turtleback) Demco.

— They Came to Baghdad. large type ed. (Agatha Christie Ser.). 359p. 1990. lib. bdg. 19.95 (*0-8161-4605-5*, G K Hall Lrg Type) Mac Lib Ref.

— They Do It with Mirrors. LC 00-5504. 208p. 1992. mass mkt. 5.99 (*0-06-100376-X*, Harp PBks) HarpC.

***Christie, Agatha.** They Do It with Mirrors. (Miss Marple Mysteries Ser.). 2000. mass mkt. 5.99 (*0-451-19990-1*, Sig) NAL.

Christie, Agatha. They Do It with Mirrors. (Miss Marple Mysteries Ser.). 1992. 10.09 (*0-606-12440-3*, Pub. by Turtleback) Demco.

— They Do It with Mirrors. large type ed. 1987. 16.95 (*0-7089-1737-2*) Ulverscroft.

***Christie, Agatha.** Third Girl. (Hercule Poirot Mysteries Ser.). 272p. 2000. mass mkt. 5.99 (*0-425-17471-9*) Berkley Pub.

Christie, Agatha. Third Girl. (Hercule Poirot Mystery Ser.). 1992. 11.09 (*0-606-12536-1*, Pub. by Turtleback) Demco.

— Third Girl: A Hercule Poirot Mystery. LC 00-1983. 272p. 1992. mass mkt. 5.99 (*0-06-100382-4*, Harp PBks) HarpC.

— The Thirteen Problems. LC 93-199376. 224p. 1985. mass mkt. 5.99 (*0-425-08903-7*) Berkley Pub.

— The Thirteen Problems. (Agatha Christie Collection). 1998. mass mkt. 3.99 (*0-425-16926-X*) Berkley Pub.

***Christie, Agatha.** The Thirteen Problems. (Miss Marple Mysteries Ser.). 2000. mass mkt. 5.99 (*0-451-20020-9*, Sig) NAL.

Christie, Agatha. Three Act Tragedy. 240p. 1986. mass mkt. 5.99 (*0-425-09180-5*) Berkley Pub.

— Three Act Tragedy. (Hercule Poirot Mystery Ser.). 1984. 10.60 (*0-606-12538-8*, Pub. by Turtleback) Demco.

— Three Blind Mice & Other Stories. 224p. 1984. mass mkt. 5.99 (*0-425-06806-4*) Berkley Pub.

— Three Blind Mice & Other Stories. large type ed. (Popular Author Ser.). 338p. 1988. lib. bdg. 19.95 (*0-8161-4461-3*, G K Hall Lrg Type) Mac Lib Ref.

— Towards Zero. (Agatha Christie Collection). 1998. mass mkt. 3.99 (*0-425-16928-6*) Berkley Pub.

— The Tuesday Club Murders. large type ed. 1992. lib. bdg. 19.95 (*0-8161-4613-6*, G K Hall Lrg Type) Mac Lib Ref.

— The Underdog & Other Stories. 224p. 1984. mass mkt. 5.99 (*0-425-06808-0*) Berkley Pub.

— The Unexpected Guest: A Novel. (Illus.). 224p. 1999. text 23.95 (*0-312-24262-X*) St Martin.

***Christie, Agatha.** The Unexpected Guest: A Novel. 304p. 2000. pap. 6.99 (*0-312-97512-0*) St Martin.

Christie, Agatha. What Mrs. McGillicuddy Saw! large type ed. (Agatha Christie Ser.). 342p. 1990. lib. bdg. 12.95 (*0-8161-4617-9*, G K Hall Lrg Type) Mac Lib Ref.

— Why Didn't They Ask Evans? 1984. 11.09 (*0-606-00963-9*, Pub. by Turtleback) Demco.

— Witness for the Prosecution & Other Stories. 240p. 1984. pap. 5.99 (*0-425-06809-9*) Berkley Pub.

— Witness for the Prosecution & Other Stories. 1996. 11.09 (*0-606-00961-2*, Pub. by Turtleback) Demco.

— Witness for the Prosecution & Other Stories. large type ed. (Popular Author Ser.). 375p. 1988. 21.95 (*0-8161-4619-5*, G K Hall Lrg Type) Mac Lib Ref.

— 4: 50 from Paddington. 272p. 1992. mass mkt. 5.99 (*0-06-100383-2*, Harp PBks) HarpC.

Christie, Agatha & Chesterton. The Floating Admiral. 320p. (Orig.). 1993. mass mkt. 4.99 (*0-515-11023-X*, Jove) Berkley Pub.

Christie, Agatha & Verner, Gerald. Towards Zero. 1957. pap. 5.25 (*0-8222-1162-9*) Dramatists Play.

Christie, Agatha, et al. The Scoop. 208p. 1984. pap. 2.95 (*0-441-75505-4*, DiamondBks) Berkley Pub.

Christie, Agatha, see Westmacott, Mary, pseud.

Christie, Alan M. Software Process Automation: The Technology & Its Adoption. LC 95-2780. 1995. write for info. (*0-387-58414-5*) Spr-Verlag.

Christie, Alice M., ed. see Perez, Bernard.

***Christie, Amanda.** Middle Sister. LC 99-68957. (7th Heaven Ser.). 132p. (J). (gr. 3-7). 2000. pap. 3.99 (*0-375-80336-X*, Pub. by Random Bks Yng Read) Random.

— Mr. Nice Guy. (7th Heaven Ser.). 132p. (J). (gr. 3-7). 2000. pap. 3.99 (*0-375-80338-6*, Pub. by Random Bks Yng Read) Random.

— The New Me. (Seventh Heaven Ser.). (Illus.). 132p. (J). (gr. 4-7). 2000. pap. 3.99 (*0-375-81161-3*, Pub. by Random Bks Yng Read) Random.

— Nobody's Perfect. 1999. pap. 4.99 (*0-375-80433-1*) Random.

— Rivals. (7th Heaven Ser.). 176p. 2000. pap. 3.99 (*0-375-80337-8*, Pub. by Random Bks Yng Read) Random.

— Secrets. 176p. (YA). (gr. 5-8). 2000. pap. 4.99 (*0-375-80340-8*, Pub. by Random Bks Yng Read) Random.

Christie, Amanda. Seventh Heaven: Nobody's Perfect. (J). 1998. pap. 3.99 (*0-679-89123-4*) Random.

***Christie, Amanda.** Seventh Heaven Secrets. (Illus.). (J). 2000. mass mkt. 4.99 (*0-553-49359-0*) Random.

— Sister Trouble. (Seventh Heaven Ser.). (Illus.). (J). 2000. mass mkt. 4.99 (*0-375-81158-3*, Pub. by Random Bks Yng Read) Random.

Christie, Andrew & Gare, Stephen. Blackstone's Statues on Intellectual Property. 2nd ed. 388p. 1995. pap. 34.00 (*1-85431-386-X*, Pub. by Blackstone Pr) Gaunt.

Christie, Andrew & Gare, Stephen, eds. Blackstone's Statutes on Intellectual Property. 3rd ed. 439p. 1997. pap. 36.00 (*1-85431-618-4*, Pub. by Blackstone Pr) Gaunt.

— Blackstone's Statutes on Intellectual Property. 4th ed. 480p. 1998. pap. 36.00 (*1-85431-871-3*) Gaunt.

Christie, Archibald H. Pattern Design: An Introduction to the Study of Formal Ornament. 2nd ed. 313p. 1969. reprint ed. pap. 9.95 (*0-486-22221-7*) Dover.

Christie, Barbara J. Sowing the Seeds of Time: A History of the Jefferson Family in the Parishes of Lythe & Hinderwell in the North Riding of Yorkshire, 1631-1994. LC 94-76674. (Illus.). 200p. 1994. 29.95 (*0-9641758-0-0*); pap. 17.95 (*0-9641758-1-9*) Jefferson WA.

Christie-Blick, Nicholas, jt. ed. see Biddle, Kevin T.

Christie, Bruce. Face to File Communication: A Psychological Approach to Information Systems. LC 80-41686. (Wiley Series in Information Processing). 318p. reprint ed. pap. 98.60 (*0-8357-4954-1*, 203788600009) Bks Demand.

Christie, Bruce, ed. Human Factors of Information Technology in the Office. LC 84-20903. (Wiley Series in Information Processing). 364p. reprint ed. pap. 112.90 (*0-7837-0191-8*, 204048700017) Bks Demand.

Christie, Bruce, jt. ed. see Gale, Anthony.

Christie, Bruce, jt. ed. see Gardiner, Margaret M.

Christie, C. R. Poetry & Doubt in the Work of Jose Angel Valente & Guillermo Carnero. LC 95-19530. 290p. 1996. text 89.95 (*0-7734-8901-0*) E Mellen.

Christie, Carl A. Ocean Bridge: The History of RAF Ferry Command. (Illus.). 458p. 1995. reprint ed. 39.95 (*0-8020-0638-8*) U of Toronto Pr.

Christie, Carl A. Ocean Bridge: The History of RAF Ferry Command. (Illus.). 458p. 1997. reprint ed. pap. 19.95 (*0-8020-8131-2*) U of Toronto Pr.

Christie, Catherine, et al. Smart Cookies Don't Get Stale: Eat to Stay Young & Stress Free. 288p. 1999. text 22.00 (*1-57566-412-7*) Kensgtn Pub Corp.

***Christie, Catherine, et al.** Smart Cookies Don't Get Stale: Eat to Stay Young & Stress Free. 288p. 2000. 13.00 (*1-57566-542-5*, Knsington) Kensgtn Pub Corp.

***Christie, Christopher.** The British Country House in the Eighteenth Century. 2000. pap. 29.95 (*0-7190-4725-0*, Pub. by Manchester Univ Pr); text 69.95 (*0-7190-4724-2*, Pub. by Manchester Univ Pr) St Martin.

Christie, Clare, jt. ed. see O'Brien, Mary.

Christie, Claudia M., jt. auth. see Goodfriend, Joyce D.

Christie, Clive, ed. Race & Nation, Vol. 1. 256p. 1998. pap. 19.95 (*1-86064-194-6*, Pub. by I B T); text 59.50 (*1-86064-195-4*, Pub. by I B T) St Martin.

Christie, Clive J. A Modern History of Southeast Asia: Decolonization, Nationalism & separatism. 288p. 1996. text 65.00 (*1-85043-997-4*, Pub. by I B T) St Martin.

— Modern History Southeast Asia: Decolonization, Nationalism & Separatism. 312p. 1998. pap. 19.95 (*1-86064-354-X*, Pub. by I B T) St Martin.

— Southeast Asia. LC 98-48804. 240p. 1998. pap. 19.95 (*1-86064-075-3*, Pub. by I B T) St Martin.

Christie, Cort W. Incorporating in Nevada. 2nd rev. ed. 192p. 1997. pap. 29.95 (*1-882180-85-2*) Griffin CA.

Christie, Cort W., jt. auth. see Bennington, Robert.

Christie, D., ed. see Vegotsky, Ken.

Christie, Dave, ed. see Vegotsky, Ken.

Christie, David, et al. Epidemiology. 116p. (C). 1987. pap. 23.95 (*0-86840-186-2*, Pub. by New South Wales Univ Pr) Intl Spec Bk.

— Epidemiology: An Introductory Text for Medical & Other Health Science Students. 2nd rev. ed. 136p. 1996. pap. 29.95 (*0-86840-400-4*, Pub. by New South Wales Univ Pr) Intl Spec Bk.

Christie, David, tr. see Jonsson, Lars.

Christie, David A., tr. & pref. see Alerstam, Thomas.

Christie, Dolores L. Adequately Considered: An American Perspective on Louis Janssens' Personalist Morals. (Louvain Theological & Pastoral Monographs). 200p. (Orig.). 1992. pap. 25.00 (*0-8028-0564-7*) Eerdmans.

***Christie, Donald.** A Dictionary of French Usage: For All English-Speaking Users of French. 1999. pap. 17.50 (*1-902587-01-4*, Pub. by Opal Books) Brit Bk Co Inc.

Christie, Donald, jt. auth. see Warden, David.

Christie, Donna R. Coastal & Ocean Management Law in a Nutshell. LC 93-48713. (Nutshell Ser.). 377p. (C). 1994. pap. text. write for info. (*0-314-03353-X*) West Pub.

— Florida Coastal Law & Policy: Cases & Readings. 403p. 1985. write for info. (*0-318-60281-4*) U Fla Law.

Christie, Folla, jt. auth. see Martin, Barbara.

***Christie, Frances.** Genre & Institutions: Social Processes in the Workplace & School. 2000. pap. text 29.95 (*0-8264-4740-6*) Continuum.

Christie, Frances. Language Education. (C). 1985. pap. 39.00 (*0-7300-0305-1*, ECS805, Pub. by Deakin Univ) St Mut.

— Language Education. (Language Education Ser.). 64p. 1989. pap. text 9.95 (*0-19-437152-2*) OUP.

— Literacy for a Changing World. (C). 1990. 60.00 (*0-86431-059-5*, Pub. by Aust Council Educ Res) St Mut.

Christie, Frances. Pedagogy & the Shaping of Consciousness: Linguistic & Social Processes. LC 97-32854. (Open Linguistics Ser.). 320p. 1998. 75.00 (*0-304-70228-5*) Continuum.

***Christie, Frances.** Pedagogy & the Shaping of Consciousness: Linguistic & Social Processes. (Open Linguistics Ser.). 2000. pap. text 31.95 (*0-8264-4747-3*) Continuum.

Christie, Frances & Martin, J. R. Genre & Institutions: Social Processes in the Workplace & School. LC 96-22204. (Open Linguistics Ser.). (Illus.). 288p. 1997. 95.00 (*0-304-33766-8*) Continuum.

An Asterisk (*) at the beginning of an entry indicates that the title is appearing for the first time.

Christie, Frances & Misson, Ray. Literacy & Schooling. LC 97-47649. 200p. (C). 1998. 65.00 (*0-415-17017-6*); pap. 20.99 (*0-415-17018-4*) Routledge.

Christie, Francis M., ed. Scenario for a Magnitude 7.0 Earthquake on the Hayward Fault. (Illus.). 109p. (C). 1997. pap. text 40.00 (*0-7881-4603-3*) DIANE Pub.

Christie, G. C. Systems for Business Success in Mexico. LC 98-50490. 1999. write for info. (*0-7890-0583-2*) Haworth Pr.

***Christie, G. C.** Systems for Business Success in Mexico. LC 98-50490. 1999. write for info. (*0-7890-0582-4*) Haworth Pr.

Christie, Gayle. Why Send Red Roses? LC 96-219615. (Illus.). 120p. 1997. write for info. (*1-887918-08-6*) Brockton Pubng.

***Christie, George C.** The Notion of an Ideal Audience in Legal Argument. 232p. 2000. 104.00 (*0-7923-6283-7*, Kluwer Plenum) Kluwer Academic.

Christie, George C. Text & Readings on Jurisprudence: The Philosophy of Law. 1056p. 1989. reprint ed. text 48.50 (*0-314-28171-1*) West Pub.

Christie, George C. & Martin, Patrick H. Jurisprudence-Text & Readings on the Philosophy of Law. 2nd ed. LC 95-3414. (American Casebook Ser.). 1202p. (C). 1995. text 62.50 (*0-314-05617-3*) West Pub.

Christie, George C. & Phillips, Jerry J. Torts. Tenen, Peter & Goldenberg, Norman S., eds. LC 98-114181. (Law Outlines Ser.). 320p. (Orig.). 1996. pap. text. write for info. (*0-87457-177-4*, 5000) Casenotes Pub.

Christie, George C., et al. Cases & Materials on the Law of Torts. 3rd ed. LC 97-10156. (Paralegal). 1345p. 1997. text 49.25 (*0-314-21113-6*) West Pub.

Christie, Gregory, jt. auth. see Joosse, Barbara M.

Christie, Iain. Samora Machel: A Biography. LC 89-25035. (Panaf Great Lives Ser.). (Illus.). 224p. (C). 1989. pap. 15.00 (*0-901787-52-3*, Pub. by Zed Books); text 49.95 (*0-901787-51-5*, Pub. by Zed Books) St Martin.

Christie, Ian. Cleaner Production in Industry: Integrating Business Goals & Environmental Management. LC 95-210856. 267p. (C). 1995. pap. 17.95 (*0-85374-619-2*, Pub. by Pol Studies Inst) Brookings.

— The Last Machine: Early Cinema & the Birth of the Modern World. (Illus.). 128p. 1995. pap. 9.95 (*0-85170-505-7*) Ind U Pr.

— A Matter of Life & Death. 80p. 2000. pap. 10.95 (*0-85170-479-4*, Pub. by British Film Inst) Ind U Pr.

Christie, Ian & Dodd, Philip, eds. Spellbound: Art & Film in Britain. (Distributed for the British Film Institute Ser.). (Illus.). 180p. 1996. pap. 39.95 (*0-85170-610-X*, Pub. by British Film Inst) Ind U Pr.

Christie, Ian & Taylor, Richard, eds. Eisenstein Rediscovered: Soviet Cinema of the 20's & 30's. LC 92-26363. (Soviet Cinema Ser.). (Illus.). 288p. (C). (gr. 13). 1993. 70.00 (*0-415-04950-4*, A7903) Routledge.

Christie, Ian, jt. auth. see Carley, Michael.

Christie, Ian, jt. auth. see Hughes, Kirsty.

Christie, Ian, jt. auth. see Taylor, Richard.

Christie, Ian, ed. see Gilliam, Terry.

Christie, Ian, jt. ed. see Taylor, Richard.

Christie, Ian, jt. ed. see Thompson, David.

Christie, Ian R. The Benthams in Russia, 1780-1791. (Anglo-Russia Affinity Ser.). 272p. 1993. text 47.50 (*0-85496-816-4*) Berg Pubs.

Christie, Ian R. British "Non-elite" MPs 1715-1820. 230p. 1995. text 49.95 (*0-19-820557-0*) OUP.

Christie, Ian R. Crisis of Empire: Great Britain & the American Colonies 1754-1783. (Foundations of Modern History Ser.). (C). 1966. pap. text 11.25 (*0-393-09650-5*) Norton.

— Wars & Revolutions: Britain, 1760-1815. (New History of England Ser.). (Illus.). 368p. 1982. 37.50 (*0-674-94760-6*) HUP.

Christie, Ian R., jt. auth. see Brown, Lucy M.

Christie, Jack. Inside Out British Columbia: A Best Places Guide to the Outdoors. 624p. 1998. pap. 21.95 (*1-57061-133-5*) Sasquatch Bks.

— Whistler Outdoor Guide. 224p. 1997. pap. 12.95 (*1-55054-478-0*, Pub. by DGL) Orca Bk Pubs.

Christie, James. The Fastest Man on Earth. 1988. 26.95 (*0-7704-2267-5*) Bantam.

Christie, James F., et al. Teaching Language & Literacy: Preschool Through the Elementary Grades. LC 96-14141. 1996. text 25.00 (*0-06-501852-4*) Addson-Wesley Educ.

Christie, James F., jt. ed. see Roskos, Kathleen.

Christie, Janet, jt. auth. see Boynton, Wendy.

***Christie, Jean.** Lester the Lazy Lion. (Felt Lift the Flap Bks.). (Illus.). (J). 2000. 4.95 (*1-58646-007-2*) Polka Dot.

— Sylvia the Sleepy Elephant. (Felt Lift the Flap Bks.). (Illus.). (J). 2000. 4.95 (*1-58646-006-4*) Polka Dot.

Christie, John. Do You Come Here Often? (Orig.). 1982. pap. 12.95 (*0-918263-00-X*) Cragg Pub.

Christie, John A. Thoreau As World Traveler. (Special Publication Ser.: No. 37). (Illus.). 358p. 1965. 25.00 (*0-318-12736-9*) Am Geographical.

Christie, John S. Latino Fiction & the Modernist Imagination: Literature of the Borderlands. LC 98-31294. (Latino Communities Ser.). 224p. 1998. 53.00 (*0-8153-3246-7*) Garland.

Christie, Kate. Apparitions: An Autobiographical Study in Parapsychology. 1965. 49.50 (*0-614-01803-X*) Elliots Bks.

Christie, Kathryn. The Gift of an Aching Back. LC 98-73945. (Illus.). 240p. 1999. pap. 13.95 (*1-883697-16-6*) Hara Pub.

Christie, Kenneth. Ethnic Conflict, Tribal Politics: A Global Perspective. 288p. 1999. text 55.00 (*0-7007-1097-3*, Pub. by Curzon Pr Ltd); pap. text 27.95 (*0-7007-1118-X*, Pub. by Curzon Pr Ltd) UH Pr.

***Christie, Kenneth.** The South African Truth Commission. LC 99-86157. 2000. text 65.00 (*0-312-23332-9*) St Martin.

***Christie, Kenneth & Roy, Denny.** The Politics of Human Rights in East Asia. LC 00-9420. 2001. write for info. (*0-7453-1419-8*, Pub. by Pluto GBR) Stylus Pub VA.

Christie, Laird, jt. ed. see Gough, Barry.

***Christie, Les.** Have You Ever Eaten French Fries in Finland? LC 98-171932. 1998. pap. 7.99 (*0-310-22439-X*) HarpC.

Christie, Les. How to Work with Rude, Obnoxious & Apathetic Kids. rev. ed. 144p. 1994. pap. 9.99 (*1-56476-351-X*, 6-3351, Victor Bks) Chariot Victor.

— Take the Journey: 34 Daily Devotions to Help You Go Against the Flow. 130p. (Orig.). 1997. pap. 5.99 (*0-89900-714-7*) College Pr Pub.

— Unfinished Sentences: 450 Tantalizing Statement-Starters to Get Teenagers Talking & Thinking. 2000. pap. 7.99 (*0-310-23093-4*) HarpC.

— Unsung Heroes: How to Recruit & Train Volunteers. 176p. 1987. 13.99 (*0-310-35150-2*, 10780) Zondervan.

— What If . . . ? 450 Thought-Provoking Questions to Get Teenagers Talking, Laughing & Thinking. 112p. (YA). 1996. pap. 7.99 (*0-310-20776-2*) Zondervan.

Christie, M. A., et al, eds. ECMOR Three: Third European Conference on the Mathematics of Oil Recovery. 437p. (Orig.). 1992. pap. 87.50 (*90-6275-785-5*, Pub. by Delft U Pr) Coronet Bks.

Christie, Margaret, jt. auth. see French, Davina.

Christie, Margaret J. & Mellett, Peter G., eds. Foundations of Psychosomatics. LC RC0049.F6. 440p. reprint ed. pap. 136.40 (*0-7837-0111-X*, 204038800016) Bks Demand.

Christie, Margaret J., jt. auth. see Venables, Peter H.

Christie, Mary L. My Rottweiler Babe: A Collection of Poems. unabridged ed. (Illus.). 47p. (Orig.). 1995. pap. 13.95 (*0-9651756-0-X*) M L Christie.

Christie, Melba M. Lifted up on Wings of Faith. 56p. 1995. pap. 6.00 (*0-9638434-1-9*) Heavenly Mess.

— Words of Strength & Courage. Hooker, Jackie, ed. (Orig.). 1993. pap. 5.95 (*0-9638434-0-0*) Heavenly Mess.

Christie, Michael G. Aboriginal Perspectives on Experience & Learning: The Role of Language in Aboriginal Education. (Role of Language in Aboriginal Education Ser.). 111p. (C). 1995. pap. 38.00 (*0-7300-0346-9*, ECS806, Pub. by Deakin Univ) St Mut.

— Breach of the Peace. 100p. 1990. pap. 32.00 (*0-406-14430-3*, UK, MICHIE) LEXIS Pub.

***Christie, Michael G.** Olive the Orphan Reindeer. LC 99-88346. 1999. pap. 9.95 (*1-889658-16-2*) New Canaan Pub.

Christie, Nancy & Gauvreau, Michael. A Full-Orbed Christianity: The Protestant Churches & Social Welfare in Canada, 1900-1940. LC 96-229053. (McGill-Queen's Studies in the History of Religion Ser.). 384p. 1996. 49.95 (*0-7735-1397-3*, HN39, Pub. by McG-Queens Univ Pr) CUP Services.

Christie, Neil. The Lombards. LC 95-155447. 320p. 1995. 62.95 (*0-631-18238-1*) Blackwell Pubs.

— The Lombards. (Peoples of Europe Ser.). (Illus.). 264p. 1998. reprint ed. pap. 24.95 (*0-631-21197-7*) Blackwell Pubs.

Christie, Neil, ed. Settlement & Economy in Italy, 1500 BC to AD 1500: Papers of the 5th Conference of Italian Archaeology. (Oxbow Monographs in Archaeology: No. 41). (Illus.). 625p. 1995. 145.00 (*0-946897-89-1*, Pub. by Oxbow Bks) David Brown.

— Three South Etrurian Churches. (British School at Rome Archaeological Monographs). (Illus.). 374p. 1991. pap. 99.00 (*0-904152-17-0*, Pub. by British Schl Rome) David Brown.

Christie, Neil & Loseby, S. T., eds. Towns in Transition: Urban Evolution in Late Antiquity & the Early Middle Ages. (Illus.). 325p. 1996. text 83.95 (*1-85928-107-9*, Pub. by Scolar Pr) Ashgate Pub Co.

Christie, Nils. Crime Control As Industry. 2nd ed. LC 95-109130. 192p. (C). 1994. pap. 24.99 (*0-415-12539-1*, B7227) Routledge.

Christie, O. French Manners. (Orig.). 1997. mass mkt. 5.95 (*0-352-33214-X*, Pub. by BLA4) London Brdge.

Christie, Octavius F. Johnson, the Essayist: His Opinions of Men, Morals & Manners. LC 68-688. (Studies in Scandinavian Life & Literature: No. 18). 1969. reprint ed. lib. bdg. 75.00 (*0-8383-0527-X*) M S G Haskell Hse.

Christie, Olivia. Dance of Obsession. (Black Lace Ser.). 300p. 1996. mass mkt. 5.95 (*0-352-33101-1*, Pub. by Virgin Bks) London Brdge.

Christie, Pan, jt. auth. see Jansen, Jonathan.

Christie, R. H. The Law of Contract. LC 95-182395. (Key to Knowledge Ser.). 152p. 1995. pap. write for info. (*0-409-03788-5*, MICHIE) LEXIS Pub.

***Christie, R. M., et al.** The Chemistry of Colour Application LC 99-42716. 1999. write for info. (*0-632-04782-8*) Blackwell Sci.

Christie, Richard C. Etienne Dolet the Martyr of the Renaissance, 1508-1546: A Biography. 1977. 23.95 (*0-8369-6999-5*, 7876) Ayer.

Christie, Richard G., jt. auth. see Edwardson, John R.

Christie, Rosemary, jt. auth. see Hague, Douglas B.

Christie, Ruth, et al. The Scripted Self: Textual Identities in Contemporary Spanish Narrative. (Re-Reading Hispanic Literature Ser.). 208p. (Orig.). 1995. pap. 20.00 (*0-85668-664-6*, Pub. by Aris & Phillips) David Brown.

Christie, Ruth, jt. auth. see Tekin, Latife.

Christie, Ruth, tr. see Tekin, Latife.

Christie-Seely, Janet. Working with the Family in Primary Care: A Systems Approach to Health & Illness. LC 83-17772. 584p. 1984. 79.50 (*0-275-91424-0*, C1424, Praeger Pubs) Greenwood.

Christie, Sherry, jt. auth. see Mellan, Olivia.

Christie, Stanton E. The New Investors' Bible Vol 1: Become Wealthy Starting at Any Age. LC 99-217172. (Illus.). 160p. 1998. pap. 19.95 (*0-9664802-0-.*) WEALTH Inc.

***Christie, Stanton E.** The New Investors' Bible Vol. 1: Become Wealthy Starting at Any Age. (Illus.). 160p. 1998. 23.95 (*0-9664802-1-X*) WEALTH Inc.

Christie, Susana, jt. auth. see Carlisi, Karen.

Christie, Thomas. More Mysteries of Science: Research Activities for Investigating Scientific Fact & Fiction. (Illus.). 64p. (J). (gr. 4-8). 1994. 8.99 (*0-8665?-820-8*, GA1512) Good Apple.

— Mysteries of Science: Research Activities for Investigating Scientific Fact & Fiction. (Illus.). 64p. (J). (gr. 4-8). 1994. 8.99 (*0-86653-796-1*, GA1490) Good Apple.

Christie, Tom. Global Alert! (Illus.). 112p. (J). (gr. 5-8). 1992. student ed. 12.99 (*0-86653-692-2*, 1426) Good Apple.

Christie, Tom, jt. ed. see Boyle, Bill.

***Christie, Vance.** Hudson Taylor: Founder, China Inland Mission. (Heroes of the Faith Ser.). 208p. 1999. pap. 3.97 (*1-57748-604-8*) Barbour Pub.

Christie, W. W. Lipid Analysis: Isolation, Separation, Identification & Structural Analysis of Lipids. 2nd ed. LC 82-491. (Illus.). 224p. 1982. pap. text 42.00 (*0-08-023792-4*, Pergamon Pr) Elsevier.

Christie, Walter. Treaty Issues. LC 97-206731. 188p. 1997. write for info. (*0-473-04307-6*) The Bradbury Hse.

Christie, Warren. Jennie Passing By. 248p. 1995. 20.95 (*0-9647850-0-5*) Caumsett-Lloyd.

***Christie, William.** Mercy Mission. 368p. 2000. pap. 5.50 (*0-8439-4753-5*, Leisure Bks) Dorchester Pub Co.

Christie, William. The Warriors of God. 1995. mass mkt. 4.99 (*0-312-95393-3*) St Martin.

Christie, William M., Jr. Preface to a Neo-Firthian Linguistics. LC 80-21016. (Edward Sapir Monographs in Language, Culture & Cognition: No. 7). viii, 70p. (Orig.). (C). 1980. pap. 18.00 (*0-933104-11-.*) Jupiter Pr.

— A Stratificational View of Linguistic Change. LC 79-115787. (Edward Sapir Monographs in Language, Culture & Cognition: No. 4). viii, 71p. (Orig.). (C). 1977. pap. 18.00 (*0-933104-04-9*) Jupiter Pr.

Christie, William W. Gas Chromatography & Lipids: A Practical Guide. (Illus.). 300p. 1989. 60.00 (*0-9514171-0-X*, Pub. by Oily Pr) Matreya.

Christie, William W., ed. Advances in Lipid Methodology - One. (Oily Press Lipid Library: Vol. 2). (Illus.). 370p. 1992. 63.00 (*0-9514171-1-8*, Pub. by Oily Pr) Matreya.

— Advances in Lipid Methodology II. (Illus.). 325p. (C). 1993. 67.00 (*0-9514171-3-4*, Pub. by Oily Pr) Matreya.

— Advances in Lipid Methodology-Three. (Oily Press Lipid Library). (Illus.). 377p. (C). 1996. 76.00 (*0-9514171-6-9*, Pub. by Oily Pr) Matreya.

Christie, William W., jt. ed. see Sebedio, Jean L.

Christienne, Charles, et al. French Military Aviation: A Bibliographical Guide. LC 88-33470. (Military History Bibliographies Ser.). 282p. 1989. text 20.00 (*0-8240-8518-3*) Garland.

— A History of French Military Aviation. Kianka, Frances, tr. from FRE. LC 85-600032. (Illus.). 552p. 1986. text 85.00 (*0-87474-310-9*, CHHF) Smithsonian.

Christiernin, P. N. The Swedish Bullionist Controversy: P. N. Christiernin's Lectures on the High Price of Foreign Exchange in Sweden, 1761. Eagly, Robert V., ed. LC 74-161990. (American Philosophical Society, Memoirs Ser.: Vol. 87). 129p. reprint ed. pap. 40.00 (*0-608-13243-8*, 202513700042) Bks Demand.

Christierson, Frank Von, see Von Christierson, Frank.

Christies, George C. & Meeks, James E. Cases & Materials on the Law of Torts. 2nd ed. (American Casebook Ser.). 1264p. 1990. text 54.50 (*0-314-69371-8*) West Pub.

Christilian, J. D. Scarlet Women. 384p. 1997. mass mkt. 5.99 (*0-451-19096-3*) NAL.

— Scarlet Women. large type ed. LC 96-18994. Date not set. 25.95 (*1-56895-349-6*) Wheeler Pub.

Christin, Pierre. Heroes of the Equinox: Valerian Spatiotemporal Agent.Tr. of Les Heros de l'Equinoxe. (ENG & FRE., Illus.). 48p. (Orig.). (YA). (gr. 7-12). 1996. pap. 8.95 (*1-887911-58-8*) Fantsy Flight.

Christina, Martha. Staying Found. LC 97-75337. 60p. 1998. pap. 10.00 (*0-9652520-1-9*) Fleur-de-lis Pr

Christina, Robert W. & Corcos, Daniel M. Coaches Guide to Teaching Sport Skills. LC 87-19687. (Illus.). 168p. 1987. pap. text 24.00 (*0-87322-020-X*, BCHR0020) Human Kinetics.

Christina, Robert W. & Eckert, Helen M., eds. Enhancing Human Performance in Sport: New Concepts & Developments. (American Academy of Physical Education Papers: No. 25). 168p. 1992. pap. text 10.00 (*0-87322-353-5*, BCHR0353) Human Kinetics.

Christina, Robert W., ed. see North American Society for the Psychology of Sport.

Christine, Anita. An Elders Christmas Miracle. 1999. pap. 3.00 (*1-57514-336-4*, 3109) Encore Perform Pub.

Christine, Deborah & Mack, Stevie. The Master a Month. (Programs Ser.). 251p. (YA). (gr. 7-12). 1987. pap. 299.00 (*0-945666-61-6*) Crizmac.

— The Master Pack. (Programs Ser.). 46p. 1987. pap. 209.00 incl. audio, VHS (*0-945666-00-4*) Crizmac.

— Tribal Design. (Programs Ser.). 50p. (J). (gr. 4-12). 1988. pap. 249.00 (*0-945666-09-8*) Crizmac.

Christine, France. Margaret Olley. (Illus.). 180p. 1990. text 37.00 (*0-947131-36-1*) Gordon & Breach.

Christine, Lou, ed. Kill 'Em with Kindness. 288p. (Orig.). pap. 7.95 (*0-9637581-0-1*) Franklin HI.

Christine, Nicole. Temple of the Living Earth. 126p. 1995. pap. write for info. (*0-9647306-0-X*) Earth Song Pubns.

Christing, Adam, compiled by. Comedy Comes Clean: A Collection of Wholesome Jokes, Quotes, & One-Liners. 128p. 1996. pap. 8.00 (*0-517-88736-3*) Crown Pub Group.

Christini, Ed, jt. auth. see Clark, Laurie.

Christini, Ed, jt. auth. see Rooney, Liam.

Christini, Ed, ed. see Averill, Harry.

***Christino, Karen.** Forseeing the Future: Evangeline Adams & Astrology in America. 200p. 2000. pap. 12.95 (*0-9628031-6-2*) One Reed Pubns.

Christiphori, Ioannis & Stellae, Calveti. De Rubus Indicis: Ad Philippum Catholicum Hispaniarum et Indiarum Regem Libri Septem. Martos, Juan J., ed. (LAT.). 852p. 1999. 185.00 (*3-8154-1129-7*, T1129, Pub. by B G Teubner) U of Mich Pr.

***Christison, Kathleen.** Perceptions of Palestine: Their Influence on U.S. Middle East Policy. LC 98-41413. Orig. Title: U.S. Policy on the Palestinians & Israel. 380p. 1999. 40.00 (*0-520-21717-9*, Pub. by U CA Pr) Cal Prin Full Svc.

Christison, M. & Bassano, Sharron. Earth & Physical Science: Content & Learning Strategies (Science Through Active Reading) (Science Through Active Reading Ser.). 128p. 1992. pap. 16.35 (*0-8013-0348-6*, 78123) Longman.

— Life Science: Content & Learning Strategies. (Science Through Active Reading Ser.). 128p. 1992. pap. 16.35 (*0-8013-0347-8*, 78122) Longman.

— Life Science for ESL. (Science Through Active Reading Ser.). 128p. 1992. teacher ed. 11.21 (*0-685-59058-5*, 79278) Longman.

— Physical Science for ESL. (Science Through Active Reading Ser.). 128p. 1991. teacher ed. 11.21 (*0-685-59057-7*, 79277) Longman.

Christison, Mary A. & Bassano, Sharron. Look Who's Talking! Strategies for Developing Group Interaction. (Illus.). 108p. 1995. pap. text 16.95 (*1-882483-33-2*) Alta Bk Ctr.

— Purple Cows & Potato Chips: Multi-Sensory Language Acquisition Activities. (Illus.). viii, 104p. 1995. pap. text 16.95 (*1-882483-31-6*) Alta Bk Ctr.

Christison, Mary A. & Stoller, Fredricka H., eds. A Handbook for Language Program Administrators. (Illus.). xii, 347p. 1997. pap. text 36.50 (*1-882483-62-6*) Alta Bk Ctr.

Christison, Mary A., jt. auth. see Bassano, Sharron.

Christison, Mary Ann. English Through Poetry. (Illus.). 130p. (J). (gr. 3-6). 1982. pap. text 8.95 (*0-88084-002-1*) Alemany Pr.

***Christison, Randall B., et al.** California Trial Practice Vol. 3: Civil Procedure During Trial, 3/98 Update. 3rd ed. Russell, Linda W., ed. LC 94-68059. 921p. 1998. ring bd. 78.00 (*0-7626-0196-5*, CP-32193) Cont Ed Bar-CA.

— California Trial Practice - Civil Procedure During Trial: March 2000 Update. 3 vols. 3rd ed. Compton, Linda, ed. LC 94-68059. 1990p. 2000. 137.00 (*0-7626-0411-5*) Cont Ed Bar-CA.

Christison, Robert. Treatise on Poisons in Relation to Medical Jurisprudence, Physiology & the Practice of Physic. LC 79-156011. reprint ed. 67.50 (*0-404-09111-3*) AMS Pr.

Christitch, Nicolas, jt. ed. see Vajou, Michael.

Christl, Cliff, jt. auth. see D'Amato, Gary.

Christl, J. The Unemployment - Vacancy Curve: Theoretical Foundation & Empirical Relevance. (Studies in Empirical Economics). (Illus.). xvi, 152p. 1992. 69.00 (*0-387-91424-2*) Spr-Verlag.

Christle, Joe, jt. auth. see Costello, John.

Christlieb, Anthony, ed. see Christlieb, Don.

Christlieb, Benjamin F. Christlieb Family. 52p. 1994. reprint ed. pap. 11.00 (*0-8328-4202-8*) Higginson Bk Co.

Christlieb, Don. Recollections of a First Chair Bassoonist: 52 Years in the Hollywood Studio Orchestras. unabridged ed. Christlieb, Anthony & Beck, Carolyn, eds. LC 96-96415. (Illus.). ix, 152p. (Orig.). 1996. pap. 24.95 (*0-9653870-0-3*) Christlieb Prod.

***Christlieb, Ward.** If Only the Walls Could Talk: The Architectural Heritage of Cooper, Michigan. (Illus.). 176p. 2000. 25.00 (*1-886167-16-8*); pap. 19.95 (*1-886167-15-X*) Priscilla Pr.

Christman. Foot & Ankle Radiology. 1999. text 115.00 (*0-443-08782-2*, W B Saunders Co) Harcrt Hlth Sci Grp.

Christman, Adam. Ann Arbor the Changing Scene. (Illus.). 151p. (Orig.). 1983. pap. 8.95 (*1-882574-03-6*) Ann Arbor Hist.

Christman, Al. Target Hiroshima: Deak Parsons & the Creation of the Atomic Bomb. LC 98-2553. (Illus.). 305p. 1998. 29.95 (*1-55750-120-3*) Naval Inst Pr.

***Christman, Alan.** NC Compendium: NC Software for Manufacturing Organizations. (Illus.). 200p. 1999. ring bd. 795.00 (*1-889760-12-9*) CIMdata Inc.

— NC Software Buyer's Guide: The Authoritative Guide to NC Software & Services. 5th rev. ed. (Illus.). 800p. 1998. ring bd. (*1-889760-09-9*) CIMdata Inc.

Christman, Brian. Power Music: Music & Trance in the Shamanic Universe. 44p. (Orig.). 1993. pap. 8.25 (*0-933421-38-9*) Redwood Seed.

Christman, Calvin L., ed. America at War: An Anthology of Articles from MHQ: The Quarterly Journal of Military History. LC 95-11131. 672p. 1995. 21.95 (*1-55750-036-3*) Naval Inst Pr.

Christman, Carolyn J. Noah's Ark Today: Saving Rare Form Animal Breeds from Extinction. 78p. (J). (gr. k-6). 1996. pap. text 130.00 (*1-887316-01-9*) Am Livestock.

***Christman, Carolyn J. & Hawes, Robert O.** Birds of a Feather: Saving Rare Turkeys from Extinction. (Illus.). 96p. 1999. pap. text 21.95 (*1-887316-03-5*) Am Livestock.

Christman, Carolyn J., et al. A Rare Breeds Album of American Livestock. LC 98-210010. (Illus.). 144p. 1997. pap. text 29.95 (*1-887316-02-7*) Am Livestock.

C

Christman, Carolyn J., jt. auth. see Sponenberg, D. Phillip.
Christman, Catherine A., jt. auth. see Christman, Ernest H.
Christman-Clark, Amber, ed. see Fielder, Anita L.
Christman-Clark, Amber, ed. see Klender, Jeane S.
Christman, E. Daniel. Danny's Travel Journals: Eight Stories, Level Four, Progressive Phonics. LC 90-71309. (Illus.). 56p. (J). 1990. pap. text, per. 10.95 (*0-912329-13-0*) Tutorial Press.
Christman, Enos. One Man's Gold: The Letters & Journals of a Forty-Niner. (American Biography Ser.). 278p. 1991. reprint ed. lib. bdg. 69.00 (*0-7812-8068-0*) Rprt Serv.
Christman, Ernest. Dr. Christman's Learn to Read Book. (Illus.). 256p. (Orig.). (J). 1990. pap. 15.95 (*0-933025-17-3*) Blue Bird Pub.
Christman, Ernest H. Cat, Kite, Bike, Cave: Four Stories, Level One, Progressive Phonics. LC 90-71307. (Illus.). 52p. (J). 1990. pap. text, per. 10.95 (*0-912329-07-6*) Tutorial Press.
— Prescription for Reading: Teach Them Phonics. LC 83-70696. (Illus.). 290p. (Orig.). 1984. reprint ed. 22.95 (*0-912329-01-7*); reprint ed. pap. 15.95 (*0-912329-00-9*) Tutorial Press.
— Progressive Phonics, Level 1. LC 90-71304. (Illus.). 84p. (J). 1990. per. 15.95 (*0-912329-06-8*) Tutorial Press.
— Progressive Phonics, Level 2. LC 90-71304. (Illus.). 48p. (J). 1990. per. 12.95 (*0-912329-03-3*) Tutorial Press.
— Progressive Phonics, Level 3. LC 90-71304. (Illus.). 44p. (J). 1990. per. 10.95 (*0-912329-09-2*) Tutorial Press.
— Progressive Phonics, Level 4. LC 90-71304. (Illus.). 48p. (J). 1990. per. 10.95 (*0-912329-12-2*) Tutorial Press.
— Progressive Phonics, Level 5. LC 90-71304. (Illus.). 40p. (J). 1990. per. 10.95 (*0-912329-15-7*) Tutorial Press.
— Video-Read Package, 2 cass.; set, Level 1. (Illus.). 1991. 145.00 incl. VHS (*0-912329-05-X*) Tutorial Press.
— Video-Read Package, 2 cass.; set, Level 2. (Illus.). 1990. 140.00 incl. VHS (*0-912329-02-5*) Tutorial Press.
— Video-Read Package, Level 3. (Illus.). 1990. 90.00 incl. VHS (*0-912329-08-4*) Tutorial Press.
— Video-Read Package, Level 4. (Illus.). 1990. 85.00 incl. VHS (*0-912329-11-4*) Tutorial Press.
— Video-Read Package, Level 5. (Illus.). 1990. 75.00 incl. VHS (*0-912329-14-9*) Tutorial Press.
Christman, Ernest H. & Christman, Catherine A. Darby's Friends: Fourteen Stories, Level Three, Progressive Phonics. LC 90-71308. (Illus.). 60p. (J). 1990. pap. text, per. 10.95 (*0-912329-10-6*) Tutorial Press.
— Darby's Stable: Cartoons & Stories, Level Two, Progressive Phonics. LC 84-50859. (Illus.). 88p. (Orig.). (J). (gr. k-12). 1984. pap. text 7.50 (*0-912329-04-1*) Tutorial Press.
Christman, Florence. The Romance of Balboa Park. 4th ed. (Illus.). 136p. 1985. pap. 9.50 (*0-918740-03-7*) San Diego Hist.
Christman, Harry M., jt. auth. see Gish, Ira.
Christman, Henry M., ed. see Altgeld, John P.
Christman, Henry M., ed. see Dennett, John R.
Christman, Henry M., ed. see Lenin, Vladimir Il'ich.
Christman, Henry M., ed. see Nation Magazine Staff.
Christman, Henry M., ed. see Warren, Earl.
Christman, Henry M., ed. see Whitman, Walt.
Christman, J. Richard. Fundamentals of Solid State Physics. 528p. 1987. text 93.95 (*0-471-81095-9*) Wiley.
Christman, John. The Myth of Property: Toward an Egalitarian Theory of Ownership. LC 93-31713. 240p. 1994. text 45.00 (*0-19-508594-9*) OUP.
Christman, John H., jt. auth. see Sennewald, Charles A.
Christman, Luther, jt. auth. see Georgopoulos, Basil S.
Christman, Marcia, ed. see Yeates, Jennifer L.
Christman, Margaret C. 1846: Portrait of the Nation. (Illus.). 224p. 1996. pap. 29.95 (*1-56098-674-3*) Smithsonian.
Christman, R., et al. The Natural Environment: Wastes & Control. LC 74-18363. 256p. reprint ed. pap. 79.40 (*0-608-11590-8*, 200775500064) Bks Demand.
Christman, R. F., ed. see Dahlem Workshop on Humic Substances & Their Role i.
Christman, Rick. Falling in Love at the End of the World: A Collection of Stories. LC 93-83977. (Minnesota Voices Project Ser.: Vol. 62). 117p. (Orig.). 1994. pap. 9.95 (*0-89823-154-X*) New Rivers Pr.
Christman, Rutch C., ed. see American Association for the Advancement of Science Staff.
Christman, Stephen. Cerebral Asymmetries in Sensory & Perceptual Processing. LC 97-43233. (Advances in Psychology Ser.: Vol. 123). 580p. 1997. 149.50 (*0-444-82510-X*, North Holland) Elsevier.
Christman, Terri, jt. auth. see Rothlein, Liz C.
Christman, Trent. Brass Button Broadcasters: A Lighthearted Look at Fifty Years of Military Broadcasting. 208p. 1992. 34.95 (*1-56311-086-5*) Turner Pub KY.
Christmann, Alexander. Untersuchungen Zum Haushalt der Hormone Ethylen, Abscisinsaeure und Indol-3-Essigsaeure In Nadelbaeumen Aus Waldschadensgebieten Suedwestdeutschlands. (Dissertationes Botanicae Ser.: Band 199). (Illus.). xx, 332p. 1993. pap. 83.00 (*3-443-64111-3*, Pub. by Gebruder Borntraeger) Balogh.
Christmann, Edwin P. The Effectiveness of Computer-Assisted Instruction: What Research Tells Us. LC 97-28328. (What Research Tells Us Ser.). (Illus.). 20p. 1997. pap. 2.00 (*0-912099-32-1*, 403) Kappa Delta Pi.
Christmann, K. Introduction to Surface Physical Chemistry. (Topics in Physical Chemistry Ser.: Vol. 1). (Illus.). 280p. 1991. 54.00 (*0-387-91405-6*) Spr-Verlag.
***Christmas-Beattie, Ginger L.** 8 Generations after Thomas Cross Christmas 1690-1769. (Illus.). xviii, 274p. 2000. pap. 29.95 (*0-9701266-5-4*) Ancestral.
— Warren County, North Carolina Minutes to the Court of Pleas & Quarter Sessions, 1780-1786, Vol. I. Taylor, Mary Lib, ed. (Illus.). xiv, 194p. 2000. pap. 23.95 (*0-9701266-0-3*) Ancestral.
— Warren County, North Carolina Minutes to the Court of Pleas & Quarter Sessions, 1787-1792, Vol. II. Taylor, Mary Lib, ed. (Illus.). xiv, 194p. 2000. pap. 23.95 (*0-9701266-1-1*) Ancestral.
— Warren County, North Carolina Minutes to the Court of Pleas & Quarter Sessions, 1793-1796, Vol. III. Taylor, Mary Lib, ed. LC 00-104293. (Illus.). xiv, 194p. 2000. pap. 23.95 (*0-9701266-2-X*) Ancestral.
— Warren County, North Carolina Minutes to the Court of Pleas & Quarter Sessions, 1797-1800, Vol. IV. Taylor, Mary Lib, ed. LC 00-104293. xiv, 194p. 2001. pap. 23.95 (*0-9701266-3-8*) Ancestral.
— Warren County, North Carolina Minutes to the Court of Pleas & Quarter Sessions, 1801-1805, Vol. V. Taylor, Mary Lib, ed. (Illus.). xiv, 194p. 2000. pap. 23.95 (*0-9701266-4-6*) Ancestral.
Christmas, Carolyn. Rodale's Visual Encyclopedia of Needlecrafts: Applique, Crochet, Cross-Stitch, Duplicate Stitch . . . LC 95-29999. (Illus.). 256p. 1996. 27.95 (*0-87596-718-3*) Rodale Pr Inc.
Christmas, Carolyn, ed. Afghans to Treasure. LC 94-79282. (Illus.). 160p. 1995. 19.95 (*1-882138-09-0*) Hse White Birches.
Christmas, Charles E., Jr. Off the Floor & into Your Soup? An Expose of What Happens Behind the Closed Doors of Restaurant Kitchens. LC 91-67062. 128p. 1992. pap. 7.95 (*0-914984-38-1*) Starburst.
Christmas, Dewey A., Jr., jt. auth. see Krouse, John H.
Christmas, Henry, tr. see Calmet, Dom A.
***Christmas, Joyce.** A Better Class of Murder. 2000. mass mkt. 6.50 (*0-449-15013-5*) Ballantine Pub Grp.
Christmas, Joyce. Down-Sized to Death. LC 97-90575. 199p. 1997. mass mkt. 5.99 (*0-449-14802-5*, GM) Fawcett.
***Christmas, Joyce.** Dying Well. 224p. 2000. mass mkt. 6.50 (*0-449-15011-9*) Fawcett.
— Mood to Murder. 1999. 5.99 (*0-449-15012-7*) Fawcett.
Christmas, Joyce. Mourning Gloria. 232p. 1996. mass mkt. 4.99 (*0-449-14704-5*) Fawcett.
Christmas, P. EDI Implementation & Security. LC 95-131332. 200p. 1993. 288.50 (*1-85617-183-3*, Pergamon Pr) Elsevier.
Christmas, P., et al. Network Security Manager. 138p. 1992. 307.00 (*1-85617-126-4*, Pub. by Elsvr Adv Tech) Elsevier.
Christmas, Ron & King, Amy. Kauai Calling. unabridged ed. LC 98-87531. 160p. 1998. pap. 31.00 (*0-9667110-0-9*) Paradise Works.
Christmas, Terri, jt. auth. see Rothlein, Liz C.
Christmas, Timothy J., jt. auth. see Chapple, Christopher R.
Christner, Anne M., ed. Dealing with Dementia: Optimizing Functional & Life-Quality Outcomes. 150p. (Orig.). 1997. pap. 69.00 (*1-884937-44-6*) Manisses Communs.
— End-of-Life Decisions: Facing the Challenges of Medical & Ethical Choices. 56p. (Orig.). 1995. pap. 29.95 (*1-884937-36-5*) Manisses Communs.
— Measuring Outcomes: Desktop Reference for Behavioral Healthcare Providers. 3rd rev. ed. 550p. 1998. 149.00 (*1-884937-51-9*) Manisses Communs.
— Outcomes Evaluation in Children's Services: A Guide for Mental Health, Child Welfare, Juvenile Justice, & Special Education Specialists. 150p. 1997. 75.00 (*1-884937-49-7*) Manisses Communs.
Christner, Anne M., ed. see Seltzer, Barbara B.
Christner, Barbara, jt. auth. see Hershberger, Mary.
Christner, David W. Let It Rain. 105p. 1980. pap. 5.50 (*0-87129-179-7*, L42) Dramatic Pub.
Christner, Susie. Old Fashioned Amish-Mennonite Cookin' A Collection of Sugarless Favorites. (Illus.). 240p. 1995. spiral bd. 12.95 (*0-9647582-0-X*) Favorite Cookbks.
Christo. Umbrellas, 2 Vols. limited ed. LC 99-194730. 1998. 950.00 (*3-8228-7477-9*) Taschen Amer.
Christo, Carlos. Against Principalities & Powers: Letters from a Brazilian Jail. Drury, John, tr. LC 76-43030. 255p. reprint ed. pap. 79.10 (*0-8357-8794-X*, 203355600086) Bks Demand.
Christo, Cyril. The Dream of the Earth: Poems. Schultz, Patricia, ed. LC 90-6403. (Lewiston Poetry Ser.: Vol. 13). 96p. 1990. pap. 14.95 (*0-88946-846-X*) E Mellen.
— Hiroshima, My Love. LC 97-37509. 96p. 1997. pap. 14.95 (*0-7734-2819-4*, Mellen Poetry Pr) E Mellen.
— Iguana at the Millennium: Poems. Schultz, Patricia, ed. LC 90-6402. (Lewiston Poetry Ser.: Vol. 14). 96p. 1991. pap. 14.95 (*0-88946-845-1*) E Mellen.
Christo, Cyril. The Twilight Language. 56p. 1996. pap. 12.00 (*1-886435-05-7*) Canios Edit.
Christo, Cyril. The Whispering Veils: Poems on Christo's Art. (Illus.). 24p. 1988. 15.00 (*0-88363-023-0*) H L Levin.
Christo, Doris H., compiled by. National Directory of Education Libraries & Collections. LC 89-13936. 280p. 1990. lib. bdg. 115.00 (*0-313-28051-7*, CNG/, Greenwood Pr) Greenwood.
Christo, Gus G. Martyrdom According to John Chrysostom: To Live Is Christ, to Die Is Gain. LC 96-37777. 228p. 1997. text 89.95 (*0-7734-2290-0*) E Mellen.
Christo, Gus G., tr. see St. John Chrysostom.
Christo, Mary Lou. Support for Life's Journey. (Illus.). 64p. 1999. pap. 5.99 (*0-9651756-1-8*) M L Christie.
Christo, Steve. Sydney Swans. 80p. 1996. pap. 19.95 (*0-86840-424-1*, Pub. by New South Wales Univ Pr) Intl Spec Bk.
Christodoulakis, D. ADA: The Choice for Ninety-Two: ADA-Europe International Conference Athens, Greece, May 13-17, 1991 Proceedings. Goos, G. & Hartmanis, J., eds. (Lecture Notes in Computer Science Ser.: Vol. 499). vi, 411p. 1991. 44.95 (*0-387-54092-X*) Spr-Verlag.
Christodoulakis, Dimitrios, jt. auth. see International Conference on Natural Language Processing Staff.
Christodoulakis, N. M., ed. Dynamic Modelling & Control of National Economies, 1989. (IFAC Proceedings Ser.: No. 9004). 600p. 1990. 281.00 (*0-08-037538-3*, Pergamon Pr) Elsevier.
Christodoulidis, Emilios A. Law & Reflexive Politics. LC 98-9204. (Law & Philosophy Library). 1998. 119.00 (*0-7923-4954-7*) Kluwer Academic.
Christodoulidis, Emilios A., ed. Communitarianism & Citizenship. (ALSP (Association for Legal & Social Philosophy) Ser.). 6p. 1998. text 67.95 (*1-84014-872-1*, Pub. by Ashgate Pub) Ashgate Pub Co.
***Christodoulou, Demetrios.** The Action Principle & Partial Differential Equations. LC 99-44795. 2000. text 89.50 (*0-691-04956-4*, Pub. by Princeton U Pr); pap. text 24.95 (*0-691-04957-2*, Pub. by Princeton U Pr) Cal Prin Full Svc.
Christodoulou, Demetrios. The Unpromised Land: Agrarian Reform & Conflict Worldwide. LC 88-31885. 256p. (C). 1990. pap. 19.95 (*0-86232-779-2*, Pub. by Zed Books); text 55.00 (*0-86232-778-4*, Pub. by Zed Books) St Martin.
Christodoulou, Demetrios & Klainerman, Sergiu. The Global Nonlinear Stability of the Minkowski Space. (Mathematical Ser.: No. 41). 432p. 1993. text 79.50 (*0-691-08777-6*, Pub. by Princeton U Pr) Cal Prin Full Svc.
Christodoulou, G. N. The Delusional Misidentification Syndromes. (Bibliotheca Psychiatrica Ser.: No. 164). (Illus.). x, 154p. 1986. 85.25 (*3-8055-4213-5*) S Karger.
Christodoulou, G. N., ed. Psychosomatic Medicine: Past & Future. LC 87-29075. (Illus.). 396p. 1988. 95.00 (*0-306-42780-X*, Plenum Trade) Perseus Pubng.
Christodoulou, G. N. & Kontaxakis, V., eds. Topics in Preventive Psychiatry. (Bibliotheca Psychiatrica Ser.: No. 165). (Illus.). viii, 152p. 1994. 121.75 (*3-8055-5877-5*) S Karger.
Christodoulou, George N., et al, eds. Issues in Preventive Psychiatry. LC 99-35333. (Illus.). x, 148p. 1999. 97.50 (*3-8055-6912-2*) S Karger.
Christodoulou, Manoulis A., jt. auth. see Rovithakis, George A.
Christodoulou, Panikos. Inward Investment: An Overview & Guide to the Literature. (Keynote Ser.). 128p. 1996. pap. 52.00 (*0-7123-0830-X*, Pub. by SRIS) L Erlbaum Assocs.
Christof-Fuchsle, Martin. Rajputentum und Puranische Geschichtsschreibung. X, 322p. 1997. 57.95 (*3-631-31590-2*) P Lang Pubng.
Christofell, Douglas, et al. Restoring Praise & Worship to the Church. 176p. 1989. pap. 10.99 (*0-938612-40-9*) Destiny Image.
Christoff, jt. auth. see Pogue.
***Christoff, Evelyn.** What's in That Box? A Spiritual War Story. 2000. 18.00 (*0-8059-4979-8*) Dorrance.
Christoff, Joseph. Surface Infrastructure: High-Speed Rail Projects in the United States. (Illus.). 53p. (C). 1999. pap. text 20.00 (*0-7881-8154-8*) DIANE Pub.
***Christoff, Joseph.** Surface Transportation: Moving into the 21st Century. (Illus.). 83p. (C). 2000. pap. text 20.00 (*0-7881-8895-X*) DIANE Pub.
Christoff, Joseph A. Rail Transportation: Federal Railroad Administration's New Approach to Railroad Safety. (Illus.). 70p. (C). 1998. pap. text 20.00 (*0-7881-4941-5*) DIANE Pub.
Christoff, Peter K. An Introduction to Nineteenth Century Russian Slavophilism: A Study in Ideas, Vol. 2. (Slavistic Printings & Reprintings Ser.). 1972. text 90.80 (*90-279-2297-7*) Mouton.
— K. S. Aksakov: A Study in Ideas. LC 63-45564. (Introduction to Nineteenth-Century Russian Slavophilism Ser.: Vol. 3). 491p. 1982. reprint ed. pap. 152.30 (*0-7837-9318-9*, 206005800004) Bks Demand.
Christoffel, E. G. Laboratory Studies of Heterogeneous Catalytic Processes. (Studies in Surface Science & Catalysis: No. 42). viv,260p. 1989. 246.00 (*0-444-43025-3*) Elsevier.
Christoffel, Katherine T. Cypress Rain. LC 96-61235. 160p. (Orig.). 1997. pap. 11.95 (*0-9654569-1-9*) Thunder Rain.
Christoffel, Katherine T. & Mizzell, Thurman E., Jr. Beyond Magnolias: A Collection of Poetry in True Conscience. 108p. (Orig.). 1996. pap. 19.95 (*0-9654569-0-0*) Thunder Rain.
Christoffel, R. Zwingli or the Rise of the Reformation in Switzerland. 1977. lib. bdg. 59.95 (*0-8490-2859-0*) Gordon Pr.
Christoffel, Tom & Gallagher, Susan S. Injury Prevention & Public Health: Practical Knowledge, Skills, & Strategies. 424p. 1999. 49.00 (*0-8342-0840-7*, 08407) Aspen Pub.
Christoffel, Tom & Teret, Stephen P. Protecting the Public: Legal Issues in Injury Prevention. LC 92-36159. (Illus.). 248p. 1993. text 45.00 (*0-19-507368-1*) OUP.
Christoffel von Grimmelshausen, Hans J. The Singular Life Story of Heedless Hopalong. Hiller, Robert L. & Osborne, John C., trs. LC 81-10446. (Illus.). 286p. reprint ed. pap. 88.70 (*0-608-10612-7*, 207123400009) Bks Demand.
Christoffer, V. F. Handbook of Electrical Tables & Design Criteria. LC 98-10517. 512p. 1998. 64.95 incl. cd-rom (*0-07-913722-9*) McGraw.
Christoffers, Henry, tr. see Boltyanskii, Vladimir G. & Gokhberg, Izrail T.
Christoffersen, Erik E. The Actor's Way. LC 92-21086. (Illus.). 240p. (C). 1993. pap. 25.99 (*0-415-08796-1*) Routledge.
— The Actor's Way. Fowler, Richard, tr. LC 92-21086. (Basic Essentials Ser.). (Illus.). 240p. (C). (gr. 13). 1993. 90.00 (*0-415-08795-3*, B0358) Routledge.
Christoffersen, Hans, tr. see Stinissen, Wilfrid.
Christoffersen, M. & Henten, A., eds. Telecommunication - Limits to Deregulation. LC 93-77462. (European Communication Policy Research Ser.). 200p. (gr. 12). 1993. pap. 78.00 (*90-5199-128-2*, Pub. by IOS Pr) IOS Press.
Christoffersen, Peter W. French Music in the Early Sixteenth Century. 845p. 1994. 141.00 (*87-7289-242-0*, Pub. by Mus Tusculanum) Paul & Co Pubs.
Christoffersen, R. E. Basic Principles & Techniques of Molecular Quantum Mechanics. (Advanced Texts in Chemistry Ser.). (Illus.). xvi, 686p. 1989. 99.95 (*0-387-96759-1*, 2687) Spr-Verlag.
Christoffersen, Ralph E., ed. Algorithms for Chemical Computations. LC 77-5030. (ACS Symposium Ser.: Vol. 46). 159p. 1977. reprint ed. pap. 49.30 (*0-608-03837-7*, 206428400008) Bks Demand.
Christoffersen, Ralph E. & Olson, Edward C., eds. Computer-Assisted Drug Design. LC 79-21038. (ACS Symposium Ser.: No. 112). 1979. 65.95 (*0-8412-0521-3*) Am Chemical.
Christoffersen, Ralph E., jt. ed. see Olson, Edward C.
Christofferson, April. After the Dance. LC 94-68379. 488p. (Orig.). 1994. pap. 5.99 (*0-89716-524-1*, Peanut Btr Pubng) Elton-Wolf Pub.
***Christofferson, April.** Clinical Trial. 304p. 2000. text 24.95 (*0-312-86899-5*) St Martin.
Christofferson, April. Edgewater. 1998. mass mkt. 5.99 (*0-8125-9045-7*, Pub. by Forge NYC) St Martin.
***Christofferson, April.** The Protocol. LC 99-33234. 304p. 1999. 23.95 (*0-312-86638-0*, Pub. by Forge NYC) St Martin.
— The Protocol. 384p. 2000. mass mkt. 6.99 (*0-8125-6188-0*) Tor Bks.
Christofferson, Thomas R. French Socialists in Power, Nineteen Eighty-One to Nineteen Eighty-Six: From Autogestion to Cohabitation. LC 89-40765. 272p. 1991. 45.00 (*0-87413-403-X*) U Delaware Pr.
Christoffersson, Britt-Marie. Swedish Sweaters. Kelsey, John, ed. LC 90-11129. (Illus.). 144p. 1990. 17.95 (*0-942391-80-2*, 070126) Taunton.
Christoffersson, Olle. The Earnest Expectation of the Creature: The Flood-Tradition As Matrix of Romans 8: 18-27. (Coniectanea Biblica. New Testament Ser.: No. 23). 174p. (Orig.). 1990. pap. 49.50 (*91-22-00988-4*) Coronet Bks.
Christofides, Constantinos & Chibaudo, Gerard, eds. Semiconductors & Semimetals Vol. 46: Effect of Disorder & Defects in Ion-Implanted Semiconductors: Optical & Photo-Thermal Characterization. (Illus.). 316p. 1997. text 125.00 (*0-12-752146-1*) Morgan Kaufmann.
Christofides, Constantinos, jt. auth. see Mandelis, Andreas.
Christofides, Nicos, et al, eds. Combinatorial Optimization. LC 78-11131. 435p. reprint ed. pap. 134.90 (*0-8357-3396-3*, 203965300013) Bks Demand.
***Christofides, Panagiotis D.** Nonlinear & Robust Control of PDE Systems: Methods & Applications to Transport-Reaction Problems. 2000. 59.95 (*0-8176-4156-4*) Spr-Verlag.
Christofis, Lee. Kelvin Coe: A Dancer's Life. 240p. 1996. 39.95 (*0-522-84616-5*, Pub. by Melbourne Univ Pr) Paul & Co Pubs.
Christoforidis, Alexander. Neotraditional Developments: The New Urbanism. LC 95-38689. (CPL Bibliographies Ser.: Vol. 322). 30p. 1995. pap. 10.00 (*0-86602-322-4*, Sage Prdcls Pr) Sage.
Christol, Carl Q. The Modern International Law of Outer Space. (Policy Studies on International Politics). (Illus.). 945p. 1982. 210.00 (*0-08-029367-0*, K130, Pergamon Pr) Elsevier.
— Space Law: Past, Present & Future. 280p. 1991. pap. 103.00 (*90-6544-475-0*) Kluwer Law Intl.
Christopeit, N., et al, eds. Stochastic Differential Systems. (Lecture Notes in Control & Information Sciences: Vol. 78). (Illus.). v, 365p. 1986. 50.95 (*0-387-16228-3*) Spr-Verlag.
Christopeit, N., jt. ed. see Kohlmann, M.
Christoper, Barbara. Iron on Transfer Patterns-Audubon Birds. 1980. text 4.95 (*0-486-23767-2*) Dover.
Christoph, jt. see Brown.
Christoph, jt. auth. see Brown.
Christoph, jt. contrib. by see Brown.
Christoph, Florence A. Upstate New York in the 1760s. LC 91-68234. (Illus.). 320p. 1992. 39.50 (*0-929539-90-7*, 1328) Picton Pr.
— Vital Records of Jerusalem Reformed Church: Baptisms, 1792-1886; Marriages, 1822-1885; Deaths, 1851-1890; Feura Bush, Albany County, NY. Kelly, Arthur C., ed. (Palatine Transcripts Ser.). 140p. 1987. lib. bdg. 28.00 (*1-56012-082-7*, 81) Kinship Rhinebeck.
Christoph, Florence A. & Christoph, Peter R., eds. The Andros Papers, 1674-1676. Gehring, Charles T., tr. from DUT. (New York Historical Manuscripts). 664p. 1989. text 75.00 (*0-8156-2457-3*) Syracuse U Pr.
Christoph, Florence A., jt. ed. see Christoph, Peter R.
Christoph, James B. Capital Punishment & British Politics. LC 62-12639. 200p. reprint ed. pap. 62.00 (*0-8357-9644-2*, 201575200002) Bks Demand.
Christoph, Peter R. Bradt Family: A Norwegian Family in Colonial America. 3rd ed. 250p. 1995. reprint ed. pap. 37.50 (*0-8328-4449-7*); reprint ed. lib. bdg. 47.50 (*0-8328-4448-9*) Higginson Bk Co.
— New York Historical Manuscripts: Dutch Kingston Papers, 2 vols. Scott, Kenneth & Stryker-Rodda, Kenn, eds. Versteeg, Dingman, tr. LC 75-5971. (Illus.). xxii, 849p. 1999. pap. 60.00 (*0-8063-0720-X*) Clearfield Co.

An Asterisk (*) at the beginning of an entry indicates that the title is appearing for the first time.

Christoph, Peter R., ed. The Andros Papers, 1677-1678. (New York Historical Manuscripts). (Illus.). 450p. 1990. text 75.00 (*0-8156-2496-4*) Syracuse U Pr.
— The Dongan Papers, 1683-1688, Pt. 1. (New York Historical Manuscripts). 200p. 1993. 55.00 (*0-8156-2570-7*) Syracuse U Pr.
— The Dongan Papers, 1683-1688: Files of the Provincial Secretary of New York During the Administration of Governor Thomas Dongan, Pt. 2. LC 93-7727. (New York Historical Manuscripts: Vol. 35). xxxv, 560p. 1996. 75.00 (*0-8156-2624-X*) Syracuse U Pr.
***Christoph, Peter R., ed.** The Leisler Papers, 1689-1691: Files of the Provincial Secretary of New York Relating to the Administration of Lieutenant-Governor Jacob Leisler. LC 99-48622. 656p. 1999. 90.00 (*0-8156-2820-X*) Syracuse U Pr.
Christoph, Peter R. & Christoph, Florence A., eds. The Andros Papers, Sixteen Seventy-Nine to Sixteen Eighty. Gehring, Charles T., tr. from DUT. (New York Historical Manuscripts Ser.). 584p. 1991. text 75.00 (*0-8156-2520-0*) Syracuse U Pr.
Christoph, Peter R., jt. ed. see Christoph, Florence A.
Christoph, Peter R., ed. see Whittelsey, Henry Edgar.
Christoph, Richard T., jt. auth. see Smith, Glenn T.
Christophe. Christophe's Book of Hair & Beauty. 2000. 50.00 (*0-06-019320-4*) HarpC.
***Christophe, Armand B. & DeVriese, Stephanie.** Fat Digestion & Absorption. LC 00-25386. 448p. 2000. 130.00 (*1-893997-12-X*) Am Oil Chemists.
Christophe, Armond, ed. Structural Modified Food Fats: Synthesis, Biochemistry & Use. LC 98-17717. (Illus.). 256p. 1998. lib. bdg. 90.00 (*0-935315-93-4*, PC114) Am Oil Chemists.
***Christophe, Francine.** From a World Apart: A Little Girl in the Concentration Camps. Burls, Christine, tr. LC 99-46937. (Illus.). 160p. 2000. pap. 15.00 (*0-8032-6402-X*, A Bison Orig) U of Nebr Pr.
Christophe, Marc A. Le Pain de l'Exil. LC 88-80261. (FRE.). 95p. (Orig.). 1988. pap. 10.95 (*0-945306-00-8*) W F Garnett.
Christopher. An Attitude of Giving: Notes & Other Things. 2nd ed. (Illus.). 1975. pap. 1.00 (*0-916940-02-0*) World Light.
— A Good Feeling. 1978. pap. 1.00 (*0-916940-03-9*) World Light.
— Our New Age: Words for the People. LC 77-72309. (Illus.). (Orig.). 1977. pap. 2.95 (*0-916940-01-2*) World Light.
***Christopher.** Stranger in Right Field: A Peach Street Mudders Story. 64p. 2000. pap. 4.50 (*0-316-10677-1*) Little.
— A Trip to the Stars. 2001. write for info. (*0-7432-0330-5*) S&S Trade.
Christopher. Wing on Ice. (J). 1997. pap. 3.95 (*0-316-13727-8*) Little.
Christopher, et al. Arrogantly Crabby. (Illus.). 88p. (Orig.). 1990. pap. 5.95 (*0-9622988-0-8*) Seaglass Pubns.
Christopher, A. J. The Atlas of Apartheid. LC 93-24510. (Illus.). 224p. (C). 1993. pap. 27.99 (*0-415-10268-5*) Routledge.
***Christopher, A. J.** Atlas of States: Global Change, 1900-2000. (Illus.). 286p. 1999. 250.00 (*0-471-98613-5*) Wiley.
Christopher, A. J. South Africa. LC 81-8254. (World's Landscapes Ser.). (Illus.). 255p. (Orig.). reprint ed. pap. 79.10 (*0-8357-3545-1*, 203449400090) Bks Demand.
Christopher, Amanda J., ed. see Smith, Stanley R.
Christopher, Andre. Top 10 Men's Tennis Players. LC 97-19979. (Sports Top 10 Ser.). (Illus.). 48p. (J). (gr. 4-10). 1998. lib. bdg. 18.95 (*0-7660-1009-0*) Enslow Pubs.
Christopher, Barbara. Butterfly Iron-on Transfer Patterns. 81st ed. (Illus.). 48p. (Orig.). 1992. pap. 3.95 (*0-486-26908-6*) Dover.
— Charted Seashell Designs. (Illus.). 48p. 1990. pap. 3.95 (*0-486-26286-3*) Dover.
— Decorative Alphabets Charted Designs. (Illus.). 48p. (Orig.). 1988. pap. 3.95 (*0-486-25631-6*) Dover.
— Easy to Make Cross Stitch Samplers & Mottoes: One Hundred & Thirty-Eight Lithographs, Etchings & Woodcuts. 32p. 1984. pap. 2.95 (*0-486-24664-7*) Dover.
— Elegant Christmas Ornaments to Crochet. LC 94-45593. 32p. 1995. pap. 3.95 (*0-486-28596-0*) Dover.
— Nautical Charted Designs. (Illus.). 48p. 1990. pap. 3.95 (*0-486-26129-8*) Dover.
— Old-Fashioned Christmas Charted Designs. LC 92-5583. (Needlework Ser.). 48p. 1992. pap. 3.50 (*0-486-27153-6*) Dover.
— Old-Fashioned Floral Charted Designs. (Illus.). 48p. 1990. pap. 3.95 (*0-486-26302-9*) Dover.
— Quick & Easy Christmas Charted Designs. 48p. 1990. pap. 3.50 (*0-486-26419-X*) Dover.
— Quick-&-Easy Christmas Crochet. (Illus.). 32p. 1991. pap. 2.95 (*0-486-26805-5*) Dover.
— Quick & Easy Miniature Samplers for Cross-Stitch. 32p. 1986. pap. 2.95 (*0-486-25209-4*) Dover.
Christopher, Barbara. Sixty Crocheted Snowflakes. 32p. (Orig.). 1987. pap. 3.95 (*0-486-25393-7*) Dover.
Christopher, Barbara. Tropical Fish Charted Designs. LC 92-24968. (Needlework Ser.). 48p. 1992. 3.50 (*0-486-27341-5*) Dover.
— Victorian Crocheted Christmas Ornaments: 33 Quick-&-Easy Projects. LC 93-13773. (Needlework Ser.). 32p. 1993. pap. 3.50 (*0-486-27627-9*) Dover.
Christopher, Barbara, jt. auth. see Christopher, William.
Christopher, Bill, ed. see Black, John R.
Christopher, Bill, ed. see Block, Thomas A. & Frame, J. Davidson.
Christopher, Bill, ed. see Bowers, David A.
Christopher, Bill, ed. see Bundy, Wayne M.
Christopher, Bill, ed. see Christopher, William F.
Christopher, Bill, ed. see Drake, John D.
Christopher, Bill, ed. see Fitz-Enz, Jac & Phillips, Jack J.
Christopher, Bill, ed. see Langevin, Roger G.
Christopher, Bill, ed. see Mason, Stanley I., Jr.
Christopher, Bill, ed. see McClure, Paul.
Christopher, Bill, ed. see Oxenfeldt, Alfred R.
Christopher, Bill, ed. see Poltorzycki, Stephen.
Christopher, Bill, ed. see Rubinyl, Paul.
Christopher, Bill, ed. see Sakurai, Michiharu & Scarbrough, D. Paul.
Christopher, Bill, ed. see Scheuing, Eberhard E.
Christopher, Bill, ed. see Sorenson, David P.
Christopher, Bill, ed. see Thor, Cari G.
Christopher, Bill, ed. see Watanabe, Ichigen.
Christopher, Bob & Christopher, Ellen. Christopher's America on Fifteen to Twenty-Five Dollars a Night Dining: Mid-West States. 80p. (Orig.). 1983. pap. 4.95 (*0-930570-04-9*) Travel Discover.
— Christopher's America on Fifteen to Twenty-Five Dollars a Night Dining: Northwest States. 80p. (Orig.). 1983. pap. 4.95 (*0-930570-06-5*) Travel Discover.
— Christopher's America on Fifteen to Twenty-Five Dollars a Night Dining & Lodging Guide: Northeast States. 80p. (Orig.). 1983. pap. 4.95 (*0-930570-02-2*) Travel Discover.
— Christopher's America on Fifteen to Twenty-Five Dollars a Night Dining & Lodging Guide: Southern States. 80p. (Orig.). 1983. pap. 4.95 (*0-930570-03-0*) Travel Discover.
— Christopher's America on Fifteen to Twenty-Five Dollars a Night Dining & Lodging Guide: Southwest States. 80p. (Orig.). 1983. pap. 4.95 (*0-930570-05-7*) Travel Discover.
— Christopher's Bed & Breakfast Guide to U. S. & Canada. 80p. (Orig.). 1983. pap. 4.95 (*0-930570-07-3*) Travel Discover.
***Christopher, Brian.** The Detective Poems. 32p. 2000. pap. 4.00 (*1-882550-30-7*, Pandemonium Pr) Quiet Lion Pr.
***Christopher, Brooke.** Middle Ages. 3rd ed. 464p. 2000. 79.95 (*0-582-36905-3*) Longman.
Christopher, Carol W., ed. Paul Caponigro "Masterworks from 40 Years" LC 93-84343. (Illus.). 140p. 1993. 100.00 (*0-9616515-5-5*) Photog West Graphics.
Christopher, Carol W., ed. see Jordan, Jim.
Christopher, Carol W., ed. see Newhall, Beaumont, et al.
Christopher, Carol W., ed. see Thompson, Dody.
Christopher, Carol W., ed. see Weston, Brett.
Christopher, Catherine. The Complete Book of Doll Making & Collecting. 2nd rev. ed. LC 76-102176. (Illus.). 288p. 1971. reprint ed. pap. 9.95 (*0-486-22066-4*) Dover.
Christopher, Cathy. This Time, for Sure. large type ed. (Romance Ser.). 272p. 1995. pap. 16.99 (*0-7089-7675-1*, Linford) Ulverscroft.
Christopher, Cindy J. Building Parent-Teacher Communication: An Educator's Guide. 157p. 1996. pap. 24.95 (*1-56676-380-0*, 763800) Scarecrow.
— Nuts & Bolts: Survival Guide for Teachers. LC 91-6691. 140p. 1997. pap. text 24.95 (*0-87762-858-0*) Scarecrow.
Christopher, Curtis P. Birmingham. 1996. 20.95 (*0-385-31737-9*) Doubleday.
— Watsons Birmingham. (J). 1995. 20.95 (*0-385-31004-8*) BDD Bks Young Read.
— Watsons of Birmingham. 1996. 20.95 (*0-385-44651-9*) Bantam.
Christopher, Daniel S., ed. Text & Experience: Towards a Cultural Exegesis of the Bible. LC 96-147571. (Biblical Seminar Ser.: No. 35). 354p. 1995. pap. text 28.50 (*1-85075-740-2*, Pub. by Sheffield Acad) CUP Services.
***Christopher, David.** British Culture: Introduction. LC 99-36124. 224p. 1999. pap. 20.99 (*0-415-14218-0*) Routledge.
Christopher, David. Desk Stress. 16p. 1991. pap. 1.00 (*1-880745-00-3*) Global City.
Christopher, David, jt. auth. see Ellis, Sandra K.
Christopher, David L. Handicap! Finding the Key Horse: Finding the Key Horse. 2nd ed. 170p. (Orig.). 1997. pap. 12.95 (*0-89709-201-5*) Liberty Pub.
— Inside Thoroughbred Racing. 192p. (Orig.). 1987. pap. 14.95 (*0-89709-160-4*) Liberty Pub.
— Winning at the Track. LC 83-81134. (Illus.). 160p. 1991. pap. 9.95 (*0-89709-195-7*) Liberty Pub.
— Winning at the Track. LC 83-81134. (Illus.). 160p. 1997. disk 59.95 (*0-89709-215-5*) Liberty Pub.
— Winning at the Track. 4th ed. 158p. 1994. pap. 9.95 (*0-89709-211-2*) Liberty Pub.
Christopher, Dean A. Manual Communication: A Basic Text & Workbook with Practical Exercises. LC 75-38884. (Illus.). 544p. 1976. pap. 39.00 (*0-936104-63-5*, 1107) PRO-ED.
Christopher, Debbonnaire. The Day the Ohio Canal Turned Eerie. LC 93-6614. (Illus.). (J). 1993. 3.00 (*1-880443-10-4*) Roscoe Village.
— Eliza Johnson's Kitchen Book. LC 91-47610. Orig. Title: Roscoe Village Recipes. (Illus.). 48p. 1992. reprint ed. pap. 4.00 (*1-880443-02-3*) Roscoe Village.
— Eliza Johnson's Kitchen Book: Being a Collection of Receipts for Cookery ... Housewifery, Economy, the Duties of the Family ... from the Journal of a Young Housewife. (Illus.). 60p. (Orig.). 1992. pap. 3.95 (*1-880443-09-0*) Roscoe Village.
***Christopher, Doris.** Come to the Table: A Celebration of Family Life. LC 99-26604. 320p. 1999. 22.95 (*0-446-52428-X*, Pub. by Warner Bks) Little.
— Come to the Table: A Celebration of Family Life. 2000. pap. 12.95 (*0-446-67623-3*) Warner Bks.
Christopher, Elizabeth M. & Smith, Larry M. Leadership Training: A Sourcebook of Activities. LC 93-34128. 250p. 1993. pap. 49.95 (*0-7494-0988-6*, Kogan Pg Educ) Stylus Pub VA.
Christopher, Ellen, jt. auth. see Christopher, Bob.
Christopher, Ellen, jt. auth. see Christopher, Robert.
***Christopher, Elphis & Solomon, Hester, eds.** Jungian Thought in the Modern World. 260p. 1999. 55.00 (*1-85343-466-3*, Pub. by Free Assoc Bks); pap. 25.00 (*1-85343-467-1*, Pub. by Free Assoc Bks) Intl Spec Bk.
***Christopher, F. Scott.** To Dance the Dance: A Symbolic Interactional Exploration of Premarital Sexuality. LC 00-44247. (Series on Personal Relationships). 2000. write for info. (*0-8058-3710-8*) L Erlbaum Assocs.
Christopher, Frederick J. Basketry. (Illus.). 111p. 1952. pap. 3.95 (*0-486-20677-7*) Dover.
Christopher, G. Amber Brown Is Not a Crayon: A Study Guide. Friedland, J. & Kessler, R., eds. (Novel-Ties Ser.). (J). (gr. 3-6). 1997. pap. text 15.95 (*0-7675-0150-0*) Lrn Links.
— Flat Stanley: A Study Guide. Friedland, J. & Kessler, R., eds. (Novel-Ties Ser.). (J). (gr. 1-3). 1997. pap. text 15.95 (*0-7675-0148-9*) Lrn Links.
— Franklin Fibs: A Study Guide. Friedland, J. & Kessler, R., eds. (Little Novel-Ties Ser.). (J). (gr. k-2). 1997. pap. text 14.95 (*0-7675-0169-1*) Lrn Links.
— Ox-Cart Man: A Study Guide. Friedland, J. & Kessler, R., eds. (Little Novel-Ties Ser.). (J). (gr. k-2). 1997. pap. text 14.95 (*0-7675-0170-5*) Lrn Links.
Christopher, Garrett. Abby: A Study Guide. Friedland, J. & Kessler, R., eds. (Little Novel-Ties Ser.). (J). (gr. k-2). 1994. pap. text, student ed. 14.95 (*1-56982-080-5*) Lrn Links.
— Aldo Applesauce: A Study Guide. Friedland, J. & Kessler, R., eds. (Novel-Ties Ser.). (J). (gr. 2-4). 1998. pap. text, student ed. 15.95 (*0-7675-0295-7*) Lrn Links.
— Alexander & the Terrible, Horrible, No Good, Very Bad Day: A Study Guide. Friedland, J. & Kessler, R., eds. (Little Novel-Ties Ser.). (J). 1992. pap. text, student ed. 14.95 (*0-88122-732-3*) Lrn Links.
— Alexander, Who Used to Be Rich Last Sunday: A Study Guide. Friedland, J. & Kessler, R., eds. (Novel-Ties Ser.). (J). (gr. k-2). 1998. pap. text, student ed. 14.95 (*0-7675-0323-6*) Lrn Links.
— Amelia Bedelia: A Study Guide. Friedland, J. & Kessler, R., eds. (Little Novel-Ties Ser.). (J). (gr. k-3). 1994. pap. text, student ed. 14.95 (*1-56982-084-8*) Lrn Links.
— Anansi the Spider: A Study Guide. Friedland, J. & Kessler, R., eds. (Little Novel-Ties Ser.). (J). (gr. k-2). 1994. pap. text, student ed. 14.95 (*1-56982-076-7*) Lrn Links.
— Annie & the Old One: A Study Guide. Friedland, Joyce & Kessler, Rikki, eds. (Novel-Ties Ser.). (J). (gr. 1-4). 1991. pap. text 15.95 (*0-88122-564-9*) Lrn Links.
— Arthur's Baby: A Study Guide. Friedland, J. & Kessler, R., eds. (Little Novel-Ties Ser.). (J). (gr. k-2). 1995. pap. text, student ed. 14.95 (*1-56982-235-2*) Lrn Links.
— The Best Christmas Pageant Ever: A Study Guide. Friedland, J. & Kessler, R., eds. (Novel-Ties Ser.). (J). (gr. 3-5). 1998. pap. text, student ed. 15.95 (*0-7675-0297-3*) Lrn Links.
— A Big Fat Enormous Lie: A Study Guide. Friedland, J. & Kessler, R., eds. (Little Novel-Ties Ser.). (J). (gr. k-2). 1994. pap. text, student ed. 14.95 (*1-56982-078-3*) Lrn Links.
— Biography: A Study Guide. Friedland, J. & Kessler, R., eds. (Novel-Ties Ser.). (J). (gr. 5-8). 1987. pap. text, student ed. 15.95 (*0-88122-866-4*) Lrn Links.
— Blackberries in the Dark: A Study Guide. Friedland, J. & Kessler, R., eds. (Novel-Ties Ser.). (J). (gr. 2-4). 1995. pap. text, student ed. 15.95 (*1-56982-262-X*) Lrn Links.
— The Boxcar Children: A Study Guide. Friedland, J. & Kessler, R., eds. (Novel-Ties Ser.). (J). (gr. 2-5). 1993. pap. text, student ed. 15.95 (*0-88122-879-6*) Lrn Links.
— Caps for Sale: A Study Guide. Friedland, Joyce & Kessler, Rikki, eds. (Little Novel-Ties Ser.). (J). (gr. k-3). 1991. pap. text 14.95 (*0-88122-587-8*) Lrn Links.
— A Chair for My Mother: A Study Guide. Friedland, J. & Kessler, R., eds. (Little Novel-Ties Ser.). (J). (gr. k-2). 1993. pap. text, student ed. 14.95 (*0-88122-950-4*) Lrn Links.
— Clifford, the Big Red Dog: A Study Guide. Friedland, J. & Kessler, R., eds. (Little Novel-Ties Ser.). (J). (gr. k-2). 1992. pap. text, student ed. 14.95 (*0-88122-733-1*) Lrn Links.
— Clifford the Small Red Puppy: A Study Guide. Friedland, J. & Kessler, R., eds. (Novel-Ties Ser.). (J). (gr. k-2). 1998. pap. text, student ed. 14.95 (*0-7675-0324-4*) Lrn Links.
— Corduroy: A Study Guide. Friedland, Joyce & Kessler, Rikki, eds. (Little Novel-Ties Ser.). (J). (gr. k-2). 1991. pap. text 14.95 (*0-88122-588-6*) Lrn Links.
— Courage of Sarah Noble: A Study Guide. Friedland, J. & Kessler, R., eds. (Novel-Ties Ser.). (J). (gr. 2-4). 1992. pap. text, student ed. 15.95 (*0-88122-722-5*) Lrn Links.
— Curious George: A Study Guide. Friedland, J. & Kessler, R., eds. (Little Novel-Ties Ser.). (J). (gr. k-2). 1993. pap. text, student ed. 14.95 (*0-88122-945-8*) Lrn Links.
— Dandelion: A Study Guide. Friedland, J. & Kessler, R., eds. (Little Novel-Ties Ser.). (J). (gr. k-2). 1994. pap. text, student ed. 14.95 (*1-56982-077-5*) Lrn Links.
— A Gathering of Days: A Study Guide. Friedland, J. & Kessler, R., eds. (Novel-Ties Ser.). 24p. (J). (gr. 4-6). 1992. pap. text 15.95 (*0-88122-698-X*) Lrn Links.
— Gilberto & the Wind: A Study Guide. Friedland, J. & Kessler, R., eds. (Little Novel-Ties Ser.). (J). (gr. k-2). 1994. pap. text, student ed. 14.95 (*1-56982-079-1*) Lrn Links.
— Goodnight Moon: A Study Guide. Friedland, J. & Kessler, R., eds. (Little Novel-Ties Ser.). (J). (gr. k-2). 1992. pap. text, student ed. 14.95 (*0-88122-734-X*) Lrn Links.
— Gregory the Terrible Eater. Friedland, Joyce & Kessler, Rikki, eds. (J). (gr. k-2). 1991. pap. text, student ed. 14.95 (*0-88122-589-4*) Lrn Links.
— Humphrey's Bear: A Study Guide. Friedland, J. & Kessler, R., eds. (Little Novel-Ties Ser.). (J). (gr. k-2). 1995. pap. text, student ed. 14.95 (*1-56982-236-0*) Lrn Links.
— The Indian School: A Study Guide. Friedland, J., ed. (Novel-Ties Ser.). (J). (gr. 2-4). 1998. pap. text, student ed. 15.95 (*0-7675-0307-4*) Lrn Links.
— Ira Sleeps Over: A Study Guide. Friedland, Joyce & Kessler, Rikki, eds. (Little Novel-Ties Ser.). (J). (gr. k-2). 1991. pap. text 14.95 (*0-88122-590-8*) Lrn Links.
— Jennifer, Hecate, Macbeth, William McKinley & Me, Elizabeth: A Study Guide. Friedland, J. & Kessler, R., eds. (Novel-Ties Ser.). (J). (gr. 3-5). 1993. pap. text, student ed. 15.95 (*0-88122-899-0*) Lrn Links.
— The Last Puppy: A Study Guide. Friedland, J. & Kessler, R., eds. (Little Novel-Ties Ser.). (J). (gr. k-2). 1993. pap. text, student ed. 14.95 (*0-88122-947-4*) Lrn Links.
— The Legend of the Bluebonnet: A Study Guide. Friedland, J. & Kessler, R., eds. (Novel-Ties Ser.). (J). (gr. k-2). 1998. pap. text, student ed. 14.95 (*0-7675-0325-2*) Lrn Links.
— Leo the Late Bloomer: A Study Guide. Friedland, Joyce & Kessler, Rikki, eds. (Little Novel-Ties Ser.). (J). (gr. k-2). 1991. pap. text 14.95 (*0-88122-591-6*) Lrn Links.
— The Little Island: A Study Guide. Friedland, Joyce & Kessler, Rikki, eds. (Little Novel-Ties Ser.). (J). (gr. k-2). 1991. pap. text 14.95 (*0-88122-592-4*) Lrn Links.
— Lyle, Lyle, Crocodile. Friedland, J. & Kessler, R., eds. (Little Novel-Ties Ser.). (J). (gr. k-2). 1994. pap. text, student ed. 14.95 (*1-56982-083-X*) Lrn Links.
— Madeline: A Study Guide. Friedland, J. & Kessler, R., eds. (Little Novel-Ties Ser.). (J). (gr. k-2). 1992. pap. text 14.95 (*0-88122-735-8*) Lrn Links.
— Make Way for Ducklings: A Study Guide. Friedland, Joyce & Kessler, Rikki, eds. (Little Novel-Ties Ser.). (J). (gr. k-2). 1991. pap. text 14.95 (*0-88122-593-2*) Lrn Links.
— May I Bring a Friend: A Study Guide. Friedland, J. & Kessler, R., eds. (Little Novel-Ties Ser.). (J). (gr. k-2). 1994. pap. text, student ed. 14.95 (*1-56982-081-3*) Lrn Links.
— Mike Mulligan & His Steam Shovel: A Study Guide. Friedland, J. & Kessler, R., eds. (Little Novel-Ties Ser.). (J). (gr. k-2). 1995. pap. text, student ed. 14.95 (*1-56982-237-9*) Lrn Links.
— Miss Nelson Is Missing! A Study Guide. Friedland, J. & Kessler, R., eds. (Little Novel-Ties Ser.). (J). (gr. k-2). 1993. pap. text, student ed. 14.95 (*0-88122-948-2*) Lrn Links.
— Miss Rumphius: A Study Guide. Friedland, J. & Kessler, R., eds. (Little Novel-Ties Ser.). (J). (gr. k-2). 1995. pap. text, student ed. 14.95 (*1-56982-238-7*) Lrn Links.
— Missing May: A Study Guide. Friedland, J. & Kessler, R., eds. (Novel-Ties Ser.). (J). (gr. 4-6). 1994. pap. text, student ed. 15.95 (*1-56982-060-0*) Lrn Links.
— Pinkerton, Behave: A Study Guide. Friedland, J. & Kessler, R., eds. (Little Novel-Ties Ser.). (J). (gr. k-2). 1994. pap. text, student ed. 14.95 (*1-56982-082-1*) Lrn Links.
— Roxaboxen: A Study Guide. Friedland, J. & Kessler, R., eds. (Little Novel-Ties Ser.). (J). (gr. k-2). 1997. pap. text 14.95 (*0-7675-0171-3*) Lrn Links.
— Stevie: A Study Guide. Friedland, J. & Kessler, R., eds. (Little Novel-Ties Ser.). (J). (gr. k-2). 1993. pap. text, student ed. 14.95 (*0-88122-949-0*) Lrn Links.
— Stone Soup (Brown) A Study Guide. Friedland, J. & Kessler, R., eds. (Little Novel-Ties Ser.). (J). (gr. k-2). 1995. pap. text, student ed. 14.95 (*1-56982-239-5*) Lrn Links.
— The Story of Ferdinand: A Study Guide. Friedland, Joyce & Kessler, Rikki, eds. (Little Novel-Ties Ser.). (J). (gr. k-2). 1991. pap. text 14.95 (*0-88122-594-0*) Lrn Links.
— Strega Nona: A Study Guide. Friedland, J. & Kessler, R., eds. (Little Novel-Ties Ser.). (J). (gr. k-2). 1995. pap. text, student ed. 14.95 (*1-56982-240-9*) Lrn Links.
— Sylvester & the Magic Pebble: A Study Guide. Friedland, Joyce & Kessler, Rikki, eds. (Little Novel-Ties Ser.). (J). (gr. k-2). 1991. pap. text 14.95 (*0-88122-595-9*) Lrn Links.
— Tales of a Fourth Grade Nothing: A Study Guide. Friedland, Joyce & Kessler, Rikki, eds. (Novel-Ties Ser.). (J). (gr. 3-5). 1991. pap. text 15.95 (*0-88122-575-4*) Lrn Links.
— Tye May & the Magic Brush: A Study Guide. Friedland, J. & Kessler, R., eds. (Novel-Ties Ser.). (J). (gr. 1-3). 1994. pap. text, student ed. 15.95 (*1-56982-055-4*) Lrn Links.
— Umbrella: A Study Guide. Friedland, J. & Kessler, R., eds. (Little Novel-Ties Ser.). (J). (gr. k-2). 1992. pap. text, student ed. 14.95 (*0-88122-736-6*) Lrn Links.
— Where the Wild Things Are: A Study Guide. Friedland, J. & Kessler, R., eds. (Little Novel-Ties Ser.). (J). (gr. k-2). 1992. pap. text, student ed. 14.95 (*0-88122-737-4*) Lrn Links.
— Whistle for Willie: A Study Guide. Friedland, Joyce & Kessler, Rikki, eds. (Little Novel-Ties Ser.). (J). (gr. k-2). 1991. pap. text 14.95 (*0-88122-596-7*) Lrn Links.
— Why Mosquitoes Buzz in People's Ears: A Study Guide. Friedland, J. & Kessler, R., eds. (Little Novel-Ties Ser.). (J). (gr. k-2). 1993. pap. text 14.95 (*0-88122-946-6*) Lrn Links.
Christopher, H., et al. Heat Mining. 400p. 1986. text 89.95 (*0-419-12230-3*, 6774, E & FN Spon) Routledge.
Christopher, H., jt. auth. see Longuet-Higgins, H.
Christopher, Helen G. Double Entry. LC 96-68667. (Illus.). 127p. 1997. pap. 14.95 (*1-881908-15-1*) PanPress.
Christopher, J. Clif & Mather, Herb. Holy Smoke! Whatever Happened to Tithing. LC 99-61197. 112p. 1999. pap. 15.95 (*0-88177-284-4*, DR284, Pub. by Discipleship Res) P B D Inc.
***Christopher, James.** Elizabeth Taylor: The Biography. LC 00-23442. 2000. write for info. (*0-7862-2587-4*) Thorndike Pr.

C

— Elizabeth Taylor: The Illustrated Biography. (Illus.). 192p. 2000. 29.95 (*0-233-99620-6*, Pub. by Andre Deutsch) Trafalgar.

Christopher, James. Escape from Nicotine Country: How to Stop Smoking Painlessly. LC 99-41267. 360p. 1999. pap. 16.95 (*1-57392-751-1*) Prometheus Bks.

— How to Stay Sober: Recovery Without Religion. LC 88-1139. 191p. 1988. pap. 19.95 (*0-87975-457-5*) Prometheus Bks.

— S. O. S. Sobriety: The Proven Alternative to 12-Step Programs. LC 92-7772. 240p. (C). 1992. pap. 17.95 (*0-87975-726-4*) Prometheus Bks.

— Unhooked: Staying Sober & Drug-Free. LC 89-62703. 184p. 1989. pap. 17.95 (*0-87975-564-4*) Prometheus Bks.

Christopher, James W. Conflict in the Far East: American Diplomacy in China from 1928-1933. LC 77-111736. (American Imperialism: Viewpoints of United States Foreign Policy, 1898-1941 Ser.). 1970. reprint ed. 23.95 (*0-405-02007-4*) Ayer.

Christopher, Jay. Runaways. 72p. (YA). 1980. pap. 5.50 (*0-87129-666-7*, R25) Dramatic Pub.

Christopher, Jess. Alana's Secret Friend. LC 93-74754. (Little Mermaid Novels Ser.: No. 12). (Illus.). 80p. (J). (gr. 1-4). 1994. pap. 3.50 (*0-7868-4002-1*, Pub. by Disney Pr) Time Warner.

Christopher, Joe R. C. S. Lewis. (Twayne's English Authors Ser.). 160p. 1987. 28.95 (*0-8057-6944-7*, TEAS 442, Twyne) Mac Lib Ref.

Christopher, Joe R., ed. Dark Fantasy: Essays on Gothic & Modern Horror Fiction. (Illus.). 120p. 1998. pap. 9.95 (*0-910619-08-5*) Niekas Pubns.

Christopher, Joe R. & Ostling, Joan K. C. S. Lewis: An Annotated Checklist of Writings about Him & His works. LC 73-76556. (Serif Series: Bibliographies & Checklists: No. 30). 407p. reprint ed. pap. 126.20 (*0-7837-0567-0*, 204091100019) Bks Demand.

Christopher, John. Beyond the Burning Lands. 2nd ed. (Sword of the Spirits Trilogy Ser.). (J). 1989. 9.60 (*0-606-02267-8*, Pub. by Turtleback) Demco.

— Beyond the Burning Lands: The Sword of the Spirits Trilogy. 2nd ed. LC 78-152288. 180p. (J). (gr. 5-9). 1989. reprint ed. mass mkt. 4.50 (*0-02-042572-4*) Macmillan.

— Career Mathematics. (Illus.). 352p. (C). 1985. pap. text 57.00 (*0-13-114943-1*) P-H.

***Christopher, John.** The City of Gold & Lead. (YA). (gr. 5-9). 2000. 19.25 (*0-8446-7141-X*) Peter Smith.

Christopher, John. City of Gold & Lead. 1970. 9.05 (*0-606-02718-1*, Pub. by Turtleback) Demco.

— The City of Gold & Lead. 2nd ed. LC 88-16118. (Tripods Trilogy Ser.). (Illus.). 224p. (YA). (gr. 5-9). 1988. mass mkt. 3.95 (*0-02-042701-8*) Macmillan.

— The Death of Grass. (Orig.). 1993. reprint ed. lib. bdg. 18.95 (*0-89968-335-5*, Lghtyr Pr) Buccaneer Bks.

— A Dusk of Demons. LC 92-31730. 176p. (J). (gr. 5-9). 1994. lib. bdg. 14.95 (*0-02-718425-0*, Mac Bks Young Read) S&S Childrens.

— Dusk of Demons. 1996. mass mkt. 3.99 (*0-689-80633-7*) S&S Childrens.

— Dusk of Demons. 1996. 9.09 (*0-606-10793-2*, Pub. by Turtleback) Demco.

— Introductory Technical Mathematics. 2nd ed. 672p. (C). 1990. text 63.00 (*0-13-485665-1*) P-H.

— Lords of the Cold: Mountaineering Tales in Verse. LC 93-84082. 64p. (Orig.). 1993. pap. 11.95 (*0-9630779-5-3*) PPC Bks.

— The Pool of Fire. large type ed. 280p. (J). (gr. 3 up). 1990. 18.95 (*0-7451-1176-9*, G K Hall Lrg Type) Mac Lib Ref.

— The Pool of Fire. 2nd ed. LC 88-16117. (Tripods Trilogy Ser.). 192p. (YA). (gr. 5-9). 1988. mass mkt. 4.50 (*0-02-042721-2*) Macmillan.

— Pool of Fire. 2nd ed. (Tripods Triology Ser.). (J). 1988. 9.05 (*0-606-04360-8*, Pub. by Turtleback) Demco.

— The Prince in Waiting. (J). (gr. 5-9). 1984. 18.25 (*0-8446-6157-0*) Peter Smith.

— The Prince in Waiting. 1990. reprint ed. lib. bdg. 25.95 (*0-89966-668-X*) Buccaneer Bks.

Christopher, John. Prince in Waiting. 2nd ed. (Sword of the Spirits Trilogy Ser.). (J). 1989. 9.05 (*0-606-02269-4*, Pub. by Turtleback) Demco.

Christopher, John. The Prince in Waiting. 2nd ed. (Sword of the Spirits Trilogy Ser.). (Illus.). 192p. (YA). (gr. 5-9). 1989. reprint ed. mass mkt. 3.95 (*0-02-042573-2*) Macmillan.

— The Sword of the Spirits Trilogy. Incl. Beyond the Burning Lands. 1980. pap. Prince in Waiting. 1980. pap. (J). (gr. 6 up). 1980. Set pap. 7.95 (*0-02-042770-0*, Collier Bks Young) S&S Childrens.

— The Tripods Trilogy, 3 bks. (Illus.). (YA). (gr. 7 up). 1999. boxed set 17.95 (*0-689-00852-X*) Aladdin.

— The Tripods Trilogy, 3 bks. 2nd ed. 224p. (YA). (gr. 7 up). 1988. boxed set 13.50 (*0-02-042571-6*) Aladdin.

— When the Tripods Came. (Tripods Triology Ser.). (J). 1990. 9.05 (*0-606-04581-3*, Pub. by Turtleback) Demco.

— When the Tripods Came. LC 90-1436. (Prequel to the Tripods Trilogy Ser.). 160p. (YA). (gr. 7 up). 1990. reprint ed. mass mkt. 4.50 (*0-02-042575-9*) Macmillan.

— The White Mountains. LC 67-10362. 172p. (J). (gr. 5-9). 1967. lib. bdg. 16.00 (*0-02-718360-2*, Mac Bks Young Read) S&S Childrens.

Christopher, John. White Mountains. 1970. 9.05 (*0-606-05083-3*, Pub. by Turtleback) Demco.

Christopher, John. The White Mountains. large type ed. 256p. (J). (gr. 3 up). 1990. 16.95 (*0-7451-1043-6*, G K Hall Lrg Type) Mac Lib Ref.

— The White Mountains. 2nd ed. LC 88-16119. (Tripods Trilogy Ser.). (Illus.). 224p. (YA). (gr. 7 up). 1988. mass mkt. 3.95 (*0-02-042711-5*) Macmillan.

Christopher, John R. Capsicum. Bailey, Lotus, ed. LC 81-204342. (Illus.). 166p. 1980. per. 6.95 (*1-879436-09-4*, 99109) Christopher Pubns.

— The Cold Sheet Treatment. 1991. pap. 2.00 (*1-879436-07-8*, 99107) Christopher Pubns.

— Dr. Christopher Talks on Rejuvenation Through Elimination. 1994. pap. 2.00 (*1-879436-06-X*, 99106) Christopher Pubns.

— Dr. Christopher's Three-Day Cleansing Program. 32p. 1994. pap. 2.00 (*1-879436-04-3*, 99104) Christopher Pubns.

— Herbal Home Health Care. 2nd ed. LC 90-205302. (Illus.). 196p. 1976. per. 12.95 (*1-879436-03-5*, 99103) Christopher Pubns.

— The Incurables. 1991. pap. 2.00 (*1-879436-08-6*, 99108) Christopher Pubns.

— Just What Is the Word of Wisdom? 1991. pap. 2.00 (*1-879436-05-1*, 99105) Christopher Pubns.

— Regenerative Diet. LC 90-205281. 275p. 1982. per. 9.95 (*1-879436-00-0*, 99111) Christopher Pubns.

— School of Natural Healing. LC 90-205323. 724p. 1996. 39.95 (*1-879436-01-9*, 99101) Christopher Pubns.

Christopher, John R. & Gileadi, Cathy. Every Woman's Herbal. LC 90-20536. (Illus.). 225p. 1994. per. 14.95 (*1-879436-10-8*, 99110) Christopher Pubns.

Christopher, Joseph P., tr. see Augustine, Saint.

Christopher, Kay. Search for a Shadow. large type ed. 416p. 31.99 (*0-7089-4046-3*) Ulverscroft.

Christopher, Ken W. & Wright, Mary P. Os/2 Warp PowerPc: New Frontie. 476p. 1995. pap. 29.99 (*1-56884-458-1*) IDG Bks.

Christopher, Kenneth, ed. A Sampler of Devotional Poems. LC 96-51591. (Spiritual Samplers Ser.). 96p. (Orig.). 1997. pap. 1.95 (*0-8091-3721-6*) Paulist Pr.

Christopher, Kevin, et al. Fundamentals of 3D Studio Viz Instructor Guide. Keller, Drew, ed. (Illus.). 88p. 1997. pap. text, teacher ed. 25.00 (*1-890484-27-X*, KnowledgeWorks) HTR Inc.

— Fundamentals of 3D Studio Viz Student Guide, 2 vols. Keller, Drew, ed. (Illus.). 621p. 1997. pap. text, student ed., spiral bd. 150.00 (*1-890484-25-3*, KnowledgeWorks) HTR Inc.

— Update/Introduction to 3D Studio Viz Student Guide. Keller, Drew, ed. (Illus.). 256p. 1997. pap. text, student ed. 100.00 (*1-890484-30-X*, KnowledgeWorks) HTR Inc.

— Update/Introduction to 3D Studio Viz Instructor Guide. Keller, Drew, ed. (Illus.). 44p. 1997. pap. text, teacher ed., spiral bd. 25.00 (*1-890484-26-1*, KnowledgeWorks) HTR Inc.

Christopher, M. G. Parents & the Three R's for an Educated America: How to Help Your Child Succeed at School in Minutes a Day, Vol. 1 Primary Grades. (Illus.). 139p. (Orig.). 1990. pap. 16.95 (*0-9624022-1-4*) Venture Bk Pubns.

— Parents & the Three R's for an Educated America, Vol. 2: How to Help Your Child Succeed at School in Minutes a Day, Intermediate Grades. (Illus.). 140p. (Orig.). 1992. pap. 16.95 (*0-9624022-0-6*) Venture Bk Pubns.

— Parents & the Three R's for an Educated America, Vol. 2: How to Help Your Child Succeed at School in Minutes a Day, Intermediate Grades, Set. (Illus.). 140p. (Orig.). 1992. pap. write for info. (*0-9624022-2-2*) Venture Bk Pubns.

Christopher, Martin. Marketing Logistics. LC 97-179025. 192p. 1997. pap. text 37.95 (*0-7506-2209-1*) Buttrwrth-Heinemann.

— The Strategy of Distribution Management. LC 84-18214. (Illus.). 192p. 1985. 42.95 (*0-89930-114-2*, CSD/, Quorum Bks) Greenwood.

***Christopher, Martin, et al.** Relationship Marketing. 256p. 2000. pap. 39.95 (*0-7506-4839-2*) Buttrwrth-Heinemann.

Christopher, Martin, et al. Relationship Marketing: Bringing Quality, Customer Service & Marketing Together. (CIM Professional Development Ser.). 204p. 1993. pap. text 39.95 (*0-7506-0978-8*) Buttrwrth-Heinemann.

— Relationship Marketing: Strategy & Implementation. LC 99-231549. 509p. 1999. text 34.95 (*0-7506-3626-2*) Buttrwrth-Heinemann.

Christopher, Martin, jt. auth. see Wentworth, Felix.

Christopher, Mary. Harvest of Desire. large type ed. 304p. 1985. 27.99 (*0-7089-1238-9*) Ulverscroft.

— Songs for the Journey. (Illus.). 158p. (Orig.). 1988. pap. 7.98 (*0-943699-00-2*) Entheo Bks.

Christopher, Matt. All-Star Fever: A Peach Street Mudders Story. 1995. 9.15 (*0-606-11030-5*, Pub. by Turtleback) Demco.

— All Star Fever: A Peach Street Mudders Story. (Illus.). 64p. (J). (gr. k-3). 1997. pap. 4.50 (*0-316-14198-4*) Little.

— At the Plate with--Ken Griffey, Jr. LC 96-40974. 144p. (J). 1997. pap. 4.50 (*0-316-14233-6*) Little.

Christopher, Matt. At the Plate with--Ken Griffey, Jr. 1997. 9.60 (*0-606-11062-3*, Pub. by Turtleback) Demco.

Christopher, Matt. At the Plate with--Mo Vaughn. LC 96-48457. 144p. (J). 1997. pap. 4.50 (*0-316-14192-5*) Little.

— At the Plate with--Mo Vaughn. (Matt Christopher Sports Biographies Ser.). (J). 1997. 9.60 (*0-606-12621-X*, Pub. by Turtleback) Demco.

***Christopher, Matt.** At the Plate with Mark McGwire. LC 99-13728. 128p. (J). (gr. 3-7). 1999. pap. 4.95 (*0-316-13457-0*) Little.

— At the Plate with Sammy Sosa. LC 99-20562. 128p. (J). (gr. 3-7). 1999. pap. 4.95 (*0-316-13477-5*) Little.

Christopher, Matt. Baseball, Vol. II. (J). (gr. 4-7). 1991. pap. 11.85 (*0-316-14075-9*) Little.

— Baseball Flyhawk. (Illus.). 94p. (J). (gr. 4-7). 1995. pap. 3.95 (*0-316-14120-8*) Little.

— Baseball Flyhawk. 1995. 9.05 (*0-606-07264-0*, Pub. by Turtleback) Demco.

— Baseball Flyhawk Special. 1998. pap. 3.95 (*0-316-13678-6*) Little.

— Baseball Jokes & Riddles. LC 95-19883. (Illus.). 48p. (J). (gr. k-3). 1996. pap. 4.50 (*0-316-14081-3*) Little.

— Baseball Jokes & Riddles. 1996. 9.15 (*0-606-08694-3*, Pub. by Turtleback) Demco.

— Baseball Pals. (Illus.). 117p. (J). (gr. 4-6). 1990. pap. 3.95 (*0-316-14005-8*) Little.

— Baseball Pals. (J). 1984. 9.05 (*0-606-03050-6*, Pub. by Turtleback) Demco.

— Baseball Turnaround. LC 96-53116. 160p. (J). (gr. 4-6). 1997. pap. 3.95 (*0-316-14264-6*) Little.

— Baseball Turnaround. (Matt Christopher Sports Classics Ser.). 1997. 9.05 (*0-606-11093-3*, Pub. by Turtleback) Demco.

— The Basket Counts. (Illus.). 125p. (J). (gr. 4-6). 1991. pap. 3.95 (*0-316-14076-7*) Little.

— The Basket Counts. 1991. 9.05 (*0-606-00302-9*, Pub. by Turtleback) Demco.

— The Captain Contest. LC 98-33802. (Soccer' Cats Ser.: No. 1). (Illus.). 64p. (J). (gr. 2-4). 1999. 13.95 (*0-316-14169-0*) Little.

— Catch That Pass! (J). 1969. 9.15 (*0-606-04182-6*, Pub. by Turtleback) Demco.

— Catch That Pass!, Vol. 1. LC 77-77442. (Illus.). 130p. (J). (gr. 4-6). 1989. pap. 3.95 (*0-316-13924-6*) Little.

— Catcher with a Glass Arm. (Illus.). 61406p. (J). (gr. 4-6). 1985. pap. 3.95 (*0-316-13985-8*) Little.

Christopher, Matt. Catcher with a Glass Arm. (J). 1985. 9.05 (*0-606-04066-8*, Pub. by Turtleback) Demco.

— The Catcher's Mask: A Peach Street Mudders Story. LC 97-40052. (Illus.). 64p. (J). (gr. k-3). 1998. 13.95 (*0-316-14186-0*) Little.

Christopher, Matt. The Catcher's Mask: A Peach Street Murders Story. (Illus.). 64p. (J). (gr. k-3). 1999. pap. 4.50 (*0-316-14185-2*) Little.

— Center Court Sting. LC 98-16835. 160p. (J). (gr. 4-6). 1998. 15.95 (*0-316-14278-6*) Little.

— Center Court Sting. LC 98-16835. 160p. (J). (gr. 4-8). 1998. pap. 3.95 (*0-316-14205-0*) Little.

— Centerfield Ballhawk. (Illus.). 59p. (J). (gr. k-3). 1994. pap. 4.50 (*0-316-14272-7*) Little.

— Centerfield Ballhawk. LC 91-28989. (Springboard Bks.). 1992. 9.15 (*0-606-06270-X*, Pub. by Turtleback) Demco.

— Centering Court Sting. 1998. 9.05 (*0-606-13260-0*, Pub. by Turtleback) Demco.

— Challenge at Second Base. (Illus.). 111p. (J). (gr. 4-6). 1992. pap. 3.95 (*0-316-14249-2*) Little.

— Challenge at Second Base. (J). 1992. 9.05 (*0-606-01421-7*, Pub. by Turtleback) Demco.

— The Comeback Challenge. LC 95-22346. (Illus.). 176p. (J). (gr. 3-7). 1996. 15.95 (*0-316-14090-2*) Little.

— The Comeback Challenge. LC 95-22346. (Illus.). 176p. (J). (gr. 4-7). 1996. pap. 3.95 (*0-316-14152-6*) Little.

— Comeback Challenge. 1996. 9.05 (*0-606-08716-8*, Pub. by Turtleback) Demco.

— The Counterfeit Tackle. 150p. (J). (gr. 4-6). 1990. pap. 3.95 (*0-316-14243-3*) Little.

— Counterfeit Tackle. (J). 1965. 9.05 (*0-606-04642-9*, Pub. by Turtleback) Demco.

— Crackerjack Halfback. LC 96-222442. (Matt Christopher Ser.). (Illus.). 160p. (J). (gr. 4-6). 1996. pap. 3.95 (*0-316-13795-2*) Little.

— Crackerjack Halfback. 1996. 9.05 (*0-606-10164-0*, Pub. by Turtleback) Demco.

— Crackerjack Halfback - Pages. 1997. pap. 3.95 (*0-316-13728-6*) Little.

— Diamond Champs. 120p. (J). (gr. 4-7). 1990. pap. 3.95 (*0-316-14006-6*) Little.

Christopher, Matt. Diamond Champs. (J). 1977. 9.05 (*0-606-03204-5*, Pub. by Turtleback) Demco.

Christopher, Matt. Dirt Bike Racer. LC 79-745. (Matt Christopher Sports Classics Ser.). (Illus.). 149p. (J). (gr. 3-7). 1986. pap. 3.95 (*0-316-14053-8*) Little.

— Dirt Bike Racer. (J). 1979. 9.05 (*0-606-03302-5*, Pub. by Turtleback) Demco.

— Dirt Bike Runaway. LC 83-13538. Vol. 37. (Illus.). 149p. (J). (gr. 3-7). 1989. pap. 3.95 (*0-316-14002-3*) Little.

— Dirt Bike Runaway. (J). 1983. 9.05 (*0-606-04201-6*, Pub. by Turtleback) Demco.

— The Dog That Called the Pitch. LC 97-28224. (Illus.). 48p. (J). (gr. k-3). 1998. 14.95 (*0-316-14207-7*) Little.

— The Dog That Pitched a No-Hitter. 42p. (J). (gr. k-3). 1993. pap. 3.95 (*0-316-14103-8*) Little.

— The Dog That Pitched a No-Hitter. (J). 1988. 9.15 (*0-606-05238-0*, Pub. by Turtleback) Demco.

— The Dog That Stole Football Plays. (J). 1997. pap. write for info. (*0-316-13746-4*) Little.

— The Dog That Stole Football Plays. (J). 1997. 9.15 (*0-606-12677-5*, Pub. by Turtleback) Demco.

— The Dog That Stole Football Plays. (Illus.). 48p. (J). (gr. k-3). 1997. reprint ed. pap. 4.95 (*0-316-13423-6*) Little.

— The Dog That Stole Home. 48p. (J). (gr. k-3). 1996. pap. 4.95 (*0-316-14187-9*) Little.

— The Dog That Stole Home. LC 92-15613. 1993. 9.15 (*0-606-08726-5*, Pub. by Turtleback) Demco.

— Double Play at Short. 160p. (J). 1997. pap. 3.95 (*0-316-14201-8*) Little.

— Double Play at Short. LC 94-39170. 1995. 9.05 (*0-606-11273-1*, Pub. by Turtleback) Demco.

— Face-Off. (J). 1972. 9.05 (*0-606-04219-9*, Pub. by Turtleback) Demco.

— Face Off, Vol. 1. 131p. (J). 1989. pap. 3.95 (*0-316-13994-7*) Little.

— Fighting Tackle. LC 94-19680. 1995. 9.05 (*0-606-10184-5*, Pub. by Turtleback) Demco.

— Football Fugitive. (Illus.). 119p. (J). (gr. 4-6). 1988. pap. 3.95 (*0-316-14064-3*) Little.

Christopher, Matt. Football Fugitive. (J). 1976. 9.05 (*0-606-04067-6*, Pub. by Turtleback) Demco.

Christopher, Matt. Football Jokes & Riddles: 50+ Facts & Funnies to Keep You Laughing 1997. 9.15 (*0-606-13395-X*, Pub. by Turtleback) Demco.

— The Fox Steals Home. LC 78-17526. (Illus.). 178p. (J). (gr. 4-6). 1985. pap. 3.95 (*0-316-13986-6*) Little.

Christopher, Matt. The Fox Steals Home. (J). 1978. 9.05 (*0-606-04068-4*, Pub. by Turtleback) Demco.

Christopher, Matt. Great Moments in Baseball History. LC 95-36956. 104p. (J). (gr. 3-7). 1996. pap. 4.95 (*0-316-14130-5*) Little.

— Great Moments in Baseball History. (J). 1996. 10.05 (*0-606-08756-7*, Pub. by Turtleback) Demco.

— Great Moments in Football History. LC 97-1603. (Illus.). 128p. (J). (gr. 3-7). 1997. pap. 4.95 (*0-316-14196-8*) Little.

— Great Moments in Football History. 1997. 10.05 (*0-606-13451-4*, Pub. by Turtleback) Demco.

— The Great Quarterback Switch. (Illus.). 97p. (J). (gr. 3-6). 1991. pap. 3.95 (*0-316-14077-5*) Little.

— The Great Quarterback Switch. (J). 1984. 9.05 (*0-606-00488-2*, Pub. by Turtleback) Demco.

Christopher, Matt. Hard Drive to Short. LC 69-10653. (Illus.). 145p. 1969. 9.05 (*0-606-04929-0*, Pub. by Turtleback) Demco.

— Hat Trick. LC 99-36649. (Soccer' Cats Ser.: Vol. 4). (Illus.). 64p. (J). 2000. 13.95 (*0-316-10669-0*) Little.

Christopher, Matt. Header Back. (J). 2000. write for info. (*0-316-13730-8*) Little.

— The Hit-Away Kid. (Illus.). 64p. (J). (gr. 4-7). 1988. 12.95 (*0-316-13995-5*) Little.

— The Hit-Away Kid. (Illus.). 60p. (J). (gr. 4-7). 1990. pap. 4.50 (*0-316-14007-4*) Little.

— The Hit-Away Kid. (Peach Street Mudders Story Ser.). 1990. 9.15 (*0-606-12335-0*, Pub. by Turtleback) Demco.

— The Hockey Machine. (Illus.). (J). (gr. 4 up). 1986. 15.95 (*0-316-14055-4*) Little.

— Hockey Machine. 137p. (J). (gr. 4-7). 1992. pap. 3.95 (*0-316-14087-2*) Little.

— Hockey Machine. (J). 1986. 9.05 (*0-606-02231-7*, Pub. by Turtleback) Demco.

— Ice Magic. (Illus.). 151p. (J). (gr. 4-6). 1987. pap. 3.95 (*0-316-13991-2*) Little.

— Ice Magic. (J). 1973. 9.05 (*0-606-03826-4*, Pub. by Turtleback) Demco.

— In the Huddle with . . . Steve Young. (Illus.). 128p. (J). (gr. 3-7). 1996. pap. 4.50 (*0-316-13793-6*) Little.

— In the Huddle with . . . Steve Young. LC 96-12553. 1996. 9.60 (*0-606-10223-X*, Pub. by Turtleback) Demco.

***Christopher, Matt.** In the Huddle with John Elway. (J). 1999. pap. 4.50 (*0-316-13441-4*, Pub. by Little) Time Warner.

Christopher, Matt. In the Huddle with...Emmitt Smith. (J). 1997. pap. 4.50 (*0-316-13673-5*) Little.

— In the Huddle with...John Elway. LC GV939.E48C57 1999. 128p. (J). (gr. 3-7). 1999. pap. 4.50 (*0-316-13355-8*) Little.

— Johnny Long Legs. (Illus.). 133p. (J). (gr. 3-6). 1988. pap. 3.95 (*0-316-14065-1*) Little.

Christopher, Matt. Johnny Long Legs. (J). 1970. 9.05 (*0-606-04069-2*, Pub. by Turtleback) Demco.

Christopher, Matt. Kid Who Hit Homers Special. 1998. pap. 3.95 (*0-316-13692-1*) Little.

— The Kid Who Only Hit Homers. (Matt Christopher Sports Classics Ser.). (Illus.). 151p. (J). (gr. 3-7). 1986. pap. 3.95 (*0-316-13987-4*) Little.

Christopher, Matt. Kid Who Only Hit Homers. 145p. (J). (gr. 3-5). pap. 145.00 (*0-8072-1464-7*) Listening Lib.

Christopher, Matt. Latch Key Guard. (J). 1999. pap. write for info. (*0-316-14208-5*) Little.

— Little Lefty. (J). 1993. 9.05 (*0-606-05718-8*, Pub. by Turtleback) Demco.

— Long Arm Quarterback. LC 99-26049. 144p. (J). (gr. 3-7). 1999. pap. 3.95 (*0-316-10562-7*) Little.

***Christopher, Matt.** Long Arm Quarterback. LC 99-26049. 144p. (J). (gr. 3-7). 1999. 15.95 (*0-316-10571-6*) Little.

Christopher, Matt. Long Shot for Paul. 155p. (J). (gr. 3-7). 1990. pap. 3.95 (*0-316-14244-1*) Little.

— Long Shot for Paul. (J). 1966. 9.05 (*0-606-04732-8*, Pub. by Turtleback) Demco.

— Long Stretch at First Base. (J). 1993. 9.05 (*0-606-05719-6*, Pub. by Turtleback) Demco.

— Look Who's Playing First Base. (Illus.). 131p. (J). (gr. 4-6). 1987. pap. 3.95 (*0-316-13989-0*) Little.

— Look Who's Playing First Base. (J). 1971. 9.05 (*0-606-02401-8*, Pub. by Turtleback) Demco.

— Lucky Baseball Bat. 58p. (J). (gr. k-3). 1993. pap. 4.50 (*0-316-14260-3*) Little.

— Lucky Baseball Bat. (Springboard Bks.). (J). 1991. 9.70 (*0-606-05720-X*, Pub. by Turtleback) Demco.

— Man Out at First. (Peach Street Mudders Story). (J). 1993. 9.40 (*0-606-07836-3*) Turtleback.

— Man Out at First: A Peach Street Mudders Story. (Illus.). 64p. (J). (gr. 2-4). 1995. pap. 3.95 (*0-316-14122-4*) Little.

— Matt Christopher's All-Star Lineup: "The Kid Who Only Hits Homers," "Return of the Home Run Kid," "Baseball Pals", "Catcher with a Glass Arm," "Challenge at Second Base" LC 96-52601. (Illus.). 704p. (J). (gr. 3-7). 1997. 9.98 (*1-884822-68-1*) Blck Dog & Leventhal.

— Matt Christopher's Book of Baseball Jokes & Riddles. (Illus.). (J). (ps-3). 1996. pap. 3.95 (*0-614-15671-8*) Little.

— Miracle at the Plate. (Illus.). 129p. (J). (gr. 3-6). 1989. pap. 3.95 (*0-316-13926-2*) Little.

— Miracle at the Plate. (J). 1967. 9.05 (*0-606-04275-X*, Pub. by Turtleback) Demco.

— Mountain Bike Mania. LC 98-24050. 160p. (J). (gr. 2-7). 1998. 15.95 (*0-316-14355-3*) Little.

An Asterisk (*) at the beginning of an entry indicates that the title is appearing for the first time.

— Mountain Bike Mania. LC 98-24050. 160p. (J). (gr. 3-7). 1998. pap. 3.95 (0-316-14292-1) Little.

— No Arm in Left Field. (Illus.). 131p. (J). (gr. 4-6). 1987. pap. 3.95 (0-316-13990-4) Little.

— No Arm in Left Field. (J). 1974. 9.05 (0-606-03046-8, Pub. by Turtleback) Demco.

— Olympic Dream. LC 95-45653. (Illus.). 160p. (J). (gr. 3-7). 1996. 15.95 (0-316-14048-1); pap. 3.95 (0-316-14163-1) Little.

— Olympic Dream. LC 95-45653. (J). 1996. 9.05 (0-606-09707-4, Pub. by Turtleback) Demco.

***Christopher, Matt.** On the Course with--Tiger Woods. LC 97-36990. (Illus.). 128p. (J). (gr. 3-7). 1998. pap. 4.95 (0-316-13445-7) Little.

Christopher, Matt. On the Course With...Tiger Woods. 1998. 9.60 (0-606-13676-2, Pub. by Turtleback) Demco.

Christopher, Matt. On the Court with - Andre Agassi. (Matt Christopher Sports Biographies Ser.). 1997. 9.60 (0-606-11704-0, Pub. by Turtleback) Demco.

Christopher, Matt. On the Court with - Grant Hill. LC 96-22360. (Illus.). 128p. (J). (gr. 3-7). 1996. pap. 4.95 (0-316-13790-1) Little.

— On the Court with - Grant Hill. LC 96-22360. 1996. 9.60 (0-606-10273-6, Pub. by Turtleback) Demco.

— On the Court with - Hakeem Olajuwon. LC 97-21551. 144p. (J). 1997. pap. 4.50 (0-316-13721-9) Little.

— On the Court with - Michael Jordan. LC 96-971. 1996. 9.60 (0-606-10274-4, Pub. by Turtleback) Demco.

***Christopher, Matt.** On the Court with... Lisa Leslie, Vol. 1. LC 98-21711. 128p. (J). (gr. 3-7). 1998. pap. 4.50 (0-316-14216-6) Little.

Christopher, Matt. On the Court With...Hakeem Olajuwon. 1997. 9.60 (0-606-13677-0, Pub. by Turtleback) Demco.

— On the Court with....Michael Jordan. LC 96-971. (Matt Christopher Sports Biographies Ser.). (Illus.). 128p. (J). (gr. 3-7). 1996. pap. 4.95 (0-316-13792-8) Little.

***Christopher, Matt.** On the Field With . . . Mia Hamm. LC 98-14937. 128p. (J). (gr. 3-7). 1998. pap. 4.95 (0-316-14217-4) Little.

Christopher, Matt. On the Field With . . . Mia Hamm. (Matt Christopher Sports Biographies Ser.). 1998. 9.60 (0-606-13678-9, Pub. by Turtleback) Demco.

— On the Field with - Emmitt Smith. LC 97-12530. 144p. (J). (gr. 3-7). 1997. pap. 4.50 (0-316-13722-7) Little.

— On the Field with - Emmitt Smith. (Matt Christopher Sports Biographies Ser.). (J). 1997. 9.60 (0-606-12786-0, Pub. by Turtleback) Demco.

***Christopher, Matt.** On the Field with Briana Scurry. (On the Field with... Ser.). (Illus.). 144p. (J). (gr. 3-7). 2000. pap. 4.95 (0-316-13507-0) Little.

— On the Field with Derek Jeter. (On the Field with... Ser.). 144p. (J). (gr. 3-7). 2000. pap. 4.95 (0-316-13508-9) Little.

— On the Field with Julie Foudy. LC 99-47174. (Illus.). 128p. (J). (gr. 3-7). 2000. pap. 4.95 (0-316-13577-1) Little.

— On the Field with Mia Hamm. (J). 1999. pap. 4.95 (0-316-13484-8, Pub. by Little) Time Warner.

— On the Field with Terrell Davis. LC 99-41273. (Illus.). 128p. (J). (gr. 3-7). 2000. pap. 4.95 (0-316-13552-6) Little.

Christopher, Matt. On the Ice with . . . Wayne Gretzky. LC 96-3042. (Illus.). 128p. (J). (gr. 3-7). 1997. pap. 4.50 (0-316-13789-8) Little.

— On the Ice with . . . Wayne Gretzky. LC 96-3042. 1997. 9.60 (0-606-10275-2, Pub. by Turtleback) Demco.

— On the Mound With - Randy Johnson. LC 97-32500. 128p. (J). (gr. 3-7). 1998. pap. 4.50 (0-316-14221-2) Little.

— On the Mound with--Greg Maddux. LC 96-40973. (Illus.). 144p. (J). 1997. pap. 4.95 (0-316-14191-7) Little.

Christopher, Matt. On the Mound with--Greg Maddux. (Matt Christopher Sports Biographies Ser.). 1997. 9.60 (0-606-11705-9, Pub. by Turtleback) Demco.

Christopher, Matt. Operation Baby-Sitter. LC PZ7.C458Op 1999. (Soccer' Cats Ser.: Vol. 2). (Illus.). 64p. (J). (gr. 2-4). 1999. 13.95 (0-316-13723-5) Little.

— Penalty Shot. LC 96-9741. (Illus.). 176p. (J). (gr. 3-7). 1997. 15.95 (0-316-13787-1); pap. 3.95 (0-316-14190-9) Little.

Christopher, Matt. Penalty Shot. 1997. 9.05 (0-606-11728-8, Pub. by Turtleback) Demco.

Christopher, Matt. Power Play. (J). 1992. pap. write for info. (0-316-14088-0) Little.

— Pressure Play. (Illus.). 168p. (J). (gr. 3-7). 1995. pap. 3.95 (0-316-14121-6) Little.

— Pressure Play. 1993. 9.30 (0-606-08042-2) Turtleback.

— Prime Time Pitcher, 59. (Matt Christopher Sports Classics Ser.). 1998. 9.05 (0-606-13722-X, Pub. by Turtleback) Demco.

— Prime Time Pitcher: Can Koby Handle the Spotlight? LC 97-46394. 160p. (J). (gr. 3-7). 1998. 15.95 (0-316-14215-8) Little.

— Prime Time Pitcher: Can Koby Handle the Spotlight? LC 97-46394. (Illus.). 160p. (J). (gr. 3-7). 1998. pap. 3.95 (0-316-14213-1) Little.

— Red-Hot Hightops. 148p. (J). (gr. 4-7). 1992. pap. 3.95 (0-316-14089-9) Little.

— Red-Hot Hightops. (J). 1987. 9.05 (0-606-02233-3, Pub. by Turtleback) Demco.

— The Reluctant Pitcher. (Matt Christopher Sports Classics Ser.). 1997. 9.05 (0-606-13735-1, Pub. by Turtleback) Demco.

— The Reluctant Pitcher, 57 vols., Vol. 54. (Matt Christopher Sports Classics Ser.). (Illus.). 96p. (J). (gr. 3-7). 1997. reprint ed. pap. 3.95 (0-316-14127-5) Little.

— Return of the Home Run Kid. 168p. (J). (gr. 4-7). 1994. pap. 3.95 (0-316-14273-5) Little.

Christopher, Matt. Return of the Home Run Kid. LC 91-30817. 1992. 9.05 (0-606-06695-0, Pub. by Turtleback) Demco.

— Roller Hockey. 160p. (J). (gr. 3-7). 1998. 15.95 (0-316-13739-1) Little.

— Roller Hockey Radicals. LC 97-33071. (Illus.). 160p. (J). (gr. 3-7). 1998. pap. 3.95 (0-316-13675-1) Little.

Christopher, Matt. Roller Hockey Radicals, 58. (Matt Christopher Sports Classics Ser.). 1998. 9.05 (0-606-13747-5, Pub. by Turtleback) Demco.

— Run, Billy, Run. 145p. (J). (gr. 3-6). 1988. pap. 3.95 (0-316-13993-9) Little.

— Run, Billy, Run. (J). 1980. 9.05 (0-606-03906-6, Pub. by Turtleback) Demco.

— Secret of Rock Island. (J). (gr. 3-7). 1995. 14.00 (0-922242-90-9) Bepuzzled.

— Secret Weapon. LC 99-31363. (J). 1999. write for info. (0-316-14170-4) Little.

***Christopher, Matt.** Secret Weapon. (Soccer' Cats Ser.: Vol. 3). (Illus.). 64p. (J). 2000. 13.95 (0-316-13458-9) Little.

Christopher, Matt. Shadow over My Heart. (Illus.). 64p. (J). (gr. k-3). 1998. pap. 3.95 (0-316-14204-2) Little.

— Shadow over Second: A Peach Street Mudders Story. LC 95-36024. (Illus.). 64p. (J). (gr. k-3). 1996. 13.95 (0-316-14078-3) Little.

— Shoot for the Hoop. LC 95-223556. (Illus.). 128p. (J). (gr. 3-7). 1995. pap. 3.95 (0-316-14125-9) Little.

Christopher, Matt. Shoot for the Hoop. 1995. 9.05 (0-606-08871-7, Pub. by Turtleback) Demco.

Christopher, Matt. Shortstop from Tokyo. (Illus.). 121p. (J). (gr. 3-6). 1988. pap. 3.95 (0-316-13992-0) Little.

— Shortstop from Tokyo. 1970. 9.05 (0-606-03915-5, Pub. by Turtleback) Demco.

***Christopher, Matt.** Skateboard Renegade. 144p. (J). 2000. 15.95 (0-316-13487-2) Little.

— Skateboard Renegade. 144p. (J). (gr. 3-7). 2000. pap. 4.50 (0-316-13549-6) Little.

Christopher, Matt. Skateboard Tough. (Matt Christopher Ser.). (Illus.). 168p. (J). (gr. 3-7). 1994. pap. 3.95 (0-316-14241-7) Little.

— Skateboard Tough. 1991. 9.05 (0-606-06741-8, Pub. by Turtleback) Demco.

— Snowboard Maverick. LC 97-18916. 160p. (J). 1997. 15.95 (0-316-14261-1); pap. 3.95 (0-316-14203-4) Little.

— Snowboard Maverick. (Matt Christopher Sports Classics Ser.). 1997. 9.05 (0-606-13781-5, Pub. by Turtleback) Demco.

— Snowboard Showdown. LC 99-27487. 144p. (J). (gr. 3-7). 1999. 15.95 (0-316-13536-4); pap. 3.95 (0-316-13512-7) Little.

— Soccer Convert. (J). 2000. write for info. (0-316-13732-4) Little.

***Christopher, Matt.** Soccer Duel. LC 99-48070. 144p. (J). (gr. 3-7). 2000. pap. 3.95 (0-316-13406-6) Little.

— Soccer Duel. LC 99-48070. (Illus.). 144p. (J). 2000. 15.95 (0-316-13474-0) Little.

Christopher, Matt. Soccer Halfback. (Illus.). 182p. (J). (gr. 4-6). 1985. pap. 3.95 (0-316-13981-5) Little.

Christopher, Matt. Soccer Halfback. (J). 1978. 9.05 (0-606-04071-4, Pub. by Turtleback) Demco.

Christopher, Matt. Soccer Scoop, 57. (Matt Christopher Sports Classics Ser.). 1998. 9.05 (0-606-13784-X, Pub. by Turtleback) Demco.

— Soccer Scoop, 57 vols., Vol. 57. LC 97-24455. (Matt Christopher Sports Classics Ser.). 160p. (J). 1998. 15.95 (0-316-14206-9); pap. 3.95 (0-316-18896-4) Little.

— Spike It! LC PZ7.C458Sop 1999. 144p. (J). (gr. 3-7). 1999. 15.95 (0-316-13451-1); pap. 3.95 (0-316-13401-5) Little.

— The Spy on Third Base. (J). 1990. 9.70 (0-606-12527-2, Pub. by Turtleback) Demco.

— The Spy on Third Base, Vol. 1. (Illus.). 62p. (J). (gr. 4-7). 1990. pap. 4.50 (0-316-14008-2) Little.

— Stranger in Right Field: A Peach Street Mudders Story. LC 96-49014. (Illus.). 64p. (J). (gr. k-3). 1997. 13.95 (0-316-14111-9) Little.

— Striker Courage. (J). 2001. write for info. (0-316-13729-4) Little.

— The Submarine Pitch. Vol. 15. (Illus.). 137p. (J). (gr. 3-7). 1992. pap. 3.95 (0-316-14250-6) Little.

— Supercharged Infield. 120p. (J). (gr. 4-7). 1994. pap. 3.95 (0-316-14277-8) Little.

Christopher, Matt. Supercharged Infield. 1985. 9.05 (0-606-06774-4, Pub. by Turtleback) Demco.

— Tackle Without a Team. 1989. 9.05 (0-606-06045-6, Pub. by Turtleback) Demco.

Christopher, Matt. Tara Lipinski. LC 98-36098. 128p. (J). (gr. 3-7). 1999. pap. 4.50 (0-316-14257-3) Little.

Christopher, Matt. The Team That Couldn't Lose. (Matt Christopher Sports Classics Ser.). (J). 1997. 9.05 (0-606-13841-2, Pub. by Turtleback) Demco.

Christopher, Matt. The Team That Couldn't Lose, 57 vols., Vol. 55. (Matt Christopher Sports Classics Ser.). 112p. (J). (gr. 3-7). 1997. reprint ed. pap. 3.95 (0-316-14167-4) Little.

***Christopher, Matt.** Tennis Ace. LC PZ7.C458Th 2000. 144p. (J). (gr. 3-7). 2000. pap. 3.95 (0-316-13491-0) Little.

— Tennis Ace. LC 99-48067. (Illus.). 144p. (J). 2000. 15.95 (0-316-13519-4) Little.

Christopher, Matt. Tie Breaker. (J). 1999. write for info. (0-316-13731-6) Little.

— Tight End. (J). (gr. 4-6). 1986. write for info. (0-318-61361-1); pap. 3.95 (0-316-14054-6) Little.

— Tight End. (J). 1981. 9.05 (0-606-03309-2, Pub. by Turtleback) Demco.

— Too Hot to Handle. 127p. (J). (gr. 4-7). 1991. pap. 3.95 (0-316-14074-0) Little.

— Too Hot to Handle. 1965. 9.05 (0-606-05034-5, Pub. by Turtleback) Demco.

— Top Wing. (Illus.). 176p. (J). (gr. 3-7). 1995. pap. 3.95 (0-316-14126-7) Little.

— Top Wing. (J). 1994. 9.05 (0-606-08315-4, Pub. by Turtleback) Demco.

— Touchdown for Tommy. (Illus.). 145p. (J). (gr. 4-6). 1985. pap. 3.95 (0-316-13982-3) Little.

Christopher, Matt. Touchdown for Tommy. (J). 1959. 9.05 (0-606-04072-2, Pub. by Turtleback) Demco.

Christopher, Matt. Touchdown Special Troll. 1998. pap. 3.95 (0-316-13699-9) Little.

Christopher, Matt. Tough to Tackle. 139p. (J). (gr. 3-5). pap. 3.95 (0-8072-1463-9) Listening Lib.

Christopher, Matt. Tough to Tackle. (Illus.). 139p. (YA). (gr. 4-6). 1987. pap. 3.95 (0-316-14058-9) Little.

— Tough to Tackle. LC 87-3714. (J). 1987. 9.05 (0-606-03938-4, Pub. by Turtleback) Demco.

— Undercover Tailback. 1992. 9.05 (0-606-06838-4, Pub. by Turtleback) Demco.

— Underdog. (J). 1998. write for info. (0-316-14212-3); pap. write for info. (0-316-14211-5) Little.

***Christopher, Matt.** Wheel Wizards. 144p. 2000. pap. 4.50 (0-316-13733-2) Little.

— Wheel Wizards. 144p. (J). (gr. 3-7). 2000. 15.95 (0-316-13611-5) Little.

Christopher, Matt. Wingman on Ice. 126p. (J). (gr. 4-7). 1993. pap. 3.95 (0-316-14269-7) Little.

— Wingman on Ice. 1993. 9.05 (0-606-06104-5, Pub. by Turtleback) Demco.

— Winning Stroke. (J). 1996. pap. 3.95 (0-316-14232-8) Little.

— Winning Stroke. LC 93-40257. (J). 1994. 9.05 (0-606-10076-8, Pub. by Turtleback) Demco.

— The Year Mom Won the Pennant. (Illus.). 147p. (J). (gr. 4 up). 1986. pap. 3.95 (0-316-13988-2) Little.

Christopher, Matt. The Year Mom Won the Pennant. (J). 1968. 9.05 (0-606-04073-0, Pub. by Turtleback) Demco.

Christopher, Matt. Zero's Slider. (Illus.). 64p. (J). (gr. 2-4). 1996. pap. 3.95 (0-316-14129-1) Little.

— Zero's Slider. LC 93-21177. (J). 1994. 9.15 (0-606-10104-7, Pub. by Turtleback) Demco.

Christopher, Matt. Zero's Slider- Book Fair. 1997. pap. 3.95 (0-316-13446-5) Little.

Christopher, Matthew. John Elway. (J). 1999. pap. write for info. (0-316-14283-2) Little.

— Kid Who Only Hit Homers. (J). 1986. 8.80 (0-606-04070-6, Pub. by Turtleback) Demco.

***Christopher, Maurine.** The Artistic World of Zula Pangle Brooks. Dawes, Geri-Lynn, ed. (Illus.). 24p. 2000. fiche Price not set. (0-9700559-0-0) Three-D Comm.

Christopher, Michael St., see St. Christopher, Michael.

Christopher, Milbourne. Houdini: The Untold Story. (Illus.). 378p. reprint ed. lib. bdg. 25.95 (0-89190-931-8, Rivercity Pr) Amereon Ltd.

— Illustrated History of Magic. LC 96-32984. (Illus.). 484p. 1996. 49.95 (0-435-07016-9) Heinemann.

— Magic, a Pictoral History. (Illus.). 224p. 1991. pap. 14.95 (0-486-26373-8) Dover.

Christopher, Nancy G. Right of Passage: The Heroic Journey to Adulthood. xii, 291p. (Orig.). 1996. pap. 15.00 (0-9652719-2-7) Cornell Press.

Christopher, Nicholas. Atomic Field: Two Poems. LC 99-45142. 112p. 2000. 23.00 (0-15-100553-2) Harcourt.

— The Creation of the Night Sky. LC 97-36881. 112p. 1998. 22.00 (0-15-100344-0) Harcourt.

— The Creation of the Night Sky: Poems. 112p. (C). 1999. pap. 13.00 (0-15-600565-4) Harcourt.

— Somewhere in the Night. LC 97-41597. 304p. 1998. 13.95 (0-8050-5699-8, Owl) H Holt & Co.

— Somewhere in the Night: Film Noir & the American City. 1997. 22.95 (0-02-922915-4); 24.50 (0-684-82803-0) Free Pr.

— A Trip to the Stars. LC 99-56181. 512p. 2000. 24.95 (0-385-31804-9, Dial Pr) Dell.

Christopher, Nicholas. Veronica. 400p. 1997. mass mkt. 6.99 (0-380-72918-0, Avon Bks) Morrow Avon.

***Christopher, Nicholas.** Veronica. LC 95-18083. 336p. 2000. pap. 12.50 (0-380-80657-6, Avon Bks) Morrow Avon.

Christopher, Noreen. Enjoy Santa Clara Valley: A Guide of Places to Go & Things to Do. 3rd ed. (Illus.). 134p. (Orig.). 1980. pap. 5.95 (0-9606134-0-4) A N C Ent.

Christopher, Paul. Alien Intervention: The Spiritual Mission of UFOs. LC 97-77563. 208p. 1998. pap. 11.99 (1-56384-148-7, Pub. by Huntington Hse) BookWorld.

— The Ethics of War & Peace: An Introduction to Legal & Moral Issues. 2nd ed. LC 97-52775. 259p. (C). (gr. 1). 1998. pap. text 30.00 (0-13-786278-4) P-H.

Christopher, Paul & Mecherle, G. Stephen, eds. Wireless Technologies & Systems Vol. 3232: Millimeter-Wave & Optical. LC 98-145680. 188p. 1998. 48.00 (0-8194-2665-2) SPIE.

Christopher, Peter, jt. auth. see Skinulis, Richard.

Christopher, Renny. The Viet Nam War - The American War: Images & Representations in Euro-American & Vietnamese Exile Narratives. LC 95-19687. 360p. (C). 1996. text 55.00 (1-55849-008-6) U of Mass Pr.

— The Vietnam War - The American War: Images & Representations in Euro-American & Vietnamese Exile Narratives. LC 95-19687. 360p. (C). 1996. pap. 19.95 (1-55849-009-4) U of Mass Pr.

Christopher, Robert & Christopher, Ellen. America's Favorite Restaurants & Inns: From Budget to Luxury. 1024p. 1980. pap. 11.95 (0-930570-01-4) Travel Discover.

Christopher, Robert C. The Japanese Mind. 320p. 1984. pap. 11.00 (0-449-90120-3, Columbine) Fawcett.

Christopher, Shirley A. Shirley's Book: Poems for Practicing Vertical Print. 80p. (Orig.). 1994. pap. text, teacher ed. 7.95 (1-890666-14-9, SB1) Peterson Direct.

— Shirley's Book Vol. 2: Poems for Practicing Slanted Print. 80p. (Orig.). 1994. pap. text, teacher ed. 7.95 (1-890666-15-7, SB2) Peterson Direct.

— Shirley's Book Vol. 3: Poems for Printing Practice. 80p. (Orig.). 1994. pap. text, teacher ed. 7.95 (1-890666-16-5, SB3) Peterson Direct.

— Shirley's Book Vol. 4: Poems for Practicing Beginning Cursive. (Illus.). 48p. (Orig.). 1994. pap. text, teacher ed. 7.95 (1-890666-17-3, SB4) Peterson Direct.

Christopher, T., jt. auth. see Asher, M.

Christopher, Thomas. Easy Roses for North American Gardens. LC 98-30638. (Illus.). 224p. 1999. 29.95 (0-7621-0123-7, Pub. by RD Assn) Penguin Putnam.

Christopher, Thomas, jt. auth. see Ruggiero, Michael A.

Christopher, Tom, jt. auth. see Asher, Marty.

Christopher, Tom, jt. auth. see Carroll, Margie K.

***Christopher, Warren.** Chances of a Lifetime. 2001. 26.00 (0-684-83024-8) Scribner.

Christopher, Warren. In the Stream of History: Shaping Foreign Policy for a New Era. LC 98-3772. 586p. 1998. 60.00 (0-8047-3225-6) Stanford U Pr.

— In the Stream of History: Shaping Foreign Policy for a New Era. LC 98-3772. 624p. 1998. pap. 22.95 (0-8047-3468-2) Stanford U Pr.

Christopher, Warren, ed. Report of the Independent Commission on the Los Angeles Police Department. (Illus.). 257p. (C). 1998. pap. text 45.00 (0-7881-4913-X) DIANE Pub.

Christopher, William & Christopher, Barbara. Mixed Blessings. 240p. 1990. mass mkt. 4.95 (0-380-70999-6, Avon Bks) Morrow Avon.

Christopher, William F. Management for the 1980s. rev. ed. LC 79-55061. 303p. reprint ed. pap. 94.00 (0-608-13026-5, 202352900033) Bks Demand.

— The New Management Accounting. Christopher, Bill, ed. LC 97-68250. (Management Library: No. 9). 88p. 1997. pap. 12.95 (1-56052-444-8) Crisp Pubns.

Christopher, William F. & Thor, Carl G., eds. Handbook for Productivity Measurement & Improvement. LC 92-20949. 1344p. 1993. 90.00 (1-56327-007-2) Productivity Inc.

Christopher, William F., ed. see Baker, Edwart Martin.

Christopher, William F., jt. ed. see Scheuing, Eberhard E.

Christophers. Day by Day with Jesus. 1994. pap. 6.00 (0-939055-06-6) Chrstphrs NY.

Christophers. Geosystems. 3rd ed. 1996. pap. text, teacher ed. write for info. (0-13-505330-7) Allyn.

Christophers. Para que Vuestro Gozo Sea Colmado. Casamada, Jose, tr. (SPA.). 158p. 1986. pap. 4.00 (0-317-46550-3) Chrstphrs NY.

— Three Minutes a Day, Vol. 32. 1997. pap. 6.00 (0-939055-16-3) Chrstphrs NY.

— Three Minutes a Day, Vol. 33. 1998. pap. 6.00 (0-939055-19-8) Chrstphrs NY.

Christophers, Brett. Positioning the Missionary: John Booth Good & the Colonial Confluence of Cultures in Nineteenth-Century Britiah Columbia. 224p. 1999. pap. 24.95 (0-7748-0655-9) U B C Pr.

Christophers, Enno, et al, eds. Topical Corticosteroid Therapy: A Novel Approach to Safer Drugs. LC 88-6537. (Illus.). 213p. 1988. reprint ed. pap. 66.10 (0-608-07218-4, 206744300009) Bks Demand.

Christophers, Mike, jt. auth. see Macmillan, Hugh.

Christophers, Richard A. George Abbot, Archbishop of Canterbury, 1562-1633: A Bibliography. LC 65-27845. 236p. reprint ed. pap. 73.20 (0-608-11181-3, 201644000004) Bks Demand.

Christophers, S. Diptera: Diptera, Family Culicidae, Tribe Anophelini, Vol. 4. (Fauna of British India Ser.). (Illus.). vi, 372p. 1977. reprint ed. 30.00 (0-88065-042-7) Scholarly Pubns.

— Diptera: Family Culicidae, Tribe Anophelini, Vol. 4. (Fauna of British India Ser.). 1977. reprint ed. 30.00 (0-88065-043-5, Pub. by Today Tomorrow) Scholarly Pubns.

Christophersen, C. & Anthoni, U. Organic Sulfur Compounds from Marine Organisms, Vol. 4. Senning, Alexander, ed. (Sulfer Reports: Vol. 4, No. 9). 91p. 1986. pap. text 98.00 (3-7186-0337-3) Gordon & Breach.

Christophersen, E. Flowering Plants of Samoa, 2 Vols. 128. (BMB Ser.). 1972. reprint ed. 60.00 (0-527-02234-9) Periodicals Srv.

— Flowering Plants of Samoa, 2 Vols, 154. (BMB Ser.). 1972. reprint ed. 20.00 (0-527-02262-4) Periodicals Srv.

Christophersen, E. & Caum, E. L. Vascular Plants of the Leeward Island, Hawaii. (BMB Ser.). 1974. reprint ed. 25.00 (0-527-02187-3) Periodicals Srv.

Christophersen, Edward. Beyond Discipline: Parenting That Lasts a Lifetime. 2nd rev. ed. (Illus.). 143p. 1997. pap. 9.95 (0-930851-06-4) Overland Pr.

— Little People: Guidelines for Common Sense Child Rearing. 4th rev. ed. (Illus.). 198p. 1997. pap. 12.95 (0-930851-05-6) Overland Pr.

Christophersen, Edward R. Baby Owner's Manual: What to Expect & How to Survive the First Year. 3rd rev. ed. Orig. Title: The Baby Owner's Manual: What to Expect & How to Survive the First 30 Days. (Illus.). 79p. 1988. pap. 7.95 (0-933701-31-4) Westport Pubs.

— Beyond Discipline: Parenting That Lasts a Lifetime. LC 90-50485. 152p. (Orig.). 1990. pap. 9.95 (0-933701-48-9) Westport Pubs.

— Little People: Guidelines for Common Sense Child Rearing. 3rd ed. LC 88-20789. (Illus.). 216p. 1988. pap. 12.95 (0-933701-32-2) Westport Pubs.

Christophersen, Erling. Soil Reaction & Plant Distribution in the Sylene National Park, Norway. (Connecticut Academy of Arts & Sciences Ser., Trans.: Vol. 27). 1925. pap. 75.00 (0-685-22814-2) Elliots Bks.

— Vegetation of Pacific Equatorial Islands. (BMB Ser.). (Illus.). 1974. reprint ed. 25.00 (0-527-02147-4) Periodicals Srv.

Christophersen, Merrill G. Biography of an Island: General C. C. Pinckney's Sea Island Plantation. Westburg, John E., ed. LC 76-18611. (Illus.). 1976. pap. 10.00 (*0-87423-020-9*) Westburg.

— The Heron & Other Poems, or Furwick Poems II. LC 80-54738. (Illus.). vii, 48p. 1980. pap. 10.00 (*0-87423-027-6*) Westburg.

Christophersen, Merrill G. & Leon, Adolfo. Cidean Ballads, Ballads About the Great Spanish Hero, El Cid. 2nd ed. Westburg, John E., ed. LC 74-24580. (Comparative Literature Studies). 180p. pap. 14.00 (*0-87423-012-8*) Westburg.

Christophersen, Susan & Farr, J. Michael. Career Preparation: Getting the Most from Training & Education. Croy, Greg, ed. (Career & Life Skills Ser.). (Illus.). 58p. (YA). (gr. 7-12). 1990. pap. 5.95 (*0-942784-59-6*, CP) JIST Works.

— Knowing Yourself: Learning about Your Skills, Values & Planning Your Life. Croy, Greg, ed. (Career & Life Skills Ser.). (Illus.). 58p. (YA). (gr. 9-12). 1990. pap. 5.95 (*0-942784-58-8*, KY) JIST Works.

— Your Career: Thinking about Jobs & Careers. Croy, Greg, ed. (Career & Life Skills Ser.). (Illus.). 58p. (YA). (gr. 9-12). 1991. pap. 5.95 (*0-942784-60-X*, YC) JIST Works.

Christophersen, Susan, jt. auth. see Farr, J Michael.

Christophersen, Susan, jt. auth. see Farr, J. Michael.

Christophersen, Susan, ed. see Johnson, Darlene.

*__Christopherson.__ Elemental Geosystems: Study Guide. 3rd ed. 2000. pap., suppl. ed. 29.33 (*0-13-016815-7*) P-H.

— Geosystems: An Introduction to Physical Geography. 4th ed. 1999. suppl. ed. write for info. (*0-13-018822-0*) P-H.

Christopherson, A. L. Canal Capers: Pun-ting about the English Midlands. (Illus.). 42p. (Orig.). 1991. pap. text 2.95 (*0-9601372-0-3*) Christopherson.

Christopherson, Dean, jt. auth. see Carrier, George B.

Christopherson, Edward R. Pediatric Compliance: A Guide for the Primary Care Physician. LC 93-41063. (Critical Issues in Developmental & Behavioral Pediatrics Ser.). (Illus.). 492p. (C). 1994. text 60.00 (*0-306-44454-2*, Kluwer Plenum) Kluwer Academic.

Christopherson, Georgia. The Lamb's Gate Trilogy: Life in the Present Within Freedom & Unified. LC 98-60753. 224p. (C). 1998. pap. 10.99 (*1-57921-120-8*, Pub. by WinePress Pub) BookWorld.

Christopherson, Jim, et al. Working with Sexually Abused Boys: An Introduction for Practitioners. 65p. 1994. pap. 14.95 (*0-902817-51-5*, Pub. by Natl Childrens Bur) Paul & Co Pubs.

Christopherson, Marie. Driftwood in a Time of War. (Prairie Plains Ser.). (Illus.). 400p. (Orig.). 1995. pap. 13.95 (*0-931170-60-5*) Ctr Western Studies.

Christopherson, Pat. Feeling Good about Feeling Bad. 160p. (Orig.). 1987. pap. 7.95 (*0-9618469-0-9*) Golden Egg.

Christopherson, Paul, tr. see Bang, Herman.

*__Christopherson, R.__ Beverly Hills Women. 184p. 2000. mass mkt. 9.95 (*0-914597-06-X*) Pubs West AZ.

— Beyond Science & Religion - The Greater Reality. 184p. 2000. mass mkt. 9.95 (*0-914597-04-3*) Pubs West AZ.

— Circles in the Sand. 89p. 2000. mass mkt. 6.95 (*0-914597-05-1*) Pubs West AZ.

— A Little Bit of Anarchy. 184p. 2000. mass mkt. 9.95 (*0-914597-02-7*) Pubs West AZ.

— Monkey in a Tree. 180p. 2000. mass mkt. 9.95 (*0-914597-07-8*) Pubs West AZ.

— Out of the Fire Mist. 184p. 2000. mass mkt. 9.95 (*0-914597-03-5*) Pubs West AZ.

Christopherson, Ragnar, tr. see Madsen, Stephan T.

Christopherson, Richard I. & Lyons, Stephen D. Nucleotide Antagonists As Anticancer Drugs. 2000. boxed set 95.00 (*0-8493-4309-7*) CRC Pr.

Christopherson, Robert W. Elemental Geosystems. 240p. (C). 1997. pap. text, student ed. 25.67 (*0-13-754086-8*) P-H.

— Elemental Geosystems. 2nd ed. LC 97-11394. 534p. 1997. pap. text 68.00 (*0-13-743535-5*) P-H.

*__Christopherson, Robert W.__ Elemental Geosystems. 2nd ed. (Illus.). 1999. pap. text 67.75 (*0-13-016136-5*) P-H.

— Elemental Geosystems. 2nd ed. 1999. suppl. ed. write for info. (*0-13-018811-5*) P-H.

— Elemental Geosystems. 3rd ed. LC 99-89102. (Illus.). 496p. 2000. 66.67 (*0-13-016800-9*) P-H.

*__Christopherson, Robert W., ed.__ Geosystems: An Intoduction to Physical Geography. 4th ed. LC 99-30922. 667p. (C). 1999. text 78.00 incl. audio compact disk (*0-13-010845-6*) P-H.

Christopherson, Robert W. & Hobbs, Gail. Applied Physical Geography. 2nd ed. LC 97-206121. 1997. pap. text, wbk. ed. 35.80 (*0-13-505405-2*) P-H.

Christopherson, Roger. The Love Experience. Hirst, Sheri, ed. 124p. (Orig.). 1984. pap. 5.95 (*0-914597-01-9*) Pubs West AZ.

Christopherson, Terry L. Let It Be Hot. unabridged ed. 80p. 1998. pap. 7.95 (*0-9666898-0-1*) IFF Inc.

Christopherson, Victor A. Child Rearing in Today's Christian Family. LC 85-23878. (Judson Family Life Ser.). 144p. 1985. reprint ed. pap. 44.70 (*0-608-00221-6*, 206101600006) Bks Demand.

Christopherson, William M., et al, eds. Golden Anniversary Anatomic Pathology Slide Seminar: Proceedings of the Forty Ninth Annual Anatomic Pathology Slide Seminar of the ASCP. 155p. 1985. 35.00 (*0-89189-191-9*) Am Soc Clinical.

Christophilopoulou, A. Byzantine History: 324-610, Vol. 1. Phelps, W. W., tr. from GRE. (ENG.). viii, 411p. 1986. text 117.50 (*0-317-57955-X*, Pub. by AM Hakkert) Coronet Bks.

Christophilopoulou, Aikaterina. Byzantine History, Vol. II: 610-867. Cullen, Timothy, tr. xxii, 534p. 1993. pap. 140.00 (*90-256-1044-7*, Pub. by AM Hakkert) BookLink Distributors.

*__Christophorou, L. G.__ Gases for Electrical Insulation & Arc Interruption: Possible Present & Future Alternatives. 50p. 1998. pap. 5.00 (*0-16-060869-4*) USGPO.

Christophorou, L. G. & James, D. R. Gaseous Dielectrics, Vol. 7. LC 95-5239. (Illus.). 716p. (C). 1995. text 159.50 (*0-306-44984-6*, Kluwer Plenum) Kluwer Academic.

Christophorou, L. G. & Sauers, I. Gaseous Dielectrics, Vol. 6. (Illus.). 664p. (C). 1991. 145.00 (*0-306-43894-1*, Plenum Trade) Perseus Pubng.

Christophorou, L. G., et al. Linking the Gaseous & Condensed Phases of Matter: The Behavior of Slow Electrons. (NATO ASI Ser.: Vol. 326). (Illus.). 606p. (C). 1994. 149.50 (*0-306-44800-9*, Kluwer Plenum) Kluwer Academic.

Christophorou, Loucas G. Atomic & Molecular Radiation Physics. LC 72-129159. (Wiley Monographs in Chemical Physics). 682p. reprint ed. pap. 200.00 (*0-8357-5852-4*, 202399900035) Bks Demand.

Christophorou, Loucas G., ed. Electron & Ion Swarms: Proceedings of the Second International Swarm Seminar. (Illus.). 279p. 1981. 56.00 (*0-08-028084-6*, Pergamon Pr) Elsevier.

— Gaseous Dielectrics V: Proceedings of the 5th International Symposium, Knoxville, TN, USA, 3-7 May 1987. (Illus.). 750p. 1987. 125.00 (*0-317-66335-6*, Pergamon Pr) Elsevier.

Christophorou, Loucas G. & Olthoff, James K., eds. Gaseous Dielectrics VIII. (Illus.). 639p. (C). 1999. 165.00 (*0-306-46056-4*, Kluwer Plenum) Kluwer Academic.

Christophorou, Loucas G. & Pace, M. O., eds. Gaseous Dielectrics: Proceedings of the Fourth International Symposium on Gaseous Dielectrics, Knoxville, Tennessee, U. S. A., April 29-May 3, 1984, No. IV. LC 84-18997. (Illus.). 624p. 1984. 230.00 (*0-08-031570-4*, Pergamon Pr) Elsevier.

Christophory, Jul & Thoma, Emile. Luxembourg, Vol. 23. 2nd rev. ed. LC 97-188274. (World Bibliographical Ser.). 361p. 1997. lib. bdg. 90.00 (*1-85109-249-8*) ABC-CLIO.

Christopoulos, Christos. Principles & Techniques of Electromagnetic Compatibility. LC 94-26751. (Electronic Mail Ser.). 336p. 1995. boxed set 119.95 (*0-8493-7892-3*) CRC Pr.

— The Transmission-Line Modeling Method: TLM. LC 94-45582. (IEEE-OUP Series on Electromagnetic Waves Theory). 232p. 1995. 69.95 (*0-7803-1017-9*, PC3665) Inst Electrical.

— The Transmission-Line Modeling Method: TLM. (IEEE/OUP Series on Electromagnetic Wave Theory). (Illus.). 232p. (C). 1995. text 65.00 (*0-19-856533-X*) OUP.

Christopoulos, Christos, jt. auth. see Wright, A.

Christopoulos, George A. & Bastias, John C., eds. The Archaic Period, Eleven Hundred to Four Hundred Seventy-Nine B C. Sherrard, Philip, tr. LC 75-27171. (History of the Hellenic World Ser.: Vol. 2). (Illus.). 620p. 1977. 65.00 (*0-271-01214-5*) Pa St U Pr.

— Prehistory & Protohistory to Eleven Hundred B.C. Sherrard, Philip, tr. LC 75-18610. (History of the Hellenic World Ser.: Vol. 1). (Illus.). 420p. 1975. 56.50 (*0-271-01199-8*) Pa St U Pr.

Christopoulos, Theodore K., jt. ed. see Diamandis, Eleftherios P.

Christos, Edith M. Roman Worlds - Old & New: Index of New Information. 150p. 1998. 47.50 (*0-7883-1702-4*); pap. 44.50 (*0-7883-1703-2*) ABBE Pubs Assn.

Christos, Edith Marie. Marriage-Analysis, Treatment & Results: Index of New Information with Authors & Subjects. (Illus.). 180p. 1992. 47.50 (*1-55914-696-6*); pap. 44.50 (*1-55914-697-4*) ABBE Pubs Assn.

Christos, George A. Criminal & Non-Criminal Homicide-Medical Guide-Book for Reference & Research. 161p. 1997. 47.50 (*0-7883-1643-5*); pap. 44.50 (*0-7883-1644-3*) ABBE Pubs Assn.

Christou. International Agency, Distribution & Licensing Agreements. 1990. text. write for info. (*0-85121-668-4*) Addison-Wesley.

Christou, A. Semiconductor Device. 1990. text 303.50 (*0-7923-0536-1*) Kluwer Academic.

Christou, Aristos. Integrating Reliability into Microelectronics Manufacturing. (Design & Measurement in Electronic Engineering Ser.). 362p. 1994. text 225.00 (*0-471-94407-6*) Wiley.

Christou, Aristos, ed. Electromigration & Electronic Device Degradation. LC 93-16841. 343p. 1993. 130.00 (*0-471-58489-4*) Wiley.

Christou, Nikolaos T., jt. ed. see Vanicek, Petr.

Christou, Paul. Biotechnology of Food Crops: Rice Biotechnology & Genetic Engineering. LC 94-60643. 210p. 1994. pap. text 49.95 (*1-56676-150-6*) Technomic.

— Genetic Engineering & in Vitro Culture of Crop Legumes. LC 92-56464. 310p. 1992. text 49.95 (*0-87762-946-3*) Technomic.

— Particle Bombardment for Genetic Engineering of Plants. (Biotechnology Intelligence Unit Ser.). 1996. text 69.95 (*0-12-174410-8*) Acad Pr.

— Particle Bombardment for Genetic Engineering of Plants. LC 96-21774. (Biotechnology Intelligence Unit Ser.). 173p. 1996. 79.00 (*1-57059-357-4*) Landes Bioscience.

Christoulas, jt. auth. see Andreadakis.

Christov-Bakargiev, Carolyn. Arte Povera. LC 99-231677. (Illus.). 304p. 1999. 59.95 (*0-7148-3413-0*, Pub. by Phaidon Press) Phaidon Pr.

Christov-Bakargiev, Carolyn, et al, texts. La Ville, le Jardin, la Memoire: 1998-2000. (Illus.). 318p. spiral bd. 60.00 (*88-8158-181-7*, Pub. by Charta) Dist Art Pubs.

Christov, C. I., jt. auth. see Vlarde, M. G.

Christovale, Cindy. Your Real Beauty. 80p. (Orig.). 1983. pap. 2.95 (*0-88144-018-3*, CPS-018) Christian Pub.

Christovich, et al. The American Sector. (New Orleans Architecture Ser.: Vol. II). (Illus.). 256p. 1998. pap. 22.50 (*1-56554-373-4*) Pelican.

Christovich, Mary Louise, et al. New Orleans Architecture Vol. IV: Creole Faubourgs. LC 74-16744. (New Orleans Architecture Ser.). (Illus.). 200p. 1974. reprint ed. 32.50 (*0-88289-037-9*) Pelican.

— New Orleans Architecture Vol. V: The Esplanade Ridge. (Illus.). 192p. (Orig.). 1995. pap. 22.50 (*1-56554-072-7*) Pelican.

Christovich, Mary Louise, jt. auth. see Toledano, Roulhac B.

Christy. American Aviation. 2nd ed. 1994. 29.95 (*0-07-022014-X*) McGraw.

*__Christy.__ College Algebra. 3rd ed. 1998. pap. 10.20 (*0-536-00969-4*) Pearson Custom.

Christy & Rosenfeld. Essentials of Precalculus, Algebra & Triganometry. 1998. pap. text 48.00 (*0-536-00260-6*) Pearson Custom.

Christy, Albert. Numeral Philosophy. 82p. 1983. pap. 8.00 (*0-89540-141-X*, SB-141) Sun Pub.

— Numeral Philosophy. 30p. 1993. reprint ed. spiral bd. 8.00 (*0-7873-0170-1*) Hlth Research.

Christy, Arthur, ed. see Thoreau, Henry David.

Christy, Arthur E. & Wells, Henry W., eds. World Literature. LC 77-149100. (Granger Index Reprint Ser.). 1977. 63.95 (*0-8369-6225-7*) Ayer.

Christy, Betty. Christmas Silhouettes. (Illus.). 1994. pap. 3.95 (*0-486-28106-X*) Dover.

— Easy-to-Cut Silhouettes. 81st ed. (Paper Craft Ser.). (Illus.). 48p. (Orig.). 1991. pap. 3.50 (*0-486-26628-1*) Dover.

— Easy-to-Cut Silhouettes. (Illus.). 1986. pap. 4.95 (*0-486-25061-X*) Dover.

Christy, Carol. Sex Differences in Political Participation: Processes of Change in Fourteen Nations. LC 87-9336. 208p. 1987. 57.95 (*0-275-92433-5*, C2433, Praeger Pubs) Greenwood.

Christy, David. Cotton Is King: Or, the Culture of Cotton, & Its Relation to Agriculture, Manufactures & Commerce. 2nd enl. rev. ed. LC 70-136634. (Reprints of Economic Classics Ser.). xxiii, 298p. 1975. reprint ed. 45.00 (*0-678-00807-8*) Kelley.

— Ethiopia: Her Gloom & Glory. LC 73-75550. 255p. 1969. reprint ed. lib. bdg. 35.00 (*0-8371-1016-5*, CHR&) Greenwood.

Christy, Deborah Alyne. Microsoft Word 2000 Exam Cram. 1999. pap. text 26.99 (*1-57610-513-X*) Coriolis Grp.

Christy, Dennis T. Algebra & Trigonometry. 4th ed. 688p. (C). 1988. text 55.00 (*0-697-05322-9*, WCB McGr Hill) McGrw-H Hghr Educ.

— Algebra & Trigonometry. 4th ed. 688p. (C). 1989. text 23.75 (*0-697-05625-2*, WCB McGr Hill) McGrw-H Hghr Educ.

— College Algebra. 496p. (C). 1988. text 38.75 (*0-697-05324-5*, WCB McGr Hill) McGrw-H Hghr Educ.

— College Algebra. 496p. (C). 1988. text, student ed. 20.63 (*0-697-05627-9*, WCB McGr Hill) McGrw-H Hghr Educ.

— College Algebra. 2nd ed. 496p. (C). 1992. text, suppl. ed. 17.50 (*0-697-16429-2*, WCB McGr Hill) McGrw-H Hghr Educ.

— College Algebra. 2nd ed. 100p. (C). 1992. text, suppl. ed. 17.50 (*0-697-17095-0*, WCB McGr Hill) McGrw-H Hghr Educ.

— College Algebra. 2nd ed. 496p. (C). 1992. text, student ed. 22.50 (*0-697-12354-5*, WCB McGr Hill) McGrw-H Hghr Educ.

— Essentials of Precalculus, Algebra & Trigonometry. 5th ed. 736p. (C). 1992. text 56.25 (*0-697-12340-5*) Brown & Benchmark.

— Fundamentals of Algebra & Trigonometry. 640p. (C). 1988. text 55.00 (*0-697-05323-7*, WCB McGr Hill) McGrw-H Hghr Educ.

— Fundamentals of Algebra & Trigonometry. 640p. (C). 1988. text, student ed. 23.75 (*0-697-05626-0*, WCB McGr Hill) McGrw-H Hghr Educ.

— Precalculus. 2nd ed. 672p. (C). 1992. text 17.50 (*0-697-16431-4*, WCB McGr Hill) McGrw-H Hghr Educ.

— Precalculus. 2nd ed. 672p. (C). 1992. text 56.25 (*0-697-12345-6*, WCB McGr Hill) McGrw-H Hghr Educ.

— Precalculus. 2nd ed. 672p. (C). 1992. text, student ed. 22.50 (*0-697-12349-9*, WCB McGr Hill) McGrw-H Hghr Educ.

Christy, Dennis T. & Levine, Deborah R. Essentials of Precalculus, Algebra & Trigonometry. 5th ed. 240p. (C). 1992. text, student ed. 22.50 (*0-697-12342-1*, WCB McGr Hill) McGrw-H Hghr Educ.

Christy, Dennis T. & Paulling, John. The Calculator View of Essentials of Precalculus Algebra & Trigonometry Using the Casio FX-7700G. 5th ed. 116p. (C). 1992. text 17.50 (*0-697-17096-9*, WCB McGr Hill) McGrw-H Hghr Educ.

— The Calculator View of Essentials of Precalculus Algebra & Trigonometry Using the TI-81. 5th ed. 120p. (C). 1992. text 17.50 (*0-697-16430-6*, WCB McGr Hill) McGrw-H Hghr Educ.

— The Calculator View of Precalculus Using the Casio FX-7700G. 2nd ed. 116p. (C). 1992. text 17.50 (*0-697-17097-7*, WCB McGr Hill) McGrw-H Hghr Educ.

Christy, Dennis T. & Rosenfeld, Robert. Beginning Algebra. 496p. (C). 1993. text 53.13 (*0-697-12588-2*, WCB McGr Hill); text, student ed. 19.38 (*0-697-12590-4*, WCB McGr Hill) McGrw-H Hghr Educ.

— Intermediate Algebra. 608p. (C). 1994. text 53.13 (*0-697-12592-0*, WCB McGr Hill) McGrw-H Hghr Educ.

— Intermediate Algebra. 608p. (C). 1994. text, student ed. 19.38 (*0-697-12594-7*, WCB McGr Hill) McGrw-H Hghr Educ.

Christy, Diane & Sarafconn, Carol A. Pacing Yourself: Steps to Help Save Your Energy. (Illus.). 128p. (Orig.). 1990. pap. 10.95 (*0-915708-31-0*) Cheever Pub.

Christy, Francis T., Jr. & Scott, Anthony. The Common Wealth in Ocean Fisheries: Some Problems of Growth & Economic Allocation. LC 65-26177. (Illus.). 315p. reprint ed. pap. 97.70 (*0-7837-3547-2*, 204284200009) Bks Demand.

Christy, Francis T., jt. auth. see Potter, Neal.

*__Christy, Gary L.__ Good Wyoming Stock, the Legacy of Joe & Arlene Watt: Illustrated with Historic Wyoming Photographs. LC 99-16806. (Illus.). 256p. 2000. 30.00 (*0-938075-78-0*); pap. 13.95 (*0-938075-77-2*) Ocean View Bks.

Christy, Geraldine. Step-by-Step Art School: Ceramics. 1991. 14.98 (*1-55521-739-7*) Bk Sales Inc.

— Step-by-Step Art School: Pastels. 1992. 14.98 (*1-55521-759-1*) Bk Sales Inc.

Christy, Howard A., ed. see Lundberg, Gary B. & Lundberg, Joy S.

Christy, Howard C. The American Girl. LC 76-10821. 1976. reprint ed. pap. 8.95 (*0-306-80042-X*); reprint ed. lib. bdg. 42.50 (*0-306-70854-X*) Da Capo.

Christy, James. The Puppet Ministry. 80p. 1978. pap. 7.99 (*0-8341-0532-2*) Beacon Hill.

Christy, Jim. Buk Book: Musings on Charles Bukowski. LC 97-158645. (Illus.). 64p. 1997. pap. text 12.95 (*1-55022-295-3*) LPC InBook.

— Long Slow Death of Jack Kerouac. LC 99-188146. (Illus.). 96p. 1998. pap. 12.95 (*1-55022-357-7*, Pub. by ECW) Genl Dist Srvs.

Christy, Joe. American Air Power: The First Seventy-Five Years. (Illus.). 208p. 1982. 21.95 (*0-8306-2327-2*, 2327) McGraw-Hill Prof.

— American Aviation: An Illustrated History. (Illus.). 400p. 1987. pap. 25.95 (*0-8306-2497-X*, 2497) McGraw-Hill Prof.

— American Aviation: An Illustrated History. 2nd ed. (Illus.). 1994. pap. 29.95 (*0-8306-4480-6*) McGraw-Hill Prof.

— ARV Flyer's Handbook. LC 85-12725. (Illus.). 192p. 1985. pap. 12.95 (*0-8306-2407-4*, 2407) McGraw-Hill Prof.

— Build Your Own Low-Cost Hangar. (Illus.). 126p. (Orig.). 1983. pap. 9.25 (*0-8306-2357-4*, 2357) McGraw-Hill Prof.

— The Complete Guide to Single - Engine Cessnas. 3rd ed. (Illus.). 1979. 9.95 (*0-8306-9800-0*); pap. 10.95 (*0-8306-2268-3*, 2268) McGraw-Hill Prof.

— Good Approaches, Good Landings. (Illus.). 224p. 1988. 21.95 (*0-8306-0387-5*, 2487) McGraw-Hill Prof.

— Good Takeoffs & Good Landings. 2nd rev. ed. George, Ken, ed. (Practical Flying Ser.). (Illus.). 208p. 1991. pap. 15.95 (*0-8306-3611-0*) McGraw-Hill Prof.

— Illustrated Handbook of Aviation & Aerospace Facts. (Illus.). 720p. (Orig.). 1984. pap. 29.50 (*0-8306-2397-3*, 2397) McGraw-Hill Prof.

— Lightplane Refurbishing Techniques. (Illus.). 160p. 1986. 18.95 (*0-8306-0337-9*, NO. 2437) McGraw-Hill Prof.

— One Thousand One Flying Facts & Firsts. (Illus.). 224p. 1989. 24.95 (*0-8306-9228-2*, 2428); pap. 15.95 (*0-8306-9428-5*, 2428P) McGraw-Hill Prof.

— The Piper Classics. (Illus.). 160p. 1988. 19.95 (*0-8306-9457-9*, 2457); pap. 13.95 (*0-8306-2457-0*) McGraw-Hill Prof.

— Racing Planes & Pilots. (Illus.). 208p. 1982. pap. 8.95 (*0-8306-2322-1*, 2322) McGraw-Hill Prof.

— Your Pilot's License. 5th ed. LC 93-44633. 1994. pap. 14.95 (*0-07-019281-2*) McGraw-Hill Prof.

Christy, Joe & Dooley, Brian A. The Complete Guide to Single - Engine Cessnas. 4th rev. ed. (Illus.). 144p. 1992. pap. 12.95 (*0-8306-4224-2*, 4274) McGraw-Hill Prof.

Christy, Joe & Dooley, Brian J. The Complete Guide to Single - Engine Cessnas. 4th ed. (Illus.). 144p. 1993. pap. 14.95 (*0-07-017766-X*) McGraw.

Christy, Joe & Johnson, Clay. Your Pilot's License. 4th ed. (Illus.). 160p. 1988. pap. 13.95 (*0-8306-2477-5*, 2477P) McGraw-Hill Prof.

Christy, Joe, ed. see Birch, Neville H. & Bramson, A. E.

Christy, K., frwd. Exotique, 3 vols. (Illus.). 2444p. 1998. reprint ed. boxed set 49.99 (*3-8228-7436-1*) Taschen Amer.

Christy, Marian. Conversations: Famous Women Speak Out. LC 98-20030. 224p. 1998. pap. 15.95 (*1-57129-061-3*, Lumen Eds) Brookline Bks.

Christy, Martha M. Healing Yourself with Homeopathy: How to Use the Hidden Key to Homeopathy: Get Great Results! LC 94-62058. (Natural Health at Home Ser.). (Illus.). 254p. (Orig.). 1994. pap. 15.95 (*0-9632091-2-4*) Wishland Inc.

— MSM - The Super-Supplement of the Decade. 31p. 1997. mass mkt. 3.95 (*0-9632091-4-0*) Wishland Inc.

— Your Own Perfect Medicine. LC 94-71171. (Illus.). 221p. (Orig.). 1994. pap. 19.95 (*0-9632091-1-6*) Wishland Inc.

Christy, Martha M., ed. see Cowger, Barry D.

Christy, Mary. Chicken Tonight - Feathers Tomorrow. LC 99-90488. 365p. 1999. 25.00 (*0-7388-0422-3*); pap. 15.00 (*0-7388-0423-1*) Xlibris Corp.

An Asterisk (*) at the beginning of an entry indicates that the title is appearing for the first time.

Christy, Ralph D. & Williamson, Lionel, eds. A Century of Service: Land-Grant Colleges & Universities, 1890-1990. 124p. (C). 1991. text 34.95 (*1-56000-002-3*) Transaction Pubs.

Christy, Ronald, jt. auth. see Jones, Billy M.

Christy, Teresa E. Cornerstone for Nursing Education: A History of the Division of Nursing Education at Teachers College, Columbia University, 1899-1947. LC 79-96868. 137p. reprint ed. pap. 42.50 (*0-608-16146-2*, 205212600036) Bks Demand.

Christy, Van Ambrose. Evaluation of Choral Music. LC 75-176698. (Columbia University. Teachers College. Contributions to Education Ser.: No. 885). reprint ed. 37.50 (*0-404-55885-2*) AMS Pr.

Christy, Van Ambrose & Paton, John G. Expressive Singing Song Anthology. 3rd ed. 228p. (C). 1990. text. write for info. (*0-697-10683-7*); text. write for info. (*0-697-10684-5*) Brown & Benchmark.

Christy, Van Ambrose & Paton, John G. Expressive Singing Song Anthology. 3rd ed. 228p. (C). 1990. text. write for info. (*0-697-10682-9*) Brown & Benchmark.

Christy, Van Ambrose & Paton, John G. Foundations in Singing: A Basic Textbook in Vocal Technique & Song Interpretation - Medium-High Voice Edition. 5th ed. 288p. (C). 1990. text. write for info. (*0-697-05846-8*) Brown & Benchmark.

Chriswell, M. Irving. Within My Sacred Lodge. (Illus.). vi, 19p. 1981. reprint ed. pap. 2.00 (*0-88053-006-5*, M-012) Macoy Pub.

Chritcher, Chas, jt. auth. see Waddington, David.

Chritian, Eugene. Uncooked Foods & How to Use Them. 246p. 1993. reprint ed. spiral bd. 20.00 (*0-7873-0171-X*) Hlth Research.

Chrnalogar, Mary A. Twisted Scriptures: A Path to Freedom from Abusive Churches. 2nd rev. ed. Brauns, Tim et al, eds. LC 96-84980. (Illus.). (Orig.). 1998. mass mkt. 12.99 (*0-9649588-0-5*) Control Technques.

***Chrnalogar, Mary Alice.** Twisted Scripture. 2000. pap. 12.99 (*0-310-23408-5*) Zondervan.

Chrodegang. The Old English Version of the Enlarged Rule of Chrodegang. (EETS, OS Ser.: No. 150). 1974. reprint ed. 36.00 (*0-527-00146-5*) Periodicals Srv.

Chroley, R. J., jt. auth. see Bennett, Robert J.

Chroma, Marta. Czech to English Law Dictionary. (CZE & ENG.). 1997. 150.00 (*0-320-00420-1*) Fr & Eur.

Chromaparke, E. V., jt. ed. see Die Gestalten Staff.

Chromecek, M. Women's Health Care Nurse Pratitioner Certification Study Question. LC 99-22640. 300p. 1999. pap. text 35.00 (*1-878028-22-7*) Hlth Lead Assoc.

Chromey, Frederick R., ed. Proceedings of the 1990 Undergraduate Symposium on Research in Astronomy. 74p. (C). 1991. pap. text. write for info. (*1-882334-00-0*) Keck NE Astron.

Chromey, Rick. Children's Ministry Guide for Smaller Churches. Wolf, Beth R., ed. (Illus.). 156p. 1995. pap. 14.99 (*1-55945-600-0*) Group Pub.

— Youth Ministry in Small Churches: Creative How-Tos, Plus 28 Involving Activities. 168p. 1990. pap. 14.99 (*0-931529-76-X*, Group Bks) Group Pub.

Chrone, Cindy, jt. auth. see Watnik, Webster.

Chronic Diseases Scenario Committee Staff. Chronic Diseases in the Year Two Thousand Five Vol. 2: Scenarios on Chronic Non-Specific Lung Diseases 1990-2005 Scenario Report Commissioned by the Steering Committee on Future Health Scenarios. 245p. (C). 1993. pap. text 102.50 (*0-7923-2354-8*) Kluwer Academic.

Chronic Diseases Scenario Committee Staff & Casparie, A. F. Chronic Diseases in the Year 2005, Vol. 1. (C). 1991. pap. text 97.50 (*0-7923-1377-1*) Kluwer Academic.

Chronic, Halka. Pages of Stone: Geology of Western National Parks & Monuments: Grand Canyon & the Plateau Country, Vol. 4. LC 82-422. (Illus.). 182p. (Orig.). 1988. pap. 16.95 (*0-89886-155-1*) Mountaineers.

— Roadside Geology of Arizona. LC 83-2233. (Roadside Geology Ser.). 335p. 1983. pap. 18.00 (*0-87842-147-5*) Mountain Pr.

— Roadside Geology of Colorado. LC 79-11148. (Roadside Geology Ser.). (Illus.). 336p. 1980. pap. 16.00 (*0-87842-105-X*) Mountain Pr.

— Roadside Geology of New Mexico. Alt, David & Hyndman, Donald W., eds. LC 86-21748. (Roadside Geology Ser.). (Illus.). 260p. (Orig.). 1987. pap. 16.00 (*0-87842-209-9*) Mountain Pr.

— Roadside Geology of Utah. LC 89-48790. (Roadside Geology Ser.). 325p. 1990. pap. 16.00 (*0-87842-228-5*) Mountain Pr.

Chronicle Books Staff. Art Deco. 1997. 17.95 (*0-8118-1477-7*) Chronicle Bks.

— Art. Rage. Us: Art & Writing by Women with Breast Cancer. LC 98-9233. (Illus.). 176p. 1998. pap. 24.95 (*0-8118-2130-7*) Chronicle Bks.

— Art, Rage, Us: Art & Writing by Women with Breast Cancer. LC 98-9233. (Illus.). 176p. 1998. 40.00 (*0-8118-2146-3*) Chronicle Bks.

***Chronicle Books Staff.** Baby Book. 2000. 17.95 (*0-8118-2742-9*) Chronicle Bks.

Chronicle Books Staff. Bordertown. (Illus.). 152p. 1998. 29.95 (*0-8118-1964-7*) Chronicle Bks.

— Desire Journal. (Illus.). 144p. 1998. 19.95 (*0-8118-2033-5*) Chronicle Bks.

***Chronicle Books Staff.** Destinations. (Illus.). 2000. 19.95 (*0-8118-2497-7*) Chronicle Bks.

— Genuine Harley-Davidson Black Book. 2000. 18.95 (*0-8118-2577-9*) Chronicle Bks.

— Greetings from the French Riveria, Vol. 40. (Illus.). 2000. 15.95 (*0-8118-2535-3*) Chronicle Bks.

— Guest Book. 1997. 18.95 (*0-8118-1607-9*) Chronicle Bks.

— Pattern Book: 64,000 Pattern Combinations for Your Home. LC 99-89459. (Illus.). 96p. 2000. 24.95 (*0-8118-2557-4*) Chronicle Bks.

Chronicle Books Staff. Road Trip. 1997. spiral bd. 16.95 (*0-8118-1601-X*) Chronicle Bks.

***Chronicle Books Staff.** Shapes: Jigsaw Books, 6 vols. (Jigsaw Bks.). (Illus.). 8p. (J). 2000. bds. 9.95 (*0-8118-2828-X*) Chronicle Bks.

Chronicle Books Staff. Superman Notecards. 1999. pap. 12.95 (*0-8118-2195-1*) Chronicle Bks.

Chronicle Books Staff, compiled by. Everything Reverberates: Thoughts on Design. LC 97-36634. (Illus.). 108p. 1998. 12.95 (*0-8118-1934-5*) Chronicle Bks.

Chronicle Guidance Publications, Inc. Staff. Chronicle Financial Aid Guide. 1997. pap. text 28.09 (*1-55631-269-5*) Chron Guide.

— Chronicle Occupations Guidebook Library, 8 vols., Set. (Illus.). 1996. text 702.90 (*1-55631-262-8*) Chron Guide.

Chronicle of Higher Education Editors Staff. The Almanac of Higher Education, 1989-90. (Illus.). 256p. 1994. pap. text 14.95 (*0-226-18455-2*) U Ch Pr.

— The Almanac of Higher Education, 1991. 264p. 1993. pap. text 18.95 (*0-226-18456-0*) U Ch Pr.

— The Almanac of Higher Education, 1992. viii, 336p. 1993. pap. text 18.95 (*0-226-18457-9*) U Ch Pr.

— The Almanac of Higher Education, 1993. 376p. (C). 1994. pap. text 18.95 (*0-226-18458-7*) U Ch Pr.

— The Almanac of Higher Education, 1994. 376p. 1995. pap. text 18.95 (*0-226-18459-5*) U Ch Pr.

— The Almanac of Higher Education, 1995. 398p. 1995. pap. text 18.95 (*0-226-18460-9*) U Ch Pr.

***Chronicle Staff.** Fosforos Cubanos, 24 vols. 1999. pap. 12.95 (*0-8118-2428-4*) Chronicle Bks.

— Genuine Hog Log: A Journal for the Motorcycle Enthusiast. 1999. 19.95 (*0-8118-2504-3*) Chronicle Bks.

— Harley-Davidson, 40 vols. 1999. pap. 15.95 (*0-8118-2505-1*) Chronicle Bks.

— Japanese Box, 24 vols. 1999. pap. 12.95 (*0-8118-2427-6*) Chronicle Bks.

— Mystic Fan. 1999. 9.95 (*0-8118-2399-7*) Chronicle Bks.

Chronicles of England Staff. The Brut: Part II. (EETS, OS Ser.: No. 136). 1972. reprint ed. 55.00 (*0-527-00134-1*) Periodicals Srv.

Chronicon Petroburgense Staff. Nunc Primum Typis Mandatum, Curante Thoma Stapleton. (Camden Society, London. Publications, First Ser.: No. 47). reprint ed. 49.00 (*0-404-50147-8*) AMS Pr.

Chroninger, Ruby. Teach Your Kids about Music: An Activity Handbook for Parents & Teachers Using Children's Literature. LC 93-8081. 176p. (Orig.). 1994. 22.95 (*0-8027-1280-0*) Walker & Co.

***Chronister, Bob.** Dr. Bob's Microsoft Windows 2000 Hints & Hacks. 350p. 2000. pap. 19.99 (*0-7897-1918-5*) Que.

Chronister, Bob. Unveiling Windows NT X. 600p. 1997. 39.99 (*0-7897-1329-2*) Que.

Chronister, Jay L. Retirement & Other Departure Plans of Instructional Faculty & Staff in Higher Education Institutions. LC 98-109863. 157p. 1997. pap. 15.00 (*0-16-049312-9*) USGPO.

Chronister, Jay L., jt. auth. see Baldwin, Roger G.

Chronister, R. B. & De France, J. F., eds. The Neurobiology of the Nucleus Accumbens. (Illus.). 380p. (Orig.). 1981. pap. 39.95 (*0-940090-00-7*) Haer Inst.

Chronister, Richard, jt. ed. see Kraehenbuehl, David.

Chrost, Ryszard J., ed. Microbial Enzymes in Aquatic Environments. (Contemporary Bioscience Ser.). (Illus.). xviii, 317p. 1991. 128.00 (*0-387-97452-0*) Spr-Verlag.

Chrost, Ryszard J., jt. ed. see Overbeck, Jurgen.

Chrostowski, Jacek & Terry, J. Photonic Networks, Components & Applications. (Series in Optics & Photonics: Vol. 2). 464p. 1991. text 118.00 (*981-02-0483-3*) World Scientific Pub.

Chrouch, Wallace M. Mego Toys: An Illustrated Value Guide. 1995. pap. 15.95 (*0-89145-592-2*, 3823) Collector Bks.

***Chrousos, George P.** Stress: Basic Mechanisms & Clinical Implications. (Annals of the New York Academy of Science Ser.). 2000. pap. 34.95 (*0-8018-6547-6*) Johns Hopkins.

Chrousos, George P., et al, eds. Mechanisms of Physical & Emotional Stress. LC 88-28384. (Illus.). 542p. 1988. 125.00 (*0-306-43017-7*, Plenum Trade) Perseus Pubng.

— Steroid Hormone Resistance: Mechanisms & Clinical Aspects. LC 85-23250. (Advances in Experimental Medicine & Biology Ser.: Vol. 196). 454p. 1986. 95.00 (*0-306-42229-8*, Plenum Trade) Perseus Pubng.

— Stress - Basis Mechanisms & Clinical Implications: Proceedings of the First World Congress on Stress, Held October 2-7, 1994, Vol. 771. 1995. pap. 165.00 (*0-89766-944-4*) NY Acad Sci.

Chrousos, George P., jt. ed. see Margioris, Andrew N.

Chrubasik, J., et al, eds. Advances in Pain Therapy I. 1992. write for info. (*0-318-69521-9*) Spr-Verlag.

— Advances in Pain Therapy One. (Illus.). 96p. 1992. 49.95 (*0-387-55536-6*) Spr-Verlag.

Chrubasik, J., et al. Advances in Pain Therapy II. (Illus.). 230p. 1993. pap. write for info. (*3-540-56917-0*) Spr-Verlag.

— Postoperative Epidural Opioids. LC 93-25591. 1993. 35.00 (*0-387-56871-9*) Spr-Verlag.

— Postoperative Epidural Opioids. (Illus.). 115p. 1993. pap. write for info. (*3-540-56871-9*) Spr-Verlag.

Chruch, Connie, et al. Listen up Girlfriends. 1996. mass mkt. 5.99 (*0-312-95790-4*, Pub. by Tor Bks) St Martin.

Chruchill, Edwin A. Hail Britannia: Maine Pewter & Silverplate: An Exhibition of Maine Britannia Ware & Silverplate, 1829-1941, in the Collections of the Maine State Museum, May 15, 1992 - May 15, 1993. (Illus.). 90p. (Orig.). 1992. 20.00 (*0-913764-21-3*) Maine St Mus.

Chruchman, Charles W. Prediction & Optimal Decision: Philosophical Issues of a Science Values. LC 82-6264. (International Management Ser.). 394p. 1982. reprint ed. lib. bdg. 79.50 (*0-313-23418-3*, CHUP, Greenwood Pr) Greenwood.

Chruden. Administracion De Personal. (C). 1997. 17.33 (*0-673-19272-5*) Addison-Wesley.

Chruscie, T. L. & Chrusciel, M. Selected Bibliography on Detection of Dependence-Producing Drugs in Body Fluids. (Offset Publications: No. 17). 1975. pap. text 15.00 (*92-4-052004-X*, 1120017) World Health.

Chrusciel, M., jt. auth. see Chruscie, T. L.

***Chrustowski, Rick.** Bright Beetle. LC 99-31777. 32p. 2000. text 15.95 (*0-8050-6058-8*) St Martin.

Chrysander, Friedrich. Georg Friedrich Handel, 3 vols. in 2. 1967. reprint ed. 190.00 (*0-318-71895-2*) G Olms Pubs.

Chrysander, Friedrich, ed. see Corelli, Arcangelo.

Chrysander, Friedrich, ed. see Handel, George Frideric.

Chrysanthis, Panos K., jt. auth. see Ramamritham, Krithi.

Chrysler, Walter P., Jr., frwd. The Gift of American Naive Paintings from the Collection of Edgar William & Bernice Chrysler Garbisch: 48 Masterpieces. LC 75-13524. (Illus.). 68p. 1975. pap. 5.00 (*0-940744-09-0*) Chrysler Museum.

Chrysler, Arthur B. The City of David Dig - The Journal of a Volunteer. LC 92-93447. 1996. pap. 5.95 (*0-9633908-5-6*) Chrysler Bks.

Chrysler, C. Donald. The Handbook of Fulfilled Bible Prophecy. LC 92-93537. 1996. pap. 8.95 (*0-9633908-7-2*) Chrysler Bks.

— The Handbook of Unfulfilled Bible Prophecy. LC 92-93537. 1994. pap. 9.95 (*0-9633908-2-1*) Chrysler Bks.

— The King of the North & the Ten Horns of the Beast. 1992. pap. 7.95 (*0-9633908-0-5*) Chrysler Bks.

— Sourdough Schoolmarm: An Alaskan Adventure. LC 92-90425. 178p. 1992. pap. 7.95 (*0-9633908-1-3*) Chrysler Bks.

Chrysler, John & Escobar, Thomas. Masonry Codes & Specifications Handbook, 1997. 464p. 1997. per. 29.95 (*0-8493-7549-5*); boxed set 54.95 (*0-8493-7548-7*) CRC Pr.

Chrysler, John, jt. auth. see Amrhein, James E.

Chrysler Learning, Inc. Weldtech Series in Welding: Oxyacetylene Welding, Cutting, & Brazing. (Illus.). 80p. 1983. pap. text 17.00 (*0-13-948091-9*) P-H.

Chrysler, Stephen A. The Fun Course: A Home Study Course Work Book to Add Color & Fun to Your Life. (Illus.). 256p. (Orig.). 1992. pap. 19.95 (*1-880740-13-3*) Chrysler Labs.

Chrysler, Walter P. Life of an American Workman. (American Biography Ser.). 219p. 1991. reprint ed. lib. bdg. 69.00 (*0-7812-8069-9*) Rprt Serv.

Chrysos, Euangelos K. & Wood, I. N. East & West: Modes of Communication: Proceedings of the First Plenary Conference at Merida LC 99-23080. (Transformation of the Roman World Ser.). 1999. write for info. (*90-04-10929-3*) Brill Academic Pubs.

Chrysostom, J. & Mozart, Wolfgang Amadeus. The Letters of Mozart & His Family. 2p. reprint ed. lib. bdg. 108.00 (*0-685-14765-7*) Rprt Serv.

Chrysostom, John. Alms & Charity. 1990. pap. 1.95 (*0-89981-216-3*) Eastern Orthodox.

***Chrysostom, John.** Commentary on the Psalms, 2 vols. Hill, Robert C., tr. 1998. pap. 34.95 (*1-58438-013-6*, Pub. by Greek Orth) BookWorld.

Chrysostom, John. Commentary on the Psalms, Vol. 1. Hill, Robert C., tr. from ENG. LC 98-18465. 1998. pap. 19.95 (*1-885652-12-7*, Pub. by Holy Cross Orthodox) BookWorld.

***Chrysostom, John.** Commentary on the Psalms, Vol. 2. Hill, Robert C., tr. 1998. pap. 19.95 (*1-885652-25-9*, Pub. by Holy Cross Orthodox) BookWorld.

Chrysostom, John. A Comparison Between a King & a Monk & Against the Opponents of the Monastic Life. Hunter, David G., tr. from GRE. & intro. by. LC 88-24463. (Studies in Bible & Early Christianity: Vol. 13). 195p. 1989. lib. bdg. 79.95 (*0-88946-613-0*) E Mellen.

— The Devil. 1987. pap. 2.95 (*0-89981-203-1*) Eastern Orthodox.

— The Divine & Holy Liturgy of St. John Chrysostom. (ARA & ENG., Illus.). 102p. 1978. pap. 6.75 (*0-911726-39-X*, CODE CAE) Alleluia Pr.

— Duties of Parents & Children to One Another. 1987. pap. 0.25 (*0-89981-016-0*) Eastern Orthodox.

— On Living Simply: The Golden Voice of Saint John Chrysostom. LC 96-39148. 96p. 1997. pap. 7.00 (*0-7648-0056-6*, Liguori Triumph) Liguori Pubns.

— On the Priesthood. 160p. 1977. pap. 8.95 (*0-913836-38-9*) St Vladimirs.

Chrysostom Society Staff. Once upon a Christmas. (Illus.). 1993. 9.50 (*0-8378-5922-0*) Gibson.

***Chrysostomides, Kypros.** The Republic of Cyprus: A Study in International Law. LC 99-89691. (Developments in International Law Ser.: Vol. 35). 652p. 1999. text 117.00 (*90-411-1338-X*) Kluwer Law Intl.

Chrysostomos. Orthodox Liturgical Dress. 73p. 1998. reprint ed. pap. 8.95 (*1-886412-22-7*) Preserv Press.

— Passions & Perfection in Christ: Narratives from Evergentinos by the Desert Fathers. 200p. 1998. pap. 15.95 (*1-886412-24-3*) Preserv Press.

— Understanding the Psychology of the Ancient Fathers: Themes on Humility, Repentence, Obedience, Love. 294p. 1998. pap. 22.95 (*1-886412-23-5*) Preserv Press.

Chrysostomos, Archimandrite. The Ancient Fathers of the Desert, Vol. 2. 90p. 1986. pap. 5.95 (*0-917653-22-X*) Holy Cross Orthodox.

Chrysostomos, Archimandrite, tr. The Ancient Fathers of the Desert, No. 2. 90p. (C). 1986. pap. text 3.00 (*0-917653-26-2*) Hellenic Coll Pr.

Chrysostomos, Archimandrite & Ambrosios, Hieromonk. Obedience. Young, Alexey & Derugin, Vladimir, eds. 90p. 1984. pap. text 3.00 (*0-916586-23-5*) Holy Cross Orthodox.

Chrysostomus. Chrysostomus - Indices Chrysostomici Vol. 1: Lettres a Olympias. Lettre d'Exil. Sur La Providence De Dieu. Malingrey, A. M., ed. (Alpha-Omega, Reihe A Ser.: Vol. XXXI). (GER.). xv, 462p. 1978. 95.00 incl. 3.5 hd (*3-487-06635-1*) G Olms Pubs.

— Chrysostomus - Indices Chrysostomici Vol. II: De Sacerdotio. Malingrey, A. M., ed. (Alpha-Omega, Reihe A Ser.: Vol. XXXI). (GER.). x, 330p. 1988. 95.00 incl. 3.5 hd (*3-487-06636-X*) G Olms Pubs.

Chrysostomus, Dio. Orations VIII, XII & XXXVI. Russell, D. A., ed. (Greek & Latin Classics - Imperial Library). 274p. (C). 1992. text 65.00 (*0-521-37548-7*); pap. text 24.95 (*0-521-37696-3*) Cambridge U Pr.

Chryssafis, G. A Textual & Stylistic Commentary on Theocritus' Idyll XXV. (London Studies in Classical Philology: Vol. I). 289p. (C). 1981. pap. 80.00 (*90-70265-21-4*, Pub. by Gieben) J Benjamins Pubng Co.

***Chryssavgis, John.** Beyond the Shattered Image: Insights into an Orthodox Ecological World View. LC 98-75639. 192p. 1999. pap. 12.95 (*1-880971-42-9*) Light&Life Pub Co MN.

Chryssavgis, John. Fire & Light. 1987. pap. 6.95 (*0-937032-46-8*) Light&Life Pub Co MN.

— Love, Sexuality, & the Sacrament of Marriage. LC 96-9464. 100p. (Orig.). (C). 1996. pap. 7.95 (*1-885652-03-8*, Pub. by Holy Cross Orthodox) BookWorld.

— Repentance & Confession in the Orthodox Church. 102p. 1996. reprint ed. pap. 5.95 (*0-917651-56-1*, Pub. by Holy Cross Orthodox) BookWorld.

— The World My Church. 58p. 1990. 9.95 (*0-917651-80-4*) Holy Cross Orthodox.

Chryssides, George D. The Elements of Unitarianism. LC 97-39390. (Elements of Ser.). 1998. pap. 9.95 (*1-86204-247-0*, Pub. by Element MA) Penguin Putnam.

***Chryssides, George D.** Exploring New Religions. LC 99-30475. (Issues in Contemporary Religion Ser.). 2000. 24.95 (*0-304-33652-1*) Continuum.

Chryssides, George D. The Path of Buddhism. 160p. (C). 1988. pap. text 45.00 (*0-7152-0619-2*) St Mut.

Chryssides, George D., ed. The Path of Buddhism. 160p. (C). 1989. pap. 32.00 (*0-7855-6806-9*, Pub. by St Andrew) St Mut.

Chryssides, George D. & Kaler, John H. Essentials of Business Ethics. LC 95-50989. 1996. pap. write for info. (*0-07-707856-X*) McGraw.

— An Introduction to Business Ethics. LC 93-17606. 600p. 1993. mass mkt. 39.95 (*0-412-46080-7*) Chapman & Hall.

Chryssides, George D., jt. auth. see Kaler, John H.

Chryssochoidis, George, et al. Internationalisation Strategies. LC 96-26116. 272p. 1997. text 55.00 (*0-312-16407-6*) St Martin.

Chryssochoou, Dimitris N. Theory & Reform in the European Union. 208p. 1999. text 69.95 (*0-7190-4991-1*) St Martin.

Chryssolouris, G. Manufacturing Systems: Theory & Practice. (Texts in Mechanical Engineering Ser.). (Illus.). xvi, 419p. 1993. 79.95 (*0-387-97754-6*) Spr-Verlag.

— Manufacturing Systems: Theory & Practice. 2nd ed. (Texts in Mechanical Engineering Ser.). (Illus.). xvi, 419p. 1993. text. write for info. (*3-540-97754-6*) Spr-Verlag.

Chryssolouris, G. & Sheng, P. Laser Machining: Theory & Practice. Ling, Frederick F., ed. (Mechanical Engineering Ser.). (Illus.). 288p. 1993. 69.95 (*0-387-97498-9*) Spr-Verlag.

Chryssostomidis, Chryssostomos. Behaviour of Offshore Structures, Vol. 3. 1744p. 1994. 342.50 (*0-08-041916-X*, Pergamon Pr) Elsevier.

— Behaviour of Offshore Structures: Geotechnics, Vol. 1. 1994. write for info. (*0-614-00700-3*, Pergamon Pr) Elsevier.

— Behaviour of Offshore Structures Vol. 2: Hydrodynamics & Cable Dynamics. 888p. 1994. 154.50 (*0-08-041914-3*, Pergamon Pr) Elsevier.

— Behaviour of Offshore Structures Vol. 3: Structures. 514p. 1994. 135.50 (*0-08-041915-1*, Pergamon Pr) Elsevier.

Chryssostomidis, Chryssostomos, ed. Automation in the Design & Manufacture of Large Marine Systems. 318p. 1990. 126.00 (*0-89116-960-1*) Hemisp Pub.

Chryssostomos, C. & Asmus, K. D., eds. Sulfur-Centered Reactive Intermediates in Chemistry & Biology, Vol. 197. LC 90-14295. (NATO ASI Ser.). (Illus.). 462p. (C). 1990. text 162.00 (*0-306-43723-6*, Kluwer Plenum) Kluwer Academic.

Chryssovitsioti. English-Greek & Greek-English Dictionary of Commerce, Banking & Financial Terms. (ENG & GRE.). 1065p. 1993. 195.00 (*0-7859-9053-4*) Fr & Eur.

Chrystal, George. Textbook of Algebra, Set, Vols. I & II. 7th ed. LC 64-21987. (YA). (gr. 9-12). text 39.90 (*0-8284-0084-9*) Chelsea Pub.

— Textbook of Algebra, Vol. I. 7th ed. LC 64-21987. (YA). (gr. 9-12). text 19.95 (*0-614-14593-7*) Chelsea Pub.

— Textbook of Algebra, Vol. II. 7th ed. LC 64-21987. (YA). (gr. 9-12). text 19.95 (*0-614-14592-9*) Chelsea Pub.

Chrystal, K. Alec, ed. Monetarism, 2 vols., Set. (Schools of Thought in Economics Ser.: Vol. 11). 964p. 1990. 360.00 (*1-85278-081-9*) E Elgar.

Chrystal, K. Alec & Lipsey, Richard G. Economics for Business & Management. LC 97-22506. 1997. write for info. (*0-19-877538-5*) OUP.

C

An Asterisk (*) at the beginning of an entry indicates that the title is appearing for the first time.

Chrystal, K. Alec, et al. Public Choice Analysis of Economic Policy. LC 98-55205. 240p. 1999. text 69.95 (*0-312-22137-1*) St Martin.

Chrystal, K. Alec, jt. see Lipsey, Richard G.

Chrystal-Smith, G. Practical Guide to Estimating for Alterations & Repairs. (Illus.). 168p. (C). (gr. 13). 1988. pap. 29.99 (*0-7198-2545-8*, E & FN Spon) Routledge.

Chrystie, Frances N. Pets: A Comprehensive Handbook for Kids. 4th rev. ed. Facklam, Margery, ed. LC 94-41229. (Illus.). 256p. (J). 1994. pap. 8.95 (*0-316-14281-6*) Little.

Chrystie, Richard & Schirn, Robert. Search Warrants. 9th ed. 264p. 1997. ring bd. 30.00 (*1-889110-05-1*) CA District Attys.

***Chrystos.** Best Lesbian Erotica 1999. (Lesbian Erotica Ser.). 200p. 1999. pap. text 14.95 (*1-57344-049-3*) Cleis Pr.

Chrystos. Dream On. 132p. 1991. pap. 11.95 (*0-88974-029-1*, Pub. by Press Gang Pubs) LPC InBook.

— Fire Power. 128p. 1995. pap. 13.95 (*0-88974-047-X*, Pub. by Press Gang Pubs) LPC InBook.

— Fugitive Colors. 70p. (Orig.). 1995. pap. 10.00 (*1-880834-11-1*) Cleveland St Univ Poetry Ctr.

— In Her I Am. 96p. 1993. pap. 12.95 (*0-88974-033-X*, Pub. by Press Gang Pubs) LPC InBook.

— Not Vanishing. 1988. pap. 10.95 (*0-88974-015-1*, Pub. by Press Gang Pubs) LPC InBook.

Chrzanowski, Gerard, jt. ed. see Arieti, Silvano.

Chrzanowski, Wojciech. On Partisan War. Orawski, Arthur T. & Tabb, Nancy, trs. from GOH. LC 95-61880. Orig. Title: O Wojnie Partyzanckiej (1835 Polish); Ueber den Partheiganger-Krieg (1839 Old German Translation). 129p. 1996. lib. bdg. 38.00 (*0-9633995-3-5*) TIPRAC.

Chu. Energy Solutions Today for the Nineties. Shih-Lung, ed. 676p. 1987. 66.00 (*0-87262-589-3*) Am Soc Civil Eng.

Chu, Kuo-Pin, jt. auth. see Leung, Priscilla Mei-Fun.

Chu, A. C. & Edelson, R. L., eds. Malignant Tumors of the Skin. (Illus.). 464p. 1999. text 175.00 (*0-340-74086-8*) OUP.

Chu, Alfred E., jt. auth. see Triebel, Walter A.

Chu, Andy, tr. see LaRouche, Lyndon H., Jr.

Chu, Anthony, jt. auth. see Darvay, Amrit.

Chu, B., ed. Selected Papers on Quasielastic Light Scattering by Nacromolecular, Supramolecular, & Fluid Systems. 736p. 1990. 45.00 (*0-8194-0374-1*, VOL. MS12/HC); pap. 35.00 (*0-8194-0375-X*, VOL. MS12) SPIE.

Chu, B. T. & Chen, S. S., eds. Intelligent Modeling, Diagnosis & Control of Manufacturing Processes. LC 92-19673. (Series in Automation: Vol. 4). 350p. (C). 1992. text 98.00 (*981-02-0817-0*) World Scientific Pub.

Chu Bon. Hym. 64p. 1987. 50.00 (*0-7212-0713-8*, Pub. by Regency Pr GBR) St Mut.

Chu, C. K. & Baker, D. C. Nucleosides & Nucleotides As Antitumor & Antiviral Agents. LC 93-13432. (Illus.). 346p. (C). 1993. text 95.00 (*0-306-44520-4*, Kluwer Plenum) Kluwer Academic.

Chu, C. K. & Cutler, H. G. Natural Products As Antiviral Agents. LC 92-27287. (Illus.). 288p. (C). 1993. text 95.00 (*0-306-44346-5*, Kluwer Plenum) Kluwer Academic.

Chu, C. W., et al. Materials, Bulk Processing & Bulk Applications: Proceedings of the 1992 TCSUH Workshop. 625p. 1992. text 137.00 (*981-02-1032-9*) World Scientific Pub.

Chu, C. Y. Cyrus. Population Dynamics: A New Economic Approach. LC 98-19032. (Illus.). 240p. 1998. text 60.00 (*0-19-512158-9*) OUP.

Chu-Carroll, Jennifer & Green, Nancy, eds. Applying Machine Learning to Discourse Processing: Papers from the 1998 Spring Symposium. (Technical Reports). (Illus.). 128p. 1998. spiral bd. 25.00 (*1-57735-046-4*, SS-98-01) AAAI Pr.

Chu, Chao-Hsien, et al. PROSIM 3 for Windows: A Production Management Simulation. 3rd rev. ed. LC 96-14308. Orig. Title: PROSIM. 224p. (C). 1996. text 25.60 (*0-256-21435-2*, Irwn McGrw-H) McGrw-H Hghr Educ.

— PROSIM 3 for Windows: A Production Management Simulation. 5th rev. ed. LC 96-9318. Orig. Title: PROSIM. 1996. teacher ed. write for info. (*0-256-21436-0*, Irwn McGrw-H) McGrw-H Hghr Educ.

Chu, Chao-Liang, et al. Nitrogen in Soils of China. LC 96-49482. (Developments in Plant & Soil Sciences Ser.). 1997. text 234.00 (*0-7923-4372-7*) Kluwer Academic.

Chu, Charles. Ch'i Pai-shih. 1967. audio 8.95 (*0-88710-011-2*) Yale Far Eastern Pubns.

Chu, Charles. China's Picasso, Ch'i Pai-Shih: His Life & Works. 1967. 9.95 (*0-88710-010-4*) Yale Far Eastern Pubns.

Chu, Charles, anno. Contemporary Chinese Writings. 1971. 12.95 (*0-88710-021-X*) Yale Far Eastern Pubns.

Chu, Chauncey C. A Discourse Grammar of Mandarin Chinese. (Berkeley Models of Grammar Ser.: Vol. 6). XVIII, 484p. (C). 1998. text 67.95 (*0-8204-3890-1*) P Lang Pubng.

Chu-Chi, W. English-Chinese Dictionary of Physical Terms. (CHI & ENG.). 218p. 1973. 49.95 (*0-8288-6290-7*, M-9258) Fr & Eur.

Chu, Chih-Chang, et al, eds. Wound Closure Biomaterials & Devices. LC 96-8975. 416p. 1996. boxed set 149.95 (*0-8493-4964-8*) CRC Pr.

Chu, Chin. Tariff Problem in China. LC 68-56650. (Columbia University. Studies in the Social Sciences: No. 169). reprint ed. 37.50 (*0-404-51169-4*) AMS Pr.

Chu, Chin-ning. Asian Mind Game: Unlocking the Hidden Agenda of the Asian Business Culture. LC 90-46045. 288p. 1991. 26.00 (*0-89256-352-4*, Rawson Assocs) Macmillan.

— The Chinese Mind Game: The Best Kept Trade Secret of the East. 288p. (Orig.). (C). 1988. pap. text 19.95 (*0-929638-19-0*) AMC Pub CA.

***Chu, Chin-ning.** Do Less, Achieve More: Discover the Hidden Power of Giving In. 2000. pap. 13.00 (*0-06-098875-4*) HarpC.

***Chu, Chin-Ning.** Do Less, Achieve More: Discover the Hidden Power of Giving In. 224p. 1998. 18.00 (*0-06-039270-3*, ReganBks) HarperTrade.

Chu, Chin-Ning. Thick Face, Black Heart: Thriving, Winning & Succeeding in Life's Every Endeavor. 400p. 1992. 26.00 (*0-929638-28-X*) AMC Pub CA.

Chu-Chong, Joseph. The Contemplative Experience: Erotic Love As an Image of Spiritual Union. LC 99-15980. 1999. pap. 14.95 (*0-8245-1781-4*) Crossroad NY.

Chu, Daniel & Shaw, Bill. Going Home to Nicodemus: The Story of an African American Frontier Town & the Pioneers Who Settled It. LC 94-27139. (Illus.). 96p. (YA). (gr. 6 up). 1995. pap. 5.95 (*0-671-88722-X*, Julian Messner); lib. bdg. 14.95 (*0-671-88723-8*, Julian Messner) Silver Burdett Pr.

Chu, Daniel & Skinner, Elliott. A Glorious Age in Africa: The Story of Three Great African Empires. LC 90-80150. (Young Reader's Ser.). (Illus.). 124p. (YA). (gr. 6-12). 1990. reprint ed. 19.95 (*0-86543-166-3*); reprint ed. pap. 9.95 (*0-86543-167-1*) Africa World.

Chu, David F., ed. see American Society of Mechanical Engineers Staff.

Chu, David K., jt. ed. see Yeung, Y. M.

Chu Djang, ed. A Complete Book Concerning Happiness & Benevolence: A Manual for Local Magistrates in Seventeenth-Century China. LC 84-2529. 672p. pap. 200.00 (*0-608-05620-0*, 206607600006) Bks Demand.

Chu, Don-chean. Patterns of Education for the Developing Nations: Tao's Work in China, 1917-1946. LC 66-5481. xi, 177p. 1966. 2.00 (*0-913973-11-4*); pap. 1.00 (*0-913973-07-6*) Inst Sino-Amer.

— Philosophic Foundations of American Education. LC 70-150045. 392p. 1971. pap. 7.00 (*0-913973-08-4*) Inst Sino-Amer.

— The Story of China. 156p. 1968. pap. write for info. (*0-913973-09-2*) Inst Sino-Amer.

Chu, Donald A. Jumping into Plyometrics. 2nd rev. ed. LC 98-17867. (Illus.). 177p. 1998. pap. 15.95 (*0-88011-846-6*, PCHU0846) Human Kinetics.

— Plyometric Exercises with the Medicine Ball. LC 89-60633. (Illus.). 136p. (Orig.). 1989. pap. 12.95 (*0-931255-05-8*) Bittersweet Pub.

— Plyometric Exercises with the Medicine Ball. 2nd rev. ed. (Illus.). (Orig.). 1999. pap. 14.95 (*0-931255-09-0*, Pub. by Bittersweet Pub) Rivers & Mnts.

— Power Tennis Training. LC 94-21325. 176p. 1994. pap. 15.95 (*0-87322-616-X*, PCHU0616) Human Kinetics.

Chu, Ellen, ed. see Ryan, John C. & Durning, Alan T.

***Chu, Ellen W. & George, Alan.** Inside the FFT Black Box. LC 99-48017. 1999. write for info. (*1-58488-131-3*) CRC Pr.

Chu, Ellen W., ed. see Durning, Alan T. & Crowther, Christopher D.

Chu, Ellen W., ed. see Ryan, John C.

Chu, Ellen W., ed. see Thein Durning, Alan & Bauman, Yoram.

***Chu, F. J.** The Mind of the Market: Spiritual Lessons for the Active Investor. LC 99-47002. 149p. 1999. 30.00 (*0-87034-133-2*) Fraser Pub Co.

Chu, Godwin C. Radical Change Through Communication in Mao's China. LC 77-3874. 352p. reprint ed. pap. 100.40 (*0-7837-0994-3*, 2041300) Bks Demand.

— Satellite Television in Indonesia. Alfian, ed. vi, 211p. (Orig.). 1981. pap. 6.00 (*0-86638-002-7*) EW Ctr HI.

Chu, Godwin C. & Hsu, Francis L., eds. China's New Social Fabric. 1983. pap. 22.50 (*0-7103-0050-6*, 00506) Routledge.

Chu, Godwin C. & Ju, Yanan. The Great Wall in Ruins: Communication & Cultural Change in China. LC 93-202. (SUNY Series, Human Communication Processes). (Illus.). 366p. (C). 1993. pap. text 21.95 (*0-7914-1622-4*) State U NY Pr.

— The Great Wall in Ruins: Communication & Cultural Change in China. LC 93-202. (SUNY Series, Human Communication Processes). (Illus.). 366p. (C). 1993. text 64.50 (*0-7914-1621-6*) State U NY Pr.

Chu, H. F. & Cutkomp, Laurence K. How to Know the Immature Insects. 2nd ed. (Pictured Key Nature Ser.). 352p. (C). 1992. text. write for info. (*0-697-05596-5*, WCB McGr Hill) McGrw-H Hghr Educ.

Chu Hsi. The Philosophy of Human Nature. Bruce, J. Percy, tr. LC 73-38057. (China Classic & Contemporary Works in Reprint Ser.: No. II). reprint ed. 49.50 (*0-404-56913-7*) AMS Pr.

Chu, I-Huey, tr. see Xin, Yang & Chengru, Zhu.

Chu-i, Po. The Selected Poems of Po Chu-I. Hinton, David, tr. from CHI. LC 99-12371. 192p. 1999. pap. 14.95 (*0-8112-1412-5*, NDP880, Pub. by New Directions) Norton.

Chu, James A. Rebuilding Shattered Lives: The Responsible Treatment of Complex Post-Traumatic & Dissociative Disorders. LC 97-32847. 288p. 1998. 47.50 (*0-471-24732-4*) Wiley.

Chu, John W. Selections from the New Testament. 1966. audio 7.95 (*0-88710-084-8*) Yale Far Eastern Pubns.

— Selections from the New Testament in Chinese. 1966. 9.95 (*0-88710-083-X*) Yale Far Eastern Pubns.

Chu, Jonathan M. Neighbors, Friends, or Madmen: The Puritan Adjustment to Quakerism in Seventeenth-Century Massachusetts Bay, 14. LC 84-29035. (Contributions to the Study of Religion Ser.: No. 14). 205p. 1985. 49.95 (*0-313-24809-5*, CNE/) Greenwood.

Chu, Ke-Young & Gupta, Sanjeev. Social Safety Nets: Issues & Recent Experiences. LC 98-19637. 1998. 22.50 (*1-55775-680-5*) Intl Monetary.

Chu, Ke-Young, jt. ed. see Blejer, Mario I.

Chu, Ke-Young, jt. ed. see Tanzi, Vito.

***Chu, Kevin.** Java 2 Programmer's Interactive Workbook. 502p. 1999. pap. text, wbk. ed. 39.99 (*0-13-016638-3*) P-H.

Chu Lin, Paul, ed. see Bugbee, Gordon P.

Chu, Louis. Eat a Bowl of Tea. 250p. 1986. pap. 10.95 (*0-8184-0395-0*) Carol Pub Group.

Chu, Luke S., et al. Acupuncture Manual: A Western Approach. LC 79-13978. (Illus.). 274p. reprint ed. pap. 85.00 (*0-608-08922-2*, 206955700005) Bks Demand.

***Chu, Madeline, ed.** Mapping the Course of the Chinese Language Field. (Monograph Ser.: Vol. III). (Illus.). xii, 350p. 1999. pap. text 20.00 (*1-891637-01-0*) Chinese Lang Teach.

Chu, Madeline M. Practical Chinese Reader I: Patterns & Exercises (Simplified Character Edition) rev. ed. LC 89-51123. (C & T Asian Language Ser.). (CHI.). 200p. (Orig.). 1992. pap., student ed. 14.95 (*0-88727-233-9*) Cheng & Tsui.

— Practical Chinese Reader I: Patterns & Exercises, Traditional Character Edition. rev. ed. LC 90-91839. (C & T Asian Language Ser.). 224p. (Orig.). (C). 1993. pap. text, student ed. 14.95 (*0-88727-187-1*) Cheng & Tsui.

Chu, P. C. & Gascard, J. C. Deep Convection & Deep Water Formation in the Oceans. (Oceanography Ser.: Vol. 57). xii,382p. 1991. 168.00 (*0-444-88764-4*) Elsevier.

Chu, Pao-liang, ed. Twentieth Century Chinese Writers & Their Pen Names, 2 vols. 2nd ed. 913p. (Orig.). 1989. pap. 75.00 (*0-88727-151-0*) Cheng & Tsui.

***Chu, Patricia P.** Assimilating Asians: Gendered Strategies of Authorship in Asian America. LC 99-33229. (New Americanists Ser.). 280p. 2000. pap. 17.95 (*0-8223-2465-2*) Duke.

***Chu, Paul Van Chi.** Me Que Huong Viet Nam D. V. D.Tr. of Mother of Vietnam Country D. V. D.. (VIE & ENG., Illus.). 15p. 1999. pap. 20.00 (*0-9663150-5-7*) P V C Chu.

— Me Que Huong Vietnam.Tr. of Mother of Vietnam Country. (VIE & ENG., Illus.). 94p. 1999. 15.00 (*0-9663150-6-5*); pap. 5.00 (*0-9663150-4-9*) P V C Chu.

Chu, Po. Tracks in the Snowy Forests. 3rd ed. Shapiro, Sidney et al, trs. from CHI. (Illus.). 559p. (C). 1978. pap. 7.95 (*0-917056-72-8*, Pub. by Foreign Lang Pr) Cheng & Tsui.

Chu, R. C., jt. auth. see Seely, John H.

Chu, Robert, et al. Complete Wing Chun. LC 98-60626. (Illus.). 168p. 1998. pap. 16.95 (*0-8048-3141-6*) Tuttle Pubng.

Chu, Ron G., tr. see Liang-tso, Hsieh.

Chu, S. N., et al, eds. State-of-the-Art Program on Compound Semiconductors XXVII. LC 97-197230. (Proceedings Ser.: Vol. 97-21). 390p. 1997. 66.00 (*1-56677-149-8*) Electrochem Soc.

Chu, S. N. G., et al, eds. Proceedings of the State-of-the-Art Program on Compound Semiconductors, 18th. LC 93-70071. (Proceedings Ser.: Vol. 93-27). 452p. 1993. 41.00 (*1-56677-069-6*) Electrochem Soc.

Chu, Samuel C. & Liu Kwang-Ching, eds. Li Hung-chang & China's Early Modernization. LC 93-31417. (Illus.). 320p. (C). (gr. 13). 1994. text 77.95 (*1-56324-242-7*, East Gate Bk); pap. text 38.95 (*1-56324-458-6*, East Gate Bk) M E Sharpe.

Chu, Show-chih Rai. Chinese for the English-Speaking Student: An Approach Through English Grammar, Vol. 1. LC 72-87136. 330p. 1973. 11.95 (*0-913973-00-9*); pap. 9.95 (*0-913973-01-7*); audio 14.95 (*0-913973-02-5*) Inst Sino-Amer.

— Chinese for the English-Speaking Student: An Approach Through English Grammar, Vol. 2. 424p. 1976. 12.95 (*0-913973-10-6*); pap. 10.95 (*0-913973-03-3*); audio 19.95 (*0-913973-04-1*) Inst Sino-Amer.

Chu Sin-Jan. Wu Leichuan: A Confucian-Christian in Republican China. LC 94-16415. (Asian Thought & Culture Ser.: Vol. 19). X, 218p. (C). 1995. text 43.95 (*0-8204-2531-1*) P Lang Pubng.

Chu, T. K., ed. see American Institute of Physics.

Chu, T. Y., jt. ed. see Chen, T. S.

Chu, Tony & Lovell, Anne. The Good Skin Doctor: A Leading Dermatologist's Guide to Beating Acne. 1999. pap. 11.00 (*0-7225-3675-5*) Thorsons PA.

Chu-tsing Li, jt. ed. see Addiss, Stephen.

Ch'u, T'ung-tsu. Han Social Structure. Dull, Jack L., ed. LC 69-14206. (Han Dynasty China Ser.: Vol. 1). 570p. 1972. 40.00 (*0-295-95068-4*) U of Wash Pr.

Chu, Valentin. The Yin-Yang Butterfly: Ancient Chinese Sexual Secrets for Western Lovers. (Illus.). 272p. 1994. pap. 16.95 (*0-87477-778-X*, Tarcher Putnam) Putnam Pub Group.

Chu, Vicky & Starr, Don. Dictionary of Basic Chinese Grammar. 320p. (C). 1998. text 49.00 (*0-7007-0435-3*, Pub. by Curzon Pr Ltd); pap. text 26.95 (*0-7007-0456-6*, Pub. by Curzon Pr Ltd) UH Pr.

***Chu, Vincent.** Beginner's Tai Chi Chuan. (Illus.). 142p. 2000. pap. 12.95 (*1-892515-17-2*, Pub. by Multi-Media Commns) Unique Pubns.

Chu-Wan Kim, jt. auth. see Man-Chung Han.

Chu, Wang Xing, tr. see Chin, Charlie.

Chu, Wen-Djang. Moslem Rebellion in Northwest China, 1862-1878. (Central Asiatic Studies: No. 5). 1966. pap. text 60.00 (*90-279-0017-5*) Mouton.

Chu, Wen Kuan, tr. see Nan, Huai-Chin.

Chu, Wesley W., ed. Distributed Systems Vol. 1: Distributed Processing Systems. LC 86-70445. (Illus.). 303p. 1986. reprint ed. pap. 94.00 (*0-7837-9642-0*, 204148400001) Bks Demand.

— Distributed Systems Vol. 2: Distributed Database Systems. LC 86-70445. 527p. 1986. reprint ed. pap. 163.40 (*0-7837-1336-3*, 204148400002) Bks Demand.

Chu, Wilson, jt. ed. see Meek, Susan.

Chu, Y. Q., jt. auth. see Lizhi, Fang.

Chu Yen. Description of Chinese Pottery & Porcelain. LC 77-38058. (China Classic & Contemporary Works in Reprint Ser.).Tr. of T'ao Shuo. reprint ed. 44.50 (*0-404-56914-5*) AMS Pr.

***Chu, Yiu Kong.** The Triads as Business. LC 99-32827. (Studies in Modern History of Asia). 1999. write for info. (*0-415-17092-3*) Routledge.

Chu-yuan Cheng. China's Allocation of Fixed Capital Investment, 1952-1957. (Michigan Monographs in Chinese Studies: No. 17). 115p. 1974. pap. text 15.00 (*0-89264-017-0*) Ctr Chinese Studies.

Chu, Yun-hen, jt. ed. see Tien, Hung-mao.

Chu, Yun-Peng & Wu, Rong-I, eds. Business Markets & Government in the Asia Pacific. LC 98-189589. (Pacific Trade & Development Conference Ser.). 232p. (C). 1998. 100.00 (*0-415-18302-2*); pap. 32.99 (*0-415-18303-0*) Routledge.

Chua, Beng-Huat. Communitarian Ideology & Democracy in Singapore. (Politics in Asia Ser.). 256p. (C). 1997. pap. 25.99 (*0-415-16465-6*) Routledge.

— Political Legitimacy & Housing: Stakeholding in Singapore. LC 97-14249. 208p. (C). 1997. 85.00 (*0-415-16690-X*) Routledge.

Chua, Cheng Lok, jt. ed. see Geok-lin Lim, Shirley.

***Chua, Daniel K.** Absolute Music & the Construction of Meaning. LC 98-42733. (New Perspectives in Music History & Criticism Ser.: No. 4). (Illus.). 250p. 1999. 54.95 (*0-521-63181-5*) Cambridge U Pr.

Chua, Daniel K. The Galitzin Quartets of Beethoven: Opus 127, 132, 130. LC 95-14421. 296p. 1996. text 47.50 (*0-691-04403-1*, Pub. by Princeton U Pr) Cal Prin Full Svc.

Chua, J. E., et al. The Management of Business. 2nd ed. 1983. text 10.00 (*0-07-099205-3*) McGraw.

Chua, Jess H., jt. auth. see Sharma, Pramodita.

Chua, John. Cliff Notes on Achebe's Things Fall Apart. (Cliffs Notes Ser.). (Illus.). 88p. (Orig.). 1996. pap. 4.95 (*0-8220-1276-6*, Cliff) IDG Bks.

— Narrative of Frederick Douglas Notes. LC 96-136125. (Cliffs Notes Ser.). 72p. 1995. pap. 4.95 (*0-8220-0872-6*, Cliff) IDG Bks.

Chua, L. O., et al. Linear & Non-Linear Circuits. 839p. (C). 1987. 104.06 (*0-07-010898-6*) McGraw.

Chua, L. O., jt. auth. see Parker, T. S.

Chua, Lawrence. Gold by the Inch. LC 97-36075. 224p. 1998. 20.00 (*0-8021-1626-4*, Grove) Grove-Atltic.

***Chua, Lawrence.** Gold by the Inch. 224p. 1999. pap. 12.00 (*0-8021-3649-4*, Grove) Grove-Atltic.

Chua, Lawrence. Muae: Contagion. 3rd ed. (Illus.). 200p. 1997. pap. 18.95 (*1-885030-23-1*) Dist Art Pubs.

Chua, Lawrence, ed. MUAE 2: Collapsing New Buildings. (Illus.). 212p. 1997. pap. 16.95 (*1-885030-22-3*, 620552) Kaya Prod.

Chua, Leon O. Cellular Neural Networks. LC 97-53185. 1998. 88.50 (*0-7923-8125-4*) Kluwer Academic.

— CNN: A Paradigm for Complexity. (World Science Series on Nonlinear Science: Vol. 31). (Illus.). 400p. 1998. 140.00 (*981-02-3483-X*) World Scientific Pub.

Chua, N. H., jt. ed. see Von Wettstein, D.

Chua, Philip S. & Nolasco, J. B. FEU United Class Nineteen Sixty-One: Thirty-Third Anniversary Yearbook. LC 94-94310. 152p. 1994. pap. write for info. (*0-9641472-2-X*); pap. text. write for info. (*0-9641472-3-8*); write for info. (*0-9641472-5-4*); write for info. (*0-9641472-6-2*); write for info. (*0-9641472-7-0*); write for info. (*0-9641472-8-9*) P S Chua.

Chua, Philip S., ed. see Nolasco, J. B.

Chua, Romulo L. & Nazareno, Rodolfo L. Ang Mahalaga sa Buhay: A Handbook of Filipino Values. 177p. (Orig.). 1992. pap. 13.75 (*971-10-0474-7*, Pub. by New Day Pub) Cellar.

Chua, Soon-Leng & Poh Choo Chua, Margaret. The Woman Warrior Notes. (Illus.). 96p. (C). 1998. pap. text, student ed. 4.95 (*0-8220-1381-9*, Cliff) IDG Bks.

Chua, T. E., ed. Coastal Area Management Education in the ASEAN Region. (ICLARM Conference Proceedings Ser.: No. 29). xi, 92 p. 1991. per. write for info. (*971-8709-00-2*, Pub. by ICLARM) Intl Spec Bk.

Chua, T. E. & Garces, L. R., eds. Waste Management in the Coastal Areas of the ASEAN Region: Roles of Governments, Banking Institutions, Donor Agencies, Private Sector & Communities. (ICLARM Conference Proceedings Ser.: No. 33). 218p. 1992. per. write for info. (*971-8709-10-X*, Pub. by ICLARM) Intl Spec Bk.

Chua, T. E. & Scura, L. F., eds. Integrative Framework & Methods for Coastal Area Management. (ICLARM Conference Proceedings Ser.: No. 37). 169p. 1992. write for info. (*971-8709-32-0*, Pub. by ICLARM) Intl Spec Bk.

Chua, T. E., et al. The Coastal Environmental Profile of Brunel Darussalam: Resource Assessment & Management Issues. (ICLARM Technical Reports: No. 18). 1988. 12.00 (*971-10-2238-9*, Pub. by ICLARM); pap. 10.00 (*971-10-2237-0*, Pub. by ICLARM) Intl Spec Bk.

Chua, T. S. & Kunii, Toshiyasu L. Multimedia Modeling (MMM '93) 300p. 1993. text 109.00 (*981-02-1518-5*) World Scientific Pub.

Chua, T. S. & Kunii, Toshiyasu L., eds. Computer Graphics International '90: Computer Graphics Around the World. (Illus.). x, 606p. 1990. 190.95 (*0-387-70062-5*) Spr-Verlag.

Chua, Wai F., jt. auth. see Wilson, Richard M. S.

Chuah, Jason. Conflict of Laws. (Q & A Ser.). 294p. 1996. 18.00 (*1-85941-142-8*, Pub. by Cavendish Pubng) Gaunt.

— International Trade Law. (Questions & Answers Ser.). 289p. 1995. 18.00 (*1-874241-31-7*, Pub. by Cavendish Pubng) Gaunt.

Chuah, Jason C. Statutes & Conventions on Private International Law. LC 98-145916. 327p. 1996. pap. 32.00 (1-85941-034-0, Pub. by Cavendish Pubng) Gaunt.

Chuah, M. I., jt. auth. see Yew, D. T.

Chuan, Goh Kim, jt. auth. see Gerber, Rod.

Chuan, Han-Sheng & Kraus, Richard A. Mid-Ch'ing Rice Markets & Trade: An Essay in Price History. LC 74-24937. (East Asian Monographs: No. 54). 185p. (Orig.). (C). 1975. pap. 20.00 (0-674-57340-4) HUP.

Chuan Kuo Jne Min Tai Piao Ta Hui. Second Session of the Second National People's Congress of the People's Republic of China (Documents), 1949. LC 79-38053. (China Classic & Contemporary Works in Reprint Ser.). 1995. reprint ed. 34.50 (0-404-56907-2) AMS Pr.

Chuan, Victor L., jt. auth. see California Continuing Education of the Bar Staff.

Chuang, C. & Yang, C. Chun, eds. Analytic Functions of One Complex Variable. LC 85-23004. (Contemporary Mathematics Ser.: Vol. 48). 254p. 1986. pap. 35.00 (0-8218-5050-4, CONM/48) Am Math.

Chuang, C. T. Normal Families of Meromorphic Functions. 488p. 1993. text 86.00 (981-02-1257-7) World Scientific Pub.

Chuang, Chi-Tai. Lectures on Complex Analysis: Proceedings of the Symposium. 420p. 1988. text 99.00 (9971-5-0707-2) World Scientific Pub.

***Chuang, Iaac l. & Nielsen, M. A.** Quantum Computation & Information. (Illus.). 700p. 2000. write for info. (0-521-63235-8); pap. write for info. (0-521-63503-9) Cambridge U Pr.

Chuang, Lily. Chinese Vegetarian Delights: Sugar & Dairy-Free Cookbook. LC 87-60146. 112p. 1987. pap. text 7.50 (0-937064-13-0) SevenStar Comm.

— One Hundred One Vegetarian Delights. LC 91-41184. 176p. 1992. pap. 12.95 (0-937064-52-1) SevenStar Comm.

Chuang, Shen-lun. Investigation of Impact of Rigid & Elastic Bodies with Water. LC 70-139810. 124p. 1970. 25.00 (0-403-04489-8) Scholarly.

Chuang, Shun L. Physics of Optoelectronic Devices. LC 94-24701. (Series in Pure & Applied Optics). 736p. 1995. 110.00 (0-471-10939-8) Wiley.

Chuang, Tsan I. & Heckard, Lawrence R. Systematics & Evolution of Cordylanthus (Scrophulariaceae-Pedicularieae) Anderson, Christiane, ed. LC 86-3546. (Systematic Botany Monographs: Vol. 10). (Illus.). 105p. 1986. pap. 13.00 (0-912861-10-X) Am Soc Plant.

Chuang, Tsu-Kung. Ripening Harvest: Mission Strategy for Mainland Chinese Intellectuals in North America. Troup, W. Lee, ed. 167p. (Orig.). 1995. pap. 7.95 (1-882324-14-5) Ambssdrs Christ.

Chuang Tzu. Chuang Tzu: Mystic, Moralist, & Social Reformer. 2nd rev. ed. Giles, Herbert A., tr. LC 70-38059. (China Classic & Contemporary Works in Reprint Ser.: No. II). reprint ed. 57.50 (0-404-56915-3) AMS Pr.

— The Complete Works of Chuang Tzu. Watson, Burton, tr. LC 68-19000. (Translations from the Oriental Classics Ser.). 397p. 1968. text 58.00 (0-231-03147-5) Col U Pr.

Chuang-Tzu. A Taoist Classic: Chuang-Tzu. Yu-Lan, Fung, tr. from CHI. 152p. (C). 1989. text 17.95 (0-8351-1970-X) China Bks.

Chuang Tzu. Wandering on the Way: Early Taoist Tales & Parables of Chuang Tzu. Mair, Victor H., tr. from CHI. LC 97-41863. (Illus.). 464p. 1997. pap. text 16.00 (0-8248-2038-X) UH Pr.

Chuang Yann Wong, jt. auth. see Cleary, Mark.

Chuang, Yao H. International Fertilizer Market Information Sources. Frederick, E. D. et al, eds. LC 84-9152. (Reference Manual Ser.: No. R-4). (Illus.). 39p. 1984. pap. text 4.00 (0-88090-049-0) Intl Fertilizer.

Chuang, Yao H., et al. The Bangladesh Fertilizer Sector. (Technical Bulletin Ser.: No. T-11). (Illus.). 61p. (Orig.). 1978. pap. 4.00 (0-88090-010-5) Intl Fertilizer.

Chuangui, Wang. Chinese Family Acupoint Massage. (Illus.). 232p. 1992. pap. 35.00 (0-8351-2569-6) China Bks.

— Chinese Family Acupoint Massage. (Illus.). 1995. 25.00 (983-9808-21-4, Pub. by Delta Edits) Weatherhill.

Chuaprasert. Laptop (IUP) pap. text 49.99 (0-471-37520-9) Wiley.

Chuaqui, R. B. Truth, Possibility & Probability: New Logical Foundations of Probability & Statistical Inference. (North Holland Mathematics Studies: 166). xx,484p. 1991. 169.50 (0-444-88840-3, MSS 166) Elsevier.

Chuaqui, Rolando. Analysis, Geometry & Probability: Proceedings of the First Chilean Symposium of Mathematics. (Lecture Notes in Pure & Applied Mathematics Ser.: Vol. 96). (Illus.). 288p. 1985. pap. text 135.00 (0-8247-7419-1) Dekker.

Chubak, Sadeq. The Patient Stone. Ghanoonparvar, Mohammad R., tr. from PER. & intro. by. (Persian Literature in Translation: No. 1). 290p. 1989. 12.95 (0-939214-62-8) Mazda Pubs.

Chubara, Yona, et al. Torah Talk: An Early Childhood Teaching Guide. LC 89-80336. 308p. 1989. pap. text 26.50 (0-86705-023-3) A R E Pub.

Chubarian, Alexander, jt. ed. see Gorodetsky, Gabriel.

***Chubarov, Alexander.** The Fragile Empire: A History of Imperial Russia. LC 99-32919. 240p. 1999. 27.50 (0-8264-1188-6) Continuum.

Chubb, Basil. The Government & Politics of Ireland. 2nd ed. LC 81-50785. 416p. 1982. 25.00 (0-8047-1115-1) Stanford U Pr.

— The Government & Politics of Ireland. 3rd ed. 360p. (C). 1995. pap. 55.00 (0-582-08624-8, 79450) Addison-Wesley.

Chubb, Bruce. Build Your Own Universal Computer Interface. (Illus.). 288p. 1989. 27.95 (0-8306-9422-6, 3122); pap. 21.95 (0-8306-3122-4, 3122) McGraw-Hill Prof.

— Build Your Own Universal Computer Interface. 2nd ed. LC 96-49215. (Illus.). 400p. 1997. text 44.95 incl. disk (0-07-912638-3) McGraw.

— Build Your Own Universal Computer Interface. 2nd ed. LC 96-49215. (Illus.). 411p. 1997. pap., pap. text 34.95 incl. disk (0-07-912639-1) McGraw.

Chubb, David A., ed. & pref. see Wilson, James F., et al.

Chubb, Edwin W. Masters of English Literature. LC 67-23194. (Essay Index Reprint Ser.). 1977. 23.95 (0-8369-0303-X) Ayer.

— Sketches of Great Painters. LC 68-55843. (Essay Index Reprint Ser.). 1977. 23.95 (0-8369-0304-8) Ayer.

— Stories of Authors, British & American. LC 68-54338. (Essay Index Reprint Ser.). 1977. 23.95 (0-8369-0305-6) Ayer.

Chubb, Hendon, tr. see Elkaim, Mony.

Chubb, John E. & Moe, Terry M. Choice Is a Panacea. 11p. 1993. 10.00 (1-886306-02-8) Nevada Policy.

— A Lesson in School Reform from Great Britain. 76p. (C). 1992. pap. 8.95 (0-8157-1411-4) Brookings.

— Politics, Markets, & America's Schools. 318p. 1990. 39.95 (0-8157-1410-6) Brookings.

— Politics, Markets, & America's Schools. 318p. 1990. pap. 18.95 (0-8157-1409-2) Brookings.

Chubb, John E. & Peterson, Paul E., eds. Can the Government Govern? 320p. 1989. 42.95 (0-8157-1408-4); pap. 18.95 (0-8157-1407-6) Brookings.

— The New Direction in American Politics. LC 85-71272. 409p. 1985. 39.95 (0-8157-1406-8); pap. 18.95 (0-8157-1405-X) Brookings.

Chubb, Judith. Patronage, Power & Poverty in Southern Italy: A Tale of Two Cities. LC 82-1325. (Cambridge Studies in Modern Political Economies). (Illus.). 304p. 1983. text 85.00 (0-521-23637-1) Cambridge U Pr.

Chubb, L. J. Geology of Galapagos, Cocos & Easter Islands. (BMB Ser.: No. 110). 1969. reprint ed. 25.00 (0-527-02216-0) Periodicals Srv.

— Geology of the Marquesas Islands. (BMB Ser.: No. 68). 1969. reprint ed. 25.00 (0-527-02174-1) Periodicals Srv.

Chubb, Thomas C. The White God & Other Poems. LC 76-144712. (Yale Series of Younger Poets: No. 5). reprint ed. 18.00 (0-404-53805-3) AMS Pr.

Chubbs, Boyd. Poems from the Burnt Woods. 72p. 1995. pap. 9.95 (1-895387-50-7) Creative Bk Pub.

Chubim, Shahram & Tripp, Charles R. Iran-Saudi Arabia Relations & Regional Order. (Adelphi Papers: No. 304). (Illus.). 88p. 1997. pap. text 29.95 (0-19-829283-X) OUP.

Chubin, Daryl, ed. Interdisciplinary Analysis & Research. LC 85-82057. 482p. 1986. 29.75 (0-912338-53-9); fiche 19.75 (0-912338-54-7) Lomond.

Chubin, Daryl E. Sociology of Sciences: An Annotated Bibliography on Invisible Colleges, 1972-1981. LC 82-48773. 216p. 1983. text 20.00 (0-8240-9223-6) Garland.

Chubin, Daryl E. & Hackett, Edward J. Peerless Science: Peer Review & U. S. Science Policy. LC 89-21855. (SUNY Series in Science, Technology, & Society). 267p. 1990. text 21.50 (0-7914-0309-2) State U NY Pr.

Chubin, Daryl E., jt. auth. see Kumar, David D.

Chubin, Shahram, ed. Domestic Political Factors. LC 81-572. (Security in the Persian Gulf Ser.: Vol. 1). 104p. 1981. pap. text 19.50 (0-86598-044-6) Rowman.

— The Role of Outside Powers. LC 80-28314. (Security in the Persian Gulf Ser.: Vol. 4). 180p. 1982. pap. 19.50 (0-86598-047-0) Rowman.

Chubin, Shahram & Tripp, Charles. Iran & Iraq at War LC 89-112947. v, 318 p. 1988. write for info. (1-85043-092-6) I B T.

Chubon, Robert A. Social & Psychological Foundations of Rehabilitation. 274p. (C). 1994. text 54.95 (0-398-05920-9); pap. text 37.95 (0-398-06042-8) C C Thomas.

***Chubykalo, Andrew E., et al, eds.** Instantaneous Action at a Distance in Modern Physics: "Pro" & "Contra" 475p. 1999. lib. bdg. 145.00 (1-56072-698-9) Nova Sci Pubs.

— The Lorentz Group, CPT & Neutrinos. 350p. 2000. 86.00 (981-02-4062-7) World Scientific Pub.

Chuckrow, Robert. The Intelligent Dieter's Guide. 78p. 1997. pap. 14.95 (0-9645919-4-4) Rising Mist.

— The Tai Chi Book: Refining & Enjoying a Lifetime of Practice. rev. ed. O'Leary, James C., ed. LC 98-60579. (Martial Arts-Internal Ser.). (Illus.). 208p. 1998. pap. 19.95 (1-886969-64-7, B032/647, Pub. by YMAA Pubn) Natl Bk Netwk.

Chuckwagon Gourmet Staff. Cheyenne Frontier Days Daddy of 'em All Cookbook. LC 96-177622. 1997. 22.95 (0-9649348-0-9) Chuckwagon Gourmet.

Chuculate, Eddie, et al, eds. Voices at Dawn: New Work for the Institute of American Indian Arts. 139p. (Orig.). (C). 1996. pap. text 8.00 (1-881396-11-8) IOA Indian Arts.

Chuculate, Eddie D., ed. Home Is in the Blood: New Work from the Institute of American Indian Arts. 280p. (Orig.). (C). 1995. pap. text 10.00 (1-881396-10-X) IOA Indian Arts.

Chud, Deborah. The Gourmet Prescription: High Flavor Recipes for Lower Carbohydrate Diets. (Illus.). 224p. 1999. 27.95 (0-912333-81-2, Pub. by BB&T Inc) Publishers Group.

Chuda, Thomas J. A Guide for Criminal Justice Training: How to Make Training Easier for Security & Law Enforcement. LC 95-13928. (Illus.). 156p. (C). 1995. text 40.95 (0-398-06525-X); pap. text 26.95 (0-398-06526-8) C C Thomas.

Chudacek, I., ed. Relationships of Polymetric Structure & Properties. (Progress in Colloid & Polymer Science Ser.: Vol. 78). 212p. 1989. 106.00 (0-387-91338-6) Spr-Verlag.

***Chudacoff, Edward & Smith, Judith E.** The Evolution of American Urban Society. 5th ed. LC 99-17555. (Illus.). 337p. 1999. pap. text 45.00 (0-13-011581-9) P-H.

Chudacoff, Howard P. The Age of the Bachelor: Creating an American Subculture. LC 98-35154. 376p. 1999. 29.95 (0-691-02796-X, Pub. by Princeton U Pr) Cal Prin Full Svc.

***Chudacoff, Howard P.** Age of the Bachelor: Creating an American Subculture. (Illus.). 376p. 2000. pap. 17.95 (0-691-07055-5) Princeton U Pr.

Chudacoff, Howard P. How Old Are You? Age Consciousness in American Culture. LC 89-3 014. (Illus.). 242p. reprint ed. pap. 75.10 (0-608-09102-2, 206973600005) Bks Demand.

— Major Problems in American Urban History: Documents & Essays. 3rd ed. 476p. (C). 1994. pap. text 29.16 (0-669-24376-0) HM Trade Div.

Chudaev, Oleg, jt. ed. see Khakara, Y. K.

Chudecki, Paul. Aston Martin & Lagonda, Vol. 2. (Collector's Guide Ser.). (Illus.). 128p. 1990. 27.95 (0-947981-41-1, Pub. by Motor Racing) Motorbooks Intl.

***Chudinov, Y. V.** Education Concept of Earth's Expansion: Main Grounds, Space-Geodetic & Paleomagnetic Evidence, Metallogenic Consequences. 130p. 1999. 132.00 (90-6764-299-1, Pub. by VSP) Coronet Bks.

***Chudinov, Yu V.** Global Education Tectonics of the Expanding Earth. 212p. 1998. 147.50 (90-6764-280-0, Pub. by VSP) Coronet Bks.

***Chudinovich, Igor & Constanda, C.** Variational & Potential Methods in the Theory of Bending of Plates with Transverse Shear Deformation. LC 00-31540. (Monographs & Surveys in Pure & Applied Mathematics). 2000. write for info. (1-58488-155-0, Chap & Hall CRC) CRC Pr.

Chudleigh. Obstetric Ultrasound. 3rd ed. 2000. pap. text 65.00 (0-443-05471-1, W B Saunders Co) Harcrt Hlth Sci Grp.

Chudleigh, Patricia. Obstetric Ultrasound. 2nd ed. 323p. (Orig.). 1992. pap. text 65.00 (0-443-04207-!) Church.

Chudley. Building Site Works. 2nd ed. 1989. pap. text. write for info. (0-582-01974-5, Pub. by Addison-Wesley) Longman.

— Building Superstructures. 2nd ed. (C). 1989. pap. text. write for info. (0-582-01969-9, Pub. by Addison-Wesley) Longman.

Chudley & Greeno. Building Construction Handbook. 3rd ed. 608p. 1998. 34.95 (0-7506-3753-6) Buttrwrth-Heinemann.

***Chudley, Carol Graham & Field, Dorothy.** Between Gardens: Seasonal Observations on Gardening, Friendship & Spirit. (Illus.). 240p. 1999. pap. 19.95 (1-896095-55-0) Polstar Bk.

Chudley, Roy. Building Finishes, Fittings & Domestic Services. 2nd ed. LC 88-39283. 276p. reprint ed. pap. 85.60 (0-608-08064-0, 206902900002) Bks Demand.

Chudley, Roy. Building Construction Handbook. 2nd ed. LC 95-232349. 1995. pap. 31.95 (0-7506-2468-X) Buttrwrth-Heinemann.

Chudnovskii, A. F., jt. auth. see Nerpin, S. V.

Chudnovsky, D. V., et al, eds. Number Theory. (Lecture Notes in Mathematics Ser.: Vol. 1240). v, 324p. 1987. 47.95 (0-387-17669-1) Spr-Verlag.

— Number Theory, New York, 1986-1988. (Lecture Notes in Mathematics Ser.: Vol. 1383). v, 256p. 1989. 41.95 (0-387-51549-6) Spr-Verlag.

Chudnovsky, D. V. & Chudnovsky, G. V. Classical & Quantum Models & Arithmetic Problems. (Lecture Notes in Pure & Applied Mathematics Ser.: 92). (Illus.). 480p. 1984. pap. text 170.00 (0-8247-1825-9) Dekker.

Chudnovsky, D. V., et al. Number Theory: A Seminar Held at the Graduate School & University Center of the City University of N.Y. 1982. (Lecture Notes in Mathematics Ser.: Vol. 1052). v, 309p. 1984. 38.70 (0-387-12909-X) Spr-Verlag.

— Number Theory: New York Seminar, 1991-1995. LC 96-24221. 272p. 1996. pap. 49.95 (0-387-94826-0) Spr-Verlag.

Chudnovsky, Daniel, ed. Transnational Corporations & Industrialization. LC 93-18761. (United Nations Library on Transnational Corporations: Vol. 11). 1993. write for info. (0-415-08544-6) Routledge.

Chudnovsky, David V. Search Theory: Some Recent Developments. (Lecture Notes in Pure & Applied Mathematics Ser.: Vol. 112). (Illus.). 176p. 1988. pap. text 135.00 (0-8247-8000-0) Dekker.

Chudnovsky, David V. & Jenks, Richard D. Computer Algebra. (Lecture Notes in Pure & Applied Mathematics Ser.: Vol. 113). (Illus.). 256p. 1989. pap. text 125.00 (0-8247-8038-8) Dekker.

Chudnovsky, David V. & Jenks, Richard D. Computers in Mathematics. (Pure & Applied Mathematics Ser.: Vol. 125). (Illus.). 432p. 1990. pap. text 155.00 (0-8247-8341-7) Dekker.

Chudnovsky, Elynne. Bare, Beautiful Feet & Other Missionary Stories. (Missionary Stories Ser.: Bk. 4). (J). (ps-6). 1992. pap. 3.99 (0-87509-485-6) Chr Pubns.

— The Potato Story & Other Missionary Stories. LC 91-78295. (Missionary Stories Ser.: Bk. 3). (J). (gr. 1-5). 1992. pap. 3.99 (0-87509-484-8) Chr Pubns.

Chudnovsky, Eugene M. & Tejada, Javier. Macroscopic Quantum Tunneling of the Magnetic Moment. LC 97-26060. (Studies in Magnetism: No. 4). (Illus.). 188p. (C). 1998. text 54.95 (0-521-47404-3) Cambridge U Pr.

Chudnovsky, G. V. Contributions to the Theory of Transcendental Numbers. LC 83-15728. (Mathematical Surveys & Monographs: No. 19). 450p. 1984. text 109.00 (0-8218-1500-8, SURV/19) Am Math.

Chudnovsky, G. V., jt. auth. see Chudnovsky, D. V.

***Chudo, Alicia.** And Quiet Flows the Vodka: or When Pushkin Comes to Shove: The Curmudgeon's Guide to Russian Literature. LC 00-8499. 232p. 2000. pap. text 14.95 (0-8101-1788-6) Northwestern U Pr.

Chudson, Walter A. The Pattern of Corporate Financial Structure: A Cross-Section View of Manufacturing, Mining, Trade, & Construction, 1937. (Financial Research Program III: Studies in Business Financing: No. 7). 165p. 1945. reprint ed. 42.90 (0-87014-135-X) Natl Bur Econ Res.

***Chudy, Harry T.** Automotive Refinishing. 3rd ed. LC 00-27424. (Illus.). 304p. 1999. 60.00 (0-13-010073-0) P-H.

Chue, S. H. Thermodynamics: A Rigorous Postulatory Approach. LC 76-44878. 286p. reprint ed. pap. 88.70 (0-608-17432-7, 202985700066) Bks Demand.

Chuen. The Personal Feng Shui Manual. LC 97-36663. (Illus.). 140p. 1998. pap. 16.95 (0-8050-5558-4, Owl) H Holt & Co.

Chuen, Lam K. Feng Shui Handbook: How to Create a Healthier Living & Working Environment. LC 95-17234. (Henry Holt Reference Bks.). (Illus.). 159p. 1996. pap. 16.95 (0-8050-4215-6) H Holt & Co.

Chuen, Lam Kam. Buccellati. (Illus.). 208p. 1999. 65.00 (0-8478-2180-3) Rizzoli Intl.

— Chi Kung: The Way of Healing. LC 98-45754. (Illus.). 160p. (Orig.). 1999. pap. 17.50 (0-7679-0339-0) Broadway BDD.

— Development Girl. LC 98-48443. 224p. 1999. pap. 10.95 (0-385-49431-9, Main St Bks) Doubleday.

— Hungarian-English Dictionary: Pocket. (ENG & HUN.). pap. 20.95 (0-87557-038-0) Saphrograph.

— It Was a Wonderful Life. 136p. 1998. 19.95 (0-9668576-0-7) S J Vetock.

— Listening to Her Understanding Him. LC 99-210829. 1997. pap. 8.99 (1-56229-112-2) Pneuma Life Pub.

— Lonely Hunter: A Biography of Carson McCullers. 1975. 12.50 (0-385-04028-8) Doubleday.

— Men of Maize. 1975. 10.00 (0-385-28644-9) Doubleday.

— Prophetic Power. 1996. pap. 7.99 (1-56229-471-7) Pneuma Life Pub.

— School Violence... Calming the Storm: A Guide to Creating a Fight-Free School Environment. Smith, Denise, ed. 171p. 1998. pap. 29.95 (1-880463-14-8, 7101) Rising Sun.

— The Venison Gourmet. xii, 43p. 1996. spiral bd. 16.95 (0-9668647-0-0) S Scheehle.

Chuen, Lam Kam, photos by. Philippine Portrait. (Illus.). 160p. 1999. 35.00 (0-8478-2169-2, Pub. by Rizzoli Intl) St Martin.

***Chuen, Lam Kam & Sin, Lam Kai.** Feng Shui Kitchen: The Philosopher's Guide to Cooking & Eating. (Illus.). 160p. 2000. pap. 17.95 (1-885203-93-4, Pub. by Jrny Editions) Tuttle Pubng.

Chuen, Lam Kam, jt. auth. see De la Huerta, Christian.

Chuen, Lam Kam, jt. auth. see Smith, Richard.

Chuen, Lam Kam, ed. see Roche, Julie A. & Del-Debbio, Andy.

Chuen-Yen, Chow. An Introduction to Computational Fluid Mechanics. rev. ed. (Illus.). 400p. 1983. reprint ed. text 35.00 (0-9612302-0-7) Seminole Pub Co.

Chuev, Felix, ed. see Molotov, V. M.

Chuev, G. N., et al. Progress in the Physics of Clusters. 500p. 1998. 88.00 (981-02-3660-3) World Scientific Pub.

Chuev, G. N., jt. ed. see Lakhno, V. D.

***Chufrin, Gennadii Illarionovich.** Russia & Asia: The Emerging Security Agenda. LC 99-57197. 550p. 2000. text 65.00 (0-19-829654-1) OUP.

Chufrin, Gennady I., jt. ed. see Scalapino, Robert A.

Chufu, Gabriel. Angels & Gods. Olaru, Victor, tr. from RUM. 20p. 1992. pap. 4.00 (1-881489-00-0) Poetry Miscellany.

Chugh, C. P. High Technology in Drilling & Exploration. (Illus.). 795p. (C). 1992. text 110.00 (90-6191-477-9, Pub. by A A Balkema) Ashgate Pub Co.

Chugh, C. P., ed. Manual of Drilling Technology. 596p. (C). 1985. text 47.00 (90-6191-553-8, Pub. by A A Balkema) Ashgate Pub Co.

Chugh, C. P., et al. Design Criteria for Drill Rigs: Equipment & Drilling Techniques. (Illus.). 412p. (C). 1996. text 91.00 (90-5410-257-8, Pub. by A A Balkema) Ashgate Pub Co.

Chugh, K. S., et al, eds. Asian Nephrology: Proceedings of the Fifth Asian Pacific Congress of Nephrology, New Delhi, India, 9-13, December 1992. (Illus.). 796p. 1995. text 160.00 (0-19-563401-2) OUP.

Chugh, Y. Paul & Davin, Donna, eds. Proceedings NMLRC Symposium, '93. (Illus.). 302p. 1994. lib. bdg. write for info. (1-885189-00-1) Coal Res Ctr.

Chughtai, Ismat. The Crooked Line. (Asian Writers Ser.). 335p. 1995. pap. 11.95 (0-435-95089-4, 95089) Heinemann.

— Hearts Break Free & the Wild One. 1993. pap. 8.00 (81-85107-70-X, Pub. by Kali for Women) S Asia.

— The Quilt & Other Stories. (C). 1996. pap. 11.00 (81-85107-10-6, Pub. by Kali for Women) S Asia.

— The Quilt & Other Stories. Naqvi, Tahira & Hameed, Syeda S., trs. LC 94-19776. 175p. 1994. pap. 14.95 (1-878818-34-1, Pub. by Sheep Meadow) U Pr of New Eng.

Chugoku Newspaper Staff. Exposure: Victims of Radiation Speak Out. McIvor, Kirsten, tr. (Illus.). 327p. 1996. pap. 12.00 (4-7700-2065-1) Kodansha.

Chuguev, Vladimir, jt. auth. see Vronskaya, Jeanne.

Chui. Wavelets in a Box. (C). 1998. 79.95 (0-12-174565-1) Acad Pr.

Chui, jt. auth. see Allen.

C

***Chui, Benjamin W.** Microcantilevers for Atomic Force Microscope Data Storage. LC 98-40855. (Microsystems Ser.). 11p. 1998. write for info. (*0-7923-8358-3*) Kluwer Academic.

Chui, C. & Chen, G. Kalman Filtering: With Real-Time Applications. 3rd ed. LC 98-41628. (Springer Series in Information Sciences). 240p. 1999. pap. 59.95 (*3-540-64611-6*) Spr-Verlag.

Chui, C. K. Discrete HN Optimization: With Applications in Signal Processing & Control Systems. 2nd ed. Huang, T. S. et al, eds. LC 97-15128. (Series in Information Sciences: No. 26). (Illus.). 288p. 1997. 79.95 (*3-540-61959-3*) Spr-Verlag.

Chui, Charles K. An Introduction to Wavelets. (Wavelet Analysis & Its Applications Ser.: Vol. 1). (Illus.). 264p. 1992. text 59.95 (*0-12-174584-8*) Acad Pr.

— Multivariate Splines. LC 88-61569. (CBMS-NSF Regional Conference Ser.: No. 54). v, 189p. (C). 1988. pap. 29.00 (*0-89871-226-2*) Soc Indus-Appl Math.

— Wavelets. (Approximations & Decomposition Ser.). 1992. text 98.00 (*981-02-1127-9*) World Scientific Pub.

— Wavelets. (Series on Approximations & Decomposition). 1993. text 58.00 (*981-02-1222-4*) World Scientific Pub.

— Wavelets: A Mathematical Tool for Signal Processing. LC 96-51635. (SIAM Monographs on Mathematical Modeling & Computation: Vol. 1). (Illus.). xviii, 210p. 1997. pap. text 39.00 (*0-89871-384-6*, MM01) Soc Indus-Appl Math.

Chui, Charles K., ed. Approximation Theory & Functional Analysis. (Illus.). 247p. 1990. text 80.00 (*0-12-174583-X*) Acad Pr.

Chui, Charles K., ed. Wavelets: A Tutorial in Theory & Applications. (Wavelet Analysis & Its Applications Ser.: Vol. 2). (Illus.). 723p. 1992. text 69.95 (*0-12-174590-2*) Acad Pr.

Chui, Charles K., et al, eds. Multivariate Approximation Theory: Proceedings of the Conference at the Mathematical Research Institute at Oberwolfach, Black Forest, Feb. 1989, No. IV. (International Series of Numerical Mathematics: No. 90). 336p. 1989. 122.00 (*0-8176-2384-1*) Birkhauser.

— Wavelets: Theory, Algorithms, & Applications. (Wavelet Analysis & Its Applications Ser.: Vol. 5). (Illus.). 627p. 1994. text 63.00 (*0-12-174575-9*) Acad Pr.

Chui, Charles K. & Chen, G. Kalman Filtering. (Information Sciences Ser.: Vol. 17). (Illus.). 210p. 1987. 39.50 (*0-387-18395-7*) Spr-Verlag.

— Kalman Filtering: With Real-Time Applications. 2nd ed. (Information Sciences Ser.: Vol. 17). 215p. 1991. 37.95 (*0-387-54013-X*) Spr-Verlag.

— Linear Systems & Optimal Control. (Information Sciences Ser.: Vol. 18). (Illus.). 120p. 1988. 75.95 (*0-387-18737-5*) Spr-Verlag.

Chui, Charles K. & Chen, Guanrong. Signal Processing & Systems Theory: Selected Topics. Huang, T. S. et al, eds. LC 92-14512. (Information Sciences Ser.: Vol. 26). (Illus.). xi, 267p. 1992. 54.50 (*0-387-55442-4*) Spr-Verlag.

Chui, Charles K. & Schumaker, Larry L., eds. Approximation Theory: Proceedings of the 8th Texas Conference, 2 vols., Set. (Series in Approximations & Decomposition). 1200p. 1996. 240.00 (*981-02-2318-8*) World Scientific Pub.

— Approximation Theory IX, 2 vols., Set. (Innovations in Applied Mathematics Ser.). (Illus.). 1998. text 100.00 (*0-8265-1327-1*) Vanderbilt U Pr.

— Approximation Theory IX: Computational Aspects, Vol. II. LC 96-51254. (Innovations in Applied Mathematics Ser.). (Illus.). 416p. 1998. text 55.00 (*0-8265-1326-3*) Vanderbilt U Pr.

— Approximation Theory IX: Theoretical Aspects, Vol. I. (Illus.). 576p. 1998. text 60.00 (*0-8265-1325-5*) Vanderbilt U Pr.

— Approximation Theory VIII: College Station, Texas, U. S. A., 8-12 January 1995, Vol. 1. LC 95-41309. (Series in Approximations & Decomposition: Vol. 6-7). 1080p. 1995. text 92.00 (*981-02-2971-2*) World Scientific Pub.

— Approximation Theory VIII: College Station, Texas, U. S. A., 8-12 January 1995, Vol. 2. LC 95-41309. (Series in Approximations & Decomposition: Vol. 6-7). 1080p. 1995. text 68.00 (*981-02-2972-0*) World Scientific Pub.

***Chui, Charles K., et al.** Wavelet Toolware. LC 98-10877. 1998. pap. 59.95 incl. cd-rom (*0-12-174595-3*) Acad Pr.

Chui, Christina. Haunted House. (Ghostwriter Ser.: Vol. 38). 1996. mass mkt. 4.75 (*0-553-54265-6*) BDD Bks Young Read.

Chui, Christopher. Did God Use Evolution to "Create"? A Critique of Biological Evolution, Geological Evolution, & Astronomical Evolution. 350p. (Orig.). 1993. pap. 12.95 (*0-9640005-0-4*) Logos Pubs.

***Chui, David.** Choosing a Career in the Post Office. LC 00-9459. (World of Work Ser.). 2000. write for info. (*0-8239-3242-7*) Rosen Group.

Chui, Pui T., jt. auth. see Chan, Siu L.

Chui, S. T., ed. Physics of the Electron Solid. (Series in Applied Physics). 258p. 1994. 42.00 (*1-57146-106-X*) Intl Pr Boston.

Chuilleanain, Eilean N. The Brazen Serpent. LC 94-61973. 50p. 1995. 13.95 (*0-916390-65-9*); pap. 7.95 (*0-916390-64-0*) Wake Forest.

— The Magdalene Sermon & Earlier Poems. LC 90-72090. 64p. 1991. pap. 8.95 (*0-916390-43-8*) Wake Forest.

— The Rose-Geranium. 44p. 1981. pap. 11.95 (*0-904011-24-0*) Dufour.

— The Second Voyage. rev. ed. LC 90-72091. 72p. (C). 1991. pap. 8.95 (*0-916390-45-4*) Wake Forest.

Chuji Hiruki, ed. Proceedings of the Second Symposium of the International Working Group on Plant Viruses with Fungal Vectors. (Illus.). 156p. (Orig.). 1993. pap. 10.00 (*0-9639572-0-1*) Am Soc Sugarbeet.

Chujoy, Anatole. The New York City Ballet. (Series in Dance). (Illus.). xxviii, 382p. 1981. reprint ed. lib. bdg. 39.50 (*0-306-76035-5*) Da Capo.

Chujoy, Anatole, tr. see Vaganova, Agrippina.

Chukanov, Kiril B. Final Quantum Revelation: General Theory of World Organisation. (Illus.). 400p. 1994. 44.95 (*0-9643579-0-9*); pap. 39.95 (*0-9643579-1-7*) Genl Energy.

Chukerman, Amy, et al, eds. Proceedings: Papers from the 19th Regional Meeting. LC 76-27943. 407p. 1983. pap. 8.00 (*0-914203-19-3*) Chicago Ling.

Chukhovskaya, Lidiya. Chukhovskaya: Sof'ya Petrovna. Murray, John, ed. (Modern Language Ser.). (RUS.). 128p. (C). 1997. pap. text 18.95 (*1-85399-510-X*, Pub. by Brist Class Pr) Focus Pub-R Pullins.

Chukhri, M. G. An Atlas of the Ultrastructure of Viruses of Lepidopteran Pests of Plants. Kothekar, V. S., tr. from RUS. (Russian Translation Ser.: No. 65). 251p. 1988. text 97.00 (*90-6191-496-5*, Pub. by A A Balkema) Ashgate Pub Co.

Chukovskaya, Lydia. Sofia Petrovna. Werth, Aline, tr. from RUS. (European Classics Ser.). 126p. 1994. pap. text 12.95 (*0-8101-1150-0*) Northwestern U Pr.

— To the Memory of Childhood. Klose, Eliza K., tr. from RUS. (Illus.). 168p. 1988. pap. 11.95 (*0-8101-0790-2*) Northwestern U Pr.

Chukovsky. Telephone. 1977. 11.25 (*0-440-08532-2*) Delacorte.

Chukovsky, Kornei. The Art of Translation: Kornei Chukovsky's A High Art. Leighton, Lauren G., ed. & tr. by. LC 83-6457. 327p. reprint ed. pap. 101.40 (*0-8357-6542-3*, 203590500097) Bks Demand.

— Chekhov, the Man. LC 74-6384. (Studies in Russian Literature & Life: No. 100). 1974. lib. bdg. 75.00 (*0-8383-1867-3*) M S G Haskell Hse.

***Chukran, Bobbi A.** Natural Dyes for Natural Fibers: A Beginner's Handbook of Dyeing Wool & Mohair with Plants. (Illus.). 52p. 1999. pap. 18.95 (*0-944577-07-5*) Limestone.

Chukran, Rudy. Performance Tuning the IBM RISC System/6000. LC 97-46800. 240p. (C). 1998. pap. text 49.95 (*0-201-63382-5*) Addison-Wesley.

Chuks-Orji, Ogonna. Names from Africa. LC 72-154523. 96p. 1972. pap. 10.95 (*0-87485-046-0*) Johnson Chicago.

Chukwo, Raymond. Blacks & Technology: The Shift of Economic Power to Blacks in the 21st Century. LC 98-70874. 93p. 1998. pap. 12.95 (*1-878647-49-0*) APU Pub Grp.

***Chukwu, Raymond.** The Curve: The Curve of Poor Medial Care for Blacks, Its Impact on Their Quality of Life & Future Solutions. 2000. pap. 12.95 (*1-878647-73-3*) APU Pub Grp.

Chukwudi Okeke Maduno. The Biafran Ideology; An African Critique of the Present World Systems. 115p. 1994. pap. text. write for info. (*0-9644596-1-2*) Ekumeku Commun.

Chukwudieze, Emmanuel, ed. African Philosophy: An Anthology. (Philosophy Anthologies Ser.: Vol. 5). 500p. (C). 1997. text 83.95 (*0-631-20337-0*); pap. text 29.95 (*0-631-20338-9*) Blackwell Pubs.

Chukwumerije, Okezie. Choice of Law in International Commercial Arbitration. LC 93-49035. 240p. 1994. 69.50 (*0-89930-878-3*, Quorum Bks) Greenwood.

Chula. Cucumber Seeds Don't Sprout Radishes. LC 91-30644. (Illus.). 112p. (Orig.). 1992. pap. 9.00 (*1-56474-044-7*) Fithian Pr.

— Joy Can Be Your Favorite Song: Tools & Affirmations. LC 92-17285. 112p. (Orig.). 1992. pap. 9.00 (*1-56474-031-5*) Fithian Pr.

Chula, Margaret. Grinding My Ink: Haiku. LC 93-80026. (Illus.). 100p. (Orig.). 1993. pap. 14.95 (*0-9638551-9-0*) Katsura Pr.

— This Moment: Tea Ceremony Haiku. 32p. 1995. pap. 10.00 (*0-9638551-7-4*) Katsura Pr.

***Chula, Margaret & Youmans, Rich.** Shadow Lines: Linked Haibun. (Illus.). 45p. 1999. pap. 12.00 (*0-9638551-4-X*, Pub. by Katsura Pr) Partners-West.

Chula Vista Historical Society Staff. Chula Vista - The Early Years, Vol. 4. Rojas, John, Jr., ed. (Illus.). 70p. (Orig.). 1995. pap. 7.95 (*0-938711-33-4*) Tecolote Pubns.

Chulaki, Sergei, tr. see Edberg, Rolf & Yablokov, Alexei.

Chulay, Marianne. AACN Handbook of Critical Care Nursing. 752p. (C). 1997. pap. 44.95 (*0-8385-0346-2*, A-0346-5, Apple Lange Med) McGraw.

— AACN Pocket Handbook of Critical Care Nursing. 240p. (C). 1997. spiral bd. 21.95 (*0-8385-0322-5*, A-0322-6, Apple Lange Med) McGraw.

Chuleshkar, A. V. Indian Economy in Transition. (C). 1992. 48.50 (*0-8364-2814-5*, Pub. by Anmol) S Asia.

Chulia, Dominique, et al. Powder Technology & Pharmaceutical Processes. LC 93-41271. (Handbook of Powder Technology Ser.: 9). 584p. 1993. 288.50 (*0-444-81533-3*) Elsevier.

Chulick, Irene. A House Full of Women. 32p. 1997. pap. 7.00 (*0-8059-4015-4*) Dorrance.

***Chulos, Chris, et al, eds.** The Fall of an Empire, the Birth of a Nation: National Identities in Russia. (Nationalism & Fascism in Russia Ser.). 238p. 2000. text 69.95 (*1-85521-902-6*, Pub. by Ashgate Pub) Ashgate Pub Co.

Chultz. Path of the Warrior. 1998. text 14.95 (*0-312-18444-1*) St Martin.

Chum, Helena L., ed. Polymers from Biobased Materials. LC 90-23203. (Illus.). 169p. 1991. 109.00 (*0-8155-1271-6*) Noyes.

Chum, Y. M. Recent Developments in Nonperturbative Quantum Field Theory: Proceedings of the APCTP-ICTP Joint International Conference '97, APCTP, Seoul, Korea, 26-30 May 1997. LC 98-28571. 1998. 86.00 (*981-02-3585-2*) World Scientific Pub.

Chumacero, Ali. Paramo de Suenos. (Fondo 2000 Ser.). (SPA.). pap. 2.99 (*968-16-5071-9*, Pub. by Fondo) Continental Bk.

Chumak, George, jt. auth. see Hodges, Linda.

Chumakov, N. M. The Problems of Old Glaciations, Pre-Pleistocene Glaciogeology in the U. S. S. R., Vol. 1. (Soviet Scientific Reviews Ser.). 210p. 1992. pap. text 267.00 (*3-7186-5358-3*, Harwood Acad Pubs) Gordon & Breach.

Chuman, Frank F. The Bamboo People: The Law & Japanese-Americans. LC 76-4117. (Illus.). 400p. 1976. 12.25 (*0-89163-013-9*) Japanese Am Citizens.

Chumas-Ernst, Mary. My Mother Had One Like That: An Easy Handbook to Learn the Worth of Your Heirlooms, Antiques & Treasures. (Illus.). 32p. (Orig.). 1995. pap. text 9.95 (*1-880971-09-7*) Light&Life Pub Co MN.

Chumbley, George L. Colonial Justice in Virginia: The Development of a Judicial System, Typical Laws & Cases of the Period. LC 97-74795. 174p. 1997. reprint ed. 60.00 (*1-56169-338-3*) Gaunt.

Chumbley, Jane. Cystic Fibrosis: A Family Affair. 1999. pap. text 11.95 (*0-85969-771-1*) S C K Pubns.

***Chumbley, Peggy Lucinda.** Mommy & Daddy Take Me to Church. LC 99-64695. (Illus.). 32p. (J). 1999. pap. 9.95 (*0-9672309-0-X*) PLC Pubng.

Chumley, Norris J. Full: The Permanent Weight Control Plan. (Illus.). 38p. 1998. pap. text 39.95 incl. audio (*0-9665112-0-4*) Magnetic Arts.

***Chumley, Norris J.** The Joy of Weight Loss. 2000. pap. 14.00 (*1-930051-19-0*) Lantern Books.

***Chumney, Edward.** Restoring the Two Houses of Israel. 520p. 1999. pap. 19.99 (*1-884369-77-4*) McDougal Pubng.

Chumney, Edward. The Seven Festivals of the Messiah. LC 95-136126. 238p. (Orig.). 1994. pap. 10.99 (*1-56043-767-7*, Treasure Hse) Destiny Image.

Chun. Cyber Buch: Spanish, Vol. 1. 1998. pap. 13.95 (*0-312-18422-0*) St Martin.

— Cyberbuch. 1997. pap. text 22.95 incl. audio (*0-312-18255-4*) St Martin.

— Wing Chun Kung Fu. 3rd ed. LC 99-236279. 144p. 1998. pap. 13.95 (*0-312-18776-9*) St Martin.

***Chun, Allen.** Unstructuring Chinese Society: The Fictions of Colonial Practice & the Changing Realities of "Land" in the New Territories of Hong Kong. (Studies in Anthropology & History: Vol. 27). 364p. 2000. text 62.00 (*90-5702-450-0*, Harwood Acad Pubs) Gordon & Breach.

Chun, Bang J. The Impact of Solidarity or Conflict on Participation in a Labor Union. rev. ed. LC 96-30017. (Studies in the History of American Labor). (Illus.). 214p. 1997. text 61.00 (*0-8153-2672-6*) Garland.

***Chun, Clayton K. S.** Shooting down a Star: America's THOR Program 437, Nuclear ASAT & Copycat Killers. LC 99-50056. (Cadre Paper Ser.). 1999. write for info. (*1-58566-071-X*) Air Univ.

Chun, Elsje. Preparing for Baptism. (Illus.). 28p. (Orig.). 1995. pap. 2.95 (*1-57665-015-4*) Muggli Graphics.

— Sariah: Mother of Nations. (Noble Women Ser.). (Illus.). 52p. (Orig.). (J). (gr. 1-6). 1995. pap. 5.95 (*1-57665-014-6*) Muggli Graphics.

***Chun, Gloria H.** Of Orphans & Warriors: Inventing Chinese-American Culture & Identity. LC 99-33563. 208p. 2000. text 50.00 (*0-8135-2708-2*); pap. text 19.00 (*0-8135-2709-0*) Rutgers U Pr.

Chun-Han Zhu. Clinical Handbook of Chinese Prepared Medicine. Feit, Richard, ed. 1995. pap. text 27.00 (*0-912111-43-7*) Paradigm Publns.

Chun, Janis Y. Precious to Precocious: The Humor of Parenting Birth Through Age 12. limited ed. Stone, Bill, ed. LC 97-92822. (Illus.). 128p. 1998. pap. 12.95 (*0-9663551-0-5*) JYC Co.

Chun, Jerold J., jt. ed. see Zhu, Li.

***Chun, Jin-Hee, et al.** Hanoak: Traditional Korean Homes. LC 99-65246. (Illus.). 239p. 1999. 49.95 (*1-56591-102-4*) Hollym Intl.

Chun, Jinsuk. Interregional Migration & Regional Development. LC 96-85507. (Bruton Center for Development Studies). 194p. 1996. text 68.95 (*1-85972-461-2*, Pub. by Avebry) Ashgate Pub Co.

Chun, Kanoenani, ed. see Reece, Kim T.

Chun, Kevin M., jt. ed. see Balls-Organista, Pamela.

Chun, Kevin M., jt. ed. see Balls-Organista, Pamela.

Chun Koh, Hesung, ed. Korean & Japanese Women: An Analytic Bibliographical Guide. LC 81-80305. (Illus.). 904p. 1982. lib. bdg. 125.00 (*0-313-23387-X*, KJW, Greenwood Pr) Greenwood.

Chun, Kyung-Ja, jt. auth. see Wanso, Pak.

Chun, Kyung-Ja, tr. see Wanso, Pak.

Chun, Laurianne, ed. Asian Studies in Hawai'i: A Guide to Theses & Dissertations. LC 97-41209. 576p. 1998. pap. text 48.00 (*0-8248-2049-5*) UH Pr.

Chun, Lin. The British New Left. 256p. 1994. 55.00 (*0-7486-0422-7*, Pub. by Edinburgh U Pr) Col U Pr.

Chun-Lum, Sharlene & Agard, Lesley. Legacy: A Portrait of the Young Men & Women of Kamehameha Schools 1887-1987. (Illus.). 150p. 1987. 24.95 (*0-87336-009-5*) Kamehameha Schools.

Chun, Malcolm N., jt. auth. see Ching, Linda.

Chun, Malcolm N., ed. see Malo, David.

Chun-Nan Lo, jt. auth. see Klonglan, Gerald E.

Chun, Naomi. Hawaiian Canoe-Building Traditions. rev. ed. LC 96-132033. (Illus.). 92p. (J). (gr. 4-10). 1995. pap. 9.95 (*0-87336-043-5*) Kamehameha Schools.

Chun, Richard. Moo Duk Kwan Tae Kwon Do, Vol. 2. (Illus.). 256p. (YA). 1983. reprint ed. pap. 19.95 (*0-89750-085-7*, 422) Ohara Pubns.

— Moo Duk Kwan Tae Kwon Do, Korean Art of Self-Defense. Johnson, Gilbert et al, eds. LC 75-3784. (Korean Arts Ser.). (Illus.). 1975. pap. text 19.95 (*0-89750-015-6*, 120) Ohara Pubns.

— Tae Kwon Do: The Korean Martial Art & National Sport. LC 74-1799. (Illus.). 544p. 1976. 65.00 (*0-06-010779-0*) HarperTrade.

— Taekwon-Do. 55.00 (*0-685-70709-1*) Wehman.

Chun, Sang E. How to Do Evangelism. (KOR.). 80p. 1997. pap. 8.95 (*0-687-05455-9*) Abingdon.

Chun, Sun W. Liquid Phase Methanol (Lpmeoh) Project: Final Environmental Assessment. (Illus.). 36p. (C). 1999. reprint ed. pap. text 20.00 (*0-7881-7721-4*) DIANE Pub.

Chun, Victor. American PT Boats in World War II. LC 96-72151. 240p. 1997. 45.00 (*0-7643-0256-6*) Schiffer.

Chun Wa Wong. Introduction to Methods & Concepts of Math Physics. (Illus.). 400p. (C). 1991. text 68.00 (*0-19-504473-8*) OUP.

Chun Wei Choo, jt. ed. see Auster, Ethel.

***Chun, Wesley J.** Core Python Programming. (Open Source Technology Ser.). (Illus.). 500p. 2000. pap. text 39.99 (*0-13-026036-3*) P-H.

Chun, Yip, jt. auth. see Connor, Danny.

Chunakara, Mathews G. Militarisation of Politics & Society: Southeast Asian Experiences. 116p. 1998. reprint ed. pap. text 25.00 (*0-7881-1907-9*) DIANE Pub.

***Chunakara, Mathews G., ed.** Indochina: From Socialism to Market Economy. 125p. 1999. reprint ed. pap. text 30.00 (*0-7881-7995-0*) DIANE Pub.

Chuncai, Zhou. The Yellow Emperor's Medicine Classic: Treastice on Health & Long Life. (Illus.). 232p. 1996. pap. 14.95 (*981-3068-28-0*) China Bks.

Chung. Chinese Business Groups: In Hong Kong & Political Changes 1900-1920s in South China. LC 96-24402. 256p. 1998. text 69.95 (*0-312-16344-4*) St Martin.

— Design of Agreement. LC 98-6991. 423p. 1998. 45.00 (*0-226-10607-1*) U Ch Pr.

— Industrial Materials. (Mechanical Technology Ser.). 1990. pap., teacher ed. 10.00 (*0-8273-3937-2*) Delmar.

— Management: Critical Success Factors. 784p. 1986. student ed. 18.00 (*0-685-17394-1*, H03262); write for info. (*0-318-61498-7*, H03254) P-H.

***Chung.** Visualizing & Communicating Color. (C). 2000. pap. 35.25 (*0-8273-8343-6*) Delmar.

Chung, Alma L., jt. auth. see Handel, Peter H.

Chung, Alma L., jt. ed. see Handel, Peter H.

Chung, Arthur. Of Rats, Sparrows & Flies: A Lifetime in China. LC 94-77656. 256p. (C). 1994. text 23.95 (*0-9623048-8-3*) Heritage West.

***Chung, B. K. & Virasoro, Miguel A.** Highlights in Condensed Matter Physics: Proceedings of the APCTP-ICTP Joint International Conference, Seoul, Korea, 12-16 June 1998. LC 99-51986. 1999. write for info. (*981-02-4134-8*) World Scientific Pub.

***Chung, B. K., et al.** Yang-Baxter System, Nonlinear Models & Their Applications: Proceedings of the APCTP-NANKAI Symposium, Seoul, Korea, 20-23 October 1998. LC 99-51985. 1999. write for info. (*981-02-4132-1*) World Scientific Pub.

Chung, Byungjoo. Behind the Curtain. Chung, Norma, ed. & photos by by. (KOR., Illus.). iii, 258p. 1998. pap. 6.50 (*0-9664340-0-5*) C & C Corp.

Chung, C. F., et al, eds. Quantitative Analysis of Mineral & Energy Resources. (C). 1987. text 326.50 (*90-277-2635-3*) Kluwer Academic.

Chung, Catherine, ed. Directory of Periodicals Online: Indexed, Abstracted & Full-Text, Vol. 1. 2nd ed. 350p. (Orig.). 1986. text 125.00 (*0-932929-09-5*) Fed Doc Retrieval.

— Directory of Periodicals Online Vol. 1: Indexed, Abstracted, & Full Text, News, Law & Business. 524p. 1985. pap. 90.00 (*0-932929-00-1*) Fed Doc Retrieval.

Chung, Chai-Sik. A Korean Confucian Encounter with the Modern World: Yi Hang-No & the West. LC 94-24521. (Korea Research Monographs: No. 20). 272p. (C). 1995. pap. 20.00 (*1-55729-046-6*) IEAS.

***Chung, Chan I.** Polymer Extrusion: Theory & Practice. LC 00-35079. 2000. write for info. (*1-56990-288-7*) Hanser-Gardner.

Chung, Charles C., ed. see Anthology Staff.

Chung, Chi. Cows in the House. 32p. (J). 1998. text 14.99 (*0-7642-2096-9*) Bethany Hse.

Chung, Chongwha, ed. Korean Classical Literature: An Anthology. 200p. 1988. 45.00 (*0-7103-0279-7*) Routledge.

Chung-Chun, Yang. Factorization Theory of Meromorphic Functions, & Related Topics. LC 82-9757. (Lecture Notes in Pure & Applied Mathematics Ser.: Vol. 78). 208p. reprint ed. pap. 64.50 (*0-608-09001-8*, 206963600005) Bks Demand.

Chung-Chun, Yang, et al, eds. Probability Theory & Its Applications in China. LC 91-16143. (Contemporary Mathematics Ser.: Vol. 118). 333p. 1991. pap. 48.00 (*0-8218-5126-8*, CONM/118) Am Math.

Chung-Chun, Yang & Chi-Tai, Chuang, eds. Fix-Points & Factorization of Meromorphic Functions. 310p. (C). 1990. text 59.00 (*981-02-0008-0*) World Scientific Pub.

Chung-Chun Yang & Sheng Gong, eds. Several Complex Variables in China. LC 92-44828. (Contemporary Mathematics Ser.: Vol. 142). 173p. 1993. pap. 36.00 (*0-8218-5164-0*, CONM/142) Am Math.

Chung-Chun, Yang, jt. ed. see Xin-Hou Hua.

Chung, Chung T., jt. auth. see Kellman, Robert M.

Chung, Cristy, et al, eds. Between the Lines: An Anthology by Pacific-Asian Lesbians of Santa Cruz, California. 56p. (Orig.). 1987. pap. 6.00 (*0-9622819-0-5*) Dancing Bird.

Chung, D. D. X-Ray Diffraction at Elevated Temperatures: A Method for In Situ Process Analysis. 268p. 1993. 150.00 (*0-471-18726-7*) Wiley.

Chung, D. D., et al. X-Ray Diffraction at Elevated Temperatures: A Method for in Situ Process Analysis. LC 92-21803. 1993. 95.00 (*0-89573-745-0*, Wiley-VCH) Wiley.

***Chung, D. D. L.** Composite Materials for Electronic Functions. (Materials Science Foundations Ser.: Vol. 12). (Illus.). 88p. 2000. text 48.00 (0-87849-836-2, Pub. by Trans T Pub) Enfield Pubs NH.

***Chung, David.** Syncretism: The Religious Context of Christian Beginnings in Korea. Oh, Kang-nam, ed. (C). 2001. pap. text 19.95 (0-7914-4942-4) State U NY Pr.

— Syncretism: The Religious Context of Christian Beginnings in Korea. Oh, Kang-nam, ed. (C). 2001. text 59.50 (0-7914-4941-6) State U NY Pr.

Chung, David C. & Lam, Arthur M. Essentials of Anesthesiology. 3rd ed. Day, Lesley, ed. 400p. 1996. pap. text 32.00 (0-7216-6675-2, W B Saunders Co) Harcrt Hlth Sci Grp.

Chung, David R. Component Java. (Java Masters Ser.). (Illus.). 560p. 1998. pap. 44.95 incl. cd-rom (0-07-913690-7) McGraw.

Chung, Deborah D. Carbon Fiber Composites. LC 94-11427. 280p. 1994. text 115.00 (0-7506-9169-7) Buttrwrth-Heinemann.

— Materials for Electronic Packaging. 368p. 1995. text 155.00 (0-7506-9314-2) Buttrwrth-Heinemann.

Chung, Donald K. The Three Day Promise: A Korean Soldier's Memoirs. (Illus.). 434p. 1989. text 20.00 (0-942407-06-7) Father & Son.

Chung, E. B., jt. ed. see Ninfo, Vito.

Chung, E. K. Complex Arrhythmias: Self Assessment. (Illus.). xiv, 310p. 1985. 71.50 (3-8055-3639-9) S Karger.

Chung, Edward K. Cardiovascular Emergencies: Current Therapy. (Illus.). xii, 244p. 1985. 147.00 (3-8055-3679-8) S Karger.

— ECG Diagnosis Simplified. Gross, Steven, ed. (Illus.). 300p. (C). 1995. pap. text 34.95 (1-887174-00-1) DevCom.

— Pocket Guide to ECG Diagnosis. LC 96-3795. (Illus.). 495p. 1996. pap. text 34.95 (0-86542-499-3) Blackwell Sci.

***Chung, Edward K.** Pocket Guide to ECG Diagnosis. 2nd ed. (Illus.). 512p. 2000. pap. 36.95 (0-86542-589-2) Blackwell Sci.

Chung, Edward K. Quick Reference to Cardiovascular Diseases. 2nd ed. (Illus.). 672p. 1982. text 39.50 (0-397-50482-9, 65-06232, Lippnctt) Lppncott W & W.

Chung, Edward K., ed. Non-Invasive Cardiac Diagnosis. LC 75-38915. (Illus.). 331p. reprint ed. pap. 102.70 (0-608-17893-4, 205667800080) Bks Demand.

Chung, Edward K. & Chung, Lisa S. Introduction to Clinical Cardiology. (Continuing Education Ser.: Vol. 4). (Illus.). xiv, 546p. 1983. 85.25 (3-8055-2997-X) S Karger.

***Chung, Edward K. & Spellberg, Brad.** ECG Diagnosis: A Self-Assessment Workbook. (Illus.). 200p. 2000. pap., wbk. ed. 29.95 (0-86542-587-6) Blackwell Sci.

***Chung, Edward K. & Tighe, Dennis A.** Pocket Guide to Cardiovascular Disease. LC 98-45297. (Illus.). 1998. pap. 35.95 (0-86542-508-6) Blackwell Sci.

Chung, Edward K. & Tighe, Dennis A. Pocket Guide to Stress Testing. LC 96-40175. (Illus.). 1997. pap. 36.95 (0-86542-509-4) Blackwell Sci.

Chung, Edward Y. The Korean Neo-Confucianism of Yi T'oegye & Yi Yulgok: A Reappraisal of the "Four-Seven Thesis" & Its Practical Implications for Self-Cultivation. LC 94-25830. (SUNY Series in Korean Studies). 325p. (C). 1995. text 59.50 (0-7914-2275-5); pap. text 19.95 (0-7914-2276-3) State U NY Pr.

Chung, Ewha. Samuel Richardson's New Nation: Paragons of the Domestic Sphere & "Native" Virtue. LC 97-40682. (American University Studies IV). 162p. 1998. 36.95 (0-8204-3362-4) P Lang Pubng.

Chung, Fan & Graham, Ron. Erdos on Graphs: His Legacy of Unsolved Problems. 2nd rev. ed. (Illus.). 142p. (C). 1999. pap. text 25.00 (1-56881-111-X) AK Peters.

Chung, Fan R. Spectral Graph Theory. LC 96-45112. (Regional Conference Series in Mathematics Ser.: No. 92). 207p. 1996. pap. 25.00 (0-8218-0315-8) Am Math.

***Chung, Frances.** Crazy Melon & Chinese Apple: The Poems of Frances Chung. (Wesleyan Poetry Ser.). 150p. 2000. pap. 15.95 (0-8195-6416-8, Wesleyan Univ Pr); text 30.00 (0-8195-6415-X, Wesleyan Univ Pr) U Pr of New Eng.

***Chung, Frank H. & Smith, Deane K.** Industrial Applications of X-Ray Diffraction. LC 99-39511. 1006p. 1999. 245.00 (0-8247-1992-1) Dekker.

Chung, George & Rothrock, Cynthia. Advanced Dynamic Kicks. Lee, Mike, ed. LC 86-60095. 128p. (Orig.). 1986. pap. 12.95 (0-89750-129-2, 444) Ohara Pubns.

Chung, H. H., ed. Integrity of Structures & Fluid Systems Hazardous Release Protection Piping & Pipe Supports & Pumps & Valves. 261p. 1996. pap. text 110.00 (0-7918-1780-6, TS283) ASME Pr.

Chung, H. H., et al, eds. Structural Integrity of Pressure Vessels, Piping, & Components. LC 96-150213. (Proceedings of the 1995 ASME/JSME Pressure Vessels & Piping Conference Ser.: PVP-Vol. 318). 384p. 1995. 120.00 (0-7918-1349-5, H00981) ASME.

Chung, H. H. & Kwon, Young W., eds. Recent Advances in Solids & Structures, 1995: Proceedings of the ASME International Mechanical Engineering Congress & Exposition, 1995, San Francisco, CA. LC 95-81283. (1995 International Mechanical Engineering Congress & Exposition Ser.: PVP-Vol. 321/NE-Vol. 18). 200p. 1995. 72.00 (0-7918-1747-4, H01026) ASME.

— Recent Advances in Structural Mechanics, 1993. LC 87-71096. 181p. pap. 55.00 (0-7918-1260-X) ASME.

Chung, H. H. & Saleem, M. A., eds. Seismic, Shock & Vibration Isolation, 1996. LC 96-85626. 139p. 1996. pap. 70.00 (0-7918-1788-1) ASME Pr.

Chung, H. H., jt. ed. see Kwon, Young W.

Chung, H. W. Understanding Quality Assurance in Construction: A Practical Guide to ISO 9000 for Contractors. LC 99-20876. 1999. pap. write for info. (0-419-24950-8) Routledge.

Chung, Haeja K., ed. Harriette Simpson Arnow: Critical Essays on Her Work. LC 95-31806. 1995. 45.00 (0-87013-381-0) Mich St U Pr.

Chung-Hawks, Helena. Nosin' 'Round with Peekie Petie. (Illus.). 36p. (J). (gr. 1-2). 1997. pap. 7.95 (1-887747-12-5) Legendary Pub.

Chung, Henry. Oriental Policy of the United States. LC 70-111737. (American Imperialism: Viewpoints of United States Foreign Policy, 1898-1941 Ser.). 1977. reprint ed. 23.95 (0-405-02008-2) Ayer.

Chung, Howard H., ed. Integrity of Structures & Components, Nondestructive Evaluations, 1998: Proceedings, ASME/JSME Joint Pressure Vessels & Piping Conference (1998, San Diego, CA) LC 98-73180. 375. 177p. 1998. pap. 100.00 (0-7918-1871-3) ASME.

— Seismic, Shock, & Vibration Isolation, 1997: Proceedings ASME Pressure Vessels & Piping Conference (1997, Orlando, FL) LC 97-73605. (PVP Ser.: Vol. 357). 85p. 1997. pap. 64.00 (0-7918-1574-9) ASME.

— Seismic, Shock & Vibration Isolation, 1998: Proceedings, ASME/JSME Joint Pressure Vessels & Piping Conference (1998, San Diego, CA), Vol. 379. LC 99-191747. 379. 237p. 1998. pap. 100.00 (0-7918-1875-6) ASME.

Chung, Howard H., et al, eds. Integrity of Structures & Fluid Systems, Piping & Pipe Supports, & Pumps & Valves, 1997: Proceedings ASME Pressure Vessels & Piping Conference (1997, Orlando, FL) LC 97-73606. (PVP Ser.: Vol. 356). 163p. 1997. pap. 90.00 (0-7918-1573-0) ASME.

Chung, Howard H. & Kwon, Young W., eds. Recent Advances in Solids & Structures, 1998; Proceedings; ASME International Mechanical Engineering Congress & Exposition (1998: Anaheim, CA) LC 98-74431. 253p. 1998. pap. 100.00 (0-7918-1600-1) ASME Pr.

Chung, Howard H., jt. ed. see Kwon, Young W.

Chung-Hui, Wang, tr. see Chiang Kai-Shek.

Chung-Hwan, Yi. Yi Chung-Hwan's T'aengniji: The Korean Classic for Choosing Settlements. Yoon, Inshil C., tr. (University of Sydney East Asian Ser.: Vol. 12). 130p. 1998. pap. text 17.00 (0-9586526-3-5) UH Pr.

Chung, Hyun K. Struggle to Be the Sun Again: Introducing Asian Women's Theology. LC 90-42683. 1990. pap. 15.00 (0-88344-684-7) Orbis Bks.

***Chung, J. W.** Risk Profile Methodology of Plant Configurations & Pilot Applications: Lessons Learned. 286p. 1999. per. 23.00 (0-16-062780-X) USGPO.

***Chung, Jae Ho.** Central Control & Local Discretion in China: Leadership & Implementation During Post-Mao Decollectivization. (Studies on Contemporary China). (Illus.). 224p. 2000. text 60.00 (0-19-829777-7) OUP.

Chung, Jin-Gyun & Parhi, Keshab K. Pipelined Lattice & Wave Digital Recursive Filters. (International Series in Engineering & Computer Science, Natural Language Processing & Machine Translation: Vol. 344). 240p. (C). 1995. text 109.00 (0-7923-9656-1) Kluwer Academic.

Chung, Jin S., ed. The Proceedings of the Sixth (1996) International Offshore & Polar Engineering Conference, 4 vols. Incl. Vol. 1. LC 95-82077. (Illus.). 625p. 1996. pap. 110.00 (1-880653-23-0); Vol. 2. LC 95-82077. (Illus.). 625p. 1996. pap. 110.00 (1-880653-24-9); Vol. 3. LC 95-82077. (Illus.). 625p. 1996. pap. 110.00 (1-880653-25-7); Vol. 4. LC 95-82077. (Illus.). 625p. 1996. pap. 110.00 (1-880653-26-5); LC 95-82077. 2326p. 1996. Set pap. 360.00 (1-880653-22-2) ISOPE.

Chung, Jin S., et al, eds. The Proceedings of the Fifth (1995) International Offshore & Polar Engineering Conference, Set, Vols. I-IV. LC 94-73796. 2543p. (Orig.). 1995. pap. 340.00 (1-880653-16-8) ISOPE.

— The Proceedings of the Fifth (1995) International Offshore & Polar Engineering Conference, Vol. I. LC 94-73796. (Orig.). 1995. pap. 100.00 (1-880653-17-6) ISOPE.

— The Proceedings of the Fifth (1995) International Offshore & Polar Engineering Conference, Vol. II. LC 94-73796. (Orig.). 1995. pap. 100.00 (1-880653-18-4) ISOPE.

— The Proceedings of the Fifth (1995) International Offshore & Polar Engineering Conference, Vol. III. LC 94-73796. (Orig.). 1995. pap. 100.00 (1-880653-19-2) ISOPE.

— Proceedings of the First (1991) International Offshore & Polar Engineering Conference, 4 vols. LC 91-71635. 2148p. (Orig.). 1991. pap. 320.00 (0-9626104-5-3) ISOPE.

— Proceedings of the First (1991) International Offshore & Polar Engineering Conference, Vol. I. LC 91-71635. 476p. (Orig.). 1991. pap. 100.00 (0-9626104-6-1) ISOPE.

— Proceedings of the First (1991) International Offshore & Polar Engineering Conference, Vol. III. LC 91-71635. 546p. (Orig.). 1991. pap. 100.00 (0-9626104-8-8) ISOPE.

— The Proceedings of the Fourth International Offshore & Polar Engineering Conference, 1994, 4 vols., Set. LC 93-80555. 2589p. (Orig.). 1994. pap. 340.00 (1-880653-10-9) ISOPE.

— The Proceedings of the Fourth International Offshore & Polar Engineering Conference, 1994, Vol. I. LC 93-80555. 649p. (Orig.). 1994. pap. 100.00 (1-880653-11-7) ISOPE.

— The Proceedings of the Fourth International Offshore & Polar Engineering Conference, 1994, Vol. II. LC 93-80555. 640p. (Orig.). 1994. pap. 100.00 (1-880653-12-5) ISOPE.

— The Proceedings of the Fourth International Offshore & Polar Engineering Conference, 1994, Vol. III. LC 93-80555. 606p. (Orig.). 1994. pap. 100.00 (1-880653-13-3) ISOPE.

— Proceedings of the 2nd (1997) Ocean Mining Symposium. LC 97-74490. (Illus.). 201p. 1997. pap. 100.00 (1-880653-33-8) ISOPE.

***Chung, Jin S., et al, eds.** Proceedings of the 2nd (1999) ISOPE European Offshore Mechanics Symposium: Pipeline. (ENG & RUS., Illus.). 135p. 1999. pap. 50.00 (1-880653-44-3) ISOPE.

Chung, Jin S., et al, eds. Proceedings of the Second (1992) International Offshore & Polar Engineering Conference, 4 vols., Set. LC 91-78280. 2900p. (Orig.). 1992. pap. 340.00 (1-880653-00-1) ISOPE.

— Proceedings of the Second (1992) International Offshore & Polar Engineering Conference, Vol. I. LC 91-78280. 729p. (Orig.). 1992. pap. 100.00 (1-880653-0[illegible]-X) ISOPE.

— Proceedings of the Second (1992) International Offshore & Polar Engineering Conference, Vol. III. LC 91-78280. 724p. (Orig.). 1992. pap. 100.00 (1-880653-03-6) ISOPE.

***Chung, Jin S., et al, eds.** The Proceedings of the Tenth (2000) International Offshore & Polar Engineering Conference, 4 vols., Set. (Illus.). 2662p. 2000. pap. 420.00 incl. cd-rom (1-880653-46-X) ISOPE.

— The Proceedings of the Tenth (2000) International Offshore & Polar Engineering Conference, Vol. I. (Illus.). 775p. 2000. pap. 130.00 (1-880653-47-8) ISOPE.

— The Proceedings of the Tenth (2000) International Offshore & Polar Engineering Conference, Vol. II. (Illus.). 688p. 2000. pap. 130.00 (1-880653-48-6) ISOPE.

— The Proceedings of the Tenth (2000) International Offshore & Polar Engineering Conference, Vol. III. (Illus.). 704p. 2000. pap. 130.00 (1-880653-49-4) ISOPE.

Chung, Jin S., et al, eds. The Proceedings of the Third International Offshore & Polar Engineering Conference, 1993, 4 vols., 1. LC 92-76219. 709p. (Orig.). 1993. pap. 100.00 (1-880653-06-0) ISOPE.

— The Proceedings of the Third International Offshore & Polar Engineering Conference, 1993, 4 vols., 2. LC 92-76219. 784p. (Orig.). 1993. pap. 100.00 (1-880653-07-9) ISOPE.

— The Proceedings of the Third International Offshore & Polar Engineering Conference, 1993, 4 vols., 3. LC 92-76219. 740p. (Orig.). 1993. pap. 100.00 (1-880653-08-7) ISOPE.

— The Proceedings of the Third International Offshore & Polar Engineering Conference, 1993, 4 vols., Set. LC 92-76219. 2965p. (Orig.). 1993. pap. 340.00 (1-880653-05-2) ISOPE.

***Chung, Jin S. & Sharma, Rahul, eds.** Proceedings of the 3rd (1999) ISOPE Ocean Mining Symposium. (Illus.). 288p. 1999. pap. 100.00 (1-880653-45-1) ISOPE.

Chung, Jin S., et al. The Proceedings of the First (1990) European Offshore Mechanics Symposium. LC 90-84691. 575p. (Orig.). 1990. pap. 80.00 (0-9626104-4-5) ISOPE.

Chung, Jin S., ed. see International Offshore Mechanics & Arctic Engineer.

Chung, Jin S., jt. ed. see Li, Yu-cheng.

Chung, Jin S., ed. see Offshore Mechanics, Arctic Engineering, Deepsea Sy.

Chung, Joseph, jt. auth. see Campbell, John R.

***Chung, K. Fan & Adcock, Ian, eds.** Asthma: Mechanisms & Protocols. (Methods in Molecular Medicine Ser.: Vol. 44). 368p. 2000. 99.50 (0-89603-626-X) Humana.

Chung, K. Fan & Barnes, Peter J., eds. Pharmacology of the Respiratory Tract: Experimental & Clinical Research. (Lung Biology in Health & Disease Ser.: Vol. 67). (Illus.). 848p. 1993. text 245.00 (0-8247-8847-8) Dekker.

Chung, K. L. A New Introduction to Stochastic Processes. (CHI.). 250p. 1997. text 36.00 (981-02-2365-X) World Scientific Pub.

Chung, Kae H. & Lee, Hak C., eds. Korean Managerial Dynamics. LC 89-3960. 251p. 1989. 62.95 (0-275-93190-0, C3190, Praeger Pubs) Greenwood.

Chung, Kae H., et al. Korean Management: Global Strategy & Transformation. LC 97-22804. (Studies in Organization: Vol. 81). xiv, 266p. (C). 1997. text 74.95 (3-11-014669-X); pap. text 24.95 (3-11-014668-1) De Gruyter.

Chung, Kai L. A Course in Probability Theory. 2nd ed. (Probability & Mathematical Statistics Ser.). 1974. text 71.00 (0-12-174650-X) Acad Pr.

— Elementary Probability Theory with Stochastic Processes. (Undergraduate Texts in Mathematics Ser.). (Illus.). 1990. 39.95 (0-387-90362-3) Spr-Verlag.

— Green, Brown, & Probability. 100p. 1995. 18.00 (981-02-2453-2) World Scientific Pub.

— Lectures from Markov Processes to Brownian Motion. (Grundlehren der Mathematischen Wissenschaften Ser.). (Illus.). 256p. 1982. 95.95 (0-387-90618-5) Spr-Verlag.

Chung, Kai L. & Williams, R. J. Introduction to Stochastic Integration. 2nd ed. (Probability & Its Applications Ser.). 250p. 1993. 43.50 (0-8176-3386-3) Birkhauser.

Chung, Kai L. & Zhao, Zhongxin. From Brownian Motion to Schrodinger's Equation. LC 95-1414. (Grundlehren der Mathematischen Wissenschaften Ser.: Vol. 312). (Illus.). 287p. 1995. 108.95 (0-387-57030-6) Spr-Verlag.

Chung, Kai L., ed. see Cinlar, Erhan, et al.

Chung Kim & McPheron, Bruce A. Evolution of Insect Pests: Patterns of Variation. (Environmental Science & Technology: A Wiley-Interscience Series of Texts & Monographs). 496p. 1993. 160.00 (0-471-60077-6, Pub. by Interscience) Wiley.

Chung, Kimberly. Identifying the Food Insecure: The Application of Mixed-Method Approaches in India. LC 97-34495. (Occasional Papers). 1997. write for info. (0-89629-336-X) Intl Food Policy.

Chung, Kwang S., jt. auth. see Weston, Fred.

Chung, Kyu-Hwa, ed. see Li, Mirok.

Chung, Kyung W. Gross Anatomy. 2nd ed. (Board Review Ser.). (Illus.). 368p. 1991. 19.95 (0-683-01565-6) Lppncott W & W.

— Gross Anatomy. 2nd ed. (Board Review Ser.). 1993. 19.95 (0-685-75155-4) Lppncott W & W.

— Gross Anatomy. 3rd ed. LC 94-23875. (Board Review Ser.). (Illus.). 350p. 1995. 19.95 (0-683-01563-X) Lppncott W & W.

Chung, Kyung Won. BRS Gross Anatomy. 4th ed. 385p. 24.95 (0-683-30727-4) Lppncott W & W.

***Chung, Lawrence.** Non-Functional Requirements in Software Engineering. LC 99-46023. (International Series in Software Engineering). 1999. write for info. (0-7923-8666-3) Kluwer Academic.

***Chung, Leland W. K., et al, eds.** Prostate Cancer. (Contemporary Cancer Research Ser.). 550p. 2000. 145.00 (0-89603-868-8) Humana.

Chung-Liang Huang, Al, jt. auth. see Watts, Alan.

Chung, Lily. Path to Good Fortune: The Meng. LC 97-2437. (Illus.). 288p. (Orig.). 1997. pap. 14.95 (1-56718-133-3) Llewellyn Pubns.

Chung, Lisa S., jt. auth. see Chung, Edward K.

Chung, Nguyen B., jt. ed. see Collins, Martha.

Chung, Nguyen Ba, see Bowen, Kevin.

Chung, Nguyen Ba, tr. see Duy, Nguyen.

Chung, Norma, ed. & photos by see Chung, Byungjoo.

Chung, Norman H., jt. auth. see Rogers, David.

Chung, Okwha & Monroe, Judy M. Cooking the Korean Way. (Easy Menu Ethnic Cookbooks Ser.). (Illus.). 48p. (J). (gr. 5 up). 1998. lib. bdg. 19.93 (0-8225-0921-0, Lerner Publctns) Lerner Pub.

Chung, Ong C. Operation Matador: Britain's War Plans Against the Japanese 1918-1941. LC 97-945721. 328p. 1997. 25.00 (981-210-095-4, Pub. by Times Academic) Intl Spec Bk.

Chung, P. W., et al, eds. The Sixth International Conference on Industrial & Engineering Applications of Artificial Intelligence & Expert Systems: The City Chambers, Edinburgh, Scotland, June 1-4, 1993, Sponsored by International Society of Applied Intelligence. LC 93-1469. 546p. 1993. pap. text 128.00 (2-88124-604-4) Gordon & Breach.

***Chung, Paul.** Spirituality & Social Ethics in John Calvin: A Pneumatological Perspective. 232p. 2000. 37.00 (0-7618-1742-5) U Pr of Amer.

***Chung, Po.** Position Method Handbook: Based on the Position Method of Learning Golf. 20p. 1998. pap. 25.00 (0-9667685-3-1) Virtual Univ Educ Sys.

Chung, Riley, ed. Hokkaido-Nansei-Oki, Japan, Earthquake of July 12, 1993, Reconnaissance Report. (Illus.). 166p. 1995. pap. 15.00 (0-943198-75-5, 95-01) Earthquake Eng.

Chung, Riley M., jt. ed. see Housner, George W.

Chung, S. J., ed. Information Highways for a Smaller World & Better Living. LC 95-7930. 850p. (YA). (gr. 12). 1996. 145.00 (90-5199-240-8, 240-8) IOS Press.

Chung, S. U. & Lindenbaum, S. J., eds. Experimental Meson Spectroscopy 1980: Sixth International Conference, Brookhaven. LC 80-71123. (AIP Conference Proceedings Ser.: No. 67). 608p. 1981. lib. bdg. 37.50 (0-88318-166-5) Am Inst Physics.

Chung, S. U. & Willutzki, H. J., eds. Hadron Spectroscopy: 7th International Conference. LC 98-70965. (AIP Conference Proceedings Ser.: Vol. 432). (Illus.). 928p. 1997. 225.00 (1-56396-765-0) Am Inst Physics.

Chung, Sandra. Case Marking & Grammatical Relations in Polynesian. LC 78-56993. 415p. reprint ed. pap. 128.70 (0-8357-7732-4, 203608900002) Bks Demand.

— The Design of Agreement: The Evidence from Chamorro. LC 98-6991. 1997. pap. text 25.00 (0-226-10609-8) U Ch Pr.

Chung, Seungwha, jt. auth. see Mezias, Stephen J.

Chung, Soon M., ed. Multimedia Information Storage & Management. 483p. (C). 1996. lib. bdg. 155.00 (0-614-19147-5) Kluwer Academic.

Chung, Stanley M. Hip Disorders in Infants & Children. LC 81-1549. (Illus.). 410p. reprint ed. pap. 127.10 (0-608-17894-2, 205667900080) Bks Demand.

Chung, Suh-Urk, ed. Glueballs, Hybrids, & Exotic Hadrons. LC 89-83513. (AIP Conference Proceedings Ser.: No. 185). 760p. 1990. lib. bdg. 90.00 (0-88318-385-4) Am Inst Physics.

Chung, T. C. New Advances in Polyolefins. (Illus.). 256p. (C). 1994. text 89.50 (0-306-44588-3, Kluwer Plenum) Kluwer Academic.

Chung, T. J. Applied Continuum Mechanics. (Illus.). 262p. (C). 1996. text 54.95 (0-521-48297-6) Cambridge U Pr.

— Finite Elements in Fluids. 1992. 231.00 (0-89116-850-8) Hemisp Pub.

Chung, T. J., ed. Numerical Modeling in Combustion. (Series in Computational Methods & Physical Processes in Mechanics & Thermal Sciences). 532p. 1993. 229.00 (0-89116-822-2) Hemisp Pub.

Chung, T. J. & Karr, Gerald R. Development in Theoretical & Applied Mechanics, Vol. XI. 638p. 1982. 50.00 (0-942166-00-0) U AL Dept Mech Eng.

Chung, Tan, ed. Dunhuang Art: Through the Eyes of Duan Wenjie. LC 94-907078. (C). 1994. 135.00 (81-7017-313-2, Pub. by Abhinav) S Asia.

***Chung, Tang, ed.** East Asian Jade 3 Vols. Symbol of Excellence. 1295p. 1998. pap. 780.00 (962-85303-2-1, Pub. by Chinese Univ of Hong Kong) St Mut.

Chung, Tang & Wai-Ming, Cheng. Archaeological Investigation of HAC Sa, Coloane, Macau. 286p. 1996. 285.00 (962-201-730-4, Pub. by Chinese Univ of Hong Kong) St Mut.

Chung, Tsai Chih. Wisdom of the Zen Master: The Quest for Enlightenment. Bruya, Brian, tr. LC 98-15909. (Illus.). 128p. 1998. pap. 13.00 (0-385-48743-6) Doubleday.

C

Chung, Wendy V. Ethnicity & Organizational Diversity: A Study of Social Cognition & Psychological Climate Perception. LC 96-41350. 168p. 1996. lib. bdg. 38.00 (*0-7618-0528-1*) U Pr of Amer.

Chung, William K., jt. auth. see Denison, Edward F.

***Chung, Y. Barry.** A Practical Handbook for Interpersonal Skills Training. 98p. 2000. write for info. (*1-58692-024-3*) Copyright Mgmt.

***Chung, Y. W., et al, eds.** Advanced Materials for the 21st Century: The 1999 Julia R. Weertman Symposium. (Illus.). 586p. 1999. 145.00 (*0-87339-455-0*) Minerals Metals.

Chung, Yip-Wah, et al, eds. Surface Science Investigations in Tribology: Experimental Approaches. LC 92-1263. (ACS Symposium Ser.: No. 485). (Illus.). 253p. 1992. text 65.00 (*0-8412-2205-3*, Pub. by Am Chemical) OUP.

Chung, Yip-Wah, jt. auth. see Miyoshi, K.

Chung Yung Staff. The Conduct of Life: The Universal Order of Confucius. 1972. lib. bdg. 250.00 (*0-87968-497-6*) Krishna Pr.

Chungara, Domitila De, see De Chungara, Domitila B.

Chunghwa, Kay, jt. auth. see Nam, Park.

Chunkath, Sheela R., jt. auth. see Athreya, Venkatesh B.

Chunko, Shelby E. & Madsen, Jane M. Hablemnos de la Tala Forestal: Un Libro de Silvicultura para Jovenes. large type unabridged ed. De Banegas, Marianne N., tr. (SPA., Illus.). v, 32p. (J). (gr. 4-9). 1998. pap. 7.50 (*0-9661896-2-0*) PA Forestry.

— Let's Talk about Clearcutting: A Forestry Book for Youth. large type unabridged ed. (Illus.). v, 32p. (J). (gr. 4-9). 1998. pap. 7.50 (*0-9661896-1-2*) PA Forestry.

***Chunlang, Jiang & Zongyao Wang.** Strongly Irreducible Operators on Hilbert Space, 389. (Pitman Research Notes in Mathematics Ser.: No. 389). 256p. 1998. pap. 52.50 (*0-582-30594-2*) Addison-Wesley.

Chunli, Qu. The Life of Confucius. 645p. 1996. pap. 19.95 (*7-119-01863-9*, Pub. by Foreign Lang) China Bks.

Chunn, Calvin E. Not by Bread Alone. (Illus.). 86p. (Orig.). 1981. pap. 5.00 (*0-9606828-1-3*) Soc Descend Wash Army.

Chunn, Cloe. 50 Hikes in the Maine Mountains: Day Hikes & Backpacks in the Fabled Northern Peaks & Lake Country. 2nd ed. LC 96-48309. (50 Hikes Ser.). (Illus.). 224p. 1997. pap. 14.95 (*0-88150-390-8*, Pub. by Countryman) Norton.

Chunn, Dorothy. From Punishment to Doing Good: Family Courts & Socialized Justice in Ontario, 1880-1940. 288p. 1992. text 45.00 (*0-8020-5993-7*); pap. text 17.95 (*0-8020-6927-4*) U of Toronto Pr.

***Chunn, Dorothy E. & Lacombe, Dany, eds.** Law As a Gendering Practice. 320p. 2000. pap. 24.95 (*0-19-541295-8*) OUP.

Chunn, Eva W., jt. ed. see Smith, Willy D.

Chunn, Jay, II, et al, eds. Mental Health & People of Color: Curriculum Development & Change. LC 83-295. (Illus.). 688p. 1982. 34.95 (*0-88258-097-3*) Howard U Pr.

Chunovic, Louis. Bruce Lee: The Tao of the Dragon Warrior. (Illus.). 128p. (Orig.). 1996. pap. 15.95 (*0-312-14290-0*) St Martin.

— The Complete Quantum Leap Book. (Illus.). 192p. 1995. pap. 17.95 (*0-8065-1699-2*, Citadel Pr) Carol Pub Group.

— The Northern Exposure Book: The Official Publication of the Television Series. rev. ed. (Illus.). 224p. 1995. pap. 17.95 (*0-8065-1623-2*, Citadel Pr) Carol Pub Group.

— The Northern Exposure Book: The Official Publication of the Television Show. LC 92-37592. 1993. 16.95 (*0-8065-1409-4*) Carol Pub Group.

***Chunovic, Louis.** One Foot on the Floor: The Curious Evolution of Sex on Television from "I Love Lucy" to "South Park" (Illus.). 256p. 2000. 25.00 (*1-57500-186-1*, Pub. by TV Bks) HarpC.

Chunovic, Louis. Penny Marshall: An Unauthorized Biography. (Illus.). 256p. 1999. 22.95 (*1-58063-074-X*, Pub. by Renaissance) St Martin.

— The Quantum Leap Book: The Official Publication of the Television Series. (Illus.). 160p. 1992. pap. 16.95 (*0-8065-1374-8*, Citadel Pr) Carol Pub Group.

Chunovic, Louis. The Rocky & Bullwinkle Book. LC 96-84876. (Illus.). 224p. 1996. 50.00 (*0-553-10503-5*) Bantam.

— TV Sex: An Illustrated Guide. LC 99-59114. 192p. 2000. pap. 14.95 (*1-57500-126-8*, Pub. by TV Bks) HarpC.

Chuong, Cheng-Ming. Molecular Basis of Epithelial Appendage Morphogenesis, \. LC 98-9174. (Molecular Biology Intelligence Unit Ser.). 444p. 1998. 99.00 (*1-57059-490-2*) Landes Bioscience.

Chuong, Chung H. Vietnamese Students: Changing Patterns, Changing Needs. (Illus.). 23p. (Orig.). 1994. pap. 5.00 (*0-936434-71-6*, Many Cultures Pubng) SF Study Ctr.

Chupa, Anna M. Anne, the White Woman in Contemporary African-American Fiction: Archetypes, Stereotypes, & Characterizations, 133. LC 89-25919. (Contributions in Afro-American & African Studies: No. 133). 192p. 1990. 52.95 (*0-313-25447-8*, PWW/, Greenwood Pr) Greenwood.

Chupack, Henry. The Scarlet Letter: A Study Guide. (Novel-Ties Ser.). (YA). (gr. 9-12). 1983. pap. text, student ed. 15.95 (*0-88122-032-9*) Lrn Links.

Chupakhin, Oleg N., et al. Nucleophilic Aromatic Substitution of Hydrogen. (Illus.). 367p. 1994. text 111.00 (*0-12-174640-2*) Acad Pr.

Chupco, Lee, et al. Creek (Muscogee) New Testament Concordance. 167p. 1982. pap. 8.00 (*0-940392-10-0*) Indian U Pr OK.

Chupeau, Y., et al, eds. Androgenesis & Haploid Plants. LC 98-14360. (Illus.). x, 121p. 1998. 99.00 (*3-540-64025-8*) Spr-Verlag.

Chupela, Dolores C. Once upon a Childhood: Fingerplays, Action Rhymes, & Fun Times for the Very Young. LC 98-3301. (School Library Media Ser.: No. 16). 144p. 1998. pap. 24.00 (*0-8108-3485-5*) Scarecrow.

Chupita, Greg. Macrossan Street. 1998. pap. write for info. (*1-57553-916-0*) Watermrk Pr.

***Chupita, Greg.** Nightshades. 1999. pap. write for info. (*1-58235-355-7*) Watermrk Pr.

Chupp, E. L. Gamma-Ray Astronomy: Nuclear Transition Region. LC 76-21711. (Geophysics & Astrophysics Monographs: No. 14). 1976. pap. text 70.50 (*90-277-0696-4*); lib. bdg. 152.00 (*90-277-0695-6*) Kluwer Academic.

Chupp, Lyle D., ed. Thy Will Be Done. 448p. 1998. text 14.95 (*1-890050-20-2*) Carlisle Press.

Chupp, Nancy C. Get Ready to Learn. LC 94-16042. 1994. pap. 9.99 (*0-8407-9225-5*) Nelson.

Chupp, Sam, et al. In Nomine the Marches Vol. 2: Revelations Cycle. Haring, Scott, ed. (Revelations Cycle Ser.). (Illus.). 128p. 1997. pap. 19.95 (*1-55634-331-0*, 3305, Pub. by S Jackson Games) BookWorld.

Chupungco, Anscar J. Beyond Inculturation. (Worship Ser.). (C). 1994. pap. text 14.95 (*1-56929-018-0*, Pastoral Press) OR Catholic.

***Chupungco, Anscar J.** Handbook for Liturgical Studies: Sacraments & Sacramentals, Vol. 4. (Handbook for Liturgical Studies: Vol. IV). 416p. 2000. 49.95 (*0-8146-6164-5*, Pueblo Bks) Liturgical Pr.

— Handbook for Liturgical Studies Vol. 5: Liturgical Time & Space. 440p. 2000. 49.95 (*0-8146-6165-3*) Liturgical Pr.

Chupungco, Anscar J. Liturgies of the Future: The Process & Methods of Inculturation. 1989. pap. 9.95 (*0-8091-3095-5*) Paulist Pr.

— Progress & Tradition. (Worship Ser.). 312p. 1995. pap. text 14.95 (*1-56929-051-2*, Pastoral Press) OR Catholic.

— Shaping the Easter Feast. (NPM Studies in Church Music & Liturgy). 1992. pap. text 14.95 (*0-912405-95-3*, Pastoral Press) OR Catholic.

Chupungco, Anscar J., ed. Handbook for Liturgical Studies No. III: The Eucharist. 464p. 1999. 49.95 (*0-8146-6163-7*) Liturgical Pr.

— Handbook for Liturgical Studies Vol. 1: Introduction to the Liturgy. LC 97-20141. 464p. 1997. 49.95 (*0-8146-6161-0*) Liturgical Pr.

Chupungco, Anscar J., Jr., ed. Handbook for Liturgical Studies Vol. II: Fundamental Liturgy, Vol. II. 404p. 1998. 49.95 (*0-8146-6162-9*) Liturgical Pr.

Chupungo, Anschar J. Liturgical Inculturation: Sacramentals, Religiosity, & Catechesis. 176p. (Orig.). 1992. pap. 14.95 (*0-8146-6120-3*, Pueblo Bks) Liturgical Pr.

Chuquet, Flegg. Renaissance Mathematics. 1984. lib. bdg. 176.50 (*90-277-1872-5*) Kluwer Academic.

Chuquet, Helene. Dictionary-Lexicon of Micro-Computers: Dictionnaire-Lexique Micro-Informatique. (FRE.). 264p. 1985. pap. 55.00 (*0-8288-1352-3*, M535) Fr & Eur.

Churaev, N. V. Liquid & Vapor Flows in Porous Bodies: Surface Phenomena. Galwey, A. K., ed. 344p. 1999. text 98.00 (*90-5699-149-3*) Gordon & Breach.

Churba, Amy. Children of the Earth. LC 98-84314. (Illus.). 32p. (J). (ps-3). 1998. 15.95 (*0-9662777-0-8*) Pleiades Pub HI.

Churba, Joseph. The Washington Compromise: How Government Betrays the National Interest. (Illus.). 342p. (C). Date not set. lib. bdg. 26.00 (*0-7618-0087-5*) U Pr of Amer.

Churban, Lita, jt. auth. see Oshry, Ephraim.

Churbuck, D. C. The Book of Rowing. LC 99-11455. (Illus.). 272p. 1999. pap. 19.95 (*0-87951-709-3*, Pub. by Overlook Pr) Penguin Putnam.

Churbuck, David C. The Book of Rowing. LC 87-5818. (Illus.). 272p. 1987. 25.00 (*0-87951-292-X*, Pub. by Overlook Pr) Penguin Putnam.

— The Book of Rowing. (Illus.). 272p. 1990. pap. 15.95 (*0-87951-317-9*, Pub. by Overlook Pr) Penguin Putnam.

Church. Cracker's Bakery. (GB - Basic Business Ser.). 1993. mass mkt., wbk. ed. 17.95 (*0-538-61752-7*) S-W Pub.

Church & Synagogue Library Association Staff. Standards for Church & Synagogue Libraries: Guidelines for Measuring Effectiveness & Progress. 2nd rev. ed. (Guide Ser.: No. 6). 24p. 1993. reprint ed. pap. 8.00 (*0-915324-36-9*) CSLA.

Church, A. J. The Fall of Athens: A Story of the Peloponnesian War. pap. 20.00 (*0-8196-0393-7*) Biblo.

Church, Albert M. Conflicts over Resource Ownership: The Use of Public Policy by Private Interests. LC 82-47942. 255p. reprint ed. pap. 79.10 (*0-7837-5749-2*, 204541100006) Bks Demand.

— Taxation of Nonrenewable Resources. LC 80-8784. 349p. reprint ed. pap. 108.20 (*0-7837-3260-0*, 204327900007) Bks Demand.

Church, Alexander H. Production Factors in Cost Accounting & Works Management. LC 75-18461. (History of Accounting Ser.). (Illus.). 1979. reprint ed. 18.95 (*0-405-07545-6*) Ayer.

Church, Alexander H., Jr. The Proper Distribution of Expense Burden. Chandler, Alfred D., ed. LC 79-7538. (History of Management Thought & Practice Ser.). 1980. reprint ed. lib. bdg. 15.95 (*0-405-12323-X*) Ayer.

Church, Alfred J. The Burning of Rome. 1994. pap. 22.00 (*0-8196-1252-9*) Biblo.

— Greek Life & Story. 320p. (YA). (gr. 6-12). 1998. reprint ed. pap. 20.00 (*0-8196-2056-4*) Biblo.

— The Iliad of Homer. 1995. pap. 20.00 (*0-8196-1253-7*) Biblo.

— Lucius, Adventures of a Roman Boy. LC 60-16706. (YA). (gr. 7-11). 1969. 22.00 (*0-8196-0108-X*) Biblo.

— Roman Life in the Days of Cicero. LC 61-24994. (YA). (gr. 7-11). 1968. 30.00 (*0-8196-0105-5*) Biblo.

— Stories from the Greek Comedians: Aristophanes, Philemon, Diphilus, Mendander & Apollodorus. (Illus.). 344p. (YA). (gr. 6-12). 1998. reprint ed. pap. 20.00 (*0-8196-2081-5*) Biblo.

— Stories of the Old World. 1996. pap. 20.00 (*0-8196-1254-5*) Biblo.

Church, Alfred J. & Gilman, Arthur. Carthage: Or, the Empire of Africa. LC 72-165620. (Select Bibliographies Reprint Ser.). 1977. reprint ed. 30.95 (*0-8369-5927-2*) Ayer.

— The Story of Carthage. (Illus.). 310p. (YA). (gr. 6-12). 1998. reprint ed. pap. 20.00 (*0-8196-2057-2*) Biblo.

Church, Alice M. Church: Genealogy & History of the Church Family in America, Descended from Richard Church of Hartford, Connecticut & South Hadley, Massachusetts, with Copies of Deeds, Will & Miscellaneous Data from Chenango County, New York. 350p. 1997. reprint ed. pap. 52.50 (*0-8328-7930-4*); reprint ed. lib. bdg. 62.50 (*0-8328-7929-0*) Higginson Bk Co.

Church, Allan & Waclawski, Janine. Designing & Using Organizational Surveys. LC 97-16696. 200p. 1998. 83.95 (*0-566-07975-5*, Pub. by Gower) Ashgate Pub Co.

Church, Alonzo. The Calculi of Lambda-Conversion. LC 41-22039. (Annals of Mathematical Studies: No. 6). 83p. reprint ed. pap. 30.00 (*0-608-06635-4*, 206683200009) Bks Demand.

— Introduction to Mathematical Logic. 378p. 1956. pap. text 19.95 (*0-691-02906-7*, Pub. by Princeton U Pr) Cal Prin Full Svc.

Church, Andrew. Transportation. LC 98-34741. (Ecology Alert Ser.). (YA). 1999. 22.83 (*0-8172-5372-6*) Raintree Steck-V.

Church, Annette E. & Church, Roberta. The Robert R. Churches of Memphis: A Father & Son Who Achieved in Spite of Race. (Illus.). 322p. 1974. 15.00 (*0-937130-13-3*) Burkes Bk Store.

Church Annual Staff, ed. Episcopal Church Annual, 1999. 1999. 25.00 (*0-8192-3154-1*) Morehouse Pub.

***Church Annual Staff, ed.** Episcopal Church Annual 2000. 2000. 32.00 (*0-8192-3155-X*, 6231) Morehouse Pub.

Church, Anthea. Angels. (Illus.). 103p. (Orig.). 1997. pap. text. write for info. (*1-886872-04-X*) Brahma Kumaris.

— Inner Space. (Illus.). 119p. (Orig.). 1997. pap. text. write for info. (*1-886872-05-8*) Brahma Kumaris.

— Invocations. 80p. (Orig.), (C). 1997. pap. text. write for info. (*1-886872-03-1*) Brahma Kumaris.

Church Art Works, creator. ArtSource: Ultimate Youth Ministry. (Ultimate Youth Ministry Clip Art Ser.: Vol. 8). 96p. 1997. pap. 10.99 (*0-310-21787-3*) Youth Spec.

Church, Austin H. Mechanical Vibrations. 2nd ed. LC 63-14755. 452p. reprint ed. pap. 140.20 (*0-8357-9933-6*, 201317900085) Bks Demand.

Church, Benjamin, jt. auth. see Walker, Jeffrey B.

Church, Beverly. Entertaining Celebrations: Celebrate Each Month with Pizzazz. Petersen, Kristen, ed. (Illus.). 100p. 1997. pap. 28.00 (*0-9659817-0-3*) Entertain Celeb.

Church, Beverly R. & Bultman, Bethany E. The Joys of Entertaining. (Illus.). 336p. 1987. 50.00 (*0-89659-752-0*) Abbeville Pr.

— The Joys of Entertaining. LC 99-186181. (Illus.). 336p. 1998. pap. 29.95 (*0-7892-0355-3*) Abbeville Pr.

Church, Bob & Gathercole, Peter. Fly Fishing for Trout. (Illus.). 160p. 1996. 45.00 (*1-85223-849-6*, Pub. by Cro1wood) Trafalgar.

— Fly Fishing for Trout. (Illus.). 160p. 1998. pap. 29.95 (*1-86126-155-1*, Pub. by Cro1wood) Trafalgar.

Church, C., jt. auth. see Dolby, K.

***Church, Caroline J.** Curious Camel. (Waggy Tales Ser.). 10p. (J). (ps). 1999. bds. 5.99 (*0-7847-1116-X*, 03524) Standard Pub.

— Little Donkey. (Waggy Tales Ser.). 10p. (J). (ps). 1999. bds. 5.99 (*0-7847-1115-1*, 03523) Standard Pub.

Church, Caroline Jayne. Humpty Dumpty's Favorite Nursery Rhymes. (J). 1999. text 10.99 (*1-56799-897-6*) M Friedman Pub Grp Inc.

***Church, Caroline Jayne.** Who Is My Mommy? (Illus.). 11p. (J). 1999. bds. 11.98 (*1-58048-068-3*) Sandvik Pub.

Church, Charles A. History of Rockford & Winnebago County, from the First Settlement in 1834 to the Civil War. (Illus.). 386p. 1997. reprint ed. lib. bdg. 45.00 (*0-8328-5791-2*) Higginson Bk Co.

Church, Charles W. Church: Simeon Church of Chester, Connecticut, 1708-1792, & His Descendants. 241p. 1993. reprint ed. pap. 38.00 (*0-8328-3281-2*); reprint ed. lib. bdg. 48.00 (*0-8328-3280-4*) Higginson Bk Co.

***Church, Charlotte.** Voice of an Angel: My Story. (Illus.). 224p. 2000. 23.95 (*0-446-52710-6*, Pub. by Warner Bks) Little.

Church, Chas. A., ed. History of Winnebago County. (Illus.). 647p. 1997. reprint ed. lib. bdg. 67.50 (*0-8328-5803-X*) Higginson Bk Co.

Church, Christine. Housecat: How to Keep Your Indoor Cat Sane & Sound. LC 97-46170. (Illus.). 193p. 1998. bds. 17.95 (*0-87605-142-5*) Howell Bks.

Church, Clive H., ed. Practice & Perspective in Validation. 180p. 1983. 38.00 (*0-900868-94-5*) Taylor & Francis.

Church, Clive H. & Hendriks, Gisela. Continuity & Change in Comtemporary Europe. LC 95-19494. 312p. 1995. 90.00 (*1-85278-420-2*) E Elgar.

— Continuity & Change in Contemporary Europe. LC 95-19494. 312p. 1997. pap. 30.00 (*1-85898-414-9*) E Elgar.

Church, Connie, jt. auth. see Love, Mother.

***Church, Dave.** Under the Influence. 48p. 1999. pap. 5.00 (*1-889289-41-8*) Ye Olde Font Shoppe.

Church, David & Myers, John. Shawangunk Ridge Conservation & Design Guidebook. (Illus.). 66p. (Orig.). 1993. pap. 10.00 (*0-9616712-1-1*) Catskill Ctr.

Church, David, jt. auth. see Traub, Cori F.

Church, David C. The Ruminant Animal: Digestive Physiology & Nutrition. 2nd ed. (Illus.). 576p. 1987. text 50.00 (*0-13-783754-2*) P-H.

Church, David C., ed. The Ruminant Animal: Digestive Physiology & Nutrition. (Illus.). 564p. (C). 1993. reprint ed. text 49.95 (*0-88133-740-4*) Waveland Pr.

Church, David C., et al. Basic Animal Nutrition & Feeding. 4th ed. 624p. 1995. pap. 84.95 (*0-471-30864-1*) Wiley.

Church, David C., jt. auth. see Kellems, Richard O.

Church, Dawson. Facing Death, Finding Love: The Healing Power of Grief & Loss in One Family's Life. LC 93-38973. (Illus.). 144p. (Orig.). 1994. pap. 10.95 (*0-944031-31-5*) Aslan Pub.

Church, Doris. Tales from Woolly Acres. (Illus.). 140p. (Orig.). 1992. pap. 10.95 (*0-9627860-5-5*) Lone Oak MN.

Church, Earl & Quinn, Alfred O. Elements of Photogrammetry. rev. ed. (Illus.). (C). 1948. 26.95 (*0-8156-2002-0*) Syracuse U Pr.

Church, Earlyn, ed. The American Alpine Journal Index, 1929-1976. 214p. 1979. pap. 10.00 (*0-930410-06-8*) Amer Alpine Club.

Church, Ellen B. Counting & Numbers. 1996. pap. text 3.95 (*0-590-97701-6*) Scholastic Inc.

— Everything You Always Wanted to Know about First Grade-But Didn't Know Whom to Ask. 1996. pap. text 2.95 (*0-590-93603-4*) Scholastic Inc.

— Everything You Always Wanted to Know about Kindergarten-But Didn't Know Whom to Ask. 1996. pap. text 2.95 (*0-590-93602-6*) Scholastic Inc.

— Everything You Always Wanted to Know about Preschool-But Didn't Know Whom to Ask. 1996. pap. text 2.95 (*0-590-93601-8*) Scholastic Inc.

***Church, Ellen B.** Great Big Book of Classroom Songs, Rhymes & Cheers. (Illus.). 228p. 2000. 21.95 (*0-590-37607-1*) Scholastic Inc.

Church, Ellen B. Group Time. 63p. (J). 1997. pap. text 9.95 (*0-590-06253-0*) Scholastic Inc.

— Letters & Sounds. 1996. pap. text 3.95 (*0-590-97695-8*) Scholastic Inc.

— Recognizing Words. 1996. pap. text 3.95 (*0-590-97700-8*) Scholastic Inc.

— Shapes & Patterns. 1996. pap. text 3.95 (*0-590-97702-4*) Scholastic Inc.

Church, Ellen C. Learning Things: Games That Make Learning Fun for Children 3-8 Years Old. LC 81-82033. (J). (ps-3). 1982. pap. 15.99 (*0-8224-4268-X*) Fearon Teacher Aids.

Church, Emily, ed. see Sulavik, Christopher.

Church, Emma. The Heart Remembers. large type ed. 512p. 1983. 27.99 (*0-7089-1025-4*) Ulverscroft.

Church, F. Forrester & Mulry, Terrence J. The MacMillan Book of Earliest Christian Prayers. 256p. 1990. pap. 9.95 (*0-02-031080-3*) Macmillan.

Church, F. Forrester, jt. auth. see Buehrens, John A.

Church, F. Forrester, jt. auth. see Tillich, Paul Johannes.

Church, F. J. Phaedo Church Plato. 96p. (C). 1951. pap. text 4.60 (*0-02-322400-2*, Macmillan Coll) P-H.

Church, F. J., tr. The Trial & Death of Socrates (1906) 214p. 1998. reprint ed. pap. 16.95 (*0-7661-0204-1*) Kessinger Pub.

Church, F. J. & Cummings, Robert D. Plato: Euthyphro, Apology, Crito. 88p. (C). 1956. pap. text 8.00 (*0-02-322410-X*, Macmillan Coll) P-H.

Church, F. J., tr. see Plato.

Church, Forrest. Life Lines: Holding on (And Letting Go) LC 96-12620. 192p. 1996. 18.00 (*0-8070-2722-7*) Beacon Pr.

— Life Lines: Holding on (And Letting Go) LC 96-12620. 192p. 1997. pap. 11.00 (*0-8070-2723-5*) Beacon Pr.

***Church, Forrest.** Lifecraft: The Art of Meaning in the Everyday. LC 99-57359. 144p. 2000. 20.00 (*0-8070-7712-7*) Beacon Pr.

Church, Forrest, jt. auth. see Buehrens, John A.

Church, Forrester F. God & Other Famous Liberals: Recapturing the Bible, Flag & Family from the Far Right. 176p. 1996. pap. 11.95 (*0-8027-7483-0*) Walker & Co.

Church, Forrester F., ed. see Davies, Powell A.

Church, Francis. Is There a Santa Claus? A Little Girl's Question Answered. (Illus.). 24p. 1999. pap. 8.95 (*1-883211-23-9*, Darling & Comp) Laughing Elephant.

Church, Francis P. Yes, Virginia, There Is a Santa Claus. LC 92-12268. 32p. (J). 1992. 10.95 (*0-385-30854-X*) Delacorte.

Church, Francis P., jt. auth. see Szekeres, Cyndy.

Church, Frank C., et al, eds. Chemistry & Biology of Serpins: Proceedings of the International Symposium Held in Chapel Hill, North Carolina, April 13-16, 1996. LC 97-31140. (Advances in Experimental Medicine & Biology Ser.: Vol. 425). (Illus.). 384p. 1998. 95.00 (*0-306-45698-2*, Kluwer Plenum) Kluwer Academic.

Church, Fred. To the Circus. 216p. 1991. write for info. (*0-9630027-0-8*) R Church Co.

***Church, Frederic C., Jr.** Avoiding Surprises. 376p. 2000. 77.50 (*0-923240-30-6*) Stndrd Publishing.

Church, Frederic C., Jr. Avoiding Surprises: 8 Steps to an Efficient, Low-Cost Corporate Risk Management & Insurance Program. LC 81-71318. (Illus.). 286p. 1982. 19.95 (*0-9607398-0-7*) Boston Risk Mgmt.

Church, Frederica C. Christ Church, Frederica Cookbook. (Illus.). 301p. 1995. 20.00 (*0-9644973-0-1*) Christ Ch.

Church, Gene. 80629 a Mengele Experiment. 2nd rev. ed. LC 96-6247. 296p. 1996. pap. 12.95 (*0-9644293-2-2*) Route Sixty-Six.

Church, George E. Aborigines of South America. 1977. lib. bdg. 59.95 (*0-8490-1374-7*) Gordon Pr.

Church, Gilbert, ed. see Steiner, Rudolf.

Church, Gilbert, ed. & tr. see Steiner, Rudolf.

Church, Gilbert, tr. see Steiner, Rudolf.

Church, Glenn A., II, ed. see Midwest Plan Service Engineers Staff.

Church, Gregory. The Handbook of Assistive Technology. Glennen, Sharon L., ed. (Illus.). 394p. (Orig.). (C). 1991. pap. text 45.00 (*1-879105-53-5*, 0234) Thomson Learn.

Church Growth Institute Staff. Attendance Letters: Challenging Your Members to Faithful Attendance. Johnson, Tamara & Spear, Cindy G., eds. (Illus.). 70p. 1991. ring bd. 39.95 incl. disk (*0-941005-46-1*) Chrch Grwth VA.

— Stewardship Letters: Revitalizing Your Church's Fund-raising. Spear, Cindy G., ed. (Illus.). 84p. 1991. ring bd. 39.95 incl. disk (*0-941005-44-5*) Chrch Grwth VA.

Church, J. A. Descendants of Richard Church of Plymouth, Mass. 354p. 1993. reprint ed. pap. 45.00 (*0-8328-3020-8*); reprint ed. lib. bdg. 55.00 (*0-8328-3019-4*) Higginson Bk Co.

Church, J. M., jt. auth. see Simonds, Herbert R.

Church, J. R. Guardians of the Grail: And the Men Who Plan to Rule the World. Griffin, Ralph G. & Stearman, G. G., eds. LC 89-91688. (Illus.). 318p. (Orig.). (YA). (gr. 12). 1989. pap. 11.95 (*0-941241-02-5*) Prophecy Pubns.

— Hidden Prophecies in the Psalms. (Illus.). 400p. 1986. pap. 11.95 (*0-941241-00-9*); text. write for info. (*0-318-61895-8*) Prophecy Pubns.

— Hidden Prophecies in the Song of Moses. pap. 11.95 (*0-941241-05-X*) Prophecy Pubns.

— Mystery of the Menorah. pap. 11.95 (*0-941241-13-0*) Prophecy Pubns.

— They Pierced the Veil & Saw the Future. LC 93-83181. 1993. pap. text 11.95 (*0-941241-12-2*) Prophecy Pubns.

Church, J. W. Deep in Piney Woods. LC 70-39080. (Black Heritage Library Collection). (Illus.). 1977. reprint ed. 19.95 (*0-8369-9018-8*) Ayer.

Church, Jame M. Endoscopy of the Colon, Rectum & Anus. (Illus.). 448p. 1995. 129.50 (*0-89640-264-9*) Igaku-Shoin.

Church, James M., et al. Molecular Genetics & Colorectal Neoplasia: A Primer for the Clinician. LC 96-13339. (Illus.). 128p. 1996. pap. text 39.95 (*0-89640-299-1*) Igaku-Shoin.

Church, James M., jt. auth. see Fazio, Victor W.

Church, Jeff. Dick Whittington & His Cat: A Musical Play Based on an English Folk Tale. (Illus.). 56p. (Orig.). (J). (ps-7). 1990. pap. 4.00 (*0-88680-340-3*) I E Clark.

— The Pied Piper of New Orleans: Playscript. (J). 1993. pap. 6.00 (*0-87602-324-3*) Anchorage.

Church, Jeff, jt. auth. see Maccoby, Annie.

Church, Jeremiah. Journal of Travels. Aurand, A. Monroe, Jr., ed. 1933. reprint ed. 30.00 (*0-686-17389-9*) R S Barnes.

Church, Jim. Jim Church's Essential Guide to Composition: A Simplified Approach to Taking Better Underwater Pictures. LC 97-32170. (Illus.). 176p. 1998. pap. 19.95 (*1-881652-18-1*) Aqua Quest.

— Jim Church's Essential Guide to Nikonos Systems. rev. ed. LC 94-15325. (Illus.). 272p. (Orig.). 1998. pap. 22.95 (*1-881652-04-1*) Aqua Quest.

— Jim Church's Essential Guide to Underwater Video. 2nd rev. ed. LC 92-33722. (Illus.). 212p. (Orig.). 2000. pap. 14.95 (*1-881652-26-2*) Aqua Quest.

Church, John I. Hoosier College Poet. 48p. (Orig.). 1984. pap. 4.95 (*0-916127-00-1*) Friendly VA.

Church, John L. Pasadena Cowboy: Growing up in Southern California & Montana, 1925-1947. Smith, Lisa, ed. LC 96-85162. (Illus.). 294p. (Orig.). 1996. pap. 17.95 (*0-9653071-2-3*) Conover-Patterson.

Church, Jok. The Best of You Can with Beakman & Jax: A Collection of the Grossest, Weirdest & Coolest Experiments You Can Do. LC 97-28519. (Illus.). 256p. (Orig.). (J). (gr. 1-7). 1997. pap. 12.95 (*0-8362-3666-1*) Andrews & McMeel.

— You Can with Beakman: Science Stuff You Can Do. LC 92-24979. (You Can Write with Beakman Bk.: Science Ser.). (Illus.). 156p. (Orig.). (J). 1992. pap. 8.95 (*0-8362-7004-5*) Andrews & McMeel.

— You Can with Beakman & Jax: More Science Stuff You Can Do. (Illus.). 156p. 1994. pap. 8.95 (*0-8362-7008-8*) Andrews & McMeel.

— You Can with Beakman & Jax: Way More Science Stuff You Can Do. (Illus.). 160p. (J). 1995. pap. 8.95 (*0-8362-7043-6*) Andrews & McMeel.

Church, Jok, creator. Beakman's World: A Visit to the Hit TV Show. (Illus.). 96p. (J). 1993. pap. 8.95 (*0-8362-7005-3*) Andrews & McMeel.

Church, Joseph. Transcendent Daughters in Jewett's Country of the Pointed Firs. LC 94-214. 1995. 34.50 (*0-8386-3560-1*) Fairleigh Dickinson.

Church, Joseph, jt. auth. see Stone, L. Joseph.

Church, Kathryn. Forbidden Narratives: Critical Autobiography As Social Science. (Theory & Practice in Medical Anthropology & International Health Ser.: Vol. 2). 168p. 1996. pap. text 13.00 (*2-88449-213-5*) Gordon & Breach.

— Forbidden Narratives: Critical Autobiography As Social Science, Vol. 2. (Theory & Practice in Medical Anthropology & International Health Ser.: Vol. 2). 168p. 1996. text 27.00 (*2-88449-212-7*) Gordon & Breach.

Church, Kathryn R. Dealing with Organizational Change: A Guide for Federal Employees & Managers. (Illus.). 49p. 1998. pap. text 11.95 (*0-936295-62-7*) FPMI Comns.

Church, Kevin E. & Dailey, Thomas V. Quail III: National Quail Symposium. (Illus.). 217p. (Orig.). 1993. pap. 12.00 (*0-9639902-0-9*) KS Dept Wldlife.

Church, Leslie F., ed. see Henry, Matthew.

Church, Linda L., jt. auth. see Gunnell, Glynna M.

Church, Lisa R. Everyday Creative Play: Simple Fun Things You Can Do to Help Your Preschooler Learn. LC 98-2508. (Illus.). xi, 179 p. 1998. pap. 13.95 (*1-57749-069-X*) Fairview Press.

*__Church, Lisa R.__ How We Made the World a Better Place: A Leader's Guide. 32p. (Orig.). 1999. pap., teacher ed. 14.95 (*1-57749-080-0*) Fairview Press.

Church, Lisa R. Kids Write Through It: A Leader's Guide. 32p. (Orig.). 1999. pap., teacher ed. 14.95 (*1-57749-082-7*, Pub. by Fairview Press) Natl Bk Netwk.

— Teens Write Through It: A Leader's Guide. 40p. (Orig.). 1999. pap., teacher ed. 14.95 (*1-57749-084-3*, Pub. by Fairview Press) Natl Bk Netwk.

Church, Madeline, jt. auth. see Cissna, Catherine A.

Church, Margaret. Structure & Theme - Don Quixote to James Joyce. LC 83-2292. 219p. reprint ed. pap. 67.90 (*0-608-09660-1*, 206977500006) Bks Demand.

Church, Martin K. & Robinson, C., eds. Eicosanoids in Inflammatory Conditions of the Lung, Skin & Joints. (C). 1988. text 147.00 (*0-85200-958-5*) Kluwer Academic.

Church, Martin K., et al. Therapeutic Index of Antihistamines. 96p. 1992. 22.00 (*0-88937-082-6*) Hogrefe & Huber Pubs.

Church, Martin K., jt. auth. see Sampson, Anthony P.

Church, Martin K., jt. ed. see Langer, S. Z.

Church, Mary M., et al. Beyond the Beginning: A Reader in English. 128p. (C). 1990. pap. text 19.93 (*0-13-068164-4*) P-H.

Church, Medeline. Emma LeDoux & the Trunk Murder. (Illus.). 88p. (Orig.). 1995. pap. 9.95 (*0-9644631-1-3*) Luxemberg Publ.

Church, Mike W. Traveler's Guide to European Camping: Explore Europe with RV of Tent 2nd ed. LC 99-70202. 1999. pap. text 19.95 (*0-9652968-3-0*) Rolling Homes.

*__Church, Mike W. & Church, Terri L.__ RV Adventures in the Pacific Northwest: A Camping Guide to Washington, Oregon, & British Columbia. 2000. pap. text 14.95 (*0-9652968-4-9*) Rolling Homes.

Church, Mike W. & Church, Terri L. Traveler's Guide to Alaskan Camping: Explore Alaska & the Yukon with RV or Tent. LC 98-91216. (Illus.). 416p. 1998. pap. 19.95 (*0-9652968-2-2*) Rolling Homes.

— Traveler's Guide to European Camping: Explore Europe Economically at Your Own Pace Using RV or Tent. (Illus.). 414p. 1996. pap. 19.95 (*0-9652968-0-6*) Rolling Homes.

— Traveler's Guide to Mexican Camping: Explore Mexico with Your RV or Tent. LC 97-91646. (Illus.). 416p. 1997. pap. 19.95 (*0-9652968-1-4*) Rolling Homes.

Church Ministries Department Staff. The Pathfinders Honors: A Manual for the Requirements of All Pathfinder Honors. (Illus.). 238p. 1989. pap. 8.99 (*0-8163-0883-7*) Pacific Pr Pub Assn.

Church, Nancy & Moss, Anne. How to Survive in the U. S. A. English for Travelers & Newcomers. 144p. 1983. pap. text 17.95 (*0-521-27206-8*) Cambridge U Pr.

Church, Nancy J. Marketing for Nonprofit Cultural Organizations. LC 86-72772. (Illus.). 136p. (Orig.). 1986. pap. 5.00 (*0-9617701-0-4*) C E F Lib Syst.

Church, Naomi. One Last Souvenir. 80p. (Orig.). pap. text 9.95 (*1-881579-05-0*) Theophilus Pr.

Church, O. Station KBOE. 3rd ed. 240p. 1984. text 7.56 (*0-07-010837-4*) McGraw.

Church of All Worlds Staff. Witchcraft, Satanism & Occult Crime: Who's Who & What's What, a Reference Manual for the Professional Investigator. 5th ed. (Illus.). 24p. 1994. pap. 4.00 (*0-919345-86-7*) Phoenix WA.

Church of England. Certaine Sermons or Homilies Appointed to Be Read in the Churches in the Time of Elizabeth 1st, 1547-1571, 2 vols. in 1. LC 68-17016. 448p. 1968. reprint ed. 75.00 (*0-8201-1008-6*) Schol Facsimiles.

Church of England Staff. Articles to Be Inquired of, in the First Metropoliticall Visitation of the Most Reverend Father Richarde...Archbishop of Canterbury. LC 74-28851. (English Experience Ser.: No. 732). 1975. reprint ed. 10.00 (*90-221-0732-9*) Walter J Johnson.

— A Booke of Certaine Canons, Concernynge Some Parte of the Discipline of the Churche of England. LC 70-26475. (English Experience Ser.: No. 312). 1971. reprint ed. 15.00 (*90-221-0312-9*) Walter J Johnson.

Church of England Staff, jt. auth. see Wickman, Edward R.

*__Church of God World Harvester Executive Staff.__ Building a Church Not a Building: Minister's Guide to Establishing a New Testament Church. 52p. 1998. pap. 9.95 (*0-9672968-2-X*) CPC Press.

Church of Jesus Christ of Latter Day Saints, Santa. Blessings from the Kitchen. 1972. 6.00 (*0-686-17209-4*) Sandollar Pr.

Church of Religious Research, Inc. Staff. Psychography: A Method of Self-Discovery. Roberts, Helen & Pinkston, Isabel H., eds. LC 90-60693. (Illus.). 232p. (Orig.). 1990. pap. 9.95 (*0-915151-00-6*) Religious Res Pr.

Church of Scientology International Staff. Scientology: Theology & Practice of a Contemporary Religion. LC 99-166068. xiii, 287 p. 1998. write for info. (*1-57318-145-5*) Bridge Pubns Inc.

Church of Scotland - Committee on Public Worship &. Prayers for Contemporary Worship. 1977. pap. 4.95 (*0-7152-0351-7*) Outlook.

— Prayers for Sunday Services. 1980. pap. 6.95 (*0-7152-0456-4*) Outlook.

Church of Scotland Advisory Committee on Artistic. Cre for Your Church. 1993. pap. 21.00 (*0-7152-0562-5*) St Mut.

Church of Scotland Board of Education Staff. In Presenting Your Child for Baptism. 1993. pap. 25.00 (*0-86153-071-3*) St Mut.

Church of Scotland Board of Social Responsibility. The Future of the Family. 157p. 1993. pap. 21.00 (*0-86153-157-4*, Pub. by St Andrew) St Mut.

Church of Scotland, Board of Stewardship & Finance. Christian Stewardship Manual. 80p. (C). 1992. pap. 40.00 (*0-86153-134-5*, Pub. by St Andrew) St Mut.

Church of Scotland Committee on Church & Nation St. Housing Scotland's People: Report of the Church of Scotland's Independent Inquiry into Scottish Housing. 76p. (C). 1988. pap. text 30.00 (*0-7152-0628-1*) St Mut.

Church of Scotland Panel on Doctrine. The Church & Freemasonry. (C). 1989. pap. 20.00 (*0-86153-115-9*, Pub. by St Andrew) St Mut.

Church of Scotland Panel on Worship. Worshipping Together. 208p. (C). 1992. pap. 45.00 (*0-86153-128-0*, Pub. by St Andrew) St Mut.

Church of Scotland, Panel on Worship Staff. Children Praying.Tr. of Clann Ag Urnaigh. (C). 1992. pap. 39.00 (*0-7855-6834-4*, Pub. by St Andrew) St Mut.

— Clann Ag Urnaigh.Tr. of Children Praying. (C). 1992. pap. 39.00 (*0-86153-135-3*, Pub. by St Andrew) St Mut.

Church of Scotland Panel on Worship Staff. The Marriage Service. 1993. pap. 12.00 (*0-86153-009-8*, Pub. by St Andrew) St Mut.

— Prayers for Contemporary Worship. 128p. 1993. pap. 22.00 (*0-86153-091-8*, Pub. by St Andrew) St Mut.

— Prayers for Sunday Services. 144p. 1993. pap. 22.00 (*0-86153-088-8*, Pub. by St Andrew) St Mut.

Church of Scotland Society, Religion & Technology. Taking Out Moscow: Talking about Trident. 106p. (C). 1992. pap. 32.00 (*0-86153-148-5*, Pub. by St Andrew) St Mut.

Church of Scotland Staff. The First & Second Books of Discipline: Together with Some Acts of the General Assemblies. LC 77-7433. (English Experience Ser.: No. 893). 1977. reprint ed. lib. bdg. 20.00 (*90-221-0893-7*) Walter J Johnson.

— Register of Ministers, Exhorters & Readers & of Their Stipends. LC 71-174310. (Maitland Club, Glasgow. Publications: No. 5). reprint ed. 32.50 (*0-404-52929-1*) AMS Pr.

Church of Scotland Woman's Guild Staff. Women of Faith: Church of Scotland Woman's Guild. 160p. 1993. pap. 21.00 (*0-86153-171-X*, Pub. by St Andrew) St Mut.

Church of South India Staff. Book of Common Worship. 1964. 8.95 (*0-19-149906-4*) OUP.

Church of St. Paul the Apostle, New York Staff. Sermons Preached at the Church of St. Paul the Apostle, New York, During the Year, 1863. 1978. 35.95 (*0-405-10851-6*, 11854) Ayer.

Church of the Province of New Zealand Staff. New Zealand Prayer Book -Rev ed. He Karakia Mihinare O Aotearoa. rev. ed. LC 97-3716. (ENG & MAO.). 992p. 1997. 28.00 (*0-06-060199-X*, Pub. by Harper SF) HarpC.

Church, Olive D. CompuHelp Inc. An Office Simulation, Instructor's guide. (C). 1991. teacher ed. 8.00 (*1-56118-032-7*) Paradigm MN.

— Electronic Office Applications. 49p. 1993. mass mkt., teacher ed. 11.25 (*0-8273-5063-5*) Delmar.

— Electronic Office Applications. 5th ed. LC 92-23041. 200p. 1989. mass mkt. 25.95 (*0-8273-5062-7*) Delmar.

— Human Relations in the Electronic Office. LC 92-2388. 199p. 1993. mass mkt. 23.95 (*0-8273-5060-0*); mass mkt., teacher ed. 11.25 (*0-8273-5061-9*) Delmar.

— Shadow Mountain Lodge, Typing Practice Set. (Illus.). (gr. 9-12). 1977. text 13.24 (*0-07-010835-8*) McGraw.

Church, Olive D. & Schatz, Anne E. Office Systems & Careers: A Resource for Administrative Assistants. 780p. 1981. write for info. (*0-205-07135-X*) Allyn.

Church, Olive D., et al. Software Solutions, Inc.: A Simulation for the Electronic Office: Instructor's manual. 14.00 (*1-56118-832-8*) EMC-Paradigm.

Church, Olive D., jt. auth. see Zajas, Jay J.

Church, Pam. The Most Important Rule of All. unabridged ed. (Illus.). 48p. (Orig.). (J). (ps-6). 1997. pap. 9.95 (*0-9657000-0-3*) Prevent & Motivat.

Church, Paula, ed. see DiLeo, Vincent.

Church, Peggy Pond. House at Otowi Bridge: The Story of Edith Warner & Los Alamos. LC 60-13408. (Zia Bks.). (Illus.). 158p. 1973. reprint ed. pap. 10.95 (*0-8263-0281-5*) U of NM Pr.

— Peggy Pond Church, New & Selected Poems. 3rd ed. Trusky, Tom, ed. LC 75-29917. (Ahsahta Press Modern & Contemporary Poets of the West Ser.). 80p. 1976. pap. 6.95 (*0-916272-02-8*) Ahsahta Pr.

— This Dancing Ground of Sky: The Selected Poetry of Peggy Pond Church. LC 92-32298. 216p. 1993. pap. 12.95 (*1-878610-28-7*) Red Crane Bks.

— When Los Alamos Was a Ranch School: Historical Profile. 2nd rev. ed. Storms, Barbara G., ed. & pref. by. LC 98-35700. 68p. 1998. pap. 14.95 (*0-941232-18-2*) Los Alamos Hist Soc.

Church, Peter, ed. Focus on Southeast Asia. (Illus.). 208p. 1995. pap. 19.95 (*1-86373-940-8*) Paul & Co Pubs.

Church, Philip D. Furnace Harbor: A Rhapsody of the North Country. Poems. LC 87-27229. 136p. 1988. 9.95 (*0-252-06003-2*) U of Ill Pr.

Church, R. A. The Healthy Traveler: A Guide for Traveling in Good Health. 118p. (Orig.). 1988. pap. 8.95 (*0-924998-00-8*) Thomas-Henning.

Church, R. A. & Wrigley, E. Anthony, eds. The Industrial Revolutions, 11 vols. Incl. Vol. 1. Pre-Industrial Britain. Chartres, J. A., intro. LC 93-46608. 1994. 124.95 (*0-631-18144-X*); Vol. 10. Coal & Iron Industries. LC 93-46608. 1994. 100.00 (*0-631-18122-9*); LC 93-46608. 1994. 1606.95 (*0-631-17486-9*) Blackwell Pubs.

Church, R. W. The Beginning of the Middle Ages. 1977. lib. bdg. 59.95 (*0-8490-1484-0*) Gordon Pr.

Church, R. W., ed. see Hooker, Richard & Walton, Isaac.

Church, Ralph W. Hume's Theory of the Understanding. LC 79-55608. 238p. 1980. reprint ed. lib. bdg. 59.50 (*0-313-20651-1*, CHHU, Greenwood Pr) Greenwood.

Church, Randolph W., ed. Deterioration of Book Stock: Causes & Remedies: Two Studies on the Permanence of Book Paper Conducted by W. J. Barrow. (Illus.). 70p. 1959. text 5.00 (*0-685-62263-0*) Library of VA.

Church, Randolph W., intro. Virginia Legislative Petitions: Bibliography, Calendar, & Abstracts from Original Sources, 6 May 1776-21 June 1782. xv, 508p. 1984. 35.00 (*0-88490-114-9*) Library of VA.

Church, Richard. British Authors: A Twentieth Century Gallery. 154p. 1977. 19.95 (*0-8369-8013-1*) Ayer.

— Eight for Immortality. LC 70-90623. (Essay Index Reprint Ser.). 1977. 19.95 (*0-8369-1204-7*) Ayer.

Church, Richard W. Bacon. Morley, John, ed. LC 68-58371. reprint ed. 41.50 (*0-404-51704-8*) AMS Pr.

— The Collected Poems of Richard Church. LC 75-41058. reprint ed. 42.50 (*0-404-14522-1*) AMS Pr.

— Mary Shelley. 1977. 13.95 (*0-8369-6925-1*, 7806) Ayer.

— Spenser. Morley, John, ed. LC 68-58372. (English Men of Letters Ser.). reprint ed. lib. bdg. 41.50 (*0-404-51703-X*) AMS Pr.

— Spenser. (BCL1-PR English Literature Ser.). 188p. 1992. reprint ed. lib. bdg. 69.00 (*0-7812-7226-2*) Rprt Serv.

Church, Robert. Turtles. (Illus.). 65p. 1988. pap. 2.95 (*0-87666-226-2*, M-515) TFH Pubns.

Church, Robert J. The 4300 4-8-2's: Southern Pacific's Mt.-Class Locomotives. rev. ed. LC 96-67272. (Illus.). 176p. 1996. 49.00 (*0-9633791-4-3*) Signature CA.

Church, Robert L. Education in the United States: An Interpretive History. LC 75-22764. 1976. pap. 32.95 (*0-02-905490-7*) Free Pr.

Church, Robert L., et al. Social Sciences at Harvard, 1860-1920: From Inculcation to the Open Mind. Buck, Paul H., ed. LC 65-22059. 336p. 1965. reprint ed. pap. 104.20 (*0-7837-4451-X*, 205798100012) Bks Demand.

Church, Roberta & Walter, Ronald. Nineteenth Century Memphis Families of Color, 1850-1900. Crawford, Charles W., ed. (Illus.). 152p. 1987. pap. 8.95 (*0-937130-12-5*) Burkes Bk Store.

Church, Roberta, jt. auth. see Church, Annette E.

Church, Roy. History of the British Coal Industry, Vol. 3: Victorian Pre-Eminence. (Illus.). 850p. 1986. text 125.00 (*0-19-828284-2*) OUP.

— The Rise & Decline of the British Motor Industry. (New Studies in Economic & Social History: No. 24). 155p. (C). 1995. text 34.95 (*0-521-55283-4*); pap. text 10.95 (*0-521-55770-4*) Cambridge U Pr.

Church, Roy & Outram, Quentin. Strikes & Solidarity: Coalfield Conflict in Britain, 1889-1966. LC 97-12821. (Illus.). 334p. (C). 1998. text 69.95 (*0-521-55460-8*) Cambridge U Pr.

Church, Russell M., jt. ed. see Boe, Erling E.

Church, Ruth E. Mary Meade's Magic Recipes for the Electric Blender. LC 65-22932. 1952. 6.00 (*0-672-50745-5*, Bobbs) Macmillan.

— Mary Mead's Country Cookbook. 1993. 8.98 (*0-88365-816-X*) Galahad Bks.

Church, Ruth Ellen. Mary Meade's Country Cookbook: Traditional American Cooking. 384p. 1998. pap. 14.95 (*0-88486-206-2*, Bristol Park Bks) Arrowood Pr.

*__Church, S. D.__ The Household Knights of King John. LC 98-43694. (Cambridge Studies in Medieval Life & Thought: Fourth Series 44). 200p. (C). 1999. 54.95 (*0-521-55319-9*) Cambridge U Pr.

*__Church, S. D., ed.__ King John: New Interpretations. LC 99-14590. 288p. 1999. 75.00 (*0-85115-736-X*) Boydell & Brewer.

Church, Sally, jt. ed. see Yuan, Boping.

Church, Sharon, et al. Ut Poesis Pictura: J. M. W. Turner's Illustrations to the British Poets. Schulz, Max F., ed. (Illus.). 96p. (Orig.). 1997. pap. 20.00 (*0-945192-19-3*) USC Fisher Gallery.

Church Society Staff. An English Prayer Book. 234p. 1997. 19.95 (*0-19-110010-2*) OUP.

Church, Stephen & Harvey, Ruth, eds. Medieval Knighthood Vol. V: Papers from the Sixth Strawberry Hill Conference, 1994. (Medieval Knighthood Ser.). (Illus.). 282p. (C). 1995. 75.00 (*0-85115-628-2*) Boydell & Brewer.

Church, Susan. Permanent Cosmetics A to Z. 143p. 1998. pap. 59.95 (*1-887080-05-8*) Action Publ.

*__Church, Susan.__ Permanent Cosmetics for the Consumer. (Illus.). 85p. 1999. pap. 19.95 (*1-887080-08-2*) Action Pub.

Church, Susan M. The Future of the Whole Language: Reconstruction or Self-Destruction? LC 95-51253. 1996. pap. text 18.50 (*0-435-08882-3*) Heinemann.

Church, Terri L., jt. auth. see Church, Mike W.

Church, Thomas D., et al. Gardens Are for People. 3rd ed. (Illus.). 256p. 1995. pap. 29.95 (*0-520-20120-5*, Pub. by U CA Pr) Cal Prin Full Svc.

Church, Thomas M., ed. Marine Chemistry in the Coastal Environment. LC 75-28151. (ACS Symposium Ser.: Vol. 18). 720p. 1975. reprint ed. pap. 200.00 (*0-608-03552-1*, 206427100008) Bks Demand.

Church, Thomas W. & Heumann, Milton, eds. Speedy Disposition: Monetary Incentives & Policy Reform in Criminal Courts. LC 91-34691. 171p. (C). 1992. text 64.50 (*0-7914-1185-0*); pap. text 21.95 (*0-7914-1186-9*) State U NY Pr.

Church, Thomas W. & Nakamura, Robert T. Cleaning up the Mess: Implementation Strategies in Superfund. LC 92-39493. 209p. (C). 1993. 34.95 (*0-8157-1414-9*) Brookings.

Church, Thomas W., jt. ed. see Heumann, Milton.

Church, Virginia A. Mediterranean Gold. (Illus.). 1986. 5.95 (*0-89407-127-0*) Strawberry Hill.

Church, Virginia W., ed. International Short Stories. LC 72-5902. (Short Story Index Reprint Ser.). 1977. reprint ed. 27.95 (*0-8369-4199-3*) Ayer.

Church, Vivian. Colors Around Me. rev. ed. LC 75-154209. (Illus.). 28p. (J). (gr. k-3). 1993. pap. 6.95 (*0-910030-15-4*) African Am Imag.

Church, W. H. Edgar Cayce's Story of the Soul. 252p. (Orig.). 1991. reprint ed. pap. 13.95 (*0-87604-273-6*, 359) ARE Pr.

C

— The Lives of Edgar Cayce. rev. ed. Dunn, Joe, ed. LC 95-16827. 289p. 1995. pap. 12.95 (*0-87604-350-3*, 461) ARE Pr.

Church, W. H., jt. auth. see Gammon, Margaret.

Church, Wendy C. An African Affair. 171p. 1997. pap. 8.95 (*0-9655995-0-7*, Pub. by Heathcoat Pub) BookWorld.

— Aqua: Great Global Hot Spots. 1999. pap. 24.95 (*0-9643711-1-1*) Heathcoat Pub.

Church, Wendy C. Aqua Expeditions I: A Global Travel Guide for the Scuba Diver & Snorkeler. LC 95-201842. 320p. 1994. pap. text 24.95 (*0-9643711-0-3*) Heathcoat Pub.

Church, William C. Ulysses S. Grant & the Period of National Preservation & Reconstruction. LC 73-14437. (Heroes of the Nations Ser.). reprint ed. 64.50 (*0-404-58255-9*) AMS Pr.

Church, William F. Richelieu & Reason of State. LC 76-181518. 562p. reprint ed. pap. 174.30 (*0-608-14963-2*, 202568800045) Bks Demand.

Church, William S. A Treatise on the Writ of Habeas Corpus: Including Jurisdiction, False Imprisonment, Writ of Error, Extradition, Mandamus, Certiorari, Judgements, Etc. with Practice & Forms. 2nd enl. rev. ed. xxvii, 1025p. 1997. reprint ed. 225.00 (*1-56169-309-X*, 14624) Gaunt.

— Windingsheets of Vineleaf. 128p. 1992. pap. text 9.95 (*1-881579-03-4*) Theophilus Pr.

Churcher, C. S., ed. Athlon: Essays on Palaeontology in Honour of Loris Shano Russell. (Illus.). 292p. 42.86 (*0-88854-157-0*) Brill Academic Pubs.

Churcher, C. S. & Mills, A. J., eds. Reports from the Survey of the Dakhleh Oasis Western Desert Egypt, 1977-1987. (Oxbow Monographs: Vol. 99). (Illus.). 271p. 1999. lib. bdg. 75.00 (*1-900188-49-X*, Pub. by Oxbow Bks) David Brown.

Churcher, C. S., jt. ed. see Mills, A. J.

Churcher, Dar, jt. auth. see Leger, Diane C.

Churcher, Sharon, jt. auth. see Gaines, Steven S.

Churches Alive, Inc. Staff. Alive! God in Intimate Relationship with You. (God in You Bible Study Ser.). (Illus.). 72p. (Orig.). 1986. pap. 5.00 (*0-89109-093-2*) NavPress.

— Changed! (God in You Bible Study Ser.). (Illus.). 72p. (Orig.). 1986. pap. 5.00 (*0-89109-096-7*) NavPress.

— Fulfilled! Enjoying God's Purpose for You. (God in You Bible Study Ser.). (Illus.). 72p. (Orig.). 1986. pap. 5.00 (*0-89109-097-5*) NavPress.

— God's Family Leader's Guide Edition. LC 82-72564. 112p. 1992. pap. text 5.25 (*0-934396-35-3*) Churches Alive.

— Growing by Discipling Pastor's Handbook. rev. ed. (Illus.). 150p. 1986. pap. text 15.00 (*0-934396-09-4*) Churches Alive.

— Growth Group Leader's Guide. rev. ed. LC 80-52536. (Illus.). 110p. 1987. pap. 10.00 (*0-934396-10-8*) Churches Alive.

— Growth Group Member's Notebook. LC 80-52536. (Illus.). 105p. (Orig.). (C). 1980. pap. text 7.00 (*0-934396-11-6*) Churches Alive.

— Jesus! God in You Made Possible. (God in You Bible Study Ser.). (Illus.). 72p. (Orig.). 1986. pap. 5.00 (*0-89109-092-4*) NavPress.

— Powerful! God Enabling You. (God in You Bible Study Ser.). (Illus.). 72p. (Orig.). 1986. pap. 5.00 (*0-89109-095-9*) NavPress.

— Rich! God Meeting Your Deepest Needs. (God in You Bible Study Ser.). (Illus.). 72p. (Orig.). 1986. pap. 5.00 (*0-89109-094-0*) NavPress.

Churches Alive Ser. Celebrate! Exhalting God in Praise & Worship. (God in You Bible Study Ser.). 64p. (Orig.). 1994. pap. 5.00 (*0-89109-789-9*) NavPress.

Churches Alive Staff. Leader's Guide. rev. ed. (God in You Ser.). (Illus.). 151p. (Orig.). 1994. pap. 7.00 (*0-89109-098-3*, Diciple Jour) NavPress.

Churches, Christine, jt. auth. see Hainsworth, Roger.

Churchett, Stephen. Heritage. 96p. 1998. pap. text 11.95 (*0-571-19180-0*) Faber & Faber.

— Tom & Clem. 96p. 1997. pap. 11.95 (*0-571-19178-9*) Faber & Faber.

Churchfield, Sara. The Natural History of Shrews. LC 90-2521. (Natural History of Mammals Ser.). (Illus.). 192p. 1991. text 39.95 (*0-8014-2595-6*) Cornell U Pr.

— Shrews of the British Isles. (Natural History Ser.: No. 30). (Illus.). 24p. pap. 5.25 (*0-85263-951-1*, Pub. by Shire Pubns) Parkwest Pubns.

Churchhouse, R. F., et al, eds. Recent Developments & Applications in Mathematics & Computer Science: Proceedings of the College ICTP, Trieste, Italy 7 May-1 June 1990. 250p. 1991. text 83.00 (*981-02-0842-1*) World Scientific Pub.

Churchich, Nicholas. Marxism & Alienation. LC 88-46151. 368p. 1990. 49.50 (*0-8386-3372-2*) Fairleigh Dickinson.

***Churchich, Nicholas.** Morals in Idealistic & Naturalistic Thought. LC 99-96746. 2000. 26.95 (*0-533-13347-5*) Vantage.

***Churchich, Veronica M. Boyle.** The Position of Women in Nineteenth-Century English Literature. LC 99-98745. 2000. 18.95 (*0-533-13346-7*) Vantage.

Churchill. Logic: An Introduction. 3rd ed. (Philosophy Ser.). 1919. pap. 42.00 (*0-534-50931-2*) Wadsworth Pub.

— Marketing. 2nd ed. 1998. pap. 7.19 (*0-256-26617-4*) McGraw.

— Marketing Paper. 2nd ed. 1999. 41.60 (*0-07-236922-1*) McGraw.

— Rib Essentials. 1996. text 200.00 (*0-443-07693-6*, W B Saunders Co) Harcrt Hlth Sci Grp.

***Churchill & Fewell.** Musgrave Ritual in Latin. (Sherlockian Scholarship Ser.). 1998. 8.00 (*1-55246-136-X*) Battered Silicon.

Churchill & Fleishman. Logic: An Introduction. 3rd ed. (Philosophy Ser.). 1919. mass mkt., student ed. 13.00 (*0-534-50937-1*) Wadsworth Pub.

Churchill & Fuge. Butterfly Kiss. (J). pap. text 11.95 (*0-340-68614-6*, Pub. by Hodder & Stought Ltd) Trafalgar.

Churchill, Adele, ed. see McCann, James Z.

Churchill, Allen. Park Row. LC 73-14193. 344p. 1973. reprint ed. lib. bdg. 55.00 (*0-8371-7146-6*, CHPR, Greenwood Pr) Greenwood.

Churchill, Bruce, jt. auth. see Jordan, Lary.

Churchill, Cameron. The Law of the Office & Duties of the Sheriff: With the Writs & Forms Relating to the Office. 2nd ed. lix, 686p. 1999. reprint ed. 187.50 (*1-56169-492-4*) Gaunt.

Churchill, Caroline N. Active Footsteps. Baxter, Annette K., ed. LC 79-8781. (Signal Lives Ser.). (Illus.). 1980. reprint ed. lib. bdg. 30.95 (*0-405-12830-4*) Ayer.

Churchill, Caryl. Blue Heart. LC 98-14963. 96p. 1998. pap. 10.95 (*1-55936-154-9*) Theatre Comm.

— Churchill Plays: One. 320p. 1985. pap. 13.99 (*0-415-90196-0*, 9499) Routledge.

— Cloud Nine. 111p. 1984. pap. 10.99 (*0-415-90135-9*, NO. 4016) Routledge.

— Cloud 9. 88p. (Orig.). 1995. pap. 9.95 (*1-55936-099-2*) Theatre Comm.

— Hotel. (Nick Hern Bks.). 96p. 1997. pap. 13.95 (*1-85459-337-4*, Pub. by N Hern Bks) Theatre Comm.

— Light Shining in Buckinghamshire. 80p. (Orig.). 1997. pap. 10.95 (*1-55936-130-1*) Theatre Comm.

— Lives of Great Poisoners. 171p. (C). 1993. write for info. (*0-413-67070-8*, A0669, Methuen Drama) Methn.

— Mad Forest: A Play from Romania. 96p. 1996. pap. text 9.95 (*1-55936-114-X*) Theatre Comm.

***Churchill, Caryl.** Plays. LC 85-186277. 2000. pap. 14.95 (*0-413-56670-6*, Methuen Drama) Methn.

Churchill, Caryl. Serious Money. (Royal Court Writers Ser.). 112p. (C). 1988. pap. write for info. (*0-413-16660-0*, A0261, Methuen Drama) Methn.

— Serious Money. 114p. 1995. pap. 9.95 (*0-413-64190-2*, AO485, Methuen Drama) Methn.

— The Skriker. LC 94-17131. 64p. (Orig.). 1994. pap. 9.95 (*1-55936-097-6*) Theatre Comm.

— Softcops & Fen. (Methuen Modern Plays Ser.). 98p. (Orig.). (C). 1988. pap. write for info. (*0-413-41200-8*, A0266, Methuen Drama) Methn.

***Churchill, Caryl.** This Is a Chair. LC 99-44744. 1999. pap. 9.95 (*1-55936-177-8*, Pub. by Theatre Comm) Consort Bk Sales.

Churchill, Caryl. Top Girls. 2nd rev. ed. 87p. (C). 1988. pap. write for info. (*0-413-55480-5*, A0298, Methuen Drama) Methn.

— Traps. 67p. 1989. pap. 11.95 (*1-85459-095-2*, Pub. by N Hern Bks) Theatre Comm.

Churchill, Caryl, tr. & intro. see Seneca, Lucius Annaeus.

Churchill, Charles, ed. The City of Beirut: A Socio-Economic Survey. 78p. 1954. pap. 12.95 (*0-8156-6023-5*, Pub. by Am U Beirut) Syracuse U Pr.

Churchill, Charles B. Adventurers & Prophets: American Autobiographers in Mexican California, 1829-1847. LC 94-47236. (Western Frontiersmen Ser.: No. 24). (Illus.). 1995. 35.00 (*0-87062-228-5*) A H Clark.

Churchill, Charles H. The Druzes & the Maronites under the Turkish Rule from 1840 to 1860. LC 73-6273. (Middle East Ser.). 1977. reprint ed. 23.95 (*0-405-05329-0*) Ayer.

— Mount Lebanon: A Ten Years' Residence, from 1842 to 1852, 3 vols., Set. LC 77-87615. reprint ed. 155.00 (*0-404-16440-4*) AMS Pr.

Churchill, Charles W. Fortunes Are for the Few Letters of a Forty-Niner. Smith, Duane A. & Weber, David J., eds. LC 77-76134. (Illus.). 136p. 1977. 12.50 (*0-918740-00-2*) San Diego Hist.

— The Italians of Newark. LC 74-17922. (Italian American Experience Ser.). (Illus.). 220p. 1979. 23.95 (*0-405-06395-4*) Ayer.

Churchill, Charles W., ed. see Lutfiyya, Abdulla H.

Churchill, Clementine, jt. auth. see Churchill, Winston L. S.

Churchill, Colin. History of the Bristish Army Infantry Collar Badges. 1998. 39.95 (*1-85753-275-9*, Pub. by Brasseys) Brasseys.

Churchill, Dale, jt. auth. see Winter, Kerrin.

Churchill, Dorothy, ed. see Churchill, Sam.

Churchill, Dorothy, ed. see Sheller, Roscoe.

Churchill, Dorothy, ed. & photos by see Sheller, Roscoe.

Churchill, Dorothy L. From Mourning to Morning. (Illus.). 28p. 1993. reprint ed. pap. 6.95 (*0-9630536-1-2*) S Dot S.

— From Mourning to Morning: Three Years Later. 48p. (Orig.). 1995. pap. 6.95 (*0-9630536-3-9*) S Dot S.

Churchill, Dorothy L., ed. see Churchill, Sam.

Churchill, Dorothy L., ed. see Churchill, Samuel J.

Churchill, Dwight D., ed. Fixed Income Management: Techniques & Practices. 133p. (Orig.). 1994. pap. text 30.00 (*1-879087-43-X*) RFICFA.

Churchill, E. Richard. Amazing Science Experiments with Everyday Materials. LC 90-20641. (Illus.). 128p. (J). (gr. 4-12). 1992. pap. 4.95 (*0-8069-7371-4*) Sterling.

— Fast & Funny Paper Toys You Can Make. LC 89-32411. (Illus.). 128p. (YA). (gr. 7-12). 1989. 14.95 (*0-8069-5770-0*) Sterling.

— Geography Flipper. 49p. (J). (gr. 5 up). 1989. reprint ed. 6.95 (*1-878383-07-8*) C Lee Pubns.

— Holiday Paper Projects. LC 92-12100. (Illus.). 128p. (J). (gr. 3-9). 1992. 14.95 (*0-8069-8512-7*) Sterling.

— How to Make Optical Illusion Tricks & Toys. LC 89-26169. (Illus.). 128p. (Orig.). (J). 1990. pap. 5.95 (*0-8069-6869-9*) Sterling.

— Paper Science Toys. LC 90-9891. (Illus.). 128p. (YA). (gr. 3-10). 1990. 14.95 (*0-8069-5834-0*) Sterling.

— Paper Tricks & Toys. LC 91-38789. 128p. (J). 1992. 16.95 (*0-8069-8416-3*) Sterling.

Churchill, E. Richard, et al. 365 Simple Science Experiments with Everyday Materials. LC 96-53239. (Illus.). 320p. (YA). (gr. 2 up). 1997. reprint ed. 12.98 (*1-884822-67-3*) Blck Dog & Leventhal.

Churchill, Edward D. Wanderjahr: The Education of a Surgeon. Scannell, J. Gordon, ed. (Illus.). xi, 213p. 1991. 18.95 (*0-88135-067-2*) F A Countway.

Churchill, Edwin A. Hail Britannia: Maine Pewter & Silverplate: An Exhibition of Maine Britannia Ware & Silverplate, 1829-1941, in the Collections of the Maine State Museum, May 15, 1992 - May 15, 1993. (Illus.). 90p. (Orig.). 1992. pap. 10.00 (*0-913764-22-1*) Maine St Mus.

— Simple Forms & Vivid Colors: Maine Painted Furniture, 1800-1850. LC 83-61807. (Illus.). 117p. 1997. reprint ed. 45.00 (*0-913764-15-9*) Maine St Mus.

Churchill, Eric R. Algebra Flipper 1. 49p. (J). (gr. 5 up). 1989. reprint ed. 6.95 (*1-878383-03-5*) C Lee Pubns.

— BASIC Programming Flipper. 49p. (YA). (gr. 8 up). 1989. 6.95 (*1-878383-10-8*) C Lee Pubns.

Churchill, Eric R., jt. auth. see Morrical, Guy.

Churchill, G. A. & Ford, Neil M. Sales Force Management. 5th ed. 800p. (C). 1996. text 67.95 (*0-256-13787-0*, Irwn McGrw-H) McGrw-H Hghr Educ.

Churchill, Gardner A. & Churchill, Nathaniel W. The Churchill Family in America. Badge, G. M., ed. (Illus.). 722p. 1989. reprint ed. pap. 89.50 (*0-8328-0401-0*); reprint ed. lib. bdg. 99.50 (*0-8328-0400-2*) Higginson Bk Co.

Churchill, Gilbert A. Basic Marketing Research. 3rd ed. (C). 1995. text 90.50 (*0-03-098367-3*, Pub. by Harcourt Coll Pubs); pap. text, teacher ed. 45.00 (*0-03-016324-2*); pap. text, teacher ed., suppl. ed. 35.50 (*0-03-016327-7*, Pub. by Harcourt Coll Pubs); 3.5 hd 222.25 (*0-03-016334-X*) Harcourt Coll Pubs.

— Basic Marketing Research. 4th ed. (C). 1999. text 90.50 (*0-03-021104-2*, Pub. by Harcourt Coll Pubs) Harcourt.

— Marketing Research. 6th ed. 824p. (C). 1994. pap. text, teacher ed. 49.75 (*0-03-006888-6*) Harcourt Coll Pubs.

— Marketing Research: Methodological Foundations. 6th ed. 1117p. (C). 1994. text 91.00 (*0-03-098366-5*) Dryden Pr.

Churchill, Gilbert A., Jr. Marketing Research: Methodological Foundations. 6th ed. 444p. (C). 1995. pap. text, teacher ed. 40.00 (*0-03-006889-4*, Pub. by Harcourt Coll Pubs) Harcourt.

Churchill, Gilbert A. Marketing Research: Methodological Foundations. 7th ed. LC 98-71246. 1998. text 91.50 (*0-03-023816-1*, Pub. by Harcourt Coll Pubs) Harcourt.

Churchill, Gilbert A., Jr. Marketing Research: Methodological Foundations. 7th ed. (C). 1998. pap. text 74.00 (*0-03-023818-8*) Harcourt Coll Pubs.

***Churchill, Gilbert A.** Sales Force Management 6th ed. LC 99-15440. 2000. write for info. (*0-07-027555-6*) McGrw-H Hghr Educ.

Churchill, Gilbert A. & Peter, J. Paul. Marketing. 304p. (C). 1995. text, student ed. 26.25 (*0-256-17474-1*, Irwn McGrw-H) McGrw-H Hghr Educ.

— Marketing: Creating Customer Value. LC 94-8479. (C). 1994. text 68.95 (*0-256-12539-2*, Irwn McGrw-H) McGrw-H Hghr Educ.

— Marketing: Creating Value for Customers. 2nd ed. LC 97-13807. 704p. (C). 1997. text 87.25 (*0-256-22877-9*, Irwn McGrw-H) McGrw-H Hghr Educ.

Churchill, Helen. Caesarean Birth: Experience, Practice & History. LC 97-204566. 120p. 1997. pap. text 30.00 (*1-898507-51-1*, RG761) Buttrwrth-Heinemann.

Churchill, J., jt. auth. see Witcomb, John.

Churchill, James. Basic Essentials: Survival. 2nd ed. LC 99-29197. (Illus.). 80p. 1999. pap. text 7.95 (*0-7627-0525-6*) Globe Pequot.

— The Complete Book of Tanning Skins & Furs. LC 83-9151. 224p. 1983. 18.95 (*0-8117-1719-4*) Stackpole.

— Field Dressing Big Game. LC 88-32369. (Illus.). 96p. (Orig.). 1989. pap. 10.95 (*0-8117-2282-1*) Stackpole.

Churchill, James S., tr. see Heidegger, Martin.

Churchill, James S., tr. see Husserl, Edmund.

***Churchill, Jan.** Classified Secret: Controlling Airstrikes in the Clandestine War in Laos. (Illus.). 176p. 2000. pap. 23.95 (*0-89745-241-0*) Sunflower U Pr.

Churchill, Jan. Hit My Smoke: Forward Air Controllers in Southeast Asia. LC 98-120475. (Illus.). 250p. 1997. pap. 24.95 (*0-89745-215-1*) Sunflower U Pr.

— Hit My Smoke: Forward Air Controllers in Southeast Asia. (Illus.). 250p. 1997. 41.95 (*0-89745-216-X*) Sunflower U Pr.

— On Wings to War: Teresa James, Aviator. 2nd ed. (Illus.). 184p. (Orig.). 1997. reprint ed. pap. 14.95 (*0-89745-130-9*) Sunflower U Pr.

***Churchill, Jane.** Complete Book of Soft Furnishings. (Illus.). 208p. 1999. pap. text 24.95 (*0-00-414049-4*) HarpC.

Churchill, Jane & Charlton, Annie. Decorating with Jane Churchill & Annie Charlton: Distinctive Ideas for Your Home from Two of Britain's Most Popular Decorators. LC 95-34372. (Illus.). 144p. 1996. 29.95 (*0-8109-3231-8*, Pub. by Abrams) Time Warner.

Churchill, Janet I. The New Labrador Retriever. LC 94-24401. (Illus.). 320p. 1995. 27.95 (*0-87605-206-5*) Howell Bks.

Churchill, Jeremy & Coombs, Mark. Honda VFR750 & 700 V-Fours 1986 Thru 1997. LC 97-75028. (Illus.). 266p. 2000. pap. 23.95 (*1-85960-365-3*, 129784AM, Pub. by J H Haynes & Co) Motorbooks Intl.

Churchill, Jill. Anything Goes: A Grace & Favor Mystery. LC 98-91018. 264p. 1999. mass mkt. 5.99 (*0-380-80244-9*, Avon Bks) Morrow Avon.

— Class Menagerie. LC 93-91667. 224p. 1999. mass mkt. 5.99 (*0-380-77380-5*, Avon Bks) Morrow Avon.

— Farewell to Yarns. LC 91-92067. 224p. 1991. mass mkt. 6.50 (*0-380-76399-0*, Avon Bks) Morrow Avon.

Churchill, Jill. Fear of Frying. LC 97-3188. 224p. 1997. pap. 22.00 (*0-380-97324-3*, Avon Bks) Morrow Avon.

Churchill, Jill. Fear of Frying: A Jane Jeffry Mystery. (Jane Jeffry Mystery Ser.). 256p. 1998. mass mkt. 5.99 (*0-380-78707-5*, Avon Bks) Morrow Avon.

— From Here to Paternity. 256p. (Orig.). 1995. mass mkt. 6.50 (*0-380-77715-0*, Avon Bks) Morrow Avon.

— Grime & Punishment. 192p. (Orig.). 1992. mass mkt. 6.50 (*0-380-76400-8*, Avon Bks) Morrow Avon.

***Churchill, Jill.** A Groom with a View: A Jane Jeffry Mystery. 256p. 2000. mass mkt. 6.50 (*0-380-79450-0*, Avon Bks) Morrow Avon.

— A Groom with a View: A Jane Jeffry Mystery. large type ed. LC 99-88722. (Americana Series). 293p. 2000. 27.95 (*0-7862-2454-1*) Thorndike Pr.

— A Groom with a View: A Jane Jeffry Mystery, Vol. 1. LC 99-16666. (Jane Jeffry Mystery Ser.). 224p. 1999. 22.00 (*0-380-97570-X*, Avon Bks) Morrow Avon.

— In the Still of the Night. LC 99-96769. 272p. 2000. mass mkt. 6.99 (*0-380-80245-7*, Avon Bks) Morrow Avon.

— Jane Jeffry 13. 2001. write for info. (*0-380-97736-2*) Morrow Avon.

— A Knife to Remember. 224p. (Orig.). 1999. mass mkt. 5.99 (*0-380-77381-3*, Avon Bks) Morrow Avon.

— The Merchant of Menace. 256p. 1999. mass mkt. 6.50 (*0-380-79449-7*, Avon Bks) Morrow Avon.

Churchill, Jill. The Merchant of Menace: A Jane Jeffry Mystery. LC 98-4493. 224p. 1998. 21.00 (*0-380-97569-6*, Avon Bks) Morrow Avon.

***Churchill, Jill.** Mulch Ado About Nothing: A Jane Jeffry Mystery. 224p. 2000. 23.00 (*0-380-97735-4*, Wm Morrow) Morrow Avon.

Churchill, Jill. Quiche Before Dying. LC 92-90438. (Jane Jeffry Mystery Ser.). 192p. 1993. mass mkt. 5.99 (*0-380-76932-8*, Avon Bks) Morrow Avon.

— Silence of the Hams. 224p. 1996. mass mkt. 6.50 (*0-380-77716-9*, Avon Bks) Morrow Avon.

— War & Peas. 224p. 1996. mass mkt. 20.00 (*0-380-97323-5*, Avon Bks) Morrow Avon.

— War & Peas. 256p. 1997. mass mkt. 6.50 (*0-380-78706-7*, Avon Bks) Morrow Avon.

— War & Peas. large type ed. LC 96-54878. (Americana Series). 275p. 1997. 24.95 (*0-7862-1049-4*) Thorndike Pr.

Churchill, John C., et al, eds. Landmarks of Oswego County, N. Y. with Biographies. (Illus.). 1191p. 1995. reprint ed. lib. bdg. 115.00 (*0-8328-4475-6*) Higginson Bk Co.

***Churchill, Karen L. & Burgess, Nancy.** The Sharlot Hall Museum Souvenir Book. (Illus.). 2000. pap. write for info. (*0-927579-10-3*) Sharlot Hall Mus Pr.

Churchill, Larry. Self-Interest & Universal Health Care: Why Well-Insured Americans Should Support Coverage for Everyone. LC 94-14568. 112p. 1994. text 22.95 (*0-674-80092-3*, CHUSEL) HUP.

Churchill, Larry R. Rationing Health Care in America: Perceptions & Principles of Justice. LC 86-40582. (C). 1987. pap. text 13.00 (*0-268-01631-3*) U of Notre Dame Pr.

Churchill, Larry R., jt. auth. see Smith, Harmon L.

Churchill, Lee, ed. see Hooker, Dennis.

Churchill, Lida A. The Magic Seven. 90p. 1996. reprint ed. spiral bd. 10.00 (*0-7873-1131-6*) Hlth Research.

— The Magic Seven, 1901. 88p. 1996. reprint ed. pap. 8.95 (*1-56459-964-7*) Kessinger Pub.

Churchill, Linda. Shetland Sheepdogs: A New Owner's Guide. LC 99-199906. 1998. 12.95 (*0-7938-2793-0*) TFH Pubns.

Churchill Livingstone Staff. Churchill Livingstone Nurse's Dictionary. 16th ed. 480p. 1989. pap. text 7.00 (*0-443-02242-9*) Church.

Churchill, Louise, tr. see Badiou, Alain.

Churchill, Mark, ed. Painting Masterpieces: Recreating 30 Works by Famous Artists. LC 98-48460. (Illus.). 160p. 1998. pap. 17.95 (*0-8069-3768-8*) Sterling.

Churchill, Nathaniel W., jt. auth. see Churchill, Gardner A.

Churchill, Neil C., et al, eds. Frontiers of Entrepreneurship Research, 1987: Proceedings of the 7th Annual Entrepreneurship Research Conference. 666p. 1987. pap. text 65.00 (*0-910897-08-5*) Babson College.

— Frontiers of Entrepreneurship Research, 1989: Proceedings of the 9th Annual Entrepreneurship Research Conference. 609p. (Orig.). 1989. pap. text 65.00 (*0-910897-10-7*) Babson College.

— Frontiers of Entrepreneurship Research, 1990: Proceedings of the 10th Annual Entrepreneurship Research Conference. (Illus.). 620p. (Orig.). (C). 1991. pap. text 65.00 (*0-910897-11-5*) Babson College.

— Frontiers of Entrepreneurship Research, 1991: Procedures of the 11th Annual Entrepreneurship Research Conference. (Illus.). 698p. (C). 1992. pap. text 65.00 (*0-910897-12-3*) Babson College.

— Frontiers of Entrepreneurship Research 1992 Frontiers of: Proceedings of the 12th Annual Entrepreneurship Research Conference. (Illus.). 677p. (C). 1994. pap. text 65.00 (*0-910897-13-1*) Babson College.

Churchill, Nicholas. Literary Eidetics. (Orig.). 1990. pap. 4.44 (*0-913412-32-5*) Brandon Hse.

Churchill-Peter. Marketing: Business Week Edition. 2nd ed. 1998. 72.74 (*0-07-013748-X*) McGraw.

Churchill, Peter. Pak: Small Business Management. 400p. (C). 1995. 56.95 (*0-7872-0449-8*) Kendall-Hunt.

Churchill, R. Elliott, jt. ed. see Teutsch, Steven M.

Churchill, R. R. EEC Fisheries Law. LC 87-12217. 1987. lib. bdg. 130.50 (*90-247-3545-9*) Kluwer Academic.

Churchill, R. R. & Lowe, A. V. The Law of the Sea. 2nd ed. LC 88-10276. (Illus.). 400p. 1988. text 59.95 (*0-7190-2634-2*, Pub. by Manchester Univ Pr) St Martin.

Churchill, R. V., ed. see Applied Mathematics Symposium Staff, et al.

Churchill, Randal. Become the Dream: The Transforming Power of Hypnotic Dreamwork. Canfield, Cheryl, ed. 1997. 29.95 (*0-9656218-0-4*) Transforming Pr.

— Regression Hypnotherapy: Transcripts of Transformation. Canfield, Cheryl, ed. 320p. 1999. 39.95 (*0-9656218-1-2*) Transforming Pr.

Churchill, Randolph S., ed. see Churchill, Winston L. S.

Churchill, Reginald C. English Literature of the Nineteenth Century. LC 75-140351. (Select Bibliographies Reprint Ser.). 1977. 18.95 (*0-8369-5594-3*) Ayer.

Churchill, Robert, jt. ed. see Sundermeier, Michael.

Churchill, Robert K. Lest We Forget: A Personal Reflection on the Formation of the Orthodox Presbyterian Church. 3rd ed. (Illus.). 135p. 1997. reprint ed. pap. 7.95 (*0-934688-34-6*) Comm Hist Orthodox.

Churchill, Robert P., ed. see Cordes, Joseph J.

Churchill, Robin. International Law & Global Climate Change: International Legal Issues & Implications. 512p. (C). 1992. lib. bdg. 183.50 (*1-85333-629-7*) Kluwer Academic.

Churchill, Robin & Ulfstein, Geir. Marine Management in Disputed Areas: The Case of the Barents Sea. LC 91-37180. (Ocean Management & Policy Ser.). 208p. (C). 1992. 100.00 (*0-415-03811-1*, A7209) Routledge.

Churchill, Robin, jt. ed. see Brown, E. D.

Churchill, Rogers P. The Anglo-Russian Convention of Nineteen Seven. LC 72-73. (Select Bibliographies Reprint Ser.). 1977. reprint ed. 21.95 (*0-8369-9956-8*) Ayer.

— The Anglo-Russian Convention of 1907. 1939. 30.00 (*0-686-17413-5*) R S Barnes.

Churchill, Ron. The Paris Interview. 347p. 1994. 24.00 (*0-9642455-0-7*); pap. 13.00 (*0-9642455-8-2*) Ave A Pr.

Churchill, Ruel V. Operational Mathematics. 3rd ed. 484p. (C). 1971. 96.56 (*0-07-010870-6*) McGraw.

Churchill, Ruel V. & Brown, James W. Complex Variables & Applications. 5th ed. (C). 1989. text 74.00 (*0-07-010905-2*) McGraw.

Churchill, Ruel V., jt. auth. see Brown, James W.

Churchill, Ruel Vance, jt. auth. see Brown, James Ward.

Churchill, Ryan & Churchill, Ward. Pacifism As Pathology: Reflections on the Role of Armed Struggle in North America. LC 99-160610. 170p. 1999. pap. 9.95 (*1-894037-07-3*) Arbeiter Ring.

Churchill, S. P., et al, eds. Biodiversity & Conservation of Neotropical Montane Forests: Proceedings of the Neotropical Forest Biodiversity & Conservation Symposium. (Illus.). 702p. 1995. text 85.00 (*0-89327-400-3*) NY Botanical.

Churchill, S. W. Practical Use of Theory in Fluid Flow Bk. 1: Inertial Flows. 155p. 1988. text 66.95 (*0-936282-01-0*) Buttrwrth-Heinemann.

Churchill, Sam. Big Sam. 184p. 1998. pap. 14.95 (*0-9630536-6-3*) S Dot S.

— Big Sam: The True Story of a Timberman & His Family in the Heyday of Northwest Logging. 2nd ed. Churchill, Dorothy, ed. LC 65-13975. (Illus.). 208p. 1998. reprint ed. pap. 14.95 (*0-8323-0476-X*) Binford Mort.

— Don't Call Me Ma. Churchill, Dorothy L., ed. 201p. 1998. pap. 14.95 (*0-9630536-7-1*) S Dot S.

Churchill, Sam, photos by see Sheller, Roscoe.

Churchill, Samuel J. Churchill: Genealogy & Biography of the Connecticut Branch of the Churchill Family in America, Containing Eleven Generations. (Illus.). 109p. 1997. reprint ed. pap. 17.00 (*0-8328-7932-0*); reprint ed. lib. bdg. 27.00 (*0-8328-7931-2*) Higginson Bk Co.

— Say It Again Sam. Churchill, Dorothy L., ed. 196p. (Orig.). 1991. pap. 9.95 (*0-9630536-0-4*) S Dot S.

Churchill, Sarah. The Prince with Many Castles & Other Stories. LC 68-93638. (Illus.). 5-60 p. (J). 1967. write for info. (*0-09-084550-1*, Pub. by Arrow Bks) Trafalgar.

***Churchill, Sharal.** The Indie Guidebook to Music Supervision for Films. 2000. 55.00 (*0-9679336-0-9*) Filmic Pr.

Churchill, Spencer. Classic Georgian Style. LC 97-66475. 1997. 45.00 (*0-8478-2042-4*, Pub. by Rizzoli Intl) St Martin.

Churchill, Stacy. The Education of Linguistic & Cultural Minorities in the OECD Countries. 175p. 1986. 99.00 (*0-905028-34-1*, MM13, Pub. by Multilingual Matters); pap. 44.95 (*0-905028-33-3*, Pub. by Multilingual Matters) Taylor & Francis.

Churchill, Stephen. The Reincarnation: From the Files of Adam Rheinhart, Parapsychologist. LC 98-39555. Orig. Title: Fridericus. 254p. 1998. pap. 12.95 (*1-57826-021-3*, Pub. by Hatherleigh) Norton.

Churchill, Steven P. The Mosses of Amazonian Ecuador. Balslev, Henrik, ed. (AAU Reports: No. 35). (Illus.). 211p. (C). 1995. pap. text 12.95 (*87-87600-62-5*, Pub. by Aarhus Univ Pr) David Brown.

Churchill, Stuart W. & Brenner, Howard. Viscous Flows: The Practical Use of Theory. (Illus.). 602p. 1988. text 99.95 (*0-409-95185-4*) Buttrwrth-Heinemann.

***Churchill, Sue.** Australian Bats. 1999. pap. 24.95 (*1-876334-07-X*) Sterling.

Churchill, Susanne E., ed. Fundamentals of Space Life Sciences, 2 vols., Set. LC 95-15029. (Orbit Series Book). (Illus.). 398p. (C). 1997. 125.00 (*0-89464-051-8*) Krieger.

Churchill-Taylor, Samuel E. Tea & Sects. 64p. (Orig.). 1975. pap. 3.95 (*0-938758-01-2*) MTM Pub Co.

Churchill, Thomas. Centralia Dead March. LC 79-9146. 213p. 1980. pap. 9.95 (*0-915306-17-4*) Curbstone.

— Commando Crusade, 1943-44. (C). 1986. text 140.00 (*0-7855-5305-3*, Pub. by Maritime Bks) St Mut.

— Triumph over Marcos: A True Story Based on the Lives of Gene Viernes & Silme Domingo, Filipino American Cannery Union Organizers, Their Assassination & the Trial That Followed. LC 94-47968. 1995. pap. 14.95 (*0-940880-52-0*) Open Hand.

Churchill, Ward. Fantasies of the Master Race: Literature, Cinema & the Colonization of American Indians. 2nd rev. ed. LC 98-36247. 192p. 1998. pap. 16.95 (*0-87286-348-4*) City Lights.

— From a Native Son: Selected Essays on Indigenism, 1985-1995. LC 96-26168. 588p. 1996. 40.00 (*0-89608-554-6*); pap. 22.00 (*0-89608-553-8*) South End Pr.

— A Little Matter of Genocide: Holocaust & Denial in the Americas 1492 to the Present. 260p. 1997. 37.50 (*0-87286-343-3*); pap. 19.95 (*0-87286-323-9*) City Lights.

— Since Predator Came: Notes from the Struggle for American Indian Liberation. (Illus.). 448p. (Orig.). 1995. pap. 18.00 (*1-883930-03-0*); lib. bdg. 30.00 (*1-883930-04-9*) AIGIS Pubns.

— Struggle for the Land: Native North American Resistance to Genocide, Ecocide & Colonization. 556p. pap. 19.95 (*1-894037-04-9*) Arbeiter Ring.

Churchill, Ward & Vander Wall, James. Agents of Repression: The FBI's Secret Wars Against the Black Panther Party & the American Indian Movement. LC 88-16844. 509p. 1988. 40.00 (*0-89608-294-6*) South End Pr.

— COINTELPRO Papers: Documents from the FBI's Secret Wars Against Dissent in the United States. 468p. (Orig.). 1990. pap. 22.00 (*0-89608-359-4*) South End Pr.

— Cointelpro Papers: Documents from the FBI's Secret Wars Against Dissent in the United States. 468p. 1990. pap. text 40.00 (*0-89608-360-8*) South End Pr.

Churchill, Ward & Vander Wall, Jim. Agents of Repression: The FBI's Secret Wars Against the Black Panther Party & the American Indian Movement. LC 88-16844. 509p. 1988. pap. 22.00 (*0-89608-293-8*) South End Pr.

Churchill, Ward, jt. auth. see Churchill, Ryan.

Churchill, William A. Beach-la-Mar, the Jargon or Trade Speech of the Western Pacific. LC 75-32806. reprint ed. 34.50 (*0-404-14110-2*) AMS Pr.

— Easter Island: The Rapanui Speech & the Peopling of Southeast Polynesia. LC 75-34642. reprint ed. 42.50 (*0-404-14214-1*) AMS Pr.

— The Polynesian Wanderings. LC 75-35186. reprint ed. 45.00 (*0-404-14215-X*) AMS Pr.

— Sissano, Movements of Migration Within & Through Melanesia. LC 16-23055. (Carnegie Institution of Washington Publication Ser.: No. 244). (Illus.). 89p. reprint ed. pap. 30.00 (*0-608-11015-9*, 201570600095) Bks Demand.

— Weather Words of Polynesia. LC 08-11468. (AAA Memoirs: No. 7). 1907. 25.00 (*0-527-00506-1*) Periodicals Srv.

Churchill, Winston L. S. Amid These Storms: Thoughts & Adventures. LC 72-5698. (Essay Index Reprint Ser.). 1977. reprint ed. 27.95 (*0-8369-2985-3*) Ayer.

— The Chartwell Bulletins: January-June 1935. Gilbert, Martin, ed. (Churchill Ser.: No. 2). (Illus.). 68p. 1989. pap. text 12.00 (*0-943879-03-5*) Churchill Ctr.

— Churchill & Roosevelt: The Complete Correspondence, Vol. 1. Kimball, Warren F., ed. LC 83-43080. (Illus.). 843p. 1987. reprint ed. pap. 200.00 (*0-608-04526-8*, 206527100001) Bks Demand.

— Churchill & Roosevelt: The Complete Correspondence, Vol. 2. Kimball, Warren F., ed. LC 83-43080. (Illus.). 784p. 1987. reprint ed. pap. 200.00 (*0-608-04527-6*, 206527100002) Bks Demand.

— Churchill & Roosevelt: The Complete Correspondence, Vol. 3. Kimball, Warren F., ed. LC 83-43080. (Illus.). 753p. 1987. reprint ed. pap. 200.00 (*0-608-04528-4*, 206527100003) Bks Demand.

Churchill, Winston L. S. Churchill in His Own Voice: And the Voices of His Contemporaries. abr. ed. 1994. audio 18.00 (*1-55994-999-6*, CPN 2018) HarperAudio.

Churchill, Winston L. S. Closing the Ring, 001. 673p. 1986. pap. 18.00 (*0-395-41059-2*) HM.

— Coniston. LC 72-96877. (Illus.). 543p. reprint ed. lib. bdg. 29.00 (*0-8398-0264-1*) Irvington.

— Crossing. 1976. 34.95 (*0-8488-0964-5*) Amereon Ltd.

— The Dream. (Churchill Ser.: No. 1). (Illus.). 36p. 1994. pap. 15.00 (*0-943879-00-0*) Churchill Ctr.

— End of the Beginning: War Speeches. LC 72-4588. (Essay Index Reprint Ser.). 1977. reprint ed. 21.95 (*0-8369-2939-X*) Ayer.

— A Far Country. (BCL1-PS American Literature Ser.). 509p. 1992. reprint ed. lib. bdg. 99.00 (*0-7812-6685-8*) Rprt Serv.

— For Free Trade. LC 76-26306. (Illus.). 119p. 1977. reprint ed. 18.50 (*0-917684-06-0*) Churchilliana.

— The Gathering Storm, 001. 724p. 1986. pap. 18.00 (*0-395-41055-X*) HM.

— The Grand Alliance, 001. 818p. 1986. pap. 18.00 (*0-395-41057-6*) HM.

— The Great Democracies. 1994. lib. bdg. 29.95 (*1-56849-507-2*) Buccaneer Bks.

— Great Democracies. 334p. Date not set. 25.95 (*0-8488-2643-4*) Amereon Ltd.

— The Hinge of Fate, 001. 917p. 1986. pap. 18.00 (*0-395-41058-4*) HM.

— His Father's Son: The Life of Randolph Churchill. LC 97-135484. (Illus.). 514p. 1997. 40.00 (*0-297-81640-3*, Pub. by Orion Pubng Grp) Trafalgar.

— India. 186p. 1990. 35.00 (*0-9606148-3-4*) Dragonwyck Pub.

— Liberalism & the Social Problem. LC 72-3299. (British History Ser.: No. 30). 1972. reprint ed. lib. bdg. 75.00 (*0-8383-1528-3*) M S G Haskell Hse.

— Memoirs of the Second World War. 1088p. 1991. pap. 29.95 (*0-395-59968-7*) HM.

— Mr. Brodrick's Army. deluxe ed. LC 76-26305. (Illus.). 120p. 1973. 18.50 (*0-917684-03-6*) Churchilliana.

— Mr. Brodrick's Army & For Free Trade, 2 bks. LC 76-26306. (Facsimile Set Editions Ser.). (Illus.). 1977. reprint ed. lib. bdg. 28.50 (*0-685-87406-0*) Churchilliana.

— Mr. Crewe's Career. (BCL1-PS American Literature Ser.). 498p. 1992. reprint ed. lib. bdg. 99.00 (*0-7812-6686-6*) Rprt Serv.

— My Early Life: A Roving Commission. (Illus.). 384p. 1987. pap. 15.00 (*0-684-18803-1*, Scribners Ref) Mac Lib Ref.

— My Early Life: A Roving Commission. (Illus.). 385p. 1989. reprint ed. 24.95 (*0-85052-257-9*, Pub. by Leo Cooper) Trans-Atl Phila.

— My Early Life, 1874-1904. 400p. 1996. per. 14.00 (*0-684-82345-4*) S&S Trade Pap.

— The New World. 1994. lib. bdg. 29.95 (*1-56849-505-6*) Buccaneer Bks.

— Richard Carvel. (BCL1-PS American Literature Ser.). 560p. 1992. reprint ed. lib. bdg. 99.00 (*0-7812-6687-4*) Rprt Serv.

***Churchill, Winston L. S.** The River War. (Illus.). 380p. 2000. pap. 14.00 (*0-7867-0751-8*, Pub. by Carroll & Graf) Publishers Group.

Churchill, Winston L. S. The River War. (Lost Treasure Ser.). (Illus.). 270p. 1997. pap. 19.95 (*1-85375-264-9*) Prion.

— Savrola. 241p. 1976. reprint ed. lib. bdg. 24.95 (*0-88411-074-5*, Queens House) Amereon Ltd.

— Savrola: A Tale of the Revolution in Laurania. 212p. 1990. 24.95 (*0-85052-255-2*, Pub. by Leo Cooper) Trans-Atl Phila.

— The Second War, 6 vols. 1985. write for info. (*0-318-60284-9*) HM.

— The Second World War, 6 vols., Vols. I-VI. 4532p. 1986. boxed set 100.00 (*0-395-41685-X*) HM.

— Shall We Commit Suicide? (Churchill Ser.: No. 3). 20p. 1994. pap. 10.00 (*0-614-04946-6*) Churchill Ctr.

— The Sinews of Peace, Post-War Speeches. Churchill, Randolph S., ed. LC 83-45733. reprint ed. 30.00 (*0-404-20059-1*) AMS Pr.

— Step by Step, 1936-1939. LC 72-156631. (Essay Index Reprint Ser.). 1977. reprint ed. 21.95 (*0-8369-2310-3*) Ayer.

— Their Finest Hour, 001. 1986. pap. 18.00 (*0-395-41056-8*) HM.

— Triumph & Tragedy, 6 vols. 716p. 1986. pap. 18.00 (*0-395-41060-6*) HM.

— While England Slept: A Survey of World Affairs, 1932-1938. LC 76-165621. (Select Bibliographic Reprint Ser.). 415p. 1982. reprint ed. lib. bdg. 22.00 (*0-8290-0804-7*) Irvington.

***Churchill, Winston L. S., ed.** The Great Republic: A History of the United States. LC 99-28511. 520p. 1999. 25.00 (*0-375-50320-X*) Random House.

— The Great Republic: A History of the United States. large type ed. LC 99-32486. 512p. 1999. 25.00 (*0-375-40856-8*) Wheeler Pub.

Churchill, Winston L. S. & Churchill, Clementine. Winston & Clementine: The Personal Letters of the Churchills. Soames, Mary, ed. LC 99-18699. (Illus.). 702p. 1999. 35.00 (*0-395-96319-2*) HM.

Churchill, Winston L. S., et al. Winston Churchill & Emery Reves: Correspondence, 1937-1965. Gilbert, Martin, ed. & intro. by. LC 97-14310. (Illus.). 432p. 1997. 39.95 (*0-292-71201-4*) U of Tex Pr.

***Churchill, Winston S.** Great Republic. 2000. mass mkt. (*0-375-75440-7*) Random House.

Churchland, Patricia S. Neurophilosophy: Toward a Unified Science of the Mind-Brain. (Illus.). 384p. 1986. 50.00 (*0-262-03116-7*, Bradford Bks) MIT Pr.

— Neurophilosophy: Toward a Unified Science of the Mind-Brain. (Illus.). 384p. 1989. pap. text 24.50 (*0-262-53085-6*, Bradford Bks) MIT Pr.

Churchland, Patricia S. & Sejnowski, Terrence J. The Computational Brain. (Illus.). 576p. 1992. 52.50 (*0-262-03188-4*, Bradford Bks) MIT Pr.

Churchland, Patricia S., et al. The Computational Brain. (Computational Neuroscience Ser.). (Illus.). 576p. 1994. pap. text 22.00 (*0-262-53120-8*, Bradford Bks) MIT Pr.

Churchland, Patricia S., jt. auth. see Churchland, Paul M.

Churchland, Patricia S., jt. ed. see Christen, Yves.

Churchland, Patricia S., jt. ed. see Llinas, Rodolfo R.

Churchland, Paul M. The Engine of Reason, the Seat of the Soul: A Philosophical Journey into the Brain. LC 94-30750. (Illus.). 330p. 1995. 38.50 (*0-262-03224-4*, Bradford Bks) MIT Pr.

— Engine of Reason, the Seat of the Soul: A Philosophical Journey into the Brain. (Illus.). 344p. 1996. pap. text 18.50 (*0-262-53142-9*, Bradford Bks) MIT Pr.

— Matter & Consciousness. rev. ed. (Illus.). 192p. 1988. pap. text 14.95 (*0-262-53074-0*, Bradford Bks) MIT Pr.

— A Neurocomputational Perspectives: The Nature of Mind & the Structure of Science. (Illus.). 344p. 1992. pap. text 20.00 (*0-262-53106-2*, Bradford Bks) MIT Pr.

— Scientific Realism & the Plasticity of Mind. LC 78-73240. (Illus.). 168p. 1986. pap. text 22.95 (*0-521-33827-1*) Cambridge U Pr.

Churchland, Paul M. & Churchland, Patricia S. On the Contrary: Critical Essays, 1987-1997. LC 97-40386. (Illus.). 320p. 1998. 30.00 (*0-262-03254-6*, Bradford Bks) MIT Pr.

— On the Contrary: Critical Essays, 1987-1997 (Illus.). 368p. 1999. pap. 16.00 (*0-262-53165-8*, Bradford Bks) MIT Pr.

Churchman, A., jt. auth. see Altman, I.

Churchman, Arza, ed. Victoria Plaza Revisited: Lessons for the Evaluation of Housing for the Elderly. (Illus.). (C). 1995. per. 15.00 (*0-938744-88-7*, R94-7) U of Wis Ctr Arch-Urban.

Churchman, C. W. & Verhulst, M. Management Sciences - Models & Techniques: Proceedings of the 6th International Management Institute on Management Sciences, Paris, September, 1959, 2 vols., Set. LC 60-14193. 1960. 486.00 (*0-08-009429-5*, Pub. by Pergamon Repr) Franklin.

Churchman, C. West. Thought & Wisdom. (Systems Inquiry Ser.). 150p. 1982. pap. text 10.95 (*0-914105-03-5*) Intersystems Pubns.

Churchman, C. West, ed. The Well-Being of Organizations. (Systems Inquiry Ser.). 380p. 1987. pap. text 15.95 (*0-914105-39-6*) Intersystems Pubns.

Churchman, C. West, frwd. Similarities, Connections & Systems: The Search for a New Rationality for Planning & Management. LC 97-44546. 192p. 1999. 52.00 (*0-7391-0000-9*) Lxngtn Bks.

Churchman, David. Negotiation: Process, Tactics, Theory. 2nd rev. ed. LC 95-10748. Orig. Title: Negotiation Tactics. 104p. (C). 1995. pap. text 16.00 (*0-8191-9947-8*); lib. bdg. 37.50 (*0-8191-9946-X*) U Pr of Amer.

Churchman, Deborah. Cross a Dark Bridge: A Novel. LC 95-34124. 132p. 1996. 14.95 (*0-918056-08-X*, Pub. by Ariadne Pr) Seven Hills Bk.

Churchman, G. J., et al, eds. Clays: Controlling the Environment. LC 96-225074. (Illus.). 526p. 1996. pap. 130.00 (*0-643-05536-3*, Pub. by CSIRO) Accents Pubns.

Churchman, Michael & Erbes, Scott. High Ideals & Aspirations: The Nelson-Atkins Museum of Art 1933-1993. Conrads, David, ed. (Illus.). 158p. (Orig.). (C). 1993. pap. 14.95 (*0-942614-22-4*) Nelson-Atkins.

Churchman, Michael, ed. see Leung, Tao & Anderson, Shelli.

***Churchouse, Chris.** Management Projects. LC 98-47108. 1999. pap. 33.95 (*0-566-08098-2*) Ashgate Pub Co.

Churchouse, Chris, jt. auth. see Churchouse, Jane.

Churchouse, Jane & Churchouse, Chris. Managing People. LC 98-3178. (Management Workbook Ser.). 207p. 1998. pap. 33.95 (*0-566-08015-X*, Pub. by Gower) Ashgate Pub Co.

Churchward, Albert. The Arcana of Freemasonry. 327p. (Orig.). 1992. reprint ed. pap. 27.50 (*1-56459-106-9*) Kessinger Pub.

— The Origin & Antiquity of Freemasonry. 75p. (Orig.). 1992. reprint ed. pap. 12.95 (*1-56459-107-7*) Kessinger Pub.

— The Origin & Evolution of Freemasonry Connected with the Origin & Evolution of the Human Race. Obaba, Al I., ed. (Illus.). 250p. 1990. pap. text 25.00 (*0-916157-48-2*) African Islam Miss Pubns.

— The Origin & Evolution of Freemasonry Connected with the Origin & Evolution of the Human Race. (African Heritage Classical Research Studies). pap. 25.00 (*0-938818-59-7*) ECA Assoc.

— The Origin & Evolution of Freemasonry Connected with the Origin & Evolution of the Human Race. 239p. 1996. reprint ed. spiral bd. 38.00 (*0-7873-0172-8*) Hlth Research.

— The Origin & Evolution of Freemasonry Connected with the Origin & Evolution of the Human Race. 239p. 1992. reprint ed. pap. 19.95 (*1-56459-104-2*) Kessinger Pub.

— Origin & Evolution of Primitive Man (1912) 136p. 1999. reprint ed. pap. 24.95 (*0-7661-0831-7*) Kessinger Pub.

— The Origin & Evolution of Religion. 421p. 1996. reprint ed. spiral bd. 62.00 (*0-7873-0174-4*) Hlth Research.

— The Origin & Evolution of Religion. 422p. 1992. reprint ed. pap. 37.00 (*1-56459-203-0*) Kessinger Pub.

— The Origin & Evolution of Religion, Vol. 1. Obaba, Al I., ed. (Illus.). 172p. 1924. pap. text 22.00 (*0-916157-27-X*) African Islam Miss Pubns.

— The Origin & Evolution of Religion, Vol. 2. Obaba, Al I., ed. (Illus.). 114p. 1924. pap. text 12.00 (*0-916157-28-8*) African Islam Miss Pubns.

— The Origin & Evolution of Religion, Vol. 3. Obaba, Al I., ed. 250p. 1924. pap. text 30.00 (*0-685-38272-9*) African Islam Miss Pubns.

— The Origin & Evolution of the Human Race. (Illus.). 600p. 1994. reprint ed. pap. 39.95 (*1-56459-427-0*) Kessinger Pub.

— The Origin & Evolution of the Human Race, Vol. I. Obaba, Al I., ed. (Illus.). 146p. 1990. pap. text 22.00 (*0-916157-39-3*) African Islam Miss Pubns.

— The Origin & Evolution of the Human Race, Vol. II. Obaba, Al I., ed. (Illus.). 144p. 1990. pap. text 22.00 (*0-916157-40-7*) African Islam Miss Pubns.

— The Origin & Evolution of the Human Race, Vol. III. Obaba, Al I., ed. (Illus.). 142p. 1990. pap. text 22.00 (*0-916157-41-5*) African Islam Miss Pubns.

— The Origin & Evolution of the Human Race, Vol. IV. Obaba, Al I., ed. (Illus.). 224p. 1990. pap. text 22.00 (*0-916157-42-3*) African Islam Miss Pubns.

— The Origin & Evolution of the Human Race, Vol. V. Obaba, Al I., ed. (Illus.). 116p. 1990. pap. text 22.00 (*0-916157-43-1*) African Islam Miss Pubns.

— Origins & Evolution of Religion. (African Heritage Classical Research Studies). 422p. reprint ed. 60.00 (*0-938818-61-9*) ECA Assoc.

— Signs & Symbols of Primordial Man. 1991. lib. bdg. 499.99 (*0-87700-998-8*) Revisionist Pr.

— The Signs & Symbols of Primordial Man. 501p. 1986. reprint ed. spiral bd. 62.00 (*0-7873-0173-6*) Hlth Research.

— Signs & Symbols of Primordial Man. (African Heritage Classical Research Studies). 449p. reprint ed. 60.00 (*0-938818-60-0*) ECA Assoc.

— The Signs & Symbols of Primordial Man, Vol. I. 232p. 1990. pap. text 24.00 (*0-916157-44-X*) African Islam Miss Pubns.

— The Signs & Symbols of Primordial Man, Vol. II. 200p. 1990. pap. text 24.00 (*0-916157-45-8*) African Islam Miss Pubns.

C

— The Signs & Symbols of Primordial Man. Vol. III. 186p. 1990. pap. text 24.00 (*0-916157-46-6*) African Islam Miss Pubns.

— The Signs & Symbols of Primordial Man: The Evolution of Religious Doctrines from the Eschatology of the Ancient Egyptians. 501p. (Orig.). 1994. pap. text 16.95 (*1-881316-73-4*) A&B Bks.

— The Signs & Symbols of Primordial Man: The Evolution of Religious Doctrines from the Eschatology of the Ancient Egyptians. 500p. (Orig.). 1992. reprint ed. pap. 39.95 (*1-56459-105-0*) Kessinger Pub.

Churchward, Clerk M. Rotuman Grammar & Dictionary. LC 75-32808. reprint ed. 42.50 (*0-404-14112-9*) AMS Pr.

Churchward, James. The Books of the Golden Age: The Sacred & Inspired Writings of Mu, the Origin of the Bible, the Origin of Freemasonry, Pearls of Wisdom, Wisdom from the Ancients. (Illus.). 294p. 1997. 85.00 (*0-914732-38-2*) Bro Life Inc.

— The Children of Mu. 1991. lib. bdg. 300.00 (*0-8490-4803-6*) Gordon Pr.

— The Children of Mu. (Illus.). 279p. 1988. reprint ed. pap. 15.95 (*0-914732-22-6*) Bro Life Inc.

— Cosmic Forces of Mu, Vol. 1. 246p. 1992. reprint ed. pap. 17.95 (*0-914732-27-7*) Bro Life Inc.

— Cosmic Forces of Mu, Vol. 2. 270p. 1992. reprint ed. pap. 17.95 (*0-914732-28-5*) Bro Life Inc.

— The Lost Continent of Mu. 1991. lib. bdg. 300.00 (*0-8490-4801-X*) Gordon Pr.

— The Lost Continent of Mu. (Illus.). 335p. 1998. reprint ed. pap. 21.95 (*0-914732-19-6*) Bro Life Inc.

— The Sacred Symbols of Mu. 1991. lib. bdg. 79.50 (*0-8490-4802-8*) Gordon Pr.

— The Sacred Symbols of Mu. (Illus.). 307p. 1988. reprint ed. pap. 15.95 (*0-914732-24-2*) Bro Life Inc.

***Churchwell, Gordon.** Expecting: One Man's Uncensored Memoir of Pregnancy. LC 99-89720. 304p. 2000. 24.00 (*0-06-039345-9*, ReganBks) HarperTrade.

Churchwell, Jo. The Cabin on Sawmill Creek: A Western Walden. Cornell, Wayne, ed. LC 97-20584. (Illus.). 250p. (Orig.). 1997. pap. 12.95 (*0-87004-380-3*) Caxton.

Churchwood, James. Children of Mu. 1996. write for info. (*0-85207-200-7*, Pub. by C W Daniel) Natl Bk Netwk.

— Cosmic Forces of Mu. 1996. write for info. (*0-85207-243-0*, Pub. by C W Daniel) Natl Bk Netwk.

— Cosmic Forces of Mu, Bk. 2. 1996. write for info. (*0-85207-245-7*, Pub. by C W Daniel) Natl Bk Netwk.

— The Lost Continent of Mu. write for info. (*0-85435-293-7*, Pub. by C W Daniel) Natl Bk Netwk.

— The Sacred Symbols of Mu. 1996. write for info. (*0-85207-198-1*, Pub. by C W Daniel) Natl Bk Netwk.

Churchyard, T., tr. see Van Meteren, Emanuel.

Churchyard, Thomas. A Lamentable & Pitifull Description of the Wofull Warres in Flaunders. LC 76-57372. (English Experience Ser.: No. 790). 1977. reprint ed. lib. bdg. 15.00 (*90-221-0790-6*) Walter J Johnson.

Churella, Albert J. From Steam to Diesel: Managerial Customs & Organizational Capabilities in the Twentieth-Century American Locomotive Industry. LC 97-51800. (Studies in Business & Technology). 224p. 1998. text 45.00 (*0-691-02776-5*, Pub. by Princeton U Pr) Cal Prin Full Svc.

Churg. Pathology Occupational Lung Disease. 2nd ed. 95.00 (*0-683-30386-4*) Lppncott W & W.

Churg, Andrew & Green, Francis H. Pathology of Occupational Lung Disease. 2nd ed. LC 97-33344. 1998. write for info. (*0-683-30342-2*) Lppncott W & W.

Churg, Andrew M. Pathology of Occupational Lung Disease. LC 87-3296. (Illus.). 416p. 1988. 98.50 (*0-89640-121-9*) Igaku-Shoin.

Churg, Andrew M. & Katzenstein, Anna-Luise A., eds. Current Topics in Lung Pathology: Based on the 1993, IAP Annual Long Course. LC 93-5319. (Monographs in Pathology: No. 36). (Illus.). 300p. 1994. write for info. (*0-683-01683-0*) Lppncott W & W.

Churg, Andrew M., ed. see Churg, Jacob.

Churg, Andrew M., jt. ed. see Thurlbeck, William M.

Churg, Jacob. Systemic Vasculitides. Churg, Andrew M., ed. LC 90-15649. (Illus.). 408p. 1991. 192.50 (*0-89640-195-2*) Igaku-Shoin.

Churg, Jacob, et al. Renal Disease: Classification & Atlas of Glomerular Diseases. 2nd ed. LC 94-22200. (Illus.). 541p. 1995. 159.95 (*0-89640-257-6*) Igaku-Shoin.

Churgin, Bathia, jt. ed. see Jenkins, Newell.

Churgin, Jonah R. The New Woman & the Old Academe: Sexism & Higher Education. LC 77-91470. 1979. 15.00 (*0-87212-076-7*) Libra.

— Rodgers' Child. LC 90-62549. 1991. 10.50 (*0-87212-243-3*) Libra.

Churgin, Pinchas, et al. Studies in Targum Jonathan to the Prophets. 59.50 (*0-87068-109-5*) Ktav.

Churgin, Pinkos. Targum Jonathan to the Prophets. LC 78-63558. (Yale Oriental Series: Researches: No. 14). reprint ed. 32.50 (*0-404-60284-3*) AMS Pr.

Churilla, Kenneth R., ed. The Computer Industry Directory. 392p. (Orig.). 1991. pap. 49.95 (*0-9629446-0-2*) Mentor Market.

Churilla, Kenneth R., ed. see Morin, Thomas, II.

Churilov, A., jt. auth. see Gelig, A. K.

Churilov, Alexander N., jt. auth. see Gelig, Arkadi I.

Churinoff, George, tr. see Dalai Lama XIV.

Churma. Surviving Your First Year of Teaching: Guidelines for Success. LC 99-175750. (C). 1998. text 8.00 (*0-13-973835-5*) P-H.

***Churma, Michelle & Stollenwerk, Debra A.** A Guide to Integrating Technology Standards into the Curriculum LC 99-179367. (Student Enrichment Ser.). 93p. 1999. write for info. (*0-13-974114-3*) P-H.

Churms, Shirley C. Carbohydrates. LC 80-29541. (Handbook of Chromatography Ser.). 288p. 1982. 161.00 (*0-8493-3061-0*, QD117, CRC Reprint) Franklin.

— Handbook of Chromatography, Vol. 2: Carbohydrates. 312p. 1990. lib. bdg. 249.00 (*0-8493-3062-9*, QD117) CRC Pr.

Churn, Serenus T. And I'll See You in the Morning: An Anthology of Funeral Messages, Helps for Sermon Development, Family Visit, Funeral & Grave Side Services. LC 98-219520. 73 p. 1998. write for info. (*1-55630-871-X*) Brentwood Comm.

Churney, Marie & Williams, Susan. Bogs, Meadows, Marshes, & Swamps: A Guide to 25 Wetland Sites of Washington State. (Illus.). 192p. 1996. pap. text 14.95 (*0-89886-476-3*) Mountaineers.

***Churns, S.** World Prize Mathematics. 2000. 86.00 (*981-02-3945-9*) World Scientific Pub.

Churruarin, Juan J. Ministerio Profetico. 1998. pap. text 5.99 (*0-8297-0724-7*) Vida Pubs.

***Churruarin, Juan J.** El Precio de la Uncion. (SPA.). 1999. pap. text 6.99 (*0-8297-0913-4*) Vida Pubs.

Churton, Annette, et al. Teaching Children with Diversity. LC 97-17563. 255p. 1997. pap. text 53.00 (*0-205-18344-1*) P-H.

Churton, Michael W., et al. Teaching Children with Diverse Abilities: Instructor's Manual with Test Items. 144p. (C). 1998. pap. text, teacher ed. write for info. (*0-205-27792-6*, T7792-9) Allyn.

***Churukian, George A. & Lock, Corey R.** International Narratives on Becoming a Teacher Educator: Pathways to a Profession. LC 99-21897. (Studies in Education: Vol. 42). 186p. 1999. text 79.95 (*0-7734-8015-3*) E Mellen.

***Chuse, Patricia J.** The GodSelf Workbook. 150p. (Orig.). 1999. mass mkt. write for info. (*0-9667560-1-0*) P Chuse.

Chuse, Patricia Jepsen. The Godself: Revelation for the New Millennium. LC 98-96820. 279p. 1999. 17.95 (*0-9667560-0-2*) P Chuse.

Chuse, Robert & Carson, Bryce E., Sr. Pressure Vessels: The ASME Code Simplified. 7th ed. LC 92-17243. 323p. 1992. 69.95 (*0-07-010939-7*) McGraw.

Chused, Richard. Cases, Materials & Problems in Property. 1988. teacher ed. write for info. (*0-8205-0242-1*) Bender.

Chused, Richard H. Cases, Materials, & Problems in Property. 2nd ed. LC 99-22124. (Casebook Ser.). 1999. 58.00 (*0-8205-4135-4*) Bender.

— Private Acts in Public Places: A Social History of Divorce in the Formative Era of American Family Law. LC 94-1335. 248p. (C). 1994. text 34.50 (*0-8122-3202-X*) U of Pa Pr.

Chused, Richard H., ed. A Copyright Anthology: The Technology Frontier. 504p. (C). 1998. pap. text 29.95 (*0-87084-190-4*) Anderson Pub Co.

— A Property Anthology. 2nd ed. 625p. (C). 1997. pap. 29.95 (*0-87084-735-X*) Anderson Pub Co.

Chushian, Tsai. Fukien Ground Boxing: Nan Sholing Leg Techniques. 150p. (Orig.). 1993. pap. 29.00 (*0-87040-924-7*) Japan Pubns USA.

Chushkin, Pavel I., jt. auth. see Dorodnicyn, Anatoly A.

Chusid. Verdi's Middle Period 1849-1859. LC 96-31949. 1997. lib. bdg. 100.00 (*0-226-10658-6*) U Ch Pr.

***Chusid, Irwin.** Songs in the Key of Z: The Curious Universe of Outsider Music. LC 99-57640. (Illus.). 272p. 2000. pap. 16.95 (*1-55652-372-6*, Pub. by A Cappella Bks) IPG Chicago.

***Chusid, Martin.** A Companion to Schubert's Schwanengesang: History, Poets, Analysis, Performance. LC 99-27829. (Illus.). 300p. 2000. 35.00 (*0-300-07289-9*) Yale U Pr.

Chusid, Martin, ed. see Schubert, Franz.

Chusid, Martin, ed. see Verdi, Giuseppe.

Chusid, Martin, jt. ed. see Weaver, William.

Chusid, Nancy. Favorite Folk Songs. (Sing along for Little Ones Ser.). (Illus.). 32p. (J). (ps-2). 1990. audio 6.95 (*1-878624-07-5*, McClanahan Book) Learn Horizon.

— Favorite Lullabies. (Sing along for Little Ones Ser.). (Illus.). 32p. (J). (ps-2). 1990. audio 6.95 (*1-878624-06-7*, McClanahan Book) Learn Horizon.

***Chusid, Nancy.** Favorite Nursery Songs. (Sing along for Little Ones Ser.). (Illus.). 32p. (J). (ps-2). 1998. pap. 6.95 incl. audio (*1-878624-05-9*, McClanahan Book) Learn Horizon.

***Chuska, Jeff.** Aristotle's Best Regime Vol. VII, Nos. 1-10: A Reading of Aristotle's Politics. LC 00-36419. 392p. 2000. 54.50 (*0-7618-1706-9*) U Pr of Amer.

Chuska, Kenneth R. Gifted Learners K-12: A Practical Guide to Effective Curriculum & Teaching. 87p. (Orig.). 1989. pap. 19.95 (*1-879639-14-9*) Natl Educ Serv.

Chuska, Kenneth R. Improving Classroom Questions. 88p. 1995. pap. 9.00 (*0-87367-474-X*) Phi Delta Kappa.

Chusod, Martin. Verdi's Middle Period 1849-1859. Hansell, Kathleen K. & Gossett, Philip, eds. LC 96-31949. 1997. pap. text 45.00 (*0-226-10659-4*) U Ch Pr.

Chuta, E. & Sethuraman, S. V., eds. Rural Small-Scale Industries & Employment in Africa & Asia: A Review of Problemes & Policies. x, 160p. (Orig.). 1983. pap. 22.50 (*92-2-103513-1*) Intl Labour Office.

Chute. Maclab for Psych 3.0 - Documentation. 3rd ed. (Psychology Ser.). 1994. pap. 14.00 (*0-534-23869-6*) Wadsworth Pub.

Chute. Maclab for Psychology V3.0: Student Lab Manual, Version 3. 3rd ed. (Psychology Ser.). 1994. mass mkt., lab manual ed. 25.50 (*0-534-23198-5*) Brooks-Cole.

— Maclab-Powerlab for Mac-Documentation. LC 98-102058. (Psychology Ser.). 1996. pap. 60.75 (*0-534-34132-2*) Wadsworth Pub.

Chute, Adrienne. Public Libraries in the United States: Fy 1994. 127p. 1997. pap. 11.00 (*0-16-049059-6*) USGPO.

— Public Libraries in the United States: FY 1995. 140p. 1998. per. 14.00 (*0-16-063669-8*) USGPO.

Chute, Alan, et al. The McGraw-Hill Handbook of Distance Learning. (Illus.). 300p. 1998. 39.95 (*0-07-012028-5*) McGraw-Hill Prof.

Chute, Carolyn. The Beans of Egypt, Maine. LC 94-37244. 304p. 1995. pap. 12.00 (*0-15-600188-8*, Harvest Bks) Harcourt.

— The Beans of Egypt, Maine. 256p. 1986. mass mkt. 6.50 (*0-446-30010-1*, Pub. by Warner Bks) Little.

— Letourneau's Used Auto Parts. LC 94-37243. (Harvest American Writing Ser.). 256p. 1995. pap. 11.00 (*0-15-600189-6*, Harvest Bks) Harcourt.

— Letourneau's Used Auto Parts. 224p. 1988. 16.45 (*0-89919-500-8*, Pub. by Ticknor & Fields) HM.

— Merry Men. LC 93-11028. 712p. 1995. pap. 16.00 (*0-15-600191-8*) Harcourt.

Chute, Carolyn. Snow Man. LC 98-35539. 256p. 1999. 23.00 (*0-15-100390-4*) Harcourt.

***Chute, Carolyn.** Snow Man. (Illus.). 256p. (J). 2001. pap. 14.00 (*0-15-601140-9*, Harcourt Child Bks) Harcourt.

Chute, Christopher G. Electronic Medical Record Infrastructures: An Overview of Critical Standards & Classifications. 320p. 1997. 49.00 (*0-387-94864-3*) Spr-Verlag.

Chute, David, et al. The Making of Judge Dredd. LC 99-233628. (Illus.). 192p. (J). 1995. pap. 15.95 (*0-7868-8106-2*, Pub. by Hyperion) Time Warner.

Chute, Janet. The Legacy of Shingwaukonse: A Century of Native Leadership. LC 98-205034. (Illus.). 400p. 1998. text 60.00 (*0-8020-4273-2*); pap. text 24.95 (*0-8020-8108-8*) U of Toronto Pr.

Chute, M. The End of the Search. 1979. pap. 8.95 (*0-933062-05-2*) R H Sommer.

— Jesus of Israel. 1988. pap. 8.95 (*0-933062-26-5*) R H Sommer.

— The Search for God. 1979. pap. 11.95 (*0-933062-04-4*) R H Sommer.

Chute, Marchette. The End of the Search: Discovery & Encounter with the Divine. LC 97-52672. 132p. 1998. reprint ed. pap. 9.95 (*1-889051-28-4*) Acrpls Bks CO.

— Stories from Shakespeare. 1959. pap. 11.95 (*0-452-01061-6*, Mer) NAL.

Chute, Patricia M., jt. auth. see Nevins, Mary E.

Chute, Robert M. Androscoggin Too. Page, Carolyn, ed. (Poetry Bks.). (Illus.). 48p. (Orig.). 1997. pap. 9.95 (*1-879205-71-8*) Nightshade Pr.

— Barely Time to Study Jesus: The Nat "Turner" Revolt. 1997. pap., spiral bd. 6.00 (*0-9624912-2-5*) Ciderpress.

— Samuel Sewall Sails for Home. (Illus.). 36p. (Orig.). 1986. pap. 5.95 (*0-913341-10-X*) Coyote Love.

— Samuel Sewall Sails for Home: Poetry by Robert Chute. 22p. 1986. pap. 5.95 (*0-614-14603-8*) Maine Writers.

***Chute, Robert M.** Sweeping the Sky: Soviet Women Pilots in Combat. (Illus.). 30p. 2000. pap. 12.50 (*0-9624912-4-1*) Ciderpress.

Chute, Robert M. Thirteen Moons. 72p. 1982. 12.95 (*0-920806-29-5*, Pub. by Penumbra Pr); pap. 7.95 (*0-920806-23-6*, Pub. by Penumbra Pr) U of Toronto Pr.

— Uncle George: Poems from a Maine Boyhood. 2nd rev. ed. (Illus.). 54p. (Orig.). 1990. reprint ed. per. 10.00 (*0-9624912-0-9*) Ciderpress.

— Woodshed on the Moon: Thoreau Poems. Zarucchi, Roy & Page, Carolyn, eds. (Chapbook Ser.). (Illus.). 48p. (Orig.). 1991. pap. 9.95 (*1-879205-10-6*) Nightshade Pr.

Chute, Robert M., ed. see Zarucchi, Roy.

Chuter, David. Humanity's Soldier: France & International Security, 1919-2001. LC 96-9584. (Contemporary France Ser.: Vol. 1). 368p. 1997. 59.95 (*1-57181-893-6*) Berghahn Bks.

***Chuter, Timothy A., et al, eds.** Endoluminal Vascular Prostheses. 2nd ed. (Illus.). 2001. 98.00 (*0-87993-642-8*) Futura Pub.

Chutia, Dharmeswar, jt. ed. see Goswmi, Ashok K.

Chutkow, Paul, jt. auth. see Mondavi, Robert.

Chuto, Jacques. James Clarence Mangan: A Bibliography of His Works. 208p. 1999. 55.00 (*0-7165-2578-X*, Pub. by Irish Acad Pr) Intl Spec Bk.

Chuto, Jacques, et al, eds. The Collected Prose of James Clarence Mangan. 500p. 1997. 55.00 (*0-7165-2577-1*, Pub. by Irish Acad Pr) Intl Spec Bk.

Chuto, Jacques, ed. see Shannon-Mangan, Ellen.

Chuun, Calvin E. Not for Bread Alone. (Illus.). 64p. 1981. 3.00 (*0-318-16568-6*) Soc Descend Wash Army.

Chuvala, John, 3rd. Pak: Security. (C). 1995. pap. text 44.95 (*0-7872-1584-8*, 41158401) Kendall-Hunt.

***Chuvala, John, 3rd & Fischer, Robert.** Suggested Preparation for Careers in Security - Loss Prevention. 2nd ed. 170p. (C). 1999. per. 38.95 (*0-7872-5883-0*, 41588301) Kendall-Hunt.

***Chuvieco, E., ed.** Remote Sensing of Large Wildfires: In the European Mediterranean Basin. (Illus.). xiv, 212p. 1999. 109.00 incl. cd-rom (*3-540-65767-3*) Spr-Verlag.

Chuvin, Pierre. A Chronicle of the Last Pagans. Archer, B. A., tr. (Revealing Antiquity Ser.: No. 4). 192p. 1990. 35.00 (*0-674-12970-9*) HUP.

Chuzeville, Jean, ed. see De Vigny, Alfred.

Chuzi, George M., jt. auth. see Hadley, Ernest C.

Chval, Kathryn, jt. auth. see Page, David A.

Chvala, M. The Empidoides (Diptera) of Fennoscandia & Denmark Pt. 2: General Part. The Families Hybotidae, Atelestidae & Microphoridae. (Fauna Entomologica Scandinavica Ser.: No. 12). (Illus.). 281p. 1983. pap. 75.00 (*87-87491-07-9*) Lubrecht & Cramer.

— The Tachydromiinae (Diptera Empididae) of Fennoscandia & Denmark. (Fauna Entomologica Scandinavica Ser.: No. 3). (Illus.). 336p. 1975. pap. 50.00 (*87-87491-04-4*) Lubrecht & Cramer.

Chvala, Richard J., jt. auth. see Johnson, William C.

Chvalovsky, Vaclav & Bellama, J. Michael, eds. Carbon-Functional Organosilicon Compounds. LC 84-3438. (Modern Inorganic Chemistry Ser.). 318p. 1984. 85.00 (*0-306-41671-9*, Plenum Trade) Perseus Pubng.

Chvany, Catherine V. Selected Essays of Catherine V. Chvany. Yokoyama, Olga T. & Klenin, Emily, eds. LC 97-165689. 391p. 1997. pap. 24.95 (*0-89357-269-1*) Slavica.

Chvany, Catherine V., jt. ed. see Crone, Anna L.

Chvatal, Vasek. Linear Programming. LC 82-21132. (Illus.). 478p. (C). 1983. pap. text 47.95 (*0-7167-1587-2*) W H Freeman.

Chvostal, Phyllis. Accent on Music: Student Puzzles, 3 vols. unabridged ed. (Illus.). (Orig.). (J). (gr. 1-7). 1999. pap. 12.00 (*0-9631050-4-3*) Safe Harbour.

— Kreative Keyboard: Don't Just Sit There... Exercise. unabridged ed. (Illus.). 28p. (Orig.). 1999. pap. 6.00 (*0-9631050-3-5*) Safe Harbour.

— Kreative Keyboard: Guide to Music Theory. unabridged ed. (Illus.), (Orig.). (J). 1999. pap. 12.00 (*0-9631050-9-4*) Safe Harbour.

— Magic of Chording, 3 vols. unabridged ed. (Illus.). 28p. (Orig.). (J). 1998. pap. 6.00 (*0-9631050-7-8*) Safe Harbour.

— My First Lessons. (Illus.). (Orig.). 1993. pap. 6.00 (*0-9631050-6-X*) Safe Harbour.

Chwa, K. Y. & Ibara, O., eds. Algorithms & Computation: Proceedings of the 9th International Symposium, ISAAC '98, Taejon, Korea, December 14-16, 1998. (Lecture Notes in Computer Science Ser.: Vol. 1533). xiii, 478p. 1998. pap. 69.00 (*3-540-65385-6*) Spr-Verlag.

Chwalek, Kazimierz, jt. auth. see O'Connor, Shaun.

Chwang, A. T., et al, eds. Hydrodynamics - Theory & Applications: Proceedings of the Second International Conference on Hydrodynamics, Hong Kong, 16-19 December 1996, 2 vols. (Illus.). 1396p. (C). 1996. text 246.00 (*90-5410-860-6*, Pub. by A A Balkema) Ashgate Pub Co.

Chwast, Seymour. Alphabet Parade. LC 90-47193. (Illus.). 32p. (J). (ps-2). 1991. 13.95 (*0-15-200351-7*, Gulliver Bks) Harcourt.

— Bra Fashions by Stephanie. 64p. (Orig.). 1994. mass mkt. 4.99 (*0-446-67050-2*, Pub. by Warner Bks) Little.

— The Left-Handed Designer. Heller, Steven, ed. LC 85-3922. (Illus.). 143p. 1985. 49.50 (*0-8109-1289-9*, Pub. by Abrams) Time Warner.

— Traffic Jam. LC 98-45865. (Illus.). 32p. (J). (ps-3). 1999. 15.00 (*0-395-97495-X*, W Lorraine) HM.

— The Twelve Circus Rings. LC 92-13576. (Illus.). 40p. (J). 1996. pap. 6.00 (*0-15-201361-X*) Harcourt.

— Twelve Circus Rings. LC 92-13576. 1996. 10.90 (*0-606-11010-0*, Pub. by Turtleback) Demco.

Chwast, Seymour, et al. Trylon & Perisphere: The 1939-40 World's Fair. (Illus.). 196p. 1989. 24.95 (*0-318-32472-5*) Abrams.

Chwast, Seymour, jt. auth. see Heller, Steven.

Chwast, Seymour, jt. auth. see Holland, D. K.

Chwatsky, Ann. Out of Bounds: Contemporary Long Island Photographs. (Illus.). 30p. 1989. pap. 5.00 (*0-933793-11-1*) Guild Hall.

***Chweh, Crystal R.** Readings on Cyrano de Bergerac. LC 00-41074. (Literary Companion to World Literature Ser.). 2001. pap. write for info. (*0-7377-0434-9*) Greenhaven.

Chwialkowski, Jerzy. The Da Capo Catalog of Classical Music Compositions. 1412p. (Orig.). 1996. pap. 35.00 (*0-306-80701-7*); lib. bdg. 29.50 (*0-306-79666-X*) Da Capo.

Chwialkowski, Paul. The Forgotten Fighting General: The Life & Career of Robert L. Eichelberger, 141. LC 92-35928. (Contributions in Military Studies Ser.: No. 141). 248p. 1993. 65.00 (*0-313-28605-1*, CKN/) Greenwood.

Chyet, Stanley & Gilbert, Barbara C. Israel Through American Eyes: A Century of Photography. (Illus.). 48p. 1998. pap. write for info. (*0-9651640-6-3*) Skirball Cultural.

Chyet, Stanley F., ed. see Ezekiel, Moses J.

Chyet, Stanley F., ed. & tr. see Gouri, Haim.

Chyet, Stanley F., jt. tr. see Bargad, Warren.

Chyi, L. L. & Chou, C. L., eds. Recent Advances in Coal Geochemistry. (Special Papers: No. 248). (Illus.). 112p. 1990. pap. 11.00 (*0-8137-2248-9*) Geol Soc.

Chylinska, Teresa. Karol Szymanowski: His Life & Works. Glowacki, John, tr. from POL. LC 93-30221. (Polish Music History Ser.: No. 5). (Illus.). 355p. 1993. 30.00 (*0-916545-00-8*) Friends of Pol Mus.

— Szymanowski. Jordan, A. T., tr. (Library of Polish Studies: Vol. 1). (Illus.). 1973. text 10.00 (*0-917004-04-3*) Kosciuszko.

***Chyna.** Chyna. 304p. 2000. 26.00 (*0-06-039329-7*, ReganBks) HarperTrade.

***Chynn, Emil W.** Chinese Proverbs for Today's World: Mini Edition. 2000. 4.95 (*0-7407-0510-5*) Andrews & McMeel.

Chynn, K. Y. & Finby, N. Manual of Cranial Computerized Tomography. (Illus.). vi, 106p. 1982. 172.25 (*3-8055-3432-9*) S Karger.

Chynoweth, A. G., ed. see American Physical Society Conference, New York Cit.

Chynoweth, Alan G., jt. auth. see Miller.

Chynoweth, Judith K. A Guide to Community-Based, Collaborative Strategic Planning. LC 93-38729. 1993. 15.95 (*0-934842-63-9*) CSPA.

Chypre, John. Gotta Go. (Illus.). 134p. 1997. pap. 6.50 (*0-9660807-0-X*) Bedlam Bks.

Chysler Corp. (pentastar Electronics, Inc.) Staff. Direct-Hydrogen-Fueled Proton-Exchange-Membrane Fuel Cell System for Transportation Applications:

C

An Asterisk (*) at the beginning of an entry indicates that the title is appearing for the first time.

Conceptual Design Report (3/97) (Fuel Cell Information Ser.: Vol. XVII). (Illus.). 157p. Date not set. lib. bdg. 135.00 (*0-89934-354-6*, BT-988) Bus Tech Bks.

Chytil, M. P. Mathematical Foundations of Computer Science, 1981. Gruska, J., ed. (Lecture Notes in Computer Science Ser.: Vol. 118). 589p. 1981. 43.00 (*0-387-10856-4*) Spr-Verlag.

Chytil, M. P., et al, eds. Mathematical Foundations of Computer Science, 1988. (Lecture Notes in Computer Science Ser.: Vol. 324). ix, 562p. 1988. 61.00 (*0-387-50110-X*) Spr-Verlag.

Chytil, M. P., et al. Mathematical Foundations of Computer Science, 1984: Praha, Czechoslovakia, September 3-8, 1984. (Lecture Notes in Computer Science Ser.: Vol. 176). xi, 581p. 1984. 55.00 (*0-387-13372-0*) Spr-Verlag.

Chytraeus, David & Melanchthon, Philip. A Summary of the Christian Faith. McCain, Paul, ed. Dinda, Richard, tr. from LAT. 168p. 1997. 20.00 (*1-891469-04-5*) Repristination.

Chytraeus, Nathan. Nomenclator Lationsaxonicus. (Documenta Linguistica, Reihe I Ser.). xvi, 626p. 1974. reprint ed. 130.00 (*3-487-05277-6*) G Olms Pubs.

Chyu, M. K., ed. Heat Transfer in Gas Turbines: 1994 International Mechanical Engineering Congress & Exposition, Chicago, Illinois - November 6-11, 1994. LC 94-79142. (HTD Ser.: Vol. 300). 188p. 1994. 74.00 (*0-7918-1440-8*, G00935) ASME.

Chyutin, Michael. The New Jerusalem Scroll from Qumran: A Comprehensive Reconstruction. (JSP Supplement Ser.: Vol. 25). 167p. 1997. 52.50 (*1-85075-683-X*, Pub. by Sheffield Acad) CUP Services.

Chyzowych, Walter. The Official Soccer Book of the United States Soccer Federation. (Illus.). 256p. 13.00 (*0-318-16829-4*); pap. 7.00 (*0-318-16830-8*) US Soccer Fed.

Ci, Jiwei. Dialectic of the Chinese Revolution: From Utopianism to Hedonism. LC 94-2558. ix, 281p. 1994. 39.50 (*0-8047-2354-0*); pap. 15.95 (*0-8047-2373-7*) Stanford U Pr.

Ci, Longjun. Land Evaluation & Expert System for Combating Desertification. LC 98-190206. 201p. 1997. write for info. (*7-5038-1824-7*) China Forest.

Ci, Y., et al. New Generation Computer: Proceedings of International Symposium on New Generation Computer, Beijing, 7-11 December, 1988. (International Academic Publishers Ser.). 500p. 1989. 145.00 (*0-08-037041-1*, Pergamon Pr) Elsevier.

CIA Staff. Atlas of the Polar Regions. 66p. 1985. reprint ed. text 250.00 (*0-86720-061-8*) Jones & Bartlett.

— Cooking Essentials New Professional. (Culinary Arts Ser.). 1997. pap. write for info. (*0-442-02464-9*, VNR) Wiley.

— Cooking Essentials New Professional. 6th ed. (Culinary Arts Ser.). 1997. pap. 22.50 (*0-442-02467-3*, VNR) Wiley.

— Energy Atlas of the U. S. S. R. 78p. 1985. reprint ed. 250.00 (*0-86720-060-X*) Jones & Bartlett.

***CIA Staff.** From Our Kitchens (Special Edi. 1999. pap. text. write for info. (*0-471-36258-1*) Wiley.

CIA Staff. New Professional Chef: Academy Edition. 5th ed. 1997. 54.95 (*0-442-01143-1*, VNR) Wiley.

— Professional Chef No. 6: Exploring Wine Set. 1997. 75.95 (*0-442-02303-0*, VNR) Wiley.

— The Professional Chef's Knife Kit. 2nd ed. LC 99-24635. 160p. 1999. pap. 34.95 (*0-471-34997-6*) Wiley.

— Rote Kapelle. Kesaris, Paul, ed. LC 79-51270. 390p. 1979. lib. bdg. 55.00 (*0-313-27051-1*, U7051, Greenwood Pr) Greenwood.

— The Secret Cuban Missile Crisis Documents. 414p. 1993. 38.00 (*0-02-881082-1*); pap. 21.00 (*0-02-881083-X*) Brasseys.

CIA Staff. Techniques of Healthy Cooking. pap. text, teacher ed. write for info. (*0-471-37955-7*) Wiley.

CIA Staff. The World Factbook, 1998-99. (Illus.). 572p. 1998. 38.95 (*1-57488-162-0*) Brasseys.

— The World Factbook, 1995-96. (Association of the U. S. Army Book Ser.). (Illus.). 526p. 1995. 32.95 (*0-02-881053-8*) Brasseys.

— The World Factbook, 1994-95. 512p. 1994. 32.00 (*0-02-881052-X*) Brasseys.

***CIA Staff.** The World Factbook, 1999. (Illus.). 572p. 1999. 42.50 (*1-57488-163-9*) Brasseys.

CIA Staff. The World Factbook, 1997-98. (Illus.). 640p. 1997. 34.95 (*1-57488-100-0*) Brasseys.

— The World Factbook, 1996-97. 572p. 1996. 32.95 (*1-57488-014-4*) Brasseys.

— The World Factbook, 1993-94. 464p. 1993. 30.00 (*0-02-881044-9*, 4149M) Brasseys.

CIA Staff & Sonnensc. Pro Hea Cook Garde Mg Prof Che. 1997. 139.95 (*0-442-01475-9*, VNR) Wiley.

Ciabattari, Mark. The Literal Truth: Rizzoli Dreams of Eating the Apple of Earthly Delights. LC 94-70904. 128p. (Orig.). 1994. pap. 12.00 (*0-9630164-7-4*) Canios Edit.

Ciabotti, Patricia. Gaming It up with Shakespeare: A Combined Study of Drama & Theatre. Smith, Linda H., ed. (Triad Prototype Ser.). 1980. pap. 5.00 (*0-936386-09-6*) Creative Learning.

Ciabotti, Patricia A. & Crocker, Herbert L. Career Awareness Day: A Prescription for Creating Job Awareness in Elementary & Intermediate School Students. 1981. pap. 14.95 (*0-936386-15-0*) Creative Learning.

Ciaccia, Maria, jt. auth. see Dornemann, Joan.

Ciaccio, Leonard L. Water & Water Pollution Handbook, Vol. 1. (Illus.). 480p. 1971. text 225.00 (*0-8247-1104-1*) Dekker.

— Water & Water Pollution Handbook, Vol. 3. (Illus.). 528p. 1972. text 225.00 (*0-8247-1117-3*) Dekker.

— Water & Water Pollution Handbook, Vol. 4. (Illus.). 648p. 1973. text 225.00 (*0-8247-1118-1*) Dekker.

Ciaccio, Leonard L., ed. Water & Water Pollution Handbook, Vol. 2. LC 78-134780. (Illus.). 362p. reprint ed. pap. 112.30 (*0-7837-7134-7*, 205252800002) Bks Demand.

Ciach, R. Advanced Light Alloys & Composites: Proceedings of the NATO Advanced Study Institute, Zakopane, Poland, September 5-15, 1997. LC 98-29275. (NATO Science Ser.). 1998. 238.00 (*0-7923-5222-X*) Kluwer Academic.

Ciacillo, Billie. Best Bible Crafts. LC 98-67796. 48p. (J). (gr. k-8). 1998. pap. 9.95 (*0-9652041-1-1*) Pack-O-Fun.

Ciafalo, Andrew, jt. auth. see Dobler, Judy.

Ciaffa, Jay A. Max Weber & the Problems of Value-Free Social Science: A Critical Examination of the "Werturteilsstreit" LC 97-51645. 192p. 1998. 34.50 (*0-8387-5395-7*) Bucknell U Pr.

Ciaffone, Bob. Improve Your Poker. 220p. 1997. pap. 20.00 (*0-9661007-0-0*) B Ciaffone.

— Omaha Holdem Poker. 106p. 1999. reprint ed. pap. 20.00 (*0-9661007-2-7*) B Ciaffone.

***Ciaffone, Bob & Finegold, Im Ben.** Smith-Morra Gambit Finegold Defense. 140p. 2000. pap. 12.00 (*0-9661007-3-5*) B Ciaffone.

Ciaffone, Bob & Reuben, Stewart. Pot-Limit & No-Limit Poker. 2nd rev. ed. 224p. 1999. pap. 25.00 (*0-9661007-1-9*) B Ciaffone.

***Ciaglia, Joseph.** Introduction to Digital Imaging. 128p. 2001. pap. 33.33 (*0-13-032136-2*, Prentice Hall) P-H.

Ciagne, Marc, jt. ed. see Kapner, Bill.

Cialdini, Robert B. Influence. 1980. 13.00 (*0-8176-0617-3*) Birkhauser.

Cialdini, Robert B. Influence: Science & Practice. 3rd ed. LC 92-26230. 253p. (C). 1997. pap. 37.00 (*0-673-46751-1*) Addson-Wesley Educ.

Cialdini, Robert B. Influence: Science & Practice. 4th ed. 260p. (C). 2000. pap. 21.99 (*0-321-01147-3*) Addson-Wesley Educ.

— Influence (rev) The Psychology of Persuasion. rev. ed. LC 93-2549. (Illus.). 304p. 1998. pap. 15.00 (*0-688-12816-5*, Quil) HarperTrade.

Cialowicz, Krzysztof, jt. auth. see Adams, Barbara.

Ciambella, Franca, jt. auth. see Davidson, Paul.

Ciambrone, David F. Environmental Life Cycle Analysis. LC 97-8058. 145p. 1997. lib. bdg. 65.00 (*1-56670-214-3*) Lewis Pubs.

— Waste Minimization As a Strategic Weapon. LC 95-14778. 272p. 1995. lib. bdg. 85.00 (*1-56670-135-X*, L1135) Lewis Pubs.

Ciammitti, Luisa, et al, eds. Dosso's Fate: Painting & Court Culture in Renaissance Italy. LC 98-4758. (Issues & Debates Ser.). (Illus.). 1998. pap. 50.00 (*0-89236-505-6*, Pub. by J P Getty Trust) OUP.

Ciampa. Local Area Networks. (Management Information Systems Ser.). 1996. pap. 34.95 (*0-7895-0585-1*) Course Tech.

— Local Area Networks. (Management Information Systems Ser.). 1996. pap. 37.95 (*0-534-20712-X*) S-W Pub.

— Microsoft Frontpage 98. (Computer Applications Ser.). 1998. pap. 27.95 (*0-538-68601-4*) S-W Pub.

— Networking Basics. (Computer Applications Ser.). 1999. pap. 12.00 (*0-538-69043-7*) Thomson Learn.

— Networking Basics. (Computer Applications Ser.). 1999. pap. 40.95 (*0-538-69042-9*) Thomson Learn.

Ciampa, Dan. Calidad Total Guia para Su Implantacion. (SPA.). 312p. (C). 1993. pap. text 9.00 (*0-201-60118-4*) Addison-Wesley.

Ciampa, Dan & Watkins, Michael. Right from the Start: Taking Charge in a New Leadership Role. LC 98-55292. (Illus.). 316p. 1999. 24.95 (*0-87584-750-1*) Harvard Busn.

Ciampa, Leanne H. Friends & Followers in the Bible, Vol. II. 80p. 1993. pap. 2.78 (*0-687-13500-1*) Abingdon.

***Ciampa, Mark D.** Microsoft Frontpage 2000. LC 99-231659. 192p. 1999. pap. 31.95 (*0-538-69092-5*) Sth-Wstrn College.

— Microsoft Photodraw 2000: Beginning Course. LC 00-23848. (Illus.). 2001. pap. 133.95 (*0-538-72428-5*) S-W Pub.

Ciampa, Roy E. The Presence & Function of Scripture in Galatians 1 & 2. (Wissenshaftliche Untersuchungen zum Neuen Testament Ser.: No. 102). 461p. 1998. pap. 95.00 (*3-16-146895-3*, Pub. by JCB Mohr) Coronet Bks.

***Ciampi, Maria L. & Manz, William H.** The Question Presented: Model Appellate Briefs. LC 99-89984. 2000. pap. text 25.00 (*0-87084-419-9*) Anderson Pub Co.

Ciampi, Maria L., et al. The Citation Workbook: How to Beat the Citation Blues. 2nd ed. 108p. (C). 1997. pap. 13.95 (*0-87084-139-4*) Anderson Pub Co.

— The Citation Workbook: How to Beat the Citation Blues, Teacher's Manual. 2nd ed. 160p. (C). 1997. pap. text 13.95 (*0-87084-147-5*) Anderson Pub Co.

Ciampi, Pam. Gardening by the Light of the Moon. (Illus.). 60p. 1998. pap. 6.99 (*1-57532-182-3*) Press-Tige Pub.

Ciampolini, Anna Foschi, jt. ed. see Minni, C. D.

Ciancarini, Paolo. Object-Based Models & Languages for Concurrent Systems: ECOOP '94 Workshop on Models & Languages for Coordination of Parallelism & Distribution, Bologna, Italy, July 5, 1994: Selected Papers. Yonezawa, Akinori et al, eds. (Lecture Notes in Computer Science Ser.: Vol. 924). 1995. write for info. (*0-387-59450-7*) Spr-Verlag.

Ciancarini, Paolo, et al, eds. Object-Based Models & Languages for Concurrent Systems: ECOOP '94 Workshop on Models & Languages for Coordination of Parallelism & Distribution, Bologna, Italy, July 5, 1994: Selected Papers. (Lecture Notes in Computer Science Ser.: Vol. 924). 193p. 1995. 36.00 (*3-540-59450-7*) Spr-Verlag.

Ciancarini, Paolo & Hankin, Chris, eds. Coordination, Languages & Models: Proceedings of the First International Conference COORDINATION '96, Cesena, Italy, April 1996. (Lecture Notes in Computer Science Ser.: Vol. 1061). 443p. 1996. pap. 75.00 (*3-540-61052-9*) Spr-Verlag.

Ciancarini, Paolo, et al. Formal Methods for Open Object-based Distributed Systems: Ifip Tc6/wg6.1 3rd International Conference on Formal Methods for Open Object-based Distributed Systems (fmoods) : February 15-18, 1999, Florence, Italy. LC 98-51608. 11p. 1999. write for info. (*0-7923-8429-6*) Kluwer Academic.

Cianci, Maria. The Best of California. (Illus.). 96p. 1994. 16.95 (*0-00-255478-X*) Collins SF.

Cianci, R., et al, eds. General Relativity & Gravitational Physics: Proceedings of the 9th Italian Conference. 728p. (C). 1991. text 130.00 (*981-02-0765-4*) World Scientific Pub.

Cianci, Roberto, et al, eds. General Relativity & Gravitational Physics: Proceedings of the 7th Italian Conference, Rapallo, Genoa, September 3-6, 1986. 528p. 1987. pap. 59.00 (*9971-5-0258-5*); text 144.00 (*9971-5-0257-7*) World Scientific Pub.

Ciancio, Sebastian G. ADA Guide to Dental Therapeutics. LC 98-194771. (Illus.). 600p. 1998. pap. text 59.00 (*1-891748-00-9*) ADA Publng.

***Cianciolo, Patricia J.** Informational Picture Books for Children. LC 99-39597. (Illus.). 192p. 1999. pap. 38.00 (*0-8389-0774-1*) ALA.

Cianciolo, Patricia J. Picture Books for Children. 4th ed. LC 96-51538. (Illus.). 288p. 1997. 40.00 (*0-8389-0701-6*) ALA.

Cianciulli, A. E., jt. auth. see Zolli, Frank.

***Ciancutti, Arthur R. & Steding, Thomas L.** Built on Trust: Gaining Competitive Advantage in Any Organization. LC 00-24463. 256p. 2000. 24.95 (*0-8092-2446-1*, Contemporary Bks) NTC Contemp Pub Co.

Ciangio, Donna L. & Smith, Karen S. Organizing Manual. (Follow Me! Ser.). 32p. 1997. pap. 15.95 (*1-881307-03-4*, B7034) Natl Pastoral LC.

— Small Group Handbook. (Follow Me! Ser.). 32p. 1997. pap. 9.95 (*1-881307-04-2*, B7042) Natl Pastoral LC.

Ciangio, Donna L., jt. auth. see Smith, Karen S.

Ciangion, Donna L., jt. auth. see Smith, Karen S.

Ciani, Alfred J., ed. see International Reading Association Staff.

Ciani, Maria G., ed. Lycophron - Lexicon Zu Lycophron. (Alpha-Omega, Reihe A Ser.: Bd. XXII). iv, 359p. 1975. 80.00 (*3-487-05593-7*) G Olms Pubs.

Ciani, Maria Grazia. The Regions of Silence: Studies on the Difficulty of Communicating. (London Studies in Classical Philology: Vol. 17). viii, 160p. (C). 1987. 40.00 (*90-70265-17-6*, Pub. by Gieben) J Benjamins Pubng Co.

Ciani, Suzanne. Suzanne Ciani: Dream Songs. 88p. 1995. per. 14.95 (*0-7935-4393-2*, 00306027) H Leonard.

Ciano, Galeazzo. Ciano's Diplomatic Papers. Muggeridge, Malcolm, ed. Head, Stuart, tr. LC 83-45734. reprint ed. 41.50 (*0-404-20060-5*, DG575) AMS Pr.

Ciano, Jim. Ciano, Family Genealogy. (Illus.). 300p. 1994. pap. write for info. (*1-888672-02-1*) J Ciano Pubng.

— Howdy Pardner Pull up a Computer. (Illus.). 150p. 1997. 29.95 (*1-888672-15-3*); pap. 19.95 (*1-888672-14-5*) J Ciano Pubng.

— Pardon Me, Do You Speak Computer? (Illus.) 120p. (Orig.). 1994. pap. 19.95 (*1-888672-04-8*) J Ciano Pubng.

— Phi Sigma Omega, 1991-1992. (Illus.). 145p. (Orig.). 1994. pap. 25.00 (*1-888672-00-5*) J Ciano Pubng.

— User Friendly. 75p. (Orig.). 1994. pap. 9.95 (*1-888672-01-3*) J Ciano Pubng.

Ciano, Jim, ed. see Chevalier, Paul.

Ciano, Jim, ed. see Hull-Schario, Mary.

Ciano, Jim, ed. see McCleary, Marguerite D.

Ciapalo, Roman T., ed. Postmodernism & Christian Philosophy. LC 96-49919. 294p. 1997. pap. 15.00 (*0-8132-0881-5*) Cath U Pr.

***Ciappelli, Giovanni & Rubin, Patricia L., eds.** Art, Memory & Family in Renaissance Florence. LC 99-24200. (Illus.). 400p. 2000. 90.00 (*0-521-64300-7*) Cambridge U Pr.

Ciapponi, Lucia A., ed. see Beroaldo, Filippo.

Ciaraldi, S., jt. ed. see Kolts, J.

Ciaramicoli, Arthur P. Treatment of Abuse & Addiction: A Holistic Approach. LC 97-11439. 264p. 1997. 50.00 (*0-7657-0087-5*) Aronson.

***Ciaramicoli, Arthur P. & Ketcham, Katherine.** The Power of Empathy: A Practical Guide to Creating Intimacy, Self-Understanding & Lasting Love in Your Life. LC 99-89849. 288p. 2000. 24.95 (*0-525-94511-3*, Dutt) Dutton Plume.

Ciaramitaro, Vivian, jt. auth. see Blass, Elliot M.

Ciaran, Fiona. Stained Glass Windows of Canterbury, New Zealand. LC 98-119270. (Illus.). 224p. 1997. pap. 79.95 (*1-877133-39-6*, Pub. by Univ Otago Pr) Intl Spec Bk.

***Ciaravino, Helene.** How to Publish Your Poetry: A Complete Guide to Finding the Right Publishers for Your Work. 2000. pap. 14.95 (*0-7570-0001-0*) Square One.

Ciarcia, Steve. The Best of Ciarcia's Cellar. 453p. 1992. 40.00 (*0-07-011019-0*) McGraw.

Ciarcia, Steve & Laurencot, Elizabeth, eds. Circuit Cellar Project File, Vol. II. (Illus.). 178p. (C). 1993. pap. text 17.95 (*0-9630133-1-9*) Circuit Cellar.

Ciarcia, Steve, jt. auth. see Dahmke, Mark.

Ciardelli, F., et al, eds. Macromolecule-Metal Complexes. (Illus.). 276p. 1995. 163.95 (*3-540-59383-7*) Spr-Verlag.

Ciardelli, F. & Giusti, P. Structural Order in Polymers: International Symposium on Macromolecules, Florence, Italy, 7-12 September 1980. (IUPAC Symposium Ser.). (Illus.). 260p. 1981. 113.00 (*0-08-025296-6*, Pub. by Pergamon Repr) Franklin.

Ciardelli, F., ed. see Advanced Study Institute on ORD & CD (1971: Tierre.

Ciardelli, I., jt. ed. see Lenz, R. W.

Ciardha, Eamonn O., jt. ed. see Ohlmeyer, Jane.

Ciardi, Charmaine L., et al. The Magic of Grandparenting. LC 95-7659. 1995. pap. 9.95 (*0-8050-4075-7*) H Holt & Co.

Ciardi, J. E., et al. Genetically Engineered Vaccines. LC 92-48784. (Advances in Experimental Medicine & Biology Ser.: Vol. 327). (Illus.). 336p. (C). 1993. text 105.00 (*0-306-44349-X*, Kluwer Plenum) Kluwer Academic.

Ciardi, John. The Birds of Pompeii. LC 84-28077. 80p. 1985. pap. 14.00 (*0-938626-45-0*) U of Ark Pr.

— Ciardi Himself: Fifteen Essays in the Reading, Writing, & Teaching of Poetry. LC 89-31386. 155p. 1989. pap. 14.00 (*1-55728-085-1*) U of Ark Pr.

— The Collected Poems of John Ciardi. Cifelli, Edward M., ed. LC 96-46331. 456p. 1997. pap. 30.00 (*1-55728-449-0*) U of Ark Pr.

— Doodle Soup. 64p. (J). (gr. 4-7). 1992. pap. 5.95 (*0-395-61617-4*) HM.

— Doodle Soup: Poems. 1985. 11.15 (*0-606-01438-1*, Pub. by Turtleback) Demco.

— Echoes: Poems Left Behind. LC 88-21927. 80p. (Orig.). 1989. pap. 14.00 (*1-55728-063-0*) U of Ark Pr.

— Hopeful Trout & Other Limericks. 64p. (J). (gr. 4-7). 1992. pap. 5.95 (*0-395-61616-6*) HM.

— Hopeful Trout & Other Limericks. 1989. 11.15 (*0-606-01437-3*, Pub. by Turtleback) Demco.

— Man Who Sang the Sillies. LC 61-11734. (Illus.). (J). (gr. 4-6). 1961. lib. bdg. 11.89 (*0-397-30569-9*) HarpC Child Bks.

— The Monster Den: or Look What Happened at My House - And to It. LC 90-85904. (Illus.). 64p. (J). (gr. k up). 1991. reprint ed. 13.95 (*1-878093-35-5*, Wordsong) Boyds Mills Pr.

— Poems of Love & Marriage. LC 88-17229. 48p. (Orig.). 1989. 16.00 (*1-55728-053-3*) U of Ark Pr.

— The Reason for the Pelican. LC 93-61163. (Illus.). 64p. (J). (gr. 1 up). 1994. 13.95 (*1-56397-370-7*, Wordsong) Boyds Mills Pr.

— Saipan: The War Diary of John Ciardi. LC 87-25564. 155p. 1988. pap. 14.00 (*1-55728-018-5*) U of Ark Pr.

— Someone Could Win a Polar Bear. LC 92-61179. (Illus.). 64p. (J). (ps-3). 1993. 13.95 (*1-56397-205-0*, Wordsong) Boyds Mills Pr.

— Stations of the Air. LC 92-8657. 64p. 1993. 10.50 (*0-933532-86-5*) BkMk.

— You Know Who. LC 90-85903. (Illus.). 64p. (J). (gr. k up). 1991. reprint ed. 13.95 (*1-878093-34-7*, Wordsong) Boyds Mills Pr.

— You Read to Me, I'll Read to You. LC 62-16296. (Illus.). 64p. (J). (gr. k-6). 1961. lib. bdg. 12.89 (*0-397-30646-6*) HarpC Child Bks.

— You Read to Me, I'll Read to You. (J). 1987. 12.15 (*0-606-03510-9*, Pub. by Turtleback) Demco.

— You Read to Me, I'll Read to You. LC 62-16296. (Trophy Nonfiction Bk.). (Illus.). 64p. (J). (ps-3). 1987. reprint ed. pap. 7.95 (*0-06-446060-6*, HarpTrophy) HarpC Child Bks.

Ciardi, John, tr. Purgatorio by Dante. 1961. mass mkt. 7.99 (*0-451-62714-8*, Ment) NAL.

Ciardi, John, jt. auth. see Asimov, Isaac.

Ciardi, John, tr. see Dante Alighieri.

***Ciardi, Margaret Russell, et al.** A Guide to School Wide Programs & Practices for Improving Early Literacy. 200p. 1999. pap. 13.00 (*0-89292-291-5*) Educ Dev Ctr.

Ciardiello, Jean A. & Bell, Morris D., eds. Vocational Rehabilitation of Persons with Prolonged Psychiatric Disorders. LC 87-26082. (Contemporary Medicine & Public Health Ser.). 320p. 1988. text 48.50 (*0-8018-3635-2*) Johns Hopkins.

Ciardullo, Carmen V. Micro Action Chemistry. (Illus.). (Orig.). 1990. pap., teacher ed. write for info. (*1-877991-23-6*, AP2044); pap., student ed. write for info. (*1-877991-22-8*, AP2042) Flinn Scientific.

Ciarlante, Deanna, jt. auth. see Sch Utte, Hellmut.

Ciarlet, P. G. Lectures on Three-Dimensional Elasticity. (Tata Institute Lectures on Mathematics). 160p. 1984. 26.95 (*0-387-12331-8*) Spr-Verlag.

— Mathematical Elasticity Vol. 1: Three-Dimensional Elasticity. (Studies in Mathematics & Its Applications: Vol. 20). 496p. 1994. pap. 98.50 (*0-444-81776-X*, North Holland) Elsevier.

— Mathematical Elasticity Vol. II: Theory of Plates. 262p. 1997. 166.50 (*0-444-82570-3*, North Holland) Elsevier.

— Numerical Linear Algebra & Optimisation. (Cambridge Texts in Applied Mathematics Ser.: No. 2). 452p. 1989. pap. text 44.95 (*0-521-33984-7*) Cambridge U Pr.

— Plates & Junctions in Elastic Multi-Structures: An Asymptotic Analysis. Lions, J. L., ed. (Recherches en Mathematiques Appliquees Ser.: Vol. 14). vii, 215p. 1990. 44.95 (*0-387-52917-9*) Spr-Verlag.

Ciarlet, P. G. & Lions, J. L. Handbook of Numerical Analysis: Pt. 2, Techniques of Scientific Computing; Pt. 3, Numerical Methods for Solids, Vol. V. 828p. Date not set. 172.50 (*0-444-82278-X*, North Holland) Elsevier.

— Handbook of Numerical Analysis Vol. III: Techniques of Scientific Computing (Pt. 1), Numerical Methods for Solids (Pt. 1), Solution of Equations in Rn (Pt. 2) 788p. 1994. 171.50 (*0-444-89928-6*, North Holland) Elsevier.

Ciarlet, P. G. & Lions, J. L., eds. Handbook of Numerical Analysis: Finite Element Methods (Part 2), Numerical Methods for Solids (Part 2) 984p. 1995. 190.00 (*0-444-81794-8*, North Holland) Elsevier.

C

An Asterisk (*) at the beginning of an entry indicates that the title is appearing for the first time.

— Handbook of Numerical Analysis Vol. 2: Finite Element Methods, Pt. I. 928p. 1991. 190.00 (*0-444-70365-9*, North Holland) Elsevier.

Ciarlet, P. G., et al. Finite Difference Methods: Solution of Equations in RN. (Handbook of Numerical Analysis Ser.: Vol. 1). 652p. 1990. 166.50 (*0-444-70366-7*) Elsevier.

Ciarlet, P. G., ed. see Crouzeix, M. & Rappaz, J.

Ciarlet, P. G., ed. see Grisvard, P.

Ciarlet, P. G., ed. see Le Tallec, P. V.

Ciarlet, P. G., ed. see Rabier, P. J. & Oden, J. Tinsley.

Ciarlet, Philippe G., et al, eds. Asymptotic Methods for Elastic Structures: Proceedings: International Conference on Asymptotic Methods for Elastic Structures (1993: Lisbon, Portugal) LC 95-7856. 291p. (C). 1995. 141.95 (*3-11-014731-9*) De Gruyter.

Ciarletta, Michele & Iesan, Dorin. Non-Classical Elastic Solids. LC 93-4718. (Pitman Research Notes in Mathematics Ser.). 1993. lib. bdg. write for info. (*0-582-22716-X*) Longman.

***Ciarlini, P.** Advanced Mathematical & Computational Tools in Metrology IV. LC 99-89211. (Series on Advances in Mathematics for Applied Sciences). 2000. write for info. (*981-02-4216-6*) World Scientific Pub.

Ciarlini, P. Advanced Mathematical Tools in Metrology II: Oxford, U.K., 27-30 September 1995. LC 96-2907. (Series on Advances in Mathematics for Applied Sciences). 304p. 1996. write for info. (*981-02-2618-7*) World Scientific Pub.

Ciarlini, P., et al. Advanced Mathematical Tools in Metrology: Proceedings of the International Workshop. (Series on Advances in Mathematics). 288p. 1994. text 86.00 (*981-02-1758-7*) World Scientific Pub.

Ciarlo, Hector O. El Camino de Occidente: Introduccion a las Humanidades. LC 82-7003. (SPA.). 258p. (Orig.). (C). 1984. pap. 5.00 (*0-8477-3504-4*) U of PR Pr.

— Critica de la Razon Poetica. 170p. (Orig.). (C). 1982. pap. 3.50 (*0-8477-2824-2*) U of PR Pr.

— El Escritor y su Obra: Al Encuentro de Concha Melendez y otros ensayos. LC 82-6894. (SPA.). 138p. (Orig.). 1982. pap. 3.50 (*0-8477-3509-5*) U of PR Pr.

Ciarloni, Diane, et al. Legends Vol. 3: Outstanding Quarter Horse Stallions & Mares. 3rd ed. (Illus.). 207p. 1997. pap. 15.95 (*0-911647-40-6*) Western Horseman.

Ciaro, M. & Hendershot, Denton. Choices: Ending Abuse in Intimate Relationships. (Illus.). (Orig.). 1991. pap. write for info. (*0-9629030-0-0*) Denton Consulting.

Ciarrapico, Anna M. Country Risk: A Theoretical Framework of Analysis. (Luiss Ser.: No. 4). 137p. 1992. 77.95 (*1-85521-099-1*, Pub. by Dartmth Pub) Ashgate Pub Co.

Ciarrocchi, Joseph W. The Doubting Disease: Help for Scrupulosity & Religious Compulsions. LC 94-25222. (Integration Bks.). 208p. (Orig.). 1995. pap. 14.95 (*0-8091-3553-1*) Paulist Pr.

— A Minister's Handbook of Mental Disorders. LC 93-11092. (Integration Bks.). 224p. 1993. pap. 16.95 (*0-8091-3403-9*) Paulist Pr.

— Why Are You Worrying? LC 95-3039. (Illumination Bks.). (Illus.). 80p. (Orig.). 1995. pap. 5.95 (*0-8091-3561-2*) Paulist Pr.

Ciarrocchi, Joseph W. & Wicks, Robert J. Psychotherapy with Priests, Protestant Clergy & Catholic Religious: A Practical Guide. 250p. 2000. 40.00 (*1-887841-22-9*, 65430, Psychosocial) Intl Univs Pr.

Ciattini, Saverio, et al. Ferrari Mugello. (Illus.). 160p. 1991. 65.00 (*88-7911-067-5*, Pub. by Giorgio Nada Editore) Howell Pr VA.

Ciavaroli, Jules. AEC Drafting Fundamentals. LC 93-48079. 272p. (C). 1994. mass mkt. 33.00 (*0-314-93452-9*) West Pub.

Ciavolella, Massimo & Beecher, Donald A., trs. Annibal Caro, the Scruffy Scoundrels. 125p. 1989. pap. 6.95 (*0-88920-103-X*, PDH45, Pub. by Dovehouse) Sterling.

Ciavolella, Massimo & Iannucci, Amilcare, eds. Saturn: From Antiquity to the Renaissance. 181p. 1992. 28.00 (*1-895537-01-0*, DH89, Pub. by Dovehouse) Sterling.

Ciavolella, Massimo, jt. ed. see Beecher, Donald.

Ciavolella, Massimo, ed. see Ferrand, Jacques.

Ciavolella, Massimo, ed. & tr. see Bernini, Gian Lorenzo.

Ciavolella, Massimo, ed. & tr. see Ferrand, Jacques.

Ciavonne, Jean. Carlos, Light the Farolito. LC 94-24510. (Illus.). 32p. (J). (gr. k-3). 1995. 14.95 (*0-395-66759-3*, Clarion Bks) HM.

***CIB Publishing Staff.** Getting into Financial Services. 200p. 1998. pap. 24.00 (*0-85660-378-3*, Pub. by Chartered Bank) St Mut.

CIB Staff, ed. Learning Banking. (C). 1989. 50.00 (*0-85297-216-4*, Pub. by Chartered Bank) St Mut.

***CIB W89 International Conference on Building Education and Research, et al.** Building Education & Research: Proceedings of the CIB W89 International Conference on Building Education & Research (BEAR'98), 8-10 July 1998, Brisbane, Australia. LC 98-218260. (Illus.). 1998. write for info. (*0-419-23800-X*, E & FN Spon) Routledge.

CIBA Foundation Staff. Abortion: Medical Progress & Social Implication - Symposium, No. 115. (CIBA Foundation Symposium Ser.). 320p. 1985. 128.00 (*0-471-91084-8*) Wiley.

— Acute Diarrhea in Childhood. LC 76-13875. (CIBA Foundation Symposium: New Ser.: No. 42). 385p. reprint ed. pap. 119.40 (*0-8357-5089-2*, 202217000024) Bks Demand.

— Adhesion & Microorganism Pathogenicity. LC 81-19829. (Ciba Foundation Symposium: New Ser.: No. 80). (Illus.). 356p. reprint ed. pap. 110.40 (*0-8357-8780-X*, 203361000086) Bks Demand.

— Antidepressants & Receptor Function. (CIBA Foundation Symposium Ser.: No. 123). 304p. 1986. 128.00 (*0-471-91089-9*) Wiley.

— Applications of Plant Cell & Tissue Culture. LC 88-10687. (CIBA Foundation Symposium Ser.: No. 137). 280p. 1988. 128.00 (*0-471-91886-5*) Wiley.

— Aromatic Amino Acids in the Brain. LC 73-91643. (Ciba Foundation Symposium: New Ser.: No. 22). 406p. reprint ed. pap. 125.90 (*0-8357-5752-8*, 202215200024) Bks Demand.

— Atherogenesis: Initiating Factors. LC 73-76974. (CIBA Foundation Symposium: New Ser.: No. 12). 296p. reprint ed. pap. 91.80 (*0-8357-5830-3*, 202214300024) Bks Demand.

— Autoimmunity & Autoimmune Disease. LC 87-10493. (CIBA Foundation Symposium Ser.: No. 129). 288p. 1987. 128.00 (*0-471-91095-3*) Wiley.

— Bioactive Compounds from Plants - Symposium No. 154. LC 90-40978. (CIBA Foundation Symposium Ser.: No. 154). 254p. 1990. 160.00 (*0-471-92691-4*) Wiley.

— Biochemistry & Pharmacology of Platelets. LC QP0097.. (Ciba Foundation Symposium: New Ser.: No. 35). 360p. reprint ed. pap. 111.60 (*0-8357-7217-9*, 202216300025) Bks Demand.

— Biochemistry of Macrophages: Symposium on Biochemistry of Macrophages Held at the CIBA Foundation, 16-18 April 1985. LC QR0185.8.M3B. (Ciba Foundation Symposium: New Ser.: No. 118). (Illus.). 266p. reprint ed. pap. 82.50 (*0-8357-4562-7*, 203746400008) Bks Demand.

— Biological Asymmetry & Handedness - Symposium No. 162. LC 91-22440. (CIBA Foundation Symposium Ser.: No. 162). 338p. 1991. 128.00 (*0-471-92961-1*) Wiley.

— Biological Roles of Copper. LC 80-23396. (Ciba Foundation Symposium: New Ser.: No. 79). 351p. reprint ed. pap. 108.90 (*0-8357-7235-7*, 202219800024) Bks Demand.

— The Biology of Hyaluronan. LC 89-30662. (CIBA Foundation Symposium Ser.: No. 143). 308p. 1989. 128.00 (*0-471-92305-2*) Wiley.

— The Biology of Nicotine Dependence. LC 90-12213. (CIBA Foundation Symposium Ser.: No. 152). 274p. 1990. 147.95 (*0-471-92688-4*) Wiley.

— Blood Cells & Vessel Walls: Functional Interactions. LC 79-26528. (CIBA Foundation Symposium: New Ser.: No. 71). 369p. reprint ed. pap. 114.40 (*0-8357-7325-6*, 202219000024) Bks Demand.

— Breast-Feeding & the Mother. LC 76-44816. (CIBA Foundation Symposium: New Ser.: No. 45). 288p. reprint ed. pap. 89.30 (*0-8357-7396-5*, 202217300024) Bks Demand.

— Calcium & the Cell. LC 86-9246. (CIBA Foundation Symposium Ser.: No. 122). 310p. 1986. 128.00 (*0-471-91088-0*) Wiley.

CIBA Foundation Staff. Carbohydrate Recognition in Cellular Function - Symposium No. 145. LC 89-9153. (CIBA Foundation Symposium Ser.: No. 145). 304p. 1989. 128.00 (*0-471-92307-9*) Wiley.

CIBA Foundation Staff. Carbon-Fluorine Compounds: Chemistry, Biochemistry & Biological Activities. LC 72-76005. (CIBA Foundation Symposium: New Ser.: No. 2). 425p. reprint ed. pap. 131.80 (*0-608-13515-1*, 202213500024) Bks Demand.

— Catalytic Antibodies - Symposium No. 159. (CIBA Foundation Symposium Ser.: No. 159). 270p. 1991. 155.00 (*0-471-92962-X*, Wiley-Interscience) Wiley.

— Cell & Molecular Biology of Vertebrate Hard Tissues. LC 87-10776. (CIBA Foundation Symposium Ser.: No. 136). 318p. 1988. 128.00 (*0-471-91885-7*) Wiley.

— Cell Patterning. LC 78-304197. (CIBA Foundation Symposium: New Ser.: No. 29). 364p. reprint ed. pap. 112.90 (*0-608-13981-5*, 202215700024) Bks Demand.

— Cellular Basis of Morphogenesis - Symposium No. 144. LC 89-5831. (CIBA Foundation Symposium Ser.: No. 144). 316p. 1989. 128.00 (*0-471-92306-0*) Wiley.

— Cerebral Vascular Smooth Muscle & Its Control. LC 77-28855. (CIBA Foundation Symposium: New Ser.: No. 56). 408p. reprint ed. pap. 126.50 (*0-608-14306-5*, 202218100024) Bks Demand.

— Child Sexual Abuse Within the Family. 1993. pap. 17.95 (*0-415-04292-5*) Routledge.

— Child Sexual Abuse Within the Family. 176p. 1984. 29.95 (*0-422-79280-2*, 9325, Pub. by Tavistock); pap. 15.95 (*0-685-10150-9*, 9326, Pub. by Tavistock) Routldge.

— The Childhood Environment & Adult Disease. LC 90-13144. (CIBA Foundation Symposium Ser.: No. 156). 252p. 1991. 128.00 (*0-471-92957-3*) Wiley.

— Chronic Fatigue Syndrome - Symposium No. 173. LC 00-92. (CIBA Foundation Symposium Ser.: No. 173). 376p. 1993. 128.00 (*0-471-93618-9*) Wiley.

— Civilization & Science in Conflict or Collaboration? LC 77-188826. (CIBA Foundation Symposium: New Ser.: No. 1). 237p. reprint ed. pap. 73.50 (*0-608-13517-8*, 202213400024) Bks Demand.

— Clinical Applications of TGF- - Symposium No. 157. LC 90-13139. (CIBA Foundation Symposium Ser.: No. 157). 264p. 1991. 128.00 (*0-471-92811-9*) Wiley.

— Cocaine: Scientific & Social Dimensions. Edwards, Griffith, ed. (CIBA Foundation Symposium Ser.: No. 166). 316p. 1992. 128.00 (*0-471-93179-9*, Wiley-Interscience) Wiley.

— Communicating Science to the Public. LC 87-8261. (CIBA Foundation Symposium Ser.). 224p. 1987. 140.00 (*0-471-91511-4*) Wiley.

— Congenital Disorders of Erythropoiesis. LC RC0647.E7. (CIBA Foundation Symposium: New Ser.: No. 37). 416p. reprint ed. pap. 129.00 (*0-608-13975-0*, 202216500025) Bks Demand.

— Corneal Graft Failure. LC 73-82445. (CIBA Foundation Symposium: New Ser.: No. 15). 371p. reprint ed. pap. 115.10 (*0-608-13501-1*, 202214600024) Bks Demand.

— Corticotropin-Releasing Factor - Symposium No. 172. LC 92-36532. (CIBA Foundation Symposium Ser.: No. 172). 368p. 1993. 128.00 (*0-471-93448-8*) Wiley.

— Development of Mammalian Absorptive Processes. LC 79-20804. (Ciba Foundation Symposium: New Ser.: No. 70). 350p. reprint ed. pap. 108.50 (*0-608-14293-X*, 202218900024) Bks Demand.

— Development of the Autonomic Nervous System. LC 81-9464. (CIBA Foundation Symposium: New Ser.: No. 83). (Illus.). 399p. reprint ed. pap. 123.70 (*0-8357-8860-1*, 203361100086) Bks Demand.

— Drug Concentrations in Neuropsychiatry. LC 80-11309. (CIBA Foundation Symposium: New Ser.: No. 74). 274p. reprint ed. pap. 85.00 (*0-608-14286-7*, 202219300024) Bks Demand.

— Embryogenesis in Mammals. LC 76-7009. (CIBA Foundation Symposium: New Ser.: No. 40). 316p. reprint ed. pap. 98.00 (*0-608-14316-2*, 202216800024) Bks Demand.

— Energy Transformation in Biological Systems. LC 76-350357. (CIBA Foundation Symposium: New Ser.: No. 31). 426p. reprint ed. pap. 132.10 (*0-608-13979-3*, 202215900024) Bks Demand.

— Environmental Chemicals, Enzyme Function & Human Disease. LC 80-18000. (CIBA Foundation Symposium: New Ser.: 76). 390p. reprint ed. pap. 120.90 (*0-608-14282-4*, 202219500024) Bks Demand.

— Enzyme Defects & Immune Dysfunction. LC 79-17092. (CIBA Foundation Symposium: New Ser.: No. 68). 299p. reprint ed. pap. 92.70 (*0-608-14295-6*, 202218800024) Bks Demand.

— Enzymes in Organic Synthesis. LC 85-115658. (CIBA Foundation Symposium: New Ser.: No. 111). 256p. reprint ed. pap. 79.40 (*0-8357-8870-9*, 203361400086) Bks Demand.

— Evolution of Hydrothermal Ecosystems on Earth & Mars - Symposium No. 202. LC 96-31351. (CIBA Foundation Symposium Ser.). 346p. 1996. 128.00 (*0-471-96509-X*) Wiley.

— Exploring Brain Functional Anatomy with Positron Tomography - Symposium No. 163. Porter, R., ed. LC 91-40214. (CIBA Foundation Symposium Ser.: No. 163). 298p. 1992. 128.00 (*0-471-92970-0*, Wiley-Interscience) Wiley.

— Filariasis. LC 86-28154. (CIBA Foundation Symposium Ser.: No. 127). 316p. 1987. 128.00 (*0-471-91093-7*) Wiley.

— The Freezing of Mammalian Embryos. LC 77-10122. (CIBA Foundation Symposium: New Ser.: No. 52). 340p. reprint ed. pap. 105.40 (*0-608-14308-1*, 202217700024) Bks Demand.

— Functions of the Proteoglycans. LC 86-18886. (CIBA Foundation Symposium Ser.: No. 124). 310p. 1986. 128.00 (*0-471-91090-2*) Wiley.

— Further Perspectives in Organic Chemistry. LC QD0241.F87. (CIBA Foundation Symposium: New Ser.: No. 53). 220p. reprint ed. pap. 68.20 (*0-608-10061-7*, 202217800024) Bks Demand.

— The Future As an Academic Discipline. LC 76-363694. (CIBA Foundation Symposium: New Ser.: No. 36). 240p. reprint ed. pap. 74.40 (*0-608-13976-9*, 202216400024) Bks Demand.

— The Future of Philanthropic Foundations. LC 75-398199. (CIBA Foundation Symposium: New Ser.: No. 30). 248p. reprint ed. pap. 76.90 (*0-608-13980-7*, 202215800024) Bks Demand.

— Genetic Analysis of Tumour Suppression - Symposium No. 142. (CIBA Foundation Symposium Ser.: No. 142). 268p. 1989. 128.00 (*0-471-92299-4*) Wiley.

— Growth Factors in Biology & Medicine. (CIBA Foundation Symposium Ser.: No. 116). 320p. 1985. 128.00 (*0-471-91085-6*) Wiley.

— Haemopoietic Stem Cells. LC 73-76975. (CIBA Foundation Symposium: New Ser.: No. 13). 355p. reprint ed. pap. 110.10 (*0-608-13503-8*, 202214400024) Bks Demand.

— Hard Tissue Growth, Repair & Remineralization. LC 72-97287. (CIBA Foundation Symposium: New Ser.: No. 11). 466p. reprint ed. pap. 144.50 (*0-608-13505-4*, 202214200024) Bks Demand.

— Health & Disease in Tribal Societies. LC 77-9478. (CIBA Foundation Symposium: New Ser.: No. 49). 352p. reprint ed. pap. 109.20 (*0-608-14310-3*, 202217500024) Bks Demand.

— Health & Industrial Growth. LC 76-370643. (CIBA Foundation Symposium: New Ser.: No. 32). 275p. reprint ed. pap. 85.30 (*0-608-13978-5*, 202216000024) Bks Demand.

— Health Care in a Changing Setting: The U. K. Experience. LC 76-15417. (CIBA Foundation Symposium: New Ser.: No. 43). 196p. reprint ed. pap. 60.80 (*0-608-14314-6*, 202217100024) Bks Demand.

— Host-Guest Molecular Interactions: From Chemistry to Biology. LC 91-330. (CIBA Foundation Symposium Ser.: No. 158). 288p. 1991. 155.00 (*0-471-92958-1*) Wiley.

— Human Genetic Information: Science, Law & Ethics. LC 89-70550. (CIBA Foundation Symposium Ser.: No. 149). 229p. 1990. 128.00 (*0-471-92624-8*) Wiley.

— The Human Lens: In Relations to Cataract. LC 73-85703. (CIBA Foundation Symposium: New Ser.: No. 19). 336p. reprint ed. pap. 104.20 (*0-608-13495-3*, 202215000024) Bks Demand.

— Human Muscle Fatigue: Physiological Mechanisms. LC 81-7472. (CIBA Foundation Symposium: New Ser.: No. 82). (Illus.). 324p. reprint ed. pap. 100.50 (*0-8357-6148-7*, 203421800089) Bks Demand.

— IgE, Mast Cells & the Allergic Response. LC 89-24895. (CIBA Foundation Symposium Ser.: No. 147). 292p. 1990. 128.00 (*0-471-92309-5*) Wiley.

— Immunopotentiation. LC 73-84990. (CIBA Foundation Symposium: New Ser.: No. 18). 365p. reprint ed. pap. 113.20 (*0-608-13496-1*, 202214900024) Bks Demand.

— Interactions Among Cell Signalling Systems - Symposium No. 164. LC 92-95. (CIBA Foundation Symposium Ser.: No. 164). 280p. 1992. 128.00 (*0-471-93073-3*) Wiley.

— Iron Metabolism. LC 77-24153. (CIBA Foundation Symposium: New Ser.: No. 51). 401p. reprint ed. pap. 124.40 (*0-608-14309-X*, 202217600024) Bks Demand.

— Junctional Complexes of Epithelial Cells: Symposium No. 125. (CIBA Foundation Symposium Ser.). 284p. 1987. 128.00 (*0-471-91091-0*) Wiley.

— Law & Ethics of A. I. D. & Embryo Transfer. LC 73-80904. (CIBA Foundation Symposium: New Ser.: No. 17). 118p. reprint ed. pap. 36.60 (*0-608-13497-X*, 202214800024) Bks Demand.

— Locomotion of Tissue Cells. LC 73-80386. (CIBA Foundation Symposium: New Ser.: No. 14). 389p. reprint ed. pap. 120.60 (*0-608-13502-X*, 202214500024) Bks Demand.

— Lung Liquids. LC 76-870. (CIBA Foundation Symposium: New Ser.: No. 38). 340p. reprint ed. pap. 105.40 (*0-608-14317-0*, 202216600024) Bks Demand.

— Major Mental Handicap: Methods & Costs of Prevention. LC 78-15495. (CIBA Foundation Symposium: New Ser.: No. 59). 234p. reprint ed. pap. 72.60 (*0-608-14301-4*, 202218300024) Bks Demand.

— Medical Care of Prisoners & Detainees. LC 73-82148. (CIBA Foundation Symposium: New Ser.: No. 16). 246p. reprint ed. pap. 76.30 (*0-608-13499-6*, 202214700024) Bks Demand.

— Medical Research Systems in Europe: A Joint Welcome Trust-Ciba Foundation Symposium. LC 73-86342. (CIBA Foundation Symposium: New Ser.: No. 21). 343p. reprint ed. pap. 106.40 (*0-608-13986-6*, 202215100024) Bks Demand.

— Melatonin & the Pineal: Symposium No. 117. 320p. 1985. 128.00 (*0-471-91086-4*) Wiley.

— Metabolic Activities of the Lung. LC 80-20318. (CIBA Foundation Symposium: New Ser.: No. 78). 411p. reprint ed. pap. 127.50 (*0-608-14278-6*, 202219700024) Bks Demand.

— Metastasis. LC 88-8494. (CIBA Foundation Symposium Ser.: No. 141). 266p. 1989. 128.00 (*0-471-91513-0*) Wiley.

— Microbial Toxins & Diarrhoeal Disease. LC 85-193279. (CIBA Foundation Symposium: New Ser.: No. 112). (Illus.). 296p. reprint ed. pap. 91.80 (*0-8357-6212-2*, 203421900089) Bks Demand.

— Molecular Approaches to Human Polygenic Diseases. LC 87-13374. (CIBA Foundation Symposium Ser.: No. 130). 284p. 1987. 128.00 (*0-471-91096-1*) Wiley.

— Molecular Control of Haemopoiesis - Symposium No. 148. LC 89-24869. (CIBA Foundation Symposium Ser.: No. 148). 242p. 1990. 128.00 (*0-471-92561-6*) Wiley.

— Molecular Interactions & Activity in Proteins. LC 78-14500. (CIBA Foundation Symposium: New Ser.: No. 60). 287p. reprint ed. pap. 89.00 (*0-608-14299-9*, 202218400024) Bks Demand.

— Monoamine Oxidase & Its Inhibition. LC 76-10396. (CIBA Foundation Symposium: New Ser.: No. 39). 427p. reprint ed. pap. 132.40 (*0-608-14595-5*, 202216700024) Bks Demand.

— Myopia & the Control of Eye Growth - Symposium No. 155. LC 90-13012. (CIBA Foundation Symposium Ser.: No. 155). 266p. 1991. 128.00 (*0-471-92692-2*) Wiley.

— The Nature & Origin of Amyloid Fibrils: Symposium, No. 199. LC 96-2872. (CIBA Foundation Symposium Ser.). 266p. 1996. 128.00 (*0-471-96361-5*) Wiley.

— Neural Tube Defects, No. 181. (CIBA Foundation Symposium Ser.: Vol. 181). 310p. 1994. 128.00 (*0-471-94172-7*) Wiley.

— Neurobiology of Incontinence - Symposium No. 151. LC 90-12321. (CIBA Foundation Symposium Ser.: No. 151). 346p. 1990. 128.00 (*0-471-92687-6*) Wiley.

— Novel Diarrhea Viruses: Symposium. LC 86-32597. (CIBA Foundation Symposium Ser.: No. 128). 280p. 1987. 128.00 (*0-471-91094-5*) Wiley.

— Novel Infectious Agents & the Central Nervous System. LC 87-31740. (CIBA Foundation Symposium Ser.: No. 135). 288p. 1988. 128.00 (*0-471-91512-2*) Wiley.

— Ontogeny of Acquired Immunity. LC 72-81001. (CIBA Foundation Symposium: New Ser.: No. 5). 293p. reprint ed. pap. 90.90 (*0-608-13513-5*, 202213700024) Bks Demand.

— Origins & Consequences of Obesity: Symposium No. 201. LC 96-24161. (CIBA Foundation Symposium Ser.). 288p. 1996. 128.00 (*0-471-96506-5*) Wiley.

— Outcome of Severe Damage to the Central Nervous System. LC 76-361019. (CIBA Foundation Symposium: New Ser.: No. 34). 364p. reprint ed. pap. 112.90 (*0-608-13977-7*, 202216200024) Bks Demand.

— Papillomaviruses. (CIBA Foundation Symposium Ser.: No. 120). 268p. 1986. 128.00 (*0-471-99837-0*) Wiley.

— Parasites in the Immunized Host: Mechanisms of Survival. LC 75-311586. (CIBA Foundation Symposium: New Ser.: No. 25). 288p. reprint ed. pap. 89.30 (*0-608-13984-X*, 202215400024) Bks Demand.

— Parent-Infant Interaction. LC 77-676760. (CIBA Foundation Symposium: New Ser.: No. 33). 336p. reprint ed. pap. 104.20 (*0-608-10681-X*, 202216100024); reprint ed. pap. 95.80 (*0-608-30668-1*, 2022161) Bks Demand.

— Pathogenic Mycoplasmas. LC 72-88563. (CIBA Foundation Symposium: New Ser.: No. 6). 414p. reprint ed. pap. 128.40 (*0-608-13512-7*, 202213800024) Bks Demand.

— Peptide Transport in Bacteria & Mammalian Cut. LC 72-76006. (Ciba Foundation Symposium: New Ser.: No. 4). 170p. reprint ed. pap. 52.70 (*0-608-13514-3*, 202213600024) Bks Demand.

— Perinatal Infections. LC 80-23631. (CIBA Foundation Symposium: New Ser.: No. 77). 304p. reprint ed. pap. 94.30 (*0-608-14280-8*, 202219600024) Bks Demand.

— Phosphorus in the Environment: Its Chemistry & Biochemistry. LC 78-4289. (CIBA Foundation Symposium: New Ser.: No. 57). 330p. reprint ed. pap. 102.30 (*0-608-14304-9*, 202218200024) Bks Demand.

An Asterisk (*) at the beginning of an entry indicates that the title is appearing for the first time.

— The Physiological Basis of Starling's Law of the Heart. LC 74-77177. (CIBA Foundation Symposium: New Ser.: No. 24). 308p. reprint ed. pap. 95.50 (*0-608-13985-8*, 202215300024) Bks Demand.
— Physiology, Emotion & Psychosomatic Illness. LC 72-93253. (CIBA Foundation Symposium: New Ser.: No. 8). 430p. reprint ed. pap. 133.30 (*0-608-13508-9*, 202214000024) Bks Demand.
— Plant Resistance to Viruses: Symposium No. 133. (CIBA Foundation Symposium Ser.). 226p. 1987. 152.00 (*0-471-91263-8*) Wiley.
— The Poisoned Patient: The Role of the Laboratory. LC 75-317672. (CIBA Foundation Symposium: New Ser.: No. 26). 333p. reprint ed. pap. 103.30 (*0-608-13983-1*, 202215500024) Bks Demand.
— Polymerization in Biological Systems. LC 72-86558. (CIBA Foundation Symposium: New Ser.: No. 7). 322p. reprint ed. pap. 99.90 (*0-608-13510-0*, 202213900024) Bks Demand.
— Polypeptide Hormones: Molecular & Cellular Aspects. LC 76-2666. (CIBA Foundation Symposium: New Ser.: No. 41). 400p. reprint ed. pap. 124.00 (*0-608-14315-4*, 202216900024) Bks Demand.
— Post-Implantation Development in the Mouse. LC 92-113. (CIBA Foundation Symposium Ser.: No. 165). 326p. 1992. 128.00 (*0-471-93384-8*, Wiley-Interscience) Wiley.
— Protein Conformation - Symposium No. 161. LC 91-22448. (CIBA Foundation Symposium Ser.: No. 161). 282p. 1991. 128.00 (*0-471-92969-7*, Wiley-Interscience) Wiley.
— Protein Degradation in Health & Disease. LC 80-15308. (CIBA Foundation Symposium: New Ser.: No. 75). 428p. reprint ed. pap. 132.70 (*0-608-14283-2*, 202219400024) Bks Demand.
— Protein Turnover. LC 72-96519. (CIBA Foundation Symposium: New Ser.: No. 9). 327p. reprint ed. pap. 101.40 (*0-608-13507-0*, 202214100024) Bks Demand.
— Proto-Oncogenes in Cell Development - Symposium No. 150. LC 90-11986. (CIBA Foundation Symposium Ser.: No. 150). 306p. 1990. 128.00 (*0-471-92686-8*) Wiley.
— Proton Passage Across Cell Membranes. LC 88-25026. (CIBA Foundation Symposium Ser.: No. 139). 278p. 1988. 128.00 (*0-471-91903-9*) Wiley.
— Purine & Pyrimidine Metabolism. LC 76-52420. (CIBA Foundation Symposium: New Ser.: No. 48). 381p. reprint ed. pap. 118.20 (*0-608-14311-1*, 202217400024) Bks Demand.
— Regeneration of Vertebrate Sensory Receptor Cells - Symposium No. 160. LC 91-21619. (CIBA Foundation Symposium Ser.: No. 160). 352p. 1991. 128.00 (*0-471-92960-3*, Wiley-Interscience) Wiley.
— Regulation of the Eukaryotic Cell Cycle - Symposium No. 170. LC 92-28930. (CIBA Foundation Symposium Ser.: No. 170). 300p. 1992. 128.00 (*0-471-93446-1*) Wiley.
— Research & Medical Practice: Their Interaction. LC 76-24846. (CIBA Foundation Symposium: New Ser.: No. 44). 228p. reprint ed. pap. 70.70 (*0-608-14313-8*, 202217200024) Bks Demand.
— Research & the Ageing Population: Symposium No. 134. LC 87-29440. (CIBA Foundation Symposium Ser.). 280p. 1988. 128.00 (*0-471-91420-7*) Wiley.
— Respiratory Tract Mucus. LC 77-16019. (CIBA Foundation Symposium: New Ser.: No. 54). 342p. reprint ed. pap. 106.10 (*0-608-14307-3*, 202217900024) Bks Demand.
— Secondary Metabolites: Their Function & Evolution. (CIBA Foundation Symposium Ser.: Vol. 171). 328p. 1993. 128.00 (*0-471-93447-X*) Wiley.
— Selective Neuronal Death. LC 86-28082. (CIBA Foundation Symposium Ser.: No. 126). 292p. 1987. 128.00 (*0-471-91092-9*) Wiley.
— Sex, Hormones & Behaviour. LC QP0251.. (CIBA Foundation Symposium: New Ser.: No. 62). 390p. reprint ed. pap. 120.90 (*0-608-14298-0*, 202218500025) Bks Demand.
— Silicon Biochemistry: Symposium, No. 121. LC 86-4095. 272p. 1986. 128.00 (*0-471-91025-2*) Wiley.
— Steroids & Neuronal Activity - Symposium No. 153. LC 90-12763. (CIBA Foundation Symposium Ser.: No. 153). 294p. 1990. 128.00 (*0-471-92689-2*) Wiley.
— The Structure & Function of Chromatin. LC 76-357416. (CIBA Foundation Symposium: New Ser.: No. 28). 378p. reprint ed. pap. 117.20 (*0-608-13982-3*, 202215600024) Bks Demand.
— Submolecular Biology & Cancer. LC 79-14324. (CIBA Foundation Symposium: New Ser.: No. 67). 360p. reprint ed. pap. 111.60 (*0-608-14296-4*, 202218700024) Bks Demand.
— Sulphur in Biology. LC 79-24939. (CIBA Foundation Symposium: New Ser.: No. 72). 324p. reprint ed. pap. 100.50 (*0-608-14290-5*, 202219100024) Bks Demand.
— Synthetic Peptides As Antigens. (CIBA Foundation Symposium Ser.: No. 119). 318p. 1986. pap. 128.00 (*0-471-91203-4*) Wiley.
— Tinnitus. LC 81-25761. (CIBA Foundation Symposium: New Ser.: No. 85). 333p. reprint ed. pap. 103.30 (*0-8357-7056-7*, 203361200086) Bks Demand.
— Trends in Enzyme Histochemistry & Cytochemistry. LC 80-11757. (CIBA Foundation Symposium: New Ser.: No. 73). 322p. reprint ed. pap. 99.90 (*0-608-14288-3*, 202219200024) Bks Demand.
— Tumor Necrosis Factor & Related Cytotoxins. LC 87-18975. (CIBA Foundation Symposium Ser.: No. 131). 252p. 1987. 128.00 (*0-471-91097-X*) Wiley.
— Vaccines Against Virally Induced Cancers: Symposium No. 187. LC 94-33207. (CIBA Foundation Symposium Ser.: Vol. 187). 292p. 1995. 128.00 (*0-471-95026-2*) Wiley.
— The Value of Preventive Medicine. LC 84-41915. (CIBA Foundation Symposium: New Ser.: No. 110). (Illus.). 266p. reprint ed. pap. 82.50 (*0-8357-7067-2*, 203361300086) Bks Demand.
CIBA Foundation Staff & Slavkin, Hal. C. Dental Enamel, Vol. 205. LC 96-42297. (CIBA Foundation Symposium Ser.). 284p. 1997. 128.00 (*0-471-96872-2*) Wiley.
CIBA Foundation Staff, et al. Variation in the Human Genome. LC 95-54159. (Ciba Foundation Symposium Ser.: Vol. 197). 340p. 1996. 128.00 (*0-471-96152-3*) Wiley.
CIBA Foundation Symposia Staff. The Biosynthesis of the Tetrapyrrole Pigments. LC 97-203019. (CIBA Foundation Symposium Ser.: No. 180). 366p. 1994. 128.00 (*0-471-93947-1*) Wiley.
CIBA Foundation Symposium Staff. Antimicrobial Peptides: Symposium No. 186. LC 94-21647. (Ciba Foundation Symposium Ser.: 186). 292p. 1995. 128.00 (*0-471-95025-4*) Wiley.
— Calcium, Waves, Gradients & Oscillations: Symposium No. 188. LC 94-42856. (Ciba Foundation Symposium Ser.: Vol. 188). 302p. 1995. 128.00 (*0-471-95234-6*) Wiley.
— Cell Adhesion & Human Disease: Symposium No. 189. LC 94-39499. (CIBA Foundation Symposium Ser.: Vol. 189). 254p. 1995. 128.00 (*0-471-95279-6*) Wiley.
— Circadian Clocks & Their Adjustment: Symposium No. 183. LC 94-37788. (IBA Foundation Symposia Ser.: No. 183). 348p. 1995. 128.00 (*0-471-94305-3*) Wiley.
— The Molecular Biology & Pathology of Elastic Tissues: Symposium. (CIBA Foundation Symposium Ser.: No. 192). 374p. 1995. 128.00 (*0-471-95718-6*) Wiley.
— Non-Reproductive Actions of Sex Steroids: Symposium No. 191. LC 95-6957. (Ciba Foundation Symposium Ser.: Vol. 191). 307p. 1995. 128.00 (*0-471-95513-2*) Wiley.
— Somatostatin & Its Receptors, Symposium No. 190. LC 94-43530. (CIBA Foundation Symposium Ser.: Vol. 190). 284p. 1995. 128.00 (*0-471-95382-2*) Wiley.
CIBA Foundation Symposium Staff & Holgate, Stephen T. The Rising Trends in Asthma - Symposium, No. 206. LC 96-40339. (CIBA Foundation Symposium Ser.: Vol. 206). 290p. 1997. 128.00 (*0-471-97012-3*) Wiley.
Cibak, Venita. Love & Cooking. 1991. 21.95 (*0-9629320-0-0*) Cibak & Assocs.
Cibas, Edmund S. & Ducantman, Barbara S. Cytology: Diagnostic Principles & Clinical Correlates. (Illus.). 528p. 1995. text 115.00 (*0-7216-4069-9*, W B Saunders Co) Harcrt Hlth Sci Grp.
***Cibbarelli, Pamela, ed.** Directory of Library Automation Software, Systems & Services, 2000-2001 Edition. 354p. 2000. pap. 89.00 (*1-57387-088-9*) Info Today Inc.
Cibbarelli, Pamela, ed. Directory of Library Automation Software, Systems, & Services: 1998 Edition. 448p. 1997. pap. 89.00 (*1-57387-044-7*) Info Today Inc.
Cibbarelli, Pamela A., ed. IOLS, '95: Proceedings of the 10th Integrated Online Library Systems Meeting. 200p. 1995. pap. 30.00 (*1-57387-005-6*) Info Today Inc.
***Cibbarelli, Pamela R., ed.** IOLS '98: Proceedings of the 13th Integrated Online Library Studies Meeting, May 13-14, 1998. 1998. pap. 30.00 (*1-57387-058-7*) Info Today Inc.
Cibbarelli, Pamela R., ed. IOLS, '94: Proceedings of the 9th Integrated Online Library Systems Conference. 240p. 1994. pap. 30.00 (*0-938734-83-0*) Info Today Inc.
— IOLS '97: Proceedings of the 12th Integrated Online Library Systems Meeting, 1997. 175p. 1997. pap. 30.00 (*1-57387-042-0*) Info Today Inc.
— IOLS, '96: Proceedings of the 11th Integrated Online Library Systems Meeting. 124p. 1996. pap. 30.00 (*1-57387-025-0*) Info Today Inc.
— IOLS, '93: Proceedings of the 8th Integrated Online Library Systems Meeting. 163p. 1993. pap. 30.00 (*0-938734-72-5*) Info Today Inc.
***Cibbarelli, Pamela R., ed.** IOLS '99: Proceedings of the 14th Integrated Online Library Systems Meeting May 19-20, 1999. 13p. 1999. 30.00 (*1-57387-085-4*) Info Today Inc.
Cibber, Colley. Apology for the Life of Colley Cibber Written by Himself, 2 vols. rev. ed. Lowe, R. W., ed. LC 25-7679. reprint ed. 125.00 (*0-404-01544-1*) AMS Pr.
— The Careless Husband. Appleton, William W., ed. LC 66-15482. (Regents Restoration Drama Ser.). xvi, 135p. 1966. text 17.95 (*0-8032-0352-7*); pap. text 7.95 (*0-8032-5352-4*) U of Nebr Pr.
— Dramatic Works, 5 vols. Baker, D. E., ed. reprint ed. 385.00 (*0-404-01590-5*) AMS Pr.
— A Letter from Mr. Cibber, to Mr. Pope. LC 92-25030. (Augustan Reprints Ser.: No. 158). 1973. reprint ed. 14.50 (*0-404-70158-2*, PR3347) AMS Pr.
— The Plays of Colley Cibber. LC 99-54768. 2000. write for info. (*0-8386-3624-1*) Fairleigh Dickinson.
Cibber, Colley, jt. auth. see Vanbrugh, John.
Cibber, Theophilus. The Harlot's Progress: or The Ridotto Al'Fresco: A Grotesque Pantomime Entertainment: And the Rake's Progress. LC 92-23677. (Augustan Reprints Ser.: No. 181). 1993. reprint ed. 14.50 (*0-404-70181-7*, PR1269) AMS Pr.
— The Lives of the Poets of Great Britain & Ireland to the Time of Dean Swift, 5 vols., Set. 1770p. 1968. reprint ed. 320.00 (*0-317-05065-6*, 05102038) G Olms Pubs.
Cibils, Luis A. Gynecologic Laparoscopy: Diagnostic & Operatory. LC 75-9554. (Current Concepts in Obstetrics & Gynecology Ser.). 185p. reprint ed. pap. 57.40 (*0-608-13436-8*, 201453200093) Bks Demand.
Cibils, Luis A., ed. Surgical Diseases in Pregnancy. (Clinical Perspectives in Obstetrics & Gynecology Ser.). (Illus.). xi, 208p. 1990. 89.00 (*0-387-97203-X*) Spr-Verlag.
Cibinic, John, Jr. & Nash, Ralph C., Jr. Administration of Government Contracts. 3rd ed. LC 94-39185. 1402p. 1995. pap., per. 90.00 (*0-935165-32-0*); boxed set 150.00 (*0-935165-33-9*) GWU Gov Contracts.
— Cost Reimbursement Contracting. 2nd ed. 1268p. 1993. pap., per. 90.00 (*0-935165-28-2*); boxed set 150.00 (*0-935165-20-7*) GWU Gov Contracts.
— Formation of Government Contracts. 2nd ed. 1046p. 1986. pap., per. 35.00 (*0-935165-08-8*); boxed set 55.00 (*0-935165-07-X*) GWU Gov Contracts.
— Formation of Government Contracts. 3rd ed. LC 98-70436. 1997. pap., per. 90.00 (*0-935165-42-8*); boxed set 150.00 (*0-935165-41-X*) GWU Gov Contracts.
Cibinic, John, Jr., et al. Construction Contracting. LC 91-4129. 1848p. 1991. boxed set 125.00 (*0-935165-18-5*) GWU Gov Contracts.
Cibinic, John, Jr., jt. auth. see Nash, Ralph C., Jr.
Ciborowski, Jean. Textbooks & the Students Who Can't Read Them: A Guide for the Teaching of Content. 102p. 1998. pap. text 21.95 (*0-914797-57-3*) Brookline Bks.
Ciborowski, Paul J. The Changing Family. (Focus on Behavior Ser.: No. 2). (Illus.). (Orig.). 1986. teacher ed. 12.75 (*0-935465-03-0*) Stratmar Ed Sys.
— The Changing Family: Group Manual. (Focus on Behavior Ser.: No. 1). (Illus.). 52p. (Orig.). 1984. student ed. 8.25 (*0-935465-00-6*) Stratmar Ed Sys.
— The Changing Family: Group Manual. (Focus on Behavior Ser.: No. 2). (Illus.). (Orig.). 1986. pap. 8.25 (*0-935465-02-2*) Stratmar Ed Sys.
— The Changing Family: Leader's Guide. (Focus on Behavior Ser.: No. 1). (Illus.). 68p. (Orig.). 1984. student ed. 12.75 (*0-935465-01-4*) Stratmar Ed Sys.
— Survival Skills for Single Parents. 182p. 1988. 14.95 (*0-935465-04-9*) Stratmar Ed Sys.
Ciborra. Words of Wisdom. write for info. (*0-471-87723-9*) Wiley.
Ciborra, Claudio. Groupware & Teamwork. LC 95-31547. (Information Systems Ser.). 254p. 1997. 87.95 (*0-471-97064-6*) Wiley.
***Ciborra, Claudio U.** From Control to Drift: The Dynamics of Corporate Information Infrastructures. (Illus.). 256p. 2000. text 52.00 (*0-19-829734-3*) OUP.
Ciborra, Claudio U. Teams, Markets & Systems: Business Innovation & Information Technology. 260p. 1996. pap. text 21.95 (*0-521-57465-X*) Cambridge U Pr.
Cibula, Matt. The Contrary Kid. LC 95-20323. (Illus.). 32p. (J). (ps-5). 1995. 16.95 (*1-55933-177-1*) Zino Pr.
— Slumgullion, the Executive Pig. (Illus.). 32p. (J). (ps-5). 1994. 14.95 (*1-55933-149-6*) Zino Pr.
Cibula, Matt S. What's up with You, Taquandra Fu? LC 97-13617. (Illus.). 32p. (J). (gr. k-2). 1998. 16.95 (*1-55933-212-3*) Zino Pr.
Cibula, Matt S. & Strassburg, Brian. How to be the Greatest Writer in the World. LC 99-27178. 92p. (J). (gr. 4-8). 1999. 11.95 (*1-55933-276-X*) Zino Pr.
Cibula, William G. An Ecological & Taxonomic Study of Selected Higher Fungi in Northeastern Ohio. (Biological Notes Ser.: No. 7). 1974. pap. text 6.00 (*0-86727-075-6*) Ohio Bio Survey.
Cibulka, Frank, jt. ed. see Valenta, Jiri.
Cibulka, James G., et al, eds. The Politics of Urban Education in the United States: The Politics of Education Association Yearbook, 1991. 210p. 1992. pap. 29.95 (*0-7507-0090-4*, Falmer Pr) Taylor & Francis.
Cibulka, James G. & Kritek, William J., eds. Coordination among Schools, Families, & Communities: Prospects for Educational Reform. LC 95-8929. (SUNY Series, Educational Leadership). 456p. (C). 1996. text 74.50 (*0-7914-2857-5*); pap. text 24.95 (*0-7914-2858-3*) State U NY Pr.
Cibulka, James G., et al. Inner-City Private Elementary Schools: A Study. LC 82-232927. (Illus.). 240p. 1982. reprint ed. pap. 74.40 (*0-608-04194-7*, 206492900011) Bks Demand.
Cicala, John A., jt. ed. see Stern, Stephen.
Cicala, Roger. The Heart Disease Sourcebook. LC 97-38624. 336p. 1997. reprint ed. 25.00 (*1-56565-635-0*, 06350W, Pub. by Lowell Hse) NTC Contemp Pub Co.
— The Heart Disease Sourcebook: A Complete Guide from Preconception to Postdelivery. LC 97-38624. (Illus.). 336p. 1998. reprint ed. pap. 18.00 (*0-7373-0020-5*, 00205W) NTC Contemp Pub Co.
***Cicala, Roger.** The Methodist Comprehensive Pain Institute's Cancer Pain Sourcebook. 2001. pap. 17.95 (*0-7373-0423-5*, Pub. by Lowell Hse) NTC Contemp Pub Co.
Cicarelli, James & Cicarelli, Julianne. Joan Robinson: A Bio-Bibliography, 2. LC 96-23236. (Bio-Bibliographies in Economics Ser.: No. 2). 200p. 1996. lib. bdg. 72.95 (*0-313-25844-9*, Greenwood Pr) Greenwood.
Cicarelli, Julianne, jt. auth. see Cicarelli, James.
***Cicatrix, Julius.** Imperial Exits: Being an Account of the Varied & Violent Deaths of the Roman Emperors. (Illus.). 114p. 2000. reprint ed. text 16.00 (*0-7881-9281-7*) DIANE Pub.
Ciccantell, Paul S. & Bunker, Stephen G., eds. Space & Transport in the World-System, 191. LC 97-16715. (Contributions in Economics & Economic History: Vol. 191). 264p. 1998. 65.00 (*0-313-30502-1*, Greenwood Pr) Greenwood.
Ciccarelli, G. Detonation Cell Size Measurements in High Temperature Hydrogen-air-steam Mixtures at the BNL High Temperature Combustion Facility. 83p. 1997. pap. 8.50 (*0-16-062871-7*) USGPO.
— Effect of Initial Temperature on Flame Acceleration & Deflagration to Detonation Transition Phenomenon. 73p. 1998. pap. 6.00 (*0-16-062922-5*) USGPO.
— Lateral Venting of Deflagration-to- Detonation Transition in Hydrogen-Air-Steam Mixtures at Various Initial Temperatures. 69p. 1998. pap. 6.00 (*0-16-062973-X*) USGPO.
***Ciccarelli, Patrick & Faulkner, Christina.** Cisco Jumpstart: Networking & Internetworking Basics. (Illus.). 377p. 1999. pap. 19.99 (*0-7821-2592-1*) Sybex.
Ciccarelli, Sheryl, jt. ed. see Napierkowski, Marie Rose.
Cicchelli, Terry & Ashby-Davis, Claire. Teaching Exceptional Children & Youth in the Regular Classroom. 368p. 1986. text 39.95 (*0-8156-2341-0*) Syracuse U Pr.
Cicchetti, jt. auth. see Sparrow.
Cicchetti, Charles J. & Sepetys, Kristina. Restructuring Electricity Markets: A World Perspective. 209p. (Orig.). 1995. 64.00 (*1-885750-02-1*, REM-96) Visions Communs.
***Cicchetti, Dante.** The Promotion of Wellness in Children & Adolescents. LC 00-30364. 2000. write for info. (*0-87868-791-2*, CWLA Pr) Child Welfare.
Cicchetti, Dante, ed. The Emergence of a Discipline: Rochester Symposium on Developmental Psychopathology, Vol. 1. 320p. 1990. 89.95 (*0-8058-0553-2*) L Erlbaum Assocs.
— Internalizing & Externalizing Expressions of Dysfunction: Rochester Symposium on Developmental Psychopathology, Vol. 2. 328p. (C). 1991. text 79.95 (*0-8058-0933-3*) L Erlbaum Assocs.
Cicchetti, Dante, et al, eds. Child Abuse, Child Development, Social Policy. (Advances in Applied Developmental Psychology Ser.: Vol. 8). 468p. 1993. 83.50 (*1-56750-042-0*) Ablx Pub.
Cicchetti, Dante & Beeghly, Marjorie, eds. Children with Downs Syndrome: A Developmental Perspective. (Illus.). 486p. (C). 1990. pap. text 32.95 (*0-521-38667-5*) Cambridge U Pr.
— The Self in Transition: Infancy to Childhood. LC 90-35059. (John D. & Catherine T. MacArthur Foundation Series on Mental Health & Development). (Illus.). 412p. 1990. 41.95 (*0-226-10662-4*) U Ch Pr.
Cicchetti, Dante & Carlson, Vicki K., eds. Child Maltreatment: Theory & Research on the Causes & Consequences of Child Abuse & Neglect. (Illus.). 816p. (C). 1989. pap. text 39.95 (*0-521-37969-5*) Cambridge U Pr.
Cicchetti, Dante & Cohen, Donald J., eds. Developmental Psychopathology, 2 vols. Incl. Risk, Disorder, & Adaptation. LC 94-36391. (Illus.). 928p. 1995. 175.00 (*0-471-53244-4*); Theory & Methods. LC 94-36391. (Illus.). 787p. 1995. 175.00 (*0-471-53243-6*); LC 94-36391. (Series on Personality Processes). 1695p. 1995. 350.00 (*0-471-53257-6*) Wiley.
Cicchetti, Dante & Grove, William M. Thinking Clearly about Psychology Vol. 1: Essays on Matters of Public Interest, Vol. 2. 320p. 1991. text 44.95 (*0-8166-1892-5*) U of Minn Pr.
Cicchetti, Dante & Grove, William M., eds. Thinking Clearly about Psychology, 2 vols. 864p. 1991. text 59.95 (*0-8166-1918-2*) U of Minn Pr.
Cicchetti, Dante & Toth, Sheree L., eds. Adolescence: Opportunities & Challenges. LC 96-28192. (Rochester Symposium on Developmental Psychopathology Ser.: Vol. 7). 440p. 1996. 95.00 (*1-878822-67-5*) Univ Rochester Pr.
— Developmental Approaches to Prevention & Intervention. LC 98-33332. (Symposium on Developmental Psychopathology Ser.: No. 1056-6511). 411p. 1999. 99.00 (*1-58046-035-6*) Univ Rochester Pr.
— Developmental Perspectives on Depression. LC 92-18117. (Rochester Symposium on Developmental Psychopathology Ser.: Vol. 4). (Illus.). 418p. (C). 1992. 90.00 (*1-878822-16-0*) Univ Rochester Pr.
— Developmental Perspectives on Trauma Vol. 8: Theory, Research & Intervention. LC 97-24123. (Rochester Symposium on Developmental Psychopathology Ser.: Vol. 1056-6511). 632p. 1998. 120.00 (*1-878822-97-7*) Univ Rochester Pr.
— Disorders & Dysfunctions of the Self. LC 93-24573. (Rochester Symposium on Developmental Psychopathology Ser.: Vol. 5). 460p. (C). 1994. 100.00 (*1-878822-31-4*) Univ Rochester Pr.
— Emotion, Cognition, & Representation: Rochester Symposium on Developmental Psychopathology VI. (Rochester Symposium on Developmental Psychopathology Ser.: Vol. 6). (Illus.). 360p. (C). 1995. 90.00 (*1-878822-49-7*, Pub. by Univ Rochester Pr) Boydell & Brewer.
— Models & Integrations Vol. 3: Rochester Symposium on Developmental Psychopathology. (Illus.). 352p. 1991. 85.00 (*1-878822-04-7*) Univ Rochester Pr.
Cicchetti, Dante, jt. ed. see Grove, William M.
Cicchetti, Mark, jt. auth. see Cicchetti, Wendy.
Cicchetti, Wendy & Cicchetti, Mark. Words of Love for Men: Secret Formulas for Mastering Intimate Relationships. Date not set. pap. 12.95 (*0-9700962-0-8*) Celestial Design.
Cicci, Regina. What's Wrong with Me? Learning Disabilities at Home & School. LC 95-40227. 253p. 1995. pap. 26.50 (*0-912752-38-6*) York Pr.
Cicciarella, Charles F. The Computer in Measurement & Evaluation in Physical Education & Sport. 74p. (Orig.). 1987. pap. text 7.95 (*0-926152-55-6*) Persimmon Soft.
— Microelectronics in the Sport Science. LC 86-287. (Illus.). 111p. 1986. reprint ed. pap. 34.50 (*0-608-07111-0*, 206733800009) Bks Demand.
— On Teaching Swimming. (Orig.). 1987. pap. text 11.95 (*0-926152-56-4*) Persimmon Soft.
— Research in Physical Education, Exercise Science & Sport: An Introduction. 304p. (C). 1996. pap. text 52.00 (*0-13-776568-1*) Allyn.
— Sport Competition Structures. 72p. 1992. pap. 15.00 (*0-926152-72-6*) Persimmon Soft.
— The Sport of Skin Diving. (Illus.). 68p. (Orig.). (C). 1982. pap. text 9.95 (*0-89641-100-1*) American Pr.
— Water Polo. 2nd ed. 132p. 1994. pap. text 11.95 (*0-89641-066-8*) American Pr.
Cicciarelli, Joellyn T. Apron Annie in the Garden, Vol. 4149. Graves, Kimberlee, ed. (Science Ser.). (Illus.). 16p. (J). (gr. k-1). 1997. pap. 2.75 (*1-57471-312-4*, 4149) Creat Teach Pr.

C

— Maps, Vol. 3929. Williams, Rozanne L., ed. (Social Studies Learn to Read Ser.). (Illus.). 16p. (J). (ps-2). 1996. pap. 2.75 (*1-57471-134-2*, 3929) Creat Teach Pr.

— Maps, Vol. 3973. Williams, Rozanne L., ed. (Social Studies Big Bks.). (Illus.). 16p. (J). (ps-2). 1997. pap. 12.98 (*1-57471-180-6*, 3972) Creat Teach Pr.

Cicciarelli, Joellyn T., ed. see Albright, Patricia, et al.

Cicciarelli, Joellyn T., ed. see DuVall, Rick.

Cicciarelli, Joellyn T., ed. see Hill, Sandi.

Cicciarelli, Joellyn T., ed. see Learning Letter Staff.

Cicciarelli, Joellyn T., ed. see Schomburg, Roberta & Sharapan, Hedda B.

Cicciarelli, Joellyn Thrall, see Thrall Cicciarelli, Joellyn, ed.

Cicciolina, La, see La Cicciolina, intro.

Ciccione. Teletexte. (College French Ser.). (C). 1992. mass mkt., suppl. ed. 6.95 (*0-8384-3672-2*) Heinle & Heinle.

— Teletexte. (College French Ser.). (C). 1993. mass mkt., teacher ed. 21.95 (*0-8384-3884-9*) Heinle & Heinle.

Ciccione & Meyer. Teletexte. (C). 1992. VHS 113.95 (*0-8384-3670-6*) Heinle & Heinle.

— Teletexte. (C). 1996. 15.95 (*0-8384-3667-6*) Heinle & Heinle.

Ciccolella, Erasmo S. Vibrant Life, 1866-1942: Trenton's Italian Americans. LC 86-6828. 165p. 1986. pap. 5.00 (*0-934733-00-7*) CMS.

Ciccone, Charles D. Pharmacology. 158p. 1995. pap. 21.00 (*1-887759-00-X*, P-115) Am Phys Therapy Assn.

— Pharmacology in Rehabilitation. 2nd ed. LC 95-22130. (Contemporary Perspectives in Rehabilitation Ser.). (Illus.). 642p. (C). 1995. text 49.95 (*0-8036-0030-5*) Davis Co.

Ciccone, Dana B. What Works: William J. Bennett's Research about Teaching & Learning. 3rd ed. LC 96-41073. 112p. 1996. pap. 10.00 (*1-888683-27-9*) Wooster Bk.

***Ciccone, Diane.** Heal Thyself Natural Living Cookbook: A Complete Guide to Natural Living Through Vegetarian Cooking & Holistic Juicing. 3rd rev. ed. LC 99-24334. Orig. Title: Heal Thyself Cookbook. (Illus.). 160p. 1999. pap. 10.95 (*1-886433-05-4*) A&B Bks.

Ciccone, Donald, jt. ed. see Grzesiak, Roy C.

Ciccone, F. Richard. Chicago & the American Century. LC 98-26990. 464p. 1999. 27.95 (*0-8092-2675-8*, 267580, Contemporary Bks) NTC Contemp Pub Co.

***Ciccone, F. Richard.** Chicago & the American Century. 384p. 2000. pap. 17.95 (*0-8092-2329-5*, 232950, Contemporary Bks) NTC Contemp Pub Co.

Ciccone, Kathleen R. & Chesnut, Thomas J. Medical Technology Assessment: A Model for Informed Decision Making. rev. ed. 100p. 1992. student ed. 100.00 (*0-915963-09-4*) Bader Assoc Inc.

Ciccone, Zack, jt. auth. see DeMassa, Thomas A.

***Ciccotosto, Emma & Bosworth, Michal.** Emma: A Recipe for Life. (Illus.). 304p. 1999. pap. 16.95 (*1-86368-230-9*) Intl Spec Bk.

Ciccotti, G., et al, eds. Simulation of Liquids & Solids: Molecular Dynamics & Monte Carlo Methods in Statistical Mechanics. (North-Holland Personal Library). xii, 482p. 1990. reprint ed. pap. 69.00 (*0-444-87061-X*, North Holland) Elsevier.

Cicellis, Kay, tr. see Lorenzatos, Zissimos.

Cicellis, Kay, tr. & frwd. see Galanaki, Rhea.

Cicely. Romancing Your Wind. (Illus.). 117p. (Orig.). 1996. pap. 9.95 (*0-9654770-0-2*) Empowermnt Pr.

Ciceri, Corrado & Vanin, Dino. Gold in the Mountains: The Mountain Tribes of Thailand. LC 96-70269. (Illus.). 82p. 1996. pap. 8.00 (*0-9642010-2-X*) Pime Wrld Pr.

Ciceri, Marcella, ed. see Martinez de Toledo, Alfonso.

Cicero, Bruce. W. H. Auden's Moral Imagination. LC 98-3086. 112p. 1998. text 59.95 (*0-7734-2237-4*) E Mellen.

Cicero, Carla. Sibling Species of Titmice in the Parus Inorntus Complex: Aves: Paridae. LC 95-46527. (Publications in Zoology: Vol. 128). (Illus.). 232p. (C). 1996. pap. 27.00 (*0-520-09808-0*, Pub. by U CA Pr) Cal Prin Full Svc.

Cicero, Chic & Cicero, Sandra T. The Golden Dawn Magical System: A Complete Tarot Set. Incl. 79 cards. (Illus.). 256p. 1999. pap. 34.95 (*1-56718-134-1*, 112770T) Llewellyn Pubns.

— The New Golden Dawn Ritual Tarot: Keys to the Rituals, Symbolism, Magic & Divination. LC 91-10428. (New Age Tarot Ser.). (Illus.). 256p. (Orig.). 1999. pap. 14.95 (*0-87542-139-3*) Llewellyn Pubns.

— Secrets of a Golden Dawn Temple: The Alchemy & Crafting of Magickal Implements. LC 92-10006. (Llewellyn's Golden Dawn Ser.). (Illus.). 592p. 1992. pap. 19.95 (*0-87542-150-4*) Llewellyn Pubns.

Cicero, Chic & Cicero, Sandra T., eds. The Golden Dawn Journal Bk. 1: Divination. LC 94-39664. (Illus.). 304p. 1994. pap. 12.00 (*1-56718-850-8*) Llewellyn Pubns.

Cicero, Chic & Cicero, Sandra Tabatha. Creating Magical Tools: The Magician's Craft. 2nd ed. LC 99-22890. 384p. 1999. pap. 16.95 (*1-56718-142-2*) Llewellyn Pubns.

***Cicero, Chic & Cicero, Sandra Tabatha.** Ritual Use of Magical Tools: The Magician's Art. 2nd ed. LC 99-24470. 336p. 2000. 14.95 (*1-56718-143-0*) Llewellyn Pubns.

Cicero, Chic, et al. Experiencing the Kabbalah: A Simple Guide to Spiritual Wholeness. LC 97-24732. (Illus.). 264p. 1997. pap. text 9.95 (*1-56718-138-4*) Llewellyn Pubns.

— Self-Initiation into the Golden Dawn Tradition: A Complete Curriculum of Study for Both the Solitary Magician & the Working Magical Group. LC 95-1118. (New Age Tarot Ser.). (Illus.). 784p. 1995. pap. 29.95 (*1-56718-136-8*) Llewellyn Pubns.

Cicero, Chic, ed. see Regardie, Israel.

Cicero, Christina, ed. see Ochs, Cathy & Perry, Marge.

Cicero, Ciceron. Les Aratea. xi, 542p. 1966. reprint ed. 95.00 (*0-318-71329-2*) G Olms Pubs.

Cicero, Marcus Tullius. Academica. x, 371p. 1984. reprint ed. lib. bdg. 70.00 (*3-487-01409-2*) G Olms Pubs.

— Ad M. Brutum Orator. xcix, 257p. 1973. reprint ed. lib. bdg. 70.00 (*3-487-04591-5*) G Olms Pubs.

— Back from Exile: Six Speeches upon His Return. Bailey, D. R., tr. 278p. 1991. pap. 19.95 (*1-55540-627-0*) OUP.

— Brutus. xxvi, 310p. 1964. 70.00 (*3-296-11500-5*) G Olms Pubs.

— Brutus. (Loeb Classical Library: No. 342). (ENG & LAT.). 15.50 (*0-674-99377-2*) HUP.

— Cato Maior de Senectute. Powell, J. G., ed. (Cambridge Classical Texts & Commentaries Ser.: No. 28). (Illus.). 320p. 1988. text 80.00 (*0-521-33501-9*) Cambridge U Pr.

— Cato Major. Kastenbaum, Robert J., ed. LC 78-22193. (Aging & Old Age Ser.). 1979. reprint ed. lib. bdg. 17.95 (*0-405-11810-4*) Ayer.

Cicero, Marcus Tullius. Cicero. Caplan, Harry, tr. 1981. 19.95 (*0-674-99444-2*) HUP.

Cicero, Marcus Tullius. Cicero: Laelius on Friendship & the Dream of Scipio. Powell, I. G. F., ed. 1991. pap. 22.00 (*0-85668-441-4*, Pub. by Aris & Phillips) David Brown.

— Cicero: Letters to Atticus. Shackleton Bailey, D. R., ed. & tr. by. LC 98-8779. (Loeb Classical Library: Vol. 1). 384p. 1998. 19.95 (*0-674-99571-6*, L007) HUP.

— Cicero: Letters to Atticus. Shackleton Bailey, D. R., ed. & tr. by. LC 98-8779. (Loeb Classical Library: Vol. 2). 384p. 1998. 19.95 (*0-674-99572-4*) HUP.

— Cicero: Letters to Atticus. Shackleton Bailey, D. R., ed. & tr. by. LC 98-8779. (Loeb Classical Library: Vol. 3). 384p. 1998. 19.95 (*0-674-99573-2*) HUP.

— Cicero: Letters to Atticus. Shackleton Bailey, D. R., ed. & tr. by. LC 98-8779. (Loeb Classical Library: Vol. 4). 384p. 1998. 19.95 (*0-674-99540-6*) HUP.

— Cicero: On Duties. 241p. 1991. text 44.95 (*0-521-34338-0*) Cambridge U Pr.

— Cicero: On Friendship & the Dream of Scipio. Powell, I. G. F., ed. (Classical Texts Ser.). 1991. 59.99 (*0-85668-440-6*, Pub. by Aris & Phillips) David Brown.

— Cicero: On Stoic Good & Evil. Wright, ed. (Classical Texts Ser.). 1991. 59.99 (*0-85668-467-8*, Pub. by Aris & Phillips); pap. 28.00 (*0-85668-468-6*, Pub. by Aris & Phillips) David Brown.

— Cicero: On the Commonwealth & On the Laws. Zetzel, James E., ed. (Cambridge Texts in the History of Political Thought Ser.). 241p. (C). 1999. 59.95 (*0-521-45344-5*) Cambridge U Pr.

— Cicero: Philippics. Shackleton Bailey, D. R., ed. & tr. by. LC 85-1029. xviii, 402p. 1986. 59.95 (*0-8078-1657-4*) U of NC Pr.

— Cicero: Philippics II. Lacey, W. K., ed. (Classical Texts Ser.). 1986. 59.99 (*0-85668-254-3*, Pub. by Aris & Phillips); pap. 28.00 (*0-85668-255-1*, Pub. by Aris & Phillips) David Brown.

— Cicero: Pro P. Sulla Oratio. Berry, D. H., ed. (Classical Texts & Commentaries Ser.: Vol. 30). 361p. (C). 1996. text 69.95 (*0-521-48174-0*) Cambridge U Pr.

— Cicero: The Letters of January to April 43 BC. Wilcock, Malcolm M., ed. & tr. by. from LAT. (Classical Texts Ser.). 160p. 1995. 59.99 (*0-85668-631-X*, Pub. by Aris & Phillips); pap. 22.00 (*0-85668-632-8*, Pub. by Aris & Phillips) David Brown.

— Cicero: Tusculan Didputations I. Douglas, Cicero, ed. (Classical Texts Ser.). 1985. 59.99 (*0-85668-250-0*, Pub. by Aris & Phillips) David Brown.

— Cicero: Tusculan Disputations I. Douglas, ed. (Classical Texts Ser.). 1985. pap. 22.00 (*0-85668-251-9*, Pub. by Aris & Phillips) David Brown.

— Cicero: Tusculan Disputations II & V. Douglas, A. E., ed. (Classical Texts Ser.). 1989. 59.99 (*0-85668-432-5*, Pub. by Aris & Phillips); pap. 22.00 (*0-85668-433-3*, Pub. by Aris & Phillips) David Brown.

— Cicero: Verrines II.1. Mitchell, T. N., ed. (Classical Texts Ser.). 1986. 59.99 (*0-85668-252-7*, Pub. by Aris & Phillips) David Brown.

— Cicero: Verrines II.1. Mitchell, ed. (Classical Texts Ser.). 1986. pap. 28.00 (*0-85668-253-5*, Pub. by Aris & Phillips) David Brown.

— Cicero on Oratory & Orators. 2nd ed. Watson, J. S., ed. LC 85-26258. (Landmarks in Rhetoric & Public Address Ser.). 432p. (C). 1986. reprint ed. pap. text 19.95 (*0-8093-1293-X*) S Ill U Pr.

— Cicero Pro Archia. 160p. 1998. pap. 15.00 (*0-86516-402-9*) Bolchazy-Carducci.

— Ciceron, les Aratea. xx, 403p. 1966. reprint ed. 95.00 incl. 3.5 hd (*0-318-71089-7*) G Olms Pubs.

— Ciceronis, M. Tulli. Bailey, Shackleton, ed. (LAT.). 1988. 49.50 (*3-519-01211-1*, T1211, Pub. by B G Teubner) U of Mich Pr.

— Ciceronis, M. Tulli. Reeve, ed. (LAT.). 1992. pap. 24.95 (*3-8154-1175-0*, T1175, Pub. by B G Teubner) U of Mich Pr.

— Ciceronis, M. Tulli, Vol. I. Bailey, Shackleton, ed. (LAT.). 1987. 89.50 (*3-519-01208-1*, T1208, Pub. by B G Teubner) U of Mich Pr.

— Ciceronis, M. Tulli, Vol. II. Bailey, Shackleton, ed. (LAT.). 1987. 110.00 (*3-519-01209-X*, T1209, Pub. by B G Teubner) U of Mich Pr.

— Ciceronis, M. Tulli Fascicule 22: Pro P. Sestio. Maslowski, Tadeusz, ed. (LAT.). 1986. 26.95 (*3-322-00268-3*, T1193, Pub. by B G Teubner) U of Mich Pr.

— Ciceronis Orationum Scholiastae. 351p. 1964. reprint ed. 80.00 (*0-318-71090-0*) G Olms Pubs.

— Cicero's Brutus: Or, History of Famous Orators. Jones, Ernest, tr. LC 72-158313. (Augustan Translators Ser.). reprint ed. 62.00 (*0-404-54106-2*) AMS Pr.

— Cicero's Caesarian Speeches: A Stylistic Commentary. Gotoff, Harold C., ed. LC 92-50816. xlvi, 310p. (C). 1993. 55.00 (*0-8078-2075-X*); pap. text 22.50 (*0-8078-4407-1*) U of NC Pr.

— Cicero's First Catilinarian Oration: With Introduction, Vocabulary & Notes. LC 96-49454. (Illus.). xviii, 62p. (Orig.). 1997. pap. text 15.00 (*0-86516-341-3*) Bolchazy-Carducci.

— Cicero's Letters to His Friends. Bailey, D. R., tr. 1989. pap. 20.95 (*1-55540-264-X*, 40 07 01) OUP.

— Cicero's Pro Caelio AP Edition. Ciraolo, Stephen N., ed. (ENG & LAT.). 232p. 1997. pap. text, teacher ed. 19.00 (*0-86516-264-6*) Bolchazy-Carducci.

— Cicero's Verrine Oration No. II.4: With Notes & Vocabulary. LC 92-9058. (Classical Studies: Pedagogy Ser.). (LAT.). 270p. (C). 1992. pap. 19.95 (*0-8143-2382-0*) Wayne St U Pr.

— The Correspondence of M. Tullius Cicero, 7 vols. 1969. reprint ed. 865.00 incl. 3.5 hd (*0-318-71091-9*) G Olms Pubs.

— De Finibus. (Loeb Classical Library: No. 40). 534p. 1914. 15.50 (*0-674-99044-7*) HUP.

— De Finibus Bonorum et Malorum: Libri Quinque. Reynolds, L. D., ed. (Oxford Classical Texts Ser.). 262p. 1998. text 35.00 (*0-19-814670-1*) OUP.

— De Finibus Bonorum et Malorum libri, I, II. Reid, J. S., ed. viii, 239p. 1968. reprint ed. 63.50 incl. 3.5 hd (*0-318-71092-7*) G Olms Pubs.

— De Inventione. Warmington, E. H., ed. (Loeb Classical Library: No. 386). (ENG & LAT.). (C). 15.50 (*0-674-99425-6*) HUP.

— De Legibus Libri Tres. xxx, 793p. 1977. reprint ed. 160.00 incl. 3.5 hd (*3-487-04628-8*) G Olms Pubs.

— De Natura Deorum. (Loeb Classical Library: No. 268). 15.50 (*0-674-99296-2*) HUP.

— De Officiis. (Loeb Classical Library: No. 30). 442p. 1913. 18.95 (*0-674-99033-1*) HUP.

— De Officiis. Winterbottom, Michael, ed. (Classical Texts Ser.). (LAT.). 190p. 1994. text 24.00 (*0-19-814673-6*) OUP.

— De Oratore, Vol. 4, Bk. 3. (Loeb Classical Library: No. 349). 15.50 (*0-674-99384-5*) HUP.

— De Oratore, Bks 1 & 2, Vol. 3. (Loeb Classical Library: No. 348). 508p. 1942. 18.95 (*0-674-99383-7*) HUP.

— De Oratore Libri Tres. (Olms Paperbacks Ser.: Vol. 9). viii, 573p. 1990. reprint ed. pap. 95.00 (*3-487-05025-0*) G Olms Pubs.

— De Re Publica. (Loeb Classical Library: No. 213). (ENG & LAT.). (C). 1928. 15.50 (*0-674-99235-0*) HUP.

— De re publica: Selections. Zetzel, James E., ed. (Cambridge Greek & Latin Classics Ser.). 280p. (C). 1995. text 65.00 (*0-521-34465-4*); pap. text 22.95 (*0-521-34896-X*) Cambridge U Pr.

— De Senectute. Shuckburgh, E. S., ed. (College Classical Ser.). pap. text 17.50 (*0-89241-348-4*) Caratzas.

— De Senectute. (Loeb Classical Library: No. 154). (ENG & LAT.). (C). 15.50 (*0-674-99170-2*) HUP.

— De Senectute: De Amicicia. LC 77-6867. (English Experience Ser.: No. 861). 1977. reprint ed. lib. bdg. 45.00 (*90-221-0861-9*) Walter J Johnson.

***Cicero, Marcus Tullius.** Epistulae Ad Familiares, Vol. 1. 16th ed. Shackleton Bailey, D. R., ed. (Illus.). (C). 1998. text 155.00 (*3-519-01210-3*) U of Mich Pr.

Cicero, Marcus Tullius. Gazae, Theodori: M. Tullii Ciceronis Liber De Senectute in Graecum. Salanitro, Ioannes, ed. (GRE.). 1987. 42.50 (*3-322-00360-4*, T1361, Pub. by B G Teubner) U of Mich Pr.

— In Catilinam, 1-4. (Loeb Classical Library: No. 324). (ENG & LAT.). (C). 15.50 (*0-674-99358-6*) HUP.

— In Vatinium. 206p. 1928. reprint ed. lib. bdg. 42.50 (*0-685-13366-4*, Pub. by AM Hakkert) Coronet Bks.

— Laelius (Sive) De Amicitia Dialogus. xii, 58p. 1965. reprint ed. 110.00 (*0-318-71095-1*); reprint ed. pap. 51.00 (*0-318-71096-X*) G Olms Pubs.

— Letters to Atticus, 3 vols., Bks. 1-6. (Loeb Classical Library: No. 7, 8, 97). 570p. 1912. 18.95 (*0-674-99008-0*) HUP.

— Letters to Atticus, 3 vols., Bks. 7-11. (Loeb Classical Library: No. 7, 8, 97). 458p. 1913. 18.95 (*0-674-99009-9*) HUP.

— Letters to Atticus, 3 vols., Bks. 12-16. (Loeb Classical Library: No. 7, 8, 97). 470p. 1918. 18.95 (*0-674-99108-7*) HUP.

— Letters to His Brother Quintus. (Loeb Classical Library: No. 462). 15.50 (*0-674-99509-0*) HUP.

— Letters to His Friends, 3 vols., Bks. 1-6. (Loeb Classical Library: No. 205, 216, 230). 562p. 1927. 18.95 (*0-674-99225-3*) HUP.

— Letters to His Friends, 3 vols., Bks. 7-12. (Loeb Classical Library: No. 205, 216, 230). 670p. 1929. 18.95 (*0-674-99238-5*) HUP.

— Letters to His Friends, 3 vols., Bks. 13-16. (Loeb Classical Library: No. 205, 216, 230). 424p. 1929. 18.95 (*0-674-99253-9*) HUP.

— M. Tulli Ciceronis Ad M Brutum Orator. Connor, W. R. & Sandys, John E., eds. LC 78-67148. (Latin Texts & Commentaries Ser.). (ENG & LAT.). 1979. reprint ed. lib. bdg. 28.95 (*0-405-11616-0*) Ayer.

— M. Tulli Ciceronis de Divinatione, 2 vols. Connor, W. R., ed. LC 78-67146. (Latin Texts & Commentaries Ser.). (ENG & LAT.). 1979. reprint ed. lib. bdg. 48.95 (*0-405-11614-4*) Ayer.

— M. Tulli Ciceronis de Domo Sua Ad Pontifices Oratio. Connor, W. R. & Nisbert, Robert G., eds. LC 78-67143. (Latin Texts & Commentaries Ser.). (ENG & LAT.). 1979. reprint ed. lib. bdg. 29.95 (*0-405-11612-8*) Ayer.

— M. Tulli Ciceronis de Natura Deorum, 2 vols., Set. Connor, W. R., ed. LC 78-67145. (Latin Texts & Commentaries Ser.). 1979. reprint ed. lib. bdg. 82.95 (*0-405-11613-6*) Ayer.

— M. Tulli Ciceronis de Oratore, 3 vols. Connor, W. R., ed. LC 78-67162. (Latin Texts & Commentaries Ser.). (ENG & LAT.). 1979. reprint ed. lib. bdg. 56.95 (*0-405-11624-1*) Ayer.

— M. Tulli Ciceronis de Provinciis Consularibus Oratio Ad Senatum. Connor, W. R., ed. LC 78-67125. (Latin Texts & Commentaries Ser.). (ENG & LAT.). 1979. reprint ed. lib. bdg. 23.95 (*0-405-11596-2*) Ayer.

— M. Tulli Ciceronis Tusculanarum Disputationum Libra Quinque, 2 vols. Connor, W. R., ed. LC 78-67129. (Latin Texts & Commentaries Ser.). (ENG & LAT.). 1979. reprint ed. lib. bdg. 66.95 (*0-405-11599-7*) Ayer.

— M. Tullius Cicero, the Fragmentary Speeches. 2nd ed. LC 94-41803. (American Philological Association American Classical Studies : No. 37). 350p. 1994. pap. 34.95 (*0-7885-0075-9*) OUP.

— Marcus Tullius Ciceroes Thre Bokes of Duties. O'Gorman, Gerald, ed. Grimalde, Nicolas, tr. LC 86-46408. (Renaissance English Text Society Ser.: No. 12). (Illus.). 272p. 1990. 37.50 (*0-918016-93-2*) Folger Bks.

— Murder at Larinum. Grose-Hodge, Humfrey, ed. 1932. text 5.95 (*0-521-04648-3*) Cambridge U Pr.

— Murder Trials. Grant, Michael, tr. (Classics Ser.). 368p. 1975. pap. 13.95 (*0-14-044288-X*, Penguin Classics) Viking Penguin.

— The Nature of the Gods. Walsh, Patrick G., tr. & intro. by. LC 96-34884. 286p. (C). 1997. text 70.00 (*0-19-815040-7*) OUP.

— The Nature of the Gods. McGregor, H. C., tr. (Classics Ser.). 280p. 1972. pap. 11.95 (*0-14-044265-0*, Penguin Classics) Viking Penguin.

— The Nature of the Gods. Walsh, P. G., tr. & intro. by. (Oxford World's Classics Ser.). 286p. 1998. reprint ed. pap. 9.95 (*0-19-282511-9*) OUP.

— The Nature of the Gods & on Divination. Yonge, C. D., tr. from GRE. LC 97-34300. 273p. 1997. pap. text 6.95 (*1-57392-180-7*) Prometheus Bks.

— On Government. Grant, Michael, tr. & intro. by. 432p. 1994. pap. 13.95 (*0-14-044595-1*, Penguin Classics) Viking Penguin.

— On the Good Life. Grant, Michael, tr. LC 77-30399. (Classics Ser.). 384p. 1971. pap. 16.99 (*0-14-044244-8*, Penguin Classics) Viking Penguin.

— Orator. Kroll, Wilhelm, ed. vii, 228p. 1971. 55.00 (*3-296-11600-1*) G Olms Pubs.

— Philippics. (Loeb Classical Library: No. 189). 670p. 1926. 18.95 (*0-674-99208-3*) HUP.

— The Poems of Cicero. Eubank, W., ed. (LAT.). 280p. 1997. pap. text 29.95 (*1-85399-529-0*, Pub. by Brist Class Pr) Focus Pub-R Pullins.

— The Poems of Cicero. ix, 267p. write for info. (*0-318-71097-8*) G Olms Pubs.

— Pro Archia. (Loeb Classical Library: No. 158). (ENG & LAT.). (C). 14.50 (*0-674-99174-5*) HUP.

— Pro Caelio. (Loeb Classical Library: No. 447). 15.50 (*0-674-99492-2*) HUP.

— Pro Lege Manilia. (Loeb Classical Library: No. 198). (ENG & LAT.). 15.50 (*0-674-99218-0*) HUP.

Cicero, Marcus Tullius. Pro M Caelio Oratio. 3rd ed. Austin, R. G., ed. 212p. 1988. pap. text 24.00 (*0-19-814062-2*) OUP.

Cicero, Marcus Tullius. Pro Milone. (Loeb Classical Library: No. 252). 15.50 (*0-674-99278-4*) HUP.

— Pro Quinctio. (Loeb Classical Library: No. 240). (ENG & LAT.). 15.50 (*0-674-99265-2*) HUP.

— Pro Sestio. (Loeb Classical Library: No. 309). 15.50 (*0-674-99341-1*) HUP.

— The Republic & the Laws. Powell, Jonathan, ed. Rudd, Niall, tr. (Oxford World's Classics Ser.). 286p. 1998. pap. 10.95 (*0-19-283236-0*) OUP.

— Rhetorica, 2 vols. Wilkins, A. S., ed. Incl. Vol. 1. Libros de Oratore Tres. 260p. 1922. text 32.00 (*0-19-814615-9*); Vol. 2. Brutus, Orator, De Optimo Genere Oratorum, Partitiones Oratoriae, Topica. 276p. 1922. text 29.95 (*0-19-814616-7*); (Oxford Classical Texts Ser.). write for info. (*0-318-54887-9*) OUP.

***Cicero, Marcus Tullius.** Scripta Quae Manserunt Omnia, Fasc. 42: Academicorum Reliquiae Cum Lucullo. Plasberg, O., ed. (Illus.). (C). 1998. pap. text 29.95 (*3-519-11218-3*) U of Mich Pr.

Cicero, Marcus Tullius. Select Letters. Bailey, D. R., ed. LC 78-67430. (Cambridge Greek & Latin Classics Ser.). 244p. 1980. pap. text 22.95 (*0-521-29524-6*) Cambridge U Pr.

— Select Letters, 2 vols., Vol. 1. How, Walter W., ed. 1925. 26.00 (*0-19-814403-2*) OUP.

— Selected Political Speeches. Grant, Michael, tr. (Classics Ser.). 336p. 1977. pap. 12.95 (*0-14-044214-6*, Penguin Classics) Viking Penguin.

— Selected Works. Grant, Michael, tr. Incl. Against Verres. 1960. pap. Old Age. 1960. pap. On Duties. 1960. pap. Second Philippic Against Anthony. 1960. pap. Twenty Three Letters. 1960. pap. (Classics Ser.). 272p. (Orig.). (gr. 9 up). 1960. Set pap. 18.99 (*0-14-044099-2*, Penguin Classics) Viking Penguin.

— Tusculan Disputations. (Loeb Classical Library: No. 141). 630p. 1927. 18.95 (*0-674-99156-7*) HUP.

— Verrine Orations, 2 Vols, I. (Loeb Classical Library: No. 221, 293). 530p. 1928. 18.95 (*0-674-99243-1*) HUP.

— Verrine Orations, 2 Vols, II. (Loeb Classical Library: No. 221, 293). 704p. 1935. 18.95 (*0-674-99323-3*) HUP.

Cicero, Marcus Tullius & Boethius, Anicius Manlius Severinus. Cicero: On Fate with Boethius Consolation of Philosophy. Sharples, ed. 1992. 59.99 (*0-85668-475-9*, Pub. by Aris & Phillips); pap. 28.00 (*0-85668-476-7*, Pub. by Aris & Phillips) David Brown.

***Cicero, Marcus Tullius & Walsh, P. G.** On Obligations. LC 99-56114. 240p. 2000. text 70.00 (*0-19-924018-3*) OUP.

An Asterisk (*) at the beginning of an entry indicates that the title is appearing for the first time.

C

Cicero, Marcus Tullius & Zetzel, James E. Cicero: On the Commonwealth & On the Laws. LC 98-49660. (Cambridge Texts in the History of Political Thought Ser.). 241p. (C). 1999. pap. 24.95 (*0-521-45959-1*) Cambridge U Pr.

Cicero, Marcus Tullius, jt. auth. see Cerutti, Steven M.

Cicero, Marcus Tullius, jt. auth. see Hunt, Terence J.

***Cicero, Sandra T.** Golden Dawn Magical Tarot. 1vol. 2000. pap. text 19.95 (*1-56718-125-2*) Llewellyn Pubns.

Cicero, Sandra T., et al, eds. The Magical Pantheons: A Golden Dawn Journal. (Golden Dawn Journal Ser.: Vol. 4). 348p. (Orig.). 1999. pap. 14.95 (*1-56718-861-3*) Llewellyn Pubns.

Cicero, Sandra T., jt. auth. see Cicero, Chic.

Cicero, Sandra T., jt. ed. see Cicero, Chic.

Cicero, Sandra T., ed. see Regardie, Israel.

Cicero, Sandra Tabatha, jt. auth. see Cicero, Chic.

Cicero, Sandra Tabatha, ed. see Regardie, Israel.

Ciceron, Marco Tulio. Las Leyes. (Biblioteca De Cultura Basica Ser.). 204p. 1968. 1.50 (*0-8477-0702-4*) U of PR Pr.

Ciceron, Marcos T. Deberes. Samaranch, Francisco, tr. (Biblioteca De Cultura Basica Ser.). (SPA.). 248p. 1993. 5.25 (*0-8477-0701-6*) U of PR Pr.

Cicerone, Keith D. Counseling Interactions with Traumatically Brain Injured Clients. Fraser, Robert & Clemmons, David, eds. LC 91-73658. (Traumatic Brain Injury Rehabilitation Training Ser.). 46p. 1991. spiral bd. 36.95 (*1-878205-20-X*) St Lucie Pr.

Cicerone, Keith D., jt. ed. see Tupper, David E.

Cichantk, Elaine, ed. see Everywoman, Catherine.

Cichelli, David J., jt. auth. see Colletti, Jerome A.

Cichester, D. G. Daredevil: Fall from Grace. (Illus.). 208p. 1994. pap. 19.95 (*0-7851-0024-5*) Marvel Entrprs.

Cichetti, Stephen, jt. auth. see Bredenberg, Fly.

Cichetti, V., et al, eds. Perspectives of Antioxidant Treatment of Emphysema with N-Acetyloysteine: Journal: Respiration, Vol. 50, Suppl. 1, 1986. vi, 74p. 1986. pap. 24.50 (*3-8055-4514-2*) S Karger.

Cichock, Mark A. Russian Politics. (C). 2001. pap. 32.00 (*0-205-18945-8*, Macmillan Coll) P-H.

Cichock, Mark A., jt. ed. see Bukowski, Charles J.

Cichocki, A., jt. auth. see Ubehauen, R.

Cichocki, Andrzej, et al. Workflow & Process Automation: Concepts & Technology. LC 97-43179. (Series in Engineering & Computing). 121p. 1998. text 88.00 (*0-7923-8099-1*) Kluwer Academic.

Cichoke, Anthony. All about Enzymes: Frequently Asked Questions. (FAQs All about Health Ser.). 96p. 1999. mass mkt. 2.99 (*0-89529-968-2*, Avery) Penguin Putnam.

— The Back Pain Bible. LC 99-31339. 336p. 1998. pap. 16.95 (*0-87983-903-1*, 39031K, Keats Publng) NTC Contemp Pub Co.

— Complete Book of Enzyme Therapy: A Practical Guide to Using the Power of Enzymes. LC 98-21195. 296p. 1998. pap. text 19.95 (*0-89529-817-1*, Avery) Penguin Putnam.

***Cichoke, Anthony.** Enzymes & Enzyme Therapy: How to Jump-Start Your Way to Lifelong Good Health. (Illus.). 320p. 2000. pap. 18.95 (*0-658-00290-2*, 002902, Keats Publng) NTC Contemp Pub Co.

Cichoke, Anthony J. Bromelain. (Good Health Guides Ser.). 1998. pap. 3.95 (*0-87983-835-3*, 38353K, Keats Publng) NTC Contemp Pub Co.

— Enzymes: Nature's Energizers. (Good Health Guides Ser.). 48p. (Orig.). 1997. pap. 3.95 (*0-87983-724-1*, 37241K, Keats Publng) NTC Contemp Pub Co.

— Enzymes & Enzyme Therapy: How to Jump Start Your Way to Lifelong Good Health. 320p. (Orig.). 1994. pap. 17.95 (*0-87983-635-0*, Keats Publng) NTC Contemp Pub Co.

Cichoki, A. & Unbehauen, Rolf. Neural Networks for Optimization & Signal Processing. LC 92-46543. 544p. 1993. 220.00 (*0-471-93010-5*) Wiley.

Cicholas, Shirley T. The Long Recess. LC 82-24389. 223p. 1985. 13.95 (*0-87949-235-X*) Ashley Bks.

***Cichon, Michael.** Modelling in Health Care Finance A Compendium of Quantitative Techniques for Health Care Finance. 1999. 60.00 (*92-2-110862-7*) Intl Labour Office.

***Cichon, Michael, et al.** Social Budgeting. 300p. 2000. 49.95 (*92-2-110861-9*, Pub. by ILO) ILO Pubns Ctr.

Cichonski, Thomas J. & Hill, Karen, eds. Recycling Sourcebook. (Environmental Library). 563p. 1992. 90.00 (*0-8103-8855-3*, 101455) Gale.

Cichorius, Conrad. Untersuchungen Zu Lucilius. ix, 364p. 1964. 80.00 (*3-296-11610-9*) G Olms Pubs.

Cichowicz, Judith A. How to Control Costs in Your Pollution Prevention Program. LC 96-51065. 445p. 1997. 110.00 (*0-471-18015-7*) Wiley.

Cichowicz, Ron. I'm Not over the Hill, I'm Simply Too Old to Climb It. 168p. (Orig.). 1994. pap. 5.95 (*1-56245-091-3*) Great Quotations.

Cichowlas, Jeazy. Teczowa Nowina: Czyliwprowadzemie do Evangelii Wienxzem. LC 93-74281. 300p. 1994. pap. write for info. (*0-9639577-3-2*) J Cichowlas.

Cichy, Helen Joos. Wagon Trails: The Defrosting of Minnesota. 2nd ed. LC 77-86170. 350p. 1977. reprint ed. pap. 15.00 (*0-9619663-4-3*, 1) Van Amber Pubs.

Cichy, Ronald F. Quality Sanitation Management. LC 94-16272. (Illus.). 448p. 1994. write for info. (*0-86612-084-X*) Educ Inst Am Hotel.

Cichy, Ronald F. & Wise, Paul E. Food & Beverage Service. 2nd rev. ed. LC 99-179543. (Illus.). (C). 1998. pap. 47.00 (*0-86612-095-5*) Educ Inst Am Hotel.

— Managing Service in Food & Beverage Operations. 2nd ed. LC 98-28430. (Illus.). 597p. (C). 1998. pap. write for info. (*0-86612-077-7*) Educ Inst Am Hotel.

Ciciani, Bruno, ed. Manufacturing Yield Evaluation of VLSI - WSI Systems. LC 94-20185. 448p. 1995. pap. 58.00 (*0-8186-6292-1*, BP06292) IEEE Comp Soc.

— Tutorial on Manufacturing Yield Evaluation of VLSI - WSI Systems. LC 94-20185. 1994. pap. write for info. (*0-8186-6290-5*); fiche. write for info. (*0-8186-6291-3*) IEEE Comp Soc.

Ciciarelli, John A. Practical Physical Geology: Problems & Solutions. x, 264p. 1986. text 195.00 (*2-88124-098-4*); pap. text 75.00 (*2-88124-065-8*) Gordon & Breach.

Cicile, J. Terminologie Bancaire, Financier et Economique Francais-Anglais. (FRE.). 192p. 1995. 110.00 (*0-7859-9880-2*) Fr & Eur.

Cicin-Sain, Biliana & Knecht, Robert. The Future of U. S. Open Policy: Choices for the Next Century. LC 99-37170. 400p. (C). 2000. pap. 25.00 (*1-55963-676-9*); text 50.00 (*1-55963-675-0*) Island Pr.

Cicin-Sain, Biliana & Knecht, Robert W. Integrated Coastal & Ocean Management: Concepts & Practices. LC 98-12593. 416p. 1998. text 65.00 (*1-55963-603-3*); pap. text 32.50 (*1-55963-604-1*) Island Pr.

Cicioni, Mirna. Primo Levi: Bridges of Knowledge. Flower, John E., ed. (New Directions in European Writing Ser.). 224p. 1995. 49.50 (*1-85973-058-2*); pap. 19.50 (*1-85973-063-9*) Berg Pubs.

Cicioni, Mirna & Prunster, Nicole, eds. Visions & Revisions: Women in Italian Culture. LC 92-16782. (European Studies Ser.). 224p. 1993. 25.00 (*0-85496-710-9*) Berg Pubs.

Ciciora, Walter, et al. Modern Cable Television Technology: Video, Voice & Data Communication. LC 98-35328. 800p. (Orig.). (C). 1998. pap. 79.95 (*1-55860-416-2*) Morgan Kaufmann.

Ciciotti, E., et al, eds. Technological Change in a Spatial Context: Theory, Empirical Evidence & Policy. (Illus.). xi, 400p. 1990. 107.95 (*0-387-52948-9*) Spr-Verlag.

Cicirelli, Victor G. Family Caregiving: Autonomous & Paternalistic Decision Making. LC 91-11256. (Sage Library of Social Research: Vol. 186). 264p. 1992. reprint ed. pap. 81.90 (*0-608-03003-1*, 206345300006) Bks Demand.

— Helping Elderly Parents: The Role of Adult Children. LC 81-10880. 215p. 1981. 24.95 (*0-86569-080-4*, Auburn Hse) Greenwood.

— Sibling Relationships Across the Life Span. (Illus.). 268p. (C). 1995. 45.00 (*0-306-45025-9*, Kluwer Plenum) Kluwer Academic.

Cicla, Roger S. Brain Disorders Sourcebook. LC 99-15345. 432p. 1999. pap. 19.95 (*0-7373-0093-0*, 00930WW) NTC Contemp Pub Co.

Cicogna, Caterina. Un Proverbio al Giorno - A Proverb a Day. (Italian Linguistics & Language Pedagogy Ser.). (Illus.). 160p. (C). 1992. pap. text, teacher ed. 19.95 (*0-8020-7379-4*); pap. text, student ed. 19.95 (*0-8020-7678-5*) U of Toronto Pr.

***Cicogna, Giampaolo & Gaeta, Giuseppe.** Symmetry & Perturbation Theory in Nonlinear Dynamics. LC 99-49856. (Lecture Notes in Physics Ser.: Vol. 57). xi, 208p. 1999. 39.95 (*3-540-65904-8*) Spr-Verlag.

Ciconia, Johannes. "Nova Musica" & "De Proportionibus" Ellsworth, Oliver B., ed. LC 93-34080. (Greek & Latin Music Theory Ser.: Vol. 8). (Illus.). x, 532p. 1993. text 50.00 (*0-8032-1465-0*) U of Nebr Pr.

Ciconte, Barbara Kushner & Jacob, Jeanne G. The Fundmentals of Fundraising. 250-300p. 1996. 59.00 (*0-8342-0793-1*) Aspen Pub.

Ciconte, Marie, ed. see Shles, Larry.

Cicora, Ken. One Hundred Twenty-Five Ideas for Successful Events. 171p. 24.95 (*0-914951-74-2*) LERN.

***Cicora, Mary A.** Modern Myths & Wagnerian Deconstructions: Literary-Critical Approaches to Wagner's Music-Dramas, 57. LC 99-31628. Vol. 57. 232p. 2000. 65.00 (*0-313-30539-0*) Greenwood.

Cicora, Mary A. Mythology As Metaphor: Romantic Irony, Critical Theory & Wagner's Ring, 46. LC 98-9606. (Contributions to the Study of Music & Dance Ser.: Vol. 46). 184p. 1998. 59.95 (*0-313-30528-5*, Greenwood Pr) Greenwood.

— Wagner's Ring & German Drama: Comparative Studies in Mythology & History in Drama, 52. LC 98-37782. (Contributions to the Study of Music & Dance: Vol. 52). 200p. 1999. 59.95 (*0-313-30529-3*, Greenwood Pr) Greenwood.

Cicotello, Louis, jt. auth. see Sassower, Raphael.

Cicourel, Aaron V. The Social Organization of Juvenile Justice. LC 94-17406. 362p. (C). 1994. reprint ed. pap. 24.95 (*1-56000-779-6*) Transaction Pubs.

Cicovacki, Predrag. Anamorphosis: Kant on Knowledge & Ignorance. LC 97-8016. 336p. 1997. 46.00 (*0-7618-0742-X*) U Pr of Amer.

— Anamorphosis: Kant on Knowledge & Ignorance. LC 97-8016. 336p. 1997. pap. 34.50 (*0-7618-0790-X*) U Pr of Amer.

Cicovacki, Predrag, ed. Essays by Lewis White Beck: Five Decades As a Philosopher. LC 98-30651. 224p. 1999. 59.95 (*1-58046-042-9*) Univ Rochester Pr.

Cid-Arregui, Angel & Garcia-Carranca, Alejandro, eds. Microinjection & Transgenesis: Strategies & Protocols. LC 97-27747. (Lab Manual Ser.). (Illus.). 400p. 1997. 104.00 (*3-540-61895-3*) Spr-Verlag.

Cid, Jordi, tr. see Greenberger, Dennis & Padesky, Christine A.

Cid, Xose F. Diccionario da Lingua Galega, 3 vols., Set. deluxe ed. (SPA.). 2086p. 1986. 450.00 (*0-7859-3367-0*, 8476800002) Fr & Eur.

Ciddor, Anna. Unplugged! The Bare Facts on Toilets Through the Ages. (True Stories Ser.). (Illus.). 100p. (J). (gr. 3-8). 1997. pap. 6.95 (*1-86448-454-3*, Pub. by Allen & Unwin Pty) IPG Chicago.

Cie, jt. auth. see Gumuchian.

CIE Electronic Components Society Staff, ed. Electronic Components & Materials: Proceedings of the International Conference on Electronic Components & Materials, Beijing, China, 7-10 November 1989. (International Academic Publishers Ser.). 590p. 1990. 175.00 (*0-08-040175-9*, 1603; 1601; 1105, Pub. by IAP) Elsevier.

Ciechanowicz, Z. J., jt. ed. see Wichmann, Briar A.

Ciee. Adventure. 1999. pap. 13.95 (*0-312-08127-8*) St Martin.

Ciegler, Alex, jt. auth. see Bennett, J. W.

Ciehanover, Aaron J. & Schwartz, Alan L., eds. Cellular Proteolytic System. (Modern Cell Biology Ser.: Vol. 15). 233p. 1994. 159.95 (*0-471-02189-X*) Wiley.

CIEL UK Staff. The Veneration & Administration of the Eucharist: Proceedings of the Second International Colloquium of Historical, Carmical & Theological Studies on the Roman Catholic Liturgy. 255p. 1997. pap. 22.95 (*1-901157-15-6*) St Austin.

Cielec, Greg. My Cleveland Story. LC 98-96292. 288p. 1998. 22.00 (*0-9665724-0-8*) Pink Flamngo Pr.

Cielo, Astra. Fortunes & Dreams. 225p. 1996. reprint ed. spiral bd. 19.50 (*0-7873-0176-0*) Hlth Research.

— Fortunes & Dreams: A Practical Manual of Fortune Telling, Divination & the Interpretation of Dreams, Signs & Omens. 226p. 1996. reprint ed. pap. 17.95 (*1-56459-847-0*) Kessinger Pub.

— Signs, Omens & Superstitions. 1991. lib. bdg. 75.00 (*0-8490-5003-0*) Gordon Pr.

— Signs, Omens & Superstitions. 159p. 1996. reprint ed. spiral bd. 14.50 (*0-7873-0175-2*) Hlth Research.

— Signs, Omens & Superstitions (1918) 163p. 1996. reprint ed. pap. 14.00 (*1-56459-899-3*) Kessinger Pub.

Cielo, Bob. Winning Hockey: Systems & Strategies for All 3 Zones. (Illus.). 128p. (Orig.). 1996. pap. 12.95 (*1-57028-076-2*, 80762H, Mstrs Pr) NTC Contemp Pub Co.

Cielo, P., ed. Optical Techniques for Industrial Inspection. 606p. 1988. text 138.00 (*0-12-174655-0*) Acad Pr.

Cielo, Paolo G. Selected Papers on Optical Techniques for Industrial Inspection. LC 97-3031. (Milestone Ser.). 1997. write for info. (*0-8194-2531-1*) SPIE.

Cienciala, Anna & Komarnicki, Titus. From Versailles to Locarno: Keys to Polish Foreign Policy, 1919-1925. LC 84-2302. xviii, 390p. 1984. 40.00 (*0-7006-0247-X*) U Pr of KS.

Ciencin, Scott. Ancient Games, Vol. 2. (The Eleven Ways Ser.). 1997. mass mkt. 5.99 (*0-380-77981-1*, Avon Bks) Morrow Avon.

***Ciencin, Scott.** Beverly Hills Brontosaurus Vol. 5. (Dinoverse Ser.: Vol. 5). (Illus.). 192p. (J). (gr. 4-7). 2000. pap. 4.99 (*0-375-80595-8*, Pub. by Random Bks Yng Read) Random.

— Dinosaurs Ate My Homework. (Dinoverse Ser.: Vol. 6). (Illus.). (J). 2000. pap. 4.99 (*0-375-80596-6*, Pub. by Random Bks Yng Read) Random.

Ciencin, Scott. I Was a Teenage T. Rex. 192p. (J). 2000. pap. 4.99 (*0-679-88843-8*) Random.

— Incarnate. (Lurker Files Ser.). (YA). (gr. 5 up). 1997. pap. 6.99 (*0-614-28944-0*) Random Bks Yng Read.

— Lost City. LC 94-44454. (Dinotopia Ser.). (YA). (gr. 5-8). 1996. pap. 3.99 (*0-679-86983-2*, Pub. by Random Bks Yng Read) Random.

— Lost City. (Dinotopia Ser.). (YA). (gr. 5-8). 1996. 9.09 (*0-606-08564-5*, Pub. by Turtleback) Demco.

— The Lotus & the Rose. 304p. (Orig.). 1993. mass mkt. 4.99 (*0-446-36249-2*, Pub. by Warner Bks) Little.

— The Mask: Mars Needs Chocolate. (Tattoo Tales Ser.). (Illus.). (J). (ps-6). 1997. pap. 5.99 (*0-614-28930-0*) Random Bks Yng Read.

— Nemesis. (Lurker Files Ser.). (YA). (gr. 5 up). 1997. pap. 6.99 (*0-614-28943-2*) Random Bks Yng Read.

— Night of Glory. (Eleven Ways Ser.: No. 3). 256p. 1998. mass mkt. 5.99 (*0-380-77983-8*, Eos) Morrow Avon.

— Please Don't Eat the Teacher! (Dinoverse Ser. No. 4). (Illus.). 192p. (YA). (gr. 4-7). 2000. pap. 4.99 (*0-679-88846-2*, Pub. by Random Bks Yng Read) Random.

— Raptor Without a Cause. (Dinoverse Ser.: No. 3). 192p. (J). (gr. 4). 2000. pap. 4.99 (*0-679-88845-4*, Pub. by Random Bks Yng Read) Random.

***Ciencin, Scott.** Return to Lost City. (Dinotopia Ser.). (Illus.). (YA). (gr. 5-8). 2000. pap. 3.99 (*0-375-81018-8*) Random.

Ciencin, Scott. Sky Dance. (Dinotopia Ser.). (Illus.). 264p. (YA). (gr. 5-8). 1999. pap. 4.99 (*0-679-80417-X*) Random.

***Ciencin, Scott.** Sky Dance. (Dinotopia Ser.). (Illus.). (YA). (gr. 5-8). 1999. pap. 4.99 (*0-375-80417-X*, Pub. by Random Bks Yng Read) Random.

Ciencin, Scott. The Teens Time Forgot, Vol. 2. 192p. (J). 2000. pap. 4.99 (*0-679-88844-6*) Random.

— Thunder Falls. LC 96-67485. (Dinotopia Ser.). (YA). (gr. 5-8). 1997. pap. 3.99 (*0-679-88256-1*, Pub. by Random Bks Yng Read) Random.

— Thunder Falls. LC 96-607485. (Dinotopia Ser.). (YA). (gr. 5-8). 1996. 9.09 (*0-606-10953-6*, Pub. by Turtleback) Demco.

— The Vampire Odyssey. 416p. 1992. mass mkt. 4.50 (*0-8217-3853-4*, Zebra Kensgtn) Kensgtn Pub Corp.

— Windchaser. (Dinotopia Ser.). (YA). (gr. 5-8). 1995. pap. 3.99 (*0-679-86981-6*) Random.

Ciencin, Scott. Windchaser. (Dinotopia Ser.). (YA). (gr. 5-8). 1995. 9.09 (*0-606-08387-1*, Pub. by Turtleback) Demco.

Ciencin, Scott. The Wolves of Autumn. 304p. (Orig.). 1992. mass mkt. 4.99 (*0-446-36248-4*, Pub. by Warner Bks) Little.

Cienfuegos, Sabina, tr. see Valdes, Zoe.

Cienik, Andy, jt. auth. see Merritt, Susan E.

Cienkus. Mentors & Mentoring: A Special Issue of the Peabody Journal of Education, Vol. 71, No. 1. 1996. pap. 20.00 (*0-8058-9932-4*) L Erlbaum Assocs.

Cientificas y Tecnic Staff. Diccionario Terminologico de Ciencias Medicas. (SPA.). 1424p. 1991. 150.00 (*0-7859-6042-2*, 8445800701) Fr & Eur.

Cieplak, Tadeusz N., ed. Poland since 1956: Readings & Essays on Polish Government & Politics. LC 79-125262. 482p. 1972. text 42.50 (*0-8290-0193-X*); pap. text 19.50 (*0-8290-0374-6*) Irvington.

Cieplinski, Feigue. Jewish Identity Through Literature. 142p. 1993. pap. 12.95 (*1-889534-20-X*) Jay St Pubs.

Cieraad, Irene. At Home: An Anthropology of Domestic Space. LC 98-31882. (Space, Place, & Society Ser.). 3p. 1999. 34.95 (*0-8156-0562-5*) Syracuse U Pr.

Cieri, Marie, et al, contrib. by. 19 Projects: Artists-in-Residence at the MIT List Visual Arts Center, Marina Abramovic & Ulay. LC 95-47172. 1996. pap. 25.00 (*0-938437-51-8*) MIT List Visual Arts.

Cierjacks, S. W., ed. Neutron Sources: For Applied & Pure Nuclear Research. (Neutron Physics & Nuclear Data in Science & Technology Ser.: Vol. 2). 370p. 1983. 160.00 (*0-08-029351-4*, Pub. by Pergamon Repr) Franklin.

Cierley, Randy S. So, You Got Talent - Now What? A Musician's Guide to the Music Business. (Illus.). (Orig.). 1989. pap. text. write for info. (*0-318-66597-2*) String Pub CA.

Cierna, et al. Nemecko-Slovensky Slovnik. (SLO.). 968p. 1996. write for info. (*80-08-01408-3*, Pub. by Slov Pegagog Naklad) IBD Ltd.

Cierna, jt. auth. see Kolesarova.

Ciernick, Bernard & Santiago, Louise J. The All-Purpose Hands-on Confirmation Director's Manual. 176p. 1996. teacher ed., ring bd. 39.95 (*0-937997-30-7*) Hi-Time Pflaum.

Ciervo, Joseph. Gort - Klatuu, Berada, Nictoe. 32p. 1999. pap. 8.00 (*0-8059-4566-0*) Dorrance.

Ciervo, Ray. Getting the Job Done: A Handbook for Christian Leaders. 96p. (Orig.). 1995. pap. 5.95 (*0-9637311-3-0*) Genesis Comm Inc.

Cieryca, Shirley A. A Collection of Time. Kost, Loretta L., ed. & illus. by. 47p. (Orig.). 1998. reprint ed. pap. 12.00 (*0-9658960-0-5*) Line Graphics Pub.

Cierzniak, Mark. Big Basic Web Site Directory. Wolin, Henly & Ryan, Tim, eds. LC 97-68674. 218p. 1997. 14.99 (*0-7897-1422-1*) Macmillan.

Ciesielski, Dennis. Between Philosophy & Rhetoric: Aesthetics & Meaning in the Postmodern Composition Classroom. LC 96-24056. (Rethinking Childhood Ser.: Vol. 6). 187p. (C). 1998. text 42.95 (*0-8204-3468-X*) P Lang Pubng.

Ciesielski, Krzysztof. Set Theory for the Working Mathematician. (London Mathematical Society Student Texts Ser.: Vol. 39). 248p. (C). 1997. text 59.95 (*0-521-59441-3*); pap. text 20.95 (*0-521-59465-0*) Cambridge U Pr.

Ciesielski, Krzysztof, et al. I-Density Continuous Functions. LC 93-39028. (Memoirs of the American Mathematical Society Ser.: No. 515). 133p. 1994. pap. 32.00 (*0-8218-2579-8*, MEMO/107/515) Am Math.

Ciesielski, Paula. Wellness: Major Chronic Diseases. 176p. (C). 1991. text 13.50 (*0-87967-873-9*, Dshkn McG-Hill) McGrw-H Hghr Educ.

Ciesielski, Z., ed. see Mathematical Institute of the Polish Academy of Sc & Institute of Mathematics of the Adam Mickiewicz Un.

Ciesla, Bill. Stranieri: An Italian Odyssey. 306p. 1998. pap. 14.00 (*1-57502-967-7*, PO2650) Morris Pubng.

Ciesla, Burghard & Judt, Matthias. Technology Transfer Out of Germany after 1945. (Studies in the History of Science, Technology & Medicine Ser.). 169p. 1996. text 27.00 (*3-7186-5822-4*) Gordon & Breach.

Ciesla-Korytowska, Maria, ed. The Slavs in the Eyes of the Occident: The Occident in the Eyes of the Slavs. 200p. (C). 1993. text 31.00 (*0-88033-252-2*, 355, Pub. by East Eur Monographs) Col U Pr.

Ciesla, Regina, jt. auth. see Ciesla, Thomas.

Ciesla, Thomas & Ciesla, Regina. Touring TX Wineries. LC 98-14790. 198p. 1997. pap. 18.95 (*0-88415-376-2*, 5376) Gulf Pub.

Ciesla, William & Danaubauer, Edwin. Decline & Dieback of Trees & Forests: A Global Overview. (Forestry Papers: No. 120). 100p. 1994. pap. 14.00 (*92-5-103502-4*, F35024, Pub. by FAO) Bernan Associates.

Cieslak, M. J., et al, eds. The Metal Science of Joining: Proceeding of a Symposium Sponsored by the TMS Solidification Committee/MDMD & the Physical Metallurgy Committee/SMD, This Symposium Was Held October 20-24, 1991 at the TMS Fall Meeting in Cincinnati, Ohio. LC 92-80699. (Illus.). 339p. 1992. pap. 105.10 (*0-608-04985-9*, 206560300004) Bks Demand.

***Cieslak, W. R., et al.** Selected Battery Topics. 692p. 1999. 98.00 (*1-56677-208-7*, PV 98-15) Electrochem Soc.

Cieslak, William. Console One Another: Commentary on the Order of Christian Funerals. 128p. 1990. pap. 9.95 (*0-912405-68-6*, Pastoral Press) OR Catholic.

Cieslawski, Steve, compiled by. At the Crack of the Bat. LC 91-28946. (Illus.). 64p. (J). (gr. 4-7). 1992. lib. bdg. 15.49 (*1-56282-177-6*, Pub. by Hyprn Child) Little.

Cieslicki, Aaron. Scenic Driving Wisconsin. LC 97-9801. (Illus.). 184p. (Orig.). 1997. pap. 14.95 (*1-56044-558-0*) Falcon Pub Inc.

Cieslik, Dietmar. Steiner Minimal Trees. LC 98-9332. (Nonconvex Optimization & Its Applications Ser.). 319p. 1998. 140.00 (*0-7923-4983-0*) Kluwer Academic.

Cieslik, Jurgen & Cieslik, Marianne. Button in Ear: The History of the Teddy Bear & His Friends. Freisberg, Laraine, tr. from GER. (Illus.). 264p. 1989. 47.00 (*3-921844-18-5*, BB-125) Gold Horse.

C

***Cieslik, Jurgen & Cieslik, Marianne.** German Doll Studies: Historic Doll Research for the Published Archives of Cieslik's Puppenmagazin. (Illus.). 332p. 1999. 75.00 (*0-912823-88-7*, BT-183, Pub. by Gold Horse) Dollmasters.

— Teddy Bear Encyclopedia: Makers, Dates, Descriptions to over 270 German Manufacturers. (Illus.). 239p. 1998. 69.00 (*0-912823-78-X*, BB-491, Pub. by Gold Horse) Dollmasters.

Cieslik, Marianne, jt. auth. see Cieslik, Jurgen.

***Cieslinski, Michael.** Dynasty League Baseball 1999 Season: 2000 Edition. 116p. 2000. pap. 49.95 (*0-9670323-1-8*) Design Depot.

Cieszynski, Joe & Fox, Dave. Electronics for Service Engineers. LC 99-234061. (Illus.). 288p. 1999. pap. text 37.95 (*0-7506-3476-6*, Newnes) Buttrwrth-Heinemann.

Cifarelli, L., et al, eds. Perspectives for New Detectors in Future Supercolliders: Proceedings of the 9th Workshop of the INFN Eloisatron Project, Erice, Italy, 17-24 October 1990. 252p. (C). 1991. text 89.00 (*981-02-0652-6*) World Scientific Pub.

Cifarelli, L. & Dokshitzer, Y., eds. QCD at 200 TeV. (Ettore Majorana International Science Ser., Life Sciences: Vol. 60). (Illus.). 304p. (C). 1992. text 126.00 (*0-306-44222-1*, Kluwer Plenum) Kluwer Academic.

Cifarelli, L. & Khoze, V. A. Properties of Susy Particles. 500p. 1994. text 121.00 (*981-02-1424-3*) World Scientific Pub.

Cifarelli, L. & Ypsilantis, T., eds. New Technologies for Supercolliders. (Ettore Majorana International Science Ser., Life Sciences: Vol. 57). (Illus.). 408p. (C). 1992. text 155.00 (*0-306-44058-X*, Kluwer Plenum) Kluwer Academic.

Cifarelli, L., jt. auth. see Ali, A.

Cifarelli, Luisa, et al, eds. Universality Features in Multihadron Production & the Leading Effect: Proceedings of the 33rd Workshop of the INFN Eloisatron Project Erice, Italy 19-25 October, 1996. LC 98-162252. (Science & Culture Ser.). 400p. 1998. 84.00 (*981-02-3340-X*) World Scientific Pub.

***Cifarelli, Luisa & Maritato, Luigi, eds.** Superconducting Materials for High Energy Colliders. (Science & Culture Ser.). 450p. 2000. 96.00 (*981-02-4319-7*) World Scientific Pub.

Cifelli, Edward, ed. The Selected Letters of John Ciardi. 504p. 1991. text 40.00 (*1-55728-171-8*) U of Ark Pr.

Cifelli, Edward M. John Ciardi: A Biography. LC 97-5394. 1998. pap. 28.00 (*1-55728-539-X*) U of Ark Pr.

Cifelli, Edward M. & Zulauf, Sander W. Index to American Periodical Verse: 1978. LC 73-3060. 432p. 1980. lib. bdg. 21.00 (*0-8108-1301-7*) Scarecrow.

Cifelli, Edward M., jt. auth. see Zulauf, Sander W.

Cifelli, Edward M., ed. see Ciardi, John.

Cifelli, Richard & Scott, George. Stratigraphic Record of the Neogene Globorotalidradiation (Planktonic Foraminiferida) LC 84-600360. (Smithsonian Contributions to Paleobiology Ser.: No. 58). 105p. reprint ed. pap. 32.60 (*0-608-17113-1*, 202713500054) Bks Demand.

***Ciferri, A.** Supramolecular Polymers. LC 00-29028. 2000. write for info. (*0-8247-0252-2*) Dekker.

Ciferri, Alberto, ed. Liquid Crystallinity in Polymers: Principles & Fundamental Properties. 438p. 1991. 95.00 (*0-89573-771-X*, Wiley-VCH) Wiley.

Ciferri, Alberto, ed. Liquid Crystallinity in Polymers: Principles & Fundamental Properties. 438p. 1991. 155.00 (*0-471-18736-4*) Wiley.

***Ciferri, Orio, et al.** Of Microbes & Art: The Role of Microbial Communities in the Degradation & Protection of Cultural Heritage. LC 00-23508. 2000. write for info. (*0-306-46377-6*, Kluwer Plenum) Kluwer Academic.

Ciffolillo, Kathryn, ed. Invitation to Change 1993 Winners: Better Government Competition on Policies Affecting Children. (Better Government Competition Ser.). 100p. (Orig.). 1993. pap. 10.00 (*0-929930-11-8*) Pioneer Inst.

Ciffolillo, Kathryn, ed. see Armor, David J. & Peiser, Brett M.

Ciffolillo, Kathryn, jt. ed. see Brown, Linda.

Ciffolillo, Kathryn, ed. see Chelius, James R. & Muscovitch, Edward.

Ciffolillo, Kathryn, ed. see Rossell, Christine H. & Baker, Keith.

Cifields, Louis. Baltimore Metropolitan African-American Resource & Tourist Guide. (Illus.). 132p. (Orig.). 1996. pap. write for info. (*0-9655741-0-5*) BAATC.

CIFOPE Staff. Energy Development in South-East Asia & Cooperation with the European Communities: Pattaya, Thailand, 27 February 3-March 1989. (Illus.). 408p. (C). 1989. 350.00 (*974-8201-81-3*, Pub. by Edits Technip) Enfield Pubs NH.

Cifuentes, A. O. Using MSC-NASTRAN: Statics & Dynamics. (Illus.). xiv, 458p. 1989. 72.95 (*0-387-97032-0*) Spr-Verlag.

Cifuentes, Carlos L. El Nuevo Empresario en Mexico (Mexico's New Entrepeneur) (SPA.). 322p. 1994. pap. 11.99 (*968-16-4507-3*, Pub. by Fondo) Continental Bk.

Cifuentes Delatte, L., ed. see Renal Stone Research Symposium Staff.

Cifuentes, Hugo. Sendas Del Ecuador (Paths of Ecuador) (SPA., Illus.). 72p. 1988. pap. 8.99 (*968-16-2855-1*, Pub. by Fondo) Continental Bk.

Cifuentes, Juan L. El Oceano y Sus Recursos VIII: Approvechamiento de Recursos. (Ciencia para Todos Ser.). (SPA.). pap. 6.99 (*968-16-2864-0*, Pub. by Fondo) Continental Bk.

— El Oceano y Sus Recursos XI: Acuicultura. (Ciencia para Todos Ser.). (SPA.). pap. 6.99 (*968-16-3433-0*, Pub. by Fondo) Continental Bk.

— El Oceano y Sus Recursos V: Plancton. (Ciencia para Todos Ser.). (SPA.). pap. 6.99 (*968-16-2653-2*, Pub. by Fondo) Continental Bk.

— El Oceano y Sus Recursos I: Panorama Oceanico. (Ciencia para Todos Ser.). (SPA.). pap. 6.99 (*968-16-2389-4*, Pub. by Fondo) Continental Bk.

— El Oceano y Sus Recursos IV: Bilogia. (Ciencia para Todos Ser.). (SPA.). pap. 6.99 (*968-16-2539-0*, Pub. by Fondo) Continental Bk.

— El Oceano y Sus Recursos IX: La Pesca. (Ciencia para Todos Ser.). (SPA.). pap. 6.99 (*968-16-4815-3*, Pub. by Fondo) Continental Bk.

— El Oceano y Sus Recursos II: Geologia y Quimica. (Ciencia para Todos Ser.). (SPA.). pap. 6.99 (*968-16-2455-6*, Pub. by Fondo) Continental Bk.

— El Oceano y Sus Recursos VII: Flujos de Energia. (Ciencia para Todos Ser.). (SPA.). pap. 6.99 (*968-16-2863-2*, Pub. by Fondo) Continental Bk.

— El Oceano y Sus Recursos VI: Bentos y Necton. (Ciencia para Todos Ser.). (SPA.). pap. 6.99 (*968-16-2704-0*, Pub. by Fondo) Continental Bk.

— El Oceano y Sus Recursos X: Pesquerias. (Ciencia para Todos Ser.). (SPA.). pap. 6.99 (*968-16-3429-2*, Pub. by Fondo) Continental Bk.

— El Oceano y Sus Recursos III: Fisica, Matematicas & Ingenieria. (Ciencia para Todos Ser.). (SPA.). pap. 6.99 (*968-16-2456-4*, Pub. by Fondo) Continental Bk.

— El Oceano y Sus Recursos XII: El Futuro. (Ciencia para Todos Ser.). (SPA.). pap. 6.99 (*968-16-3434-9*, Pub. by Fondo) Continental Bk.

Cifuentes, Luis F., jt. ed. see Molloy, Sylvia.

Cifuentes, Marcela Campuzano, see Llano Restrepo, Maria C. & Campuzano Cifuentes, Marcela.

Cigan, John M., ed. see World Symposium on Metallurgy & Environmental Cont.

Cigar, Norman. Genocide in Bosnia: The Policy of "Ethnic Cleansing" LC 94-32948. (Eastern European Studies: No. 1). (Illus.). 240p. 1995. 32.95 (*0-89096-638-9*) Tex A&M Univ Pr.

Cigard, Jane, ed. see Sink, Kevin.

Cigarette Card Co of London Staff, ed. Complete Catalogue of British Cigarettes. 2nd ed. 1983. 25.95 (*0-03-063533-0*) Holt R&W.

Ciges, M & Campos, A., eds. Inner Ear Pathobiology. (Advances in OtoRhinoLaryngology Ser.: Vol. 45). (Illus.). x, 224p. 1990. 198.50 (*3-8055-5203-3*) S Karger.

***Ciggaar, K. N. & Teule, H. G. B.** East & West in the Crusader States. Context - Contacts - Confrontations II: Acts of the Congress Held at Hernen Castle in May 1997. xiv, 218p. 1999. 42.00 (*90-429-0786-X*, Pub. by Peeters Pub) Bks Intl VA.

Ciggaar, Krijnie N. Western Travellers to Constantinople: The West & Byzantium, 962-1204: Cultural & Political Relations. LC 96-19020. (Medieval Mediterranean, x0928-5520 Ser.). (Illus.). 368p. 1996. 149.00 (*90-04-10637-5*) Brill Academic Pubs.

Cigler. American Politics. 4th ed. LC 97-72452. (C). 1998. pap. text 28.36 (*0-395-87538-2*) HM.

Cigler, Allan J. & Loomis, Bardett A. Interest Group Politics. 4th ed. LC 94-33764. 435p. (YA). 1994. text 29.95 (*0-87187-801-1*) Congr Quarterly.

Cigler, Allan J. & Loomis, Burdett A. American Politics: Classic & Contemporary Readings. LC 88-81326. 1989. teacher ed. 2.76 (*0-318-36887-0*) HM.

— American Politics: Classic & Contemporary Readings, 3 vols. 3rd ed. (C). 1995. text, teacher ed. 11.96 (*0-395-70834-6*); pap. text 28.36 (*0-395-70833-8*) HM.

— Interest Group Politics. 5th ed. LC 98-30202. 400p. 1998. pap. text 30.95 (*1-56802-159-3*) Congr Quarterly.

Cigler, Allan J., jt. ed. see Browne, William P.

***Cigliano, Jan.** Bungalow: American Restoration Style. LC 98-13420. (Illus.). 112p. 1998. pap. 21.95 (*0-87905-852-8*) Gibbs Smith Pub.

Cigliano, Jan. Private Washington: Residences in the Nation's Capital. LC 98-26054. (Illus.). 176p. 1998. 50.00 (*0-8478-2024-6*, Pub. by Rizzoli Intl) St Martin.

— Showplace of America: Cleveland's Euclid Avenue, 1850-1910 c. LC 91-9019. (Illus.). 416p. 1991. 45.00 (*0-87338-445-8*) Kent St U Pr.

Cigman, Gloria, ed. Lollard Sermons: Edited from British Library MS Additional 41321; Bodleian Library MS Rawlinson C. 751; Manchester, John Rylands Library MS English 412. (OS 294 Ser.: No. 294). 416p. 1989. 69.00 (*0-19-722296-X*) OUP.

Cigman, Gloria, ed. see Chaucer, Geoffrey.

Cignetti, Pamela B., jt. auth. see Campbell, Dorothy M.

***Cigno & Bourn.** Cognitive Behavioral Social Work in Practice. 304p. 1998. pap. 33.95 (*1-85742-374-7*) Ashgate Pub Co.

Cigno, Alessandro. The Economics of the Family. (Illus.). 224p. 1994. reprint ed. pap. text 24.95 (*0-19-828871-9*) OUP.

Cigno, Katy & Bourn, Diana, eds. Cognitive Behavioural Social Work in Practice. 288p. 1998. text 67.95 (*1-85742-373-9*, Pub. by Ashgate Pub) Ashgate Pub Co.

Cigno, Katy, jt. auth. see Burke, Peter.

***Cignoli, Roberto, et al.** Algebraic Foundations of Many-Valued Reasoning. LC 99-52098. (Trends in Logic Ser.). 244p. 1999. 100.00 (*0-7923-6009-5*) Kluwer Academic.

Cigrand, B. J. Crispe. History of the Crispe Family . . . in the Old War . . . & the New World. (Illus.). 409p. 1997. reprint ed. pap. 61.50 (*0-8328-8142-2*); reprint ed. lib. bdg. 71.50 (*0-8328-8141-4*) Higginson Bk Co.

***Cigrand, Mariann.** Easy Literature-Based Quilts Around the Year. (Illus.). 72p. (J). 2000. pap. 10.95 (*0-439-13898-1*) Scholastic Inc.

Cihac, Alexandre de. Dictionnaire d'Etymologie Daco-Romane, 2 vols., Set. fac. ed. (FRE.). 1188p. 1978. 695.00 (*0-7859-8457-7*, 3764802049) Fr & Eur.

Cihak, Kathryn. Thones: Thirty-Four Calligraphic Meditations from a Westerner's Pen. LC 93-80617. 34p. (Orig.). 1994. pap. 10.95 (*0-9631750-3-3*) Muse Pubns.

Cihak, Mary K. & Heron, Barbara J. Games Children Should Play: Sequential Lessons for Teaching Communication Skills in Grades K-6. (Illus.). 240p. (Orig.). 1980. pap. 15.95 (*0-673-16370-9*, GoodYrBooks) Addson-Wesley Educ.

Cihak, R., jt. ed. see Christ, B.

Cihlar, Josef, ed. The Use of Landsat Data in Forestry, Vol. 2. (Remote Sensing Reviews Ser.: Vol. 1, Pt. 3). 258p. 1986. pap. text 267.00 (*3-7186-0307-1*) Gordon & Breach.

Cihlar, Many, ed. Mystics at Prayer. LC 36-17108. 83p. 1931. pap. 9.95 (*0-912057-58-0*, 501650) GLELJ AMORC.

Ciholas, Paul. Consider My Servant Job: Meditations on Life's Struggles & God's Faithfulness. LC 98-8340. 272p. 1998. 16.95 (*1-56563-372-5*) Hendrickson MA.

Cihon, Patrick J. & Castagnera, James O. Employment & Labor Law. 3rd ed. LC 98-5637. (LG - Labor Law Ser.). 1998. pap. 89.95 (*0-538-85443-X*) S-W Pub.

— Labor & Employment Law. (SWC-Business Law). 690p. (C). 1988. mass mkt. 51.75 (*0-534-07842-7*) PWS Pubs.

— Labor & Employment Law. 2nd ed. 675p. 1992. mass mkt. 79.95 (*0-534-92816-1*) S-W Pub.

Cihui, Y., jt. auth. see Dongwuxue.

Cihylik, Nancy, jt. auth. see Stoddard, Elga.

CIIR & Latin America Bureau, jt. ed. see Painter, James.

CIIR Staff. Black Christians & the Church in South Africa (Bishop Zwane of Swaziland) 1979. 20.00 (*0-904393-43-7*) Cath Inst Inter.

***Cijntje, Dennis E., ed.** Netherlands Antilles Business Law. 624p. 1999. 159.00 (*90-411-1248-0*) Kluwer Law Intl.

Cikanova, Karla. Having Fun with Yarn & Fabric. (Illus.). 128p. 1996. text 22.50 (*976-641-071-2*) Gordon & Breach.

***Cikanova, Karla.** Let's Talk with the World: A Child's Guide to Art & the Natural World. (Illus.). 128p. 1998. text 22.50 (*90-5703-311-9*, Harwood Acad Pubs) Gordon & Breach.

Cikanova, Karla. Teaching Children to Paint. 128p. (J). (gr. 3-7). 1993. text 14.00 (*976-8097-39-6*) Gordon & Breach.

Cikes, I., ed. Echocardiography in Cardiac Interventions. (Developments in Cardiovascular Medicine Ser.). (C). 1989. text 420.50 (*0-7923-0088-2*) Kluwer Academic.

Cikins, Warren I. & Sevick, James R., eds. Constructing Correctional Facilities: Is There a Role for the Private Sector? (Dialogues on Public Policy Ser.). 60p. 1987. pap. 10.95 (*0-8157-1415-7*) Brookings.

Cikins, Warren I., jt. ed. see Baily, Mary A.

Cikins, Warren I., jt. ed. see Falco, Mathea.

Cikovsky, Jr., Nicolai, et al. Winslow Homer. LC 95-19025. (Illus.). 464p. 1995. 60.00 (*0-300-06555-8*) Yale U Pr.

Cikovsky, Nicolai, Jr. George Inness. LC 93-18308. (Library of American Art). (Illus.). 144p. 1993. 45.00 (*0-8109-3462-0*, Pub. by Abrams) Time Warner.

— Raphaelle Peale Still Lifes. (Illus.). 132p. 1989. 30.00 (*0-8109-1474-3*, Pub. by Abrams) Time Warner.

— Winslow Homer. (Library of American Art). (Illus.). 160p. 1990. 45.00 (*0-8109-1193-0*, Pub. by Abrams) Time Warner.

Cikovsky, Nicolai, Jr., ed. Studies in the History of Art: Winslow Homer: A Symposium. LC 72-600309. (Symposium Papers XI: Vol. 26). (Illus.). 140p. (Orig.). 1989. pap. 25.00 (*0-89468-132-X*) Natl Gallery Art.

— Winslow Homer: A Symposium. 1996. 30.00 (*0-300-07520-0*) Yale U Pr.

Cikovsky, Nicolai, Jr., frwd. Lewis Rubenstein: The Hudson Valley Painter. LC 93-19589. (Illus.). 1993. 29.95 (*0-87951-515-5*, Pub. by Overlook Pr) Penguin Putnam.

Cikovsky, Nicolai, Jr. & Kelly, Franklin. Winslow Homer. LC 95-19025. 1995. write for info. (*0-89468-217-2*) Natl Gallery Art.

Cikovsky, Nicolai & National Gallery of Art (U. S.) Staff. American Impressionism & Realism: The Margaret & Raymond Horowitz Collection. LC 98-38978. 1998. pap. write for info. (*0-89468-239-3*) Natl Gallery Art.

Cikovsky, Nicolai & Robinson, William, eds. Paintings from the C. R. Smith Collection. (Illus.). 1970. pap. 5.00 (*0-87959-030-0*) U of Tex H Ransom Ctr.

Cikovsky, Nicolai, Jr., et al. Celebrate America: 19th Century Paintings from the Manoogian Collection. (Illus.). 132p. 1999. write for info. (*0-945064-02-0*) Dixon Gallery.

Cilag-Chemie, ed. Toxikologische, Endokrinologische und Klinische Aspekte bei der Pruefung eines neuen Neuroleptikums. Ein wissenschaftliches Gespraech. (International Pharmacopsychiatry Ser.: Vol. 13, Suppl. 1). (Illus.). 1978. pap. 25.25 (*3-8055-2931-7*) S Karger.

Cilella, Salvatore G., ed. see Mandel, Richard D.

Cilento, Raphael W. Causes of Depopulation in the Western Islands of the Territory of New Guinea. LC 75-32809. reprint ed. 32.50 (*0-404-14113-7*) AMS Pr.

Cilento, Ruth. Heal Cancer: Choose Your Own Path. 420p. (Orig.). 1994. pap. 15.95 (*0-85572-213-4*, Pub. by Hill Content Pubng) Seven Hills Bk.

Cilento, V., ed. see Marien, Bert.

Cilescu, V. Vixens of Night. 1997. mass mkt. 6.95 (*0-7472-5582-2*, Pub. by Headline Bk Pub) Trafalgar.

Cilescu, Valentina. Body & Soul: Mistress with a Maid, Vol. 3. (Orig.). 1997. mass mkt. 6.50 (*1-56333-515-8*, Rosebud) Masquerade.

— Dark Venus. (Orig.). 1997. mass mkt. 6.50 (*1-56333-481-X*, Rosebud) Masquerade.

— Mistress Mine. 3rd ed. (Orig.). 1997. reprint ed. mass mkt. 6.50 (*1-56333-502-6*, Rosebud) Masquerade.

CILETTI. Modeling Synthesis & Rapid Prototyping with the VERILOG HDL. LC 99-10494. 727p. 1999. text 105.00 (*0-13-977398-3*) S&S Trade.

***Ciletti, Barbara.** Creative Pickling: From Classic Dills to Ginger Pears, 50 Sweet, Savory, & Tangy Recipes. LaFerla, Jane, ed. LC 99-86889. (Classic Kitchen Crafts Ser.). (Illus.). 128p. 2000. write for info. (*1-57990-177-8*, Pub. by Lark Books) Sterling.

Ciletti, Barbara. Making Great Cheese: 30 Simple Recipes from Cheddar to Chevre, Plus 18 Scrumptious Dishes. LC 98-53253. (Illus.). 144p. 1999. 24.95 (*1-57990-109-3*, Pub. by Lark Books) Random.

— The Onion Harvest Cookbook. (Illus.). 176p. 1998. pap. 19.95 (*1-56158-245-X*, 070370) Taunton.

— The Pepper Harvest Cookbook. LC 97-10086. (Illus.). 172p. 1997. 24.95 (*1-56158-195-X*, 70323) Taunton.

— The Pepper Harvest Cookbook. (Illus.). 176p. 1998. pap. 19.95 (*1-56158-276-X*, 070408) Taunton.

Ciletti, Michael D. Circuit Master: Circuit Simulation Program & Study Guide. (Illus.). 312p. (C). 1995. pap. text, student ed. 45.00 (*0-03-070566-5*) OUP.

— Introduction to Circuit Analysis & Design & Circuit Master: Circuit Simulation Program & Study Guide. (Illus.). 1014p. 1995. text 84.00 (*0-03-020788-6*) OUP.

CILF Staff. Dictionnaires de Genetique.Tr. of Genetics Dictionary with English-French Index. (ENG & FRE.). 352p. 1991. pap. 125.00 (*0-8288-6166-8*, F116440) Fr & Eur.

— French-Arabic Agricultural Dictionary: Dictionnaire d'Agriculture Francais-Arabe. (ARA & FRE.). 606p. 1985. pap. 95.00 (*0-8288-0756-6*, M14595) Fr & Eur.

— Quadrilingual Dictionary of the Press & Media (Dictionnaire Quadrilingue de la Presse et des Medias) (FRE, ITA, POR & SPA.). 304p. 1990. 95.00 (*0-7859-4580-6*, 2853192210) Fr & Eur.

— Technical Vocabulary of Tobacco: Vocabulaire Technique du Tabac. (ENG, FRE & GER.). 320p. 1982. pap. 49.95 (*0-8288-0761-2*, M14591) Fr & Eur.

— Vocabulaire d'Astronomie. (DUT, ENG, FRE, GER & ITA.). 320p. 1980. pap. 49.95 (*0-8288-0773-6*, M6555) Fr & Eur.

— Vocabulaire de la Micrographie. (ENG, FRE & GER.). 230p. 1980. pap. 49.95 (*0-8288-0187-8*, M 14590) Fr & Eur.

— Vocabulaire de L'Equitation et des Courses. (FRE.). 1984. pap. 22.50 (*0-8288-2338-3*, M14596) Fr & Eur.

Cilia, John P. A Guide for Building & Facility Automation Systems. 220p. 1991. 67.00 (*0-88173-082-3*) Fairmont Pr.

Cilia, John P., jt. auth. see Fairmont Press Staff.

Ciliberti, Anthony. Bank Internal Auditing Manual. 1984. 295.00 (*0-88712-132-2*) Warren Gorham & Lamont.

Ciliberti, Charles. Backstairs Mission in Moscow: American Autobiography. 127p. 1995. lib. bdg. 69.00 (*0-7812-8479-1*) Rprt Serv.

Ciliberto, Ciro, et al, eds. Classification of Algebraic Varieties: Proceedings of the Algebraic Geometry Conference on Classification of Algebraic Varieties, May 22-30, 1992, University of L'Aquila, L'Aquila, Italy. LC 93-44549. (Contemporary Mathematics Ser.: No. 162). 410p. 1994. pap. 39.00 (*0-8218-5179-9*, CONM/162) Am Math.

Ciliberto, Ciro, jt. auth. see Ballico, E.

***Ciliberto, Enrico & Spoto, Giuseppe.** Art & Archaeology, Vol. 154. LC 99-57435. 736p. 2000. 145.00 (*0-471-29361-X*) Wiley.

Ciliga, Ante. The Russian Enigma. Renier, Fernand G. et al, trs. from RUS. 588p. 1989. pap. text 15.95 (*0-906133-23-8*) Routledge.

— Sve i Odmah. Arapovic, Rudolf et al, eds. LC 98-216625. (CRO., Illus.). 128p. 1999. pap. 7.00 (*0-9669561-0-9*, 078) Hrvatski.

Cilingiroglu, A. & French, D. H., eds. Anatolian Iron Ages, Vol. 2. (British Institute of Archaeology at Ankara, Monograph Ser.: No. 13). (Illus.). 192p. 1991. pap. 42.00 (*0-946897-38-7*, Pub. by Brit Sch Archaeol Iraq) David Brown.

— Anatolian Iron Ages, Vol. 3. (Illus.). 314p. 1994. 54.00 (*1-898249-05-9*, Pub. by Brit Inst Arch) David Brown.

Cilingiroglu, Ugur. Systematic Analysis of Bipolar & MOS Transistors. LC 92-43084. (Materials Ser.). 220p. 1993. text 29.00 (*0-89006-625-6*) Artech Hse.

Ciliotta, Claire & Livingston, Carole. Why Am I Going to the Hospital? (Where Did I Come From Ser.). (Illus.). (J). (gr. k-7). 1992. pap. 8.95 (*0-8184-0568-6*, L Stuart) Carol Pub Group.

Ciliotta, Claire, jt. auth. see Livingston, Carole.

Ciliska, Donna. Beyond Dieting: Psychoeducational Interventions for Chronically Obese Women - A Non-Dieting Approach. LC 90-1533. (Eating Disorders Monographs: No. 5). (Illus.). 192p. 1990. text 33.95 (*0-87630-583-4*) Brunner-Mazel.

***Cilla, Raul Homero.** Barrio-Logos: Space & Place in Urban Chicano Literature & Culture. (CMAS History Culture Ser.). (Illus.). 288p. 2000. 35.00 (*0-292-78741-3*) U of Tex Pr.

Cillario, Simona, jt. auth. see Schiatti, Lamberto.

Cillers, H. S. Close Corporations: A Comprehensive Guide. 2nd ed. 280p. 1993. pap. 63.00 (*0-409-01997-6*, SA, MICHIE) LEXIS Pub.

— Company Law. 4th ed. 816p. 1982. pap. 110.00 (*0-409-01936-4*, SA, MICHIE) LEXIS Pub.

— Corporate Law. 2nd ed. 816p. 1992. pap. 59.00 (*0-409-01968-2*, SA, MICHIE); pap. 92.00 (*0-409-01969-0*, SA, MICHIE) LEXIS Pub.

— Entrepreneurial Law. write for info. (*0-409-01978-X*, SA, MICHIE) LEXIS Pub.

***Cillessen, F. & Van Der Meen, W., eds.** Atlas of Urine Sediments: Interactive Reference on Cd-Rom. 1999. 330.50 (*0-444-50177-0*, Pergamon Pr) Elsevier.

Cilley, Dean & Cilley, Susan, eds. Appalachian Trail Guide to Maine. 13th ed. (Illus.). 184p. 1996. pap. 24.95 (*0-917953-90-8*) Appalachian Trail.

Cilley, G. & Cilley, J. P. Gamble: The Mount Desert Widow: Genealogy of the Maine Gamble Family from the First Landing on the Coast of Mt. Desert down to the Present Day. 196p. 1992. reprint ed. pap. 30.00 (*0-8328-6563-X*); reprint ed. lib. bdg. 40.00 (*0-8328-6562-1*) Higginson Bk Co.

Cilley, J. P., jt. auth. see Cilley, G.

Cilley, Susan, jt. ed. see Cilley, Dean.

Cillia, Rudolf De, see De Cillia, Rudolf.

Cillian, David J. Resume Kit, Do-It-Yourself. (Illus.). 9.95 (*1-880398-04-4*, 01014) SJT Enterprises.

Cillie, Burger. Pocket Guide to Southern African Mammals. (Illus.). 124p. 1999. pap. 14.95 (*0-627-01686-3*, Pub. by J L Van Schaik) BHB Intl.

***Cillie, Burger & Oberprieler, Ulrich.** Pocket-Guide to Southern African Birds. 2000. pap. 14.95 (*0-627-01979-X*, Pub. by J L Van Schaik) BHB Intl.

Cillie, LaCheryl B. & Powell, Yolanda W. From Darkness to Light: A Modern Guide to Recapturing Historical Riches - Understanding Auctions, Collectibles & Estate Sales. LC 97-92326. (Illus.). 210p. (Orig.). 1998. pap. 16.95 (*0-9658908-0-5*) Creat Inspirations.

Cilliers, H. C., et al. Extracts from Entrepreneurial Law. 152p. 1994. pap. write for info. (*0-409-01980-1*, MICHIE) LEXIS Pub.

Cilliers, H. S., et al. Close Corporations Service - Beslote Korporasiesdiens. (AFR & ENG.). write for info. (*0-409-01995-X*, R220.02, MICHIE) LEXIS Pub.

— Korporatiewe Finansiele Verslagdoening. write for info. (*0-409-07159-5*) Buttrwrth-Heinemann.

— Ondernemingsreg. (AFR.). 459p. 1993. pap. write for info. (*0-409-01979-8*, MICHIE) LEXIS Pub.

— Uittreksels Uit Ondernemingsreg. (AFR.). 152p. 1994. pap. write for info. (*0-409-01981-X*, MICHIE) LEXIS Pub.

Cilliers, Hendrik S., et al. Close Corporations Law. 3rd ed. LC 98-214124. vii, 342 p. 1998. write for info. (*0-409-01991-7*) Buttrwrth-Heinemann.

Cilliers, Johan. Korrels Van Die Koninkryk: Grepe Uit Die Gelykenisse Van Jesus. LC 98-140275. 103 p. 1998. write for info. (*0-627-02307-X*) J L Van Schaik.

Cilliers, Paul. Complexity & Postmodernism: Understanding Complex Systems. LC 97-18224. (Illus.). 176p. (C). 1998. 70.00 (*0-415-15286-0*); pap. 21.99 (*0-415-15287-9*) Routledge.

Cilluffo, Frank, et al, eds. The Nuclear Black Market: Global Organized Crime Project. LC 96-20400. (CSIS Report Ser.). 49p. (C). 1996. pap. text 16.95 (*0-89206-287-8*) CSIS.

Cilluffo, Frank J., ed. Cybercrime... Cyberterrorism... Cyberwarfare: Averting a Electronic Waterloo. LC 99-164238. 96p. (C). 1998. pap. text 21.95 (*0-89206-295-9*) CSIS.

— Russian Organized Crime. LC 97-33442. (Panel Report Ser.). 94p. 1997. pap. 21.95 (*0-89206-293-2*) CSIS.

Cilluffo, Frank J & Raine, Linnea P., eds. Global Organized Crime: The New Empire of Evil. LC 94-41954. (CSIS Report Ser.). 185p. (C). 1994. pap. text 24.95 (*0-89206-312-2*) CSIS.

Cilton, Michael. USFTL Rule Book & Official's Manual, 5. 5th rev. ed. (USFTL Rule Book & Official's Manual). (Illus.). 208p. 1988. pap. 20.00 (*0-9672456-0-5*) USFTL.

Cilurzo, Mary J., ed. Health Industry QuickSource: A Complete Descriptive Reference to Health Care Information Resources. 1100p. (Orig.). 1995. pap. 225.00 (*1-886515-08-5*) QuickSource Pr.

Cilwa, Paul. Borland C++ Insider. 457p. 1995. pap. 26.95 (*0-471-30338-0*) Wiley.

— Borland Pascal 7 Insider. Duntemann, Jeff, ed. LC 93-15005. 560p. 1993. pap. 26.95 (*0-471-59894-1*) Wiley.

Cima, Alex. Click Tables: In Beats per Minute & Frames per Beat. 460p. 1988. pap. text 39.95 (*0-928448-00-2*) Neuron Music.

Cima, Bill. Rest Area Guide to the United States & Canada, Vol. 5. 5th rev. ed. (Illus.). 248p. 1977. pap. 13.95 (*0-937877-25-5*) Cottage Pubns Inc.

Cima, Bill & Cima, Saundra. Sunset California Freeway: Exit Guide. (Illus.). 352p. (Orig.). 1985. pap. 9.95 (*0-936929-01-4*) Am Travel Pubns.

Cima Communications Staff, ed. see Martinez, Jose F.

Cima, Gay G. Performing Women: Female Characters, Male Playwrights, & the Modern Stage. (Illus.). 240p. 1993. text 39.95 (*0-8014-2874-2*) Cornell U Pr.

— Performing Women: Female Characters, Male Playwrights, & the Modern Stage. (Illus.). 248p. 1996. pap. text 15.95 (*0-8014-8337-9*) Cornell U Pr.

Cima, James P. Achieving Unlimited Health: The Elusive Fountain of Youth. 150p. (Orig.). 1997. pap. 19.95 (*0-9659476-0-2*) JPC Pubng.

— How to Eat More & Lose Weight & Never Diet Again. Hurst, Elizabeth, ed. 158p. (Orig.). 1997. pap. 19.95 (*0-9659476-1-0*) JPC Pubng.

— Stress, You Can't Live with It & You Can't Live Without It: Changing Stress into Success. 150p. (Orig.). 1997. pap. 19.95 (*0-9659476-2-9*) JPC Pubng.

***Cima, Joseph A. & Ross, William T.** The Backward Shift on the Hardy Space. (SURV Ser.: Vol. 79). 199p. 2000. 49.00 (*0-8218-2083-4*) Am Math.

Cima, Ronald J., ed. Vietnam: A Country Study. LC 88-600482. (Illus.). 432p. (Orig.). 1990. boxed set 23.00 (*0-16-018143-7*, 008-020-01190-8) USGPO.

— Vietnam: A Country Study. (Illus.). 386p. (Orig.). (C). 1995. reprint ed. text 45.00 (*0-7881-1876-5*) DIANE Pub.

Cima, Saundra, jt. auth. see Cima, Bill.

Cimaglia, Alice R. The Art & Science of Manicuring. (Illus.). 144p. pap. 10.13 (*0-685-40006-9*) Milady Pub.

— The Art & Science of Manicuring. (Illus.). 144p. 1986. pap. 23.95 (*0-87350-409-7*) Milady Pub.

— Cuaderno sobre el Arte y la Ciencia de la Manicura. (SPA.). 96p. 1987. pap. 16.95 (*0-87350-380-5*) Milady Pub.

Cimarosti, Adriano. The Complete History of Grand Prix Motor Racing. (Illus.). 504p. 1997. 50.00 (*1-85410-500-0*, Pub. by Aurum Pr) London Brdge.

***Cimarrusti, Marianna Neverka.** A Gift - Poems from Spiritual Experiences. 120p. 2000. pap. 8.95 (*0-533-13286-X*) Vantage.

Cimarusti, Marie Torres. Peek-A-Moo! (Illus.). 10p. (J). (ps up). 1998. 9.99 (*0-525-46083-7*, Dutton Child) Peng Put Young Read.

Cimasi, Robert J. A Guide to Consulting Services for Emerging Healthcare Organizations. LC 98-52741. 501p. 1999. 75.00 (*0-471-31625-3*) Wiley.

Cimasoni, Geneve. The Crevicular Fluid. (Monographs in Oral Science: Vol. 3). 121p. 1974. 48.75 (*3-8055-1699-1*) S Karger.

— Crevicular Fluid Updated. (Monographs in Oral Science: Vol. 12). (Illus.). viii, 152p. 1983. 101.00 (*3-8055-3705-0*) S Karger.

Cimbais, James. In Nomine Infernal Player's Guide. Hartsock, Nettie, ed. (Illus.). 128p. 1998. pap. 19.95 (*1-55634-344-2*, 3309, Pub. by S Jackson Games) BookWorld.

Cimbais, James. In Nomine Angelic Player's Guide. Hartsock, Nettie, ed. (Illus.). 128p. 1997. pap. 19.95 (*1-55634-340-X*, 3307) S Jackson Games.

Cimbala, Paul & Miller, Randall, eds. The Freedmans Bureau & Reconstruction: Essays on an Institution & Its Failures. LC 99-34974. (Reconstructing America Ser.: Vol. 4). 352p. 1999. 35.00 (*0-8232-1934-8*, Pub. by Fordham) BookMasters.

— The Freedmans Bureau & Reconstruction: Essays on an Institution & Its Failures. LC 99-34974. (Reconstructing America Ser.: Vol. 4). 1999. pap. 19.95 (*0-8232-1935-6*, Pub. by Fordham) BookMasters.

Cimbala, Paul A. The Freedmen's Bureau. Date not set. pap. write for info. (*1-57524-094-7*) Krieger.

— Under the Guardianship of the Nation: The Freedmen's Bureau & the Reconstruction of Georgia, 1865-1870. LC 96-31225. 1997. 50.00 (*0-8203-1891-4*) U of Ga Pr.

Cimbala, Paul A. & Himmelberg, Robert F., eds. Historians & Race: Autobiography & the Writing of History. LC 96-24749. (Blacks in the Diaspora Ser.). 160p. 1996. 25.00 (*0-253-33235-4*); pap. 12.95 (*0-253-21101-8*) Ind U Pr.

Cimbala, Paul A. & Miller, Randall M., eds. Against the Tide: Women Reformers in American Society. LC 96-47662. 192p. 1997. pap. 20.95 (*0-275-95806-X*, Praeger Pubs) Greenwood.

Cimbala, Paul A., jt. ed. see Miller, Randall M.

Cimbala, Stephen. The Politics of Warfare: The Great Powers in the Twentieth Century. LC 96-6450. 208p. 1997. pap. 18.95 (*0-271-01598-5*) Pa St U Pr.

Cimbala, Stephen J. Challenges to Deterrence: Resources, Technology & Policy. LC 87-2227. 327p. 1987. 59.95 (*0-275-92350-9*, C2350, Praeger Pubs) Greenwood.

***Cimbala, Stephen J.** Clausewitz & Chaos: Friction in War & Military Policy. LC 00-39173. 240p. 2000. 59.00 (*0-275-96951-7*, Praeger Pubs) Greenwood.

Cimbala, Stephen J. Clausewitz & Escalation: Classical Perspective on Nuclear Strategy. 218p. 1991. text 42.50 (*0-7146-3420-4*, Pub. by F Cass Pubs) Intl Spec Bk.

— Clinton & Post-Cold War Defense. LC 95-30659. 216p. 1996. 57.95 (*0-275-95006-9*, Praeger Pubs) Greenwood.

— Coercive Military Strategy. LC 98-22791. 229p. 1998. 39.95 (*0-89096-836-5*) Tex A&M Univ Pr.

— Collective Insecurity: U. S. Defense Policy & the New World Disorder, 162. LC 95-7511. (Contributions in Military Studies Ser.: No. 162). 240p. 1995. 59.95 (*0-313-29656-1*, Greenwood Pr) Greenwood.

— Conflict Termination in Europe: Games Against War. LC 89-77107. 296p. 1990. 65.00 (*0-275-93592-2*, C3592, Praeger Pubs) Greenwood.

— First Strike Stability: Deterrence after Containment, 101. LC 90-32456. (Contributions in Military Studies Ser.: No. 101). 232p. 1990. 62.95 (*0-313-27448-7*, CND/, Greenwood Pr) Greenwood.

— Force & Diplomacy in the Future. LC 91-31504. 256p. 1992. 59.95 (*0-275-94109-4*, C4109, Praeger Pubs) Greenwood.

— Military Persuasion: Deterrence & Provocation in Crisis & War. LC 93-1202. 1994. 50.00 (*0-271-01005-3*); pap. 18.95 (*0-271-01006-1*) Pa St U Pr.

— Nuclear Endings: Stopping War on Time. LC 88-27441. 318p. 1989. 65.00 (*0-275-93165-X*, C3165, Praeger Pubs) Greenwood.

— Nuclear Strategizing: Deterrence & Reality. LC 87-38496. 316p. 1988. 59.95 (*0-275-92987-6*, C2987, Praeger Pubs) Greenwood.

***Cimbala, Stephen J.** Nuclear Strategy in the Twenty-first Century. LC 99-52984. 224p. 2000. 65.00 (*0-275-96869-3*, Praeger Pubs) Greenwood.

Cimbala, Stephen J. Nuclear War & Nuclear Strategy: Unfinished Business, 68. LC 87-12003. (Contributions in Military Studies Ser.: No. 68). 299p. 1987. 59.95 (*0-313-26015-X*, CNW/, Greenwood Pr) Greenwood.

— The Past & Future of Nuclear Deterrence. LC 97-49280. 248p. 1998. 55.00 (*0-275-96239-3*, Praeger Pubs) Greenwood.

— The Politics of Warfare: The Great Powers in the Twentieth Century. LC 96-6450. 208p. 1997. 50.00 (*0-271-01597-7*) Pa St U Pr.

— Rethinking Nuclear Strategy. LC 87-28702. 288p. 1988. 45.00 (*0-8420-2294-5*) Scholarly Res Inc.

— Strategic Impasse: Offense, Defense, & Deterrence Theory & Practice, 89. LC 89-2166. (Contributions in Military Studies Ser.: No. 89). 287p. 1989. 69.50 (*0-313-26516-X*, CSI/, Greenwood Pr) Greenwood.

— Strategy after Deterrence. LC 90-39027. 288p. 1991. 65.00 (*0-275-93741-0*, C3741, Praeger Pubs) Greenwood.

— U. S. Military Policy & the Cold War Endgame. LC 94-17487. 280p. 1995. 47.50 (*0-7146-4556-7*, Pub. by F Cass Pubs); pap. 24.50 (*0-7146-4117-0*, Pub. by F Cass Pubs) Intl Spec Bk.

— U. S. Nuclear Strategy in the New World. 259p. 1994. 46.95 (*1-56924-986-5*) Marlowe & Co.

***Cimbala, Stephen J., ed.** Deterrence & Nuclear Proliferation in the Twenty-First Century. LC 00-38526. 240p. 2000. 59.00 (*0-275-96698-4*) Greenwood.

— Mysteries of the Cold War. LC 98-31001. (Policy Studies Organization Ser.). 200p. 1999. text 78.95 (*1-84014-425-4*, Pub. by Ashgate Pub) Ashgate Pub Co.

Cimbala, Stephen J., ed. National Security Strategy: Choices & Limits. LC 84-6845. (Foreign Policy Issues: A Foreign Policy Research Institute Ser.). 371p. 1984. 49.95 (*0-275-91138-1*, C1138, Praeger Pubs) Greenwood.

— The Reagan Defense Program: An Interim Assessment. LC 86-962. 215p. (C). 1986. 45.00 (*0-8420-2243-0*); pap. 17.95 (*0-8420-2262-7*) Scholarly Res Inc.

— Soviet C3. LC 87-26967. (AFCEA Signal Magazine C3I Ser.: Vol. VII). (Illus.). 472p. 1987. text 39.95 (*0-916159-15-9*) AFCEA Intl Pr.

— Strategic Air Defense. LC 88-26079. 275p. 1989. 45.00 (*0-8420-2285-6*) Scholarly Res Inc.

— Strategic Arms Control after SALT. LC 88-35254. 233p. 1989. 45.00 (*0-8420-2290-2*) Scholarly Res Inc.

— Strategic War Termination. LC 86-91508. 244p. 1986. 55.00 (*0-275-92239-1*, C2239, Praeger Pubs) Greenwood.

Cimbala, Stephen J. & Starron, John, Jr., eds. The Soviet Challenge in the 1990s. LC 89-16128. 325p. 1989. 65.00 (*0-275-92788-1*, C2788, Praeger Pubs) Greenwood.

Cimbala, Stephen J. & Waldman, Sidney R., eds. Controlling & Ending Conflict: Issues Before & after the Cold War, 119. LC 91-27741. 296p. 1991. 65.00 (*0-313-27477-0*, CCQ, Greenwood Pr) Greenwood.

Cimbalik, Kari, ed. Take Good Care of Me: What Kids Think Every Grown-Up Needs to Know about Being a Parent. LC 98-33195. (Illus.). 96p. 1999. pap. 9.95 (*1-57071-442-8*) Sourcebks.

Cimbola, Stephen J., ed. Intelligence & Intelligence Policy in Democratic Society. 260p. (C). 1987. lib. bdg. 45.00 (*0-941320-44-8*) Transnatl Pubs.

Cimbolic, Peter & Jobes, David A., eds. Youth Suicide: Issues, Assessment, & Intervention. 138p. 1990. pap. 18.95 (*0-398-06057-6*) C C Thomas.

— Youth Suicide: Issues, Assessment, & Intervention. 138p. (C). 1990. text 33.95 (*0-398-05706-0*) C C Thomas.

Cimbuna, Al, jt. auth. see Avery, Constance.

Ciment, James. Algeria: The Fundamentalist Challenge. LC 96-48372. (Conflict & Crisis in the Post-Cold War World Ser.). 176p. 1997. 23.95 (*0-8160-3340-4*) Facts on File.

— Angola & Mozambique: Postcolonial Wars in Southern Africa. LC 96-29643. (Conflict & Crisis in the Post-Cold War World Ser.). 1997. 23.95 (*0-8160-3525-3*) Facts on File.

— The Kurds: State & Minority in Turkey, Iraq, & Iran. LC 95-9595. (Conflict & Crisis in the Post-Cold War World Ser.). 1996. 23.95 (*0-8160-3339-0*) Facts on File.

— Law & Order. LC 94-42471. (Life in America 100 Years Ago Ser.). (Illus.). 100p. (YA). (gr. 5 up). 1995. lib. bdg. 19.95 (*0-7910-2843-7*) Chelsea Hse.

— Palestine/Israel: The Long Conflict. LC 96-48371. (Conflict & Crisis in the Post-Cold War World Ser.). 1997. 23.95 (*0-8160-3526-1*) Facts on File.

— Scholastic Encyclopedia of the North American Indian. LC 95-26171. 224p. (J). (gr. 4-7). 1996. 17.95 (*0-590-22790-4*, Scholastic Ref) Scholastic Inc.

Ciment, James, ed. Encyclopedia of Conflicts since World War II, 4 vols., Set. LC 98-28374, (Illus.). 1400p. (C). 1999. text 399.00 (*0-7656-8004-1*, Sharpe Prof) M E Sharpe.

***Ciment, James & Ness, Immanuel.** Encyclopedia of American Immigration. LC 00-26560. 2000p. 2000. text 399.00 (*0-7656-8028-9*, Sharpe Ref) M E Sharpe.

Ciment, James, jt. auth. see Ness, Immanuel.

Ciment, Jill. Half a Life. LC 97-10815. 224p. 1997. pap. 12.95 (*0-385-48891-2*, Anchor NY) Doubleday.

***Ciment, Jill.** Teeth of the Dog. LC 98-26453. 224p. 1999. 22.00 (*0-517-70202-9*, Crown) Crown Pub Group.

Ciment, Michel. Dictionnaire du Cinema Americain (A-K) (FRE.). 1988. lib. bdg. 35.00 (*0-8288-2498-3*) Fr & Eur.

— Dictionnaire du Cinema Americain (K-Z) (FRE.). 1988. lib. bdg. 35.00 (*0-8288-2499-1*) Fr & Eur.

Cimet, Adina. Ashkenazi Jews in Mexico: Ideologies in the Structuring of a Community. LC 95-5161. (SUNY Series in Anthropology & Judaic Studies). 248p. (C). 1997. text 59.50 (*0-7914-3179-7*); pap. text 19.95 (*0-7914-3180-0*) State U NY Pr.

Ciminero, Anthony R., et al. Handbook of Behavioral Assessment. 2nd ed. LC 86-11010. (Personality Processes Ser.). 789p. 1986. 195.00 (*0-471-88849-4*) Wiley.

Ciminero, Sandra E. Planning a Model Boat Regatta, 2 Vols., No. 1. (Boat Book Series: Vol. 1). (Illus.). 32p. 1999. pap. 9.95 (*0-9669513-1-X*) ArtsyKids.

Cimino. Oasis Chronicles. 1997. pap. text 24.95 (*1-901674-02-9*) Arrowhead Bks.

Cimino, Al. Great Record Labels. 1992. 17.98 (*1-55521-787-7*) Bk Sales Inc.

— 101 All Time Best Loved Songs: For Piano & Guitar. 256p. 1997. pap. text 16.95 (*1-878427-54-7*, XC7700) Cimino Pub Grp.

Cimino, Carol. Ensuring a Future Full of Hope: A Board's & Parent's Guide to Active Participation in the School's Recruitment Effort. (Illus.). 35p. (Orig.). 1992. pap. 4.00 (*1-55833-080-1*) Natl Cath Educ.

Cimino, Esther R. The Touchstone & Me: Experiences of a Missionary Wife. 275p. (Orig.). 1993. write for info. (*0-9639059-0-2*) E R Cimino.

Cimino, F., et al. Human Tumor Markers: Proceedings of the International Conference Lacco Ameno d'Ischia, 3rd, Napoli, Italy, April 23-26, 1986. xiv, 922p. (C). 1987. lib. bdg. 292.35 (*3-11-010935-2*) De Gruyter.

Cimino, James D. Intranets: The Surf Within. (Illus.). 500p. 1996. pap. 39.95 (*1-886801-40-1*) Thomson Learn.

— Webmaster's Guide to Lotus Domino. (Illus.). 400p. (Orig.). 1997. pap. 39.95 (*1-886801-11-8*) Chrles River Media.

Cimino, James E. & Brescia, Michael, eds. Calvary Hospital: A Model for Pallitaive Care in Advanced Cancer. LC 98-71723. 180p. 1998. text 49.95 (*0-930194-98-5*) Ctr Thanatology.

Cimino, James E. & Kutscher, Austin H., eds. Management of Intercurrent Illness & Complicated Advanced Disease: Advanced Cancer & Stroke As a Model. LC 98-71723. 120p. 1999. pap. 18.95 (*0-930194-34-9*) Ctr Thanatology.

Cimino, John A. Be Your Own Lawyer Videos: Chapter Seven Bankruptcy. 1992. write for info. incl. VHS (*1-879833-07-7*) Be Own Lawyer.

Cimino, Judith. Walking on Eggshells. 198p. Date not set. mass mkt. 5.99 (*1-55197-059-7*) Picasso Publ.

Cimino, Moyra. A Servant of the Stuarts. 1982. 40.00 (*0-7223-1557-0*, Pub. by A H S Ltd) St Mut.

Cimino Publishing Group Staff. British Isles. (Real Exploring Guides Ser.). (Illus.). 96p. 1997. pap. text 14.95 (*1-901438-00-7*) Cimino Pub Grp.

— France. (Real Exploring Guides Ser.). (Illus.). 96p. 1997. pap. text 14.95 (*1-901438-01-5*) Cimino Pub Grp.

— Kurt Cobain Files. 1998. pap. text 24.95 (*1-901674-01-0*) Arrowhead.

— Madonna Diaries. 1997. pap. text 24.95 (*1-901674-03-7*, Pub. by Arrowhead) Cimino Pub Grp.

— Metallica Files. 1998. pap. text 24.95 (*1-901674-00-2*) Arrowhead.

— X-Files Files. 1998. pap. text 24.95 (*1-901674-19-3*) Arrowhead.

Cimino, Richard & Lattin, Don. Shopping for Faith: American Religion in the New Millenium. LC 98-19707. (Religion in Practice Ser.). 224p. 1998. 22.00 incl. cd-rom (*0-7879-4170-0*) Jossey-Bass.

Cimino, Richard P. Against the Stream: The Adoption of Traditional Christian Faiths by Young Adults. LC 96-35834. 146p. 1996. pap. text 26.00 (*0-7618-0575-3*); lib. bdg. 46.00 (*0-7618-0574-5*) U Pr of Amer.

Cimino, Rosa M. Ancient Rome & India: Commercial & Cultural Contacts Between the Roman World & India. (Illus.). 264p. 1994. 47.50 (*81-215-0676-X*, Pub. by M Manoharial) Coronet Bks.

Cimmino, Marion, jt. auth. see Edwards, Gabrielle I.

***Cimolai, Nevio.** Serodiagnosis of the Infectious Diseases: Mycoplasma Pneumoniae. LC 99-33336. 117p. 1999. write for info. (*0-7923-8568-3*) Kluwer Academic.

***Cimoli, Mario, ed.** Developing Innovation Systems: Mexico in a Global Context. LC 00-35835. (Science, Technology & International Political Economy Ser.). 224p. 2000. pap. 82.95 (*0-8264-4768-6*) Continuum.

Cimono Publishing Staff. Favorite Classical Melodies: Hundred Songs for Easy Piano. 124p. (YA). 1992. pap. 14.95 (*0-943748-55-0*, PF0793) Ekay Music.

Cimorell-Strong, Jacqueline M. Language Facilitation: A Complete Cognitive Therapy Program. LC 83-1075. 208p. (C). 1983. spiral bd. 34.00 (*0-936104-96-1*, 1246) PRO-ED.

Cimorelli, Lynne. Playing on the Keys, Prep Bk. C. large type ed. (Illus.). 88p. (Orig.). (J). (gr. 1-5). 1997. pap. text 10.95 (*0-9657845-2-5*) Alex Pub.

— Playing on the Keys, Prep Bk. A. large type ed. (Illus.). 102p. (Orig.). (J). (gr. 1-5). 1997. pap. text 10.95 (*0-9657845-0-9*) Alex Pub.

— Playing on the Keys, Prep Bk. B. large type ed. (Illus.). 94p. (Orig.). (J). (gr. 1-5). 1997. pap. text 10.95 (*0-9657845-1-7*) Alex Pub.

***Cimorosi, Tony.** World Beat Grooves for Bass. 40p. 1999. pap. 14.95 incl. audio compact disk (*0-7935-9836-2*) H Leonard.

Cimorra, Ana M. Atlas of Nursing: Atlas de la Enfermera. (SPA., Illus.). 86p. 1987. pap. 19.95 (*0-7859-4943-7*) Fr & Eur.

Cimperman, Wayne, jt. auth. see Passport Publications Staff.

Cimprich, John. Slavery's End in Tennessee, 1861-1865. LC 84-16200. (Illus.). 202p. 1985. reprint ed. pap. 62.70 (*0-608-01663-2*, 206231800002) Bks Demand.

Cin, Mario D., jt. ed. see Bode, Arndt.

Cinader, Bernard, ed. Immunology of Receptors. LC 77-14020. (Immunology Ser.: No. 6). 540p. reprint ed. pap. 167.40 (*0-7837-3349-6*, 204330700008) Bks Demand.

Cinader, Martha. When the Body Calls: Poems. 128p. 1998. pap. 12.00 (*0-86316-279-7*) Writers & Readers.

Cinca, Silvia. Comrade Dracula. LC 87-92212. 250p. (Orig.). 1988. pap. 8.88 (*0-9619930-0-6*) Moonfall Pr VA.

— Forest of Angels. Date not set. pap. 14.99 (*0-9623183-4-5*) Moonfall Pr VA.

— Homo Spiritus: Journeys of Our Magic. LC 88-90647. 224p. 1988. pap. 12.88 (*0-9619930-1-4*) Moonfall Pr VA.

— Hoot of the Owl. 1996. pap. 12.95 (*0-9619930-4-9*) Moonfall Pr VA.

— Strigat (Scream) Silvia Cinca. (RUM.). 1990. pap. 14.99 (*0-9623183-1-0*) Moonfall Pr VA.

— X-Ray for Love. LC 91-90111. (Orig.). 1991. pap. 15.00 (*0-9619930-2-2*) Moonfall Pr VA.

Cinca, Silvia. X-Ray for Success. 1991. pap. 14.99 (*0-9619930-7-3*) Moonfall Pr VA.

Cincel Staff. Pequeno Diccionario Kapelusz de la Lengua Espanola. (SPA.). 612p. 1980. pap. 9.95 (*0-8288-2025-2*, S32728) Fr & Eur.

Cincerelli, Carol J. A Russian Folktale - My Mother Is the Most Beautiful Woman in the World. (Integrating Literature, Language & the Arts Ser.). 96p. (J). (gr. 1-6). teacher ed. 6.99 (*0-86653-539-X*, GA1162) Good Apple.

— The Selfish Giant by Oscar Wilde. (Integrating Literature, Language & the Arts Ser.). 96p. (J). (gr. 1-6). teacher ed. 6.99 (*0-86653-537-3*, GA1158) Good Apple.

— The Tales of the Brothers Grimm. (Integrating Literature, Language & the Arts Ser.). 96p. (J). (gr. 1-6). teacher ed. 7.99 (*0-86653-562-4*, GA1160) Good Apple.

Cincinnati Art Galleries Staff. The Glover Collection: Rookwood Pottery. (Illus.). 288p. (Orig.). 1991. pap. 45.00 (*0-943633-01-X*) Cinc Art Gal.

Cincinnati Zoo Volunteer Program Staff. Cooking on the Wild Side with the Cincinnati Zoo & Botanical Garden. Brooke, Patricia S., ed. (Illus.). 205p. 1995. 12.00 (*0-9636552-1-3*) Cinc Zoo.

Cincinnatus. Chernobyl in Judea. 56p. 1995. 10.00 (*965-229-151-X*, Pub. by Gefen Pub Hse) Gefen Bks.

Cinderella, Joe & Renda, Sandy. Chord Melody Playing for the Guitarist Musician. Stang, Aaron, ed. 52p. (C). 1990. pap. text 9.95 (*0-7692-1351-0*, GF0342) Wrner Bros.

Cindrich, Ivan & Lee, Sing H., eds. Diffractive & Holographic Device Technologies & Applications IV, Vol. 3010. LC 97-200961. 384p. 1997. 80.00 (*0-8194-2421-8*) SPIE.

— Diffractive & Holographic Device Technologies & Applications V. LC 99-165382. (Proceedings of SPIE Ser.: Vol. 3291). 246p. 1998. 69.00 (*0-8194-2730-6*) SPIE.

***Cindrich, Ivan, et al, eds.** Diffractive & Holographic Technologies, Systems, & Spatial Light Modulators VI. 316p. 1999. pap. text 72.00 (*0-8194-3103-6*) SPIE.

Cindrich, Robert J., et al. Federal Civil Procedure Before Trial: Federal Practice Guide. LC 96-77616. (American Inns of Court Ser.). 2200p. 1996. text. write for info. (*0-7620-0096-1*) West Group.

Cindro, N., et al, eds. Frontiers of Heavy-Ion Physics: Proceedings of the 6th International Adriatic Conference on Nuclear Physics, Dubrovnik, Yugoslavia, 15-19 June 1987. 564p. (C). 1988. text 141.00 (*9971-5-0392-1*) World Scientific Pub.

— Fundamental Problems in Heavy-Ion Collisions: Proceedings of the 5th Adriatic Conference on Nuclear Physics, Croatia, Yugoslavia, September, 1984. 588p. 1985. 115.00 (*9971-978-16-4*) World Scientific Pub.

Cindy the Songlady. Kid-Fun Circle Games. 18p. 1992. teacher ed. 10.00 (*0-9628207-1-7*) Kid-Fun Prods.

Cine Books Staff. The Motion Picture Guide, 1994 Annual: THe Films of 1993. 600p. 1994. 99.50 (*0-933997-33-7*) CineBks.

Cine Books Staff, ed. The Motion Picture Guide, 1991 Annual: The Films of 1990. 460p. 1991. 99.50 (*0-918432-92-8*) CineBks.

Cineas, Jean-Baptiste. Le Choc en Retour. (B. E. Ser.: No. 48). (FRE.). 1948. 30.00 (*0-8115-2999-1*) Periodicals Srv.

— Le Drame de la Terre. (B. E. Ser.: No. 46). (FRE.). 1933. 25.00 (*0-8115-2997-5*) Periodicals Srv.

— L' Heritage Sacre. (B. E. Ser.: No. 47). (FRE.). 1945. 35.00 (*0-8115-2998-3*) Periodicals Srv.

Cinebell, Howard. Asesoramiento y Cuidado Pastoral. (SPA.). 480p. 19.00 (*1-55883-403-6*, 6792-0004C) Libros Desafio.

Cinebooks Editors. Movie Guide: The Most Comprehensive Film Reference of Its Kind. LC 97-38975. 832p. 1998. pap. 24.95 (*0-399-52393-6*, Perigee Bks) Berkley Pub.

CineBooks Staff. Family Classics. LC 88-62980. (CineBooks Home Library Ser.: No. 2). 260p. (Orig.). 1997. pap. 9.95 (*0-933997-19-1*) CineBks.

— Foreign Films. LC 89-60765. (CineBooks Home Library Ser.: No. 3). 288p. 1997. pap. 9.95 (*0-933997-22-1*) CineBks.

— Horror Movies. LC 89-60764. (CineBooks Home Library Ser.: No. 4). 336p. 1997. pap. 9.95 (*0-933997-23-X*) CineBks.

— The Motion Picture Guide, 1998 Annual: The Films of 1997. 1998. 179.95 (*0-933997-41-8*) CineBks.

— The Motion Picture Guide, 1997 Annual: The Films of 1996. 1997. 99.50 (*0-933997-39-6*) CineBks.

— MPG Consumer Annual 1989 (Films of 1988) (Illus.). 320p. 1997. pap. 19.95 (*0-933997-21-3*) CineBks.

— MPG Consumer Annual 1990 (Films of 1989) (Illus.). 340p. 1997. pap. 19.95 (*0-933997-28-0*) CineBks.

— Spies & Sleuths. LC 88-71573. (CineBooks Home Library Ser.: No. 1). 224p. (Orig.). 1997. pap. 8.95 (*0-933997-18-3*) CineBks.

— Sports Movies. LC 89-60763. (CineBooks Home Library Ser.: No. 5). 256p. (Orig.). 1997. pap. 9.95 (*0-933997-24-8*) CineBks.

— War Movies. LC 89-60760. (CineBooks Home Library Ser.: No. 6). 256p. (Orig.). 1997. pap. 9.95 (*0-933997-25-6*) CineBks.

CineBooks Staff, ed. The Motion Picture Guide 1996 Annual: The Films of 1995. 1997. 99.50 (*0-933997-37-X*) CineBks.

Cinel, Dino. From Italy to San Francisco: The Immigrant Experience. LC 80-53224. (Illus.). 360p. 1982. 47.50 (*0-8047-1117-8*) Stanford U Pr.

— The National Integration of Italian Return Migration, 1870-1929. (Interdisciplinary Perspectives on Modern History Ser.). 288p. (C). 1991. text 64.95 (*0-521-40058-9*) Cambridge U Pr.

Cinelli, Janet M., ed. see Smith, Gary M.

Cinema Commission of Inquiry. Cinema: Its Present Position & Future Possibilities. LC 78-124002. (Literature of Cinema Ser.). 1970. reprint ed. 30.95 (*0-405-01608-5*) Ayer.

Cinematheque Ontario Staff, jt. auth. see Elder, Kathryn.

Cinevisions Inc. Staff & Gibson, William. Johnny Mnemonic. 176p. (Orig.). 1995. pap. 12.00 (*0-441-00234-X*) Ace Bks.

Cingaranelli, David L., ed. Human Rights: Theory & Measurement. LC 88-4508. (Policy Studies Organization). 256p. 1988. text 39.95 (*0-312-01612-3*) St Martin.

Cingel, N. A. Van der, see Van der Cingel, N. A.

Cingolani, Gabriele. Gabriel of Our Lady of Sorrows: Life & Prayers. Zak, S. B., tr. from ITA. LC 97-8089. Orig. Title: Gabriele Dell'Addolorata: Vita e Preghiere. 86p. (Orig.). 1997. mass mkt. 4.95 (*0-8189-0791-6*) Alba.

— Saint Gabriel Possenti, Passionist: A Young Man in Love. Zak, S. B., tr. from ITA. LC 97-3129.Tr. of Gabriele Dell'Addolorata. (Illus.). 124p. (Orig.). 1997. pap. 12.95 (*0-8189-0790-8*) Alba.

Cingranelli, David L., ed. Comparative Human Rights Policies. 212p. (Orig.). 1986. pap. 15.00 (*0-918592-90-9*) Pol Studies.

Cini, M. & Levy-Leblond, Jean-Marc, eds. Quantum Theory Without Reduction. (Illus.). 180p. 1990. 66.00 (*0-7503-0031-0*) IOP Pub.

Cini, Michelle & McGowan, Lee. Competition Policy in the European Union. LC 98-13815. (European Union Ser.). 272p. 1998. text 59.95 (*0-312-21505-3*) St Martin.

Ciniglio, Jay. Jay Walking: The Ultimate Fitness Journey. LC 98-222971. 160p. 1998. pap. 12.95 (*0-425-16310-5*) Berkley Pub.

Cinlar, Erhan. Introduction to Stochastic Processes. (Illus.). 448p. (C). 1974. text 64.60 (*0-13-498089-1*) P-H.

Cinlar, Erhan, ed. Seminar on Stochastic Processes, 1985. (Progress in Probability & Statistics Ser.: Vol. 12). 336p. 1986. 69.00 (*0-8176-3331-6*) Birkhauser.

Cinlar, Erhan, et al, eds. Seminar on Stochastic Processes, 1987. (Progress in Probability & Statistics Ser.: No. 15). 250p. 1988. 69.00 (*0-8176-3381-2*) Birkhauser.

— Seminar on Stochastic Processes, 1988. (Progress in Probability Ser.: No. 17). 250p. 1989. 69.00 (*0-8176-3422-3*) Birkhauser.

— Seminar on Stochastic Processes, 1989. (Progress in Probability Ser.: No. 18). 224p. 1989. 69.00 (*0-8176-3457-6*) Birkhauser.

Cinlar, Erhan & Sharpe, M. J., eds. Seminar on Stochastic Processes, 1991. (Progress in Probability Ser.: Vol. 29). viii, 247p. 1992. 90.50 (*0-8176-3628-5*) Birkhauser.

Cinlar, Erhan, et al. Seminar on Stochastic Processes: Proceedings from 12th Seminar on Stochastic Processes, 1992, University of Washington. Chung, Kai L. & Sharpe, M. J., eds. LC 93-22016. (Progress in Probability Ser.: Vol. 33). vii, 276p. 1993. 90.50 (*0-8176-3649-8*) Birkhauser.

Cinnaissane des Arts Editorial Staff. French Cabinetmakers of the 18th Century. (Connaissance des Arts Collection). (FRE.). 280p. 1966. 150.00 (*0-8288-6721-6*) Fr & Eur.

Cinnamon, Barry, jt. auth. see Green, Hugh R.

***Cinnamon, Gayle.** Internet Security for Business Applications. McKenna, Jill et al, eds. (Illus.). 1999. pap. write for info. (*1-58143-005-1*, PSG1ISBA) Prosoft I-net.

Cinnamon, Jerry. Climbing Rock & Ice: Learning the Vertical Dance. (Illus.). 308p. 1993. pap. 20.95 (*0-07-011078-6*) McGraw.

— Climbing Rock & Ice: Learning the Vertical Dance. (Illus.). 320p. 1993. text 19.95 (*0-87742-405-5*, Ragged Mntain) McGraw-Hill Prof.

— Climbing Rock & Ice: Learning the Vertical Dance. 2nd ed. 352p. 2000. pap. 22.95 (*0-07-135755-6*) McGraw.

Cinnamon, Kenneth & Farson, Dave. Cults & Cons: The Exploitation of the Emotional Growth Consumer. LC 79-1174. 128p. 1979. pap. text 27.95 (*0-88229-456-3*) Burnham Inc.

Cinneide, Tomas O. The Wild Rover: The Autobiography of Tomas O. Cinneide. LC 97-189501. 176p. 1997. pap. 12.95 (*1-85635-182-3*, Pub. by Mercier Pr) Irish Amer Bk.

***Cinningham, Noble E. Jr.** Thomas Jefferson Versus Alexander Hamilton: Confrontations. 176p. 2000. text 35.00 (*0-312-22821-X*) St Martin.

Cinoman, Susan. Fitting Rooms. 54p. 1996. pap. 10.00 (*0-929741-16-1*) Playsmith.

Cinotti, G. A., jt. ed. see Massry, Shaul G.

Cinqualbre, J., jt. ed. see Bollack, C. G.

Cinquanti, Michael, jt. auth. see Roy, Peter A.

Cinque, Guglielmo. Adverbs & Functional Heads: A Cross-Linguistic Approach. LC 98-21411. (Oxford Studies in Comparative Syntax). 288p. 1999. pap. 45.00 (*0-19-511527-9*) OUP.

— Adverbs & Functional Heads: A Cross-Linguistic Approach. LC 98-21411. (Oxford Studies in Comparative Syntax). 288p. 1999. 65.00 (*0-19-511526-0*) OUP.

— Italian Syntax & Universal Grammer. (Studies in Linguistics: No. 77). 340p. (C). 1996. text 69.95 (*0-521-47513-9*) Cambridge U Pr.

— Paths Towards Universal Grammar: Studies in Honor of Richard S. Kayne. Koster, Jan et al, eds. LC 94-23291. (Georgetown Studies in Romance Linguistics). (Illus.). 507p. reprint ed. pap. 157.20 (*0-608-08036-5*, 206900100002) Bks Demand.

Cinque, Guglielmo & Giusti, Giuliana, eds. Advances in Roumanian Linguistics. LC 95-9960. (Linguistik Aktuell/Linguistics Today Ser.: No. 10). xi, 172p. 1995. 53.00 (*1-55619-228-2*) J Benjamins Pubng Co.

Cinque, Ralph. Quit for Good. 160p. 1994. 8.95 (*1-895952-04-2*, Pub. by Monrch Bks) BookWorld.

Cinquemani, A.M. Glad to Go for a Feast: Milton, Buonmattei & the Florentine "Accademici" LC 97-47420. (Studies in Italian Culture). XXII, 186p. 1998. 44.95 (*0-8204-3974-6*) P Lang Pubng.

Cinquini, Adolph. Index Phaedrianus. 87p. 1964. reprint ed. 20.00 (*0-318-71098-6*) G Olms Pubs.

Cinquino, J. C., jt. auth. see Ali, Amina I.

Cinquino, J. C., ed. see Ali, Amina I.

Cintas, Holly M., jt. auth. see Long, Toby M.

Cintas, P. & Sullivan, Navin. Activated Metals in Organic Synthesis. 256p. 1993. boxed set 99.95 (*0-8493-7863-X*, QD262) CRC Pr.

Cinthio. Cleopatra Tragedia. Morrison, ed. (Exeter Italian Text Ser.: No. 6). (ITA.). 133p. Date not set. pap. text 17.95 (*0-85989-236-0*, Pub. by Univ Exeter Pr) Northwestern U Pr.

Cinthio, Erik, et al, eds. Church Building in Sweden, 1760-1860 Vol. 1: Skane & Blekinge. (ENG & SWE., Illus.). 296p. 1989. 77.50 (*91-7192-774-3*) Coronet Bks.

Cinti, D. Dictionary of Synonyms & Antonyms Italian. (ITA.). 702p. 1995. 47.00 incl. disk (*88-415-1989-4*, Pub. by De Agostini) IBD Ltd.

Cinti, Decio. Dictionary of Synonyms & Antonyms: Dizionario dei Sinonimi e dei Contrari. (ENG & ITA.). 587p. 1983. 49.95 (*0-8288-1987-4*, M14419) Fr & Eur.

— Dizionario dei Sinonimi e dei Contrari. (ITA.). 1990. lib. bdg. 49.95 (*0-8288-3330-3*, M14419) Fr & Eur.

Cinti, Decio, ed. Dizionario dei Sinonimi e dei Contrari. (ITA.). 702p. 1995. 59.00 (*0-913298-75-1*) S F Vanni.

Cintron, jt. auth. see Weber.

Cintron, David. Fast Track Web Programming: A Programmer's Guide to Mastering Web Technologies. LC 98-50462. (Illus.). 448p. 1999. pap. 39.99 (*0-471-32426-4*) Wiley.

Cintron, Esperanza, ed. Seeds: The Literary Journals of the Sisters of Color, Vol. V. unabridged ed. Date not set. pap. write for info. (*1-892730-00-6*) Sisters of Color.

— Seeds: The Literary Journals of the Sisters of Color, Vol. VII. unabridged ed. Date not set. pap. write for info. (*1-892730-02-2*) Sisters of Color.

— Seeds: The Literary Journals of the Sisters of Color, Vol. VIII. unabridged ed. Date not set. pap. write for info. (*1-892730-03-0*) Sisters of Color.

— Seeds: The Literary Journals of the Sisters of Color, Vol. IX. unabridged ed. Date not set. pap. write for info. (*1-892730-04-9*) Sisters of Color.

— Seeds: The Literary Journals of the Sisters of Color, Vol. X. unabridged ed. Date not set. pap. write for info. (*1-892730-05-7*) Sisters of Color.

— Seeds: The Literary Journals of the Sisters of Color, Vol. XI. unabridged ed. Date not set. pap. write for info. (*1-892730-06-5*) Sisters of Color.

— Seeds: The Literary Journals of the Sisters of Color, Vol. XII. unabridged ed. Date not set. pap. write for info. (*1-892730-07-3*) Sisters of Color.

— Seeds: The Literary Journals of the Sisters of Color, Vol. XIII. unabridged ed. Date not set. pap. write for info. (*1-892730-08-1*) Sisters of Color.

— Seeds: The Literary Journals of the Sisters of Color, Vol. XIV. unabridged ed. Date not set. pap. write for info. (*1-892730-09-X*) Sisters of Color.

Cintron, Esperanza, et al, eds. Seeds - The Literary Journal of the Sisters of Color Vol. VI: Wild Women, Wild Times - Millennium Edition. unabridged ed. (Illus.). 2000. pap. 10.00 (*1-892730-01-4*) Sisters of Color.

Cintron, Gilberto, jt. auth. see Bossi, Richard.

Cintron, Myrna, jt. ed. see McCandless, N. Jane.

Cintron, Nelida A. Religion y Cambio Social en P. R. (1898-1940) LC 96-85613. 168p. 1996. pap. 9.25 (*0-929157-39-7*) Ediciones Huracan.

Cintron, Ralph. Angels' Town: Chero Ways, Gang Life, & Rhetorics of the Everyday. Chasman, Deborah, ed. 288p. 1998. pap. 18.00 (*0-8070-4637-X*) Beacon Pr.

Cinworth, Michael W. Inside Japan's Defense: Technology, Economics & Strategy. LC 92-8390. (Association of the U. S. Army Book Ser.). 267p. 1992. 26.00 (*0-02-881038-4*, 4138M) Brasseys.

Ciob. Code of Practice for Project Management for Construction & Development. 2nd ed. (C). 1996. pap. text. write for info. (*0-582-27680-2*, Pub. by Addison-Wesley) Longman.

— Handbook of Facilities Management. (C). 1994. pap. text. write for info. (*0-582-25742-5*, Pub. by Addison-Wesley) Longman.

Ciobanu. Preliminary Objections. 1976. pap. text 121.50 (*90-247-1774-4*, Pub. by M Nijhoff) Kluwer Academic.

***Ciobanu, Gabriel, et al, eds.** Fundamentals of Computation Theory: 12th International Symposium, FCT'99, Iasi, Romania, August 30-September 3, 1999, Proceedings, LC 99-40196. (Lecture Notes in Computer Science Ser.: Vol. 1684). xi, 570p. 1999. pap. 85.00 (*3-540-66412-2*) Spr-Verlag.

Ciocaltea, Georgeta, tr. see Dancu, Juliana & Dancu, Dumitru.

Ciocca, Pierluigi. The High Price of Money: An Interpretation of International Interest Rates, with an Essay on "The Main Trends of Real Interest Rates (1960-1994)" Keates, Timothy, tr. (ITA., Illus.), 204p. (C). 1996. text 55.00 (*0-19-828949-9*, Clarendon Pr) OUP.

Ciocci, F. Insertion Devices for Synchrotron Radiation & Free Electron Laser. (Series on Synchrotron Radiation Techniques & Applications). 400p. 1999. 68.00 (*981-02-3832-0*) World Scientific Pub.

Ciocco, A. Hearing of School Children. (SRCD M Ser.: Vol. 6, No. 3). 1941. pap. 25.00 (*0-527-01519-9*) Periodicals Srv.

Ciocco, Margaret C., ed. see Baran, Paula.

Ciocco, Margaret C., ed. see Feinen, Cynthia & Coleman, Winifred.

Ciochon, Russell C. & Fleagle, John J. The Human Evolution Source Book. 675p. (C). 1992. pap. text 49.00 (*0-13-446097-9*) P-H.

Ciochon, Russell L. & Corruccini, Robert S., eds. New Interpretations of Ape & Human Ancestry. (Advances in Primatology Ser.). 850p. 1983. 165.00 (*0-306-41072-9*, Plenum Trade) Perseus Pubng.

Ciochon, Russell L. & Fleagle, John G., eds. Primate Evolution & Human Origins. (Evolutionary Foundations of Human Behavior Ser.). (Illus.). 406p. 1987. reprint ed. pap. text 36.95 (*0-202-01175-5*) Aldine de Gruyter.

Ciochon, Russell L. & Nisbett, Richard. Primate Reader. LC 97-26732. 246p. 1997. pap. text 32.80 (*0-13-613845-4*) P-H.

Ciochon, Russell L., jt. auth. see Corruccini, Robert S.

Ciociola, Gail. Wendy Wasserstein: Dramatizing Women, Their Choices & Their Boundaries. LC 98-12339. 176p. 1998. lib. bdg. 29.50 (*0-7864-0523-6*) McFarland & Co.

Ciofalo, Andrew, ed. Internships: Perspectives on Experiential Learning. LC 91-26331. 278p. (C). 1992. pap. text 22.50 (*1-57524-129-3*) Krieger.

— Internships: Perspectives on Experiential Learning. 278p. (C). 1992. lib. bdg. 34.50 (*0-89464-581-1*) Krieger.

***Ciofalo, John J.** The Self-Portraits of Francisco Boys. (Illus.). 256p. 2001. write for info. (*0-521-77136-6*) Cambridge U Pr.

Ciofalo, Michele, et al. Nanoscale Fluid Dynamics in Physiological Processes: A Review Study. (Advances in Computational Bioengineering Ser.: Vol. 2). (Illus.). 360p. 1999. 149.00 (*1-85312-586-5*, 5865) Computational Mech MA.

Cioffari, Angelina G., jt. auth. see Cioffari, Vincenzo.

Cioffari, Vincenzo. Beginning Italian. 3rd ed. (ENG & ITA.). 327p. (C). 1979. student ed. 29.16 (*0-669-00581-9*) HM Trade Div.

Cioffari, Vincenzo & Cioffari, Angelina G. Graded Italian Reader: Prima Tappa. 3rd ed. LC 90-81987. (ENG & ITA.). 246p. (C). 1991. pap. text 31.56 (*0-669-20296-7*) HM Trade Div.

— Graded Italian Reader: Seconda Tappa. 2nd ed. (ENG & ITA.). 218p. (C). 1984. pap. text 31.56 (*0-669-06325-8*) HM Trade Div.

Cioffari, Vincenzo & Gonzalez, Emilio. Repaso Pratico y Cultural. 4th ed. (ENG & SPA.). 301p. (C). 1977. text 45.56 (*0-669-96461-1*) HM Trade Div.

Cioffi, Alfred. The Fetus As Medical Patient: Moral Dilemmas in Prenatal Diagnosis from a Catholic Perspective. LC 94-24378. 334p. (C). 1995. lib. bdg. 42.50 (*0-8191-9780-7*) U Pr of Amer.

Cioffi, Frank. Formula Fiction? An Anatomy of American Science Fiction, 1930-1940, 3. LC 82-6112. (Contributions to the Study of Science Fiction & Fantasy Ser.: No. 3). 181p. 1982. 45.00 (*0-313-23326-8*, CIF/, Greenwood Pr) Greenwood.

— Freud & the Question of Pseudoscience. LC 98-26764. 340p. 1998. pap. 26.95 (*0-8126-9385-X*) Open Court.

— Wittgenstein on Freud & Frazer. LC 97-29411. 320p. (C). 1998. text 59.95 (*0-521-59307-7*); pap. text 19.95 (*0-521-62624-2*) Cambridge U Pr.

Cioffi, George A. & Devers Eye Institute Staff. The Devers Manual: Ophthalmology for the Health Care Professional. LC 97-2483. 300p. 1997. 45.00 (*0-683-01690-3*) Lppncott W & W.

Cioffi, Kathleen. Alternative Theatre in Poland: 1954-1989. (Polish Theatre Archive Ser.: Vol. 2). 288p. 1996. text 60.00 (*3-7186-5853-4*, ECU56, Harwood Acad Pubs); pap. text 26.00 (*3-7186-5854-2*, ECU28, Harwood Acad Pubs) Gordon & Breach.

Cioffi, Luigi A., et al, eds. The Body Weight Regulatory System: Normal & Disturbed Mechanisms. LC 81-17894. 398p. 1981. reprint ed. pap. 123.40 (*0-608-00389-1*, 206110300007) Bks Demand.

Cioffi, Michael I., et al. Sixth Circuit Federal Practice Manual. 2nd rev. ed. 212p. 1993. pap. 35.00 (*1-58360-101-5*) Anderson Pub Co.

Cioffi, Michael L. Ohio Pretrial Litigation. 2nd ed. 346p. 1998. pap. 62.00 (*0-87084-672-8*) Anderson Pub Co.

Cioffi-Revilla, Claudio. Politics & Uncertainty: Theory, Models & Applications. LC 97-23646. (Illus.). 364p. (C). 1998. text 64.95 (*0-521-58121-4*); pap. text 23.95 (*0-521-58915-0*) Cambridge U Pr.

— The Scientific Measurement of International Conflict: Handbook of Datasets on Crises & Wars, 1495-1988 A. D. LC 89-39491. 88p. 1990. pap. text 15.95 (*1-55587-194-1*) L Rienner.

Cioffi-Revilla, Claudio, et al, eds. Communication & Interaction in Global Politics. LC 85-14487. (Advances in Political Science Ser.: No. 5). (Illus.). 271p. 1987. reprint ed. pap. 84.10 (*0-608-01105-3*, 205941400001) Bks Demand.

Ciolek-Torrello, Richard, ed. Early Farmers of the Sonoran Desert: Archaeological Investigations at the Houghton Road Site, Tucson, Arizona. (Statistical Research Technical Ser.: Vol. 72). (Illus.). 364p. 1998. pap. text, per. 25.00 (*1-879442-69-8*) Stats Res.

***Ciolek-Torrello, Richard, et al, eds.** Investigations at Sunset Mesa Ruin: Archaeology at the Confluence of the Santa Cruz & Rillito Rivers. (Technical Ser.: Vol. 66). (Illus.). 328p. 1999. pap. 25.00 (*1-879442-63-9*) Stats Res.

Ciolek-Torrello, Richard & Swanson, Mark T., eds. Pit House, Presidio, & Privy: 1,400 Years of Archaeology & History on Block 180, Tucson, Arizona. (Statistical Research Technical Ser.: Vol. 63). (Illus.). 762p. 1997. per. 45.00 (*1-879442-60-4*) Stats Res.

Ciolek-Torrello, Richard S. A Cultural Resources Testing Program, Holbrook, Arizona. (Statistical Research Technical Ser.: No. 18). 151p. 1989. spiral bd. 12.50 (*1-879442-16-7*) Stats Res.

— A Cultural Resources Testing Program, Holbrook, Arizona.

C

An Asterisk (*) at the beginning of an entry indicates that the title is appearing for the first time.

fac. ed. (Statistical Research (Tucson, Arizona) Technical Ser.: No. 18). (Illus.). 161p. 1989. reprint ed. pap. text 17.50 (*1-55567-573-5*) Coyote Press.

Ciolek-Torrello, Richard S. & Homburg, Jeffrey A. Cultural Resources Surveys & Overviews of the Rillito River Drainage Area, Pima County, Arizona: Cultural Resources Survey & Archival Search along the Rillito River, Pima County, Arizona; Cultural Resources Survey & Archival Search at the 49'ers Country Club, along Tanque Verde Wash, Pima County, Arizona. (Statistical Research Technical Ser.: No. 20). (Illus.). 173p. 1990. reprint ed. spiral bd. 13.75 (*1-879442-18-3*) Stats Res.

Ciolek-Torrello, Richard S. & Welch, John R. The Roosevelt Rural Sites Study Vol. 3: Changing Land Use in the Tonto Basin, 3 vols., Set. (Statistical Research Technical Ser.: No. 28). (Illus.). 692p. (Orig.). 1994. per. 35.00 (*1-879442-43-4*) Stats Res.

Ciolek-Torrello, Richard S., et al. The Roosevelt Rural Sites Study Vol. 2: Prehistoric Rural Settlements in the Tonto Basin, 3 vols., Set. (Statistical Research Technical Ser.: No. 28). (Illus.). 750p. (Orig.). 1994. per. 35.00 (*1-879442-42-6*) Stats Res.

— The Roosevelt Rural Sites Study, Vol. 1: Research Design, 3 vols., Set. (Statistical Research Technical Ser.: No. 28). (Illus.). 75p. 1991. reprint ed. spiral bd. 7.50 (*1-879442-26-4*) Stats Res.

Ciolek-Torrello, Richard S., jt. auth. see Harry, Karen G.

Ciolek-Torrello, Richard S., jt. auth. see Whittlesey, Stephanie M.

***Ciolino, Paul J. & Castle, Grace Elting, eds.** Advanced Forensic Criminal Defense Investigations. LC 99-48194. 322p. 2000. 99.00 (*0-913875-55-4*, 5554-N) Lawyers & Judges.

Ciolkosz, E. J., jt. ed. see Smeckand, N. E.

***Ciolowski, Jerzy.** Many-Electron Densities & Reduced Density Matrices. LC 00-42336. (Mathematical & Computational Chemistry Ser.). 2000. write for info. (*0-306-46454-3*) Plenum.

CIOM-WHO-UNESCO Conference Staff. Medical Research - Priorities & Responsibilities: Proceedings of the Round Table Conference of CIOM-WHO-UNESCO, Geneva, Oct., 1969. 156p. 1970. pap. text 7.20 (*92-4-156031-2*, 1830004) World Health.

Ciompi, Luc. The Psyche & Schizophrenia: The Bond Between Affect & Logic. Schneider, Deborah L., tr. LC 88-6768. (Illus.). 320p. 1988. 52.95 (*0-674-71990-5*) HUP.

CIOMS Round Table Conference Staff. Training of Research Workers in the Medical Sciences: Proceedings of the CIOMS Round Table conference, Geneva, 1970. 186p. 1972. pap. text 24.00 (*92-4-156040-1*, 1830005) World Health.

Cionca, John. Inviting Volunteers to Minister: Stories & Strategies from Seven Effective Churches. Perrigo, Lynn, ed. LC 99-200240. (Illus.). 144p. 1999. pap. text 14.99 (*0-7847-0947-5*, 03587) Standard Pub.

Ciongoli, A. Kenneth & Parini, Jay, eds. Beyond "The Godfather" Italian American Writers on the Real Italian American Experience. LC 97-19535. 334p. 1997. text 40.00 (*0-87451-845-8*) U Pr of New Eng.

— Beyond "The Godfather" Italian American Writers on the Real Italian American Experience. LC 97-19535. (Illus.). 338p. 1998. pap. 17.95 (*0-87451-888-1*) U Pr of New Eng.

Cionso, Pierre. La Gestion Financiee de l'Enterprise Vol. 2: Politique Financiers. 7th ed. (FRE.). 1985. pap. 49.95 (*0-7859-3947-4*) Fr & Eur.

Cioran, E. M. Anathemas & Admirations.Tr. of Aveux et Anathemes. 264p. 1998. pap. 13.95 (*1-55970-461-6*, Pub. by Arcade Pub Inc) Time Warner.

— Aveux et Anathemes. (FRE.). 1986. pap. 13.95 (*0-7859-2937-1*) Fr & Eur.

— Aveux et Anathemes. (Arcades Ser.). (FRE.). 145p. 1987. pap. 15.95 (*2-07-070830-6*) Schoenhof.

— De l'Inconvenient d'Etre Ne. (FRE.). 1989. pap. 10.95 (*0-7859-2808-1*) Fr & Eur.

— De l'Inconvenient d'Etre Ne. (Folio Essais Ser.: No. 80). (FRE.). 243p. 1973. pap. 8.95 (*2-07-032448-6*) Schoenhof.

— Des Larmes et des Saints. (FRE.). 1988. pap. 10.95 (*0-7859-3143-0*, 2253046833) Fr & Eur.

— Drawn & Quartered. Howard, Richard, tr. from FRE. LC 98-21995.Tr. of Ecartelement. 192p. 1998. pap. 13.95 (*1-55970-463-2*, Pub. by Arcade Pub Inc) Time Warner.

— Exercices d'Admiration: Essais et Portraits. (FRE.). 1986. pap. 19.95 (*0-7859-2935-5*) Fr & Eur.

— Histoire et Utopie. (FRE.). 1977. pap. 10.95 (*0-7859-2848-0*) Fr & Eur.

— Histoire et Utopie. (Folio Essais Ser.: No. 53). (FRE.). 147p. 1987. pap. 8.95 (*2-07-032407-9*) Schoenhof.

— History & Utopia. Howard, Richard, tr. from FRE. LC 86-31645.Tr. of Histoire et Utopie. 1987. 16.95 (*0-8050-0391-6*) Seaver Bks.

— History & Utopia. Howard, Richard, tr. LC 98-11068.Tr. of Histoire et Utopie. 118p. 1998. pap. 11.00 (*0-226-10676-4*) U Ch Pr.

— Le Livre des Leurres. (FRE.). 1992. pap. 23.95 (*0-7859-2955-X*, 2070728013) Fr & Eur.

— On the Heights of Despair. Zarifopol-Johnston, Ilinca, tr. LC 91-35173. 150p. 1992. 18.95 (*0-226-10670-5*) U Ch Pr.

— On the Heights of Despair. Zaripofol-Johnston, Ilinca, tr. xxii, 128p. 1996. pap. 10.95 (*0-226-10671-3*) U Ch Pr.

— Precis de Decomposition. (FRE.). 1978. pap. 18.95 (*0-7859-2749-2*) Fr & Eur.

— A Short History of Decay. Howard, Richard, tr. from FRE. LC 98-21994. 192p. 1998. pap. 13.95 (*1-55970-464-0*, Pub. by Arcade Pub Inc) Time Warner.

— Sur les Cimes du Desespoir. (FRE.). 1991. pap. 12.95 (*0-7859-3166-X*, 22530577819) Fr & Eur.

— Syllogismes de l'Amertume. (FRE.). 1987. pap. 10.95 (*0-7859-2809-X*, 2070324494) Fr & Eur.

— Syllogismes de l'Amertume. (Folio Essais Ser.: No. 79). (FRE.). pap. 8.95 (*2-07-032449-4*) Schoenhof.

— Tears & Saints. Zarifopol-Johnston, Ilinca, tr. LC 95-8428. 154p. 1995. 18.95 (*0-226-10672-1*) U Ch Pr.

— Tears & Saints. Zarifopol-Johnston, Ilinca, tr. 128p. 1998. pap. 12.00 (*0-226-10674-8*) U Ch Pr.

— Temptation to Exist. Howard, Richard, tr. LC 98-5161. 222p. 1998. pap. 14.00 (*0-226-10675-6*) U Ch Pr.

— La Tentation D'Exister. (FRE.). 1986. pap. 15.95 (*0-7859-2934-7*) Fr & Eur.

— The Trouble with Being Born. LC 98-21993. Orig. Title: L' Inconvenient d'Etre Ne. 224p. 1998. pap. 13.95 (*1-55970-462-4*, Pub. by Arcade Pub Inc) Time Warner.

Cioran, E.M. All Gall Is Divided: Gnomes & Apothegms. Howard, Richard, tr. from FRE. & intro. by. LC 98-43656. Orig. Title: Syllogismes de l'amertune. 128p. 1999. 14.95 (*1-55970-471-3*, Pub. by Arcade Pub Inc) Time Warner.

Cioran, Samuel D. RussianAlive! An Introduction to Russian. 2nd ed. (ENG & RUS., Illus.). 428p. (C). 1993. reprint ed. pap. text 37.95 (*0-87501-102-0*) Ardis Pubs.

Cioran, Samuel D. & Kalinin, Gennadi A. The General's Daughter: First Year Russian Reader. 1993. pap. 15.95 (*0-87501-109-8*) Ardis Pubs.

Cioran, Samuel D. & Kalinin, Gennadi A., eds. Welcome to Divnograd: An Illustrated Workbook for Students of Russian. 2nd ed. (ENG & RUS., Illus.). 180p. (Orig.). (C). 1994. reprint ed. pap. text 22.95 (*0-87501-103-9*) Ardis Pubs.

Cioran, Samuel D., jt. auth. see Nxumalo, Thandiwe.

Cioran, Samuel D., tr. see Dostoyevsky, Fyodor.

Cioran, Samuel D., tr. see Saltykov-Shchedrin, Mikhail Evgrafovich.

Cioran, Samuel D., tr. see Sologub, Fedor, pseud.

Cioranesco. Bibliographie de la Litterature Francaise du Dix-Huitieme Siecle: Vol. 2, E-Q. (FRE.). 690p. 1969. lib. bdg. 79.95 (*0-7859-3637-8*, 2222011981) Fr & Eur.

— Bibliographie de la Litterature Francaise du XVIIe Siecle, 3 vols., Tome 2: D-M. (FRE.). 74.95 (*0-8288-9105-2*, F125001) Fr & Eur.

— Bibliographie de la Litterature Francaise du XVIIe Siecle, Tome 3: N-Z, Tables. 2nd ed. (FRE.). 724p. 1969. 79.95 (*0-7859-4619-5*) Fr & Eur.

— Bibliographie de la Litterature Francaise du XVIIIe Siecle, 3 tomes. (FRE.). 772p. 1969. 79.95 (*0-318-72614-9*) Fr & Eur.

— Bibliographie de la Litterature Francaise du XVIIIe Siecle. (FRE.). 704p. 1970. 79.95 (*0-7859-3638-6*) Fr & Eur.

— Bibliographie de la Litterature Francaise du XVIIIe Siecle, Tome 1: A-D. (FRE.). 1970. write for info. (*0-318-51933-X*) Fr & Eur.

— 1972, 3 vols., Tome 1: A-C. (FRE.). 54.95 (*0-8288-9104-4*, F125000) Fr & Eur.

Cioranescu, Alexandre. Vasile Alecsandri. LC 79-169637. (Twayne's World Authors Ser.). 1973. lib. bdg. 20.95 (*0-8057-2020-0*) Irvington.

Cioranescu, D. & Lions, J. L., eds. Nonlinear Partial Differential Equations & Their Applications. (Pitman Research Notes in Mathematics Ser.: No. 391). 352p. 1998. pap. 60.00 (*0-582-36926-6*, LM0646, Chap & Hall CRC) Addison-Wesley.

Cioranescu, Diona & Donato, Patrizia. An Introduction to Homogenization. LC 99-33467. (Oxford Lecture Series in Mathematics & Its Applications: Vol 17). (Illus.). 240p. 2000. text 70.00 (*0-19-856554-2*) OUP.

Cioranescu, Doina. Homogenization of Lattice-Type Structures. LC 98-45796. 375p. 1999. 69.95 (*0-387-98634-0*) Spr-Verlag.

Cioranescu, Ioana. Geometry of Banach Spaces, Duality Mappings & Nonlinear Problems. (C). 1990. text 182.50 (*0-7923-0910-3*) Kluwer Academic.

***Ciorra, Anna Giuseppe, ed.** New Italian Architecture. (Library of Architecture). (Illus.). 184p. 2000. pap. text 19.95 (*88-8118-654-3*, Pub. by Skira IT) Abbeville Pr.

Ciorra, Anthony J. Everyday Mysticism: Cherishing the Holy. 176p. (Orig.). 1995. pap. 14.95 (*0-8245-1483-1*) Crossroad NY.

Ciorra, Anthony J. & Keating, James. Moral Formation in the Parish: With Your Whole Heart Turn to God. LC 98-5365. 200p. 1998. pap. 12.95 (*0-8189-0815-7*) Alba.

Ciorra, Pippo. Antonio Citterio, Terry Dwan: Ten Years of Architecture & Design. (Illus.). 192p. 1996. pap. text 45.00 (*3-7643-5597-2*, Pub. by Birkhauser) Princeton Arch.

Ciorra, Pippo, jt. auth. see Campi, Mario.

Ciorra, Pippo, jt. ed. see Campi, Mario.

Cios, Krzysztof J., et al. Data Mining Methods for Knowledge Discovery. LC 98-29384. (International Series in Engineering & Computer Science). xxi, 495p. 1998. write for info. (*0-7923-8252-8*) Kluwer Academic.

Ciotti, Paul, jt. auth. see Spare, Anthony E.

Ciottone, Robert A. & Madonna, John M. Play Therapy with Sexually Abused Children: A Synergistic Clinical-Developmental Approach. LC 95-42102. 240p. 1996. 50.00 (*1-56821-571-1*) Aronson.

CIP Group Staff, ed. The Munich Project CIP. (Lecture Notes in Computer Science Ser.: Vol. 183). (Illus.). xi, 275p. 1985. pap. 33.00 (*0-387-15187-7*) Spr-Verlag.

Cipani, Ennio. Classroom Management: Eleven Effective Plans. LC 97-27671. 168p. 1997. pap., teacher ed. 36.00 (*0-13-520933-1*) P-H.

— Disruptive Behavior: Three Techniques to Use in Your Classroom. LC 93-28966. 1993. pap. text 11.40 (*0-86586-243-5*, P390) Coun Exc Child.

***Cipani, Ennio.** A Functional Analysis of Behavior (FAB) Model for School Settings. 67p. 2000. text, wbk. ed. 120.00 incl. audio (*1-929736-01-0*) Cipani & Assocs.

Cipani, Ennio. Helping Parents Help Their Kids: A Clinical Guide to Six Child Problem Behaviors. LC 98-28099. 1998. 49.95 (*0-87630-951-1*); pap. 27.95 (*0-87630-952-X*) Brunner-Mazel.

— Non-Compliance: Four Strategies That Work. LC 93-26753. 1993. pap. text 11.40 (*0-86586-238-9*, P389) Coun Exc Child.

Cipani, Ennio, ed. Transitioning Exceptional Child & Youth into the Community: Research & Practice. LC 88-852. (Child & Youth Services Ser.: Vol. 10, No. 2). (Illus.). 202p. 1989. text 39.95 (*0-86656-733-X*) Haworth Pr.

Cipani, Ennio & Spooner, Fred. Curricular & Instructional Approaches for Persons with Severe Disabilities. LC 93-38165. 512p. 1993. pap. text 93.00 (*0-205-14090-4*) Allyn.

***Cipani, Ennio Ciro.** A Functional Analysis of Behavior (FAB) Model for School Settings. 124p. (C). 1999. pap. text 22.00 (*1-929736-00-2*) Cipani & Assocs.

Cipes, Robert M. Rules of Criminal Procedure, 4 vols. Waxner, Marvin & Eisenstein, Michael, eds. 1965. ring bd. 1290.00 (*0-8205-1201-X*) Bender.

Cipielewski, James, jt. auth. see Devers, William J., III.

Cipkowski, Peter. Revolution in Eastern Europe: Understanding the Collapse of Communism in Poland, Hungary, East Germany, Czechoslovakia, Romania & the Soviet Union. LC 90-26990. 184p. 1991. 45.00 (*0-471-53967-8*); pap. 10.95 (*0-471-53968-6*) Wiley.

— Understanding the Crisis in the Persian Gulf. LC 91-39259. 192p. (J). 1992. pap. 12.95 (*0-471-54816-2*) Wiley.

Cipolla, Carlo M. Before the Industrial Revolution: European Society & Economy, 1000-1700. 3rd ed. LC 94-2708. 1994. pap. 15.95 (*0-393-31198-8*) Norton.

— Before the Industrial Revolution: European Society & Economy, 1000-1700. 3rd ed. LC 93-6919. 1993. pap. write for info. (*0-415-09005-9*) Routledge.

— Between Two Cultures: An Introduction to Economic History. 224p. 1992. pap. 10.95 (*0-393-30816-2*) Norton.

— Faith, Reason & the Plague in Seventeenth-Century Tuscany. 128p. 1981. reprint ed. pap. 9.95 (*0-393-00045-1*) Norton.

— Fighting the Plague in Seventeenth-Century Italy. (Curti Lectures). 136p. 1981. pap. 14.95 (*0-299-08344-6*) U of Wis Pr.

— Fighting the Plague in Seventeenth-Century Italy. (Curti Lectures). 136p. 1981. 30.00 (*0-299-08340-3*) U of Wis Pr.

— Guns, Sails & Empires: Technological Innovations & the Early Phases of European Expansion, 1400-1700. (Illus.). 192p. 1996. reprint ed. pap. 13.95 (*0-89745-071-X*) Sunflower U Pr.

— Miasmas & Disease: Public Health & Environment in the Pre-Industrial Age. Potter, Elizabeth, tr. from ITA. 144p. (C). 1992. 32.00 (*0-300-04806-8*) Yale U Pr.

— Money in Sixteenth-Century Florence. 1989. 45.00 (*0-520-06222-1*, Pub. by U CA Pr) Cal Prin Full Svc.

— Money, Prices & Civilization in the Mediterranean World. LC 67-18440. (Illus.). 75p. 1967. reprint ed. 20.00 (*0-87752-021-6*) Gordian.

— Money, Prices & Civilization in the Mediterranean World. LC 67-18440. (Illus.). 75p. 1967. reprint ed. pap. 15.00 (*0-686-86000-4*) Gordian.

— Public Health & the Medical Profession in the Renaissance. LC 75-22984. 144p. reprint ed. pap. 41.10 (*0-608-15704-X*, 2031631) Bks Demand.

Cipolla, Daniel. Cabeza y No Cola (Head & Not Tail) (What You Need to Know about ... in 12 Lessons Ser.) (SPA & ENG.). 160p. 8.99 (*0-88113-546-1*) Caribe Betania.

Cipolla, Frank J. & Hunsberger, Donald, eds. The Wind Ensemble: And Its Repertoire. 324p. (C). 1997. pap. text 29.95 (*1-57623-983-7*, DHBK01) Wrner Bros.

Cipolla, Frank J. & Hunsberger, Donald R., eds. The Wind Ensemble & Its Repertoire: Essays on the Fortieth Anniversary of the Eastman Wind Ensemble. LC 94-29156. (Illus.). 320p. (C). 1995. 75.00 (*1-878822-46-2*) Univ Rochester Pr.

Cipolla, Gaetano. Labyrinth: Studies on an Archetype. (Literary Criticism Ser.: Vol. 1). 160p. (Orig.). (C). 1987. pap. 12.00 (*0-921252-00-5*) LEGAS.

— What Italy Has Given to the World. (Illus.). 32p. (C). 1994. pap. 3.00 (*1-881901-04-1*) LEGAS.

— What Makes a Sicilian? (Illus.). 32p. (Orig.). 1996. 3.00 (*1-881901-11-4*) LEGAS.

Cipolla, Gaetano, tr. from ITA. The Poetry of Nino Martoglio: Selections from Centona. LC 93-28682. (Poets of Arba Sicula Ser.). (ENG & ITA.). 304p. (Orig.). (C). 1993. pap. 10.00 (*1-881901-03-3*) LEGAS.

Cipolla, Gaetano, ed. see Bazbera, Henry.

Cipolla, Gaetano, ed. see Morreale, Ben.

Cipolla, Gaetano, ed. & tr. see Meli, Giovanni.

Cipolla, Gaetano, ed. & tr. see Provenzano, Antonino.

Cipolla, Gaetano, tr. see Ancona, Vincenzo.

Cipolla, Gaetano, tr. & intro. see Meli, Giovanni.

Cipolla, Roberto. Active Visual Inference of Surface Shape. LC 95-48031. (Lecture Notes in Computer Science Ser.: Vol. 1016). 194p. 1995. pap. 43.00 (*3-540-60642-4*) Spr-Verlag.

Cipolla, Roberto & Giblin, Peter. Visual Motion of Curves & Surfaces. LC 99-36404. (Illus.). 192p. (C). 2000. text 49.95 (*0-521-63251-X*) Cambridge U Pr.

Cipolla, Roberto & Pentland, Alexander, eds. Computer Vision for Human-Machine Interaction. LC 98-22043. (Illus.). 360p. (C). 1998. text 64.95 (*0-521-62253-0*) Cambridge U Pr.

Cipolla, Roberto, jt. ed. see Buxton, Bernard.

Cipollaro, Anthony C. & Crossland, Paul M. X-Rays & Radium in the Treatment of Diseases of the Skin. LC 66-23240. (Illus.). 830p. reprint ed. pap. 200.00 (*0-8357-9425-3*, 201453300092) Bks Demand.

Cipolle, Robert J., et al. Pharmaceutical Care Practice. LC 97-52763. (Illus.). 384p. 1998. pap. text 42.00 (*0-07-012046-3*) McGraw-Hill HPD.

Cipollone, Diana B., jt. ed. see Alves, Pericles G.

Cipolloni, David C. An Extraordinary Silence: The Emergence of a Deeply Disturbed Child. LC 93-15184. 160p. 1993. 49.95 (*0-89789-357-3*, H357, Bergin & Garvey) Greenwood.

Cipparone, Salvatore. From Dusk to Dawn. 4.95 (*0-686-20574-X*) Ivory Scroll.

— From the Fountain of Life. 4.95 (*0-686-20576-6*) Ivory Scroll.

— Sayings of the Hour. 4.95 (*0-686-20575-8*) Ivory Scroll.

— Sorrow, Grief & God. 4.95 (*0-686-20577-4*) Ivory Scroll.

— Yet I Weep, Yet I Joy. 4.95 (*0-686-20578-2*) Ivory Scroll.

Cippico, A., et al, eds. Dante: Essays in Commemoration, 1321-1921. LC 68-16923. (Essay Index Reprint Ser.). 1977. 20.95 (*0-8369-0360-9*) Ayer.

Cippriani, Curzio & Borelli, Alessando. Simon & Schuster's Guide to Gems & Precious Stones. Lyman, Kennie, ed. 384p. 1986. pap. 14.00 (*0-671-60430-9*) S&S Trade.

Cipra, Barry. Misteaks & How to Find Them Before the Teacher Does. 70p. 1983. pap. text 5.95 (*0-8176-3083-X*) Birkhauser.

— Misteaks & How to Find Them Before the Teacher Does. 2nd ed. 66p. 1989. pap. text 13.00 (*0-12-174695-X*) Acad Pr.

***Cipra, Barry.** Misteaks [sic] & How to Find Them Before the Teacher Does: A Calculus Supplement. 3rd ed. LC 00-24778. (Illus.). 88p. 2000. 5.95 (*1-56881-122-5*) AK Peters.

Cipra, Barry. What's Happening in the Mathematical Sciences, Vol. 2. 51p. 1994. 8.00 (*0-8218-8998-2*, HAPPENING/2C) Am Math.

— What's Happening in the Mathematical Sciences, 1995-1996, Vol. 3. 111p. 1996. reprint ed. 12.00 (*0-8218-0355-7*, HAPPENING/3C) Am Math.

— What's Happening in the Mathematical Sciences, 1998-1999. (What's Happening in the Mathematical Sciences Ser.: Vol. 4). 120p. 1998. pap. 14.00 (*0-8218-0766-8*) Am Math.

Cipra, Barry A. What's Happening in the Mathematical Sciences, Vol. 1. 47p. 1993. 7.00 (*0-8218-8999-0*, HAPPENING/1C) Am Math.

Cipra, David G. Lighthouses, Lightships, & the Gulf of Mexico. LC 96-72414. (Illus.). 260p. (Orig.). 1997. pap. 24.95 (*0-9636412-1-2*) Cypress Communs.

Cipraini, Arrigo. The Harry's Bar Cookbook. 304p. 1991. 45.00 (*0-553-07030-4*) Bantam.

Cipriane, John L., Jr., jt. auth. see Nathanson, William S.

Cipriani, Arrigo. Harry's Bar: Watering Hole to the Rich & Famous. (Illus.). 192p. 1996. 21.45 (*1-55970-259-1*, Pub. by Arcade Pub Inc) Time Warner.

Cipriani, Giovanni. Cesare e la Retorica dell'Assedio. (London Studies in Classical Philology: Vol. 16). (ITA.). 101p. (C). 1987. pap. 24.00 (*90-70265-59-1*, Pub. by Gieben) J Benjamins Pubng Co.

Cipriani, N. J. A Brother's Love. 100p. (J). 1998. pap. 5.95 (*0-9653570-5-8*) N J Cipriani.

Cipriani, Nicholas. A World Forgotten. LC 98-87026. 192p. 1999. pap. 11.95 (*1-56315-176-6*) SterlingHse.

Cipriani, Nicholas J. A Message to the Children. 78p. (Orig.). 1997. pap. 8.95 (*0-9653570-1-5*) N J Cipriani.

— Mythology: A Short Story about Creation, Gods, & Revenge. 34p. (Orig.). 1996. pap. 5.95 (*0-9653570-2-3*) N J Cipriani.

***Cipriani, Roberto.** The Sociology of Religion: An Historical Introduction. Ferrarotti, Laura, tr. 304p. 2000. pap. text 23.95 (*0-202-30592-9*); lib. bdg. 47.95 (*0-202-30591-0*) Aldine de Gruyter.

Cipriano, A. G. Bertie. 294p. (YA). (gr. 6-12). 1999. pap. 5.99 (*0-9672074-0-1*) Gold Lace.

Cipriano, Jeri. The Good Apple Homework Helper. 112p. 1996. teacher ed. 13.99 (*1-56417-854-4*, GA1562) Good Apple.

***Cipriano, Jeri S.** Arithetricks. (Illus.). (J). 1999. pap. 14.95 (*0-673-58896-3*, GoodYrBooks) Addson-Wesley Educ.

Cipriano, Joseph J. Photographic Manual of Regional Orthopaedics & Neurological Testing. 2nd ed. (Illus.). 346p. 1991. 60.00 (*0-683-01701-2*) Lppncott W & W.

Cipriano, Joseph J., et al. Photographic Manual of Regional Orthopaedic & Neurological Testing. 3rd ed. LC 96-43896. (Illus.). 456p. 1997. 65.00 (*0-683-18100-9*) Lppncott W & W.

Cipro, Sil. Campfire Cats: Blue Ridge Smoky Mountain Hiking Guide & Journal. 1991. pap. 5.95 (*0-9631613-1-8*) Campfire Cats.

***Ciprut, Jose V.** The Art of the Feud: Reconceptualizing International Relations. LC 99-45993. 2000. write for info. (*0-275-96854-5*, Praeger Pubs) Greenwood.

— Of Fears & Foes: Security & Insecurity in an Evolving Global Political Economy. LC 99-45990. 2000. write for info. (*0-275-96855-3*, Praeger Pubs) Greenwood.

Cipullo, Thomas. Take It & Like It. 106p. (Orig.). 1997. pap. 10.95 (*0-9655112-7-8*) A T Cipullo.

Cirafesi, Wally. English in Action: A Fast & Fun Way to Learn English. 3rd ed. (Illus.). 136p. 1995. pap. text, student ed. 9.95 (*0-9638273-1-6*) Eng Outreach.

— English in Action: Learn How to Teach English Using the Bible. 3rd ed. (Illus.). 208p. 1995. pap. text, teacher ed. 14.95 (*0-9638273-0-8*) Eng Outreach.

Cirafici, John L. Airhead Operations - Where AMC Delivers: The Linchpin of Rapid Force Projection. LC 95-6191. (Illus.). 109p. 1995. pap. 6.50 (*1-58566-057-4*) Air Univ.

Ciranna, Alfonso. Giacomo Manzu: Cataloque of the Graphic Work. (ITA., Illus.). 295p. 1968. 400.00 (*0-915346-48-6*) A Wofsy Fine Arts.

C

Ciranowicz, Marlene. Instructor's Manual for Clinical Pharmacology & Nursing. 3rd ed. 240p. 1996. teacher ed. write for info. (*0-87434-773-4*) Springhouse Corp.

***Ciraolo, Stephen N., ed.** Cicero: Pro Caelio. 2nd ed. LC 99-38708. xxi, 198p. (C). 1999. pap. 24.00 (*0-86516-461-4*) Bolchazy-Carducci.

Ciraolo, Stephen N., ed. see Cicero, Marcus Tullius.

Cirasa, Robert J. The Lost Works of William Carlos Williams: The Volumes of Collected Poetry as Lyrical Sequence. LC 94-41572. 344p. 1995. 49.50 (*0-8386-3576-8*) Fairleigh Dickinson.

Ciraulo, Domenic A. Drug Interactions in Psychiatry. 2nd ed. (Illus.). 352p. 1995. pap. 35.00 (*0-683-01944-9*) Lppncott W & W.

Ciraulo, Domenic A. & Shader, Richard I., eds. Clinical Manual of Chemical Dependence. LC 90-14511. 420p. 1991. spiral bd. 48.50 (*0-88048-280-X*, 8280) Am Psychiatric.

***Ciraulo, Donald.** World Philosophers on Death. 272p. (C). 2000. per. 52.95 (*0-7872-7184-5*) Kendall-Hunt.

Ciravegna, Nino, jt. auth. see Galbiati, Fermo.

Circa Press. The Family Passover Haggadah. (Prince of Egypt Ser.). (Illus.). 90p. 1999. pap. text 12.99 (*1-892731-17-7*) Circa Pr.

***Circa, Silvia.** Mesagerul Sperantei. 1999. 14.99 (*0-9623183-9-6*) Moonfall Pr VA.

Circa, Silvia. Oceanul (The Ocean) 160p. 1993. pap. 14.95 (*0-9623183-0-2*) Moonfall Pr VA.

Circirelli, Victor G. Family Caregiving: Autonomous & Paternalistic Decision Making. (Library of Social Research: Vol. 186). (Illus.). 320p. 1991. text 59.95 (*0-8039-3906-X*); pap. text 26.00 (*0-8039-3907-8*) Sage.

***Circle, Homer.** Bass Wisdom. LC 99-45220. 2000. pap. 16.95 (*1-58574-036-5*) Lyons Pr.

Circle, Homer. Circle on Bass: Bass Wisdom from a Master. LC 96-31356. (Illus.). 304p. 1996. 24.95 (*1-55821-463-1*) Lyons Pr.

Circo, Carl J. & Little, Christopher H. Construction & Design Law. LC 98-38838. 1998. write for info. (*1-57073-618-9*) Amer Bar Assn.

Circo, Carl J., jt. ed. see Heaven, Lewis A.

Circulation Liaison Committee Staff. Circulation Information Systems. 52p. (Orig.). 1985. pap. 49.95 (*1-877888-03-6*) Intl Newspaper.

Circum-Pacific Energy & Mineral Resources Conferen. Circum-Pacific Energy & Mineral Resources: Papers from the Circum-Pacific Energy & Mineral Resources Conference, Held August 26-30, 1974, Honolulu, Hawaii. Halbouty, Michel et al, eds. LC 76-41597. (American Association of Petroleum Geologists. Memoir Ser.: Vol. 25). (Illus.). 624p. reprint ed. pap. 193.50 (*0-608-17831-4*, 203258400079) Bks Demand.

Circus, Philip J. Circus: Sales Promotion Law - a Practical Guide. 2nd ed. 1995. pap. write for info. (*0-406-04803-7*, CSPL2, MICHIE) LEXIS Pub.

— Sales Promotion Law - A Practical Guide. 1989. pap. 64.00 (*0-406-11800-0*, MICHIE) LEXIS Pub.

Cird, T. H., jt. auth. see Fuller, F. D.

***Cirelli, Lawrence.** Harvesting Ice. LC 99-63778. 1999. pap. 12.00 (*1-892657-09-0*) Town Bk Pr.

Cirese, Eugenio. Molisan Poems: Selected Poems. Bonaffini, Luigi, tr. from ITA. (Essential Poets Ser.: Vol. 83). 154p. 2000. pap. 13.00 (*1-55071-075-3*) Guernica Editions.

Cirese, Sarah, jt. auth. see Wade, Carole.

Ciresi, Rita. Blue Italian. 304p. 1997. pap. 11.95 (*0-385-31940-1*) Doubleday.

— Blue Italian: A Novel. LC 96-10176. 256p. 1996. 22.00 (*0-88001-515-2*) HarpC.

— Mother Rocket: Stories. LC 92-22666. (Flannery O'Connor Award for Short Fiction Ser.). 160p. 1993. 19.95 (*0-8203-1508-7*) U of Ga Pr.

— Pink Slip. LC 98-21130. 368p. 1998. 22.95 (*0-385-32362-X*) Dell.

***Ciresi, Rita.** Pink Slip. 416p. 1999. pap. 11.95 (*0-385-32363-8*) Dell.

— Sometimes I Dream in Italian. 224p. 2000. 23.95 (*0-385-33493-1*) Delacorte.

Ciria, Alberto. Parties & Power in Modern Argentina, 1930-1946. Astiz, Carlos A. & McCarthy, Mary F., trs. LC 70-129642. 357p. (C). 1974. text 24.50 (*0-87395-079-8*) State U NY Pr.

***Ciriacono, Salvatore, ed.** Land Drainage & Irrigation. LC 98-23062. (Studies in the History of Civil Engineering: No. 3). (Illus.). 1998. text 157.95 (*0-86078-752-4*) Ashgate Pub Co.

Ciriani, Henri E. Luciana Miotto. 1998. pap. 7.99 (*88-86502-88-5*, Pub. by Canal & Stamperia) Antique Collect.

***Ciriani, Tito A.** Operational Research in Industry. LC 99-26098. 1999. 62.95 (*1-55753-172-2*, Ichor Busn Bks) Purdue U Pr.

Cirici-Pellicer, Alexandre. Les Tresors de l'Espagne. (Tresors du Monde Ser.). (FRE., Illus.). 242p. 1965. lib. bdg. 95.00 (*0-8288-3995-6*) Fr & Eur.

Ciriello, Janet, jt. auth. see Schave, Barbara.

Ciriello, John, jt. ed. see Kunos, George.

Ciriello, Maria, ed. Formation & Development for Catholic School Leaders Vol. III: The Principal As Managerial Leader. 2nd ed. 340p. 1998. pap. text 29.95 (*1-57455-079-9*) US Catholic.

— The Principal As Educational Leader, Vol. 1. 2nd ed. (Formation & Development for Catholic School Leaders Ser.). 480p. 1998. pap. 29.95 (*1-57455-077-2*) US Catholic.

Ciriello, Maria J., ed. Expectations for the Catholic School Principal: A Handbook for Pastors & Parish School Committees. 160p. (Orig.). 1996. pap. 9.95 (*1-57455-054-3*) US Catholic.

Ciriello, Maria J., et al. Formation & Development for Catholic School Leaders Vol. II: A Three Volume Preparation Program for Future & Neophyte Principals: The Principal As Spiritual Leader. 2nd ed. 290p. (Orig.). 1996. pap. 29.95 (*1-57455-078-0*) US Catholic.

Ciriello, Maria J., jt. auth. see Convey, John J.

Cirigliano, Marc, ed. & tr. see Dante Alighieri.

Cirigliano, Marc, tr. see Dooyeweerd, Herman.

Cirigliano, Marc A., tr. & intro. see Cavalcanti, Guido.

Cirignano, John, tr. see Mazzoni, Cristina, ed.

Cirillo, Dexter. Across Frontiers: Hispanic Crafts of New Mexico. LC 97-33258. 1998. 35.00 (*0-8118-1793-8*); pap. 22.95 (*0-8118-1774-1*) Chronicle Bks.

— Southwestern Indian Jewelry. (Illus.). 240p. 1995. 49.95 (*1-55859-282-2*) Abbeville Pr.

Cirillo, Jim. Guns, Bullets & Gunfights: Lessons & Tales from a Modern-Day Gunfighter. (Illus.). 136p. 1996. pap. 16.00 (*0-87364-877-3*) Paladin Pr.

***Cirillo, Joan.** The Complete Idiot's Guide to Cooking with Kids. (Complete Idiot's Guide Ser.). 352p. 1999. pap. 16.95 (*0-02-863897-2*, Alpha Ref) Macmillan Gen Ref.

Cirillo, JoAnn. Liver Transplant. LC 94-70677. 1994. pap. 9.95 (*1-55673-930-3*, Fairway Pr) CSS OH.

Cirillo, L. Fathers of the Church Coloring Book. (J). 1995. pap. 3.95 (*0-935952-26-8*) Angelus Pr.

Cirillo, Lee M. The Italian Bakery: Featuring: the Italian Wedding Cookie Cake. (Illus.). 204p. (Orig.). 1984. pap. 13.50 (*0-9623225-1-2*) SCP Rochester.

— Lite Sweet Delites: Sweetened with Sugar Substitutes. LC 89-91755. (Illus.). 226p. (Orig.). 1989. pap. 13.50 (*0-9623225-0-4*) SCP Rochester.

Cirillo, Leonard, et al, eds. Emotions in Ideal Human Development. 184p. 1989. 39.95 (*0-8058-0473-0*) L Erlbaum Assocs.

Cirillo, Leonard & Wapner, Seymour. Value Presuppositions in Theories of Human Development. 184p. 1986. text 39.95 (*0-89859-753-6*) L Erlbaum Assocs.

Cirillo, R. Economics of Vilfredo Pareto. 148p. 1979. 32.50 (*0-7146-3100-0*, Pub. by F Cass Pubs) Intl Spec Bk.

Cirillo, Roger, ed. see Steury, Donald P.

Cirillo, Stefano & DiBlasio, Paola. Families That Abuse: Diagnosis & Therapy. Neugroschel, Joachim, tr. 192p. 1992. 22.95 (*0-393-70122-0*) Norton.

Cirillo, Susan E., ed. see Library Administration & Management Association Pr.

Cirincione, Diane V. Sounds of the Morning Sun. LC 93-33200. 192p. 1993. 15.00 (*1-56170-073-8*, 113) Hay House.

Cirincione, Diane V., jt. auth. see Jamplosky, Gerald G.

Cirincione, Diane V., jt. auth. see Jampolsky, Gerald G.

***Cirincione, Joseph.** Repairing the Regime: Preventing the Spread of Weapons of Mass Destruction. LC 99-56509. 304p. 2000. pap. write for info. (*0-415-92596-7*) Routledge.

Cirincione, Joseph, ed. Central America & the Western Alliance. LC 84-19770. 225p. 1985. 40.00 (*0-8419-1003-0*) Holmes & Meier.

Cirino, Andre & Raischl, Josef, eds. Franciscan Solitude. (History Ser.). 370p. 1995. pap. 25.00 (*1-57659-006-2*) Franciscan Inst.

Cirino, Anna M., jt. auth. see Dickmeyer, Nathan.

Cirino, Antonio, jt. auth. see Rose, Augustus F.

Cirino, Leonard. 96 Sonnets Facing Conviction. 72p. 1999. pap. 10.00 (*1-891812-20-3*, 99-002) Cedar Hill Pubns.

***Cirino, Leonard.** War Horses. (Poetry Chapbks.: No. 2). 30p. 2000. pap. 8.00 (*1-930259-01-8*) Anabasis.

Cirino, Leonard J. The Terrible Wilderness of Self. unabridged ed. 84p. 1998. pap. 11.00 (*1-891812-00-9*, 98-001) Cedar Hill Pubns.

Cirino, Leonard J., et al. Jam. viii, 43p. 1998. pap. 10.00 (*1-891812-05-X*, 98-005) Cedar Hill Pubns.

— 2000: Here's to Humanity. Richburg, Shirley, ed. 2000. write for info. (*0-9658432-4-6*) Peoples MD.

Cirino, Leonard J., ed. see Seffron, Richard A.

Cirino, Linda D. Eva's Story. LC 99-24388. Orig. Title: The Egg Woman (British Edition). 167p. 1999. pap. 12.95 (*0-86538-097-X*) Ontario Rev NJ.

— On Your Own Terms: The Seniors' Guide to an Independent Life. large type ed. 470p. 1996. pap. 23.95 (*0-7838-1594-8*, G K Hall Lrg Type) Mac Lib Ref.

Cirino, Mark. Name the Baby. LC 97-41134. 224p. 1998. pap. 12.00 (*0-385-49159-X*) Doubleday.

Ciriscioli, Peter R. & Mantell, Susan C., eds. Composites, Design & Manufacture for Cost Effectiveness: Proceedings: International Mechanical Engineering Congress & Exposition (1994: Chicago, IL) LC 94-78962. (MD Ser.: Vol. 48). 81p. 1995. pap. 40.00 (*0-7918-1388-6*, G00883) ASME Pr.

Ciriscioli, Peter R. & Springer, George S. Smart Autoclave Cure of Composites. LC 90-71382. 172p. 1990. 24.95 (*0-87762-802-5*) Technomic.

Cirker. Masterpieces of Flower Painting. 1998. pap. 4.95 (*0-486-29531-1*) Dover.

— Mortised Cuts. 1998. pap. 1.00 (*0-486-27918-9*) Dover.

Cirker, Blanche. The Book of Kells: Selected Plates in Full Color. (Fine Art, History of Art Ser.). (Illus.). 32p. 1982. reprint ed. pap. 5.95 (*0-486-24345-1*) Dover.

— Complete Masters of the Poster. 1990. pap. 29.95 (*0-486-26309-6*) Dover.

Cirker, Blanche, ed. Victorian House Designs in Authentic Full Color: 75 Plates from the Scientific American - Architects & Builders Edition, 1886-1894. LC 96-47807. (Illus.). 80p. (Orig.). 1999. pap. text 17.95 (*0-486-29438-2*) Dover.

Cirker, Blanche, jt. auth. see Cirker, Hayward.

Cirker, Blanche, ed. see B. Altman & Co. Staff.

Cirker, Blanche, ed. see Bewick, Thomas.

Cirker, Blanche, jt. ed. see Cirker, Hayward.

Cirker, H. Great Painting by Women Artists. 1998. pap. text 4.95 (*0-486-40213-4*) Dover.

Cirker, Hayward. Hebrew Picture Word Book. (HEB & ENG., Illus.). 32p. 1995. pap. 2.95 (*0-486-28213-9*) Dover.

— Italian Picture Word Book. LC 95-140476. (ITA., Illus.). 32p. 1994. pap. 2.95 (*0-486-28202-3*) Dover.

— New York Paintings Postcards. 1996. pap. text 4.95 (*0-486-29058-1*) Dover.

Cirker, Hayward & Cirker, Blanche. Dictionary of American Portraits. Dover Staff, ed. 756p. 1967. 80.00 (*0-486-21823-6*) Dover.

— Monograms & Alphabetic Devices. (Illus.). 226p. (Orig.). 1970. pap. 10.95 (*0-486-22330-2*) Dover.

Cirker, Hayward & Cirker, Blanche, eds. Masterpieces of the Poster from the Belle Epoque: 48 Full-Color Plates from "Les Maitres de L'Affiche" (Fine Art Ser.). 48p. 1984. reprint ed. pap. 6.95 (*0-486-24549-7*) Dover.

Cirker, Hayward & Steadman, Barbara. English Picture Word Book: Learn over Five Hundred Commonly Used English Words Through Pictures. (Illus.). 32p. (Orig.). 1994. pap. text 2.95 (*0-486-27776-3*) Dover.

— French Picture Word Book: Learn over Five Hundred Commonly Used French Words Through Pictures. (ENG & FRE., Illus.). 32p. (Orig.). (J). 1994. pap. text 2.95 (*0-486-27777-1*) Dover.

— German Picture Word Book: Learn over Five Hundred Commonly Used German Words Through Pictures. (ENG & GER., Illus.). 32p. (Orig.). (J). 1994. pap. text 2.95 (*0-486-27778-X*) Dover.

— Spanish Picture Word Book: Learn over Five Hundred Commonly Used Spanish Words Through Pictures. (ENG & SPA., Illus.). 32p. (Orig.). (J). 1994. pap. text 2.95 (*0-486-27779-8*) Dover.

Cirlot, J. C. Dictionary of Symbols. (Illus.). 476p. (C). 1983. pap. 20.99 (*0-415-03649-6*) Routledge.

Cirlot, Juan Eduardo C. Diccionario de Simbolos. 8th ed. (SPA.). 476p. 1991. pap. 34.95 (*0-7859-5921-1*, 8433535048) Fr & Eur.

Cirlot, Juan-Eduardo C. Diccionario Universal del Arte y los Artistas, 9 vols., Set.Tr. of Universal Dictionary of Art & Artists. (SPA.). 2794p. 1969. 229.50 (*0-8288-6582-5*) Fr & Eur.

Cirn, John T., et al. Long-Term Care Human Resources Management: The Personnel Touch. (Learning the Continuum: AUPHA Modules for Management Education Ser.). (Illus.). (Orig.). (C). 1989. pap. text 20.00 (*0-910591-20-2*) AUPHA Pr.

Cirni, Jim. The Big Squeeze. LC 90-19851. (Soho Crime Ser.). 224p. 1996. pap. 12.00 (*1-56947-058-8*) Soho Press.

— The Come On. LC 89-6269. (Soho Crime Ser.). 216p. 1995. pap. 10.00 (*1-56947-037-5*) Soho Press.

— The Kiss Off. 256p. 1989. pap. 3.95 (*0-380-70561-3*, Avon Bks) Morrow Avon.

— The Kiss Off. LC 87-9184. (Soho Crime Ser.). 266p. 1995. pap. 10.00 (*1-56947-036-7*) Soho Press.

Cirone, jt. auth. see Girsberger, Russ.

Cirone, Anthony. The Concerto: Solo Music for Marimba & Piano. (Music of the Masters Ser.: Vol. 8). 72p. (YA). 1997. pap. text 14.95 (*0-7692-1434-7*, 0102B) Wrner Bros.

Cirone, Anthony J. Japanese Impressions. (Percussion Ensemble Ser.). 40p. (YA). 1997. pap. text 14.95 (*0-7692-1483-5*, 0113B) Wrner Bros.

— Portraits in Rhythm: 50 Studies for Snare Drum. 56p. (Orig.). 1997. pap. 12.95 (*0-7692-1439-8*, HAB00101) Wrner Bros.

Cirone, Etta. Flash in the Pan: Generations of Original Recipes with an Italian Flavor. 1995. pap. 16.95 (*0-533-11159-5*) Vantage.

Cirou, Alain. Incredibly Far. LC 93-20078. (Frontiers of the Invisible Ser.). (Illus.). 48p. (YA). (gr. 6 up). 1993. lib. bdg. 22.00 (*0-02-718650-4*, Mac Bks Young Read) S&S Childrens.

Cirou, Joseph, et al. The Johannine Hymnal. LC 75-14542. 1970. 39.95 (*0-915866-00-5*) Am Cath Pr.

— Leaflet Missal Organ Accompaniment. 1987. 34.95 (*0-915866-09-9*) Am Cath Pr.

CIRP International Design Seminar, et al. Integration of Process Knowledge into Design Support Systems: Proceedings of the 1999 Cirp International Design Seminar, University of Twente, Enschede, the Netherlands, 24-26 March 1999. LC 99-14199. 1999. write for info. (*0-7923-5655-1*) Kluwer Academic.

CIRP International Seminar on Computer-Aided Tolerancing Staff, et al. Global Consistency of Tolerances: Proceedings of the 6th CIRP International Seminar on Computer-Aided Tolerancing, University of Twente, Enschede, the Netherlands, 22-24 March 1999. LC 99-18974. xi, 438 p. 1999. write for info. (*0-7923-5654-3*) Kluwer Academic.

Cirre, Jose F. Espana y los Espanoles. 2nd ed. (C). 1996. pap. text 37.50 (*0-15-504515-6*) Harcourt Coll Pubs.

Cirre, Jose F. & Cirre, Manuela M. Espana y los Espanoles. 2nd ed. LC 80-23274. (SPA.). 190p. (C). 1981. pap. text 23.50 (*0-03-058051-X*) Harcourt Coll Pubs.

Cirre, Manuela M., jt. auth. see Cirre, Jose F.

Cirrincione, J. A. & Nelson, Thomas Allen. The Forgotten Secret of Fatima: And the Silent Apostolate. LC 88-50579. 52p. 1988. pap. 1.50 (*0-89555-337-6*) TAN Bks Pubs.

Cirrincione, James F. Taking Depositions. LC 94-29467. 476p. 1994. pap. 38.50 (*0-934753-38-5*) LRP Pubns.

Cirrincione, Joseph A. Fatima's Message for Our Times. LC 90-70660. 72p. (Orig.). 1990. pap. 2.00 (*0-89555-403-8*) TAN Bks Pubs.

— Ven. Francisco Marto of Fatima. 43p. 1995. pap. 1.50 (*0-89555-511-5*) TAN Bks Pubs.

— Ven. Jacinta Marto of Fatima. LC 92-61353. 71p. (Orig.). 1992. pap. 2.00 (*0-89555-480-1*) TAN Bks Pubs.

Cirrincione, Joseph A. & Nelson, Thomas A. St. Joseph, Fatima & Fatherhood: Reflections on the Miracle of the Sun. LC 89-50766. 62p. (Orig.). 1989. pap. 1.50 (*0-89555-384-8*) TAN Bks Pubs.

Cirrito, William, jt. auth. see Arrowood, David.

Cirtautas, Arista M. The Polish Solidarity Movement: Revolution, Democracy & Natural Rights. LC 97-5239. (Routledge Studies of Societies in Transition). 336p. (C). 1997. 90.00 (*0-415-16940-2*) Routledge.

Ciruenwald, Mark, ed. see Schuller, Catherine.

Ciscel, Dennis. Patting the Air. (Illus.). 100p. Date not set. 12.95 (*0-911051-68-6*) Plain View.

— Tiny Stories. (Illus.). 100p. Date not set. 11.95 (*0-911051-62-7*) Plain View.

Cisco, Bob. The Ultimate Game of Golf: Mental & Strategic Tips for Your Best Game. Makovsky, Andre, ed. (Illus.). 200p. (Orig.). 1993. pap. 19.95 (*1-882180-38-0*) Griffin CA.

Cisco, Cheyenne. The Lion & the Mouse: Big Book. large type ed. (Little Books & Big Bks.). (Illus.). 16p. (J). (gr. 1-3). 1997. pap. text 29.85 (*0-8215-0984-5*) Sadlier.

— Why Coyote Howls at Night: Big Book. large type ed. (Little Books & Big Bks.). (Illus.). 16p. (J). (gr. 1-3). 1997. pap. text 29.85 (*0-8215-0971-3*) Sadlier.

Cisco, Dan. Hawaii Sports: History, Facts & Statistics. LC 98-48396. 544p. (Orig.). 1999. pap. 24.95 (*0-8248-2121-1*, Latitude Twenty) UH Pr.

Cisco, Jay G. Historic Sumner Co., TN: With Genealogies of the Bledsoe, Cage, & Douglass Families, & Genealogical Notes of Other Sumner Co. Families. (Illus.). 340p. (Orig.). 1994. reprint ed. pap. text 25.00 (*1-55613-948-9*) Heritage Bk.

— Historic Sumner County, Tennessee with Genealogies of the Bledsoe, Cage & Douglass Families. 319p. 1993. reprint ed. lib. bdg. 37.00 (*0-8328-3500-5*) Higginson Bk Co.

Cisco, Michael. The Divinity Student. (Illus.). 160p. 1999. pap. 12.99 (*0-9652200-1-X*) Buzzcity Pr.

Cisco, Perry. Keeper of the Inn. LC 94-70286. 1994. pap. 6.95 (*1-55673-926-5*, Fairway Pr) CSS OH.

Cisco, Perry R. The Unforgivable Betrayal: An Account of the Life of Judas Iscariot. LC 99-164379. 331p. 1998. write for info. (*1-884707-82-3*) Lifestyles.

***Cisco Press Staff.** Cisco IOS 12.0 Solutions for Network Protocols Vol. II: IPX, Appletalk & More. (Illus.). 1999. 50.00 (*1-57870-164-3*) Cisco Press.

Cisco Press Staff. Cisco IOS Wide Area Networking Solutions. LC 97-80681. 558p. 1998. pap. text 50.00 (*1-57870-054-X*) Cisco Press.

Cisco, Susan, ed. see Waegemann, C. Peter.

Cisco, Susan L., jt. auth. see Dale, Tom.

Cisco Systems Inc. CCDA Exam Certification Guide. 1999. 49.95 (*0-7357-0074-5*) New Riders Pub.

— Cisco CCNA Training Kit. 1999. 149.99 (*0-7357-0879-7*) Cisco Press.

***Cisco Systems, Inc.** Cisco Ios 12.0 Configuration Fundamentals. 1158p. 1999. text 50.00 (*1-57870-155-4*) Cisco Press.

— Cisco Ios 12.0 Quality of Service. 500p. 1999. text 40.00 (*1-57870-161-9*) Cisco Press.

— Cisco Networking Academy: First Year Companion Guide. Amato, Vito, ed. 438p. 1999. pap. text 50.00 (*1-57870-126-0*) Cisco Press.

— Cisco Networking Academy: Second Year Companion Guide. Amato, Vito, ed. 450p. 1999. pap. text 50.00 (*1-57870-169-4*) Cisco Press.

***Cisco Systems Inc. Publishing Company Staff.** Cisco Internetwork Design. 600p. 1999. 60.00 (*1-57870-171-6*) Macmillan Tech.

Cisco Systems, Inc. Staff. Cisco IOS Configuration Fundamentals. LC 97-81047. 1100p. 1997. pap. 60.00 (*1-57870-044-2*) Cisco Press.

***Cisco Systems, Inc. Staff.** Cisco IOS Documentation Assortment I. 1998. write for info. (*1-57870-121-X*) Macmillan Tech.

— Cisco IOS 12.0 Interface Configuration. (Cisco IOS Reference Library). 1999. 45.00 (*1-57870-156-2*) Cisco Press.

Cisco Systems, Inc. Staff, jt. auth. see Chappell, Laura.

***Cisco Systems Staff.** Building Cisco Multilayer Switched Networks. 700p. 2000. 60.00 (*1-57870-093-0*) Cisco Press.

Cisco Systems Staff. Cisco CCIE Fundamentals: Network Design & Case Studies. LC 98-84211. (CCIE Preparations Guides Ser.). 1998. 50.00 (*1-57870-066-3*) Cisco Press.

— Cisco CCNA Preparation Library. 1998. 90.00 (*1-57870-125-2*) Macmillan Tech.

— Cisco Internetwork Troubleshooting. 1999. 60.00 (*1-57870-092-2*) Cisco Press.

— Cisco IOS Bridging & IBM Network Solutions. LC 98-84217. 1998. pap. text 60.00 (*1-57870-051-5*) Macmillan Tech.

— Cisco IOS Dial Solutions. LC 97-80684. 1568p. 1998. pap. text 60.00 (*1-57870-055-8*) Cisco Press.

— Cisco IOS Solutions for Network Protocols. LC 98-84216. 1998. pap. text 60.00 (*1-57870-049-3*) Macmillan Tech.

— Cisco IOS Solutions for Network Protocols, 2. LC 98-84216. 1998. pap. text 60.00 (*1-57870-050-7*) Macmillan Tech.

— Cisco IOS Switching Services. LC 97-80673. 1998. pap. text 50.00 (*1-57870-053-1*) Cisco Press.

— Cisco IOS 12.0 Bridging & IBM Network Solutions, Vol. 1. (Cisco IOS Reference Library). 1999. 60.00 (*1-57870-162-7*) Cisco Press.

***Cisco Systems Staff.** Cisco IOS 12.0 Solutions for Network Protocols, 1. LC 99-60044. (Illus.). 976p. 1999. 50.00 (*1-57870-154-6*) Cisco Press.

C

An Asterisk (*) at the beginning of an entry indicates that the title is appearing for the first time.

Cisco Systems Staff. Cisco IOS 12.0 Switching Services, 1. LC 99-60809. (Cisco Ios Reference Library Ser.). (Illus.). 421p. 1999. 40.00 (*1-57870-157-0*) Macmillan Tech.

— Cisco IOS 12.0 Wide Area Network Solutions, 1. LC 99-60810. (Cisco Ios Reference Library Ser.). 618p. 1999. 45.00 (*1-57870-158-9*) Macmillan Tech.

— Cisco Router Security. 1998. 50.00 (*1-57870-057-4*) Macmillan Tech.

— Configuring, Monitoring & Troubleshooting Dial Up Services. 1999. 60.00 (*1-57870-091-4*) Cisco Press.

— Internetworking Troubleshooting Handbook. LC 98-85488. 1998. pap. 50.00 (*1-57870-024-8*) Macmillan Tech.

Cisco Systems Staff, ed. CCIE Fundamentals: Network Design & Case Studies. 2nd ed. 1000p. 1999. pap. 50.00 (*1-57870-167-8*) Cisco Press.

Cisco Systems Staff, jt. auth. see Lew, H. Kim.

***Cisco, Walter Brian.** Taking a Stand: Portraits from the Southern Secession Movement. (Illus.). 151p. 2000. pap. 14.95 (*1-57249-210-4*, Burd St Pr) White Mane Pub.

Cise, Philip S. Van, see Van Cise, Philip S.

Cisek, David E., compiled by. The Longshore Textbook. 3rd ed. 400p. 1993. 49.00 (*0-88450-086-1*, 0861) Lawyers & Judges.

Cisek, Eugene & Persky, Robert S. Penny Wonder Drug: What the Label on Your Aspirin Bottle Doesn't Tell You. Levy, Susan P., ed. 128p. (Orig.). 1993. pap. 9.95 (*0-913069-31-0*) Consultant Pr.

Cisek, James & George, Anthea. Finding Solutions: How to Get "IDEAL" Answers to Problems & Decisions. rev. ed. (Illus.). 60p. 1985. pap. 4.95 (*0-9604510-8-0*) Life Skills.

— Life Skills: Teaching Attitudes & Behaviors for Success in Life. 280p. 1985. teacher ed. 59.95 incl. digital audio (*0-9604510-9-9*) Life Skills.

— Loosening Up: Getting Rid of Those Uptight Feelings. (Illus.). 40p. 1985. reprint ed. pap. 4.25 (*0-9604510-7-2*) Life Skills.

***Cisilino, Adrian P.** Linear & Nonlinear Crack Growth Using Boundary Elements. (Topics in Engineering Ser.: Vol. 36). 208p. 1999. 126.00 (*1-85312-700-0*, 7000, Pub. by WIT Pr) Computational Mech MA.

Ciskowski, R. D. & Brebbia, C. A., eds. Boundary Element Methods in Acoustics. 292p. 1995. reprint ed. 137.00 (*1-85312-104-5*) Computational Mech MA.

Ciskowski, R. D. & Brebbia, Carlos A., eds. Boundary Element Methods in Acoustics. LC 91-70445. (Computational Engineering Ser.). 155p. 1991. 155.00 (*0-945824-87-4*, 1045) Computational Mech MA.

Cislak, Lucille. Treasured Moments with God: Words of Challenge & Encouragement from our Father & Creator. 132p. 1999. pap. 7.99 (*1-58169-014-2*) Genesis Comm Inc.

Cisler, Valerie C. Alfred's Basic Piano Composition Book, Level 1B. (Alfred's Basic Piano Library Ser.). 1996. pap. 5.95 (*0-7390-0002-0*, 14511) Alfred Pub.

CISM (International Center for Mechanical Sciences. Channel Coding Theory: Proceedings of CISM, Department of Automation & Information, 1970. Csiszar, I., ed. (CISM Publications: No. 29). 79p. 1974. 19.95 (*0-387-81089-7*) Spr-Verlag.

— Examples to Extremum & Variational Principles in Mechanics. Besdo, D., ed. (CISM International Centre for Mechanical Sciences Ser.: No. 65). (Illus.). 236p. 1974. 41.95 (*0-387-81230-X*) Spr-Verlag.

— Extremum & Variational Principles in Mechanics: Proceedings of the CISM, Department for General Mechanics, Technical Univ. of Brunswick, 1970. Lippmann, H., ed. (CISM Publications: No. 54). (Illus.). ii, 239p. 1978. 50.95 (*0-387-81115-X*) Spr-Verlag.

— Fluidic Sensors & Some Large Scale Devices. Jacobs, B. E., ed. (CISM International Centre for Mechanical Sciences Ser.: No. 52). (Illus.). 41p. 1974. 9.95 (*0-387-81228-8*) Spr-Verlag.

— Information Transmission with Symbols of Different Cost. Csiszar, I., ed. (CISM Publications: No. 136). 36p. 1973. 8.95 (*0-387-81136-2*) Spr-Verlag.

— An Introduction to the Design of Pattern Recognition Devices: Proceedings of the CISM, Department of Automation & Information, Denmark, 1971. Becker, P. W., ed. (CISM Publications: No. 83). (Illus.). 188p. 1973. 43.95 (*0-387-81153-2*) Spr-Verlag.

— On Theory & Practice of Robots & Manipulators: Proceedings of CISM, IFTOMM Symposium, 1st, 1972. (CISM International Centre for Mechanical Sciences Ser.: No. 201). (Illus.). 668p. 1974. 85.95 (*0-387-81252-0*) Spr-Verlag.

— Photoelasticity in Theory & Practice: Proceedings of CISM, Department for Mechanics of Defable Bodies, 1970. Brcic, V., ed. (CISM International Centre for Mechanical Sciences Ser.: No. 59). (Illus.). 242p. 1975. 41.95 (*0-387-81081-1*) Spr-Verlag.

— Random Processes in Mechanical Sciences. Parkus, H., ed. (CISM Publications: No. 9). (Illus.). vi, 169p. 1973. 35.95 (*0-387-81086-2*) Spr-Verlag.

— Theory of Popular Elasticity: Proceedings of the CISM, Department of Mechanics of Deformable Bodies, 1970. Nowacki, Wojoiech K., ed. (CISM Publications: No. 25). (Illus.). 286p. 1974. 47.95 (*0-387-81078-1*) Spr-Verlag.

— The Tragicomedy of Classical Thermodynamics: Proceedings of CISM, Department of Solids, 1971. Truesdell, Clifford A., ed. (CISM Publications: No. 70). (Illus.). 41p. 1973. 15.95 (*0-387-81114-1*) Spr-Verlag.

CISM (International Center for Mechanical Sciences, et al, eds. Radiation Damage: Proceedings of CISM, Department for Mechanics of Defamable Bodies, Univ. of Vienna, 1970. Incl. Behavior of Insonated Metals. 1973. (CISM Publications: No. 64). (Illus.). 88p. 1973. 10.60 (*0-387-81124-9*) Spr-Verlag.

Cismaru, Alfred. Marivaux & Moliere: A Comparison. 139p. 1977. 12.95 (*0-89672-055-1*) Tex Tech Univ Pr.

***Cisnero, Isabel.** Spanish in Three Months. LC 97-47225. (SPA.). 1998. pap. 29.95 incl. audio (*0-7894-3228-5*) DK Pub Inc.

Cisneros, Antonio. At Night the Cats. Ahern, Maureen et al, trs. from SPA. LC 85-60358. (ENG & SPA.). 250p. 1985. 14.95 (*0-87376-044-1*) Red Dust.

— Helicoptors in the Kingdom of Peru. (C). 1988. 30.00 (*0-904524-25-6*, Pub. by Rivelin Grapheme Pr) St Mut.

Cisneros, C. & Morgan, T. J., eds. Atomic & Molecular Physics: Third U. S.-Mexico Symposium, Morelos, Mexico, 13-16 March 1991. 450p. 1991. text 118.00 (*981-02-0843-X*) World Scientific Pub.

Cisneros, Florencio G. Maximo Gomez, Caudillo o Dictador? (SPA.). 185p. (Orig.). 1987. pap. 9.95 (*0-9617456-0-6*) F Garcia-Cisneros.

Cisneros, G., et al, eds. Computational Chemistry & Chemical Engineering. LC 97-26421. 400p. 1997. text 84.00 (*981-02-3220-9*) World Scientific Pub.

Cisneros, Henry, jt. auth. see Wolff, Nelson W.

Cisneros, Henry G. Empowerment: A New Covenant with America's Communities: President Clinton's National Urban Policy Report. (Illus.). 68p. (C). 1998. reprint ed. pap. text 25.00 (*0-7881-3501-5*) DIANE Pub.

— Interwoven Destinies. (C). 1994. pap. text 13.00 (*0-393-96582-1*, Norton Paperbks) Norton.

— Regionalism: The New Geography of Opportunity. 29p. (Orig.). 1995. pap. text 15.00 (*0-7881-2202-9*) DIANE Pub.

— Renewing America's Communities from the Ground Up: The Plan to Complete the Transformation of HUD. 85p. 1996. reprint ed. pap. text 30.00 (*0-7881-3103-6*) DIANE Pub.

Cisneros, Henry G., ed. Interwoven Destinies: The Cities & the Nation. 288p. 1993. 25.00 (*0-393-03571-9*) Norton.

Cisneros, Isabel. Hugo Latin American Spanish in Three Months: Simplified Language Course. LC 98-48008. (Hugo Ser.). (SPA & ENG.). 1999. 29.95 incl. audio (*0-7894-4221-3*) DK Pub Inc.

— Latin American Spanish in Three Months. LC 98-48008. (Hugo Three Month Language Courses Ser.). 256p. 1999. pap. text 14.95 (*0-7894-4215-9*) DK Pub Inc.

Cisneros, Kathy. Bottle Cap Activities: Recycled Crafts for All Ages. (Illus.). 208p. 1998. 26.95 (*0-89334-288-2*); lib. bdg. 26.95 (*0-89334-282-3*) Humanics Ltd.

Cisneros-Lavaller, Alberto. The Geopolitics of Oil in the Middle East: An Overview. 20p. 1990. pap. 10.00 (*0-918714-22-2*) Intl Res Ctr Energy.

Cisneros, Milagros. Respectful Engagement: Cuban NGO Cooperation with Latin America, Europe & Canada. 1996. pap. 7.00 (*0-910082-32-4*) Am Fr Serv Comm.

Cisneros, Phil. Gabriela Gecko, the Story of Belonging. (Illus.). 22p. (J). (gr. 1-6). 1996. pap. 8.00 (*0-9651804-1-7*, 102) New Horizons Unlimited.

— Raking the Rocks. 100p. (J). (gr. 4-8). 1996. pap. 8.00 (*0-9651804-2-5*, 103) New Horizons Unlimited.

— Snowy, the Story of a Reluctant Snowflake. large type ed. (Illus.). 22p. (Orig.). (J). (gr. k-4). 1993. pap. 8.00 (*0-9651804-0-9*, 101) New Horizons Unlimited.

Cisneros, Sandra. El Arroyo de la llorona y otros cuentos.Tr. of Woman Hollering Creek & Other Stories. (ENG & SPA.). 191p. 1996. pap. 11.00 (*0-679-76804-1*) Vin Bks.

— La Casa en Mango Street.Tr. of House on Mango Street. (SPA.). 128p. 1994. pap. 9.95 (*0-679-75526-8*) Vin Bks.

— Hairs: Pelitos. (J). 1997. pap. 6.99 (*0-679-89007-6*, Pub. by Random Bks Yng Read) Random.

Cisneros, Sandra. Hairs: Pelitos. (J). 1997. 13.30 (*0-606-12960-X*, Pub. by Turtleback) Demco.

Cisneros, Sandra. The House on Mango Street. LC 90-50593. 112p. 1991. pap. 9.95 (*0-679-73477-5*) Knopf.

— The House on Mango Street. 144p. 1994. 24.00 (*0-679-43335-X*) Random.

— The House on Mango Street. (Vintage Contemporaries Ser.). (J). 1991. 15.05 (*0-606-05352-2*, Pub. by Turtleback) Demco.

— Loose Woman. LC 93-35937. 115p. 1994. 22.50 (*0-679-41644-7*) Knopf.

— Loose Woman. LC 93-35937. 1995. pap. 10.00 (*0-679-75527-6*) Vin Bks.

— My Wicked, Wicked Ways. LC 92-14852. (Orig.). 1992. 24.00 (*0-679-41821-0*) Random.

— Woman Hollering Creek & Other Stories. (Vintage Contemporaries Ser.). 165p. 1992. pap. 11.00 (*0-679-73856-8*) Vin Bks.

Cisse, M. Dictionary French to Wolof. (FRE & WOL.). 1998. 59.95 (*0-320-00284-5*) Fr & Eur.

Cissell, James. Federal Criminal Trials, 1996. 4th ed. LC 96-79662. 798p. 1996. text 105.00 (*1-55834-451-9*, 60877-11, MICHIE) LEXIS Pub.

Cissell, James C. Federal Criminal Trials. 786p. 1993. suppl. ed. 95.00 (*1-55834-001-7*, MICHIE) LEXIS Pub.

***Cissell, James C.** Federal Criminal Trials. 5th ed. 773p. 1999. 115.00 (*0-327-04907-3*, 6087812) LEXIS Pub.

Cissell, James C. Federal Criminal Trials: 1998 Supplement. 4th ed. 200p. 1998. write for info. (*0-327-00632-3*, 6087814) LEXIS Pub.

Cissell, Robert, et al. Mathematics of Finance, 8 vols. 8th ed. (C). 1989. pap. text 3.96 (*0-395-52652-3*) HM.

— Mathematics of Finance, 8 vols. 8th ed. (C). 1990. text 69.96 (*0-395-43324-X*) HM.

Cissell, William B., jt. ed. see Patton, Robert D.

Cissik, John M. The Basics of Strength Training. 1998. pap. 12.19 (*0-07-027465-X*) McGraw.

— An Introduction to Olympic-Style Weightlifting. 2nd ed. 1998. pap. 17.19 (*0-07-043488-3*) McGraw.

Cissna, Catherine A. & Church, Madeline. A Few of Our Friends in the Amador County Cemeteries. 87p. 1994. pap. 12.95 (*0-9644631-0-5*) Luxemberg Publ.

Cissna, Kenneth N., ed. Applied Communication in the Twenty-First Century. LC 95-2003. (LEA's Communication Ser.). 232p. 1995. pap. 27.50 (*0-8058-1852-9*) L Erlbaum Assocs.

— Applied Communication in the 21st Century. LC 95-2003. (LEA's Communication Ser.). 232p. 1995. text 45.00 (*0-8058-1475-2*) L Erlbaum Assocs.

Cissna, Kenneth N., jt. auth. see Anderson, Rob.

Cist, Charles. Cincinnati Miscellany, or Antiquities of the West: Pioneer History & General & Local Statistics Compiled from the Western General Advertiser, 2 vols. LC 72-146381. (First American Frontier Ser.). 1971. reprint ed. 47.95 (*0-405-02832-6*) Ayer.

Cist, O., jt. auth. see Hardy, Gilbert G.

Cist, Richard. The English Ceivil War. Hughes, Ann, ed. LC 97-152036. (Arnold Readers in History Ser.). 384p. 1997. pap. text 19.95 (*0-340-63173-2*, Pub. by E A) OUP.

Cistercian Abbey of las Huelgas, Burgos, Spain Sta. El Codex Musical de las Huelgas, 3 vols., Set. LC 71-178510. (Publications del Departament de Musica, Biblioteca de Catalunya: No. 6). (Illus.). reprint ed. 295.00 (*0-404-56504-2*) AMS Pr.

Cistjakov, G. P., et al, eds. Eighteen Papers on Statistics & Probability. LC 61-9803. (Selected Translations in Mathematical Statistics & Probability Ser.: Vol 15). 317p. 1982. 79.00 (*0-8218-1465-6*, STAPRO/15) Am Math.

Cistogradov, D. English-Russian Serbocroat Dictionary of Aviation. 440p. (C). 1988. 295.00 (*0-7855-6447-0*, Pub. by Collets) St Mut.

Ciszek, Henry. Obey God Rather Than Man. 322p. 1993. pap. 14.95 (*1-56794-030-7*, C2290) Star Bible.

Ciszek, Walter J. He Leadeth Me. LC 94-73067. 202p. pap. 11.95 (*0-89870-546-0*) Ignatius Pr.

— With God in Russia: My 23 Years in Siberian Prison Camps. LC 96-76024. 1997. pap. text 14.95 (*0-89870-574-6*) Ignatius Pr.

Citati, Pietro. Kafka. (FRE.). 1991. pap. 16.95 (*0-7859-2173-7*, 2070384179) Fr & Eur.

Citation Directories, Ltd., Inc. Staff. Citation's Who's Who among Rising Young Americans, 1991, Vol. 1. Peed, Joseph W. & Riley, Marilyn A., eds. 1991. lib. bdg. 99.95 (*1-880486-00-8*) Citation Direct.

— Citation's Who's Who among Rising Young Americans, 1992, Vol. 2. Peed, Joseph W. & Riley, Marilyn A., eds. 1992. lib. bdg. 119.95 (*1-880486-01-6*) Citation Direct.

— Citation's Who's Who Environmental Registry, 1992. Peed, Joseph W. & Riley, Marilyn A., eds. (Environmental Ser.: Vol. 1). 750p. 1992. pap. 239.95 (*1-880486-02-4*) Citation Direct.

Citation Directories, Ltd. Inc. Staff. Citation's Who's Who Registry of Rising Young Americans, 1993. Peed, Joseph W. & Riley, Marilyn A., eds. (Young American Ser.: Vol. 3). 1993. lib. bdg. 119.95 (*1-880486-03-2*) Citation Direct.

Citeno, Rocco J. Northeast Boaters Almanac. rev. ed. Orig. Title: Boat Owners. (Illus.). 512p. 1999. pap. 12.95 (*0-9659325-0-8*) Northeast Boat.

Citi, Sandra, ed. Molecular Mechanisms of Epithelial Cell Junctions: From Development to Disease. (Molecular Biology Intelligence Unit Ser.). 118p. 1994. 99.00 (*1-57059-091-5*, LN9091) Landes Bioscience.

Citicorp Staff. Interest Rate Spreads Market Analysis: Tools for Managing & Reducing Rate Exposure in Global Markets. 8th ed. 224p. 1996. 65.00 (*0-7863-0970-9*, Irwn Prfssnl) McGraw-Hill Prof.

Citino, David. The Appassionata Doctrines. 97p. (Orig.). 1986. 12.00 (*0-914946-57-9*); pap. 6.00 (*0-914946-56-0*) Cleveland St Univ Poetry Ctr.

— The Book of Appassionata: Collected Poems. LC 98-4326. 199p. 1998. pap. 19.00 (*0-8142-0774-X*, CITAPX); text 35.00 (*0-8142-0773-1*, CITAPP) Ohio St U Pr.

— Broken Symmetry. LC 96-37496. 92p. 1997. pap. 15.00 (*0-8142-0731-6*) Ohio St U Pr.

— The Weight of the Heart. (QRL Poetry Bks.: Vol. XXXV). 1996. 20.00 (*0-614-15861-3*) Quarterly Rev.

Citino, Robert M. Armored Forces: History & Sourcebook. LC 94-4784. (Histories & Sourcebooks on Combat Forces Ser.). 328p. 1994. lib. bdg. 79.50 (*0-313-28500-4*, Greenwood Pr) Greenwood.

— The Evolution of Blitzkrieg Tatics: Germany Defends Itself Against Poland, 1918-1933, 61. LC 87-5. (Contributions in Military Studies Ser.: No. 61). 223p. 1987. 57.95 (*0-313-25631-4*, CEN/, Greenwood Pr) Greenwood.

— Germany & the Union of South Africa in the Nazi Period, 27. LC 90-23211. (Contributions to the Study of World History Ser.: No. 27). 256p. 1991. 65.00 (*0-313-27789-3*, CGY, Greenwood Pr) Greenwood.

***Citino, Robert M.** The Path to Blitzkrieg: Doctrine & Training in the German Army, 1920-1939. LC 98-5251. 286p. 1999. lib. bdg. 55.00 (*1-55587-714-1*) L Rienner.

Citizen, John. The Twentieth-Eighth Amendment: The People's Voting Network. 32p. 1992. 5.00 (*1-882350-00-6*) Whte Horse Pub.

Citizens' Association of New York Staff. Report of the Council of Hygiene & Public Health of the Citizens' Association of New York Upon the Sanitary Condition of the City. LC 77-112532. (Rise of Urban America Ser.). (Illus.). 1976. reprint ed. 51.95 (*0-405-02443-6*) Ayer.

Citizens Clearinghouse for Hazardous Waste Staff, jt. auth. see Gibbs, Lois M.

Citizens' Commission on Civil Rights. Lost Opportunities: The Civil Rights Record of the Bush Administration Mid-Term. Liss, Susan M. & Taylor, William L., eds. LC 91-70979. 251p. (Orig.). 1991. pap. text 15.00 (*0-9622865-1-6*) CCCR.

Citizens Committee for New York City. New York Self Help. 1978. pap. 4.95 (*0-9601496-1-9*) Citizens Comm NY.

Citizens Crime Commission of New York City Staff & Regional Plan Association Staff. Downtown Safety, Security & Economic Development. (Regional Plan Technical Reports: No. 3). 105p. 1986. pap. text 45.00 (*0-318-19016-8*) Regional Plan Assn.

Citizens Crime Commission of New York City Staff & Regional Plan Association Staff. Downtown Safety, Security & Economic Development. LC 86-50000. (Illus.). 148p. (Orig.). 1986. pap. 38.00 (*0-915910-22-5*) Downtown Res.

***Citizens for Independent Courts Staff & Century Foundation Staff.** Uncertain Justice: Politics & America's Courts: The Reports of the Task Forces of Citizens for Independent Courts. LC 00-8494. 2000. pap. write for info. (*0-87078-448-X*) Century Foundation.

Citizens' Police Committee. Chicago Police Problems. LC 69-16230. (Criminology, Law Enforcement, & Social Problems Ser.: No. 89). 1969. reprint ed. 25.00 (*0-87585-089-8*) Patterson Smith.

Citizenship Foundation Staff, jt. auth. see Rowe, Don.

***Citow.** Comprehensive Neurosurgery Board Review. (Illus.). 392p. 2000. pap. 79.00 (*0-86577-889-2*) Thieme Med Pubs.

***Citra, Becky.** Ellie's New Home. LC 99-65483. (Young Reader Ser.). 112p. (J). (gr. 2-5). 2000. pap. 4.50 (*1-55143-164-5*) Orca Bk Pubs.

Citrenbaum, Charles M. Weight Control Through Trance & Self-Hypnosis. 1985. student ed. 10.95 incl. audio, reel tape (*0-393-70016-X*) Norton.

Citrenbaum, Charles M., jt. auth. see King, Mark E.

Citret, Mark, photos by. Along the Way. LC 98-47156. (Illus.). 132p. 1999. 55.00 (*1-881529-34-7*) Custom & Limited.

— Along the Way. limited ed. LC 98-47156. (Illus.). 132p. 1999. 400.00 (*1-881529-35-5*) Custom & Limited.

Citrin, D. A., ed. Radiative Processes & Dephasing in Semiconductors. LC 97-81323. (Trends in Optics & Photonics Ser.: Vol. 18). (Illus.). 154p. 1998. pap. 55.00 (*1-55752-525-0*) Optical Soc.

Citrin, Daniel A. & Lahiri, Ashok K., eds. Policy Experiences & Issues in the Baltic Countries, Russia & Other FSU Countries. LC 96-118846. (Occasional Papers: No. 133). 1995. pap. 15.00 (*1-55775-518-3*) Intl Monetary.

Citrin, Jack, jt. auth. see Sears, David O.

Citrin, Paul J. Joseph's Wardrobe. (Illus.). (J). (gr. 4-6). 1987. pap. 6.95 (*0-8074-0319-9*, 123924) UAHC.

— Joseph's Wardrobe. 1987. pap., teacher ed. 5.00 (*0-8074-0320-2*, 201351) UAHC.

Citrin, Richard, jt. auth. see Sanborn, Robert.

Citrine, W. M. Men & Work: An Autobiography. LC 75-36094. (Illus.). 384p. 1976. reprint ed. lib. bdg. 38.50 (*0-8371-8613-7*, CIMW, Greenwood Pr) Greenwood.

Citriniti, Michael E. & Juzwick, Michael D. The Original Intent of the First Amendment - According to the Founding Fathers: The Profane Wresting of United States Federal Law. 2nd ed. (Illus.). 128p. 1997. pap. 13.25 (*1-887412-00-X*) Light Eternal Pubns.

Citro, Constance F. & Cohen, Michael L., eds. The Bicentennial Census: New Directions for Methodology in 1990. LC 85-51816. (Illus.). 420p. reprint ed. pap. 130.20 (*0-7837-2595-7*, 204275800006) Bks Demand.

***Citro, Constance F. & Kalton, Graham, eds.** Small-Area Estimates of School-Age Children in Poverty. LC 99-191113. 134p. 1999. 30.50 (*0-309-06395-7*) Natl Acad Pr.

Citro, Constance F., et al. Assessing Policies for Retirement Income: Needs for Data, Research, & Models. LC 96-51696. 1997. pap. text 49.00 (*0-309-05627-6*) Natl Acad Pr.

Citro, Constance F., ed. see National Research Council, Panel on Poverty & Fami.

Citro, Constance F., ed. see National Research Council, Panel to Evaluate the S.

Citro, Constance F., ed. see National Research Council Staff.

Citro, Constance F., ed. see NRC Staff.

Citro, Joseph. Passing Strange: True Tales of New England Hauntings & Horrors. LC 97-9702. (Illus.). 320p. 1997. pap. 13.00 (*1-57630-059-5*, Chapters Bks) HM.

***Citro, Joseph A.** The Gore: A Novel. LC 00-9306. (Hardscrabble Bks.). 2000. write for info. (*1-58465-053-2*) U Pr of New Eng.

Citro, Joseph A. Green Mountain Ghosts, Ghouls & Unsolved Mysteries. LC 94-25962. (Illus.). 240p. 1994. pap. 13.00 (*1-881527-50-6*, Chapters Bks) HM.

***Citro, Joseph A.** Green Mountains, Dark Tales. LC 98-33105. 249p. 1999. 19.95 (*0-87451-863-6*) U Pr of New Eng.

— Guardian Angels. LC 99-23470. (Hardscrabble Bks.). 358p. 1999. reprint ed. pap. 13.95 (*1-58465-002-8*) U Pr of New Eng.

Citro, Joseph A. Shadow Child. LC 98-24018. (Hardscrabble Bks.). 296p. 1998. reprint ed. pap. 12.95 (*0-87451-884-9*) U Pr of New Eng.

***Citro, Joseph A.** The Vermont Ghost Guide. LC 99-55973. (Illus.). 115p. 2000. pap. 12.95 (*1-58465-009-5*) U Pr of New Eng.

Citron, Howard. Families Make a Difference. 12p. (J). (gr. 3-6). 1993. pap. text 1.30 (*0-9639216-0-6*) Educ Research.

Citron, Kathye J., jt. auth. see Citron, Ronald S.

Citron, Leslie. The Manifesto of Freedom. 160p. (C). 1993. text 25.50 (*0-88033-254-9*, 357, Pub. by East Eur Monographs) Col U Pr.

Citron, Marcia J. Cecile Chaminade: A Bio-Bibliography, 15. LC 88-21315. (Bio-Bibliographies in Music Ser.: No. 15). 257p. 1988. lib. bdg. 59.95 (*0-313-25319-6*, CCA/, Greenwood Pr) Greenwood.

***Citron, Marcia J.** Gender & the Musical Canon. 328p. 2000. 17.95 (*0-252-06916-1*) U of Ill Pr.

C

Citron, Marcia J. The Letters of Fanny Mendelssohn Hensel to Felix Mendelssohn. LC 84-26364. (ENG & GER.). 600p. 1987. lib. bdg. 83.00 (*0-918728-52-5*) Pendragon NY.

*__Citron, Marcia J.__ Opera on Screen. LC 99-48686. 336p. 2000. 35.00 (*0-300-08158-8*) Yale U Pr.

Citron, Michelle. Home Movies & Other Necessary Fictions. LC 98-29233. 1998. pap. 19.95 (*0-8166-3262-6*) U of Minn Pr.

— Home Movies & Other Necessary Fictions. (Visible Evidence Ser.: Vol. 4). (Illus.). 216p. 1998. 49.95 (*0-8166-3261-8*) U of Minn Pr.

*__Citron, Neil.__ Complications in Orthopaedics. (Illus.). 192p. 2000. 45.00 (*0-7506-2922-3*) Buttrwrth-Heinemann.

Citron, Pierre, jt. auth. see Balzac, Honore de.

Citron, Pierre, ed. see Balzac, Honore de.

Citron, Renee. Order & Reality: Supplemental Science Experiments & Activities. (Illus.). 45p. (J). (gr. k-7). 1997. pap. text 5.95 (*1-57896-011-8*, 2409) Hewitt Res Fnd.

Citron, Ronald S. Dr. Citron's Evolutionary Diet. (Illus.). 368p. 1998. pap. text 14.95 (*1-56170-522-5*) Hay House.

Citron, Ronald S. & Citron, Kathye J. Dr. Citron's Evolutionary Diet. LC 96-33164. 350p. 1997. 14.95 (*1-56170-354-0*, 841) Hay House.

Citron, Samuel J. Dramatics for Creative Teaching. (Illus.). 1961. 9.50 (*0-8381-0212-3*) USCJE.

Citron, Stephen. The Musical from the Inside Out. 336p. 1992. text 27.50 (*0-929587-79-0*) I R Dee.

— The Musical from the Inside Out. LC 97-19905. 312p. 1997. pap. 14.95 (*1-56663-176-9*, Elephant Paperbacks) I R Dee.

— Songwriting: A Complete Guide to the Craft. LC 89-49700. (Illus.). 352p. 1990. reprint ed. pap. 15.95 (*0-87910-137-7*) Limelight Edns.

Citron, Sterna. Hirsh's Secret: A Baal Shem Tov Story. large type ed. LC 96-78003. (Children's Ser.). (Illus.). 24p. (J). (gr. k-2). 1996. 12.95 (*1-889727-16-4*) Kerem Pubng.

— The Shepherd Boy Who Loved God: A Baal Shem Tov Story. LC 96-78002. (Children's Ser.). (Illus.). 24p. (J). (gr. k-2). 1996. 12.95 (*1-889727-15-6*) Kerem Pubng.

— Zushe's Find: A Story about the Rebbe Reb Zushe. LC 96-78004. (Children's Ser.). (Illus.). 24p. (J). (gr. k-2). 1996. 12.95 (*1-889727-17-2*) Kerem Pubng.

C

Cittadini, A., et al, eds. Molecular Oncology & Clinical Applications. LC 93-2395. (Molecular & Cell Biology Updates Ser.). (Illus.). 448p. 1993. 119.00 (*0-8176-2915-7*) Birkhauser.

Cittadini, E. & Rossi, T. Celioscopy & Ancillary Techniques in the Study of Gynecological Pathology. 96p. 1974. text 32.00 (*1-57235-058-X*) Piccin Nuova.

Cittadini, E., et al. The Surgical Management of Sterility. 150p. 1976. text 24.00 (*1-57235-057-1*) Piccin Nuova.

Cittadini, Giorgio. Double Contrast Barium Enema: The Genoa Approach. LC 97-40608. 1997. 69.00 (*88-470-0003-3*) Spr-Verlag.

Citti, Vittorio, et al, eds. An Index to the Anthologia Graeca (Anthologia Palatina & Planudea), 4 vols., Set. 897p. (Orig.). 1990. pap. 495.00 (*90-256-0912-0*, Pub. by AM Hakkert) Coronet Bks.

— An Index to the Griechische Vers-Inschriften, Vol. 1. (GRE.). 151p. 1995. pap. 48.00 (*90-256-1084-6*, Pub. by AM Hakkert) BookLink Distributors.

Cituk, Kathy & Finnegan, John. Natural Foods & Good Cooking. (Illus.). 128p. (Orig.). 1989. pap. 8.00 (*0-927425-01-7*) Elysian Arts.

City & Company Staff. Restoration Directory: A Listing of Services in the New York City Area. 7th ed. 1998. pap. 25.00 (*0-9647061-3-X*) NY Landmarks.

City & Suburban Kids Staff. The Sky Is a Long Way to Jump! Poem Exchange by City & Suburban Kids. Woodrich, Mary N., ed. LC 96-175576. (Illus.). 60p. (Orig.). (J). (gr. 3-6). 1995. pap. 8.00 (*0-913678-29-5*) New Day Pr.

City Beautiful Council of Dayton Ohio & Wright State University Staff. Quintessence--The Alternative Spaces Residency Program, the City Beautiful Council of Dayton, Ohio, the Wright State University, Department of Art, Vols. 2-3. LC 78-64851. 1978. write for info. (*0-9602550-0-1*) City Beautiful Council.

*__City Council of Baltimore Staff.__ First Records of Baltimore Town & Jonestown, 1729-1797. (Illus.). 142p. 1999. pap. 15.00 (*0-7884-1339-2*, C379) Heritage Bk.

City Family Magazine Staff. New Americans' Legal Guide. 1997. pap. 9.95 (*0-8050-4800-6*) H Holt & Co.

— New Americans' Medical Guide. 1997. pap. 9.95 (*0-8050-4801-4*) H Holt & Co.

City Literary Institute of London Staff. Tradition & Experiment in Present-Day Literature. LC 68-20290. (Essay Index Reprint Ser.). 1977. reprint ed. 18.95 (*0-8369-0307-2*) Ayer.

*__City of Ann Arbor Natural Area Preservation Division Satff.__ Along the Huron: The Natural Communities of the Huron River Corridor in Ann Arbor, Michigan. (Illus.). 136p. (C). 1999. pap. 2.95 (*0-472-08674-X*, 08674) U of Mich Pr.

City of Fairfax Round Table (Fairfax, Va.), jt. auth. see Netherton, Nan.

City of Toledo, Division of Water Staff, et al. Controlling Zebra Mussels at Water Treatment Intakes. LC 97-208051. (Illus.). 86p. 1997. pap. 125.00 (*0-89867-910-9*, 90612) Am Water Wks Assn.

City University Staff & Shaw, Roger C. Safety & Reliability of Software Based Systems: Twelfth Annual CSR Workshop (Bruges 12-15 September 1995) LC 96-29238. (Illus.). 461p. 1996. pap. 89.50 (*3-540-76034-2*) Spr-Verlag.

Citykids Staff & Mitchell, Carolyn B. City Kids Speak on Prejudice. (City Kids Speak Ser.). (Illus.). 48p. (J). (gr. 3-7). 1995. pap. 5.99 (*0-679-86552-7*, Pub. by Random Bks Yng Read) Random.

— City Kids Speak on Relationships. (City Kids Speak Ser.). (Illus.). 48p. (J). (gr. 3-7). 1995. pap. 5.99 (*0-679-86553-5*, Pub. by Random Bks Yng Read) Random.

Ciuba, Edward J. Who Do You Say That I Am? An Adult Inquiry Into the First Three Gospels. 2nd rev. ed. LC 92-37734. 172p. 1993. pap. 7.95 (*0-8189-0638-3*) Alba.

Ciuba, German, tr. see Keller, Ludmila.

*__Ciuba, Ted.__ Mail & Grow Rich: How to Get Rich in Mail Order in the Information Age. 224p. 2000. pap. 19.97 (*0-9672414-0-5*, Pub. by Parthenon Mktg) ACCESS Pubs Network.

Ciucci. Giuseppe Terragni: Opera Completa. (ITA., Illus.). 650p. 1997. pap. 78.00 (*88-435-5782-3*, Pub. by Art Bks Intl) Partners Pubs Grp.

Ciudad, Ricardo, ed. Nautical Dictionary in English, Spanish & French. (ENG, FRE & SPA.). 1992. 150.00 (*0-320-03697-9*) Fr & Eur.

Ciurena. Latino Periodicals: A Selection Guide. 1995. 40.00 (*0-8161-7334-6*, G K Hall & Co) Mac Lib Ref.

Ciuffreda, A. R., ed. see Energy Sources Technology Conference & Exhibition.

Ciuffreda, A. R., ed. see International Symposium on Aboveground Storage Tan.

Ciuffreda, Kenneth J. & Tannen, Barry. Eye Movement Basics for the Clinician. (Illus.). 280p. (C). (gr. 13). 1994. text 45.00 (*0-8016-6843-3*, 06843) Mosby Inc.

Ciuffreda, Kenneth J., jt. auth. see Ong, Editha.

Ciuffreda, Lillian, ed. see Erben, Karel J.

Ciufolini, Ignazio & Wheeler, John A. Gravitation & Intertia. LC 94-29874. (Series in Physics). 576p. 1995. text 49.50 (*0-691-03323-4*, Pub. by Princeton U Pr) Cal Prin Full Svc.

Ciufolini, Ignazio, jt. auth. see Ruffini, Remo.

Ciufolini, Marco A., jt. ed. see Billups, W. Edward.

Ciufolini, Marco A., jt. ed. see Billups, W. E.

Ciulla, A. J., ed. see Akel, Abdullatif A.

Ciulla, Andrew J. Papa Was a Riot. LC 83-61413. (Illus.). 212p. 1983. pap. 5.95 (*0-913791-00-8*) Rubicon Bks.

Ciulla, Joanne B. Ethics, the Heart of Leadership. LC 97-13410. 216p. 1998. 59.95 (*1-56720-175-X*, Quorum Bks); pap. 22.95 (*0-275-96120-6*, Praeger Pubs) Greenwood.

*__Ciulla, Joanne B.__ Honest Work. 2000. 25.00 (*0-394-56007-8*) Random.

Ciulla, Joanne B. The Working Life: Working to Live & Living to Work. LC 99-15768. 240p. 2000. 25.00 (*0-8129-2901-2*, Times Bks) Crown Pub Group.

Ciulla, Joanne B., et al. Ethics & Leadership Working Papers. Adams, Bruce & Webster, Scott, eds. (Kellogg Leadership Studies Project). 90p. 1996. pap. write for info. (*1-891464-01-9*) J M Burns Academy.

Ciulla, Thomas A. & Baker, Ann Sullivan, eds. Massachusetts Eye & Ear Infirmary Residents' Guide to Ocular Antimicrobial Therapy. 88p. (C). 1996. pap. text 9.95 (*1-56881-062-8*) AK Peters.

Ciullo, Jerome V. Shoulder Injuries in Sport: Evaluation, Treatment, & Rehabilitation. LC 95-41120. (Illus.). 304p. 1996. text 59.00 (*0-87322-651-8*, BCIU0651) Human Kinetics.

Ciullo, Peter A. Baking Soda Bonanza. LC 95-72. 176p. 1995. pap. 10.00 (*0-06-095097-8*, Perennial) HarperTrade.

— Bicarb: Buffers, Bubbles, Biscuits & EarthBurps. LC 97-93485. (Illus.). 80p. (Orig.). (YA). (gr. 9-11). 1997. pap. 10.00 (*0-9626043-7-2*) Maradia Pr.

— Industrial Minerals & Their Uses: A Handbook & Formulary. LC 96-29173. 632p. 1996. 145.00 (*0-8155-1408-5*) Noyes.

— Low Impact Service - A Guide to Automotive Service & Warranty Complaints, How to Avoid Them, How to Resolve Them: The Complete Handbook & Directory for the Mechanically Disinclined. LC 92-80997. 176p. (Orig.). 1992. pap. 12.95 (*0-9626043-6-4*) Maradia Pr.

— Save Big Money on a New Car: A Common Sense Buyers Guide. LC 90-91633. 64p. (Orig.). 1990. pap. 6.95 (*0-9626043-4-8*) Maradia Pr.

*__Ciuraru, Carmela, ed.__ First Loves: Poets Introduce the Essential Poems That Captivated & Inspired Them. LC 99-89937. (Illus.). 272p. 2000. 21.50 (*0-684-86438-X*, Scb1) S&S Trade.

Ciurczak, E. W. & Drennen, J. Near Infrared Spectroscopy in Pharmaceutical & Medical Applications. (Practical Spectroscopy Ser.). (Illus.). Date not set. text. write for info. (*0-8247-9453-2*) Dekker.

Ciurczak, Emil W. Molecular Spectroscopy Workbench: Advances, Applications & Practical Advice on Modern Spectroscopic Analysis. LC 97-24060. 476p. 1998. 79.95 (*0-471-18081-5*) Wiley.

Ciurczak, Emil W., jt. ed. see Burns, Donald A.

Ciureanu, P. & Middelhoek, S., eds. Thin Film Resistive Sensors. (Sensors Ser.). (Illus.). 512p. 1992. 220.00 (*0-7503-0173-2*) IOP Pub.

Civalleri, Paolo, jt. auth. see Carlin, Herbert J.

Civan, et al. Haitians, History & Culture. 42p. (YA). (gr. 5-12). Date not set. pap. 7.50 (*1-881839-46-X*) Educa Vision.

*__Civan, Faruk.__ Reservoir Formation Damage: Fundamentals, Modeling, Assessment & Mitigation. LC 00-27480. 744p. 2000. 150.00 (*0-88415-301-0*) Gulf Pub.

Civan, Mortimer M., ed. Current Topics in Membranes Vol. 45: The Eye's Aqueous Humor: From Secretion to Glaucoma. LC 97-213196. (Illus.). 288p. 1997. text 89.95 (*0-12-153345-X*) Morgan Kaufmann.

— Current Topics in Membranes Vol. 45: The Eye's Aqueous Humor: From Secretion to Glaucoma. LC 97-213196. (Illus.). 288p. 1998. pap. text 49.95 (*0-12-174675-5*) Morgan Kaufmann.

Civanla, Seyhanr, et al, eds. Internet Routing & Quality of Service, Vol. 3529. LC 99-192223. 1999. 80.00 (*0-8194-2990-2*) SPIE.

*__Civanlar, Seyhan, et al, eds.__ Internet II. 1999. pap. text 72.00 (*0-8194-3435-3*) SPIE.

Civanlar, Seyhan, et al. Broadband Networking Technologies: 2-3 November 1997, Dallas, Texas. LC 98-122106. (Proceedings Series). 380 p. 1997. 80.00 (*0-8194-2666-0*) SPIE.

Civardi. Going to the Doctor. (First Experiences Ser.). (Illus.). 16p. (ps-3). 1989. pap. 4.50 (*0-7460-1505-4*, Usborne) EDC.

Civardi, Anne. Going on a Plane. (Illus.). 16p. (ps-3). 1989. pap. 4.50 (*0-7460-1507-0*, Usborne) EDC.

*__Civardi, Anne.__ Going to the Doctor. (First Experiences Ser.). (Illus.). 16p. (YA). (ps up). 2000. pap. 4.95 (*0-7460-4117-9*, Usborne) EDC.

Civardi, Anne. Moving House. (Illus.). 16p. (J). (ps-3). 1993. pap. 4.50 (*0-7460-1281-0*, Usborne) EDC.

— Things People Do. (Illus.). 38p. (J). (ps-4). 1986. 12.95 (*0-86020-864-8*, Usborne) EDC.

— Word Finders in English. (Word Finders Bks.). 48p. (J). (gr. 2-6). 1984. pap. 9.95 (*0-7460-0392-7*) EDC.

Civardi, Anne & Cartwright, Stephen. Going to the Dentist. (First Experiences Ser.). (Illus.). 16p. (J). (ps-3). 1987. pap. 4.50 (*0-7460-1515-1*) EDC.

— Going to the Hospital. (First Experiences Ser.). (Illus.). 16p. (J). (ps-3). 1987. pap. 4.50 (*0-7460-1511-9*) EDC.

Civardi, Anne, et al. Detective's Handbook (B - U) (Detective Guides Ser.). (Illus.). 192p. (J). (gr. 3-6). 1992. pap. 9.95 (*0-86020-278-X*) EDC.

— Viking Raiders. (Time Traveller Ser.). (Illus.). 32p. (J). (gr. 3-6). 1998. lib. bdg. 14.95 (*0-88110-973-8*, Usborne) EDC.

— Viking Raiders. rev. ed. (Time Traveller Ser.). (Illus.). 32p. (J). (gr. 3-6). 1998. pap. 6.95 (*0-7460-3073-8*, Usborne) EDC.

Civardi, Anne, jt. auth. see Thomson, Ruth.

Civardi, Annie. The Secrets of Santa. LC 91-130. (Illus.). 32p. (J). (ps-1). 1991. pap. 13.95 (*0-671-74270-1*) S&S Bks Yung.

Civardi, Giovanni. Drawing the Female Nude. (Illus.). 104p. 1995. pap. 14.95 (*0-289-80090-0*, Pub. by SVista Bks) Sterling.

Civardi, Luigi. How Christ Changed the World: The Social Principles of the Catholic Church. Andriano, Sylvester, tr. from ITA. LC 91-65350. Orig. Title: Christianity & Social Justice. 111p. 1991. reprint ed. pap. 8.00 (*0-89555-443-7*) TAN Bks Pubs.

Civello, Catherine A. Patterns of Ambivalence: The Poetry & Fiction of Stevie Smith. LC 97-24267. (Studies in English & American Literature, Linguistics, & Culture). 145p. 1997. 45.00 (*1-57113-119-1*) Camden Hse.

Civerolo, E. L., Jr., et al, eds. Plant Pathogenic Bacteria. (Current Plant Science & Biotechnology in Agriculture Ser.). 1987. text 445.50 (*90-247-3476-2*) Kluwer Academic.

Civetta, Joseph M., et al. Critical Care. 3rd ed. 2224p. 1996. text 187.00 (*0-397-51527-8*) Lppncott W & W.

Civic Federation of Chicago, Chicago Staff. Chicago Conference on Trusts: Proceedings of Civic Federation of Chicago, Chicago Conference on Trusts, Sept. 1899. LC 73-1996. (Big Business; Economic Power in a Free Society Ser.). 1973. reprint ed. 42.95 (*0-405-05078-X*) Ayer.

Civic, Jed & Civic, Susan. The Vegetarian Traveler: Where to Stay If You're Vegetarian, Vegan, Environmentally Sensitive. LC 96-6749. 36p. (Illus.). 300p. (Orig.). 1997. pap. 15.95 (*0-943914-79-5*) Larson Pubns.

Civic, Susan, jt. auth. see Civic, Jed.

*__CIVICUS Staff.__ Civil Society at the Millennium. Naidoo, Kumi, ed. LC 99-34944. 224p. 1999. pap. 18.95 (*1-56549-101-7*, Frog Bks) Kumarian Pr.

CIVICUS Staff, ed. Building Civil Society Worldwide: Strategies for Successful Communications. (Illus.). 95p. 1997. pap. 15.00 (*0-9644001-5-4*) CIVICUS.

— The New Civic Atlas: Profiles of Civil Society in 60 Countries. (Illus.). 177p. 1997. pap. 15.00 (*0-9644001-6-2*) CIVICUS.

Cividini, A., ed. Application of Numerical Methods to Geotechnical Problems: Proceedings of the 4th European Conference on Numerical Methods in Geotechnical Engineering - NUMGE98, Udine, Italy, October 14-16, 1998. (CISM International Centre for Mechanical Sciences Ser.: Vol. 397). xv,765p. 1998. pap. 135.00 (*3-211-83141-X*) Spr-Verlag.

Civikly, Jean M., ed. Communicating in College Classrooms. LC 85-81904. (New Directions for Teaching & Learning Ser.: No. TL 26). (Orig.). 1986. pap. 22.00 (*0-87589-736-3*) Jossey-Bass.

*__Civil, Diana.__ Inspirations: Waxwork. 2000. pap. 12.95 (*1-84215-052-9*) Anness Pub.

Civil Aeronautics Authority Staff. Airports Survey. LC 77-74965. (American Federalism Ser.). (Illus.). 1978. reprint ed. lib. bdg. 23.95 (*0-405-10507-X*) Ayer.

Civil-Brown, Sue. Carried Away. 384p. 1997. mass mkt. 5.99 (*0-380-72774-9*, Avon Bks) Morrow Avon.

*__Civil-Brown, Sue.__ Catching Kelly. LC 99-95338. 384p. 2000. mass mkt. 5.99 (*0-380-80061-6*, Avon Bks) Morrow Avon.

Civil-Brown, Sue. Chasing Rainbow. LC 98-93534. 384p. 1999. mass mkt. 5.99 (*0-380-80060-8*, Avon Bks) Morrow Avon.

— Letting Loose. 384p. 1998. mass mkt. 5.99 (*0-380-72775-7*, Avon Bks) Morrow Avon.

*__Civil-Brown, Sue.__ Tempting Mr. Wright. 384p. 2000. mass mkt. 5.99 (*0-380-81179-0*, Avon Bks) Morrow Avon.

Civil Comp Editors. The Application of Artificial Intelligence Techniques to Civil & Structural Engineering. 152p. 1987. pap. 245.00 (*0-948749-06-7*, Pub. by Civil-Comp) St Mut.

— Artificial Intelligence & Civil Engineering. 313p. 1991. pap. 185.00 (*0-948749-14-8*, Pub. by Civil-Comp) St Mut.

— Artificial Intelligence & Structural Engineering. 320p. 1991. pap. 245.00 (*0-948749-15-6*, Pub. by Civil-Comp) St Mut.

— Artificial Intelligence Tools & Techniques for Civil & Structural Engineers. 303p. 1989. pap. 245.00 (*0-948749-13-X*, Pub. by Civil-Comp) St Mut.

— Development in Structural Engineering Computing. 1993. pap. 245.00 (*0-948749-20-2*, Pub. by Civil-Comp) St Mut.

— Developments in Civil & Construction Engineering Computing. 1990. pap. 245.00 (*0-948749-17-2*, Pub. by Civil-Comp) St Mut.

— Developments in Computational Engineering Mechanics. 1993. pap. 245.00 (*0-948749-21-0*, Pub. by Civil-Comp) St Mut.

— Knowledge Based Systems for Civil & Structural Engineering. 1993. pap. 245.00 (*0-948749-19-9*, Pub. by Civil-Comp) St Mut.

— Neural Networks & Combinatorial Optimization in Civil & Structural Engineering. 1993. pap. text 245.00 (*0-948749-18-0*, Pub. by Civil-Comp) St Mut.

— Proceedings of the Fourth International Conference on Civil & Structural Engineering Computing, 2 vols., Set. 1989. pap. text 245.00 (*0-948749-10-5*, Pub. by Civil-Comp) St Mut.

— Proceedings of the International Conference on the Design & Construction of Non-Conventional Structures, 2 vols., Set. 1987. pap. 245.00 (*0-948749-07-5*, Pub. by Civil-Comp) St Mut.

— Proceedings of the Second International Conference on Civil & Structural Engineering Computing, Set. 1985. pap. 245.00 (*0-948749-00-8*, Pub. by Civil-Comp) St Mut.

— Proceedings of the Third International Conference on Civil & Structural Engineering Computing, Set. 1987. pap. 245.00 (*0-948749-03-2*, Pub. by Civil-Comp) St Mut.

Civil Engineering Research Association Staff. Creating the 21st Century Through Innovation. LC 96-22147. 68p. 1996. 27.00 (*0-7844-0185-3*) Am Soc Civil Eng.

Civil Engineering Research Foundation. Construction Industry Research Prospectuses for the 21st Century. LC 96-9205. 140p. 1996. 82.00 (*0-7844-0186-1*) Am Soc Civil Eng.

— A Nationwide Survey of Civil Engineering Related R&D: Prepared by the Civil Engineering Research Foundation. LC 93-5108. 64p. 1993. 7.00 (*0-87262-970-8*) Am Soc Civil Eng.

Civil Engineering Research Foundation Staff. Action Plan: An Enhanced Building Technology Evaluation Process: The Partnership for Building Innovation: Enhancing the Process for Implementing New Technology. LC 96-30997. 44p. 1996. 21.00 (*0-7844-0198-5*) Am Soc Civil Eng.

— An Evaluation of Laboratory Test Results for the U. S. Gypsum Sight & Sound Screen System. LC 96-43025. 22p. 1997. 20.00 (*0-7844-0200-0*) Am Soc Civil Eng.

— Guidelines for Evaluating the Performance of Highway Sound Barriers. LC 96-43024. 56p. 1996. 21.00 (*0-7844-0199-3*) Am Soc Civil Eng.

— Guidelines for Field Evaluations of Pothole Repairs. 56p. 1995. pap. 27.00 (*0-7844-0090-3*) Am Soc Civil Eng.

— Guidelines for the Testing of Seismic Isolation & Energy Dissipating Devices. LC 96-6749. 36p. 1996. pap. 21.00 (*0-7844-0162-4*) Am Soc Civil Eng.

— International Sourcebook for Construction Industry Product Assessment. LC 96-21796. 78p. 1996. 20.00 (*0-7844-0173-X*) Am Soc Civil Eng.

— Materials for Tomorrow's Infrastructure: A Ten-Year Plan for Using High-Performance Construction Materials & Systems. LC 94-44437. 55p. 1994. 43.00 (*0-7844-0066-0*) Am Soc Civil Eng.

— Opportunities in Asia: An Assessment of Construction Trends, Needs & Potential Collaboration. LC 97-20863. 276p. 1997. 75.00 (*0-7844-0257-4*) Am Soc Civil Eng.

Civil Engineering Research Foundation Staff, compiled by. Federal Public Works Infrastructure R&D: A New Perspective. LC 93-9907. 76p. 1993. 6.00 (*0-87262-943-0*) Am Soc Civil Eng.

Civil Engineering Research Foundation Staff, ed. Improving Development Characteristics of Reinforcing Bars. LC 94-41542. 50p. 1994. 21.00 (*0-7844-0062-8*) Am Soc Civil Eng.

Civil Engineering Research Foundation Staff & Highway Innovative Technology Evaluation Center Staff. Guidelines for Evaluating Composite Column Wrap Systems for Seismic Retrofit. LC 98-48553. (Technology Evaluation Guidelines Ser.). 1998. 40.00 (*0-7844-0409-7*) Am Soc Civil Eng.

Civil Engineering Research Foundation Staff, jt. auth. see Environmental Technology Evaluation Center (U. S.

Civil Engineering Research Foundation Staff, jt. auth. see Highway Innovative Technology Evaluation Center (H.

*__Civil, Jean.__ Assertiveness. 96p. 2000. pap. 12.95 (*1-85835-529-X*, Pub. by Stylus Pub VA) LPC InBook.

Civil, Jean. Sexuality at Work: How Does It Affect You? LC 99-216971. 1998. 39.95 (*0-7134-8370-9*, Pub. by B T B) Branford.

*__Civil, Jean.__ Stress Management. 96p. 2000. pap. 12.95 (*1-85835-524-9*, Pub. by Stylus Pub VA) LPC InBook.

Civil Liberty Panel on Criminal Justice Staff. Jusice on Trial No. AJ2: Report of the Independent. 1992. pap. 15.00 (*0-900137-38-X*, Pub. by NCCL) St Mut.

Civil, Miguel. Mesopotamian Lexicography. (Handbook of Oriental Studies: Pt. 1A, 37). 300p. 1999. 104.00 (*90-04-11007-0*) Brill Academic Pubs.

An Asterisk (*) at the beginning of an entry indicates that the title is appearing for the first time.

Civil Rights Congress (U.S.), et al. Papers of the Civil Rights Congress: Manuscript Collections from the Schomburg Ce. LC 89-24822. (Black Studies Research Sources). 125 p. 1989. write for info. (*1-55655-065-0*) U Pubns Amer.

Civil War Society. The American Civil War: A Multicultural Encyclopedia, 7 vols. (Illus.). 1994. lib. bdg. 209.00 (*0-7172-7348-2*) Grolier Educ.

Civil War Society Staff. Civil War Battles. LC 98-33254. 1999. 6.99 (*0-517-20292-1*) Random Hse Value.

— Civil War Generals. LC 98-33253. 1999. 6.99 (*0-517-20288-3*) Random Hse Value.

Civil War Trust Staff & Braselton, Susan C. The Civil War Trust's Official Guide to the Civil War Discovery Trail. 3rd ed. LC E641.C59 1999. 336p. 1998. 13.95 (*0-02-862144-1*, Pub. by Macmillan) S&S Trade.

Civille, Gail V. & Lyon, Brenda G., eds. Aroma & Flavor Lexicon for Sensory Evaluation: Terms, Definitions, References, & Examples. LC 96-6909. (DS66 Ser.: Vol. 6666). (Illus.). 160p. 1996. pap. text 99.00 (*0-8031-2072-9*, DS66) ASTM.

Civille, John R., jt. auth. see Duggan, William R.

***Civin, Michael A.** Male, Female, Email: The Struggle for Relatedness in a Paranoid Society. LC 99-43547. 240p. 2000. 25.95 (*1-892746-30-1*) Other Pr LLC.

***Civitello, Andrew.** Construction Operations Manual of Policies & Procedures. 3rd ed. (Illus.). 368p. 2000. 89.95 (*0-07-135495-6*) McGraw-Hill Prof.

Civitello, Andrew, Jr. Construction Safety & Loss Control Program Manual. LC 97-30499. 364p. 1998. text 94.95 (*0-7656-0181-8*, Sharpe Prof) M E Sharpe.

Civitello, Andrew M., Jr. The Builder's & Contractor's Yearbook: The Construction Yearbook, 1987. 704p. 1987. text 59.95 (*0-13-085929-X*) P-H.

Civitello, Andrew M. Complete Contracting: A to Z Guide to Controlling Projects. LC 96-39020. (Illus.). 432p. 1996. 65.00 (*0-07-011354-8*) McGraw.

Civitello, Andrew M., Jr. The Construction Manager - 1989. 448p. 1989. text 32.50 (*0-13-168154-0*) P-H.

— The Construction Manager - 1991. 448p. 1991. text 32.50 (*0-13-173535-7*) P-H.

— The Construction Manager, 1988. 448p. 1988. text 32.50 (*0-13-169525-8*, Busn) P-H.

— The Construction Manager, 1990. 448p. 1990. text 32.50 (*0-13-171281-0*) P-H.

— Construction Operations Manual of Policies & Procedures. 2nd ed. LC 94-2651. 336p. 1994. 89.95 (*0-07-011048-4*) McGraw.

***Civitello, Andrew M.** Construction Operations Manual of Policies & Procedures. 3rd ed. LC 00-31876. 2000. write for info. (*0-07-136306-8*) McGraw.

— Construction Planning & Scheduling Manual. (Illus.). 2000. 79.95 (*0-07-012061-7*) McGraw.

Civitello, Andrew M., Jr. Contractor's Guide to Change Orders: The Art of Finding, Pricing, & Getting Paid for Contract Changes & the Damages They Cause. 400p. (C). 1987. text 69.95 (*0-13-171588-7*) P-H.

Civitello, Andrew M. 1997 Construction Manager. 480p. 1996. text 39.95 (*0-07-011782-9*) McGraw.

Cixous, Helen & Calle-Grubar, Mireille. Helene Cixous, Rootprints: Memory & Life Writings. Prenowitz, Eric, tr. from FRE. LC 96-44588. (Illus.). 272p. 1997. pap. 19.99 (*0-415-15542-8*) Routledge.

Cixous, Helene. The Book of Promethea. Wing, Betsy, tr. from FRE. LC 90-41111. (European Women Writers Ser.). xiv, 211p. 1991. pap. 14.00 (*0-8032-6343-0*, Bison Books) U of Nebr Pr.

— The Book of Promethea. Wing, Betsy, tr. from FRE. LC 90-41111. (European Women Writers Ser.). xiv, 211p. 1991. text 40.00 (*0-8032-1443-X*) U of Nebr Pr.

— Coming to Writing & Other Essays. Jenson, Deborah, ed. Cornell, Sarah et al, trs. 232p. (C). 1991. text 33.95 (*0-674-14436-8*) HUP.

— Coming to Writing & Other Essays. Jenson, Deborah, ed. & tr. by. from FRE. Liddle, Ann et al, trs. from FRE. 240p. 1992. pap. text 13.95 (*0-674-14437-6*) HUP.

— La Femmes. (FRE.). 1976. pap. 19.95 (*0-7859-3302-6*, 2721001507) Fr & Eur.

— The First Days of the Year. MacGillivray, Catherine A., tr. LC 98-9302. 192p. 1998. 42.95 (*0-8166-2116-0*); pap. 16.95 (*0-8166-2117-9*) U of Minn Pr.

— Manna: For the Mandelstams for the Mandelas. MacGillivray, Catherine A., tr. from FRE. & intro. by. LC 93-34674. (Emergent Literatures Ser.). 1994. 24.95 (*0-8166-2114-4*) U of Minn Pr.

— Reading with Clarice Lispector. Conley, Verena A., tr. & intro. by. (Theory & History of Literature Ser.: Vol. 73). (Illus.). 187p. (C). 1990. pap. 14.95 (*0-8166-1829-1*) U of Minn Pr.

— Readings: The Poetics of Blanchot, Joyce, Kafka, Kleist, Lispector, & Tsvetayeva. Conley, Verena A., tr. from FRE. & intro. by. (Theory & History of Literature Ser.: Vol. 77). 192p. (C). 1991. text 39.95 (*0-8166-1940-9*) U of Minn Pr.

— Readings: The Poetics of Blanchot, Joyce, Kafka, Kleist, Lispector, & Tsvetayeva. Conley, Verena A., tr. from FRE. & intro. by. (Theory & History of Literature Ser.: Vol. 77). 192p. (C). 1991. pap. 15.95 (*0-8166-1941-7*) U of Minn Pr.

— La Risa de la Medusa. (SPA.). 208p. 1995. pap. 14.95 (*0-614-16494-X*) U of PR Pr.

— Stigmata: Escaping Texts. LC 98-17127. (Illus.). 198p. 1998. pap. 19.99 (*0-415-17979-3*) Routledge.

— Stigmata: Escaping Texts. LC 98-17127. (Illus.). 224p. (C). 1998. 65.00 (*0-415-17978-5*) Routledge.

— The Terrible but Unfinished Story of Norodom Sihanouk, King of Cambodia. MacCannell, Juliet F. et al, trs. LC 93-1916. (European Women Writers Ser.).Tr. of Histoire Terrible Mais Inachevee de Nordorodom Sihanouk, roi du Cambodge. (ENG & FRE.). xxvii, 233p. 1994. pap. 13.95 (*0-8032-6361-9*, Bison Books) U of Nebr Pr.

— The Third Body. Cohen, Keith, tr. from FRE. LC 99-27406. 168p. 1999. 24.95 (*0-8101-1687-1*, Hydra Bks) Northwestern U Pr.

— Three Steps on the Ladder of Writing. 1994. pap. 15.00 (*0-231-07659-2*) Col U Pr.

Cixous, Helene & Calle-Grubar, Mireille. Helene Cixous, Rootprints: Memory & Life Writings. Prenowitz, Eric, tr. from FRE. LC 96-44588. (Illus.). 272p. (C). 1997. 75.00 (*0-415-15541-X*) Routledge.

Cixous, Helene & Clement, Catherine. Newly Born Woman. Wing, Betsy, tr. from FRE. LC 85-30898. (Theory & History of Literature Ser.: Vol. 24).Tr. of La/Jeune Nee. 186p. (Orig.). 1986. pap. 13.95 (*0-8166-1466-0*); text 42.95 (*0-8166-1465-2*) U of Minn Pr.

Cizakca, Murat. A Comparative Evolution of Business Partnerships: The Islamic World & Europe, with Specific Reference to the Ottoman Archive. Vol. 8. (Illus.). xxvi, 232p. 1996. 84.00 (*90-04-10601-4*) Brill Academic Pubs.

Cizek, Gregory J. Handbook of Educational Policy. LC 98-88526. (Illus.). 584p. (C). 1999. 84.95 (*0-12-174698-4*) Acad Pr.

Cizek, Gregory H. Cheating on Tests: How to Do It, Detect It & Prevent It. LC 99-20275. 288p. 1999. 59.95 (*0-8058-3144-4*); pap. 29.95 (*0-8058-3145-2*) L Erlbaum Assocs.

Cizek, V., ed. Discrete Fourier Transforms & Their Applications. (Illus.). 141p. 1986. 54.00 (*0-85274-800-0*) IOP Pub.

Cizevska, Tatana. Glossary of the Igor Tale. (S P R Ser.: No. 53). 1966. text 88.50 (*90-279-0198-8*) Mouton.

Cizevskij, Dimitry. History of Russian Literature. 3rd ed. (Slavistic Printings & Reprintings Ser.: No. 12). 1971. text 50.00 (*90-279-1917-8*) Mouton.

Cizevskij, Dmitry. Comparative History of Slavic Literatures. Porter, Richard N. & Rice, Martin P., trs. from GER. LC 74-124115. Orig. Title: Vergleichende Geschichte der Slavischen Literaturen. 225p. 1971. 17.50 (*0-8265-1159-7*) Vanderbilt U Pr.

Cizmar, Paula. Candy & Shelley Go to the Desert. 1988. pap. 5.25 (*0-8222-0179-8*) Dramatists Play.

Cizmar, Paula, jt. auth. see Suzuki, Sylvester.

Cizmar, Paula, ed. see Malmuth, Mason.

Cizmar, Paula, ed. see Paymar, Dan, et al.

Cizmar, Paula, ed. see Sklansky, David & Malmuth, Mason.

CJCLDS Mason County Staff. Mason County, Illinois: Lutheran Church Records to 1904. 53p. 1990. pap. 5.00 (*1-877869-23-6*) Mason Cnty Hist Proj.

Cjetti, David Chier. Edith Head. 2000. 37.50 (*0-06-019390-5*) HarpC.

CJH Enterprises Staff, ed. see Tarvin, Al.

Cjl, ed. see Kinkade, Thomas.

CJS, Inc. Staff. Colorado Business Directory, 1999 Edition. 10th ed. 483p. 1998. pap. 65.00 (*1-882538-65-X*) CJS.

— Dallas - Ft. Worth Metro Business Directory, 1999 Edition. 3rd ed. 428p. 1998. pap. 85.00 (*1-882538-67-6*) CJS.

— Houston Business Directory, 1999 Edition. 3rd ed. 472p. 1998. pap. 85.00 (*1-882538-66-8*) CJS.

— Maryland Business Directory, 1999 Edition. 5th ed. 408p. 1998. pap. 65.00 (*1-882538-68-4*) CJS.

Cla Dias, Joao S. Antonio Royo Marin, O. P. A Master on the Spiritual Life, a Brilliant Preacher, & a Famous Writer. (ENG & SPA., Illus.). 62p. (Orig.). (C). 1987. pap. 5.00 (*1-877905-05-4*) Am Soc Defense TFP.

— Cardinal Stickler: Salesian, Erudite & Librarian of the Holy Catholic Church. (Illus.). 46p. (Orig.). (C). 1987. pap. 5.00 (*1-877905-03-8*) Am Soc Defense TFP.

Claar, James & Schullery, Paul D., eds. Bears: Their Biology & Management. (Illus.). 586p. 1994. pap. text 45.00 (*0-944740-04-9*) Intl Assn Bear Res.

Claar, Terry D., ed. see Symposium on Molten Carbonate Fuel Cell Technology.

***Claasen, Adam R. A.** Hitler's Northern War: The Luftwaffe's Ill-Fated Campaign, 1940-1945. 2001. 39.95 (*0-7006-1050-2*) U Pr of KS.

Claasen, Johannes. Ludwig von Saint-Martin, Vol. V. 456p. reprint ed. write for info. (*0-318-71433-7*) G Olms Pubs.

Claasen, M., jt. auth. see Fruehmorgen, P.

Claasens, Geert & Johnson, David. Arthurian Archives: Middle Dutch. Lacy, Norris J., ed. 1500p. 1998. text 125.00 (*0-8153-2040-X*) Garland.

Claassen, C. J. Dictionary of Legal Words & Phrases, Vol. 1. boxed set 114.00 (*0-409-01890-2*, SA, MICHIE) LEXIS Pub.

— Dictionary of Legal Words & Phrases, Vol. 2. boxed set 114.00 (*0-409-01891-0*, SA, MICHIE) LEXIS Pub.

— Dictionary of Legal Words & Phrases, Vol. 3. boxed set 114.00 (*0-409-01892-9*, SA, MICHIE) LEXIS Pub.

— Dictionary of Legal Words & Phrases, Vol. 4. boxed set 114.00 (*0-409-01893-7*, SA, MICHIE) LEXIS Pub.

Claassen, Cheryl. Shells. LC 97-35274. (Cambridge Manuals in Archaeology). (Illus.). 292p. (C). 1998. text 74.95 (*0-521-57036-0*); pap. text 27.95 (*0-521-57852-3*) Cambridge U Pr.

Claassen, Cheryl, ed. Women in Archaeology. LC 94-8818. (Illus.). 264p. (Orig.). (C). 1994. text 39.95 (*0-8122-3277-1*) U of Pa Pr.

Claassen, Cheryl, ed. Women in Archaeology. LC 94-8818. (Illus.). 264p. (Orig.). (C). 1994. pap. text 17.95 (*0-8122-1509-5*) U of Pa Pr.

Claassen, Cheryl & Joyce, Rosemary, eds. Women in Prehistory: North America & Mesoamerica. LC 96-3455. (Illus.). 288p. 1996. text 39.95 (*0-8122-3381-6*); pap. text 18.50 (*0-8122-1602-4*) U of Pa Pr.

Claassen, David J. Object Lessons for a Year: 52 Talks for the Children's Sermon Time. (Object Lesson Ser.). 114p. (gr. 11). 1986. pap. 6.99 (*0-8010-2514-1*) Baker Bks.

Claassen, Emil-Maria. Exchange Rate Policies in Developing & Post-Socialist Countries. 552p. 1992. pap. 19.95 (*1-55815-146-X*) ICS Pr.

— Global Monetary Economics. LC 95-49774. (Illus.). 342p. 1997. pap. text 19.95 (*0-19-877465-6*) OUP.

Claassen, Emil-Maria, ed. International & European Monetary Systems. LC 89-3916. 232p. 1990. 67.95 (*0-275-93284-2*, C3284, Greenwood Pr) Greenwood.

Claassen, Eric & Jeurissen, Suzan H. Histophysiology Immunology of Lymphoid Tissues. 1999. 80.00 (*0-8493-9220-9*) CRC Pr.

***Claassen, Jo-Marie.** Displaced Persons: The Literature of Exile from Cicero to Boethius. LC 99-29892. (Wisconsin Studies in Classics). 360p. (Orig.). 1999. text 49.95 (*0-299-16640-6*); pap. text 19.95 (*0-299-16644-9*) U of Wis Pr.

Claassen, Lynda C. Finders' Guide to Prints & Drawings in the Smithsonian Institution. LC 81-607070. (Finders' Guides to Works in the Smithsonian Institution Ser.). (Illus.). 210p. 1981. pap. text 19.95 (*0-87474-317-6*, CLFGP) Smithsonian.

Claassen, R. D. Dictionary of Legal Words & Phrases: Fifth Cumulative Supplement. (AFR & ENG.). 252p. 1991. pap., suppl. ed. write for info. (*0-409-01899-6*, MICHIE) LEXIS Pub.

Claassen, Volkert. Neglected Factors in Pharmacology & Neuroscience Research. LC 94-16419. (Techniques in the Behavioral & Neural Sciences Ser.: Vol. 12). 496p. 1994. 247.50 (*0-444-81871-5*) Elsevier.

Claassen, Volkert, ed. Neglected Factors in Pharmacology & Neuroscience Research. (Techniques in the Behavioral & Neural Sciences Ser.: Vol. 12). 496p. 1994. pap. 88.50 (*0-444-81907-X*) Elsevier.

Claassens, Geert H. M., jt. ed. see Johnson, David F.

Clabaugh, Gary K. & Rozycki, Edward G. Analyzing Controversy: An Introductory Guide. (Illus.). 192p. 1997. pap. text 11.90 (*0-697-34335-9*, Dshkn McG-Hill) McGrw-H Hghr Educ.

— Preventing Plagiarism & Cheating: An Instructor's Guide. 1999. pap., teacher ed. 6.95 (*1-929463-01-4*) NewFound.

Clabaugh, Gary K., jt. auth. see Rozycki, Edward G.

Clabaugh, Maurice G., Jr. & Forbes, Jesse L. Experimental Exercises in Relationship Selling. Leyh, ed. 182p. (C). 1992. pap. text 19.00 (*0-314-93451-0*) West Pub.

— Practical Selling: A Relationship Approach. Leyh, ed. 535p. (C). 1992. text 61.50 (*0-314-88422-X*) West Pub.

Clabaugh, Maurice G., Jr., et al. Practical Selling: A Case Approach. Leyh, ed. 528p. (C). 1992. pap. text 27.75 (*0-314-93311-5*) West Pub.

Clabburn, Pamela. Beadwork, 1989. (Album Ser.: No. 57). (Illus.). 32p. 1989. pap. text 4.95 (*0-685-54429-X*, Pub. by Shire Pubns) Lubrecht & Cramer.

— The Norwich Shawl: Its History & a Catalogue of the Collection at Strangers Hall Museum, Norwich. (Illus.). 145p. 1995. 40.00 (*0-11-701591-1*, Pub. by Statnry Office); pap. 26.00 (*0-11-701584-9*, Pub. by Statnry Office) Balogh.

— Patchwork. 1989. pap. 25.00 (*0-85263-631-8*, Pub. by Shire Pubns) St Mut.

— Sampler. (Illus.). 40p. 1998. pap. 8.50 (*0-7478-0365-X*, Pub. by Shire Pubns) Parkwest Pubns.

Clabby, J. The History of the RAVC, 1919-1961. (Illus.). 244p. 1990. 60.00 (*0-85131-082-6*, Pub. by J A Allen) St Mut.

Clabeaux, John J. A Lost Edition of the Letters of Paul: A Reassessment of the Text of the Pauline Corpus Attested by Marcion. LC 88-28511. (Catholic Biblical Quarterly Monographs: No. 21). xiv, 181p. 1989. pap. 8.50 (*0-915170-20-5*) Catholic Bibl Assn.

Clabes, Judith G. By Judy! About Working Moms & Other Human Things. 180p. (Orig.). 1990. pap. 9.95 (*0-9624673-2-4*) Picture This Bks.

Clabes, Judith G., ed. New Guardians of the Press: Selected Profiles of America's Women Newspaper Editors. LC 83-71282. 140p. 1983. 18.95 (*0-89730-106-4*) R J Berg.

Clabo, Margo J. The Ultimate Book of Quilt Labels. White, Janet, ed. LC 97-48429. (Joy of Quilting Ser.). (Illus.). 64p. 1998. pap. 12.95 (*1-56477-146-6*, B320, That Patchwrk Pl) Martingale & Co.

Clabon, George D. Potbellied Stove. LC 97-60486. (Illus.). 64p. 1997. pap. 10.00 (*1-890459-00-3*) TA Pubns.

Claborn, Jimmy W., jt. auth. see Henderson, William D.

Claborn, Jo C., jt. auth. see Zerwekh, JoAnn.

Claborn, Jo C., jt. ed. see Zerwekh, JoAnn.

Claborn, Jo Carol, jt. auth. see Zerwekh, Jo Ann.

Claborn, Jo Carol, jt. auth. see Zerwekh, JoAnn.

Claborn, Jo Carol, jt. auth. see Zerwekh, Joann.

Claborn, Jo Carol, jt. auth. see Zerwekh, JoAnn.

Clabough, Jean. Matty's Heart: A Child's & Parents' Guide to Open Heart Surgery. Polk, Debbie & Cocalis, M. W., eds. LC 94-71677. (Child's & Parent's Medical Storybooks Ser.: Vol. 1). (Illus.). 55p. (J). (gr. k-6). 1995. lib. bdg. 14.95 (*0-9638662-3-0*) Aletheia CA.

Clabough, Jean. Matty's Heart Cath: Story & Coloring Book. (Illus.). 20p. (J). (gr. k-6). 1995. pap., wbk. ed. 3.99 (*0-9638662-0-6*) Aletheia CA.

Clack, Beverly, ed. Misogyny in the Western Philosophical Tradition: A Reader. LC 98-34341. 320p. (C). 1999. pap. 22.99 (*0-415-92182-1*, D5989) Routledge.

— Misogyny in the Western Philosophical Tradition: A Reader. LC 98-34341. 320p. (C). (gr. 13). 1999. 75.00 (*0-415-92181-3*, D5985) Routledge.

Clack, Beverly & Clack, Brian R. The Philosophy of Religion: A Critical Introduction. LC 98-36041. 209p. (Orig.). 1999. pap. 22.95 (*0-7456-1738-7*) Blackwell Pubs.

Clack, Beverly & Taylor, Scott W. The Philosophy of Religion: A Critical Introduction. LC 98-36041. 209p. (Orig.). 1999. 54.95 (*0-7456-1737-9*) Blackwell Pubs.

***Clack, Brian R.** An Introduction to Wittgenstein's Philosophy of Religion. 192p. 2000. pap. text 25.00 (*0-7486-0939-3*) Col U Pr.

Clack, Brian R., jt. auth. see Clack, Beverly.

Clack, C., et al, eds. Implementation of Functional Languages: 9th International Workshop, IFL'97, St. Andrews, Scotland, U. K., September 10-12, 1997, Selected Papers, Vol. 146. LC 98-30692. (Lecture Notes in Computer Science Ser.: Vol. 1467). x, 375p. 1998. pap. 59.00 (*3-540-64849-6*) Spr-Verlag.

Clack, Doris H. Authority Control: Principles, Applications & Instructions. LC 89-33240. 247p. 1990. reprint ed. pap. 76.60 (*0-608-01443-5*, 206220600002) Bks Demand.

— Black Literature Resources: Analysis & Organization. LC 75-23582. (Books in Library & Information Science: No. 16). 217p. reprint ed. pap. 67.30 (*0-8357-6043-X*, 203452300090) Bks Demand.

Clack, Jerry, ed. Meleagen - The Poems. (GRE.). vii, 160p. (Orig.). (C). 1992. pap. text 18.00 (*0-86516-254-9*) Bolchazy-Carducci.

Clack, Linda, jt. auth. see Josey, Martha.

Clack, Louise. General Lee & Santa Claus: Christmas Gifts to Her Little Southern Friends. 88p. (J). (gr. 2-5). 1996. reprint ed. pap. 9.95 (*1-55793-106-2*) Guild Bindery Pr.

Clack, Mary E., jt. ed. see Chatterton, Leigh A.

Clack, R. Bertrand Russell's Philosophy of Language. 100p. 1972. pap. text 66.50 (*90-247-0031-0*) Kluwer Academic.

Clack, R. James, jt. auth. see Conyne, Robert K.

***Clack, Randall A.** The Marriage of Heaven & Earth: Alchemical Regeneration in the Works of Taylor, Poe, Hawthorne & Fuller, 6. LC 99-58878. (Contributions to the Study of American Literature: Vol. 5). 176p. 2000. 59.95 (*0-313-31269-9*, Greenwood Pr) Greenwood.

Clack, Robert W. Celestial Symphonies: A History of Chinese Music. 1975. lib. bdg. 250.00 (*0-87968-447-X*) Gordon Pr.

— The Herd Boy & the Weaver Maid: A Definitive Anthology of Chinese Love Songs & Poetry. 1975. lib. bdg. 250.00 (*0-87968-461-5*) Gordon Pr.

— Millenniums of Moonbeams: A Definitive History & Anthology of Chinese Poetry, 3 vols., Set. 995p. 1975. lib. bdg. 900.00 (*0-87968-445-3*) Gordon Pr.

— The Soul of Yamato: A History & Anthology of Japanese Poetry, 2 vols., Set. 1975. lib. bdg. 600.00 (*0-87968-446-1*) Gordon Pr.

Clackett, Dave. Handbook of Midi Sequencing. 224p. 1996. pap. 17.95 (*1-870775-38-4*, Pub. by PC Pubg) Cimino Pub Grp.

Clackson, James. The Linguistic Relationship Between Armenian & Greek. LC 94-26076. (Publications of the Philological Society). 276p. (Orig.). (C). 1995. pap. 37.95 (*0-631-19197-6*) Blackwell Pubs.

Clad, James, jt. auth. see Clarke, Jonathan.

Clader, Timothy. Royal Hours of Nativity: Complete Texts & Music. Campbell, Laurence & Lambertsen, Isaac E., trs. from SLA. 57p. 1996. pap. 12.00 (*0-912927-66-6*, D032) St John Kronstadt.

Clader, Timothy, ed. The Eight Tones: Selection of Introductory Verses. Lambertsen, Isaac E. & Campbell, Laurence, trs. from GRE. 64p. (Orig.). 1992. spiral bd. 12.00 (*0-912927-49-6*, D012) St John Kronstadt.

— Music for a Pannykhida: The Orthodox Service for the Departed. Campbell, Laurence, tr. from SLA. 60p. 1994. spiral bd. 10.00 (*0-912927-84-4*, D021) St John Kronstadt.

— Music for Daily Vespers & Matins. Holy Transfiguration Monastery Staff et al, trs. from SLA. 98p. 1996. pap., spiral bd. 20.00 (*0-912927-73-9*, D038) St John Kronstadt.

— Music for the Divine Liturgy: Multiple Settings for the Unvarying Portions of the Divine Liturgy. Holy Transfiguration Monastery Staff et al, trs. from SLA. 332p. 1996. pap., spiral bd. 55.00 (*0-912927-75-5*, D040) St John Kronstadt.

— Music for the Divine Liturgy of the Presanctified Gifts. Lambertsen, Isaac E. & Campbell, Laurence, trs. from GRE. 73p. 1994. pap. 12.00 (*0-912927-59-3*, D019) St John Kronstadt.

— Music for the Eleven Evangelical Stichera. Lambertsen, Isaac, tr. from SLA. 58p. 1997. spiral bd. 12.00 (*0-912927-83-6*, D020) St John Kronstadt.

— Music for the Paschal Canon: According to the Liturgy of the Orthodox Church, As Chanted During Paschaltide. Campbell, Laurence, tr. from SLA. 98p. 1994. spiral bd. 15.00 (*0-912927-85-2*) St John Kronstadt.

— Music for the Sunday Vigil in the Eight Tones, 8 vols., Set. Lambertsen, Isaac E. & Campbell, Laurence, trs. from GRE. (Orig.). 1992. spiral bd. 100.00 (*0-912927-47-X*, D010) St John Kronstadt.

— Music for the Vigil Service: Multiple Settings for the Unvarying Portions of the Vigil Service. Holy Transfiguration Monastery Staff et al, trs. from SLA. 196p. 1996. pap., spiral bd. 40.00 (*0-912927-74-7*, D039) St John Kronstadt.

— Vespers for Holy Nativity: Complete Texts & Music. Campbell, Laurence & Lambertsen, Isaac E., trs. from SLA. 45p. 1996. pap. 10.00 (*0-912927-67-4*, D033) St John Kronstadt.

— Vigil of Holy Nativity: The Order of Great Compline & Matins, & Music for the Divine Liturgy. Campbell, Laurence & Lambertsen, Isaac E., trs. from SLA. 185p. 1996. 35.00 (*0-912927-68-2*, D034) St John Kronstadt.

Cladis, George. Leading the Team-based Church: How Pastors & Church Staffs Can Grow Together into a Powerful Faith. LC 98-40264. 1999. 21.95 (*0-7879-4119-0*) Jossey-Bass.

Cladis, Mark S. Communitarian Defence of Liberalism: Emile Durkheim & Contemporary Social Theory. xii, 339p. 1994. pap. 16.95 (*0-8047-2365-6*) Stanford U Pr.

C

— A Communitarian Defense of Liberalism: Emile Durkheim & Contemporary Social Theory. LC 92-10125. (Series in Philosophy). 360p. (C). 1993. 47.50 (*0-8047-2042-8*) Stanford U Pr.

Cladis, P. E. Spatio-Temporal Patterns in Nonequilibrium Complex Systems - NATO Advanced Research Workshop: Proceedings of the NATO Advanced Research Workshop on Spatio-Temporal Patterns in Nonequilibrium Complex Systems, Held April 13-17, 1993, in Santa Fe, NM. LC 94-43003. (Santa Fe Institute Studies in the Sciences of Complexity: Vol. 21). (C). 1995. pap. 57.00 (*0-201-40987-9*) Addison-Wesley.

***Cladis, Patricia E., ed.** Dynamics & Defects in Liquid Crystals: A Festschrift in Honor of Alfred Saupe. 480p. 1998. text 125.00 (*90-5699-649-5*) Gordon & Breach.

***Claerbaut, David.** Durocher's Cubs: The Greatest Team That Didn't Win. (Illus.). 2000. 22.95 (*0-87833-177-8*) Taylor Pub.

Claerbaut, David. The 1999 NBA Analyst: A Revolutionary Method for Evaluating NBA Players & Teams. LC 98-38723. 192p. 1998. pap. 16.95 (*0-87833-210-3*) Taylor Pub.

Claerbaut, David P. Black Jargon in White America. LC 72-77176. 89p. reprint ed. pap. 30.00 (*0-8357-7290-X*, 201285800083) Bks Demand.

Claerbaut, David P. Urban Ministry. 224p. 1983. mass mkt. 14.99 (*0-310-45961-3*, 12605P) Zondervan.

Claerbout, Jon F. Earth Soundings Analysis. (Illus.). 320p. 1991. 65.00 (*0-86542-210-9*) Blackwell Sci.

***Claes, Dag Harald.** Politics of Oil-producer Cooperation. 270p. 2000. 70.00 (*0-8133-6843-X*, Pub. by Westview) HarpC.

Claes, Frans M., compiled by. A Bibliography of Netherlandic (Dutch, Flemish) Dictionaries: An Exhaustive Bibliography of Netherlandic Dictionaries from the Outset of Printing to the Present Day. xvi, 314p. (C). 1980. 68.00 (*3-262-02024-9*) J Benjamins Pubng Co.

Claes, Hubert. Research on Venous Outflow Reduction in Erectile Dysfunction. (Acta Biomedica Lovaniensia Ser.: Vol. 108). 152p. (Orig.). 1995. pap. 39.50 (*90-6186-678-2*, Pub. by Leuven Univ) Coronet Bks.

Claes, Stephan. Localization of Genetic Factors for Nonspecific & Syndromic X-Linked Mental Retardation. (Acta Biomedica Lovaniensia Ser.: No. 160). (Illus.). 100p. 1997. pap. 34.50 (*90-6186-853-X*, Pub. by Leuven Univ) Coronet Bks.

C

Claesen, Luc J., ed. VLSI Design Methods, Vol. I: Formal VLSI Specification & Synthesis; Vol. II: Formal VLSI Correctness Verification: Proceedings of the IFIP WG10.2 WG10.5 International Workshop on Applied Formal Methods for Correct VLSI Design. 1990. 222.50 (*0-444-88689-3*, North Holland) Elsevier.

Claesges. Edmund Husserls Theorie der Raumkonstition. (Phaenomenologica Ser.: No. 19). 158p. 1965. lib. bdg. 120.00 (*90-247-0251-8*, Pub. by M Nijhoff) Kluwer Academic.

Claesges, U. & Held, K. Perspektiven Transzendental-Phanomelogischer Forschung. (Phaenomenologica Ser.: No. 49). 306p. 1972. lib. bdg. 112.50 (*90-247-1313-7*, Pub. by M Nijhoff) Kluwer Academic.

Claeson, Eva, tr. see Ekstrom, Margareta.

Claeson, Eva, tr. see Jarring, Gunnar.

Claeson, G., et al. The Design of Synthetic Inhibitors of Thrombin. (Advances in Experimental Medicine & Biology Ser.: Vol. 340). (Illus.). 256p. (C). 1994. text 95.00 (*0-306-44593-X*, Kluwer Plenum) Kluwer Academic.

Claessen, Henri J., et al, eds. Development & Decline: The Evolution of Sociopolitical Organization. LC 84-28258. 381p. (C). 1985. 69.50 (*0-89789-075-2*, Bergin & Garvey) Greenwood.

Claessen, Henri J. & Oosten, Jarich G., eds. Ideology & the Formation of Early States. (Studies in Human Society: Vol. 11). 456p. 1996. 112.50 (*90-04-10470-4*) Brill Academic Pubs.

Claessen, Henri J. & Skalnik, Peter, eds. The Early State. (New Babylon Ser.: No. 32). 1976. 130.80 (*90-279-7904-9*) Mouton.

— The Study of the State. (New Babylon Studies in the Social Sciences: No.35). 535p. 1981. 80.80 (*90-279-3348-0*) Mouton.

Claessen, Henri J. & Van de Velde, Pieter, eds. Early State Economics Vol. 8: Political Anthropology. (Political Anthropology Ser.: Vol. 9). 247p. (C). 1991. 44.95 (*0-88738-402-1*); pap. 24.95 (*0-88738-885-X*) Transaction Pubs.

Claessen, Henry J., jt. ed. see Seaton, S. Lee.

Claessens, P. L. & Harris, G. B. Electrometallurgical Plant Practice: Proceedings of the International Symposium on Electrometallurgical Plant Practice, Montreal, Quebec, Canada, October 21-24, 1990. (Proceedings, Metallurgical Society of the Canadian Institute of Mining & Metallurgy Ser.: No. 24). 342p. 1991. 146.00 (*0-08-040430-8*, Pergamon Pr) Elsevier.

Claessens, Sharon S. The No-Tofu Vegetarian Cookbook. LC 96-52652. 272p. 1997. pap. 14.00 (*1-55788-269-X*, HP Books) Berkley Pub.

Claessens, Sharon S. & Rodale Food Center Staff. The Lose Weight Naturally Cookbook. (Illus.). 392p. 1994. 13.98 (*1-56731-043-5*, MJF Bks) Fine Comms.

Claessens, Stijn. Risk Management in Developing Countries. LC 93-34713. (Technical Papers: No. 235). 87p. 1993. pap. 22.00 (*0-8213-2668-6*, 12668) World Bank.

Claessens, Stijn & Duncan, Ronald C., eds. Managing Commodity Price Risk in Developing Countries. (World Bank Research Publications). 480p. 1994. text 39.95 (*0-8018-4662-5*, 44662) Johns Hopkins.

Claessens, Stijn & Gooptu, Sudarshan, eds. Portfolio Investment in Developing Countries. LC 93-44215. (Discussion Papers: Vol. 228). 502p. 1993. pap. 26.00 (*0-8213-2747-X*) World Bank.

Claessens, Stijn, et al. Market-Based Debt Reduction for Developing Countries: Principles & Prospects. (Policy & Research Ser.: No. 16). 72p. 1991. pap. 22.00 (*0-8213-1732-6*, 11732) World Bank.

Claesson-Welsh, L., et al, eds. Vascular Growth Factors & Angiogenesis. (Current Topics in Microbiology & Immunology Ser.: Vol. 237). (Illus.). 190p. 1999. 129.00 (*3-540-64731-7*) Spr-Verlag.

Claeys. Chartist Movement in Britain 1838-1850, Vol. 6. 795.00 (*1-85196-330-8*) Ashgate Pub Co.

Claeys. Medical Filing. (Medical Assisting Ser.). 1993. pap. 14.95 (*0-538-70675-9*) S-W Pub.

Claeys & Philp. Works of Thomas Paine, Vol. 8. 795.00 (*1-85196-200-X*) Ashgate Pub Co.

Claeys, C., et al, eds. Gettering & Defect Engineering in Semiconductor Technology: GADEST '97. (Solid State Phenomena Ser.: Vols. 57-58). (Illus.). 556p. (C). 1998. text 196.00 (*3-908450-27-6*, Pub. by Scitec Pubns) Enfield Pubs NH.

— High Purity Silicon IV. LC 95-83758. (Proceedings Ser.: Vol. 96-13). (Illus.). 586p. 1996. 76.00 (*1-56677-156-0*) Electrochem Soc.

— Low Temperature Electronics & High Temperature Superconductivity: 4th International Symposium. LC 97-197087. (Proceedings Ser.: Vol. 97-2). (Illus.). 412p. 1997. 64.00 (*1-56677-129-3*) Electrochem Soc.

Claeys, C. L., et al, eds. High Purity Silicon V. LC 99-160997. (Proceedings Ser.: Vol. 98-13). (Illus.). 478p. 1998. 63.00 (*1-56677-207-9*) Electrochem Soc.

***Claeys, C. L., et al, eds.** ULSI Process Integration. 385p. 1999. 65.00 (*1-56677-241-9*, PV 99-18) Electrochem Soc.

Claeys, C. L., et al. Low Temperature Electronics & High Temperature Superconductivity. (Proceedings Ser.: Vol. 95-9). 446p. 1995. 62.00 (*1-56677-103-X*) Electrochem Soc.

Claeys, Gregory. Machinery, Money & the Millennium: From Moral Economy to Socialism, 1815-1860. LC 87-2372. 275p. 1987. reprint ed. pap. 85.30 (*0-7837-9497-5*, 206024100004) Bks Demand.

— The Political Writings of the 1790s: French Revolution Debate in Britain, 8 vols. 353p. 1995. 880.00 (*1-85196-320-0*) Ashgate Pub Co.

***Claeys, Gregory.** Restoration & Augustan British Utopias. LC 99-46752. 416p. 1999. pap. text 45.00 (*0-8156-2824-2*) Syracuse U Pr.

Claeys, Gregory, ed. Modern British Utopias, 1700-1850, 8 vols. LC 96-23444. 4128p. 1997. 880.00 (*1-85196-319-7*, Pub. by Pickering & Chatto) Ashgate Pub Co.

— The Politics of English Jacobinism: Writings of John Thelwall. LC 94-20695. 608p. 1995. 85.00 (*0-271-01347-8*); pap. 25.00 (*0-271-01348-6*) Pa St U Pr.

— Utopias of the British Enlightenment. (Cambridge Texts in the History of Political Thought Ser.). 349p. (C). 1994. text 59.95 (*0-521-43084-4*); pap. text 21.95 (*0-521-45590-1*) Cambridge U Pr.

Claeys, Gregory & Sargent, Lyman T., eds. The Utopia Reader. LC 99-6660. 432p. 1999. pap. 22.95 (*0-8147-1571-0*); text 55.00 (*0-8147-1570-2*) NYU Pr.

Claeys, Gregory, ed. see Owen, Robert.

Claeys, L., jt. ed. see Horsch, S.

Claeys, Terese. Medical Filing. 2nd ed. 112p. 1996. pap., teacher ed. write for info. (*0-8273-8178-6*) Delmar.

— Medical Filing. 2nd ed. LC 96-9526. (Illus.). 128p. 1996. mass mkt. 29.95 (*0-8273-8177-8*) Delmar.

Claeys, Tracy, jt. auth. see Smith-Kiewel, Linda.

Claeyssens, M., et al, eds. Carbohydrases from Trichoderma Reesei & Other Micro-Organisms. xvi, 350p. 1998. 145.00 (*0-85404-713-1*) Spr-Verlag.

Claff, Chester E., Jr., tr. see Hilberg, Wolfgang.

Claffey, Tom. And the Angels Cried. 156p. 1999. pap. 8.95 (*1-891929-08-9*) Four Seasons.

— Ladies & Gentlemen of the Jury. ix, 138p. (Orig.). 1997. pap. 14.95 (*0-9656375-0-6*) Coyote Junction.

***Clafin, Donald.** I Push the Pen. 140p. 2001. pap. 12.95 (*1-57532-242-0*) Press-Tige Pub.

Claflin, Edward, ed. The Experts Book of Practical Secrets: From the People Who Know - over 1,200 Hints & Tips to Save Money, Avoid Ripoffs, Heal Health Problems, & Solve Hundreds of Other Everyday Hassles. LC 93-7360. 512p. 1993. 27.95 (*0-87596-150-9*, 03-066-0) Rodale Pr Inc.

Claflin, Edward, jt. auth. see Conner, Dennis.

Claflin, Edward B., ed. see Broder, Michael S.

Claflin, Edward Beecher. Sojourner Truth & the Struggle for Freedom. LC 87-19325. (Henry Steele Commager's Americans Ser.). (Illus.). 144p. (J). (gr. 3-6). 1987. pap. 5.95 (*0-8120-3919-X*) Barron.

— Sojourner Truth & the Struggle for Freedom. (Henry Steele Commager's Americans Ser.). (J). 1987. 11.05 (*0-606-02937-0*, Pub. by Turtleback) Demco.

Claflin, Edward Beecher & Prevention Health Books Editors. Age Protectors: Stop Aging Now with the Latest Breakthroughs. LC 97-46595. (Illus.). 560p. 2000. pap. 16.95 (*0-87596-455-9*) Rodale Pr Inc.

Claflin, Jackie. Windows of My World, Vol. 4. 63p. 1996. pap. 10.50 (*1-56770-359-3*) S Scheewe Pubns.

— Windows of My World, Vol. 5. 72p. 1999. pap. 10.50 (*1-56770-447-6*) S Scheewe Pubns.

***Claflin, Jackie.** Windows of My World 6. (Illus.). 60p. 1999. pap. 10.50 (*1-56770-464-6*) S Scheewe Pubns.

Claflin, James V. Sheriffs' Insignia of the United States: A Guide to the Uniform Emblems Worn by the Nation's Sheriffs. LC 96-75680. (Illus.). 144p. 1997. 49.95 (*1-882824-17-2*); pap. 32.95 (*1-882824-16-4*) Graphic Pubs.

Claflin, James W. Lighthouses & Lifesaving Along the Massachusetts Coast. LC 98-88060. (Images of America Ser.). (Illus.). 228p. 1998. pap. 18.99 (*0-7524-1372-4*) Arcadia Publng.

Claflin, W. H. Stalling's Island Mound, Columbia County, Georgia. (HU PMP Ser.). 1931. 25.00 (*0-527-01232-7*) Periodicals Srv.

Clagett, Alice B. & Meredith, Elandra K., eds. Yoga for Health & Healing: From the Teachings of Yogi Bhajan, Ph.D. (Illus.). 144p. (Orig.). 1995. pap. 18.95 (*0-940992-01-9*) A B Clagett.

Clagett, Helen L. A Guide to the Law & Legal Literature of Argentina. 1977. lib. bdg. 250.00 (*0-8490-1921-4*) Gordon Pr.

— A Guide to the Law & Legal Literature of Bolivia. 1977. lib. bdg. 250.00 (*0-8490-1918-4*) Gordon Pr.

— A Guide to the Law & Legal Literature of Paraguay. 1977. 250.00 (*0-8490-1919-2*) Gordon Pr.

— A Guide to the Law & Legal Literature of the Mexican States. 1977. 250.00 (*0-8490-1922-2*) Gordon Pr.

— A Guide to the Law & Legal Literature of Uruguay. 1977. lib. bdg. 250.00 (*0-8490-1920-6*) Gordon Pr.

Clagett, Helen L., jt. auth. see Vance, John T.

Clagett, Leslie P., jt. auth. see Locktov, JoAnn.

Clagett, Marshall. Ancient Egyptian Science, Vol. 1. LC 89-84668. (Memoirs Ser.: Vol. 184). (Illus.). 863p. (C). 1992. pap. 30.00 (*0-87169-184-1*, M184-PAP) Am Philos.

— Ancient Egyptian Science, Vol. 2. LC 89-84668. (Memoirs Ser.: Vol. 214). (Illus.). 518p. (C). 1994. pap. 30.00 (*0-87169-214-7*, M214-pap) Am Philos.

***Clagett, Marshall.** Ancient Egyptian Science: A Source Book. LC 89-84668. (Ancient Egyptian Mathematics Ser.: Vol. 232). 462p. 1999. 30.00 (*0-87169-232-5*) Am Philos.

Clagett, Marshall. Archimedes in the Middle Ages, Vol. 1. Arabo-Latin Tradition. LC 62-7218. (Medieval Science Pubns., No. 6). (Illus.). 752p. reprint ed. 200.00 (*0-8357-9771-6*, 201262900082) Bks Demand.

— Greek Science in Antiquity. LC 77-142615. (Essay Index Reprint Ser.). 1977. 25.95 (*0-88143-073-0*) Ayer.

— Greek Science in Antiquity. (Illus.). 256p. (C). 1988, reprint ed. pap. text 12.95 (*0-945726-10-4*) Scholars Bookshelf.

Clagett, Marshall, ed. Critical Problems in the History of Science. LC 59-5304. 569p. reprint ed. pap. 176.40 (*0-8357-9773-2*, 201535700093) Bks Demand.

Clagett, Marshall, ed. see Oresme, Nicole.

Clagg, Sam E. The Cam Henderson Story - His Life & Times. 400p. 1981. 18.00 (*0-87012-431-5*) McClain. Covers much of the athletic history & scholastic endeavor in the first half of the 20th century. It does so through the life story of Cam Henderson & his wife, Roxie. *Publisher Paid Annotation.*

–The Marine Way. McClain Printing Co., Staff, ed. (Illus.). 588p. 1989. 24.95 (*0-9623827-0-1*) McClain. This is a factual story of Marine training & military activities in the Pacific during World War II. The detailed relating was made possible by over 900 pages of material personally logged at the time of the actual events. A portion of the content has been embellished in an effort to generate reader interest & to maintain continuity. Time may have eroded the specifics from the minds of most, but all warriors past & present should be able to identify with THE MARINE WAY. The work, accurate & in place & chronology, is approached in the manner of oral history. *Publisher Paid Annotation.*

Clagg, Sam E., ed. West Virginia Historical Almanac. (Illus.). 180p. 1975. pap. 8.00 (*0-87012-231-2*) McClain.

A significant publication for persons interested in the heritage & history of West Virginia. Entries for each day of the year & over 1,300 total happenings are provided. The book has an index of almost 3,000 references. Some 300 line drawings & maps are included. *Publisher Paid Annotation.*

Claggett, Fran & Brown, Joan. Drawing Your Own Conclusions: Graphic Strategies for Reading, Writing & Thinking. LC 92-28860. 184p. (YA). 1992. pap. text 25.00 (*0-86709-293-9*, 0293, Pub. by Boynton Cook Pubs) Heinemann.

Claggett, Fran, et al. Learning the Landscape: Inquiry-Based Activities for Comprehending & Composing. LC 96-20849. 176p. 1996. pap. text 19.50 (*0-86709-395-1*, 0395, Pub. by Boynton Cook Pubs) Heinemann.

— Recasting the Text: Inquiry-Based Activities for Comprehending & Composing. LC 96-24629. 192p. 1996. pap. text 19.50 (*0-86709-402-8*, 0402, Pub. by Boynton Cook Pubs) Heinemann.

***Claggett, Hilary D.** The 21st Century. LC 99-462343. (Reference Shelf Ser.). 1999. write for info. (*0-8242-0966-4*) Wilson.

Claggett, Hilary D., ed. Wildlife Conservation. LC 97-14000. (Reference Shelf Ser.: Vol. 69, No. 2). 1997. pap. 25.00 (*0-8242-0915-X*) Wilson.

Claggett, Hilary D., jt. ed. see Thompson, Clifford.

***Claggett, Laurence.** Easton. (Images of America Ser.). (Illus.). 128p. 1999. pap. 18.99 (*0-7385-0171-9*) Arcadia Publng.

Claggett, Marshall, ed. see Archimedes.

Claggett, Mary. A Measure of Success: From Assignment to Assessment in Language Arts. LC 95-33583. 215p. 1996. pap. text 21.50 (*0-86709-373-0*, 0373, Pub. by Boynton Cook Pubs) Heinemann.

Claggett, William J., jt. auth. see Shafer, Byron E.

Claghorn, Charles E. Naval Officers of the American Revolution: A Concise Biographical Dictionary. LC 87-35410. (Illus.). 383p. 1988. 58.00 (*0-8108-2096-X*) Scarecrow.

— Popular Bands & Performers. LC 94-42655. 480p. 1995. 79.00 (*0-8108-2976-2*) Scarecrow.

— Women Patriots of the American Revolution: A Biographical Dictionary. LC 91-15495. (Illus.). 519p. 1991. 60.00 (*0-8108-2421-3*) Scarecrow.

Claghorn, Gene. Women Composers & Songwriters: A Concise Biographical Dictionary. LC 95-51308. 368p. 1996. text 68.00 (*0-8108-3130-9*) Scarecrow.

Claghorn, George S., ed. see Edwards, Jonathan.

Claghorn, Kate. Immigrant's Day in Court. LC 69-18765. (American Immigration Collection. Series 1). 1969. reprint ed. 24.95 (*0-405-00513-X*) Ayer.

Clagne, Yelone. The American Way: More Than Skin Deep. LC 92-85168. 132p. (Orig.). 1993. pap. 9.95 (*0-939644-92-4*, Midgrd Press) Media Pub.

Clague, Christopher K., ed. Institutions & Economic Development: Growth & Governance in Less-Developed & Post-Socialist Countries. LC 97-5135. (Studies in Development). 390p. 1997. text 48.50 (*0-8018-5492-X*); pap. text 18.95 (*0-8018-5493-8*) Johns Hopkins.

Clague, Ewan, jt. ed. see Kramer, Leo.

Clague, Mary H. Fort Brooke Drummer Boy: A Story of Old Florida. LC 98-174413. 93p. (J). 1998. pap. 6.99 (*1-57502-747-X*, PO2075) Morris Pubng.

Clague, Michael, jt. ed. see Wharf, Brian.

Clahsen, Harald. Child Language & Developmental Dysphasia: Linguistic Studies of the Acquisition of German. Richman, Karin, tr. from GER. LC 91-22437. (Studies in Speech Pathology & Clinical Linguistics: Vol. 2). x, 350p. 1991. 100.00 (*1-55619-388-2*) J Benjamins Pubng Co.

— Generative Perspectives on Language Acquisition: Empirical Findings, Theoretical Considerations & Crosslinguistic Comparisons. LC 96-22417. (Language Acquisition & Language Disorders Ser.: Vol. 14). xxviii, 499p. 1996. 115.00 (*1-55619-777-2*, JB1214) J Benjamins Pubng Co.

— Normale und Gestorte Kindersprache: Linguistische Untersuchungen zum Erwerb von Syntax und Morphologie. LC 87-34651. ix, 340p. (C). 1988. 74.00 (*90-272-2052-2*); pap. 22.95 (*90-272-2053-0*) J Benjamins Pubng Co.

Clahsen, Harald, ed. Generative Perspectives on Language Acquisition: Empirical Findings, Theoretical Considerations & Crosslinguistic Comparisons. LC 96-22417. (Language Acquisition & Language Disorders (LALD) Ser.: Vol. 14). xxviii, 499p. 1996. pap. 29.95 (*1-55619-780-2*, JB1214) J Benjamins Pubng Co.

***Claiborne, Craig.** The Best of Craig Claiborne: More Than 1,000 Recipes from His Cooking Columns in the New York Times. 1999. pap. write for info. (*0-8129-3090-8*, Times Bks) Crown Pub Group.

— Cooking with Herbs & Spices. (Illus.). 368p. 2000. 9.99 (*1-57866-105-6*) Galahad Bks.

Claiborne, Craig. Craig Claiborne's Kitchen Primer. LC 68-23951. (Illus.). 1972. pap. 10.00 (*0-394-71854-2*) Knopf.

— The New York Times Cookbook. Incl. New York Times Menu Cookbook. 1975. (Illus.). 1975. 30.50 (*0-06-010775-8*) HarperTrade.

— New York Times Cookbook. rev. ed. LC 89-45640. 800p. 1990. 32.50 (*0-06-016010-1*) HarperTrade.

— The New York Times Cookbook: The Classic Gourmet Cookbook for the Home Kitchen with Hundreds of New Recipes. rev. ed. 1990. reprint ed. 25.00 (*0-317-99579-0*) HarperTrade.

Claiborne, Craig & Franey, Pierre. The Best of Craig Claiborne: More Than 1,000 Recipes from His Cooking Columns in the New York Times. Whitman, Joan, ed. LC 99-12087. 960p. 1999. 35.00 (*0-8129-3089-4*, Times Bks) Crown Pub Group.

Claiborne, Denise K., et al. Ergonomics & Cumulative Trauma Disorders: A Handbook for Occupational Therapists. LC 98-50553. 10p. (Orig.). 1999. pap. 39.95 (*0-7693-0024-3*, 2026) Thomson Learn.

Claiborne, Gay D. Japanese & American Rhetoric: A Contrastive Study. LC 93-48389. 210p. 1994. 64.95 (*1-883255-31-7*) Intl Scholars.

Claiborne, Jack. The Charlotte Observer: Its Time & Place, 1869-1986. LC 86-40026. xv, 391p. 1986. 29.95 (*0-8078-1712-0*) U of NC Pr.

Claiborne, Jack & Price, William, eds. Discovering North Carolina: A Tar Heel Reader. LC 90-50009. xviii, 372p. (C). 1991. 34.95 (*0-8078-1931-X*) U of NC Pr.

— Discovering North Carolina: A Tar Heel Reader. LC 90-50009. xviii, 372p. 1993. reprint ed. pap. 17.95 (*0-8078-4434-9*) U of NC Pr.

Claiborne, John F. Mississippi As a Province, Territory & State, with Biographical Notices of Eminent Citizens. LC 78-2291. (Illus.). 568p. 1999. reprint ed. 45.00 (*0-87152-264-0*) Reprint.

Claiborne, John H. Seventy-Five Years in Old Virginia. (Illus.). 360p. (Orig.). 1994. pap. text 24.00 (*0-7884-0010-X*) Heritage Bk.

Claiborne, Michele. Light & Illusion. (DK Action Packs Ser.). (Illus.). 16p. (J). (gr. 3 up). 1995. pap. 19.95 (*1-56458-897-1*, 5-70552) DK Pub Inc.

— Pyramid: An Interactive Guide to the Pyramids of Ancient Egypt. (DK Action Packs Ser.). (Illus.). (J). (gr. 3-7). 1994. pap. 19.95 (*1-56458-684-7*) DK Pub Inc.

— Rome: An Interactive Guide to Ancient Rome. (DK Action Packs Ser.). (Illus.). 16p. (J). (gr. 3 up). 1995. pap. 19.95 (*1-56458-896-3*, 5-70551) DK Pub Inc.

Claiborne, Michele, jt. auth. see Bown, Deni.

Claiborne, Nathaniel H. Notes on the War in the South: With Biographical Sketches of the Lives of Montgomery, Jackson, Sevier, Late Governor Claiborne & Others. LC 76-146382. (First American Frontier Ser.). 1977. reprint ed. 24.95 (*0-405-02833-4*) Ayer.

Claiborne, Robert. God or Beast: Evolution & Human Nature. (Illus.). 1974. 7.95 (*0-393-06399-2*) Norton.

Claiborne, William C. Official Letter Books, 1801 to 1816, 6 vols. Rowland, Dunbar, ed. LC 72-980. reprint ed. 575.00 (*0-404-01600-6*) AMS Pr.

Claigh, Roberleigh H. Numerology for Personal Transformation: Easy As A B C 1 2 3, Empower the Real You & All You Are to Become by Understanding & Manifesting the Potential in Your Name & Birthdate to Bring Out Your Best! (Illus.). 163p. 1997. reprint ed. pap. 13.95 (*0-9631405-1-5*) Liv Wellness.

— The Star Gazer: A Hawaiian Astrological Tale. (Illus.). 123p. 1996. pap. 12.50 (*0-9631405-4-X*) Liv Wellness.

Claik, Charles S., jt. ed. see Cleland, Jeffery Lynn.

Claims Provide of America Staff. The National Directory of Expert Witnesses, 1998. 384p. 1998. pap. 45.00 (*1-890714-02-X*) Claims Providers.

Clain, Allan, jt. auth. see Lumley, J. S.

Clain-Stefanelli, E. Italian Coin Engravers since 1800. (Illus.). 1965. pap. 8.00 (*0-932106-08-0*) S J Durst.

Clain-Steffanelli, E. Select Numismatic Bibliography. (Illus.). 1965. lib. bdg. 20.00 (*0-932106-09-9*) S J Durst.

Clair, Alicia A. Therapeutic Uses of Music with Older Adults. LC 96-16282. (Illus.). 336p. (Orig.). 1996. pap. text 30.95 (*1-878812-32-7*) Hlth Prof Pr.

Clair, Bernard E. & Daniele, Anthony. The Ex-Factor: The Complete Do-It-Yourself Post-Divorce Handbook. 320p. 1987. mass mkt. 12.95 (*0-446-38414-3*, Pub. by Warner Bks) Little.

Clair, Bevan. Run Roadrunner. LC 80-82912. (J). (ps-6). 1980. pap. 1.50 (*0-686-30719-4*) B A Scott.

Clair, Burl St., see St. Clair, Burl.

Clair, Charles Le, see Le Clair, Charles.

Clair, Cherie. Cajun Dream, 1. (Zebra Splendor Historical Romances Ser.). 320p. 1999. mass mkt. 12.95 (*0-8217-6252-4*) Kensgtn Pub Corp.

Clair, Daphne. Amarga Separacion: Edge of Deception. (SPA.). 1997. per. 3.50 (*0-373-33397-8*, 1-33397-0) Harlequin Bks.

— And Then Came Morning: Year Down Under. (Presents Ser.). 1993. per. 2.99 (*0-373-11586-5*, 1-11586-4) Harlequin Bks.

— Dark Mirror. 1994. per. 2.99 (*0-373-11688-8*, 1-11688-8) Harlequin Bks.

— Edge of Deception. LC 95-13567. (Presents Ser.). 189p. 1995. per. 3.25 (*0-373-11749-3*, 1-11749-8) Harlequin Bks.

***Clair, Daphne.** Une Etrange Attirance. (Azur Ser.: No. 808). (FRE.). 2000. mass mkt. 3.99 (*0-373-34808-8*, 1-34808-5, Harlequin French) Harlequin Bks.

Clair, Daphne. Flame on the Horizon. 1994. per. 2.99 (*0-373-11648-9*) Harlequin Bks.

— Flame on the Horizon. large type ed. (Harlequin Ser.). 1994. lib. bdg. 19.95 (*0-263-13719-8*) Mac Lib Ref.

— Grounds for Marriage. 1997. per. 3.50 (*0-373-11866-X*, 1-11866-0) Harlequin Bks.

— Infamous Bargain. large type ed. (Harlequin Romance Ser.). 1995. lib. bdg. 18.95 (*0-263-13964-6*) Thorndike Pr.

— Lovers' Lies. (Presents Ser.: Vol. 1970). 1998. per. 3.75 (*0-373-11970-4*, 1-11970-0) Harlequin Bks.

— Lover's Lies. large type ed. (Mills & Boon Large Print Ser.). 288p. 1997. 23.99 (*0-263-15166-2*, Pub. by Mills & Boon) Ulverscroft.

— Marriage in Jeopardy. LC 95-4580. (Presents Ser.). 189p. 1995. per. 3.25 (*0-373-11730-2*, 1-11730-8) Harlequin Bks.

***Clair, Daphne.** La Memoire Endormie. 1999. mass mkt. 3.99 (*0-373-34804-5*) Silhouette.

Clair, Daphne. Menteuse par Amour. (Azur Ser.: Vol.754). (FRE.). 1999. mass mkt. 3.50 (*0-373-34754-5*, 1-34754-1) Harlequin Bks.

— No Winner. large type ed. 280p. 1993. 27.99 (*0-7505-0443-9*, Pub. by Mgna Lrg Print) Ulverscroft.

***Clair, Daphne.** Nuits de Chine. (Azur Ser.: No. 796). (FRE.). 1999. mass mkt. 3.99 (*0-373-34796-0*, 1-34796-2, Harlequin French) Harlequin Bks.

Clair, Daphne. Pasion en Verano. (Harlequin Bianca Ser.).Tr. of Summer Passion. (SPA.). 156p. 1999. per. 3.50 (*0-373-33504-0*, 1-33504-1) Harlequin Bks.

— A Streak of Gold. large type ed. (Linford Romance Library). 336p. 1984. pap. 16.99 (*0-7089-6039-1*) Ulverscroft.

— Summer Seduction. 1999. mass mkt. 3.75 (*0-373-18709-2*, 1-18709-5) Harlequin Bks.

— The Wayward Bride. large type ed. 1994. 26.95 (*0-685-73035-2*, Pub. by Mgna Lrg Print) Ulverscroft.

— The Wayward Bride. large type ed. (Magna Large Print Ser.). 1994. 27.99 (*0-7505-0660-1*, Pub. by Mgna Lrg Print) Ulverscroft.

— Wilde Heart. (Weddings by DeWilde Ser.). 1996. per. 4.50 (*0-373-82540-4*, 1-82540-5) Harlequin Bks.

— A Wilder Shore. large type ed. (Linford Romance Library). 336p. 1985. pap. 16.99 (*0-7089-6049-9*) Ulverscroft.

Clair, Daphne, jt. auth. see Lamb, Charlotte.

Clair, Guy St., see St. Clair, Guy.

Clair, Guy St., see Berner, Andrew & St. Clair, Guy.

Clair, Guy St., see St. Clair, Guy.

Clair, J. Identity & Alterity: A Brief History of the Human Body, 1895-1995. 589p. 1995. 55.00 (*1-56886-019-6*) Marsilio Pubs.

Clair, Jean. Lost Paradise. LC 96-135279. (Illus.). 600p. 1995. 125.00 (*2-89192-194-1*) Mont Mus Fine Arts.

Clair, Jean, ed. Cosmos: From Romanticism to Avant-Garde, 1801-2001. LC 99-232451. (Illus.). 320p. 1999. 75.00 (*3-7913-2089-0*) Prestel.

Clair, Jean, ed. see Monnier, Virginie.

***Clair, Jeffrey M. & Allman, Richard M.** The Gerontological Prism: Developing Interdisciplinary Bridges LC 99-32264. (Society & Aging Ser.). 1999. write for info. (*0-89503-226-0*) Baywood Pub.

Clair, Jeffrey M. & Allman, Richard M., eds. Sociomedical Perspectives on Patient Care. LC 92-48516. 304p. (C). 1993. pap. text 19.00 (*0-8131-0819-5*) U Pr of Ky.

— Sociomedical Perspectives on Patient Care Relationships. LC 92-48516. 304p. (C). 1993. text 39.95 (*0-8131-1815-8*) U Pr of Ky.

Clair, Jeffrey M., et al. Experiencing the Life Cycle: A Social Psychology of Aging. 2nd ed. (Illus.). 274p. 1993. pap. 38.95 (*0-398-06059-2*) C C Thomas.

— Experiencing the Life Cycle: A Social Psychology of Aging. 2nd ed. (Illus.). 274p. (C). 1993. text 57.95 (*0-398-05876-8*) C C Thomas.

***Clair, Jeffrey Michael, et al, eds.** The Gerontological Prism: Developing Interdisciplinary Bridges. (Society & Aging Ser.). 315p. 2000. text 48.95 (*0-89503-201-5*) Baywood Pub.

Clair, Joan B. Wind-of-Fire: The Story of an Untouchable. LC 95-90409. 152p. (Orig.). 1999. pap. 10.95 (*0-9635834-0-9*) Wind-of-Fire.

Clair, John B. St., see St. Clair, John B.

Clair, Joy St., see St. Clair, Joy.

***Clair, Kate.** A Typographic Workbook: A Primer to History, Techniques, & Artistry. LC 99-14424. (Illus.). 384p. 1999. pap. 34.95 (*0-471-29237-0*) Wiley.

Clair, Mary Le, see Le Clair, Mary.

Clair, Maxine. Coping with Gravity. LC 87-37162. 1988. pap. 7.00 (*0-931846-32-3*) Wash Writers Pub.

— Rattlebone. LC 93-50114. 224p. 1994. 19.00 (*0-374-24716-1*) FS&G.

— Rattlebone. 224p. 1995. pap. 10.95 (*0-14-024825-0*, Penguin Bks) Viking Penguin.

Clair, Nancy. The Grammar Handbook Part Two: Intermediate ESL. Clark, Raymond C., ed. (Interplay ESL Ser.). (Illus.). 168p. (Orig.). 1986. pap. text 14.00 (*0-86647-017-4*) Pro Lingua.

Clair, Rene. Four Screenplays. Bozzetti, Piergiuseppe, tr. from FRE. LC 70-86125. (Illus.). 439p. 1970. 19.95 (*0-910278-06-7*) Boulevard.

Clair, Robert C. Le, see Le Clair, Robert C.

Clair, Robert N. St., see St. Clair, Robert N.

Clair, Robert N. St., see Ishii, Hiroshi.

Clair, Robert N. St., see Ishii, Hiroshi & St. Clair, Robert N.

Clair, Robin P. Organizing Silence: A World of Possibilities. LC 97-47048. (Series in Speech Communication). 288p. (C). 1998. text 59.50 (*0-7914-3941-0*); pap. text 19.95 (*0-7914-3942-9*) State U NY Pr.

Clair Tisdall, W. M. Simplified Grammar of the Gujarati Language. (ENG & GUJ.). 1986. 29.95 (*0-8288-8429-3*) Fr & Eur.

Clairborne, Gay D. Japanese & American Rhetoric: A Contrastive Study. LC 93-48389. 210p. 1994. pap. 49.95 (*1-883255-30-9*) Intl Scholars.

***Clairday, Robynn.** Expect the Unexpected. (Illus.). (J). 2000. pap. 4.50 (*0-439-21581-1*) Scholastic Inc.

Clairday, Robynn. Tell Me This Isn't Happening!, 1 vol. 144p. (gr. 3-7). 1999. pap. text 4.50 (*0-439-09502-6*) Scholastic Inc.

***Claire, Cherie.** Emilie. 2000. mass mkt. 5.50 (*0-8217-6648-1*, Zebra Kensgtn) Kensgtn Pub Corp.

Claire, Cherie. Snow Angels. 1999. mass mkt. 5.99 (*0-8217-6383-0*, Zebra Kensgtn) Kensgtn Pub Corp.

Claire, Edie. Never Buried. 256p. 1999. mass mkt. 5.99 (*0-451-19788-7*, Sig) NAL.

***Claire, Edie.** Never Preach Past Noon. (Leigh Koslow Mysteries Ser.). 2000. mass mkt. 5.99 (*0-451-20144-2*, Sig) NAL.

— Never Sorry. 272p. 1999. mass mkt. 5.99 (*0-451-19885-9*, Sig) NAL.

Claire, Elizabeth. All Around Me. (ESL Wonder Workbooks Ser.: Vol. 2). (Illus.). vii, 104p. (J). (gr. k-6). 1991. pap. text 8.50 (*1-882483-51-0*) Alta Bk Ctr.

— The Classroom Teacher's ESL Survival Kit, No. 2. 224p. (C). 1995. pap. 37.80 (*0-13-299876-9*) P-H.

— ESL Teacher's Activities Kit. 288p. (C). 1998. pap. 29.50 (*0-13-080478-9*, Parker Publishing Co) P-H.

— ESL Teachers Activities Kit. 6th ed. 288p. (C). 1987. pap. text 29.95 (*0-13-283979-2*, Busn) P-H.

— ESL Teachers Holiday Activities Kit. LC 90-41346. 232p. (C). 1990. pap. text 29.95 (*0-87628-305-9*) P-H.

— ESL Wonder Workbook, No. 1: This Is Me. Flamm, Jackie, ed. (Illus.). 104p. (Orig.). (J). (gr. 1-6). 1990. pap. 7.65 (*1-878598-00-7*) Alta Bk Co Pubs.

— ESL Wonder Workbook, No. 2: All Around Me. Chapman, Charles, ed. (Illus.). 104p. (Orig.). (J). (gr. 1-6). 1991. pap. write for info. (*1-878598-01-5*) Alta Bk Co Pubs.

— An Indispensable Guide to Dangerous English: For Language Learners & Others. 2nd ed. (Illus.). 127p. (C). 1990. pap. text 9.95 (*0-937354-47-3*) Delta Systems.

— The Little Brown Jay: A Tale from India. LC 94-14366. (Mondo Folktales Ser.). (Illus.). 24p. (Orig.). (J). (gr. k-4). 1994. pap. 4.95 (*1-879531-23-2*); lib. bdg. 9.95 (*1-879531-44-5*) Mondo Pubng.

— The Sun, the Wind & Tashira: A Hottentot Tale from Africa. LC 94-8129. (Mondo Folktales Ser.). (Illus.). 24p. (J). (gr. k-4). 1994. pap. 4.95 (*1-879531-20-8*); lib. bdg. 9.95 (*1-879531-41-0*) Mondo Pubng.

— This Is Me. (ESL Wonder Workbooks Ser.: Vol. 1). (Illus.). ix, 104p. (J). (gr. k-6). 1990. pap. text 8.50 (*1-882483-50-2*) Alta Bk Ctr.

— Three Little Words: A, An, & The: A Foreign Student's Guide to English Articles. (Illus.). 62p. (Orig.). (C). 1988. pap. text 9.95 (*0-937354-46-5*) Delta Systems.

Claire, Elizabeth & Haynes, Judith L. Classroom Teacher's ESL Survival Kit Number One. Chapman, John, ed. LC 94-7447. (Illus.). 208p. (C). 1994. pap. 37.80 (*0-13-137613-6*) P-H.

Claire, Hilary, et al, eds. Equality Matters: Case Studies from the Primary School. LC 92-38457. 108p. 1993. 74.95 (*1-85359-181-5*, Pub. by Multilingual Matters); pap. 29.95 (*1-85359-180-7*, Pub. by Multilingual Matters) Taylor & Francis.

Claire, Jean. The Latin Liturgical Repertories Before the Octoechos: The Romano-Frankish Daily Office. (Etudes Gregoriennes Ser.: Vol. XV). (FRE.). 110p. (C). reprint ed. pap. 28.95 (*1-55725-035-9*, 4031, Pub. by Abbey St Peter Solesmes) Paraclete MA.

Claire, Jo. Magic Carpetry: Flying Your Car with Your Mind. LC 90-85490. (Orig.). 1991. pap. 9.50 (*0-9628554-0-5*) Eureka Bks.

Claire, John La, see Bold, Harold C. & La Claire, John.

Claire, Linda. Acronyms of Light: Letting Inner Guidance Help Teach. (Good News about You! Ser.). 79p. 1987. pap. 4.99 (*0-9644324-0-4*) Clarity Prods.

Claire, Miriam. The Abortion Dilemma: Personal Views on a Public Issue. (Illus.). 312p. (C). 1995. 24.95 (*0-306-45080-1*, Plenum Trade) Perseus Pubng.

Claire, Olivia. 203 Maneras de Volverlo Loco. 1997. pap. text 10.98 (*968-890-110-5*) Edit Diana.

Claire, Regi. Inside-Outside. 128p. 1994. pap. 21.00 (*1-84017-023-9*) St Mut.

***Claire, Rodger.** Entertainment 101: An Industry Primer. 232p. 1999. pap. 16.95 (*0-938817-16-7*) Pomegranate Pr.

Claire, Rosine. French Vegetarian Cosmetics. LC 78-50439. (Illus.). 128p. (Orig.). 1979. pap. 5.95 (*0-89407-016-9*) Strawberry Hill.

***Claire, Sylvia.** Trusting Your Intuition: Rediscover Your True Self to Achieve a Richer, More Rewarding Life. (Pathways Ser.: No. 6). 208p. 2000. pap. 15.95 (*1-85703-393-0*, Pub. by How To Bks) Midpt Trade.

Claire, Thomas. Bodywork: What Type of Massage to Get--& How to Make the Most of It. 1995. 25.00 (*0-688-12581-6*, Wm Morrow) Morrow Avon.

— Bodywork: What Type of Massage to Get--& How to Make the Most of It. 464p. 1996. pap. 15.00 (*0-688-14952-9*, Wm Morrow) Morrow Avon.

— Songs of Surrender: Poems. LC 92-18520. 80p. (Orig.). 1991. pap. 8.95 (*0-931832-94-2*) Fithian Pr.

Claire, W. God, Help Me Stop! Break Free from Addiction & Compulsion. LC 87-72964. 120p. (Orig.). 1988. pap. 13.95 (*0-9619383-2-3*) Books West CA.

Claire, William F., ed. see Van Doren, Mark.

Claire, William H., ed. Innovative & Affordable Residential Development: Proceedings of a Session Sponsored by the Committee on Housing of the Urban Planning & Development Division. 40p. 1984. 5.00 (*0-87262-420-X*) Am Soc Civil Eng.

Clairk. Typographic. (Design & Graphic Design Ser.). 1997. pap., wbk. ed. 34.95 (*0-442-02520-3*, VNR) Wiley.

***Clairmont.** Embracing Grace. LC 99-49216. 1999. 14.99 (*0-310-23125-6*) Zondervan.

Clairmont, jt. auth. see Johns.

Clairmont, Christoph W. The Glass Vessels: Final Report IV, Part V. LC 43-2669. 38.00 (*0-685-71743-7*) J J Augustin.

Clairmont, Claire. The Journals of Claire Clairmont. Stocking, Marion K. & Stocking, David M., eds. LC 68-17634. (Illus.). 591p. 1968. 55.50 (*0-674-48500-9*) HUP.

Clairmont, Frederic F. The Rise & Fall of Economic Liberalism: The Making of the Economic Gulag. rev. ed. 356p. 1996. pap. 15.00 (*0-945257-85-6*) Apex Pr.

Clairmont, Leonard. Tahitian-English, English-Tahitian Dictionary. 64p. 29.50 (*0-87559-053-5*) Shalom.

Clairmont, Patsy. The Best of Patsy Clairmont. 512p. 1999. 12.99 (*0-88486-250-X*) Galahad Bks.

— God Uses Cracked Pots. 1991. pap. 9.99 (*1-56179-051-6*) Focus Family.

— God Uses Cracked Pots: A Lighthearted Look at Life's Foibles & Fears. 152p. 1999. pap. 10.99 (*1-56179-584-4*) Focus Family.

— I Love Being a Woman. LC 99-35717. (Focus on the Family Ser.). (Illus.). 203p. 1999. pap. 12.99 (*1-56179-678-6*) Focus Family.

— It's about Home: Creating a Place to Cherish. LC 98-21724. 112p. 1998. 14.99 (*1-56955-101-4*) Servant.

— Joyful Journey: Daybreak. 1997. pap. text 9.99 (*0-310-97282-5*) Zondervan.

— Normal Is Just a Setting on Your Dryer. LC 93-3380. 1993. pap. 9.99 (*1-56179-112-1*) Focus Family.

***Clairmont, Patsy.** Normal Is Just a Setting on Your Dryer: Pithy Parables about People's Perilous Pursuits of Normalcy. 1998. pap. 15.99 incl. audio (*1-56179-594-1*) Focus Family.

Clairmont, Patsy. Normal Is Just a Setting on Your Hair Dryer. 140p. 1999. pap. 10.99 (*1-56179-585-2*) Focus Family.

— Sportin' a 'Tude: What Your Attitude Says When You're Not Looking. LC 96-15378. 1996. pap. 10.99 (*1-56179-470-8*) Focus Family.

— Sportin' a 'Tude: What Your Attitude Says When You're Not Looking, 2. 1998. audio 15.99 (*1-56179-647-6*) Focus Family.

— Sportin' A 'Tude: What Your Attitude Says When You're Not Looking. 213p. 1998. pap. 10.99 (*1-56179-646-8*) Focus Family.

***Clairmont, Patsy.** Stardust on My Pillow: Stones to Sleep On. LC 00-21926. 208p. 2000. 14.95 (*1-57856-369-0*) Waterbrook Pr.

— Stepping Stones: A Garden Path. 2001. write for info. (*1-56955-150-2*) Servant.

Clairmont, Patsy. Tea with Pasty Clairmont. LC 97-16862. 1997. 9.97 (*1-56955-039-5*) Servant.

— Under His Wings: And Other Places of Refuge. LC 94-3499. 1994. 14.99 (*1-56179-279-9*) Focus Family.

Clairmont, Patsy, et al. Joy Breaks: 90 Devotions to Celebrate, Simplify & Add Laughter to Your Life. LC 97-1602. (Women of Faith Ser.). 224p. 1997. 14.99 (*0-310-21345-2*) Zondervan.

— The Joyful Journey. LC 96-39584. (Women of Faith Ser.). 208p. 1997. 16.99 (*0-310-21344-4*) Zondervan.

— The Joyful Journey: With Wisdom & Laughter, Women of Faith Share Their Secrets to Finding Joy in Life's Journey. large type ed. LC 97-47671. 296p. 1998. pap. 14.95 (*0-8027-2730-1*) Walker & Co.

— We Brake for Joy! 90 Devotions to Joyproof Your Soul. LC 98-17614. 288p. 1998. 14.99 (*0-310-22042-4*) Zondervan.

Clairmonte, Glenn. Truth to Tell. LC 78-66006. 280p. 1979. 3.48 (*0-87159-155-3*) Unity Bks.

Clairon, Hippolyte. Memoirs of Hippolyte Clairon, 2 vols., 1 bk. LC 79-82821. 1972. 27.95 (*0-405-08359-9*, Pub. by Blom Pubns) Ayer.

Clairvoyant. Banana Republic: A Political Thriller of Love, Power & the White House. 144p. 1996. pap. write for info. (*1-885778-17-1*) Seaburn.

Claisse-Walford, Nancy L. De, see De Claisse-Walford, Nancy L.

***Claitors Publishing Co. Staff.** Official Congressional Directory 1999-2000. 1100p. 1999. 45.00 (*1-57980-444-6*) Claitors.

— Statistical Abstract of U. S. A. 1999. 1999. pap. 39.00 (*1-57980-467-5*) Claitors.

— United States Government Manual 1999-2000. 1999. pap. 46.00 (*1-57980-442-X*) Claitors.

Claitors Publishing Staff. Agricultural Statistics: 1998 Edition. 1998. pap. 25.00 (*1-57980-302-4*) Claitors.

***Claitors Publishing Staff.** Budget of the United States Government 2001. 2000. 38.00 (*1-57980-488-8*); pap. 28.00 (*1-57980-491-8*) Claitors.

— Economic Report of the President 2000. 2000. pap. 25.00 (*1-57980-492-6*) Claitors.

— Official Congressional Directory 1999-2000. 1100p. 1999. pap. 32.00 (*1-57980-443-8*) Claitors.

— Statistical Abstract of the United States 1999. 19th ed. 1999. 46.00 (*1-57980-468-3*) Claitors.

— Statistical Abstract of U. S. 98. 38.00 (*1-57980-353-9*) Claitors.

Clajus, Martin, tr. see Kinzel, Wolfgang & Reents, Georg.

Clake, Hyde & Wake, C. Staniland. Serpent & Siva Worship & Mythology in Central America, Africa, & Asia & the Origin of Serpent Worship. 54p. 1998. reprint ed. pap. 9.95 (*0-7661-0472-9*) Kessinger Pub.

Clam, DuPaty De, see De Clam, DuPaty.

Claman, Elizabeth. Peripheral Visions. 1989. pap. 4.00 (*0-9618409-2-7*) Five Fingers.

Claman, Elizabeth, ed. Each in Her Own Way: Women Writing on Menopause & Other Aspects of Aging. LC 93-86396. 192p. 1994. pap. 10.95 (*0-9638992-0-1*) Queen of Swords.

— Writing Our Way Out of the Dark: An Anthology by Child Abuse Survivors. LC 95-68828. (Illus.). 308p. (Orig.). 1995. pap. 16.95 (*0-9638992-2-8*) Queen of Swords.

Claman, Elizabeth, ed. Hard Love: Writings on Violence & Intimacy. LC 96-70556. 304p. (Orig.). 1997. pap. 17.50 (*0-9638992-3-6*) Queen of Swords.

Claman, Elizabeth, et al. Passionate Lives: Eight Autobiographical Poem Cycles. LC 98-66538. 216p. 1998. pap. 12.99 (*0-9638992-4-4*) Queen of Swords.

Claman, Elizabeth, tr. see Le Goff, Jacques.

Claman, Henry N. The Immunology of Human Pregnancy. LC 92-49012. 232p. 1993. 75.00 (*0-89603-251-5*) Humana.

***Claman, Henry N.** Jewish Images in the Christian Church: Art as the Mirror of the Jewish-Christian Conflict, 200-1250CE. 2000. 39.95 (*0-86554-695-9*, H514) Mercer Univ Pr.

Claman, Marcy. Rise & Dine America: Savory Secrets from America's Bed & Breakfast Inns. 2nd rev. ed. (Illus.). 400p. 1998. pap. 16.95 (*1-896511-09-0*, Pub. by Callawind) Firefly Bks Ltd.

***Claman, Marcy.** Rise & Dine Canada: Savory Secrets from Canada's Bed & Breakfast Inns. 2nd rev. ed. (Illus.). 340p. 1999. pap. 21.95 (*1-896511-11-2*, Pub. by Callawind) Firefly Bks Ltd.

Claman, Priscilla H. & Claman, Victor N. Sixty-Plus in Massachusetts: The Guide to Benefits, Bargains & Better Living for People over Sixty. 2nd ed. (Illus.). 92p. 1985. pap. 8.95 (*0-939532-01-8*) Ctr Info Sharing.

Claman, Victor N., et al. Acting on Your Faith: Congregations Making a Difference: A Guide to Success in Service & Social Action. LC 94-75418. (Illus.). 194p. (Orig.). 1994. pap. 25.00 (*0-9639701-0-0*) Insights MA.

Claman, Victor N., jt. auth. see Claman, Priscilla H.

Clammer, John. Contemporary Urban Japan: A Sociology of Consumption. (Studies in Urban & Social Change). 256p. (C). 1997. text 57.95 (*0-631-20301-X*, Pub. by Polity Pr); pap. text 26.95 (*0-631-20302-8*, Pub. by Polity Pr) Blackwell Pubs.

— Difference & Modernity: Social Theory & Contemporary Japanese Society. LC 94-44931. (Japanese Studies). 1995. write for info. (*0-7103-0507-9*) Routledge.

— Race & State in Independent Singapore: The Cultural Politics of Pluralism in a Multiethnic Society. LC 98-3169. 296p. 1998. text 68.95 (*1-84014-029-1*, DS610.C55) Ashgate Pub Co.

C

— Singapore: Ideology, Society, Culture. 178p. (C). 1986. text 32.50 (*0-317-43158-7*, Pub. by Chopmen Singapore) Advent Bks Div.

Clammer, John, jt. auth. see Ashekenzai, Michael.

Clamon, Judy. MaxNotes Romeo & Juliet. (MaxNotes Ser.). 104p. 1999. pap. text. write for info. (*0-87891-990-2*) Res & Educ.

***Clamorgan, Cyprian.** The Colored Aristocracy of St. Louis. Winch, Julie, ed. & intro. by. LC 99-29777. (Illus.). 122p. 1999. 27.50 (*0-8262-1236-0*) U of Mo Pr.

Clamp. Magic Knight Rayearth. Vol. 1. (Illus.). 192p. (YA). (gr. 3 up). 1999. pap. 11.95 (*1-892213-00-1*) Mixx Enter Inc.

***Clamp.** Magic Knight Rayearth, No. 2 (YA). (gr. 4 up). 1999. pap. 11.95 (*1-892213-08-7*, Mixx Manga) Mixx Enter Inc.

Clamp. Magic Knight Rayearth, Vol. 3. (Illus.). 208p. (YA). (gr. 4 up). 1999. pap. 11.95 (*1-892213-16-8*, Mixx Manga) Mixx Enter Inc.

***Clamp.** Magic Knight Rayearth, Vol. 4. (Illus.). 2000. pap. 11.95 (*1-892213-43-5*) Mixx Enter Inc.

— Magic Knight Rayearth, Vol. 5. (Illus.). (J). 2000. pap. 11.95 (*1-892213-52-4*) Talisman Hse.

Clamp. Overture. (Illus.). 184p. 1997. pap. text 15.95 (*1-56931-189-7*, Viz Comics) Viz Commns Inc.

***Clamp.** Serenade, 1999. 1999. pap. 15.95 (*1-56931-407-1*) Viz Commns Inc.

Clamp. X-1999: Sonata. (Illus.). 184p. 1997. pap. text 15.95 (*1-56931-227-3*, Viz Comics) Viz Commns Inc.

***Clamp.** X/1999: Duet. 2000. pap. 15.95 (*1-56931-474-8*) Viz Commns Inc.

Clamp. X/1999: Intermezzo. (Illus.). 186p. 1998. pap. text 15.95 (*1-56931-264-8*, Viz Comics) Viz Commns Inc.

— X/1999: Prelude. (Illus.). 184p. 1996. pap. text 15.95 (*1-56931-138-2*, Viz Comics) Viz Commns Inc.

Clamp, Betty A., et al. Problem-Solving Exercises for Nutrition. 5th rev. ed. (Illus.). 1997. pap. text, spiral bd. 23.95 (*1-890871-00-1*) Holcomb Hath.

***Clamp, Cynthia.** Resources for Nursing Research. 1999. pap. text. write for info. (*0-7619-6066-X*, Sage Prdcls Pr) Sage.

Clamp, Hugh. Landscape Professional Practice. 200p. 1988. text 63.95 (*0-291-39721-2*, Pub. by Gower) Ashgate Pub Co.

— The Shorter Forms of Building Contract. 3rd ed. 208p. 1993. 64.95 (*0-632-03384-3*) Blackwell Sci.

Clamp, Hutch. Landscape Professional Practice: A Guide to Legislation, Conduct, Appointment Practices & Contract Procedures. 2nd ed. LC 98-38680. 200p. 1999. 96.95 (*0-566-08071-0*) Ashgate Pub Co.

Clamp, Liz, jt. auth. see Bohdanowicz, Janet.

Clamp, Michael, ed. see Shakespeare, William.

***Clamp Staff.** Cardcaptor Sakura. (Illus.). 192p. (gr. 7-12). 2000. pap. 9.95 (*1-892213-36-2*) Mixx Enter Inc.

Clampett, Frederick W. Luther Burbank, Our Beloved Infidel, His Religion of Humanity. LC 73-109720. (Illus.). 144p. 1970. reprint ed. lib. bdg. 35.00 (*0-8371-4210-5*, CLLB, Greenwood Pr) Greenwood.

Clampitt, Amy. The Collected Poems of Amy Clampitt. 496p. 1999. pap. 19.95 (*0-375-70064-1*) Knopf.

— Predecessors, et Cetera. (Poets on Poetry Ser.). 184p. (C). 1991. pap. 13.95 (*0-472-06457-6*, 06457); text 39.50 (*0-472-09457-2*, 09457) U of Mich Pr.

— A Silence Opens: Poems. 112p. 1996. pap. 13.00 (*0-679-75022-3*) McKay.

— Westward. 1990. pap. 15.00 (*0-679-72867-8*) Knopf.

Clampitt, Amy, intro. The Essential Donne. (Essential Poets Ser.: Vol. 8). 120p. (Orig.). (C). 1988. 15.50 (*0-88001-205-6*) HarpC.

Clampitt, Phillip G. Communicating for Managerial Effectiveness. (Illus.). 320p. 1991. 58.00 (*0-8039-3759-8*); pap. 26.50 (*0-8039-3760-1*) Sage.

***Clampitt, Phillip G.** Communicating for Managerial Effectiveness. 2nd ed. LC 00-9550. 2001. pap. write for info. (*0-7619-2153-2*) Sage.

Clampitt, William H. & Potempa, John. Employee Compensation Basics: Developing the Direct Pay Component of Total Compensation. (Building Blocks Ser.: Vol. 16). (Illus.). 20p. (Orig.). 1994. pap. 24.95 (*1-57963-019-7*, A0036) Am Compensation.

Clamurro, William. Language & Ideology in the Prose of Quevedo. 201p. 1992. 18.50 (*0-936388-50-1*) Juan de la Cuesta.

Clamurro, William H. Beneath the Fiction: The Contrary Worlds of Cervantes's "Novelas Ejemplares" LC 97-11704. (Studies on Cervantes & His Times: Vol. 7). XIV, 317p. (C). 1998. text 54.95 (*0-8204-3820-0*) P Lang Pubng.

Clancey, Eleanor, jt. auth. see Diggs, Richard.

Clancey, K. Wordsworth's Prelude As a Study of Education. LC 99-43170. 248p. 1999. text 65.00 (*0-312-22560-1*, St Martins Paperbacks) St Martin.

Clancey, Lisa, ed. see Cusizk, Richie T.

Clancey, Lisa, ed. see Reisfeld, Randi.

Clancey, Noni, illus. see Diggs, Richard N.

Clancey, William J. Conceptual Coordination: How the Mind Orders Experience in Time. LC 99-28055. 432p. 1999. 89.95 (*0-8058-3143-6*) L Erlbaum Assocs.

— Readings in Medical Artificial Intelligence: The First Decade. 1984. 33.29 (*0-201-10854-2*) Addison-Wesley.

— Situated Cognition: On Human Knowledge & Computer Representations. LC 96-35839. (Learning in Doing: Social, Cognitive & Computational Perspectives Ser.). (Illus.). 424p. (C). 1997. text 69.95 (*0-521-44400-4*); pap. text 27.95 (*0-521-44871-9*) Cambridge U Pr.

Clancey, William J., et al, eds. Contemplating Minds: A Forum for Artificial Intelligence. LC 93-35759. (Artificial Intelligence Ser.). 559p. 1994. pap. text 37.50 (*0-262-53119-4*) MIT Pr.

Clancey, William J. & Soloway, Elliot, eds. Artificial Intelligence & Learning Environments. 168p. 1990. pap. text 25.00 (*0-262-53090-2*) MIT Pr.

Clanchy, John & Ballard, Brigid. How to Write Essays. 1992. pap. text. write for info. (*0-582-87497-1*, Pub. by Addison-Wesley) Longman.

Clanchy, John J. Homecoming. 150p. (Orig.). 1989. pap. 16.95 (*0-7022-2260-7*, Pub. by Univ Queensland Pr) Intl Spec Bk.

— Lie of the Land. 245p. (C). 1990. 35.00 (*0-9592104-6-6*, Pub. by Pascoe Pub) St Mut.

***Clanchy, Kate.** Samarkand: A Poetry Collection. LC 99-490358. 68p. 1999. pap. 16.95 (*0-330-37194-0*, Pub. by Picador) Trans-Atl Phila.

Clanchy, M. T. Abelard: A Medieval Life. 432p. 1999. reprint ed. pap. 29.95 (*0-631-21444-5*) Blackwell Pubs.

— England & Its Rulers, 1066-1272. 2nd ed. (Illus.). 288p. 1998. 62.95 (*0-631-20556-X*); pap. 26.95 (*0-631-20557-8*) Blackwell Pubs.

— From Memory to Written Record, England, 1066-1307. 2nd ed. LC 92-20180. 1993. pap. 28.95 (*0-631-16857-5*) Blackwell Pubs.

Clancy. Core Java Corba. (C). Date not set. 44.95 (*0-13-080726-5*, Macmillan Coll) P-H.

— Design Pascal. 209p. (C). 1992. text 12.00 (*0-7167-8264-2*) W H Freeman.

— Most Wanted, Vol. 3. (J). Date not set. pap. write for info. (*0-671-03288-7*) PB.

Clancy, ed. Acquisition of Japanese. (Crosslinguistic Study of Language Acquisition Ser.). 176p. 1986. pap. 24.50 (*0-89859-843-5*) L Erlbaum Assocs.

Clancy, et al. Info Tech 2000. 1993. pap. write for info. (*0-7299-0258-7*) Addison-Wesley.

Clancy, jt. auth. see Andersen.

Clancy, Ambrose & Donahoe, Peter M. The Night Line. (Illus.). 127p. 27.00 (*0-941533-45-X*, NAB) I R Dee.

Clancy, Bernard. Best We Forget. 420p. 1998. pap. 19.95 (*0-9587718-9-8*, Pub. by Indra Pub) Intl Spec Bk.

Clancy, Cassandra S. Ohio Nature Reflections: Home-Grown Guidance from Mother Nature. LC 93-79004. (Illus.). 82p. (Orig.). 1994. pap. 9.95 (*0-9637114-0-7*) Inky Pr OH.

Clancy, Catherine. Entree to Catalunya: An Eat & Sleep Guide. 1995. pap. 11.95 (*1-899163-04-2*) Cimino Pub Grp.

— Madrid & Castile. (Crowood Travel Guides Ser.). (Illus.). 352p. 1991. pap. 24.95 (*1-85223-468-7*, Pub. by Cro1wood) Trafalgar.

***Clancy, Christopher E. & Winter, Toar G.** Get Stoned & Read This Book. (Illus.). 72p. 1999. 34.95 (*0-9673537-1-8*) G G Gourd Inc.

Clancy, Christopher H., jt. auth. see Jennings, E. J.

***Clancy, David.** Roses & Rust: Redifining the Essence of Leadership in a New Age. 2nd ed. 244p. 1999. pap. 24.95 (*1-875680-37-3*) Business Prof of Amer.

Clancy, Deirdre. Costume Since 1945: Couture, Street Style, & Anti-Fashion. LC 96-9362. 1996. pap. 24.95 (*0-89676-146-0*, Costume & Fashion Pr) QSMG Ltd.

Clancy Dollinger, Stephanie M. Assessment of Biological Mechanisms Across the Lifespan. DiLalla, Lisabeth F., ed. 216p. 1995. 39.95 (*0-8058-1486-8*) L Erlbaum Assocs.

Clancy, Flora Simmons. Pyramids. LC 94-18949. (Exploring the Ancient World Ser.). (Illus.). 176p. 1995. text 24.95 (*0-89599-039-3*) Smithsonian.

***Clancy, Flora Simmons.** Sculpture in the Ancient Maya Plaza: The Early Classic Period. LC 98-46528. 1999. 65.00 (*0-8263-1787-1*) U of NM Pr.

***Clancy, Gary.** The Complete Hunter Hunting Whitetail Deer: Innovative Techniques for Any Situation. (Complete Hunter Ser.). (Illus.). 2000. pap. 12.95 (*0-86573-121-7*) Creat Pub Intl.

— Rattling, Calling & Decoying Whitetails: How to Consistently Coax Big Bucks Into Range. Durkin, Patrick, ed. LC 99-67145. (Illus.). 208p. 2000. pap. 19.95 (*0-87341-833-6*) Krause Pubns.

Clancy, Gary & Cy DeCosse Incorporated Staff. Wild Turkey. LC 96-43709. (Hunting & Fishing Library). (Illus.). 128p. 1996. 19.95 (*0-86573-062-8*) Creat Pub Intl.

Clancy, Gary & Nelson, Larry R. White-Tailed Deer. LC 91-16959. (Hunting & Fishing Library). (Illus.). 160p. 1991. 19.95 (*0-86573-036-9*) Creat Pub Intl.

Clancy, Gary, jt. auth. see Spomer, Ron L.

Clancy, Gertrude. The Cup & the Mask. 70p. (J). (gr. 4). 1998. pap. 10.95 (*0-8464-4833-5*) Beekman Pubs.

Clancy, Helen. Occupational Therapy with Children. (Illus.). 320p. 1990. pap. text 35.00 (*0-443-03437-0*) Church.

Clancy-Hepburn, Meghan, et al. Issues in Resource Conservation. LC 98-91462. (Briefing Ser.: No. 1). 50p. 1998. pap. 10.00 (*0-936758-37-6*) Ctr Responsive Law.

***Clancy, Jennifer L. & AWWA Research Foundation Staff.** Cryptosporidium Viability & Infectivity Methods. LC 00-42131. 2000. write for info. (*1-58321-028-8*) Am Water Wks Assn.

Clancy, Jennifer L., jt. auth. see Schaefer, Frank W., III.

Clancy, Jo. Anger & Addiction: Breaking the Relapse Cycle - A Teaching Guide for Professionals. LC 96-7939. 200p. 1996. 29.50 (*1-887841-02-4*, BN 60155, Psychosocial) Intl Univs Pr.

Clancy, Jo. Anger & Relapse: Breaking the Cycle. LC 96-53387. 1997. pap. 24.95 (*1-887841-05-9*, Psychosocial) Intl Univs Pr.

Clancy, Jo. Desperate Disguises: Living in the Shadow of Psychiatric Illness. LC 97-21397. 1998. pap. 32.50 (*1-887841-09-1*, Psychosocial) Intl Univs Pr.

— What Love Is: Lessons from the Heart. LC 98-55526. 135p. 1999. pap. 25.95 (*1-887841-24-5*, 66825, Psychosocial) Intl Univs Pr.

***Clancy, Joe & Rebedy, Lucy.** Electricity in Households & Microenterprises. 80p. 2000. pap. 18.00 (*1-85339-501-3*, Pub. by Intermed Tech) Stylus Pub VA.

Clancy, John, Jr. Basic Concepts in Immunology: A Student's Survival Guide. LC 97-25668. (Basic Concepts Ser.). (Illus.). 216p. 1997. text 25.95 (*0-07-011371-8*) McGraw-Hill HPD.

Clancy, John. Freelance Dee-Jaying: How to Become a Successful Discotheque & Radio Jock. (Jobs & Careers Ser.). (Illus.). 136p. 1996. pap. 19.95 (*1-85703-402-3*, Pub. by How To Bks) Trans-Atl Phila.

Clancy, John & McVicar, Andrew. Physiology & Anatomy: A Homeostatic Approach. (Illus.). 736p. (Orig.). 1995. pap. text 47.99 (*1-56593-614-0*, 1274) Singular Publishing.

Clancy, John, ed. see Suoboda, Robert E.

***Clancy, John J.** The Invisible Powers: The Language of Business. 352p. 1999. 29.95 (*0-7391-0073-4*) Lxngtn Bks.

Clancy, John J. The Old Dispensation: Loyalty in Business. LC 98-7073. 344p. 1998. 48.50 (*0-8386-3793-0*) Fairleigh Dickinson.

Clancy, Joseph C. Special Needs Software & Resources: A Guide & Directory. 4th ed. (For the Apple II Series Computers). 445p. 1991. pap. text 49.95 (*0-9627249-0-4*) SW & Resources.

Clancy, Joseph P. Odes & Epodes. LC 60-10659. 262p. 1960. pap. text 17.95 (*0-226-10679-9*, P47) U Ch Pr.

***Clancy, Joseph P.** Other Words: Essays on Poetry & Translation. 146p. 2000. 39.95 (*0-7083-1558-5*, Pub. by U Wales Pr) Paul & Co Pubs.

Clancy, Joseph P. The Significance of Flesh. 159p. (C). 1984. pap. 30.00 (*0-86383-061-7*, Pub. by Gomer Pr) St Mut.

Clancy, Joseph P., tr. from WEL. The World of Kate Roberts: Selected Stories, 1925-1981. (Border Lines: Works in Translation Ser.). 1991. 59.95 (*0-87722-794-2*); pap. 19.95 (*0-87722-795-0*) Temple U Pr.

Clancy, Judith. The Ecotopian Sketchbook. 48p. 1981. pap. 4.25 (*0-9604320-2-7*) Synergistic Pr.

— Exploring Kyoto: On Foot Through the Ancient Capital. LC 97-3726. (Illus.). 256p. 1997. pap. 19.95 (*0-8348-0383-6*) Weatherhill.

— Last Look at the Old Met. LC 79-103983. (Illus.). 54p. 1969. bds. 9.95 (*0-912184-10-8*) Synergistic Pr.

Clancy, Judith & Fisher, M. F. K. Not a Station but a Place. LC 79-20885. (Illus.). 72p. 1979. pap. 7.95 (*0-912184-02-7*); bds. 9.95 (*0-912184-08-6*) Synergistic Pr.

Clancy, Judith, et al. Paris Alive, the Point of View of an American. Orig. Title: Paris Vivant. (ENG & FRE., Illus.). 72p. 1986. pap. 10.00 (*0-912184-06-X*) Synergistic Pr.

Clancy, Judith, ed. see Spector, Herman.

Clancy, Kevin J. Marketing Revolution: A Radical Manifesto for Dominating the Marketplace. 1992. 22.00 (*0-88730-481-8*, HarpBusn) HarpInfo.

***Clancy, Kevin J. & Krieg, Peter C.** Counterintuitive Marketing: How Great Results Come from Uncommon Sense. 368p. 2000. text 27.50 (*0-684-85555-0*) Free Pr.

Clancy, Kevin J. & Lloyd, David W. Uncover the Hidden Power of Television Programming: And Get the Most from Your Advertising Budget / LC 99-6227. 1999. write for info. (*0-7619-1582-6*) Sage.

***Clancy, Kevin J. & Lloyd, David W.** Uncover the Hidden Power of Television Programming: And Get the Most from Your Advertising Budget. LC 99-6227. 236p. 1999. 66.00 (*0-7619-1581-8*) Sage.

Clancy, Kevin J. & Shulman, Robert S. Marketing Myths That Are Killing Business: The Cure for Death Wish Marketing. 308p. 1995. pap. 14.95 (*0-07-011361-0*) McGraw.

Clancy, Kevin J., et al. Simulated Test Marketing: Technology for Launching Successful New Products. LC 94-17718. 306p. 1994. 41.95 (*0-02-905505-9*) U Pr of Amer.

Clancy, L. J. Aerodynamics. LC 87-9847. 628p. 1991. reprint ed. pap. 194.70 (*0-608-03618-8*, 206444400009) Bks Demand.

Clancy, Laurie. A Reader's Guide to Australian Fiction. 382p. 1993. pap. text 35.00 (*0-19-554620-2*) OUP.

Clancy, Lisa, ed. The Boy-Oh-Boy Next Door. (Full House Stephanie Ser.). 128p. (J). (gr. 4-6). 1993. per. 3.99 (*0-671-88121-3*, Minstrel Bks) PB.

— Getting Even with the Flamingoes. (Full House Stephanie Ser.). 144p. (J). (gr. 4-6). 1995. per. 3.99 (*0-671-52273-6*, Minstrel Bks) PB.

Clancy, Lisa, ed. see Auch, Mary J.

Clancy, Lisa, ed. see Cusick, Richie T.

Clancy, Lisa, ed. see Ellis, Carol & Carroll, Jacqueline.

Clancy, Lisa, ed. see Friedman, Michael J.

Clancy, Lisa, ed. see Gelb, Alan.

Clancy, Lisa, ed. see Gilden, Mel & Pedersen, Ted.

Clancy, Lisa, ed. see Gorman, S. S.

Clancy, Lisa, ed. see Gutman, Bill.

Clancy, Lisa, ed. see Hall, Katy.

Clancy, Lisa, ed. see Hall, Katy & Eisenberg, Lisa.

Clancy, Lisa, ed. see Lawlor, Laurie.

Clancy, Lisa, ed. see Meacham, Margaret.

Clancy, Lisa, ed. see Nash, Bruce & Zullo, Allan.

Clancy, Lisa, ed. see Peel, John.

Clancy, Lisa, ed. see Reisfeld, Randi.

Clancy, Lisa, ed. see Speregen, Devra Newberger.

Clancy, Lisa, ed. see Stine, Megan.

Clancy, Lisa, ed. see Strickland, Bard.

Clancy, Lisa, ed. see Tankersley-Cusick, Richie.

Clancy, Lisa, ed. see Thomas, Linda.

Clancy, Lisa, ed. see Vornholt, John.

Clancy, Lisa, ed. see Wright, Mary.

Clancy, Lorraine. Preschool Teachers Month by Month Activities Program. 304p. 1991. pap. text 27.95 (*0-87628-632-5*) Ctr Appl Res.

— Ready-to-Use Discovery Center Activities for Preschool Children. 340p. 1993. pap. text 27.95 (*0-87628-810-7*) Ctr Appl Res.

Clancy, M. Colleen. California Liability Insurance Practice: Claims & Litigation: June 1993 Update, Set, Vols. 1 & 2. LC 90-4639. 470p. 1993. 50.00 (*0-88124-657-3*, CP-39262) Cont Ed Bar-CA.

— California Liability Insurance Practice: Claims & Litigation: May 1992 Update, 2 vols., Set. LC 90-84639. 452p. 1992. ring bd. 52.00 (*0-88124-503-8*, CP-39261) Cont Ed Bar-CA.

Clancy, M. Colleen, ed. California Liability Insurance Practice: Claims & Litigation, Vols. 1 & 2. LC 90-84639. 1155p. 1991. ring bd. 160.00 (*0-88124-332-9*, CP-39260) Cont Ed Bar-CA.

Clancy, Marilyn D. Chicago. LC 95-20329. (Citylife Pictorial Guide Ser.). (Illus.). 96p. 1999. 24.95 (*0-89658-436-4*) Voyageur Pr.

Clancy, Mark. The Art & Science of Raising a Million in 120 Days: A Step-by-Step Practitioner's Guide to Write, File & Sell a Small Corporate Offering Registration $1,000,000 Public Offering. Toups, Leon & Toups, Michael, eds. LC 95-120164. 288p. (Orig.). 1994. pap. 39.95 (*0-9644544-2-4*) DMV.

Clancy, Michael J. Designing Pascal Solutions, Vol. II. 450p. (C). 1996. text 30.95 (*0-7167-8260-X*) W H Freeman.

Clancy, Michael J. & Linn, Marcia C. Designing Pascal Solutions: A Case Study Approach. (Illus.). 448p. (C). 1992. pap. text 30.95 (*0-7167-8258-8*) W H Freeman.

***Clancy, Padraigin.** Celtic Threads: Exploring the Wisdom of Our Heritage. 220p. 1999. pap. 12.95 (*1-85390-499-6*, Pub. by Veritas Pubns) Irish Bks Media.

Clancy, Pat & Nels, Rebecca. Internet Essentials, Instructor's Manual. 1996. pap. text, teacher ed. 49.99 (*1-57576-287-0*) Que Educ & Trng.

Clancy, Pat, et al. Internet Essentials for Windows. 1996. pap. text 22.99 (*1-57576-286-2*) Que Educ & Trng.

Clancy, Patricia & Allen, Jeanne, eds. The French Consul's Wife: Memoirs of Celeste de Chabrillan in Gold-Rush Australia. LC 98-221547. 320p. 1998. 49.95 (*0-522-84775-7*, Pub. by Melbourne Univ Pr) Paul & Co Pubs.

Clancy, Patricia, tr. see Kauffmann, Jean-Paul.

Clancy, Patricia, tr. see Leys, Simon.

Clancy, Patricia Marie, tr. see Kauffman, Jean-Paul.

Clancy, Patrick E., jt. auth. see Coleman, Lee.

Clancy, Paul, jt. auth. see Dickson, Paul.

Clancy, Paul R. Just a Country Lawyer: A Biography of Senator Sam Ervin. LC 73-16528. (Illus.). 332p. reprint ed. pap. 103.00 (*0-8357-9221-8*, 205521400011) Bks Demand.

Clancy, Peter L., jt. ed. see Sandberg, L. Anders.

Clancy-Smith, Julia A. Rebel & Saint: Muslim Notables, Populist Protest, & Colonial Encounters - Algeria & Tunisia, 1800-1904. LC 93-17223. (Comparative Studies on Muslim Societies: Vol. 18). 1994. 50.00 (*0-520-08242-7*, Pub. by U CA Pr) Cal Prin Full Svc.

— Rebel & Saint: Muslim Notables, Populist Protest, Colonial Encounters. 370p. 1996. 45.00 (*0-614-21169-7*, 1062) Kazi Pubns.

— Rebel & Saint: Muslim Notables, Populist Protest, Colonial Encounters (Algeria & Tunisia) 1997. pap. text 17.95 (*0-520-21216-9*, Pub. by U CA Pr) Cal Prin Full Svc.

Clancy-Smith, Julia A. & Gouda, Frances, eds. Domesticating the Empire: Race, Gender, & Family Life in French & Dutch Colonialism. LC 97-39064. 364p. 1998. text 59.50 (*0-8139-1780-8*); pap. text 19.50 (*0-8139-1781-6*) U Pr of Va.

Clancy, Thomas H. The Conversational Word of God: A Commentary on the Doctrine of St. Ignatius of Loyola Concerning Spiritual Conversation, with Four Early Jesuit Texts. LC 78-51343. (Studies on Jesuit Topics IV: No. 8). xii, 71p. 1978. 5.00 (*0-912422-33-5*); pap. 2.50 (*0-912422-34-3*) Inst Jesuit.

— English Catholic Books, 1641-1700: A Bibliography. rev. ed. LC 96-12614. 230p. 1996. 74.95 (*1-85928-329-2*, Pub. by Scolar Pr) Ashgate Pub Co.

— A Literary History of the English Jesuits: A Century of Books, 1615-1714. LC 93-41584. 284p. 1996. 69.95 (*1-883255-25-2*); 49.95 (*1-883255-24-4*) Intl Scholars.

Clancy, Thomas O. The Triumph Tree: Scotland's Earliest Poetry. 1999. pap. 15.00 (*0-86241-787-2*) Interlink Pub.

Clancy, Thomas O. & Markus, Gilbert. Iona: The Earliest Poetry of a Celtic Monastery. 200p. 1995. pap. 25.00 (*0-7486-0531-2*, Pub. by Edinburgh U Pr) Col U Pr.

Clancy, Thomas Owen, jt. ed. see Broun, Dauvit.

Clancy, Tom. Airborne: A Guided Tour of an Airborne Task Force. LC 97-224023. 352p. 1997. pap. 16.00 (*0-425-15770-9*) Berkley Pub.

***Clancy, Tom.** Airborne: A Guided Tour of an Airborne Task Force. (Illus.). 326p. 1999. reprint ed. pap. text 16.00 (*0-7881-6159-8*) DIANE Pub.

Clancy, Tom. Armored Cav: A Guided Tour of an Armored Cavalry Regiment. 352p. (Orig.). 1994. pap. 15.00 (*0-425-15836-5*) Berkley Pub.

***Clancy, Tom.** The Bear & the Dragon. 752p. 2000. 28.95 (*0-399-14563-X*) Putnam Pub Group.

— The Bear & the Dragon. large type ed. LC 00-21644. 1200p. 2000. 28.95 (*0-375-43069-5*) Random Hse Lrg Prnt.

Clancy, Tom. The Cardinal of the Kremlin. LC 88-5818. 544p. 1988. 24.95 (*0-399-13345-3*, G P Putnam) Peng Put Young Read.

— The Cardinal of the Kremlin. 1989. 13.09 (*0-606-00979-5*, Pub. by Turtleback) Demco.

An Asterisk (*) at the beginning of an entry indicates that the title is appearing for the first time.

— The Cardinal of the Kremlin. large type ed. 1991. pap. 16.95 (*0-89621-244-0*, G K Hall Lrg Type) Mac Lib Ref.
— The Cardinal of the Kremlin. large type ed. LC 88-26768. 871p. 1991. lib. bdg. 22.95 (*0-89621-232-7*) Thorndike Pr.
***Clancy, Tom.** Carrier: A Guided Tour of an Aircraft Carrier. LC 99-174425. (Illus.). 348p. 1999. pap. 16.00 (*0-425-16682-1*) Berkley Pub.
— Caza del Submarino Ruso. pap. 12.95 (*950-04-0549-0*) Emece.
Clancy, Tom. Clear & Present Danger. 544p. 1989. 25.95 (*0-399-13440-9*, G P Putnam) Peng Put Young Read.
— Clear & Present Danger. 1990. 13.09 (*0-606-00980-9*, Pub. by Turtleback) Demco.
— Clear & Present Danger. large type ed. LC 89-27153. 1209p. 1991. lib. bdg. 23.95 (*0-89621-930-5*) Thorndike Pr.
— Debt of Honor. 1008p. 1997. mass mkt. 7.99 (*0-425-14758-4*) Berkley Pub.
— Debt of Honor. 640p. 1994. 25.95 (*0-399-13954-0*, G P Putnam) Peng Put Young Read.
— Debt of Honor. large type ed. LC 94-34297. 1248p. 1994. lib. bdg. 29.95 (*0-7862-0335-8*) Thorndike Pr.
— Debt of Honor. limited ed. 640p. 1994. 150.00 (*0-399-13960-5*, G P Putnam) Peng Put Young Read.
***Clancy, Tom.** Deuda de Honor. Orig. Title: Debt of Honor. 1998. pap. 16.95 (*84-08-02191-5*) Planeta.
— Duel Identity, (Tom Clancy's Net Force Ser.: Vol. 12). 2000. mass mkt. 4.99 (*0-425-17634-7*) Berkley Pub.
— Equilibrio De Poder. 1999. 26.95 (*84-08-02891-X*) Planeta.
Clancy, Tom. Executive Orders. 1376p. (YA). 1997. mass mkt. 7.50 (*0-425-16057-2*) Berkley Pub.
— Executive Orders. 1376p. (YA). 1997. mass mkt. 7.99 (*0-425-15863-2*) Berkley Pub.
— Executive Orders. large type ed. LC 96-3403. (YA). 1996. 28.95 (*0-7862-0855-4*) Thorndike Pr.
— Fighter Wing: A Guided Tour of an Air Force Combat Wing. LC 95-232282. 352p. 1995. pap. 15.00 (*0-425-14957-9*) Berkley Pub.
— The Hunt for Red October. LC 84-16569. 388p. 1984. 24.95 (*0-87021-285-0*) Naval Inst Pr.
— The Hunt for Red October. 1984. 13.09 (*0-606-03908-2*, Pub. by Turtleback) Demco.
***Clancy, Tom.** The Hunt for Red October. 15th ed. 1999. pap. 13.95 (*0-425-17290-2*) Berkley Pub.
— Juegos de Patriotas. (SPA.). pap. 13.95 (*950-04-0857-0*) Emece.
Clancy, Tom. Living the Word: Reflections on the Gospels of the Three-Year Cycle. 224p. (Orig.). 1996. pap. 14.95 (*1-85607-156-1*, Pub. by Columba Press) Whitecap Bks.
— Marine: A Guided Tour of a Marine Expeditionary Unit. LC 96-224067. 352p. 1996. pap. 16.00 (*0-425-15454-8*) Berkley Pub.
— Net Force. (Tom Clancy's Net Force Ser.). 384p. (YA). 1999. mass mkt. 7.99 (*0-425-16172-2*) Berkley Pub.
Clancy, Tom. Net Force. 384p. write for info. (*0-7278-5511-5*) Severn Hse.
— Op-Center. 1997. pap. 11.95 (*84-08-02019-6*) Planeta.
— Op-Center: El Silencio del Kremlin. 1998. pap. 9.95 (*84-08-02117-6*) Planeta.
Clancy, Tom. Op-Center: Juegos del Estado. 1998. pap. 9.95 (*84-08-02368-3*) Planeta.
***Clancy, Tom.** Op Center: State of Siege. large type ed. LC 99-55761. (Basic Ser.). 1999. 29.95 (*0-7862-2318-9*) Thorndike Pr.
Clancy, Tom. Op-Center: Actos de Guerra. 1999. 29.95 (*84-08-02717-4*) Planeta.
— Ordenes Ejecutivas I. 1998. 34.95 (*84-08-02448-5*) Planeta.
— Ordenes Ejecutivas II. 1998. 29.95 (*84-08-02449-3*) Planeta.
— Patriot Games. 512p. 1988. mass mkt. 7.50 (*0-425-10972-0*) Berkley Pub.
— Patriot Games. 416p. 1987. 25.95 (*0-399-13241-4*, G P Putnam) Peng Put Young Read.
— Patriot Games. 1992. 14.00 (*0-606-00982-5*, Pub. by Turtleback) Demco.
— Peligro Imminente. Orig. Title: Clear & Present Danger. 1998. pap. 8.50 (*84-01-49525-3*) Lectorum Pubns.
— Rainbow Six. LC 98-22301. 752p. 1998. 27.95 (*0-399-14390-4*, G P Putnam) Peng Put Young Read.
— Rainbow Six. large type ed. LC 98-26251. 800p. 1998. pap. 27.95 (*0-375-70324-1*) Random.
***Clancy, Tom.** Rainbow Six. limited ed. 800p. 1998. 150.00 (*0-399-14413-7*, G P Putnam) Peng Put Young Read.
Clancy, Tom. Rainbow Six, 1 vol. 897p. 1999. reprint ed. mass mkt. 8.50 (*0-425-17034-9*) Berkley Pub.
— Red Storm Rising. 725p. 1987. pap. 7.99 (*0-425-10107-X*) Berkley Pub.
— Red Storm Rising. 480p. 1986. 25.95 (*0-399-13149-3*, G P Putnam) Peng Put Young Read.
— Red Storm Rising. 1987. 13.09 (*0-606-00983-3*, Pub. by Turtleback) Demco.
— Red Storm Rising. large type ed. LC 89-20219. 1289p. 1991. lib. bdg. 22.95 (*0-89621-885-6*) Thorndike Pr.
***Clancy, Tom.** Safe House. (Tom Clancy's Net Force Ser.: Vol. 10). 186p. (YA). (gr. 7-12). 2000. mass mkt. 4.99 (*0-425-17431-X*) Berkley Pub.
— Shadow Watch. 1999. audio 18.00 (*0-671-04557-1*) S&S Audio.
— Special Ops. 2000. pap. 15.00 (*0-425-17268-6*) Berkley Pub.
— SSN: A Strategic Guide to Submarine Warfare. 2000. reprint ed. mass mkt. 7.99 (*0-425-17353-4*) Berkley Pub.
Clancy, Tom. SSN: Strategies of Submarine Warfare. LC 97-106633. 1996. pap. 15.00 (*0-425-15911-6*) Berkley Pub.
— Submarine: A Guided Tour Inside a Nuclear Warship. 352p. 1993. pap. 14.95 (*0-425-13873-9*) Berkley Pub.
— The Sum of All Fears. 928p. 1992. mass mkt. 7.99 (*0-425-13354-0*) Berkley Pub.
— The Sum of All Fears. 640p. 1991. 24.95 (*0-399-13615-0*, G P Putnam) Peng Put Young Read.
— The Sum of All Fears. 1992. 12.60 (*0-606-00978-7*, Pub. by Turtleback) Demco.
— The Sum of All Fears. large type ed. 1507p. 1991. lib. bdg. 25.95 (*1-56054-258-6*) Thorndike Pr.
— The Sum of All Fears. large type ed. 1507p. 1992. pap. 17.95 (*1-56054-947-5*) Thorndike Pr.
— Three Complete Novels. LC 93-31270. 1456p. 1994. pap. 14.98 (*0-399-13935-4*, G P Putnam) Peng Put Young Read.
Clancy, Tom. Tormenta Roja. (SPA.). 14.50 (*950-04-0754-X*) Emece.
Clancy, Tom. Two Complete Novels. LC 92-39237. 880p. 1993. 11.98 (*0-399-13841-2*, G P Putnam) Peng Put Young Read.
— Virtual Vandals. (Tom Clancy's Net Force Ser.). 181p. (YA). (gr. 7-12). 1999. mass mkt. 4.99 (*0-425-16173-0*, JAM) Berkley Pub.
— Without Remorse. LC 93-13940. 640p. 1993. 24.95 (*0-399-13825-0*, G P Putnam) Peng Put Young Read.
Clancy, Tom. Without Remorse. 1994. 13.09 (*0-606-06889-9*, Pub. by Turtleback) Demco.
Clancy, Tom. Without Remorse. 768p. 1994. reprint ed. mass mkt. 7.99 (*0-425-14332-5*) Berkley Pub.
Clancy, Tom & Franks, Frederick M., Jr. Into the Storm. 544p. 1998. pap. 16.95 (*0-425-16308-3*) Berkley Pub.
— Into the Storm: A Study in Command. LC 96-38068. 1997. 27.50 (*0-399-14236-3*, G P Putnam) Peng Put Young Read.
Clancy, Tom & Franks, Frederick M., Jr. Into the Storm: A Study in Command, Set. abr. ed. 1997. 25.00 incl. audio (*0-671-57661-5*, 595370, Pub. by S&S Audio) Lndmrk Audiobks.
***Clancy, Tom & Greenberg, Martin.** Private Lives. (Tom Clancy's Net Force Ser.: No. 9). (YA). 2000. mass mkt. 4.99 (*0-425-17367-4*) Berkley Pub.
— Shadow Watch. (Tom Clancy's Power Plays Ser.: No. 3). 1999. pap. 7.99 (*0-425-17188-4*) Berkley Pub.
Clancy, Tom & Greenberg, Martin, creators. Tom Clancy's Power Plays: Politika. 1997. mass mkt. 7.50 (*0-425-16278-8*) Berkley Pub.
Clancy, Tom & Horner, Chuck. Every Man a Tiger. LC 98-53339. (Commander's Ser.). (Illus.). 564p. 1999. 27.95 (*0-399-14493-5*, G P Putnam) Peng Put Young Read.
Clancy, Tom & Pieczenik, Steve. The Deadliest Game. (Tom Clancy's Net Force Ser.). 182p. (YA). (gr. 7-12). 1998. mass mkt. 4.99 (*0-425-16174-9*) Berkley Pub.
***Clancy, Tom & Pieczenik, Steve.** Divide & Conquer. (Op-Center Ser.: 7). 384p. 2000. mass mkt. 7.99 (*0-425-17480-8*) Berkley Pub.
— The End Game, vol. 1, (Net Force Ser.: Vol. 6). 1999. mass mkt. 4.99 (*0-425-17113-2*) Berkley Pub.
— Gameprey. (Net Force Ser.: No. 11). (YA). 2000. mass mkt. 4.99 (*0-425-17514-6*) Berkley Pub.
Clancy, Tom & Pieczenik, Steve. Hidden Agendas. (Tom Clancy's Net Force Ser.). 384p. (YA). 1999. mass mkt. 7.99 (*0-425-17139-6*) Berkley Pub.
***Clancy, Tom & Pieczenik, Steve.** Net Force. large type ed. 2000. pap. 11.95 (*1-56895-966-4*) Wheeler Pub.
— One Is the Loneliest Number. (Tom Clancy's Net Force Ser.). (Orig.). (YA). 1999. mass mkt. 4.99 (*0-425-16417-9*, JAM) Berkley Pub.
Clancy, Tom & Pieczenik, Steve. State of Seige: Tom Clancy's Op-Center, Vol. VI. (Op-Center Ser.). 448p. 1999. mass mkt. 7.99 (*0-425-16822-0*) Berkley Pub.
***Clancy, Tom & Pieczenik, Steve.** Tom Clancy's Net Force: Night Moves. (Net Force Ser.: No. 3). 384p. (YA). (gr. 7-12). 2000. mass mkt. 7.99 (*0-425-17400-X*) Berkley Pub.
Clancy, Tom & Pieczenik, Steve. Tom Clancy's Net Force No. 5: The Great Race. 1999. mass mkt. 4.99 (*0-425-16991-X*, JAM) Berkley Pub.
— The Ultimate Escape. (Tom Clancy's Net Force Ser.). (YA). 1999. mass mkt. 4.99 (*0-425-16939-1*, JAM) Berkley Pub.
***Clancy, Tom & Pieczenik, Steve, creators.** Cyberspy. (Tom Clancy's Net Force Ser.: No. 7). (YA). 1999. mass mkt. 4.99 (*0-425-17191-4*, JAM) Berkley Pub.
— Shadow of Honor. (Tom Clancy's Net Force Ser.: No. 8). (YA). 2000. mass mkt. 4.99 (*0-425-17303-8*, JAM) Berkley Pub.
Clancy, Tom & Pieczenik, Steve R. Acts of War. (Tom Clancy's Op Center Ser.). 492p. 1997. mass mkt. 7.50 (*0-425-15601-X*) Berkley Pub.
***Clancy, Tom & Pieczenik, Steve R.** Tom Clancy's Net Force LC 99-27784. (Large Print Book Ser.). 1999. 26.95 (*1-56895-761-0*) Wheeler Pub.
Clancy, Tom & Pieczenik, Steve R. Tom Clancy's Op-Center: Acts of War. large type ed. LC 97-28191. (Op-Center Ser.). 678p. 1997. 27.95 (*0-7862-1218-7*) Thorndike Pr.
— Tom Clancy's Op-Center: Balance of Power. (Op-Center Ser.). 352p. 1998. mass mkt. 7.50 (*0-425-16556-6*, Prime Crime) Berkley Pub.
Clancy, Tom & Pieczenik, Steve R. Tom Clancy's Op-Center: Games of State. large type ed. LC 96-41769. (Basic Ser.). 632p. 1996. lib. bdg. 26.95 (*0-7862-0912-7*) Thorndike Pr.
Clancy, Tom & Pieczenik, Steve R. Tom Clancy's Op-Center: Games of State. large type ed. LC 96-41769. 1997. pap. 24.95 (*0-7862-0913-5*) Thorndike Pr.
— Tom Clancy's Op-Center: Mirror Image. large type ed. (Thorndike Basic Ser.). 1996. text 25.95 (*0-7862-0617-9*) Thorndike Pr.
— Tom Clancy's Op-Center: Mirror Image. large type ed. (Thorndike Basic Ser.). 1996. pap. 23.95 (*0-7862-0618-7*) Thorndike Pr.
— Tom Clancy's Op-Center: Mirror Image, Vol. II. (Op-Center Ser.). 448p. 1995. mass mkt. 7.50 (*0-425-15014-3*) Berkley Pub.
***Clancy, Tom & Pieczenik, Steve R.** Tom Clancy's Op-Center: State of Siege. abr. ed. 1999. audio 24.00 (*0-671-04559-8*) S&S Audio.
Clancy, Tom & Pieczenik, Steve R., creators. Tom Clancy's Op-Center. (Op-Center Ser.). 387p. 1995. mass mkt. 7.50 (*0-425-14736-3*) Berkley Pub.
— Tom Clancy's Op-Center. large type ed. (Op-Center Ser.). 1995. 25.95 (*0-7862-0491-5*) Thorndike Pr.
— Tom Clancy's Op-Center I. large type ed. LC 95-17609. (Op-Center Ser.). 1996. lib. bdg. 22.95 (*0-7862-0492-3*) Thorndike Pr.
Clancy, William, jt. auth. see Iannacci, Jerry.
Clancy, William G., ed. see Andrews, James R.
Clandestine Press Staff. The Code Book of America: 1997-1998. 4th ed. 96p. 1997. pap. text 6.95 (*0-929150-64-3*, Clandestine Pr) Castalia CA.
Clandinin, D. Jean. Classroom Practice: Teacher Images in Action. 190p. 1986. 69.95 (*1-85000-037-9*, Falmer Pr) Taylor & Francis.
Clandinin, D. Jean, jt. ed. see Connelly, F. Michael.
Clandinin, Jean D., et al, eds. Learning to Teach, Teaching to Learn: Stories of Collaboration in Teacher Education. LC 92-35077. 256p. (C). 1993. text 39.00 (*0-8077-3224-9*); pap. text 19.95 (*0-8077-3223-0*) Tchrs Coll.
***Clandinin, Jean D. & Connelly, F. Michael.** Narrative Inquiries: The Use of Storytelling in Qualitative Research. LC 99-6680. 256p. 1999. 29.95 (*0-7879-4343-6*) Jossey-Bass.
Clandinin, Jean D. & Connelly, F. Michael, eds. Teachers Professional Knowledge Landscapes. (Advances in Contemporary Educational Thought Ser.). 1925. (C). 1995. text 40.00 (*0-8077-3419-5*); pap. text 17.95 (*0-8077-3418-7*) Tchrs Coll.
Clandinin, Jean D., jt. auth. see Connelly, F. Michael.
Clandinin, M. T., jt. ed. see Jumpsen, J.
Clanin, Gloria. In the Days of Noah. (Illus.). 80p. (J). 1996. boxed set 14.95 (*0-89051-205-1*, DAYNOA) Master Bks.
— Noah's Ark & the Great Flood. (Illus.). 32p. (J). (gr. 1-5). 1996. pap. 6.95 (*0-89051-213-2*, NOAGFL) Master Bks.
— The Tower of Babel. 32p. (J). (gr. 1-5). 1996. pap. 6.95 (*0-89051-214-0*, TOWBAB) Master Bks.
Clans, Heather M. Sew Far Sew Good: The Comprehensive Sourcebook for Home & Professional Sewers, Quilters, Beaders, Needleworkers, Weavers, Knitters & Other Creative Persons. Moser, Grant, ed. (Illus.). 416p. (Orig.). 1996. pap. 29.95 (*0-9652103-5-9*) Oracle Publns.
Clanton, Charles. I Surrender All. rev. ed. (Illus.). 334p. 1998. pap. 12.00 (*1-56722-227-7*) Word Aflame.
Clanton, Arthur L. & Clanton, Charles E. United We Stand. rev. ed. LC 95-24156. 336p. 1995. text 14.99 (*1-56722-134-3*) Word Aflame.
Clanton, Candace & Cruice, Gary, Jr. Communication: A Common Sense Approach. 288p. (C). 1995. pap. text, per. 35.95 (*0-7872-1832-4*) Kendall-Hunt.
Clanton, Charles E., jt. auth. see Clanton, Arthur L.
Clanton, Charles E., ed. see Freeman, Nona.
Clanton, Gene. Congressional Populism & Crisis of the 1890s. LC 98-20605. 240p. 1999. 35.00 (*0-7006-0913-X*) U Pr of KS.
— Populism: The Humane Preference in America, 1890-1900. (Twayne's Social Movements Past & Present Ser.). 208p. 1991. pap. 15.95 (*0-8057-9744-0*, Twayne); text 24.95 (*0-8057-9743-2*, Twayne) Mac Lib Ref.
Clanton, Gordon & Smith, Lynn G., eds. Jealousy. 274p. (C). 1987. reprint ed. pap. text 23.00 (*0-8191-5693-0*) U Pr of Amer.
— Jealousy. 3rd ed. LC 97-41213. 344p. (C). 1997. pap. 23.00 (*0-7618-0949-X*) U Pr of Amer.
Clanton, Jann A. Counseling People with Cancer. LC 97-28816. (Counseling & Pastoral Theology Ser.). 176p. 1998. pap. 17.00 (*0-664-25666-X*) Westminster John Knox.
***Clanton, Karen.** Dear Sisters, Dear Daughters. LC 00-44754. 2000. write for info. (*1-57073-815-7*) Amer Bar Assn.
Clanton, Karen, ed. see Garner, Bryan A.
Clanton, Nancy, et al. The Sustainable Grand Canyon Workshop. (Illus.). 116p. (C). 1996. reprint ed. pap. text 35.00 (*0-7881-3476-0*) DIANE Pub.
Clanton, Phil, jt. auth. see Waddell, Dottie.
Clanton, Reita E. & Dwight, Mary P. Team Handball: Steps to Success. LC 96-15149. (Steps to Success Activity Ser.). 168p. (Orig.). 1996. pap. 15.95 (*0-87322-411-6*, PCLA0411) Human Kinetics.
Clanton, Robert, jt. auth. see Beck, Johannes.
Claove, Charles, ed. Laser & Conventional Refractive Surgery. 416p. 1996. text 52.00 (*0-7279-0918-5*, Pub. by BMJ Pub) Login Brothers Bk Co.
Clap, Roger. Memoirs of Roger Clap: Collections of the Dorchester Antiquarian & Historical Society. No. 1. LC 73-150176. (Select Bibliographies Reprint Ser.). 1977. reprint ed. 15.95 (*0-8369-5689-3*) Ayer.
Claparede, Edouard. Experimental Pedagogy & the Psychology of the Child. 344p. 90.00 (*1-85506-696-3*) Thoemmes Pr.
Claparede, Edouard. Experimental Pedagogy & the Psychology of the Child. Louch, Mary & Holman, Henry, trs. from FRE. LC 74-21404. (Classics in Child Development Ser.). 344p. 1975. reprint ed. 29.95 (*0-405-06457-8*) Ayer.
Clapes, Anthony L. Software, Copyright, & Competition: The "Look & Feel" of the Law. LC 89-10477. (Illus.). 247p. 1989. 55.00 (*0-89930-507-5*, CCJ/, Quorum Bks) Greenwood.
— Softwars: The Legal Battles for Control of the Global Software Industry. LC 92-24223. 336p. 1993. 55.00 (*0-89930-597-0*, CRX, Quorum Bks) Greenwood.
Clapesattle, Helen. Dr. Webb of Colorado Springs. LC 84-70852. (Illus.). 518p. reprint ed. pap. 160.60 (*0-8357-5520-7*, 203513600093) Bks Demand.
Clapham, Adam & Constable, Robin. As Nature Intended: A Pictorial Historial of the Nudists. 120p. 1986. 29.95 (*0-434-98026-9*, Pub. by W Heinemann) Bentley Pubs.
Clapham, Alfred W., jt. auth. see Reddan, Minnie.
Clapham, Andrew. Homosexuality in the European Community: A Report on the Legal & Social Situation of Lesbians & Gay Men in the Single European Market. Waaldijk, Kees, ed. LC 92-34502. (International Studies in Human Rights: No. 26). 1993. lib. bdg. 111.00 (*0-7923-2038-7*) Kluwer Academic.
— Human Rights in the Private Sphere. (Oxford Monographs in International Law). 424p. 1996. pap. text 35.00 (*0-19-876431-6*) OUP.
Clapham, Arthur R., et al. Excursion Flora of the British Isles. 3rd ed. LC 79-51679. 536p. 1981. text 44.95 (*0-521-23290-2*) Cambridge U Pr.
Clapham, Caroline. Studies in Language Testing 4: The Development of IELTS: A Study of the Effect of Background Knowledge on Reading Comprehension. (Illus.). 316p. (C). 1996. text 59.95 (*0-521-56199-X*); pap. text 28.95 (*0-521-56708-4*) Cambridge U Pr.
Clapham, Caroline & Corson, David. Language Testing & Assessment. LC 97-30205. (Encyclopedia of Language & Education Ser.). 1997. lib. bdg. write for info. (*0-7923-4702-1*) Kluwer Academic.
Clapham, Christopher. Africa & the International System: The Politics of State Survival. (Cambridge Studies in International Relations: No. 50). 351p. (C). 1996. pap. text 22.95 (*0-521-57668-7*) Cambridge U Pr.
— Africa & the International System: The Politics of State Survival. (Cambridge Studies in International Relations: No. 50). 352p. (C). 1996. text 59.95 (*0-521-57207-X*) Cambridge U Pr.
— African Guerrillas. LC 98-15631. 224p. 1998. 39.95 (*0-253-33466-7*) Ind U Pr.
Clapham, Christopher. Concise Oxford Dictionary of Mathematics. 1990. 15.05 (*0-606-03162-6*, Pub. by Turtleback) Demco.
Clapham, Christopher. The Concise Oxford Dictionary of Mathematics. 2nd ed. (Oxford Paperback Reference Ser.). (Illus.). 320p. 1996. pap. 11.95 (*0-19-280041-8*) OUP.
— Third World Politics: An Introduction. 256p. 1985. pap. text 17.95 (*0-299-10334-X*) U of Wis Pr.
Clapham, Christopher S. African Guerrillas. LC 98-15631. 224p. 1998. pap. 17.95 (*0-253-21243-X*) Ind U Pr.
— Liberia & Sierra Leone: An Essay in Comparative Politics. LC 75-32447. (African Studies: No. 20). 164p. reprint ed. pap. 46.80 (*0-608-15705-8*, 2031632) Bks Demand.
Clapham, David & Hegedus, Jozsef, eds. Housing Privatization in Eastern Europe, 117. LC 96-10741. (Contributions in Sociology Ser.: Vol. 117). 224p. 1996. 67.95 (*0-313-27214-X*, Praeger Pubs) Greenwood.
Clapham, David, jt. auth. see Hutson, Susan.
Clapham, John H. A Concise Economic History of Britain, from the Earliest Times to 1750. LC 75-41059. (BCL Ser.: No. II). 1976. reprint ed. 34.50 (*0-404-14654-6*) AMS Pr.
***Clapham, Mark & Miller, John.** Twilight of the Gods. 256p. 2000. mass mkt. 6.95 (*0-426-20536-7*, Pub. by Virgin Bks) London Brdge.
Clapham, Mark, jt. auth. see Bucher-Jones, Simon.
Clapham, Phil. Humpback Whales. LC 95-46052. (WorldLife Library). (Illus.). 72p. (YA). 1995. pap. 16.95 (*0-89658-296-5*) Voyageur Pr.
— Whales of the World. LC 97-1860. (Illus.). 120p. 1997. 29.95 (*0-89658-359-7*) Voyageur Pr.
Clapham, Sidney. Fuchsias for House & Garden. LC 82-8401. (Illus.). 152p. 1982. text 15.00 (*0-87663-404-8*, Pub. by Universe) St Martin.
Clapham, V. M., ed. see International Conference on Solid State Nuclear Tr.
Clapin, Sylva. Dictionnaire Canadien-Francais. (FRE.). 394p. 1974. 49.95 (*0-8288-6009-2*, M6587) Fr & Eur.
Clapin, Sylvia. A New Dictionary of Americanisms. 1973. 59.95 (*0-8490-0721-6*) Gordon Pr.
Clapinson, Mary & Rogers, T. D. Summary Catalogue of Post-Medieval Western Manuscripts in the Bodleian Library, Oxford: Acquisitions 1916-1975 (SC 37300-55936), 3 vols., Set. 2,214p. 1992. text 700.00 (*0-19-952109-3*) OUP.
Clapman, Arnold. Angel the Pig. LC 94-20302. (Illus.). 32p. (J). 1994. pap. 4.95 (*0-382-24662-4*) Silver Burdett Pr.
Clapp. The Next Bible. 2nd ed. 1991. pap. 29.95 (*0-13-617200-8*) P-H.
— Next Software Guide. 1991. pap. 29.95 (*0-13-617218-0*) P-H.
Clapp, jt. auth. see Brown.
Clapp, Alfred C. & Mears, William H. Planning for the Elderly. LC 98-184320. (Personal Financial Planning Portfolio Ser.). viii, 104p. 1996. write for info. (*0-15-601848-9*) Harcourt Legal.
Clapp, Allan L., ed. Practical Utility Safety: A Collection of Discussions & Calculation Aids for Power, Telephone & CATV Utilities. (Illus.). 360p. 1999. pap. write for info. (*0-7392-0162-X*, PO3116) Morris Pubng.
Clapp, Allen L., ed. National Electrical Safety Code Handbook: A Discussion of the Grounding Rules, General Rules, & Pts. 1, 2, 3, & 4 of the 3rd 1920-1990

C

Editions of the National Electrical Safety Code American National Standard C2. LC 91-12657. (Illus.). 436p. (Orig.). 1991. pap. 55.00 (*1-55937-081-5*, SP00018) IEEE Standards.

— National Electrical Safety Code Handbook: A Discussion of the Grounding Rules, General Rules, & Pts. 1, 2, 3, & 4 of the 3rd 1920-1990 Editions of the National Electrical Safety Code American National Standard C2. 3rd ed. LC 92-18434. (Orig.). 1992. write for info. (*1-55937-211-7*) IEEE Standards.

Clapp, Allen L. & American National Standards Institute Staff. National Electrical Safety Code Handbook (NESC) A Discussion of the Grounding Rules, General Rules, & Parts 1, 2, 3, & 4 of the 3rd (1920) Through 1977 Editions of the National Electrical Safety Code, American National Standard C2. 4th ed. LC 96-9505. 456p. 1997. pap. 89.00 (*1-55937-724-0*, SP1105) IEEE Standards.

Clapp, Ann D. The Painting of T'Ang Yin. (Illus.). 320p. 1991. 57.50 (*0-226-10699-3*) U Ch Pr.

Clapp, Anne F. Curatorial Care of Works of Art on Paper. (Illus.). 201p. 1978. pap. 18.95 (*0-941130-31-2*, 50263) Lyons Pr.

Clapp, B. W. An Environmental History of Britain Since the Industrial Revolution. LC 93-13073. 1994. pap. text. write for info. (*0-582-22626-0*) Longman.

Clapp, C. E., et al, eds. Sewage Sludge: Land Utilization & the Environment. LC 94-29183. 254p. 1994. pap. 30.00 (*0-89118-813-4*) Am Soc Agron.

Clapp, Charles L. The Congressman: His Work As He Sees It. LC 79-28559. 452p. 1980. reprint ed. lib. bdg. 55.00 (*0-313-22296-7*, CLCG, Greenwood Pr) Greenwood.

Clapp, Deborah, jt. auth. see Clapp, Robert D.

Clapp, E., ed. The Clapp Memorial Record of the Clapp Family Containing Sketches of the Original Six Emigrants & a Genealogy of Their Descendants Bearing That Name: With Supplement & Proceedings at Two Family Meetings. (Illus.). 536p. 1989. reprint ed. pap. 77.00 (*0-8328-0403-7*); reprint ed. lib. bdg. 87.00 (*0-8328-0402-9*) Higginson Bk Co.

Clapp, Elizabeth J. Mothers of All Children: Women Reformers & the Rise of Juvenile Courts in Progressive Era America. LC 97-49129. 256p. 1998. 55.00 (*0-271-01777-5*); pap. 18.95 (*0-271-01778-3*) Pa St U Pr.

C

Clapp, Elsie R. Community Schools in Action. LC 78-165714. (American Education, Ser, No. 2). 1978. reprint ed. 29.95 (*0-405-03703-1*) Ayer.

Clapp, Frederick M. A History of the Seventeenth Aero Squadron. (Great War Ser.: No. 2). (Illus.). 171p. 1990. reprint ed. 29.95 (*0-89839-140-7*) Battery Pr.

Clapp, Genevieve. Divorce & New Beginnings: A Complete Guide to Recovery, Solo Parenting & Step Families. LC 91-27824. 400p. 1992. pap. 22.00 (*0-471-52631-2*) Wiley.

***Clapp, Genevieve.** Divorce & New Beginnings: A Complete Guide to Recovery, Solo Parenting, Co-Parenting & Stepfamilies. 2nd ed. LC 00-25516. 380p. 2000. pap. 19.95 (*0-471-32648-8*) Wiley.

Clapp, Henry A. Reminiscences of a Dramatic Critic: With an Essay on the Art of Henry Irving. LC 72-5536. (Select Bibliographies Reprint Ser.). 1977. reprint ed. 23.95 (*0-8369-6902-2*) Ayer.

Clapp, Henry L. Clapp Pts. I & II: Fifty Ancestors of Henry Lincoln Clapp, Who Came to New England, from 1620-1650. (Illus.). 140p. 1997. reprint ed. pap. 25.00 (*0-8328-7936-3*); reprint ed. lib. bdg. 35.00 (*0-8328-7935-5*) Higginson Bk Co.

Clapp, James A. New Towns: An Emphasis on the American Enterprise, No. 982. 1976. 10.00 (*0-686-20387-9*, Sage Prdcls Pr) Sage.

Clapp, James E. Random House Legal Dictionary. 320p. 1996. pap. 6.99 (*0-679-76435-6*) Random Ref & Info.

— Random House Webster's Legal Dictionary. 640p. 2000. pap. 17.95 (*0-375-70239-3*) Random Ref & Info.

— Random House Webster's Legal Spell Check. LC 98-27428. 1998. pap. 10.95 (*0-375-40155-5*) Random Ref & Info.

Clapp, James T., III. Exercising Through Your Pregnancy. LC 98-12426. (Illus.). 256p. (Orig.). 1998. pap. 16.95 (*0-87322-941-X*, BCLA0941) Human Kinetics.

Clapp, Jamie, ed. see Kerl, Mary A. & D'Queue, Jay.

Clapp, Jeanie J. & Bliss, Mary L., eds. The American Bench: Judges of the Nation. 10th ed. 2500p. 1999. 350.00 (*0-931398-39-8*) Forster-Long.

***Clapp, Jeanie J. & Irvine, Diana R., eds.** The American Bar - The Canadian Bar - The Mexican Bar - The International Bar. 81st ed. 4050p. 1999. 360.00 (*0-931398-40-1*) Forster-Long.

Clapp, Jeanie J. & Irvine, Diana R., eds. The American Bar - The Canadian Bar - The Mexican Bar - The International Bar, 1997. 79th ed. 3870p. 1997. 340.00 (*0-931398-36-3*) Forster-Long.

— The American Bar--The Canadian Bar--The Mexican Bar--The International Bar, 1998 Edition. 80th ed. 3915p. 1998. 350.00 (*0-931398-38-X*) Forster-Long.

Clapp, Jeanie J. & Kennedy, Ruth A., eds. The American Bench: Judges of the Nation 1997/1998 Edition. 9th ed. 2500p. 1997. 340.00 (*0-931398-37-1*) Forster-Long.

Clapp, Jennifer. Adjustment & Agriculture in Africa: Farmers, the State & the World Bank in Guinea. LC 96-18825. (International Political Economy Ser.). 192p. 1997. text 59.95 (*0-312-16341-X*) St Martin.

Clapp, John, jt. auth. see Cooper, Susan.

Clapp, John B. & Edgett, Edwin F. Players of the Present, 3 vols., 1 bk. LC 72-91897. (Illus.). 432p. 1972. 32.95 (*0-405-08360-2*, Pub. by Blom Pubns) Ayer.

— Plays of the Present. LC 73-83498. (Illus.). 331p. 1972. 24.95 (*0-405-08361-0*, Pub. by Blom Pubns) Ayer.

Clapp, John M. Dynamics of Office Markets: Empirical Findings & Research Issues. (AREUEA Monograph Ser.). (Illus.). 212p. (C). 1993. pap. text 27.50 (*0-87766-606-7*) Urban Inst.

Clapp, John M. & Messner, Stephen D., eds. Real Estate Market Analysis: Methods & Applications. LC 87-15832. 367p. 1988. 75.00 (*0-275-92414-9*, C2414, Praeger Pubs) Greenwood.

Clapp, Judith A. & Cerino, Deborah A. Software Quality Control, Error Analysis, & Testing. LC 94-35136. (Advanced Computing & Telecommunications Ser.). (Illus.). 392p. 1995. 54.00 (*0-8155-1363-1*) Noyes.

Clapp, Justin P., ed. Species Diagnostics Protocols: PCR & Other Nucleic Acid Methods. LC 95-24805. (Methods in Molecular Biology Ser.: Vol. 50). (Illus.). 440p. 1995. 84.50 (*0-89603-323-6*) Humana.

Clapp, Katie, ed. see Kroll, Mary.

Clapp, Larry. Prostate Health in 90 Days: Without Drugs Or Surgery. (Illus.). 323p. 1997. pap. 14.95 (*1-56170-460-1*) Hay House.

Clapp, Michael & Southby-Tailyour, Ewen. Amphibious Assault, Falklands. LC 96-69151. (Illus.). 272p. 1996. 27.95 (*1-55750-028-2*) Naval Inst Pr.

— Amphibious Assault Falklands: The Battle of San Carlos Water. (Illus.). 300p. 1996. 54.50 (*0-85052-420-2*, Pub. by Leo Cooper) Trans-Atl Phila.

Clapp, Neal K. A Primate Model for the Study of Colitis & Colonic Carcinoma: The Cotton Top Tamarin (Saguinus Oedipus) 352p. 1993. lib. bdg. 225.00 (*0-8493-5363-7*, RC862) CRC Pr.

Clapp, Nicholas. The Road to Ubar: Finding the Atlantis of the Sands. LC 97-36640. (Illus.). 331p. 1998. 24.00 (*0-395-87596-X*) HM.

— The Road to Ubar: Finding the Atlantis of the Sands. (Illus.). 288p. 1999. pap. 14.00 (*0-395-95786-9*) HM.

Clapp, Patrici C. The Invisible Dragon. 1972. pap. 3.50 (*0-87129-377-3*, I27) Dramatic Pub.

Clapp, Patricia. The Toys Take over Christmas. 1977. 3.95 (*0-87129-545-8*, T46) Dramatic Pub.

Clapp, Patricia C. Constance. LC 85-43127. 256p. (YA). (gr. 4-7). 1991. reprint ed. mass mkt. 5.95 (*0-688-10976-4*, Wm Morrow) Morrow Avon.

— Constance: A Story of Early Plymouth. (J). (gr. 5-9). 1993. 20.25 (*0-8446-6647-5*) Peter Smith.

— The Tamarack Tree. LC 86-108. 224p. (YA). (gr. 7 up). 1986. 16.00 (*0-688-02852-7*) Lothrop.

Clapp, Patricia C., et al. The Magic Toyshop - Musical. 1995. 5.95 (*0-87129-505-9*, M07) Dramatic Pub.

Clapp, Priscilla & Halperin, Morton H., eds. United States-Japanese Relations: The 1970s. LC 74-80441. 256p. (C). 1974. 37.95 (*0-674-92571-8*) HUP.

***Clapp, Robert D. & Clapp, Deborah.** Bankruptcy Is Not Your Only Option! Your Step-by-Step Guide to Financial Rehabilitation. (Illus.). 92p. 1999. 29.95 (*0-9673610-0-1*) Clapp & Affil.

***Clapp, Rodney.** Border Crossings: Christian Trespasses on Popular Culture & Public Affairs. LC 00-40352. 2000. pap. 16.99 (*1-58743-003-7*) Brazos.

Clapp, Rodney. Families at the Crossroads: Beyond Traditional & Modern Options. LC 93-21559. 208p. (Orig.). 1993. pap. 13.99 (*0-8308-1655-0*, 1655) InterVarsity.

— A Peculiar People: The Church As Culture in a Post-Christian Society. 276p. (Orig.). 1996. pap. 14.99 (*0-8308-1990-8*, 1990) InterVarsity.

Clapp, Rodney, ed. The Consuming Passion: Christianity & the Culture of Consumption. LC 97-44349. 224p. 1997. pap. 14.99 (*0-8308-1897-9*, 1897) InterVarsity.

Clapp, Rodney, jt. auth. see Webber, Robert.

Clapp, Steve. The Bible & Major Issues. 145p. 1990. pap. 14.95 (*0-87178-098-4*, 8984) Brethren.

— Christian Education As Evangelism. 154p. (Orig.). 1982. pap. 9.00 (*0-914527-11-8*) C-Four Res.

— Fifty Ways to Reach Young Singles, Couples & Families. 60p. 1995. pap. 8.00 (*0-9637206-2-7*) LifeQuest IN.

— Ministerial Competency Report. (Practice of Ministry Ser.). 123p. (Orig.). 1982. pap. 8.00 (*0-914527-10-X*) C-Four Res.

— Overcoming Barriers to Church Growth. 128p. 1995. pap. 14.00 (*0-9637206-3-5*) LifeQuest IN.

— Plain Talk about Church Growth. LC 89-49600. 183p. 1990. reprint ed. pap. 56.80 (*0-608-02155-5*, 206282400004) Bks Demand.

— Promising Results: Passing on the Promise & the Pilgrimage Toward Growth. LC BV0652.25.C5. 96p. 1993. reprint ed. pap. 30.00 (*0-608-02156-3*, 206282500004) Bks Demand.

— Retreat Guide I. 20p. (Orig.). 1981. pap. 2.00 (*0-914527-04-5*) C-Four Res.

— Retreat Guide II. (C-4 Journals Ser.). 29p. (Orig.). 1982. pap. 2.00 (*0-914527-13-4*) C-Four Res.

— Sermons on Shalom. 79p. (Orig.). 1982. pap. 8.00 (*0-914527-37-1*) C-Four Res.

— Shalom: Hope for the World. 178p. (Orig.). 1982. pap. 8.00 (*0-914527-35-5*) C-Four Res.

— Who's In? Who's Out? A Look at Jonah & Ruth. (Generation Why Ser.: Vol. 1:1). 32p. (YA). (gr. 9-12). 1995. pap. 12.95 (*0-87303-257-8*) Faith & Life.

Clapp, Steve, ed. Prayer & the Christian Life: C-4 Devotional Journal II. (C-4 Journals Ser.). 126p. (Orig.). 1982. pap. 6.00 (*0-914527-12-6*) C-Four Res.

Clapp, Steve, frwd. Mid-Winter Festivals: Anthology of Stories, Traditions & Poems. (Family Reading Ser.). 211p. (Orig.). 1983. pap. 10.00 (*0-914527-01-0*) C-Four Res.

Clapp, Steve & Cook, Jerry O. Reaching Out Through Christian Education. 144p. 1995. pap. 14.00 (*0-9637206-4-3*) LifeQuest IN.

— Youth Workers' Handbook. 280p. 1981. pap. 11.00 (*0-914527-05-3*) C-Four Res.

— Youth Workers' Handbook. rev. ed. 224p. 1992. reprint ed. pap. 16.95 (*0-87178-979-5*) Brethren.

Clapp, Steve & Detwiler, Sam. Peer Evangelism. (FaithQuest Youth Resources Ser.). 100p. 1993. pap. 16.95 (*0-87178-693-1*, 8931) Brethren.

— Sharing Living Water: Evangelism As Caring Friendship. 176p. 1996. pap. 14.00 (*0-9637206-8-6*) LifeQuest IN.

Clapp, Steve & Mauck, Sue I. A Primer for Angry Christians. (Illus.). 138p. (Orig.). 1981. pap. 6.00 (*0-914527-09-6*) C-Four Res.

— Repairing Christian Lifestyles. 2nd ed. (Repairing Christian Lifestyles Ser.). (Illus.). 174p. (YA). (gr. 7-12). 1983. pap. 6.00 (*0-914527-26-6*); pap., teacher ed. 5.00 (*0-914527-27-4*) C-Four Res.

— Through the Bible, Vol. I. (C-Four Youth Bible Materials Ser.). (Illus.). 138p. (Orig.). 1982. pap. 10.00 (*0-914527-15-0*) C-Four Res.

Clapp, Steve & Peterson, Gerald W. Forming Bible Study Groups. LC 90-40628. (Covenant Bible Studies). 32p. 1990. pap. 3.95 (*0-87178-293-6*, 8936) Brethren.

Clapp, Steve & Snider, Cindy H. Creating Quality in Ministry: Insights on How Quality Can Sharpen & Focus Today's Local Church Ministry. 160p. 1996. pap. 14.00 (*0-9637206-6-X*) LifeQuest IN.

Clapp, Steve, et al. The Desires of Your Heart: Financial Giving & the Spiritual Life. (Illus.). 192p. 1998. pap. 19.00 (*0-9637206-5-1*) LifeQuest IN.

— Preaching, Planning & Plumbing: Discovering God's Call to Service & Joy. (Illus.). 128p. 1999. pap. 12.00 (*1-893270-02-5*, Chrstn Commnty) LifeQuest IN.

— Youth Experiential Annual Resource 1. 122p. (Orig.). 1981. pap. 10.00 (*0-914527-42-8*) C-Four Res.

Clapp, Steve, jt. auth. see Bernhard, Fred.

Clapp, Steve, jt. auth. see Conn, Robert.

Clapp, Steve, jt. auth. see Davis, Dennis M.

Clapp, Steve, jt. auth. see Snider, Cindy H.

Clapp, Steve, ed. see Andrew Center Staff Members.

Clapp, Sue C. Teams with Style (Facilitator Guide) Tapping the Power of Personality Style in Workplace Teams. 2nd ed. Sullivan, Joseph R., ed. (Illus.). 92p. Date not set. reprint ed. pap. 195.00 (*1-929112-10-6*) Personality Res.

Clapp, Susannah. With Chatwin: Portrait of a Writer. LC 97-73722. 241p. 1997. 23.00 (*0-679-41033-3*) Knopf.

— With Chatwin: Portrait of a Writer. LC 97-73722. 241p. 1999. pap. 12.95 (*0-14-027645-9*) Viking Penguin.

Clapp, Theodore. Autobiographical Sketches & Recollections. (American Biography Ser.). 419p. 1991. reprint ed. lib. bdg. 99.00 (*0-7812-8070-2*) Rprt Serv.

— Autobiographical Sketches & Recollections: During a 35 Years Residence in New Orleans. LC 77-38346. (Select Bibliographies Reprint Ser.). 1977. reprint ed. 25.95 (*0-8369-6763-1*) Ayer.

Clapp, Tom. Dracula: A New Stage Version. rev. ed. LC 91-51165. 1985. pap. 6.00 (*0-88734-202-7*) Players Pr.

— The Open Boat. LC 96-22481. 55p. (Orig.). 1996. reprint ed. pap. 6.00 (*0-88734-200-0*) Players Pr.

— Tomorrow or the Next Day. LC 96-27702. 55p. (Orig.). 1996. pap. 6.00 (*0-88734-279-5*) Players Pr.

Clapp, Wiley M., jt. auth. see Grennell, Dean A.

Clapp, William W. Record of the Boston Stage. LC 11-19303. 1853. 12.00 (*0-403-00473-X*) Scholarly.

— Record of the Boston Stage. LC 68-58197. 1972. reprint ed. 36.95 (*0-405-08362-9*, Pub. by Blom Pubns) Ayer.

Clappe, Louise. The Shirley Letters. LC 77-141468. (Illus.). 224p. 1970. pap. 14.95 (*0-87905-004-7*) Gibbs Smith Pub.

Clappe, Louise A. The Shirley Letters: From the California Mines, 1851-1852. LC 97-43472. (Illus.). 240p. 1998. reprint ed. pap. 12.95 (*1-890771-00-7*) Heyday Bks.

Clapper, Gregory S. As If the Heart Mattered: A Wesleyan Spirituality. LC 97-11415. 112p. 1997. pap. 10.00 (*0-8358-0820-3*, UR 820) Upper Room Bks.

— John Wesley on Religious Affections: His Views on Experience & Emotion & Their Role in the Christian Life & Theology. LC 89-39661. (Pietist & Wesleyan Studies: No. 1). 223p. 1989. 26.50 (*0-8108-2267-9*) Scarecrow.

— When the World Breaks Your Heart: Spiritual Ways of Living with Tragedy. LC 98-19154. 112p. 1999. 10.00 (*0-8358-0842-4*) Upper Room Bks.

Clapper, M. L. & Houser, D. A Boundary Element Procedure for Predicting Helical Gear Root Stresses & Load Distribution Factors. (Nineteen Ninety-Four Fall Technical Meeting Ser.: Vol. 94FTM6). (Illus.). 8p. 1994. pap. text 30.00 (*1-55589-640-5*) AGMA.

Clapper, Petie. Natural Guide to Better Health. 1990. 19.95 (*0-685-29021-2*) Orange Bl Pr.

Clapper, Raymond. Racketeering in Washington: An Account of the Grafting in Small & Great Things by Our Senators & Members of the House of Representatives & Executives in Public Departments. LC 73-19138. (Politics & People Ser.). 356p. 1974. reprint ed. 26.95 (*0-405-05863-2*) Ayer.

— Watching the World. (FDR & the Era of the New Deal Ser.). 1975. reprint ed. 45.00 (*0-306-70730-6*) Da Capo.

Clapperton. People Like Us. Date not set. 14.95 (*0-06-016762-9*) HarperTrade.

Clapperton, C. M. Quaternary Geology & Geomorphology of South America. LC 93-5243. 796p. 1993. 241.00 (*0-444-88247-2*) Elsevier.

Clapperton, H. Journal of a Second Expedition into the Interior of Africa from the Bight of Benin to Soccatoo. 355p. 1966. reprint ed. 75.00 (*0-7146-1798-9*, Pub. by F Cass Pubs) Intl Spec Bk.

Clapsaddle-Counts, Ruth. Four Corners. LC 97-69231. 200p. 1998. 19.95 (*1-57197-079-7*) Pentland Pr.

Clapson. Invincible Green Suburbs, Brave New Towns: Social Change & Urban Disperalin in Post-War England. LC 97-24841. 224p. 1998. text 69.95 (*0-7190-4135-X*) St Martin.

Clapton, Eric. Classic Songs Transcribed from the Recordings of Eric Clapton. 184p. (Orig.). 1995. pap. 19.95 (*1-56922-072-7*, 07-4055) Creat Cncpts.

— The Cream of Clapton. 64p. 1996. pap. 9.95 (*0-7935-6557-X*) H Leonard.

— Eric Clapton: The Best of Signature Licks. (Guitar Signature Licks Ser.). 88p. 1996. pap. 19.95 incl. audio compact disk (*0-7935-5801-8*) H Leonard.

Clapton, M. J. Aikido: An Introduction to Tomiki Style. 88p. 1995. pap. 15.95 (*0-901764-23-X*, 93308) P H Crompton.

Claquin, Pierre, et al. Surveillance of Morbidity & Mortality Module 4: User's Guide. (Primary Health Care Management Advancement Programme (PHC MAP) Modules Ser.). 126p. 1993. pap. text. write for info. (*1-882839-15-3*) Aga Khan Fnd.

Clar, C. Raymond. Out of the River Mist. 3rd ed. (Illus.). 135p. 1984. pap. 7.00 (*0-9613635-0-9*) C R Clar.

Clar, Erich J. The Aromatic Sextet. LC 72-616. 138p. reprint ed. pap. 42.80 (*0-8357-5753-6*, 202399800035) Bks Demand.

Clar, Lawrence. Pak: Mathematics for Business & Personal Finance. 2nd ed. 792p. (C). 1997. 65.95 (*0-7872-4233-0*) Kendall-Hunt.

Clar, Lawrence & Hart, James. Pak: Mathematics for Business. 752p. (C). 1995. 58.95 (*0-7872-0820-5*) Kendall-Hunt.

Clar, Lawrence M. & Hart, James A. Calculus with Analytic Geometry for the Technologies. (Technological Mathematics Ser.). (Illus.). 1980. text 35.65 (*0-13-111856-0*) P-H.

Clar, Raymond C. Quarterdecks & Spanish Grants. (Illus.). 156p. 1984. pap. 30.00 (*0-910845-23-9*, 909) Landmark Ent.

Clarage, Elizabeth C., jt. auth. see Brennan, Elizabeth A.

***Claramunt, Marc.** Pages Paysages: In the Meantime. (Illus.). 192p. 2000. pap. 42.00 (*3-7643-6322-3*) Birkhauser.

Claraso, N. Vademecum del Arquitecto de Jardines. (SPA.). 256p. 1977. pap. 19.95 (*0-8288-5528-5*, S35347) Fr & Eur.

Claraso, V. Diccionario Humoristico. (SPA.). 297p. 1966. 35.00 (*0-8288-6706-2*, S-37662) Fr & Eur.

Clarc, Michel. Les Meteques Atheniens. Vlastos, Gregory, ed. LC 78-15862. (Morals & Law in Ancient Greece Ser.). 1979. reprint ed. lib. bdg. 37.95 (*0-405-11533-4*) Ayer.

Clard, Harrison. All Cloudless Glory. 483p. 1998. pap. 22.50 (*0-89526-372-6*) Regnery Pub.

Clardy, Alan B. Managing Human Resources: Exercises, Experiments, & Applications, Set, incl. tchr's. manual. 136p. (C). 1995. pap., student ed. write for info. (*0-8058-1749-2*) L Erlbaum Assocs.

— Managing Human Resources: Exercises, Experiments, & Applications, Set, incl. tchr's. manual. 176p. (C). 1995. student ed. 19.95 (*0-8058-1748-4*) L Erlbaum Assocs.

— Studying Your Workforce: Applied Research Methods & Tools for the Training & Development Practitioner. LC 97-4672. 208p. 1997. 45.00 (*0-8039-7321-7*); pap. 21.95 (*0-8039-7322-5*) Sage.

Clardy, Andrea F. Dusty Was My Friend. (Illus.). 32p. (J). (gr. 5 up). 1984. 16.95 (*0-89885-141-6*, Kluwer Acad Hman Sci) Kluwer Academic.

Clardy, Jonell, tr. see Baker, Ron.

Clardy, Mary K. Flute Fundamentals: The Building Blocks of Technique. (Illus.). 44p. (C). 1993. pap. text 9.95 (*0-913574-98-8*, EA730) Eur-Am Music.

Clare. Information Systems: Strategy to Design. (ITCP US Computer Science). 1994. mass mkt. 31.00 (*0-412-57670-8*, VNR) Wiley.

— Voyages of Christopher Columbus. 1997. pap. 16.95 (*0-15-201674-0*) Harcourt.

Clare & Stutley. Information Systems Strat to Design. (ITCP-UK Computer Science Ser.). 1996. pap., student ed. 29.95 (*1-85032-229-5*) Thomson Learn.

Clare, A. W. & Lader, Malcolm H., eds. Psychiatry & General Practice. 1982. text 104.00 (*0-12-174720-4*) Acad Pr.

Clare, Alexis G. & Jones, Linda, eds. Advances in Fusion & Processing of Glass II: Proceedings, 5th International Symposium on the Advances in Fusion & Processing of Glass, Toronto, Canada, 1997. (Ceramic Transactions Ser.: Vol. 82). 487p. 1998. 111.00 (*1-57498-045-9*, CT082) Am Ceramic.

Clare, Alys. Fortune Like the Moon. mass mkt. write for info. (*0-312-97630-5*) St Martin.

— Fortune Like the Moon. 256p. 2000. text 22.95 (*0-312-26162-4*, Minotaur) St Martin.

Clare, Anthony. In the Psychiatrist's Chair. 192p. 1985. 16.95 (*0-7011-2793-7*, Pub. by Chatto & Windus) Random House.

— Lovelaw: Love, Sex, & Marriage Around the World. (Illus.). 200p. 1988. pap. 14.95 (*0-563-20412-5*, Pub. by BBC) Parkwest Pubns.

***Clare, Baxter.** Bleeding Out. 304p. 2000. pap. 13.95 (*1-56341-118-0*, Pub. by Firebrand Bks); lib. bdg. 26.95 (*1-56341-119-9*, Pub. by Firebrand Bks) LPC InBook.

Clare, Cathleen. Clarissa. 256p. (Orig.). 1993. mass mkt. 3.99 (*0-380-77179-9*, Avon Bks) Morrow Avon.

— A Delectable Dilemma. 224p. (Orig.). 1995. mass mkt. 3.99 (*0-380-78126-3*, Avon Bks) Morrow Avon.

— An Elusive Groom. 1996. mass mkt. 4.50 (*0-8217-5295-2*, Zebra Kensgtn) Kensgtn Pub Corp.

***Clare, Cathleen.** Elusive Groom. (Regency Romance Ser.). 2000. mass mkt. 4.99 (*0-8217-7074-8*) Kensgtn Pub Corp.

— Family Affair. (Regency Romance Ser.). 2000. mass mkt. 4.99 (*0-8217-6482-9*, Zebra Kensgtn) Kensgtn Pub Corp.

Clare, Cathleen. Felicia. 224p. (Orig.). 1993. mass mkt. 3.99 (*0-380-76816-X*, Avon Bks) Morrow Avon.

An Asterisk (*) at the beginning of an entry indicates that the title is appearing for the first time.

— Letitia. (Regency Romance Ser.). 256p. (Orig.). 1994. mass mkt. 3.99 (*0-380-77667-7*, Avon Bks) Morrow Avon.

— Lord Montjoy's Country Inn. (Zebra Regency Romance Ser.). 256p. 1998. mass mkt. 4.99 (*0-8217-5902-7*, Zebra Kensgtn) Kensgtn Pub Corp.

— Lord Scandal's Lady. 256p. 1997. mass mkt. 4.99 (*0-8217-5591-9*, Zebra Kensgtn) Kensgtn Pub Corp.

— Midwinter's Bliss. 240p. (Orig.). 1995. mass mkt. 3.99 (*0-380-77668-5*, Avon Bks) Morrow Avon.

— Mistress of Mishap. 256p. (Orig.). 1992. mass mkt. 3.99 (*0-380-76815-1*, Avon Bks) Morrow Avon.

— A Priceless Acquisition. 256p. 1997. mass mkt. 4.99 (*0-8217-5790-3*, Zebra Kensgtn) Kensgtn Pub Corp.

— Tournament of Hearts. 256p. (Orig.). 1994. mass mkt. 3.99 (*0-380-77432-1*, Avon Bks) Morrow Avon.

Clare, Cathleen, et al. Sweet Delights, 1. 256p. 1999. mass mkt. 4.99 (*0-8217-6324-5*) Kensgtn Pub Corp.

Clare, Cathryn. The Angel & the Renegade. (Intimate Moments Ser.: No. 599). 1994. per. 3.50 (*0-373-07599-5*) Silhouette.

— The Baby Assignment. (Intimate Moments Ser.: No. 726). 1996. per. 3.99 (*0-373-07726-2*, 1-07726-2) Silhouette.

— Chasing Destiny. (Intimate Moments Ser.). 1993. per. 3.50 (*0-373-07503-0*, 5-07503-1) Silhouette.

— Entente Forcee. (Amours d'Aujourd'Hui Ser.: No. 310). (FRE.). 1998. mass mkt. 4.99 (*0-373-38310-X*, 1-38310-8) Harlequin Bks.

— Gunslinger's Child. (Intimate Moments Ser.). 1995. per. 3.75 (*0-373-07629-0*, 1-07629-8) Silhouette.

— The Honeymoon Assignment. (Intimate Moments Ser.). 1996. per. 3.99 (*0-373-07714-9*, 1-07714-8) Silhouette.

— A Marriage to Remember. (Intimate Moments Ser.: No. 795). 1997. per. 3.99 (*0-373-07795-5*, 1-07795-7) Silhouette.

— The Quiet One (The Guiness Gang) LC 96-7311. (Intimate Moments Ser.). 248p. 1996. per. 3.99 (*0-373-07701-7*, 1-07701-5) Silhouette.

— Sun & Shadow. (Shadows Ser.). 1994. per. 3.50 (*0-373-07558-6*, 5-07558-5) Silhouette.

— The Wedding Assignment: Assignment: Romance. (Intimate Moments Ser.). 1996. per. 3.99 (*0-373-07702-5*, 1-07702-3) Silhouette.

Clare, Chris P. Information Systems Design. (Illus.). 500p. 1996. mass mkt. 29.95 (*1-85032-175-2*) ITCP.

Clare, Elizabeth. The Enchanted Way. large type ed. 1990. 27.99 (*0-7089-2165-5*) Ulverscroft.

— Exile & Pride: Disability, Queerness & Liberation. LC 99-36063. 150p. 1999. 40.00 (*0-89608-606-2*, Pub. by South End Pr); pap. 14.00 (*0-89608-605-4*, Pub. by South End Pr) Consort Bk Sales.

— In Spring Time. large type ed. 267p. 1989. 27.99 (*0-7089-1971-5*) Ulverscroft.

— A Land of Stars. large type ed. 384p. 1988. 27.99 (*0-7089-1894-8*) Ulverscroft.

— A Song to the Sun. large type ed. 1990. 27.99 (*0-7089-2214-7*) Ulverscroft.

Clare, Ellen. Ripening Vine. large type ed. 280p. 1995. 11.50 (*0-7505-0886-8*, Pub. by Mgna Lrg Print) Ulverscroft.

Clare, Francis. Glory to Glory: Into the Millennium & Beyond. 208p. 1998. pap. 10.95 (*1-878718-46-0*, Resurrection Pr) Catholic Bk Pub.

— Wow God. 192p. 1998. reprint ed. pap. 8.95 (*1-878718-55-X*, Resurrection Pr) Catholic Bk Pub.

— Your Move God. 144p. 1998. reprint ed. pap. 7.95 (*1-878718-47-9*, Resurrection Pr) Catholic Bk Pub.

Clare, George. ABC of the Foreign Exchanges. Wilkins, Mira, ed. LC 78-3905. (International Finance Ser.). (Illus.). 1979. reprint ed. lib. bdg. 19.95 (*0-405-11210-6*) Ayer.

— Berlin Days, 1946-47. 230p. 1994. pap. 24.00 (*0-333-60587-X*, Pub. by Papermac) Trans-Atl Phila.

Clare, Israel S. A Brief History of Lancaster County, Pennsylvania. (Illus.). 317p. 1994. reprint ed. lib. bdg. 32.50 (*0-8328-4004-1*) Higginson Bk Co.

Clare, J. N. & Sinclair, M. A., eds. Search & the Human Observer. (Illus.). 198p. 1979. pap. 31.00 (*0-85066-193-5*) Taylor & Francis.

***Clare, Janet.** Art Made Tongue-tied by Authority: Elizabethan & Jacobean Dramatic Censorship. 2nd ed. 1999. pap. text 24.95 (*0-7190-5695-0*, Pub. by Manchester Univ Pr) St Martin.

Clare, Jini. Naperville: Reflections of Community. (Illus.). 150p. 1997. 34.95 (*1-890291-03-X*) Platinum Pubng.

***Clare, Jini L. & Clare, Kelli M.** Naperville Area Handbook & Guide: An Introduction to the Community. 82p. 1999. pap. 9.95 (*0-9676084-0-6*) Clare Commns.

Clare, Johanne. John Clare & the Bounds of Circumstance. 240p. 1987. 65.00 (*0-7735-0606-3*, Pub. by McG-Queens Univ Pr) CUP Services.

Clare, John. By Himself. LC 97-102496. 364p. 1997. pap. 18.95 (*1-85754-288-6*, Pub. by Carcanet Pr) Paul & Co Pubs.

***Clare, John.** A Champion for the Poor: Political Verse & Prose. 220p. 2000. pap. 24.95 (*1-85754-423-4*, Pub. by Carcanet Pr) Paul & Co Pubs.

Clare, John. Classical Rome. LC 92-30502. (Illus.). 64p. 1996. pap. 9.00 (*0-15-201321-0*) Harcourt.

— The Early Poems of John Clare, 1804-1822, Vol. I. Robinson, Eric et al, eds. (Oxford English Texts Ser.). 634p. 1989. text 180.00 (*0-19-812314-0*) OUP.

— John Clare: Poems of the Middle Period: 1822-1837, Vols. III & IV. Robinson, Eric et al, eds. (Oxford English Texts Ser.). 1336p. 1998. 300.00 (*0-19-818298-8*) OUP.

Clare, John. The Later Poems of John Clare, 1837-1864, Set, Vols. I & II. Robinson, Eric et al, eds. (Oxford English Texts Ser.). (Illus.). 1984. 225.00 (*0-19-811874-0*) OUP.

Clare, John. The Letters of John Clare. Storey, Mark, ed. 748p. 1986. text 79.00 (*0-19-812669-7*) OUP.

— The Natural History Prose Writings of John Clare. Grainger, Margaret, ed. (Illus.). 460p. 1984. text 100.00 (*0-19-818517-0*) OUP.

— Poems of the Middle Period, 1822-1837, Vol. I. Powell, David et al, eds. (Oxford English Texts Ser.). 406p. 1996. text 110.00 (*0-19-812340-X*) OUP.

— Poems of the Middle Period, 1822-1837, Vol. II. Robinson, Eric et al, eds. (English Texts Ser.). 416p. 1996. text 105.00 (*0-19-812387-6*) OUP.

— Selected Letters. Storey, Mark, ed. (Illus.). 284p. 1988. text 55.00 (*0-19-818585-5*) OUP.

— The Shepherd's Calendar. 2nd ed. Robinson, Eric et al, eds. LC 92-44091. (Illus.). 1993. 10.00 (*0-19-283154-2*) OUP.

— The Shepherd's Calendar, 1827. LC 91-30167. (Revolution & Romanticism Ser.). 258p. 1991. reprint ed. 48.00 (*1-85477-062-4*) Continuum.

Clare, John, ed. Poems Descriptive of Rural Life & Scenery. 176p. 1986. 45.00 (*0-948697-01-6*, Pub. by Lark Pubns) St Mut.

Clare, John & Brennan, Gail. Bodgie Dada & the Cult of Cool: Jazz in Australia since the 1940s. 1995. 39.95 (*0-86840-103-X*, Pub. by New South Wales Univ Pr) Intl Spec Bk.

Clare, John D. Fourteenth-Century Towns. LC 92-13760. (Illus.). 64p. 1996. pap. 9.00 (*0-15-201320-2*) Harcourt.

— Growing up in the People's Century: Children's Eyewitness Accounts of the 20th Century. LC 98-70039. 144p. (YA). 1998. 23.95 (*0-563-40410-8*, BBC-Parkwest) Parkwest Pubns.

— Knights in Armor. LC 91-2766. (Illus.). 64p. (J). (gr. 2-7). 1996. pap. 10.00 (*0-15-201308-3*, Gulliver Bks) Harcourt.

— The Vikings. LC 91-24146. (Illus.). 64p. (J). (gr. 2-7). 1996. pap. 9.00 (*0-15-201309-1*, Gulliver Bks) Harcourt.

Clare, John D., ed. Ancient Greece. LC 93-6267. (Living History Ser.). (Illus.). 64p. (J). (gr. 2-7). 1994. 16.95 (*0-15-200516-1*, Gulliver Bks) Harcourt.

— Classical Rome. LC 92-30502. (Living History Ser.). (Illus.). 64p. (J). (gr. 2-7). 1993. 16.95 (*0-15-200513-7*, Gulliver Bks) Harcourt.

— The First World War. LC 94-7875. (Living History Ser.). (Illus.). 64p. (J). (gr. 3-7). 1995. 16.95 (*0-15-200087-9*, Gulliver Bks) Harcourt.

— Fourteenth-Century Towns. LC 92-13760. (Living History Ser.). (Illus.). 64p. (J). (gr. 4-7). 1993. 16.95 (*0-15-200515-3*, Gulliver Bks) Harcourt.

***Clare, John D., ed.** Fourteenth-Century Towns. (Illus.). 64p. (J). (gr. 5-7). 1999. reprint ed. text 17.00 (*0-7881-6657-3*) DIANE Pub.

Clare, John D., ed. Italian Renaissance. LC 94-26637. (Living History Ser.). (Illus.). 64p. (J). (gr. 4-7). 1995. 16.95 (*0-15-200088-7*, Gulliver Bks) Harcourt.

— Knights in Armor. LC 91-2766. (Living History Ser.). (Illus.). 64p. (J). (gr. 4-7). 1992. 17.00 (*0-15-200508-0*, Gulliver Bks) Harcourt.

— Pyramids of Ancient Egypt. abr. ed. LC 91-11735. (Living History Ser.). (Illus.). 64p. (J). (gr. 2-7). 1992. 16.95 (*0-15-200509-9*, Gulliver Bks) Harcourt.

— Vikings. LC 91-24146. (Living History Ser.). (Illus.). 64p. (J). (gr. 2-7). 1992. 16.95 (*0-15-200512-9*, Gulliver Bks) Harcourt.

— Voyages of Christopher Columbus. LC 91-75998. (Living History Ser.). (Illus.). 64p. (J). (gr. 2-7). 1992. 16.95 (*0-15-200507-2*, Gulliver Bks) Harcourt.

Clare, Josephine. Deutschland & Other Places. 52p. (Orig.). 1974. pap. 3.00 (*0-913028-22-3*) North Atlantic.

— Mammatocumulus. LC 76-58627. (Poetry Ser.). 1977. pap. 4.50 (*0-685-75802-8*) Ocotillo.

Clare, Kelli M., jt. auth. see Clare, Jini L.

Clare, Liam. Victorian Bray: A Town Adapts to Changing Times. LC 99-220301. (Maynooth Studies in Local History). 88p. 1998. pap. 9.95 (*0-7165-2700-6*) Intl Spec Bk.

Clare, Lilian A., tr. see Levy-Bruhl, Lucien.

***Clare, Mark K.** 2000 Practical Guide to Knowledge Assets. 500p. 2000. pap. 119.00 (*0-15-607000-6*) Harcourt.

Clare, Mary. Encountering the Depths: Prayers, Solitude, & Contemplation. rev. ed. LC 95-39. 112p. 1995. pap. 8.95 (*0-8192-1639-9*) Morehouse Pub.

Clare, Maryanne. The Splintered Soul: Shamanic Journeys to Heal the Inner Darkness. LC 97-212645. 208p. 1997. pap. 12.95 (*1-57174-070-8*) Hampton Roads Pub Co.

***Clare, Mason.** Spiritual Years: Personal & Spiritual Numerology. LC 99-91660. 2000. 25.00 (*0-7388-1166-1*); pap. 18.00 (*0-7388-1167-X*) Xlibris Corp.

Clare, Norman. Billiards & Snooker Bygones. (Handbook Ser.: No. 201). (Illus.). 32p. 1999. pap. 4.75 (*0-85263-730-6*, Pub. by Shire Pubns) Parkwest Pubns.

Clare, Patricia. The Struggle for the Great Barrier Reef. LC 77-159515. 223 p. 1971. write for info. (*0-8027-0352-6*) Walker & Co.

Clare, Paul K. Racketeering in Northern Ireland: A New Version of the Patriot Game. 55p. (C). 1989. pap. text 4.95 (*0-942511-19-0*) OICJ.

Clare, Philippa, jt. auth. see Potter, Shelia.

Clare, R., ed. Tidal Power: Trends & Developments: Proceedings of the 4th Conference on Tidal Power, Organized by the Institution of Civil Engineers, London, March 19-20, 1992. 332p. 1992. 10.00 (*0-7277-1905-X*) Am Soc Civil Eng.

Clare, Samantha. Heron's Keep. large type ed. 288p. 1985. 27.99 (*0-7089-1251-6*) Ulverscroft.

Clare, Sylvia. Raising the Successful Child: How to Encourage Your Child on the Road to Emotional & Learning Competence. 144p. 2000. pap. 14.95 (*1-85703-353-1*, Pub. by How To Bks) Midpt Trade.

***Clare, Sylvia.** Releasing Your Child's Potential: Empower Your Child to Set & Reach Their Own Goals. (Pathways Ser.). (Illus.). 208p. 2000. pap. 24.50 (*1-85703-571-2*, Pub. by How To Bks) Midpt Trade.

***Clare, Sylvia & Hughes, David.** Living the Life You Want: Your Personal Key to True Abundance & the Richness of Everyday Experience. 208p. 2000. pap. 15.95 (*1-85703-595-X*, Pub. by How To Bks) Midpt Trade.

Clarebrough, L. M. & Forwood, C. T. Electron Microscopy of Interfaces in Metals & Alloys. (Microscopy in Materials Science Ser.). (Illus.). 436p. 1991. 210.00 (*0-7503-0116-3*) IOP Pub.

Clarement, Chris. X-Men, Enter the Phoenix, No. 2. Vol. 2. 1996. mass mkt. 3.99 (*0-8125-4325-4*, Pub. by Tor Bks) St Martin.

Claremon, Neil. Zen in Motion: Lessons from a Master Archer on Breath, Posture, & the Path of Intuition. (Illus.). 144p. (Orig.). 1992. pap. 10.95 (*0-89281-361-X*) Inner Tradit.

Claremont. WildC.A.T.S. A Gathering of Eagles. 112p. pap. 9.95 (*1-56389-585-4*) DC Comics.

Claremont, Chris. The Black Dragon. unabridged ed. (Illus.). 184p. (Orig.). (YA). (gr. 7 up). 1996. pap. 17.95 (*1-56971-042-2*) Dark Horse Comics.

— Essential Wolverine. (Illus.). 528p. 1997. pap. text 12.99 (*0-7851-0257-4*) Marvel Entrprs.

— Essential Wolverine, Vol. 1. (Illus.). 528p. 1998. pap. text 12.95 (*0-7851-0595-6*) Marvel Entrprs.

— Essential X-Men, Vol. III. (Essential Ser.). (Illus.). 528p. 1998. pap. 12.95 (*0-7851-0661-8*) Marvel Entrprs.

— Essential X-Men II. (Illus.). 528p. 1997. pap. text 14.95 (*0-7851-0298-1*) Marvel Entrprs.

— First Flight. 256p. (Orig.). 1987. mass mkt. 5.99 (*0-441-23584-0*) Ace Bks.

— Grounded! 1991. mass mkt. 5.99 (*0-441-30416-8*) Ace Bks.

— Shadow Moon. 464p. 1995. pap. 12.99 (*0-593-03926-2*) Bantam.

***Claremont, Chris.** Shadow Star. 35p. 2000. mass mkt. 6.50 (*0-553-57288-1*) Bantam.

Claremont, Chris. Sovereign Seven. Kahan, Bob & Turner, Dwayne, eds. LC 97-141359. (Illus.). 208p. 1996. pap. 12.95 (*1-56389-269-3*, Pub. by DC Comics) Time Warner.

— Sundowner. 352p. (Orig.). 1994. pap. text 5.50 (*0-441-00070-3*) Ace Bks.

— X-Men: Crossroads. (Finest Ser.). (Illus.). 128p. 1998. pap. 15.95 (*0-7851-0662-6*) Marvel Entrprs.

— X-Men: God Loves, Man Kills Bookshelf Edition. (X-Men Ser.). (Illus.). 64p. 1994. pap. 6.95 (*0-7851-0039-3*) Marvel Entrprs.

— X-Men: Inferno. (Illus.). 208p. 1996. pap. text 19.95 (*0-7851-0222-1*) Marvel Entrprs.

— X-Men: Mutations. (Illus.). 176p. 1996. pap. text 19.95 (*0-7851-0197-7*) Marvel Entrprs.

— X-Men Visionaries: Chris Claremont, Vol. 1. (Illus.). 240p. 1998. pap. text 24.95 (*0-7851-0598-0*) Marvel Entrprs.

Claremont, Chris, text. Shadow Star. LC 99-33250. Vol. 3. 304p. 1999. 24.95 (*0-553-09598-6*) Bantam.

Claremont, Chris & Lucas, George. Shadow Moon. 464p. 1996. mass mkt. 5.99 (*0-553-57285-7*) Bantam.

Claremont, Chris & Simonson, Louise. X-Men: X-Tinction Agenda. (Illus.). 224p. 1992. pap. 24.95 (*0-87135-922-7*) Marvel Entrprs.

Claremont, Chris & Thomas, Roy. Greatest Battles of The X-Men. (Illus.). 176p. 1994. pap. 15.95 (*0-7851-0042-3*) Marvel Entrprs.

Claremont, Chris, et al. The All-New, All-Different X-Men: Masterworks, Vol. 1. (Illus.). 122p. 1993. 12.95 (*0-87135-988-X*) Marvel Entrprs.

— Wolverine. (Spiderman Ser.). (Illus.). 96p. 1987. pap. 12.95 (*0-87135-277-X*) Marvel Entrprs.

— X-Men. (Marvel Masterworks Ser.: Vol. 12). 183p. 1990. 34.95 (*0-87135-628-7*) Marvel Entrprs.

— X-Men: Days of Future Past. (Illus.). 48p. 1989. 15.95 (*0-87135-582-5*) Marvel Entrprs.

— X-Men: The Dark Phoenix Saga. (Spiderman Ser.). (Illus.). 192p. 1984. pap. 15.95 (*0-939766-96-5*) Marvel Entrprs.

Claremont, Chris, jt. auth. see Conway, Gerry.

Claremont, Chris, jt. auth. see Lucas, George.

Claremont de Castillejo, Irene. Knowing Woman: A Feminine Psychology. LC 72-80470. 1973. 12.00 (*0-913430-01-3*) C G Jung Foun.

Claremont Graduate School, Symposium on Applied So. Interpersonal Processes: The Claremont Symposium on Applied Social Psychology. Oskamp, Stuart & Spacapan, Shirlynn, eds. LC 87-16435. 232p. reprint ed. pap. 72.00 (*0-7837-4574-5*, 204410300003) Bks Demand.

Claremont, Lewis De, see De Claremont, Lewis.

Claremont McKenna College Staff, jt. auth. see Haley, P. Edward.

Claremont Symposium on Applied Social Psychology S. The Social Psychology of Health. Spacapan, Shirlynn & Oskamp, Stuart, eds. LC 87-35339. 251p. reprint ed. pap. 77.90 (*0-7837-6718-8*, 204634500011) Bks Demand.

Claremount, Chris. X-Men: Mutant Massacre. (Illus.). 256p. 1996. pap. text 24.95 (*0-7851-0224-8*) Marvel Entrprs.

Clarenbach, Kathryn F. & Kamarck, Edward L., eds. The Green Stubborn Bud: Women's Culture at Century's Close. LC 86-31649. 406p. 1987. 34.50 (*0-8108-1981-3*) Scarecrow.

Clarenburg, Rudolf. Physiological Chemistry of Domestic Animals. (Illus.). 448p. (gr. 13). 1992. pap. text 56.00 (*0-8016-6953-7*, 06953) Mosby Inc.

Clarence Lee Design & Associates Staff, tr. & photos by see Martin, Lynn J., ed.

Clarence, Margaret. A Glimpse of China. (C). 1990. 60.00 (*0-947333-18-5*, Pub. by Pascoe Pub) St Mut.

Clarence-Smith, W. G., ed. Cocoa Pioneer Fronts since 1800: The Role of Smallholders, Planters & Merchants. 240p. 1996. text 69.95 (*0-312-15847-5*) St Martin.

Clarence-Smith, Wilhelm G. Economics of the Indian Ocean Slave Trade in the Nineteenth Century. 1989. lib. bdg. 39.50 (*0-7146-3359-3*, F3359, Pub. by F Cass Pubs) Intl Spec Bk.

— Slaves, Peasants, & Capitalists in Southern Angola, 1840-1926. LC 78-67805. (African Studies: No. 27). 142p. reprint ed. pap. 40.50 (*0-608-15706-6*, 2031633) Bks Demand.

Clarence-Smith, William G., jt. auth. see Freitag, Ulrike.

Clarence, V., ed. China in World Affairs. (Illus.). 245p. (C). 1996. lib. bdg. 85.00 (*1-56072-359-9*) Nova Sci Pubs.

Clarendon, Colin & Strock, Sylvia. Clarendon Guide to Kansas City Restaurants. (Illus.). 195p. (Orig.). pap. 7.50 (*0-9609028-0-5*) C&S Ent.

Clarens, Carlos. Crime Movies. LC 96-47922. (Illus.). 373p. 1997. pap. 15.95 (*0-306-80768-8*) Da Capo.

— An Illustrated History of Horror & Science Fiction Films: The Classic Era, 1895-1967. LC 97-19406. Orig. Title: An Illustrated History of the Horror Film. (Illus.). 328p. 1997. reprint ed. pap. 14.95 (*0-306-80800-5*) Da Capo.

Clarensau, Michael H. Journey to Integrity. 128p. 1997. pap., teacher ed. 9.95 (*0-88243-220-6*) Gospel Pub.

— Journey to Integrity: Developing Christian Character. (Spiritual Discovery Ser.). 112p. 1997. pap., student ed. 4.95 (*0-88243-120-X*, 02-0120) Gospel Pub.

— The Sanctity of Life. (Spiritual Discovery Ser.). (Illus.). 112p. 1996. pap., student ed. 4.95 (*0-88243-110-2*, 02-0110) Gospel Pub.

— The Sanctity of Life. (Spiritual Discovery Ser.). (Illus.). 128p. 1996. pap., teacher ed. 9.95 (*0-88243-210-9*, 02-0210) Gospel Pub.

— Your New Life in Christ: A Twelve-Week Self-Study on Basic Bible Doctrines. LC 90-83497. 112p. 1991. pap., student ed. 6.95 (*0-88243-766-6*, 02-0766) Gospel Pub.

Clarensau, Michael H., et al. We Build People: Making Disciples for the 21st Century. 144p. 1996. pap. 4.95 (*0-88243-698-8*, 02-0698) Gospel Pub.

Clareson, Thomas, ed. Voices for the Future: Essays on Major Science Fiction Writers, Vol. 2. LC 78-61202. 1979. 14.95 (*0-87972-135-9*); pap. 8.95 (*0-87972-136-7*) Bowling Green Univ Popular Press.

Clareson, Thomas & Wymer, Thomas, eds. Voices for the Future: Essays on Major Science Fiction Writers, Vol. 3. LC 76-10939. 1983. 20.95 (*0-87972-251-7*); pap. 9.95 (*0-87972-252-5*) Bowling Green Univ Popular Press.

Clareson, Thomas D. Frederik Pohl. Schlobin, Roger C., ed. LC 86-14587. (Starmont Reader's Guide Ser.: Vol. 39). x, 173p. 1987. pap. 21.00 (*0-930261-33-X*) Millefleurs.

— Robert Silverberg. Schlobin, Roger C., ed. LC 83-542. (Starmont Reader's Guide Ser.: Vol. 18). 96p. 1983. pap. 17.00 (*0-916732-47-9*) Millefleurs.

— Science Fiction Criticism: An Annotated Checklist. LC 71-181084. (Serif Series: Bibliographies & Checklists: No. 23). 239p. reprint ed. pap. 74.10 (*0-7837-0568-9*, 204091200019) Bks Demand.

— Some Kind of Paradise: The Emergence of American Science Fiction, 16. LC 84-29060. (Contributions to the Study of Science Fiction & Fantasy Ser.: No. 16). 248p. 1985. 59.95 (*0-313-23167-2*, CSK/, Greenwood Pr) Greenwood.

— Understanding Contemporary American Science Fiction: The Formative Period, 1926-1970. Bruccoli, Matthew J., ed. LC 89-49088. (Understanding Contemporary American Literature Ser.). 307p. 1992. pap. 12.95 (*0-87249-870-0*) U of SC Pr.

Clareson, Thomas D., compiled by. Science Fiction in America, 1870s-1930s: An Annotated Bibliography of Primary Sources, 1. LC 84-8934. (Bibliographies & Indexes in American Literature Ser.: No. 1). 305p. 1984. lib. bdg. 69.50 (*0-313-23169-9*, CSF/) Greenwood.

Clareson, Thomas D., ed. Many Futures, Many Worlds: Theme & Form in Science Fiction. LC 76-42448. 313p. reprint ed. pap. 97.10 (*0-7837-1357-6*, 204150500020) Bks Demand.

— SF: the Other Side of Realism. 370p. 1971. 15.95 (*0-87972-022-0*); pap. 9.95 (*0-87972-023-9*) Bowling Green Univ Popular Press.

— Voices for the Future: Essays on Major Science Fiction Writers, Vol. 1. 1976. pap. 8.95 (*0-87972-120-0*) Bowling Green Univ Popular Press.

Claret, Anthony M. The Autobiography of St. Anthony Mary Claret. LC 85-51661. (Illus.). 227p. 1989. pap. 13.00 (*0-89555-284-1*) TAN Bks Pubs.

Claret de la Touche, Margaret Louise Margaret. The Love & Service of God, Infinite Love. O'Connell, Patrick, tr. from FRE. LC 86-51580. 230p. 1994. reprint ed. pap. 12.50 (*0-89555-310-4*) TAN Bks Pubs.

Claret, Maria. The Chocolate Rabbit. LC 84-24610. (Illus.). 28p. (J). (ps-3). 1985. 7.95 (*0-8120-5624-8*); pap. 5.95 (*0-8120-4926-8*) Barron.

— The Chocolate Rabbit. 1992. 11.15 (*0-606-01619-8*, Pub. by Turtleback) Demco.

Claretie, Jules. The Crime of the Boulevard. Kingsbury, Carlton A., tr. LC 75-32739. (Literature of Mystery & Detection Ser.). 1976. reprint ed. 21.95 (*0-405-07867-6*) Ayer.

Clareus, Ingrid, ed. Scandinavian Women Writers: An Anthology from the 1880s to the 1980s, 95. LC 89-2147. (Contributions in Women's Studies: No. 95). 246p. 1989. 57.95 (*0-313-25884-8*, CSV/, Greenwood Pr) Greenwood.

***Clarey, Alison.** Discreet Madness. LC 99-91949. 2000. 25.00 (*0-7388-1436-9*); pap. 18.00 (*0-7388-1437-7*) Xlibris Corp.

***Clarey, Christopher.** Davis Cup: A Year in Tennis; The International Tennis Federation. 2000. 35.00 (*0-7893-0384-1*, Pub. by Universe) St Martin.

C

An Asterisk (*) at the beginning of an entry indicates that the title is appearing for the first time.

Clarey, Christopher. The Davis Cup Yearbook 1996. 128p. 1999. 35.00 (0-7893-0253-5, Pub. by Universe) St Martin.

— Davis Cup Yearbook 1997. 128p. 1998. 35.00 (0-7893-0125-3, Pub. by Universe) St Martin.

Clarey, JoEllen, jt. ed. see Lohafer, Susan.

Clarey, M. Elizabeth & Dixson, Robert J. Pronunciation Exercises in English. rev. ed. 144p. 1987. pap. text 18.07 (0-13-730854-X) P-H.

Clarey, Tim, jt. illus. see Hull, Robert.

Clarfield, Gerard H. Security with Solvency: Dwight D. Eisenhower & the Shaping of the American Military Establishment. LC 98-50241. 288p. 1999. 59.95 (0-275-96445-0) Greenwood.

— Timothy Pickering & the American Republic. LC 79-24326. 328p. 1980. reprint ed. pap. 101.70 (0-608-00901-6, 206169500010) Bks Demand.

— United States Diplomatic History Vol. 1: From Revolution to Empire to 1914. 368p. (C). 1991. pap. text 26.80 (0-13-029190-0) P-H.

— United States Diplomatic History Vol. 2: The Age of Ascendancy since 1900, Vol. 2. 512p. (C). 1991. pap. text 33.00 (0-13-029232-X) P-H.

Clarfield, Ingrid J. Beethoven/Moonlight Sonata. (Artistic Preparation & Performance Ser.). Date not set. pap. write for info. (0-7390-0805-6, 16745) Alfred Pub.

Clarfield, Ingrid J. & Guy, Suzanne. From Mystery to Mystery, Bk. 2. 96p. 1996. pap. 12.95 (0-7390-0784-X, 14710) Alfred Pub.

Clarholm, M. & Bergstrom, L., eds. Ecology of Arable Land-Perspectives & Challenges. (C). 1989. text 239.50 (0-7923-0424-1) Kluwer Academic.

Clari, M., jt. auth. see Love, C. E.

Clari, Robert De, see De Clari, Robert.

Clarida, Vincent, jt. auth. see Atwell, Cheryl.

Claridge, Amanda. Rome: An Oxford Archaeological Guide. (Oxford Archaeological Guides Ser.). (Illus.). 480p. 1998. pap. 19.95 (0-19-288003-9) OUP.

Claridge, Amanda & Gallina-Zevi, Anna, eds. Roman Ostia Revisited. (Illus.). 1996. 63.00 (0-904152-29-4, Pub. by British Schl Rome) David Brown.

Claridge, Amanda, jt. auth. see Osborne, John.

Claridge, David E. & Pacheco, James E., eds. Solar Engineering: Proceedings, International Solar Energy Conference, 1997: Washington, D. C. LC 96-83948. 450p. 1997. pap. 140.00 (0-7918-1555-2) ASME Pr.

Claridge, Edward. Animal Signatures: How to Recognize & Interpret Animal Signs. (Illus.). 80p. 1993. pap. 6.95 (1-55109-048-1) Nimbus Publ.

Claridge, G. Cyril. Wild Bush Tribes of Tropical Africa. LC 74-90111. (Illus.). 314p. 1969. reprint ed. lib. bdg. 59.50 (0-8371-2029-2, CLB&, Greenwood Pr) Greenwood.

Claridge, Gordon. Origins of Mental Illness: Temperament, Deviance & Disorder. 2nd ed. 293p. 1995. pap. 15.00 (1-883536-01-4, Malor Bks) ISHK.

Claridge, Gordon, ed. Schizotypy: Implications for Illness & Health. LC 96-45523. (Illus.). 354p. 1997. text 115.00 (0-19-852353-X) OUP.

Claridge, Gordon, et al. Sounds from the Bell Jar: Ten Psychotic Authors. 2nd ed. LC 98-23264. 276p. 1998. reprint ed. pap. 15.00 (1-883536-15-4, Malor Bks) ISHK.

Claridge, Gordon S., et al. Personality Differences & Biological Variations: A Study of Twins. LC 72-10132. (C). 1973. 84.00 (0-08-017124-9, Pub. by Pergamon Repr) Franklin.

Claridge, Henry, ed. F. Scott Fitzgerald: Critical Assessments, 4 vols., Set. (Critical Assessments of Writers in English Ser.). (Illus.). 2040p. (C). (gr. 13 up). 1992. text, boxed set 535.00 (1-873403-02-X) Routledge.

Claridge, Laura. Romantic Potency: The Paradox of Desire. LC 91-55556. 288p. 1992. 45.00 (0-8014-2696-0); pap. text 16.95 (0-8014-8016-7) Cornell U Pr.

— Tamara de Lempicka: A Life of Deco & Decadence. LC 99-19700. 448p. 1999. 35.00 (0-517-70557-5) Crown Pub Group.

Claridge, Laura & Langland, Elizabeth, eds. Out of Bounds: Male Writers & Gender(ed) Criticism. LC 90-35674. 360p. 1990. 42.50 (0-87023-734-9); pap. 19.95 (0-87023-735-7) U of Mass Pr.

Claridge, Laura, et al. Don Juan. Wood, Nigel, ed. LC 92-32424. (Theory in Practice Ser.). 176p. 1993. pap. 29.95 (0-335-09625-5) OpUniv Pr.

Claridge, M. Geography Quizbook. (Quizbooks Ser.). (Illus.). 32p. (J). (gr. 4 up). 1993. pap. 7.95 (0-7460-0710-8, Usborne) EDC.

— Geography Quizbook. (Quizbooks Ser.). (Illus.). 32p. (J). (gr. 4 up). 1999. lib. bdg. 15.95 (0-88110-535-X, Usborne) EDC.

— History Quizbook. (Quizbooks Ser.). (Illus.). 32p. (J). (gr. 4-7). 1992. pap. 7.95 (0-7460-0641-1, Usborne) EDC.

— History Quizbook. (Quizbooks Ser.). (Illus.). 32p. (J). (gr. 4 up). 1999. lib. bdg. 15.95 (0-88110-534-1, Usborne) EDC.

— How to Draw Buildings. (Young Artist Ser.). (Illus.). 32p. (J). (gr. 4 up). 1992. pap. 4.95 (0-7460-0747-7, Usborne); lib. bdg. 12.95 (0-88110-539-2, Usborne) EDC.

— How to Draw Dinosaurs. (Young Artist Ser.). (Illus.). 32p. (J). (gr. 4 up). 1991. lib. bdg. 12.95 (0-88110-502-3, Usborne) EDC.

— How to Draw Dinosaurs. (Young Artist Ser.). (Illus.). 32p. (J). (gr. 4-7). 1991. pap. 4.95 (0-7460-0673-X, Usborne) EDC.

Claridge, M. & Dowswell, P. Animal Quizbook. (Quizbooks Ser.). (Illus.). 32p. (J). (gr. 4-7). 1993. lib. bdg. 15.95 (0-88110-536-8, Usborne) EDC.

— Animal Quizbook. (Quizbooks Ser.). (Illus.). 32p. (J). (gr. 4-12). 1993. pap. 7.95 (0-7460-0720-5, Usborne) EDC.

Claridge, M., et al. Questions & Answers. (Quizbooks Ser.). (Illus.). 128p. (J). (gr. 4-7). 1994. pap. 12.95 (0-7460-1359-0, Usborne) EDC.

Claridge, M., jt. auth. see Dowswell, P.

Claridge, M. F., et al, eds. Species: The Units of Biodiversity. LC 96-70872. (Systematics Association Ser.). (Illus.). 456p. (C). 1997. write for info. (0-412-63120-2) Kluwer Academic.

Claridge, M. F., jt. auth. see Wilson, M. R.

Claridge, Marten. Nobody's Fool. 312p. 1991. 19.95 (0-8027-5793-6) Walker & Co.

Claridge, Mary. Margaret Clitherow, 1556-1586. LC 66-19228. 208p. reprint ed. pap. 64.50 (0-7837-5595-3, 204550100005) Bks Demand.

Claridge, R. F. & Dohrmann, J. Molecules & Radicals Vol. 18, Group II: Radical Reaction Rates in Liquids. Martienssen, W. & Fischer, H., eds. xvi, 478p. 1997. 1931.00 (3-540-57262-7) Spr-Verlag.

Claridge, Steve & Ridley, Ian. Tales from the Boot Camps. (Illus.). 240p. 1998. pap. 15.95 (0-575-60185-X, Pub. by Vista) Trafalgar.

Claridge, Timothy D., jt. auth. see Harwood, L. M.

***Claridge, Timothy D. W.** High-resolution NMR Techniques in Organic Chemistry. LC 99-57319. (Tetrahedron Organic Chemistry Ser.). 384p. 1999. 134.50 (0-08-042799-5, Pergamon Pr); 49.50 (0-08-042798-7, Pergamon Pr) Elsevier.

Clarie, Thomas C. Occult Bibliography: An Annotated List of Books Published in English, 1971 Through 1975. LC 78-17156. 482p. 1978. 37.00 (0-8108-1152-9) Scarecrow.

— Occult-Paranormal Bibliography: An Annotated List of Books Published in English, 1976-1981. LC 83-20319. 579p. 1984. 45.00 (0-8108-1674-1) Scarecrow.

Clarin, Leo. '60's Children. Pearson, Anita & Knox, W. B., eds. (Illus.). 300p. (Orig.). 1996. pap. 12.95 (1-881116-68-9) Black Forest Pr.

***Clarin, Leopoldo A.** Cuentos. 1999. 13.00 (84-481-0951-1, McGrw-H College) McGrw-H Hghr Educ.

Clarin, Leopoldo A. Cuentos Morales. (SPA.). pap. 9.95 (84-206-1457-2, Pub. by Alianza Editorial) Continental Bk.

— El Senor y lo Demas, Son Cuentos. (Nueva Austral Ser.: Vol. 43). (SPA.). 1991. pap. text 24.95 (84-239-1843-2) Elliots Bks.

— Su Unico Hijo. Richmond, Carolyn, ed. (Nueva Austral Ser.: Vol. 104). (SPA.). 1991. pap. text 24.95 (84-239-1904-8) Elliots Bks.

***Clarin, Leopoldo Alas.** Ten Tales. Fedorchek, Robert M., tr. from SPA. LC 99-36769. 208p. 2000. 38.50 (0-8387-5436-8) Bucknell U Pr.

Claringbloud, M. H., ed. International Transport Treaties. 1983. ring bd. 255.00 (90-6544-903-5, 90P1312003) Kluwer Law Intl.

Claringbould, M. & Sandee, H., eds. International Transport Treaties. 1985. 228.00 (0-685-16609-0) Kluwer Academic.

Claringbould, Michael J. & Hickey, Lawrence J. Rampage of the Roarin' Twenties: The Illustrated History of the 312th Bombardment Group During WWII. LC 89-84159. (Eagles over the Pacific Ser.: Vol. 4). (Illus.). 352p. 1997. 70.00 (0-913511-03-X) Intl Res & Pub.

Clariodus. Clariodus: A Metrical Romance. Irving, David, ed. LC 72-1035. (Maitland Club, Glasgow. Publications: No. 9). reprint ed. 49.50 (0-404-52937-2) AMS Pr.

Claris & Coleman. Macwrite Guidebook. 1992. pap. 38.40 incl. cd-rom (0-673-46723-6) Addson-Wesley Educ.

ClarisWorks Users Group Staff. The Complete Guide to ClarisWorks, Vol. 1. (Illus.). 445p. (Orig.). (C). 1995. pap. 39.95 (0-9620807-6-4) Natl AppleWrks.

Clarizio, Harvey F. Assessment & Treatment of Depression in Children & Adolescents. 2nd ed. LC 89-90917. 250p. 1994. pap. 31.95 (0-88422-103-2) Clinical Psych.

— Assessment & Treatment of Depression in Children & Adolescents. 2nd ed. 258p. 1996. pap. 75.00 (0-471-16193-4) Wiley.

Clarizio, Harvey F., et al. Contemporary Issues in Educational Psychology. 6th ed. LC 93-37335. 384p. (C). 1993. 52.19 (0-07-011132-4) McGraw.

Clarizio, Tony V., jt. auth. see Rubin, Stephen M.

Clark. Abnormal Psychology, Vol. 1. 3rd ed. 1997. pap. 24.00 (0-7167-3131-2) St Martin.

— Animals & Their Moral Standing. LC 96-39502. 208p. (C). 1997. 70.00 (0-415-13559-1) Routledge.

— Argument Rhetoric. (C). 1997. pap. text, teacher ed. 28.00 (0-15-503531-2) Harcourt Coll Pubs.

— Atlas of Neonatology. LC 99-11887. (C). 1999. text. write for info. (0-7216-7636-7, W B Saunders Co) Harcrt Hlth Sci Grp.

— Best of the Delineator. 1976. 30.95 (0-8488-1532-7) Amereon Ltd.

***Clark.** Cases & Materials on Gratuitous Transfers. 4th ed. LC 99-210294. (Paralegal Ser.). (C). 1999. pap. 47.25 (0-314-21112-8) West Pub.

Clark. Community Health Nursing Handbook. LC 98-37952. (Illus.). 256p. (C). 1998. pap. text 24.95 (0-8385-1070-1) Appleton & Lange.

— Discovering the Universe. 5th ed. 1999. pap. write for info. (0-7167-3578-4); text. write for info. (0-7167-3576-8) W H Freeman.

— Economics: The Science of Cost, Benefit. (HB - Economics Ser.). 1984. text 61.95 (0-538-08280-1) S-W Pub.

— Economics: The Science of Cost, Benefit. 3rd ed. (HB - Economics Ser.). 1992. mass mkt. 61.95 (0-538-61400-5) S-W Pub.

— Flights of Fancy. 1998. pap. 15.00 (0-226-10778-7) U Ch Pr.

— General Chemistry Pearls of Wisdom. (Pearls of Wisdom Ser.). 1999. pap. 18.00 (1-890369-22-5) Boston Medical.

— Getting & Keeping the Job: Success in Business & Technical Careers. LC 98-30268. 210p. (C). 1998. pap. text 17.95 (0-205-28920-7) Allyn.

— Handbook for Office Workers. 9th ed. (SWC-Business Communication Ser.). 2000. pap., wbk. ed. 12.00 (0-324-01360-4) Thomson Learn.

— Information Processing: Concepts, Principles. 3rd ed. (DC - Introduction to Computing Ser.). 1984. mass mkt. 48.95 (0-538-10540-2) S-W Pub.

Clark. International Finance. 1993. pap. write for info. (1-86152-382-3, Pub. by ITBP) Thomson Learn.

— International Trading. 1969. text 49.95 (0-471-85210-4) Wiley.

Clark. Law & Business. 4th ed. 1993. teacher ed. 57.81 (0-07-035165-1) McGraw.

— Managing Operations. (Illus.). 352p. 1997. text. write for info. (0-412-74990-4, Chap & Hall NY) Chapman & Hall.

— Managing the Florida Condominium 99-1. 394p. 1999. ring bd. write for info. (0-327-01167-X, 8089018) LEXIS Pub.

— Murder at the Howard Johnson's. 1980. pap. 4.00 (0-573-61202-1) French.

— The Negro Leagues Book. Lester, ed. 1994. 49.95 (0-910137-59-5) Soc Am Baseball Res.

— Negro Leagues Book Signed. Lester, ed. 1994. 150.00 (0-910137-60-9) Soc Am Baseball Res.

— Organizational Theory of Education. 2000. 55.00 (0-07-011161-8) McGraw.

— Organizational Theory of Education. 2001. 55.00 (0-07-011162-6) McGraw.

— Pediatric Emergencies. 2nd ed. 1997. pap., teacher ed. 46.00 (0-8359-5129-4) P-H.

— Perplexity & Knowledge. 1972. lib. bdg. 94.00 (90-247-1289-0, Pub. by M Nijhoff) Kluwer Academic.

— Printed Circuit Engineering. 1989. 44.00 (0-07-158621-0) McGraw.

— Product Development Challenge. 1995. 32.50 (0-07-103619-9) McGraw.

— Product Devlopment Performance. 350p. 1991. 39.95 (0-07-103291-6) McGraw.

Clark. Researchers Notebook. 1997. cd-rom 52.00 (0-673-46714-7) Longman.

Clark. Restructuring Corporate America. (C). 1996. pap. text, teacher ed. 36.75 (0-03-006304-3) Harcourt Coll Pubs.

***Clark.** Sciences in Enlightened Europe. LC 98-51992. 1999. pap. text 27.50 (0-226-10940-2) U Ch Pr.

Clark. Structured BASIC: Apple Version Textbook. 2nd ed. (DG - Computer Programming Ser.). 1988. text 45.95 (0-538-10812-6) S-W Pub.

— Supplement T/a State & Market. 1999. pap. 1.50 (0-07-234399-0) McGraw.

— Survey of Economics. LC 96-33129. (AB - Accounting Principles Ser.). (C). 1996. 67.95 (0-538-84677-1) S-W Pub.

— Theory of Inspiration. LC 96-29805. 1997. text 69.95 (0-7190-5064-2) St Martin.

— A Thousand & More Feature Story Ideas. rev. ed. 1994. 2.00 (0-318-19214-4) Quill & Scroll.

— Top down Programming Using Turbo Pascal. (De-Computer Science Ser.). 224p. 1997. pap. text 27.95 (0-340-66287-5, VNR) Wiley.

— Twin Block Funct Therapy. 1995. text 147.00 (0-7234-2120-X) Wolfe Pubng AZ.

— U. S. History to 1877 rev. ed. 1997. 5.74 (0-07-218822-7) McGraw.

Clark. VTI Introductory Algebra Instructor's Solution Manual. 1995. pap. text, teacher ed. 25.20 (0-201-88991-9) Addison-Wesley.

— VTI Introductory Algebra Student's Solution Manual. 1995. pap. text, student ed. 27.40 (0-201-88992-7) Addison-Wesley.

— VTI Prealgebra Instructor's Solution. 1995. pap. text, teacher ed. 17.60 (0-201-88979-X) Addison-Wesley.

Clark. Wound Care. 2000. text. write for info. (0-7216-7104-7) Harcrt Hlth Sci Grp.

— Writing about Diversity. (C). 1993. pap. text, teacher ed. 33.75 (0-15-500950-8) Harcourt Coll Pubs.

Clark, ed. Central & Southern Appalachian Geomorphology Tennessee, Virginia, & West Virginia. (IGC Field Trip Guidebooks Ser.). 112p. 1989. 28.00 (0-87590-659-1, T150) Am Geophysical.

***Clark & Clark.** Cyberstyle! 2000. pap. 24.95 (0-324-07073-X) Sth-Wstrn College.

Clark & Clinton. Effective Speech Communication 1994: Teacher's Wraparound Edition. 3rd ed. 1999. teacher ed. 51.10 (0-02-659894-9) Glencoe.

Clark & Goss. Contemporary Piano Literature. 64p. 1953. pap. text 9.95 (0-87487-109-3) Summy-Birchard.

— Contemporary Piano Literature. 28p. 1955. pap. text 5.95 (0-87487-108-5) Summy-Birchard.

— Contemporary Piano Literature. 24p. 1961. pap. text 5.95 (0-87487-107-7) Summy-Birchard.

Clark & Goss, eds. I Remember Gurlitt, Bk. 1. 16p. 1984. pap. text 3.50 (0-913277-14-2) Summy-Birchard.

— I Remember Gurlitt, Bk. 2. 16p. 1984. pap. text 3.50 (0-913277-15-0) Summy-Birchard.

Clark & Hashimoto. Communications Workbook: Spelling. 119p. (C). 1984. pap. text 12.25 (0-89702-056-1, Irwn McGrw-H) McGrw-H Hghr Educ.

Clark & Hixson. My Acres of Diamonds Prosperity Workbook. 192p. 1985. pap. 14.50 (0-8187-0064-5) Harlo Press.

Clark & Neave, Guy. Encyclopedia of Higher Education, 4 vols., Set. 1992. 1250.00 (0-08-041027-8, Pergamon Pr) Elsevier.

***Clark & Scanlan.** Asne Best Newspaper Writing. 2000. pap. text. write for info. (0-312-25096-7) St Martin.

Clark, et al. Clinical Pharmacology in Dental Practice. 4th ed. (Illus.). 624p. (C). (gr. 13). 1987. pap. text 43.95 (0-8016-2260-3, 02260) Mosby Inc.

Clark, et al. Computers & Information Process: Concepts & Applications. 2nd ed. 1989. text 370.00 (0-538-60139-6) Thomson Learn.

Clark, et al. New Themes in Palliative Care. LC 97-12123. 306p. 1997. 105.00 (0-335-19606-3) OpUniv Pr.

Clark, et al. Organization & Identities. 1994. pap. write for info. (1-86152-529-X) Thomson Learn.

Clark, jt. auth. see Afifi, A. A.

Clark, jt. auth. see Ashworth.

Clark, jt. auth. see Ashworth, Clark.

Clark, jt. auth. see Baglan.

Clark, jt. auth. see Chenery.

Clark, jt. auth. see Clark.

Clark, jt. auth. see Hicks.

Clark, jt. auth. see Martin.

Clark, Barton B., jt. auth. see MacHarg, Marcia L.

Clark, Jeanne E. Ohio Blue Tips. LC 98-51955. (Akron Series in Poetry). 77p. 1999. 24.95 (1-884836-43-7); pap. 12.95 (1-884836-44-5) U Akron Pr.

Clark, A., et al, eds. Connectionism in Context. (Artificial Intelligence & Society Ser.). (Illus.). 192p. 1992. pap. 59.00 (0-685-54831-7) Spr-Verlag.

Clark, A., ed. see Godstow Nunnery Staff.

Clark, A. H. Ophiuroidea of the Hawaiian Islands. (BMB Ser.: No. 195). 1974. reprint ed. 25.00 (0-527-02303-5) Periodicals Srv.

Clark, A. J. General Pharmacology. LC 75-105699. (Handbook of Experimental Pharmacology Ser.: Vol. 4). (Illus.). 1970. reprint ed. 76.95 (0-387-04845-6) Spr-Verlag.

Clark, A. J., ed. Animal Breeding: Technology for the 21st Century. (Modern Genetics Ser.: Vol. 4). (Illus.). 268p. 1998. text 60.00 (90-5702-292-3, ECU63, Harwood Acad Pubs) Gordon & Breach.

Clark, A. J. L., jt. ed. see Hughes, I. A.

Clark, A. Kim. The Redemptive Work: Railway & Nation in Ecuador, 1895-1930. LC 97-14679. (Latin American Silhouettes Ser.). (Illus.). 236p. (C). 1998. 48.00 (0-8420-2674-6) Scholarly Res Inc.

Clark, A. L. Economics & Development Potential of Manganese Nodules Within the Cook Islands Exclusive Economic Zone (EEZ) LC 94-40814. 1995. write for info. (0-86638-167-8) EW Ctr HI.

Clark, A. McFadyen. Who Lived in This House? A Study of Koyukuk River Semisubterranean Houses. (Mercury Ser.: ASC No. 153). (Illus.). 282p. 1996. pap. 24.95 (0-660-15958-9, Pub. by CN Mus Civilization) U of Wash Pr.

Clark, A. McFadyen, jt. auth. see Clark, Donald W.

Clark, A. W. Clark Family Genealogy in the U. S., 1541-1907: Genealogical Record Showing Sources of the English Ancestors, Also Illustrations & Biographical Sketches, Etc. (Illus.). 149p. 1997. reprint ed. pap. 25.00 (0-8328-7940-1); reprint ed. lib. bdg. 35.00 (0-8328-7939-8) Higginson Bk Co.

***Clark, A. W.** Clarke Family Genealogy in the U. S., 1541-1907: Genealogical Record Showing Sources of the English Ancestors. fac. ed. (Illus.). 149p. 1999. reprint ed. 35.00 (0-8328-9956-9); reprint ed. pap. 25.00 (0-8328-9957-7) Higginson Bk Co.

Clark, Admont G. Lighthouses of Cape Cod, Nantucket, Martha's Vineyard: Their History & Lore. LC 91-68256. (Illus.). 258p. (Orig.). 1992. 29.95 (0-940160-54-4) Parnassus Imprints.

***Clark, Admont G.** Sea Stories of Cape Cod & the Islands. unabridged ed. LC 00-90746. (Illus.). 262p. 2000. 40.00 (0-936972-17-3) Lower Cape.

Clark, Admont G. They Built Clipper Ships in Their Back Yard. 1998. pap. 7.95 (0-940160-58-7) Parnassus Imprints.

Clark, Agnes. Dutchess County Days: A Memoir. (Illus.). 144p. (Orig.). 1996. pap. 10.00 (1-56474-170-2) Fithian Pr.

Clark, Ailsa M., jt. ed. see Yulin Liao.

Clark, Al. Raymond Chandler in Hollywood. (Illus.). 229p. (Orig.). 1996. pap. 19.95 (1-879505-29-0) Silman James Pr.

Clark, Alan. Barbarossa: The Russian-German Conflict, 1941-1945. LC 85-502. (Illus.). 528p. 1985. reprint ed. pap. 15.00 (0-688-04268-6, Quil) HarperTrade.

— Battles on the Eastern Front 1914-18: Suicide of the Empires. 1999. pap. text 21.95 (1-900624-23-0) Windrush Pr.

— Dictionary of British Comic Artists, Writers & Editors. (Illus.). 300p. 1997. 80.00 (0-7123-4521-3) U of Toronto Pr.

— The Donkeys. (Illus.). 216p. 1993. reprint ed. pap. 19.95 (0-7126-5035-0, Pub. by Pimlico) Trafalgar.

— The Fall of Crete. (Illus.). 224p. 1999. 29.95 (0-304-35226-8, Pub. by Cassell) Sterling.

— Mrs. Thatcher's Minister: The Private Diaries of Alan Clark. LC 94-6701. 1994. 30.00 (0-374-13917-2) FS&G.

***Clark, Alan.** Tories & the Nation State: The Conservative Party in Power, 1922-1997. (Illus.). 480p. 1998. 45.00 (0-297-81849-X, Pub. by Weidenfeld & Nicolson) Trafalgar.

Clark, Alan F., jt. ed. see Reed, Richard P.

Clark, Alan J., ed. see Jackson, Laura R.

Clark, Alexander, ed. Schoolday Dialogues. LC 72-103085. (Granger Index Reprint Ser.). 1977. 19.95 (0-8369-6100-5) Ayer.

— Standard Dialogues. LC 77-109137. (Granger Index Reprint Ser.). 1977. 18.95 (0-8369-6121-8) Ayer.

Clark, Alice. Working Life of Women in the Seventeenth Century. 368p. 1982. pap. 14.95 (0-7100-9045-5, Routledge Thoemms) Routledge.

— Working Life of Women in the Seventeenth Century. 328p. 1968. reprint ed. 45.00 (0-7146-1291-X, BHA-01291, Pub. by F Cass Pubs) Intl Spec Bk.

An Asterisk (*) at the beginning of an entry indicates that the title is appearing for the first time.

— Working Life of Women in the Seventeenth Century. LC 67-31558. (Reprints of Economic Classics Ser.). 328p. 1968. reprint ed. 45.00 (*0-678-05039-2*) Kelley.

Clark, Alice B. Briards. (Illus.). 192p. 9.95 (*0-7938-1058-2*, KW231) TFH Pubns.

Clark, Alice S. Managing Curriculum Materials in the Academic Library. LC 81-16574. 227p. 1982. 30.00 (*0-8108-1482-X*) Scarecrow.

Clark, Alice S., jt. ed. see Hoadley, Irene B.

Clark, Alice W., ed. Gender & Political Economy: Explorations of South Asian Systems. (Oxford India Paperbacks Ser.). (Illus.). 384p. 1995. pap. text 11.95 (*0-19-563461-6*) OUP.

Clark, Alistair M. Company & Commercial Law in Scotland. 708p. 1994. boxed set 154.00 (*0-406-11716-0*, UK, MICHIE) LEXIS Pub.

Clark, Allan. Elements of Abstract Algebra. 205p. 1984. reprint ed. pap. 8.95 (*0-486-64725-0*) Dover.

Clark, Allen L., jt. ed. see Fesharaki, Fereidun.

Clark, Allison & Kohler, Paul. Property Law: Texts & Materials. 480p. 1996. pap. text 52.95 (*0-406-05191-7*, MICHIE) LEXIS Pub.

***Clark, Alson & Neff, Wallace.** Wallace Neff, Architect of California's Golden Age. LC 00-26769. (California Architecture & Architects Ser.). (Illus.). 2000. write for info. (*0-940512-24-6*) Hennessey.

Clark, Alson, et al. Wallace Neff, 1895-1982: The Romance of Regional Architecture. LC 98-28885. (California Architecture & Architects Ser.: Vol. 15). (Illus.). 144p. 1998. reprint ed. pap. 29.95 (*0-940512-13-0*) Hennessey.

Clark, Alvin L., Jr., et al, eds. Mastery & Elegance: Two Centuries of French Drawings from the Collection of Jeffrey E. Horvitz. LC 98-45920. (Illus.). 1998. pap. 40.00 (*1-891771-02-7*, Pub. by Harvard Art Mus) U of Wash Pr.

Clark, Amalia R., jt. auth. see Clark, Tomas.

Clark, Amanada. Le Chalet du Bonheur. (Horizon Ser.: No. 519). (FRE.). 1999. mass mkt. 3.99 (*0-373-39519-1*, 1-39519-3) Harlequin Bks.

Clark, Amanda. Early Harvest. (Romance Ser.). 1994. per. 2.99 (*0-373-03321-4*, 1-03321-6) Harlequin Bks.

— Early Harvest. large type ed. 1994. per. 2.99 (*0-373-15567-0*) Harlequin Bks.

— First Love, Second Chance: (Family Man) LC 95-6887. (Superromance Ser.). 297p. 1995. per. 3.75 (*0-373-70640-5*, 1-70640-7) Harlequin Bks.

— Flower of the Sea, No. 27. (Serenade Serenata Ser.). 1985. pap. 2.50 (*0-310-46882-5*, 15547P) Zondervan.

— Sullivan's Law. 1994. per. 2.99 (*0-373-03333-8*, 1-03333-1) Harlequin Bks.

Clark, Amee Stambaugh, jt. auth. see Good, E. Perry.

Clark, Amy, jt. auth. see Clark, Andy.

Clark, Andrew. Corpus Vasorum Antiquorum, United States of America, Fascicule 25: The J. Paul Getty Museum, Fascicule 2. LC 88-12781. (Illus.). 100p. 1990. 90.00 (*0-89236-170-0*, Pub. by J P Getty Trust) OUP.

— Hey's Mineral Index: Mineral Species, Varieties & Synonyms. 2nd ed. LC 92-47371. 848p. (C). (gr. 13). 1993. lib. bdg. 149.95 (*0-412-39950-4*, A9489) Chapman & Hall.

***Clark, Andrew.** Riffs & Choruses: A New Jazz Anthology. 448p. 2001. 123.95 (*0-8264-4755-4*); pap. 29.95 (*0-8264-4756-2*) Continuum.

Clark, Andrew. Stand & Deliver. LC 97-174512. 256p. 1997. 29.95 (*0-385-25602-7*) Doubleday.

— Stand & Deliver: Inside Canadian Comedy. 272p. 1998. pap. write for info. (*0-385-25700-7*) Doubleday.

Clark, Andrew, jt. auth. see Clark, David.

Clark, Andrew, jt. auth. see Fallowfield, Lesley.

Clark, Andrew F. From Frontier to Backwater: Economy & Society in the Upper Senegal Valley (West Africa), 1850-1920. 296p. 1999. 47.00 (*0-7618-1438-8*) U Pr of Amer.

Clark, Andrew F. & Lucie C.Phillips. Historical Dictionary of Senegal. 2nd ed. LC 93-27031. (African Historical Dictionaries Ser.: No. 65). (Illus.). 370p. 1994. 50.00 (*0-8108-2747-6*) Scarecrow.

Clark, Andrew G., jt. auth. see Hartl, Daniel L.

Clark, Andrew H. Acadia: The Geography of Early Nova Scotia to 1760. LC 68-9829. (Illus.). 470p. reprint ed. pap. 145.70 (*0-8357-6000-6*, 203427500089) Bks Demand.

— Three Centuries & the Island: A Historical Geography of Settlement & Agriculture in Prince Edward Island, Canada. LC 59-2157. 300p. reprint ed. pap. 93.00 (*0-608-13300-0*, 205581700038) Bks Demand.

Clark, Andrew J. Corpus Vasorum Antiquorum, United States of America, Fascicule 23: The J. Paul Getty Museum, Fascicule 1. LC 88-12781. (Illus.). 88p. 1988. 90.00 (*0-89236-134-4*, Pub. by J P Getty Trust) OUP.

Clark-Andrews, jt. auth. see Andrews, Isabelle.

Clark, Andy. Associative Engines: Connectionism, Concepts, & Representational Change. LC 93-18722. (Illus.). 272p. 1993. 35.00 (*0-262-03210-4*, Bradford Bks) MIT Pr.

***Clark, Andy.** Athletic Scholarships: Thousands of Grants--And over $400 Million--For College-Bound Athletes. 4th ed. 2000. pap. 16.95 (*0-8160-4309-4*, Checkmark) Facts on File.

Clark, Andy. Being There: Putting Brain, Body, & World Together Again. (Illus.). 308p. 1998. reprint ed. pap. text 16.50 (*0-262-53156-9*, Bradford Bks) MIT Pr.

— Microcognition: Philosophy, Cognitive Science, & Parallel Distributed Processing. 240p. 1989. 35.00 (*0-262-03148-5*) MIT Pr.

— Microcognition: Philosophy, Cognitive Science & Parallel Distributed Processing. 248p. 1991. reprint ed. pap. text 20.00 (*0-262-53095-3*, Bradford Bks) MIT Pr.

***Clark, Andy.** Mindware: An Introduction to the Philosophy of Cognitive Science. (Illus.). 240p. (C). 2000. pap. 18.95 (*0-19-513857-0*); text 45.00 (*0-19-513856-2*) OUP.

Clark, Andy & Clark, Amy. Athletic Scholarships: Thousands of Grants & Over 400 Million Dollars for College-Bound Athletes. 3rd ed. LC 93-16812. Orig. Title: The Directory of Athletic Scholarships. 336p. 1993. reprint ed. 26.95 (*0-8160-2892-3*) Facts on File.

Clark, Andy & Millican, Peter, eds. Connectionism, Concepts, & Folk Psychology: The Legacy of Alan Turing, Vol. II. (Mind Association Occasional). (Illus.). 290p. 1997. text 55.00 (*0-19-823594-1*) OUP.

— Connectionism, Concepts & Folk Psychology: The Legacy of Alan Turing, Vol .2. (Illus.). 292p. 1999. pap. text 24.95 (*0-19-823875-4*) OUP.

***Clark, Andy, et al.** Athletic Scholarships: Thousands of Grants & over $400 Million--For College-Bound Athletes. 4th ed. LC 00-22078. 352p. 2000. 35.00 (*0-8160-4308-6*) Facts on File.

Clark, Andy, jt. compiled by see Mead, Hayden.

Clark, Andy, jt. ed. see Millican, Peter.

Clark, Andy L. & Ezquerro, Jesus. Philosophy & Cognitive Science: Categories, Consciousness, & Reasoning: Proceedings of the Second International Colloquium on Cognitive Science. LC 96-1802. (Philosophical Studies). 1996. text 140.00 (*0-7923-4068-X*) Kluwer Academic.

Clark, Angela, tr. see Goma, Paul.

Clark, Angus. The Complete Illustrated Guide to Tai Chi: A Practical Approach to the Ancient Chinese Movement for Health & Well-Being. (Illus.). 192p. 1999. pap. 24.95 (*1-86204-452-X*, Pub. by Element MA) Penguin Putnam.

***Clark, Angus.** The Complete Illustrated Guide to Tai Chi: A Practical Approach to the Ancient Chinese Movement for Health & Well-Being. (Illus.). 2000. pap. 24.95 (*1-86204-451-1*, Pub. by Element MA) Penguin Putnam.

Clark, Ann & Clark, Johnie E. Apples, Apples, Apples. 112p. 1991. pap. 7.00 (*0-9632073-0-X*) Apples.

Clark, Ann & Millard, Elaine. Gender in the Secondary Curriculum: Balancing the Books. LC 97-32353. 280p. (C). 1998. 85.00 (*0-415-16701-9*); pap. 25.99 (*0-415-16702-7*) Routledge.

Clark, Ann D. & Perkins, Patt. Surviving Your Boss: How to Cope with Office Politics & Get on with Your Job. 224p. 1996. 19.95 (*1-55972-336-X*, Birch Ln Pr) Carol Pub Group.

— Surviving Your Boss: How To Cope with Office Politics & Get on with Your Job. 224p. 1996. pap. 12.95 (*0-8065-1803-0*, Citadel Pr) Carol Pub Group.

Clark, Ann L. & Mandell, Steven L. A Short Course in PL-1 PL-C. (Data Processing & Information Systems Ser.). 190p. 1978. write for info. (*0-8299-0465-4*) West Pub.

Clark, Ann N. In My Mother's House. (Picture Puffin Ser.). (Illus.). (J). 1992. 10.19 (*0-606-00517-X*, Pub. by Turtleback) Demco.

— Little Boy with Three Names: Stories of Taos Pueblo. LC 89-81747. (Illus.). 80p. (J). (gr. 3 up). 1990. reprint ed. pap. 8.95 (*0-941270-59-9*) Ancient City Pr.

— Little Boy with Three Names & Other Stories. rev. ed. (Illus.). 48p. (J). (gr. k-7). 1999. pap. 6.95 (*1-885772-16-5*) Kiva Pubng.

— Little Herder in Autumn. Harrington, John P., ed. Young, Robert W., tr. LC 88-70848. (ENG & NAV., Illus.). 96p. (J). (gr. 3 up). 1988. reprint ed. pap. 9.95 (*0-941270-46-7*) Ancient City Pr.

— Secret of the Andes. (J). (gr. 4-8). 1976. 10.80 (*0-606-01802-6*, Pub. by Turtleback) Demco.

— Sun Journey: A Story of Zuni Pueblo. LC 88-70955. (Illus.). 96p. (J). (gr. 3 up). 1988. reprint ed. pap. 9.95 (*0-941270-48-3*) Ancient City Pr.

— There Still Are Buffalo. Beatty, Willard W., ed. LC 90-85645. (Illus.). 50p. (J). (gr. 2 up). 1992. reprint ed. pap. 8.95 (*0-941270-67-X*) Ancient City Pr.

— Who Wants to Be a Prairie Dog? Haisha'taa K'ad Dloo' Silii? 64p. (J). (gr. 2-4). 1994. pap. 9.00 (*0-9644189-0-8*) Salina Bkshelf.

— Young Hunter of Picuris. rev. ed. (Illus.). 32p. (J). (gr. k-5). 1999. pap. 6.95 (*1-885772-15-7*) Kiva Pubng.

***Clark, Ann Nolan.** Bringer of the Mystery Dog. LC 99-89874. (Illus.). 48p. (J). (gr. k-5). 2000. pap. 6.95 (*1-885772-20-3*) Kiva Pubng.

Clark, Anna. The Struggle for the Breeches: Gender & the Making of the British Working Class. LC 93-50835. (Studies on the History of Society & Culture: No. 23). 1995. 45.00 (*0-520-08624-4*, Pub. by U CA Pr) Cal Prin Full Svc.

— Struggle for the Breeches: Gender & the Making of the British Working Class. LC 93-50835. (Studies on the History of Society & Culture: Vol. 23). (Illus.). 1997. pap. 19.95 (*0-520-20883-8*, Pub. by U CA Pr) Cal Prin Full Svc.

— Women's Silence, Men's Violence: Sexual Assault in England, 1770-1845. 1987. 10.95 (*0-86358-103-X*, Pub. by Pandora) Harper SF.

***Clark, Anna & Richardson, Sarah.** History of Suffrage, 1760-1867, 6 vols. 2100p. 1999. 780.00 (*1-85196-706-0*, Pub. by Pickering & Chatto) Ashgate Pub Co.

Clark, Anne. Australian Adventure: Letters from an Ambassador's Wife. LC 73-97905. 262p. reprint ed. pap. 81.30 (*0-7837-1011-9*, 204132200020) Bks Demand.

Clark, Anne, et al. Hanukkah. LC 97-29998. (World of Holidays Ser.). (J). 1998. lib. bdg. 22.83 (*0-8172-4614-2*) Raintree Steck-V.

Clark, Anne B., jt. auth. see Klein, Donald.

Clark, Anne L. Elisabeth of Schonau: A Twelfth-Century Visionary. LC 92-12937. (Middle Ages Ser.). 224p. (C). 1992. text 32.50 (*0-8122-3123-6*) U of Pa Pr.

***Clark, Anne L., tr.** Elisabeth of Schonau: The Complete Works. (Classics of Western Spirituality Ser.). 384p. 2000. 34.95 (*0-8091-0521-7*); pap. 24.95 (*0-8091-3959-6*) Paulist Pr.

Clark, Anne R. & Brace, Andrew. The International Encyclopedia of Dogs. LC 95-30193. (Illus.). 496p. 1995. 49.95 (*0-87605-624-9*) Howell Bks.

Clark, Anthony, jt. auth. see Schaeffer, John.

***Clark, Antoinette.** Prairie Prose... And Cons. 2nd ed. 1999. reprint ed. 13.00 (*0-9700848-1-1*) J Hilderbrant Enter.

— Prairie Prose... And Cons. 2nd ed. 53p. 1999. reprint ed. pap. 8.00 (*0-9700848-0-3*) J Hilderbrant Enter.

Clark, Arnold M., et al. Aging in Insects. (Aging Ser.). 201p. 1976. text 24.50 (*0-8422-7269-0*) Irvington.

Clark, Arthur. Su Pasaporte Al Exito. (SPA.). 1997. pap. text 15.98 (*968-409-751-4*) Edamex.

Clark, Arthur B. & Skouras, Cassandra. Finding Your Perfect Love: Within & Without. LC 97-92309. 180p. 1998. pap. 9.85 (*0-9652769-0-2*) Rosebud Pr NM.

Clark, Arthur E., Jr., jt. ed. see Caswell, C. Wayne.

Clark, Arthur J. Defense Mechanisms in the Counseling Process. LC 97-45280. 255p. 1998. write for info. (*0-7619-0660-6*); pap. write for info. (*0-7619-0661-4*) Sage.

Clark, Arthur M. Realistic Revolt in Modern Poetry. (Studies in Comparative Literature: No. 35). (C). 1970. reprint ed. pap. 27.95 (*0-8383-0087-1*) M S G Haskell Hse.

Clark, Arthur R., et al. Contributions to the Natural Sciences & Anthropology: A Festschrift in Honor of George F. Goodyear. Both, Ernst E., ed. LC 97-40902. (Bulletin of the Buffalo Society of Natural Sciences Ser.: Vol. 36). (Illus.). 252p. 1998. 32.00 (*0-944032-56-7*) Buffalo SNS.

Clark, Arthur W. The Primary Degenerative Dementias Other Than Alzheimer's Disease. LC 97-38212. 400p. 1998. pap. write for info. (*0-89089-713-1*) Carolina Acad Pr.

Clark, Asa A., IV & Lilley, John F., eds. Defense Technology. LC 88-27575. 320p. 1989. 67.95 (*0-275-93078-5*, C3078, Praeger Pubs) Greenwood.

Clark, Asa C., IV, et al, eds. The Defense Reform Debate: Issues & Analysis. LC 83-49196. (Illus.). 389p. 1984. reprint ed. pap. 120.60 (*0-608-05933-1*, 206626900008) Bks Demand.

Clark, Aubert J. The Movement for International Copyright in Nineteenth Century America. LC 73-9209. x, 215p. 1973. reprint ed. lib. bdg. 22.50 (*0-8371-6980-1*, CLIC, Greenwood Pr) Greenwood.

Clark, Audrey N. Longman Dictionary of Geography. (C). 1986. pap. text 36.95 (*0-582-35261-4*) Longman.

— Longman Dictionary of Geography. 750p. 1989. pap. 25.60 (*0-582-01779-3*, 78043) Longman.

— New Penguin Dictionary of Geography. 2nd ed. LC 99-187508. (Penguin Reference Ser.). 464p. 1998. pap. 14.95 (*0-14-051388-4*) Viking Penguin.

Clark, Audria. Clark: Ebenezer Clark Family History. (Illus.). 38p. 1997. reprint ed. pap. 8.00 (*0-8328-7958-4*); reprint ed. lib. bdg. 18.00 (*0-8328-7957-6*) Higginson Bk Co.

Clark, Augusta, et al. C est a toi!, Level Three: Workbook. 10.95 (*0-8219-1751-X*) EMC-Paradigm.

— C est a toi!, Level Three: Workbook teacher's edition. 15.95 (*0-8219-1752-8*) EMC-Paradigm.

— C'est a toi!, Level 3: Annotated teacher's edition. annot. ed. text, teacher ed. 54.95 (*0-8219-1704-8*) EMC-Paradigm.

Clark, Austen. Psychological Models & Neural Mechanisms: An Examination of Reductionism in Psychology. (CLLP Ser.). (Illus.). 216p. (C). 1980. text 70.00 (*0-19-824422-3*) OUP.

— Sensory Qualities. (Clarendon Library of Logic & Philosophy). (Illus.). 264p. 1993. text 49.95 (*0-19-824001-5*) OUP.

— Sensory Qualities. (Clarendon Library of Logic & Philosophy). (Illus.). 264p. 1996. reprint ed. pap. text 21.00 (*0-19-823680-8*, Clarendon Pr) OUP.

***Clark, Austen.** A Theory of Sentience. LC 99-59001. 296p. 2000. text 45.00 (*0-19-823851-7*) OUP.

Clark, Ave. Lights in the Darkness: For Survivors & Healers of Sexual Abuse. LC 92-82000. 150p. (Orig.). 1993. pap. 8.95 (*1-878718-12-6*, Resurrection Pr) Catholic Bk Pub.

Clark, B. The Past, Present, & Future in Prose & Poetry. LC 72-947. reprint ed. 39.50 (*0-404-00015-0*) AMS Pr.

Clark, B. H., tr. see Augier, Emile.

Clark, B. J. Chuck & the Little Yellow-Haired Girls: A Wondrous Story of Puppy Love. large type ed. (Illus.). 24p. (J). (gr. 4 up). 1997. pap. 7.95 (*0-9663105-0-8*, ESA Intl) ESA Serv.

Clark, Barbara. Growing up Gifted: Developing the Potential of Children at Home & at School. 5th ed. LC 96-46522. 607p. (C). 1997. 75.00 (*0-13-569658-5*) P-H.

— Jin Shin Acutouch Bk. 1: The Tai Chi of Healing Touch. rev. ed. (Illus.). 350p. (C). 1989. pap. text 42.00 (*0-9618179-4-1*) IPSB Pubns.

— Jin Shin Acutouch Bk. 2: The Tai Chi of Healing Touch. rev. ed. (Illus.). 200p. (C). 1995. pap. text 42.00 (*0-9618179-9-2*) IPSB Pubns.

— Jin Shin Acutouch - Self Help: The Tai Chi of Healing Touch. rev. ed. (Illus.). 100p. (C). 1987. pap. text 10.00 (*0-9618179-3-3*) IPSB Pubns.

— Optimizing Learning: The Integrative Education Model in the Classroom. 256p. (C). 1990. pap. 45.80 (*0-675-20482-8*, Merrill Coll) P-H.

— Pieces. 72p. 1985. pap. 6.95 (*0-9612296-3-2*) Williams SC.

Clark, Barbara, intro. Conversations & Constructions. 64p. (J). (gr. k-12). 1978. pap. 4.95 (*0-945349-01-7*) Journeys Into Language.

Clark, Barbara & Spohr, Susan. Guide to Post-Production for TV & Film: Managing the Process. LC 98-9165. 256p. 1998. pap. 32.95 (*0-240-80322-1*, Focal) Buttrwrth-Heinemann.

Clark, Barbara B., jt. auth. see Clark, Barkley.

Clark, Barbara R., et al. Reflections. Davis, Ruby et al, eds. 72p. (Orig.). (J). (gr. 4-12). 1982. pap. 4.95 (*0-686-37922-5*) Williams SC.

Clark, Barkley. Law of Bank Deposits, Collections & Credit Cards. 1990. suppl. ed. 145.00 (*0-7913-0484-1*) Warren Gorham & Lamont.

— Law of Bank Deposits, Collections & Credit Cards. 1991. suppl. ed. 48.00 (*0-7913-1050-7*) Warren Gorham & Lamont.

— The Law of Secured Transactions under the Uniform Commercial Code. 2nd ed. 1988. suppl. ed. 145.00 (*0-7913-0070-6*) Warren Gorham & Lamont.

— The Law of Secured Transactions under the Uniform Commercial Code, Suppl. 2. 2nd ed. 1988. suppl. ed. 66.00 (*0-7913-1195-3*) Warren Gorham & Lamont.

Clark, Barkley & Clark, Barbara B. Clarks' Secured Transactions Monthly. 160.00 (*0-685-69620-0*, SLA) Warren Gorham & Lamont.

Clark, Barkley & Smith, Christopher. Law of Product Warranties, No. 0622. annuals 1056p. 1984. boxed set, suppl. ed. 155.00 (*0-88712-098-9*) Warren Gorham & Lamont.

— Law of Product Warranties, No. 0622. 1056p. 1992. suppl. ed. 155.00 (*0-7913-0997-5*) Warren Gorham & Lamont.

Clark, Barrett & Vincent, Thomas M. The Heart of the Hudson No. 1: Travel Discovery Kit. (Illus.). 208p. 1998. pap. 24.95 (*0-9662059-0-1*) Mktg A La Carte.

Clark, Barrett H. Blush of Shame: A Few Considerations on Verbal Obscenity in the Theatre. 1932. pap. 4.00 (*0-910664-01-3*) Gotham.

— The British & American Drama of Today: Outlines for Their Study. (BCL1-PR English Literature Ser.). 317p. 1992. reprint ed. lib. bdg. 89.00 (*0-7812-7110-X*) Rprt Serv.

— Paul Green. LC 74-1164. (Studies in Drama: No. 39). 1974. lib. bdg. 49.00 (*0-8383-2016-3*) M S G Haskell Hse.

Clark, Barrett H., ed. World Drama Vol. 1: Ancient Greece, Rome, India, China, Japan, Medieval Europe, England. 1956. pap. 13.95 (*0-486-20057-4*) Dover.

— World Drama Vol. 2: Italy, Spain, France, Germany, Denmark, Russia, Norway. 1956. pap. 13.95 (*0-486-20059-0*) Dover.

Clark, Barrett H., jt. ed. see Sanborn, Ralph.

Clark, Barry. Political Economy: A Comparative Approach. 2nd ed. LC 98-15657. 376p. 1998. 69.50 (*0-275-95869-8*, Praeger Pubs); pap. 24.95 (*0-275-96370-5*, Praeger Pubs) Greenwood.

Clark, Barry, tr. see Dalai Lama XIV.

Clark, Bates, jt. auth. see Giddings, Franklin H.

Clark, Beatrice S., tr. see Capecia, Mayotte.

Clark-Bekederemo, J. P. Collected Plays & Poems, 1958-1988. LC 91-14580. 1991. 34.95 (*0-88258-128-7*); pap. 17.95 (*0-88258-136-8*); pap. 17.95 (*0-88258-129-5*) Howard U Pr.

Clark, Ben. Client/Server Database Performance Tuning. (Illus.). 732p. (Orig.). 1996. 49.99 (*0-7897-0190-1*) Que.

Clark, Benjamin, tr. see Massignon, Louis.

Clark, Benjamin R. Delight for a Wretched Man. 1993. pap. 8.99 (*0-85234-311-6*, Pub. by Evangelical Pr) P & R Pubng.

Clark, Bernadine. Fanfare for Words: Bookfairs & Book Festivals in North America. 108p. (C). 1993. pap. text 20.00 (*1-56806-595-7*) DIANE Pub.

— Fanfare for Words: Bookfairs & Book Festivals in North America. LC 90-21318. 108p. 1991. 6.95 (*0-8444-0711-9*) Lib Congress.

Clark, Bertha W. Haxton Genealogy. 167p. 1997. reprint ed. pap. 25.00 (*0-8328-9060-X*); reprint ed. lib. bdg. 35.00 (*0-8328-9059-6*) Higginson Bk Co.

Clark, Bess V. Twiggs County Georgia Abstracts: Records of a Burned County. 1988. 25.00 (*0-9619864-0-9*) B V Clark.

Clark, Beth. Anne Hutchinson. (Colonial Leaders Ser.). (Illus.). 80p. (J). (gr. 3 up). 1999. pap. 8.95 (*0-7910-5685-6*) Chelsea Hse.

— Anne Hutchinson: Religious Leader. LC 99-21553. (Illus.). 80p. (J). 1999. 16.95 (*0-7910-5342-3*) Chelsea Hse.

***Clark, Beth K. & Clark, Charles R.** Law & Mental Health Professionals: Michigan. 2000. write for info. (*1-55798-715-7*) Am Psychol.

Clark, Bettie. A Ham for All Seasons. LC 85-61032. (Illus.). 128p. (Orig.). 1985. pap. 7.95 (*0-933050-27-5*) New Eng Pr VT.

Clark, Betty. Coping on a Tight Budget. (Coping Ser.). (YA). (gr. 7-12). 1990. lib. bdg. 17.95 (*0-8239-1184-5*, D1143-8) Rosen Group.

— Too Many Toys. LC 96-75798. (Illus.). 32p. (J). (ps-3). 1996. 15.95 (*0-9641285-5-1*) Little Frnd.

— When Your Parents Divorce: A Handbook for Children Whose Parents Are Divorcing. LC 98-72127. (Illus.). 96p. (J). (gr. 8 up). 1998. pap. 7.95 (*0-932796-89-3*) Ed Media Corp.

Clark, Beverly. All about Her: A Personal Reference from the Woman in My Life. 96p. 1995. pap. 7.95 (*0-934081-10-7*) Wlshre Pubns.

— All about Him: A Personal Reference from the Man in My Life. 96p. 1995. pap. 7.95 (*0-934081-11-5*) Wlshre Pubns.

— Beverly Clark's Book of Wedding Cakes. 1999. 4.95 (*0-7624-0628-3*) Running Pr.

— Beverly Clark's for My Bridesmaid. 1999. 4.95 (*0-7624-0627-5*) Running Pr.

***Clark, Beverly.** Beverly Clark's for the Bride. 2000. pap. 4.95 (*0-7624-0735-2*, Courage) Running Pr.

Clark, Beverly. Beverly Clark's I Love You Because. 1999. 4.95 (*0-7624-0626-7*) Running Pr.

***Clark, Beverly.** Beverly Clark's Wedding Toasts. 2000. pap. 4.95 (*0-7624-0736-0*, Courage) Running Pr.

C

Clark, Beverly. Beverly Clark's Weddings A Celebration. 1999. 4.95 (*0-7624-0625-9*) Running Pr.

***Clark, Beverly.** Bound by Love. 2000. pap. 8.95 (*1-58571-016-4*, Pub. by Genesis Press) BookWorld.

— Bridal Showers: Special Touches & Unique Ideas for Throwing a Fabulous Shower. 2nd ed. (Illus.). 166p. 1999. pap. 12.95 (*0-934081-18-2*) Wlshre Pubns.

Clark, Beverly. Como Planear una Boda Inolvidable: Planning a Wedding to Remember. (SPA.). 248p. 1993. pap. 15.95 (*0-934081-07-7*) Wlshre Pubns.

— A Love to Cherish. LC 98-206080. (Indigo Love Stories Ser.). 287p. 1998. 15.95 (*1-885478-35-6*, Pub. by Genesis Press) BookWorld.

— Planning a Wedding to Remember: Special & Unique Ideas. rev. ed. (Illus.). 250p. 1989. pap. 12.95 (*0-934081-06-9*) Wlshre Pubns.

— The Price of Love. (Indigo Love Stories Ser.). 239p. 1999. pap. 8.95 (*1-885478-61-5*, Pub. by Genesis Press) BookWorld.

— Recuerdos de la Boda: Wedding Memories. (SPA., Illus.). 72p. 1994. 16.95 (*0-934081-08-5*) Wlshre Pubns.

— Showers: The Complete Guide to Hosting a Perfect Bridal or Baby Shower. Burk, Celine, ed. (Illus.). 168p. (Orig.). 1989. pap. 8.95 (*0-934081-03-4*) Wlshre Pubns.

— Wedding Memories. (Illus.). 64p. 1990. 16.95 (*0-934081-05-0*) Wlshre Pubns.

— Weddings. LC 96-61134. (Illus.). 256p. 1996. 60.00 (*0-934081-14-X*) Wlshre Pubns.

— Yesterday Is Gone. LC 97-216923. 293p. 1997. pap. 10.95 (*1-885478-12-7*, Pub. by Genesis Press) BookWorld.

***Clark, Beverly, intro.** Planning a Wedding to Remember: The Perfect Wedding Planner. 5th rev. ed. (Illus.). 248p. 1999. pap. 18.95 (*0-934081-17-4*) Wlshre Pubns.

Clark, Beverly L. Lewis Carroll. Schlobin, Roger C., ed. LC 87-16032. (Starmont Reader's Guide Ser.: Vol. 47). viii, 96p. 1990. pap. 17.00 (*1-55742-030-0*) Millefleurs.

— A Love to Cherish. unabridged ed. 287p. 1999. pap. 8.95 (*1-885478-84-4*, Pub. by Genesis Press) BookWorld.

— Regendering the School Story: Sassy Sissies & Tattling Tomboys. Zipes, Jack D., ed. LC 96-19804. (Children's Literature & Culture Ser.: Vol. 3). (Illus.). 312p. 1996. text 60.00 (*0-8153-2116-3*, SS1060) Garland.

— Talking about Writing: A Guide for Tutor & Teacher Conferences. (Illus.). 240p. 1985. pap. text 19.95 (*0-472-08062-8*, 08062) U of Mich Pr.

Clark, Beverly L., et al, eds. Little Women & the Feminist Imagination: Criticism, Controversy, Personal Essays. LC 98-26670. (Children's Literature & Culture Ser.: Vol. 6). 496p. 1998. reprint ed. 75.00 (*0-8153-2049-3*, H1974) Garland.

***Clark, Beverly Lyon.** Girls, Boys, Books, Toys: Gender in Children's Literature & Culture. (Illus.). 312p. 2000. pap. 19.95 (*0-8018-6526-3*) Johns Hopkins.

Clark, Beverly Lyon & Higonnet, Margaret R. Girls, Boys, Books, Toys: Gender in Children's Literature & Culture. LC 99-22652. (Illus.). 336p. 1999. 45.00 (*0-8018-6053-9*) Johns Hopkins.

Clark, Beverly Lyon, ed. see Friedman, Melvin J.

Clark, Bill. The Cessna One Hundred Fifty & One Hundred Fifty-Two. (Illus.). 272p. (Orig.). 1987. 19.95 (*0-8306-9022-0*, 2422); pap. 13.95 (*0-8306-0222-4*) McGraw-Hill Prof.

Clark, Bill, jt. auth. see Milch, David.

***Clark, Billy C.** By Way of the Forked Stick. LC 00-8431. 160p. 2000. 22.50 (*1-57233-094-5*, Pub. by U of Tenn Pr) U Ch Pr.

Clark, Billy C. Goodbye Kate. LC 94-2193. (Illus.). 288p. (J). (gr. 6 up). 1994. reprint ed. 20.00 (*0-945084-41-2*) J Stuart Found.

— A Long Row to Hoe. limited rev. ed. Gifford, James M., ed. LC 91-40399. (Illus.). 285p. (YA). (gr. 6 up). 1992. reprint ed. 30.00 (*0-945084-28-5*) J Stuart Found.

— A Long Row to Hoe. rev. ed. Gifford, James M., ed. LC 91-40399. (Illus.). 285p. 1992. reprint ed. 22.00 (*0-945084-27-7*) J Stuart Found.

— Mooneyed Hound. 2nd ed. Gifford, James M. & Hall, Patricia A., eds. LC 95-7143. (Illus.). 128p. (J). (gr. 4 up). 1995. pap. 8.50 (*0-945084-49-8*) J Stuart Found.

— Riverboy. Besmark, Tracey, ed. LC 97-25377. (Illus.). 160p. 1997. reprint ed. pap. 9.95 (*0-945084-65-X*) J Stuart Found.

— Song of the River. rev. ed. Gifford, James M. et al, eds. LC 92-31483. (Illus.). 144p. (YA). 1994. pap. 10.00 (*0-945084-46-3*) J Stuart Found.

— To Leave My Heart at Catlettsburg. LC 99-23489. (Illus.). 80p. 1999. pap. 9.95 (*0-945084-75-7*) J Stuart Found.

— Trail of the Hunter's Horn. 2nd ed. Gifford, James M. & Hall, Patricia A., eds. LC 95-7143. (Illus.). 80p. (J). (gr. 4 up). 1995. pap. 6.00 (*0-945084-48-X*) J Stuart Found.

— Useless Dog. 2nd ed. LC 96-14489. (Illus.). (YA). (gr. 4 up). 1996. reprint ed. pap. 8.50 (*0-945084-57-9*) J Stuart Found.

Clark, Blake. Remember Pearl Harbor. 6th ed. 266p. 1987. reprint ed. mass mkt. 4.95 (*0-935180-49-4*) Mutual Pub HI.

Clark, Blue. Lone Wolf vs. Hitchcock: Treaty Rights & Indian Law at the End of the Nineteenth Century. LC 94-7735. (Law in the American West Ser.: Vol. 5). (Illus.). 198p. 1994. text 45.00 (*0-8032-1466-9*) U of Nebr Pr.

— Lone Wolf vs. Hitchcock: Treaty Rights & Indian Law at the End of the Nineteenth Century. LC 94-7735. (Law in the American West Ser.). (Illus.). 198p. 1999. pap. text 15.00 (*0-8032-6401-1*) U of Nebr Pr.

Clark Boardman Callaghan Staff. Environmental Compliance Desk Reference, 3 vols., Set. (Environmental Law Ser.). 1995. ring bd. write for info. (*0-614-06265-9*) West Group.

Clark, Bob. Scenic Driving Idaho. LC 98-5872. (Illus.). 168p. 1998. pap. 15.95 (*1-56044-621-8*) Falcon Pub Inc.

Clark, Bobby & Huffman, Florence, eds. The Kentucky Directory Gold Book, 1996. 803p. 1996. write for info. (*0-614-10960-4*, 2001) Clark Pub KY.

Clark, Boden, ed. see Bloomberg, Marty & Barrett, Buckley B.

Clark, Bradbury R., ed. Ballantine & Sterling California Corporation Laws. 4th ed. 50p. 1993. suppl. ed. 215.00 (*0-685-67727-3*, MICHIE) LEXIS Pub.

Clark, Brenda. Little Fingerling. LC 92-85. 32p. (J). (gr. k-3). 1992. 13.95 (*0-8249-8553-2*, Ideals Child) Hambleton-Hill.

Clark, Brenda. Little Fingerling: A Japanese Folk Tale. 32p. (J). 1989. pap. 4.95 (*1-55074-075-X*) Kids Can Pr.

Clark, Brenda, jt. see Bourgeois, Paulette.

Clark, Brenda, jt. auth. see Bougeois, Paulette.

Clark, Brenda, jt. auth. see Bourgeois, Paulette.

Clark, Brenda, jt. auth. see Staunton, Ted.

Clark, Brian. Sibling Constellation. 272p. 1999. pap. 12.95 (*0-14-019564-5*, PuffinBks) Peng Put Young Read.

— Whose Life Is It Anyway? Female Version. 1980. pap. 5.95 (*0-87129-371-4*, W48) Dramatic Pub.

— Whose Life Is It Anyway? Male Version. 1980. pap. 5.95 (*0-87129-329-3*, W43) Dramatic Pub.

Clark, Brian, jt. auth. see Reneau, Mike.

***Clark, Brian Charles.** Splitting. 172p. 2000. pap. 9.00 (*1-877655-30-9*, Pub. by Wordcraft Oregon) SPD-Small Pr Dist.

Clark, Brian D., et al. Perspectives on Environmental Impact Assessment. 1984. text 237.50 (*90-277-1753-2*) Kluwer Academic.

Clark, Brian F., ed. see NATO Advanced Research Workshop on RNA: Biochemistry & Biotechnology Staff.

Clark, Brooks. Kids' Book of Soccer: Skills, Strategies & the Rules of the Game. LC 97-19658. (Illus.). 160p. (J). 1997. pap. 9.95 (*0-8065-1916-9*) Carol Pub Group.

Clark, Bruce. Native Liberty, Crown Sovereignty: The Existing Aboriginal Right of Self-Government in Canada. (McGill-Queen's Native & Northern Ser.). 288p. (C). 1990. text 65.00 (*0-7735-0767-1*, Pub. by McG-Queens Univ Pr) CUP Services.

— Native Liberty, Crown Sovereignty: The Existing Aboriginal Right of Self-Government in Canada. (McGill-Queen's Native & Northern Ser.). 288p. (C). 1992. pap. 24.95 (*0-7735-0946-1*, Pub. by McG-Queens Univ Pr) CUP Services.

Clark, Bruce & Chan, Susan D., eds. Handbook of Zoonotic Diseases, A Summary of the More Common Maladies Afflicting Animals & Man. 2nd rev. ed. 40p. 1990. pap. 10.00 (*1-929672-01-2*) Am Assn Zoo Keep.

***Clark, Bruce A.** Justice in Paradise. 440p. 1999. text 29.95 (*0-7735-2001-5*, Pub. by McG-Queens Univ Pr) CUP Services.

Clark, Bruce M. ADA Resource Directory: A Guide to Accessibility in Hawaii. 108p. 1994. pap. 26.95 (*0-9641990-0-9*) Access Planning.

Clark, Bruce T. The Custer Legacy. aut. ed. 640p. 1997. 24.95 (*1-885857-20-9*) Four Wnds Pubng.

Clark, Buny C., et al, eds. Relativistic Nuclear Many-Body Physics: Proceedings. 698p. 1989. text 131.00 (*9971-5-0680-7*) World Scientific Pub.

Clark, Burton R. Academic Power in Italy: Bureaucracy & Oligarchy in National University System. LC 77-4010. (Illus.). 1977. 18.00 (*0-226-10847-3*) U Ch Pr.

— Adult Education in Transition: A Study of Institutional Insecurity. Zuckerman, Harriet & Merton, Robert K., eds. LC 79-8982. (Dissertations on Sociology Ser.). 1980. lib. bdg. 18.95 (*0-405-12957-2*) Ayer.

— Creating Entrepreneurial Universities: Organizational Pathways of Transformation. LC 97-42123. (Issues in Higher Education Ser.). 200p. 1998. 79.50 (*0-08-043342-1*, Pergamon Pr) Elsevier.

— Creating Entrepreneurial Universities: Organizational Pathways of Transformation. LC 97-42123. (Issues in Higher Education Ser.: 12). 200p. 1998. pap. write for info. (*0-08-043354-5*, Pergamon Pr) Elsevier.

— The Distinctive College: Antioch, Reed & Swarthmore. 292p. (C). 1999. pap. 24.95 (*1-56000-592-0*) Transaction Pubs.

— The Higher Education System: Academic Organization in Cross-National Perspective. LC 82-13521. (C). 1983. pap. 20.00 (*0-520-05892-5*, Pub. by U CA Pr) Cal Prin Full Svc.

— Places of Inquiry: Research & Advanced Education in Modern Universities. LC 94-25325. 1995. 48.00 (*0-520-08762-3*, Pub. by U CA Pr) Cal Prin Full Svc.

Clark, Burton R., ed. The Research Foundations of Graduate Education: Germany, Britain, France, United States, Japan. LC 92-13407. (C). 1993. 55.00 (*0-520-07997-3*, Pub. by U CA Pr) Cal Prin Full Svc.

Clark, Burton R. & Neave, Guy, eds. Encyclopedia of Higher Education, 4 vols. 2600p. 1992. 1250.00 (*0-685-53438-3*, Pergamon Pr) Elsevier.

— Encyclopedia of Higher Education, 4 vols., Set. 2530p. 1992. 1358.75 (*0-08-037251-1*, Pergamon Pr) Elsevier.

Clark, Byron N. A List of Pensioners of the War of 1812 (Vermont Claimants) (Illus.). 171p. 1996. reprint ed. pap. 18.00 (*0-8063-0074-4*, 1000) Clearfield Co.

Clark, C., jt. ed. see Lowyck, J.

Clark, C. A. & Moyer, J. W. Compendium of Sweet Potato Diseases. LC 88-70995. (Disease Compendium Ser.). (Illus.). 96p. (Orig.). 1988. pap. 42.00 (*0-89054-089-6*) Am Phytopathol Soc.

Clark, C. E., Jr., ed. Concise Dictionary of American Literary Biography Supplement. (Illus.). 1998. 80.00 (*0-7876-1695-8*, GML00298-111096) Gale.

Clark, C. E., jt. ed. see Bruccoli, Matthew J.

Clark, C. E. Frazer, ed. Nathaniel Hawthorne Journal. Incl. Nathaniel Hawthorne Journal: 1974. 1974. 25.00 (*0-910972-50-8*); write for info. (*0-318-51241-6*) Bruccoli.

— Nathaniel Hawthorne Journal: 1972. 1972. 25.00 (*0-910972-33-8*) Bruccoli.

— Nathaniel Hawthorne Journal: 1973. 1973. 25.00 (*0-910972-39-7*) Bruccoli.

Clark, C. F., ed. see Crow, Little.

Clark, C. F., ed. see Little Crow.

Clark, C. Frazer, Jr. Nathaniel Hawthorne: A Descriptive Bibliography. LC 76-50885. (Series in Bibliography). 328p. 1978. 100.00 (*0-8229-3343-8*) U of Pittsburgh Pr.

Clark, C. W. Clark: History of the Descendants of Cephas Clark, Born in Medfield, Massachusetts, 1745, with Some Account of His Ancestry from Their Advent in America. 102p. 1993. reprint ed. pap. 19.00 (*0-8328-3283-9*); reprint ed. lib. bdg. 29.00 (*0-8328-3282-0*) Higginson Bk Co.

Clark, C. W., jt. ed. see Nayfeh, Munir H.

Clark, Cal. Taiwan's Development: Implications for Contending Political Economy Paradigms, 100. LC 89-7494. (Contributions in Economics & Economic History Ser.: No. 100). 283p. 1989. 59.95 (*0-313-25448-6*, CTE, Greenwood Pr) Greenwood.

Clark, Cal & Chan, Steve, eds. The Evolving Pacific Basin in the Global Political Economy: Domestic & International Linkages. LC 92-4871. 226p. 1992. lib. bdg. 42.00 (*1-55587-271-9*) L Rienner.

Clark, Cal & Farlow, Robert L. Comparative Patterns of Foreign Policy & Trade: The Communist Balkans in International Politics. LC 76-9078. (Studies in East European & Soviet Planning, Development, & Trade: No. 23). (Illus.). 1976. pap. 6.00 (*0-89249-016-0*) Intl Development.

Clark, Cal & Roy, K. C. Comparing Development Patterns in Asia. LC 96-3462. 216p. 1996. lib. bdg. 49.95 (*1-55587-307-3*, 873073) L Rienner.

Clark, Cal, jt. ed. see Chai, Winberg.

Clark, Cal, jt. ed. see Lee, Rose J.

Clark, Cal M., jt. ed. see Roy, Kartik C.

***Clark, Cammy.** Paul Kariya: Maine Man. (SuperStar Series: Vol. 3). 96p. 1999. pap. 4.95 (*1-58261-150-5*, Pub. by Sprts Pubng) Partners-West.

Clark, Candace. Misery & Company. LC 96-34946. 300p. (C). 1997. 29.95 (*0-226-10756-6*) U Ch Pr.

— Misery & Company: Sympathy in Everyday Life. LC 96-34946. 1998. pap. text 18.00 (*0-226-10757-4*) U Ch Pr.

Clark, Candace & Robboy, Howard. Social Interaction: Readings in Sociology. 4th ed. LC 90-63538. 611p. (C). 1992. pap. text 23.95 (*0-312-05665-6*) St Martin.

Clark, Carl D. & Essary, Loris. Semi-Constructs of the Secretaire De Registre. 1980. pap. 2.00 (*0-918406-07-2*) Future Pr.

***Clark, Carl E.** Pieces from My Mind. LC 99-64938. 188p. 2000. pap. 13.95 (*0-88739-307-1*) Creat Arts Bk.

Clark, Carol. American Drawings & Watercolors. (Robert Lehman Collection: Vol. 8). (Illus.). 272p. 1992. pap. 45.00 (*0-87099-640-1*) Metro Mus Art.

— The Robert Lehman Collection at the Metropolitan Museum of Art: American Drawings & Watercolors, Vol. 8. (Illus.). 268p. 1992. text 95.00 (*0-691-03208-4*, Pub. by Princeton U Pr) Cal Prin Full Svc.

— Tropical Gemstones. (Nature Guides Ser.). (Illus.). 64p. 1998. 9.95 (*962-593-184-8*, Periplus Eds) Tuttle Pubng.

— The Web of Metaphor: Studies in the Imagery of Montaigne's Essays. LC 77-93404. (French Forum Monographs: No. 7). 191p. (Orig.). 1978. pap. 10.95 (*0-917058-06-2*) French Forum.

Clark, Carol, et al. Maurice Brazil Prendergast - Charles Prendergast: A Catalogue Raisonne. (Illus.). 812p. 1990. 285.00 (*3-7913-0965-X*, Pub. by Prestel) te Neues.

Clark, Carol, ed. see Baudelaire, Charles.

Clark, Carol, tr. see Baudelaire, Charles.

Clark, Carol Higgins. Decked: A Regan Reilly Mystery. (Dove Bk.). 288p. 1993. mass mkt. 7.50 (*0-446-36470-3*, Pub. by Warner Bks) Little.

— Decked: A Regan Reilly Mystery. 1999. mass mkt. 4.50 (*0-446-60777-0*, Pub. by Warner Bks) Little.

— Fleeced. 272p. 1999. 22.00 (*0-446-52292-9*, Pub. by Warner Bks) Little.

— Iced. 320p. 1996. mass mkt. 7.50 (*0-446-60198-5*, Pub. by Warner Bks) Little.

***Clark, Carol Higgins.** Iced. 306p. 1999. mass mkt. 4.50 (*0-446-60778-9*) Warner Bks.

Clark, Carol Higgins. Snagged. 320p. 1994. mass mkt. 7.50 (*0-446-60076-8*, Pub. by Warner Bks) Little.

— Twanged. 336p. 1999. mass mkt. 7.50 (*0-446-60536-0*, Pub. by Warner Bks) Little.

— Twanged. large type ed. LC 98-5235. (Basic Ser.). 504p. 1998. 27.95 (*0-7862-1417-1*) Mac Lib Ref.

Clark, Carol L. Interconnections: Writer, Culture, & Environment. LC 96-76422. 768p. (C). 1996. pap. text 34.00 (*0-15-503298-4*, Pub. by Harcourt Coll Pubs) Harcourt.

— The Red Tape Cutter's Handbook: A Working Tool for Dealing with Bureaucracies. LC 80-21193. 326p. reprint ed. pap. 101.10 (*0-8357-4256-3*, 203704500007) Bks Demand.

— A Student Guide to the Internet. LC 95-35805. 192p. 1995. pap. text, student ed. 22.00 (*0-13-442310-0*, Pub. by P-H) S&S Trade.

— Working the Web: A Student's Guide. LC 96-78585. 240p. (C). 1996. pap. text, student ed. 22.50 (*0-15-504060-X*, Pub. by Harcourt Coll Pubs) Harcourt.

Clark, Carol R., jt. auth. see Schallert, William F.

Clark, Carolyn C. Cast into the Fire. Liotta, Mary A., ed. LC 94-60685. (Illus.). 224p. 1994. pap. 14.95 (*1-880254-19-0*) Vista.

— Creating a Climate for Power Learning: 36 Mind-Stretching Activities. LC 96-51246. 1997. 21.95 (*1-57025-139-8*) Whole Person.

— Dangerous Alibis. Liotta, Mary A., ed. LC 94-60517. 160p. 1994. pap. 9.95 (*1-880254-16-6*) Vista.

— Deadlier Than Death. Rezvan, Jerina B., ed. LC 93-60315. 186p. 1993. pap. 9.95 (*1-880254-06-9*) Vista.

***Clark, Carolyn C.** Integrating Complementary Health Procedures into Practice. LC 99-28875. (Illus.). 352p. 1999. text 38.95 (*0-8261-1288-9*) Springer Pub.

Clark, Carolyn C. The Nurse As Group Leader. 3rd ed. LC 94-3104. (Teaching of Nursing Ser.: Vol. 3). 304p. (C). 1994. text 32.95 (*0-8261-2333-3*) Springer Pub.

— Wellness Practitioner: Concepts, Research, & Strategies. 2nd expanded rev. ed. LC 95-47784. (Illus.). 368p. 1996. 46.95 (*0-8261-5151-5*) Springer Pub.

***Clark, Carolyn C., et al, eds.** Encyclopedia of Complementary Health Practice. LC 99-25832. (Illus.). 664p. 1999. text 119.00 (*0-8261-1237-4*); pap. text 64.00 (*0-8261-1239-0*) Springer Pub.

Clark, Carolyn M., ed. see Korab, Balthazar.

Clark-Carter, David. Doing Qualitative Psychology Research: From Design to Report. LC 98-152418. 1997. pap. text 32.00 (*0-86377-789-9*) L Erlbaum Assocs.

— Doing Qualitative Psychology Research: From Design to Report. LC 98-152418. 672p. 1997. 72.00 (*0-86377-788-0*) L Erlbaum Assocs.

Clark, Catherine. The Day I Met Him. (Love Stories Ser.). 192p. (YA). (gr. 7-12). 1995. mass mkt. 4.50 (*0-553-56664-4*) Bantam.

— Educating Able Children: Resource Issues & Processes for Teachers. 1998. pap., pap. text 25.95 (*1-85346-537-2*) Taylor & Francis.

— Flamingoes Forever? (Full House Club Stephanie Ser.: Vol. 9). 144p. (J). (gr. 3-6). 1999. per. 3.99 (*0-671-02159-1*) PB.

— My So-Called Life. (Illus.). 176p. (YA). (gr. 9). 1995. pap. 4.99 (*0-679-87789-4*) McKay.

***Clark, Catherine.** Truth or Dairy. LC 99-96351. 272p. (YA). (gr. 8 up). 2000. pap. 6.95 (*0-380-81443-9*, Avon Bks) Morrow Avon.

Clark, Catherine. What's So Funny about Ninth Grade? LC 91-2494. (Midway Junior High Ser.). 128p. (J). (gr. 6-9). 1996. pap. 2.95 (*0-8167-2397-4*) Troll Communs.

Clark, Catherine, et al, eds. Towards Inclusive Schools? LC 95-5706. (Special Education Ser.: Vol. 16). 280p. (C). 1995. pap. text 22.95 (*0-8077-3461-6*) Tchrs Coll.

Clark, Catherine, et al. A Decade of Change: Public Education Reform in Texas 1981-1992. (Special Project Reports). 82p. 1993. pap. 9.95 (*0-89940-874-5*) LBJ Sch Pub Aff.

— Preparing for the Twenty-First Century: Public Education Reform in Texas. (Policy Research Project Report: No. 107). 107p. 1994. pap. 10.50 (*0-89940-715-3*) LBJ Sch Pub Aff.

— Theorising Special Education. LC 97-43773. 216p. (C). 1998. 75.00 (*0-415-14750-6*); pap. 22.99 (*0-415-14751-4*) Routledge.

Clark, Catherine C. The Saturday Treat. large type ed. (Magna Large Print Ser.). 1994. 27.99 (*0-7505-0649-0*, Pub. by Mgna Lrg Print) Ulverscroft.

Clark, Catherine H. Annual Church Review Procedure: The Church's Ministry & the Minister. pap. 12.00 (*1-56699-060-2*) Alban Inst.

Clark, Caven P., et al. Late Archaic & Early Woodland Adaptation in the Lower St. Joseph River Valley, Berrien County, MI, Vol. 2. (Michigan Cultural Resource Investigation Ser.). 507p. (C). 1990. pap. text. write for info. (*0-9623670-1-X*) MI Dept Trans.

Clark, Cecily. Words, Names & History: Selected Writings of Cecily Clark. Jackson, Peter, ed. (Illus.). 476p. (C). 1996. text 125.00 (*0-85991-402-X*) Boydell & Brewer.

Clark, Champ. My Quarter Century of American Politics, 2 vols., Set. (History - United States Ser.). 1992. reprint ed. lib. bdg. 150.00 (*0-7812-6195-3*) Rprt Serv.

Clark, Chap. Creative Bible Lessons in Romans: Faith on Fire!: Twelve Ready-to-Use Bible Lessons for Youth Ministry. LC 95-41227. 96p. 1996. pap. 12.99 (*0-310-20777-0*) Zondervan.

***Clark, Chap.** Lecciones Biblicas Creativas para Jovenes Sobre Romanos: Fe al Rojo Vivo! (SPA.). 2000. pap. 10.99 (*0-8297-2887-2*) Vida Pubs.

Clark, Chap. Next Time I Fall in Love. 1992. 29.99 incl. VHS (*0-310-54518-8*) Zondervan.

— The Youth Worker's Handbook of Family Ministry: Strategies & Practical Ideas for Reaching Your Students' Families. LC 97-13808. 1997. pap. 15.99 (*0-310-22025-4*) Youth Spec.

Clark, Chap & Clark, Dee. Daughters & Dads: Building a Lasting Relationship. LC 97-44063. 1998. 11.00 (*1-57683-048-9*) NavPress.

Clark, Charles. Brainstorming: How to Create Successful Ideas. 1989. pap. 10.00 (*0-87980-423-8*) Wilshire.

— Publishing Agreements: A Book of Precedents. 3rd ed. 1990. text 44.95 (*0-04-440237-6*) Routledge.

— Publishing Agreements: A Book of Precedents. 3rd rev. ed. 238p. (C). 1989. 30.00 (*0-941533-56-5*, NAB) I R Dee.

— Publishing Agreements: A Book of Precedents. 4th ed. 270p. 1993. boxed set 75.00 (*0-406-02094-9*, U.K., MICHIE) LEXIS Pub.

Clark, Charles & Parker, David. Selling New Homes. LC 89-34605. 160p. 1989. pap. 7.50 (*0-86718-336-5*) Home Builder.

Clark, Charles, et al. Clark: Publishing Agreements. 5th ed. 1997. write for info. (*0-406-00923-6*, CPA5, MICHIE) LEXIS Pub.

Clark, Charles E. The Meetinghouse Tragedy: An Episode in the Life of a New England Town. LC 98-23577. (Illus.). 170p. 1998. pap. 14.95 (*0-87451-872-5*); text 30.00 (*0-87451-887-3*) U Pr of New Eng.

— New Hampshire Newspapers & the Constitution, 1787-1788. (Illus.). 80p. (Orig.). 1989. pap. 15.00 (*0-317-93998-X*) NH Human Council.

***Clark, Charles E.** Uprooting Otherness: The Literacy Campaign in Nep-Era Russia. LC 99-33547. 240p. 2000. 41.00 (*1-57591-030-6*) Susquehanna U Pr.

An Asterisk (*) at the beginning of an entry indicates that the title is appearing for the first time.

C

An Asterisk (*) at the beginning of an entry indicates that the title is appearing for the first time.

Clark, David, ed. see Walrand, Jean & Varaiya, Pravin.

Clark, David A. Coronary Angioplasty. 2nd ed. 316p. 1991. text 595.00 incl. VHS (*0-471-56109-6*, Wiley-Interscience) Wiley.

— True Blood. 1997. 40.00 (*0-86719-447-2*) Last Gasp.

— True Blood. (Illus.). 48p. 1997. pap. text 19.95 (*0-86719-443-X*) Last Gasp.

Clark, David A., ed. Coronary Angioplasty. 2nd ed. LC 90-13100. 316p. 1991. 150.00 (*0-471-56074-X*) Wiley.

Clark, David A. & Taormino, Tristan, eds. Ritual Sex. (Orig.). 1996. mass mkt. 6.95 (*1-56333-391-0*, Rhinoceros) Masquerade.

Clark, David A., et al. Scientific Foundations of Cognitive Theory & Therapy of Depression. LC 98-44674. 504p. 1999. 57.50 (*0-471-18970-7*) Wiley.

Clark, David A., jt. auth. see Ensher, Gail L.

***Clark, David Aaron.** The Fallen. Kim, Miran, ed. (Illus.). 48p. 1999. pap. 8.95 (*1-56163-233-3*) NBM.

Clark, David C., ed. Clergy Response to Suicidal Persons & Their Family Members: An Interfaith Resource Book for Clergy & Congregations. LC 93-72090. (Studies in Ministry & Parish Life). x, 219p. 1993. text 30.95 (*0-913552-49-6*); pap. text 19.95 (*0-913552-50-X*) Exploration Pr.

Clark, David E., et al, eds. Microwaves: Theory & Application in Materials Processing II. (Ceramic Transactions Ser.: Vol. 36). 596p. 1993. 74.00 (*0-944904-66-1*, CT036) Am Ceramic.

— Microwaves: Theory & Application in Materials Processing III. LC 95-43601. (Ceramic Transactions Ser.: Vol. 59). 592p. 1995. 95.00 (*1-57498-002-5*, CT059) Am Ceramic.

Clark, David E., et al, eds. Microwaves: Theory & Application in Materials Processing IV: First World Congress on Microwave Processing & RF Technology from Science to Application. (Ceramic Transactions Ser.: Vol. 80). 731p. 1997. text 95.00 (*1-57498-025-4*, CT080) Am Ceramic.

Clark, David E. & Zoitos, Bruce K., eds. Corrosion of Glass, Ceramics & Ceramic Superconductors: Principles, Testing, Characterization & Applications. LC 91-16010. (Illus.). 672p. 1992. 169.00 (*0-8155-1283-X*) Noyes.

Clark, David F. Ammon & the Battle at Riplah. 96p. (YA). (gr. 7-12). 1997. pap. 9.95 (*1-890830-42-9*, Pub. by Riplah Pub) Origin Bk Sales.

— The First Mission. (Ammon Adventures Ser.: Vol. 2). 96p. (J). (gr. 6-12). 1997. pap. 7.95 (*1-890830-57-7*, Pub. by Riplah Pub) Origin Bk Sales.

— In the Enemy's Camp. (Ammon Adventures Ser.: Vol. 3). 128p. (J). (gr. 6-12). 1997. pap. 7.95 (*1-890830-58-5*, Pub. by Riplah Pub) Origin Bk Sales.

***Clark, David F. & Clark, Trina W.** A Witness at the Cross. 96p. 1999. 14.95 (*1-890830-70-4*, Pub. by Riplah Pub) Origin Bk Sales.

Clark, David H. The Cosmos from Space. fac. ed. LC 87-34410. 178p. reprint ed. pap. 55.20 (*0-7837-8002-8*, 204775800008) Bks Demand.

— The Story of a Mental Hospital: Fulbourn 1858-1983. 1996. pap. 29.95 (*1-899209-03-4*, Pub. by Process Pr) Intl Spec Bk.

Clark, David H., jt. auth. see Stephenson, Francis R.

Clark, David J. & Hatton, Howard A. A Handbook on the Books of Nahum, Habakkuk, & Zephaniah. LC 93-36507. (UBS Handbook Ser.). Orig. Title: Translators Handbook on the Books of Nahum, Habakkuk & Zephaniah. ix, 221p. 1989. pap. 13.99 (*0-8267-0141-8*, 102694) Untd Bible Soc.

Clark, David J., et al. A Handbook on the Books of Obadiah, Jonah & Micah. LC 93-25085. 290p. 1993. 19.99 (*0-8267-0132-9*, 105180) Untd Bible Soc.

Clark, David J., jt. ed. see Chan, Ming K.

Clark, David K. & Rakestraw, Robert V., eds. Readings in Christian Ethics: Issues & Applications, 2. LC 93-30274. 496p. 1995. pap. 29.99 (*0-8010-2056-5*) Baker Bks.

— Readings in Christian Ethics: Theory & Method, 2. LC 93-30274. 880p. 1994. pap. 49.99 (*0-8010-2094-8*) Baker Bks.

Clark, David L. Charles Brockden Brown: Pioneer Voice of America. LC 75-181909. (BCL Ser.). reprint ed. 34.50 (*0-404-01548-4*) AMS Pr.

— Database Design: Applications of Library Cataloging Techniques. (Illus.). 352p. 1990. 34.95 (*0-8306-3443-6*, 3443) McGraw-Hill Prof.

— L. A. on Foot. (Illus.). 1985. pap. 4.95 (*0-913290-03-3*) Camaro Pub.

— Stratigraphy & Glacial-Marine Sediments of the Amerasian Basin, Central Arctic Ocean. LC 80-65270. (Geological Society of America, Special Paper: No. 181). 95p. (Orig.). reprint ed. pap. 30.00 (*0-608-13242-X*, 202545300044) Bks Demand.

Clark, David L., ed. Conodont Biofacies & Provincialism. LC 84-21231. (Geological Society of America Ser.: Vol. 196). (Illus.). 346p. reprint ed. pap. 107.30 (*0-608-07725-9*, 206781300010) Bks Demand.

— Shelley's Prose. LC 54-6517. 1954. 20.00 (*0-8263-0015-4*) Lib Soc Sci.

***Clark, David L. & Boutros, Nashaat N.** The Brain & Behavior: An Introduction to Behavioral Neuroanatomy. LC 99-21428. (Illus.). 1999. pap. 34.95 (*0-632-04295-8*) Blackwell Sci.

Clark, David L. & Coellnicht, Donald C., eds. New Romanticisms: Theory & Critical Practice. (Theory - Culture Ser.). 144p. 1994. text 55.00 (*0-8020-2890-X*) U of Toronto Pr.

Clark, David L., ed. see Cooper, et al.

Clark, David L., ed. see Giroux, Henry A.

Clark, David L., jt. ed. see Rajan, Tilottama.

Clark, David Leon. Managing Virtual Private Networks. LC 99-35354. 1999. pap. text 55.00 (*0-07-135202-3*) McGraw.

Clark, David Lindsey. Appraisals of Original Wind Music: A Survey & Guide, 77. LC 98-51908. (Music Reference Collection: Vol. 77). 576p. 1999. lib. bdg. 89.50 (*0-313-30906-X*) Greenwood.

Clark, David M. & Davey, Brian A. Natural Dualities for the Working Algebraist. LC 97-46777. 368p. 1999. text 64.95 (*0-521-45415-8*) Cambridge U Pr.

Clark, David M. & Fairburn, Christopher G., eds. The Science & Practice of Cognitive Behaviour Therapy. (Illus.). 452p. 1996. pap. text 51.95 (*0-19-262725-2*) OUP.

Clark, David R. That Black Day: Manuscripts of Crazy Jane on the Day of Judgement. (Illus.). 55p. 1980. pap. 10.95 (*0-318-39998-9*, Pub. by Smyth) Dufour.

— Yeats at Songs & Choruses. LC 81-16096. (Illus.). 308p. 1983. lib. bdg. 35.00 (*0-87023-358-0*) U of Mass Pr.

Clark, David R. & McGuire, James B. W. B. Yeats: The Writing of Sophocles' King Oedipus. LC 86-72889. (Memoirs Ser.: Vol. 175). (Illus.). (C). 1989. 20.00 (*0-87169-175-2*, M175-CLD) Am Philos.

Clark, David R., et al. Druid Craft: The Writing of "The Shadowy Waters" LC 74-103474. 376p. 1971. 40.00 (*0-87023-068-9*) U of Mass Pr.

Clark, David R., et al. W. B. Yeats & the Theatre of Desolate Reality: Including Vivien & Time, The Irish National Theatre & The Poet & the Actress. rev. ed. LC 92-25035. (Critical Studies in Irish Literature: Vol. 3). (Illus.). 288p. (C). 1993. reprint ed. 49.95 (*0-8132-0773-8*); reprint ed. pap. 19.95 (*0-8132-0774-6*) Cath U Pr.

Clark, David R., ed. see Yeats, William Butler.

Clark, David S. Introduction to U. S. Law. 1993. pap. text 53.00 (*90-6544-688-5*) Kluwer Academic.

Clark, David S. & Ansay, Tugrul, eds. Introduction to the Law of the United States. LC 92-35806. 1993. 108.00 (*90-6544-655-9*) Kluwer Law Intl.

Clark, David S. & D'Amato, Anthony, eds. International Civil Litigation Anthology. (C). 2000. pap. text. write for info. (*0-87084-386-9*) Anderson Pub Co.

Clark, David S., jt. auth. see Merryman, John H.

Clark, David T. & Feast, W. J., eds. Polymer Surfaces. LC 77-17426. (Illus.). 457p. reprint ed. pap. 141.70 (*0-608-30010-1*, 202210100024) Bks Demand.

***Clark, Dawn E.** Gifts for the Soul: A Guided Journey of Discovery, Transformation & Infinite Possibilities. LC 99-61373. (Illus.). 192p. 1999. 23.00 (*1-928532-00-4*) Aarron Pubg.

— Perceiving Energy: Beyond the Physical Form. LC 99-90425. (Illus.). 128p. 1999. pap. 12.95 (*1-928532-02-0*) Aarron Pubg.

***Clark, Debbie.** Beyond Our Mega Dawn. LC 99-96661. 1999. pap. 12.95 (*0-533-13280-0*) Vantage.

***Clark, Deborah.** Antipodeans: Challenge & Response in Australian Art, 1955-1965. (Illus.). 48p. 2000. pap. 18.95 (*0-642-54158-2*) Natl Gallery.

Clark, Deborah M., jt. auth. see Murphy, Earline M.

Clark, Dee, jt. auth. see Clark, Chap.

Clark, Della R. Quiet One. LC 92-70830. (Illus.). 64p. (J). (ps-5). 1992. 15.00 (*0-9631252-0-6*) Desert Rose.

Clark, Dennis. Erin's Heirs: Irish Bonds of Community. LC 90-25249. 248p. 1991. reprint ed. pap. 76.90 (*0-7837-9581-5*, 206033000005) Bks Demand.

— Hibernia America: The Irish & Regional Cultures, 14. LC 85-27230. (Contributions in Ethnic Studies: No. 14). 230p. 1986. 59.95 (*0-313-25252-1*, CHB/, Greenwood Pr) Greenwood.

— The Irish in Philadelphia: Ten Generations of Urban Experience. LC 81-18343. 264p. 1982. pap. 19.95 (*0-87722-227-4*) Temple U Pr.

— The Irish Relations: Trials of an Immigrant Tradition. LC 81-65293. 356p. 1982. 34.50 (*0-8386-3083-9*) Fairleigh Dickinson.

Clark, Dennis, jt. ed. see England, Eugene.

Clark, Dennis R. Sunday Morning: Reflections on the Word. LC 97-150158. 160p. (Orig.). 1996. pap. 24.95 (*1-55612-861-4*, LL1861) Sheed & Ward WI.

Clark, Dexter, jt. auth. see Clark, Lynette.

Clark, Diana B. & Uhry, Joanna K. Dyslexia: Theory & Practice of Remedial Instruction. 2nd ed. LC 95-33423. (Orig.). 1995. pap. 28.00 (*0-912752-43-2*) York Pr.

***Clark, Dick.** Dicks Clarks Amern Band Lit G. 2000. 40.00 (*0-06-757529-3*) HarpC.

Clark, Dick. A Foreign Policy for the United States in the 1980s & 1990s. 54p. 1983. pap. text 10.50 (*0-8191-5867-4*) U Pr of Amer.

— Looking Great, Staying Young. LC 80-684. 256p. 1980. 11.95 (*0-672-52657-3*, Bobbs) Macmillan.

— The Negro Leagues Book. 1994. pap. 24.95 (*0-910137-55-2*) Soc Am Baseball Res.

Clark, Dick & Aspen Institute. The Convergence of U.S. National Security & the Global Environment: Second Conference, March 31-April 5, 1997. LC 98-127958. 1997. write for info. (*0-89843-210-3*) The Aspen Inst.

— Education & the Development of American Youth: Fifth Conference, February 13-16, 1998. LC 99-163681. 1998. write for info. (*0-89843-234-0*) The Aspen Inst.

— Ensuring Our Children's Future: Fourth Conference, February 14-17, 1997. LC 98-207895. 1997. write for info. (*0-89843-207-3*) The Aspen Inst.

Clark, Dick & Bronson, Fred. Dick Clark's American Bandstand. LC 96-45007. 192p. 1997. pap. 20.00 (*0-06-757456-4*) HarpC.

***Clark, Dick & Bronson, Fred.** Dick Clark's American Bandstand. (Illus.). 189p. 1999. reprint ed. pap. text 20.00 (*0-7881-6582-8*) DIANE Pub.

Clark, Dick & Francis, Paul. Murder on Tour: A Rock 'n Roll Mystery. 224p. 1989. 16.95 (*0-89296-286-0*) Mysterious Pr.

— Murder on Tour: A Rock 'n Roll Mystery. 1990. mass mkt. 4.50 (*0-445-40856-1*, Pub. by Warner Bks) Little.

Clark, Dollie, ed. Best of Bayou Cuisine. rev. ed. LC 97-39802. Orig. Title: Bayou Cuisine. (Illus.). 288p. 1997. pap. 14.95 (*0-937552-78-X*) Quail Ridge.

Clark, Domini. Canada: The Culture. (Lands, Peoples, & Cultures Ser.). (Illus.). (J). 1993. 7.95 (*0-606-18051-6*) Turtleback.

— South Africa the Culture. LC 99-44280. (Lands, Peoples, & Cultures Ser.). (Illus.). 32p. (YA). (gr. 4-9). 1999. pap. 7.95 (*0-86505-317-0*); lib. bdg. 20.60 (*0-86505-237-9*) Crabtree Pub Co.

— South Africa the Land. LC 99-42506. (Lands, Peoples & Cultures Ser.). (Illus.). 32p. (YA). (gr. 4-9). 1999. pap. 7.95 (*0-86505-315-4*); lib. bdg. 20.60 (*0-86505-235-2*) Crabtree Pub Co.

— South Africa the People. LC 99-44281. (Lands, Peoples & Cultures Ser.). (Illus.). 32p. (YA). (gr. 4-9). 1999. lib. bdg. 20.60 (*0-86505-236-0*) Crabtree Pub Co.

***Clark, Domini & Kalman, Bobbie.** South Africa the People. LC 99-44281. (Lands, Peoples & Cultures Ser.). (Illus.). 32p. (YA). (gr. 4-9). 1999. pap. 7.95 (*0-86505-316-2*) Crabtree Pub Co.

Clark, Dominic & Krause, Paul. Representing Uncertain Knowledge: An AI Approach. 288p. (Orig.). 1993. pap. text 22.95 (*1-871516-17-X*, Pub. by Intellect) Cromland.

Clark, Don. Loving Someone Gay. rev. ed. LC 87-13846. 290p. 1995. pap. 9.95 (*0-89087-505-7*) Celestial Arts.

— Loving Someone Gay. 3rd ed. LC 97-13372. 256p. 1997. pap. 14.95 (*0-89087-837-4*) Celestial Arts.

— Magy la Magnifica. 1994. pap. 19.95 (*1-884321-02-X*); disk 9.95 (*1-884321-03-8*) Big Sky Orig.

— Sunday in Sudan. 230p. (Orig.). 1993. pap. 19.95 (*1-884321-00-3*); disk 9.95 (*1-884321-01-1*) Big Sky Orig.

Clark, Donald. Field Experience in Teacher Education: A Model for Industrial Arts-Technology Education. 73p. 1985. 7.25 (*0-318-20413-4*, SN52) Ctr Educ Trng Employ.

Clark, Donald & Andersen, Christopher. John Wayne's "The Alamo" The Making of John Wayne's 1960 Epic Film. LC 95-105156. (Illus.). 172p. (Orig.). 1994. pap. 17.95 (*0-9640338-0-1*) R & G Prods.

— John Wayne's "The Alamo" The Making of the Epic Film. (Illus.). 172p. 1995. pap. 17.95 (*0-8065-1625-9*, Citadel Pr) Carol Pub Group.

Clark, Donald & Friends of Thornton W. Burgess Society Committee. Flavors of Cape Cod. 6th ed. (Illus.). 1988. pap. text 9.95 (*0-9621171-0-2*) T W Burgess Society.

Clark, Donald, et al. U. S.-Korean Relations. (Keck Center for International & Strategic Studies: No. 8). viii, 117p. 1995. pap. 10.95 (*0-930607-19-8*) Regina Bks.

Clark, Donald C., jt. auth. see Clark, Sally N.

Clark, Donald C., jt. auth. see Georgiades, William D.

Clark, Donald L. Rhetoric in Greco-Roman Education. LC 77-21723. 285p. 1977. reprint ed. lib. bdg. 62.50 (*0-8371-9790-2*, CLRH, Greenwood Pr) Greenwood.

Clark, Donald M. Displaced Workers: A Challenge for Vocational Education. 37p. 1983. 4.25 (*0-318-22078-4*, IN255) Ctr Educ Trng Employ.

Clark, Donald N. Christianity in Modern Korea. LC 86-9092. (Asian Agenda Reports: No. 5). 70p. (Orig.). (C). 1986. pap. text 12.50 (*0-8191-5385-0*); lib. bdg. 27.00 (*0-8191-5384-2*) U Pr of Amer.

***Clark, Donald N.** Culture & Customs of Korea. (Culture & Customs of Asia Ser.). 208p. 2000. 45.00 (*0-313-30456-4*, GR0456, Greenwood Pr) Greenwood.

Clark, Donald N., ed. & rev. see Macdonald, Donald S.

Clark, Donald T. Monterey County Place Names: A Geographical Dictionary. LC 91-32260. 800p. 1991. 29.95 (*1-880478-01-3*); pap. 21.95 (*1-880478-00-5*) Kestrel Pr.

— Santa Cruz County Place Names: A Geographical Dictionary. LC 86-24840. (Illus.). 624p. 1986. 33.95 (*0-940283-00-X*); pap. 23.95 (*0-940283-01-8*) Santa Cruz Hist.

Clark, Donald W. The Early Kachemak Phase on Kodiak Island at Old Kiavak. LC 96-901071. (Mercury Ser.: ASC No. 155). (FRE & ENG., Illus.). 129p. 1997. pap. 21.95 (*0-660-15967-8*) U of Wash Pr.

— Fort Reliance, Yukon: An Archaeological Assessment, Vol. 2. LC 96-117973. (Mercury Ser.: ASC No. 150). (FRE & ENG., Illus.). 262p. 1995. pap. 24.95 (*0-660-14032-2*, Pub. by CN Mus Civilization) U of Wash Pr.

Clark, Donald W. & Clark, A. McFadyen. Batza Tena, Trail to Obsidian: Archaeology at an Alaskan Obsidian Source. (Mercury Ser.: ASC No. 147). (Illus.). 332p. 1994. pap. 27.95 (*0-660-14016-0*, Pub. by CN Mus Civilization) U of Wash Pr.

Clark, Donna. Queer Street Cookbook. (Sexual Politics Ser.). (Illus.). 160p. 1996. pap. 14.95 (*0-304-33812-5*) Continuum.

Clark, Donna, jt. auth. see Haven, Kendall.

***Clark, Doris C.** Feed All My Sheep: A Guide & Curriculum for Adults with Developmental Disabilities. LC 99-47555. (Illus.). 128p. 2000. pap. 21.95 (*0-664-50113-3*, Pub. by Geneva Press) Presbyterian Pub.

Clark, Dorothy. Country Mediterranean Cooking: Over 50 Inspiring Recipes for Authentic Regional Dishes. 1997. 12.98 (*1-901289-93-1*, Pub. by Hermes Hse) Random.

Clark, Dorothy C. Vincente Espinel "Diversas Rimas" 204p. 1956. 4.50 (*0-318-22353-8*) Hispanic Inst.

Clark, Doug. Doug Clark's Loose Clark Journals: A Collection of Columns by Doug Clark. Higgins, Shaun O., ed. LC 99-187319. 325p. 1998. 23.95 (*0-923910-10-7*) NMV.

Clark, Doug. Unkindest Cut. 336p. 1996. mass mkt. 7.99 (*0-7710-2117-8*) McCland & Stewart.

Clark, Dougan. Instructions to Christian Converts. 1990. pap. 3.99 (*0-88019-072-8*) Schmul Pub Co.

— The Theology of Holiness. unabridged ed. 112p. 1996. reprint ed. pap. 7.99 (*0-88019-347-6*) Schmul Pub Co.

Clark, Douglas. Dead Letter: A Masters & Green Mystery. large type ed. 379p. 1989. 27.99 (*0-7089-1972-3*) Ulverscroft.

— Doone Walk. large type ed. (Linford Mystery Library). 368p. 1987. pap. 16.99 (*0-7089-6394-3*, Linford) Ulverscroft.

— Plain Sailing: A Masters & Green Mystery. large type ed. 384p. 1989. 27.99 (*0-7089-2008-X*) Ulverscroft.

Clark, Douglas A. Aerospace Historian: Cumulative Index by Author, Book Review, Title & Subject 1974-1983. 127p. 1985. pap. text 27.95 (*0-89126-124-9*) MA-AH Pub.

Clark, Douglas R. & Brunt, John C., eds. Introducing the Bible Vol. I: The Old Testament & Interestamental Literature. (Illus.). 648p. (C). 1997. 69.00 (*0-7618-0804-3*); pap. 32.50 (*0-7618-0805-1*) U Pr of Amer.

Clark, Douglas R., jt. ed. see Brunt, John C.

Clark, Douglas S., jt. auth. see Blanch, Harvey W.

Clark, Douglas S., jt. ed. see Blanch, Harvey W.

Clark, Douglas S., jt. ed. see Burrington, James D.

Clark, Douglas W. Alchemy Unlimited. 320p. 1990. pap. 3.50 (*0-380-75726-5*, Avon Bks) Morrow Avon.

— Rehearsal for a Renaissance. 1992. mass mkt. 4.50 (*0-380-76310-9*, Avon Bks) Morrow Avon.

— Whirlwind Alchemy. 320p. (Orig.). 1993. mass mkt. 4.99 (*0-380-76309-5*, Avon Bks) Morrow Avon.

Clark, Duncan W. & Macmahon, Brian, eds. Preventive & Community Medicine. 2nd ed. 1981. 65.00 (*0-316-14596-3*, Little Brwn Med Div) Lppncott W & W.

Clark, Dymphna, ed. New Holland Journal: Baron Charles von Hugel November 1833-October 1834. (Miegunyah Press Ser.: No. 1:17). (Illus.). 240p. 1995. 49.95 (*0-522-84474-X*, Pub. by Melbourne Univ Pr) Paul & Co Pubs.

Clark, E. Ann, et al. The Contribution of Managed Grasslands to Sustainable Agriculture in the Great Lakes Basin. LC 96-42369. (Journal of Sustainable Agriculture Ser.: Vol. 8, Nos. 2/3). 189p. (C). 1997. text 69.95 (*1-56022-056-2*) Haworth Jrnl Co-Edits.

Clark, E. C. Analysis of Criminal Liability. xii, 115p. 1983. reprint ed. 27.50 (*0-8377-0446-4*, Rothman) W S Hein.

— Early Roman Law: The Regal Period. v, 151p. 1987. reprint ed. 32.50 (*0-8377-2011-7*, Rothman) W S Hein.

— History of Roman Private Law, 3 vols. in 4 bks., Set. LC 90-55179. 1652p. 1990. reprint ed. 245.00 (*0-912004-80-0*) Gaunt.

— Practical Jurisprudence: A Comment on Austin. xii, 403p. 1980. reprint ed. 42.50 (*0-8377-0427-8*, Rothman) W S Hein.

Clark, E. Culpepper. Francis Warrington Dawson & the Politics of Restoration: South Carolina, 1874-1889. LC 79-27884. 260p. 1980. reprint ed. pap. 80.60 (*0-608-01664-0*, 206231900002) Bks Demand.

— The Schoolhouse Door: Segregation's Last Stand at the University of Alabama. (Illus.). 352p. 1995. pap. text 21.00 (*0-19-509658-4*) OUP.

Clark, E. D., et al. La Fabrication des Plates et Papiers (Pulp & Paper Manufacture) Les Fibres Secondaires (Secondary Fibers) Traductions de Villers-Cote, Inc. Staff, tr. (FRE.). 164p. (C). 1991. pap. text (*2-9801486-4-4*) CA66.

Clark, E. Douglas & Clark, Robert S. Fathers & Sons in the Book of Mormon. LC 91-35112. xviii, 334p. 1992. 14.95 (*0-87579-567-6*) Deseret Bk.

Clark, E. Eugene & Livermore, John. Australian Marketing Law. LC 94-208297. 400p. 1994. text 49.00 (*0-455-21055-1*, Pub. by LawBk Co) Gaunt.

Clark, E. Harrison. All Cloudless Glory Vol. 1: The Life of George Washington: From Boyhood to Valley Forge, 2 vols., Set. (Illus.). 16p. (C). 1995. 39.95 (*0-89526-466-8*) Regnery Pub.

Clark, E. Nelson & Kasar, Jack. Developing Professional Behaviors. LC 99-57166. 220p. 2000. pap. 25.00 (*1-55642-316-0*, 33160) SLACK Inc.

Clark, E. Ray & Canter, Larry W., eds. Environmental Policy & NEPA: Past, Present & Future. LC 97-173383. (Illus.). 360p. 1997. boxed set 74.95 (*1-57444-072-1*) St Lucie Pr.

Clark, Earl E. Name Thang Baby Name Book: Over 15,000 English Names with Spanish & French Translations. 1997. pap. text 5.95 (*0-9646643-0-5*) New Vis Dist.

Clark, Ed & Soulsby, Anna. Organizational Change in Post-Communist Europe: Management & Transformation in the Czech Republic. LC 98-35445. (Studies of Societies in Transition). 1998. write for info. (*0-415-20333-3*) Routledge.

Clark, Eddie, et al, eds. Attention, Attitude & Effect in Response to Advertising. (Advertising & Consumer Psychology Ser.). 336p. 1993. text 79.95 (*0-8058-0756-X*) L Erlbaum Assocs.

Clark, Edie. The Place He Made. large type ed. (General Ser.). 1996. pap. 20.95 (*0-7862-0668-3*) Thorndike Pr.

Clark, Edie, ed. The Forgotten Arts, Bk. 4. LC 75-10770. (Forgotten Arts Ser.). (Illus.). 64p. (Orig.). 1979. pap. 6.95 (*0-911658-95-5*, 80-250-5) Yankee Bks.

Clark Editorial & Design Staff, ed. see Amerikaner, Phyllis.

Clark Editorial & Design Staff, ed. see Bollinger, Taree & Seeman, Cary.

Clark Editorial & Design Staff, ed. see Costello, Cynthia.

Clark Editorial & Design Staff, ed. see Falstein, Mark.

Clark Editorial & Design Staff, ed. see Fox, Nancy.

Clark Editorial & Design Staff, ed. see Jaffee, Charlotte & Doherty, Barbara.

Clark Editorial & Design Staff, ed. see Johmann, Carol & Rieth, Elizabeth.

Clark Editorial & Design Staff, ed. see Klawitter, Pamela Amick.

An Asterisk (*) at the beginning of an entry indicates that the title is appearing for the first time.

Clark Editorial & Design Staff, ed. see Learning Works Staff & Schwartz, Linda.

Clark Editorial & Design Staff, ed. see Otto, Ramona & Balaban, Jocelyn.

Clark Editorial & Design Staff, ed. see Schwartz, Linda.

Clark Editorial & Design Staff, ed. see Sylvester, Diane.

Clark Editorial & Design Staff, ed. & des. see Schwartz, Linda.

Clark Editorial & Design Staff, ed. & des. see Sylvester, Diane.

Clark, Edna. Ohio Art & Artists. 1993. reprint ed. lib. bdg. 89.00 (*0-7812-5350-0*) Rprt Serv.

Clark, Edward. Black Writers in New England. (Illus.). 76p. (Orig.). (C). 1985. pap. 10.00 (*0-934441-01-4*) Boston Afro Am.

— Dictionary Catalog of the Collection of African American Literature in the Mildred F. Sawyer Library of Suffolk University. LC 95-73090. (Illus.). xxvi, 220p. (Orig.). 1996. pap. 20.00 (*0-9650710-0-6*) Boston Afro Am.

Clark, Edward A., ed. see Shaw, Michael & Lee, Victoria.

***Clark, Edward B., et al, eds.** Etiology & Morphogenesis of Congenital Heart Disease: Twenty Years of Progress in Genetics & Developmental Biology. (Illus.). 350p. 2000. 150.00 (*0-87993-447-6*) Futura Pub.

Clark, Edward B., jt. ed. see Neill, Catherine A.

Clark, Edward S. Stephens Family with Collateral Branches. (Illus.). 185p. 1994. reprint ed. pap. 29.50 (*0-8328-4385-7*) Higginson Bk Co.

— Stephens Family with Collateral Branches. (American Genealogical Record Ser.: Vol. I). (Illus.). 185p. 1994. reprint ed. lib. bdg. 39.50 (*0-8328-4384-9*) Higginson Bk Co.

Clark, Edward W. Five Great Catholic Ideas. LC 98-9515. 160p. 1998. pap. 13.95 (*0-8245-1751-2*, Crsrd) Crossroad NY.

Clark, Edward W., jt. ed. see Vaughan, Alden T.

Clark, Edwin C. History of Roman Private Law: Sources, Jurisprudence & Regal, 3 vols. LC 64-13392. 2036p. 1906. 65.00 (*0-8196-0146-2*) Biblo.

— Jurisprudence, 2 vols., Vol. 2. LC 64-13392. 1234p. 1906. write for info. Biblo.

— Regal, Vol. 3. LC 64-13392. 634p. 1906. write for info. Biblo.

— Source, Vol. 1. LC 64-13392. 168p. 1906. write for info. Biblo.

Clark, Edwin H. & Cherry, Philip J. Groundwater: Managing the Unseen Resource: A Handbook for States. LC 92-195880. 45p. 1992. reprint ed. pap. 30.00 (*0-608-04235-8*, 206499200012) Bks Demand.

Clark, Elaine A. There's Money Where Your Mouth Is: An Insider's Guide to a Career in Voice-overs. LC 95-17341. (Illus.). 208p. 1995. pap. 16.95 (*0-8230-7703-9*, Back Stage Bks) Watsn-Guptill.

***Clark, Elaine A.** There's Money Where Your Mouth Is: An Insider's Guide to a Career in Voice-Overs. 2nd enl. ed. (Illus.). 240p. 2000. pap. write for info. (*0-8230-7702-0*, Back Stage Bks) Watsn-Guptill.

Clark, Eleanor. The Oysters of Locmariaquer. LC 77-82670. (Illus.). 1978. pap. 3.95 (*0-226-10763-9*, P752) U Ch Pr.

***Clark, Eleanor.** Rome & a Villa. (Illus.). 450p. 2000. pap. 18.00 (*1-883642-51-5*, Pub. by Steerforth Pr) Publishers Group.

Clark, Eleanor. The Song of Roland. 1999. lib. bdg. 19.95 (*1-56723-205-1*) Yestermorrow.

Clark, Eleanor, jt. auth. see Eddy, Jackie.

Clark, Elias, et al. Gratuitous Transfers, Wills Intestate Succession, Trusts, Gifts & Future Interests. 3rd ed. LC 85-10571. (American Casebook Ser.). 969p. (C). 1985. reprint ed. text 52.00 (*0-314-91766-7*) West Pub.

Clark, Elias, jt. auth. see Bittker, Boris I.

Clark, Eliza. What You Need. 176p. pap. 19.95 (*1-895897-11-4*) Somerville Hse.

— What You Need: Collector's Edition. 176p. 35.00 (*1-895897-13-0*) Somerville Hse.

***Clark, Eliza & Krykorka, Vladyana.** Seeing & Believing. 2000. 17.95 (*0-00-648190-6*) HarpC.

Clark, Elizabeth Ann. Clement's Use of Aristotle: The Aristotelian Contribution of Clement of Alexandria's Refutation of Gnosticism. LC 77-93913. (Texts & Studies in Religion: Vol. 1). 192p. 1977. lib. bdg. 79.95 (*0-88946-984-9*) E Mellen.

— Jerome, Chrysostom, & Friends: Essays & Translations. LC 79-66374. (Studies in Women & Religion: Vol. 2). xi, 270p. 1979. lib. bdg. 89.95 (*0-88946-548-7*) E Mellen.

— The Life of Melania the Younger: Introduction, Translation & Commentary. LC 84-20635. (Studies in Women & Religion: Vol. 14). 305p. 1984. lib. bdg. 99.95 (*0-88946-535-5*) E Mellen.

— The Origenist Controversy: The Cultural Construction of an Early Christian Debate. 352p. 1992. text 52.50 (*0-691-03173-8*, Pub. by Princeton U Pr) Cal Prin Full Svc.

***Clark, Elizabeth Ann.** Reading Renunciation: Asceticism & Scripture in Early Christianity. LC 98-55313. 360p. 1999. 65.00 (*0-691-00511-7*, Pub. by Princeton U Pr) Cal Prin Full Svc.

Clark, Elizabeth Ann. Reading Renunciation: Asceticism & Scripture in Early Christianity. LC 98-55313. 360p. 1999. pap. 21.95 (*0-691-00512-5*, Pub. by Princeton U Pr) Cal Prin Full Svc.

— Women in the Early Church. Halton, Thomas, ed. LC 83-81477. (Message of the Fathers of the Church Ser.: Vol. 13). 250p. 1984. pap. 14.95 (*0-8146-5332-4*) Liturgical Pr.

Clark, Elizabeth Ann, ed. Supplier Profiles Directory of SCADA Products, Systems, Services. 364p. 1994. pap. 75.00 (*0-9644786-0-9*) GITA.

Clark, Elizabeth Ann & Hatch, Diane F. The Golden Bough, the Oaken Cross: The Virgilian Cento of Faltonia Betitia Proba. LC 81-5081. (American Academy of Religion: Vol. 5). 259p. 1981. reprint ed. pap. 80.30 (*0-608-05668-5*, 206618400006) Bks Demand.

Clark, Elizabeth Ann, ed. see Augustine, Saint.

Clark, Elizabeth J., et al, eds. Clinical Sociological Perspectives in Illness & Loss: The Linkage of Theory & Practice. LC 90-1529. 348p. 1990. pap. 21.95 (*0-914783-41-6*) Charles.

Clark, Elizabeth J. & Kutscher, Austin H., eds. The Thanatology Community & the Needs of the Movement. LC 92-10750. (Loss, Grief & Care Ser.: Vol. 6, No. 1). 125p. 1992. text 39.95 (*1-56024-218-3*) Haworth Pr.

Clark, Elizabeth L., jt. auth. see Wentworth, Michael.

Clark, Elizabeth W. Addicted to Baskets: 20 Original Baskets with Step by Step Instructions. (Illus.). 124p. 1997. pap. 16.98 (*0-9663737-0-7*) E W Clark.

Clark, Ella. Guardian Spirit Quest. (Indian Culture Ser.). 50p. (J). (gr. 5-10). 1997. pap. 6.95 (*0-89992-144-2*) Coun India Ed.

Clark, Ella E. Indian Legends from the Northern Rockies. LC 66-13421. (Civilization of the American Indian Ser.: No. 82). (Illus.). 416p. 1988. reprint ed. pap. 14.95 (*0-8061-2087-8*) U of Okla Pr.

— Indian Legends of the Pacific Northwest. (Illus.). (YA). 1953. pap. 15.95 (*0-520-00243-1*, Pub. by U CA Pr) Cal Prin Full Svc.

Clark, Ella E. & Edmonds, Margot. Sacagawea of the Lewis & Clark Expedition. LC 78-65466. 1979. pap. 15.95 (*0-520-05060-6*, Pub. by U CA Pr) Cal Prin Full Svc.

Clark, Ella E., jt. auth. see Edmonds, Margot.

Clark, Elmer S. Clark of Elizabethtown in Jersey. (Illus.). 223p. 1997. reprint ed. pap. 34.50 (*0-8328-7942-8*); reprint ed. lib. bdg. 44.50 (*0-8328-7941-X*) Higginson Bk Co.

Clark, Elmer T. Charles Wesley. 3rd ed. 20p. 1976. reprint ed. pap. 1.00 (*1-880927-02-0*) Gen Comm Arch.

— Francis Asbury: The Prophet of the Long Road. 4th ed. 19p. 1984. reprint ed. pap. 1.00 (*1-880927-04-7*) Gen Comm Arch.

***Clark, Elmer T.** The Small Sects in America. rev. ed. 256p. 1999. reprint ed. text 20.00 (*0-7881-6404-X*) DIANE Pub.

Clark, Elsie, ed. see Thomas, Mady, III.

Clark, Emery. Recipes & Reminiscences of New Orleans. 237p. (Orig.). 1971. pap. 9.95 (*0-9604718-0-4*) Ursuline.

Clark, Emilie, jt. auth. see Shaw, Lytle.

Clark, Emilie, ed. see Cory, Alex & Hejinian, Lyn.

Clark, Emily. The Gingerbread Man: Easy Readers Tales & Rhymes. (Easy Readers Ser.). 16p. (J). (ps-k). 1997. pap. 2.49 (*1-57690-288-9*) Tchr Create Mat.

— The Little Red Hen: Easy Readers Tales & Rhymes. (Easy Readers Ser.). 16p. (J). (ps-1). 1997. pap. 2.49 (*1-57690-286-2*) Tchr Create Mat.

— Stuffed Peacocks. LC 75-110181. (Short Story Index Reprint Ser.). 1977. 20.95 (*0-8369-3332-X*) Ayer.

— The Three Billy Goats Gruff. (Easy Reader Ser.). (Illus.). (J). 1997. pap., teacher ed. 2.49 (*1-57690-287-0*, TCM2287) Tchr Create Mat.

Clark, Emma. Underneath Which Rivers Flow: The Symbolism of the Islamic Garden. 48p. 1996. pap. 16.95 (*1-898465-06-1*) Intl Spec Bk.

Clark, Emma C. Across the Blue Mountains. LC 93-12118. (Illus.). 32p. (J). (ps-3). 1993. 14.95 (*0-15-201220-6*) Harcourt.

— The Bouncing Dinosaur. LC 89-46429. (Illus.). 32p. (J). (ps-3). 1990. 13.95 (*0-374-30912-4*) FS&G.

— Catch That Hat! LC 89-34881. (Illus.). (J). (ps-2). 1990. 12.95 (*0-316-14496-7*) Little.

— Little Miss Muffet's Count-Along Surprise. LC 97-204886. (Illus.). 32p. (J). (ps-1). 1997. 15.95 (*0-385-32517-7*, DD Bks Yng Read) BDD Bks Young Read.

Clark, Emma C. A Thousand Yards of Sea. LC 91-35687. 80p. (J). (ps up). 1993. 18.00 (*0-688-11437-7*, Grenwillow Bks) HarpC Child Bks.

***Clark, Emma Chichester.** I Love You Blue Kangaroo. (J). 2001. pap. 6.99 (*0-440-41549-7*) BDD Bks Young Read.

— Little Miss Muffet's Count-Along Surprise. (Illus.). 32p. (J). (ps-1). 2000. pap. 6.99 (*0-440-41414-8*, Yearling) BDD Bks Young Read.

— Little Miss Muffet's Count-Along Surprise. (Illus.). (J). 2000. 12.44 (*0-606-18000-1*) Turtleback.

Clark, Emma Chichester. More! LC 98-45497. (Illus.). 32p. (J). 1999. 15.95 (*0-385-32630-0*) BDD Bks Young Read.

***Clark, Emma Chichester.** Where Are You Blue Kangaro. (J). 2001. mass mkt. (*0-385-90003-1*) BDD Bks Young Read.

— Where Are You Blue Kangaroo. (J). 2001. mass mkt. (*0-385-32797-8*) BDD Bks Young Read.

Clark, Ephraim. Managing Risk in International Business: Techniques & Applications. LC 96-38876. 304p. (gr. 13). 1996. mass mkt. 50.00 (*0-412-59720-9*) Chapman & Hall.

Clark, Ephraim, et al. International Finance. LC 93-10860. (Accounting & Finance Ser.). 640p. (gr. 13). 1994. mass mkt. 29.95 (*0-412-40930-5*) Chapman & Hall.

Clark, Eric. Chinese Burn. large type ed. 528p. 1986. 27.99 (*0-7089-1454-3*) Ulverscroft.

— The Sleeper. large type ed. 432p. 1987. 27.99 (*0-7089-1623-6*) Ulverscroft.

Clark, Erica R., jt. auth. see Rogers, William W.

Clark, Erlinda. Intermediate Accounting: Selected Topics 2nd ed. 350p. (C). 1994. text 51.00 (*0-536-58706-X*) Pearson Custom.

***Clark, Erskine, ed.** Exilic Preaching: Testimony for Christian Exiles in an Increasingly Hostile Culture. LC 98-41028. 144p. 1998. pap. 13.00 (*1-56338-246-6*) TPI PA.

Clark, Etta. Growing Old Is Not for Sissies II: Portraits of Senior Athletes. LC 95-24277. (Illus.). 120p. (Orig.). 1995. pap. 22.95 (*0-87654-478-2*) Pomegranate Calif.

Clark, Eugene, ed. When Conscience & Politics Meet: A Catholic View. LC 93-78818. 104p. (Orig.). 1993. pap. 8.95 (*0-89870-477-4*) Ignatius Pr.

Clark, Eunice, tr. see La Fontaine, Jean de & Calder, Alexander.

Clark, Eunice N. Clarks from Pennsylvania & Allied Families from Early 1700s to 1984. LC 84-62534. (Illus.). 420p. (C). 1984. 35.00 (*0-9614199-0-3*) E N Clark.

— Six American Colonists - Thomas Newbold, William Rodney, George Hufford, Eberhard Ream, Edward Painter, Richard Bridgeford - & Their Descendants, Vol. 1. LC 95-69865. (Illus.). 836p. 1995. lib. bdg. 40.00 (*0-9614199-1-1*) E N Clark.

Clark, Eva T. Clark: Jacob Clark of Abbeville, S. C., & Some of His Descendants; Notes on Allied Families & Letters of Rev. Jacob Clark: A Family Memorial. (Illus.). 121p. 1997. reprint ed. pap. 28.50 (*0-8328-7954-1*); reprint ed. lib. bdg. 28.50 (*0-8328-7953-3*) Higginson Bk Co.

— Gill. Abstracts from Records in Southern States & Genealogical Notes. (Illus.). 196p. 1997. reprint ed. pap. 29.50 (*0-8328-8744-7*); reprint ed. lib. bdg. 39.50 (*0-8328-8743-9*) Higginson Bk Co.

— Man Who Was Shakespeare. LC 75-113577. reprint ed. 24.00 (*0-404-01549-2*) AMS Pr.

Clark, Evans. Financing the Consumer. LC 75-39239. (Getting & Spending: The Consumer's Dilemma Ser.). (Illus.). 1976. reprint ed. 31.95 (*0-405-08016-6*) Ayer.

Clark, Eve. The Proceedings of the 27th Annual Child Language Research Forum. 241p. 1996. 69.95 (*1-57586-021-X*); pap. 22.95 (*1-57586-020-1*) CSLI.

Clark, Eve, ed. The Proceedings of the Twenty-Ninth Annual Child Language Research Forum. 310p. (C). 1998. 64.95 (*1-57586-119-4*); pap. 24.95 (*1-57586-118-6*) CSLI.

***Clark, Eve V., ed.** Proceedings of the Thirtieth Child Language Research Forum. LC 99-462363. 330p. (C). 2000. pap. 24.95 (*1-57586-242-5*, Pub. by CSLI); text 64.95 (*1-57586-241-7*, Pub. by CSLI) Cambridge U Pr.

Clark, Eve V., ed. The Proceedings of the Twenty-Fourth Annual Child Language Research Forum. LC 92-43908. ix, 288p. 1993. 49.95 (*1-881526-05-4*); pap. 19.95 (*1-881526-04-6*) CSLI.

— 26th Annual Child Language Research Forum: Proceedings. (CSLI Lecture Notes Ser.). 1995. pap. 22.95 (*0-521-52657-4*) Cambridge U Pr.

Clark, Eve V., ed. The Proceedings of the Twenty-Eighth Annual Child Language Research Forum. 308p. (C). 1997. 69.95 (*1-57586-063-5*); pap. 24.95 (*1-57586-062-7*) CSLI.

— The Proceedings of the Twenty-Sixth Annual Child Language Research Forum. 261p. 1995. pap. 22.95 (*1-881526-57-7*) CSLI.

Clark, Eve V., intro. The Proceedings of the Twenty-Fifth Annual Child Language Research Forum. 1993. 54.95 (*1-881526-32-1*); pap. 23.95 (*1-881526-31-3*) CSLI.

Clark, Eve V., jt. auth. see Clark, Herbert H.

Clark, F. The Pseudo-Gregorian Dialogues, Set, Vols. 1 & 2. (Studies in the History of Christian Thought: No. 37-38). 1987. 205.50 (*90-04-07773-1*) Brill Academic Pubs.

Clark, F. C. & Schmitt, Conrad J. Schaum's Outline of Italian Vocabulary. (Schaum's Outline Ser.). 237p. (C). 1997. pap. 15.95 (*0-07-023032-3*) McGraw.

Clark, Faye. Through the Looking Glasses II. LC 93-80576. 72p. 1993. pap. 8.95 (*0-9639110-0-7*) Lavender Lady.

Clark, Ferdinand L. Growing Old in a Mechanized World. Stein, Leon, ed. LC 79-8663. (Growing Old Ser.). (Illus.). 1980. reprint ed. lib. bdg. 17.95 (*0-405-12780-4*) Ayer.

Clark-Fletcher, Tribeniea M. True Feelings. 40p. 1999. pap. 8.00 (*0-8059-4650-0*) Dorrance.

Clark, Flora K. Steal Away. 1999. mass mkt. 6.50 (*0-449-00319-1*) Fawcett.

Clark, Florence M., jt. auth. see Epstein, Ralph C.

Clark, Floyd B. The Constitutional Doctrines of Justice Harlan. LC 74-87560. (Law, Politics & History Ser.). 1969. reprint ed. lib. bdg. 29.50 (*0-306-71391-8*) Da Capo.

Clark, Forrest D. & Lorenzoni, A. B. Applied Cost Engineering. LC 78-15949. (Cost Engineering Ser.: No. 1). (Illus.). 309p. reprint ed. pap. 95.80 (*0-8357-6022-7*, 203452400090) Bks Demand.

Clark, Forrest D., et al. Applied Cost Engineering. 3rd ed. LC 96-36592. (Cost Engineering Ser.: Vol. 28). (Illus.). 432p. 1996. text 69.75 (*0-8247-9800-7*) Dekker.

Clark, Fran. Integrating Technology into the Social Studies Curriculum. 144p. (J). (gr. 1-3). 1997. pap. 14.95 (*1-57690-430-X*) Tchr Create Mat.

Clark, Francelia M. Theme in Oral Epic & in Beowulf. LC 94-43067. (Milman Parry Studies in Oral Tradition). 1995. 649.00 (*0-8153-1235-0*) Garland.

Clark, Frances. ABC Papers. 32p. (gr. k-6). 1947. pap. text 5.95 (*0-87487-198-0*) Summy-Birchard.

— Leadership for Quality: Strategies for Action. LC 95-37231. 1995. pap. write for info. (*0-07-707828-4*) McGraw.

— Look & Listen, Pt. C. (Frances Clark Library for Piano Students). 48p. (Orig.). (J). (gr. k-12). 1962. pap. text 6.95 (*0-87487-178-6*) Summy-Birchard.

— Look & Listen, Pt. D. (Frances Clark Library for Piano Students). 48p. (Orig.). (J). (gr. k-12). 1962. pap. text 6.95 (*0-87487-179-4*) Summy-Birchard.

— Look & Listen, Pt. A. (Frances Clark Library for Piano Students). 48p. (Orig.). (J). (gr. k-6). 1962. pap. text 6.95 (*0-87487-176-X*) Summy-Birchard.

— Look & Listen, Pt. B. (Frances Clark Library for Piano Students). 48p. (Orig.). (J). (gr. k-12). 1962. pap. text 6.95 (*0-87487-177-8*) Summy-Birchard.

— Pencil Play, Pt. C. (Frances Clark Library for Piano Students). 24p. (Orig.). 1962. pap. text 3.95 (*0-87487-672-9*) Summy-Birchard.

— Pencil Play, Pt. D. (Frances Clark Library for Piano Students). 16p. (Orig.). 1962. pap. text 3.50 (*0-87487-673-7*) Summy-Birchard.

— Pencil Play, Pt. A. (Frances Clark Library for Piano Students). 32p. (Orig.). 1962. pap. text 4.95 (*0-87487-670-2*) Summy-Birchard.

— Pencil Play, Pt. B. (Frances Clark Library for Piano Students). 24p. (Orig.). 1962. pap. text 3.95 (*0-87487-671-0*) Summy-Birchard.

— Piano Literature of the 17th, 18th, & 19th Centuries, Bk. 6B. (Frances Clark Library for Piano Students). (Illus.). 64p. 1956. pap. text 9.95 (*0-87487-130-1*) Summy-Birchard.

— Questions & Answers. 1992. 26.00 (*0-317-05202-0*) Instrumental.

— Reader, Pt. C. 16p. 1970. pap. text 3.50 (*0-87487-676-1*) Summy-Birchard.

— Reader, Pt. D. 16p. 1970. pap. text 3.50 (*0-87487-677-X*) Summy-Birchard.

— Reader, Pt. B. 16p. 1969. pap. text 3.50 (*0-87487-675-3*) Summy-Birchard.

Clark, Frances & Goss, Louise. Contemporary Piano Literature, Bks. 5 & 6. (Frances Clark Library for Piano Students). 64p. 1957. pap. text 9.95 (*0-87487-110-7*) Summy-Birchard.

— Keyboard Musician for the Adult Beginner. 208p. (Orig.). 1980. pap. text 24.95 (*0-87487-103-4*) Summy-Birchard.

— Music Maker, Pt. A. (Music Maker Ser.). (Illus.). 56p. (J). (gr. 2 up). 1986. pap. text, student ed. 6.95 (*0-913277-20-7*) Summy-Birchard.

— Music Maker, Pt. B. (Music Maker Ser.). 56p. 1987. pap. text 6.95 (*0-913277-21-5*) Summy-Birchard.

— The Music Tree, 3 pts. 1993. write for info. (*0-318-55882-3*) Summy-Birchard.

— The Music Tree, Pt. C. 1973. 9.95 (*0-87487-123-9*) Summy-Birchard.

— The Music Tree, Pt. C. 56p. 1995. pap. text, wbk. ed. 7.95 (*0-87487-952-3*) Summy-Birchard.

— The Music Tree, Pt. C. rev. ed. 72p. 1994. pap. text 7.95 (*0-87487-688-5*) Summy-Birchard.

— The Music Tree, Pt. A. 1973. 9.95 (*0-87487-121-2*) Summy-Birchard.

— The Music Tree, Pt. A. rev. ed. 64p. 1993. pap. text 7.95 (*0-87487-686-9*) Summy-Birchard.

— The Music Tree, Pt. B. 1973. 9.95 (*0-87487-122-0*) Summy-Birchard.

— The Music Tree, Pt. B. rev. ed. 64p. 1993. pap. text 7.95 (*0-87487-687-7*) Summy-Birchard.

— The Music Tree: Workbook, Pt. A. 64p. 1993. pap. text 7.95 (*0-87487-950-7*) Summy-Birchard.

— The Music Tree B Workbook. 64p. 1994. pap. text 7.95 (*0-87487-951-5*) Summy-Birchard.

— The Music Tree Time to Begin. rev. ed. 72p. 1993. reprint ed. pap. text 7.95 (*0-87487-685-0*) Summy-Birchard.

— Piano Literature of the 17th, 18th, & 19th Centuries, Bk. 1. (Frances Clark Library for Piano Students). 32p. 1964. pap. text 5.95 (*0-87487-125-5*) Summy-Birchard.

— Piano Literature of the 17th, 18th, & 19th Centuries, Bk. 2. (Frances Clark Library for Piano Students). (Illus.). 32p. 1954. pap. text 5.95 (*0-87487-126-3*) Summy-Birchard.

— Piano Literature of the 17th, 18th, & 19th Centuries, Bk. 5B. (Frances Clark Library for Piano Students). (Illus.). 48p. 1957. pap. text 7.95 (*0-87487-129-8*) Summy-Birchard.

— Piano Literature of the 17th, 18th, & 19th Centuries, Bks. 3, 4A & 4B. (Frances Clark Library for Piano Students). (Illus.). 64p. 1957. pap. text 9.95 (*0-87487-127-1*) Summy-Birchard.

— Piano Literature of the 17th, 18th, & 19th Centuries, Bks. 5A & 6A. (Frances Clark Library for Piano Students). (Illus.). 48p. 1974. pap. text 7.95 (*0-87487-128-X*) Summy-Birchard.

— Piano Technic, Bk. 1. (Frances Clark Library for Piano Students). 48p. 1954. pap. text 7.95 (*0-87487-131-X*) Summy-Birchard.

— Piano Technic, Bk. 2. (Frances Clark Library for Piano Students). 40p. 1954. pap. text 7.95 (*0-87487-132-8*) Summy-Birchard.

— Piano Technic, Bk. 3. (Frances Clark Library for Piano Students). 40p. 1954. pap. text 7.95 (*0-87487-133-6*) Summy-Birchard.

— Piano Technic, Bk. 4. (Frances Clark Library for Piano Students). 40p. 1960. pap. text 7.95 (*0-87487-134-4*) Summy-Birchard.

— Piano Technic, Bk. 5. (Frances Clark Library for Piano Students). 40p. 1960. pap. text 7.95 (*0-87487-135-2*) Summy-Birchard.

— Piano Technic, Bk. 6. (Frances Clark Library for Piano Students). 40p. 1960. pap. text 7.95 (*0-87487-136-0*) Summy-Birchard.

— Teaching the Music Tree: A Handbook for Teachers. (Frances Clark Library for Piano Students). 24p. 1973. pap. text 5.95 (*0-87487-124-7*) Summy-Birchard.

— Time to Begin: Teacher's Handbook. 25p. 1993. reprint ed. pap. text 3.95 (*0-87487-954-X*) Summy-Birchard.

— Write & Playtime, Pt. A. (Frances Clark Library for Piano Students). 64p. (Orig.). (J). (gr. k-6). 1974. pap. text 9.95 (*0-87487-196-4*) Summy-Birchard.

— Write & Playtime, Pt. B. (Frances Clark Library for Piano Students). 64p. (Orig.). 1957. pap. text 7.95 (*0-87487-197-2*) Summy-Birchard.

C

Clark, Frances & Goss, Louise, contrib. by. The Music Tree: A Handbook for Teachers, A, B, C. 72p. 1996. pap. text 4.95 (0-87487-955-8) Summy-Birchard.

Clark, Frances & Goss, Louise, eds. Minor Masters, Bk. 1. 16p. 1983. pap. text 3.50 (0-913277-05-3) Summy-Birchard.

— Minor Masters, Bk. 2. 16p. 1983. pap. text 3.50 (0-913277-06-1) Summy-Birchard.

— Minor Masters, Bk. 3. 16p. 1983. pap. text 3.50 (0-913277-07-X) Summy-Birchard.

— Playtime: Supplementary Music, Pt. A. 5th ed. (Frances Clark Library for Piano Students). 16p. (J). (gr. 1-3). 1976. reprint ed. pap. 5.95 (0-87487-137-9, 0137) Summy-Birchard.

Clark, Frances, et al. Keyboard Theory, Bk. 1. (Frances Clark Library for Piano Students). 48p. 1978. pap. text 7.95 (0-87487-115-8) Summy-Birchard.

— Keyboard Theory, Bk. 2. (Frances Clark Library for Piano Students). 48p. 1965. pap. text 7.95 (0-87487-116-6) Summy-Birchard.

— Keyboard Theory, Bk. 3. (Frances Clark Library for Piano Students). 48p. 1965. pap. text 7.95 (0-87487-117-4) Summy-Birchard.

— Keyboard Theory, Bk. 4. (Frances Clark Library for Piano Students). 48p. 1965. pap. text 7.95 (0-87487-118-2) Summy-Birchard.

— Keyboard Theory, Bks. 5 & 6. (Frances Clark Library for Piano Students). 64p. 1966. pap. text 9.95 (0-87487-119-0) Summy-Birchard.

— Musical Fingers, Bk. 1. (Illus.). 32p. 1983. pap. 4.95 (0-913277-09-6) Summy-Birchard.

— Musical Fingers, Bk. 2. (Illus.). 40p. 1984. pap. 4.95 (0-913277-10-X) Summy-Birchard.

— Musical Fingers, Bk. 3. (Illus.). 40p. 1985. pap. 4.95 (0-913277-11-8) Summy-Birchard.

— Musical Fingers, Bk. 4. (Illus.). 48p. 1986. pap. 5.95 (0-913277-12-6) Summy-Birchard.

— Piano Etudes: For the Development of Musical Fingers, Bk. 1. 24p. 1990. pap. 4.95 (0-913277-24-X) Summy-Birchard.

— Piano Etudes: For the Development of Musical Fingers, Bk. 2. 24p. 1990. pap. 4.95 (0-913277-25-8) Summy-Birchard.

— Piano Etudes: For the Development of Musical Fingers, Bk. 3. 24p. 1990. pap. 4.95 (0-913277-26-6) Summy-Birchard.

— Piano Etudes: For the Development of Musical Fingers, Bk. 4. 32p. 1990. pap. 5.95 (0-913277-27-4) Summy-Birchard.

Clark, Frances, ed. see Caramia, Tony.

Clark, Frances, ed. see Kraehenbuehl, David, et al.

Clark, Frances, ed. see Telfel, Nancy.

***Clark, Francis.** Godfaring: On Reason, Faith, & Sacred Being. LC 99-36505. 2000. 19.95 (0-8132-0959-5) Cath U Pr.

Clark, Francis, ed. see Grove, Roger, et al.

Clark, Francis E. New Way Around an Old World. LC 70-115519. (Russia Observed, Series I). 1970. reprint ed. 23.95 (0-405-03014-2) Ayer.

— Our Italian Fellow Citizens in Their Old Homes & Their New. LC 74-17923. (Italian American Experience Ser.). (Illus.). 260p. 1975. reprint ed. 21.95 (0-405-06396-2) Ayer.

Clark, Francis E., jt. auth. see Paul, Eldor A.

Clark, Frank E. & Faucher, Marybeth. Around Somersworth. (Images of America Ser.). 128p. 1995. pap. 18.99 (0-7524-0094-0) Arcadia Publng.

Clark, Frank Emerson. Treatise on the Law of Surveying & Boundaries. 4th ed. 1976. 27.50 (0-672-82326-8) Sams.

Clark, Frank J. The Accountant & the Personal Computer. (Illus.). 176p. 1986. pap. text 30.00 (0-13-001322-6) P-H.

Clark, Frank L. & Warren-Clark, Sandra L. Inspection: Sexually Transmitted Diseases. Koopman, Joel E., ed. (Illus.). 124p. (Orig.). 1988. pap. 14.95 (0-923944-00-1) Pub Partners.

Clark, Frank M. Sandpapers: The Lives & Letters of Eugene Rhodes & Charles Lummis. (Illus.). 160p. (Orig.). 1994. pap. 14.95 (0-86534-211-3) Sunstone Pr.

Clark, Frank P. Special Effects in Motion Pictures. (Illus.). 238p. 1982. reprint ed. pap. text 20.00 (0-940690-00-4) Soc Motion Pic & TV Engrs.

Clark, Frank P., ed. see Society of Photographic Scientists & Engineers Sta.

Clark, Frank W., et al, eds. The Pursuit of Competence in Social Work. LC 79-83570. (Jossey-Bass Social & Behavioral Science Ser.). 352p. reprint ed. pap. 109.20 (0-8357-4973-8, 203790600009) Bks Demand.

Clark, Franklin & Diliberto, Ken. Investigating Computer Crime. (Practical Aspects of Criminal & Forensic Investigations Ser.). 256p. 1996. boxed set 64.95 (0-8493-8158-4) CRC Pr.

Clark, Franklin, jt. auth. see Olsen, Alfred O.

Clark, Fred A. Teenage Street Gangs: Differences, Membership & Intervention. unabridged ed. Curry, Lee S., ed. (Illus.). 186p. (Orig.). 1996. pap. text 39.95 (0-9651587-0-5) Clarco Ent.

Clark, Fred E. Principles of Marketing. Assael, Henry, ed. LC 78-255. (Century of Marketing Ser.). 1979. reprint ed. lib. bdg. 51.95 (0-405-11158-4) Ayer.

Clark, Fred G. Camp Tecumseh: 1903-1993. LC 94-8224. (Illus.). 160p. 1994. 30.00 (0-914659-70-7) Phoenix Pub.

Clark, Fred M. Impermanent Structures: Semiotic Readings of Nelson Rodrigues' Vestido de Noiva, Album de Familia, & Anjo Negro. LC 91-19885. (North Carolina Studies in the Romance Languages & Literatures: No. 238). 132p. reprint ed. pap. 41.00 (0-608-20075-1, 207134700011) Bks Demand.

***Clark, Freddie.** Agents by Moonlight: The Secret History of RAF Tempsford During World War II. (Military History Ser.). (Illus.). 360p. (C). 1999. 34.99 (0-7524-1691-X, Tempus Publng) Arcadia Publng.

Clark, Frederick L. & Pirie, Norman W., eds. Four Thousand Million Mouths. LC 71-117768. (Essay Index Reprint Ser.). 1977. 21.95 (0-8369-1746-4) Ayer.

Clark, G. A., ed. The North Burgos Archaeological Survey: Bronze & Iron Age Archaeology on the Meseta del Norte (Province of Burgos, North-Central Spain) (Anthropological Research Papers: No. 19). (Illus.). xviii, 307p. 1979. pap. 20.00 (0-685-19302-0) AZ Univ ARP.

Clark, G. C., Jr. & Cain, J. B. Error-Correction Coding for Digital Communications. LC 81-1630. (Applications of Communications Theory Ser.). (Illus.). 436p. (C). 1981. 95.00 (0-306-40615-2, Plenum Trade) Perseus Pubng.

Clark, G. H. Industrial & Marine Fuels Handbook. (Illus.). 143p. 1988. 300.00 (0-408-01488-1) Buttrwrth-Heinemann.

Clark, G. J. Great Sayings by Great Lawyers: Immortal Thoughts Snatched from Oblivion. xvi, 801p. 1992. reprint ed. 85.00 (0-8377-2020-6, Rothman) W S Hein.

— Memoirs of Jeremiah Mason: Reproduction of Privately Printed Edition of 1873 Illustrated & Annotated, with Enlarged Index. (Illus.). xv, 491p. 1997. reprint ed. 152.00 (1-56169-350-2) Gaunt.

Clark, G. Kitson. The Critical Historian. Winks, Robin W., ed. LC 83-49175. (History & Historiography Ser.). 267p. 1985. lib. bdg. 35.00 (0-8240-6354-6) Garland.

Clark, G. M., et al. The University of Melborune - Nucleus Multi-Electrode Cochlear Implant. (Advances in OtoRhinoLaryngology Ser.: Vol. 38). (Illus.). x, 190p. 1987. 116.75 (3-8055-4575-4) S Karger.

Clark, G. V. Four Captains. (C). 1987. 100.00 (0-85174-247-5) St Mut.

— Last of the Whaling Captains. (C). 1987. 120.00 (0-85174-498-2) St Mut.

— Yarns of a Cyprus Pilot. 192p. (C). 1989. text 65.00 (1-872795-08-0, Pub. by Pentland Pr) St Mut.

Clark, Gail. It Can Begin with Me: I Like Me. Drake, Alice & Erickson, Beverly H., eds. LC 94-61209. (Illus.). 24p. (J). (gr. k-2). 1995. pap. 3.95 (1-885527-00-4) Feather Fables.

Clark, Gail I. Puppy Parenting. LC 98-34718. 292p. 1999. pap. 16.95 (1-57779-012-X) Alpine Pubns.

Clark, Gail I. & Boyer, William N. Mentally Sound Dog: How to Shape, Train & Change Canine Behavior. Carriera, Joanne, ed. LC 95-15516. (Illus.). 280p. 1995. pap. 21.95 (0-931866-67-7) Alpine Pubns.

Clark, Galen. Indians of the Yosemite. (Illus.). 132p. 1988. reprint ed. pap. 9.95 (0-9607520-1-3) Diablo Bks.

Clark, Garth. American Ceramics: Eighteen Seventy-Six to the Present. exp. rev. ed. Orig. Title: A Century of Ceramics in the United States: 1878-1978. (Illus.). 352p. 1988. 75.00 (0-89659-743-1) Abbeville Pr.

— The Book of Cups. (Illus.). 96p. 1996. pap. 9.95 (0-7892-0170-4) Abbeville Pr.

— The Eccentric Teapot: Four Hundred Years of Invention. (Illus.). 120p. 1996. pap. 29.95 (0-89659-923-X) Abbeville Pr.

— Markborough Decision. 25.00 (0-614-05188-6, PECO191.5M) ASFE.

— The Potter's Art: A Complete History of Pottery in Britain. (Illus.). 240p. (C). 1995. text 59.95 (0-7148-3202-2, Pub. by Phaidon Press) Phaidon Pr.

***Clark, Garth & Lauria, Jo.** Color & Fire: Defining Moments in Studio Ceramics, 1950-2000. (Illus.). 252p. 2000. text 40.00 (0-8478-2254-0) Rizzoli Intl.

Clark, Garth, et al. The Mad Potter of Biloxi: The Art & Life of George E. Ohr. (Illus.). 192p. 1989. 85.00 (0-89659-927-2) Abbeville Pr.

Clark, Garth, jt. auth. see Sims, Patterson.

Clark, Gary. Night-Limited Visibility Diving. (Specialty Diver Ser.). 30p. 1990. teacher ed. 6.95 (1-880229-01-3); pap. text 10.95 (0-943717-98-1) Concept Sys.

Clark, Gary, jt. auth. see Humpal, Laurie.

Clark, Gary, jt. auth. see Miller, Geoffrey.

Clark, Gary B. Systematic Quality Management. 1996. 65.00 (0-89189-312-1) Am Soc Clinical.

Clark, Gary B., ed. see Clark, Sue A.

Clark, Gary M. Assessment for Transitions Planning: A Guide for Special Education Teachers & Related Services Professionals. LC 97-42871. (Series on Transition). 143p. 1998. pap. 14.00 (0-89079-755-2, 8547) PRO-ED.

— Career Education for the Handicapped Child in the Elementary Classroom. LC 78-78028. 1979. pap. 19.95 (0-89108-092-9) Love Pub Co.

***Clark, Gary M., et al.** Informal Assessments for Transition Planning. LC 99-86985. 2000. pap. write for info. (0-89079-849-4) PRO-ED.

Clark, Gary R. Boat Diving Manual. (Specialty Diver Ser.). 80p. 1990. pap. text 10.95 (0-943717-97-3) Concept Sys.

Clark, Gaylord L., ed. Hand Rehabilitation: A Practical Guide. 2nd ed. LC 96-48429. 1996. pap. text 54.95 (0-443-07642-1) Church.

Clark, Gene E. Let's Talk about You. 109p. 1982. reprint ed. pap. 3.50 (0-87516-478-1) DeVorss.

Clark, Geoffrey. All the Way Home. LC 97-2126. 160p. (Orig.). 1997. pap. 15.00 (1-888105-18-6) Avisson Pr.

— Betting on Lives: The Culture of Life Insurance in England, 1695-1775. 1999. 69.95 (0-7190-5675-6, Pub. by Manchester Univ Pr) St Martin.

— Jackdog Summer. LC 96-76626. 240p. 1996. pap. 15.00 (1-57650-083-7) Hi Jinx Pr.

— Schooling the Spirit: Stories. LC 92-72709. 208p. 1993. pap. 11.95 (1-878580-36-1) Asylum Arts.

Clark, Geoffrey, ed. Trial of James Camb: The Port-Hole Murder, No. 1. (Notable British Trials Ser.). 255p. 1995. reprint ed. 80.00 (1-56169-188-7) Gaunt.

Clark, Geoffrey A. The Asturian of Cantabria: Early Holocene Hunter-Gatherers in Northern Spain. LC 83-1052. (Anthropological Papers: No. 41). 171p. 1983. pap. 20.95 (0-8165-0800-3) U of Ariz Pr.

Clark, Geoffrey A., ed. Perspectives on the Past: Theoretical Biases in Mediterranean Hunter-Gatherer Research. LC 91-16444. (Illus.). 560p. (C). 1991. text 47.95 (0-8122-8190-X) U of Pa Pr.

Clark, Geoffrey A. & Willermet, Cathy M. Conceptual Issues in Modern Human Origins Research. LC 96-33415. (Evolutionary Fouondations of Human Behavior Ser.). 521p. (C). 1997. pap. text 45.95 (0-202-02040-1); lib. bdg. 89.95 (0-202-02039-8) Aldine de Gruyter.

Clark, Geoffrey A., et al. The Archaeology of the Wadi al-Hasa, West-Central Jordan Vol. I: Surveys, Settlement Patterns & Paleoenvironments. Coinman, Nancy R., ed. LC 98-71899. (Arizona State University Anthropological Research Papers: No. 50). (Illus.). v, 228p. 1998. pap. 25.00 (0-936249-14-5, ARP #50) AZ Univ ARP.

Clark, Geoffrey A., jt. ed. see Straus, Lawrence G.

***Clark, Geoffry.** Rabbit Fever. LC 99-71824. 144p. 2000. pap. 15.00 (1-888105-39-9) Avisson Pr.

Clark, George. Hydronics: The Art of Heating, Cooling with Water. Busby, Harry, ed. LC 86-4174. 123p. 1973. pap. 6.95 (0-912524-37-5) Busn News.

— The Small Bees' Honey. 196p. 1997. pap. 14.00 (1-877727-74-1) White Pine.

***Clark, George & Timmons, Daniel.** J.R.R. Tolkien & His Literary Resonances: Views of Middle-earth, 89. LC 99-56047. (Contributions to the Study of Science Fiction & Fantasy Ser.). 2000. write for info. (0-313-30845-4, Greenwood Pr) Greenwood.

Clark, George B. Basic Properties of Ammonium Nitrate Fuel Oil Explosives (ANFO) Raese, Jon W., ed. LC 81-38436. (Colorado School of Mines Quarterly Ser.: Vol. 76, No. 1). (Illus.). 32p. 1981. pap. text 10.00 (0-686-46975-5) Colo Sch Mines.

— Devil Dogs: Fighting Marines of World War I. LC 98-21853. (Illus.). 576p. 1999. 39.95 (0-89141-653-6, Pub. by Presidio Pr) Natl Bk Netwk.

— Geotechnical Centrifuges for Model Studies & Physical Property Testing of Rock & Rock Structures. Raese, Jon W., ed. LC 81-21614. (Colorado School of Mines Quarterly Ser.: Vol. 76, No. 4). (Illus.). 63p. 1982. pap. text 12.00 (0-686-79746-9) Colo Sch Mines.

— Industrial High Explosives: Composition & Calculations for Engineers. Raese, Jon W., ed. LC 80-18063. (Colorado School of Mines Quarterly Ser.: Vol. 75, No. 1). (Illus.). 47p. (Orig.). 1980. pap. 8.00 (0-686-63161-7) Colo Sch Mines.

— Principles of Rock Drilling & Bit Wear, Pt. 1. Raese, Jon W., ed. LC 82-1148. (Colorado School of Mines Quarterly Ser.: Vol. 77, No. 1). (Illus.). 118p. 1982. 12.00 (0-685-06987-7) Colo Sch Mines.

— Principles of Rock Drilling & Bit Wear, Pt. 2. rev. ed. Raese, Jon W., ed. LC 82-1148. (Colorado School of Mines Quarterly Ser.: Vol. 77 No. 2). (Illus.). 42p. 1982. pap. text 10.00 (0-686-79748-5) Colo Sch Mines.

***Clark, George B.** Treading Softly: U.S. Marines in China, 1819-1949. 2001. write for info. (0-275-97078-7) Greenwood.

Clark, George F. A History of the Town of Norton, Massachusetts. (Illus.). 608p. 1993. reprint ed. text 45.00 (1-55613-850-4) Heritage Bk.

Clark, George H., ed. The New Treasury of War Poetry: Poems of the Second World War. 1977. 18.95 (0-8369-6009-2) Ayer.

Clark, George N. Later Stuarts, 1660-1714. 2nd ed. (Oxford History of England Ser.: Vol. 10). (Illus.). 504p. 1956. text 75.00 (0-19-821702-1) OUP.

Clark, George N. War & Society in the Seventeenth Century. LC 85-12551. 157p. 1985. reprint ed. lib. bdg. 43.75 (0-313-24948-2, CWSO, Greenwood Pr) Greenwood.

— The Wealth of England from 1496 to 1760. LC 85-27270. (Home University of Modern Knowledge Ser.). 199p. 1986. reprint ed. lib. bdg. 65.00 (0-313-25045-6, CLWE, Greenwood Pr) Greenwood.

Clark, George P., ed. Into the Old Northwest: Journeys with Charles H. Titus, 1841-1846. LC 93-41405. 184p. 1994. 27.95 (0-87013-343-8) Mich St U Pr.

Clark, George R. Col. George Rogers Clark's Sketch of His Campaign in the Illinois in 1778-9 with an Introduction by Hon. Henry Pirtle. LC 73-146384. (First American Frontier Ser.). 1975. reprint ed. 24.95 (0-405-02835-0) Ayer.

— The Conquest of the Illinois. (BCL1 - U. S. History Ser.). 190p. 1991. reprint ed. lib. bdg. 69.00 (0-7812-6115-5) Rprt Serv.

— History of the U. S. Navy. 1972. lib. bdg. 75.00 (0-8490-2008-5) Gordon Pr.

— Papers, 1771 to 1784, 2 vols. James, James A., ed. LC 72-444. reprint ed. 215.00 (0-404-01556-5) AMS Pr.

Clark, George T., jt. auth. see Chek-Chart Staff.

Clark, George W. Clark: History & Genealogy of One Branch of the Clark Family & Its Connections, with the Shattucks on My Father's Side, the Smiths on My Mother's Side & the Elliotts on My Wife's Side. (Illus.). 74p. 1997. reprint ed. pap. 15.00 (0-8328-7946-0); reprint ed. lib. bdg. 25.00 (0-8328-7945-2) Higginson Bk Co.

Clark, Gertrude M., tr. see Kant, Immanuel.

Clark, Gilbert, et al. Understanding Art Testing: Past Influences, Norman C. Meier's Contributions, Present Concerns, & Future Possibilities. 128p. (C). 1987. pap. 17.00 (0-937652-40-7, 223) Natl Art Ed.

Clark, Gilbert A. & Zimmerman, Enid. Programming Opportunities for Students Gifted & Talented in the Visual Arts. 51p. 1998. reprint ed. pap. text 20.00 (0-7881-7210-7) DIANE Pub.

Clark, Gilbert A. & Zimmerman, Enid D. Resources for Educating Artistically Talented Students. LC 86-23183. (Illus.). 192p. 1987. text 34.95 (0-8156-2401-8) Syracuse U Pr.

Clark, Gilbert J. Life Sketches of Eminent Lawyers: American, English & Canadian, to Which Is Added Thoughts, Facts & Facetiae, 2 vols., Vol. 1. (Illus.). xi, 368p. 1983. reprint ed. 95.00 (0-8377-0447-2, Rothman) W S Hein.

— Life Sketches of Eminent Lawyers, American, English & Canadian, to Which Is Added Thoughts, Facts & Facetiae, 2 vols., Vol. 2. (Illus.). xi, 384p. 1983. reprint ed. write for info. (0-318-57042-4) W S Hein.

Clark, Giles. Inside Book Publishing. 2nd ed. (Blueprint Ser.). 232p. (C). 1994. pap. 24.99 (0-415-13663-6) Routledge.

Clark, Giles N. Inside Book Publishing: A Career Builder's Guide. 192p. 1991. pap. 20.95 (0-948905-25-5) Chapman & Hall.

Clark, Gillian. Women in Late Antiquity: Pagan & Christian Lifestyles. (Illus.). 174p. 1994. reprint ed. pap. text 17.95 (0-19-872166-8) OUP.

Clark, Gillian, tr. One Moonlit Night. 107p. (J). (gr. 4). 1991. 38.95 (0-8464-4831-9) Beekman Pubs.

Clark, Gillian, tr. from LAT. Iamblichus: On the Pythagorean Life. (Translated Texts for Historians Ser.). 154p. (Orig.). 1992. reprint ed. pap. text 16.50 (0-85323-326-8, Pub. by Liverpool Univ Pr) U of Pa Pr.

Clark, Gillian, jt. auth. see Porphyry.

Clark, Gillian, ed. see Augustine, Saint.

Clark, Gina. Through My Eyes. 1998. pap. write for info. (1-58235-003-5) Watermrk Pr.

Clark, Gina, ed. see Blackman, Tannis.

Clark, Gina, ed. see Righteous Mother.

***Clark, Gina Beth.** Arty, the Love Angel. LC 99-91627. 2000. 25.00 (0-7388-1144-0); pap. 18.00 (0-7388-1145-9) Xlibris Corp.

— Montana Moon Lady. LC 99-91962. 2000. 25.00 (0-7388-1420-2); pap. 18.00 (0-7388-1421-0) Xlibris Corp.

— Sylva's Pursuit. 1999. pap. 3.50 (1-929017-14-6) Gemini Bks AR.

Clark, Ginny. Ansel Adams Wilderness. (Illus.). 128p. 2000. pap. 13.95 (0-931532-27-2) West Trails Pubns.

— Catch Em' & Eat Em' A Fish Cookbook. (Illus.). 128p. 1988. pap., spiral bd. 6.95 (0-931532-22-1) West Trails Pubns.

— High Mountains & Deep Valleys. 1981. pap. 9.95 (0-931532-05-1) West Trails Pubns.

— John Muir Trail Country. 1977. pap. 9.95 (0-931532-02-7) West Trails Pubns.

— Lighten Up! Low-Fat Cooking in 15 Minutes. LC 98-34059. (Illus.). 177p. 1999. mass mkt. 10.99 (0-446-67507-5, Pub. by Warner Bks) Little.

— Yosemite Trails. 1980. pap. 12.95 (0-931532-01-9) West Trails Pubns.

Clark, Gladys L., jt. auth. see Greene, John C.

Clark, Glenn. Creative Peace. 1989. pap. 5.95 (0-910924-94-5) Macalester.

— From Crime to Christ. pap. 3.95 (0-910924-61-9) Macalester.

— Lord's Prayer. pap. 1.95 (0-910924-08-2) Macalester.

— Man Who Talks with the Flowers. pap. 4.95 (0-910924-09-0) Macalester.

— The Man Who Tapped the Secrets of the Universe. pap. 4.95 (0-910924-10-4) Macalester.

— The Man Who Tapped the Secrets of the Universe. (Illus.). 61p. 1999. reprint ed. 5.00 (1-879605-07-4) U Sci & Philos.

— Man's Reach. 1977. reprint ed. pap. 11.00 (0-910924-82-1) Macalester.

— Man's Reach: American Autobiography. 314p. 1995. lib. bdg. 89.00 (0-7812-8480-5) Rprt Serv.

— The Soul's Sincere Desire. 128p. Date not set. pap. 7.95 (1-886158-09-6) Macalester.

— The Soul's Sincere Desire. 1988. pap. 9.95 (0-910924-93-7) Macalester.

— Three Mysteries of Jesus. 1978. pap. 1.95 (0-910924-85-6) Macalester.

— Water of Life. 1979. pap. 5.95 (0-910924-86-4) Macalester.

Clark, Glenn, ed. I Will Lift up Mine Eyes. (C). 1990. pap. 40.00 (0-85305-257-3, Pub. by Arthur James) St Mut.

***Clark, Glenn Slade, Jr.** Cry, Wolf. LC 99-90878. 1999. 25.00 (0-7388-0558-0); pap. 18.00 (0-7388-0559-9) Xlibris Corp.

Clark, Glenn T., et al. Modern Diagnostic & Surgical Arthroscopy of the Temporomandibular Joint. LC 92-11625. (Illus.). 192p. 1992. text 165.00 (0-7216-6591-8, W B Saunders Co) Harcrt Hlth Sci Grp.

Clark, Gloria J. A Synergy of Styles: Art & Artifact in Gabriel Garcia Marquez. LC 99-25070. 160p. 1999. 35.00 (0-7618-1408-6) U Pr of Amer.

Clark, Gordon. Housing & Planning in the Countryside. LC 82-292. (Geography & Public Policy Research Studies: No. 2). (Illus.). 175p. reprint ed. pap. 54.30 (0-8357-6146-0, 203422000089) Bks Demand.

Clark, Gordon, et al. Accountability & Corruption: Public Sector Ethics. 224p. 1998. pap. 24.95 (1-86448-423-3, Pub. by Allen & Unwin Pty) Paul & Co Pubs.

— Surfboard. rev. ed. Shaw, Eric, ed. (JPN., Illus.). 72p. (YA). (gr. 8 up). 1993. 14.95 (0-912750-04-9) Transmedia.

***Clark, Gordon B.** The Loyalties of Lieutenant Hawk. LC 98-94263. viii, 349p. 1999. per. write for info. (0-9661371-2-4) Long Pt Pr.

An Asterisk (*) at the beginning of an entry indicates that the title is appearing for the first time.

Clark, Gordon B. The Loyalties of Lieutenant Hawk. 224p. 1997. pap. 9.95 (*1-882265-52-1*) Tandem Alley.

Clark, Gordon H. Ancient Philosophy. Robbins, John W., ed. & intro. by. 500p. 1996. pap. 24.95 (*0-940931-49-4*) Trinity Found.

— The Atonement. 2nd rev. ed. Robbins, John W., ed. & intro. by. 163p. 1996. pap. 8.95 (*0-940931-87-7*) Trinity Found.

— Behaviorism & Christianity. Robbins, John W., ed. & intro. by. 130p. 1982. pap. 5.95 (*0-940931-04-4*) Trinity Found.

— The Biblical Doctrine of Man. (Trinity Papers: No. 7). 127p. 1984. pap. 6.95 (*0-940931-07-9*) Trinity Found.

— The Biblical Doctrine of Man. 2nd ed. Robbins, John W., ed. & intro. by. 127p. 1992. pap. 6.95 (*0-940931-91-5*) Trinity Found.

***Clark, Gordon H.** A Christian Philosophy of Education Vol. 10: The Works of Gordon Haddon Clank. rev. ed. Robbins, John W., ed. (Illus.). 200p. 2000. 18.95 (*1-891777-06-8*); pap. 12.95 (*1-891777-07-6*) Trinity Found.

Clark, Gordon H. A Christian View of Men & Things: An Introduction to Philosophy. 3rd rev. ed. Robbins, John W., ed. & intro. by. (Works of Gordon Haddon Clark: No. 1). (Illus.). 275p. 1998. 29.95 (*1-891777-00-9*) Trinity Found.

— A Christian View of Men & Things: An Introduction to Philosophy. 3rd rev. ed. Robbins, John W., ed. & intro. by. (Works of Gordon Haddon Clark: No. 2). (Illus.). 275p. 1998. pap. 14.95 (*1-891777-01-7*) Trinity Found.

— Clark Speaks from the Grave. Robbins, John W., ed. & intro. by. 77p. (Orig.). 1986. pap. 3.95 (*0-940931-12-5*) Trinity Found.

— Colossians. 2nd ed. Robbins, John W., ed. & intro. by. 149p. 1989. pap. 6.95 (*0-940931-25-7*) Trinity Found.

— Ephesians. Robbins, John W., ed. & intro. by. 213p. (Orig.). 1985. pap. 8.95 (*0-940931-11-7*) Trinity Found.

— Essays on Ethics & Politics. Robbins, John W., ed. & intro. by. 221p. (Orig.). 1992. pap. 10.95 (*0-940931-32-X*) Trinity Found.

— Faith & Saving Faith. 2nd ed. Robbins, John W., ed. & intro. by. 132p. 1990. pap. 8.95 (*0-940931-95-8*) Trinity Found.

— First & Second Thessalonians. Robbins, John W., ed. & intro. by. 175p. (Orig.). 1986. pap. 5.95 (*0-940931-14-1*) Trinity Found.

— First Corinthians: A Contemporary Commentary. 2nd ed. Robbins, John W., ed. & intro. by. 349p. 1991. pap. 10.95 (*0-940931-29-X*) Trinity Found.

— First John. 2nd ed. Robbins, John W., ed. & intro. by. 184p. 1992. pap. 10.95 (*0-940931-94-X*) Trinity Found.

— God & Evil: The Problem Solved. Robbins, John W., ed. 60p. 1996. pap. 4.95 (*0-940931-46-X*) Trinity Found.

— God's Hammer: The Bible & Its Critics. 3rd rev. ed. Robbins, John W., ed. & intro. by. Lindsell, Harold, intro. 215p. 1995. pap. 10.95 (*0-940931-88-5*) Trinity Found.

— Historiography: Secular & Religious. 2nd ed. Robbins, John W., ed. & intro. by. 366p. 1994. pap. 13.95 (*0-940931-39-7*) Trinity Found.

— The Holy Spirit. Robbins, John W., ed. & intro. by. 129p. 1993. pap. 8.95 (*0-940931-37-0*) Trinity Found.

— The Incarnation. Robbins, John W., ed. & intro. by. 91p. (Orig.). 1988. pap. 8.95 (*0-940931-23-0*) Trinity Found.

— An Introduction to Christian Philosophy. Robbins, John W., ed. & intro. by. 136p. 1993. pap. 8.95 (*0-940931-38-9*) Trinity Found.

— The Johannine Logos. 2nd ed. Robbins, John W., ed. & intro. by. 138p. 1989. pap. 5.95 (*0-940931-22-2*) Trinity Found.

— Karl Barth's Theological Method. rev. ed. Robbins, John W., ed. & intro. by. 320p. 1997. pap. 18.95 (*0-940931-51-6*) Trinity Found.

— Language & Theology. 2nd ed. Robbins, John W., ed. & intro. by. 175p. 1993. pap. 9.95 (*0-940931-90-7*) Trinity Found.

— Logic. 3rd rev. ed. Robbins, John W., ed. & frwd. by. 160p. 1998. text 16.95 (*0-940931-81-8*); pap. text 10.95 (*0-940931-80-X*) Trinity Found.

— Logical Criticisms of Textual Criticism. (Trinity Papers: No. 16). 60p. 1986. pap. 3.25 (*0-940931-16-8*) Trinity Found.

— Logical Criticisms of Textual Criticism. 2nd ed. Robbins, John W., ed. & intro. by. 60p. 1990. pap. 3.25 (*0-940931-93-1*) Trinity Found.

— New Heavens, New Earth: A Commentary on First & Second Peter. Robbins, John W., ed. & intro. by. 250p. 1993. pap. 10.95 (*0-940931-36-2*) Trinity Found.

— The Pastoral Epistles. 2nd rev. ed. Robbins, John W., ed. & intro. by. (Works of Gordon Haddon Clark). (Illus.). 250p. 1998. pap. 14.95 (*1-891777-05-X*) Trinity Found.

— The Pastoral Epistles. 2nd rev. ed. Robbins, John W., ed. & intro. by. (Works of Gordon Haddon Clark). (Illus.). 250p. 1999. 29.95 (*1-891777-04-1*) Trinity Found.

— Philippians. 100p. 1996. pap. 8.95 (*0-940931-47-8*) Trinity Found.

— The Philosophy of Science & Belief in God. 3rd rev. ed. Robbins, John W., ed. & intro. by. 138p. 1996. pap. 8.95 (*0-940931-85-0*) Trinity Found.

— Predestination. LC 87-16815. 224p. (Orig.). 1987. pap. 9.99 (*0-87552-169-X*) P & R Pubng.

— Religion, Reason & Revelation. 3rd rev. ed. Robbins, John W., ed. & intro. by. 264p. 1995. pap. 10.95 (*0-940931-86-9*) Trinity Found.

— Sanctification. Robbins, John W., ed. & intro. by. 112p. (Orig.). 1992. pap. 8.95 (*0-940931-33-8*) Trinity Found.

***Clark, Gordon H.** Thales to Dewey: A History of Philosophy. Robbins, Joan W., ed. (Works of Gordon Haddon Clark: Vol. 3). (Illus.). 475p. (C). 2000. pap. 19.95 (*1-891777-09-2*) Trinity Found.

— Thales to Dewey: A History of Philosophy. rev. ed. Robbins, John W., ed. (Works of Gordon Haddon Clark: Vol. 3). (Illus.). 475p. (C). 2000. 29.95 (*1-891777-08-4*) Trinity Found.

Clark, Gordon H. Three Types of Religious Philosophy. 2nd ed. Robbins, John W., ed. & intro. by. 155p. 1989. pap. 6.95 (*0-940931-21-4*) Trinity Found.

— The Trinity. (Trinity Papers: No. 8). 157p. 1985. pap. 8.95 (*0-940931-08-7*) Trinity Found.

— The Trinity. 2nd ed. Robbins, John W., ed. & intro. by. 157p. 1990. pap. 8.95 (*0-940931-92-3*) Trinity Found.

— What Do Presbyterians Believe? LC 65-27481. 1965. pap. 9.99 (*0-87552-168-1*) P & R Pubng.

— William James & John Dewey. Robbins, John W., ed. & intro. by. 141p. 1995. pap. 8.95 (*0-940931-43-5*) Trinity Found.

Clark, Gordon H., ed. Selections from Hellenistic Philosophy. LC 40-31306. 1964. pap. text 11.95 (*0-89197-396-6*) Irvington.

Clark, Gordon H. & Augustine, Aurelius. Lord God of Truth & Concerning the Teacher. Robbins, John W., ed. & intro. by. 110p. 1994. pap. 7.95 (*0-940931-40-0*) Trinity Found.

Clark, Gordon H. & Warfield, Benjamin B. What Christians Believe: The Westminster Confession Yesterday & Today. 3rd rev. ed. Robbins, John W., ed. & intro. by. (Works of Gordon Haddon Clark: No. 2). Orig. Title: What Presbyterians Believe, What Do Presbyterians Believe?. (Illus.). 500p. Date not set. 29.95 (*1-891777-02-5*); pap. 19.95 (*1-891777-03-3*) Trinity Found.

Clark, Gordon H., et al. Against the World: The Trinity Review, 1978-1988. Robbins, John W., ed. 350p. 1996. 34.95 (*0-940931-45-1*) Trinity Found.

Clark, Gordon H., Jr., jt. ed. see Vaccaro, Jerome V.

Clark, Gordon L. Judges & the Cities: Interpreting Local Autonomy. LC 85-1018. (Illus.). xxvi, 264p. 1985. 30.00 (*0-226-10753-1*) U Ch Pr.

***Clark, Gordon L.** Pension Fund Capitalism. LC 99-45918. 320p. 2000. 72.00 (*0-19-924047-7*); 29.95 (*0-19-924048-5*) OUP.

Clark, Gordon L. Pensions & Corporate Restructuring in American Industry: A Crisis of Regulation. LC 92-34553. 304p. (C). 1993. text 39.95 (*0-8018-4523-8*) Johns Hopkins.

— Unions & Communities under Siege: American Communities & the Crisis of Organized Labor. (Cambridge Human Geography Ser.). (Illus.). 328p. (C). 1989. text 69.95 (*0-521-36516-3*) Cambridge U Pr.

***Clark, Gordon L., et al, eds.** The Oxford Handbook of Economic Geography. (Illus.). 760p. 2000. text 98.00 (*0-19-823410-4*) OUP.

Clark, Gordon L. & Won Bae Kim. Asian NIEs & the Global Economy: Industrial Restructuring & Corporate Strategy in the 1990s. 360p. 1996. text 48.50 (*0-8018-5105-X*) Johns Hopkins.

Clark, Gordon L., et al. Regional Dynamics: Studies in Adjustment Theory. 350p. (C). 1986. text 75.00 (*0-04-330353-6*); pap. text 29.95 (*0-04-330354-4*) Routledge.

Clark, Gracia. Onions Are My Husband: Survival & Accumulation by West African Market Women. LC 94-1907. 488p. 1994. pap. text 22.95 (*0-226-10780-9*); lib. bdg. 59.95 (*0-226-10779-5*) U Ch Pr.

Clark, Graeme M., et al, eds. Cochlear Prostheses. (Illus.). 288p. 1990. text 79.95 (*0-443-03582-2*) Church.

Clark, Graeme R., et al, eds. Cochlear Implantation for Infants & Children. LC 96-49000. 288p. 1997. 84.95 (*1-56593-727-9*, 1412) Thomson Learn.

Clark, Graham. Davie Cooper: Tribute to a Legend. (Illus.). 144p. 1996. 34.95 (*1-85158-789-6*, Pub. by Mainstream Pubng) Trafalgar.

Clark, Graham, ed. Henry James: Critical Assessments, 4 vols., Set. (Critical Assessments of Writers in English Ser.). (Illus.). 2064p. (C). (gr. 13 up). 1992. text, boxed set 535.00 (*1-873403-01-1*) Routledge.

Clark, Graham, jt. auth. see Armistead, Colin G.

Clark, Graham, jt. auth. see Longley, Paul.

Clark, Graham, jt. auth. see McAllister, Gary.

Clark, Grahame. Space, Time & Man: A Prehistorian's View. (Canto Book Ser.). (Illus.). 181p. (C). 1994. pap. 10.95 (*0-521-46762-4*) Cambridge U Pr.

— Symbols of Excellence: Precious Materials As Expressions of Status. (Illus.). 138p. 1986. text 42.95 (*0-521-30264-1*) Cambridge U Pr.

Clark, Grata J. The Jeter Mosaic: Seven Centuries in the History of a Family. (Illus.). 847p. 1987. 55.00 (*0-9619337-0-4*) Arcadia Clark Inc.

— The Jeter Mosaic Vol. 2: Connecting Lines. (Illus.). 440p. 1988. 42.00 (*0-9619337-1-2*) Arcadia Clark Inc.

Clark, Grata J. & Clark, Jeffrey S., eds. A Soldier's Dream of Home: The Civil War Letters of John C. Hughes to His Wife, Harriet. unabridged ed. (Illus.). 110p. 1996. 19.95 (*0-9619337-2-0*) Arcadia Clark Inc.

Clark, Gregory. A Bar'l of Apples: A Gregory Clark Omnibus. LC 72-183911. 326 p. 1971. write for info. (*0-07-092952-1*) McGraw.

— Dialogue, Dialectic, & Conversation: A Social Perspective on the Function of Writing. LC 89-6214. 120p. (C). 1989. pap. text 14.95 (*0-8093-1579-3*) S Ill U Pr.

Clark, Gregory & Halloran, S. Michael, eds. Oratorical Culture in Nineteenth-Century America: Transformations in the Theory & Practice of Rhetoric. LC 92-42230. (Illus.). 304p. (C). 1993. 36.95 (*0-8093-1739-7*) S Ill U Pr.

Clark, Gregory, et al. A Tribute to Robert A. Koch: Studies in the Northern Renaissance. LC 94-22519. (Illus.). 193p. 1995. 42.50 (*0-691-04340-X*) Princeton A & A.

Clark, Gregory R. Words of the Vietnam War: The Slang, Jargon, Abbreviations, Acronyms, Nomenclature, Nicknames, Pseudonyms, Slogans, Specs, Euphemisms, Double-talk, Chants & Names & Places of the Era of United States Involvement in Vietnam. LC 89-43639. 614p. 1990. lib. bdg. 55.00 (*0-89950-465-5*) McFarland & Co.

Clark, Grenville. World Peace Through World Law: Two Alternative Plans. 3rd ed. LC 66-21198. 589p. reprint ed. pap. 182.60 (*0-608-30691-6*, 200300600017) Bks Demand.

Clark, Grenville & Sohn, Louis B. World Peace Through World Law. 2nd rev. ed. 388p. 1960. 34.95 (*0-87855-358-4*) Transaction Pubs.

Clark, Grenville, jt. auth. see Sohn, Louis B.

Clark, Grover. The Great Wall Crumbles. LC 70-175694. (Select Bibliographies Reprint Ser.). 1977. reprint ed. 35.95 (*0-8369-6609-0*) Ayer.

Clark, H., tr. see Favre, Jules.

Clark, H. Jackson. Glass Plates & Wagon Ruts: Images of the Southwest by Lisle Updike & William Pennington. LC 98-26196. 1998. 32.50 (*0-87081-495-8*) Univ Pr Colo.

— The Owl in Monument Canyon: And Other Stories from Indian Country. (Illus.). 192p. 1993. 24.95 (*0-87480-438-8*); pap. 14.95 (*0-87480-439-6*) U of Utah Pr.

Clark, H. Nichols & Gerdts, William H. A Marble Quarry: The James H. Ricau Collection of Sculpture at the Chrysler Museum of Art. LC 97-15397. (Illus.). 280p. 1997. 75.00 (*1-55595-131-7*, Pub. by Hudson Hills) Natl Bk Netwk.

Clark, H. Nichols, jt. auth. see Clark, Trinkett.

Clark, Hal. OGI Pascal Development System Version 2: OGI Pascal2. (Education Ser.). 1989. 65.00 (*0-918667-08-9*); student ed. 275.00 (*0-685-40820-5*) On-Going Ideas.

Clark, Hal G. & Lorensen, Leonard. Illustrations of Accounting for Income Taxes: A Survey of the Application of FASB Statement No. 96. fac. ed. LC 89-401. (Financial Report Survey Ser.: No. 37). 137p. 1989. reprint ed. pap. 42.50 (*0-7837-8221-7*, 204798100009) Bks Demand.

— Illustrations of Departures from the New Standard Auditor's Report on Financial Statements of Business Enterprises: A Survey of the Application of SAS No. 58. fac. ed. LC 90-741. (Financial Report Survey Ser.: No. 41). 142p. 1990. reprint ed. pap. 44.10 (*0-7837-8220-9*, 204798000009) Bks Demand.

— Illustrations of the Disclosure of Related-Party Transactions: A Survey of the Application of FASB Statement No. 57. fac. ed. LC 90-1036. (Financial Report Survey Ser.: No. 42). 104p. 1990. pap. 32.30 (*0-7837-8228-4*, 204798800009) Bks Demand

— Illustrations of the Presentation of Financial Information about Consolidated Nonhomogeneous Subsidiaries: A Survey of the Application of FASB Statement No. 94. fac. ed. LC 90-632. (Financial Report Survey Ser.: No. 40). 118p. 1990. reprint ed. pap. 36.60 (*0-7837-8224-1*, 204798400009) Bks Demand.

— Quasi-Reorganizations: A Survey of Quasi-Reorganizations Disclosed in Corporate Annual Reports to Shareholders. fac. ed. LC 89-17656. (Financial Report Survey Ser.: No. 39). 179p. 1989. pap. 55.50 (*0-7837-8229-2*, 204798900009) Bks Demand.

— Updated Illustrations of Reporting Accounting Changes: A Survey of the Application of APB Opinion No. 20, As Amended. fac. ed. LC 88-137081. (Financial Report Survey Ser.: No. 36). 92p. 1987. reprint ed. pap. 30.00 (*0-7837-8223-3*, 204798300009) Bks Demand.

Clark, Hal G., et al. Illustrations of Accounting Policy Disclosure: A Survey of the Applications of APB Opinion No. 22. rev. ed. LC HF5681.B2C42. (Financial Report Survey Ser.: No. 36). 196p. 1988. reprint ed. pap. 60.80 (*0-7837-8222-5*, 204798200009) Bks Demand.

Clark, Hale C. The Great American Barbecue Instruction Book. Frank, Judy B., ed. (Illus.). 158p. 1985. pap. 10.95 (*0-936171-00-6*) Abacus Pub.

Clark, Harold F. The Cost of Government & the Support of Education: An Intensive Study of New York State with Results Applicable Over the Entire Country. LC 79-17668. (Columbia University. Teachers College. Contributions to Education Ser.: No. 145). reprint ed. 37.50 (*0-404-55145-9*) AMS Pr.

— Economic Theory & Correct Occupational Distribution. Stein, Leon, ed. LC 77-70488. 1977. reprint ed. lib. bdg. 21.95 (*0-405-10160-0*) Ayer.

Clark, Harold P., et al. History of the Tazewell House: Talisman from the Wishing Oak. Tazewell, Calvert W., ed. & intro. by Grigsby, Hugh B., intro. LC 90-80409. (Illus.). 130p. (Orig.). 1991. pap. 14.00 (*1-878515-12-8*) W S Dawson.

Clark, Harrison. All Cloudless Glory, 2 vols., Set. (Illus.). 1996. 69.95 (*0-89526-441-2*) Regnery Pub.

— All Cloudless Glory, Vol. II. 591p. 1998. pap. 22.50 (*0-89526-371-8*) Regnery Pub.

— All Cloudless Glory: Making a Nation, Vol. II. (Illus.). 608p. 1996. 39.95 (*0-89526-445-5*, Gateway Editions) Regnery Pub.

Clark, Harry H. American Literature: Poe Through Garland. LC 77-137641. (Goldentree Bibliographies Series in Language & Literature). (C). 1971. text 15.95 (*0-88295-509-8*); pap. text 6.95 (*0-88295-508-X*) Harlan Davidson.

— The Literary Influences of Philip Freneau. 33p. (Orig.). (C). 1925. reprint ed. pap. 39.95 (*0-8383-0014-6*) M S G Haskell Hse.

Clark, Harry H., jt. ed. see Wilson, Gay W.

Clark, Hazel. An Informal History of the Everett Public Library. 148p. 1996. pap. 19.95 (*1-881147-22-3*) Lowell Print.

— Textile Printing. (Album Ser.: No. 135). (Illus.). 32p. 1999. pap. 5.25 (*0-85263-729-2*, Pub. by Shire Pubns) Parkwest Pubns.

Clark, Heather, et al, eds. Organization & Identities: Text & Readings in Organizational Behavior. LC 94-70255. 456p. 1994. mass mkt. 34.95 (*0-412-56410-6*) Chapman & Hall.

Clark, Henry. Altering Behavior: The Ethics of Controlled Experience. LC 86-3710. 236p. 1987. reprint ed. pap. 73.20 (*0-608-01088-X*, 205939700001) Bks Demand.

— The Church & Residential Desegregation. 1965. 22.95 (*0-8084-0076-2*) NCUP.

— The Irony of American Morality. 1972. pap. 15.95 (*0-8084-0037-1*) NCUP.

Clark, Henry B., II. Freedom of Religion in America: Historical Roots, Philosophical Concepts, Contemporary Problems. 143p. 1982. pap. 24.95 (*0-87855-925-6*) Transaction Pubs.

Clark, Henry B. Practical Oral Surgery. 3rd ed. LC 65-19426. 503p. reprint ed. pap. 156.00 (*0-608-13438-4*, 201453400094) Bks Demand.

— Serenity, Courage & Wisdom: The Enduring Legacy of Reinhold Niebuhr. LC 94-21482. (Illus.). 208p. (Orig.). 1994. pap. 14.95 (*0-8298-1004-8*) Pilgrim OH.

Clark, Henry W. Clark: Genealogies of the Clark, Parks, Brockman & Dean Families, 3 pts. (Illus.). 371p. 1997. pap. 56.50 (*0-8328-7948-7*) Higginson Bk Co.

— Clark: Genealogies of the Clark, Parks, Brockman & Dean Families, 3 pts. (Illus.). 371p. 1997. reprint ed. lib. bdg. 66.50 (*0-8328-7947-9*) Higginson Bk Co.

— Davis: Genealogies of the Davis & Goss Families, 2 pts. (Illus.). 141p. 1993. reprint ed. pap. 59.50 (*0-8328-2983-8*); reprint ed. lib. bdg. 69.50 (*0-8328-2982-X*) Higginson Bk Co.

— History of Alaska. LC 72-37877. (Select Bibliographies Reprint Ser.). 1977. reprint ed. 25.95 (*0-8369-6714-3*) Ayer.

Clark, Herbert. Characteristic Studies of the Cornet. (Illus.). 64p. 1915. pap. 10.95 (*0-8258-0250-4*, 0-2281) Fischer Inc NY.

Clark, Herbert H. Arenas of Language Use. LC 92-38874. 440p. (C). 1993. lib. bdg. 47.50 (*0-226-10781-7*) U Ch Pr.

— Semantics & Comprehension. (Janua Linguarum, Series Minor: No. 187). 148p. 1976. pap. text 32.35 (*90-279-3384-7*) Mouton.

— Using Language. 343p. (C). 1996. text 59.95 (*0-521-56158-2*); pap. text 19.95 (*0-521-56745-9*) Cambridge U Pr.

Clark, Herbert H. & Clark, Eve V. Psychology & Language: An Introduction to Psycholinguistics. (Illus.). 608p. (C). 1977. write for info. (*0-318-52974-2*) Harcourt Coll Pubs.

***Clark, Hewitt B. & Davis, Maryann.** Transition to Adulthood. LC 99-47610. (Systems of Care for Children's Mental Health Ser.). 2000. write for info. (*1-55766-454-4*) P H Brookes.

Clark, Hilary. The Fictional Encyclopedia: Joyce, Poond, Sollers. LC 90-38188. (Studies in Comparative Literature). 216p. 1990. reprint ed. 15.00 (*0-8240-0006-4*) Garland.

Clark, Hilary, jt. ed. see Adamson, Joseph.

Clark, Homer H., Jr. Domestic Relations in the United States: Practitioner's Edition, 2 vols. 2nd ed. (Hornbook Ser.). 1529p. (C). 1987. 178.00 (*0-314-05472-3*) West Pub.

— Hornbook on the Law of Domestic Relations in the United States. 2nd ed. (Hornbook Ser.). 1050p. (C). 1988. reprint ed. 41.00 (*0-314-61281-5*) West Pub.

— The Law of Domestic Relations in the United States, Vol. 1. 826p. (C). 1990. reprint ed. text. write for info. (*0-318-67350-9*) West Pub.

Clark, Homer H., Jr. & Glowinsky, Carol. Cases & Problems on Domestic Relations. 5th ed. LC 95-17814. (American Casebook Ser.). 1151p. (C). 1995. 65.00 (*0-314-05905-9*) West Pub.

— Domestic Relations: Cases & Materials On. 4th ed. 900p. 1993. reprint ed. text 51.00 (*0-314-73781-2*) West Pub.

— Domestic Relations, Fourth Edition, Cases & Problems On: 1992 Supplement. 4th ed. (American Casebook Ser.). 160p. (C). 1992. pap. text 10.50 (*0-314-01121-8*) West Pub.

— Domestic Relations Teacher's Manual. 4th ed. (American Casebook Ser.). 304p. 1990. pap. text, teacher ed. write for info. (*0-314-81132-X*) West Pub.

— Domestic Relations, Teacher's Manual to Accompany Cases & Problems On. 5th ed. (American Casebook Ser.). 252p. 1995. pap. text. write for info. (*0-314-07231-4*) West Pub.

***Clark, Howard.** Civil Resistance in Kosovo. 224p. 2000. 59.95 (*0-7453-1574-7*, Pub. by Pluto GBR); pap. 19.95 (*0-7453-1569-0*, Pub. by Pluto GBR) Stylus Pub VA.

Clark, Hugh R. Community, Trade, & Networks: Southern Fujian Province from the Third to the Thirteenth Centuries. (Studies in Chinese History, Literature & Institutions). (Illus.). 278p. (C). 1991. text 69.95 (*0-521-39029-X*) Cambridge U Pr.

Clark, Hulda R. The Cure for All Cancers: With 100 Case Histories. rev. ed. (Illus.). 623p. (Orig.). 1993. pap. 19.95 (*0-9636328-2-5*) ProMotion Pub.

— The Cure for All Diseases. rev. ed. (Illus.). 604p. 1995. pap. 21.95 (*1-887314-02-4*) ProMotion Pub.

— The Cure for HIV & AIDS. rev. ed. (Illus.). 543p. 1996. pap. 19.95 (*0-9636328-3-3*) ProMotion Pub.

***Clark, Hulda Regehr.** The Cure for All Advanced Cancers. large type ed. (Illus.). 610p. 1999. pap. 21.95 (*1-890035-16-5*) New Centry Pr.

Clark, Hulda Regehr. The Cure for All Cancers: With 100 Case Histories. 16th large type ed. (Illus.). 623p. 1993. pap. 19.95 (*1-890035-00-9*) New Centry Pr.

— The Cure for All Diseases: With Many Case Histories. 17th large type ed. (Illus.). 604p. 1995. pap. 21.95 (*1-890035-01-7*) New Centry Pr.

C

— The Cure for HIV & AIDS: With over 75 Case Histories. 7th large type ed. (Illus.). 543p. 1993. pap. 19.95 (1-890035-02-5) New Centry Pr.
— Heilverfahren Aller Krebsarten (The Cure for All Cancers) Mit uber 100 Fallgeschichten Geheilter Personen. 3rd ed. (GER., Illus.). 589p. 1993. reprint ed. 19.95 (1-890035-03-3) New Centry Pr.
Clark, Hunter R. Justice Brennan: The Great Conciliator. LC 94-16681. (Illus.). 368p. 1994. 22.50 (1-55972-261-4, Birch Ln Pr) Carol Pub Group.
— Justice Denied: Why Our Jury System Doesn't Work. 1997. 22.50 (0-614-28009-5, Birch Ln Pr) Carol Pub Group.
— Race. 304p. Date not set. 23.00 (0-465-06808-1, Pub. by Basic); pap. write for info. (0-465-06809-X) Basic.
— Why Our Jury System Doesn't Work. 224p. 1997. 22.50 (1-55972-410-2, Birch Ln Pr) Carol Pub Group.
Clark, Hunter R., jt. auth. see Davis, Michael D.
Clark, I. Forever Young. 109p. (Orig.). 1994. pap. 9.95 (0-929385-53-5) Light Tech Pubng.
Clark, I. E. Christmas Dream: Director's Script. (Illus.). 21p. 1970. pap. 5.00 (0-88680-026-9) I E Clark.
— Christmas Dream: Dramatiztion of a Poem by Edwin Markham. (Illus.). 21p. 1970. pap. 3.00 (0-88680-025-0) I E Clark.
— Cyrano de Bergerac: One-Act Adaptation. (Illus.). 31p. 1968. pap. 3.25 (0-88680-032-3) I E Clark.
— Cyrano de Bergerac: One-Act Adaptation (Director's Script) (Illus.). 31p. 1968. pap. 10.00 (0-88680-033-1) I E Clark.
— Gammer Gurton's Needle: One-Act Adaptation. (Illus.). 40p. 1965. pap. 3.25 (0-88680-064-1) I E Clark.
— Gammer Gurton's Needle: One-Act Adaptation - Director's Script. (Illus.). 40p. 1965. pap. 10.00 (0-88680-065-X) I E Clark.
— Hansel & Gretel: Director's Script. (Illus.). 38p. (J). (ps up). 1970. pap. 15.00 (0-88680-076-5) I E Clark.
— Hansel & Gretel: 3-Act Dramatization. (Illus.). 38p. (J). (ps up). 1970. pap. 4.00 (0-88680-075-7) I E Clark.
— Hansel & Gretel in One Act. (Illus.). 22p. (Orig.). 1996. pap. 3.25 (0-88680-432-9) I E Clark.
— The Happy Scarecrow: A One-Act Fantasy. (Illus.). 17p. (J). (gr. 5-12). 1966. pap. 3.25 (0-88680-077-3) I E Clark.
— The Happy Scarecrow: Director's Script. (Illus.). 17p. (Orig.). (J). (gr. 5-12). 1966. 7.50 (0-88680-078-1) I E Clark.
— I Hate War: A One-Act Comedy. (Illus.). 26p. 1970. pap. 3.25 (0-88680-086-2) I E Clark.
— I Hate War: Director's Script. (Illus.). 26p. 1970. pap. 10.00 (0-88680-087-0) I E Clark.
— Once upon a Texas: With Pecos Bill & the Texas Stars. (Illus.). 44p. 1985. pap. 4.25 (0-88680-238-5) I E Clark.
— Pandora & the Magic Box: After Nathaniel Hawthorne. (Illus.). 20p. (J). (gr. 2 up). 1968. pap. 3.00 (0-88680-147-8) I E Clark.
— Pandora & the Magic Box: Director's Script. (Illus.). 20p. (J). (gr. 2 up). 1968. pap. 7.50 (0-88680-148-6) I E Clark.
— Ragweed Cowboy Joe: A Sneeze in 2-Acts. (Illus.). 24p. 1974. pap. 3.50 (0-88680-159-1) I E Clark.
— Ragweed Cowboy Joe: Director's Script. (Illus.). 24p. 1974. pap. 10.00 (0-88680-160-5) I E Clark.
— The Saga of Sagebrush Sal: Director's Script. (Illus.). 20p. 1972. pap. 10.00 (0-88680-168-0) I E Clark.
— The Saga of Sagebrush Sal: Wild-West Melodrama in 2-Acts. (Illus.). 20p. 1972. pap. 3.50 (0-88680-167-2) I E Clark.
— The Shaky Tale of Dr. Jakey: A Comic Melodrama. (Illus.). 40p. 1984. pap. 3.50 (0-88680-228-8) I E Clark.
— The Shaky Tale of Dr. Jakey: Director's Production Script. (Illus.). 40p. 1984. 10.00 (0-88680-229-6) I E Clark.
— Stagecrafters' Handbook. 3rd ed. (Illus.). 56p. 1977. pap. 5.00 (0-88680-182-6) I E Clark.
— Stagecrafters' Handbook: A Guide for Theatre Technicians. 3rd ed. LC 94-39528. (Illus.). 96p. (Orig.). 1995. pap. 10.00 (0-88734-649-9) Players Pr.
— El Sueno Navideno: The Christmas Dream. Barranco, David, tr. from ENG.Tr. of Christmas Dream. (SPA.). 17p. 1974. pap. 2.25 (0-88680-027-7) I E Clark.
— Twelve Dancing Princesses: Director's Script. 40p. (J). (ps up). 1969. pap. 15.00 (0-88680-198-2) I E Clark.
— Twelve Dancing Princesses: 2-Act Comedy Based on the Story by the Brothers Grimm. 40p. (J). (ps up). 1969. pap. 4.00 (0-88680-197-4) I E Clark.
Clark, I. E., adapted by. Cain: A Mystery Director's Script. (Illus.). 40p. 1970. pap. 10.00 (0-88680-017-X) I E Clark.
— Importance of Being Earnest: One-Act Adaptation - Director's Script. (Illus.). 35p. 1965. pap. 10.00 (0-88680-090-0) I E Clark.
Clark, I. E. & Byron, adapted by. Cain: A Mystery in One-Act Involving the World's First Murder. (Illus.). 40p. 1970. pap. 3.25 (0-88680-016-1) I E Clark.
Clark, I. E. & Carter, Kit. It's a Dungaree World: Director's Script. (Illus.). 40p. (J). (ps up). 1974. pap. 15.00 (0-88680-099-4) I E Clark.
— It's a Dungaree World: 2-Act Musical Comedy. (Illus.). 40p. (J). (ps up). 1974. pap. 4.50 (0-88680-097-8) I E Clark.
Clark, I. E., tr. see Moliere.
Clark, I. E., tr. see Sachs, Hans.
Clark, I. Edward. The Royal Secret. (Illus.). 363p. 1995. reprint ed. pap. 27.95 (1-56459-494-7) Kessinger Pub.
Clark, Ian. Classical Theories in International Relations. (St. Antony's Ser.). 1999. pap. 21.95 (0-312-21926-1) St Martin.
— Globalization & Fragmentation: International Relations in the Twentieth Century. LC 97-181236. 230p. (C). 1997. pap. text 26.95 (0-19-878166-0) OUP.
— Globalization & International Relations Theory. LC 99-21478. 216p. (C). 1999. text 69.95 (0-19-878210-1); pap. text 26.95 (0-19-878209-8) OUP.
— The Hierarchy of States: Reform & Resistance in the International Order. (Cambridge Studies in International Relations: No. 7). 264p. (C). 1989. text 59.95 (0-521-37252-6); pap. text 21.95 (0-521-37861-3) Cambridge U Pr.
— Nuclear Diplomacy & the Special Relationship: Britain's Deterrent & America, 1957-1962. LC 93-30705. 470p. 1994. text 85.00 (0-19-827370-3, Clarendon Pr) OUP.
— Waging War: A Philosophical Introduction. 160p. 1991. reprint ed. pap. 21.00 (0-19-827759-8) OUP.
Clark, Ian & Wheeler, Nicholas J. The British Origins of Nuclear Strategy, 1945-1955. 272p. 1989. text 59.00 (0-19-827541-2) OUP.
Clark, Ian C. Arte Indio y Esquimal del Canada. (ENG, FRE, GER & SPA., Illus.). 212p. 1993. 100.00 (84-343-0053-2) Elliots Bks.
Clark, Ian D. Scars in the Landscape: A Register of Massacre Sites in Western Victoria, 1803-1859. LC 96-134441. (Report Series/Australian Institute of Aboriginal & Torres Strait Islander Studies). x, 199 p. 1995. write for info. (0-85575-281-5) AIB & TSIS.
Clark, Ian D. & Fritz, P. Environmental Isotopes in Hydrogeology. LC 97-21889. 352p. 1997. boxed set 84.95 (1-56670-249-6) CRC Pr.
Clark, Ian M., ed. Matrix Metalloproteinase Protocols. LC 99-87618. (Methods in Molecular Biology Ser.: Vol. 151). 600p. 2000. 99.50 (0-89603-733-9) Humana.
Clark, Ira. Christ Revealed: The History of the Neotypological Lyric in the English Renaissance. LC 82-2696. (University of Florida Humanities Monographs: No. 51). xiv, 218p. 1982. 24.95 (0-8130-0712-7) U Press Fla.
— The Moral Art of Philip Massinger. LC 91-58964. 320p. 1993. 42.50 (0-8387-5225-X) Bucknell U Pr.
— The Professional Playwrights: Massinger, Ford, Shirley, & Brome. LC 91-45853. 240p. 1992. 29.95 (0-8131-1787-9) U Pr of Ky.
Clark, Ira G. Water in New Mexico: A History of Its Management & Use. LC 86-30819. (Illus.). 857p. 1987. reprint ed. pap. 200.00 (0-608-04151-3, 2064884000 11) Bks Demand.
Clark, Irene. Writing in the Center. 3rd ed. 208p. (C). 1998. per. 37.95 (0-7872-4614-X, 41461401) Kendall-Hunt.
Clark, Irene L. The Genre of Argument. LC 97-71706. 408p. (C). 1997. pap. text 33.50 (0-15-502184-2, Pub. by Harcourt Coll Pubs) Harcourt.
— The Informed Citizen: Argument & Analysis. LC 96-77232. 576p. (C). 1996. pap. text 39.50 (0-15-503785-4, Pub. by Harcourt Coll Pubs) Harcourt.
— Taking a Stand: A Guide to the Research Paper with Readings. (C). 1997. pap. text 35.80 (0-673-46027-4) Addson-Wesley Educ.
— Taking a Stand IE. 2nd ed. 752p. 1997. text, teacher ed. 7.25 (0-673-99510-0) Addson-Wesley Educ.
Clark, Irene L. Taking Stand. 2nd ed. (Illus.). 640p. (C). 1997. pap. text 49.00 (0-673-99509-7) Addson-Wesley Educ.
Clark, Irene L. Writing about Diversity. 2nd ed. 92p. (C). 1996. pap. text, teacher ed. 28.00 (0-15-503564-9) Harcourt Coll Pubs.
— Writing about Diversity: An Argument Reader & Guide. 2nd ed. LC 96-76633. 784p. (C). 1996. pap. text 37.50 (0-15-503563-0, Pub. by Harcourt Coll Pubs) Harcourt.
— Writing in the Center: Teaching in a Writing Center Setting. LC 85-80256. 84 p. 1985. write for info. (0-8403-3601-2) Kendall-Hunt.
— Writing in the Center: Teaching in a Writing Center Setting. 2nd ed. 180p. 1994. per. 26.95 (0-8403-7558-1) Kendall-Hunt.
Clark, J. Advanced Structured Basic Programming Manual. (DG - Computer Programming Ser.). 1985. mass mkt. 42.95 (0-538-27141-8) S-W Pub.
— The Care of Books. 1976. lib. bdg. 59.95 (0-8490-1572-3) Gordon Pr.
— Computer Confidence. (DC - Introduction to Computing Ser.). 1985. mass mkt., student ed. 15.95 (0-538-10011-7) S-W Pub.
— Computer Confidence: A Challenge for Today. 2nd ed. (DA - Computer Education Ser.). 1991. pap., student ed. 12.95 (0-538-60185-X) S-W Pub.
— Computer Confidence: A Challenge for Today. 2nd ed. (DA - Computer Education Ser.). (J). (gr. k-8). 1991. 141.95 (0-538-61423-4) S-W Pub.
— Computer Confidence: A Challenge for Today Deskmate. 2nd ed. (DA - Computer Education Ser.). 1991. 79.95 (0-538-61429-3); 79.95 (0-538-61430-7) S-W Pub.
— Computer Confidence: A Challenge for Today Microtools. 2nd ed. (DA - Computer Education Ser.). 1991. 79.95 (0-538-60188-4) S-W Pub.
— Computer Confidence: A Challenge for Today Microtools. 2nd ed. (DA - Computer Education Ser.). (J). (gr. k-8). 1991. 79.95 (0-538-61425-0) S-W Pub.
— Computer Confidence: A Challenge for Today MS-Works. 2nd ed. (DA - Computer Education Ser.). (J). (gr. k-8). 1991. 79.95 (0-538-61426-9) S-W Pub.
— Computer Information Processing. 2nd ed. (DC - Introduction to Computing Ser.). 1990. 112.95 (0-538-60135-3) S-W Pub.
— Computers & Information Processing. 2nd ed. (DC - Introduction to Computing Ser.). 1989. mass mkt. 51.95 (0-538-60131-0) S-W Pub.
— Economics: The Science of Cost, Benefit. 3rd ed. (HB - Economics Ser.). 1991. mass mkt., wbk. ed. 16.95 (0-538-61401-3) S-W Pub.
— Economics: The Science of Cost, Benefits. 2nd ed. (HB - Economics Ser.). 1988. 158.95 (0-538-08294-1) S-W Pub.
— The Great Arc of the Wild Sheep. (Illus.). 247p. 1995. 24.95 (1-57157-013-6) Safari Pr.
— Handbook for Office Workers. 8th ed. (EC - HS Communication/English Ser.). 1997. text 13.95 (0-538-86320-X) S-W Pub.
Clark, J. Handbook for Office Workers. 8th ed. LC 97-17711. (EC - HS Communication/English Ser.). (Illus.). 517p. 1997. pap. 29.95 (0-538-86319-6) S-W Pub.
Clark, J. How 7: A Handbook for Office Workers. 7th ed. (GE - Office Management Ser.). 1995. mass mkt., wbk. ed. 16.95 (0-538-85043-4) S-W Pub.
— Information Processing Study Guides & Applications. 3rd ed. (DC - Introduction to Computing Ser.). 1984. mass mkt., suppl. ed. 11.95 (0-538-10541-0) S-W Pub.
— Records of the Descendants of Hugh Clark of Watertown, Mass. 1640-1866. (Illus.). 261p. 1993. reprint ed. pap. 39.00 (0-8328-1349-4); reprint ed. lib. bdg. 49.00 (0-8328-1348-6) Higginson Bk Co.
— Structured Basic. 2nd ed. (DG - Computer Programming Ser.). 1988. teacher ed. 31.95 (0-538-28727-6) S-W Pub.
— Structured BASIC: Apple Version. 3rd ed. (DG - Computer Programming Ser.). 1994. pap., wbk. ed. 15.95 (0-538-61803-5) S-W Pub.
— Structured BASIC: IBM PC, TRS 80. 2nd ed. 1988. mass mkt. 45.95 (0-538-10840-1) S-W Pub.
— Structured BASIC: IBM Version. 3rd ed. (DG - Computer Programming Ser.). 1994. pap., wbk. ed. 15.95 (0-538-61802-7) S-W Pub.
— Structured BASIC Programming. (DG - Computer Education Ser.). 1983. pap., wbk. ed. 15.50 (0-538-10801-0) S-W Pub.
— Structured BASIC Texas Manual. 2nd ed. (DG - Computer Programming Ser.). 1991. 39.95 (0-538-28246-0) S-W Pub.
— Survey of Economics. (Miscellaneous/Catalogs Ser.). (C). 1996. 19.00 (0-538-86853-8) S-W Pub.
— Workbook for Computers & Information Processing. 2nd ed. (DC - Introduction to Computing Ser.). 1989. mass mkt., wbk. ed. 16.95 (0-538-60132-9) S-W Pub.
Clark, J. & Klooster, Dale H. Technology for Production & Decision Making. 3rd ed. (DC - Introduction to Computing Ser.). 1996. mass mkt., wbk. ed. 16.95 (0-538-64988-7) S-W Pub.
— Technology for Productivity & Decision Making. 3rd ed. (DC - Introduction to Computing Ser.). 1996. text 47.95 (0-538-64986-0) S-W Pub.
Clark, J., jt. auth. see Bux.
Clark, J., jt. auth. see Downing, D.
Clark, J. B., jt. ed. see Edmon, J.
Clark, J. Brent. Sooner Century: 100 Glorious Years of Oklahoma Football. Smith, Susan, ed. (Illus.). 256p. 1995. 39.50 (1-885758-04-9) Quality Sports.
— 3rd down & Forever. 1997. mass mkt. 5.99 (0-312-96148-0) St Martin.
Clark, J. Bunker. The Dawning of American Keyboard Music, 12. LC 88-3095. (Contributions to the Study of Music & Dance Ser.: No. 12). 433p. 1988. 65.00 (0-313-25581-4, CEK/, Greenwood Pr) Greenwood.
— Music at KU: A History of the University of Kansas Music Department. 196p. (Orig.). 1985. write for info. (0-318-60139-7) U KS Dept Mus Dance.
Clark, J. Bunker, ed. see Carr, Benjamin, et al.
Clark, J. C. The Language of Liberty, 1660-1832: Political Discourse & Social Dynamics in the Anglo-American World. 422p. (C). 1993. pap. text 24.95 (0-521-44957-X) Cambridge U Pr.
— Samuel Johnson: Literature, Religion & English Cultural Politics from the Restoration to Romanticism. (Illus.). 284p. (C). 1994. pap. text 18.95 (0-521-47885-5) Cambridge U Pr.
*__Clark, J. C. D.__ English Society, 1660-1832: Religion, Ideology & Politics During the Ancient Regime. 2nd ed. LC 99-45513. (Illus.). 580p. (C). 2000. 74.95 (0-521-66180-3) Cambridge U Pr.
— English Society, 1660-1832: Religion, Ideology & Politics During the Ancien Regime. 2nd ed. (Illus.). 580p. (C). 2000. pap. 27.95 (0-521-66627-9) Cambridge U Pr.
*__Clark, J. Desmond, et al, eds.__ Kalambo Falls Prehistoric Site Vol. 3: The Earlier Cultures: Middle & Earlier Stone Age. (Illus.). 400p. (C). 2000. 120.00 (0-521-20071-7) Cambridge U Pr.
Clark, J. Desmond, jt. ed. see Bishop, Walter W.
Clark, J. E. & Copcutt, L., eds. Management for Nurses & Health Care Professionals. (Illus.). 242p. 1996. pap. write for info. (0-443-05091-0) Church.
Clark, J. H. Catalysis of Organic Reactions by Supported Inorganic Reagents. 126p. 1994. 98.95 (0-471-18560-4) Wiley.
*__Clark, J. H. & Rhodes, C. N.__ Clean Synthesis Using Porous Inorganic Solid Catalysts & Supported Reagents. 124p. 2000. 115.00 (0-85404-526-0, Pub. by Royal Soc Chem) Spr-Verlag.
*__Clark, J. H., et al.__ Feedstock Recycling of Plastic Wastes. 220p. 1999. 120.00 (0-85404-531-7, Pub. by Royal Soc Chem) Spr-Verlag.
— Supported Reagents: Preparation, Analysis & Applications. 152p. 1992. 89.95 (0-471-18779-8) Wiley.
Clark, J. H., jt. ed. see Roy, A. K.
Clark, J. Kent. Goodwin Wharton. 1984. 34.00 (0-19-212234-7) OUP.
Clark, J. L., jt. auth. see Cracknell, Arthur P.
Clark, J. Marshall, ed. Molecular Action of Insecticides on Ion Channels. LC 95-6612. (ACS Symposium Ser.: No. 591). (Illus.). 356p. 1995. text 110.00 (0-8412-3165-6, Pub. by Am Chemical) OUP.
Clark, J. Marshall & Matsumura, Fumio, eds. Membrane Receptors & Enzymes As Targets of Insecticidal Action. LC 86-4908. 266p. 1986. 65.00 (0-306-42239-5, Plenum Trade) Perseus Pubng.
*__Clark, J. Marshall & Yamaguchi, Isamu, eds.__ Pesticide Science: Pesticide Resistance. (ACS Symposium Series). (Illus.). 306p. 2001. text 115.00 (0-8412-3723-9, Pub. by Am Chemical) OUP.
Clark, J. Michael. A Defiant Celebration: Theological Ethics & Gay Sexuality. LC 90-30837. 200p. (Orig.). 1990. pap. 10.00 (0-934667-08-X) Tangelwuld.
— Defying the Darkness: Gay Theology in the Shadows. LC 96-40134. 128p. (Orig.). 1997. pap. 12.95 (0-8298-1163-X) Pilgrim OH.
— Gay Being, Divine Presence: Essays in Gay Spirituality (The Ganymede Papers) LC 87-6431. (Illus.). ix, 95p. (Orig.). 1987. pap. 8.00 (0-934667-03-9) Tangelwuld.
Clark, J. R. & Brown, G. E., eds. Chemistry & Physics of Minerals. (Transactions of the American Crystallographic Association Ser.: Vol. 15). 120p. 1979. pap. 25.00 (0-686-60385-0) Polycrystal Bk Serv.
Clark, J. R., et al. Macroeconomics for Managers. 600p. 1990. teacher ed. write for info. (0-318-66333-3, H22114); student ed. 18.00 (0-685-29826-4, H22122); disk 13.33 (0-685-29827-2, H24342) P-H.
Clark, J. R., jt. ed. see Snow, Gordon B.
Clark, J. Reuben, Jr. To Them of the Last Wagon & Who Was This Jesus? LC 97-78188. 51 p. 1998. write for info. (0-87579-975-2) Deseret Bk.
Clark, J. S. & De Corso, S. M., eds. Stationary Gas Turbine Alternative Fuels - STP 809. LC 82-73767. 360p. 1983. 43.00 (0-8031-0258-5, STP809) ASTM.
*__Clark, J. W.__ SSS. LC 00-190645. 528p. 2000. 25.00 (0-7388-1894-1); pap. 18.00 (0-7388-1895-X) Xlibris Corp.
Clark, J. W., et al, eds. Scientific Applications of Neural Nets: Proceedings of the 194th W. E. Heraeus Seminar Held at Bad Honnef, Germany, 11-13 May 1998. LC 99-14728. (Lecture Notes in Physics Ser.: Vol. 522). xiii, 288p. 1999. 62.00 (3-540-65737-1) Spr-Verlag.
Clark, J. W. & Ristig, M. L. Theory of Spin Lattices & Lattice Gauge Models: Proceedings of the 165th We-Heraeus-Seminar Held at the Physikzentrum, Bad Honnef, Germany, 14-16 October 1996, Vol. 494. LC 97-22630. (Lecture Notes in Physics). xi, 194p. 1997. write for info. (3-540-63207-7) Spr-Verlag.
Clark, Jacquelin, jt. auth. see Farrow, Joanna.
*__Clark, Jacqueline & Farrow, Joanna.__ Mediterranean Country Kitchen. 96p. 2000. pap. 12.95 (0-7548-0305-8) Anness Pub.
— Taste of the Mediterranean. 256p. 2000. pap. 19.95 (1-84215-019-7) Anness Pub.
Clark, Jacquie. News 4 You. 400p. (J). (ps-6). 1996. spiral bd. 32.00 (1-884135-29-3) Mayer-Johnson.
Clark, Jama. What the Hell Do Women Really Want? A Practical & Scientific Guide for Men in the 90s. 2nd rev. ed. 260p. 1997. 22.95 (0-9642254-1-7) Islnd Flower.
*__Clark, James.__ The Spirit of Revolt & the Quest for Freedom in the Cinema of the 60's. 2000. pap. 15.00 (1-58790-000-9) Regent Pr.
Clark, James & Clark, Lyn. Clarks' Online Reference Manual: How 7. 500p. 1995. 40.95 incl. disk (0-538-85689-0) S-W Pub.
— How 8 Reference Guide & Clarks' Online Reference Manual. 8th ed. 496p. 1997. 33.75 (0-538-88140-2) Sth-Wstrn College.
Clark, James & Matheny, Nelda. A Handbook of Hazard Tree Evaluation for Utility Arborists. (Illus.). 34p. 1993. pap. text 5.00 (1-881956-05-9) Int Soc Arboricult.
Clark, James, jt. auth. see Matheny, Nelda.
Clark, James A. A Woman's Guide to Divorce: A Practical Handbook. LC 97-18834. 224p. (Orig.). 1998. pap. 14.95 (1-880090-44-9) Galde Pr.
Clark, James A., ed. see Halbouty, Michel T.
Clark, James Anthony & Halbouty, Michael T. Spindletop: The True Story of the Oil Discovery That Changed the World. anniversary ed. LC 99-13006. (Illus.). 322p. 2000. 26.95 (0-88415-813-6) Gulf Pub.
Clark, James C. Faded Glory: Presidents Out of Power. LC 84-18327. 204p. 1985. 49.95 (0-275-90075-4, C0075, Praeger Pubs); pap. 12.95 (0-275-91802-5, B1802, Praeger Pubs) Greenwood.
— Last Train South: The Flight of the Confederate Government from Richmond. LC 84-42610. (Illus.). 192p. 1997. pap. 25.00 (0-7864-0469-8) McFarland & Co.
*__Clark, James C.__ 200 Quick Looks at Florida History. (Illus.). 2000. pap. write for info. (1-56164-200-2) Pineapple Pr.
Clark, James d'A. Pulp Technology & Treatment for Paper. 2nd ed. LC 85-62603. (Illus.). 872p. 1985. 97.00 (0-87930-164-3) Miller Freeman.
Clark, James F. & Drum, William O. Structured BASIC: Apple Version. 3rd ed. LC 93-4720. 1994. mass mkt. 48.95 (0-538-61801-9) S-W Pub.
— Structured BASIC: DOS Version. 3rd ed. LC 93-1153. 1994. mass mkt. 48.95 (0-538-61800-0) S-W Pub.
Clark, James F. & Xerox Corporation Staff. Power Publishing with Ventura (IBM) 240p. (C). 1992. text 33.35 (0-697-16511-6) Bus & Educ Tech.
Clark, James F., et al. Technology for Productivity & Decision Making: A Brief Course. 3rd ed. LC 96-43281. 1997. mass mkt. 22.95 (0-538-67526-8) S-W Pub.
Clark, James H., et al. Aromatic Fluorination. LC 96-14024. 208p. 1996. boxed set 129.95 (0-8493-7867-2) CRC Pr.
— Catalysis of Organic Reactions by Supported Inorganic Reagents. LC 94-2230. (Illus.). xii, 126p. 1994. 65.00 (1-56081-507-8, Wiley-VCH) Wiley.
Clark, James I. & Remini, Robert O. Freedom Frontiers: The Story of the American People. 1975. write for info. (0-02-640660-8, 64066); teacher ed. write for info. (0-02-640670-5, 64067) Macmillan.
Clark, James J. & Yuille, Alan L. Data Fusion for Sensory Information Processing Systems. (C). 1990. text 113.50 (0-7923-9120-9) Kluwer Academic.

An Asterisk (*) at the beginning of an entry indicates that the title is appearing for the first time.

Clark, James L. The Great Arc of the Wild Sheep. LC 94-9424. (Illus.). 247p. 1994. pap. 15.95 (*0-8061-1472-X*) U of Okla Pr.

Clark, James L. & Clark, Lyn R. Clarks' Online Reference Manual for Windows: Includes HOW 7 on 3.5" Disks. LC 95-9559. 1995. text. write for info. incl. disk (*0-538-85904-0*) S-W Pub.

— How Seven: A Handbook for Office Workers. 7th ed. LC 94-31764. (C). 1994. pap. 24.95 (*0-538-84632-1*) S-W Pub.

Clark, James L. & Clark, Lyn R. How To Handbook For Office Work. 3rd ed. (SWC-Business Communication). 297p. 1982. mass mkt. 11.75 (*0-534-01116-0*) PWS Pubs.

— How To Handbook For Office Workers. 2nd ed. (SWC-Business Communication). 280p. (C). 1979. pap. 9.00 (*0-534-00635-3*) PWS Pubs.

Clark, James L. & Clark, Lyn R. How 4: A Handbook For Office Workers. 4th ed. LC 84-23366. (SWC-Business Communication). 336p. (C). 1984. mass mkt. 13.25 (*0-534-04542-1*) PWS Pubs.

— How 5: Handbook For Office Workers. 5th ed. (SWC-Business Communication). 352p. (C). 1987. mass mkt. 17.00 (*0-534-87144-5*) PWS Pubs.

Clark, James L. & Clark, Lynn R. How 6: Handbook For Office Workers. 6th ed. (SWC-Business Communication). 439p. (C). 1991. mass mkt. 20.00 (*0-534-92556-1*) S-W Pub.

***Clark, James Leland & Clark, Lyn.** How 9: A Handbook for Office Workers. 9th ed. LC 00-34439. 2001. pap. 30.95 (*0-324-01357-4*) Sth-Wstrn College.

Clark, James M. Teachers & Politics in France: A Pressure Group Study of the Federation de l'Education Nationale. LC 67-13494. 215p. reprint ed. pap. 66.70 (*0-8357-3981-3*, 203667900005) Bks Demand.

Clark, James P., et al. Antitrust Laws & Trade Regulation: Desk Edition, 2 vols. 1981. ring bd. 600.00 (*0-8205-1763-1*) Bender.

***Clark, James R.** Fat Free Forever: A Comprehensive Program for Reducing Body Fat & Keeping It Off. 184p. 1998. pap. 23.95 (*1-56072-561-3*, Nova Kroshka Bks) Nova Sci Pubs.

Clark, James R., jt. auth. see Matheny, Nelda.

Clark, James W., Jr., ed. see Wolfe, Thomas.

Clark, Jan. Earth Herald. 256p. 1998. mass mkt. 5.99 (*0-451-45638-6*, ROC) NAL.

— Prodigy. 1997. mass mkt. 5.99 (*0-451-45615-7*, ROC) NAL.

Clark, Janan. Sexocize: A Female Genitourinary Program. 2nd ed. (Illus.). 41p. 1998. pap. 12.95 (*0-929593-01-4*) West Pine Pub.

***Clark, Jane, et al.** A Garden for All Seasons: An Artist's View of the Royal Botanic Gardens. (Illus.). 128p. 1998. text 65.00 (*90-5703-861-7*, Harwood Acad Pubs) Gordon & Breach.

Clark, Jane, jt. ed. see Harman, Willis.

Clark, Jane C. & McGee, Rose F., eds. Core Curriculum for Oncology Nursing. 2nd ed. (Illus.). 255p. 1992. pap. text, student ed. 31.95 (*0-7216-3487-7*, W B Saunders Co) Harcrt Hlth Sci Grp.

Clark, Jane E. & Humphrey, James H., eds. Advances in Motor Development Research, 4 vols. LC 86-47829. (Illus.). 1993. 37.50 (*0-404-63450-8*) AMS Pr.

Clark, Jane E., jt. ed. see Kelso, J. Scott.

Clark, Jane P. Deportation of Aliens from the United States to Europe. LC 69-18766. (American Immigration Collection. Series 1). 1969. reprint ed. 23.95 (*0-405-00514-8*) Ayer.

Clark, Janice, jt. auth. see Hart, C. W., Jr.

Clark, Janie. Full Life Fitness: A Complete Exercise Program for Mature Adults. LC 92-2860. 191p. 1992. pap. 14.95 (*0-87322-391-8*, PCLA0391) Human Kinetics.

Clark, Janie, ed. Exercise Programming for Older Adults. LC 96-7978. (Activities, Adaptation & Aging Ser.: Vol. 20, No. 3). 100p. 1996. 39.95 (*1-56024-805-X*) Haworth Pr.

Clark, Janine, jt. auth. see Clark, Dareld.

Clark, Janine A., jt. auth. see Kleinberg, Remonda B.

***Clark, Jason & Richter, Jeffrey M.** Programming Services for Microsoft Windows. 2000. pap. 49.99 (*0-7356-0753-2*) Microsoft.

Clark, Jay. Algebra Flipper 2, Vol. 2. 49p. (YA). (gr. 8 up). 1993. 6.95 (*1-878383-21-3*) C Lee Pubns.

Clark, Jay, ed. Voyages: The World's 100 Most Exciting Ports of Call Selected by the World's Leading Travel Writers. (Illus.). 248p. 1998. 39.95 (*0-7370-0033-3*) Tme Inc.

Clark, Jayne & Wingenbach, Gerry. Go Guide: Two-Day Getaways from Pittsburgh. Merriman, Woodene, ed. Date not set. pap. 12.95 (*0-9657325-0-9*) Pittsbrgh Post-Gazette.

Clark, Jean. Ongoing Record Review: A Guide to JCAHO Compliance & Best Practice. (Illus.). 120p. 1998. pap. text 87.00 (*1-57839-038-9*) Opus Communs.

Clark, Jeanne. California Wildlife Viewing Guide. rev. ed. (Illus.). 192p. 1996. pap. 12.95 (*1-56044-494-0*) Falcon Pub Inc.

Clark, Jeanne L. Nevada Wildlife Viewing Guide. LC 93-17494. (Watchable Wildlife Ser.). (Illus.). 88p. (Orig.). 1993. pap. 6.95 (*1-56044-207-7*) Falcon Pub Inc.

Clark, Jeff. The Little Door Slides Back, Vol. 32. (New American Poetry Ser.). 120p. 1998. pap. text 10.95 (*1-55713-314-X*) Sun & Moon CA.

Clark, Jeff, jt. auth. see Downing, Douglas.

***Clark, Jeffery J., et al.** Archaeological Investigations along Tonto Creek: Introduction, Slate Creek & Sycamore Creek Sections. (Anthropological Papers: No. 22, Vol. 1). (Illus.). 1999. pap. write for info. (*1-886398-34-8*) Desert Archaeol.

— Archaeological Investigations along Tonto Creek No. II: Punkin Center Section. (Anthropological Papers: No. 22, Vol. 2). (Illus.). 2000. pap. write for info. (*1-886398-41-0*) Desert Archaeol.

Clark, Jeffery J., jt. ed. see Elson, Mark D.

Clark, Jeffery J., ed. see Hall, Susan, et al.

Clark, Jeffery J., ed. see Sliva, R. Jane, et al.

Clark, Jeffery J., jt. ed. see Yoffee, Norman.

Clark, Jeffrey, jt. auth. see Evans, G. Edward.

Clark, Jeffrey S., jt. ed. see Clark, Grata J.

Clark, Jenness. An Unobstructed View. Goodfellow, Pamela R., ed. (Illus.). 250p. 1998. pap. 12.99 (*1-891761-02-1*) Goodfellow Pr.

Clark, Jennifer. Video Training Resource Guide. 36p. 1996. pap. 25.00 (*1-892663-02-3*) WERC.

Clark, Jennifer, jt. auth. see Clark, Peter.

***Clark, Jeramy.** I Gave Dating a Chance: A Biblical Perspective to Balance the Extremes. LC 99-59022. 192p. 2000. pap. 9.95 (*1-57856-329-1*) Waterbrook Pr.

Clark, Jerome. The Emergence of a Phenomenon: UFOs from the Beginning Through 1959. (UFO Encyclopedia Ser.: Vol. 2). 433p. 1992. lib. bdg. 95.00 (*1-55888-741-5*) Omnigraphics Inc.

— Encyclopedia of Strange & Unexplained Physical Phenomena. LC 93-16958. 400p. 1993. 65.00 (*0-8103-8843-X*, 101433) Gale.

— High Strangeness: UFOs 1960-1979. LC 96-231631. (UFO Encyclopedia Ser.: Vol. 3). (Illus.). 777p. 1996. lib. bdg. 95.00 (*1-55888-742-3*) Omnigraphics Inc.

— The UFO Book: Encyclopedia of the Extraterrestrial. LC 97-35767. (Illus.). 705p. 1997. 19.95 (*1-57859-029-9*, 00157411) Visible Ink Pr.

— UFOs in the 1980s. (UFO Encyclopedia Ser.: Vol. 1). 234p. 1990. lib. bdg. 95.00 (*1-55888-301-0*) Omnigraphics Inc.

***Clark, Jerome.** Unexplained! 347 Strange Sightings, Incredible Occurrences & Physical Phenomena. (Illus.). 443p. 2000. reprint ed. pap. text 15.00 (*0-7881-9033-4*) DIANE Pub.

Clark, Jerome. Unexplained! Strange Sightings, Incredible Occurences & Puzzling Physical Phenomena. 2nd rev. ed. LC 99-168445. (Illus.). 650p. 1998. text 19.95 (*1-57859-070-1*) Visible Ink Pr.

Clark, Jerome & Pear, Nancy, eds. Strange & Unexplained Happenings: When Nature Breaks the Rules of Science, 3 vols., Vol. 3. (Illus.). 538p. (YA). (gr. 5 up). 1995. text 69.00 (*0-8103-9780-3*, UXL) Gale.

Clark, Jerome, jt. auth. see Coleman, Loren.

Clark, Jerome C., ed. UFO Encyclopedia: The Phenomenon from the Beginning. 2nd ed. LC 98-15930. 1178p. 1997. lib. bdg. 140.00 (*0-7808-0097-4*) Omnigraphics Inc.

Clark, Jerome L. 1844 Religious Movements, Vol. I. fac. ed. LC 68-20556. 400p. 1996. reprint ed. per. 14.95 (*1-57258-067-4*) Teach Servs.

— 1844 Religious Movements, Vol. II. fac. ed. LC 68-20556. 368p. 1996. reprint ed. per. 14.95 (*1-57258-068-2*) Teach Servs.

— 1844 Religious Movements, Vol. III. fac. ed. LC 68-20556. 240p. 1996. reprint ed. per. 14.95 (*1-57258-069-0*) Teach Servs.

***Clark, Jerry.** Reflections. 2000. pap. write for info. (*1-58235-437-5*) Watermrk Pr.

***Clark, Jerry & Huba, Fritz.** Seven Lifetime Sports. 2nd ed. 238p. 1998. pap. 34.95 (*0-945483-90-2*) E Bowers Pub.

Clark, Jerry E. Anson to Zuber: Iowa Boys in the Major Leagues. vi, 228p. 1992. pap. 20.00 (*0-9631699-1-2*) Making Hist.

— The Shawnee. LC 93-14114. 120p. 1993. 18.00 (*0-8131-1839-5*) U Pr of Ky.

Clark, Jerry E. & Webb, Martha E. Alexander the Great: The Story of Grover Cleveland Alexander. (Illus.). vii, 59p. (Orig.). 1993. pap. 11.00 (*0-9631699-2-0*) Making Hist.

Clark, Jesse. Don't Throw Out That Pizza. 128p. 1998. pap. 6.95 (*0-9645727-3-7*) Pine Orchard.

Clark, Jewell T. & Long, Elizabeth T., compiled by. A Guide to Church Records in the Archives Branch, Virginia State Library & Archives. x, 271p. 1988. reprint ed. pap. 10.00 (*0-88490-146-7*) Library of VA.

Clark, Jill N. Needle Lace: Techniques & Inspiration. (Illus.). 144p. 1999. 29.99 (*0-9658248-5-3*) GUILDcom.

***Clark, Jill Nordfors.** Needle Lace: Techniques & Inspiration. (Illus.). 144p. 1999. 35.00 (*0-85532-897-5*, 8975, Pub. by Srch Pr) A Schwartz & Co.

Clark, Jillian, jt. auth. see Harris, Mark.

Clark, Jim. Courage in Crisis: Finding Harbors of Hope in the Stroms of Life. 1999. pap. write for info. (*0-88965-172-8*) Chr Pubns.

— Cycling the U. S. Parks: Scenic Bicycle Tours in National Parks. LC 92-83825. (Active Travel Ser.). (Illus.). 224p. 1996. pap. 12.95 (*0-933201-56-7*) MBI Pubg.

— Daily Courage. 1999. pap. 9.99 (*0-88965-152-3*) Chr Pubns.

— Dancing on Canaan's Ruins: Poems by Jim Clark. 64p. 1997. reprint ed. pap. 8.95 (*0-9661862-0-6*) Eternal Delight.

— Handiwork. 88p. 1998. pap. 10.00 (*1-879934-59-0*) St Andrews NC.

— How to Build Hot Rod Trucks. (Illus.). 200p. 1993. pap. 22.95 (*1-884089-00-3*) CarTech.

— Mountain Biking the National Parks: Off-Road Cycling Adventures in America's National Parks. LC 95-76297. (Active Travel Ser.). (Illus.). 208p. (Orig.). 1996. pap. 12.95 (*0-933201-69-9*) MBI Pubg.

***Clark, Jim, ed.** Swagazine 7. iv, 60p. 1999. pap. 8.95 (*1-930050-01-1*, Swagazine) Lip Think Pr.

Clark, Jim, photos by. West Virginia: The Allegheny Highlands. LC 98-3437. (Illus.). 128p. 1998. 39.95 (*1-56579-296-3*) Westcliffe Pubs.

Clark, Jim & Beck, Kenneth. The All-American Cowboy Cookbook. LC 95-24938. (Illus.). 256p. 1995. spiral bd. 14.95 (*1-55853-365-6*) Rutledge Hill Pr.

— Aunt Bee's Mayberry Cookbook. Pitkin, Julia M., ed. LC 91-3047. (Illus.). 244p. 1991. pap. 14.95 (*1-55853-098-3*) Rutledge Hill Pr.

— Granny's Beverly Hillbillies Cookbook. LC 94-8430. (Illus.). 256p. 1994. spiral bd. 12.95 (*1-55853-271-4*) Rutledge Hill Pr.

— Postcards from Aunt Bee's Mayberry Cookbook. (Illus.). 1993. pap. 8.95 (*1-55853-231-5*) Rutledge Hill Pr.

***Clark, Jim & Edwards, Owen.** Netscape Time: The Making of the Billion-Dollar Start-Up That Took on Microsoft. 288p. 2000. pap. 14.95 (*0-312-26361-9*, St Martin Griffin) St Martin.

Clark, Jim, et al. Le Peintre Sumida: Persistence of Vision. Lenning, Janet, ed. Met, Philippe & Watanabe, Kayko, trs. from ENG. (FRE & JPN., Illus.). 1991. 45.00 (*1-879138-47-6*) Beaux-Arts Coterie.

***Clark, Jim, et al.** Swagazine 6. viii, 101p. 1998. pap. 8.95 (*1-930050-00-3*) Lip Think Pr.

— Swagazine 8. (Illus.). 100p. 2000. pap. 5.00 (*1-930050-02-X*, Swagazine) Lip Think Pr.

Clark, Jim, jt. auth. see Beck, Ken.

Clark, Jim, jt. auth. see Beck, Kenneth.

Clark, Jim, jt. auth. see Edwards, Owen.

Clark, Jim, ed. see Early, Donna P. & Hand, Edie.

Clark, Jim, ed. see Hemphill, Bethni & McClain, Brenda.

Clark, Jo, jt. auth. see Fearing, Virginia G.

Clark, Joan. The Hand of Robin Squires. unabridged ed. 160p. (YA). (gr. 7-12). 1996. mass mkt. 5.99 (*0-7736-7426-8*) STDK.

Clark, Joanne, ed. Marconi's International Register: 98th Annual. annuals 99th rev. ed. LC 31-15824. 1300p. 1998. pap. 150.00 (*0-916446-23-9*) Tele Cable.

Clark, Joe. Tennessee Hill Folk. LC 72-2880. (Illus.). 96p. 1972. 14.95 (*0-8265-1183-X*) Vanderbilt U Pr.

Clark, Joe, photos by. Up the Hollow from Lynchburg. (Illus.). 128p. 1975. 15.00 (*0-07-062210-8*) McGraw.

Clark, John. Democratizing Development: The Role of Voluntary Organizations. LC 91-7371. (Library of Management for Development). 226p. 1991. pap. 18.95 (*0-931816-91-2*) Kumarian Pr.

***Clark, John.** Dictionary of Accounting Terms. 2000. 55.00 (*0-8144-0618-1*) AMACOM.

— Dictionary of Banking & Finance Terms: "AAA to Zloty" 350p. 1998. pap. 60.00 (*0-85297-493-0*, Pub. by Chartered Bank) St Mut.

— Dictionary of Insurance & Finance Terms: A1 to Zero-Rated. 350p. 1998. pap. 60.00 (*0-85297-494-9*, Pub. by Chartered Bank) St Mut.

Clark, John. History of Epic Poetry: Post-Virgilian. LC 65-15876. (Studies in Poetry: No. 38). 1969. reprint ed. lib. bdg. 75.00 (*0-8383-0528-8*) M S G Haskell Hse.

***Clark, John.** The International Dictionary of Banking & Finance. 355p. 1999. 50.00 (*0-8144-0533-9*) AMACOM.

— International Dictionary of Banking & Finance. 325p. 1999. 50.00 (*1-888998-65-2*, 98-65-2) Glenlake Pub.

Clark, John. The International Dictionary of Insurance & Finance. 450p. 1999. 50.00 (*0-8144-0532-0*) AMACOM.

***Clark, John.** The International Dictionary of Insurance & Finance. 345p. 2000. 50.00 (*1-888998-69-5*, 98-69-5) Glenlake Pub.

Clark, John. The Macmillan Dictionary of Measurement. 512p. 1994. 27.50 (*0-02-525750-1*) Macmillan.

— Managing Innovation & Change: People, Technology, & Strategy. LC 95-74574. 304p. 1995. 75.00 (*0-8039-8944-X*); pap. 28.50 (*0-8039-8945-8*) Sage.

***Clark, John.** Modern Asian Art. (Illus.). 344p. 1998. text 56.00 (*90-5704-041-7*, Harwood Acad Pubs) Gordon & Breach.

Clark, John. Modern Asian Art. LC 98-26254. (Illus.). 368p. (C). 1998. text 48.00 (*0-8248-2142-4*) UH Pr.

— There Are No Poets in the Yellow Pages. LC 93-648. 100p. (Orig.). 1993. pap. 9.00 (*1-882979-11-7*) Tribe Heart.

***Clark, John, ed.** International Dictionary of Banking & Finance. 360p. 1999. 55.00 (*1-57958-099-8*) Fitzroy Dearborn.

— International Dictionary of Insurance & Finance. 342p. 1999. 55.00 (*1-57958-161-7*) Fitzroy Dearborn.

Clark, John, ed. Matter & Energy: Physics in Action. (New Encyclopedia of Science Ser.). (Illus.). 160p. 1995. 39.95 (*0-19-521085-9*) OUP.

— Modernity in Asian Art. (University of Sydney East Asian Ser.: No. 7). (Illus.). 210p. (C). 1993. pap. text 28.00 (*0-646-14773-0*, Pub. by Wild Peony Pty) UH Pr.

— PlopLop, No. 2. (Adventures of PlopLop Ser.). 16p. 1992. pap. 5.00 (*1-885710-01-1*) Geekspeak Unique.

Clark, John & Allison, Caroline. Zambia: Debt & Poverty. 80p. (C). 1989. pap. 9.95 (*0-85598-115-6*, Pub. by Oxfam Pub) Stylus Pub VA.

— Zambia: Debt & Poverty. 80p. (C). 1989. text 80.00 (*0-85598-114-8*, Pub. by Oxfam Pubns) St Mut.

Clark, John & Cole, Daniel H., eds. Environmental Protection in Transition: Economic, Legal & Socio-Political Perspectives on Poland. LC 98-6528. (Illus.). 156p. 1998. text 68.95 (*1-84014-422-X*, Pub. by Ashgate Pub) Ashgate Pub Co.

Clark, John & Dantzler, John. Hiking South Carolina. (Falcon Guides Ser.). (Illus.). 224p. 1998. pap. 14.95 (*1-56044-602-1*) Falcon Pub Inc.

Clark, John & Franke, Scott, eds. PlopLop, No. 1. (Adventures of PlopLop Ser.). 16p. 1991. pap. 5.00 (*1-885710-00-3*) Geekspeak Unique.

Clark, John & Wildavsky, Aaron. The Moral Collapse of Communism: Poland As a Cautionary Tale. 400p. 1990. 24.95 (*1-55815-121-4*) ICS Pr.

Clark, John, et al. Global Simulation Models: A Comparative Study. LC 74-32231. 145p. reprint ed. pap. 45.00 (*0-608-18443-8*, 203265500080) Bks Demand.

Clark, John, jt. auth. see Pirie, Gayle.

Clark, John, jt. auth. see Ring, Tony.

Clark, John, ed. see Alford, John.

Clark, John, ed. see Andis, Kitrell, et al.

Clark, John, jt. ed. see Daintith, John.

Clark, John, ed. see Gardinier, David.

Clark, John, ed. & illus. see Andis, Kitrell, et al.

Clark, John, ed. & illus. see Niditch, B. Z., et al.

Clark, John A. Gleanings by the Way. 352p. 1991. reprint ed. pap. 17.50 (*0-89981-207-4*) Eastern Orthodox.

— HO Slot Car Identification & Price Guide. (Illus.). 139p. (Orig.). 1995. pap. 19.95 (*0-89538-030-7*) L-W Inc.

— Mormon Origins: An Eyewitness Account. 1991. reprint ed. pap. 12.50 (*0-89979-058-5*) British Am Bks.

Clark, John A. & Freidlich, Mark L. How to Save Time & Taxes in Handling Estates, Vol. 1. 2nd ed. (How to Save Time & Taxes Ser.). 1966. ring bd. 235.00 incl. cd-rom (*0-8205-1203-6*) Bender.

Clark, John B. Capital & Its Earnings. (Foundations of Accounting Ser.: No. 4). 80p. 1988. text 10.00 (*0-8240-6123-3*) Garland.

— The Distribution of Wealth: A Theory of Wages, Income & Profits. LC 65-19641. (Reprints of Economic Classics Ser.). xxviii, 445p. 1965. reprint ed. 49.50 (*0-678-00078-6*) Kelley.

Clark, John B. & Clark, John M. The Control of Trusts. enl. ed. LC 70-108000. (Reprints of Economic Classics Ser.). xi, 202p. 1971. reprint ed. lib. bdg. 35.00 (*0-678-00606-7*) Kelley.

Clark, John B, jt. auth. see Giddings, Franklin H.

Clark, John B., jt. ed. see Edmond, John.

Clark, John B., jt. ed. see Speich, Gilbert R.

Clark, John D. The Federal Trust Policy. LC 78-64285. (Johns Hopkins University. Studies in the Social Sciences. Thirtieth Ser. 1912: 15). 312p. 1982. reprint ed. 45.00 (*0-404-61385-3*) AMS Pr.

— Ignition: An Informal History of Liquid Rocket Propellants. LC 72-185390. (Illus.). 232p. reprint ed. pap. 72.00 (*0-8357-4395-0*, 205233800007) Bks Demand.

***Clark, John E. & Pye, Mary E., eds.** Olmec Art & Archaeology in Meso-America. (Illus.). 344p. 2000. 50.00 (*0-300-08522-2*) Yale U Pr.

Clark, John G. The ABCs to Better Hearing. (Illus.). 87p. 1992. pap. text 9.95 (*0-9632001-0-0*) Hearcare.

— Energy & the Federal Government: Fossil Fuel Policies, 1900-1946. LC 85-20505. 536p. 1987. text 44.95 (*0-252-01295-X*) U of Ill Pr.

— The Grain Trade in the Old Northwest. LC 80-18227. (Illus.). xi, 324p. 1980. reprint ed. lib. bdg. 75.00 (*0-313-22419-6*, CLGT, Greenwood Pr) Greenwood.

— The Mesolithic Age in Britain. LC 76-44704. reprint ed. 40.00 (*0-404-15914-1*) AMS Pr.

— The Political Economy of World Energy: A Twentieth-Century Perspective. LC 90-37657. 417p. 1990. reprint ed. pap. 129.30 (*0-608-08015-2*, 206798000001) Bks Demand.

— The Political Economy of World Energy: A 20th-Century Perspective. LC 90-37657. xx, 397p. (C). 1991. pap. 19.95 (*0-8078-4306-7*) U of NC Pr.

— La Rochelle & the Atlantic Economy During the Eighteenth Century. LC 80-29275. (Illus.). 302p. reprint ed. pap. 93.70 (*0-8357-6607-1*, 203525200094) Bks Demand.

— World Prehistory in New Perspective. 3rd ed. LC 76-51318. (Illus.). 554p. 1977. pap. text 37.95 (*0-521-29178-X*) Cambridge U Pr.

Clark, John G. & Carter, Daniel L. 96 Ways You Can Save Taxes in '96: Grand Rapids, MI Edition. 128p. (Orig.). Date not set. pap. 9.95 (*0-9644913-5-4*) Loopholes Pr.

Clark, John G., jt. ed. see Martin, Frederick N.

Clark, John Greer & Martin, Frederick N., eds. Effective Counseling in Audiology: Perspectives & Practice. LC 93-1240. 336p. 1993. 52.00 (*0-13-181348-X*) P-H.

Clark, John H. Dictionary of Practical Materia Medica. 3rd ed. 1635p. 1991. 225.00 (*0-8464-4505-0*) Beekman Pubs.

— God of Shelley & Blake. (English Literature Ser.: No. 33). 1970. reprint ed. lib. bdg. 59.00 (*0-8383-0342-0*) M S G Haskell Hse.

— Trader Clark: Six Decades of Racing Lore. 336p. 1991. 22.95 (*1-879850-00-1*) Thrghbred Times.

Clark, John J. Restructuring Corporate America. (C). 1996. text 84.50 (*0-03-097667-7*, Pub. by Harcourt Coll Pubs) Harcourt.

Clark, John J. & Clark, Margaret T. A Statistics Primer for Managers: How to Ask the Right Questions About Forecasting, Control & Investment. (Illus.). 272p. write for info. (*0-318-56699-0*) Macmillan.

Clark, John J. & Gerlach, John. Restructuring Corporate America. 2nd ed. 638p. (C). 1990. pap. 78.00 (*0-536-57883-4*) Pearson Custom.

Clark, John J., et al. Sustainable Corporate Growth: A Model & Management Planning Tool. LC 88-6755. 322p. 1989. 69.50 (*0-89930-238-6*, CKS/, Quorum Bks) Greenwood.

Clark, John L. Guffaw: Poems & Drawings. (Illus.). 16p. 1996. pap. 3.00 (*1-885710-16-X*) Geekspeak Unique.

Clark, John L., see Aubu, pseud.

Clark, John M. Competition As a Dynamic Process. LC 79-26651. 501p. 1980. reprint ed. lib. bdg. 48.50 (*0-313-22300-9*, CLCD, Greenwood Pr) Greenwood.

— The Costs of the World War to the American People. LC 68-55507. (Reprints of Economic Classics Ser.). xii, 316p. 1970. reprint ed. 45.00 (*0-678-00662-8*) Kelley.

— Economic Institutions & Human Welfare. LC 77-27310. 285p. 1978. reprint ed. lib. bdg. 65.00 (*0-313-20184-6*, CLEI, Greenwood Pr) Greenwood.

— Economics of Planning Public Works: A Study Made for

C

the National Planning Board of the Federal Emergency Administration. LC 65-19647. (Reprints of Economic Classics Ser.). vi, 194p. 1965. reprint ed. 35.00 (*0-678-00099-9*) Kelley.

— Emergency & High Speed Driving Techniques. LC 76-1675. 142p. reprint ed. pap. 44.10 (*0-608-12785-X*, 202431100037) Bks Demand.

— Preface to Social Economics: Essays on Economic Theory & Social Problems. LC 67-28453. (Reprints of Economic Classics Ser.). (Illus.). xxi, 435p. 1967. reprint ed. 49.50 (*0-678-00333-5*) Kelley.

— The Social Control of Business. 2nd ed. LC 68-55508. (Reprints of Economic Classics Ser.). (Illus.). xvi, 537p. 1969. reprint ed. 57.50 (*0-678-00526-5*) Kelley.

— Standards of Reasonableness in Local Freight Discriminations. LC 68-56651. (Columbia University. Studies in the Social Sciences: No. 97). reprint ed. 32.50 (*0-404-51097-3*) AMS Pr.

— Strategic Factors in Business Cycles. 234p. 1963. reprint ed. 35.00 (*0-678-00016-6*) Kelley.

— Strategic Factors in Business Cycles. (General Ser.: No. 24). 256p. 1934. reprint ed. 66.60 (*0-87014-023-X*) Natl Bur Econ Res.

Clark, John M., Jr. & Switzer, Robert L. Experimental Biochemistry. 2nd ed. (Illus.). 335p. (C). 1977. pap. text 31.00 (*0-7167-0179-0*) W H Freeman.

Clark, John M., et al. Adam Smith, 1776-1926: Lectures to Commemorate the Sesquicentennial of the Publication of "The Wealth of Nations" LC 88-32065. (Reprints of Economic Classics Ser.). ix, 241p. 1989. reprint ed. 39.50 (*0-678-00138-3*) Kelley.

Clark, John M., jt. auth. see Clark, John B.

Clark, John M., jt. auth. see Ward, Alfred D.

Clark, John Marshall & Kenna, Michael P. Fate of Management of Turfgrass Chemicals. LC 99-38608. (ACS Symposium Ser.: No. 743). (Illus.). 448p. 1999. text 140.00 (*0-8412-3624-0*, Pub. by Am Chemical) OUP.

Clark, John O. Word Wise: A Dictionary of English Idioms. 608p. 1995. pap. 14.95 (*0-8050-1456-X*, Owl) H Holt & Co.

Clark, John O. & Holton, Derek A. A First Look at Graph Theory. 352p. (C). 1991. text 67.00 (*981-02-0489-2*); pap. text 32.00 (*981-02-0490-6*) World Scientific Pub.

Clark, John O., jt. ed. see Daintith, John.

Clark, John O., tr. see Vegetius Renatus, Flavia.

***Clark, John O. E. & Stiegeler, Stella E.** The Facts on File Dictionary of Earth Science. (Illus.). 336p. 2000. 45.00 (*0-8160-4287-X*); pap. 17.95 (*0-8160-4288-8*, Checkmark) Facts on File.

Clark, John O. E., jt. auth. see Illingworth, Valerie.

Clark, John P. The Anarchist Moment: Reflections on Culture, Nature, & Power. LC 85-112261. 256p. 1984. reprint ed. pap. 79.40 (*0-608-00451-0*, 206127000007) Bks Demand.

— Max Stirner's Egoism. 111p. (Orig.). 1976. pap. 5.00 (*0-900384-14-X*) Left Bank.

Clark, John P., ed. The Ozidi Saga. 1979. 59.00 (*0-19-575558-8*) OUP.

Clark, John P. & Dorward, Rosemary, trs. Walter Hilton: The Scale of Perfection. annot. ed. (Classics of Western Spirituality Ser.). 1990. 24.95 (*0-8091-0440-7*); pap. 17.95 (*0-8091-3194-3*) Paulist Pr.

Clark, John P., ed. see Reclus, Elisee.

Clark, John R. Beaches of Kaua'i & Ni'ihau. LC 89-36116. (Illus.). 144p. 1990. pap. 13.95 (*0-8248-1260-3*, Kolowalu Bk) UH Pr.

— The Beaches of Maui County. rev. ed. LC 89-4794. (Illus.). 168p. 1989. pap. 13.95 (*0-8248-1246-8*, Kolowalu Bk) UH Pr.

— The Beaches of O'ahu. LC 77-8244. (Illus.). 210p. (Orig.). 1977. pap. 14.95 (*0-8248-0510-0*, Kolowalu Bk) UH Pr.

— Beaches of the Big Island. LC 85-13971. (Illus.). 204p. 1985. pap. 13.95 (*0-8248-0976-9*, Kolowalu Bk) UH Pr.

— Coastal Ecosystems: Ecological Considerations for Management of the Coastal Zone. LC 74-77717. (Illus.). 192p. reprint ed. pap. 59.60 (*0-608-08705-X*, 206927300006) Bks Demand.

***Clark, John R.** Coastal Seas: The Conservation Challenge. LC 98-11892. (Illus.). 133p. 1998. pap. 19.95 (*0-632-04955-3*) Blackwell Sci.

Clark, John R. Coastal Zone Management Handbook. 720p. 1995. lib. bdg. 99.95 (*1-56670-092-2*, L1092) Lewis Pubs.

— Commentary on Agreements for Engineering Services & Contract Documents. 98p. 1986. 25.00 (*0-686-48322-7*) Am Consul Eng.

— Hawaii's Best Beaches. LC 98-30326. (Illus.). 176p. 1999. pap. 19.95 (*0-8248-2116-5*, Latitude Twenty) UH Pr.

— Joseph Priestley: A Comet in the System. 253p. (Orig.). 1994. pap. 12.95 (*0-9642064-0-4*) Frnds J Priestley.

— The Modern Satiric Grotesque & Its Traditions. LC 90-27474. 224p. 1991. text 29.95 (*0-8131-1744-5*) U Pr of Ky.

— Snorkeling: A Complete Guide to the Underwater Experience. LC 85-9397. 191p. 1986. 18.95 (*0-13-815192-X*) P-H.

Clark, John R., ed. Coastal Resources Management: Development Case Studies. (Renewable Resources Information Series: Coastal Management Publication: No. 3). 749p. 1985. pap. write for info. (*0-931531-02-0*) Res Plan Inst.

Clark, John R., jt. auth. see Motto, Anna Lydia.

Clark, John R., jt. ed. see Kaske, Carol V.

Clark, John R., jt. ed. see Motto, Anna Lydia.

Clark, John S. & Odell, John P. Study of English & American Writers: A Laboratory Method. LC 72-1070. reprint ed. 74.50 (*0-404-01559-X*) AMS Pr.

Clark, John T. & Clark, Nicole K. Adventures in Dreamtime. large type ed. LC 98-96326. (Illus.). 32p. (J). (gr. k-2). 1998. 15.95 (*1-892176-12-2*) PremaNations.

— A Journey Through Your Heart-3D. large type ed. (Illus.). 32p. (J). (ps-4). 2000. 17.95 (*1-892176-14-9*) PremaNations.

Clark, John T., jt. auth. see Clark, Nicole K.

***Clark, John W.** Competition Law & Policy in the Baltic Countries. 128p. 2000. pap. 30.00 (*92-64-17163-0*, 14 1999 12 1 P, Pub. by Org for Econ) OECD.

Clark, John W., et al, eds. Condensed Matter Theories, Vol. 9. (Illus.). 495p. (C). 1994. lib. bdg. 175.00 (*1-56072-181-2*) Nova Sci Pubs.

Clark, John W. & Panat, P. V., eds. Condensed Matter Theories, Vol. 12. 277p. 1997. 165.00 (*1-56072-529-X*) Nova Sci Pubs.

Clark, John W., jt. auth. see Partridge, Eric.

Clark, John W., jt. auth. see Willis, Robert.

Clark, Johnie E., jt. auth. see Clark, Ann.

Clark, Jon, ed. Human Resource Management & Technical Change. (Illus.). 256p. 1993. 65.00 (*0-8039-8786-2*); pap. 21.95 (*0-8039-8787-0*) Sage.

— James S. Coleman. LC 95-26507. (Falmer Sociology of Education Ser.). 550p. 1996. pap. 37.95 (*0-7507-0512-4*, Falmer Pr) Taylor & Francis.

— James S. Coleman: Seventeenth Century England. LC 95-26507. (Falmer Sociology of Education Ser.). 452p. 1996. 99.50 (*0-7507-0511-6*, Falmer Pr) Taylor & Francis.

Clark, Jon, et al, eds. John Goldthorpe: Consensus & Controversy. 402p. 1990. pap. 60.00 (*1-85000-984-8*, Falmer Pr) Taylor & Francis.

— Robert Merton: Consensus & Controversy. 520p. 1990. pap. 69.95 (*1-85000-982-1*, Falmer Pr) Taylor & Francis.

Clark, Jon & Diani, Marco, eds. Alain Touraine. LC 96-26507. (Falmer Sociology Ser.). 450p. 1996. 99.95 (*0-7507-0552-3*, Falmer Pr) Taylor & Francis.

Clark, Jon & Hoffer, Jeffrey A. Physical Data Base Record Design. LC 79-113431. (QED Monograph Series. Data Base Management: No. 7). 118p. reprint ed. pap. 36.60 (*0-608-15622-1*, 203175100076) Bks Demand.

Clark, Jon, jt. auth. see McLoughlin, Ian.

Clark, Jon D. Data Base Selection, Design & Administration. LC 80-607121. 233p. 1980. 59.95 (*0-275-91687-1*, C1687, Praeger Pubs) Greenwood.

Clark, Jonas. Exposing Spiritual Witchcraft: Breaking Controlling Powers. 2nd ed. 138p. (Orig.). 1995. reprint ed. pap. 8.99 (*1-886885-00-1*) Spirit Life.

— Jezebel, Seducing Goddess of War. LC 98-93152. (Illus.). 235p. 1998. pap. 11.99 (*1-886885-04-4*) Spirit Life.

— Prophetic Operations: Walking Through Prophetic Ministry. 2nd ed. (Illus.). 124p. (Orig.). 1996. reprint ed. pap. 8.00 (*1-886885-02-8*) Spirit Life.

— Religious Spirits: Having a Form of Godliness. 2nd ed. 75p. (Orig.). 1995. reprint ed. pap. 6.00 (*1-886885-01-X*) Spirit Life.

— Spiritual Productivity. (Illus.). pap. 8.00 (*1-886885-05-2*) Spirit Life.

Clark, Jonas B. Casting down Imaginations. (Illus.). 100p. (Orig.). pap. 8.00 (*1-886885-03-6*) Spirit Life.

Clark, Jonathan. Painting. LC 99-181873. (Easy-Step Ser.). 64p. (Orig.). 1998. pap. 4.95 (*0-8069-7057-X*) Sterling.

Clark, Jonathan & Clark, Susan. How to Make the Most of Your Workday. LC 94-26669. 304p. (Orig.). 1994. pap. 16.95 (*1-56414-143-8*) Career Pr Inc.

Clark, Jonathan P., Jr., ed. see Otto, Karl F.

Clark-Jones, Melissa. A Staple State: Canadian Industrial Resources in Cold War. 1987. pap. 19.95 (*0-8020-6626-7*); text 38.50 (*0-8020-5700-4*) U of Toronto Pr.

Clark, Joseph. Jungle Wedding: Stories. LC 98-17126. 192p. 1998. 22.95 (*0-393-04526-9*) Norton.

Clark, Joseph. Proclaming Bible Truth Vol. 3: Sermons for Hurting People. 1997. 19.95 (*1-882449-27-4*, 130124) Messenger Pub.

Clark, Joseph F. & Conway, Michael, eds. Creatine & Creatine Phosphate: Scientific & Clinical Aspects. (Illus.). 256p. 1996. text 69.00 (*0-12-186340-9*) Acad Pr.

Clark, Joseph G. Lights & Shadows of Sailor Life. LC 70-169754. (Select Bibliographies Reprint Ser.). 1977. reprint ed. 24.95 (*0-8369-5974-4*) Ayer.

Clark, Joseph H., jt. auth. see Fitzgerald, Joseph F.

Clark, Joseph S., et al. The Senate Establishment. LC 83-26395. 138p. 1984. reprint ed. lib. bdg. 55.00 (*0-313-24285-2*, CLSE, Greenwood Pr) Greenwood.

Clark, Joshua V. Onondaga, or Reminiscences of Earlier & Later Times, Being a Series of Historical Sketches Relative to Onondaga; with Notes on the Several Towns in the County, & Oswego, 2 vols. (Illus.). 1800p. 1997. reprint ed. lib. bdg. 82.00 (*0-8328-6189-8*) Higginson Bk Co.

Clark, Joy L., et al. Current Regional Issues: Alabama, Arkansas, Georgia, Kentucky, Louisiana, Mississippi, Tennessee, West Virginia. 61p. (C). 1994. pap. text 19.00 (*0-03-002049-2*) Dryden Pr.

Clark, Juan. Cuba: Mito y Realidad. (SPA., Illus.). 769p. 1990. pap. 50.00 (*0-917049-16-0*) Saeta.

— Los Derechos Humanos en Cuba: Una Perspectiva Vivencial. (SPA.). 100p. (Orig.). 1990. pap. 5.00 (*0-917049-25-X*) Saeta.

— Human Rights in Cuba: An Experiential Perspective. Saeta Ediciones Staff, ed. 100p. (Orig.). 1990. pap. 5.00 (*0-917049-26-8*) Saeta.

Clark, Judith. Almanac of American Women in the 20th Century. (Illus.). 320p. (Orig.). 1987. pap. 15.95 (*0-685-18014-X*) P-H.

— Too Many Animals Sleep in My Bed. (Illus.). (J). (ps). 1993. write for info. (*1-56156-264-5*) Kidsbks.

Clark, Judith F. Massachusetts: From Colony to Commonwealth. (Illus.). 328p. 1987. 32.95 (*0-89781-216-6*) Am Historical Pr.

Clark, Judith S., ed. see Shankar, Sri Sri Ravi.

Clark, Judy. Feminine, Femme Fatale, Feminist: Who Is the Real Woman? (Inter Acta Ser.). (Illus.). 6p. (C). 1994. teacher ed., ring bd. 1.25 (*1-885702-29-9*, 741-028t, Inter Acta); student ed., ring bd. 3.25 (*1-885702-28-0*, 741-028s, Inter Acta) WSN Pr.

Clark, Judy, jt. auth. see Kime, Linda A.

Clark, Judy, jt. auth. see Kime, Linda Almgren.

Clark, Julia & National Portrait Gallery (Australia) Staff. Australians of the Year. LC 97-229486. 45p. 1995. write for info. (*0-642-10664-9*, Pub. by Aust Gov Pub) Accents Pubns.

Clark, Julia F. & Queener, Sherry F. Pharmacologic Basis of Nursing Practice. 5th ed. 96p. (C). (gr. 13). 1996. pap. text, student ed. 14.95 (*0-8151-1510-5*, 28264) Mosby Inc.

Clark, Julia F., et al. Pharmacologic Basis of Nursing Practice. 5th ed. teacher ed., suppl. ed. write for info. (*0-8151-2124-5*) Mosby Inc.

— Pharmacologic Basis of Nursing Practice. 5th ed. (C). 1997. text. write for info. (*0-323-00701-5*) Mosby Inc.

***Clark, Julia F., et al.** Pharmacologic Basis of Nursing Practice. 6th ed. (Illus.). (C). 1999. teacher ed. write for info. (*0-323-00722-8*); pap. text 52.00 (*0-323-00684-1*) Mosby Inc.

— Pharmacologic Basis of Nursing Practice: Text & Student Learning Guide Package, Set. 5th ed. (C). 1997. text, student ed. write for info. (*0-8151-1511-3*) Mosby Inc.

Clark, Julia V. Redirecting Science Education: Reform for a Culturally Diverse Classroom. 88p. 1996. 31.95 (*0-8039-6275-4*); pap. 14.95 (*0-8039-6276-2*) Corwin Pr.

Clark, Julie A. Defense Spending in Transition. 68p. (Orig.). (C). 1994. pap. text 25.00 (*1-56806-166-8*) DIANE Pub.

Clark, K. Civilization: A Personal View. 1972. pap. 9.95 (*0-06-010801-0*) HarpC.

Clark, Karen K. Grow Deep, Not Just Tall. LC 84-70372. (Illus.). 109p. 1984. reprint ed. pap. 11.95 (*0-9626467-1-7*) Ctr Exec Planning.

— Life Is Change, Growth Is Optional. (Illus.). 247p. 1993. pap. 15.95 (*0-9626467-2-5*) Ctr Exec Planning.

— Where Have All the Children Gone? Gone to Grown Ups Everyone! (Illus.). 67p. 1997. reprint ed. pap. 9.95 (*0-9626467-0-9*) Ctr Exec Planning.

Clark, Kate. White Butterflies & Other Stories. LC 75-103505. (Short Story Index Reprint Ser.). 1977. 20.95 (*0-8369-3247-1*) Ayer.

Clark, Kate M. Maori Tales & Legends. LC 78-67696. (Folktale Ser.). (Illus.). reprint ed. 32.50 (*0-404-16067-0*) AMS Pr.

Clark, Katerina. Petersburg: Crucible of Cultural Revolution. LC 95-17161. 368p. (C). 1995. 44.00 (*0-674-66335-7*) HUP.

— Petersburg: Crucible of Cultural Revolution. 384p. 1998. pap. text 18.95 (*0-674-66336-5*) HUP.

— The Soviet Novel: History As Ritual. LC 80-18758. xvi, 302p. 1985. pap. text 11.95 (*0-226-10767-1*) U Ch Pr.

— The Soviet Novel: History As Ritual. 2nd rev. ed. LC 86-214133. 317p. reprint ed. pap. 98.30 (*0-608-09283-5*, 205415700004) Bks Demand.

***Clark, Katerina.** The Soviet Novel: History As Ritual. 3rd ed. 352p. 2000. lib. bdg. 39.95 (*0-253-33703-8*) Ind U Pr.

— The Soviet Novel: History as Ritual. 3rd ed. LC 00-38290. 352p. 2000. pap. 19.95 (*0-253-21367-3*) Ind U Pr.

Clark, Katerina & Holquist, Michael. Mikhail Bakhtin. (Illus.). 416p. 1986. pap. 18.95 (*0-674-57417-6*) Belknap Pr.

Clark, Katherine S., et al. Meeting Statuary Deadlines: Contractual & Financial Injury Litigation Action Guide - Winter 1997. Waxman, Robert, ed. 100p. 1997. pap. 58.00 (*0-7626-0051-9*) Cont Ed Bar-CA.

Clark, Kathryn, jt. auth. see Solnit, Rebecca.

Clark, Kathy. Cody's Last Stand. (American Romance Ser.: No. 442). 1992. per. 3.39 (*0-373-16442-4*, 1-16442-5) Harlequin Bks.

— Five Flamingo Summer. (Full House Club Stephanie Ser.). (J). (gr. 4-6). 1999. pap. 3.99 (*0-671-02157-5*) PB.

— Forget It, Flamingoes! (Full House Club Stephanie Ser.: Vol. 8). 112p. (J). (gr. 3-6). 1999. pap. 3.99 (*0-671-02158-3*) PB.

— Good Morning, Miss Greene. (American Romance Ser.: No. 428). 1992. per. 3.29 (*0-373-16428-9*, 1-16428-4) Harlequin Bks.

— Goodbye, Desperado. (American Romance Ser.). 1993. per. 3.39 (*0-373-16481-5*, 1-16481-3) Harlequin Bks.

— Groom Unknown. (American Romance Ser.). 1994. per. 3.50 (*0-373-16536-6*) Harlequin Bks.

***Clark, Kathy.** The Real Thing. (Full House Club Stephanie Ser.: Vol. 12). 144p. (J). (gr. 3-6). 2000. per. 3.99 (*0-671-04193-2*, Minstrel Bks) PB.

Clark, Kathy. Stand by Your Man. (Crystal Creek Ser.). 1993. per. 3.99 (*0-373-82522-6*, 1-82522-3) Harlequin Bks.

— Stroke of Midnight. LC 95-4592. (American Romance Ser.). 248p. 1995. per. 3.50 (*0-373-16571-4*, 1-16571-1) Harlequin Bks.

***Clark, Kathy.** Summertime Secrets. (Full House Club Stephanie Ser.). 160p. (J). (gr. 4-6). 2000. per. 3.99 (*0-671-04192-4*, Minstrel Bks) PB.

— Truth or Dare. (Full House Club Stephanie Ser.: Vol. 10). 160p. (J). (gr. 3-7). 2000. per. 3.99 (*0-671-04126-6*, Minstrel Bks) PB.

Clark, Kathy, jt. auth. see Silberman, Mel.

Clark, Katia. Hidden Lovers: A Black & White Romance Novel. (Illus.). 176p. (Orig.). 1988. pap. 4.95 (*0-685-22647-6*) Rack Bks.

Clark, Kay, jt. auth. see Drolet, Judy C.

Clark, Kay, jt. ed. see Nelson, Mary.

Clark, Keith. International Communications, the American Attitude. LC 68-58559. (Columbia University. Studies in the Social Sciences: No. 340). reprint ed. 27.50 (*0-404-51340-9*) AMS Pr.

Clark, Keith & Tiller, Lowell. Terrible Trail: The Meek Cutoff, 1845. rev. ed. LC 93-16761. (Illus.). 250p. 1993. reprint ed. pap. 14.95 (*0-89288-233-6*) Maverick.

Clark, Kelly J. Return to Reason: A Critique of Enlightment Evidentialism & a Defense of Reason & Belief. 1990. pap. 12.00 (*0-8028-0456-X*) Eerdmans.

— When Faith Is Not Enough. LC 97-17758. 204p. 1997. pap. 18.00 (*0-8028-4354-9*) Eerdmans.

Clark, Kelly J., ed. Our Knowledge of God: Essays on Natural & Philosophical Theology. (Studies in Philosophy & Religion). 240p. (C). 1992. lib. bdg. 152.50 (*0-7923-1485-9*, Pub. by Kluwer Academic) Kluwer Academic.

— Philosophers Who Believe: The Spiritual Journeys of Eleven Leading Thinkers. 284p. 1997. reprint ed. pap. 17.99 (*0-8308-1543-0*, 1543) InterVarsity.

***Clark, Kelly James.** Readings in the Philosophy of Religion. 2000. 29.95 (*1-55111-246-9*) Broadview.

Clark, Ken & Steen, Charlie. Making Sense of the Episcopal Church: Leader's Guide. 33p. (Orig.). 1996. pap., teacher ed. 10.95 (*0-8192-1667-4*) Morehouse Pub.

Clark, Kenneth. The Gothic Revival: An Essay in the History of Taste: New Edition. (Illus.). 256p. 1996. pap. 24.95 (*0-7195-5454-3*, Pub. by John Murray) Trafalgar.

— Leonardo da Vinci. 1989. pap. 21.95 (*0-14-016982-2*) Viking Penguin.

— The Nude. (Illus.). 458p. 1996. reprint ed. 17.98 (*1-56731-123-7*, MJF Bks) Fine Comms.

— One Hundred Details. (Illus.). 120p. 1991. write for info. (*0-318-68195-1*) HUP.

— One Hundred Details. (Illus.). 120p. 1991. pap. text 22.00 (*0-674-63863-8*, CLAONX) HUP.

— Potter's Manual. (Illus.). 208p. 1990. pap. 14.98 (*0-89009-674-0*) Bk Sales Inc.

Clark, Kenneth & Bergman-Taney, Janet. The Insiders' Guide to the Pocono Mountains. 2nd ed. (Insiders' Guide Travel Ser.). (Illus.). 495p. 1997. pap. 14.95 (*1-57380-045-7*, The Insiders Guide) Falcon Pub Inc.

Clark, Kenneth & Dieterle, Martin, texts. Corot: Late Paintings. (Illus.). 79p. 1996. pap. 30.00 (*1-58821-010-3*) Salander OReilly.

Clark, Kenneth, jt. auth. see Moore, Henry.

Clark, Kenneth A. Martin, Descendants of John Martin of Brunswick & Old Bristol, Maine. (Illus.). 81p. 1993. pap. 16.00 (*0-8328-3579-X*); lib. bdg. 26.00 (*0-8328-3578-1*) Higginson Bk Co.

Clark, Kenneth B. Dark Ghetto: Dilemmas of Social Power. 2nd ed. LC 89-34554. 296p. 1989. pap. 19.95 (*0-8195-6226-2*, Wesleyan Univ Pr) U Pr of New Eng.

— Prejudice & Your Child. LC 85-17862. 327p. 1988. reprint ed. pap. 19.95 (*0-8195-6155-X*, Wesleyan Univ Pr) U Pr of New Eng.

Clark, Kenneth B., ed. Traditional Black Music, 10 vols., Set. (Illus.). 80p. (YA). (gr. 5 up). 1993. lib. bdg. 189.50 (*0-7910-1826-1*) Chelsea Hse.

Clark, Kenneth E., et al, eds. Impact of Leadership. LC 92-81214. 559p. text 30.00 (*0-912879-95-5*) Ctr Creat Leader.

Clark, Kenneth E. & Clark, Miriam B. Choosing to Lead. 2nd rev. ed. LC 95-46696. 290p. 1996. 25.00 (*1-882197-12-7*, 327) Ctr Creat Leader.

Clark, Kenneth E. & Clark, Miriam B., eds. Measures of Leadership. LC 90-32042. 636p. 1990. 59.50 (*1-878435-00-0*) Leadership Lib Amer.

Clark, Kenneth M. The Artist Grows Old. LC 72-898082. (Rede Lecture). (Illus.). 36p. reprint ed. pap. 25.00 (*0-8357-5776-5*, 2051371) Bks Demand.

— The Nude: A Study in Ideal Form. (A. W. Mellon Lectures in the Fine Arts, 1989: Vol. 34, No. 2). (Illus.). 458p. 1956. pap. text 27.95 (*0-691-01788-3*, Pub. by Princeton U Pr) Cal Prin Full Svc.

***Clark, Kerry.** A Celebration of Harvest Wild: A Wild Country Fish & Game Cookbook. (Illus.). 117p. 1999. spiral bd. 12.95 (*0-9674986-0-0*) Wildwing.

Clark, Kevin. Widow under a New Moon. 30p. 1990. pap. 7.00 (*0-937669-38-5*) Owl Creek Pr.

Clark, Kevin E. Wholly Men: Keys to Manhood. 50p. 1999. pap. 9.95 (*0-9653264-4-6*) Noisemaker Pub.

Clark, Kim B. & Fujimoto, Takahiro. Product Development Performance: Strategy, Organization, & Management in the World Auto Industry. 409p. 1991. 35.00 (*0-87584-245-3*) Harvard Busn.

Clark, Kim B. & Wheelwright, Steven C. Managing New Product & Process Development: Text & Cases. LC 92-29067. 1992. 60.00 (*0-02-905517-2*) Free Pr.

— The Product Development Challenge: Competing Through Speed, Quality, & Creativity. LC 94-44895. (Harvard Business Review Book Ser.). 448p. 1995. 32.50 (*0-87584-609-2*) Harvard Busn.

Clark, Kim B., jt. auth. see Baldwin, Carliss Y.

Clark, Kim B., jt. auth. see Wheelwright, Steven C.

Clark, Kimberley, ed. see Costello, Cynthia.

Clark, Kimberley, ed. see Dever, Barbara.

Clark, Kimberley, ed. see Harbaugh, Kathy.

Clark, Kimberley, ed. see Klawitter, Pamela Amick.

Clark, Kimberley, ed. see Peters, Stephanie T.

Clark, Kimberley, ed. see Schwartz, Linda.

Clark, Kimberley, jt. ed. see Schwartz, Linda.

Clark, Kimberly. Three Is the Perfect Number. (Illus.). 16p. (J). (ps-k). 1998. pap. 5.95 (*1-891846-01-9*) Busn Word.

Clark, Kimberly, ed. see Dever, Barbara.

Clark, Kimberly, ed. see Johmann, Carol & Rieth, Elizabeth.

Clark, Kimberly, ed. see Konczal, Dee & Getskow, Veronica.

Clark, Kimberly, ed. see Markham, Lois.

An Asterisk (*) at the beginning of an entry indicates that the title is appearing for the first time.

Clark, Kimberly, ed. see Schwartz, Linda.

Clark, Kimn B., et al. The Uneasy Alliance: Managing the Productivity-Technology Dilemma. 1985. text 32.95 (*0-07-103222-3*) McGraw.

Clark, L. A., jt. ed. see Cope, R. J.

Clark, L. H., jt. auth. see Ruttenber, E. M.

Clark, L. H., jt. compiled by see Ruttenber, E. M.

Clark, Laban. Laban Clark: Autobiography about His Early Life from 1778 to 1804. Sharp, E. Farley, ed. LC 87-72058. (Illus.). 48p. (Orig.). 1987. pap. 8.95 (*0-914960-66-0*) Academy Bks.

Clark, Lance R. & Sampson, R. Neil. A Science & Policy Reader. write for info. (*0-614-16429-X*) Am Forests.

Clark-Langager, Sarah. Sculpture Space Recent Trends. (Illus.). 48p. 1984. pap. 5.00 (*0-915895-01-3*) Munson Williams.

Clark-Langager, Sarah A., jt. auth. see De-Almeida, Cristina.

Clark, Larry. Heroin. (Illus.). 336p. 1999. pap. 100.00 (*1-57687-030-8*, pwerHse Bks) pwerHse Cultrl.

— The Recruiter. LC 98-90811. 1999. pap. 14.95 (*0-533-12928-1*) Vantage.

*__Clark, Larry.__ Tulsa. (Illus.). 2000. 39.95 (*0-8021-1677-9*, Grove) Grove-Atltic.

— Tulsa. 2000. reprint ed. pap. write for info. (*0-8021-3748-2*, Pub. by Grove-Atltic) Publishers Group.

Clark, Larry, ed. Advanced Ear Training for Jazz Musicians. 68p. (C). 1996. pap. text 19.95 (*1-57623-607-2*, SB34A) Wrner Bros.

— Jimmy Dorsey - Saxophone Method. 100p. (Orig.). (C). 1979. pap. text 12.95 (*0-7692-0745-6*, TPF0103) Wrner Bros.

— John Coltrane - Improvised Saxophone Solos. 48p. (Orig.). (C). 1986. pap. text 12.95 (*0-7692-0744-8*, SB267) Wrner Bros.

— New Concepts in Linear Improvisation. (Orig.). (C). 1996. pap. text 24.95 (*1-57623-757-5*, SB32CD) Wrner Bros.

Clark, Larry & Korine, Harmony. Kids: The Screenplay. (Illus.). 160p. 1995. pap. 19.95 (*0-8021-3438-6*, Grove) Grove-Atltic.

Clark, Larry, ed. see Mintzer, Bob.

Clark, Larry, ed. see Rizzo, Jacques.

Clark, Larry, ed. see Thomas, Wilie.

Clark, Larry, ed. see Thomas, Willie.

Clark, Larry V., ed. see Permanent International Altaistic Conference Staff.

Clark, Laura A. & Moon, Maxine L. Personal Health Profile: Health Information Organizer System. 130p. 1997. ring bd. 19.95 (*0-9671911-0-6*) Health InFacts.

*__Clark, Laura S. & Shippe, Dave.__ The Donut Repair Club Helps Out. Caldwell, Lise, ed. (Happy Day Book Ser.). (Illus.). 24p. (ps-1). 1999. pap. 1.99 (*0-7847-1089-9*, 04285, Bean Sprouts) Standard Pub.

Clark, Laura S., jt. auth. see Shippe, Dave.

Clark, Laura V. A Study of the Relationship Between the Vocational Home Economics Teacher Training Curricula of a Group of Women's Colleges & Expected Responsibilities of Beginning Teachers. LC 72-176649. (Columbia University. Teachers College. Contributions to Education Ser.: No. 586). reprint ed. 37.50 (*0-404-55586-1*) AMS Pr.

Clark, Lauren. Marblesized Paper Patterns in Full Color. LC 92-12032. (Pictorial Archive Ser.). 64p. 1992. pap. 9.95 (*0-486-27220-6*) Dover.

Clark, Laurie & Christini, Ed. Scuba Skills Update Field Guide. 43p. 1988. pap. text 5.95 (*0-943717-59-0*) Concept Sys.

— Scuba Skills Update Instructor Outline. 34p. 1988. pap. text 8.95 (*0-943717-60-4*) Concept Sys.

Clark, Laurie, ed. see Clark, Thomas A.

Clark, Laurie K. & Pulley, Dennis. Diver Stress & Rescue Instructor Manual. 60p. 1990. pap. text 19.95 (*0-943717-85-X*) Concept Sys.

Clark, LaVerne H. The Deadly Swarm & Other Stories. LC 85-61099. (Illus.). 136p. (Orig.). 1985. pap. 5.00 (*0-9605008-2-0*) Hermes Hse Pr.

— Focus One Hundred One: An Illustarted Biography of 101. LC 78-57156. (Illus.). 146p. 1979. pap. text 7.95 (*0-918606-03-9*) Heidelberg Graph.

— Keepers of the Earth. LC 97-340. (Hell Yes! Texas Women's Ser.). 356p. (Orig.). 1997. pap. 14.95 (*0-938317-28-8*) Cinco Puntos.

Clark, LaVerne H. & MacArthur, Mary, eds. The Face of Poetry: 101 Poets of the 60s & 70s. 2nd ed. LC 79-17351. (Illus.). 302p. 1979. reprint ed. pap. text 8.95 (*0-918606-04-7*) Heidelberg Graph.

Clark, Lawrence P. Designs for Evaluating Social Programs. (Learning Packages in the Policy Sciences Ser.: No. 11). 44p. (C). 1979. pap. text 8.75 (*0-936826-00-2*) PS Assocs Croton.

— Introduction to Surveys & Interviews. (Learning Packages in the Policy Sciences Ser.: No. 12). (Illus.). 56p. (C). 1978. pap. text 9.50 (*0-936826-01-0*) PS Assocs Croton.

Clark, Lawrence S., et al. Law & Business: The Regulatory Environment. 4th ed. LC 93-24356. (C). 1993. pap., student ed. 28.13 (*0-07-035163-5*) McGraw.

— Law & Business: The Regulatory Environment. 4th ed. LC 93-24356. 1248p. (C). 1994. 92.19 (*0-07-035162-7*) McGraw.

Clark, Lea, et al. Quest: The Search for Heroes. Crane, Carla, ed. (Next Level Preteen Electives Ser.). (Illus.). 128p. 1996. teacher ed. 14.99 (*0-7847-0503-8*, 42103) Standard Pub.

*__Clark, Lee & Warren, Joe.__ Fly Tying with Poly Yarn. (Illus.). 56p. 2000. pap. 19.95 (*1-57188-201-4*) F Amato Pubns.

Clark, Leigh. Carnivore. 368p. (Orig.). 1997. mass mkt. 4.99 (*0-8439-4225-8*) Dorchester Pub Co.

— Evil Reincarnate. 384p. 1996. mass mkt. 4.99 (*0-614-05532-6*); mass mkt. 5.99 (*0-8125-2371-7*, Pub. by Tor Bks) St Martin.

— Shock Radio. 352p. 1998. mass mkt. 6.99 (*0-8125-2372-5*, Pub. by Tor Bks) St Martin.

Clark, Len, jt. auth. see Bakker, Gerald.

Clark, Leon E. Through African Eyes: Culture & Society: Continuity & Change, Vol. 2. (Illus.). 358p. (YA). (gr. 11 up). 2000. pap. text 21.95 (*0-938960-28-8*); lib. bdg. 44.00 (*0-938960-45-8*) CITE.

— Through African Eyes: Teaching Strategies, Vol. 1. (Illus.). 81p. 1989. pap. 9.95 (*0-938960-32-6*) CITE.

— Through African Eyes: The Past: The Road to Independence. 2nd rev. ed. (Illus.). 288p. (YA). (gr. 11 up). 1991. lib. bdg. 39.50 (*0-938960-44-X*) CITE.

— Through African Eyes Vol. 1: The Past: The Road to Independence. rev. ed. (Illus.). 294p. (YA). (gr. 11 up). 1991. pap. text 21.95 (*0-938960-27-X*) CITE.

— Through Indian Eyes: Teaching Strategies. 81p. 1995. pap. text 9.95 (*0-938960-40-7*) CITE.

Clark, Leon E. & Fleck, Chadwick. Through African Eyes Vol. 2: Teaching Strategies. 174p. 2000. pap. 11.95 (*0-938960-33-4*) CITE.

Clark, Leon E. & Strauss, Jack. Through Japanese Eyes: Teaching Strategies. (Illus.). 179p. (Orig.). 1995. pap. text, teacher ed. 11.95 (*0-938960-37-7*) CITE.

Clark, Leon E., jt. auth. see Pearson, Robert P.

Clark, Leon E., ed. see Minear, Richard H.

Clark, Leon E., ed. see Seybolt, Peter J.

Clark, Leonard. Alfred Williams: His Life & Work. LC 69-13754. (Illus.). xv, 206p. 1969. reprint ed. 35.00 (*0-678-05512-2*) Kelley.

Clark, Leonard & Starr, Irving S. Secondary & Middle School Teaching Methods. 7th ed. (Illus.). 477p. (C). 1995. pap. text 60.00 (*0-02-322871-7*, Macmillan Coll) P-H.

Clark, Leslie. Frog & Toad Together Study Guide. 34p. (J). (gr. k-2). 1995. student ed., ring bd. 9.99 (*1-58609-125-5*) Progeny Pr WI.

— Wagon Wheels Study Guide. 30p. (J). (gr. 1-3). 1993. student ed., ring bd. 9.99 (*1-58609-119-0*) Progeny Pr WI.

Clark, Leslie F., jt. auth. see Graesser, Arthur C.

Clark, Leslie L., ed. see Kusajima, Tokisuke.

Clark, Leslie L., ed. see Research Conference on Geriatric Blindness & Severe Visual Impairment Staff.

Clark-Lewis, E. Win-Win. 5.00 (*0-614-05198-3*, WW12792M) ASFE.

Clark-Lewis, Elizabeth. Living in, Living Out: African American Domestics & the Great Migration. Baker, Deborah, ed. (Illus.). 256p. 1996. pap. 15.00 (*1-56836-124-6*, Kodansha Globe) Kodansha.

— Living in, Living Out: African American Domestics in Washington, D. C., 1910-1940. LC 94-14415. (Illus.). 192p. 1994. text 29.95 (*1-56098-362-0*) Smithsonian.

Clark, Lewis H. Military History of Wayne County: The County in the Civil War. (Illus.). 924p. 1997. reprint ed. lib. bdg. 92.50 (*0-8328-6272-X*) Higginson Bk Co.

Clark, Lincoln H. & Assael, Henry, eds. Consumer Behavior. LC 78-294. (Century of Marketing Ser.). (Illus.). 1979. reprint ed. lib. bdg. 42.95 (*0-405-11166-5*) Ayer.

Clark, Linda. Are You Radioactive? LC 73-76155. 128p. 1973. pap. 9.95 (*0-8159-5013-6*) Devin.

— Get Well Naturally. 1974. reprint ed. 12.95 (*0-8159-5605-3*) Devin.

— Handbook of Natural Remedies for Common Ailments. LC 75-13349. 292p. 1976. 14.95 (*0-8159-5710-6*) Devin.

— Help Yourself to Health. 2nd rev. ed. 268p. 1990. reprint ed. pap. 12.95 (*0-8159-5722-X*) Devin.

— Know Your Nutrition. LC 80-84437. 276p. 1984. reprint ed. pap. 4.95 (*0-87983-401-3*, 34013K, Keats Publng) NTC Contemp Pub Co.

— Linda Clark's Cookbook. LC 77-8716. (Illus.). 128p. (Orig.). 1977. pap. 5.95 (*0-89407-009-6*) Strawberry Hill.

— Rejuvenation. 1978. 12.95 (*0-8159-6718-7*) Devin.

Clark, Linda & Martine, Yvonne. Health, Youth, & Beauty Through Color Breathing. LC 75-28754. 96p. 1995. pap. 5.95 (*0-89087-113-2*) Celestial Arts.

Clark, Linda, et al. Your Natural Beauty Sampler. LC 77-92810. 1978. pap. 1.95 (*0-87983-168-5*, Keats Publng) NTC Contemp Pub Co.

Clark, Linda A. Secrets of Health & Beauty: How to Make Yourself Over. 1969. 14.95 (*0-8159-6807-8*) Devin.

Clark, Linda J. Music in Churches: Nourishing Your Congregation's Musical Life. LC 94-78334. 140p. 1994. pap. 13.25 (*1-56699-134-X*, AL155) Alban Inst.

*__Clark, Linda L.__ The Rise of Professional Women in France: Gender & Public Admnistration Since 1830. (Illus.). 344p. 2001. write for info. (*0-521-77344-X*) Cambridge U Pr.

Clark, Linda L. Schooling the Daughters of Marianne: Textbooks & the Socialization of Girls in Modern French Primary Schools. LC 83-5035. 224p. (C). 1984. text 74.50 (*0-87395-787-3*); pap. text 24.95 (*0-87395-786-5*) State U NY Pr.

— Social Darwinism in France. LC 82-21795. 275p. 1984. pap. 85.30 (*0-7837-8366-3*, 205917600009) Bks Demand.

Clark, Liz. Fresh Bread Companion. Colby, J. & Vorbeck, Jill, eds. (Traditional Country Life Recipes Ser.). (Illus.). 110p. (Orig.). 1997. pap. 9.95 (*1-883283-11-6*) Brick Tower.

Clark, Liz, jt. auth. see Vorbeck, Jill.

Clark, Lorenne & Lange, Lynda, eds. The Sexism of Social & Political Theory: Women & Reproduction from Plato to Nietzsche. LC 79-17862. 1979. pap. text 14.95 (*0-8020-6375-6*) U of Toronto Pr.

Clark, Lori. The Denver Bargain Hunter's Guide: Shopping in the 90's. LC 93-71451. 260p. (Orig.). pap. 12.95 (*0-9637251-0-6*) ConsumerWise.

Clark, Lorna J., ed. see Burney, Sarah H.

Clark, Lorraine. Blake, Kierkegaard, & the Spectre of Dialectic. 250p. (C). 1991. text 64.95 (*0-521-39509-7*) Cambridge U Pr.

Clark, Louis H. The Complete Guide for the Manufacturer's Rep: How to Get & Hold Key Accounts. 264p. 1977. text 37.50 (*0-07-011160-X*) McGraw.

*__Clark, Louise.__ Pretender's Games. 320p. 1999. mass mkt. 4.99 (*0-8439-4514-1*, Leisure Bks) Dorchester Pub Co.

Clark, Lovel D. A Bright Tragic Thing: A Tale of Civil War Texas. LC 91-78329. 304p. (Orig.). 1992. pap. 14.95 (*0-938317-17-2*); pap. text 24.95 (*0-938317-18-0*) Cinco Puntos.

— Civil War Recollections of James Lemuel Clark: And the Great Hanging at Gainesville, Texas In... (Military History Ser.). 130p. 1996. pap. 12.95 (*1-55622-505-9*, Rep of TX Pr) Wordware Pub.

— The Fifth Wind. 128p. 1981. 15.00 (*0-933188-18-8*); pap. 6.95 (*0-933188-17-X*) Blue Moon Pr.

— The Guibord Affair: Canadian Studies. LC 73-156119. (Canadian History Through the Press Ser.). xvi, 126 p. 1971. write for info. (*0-03-925851-3*) Holt R&W.

— Is This Naomi & Other Stories: A Cycle of Rural Life. (Fiction Ser.). (Illus.). (Orig.). 1979. pap. 6.95 (*0-933188-11-0*) Blue Moon Pr.

— The Minoan Distance: The Symbolism of Travel in D. H. Lawrence. LC 80-18844. 428p. 1980. 42.00 (*0-8165-0707-4*) U of Ariz Pr.

Clark, Lucy. A Surgeon's Care. large type ed. (Mills & Boon Large Print Ser.). 288p. 1997. 23.99 (*0-263-15004-6*) Ulverscroft.

*__Clark, Lygia.__ The Experimental Exercise of Freedom. 264p. 2000. pap. 34.95 (*0-914357-64-6*) Los Angeles Mus Contemp.

Clark, Lyn. Business English & Communication. 8th ed. 1995. pap. text 25.95 (*0-02-800996-7*) Glencoe.

Clark, Lyn, et al. Business English & Communication. 7th ed. 672p. 1987. text, student ed. 22.96 (*0-07-061432-6*) McGraw.

*__Clark, Lyn, et al.__ Business English & Communication: Teacher's Annotated Edition. annot. ed. 1999. teacher ed. 42.00 (*0-02-800991-6*) Glencoe.

Clark, Lyn, jt. auth. see Clark, James.

Clark, Lyn, jt. auth. see Clark, James Leland.

Clark, Lyn R., jt. auth. see Clark, James L.

Clark, Lynette & Clark, Dexter. On Golden Ground: Our Journey to the Eldorado. LC 97-70712. (Illus.). 160p. (Orig.). (J). 1997. pap. 13.95 (*0-9657676-0-4*) Larson & Larrigan.

Clark, Lynn. SOS Help for Emotions: Managing Anxiety, Anger, & Depression. LC 97-42925. (Illus.). 280p. (Orig.). 1997. pap. 13.50 (*0-935111-50-6*) Parents Pr KY.

Clark, Lynn F. SOS: Help for Parents. rev. ed. LC 95-47640. (Illus.). 254p. 1996. pap. 12.00 (*0-935111-20-4*) Parents Pr KY.

Clark, Lynn G. Systematics of Chusquea Section Swallenochloa, Section Verticillatae, Section Serpentes, & Section Longifoliae (Poaceae-Bambusoideae) Anderson, Christiane, ed. (Systematic Botany Monographs: Vol. 27). (Illus.). 127p. (Orig.). 1989. pap. 15.00 (*0-912861-27-4*) Am Soc Plant.

Clark, Lynn G. & Pohl, Richard W. Agnes Chase's First Book of Grasses: The Structure of Grasses Explained for Beginners. 4th rev. ed. LC 95-33321. 176p. 1996. pap. 16.95 (*1-56098-656-5*) Smithsonian.

Clark, Lynn R., jt. auth. see Clark, James L.

*__Clark, Lynne W.__ Smile-A-While. 2000. 4.99 (*1-56245-409-9*) Great Quotations.

Clark, M. Interpersonal Skills for Hospitality Management. (Illus.). 224p. 1995. mass mkt. 17.99 (*0-412-57330-X*) Chapman & Hall.

— Plant Molecular Biology: Springer Lab Manual. 520p. 1997. pap. text 89.50 (*3-540-58405-6*) Spr-Verlag.

— Practical Nursing. 14th ed. (Illus.). 416p. 1991. pap. text 19.95 (*0-7020-1411-7*) Bailliere Tindall.

*__Clark, M., et al, eds.__ Early Childhood Nutrition Resource Guide: June 1998. (Illus.). 44p. 1998. pap. write for info. (*1-57285-048-5*) Nat Ctr Educ.

Clark, M. & Thyen, O., eds. The Pocket Oxford-Duden German Dictionary. 2nd rev. ed. LC 99-174797. 856p. 1998. pap. 11.95 (*0-19-860131-X*) OUP.

Clark, M. Carolyn, jt. auth. see Merriam, Sharan B.

Clark, M. Diane, jt. ed. see Marschark, Marc.

Clark, M. Douglas. Managing the Troubled Employee. LC 79-91188. (Illus.). 77p. ring bd. 69.50 (*0-88061-009-3*) Intl Loss Cntrl.

— Risk Control for Churches. LC 81-86316. (Illus.). ring bd. 39.50 (*0-88061-007-7*) Intl Loss Cntrl.

Clark, M. Douglas, ed. Practical Leadership Skills: Accident-Incident Investigation. 1986. ring bd. 180.00 (*0-88061-056-5*) Intl Loss Cntrl.

— Practical Leadership Skills: Causes & Effects of Loss. 1986. ring bd. 180.00 (*0-88061-055-7*) Intl Loss Cntrl.

— Practical Leadership Skills: Group Meetings. 1986. ring bd. 180.00 (*0-88061-060-3*) Intl Loss Cntrl.

— Practical Leadership Skills: Job Pride Development. 1986. ring bd. 180.00 (*0-88061-074-3*) Intl Loss Cntrl.

— Practical Leadership Skills: Job-Task Analysis & Procedures. 1986. ring bd. 180.00 (*0-88061-059-X*) Intl Loss Cntrl.

— Practical Leadership Skills: Management Control. 1986. ring bd. 180.00 (*0-88061-075-1*) Intl Loss Cntrl.

— Practical Leadership Skills: Personal Communications. 1986. ring bd. 180.00 (*0-88061-061-1*) Intl Loss Cntrl.

— Practical Leadership Skills: Planned Inspections. 1986. ring bd. 180.00 (*0-88061-057-3*) Intl Loss Cntrl.

— Practical Leadership Skills: Planned Job-Task Observation. 1986. ring bd. 180.00 (*0-88061-058-1*) Intl Loss Cntrl.

Clark, M. M. Understanding Research in Early Education. x, 132p. 1989. pap. text 28.00 (*2-88124-730-X*) Gordon & Breach.

Clark, M. P. Managing to Communicate: Using Telecommunications for Increased Business Efficiency. LC 93-30453. 182p. 1994. pap. 79.95 (*0-471-94188-3*) Wiley.

Clark, M. R. & Holman, M. P. Evergreen Valley Project Archaeological Evaluation & Impact Assessment Report: Sites CA-SCL-63, 428, & 286. (Illus.). 122p. (C). 1980. reprint ed. pap. text 13.75 (*1-55567-437-2*) Coyote Press.

Clark, M. R., et al. Archaeological Investigations at the Keller Ranch Site Pt. I & II: An Ethnographic Study of the Clayton Area, Contra Costa County, California. (Illus.). 206p. (C). 1982. reprint ed. pap. text 21.88 (*1-55567-438-0*) Coyote Press.

Clark, M. S. & Wallace, W. J. Chromosomes: The Complex Code. 360p. 1996. write for info. (*0-412-75210-7*) Kluwer Academic.

Clark, M. Ursula. Cult of Enthusiasm in French Romanticism. LC 70-94179. (Catholic University of America. Studies in Romance Languages & Literatures: No. 37). reprint ed. 37.50 (*0-404-50337-3*) AMS Pr.

Clark, M. W. PC: Portable Standard FORTRAN 77. (Computers & Their Applications Ser.). 228p. 1986. text 36.95 (*0-470-20756-6*) P-H.

Clark, Madeline A. & Mazza, Virginia S. Health Unit Coordinating: Expanding the Scope of Practice. Pfeiffer, Maureen, ed. LC 98-24850. (Illus.). 655p. 1999. pap. text. write for info. (*0-7216-7036-9*, W B Saunders Co) Harcrt Hlth Sci Grp.

Clark, Malcolm. A Plain TEX Primer. (Illus.). 490p. 1993. pap. text 35.00 (*0-19-853724-7*) OUP.

Clark, Malcolm, Jr. & Porter, Kenneth W. War on the Webfoot Saloon & Other Tales of Feminine Adventures. (Illus.). 54p. 1969. pap. 2.95 (*0-87595-023-X*) Oregon Hist.

Clark, Manning. Henry Lawson. LC 96-169202. 192p. 1996. pap. 19.95 (*0-522-84695-5*, Pub. by Melbourne Univ Pr) Paul & Co Pubs.

Clark, Manning. A Historian's Apprenticeship. 127p. 1994. pap. 16.95 (*0-522-84631-9*, Pub. by Melbourne Univ Pr) Paul & Co Pubs.

— A History of Australia, Vol. V & VI. 2000. pap. 39.95 (*0-522-84899-0*, Pub. by Melbourne Univ Pr) Paul & Co Pubs.

— A History of Australia, Vols. I & II. 2000. pap. 39.95 (*0-522-84897-4*, Pub. by Melbourne Univ Pr) Paul & Co Pubs.

— A History of Australia, Vols. III & IV. 2000. pap. 39.95 (*0-522-84898-2*, Pub. by Melbourne Univ Pr) Paul & Co Pubs.

Clark, Marceal. Losing, Leaving, & Letting Go: Surviving the Change Points of Life. LC 94-6853. 144p. (Orig.). 1994. pap. 3.99 (*1-56722-022-3*) Word Aflame.

Clark, Marcia. The World Is Round: Contemporary Panoramas. LC 87-31092. (Illus.). 64p. (Orig.). 1987. pap. 7.50 (*0-943651-03-4*) Hudson Riv.

Clark, Marcia & Carpenter, Teresa. Without a Doubt. LC 98-171512. 528p. 1998. pap. 13.95 (*0-14-025977-5*) Viking Penguin.

Clark, Marcus R., ed. Forest Service: Barriers to Generating Revenue or Reducing Costs. (Illus.). 118p. (C). 1998. pap. text 20.00 (*0-7881-7342-1*) DIANE Pub.

Clark, Marden J. Liberating Form: Mormon Essays on Religion & Literature. LC 92-32725. 1992. pap. 9.95 (*1-56236-206-2*, Pub. by Aspen Bks) Origin Bk Sales.

*__Clark, Margaret.__ Care Factor Zero. LC 99-95319. 192p. (J). (gr. 4-6). 2000. mass mkt. 6.99 (*0-380-81390-4*) Morrow Avon.

Clark, Margaret. Children under Five: Educational Research & Evidence. x, 303p. 1988. pap. text 52.00 (*2-88124-680-X*) Gordon & Breach.

— Writing for Children. 2nd ed. 120p. 1997. pap. write for info. (*0-7136-4622-5*, Pub. by A & C Blk) Midpt Trade.

Clark, Margaret & Anderson, Barbara G. Culture & Aging. Stein, Leon, ed. LC 79-8827. (Growing Old Ser.). (Illus.). 1980. reprint ed. lib. bdg. 48.95 (*0-405-12781-2*) Ayer.

Clark, Margaret & Clark, Virginia. Cooking with Strawberries: Delicious Ways to Eat Strawberries. LC 94-37121. (Illus.). 112p. (Orig.). 1994. pap. text 10.95 (*1-879415-26-7*) Mtn n Air Bks.

Clark, Margaret, ed. see DeMatteis, J. M.

Clark, Margaret, jt ed. see Fletcher, Garth.

Clark, Margaret, ed. see Hempel, Marc.

Clark, Margaret, ed. see McDuffie, Dwayne.

Clark, Margaret, ed. see Simonson, Walter & Simonson, Louise.

Clark, Margaret G. Freedom Crossing. 160p. (J). (gr. 4-7). 1991. 3.50 (*0-590-44569-3*) Scholastic Inc.

Clark, Margaret S., ed. Emotion. (Review of Personality & Social Psychology Ser.: Vol. 13). (Illus.). 328p. 1992. 58.00 (*0-8039-4613-9*); pap. 26.00 (*0-8039-4614-7*) Sage.

— Emotion. LC 80-649712. 336p. reprint ed. pap. 104.20 (*0-608-09779-9*, 206995300007) Bks Demand.

— Emotion & Social Behavior. (Review of Personality & Social Psychology Ser.: Vol. 14). (Illus.). 336p. 1992. 58.00 (*0-8039-4744-5*); pap. 26.00 (*0-8039-4745-3*) Sage.

— Emotion & Social Behavior. LC 80-649712. (Review of Personality & Social Psychology Ser.: Vol. 14). 323p. 1992. reprint ed. pap. 100.20 (*0-608-01714-0*, 206236900003) Bks Demand.

C

— Prosocial Behavior. (Review of Personality & Social Psychology Ser.: Vol. 12). (Illus.). 320p. (C). 1990. text 58.00 (*0-8039-4071-8*); pap. text 26.00 (*0-8039-4072-6*) Sage.

— Prosocial Behavior. LC 80-649712. (Review of Personality & Social Psychology Ser.: No. 12). (Illus.). 327p. 1991. reprint ed. pap. 101.40 (*0-608-04305-2*, 206508400012) Bks Demand.

Clark, Margaret S. & Fiske, Susan T., eds. Affect & Cognition: Seventeenth Annual Carnegie Symposium on Cognition. (Ongoing Ser.). 368p. (C). 1982. text 89.95 (*0-89859-212-7*) L Erlbaum Assocs.

Clark, Margaret S., jt. ed. see Hendrick, Clyde.

Clark, Margaret T., jt. auth. see Clark, John J.

Clark, Marge. The Best of Thymes. Mauck, Sheila, ed. LC 97-60074. (Illus.). 416p. 1997. 25.00 (*0-9640514-1-9*) Thyme Ckbks.

— Christmas Thyme at Oak Hill Farm. LC 94-90065. (Illus.). 176p. 1994. 20.00 (*0-9640514-5-1*) Thyme Ckbks.

— It's about Thyme! An Herb Manual & Cookbook of Herb & Non-Herb Recipes. rev. ed. LC 88-92078. (Illus.). 320p. 1988. 15.00 (*0-9620692-0-5*) Thyme Ckbks.

Clark, Margery. Poppy Seed Cakes. (Books for Young Readers). (J). (ps-1). 1986. 9.95 (*0-385-07457-3*) Doubleday.

***Clark, Margot.** Strokework Flowers, Step by Step. LC 99-54238. (Illus.). 128p. 2000. pap. 23.99 (*0-89134-926-X*, North Lght Bks) F & W Pubns Inc.

Clark, Marian. A Little Irish Birthday Book. (Illus.). 125p. 1994. 13.95 (*0-86281-458-8*, Pub. by Appletree Pr) Irish Bks Media.

— Little Scottish Birthday Book. (Illus.). 124p. 1998. 13.95 (*0-86281-704-8*, Pub. by Appletree Pr) Irish Bks Media.

— Main Street of America Cookbook. LC 97-28528. 308p. (Orig.). 1997. pap. 14.95 (*1-57178-024-6*) Coun Oak Bks.

— The Route 66 Cookbook. (Illus.). 237p. 1995. pap. 17.95 (*1-57178-020-3*) Coun Oak Bks.

***Clark, Marian.** The Route 66 Cookbook: Comfort Food from the Mother Road. 75th deluxe anniversary ed. (Illus.). 272p. 2000. 24.95 (*1-57178-095-5*) Coun Oak Bks.

Clark, Marilyn A. Fantaisie Impromptu. LC 97-90908. 1998. pap. 8.95 (*0-533-12523-5*) Vantage.

Clark, Marilyn F. & Keiser, Linda H. Teaching Guide Imagery & Music: An Experiential - Didactic Approach. 214p. 1989. teacher ed. 100.00 (*0-944135-00-5*) Archedigm Pubns.

Clark, Marilyn N. Travel on Your Own: Go Now, Here's How: An Adventure in Discovery, Solo Travel Can Be Fun. LC 93-87063. 224p. 1994. pap. 12.95 (*1-884617-24-7*) Primrose.

Clark, Marjorie G., ed. Eighteen Fifty-Seven Plat Map Transcription Oakland County, Michigan. (Illus.). 193p. (Orig.). 1993. pap. 16.00 (*1-879766-20-5*) OCG Society.

Clark, Mark. Transport Modeling for Environmental Engineers & Scientists. LC 96-4814. (Environmental Science & Technology Ser.). 559p. 1996. 84.95 (*0-471-12348-X*) Wiley.

Clark, Marlene, jt. ed. see Morrow, Nancy.

Clark, Marnie, et al, eds. Lighting Candles in the Dark. (Illus.). 215p. (Orig.). (YA). 1992. pap. 9.50 (*0-9620912-3-5*) Friends Genl Conf.

Clark, Marsha, jt. auth. see Bradshaw, Thomas I.

Clark, Martin. Antonio Gramsci & the Revolution That Failed. LC 76-49754. 267p. reprint ed. pap. 82.80 (*0-7837-3289-9*, 205769100006) Bks Demand.

— Italian Risorgimento Seminar Studies in History. LC 97-42541. (Seminar Studies in History). 160p. (C). 1998. pap. 15.93 (*0-582-00353-9*) Longman.

— The Many Aspects of Mobile Home Living: A Novel. 352p. 2000. 24.00 (*0-375-40725-1*) Knopf.

— MODERN ITALY 1871 1982. (Longman History of Italy Ser.). (Illus.). 444p. (C). 1984. pap. text 28.50 (*0-582-48362-X*, 73226) Longman.

— MODERN ITALY 1871 1995. 2nd ed. LC 95-53742. (History of Italy Ser.). 488p. (C). 1996. pap. text 28.13 (*0-582-05126-6*, Pub. by Addison-Wesley) Longman.

Clark, Martin E. Choosing Your Career: The Christian's Decision Manual. 1981. pap. 7.99 (*0-87552-205-X*) P & R Pubng.

Clark, Martin E., jt. auth. see Morris, Henry M.

Clark, Martin P. ATM Networks: Principles & Use. LC 96-11992. 244p. 1996. pap. 74.95 (*0-471-96701-7*) Wiley.

— Networks & Telecommunications: Design & Operation. LC 97-9248. 958p. 1997. 175.00 (*0-471-97346-7*) Wiley.

***Clark, Martin P.** Wireless Access Networks: Fixed Wireless Access & Wll Networks--Design & Operation. LC 00-33016. 2000. write for info. (*0-471-49298-1*) Wiley.

Clark, Marvin. Reverberations: Echoes from the Head & Heart. 100p. 1999. per. 9.95 (*0-9671244-0-9*) Chicago Ave Pubns.

— Track of the Kodiak. (Illus.). 224p. 1984. reprint ed. pap. 19.95 (*0-937708-02-X*) Great Northwest.

Clark, Marvin, ed. see Warbelow, Willy L.

Clark, Marvin, ed. see Wilson, Jack E.

Clark, Marvin H., Jr. Pinnell & Talifson: Last of the Great Brown Bear Men. (Illus.). 224p. (C). 1980. 39.95 (*0-937708-00-3*) Great Northwest.

— Pinnell & Talifson: Last of the Great Brown Bear Men. (Illus.). 224p. 1985. reprint ed. pap. 19.95 (*0-937708-03-8*) Great Northwest.

— Track of the Kodiak. (Illus.). 224p. 1984. reprint ed. 39.95 (*0-937708-01-1*) Great Northwest.

Clark, Mary. Biological & Health Sciences: Report of the Project 2061 Phase I Biological & Health Science Panel. LC 89-76. 34p. 1989. pap. 8.00 (*0-87168-343-1*, 89-02S) AAAS.

***Clark, Mary.** Dieting. (Collins Gem Ser.). (Illus.). 256p. 2000. pap. 7.95 (*0-00-472306-6*, Pub. by HarpC) Trafalgar.

— Hell's Kitchen: Slices of Life. (Illus.). 72p. 1999. pap. 3.95 (*0-9611738-0-7*) Public Pr.

Clark, Mary. Pocket Prophecy: I Ching. LC 98-22601. (Illus.). 64p. 1998. 7.95 (*1-86204-265-9*, Pub. by Element MA) Penguin Putnam.

Clark, Mary, tr. see De Leon Paiva, Anton P.

Clark, Mary A. Milady's Workbook for the Professional Instructor - Answers. 105p. 1994. 28.00 (*1-56253-233-2*) Milady Pub.

***Clark, Mary B.** Reconnections. LC 99-88533. 2000. pap. write for info. (*1-880090-87-2*) Galde Pr.

Clark, Mary C. Japanese Folded Patchwork. LC 97-73023. (Illus.). 128p. (Orig.). 1997. pap. 21.95 (*0-8019-9046-7*, JFPA) Krause Pubns.

— Story Quilts & How to Make Them. LC 95-34185. (Illus.). 128p. 1995. 27.95 (*0-8069-1316-9*) Sterling.

Clark, Mary E. Ariadne's Thread: In Search of a Greener Future. 400p. 1989. pap. 24.95 (*0-312-01586-0*) St Martin.

— Discipleship of Nonviolence. 24p. 1996. pap. 1.95 (*1-55612-869-X*) Sheed & Ward WI.

— Peter Porcupine in America: The Career of William Cobbett. (American Newspapermen 1790-1933 Ser.). v, 193p. 1974. reprint ed. 18.00 (*0-8464-0026-X*) Beekman Pubs.

Clark, Mary E. & Wawrytko, Sandra A., eds. Rethinking the Curriculum: Toward an Integrated, Interdisciplinary College Education, 40. LC 89-78404. (Contributions to the Study of Education Ser.: No. 40). 296p. 1990. 49.95 (*0-313-27306-5*, CRJ/, Greenwood Pr) Greenwood.

Clark, Mary F. Hiding, Hurting, Healing. 176p. (Orig.). 1985. pap. 3.95 (*0-310-30551-9*, 11612P) Zondervan.

Clark, Mary Higgins. All Around the Town. 1994. reprint ed. lib. bdg. 32.95 (*1-56849-264-2*) Buccaneer Bks.

— All Around the Town. Rubenstein, Julie, ed. 352p. 1993. reprint ed. per. 7.99 (*0-671-79348-9*) PB.

— All Through the Night. 1999. per. 7.99 (*0-671-02712-3*) PB.

— All Through the Night. LC 98-36927. 160p. 1998. 17.00 (*0-684-85660-3*) S&S Trade.

— All Through the Night. large type ed. 1998. pap. 17.00 (*0-684-85783-9*) S&S Trade.

— The Anastasia Syndrome. Rubenstein, Julie, ed. 320p. 1991. reprint ed. per. 7.99 (*0-671-70123-1*) PB.

— The Anastasia Syndrome & Other Stories. 1991. 12.35 (*0-606-04606-2*, Pub. by Turtleback) Demco.

— The Anastasia Syndrome & Other Stories. 1991. reprint ed. lib. bdg. 35.95 (*1-56849-073-9*) Buccaneer Bks.

— Aspire to the Heavens. 216p. 1986. reprint ed. lib. bdg. 31.95 (*0-89966-533-0*) Buccaneer Bks.

***Clark, Mary Higgins.** Before I Say Good-Bye. 336p. 2000. 25.50 (*0-684-83598-3*) Simon & Schuster.

— Before I Say Good-Bye. large type ed. 480p. 2000. pap. 25.50 (*0-7432-0046-2*) S&S Trade.

Clark, Mary Higgins. The Cradle Will Fall. Rubenstein, Julie, ed. 432p. 1991. per. 7.99 (*0-671-74119-5*) PB.

— The Cradle Will Fall. 1995. reprint ed. lib. bdg. 35.95 (*0-89968-448-3*, Lghtyr Pr) Buccaneer Bks.

— A Cry in the Night. 352p. 1993. per. 7.99 (*0-671-88666-5*) PB.

— A Cry in the Night. 1994. 13.09 (*0-606-06961-5*, Pub. by Turtleback) Demco.

— A Cry in the Night. 1993. reprint ed. lib. bdg. 32.95 (*0-89968-447-5*, Lghtyr Pr) Buccaneer Bks.

— Donde Estan los Ninos? (SPA.). 272p. 1992. pap. 3.95 (*1-56780-055-6*) La Costa Pr.

Clark, Mary Higgins. I'll Be Seeing You. LC 93-16584. 1993. 12.60 (*0-606-06490-7*, Pub. by Turtleback) Demco.

Clark, Mary Higgins. I'll Be Seeing You. 1997. reprint ed. lib. bdg. 32.95 (*1-56849-603-6*) Buccaneer Bks.

— I'll Be Seeing You. Rubenstein, Julie, ed. 320p. 1994. reprint ed. per. 7.99 (*0-671-88858-7*) PB.

— Let Me Call You Sweetheart. 320p. 1996. per. 7.50 (*0-671-56817-5*) Thorndike Pr.

— Let Me Call You Sweetheart. LC 95-7331. 1996. 12.60 (*0-606-09540-3*, Pub. by Turtleback) Demco.

— Let Me Call You Sweetheart. enl. ed. 1995. 7.50 (*0-684-80396-8*) Thorndike Pr.

— The Lottery Winner. 304p. 1995. mass mkt. 7.99 (*0-671-86717-2*, Pocket Books) PB.

— The Lottery Winner. 1997. reprint ed. lib. bdg. 32.95 (*1-56849-588-9*) Buccaneer Bks.

— The Lottery Winner: Alvirah & Willy Stories. 256p. 1994. 22.00 (*0-671-86716-4*) S&S Trade.

— Loves Music, Loves to Dance. 1996. reprint ed. lib. bdg. 35.95 (*1-56849-265-0*) Buccaneer Bks.

— Loves Music, Loves to Dance. Rubenstein, Julie, ed. 336p. 1992. reprint ed. per. 7.99 (*0-671-75889-6*) PB.

— Lucky Day. abr. ed. 1992. pap. 11.00 incl. audio (*0-671-76017-3*) PB.

— Mary Higgins Clark: Boxed Set, 3 vols. 1990. pap., boxed set 14.85 (*0-440-36009-9*) Dell.

— Mary Higgins Clark: Three Complete Novels. 560p. 1991. 13.99 (*0-517-06462-6*) Random Hse Value.

— Mary Higgins Clark: Three New York Times Bestselling Novels. 704p. 1996. 13.99 (*0-517-18368-4*) Random Hse Value.

Clark, Mary Higgins. The Mary Higgins Clark Audio Double Feature: While My Pretty One Sleeps; Weep No More, My Lady. abr. ed. 1992. audio 25.00 (*0-671-77677-0*) S&S Audio.

Clark, Mary Higgins. Mi Querida Sunday. 1998. pap. 6.50 (*84-01-49316-1*) Lectorum Pubns.

— Moonlight Becomes You. 339p. 1997. per. 7.99 (*0-671-86711-3*) PB.

— Moonlight Becomes You. large type ed. 320p. 1996. pap. 24.00 (*0-684-83127-9*) Simon & Schuster.

— Moonlight Becomes You: A Novel. 336p. 1996. 24.00 (*0-684-81038-7*) Simon & Schuster.

Clark, Mary Higgins. Moonlight Becomes You, a Novel. LC 96-11529. 1996. 13.09 (*0-606-11638-9*, Pub. by Turtleback) Demco.

Clark, Mary Higgins. My Gal Sunday. 1997. per. 6.99 (*0-671-01491-9*) PB.

— My Gal Sunday. LC 96-230890. 240p. 1996. 23.00 (*0-684-83229-1*) S&S Trade.

— My Gal Sunday. 1997. 11.60 (*0-606-13632-0*, Pub. by Turtleback) Demco.

— My Gal Sunday: Henry & Sunday Stories. 1996. pap. text 23.00 (*0-684-83238-0*, Scribner Pap Fic) S&S Trade Pap.

***Clark, Mary Higgins.** Ni Vue, Ni Connue. 1999. pap. 12.95 (*2-253-17056-9*) Midwest European Pubns.

Clark, Mary Higgins. Perseguida Por Toda La Ciudad. 1998. pap. 6.50 (*84-01-49310-2*) Lectorum Pubns.

— Pretend You Don't See Her. LC 97-150693. 320p. 1997. 25.00 (*0-684-81039-5*) S&S Trade.

— Pretend You Don't See Her. 1998. per. 7.99 (*0-671-86715-6*) S&S Trade.

— Pretend You Don't See Her. 1998. 13.09 (*0-606-13721-1*, Pub. by Turtleback) Demco.

— Pretend You Don't See Her. large type ed. 1997. 25.00 (*0-684-83416-2*) S&S Trade.

— Remember Me. 352p. 1995. per. 7.99 (*0-671-86709-1*) PB.

— Remember Me. 1994. 23.50 (*0-671-86708-3*) S&S Trade.

— Remember Me. 1997. reprint ed. lib. bdg. 32.95 (*1-56849-589-7*) Buccaneer Bks.

— Selected from The Lost Angel: Writer's Voices. abr. ed. Literacy Volunteers of New York City Staff, ed. (Writers' Voices Ser.). 64p. (Orig.). 1990. pap. 3.95 (*0-929631-13-7*, Signal Hill) New Readers.

— Silent Night. LC 95-36717. 177p. 1996. mass mkt. 6.50 (*0-671-00042-X*) PB.

— Silent Night. LC 95-36717. 160p. 1995. 16.00 (*0-684-81545-1*) S&S Trade.

Clark, Mary Higgins. Silent Night. LC 95-36717. 1996. 11.09 (*0-606-11843-8*, Pub. by Turtleback) Demco.

Clark, Mary Higgins. Silent Night. large type ed. 176p. 1995. 18.00 (*0-684-81546-X*) S&S Trade.

— Stillwatch. 368p. 1997. per. 7.99 (*0-671-52820-3*, Pocket Books) PB.

— Stillwatch. 1997. 13.09 (*0-606-11914-0*, Pub. by Turtleback) Demco.

— Stillwatch. 1991. reprint ed. lib. bdg. 31.95 (*1-56849-070-4*) Buccaneer Bks.

***Clark, Mary Higgins.** Stowaway & Milk Run: Two Unabridged Stories from Mary Higgins Clark. abr. ed. 1999. audio 18.00 (*0-671-04624-1*) S&S Audio.

Clark, Mary Higgins. A Stranger Is Watching. Rubenstein, Julie, ed. 283p. 1991. mass mkt. 7.99 (*0-671-74120-9*) PB.

— A Stranger Is Watching. 1991. reprint ed. lib. bdg. 31.95 (*1-56849-071-2*) Buccaneer Bks.

— Testigo en la Sombra. (SPA.). 224p. 1998. pap. 16.95 (*0-553-06089-9*) Bantam.

— Weep No More, My Lady. 384p. 1997. pap. 11.95 (*0-385-31921-5*) Doubleday.

— Weep No More, My Lady. 307p. 1998. per. 7.99 (*0-671-02558-9*, Pocket Books) PB.

— Weep No More, My Lady. 1987. 12.09 (*0-606-04108-7*, Pub. by Turtleback) Demco.

— Weep No More, My Lady. 1993. reprint ed. lib. bdg. 37.95 (*0-89968-446-7*, Lghtyr Pr) Buccaneer Bks.

— Weep No More, My Lady. 384p. 1993. reprint ed. mass mkt. 6.99 (*0-440-20098-9*) Dell.

— We'll Meet Again. LC 99-20134. 314p. 1999. 25.00 (*0-684-83597-5*) S&S Trade.

— We'll Meet Again. large type ed. 480p. 1999. 24.50 (*0-684-86211-5*) S&S Trade.

***Clark, Mary Higgins.** We'll Meet Again. 400p. 2000. reprint ed. per. 7.99 (*0-671-00456-5*, Pocket Books) PB.

Clark, Mary Higgins. Where Are the Children? Rubenstein, Julie, ed. 304p. 1992. per. 7.99 (*0-671-74118-7*) PB.

***Clark, Mary Higgins.** Where Are the Children? LC 98-55511. (Classic Editions Ser.). 272p. 1999. 24.50 (*0-684-86356-1*) S&S Trade.

Clark, Mary Higgins. Where Are the Children? 1992. 12.60 (*0-606-12084-X*, Pub. by Turtleback) Demco.

— Where Are the Children? 192p. 1991. reprint ed. lib. bdg. 27.95 (*0-89966-780-5*) Buccaneer Bks.

Clark, Mary Higgins. Where Are the Children?, Set. abr. ed. 1992. audio 17.00 (*0-671-75336-3*, Pub. by S&S Audio) Lndmrk Audiobks.

Clark, Mary Higgins. Where Are the Children? - The Cradle Will Fall - A Stranger Is Watching. 1996. per. 22.50 (*0-671-85157-8*) PB.

— While My Pretty One Sleeps. 1989. 13.09 (*0-606-04584-8*, Pub. by Turtleback) Demco.

— While My Pretty One Sleeps. 1991. reprint ed. lib. bdg. 31.95 (*1-56849-072-0*) Buccaneer Bks.

— While My Pretty One Sleeps. Rubenstein, Julie, ed. 320p. 1990. reprint ed. per. 7.99 (*0-671-67368-8*) PB.

— You Belong to Me. 1999. per. 7.99 (*0-671-00454-9*) S&S Trade.

— You Belong to Me. abr. large type ed. LC 98-13064. 320p. 1998. 25.00 (*0-684-83595-9*) S&S Trade.

— You Belong to Me. large type ed. 448p. 1998. 24.50 (*0-684-84330-7*) S&S Trade.

***Clark, Mary Higgins, ed.** Mary Higgins Clark Presents: The Plot Thickens. large type ed. 268p. 2000. lib. bdg. 25.95 (*1-58547-048-1*) Ctr Point Pubg.

— The Night Awakens: A Mystery Writers of America Anthology. 320p. 2000. reprint ed. per. 6.99 (*0-671-51918-2*, Pocket Star Bks) PB.

Clark, Mary Higgins, ed. The Plot Thickens. 1997. per. 5.99 (*0-671-01557-5*) PB.

Clark, Mary Higgins, ed. Bad Behavior. LC 94-43344. 320p. 1995. 20.00 (*0-15-200179-4*, Gulliver Bks) Harcourt.

Clark, Mary Higgins, et al, eds. Malice Domestic No. 2: An Anthology of Original Traditional Mystery Stories. 272p. 1993. per. 5.99 (*0-671-73827-5*) PB.

Clark, Mary Higgins, et al. Missing in Manhattan. 1994. mass mkt. 4.99 (*0-425-14203-5*) Berkley Pub.

— Mother. O'Keefe, Claudia, ed. 1996. pap. 12.00 (*0-614-97652-9*, Pocket Books) PB.

Clark, Mary J. The Commonwealth of Independent States. LC 92-20745. (Headliners Ser.). (Illus.). 64p. (J). (gr. 5-8). 1992. lib. bdg. 23.40 (*1-56294-081-3*) Millbrook Pr.

— Computerized Testbank for Nursing in the Community: IBM Version. 2nd ed. (C). 1995. write for info. (*0-8385-7106-9*, A7106) Appleton & Lange.

— Instructor's Guide for Nursing in the Community. 2nd ed. (C). 1995. write for info. (*0-8385-7092-5*, A7902-8) Appleton & Lange.

— Nursing in the Community. 2nd ed. LC 95-11594. (Illus.). 1160p. (C). 1995. pap. text 49.95 (*0-8385-7091-7*, A7091-0) Appleton & Lange.

Clark, Mary Jane. Do You Promise Not to Tell ? LC 99-33393. 304p. 1999. text 23.95 (*0-312-20527-9*) St Martin.

***Clark, Mary Jane.** Do You Promise Not to Tell? 1999. mass mkt. write for info. (*0-312-97148-6*) St Martin.

— Do You Promise Not to Tell? 2000. mass mkt. 6.99 (*0-312-97424-8*) St Martin.

— Do You Promise Not to Tell? large type ed. LC 99-40364. (Core Ser.). 1999. 28.95 (*0-7838-8771-X*, G K Hall & Co) Mac Lib Ref.

Clark, Mary Jane. Do You Want to Know a Secret? LC 98-21115. 304p. 1998. text 23.95 (*0-312-19260-6*) St Martin.

— Do You Want to Know a Secret? 320p. 1999. mass mkt. 6.50 (*0-312-96924-4*, St Martins Paperbacks) St Martin.

— Do You Want to Know a Secret? large type ed. (G. K. Hall Core Ser.). 1999. 28.95 (*0-7838-8530-X*, G K Hall Lrg Type) Mac Lib Ref.

***Clark, Mary Jane.** Let Me Whisper in Your Ear. 304p. 2000. 22.95 (*0-312-26191-8*) St Martin.

***Clark, Mary Jo.** Community Health Nursing Handbook. 1998. pap. 24.95 (*0-8385-1071-X*, Medical Exam) Appleton & Lange.

Clark, Mary Jo Dummer. Nursing in the Community: Dimensions of Community Health Nursing. 3rd ed. 1103p. (C). 1998. pap. text 51.95 (*0-8385-6984-6*) Appleton & Lange.

Clark, Mary K. Catholic Home Schooling: A Handbook for Parents. LC 93-60757. 448p. (Orig.). 1993. pap. 18.00 (*0-89555-494-1*, 1227) TAN Bks Pubs.

Clark, Mary K., ed. Endangered, Threatened & Rare Fauna of North Carolina Pt. 1: A Re-evaluation of the Mammals. (Occasional Papers of the North Carolina Biological Survey: No. 1987-3). (Illus.). 52p. (Orig.). 1987. pap. text 5.00 (*0-917134-14-1*) NC Natl Sci.

Clark, Mary L. Dinosaurs. LC 81-7750. (New True Books Ser.). (Illus.). 48p. (J). (ps-3). 1981. lib. bdg. 21.00 (*0-516-01612-1*) Childrens.

Clark, Mary M. The Tonal System of Igbo. (Publications in African Languages & Linguistics). 324p. 1990. pap. 106.15 (*3-11-013041-6*) Mouton.

Clark, Mary N. Bear Fetishes among the Zuni: A Study in Form & Imagery. (Illus.). 112p. (C). 1997. pap. text 12.50 (*1-55567-836-X*) Coyote Press.

Clark, Mary S. The Old Middlesex Canal. LC 87-29957. 191p. 1987. reprint ed. 14.00 (*0-930973-05-4*); reprint ed. pap. 6.00 (*0-930973-06-2*) H M Historical.

Clark, Mary T. Augustine. LC 93-36685. 160p. (C). 1994. pap. 17.95 (*0-225-66681-2*, Pub. by G Chapman) Morehouse Pub.

Clark, Mary T., ed. An Aquinas Reader: Selections from the Writings of Thomas Aquinas. 2nd ed. LC 72-76709. 597p. (C). 1988. pap. text 17.95 (*0-8232-1206-8*) Fordham.

***Clark, Mary T., ed.** An Aquinas Reader: Selections from the Writings of Thomas Aquinas. 3rd rev. ed. 640p. 2000. pap. text 19.95 (*0-8232-2029-X*, Pub. by Fordham) BookMasters.

Clark, Mary T., tr. see Augustine, Saint.

***Clark, Marylyn.** Which Came First... Addiction or Disease? (Illus.). 132p. 1999. pap. 15.95 (*1-893780-00-7*) Granite Dells.

Clark, Mason A., ed. The Healing Wisdom of Doctor P. P. Quimby. LC 82-24232. (Illus.). 128p. (Orig.). 1982. pap. text 8.95 (*0-931400-02-3*) Frontal Lobe.

***Clark, Matityahu & Hirsch, Samson Raphael.** Etymological Dictionary of Biblical Hebrew: Based on the Commentaries of Rabbi Samson Raphael Hirsch. LC 00-29424. 2000. write for info. (*1-58330-431-2*) Feldheim.

Clark, Matthew. Out of Line: Homeric Composition Beyond the Hexameter. LC 97-35673. (Greek Studies). 224p. 1997. 61.00 (*0-8476-8697-3*); pap. 24.95 (*0-8476-8698-1*) Rowman.

Clark, Maudemarie. Nietzsche on Truth & Philosophy. (Modern European Philosophy Ser.). 312p. (C). 1991. text 64.95 (*0-521-34368-2*) Cambridge U Pr.

— Nietzsche on Truth & Philosophy. (Modern European Philosophy Ser.). 312p. (C). 1991. pap. text 20.95 (*0-521-34850-1*) Cambridge U Pr.

Clark, Maudemarie, ed. see Nietzsche, Friedrich Wilhelm.

Clark, Maudemarie, tr. see Nietzsche, Friedrich Wilhelm.

Clark, Maudmarie, tr. see Nietzsche, Friedrich Wilhelm.

Clark, Max S. Letters to George. 208p. 1997. pap. 22.95 (*1-85459-317-X*) N Hern Bks.

An Asterisk (*) at the beginning of an entry indicates that the title is appearing for the first time.

Clark, Maxine. The Book of Light Italian Dishes. 96p. 1997. pap. 12.00 (*1-55788-268-1*, HP Books) Berkley Pub.
— Pasta & Pizza Presto: 100 of the Best, Most Authentic Italian Favourites Made Simple. (Illus.). 192p. 1996. pap. text 16.95 (*1-85967-279-5*, Lorenz Bks) Anness Pub.
Clark, Maxine, jt. auth. see Newdick, Jane.
Clark, Maynard. The Art of Airbrushing. LC 90-63279. 54p. 1990. pap. 5.95 (*0-916809-46-3*) Scott Pubns MI.
Clark-McDowell, Tricia, jt. auth. see McDowell, C. Forrest.
Clark, Mei. Flying Away. 2nd rev. ed. 136p. 1998. pap. 13.99 (*0-9668523-0-3*) Mei Clark.
Clark, Melanie M., et al, eds. The Family Guide to Omaha: The Handy Guide That Keeps Local Family Resources at Your Fingertips. 2nd ed. (Illus.). 126p. 1990. 5.95 (*0-9628451-0-8*) J&J Pubns NE.
Clark, Melanie M., ed. see Braddock, Suzanne, et al.
***Clark, Melanie Y. W.** Heartfelt: Poems by Melanie. 100p. 1999. pap. write for info. (*0-7392-0445-9*, PO3731) Morris Pubng.
Clark, Melissa. The Bread Machine Cookbook. (Orig.). 1993. pap. 4.99 (*0-425-13734-1*); mass mkt. 5.99 (*0-425-13733-3*) Berkley Pub.
— Champagne & Caviar: A Connoisseur's Guide to Survival. LC 99-36142. 1999. text 20.00 (*1-56799-743-0*, Friedman-Fairfax) M Friedman Pub Grp Inc.
— The Coffee Book. 272p. (Orig.). 1994. pap. 4.99 (*0-425-14121-7*) Berkley Pub.
— Ice Cream Machine Cookbook, 1 vol. 1999. mass mkt. 6.99 (*0-425-16820-4*) Berkley Pub.
— A Kitchen Primer. LC 97-183790. 288p. 1997. mass mkt. 5.99 (*0-425-15720-2*) Berkley Pub.
— The Sweet Bread Machine Cookbook. 192p. 1997. mass mkt. 5.99 (*0-425-15695-8*) Berkley Pub.
Clark, Melody, ed. In Situ Hybridization. 1996. mass mkt. 82.95 (*3-8261-0038-7*, Chap & Hall NY) Chapman & Hall.
Clark, Merry, ed. see Baldwin, Judith M.
Clark, Mia. Coming Alive: User's Guide for a Worksite Exercise Program. 2nd ed. 65p. 1991. reprint ed. pap. 19.50 (*1-879552-18-3*) SCRDP.
Clark, Michael. Badgers. (Illus.). 128p. text 19.95 (*0-905483-65-0*, Pub. by Whittet Bks) Diamond Farm Bk.
— Corot & the Art of Landscape. (Illus.). 160p. 1991. 45.00 (*1-55859-223-7*, Cross Riv Pr) Abbeville Pr.
— Dos Passos's Early Fiction, 1912-1938. LC 85-63015. 172p. 1987. 32.50 (*0-941664-18-X*) Susquehanna U Pr.
— Jacques Lacan: An Annotated Bibliography. LC 84-45394. (Modern Critics & Critical Schools Ser.). 400p. 1988. text 20.00 (*0-8240-8848-4*) Garland.
***Clark, Michael.** Oxford-Duden German Dictionary. 2nd ed. 1,728p. 1999. 45.00 (*0-19-860248-0*) OUP.
Clark, Michael. Reason to Believe: A Practical Guide to Psychic Phenomena. LC 96-96925. 224p. (Orig.). 1997. mass mkt. 5.99 (*0-380-78474-2*, Avon Bks) Morrow Avon.
***Clark, Michael.** Revenge of the Aesthetic: The Place of Literature in Theory Today LC 99-29827. 280p. 2000. 19.95 (*0-520-22004-8*, Pub. by U CA Pr) Cal Prin Full Svc.
— Revenge of the Aesthetic: The Place of Literature in Theory Today. LC 99-29827. 274p. 2000. 50.00 (*0-520-22002-1*, Pub. by U CA Pr) Cal Prin Full Svc.
Clark, Michael, ed. Brassey's Defence Yearbook 1996: Centre for Defence Studies. 432p. 1996. 55.00 (*1-85753-124-8*, Pub. by Brasseys) Brasseys.
Clark, Michael. From Head to Soul for Men. rev. ed. (From Head to Soul Ser.). pap. 19.95 (*0-9639996-1-3*) ImageMaker.
Clark, Michael & Crawford, Catherine, eds. Legal Medicine in History. LC 93-11582. (Cambridge History of Medicine Ser.). 378p. (C). 1994. text 69.95 (*0-521-39514-3*) Cambridge U Pr.
***Clark, Michael & Kumar, Parveen.** Acute General Medicine: Self Assessment Workbook. 188p. 2000. pap. 19.95 (*1-873207-07-7*) Buttrwrth-Heinemann.
— Acute General Medicine: The Essentials. (Illus.). 500p. 2000. 44.95 (*1-873207-02-6*, Pub. by Joint Centre for Education in Medicine) Buttrwrth-Heinemann.
Clark, Michael & Sabin, Philip, eds. British Defence Choices for the Twenty-First Century: A Centre for Defence Studies Book. 200p. 1993. 45.00 (*1-85753-088-8*, Pub. by Brasseys) Brasseys.
***Clark, Michael & Thyen, Olaf, eds.** The Concise Oxford-Duden German Dictionary. 2nd ed. 1264p. 2000. 27.95 (*0-19-864230-X*) OUP.
Clark, Michael & Thyen, Olaf, eds. The Concise Oxford-Duden German Dictionary: English-German, German-English. 2nd rev. ed. LC 98-114283. (ENG & GER.). 1424p. 1997. 25.00 (*0-19-860133-6*) OUP.
— The Oxford-Duden German Desk Dictionary. rev. ed. LC 97-193253. 864p. 1997. 14.95 (*0-19-860147-6*) OUP.
***Clark, Michael & Thyen, Olaf, eds.** The Oxford-Duden German Dictionary. 2nd ed. (Illus.). 1,728p. 1999. 45.00 (*0-19-860226-X*) OUP.
Clark, Michael, jt. auth. see Cummings, Joe.
Clark, Michael, ed. see Dos Passos, John.
Clark, Michael, ed. see Dudenredaktion (Bibliographisches Institut) & Oxford University Press. Dictionary Dept. German Section.
Clark, Michael A., et al, eds. Youth Baseball: A Complete Handbook. (Illus.). 528p. (Orig.). 1993. pap. 30.00 (*1-884125-01-8*) Cooper Pubng.
Clark, Michael B. & Riddle, Michael R. Biology Lab Book. rev. ed. (Illus.). 270p. (C). 1994. pap. text, spiral bd., wbk. ed. 20.00 (*1-885380-50-X*) Suspended Animat.
— Human Biology Lab Book. rev. ed. (Illus.). 302p. (C). 1995. pap. text, spiral bd., wbk. ed. 23.00 (*1-885380-52-6*) Suspended Animat.
— Laboratory Investigations: A Manual for General Biology. (Illus.). 350p. (C). 1998. pap. text, spiral bd., wbk. ed. 27.00 (*1-885380-57-7*) Suspended Animat.
Clark, Michael D. Coherent Variety: The Idea of Diversity in British & American Conservative Thought, 86. LC 82-9228. (Contributions in Political Science Ser.: No. 86). 228p. 1983. 55.00 (*0-313-23284-9*, CCV/, Greenwood Pr) Greenwood.
Clark, Michael J. Advances in Periglacial Geomorphology. LC 86-28148. 505p. 1988. reprint ed. pap. 156.60 (*0-608-05296-5*, 206583400001) Bks Demand.
Clark, Michael J., et al. Horizons in Physical Geography. (Illus.). 430p. 1987. 69.50 (*0-389-20752-7*, N 8311) B&N Imports.
Clark, Michael L. Ride in Pursuit of Happiness. LC 95-92359. 204p. (Orig.). 1995. pap. 6.95 (*0-9647242-0-0*) Wet Saddleblankets Pubns.
— Ride in Pursuit of Happiness: Sonya's Story. 144p. Date not set. pap. text. write for info. (*0-9647242-1-9*) Wet Saddleblankets Pubns.
Clark, Michael R. Condition Yourself for Success: Daily Meditations & Inspiring Thoughts to Help You Reach Your Goals. 126p. 1997. pap. 12.95 (*0-9636042-1-X*) Clark Assoc Busn.
— The Struggle Stops Here: When You Believe in You. LC 92-97390. 82p. 1993. pap. 8.95 (*0-9636042-0-1*) Clark Assoc Busn.
***Clark, Michael T.** Thinking about World Change. 170p. 2000. reprint ed. pap. text 30.00 (*0-7881-8940-9*) DIANE Pub.
Clark, Michele, jt. auth. see Danzberger, Jacqueline.
Clark, Miles. The Man Who Tapped the Secrets of Creative Power: The Spiritual Journey of Glenda Clark. 170p. (Orig.). pap. write for info. (*0-9619579-0-5*) Lorkot Pr.
— Skydiving in 8 Days. (Illus.). 136p. 1995. per. 14.95 (*0-9607814-0-4*) AeroGraphics.
Clark, Millard W. Florida State & Local Taxation, 2 vols., Set. 118p. 1997. ring bd. 38.00 (*0-409-26176-9*, 83115-10, MICHIE) LEXIS Pub.
Clark, Miriam B., jt. auth. see Clark, Kenneth E.
Clark, Miriam B., jt. ed. see Clark, Kenneth E.
Clark, Mona, et al. Researching & Writing Dissertations in Hospitality & Tourism. 192p. 1998. pap. 21.99 (*1-86152-046-8*) Thomson Learn.
Clark, Murtie J. Loyalists in the Southern Campaign of the Revolutionary War Vol. 1: Official Rolls of Loyalists Recruited from North & South Carolina, Georgia, Florida, Mississippi, & Louisiana. LC 80-84321. 635p. 1999. pap. 47.50 (*0-8063-0924-5*) Clearfield Co.
— Loyalists in the Southern Campaign of the Revolutionary War Vol. II: Official Rolls of Loyalists Recruited from Maryland, Pennsylvania, Virginia, & Those Recruited from Other Colonies. LC 80-84321. 687p. 1999. pap. 49.95 (*0-8063-0941-5*) Clearfield Co.
— Loyalists in the Southern Campaign of the Revolutionary War Vol. III: Official Rolls of Loyalists Recruited from the Middle Atlantic Colonies, with Lists of Refugees from Other Colonies. LC 80-84321. 484p. 1999. pap. 37.50 (*0-8063-0952-0*) Clearfield Co.
— The Pension Lists of 1792-1795: With Other Revolutionary War Pension Records. 216p. 1996. 25.00 (*0-8063-1318-8*, 1008) Genealog Pub.
Clark, Myrtle, jt. auth. see Schroeder, Richard G.
Clark, Myrtle B. Jones Genealogy, Being a Record of the Descendants of Hugh Jones of Salem, Mass., Emigrant from Wincanton, England, 1635-1931. (Illus.). 219p. 1997. reprint ed. pap. 33.00 (*0-8328-9357-9*); reprint ed. lib. bdg. 43.00 (*0-8328-9356-0*) Higginson Bk Co.
Clark, N. Como Hallar el Amor en Tu Vida.Tr. of Finding the Love of Your Life. (SPA.). 178p. 2001. 6.99 (*1-56063-569-X*, 498592) Editorial Unilit.
Clark, N. A., et al. Ferroelectric Liquid Crystals: Principles, Properties & Applications, Vol. 7. Goodby, J. W. & Blinc, R., eds. (Ferroelectricity & Related Phenomena Ser.). 474p. 1991. text 348.00 (*2-88124-282-0*) Gordon & Breach.
Clark, N. A., jt. ed. see Scott, J. F.
Clark, N. J., jt. auth. see McColm, I. J.
Clark, N. Laurie. Bringing Grandy Home: For End-of-Life Care with Family with Year 2000 Update Form. large type rev. ed. LC 94-94607. (Illus.). 250p. 1994. pap. 18.95 (*0-9641197-0-6*) Clark Pubs.
— It's Wesley! The Adirondack Guide. (Illus.). 32p. (J). (gr. k up). 1998. per. 14.95 (*0-9641197-1-4*) Clark Pubs.
Clark, Nan. Harker's Hard Hat. Alward, Edgar C., ed. (Illus.). 58p. (YA). 1995. pap. text 12.95 (*1-880836-06-8*) Pine Isl Pr.
— The World's Greatest Star Trek Quiz: Commemorating the 30th Anniversary of the Original TV Series. LC 96-77424. 221p. 1997. pap. 14.95 (*1-878044-33-8*) Mayhaven Pub.
Clark, Nancy. Nancy Clark's Sports Nutrition Guidebook. 2nd ed. LC 96-11313. (Illus.). 464p. (Orig.). 1996. pap. 16.95 (*0-87322-730-1*, PCLA0730) Human Kinetics.
Clark, Nancy, et al, eds. A Dictionary of the Bible & Christian Doctrine in Everyday English. 360p. (Orig.). 1986. 14.99 (*0-8341-1075-X*) Beacon Hill.
Clark, Nancy & Crull, Anna. Bioremediation of Hazardous Wastes, Wastewater, & Municipal Waste. LC 97-162293. 253p. 1997. 2850.00 (*1-56965-366-6*, C-110U) BCC.
Clark, Nancy, et al. Ventilation: A Practical Guide. LC 84-12680. (Illus.). 128p. (Orig.). 1984. pap. text 18.95 (*0-918875-00-5*) Ctr Occupational Hazards.
— Ventilation: A Practical Guide for Artists, Craftspeople & Others in the Arts. 128p. 1987. reprint ed. pap. 18.95 (*0-941130-44-4*) Lyons Pr.
Clark, Nancy, ed. see Lodo, Venerable L.
Clark, Nancy A. Earth in Ascension.Tr. of Vzostup Zeme. (SLO.). 176p. (Orig.). 1995. pap. text 14.95 (*0-9648307-6-0*) Violet Fire Pubns.
Clark, Nancy H. How to Cut Kids' Hair. LC 83-25837. (Kid Care Ser.). (Illus.). 64p. 1984. pap. write for info. (*0-201-10811-9*) Addison-Wesley.
Clark, Nancy L. Manufacturing Apartheid: State Corporations in South Africa. LC 93-48316. (Yale Historical Publications). 264p. 1994. 40.00 (*0-300-05638-9*) Yale U Pr.
Clark, Nancy P. & Lippman, Marcia Z. Developmental Psychology: Childhood & Adolescence, Test Item Bank & Test File. 4th ed. 1995. pap. write for info. (*0-534-26438-7*) Brooks-Cole.
Clark, Naomi. Burglaries & Celebrations. 1977. 6.95 (*0-685-80001-6*); 2.95 (*0-685-80002-4*) Oyez.
— The Single Eye. (QRL Poetry Bks.: Vol. XXXI). 1992. 20.00 (*0-614-06450-3*) Quarterly Rev.
— When I Kept Silence. LC 88-71363. (CSU Poetry Ser.: No. XXVI). 80p. (Orig.). 1988. 12.00 (*0-914946-68-4*); pap. 6.00 (*0-914946-69-2*) Cleveland St Univ Poetry Ctr.
Clark, Nate, Jr., jt. auth. see Lorenzo, Robert.
Clark, Neal. Birds on the Move: A Guide to New England's Avian Invaders. LC 88-15216. (Illus.). 196p. (Orig.). 1988. pap. 8.95 (*0-945980-04-3*) Nrth Country Pr.
— Eastern Birds of Prey: A Guide to the Private Lives of Eastern Raptors. LC 83-4775. (Illus.). 174p. 1983. pap. 8.95 (*0-945980-27-2*) Nrth Country Pr.
Clark, Neil. Dinosaurs: A Unique First Visual Reference. (Look Inside Ser.). (Illus.). 20p. (J). (gr. 4-6). 1995. 10.99 (*0-89577-689-8*) Rdrs Digest.
Clark, Neil & Fraser, Tony. The Gestalt Approach. 2nd ed. (Illus.). 56p. (C). 1991. reprint ed. pap. text 8.00 (*0-939266-12-1*) Gestalt Journal.
Clark, Neil & Lindsay, William. Dinosaurs. LC 93-48880. (DK Pockets Ser.). (Illus.). 128p. (YA). (gr. 7 up). 1995. pap. 6.95 (*1-56458-662-6*) DK Pub Inc.
Clark, Neil, et al. Unfinished Business: The Theory & Practice of Personal Process Work in Training. LC 84-8134. 200p. 1984. text 63.95 (*0-566-02514-0*) Ashgate Pub Co.
Clark, Neil M., ed. see Harshman, James H.
Clark, Nicholas. Melozzo Da Forli. (Illus.). 160p. 1990. 95.00 (*0-85667-371-4*, Pub. by P Wilson) Hcovers TX.
Clark, Nicholas L., intro. Woodland Peoples: An Educational Unit. 32p. (Orig.). 1993. pap. write for info. (*0-9623291-6-9*) Minnetrista.
Clark, Nick. Duotones, Tritones, & Quadtones: A Complete Visual Guide to Enhancing Two-, Three-, & Four-Color Images. LC 97-105690. (Illus.). 144p. 1996. pap. 24.95 (*0-8118-1426-2*) Chronicle Bks.
— Duotones, Tritones & Quadtones: A Complete Visual Guide to Enhancing Two, Three & Four Color Images. (Illus.). 144p. 1996. pap. text 47.95 (*0-240-51490-4*, Focal) Buttrwrth-Heinemann.
Clark, Nicole, ed. see Crawford, L. Ann & Crawford, William R., Sr.
Clark, Nicole K. Pigment the Rainbow Pig. (Illus.). (J). (ps-2). Date not set. write for info. (*1-892176-18-1*) PremaNations.
***Clark, Nicole K. & Clark, John T.** The Oceans of Emotions-3D. large type ed. (Illus.). 32p. (J) (ps-4). 1999. 17.95 (*1-892176-13-0*) PremaNations.
Clark, Nicole K., jt. auth. see Clark, John T.
Clark, Nina. The Politics of Physician Assisted Suicide. rev. ed. LC 96-48392. (Studies on the Elderly in America). (Illus.). 148p. 1997. text 33.00 (*0-8153-2645-9*) Garland.
Clark, Noel. The Millionaire Sourcebook. 1971. 15.00 (*0-579-80030-X*) Claitors.
Clark, Noel, tr. see Fredro, Aleksander.
Clark, Noel, tr. see Wypianski, Stanislaw.
Clark, Noel A., jt. ed. see Safran, Samuel A.
Clark, Noreen & McCaffery, James. Demystifying Evaluation. LC 78-65627. (Illus.). 69p. 1979. pap. 10.00 (*0-914262-11-4*) World Educ.
Clark, Norma L. The Marriage Mart. 240p. 1990. pap. 3.50 (*0-318-50081-7*, Sig) NAL.
Clark, Norman. Deliver Us from Evil: An Interpretation of American Prohibition. (Essays in American History Ser.). (C). 1976. pap. text 12.50 (*0-393-09170-8*) Norton.
Clark, Norman & Juma, Calestous. Long-Run Economics: An Evolutionary Approach to Economic Growth. 230p. 1992. pap. text 19.50 (*1-85567-062-3*) St Martin.
— Long-Run Economics: An Evolutionary Approach to Economics. 230p. 1992. 49.00 (*0-86187-903-1*) St Martin.
Clark, Norman, et al. Evolutionary Dynamics & Sustainable Development: A Systems Approach. LC 95-13219. 196p. 1995. 90.00 (*1-85898-273-1*) E Elgar.
Clark, Norman H. The Dry Years. rev. ed. LC 86-26741. (Illus.). 352p. 1987. pap. 14.95 (*0-295-96465-9*) U of Wash Pr.
Clark, Norton D., jt. auth. see Humphrey, Thomas J.
Clark, O. & Roeher, H. D., eds. Thyroid Tumors. (Progress in Surgery Ser.: Vol. 19). (Illus.). viii, 228p. 1988. 165.25 (*3-8055-4713-7*) S Karger.
Clark, Olive I. Along the Way. (Illus.). 48p. 1996. pap. 8.00 (*0-8059-3978-4*) Dorrance.
Clark, Opal B. A Fool's Enterprise: The Life of Charles Page. (Illus.). 272p. 1988. text 16.95 (*0-9621444-0-1*) Dexter Pubs.
***Clark, Orio H., et al.** Endocrine Tumors. (ACS Atlas of Clinical Oncology Ser.). 300p. 2000. boxed set 89.95 incl. cd-rom (*1-55009-134-4*) DEKR.
Clark, Orlo H. & Duh, Quan-Yang. Textbook of Endocrine Surgery. McGrew, Larry, ed. (Illus.). 560p. 1997. text 155.00 (*0-7216-5882-2*, W B Saunders Co) Harcrt Hlth Sci Grp.
***Clark, Orlo H. & Noguchi, Shiro, eds.** Thyroid Cancer: Diagnosis & Treatment. LC 99-57674. (Illus.). 447p. 2000. text 99.00 (*1-57626-116-6*) Quality Med Pub.
***Clark, Orville & Hull, Wayne.** Good Thinking: Helping Students to Reframe Their Thinking Patterns. 2nd ed. (Illus.). 508p. 1999. ring bd. 59.00 (*1-57035-199-6*) Sopris.
Clark, Oz, contrib. by. Oz Clark's Encyclopedia of World Wines. LC 93-1948. 1994. 22.50 (*0-671-79294-6*) S&S Trade.
***Clark, P.** Promoting Palliative Care: Sociological & Policy Perspectives. LC 98-28627. (Facing Death Ser.). 1999. 85.00 (*0-335-19455-9*) OpUniv Pr.
Clark, P., jt. ed. see Aerts, E.
Clark, P., tr. see Badr, Liyana.
Clark, P. M. & Kricka, Larry J. Biochemistry of Alcohol & Alcoholism. LC 79-40252. (Chemical Science Ser.). 285p. 1979. text 104.95 (*0-470-26712-7*) P-H.
Clark, P. U. & Lea, P. D., eds. The Last Interglacial-Glacial Transition in North America. (Special Papers: No. 270). (Illus.). 1992. pap. 31.25 (*0-8137-2270-5*) Geol Soc.
Clark Parker Associates Staff. Marketing New Homes. 129p. 1989. pap. 22.00 (*0-86718-332-2*) Home Builder.
***Clark, Pat.** Little Hummingbird. (Illus.). 36p. (J). 2000. pap. 22.95 (*1-57532-289-7*) Press-Tige Pub.
Clark, Patch. Intergenerational Arts in the Nursing Home: A Handbook. LC 91-138. 200p. 1991. lib. bdg. 55.00 (*0-313-25965-8*, CKI, Greenwood Pr) Greenwood.
Clark, Patricia. Current Research in British Studies, Vol. 9. 9th ed. Donovan, Robert K., ed. 106p. (Orig.). 1988. pap. 29.95 (*0-89126-167-2*) MA-AH Pub.
— North of Wondering. Dallman, Elaine, ed. LC 98-61315. 72p. 1999. pap. text 13.50 (*0-935634-16-9*) Women-in-Lit.
Clark, Patricia, jt. auth. see Kallet, Marilyn.
Clark, Patricia A. & Osgood, Nancy J. Seniors on Stage: The Impact of Applying Theatre Techniques on the Elderly. LC 85-9347. 218p. 1985. 55.00 (*0-275-90198-X*, C0198, Praeger Pubs) Greenwood.
Clark, Patrick S. Light Verse from an Island Parish. (Illus.). 90p. (Orig.). 1996. pap. write for info. (*1-57502-254-0*, P0936) Morris Pubng.
***Clark, Paul.** Building More Effective Unions. 2000. pap. 19.95 (*0-8014-8705-6*, ILR Press) Cornell U Pr.
Clark, Paul. Phone: An Appreciation, 4 vols. LC 97-35667. (Design Icons Ser.). 1997. 4.99 (*1-57145-616-3*, Laurel Glen Pub) Advantage Pubs.
— The Watch. (Illus.). 1999. pap. 9.95 (*1-85410-598-1*, Pub. by Aurum Press Ltd) London Brdge.
Clark, Paul, contrib. by. Folk Tunes of Austria. 1976. 4.00 (*0-913334-32-4*, CM1037) Consort Music.
***Clark, Paul & Freeman, Julian.** Design: A Crash Course. (Illus.). 144p. 2000. write for info. (*0-8230-0983-1*) Watsn-Guptill.
Clark, Paul C. The United States & Somoza, 1933-1956: A Revisionist Look. LC 92-8399. 264p. 1992. 55.00 (*0-275-94334-8*, C4334, Praeger Pubs) Greenwood.
Clark, Paul C., jt. auth. see Moseley, Edward H.
Clark, Paul F. The University of Wisconsin Medical School: A Chronicle, 1848-1948. LC 67-12004. (Illus.). 311p. reprint ed. pap. 96.50 (*0-8357-4742-5*, 203766300009) Bks Demand.
Clark, Paul F., et al, eds. Forging a Union of Steel: Philip Murray, S W O C & the United Steelworkers. LC 87-21508. 168p. 1987. pap. text 12.95 (*0-87546-135-2*, ILR Press) Cornell U Pr.
Clark, Paul O. Gulliver Dictionary. LC 75-100739. (Studies in Comparative Literature: No. 35). (C). 1970. reprint ed. pap. 22.95 (*0-8383-0015-4*) M S G Haskell Hse.
Clark, Peggy. Microenterprise & the Poor: Findings from the Self-Employment Learning Project 5 Year Survey of Microentrepreneurs. (Economic Opportunities Program Ser.). 84p. pap. 15.00 (*0-89843-260-X*) The Aspen Inst.
Clark, Peggy, et al. Isozymes: Biochemical & Genetic Studies. LC 73-10223. 242p. (C). 1973. text 30.50 (*0-8422-7126-0*) Irvington.
Clark, Penny. A Coloring Book of Bible Proverbs: KJV. 32p. (J). (ps-5). 1988. ring bd. 2.50 (*0-9618608-2-0*) Lynns Bookshelf.
Clark, Pernell, jt. auth. see Naylor, Barbara.
Clark, Peter. Black Brigade of Cincinnati: Being a Report of Its Labors & a Muster-Roll of Its Members: Together with Various Orders, Speeches, Etc. Relating to It. LC 73-92227. (American Negro: His History & Literature. Series 3). 1970. reprint ed. 11.95 (*0-405-01917-3*) Ayer.
***Clark, Peter.** British Clubs & Societies C1580-1800: The Origins of an Associational World. LC 99-16109. 536p. 2000. 98.00 (*0-19-820376-4*) OUP.
Clark, Peter. European Financial Reporting: Luxembourg. LC 93-25764. (European Financial Reporting Ser.). (Illus.). 345p. (C). (gr. 13). 1993. pap. 114.95 (*0-415-06661-1*, B0284) Thomson Learn.
— FRW (Fire Retardant Workwear) Handbook. 1993. pap. 47.95 (*0-317-05932-7*) Phoenix Soc.
— O'Neill's Plays Notes. (Cliffs Notes Ser.). 112p. (Orig.). 1966. pap. 4.50 (*0-8220-0910-2*, Cliff) IDG Bks.
— Zorastrianism: An Introduction to Ancient Faith. LC 98-27763. 232p. 1998. pap. 24.95 (*1-898723-78-8*, Pub. by Sussex Acad Pr) Intl Spec Bk.
***Clark, Peter, ed.** The Cambridge Urban History of Britain Vol. 2: 1540-1840. (Illus.). 936p. 2000. 125.00 (*0-521-43141-7*) Cambridge U Pr.
Clark, Peter, ed. The European Crisis of the Fifteen Nineties: Essays in Comparative History. 352p. 1985. text 65.00 (*0-04-940074-6*) Routledge.
— Small Towns in Early Modern Europe. (Themes in International Urban History Ser.: No. 3). (Illus.). 330p. (C). 1995. text 69.95 (*0-521-46463-3*) Cambridge U Pr.
Clark, Peter & Clark, Jennifer. The Boston Assembly Minutes, Fifteen Forty-Five to Fifteen Seventy-Five. (Publications of the Lincoln Record Society). 1988. 45.00 (*0-901503-50-9*) Boydell & Brewer.

C

Clark, Peter & Fry, Don. Coaching Writers: Editors & Reporters Working Together. LC 91-61444. 182p. (Orig.). (C). 1991. pap. 30.95 (*0-312-04937-4*) St Martin.

Clark, Peter & Hale, Bob, eds. Reading Putnam. (Illus.). 310p. 1994. 58.95 (*0-631-17907-0*) Blackwell Pubs.

Clark, Peter & Lepetit, Bernard, eds. Capital Cities & Their Hinterlands in Early Modern Europe. LC 95-50649. (Historical Urban Studies). (Illus.). 272p. 1996. 86.95 (*1-85928-224-5*, Pub. by Scolar Pr) Ashgate Pub Co.

Clark, Peter & Starkey, Ken. Organization Transitions & Innovation Design. 252p. 1993. 49.95 (*0-86187-646-6*, Pub. by P P Pubs) Cassell & Continuum.

Clark, Peter & Staunton, Neil. Innovation in Technology & Organisation. 256p. 1993. pap. 19.95 (*0-415-09014-8*, B0287) Routledge.

— Innovation in Technology & Organization. 256p. (C). 1993. pap. 29.95 (*0-415-09318-X*) Thomson Learn.

Clark, Peter & Stephenson, Graham. SWOT Law of Torts. 178p. (C). 1990. 92.00 (*1-85431-029-1*, Pub. by Blackstone Pr) St Mut.

— SWOT Law of Torts. 4th ed. 168p. 1995. pap. 22.00 (*1-85431-343-6*, Pub. by Blackstone Pr) Gaunt.

Clark, Peter, et al. Exchange Rates & Economic Fundamentals: A Framework for Analysis. LC 94-24052. (Occasional Paper Ser.: Vol. 116). 1994. 15.00 (*1-55775-451-9*) Intl Monetary.

— Improving the International Monetary System. (Occasional Paper Ser.: No. 116). 55p. 1995. pap. 15.00 (*1-55775-444-6*) Intl Monetary.

Clark, Peter, jt. auth. see Gervae, Nik.

Clark, Peter, jt. auth. see Stephenson, Graham.

Clark, Peter, jt. ed. see Stephenson, Graham.

Clark, Peter, tr. see Idilbi, Ulfat.

Clark, Peter, tr. see Murr, Muhammed A.

Clark, Peter A. Anglo-American Innovation. (Studies in Organization: No. 9). 404p. (C). 1987. lib. bdg. 82.95 (*3-11-010572-1*) De Gruyter.

***Clark, Peter A.** Organisations in Action: Competition Between Contexts LC 99-17479. 1999. pap. write for info. (*0-415-18231-X*) Routledge.

— Organisations in Action: Competition Between Contexts. LC 99-17479. 256p. (C). 1999. text. write for info. (*0-415-18230-1*) Routledge.

Clark, Peter J. Beyond the Deal: Optimizing Merger & Acquisition Value. 326p. 1991. 39.95 (*0-88730-440-0*, HarpBusn) HarpInfo.

***Clark, Peter J. & Neill, Stephen.** Net Value: Valuing Dot-Com Companies - Uncovering the Reality Behind the Hype. 2000. 27.95 (*0-8144-0604-1*) AMACOM.

— The Value Mandate: Maximizing Shareholder Value Across the Corporation. 2000. 40.00 (*0-8144-0605-X*) AMACOM.

Clark, Peter U., ed. see Keigwin, Lloyd D.

Clark, Philip. American Civil War: Wars That Changed the World. (Illus.). 31p. (J). (gr. 5-8). 1998. text 9.00 (*0-7881-5896-1*) DIANE Pub.

— Jane's Space Directory, 1997-98: Keep Up-to-Date on the Latest Space Programs. 13th ed. 1997. 320.00 (*0-7106-1560-4*) Janes Info Group.

Clark, Philip J., jt. auth. see Dice, Lee R.

Clark, Philip M. Microcomputer Spreadsheet Models for Libraries: Preparing Documents, Budgets, & Statistical Reports. LC 84-20470. 132p. 1985. reprint ed. pap. 41.00 (*0-7837-9678-1*, 206040600005) Bks Demand.

Clark, Phillip G., jt. auth. see Drinka, Theresa J. K.

Clark, Phillip G., jt. ed. see Callahan, Daniel.

Clark, Priscilla P. Literary France: The Making of a Culture. 289p. 1987. 50.00 (*0-520-05703-1*, Pub. by U CA Pr) Cal Prin Full Svc.

— Literary France: The Making of a Culture. (Illus.). 289p. 1991. pap. 15.95 (*0-520-07397-5*, Pub. by U CA Pr) Cal Prin Full Svc.

***Clark Publishing Staff.** Kentucky Directory Gold Book. 1999. pap. 60.00 (*1-883589-43-6*) Clark Pub KY.

Clark Publishing Staff. Kentucky Directory Gold Book, 1998 Ed. 1998. pap. text 50.00 (*1-883589-38-X*) Clark Pub KY.

Clark, R. A Procedure for Commissioning Variable Air Volume Systems. (C). 1988. 100.00 (*0-86022-222-5*, Pub. by Build Servs Info Assn) St Mut.

— The Security, Audit & Control of Databases. Holloway, S. R. & List, W., eds. 170p. 1991. text 72.95 (*1-85628-168-X*, Pub. by Avebry) Ashgate Pub Co.

Clark, R., ed. Dumas Fils: La Dame Aux Camelias. (Bristol French Texts Ser.). (FRE.). 215p. 1994. pap. 18.95 (*1-85399-401-4*, Pub. by Brist Class Pr) Focus Pub-R Pullins.

Clark, R. A. & Henson, P. M., eds. The Molecular & Cellular Biology of Wound Repair. LC 87-37683. (Illus.). 620p. 1988. 125.00 (*0-306-42716-8*, Plenum Trade) Perseus Pubng.

Clark, R. B. The Waters Around the British Isles: Their Conflicting Uses. (Illus.). 386p. 1987. 90.00 (*0-19-828492-6*) OUP.

Clark, R. B., jt. ed. see Heywood, Vernon H.

Clark, R. Bradbury, ed. Ballantine & Sterling, California Corporation Laws. text 1350.00 (*0-8205-2014-4*) Bender.

Clark, R. Bradbury, ed. Ballantine & Sterling California Corporation Laws, 7 vols., Set. 4th ed. 1995. spiral bd. 1160.00 (*0-8205-1050-5*, MICHIE) LEXIS Pub.

Clark, R. J. & Hester, R. E. Spectroscopy for Surface Science. LC 97-29175. (Advances in Spectroscopy Ser.). 430p. 1998. 495.00 (*0-471-97423-4*) Wiley.

Clark, R. J. & Hester, R. E., eds. Biomedical Applications of Spectroscopy. LC 95-42360. (Advances in Spectroscopy Ser.: Vol. 25). 402p. 1996. 368.00 (*0-471-95918-9*) Wiley.

— Spectroscopy of Matrix Isolated Species, Vol. 17. LC 88-38320. (Advances in Spectroscopy Ser.). 530p. 1989. 900.00 (*0-471-92170-X*) Wiley.

Clark, R. J. & Long, D. A., eds. Eleventh International Conference on Raman Spectroscopy: Proceedings of the Eleventh International Conference on Raman Spectroscopy, 5-9 September 1988, London, England. LC 88-20873. (Illus.). 1088p. 1988. pap. 200.00 (*0-608-05257-4*, 206579500001) Bks Demand.

Clark, R. J., jt. auth. see Quigley, Hugh.

Clark, R. L. & Rushforth, S. R. Diatom Studies of the Headwaters of Henrys Fork of the Snake River, Island Park, Idaho, U. S. A. (Bibliotheca Phycologica Ser.: No. 33). 1977. pap. text 50.00 (*3-7682-1149-5*) Lubrecht & Cramer.

Clark, R M. Dodge Viper. 2nd ed. 1998. pap. text 19.95 (*1-85520-472-X*) Brooklands Bks.

Clark, R. T. Myth & Symbol in Ancient Egypt. 1991. pap. 15.95 (*0-500-27112-7*, Pub. by Thames Hudson) Norton.

Clark, R. T., tr. see Ritter, Gerhard A.

Clark, Rabia L. Past Life Therapy: The State of the Art. 233p. 1995. pap. 14.95 (*0-9646141-0-3*) Rising Star.

Clark, Rae. Ben, Friends, & Heart-Tears. LC 93-74619. (Gramma Rae Story Ser.). (Illus.). 32p. (J). (ps-3). 1994. 14.00 (*0-9631252-1-4*) Desert Rose.

Clark, Ralph E. Treatise on the Law & Practice of Receivers (Clark on Receivers) 3rd ed. 2372p. 1992. reprint ed. 360.00 (*0-89941-811-2*, 307670) W S Hein.

Clark, Ralph W. Introduction to Moral Reasoning: Applying Basic Moral Principles to Selected Readings. 404p. (C). 1986. pap. text 41.00 (*0-314-93161-9*) West Pub.

— Introduction to Philosophical Thinking: Readings & Commentary. LC 86-15822. 612p. (C). 1987. text 48.00 (*0-314-29524-0*) West Pub.

Clark, Ralph W. & Lattal, Alice D. Workplace Ethics: Winning the Integrity Revolution. 176p. (Orig.). (C). 1992. pap. text 18.95 (*0-8226-3020-6*) Rowman.

Clark, Ramsey. Challenge to Genocide: Let Iraq Live. LC 98-14187. 1998. 12.95 (*0-9656916-4-0*) Intl Action Ctr.

— The Children Are Dying: The Impact of Sanctions on Iraq. LC 96-16232. 168p. 1996. 11.95 (*0-89567-127-1*) World View Forum.

Clark, Ramsey, et al. Metal of Dishonor: How Depleted Uranium Penetrates Steel, Radiates People & Contaminates the Environment. unabridged ed. LC 97-70773. (Illus.). 200p. (Orig.). 1997. pap. 12.95 (*0-9656916-0-8*) Intl Action Ctr.

— NATO in the Balkans: Voice of Opposition. LC 97-42683. (Illus.). 220p. 1998. pap. 15.95 (*0-9656916-2-4*) Intl Action Ctr.

— War Crimes: A Report on United States War Crimes Against Iraq. LC DS79.736.W37. (Illus.). 300p. (Orig.). 1992. pap. text 12.95 (*0-944624-15-4*) Maisonneuve Pr.

Clark, Randall. At a Theater or Drive-in Near You: The History, Culture, & Politics of the American Exploitation Film. rev. ed. LC 94-39322. (Studies in American Popular History & Culture). 248p. 1995. text 58.00 (*0-8153-1951-7*) Garland.

Clark, Randall, ed. American Screenwriters, Vol. 44. (Dictionary of Literary Biography Ser.: Vol. 44, Pt. 2). 350p. 1986. text 155.00 (*0-8103-1722-2*) Gale.

Clark, Randolph. Reminiscences, Biographical & Historical. LC 86-1286. 92p. 1986. reprint ed. 25.00 (*0-87565-064-3*) Tex Christian.

Clark, Randolph L. & Howe, Clifton D., eds. Cancer Patient Care at M. D. Anderson Hospital & Tumor Institute, the University of Texas. LC 76-9374. 862p. reprint ed. pap. 200.00 (*0-608-15496-2*, 202973400064) Bks Demand.

Clark, Randy. Essential Chords for Alternative Rock Guitar. 1996. pap. 5.95 (*0-8256-1492-9*, AM931293) Music Sales.

— God Can Use Little Ole Me. 1998. pap. 10.99 (*1-56043-696-4*, Revival Pr) Destiny Image.

— Lighting Fires. LC 97-20075. 1998. pap. 9.99 (*0-88419-478-7*) Creation House.

— Power/Holiness/Evangelism: Rediscovering God's Purity, Power... 1999. pap. 11.99 (*1-56043-345-0*) Destiny Image.

— Your New Beginning. 35p. 1997. 1.25 (*0-9652425-0-1*) Randy Clark.

Clark, Randy & Koehler, Stephen. The UCSD Pascal Handbook. (Software Ser.). (Illus.). 384p. 1982. 24.95 (*0-13-935536-7*); text 32.00 (*0-13-935544-8*) P-H.

***Clark, Ray.** Commercial Metal Stud Framing. LC 99-50302. (Illus.). 208p. 1999. pap. 45.00 (*1-57218-079-X*) Craftsman.

Clark, Ray & Goff, Mervyn, eds. Recent Developments in Medical & Physiological Imaging. 180p. 1986. pap. text 25.00 (*0-85066-955-3*) Taylor & Francis.

Clark, Raymond A. Utopia Falls. LC 97-90871. 219p. 1998. pap. 8.50 (*0-533-12501-4*) Vantage.

Clark, Raymond C. Language Teaching Techniques. rev. ed. LC 80-84109. (Language Resource Handbook Ser.: No. 1). (Illus.). 128p. (Orig.). 1987. pap. text 14.00 (*0-86647-023-9*) Pro Lingua.

***Clark, Raymond C.** Living in the United States: How to Feel at Home, Make Friends & Enjoy Everyday Life: A Brief Introduction to the Culture for Visitors, Students & Business Travelers. 1999. pap. 9.95 (*0-86647-114-6*) Pro Lingua.

Clark, Raymond C. Money: Exploring the Ways We Use It. (Vocabureader Workbook Ser.: No. 4). (Illus.). 96p. 1989. pap. text 12.50 (*0-86647-029-8*) Pro Lingua.

— More Index Card Games & Activities for English. (Supplementary Materials Handbook Ser.: No. 9). (Illus.). 104p. (Orig.). 1993. pap. text 12.50 (*0-86647-075-1*) Pro Lingua.

— Potluck: Exploring American Foods & Meals. rev. ed. (Vocabureader Workbook Ser.: No. 2). (Illus.). 128p. (Orig.). 1994. pap. text 10.50 (*0-86647-084-0*) Pro Lingua.

— Story Cards: Aesop's Fables. (Illus.). 32p. (Orig.). 1995. pap. text 14.50 (*0-86647-086-7*) Pro Lingua.

— Story Cards: The Tales of Nasreddin Hodja - Pairwork Conversation Activities. (Illus.). 44p. 1991. pap. text 14.50 (*0-86647-044-1*) Pro Lingua.

Clark, Raymond C., ed. Max in America Pt. 2: Communcating in the Culture. (Illus.). 128p. 1987. pap. text 2.00 (*0-86647-025-5*) Pro Lingua.

— Max in America, Posters: Communcating in the Culture. (Illus.). 26p. 1987. pap. text 12.50 (*0-86647-027-1*) Pro Lingua.

— Max in America, Teacher's Handbook: Communcating in the Culture. (Illus.). 160p. 1987. pap. text, teacher ed. 2.00 (*0-86647-026-3*) Pro Lingua.

Clark, Raymond C. & Clark, Susannah J. Wheels & Wings: Exploring the Word of Transportation & Travel. (Vocabureader Workbook Ser.: No. 6). (Illus.). 104p. (Orig.). 1992. pap. text 10.50 (*0-86647-053-0*) Pro Lingua.

Clark, Raymond C. & Duncan, Janie L. Getting a Fix on Vocabulary, Using Words in the News: The System of Affixation & Compounding in English. (Illus.). 96p. (J). 1991. 11.00 (*0-86647-038-7*) Pro Lingua.

Clark, Raymond C. & Jerald, Michael. Summer Olympic Games: Exploring International Athletic Competition. (Vocabureader Workbook Ser.: No. 5). (Illus.). 96p. 1987. pap. text 2.00 (*0-86647-021-2*) Pro Lingua.

Clark, Raymond C. & Mussman, Anna. Cue Cards: Nations of the World. (Supplementary Materials Handbook Ser.: No. 7). (Illus.). 110p. (Orig.). 1993. pap. text 14.00 (*0-86647-076-X*) Pro Lingua.

Clark, Raymond C., et al. The ESL Miscellany: A Treasury of Cultural & Linguistic Information. 2nd rev. ed. LC 81-8581. (Language Resource Handbook Ser.: No. 2). (Illus.). 304p. 1991. pap. text 23.00 (*0-86647-043-3*) Pro Lingua.

— Index Card Games for ESL. 2nd rev. ed. LC 82-9786. (Supplementary Materials Handbook Ser.: No. 1). (Illus.). 80p. (Orig.). 1992. pap. text 11.00 (*0-86647-052-2*) Pro Lingua.

Clark, Raymond C., jt. auth. see Hawkinson, Annie.

Clark, Raymond C., jt. auth. see Jerald, Michael.

Clark, Raymond C., ed. see Burrows, Arthur A.

Clark, Raymond C., ed. see Clair, Nancy.

Clark, Raymond C., ed. see Clark, Susannah J.

Clark, Raymond C., ed. see DeWitt, Lisa F.

Clark, Raymond C., ed. see Gaston, Jan.

Clark, Raymond C., ed. see Kehe, David & Kehe, Peggy D.

Clark, Raymond C., ed. see Marcus, Arlene.

Clark, Raymond C., jt. ed. see Miller, John N.

Clark, Raymond C., ed. see Nelson, Gayle & Winter, Thomas.

Clark, Raymond C., ed. see Rein, David.

Clark, Rebecca. The Rainbow Connection. LC 82-84590. 260p. 1983. 3.48 (*0-87159-136-7*) Unity Bks.

Clark, Rebecca & Duncan, King. Minute Motivator. (Orig.). 1996. pap. write for info. (*0-936497-19-X*) Seven Worlds.

Clark, Reginald M. Family Life & School Achievement: Why Poor Black Children Succeed or Fail. LC 83-3481. (Illus.). 264p. (C). 1984. pap. text 9.95 (*0-226-10770-1*) U Ch Pr.

Clark, Richard & Pinchuck, Tony. Medicine for Beginners. 1984. 4.95 (*0-86316-006-9*); pap. 4.95 (*0-86316-007-7*) Writers & Readers.

Clark, Richard A., ed. The Molecular & Cellular Biology of Wound Repair. 2nd ed. (Illus.). 600p. (C). 1996. text 135.00 (*0-306-45159-X*, Kluwer Plenum) Kluwer Academic.

Clark, Richard B., ed. Air Power & Desert Storm. (Illus.). 92p. (Orig.). (C). 1993. pap. text 30.00 (*1-56806-446-2*) DIANE Pub.

Clark, Richard C. Technological Terrorism. 1980. 10.00 (*0-8159-6915-5*) Devin.

Clark, Richard E. Never Fear the IRS Again: A Defensive Handbook for Dealing with the IRS. 272p. 1997. pap. 29.95 (*0-9666428-0-5*) T Jefferson Pr.

Clark, Richard G., jt. auth. see Chapel, Hal J.

Clark, Richard K., et al. Wildlife Restraint Series. 250p. (C). 1992. student ed. 74.00 (*0-9634984-0-1*); lib. bdg. 74.00 (*0-9634984-1-X*) Int Wildlife.

Clark, Richard W. Creating Professional Development Schools: Attiring the Emperor. LC 98-58076. 294p. 1999. pap. 26.95 (*0-7879-4562-5*) Jossey-Bass.

— Professional Development Schools Policy & Financing: A Guide for Policymakers. 1997. pap. 7.00 (*0-89333-152-X*) AACTE.

— What School Leaders Can Do to Help Change Teacher Education. 1997. pap. 5.00 (*0-89333-072-8*) AACTE.

***Clark, Rick.** Pressure-Point Fighting: A Guide to the Secret Heart of Asian Martial Arts. (Illus.). 196p. 2000. pap. 19.95 (*0-8048-3217-X*) Tuttle Pubng.

Clark, Ricky. Quilted Gardens: Floral Quilts of the Nineteenth Century. LC 94-2444. (Illus.). 128p. (Orig.). 1994. pap. 19.95 (*1-55853-272-2*) Rutledge Hill Pr.

Clark, Robert. Corporate Law. 880p. 1986. 43.00 (*0-316-14494-0*, Aspen Law & Bus) Aspen Pub.

— In the Deep Mid Winter. 288p. 1998. pap. 12.00 (*0-312-18114-0*) St Martin.

— In the Deep Midwinter. 1997. 23.00 (*0-614-19882-8*, Picador USA) St Martin.

— Jiu Jitsu: Black Belt Syllabus. (Illus.). 160p. pap. 24.95 (*0-7136-3831-1*, 93160) A & C Blk.

— Jiu Jitsu: Blue Belt to Brown Belt. pap. write for info. (*0-7136-3720-X*, 92917, Pub. by A & C Blk) Midpt Trade.

— Jiu Jitsu: The Official World Jiu Jitsu Federation Training Manual. (Illus.). 160p. 1991. pap. write for info. (*0-7136-3403-0*, Pub. by A & C Blk) Midpt Trade.

— Marine Pollution. 4th ed. (Illus.). 172p. 1997. pap. text 37.00 (*0-19-850069-6*) OUP.

— Marine Pollution. 4th ed. (Illus.). 172p. (C). 1997. text 75.00 (*0-19-850070-X*) OUP.

— Mr. White's Confession. LC 98-18717. 341p. 1998. text 24.00 (*0-312-19217-7*, Picador USA) St Martin.

— Mr. White's Confession. LC 98-18717. 341p. 1999. pap. 14.00 (*0-312-20426-4*, Picador USA) St Martin.

— Mr. White's Confession. large type ed. (Basic Ser.). 436p. 1999. 27.95 (*0-7862-1733-2*) Thorndike Pr.

— My Grandfather's House. 2nd ed. LC 99-27746. 288p. 1999. text 24.00 (*0-312-20932-0*, Picador USA) St Martin.

***Clark, Robert.** My Grandfather's House: A Genealogy of Doubt & Faith. 304p. 2000. pap. 13.00 (*0-312-24314-6*, Picador USA) St Martin.

Clark, Robert. River of the West: Stories from the Columbia. LC 97-20839. 416p. 1997. reprint ed. pap. 15.00 (*0-312-16987-6*, Picador USA) St Martin.

— The Role of Private Pensions in Maintaining Living Standards in Retirement. LC 77-87188. 64p. 1977. 3.50 (*0-89068-041-8*) Natl Planning.

— The Solace of Food: A Life of James Beard. LC 96-1701. 357p. 1996. pap. 16.00 (*1-883642-04-3*) Steerforth Pr.

— Traditional Kobujutsu. 1997. pap. 17.95 (*0-7136-4381-1*, Pub. by A & C Blk) Midpt Trade.

— Who Is Jesus? Leader's Guide. Chao, Lorna Y., tr. (Basic Doctrine Ser.). 1986. pap. write for info. (*0-941598-33-0*) Living Spring Pubns.

Clark, Robert, ed. Legal Skills & System. 322p. 1996. pap. 110.00 (*0-7510-0276-3*, Pub. by HLT Pubns) St Mut.

Clark, Robert & Haltzel, Michael H., eds. Spain in the Nineteen Eighties: The Democratic Transition & a New International Role. LC 87-1304. (Wilson Center Series on International Security Studies). 224p. 1987. pap. text 14.95 (*0-88730-269-6*, HarpBusn) HarpInfo.

Clark, Robert & Summers, R. Scott, eds. Strategies & Technologies for Meeting SDWA Requirements. LC 92-56465. 400p. 1992. pap. text 94.95 (*0-87762-957-9*) Technomic.

Clark, Robert, jt. auth. see Kreps, Juanita.

Clark, Robert, ed. see Cooper, James Fenimore.

Clark, Robert, tr. see Rinpoche, H. H. Chetsang.

Clark, Robert A. Africa's Emerging Securities Markets: Developments in Financial Infrastructure. LC 98-9945. 248p. 1998. 69.50 (*1-56720-149-0*, Quorum Bks) Greenwood.

— Mental Illness in Perspective. 101p. (Orig.). 1973. 3.75 (*0-910286-34-5*); pap. 2.95 (*0-910286-29-9*) Boxwood.

Clark, Robert A. Never Let 'Em Quit: How Scuba Instructors Can Make Confident, Loyal Divers Out of Any Student. 110p. 1997. pap. 29.95 (*1-880229-41-2*, 2165) Concept Sys.

Clark, Robert A. Open Water Diver: Manual para el Instructor de Buceo en Aguas Abiertas. (SPA.). 140p. 1991. pap. 110.00 (*0-943717-71-X*) Concept Sys.

— Referral Instructor Manual. 90p. 1991. pap. text 40.00 (*0-943717-96-5*) Concept Sys.

— Six Talks on Jung's Psychology. (Orig.). 1953. pap. 4.50 (*0-910286-07-8*) Boxwood.

— SSI Open Water Diver Instructor Manual. 8th rev. ed. 5p. 1998. teacher ed., ring bd. 40.00 (*1-880229-34-X*, 2101 INS) Concept Sys.

— Talking with God. 1994. 22.50 (*0-940168-29-4*) Boxwood.

Clark, Robert A., ed. The Killing of Chief Crazy Horse. LC 87-30209. (Illus.). 152p. 1988. pap. 7.95 (*0-8032-6330-9*, Bison Books) U of Nebr Pr.

Clark, Robert A., ed. see Humpal, Laurie.

Clark, Robert A., ed. see Humpal, Laurie & Clark, Gary.

Clark, Robert A., ed. see International Symposium on Hydrometeorology Staff.

Clark, Robert A., jt. ed. see Reintgen, Douglas.

Clark, Robert C. Preventing & Handling Trouble in Closely Held Corporations. 1989. write for info. (*1-55917-556-7*, 9321); audio 115.00 (*1-55917-555-9*) Natl Prac Inst.

Clark, Robert C., jt. auth. see Cervantes, Jorge.

***Clark, Robert Charles.** Reflections of South Carolina. LC 99-6608. (Illus.). 224p. 1999. 39.95 (*1-57003-344-7*) U of SC Pr.

Clark, Robert D. The Odyssey of Thomas Condon: Irish Immigrant - Frontier Missionary - Oregon Geologist. (Illus.). 592p. 1989. 29.95 (*0-87595-200-3*) Oregon Hist.

— Rain Follows the Plow: Homesteading in Haynes County, Nebraska. LC 96-3388. (Illus.). 352p. (Orig.). 1996. per. 17.95 (*0-934988-36-6*) Foun Bks.

Clark, Robert E. Teaching Preschoolers with Confidence. 26p. 1983. ring bd. 4.25 (*0-910566-37-2*) Evang Trg Assn.

Clark, Robert E. & Johnson, Lin, eds. Christian Education: Foundations for the Future. 34.99 (*0-8024-1647-0*, 111) Moody.

Clark, Robert E., et al. Childhood Education in the Church. expanded rev. ed. 628p. 1986. 29.99 (*0-8024-1251-3*, 107) Moody.

Clark, Robert E., jt. compiled by see Clark, Thomas C.

***Clark, Robert F.** Random Assignment: A Research Thriller. LC 00-191004. 223p. 2000. pap. 18.00 (*0-7388-2192-6*) Xlibris Corp.

Clark, Robert G. Kentucky Law on Computer: Education Law Edition: Version 2.0, 1994-1996. 1993. 450.00 incl. disk (*1-883589-14-2*) Clark Pub KY.

Clark, Robert G. & Stoltz, Lenny, II. Clark's Kentucky Directory: 1988. 384p. 1988. pap. 12.50 (*1-883589-00-2*) Clark Pub KY.

— Clark's Kentucky Directory: 1989. 528p. 1989. pap. 12.50 (*1-883589-01-0*) Clark Pub KY.

— Federal Grant & Loan Catalog: Version 1.1. 1993. 99.00 incl. disk (*1-883589-16-9*) Clark Pub KY.

— The Kentucky Directory Gold Book, 1990. 544p. 1990. pap. 12.50 (*1-883589-02-9*) Clark Pub KY.

— The Kentucky Directory Gold Book, 1992. 832p. 1992. pap. 20.00 (*1-883589-04-5*) Clark Pub KY.
— The Kentucky Directory Gold Book, 1993. 832p. 1993. pap. 20.00 (*1-883589-05-3*) Clark Pub KY.
— The Kentucky Directory Gold Book on Computer, 1993. 1993. 99.00 incl. disk (*1-883589-06-1*) Clark Pub KY.
— Kentucky General Assembly "Blue Book", 1990. 96p. 1990. pap. 9.00 (*1-883589-07-X*) Clark Pub KY.
— Kentucky General Assembly "Blue Book", 1991. 96p. 1991. pap. 9.00 (*1-883589-08-8*) Clark Pub KY.
— Kentucky General Assembly "Blue Book", 1992. 100p. 1992. pap. 9.00 (*1-883589-09-6*) Clark Pub KY.
— Kentucky General Assembly "Blue Book", 1993. 96p. 1993. pap. 12.00 (*1-883589-10-X*) Clark Pub KY.
— Kentucky Law on Computer: Workers' Compensation Edition Version 1.0. 1992. 495.00 incl. disk (*1-883589-11-8*) Clark Pub KY.
— Kentucky Law on Computer: Workers' Compensation Edition Version 4.0. 1993. 495.00 incl. disk (*1-883589-12-6*) Clark Pub KY.

Clark, Robert G., jt. auth. see Wilson, Leslie B.

Clark, Robert G., jt. ed. see Rattray, Charles.

Clark, Robert J. Arts & Crafts Movement in America, 1876-1916. 295p. (C). 1972. pap. text 35.00 (*0-691-00294-0*, Pub. by Princeton U Pr) Cal Prin Full Svc.

Clark, Robert J. & Cathers, David M. Gustav Stickley's Craftsman Farms: A Pictorial History. LC 98-61873. (Illus.). 112p. 1999. pap. 12.50 (*0-940326-22-1*) Turn of Cent.

Clark, Robert L. Cost Effective Pension Planning. (Studies in Productivity: Highlights of the Literature Ser.: Vol. 20). 1982. pap. 55.00 (*0-89361-030-5*) Work in Amer.
— Retirement Systems in Japan. (Pension Research Council Publications). 120p. (C). 1991. text 32.50 (*0-256-09141-2*) U of Pa Pr.

Clark, Robert L., et al. Adaptive Structures: Dynamics & Control. LC 97-20308. 488p. 1998. 125.00 incl. disk (*0-471-12262-9*) Wiley.
— Inflation & the Economic Well-Being of the Elderly. LC 84-7863. 157p. reprint ed. pap. 48.70 (*0-7837-2195-1*, 204253300004) Bks Demand.

Clark, Robert L., Jr., jt. auth. see Cranfill, Thomas M.

Clark, Robert L., jt. tr. see Sheingorn, Pamela.

Clark, Robert M. Canadian Issues: Essays in Honour of Henry F. Angus. LC 62-53358. 393p. reprint ed. pap. 121.90 (*0-8357-6358-7*, 203571200096) Bks Demand.
— Intelligence Analysis: Estimation & Prediction. LC 96-162967. 368p. (Orig.). 1996. pap. 12.00 (*1-56167-307-2*) Am Literary Pr.

Clark, Robert M. & Adams, Jeffrey Q. Drinking Water & Groundwater Remediation Cost Evaluation: Granular Activated Carbon. 40p. 1991. lib. bdg. 124.95 incl. 5.25 hd (*0-87371-353-2*, L353) Lewis Pubs.
— EPA's Drinking Water-Ground Water Remediation Cost Evaluation: Air Stripping. 25p. 1991. ring bd. 119.00 (*0-87371-352-4*, L352) Lewis Pubs.

Clark, Robert M. & Clark, Daniel A., eds. Drinking Water Quality Management. 460p. 1994. pap. text 74.95 (*1-56676-178-6*) Technomic.

Clark, Robert M. & Grayman, W. M. Modeling Water Quality in Drinking Water Distribution Systems. LC 98-36443. 231p. 1998. write for info. (*0-89867-972-9*) Am Water Wks Assn.

Clark, Robert M. & Lykins, Benjamin W., Jr. Granular Activated Carbon: Design, Operation & Cost. (Illus.). 356p. 1989. lib. bdg. 82.00 (*0-87371-114-9*, 1114) Lewis Pubs.

Clark, Robert N. Control System Dynamics. (Illus.). 525p. (C). 1996. text 90.00 (*0-521-47239-3*) Cambridge U Pr.
— Introduction to Automatic Control Systems. (Illus.). 478p. (C). 1991. reprint ed. 97.00 (*1-878907-34-4*) TechBooks.

Clark, Robert P. The Basque Insurgents: ETA, 1952-1980. LC 83-40259. (Illus.). 352p. 1984. text 35.00 (*0-299-09650-5*) U of Wis Pr.
— The Basques: The Franco Years & Beyond. LC 79-24926. (Basque Ser.). 452p. 1980. text 35.00 (*0-87417-057-5*) U of Nev Pr.
— The Global Imperative: An Interpretive History of the Spread of Humankind. LC 96-42568. (Global History Ser.). 208p. (C). 1997. pap. text 24.00 (*0-8133-3181-1*, Pub. by Westview) HarpC.

***Clark, Robert P.** Global Life Systems: Population, Food & Disease in the Process of Globalization. LC 00-40300. 2000. pap. write for info. (*0-7425-0075-6*) Rowman.

Clark, Robert P. Negotiating with ETA: Obstacles to Peace in the Basque Country, 1975-1988. LC 90-33577. (Basque Ser.). (Illus.). 296p. 1990. text 39.95 (*0-87417-162-8*) U of Nev Pr.
— Power & Policy in the Third World. 4th ed. 224p. (C). 1990. pap. 42.00 (*0-02-322675-7*, Macmillan Coll) P-H.

Clark, Robert S. The Coven. LC 98-87846. 325p. 1998. 25.00 (*0-7388-0123-2*); pap. 15.00 (*0-7388-0124-0*) Xlibris Corp.

Clark, Robert S., jt. auth. see Clark, E. Douglas.

Clark, Robert S., jt. ed. see Glazier, Stewart E.

***Clark, Robert Swann.** Rites of Passage: The Journal of Richard Mac Cairill. LC 99-91263. 400p. 1999. 25.00 (*0-7388-0712-5*); pap. 18.00 (*0-7388-0713-3*) Xlibris Corp.

Clark, Roberta C. How to Paint Living Portraits. (Illus.). 176p. 1990. 28.99 (*0-89134-326-1*, 30230, North Lght Bks) F & W Pubns Inc.

Clark, Roberta C. Painting Vibrant Children's Portraits. (Illus.). 144p. 1997. pap. 22.99 (*0-89134-781-X*, North Lght Bks) F & W Pubns Inc.

Clark, Robin & Hester, R. E., eds. Advances in Infrared & Raman Spectroscopy, Vol. 8. LC 80-49886. 384p. reprint ed. pap. 119.10 (*0-8357-5168-6*, 205224800008) Bks Demand.

Clark, Robin A. Who's Going to Bury Me When I'm Gone?, Vol. 1. Maksen, Tammy, ed. 290p. (Orig.). 1999. pap. 9.99 (*0-9656425-9-3*) Fly Robin.

***Clark, Robin E.** Encyclopedia of Child Abuse. 2nd ed. LC 00-35384. (Library of Health & Living Ser.). (Illus.). 368p. 2000. write for info. (*0-8160-4060-5*) Facts on File.

Clark, Robin J. & Hester, R. E., eds. Advances in Infrared & Raman Spectroscopy, 4 vols., 3. LC 76-644959. (Illus.). 301p. reprint ed. pap. 93.40 (*0-8357-8784-2*, 203333100003) Bks Demand.
— Advances in Infrared & Raman Spectroscopy, 4 vols., 4. LC 76-644959. (Illus.). 369p. reprint ed. pap. 114.40 (*0-8357-8785-0*, 203333100004) Bks Demand.
— Advances in Infrared & Raman Spectroscopy, 4 vols., 5. LC 76-644959. (Illus.). 423p. reprint ed. pap. 131.20 (*0-8357-8786-9*, 203333100005) Bks Demand.
— Advances in Infrared & Raman Spectroscopy, 4 vols., Vol. 2. LC 76-644959. (Illus.). 359p. reprint ed. pap. 111.30 (*0-8357-8783-4*, 203333100002) Bks Demand.
— Advances in Infrared & Raman Spectroscopy, Vol. 12. LC 76-644959. (Wiley Heyden Publication). (Illus.). 382p. 1985. reprint ed. pap. 118.50 (*0-608-01607-1*, 203333100012) Bks Demand.

***Clark, Rod.** Redshift: Greenstreem. (Illus.). 50p. 2000. pap. 8.00 (*0-9660376-2-6*) Cambridge Bk Rev.

Clark, Rodney. The Japanese Company. 1981. pap. 26.00 (*0-300-02646-3*) Yale U Pr.

Clark, Rodney D., jt. auth. see Howley, Lara E.

Clark, Rodney S. When I Grow Up: Portraits of India's Street Children. (Illus.). 144p. 1997. pap. 27.50 (*0-9660980-0-5*) Positive Pr Intl.

Clark, Roger. Art Education: Issues in Postmodernist Pedagogy. 114p. (Orig.). 1996. pap. text 20.00 (*0-937652-94-6*, 263) Natl Art Ed.
— L' Assommoir, Zola: Critical Monographs in English. 88p. 1993. pap. 45.00 (*0-85261-268-0*, Pub. by Univ of Glasgow) St Mut.
— Sailing Basics. (Illus.). 84p. (C). 1994. pap. text 12.95 (*0-9639190-1-6*) Time Traveler.
— Somerset Anthology. (C). 1988. 37.00 (*0-900657-27-8*, Pub. by W Sessions) St Mut.
— South Dakota's Fairburn Agate. LC 98-90403. (Illus.). 80p. 1998. pap. 19.95 (*0-9664640-0-1*) Silverwind.
— Ten Minutes till Christmas. 21p. 1996. pap. 3.50 (*0-87129-706-X*, TA4) Dramatic Pub.
— Visual Astronomy of the Deep Sky. (Illus.). 376p. 1991. 39.95 (*0-933346-54-9*) Sky Pub.

Clark, Roger & Sann, Madeleine, eds. The Prosecution of International Crimes: A Critical Study of the International Tribunal for the Former Yugoslavia. 491p. 1996. text 49.95 (*1-56000-269-7*) Transaction Pubs.

Clark, Roger E. & Johnson-Swersey, Patricia. The Compleat Apple Spreadsheeter. 1986. 17.95 (*0-13-155086-1*) S&S Trade.
— The Compleat IBM Spreadsheeter. 1986. 17.95 (*0-13-155102-7*) S&S Trade.

Clark, Roger H. & Pause, Michael. Precedents in Architecture. 2nd ed. (Architecture Ser.). 274p. 1996. 54.95 (*0-471-28703-2*, VNR) Wiley.

Clark, Roger H. & Pause, Michael. Precedents in Architecture. 2nd ed. (Architecture Ser.). (Illus.). 274p. 1996. text 44.95 (*0-442-02051-1*, VNR) Wiley.

Clark, Roger R. The Musician's Survival Guide. 60p. 1993. pap. text 12.95 (*0-9639190-0-8*) Time Traveler.

Clark, Roger S. The United Nations Crime Prevention & Criminal Justice Program: Formulation of Standards & Efforts at Their Implementation. (Procedural Aspects of International Law Ser.). 352p. (C). 1994. text 47.50 (*0-8122-3269-0*) U of Pa Pr.

Clark, Roger S. & Sann, Madeleine, eds. The Case Against the Bomb: Marshall Islands, Samoa, & Solomen Islands Before the International Court of Justice in Advisory Proceedings on the Legality of the Threat or Use of Nuclear Weapons. LC 96-71727. vi, 354p. (Orig.). 1996. pap. 20.00 (*0-9655578-0-4*) Rutgers Schl.

Clark, Rolf. System Dynamics & Modeling. (Topics in Operations Research Ser.). iii, 163p. 1988. pap. 15.00 (*1-877640-08-5*) INFORMS.

Clark, Rolf H., jt. auth. see Binkin, Martin.

Clark, Romy & Ivanic, Roz. Politics of Writing. LC 97-213182. 272p. (C). 1997. pap. 24.99 (*0-415-13483-8*) Routledge.
— Politics of Writing. LC 97-213182. 272p. (C). 1997. 75.00 (*0-415-13482-X*) Routledge.

Clark, Ron. Color Computer Graphics. (Illus.). 128p. 1983. 9.95 (*0-86668-012-8*) ARCsoft.
— The Color Computer Songbook. (Illus.). 96p. 1983. 7.95 (*0-86668-011-X*) ARCsoft.
— Fifty-Five Color Computer Programs for the Home, School & Office. 128p. (Orig.). 1982. pap. 9.95 (*0-86668-005-5*) ARCsoft.
— Fifty-Five More Color Computer Programs for the Home, School & Office. (Illus.). 112p. (Orig.). 1982. pap. 9.95 (*0-86668-008-X*) ARCsoft.
— One Hundred One Color Computer Programming Tips & Tricks. 128p. (Orig.). 1982. pap. 7.95 (*0-86668-007-1*) ARCsoft.
— Sailing Through the Storms of Life - Practical Steps to Overcoming Your Crisis. LC 94-77928. 96p. (Orig.). 1994. pap. 6.00 (*0-9641920-0-4*) Liv Water Pub.

Clark, Ron, ed. My Buttons Are Blue & Other Love Poems from the Digital Heart of an Electronic Computer. (Illus.). 96p. 1983. 4.95 (*0-86668-013-6*) ARCsoft.

Clark, Ron, jt. auth. see Aidells, Bruce.

Clark, Ronald H. Brough Superior: The Rools-Royce of Motorcycles. 3rd ed. 1998. 29.95 (*1-85960-438-2*, Pub. by J H Haynes & Co) Motorbooks Intl.

Clark, Ronald W. Einstein: The Life & Times. 880p. 1994. pap. 15.00 (*0-380-72148-1*, Avon Bks) Morrow Avon.

***Clark, Ronald W.** Einstein: The Life & Times. (Illus.). 878p. 1999. mass mkt. 7.99 (*0-380-01159-X*, Avon Bks) Morrow Avon.

Clark, Ronald W. The Survival of Charles Darwin: A Biography of a Man & an Idea. 1986. mass mkt. 5.95 (*0-380-69991-5*, Avon Bks) Morrow Avon.

Clark, Rosalind. The Great Queens: Irish Goddesses from the Morrigan to Cathleen ni Houlihan. (Irish Literary Studies: No. 34). 266p. (C). 1992. 69.00 (*0-389-20928-7*) B&N Imports.

Clark, Rosalind, jt. auth. see Friedman, Donna H.

Clark, RoseMarie. There Is a Future in the Past. 155p. (YA). 1996. 20.00 (*0-9655146-0-9*) R M Clark.

***Clark, RoseMarie, et al.** The School - Savvy Parent: 365 Insider Tips to Help You Help Your Child. LC 99-29793. (Illus.). 208p. (J). 1999. pap. 12.95 (*1-57542-972-4*) Free Spirit Pub.

***Clark, Rosemary.** Sacred Tradition in Ancient Egypt: The Esoteric Wisdom. 2000. pap. 24.95 (*1-56718-129-5*) Llewellyn Pubns.

Clark, Rosie H. Let's Go Let's Go: Biography of Lorrin "Whitey" Harrison, Californias Legendary Surf Pioneer. (Illus.). 176p. 1997. 35.00 (*0-9660153-1-2*); pap. 20.00 (*0-9660153-2-0*) R H Clark.

Clark, Ross. Cambridgeshire. (Pimlico County History Guides Ser.). (Illus.). 240p. 1997. pap. 19.95 (*0-7126-7467-5*, Pub. by Pimlico) Trafalgar.
— Mastering the Marketplace, 2 vols. Incl. Taking Your Practice to the Top. LC 96-60136. 358p. 1996. pap. Not sold separately (*0-935078-57-6*); The Workbook. LC 96-60136. (Illus.). 158p. 1996. pap. Not sold separately (*0-935078-58-4*); Set pap. 89.95 (*0-935078-65-7*) Veterinary Med.

Clark, Ross D. Medical Genetic & Behavioral Aspects of Purebred Cats. 253p. 1992. 64.95 (*0-9634124-0-X*) Cortlandt Grp.

Clark, Ross D. & Stainer, Joan R. Medical & Genetic Aspects of Purebred Dogs II. 2nd ed. LC 94-1762. 687p. (C). 1994. 103.50 (*0-9641609-0-0*) Cortlandt Grp.

Clark, Ross D. & Stainer, Joan R., eds. Medical & Genetic Aspects of Purebred Dogs. LC 83-80248. (Illus.). 584p. 29.50 (*0-935078-24-X*) Veterinary Med.

Clark, Roy. My Life-In Spite of Myself. (Illus.). (J). 1995. mass mkt. 6.99 (*0-671-52686-3*) PB.

Clark, Roy & Eliot, Marc. My Life - In Spite of Myself! 1994. 22.00 (*0-671-86434-3*) S&S Trade.

Clark, Roy P. Free to Write: A Journalist Teaches Young Writers. LC 95-15792. 304p. (Orig.). 1995. pap. 21.00 (*0-435-08125-X*) Heinemann.

Clark, Rufus W. African Slave Trade. LC 70-133151. (Black Heritage Library Collection). 1977. 21.95 (*0-8369-8706-3*) Ayer.

Clark-Rugley, Vera D. From Dogs to Riches: Step-by-Step Guide to Start & Operate Your Own Mobile Cart Vending Business - Includes Merchandise & Food Carts. LC 93-92647. (Illus.). 250p. (Orig.). 1995. pap. 39.95 (*0-9636175-0-8*) MCC Pub.

***Clark, Rupert.** With Alex at War: Burma, North Africa, Sicily, Italy: 1941 - 1945. (Illus.). 2000. 36.95 (*0-85052-717-1*, Pub. by Leo Cooper) Combined Pub.

Clark, Ruth A. Studying Interpersonal Communication. (Interpersonal CommTexts Ser.: Vol. 2). 144p. 1991. 44.00 (*0-8039-3305-3*); pap. 19.95 (*0-8039-3306-1*) Sage.

Clark, Ruth C. Developing Technical Training: A Structured Approach for the Development of Classroom & Computer-Based Instructional Materials. (Illus.). 263p. (C). 1989. 37.95 (*0-201-14967-2*) Addison-Wesley.
— Developing Technical Training: A Structured Approach for the Development of Classroom & Computer-Based Instructional Materials. LC 88-34964. (Training & Development Ser.). (Illus.). 272p. (C). 1994. reprint ed. pap. text 31.95 (*0-9641045-0-4*) Buzzards Bay.

Clark, S. King Blood. 1997. mass mkt. 11.95 (*0-340-66062-7*, Pub. by Hodder & Stought Ltd) Trafalgar.
— Life on Other Worlds & How to Find It. LC 99-58201. (Series in Astronomy & Space Science). 300p. 2000. pap. 32.95 (*1-85233-097-X*, Pub. by Spr-Verlag) Spr-Verlag.
— Nailed by the Heart. 1995. mass mkt. 13.95 (*0-340-62573-2*, Pub. by Hodder & Stought Ltd) Trafalgar.
— Wasps. LC 99-219340. 1998. pap. text 11.95 (*0-88922-398-X*) Talonbks.

Clark, S., et al. How to Be Ecumenical Today: Cooperative & Convergent Ecumenism. (Illus.). 100p. (Orig.). 1996. pap. text 5.95 (*0-9636937-5-1*) Tabor Hse.

***Clark, S H.** Travel Writing & Empire: Postcolonial Theory in Transit. LC 99-24811. 1999. text 65.00 (*1-85649-627-9*) St Martin.

Clark, S. H., ed. Handbook of Best Readings. LC 72-5593. (Granger Index Reprint Ser.). 1977. reprint ed. 31.95 (*0-8369-6382-2*) Ayer.

Clark, S. H. & Campbell, W. The Federal Reserve Monster. 1979. lib. bdg. 59.95 (*0-8490-2914-7*) Gordon Pr.

Clark, S. L., ed. see Hankins, Gary D., et al.

Clark, Sally. Life Without Instruction. LC 96-106350. (Illus.). 168p. 1994. pap. 13.95 (*0-88922-347-5*, Pub. by Talonbks) Genl Dist Srvs.
— Moo. LC 90-175646. 132p. 1997. pap. text 11.95 (*0-88754-476-2*) Theatre Comm.
— Saint Frances of Hollywood. 200p. 1996. pap. 11.95 (*0-88922-366-1*) Genl Dist Srvs.

Clark, Sally & Herst, Beth. Big Time Women from Way Back When: Two Plays - Jehanne of the Witches & a Woman's Comedy. LC 94-148168. 236p. 1997. pap. 14.95 (*0-88754-493-2*) Playwrights.

Clark, Sally, jt. auth. see House Beautiful Magazine Editors.

Clark, Sally N. & Clark, Donald C. Restructuring the Middle Level School: Implications for School Leaders. LC 93-26782. (SUNY Series, Middle Schools & Early Adolescents). 316p. (C). 1994. pap. text 23.95 (*0-7914-1922-3*) State U NY Pr.
— Restructuring the Middle Level School: Implications for School Leaders. LC 93-26782. (SUNY Series, Middle Schools & Early Adolescents). 316p. (C). 1994. text 65.50 (*0-7914-1921-5*) State U NY Pr.

Clark, Sam. Independent Builder: Designing & Building a House Your Own Way. LC 96-32231. (Real Goods Independent Living Ser.). (Illus.). 520p. 1996. pap. 30.00 (*0-930031-85-7*) Chelsea Green Pub.

Clark, Samuel. State & Status: The Rise of the State & Aristocratic Power. 520p. 1996. pap. 29.95 (*0-7083-1299-3*, Pub. by Univ Wales Pr) Paul & Co Pubs.
— State & Status: The Rise of the State & Aristocratic Power in Western Europe. (Illus.). 520p. 1995. pap. 22.95 (*0-7735-1249-7*, Pub. by McG-Queens Univ Pr) CUP Services.
— State & Status: The Rise of the State & Aristocratic Power in Western Europe. (Illus.). 520p. 1995. 65.00 (*0-7735-1226-8*, Pub. by McG-Queens Univ Pr) CUP Services.

Clark, Samuel & Donnelly, James S., Jr., eds. Irish Peasants: Violence & Political Unrest, 1780-1914. LC 83-1289. 469p. 1983. reprint ed. pap. 145.40 (*0-608-06998-1*, 206720600009) Bks Demand.

Clark, Samuel, ed. see Love, John.

Clark, Samuel D. Movements of Political Protest in Canada, 1640-1840. LC 60-29. (Social Credit in Alberta Ser.: 9). 528p. reprint ed. pap. 163.70 (*0-608-13755-3*, 202651900050) Bks Demand.
— The Social Development of Canada. LC 75-41060. reprint ed. 49.50 (*0-404-14655-4*) AMS Pr.
— The Suburban Society. LC 66-1140. 243p. reprint ed. pap. 75.40 (*0-608-30203-1*, 201919300011) Bks Demand.

Clark, Sandie West. Bulletin Boards Made Easy. (Illus.). 1997. pap. 18.95 (*0-9660179-0-0*) Clark Studios.

Clark, Sandra. A Dictionary of Who, What & Where in Shakespeare. LC 97-21267. (Illus.). 304p. 1997. pap. 12.95 (*0-8442-5757-5*, 57575) NTC Contemp Pub Co.
— Elizabethan Pamphleteers: Popular Moralistic Pamphlets, 1580-1640. LC 81-72064. (Illus.). 320p. 1983. 37.50 (*0-8386-3173-8*) Fairleigh Dickinson.
— NTC's Dictionary of Shakespeare: A Comprehensive Guide to Shakespeare's Plays, Characters, & Contemporaries. (Illus.). 304p. 1994. 27.95 (*0-8442-5755-9*, 57559, Natl Textbk Co) NTC Contemp Pub Co.
— NTC's Dictionary of Shakespeare: A Comprehensive Guide to Shakespeare's Plays, Characters, & Contemporaries. (Illus.). 304p. 1996. pap. 12.95 (*0-8442-5756-7*, 57567, Natl Textbk Co) NTC Contemp Pub Co.

***Clark, Sandra.** Shakespeare Dictionary. 240p. 2000. pap. 14.95 (*0-14-051421-X*) Viking Penguin.

Clark, Sandra. Too Dangerous to Love. large type ed. 306p. 1993. 27.99 (*0-7505-0477-3*) Ulverscroft.

Clark, Sandra, ed. Shakespeare Made Fit: Restoration Adaptations of Shakespeare. (Everyman Paperback Classics). 320p. 1997. pap. 8.50 (*0-460-87746-1*, Everyman's Classic Lib) Tuttle Pubng.

Clark, Sandra R., photos by. Elysium - A Gathering of Souls: New Orleans Cemeteries. LC 97-16235. (Illus.). 144p. 1997. 39.95 (*0-8071-2228-9*) La State U Pr.

Clark, Sandy, et al. The Mac Demystified: The Uncompromised Desktop Reference. LC 98-216405. xv, 736p. 1998. write for info. (*1-56784-425-1*) Newbridge Educ.

Clark, Sara. The Capitols of Texas: A Visual History. (Illus.). 130p. 1975. 22.50 (*0-88426-046-1*) Encino Pr.

Clark, Sarah. Mealworms & Silkworms. (Thematic Units Ser.). 80p. (J). (gr. 1-3). 1997. pap. 9.95 (*1-57690-371-0*) Tchr Create Mat.
— World War I. (Thematic Unit Ser.). (Illus.). 80p. 1997. pap., teacher ed. 9.95 (*1-55734-598-8*) Tchr Create Mat.

***Clark, Sarah Kartchner.** How to Improve Your Vocabulary. Buehler, Stephanie J., ed. 48p. (YA). (gr. 6-8). 1999. pap., teacher ed. 7.95 (*1-57690-489-X*, TCM2489) Tchr Create Mat.

Clark, Sarah Kartchner, jt. auth. see Teacher Created Materials Staff.

Clark, Scott. Complete Guide to Norton Utilities. 1997. 29.99 (*0-672-31212-3*) Macmillan.
— Japan, a View from the Bath. LC 94-10877. (Illus.). (C). 1994. pap. text 18.00 (*0-8248-1657-9*) UH Pr.

Clark, Sebia, ed. Compensation 99: An Annual Report on Local Government Executive Salaries & Fringe Benefits. 1999. per. 180.00 (*0-87326-980-2*) Intl City-Cnty Mgt.

Clark, Sedgwick. Musical America 1999: International Directory of the Performing Arts. 832p. 1998. pap. 105.00 (*1-891131-01-X*) Primedia Directories.

***Clark, Sedgwick, ed.** Musical America 2000: International Directory of the Performing Arts. (Illus.). 840p. 1999. pap. 105.00 (*1-891131-05-2*) Primedia Directories.

Clark, Shannon, ed. see Graham, Mary & McGee, Michelle.

Clark, Sharon. Not Our Baby, Vol. 1. (Illus.). 149p. 1984. 17.95 (*0-920490-43-3*) Temeron Bks.

Clark, Sharon L., jt. auth. see Schurman, Nona.

***Clark, Shawn M.** The Co-Marketing Solution. LC 99-38467. (Illus.). 224p. 2000. 39.95 (*0-658-00006-3*, NTC Business Bks) NTC Contemp Pub Co.

Clark-Shedla, Sarah & Grandinetti, Debra. California. (Places & History Ser.). (Illus.). 136p. 1997. 24.95 (*1-55670-541-7*) Stewart Tabori & Chang.

Clark, Sheila. After Suicide: Help for the Bereaved. 1996. pap. text 11.95 (*0-85572-262-2*, Pub. by Hill Content Pubng) Seven Hills Bk.

C

Clark, Shelby. The Baby Care Handbook: A Practical Guide to Infant Care from Birth to 12 Months. (Illus.). 112p. (Orig.). 1994. pap. 10.00 (*0-9641324-0-0*) New Shoes.

Clark, Shelley, jt. auth. see Kadish, Ferne.

***Clark, Sheree & Lennert, Kristen.** Get Noticed! Self Promotion for Creative Professionals. LC 99-42463. (Illus.). 144p. 2000. pap. 29.99 (*0-89134-985-5*, 31499, North Lght Bks) F & W Pubns Inc.

Clark, Sheree & Lyons, Wendy. Creative Direct Mail Design: The Guide & Showcase. (Illus.). 160p. 1998. pap. text 22.99 (*1-56496-436-1*) Rockport Pubs.

— Great Design Using Non-Traditional Materials. LC 95-44960. (Illus.). 144p. 1996. 29.99 (*0-89134-656-2*, North Lght Bks) F & W Pubns Inc.

Clark, Sheree, jt. auth. see Lyon, Wendy.

Clark, Shirley A. The Best of Midwest Cooking. abr. ed. (Illus.). viii, 406p. 1998. pap. 14.95 (*0-9665490-0-7*) Clark Ent.

Clark, Shirley M. & Lewis, Darrell R., eds. Faculty Vitality & Institutional Productivity: Critical Perspectives for Higher Education. LC 84-17058. (Illus.). 303p. 1985. reprint ed. pap. 94.00 (*0-7837-8945-9*, 204965600002) Bks Demand.

Clark, Silvana. 101 Tips for Child Development Training: 101 Quick Tips for Managing a Preschool or Daycare. Bittinger, Gayle et al, eds. (101 Tips for Directors Ser.). (Illus.). 24p. (Orig.). 1996. pap. text 3.95 (*1-57029-078-4*, WPH 4006) Totline Pubns.

— 101 Tips for Resources for You & Your Center: 101 Quick Tips for Managing a Preschool or Daycare. Bittinger, Gayle et al, eds. (101 Tips for Directors Ser.). (Illus.). 24p. (Orig.). 1996. pap. text 3.95 (*1-57029-079-2*, WPH 4005) Totline Pubns.

— 101 Tips for Health & Safety: 101 Quick Tips for Managing a Preschool or Daycare. Bittinger, Gayle et al, eds. (101 Tips for Directors Ser.). (Illus.). 24p. (Orig.). 1996. pap. text 3.95 (*1-57029-076-8*, WPH 4003) Totline Pubns.

— 101 Tips for Marketing Your Center: 101 Quick Tips for Managing a Preschool or Daycare. Bittinger, Gayle et al, eds. (101 Tips for Directors Ser.). (Illus.). 24p. (Orig.). 1996. pap. text 3.95 (*1-57029-080-6*, WPH 4004) Totline Pubns.

— 101 Tips for Parent Communication: 101 Quick Tips for Managing a Preschool or Daycare. Bittinger, Gayle et al, eds. (101 Tips for Directors Ser.). (Illus.). 24p. (Orig.). 1996. pap. text 3.95 (*1-57029-077-6*, WPH 4002) Totline Pubns.

— 101 Tips for Staff & Parent Self-Esteem: 101 Quick Tips for Managing a Preschool or Daycare. Bittinger, Gayle et al, eds. (101 Tips for Directors Ser.). (Illus.). 24p. (Orig.). 1996. pap. text 3.95 (*1-57029-075-X*, WPH 4001) Totline Pubns.

***Clark, Silvana.** Parent-Tested Ways to Grow Your Child's Confidence. LC 00-24913. 160p. 2000. pap. write for info. (*0-88166-369-7*) Meadowbrook.

— Parent-Tested Ways to Grow Your Child's Confidence. 160p. 2000. per. 8.00 (*0-671-31823-3*) S&S Trade.

Clark, Silvana. Taming the Marketing Jungle: Marketing When Your Creativity Is High, & Your Budget Is Low. LC 94-78210. 112p. (Orig.). 1994. pap. 6.95 (*1-883697-78-6*) Hara Pub.

— Terrific Tips for Directors. rev. ed. Cubley, Kathleen, ed. LC 98-60799. (Terrific Tips Ser.). (Illus.). 128p. (J). (ps up). 1998. pap. 3.95 (*1-57029-235-3*, W04019) Totline Pubns.

***Clark, Simon.** Nailed by the Heart. 400p. 2000. pap. 5.99 (*0-8439-4713-6*, Leisure Bks) Dorchester Pub Co.

Clark, Slobin, ed. The Acquisition of Romance, with Special Reference to French. (Crosslinguistic Study of Language Acquisition Ser.). 120p. 1986. pap. 17.50 (*0-89859-846-X*) L Erlbaum Assocs.

Clark Smith, Barbara, jt. auth. see Peiss, Kathy.

Clark, Sondra. Craft Fun with Sondra. (J). 1998. pap. 5.95 (*1-883697-15-8*) Hara Pub.

***Clark, Sondra.** Craft Fun with Sondra. LC 99-32463. 1999. pap. text. write for info. (*0-88166-343-3*) Meadowbrook.

— Craft Fun with Sondra. (Illus.). 128p. (J). 1999. pap. 5.95 (*0-689-83069-6*, Pub. by Meadowbrook) S&S Childrens.

— Wearable Art with Sondra: Over 50 Fun & Easy Crafts Projects to Make & Wear. 4th ed. (Illus.). 2000. pap. 12.95 (*0-7615-2540-8*) Prima Pub.

***Clark, Sonja.** Choose the Right Recipes. 2000. pap. 12.95 (*0-9701597-0-6*) S N Clark.

Clark, Stanley, Jr., tr. see Leonard, Bill J.

Clark, Stella. Rough & Smooth Collies. (Illus.). 160p. 1993. 24.95 (*0-948955-82-1*, Pub. by Ringpr Bks) Seven Hills Bk.

***Clark, Stephan H.** Travel Writing & Empire. LC 99-24811. 1999. pap. 22.50 (*1-85649-628-7*) St Martin.

Clark, Stephen. Katahdin: A Guide to Baxter State Park & Katahdin. rev. ed. LC 85-2843. (Illus.). 213p. 1988. pap. 13.95 (*0-945980-00-0*) Nrth Country Pr.

— Smallpox & the Iroquois Wars: An Ethnohistorical Study of the Influence of Disease & Demographic Change in Iroquoian Culture History, 1630-1700. (Illus.). vi, 121p. 1981. reprint ed. pap. text 14.38 (*1-55567-027-X*) Coyote Press.

Clark, Stephen B. Where Has the Prophetic Movement Gone? 56p. 1993. pap. text 2.50 (*0-9636937-1-9*) Tabor Hse.

Clark, Stephen B. & Kinzer, Mark. Celebrating the Lord's Day: Participants Version. 14p. (Orig.). 1995. 1.00 (*0-9636937-3-5*) Tabor Hse.

***Clark, Stephen C.** National Guidelines for Death Investigation. (Illus.). 48p. (C). 1999. reprint ed. pap. text 25.00 (*0-7881-7896-2*) DIANE Pub.

***Clark, Stephen J. & Isea, Antonio M.** Belated Declaration of Love to Seraphine Louis: A Bilingual, Critical Edition of Denzil Romero's Short Stories; Edited & Translated by Stephen J. Clark. 144p. 2000. 46.00 (*0-7618-1755-7*) U Pr of Amer.

Clark, Stephen John, tr. see Romero, Denzil.

Clark, Stephen L., ed. & tr. see Bach, Carl P.

Clark, Stephen P. H., jt. auth. see Clark, David.

Clark, Stephen R. Animals & Their Moral Standing. LC 96-39502. 208p. (C). 1997. pap. 22.99 (*0-415-13560-5*) Routledge.

— Civil Peace & Sacred Order: Limits & Renewals, Vol. 1. 208p. 1989. text 55.00 (*0-19-824446-0*) OUP.

— God's World & the Great Awakening: Limits & Renewals 3. 256p. 1991. text 65.00 (*0-19-824284-0*) OUP.

— How to Live Forever: Science Fiction & Philosophy. LC 95-14403. 232p. (C). (gr. 13). 1995. 80.00 (*0-415-12626-6*) Routledge.

— A Parliament of Souls: Limits & Renewals, Vol. 2. 202p. 1990. text 55.00 (*0-19-824236-0*) OUP.

— The Political Animal: Biology, Ethics, & Politics. LC 98-35441. 1999. pap. 24.99 (*0-415-18911-X*) Routledge.

— The Political Animal: Biology, Ethics & Politics. LC 98-35441. 1999. 75.00 (*0-415-18910-1*) Routledge.

Clark, Stephen R. L. God, Religion, & Reality: The Case for Christian Theism. 1999. pap. text 32.95 (*0-281-05133-X*) Society Prom Christ Know.

Clark, Sterling B. How Many Miles from St. Jo? 59p. 1989. 14.95 (*0-87770-461-9*) Ye Galleon.

Clark, Steve. Alden Aaroe: Voice of the Morning. 168p. 1994. 15.95 (*0-87517-072-2*) Dietz.

— The Aristocracy of Labor: Development of the Marxist Position. 143p. pap. 8.00 (*0-87348-637-4*) Pathfinder NY.

— Baptized in the Spirit & Spiritual Gifts: A Basic Explanation of the Key Concepts & Experiences of the Charismatic Renewal. 147p. 1967. pap. 7.99 (*0-89283-033-6*, Charis) Servant.

***Clark, Steve.** Catholics & the Eucharist: A Scriptural Introduction. LC 00-21469. 304p. 2000. pap. 11.99 (*1-56955-133-2*, Charis) Servant.

Clark, Steve. Le Deuxieme Assassinat De Maurice Bishop. (FRE.). 230p. 1988. reprint ed. pap. 13.00 (*0-87348-646-3*) Pathfinder NY.

— Grenada: Workers & Farmers Government. 36p. pap. 6.00 (*0-87348-682-X*) Pathfinder NY.

— On Set: The British Television Location Guide. (Illus.). 256p. 1999. pap. 14.95 (*1-85782-391-5*, Pub. by Blake Publng) Seven Hills Bk.

Clark, Steve. The Second Assassination of Maurice Bishop. (New International Ser.: No. 6). 272p. 1989. reprint ed. pap. 15.00 (*0-87348-641-2*) Pathfinder NY.

Clark, Steve & Worrall, David, eds. Historicizing Blake. LC 93-43706. 1995. text 55.00 (*0-312-10393-X*) St Martin.

Clark, Steve, jt. auth. see Wang, Diane.

Clark, Steve, ed. see Malcolm X.

Clark, Steve, ed. see Mandela, Nelson.

Clark, Steve H. Sordid Images: The Poetry of Masculine Desire. LC 93-43826. 296p. (C). (gr. 13). 1994. 85.00 (*0-415-06801-0*, B3940) Routledge.

Clark, Steve H. & Worrall, David, eds. Blake in the Nineties. LC 98-50735. 242p. 1999. text 49.95 (*0-312-22054-5*) St Martin.

Clark, Steven, jt. auth. see Smith, Dave.

***Clark, Steven C., ed.** Professional Medicolegal Death Investigator Series Training Module A: Interacting with Federal, State & Local Agencies. 2000. wbk. ed. 5.50 (*0-9651299-2-6*) Occupat Res.

— Professional Medicolegal Death Investigator Series Training Module B: Communicating. 2000. 9.50 (*0-9651299-3-4*) Occupat Res.

— Professional Medicolegal Death Investigator Series Training Module C: Interacting with Families. 2000. 5.50 (*0-9651299-4-2*) Occupat Res.

— Professional Medicolegal Death Investigator Series Training Module D: Investigating Deaths. 2000. 10.50 (*0-9651299-5-0*) Occupat Res.

— Professional Medicolegal Death Investigator Series Training Module E: Identifying & Preserving Evidence. 2000. 3.50 (*0-9651299-6-9*) Occupat Res.

— Professional Medicolegal Death Investigator Series Training Module F: Maintaining Ethical & Legal Responsibilities. 2000. 5.50 (*0-9651299-7-7*) Occupat Res.

— Professional Medicolegal Death Investigator Series Training Module G: Demonstrating Scientific Knowledge. (Illus.). 2000. 7.50 (*0-9651299-8-5*) Occupat Res.

— Professional Medicolegal Death Investigator Series Training Module H: Coping with Job-Related Stress. (Illus.). 2000. 1.50 (*0-9651299-9-3*) Occupat Res.

— Professional Medicolegal Death Investigator Series Training Modules. (Illus.). 2000. 49.00 (*0-9651299-1-8*) Occupat Res.

Clark, Steven L., et al. Critical Care Obstetrics. 3rd ed. LC 97-5559. (Illus.). 720p. 1997. 115.00 (*0-86542-538-8*) Blackwell Sci.

— Handbook of Critical Care Obstetrics. (Illus.). 504p. 1994. pap. 46.95 (*0-86542-351-2*) Blackwell Sci.

Clark, Stewart C. & Alberta Alcohol and Drug Abuse Commission. Medical/physiological Effects of Alcohol. LC 96-218598. ii, 47 p. 1995. write for info. (*0-7732-1543-3*) APAB.

***Clark, Stuart.** The Annales School. LC 98-44048. 1999. write for info. (*0-415-15551-7*) Routledge.

Clark, Stuart. Extrasolar Planets: The Search for New Worlds. LC 97-14893. (Wiley-Praxis Series in Astronomy & Astrophysics). 238p. 1998. 110.00 (*0-471-97633-4*) Wiley.

***Clark, Stuart.** Extrasolar Planets: The Search for New Worlds. LC 97-14893. (Wiley-Praxis Series in Astronomy & Astrophysics). 238p. 1998. pap. 54.95 (*0-471-97634-2*) Wiley.

— Languages of Witchcraft: Narrative, Ideology & Meaning in Early Modern Culture. LC 00-33302. (Illus.). 2000. pap. write for info. (*0-312-23813-4*) St Martin.

— Redshift. (Building Blocks of Modern Astronomy Ser.). (Illus.). 197p. 1997. 59.95 (*0-900458-79-8*, Pub. by Univ of Herfordshire); pap. 29.95 (*0-900458-66-6*, Pub. by Univ of Herfordshire) Bold Strummer Ltd.

Clark, Stuart. Stars & Atoms: From the Big Bang to the Solar System. LC 94-30783. (New Encyclopedia of Science Ser.). (Illus.). 160p. 1995. 39.95 (*0-19-521087-5*) OUP.

— Thinking with Demons: The Idea of Witchcraft in Early Modern Europe. LC 96-16982. (Illus.). 844p. (C). 1997. text 165.00 (*0-19-820001-3*) OUP.

— Thinking with Demons: The Idea of Witchcraft in Early Modern Europe. (Illus.). 848p. 1999. pap. 39.95 (*0-19-820808-1*) OUP.

***Clark, Stuart.** Towards the Edge of the Universe: A Review of Modern Cosmology. 2nd ed. LC 99-35673. (Springer-Praxis Series in Astronomy & Space Science). 255p. 1999. pap. 39.95 (*1-85233-098-8*, Pub. by Spr-Verlag) Spr-Verlag.

Clark, Stuart, jt. auth. see Ankarloo, Bengt.

Clark, Stuart, jt. ed. see Ankarloo, Bengt.

Clark, Sue. All about All of You: Faces, Feelings, Bodies, Clothes, 4 bks. (Illus.). 16p. (J). (ps-k). 1994. 15.45 (*0-7868-0035-6*, Pub. by Hyprn Child) Time Warner.

Clark, Sue A. The Rainbow Tree. Clark, Gary B., ed. (Illus.). 18p. (J). (gr. 4-7). 1990. write for info. (*0-318-65868-2*) Point View Pr.

— Rainbow Workshop: Building Self-Esteem Through Creative Imagination & Self-Expression! Clark, Gary B., ed. (Illus.). 125p. (Orig.). 1990. pap. write for info. (*0-318-65869-0*) Point View Pr.

Clark, Sue A., jt. auth. see McPherson, Alan.

Clark, Sunie B., ed. see Herlong, Daniel W.

Clark, Sunie B., ed. see Thomas, Paul.

Clark, Susan. The Teacher's Book of Days. LC 99-15058. 384p. 1999. 15.95 (*0-7615-1700-6*) Prima Pub.

***Clark, Susan, ed.** Raddle Moon 18. (Illus.). 192p. 1999. pap. 8.00 (*0-921586-73-6*, Pub. by New Star Bks) Genl Dist Srvs.

***Clark, Susan, et al, eds.** Raddle Moon 17: 22 Vancouver Poets. (Illus.). 192p. 1998. pap. 8.00 (*0-921331-27-4*, Pub. by Tsunami Edits) Barnholden.

Clark, Susan & Laird, Robin F. Britain's Security Policy: The Modern Soviet View. (C). 1990. 50.00 (*0-907967-89-2*, Pub. by Inst Euro Def & Strat) St Mut.

Clark, Susan, jt. auth. see Clark, Jonathan.

Clark, Susan E., tr. see Tusquets, Esther.

Clark, Susan G. The Terrible Tooths: Survival Cookbook. 150p. (J). 1991. 12.95 (*0-9631133-0-5*) La Petite.

Clark, Susan L., jt. auth. see Laird, Robbin F.

Clark, Susan P., jt. auth. see Shafer, Jean.

Clark, Susannah, jt. ed. see Miller, John.

Clark, Susannah J. Story Cards: North American Indian Tales. Clark, Raymond C., ed. (Illus.). 32p. (Orig.). 1995. pap. text 14.50 (*0-86647-083-2*) Pro Lingua.

Clark, Susannah J., jt. auth. see Clark, Raymond C.

***Clark, Susanne, et al.** VB Script Programmer's Reference. 850p. 1999. pap. 29.99 (*1-86100-271-8*) Wrox Pr Inc.

Clark, Sushannah, jt. auth. see McCulley, Fred.

Clark, Suzanne. Blackboard Blackmail. 242p. (Orig.). 1988. pap. 10.95 (*1-877818-00-3*) Footstool Pubns.

***Clark, Suzanne.** Cold Warriors. LC 99-39120. 272p. 2000. 34.95 (*0-8093-2302-8*) S Ill U Pr.

Clark, Suzanne. Estates & Trusts: A Guide for Fiduciary Advisers. LC 96-23804. 210p. 1996. 145.00 (*0-471-13388-4*) Wiley.

— Sentimental Modernism: Women Writers & the Revolution of the Word. LC 90-47556. 240p. reprint ed. pap. 74.40 (*0-608-09330-0*, 205407600002) Bks Demand.

— Sketches of Home. 160p. 1998. 16.50 (*1-885767-35-8*, F-116) Canon Pr ID.

— Weather of the House. (Chapbook Ser.: No. 4). 36p. 1994. pap. 6.00 (*1-885912-01-3*) Sows Ear Pr.

Clark, Suzanne M. New England in U. S. Government Publications, 1789-1849: An Annotated Bibliography, 36. LC 98-10085. (Bibliographies & Indexes in American History Ser.: Vol. 36). 616p. 1998. lib. bdg. 125.00 (*0-313-28128-9*, Greenwood Pr) Greenwood.

***Clark, Suzanne U.** The Roar on the Other Side: A Guide for Student Poets. LC 00-9757. 2000. write for info. (*1-885767-66-8*) Canon Pr ID.

— What a Light Thing, This Stone. 68p. 1999. pap. 12.00 (*1-885912-23-4*) Sows Ear Pr.

Clark, Sydney P., Jr., et al, eds. Processes in Continental Lithospheric Deformation. LC 87-37344. (Geological Society of America Ser.: Vol. 218). (Illus.). 220p. 1988. reprint ed. pap. 68.20 (*0-608-07744-5*, 206783200010) Bks Demand.

Clark, Sylvia. The Kokoda Track. (Illus.). 32p. (J). 1998. pap. 10.95 (*0-86417-841-7*, Pub. by Kangaroo Pr) Seven Hills Bk.

Clark, T. Chemist's Electronic Book of Orbitals. 1998. 39.95 (*3-540-63726-5*) Spr-Verlag.

Clark, T., ed. Molecular Modeling Annual, 1998: CD-ROM & Print Archive Edition Journal of Molecular Modeling, Vol. 4, 1998. (Illus.). 435p. 1999. 280.00 incl. cd-rom (*3-540-14647-4*) Spr-Verlag.

— Molecular Modeling Annual, 1995: CD-ROM & Print Archive Edition of Journal of Molecular Modeling. 600p. 1996. 234.00 incl. cd-rom (*3-540-14524-9*) Spr-Verlag.

— Molecular Modeling Annual 1997: CD-ROM & Print Archive Edition. (Journal of Molecular Modeling Ser.). (Illus.). 490p. 1998. 189.00 incl. cd-rom (*3-540-14637-7*) Spr-Verlag.

— Molecular Modeling Annual, 1996: CD-ROM & Print Archive Edition Journal of Molecular Modeling. 160p. 1997. 192.00 incl. cd-rom (*3-540-14566-4*) Spr-Verlag.

Clark, T. D., et al, eds. Macroscopic Quantum Phenomena: Proceedings of the Workshop, Sussex, UK, August 23-24, 1990. 250p. 1990. pap. 32.00 (*981-02-0383-7*); text 101.00 (*981-02-0382-9*) World Scientific Pub.

***Clark, T. J.** The Absolute Bourgeois: Artists & Politics in France, 1848-1851. 224p. (Orig.). 1999. pap. 17.95 (*0-520-21744-6*, Pub. by U CA Pr) Cal Prin Full Svc.

Clark, T. J. Farewell to an Idea: Episodes from a History of Modernism. LC 98-49433. (Illus.). 450p. 1999. 45.00 (*0-300-07532-4*) Yale U Pr.

***Clark, T. J.** Image of the People: Gustave Courbet & the 1848 Revolution. 208p. 1999. pap. 17.95 (*0-520-21745-4*, Pub. by U CA Pr) Cal Prin Full Svc.

Clark, T. J. The Painting of Modern Life: Paris in the Art of Manet & His Followers. rev. ed. LC 99-29643. (Illus.). 1999. pap. 24.95 (*0-691-00903-1*, Pub. by Princeton U Pr) Cal Prin Full Svc.

Clark, T. Mich. Image Composer Web Techniques. 1997. 39.99 (*1-56205-838-X*) New Riders Pub.

***Clark, T Michael.** Illustrator X Visual Insight. (Illus.). 320p. 2000. pap. 24.99 (*1-57610-749-3*) Coriolis Grp.

Clark, T. Michael. Paint Shop Pro Web Techniques. LC 97-6578. 350p. 1997. 44.99 (*1-56205-756-1*) New Riders Pub.

— Photoshop 5 Filters F/X & Design. LC 98-26354. 377p. 1998. pap. 49.99 (*1-57610-300-5*) Coriolis Grp.

— Sams Teach Yourself Paint Shop Pro in 24 Hours. LC 98-85493. (Teach Yourself Ser.). 1998. pap. 19.99 (*0-672-31362-6*) Sams.

***Clark, T. Michael.** Sams Teach Yourself Paint Shop Pro 6 in 24 Hours. (Teach Yourself Ser.). 375p. 1999. pap. text 19.99 (*0-672-31720-6*) Sams.

Clark, T. Michael. Sams Teach Yourself Photoshop 5.0 in 21 Days. (Teach Yourself Ser.). 1998. pap. 39.99 (*0-672-31300-6*) Sams.

— Using Web Graphics. LC 97-28575. 1997. 24.99 (*0-7897-1401-9*); pap. text 19.99 (*0-7897-1397-7*) Que.

Clark, T. S. & Corlett, E. N. The Ergonomics of Workspace & Machines: A Design Manual. 2nd ed. LC 94-44731. 1995. 89.95 (*0-7484-0316-7*) Taylor & Francis.

Clark, T. S., jt. auth. see Corlett, E. N.

Clark, T. W. Introduction to Nepali: A First-Year Language Course. 1989. 150.00 (*0-7855-0276-9*, Pub. by Ratna Pustak Bhandar) St Mut.

Clark, T. W., ed. Introduction to Nepali: A First-Year Language Course. 421p. (C). 1989. 415.00 (*0-89771-077-0*, Pub. by Ratna Pustak Bhandar) St Mut.

***Clark, Taylor & Bannon, Lois Elmer.** Handbook of Audubon Prints. 4th ed. LC 99-187264. (Illus.). 128p. 1999. 16.95 (*1-56554-428-5*) Pelican.

Clark, Taylor, jt. auth. see Bannon, Lois.

Clark, Ted. The Oppression of Youth. 1990. 12.50 (*0-8446-5169-9*) Peter Smith.

Clark, Terry & Ferguson, Lorna. City Money: Political Processes, Fiscal Strain, & Retrenchment. LC 83-7375. 384p. 1983. text 87.50 (*0-231-05688-5*) Col U Pr.

Clark, Terry & Lacey, Richard. Learning by Doing: Panasonic Partnerships & Systemic School Reform. (Illus.). 168p. 1997. per. 24.95 (*1-884015-37-9*) St Lucie Pr.

Clark, Terry, et al. Research in Urban Policy, Vol. 7. 1998. 73.25 (*0-7623-0464-2*) Jai Pr.

Clark, Terry A. Collaboration to Build Competence: The Urban Superintendents' Perspective. 65p. (Orig.). (C). 1993. pap. text 35.00 (*0-7881-0150-1*) DIANE Pub.

Clark, Terry N. New Political Culture. LC 98-159745. (Urban Policy Challenges Ser.). 1998. text 65.00 (*0-8133-2814-4*, Pub. by Westview) HarpC.

— Prophets & Patrons: The French University & the Emergence of the Social Sciences. LC 72-93947. (Illus.). 320p. 1973. 37.95 (*0-674-71580-2*) HUP.

Clark, Terry N., ed. Research in Urban Policy, Vol. 1: Coping with Urban Austerity. 393p. 1984. 73.25 (*0-89232-325-6*) Jai Pr.

— Research in Urban Policy, 2 vols. in 1, Vol. 2. 1986. 146.50 (*0-89232-729-4*) Jai Pr.

— Research in Urban Policy, Vol. 4: Politics of Policy Innovation in Chicago. 232p. 1992. 73.25 (*1-55938-057-8*) Jai Pr.

— Research in Urban Policy, Vol. 5: Local Admin. in the Policy Process: An Int. 290p. 1994. 73.25 (*1-55938-361-5*) Jai Pr.

— Research in Urban Policy, Vol. 6. 1996. 73.25 (*1-55938-896-X*) Jai Pr.

— Research in Urban Policy Vol. 2, Pt. A: Fiscal Austerity & Urban Management. 264p. 1986. 73.25 (*0-89232-534-8*) Jai Pr.

— Research in Urban Policy Vol. 2, Pt. B: Managing Cities. 280p. 1986. 73.25 (*0-89232-728-6*) Jai Pr.

— Research in Urban Policy Vol. 3: Decisions on Urban Dollars. 274p. 1989. 73.25 (*0-89232-757-X*) Jai Pr.

— Urban Innovation: Creative Strategies for Turbulent Times. LC 94-13485. (Urban Innovation Ser.: Vol. 3). 348p. 1994. 49.95 (*0-8039-3800-4*); pap. 24.95 (*0-8039-3801-2*) Sage.

Clark, Terry N., jt. auth. see Ben-David, Joseph.

Clark, Terry N., jt. auth. see Leif, Irving P.

Clark, Terry N., ed. see Aron, Raymond.

Clark, Terry N., ed. see Rempel, Michael.

***Clark, Terry Nichols.** Breakdown of Class Politics: A Debate on Post-Industrial Stratification. 2000. pap. 18.95 (*0-8018-6576-X*) Johns Hopkins.

***Clark, Terry Nichols, ed.** Research in Urban Policy Vol. 8. 1999. 73.25 (*0-7623-0499-5*) Jai Pr.

Clark, Tessa, ed. Bakelite Style. 224p. 1997. 25.98 (*0-7858-0876-0*) Bk Sales Inc.

An Asterisk (*) at the beginning of an entry indicates that the title is appearing for the first time.

Clark-Thayer, Susan, ed. NADE Self-Evaluation Guides: Models for Assessing Learning Assistance - Developmental Education Programs. LC 94-73826. (Orig.). 1995. pap. 18.95 (*0-943202-49-3*) H & H Pub.

Clark, Thekla. Children in Exile: The Story of a Cross-Cultural Family. unabridged ed. LC 98-15438. 192p. 1998. text 23.00 (*0-88001-633-7*) HarpC.

— Wystan & Chester: A Personal Memoir of W. H. Auden & Chester Kallman. LC 96-8842. 1996. write for info. (*0-231-10760-9*) Col U Pr.

— Wystan & Chester: A Personal Memoir of W. H. Auden & Chester Kallman. LC 96-8842. (Illus.). 130p. 1996. 21.00 (*0-231-10706-4*) Col U Pr.

— Wystan & Chester: A Personal Memoir of W. H. Auden & Chester Kallman. (Illus.). 130p. 1997. pap. 14.00 (*0-231-10707-2*) Col U Pr.

— Wyster & Chester: A Personal Memoir of W. H. Auden & Chester Kallman. LC 96-8842. 1996. pap. write for info. (*0-231-10761-7*) Col U Pr.

Clark, Thomas. Designing Storage Area Networks: A Practical Reference for Implementing Fibre Channel SANs. LC 99-33181. 224p. (C). 1999. pap. text 19.95 (*0-201-61584-3*) Addison-Wesley.

Clark, Thomas, jt. auth. see Pugh, Harry F.

Clark, Thomas A., III. Collection Practice. (Illus.). 61p. 1992. pap. 35.00 (*0-685-14624-3*) NJ Inst CLE.

Clark, Thomas A. Proverbs of the Meadow & the Mountain. Clark, Laurie, ed. (Illus.). 62p. 1986. pap. 10.00 (*0-87924-059-8*) Membrane Pr.

— Tormentil & Bleached Bones. 1994. pap. 10.95 (*0-7486-6168-9*, Pub. by Edinburgh U Pr) Col U Pr.

Clark, Thomas A., jt. auth. see Verduin, John R., Jr.

Clark, Thomas C. Poems for Special Days & Occasions. 168p. 1977. 24.95 (*0-8369-6138-2*) Ayer.

Clark, Thomas C., ed. Master of Men. fac. ed. LC 72-116396. (Granger Index Reprint Ser.). 1977. 18.95 (*0-8369-6137-4*) Ayer.

Clark, Thomas C. & Clark, Robert E., compiled by. Poems for the Great Days. LC 72-11861. (Granger Index Reprint Ser.). 1977. reprint ed. 24.95 (*0-8369-6401-2*) Ayer.

Clark, Thomas C. & Garrison, Winfred E., eds. One Hundred Poems of Peace: An Anthology. LC 75-160902. (Granger Index Reprint Ser.). 1977. reprint ed. 15.95 (*0-8369-6265-6*) Ayer.

Clark, Thomas C. & Gillespie, Esther A., eds. New Patriotism. LC 73-108581. (Granger Index Reprint Ser.). 1977. 15.95 (*0-8369-6109-9*) Ayer.

Clark, Thomas D. Agrarian Kentucky. LC 77-73703. (Kentucky Bicentennial Bookshelf Ser.). 147p. reprint ed. pap. 45.60 (*0-7837-5821-9*, 204548800006) Bks Demand.

— Footloose in Jacksonian America: Robert W. Scott & His Agrarian World. 250p. 1990. 10.00 (*0-916968-19-7*) Kentucky Hist.

— A History of Kentucky. rev. ed. LC 92-1403. (Illus.). 531p. (C). 1992. reprint ed. text 24.95 (*0-945084-30-7*) J Stuart Found.

— Indiana University: Midwestern Pioneer, 4 vols., Set. Incl. Vol. II. In Mid-Passage. LC 74-126207. (Illus.). 448p. 1973. 7.95 (*0-253-32995-7*); Vol. III. Years of Fulfillment. LC 74-126207. (Illus.). 704p. 1977. 7.95 (*0-253-32996-5*); Vol. IV. Historical Documents since 1816. LC 74-126207. (Illus.). 704p. 1977. 5.95 (*0-253-37501-0*); LC 74-126207. (Illus.). 50.00 (*0-253-32997-3*) Ind U Pr.

— Indiana University Vol. 1: Midwestern Pioneer: The Early Years. LC 74-126207. 391p. 1970. reprint ed. pap. 121.30 (*0-608-02385-X*, 206302700001) Bks Demand.

— The Kentucky. LC 92-7528. (Illus.). 464p. 1992. 30.00 (*0-8131-1726-7*) U Pr of Ky.

— Pills, Petticoats, & Plows: The Southern Country Store. LC 64-11333. (Illus.). 336p. 1989. pap. 13.95 (*0-8061-1093-7*) U of Okla Pr.

— Power Communication. (C). 1993. mass mkt. 26.95 (*0-538-82299-6*, EH60AA) S-W Pub.

— The Rampaging Frontier. LC 75-17477. 350p. 1976. reprint ed. lib. bdg. 65.00 (*0-8371-8313-8*, CLRF, Greenwood Pr) Greenwood.

— Simon Kenton, Kentucky Scout. 2nd ed. LC 93-20718. (Illus.). 256p. (YA). (gr. 6-12). 1993. reprint ed. 17.95 (*0-945084-38-2*) J Stuart Found.

— South & the Middle West. (BCL1 - U. S. History Ser.). 350p. 1991. reprint ed. lib. bdg. 89.00 (*0-7812-6001-9*) Rprt Serv.

— The Southern Country Editor. 1992. 16.50 (*0-8446-1115-8*) Peter Smith.

— The Southern Country Editor. Sproat, John G., ed. LC 91-10189. (Southern Classics Ser.). 382p. 1991. reprint ed. text 29.95 (*0-87249-766-6*); reprint ed. pap. text 14.95 (*0-87249-767-4*) U of SC Pr.

— Travels in the New South: A Bibliography, 2 vols. LC 62-10772. (American Exploration & Travel Ser.: No. 36). (Illus.). 284p. reprint ed. pap. 90.10 (*0-608-17351-7*, 2029819) Bks Demand.

— Travels in the New South Vol. 1: A Bibliography. LC 62-10772. (American Exploration & Travel Ser.: No. 36). (Illus.). 284p. 1962. reprint ed. pap. 88.10 (*0-608-10357-8*, 202981900001) Bks Demand.

— Travels in the New South Vol. 2: A Bibliography. LC 62-10772. (American Exploration & Travel Ser.: No. 36). (Illus.). 316p. 1962. reprint ed. pap. 98.00 (*0-608-10358-6*, 202981900002) Bks Demand.

Clark, Thomas D., ed. The Great American Frontier: A History of Western Pioneering, No. 87. LC 74-28026. 376p. 1975. pap. 8.95 (*0-672-60146-X*, AHS-87, Bobbs) Macmillan.

— Travels in the Old South Vol. 1: A Bibliography. LC 56-8016. (American Exploration & Travel Ser.: No. 19). 343p. 1956. reprint ed. pap. 106.40 (*0-608-10359-4*, 201620100001) Bks Demand.

— Travels in the Old South Vol. 2: A Bibliography. LC 56-8016. (American Exploration & Travel Ser.: No. 19). 302p. 1956. reprint ed. pap. 93.70 (*0-608-10360-8*, 201620100002) Bks Demand.

— Travels in the Old South Vol. 3: A Bibliography. LC 56-8016. (American Exploration & Travel Ser.: No. 19). 417p. 1956. reprint ed. pap. 129.30 (*0-608-10361-6*, 201620100003) Bks Demand.

— The Voice of the Frontier: John Bradford's Notes on Kentucky. LC 92-28767. 424p. (C). 1993. text 39.95 (*0-8131-1801-8*) U Pr of Ky.

Clark, Thomas D. & Guice, John D. The Old Southwest, 1795-1830: Frontiers in Conflict. LC 95-42772. (Illus.). 335p. (Orig.). (C). 1996. pap. 18.95 (*0-8061-2836-4*, 2836) U of Okla Pr.

Clark, Thomas H. Unequal Protection. Stone, Linda, ed. LC 95-96013. (Illus.). 295p. 1996. 23.00 (*0-9649521-4-9*) Delta Pub MD.

Clark, Thomas L. The Dictionary of Gambling & Gaming. LC 87-82866. xxi, 263p. 1988. 48.00 (*0-936368-06-3*) Lexik Hse.

— A Guide for the Church Usher. LC 83-26211. 128p. 1984. pap. 7.99 (*0-8054-3517-4*, 4235-17) Broadman.

— Marietta, Ohio: The Continuing Erosion of a Speech Island. (Publications of the American Dialect Society: Vol. 57). 55p. 1974. pap. text 5.85 (*0-8173-0657-9*) U of Ala Pr.

— Western Lore & Language: A Dictionary for Enthusiasts of the American West. (Illus.). 320p. (C). 1996. 24.95 (*0-87480-510-4*) U of Utah Pr.

Clark, Thomas L., jt. auth. see Taulbee, Earl S.

Clark, Thomas S. Arrays: A Worktext of Musical Patterns for Aural Development. 164p. (C). 1992. text. write for info. (*0-697-14348-1*) Brown & Benchmark.

***Clark, Tim.** Charles Tomlinson. (Writers & Their Works Ser.). 112p. 1999. pap. text 19.00 (*0-7463-0903-1*, Pub. by Northcote House) U Pr of Miss.

Clark, Tim. A Handbook of Computational Chemistry: A Practical Guide to Chemical Structure & Energy Calculations. LC 84-27055. 352p. 1985. 80.95 (*0-471-88211-9*) Wiley.

— Practical Management of Asthma. 2nd ed. 176p. (C). 1996. text. write for info. (*1-85317-199-9*, Pub. by Martin Dunitz) Mosby Inc.

***Clark, Tim, ed.** TV Cartoons. (Celebrity Ser.: No. 21). * 2000. pap. 4.99 (*0-88013-013-X*, Pub. by Starlog Grp Inc) Kable News Co Inc.

— TV Cartoons. (Starlog Celebrity Ser.: No. 19). 2000. pap. 4.99 (*0-88013-009-1*, Pub. by Starlog Grp Inc) Kable News Co Inc.

Clark, Tim & Casey, Denise, eds. Tales of the Grizzly. LC 92-81304. (Illus.). 192p. (Orig.). 1992. pap. 14.95 (*0-943972-14-0*) Homestead WY.

— Tales of the Wolf. (Illus.). 256p. (Orig.). 1995. pap. 14.95 (*0-943972-40-X*) Homestead WY.

Clark, Tim & Rees, John. Practical Management. 3rd ed. 176p. (C). 1998. text. write for info. (*1-85317-587-0*, Pub. by Martin Dunitz) Mosby Inc.

Clark, Tim, jt. auth. see McArthur, Loretta.

Clark, Tim W. Averting Extinction: Reconstructing Endangered Species Recovery. LC 96-37273. 288p. 1997. 32.00 (*0-300-06847-6*) Yale U Pr.

***Clark, Tim W.** Carnivores in Ecosystems: The Yellowstone Experience. LC 99-28229. (Illus.). 400p. 1999. 37.50 (*0-300-07816-1*) Yale U Pr.

Clark, Tim W. The Natural World of Jackson Hole: An Ecological Primer. rev. ed. Casey, Denise, ed. & illus. by. Ormsby, Lawrence, illus. 79p. 1999. pap. 16.95 (*0-931895-51-0*) Grand Teton NHA.

— Wildlife Preservation Trust Special Scientific Report, No. 3: Conservation Biology of the Black-footed Ferret. LC 89-22739. (Illus.). 192p. (Orig.). (C). 1989. pap. text 15.00 (*0-9624368-0-1*) WPTI.

Clark, Tim W., et al, eds. Endangered Species Recovery: Finding the Lessons, Improving the Process. LC 94-18097. 512p. (C). 1994. text 55.00 (*1-55963-271-2*); pap. text 30.00 (*1-55963-272-0*) Island Pr.

***Clark, Tim W., et al, eds.** Foundations of Natural Resources Policy & Management. (Illus.). 368p. 2000. 37.50 (*0-300-08356-4*); pap. 18.00 (*0-300-08144-8*) Yale U Pr.

Clark, Tim W. & Minta, Steven C. Greater Yellowstone's Future. LC 93-77118. (Illus.). 128p. (Orig.). 1994. pap. 11.95 (*0-943972-20-5*) Homestead WY.

Clark, Tim W. & Seebeck, John H. Management & Conservation of Small Populations. 316p. (Orig.). 1990. pap. text 12.00 (*0-913934-16-X*) Chicago Zoo.

Clark, Tim W. & Stromberg, Mark R. Mammals in Wyoming. Collins, Joseph T., ed. (Public Education Ser.: No. 10). (Illus.). xii, 308p. 1987. 25.00 (*0-89338-026-1*) U KS Nat Hist Mus.

— Mammals in Wyoming. Collins, Joseph T., ed. (Public Education Ser.: No. 10). (Illus.). xii, 308p. 1987. pap. 12.95 (*0-89338-025-3*) U KS Nat Hist Mus.

Clark, Timothy. Actor's Image: Printmakers of the Katsukawa School. 504p. (C). 1994. text 135.00 (*0-691-03627-6*, Pub. by Princeton U Pr) Cal Prin Full Svc.

— Embodying Revolution: The Figure of the Poet in Shelley. (Oxford English Monographs). 310p. 1989. text 75.00 (*0-19-812981-5*) OUP.

Clark, Timothy. EQ vs. IQ the Six Steps to EQ Mastery: Complete Emotional Competence Video, Audio, Book Power Pack (Album) Date not set. 95.00 incl. audio, VHS (*0-9638625-1-0*) Mind Power.

Clark, Timothy. European Human Resource Management: An Introduction to Comparative Theory & Practice. LC 96-23267. (Illus.). 320p. (C). 1997. pap. 39.95 (*0-631-19368-5*) Blackwell Pubs.

— European Human Resource Management: An Introduction to Comparative Theory & Practice. LC 96-23267. (Illus.). 320p. (C). 1997. 69.95 (*0-631-19367-7*) Blackwell Pubs.

— Managing Consultants: Consultancy as the Management of Impressions. LC 95-15675. (Managing Work & Organizations Ser.). 160p. 1995. 114.95 (*0-335-19220-3*); pap. 31.95 (*0-335-19219-X*) OpUniv Pr.

— Margery Fish's Country Gardening. 1999. 39.50 (*1-870673-31-X*) Garden Art Pr.

— Maximizing Mind Power: The Art of Managing Your Greatest Asset. 197p. 1993. pap. 15.95 (*0-9638625-0-2*) Mind Power.

— Ukiyo-E Paintings: In the British Museum. LC 92-64231. (Illus.). 256p. (Orig.). 1993. pap. 45.00 (*1-56098-243-8*) Smithsonian.

Clark, Timothy, ed. Advancement in Organizational Behaviour: Essays in Honour of Derek S. Pugh. LC 96-35392. (Illus.). 400p. 1997. pap. 36.95 (*1-85521-801-1*, Pub. by Dartmth Pub); text 87.95 (*1-85521-796-1*, Pub. by Dartmth Pub) Ashgate Pub Co.

Clark, Timothy & Hogle, Jerrold E., eds. Evaluating Shelley. 320p. 1996. 69.50 (*0-7486-0843-5*, Pub. by Edinburgh U Pr) Col U Pr.

Clark, Timothy, et al. The Actor's Image: Print Makers of the Katsukawa School. Richard, Naomi N., ed. LC 93-6382. (Illus.). 504p. 1994. 135.00 (*0-86559-097-4*) Art Inst Chi.

Clark, Timothy J. Image of the People: Gustave Courbet & the 1848 Revolution. LC 81-82045. (Illus.). 208p. 1982. reprint ed. pap. 64.50 (*0-7837-8165-2*, 204787000008) Bks Demand.

— Success Through Quality: Support Guide for the Journey to Continuous Improvement. LC 98-40612. 144p. 1998. pap. 22.00 (*0-87389-441-3*, H1006) ASQ Qual Pr.

Clark, Toby. Art & Propaganda in the Twentieth Century: The Political Image in the Age of Mass Culture. LC 97-5729. (Perspectives Ser.). (Illus.). 176p. 1997. pap. 18.95 (*0-8109-2713-6*, Pub. by Abrams) Time Warner.

Clark, Toby, jt. auth. see Clark, Todd.

Clark, Todd. Creative to the Max: Outrageous Ideas for Youth Ministry. LC 96-44109. 144p. (Orig.). 1997. pap. 8.99 (*0-89900-772-4*) College Pr Pub.

— Things They Never Taught You About Youth Ministry That You Really Need to Know. LC 95-51052. 182p. 1996. pap. 8.99 (*0-89900-754-6*) College Pr Pub.

Clark, Todd & Clark, Toby. Creative to the Max 2: Outrageous Ideas for Youth Ministry. 1999. pap. text 8.99 (*0-89900-850-X*) College Pr Pub.

Clark, Tom. Apocalyptic Talkshow. (Bloody Twin Press Ser.). (Illus.). 24p. (Orig.). 1987. pap. 22.00 (*1-886350-27-2*) Bloody Twin Pr.

— At Malibu. 1975. 7.00 (*0-686-11115-X*); pap. 3.50 (*0-686-11116-8*) Kulchur Foun.

— The Border. (Morning Coffee Chapbook Ser.). (Illus.). 17p. (Orig.). 1985. pap. 7.50 (*0-918273-06-4*) Coffee Hse.

***Clark, Tom.** Charles Olson: The Allegory of a Poet's Life. (Illus.). 352p. 2000. pap. 14.95 (*1-55643-342-5*, Pub. by North Atlantic) SPD-Small Pr Dist.

Clark, Tom. Disordered Ideas. LC 87-5211. 206p. 1987. 17.50 (*0-87685-696-2*); pap. 10.00 (*0-87685-695-4*) Black Sparrow.

— Easter Sunday. LC 87-27653. 160p. (Orig.). 1987. pap. 8.95 (*0-918273-27-7*) Coffee Hse.

***Clark, Tom.** Edward Dorn: The Last Range. (Illus.). 250p. (C). 2000. 18.95 (*1-55643-348-4*) North Atlantic.

Clark, Tom. Empire of Skin. LC 97-37463. 232p. 1997. 27.50 (*1-57423-050-6*); pap. 15.00 (*1-57423-049-2*) Black Sparrow.

— Empire of Skin. limited ed. LC 97-37463. 232p. 1997. 35.00 (*1-57423-051-4*) Black Sparrow.

— Fan Poems. (Illus.). 1976. pap. 3.00 (*0-913028-45-2*) North Atlantic.

— Fractured Karma. LC 90-30676. 168p. (Orig.). 1990. 20.00 (*0-87685-792-6*) Black Sparrow.

— Fractured Karma. LC 90-30676. (Illus.). 168p. (Orig.). 1990. pap. 12.50 (*0-87685-791-8*) Black Sparrow.

— Fractured Karma, signed ed. deluxe ed. LC 90-30676. 168p. (Orig.). 1990. 30.00 (*0-87685-793-4*) Black Sparrow.

— Golden Rule Video. (C). 1997. pap. text, student ed. write for info. (*0-201-84510-5*) Addison-Wesley.

— How I Broke in & Six Modern Masters. (Illus.). 1977. 3.00 (*0-939180-06-5*) Tombouctou.

Clark, Tom. Introductory Algebra Worktext to Accompany Videotext Interactive (VTI) Series. 1995. pap. text 40.00 (*0-201-88981-1*) Addison-Wesley.

Clark, Tom. Jack Kerouac: A Biography. 2nd ed. LC 98-165790. (Illus.). 254p. 1995. pap. 12.95 (*1-56924-850-8*) Marlowe & Co.

— Junkets on a Sad Planet: Scenes from the Life of John Keats. LC 93-43557. 190p. 1994. pap. 13.00 (*0-87685-917-1*) Black Sparrow.

— The Last Gas Station & Other Stories. LC 80-36765. 220p. (Orig.). 1980. 14.00 (*0-87685-457-9*); pap. 10.00 (*0-87685-456-0*) Black Sparrow.

— The Last Gas Station & Other Stories, signed ed. deluxe ed. LC 80-36765. 220p. (Orig.). 1980. 20.00 (*0-87685-458-7*) Black Sparrow.

— Late Returns: A Personal Memoir of Ted Berrigan. 88p. 1985. pap. 7.00 (*0-939180-38-3*) Tombouctou.

— Late Returns: A Personal Memoir of Ted Berrigan. deluxe limited ed. 88p. 1985. 35.00 (*0-939180-35-9*) Tombouctou.

— Like Real People. LC 95-38813. 240p. (Orig.). (C). 1995. 25.00 (*0-87685-985-6*); pap. 13.50 (*0-87685-984-8*) Black Sparrow.

— Like Real People, signed ed. deluxe ed. LC 95-38813. 240p. (Orig.). (C). 1995. 35.00 (*0-87685-986-4*) Black Sparrow.

— Paradise Resisted: Selected Poems 1978-1984. LC 84-5524. 220p. 1984. pap. 10.00 (*0-87685-611-3*) Black Sparrow.

— Paradise Resisted: Selected Poems 1978-1984, signed ed. deluxe ed. LC 84-5524. 220p. 1984. 25.00 (*0-87685-613-X*) Black Sparrow.

— The Poetry Beat: Reviewing the 80's. 244p. 1990. pap. 13.95 (*0-472-06428-2*, 06428) U of Mich Pr.

— Robert Creeley & the Genius of the American Common Place: Together with the Poet's Own Autobiography. LC 93-793. (Illus.). 160p. 1993. 19.95 (*0-8112-1250-5*, Pub. by New Directions) Norton.

— Sleepwalker's Fate: New & Selected Poems 1965-1991. LC 92-4317. 212p. (Orig.). 1992. 25.00 (*0-87685-870-1*) Black Sparrow.

— Sleepwalker's Fate: New & Selected Poems 1965-1991. LC 92-4317. 212p. (Orig.). 1992. pap. 12.50 (*0-87685-869-8*) Black Sparrow.

— Sleepwalker's Fate: New & Selected Poems 1965-1991. limited ed. LC 92-4317. 212p. (Orig.). 1992. 30.00 (*0-87685-871-X*) Black Sparrow.

***Clark, Tom.** The Spell: A Romance. LC 00-23695. 250p. 2000. pap. 16.00 (*1-57423-123-5*) Black Sparrow.

— The Spell: A Romance. LC 00-23695. 250p. 2000. 30.00 (*1-57423-124-3*) Black Sparrow.

— The Spell: A Romance. aut. ed. LC 00-23695. 250p. 2000. 40.00 (*1-57423-125-1*) Black Sparrow.

Clark, Tom. White Thought. LC 97-44881. (Lingo Bks.). 64p. 1997. pap. 10.00 (*1-889097-20-9*) Hard Pr MA.

— Who Is Sylvia? LC 79-19070. 1979. 29.95 (*0-912652-54-3*); pap. 9.95 (*0-912652-53-5*) Blue Wind.

— Who Is Sylvia? deluxe limited ed. LC 79-19070. 1979. 49.95 (*0-912652-55-1*) Blue Wind.

Clark, Tom & Else, David. Distance Education, Electronic Networking & School Policy. (Fastback Ser.: No. 441). 53p. 1998. pap. 3.00 (*0-87367-641-6*, FB441) Phi Delta Kappa.

Clark, Tom, jt. auth. see Leach, Terry.

Clark, Tom C., jt. auth. see United States Department of Justice Staff.

Clark Tom, Tom. Pre-Algebra Student's Solutions Manual. 54p. 1995. pap. text 27.40 incl. VHS (*0-201-88978-1*) Addison-Wesley.

Clark, Tomas & Clark, Amalia R. Amalia's Special Mexican Dishes. 6th rev. ed. (Illus.). 1994. 10.00 (*0-89741-010-6*) Gila River.

Clark, Tony. Bookbinding with Adhesives. 2nd ed. LC 93-45647. 1994. write for info. (*0-07-707985-X*) McGraw.

Clark, Tosca J., jt. auth. see Kaestner, Johanna.

Clark, Tracy, et al. Take Your Mark on Vacation, Level 4. Currie, Christine et al, eds. (Summer Workbooks Ser.). (Illus.). (J). (gr. 3-4). 1994. student ed. 6.95 (*0-9641274-0-7*) TYM Pubng.

— Take Your Mark on Vacation, Level 5. Currie, Christine et al, eds. (Summer Workbooks Ser.). (Illus.). 52p. (J). (gr. 4-5). 1994. student ed. 6.95 (*0-9641274-1-5*) TYM Pubng.

Clark, Trevor. Born to Lose. 154p. (Orig.). 1989. pap. 12.00 (*1-55022-081-0*, Pub. by ECW) Genl Dist Srvs.

— A Right Honourable Gentleman. 896p. pap. text. write for info. (*0-340-56275-7*, Pub. by E A) Routldge.

— A Right Honourable Gentleman: Abubakar from the Black Rock. 896p. 1995. text 55.00 (*0-340-56189-0*, Pub. by E A) St Martin.

Clark, Tricia, ed. see Sims, Michael.

Clark, Trina W., jt. auth. see Clark, David F.

Clark, Trinkett. The Drawings of David Smith. LC 85-80543. (Illus.). 64p. (Orig.). 1988. reprint ed. pap. 14.95 (*0-295-96531-2*) U of Wash Pr.

Clark, Trinkett, intro. Land Ho! The Mythical World of Rodney Alan Greenblat. 47p. 1992. pap. 14.00 (*0-940744-64-3*) Chrysler Museum.

Clark, Trinkett & Clark, H. Nichols. Myth, Magic & Mystery: 100 Years of American Children. (Illus.). 240p. 1996. pap. 29.95 (*1-57098-079-9*) Roberts Rinehart.

Clark, Truman R. Puerto Rico & the United States, 1917-1933. LC 74-26019. (Pitt Latin American Ser.). 254p. reprint ed. pap. 78.80 (*0-608-12633-0*, 202543300043) Bks Demand.

Clark, Tyrone L., ed. see Morgan, Mary.

Clark, V. L., et al. Techniques for Starting & Maintaining an FHA - Hero Chapter. 1988. pap. 6.00 (*0-911365-28-1*, A261-08472) Family & Consumer Sci Educ.

Clark, Velma R., jt. auth. see Bennett, Paul P.

Clark, Veve, et al, eds. Antifeminism in the Academy. LC 95-32371. 288p. (C). 1996. pap. 18.99 (*0-415-91071-4*) Routledge.

— Revising the Word & the World: Essays in Feminist Literary Criticism. LC 93-10197. 288p. 1993. pap. 14.95 (*0-226-40064-6*) U Ch Pr.

— Revising the Word & the World: Essays in Feminist Literary Criticism. LC 93-10197. 288p. 1993. lib. bdg. 35.00 (*0-226-40063-8*) U Ch Pr.

Clark, VeVe A., et al. The Legend of Maya Deren, a Documentary & Collected Works, Vol. 1, Pt. 1 Vol. 1, Pt. 1: Signatures, 1917-1942. Melton, Hollis, ed. (Illus.). 514p. 1984. 40.00 (*0-911689-16-8*); pap. 22.50 (*0-911689-15-X*) Anthology Film.

Clark, Vicky A., et al. International Encounters: The Carnegie International & Contemporary Art, 1896-1996. Freshman, Phil, ed. (Illus.). 192p. (Orig.). 1996. pap. 35.00 (*0-88039-336-X*) Mus Art Carnegie.

Clark, Vicky A., ed. see Hallowell, Bay.

Clark, Victor S. History of Manufacturers in the U. S., from 1607-1928, Vols. 2 & 3. (Illus.). 1990. 20.50 (*0-8446-1116-6*) Peter Smith.

C

— History of Manufacturers in the United States, 3 vols., Set. 1993. reprint ed. lib. bdg. 270.00 (*0-7812-5210-5*) Rprt Serv.

Clark, Victor S., et al. Puerto Rico & Its Problems. LC 74-14226. (Puerto Rican Experience Ser.). (Illus.). 748p. 1975. reprint ed. 62.95 (*0-405-06216-8*) Ayer.

Clark, Virginia. Guide to Highway 395: Los Angeles to Reno. rev. ed. 1997. pap. 12.95 (*0-931532-26-4*) West Trails Pubns.

Clark, Virginia, jt. auth. see Clark, Margaret.

Clark, Virginia, jt. auth. see Dunn, Olive Jean.

Clark, Virginia A., jt. auth. see Bourque, Linda B.

Clark, Virginia A., ed. see Bridges, Nancy S.

Clark, Virginia D. Grand Canyon Country. 1986. pap. 7.95 (*0-931532-21-3*) West Trails Pubns.

Clark, Virginia L., et al, eds. Bacterial Pathogenesis Pt. B: Interaction of Pathogenic Bacteria with Host Cells. (Methods in Enzymology Ser.: Vol. 236). 642p. 1994. text 115.00 (*0-12-182137-4*) Acad Pr.

Clark, Virginia L. & Bavoil, Patrik M., eds. Bacterial Pathogenesis Pt. A: Identification & Regulation of Virulence Factors. (Methods in Enzymology Ser.: Vol. 235). (Illus.). 789p. 1994. text 115.00 (*0-12-182136-6*) Acad Pr.

Clark, Virginia L. & Pomraning, Dorothy E. Resources for Teaching Home Economics. 1986. 6.00 (*0-911365-26-5*, A261-08468) Family & Consumer Sci Educ.

Clark, Virginia L., jt. auth. see Kammermeyer, Karl.

Clark, Virginia L., jt. ed. see Iglewski, Barbara H.

Clark, Virginia M. Aldous Huxley & Film. LC 87-12308. (Filmmakers Ser.: No. 16). (Illus.). 185p. 1987. 21.00 (*0-8108-2002-1*) Scarecrow.

Clark, Virginia R. Dialectics of Religious Consciousness: An Inquiry into the Relationship Between Religion & Society. LC 89-62395. 377p. 1990. pap. 12.00 (*0-938875-19-1*) Pittenbruach Pr.

— Going Toward Jason. LC 88-60455. 560p. (Orig.). 1988. pap. 10.00 (*0-938875-11-6*) Pittenbruach Pr.

Clark, W. & Kape, J. Veneering & Wood Bending in the Furniture Industry. LC 65-97150. (Pergamon Series of Monographs on Furniture & Timber: Vol. 3). 1965. 60.00 (*0-08-011255-2*, Pub. by Pergamon Repr) Franklin.

Clark, W. A., et al, eds. Structure & Properties of Interfaces in Materials. (Symposium Proceedings Ser.: Vol. 238). 889p. 1992. text 17.50 (*1-55899-132-8*) Materials Res.

Clark, W. A. & Hosking, P. L. Statistical Methods for Geographers. LC 85-20309. 528p. 1986. text 90.95 (*0-471-81807-0*) Wiley.

Clark, W. A., jt. auth. see Blair, William A.

Clark, W. C. & Thaman, R. R., eds. Agro-Forestry in the Pacific Islands: Systems for Sustainability. 307p. 1993. pap. write for info. (*92-808-0824-9*, Pub. by UN Univ Pr) Brookings.

Clark, W. Craig, jt. ed. see Robertson, Jon H.

Clark, W. D. & Halpert, G., eds. High Power, Ambient Temperature Lithium Batteries. LC 92-81315. (Proceedings Ser.: Vol. 92-15). 200p. 1992. 40.00 (*1-56677-014-9*) Electrochem Soc.

Clark, W. E. The Fossil Evidence for Human Evolution: An Introduction to the Study of Paleoanthropology. 3rd rev. ed. Campbell, Bernard G., ed. LC 78-529. (Illus.). 1979. lib. bdg. 16.00 (*0-226-10937-2*) U Ch Pr.

— History of the Primates. 5th ed. (Illus.). 1966. pap. text 1.25 (*0-226-10936-4*, P227) U Ch Pr.

— The Tissues of the Body. 6th ed. (Illus.). 1977. pap. text 29.50 (*0-19-857163-1*) OUP.

Clark, W. Edward. Sonnets from My Lanai. 90p. 1998. pap. write for info. (*1-57502-861-1*, PO2352) Morris Pubng.

Clark, W. L., jt. auth. see Hunt, Charles W.

Clark, W. P. The Indian Sign Language. LC 81-16420. vii, 443p. 1982. reprint ed. pap. 16.95 (*0-8032-6309-0*, Bison Books) U of Nebr Pr.

Clark, W. Royce, jt. auth. see Wilson, John F.

Clark, W. V. The Track of the Cat. 25.95 (*0-88411-389-2*) Amereon Ltd.

Clark, W. W., et al, eds. Active - Passive Vibration Control & Nonlinear Dynamics of Structures: Proceedings, ASME International Symposium Mechanical Engineering Congress & Exposition, Dallas, TX, 1997. LC 97-76708. (DE - AMD Ser.: Vols. 95 & 223). 217p. 1997. pap. 140.00 (*0-7918-1829-2*, QC155) ASME Pr.

Clark, Walter. The Papers of Walter Clark, 2 vols., 1. Brooks, Aubrey L. & Lefler, Hugh T., eds. LC 48-6298. 643p. 1950. reprint ed. pap. 199.40 (*0-7837-2068-8*, 204234300001) Bks Demand.

— The Papers of Walter Clark, 2 vols., 2. Brooks, Aubrey L. & Lefler, Hugh T., eds. LC 48-6298. 634p. 1950. reprint ed. pap. 196.60 (*0-7837-2069-6*, 204234300002) Bks Demand.

Clark, Walter, ed. Two Lamaistic Pantheons, 2 vols. 1999. reprint ed. 115.00 (*81-215-0881-9*, Pub. by M Manoharial) Coronet Bks.

Clark, Walter, ed. see North Carolina General Assembly Staff.

Clark, Walter A. Hepzibah - A Lost Arcadia: or the Story of My Old Community (with Biographical Sketches) (Illus.). 200p. 1997. reprint ed. lib. bdg. 29.50 (*0-8328-6624-5*) Higginson Bk Co.

— Isaac Albeniz: A Guide to Research. Marco, Guy A., ed. LC 98-23412. (Composer Resource Manuals Ser.). (Illus.). 280p. 1998. text 60.00 (*0-8153-2095-7*) Garland.

— Issac Albeniz: Portrait of a Romantic. (Illus.). 344p. 1999. text 75.00 (*0-19-816369-X*) OUP.

Clark, Walter E. Josiah Tucker, Economist: A Study in the History of Economics. LC 77-76670. (Columbia University. Studies in the Social Sciences: No. 49). reprint ed. 37.50 (*0-404-51049-3*) AMS Pr.

Clark, Walter E., jt. auth. see Jenks, Jeremiah W.

Clark, Walter J. How to Use New Testament Greek Study Aids. LC 83-14889. 256p. 1984. pap. 9.99 (*0-87213-079-7*) Loizeaux.

Clark, Walter V. The Ox-Bow Incident. 1990. 17.50 (*0-8446-0060-1*) Peter Smith.

Clark, Walter Van Tilburg. The Ox-Bow Incident. 1960. 11.05 (*0-606-01219-2*, Pub. by Turtleback) Demco.

Clark, Warren E. Traffic Management & Collision Investigation. (Illus.). 352p. (C). 1982. text 58.51 (*0-13-926162-1*) P-H.

Clark-Watson, Jo, jt. auth. see Giles, Gordon M.

Clark, Wayne, jt. auth. see Grisham, Beverly.

Clark, Wayne C. The Meaning of Church Membership. 1950. pap. 11.00 (*0-8170-0103-4*) Judson.

Clark, Wesley C., ed. Journalism Tomorrow. LC 58-13727. 147p. reprint ed. pap. 45.60 (*0-608-15214-5*, 202740800055) Bks Demand.

Clark, Wilfrid E. Early Forerunners of Man. LC 76-44705. reprint ed. 54.50 (*0-404-15915-X*) AMS Pr.

Clark, Will. School Bells & Broken Tales: Exploring with Jack & Jill. LC 97-95063. (Illus.). 176p. (J). (gr. 3-6). 1998. pap. 14.95 (*0-9661993-5-9*) Motivat Basics.

— Who Is Blaming Who. LC 93-72225. (Illus.). 320p. (Orig.). 1993. pap. 12.95 (*1-56883-008-4*) Colonial Pr AL.

Clark, Willene B. Stained Glass Art of William Jay Bolton: The Gothic Revival in 19th Century America. LC 91-18456. (Illus.). 242p. 1992. 65.00 (*0-8156-2553-7*) Wittenborn Art.

Clark, Willene B., comment. Valleys of the Shadow: The Memoir of Confederate Captain Reuben G. Clark, Company I, 59th Tennessee Mounted Infantry. LC 93-28758. (Voices of the Civil War Ser.). (Illus.). 200p. (C). 1994. 26.00 (*0-87049-819-3*) U of Tenn Pr.

Clark, Willene B., ed. The Medieval Book of Birds: Hugh of Fouilloy's "Aviarium" (Medieval & Renaissance Texts & Studies: Vol. 80). (Illus.). 464p. 1996. reprint ed. 38.00 (*0-86698-091-1*, MR80) MRTS.

***Clark, William.** Best of Words of Life. 1998. pap. 12.99 (*0-340-71418-2*, Pub. by Hodder & Stought Ltd) Trafalgar.

Clark, William. The Boy's Own Book. LC 95-42274. (Illus.). 320p. (Orig.). (J). (gr. 2-10). 1996. reprint ed. pap. 12.95 (*1-55709-505-1*) Applewood.

— Field Notes of Captain William Clark, 1803-1805. Osgood, Ernest S., ed. 1964. 350.00 (*0-685-26708-3*) Elliots Bks.

— Firefighting Principles & Practices. 2nd ed. LC 90-50451. 1991. 43.95 (*0-912212-16-0*) Fire Eng.

— Retrofitting for Energy Conservation. LC 97-26079. (Illus.). 427p. 1997. 49.95 (*0-07-011920-1*) McGraw.

Clark, William, jt. auth. see Lewis, Meriwether.

Clark, William, jt. auth. see Sell, Edward.

Clark, William, jt. auth. see Wyka, Kenneth.

Clark, William, jt. ed. see Becker, Peter.

Clark, William, ed. see U. S. - Japan Study Group on Arms Control & Non-Pr.

Clark, William A. The California Cauldron: Immigration & the Fortunes of Local Communities. LC 98-38943. 224p. 1998. lib. bdg. 27.95 (*1-57230-403-0*) Guilford Pubns.

— Crime & Punishment in Soviet Officialdom: Combating Corruption in the Political Elite, 1965-1990. LC 92-45245. (Contemporary Soviet - Post-Soviet Politics Ser.). 256p. (C). (gr. 13). 1993. text 75.95 (*1-56324-055-6*); pap. text 42.95 (*1-56324-056-4*) M E Sharpe.

— Soviet Regional Elite Mobility from Brezhnev to Gorbachev. LC 88-36973. 217p. 1989. 57.95 (*0-275-93124-2*, C3124, Praeger Pubs) Greenwood.

— The Spirit of Amy. Richards, J., ed. LC 96-86366. 233p. (Orig.). (J). (gr. 5-10). 1996. pap. 9.98 (*1-887303-23-5*) Blu Lantern Pub.

Clark, William A. & Dieleman, Frans M. Households & Housing: Choice & Outcomes in the Housing Market. LC 95-52803. 275p. 1996. pap. 19.95 (*0-88285-156-X*) Ctr Urban Pol Res.

Clark, William A. & Moore, Eric G., eds. Residential Mobility & Public Policy. LC 80-12624. (Urban Affairs Annual Reviews Ser.: No. 19). (Illus.). 320p. 1980. reprint ed. pap. 99.20 (*0-8357-8487-8*, 203475700091) Bks Demand.

Clark, William A., jt. ed. see Kelley, Martin J.

Clark, William B. The American Vision of Robert Penn Warren. LC 90-28299. 176p. 1991. text 22.50 (*0-8131-1756-9*) U Pr of Ky.

— The First Saratoga: Being the Saga of John Young & His Sloop-of-War. 208p. 1995. pap. 14.95 (*0-939218-07-0*) Chapman Billies.

Clark, William B., jt. ed. see Machann, Clinton.

Clark, William Bedford, ed. see Warren, Robert Penn.

Clark, William C. Carbon Dioxide Review. 1982. (Illus.). 506p. 1982. pap. 65.00 (*0-19-855368-4*) OUP.

Clark, William C. Clark: Ancestors of My Children & Other Related Children of the Generations Living in the Morning of the Twentieth Century. (Illus.). 215p. 1997. reprint ed. pap. 33.00 (*0-8328-7950-9*); reprint ed. lib. bdg. 43.00 (*0-8328-7949-5*) Higginson Bk Co.

Clark, William C., jt. auth. see Johnston, Bruce F.

Clark, William D. Death Valley: The Story Behind the Scenery. 3rd rev. ed. LC 88-82822. (Illus.). 48p. (Orig.). 1989. pap. 7.95 (*0-88714-026-2*) KC Pubns.

— Landlord - Tenant Rights in Florida: What You Need to Know. (Florida Legal Ser.). 144p. 1993. pap. 12.95 (*0-88908-782-2*) Self-Counsel Pr.

— Managing the Florida Condominium. (FRE.). 116p. 1994. ring bd., suppl. ed. 42.00 (*0-614-03740-9*, MICHIE) LEXIS Pub.

— Managing the Florida Condominium, 3 vols., Set. 252p. 1996. ring bd. 105.00 (*0-409-26863-1*, 80886-10, MICHIE) LEXIS Pub.

— Managing the Florida Condominium, 98-2. 236p. 1998. ring bd. write for info. (*0-327-00613-7*, 8089017) LEXIS Pub.

Clark, William G., ed. see Shakespeare, William.

Clark, William H., II. Electrical Design Guide for Commercial Buildings. LC 98-25774. (Illus.). 400p. 1998. 59.95 (*0-07-011991-0*) McGraw-Hill Prof.

Clark, William H. Farms & Farmers. LC 75-99625. (Essay Index Reprint Ser.). 1977. 35.95 (*0-8369-1560-7*) Ayer.

— Ships & Sailors: The Story of Our Merchant Marine. LC 74-22736. (Illus.). reprint ed. 37.50 (*0-404-58488-8*) AMS Pr.

***Clark, William H., Jr. & Sell, W. Edward.** Pennsylvania Business Associations Lawsource: Relevant Sections of Titles 15 & 54 Plus Committee Comments. 654p. 1999. pap. 64.50 (*1-887024-79-4*) Bisel Co.

— Pennsylvania Nonprofit Corporations & Charities Lawsource: Relevant Sections of Titles 15, 20 & 54 on Nonprofit Corporations & Full Text of Laws on Charities. LC 99-73295. 260p. 1999. pap. 59.50 (*1-887024-80-8*) Bisel Co.

Clark, William J. Family Court Act Quizzer & Review Book for New York State Family Court Act. LC 98-228672. 2000. 15.95 (*1-889031-19-4*) Looseleaf Law.

Clark, William L. Gardens of the Streets: Poetry & Pictures of Urban Rescue Missions & the People They Serve. LC 95-77227. (Illus.). 109p. 1995. pap. 12.95 (*1-878044-40-0*) Mayhaven Pub.

Clark, William L., et al. Treatise on the Law of Crimes. 2nd ed. xxxiv, 906p. 1996. reprint ed. 87.50 (*0-8377-2059-1*, Rothman) W S Hein.

Clark, William M. The Hills of Maine: And Other Stories. LC 89-28250. 122p. (Orig.). 1990. pap. 12.95 (*0-945980-17-5*) Nrth Country Pr.

Clark, William M., ed. Model Dialogues. LC 70-109138. (Granger Index Reprint Ser.). 1977. 17.95 (*0-8369-6122-6*) Ayer.

— Sterling Dialogues. LC 76-103086. (Granger Index Reprint Ser.). 1977. 19.95 (*0-8369-6101-3*) Ayer.

Clark, William P. The Experimental Foundations of Modern Immunology. 4th ed. LC 90-13085. 506p. 1991. text 84.95 (*0-471-51707-0*) Wiley.

Clark, William R. At War Within: The Double-Edged Sword of Immunity. 1995. 22.00 (*0-614-15010-8*) OUP.

— At War Within: The Double-Edged Sword of Immunity. (Illus.). 288p. 1997. pap. 13.95 (*0-19-511568-6*) OUP.

— A Means to an End: The Biological Basis of Aging & Death. LC 98-18878. (Illus.). 256p. 1999. 27.50 (*0-19-512593-2*) OUP.

— The New Healers: The Promise & Problems of Molecular Medicine in the Twenty-First Century. LC 97-9086. (Illus.). 256p. 1997. 27.50 (*0-19-511730-1*) OUP.

— The New Healers: The Promise & Problems of Molecular Medicine in the Twenty-First Century. (Illus.). 256p. 1999. pap. 14.95 (*0-19-513084-7*) OUP.

— Savonarola, His Life & Times. LC 83-45654. reprint ed. 34.50 (*0-404-19804-X*) AMS Pr.

— Sex & the Origins of Death. (Illus.). 208p. 1996. 25.00 (*0-19-510644-X*) OUP.

— Sex & the Origins of Death. (Illus.). 208p. 1998. reprint ed. pap. 14.95 (*0-19-512119-8*) OUP.

Clark, William R., ed. & tr. see Von Hefele, Karl J.

Clark, William S. The Early Irish Stage, the Beginnings to 1720. LC 73-9262. (Illus.). 227p. 1973. reprint ed. lib. bdg. 38.50 (*0-8371-7004-4*, CLIS, Greenwood Pr) Greenwood.

— A Field Guide to the Raptors of Europe, the Middle East & North Africa. LC 98-49178. (Illus.). 496p. 1999. 100.00 (*0-19-854662-9*) OUP.

— A Field Guide to the Raptors of Europe, the Middle East & North Africa. LC 98-49178. (Illus.). 496p. 2000. pap. text 45.00 (*0-19-854661-0*) OUP.

Clark, William S., jt. auth. see Wheeler, Brian K.

Clark, William W. The Architecture of Laon Cathedral. 160p. 1983. text 68.00 (*0-905203-17-8*) Gordon & Breach.

Clark, William W., jt. auth. see Radding, Charles M.

Clark, Wilma. Family Literacy: A Profile of a Social Program in the Era of Welfare Reform. LC 98-132057. 58p. 1997. pap. 6.00 (*1-885474-08-3*) Chipp Valley.

Clark-Wilson, Jo & Giles, Gordon M. Brain Injury Rehabilitation: A Neuro-Functional Approach. LC 92-21407. (Therapy in Practice Ser.: Vol. 33). 458p. 1992. 55.00 (*1-56593-052-5*, 0300) Singular Publishing.

Clark-Wilson, Jo, jt. auth. see Muir-Giles, G.

Clark, Winifred, ed. see Mayer, Margarita.

Clark, Wm. S. F G Hawks, Vol. 1. 1999. pap. 18.00 (*0-395-93615-2*) HM.

Clark, Zane. How to Build a Galilean Ministry. (Illus.). 48p. 1989. pap. 4.75 (*0-89114-168-5*) Baptist Pub Hse.

— My Royal Service. (Illus.). 165p. (J). (gr. 4-12). 1989. pap. 12.95 (*0-89114-164-2*) Baptist Pub Hse.

Clark, Zenas R. The Recognition of Merit in Superintendents' Reports to the Public. LC 77-176650. (Columbia University. Teachers College. Contributions to Education Ser.: No. 471). reprint ed. 37.50 (*0-404-55471-7*) AMS Pr.

Clarke. Aspects of the Hague Rules. 1976. pap. text 96.00 (*90-247-1806-6*) Kluwer Academic.

— Brigden's Operating Department. LC 98-3309. (C). 1998. text 153.00 (*0-443-05188-7*, W B Saunders Co) Harcrt Hlth Sci Grp.

***Clarke.** Buyers Get Used Airplanes. 5th ed. LC 99-39006. 576p. 1999. pap. 39.95 (*0-07-135179-5*) McGraw.

— Clarkenotes for Netware 5 Administration: Course 560. LC 99-46056. (Novell Press Ser.). (Illus.). 264p. 1999. 24.99 (*0-7645-4577-9*) IDG Bks.

Clarke. Clinical Repertory. pap. 44.95 (*0-8464-4488-7*) Beekman Pubs.

— Colloquial Japanese. (Orig.). 1986. pap. 14.95 (*0-7100-0595-4*, Routledge Thoemms) Routledge.

— Critical Reading for the Reflective Practitioner. LC 99-182011. 336p. 1998. pap. text 38.50 (*0-7506-3939-3*) Buttrwrth-Heinemann.

— A Dictionary of Practical Materia Medica. 1996. 180.00 (*0-85032-084-4*, Pub. by C W Daniel) Natl Bk Netwk.

***Clarke.** Durable Reinforcement for Concrete Structures. 1998. pap. write for info. (*0-419-23470-5*) Thomson Learn.

Clarke. Getting Started with Geography. 2nd ed. LC 98-29621. (Prentice Hall Series in Geographic Information Science). 368p. 1998. 73.00 (*0-13-923889-1*) P-H.

— Manual of Equine Anaesthesia. 2nd ed. 1998. pap. text 37.00 (*0-7020-1806-6*, W B Saunders Co) Harcrt Hlth Sci Grp.

— Minimizing Emissions from MSW Incinerators. 1998. write for info. (*0-87371-629-9*, L629) Lewis Pubs.

— New Encyclopedia of Wine 1999. write for info. (*0-15-601068-2*) Harcourt.

— Novell's CNE Update to Netware 5. LC QA76.3.C62 1999. 696p. 1998. pap., student ed. 49.99 (*0-7645-4559-0*) IDG Bks.

— Ozidi Saga. 436p. 1991. pap. 24.95 (*0-88258-108-2*) Howard U Pr.

— Pocket Wine Guide 2000. 1999. write for info. (*0-15-601074-7*) Harcourt.

Clarke. The Prescriber. 31.95 (*0-8464-4495-X*) Beekman Pubs.

Clarke. Rebellion in Rhyme. per. 9.95 (*0-86543-231-7*) Africa World.

— The Rights of Nations. LC 99-28876. 1999. pap. 18.95 (*0-312-22595-4*) St Martin.

***Clarke.** Rights of Nations. LC 99-28876. 208p. 1999. text 59.95 (*0-312-22594-6*) St Martin.

Clarke & Gregory. Western Reports on Taiping. (Australian National University Press Ser.). 1996. pap. text 18.00 (*0-08-033003-7*, Pergamon Pr) Elsevier.

Clarke & Wideman. Together We Learn. 1989. pap. text 38.00 (*0-13-924556-1*) P-H.

Clarke, jt. auth. see Abel.

Clarke, jt. auth. see Shelley.

Clarke, ed. see Corneille.

Clarke, ed. see Van de Perre.

Clarke, Alison, ed. Current Issues in Insolvency Law. (Current Legal Problems Ser.). xx, 144p. 1991. reprint ed. pap. 45.00 (*0-421-44370-7*) W S Hein.

***Clarke, Alison & Sinclair, Ruth.** The Child in Focus: The Evolving Role of the Guardian Ad Litem. 132p. 2000. pap. 26.00 (*1-900990-50-4*, Pub. by Natl Childrens Bur) Paul & Co Pubs.

Clarke, Henrik, jt. auth. see Jackson, John G.

***Clarke, A.** Solving Your Company's Corporate Governance Issues. (Financial Times Management Briefings Ser.). 1998. pap. 137.50 (*0-273-63719-3*) F T P-H.

Clarke, A., ed. Genetic Testing of Children. 300p. 1997. 65.00 (*1-85996-181-9*, Pub. by Bios Sci) Coronet Bks.

Clarke, A. A. Police Uniform & Equipment. 1989. pap. 6.25 (*0-7478-0126-6*, Pub. by Shire Pubns) St Mut.

Clarke, A. A., tr. see Gauss, Christopher F.

Clarke, A. B. Travels in Mexico & California. Perry, Anne M., ed. LC 88-1490. (Elma Dill Russell Spencer Series in the West & Southwest: No. 10). (Illus.). 176p. 1988. 19.95 (*0-89096-354-1*) Tex A&M Univ Pr.

Clarke, A. Bruce & Disney, Ralph L. Probability & Random Processes: A First Course with Applications. 2nd ed. LC 84-15312. (Probability & Mathematical Statistics Ser.). 336p. 1985. text 92.95 (*0-471-08535-9*) Wiley.

Clarke, A. M., ed. Best Poems of Trinidad. 2nd ed. LC 98-54293. (Caribbean Classics Ser.: Vol. 1). xix, 66p. 1999. reprint ed. pap. 10.95 (*0-912469-36-6*) Majority Pr.

Clarke, A. Mason. A Biographical Dictionary of Fiddlers Including Performers on the Violin, Cello & Double Bass. LC 79-166225. 360p. 1895. reprint ed. 39.00 (*0-403-01352-6*) Scholarly.

— Biographical Dictionary of Fiddlers Including Performers on the Violin, Cello & Double D. 1988. reprint ed. lib. bdg. 59.00 (*0-7812-0677-4*) Rprt Serv.

— Pronouncing Dictionary of Musical Terms, Giving the Meaning, Derivation & Pronunciation. 121p. 2000. reprint ed. lib. bdg. 69.00 (*0-7812-0750-9*) Rprt Serv.

— The Violin & Old Violin Makers. 1976. lib. bdg. 45.00 (*0-403-03813-8*) Scholarly.

Clarke, A. P. Clarke's Kindred Genealogy: A Genealogical History of Certain Descendants of Joseph Clarke, Dorchester, 1630, Denice Darling, Edward Gray, & W. Horne. (Illus.). 185p. 1993. reprint ed. pap. 26.50 (*0-8328-1353-2*); reprint ed. lib. bdg. 36.50 (*0-8328-1352-4*) Higginson Bk Co.

Clarke, A. S., jt. auth. see Morison, J. D.

Clarke, Adam. Adam Clarke's Commentary on the Bible. 1360p. 1996. 39.99 (*0-529-10634-5*) World Publng.

***Clarke, Adam.** The Christian Prophet & His Work. 152p. 2000. pap. 7.99 (*0-88019-406-5*) Schmul Pub Co.

Clarke, Adam. Clarke's Christian Theology. 1990. reprint ed. pap. 18.99 (*0-88019-261-5*) Schmul Pub Co.

— Clarke's Commentary, 3 vols., Set. Incl. Vol. 1. Genesis-Esther. 1977. 39.95 (*0-687-09119-5*); Vol. 3. Matthew-Revelation. 1977. 39.95 (*0-687-09121-7*); 1977. 119.95 (*0-687-09118-7*) Abingdon.

Clarke, Adam, ed. Clarke's Commentary. abr. ed. LC 67-13093. 1967. 34.99 (*0-8010-2321-1*) Baker Bks.

Clarke, Adam, et al. Holiness Heart Talk. 1986. pap. 7.99 (*0-88019-202-X*) Schmul Pub Co.

Clarke, Adele. Disciplining Reproduction: Modernity, American Life Sciences, & "The Problem of Sex" LC 97-1114. (Illus.). 438p. 1998. 45.00 (*0-520-20720-3*, Pub. by U CA Pr) Cal Prin Full Svc.

Clarke, Adele & Olesen, Virginia L. Revisioning Women, Health & Healing: Feminist, Cultural & Technoscience Perspectives. LC 98-9685. x, 374p. (C). 1999. pap. 22.99 (*0-415-91846-4*) Routledge.

Clarke, Adele E. & Fujimura, Joan H., eds. The Right Tools for the Job: At Work in Twentieth-Century Life Sciences. (Illus.). 394p. 1992. text 42.50 (*0-691-08581-1*, Pub. by Princeton U Pr) Cal Prin Full Svc.

Clarke, Adele E. & Olesen, Virginia L., eds. Revisioning Women, Health & Healing: Feminist, Cultural & Technoscience Perspectives. 352p. (C). (gr. 13). 1998. 80.00 (*0-415-91845-6*, D2984) Routledge.

Clarke, Adrian. Legends: How to Play & Compose Like the World's Greatest Guitarists, 1. 1998. pap. text 21.95 (*1-86074-220-3*) Music Sales.

Clarke, Adrian & Sheppard, Robert, eds. Floating Capital. 124p. 1991. pap. 12.00 (*0-937013-35-8*) Potes Poets.

Clarke, Adrienne E., jt. auth. see Stone, Bruce A.

***Clarke, Aidan.** The Old English in Ireland, 1625-42. 288p. 2000. pap. 29.95 (*1-85182-552-5*, Pub. by Four Cts Pr) Intl Spec Bk.

Clarke, Aidan. Prelude to Restoration in Ireland: The End of the Commonwealth, 1659-1660. LC 98-36968. (Illus.). 280p. (C). 1999. text 59.95 (*0-521-65061-5*) Cambridge U Pr.

***Clarke, Alan.** The Economic Dimensions of Crime. 2000. text 65.00 (*0-312-23161-X*) St Martin.

Clarke, Alan. Transgenic Techniques. 2nd ed. (Methods in Molecular Biology Ser.). 400p. 1999. 79.50 (*0-89603-696-0*) Humana.

Clarke, Alan, tr. see Coelho, Paulo.

Clarke, Alan R., tr. see Coelho, Paulo.

Clarke, Alexander M., jt. ed. see Mikulecky, Donald C.

Clarke, Alison J. Tupperware: The Promise of Plastic in 1950s America. LC 99-16972. (Illus.). 256p. 1999. 24.95 (*1-56098-827-4*) Smithsonian.

Clarke, Andrew D. Secular & Christian Leadership in Corinth: A Socio-Historical & Exegetical Study of 1 Corinthians 1-6. LC 93-10139. (Arbeiten zur Geschichte des Antiken Judentums & des Urchristentums Ser.: Vol. 18). (Illus.). xii, 188p. 1993. 87.00 (*90-04-09862-3*) Brill Academic Pubs.

***Clarke, Andrew D.** Serve the Community of the Church: Christians As Leaders & Ministers. LC 99-46841. 292p. 2000. pap. 30.00 (*0-8028-4182-1*) Eerdmans.

Clarke, Angela. Bahrain Oil & Development. LC 90-84725. (Illus.). 332p. 1990. 38.00 (*0-918714-25-7*) Intl Res Ctr Energy.

Clarke, Angela, jt. auth. see Lawrence, T. E.

***Clarke, Angus.** Genetic Testing of Children. (Human Molecular Genetics Ser.). 334p. 1999. 110.00 (*0-12-220445-X*) Acad Pr.

Clarke, Angus, ed. Genetic Counselling: Practice & Principles. LC 93-5884. (Professional Ethics Ser.). (Illus.). 280p. (C). 1994. 75.00 (*0-415-08257-9*, B3413); pap. 27.99 (*0-415-08258-7*, B3417) Routledge.

Clarke, Angus J., jt. auth. see Harper, Peter S.

Clarke, Ann B. Wade Hampton Pipes: Arts & Crafts Architect in Portland, Oregon. LC 86-70205. (Illus.). 104p. 1986. pap. 14.95 (*0-8323-0451-4*) Binford Mort.

Clarke, Ann N. & Wilson, David J. Foam Flotation: Theory & Applications. LC 83-5135. (Chemical Industries Ser.: Vol. 11). (Illus.). 432p. reprint ed. pap. 134.00 (*0-608-08923-0*, 206955800005) Bks Demand.

Clarke, Ann N., jt. ed. see Wilson, David J.

Clarke, Anna. Ancient Egyptian Construction & Architecture. (Illus.). 352p. 1999. pap. 12.95 (*0-486-26485-8*) Dover.

— Case of the Anxious Aunt. 1996. mass mkt. 5.99 (*0-425-15311-8*) Berkley Pub.

— The Case of the Paranoid Patient. large type ed. LC 93-11537. (Nightingale Ser.). 300p. 1993. lib. bdg. 15.95 (*0-8161-5845-2*, G K Hall Lrg Type) Mac Lib Ref.

— Last Seen in London. large type ed. 340p. 1992. pap. 14.95 (*0-8161-5452-X*, G K Hall Lrg Type) Mac Lib Ref.

— My Search for Ruth. large type ed. (General Ser.). 263p. 1989. lib. bdg. 16.95 (*0-8161-4709-4*, G K Hall Lrg Type) Mac Lib Ref.

Clarke, Anne, et al, eds. Bringing Telecommunication Services to the People: Third International Conference on Intelligence in Broadband Services & Networks, Heraclion, Crete, Greece, October 1995: Proceedings. (Lecture Notes in Computer Science Ser.: Vol. 998). 510p. 1995. pap. 81.00 (*3-540-60479-0*) Spr-Verlag.

Clarke, Anne, jt. auth. see Torrence, Robin.

Clarke, Anne B. Adventures Bk. 1, Level 1. 64p. 1990. pap. 9.82 (*0-8442-1525-2*); pap. 9.82 (*0-8442-1540-6*) NTC Contemp Pub Co.

Clarke, Anthony & Hart, Frank D. Clinical Problems in Rheumatology. 1994. pap. 74.95 (*1-85317-125-5*, M Dunitz) Scovill Paterson.

Clarke, Anthony H., ed. A Further Range: Studies in Modern Spanish Fiction. 200p. 1998. text 75.00 (*0-85989-575-0*, Pub. by Univ Exeter Pr) Northwestern U Pr.

Clarke, Anthony J. Biodegradation of Cellulose: Enzymology & Biotechnology. LC 96-60383. 280p. 1996. text 149.95 (*1-56676-414-9*) Technomic.

Clarke, Antony B. & Coverman, Sidney H. Structural Steelwork: Limit State Design to BS 5950. 300p. (gr. 13). 1987. text 92.50 (*0-412-29660-8*) Chapman & Hall.

Clarke, Arielle, jt. auth. see Sarada, Jaya.

Clarke, Arthur C. Arthur C. Clarke & Lord Dunsany: A Correspondence. Daniels, Keith A., ed. LC 98-18688. (Illus.). 84p. 1998. pap. 19.95 (*0-9631203-0-1*) Anamnesis Pr.

— Beyond the Fall of Night. 1991. mass mkt. 5.99 (*0-441-05612-1*) Ace Bks.

— Childhood's End. 21.95 (*0-8488-0157-1*) Amereon Ltd.

— Childhood's End. LC 53-10419. 224p. 1987. mass mkt. 5.99 (*0-345-34795-1*, Del Rey) Ballantine Pub Grp.

— Childhood's End. 218p. 1996. pap. 5.99 (*0-345-90988-7*, Del Rey) Ballantine Pub Grp.

— Childhood's End. LC 53-10419. 216p. 1963. 14.95 (*0-15-117205-6*) Harcourt.

— Childhood's End. 1953. 11.09 (*0-606-00463-7*, Pub. by Turtleback) Demco.

— The City & the Stars. 1999. lib. bdg. 21.95 (*1-56723-160-8*) Yestermorrow.

***Clarke, Arthur C.** The Collected Stories of Arthur C. Clarke. 2000. write for info. (*0-312-87821-4*) Tor Bks.

Clarke, Arthur C. Earthlight. 192p. 1998. pap. 10.00 (*0-345-43070-0*, Del Rey) Ballantine Pub Grp.

***Clarke, Arthur C.** El Espectro del Titanic. (SPA.). 1998. pap. 6.50 (*84-01-49272-6*) Plaza.

Clarke, Arthur C. Expedition to Earth. 192p. 1998. pap. 10.00 (*0-345-43073-5*, Del Rey) Ballantine Pub Grp.

— The Garden of Rama. 528p. 1992. mass mkt. 6.99 (*0-553-29817-8*, Spectra) Bantam.

— The Garden of Rama. 1991. 11.60 (*0-606-00743-1*, Pub. by Turtleback) Demco.

— Greetings, Carbon Based Bipeds. LC 99-22074. 1999. text 35.00 (*0-312-19893-0*) St Martin.

— The Hammer of God. 272p. 1994. mass mkt. 6.99 (*0-553-56871-X*) Bantam.

***Clarke, Arthur C.** The Hammer of God. large type ed. (G. K. Hall Science Fiction Ser.). 2000. 25.95 (*0-7838-8979-8*, G K Hall Lrg Type) Mac Lib Ref.

Clarke, Arthur C. Islands in the Sky. Date not set. lib. bdg. 18.95 (*0-8488-2139-4*) Amereon Ltd.

— Islands in the Sky. 1994. lib. bdg. 24.95 (*1-56849-416-5*) Buccaneer Bks.

— The Lion of Comarre. LC 68-28816. 214p. 1968. 5.75 (*0-15-152524-2*) Harcourt.

— The Lion of Comarre: Against the Fall of Night. 228p. 1986. pap. 9.95 (*0-15-652517-8*) Harcourt.

— A Meeting with Medusa. 192p. 1988. 2.95 (*0-8125-3362-3*) Tor Bks.

— The Nine Billion Names of God: The Best Short Stories of Arthur C. Clarke. Date not set. lib. bdg. 23.95 (*0-8488-2181-5*) Amereon Ltd.

— The Possessed & Other Stories. 188p. reprint ed. lib. bdg. 20.95 (*0-89190-956-7*, Rivercity Pr) Amereon Ltd.

— Prelude to Space. 192p. 1986. mass mkt. 5.99 (*0-345-34102-3*, Del Rey) Ballantine Pub Grp.

— Rama Revealed. 624p. 1995. mass mkt. 6.99 (*0-553-56947-3*) Bantam.

— Reach for Tomorrow. 176p. 1998. pap. 10.00 (*0-345-43071-9*, Del Rey) Ballantine Pub Grp.

— Rendezvous with Rama. LC 73-3497. 288p. 1990. mass mkt. 6.99 (*0-553-28789-3*, Spectra) Bantam.

— Rendezvous with Rama. LC 73-3497. 1993. reprint ed. lib. bdg. 35.95 (*0-89968-449-1*, Lghtyr Pr) Buccaneer Bks.

— The Sands of Maris. 1999. lib. bdg. 21.95 (*1-56723-162-4*) Yestermorrow.

***Clarke, Arthur C.** The Sentinel. 2000. per. 14.95 (*0-7434-0721-0*, Pub. by ibooks) S&S Trade.

Clarke, Arthur C. The Songs of Distant Earth. 336p. 1987. mass mkt. 6.99 (*0-345-32240-1*, Del Rey) Ballantine Pub Grp.

— Tales from the White Hart. 20.95 (*0-89190-249-X*) Amereon Ltd.

— Tales from the White Hart. 160p. 1998. pap. 10.00 (*0-345-43072-7*, Del Rey) Ballantine Pub Grp.

— 3001, the Final Odyssey. 1998. pap. write for info. (*0-345-42133-7*, Del Rey); mass mkt. 6.99 (*0-345-42349-6*, Del Rey) Ballantine Pub Grp.

***Clarke, Arthur C.** 3001, the Final Odyssey. 263p. 1999. pap. 12.00 (*0-345-43820-5*, Del Rey) Ballantine Pub Grp.

Clarke, Arthur C. 3001, the Final Odyssey. large type ed. LC 97-10818. 464p. 1997. 25.95 (*0-7838-8190-8*, G K Hall Lrg Type) Mac Lib Ref.

— The Tribe Alasmidontini: Unionidae Anodontinae. LC 80-23747. (Smithsonian Contributions to Zoology Ser.: No. 326). 79p. reprint ed. pap. 30.00 (*0-608-12672-1*, 202511200042) Bks Demand.

***Clarke, Arthur C.** The Trigger. 704p. 2000. mass mkt. 6.99 (*0-553-57620-8*) Bantam.

Clarke, Arthur C. 2001: A Space Odyssey. 236p. 1999. mass mkt. 20.01 (*0-451-19849-2*, ROC) NAL.

— 2001: A Space Odyssey. large type ed. LC 94-29899. 325 p. 1994. lib. bdg. 22.95 (*0-8161-7486-5*, G K Hall Lrg Type) Mac Lib Ref.

— Two Thousand Sixty-One: Odyssey Three. 288p. 1989. mass mkt. 6.99 (*0-345-35879-1*, Del Rey) Ballantine Pub Grp.

— 2061: Odyssey Three. 1997. pap. 10.00 (*0-345-41398-9*) Ballantine Pub Grp.

— Two Thousand Ten: Odyssey Two. 352p. 1984. mass mkt. 6.99 (*0-345-30306-7*, Del Rey) Ballantine Pub Grp.

— 2010: Odyssey Two. LC 96-95451. 1997. pap. 10.00 (*0-345-41397-0*) Ballantine Pub Grp.

— 2010: Odyssey Two. 1984. 11.05 (*0-606-00264-2*, Pub. by Turtleback) Demco.

Clarke, Arthur C. 2010 Odyssey 2. abr. ed. LC 82-740054. 1989. audio 14.00 (*0-89845-221-X*, SWC 1709, Caedmon) HarperAudio.

Clarke, Arthur C. The View from Serendip. (A Del Rey Bk.). 1978. mass mkt. 2.95 (*0-345-27108-4*) Ballantine Pub Grp.

— The View from Serendip. (A Del Rey Bk.). 1984. mass mkt. 2.95 (*0-345-31441-7*, Ballantine) Ballantine Pub Grp.

***Clarke, Arthur C. & Baxter, Stephen.** The Light of Other Days. 320p. 1999. mass mkt. 7.99 (*0-8125-7640-3*) Tor Bks.

— The Light of Other Days. LC 99-89761. 320p. 2000. 24.95 (*0-312-87199-6*, Pub. by Tor Bks) St Martin.

Clarke, Arthur C. & Kube-McDowell, Michael P. The Trigger. LC 99-34692. 464p. 1999. 24.95 (*0-553-10458-6*) Bantam.

Clarke, Arthur C. & Kubrick, Stanley. 2001: A Space Odyssey. 1994. lib. bdg. 24.95 (*1-56849-417-3*) Buccaneer Bks.

Clarke, Arthur C. & Kubrick, Stanley. 2001: A Space Odyssey. 25th anniversary ed. LC 93-10067. 236p. 1993. pap. 12.95 (*0-451-45273-9*, ROC) NAL.

Clarke, Arthur C. & Lee, Gentry. Cradle. LC 87-40404. 416p. 1989. mass mkt. 5.99 (*0-446-35601-8*, Pub. by Warner Bks) Little.

— Rama II. 512p. 1990. mass mkt. 6.99 (*0-553-28658-7*, Spectra) Bantam.

***Clarke, Arthur C. & Preuss, Paul.** Venus Prime, Vol. 3. 320p. 2000. per. 14.00 (*0-7434-0001-1*, Pub. by ibooks) S&S Trade.

Clarke, Arthur C., et al. Arthur C. Clarke's Mysteries. 256p. 1998. pap. 10.95 (*1-85479-281-4*) Trans-Atl Phila.

Clarke, Arthur C., ed. see Wells, H. G.

Clarke, Arthur C., tr. & frwd. see Devendra, Tissa.

***Clarke, Arthur Charles.** 2001: A Space Odyssey. 2000. mass mkt. 6.99 (*0-451-45799-4*, ROC) NAL.

Clarke, Arthur G. New Testament Church Principles. 1996. pap. 6.99 (*0-946351-11-2*, Pub. by John Ritchie) Loizeaux.

Clarke, Arthur L. Bosnia: What Every American Needs to Know. 1996. mass mkt. 6.99 (*0-425-15538-2*) Berkley Pub.

Clarke, Asia. The Elder & the Younger Booth. 1977. 17.95 (*0-8369-7144-2*, 7977) Ayer.

— Unlocked Book: A Memoir of John Wilkes Booth by His Sister. LC 74-88533. (Illus.). 206p. 1972. 24.95 (*0-405-08363-7*, Pub. by Blom Pubns) Ayer.

Clarke, Asia B. John Wilkes Booth: A Sister's Memoir. 152p. 1999. reprint ed. pap. 18.00 (*1-57806-225-X*) U Pr of Miss.

Clarke, Audrey, ed. see Stamp, Dudley.

Clarke, Audrey E., jt. auth. see Shelley, Fred M.

Clarke, Austin. Celtic Twilight & the Nineties. 104p. 1970. 18.95 (*0-85105-010-7*) Dufour.

— The Collected Poems of Austin Clarke. LC 75-41061. (BCL Ser.: No. II). reprint ed. 41.50 (*0-404-14523-X*) AMS Pr.

— Echo at Coole. LC 68-26020. 78p. 1968. 15.95 (*0-8023-1155-5*) Dufour.

— Origins of Waves. LC 96-932212. 1997. pap. 19.99 (*0-7710-2127-5*) McCland & Stewart.

***Clarke, Austin.** Pig Tails 'n Breadfruit: A Culinary Memoir. 256p. 2000. 22.95 (*1-56584-580-3*, Pub. by New Press NY) Norton.

Clarke, Austin. Selected Poems. Maxton, Hugh, ed. LC 91-65935. 288p. (C). 1991. 20.00 (*0-916390-50-0*) Wake Forest.

Clarke, B. G. Pressuremeters in Geotechnical Design. LC 94-71805. 364p. 1994. 164.95 (*0-7514-0041-6*, Pub. by B Acad & Prof) Routldge.

Clarke, Barbara K., jt. auth. see Kasten, Wendy C.

Clarke, Barry. Amazing Frogs & Toads. LC 90-31882. (Eyewitness Juniors Ser.: No. 6). (Illus.). 32p. (J). (ps-3). 1990. pap. 9.99 (*0-679-80688-1*, Pub. by Knopf Bks Yng Read) Random.

— Amazing Frogs & Toads. LC 90-31882. (Eyewitness Juniors Ser.: No. 6). (Illus.). 32p. (J). (ps-3). 1991. lib. bdg. 11.99 (*0-679-90688-6*, Pub. by Knopf Bks Yng Read) Random.

— Amazing Frogs & Toads. (Eyewitness Juniors Ser.: No. 6). (J). (ps-3). 1990. 15.19 (*0-606-04602-X*, Pub. by Turtleback) Demco.

***Clarke, Barry.** Amphibian. (Eyewitness Books). (Illus.). (J). (gr. 4-7). 2000. 19.99 (*0-7894-6590-6*) DK Pub Inc.

— Amphibian. (Eyewitness Books). (J). (gr. 4-7). 2000. 15.95 (*0-7894-5754-7*) DK Pub Inc.

Clarke, Barry, et al. Coastal Forces. Till, Geoffrey, ed. (Naval Weapons, Systems & Technology Ser.: Vol. 10). (Illus.). 200p. 1994. pap. 25.00 (*0-08-040986-5*, Pub. by Brasseys) Brasseys.

Clarke, Barry O. & Spaight, Robert. The International Guide to Fly-Tying Materials. (Illus.). 189p. 1997. 34.95 (*0-07-011943-0*) McGraw.

Clarke, Barry R. Puzzles for Pleasure. (Illus.). 128p. (C). 1994. pap. 11.95 (*0-521-46634-2*) Cambridge U Pr.

Clarke, Ben, et al. Image & Imagination: Encounters with the Photography of Dorothea Lange. LC 97-614446. (Illus.). 100p. 1997. pap. 15.95 (*0-9625153-6-8*) Freedom Voices Pubns.

Clarke, Ben, ed. see Pepper, Margot.

Clarke, Ben, ed. see Robertson, Eric.

Clarke, Ben, ed. see TallMountain, Mary.

Clarke, Ben, ed. see Zapatista National Liberation Army Staff.

Clarke, Betty G. The Gackstetters from Germany. Brandt, Edward, tr. from GER. (Illus.). 352p. 1993. 31.00 (*0-9636192-0-9*) B Clarke.

Clarke, Beverly. Creek Watchers. LC 98-11148. 128p. (Orig.). (J). (gr. 7-9). 1998. pap. 7.99 (*0-8280-1312-8*) Review & Herald.

Clarke, Bill. Aviator's Guide to GPS. 2nd ed. (Tab Practical Flying Ser.). 1995. 39.95 (*0-07-011545-1*) McGraw.

— Aviator's Guide to GPS. 3rd ed. LC 97-49041. 1998. 44.95 (*0-07-009492-6*) McGraw.

— Aviator's Guide to GPS. 3rd ed. LC 97-49041. (Illus.). 304p. 1998. pap. 29.95 (*0-07-009493-4*) McGraw.

— The Caring Services. (Skills for Caring Ser.). (Illus.). 48p. (Orig.). 1992. pap. text 9.95 (*0-443-04527-5*) Church.

— Cessna One Hundred & Seventy-Two. 2nd ed. 1993. pap. 15.95 (*0-8306-4294-3*) McGraw-Hill Prof.

— The Cessna 150 & 152. 2nd ed. (Illus.). 248p. 1993. pap. 24.95 (*0-07-011269-X*) McGraw.

— The Cessna 150 & 152. 2nd ed. LC 92-35194. 1993. pap. 14.95 (*0-8306-4293-5*) McGraw-Hill Prof.

— The Cessna One Hundred Seventy Two. (Illus.). 320p. (Orig.). 1987. 19.95 (*0-8306-0912-1*, 2412) McGraw-Hill Prof.

— The Cessna 172. 2nd ed. (Illus.). 274p. 1993. pap. 24.95 (*0-07-011270-3*) McGraw.

— Cold Weather Flying. (Practical Flying Ser.). (Illus.). 160p. 1989. pap. 15.95 (*0-8306-9442-0*, 2442) McGraw-Hill Prof.

— GPS Aviation Applications. (Illus.). 301p. 1996. pap. 34.95 (*0-07-011633-4*) McGraw.

— The Illustrated Buyer's Guide to Used Airplanes. (Illus.). 288p. 1985. pap. 17.60 (*0-8306-2372-8*, 2372P) McGraw-Hill Prof.

— The Illustrated Buyer's Guide to Used Airplanes. 2nd ed. (Illus.). 304p. 1989. 27.95 (*0-07-155741-5*) McGraw.

— The Illustrated Buyer's Guide to Used Airplanes. 2nd ed. (Illus.). 320p. 1989. 27.95 (*0-8306-9462-5*) McGraw-Hill Prof.

— The Illustrated Buyer's Guide to Used Airplanes. 3rd ed. (Illus.). 368p. 1992. 29.95 (*0-8306-2571-2*, 4052); pap. 19.95 (*0-8306-2570-4*, 4052) McGraw-Hill Prof.

— The Illustrated Buyer's Guide to Used Airplanes. 4th ed. LC 97-36131. (Illus.). 516p. 1997. 44.95 (*0-07-011935-X*); pap. 28.95 (*0-07-011936-8*) McGraw.

— The Pilot's Guide to Affordable Classics. 2nd ed. LC 92-41242. 1993. 26.95 (*0-8306-4106-8*); pap. 16.60 (*0-8306-4107-6*) McGraw-Hill Prof.

— Pilots Guide to Affordable Classics. 2nd ed. 320p. 1993. pap. 19.95 (*0-07-011268-1*) McGraw.

— The Piper Indians. (Illus.). 288p. 1988. pap. 18.95 (*0-07-155369-X*) McGraw.

— The Piper Indians. (Illus.). 288p. 1987. 24.95 (*0-8306-0232-1*, 2432); pap. 17.95 (*0-8306-2432-5*) McGraw-Hill Prof.

— Professional Cleaning & Building Maintenance: How to Organize a Money Saving Business or Department for Floor & Building Care. Griffin, William R., ed. 344p. 1965. reprint ed. pap. 25.00 (*0-944352-04-9*) Cleaning Cons.

Clarke, Bob, jt. auth. see Jacobs, Frank.

***Clarke, Bob C.** Insatiable. (Illus.). 224p. 2000. 44.95 (*1-893263-13-4*) Ipso Facto.

C

Clarke, Boden & Burgess, Mary A. The Work of Katherine Kurtz: An Annotated Bibliography & Guide. LC 85-31401. (Bibliographies of Modern Authors Ser.: No. 7). 128p. 1993. pap. 17.00 (*0-89370-486-5*, 13063902) Millefleurs.

Clarke, Boden & Hopkins, James. The Work of William F. Nolan: An Annotated Bibliography & Literary Guide. 2nd rev. ed. LC 95-2762. (Bibliographies of Modern Authors Ser.: No. 14). 256p. 1997. pap. 25.00 (*0-8095-1518-0*) Millefleurs.

Clarke, Boden, ed. see Ashley, Mike.

Clarke, Boden, ed. see Bamberger, W. C.

Clarke, Boden, ed. see Bourquin, David R.

Clarke, Boden, ed. see Burgess, Michael.

Clarke, Boden, ed. see Burgess, Scott A.

Clarke, Boden, ed. see Elliot, Jeffrey M.

Clarke, Boden, ed. see Hall, Hal W.

Clarke, Boden, ed. see Mackey, Douglas A.

Clarke, Boden, ed. see Mallett, Daryl F. & Mallett, Annette Y.

Clarke, Boden, ed. see Menville, Douglas A.

Clarke, Boden, ed. see Nolan, William F.

Clarke, Boden, ed. see Wood, Martine.

Clarke, Bowman L. Language & Natural Theology. (Janua Linguarum, Ser. Minor: No. 47). (Orig.). 1966. pap. text 34.65 (*90-279-0580-0*) Mouton.

Clarke, Bowman L. & Long, Eugene T., eds. God & Temporality. (Contemporary Discussion Ser.). 189p. (C). 1986. pap. 12.95 (*0-913757-10-1*) Paragon Hse.

Clarke, Bradley. O Holy Night. (J). (ps-3). 1994. 16.99 (*1-56476-419-2*, 6-3419, Victor Bks) Chariot Victor.

Clarke, Bradley H. & Cummings, O. R. Tremont Street Subway: A Century of Public Service. LC 97-36385. (Bulletin Ser.: No. 22). (Illus.). 64p. 1997. pap. 15.95 (*0-938315-04-8*) Boston St Rwy.

Clarke, Bransby. Think Yourself Slim. 96p. (Orig.). 1995. pap. 7.95 (*0-572-01471-6*, Pub. by Foulsham UK) Assoc Pubs Grp.

***Clarke, Breena.** River, Cross My Heart. 2000. pap. 7.50 (*0-316-89816-3*) Little.

— River, Cross My Heart. LC 99-88727. 2000. pap. 28.95 (*0-7862-2432-0*) Mac Lib Ref.

— River, Cross My Heart. large type ed. LC 99-88727. (Basic Ser.). 2000. 30.95 (*0-7862-2431-2*) Thorndike Pr.

— River, Cross My Heart: A Novel. 245p. 1999. 23.00 (*0-316-89999-2*); pap. 14.95 (*0-316-89998-4*) Little.

Clarke, Brenda. The Far Morning. large type ed. 592p. 1983. 27.99 (*0-7089-8144-5*) Ulverscroft.

— Last of the Barons. 224p. 1998. 24.00 (*0-7278-5311-2*) Severn Hse.

***Clarke, Brenda.** Last of the Barons. large type ed. 360p. 1999. 31.99 (*0-7089-4143-5*) Ulverscroft.

Clarke, Brenda. A Royal Alliance. 224p. 1999. 24.00 (*0-7278-2265-9*, Pub. by Severn Hse) Chivers N Amer.

— Sisters & Lovers. 416p. 1992. reprint ed. mass mkt. 4.99 (*1-55817-655-1*, Pinncle Kensgtn) Kensgtn Pub Corp.

— Under Heaven. large type ed. 1989. 27.99 (*0-7089-2084-5*) Ulverscroft.

— The Warrior King. 224p. 1998. 24.00 (*0-7278-5376-7*) Severn Hse.

Clarke, Brian. Projects. 1999. 49.95 (*1-891475-13-4*) T Shafrazi.

Clarke, Brian & Goddard, John. The Trout & the Fly. 192p. 1996. 40.00 (*1-55821-441-0*) Lyons Pr.

Clarke, Brian, jt. auth. see Reger, Janet.

Clarke, Brian L. Running by Feeling: A Year on the Racing Comeback Trail. 320p. 1999. 24.95 (0-9663595-9-3) Competitive Running.
Clarke, Brian P. Piety & Nationalism: Lay Voluntary Associations & the Creation of an Irish-Catholic Community in Toronto, 1850-1895. 352p. 1993. 55.00 (0-7735-1130-X, Pub. by McG-Queens Univ Pr) CUP Services.
Clarke, Brian W., ed. Handbook of International Credit Management. 2nd ed. LC 95-871. 1995. 99.95 (0-566-07576-8, Pub. by Gower) Ashgate Pub Co.
Clarke, Bruce. Allegories of Writing: The Subject of Metamorphosis. LC 94-48335. (SUNY Series, the Margins of Literature). 204p. (C). 1995. text 49.50 (0-7914-2623-8); pap. text 16.95 (0-7914-2624-6) State U NY Pr.
— Dora Marsden & Early Modernism: Gender, Individualism, Science. LC 95-40679. (Studies in Literature & Science). 288p. (C). 1996. text 44.50 (0-472-10646-5, 10646) U of Mich Pr.
Clarke, Bruce. Energy Forms: Allegory & Science in the Era of Classical Thermodynamics. (Illus.). 352p. (C). text 49.50 (0-472-11174-4, 11174) U of Mich Pr.
Clarke, Bruce & Aycock, Wendell M., eds. The Body & the Text: Comparative Essays in Literature & Language. LC 90-10998. (Studies in Comparative Literature: No. 22). 1990. 24.95 (0-89672-225-2); pap. 12.95 (0-89672-226-0) Tex Tech Univ Pr.
Clarke, Bruce, jt. auth. see Collinge, John.
Clarke, Bruce B. & Gould, Ann B., eds. Turfgrass Patch Diseases Caused by Ectotrophic Root-Infecting Fungi. LC 93-72095. (Illus.). 161p. 1993. pap. 39.00 (0-89054-154-X) Am Phytopathol Soc.
Clarke, C. B. Composite Indica. 346p. (C). 1976. text 350.00 (0-89771-586-1, Pub. by Intl Bk Distr) St Mut.
Clarke, C. B., ed. Composite Indica. 347p. 1976. 225.00 (0-7855-6658-9, Pub. by Intl Bk Distr) St Mut.
Clarke, C. F., jt. auth. see Vaizey, John.
Clarke, C. G., jt. auth. see Roberts, Frank D.
Clarke, C. J. Reality Through the Looking-Glass: Science & Awareness in the Postmodern World. LC 96-147207. 1997. pap. text 19.95 (0-86315-216-3, Pub. by Floris Bks) Anthroposophic.
Clarke, C. J., jt. auth. see De Felice, F.
Clarke, Carl D. Illustration, Its Technique & Application to the Sciences. 2nd ed. (Illus.). 258p. 1949. 40.00 (0-911426-05-1) Standard Arts.
— Pictures, Their Preservation & Restoration. (Illus.). 250p. 1959. 40.00 (0-911426-06-X) Standard Arts.
— Prosthetics: Methods of Producing Facial & Body Restorations. (Illus.). 336p. 1965. 40.00 (0-911426-07-8) Standard Arts.
Clarke, Caro. The Wolf Ticket: A Novel. LC 98-14328. 216p. 1998. pap. 12.95 (1-56341-098-2); lib. bdg. 24.95 (1-56341-099-0) Firebrand Bks.
Clarke, Carol & Vanderway, Virginia. The Crisis Team: Your Guidebook for Developing a Crisis Response Program. Schilling, Dianne, ed. 135p. (Orig.). 1996. pap. text 26.95 (1-56499-030-3, IP9030) Innerchoice Pub.
Clarke, Carol, et al. Home Care Compliance Manual: Accredition & Legal Requirements. LC 99-19054. (Health Law & Compliance Center Ser.). 1999. write for info. (0-8342-1145-9) Aspen Pub.
Clarke, Caroline C. Village Life in America, 1852-1872. (American Biography Ser.). 202p. 1991. reprint ed. lib. bdg. 69.00 (0-7812-8071-0) Rprt Serv.
Clarke, Carwood G. W. T. Brown's "Scenes in My Life" Reprinted from the Rochester Post-Express, 1886. Santucci, James A. & Gomes, Michael, eds. (Theosophical History Occasional Papers: No. IV). (Illus.). i, 40p. (Orig.). 1995. reprint ed. pap. text 17.00 (1-883279-04-6) J Santucci.
Clarke, Catherine. My So-Called Life Goes On. 212p. (YA). (gr. 9-11). 1999. pap. 4.99 (0-375-80111-1, Pub. by Random Bks Yng Read) Random.
— Ninja Turtles: The Next Mutation. (J). 1998. 3.99 (0-679-89301-6, Pub. by Random Bks Yng Read) Random.
— Teenage Mutant Ninja Turtles: The Next Mutation. (J). 1998. 3.99 (0-679-89302-4, Pub. by Random Bks Yng Read) Random.
Clarke, Cathy & Swearingen, Lee. Macromedia Director Design Guide for Windows. (Illus.). 198p. (Orig.). 1995. pap. 30.00 (1-56830-202-9, Alpha Ref) Macmillan Gen Ref.
Clarke, Cathy, et al. Shocking the Web, Macintosh Edition. LC 97-138079. 464p. 1996. pap. 44.95 incl. cd-rom (0-201-88663-4) Peachpit Pr.
— Shocking the Web, Windows Edition. LC 97-163572. 464p. 1997. pap. 44.95 incl. cd-rom (0-201-88662-6) Peachpit Pr.
Clarke, Celia & Wallin, Debbie. The International Warmblood Horse: A Worldwide Guide to Breeding & Bloodlines. Kidd, Jane, ed. (Illus.). 256p. 1995. 42.95 (1-872082-71-8, Pub. by Kenilworth Pr) Half Halt Pr.
***Clarke, Chandra K.** Talamoora. LC 99-91772. 2000. 25.00 (0-7388-1256-0); pap. 18.00 (0-7388-1257-9) Xlibris Corp.
***Clarke, Charles.** The Art of Weight Loss: A Journey of Common Sense. LC 99-58868. (Illus.). 128p. 2000. pap. 7.95 (0-9644849-1-9, Pubng Cooperative) Pendleton Clay.
Clarke, Charles, jt. auth. see Bonington, Chris.
Clarke, Charles C. Shakespeare-Characters. LC 72-961. reprint ed. 49.50 (0-404-01567-0) AMS Pr.
Clarke, Charles G. Highlights & Shadows: The Memoirs of a Hollywood Cameraman. Slide, Anthony, ed. LC 89-10877. (Filmmakers Ser.: No. 21). (Illus.). 284p. 1989. 32.50 (0-8108-2237-7) Scarecrow.
***Clarke, Charles H.** Nathan's Spiritual Legacy. Fred. (Nathan Trilogy Ser.). 120p. 1999. pap. 9.99 (0-9660596-2-X) Matou Communs.
Clarke, Charlotte. A Narrative of the Life of Mrs. Charlotte Charke by Charlotte Charke. Rehder, Robert, ed. LC 97-47587. (Pickering Women's Classics Ser.). 320p. 1998. text 55.00 (1-85196-267-0, Pub. by Pickering & Chatto) Ashgate Pub Co.
Clarke, Charlotte B. Edible & Useful Plants of California. LC 76-14317. (California Natural History Guides Ser.: No. 41). (Illus.). 1978. pap. 15.95 (0-520-03267-5, Pub. by U CA Pr) Cal Prin Full Svc.
Clarke, Charlotte L., jt. auth. see Farlie, Barbara L.
***Clarke, Cheryl.** Best of the Vests. LC 98-26492. 64p. 1998. pap. 12.95 (0-7611-0000-8) Workman Pub.
Clarke, Cheryl. Experimental Love: Poetry. LC 93-32509. 88p. (Orig.). 1993. pap. 8.95 (1-56341-035-4); lib. bdg. 18.95 (1-56341-036-2) Firebrand Bks.
— Great Capes. LC 98-17408. 64p. 1998. pap. 12.95 (0-7611-0001-6) Workman Pub.
— Humid Pitch: Narrative Poetry. LC 89-23609. 132p. (Orig.). 1989. pap. 8.95 (0-932379-66-4); lib. bdg. 18.95 (0-932379-67-2) Firebrand Bks.
— Living As a Lesbian. LC 86-4648. 96p. (Orig.). 1986. pap. 7.95 (0-932379-12-5); lib. bdg. 16.95 (0-932379-13-3) Firebrand Bks.
Clarke, Christa. Collecting African Art: 1890's-1950's. (Illus.). 48p. 1996. pap. 25.00 (0-9628074-4-3) Hurst Gal.
Clarke, Christopher, ed. & illus. see Clarke, Cynthia.
Clarke, Christopher J., ed. Shareholder Value: Key to Corporate Development. LC 92-46885. (Best of Long Range Planning Ser.: Vol. 10). 132p. 1993. text 101.50 (0-08-040668-8, Pergamon Pr) Elsevier.
Clarke, Christopher M. Climbing the Mountain: In Search of the Soul of Karate. (Illus.). 42p. 1995. pap. 8.95 (1-929051-01-8) Amer Shorin-Ryu.
— Kamikaze! Japan's "Divine Wind" & the Spirit of the Martial Arts. (Illus.). 68p. 1995. pap. 8.95 (1-929051-02-6) Amer Shorin-Ryu.
— Samurai, Scoundrels & Saints: Stories from the Martial Arts. (Illus.). 165p. 1997. pap. 9.95 (1-929051-03-4) Amer Shorin-Ryu.
— Warriors & Wisemen: More Stories from the Martial Arts. (Illus.). 121p. 1998. pap. 19.95 (1-929051-04-2) Amer Shorin-Ryu.
Clarke, Clare E. Math in Stride, Bk. 3. 3rd ed. (C). 1988. text, student ed., wbk. ed. 10.95 (0-201-22371-6) Addison-Wesley.
Clarke, Clifford H. & Lipp, G. Douglas. Danger & Opportunity: Resolving Conflict in U. S.-Based Japanese Subsidiaries. LC 98-4939. 288p. 1998. 28.95 (1-877864-59-5) Intercult Pr.
***Clarke, Colin.** Class, Ethnicity & Community in Southern Mexico: Oaxaca's Peasantries. (Oxford Geographical & Environmental Studies). (Illus.). 270p. 2000. text 65.00 (0-19-823387-6) OUP.
Clarke, Colin, et al, eds. Geography & Ethnic Pluralism. 320p. 1984. pap. text 21.95 (0-04-309108-3) Routledge.
Clarke, Colin & Payne, Tony, eds. Politics, Security & Development in Small States. LC 87-1199. 238p. 1987. 55.00 (0-04-320203-9) Routledge.
Clarke, Colin C. Romantic Paradox: An Essay on the Poetry of Wordsworth. LC 78-10859. 101p. 1979. reprint ed. lib. bdg. 59.50 (0-313-20758-5, CLPA, Greenwood Pr) Greenwood.
Clarke, Colleen. Networking: How to Creatively Tap Your People Resources. xiv, 62p. (Orig.). 1993. pap. 12.95 (1-878542-41-9, 12-0011) SkillPath Pubns.
Clarke, Corita. Spirituality for Active Ministry. LC 90-61955. 88p. (Orig.). (C). 1991. pap. 6.95 (1-55612-361-2) Sheed & Ward WI.
Clarke, Cynthia. Cynthia Clarke's 60 Smoothie Sensations. Clarke, Christopher, ed. & illus. by. 144p. 1998. pap. 12.95 (0-9666091-0-7) Recreate Commun.
Clarke, Cyril, tr. see Cortot, Alfred.
Clarke, D. & Grainger, J. F. Polarized Light & Optical Measurements. 1971. 94.00 (0-08-016320-3, Pub. by Pergamon Repr) Franklin.
Clarke, D., jt. auth. see Roy, A. E.
Clarke, D. A. A London Bibliography of the Social Sciences Vols. 29-31: Eighth Supplement, 1972-1973, Set. 1768p. 1975. text 260.00 (0-7201-0454-8) Continuum.
Clarke, D. A., et al. Foundations of Analysis: With An Introduction to Logic & Set Theory. LC 73-136217. (Century Mathematics Ser.). (Illus.). (Orig.). (C). 1971. text 22.95 (0-89197-171-8) Irvington.
Clarke, D. J., jt. auth. see Minton, N. P.
Clarke, D. S. Philosophy's Second Revolution: Early & Recent Analytic Philosophy. LC 97-2863. 244p. 1997. 42.95 (0-8126-9347-7); pap. 21.95 (0-8126-9348-5) Open Court.
Clarke, D. S., Jr. Principles of Semiotic. 160p. 1987. 35.00 (0-7102-0981-9, Routledge Thoemms); pap. 14.95 (0-7102-1136-8, Routledge Thoemms) Routledge.
— Rational Acceptance & Purpose: An Outline of Pragmatist Epistemology. LC 87-37680. 158p. (Orig.). (C). 1989. 55.00 (0-8476-7599-8); pap. 23.00 (0-8476-7600-5) Rowman.
— Sources of Semiotic: Readings with Commentary from Antiquity to the Present. LC 89-26105. 240p. (C). 1990. pap. 17.95 (0-8093-1614-5) S Ill U Pr.
Clarke, D. S. & Behling, Richard. Deductive Logic: An Introduction to Evaluation Technique & Logical Theory. 2nd ed. LC 97-37708. 416p. (C). 1997. pap. 42.50 (0-7618-0922-8) U Pr of Amer.
Clarke, Dana W., Sr. TRIZ: Through the Eyes of an American TRIZ Specialist. 88p. 1997. 30.00 (1-928747-03-5) Ideation Intl.
***Clarke, Danielle.** Double Voice: Gendered Writing in Early Modern England. LC 99-88692. 224p. 2000. text 59.95 (0-312-23220-9) St Martin.
Clarke, Darral. Marketing Analysis & Decision Making: Text & Cases with Spreadsheets. 2nd ed. 480p. (C). 1992. teacher ed. write for info. (0-89426-231-9) Course Tech.
Clarke, David. The Architecture of Alienation: The Political Economy of Professional Education. LC 99-20883. 147p. (C). 1994. 34.95 (1-56000-157-7) Transaction Pubs.
— Constructive Assessment in Mathematics: Practical Steps for Classroom Teachers. 1997. pap. text 12.95 (1-55953-201-7) Key Curr Pr.
— Men Are Clams, Women Are Crowbars: Understanding Your Differences & Make Them Work. LC 99-194420. 256p. 1998. 14.99 (1-57748-450-9) Barbour Pub.
***Clarke, David.** Modern Chinese Art. LC 99-35800. (Images of Asia Ser.). (Illus.). 96p. 2000. text 16.95 (0-19-590606-3) OUP.
Clarke, David. Winning the Parenting War: A Battle Plan for Securing Victory on the Home Front. 254p. 1999. 14.99 (1-57748-574-2) Barbour Pub.
Clarke, David, ed. Tippett Studies. LC 97-41862. (Illus.). 275p. (C). 1998. 69.95 (0-521-59205-4) Cambridge U Pr.
Clarke, David & Roberts, Andy. Twilight of the Celtic Gods: An Exploration of Britain's Hidden Pagan Traditions. (Illus.). 176p. 1996. 27.95 (0-7137-2522-2, Pub. by Blandford Pr) Sterling.
Clarke, David, jt. auth. see Hegener, Karen C.
Clarke, David, jt. auth. see Sullivan, Peter.
Clarke, David, jt. ed. see Niven, Bill.
Clarke, David A. & West, Michael J., eds. Computational Astrophysics: Proceedings of the 12th Kingston Meeting on Theoretical Astrophysics Held in Halifax, Nova Scotia, Canada, October 17-19, 1996. LC 97-73640. (ASP Conference Series Proceedings: Vol. 123). 370p. 1997. 34.00 (1-886733-43-0) Astron Soc Pacific.
Clarke, David B. The Cinematic City. LC 96-31750. (Illus.). 264p. (C). 1997. 85.00 (0-415-12745-9); pap. 24.99 (0-415-12746-7) Routledge.
Clarke, David D., jt. auth. see Nerlich, Brigitte.
Clarke, David J. CNE Study Guide. 2nd ed. LC 95-70586. 145p. 1995. pap. 89.99 incl. cd-rom (0-7821-1820-8, Network Pr) Sybex.
— The CNE 3 Study Guide. 3rd ed. 1664p. 1996. pap. text, student ed. 89.99 incl. cd-rom (0-7821-1930-1, Network Pr) Sybex.
— The Complete Netware Construction Kit: A Professional Blueprint for Designing, Installing, & Managing LANs. LC 92-38970. 512p. 1993. pap. 39.95 (0-471-58259-X) Wiley.
— Novell's CNE Study Guide for Version 4.11: For Version 4.11. 2532p. 1997. pap. text 148.99 incl. cd-rom (0-7645-4533-7) IDG Bks.
Clarke, David J., 4th. Novell's CNA Study Guide for IntranetWare. LC 96-79590. 700p. 1997. 69.99 incl. cd-rom (0-7645-4513-2) IDG Bks.
Clarke, David J., IV. Novell's CNASM Study Guide for NetWare 5. LC TK5105.5.C555 1999. (Illus.). 944p. 1999. student ed. 74.99 incl. cd-rom (0-7645-4542-6) IDG Bks.
***Clarke, David J., IV.** Novell's CNE Study Guide for Netware 5. LC 99-60654. (Novell Press Ser.). 1552p. 1999. student ed., boxed set 99.99 incl. cd-rom (0-7645-4543-4) IDG Bks.
Clarke, David J., IV. Novell's CNE Study Guide for Netware 4.11. LC 96-78781. 1600p. 1997. pap. 89.99 (0-7645-4512-4) IDG Bks.
Clarke, David J., 4th. Novell's CNE Study Guide to Core Technologies. 900p. 1996. pap., student ed. 74.99 incl. cd-rom (0-7645-4501-9) IDG Bks.
***Clarke, David James.** Novell's CNE Clarke Notes for NetWare 5 Advanced Administration & Design & Implementation: Course 570 & 575. LC 99-86386. (Illus.). 400p. 2000. pap. text 34.99 (0-7645-4578-7) IDG Bks.
— Novell's CNE Clarke Notes for NetWare 5 Networking Technologies & Service & Support: Course 5. (Illus.). 400p. 2000. pap. 34.99 (0-7645-4576-0) IDG Bks.
— Novell's CNE Clarke Notes Update to NetWare 5. LC 99-48098. 264p. 1999. pap. 24.99 (0-7645-4575-2) IDG Bks.
Clarke, David James. Novell's CNE Study Set for NetWare 5. 2700p. 1999. pap. text 174.99 (0-7645-4554-X) IDG Bks.
Clarke, David L., ed. Models in Archaeology. 1972. 120.00 (0-416-16540-0, NO. 2144) Routledge.
Clarke, David L. & Merusi, Donald E. Systems Programming. LC 97-19517. 480p. 1997. pap. text 54.99 (0-13-490558-X) P-H.
Clarke, David R., ed. Transplantation Techniques & Use of Cryopreserved Allograft Cardiac Valves & Vascular Tissue. (Illus.). 237p. (C). 1989. pap. 345.00 (0-944903-03-7) Adams Pub Group.
Clarke, David W. Determining the Rate Law for the Crystal Violet - Hydroxide Ion Reaction. Schreiber, H., ed. (Modular Laboratory Program in Chemistry Ser.). 12p. (C). 1998. pap. text 1.50 (0-87540-504-5, KINE 504) Chem Educ Res.
— William Shakespeare. LC 70-179330. (Illus.). reprint ed. 49.50 (0-404-01568-9) AMS Pr.
Clarke, Deborah. Robbing the Mother: Women in Faulkner. LC 93-33642. 224p. 1994. text 30.00 (0-87805-592-4) U Pr of Miss.
— Women at Work: The Essential Guide for the Working Woman. 176p. 1992. pap. 12.95 (1-85230-109-0, Pub. by Element MA) Penguin Putnam.
Clarke, Dennis. Computer Aided Structural Design. LC 78-1511. (Illus.). 239p. 1978. reprint ed. pap. 74.10 (0-608-00192-9, 206097500006) Bks Demand.
Clarke, Desmond. Arthur Dobbs, Esquire, 1689-1765: Surveyor-General of Ireland, Prospector & Governor of North Carolina. LC 58-14501. 232p. reprint ed. pap. 72.00 (0-7837-2078-5, 204235200004) Bks Demand.
Clarke, Desmond, jt. auth. see Brown, Stephen.
Clarke, Desmond M. Occult Powers & Hypotheses: Cartesian Natural Philosophy under Louis XIV. 276p. 1989. text 85.00 (0-19-824812-1) OUP.
Clarke, Desmond M., jt. auth. see Descartes, Rene.
Clarke, Desmond M., ed. & tr. see De La Forge, Louis.
Clarke, Don & Murray, Anne, eds. Developing & Implementing a Whole-School Behavior Policy: A Practical Approach. LC 97-152996. 112p. 1996. pap. text 24.95 (1-85346-365-5, Pub. by David Fulton) Taylor & Francis.
Clarke, Donald. All or Nothing at All: A Life of Frank Sinatra. large type ed. LC 97-51266. (Americana Series). 1998. 26.95 (0-7862-1399-X) Thorndike Pr.
— All or Nothing at All: A Life of Frank Sinatra. LC 97-21885. (Illus.). 320p. 1997. reprint ed. 25.95 (0-88064-181-9) Fromm Intl Pub.
***Clarke, Donald.** All or Nothing at All: A Life of Sinatra. (Illus.). 2000. pap. 14.00 (0-88064-224-6) Fromm Intl Pub.
Clarke, Donald. Encyclopedia of Film. 1400p. 1999. text 65.00 (0-670-84667-8) Viking Penguin.
— The Rise & Fall of Popular Music. 640p. 1996. pap. 19.95 (0-312-14200-5) St Martin.
***Clarke, Donald.** The Rise & Fall of Popular Music. 620p. 1999. reprint ed. text 30.00 (0-7881-6590-9) DIANE Pub.
Clarke, Donald, ed. The Penguin Encyclopedia of Popular Music. 2nd ed. LC 99-213528. 1524p. 1999. pap. 22.95 (0-14-051370-1) Viking Penguin.
Clarke, Donald & Dartford, Mark, eds. Illustrated Encyclopedia Science & Invention: How It Works, Set. LC 93-3331. (Illus.). 3700p. (J). 1994. 349.95 (0-86307-491-X) Marshall Cavendish.
Clarke, Donald, jt. auth. see Coopey, Richard.
Clarke, Dorothy C. Juan de Mena's "Laberinto de Fortuna" Classic Epic & Mester de Clerecia. LC 73-89015. (Romance Monographs: No. 5). 1973. 22.00 (84-399-1732-5) Romance.
Clarke, Douglas A. Hierarchies of Predicates of Finite Types. LC 52-42839. (Memoirs Ser.: No. 1/51). 95p. 1964. pap. 16.00 (0-8218-1251-3, MEMO/1/51) Am Math.
— Hierarchies of Predicates of Finite Types. LC QA0241.A57. (American Mathematical Society, Memoirs Ser.: No. 51). 97p. reprint ed. pap. 30.10 (0-7837-6754-4, 204638300011) Bks Demand.
Clarke, Duncan. African Art. (Illus.). 112p. 1998. pap. 19.95 (1-57715-051-1) Knckerbocker.
— African Hats & Jewelry. 1998. 17.99 (0-7858-0984-8) Bk Sales Inc.
— The Art of African Textiles. LC 97-36666. (Illus.). 128p. 1997. 19.98 (1-57145-132-3, Thunder Bay) Advantage Pubs.
***Clarke, Duncan.** Colors of Africa. 2000. 19.98 (1-57145-264-8, Thunder Bay) Advantage Pubs.
— The History of American Slavery. 192p. 19.99 (1-57215-256-7) World Pubns.
***Clarke, Duncan, et al.** A New World: History of Immigration to the United States. 2000. 24.98 (1-57145-280-X, Thunder Bay) Advantage Pubs.
Clarke, Duncan L. American Defense & Foreign Policy Institutions: Toward a Sound Foundation. 320p. 1989. pap. 39.95 (0-88730-292-0, HarpBusn); pap. 17.95 (0-88730-296-3, HarpBusn) HarpInfo.
— American Defense & Foreign Policy Institutions: Toward a Sound Foundation. LC 92-15660. 268p. (C). 1992. reprint ed. pap. text 29.50 (0-8191-8732-1) U Pr of Amer.
Clarke, Duncan L. & Nagel, Stuart S., eds. Public Policy & Political Institutions Vol. 5: United States Defense & Foreign Policy - Policy Coordination & Integration. LC 85-12705. (Public Policy Ser.: Vol. 5). 414p. 1985. 73.25 (0-89232-374-4) Jai Pr.
Clarke, Duncan L. & O'Connor, Daniel D. Send Guns & Money: Security Assistance & U. S. Foreign Policy. LC 97-5885. 224p. 1997. 62.95 (0-275-95991-0, Praeger Pubs); pap. 21.95 (0-275-95992-9, Praeger Pubs) Greenwood.
Clarke, Duncan L., jt. ed. see Brauch, Hans G.
Clarke, E. D. Elements of Practical Geology. 4th ed. 1967. 19.95 (0-85564-029-4, Pub. by Univ of West Aust Pr) Intl Spec Bk.
Clarke, E. G. The Targum Pseudo - Jonathan of the Pentateuch. 1983. 150.00 (0-88125-015-5) Ktav.
Clarke, E. M., et al, eds. Computer-Aided Verification: 2nd International Conference, CAV '91 New Brunswick, NJ, June 18-21, 1990 Proceedings. (Lecture Notes in Computer Science Ser.: Vol. 531). xiii, 372p. 1991. 39.95 (0-387-54477-1) Spr-Verlag.
Clarke, E. M., et al. Computer-Aided Verification '90. LC 91-8815. (DIMACS Ser.: Vol. 3). 628p. 1991. text 100.00 (0-8218-6594-3, DIMACS/3) Am Math.
— Model Checking. LC 99-17979. (Illus.). 305p. 1999. 50.00 (0-262-03270-8) MIT Pr.
Clarke, Edward. Sex in Education: or A Fair Chance for the Girls. LC 74-180566. (Medicine & Society in America Ser.). 190p. 1977. reprint ed. 17.95 (0-405-03943-3) Ayer.
— The Story of My Life. viii, 439p. 1997. reprint ed. 112.50 (1-56169-344-8) Gaunt.
Clarke, Edward, jt. auth. see Walker-Smith, Derek.
Clarke, Edward D. Travels to Russia, Tartary & Turkey. LC 75-115520. (Russia Observed, Series I). 1970. reprint ed. 35.95 (0-405-03015-0) Ayer.

C

An Asterisk (*) at the beginning of an entry indicates that the title is appearing for the first time.

Clarke, Edwin & Jacyna, L. S. Nineteenth-Century Origins of Neuroscientific Concepts. 593p. (C). 1998. pap. text 17.00 (*0-7881-5669-1*) DIANE Pub.

— Nineteenth-Century Origins of Neuroscientific Concepts. (C). 1992. pap. 19.95 (*0-520-07879-9*, Pub. by U CA Pr) Cal Prin Full Svc.

Clarke, Edwin & O'Malley, C. D. The Human Brain & Spinal Cord: A Historical Study Illustrated By Writings from Antiquity to the Twentieth Century. LC 68-11275. 1019p. reprint ed. pap. 200.00 (*0-608-14441-X*, 20518650012) Bks Demand.

— The Human Brain & Spinal Cord: A Historical Study Illustrated by Writings from Antiquity to the 20th Century. 2nd ed. (Illus.). 973p. 1995. 225.00 (*0-930405-25-0*) Norman SF.

Clarke, Edwin, et al. An Illustrated History of Brain Function: Imaging the Brain from Antiquity to the Present. 2nd enl. rev. ed. (Illus.). 188p. 1995. reprint ed. 135.00 (*0-930405-65-X*) Norman SF.

Clarke, Edwin, ed. & tr. see Neuberger, Max.

Clarke, Edwin L. American Men of Letters: Their Nature & Nurture. LC 76-76714. (Columbia University. Studies in the Social Sciences: No. 168). reprint ed. 32.50 (*0-404-51168-6*) AMS Pr.

Clarke, Eileen. Classic Freshwater Fish Cooking. LC 97-28582. (Illus.). 128p. 1998. 24.95 (*0-89658-345-7*) Voyageur Pr.

— The Freshwater Fish Cookbook. LC 96-23137. (Fish & Game Kitchen Ser.). (Illus.). 128p. 1997. 24.95 (*0-89658-332-5*) Voyageur Pr.

— Queen of the Legal Tender Saloon. LC 97-4031. (Montana Novel Ser.). 288p. 1997. pap. 16.95 (*0-9626663-5-1*) Greycliff Pub.

— The Venison Cookbook. LC 96-23136. (Fish & Game Kitchen Ser.). (Illus.). 128p. 1997. 24.95 (*0-89658-331-7*) Voyageur Pr.

Clarke, Eileen & Strung, Sil. The Art of Wild Game Cooking. LC 95-22060. (Illus.). 128p. 1996. 24.95 (*0-89658-276-0*) Voyageur Pr.

Clarke, Eliza. Handel. LC 70-158201. (Studies in Music: No. 42). 1971. reprint ed. lib. bdg. 75.00 (*0-8383-1250-0*) M S G Haskell Hse.

Clarke, Elizabeth. Theory & Theology in George Herbert's Poetry: "Divinite & Poesie, Met" LC 97-9925. (Oxford Theological Monographs). 312p. 1997. text 75.00 (*0-19-826398-8*) OUP.

Clarke, Elizabeth D., et al. The Joy of Service. (Illus.). 1979. 5.95 (*0-686-26879-2*) YWCA.

Clarke-Epstein, Chris, et al. Finding Solutions to Workplace Problems: A Team's Guide to the Myers Briggs Type Indicator. 99p. 1994. ring bd. 139.00 (*0-9643933-0-1*) Link Pubns.

Clarke-Epstein, Chris, jt. auth. see Charles, C. Leslie.

Clarke-Epstein, Chris, jt. auth. see Charles, Leslie C.

Clarke, Eric & Emmerson, Simon. Music, Mind & Structure, Vol. 3, No. 1. Osborne, Nigel, ed. (Contemporary Music Review Ser.: Vol. 3, Pt. 1). iv, 236p. 1989. text 23.00 (*3-7186-4879-2*) Gordon & Breach.

***Clarke, Eric O.** Virtuous Vice: Homoeroticism & the Public Sphere. LC 99-44768. 216p. 2000. pap. 17.95 (*0-8223-2513-6*) Duke.

Clarke, Ernest. The Siege of Fort Cumberland, 1776: An Episode in the American Revolution. pap. 19.95 (*0-7735-1867-3*) McG-Queens Univ Pr.

— The Siege of Fort Cumberland, 1776: An Episode in the American Revolution. LC 96-191694. (Illus.). 304p. 1995. 49.95 (*0-7735-1323-X*, Pub. by McG-Queens Univ Pr) CUP Services.

Clarke, Ernest G. The Targum Pseudo - Jonathan Vol. 5B: Deuteronomy. LC 97-22398. 128p. 1997. 65.00 (*0-8146-5863-6*) Liturgical Pr.

Clarke, Ernst, jt. auth. see McNamara, Martin.

Clarke, Erskine. Our Southern Zion: A History of Calvanism in the South Carolina Low Country, 1690-1990. LC 95-8150. (FRE & LAT., Illus.). 448p. (C). 1996. text 44.95 (*0-8173-0757-5*) U of Ala Pr.

***Clarke, Erskine.** Wrestlin' Jacob: A Portrait of Religion in Antebellum Georgia & the Carolina Low Country. LC 99-53046. (Religion & American Culture Ser.). 256p. 2000. reprint ed. pap. text 19.95 (*0-8173-1040-1*) U of Ala Pr.

Clarke, Ethne. Autumn Gardens. LC 99-29015. (Illus.). 168p. 1999. 35.00 (*1-57959-049-7*, SOMA) BB&T Inc.

— Gardening with Foliage Plants: Leaf, Bark & Berry. LC 97-208151. (Illus.). 168p. 1997. 29.95 (*0-7892-0330-8*) Abbeville Pr.

— Gardening with Foliage Plants: Leaf, Bark, & Berry. (Illus.). 168p. 1999. 14.98 (*0-89660-109-9*, Artabras) Abbeville Pr.

— Herb Garden Design. LC 94-46523. (Illus.). 144p. 1995. 25.00 (*0-02-860358-3*, Pub. by Macmillan) S&S Trade.

***Clarke, Ethne.** Three Seasons of Summer: Gardening with Annuals & Biennials. (Illus.). 168p. 1999. 29.95 (*0-7153-0807-6*, Pub. by D & C Pub) Sterling.

***Clarke, Ethne.** Water Features for Small Gardens. 128p. 1999. pap. text 17.95 (*0-7063-7842-3*) Ward & Ward.

Clarke, Ethne. Water Features for Small Gardens. (Illus.). 128p. 1998. 27.95 (*0-7063-7706-0*, Pub. by WrLock) Sterling.

Clarke, Ethne & Wright, George. English Topiary Gardens. (Country Ser.). (Illus.). 160p. 1997. pap. 16.95 (*1-85799-928-2*) Phoenix Hse.

Clarke, F. C., tr. see German General Staff.

Clarke, F. H. Optimization & Nonsmooth Analysis. LC 90-35113. (Classics in Applied Mathematics Ser.: No. 5). xii, 308p. 1990. pap. 38.00 (*0-89871-256-4*) Soc Indus-Appl Math.

Clarke, F. H., et al, eds. Nonsmooth Optimization & Related Topics. (Ettore Majorana International Science Ser., Life Sciences: Vol. 43). (Illus.). 502p. (C). 1989. text 174.00 (*0-306-43247-1*, Kluwer Plenum) Kluwer Academic.

Clarke, F. L., et al. Corporate Collapse: Regulatory, Accounting & Ethical Failure. LC 96-39880. (Illus.). 314p. (C). 1998. pap. text 24.95 (*0-521-58523-6*) Cambridge U Pr.

Clarke, F. P. & Nahm, Milton C. Philosophical Essays in the Honor of Edgar Arthur Singer, Jr. LC 78-80394. (Essay Index Reprint Ser.). 1977. 26.95 (*0-8369-1062-1*) Ayer.

Clarke, F. R. Healey Willan: Life & Music. unabridged ed. (Illus.). 320p. 1997. reprint ed. pap. 24.95 (*0-8020-8136-3*) U of Toronto Pr.

Clarke, Frank & Dean, Graeme. Replacement Costs & Accounting Reform in Post World War I Germany. 206p. 1991. text 10.00 (*0-8153-0006-9*) Garland.

Clarke, Frank H. Methods of Dynamic & Nonsmooth Optimization. LC 89-21682. (CBMS-NSF Regional Conference Series in Applied Mathematics: No. 57). v, 90p. 1989. pap. 24.50 (*0-89871-241-6*) Soc Indus-Appl Math.

Clarke, Frank H., et al. Nonsmooth Analysis & Control Theory. LC 97-34140. (Graduate Texts in Mathematics Ser.: Vol. 178). (Illus.). 296p. 1997. 49.95 (*0-387-98336-8*) Spr-Verlag.

Clarke, Frank L. & Dean, Graeme. Contributions of Limperg & Schmidt to the Replacement Cost Debate in the 1920s. LC 90-27264. (New Works in Accounting History: Vol. 3). 350p. 1991. reprint ed. text 10.00 (*0-8153-0007-7*) Garland.

***Clarke, G.** Scratch N'Sniff. (J). 1998. pap. text 9.95 (*0-86264-810-6*, Pub. by Random) Trafalgar.

Clarke, G. C., jt. ed. see Punt, W.

Clarke, G. K. The Descendants of Nathanial Clarke & His Wife Elizabeth Somerby of Newbury, Mass. A History of Ten Generations, 1642-1902. (Illus.). 468p. 1989. reprint ed. pap. 73.00 (*0-8328-0405-3*); reprint ed. lib. bdg. 83.00 (*0-8328-0404-5*) Higginson Bk Co.

***Clarke, G. M. & Cooke, D.** A Basic Course in Statistics. 4th ed. LC 98-28794. (Arnold Publications). (Illus.). 704p. 1998. pap. text 35.00 (*0-340-71995-8*) OUP.

Clarke, G. M. & Griffiths, J. B., eds. Raw Materials for the Glass & Ceramics Industries. 210p. 1987. pap. text 84.00 (*0-947671-13-7*) Metal Bulletin.

Clarke, G. W., ed. The Letters of St. Cyprian of Carthage, Vol. IV. (Ancient Christian Writers Ser.: No. 47). 1988. 24.95 (*0-8091-0370-2*) Paulist Pr.

Clarke, G. W., tr. see Lawler, Thomas C. & Burghart, Johannes, eds.

Clarke, Garry E. Essays on American Music, 62. LC 76-52606. (Contributions in American History Ser.: No. 62). (Illus.). 259p. 1977. 65.00 (*0-8371-9484-9*, CAM/, Greenwood Pr) Greenwood.

Clarke, Geoffrey M. Statistics & Experimental Design: An Introduction for Biologists & Biochemists. 3rd ed. LC 94-35530. (An Arnold Publication). 256p. 1994. pap. 35.00 (*0-340-59324-5*, Pub. by E A) OUP.

Clarke, Geoffrey M. & Kempson, Robert E. Introduction to the Design & Analysis of Experiments. LC 97-119753. (An Arnold Publication). 352p. 1998. pap. 39.95 (*0-340-64555-5*, Pub. by E A) OUP.

Clarke, George. John Bellers: His Life, Times, & Writings. 320p. 1988. text 57.50 (*0-7102-1278-X*, Routledge Thoemms) Routledge.

***Clarke, George.** John Bellers (1654-1725) 1999. pap. 30.00 (*1-85072-136-X*, Pub. by W Sessions) St Mut.

Clarke, George. Woggle & Butter Harsies. 112p. 1990. pap. 35.00 (*0-86138-081-9*, Pub. by T Dalton) St Mut.

***Clarke, George E.** Beatrice Chancy. LC 99-61831. 160p. 1999. pap. 14.95 (*1-896095-94-1*) Polstar Bk.

Clarke, George E. Eyeing the North Star: Directions in African-Canadian Literature. LC 97-156822. 286p. 1997. pap. text 15.95 (*0-7710-2125-9*) McCland & Stewart.

Clarke, George E. & Sparks, Jeremy. Whylah Falls: The Play. 1999. pap. 14.95 (*0-88754-565-3*) Theatre Comm.

***Clarke, George Elliot.** Gold Indigoes. num. ed. Kellogg, David, ed. (Carolina Wren Press Poetry Chapbook Ser.). 32p. 2000. pap. 19.60 (*0-932112-42-0*) Carolina Wren.

— Succory. Kellogg, David, ed. LC 99-57475. (Carolina Wren Press Poetry Chapbook Ser.). 32p. 2000. 12.95 (*0-932112-41-2*) Carolina Wren.

— Succory. num. ed. Kellogg, David, ed. (Carolina Wren Press Poetry Chapbook Ser.). 32p. 2000. pap. 19.64 (*0-932112-43-9*) Carolina Wren.

***Clarke, George Elliott.** Gold Indigoes. LC 99-56663. (Carolina Wren Press Poetry Chapbook Ser.). 32p. 1999. 12.95 (*0-932112-40-4*) Carolina Wren.

— Whylah Falls: Tenth Anniversary Edition. 2nd anniversary rev. ed. (Illus.). 240p. 2000. 19.95 (*1-896095-52-6*); pap. 15.95 (*1-896095-50-X*) Polstar Bk.

Clarke, George K., ed. Epitaphs from Graveyards in Wellesley (formerly West Needham), North Natick, & Saint Mary's Churchyard in Newton Lower Falls, Massachusetts: With Genealogical & Biographical Notes. 236p. 1987. reprint ed. pap. 17.50 (*1-55613-021-X*) Heritage Bk.

***Clarke, Georgia & Crossley, Paul, eds.** Architecture & Language. LC 99-52216. (Illus.). 256p. 2000. write for info. (*0-521-65078-X*) Cambridge U Pr.

Clarke, Gerald. Capote: A Biography. 1997. pap. 14.95 (*0-345-91276-4*) Ballantine Pub Grp.

***Clarke, Gerald.** Get Happy: The Life of Judy Garland. LC 99-36285. (Illus.). 608p. 2000. 29.95 (*0-375-50378-1*) Random.

— Get Happy: The Life of Judy Garland. LC 00-42577. (Illus.). 2000. write for info. (*0-7862-2721-4*) Thorndike Pr.

Clarke, Gerard. Politics of NGO's in Southeast Asia: Participation & Protest in the Philippines. LC 97-38363. (Politics in Asia Ser.). 272p. (C). 1998. 85.00 (*0-415-17140-7*) Routledge.

Clarke, Giles. Offshore Tax Planning. LC 99-187689. xxi, 225 p. 1997. write for info. (*0-406-89924-X*, Pub. by Butterworths) LEXIS Pub.

— Offshore Tax Planning. 5th ed. LC 99-187603. xxii, 248 p. 1998. write for info. (*0-406-89923-1*, Pub. by Butterworths) LEXIS Pub.

Clarke, Giles. Pre-Roman & Roman Winchester Pt. 2: The Roman Cemetary at Lankhills. (Winchester Studies). (Illus.). 510p. 1980. text 105.00 (*0-19-813177-1*) OUP.

Clarke, Giles, ed. Butterworths Offshore Cases & Materials. 1996. ring bd., boxed set. write for info. (*0-406-05396-0*, COTSBI0, MICHIE) LEXIS Pub.

Clarke, Giles & Sumption, Anthony, compiled by. Sumption: Capital Gains Tax. 1995. ring bd. write for info. (*0-406-99840-X*, STCGASET, MICHIE) LEXIS Pub.

Clarke, Giles, ed. see Sumption, Anthony.

Clarke, Gillian. Collected Poems. LC 98-203752. 220p. 1998. pap. 18.95 (*1-85754-335-1*, Pub. by Carcanet Pr) Paul & Co Pubs.

***Clarke, Gillian.** Five Fields. 80p. 1999. pap. (*1-85754-401-3*, Pub. by Carcanet Pr) Paul & Co Pubs.

Clarke, Gillian. The Sundial. 55p. 1984. pap. 5.95 (*0-8464-4753-3*) Beekman Pubs.

— The Sundial. (C). 1984. pap. 20.00 (*0-85088-540-X*, Pub. by Gomer Pr) St Mut.

Clarke, Gillian, ed. see Augustine, Saint.

Clarke, Gillian, tr. see Elfyn, Menna.

Clarke, Gillian, tr. see Jones, T. Llew.

***Clarke, Ginjer.** Baby Alligator. LC 99-88807. (All Aboard Reading Ser.). (Illus.). 48p. (J). 2000. 13.89 (*0-448-41851-7*, G & D); pap. 3.99 (*0-448-42095-3*, G & D) Peng Put Young Read.

***Clarke, Ginjer L.** Baby Alligator. (All Aboard Reading Ser.). (Illus.). (J). 2000. 9.44 (*0-606-18463-5*) Turtleback.

Clarke, Gordon R. The Word Hesed in the Hebrew Bible. (JSOTS Ser.: Vol. 157). 286p. 1993. 80.00 (*1-85075-408-X*, Pub. by Sheffield Acad) CUP Services.

Clarke, Graehme W., tr. The Letters of St. Cyprian. (Ancient Christian Writers Ser.: Nos. 43 & 44). 416p. 1983. 24.95 (*0-8091-0341-9*) Paulist Pr.

Clarke, Graeme, ed. Reading the Past in Late Antiquity. 370p. 1990. 39.00 (*0-08-034407-0*, Pergamon Pr) Elsevier.

Clarke, Graeme W., ed. The Letters of St. Cyprian Vol. 3: Letters 55-66. (Ancient Christian Writers Ser.: No. 46). 352p. 1986. 24.95 (*0-8091-0369-9*) Paulist Pr

Clarke, Graeme W., tr. The Letters of St. Cyprian. (Ancient Christian Writers Ser.: No. 44). 352p. 1983. 22.95 (*0-8091-0342-7*) Paulist Pr.

***Clarke, Graham.** Bait Box Stew: Graham Clarke's Cornwall. (Illus.). 63p. 2000. 37.50 (*0-9536969-2-8*, Pub. by Thrd Millennium) Trans-Atl Phila.

— Graham Clarke's History of England: Before It Became Boring & Too Much Like Real Life. rev. ed. (Illus.). 80p. 1999. 26.50 (*0-9536969-1-X*, Pub. by Thrd Millennium) Trans-Atl Phila.

— Kent Book: Graham Clarke's Kent. (Illus.). 128p. 2000. 46.50 (*0-9536969-3-6*, Pub. by Thrd Millennium) Trans-Atl Phila.

Clarke, Graham. The Photograph: A Visual & Cultural History. LC 96-47645. (Oxford History of Art Ser.). (Illus.). 246p. 1997. pap. 16.95 (*0-19-284200-5*) OUP.

— The Photograph: A Visual & Cultural History. (Oxford History of Art Ser.). (Illus.). 248p. (C). 1997. 39.95 (*0-19-284248-X*) OUP.

— W. Shakespeare Gent: His Actual Nottebooke. (Illus.). 78p. 1992. pap. 20.00 (*0-9502357-2-5*, Pub. by Ebenezer Pr GBR) Trans-Atl Phila.

— Walt Whitman: The Poem As Private History. 176p. 1991. text 35.00 (*0-312-03744-9*) St Martin.

Clarke, Graham, ed. The American City: Literary & Cultural Perspectives, 3 vols., Set. (Literary Sources & Documents Ser.). (Illus.). 1872p. (C). (gr. 13). 1997. 410.00 (*1-873403-20-8*, C0549) Routledge.

— The American Landscape, 3 vol. set. (Sources & Documents Ser.). (Illus.). 1808p. (C). (gr. 13). 1993. 410.00 (*1-873403-05-4*, A9755) Routledge.

— Edgar Allen Poe: Critical Assessments, 4 vols., Set. (Illus.). 1508p. (C). (gr. 13). 1991. 535.00 (*1-873403-00-3*, A6473) Routledge.

— Walt Whitman: Critical Assessments, 4 vols., Set. (Critical Assessments of Writers in English Ser.). 2112p. (C). (gr. 13). 1994. 535.00 (*1-873403-16-X*, C0580) Routledge.

Clarke, Graham & Toogood, Alan. The Complete Book of Plant Propagation. (Illus.). 256p. 1992. pap. 19.95 (*0-7063-7079-1*, Pub. by WrLock) Sterling.

Clarke, Graham, ed. see Poe, Edgar Allan.

Clarke, Grahm, ed. Thomas Hardy: Critical Assessments, 4 vols., Set. (Critical Assessments of Writers in English Ser.). (Illus.). 1856p. (C). (gr 13 up). 1993. text, boxed set 535.00 (*1-873403-08-9*) Routledge.

Clarke, Greg, jt. auth. see Jensen, Phillip D.

Clarke, Gus. Demasiados Ositos/Too Many Teddies. 1996. pap. 7.50 (*84-480-0151-6*) Lectorum Pubns.

— Nothing but Trouble. (Illus.). 32p. 1998. pap. 9.95 (*0-86264-841-6*, Pub. by Andersen Pr) Trafalgar.

***Clarke, Gus.** Sammy's Waggy Tail. (Illus.). 6p. (J). 1999. 13.95 (*0-86264-838-6*, Pub. by Andersen Pr) Trafalgar.

Clarke, Gus. E I E I O: The Story of Old MacDonald, Who Had a Farm. LC 92-53462. (J). (gr. 3 up). 1993. 14.00 (*0-688-12215-9*) Lothrop.

— Good Night Lucy a Push & Pull Tab Book. 12p. (YA). (ps-1). 1998. per. 12.95 (*0-689-81889-0*) S&S Trade.

Clarke, H. Menu Terminology. 86p. 1982. pap. 12.95 (*0-8288-1296-9*, M13058) Fr & Eur.

Clarke, H., et al. Political Choice in Canada. 1979. text 24.95 (*0-07-082783-4*) McGraw.

***Clarke, H. B.** Biblical Law: Being a Text of the Statutes, Ordinances & Judgments Established in the Holy Bible with Many Allusions to Secular Laws--Ancient, Medieval & Modern--Documented to the Scriptures, Judicial Decisions & Legal Literature. fac. ed. LC 99-53316. 2000. write for info. (*1-58477-062-7*) Lawbk Exchange.

Clarke, H. B. Spanish Literature: A Handbook with Index. 1977. lib. bdg. 59.95 (*0-8490-2651-2*) Gordon Pr.

Clarke, H. D. & Hamamura, Motoko. Colloquial Japanese. (Colloquials Ser.). 240p. (gr. 13). 1981. pap. 18.99 (*0-415-04544-4*, A4363) Routledge.

— Colloquial Japanese. (Colloquials Ser.). 346p. (C). 1990. audio 27.99 (*0-415-04740-4*, A4359) Routledge.

— Colloquial Japanese. (Colloquials Ser.). 364p. (gr. 13). 1990. pap. 29.99 incl. audio (*0-415-04741-2*, 05954) Routledge.

Clarke, H. D., tr. see Morton, Leith, ed.

Clarke, H. J. The New Approach to Uilleann Piping. (Illus.). 85p. 1999. pap. text 26.95 (*1-900428-51-2*, OS10968) Ossian.

Clarke, H. W., tr. see Dessemontet, Francois.

Clarke, H. Wilberforce, ed. Sufi Mysticism: An Account, with a Glossary of Their Esoteric Terms. 1994. pap. 6.95 (*1-55818-300-0*, Near Eastern) Holmes Pub.

Clarke, H. Wilberforce, tr. A Dervish Textbook: Kashani's Recension of Suhrawardi's Gifts. 168p. 1990. reprint ed. 32.00 (*0-900860-73-1*, Pub. by Octagon Pr) ISHK.

Clarke, H. Wilberforce, jt. auth. see Shahab ud-Din Suhrawardi.

Clarke, H. Wilberforce, tr. see Nizami, Nizam.

Clarke, Hans T., et al. A Symposium on the Use of Isotopes in Biology & Medicine, University of Wisconsin, 1947. LC 48-2939. 468p. reprint ed. pap. 145.10 (*0-608-18665-1*, 202113100021) Bks Demand.

Clarke, Harold. Parish, Town & Community Councils: A Guide to Law & Administration. 160p. 1991. 42.00 (*0-85314-368-4*, Pub. by Tolley Pubng) St Mut.

Clarke, Harold, et al. Canadian National Election Study, 1974. 1977. write for info. (*0-89138-156-2*) ICPSR.

Clarke, Harold D. & Czudnowski, Moshe M., eds. Political Elites in Anglo-American Democracies. LC 86-21822. (International Yearbook for Studies of Leaders & Leadership Ser.). 1987. 32.00 (*0-87580-126-9*) N Ill U Pr.

Clarke, Harold D., jt. auth. see Kornberg, Allan.

Clarke, Harold G. Remembering Forward. LC 94-42345. 234p. 1995. 25.00 (*0-86554-472-7*, MUP-H370) Mercer Univ Pr.

Clarke, Helen. East Anglia. LC 72-175516. (Regional Archaeologies Ser.). 92 p. 1971. write for info. (*0-435-32972-3*) Heinemann.

Clarke, Helen & Ambrosiani, Bjorn. Towns in the Viking Age. 2nd ed. 210p. 2000. pap. 21.00 (*0-7185-1792-X*) St Martin.

Clarke, Helen A. Browning & His Century. LC 73-18248. (Studies in Browning: No. 4). 1974. lib. bdg. 75.00 (*0-8383-1734-0*) M S G Haskell Hse.

— Browning's Italy. LC 72-3566. (Studies in Browning: No. 4). (Illus.). 1972. reprint ed. lib. bdg. 75.00 (*0-8383-1546-1*) M S G Haskell Hse.

Clarke, Helen A., ed. see Browning, Elizabeth Barrett.

Clarke, Helen I. Social Legislation. 2nd ed. LC 57-6100. 1957. 29.50 (*0-8290-1656-2*) Irvington.

Clarke, Henry Austin, Jr., jt. ed. see Kimes, Beverly R.

Clarke, Henry B. The Cid Campeador & the Waning of the Crescent in the West. LC 73-14438. (Heroes of the Nations Ser.). (Illus.). reprint ed. 49.50 (*0-404-58256-7*) AMS Pr.

— Spanish Literature: A Handbook. 1980. lib. bdg. 64.50 (*0-8490-3194-X*) Gordon Pr.

Clarke, Herb, jt. auth. see Fisher, Chris.

Clarke, Herbert. An Introduction to Northern California Birds. Ort, Kathleen, ed. LC 95-2055. (Illus.). 200p. (Orig.). 1995. pap. 14.00 (*0-87842-312-5*) Mountain Pr.

— An Introduction to Southern California Birds. LC 89-30720. (Illus.). 192p. 1989. pap. 14.00 (*0-87842-233-1*) Mountain Pr.

Clarke, Herbert L. Elementary Studies for the Trumpet. (Illus.). 53p. 1936. pap. 10.95 (*0-8258-0234-2*, 0-2279) Fischer Inc NY.

— Technical Studies for the Cornet. 53p. 1934. pap. 11.50 (*0-8258-0158-3*, 02280) Fischer Inc NY.

Clarke, Herman F. John Coney, Silversmith, 1655-1722. LC 71-87562. (Architecture & Decorative Art Ser.: Vol. 38). (Illus.). lx, 104p. 1971. reprint ed. lib. bdg. 35.00 (*0-306-71393-4*) Da Capo.

Clarke, Herman F. & Foote, Henry W. Jeremiah Dummer: Colonial Craftsman & Merchant, 1645-1718. LC 75-87563. (Architecture & Decorative Art Ser.). (Illus.). 1970. reprint ed. 32.50 (*0-306-71394-2*) Da Capo.

Clarke, Hilda. From the Fens to Westminster & Back - or What Price Independence? 121p. (C). 1989. text 36.00 (*0-902662-77-5*, Pub. by R K Pubns); pap. text 21.00 (*0-902662-78-3*, Pub. by R K Pubns) St Mut.

***Clarke, Hope C.** Shadow Lover: He Heard Her Cries & Out of the Shadows He Came. 1999. pap. 15.00 (*1-929279-00-0*) A New Hope Pubg.

Clarke, Howard. Homer's Readers: A Historical Introduction to the Iliad & the Odyssey. LC 78-66824. 327p. 1981. 38.50 (*0-87413-150-2*) U Delaware Pr.

Clarke, Howard, ed. Medieval Dublin: The Living City. (Illus.). 240p. 1990. 16.95 (*0-7165-2460-0*, Pub. by Irish Acad Pr) Intl Spec Bk.

— Medieval Dublin: The Making of a Metropolis. (Illus.). 320p. 1990. 16.95 (*0-7165-2459-7*, Pub. by Irish Acad Pr) Intl Spec Bk.

Clarke, Howard, et al, eds. Ireland & Scandinavia in the Early Viking Age. 492p. 1999. 39.50 (*1-85182-235-6*, Pub. by Four Cts Pr) Intl Spec Bk.

C

Clarke, Howard & Burden, Vera. Discovering the Ridgeway. 80p. 1995. pap. 8.50 (0-7478-0267-X, Pub. by Shire Pubns) St Mut.

Clarke, Howard, ed. & intro. see Virgil.

Clarke, Howard B. Irish Cities. LC 95-229083. (Illus.). 224p. 1996. pap. 19.95 (1-85635-127-0) Dufour.

Clarke, Howard B., tr. see Duby, Georges.

Clarke, Howard W. The Art of the Odyssey. Betts, John H., ed. (Illus.). 120p. (C). 1989. reprint ed. pap. 11.00 (0-86516-236-0) Bolchazy-Carducci.

Clarke, Hugh A. Pronouncing Dictionary of Musical Terms, Giving the Meaning Derivation & Pronunciation of Italian, German, French & Other Words. 1977. reprint ed. 39.00 (0-403-07492-4) Scholarly.

Clarke, Hugh V. Fire One! LC 80-507927. 152 p. 1978. 2.15 (0-207-13620-3) Consort Bk Sales.

— A Life for Every Sleeper: A Pictorial Record of the Burma-Thailand Railway. (Illus.). 144p. 1987. 24.95 (0-04-909023-2) Routledge.

Clarke, Hyde. Memoir of the Comparative Grammar of Egyptian-Coptic & Ude. 1987. reprint ed. pap. 7.95 (0-89979-045-3) British Am Bks.

***Clarke, I. F.** British Future Fiction, 1700-1914. 2100p. 2000. 795.00 (1-85196-617-X, Pub. by Pickering & Chatto) Ashgate Pub Co.

Clarke, I. F., ed. The Great War with Germany, 1890-1914 No. 2: Fictions & Fantasies of the War-to-Come. LC 98-200137. (Illus.). 440p. 1997. 46.95 (0-85323-632-1, Pub. by Liverpool Univ Pr); pap. 18.95 (0-85323-642-9, Pub. by Liverpool Univ Pr) Intl Spec Bk.

— The Tale of the Next Great War, 1871-1914: Fictions of Future Warfare & Battles Still-to-Come. LC 95-40302. (FRE & GER., Illus.). 396p. (C). 1996. text 45.00 (0-8156-2672-X, CLTN); pap. text 19.95 (0-8156-0358-4, CLTN) Syracuse U Pr.

Clarke, Ian & Lee, Helen. Name That Flower: The Identification of Flowering Plants. (Illus.). 272p. 1994. reprint ed. pap. 29.95 (0-522-84335-2, Pub. by Melbourne Univ Pr) Paul & Co Pubs.

Clarke, Ida C. American Women & the World War. LC 74-75233. (United States in World War I Ser.). xix, 545p. 1974. reprint ed. lib. bdg. 59.95 (0-89198-096-2) Ozer.

Clarke, Isabel. Shelley & Byron. LC 74-118006. (English Literature Ser.: No. 33). 1970. reprint ed. lib. bdg. 75.00 (0-8383-1062-1) M S G Haskell Hse.

Clarke, Isabel C. Six Portraits. LC 67-26725. (Essay Index Reprint Ser.). 1977. 23.95 (0-8369-0309-9) Ayer.

Clarke, J. Al Capsella & the Watchdogs. LC 90-26090. 160p. (YA). (gr. 6 up). 1995. 14.95 (0-8050-1598-1, Bks Young Read) H Holt & Co.

— The Heroic Life of Al Capsella. LC 89-24629. 160p. (YA). (gr. 6 up). 1995. 14.95 (0-8050-1310-5, Bks Young Read) H Holt & Co.

— The Heroic Life of Al Capsella. 1997. 12.05 (0-606-13480-8, Pub. by Turtleback) Demco.

— The Heroic Life of Al Capsella. (J). (gr. 7). 1997. reprint ed. pap. 6.95 (0-8050-5541-X) H Holt & Co.

Clarke, J., ed. Large-Scale Pile Tests in Clay: Proceedings of the Conference on Recent Large-Scale Fully Instrumented Pile Tests in Clay Held at the Institution of Civil Engineers, London, June 23-24, 1992. 120p. 1993. 134.00 (0-7277-1918-1) Am Soc Civil Eng.

Clarke, J. A. Huguenot Warrior: The Life & Times of Henri de Rohan, 1579-1638. (International Archives of the History of Ideas Ser.: No. 17). 230p. 1967. lib. bdg. 163.00 (90-247-0193-7) Kluwer Academic.

Clarke, J. C. Agoraphobia: A Clinical & Personal Account. (Illus.). 202p. 1985. text 39.00 (0-08-029866-4); pap. text 21.00 (0-08-029846-X) Elsevier.

— Alcoholism & Problem Drinking: Treating Addiction or Modifying Bad Habits? 152p. 1988. text 24.51 (0-08-034432-1, Pergamon Pr); pap. text 28.00 (0-08-034433-X, Pergamon Pr) Elsevier.

Clarke, J. D. Yakubu Gowon: Faith in a United Nigeria. (Illus.). 150p. 1986. 32.50 (0-7146-3286-4, Pub. by F Cass Pubs) Intl Spec Bk.

Clarke, J. F., jt. auth. see Toro, E. F.

Clarke, J. I., jt. auth. see O'Brien, Michael J.

Clarke, J. J. The Crow of the Moon. 1987. 4.00 (0-318-64164-X) Poets Pr.

— Oriental Enlightenment: The Encounter Between Asian & Western Thought. LC 96-41067. 272p. (C). 1997. pap. 22.99 (0-415-13376-9) Routledge.

***Clarke, J. J.** Tao of the West: Taoism in Western Thought. 224p. 2000. 75.00 (0-415-20619-7) Routledge.

— Tao of the West: Western Transformation of Taoist Thought. 2000. pap. 19.99 (0-415-20620-0) Routledge.

Clarke, J. L., ed. Structural Design of Polymer Composites: Eurocomp Design Code & Background Document. 768p. (C). (gr. 13). 1996. 180.00 (0-419-19450-9) Chapman & Hall.

Clarke, J. L. & Garas, F. K., eds. Structural Design for Hazardous Loads: The Role of Physical Testing. (Illus.). 488p. 1992. mass mkt. 154.95 (0-419-17250-5, E & FN Spon) Routledge.

Clarke, Jack. From Feathers to Iron. 400p. (Orig.). 1987. pap. 10.00 (0-939180-42-1) Tombouctou.

— Life after Grief: A Soul Journey after Suicide. LC 88-90968. 192p. (Orig.). 1989. pap. 9.95 (0-929841-02-6) Prsnl Pathways.

Clarke, Jack A. Research Materials in the Social Sciences. 2nd ed. LC 67-25948. 64p. reprint ed. pap. 30.00 (0-608-12890-2, 202362900033) Bks Demand.

Clarke, Jack A., ed. see Conference on Book Publishing in Wisconsin, May 6,, et al.

Clarke, Jackie, jt. auth. see Godfrey, Kerry.

***Clarke, Jacqueline.** Fresh & Fun: Dozens of Instant & Irresistible Ideas & Activities from Creative Teachers Across the Country. (Fresh & Fun Ser.). (Illus.). 32p. (J). 2000. pap. 8.95 (0-439-05183-5) Scholastic Inc.

— Hands-on-Math Around the Year: A Super-Creative Collection of Kid-Pleasing Activities That Build. (Illus.). 11p. (J). 2000. pap. 14.95 (0-590-96725-8) Scholastic Inc.

Clarke, Jacqueline L. Nathan: The Spiritual Journey of an Uncommon Cat. (Illus.). 120p. 1997. pap. 7.99 (0-9660596-0-3) Matou Communs.

— Nathan, Spiritual Advisor to Bill & Bob: An Adult Parable by Jacqueline L. Clarke. (Illus.). 128p. 1998. pap. 9.99 (0-9660596-1-1) Matou Communs.

Clarke, James. Atlantic Pilot Atlas. 2nd ed. 80p. 1997. pap. 65.00 (0-07-011921-X) McGraw.

Clarke, James F. Anti-Slavery Days: A Sketch of the Struggle Which Ended in the Abolition of Slavery in the United States. LC 72-1050. reprint ed. 29.50 (0-404-00252-8) AMS Pr.

— Bible Societies, American Missionaries & the National Revival of Bulgaria. LC 71-135841. (Eastern Europe Collection). 1971. 23.95 (0-405-02783-4) Ayer.

— Nineteenth Century Questions. LC 71-37527. (Essay Index Reprint Ser.). 1977. reprint ed. 23.95 (0-8369-2539-4) Ayer.

Clarke, James F., jt. auth. see Jay, William.

Clarke, James W. American Assassins: The Darker Side of Politics. rev. ed. LC 90-213001. 341p. reprint ed. pap. 105.80 (0-608-09575-3, 205437700006) Bks Demand.

***Clarke, James W.** The Last Rampage: The Escape of Gary Tison. LC 99-29166. (Illus.). 336p. 1999. pap. 16.95 (0-8165-1967-6) U of Ariz Pr.

Clarke, James W. The Lineaments of Wrath: Race, Violent Crime, & American Culture. LC 97-51699. 339p. 1998. 39.95 (1-56000-358-8) Transaction Pubs.

— On Being Mad or Merely Angry: John W. Hinckley, Jr. & Other Dangerous People. 160p. 1990. text 26.95 (0-691-07852-1, Pub. by Princeton U Pr) Cal Prin Full Svc.

Clarke, James W., jt. auth. see Peterson, James A.

Clarke, Jan. The Guenegaud Theatre in Paris, 1673-1680 Vol. 1: Founding, Design & Production. LC 98-18090. (Studies in Theatre Arts: Vol. 5). 428p. 1998. 109.95 (0-7734-8392-6) E Mellen.

Clarke, Jane. Office Politics: A Survival Guide. 144p. 1999. pap. 19.95 (1-85835-532-X, Indust Soc) Stylus Pub VA.

***Clarke, Jay, ed.** Voyages: The Romance of Cruising. LC 99-152. (Illus.). 284p. 1999. 30.00 (1-887656-21-9) Tehabi Bks.

Clarke, Jean I. Self-Esteem: A Family Affair. LC 98-27064. 280p. 1998. reprint ed. pap. 14.95 (1-56838-287-1) Hazelden.

— Time-In: When Time-Out Doesn't Work. LC 98-37158. (Illus.). 64p. 1999. pap. 9.95 (1-884734-28-6); lib. bdg. 18.95 (1-884734-29-4) Parenting Pr.

— Who, Me Lead a Group? LC 98-12096. (Illus.). 128p. (Orig.). 1998. reprint ed. pap. 9.95 (1-884734-41-3) Parenting Pr.

Clarke, Jean I., et al. Platica de Autoestima - Conversations about Self-Esteem: Guia para el Lider y Novelas - Guide for the Leader & Short Stories. 268p. 1993. write for info. (1-882556-00-3); write for info. (1-882556-01-1); write for info. (1-882556-02-X); write for info. (1-882556-03-8); write for info. (1-882556-04-6); write for info. (1-882556-05-4); write for info. (1-882556-06-2); write for info. (1-882556-07-0) U WA Early Chldhood.

Clarke, Jean I., jt. auth. see Dawson, Connie.

***Clarke, Jean Illsley.** Connections: The Threads That Strengthen Families. LC 99-35167. 200p. 1999. pap. text 15.00 (1-56838-342-8) Hazelden.

Clarke, Jean M. & Bostle, Eileen, eds. Reading Therapy. LC 88-19750. 230p. 1988. reprint ed. pap. 71.30 (0-608-02482-1, 206312500004) Bks Demand.

Clarke, Jean M. & Going, Mona E. Hospital Libraries & Community Care. 4th ed. LC 91-105510. 282p. reprint ed. pap. 87.50 (0-608-08881-1, 206951800004) Bks Demand.

Clarke, Jean-Marie, tr. see Terrasse, Antoine.

Clarke, Jeanne N. Roosevelt's Warrior: Harold L. Ickes & the New Deal. LC 95-44493. (Illus.). 423p. (C). 1996. text 39.95 (0-8018-5094-0) Johns Hopkins.

Clarke, Jeanne N. & McCool, Daniel C. Staking Out the Terrain: Power & Performance among Natural Resource Agencies. 2nd ed. LC 95-45344. (SUNY Series in Environmental Politics & Policy). 279p. (C). 1996. pap. text 19.95 (0-7914-2946-6) State U NY Pr.

Clarke, Jeff, jt. auth. see Feil, Charles.

Clarke, Jeffrey J. Advice & Support: The Final Years, 1965-1973. LC 87-600379. (United States Army in Vietnam CMH Publication: CMH Pub No. 91-3). (Illus.). 583p. 1988. pap. 27.00 (0-16-001960-5, 008-029-00158-6) USGPO.

— Advice & Support: The Final Years, 1965-1973. LC 87-600379. (United States Army in Vietnam CMH Publications: No. 91-3). (Illus.). 583p. 1988. 33.00 (0-16-001959-1, 008-029-00157-8) USGPO.

Clarke, Jeffrey J. Southern France: United States Army Campaigns of World War 2. 32p. 1994. pap. 1.25 (0-16-061317-5) USGPO.

— United States Army in World War 2, European Theater of Operations: The Riviera to the Rhine. 627p. 1993. pap. text 36.00 (0-16-034746-7) USGPO.

Clarke, Jennifer F., ed. A Gathering of Wisdoms: Tribal Mental Health-A Cultural Perspective. (Illus.). 514p. 1991. pap. 19.95 (0-9631016-0-9) Swinomish Ind.

Clarke, Joan. Family Traditions in Hawaii. LC 94-68763. 112p. 1994. pap. text 16.95 (0-9643359-0-5) Namkoong Pubng.

— Local Food: What to Eat in Hawai'i. LC 97-67940. (Illus.). 80p. 1997. pap. 4.95 (0-9643359-1-3) Namkoong Pubng.

Clarke, Joan & Dods, Diane, eds. Artists/Hawaii. LC 96-11756. (Illus.). 1996. text 35.00 (0-8248-1859-8) UH Pr.

Clarke, Joe. Control Without Confusion: Trouble Shooting Screen-Printed Process Color. LC 86-21936. (Orig.). (C). 1987. pap. 19.95 (0-911380-73-6) ST Pubns.

Clarke, Joe T. A Clinical Guide to Inherited Metabolic Diseases. LC 96-36666. (Illus.). 299p. (C). 1996. pap. text 34.95 (0-521-48524-X) Cambridge U Pr.

— A Clinical Guide to Inherited Metabolic Diseases. LC 96-36666. (Illus.). 299p. (C). 1996. text 80.00 (0-521-48064-7) Cambridge U Pr.

Clarke, John. A Crisis in Care? Challenges to Social Work. (Illus.). 272p. (C). 1993. text 65.00 (0-8039-8843-5); pap. text 19.95 (0-8039-8844-3) Sage.

— Evangelism That Really Works. 176p. 1995. pap. 9.95 (0-687-85342-7) Abingdon.

***Clarke, John.** The Future of Population. (Predictions Ser.). 58p. 1999. pap. 3.95 (0-297-81923-2, Pub. by Weidenfeld & Nicolson) Trafalgar.

Clarke, John. In the Analogy. LC 95-74806. 1997. pap. 18.00 (1-880631-10-5) Shuffaloff Bks.

— In the Analogy, Bk. 1. LC 90-63754. (Local Habitations Ser.). (Illus.). 40p. 1991. 40.00 (0-9628035-2-9); pap. 10.00 (0-9628035-3-7) Shuffaloff Bks.

— Introduction to the Fernandian Tongue. LC 73-161257. (Black Heritage Library Collection). 1977. reprint ed. 16.95 (0-8369-8531-1) Ayer.

— New Times & Old Enemies: Essays on Cultural Studies & America. LC 91-40869. 224p. (C). 1992. text 55.00 (0-04-445474-0) Routledge.

***Clarke, John.** The Right Way to Write Your Own CV. 128p. 2000. pap. 6.95 (0-7160-2093-9, Pub. by Elliot RW Bks) Midpt Trade.

Clarke, John. Tibet: Caught in Time. (Illus.). 160p. 1998. 30.00 (1-873938-96-9, Pub. by Garnet-Ithaca) LPC InBook.

— The Virgin Seducer. (Foundations of the Novel Ser.: Vol. 49). 1972. lib. bdg. 61.00 (0-8240-0561-9) Garland.

Clarke, John, ed. Voices of the Earth: An Anthology of Ideas & Arguments. 198p. 1994. pap. 14.95 (0-8076-1349-5) Braziller.

Clarke, John, et al, eds. Failure of the Public Trust Exhibits: Proof of FBI & OIC Cover-Up in the Independent Counsel's Probe. (Failure of the Public Trust Ser.: Vol. 2). 650p. 1994. pap. 90.00 (0-9673521-1-8) McCabe Publishing.

Clarke, John, intro. Letters of St. Therese of Lisieux Vol. I: General Correspondence I, 1877-1890. LC 81-6474. 700p. (Orig.). 1982. pap. 16.95 (0-9600876-9-9) ICS Pubns.

— St. Therese of Lisieux: Her Last Conversations. LC 76-27207. (Illus.). 352p. 1977. pap. 11.95 (0-9600876-3-X) ICS Pubns.

Clarke, John, tr. from FRE. Letters of St. Therese of Lisieux Vol. II: General Correspondence II. LC 81-6474. (Illus.). 688p. (Orig.). 1988. pap. 16.95 (0-935216-10-3) ICS Pubns.

Clarke, John & McLoughlin, William G. Colonial Baptists: Massachusetts & Rhode Island. Gaustad, Edwin S., ed. LC 79-52586. (Baptist Tradition Ser.). 1980. lib. bdg. 19.95 (0-405-12453-8) Ayer.

Clarke, John & Newman, Janet. The Managerial State: Power, Politics, & Ideology in the Remaking of Social Welfare. 208p. 1997. 69.95 (0-8039-7611-9); pap. 21.95 (0-8039-7612-7) Sage.

***Clarke, John, et al.** Failure of the Public Trust, FBI cover-up.com: Proof of FBI & OIC Cover-Up in the Independent Counsel's Probe into the Death of Deputy White House Counsel, Vincent W. Foster, 2 vols. 510p. 1999. pap. 28.00 (0-9673521-0-X) McCabe Publishing.

Clarke, John, jt. auth. see Cochrane, Alan.

Clarke, John A. A Colour Atlas of Burn Injuries. LC 92-49022. (Medical Atlas Ser.: No. 9). (Illus.). 128p. 1992. text 89.50 (0-412-34840-3, Pub. by E A) OUP.

Clarke, John B. Manchester: Brief Record of Its Past, Also a Picture of Its Present, Including an Account of Its Settlement & of Its Growth...& Sketches of Its Representative Citizens. 463p. 1997. reprint ed. lib. bdg. 49.50 (0-8328-6010-7) Higginson Bk Co.

Clarke, John C. John Clem Clarke. LC 98-73938. 55 p. 1998. write for info. (1-882011-49-X) Allentown.

— Teacher & Friend: Memoirs of an Education Officer in Colonial Africa. (Illus.). 7p. (Orig.). 1993. pap. 15.00 (0-9639288-0-5) Allies Behav.

Clarke, John F. Pyralidae & Microlepidoptera of the Marquesas Archipelago. LC 85-600124. (Smithsonian Contributions to Zoology Ser.: No. 416). 489p. reprint ed. pap. 151.60 (0-608-15427-X, 202935700060) Bks Demand.

***Clarke, John H.** Christopher Columbus & the Afrikan Holocaust: Slavery & the Rise of European Capitalism. 128p. 1999. pap. 10.95 (1-886433-18-6) A&B Bks.

Clarke, John Henrik. African People in World History: A Lecture & Illustrated History. LC 90-82687. (Illus.). 100p. (Orig.). 1992. pap. 8.95 (0-933121-77-6) Black Classic.

— Africans at the Crossroads: Notes for an African World Revolution. LC 91-74121. 480p. 1992. 49.95 (0-86543-270-8); pap. 21.95 (0-86543-271-6) Africa World.

— A Clinical Repertory to the Dictionary of Materia Medica. 360p. 1995. 29.95 (0-85032-061-5, Pub. by C W Daniel) Natl Bk Netwk.

— Harlem Voices from the Soul of Black America. 2nd ed. 222p. 1993. reprint ed. pap. text 11.95 (1-881316-23-8) A&B Bks.

— My Life in Search of Africa. LC 97-48939. 1997. 30.00 (0-88378-158-1) Third World.

— My Life in Search of Africa. LC 97-48939. 104p. 1999. pap. 15.95 (0-88378-178-6) Third World.

— Patterns of Thinking: Integrating Learning Skills in Content Teaching. 320p. (C). 1990. 68.00 (0-205-12361-9, H23617) Allyn.

— The Prescriber. 109p. 1972. 21.00 (0-85032-088-7, Pub. by C W Daniel) Natl Bk Netwk.

— The Prescriber. 11th ed. 382p. (C). 1972. pap. 31.95 (0-8464-1041-9) Beekman Pubs.

— Rebellion in Rhyme: The Early Poetry of John Henrik Clarke. 1996. 24.95 (0-86543-230-9) Africa World.

— Who Betrayed the African World Revolution? 1996. 32.00 (0-88378-183-2) Third World.

— William Blake on the Lord's Prayer, 1757-1827. LC 70-95421. (Studies in Blake: No. 3). 1971. reprint ed. lib. bdg. 75.00 (0-8383-0967-4) M S G Haskell Hse.

Clarke, John Henrik, ed. Black American Short Stories. rev. ed. LC 92-16249. (American Century Ser.). 448p. 1993. 13.00 (0-374-52354-1) Hill & Wang.

— Malcolm X: The Man & His Times. LC 90-84761. 1991. reprint ed. 35.00 (0-86543-200-7); reprint ed. pap. 14.95 (0-86543-201-5) Africa World.

— New Dimensions in African History: From the Nile Valley to the New World. LC 91-70616. 49.95 (0-86543-226-0); pap. 16.95 (0-86543-227-9) Africa World.

— The Second Crucifixion of Nat Turner. 2nd ed. LC 96-83452. Orig. Title: William Styron's Nat Turner: Ten Black Writer's Respond. 126p. 1997. reprint ed. pap. 9.95 (0-933121-95-4) Black Classic.

— William Styron's Nat Turner: Ten Black Writers Respond. LC 87-8695. 130p. 1987. reprint ed. lib. bdg. 57.50 (0-313-25957-7, CLNT, Greenwood Pr) Greenwood.

Clarke, John Henrik, frwd. Harlem U. S. A. The Story of a City Within a City. LC 98-42697. 388p. 1992. reprint ed. pap. text 11.95 (1-881316-48-3) A&B Bks.

***Clarke, John Henrik, intro.** Our Black Seminarians: And Black Clergy Without a Black Theology. LC 96-84728. (Illus.). 109p. 1998. reprint ed. pap. 14.95 (0-933121-62-8) Black Classic.

Clarke, John Henrik & Adams, Barbara E. John Henrik Clarke Pt. I: The Early Years. (Illus.). 145p. (Orig.). 1992. pap. 10.00 (1-56411-040-0) Untd Bros & Sis.

Clarke, John Henrik & Agne, Russell M., eds. Interdisciplinary High School Teaching: Strategies for Integrated Learning. LC 96-7009. 364p. (C). 1996. pap. text 36.00 (0-205-15710-6) Allyn.

Clarke, John Henrik, et al. Critical Lessons in Slavery & the Slavetrade: Essential Studies & Commentaries on Slavery, in General & the African Slavetrade, in Particular. 2nd expanded rev. ed. LC 96-68505. (Truth & Sanity Reprint Ser.). (Illus.). 208p. 1997. reprint ed. 26.98 (1-879289-06-7); reprint ed. pap. 16.98 (1-879289-07-5) Native Sun Pubs.

— Real Questions, Real Answers: Focusing Teacher Leadership on School Improvement. LC 97-33941. 78p. 1998. pap. 14.95 (0-87120-293-X, 198007) ASCD.

***Clarke, John I.** The Human Dichotomy: The Changing Numbers of Males & Females. LC 00-34693. 2000. write for info. (0-08-043782-6, Pergamon Pr) Elsevier.

Clarke, John I. & Kosinski, Leszek A. Redistribution of Population in Africa. 212p. (C). 1982. pap. text 22.50 (0-435-95031-2, 95031) Heinemann.

Clarke, John I. & Noin, Daniel, eds. Population & Environment in Arid Regions. LC 97-17028. (Man & the Biosphere Ser.: Vol. 19). (Illus.). 410p. 1998. 75.00 (1-85070-962-9) Prthnon Pub.

Clarke, John J. Jung & the East: A Dialogue with the Orient. LC 93-8078. 224p. (C). 1994. 75.00 (0-415-07640-4) Routledge.

— Jung & the East: A Dialogue with the Orient. LC 93-8078. 224p. (C). (gr. 13). 1994. pap. 25.99 (0-415-10419-X) Routledge.

Clarke, John L., ed. Alternative Materials for the Reinforcement & Prestressing of Concrete. LC 93-1468. (Illus.). 224p. (C). 1993. 150.00 (0-7514-0007-6) Routledge.

— Structural Lightweight Aggregate Concrete Performance. LC 93-12642. 1993. write for info. (0-7514-0006-8, Pub. by B Acad & Prof) Routldge.

Clarke, John M. James Hall of Albany: Geologist & Palaeontologist, 1811-1898. Albritton, Claude C., ed. LC 77-6511. (History of Geology Ser.). (Illus.). 1978. reprint ed. lib. bdg. 51.95 (0-405-10435-9) Ayer.

Clarke, John M., et al. The Trust Business. 2nd ed. (Illus.). 289p. (C). 1988. text 43.00 (0-89982-350-5) Am Bankers.

Clarke, John R. The Houses of Roman Italy, 100 B.C.-A.D. 250: Ritual, Space, & Decoration. LC 90-48357. (Illus.). 450p. 1991. pap. 34.95 (0-520-08429-2, Pub. by U CA Pr) Cal Prin Full Svc.

— Looking at Lovemaking: Constructions of Sexuality in Roman Art, 100 B.C., A.D. 250. LC 96-40380. 406p. 1998. 39.95 (0-520-20024-1, Pub. by U CA Pr) Cal Prin Full Svc.

— Roman Black-&-White Figural Mosaics. LC 78-68553. (College Art Association Monographs: Vol. 35). (Illus.). 172p. 1985. reprint ed. 35.00 (0-271-00401-0) Pa St U Pr.

— Surgical Judgement Using Decision Sciences, 3. LC 83-24594. (Surgical Science Ser.: Vol. III). 106p. 1984. 45.00 (0-275-91425-9, C1425, Praeger Pubs) Greenwood.

Clarke, John W. A Quest for Silence. 46p. 1994. pap. 6.95 (1-877871-76-1, 6712) Ed Ministries.

— What Good Is Christianity . . . Anyhow? 56p. 1992. pap. 9.95 (1-877871-42-7, 6710) Ed Ministries.

Clarke, Jonathan & Clad, James. After the Crusade: American Foreign Policy for the Post-Superpower Age. LC 94-47399. 1995. 24.95 (1-56833-051-0) Madison Bks UPA.

Clarke, Jonathan, jt. ed. see James, Noel P.

Clarke, Joseph. Virginia Criminal Law Case Finder: 1992 Supplement. 2nd ed. 118p. 1992. write for info. (0-87473-956-X, 60905-10, MICHIE) LEXIS Pub.

Clarke, Joseph C., III. Russia & Italy Against Hitler: The Bolshevik-Fascist Rapprochement of the 1930s, 21. LC 90-43372. (Contributions to the Study of World History Ser.: No. 21). 240p. 1991. 59.95 (*0-313-27468-1*, CRY/, Greenwood Pr) Greenwood.

Clarke, Joseph M., II. Virginia Criminal Law Case Finder. 2nd ed. 1265p. 1991. 95.00 (*0-87473-763-X*, MICHIE) LEXIS Pub.

— Virginia Criminal Law Case Finder, 2 vols. 3rd ed. LC 95-77368. 1995. 125.00 (*1-55834-233-8*, 60904-11, MICHIE) LEXIS Pub.

— Virginia Criminal Law Case Finder. 3rd ed. 1996. suppl. ed. 42.00 (*0-614-25258-X*, 60905-11, MICHIE) LEXIS Pub.

— Virginia Criminal Law Case Finder, 2 vols. 4th ed. Incl. Vol. 1. 4th ed. LC 99-62451. 1999. (*0-327-01308-7*, 6090712); Vol. 2. 4th ed. LC 99-62451. 1999. (*0-327-01309-5*, 6090812); LC 99-62451. 1200p. 1999. 160.00 (*0-327-01310-9*) LEXIS Pub.

Clarke, Joseph M., 2nd. Virginia Criminal Law Case Finder: 1998 Cumulative Supplement, Vols. 1 & 2. 3rd ed. LC 95-77368. 1998. 50.00 (*0-327-00117-8*, 60905-13) LEXIS Pub.

Clarke, Joy A. Multicultural Social Studies Unit: Who Am I? (Illus.). 150p. (J). (gr. 3-8). 1991. ring bd. 45.00 (*0-9626984-1-5*) Clarke Enterprise.

— Spiritual Nourishment. (Illus.). 84p. (Orig.). 1990. pap. 9.95 (*0-9626984-0-7*) Clarke Enterprise.

Clarke, Joy P. The Bible & Life: God's Message for Today. (Intersections Small Group Ser.). 1995. pap. 5.49 (*0-8066-0127-2*, 15-162) Augsburg Fortress.

Clarke, Juanita. Making Rag Dolls. unabridged ed. LC 95-1027. (Illus.). 80p. 1995. reprint ed. pap. text 12.95 (*0-486-28684-3*) Dover.

Clarke, Juanne N. Health, Illness & Medicine in Canada. 2nd ed. 429p. 1996. pap. text 49.95 (*0-19-541206-0*) OUP.

***Clarke, Juanne Nancarrow.** Health, Illness & Medicine in Canada. 3rd ed. (Illus.). 480p. 2000. pap. text 35.00 (*0-19-541552-3*) OUP.

Clarke, Judie. I Spy Disney: An ABC Book. (Illus.). 32p. (J). Date not set. 12.99 (*0-7868-3185-5*, Pub. by Disney Pr) Little.

Clarke, Judith. Friend of My Heart. LC 95-119218. 1994. pap. 11.95 (*0-7022-2699-8*, Pub. by Univ Queensland Pr) Intl Spec Bk.

***Clarke, Judith.** The Heroic Lives of Al Capsella. 288p. 2000. pap. 14.95 (*0-7022-3061-8*, Pub. by Univ Queensland Pr) Intl Spec Bk.

— The Lost Day. LC 98-55096. 154p. (YA). (gr. 9 up). 1999. 16.95 (*0-8050-6152-5*) H Holt & Co.

— Night Train. LC 99-27966. 176p. (J). 2000. 16.95 (*0-8050-6151-7*) H Holt & Co.

Clarke, Judith. Panic Stations. (YA). 1995. 11.95 (*0-7022-2696-3*, Pub. by Univ Queensland Pr) Intl Spec Bk.

Clarke, Judy. I Spy Disney: An ABC Book. 32p. (J). Date not set. lib. bdg. 13.49 (*0-7868-5069-8*, Pub. by Disney Pr) Little.

***Clarke, Judy, ed.** Graded Vocabulary List: Grade Five. 43p. 2000. pap. write for info. (*0-9676085-7-0*) Epicenter Press.

— Graded Vocabulary List: Grade Four. 40p. 2000. pap. write for info. (*0-9676085-6-2*) Epicenter Press.

— Graded Vocabulary List: Grade Three. 35p. 2000. pap. write for info. (*0-9676085-5-4*) Epicenter Press.

— Graded Vocabulary List: Grade Two. 21p. 2000. pap. write for info. (*0-9676085-4-6*) Epicenter Press.

— Graded Vocabulary List: Pre-Primer & Grade One. 17p. 2000. pap. write for info. (*0-9676085-3-8*) Epicenter Press.

— Graded Vocabulary List: Pre-Primer Through Grade Six Master List. 27p. 2000. pap. write for info. (*0-9676085-2-X*) Epicenter Press.

***Clarke, Julia.** Crysta. large type ed. 256p. 1999. pap. 18.99 (*0-7089-5611-4*, Linford) Ulverscroft.

— Flower in the Snow. large type ed. 280p. 2000. pap. 18.99 (*0-7089-5641-6*, Linford) Ulverscroft.

— Love Across the Water. 224p. 2000. 18.99 (*0-7089-5700-5*) Ulverscroft.

Clarke, Juliette, jt. ed. see Exley, Helen.

Clarke, K., jt. auth. see Taylor, B.

Clarke, K. A. Neurophysiology: Applications in the Behavioural & Biomedical Sciences. (Ellis Horwood Series in Eurosciences). 1989. text 59.95 (*0-470-21554-2*) P-H.

Clarke, Kate, tr. see Posadskaya, Anastasia, ed.

Clarke, Katherine A. Between Geography & History: Hellenistic Constructions of the Roman World. LC 99-23235. (Oxford Classical Monographs Ser.). 300p. 2000. text 85.00 (*0-19-924003-5*) OUP.

Clarke, Kathleen & Litton, Helen. Revolutionary Woman: My Fight for Ireland's Freedom. (Illus.). 240p. 1997. pap. 15.95 (*0-86278-294-5*, Pub. by OBrien Pr) Irish Amer Bk.

Clarke, Kenneth & Kohn, Ira. Kentucky's Age of Wood. LC 76-4432. (Kentucky Bicentennial Bookshelf Ser.). (Illus.). 83p. reprint ed. pap. 30.00 (*0-7837-5819-7*, 204548600006) Bks Demand.

Clarke, Kenneth K. & Hess, Donald T. Communication Circuits: Analysis & Design. LC 78-125610. (Engineering Ser.). (C). 1971. text 48.76 (*0-201-01040-2*) Addison-Wesley.

Clarke, Kenneth L., jt. auth. see Bala, Nicholas C.

Clarke, Kenneth T. & Hess, Donald T. Communication Circuits: Analysis & Design. 670p. (C). 1994. reprint ed. lib. bdg. 75.50 (*0-89464-863-2*) Krieger.

Clarke, Kenneth W. & Clarke, Mary. The Harvest & the Reapers: Oral Traditions of Kentucky. LC 74-7872. (Kentucky Bicentennial Bookshelf Ser.). 108p. reprint ed. pap. 33.50 (*0-608-18281-8*, 203152200075) Bks Demand.

***Clarke, Kent D.** Adobe "Groundzero" for Dummies. (For Dummies Ser.). (Illus.). 384p. 2000. pap. 19.95 (*0-7645-0701-X*) IDG Bks.

Clarke, Kent D. Textual Optimism: A Critique of the United Bible Societies, Greek New Testament. (JSNTS Ser.: Vol. 138). 350p. 1997. 85.00 (*1-85075-649-X*, Pub. by Sheffield Acad) CUP Services.

Clarke, L. J. Surface Crystallography: An Introduction to Low Energy Election Diffraction. LC 84-11804. (Wiley-Interscience Publications). (Illus.). 343p. reprint ed. pap. 106.40 (*0-7837-1885-3*, 204208600001) Bks Demand.

Clarke, Laura J. & Thompson-Wise, Deborah. Urban & Regional Planning Periodicals with Book Reviews. 19p. 1993. pap. 10.00 (*0-614-25157-5*, Sage Prdcls Pr) Sage.

— Urban & Regional Planning Periodicals with Book Reviews. LC 93-42458. (CPL Bibliographies Ser.: No. 297). 1993. 10.00 (*0-86602-297-X*, Sage Prdcls Pr) Sage.

Clarke, Laurie A. Clarke's Guide to Margaret Sutton's Judy Bolton Mystery Stories. 2nd ed. 37p. 1995. spiral bd. 14.95 (*0-9639949-3-X*) SynSine Pr.

Clarke, Lee. Acceptable Risk? Making Decisions in a Toxic Environment. 1989. 50.00 (*0-520-06303-1*, Pub. by U CA Pr) Cal Prin Full Svc.

— Acceptable Risk? Making Decisions in a Toxic Environment. 242p. 1991. reprint ed. pap. 16.95 (*0-520-07657-5*, Pub. by U CA Pr) Cal Prin Full Svc.

Clarke, Lee B. Mission Improbable: Using Fantasy Documents to Tame Disasters. LC 98-40808. 216p. 1991. pap. text 14.95 (*0-226-10942-9*) U Ch Pr.

***Clarke, Lee B.** Mission Improbable: Using Fantasy Documents to Tame Disasters. LC 98-40808. 216p. 1999. 25.00 (*0-226-10941-0*) U Ch Pr.

Clarke, Lewis G. Narratives of the Sufferings of Lewis & Milton Clarke, Sons of a Soldier of the Revolution. LC 73-82186. (Anti-Slavery Crusade in America Ser.). 1978. reprint ed. 21.95 (*0-405-00624-1*) Ayer.

Clarke, Liam. Challenging Ideas in Psychiatric Nursing. LC 98-32451. 208p. 1999. pap. write for info. (*0-415-18697-8*) Routledge.

***Clarke, Liam.** Challenging Ideas in Psychiatric Nursing. LC 98-32451. 208p. 1999. text. write for info. (*0-415-18696-X*) Routledge.

— Health & Social Care for Foundation GNVQ. 2nd ed. (Illus.). 368p. 2000. pap. 42.50 (*0-7487-3509-7*, Pub. by S Thornes Pubs) Trans-Atl Phila.

— Health & Social Care for Intermediate GNVQ. 2nd ed. (Illus.). 288p. 2000. pap. 42.50 (*0-7487-3508-9*, Pub. by S Thornes Pubs) Trans-Atl Phila.

Clarke, Liam & Waltham, Peter. Foundation Health & Social Care. 320p. (Orig.). 1995. pap. 29.50 (*0-7487-2082-0*, Pub. by S Thornes Pubs) Trans-Atl Phila.

Clarke, Liam, et al. Advanced Health & Social Care. 2nd ed. 448p. (Orig.). 1995. pap. 37.50 (*0-7487-2225-4*, Pub. by S Thornes Pubs) Trans-Atl Phila.

***Clarke, Liam, et al.** Health & Social Care for Advanced GNVQ. 3rd ed. 2000. 59.50 (*0-7487-3510-0*, Pub. by S Thornes Pubs) Trans-Atl Phila.

Clarke, Liam, et al. Intermediate Health & Social Care. 336p. (Orig.). 1995. pap. 29.50 (*0-7487-1771-4*, Pub. by S Thornes Pubs) Trans-Atl Phila.

Clarke, Linda. Building Capitalism: Historical Change & the Labour Process in the Production of the Built Environment. (Illus.). 336p. (C). 1991. pap. 40.00 (*0-415-01553-7*, A6672) Routledge.

— Discrimination. 216p. 1993. 45.00 (*0-85292-528-X*, Pub. by IPM Hse) St Mut.

— Discrimination. 2nd ed. 140p. 1995. pap. 90.00 (*0-85292-625-1*, Pub. by IPM Hse) St Mut.

— Learning to Talk, Talking to Learn. 1998. pap. text 11.95 (*0-207-19100-X*) HarpC.

***Clarke, Linda, et al.** The Dynamics of Wage Relations in the New Europe. LC 99-88703. 2000. write for info. (*0-7923-7742-7*) Kluwer Academic.

Clarke, Linda, et al. Training for Employment in Western Europe & the United States. LC 94-34106. 288p. 1995. 95.00 (*1-85278-863-1*) E Elgar.

Clarke, Lindsay. Essential Celtic Mythology. 1997. pap. 12.00 (*1-85538-477-9*, Pub. by Aqm Pr) Harper SF.

***Clarke, Lindsay.** Traditional Celtic Stories. 2nd ed. 2000. pap. 12.00 (*0-7225-3983-5*) Thorsons PA.

Clarke, Loren K. & Potts, Malcolm. The AIDS Reader, Vol. I. 350p. 1988. pap. 17.95 (*0-8283-1918-9*) Branden Bks.

Clarke, M. Behavioural Research for Transport Policy: The 1985 International Conference on Travel Behaviour, the Netherlands. 504p. 1986. lib. bdg. 122.50 (*90-6764-060-3*, Pub. by VSP) Coronet Bks.

Clarke, M., ed. Shipbuilding Contracts. 2nd ed. 265p. 1992. 110.00 (*1-85044-482-X*) LLP.

Clarke, M. A. International Carriage of Goods by Road: CMR. (C). 1985. 400.00 (*0-7855-4122-5*, Pub. by Witherby & Co) St Mut.

Clarke, M. B. Bosworth, Pts. V & VI. (Illus.). 464p. 1991. reprint ed. pap. 69.50 (*0-8328-2030-X*); reprint ed. lib. bdg. 79.50 (*0-8328-2029-6*) Higginson Bk Co.

— Bosworth Genealogy: History of the Descendants of Edward Bosworth Who Arrived in America in 1634. (Illus.). 122p. 1993. reprint ed. pap. 23.00 (*0-8328-3648-6*); reprint ed. lib. bdg. 33.00 (*0-8328-3647-8*) Higginson Bk Co.

Clarke, M. J., et al, eds. Inorganic Chemistry. (Structure & Bonding Ser.: Vol. 46). (Illus.). 190p. 1981. 70.95 (*0-387-10655-3*) Spr-Verlag.

— Metallopharmaceuticals Vol. 1: DNA Interactions. LC 99-21036. (Topics in Biological Inorganic Chemistry Ser.). (Illus.). 250p. 1999. 129.00 (*3-540-64889-5*) Spr-Verlag.

***Clarke, M. J., et al, eds.** Metallopharmaceuticals II: Diagnosis & Therapy. (Topics in Biological Inorganic Chemistry Ser.: Vol. 2). (Illus.). 195p. 1999. 124.00 (*3-540-65308-2*) Spr-Verlag.

Clarke, M. J., et al, eds. Structure vs. Special Properties. (Structure & Bonding Ser.: Vol. 52). (Illus.). 204p. 1982. 86.95 (*0-387-11781-4*) Spr-Verlag.

Clarke, M. J., et al. Copper, Molybdenum, & Vanadium in Biological Systems: Structure & Bonding, Vol. 53. (Illus.). 166p. 1983. 70.95 (*0-387-12042-4*) Spr-Verlag.

Clarke, M. J., ed. see Allan, C. B., et al.

Clarke, M. L. The Noblest Roman: Marcus Brutus & His Reputation. LC 80-69178. (Aspects of Greek & Roman Life Ser.). 157p. 1981. text 37.50 (*0-8014-1393-1*) Cornell U Pr.

— Rhetoric at Rome: A Historical Survey. rev. ed. LC 96-3816. (Classical Studies). 224p. (C). 1996. pap. 24.99 (*0-415-14156-7*) Routledge.

Clarke, M. L., tr. see Von Bode, Wilhelm.

Clarke, M. S., jt. auth. see Wallace, W. J.

Clarke, Malcolm. Policies & Perceptions of Insurance: An Introduction to Insurance Law. 354p. 1997. pap. text (*0-19-876341-7*) OUP.

— Policies & Perceptions of Insurance: An Introduction to Insurance Law. (Clarendon Law Ser.). 354p. 1998. text 80.00 (*0-19-876340-9*) OUP.

Clarke, Malcolm A. The Law of Insurance Contracts. 2nd ed. 827p. 1994. 265.00 (*1-85044-551-6*) LLP.

Clarke, Malcolm R., ed. A Handbook for the Identification of Cephalopod Beaks. (Illus.). 220p. 1986. 55.00 (*0-19-857603-X*) OUP.

Clarke, Manning. Speaking Out of Turn: Lectures & Speeches, 1940-1991. LC 98-165793. 272p. 1998. pap. 29.95 (*0-522-84770-6*, Pub. by Melbourne Univ Pr) Paul & Co Pubs.

Clarke, Marcus. His Natural Life. Tulloch, Graham, ed. LC 96-33273. (The World's Classics Ser.). (Illus.). 524p. 1997. pap. 14.95 (*0-19-282418-X*) OUP.

Clarke, Margaret, jt. auth. see Bailey, Roy.

Clarke, Margaret, jt. auth. see Buss, Helen M.

Clarke, Margaret A., ed. Proceedings of the International Dextran Workshop (1984) (Workshop Ser.). (Illus.). 90p. (Orig.). 1984. pap. text 100.00 (*1-883326-06-0*) Sugar Process Res.

— Proceedings of the 1996 Sugar Processing Research Conference. (Illus.). 534p. (Orig.). 1996. pap. text 100.00 (*1-883326-05-2*) Sugar Process Res.

Clarke, Margaret A., ed. Products of Sugarbeet & Sugarcane: Proceedings of Workshop on Products of Sugarbeet & Sugarcane, 1994. (Workshop of Sugar Processing Research Institute (since 1984) Ser.). (Illus.). 307p. (Orig.). 1995. pap. text 100.00 (*1-883326-03-6*) Sugar Process Res.

— Separation Processes in the Sugar Industry. (Illus.). 307p. (Orig.). 1996. pap. 100.00 (*1-883326-04-4*) Sugar Process Res.

Clarke, Margaret A. & Borel, Beryl A., eds. Proceedings, 1994 Sugar Processing Research Conference (Proceedings Sugar Processing Research Conference (since 1982) Ser.). (Illus.). 411p. (Orig.). 1994. pap. text 100.00 (*1-883326-02-8*) Sugar Process Res.

Clarke, Margaret A. & Borel, Beryl T., eds. Analysis of Sugars in Foods: Proceedings of Workshop on Analysis of Sugars in Foods, Sugar Processing Research Institute, Inc., 1992. (Workshop of Sugar Processing Research Institute (since 1984) Ser.). (Illus.). 230p. (Orig.). 1992. pap. text 100.00 (*1-883326-01-X*) Sugar Process Res.

— Proceedings, 1992 Sugar Processing Research Conference. (Proceedings Sugar Processing Research Conference (since 1982) Ser.). (Illus.). 375p. (Orig.). 1992. pap. text 100.00 (*1-883326-00-1*) Sugar Process Res.

Clarke, Margaret C. The Wumples of Wigwump. (Illus.). (J). (gr. k-3). 1995. pap. 7.95 (*0-9614659-8-7*) Cuchullain Pubns.

Clarke, Marianne. Citywide Targeting Strategies. Bell, Stephanie, ed. 8p. (Orig.). 1978. pap. 8.00 (*0-317-04866-X*) Natl Coun Econ Dev.

Clarke, Marianne & McDonald, Jean. Increasing the Supply of Women & Minority Engineers: A State Action Agenda. Glass, Karen, ed. 55p. (Orig.). 1990. pap. text 15.00 (*1-55877-116-6*) Natl Governor.

Clarke, Marianne K. A Governor's Guide to Economic Conversion. Feinstein, Gerry, ed. 65p. (Orig.). 1992. pap. text 15.00 (*1-55877-165-4*) Natl Governor.

Clarke, Marianne K. & Dobson, Eric N. Increasing the Competitiveness of America's Manufacturers: A Review of State Industrial Extension Programs. Feinstein, Gerry, ed. 92p. (Orig.). 1991. pap. text 15.00 (*1-55877-140-9*) Natl Governor.

— Promoting Technological Excellence: The Role of State & Federal Extension Activities. Miller, Mark, ed. 78p. (Orig.). 1989. pap. text 15.00 (*1-55877-069-0*) Natl Governor.

Clarke, Marianne K., et al. Promoting Quality Businesses: A State Action Agenda. 40p. (Orig.). 1992. pap. text 15.00 (*1-55877-153-0*) Natl Governor.

Clarke, Marieke. We Are the Original People. (C). 1991. 28.00 (*81-202-0243-0*, Pub. by Ajanta) S Asia.

Clarke, Marion. Entranced. 1996. mass mkt. 4.99 (*0-8217-5292-8*, Zebra Kensgtn) Kensgtn Pub Corp.

— The Jade Pagoda. large type ed. LC 92-46345. (General Ser.). 342p. 1993. reprint ed. lib. bdg. 17.95 (*1-56054-665-4*) Thorndike Pr.

— Mystique. 1997. mass mkt. 4.99 (*0-8217-5753-9*) Kensgtn Pub Corp.

Clarke, Mark A., et al. Choice Readings. LC 96-60040. 296p. (Orig.). (C). 1996. pap. text 15.95 (*0-472-08329-5*, 08329) U of Mich Pr.

— Choice Readings Bk. 1: International Edition. LC 99-204430. (Illus.). 160p. (C). 1999. pap. text 10.95 (*0-472-08457-7*, 08457) U of Mich Pr.

— Choice Readings Bk. 2: International Edition. LC 99-204430. (Illus.). 184p. (C). 1999. pap. text 10.95 (*0-472-08458-5*, 08458) U of Mich Pr.

Clarke, Martin. Beck: A Life Less Ordinary. 1999. pap. 16.95 (*0-85965-267-X*) Plexus.

— Radiohead: Hysterical & Useless. 1999. pap. 16.95 (*0-85965-266-1*) Publishers Group.

— Verve: Crazed Highs & Horrible Lows. 144p. 1998. pap. 16.95 (*0-85965-269-6*) Plexus.

Clarke, Martin L. Greek Studies in England 1700-1830. 261p. 1945. reprint ed. lib. bdg. 48.50 (*0-685-13355-9*, Pub. by AM Hakkert) Coronet Bks.

Clarke, Mary. Little Girl Lost: The Troubled Childhood of Princess Diana by the Woman Who Raised Her. (Illus.). 256p. 1996. 19.95 (*1-55972-330-0*, Birch Ln Pr) Carol Pub Group.

— The Sadler's Wells Ballet: A History & an Appreciation. LC 77-563. (Series in Dance). 1977. reprint ed. lib. bdg. 37.50 (*0-306-70863-9*) Da Capo.

Clarke, Mary & Ashton, Frederick. Antoinette Sibley. (Illus.). 128p. (J). (gr. 8-12). 1981. 29.95 (*0-903102-64-1*, Pub. by Dance Bks) Princeton Bk Co.

Clarke, Mary & Hardiman, Nodlaig P., eds. John T. Gilbert, 1829-1898: Librarian, Historian & Archivist: A Centenary Celebration. 128p. 1999. boxed set 35.00 (*1-85182-437-5*, Pub. by Four Cts Pr) Intl Spec Bk.

Clarke, Mary, jt. auth. see Clarke, Kenneth W.

Clarke, Mary C. Complete Concordance to Shakespeare. rev. ed. LC 72-1029. reprint ed. lib. bdg. 97.50 (*0-404-01574-3*) AMS Pr.

— The Girlhood of Shakespeare's Heroines, 3 vols., Set. LC 72-1011. reprint ed. 125.00 (*0-404-01610-3*) AMS Pr.

— My Long Life: An Autobiographic Sketch. LC 12-31352. 1969. reprint ed. 25.00 (*0-403-00105-6*) Scholarly.

— My Long Life, an Autobiographic Sketch. (BCL1-PR English Literature Ser.). 276p. 1992. reprint ed. lib. bdg. 79.00 (*0-7812-7498-2*) Rprt Serv.

Clarke, Mary S. Immigration in Colonial Times. 1990. student ed. 39.00 (*1-56696-022-3*) Jackdaw.

Clarke, Mary W. Chief Bowles & the Texas Cherokees. LC 72-160490. (Civilization of the American Indian Ser.: Vol. 113). 191p. reprint ed. pap. 59.30 (*0-608-13525-9*, 201620200002) Bks Demand.

— Kentucky Quilts & Their Makers. LC 79-1502. (Illus.). 136p. 1993. reprint ed. 19.95 (*0-8131-0096-8*) U Pr of Ky.

Clarke, Mary W., ed. see Collinson, Frank.

Clarke, Mary W., jt. ed. see LeMaster, J. R.

Clarke, Mason A. The Violin & Old Violin Makers. 1988. reprint ed. lib. bdg. 49.00 (*0-7812-0486-0*) Rprt Serv.

Clarke, Matthew S. & Hall, D. A., compiled by. Legislative & Documentary History of the Bank of the United States: Including the Original Bank of North America. LC 67-23017. (Library of Money & Banking History). 832p. 1967. reprint ed. 87.50 (*0-678-00269-X*) Kelley.

Clarke, Maude V. Fourteenth Century Studies. Sutherland, L. G. & McKisack, May, eds. LC 67-30181. (Essay Index Reprint Ser.). 1977. 22.95 (*0-8369-0310-2*) Ayer.

***Clarke, Maureen.** Frommer's What the Airlines Never Tell You. (Illus.). 192p. 2000. pap. text 9.99 (*0-02-863594-9*) Macmillan Gen Ref.

Clarke, Micael M. Thackeray & Women. LC 94-36979. (Illus.). 250p. 1995. lib. bdg. 30.00 (*0-87580-197-8*) N Ill U Pr.

Clarke, Michael. Brassey's Defence Yearbook 1997: Centre for Defense Studies. 1997. 55.00 (*1-85753-215-5*, Pub. by Brasseys) Brasseys.

— British External Policy-Making in the 1990s. 339p. (C). 1992. 39.95 (*0-8157-1454-8*); pap. 18.95 (*0-8157-1453-X*) Brookings.

— Citizen's Financial Futures: The Regulation of Retail Investment Financial Services in Britain LC 98-70152. 245p. 1998. 69.95 (*1-84014-117-4*, Pub. by Ashgate Pub) Ashgate Pub Co.

***Clarke, Michael.** Flesh & Spirit in the Songs of Homer: A Study of Words & Myths. LC 99-30884. 400p. 2000. text 80.00 (*0-19-815263-9*) OUP.

Clarke, Michael. Mortgage Fraud. LC 91-26319. (Illus.). 64p. (Orig.). (C). (gr. 13). 1992. pap. text 114.00 (*0-412-45620-6*, Chap & Hall NY) Chapman & Hall.

— Regulating the City: Competition, Scandal & Reform. LC 85-29715. 192p. 1986. 69.00 (*0-335-15381-X*); pap. 25.00 (*0-335-15382-8*) OpUniv Pr.

***Clarke, Michael.** Regulation: The Social Control of Business Between Law & Politics. LC 99-53013. 256p. 2000. text 69.95 (*0-312-23104-0*) St Martin.

Clarke, Michael. Roaring Silence. 128p. 1994. pap. 13.95 (*1-874250-30-8*, 93163, Pub. by P H Crompton) Midpt Trade.

***Clarke, Michael.** Watercolor. (Eyewitness Books). 64p. (J). (gr. 4-7). 2000. 15.95 (*0-7894-5584-6*, D K Ink) DK Pub Inc.

Clarke, Michael, ed. New Perspectives on Security. 158p. 1993. text 37.00 (*0-08-041790-6*, Pub. by Brasseys) Brasseys.

— New Perspectives on Security. 158p. 1994. pap. 21.00 (*0-08-041789-2*, Pub. by Brasseys) Brasseys.

Clarke, Michael, et al, eds. Symbolic & Quantitative Approaches to Reasoning & Uncertainty: European Conference ECSQARU '93, Granada, Spain, November 8-10, 1990: Proceedings. LC 93-34942. (Lecture Notes in Computer Science Ser.: Vol. 747). 1993. 55.95 (*0-387-57395-X*) Spr-Verlag.

Clarke, Michael & White, Brian, eds. Understanding Foreign Policy: The Foreign Policy Systems Approach. 232p. 1989. text 80.00 (*1-85278-123-8*); pap. text 25.00 (*1-85278-125-4*) E Elgar.

C

Clarke, Michael, et al. Slippery Customers: Estate Agents, the Public & Regulation. 1994. text 44.00 (*1-85431-377-0*, Pub. by Blackstone Pr) Gaunt.

Clarke, Michael, jt. auth. see Smith, Steve.

Clarke, Michael, ed. see Centre for Defence Studies Staff.

Clarke, Mickey. A Book of Learnin' fer' Younguns. Halbert, Bill & Barnes, Mary, eds. 40p. (J). (gr. 4-5). 1998. write for info. (*1-929326-04-1*) Hal Bar Pubg.

— The Con. Halbert, Bill & Barnes, Mary, eds. 100p. 1998. pap. 15.00 (*1-929326-01-7*) Hal Bar Pubg.

— Death; The Illusion & the Lie: "Your Body"-A Temple of Spiritual Understanding... Halbert, Bill & Barnes, Mary, eds. 50p. 1998. spiral bd. 10.00 (*1-929326-03-3*) Hal Bar Pubg.

— The Nylexadorian Theory. Halbert, Bill & Barnes, Mary, eds. 125p. 1998. per. 15.00 (*1-929326-02-5*) Hal Bar Pubg.

— A Reader's Garden. Marusak, Kathleene et al, eds. 40p. 1997. pap. 10.00 (*1-929326-00-9*) Hal Bar Pubg.

***Clarke, Mike.** The Migration of Willie Mackerels. LC 99-66903. 160p. 2000. pap. 11.95 (*1-885003-30-7*, Pub. by R D Reed Pubs) Midpt Trade.

Clarke, Moya. Fruit Fandango Cookbook. 128p. 1994. 12.98 (*0-7858-0091-3*) Bk Sales Inc.

Clarke, Nicholas. Left Handed Guitar: Chords Especially for Lefties. (Illus.). 28p. 1992. pap. 12.95 (*0-933224-99-0*, T024) Bold Strummer Ltd.

Clarke, Nicholas, ed. see Brosnac, Donald.

***Clarke, Nick.** Alistair Cooke: The Biography. 2000. 29.95 (*1-55970-548-5*, Pub. by Arcade Pub Inc) Time Warner.

Clarke, Nick. Kai's Power Tools 3: An Illustrated Guide. LC 97-161461. 120p. 1997. pap. text 39.95 (*0-201-68809-3*) Peachpit Pr.

***Clarke, Nicky.** Hair Power. 2000. 27.50 (*1-85225-270-7*, Pub. by Transworld Publishers Ltd) Trafalgar.

Clarke, Nita. London for Beginners. 2nd ed. 1999. pap. text 11.00 (*0-86316-274-6*) Writers & Readers.

Clarke, Norm. High Hard Ones: Denver's Road to the Rockies from Inside the Newspaper War. 1993. pap. 10.95 (*0-9636394-0-4*) N D Clarke.

***Clarke, Norman F.** The Recreation & Entertainment Industries: An Information Sourcebook. 2nd ed. 312p. 2000. 55.00 (*0-7864-0797-2*) McFarland & Co.

Clarke, Oliver, jt. ed. see Niland, John.

Clarke, Oz. The Essential Wine Book. 3rd ed. LC 96-18738. 320p. 1997. per. 21.00 (*0-684-83064-7*) S&S Trade Pap.

— The Essential Wine Book: An Indispensable Guide to the Wines of the World. rev. ed. (Illus.). 300p. 1989. pap. 17.00 (*0-671-67049-2*, Fireside) S&S Trade Pap.

— Oz Clarke's Encyclopedia of Wine: An Illustrated A-to-Z Guide to Wines of the World. LC 93-17939. (Illus.). 1994. 35.00 (*0-671-79295-4*) S&S Trade.

***Clarke, Oz.** Oz Clarke's Introducing Wine. 144p. 2000. 20.00 (*0-15-100642-3*) Harcourt.

Clarke, Oz. Oz Clarke's New Encyclopedia of Wine. LC 99-33068. 416p. 1999. 40.00 (*0-15-100565-6*, Harvest Bks) Harcourt.

— Oz Clarke's Pocket Wine Guide, 1999. (Illus.). 304p. (C). 1998. 12.00 (*0-15-100430-7*) Harcourt.

***Clarke, Oz.** Oz Clarke's Pocket Wine Guide 2001. rev. ed. (Illus.). 320p. 2000. 13.00 (*0-15-100634-2*) Harcourt.

Clarke, Oz. Oz Clarke's Pocket Wine Guide 2000. 320p. 1999. 12.00 (*0-15-100571-0*, Harvest Bks) Harcourt.

— Oz Clarke's Wine Advisor, 1995: An Opinionated A-Z Guide to Wines by the World's Most Readable Wine Writer. 288p. 1994. pap. 12.00 (*0-671-88252-X*, Fireside) S&S Trade Pap.

— Oz Clarke's Wine Advisor 1999. (C). 1998. pap. 12.00 (*0-15-600628-6*) Harcourt.

— Oz Clarke's Wine Atlas: Wines & Wine Regions of the World. (Illus.). 320p. (gr. 8). 1995. 60.00 (*0-316-14697-8*) Little.

Clarke, Oz & Spurrier, Steven. Clarke & Spurrier's Fine Wine Guide: A Connoisseur's Bible. LC 98-227477. (Illus.). 320p. 1998. 30.00 (*0-15-100412-9*) Harcourt.

Clarke, P. & Krever, R. Australian Blackletter Law Series: Contract Law. 270p. 1993. pap. 35.00 (*0-409-30818-8*, Austral, MICHIE) LEXIS Pub.

Clarke, P. A. & Orchard, J. E., eds. Directory of Food Grain Standards. 1993. pap. 150.00 (*0-85954-358-7*, Pub. by Nat Res Inst) St Mut.

Clarke, P. A., et al. Quality Perceptions of Parboiled Rice Marketed in Sri Lanka. 1997. pap. 60.00 (*0-85954-479-6*, Pub. by Nat Res Inst) St Mut.

Clarke, P. B., et al, eds. Effects of Nicotine on Biological Systems II. LC 95-1165. (Advances in Pharmacological Sciences Ser.). (Illus.). xi, 403p. 1995. 129.00 (*0-8176-5083-0*) Birkhauser.

Clarke, P. B. S., et al. International Symposium on Nicotine: The Effects of Nicotine on Biological Systems II. (Abstracts Ser.). 80p. 1996. 29.50 (*0-8176-5087-3*) Birkhauser.

Clarke, P. H. 100 Soviet Chess Miniatures. LC 99-51927. 192p. 2000. pap. text 8.95 (*0-486-40844-2*) Dover.

Clarke, P. H. & Richmond, M. H., eds. Genetics & Biochemistry of Pseudomonas. LC 73-18926. (Wiley-Interscience Publications). 378p. reprint ed. pap. 117.20 (*0-608-14915-2*, 202598100048) Bks Demand.

Clarke, P. H., jt. auth. see Hoyle, Russel D.

Clarke, P. H., ed. see Suetin, A. S.

Clarke, P. H., tr. see Averbakh, Yuri.

***Clarke, Pat.** Painting Heads & Faces. LC 99-43575. (First Steps Ser.). (Illus.). 128p. 2000. pap. 18.99 (*0-89134-856-5*, North Lght Bks) F & W Pubns Inc.

Clarke, Patricia. A Colonial Woman: The Life & Times of Mary Braidwood Mowle 1827-1857. (Illus.). 316p. 1986. text 34.95 (*0-04-909025-9*) Routledge.

— Paul of Venice: Logica Magna, Fascicule 7, Pt. I. (Classical & Medieval Logic Texts Ser.: Vol. IV). (Illus.). 240p. 1982. 135.00 (*0-19-726003-9*) OUP.

— The Pioneer Writer. 272p. 1991. 29.95 (*0-04-442267-9*, Pub. by Allen & Unwin Pty) Paul & Co Pubs.

***Clarke, Patricia.** Rosa! Rosa! A Life of Rosa Praed, Novelist & Specialist. (Illus.). 250p. 2000. 39.95 (*0-522-84855-9*, Pub. by Melbourne Univ Pr) Paul & Co Pubs.

Clarke, Patricia, et al. To a Different Drumbeat: A Practical Guide to Parenting Children with Special Needs. (Lifeways Ser.). (Illus.). 240p. 1989. pap. 16.95 (*1-869890-09-4*, 1264, Pub. by Hawthorn Press) Anthroposophic.

Clarke, Patricia H. & Thompson, Rosemary. Rescue from Reality: Tour Operators & Travel Related Businesses That Are Unique and/or Almost Impossible to Find on Your Own. (Illus.). iv, 336p. 1997. pap. write for info. (*0-9660129-0-9*) Travel Pals.

Clarke, Patrick, tr. see Freire, Paulo.

***Clarke, Paul.** Learning School, Learning Systems. 2000. 74.95 (*0-304-70772-4*); pap. 24.95 (*0-304-70773-2*) Continuum.

Clarke, Paul. Lessons in Excellence from Charlie Trotter: 75 Ways One Visionary is Setting a New Standard. 208p. 1999. pap. 19.95 (*0-89815-908-3*) Ten Speed Pr.

Clarke, Paul, et al. Rural Wales Community & Marginalization. LC 97-176359. 200p. 1997. pap. 25.00 (*0-7083-1365-5*, Pub. by Univ Wales Pr) Paul & Co Pubs.

Clarke, Paul, jt. auth. see Boyle, Bill.

Clarke, Paul A., jt. auth. see Linzey, Andrew.

***Clarke, Paul B.** Autonomy Unbound. 392p. 1999. text 78.95 (*1-84014-798-9*, Pub. by Ashgate Pub) Ashgate Pub Co.

Clarke, Paul Barry. Citizenship: A Reader. LC 93-29326. 208p. (C). 1993. 70.00 (*0-7453-0585-7*, Pub. by Pluto GBR); pap. 16.95 (*0-7453-0586-5*, Pub. by Pluto GBR) Stylus Pub VA.

— Deep Citizenship. LC 95-52758. 168p. 1996. 49.95 (*0-7453-1102-4*, Pub. by Pluto GBR); pap. 17.95 (*0-7453-1101-6*, Pub. by Pluto GBR) Stylus Pub VA.

***Clarke, Pauline, contrib. by.** Writing down the Words: A Collection of Columns by Pauline Clarke Printed in the Berkshire Record from 1990-1999. 98p. 2000. 9.95 (*0-9677826-0-0*) P C Pub MA.

Clarke-Pearson, Daniel & Dawood, M. Yusoff. Green's Gynecology. 4th ed. (Illus.). 650p. 1990. pap. text 54.95 (*0-316-14490-8*, Little Brwn Med Div) Lppncott W & W.

Clarke-Pearson, Daniel L., jt. ed. see Nichols, David H.

Clarke, Peggy. Chelsea. LC 98-87777. (Images of America Ser.). (Illus.). 128p. 1998. pap. 18.99 (*0-7524-1208-6*) Arcadia Publng.

Clarke, Penny. Beneath the Oceans. LC 96-27727. (Worldwise Ser.). (Illus.). (J). 1997. pap. 7.00 (*0-531-15314-2*) Watts.

— Beneath the Oceans. LC 96-27727. (Worldwise Ser.). (Illus.). (J). (gr. 4-6). 1997. lib. bdg. 23.00 (*0-531-14437-2*) Watts.

— Insects & Spiders. (Worldwise Ser.). (Illus.). 48p. (J). (gr. 4-6). 1995. pap. 7.00 (*0-531-15282-0*); lib. bdg. 23.00 (*0-531-14365-1*) Watts.

— Rain Forest. LC 95-49026. (Worldwise Ser.). (Illus.). (J). 1996. lib. bdg. 23.00 (*0-531-14404-6*) Watts.

— Rain Forest. (Worldwise Ser.). 40p. (J). 1997. pap. 7.95 (*0-531-15296-0*) Watts.

— Volcanoes. LC 97-5965. (Worldwise Ser.). 40p. (J). 1998. 23.00 (*0-531-14462-3*) Watts.

— Volcanoes. (Worldwise Ser.). (Illus.). 40p. 1998. pap. 7.00 (*0-531-15319-3*) Watts.

Clarke, Peter. Hope & Glory: Britain in the Twentieth Century. LC 98-100813. 1997. pap. 14.95 (*0-14-014830-2*) Viking Penguin.

Clarke, Peter. The Keynesian Revolution & Its Economic Consequences: Selected Essays by Peter Clarke. LC 97-29957. 240p. 1998. 80.00 (*1-85898-590-0*) E Elgar.

— Lancashire & the New Liberalism. (Modern Revivals in History Ser.). 488p. 1993. 79.95 (*0-7512-0213-4*, Pub. by Gregg Revivals) Ashgate Pub Co.

— Liberals & Social Democrats. (Modern Revivals in History Ser.). 360p. 1993. 72.95 (*0-7512-0212-6*, Pub. by Gregg Revivals) Ashgate Pub Co.

Clarke, Peter & Evans, Susan H. How to Get First-Class Medical Care: Dealing with Doctors, Hospitals, Family, & Friends During Illness or Injury. LC 97-813. 256p. 1997. 22.50 (*1-55972-413-7*, Birch Ln Pr) Carol Pub Group.

— Surviving Modern Medicine: How to Get the Best from Doctors, Family, & Friends. LC 98-6812. (Illus.). 288p. (C). 1998. 38.00 (*0-8135-2555-1*); pap. 17.00 (*0-8135-2556-X*) Rutgers U Pr.

Clarke, Peter & Hale, Bob, eds. Reading Putnam. 302p. 1996. pap. 29.95 (*0-631-19995-0*) Blackwell Pubs.

Clarke, Peter & Trebilcock, Clive, eds. Understanding Decline: Perceptions & Realities of British Economic Performance. LC 97-8905. (Illus.). 330p. (C). 1998. text 64.95 (*0-521-56317-8*) Cambridge U Pr.

Clarke, Peter, jt. auth. see Arweck, Elisabeth B.

Clarke, Peter, jt. ed. see Kline, F. Gerald.

Clarke, Peter A. The English Nobility under Edward the Confessor. (Oxford Historical Monographs). (Illus.). 400p. 1994. 65.00 (*0-19-820442-6*) OUP.

Clarke, Peter B. Japanese New Religions in Global Perspective. (New Religious Movements Ser.). 300p. (C). 1999. text 52.00 (*0-7007-1185-6*, Pub. by Curzon Pr Ltd) UH Pr.

— Mahdism in West Africa: The Ijebu Mahdiyya Movement. 224p. 1996. 35.00 (*1-898942-06-4*, Pub. by Luzac Oriental) Weatherhill.

Clarke, Peter B. New Trends & Developments in the World of Islam. LC 97-182446. x, 400 p. 1997. 60.36 (*1-898942-17-X*, Pub. by Luzac Oriental) Weatherhill.

Clarke, Peter B., ed. Bibliography of Japanese New Religious Movements. 240p. 1998. text 55.00 (*1-873410-80-8*, Pub. by Curzon Pr Ltd) UH Pr.

— New Trends & Developments in African Religions, 186. LC 97-32006. (Contributions in Afro-American & African Studies: Vol. 186). 328p. 1998. 59.95 (*0-313-30128-X*, Greenwood Pr) Greenwood.

Clarke, Peter B. & Somers, Jeffrey, eds. Japanese New Religions in the West. LC 94-221238. (Japan Library). 164p. (C). 1996. text 42.00 (*1-873410-24-7*, Pub. by Curzon Pr Ltd) UH Pr.

Clarke, Peter B., jt. ed. see Puttick, Elizabeth.

Clarke, Peter S. Asset Based Lending: The Complete Guide to Originating, Evaluating & Managing Asset-Based Loans, Leasing & Factoring. 350p. (C). 1995. text 65.00 (*1-55738-754-0*, Irwn Prfssnl) McGraw-Hill Prof.

— The Problem Loan Problem-Solver: Step-by-Step Strategies for Resolving Bankruptcy, Lender Liability & Other Problem Loan Situations. rev. ed. 1994. text 55.00 (*1-55738-736-2*, Irwn Prfssnl) McGraw-Hill Prof.

Clarke, Peter S., jt. auth. see Robbins, Joel.

Clarke, Peyton N. Old King William Holmes & Families: Families of King William County VA. LC 98-117888. (Illus.). 211p. 1998. pap. 18.00 (*0-7884-0772-4*, C406) Heritage Bk.

— Old King William Homes & Families: An Account of Some of the Old Homesteads & Families of King William County, Virginia, from Its Earliest Settlement. (Illus.). 211p. 1995. reprint ed. pap. 21.50 (*0-8063-7956-1*, 1010) Clearfield Co.

Clarke, Philip, jt. auth. see Corones, Stephen.

Clarke, Philip H. Vertical Price Fixing in Australia. 244p. 1991. 68.00 (*1-86287-054-3*, Pub. by Federation Pr) Gaunt.

Clarke, Phyllis, et al, eds. Authority & Influence: Institutions, Concepts & Issues in Canadian Politics. (Illus.). 568p. 1994. pap. 24.95 (*0-88962-279-5*) Mosaic.

Clarke, Priscilla, jt. auth. see Siraj-Blatchford, Iram.

Clarke, R., et al, eds. Synchrotron Radiation in Materials Research Vol. 143: Materials Research Society Symposium Proceedings. 304p. 1989. text 17.50 (*1-55899-016-X*) Materials Res.

Clarke, R. Floyd. Science of Law & Lawmaking: Being an Introduction to Law, a General View of Its Forms & Substance & a Discussion of the Question of Codification. xvi, 473p. 1982. reprint ed. 48.50 (*0-8377-0437-5*, Rothman) W S Hein.

Clarke, R. H. Public Works: Engineering in Local Government. LC 96-175407. 214p. 1996. 67.00 (*0-7277-2093-7*, 2093, Pub. by T Telford) RCH.

Clarke, R. L. Coinage of Switzerland. (Illus.). 1968. lib. bdg. 8.00 (*0-932106-10-2*) S J Durst.

Clarke, R. M. AMX & Javelin Muscle Portfolio 1968-1974. (Illus.). 140p. 1994. pap. 19.95 (*1-85520-248-4*, Pub. by Brooklands Bks) Motorbooks Intl.

— Barracuda Music Port 1964-1974. (Brooklands Bks.). (Illus.). 140p. 1994. pap. 19.95 (*1-85520-259-X*) MBI Pubg.

— Camaro Muscle Portfolio, 1967-73. (Illus.). 140p. 1992. pap. 19.95 (*1-85520-145-3*) MBI Pubg.

— Charger Muscle 1966-1974 Portfolio. (Brooklands Muscle Portfolio Ser.). (Illus.). 140p. 1994. pap. 19.95 (*1-85520-261-1*) MBI Pubg.

— Chevelle & SS Muscle Portfolio 1964-72. (Brooklands Bks.). (Illus.). 140p. 1993. pap. 19.95 (*1-85520-188-7*) MBI Pubg.

— Chevrolet High Performance Tips & Techniques. (Illus.). 196p. 1991. pap. 18.95 (*1-85520-077-5*, Pub. by Brooklands Bks) Motorbooks Intl.

— Chevy II Nova & Musc., 1962-1974: Muscle Portfolio. (Brooklands Muscle Portfolio Ser.). (Illus.). 140p. 1994. pap. 19.95 (*1-85520-258-1*) MBI Pubg.

— Chrysler Engine Swapping Tips & Techniques. (Brooklands Bks.). (Illus.). 100p. 1993. pap. 16.95 (*1-85520-190-9*) MBI Pubg.

— Classic Camaro Restoration. (Illus.). 172p. 1997. pap. 18.95 (*1-85520-382-0*, Pub. by Brooklands Bks) Motorbooks Intl.

— Ducati: 1960-73 Gold Portfolio. (Illus.). 172p. 1996. pap. 24.95 (*1-85520-350-2*, Pub. by Brooklands Bks) Motorbooks Intl.

— Ducati 1974-1978. (Illus.). 172p. 1996. 24.95 (*1-85520-351-0*, Pub. by Brooklands Bks) Motorbooks Intl.

— 40 Years of Selling Volvo. 1996. pap. text 13.95 (*1-85520-318-9*) Brooklands Bks.

— Impala & SS 1958-1972 Musclecar Portfolio. (Musclecar Portfolio Ser.). (Illus.). 172p. 1996. pap. 19.95 (*1-85520-354-5*, Pub. by Brooklands Bks) Motorbooks Intl.

— Mazda Miata MX5 Performance Portfolio, 1989-1996. (Performance Portfolio Ser.). (Illus.). 140p. 1997. pap. 19.95 (*1-85520-355-3*, Pub. by Brooklands Bks) Motorbooks Intl.

— Mustang Restoration Tips & Techniques. 163p. 1986. pap. 18.95 (*0-948207-97-3*, Pub. by Brooklands Bks) Motorbooks Intl.

— Pontiac Fiero, 1984-88. (Brooklands Bks.). (Illus.). 100p. 1988. pap. 16.95 (*1-870642-01-5*, Pub. by Brooklands Bks) Motorbooks Intl.

— Shelby Cobra G. P., 1962-1969. (Gold Portfolio Ser.). (Illus.). 180p. 1990. pap. 24.95 (*1-85520-023-6*, Pub. by Brooklands Bks) Motorbooks Intl.

Clarke, R. S., jt. ed. see Trueman, Carl R.

Clarke, R. V. Suicide. (Illus.). 145p. 1989. 71.95 (*0-387-97004-5*) Spr-Verlag.

Clarke, R. V., jt. auth. see Cornish, D. B.

Clarke, R. Wallace. British Aircraft Armament: RAF Guns & Gunsights from 1914 to the Present Day, Vol. 2. Vol. 2. (Illus.). 224p. 1995. 44.95 (*1-85260-402-6*, Pub. by J H Haynes & Co) Motorbooks Intl.

Clarke, Rachel, jt. auth. see Roberts, Andrew.

Clarke, Rebecca. Sonata for Viola (Or Violincello) & Piano. (Women Composers Ser.: No. 20). 65p. 1986. reprint ed. lib. bdg. 32.50 (*0-306-76251-X*) Da Capo.

Clarke, Rena, tr. see Cortot, Alfred.

Clarke, Renfrey, tr. see Buzgalin, Alexander & Kolganov, Andre.

Clarke, Renfrey, tr. see Kagarlitsky, Boris.

Clarke, Richard. Anglo-American Collaboration in War & Peace, 1942-1949. Cairncross, Alec, ed. 1982. 34.50 (*0-19-828439-X*) OUP.

— The Guns of Peralta. LC 93-22963. 200p. 1993. 19.95 (*0-8027-1275-4*) Walker & Co.

— The Workout Manual. Miller, Ned & Behr, Joan H., eds. 64p. 1993. pap. text 50.00 (*0-936742-93-3*, 33211) Robt Morris Assocs.

Clarke, Richard & Logan, J. S. The Royal Victoria Hospital: A History, 1797-1997. LC 97-212442. 304p. 1998. 40.00 (*0-85640-601-5*, Pub. by Blackstaff Pr) Dufour.

Clarke, Richard F., ed. see Spirago, Francis.

Clarke, Richard G. Maximizing Coverage Minimizing Costs. 52p. 1993. pap. 20.00 (*0-614-05731-0*) CPCU Society.

Clarke, Richard H., ed. Triplet State ODMR Spectroscopy: Techniques & Applications to Biophysical Systems. LC 81-10486. (Illus.). 576p. reprint ed. pap. 178.60 (*0-8357-7518-6*, 203601300097) Bks Demand.

Clarke, Richard L., jt. auth. see Uncompensated Services Task Force Staff.

Clarke, Richard S. Countdown to Perfection: Take a Giant Step Forward - in This Lifetime! rev. ed. (Illus.). 256p. 1992. pap. 9.99 (*0-934363-10-2*) Lance Pubns.

Clarke, Robert. Mastering Advanced Spanish. (Mastering Languages Ser.). (Illus.). 303p. 1993. pap. 14.95 (*0-7818-0081-1*); audio 12.95 (*0-7818-0089-7*) Hippocrene Bks.

— Mastering Spanish. (Mastering Languages Ser.). (Orig.). 1991. audio 12.95 (*0-87052-067-9*) Hippocrene Bks.

— Mastering Spanish. (Mastering Languages Ser.). (Illus.). 322p. (Orig.). 1991. pap. 11.95 (*0-87052-059-8*) Hippocrene Bks.

***Clarke, Robert.** Murderers are Silent. large type ed. 296p. 1999. pap. 18.99 (*0-7089-5593-2*, Linford) Ulverscroft.

Clarke, Robert, jt. auth. see Minium, Edward W.

Clarke, Robert C. Hashish! Frank, Mel, ed. & photos by by. King, Jason, photos by. LC 97-51587. (Illus.). 378p. 1998. pap. 29.95 (*0-929349-05-9*) Red Eye Pr.

— Marijuana Botany. 3rd ed. (Illus.). 197p. 1995. pap. 24.95 (*0-914171-78-X*) Ronin Pub.

Clarke, Robert L. & Mohabat-Avin. Modern Coinage of Iran. 92p. 1974. pap. 4.00 (*1-889172-02-2*) Numismatic Intl.

Clarke, Robert W. & Lawry, Robert P., eds. The Power of the Professional Person. LC 88-840. 250p. (Orig.). (C). 1988. lib. bdg. 48.00 (*0-8191-6955-2*) U Pr of Amer.

Clarke, Roberta. Violence Against Women in the Caribbean: State & Non-State Responses. 110p. 1998. pap. 9.95 (*0-912917-50-4*) UNIFEM.

Clarke, Robin. Water: The International Crisis. LC 92-36487. (Illus.). 204p. (Orig.). (C). 1993. 35.00 (*0-262-03208-2*); pap. text 18.50 (*0-262-53116-X*) MIT Pr.

***Clarke, Robin T.** Stochastic Processes for Water Scientists: Developments & Applications. LC 97-26708. 198p. 1998. 90.00 (*0-471-97348-3*) Wiley.

Clarke, Roger. Digital Compression of Still Images & Video. LC 96-133907. (Signal Processing & Its Applications Ser.). (Illus.). 480p. 1995. text 69.00 (*0-12-175720-X*) Acad Pr.

— Harriers of the British Isles. (Natural History Ser.: No. 57). (Illus.). 24p. 1989. pap. 5.25 (*0-7478-0092-8*, Pub. by Shire Pubns) Parkwest Pubns.

— Industrial Economics. 340p. 1985. pap. 37.95 (*0-631-14305-X*) Blackwell Pubs.

— Sideways to Victory. (Illus.). 256p. 1998. 29.95 (*1-899870-27-X*, Pub. by Motor Racing) Motorbooks Intl.

Clarke, Roger, et al. Monopoly Policy in the U. K. Assessing the Evidence. LC 97-50054. 224p. 1998. 80.00 (*1-85898-585-4*) E Elgar.

Clarke, Roger A., ed. Hungary: The Second Decade of Economic Reform. (Perspectives on Eastern Europe Ser.). 172p. 1989. 25.00 (*0-582-04441-3*) St James Pr.

— Poland: The Economy in the 1980's. (Perspectives on Eastern Europe Ser.). 149p. 1989. lib. bdg. 25.00 (*1-55862-045-1*) St James Pr.

Clarke, Roger G. Options & Futures: A Tutorial. 1992. pap. text 20.00 (*0-943205-16-6*) RFICFA.

Clarke, Roger G. & Kritzman, Mark P. Currency Management: Concepts & Practices. LC 99-207578. (Orig.). 1996. pap. text 30.00 (*0-943205-33-6*) RFICFA.

Clarke, Ronald & Hope, Tim. Coping with Burglary: Research Perspectives on Policy. LC 84-3970. (International Series in Social Welfare). 1984. lib. bdg. 98.00 (*0-89838-151-7*) Kluwer Academic.

Clarke, Ronald, jt. auth. see Gottfresdon, Don.

Clarke, Ronald V. Situational Crime Prevention: Successful Case Studies. 2nd ed. LC 97-20375. (Illus.). 280p. (C). 1997. pap. text 27.50 (*0-911577-38-6*, Criminal Justice) Willow Tree NY.

— Situational Crime Prevention: Successful Case Studies. 2nd rev. ed. LC 97-20375. (Illus.). 280p. (C). 1997. text 69.90 (*0-911577-39-4*, Criminal Justice) Willow Tree NY.

Clarke, Ronald V., ed. Crime Prevention Studies, Vol. 1. (Illus.). 196p. 1993. 47.50 (*1-881798-00-3*, Criminal Justice) Willow Tree NY.

— Crime Prevention Studies, Vol. 2. (Illus.). 240p. 1998. reprint ed. pap. 37.50 (*1-881798-16-X*) Willow Tree NY.

An Asterisk (*) at the beginning of an entry indicates that the title is appearing for the first time.

— Preventing Mass Transit Crime. (Crime Prevention Studies: Vol. 6). 225p. 1996. 47.50 (*0-9606960-8-3*, Criminal Justice) Willow Tree NY.

Clarke, Ronald V. & Felson, Marcus, eds. Routine Activity & Rational Choice. (Advances in Criminological Theory Ser.: Vol. 5). 418p. (C). 1993. text 49.95 (*1-56000-087-2*) Transaction Pubs.

Clarke, Ronald V., jt. ed. see Felson, Marcus.

Clarke, Ross. The Doors: Dance on Fire. (Illus.). 224p. 1993. pap. 14.00 (*0-685-72582-0*, Pub. by Castle Communs) Viking Penguin.

Clarke, Rosy. Japanese Antique Furniture: A Guide to Evaluating & Restoring. LC 82-21916. (Illus.). 152p. (Orig.). 1983. pap. 22.50 (*0-8348-0178-7*) Weatherhill.

Clarke, Roy. Gala Week. large type ed. 352p. 1987. 27.99 (*0-7089-1682-1*) Ulverscroft.

— The Moonbather. large type ed. 307p. 1989. 27.99 (*0-7089-1926-X*) Ulverscroft.

Clarke, Roy & Rice, Jonathan. Keeping up Appearances: Hyacinth Bucket's Book of Etiquette for the Socially Less Fortunate. (Illus.). 191p. 1995. 21.95 (*0-563-36975-2*, BBC-Parkwest) Parkwest Pubns.

Clarke, Roy & Rice, Jonathan. Keeping up Appearances: Hyacinth Bucket's Book of Etiquette for the Socially Less Fortunate. LC 94-73742. (Illus.). 92p. 1996. pap. 11.95 (*0-563-37107-2*, BBC-Parkwest) Parkwest Pubns.

Clarke, Roy, jt. auth. see Rice, Jonathan.

Clarke, Roy H., jt. auth. see Spurgeon, Charles H.

Clarke, Roy H., ed. see Spurgeon, Charles H.

Clarke, Roy S., Jr., ed. The Port Orford, Oregon, Meteorite Mystery. LC 92-26788. (Smithsonian Contributions to the Earth Sciences Ser.: No. 31). 48p. reprint ed. pap. 30.00 (*0-7837-4483-8*, 204425800001) Bks Demand.

Clarke, Sally C. & Ventura, Stephanie J. Birth & Fertility Rates for States, United States, 1990. National Center for Health Statistics (U.S.) Staff, ed. LC 94-24746. (Vital & Health Statistics Ser.: Series 21, Vol. 52). iv, 53p. 1994. write for info. (*0-8406-0502-1*) Natl Ctr Health Stats.

Clarke, Sally H. Regulation & Revolution in United States Farm Productivity. (Studies in Economic History & Policy: The United States in the Twentieth Century). (Illus.). 326p. (C). 1994. text 74.95 (*0-521-44117-X*) Cambridge U Pr.

Clarke, Samuel, jt. auth. see Leibniz, Gottfried Wilhelm.

Clarke, Sandra, ed. Focus on Canada. LC 93-31907. (Varieties of English Around the World General Ser.: Vol. 11). xii, 302p. 1993. pap. 59.00 (*1-55619-442-0*) J Benjamins Pubng Co.

Clarke, Sarah. No Faith in the System. LC 96-144511. 216p. 1997. pap. 18.95 (*1-85635-128-9*, Pub. by Mercier Pr) Irish Amer Bk.

***Clarke, Sathianathan.** Dalits & Christianity: Subaltern Religion & Liberation Theology in India. 256p. 2000. pap. 10.95 (*0-19-565130-8*) OUP.

Clarke, Serafina M., tr. see Brown, Mary E., ed.

Clarke, Sidney M. The Miracle Play in England. LC 65-15874. 1970. reprint ed. lib. bdg. 75.00 (*0-8383-0529-6*) M S G Haskell Hse.

***Clarke, Sidney W. & Blind, Adolphe.** The Bibliography of Conjuring & Kindred Deceptions. 84p. 1998. reprint ed. 40.00 (*1-57898-096-8*) Martino Pubng.

***Clarke, Silvana.** Science Experiments. (Mother Nature's Ser.). (Illus.). 64p. (J). (gr. 3-7). 2001. pap. 6.95 (*0-7373-0338-7*, 03387W, Pub. by Lowell Hse) NTC Contemp Pub Co.

***Clarke, Simon.** The Formation of a Labour Market in Russia. LC 99-41672. 315p. 1999. 95.00 (*1-85898-831-4*) E Elgar.

Clarke, Simon. Keynesianism, Monetarism & the Crisis of the State. 384p. 1988. pap. 30.00 (*1-85278-434-2*) E Elgar.

— Keynesianism, Monetarism & the Crisis of the State. 384p. 1988. 95.00 (*1-85278-010-X*) E Elgar.

Clarke, Simon, ed. Conflict & Change in the Russian Industrial Enterprise. (Management & Industry in Russia Ser.). 320p. (C). 1996. text 90.00 (*1-85898-340-1*) E Elgar.

— Labour Relations in Transition: Wages, Employment & Industrial Conflict in Russia. LC 95-49536. (Management & Industry in Russia Ser.). 304p. 1996. 90.00 (*1-85898-411-4*) E Elgar.

— Management & Industry in Russia: Formal & Informal Relations in the Period of Transition. LC 95-4048. (Management & Industry in Russia Ser.). 1995. 90.00 (*1-85898-062-3*) E Elgar.

— The Russian Enterprise in Transition. LC 96-15888. (Management & Industry in Russia Ser.). 416p. 1996. 100.00 (*1-85898-341-X*) E Elgar.

— Structural Adjustment Without Mass Unemployment? Lessons from Russia. LC 97-35420. 384p. 1998. 95.00 (*1-85898-713-X*) E Elgar.

***Clarke, Simon & Palmer, Susan L.** Discussion Paper, Preparing for Elections in Sierra Leone: Summary Findings of an IFES Assessment Mission to Sierra Leone. ii, 30p. 1999. pap. 5.00 (*1-879720-69-8*) Intl Fndt Elect.

— Rapport de l'AAEA et de l'IFES sur l'Observation des Elections de Transition au Nigeria: Decembre 1998-Fevrier 1999. (FRE.). ii, 90p. 1999. 11.00 (*1-879720-65-5*) Intl Fndt Elect.

— Report of the AAEA/IFES Observation of the Transitional Elections in Nigeria: December 1998-February 1998. ii, 78p. 1999. pap. text 10.00 (*1-879720-57-4*) Intl Fndt Elect.

Clarke, Simon, et al. The Workers' Movement in Russia. LC 95-6826. (Studies of Communism in Transition). 448p. 1995. 100.00 (*1-85898-063-1*) E Elgar.

Clarke, Simone, jt. ed. see Roberts, Michael.

Clarke, Stanley C. Mughal Paintings: The School of Jahangir. Orig. Title: Indian Drawings. (Illus.). 1983. 45.00 (*0-318-36344-5*) Asia Bk Corp.

— Mughal Paintings, Being Thirty Paintings of the School of Jahangir & Four Panels of Calligraphy. (Illus.). 60p. 1983. text 32.00 (*0-89563-641-7*) Coronet Bks.

Clarke, Stephan. The Lord Peter Wimsey Companion. 1986. 49.95 (*0-89296-125-2*, Pub. by Mysterious Pr) Little.

***Clarke, Stephen.** Social Work as Community Development: A Management Model for Change. 2nd ed. 320p. 2000. pap. text 30.95 (*0-7546-1111-6*, Pub. by Ashgate Pub) Ashgate Pub Co.

Clarke, Stephen. Social Work As Community Development: A Management Model for Social Change. LC 96-84101. 288p. 1996. 69.95 (*1-85972-098-6*, Pub. by Avebry) Ashgate Pub Co.

Clarke, Stephen V. The Reconstruction of the International Monetary System: The Attempts of 1922 & 1933. LC 73-9360. (Princeton Studies in International Finance Ser.: No. 33). 52p. reprint ed. pap. 30.00 (*0-608-13811-8*, 201782300010) Bks Demand.

Clarke, Steve. Metaphysics & the Disunity of Scientific Knowledge. LC 97-78320. (Avebury Series in Philosophy). 148p. 1998. text 59.95 (*1-85972-538-4*, Pub. by Ashgate Pub) Ashgate Pub Co.

***Clarke, Steve & Lehaney, Brian.** Human Centered Methods in Information Systems: Current Research & Practice. LC 99-88689. 2000. pap. write for info. (*1-878389-75-0*) L Ashley & Joshua.

***Clarke, Steve & Lehaney, Brian, eds.** Human Centered Methods in Information Systems: Current Research & Practice. LC 99-88689. (Illus.). 300p. (C). 2000. pap. 69.95 (*1-878289-64-0*) Idea Group Pub.

***Clarke, Stevens H.** An Introduction to the County Jail. (C). 1999. pap. 15.00 (*1-56011-363-4*) Institute Government.

Clarke, Stevens H. The Law of Sentencing, Probation, & Parole in North Carolina. 2nd ed. LC 98-113057. 224p. 1997. text 38.00 (*1-56011-317-0*); pap. text 28.00 (*1-56011-307-3*, 97.06) Institute Government.

Clarke, Stevens H. & Harrison, Anita L. Recidivism of Criminal Offenders Assigned to Community Correctional Programs or Released from Prison: Final Report. 56p. (Orig.). (C). 1992. pap. text 12.00 (*1-56011-204-2*, 92.02) Institute Government.

Clarke, Stevens H. & McCormick, Kelly. Mediation in Workers' Compensation Cases: An Evaluation of Its Effects. LC 97-151586. (Special Ser.: Vol. 16). 15p. (Orig.). 1997. pap. text 14.00 (*1-56011-308-1*, SS#16) Institute Government.

Clarke, Stevens H., et al. Court-Ordered Civil Case Mediation in North Carolina: An Evaluation of Its Effects. 82p. (Orig.). (C). 1996. pap. text 15.00 (*1-56011-277-8*) Institute Government.

— Juvenile Detention Facilities in North Carolina: Use in 1993. LC 95-620133. 43p. (Orig.). (C). 1994. pap. text 13.00 (*1-56011-228-X*, 94-15) Institute Government.

— Mediation of Interpersonal Disputes in North Carolina: An Evaluation. 84p. (Orig.). (C). 1993. pap. text 16.00 (*1-56011-208-5*, 92-05) Institute Government.

Clarke-Stewart, Alison. Daycare. rev. ed. LC 92-19515. (Developing Child Ser.). 216p. 1993. 28.50 (*0-674-19405-5*) HUP.

— Daycare. rev. ed. LC 92-19515. (Developing Child Ser.). 216p. 1993. pap. text 9.95 (*0-674-19406-3*) HUP.

Clarke-Stewart, K. Alison, et al. Children at Home & in Day Care. 296p. 1994. text 59.95 (*0-8058-1484-1*) L Erlbaum Assocs.

Clarke, Stuart. Memory New Testament. (Illus.). 700p. (Orig.). 1987. pap. 9.95 (*0-9619291-0-3*) Bibles Intl.

Clarke, Stuart N., jt. auth. see Kirkpatrick, B. J.

Clarke, Sue. The Tombs of the Pharaohs: A Three-Dimensional Discovery. 10p. (J). (gr. 3 up). 1994. 16.95 (*1-56282-485-6*, Pub. by Hyprn Child) Little.

Clarke, Susan. Work of Cities. LC 98-10858. 1998. pap. 47.95 (*0-8166-2892-0*); pap. 18.95 (*0-8166-2893-9*) U of Minn Pr.

Clarke, Susan E., ed. Urban Innovation & Autonomy: Political Implications of Policy Change. LC 89-10513. (Urban Innovation Ser.: No. 1). (Illus.). 288p. 1989. pap. 89.30 (*0-608-05074-1*, 206562900005) Bks Demand.

— Urban Innovation & Autonomy: Political Implications of Policy Change. (Urban Innovation Ser.: Vol. 1). 320p. (C). 1989. text 36.00 (*0-8039-3139-5*) Sage.

Clarke, Susan E., ed. Urban Innovation & Autonomy: Political Implications of Policy Change. (Urban Innovation Ser.: Vol. 1). 320p. (C). 1989. pap. text 17.95 (*0-8039-3140-9*) Sage.

Clarke, Susan E., jt. ed. see Goetz, Edward G.

Clarke, Sylvia S., jt. ed. see Rosenberg, Gary.

Clarke, T. H. The Rhinoceros from Durer to Stubbs: An Aspect of the Exotic. LC 86-50086. (Illus.). 220p. 1988. pap. 29.95 (*0-85667-326-9*, Pub. by P Wilson) Scala Books.

Clarke, Terence. The Englewood Readings. (American Dust Ser.: No. 5). (Illus.). 64p. 1976. 6.95 (*0-913218-30-8*); pap. 2.50 (*0-913218-29-4*) Dustbooks.

— My Father in the Night. LC 90-49561. 304p. 1991. 19.95 (*0-916515-93-1*) Mercury Hse Inc.

Clarke, Theodore H., jt. auth. see West, J. Christopher.

Clarke, Thomas. The American Railway. 484p. 1972. 27.95 (*0-405-18125-6*) Ayer.

Clarke, Thomas, ed. International Privatisation: Strategies & Practices. LC 94-169. (De Grutyer Studies in Organization: No. 55). xiv, 435p. (C). 1994. lib. bdg. 72.95 (*3-11-013569-8*) De Gruyter.

Clarke, Thomas, et al. The American Railway: Its Constructon, Development, Management, & Appliances. LC 74-189048. (Illus.). reprint ed. 25.00 (*0-405-08364-5*, Pub. by Blom Pubns) Ayer.

Clarke, Thomas E. Christian Living in the U. S. Culture. 36p. 1987. pap. text 2.95 (*1-55612-075-3*) Sheed & Ward WI.

Clarke, Thomas L., ed. Distributed Interactive Simulation Systems for Simulation & Training in the Aerospace Environment. LC 95-10060. (Critical Reviews of Optical Science & Technology Ser.: Vol. CR58). 1995. pap. 66.00 (*0-8194-1850-1*) SPIE.

Clarke, Thurston. California Fault: Searching for the Spirit of a State along the San Andreas. 1997. pap. 12.95 (*0-345-40908-6*) Ballantine Pub Grp.

***Clarke, Thurston.** California Fault: Searching for the Spirit of the State along the San Andreas. 2000. 26.75 (*0-8446-7115-0*) Peter Smith.

Clarke, Thurston. Equator: A Journey. 464p. 1990. pap. 9.95 (*0-380-70855-8*, Avon Bks) Morrow Avon.

— Equator: A Journey. 464p. 1997. pap. 13.00 (*0-380-72941-5*, Avon Bks) Morrow Avon.

Clarke, Tim, jt. auth. see Robson, Michelle.

***Clarke, Tony.** Managing Health & Safety in Building & Construction. LC 99-36658. 345p. 1999. write for info. (*0-7506-4015-4*) Buttrwrth-Heinemann.

Clarke, Tony. Silent Coup: Confronting the Big Business Takeover of Canada. (Illus.). 273p. (Orig.). 1997. pap. 19.95 (*0-88627-923-2*, Pub. by J Lorimer) Formac Dist Ltd.

— Silent Coup: Confronting the Big Business Takeover of Canada. 160p. (Orig.). 1997. pap. 19.95 (*1-55028-556-4*, Pub. by J Lorimer); bds. 34.95 (*1-55028-557-2*, Pub. by J Lorimer) Formac Dist Ltd.

Clarke, Tony, jt. auth. see Barlow, Maude.

Clarke, Valerie A., et al. A Journey Through Breast Cancer: Reflections of Thirty Survivors. (Research Monographs: No. 9). 93p. 1995. pap. 50.00 (*0-7300-2058-4*, Pub. by Deakin Univ) St Mut.

Clarke, Velta, ed. see Obebe, Bolarinde, et al.

Clarke, Velta J. Aliens in a New Frontier: Caribbean Immigration into the U. S.... (Illus.). 103p. (Orig.). 1994. pap. text. write for info. (*1-878433-18-0*) Caribbean Diaspora Pr.

Clarke, Velta J. & Riviere, Emmanuel, eds. Establishing New Lives: Selected Readings on Caribbean Immigrants in New York City. (Illus.). 257p. (Orig.). 1989. pap. text 15.00 (*1-878433-00-8*) Caribbean Diaspora Pr.

Clarke, Velta J., ed. see Nunez-Harrell, Elizabeth, et al.

Clarke, Victoria. Why Angels Fall. text 29.95 (*0-312-23396-5*) St Martin.

Clarke, W. G., ed. see Prehistoric Society of East Anglia Staff.

Clarke, W. K., tr. & intro. see Basilius.

Clarke, W. M. How the City of London Works: An Introduction to Its Financial Markets. 2nd ed. (Waterlow Publications). (Illus.). 120p. 1988. pap. 16.00 (*0-08-033105-X*) Macmillan.

— How the City of London Works: An Introduction to Its Financial Markets. 3rd ed. (Waterlow Publications). (Illus.). 128p. 1991. pap. 21.90 (*0-08-040867-2*) Macmillan.

— How the City Works: An Introduction to Its Financial Markets. (Illus.). 112p. 1986. pap. 10.00 (*0-08-039235-0*, L125, Pergamon Pr) Elsevier.

Clarke, W. M., ed. Planning for Europe, 1992: Britain & the Common Internal Market. (Waterlow Publications). (Illus.). 240p. 1989. pap. 19.95 (*0-08-036903-0*, Pergamon Pr) Elsevier.

Clarke, W. Norris. Explorations in Metaphysics: Being-God-Person. LC 94-15469. (C). 1995. text 40.50 (*0-268-00696-2*); pap. text 23.00 (*0-268-00697-0*) U of Notre Dame Pr.

***Clarke, W. Norris.** The One & the Many: A Contemporary Thomistic Metaphysics. 2001. pap. 24.00 (*0-268-03707-8*, Pub. by U of Notre Dame Pr); lib. bdg. 45.00 (*0-268-03706-X*, Pub. by U of Notre Dame Pr) Chicago Distribution Ctr.

Clarke, W. Norris. Person & Being. LC 92-63402. (Aquinas Lectures). 1993. pap. 15.00 (*0-87462-160-7*) Marquette.

Clarke, W. Norris, jt. auth. see Wapnick, Kenneth.

Clarke, Walter. Learning from Somalia: The Lessons of Armed Humanitarian Intervention. LC 96-48453. (C). 1997. pap. 79.00 (*0-8133-2793-8*, Pub. by Westview) HarpC.

Clarke, Walter & Herbst, Jeffrey, eds. Learning from Somalia: The Lessons of Armed Humanitarian Intervention. LC 96-48453. 288p. (C). 1997. pap. text 28.00 (*0-8133-2794-6*, Pub. by Westview) HarpC.

Clarke, William. The Lost Fortune of Tsars. LC 96-24818. 336p. 1996. pap. 14.95 (*0-312-14672-8*) St Martin.

***Clarke, William.** Soul of the Law. 582p. 1999. reprint ed. 175.00 (*1-56169-482-7*) Gaunt.

Clarke, William. Walt Whitman. LC 77-130249. (Studies in Whitman: No. 28). 1970. reprint ed. lib. bdg. 75.00 (*0-8383-1139-3*) M S G Haskell Hse.

Clarke, William, tr. see Trapp, Joseph.

Clarke, William H. An Outline of the Structure of the Pipe Organ. (Illus.). 1977. reprint ed. pap. text 18.00 (*0-913746-09-6*) Organ Lit.

Clarke, William L., et al, eds. Methods in Diabetes Research, Vol. 2. LC 84-3714. (Illus.). 732p. reprint ed. pap. 200.00 (*0-8357-7519-4*, 203601400097) Bks Demand.

Clarke, William M. The Secret Life of Wilkie Collins. (Illus.). 256p. 1991. text 24.95 (*0-929587-51-0*) I R Dee.

— The Secret Life of Wilkie Collins. LC 97-131296. (Illus.). 256p. 1996. pap. 17.95 (*0-7509-1208-1*, Pub. by Sutton Pub Ltd) Intl Pubs Mktg.

Clarke, William P. Clarke: History of Patrick Clarke & Catherin Wade Clarke, Their Ancestors & Descendants. 138p. 1997. reprint ed. pap. 22.00 (*0-8328-7968-1*); reprint ed. lib. bdg. 32.00 (*0-8328-7967-3*) Higginson Bk Co.

Clarkin, J. J. The Art of Betting Horses & Winning Consistently. 32p. 1997. pap. 7.95 (*0-934650-08-X*) Sunnyside.

— Winning Consistently at the Greyhound Races. 32p. 1997. pap. 7.95 (*0-934650-13-6*) Sunnyside.

Clarkin, Jean, ed. see Bramson, John.

Clarkin, John F., et al, eds. Affective Disorders & the Family: Assessment & Treatment. LC 87-28175. (Family Therapy Ser.). 263p. 1988. lib. bdg. 37.95 (*0-89862-101-1*) Guilford Pubns.

— Borderline Personality Disorder: Clinical & Empirical Perspectives. LC 91-28304. (Personality Disorders Ser.). 352p. 1991. lib. bdg. 47.00 (*0-89862-262-X*) Guilford Pubns.

Clarkin, John F. & Docherty, John P., eds. Psychological & Biological Assessment at the Turn of the Century. (Review of Psychiatry Ser.: Vol. 16, Sect. V). 144p. (Orig.). 1997. pap. text 25.00 (*0-88048-449-7*, 8449) Am Psychiatric.

Clarkin, John F. & Lenzenweger, Mark F., eds. Major Theories of Personality Disorder. LC 95-53935. 402p. 1996. lib. bdg. 46.00 (*1-57230-082-5*) Guilford Pubns.

Clarkin, John F., et al. A DSM-IV Casebook of Treatment Selection. 3rd ed. 1997. text. write for info. (*0-87630-746-2*) Brunner-Mazel.

***Clarkin, John F., et al.** Psychotheraphy for Borderline Personality. LC 98-28270. 390p. 1998. 55.00 (*0-471-17042-9*) Wiley.

Clarkin, John F., jt. auth. see Beutler, Larry E.

Clarkin, John F., ed. see Glick, Ira D., et al.

Clarkin, Maura A. National Gallery of Art Activity Book. (Illus.). 112p. 1994. pap. 16.95 (*0-8109-2595-8*, Pub. by Abrams) Time Warner.

Clarkin, Mike & Brennan, Terry. Radon-Resistant Construction Techniques for New Residential Construction: Technical Guidance. (Illus.). 43p. (Orig.). (C). 1993. pap. text 20.00 (*1-56806-184-6*) DIANE Pub.

Clarksean, R., et al, eds. Proceedings of the 32nd National Heat Transfer Conference, Baltimore, Maryland, August 8-12, 1997, Vol. 10. (HTD Ser.: Vol. 348). 144p. 1997. 70.00 (*0-7918-1815-2*, H01096) ASME Pr.

Clarkson. Business Law-New York. 6th ed. Date not set. suppl. ed. write for info. (*0-314-05106-6*) West Pub.

— Business Law-Texas. 6th ed. Date not set. suppl. ed. write for info. (*0-314-05107-4*) West Pub.

— Elementary Algebra. (C). Date not set. pap. 19.96 (*0-395-87946-9*); text 58.76 (*0-395-74424-5*) HM.

— Fundamentals of College Mathematics. (C). 1993. pap. 60.36 (*0-395-69133-8*); pap. text 59.16 (*0-395-48403-0*) HM.

— Fundamentals of College Mathematics. (C). 1994. pap., teacher ed. 5.96 (*0-395-69301-2*); pap., student ed. 9.96 (*0-395-69300-4*) HM.

— Intermediate Algebra. (C). Date not set. pap. 19.96 (*0-395-87953-1*); text 58.76 (*0-395-74425-3*) HM.

— Intermediate Algebra. LC 93-78642. (C). 1994. pap. text 57.56 (*0-395-48406-5*) HM.

— Intermediate Algebra. (C). 1994. pap., student ed. 5.96 (*0-395-69303-9*) HM.

— Intermediate Algebra. (C). 1994. pap., teacher ed. 5.96 (*0-395-69305-5*) HM.

— Intermediate Algebra. (C). 1994. pap. text, student ed. 20.76 (*0-395-48407-3*) HM.

— Introduction to Algebra. (C). 1994. pap. 60.36 (*0-395-69134-6*); pap. text 59.16 (*0-395-48405-7*) HM.

— Introduction to Algebra. (C). 1994. pap. text, student ed. 20.76 (*0-395-48409-X*) HM.

— On Psychotherapy. 266p. 1993. pap. 48.00 (*1-56593-247-1*, 0313) Singular Publishing.

***Clarkson.** Web Tutor on Webct to Accompany Wests Business Law. 8th ed. 2000. pap. 19.00 (*0-324-06795-X*) Sth-Wstrn College.

— West Bus Law Handbook on Critical Thinking. 7th ed. (SWC -Business Law Ser.). 1997. pap. 6.00 (*0-538-87989-0*) Sth-Wstrn College.

Clarkson. West's Business Law. 7th ed. (LA - Business Law Ser.). (C). 1997. pap., student ed. 27.95 (*0-538-87981-5*) S-W Pub.

— West's Business Law. 7th ed. (LA - Business Law Ser.). (C). 1997. mass mkt., student ed. 27.95 (*0-538-87980-7*) S-W Pub.

***Clarkson.** West's Business Law: Test Preparation. 8th ed. (C). 2000. text, student ed. 25.00 (*0-324-05284-7*) Sth-Wstrn College.

Clarkson & Cross. Advanced Topics & Contemporary Issues, West's Business Law. 7th ed. (SWC-Business Law Ser.). 1997. pap. 21.00 (*0-538-87987-4*) Sth-Wstrn College.

Clarkson & McAllister. Early Modern England. 68.95 (*1-85928-259-8*) Ashgate Pub Co.

Clarkson & Miller. Introduction to Critical Thinking West Business Law. 6th ed. (SWC-Business Law Ser.). 1994. pap. 5.00 (*0-314-05166-X*) Thomson Learn.

— Western Business Law: Introduction to Critical Thinking. (SWC-Business Law Ser.). Date not set. 57.00 (*0-314-12435-7*) Sth-Wstrn College.

Clarkson, A. R., ed. IgA Nephropathy. (Topics in Renal Medicine Ser.). 1987. text 161.50 (*0-89838-839-2*) Kluwer Academic.

Clarkson, A. R. & Woodroffe, A. J., eds. IgA Nephropathy: Pathogenesis & Treatment. (Contributions to Nephrology Ser.: Vol. 111). (Illus.). x, 212p. 1995. 199.25 (*3-8055-6030-3*) S Karger.

Clarkson, Adrienne, intro. An Unlikely Affair: The Irving Layton - Dorothy Rath Correspondence. 230p. 1992. 8.95 (*0-88962-101-2*) Mosaic.

***Clarkson, Angela G. & Larson, Anne M.** CheckMate Classic. 2nd rev. ed. (Critical Care CheckMate Ser.). (Illus.). 206p. 1998. write for info. (*0-9700484-3-2*) NNCC.

— Critical Care CheckMate. 2nd rev. ed. (Illus.). 88p. 1998. write for info. (*0-615-11170-X*) NNCC.

C

— ER/Trauma CheckMate. 2nd rev. ed. (Critical Care CheckMate Ser.). (Illus.). 166p. 1998. write for info. (*0-9700484-0-8*) NNCC.

— Pediatric CheckMate. 2nd rev. ed. (Critical Care CheckMate Ser.). (Illus.). 108p. 1997. write for info. (*0-9700484-2-4*) NNCC.

— PeriAnesthesia CheckMate. (Critical Care CheckMate Ser.). (Illus.). 134p. 1998. write for info. (*0-9700484-1-6*) NNCC.

Clarkson, B. D. Vegetation of Egmont National Park, New Zealand. 1986. 27.50 (*0-477-06787-5*, Pub. by Manaaki Whenua) Balogh.

Clarkson, B. D., et al. Botany of Rotorua. 1991. pap. 39.95 (*0-614-07539-4*, Pub. by Manaaki Whenua) Balogh.

Clarkson, Bayard, et al, eds. Differentiation of Normal & Neoplastic Hematopoietic Cells, Bk. B. LC 78-60391. (Cold Spring Harbor Conferences on Cell Proliferation Ser.: No. 5). 480p. reprint ed. pap. 148.80 (*0-7837-2008-4*, 204228200002) Bks Demand.

Clarkson, Bayard & Baserga, Renato, eds. Control of Proliferation in Animal Cells. LC 73-88195. (Cold Spring Harbor Conferences on Cell Proliferation Ser.: No. 1). 1043p. reprint ed. pap. 200.00 (*0-7837-2007-6*, 204228100002) Bks Demand.

Clarkson, C. & Keating, H. R. F. Criminal Law: Text & Materials. 3rd ed. 1994. pap. 47.00 (*0-421-48210-9*, Pub. by Sweet & Maxwll) Gaunt.

Clarkson, C. M. & Morgan, Rod, eds. The Politics of Sentencing Reform. (Illus.). 296p. 1995. text 62.00 (*0-19-825872-0*) OUP.

Clarkson, Clay. Our 24 Family Ways Coloring Book. (Illus.). 28p. (J). (gr. 1-8). 1999. 3.95 (*1-888692-07-3*) Whole Heart.

Clarkson, Clay, ed. see Clarkson, Sally.

Clarkson, Clay, ed. see MacLead, Norman.

Clarkson, Clay, ed. see Porter, Eleanor.

Clarkson, Clay, ed. see Porter, Eleanor H.

Clarkson College of Technology Staff. Stable Colloidal Dispersions of Copper. 73p. 1972. 10.95 (*0-317-34547-8*, 174) Intl Copper.

Clarkson, D. T., jt. auth. see Cooke, D. T.

Clarkson, Donald, jt. ed. see Brock, Colin.

Clarkson, E. N. Invertebrate Palaeontology & Evolution. 2nd ed. (Illus.). 384p. 1986. text 80.00 (*0-04-560009-0*); pap. text 44.95 (*0-04-560010-4*) Routledge.

Clarkson, Edith M. All Nature Sings. LC 86-16529. 148p. (Orig.). reprint ed. pap. 45.90 (*0-7837-3194-9*, 204279800006) Bks Demand.

Clarkson, Elisabeth Hudnut. An Adirondack Archive: The Trail to Windover. LC 93-8211. 260p. 1993. 30.00 (*0-925168-17-3*) North Country.

***Clarkson, Euan N. K.** Invertebrate Palaeontology & Evolution. 4th ed. (Illus.). 1999. pap. 48.95 (*0-632-05238-4*) Blackwell Sci.

Clarkson, Ewan. Flight of the Osprey. LC 95-45791. 192p. 1996. 19.95 (*0-312-13973-X*) St Martin.

— The Flight of the Osprey. large type ed. (Large Print Ser.). 368p. 1996. 27.99 (*0-7089-3567-2*) Ulverscroft.

Clarkson, Frederick. Eternal Hostility: The Struggle Between Theocracy & Democracy. LC 96-41262. 275p. 1997. pap. 15.95 (*1-56751-088-4*) Common Courage.

— Eternal Hostility: The Struggle Between Theocracy & Democracy. LC 96-41262. 275p. 1997. lib. bdg. 29.95 (*1-56751-089-2*) Common Courage.

— Profiles in Terrorism: Twenty Years of Anti-Abortion Violence. 2000. 20.00 (*1-56751-165-1*); pap. 10.00 (*1-56751-164-3*) Common Courage.

Clarkson, G. Fairy Tales: Musical Dramas for Children. (MMB Horizon Ser.: No. 2). 48p. (J). (gr. k-6). 1986. pap. 9.00 (*0-918812-49-6*, ST 023) MMB Music.

Clarkson, George E. The Mysticism of William Law. LC 91-18018. (American University Studies: Philosophy: Ser. V, Vol. 124). 194p. (C). 1992. text 38.95 (*0-8204-1634-7*) P Lang Pubng.

Clarkson, George E., ed. Grounds for Belief in Life after Death with Paul Tillich's "Symbols of Eternal Life" (The Ingersoll Lecture, 1962) LC 87-24685. (Symposium Ser.: Vol. 24). 160p. 1987. lib. bdg. 69.95 (*0-88946-716-1*) E Mellen.

Clarkson, George F. George Whitefield & Welsh Calvinistic Methodism. LC 96-23248. (Welsh Studies: Vol. 12). (Illus.). 160p. 1996. text 69.95 (*0-7734-8758-1*) E Mellen.

Clarkson, Grosvenor B. Industrial America in the World War: The Strategy Behind the Line, 1917-1918. LC 74-75234. (United States in World War I Ser.). (Illus.). xxiii, 573p. 1974. reprint ed. lib. bdg. 60.95 (*0-89198-097-0*) Ozer.

Clarkson, Hazel. Musculoskeletal Assessment: Joint Range of Motion & Manual Muscle Strength. (Illus.). 384p. (C). 1989. pap. text 42.00 (*0-683-01711-X*) Lppncott W & W.

Clarkson, Hazel M. Musculoskeletal Assessment: Joint Range of Motion & Manual Muscle Strength. 2nd ed. LC 99-33414. 432p. 2000. pap. 48.00 (*0-683-30384-8*) Lppncott W & W.

Clarkson, J. Dunsmore. Labour & Nationalism in Ireland. LC 78-12024. (Columbia University. Studies in the Social Sciences: No. 266). reprint ed. 37.50 (*0-404-51266-6*) AMS Pr.

Clarkson, J. Shannon, jt. ed. see Russell, Letty M.

Clarkson, James. The Elastic Analysis of Flat Grillages: With Particular Reference to Ship Structures. LC 65-16200. (Cambridge Engineering Ser.). 143p. reprint ed. pap. 40.80 (*0-608-30978-8*, 2050786) Bks Demand.

Clarkson, James D. The Cultural Ecology of a Chinese Village: Cameron Highlands, Malaysia. LC 67-28490. (University of Chicago, Department of Geography, Research Paper Ser.: No. 114). (Illus.). 191p. reprint ed. pap. 59.30 (*0-608-18478-0*, 203299200082) Bks Demand.

Clarkson, Jessie D., ed. see American Historical Association Staff.

Clarkson, John. And Justice for One. 368p. 1993. mass mkt. 5.99 (*0-515-11055-8*, Jove) Berkley Pub.

— Blanche Lazzell. LC 89-61664. (Provincetown Classics in History, Literature, & Art Ser.: Vol. 2). (Illus.). 44p. 1989. reprint ed. pap. 7.00 (*0-945135-01-7*) Cape Cod Pilgrim.

***Clarkson, John.** New Lots. 2001. mass mkt. 6.99 (*0-8125-6476-6*) Tor Bks.

Clarkson, John. New Lots: A Novel. LC 98-19395. 320p. 1998. 24.95 (*0-312-85242-8*, Pub. by Forge NYC) St Martin.

— One Man's Law. 368p. (Orig.). 1994. mass mkt. 5.99 (*0-425-14249-3*) Berkley Pub.

— One Way Out. 400p. (Orig.). 1996. mass mkt. 5.99 (*0-515-11802-8*, Jove) Berkley Pub.

Clarkson, John F., ed. see St. Mary's College Jesuit Fathers, Kansas Staff.

Clarkson, Kenneth W. Catalog of Research Issues for Understanding National Economic Planning. LC 76-1551. 1976. pap. 15.00 (*0-916770-01-X*) Law & Econ U Miami.

***Clarkson, Kenneth W.** West's Business Law: Text, Cases, Legal, Ethical, Regulatory & International Environment. 8th ed. LC 00-35932. 2000. 109.95 (*0-324-01661-1*) Sth-Wstrn College.

Clarkson, Kenneth W., ed. West's Business Law. 7th ed. LC 97-25028. (C). 1997. pap. 112.95 (*0-538-87979-3*) Wadsworth Pub.

Clarkson, Kenneth W. & Meiners, Roger E. Inflated Unemployment Statistics, The Effects of Welfare Work Registration Requirements. LC 77-74738. 1977. pap. 2.50 (*0-916770-04-4*) Law & Econ U Miami.

Clarkson, Kenneth W., et al. Economics of Nonproprietary Organizations. Zerbe, Richard O., Jr., ed. (Research in Law & Economics Ser.: Vol. 1). 288p. 1980. suppl. ed. 78.50 (*0-89232-132-6*) Jai Pr.

— West's Business Law: Text, Cases, Legal & Regulatory Environment. 5th ed. Perlee, Clyde, ed. 1250p. (C). 1992. text 66.00 (*0-314-88944-2*) West Pub.

— West's Business Law 6/e. 6th ed. LC 94-22665. (SWC-Business Law). 1530p. (C). 1994. mass mkt. 63.50 (*0-314-04220-2*) West Pub.

Clarkson, L. A., et al, eds. Mapping the Great Irish Famine: An Atlas of the Famine Years. 240p. 1999. pap. 30.00 (*1-85182-357-3*, Pub. by Four Cts Pr); boxed set 60.00 (*1-85182-353-0*, Pub. by Four Cts Pr) Intl Spec Bk.

Clarkson, Lisa K., ed. see Singeltary, Theresa, et al.

Clarkson, Margaret. Destined for Glory. large type ed. (Large Print Inspirational Ser.). 1987. pap. 9.95 (*0-8027-2587-2*) Walker & Co.

— A Singing Heart. LC 87-82067. 203p. 1987. pap. 14.95 (*0-916642-31-3*, 390) Hope Pub.

Clarkson, Mark. Windows Hothouse: Creating Artificial Life with Visual C++ (Illus.). 304p. 1994. pap. 34.95 (*0-201-62669-1*) Addison-Wesley.

Clarkson, Mark. Windows Hothouse: Creative Artificial Life with Visual C Plus Plus. 1994. write for info. (*0-318-72316-6*) Addison-Wesley.

Clarkson, Mary C. Mainstreaming the Exceptional Child: A Bibliography. LC 81-84656. (Checklists in the Humanities & Education Ser.: No. 6). 250p. reprint ed. pap. 77.50 (*0-8357-6348-X*, 203562200096) Bks Demand.

Clarkson, Max B. The Corporation & Its Stakeholders: Classic & Contemporary Readings. LC 98-134568. 296p. 1998. text 55.00 (*0-8020-4300-3*); pap. text 20.00 (*0-8020-8127-4*) U of Toronto Pr.

Clarkson, Michael. Competitive Fire: Insights to Developing the Warrior Mentality of Sports Champions. LC 99-17568. (Illus.). 264p. 1999. pap. 15.95 (*0-88011-865-2*) Human Kinetics.

Clarkson, P. A. & Nijhoff, F. W., eds. Symmetries & Integrability of Difference Equations, Vol. 255. LC 99-18750. (London Mathematical Society Lecture Note Ser.). 1999. pap. text 49.95 (*0-521-59699-8*) Natural Hist Mus.

Clarkson, P. A., jt. auth. see Ablowitz, M. A.

Clarkson, P. C. Bilingualism & Mathematics Learning. 60p. (C). 1995. pap. 34.00 (*0-7300-1292-1*, ECT403, Pub. by Deakin Univ) St Mut.

Clarkson, Paul S. & Jett, R. Samuel. Luther Martin of Maryland. LC 76-94392. 348p. reprint ed. pap. 107.90 (*0-608-15144-0*, 202580900046) Bks Demand.

Clarkson, Paul S. & Warren, Clyde T. Law of Property in Shakespeare & the Elizabethan Drama. LC 68-9790. 364p. 1968. reprint ed. 75.00 (*0-87752-022-4*) Gordian.

***Clarkson, Peter.** Volcanoes. LC 00-36465. (WorldLife Library). (Illus.). 72p. (J). 2000. pap. 16.95 (*0-89658-502-6*) Voyageur Pr.

Clarkson, Peter & Stark, Henry, eds. Signal Processing Methods for Audio, Images & Telecommunications. (Signal Processing & Its Applications Ser.). (Illus.). 452p. 1995. text 53.00 (*0-12-175790-0*) Acad Pr.

Clarkson, Peter A., ed. Applications of Analytic & Geometric Methods to Nonlinear Differential Equations. LC 93-11843. (NATO Advanced Study Institutes Series C, Mathematical & Physical Sciences: No. 413). 1993. text 307.50 (*0-7923-2457-9*) Kluwer Academic.

Clarkson, Peter M. Optimal & Adaptive Signal Processing. 560p. 1993. boxed set 104.95 (*0-8493-8609-8*, TK) CRC Pr.

Clarkson, Petremeuska. Transactional Analysis Psychotherapy: An Integrated Approach. 368p. (C). 1993. pap. 27.99 (*0-415-08699-X*, B2554) Routledge.

Clarkson, Petruska. Achilles Syndrome: Overcoming the Secret Fear of Failure. LC 97-43908. 1998. pap. 13.95 (*1-86204-263-2*, Pub. by Element MA) Penguin Putnam.

— The Bystander. (Illus.). 150p. (Orig.). 1996. pap. 39.95 (*1-56593-786-4*, 1534) Singular Publishing.

— Counselling Psychology: Integration of Theory, Research, & Supervised Practice. LC 97-9536. (Illus.). 360p. (C). 1997. 85.00 (*0-415-14522-8*) Routledge.

— Counselling Psychology: Integration of Theory, Research, & Supervised Practice. LC 97-9536. (Illus.). xix, 337p. (C). 1998. pap. 29.99 (*0-415-14523-6*) Routledge.

— Ethics: Working with Ethical & Moral Dilemmas in Psychotherapy. 1999. pap. 44.95 (*1-86156-112-1*) Whurr Pub.

— Fritz Perls. (Key Figures in Counselling & Psychotherapy Ser.). (Illus.). 160p. (C). 1992. text 44.00 (*0-8039-8452-9*); pap. text 18.95 (*0-8039-8453-7*) Sage.

— Gestalt Counselling in Action. (Counselling in Action Ser.: Vol. 5). 154p. (C). 1989. text 49.95 (*0-8039-8188-0*); pap. text 21.50 (*0-8039-8189-9*) Sage.

— On Psychotherapy. LC 94-71773. 266p. 1994. pap. 45.00 (*1-56821-310-7*) Aronson.

— The Therapeutic Relationship. 400p. 1995. pap. 42.50 (*1-56593-595-0*, 1218) Singular Publishing.

Clarkson, Petruska, ed. The Sublime. 320p. 1997. 150.00 (*1-56593-879-8*, 1722) Singular Publishing.

Clarkson, Petruska & Pokorny, Michael, eds. The Handbook of Psychotherapy. LC 93-32583. 496p. (C). 1994. text 69.95 (*0-415-07722-2*) Routledge.

Clarkson, Quentin D. Handbook of Field Botany. LC 61-13273. (Illus.). 96p. 1961. pap. 3.95 (*0-8323-0350-X*) Binford Mort.

Clarkson, R. W. & Dreyer, R. J. Investigation of Techniques to Establish & Maintain Arctic Grayling & Apache Trout Lake Fisheries. rev. ed. (Arizona Game & Fish Department Technical Report: No. 12). (Illus.). 71p. 1996. pap. 5.00 (*0-917563-17-4*) AZ Game & Fish.

Clarkson, Rich. Kansas Century: 100 Years of Jayhawk Championship Basketball. LC 97-37470. 152p. 1997. 39.95 (*0-8362-5303-5*) Andrews & McMeel.

— Kansas Century: 100 Years of Jayhawk Championship Basketball. (Illus.). 144p. 1998. pap. 19.95 (*0-8362-6938-1*) Andrews & McMeel.

Clarkson, Rich, ed. World Champion Broncos: Road to the Super Bowl. LC 98-36099. (Illus.). 144p. 1998. 39.95 (*0-8362-6984-5*) Andrews & McMeel.

Clarkson, Ron. Family Matters. LC 98-154333. 224p. 1997. write for info. (*0-7459-3767-5*, Lion) Chariot Victor.

— Making Classic Chairs: A Craftsman's Chippendale Reference. (Illus.). 158p. 1997. pap. 24.95 (*1-56523-081-7*) Fox Chapel Pub.

Clarkson, Ron & Heller, Tom. Making Classic Carved Furniture: The Queen Anne Stool. LC 93-87051. (Illus.). 96p. (Orig.). 1994. pap., per. 18.95 (*0-88740-588-6*) Schiffer.

Clarkson, Ronald, jt. auth. see Heller, Thomas.

Clarkson, Rosetta E. Green Enchantment. (American Gardening Classics Ser.). (Illus.). 352p. 1991. reprint ed. text 12.95 (*0-02-009461-2*) Macmillan.

— Herbs: Their Culture & Uses. (American Gardening Classics Ser.). 256p. 1990. pap. 14.00 (*0-02-030975-9*) Macmillan.

Clarkson, Roy B., et al. Forest Wildlife Plants of the Monangahela National Forest. 1980. pap. 8.95 (*0-910286-82-5*) Boxwood.

Clarkson, S., jt. auth. see Hall, J.

Clarkson, Sally. Seasons of a Mother's Heart. Clarkson, Clay, ed. 224p. 1998. pap. 10.95 (*1-888692-03-0*) Whole Heart.

Clarkson, Sandra P. & Barone, Barbara J. Fundamentals of College Mathematics. (C). 1994. pap. text, student ed. 20.76 (*0-395-48404-9*) HM.

— Intermediate Algebra. (C). 1994. text, teacher ed. 9.96 (*0-395-69304-7*) HM.

— Introduction to Algebra. (C). 1994. pap. text, teacher ed. 9.96 (*0-395-69302-0*) HM.

Clarkson, Sandra P., jt. auth. see Altamuro, Vincent J.

Clarkson, Sarah M., jt. auth. see Burns, Deborah.

Clarkson, Sarah M., ed. see Appleton, Bonnie L.

Clarkson, Sarah M., ed. see Clegg, Peter & Watkins, Derry.

Clarkson, Sarah M., ed. see Cox, Jeff.

Clarkson, Sarah M., ed. see Hill, Lewis.

Clarkson, Sarah M., ed. see Hill, Lewis & Hill, Nancy.

Clarkson, Sarah M., ed. see Miller, Dave.

Clarkson, Sarah M., ed. see O'Keefe, John.

Clarkson, Sidney S. More Unforgettable: Enjoyable Reading for the Intellect. 104p. 1996. pap. text, per. 13.95 (*0-7872-2299-2*) Kendall-Hunt.

***Clarkson, Stephen.** The Canonical Compendium. xiv, 430p. 1999. 45.00 (*1-899562-75-3*, Calabash Pr) Ash-Tree.

Clarkson, Stephen. The Soviet Theory of Development: India & the Third World in Marxist-Leninist Scholarship. LC 78-1771. 336p. reprint ed. pap. 104.20 (*0-608-17038-0*, 202643000049) Bks Demand.

Clarkson, Stephen, jt. auth. see McCall, Christina.

Clarkson, Steve. The Sherlockian Star Chamber, 2 vols. (Illus.). 108p. 1996. 30.00 (*1-896648-71-1*) Battered Silicon.

— The Sherlockian Star Chamber, Vol. 1. (Illus.). 184p. 1996. pap. 12.00 (*1-896648-88-6*) Battered Silicon.

— The Sherlockian Star Chamber, Vol. 2. (Illus.). 292p. 1996. lib. bdg. 14.00 (*1-896648-89-4*) Battered Silicon.

Clarkson, T. W., et al, eds. Biological Monitoring of Toxic Metals. LC 87-36128. (Rochester Series on Environmental Toxicity). (Illus.). 698p. (C). 1988. text 186.00 (*0-306-42809-1*, Kluwer Plenum) Kluwer Academic.

Clarkson, Thomas. Essay on the Impolicy of the African Slave Trade, 2 Pts. LC 71-154074. (Black Heritage Library Collection). 1977. 17.95 (*0-8369-8785-3*) Ayer.

— Essay on the Slavery & Commerce of the Human Species. LC 73-93417. (Black Heritage Library Collection). 1977. 17.95 (*0-8369-8542-7*) Ayer.

— Essay on the Slavery & Commerce of the Human Species, Particularly the African. LC 72-8360. reprint ed. 37.50 (*0-404-00253-6*) AMS Pr.

— History of the Rise, Progress & Accomplishment of the Abolition of the African Slave-Trade by the British Parliament. 1968. reprint ed. 145.00 (*0-7146-1889-6*, Pub. by F Cass Pubs) Intl Spec Bk.

Clarkson, Thomas, ed. see Wilberforce, William & Wilberforce, Samuel.

Clarkson, Thomas W., et al, eds. The Cytoskeleton: A Target for Toxic Agents. LC 85-24470. (Rochester Series on Environmental Toxicity). 276p. 1986. 65.00 (*0-306-42205-0*, Plenum Trade) Perseus Pubng.

Clarkson, Wensley. Caged Heat. LC 98-164988. 1998. mass mkt. 6.50 (*0-312-96324-6*) St Martin.

***Clarkson, Wensley.** Deadlier Than the Male: Ten True Stories of Women Who Kill. 2000. mass mkt. 6.99 (*1-85782-377-X*) Blake Publng.

Clarkson, Wensley. Deadly Seduction. 1996. mass mkt. 5.99 (*0-312-95773-4*, Pub. by Tor Bks) St Martin.

— Death at Every Stop. LC 97-208520. 1997. mass mkt. 5.99 (*0-312-96636-9*) St Martin.

— Doctors of Death. 1996. mass mkt. 4.99 (*1-85782-035-5*, Pub. by Blake Publng) Seven Hills Bk.

— Doctors of Death: Ten True Crime Stories of Doctors Who Kill. LC 92-18776. 1992. 18.95 (*0-942637-66-6*) Barricade Bks.

***Clarkson, Wensley.** Doctors Who Kill: Terrifying True Stories of the World's Most Sinister Doctors. 2000. mass mkt. 6.99 (*1-85782-343-5*) Blake Publng.

Clarkson, Wensley. Eye for an Eye. 1996. mass mkt. 4.99 (*1-85782-116-5*, Pub. by Blake Publng) Seven Hills Bk.

— Hell Hath No Fury. 1996. mass mkt. 4.99 (*0-905846-93-1*, Pub. by Blake Publng) Seven Hills Bk.

— In the Name of Stan. LC 98-122048. 1998. mass mkt. 6.50 (*0-312-96389-0*) St Martin.

— John Travolta: Back in Character. LC 96-9915. (Illus.). 258p. (Orig.). 1997. pap. 15.95 (*0-87951-757-3*, Pub. by Overlook Pr) Penguin Putnam.

— Like a Woman Scorned. 1996. mass mkt. 4.99 (*1-85782-003-7*, Pub. by Blake Publng) Seven Hills Bk.

— Love You to Death, Darling. 1996. mass mkt. 4.99 (*1-85782-012-6*, Pub. by Blake Publng) Seven Hills Bk.

— Mel: The Inside Story. 1996. 24.95 (*1-85782-045-2*, Pub. by Blake Publng) Seven Hills Bk.

— Mel Gibson. 400p. 1998. pap. 13.95 (*1-56025-225-1*, Thunders Mouth) Avalon NY.

***Clarkson, Wensley.** The Mother's Day Murder. (Illus.). 232p. 2000. mass mkt. 6.50 (*0-312-97411-6*) St Martin.

— The Rail Road Killer: Tracking Down One of the Most Brutal Serial Killers in History. (Illus.). 256p. (Orig.). pap. text 6.50 (*0-312-97452-3*, St Martins Paperbacks) St Martin.

Clarkson, Wensley. Ronaldo! The True Story Behind the 90 Minutes that Shocked the World. 1998. 24.95 (*1-85782-336-2*, Pub. by Blake Publng) Seven Hills Bk.

***Clarkson, Wensley.** Slave Girls. 288p. 2000. mass mkt. 6.50 (*0-312-95870-6*) St Martin.

Clarkson, Wensley. Sting: The Secret Life of Gordon Sumner. LC 98-46736. 368p. 1999. pap. 13.95 (*1-56025-226-X*, Thunders Mouth) Avalon NY.

— Sting: The Secret Life of Gordon Sumner. 1996. 26.95 (*1-85782-125-4*, Pub. by Blake Publng) Seven Hills Bk.

— Tom Cruise: Unauthorised. 1996. 24.95 (*1-85782-086-X*, Pub. by Blake Publng) Seven Hills Bk.

— The Valkyrie Operation: The True Story of a British Agent's Battle Against the World's Deadliest Arm. (Illus.). 304p. 1998. 24.95 (*1-85782-197-1*, Pub. by Blake Publng) Seven Hills Bk.

— Whatever Mother Says. 2001. mass mkt. 6.50 (*0-312-95542-1*) St Martin.

***Clarkson, Wensley & Fielder, Mike.** Women in Chains: Murder of Rachel Nickell. 2000. mass mkt. 6.99 (*1-85782-353-2*) Blake Publng.

Clarkson, William B. & Campos, Guillermo. Buscalo! (Look It Up) A Quick Reference Guide to Spanish Grammer & Usage. 219p. 1998. pap. 14.95 (*0-471-24560-7*) Wiley.

Clarmont, et al. X-Men. (Marvel Masterworks Ser.: Vol. 11). 169p. 1989. 29.95 (*0-87135-597-3*) Marvel Entrprs.

Claro, Christopher & Klam, Julie. Comedy Central: The Essential Guide to Comedy. LC 97-143377. 272p. (Orig.). 1997. pap. 12.00 (*1-57297-108-8*) Blvd Books.

Claro, Danielle. How to Have the Wedding You Want. 261p. (Orig.). 1995. pap. 12.95 (*0-425-14578-6*) Berkley Pub.

Claro, Joe. Random House's Book Jokes & Anecdotes. 2nd ed. 272p. 1996. pap. 8.95 (*0-679-76971-4*) Random.

C

An Asterisk (*) at the beginning of an entry indicates that the title is appearing for the first time.

C

— Thukydides, Bd. 8. viii, 302p. 1982. 80.00 (*3-296-15808-1*) G Olms Pubs.
— Thukydides, Vol. 3. (GER.). iv, 285p. 1977. 95.00 (*3-296-15803-0*, Pub. by Weidmann) Lubrecht & Cramer.
— Thukydides, Vol. 5. (GER.). vii, 290p. 1999. 95.00 (*3-296-15805-7*, Pub. by Weidmann) Lubrecht & Cramer.
— Thukydides, Vol. 6. (GER.). iv, 299p. 1999. 95.00 (*3-296-15806-5*, Pub. by Weidmann) Lubrecht & Cramer.
— Thukydides, Vol. 7. (GER.). iv, 286p. 1999. 95.00 (*3-296-15807-3*, Pub. by Weidmann) Lubrecht & Cramer.
— Thukydides Bk. 1: Einleitung. (GER.). iv, 474p. 1977. 125.00 (*3-296-15801-4*, Pub. by Weidmann) Lubrecht & Cramer.

Classen, M., jt. auth. see Roesch, T.

Classen, Susan. Dewdrops on Spiderwebs: Connections Made Visible. LC 96-52277. 176p. (Orig.). (YA). 1997. pap. 10.99 (*0-8361-9066-1*) Herald Pr.
— Vultures & Butterflies: Living the Contradictions. LC 92-16148. 184p. (Orig.). 1992. pap. 9.99 (*0-8361-3607-1*) Herald Pr.

Classens, Geert H. M., jt. ed. see Johnson, David F.

Classey, Pat. The Horseman's Art of Healing: A Journal of Horseman's Remedies. Pence, Sharon, ed. (Illus.). 56p. 1983. write for info. (*0-318-64419-3*) L & P Prods.

Classic, A. T. A. T. & Friends. 1987. text 12.95 (*0-9616665-0-1*) Monarch Trails Pubns.

Classic, Carl. Secret to Hunza Superior Health. Richiusa, Gordon F., ed. 203p. (Orig.). 1991. reprint ed. pap. 7.95 (*0-9628298-7-0*) Ctr Human Natural Ntrtn.

Classic Chevy International Staff. The Tech Book. 1994. 59.95 (*0-9641464-0-1*) Classic Chevy.

Classic Companion Staff. Classic Companion Bible. 1998. 36.99 (*0-529-11063-6*); 36.99 (*0-529-11061-X*); 29.99 (*0-529-11060-1*) World Publng.
— Classic Companion Bible. 1999. 29.99 (*0-529-11062-8*) World Publng.

***Classic, Lesley.** Directory of Canadian Schools, 1999, 2 vols. Kasher, Robert, ed. 1335p. 1999. text 109.95 (*1-896537-44-8*) DAD3.
— Directory of Canadian Schools, 1999 Edition Vol. 2: Western Canadian Schools & Index. Kasher, Robert, ed. 614p. 1999. pap. 59.95 (*1-896537-40-5*) DAD3.

Classic Ref Staff. Classic Reference Holy Bible. LC 98-61548. 1999. 24.99 (*0-310-93127-4*); 39.99 (*0-310-93128-2*); 49.99 (*0-310-93129-0*); 39.99 (*0-310-93130-4*) Zondervan.

Classroom Connect Staff. Family Internet Companion. 1996. 34.95 incl. cd-rom (*0-614-20313-9*) P-H.

Claster, Barbara L., jt. auth. see Dilling, Carole.

Claster, Daniel S. Bad Guys & Good Guys: Moral Polarization & Crime, 36. LC 92-4053. (Contributions in Criminology & Penology Ser.: No. 36). 320p. 1992. 52.95 (*0-313-28489-X*, CBY/, Greenwood Pr) Greenwood.

Claster, Jill N. The Medieval Experience, 300-1400. (Illus.). 352p. (C). 1982. pap. text 22.50 (*0-8147-1381-5*) NYU Pr.

Clastres, Helene. The Land-Without-Evil: Tupi-Guarani Prophetism. Brovender, Jacqueline G., tr. LC 94-32437. 144p. 1995. text 39.95 (*0-252-02055-3*) U of Ill Pr.

Clastres, Helene & Hill, Jonathan D. The Land Without Evil: Tupi-Guarani Prophetism. Grenez Brovender, Jacqueline, tr. LC 94-32437. 144p. 1995. pap. text 13.95 (*0-252-06351-1*) U of Ill Pr.

Clastres, Pierre. The Archeology of Violence. 200p. Date not set. 12.00 (*0-936756-95-0*) Autonomedia.
— Chronicle of the Guayaki Indians. Auster, Paul, tr. LC 97-20623. (Illus.). 352p. 1998. 25.50 (*0-942299-77-9*) Zone Bks.

***Clastres, Pierre.** Chronicle of the Guayaki Indians. Auster, Paul, tr. & frwd. by. (Illus.). 352p. 2000. reprint ed. pap. 15.00 (*0-942299-78-7*, Pub. by Zone Bks) MIT Pr.

Clastres, Pierre. Society Against the State: Essays in Political Anthropology. Hurley, Robert & Stein, Abe, trs. from FRE. LC 87-50396. 218p. 1987. 24.95 (*0-942299-00-0*); pap. 12.95 (*0-942299-01-9*) Zone Bks.
— Society vs. the State. 1991. lib. bdg. 78.95 (*0-8490-4701-3*) Gordon Pr.

Clatanoff, Robert M. Valuation & Property Taxation of Nonrenewable Resources: An Annotated Bibliography. (CPL Bibliographies Ser.: No. 99). 53p. 1983. 10.00 (*0-86602-099-3*, Sage Prdcls Pr) Sage.

Clatanoff, Robert M., ed. Ad Valorem Assessment of Telecommunications Property: A Bibliography, Directory & Resource Guide. (CPL Bibliographies Ser.: No. 83). 32p. 1982. 10.00 (*0-86602-083-7*, Sage Prdcls Pr) Sage.

Claton, Rose, ed. see Kirby, Edward.

Clatterbaugh, Kenneth. Contemporary Perspectives on Masculinity: Men, Women & Politics in Modern Society. 2nd ed. 4p. (C). 1996. text 79.00 (*0-8133-2700-8*, Pub. by Westview); pap. text 26.00 (*0-8133-2701-6*, Pub. by Westview) HarpC.

Clatterbaugh, Kenneth C. The Causation Debate in Modern Philosophy, 1637-1739. LC 98-17267. 256p. (C). 1998. 75.00 (*0-415-91476-0*); pap. 21.99 (*0-415-91477-9*) Routledge.

Clatworthy, Jonathan. Good God: Green Theology & the Value of Creation. LC 98-175568. 240p. 1998. pap. 27.50 (*1-897766-37-8*, Pub. by Jon Carpenter) Paul & Co Pubs.

Clatyon & King. Biology of Marine Plants. 1990. pap. text. write for info. (*0-582-71243-2*, Pub. by Addison-Wesley) Longman.

***Clauberg, Johannes.** Johannes Clauberg (1622-1665) & Cartesian Philosophy in the Seventeenth Century (1622-1665) Verbeek, Theo, ed. (International Archives of the History of Ideas Ser.). 224p. 1999. text 103.00 (*0-7923-5831-7*) Kluwer Academic.

Claud, Fay P. Touching the Soul. 51p. (Orig.). 1995. pap. 6.95 (*1-56411-120-2*) Untd Bros & Sis.

Claude, Cristian. Information & Randomness: An Algorithmic Perspective. (Monographs on Theoretical Computer Science). 1994. write for info. (*3-540-57456-5*) Spr-Verlag.

Claude, Cristoph. Wrapped Trees: Foundation Beyeler & Berower Park, Riehen, Basel, Switzerland, 1997-98. LC 99-195001. 1999. 19.99 (*3-8228-7176-1*) Taschen Amer.

Claude, I. L. American Approaches to World Affairs: The Credibility of Institutions, Policies & Leadership, Vol. 4. Thompson, Kenneth W., ed. 80p. (Orig.). (C). 1986. pap. text 11.50 (*0-8191-5304-4*, Pub. by White Miller Center); lib. bdg. 32.00 (*0-8191-5303-6*, Pub. by White Miller Center) U Pr of Amer.

Claude, Inis L. National Minorities: An International Problem. LC 78-90486. 248p. 1969. reprint ed. lib. bdg. 49.75 (*0-8371-2283-X*, CLMN, Greenwood Pr) Greenwood.

Claude, Inis L., Jr. Swords into Plowshares: The Problems & Progress of International Organization. 4th ed. (C). 1984. pap. text 39.74 (*0-07-554636-1*) McGraw.

Claude, Juillet. Classic Patisserie: An A-Z Handbook. LC 98-184381. 236p. 1998. 29.95 (*0-7506-3815-X*) Buttrwrth-Heinemann.

Claude-Pierre, Peggy. The Secret Language of Eating Disorders: The Revolutionary Approach to Understanding & Curing Anorexia & Bulimia. (Illus.). 288p. 1999. pap. 14.00 (*0-375-75018-5*) Vin Bks.

Claude, Richard. The Supreme Court & the Electoral Process. LC 70-94885. 314p. reprint ed. pap. 97.40 (*0-608-30525-1*, 201568700095) Bks Demand.

Claude, Richard P., ed. Comparative Human Rights. LC 83-3261. 99p. reprint ed. pap. 30.70 (*0-608-08663-0*, 206918600003) Bks Demand.

Claude, Richard P. & Weston, Burns H., eds. Human Rights in the World Community: Issues & Action. 2nd ed. LC 92-15656. (Illus.). 480p. (Orig.). (C). 1992. 56.95 (*0-8122-3154-6*); pap. 24.95 (*0-8122-1396-3*) U of Pa Pr.

Claude, Richard P., jt. auth. see Andreopoulos, George J.

Claude, Richard P., jt. ed. see Andreopouos, George J.

Claude, Richard P., jt. ed. see Jabine, Thomas B.

Claudel. L' Annonce Faite a Marie. (FRE.). (C). pap. write for info. (*0-8442-1800-6*, VF1800-6) NTC Contemp Pub Co.

Claudel, Calvin A. Louisiana Creole Poems. LC 82-80025. (Illus.). 50p. (Orig.). 1982. pap. 3.50 (*0-942544-00-5*) Negative Capability Pr.

Claudel, Paul. L' Annonce Faite a Marie. (FRE.). 1972. pap. 10.95 (*0-8288-3628-0*, F93892); pap. 10.95 (*0-7859-1687-3*, 2070360261) Fr & Eur.
— L' Annonce Faite a Marie: Theatre. (Folio Ser.: No. 26). (FRE.). 1959. pap. 8.95 (*2-07-036026-1*) Schoenhof.
— Art Poetique: Connaissance du Temps, Traite de la Connaissance du Monde et de Soi-Meme, Developpement de l'Eglise. (FRE.). 1984. pap. 10.95 (*0-8288-3824-0*, F137440) Fr & Eur.
— Les Aventures de Sophie. (FRE.). 224p. 1937. pap. 10.95 (*0-7859-1113-8*, 2070215008) Fr & Eur.
— Bibliographie de la Litterature Francaise du 18eme Siecle, Vol. 1: A-D. (FRE.). 285p. 1986. pap. 29.95 (*0-7859-4715-9*) Fr & Eur.
— Breviaire Poetique. (FRE.). pap. 10.95 (*0-8288-9108-7*, F93930) Fr & Eur.
— Cent Phrases pour Eventails. (FRE.). 1942. pap. 10.95 (*0-7859-1139-1*, 2070269094) Fr & Eur.
— Les Choephores et les Eumerides d'Eschyle. 1952. pap. 8.95 (*0-686-50142-X*) Fr & Eur.
— Cinq Grandes Odes, Processional Pour Saluer le Siecle Nouveau, la Cantate a Trois Voix. (FRE.). 1966. pap. 10.95 (*0-8288-3850-X*, F93970) Fr & Eur.
— Cinq Grandes Odes' Processional pour Saluer le siecle Nouveau; la Cantate; etc. (Poesie Ser.). (FRE.). pap. 9.95 (*2-07-030074-9*) Schoenhof.
— Claudel on the Theatre. Petit, Jacques & Kempf, Jean-Pierre, eds. Trollope, Christine, tr. LC 76-121683. (Illus.). 1972. 19.95 (*0-87024-158-3*) U of Miami Pr.
— Connaissance de l'est. (Poesie Ser.). (FRE.). pap. 9.95 (*2-07-032133-9*) Schoenhof.
— Connaissance de l'Est, l'Oiseau Noir. (FRE.). 1974. pap. 10.95 (*0-8288-3851-8*, F93980) Fr & Eur.
— Contacts et Circumstances. (FRE.). 268p. 1940. pap. 10.95 (*0-7859-1116-2*, 2070215067) Fr & Eur.
— Conversations dans le Coir-et-Cher. (FRE.). 182p. 1984. pap. 10.95 (*0-7859-1157-X*, 2070701913) Fr & Eur.
— Correspondance avec Andre Gide: 1899-1926. (FRE.). 400p. 1949. pap. 10.95 (*0-7859-1128-6*, 2070215326) Fr & Eur.
— Correspondance avec Andre Suares: 1904-1938. (FRE.). 272p. 1951. pap. 10.95 (*0-7859-1129-4*, 2070215334) Fr & Eur.
— Correspondance avec Francis Jammes et Gabriel Frizeau: 1897-1938. (FRE.). 468p. 1952. pap. 10.95 (*0-7859-1130-8*, 2070215342) Fr & Eur.
— L' Echange. pap. 8.95 (*0-686-50144-6*) Fr & Eur.
— L' Echange. (FRE.). 1977. pap. 10.95 (*0-8288-3629-9*, F94090); pap. 10.95 (*0-7859-1843-4*, 2070369110) Fr & Eur.
— L' Epee et le Miroir. (FRE.). 278p. 1939. pap. 10.95 (*0-7859-1115-4*, 2070215024) Fr & Eur.
— L' Evangile d'Isale. (FRE.). 336p. 1951. pap. 10.95 (*0-7859-1124-3*, 2070215202) Fr & Eur.
— Feuilles de Saints. (FRE.). 208p. 1925. 10.95 (*0-7859-1107-3*, 2070214842) Fr & Eur.
— Figures et Paraboles. (FRE.). 264p. 1936. 10.95 (*0-7859-1111-1*, 2070214982) Fr & Eur.
— L' Histoire de Tobie et de Sara. (FRE.). 128p. 1942. 10.95 (*0-7859-1117-0*, 2070215075) Fr & Eur.
— Introduction au Livre de Ruth. (FRE.). 1953. 10.95 (*0-7859-1140-5*, 2070269108) Fr & Eur.
— Je Crois en Dieu. (FRE.). 432p. 1961. 10.95 (*0-7859-1131-6*, 2070215385) Fr & Eur.
— Jeanne d'Arc au Bucher. 94p. 1939. 8.95 (*0-686-54395-5*) Fr & Eur.
— La Jeune Fille Violaine. (FRE.). 170p. 1926. 8.95 (*0-8288-9109-5*, F94200) Fr & Eur.
— Journal, 2 tomes, Set. Vrillon & Petit, eds. (Bibliotheque de la Pleiade Ser.). 150.00 (*0-685-37275-8*) Fr & Eur.
— Journal, 1904-1932. (FRE.). 1968. 95.00 (*0-8288-3462-8*, M5085) Fr & Eur.
— Journal, 1933-1955. (FRE.). 1969. 95.00 (*0-8288-3463-6*, M5086) Fr & Eur.
— La Legende de Prakhriti: Ossements. Le Bestiaire Spirituel. 216p. 1972. 25.00 (*0-686-54398-X*) Fr & Eur.
— Le Livre de Christophe Colomb. (FRE.). 252p. 1932. 10.95 (*0-7859-1109-X*, 2070214931) Fr & Eur.
— Memoires Improvises. (FRE.). 384p. 1969. 10.95 (*0-7859-1149-9*, 2070351904) Fr & Eur.
— La Messe la-Bas. (FRE.). 132p. 1919. 10.95 (*0-7859-1105-7*, 2070214796) Fr & Eur.
— Le Monde de Vezelay. (Illus.). 200p. 27.50 (*0-686-54403-X*) Fr & Eur.

Claudel, Paul. L' Oeil Ecoute. (FRE., Illus.). 248p. 1990. pap. 13.95 (*0-7859-1148-0*, 2070325873) Fr & Eur.
— L' Oeil Ecoute. (Folio Essais Ser.: No. 127). (FRE.). 1990. pap. 14.95 (*2-07-032587-3*) Schoenhof.

Claudel, Paul. Oeuvre Poetique. deluxe ed. Petit, Jacques, ed. (FRE.). 1328p. 1957. 105.00 (*0-7859-3751-X*, 2070101436) Fr & Eur.

Claudel, Paul. Oeuvres Completes, Theatre. (FRE.). 160p. 1958. 10.95 (*0-7859-1212-6*, 207021530X) Fr & Eur.
— Oeuvres en Prose. deluxe ed. Petit, Jacques & Galperine, Charles, eds. (Pleiade Ser.). (FRE.). 1680p. 1965. write for info. (*0-7859-4540-7*) Fr & Eur.
— Oeuvres Poetiques. deluxe ed. Fumet, ed. (Pleiade Ser.). 1957. 69.95 (*2-07-010143-6*) Schoenhof.

Claudel, Paul. L' Oiseau Noir dans le Soleil Levant. 248p. 1929. 8.95 (*0-686-54405-6*) Fr & Eur.
— L' Orestie. (FRE.). 256p. 1961. 8.95 (*0-7859-1132-4*, 2070215393) Fr & Eur.
— L' Otage: Le Pain Dur - Le Pere Humilie. (FRE.). pap. 13.95 (*0-8288-3630-2*, F94322) Fr & Eur.
— L' Otage: Le Pain Dur - Le Pere Humilie. (Folio Ser.: No. 170). (FRE.). pap. 10.95 (*2-07-036170-5*) Schoenhof.
— Pages de Prose. (FRE.). 428p. 1944. 14.95 (*0-7859-1119-7*, 2070215091) Fr & Eur.
— Partage de Midi. (FRE.). 1972. pap. 10.95 (*0-8288-3631-0*, F94341) Fr & Eur.
— Partage de Midi. (Folio Ser.: No. 245). (FRE.). 160p. 1972. pap. 6.95 (*2-07-036245-0*) Schoenhof.
— Paul Claudel Interroge le Cantique des Cantiques. (FRE.). 540p. 1954. 16.95 (*0-8288-9111-7*, F94360) Fr & Eur.
— Le Pere Humile. (FRE.). 194p. 1920. 8.95 (*0-686-54414-5*); pap. 10.95 (*0-7859-1106-5*, 2070214826) Fr & Eur.
— La Perle Noire. (FRE.). 250p. 1947. 8.95 (*0-8288-9110-9*, F94390) Fr & Eur.
— Poemes et Paroles Durant la Guerre de Trente Ans. (FRE.). 216p. 1945. 10.95 (*0-7859-1120-0*, 2070215105) Fr & Eur.
— Poesies. (FRE.). 1970. pap. 10.95 (*0-8288-3852-6*, F105180) Fr & Eur.
— Poesies. (Poesie Ser.). (FRE.). pap. 7.95 (*2-07-030375-6*) Schoenhof.
— Le Poete et le Shamisen: Avec: Le Poete et le Vase d'Encens, Jules ou l'Homme-aux-deux-cravates. 368p. 1970. 30.00 (*0-686-54419-6*) Fr & Eur.
— Un Poete Regarde la Croix. (FRE.). 290p. 1938. 10.95 (*0-7859-1114-6*, 2070215016) Fr & Eur.
— Positions et Propositions, 2 vols., 1. (FRE.). 266p. 1934. pap. 12.95 (*0-685-73322-X*) Fr & Eur.
— Positions et Propositions, 2 vols., 2. (FRE.). 266p. 1934. pap. 13.95 (*0-7859-1110-3*, 2070214958) Fr & Eur.
— Prose. Petit & Galperine, Charles, eds. (Bibliotheque de la Pleiade Ser.). 1965. 80.95 (*0-685-11455-4*) Fr & Eur.
— Protee. (FRE.). 1972. 8.95 (*0-8288-9113-3*, F94450) Fr & Eur.
— Reflexions sur la Poesie. (FRE.). 192p. 1963. 6.95 (*0-8288-9115-X*, F94480) Fr & Eur.
— Le Repos du Septieme Jour. 1973. 14.95 (*0-686-54429-3*) Fr & Eur.
— Richard Wagner: Reverie d'un Poete Francais. 180p. 22.50 (*0-686-54430-7*) Fr & Eur.
— La Rose et le Rosaire. (FRE.). 272p. 1947. 10.95 (*0-7859-1122-7*, 2070215121) Fr & Eur.
— Sainte Agnes et Poemes Inedits. (Illus.). 60.00 (*0-686-54433-1*) Fr & Eur.
— Seigneur Apprenez-Nous a Prier. (FRE.). 128p. 1943. 10.95 (*0-7859-1118-9*, 2070215083) Fr & Eur.
— Les Sept Psaumes de la Penitence. (FRE.). 1945. 10.95 (*0-7859-1070-0*, 2020041235) Fr & Eur.
— Soulier de Satin. (FRE.). 1963. pap. 10.95 (*0-8288-9116-8*, F94551) Fr & Eur.
— Soulier de Satin. (Folio Ser.: No. 774). (FRE.). 1963. pap. 11.95 (*2-07-036774-6*) Schoenhof.
— Le Soulier de Satin Ou le Pire. (FRE.). 1972. pap. 13.95 (*0-8288-3632-9*, FC1197) Fr & Eur.
— Sous le Signe du Dragon. (FRE.). 232p. 1958. 10.95 (*0-7859-1127-8*, 2070215318) Fr & Eur.
— Le Symbolisme de la Salette. (FRE.). 64p. 1952. 10.95 (*0-7859-1125-1*, 2070215237) Fr & Eur.
— Tete d'Or. (FRE.). 1987. pap. 10.95 (*0-8288-3633-7*, M3266) Fr & Eur.
— Tete d'Or. (Folio Ser.: No. 308). (FRE.). 326p. 1959. pap. 8.95 (*2-07-036308-2*) Schoenhof.
— Theatre, 2 vols., 2. Madaule, ed. (Bibliotheque de la Pleiade Ser.). (FRE.). 1966. 110.00 (*0-685-73336-X*, F93762) Fr & Eur.
— Theatre, Vol. 1. (FRE.). 1966. 99.50 (*0-8288-3460-1*, F93761) Fr & Eur.
— Theatre, Vol. 2. (FRE.). 1966. 110.00 (*0-8288-3461-X*, F93762) Fr & Eur.
— Toi, Qui Es-Tu? (FRE.). 126p. 1936. 10.95 (*0-7859-1112-X*, 2070214990) Fr & Eur.
— Trois Figures Saintes. (FRE.). 148p. 1953. 10.95 (*0-7859-1126-X*, 2070215245) Fr & Eur.
— La Ville. (FRE.). 1982. pap. 10.95 (*0-8288-3634-5*, F137830) Fr & Eur.
— La Ville. (Folio Ser.: No. 1345). (FRE.). 1967. 6.95 (*2-07-037345-2*) Schoenhof.
— Visages Radieux. (FRE.). 144p. 1959. 10.95 (*0-7859-1121-9*, 2070215113) Fr & Eur.
— Une Voix sur Israel. (FRE.). 96p. 1950. 10.95 (*0-7859-1123-5*, 2070215199) Fr & Eur.
— Ways & Crossways. O'Conner, Fr. J., tr. LC 67-28732. (Essay Index Reprint Ser.). 1977. 23.95 (*0-8369-0313-7*) Ayer.

Claudel, Paul & Petit, Jacques. La Jeune Fille Violaine: Premiere et Seconde Versions, Pieces en 4 Actes. (FRE.). 170p. 1926. pap. 10.95 (*0-7859-1108-1*, 2070214869) Fr & Eur.

Clauder, Amelia C. American Commerce As Affected by the Wars of the French Revolution & Napoleon. LC 68-55509. (Reprints of Economic Classics Ser.). 264p. 1972. reprint ed. 39.50 (*0-678-00905-8*) Kelley.

Claudet, Rita R., ed. see Brumback, Roger A.

Claudet, Rita R., ed. see Hirsch, Jeffrey G.

***Claudi, Renata.** Nonindigenous Freshwater Organisms: Biology & Impact. (Illus.). 500p. 1999. text 89.95 (*0-8493-4104-3*) CRC Pr.

Claudi, Renata & Leach, Joseph H., eds. Nonindigenous Freshwater Organisms: Vectors, Biology & Impacts. LC 99-28607. 480p. 1999. boxed set 89.95 (*1-56670-449-9*) Lewis Pubs.

Claudi, Renata & Mackie, Gerald L. Practical Manual for Zebra Mussel Monitoring & Control. LC 93-5031. 240p. 1993. lib. bdg. 85.00 (*0-87371-985-9*, L985) Lewis Pubs.

Claudian. Panegyricus de Sexto Consulatu Honorii Augustii. Dewar, Michael, ed. & tr. by. LC 96-1460. (ENG & LAT.). 490p. 1997. text 105.00 (*0-19-814964-6*, Clarendon Pr) OUP.
— Poems, 2 vols. No. 135, 136. 19.95 (*0-318-53141-0*) HUP.

Claudianus. Claudianus - Concordantia in Claudinaum. Christiansen, Peder G. et al, eds. (Alpha-Omega, Reihe A Ser.: Vol. XLVII). (GER.). 438p. 1988. 110.00 incl. 3.5 hd (*3-487-07848-1*) G Olms Pubs.

Claudianus, Claudius. Claudii Claudiani Quae Exstant, 2 vols. (GER.). xlviii, 944p. 1969. reprint ed. 280.00 (*0-318-70577-X*) G Olms Pubs.

Claudin, Fernando. Communist Movement 1. 1975. text 20.00 (*0-85345-364-0*) Monthly Rev.

Claudin, Victor. General Dictionary of Communication: Diccionario General de la Comunicacion. (SPA.). 1986. 35.00 (*0-8288-1318-3*, F90200) Fr & Eur.

Claudio de la Torre, Josefina. Diccionario de la Jerga del Estudiante Universitario Puertorriqueno del Sistema Publico. LC 87-25559. 1989. 12.95 (*0-8477-2010-1*) U of PR Pr.

Claudio, Virginia S. Filipino-American Food Practices, Customs, & Holidays. LC 94-35146. (Ethnic & Regional Food Practices Ser.). 1994. pap. 9.00 (*0-88091-139-5*) Am Dietetic Assn.

Claudon, Francis, ed. Dictionnaire de l'Opera-Comique Francais. (FRE.). 536p. 1995. 71.95 (*3-906753-42-5*, Pub. by P Lang) P Lang Pubng.

Claudon, Michael, ed. World Debt Crisis: International Lending on Trial. LC 85-15781. 328p. 1985. pap. 34.95 (*0-88730-052-9*, HarpBusn) HarpInfo.

Claudon, Michael P. & Cornwall, Richard R. Incomes Policy for the United States: New Approaches. 240p. 1980. lib. bdg. 71.50 (*0-89838-048-0*) Kluwer Academic.

Claudy, Carl H. Foreign Countries: An Aid in Looking to the East (1925) 156p. 1998. reprint ed. pap. 16.95 (*0-7661-0726-4*) Kessinger Pub.
— The Old Past Master (1924) 112p. 1998. reprint ed. pap. 16.95 (*0-7661-0203-3*) Kessinger Pub.

Claudy, Carl H., ed. Foreign Countries: A Gateway to the Interpretation & Development of Certain Symbols of Freemasonry. 148p. 1988. reprint ed. text 10.50 (*0-88053-039-1*, M-88) Macoy Pub.

Claudy, Nicholas, ed. Environmental Geosciences Directory. 128p. 1996. pap. 24.50 (*0-922152-37-3*) Am Geol.

Claudy, Nicholas H., ed. Directory of Geoscience Departments. 36th ed. 600p. (Orig.). 1997. pap. 34.50 (*0-922152-42-X*) Am Geol.
— Geoscience Employment & Hiring Survey - 1990. (Illus.). 1990. pap. 20.00 (*0-922152-08-X*) Am Geol.
— Guide to Geoscience Departments in the United States & Canada. 5th ed. 560p. (Orig.). 1997. pap. 24.50 (*0-922152-43-8*) Am Geol.
— International Directory of Geoscience Organizations. 2nd ed. 176p. (Orig.). 1996. pap. 21.50 (*0-922152-40-3*) Am Geol.
— National Directory of Geoscience Data Repositories. 91p. 1998. pap. 12.50 (*0-922152-41-1*) Am Geol.
— North American Survey of Geoscientists. 132p. 1988. pap. 20.00 (*0-913312-95-9*) Am Geol.

Clauer, Allan H., ed. see Minerals, Metals & Materials Society Staff.

Clauer, N., jt. ed. see Paquet, H.

An Asterisk (*) at the beginning of an entry indicates that the title is appearing for the first time.

Clauer, Norbert & Chaudhuri, Sambhu. Clays in Crustal Environments: Isotope Dating & Tracing. LC 94-35344. 1995. 119.95 (*3-540-58151-0*) Spr-Verlag.

Clauer, Norbert & Chaudhuri, Sambhu, eds. Isotopic Signatures & Sedimentary Records. LC 92-25372. (Lecture Notes in Earth Sciences Ser.: Vol. 43). 1992. 131.95 (*0-387-55828-4*); pap. 119.00 (*3-540-55828-4*) Spr-Verlag.

Claugher, D., ed. Scanning Electron Microscopy in Taxonomy & Functional Morphology. (Systematics Association Special Volume Ser.: Vol. 41). (Illus.). 328p. 1990. text 115.00 (*0-19-857714-1*) OUP.

Claughton. Sailing Yacht Design: Practice. 352p. (C). 1999. pap. 104.67 (*0-582-36857-X*) Addison-Wesley.

— Sailing Yacht Design: Theory. 32p. (C). 1999. pap. 104.67 (*0-582-36856-1*) Addison-Wesley.

Claunch, Jerry W. & Stang, Philip D. Set-Up Reduction: Saving Dollars with Common Sense. LC 89-27627. (Illus.). 309p. 1990. text 29.95 (*0-945456-04-2*) PT Pubns.

Claunch, Lillian. Conrad & Me: Childhood Tales of Adventure During the Great Depression. LC 92-61930. (Illus.). 118p. (Orig.). 1992. pap. 9.95 (*1-880222-10-8*) Red Apple Pub.

Clauretie, Terrance M., jt. auth. see Wofford, Larry E.

Clauretie, Terrence M. Real Estate Finance: Theory & Practice. 3rd ed. LC 98-19265. 584p. 1998. pap. text 85.00 (*0-13-974916-0*) P-H.

Claus. Microbes. (C). 1989. pap. text 5.60 (*0-7167-2051-5*) W H Freeman.

Claus, Audrey, jt. auth. see Kottmeyer, William A.

Claus, Hugo. Desire. Knecht, Stacey, tr. LC 97-22190. 211p. 1997. 24.95 (*0-670-86746-2*) Viking Penguin.

***Claus, Hugo.** Desire. 224p. 1998. pap. 12.95 (*0-14-025538-9*) Viking Penguin.

Claus, Hugo. The Swordfish. Levitt, Ruth, tr. from FLE. LC 97-120905. (Unesco Collection of Representative Works, Series of Translations from the Literature of the Union of Soviet Socialist Republics). 168p. 1997. 27.95 (*0-7206-0985-2*, Pub. by P Owen Ltd) Dufour.

Claus, James R. & Claus, Karen. The Sign User's Guide: A Marketing Aid. rev. ed. Dorsey, William, ed. LC 88-201992. (Illus.). 165p. 1988. 15.00 (*0-911380-83-3*, 92) ST Pubns.

Claus, Jeff & Ogden, Curtis, eds. Service Learning for Youth Empowerment & Social Change. LC 98-37904. (Adolescent Cultures, School, & Society Ser.: Vol. 5). XII, 198p. (C). 1999. pap. text 29.95 (*0-8204-3858-8*) P Lang Pubng.

Claus, K., tr. see Justi, E. W.

Claus, Karen, jt. auth. see Claus, James R.

Claus, Konig, et al. Owls: A Guide to the Owls of the World. LC 99-60571. (Illus.). 320p. 1999. 50.00 (*0-300-07920-6*) Yale U Pr.

Claus, Lynda. Simply State It Vol. 1: Verses for You to Share. LC 92-91189. 64p. (Orig.). 1993. pap. 8.95 (*0-9635598-1-8*) Simply Stated.

Claus, Richard O., ed. Fiber Optics Sensor-Based Smart Materials & Structures: Proceedings of the Fifth Annual Smart Materials & Structures Workshop, Held in Blacksburg, Virginia, April 1992. (Smart Materials & Structures Ser.). (Illus.). 208p. 1992. 124.00 (*0-7503-0248-8*) IOP Pub.

— Smart Structures & Materials, 1997 Vol. 3042: Smart Sensing, Processing & Instrumentation. LC 98-114061. 442p. 1997. 99.00 (*0-8194-2455-2*) SPIE.

Claus, Richard O. & Spillman, William B., eds. Smart Structures & Materials, 1998: Sensory Phenomena & Measurement Instrumentation for Smart Structures & Materials. LC 98-227299. (Proceedings of SPIE Ser.: Vol. 3328). 462p. 1998. 99.00 (*0-8194-2774-8*) SPIE.

***Claus, Santa & Green, Martin I.** Santa Claus: My Life & Times: An Illustrated Autobiography. LC 98-19245. (Illus.). 128p. 1998. pap. 25.00 (*0-380-97559-9*, Avon Bks) Morrow Avon.

Claus, V., ed. Graph-Grammars & Their Application to Computer Science & Biology: Proceedings, International Workshop, Bad Honnef, October 30-November 3, 1978. (Lecture Notes in Computer Science Ser.: Vol. 73). 1979. 37.00 (*0-387-09525-X*) Spr-Verlag.

Claus, W., jt. ed. see Vogl, T. J.

Claus-Walker, Jacqueline, jt. auth. see Halstead, Lauro S.

Claus, William G. Understanding Microbes: Laboratory Textbook for Microbiology. LC 87-33152. 547p. (C). 1988. pap. text 41.95 (*0-7167-1809-X*) W H Freeman.

Clausager, A. D. Original MGA: Restorer's Guide to 1500, 1600, MKII, Twin Cam & Roadsters & Coups. (Bayview Ser.). (Illus.). 120p. 1993. 34.95 (*1-870979-31-1*) MBI Pubg.

Clausager, Anders. Essential Mini Cooper: The Cars & Their Story 1961-71 & 1990 to Date. (Essential Ser.). (Illus.). 80p. 1997. pap. 15.95 (*1-870979-86-9*, Bay View Bks) MBI Pubg.

— MG Saloon Cars - From the 1920s to the 1970s. (Illus.). 192p. 1998. 39.95 (*1-901432-06-8*, Bay View Bks) MBI Pubg.

Clausager, Anders D. Original MGT Series: Restorer's Guide to MG, TA, TB, TC, TD & TF. (Illus.). 96p. 1989. text 34.95 (*1-870979-06-0*, Bay View Bks) MBI Pubg.

Clausen, A. Country Guitar Method. 48p. 1991. pap. 6.95 (*0-7935-0883-5*, 00660129) H Leonard.

Clausen, A. Country Guitar Method. 48p. 1991. pap. 14.95 (*0-7935-0882-7*, 00660128) H Leonard.

Clausen, A. Rock Scales for Guitar: Tablature. 16p. 1986. pap. 6.95 (*0-7935-3782-7*, 00699164) H Leonard.

Clausen, Andrew. The Best Christmas Pageant Ever. 54p. (J). (gr. 4-6). 1993. student ed., ring bd. 12.99 (*1-58609-130-1*) Progeny Pr WI.

— Charlotte's Web. 58p. (J). (gr. 4-6). 2000. student ed., ring bd. 12.99 (*1-58609-169-7*) Progeny Pr WI.

— The Cricket in Times Square Study Guide. 58p. (J). (gr. 4-6). 1998. student ed., ring bd. 12.99 (*1-58609-134-4*) Progeny Pr WI.

— A Day No Pigs Would Die Study Guide. 44p. (YA). (gr. 9-12). 1994. student ed., ring bd. 14.99 (*1-58609-161-1*) Progeny Pr WI.

— The Door in the Wall Study Guide. 40p. (J). (gr. 4-6). 1993. student ed., ring bd. 12.99 (*1-58609-129-8*) Progeny Pr WI.

— The Giver Study Guide. 70p. (YA). (gr. 7-9). 1997. student ed., ring bd. 12.99 (*1-58609-150-6*) Progeny Pr WI.

— In the Year of the Boar & Jackie Robinson Study Guide. 66p. (J). (gr. 4-6). 1999. student ed., ring bd. 12.99 (*1-58609-135-2*) Progeny Pr WI.

— The Indian in the Cupboard Study Guide. 52p. (J). (gr. 4-7). 1993. ring bd. 12.99 (*1-58609-140-9*) Progeny Pr WI.

— Island of the Blue Dolphins Study Guide. 54p. (J). (gr. 5-7). 1996. student ed., ring bd. 12.99 (*1-58609-144-1*) Progeny Pr WI.

— The Lion, the Witch & the Wardrobe Study Guide. 52p. (J). (gr. 4-7). 1993. student ed., ring bd. 12.99 (*1-58609-136-0*) Progeny Pr WI.

— The Magician's Nephew Study Guide. 62p. (J). (gr. 5-7). 1997. student ed., ring bd. 12.99 (*1-58609-149-2*) Progeny Pr WI.

— Maniac Magee Study Guide. 68p. (YA). (gr. 6-8). 1999. student ed., ring bd. 12.99 (*1-58609-153-0*) Progeny Pr WI.

— Out of the Silent Planet Study Guide. 38p. (YA). (gr. 9-12). 1993. student ed., ring bd. 14.99 (*1-58609-156-5*) Progeny Pr WI.

— To Kill a Mockingbird Study Guide. 64p. (YA). (gr. 9-12). 1994. student ed., ring bd. 14.99 (*1-58609-160-3*) Progeny Pr WI.

— The Yearling Study Guide. 62p. (YA). (gr. 9-12). 1995. student ed., ring bd. 14.99 (*1-58609-163-8*) Progeny Pr WI.

Clausen, Andy. 40th Century Man: Selected Verse, 1996-1966. 190p. 1997. 8.00 (*1-57027-064-3*) Autonomedia.

— Trek to the Top of the World. 1995. pap. 3.00 (*0-929730-57-7*) Zeitgeist Pr.

Clausen, Barry & Pomeroy, Dana R. Walking on the Edge: How Infiltrated Earth First! Pickell, William, ed. LC 94-60636. (Illus.). 320p. (Orig.). 1994. pap. 14.95 (*0-936783-12-5*) Merril Pr.

Clausen, C. A. & Lovoll, Odd Sverre. A Chronicler of Immigrant Life: Svein Nilsson's Articles in Billed-Magazin, 1868-1870. (Author's Ser.). (Illus.). 171p. 1982. 15.00 (*0-87732-067-5*) Norwegian-Am Hist Assn.

Clausen, Carl J., jt. auth. see Burgess, Robert F.

***Clausen, Christopher.** Faded Mosaic: The Emergence of Post-Cultural America. LC 99-59433. 210p. 2000. text 25.00 (*1-56663-283-8*, Pub. by I R Dee) Natl Bk Netwk.

Clausen, Christopher. The Moral Imagination: Essays on Literature & Ethics. LC 86-11282. 208p. (C). 1986. text 25.95 (*0-87745-151-6*) U of Iowa Pr.

— My Life with President Kennedy. LC 94-16527. 143p. 1994. pap. 9.95 (*0-87745-485-X*) U of Iowa Pr.

— The Place of Poetry: Two Centuries of an Art in Crisis. LC 80-5172. 160p. 1981. 20.00 (*0-8131-1429-2*) U Pr of Ky.

Clausen, Clarence A., ed. see Bache, Soren.

Clausen, Dennis M. Prairie Son. LC 98-46831. (First Series). (Illus.). 239p. 1999. pap. 16.00 (*0-922811-39-3*) Mid-List.

Clausen, Edwin, et al. Out from the Shadows: The U. S. & the Third World since 1945. 200p. (C). 1999. pap. 39.00 (*0-8133-0816-X*); pap. text 14.95 (*0-8133-0817-8*) Westview.

Clausen, Edwin G., jt. ed. see Head, William P.

Clausen, J. Immunological Techniques for the Identification & Estimation of Macromolecules. rev. ed. (Laboratory Techniques in Biochemistry & Molecular Biology Ser.: Vol. 1, Pt. III). xiv,387p. 1989. pap. 58.50 (*0-444-80920-1*) Elsevier.

Clausen, Jan. Apples & Oranges: My Journey Through Sexual Identity. LC 98-47997. 288p. 1999. 24.00 (*0-395-82752-3*) HM.

— Beyond Gay or Straight: Understanding Sexual Identity. 154p. (YA). (gr. 9 up). 1996. pap. text 12.95 (*0-7910-2956-5*) Chelsea Hse.

— Beyond Gay or Straight: Understanding Sexual Identity. Duberman, Martin, ed. (Contemporary Issues Ser.). 154p. (YA). (gr. 9 up). 1996. 24.95 (*0-7910-2606-X*) Chelsea Hse.

— Books & Life. LC 88-17975. 257p. reprint ed. pap. 79.70 (*0-608-09661-X*, 206977600006) Bks Demand.

— Duration. 1983. pap. 7.00 (*0-914610-36-8*) Hanging Loose.

— A Movement of Poets: Thoughts on Poetry & Feminism. 1982. pap. 3.25 (*0-9602284-1-1*) Long Haul.

— Waking at the Bottom of the Dark. LC 78-71983. 1979. pap. 3.00 (*0-9602284-0-3*) Long Haul.

Clausen, Jean. Eagles over the River. 2nd rev. ed. Kirsch, J. Allen, ed. 1997. pap. 9.95 (*1-878569-50-3*) Badger Bks Inc.

— To Thank a River. 1996. pap. 9.95 (*1-878569-37-6*) Badger Bks Inc.

Clausen, Jeanette & Cafferty, Helen, eds. Women in German Yearbook, No. VI. 123p. (C). 1991. pap. text 17.50 (*0-8191-8127-7*); lib. bdg. 36.00 (*0-8191-8126-9*) U Pr of Amer.

— Women in German Yearbook, 5: Feminist Studies & German Culture. 150p. 1989. pap. 23.00 (*0-8191-7551-X*); lib. bdg. 46.00 (*0-8191-7550-1*) U Pr of Amer.

Clausen, Jeanette, jt. ed. see Burkhard, Marianne.

Clausen, Jeanette, tr. & intro. see Morgner, Irmtraud.

Clausen, Jens, jt. ed. see Balas, Egon.

Clausen, Jens C. Experimental Studies on the Nature of Species Vol. 5: Biosystematics, Genetics, & Physiological Ecology of the Erythranthe Section of Mimulus. LC 40-14859. (Carnegie Institution of Washington Publication Ser.: Vol. 628). (Illus.). 223p. reprint ed. pap. 69.20 (*0-608-06227-8*, 206655600005) Bks Demand.

Clausen, Jens C., et al. Experimental Studies on the Nature of Species Vol. 1: Effect of Varied Environments on Western North American Plants. LC 40-14859 (Carnegie Institution of Washington Publication Ser.: Vol. 520). (Illus.). 460p. reprint ed. pap. 142.60 (*0-608-06220-0*, 206654900001) Bks Demand.

— Experimental Studies on the Nature of Species Vol. 2: Plant Evolution Through Amphiploidy & Autoploidy with Examples from the Madiinae. LC 40-14859. (Carnegie Institution of Washington Publication Ser.: Vol. 564). (Illus.). 184p. reprint ed. pap. 57.10 (*0-608-06229-4*, 206655800002) Bks Demand.

Clausen, John A. American Lives: Looking Back at the Children of the Great Depression. LC 93-12171. 594p. 1993. text 40.00 (*0-02-905535-0*) Free Pr.

— American Lives: Looking Back at the Children of the Great Depression. LC 94-34091. 1995. pap. 15.95 (*0-520-20149-3*, Pub. by U CA Pr) Cal Prin Full Svc.

— Life Course. 1985. pap. text 24.00 (*0-13-535907-4*) P-H.

Clausen, Josie, jt. auth. see Ramos, Teresita V.

Clausen, L. W. Insect Fact & Folk Lore. 195p. 1985. pap. 175.00 (*0-7855-0366-8*, Pub. by Intl Bks & Periodicals) St Mut.

***Clausen, Lowen.** First Avenue: A Novel. 1999. 21.95 (*0-9669919-0-7*) Watershed WA.

Clausen, Marianne F., tr. see McIntyre, Sally.

Clausen, Mary, ed. see Grossman, Andrea & Curtin, Mary L.

Clausen, Meredith L. Pietro Belluschi: Modern American Architect. (Illus.). 479p. 1995. 65.00 (*0-262-03220-1*) MIT Pr.

— Pietro Belluschi: Modern American Architect. LC 94-20789. (Illus.). 479p. 1999. reprint ed. pap. 34.50 (*0-262-53167-4*) MIT Pr.

— Spiritual Space: The Religious Architecture of Pietro Belluschi. LC 92-14621. (Illus.). 208p. (C). 1992. 50.00 (*0-295-97213-0*) U of Wash Pr.

Clausen, Robert T., ed. Sedum of North America North of the Mexican Plateau. LC 75-6084. (Comstock Bk.). (Illus.). 784p. 1975. text 115.00 (*0-8014-0950-9*) Cornell U Pr.

Clausen, Russell W., jt. auth. see Homan, Hugh W.

***Clausen, Ruth R.** Wildflowers. (Fandex Family Field Guides Ser.). (Illus.). 1999. pap. 9.95 (*0-7611-1464-5*) Workman Pub.

Clausen, Ruth R. & Ekstrom, Nicolas H. Perennials for American Gardens. 631p. 1989. 50.00 (*0-394-55740-9*) Random.

Clausen, Ruth Rogers, see Courtier, Jane & Rogers Clausen, Ruth.

Clausen, Sonja. Regionalwirtschaftliche Implikationen Offentlicher Kulturforderung. (Europaische Hochschulschriften, Reihe 5: Bd. 2153). (GER., Illus.). 251p. 1997. 51.95 (*3-631-31680-1*) P Lang Pubng.

Clausen, Soren, et al, eds. Cultural Encounters: China, Japan, & the West. Essays Commemorating 25 Years of East Asian Studies at the University of Aarhus. 497p. (C). 1995. 40.00 (*87-7288-497-5*, Pub. by Aarhus Univ Pr) David Brown.

Clausen, Soren & Thogersen, Stig. The Making of a Chinese City: History & Historiography in Harbin. LC 94-30519. (Studies on Modern China Ser.). (Illus.). 252p. (C). (gr. 13). 1995. text 81.95 (*1-56324-475-6*, East Gate Bk) M E Sharpe.

Clausen, Soren & Thogersen, Stig. The Making of a Chinese City: History & Historiography in Harbin. LC 94-30519. (Studies on Modern China). (Illus.). 252p. (C). (gr. 13). 1995. pap. text 36.95 (*1-56324-476-4*, East Gate Bk) M E Sharpe.

Clausen, Sten-Erik. Applied Correspondence Analysis: An Introduction. LC 98-8883. (Quantitative Applications in the Social Sciences Ser.). 1998. pap. 10.95 (*0-7619-1115-4*) Sage.

Clausen, Suzanne R. Growing up Rootless. 112p. (Orig.). 1995. 18.95 (*1-56474-133-8*); pap. 10.00 (*1-56474-131-1*) Fithian Pr.

Clausen, W. V., ed. see Juvenal & Persius.

Clausen, W. V., jt. ed. see Kenney, Edwin J.

Clausen, W. V., ed. see Virgil.

Clausen, Wendell, ed. Harvard Studies in Classical Philology, Vol. 86. (Illus.). 296p. 1990. 30.00 (*0-674-37933-0*) HUP.

— Harvard Studies in Classical Philology, Vol. 93. LC 44-32100. (Illus.). 359p. 1991. 39.95 (*0-674-37941-1*, HSCP93) HUP.

— Harvard Studies in Classical Philology, Vol. 94. 432p. 1992. text 45.00 (*0-685-57483-0*) HUP.

— Harvard Studies in Classical Philology, Vol. 95. 422p. (C). 1994. text 45.00 (*0-674-37943-8*) HUP.

Clausen, Wendell, ed. A Commentary on Virgil, Eclogues. 360p. 1995. pap. text 29.95 (*0-19-815035-0*) OUP.

Clausens. Danish-English Technical Dictionary. (DAN & ENG.). 471p. 1997. 195.00 (*0-320-02322-2*) Fr & Eur.

Clausens. English-Danish Technical Dictionary. 461p. 1995. 116.00 (*0-7859-9554-4*) Fr & Eur.

Clauser, C. Thermal Signatures of Heat Transfer Processes in the Earth's Crust. Newcomb, C., tr. from GER. LC 99-30071. (Lecture Notes in Earth Sciences Ser.: Vol. 85). (Illus.). xii, 130p. 1999. pap. 69.95 (*3-540-65604-9*) Spr-Verlag.

Clauser, H. R. Diccionario de Materiales y Procesos de Ingenieria. (SPA.). 820p. 1970. 125.00 (*0-8288-6497-7*, S-50067) Fr & Eur.

***Clauser, Suzanne.** East of Mandalay. LC 00-102838. 366p. 2000. pap. write for info. (*1-58444-117-8*) DiscUs Bks.

— A Girl Named Sooner. 285p. 1999. pap. 17.95 (*1-58444-013-9*, Looking Glass Pr) DiscUs Bks.

Clauser, Suzanne. A Girl Named Sooner. (YA). (gr. 7 up). 1976. pap. 2.95 (*0-380-00216-7*, Avon Bks) Morrow Avon.

***Clauser, Suzanne.** The Glad Season: The True Story of George & Sam... And Henry. (Illus.). 96p. 2000. 15.95 (*1-58444-132-1*); pap. 10.95 (*1-58444-131-3*) DiscUs Bks.

Clauser, Suzanne S., jt. auth. see Thomas, Deborah.

Clausewitz, Karl Von, see Von Clausewitz, Karl.

Clausing, A., jt. auth. see Kaegi, A.

Clausing, Don P. Total Quality Development: Improved Total Development Process. 350p. 1994. 49.95 (*0-7918-0035-0*, 800350) ASME Pr.

Clausing, Donald J. Aviator's Guide to Flight Planning. (Practical Flying Ser.). (Illus.). 224p. 1989. 26.95 (*0-8306-9238-X*, 2438) McGraw-Hill Prof.

— The Aviator's Guide to Modern Navigation. (Illus.). 256p. (Orig.). 1987. 28.95 (*0-8306-0208-9*, 2408) McGraw-Hill Prof.

— Aviator's Guide to Navigation. 2nd ed. (Practical Flying Ser.). 360p. 1992. 28.95 (*0-8306-2171-7*, 3998) McGraw-Hill Prof.

— Aviator's Guide to Navigation. 3rd ed. (Practical Flying Ser.). (Illus.). 368p. 1997. 39.95 (*0-07-011791-8*); pap. 34.95 (*0-07-011792-6*) McGraw.

Clausing, Gerhard. Ubergange: Sprechen, Berichten, Diskutieren. (Bridging the Gap Ser.). (C). 1994. mass mkt. 36.95 (*0-8384-4632-9*) Heinle & Heinle.

Clausing, Gerhard & Rings, Lana. Deutsch Naturlich! (C). 1986. write for info. (*0-318-62575-X*) HM.

Clausing, Gerhard & Von Hammerstein, Katharina. Interaktion: A Text-Based Intermediate German Course. (C). 1990. 20.76 (*0-395-52918-2*) HM.

Clausing, R. E., et al. Diamond & Diamond-Like Films & Coatings. (NATO ASI Ser.: Vol. 266). (Illus.). 928p. (C). 1991. 234.00 (*0-306-44004-0*, Kluwer Plenum) Kluwer Academic.

Clausing, Roth. Roman Colonate: The Theories of Its Origin. LC 70-78011. (Columbia University. Studies in the Social Sciences: No. 260). 1969. reprint ed. 37.50 (*0-404-51260-7*) AMS Pr.

Clausius, Claudia. The Gentleman Is a Tramp: Charlie Chaplin's Comedy. XII, 194p. (C). 1989. text 38.50 (*0-8204-0459-4*) P Lang Pubng.

Clauson, Gerard. An Etymological Dictionary of Pre-Thirteenth Century Turkish. (TUR.). 1038p. 1972. text 265.00 (*0-19-864112-5*) OUP.

Clauson, James R. Quality Management Resources on the Internet. LC 99-36247. 140p. 1999. pap. 49.00 (*0-86587-665-7*) Gov Insts.

Clauson-Kaas, Jes, et al. Crowding & Health in Low Income Settlements: Kali Anyar, Jakarta. 160p. 1997. text 59.95 (*1-85972-512-0*, Pub. by Avebry) Ashgate Pub Co.

Clauson, Will M. Old-Time Cowboy Songbook. 160p. 1996. pap. 17.95 (*0-7866-0200-7*, MB95350) Mel Bay.

Clauss, Francis J. Applied Management Science & Spreadsheet Modeling. LC 95-2889. 1995. pap. 94.95 (*0-534-25842-5*) PWS Pubs.

Clauss, G., et al. Offshore Structures Vol. 1: Conceptual Design & Hydromechanics. (Illus.). 352p. (C). 1992. 185.95 (*0-387-19709-5*) Spr-Verlag.

— Offshore Structures Vol. 2: Strength & Safety for Structural Design. (Illus.). 350p. 1995. 175.00 (*0-387-19770-2*) Spr-Verlag.

Clauss, Guenther Van, see Van Clauss, Guenther.

Clauss, Gunter. Dictionary of Psychology: Woerterbuch der Psychologie. 4th ed. (ENG & GER.). 704p. 1986. 59.95 (*0-8288-2208-5*, M15378) Fr & Eur.

Clauss, J., ed. M*A*S*H: The First Five Years. reprint ed. pap. 12.95 (*0-88411-197-0*) Amereon Ltd.

— P. G. Wodehouse Checklist. 12.95 (*0-89190-843-9*) Amereon Ltd.

— Timeless Children's Tales from Around the World. (Illus.). (J). (gr. 5-6). 1976. lib. bdg. 23.95 (*0-88411-992-0*) Amereon Ltd.

Clauss, J. E. John D. MacDonald: A Checklist. reprint ed. pap. 17.95 (*0-88411-799-5*) Amereon Ltd.

— Louis L'Amour Checklist. pap. 17.95 (*0-88411-244-6*) Amereon Ltd.

— The Star Trek Guide. 1976. pap. 7.95 (*0-88411-079-6*) Amereon Ltd.

Clauss, J. E., ed. see Grey, Zane.

Clauss, J. E., ed. see Hill, Grace Livingston.

Clauss, James J. Best of the Argonauts: The Redefinition of the Epic Hero in Book One of the Apollonius' Argonautica. (C). 1993. 45.00 (*0-520-07925-6*, Pub. by U CA Pr) Cal Prin Full Svc.

Clauss, James J. & Johnston, Sarah I. Medea: Essays on Medea in Myth, Literature, Philosophy & Art. LC 96-8537. 376p. 1997. text 55.00 (*0-691-04377-9*, Pub. by Princeton U Pr) Cal Prin Full Svc.

— Medea: Essays on Medea in Myth, Literature, Philosophy& Art. LC 96-8537. 376p. 1997. pap. text 17.95 (*0-691-04376-0*, Pub. by Princeton U Pr) Cal Prin Full Svc.

Clauss, Jedediah. Confederate War Stories. Date not set. lib. bdg. 19.95 (*0-8488-1737-0*) Amereon Ltd.

— Victorian Vampires. 22.95 (*0-8488-0965-3*) Amereon Ltd.

Clauss, Jedediah, ed. A Cast of Casts: A Biographical Dictionary of Shakespeare's Characters. large type ed. 45.95 (*0-88411-199-7*) Amereon Ltd.

Clauss, Jedehiah. The Loan Book. 19.95 (*0-8488-0121-0*) Amereon Ltd.

Clauss, W., jt. auth. see Dawson, Peter H.
Clauss, W., jt. ed. see Dawson, P.
Claussen, Angelika Hartl, jt. ed. see Crittenden, Patricia McKinsey.
Claussen, Bernhard & Mueller, Horst, eds. Political Socialization of the Young in East & West. (International Studies in Political Socialization & Political Education: Vol. 5). (Illus.). 336p. 1990. pap. 69.00 (*3-631-43116-3*) P Lang Pubng.
Claussen, Claus-Frenz. Differential Diagnosis of Vertigo: Equilibrium in Patients & Research. (Proceedings of the 8th Scientific Meeting of the NES, Turku-Finland, 1979 Ser.). 617p. 1980. 92.30 (*3-11-008298-5*) De Gruyter.
Claussen, Claus-Frenz, et al, eds. Vertigo, Nausea, Tinnitus & Hearing Loss in Central & Peripheral Vestibular Diseases: Proceedings of the XXIInd Annual Meeting of the International Neurootologic & Equilibriometric Society, Hakone, Japan, 6-9 April 1995. LC 95-23632. (International Congress Ser.: No. 1087). 414p. 1995. text 214.25 (*0-444-82193-7*, Excerpta Medica) Elsevier.
Claussen, Dane S., ed. The Promise Keepers: Essays on Masculinity & Christianity. LC 99-38799. 352p. 1999. lib. bdg. 46.50 (*0-7864-0700-X*) McFarland & Co.
— Standing on the Promises: The Promise Keepers & the Revival of Manhood. LC 99-47184. 1999. pap. 19.95 (*0-8298-1307-1*) Pilgrim OH.
Claussen, Evelyn B., jt. auth. see Claussen, Martin P.
Claussen, Louise K., ed. see Pennington, Estill C. & Gruber, J. Richard.
Claussen, Martin P. Comparative History of Research & Development Policies Affecting Air Material. (USAF Historical Studies: No. 20). 196p. 1994. pap. text 33.95 (*0-89126-131-1*) MA-AH Pub.
— Comparative History of Research & Development Policies Affecting Air Materiel, 1915-1944. (USAF Historical Studies: No. 20). 189p. 1945. pap. text 26.00 (*0-89126-039-0*) MA-AH Pub.
Claussen, Martin P. & Claussen, Evelyn B. The Voice of Christian & Jewish Dissenters in America: U. S. Internal Revenue Service Hearings, December 1978. xv, 591p. 1982. pap. 25.00 (*0-685-05732-1*) Piedmont.
Claussen, Martin P. & Friis, Herman R. Descriptive Catalog of Maps Produced by Congress, 1817-1847. 104p. 1997. reprint ed. 40.00 (*1-57898-005-4*) Martino Pubng.
Claussen, Nils, ed. see International Conference on the Science & Technolo.
Claussen, W. Edmunds. The Patriots of the American Revolution. (Illus.). 202p. (Orig.). 1975. 7.00 (*0-9616068-1-9*) Boyertown Hist.
— Pioneers along the Manatawny. (Illus.). 52p. (Orig.). 1968. pap. text 5.00 (*0-9616068-4-3*) Boyertown Hist.
— The Revolutionary War Years. 2nd ed. (Illus.). 182p. 1974. 10.00 (*0-9616068-2-7*) Boyertown Hist.
— Stories of the Falls of French Creek. (Illus.). 75p. (Orig.). pap. text 2.50 (*0-9616068-3-5*) Boyertown Hist.
Claux, Agnes M. Du, see Du Claux, Agnes M.
Clavaguera, N., jt. ed. see Baro, M.
Claval, Paul, ed. Introduction to Regional Geography. Thompson, Ian, tr. LC 97-32760. 288p. 1998. 68.95 (*1-55786-732-1*); pap. 31.95 (*1-55786-733-X*) Blackwell Pubs.
***Clavel, Manuel.** Reflection in Rewriting Logic: Metalogical Foundations & Metaprogramming Applications. 192p. (C). 2000. 64.95 (*1-57586-237-9*, Pub. by CSLI); pap. 24.95 (*1-57586-238-7*, Pub. by CSLI) Cambridge U Pr.
Clavel, Maurice, jt. auth. see Sollers, Phillipe.
Clavel, Pierre. The Progressive City: Planning & Participation, 1969-1984. 300p. (C). 1986. pap. text 17.00 (*0-8135-1120-8*) Rutgers U Pr.
Clavel, Pierre & Goldsmith, William W., eds. Urban & Regional Planning in an Age of Austerity. LC 79-21416. (Policy Studies in Urban Affairs). 402p. 1980. text 100.00 (*0-08-025539-6*, Pergamon Pr); pap. text 19.50 (*0-08-025540-X*, Pergamon Pr) Elsevier.
Clavel, Pierre & Wiewel, Wim, eds. Harold Washington & the Neighborhoods: Progressive City Government in Chicago, 1893-1987. LC 91-9430. 375p. (C). 1991. text 45.00 (*0-8135-1725-7*); pap. text 19.00 (*0-8135-1726-5*) Rutgers U Pr.
Clavel, Pierre, jt. auth. see Krumholz, Norman.
Clavell, James. The Children's Story. 96p. 1989. mass mkt. 5.99 (*0-440-20468-2*) Dell.
— The Children's Story. 1981. 7.95 (*0-385-28135-8*) Doubleday.
— The Children's Story. 1966. pap. 3.25 (*0-8222-0206-9*) Dramatists Play.
***Clavell, James.** Escape: The Love Story from "Whirlwind" 584p. 1999. pap. 9.95 (*0-340-65416-3*, Pub. by Coronet) Trafalgar.
Clavell, James. Gai Jin: A Novel of Japan. LC 92-42129. 1056p. 1993. 27.50 (*0-385-31016-1*) Delacorte.
— Gai-Jin: A Novel of Japan. 1248p. 1994. mass mkt. 7.99 (*0-440-21680-X*) Dell.
— Gai-Jin: A Novel of Japan. limited ed. 1056p. 1993. 300.00 (*0-385-31022-6*) Delacorte.
— King Rat. 480p. 1974. mass mkt. 7.99 (*0-440-14546-5*) Dell.
— King Rat. 496p. 1999. pap. 14.95 (*0-385-33376-5*) Dell.
— Noble House. 1376p. 1984. mass mkt. 7.99 (*0-440-16484-2*) Dell.
— Shogun: A Novel. 1152p. (YA). 1976. mass mkt. 7.99 (*0-440-17800-2*) Dell.
— Tai-Pan. 736p. 1976. mass mkt. 7.99 (*0-440-18462-2*) Dell.
— Two Complete Novels. LC 95-17117. 1995. 13.99 (*0-517-14800-5*) Random.
— Whirlwind. 1280p. 1987. mass mkt. 6.99 (*0-380-70312-2*, Avon Bks) Morrow Avon.
Clavell, James, ed. see Sun Tzu Wu.
Clavelli, L. & Halprin, A., eds. Lewes String Theory Workshop: Lewes, Delaware, July 6-27. 1985. 312p. 1986. text 127.00 (*9971-5-0033-7*) World Scientific Pub.
Clavelli, L. & Harms, B., eds. Superstrings & Particle Theory. 364p. (C). 1990. text 130.00 (*981-02-0157-5*) World Scientific Pub.
Claveloux, Nicole, jt. auth. see Hughes, Richard A.
Claveloux, Nicole, jt. auth. see Sand, George.
Claver, Clive, et al, eds. A Guide to Evangelism. 302p. 1987. pap. 11.95 (*0-310-55221-4*, 19022P) Zondervan.
Claverhouse, Richard, tr. & intro. see Bacchylides.
Claverie, Jean. Little Lou. (Illus.). 48p. (YA). (gr. 3 up). 1990. 22.60 (*0-88682-329-3*, Creative Eds) Creative Co.
Claverie, Jean M., ed. Advances in Computational Biology, Vol. 3. Date not set. 128.50 (*0-7623-0402-2*) Jai Pr.
Claverie, Philip D. & Stuckey, James A. Louisiana Commercial Financing Forms, 2 vols. 1994. ring bd., suppl. ed. 85.00 (*0-685-74615-1*, MICHIE) LEXIS Pub.
— Louisiana Commercial Financing Forms, 2 vols., Set. 600p. 1994. spiral bd. 170.00 (*0-8342-0195-X*, 81317-10, MICHIE) LEXIS Pub.
Clavert, A., jt. ed. see Bollack, C. G.
Clavert, C., jt. auth. see Henderson, Bernard.
Clavey, Steven. Fluid Physiology & Pathology in Traditional Chinese Medicine. LC 94-39411. 1995. text 60.00 (*0-443-04362-0*) Church.
Clavien, Pierre A., jt. auth. see Killenberg, Paul G.
Clavien, Pierre-Alain & Lyerly, Kim. Malignant Liver Tumors: Current & Emerging Therapies. LC 98-49184. (Illus.). 1999. 125.00 (*0-632-04406-3*) Blackwell Sci.
Claviere, Etienne, jt. auth. see Brissot De Warville, Jean P.
Claviez, J. English-French Data Processing Dictionary. (ENG & FRE.). 256p. 1991. 95.00 (*0-8288-6966-9*, 2856080405) Fr & Eur.
Claviez, Wolfram. Seemaennisches Woerterbuch. (GER.). 1973. 75.00 (*0-8288-6329-6*, M-7620) Fr & Eur.
Clavijo, Jose D. Viera y, see Viera y Clavijo, Jose D.
Clavijo, Uva A. No Puedo Mas y Otros Cuentos. LC 88-81562. (Coleccion Caniqui). (SPA.). 98p. (Orig.). 1989. pap. 9.00 (*0-89729-495-5*) Ediciones.
— Tus Ojos y Yo. (Coleccion Espejo de Paciencia). (SPA.). 14p. (Orig.). 1985. pap. 4.50 (*0-89729-373-8*) Ediciones.
Clavin, John. The Mystery of Godliness & Other Sermons. 212p. 1999. reprint ed. 20.95 (*1-57358-094-5*) Soli Deo Gloria.
— Sermons on Galatians. Golding, Arthur, tr. 1000p. 49.95 (*0-9632557-8-9*) Old Paths Pubns.
Clavin, Patricia. The Failure of Economic Diplomacy: Britain, Germany, France & the U. S. A., 1931-36. 270p. 1996. text 65.00 (*0-312-12725-1*) St Martin.
***Clavin, Patricia.** The Great Depression in Europe, 1929-1939. LC 00-30887. 2000. pap. write for info. (*0-312-23735-9*) St Martin.
Clavin, Patricia, jt. auth. see Briggs, Asa.
Clavin, Thomas, jt. auth. see Obler, Martin.
Clavin, Tom, jt. auth. see Bubka, Bob.
Clavin, Tom, jt. auth. see LeRoy, Bridget.
Clavin, Tracy. Comida y Cocina. LC 95-30286. (Vida Latina Ser.). (SPA.). 48p. (J). (gr. 4-8). Date not set. lib. bdg. 23.93 (*0-86625-563-X*) Rourke Pubns.
— Food & Cooking. LC 95-1407. (Latino Life Ser.). 48p. (J). (gr. 4-8). 1995. lib. bdg. 23.93 (*0-86625-546-X*) Rourke Pubns.
Clavius, Christoph. Commentaria in Euclidis Elementa Geometrica: Nachdruck Nach der Ausgabe in Opera Mathematica, Band 1, 1-638 Knobloch, Eberhard, ed. (Historia Scientiarum Ser.). (GER.). xvi, 644p. 1999. reprint ed. 385.00 (*3-487-10278-1*, Pub. by G Olms Verlag) Lubrecht & Cramer.
— In Sphaeram Ioannis de Sacro Bosco Commentarius: Nachdruck Nach der Ausgabe in Opera Mathematica, Band 3, 1-317. Knobloch, Eberhard, ed. (Historia Scientiarum Ser.). (GER.). xii, 340p. 1999. reprint ed. 270.00 (*3-487-10277-3*, Pub. by G Olms Verlag) Lubrecht & Cramer.
Clawar, Stanley S. You & Your Clients: A Guide to a More Successful Law Practice Through Behavior Management. 2nd ed. LC 96-6865. (Illus.). 1996. write for info. (*1-57073-275-2*) Amer Bar Assn.
Clawson. Andean Cocaine Industry. 282p. 1998. pap. 16.95 (*0-312-17691-0*) St Martin.
— Leadership Level Three. LC 98-33824. 231p. (C). 1998. pap. text 37.80 (*0-13-010878-2*) P-H.
Clawson, Aileen. Bender Visual Motor Gestalt Test for Children: A Manual. LC 79-57294. (Illus.). 92p. 1962. pap. 42.50 (*0-87424-035-2*, W-35) Western Psych.
Clawson, C. C. Mathematical Sorcery: Revealing the Secrets of Numbers. LC QA93.C62 1999. (Illus.). 294p. (C). 1999. 26.95 (*0-306-46003-3*, Kluwer Plenum) Kluwer Academic.
— The Mathematical Traveller: Exploring the Grand History of Numbers. (Illus.). 318p. (C). 1994. 25.95 (*0-306-44645-6*, Plenum Trade) Perseus Pubng.
Clawson, C. Joseph. Thesaurus of Values: Comprehensive Index to Values That Strongly Influence People. LC 96-94303. (Illus.). x, 283p. (Orig.). 52.00 (*0-9646095-0-9*) Lake Arrowhead Pubns.
Clawson, Calvin C. Conquering Math Phobia: A Painless Primer. LC 91-41249. 304p. 1991. pap. 16.95 (*0-471-52898-6*) Wiley.
— Mathematical Mysteries: The Beauty & Magic of Numbers. (Illus.). 310p. (C). 1996. 27.95 (*0-306-45404-1*, Plenum Trade) Perseus Pubng.
***Clawson, Calvin C.** Mathematical Mysteries: The Beauty & Magic of Numbers. LC 99-66854. 328p. 1999. pap. text 17.00 (*0-7382-0259-2*, Pub. by Perseus Pubng) HarpC.
***Clawson, Charles W.** Collector's Guide to Colt .45 Service Pistols: Models of 1911 & 1911 A1. 2nd rev. enl. ed. LC 98-93273. (Illus.). 130p. 1998. 29.95 (*0-9633971-8-4*) C W Clawson.
Clawson, D. Kay & Wilson, Emery A. The Medical School Dean: Reflections & Directions. LC 99-60111. (Illus.). 256p. 1999. 21.95 (*0-913383-63-5*) McClanahan Pub.
Clawson, Dan. Bureaucracy & the Labor Process: The Transformation of U. S. Industry, 1860-1920. LC 79-3885. 284p. 1982. pap. 15.00 (*0-85345-543-0*, Pub. by Monthly Rev) NYU Pr.
Clawson, Dan, ed. Required Reading: Sociology's Most Influential Books. LC 98-11944. 232p. 1998. pap. 16.95 (*1-55849-153-8*) U of Mass Pr.
Clawson, Dan, et al. Dollars & Votes: How Business Campaign Contributions Subvert Democracy. LC 98-11172. 256p. 1998. pap. 19.95 (*1-56639-626-3*); text 59.95 (*1-56639-625-5*) Temple U Pr.
Clawson, David K. Latin America & the Caribbean: Lands & Peoples. LC 96-85795. 432p. (C). 1996. text. write for info. (*0-697-12481-9*, WCB McGr Hill) McGrw-H Hghr Educ.
***Clawson, David L.** Latin America & the Caribbean: Lands & Peoples 2nd ed. LC 99-23060. 2000. write for info. (*0-697-38492-6*) McGrw-H Hghr Educ.
— World Regional Geography: A Human Development Approach. 7th ed. 700p. 2000. 88.00 (*0-13-016821-1*) P-H.
Clawson, David L., ed. World Regional Geography: A Development Approach. 6th ed. LC 97-23645. 685p. 1997. 78.67 (*0-13-857400-6*) P-H.
Clawson, Dell M. Keeper of the Echoes. Alford, Kathy M., ed. 202p. 1999. pap. 14.95 (*0-9637274-1-9*) Lagniappe Pr.
— Sunrise Tomorrow. LC 93-79446. 200p. (Orig.). 1993. pap. 13.95 (*0-9637274-0-0*) Lagniappe Pr.
Clawson, Elmer. Activities & Investigations in Economics. (YA). 1995. pap., teacher ed. 12.95 (*0-201-49006-4*) Addison-Wesley.
— Activities & Investigations in Economics. 2nd ed. (YA). 1993. pap. text 8.35 (*0-201-49005-6*) Addison-Wesley.
Clawson, James G., et al. Self-Assessment & Career Development. 3rd ed. 480p. (C). 1991. pap. text 73.00 (*0-13-803180-0*) P-H.
Clawson, Jan. Baptism: My Promise to Jesus (Boy) (Illus.). 24p. (Orig.). (J). (gr. 1-3). 1988. pap. 5.98 (*0-88290-298-9*) Horizon Utah.
— Baptism--My Promise to Jesus: Girl. (Illus.). 24p. 1998. pap. 5.98 (*0-88290-617-8*, 1301G) Horizon Utah.
— Let's Learn about Tithing. (Illus.). 24p. (J). (gr. k-6). 1988. pap. 4.98 (*0-88290-339-X*) Horizon Utah.
— Living the Word of Wisdom: A Guide for Young Latter-Day Saints (A Storybook to Color) LC 89-85210. 32p. 1989. pap. 4.98 (*0-88290-354-3*) Horizon Utah.
Clawson, Jeff J. & Dernocoeur, Kate B. Principles of Emergency Medical Dispatch. 2nd ed. Cottle, Gordon W. & Martin, Robert L., eds. (Illus.). ix, 250p. (C). 1997. 44.99 (*0-9658890-0-9*); pap. 36.99 (*0-9658890-1-7*) Medical Priority.
***Clawson, Jeff J., et al.** Principles of Emergency Medical Dispatch. 3rd ed. Sinclair, Bob, ed. (Illus.). 450p. 2000. write for info. (*0-9658890-2-5*) Medical Priority.
Clawson, Marcy. The Beauty Within. (Illus.). 18p. (Orig.). (J). (gr. 4-6). 1997. pap. 3.00 (*0-9651584-5-4*) Wise Astro.
Clawson, Marion. America's Land & Its Uses. LC 70-167985. (Resources for the Future Ser.). (Illus.). 166p. 1972. pap. 8.95 (*0-8018-1330-1*) Johns Hopkins.
— America's Land & Its Uses. LC 70-167985. (Illus.). 178p. reprint ed. pap. 55.20 (*0-8357-5407-3*, 203019400067) Bks Demand.
— Decision Making in Timber Production, Harvest, & Marketing. LC 77-84930. (Resources for the Future. Research Paper Ser.: No. R-4). 129p. reprint ed. pap. 40.00 (*0-608-14254-9*, 201981600014) Bks Demand.
— The Economics of National Forest Management. LC 76-15939. 117p. 1976. pap. 9.95 (*0-8018-1889-3*, Pub. by Resources Future) Johns Hopkins.
— The Economics of U. S. Nonindustrial Private Forests. LC 79-2196. (RFF Research Paper Ser.: R-14). 434p. reprint ed. pap. 134.60 (*0-608-18805-0*, 203019500067) Bks Demand.
— The Federal Lands Revisited. LC 83-42904. 302p. 1983. 35.00 (*0-8018-3097-4*); pap. 15.95 (*0-8018-3098-2*) Resources Future.
— Federal Lands since Nineteen Fifty-Six: Recent Trends in Use & Management. LC 67-16034. (Resources for the Future Ser.). 128p. (Orig.). 1967. pap. 4.00 (*0-8018-0120-6*) Johns Hopkins.
— The Federal Lands since Nineteen Fifty-Six: Recent Trends in Use & Management. LC 67-16034. 127p. reprint ed. pap. 39.40 (*0-608-18806-9*, 203019600067) Bks Demand.
— Forests for Whom & for What? LC 74-24399. (Resources for the Future Ser.). 175p. 1975. pap. 14.95 (*0-8018-1751-X*, Pub. by Resources Future) Johns Hopkins.
— From Sagebrush to Sage: The Making of a Natural Resource Economist. LC 87-71568. (Illus.). 498p. (Orig.). 1987. pap. 20.00 (*0-9618941-0-5*) Ana Pubns.
— The Land System of the United States: An Introduction to the History & Practice of Land Use & Land Tenure. LC 68-10250. 155p. reprint ed. pap. 48.10 (*0-608-15675-2*, 203199100077) Bks Demand.
— New Deal Planning: The National Resources Planning Board. LC 80-8777. 376p. 1981. 32.50 (*0-8018-2595-4*, Pub. by Resources Future) Johns Hopkins.
— Suburban Land Conversion in the United States: An Economic & Governmental Process. LC 70-149239. (Resources for the Future Ser.). (Illus.). 424p. reprint ed. 131.50 (*0-8357-9287-0*, 201757100007) Bks Demand.
— Uncle Sam's Acres. LC 74-106685. 414p. 1970. reprint ed. lib. bdg. 75.00 (*0-8371-3356-4*, CLSA, Greenwood Pr) Greenwood.
— The Western Range Livestock Industry. Bruchey, Stuart, ed. LC 78-56713. (Management of Public Lands in the U. S. Ser.). (Illus.). 1979. reprint ed. lib. bdg. 31.95 (*0-405-11326-9*) Ayer.
Clawson, Marion, ed. Modernizing Urban Land Policy: Papers Presented at an RFF Forum Held in Washington, DC, 13-14 April 1972. LC 72-12365. 256p. reprint ed. pap. 79.40 (*0-7837-3143-4*, 202379200034) Bks Demand.
Clawson, Marion & Hall, Peter. Planning & Urban Growth: An Anglo-American Comparison. LC 72-12364. (Illus.). 314p. reprint ed. pap. 97.40 (*0-608-18084-X*, 203214600078) Bks Demand.
Clawson, Marion & Knetsch, Jack L. The Economics of Outdoor Recreation. LC 66-16040. 328p. 1967. pap. 15.95 (*0-8018-1302-6*) Resources Future.
Clawson, Marion & Stewart, Charles L. Land Use Information: A Critical Survey of United States Statistics, Including Possibilities for Greater Uniformity. LC 66-14380. 422p. reprint ed. pap. 130.90 (*0-7837-3141-8*, 204284600006) Bks Demand.
Clawson, Marion, jt. auth. see Held, R. Burnell.
Clawson, Marion, jt. auth. see Montgomery, Mary.
Clawson, Marion, jt. ed. see Dysart, Benjamin C., III.
Clawson, Marion, ed. see Forum on Forest Policy for the Future Staff.
Clawson, Marion, ed. see Resources for the Future, Inc. Staff & Farm Foundation Staff.
Clawson, Mary A. Constructing Brotherhood: Class, Gender, & Fraternalism. LC 88-38418. 280p. reprint ed. pap. 86.80 (*0-608-06388-6*, 206674900008) Bks Demand.
Clawson, Patrick L. Iran's Challenge to the West: How, When, & Why. LC 93-12300. (Policy Papers: No. 33). 98p. 1993. pap. 8.00 (*0-944029-24-8*) Wash Inst NEP.
Clawson, Patrick L. Iran's Strategic Intentions & Capabilities. 230p. 1994. per. 12.00 (*0-16-061163-6*) USGPO.
Clawson, Patrick L. Unaffordable Ambitions: Syria's Military Build-Up & Economic Crisis. LC 89-25113. (Policy Papers: No. 17). 57p. 1989. pap. 8.00 (*0-944029-02-7*) Wash Inst NEP.
Clawson, Patrick L., ed. Energy & National Security. 1997. pap. 14.00 (*1-57906-026-9*) Natl Defense.
— Iran's Strategic Intentions & Capabilities. 224p. (C). 1996. reprint ed. pap. text 35.00 (*0-7881-3677-1*) DIANE Pub.
— Iraq Strategy Review: Options for U. S. Policy. LC 98-23817. 168p. 1998. pap. 19.95 (*0-944029-26-4*) Wash Inst NEP.
Clawson, Patrick L. & Rosen, Howard. The Economic Consequences of Peace for Israel, the Palestinians, & Jordan. LC 91-31772. (Policy Papers: No. 25). 80p. 1991. pap. 8.00 (*0-944029-12-4*) Wash Inst NEP.
Clawson, Patrick L., et al. Dollars & Diplomacy: The Impact of U. S. Economic Initiatives on Arab-Israeli Negotiations. LC 99-11811. (Policy Paper Ser.: No. 49). 1999. pap. 19.95 (*0-944029-29-9*) Wash Inst NEP.
***Clawson, Patrick L., et al.** Iran under Khatami: A Political, Economic, & Military Assessment. LC 98-39718. 114p. 1998. pap. 19.95 (*0-944029-27-2*) Wash Inst NEP.
Clawson, Patrick L., jt. ed. see Binneddijk, Hans.
Clawson, Patrick L., jt. ed. see Binnendijk, Hans.
Clawson, Patrick L., jt. ed. see Tismaneanu, W. Vladimir.
Clawson, R. A., et al. Basic Pharmacology & Clinical Drug Use in Dentistry. 6th ed. LC 94-22240. 1995. pap. text 39.95 (*0-443-05107-0*) Church.
Clawson, Richard P. & Wolcott, Jahn A. Christmas Celebration: Santa Fe Traditions, Foods & Crafts. LC 95-32963. (Illus.). 128p. 1995. 39.95 (*0-940666-68-5*) Clear Light.
Clawson, Robert W., ed. The East-West Rivalry in the Third World: Security Issues & Regional Perspectives. LC 85-14167. 348p. 1986. 45.00 (*0-8420-2236-8*) Scholarly Res Inc.
Clawson, Robert W. & Kaplan, Lawrence S., eds. The Warsaw Pact: Political Purpose & Military Means. LC 81-86387. 297p. (C). 1982. pap. text 17.95 (*0-8420-2199-X*); lib. bdg. 45.00 (*0-8420-2198-1*) Scholarly Res Inc.
Clawson, Robert W., jt. auth. see Kaplan, Lawrence S.
Clawson, Roger. Yellowstone Reflections: An Artist's Inspiration & Canoe Flyers Love Song. LC 91-67241. (Yellowstone Ser.: No. 1). (Illus.). 1991. 30.00 (*0-9631762-0-X*) Prose Works.
Clawson, Roger & Shandera, Katherine A. Billings: The City & the People. LC 93-17652. (Illus.). 112p. (Orig.). 1993. pap. 14.95 (*1-56037-037-8*) Am Wrld Geog.
Clawson, Rudger. A Ministry of Meetings: The Apostolic Diaries of Rudger Clawson. limited ed. Larson, Stan, ed. LC 92-5901. (Significant Mormon Diaries Ser.: No. 6). (Illus.). 844p. 1993. 85.00 (*0-941214-96-6*) Signature Bks.
Clawson, Sharalee S. & Marshall, Barbara K. I Feel My Savior's Love: Themes from LDS Children's Songs in Counted Cross-Stitch. 9p. 1986. pap. 5.98 (*0-88290-515-5*) Horizon Utah.
Claxton. Caring for Children with HIV & AIDS. 222p. 1992. pap. 62.50 (*1-56593-520-9*, 0518) Singular Publishing.
— Dermatologic Core Curriculum. 154p. 1997. per. 70.00 (*0-7872-3571-7*, 41357101) Kendall-Hunt.
— Tennis. 2nd ed. 106p. 1997. pap. text 21.00 (*0-13-777855-4*) P-H.
***Claxton, Annette.** Greeting Cards. 1999. pap. 29.95 (*1-86126-296-5*, Pub. by Crolwood) Trafalgar.
Claxton, Annette. Quick Quilts. (Needleworker's Collection). (Illus.). 112p. 10.99 (*1-57215-153-6*, JG1153) World Pubns.

An Asterisk (*) at the beginning of an entry indicates that the title is appearing for the first time.

Claxton, Charles S. & Murrell, Patricia H. Learning Styles: Implications for Improving Educational Practices. Fife, Jonathan D., ed. LC 88-70151. (ASHE-ERIC Higher Education Reports: No. 87-4). 120p. (C). 1988. pap. 24.00 (*0-913317-39-X*) GWU Grad Schl E&HD.

Claxton, Eve. New York's 50 Best Bookstores for Book Lovers. LC 99-52459. (Illus.). 128p. 2000. pap. 12.00 (*1-885492-84-7*) City & Co.

***Claxton, Guy.** Hare Brain, Tortoise Mind: How Intelligence Increases When You Think Less, 272p. 2000. pap. 13.00 (*0-06-095541-4*, Ecco Press) HarperTrade.

Claxton, Guy. Hare Brain, Tortoise Mind: Why Intelligence Increases When You Think Less. LC 98-16001. (Illus.). 259p. 1999. reprint ed. 25.95 (*0-88001-622-1*) HarpC.

— The Heart of Buddhism: Practical Wisdom for an Agitated World. 191p. 1990. pap. 12.95 (*1-85274-065-5*, Pub. by Aqrn Pr) Harper SF.

— The Heart of Buddhism: Practical Wisdom for an Agitated World. 191p. 1993. reprint ed. pap. 15.00 (*1-85538-274-1*, Pub. by Aqrn Pr) Harper SF.

— Live & Learn: An Introduction to the Psychology of Growth & Change in Everyday Life. 288p. 1984. pap. 34.95 (*0-335-09809-6*) OpUniv Pr.

Claxton, Guy. Wise Up: The Challenge of Lifelong Learning. 352p. 1999. 25.95 (*1-58234-039-0*) Bloomsbury Pubg.

***Claxton, Guy.** Wise Up: The Challenge of Lifelong Learning. 388p. 2000. pap. 14.95 (*1-58234-092-7*) Bloomsbury Pubg.

Claxton, Guy, ed. Beyond Therapy: The Impact of Eastern Religions on Psychological Theory & Practice. 352p. (Orig.). 1996. reprint ed. pap. 26.95 (*1-85327-100-4*, Pub. by Prism Pr) Assoc Pubs Grp.

Claxton, Guy, ed. Growth Points in Cognition. 288p. 1988. text 49.95 (*0-415-00260-5*) Routledge.

Claxton, Guy, jt. auth. see Atkinson, Terry.

***Claxton, John.** Managing Your Personal Finances: How to Achieve Your Own Financial Security, Wealth & Independence. 3rd ed. (Illus.). 160p. (Orig.). 1999. pap. 19.95 (*1-85703-471-6*, Pub. by How To Bks) Trans-Atl Phila.

Claxton, John D., et al, eds. Consumers & Energy Conservation: International Perspectives on Research & Policy Options. LC 81-10626. 304p. 1981. 69.50 (*0-275-90595-0*, C0595, Praeger Pubs) Greenwood.

Claxton, Patricia, tr. see Lavallee, Ronald.

Claxton Stevens, C., jt. auth. see Whittington, S.

Claxton, William. Jazz Postcard Book. (Illus.). 1998. pap. 5.99 (*3-8228-7984-3*) Taschen Amer.

***Claxton, William.** Photographic Memory. 2000. 65.00 (*1-57687-085-5*, pwerHse Bks) pwerHse Cultrl.

Claxton, William, photos by. Jazz. LC 96-14968. (Illus.). 124p. 1996. pap. 22.95 (*0-8118-1351-7*) Chronicle Bks.

— Laugh: Portraits of the Greatest Comedians & the Stories They Tell Each Other. LC 99-19846. (Illus.). 112p. 1999. 30.00 (*0-688-15891-9*, Wm Morrow) Morrow Avon.

— Young Chet. (Illus.). 112p. 1999. per. 16.95 (*3-8238-9966-X*) te Neues.

***Claxton, William, photos by.** William Claxton: Steve McQueen. (Illus.). 176p. 2000. 60.00 (*1-892041-37-5*) Arena Editions.

Clay. Geschaftsdeutsch: Tape T/A Text. 1995. 9.68 (*0-07-011335-1*) McGraw.

— Information Structures. Date not set. pap. text, teacher ed. write for info. (*0-314-96601-3*) West Pub.

— The Stars That Shine. (J). (gr. 4-6). 2000. mass mkt. 22.00 (*0-689-82202-2*) S&S Childrens.

Clay & Frankel. Concept Fitness & Wellness. 88p. (C). 1998. pap. text 12.00 (*0-536-01170-2*) Pearson Custom.

***Clay, Alan B., Jr.** Freon, Section 609: Certification Test. 12p. 1999. pap., student ed. 19.95 (*0-9674609-1-3*) Vatterott Col.

Clay, Albert T. Babylonian Business Transactions of the First Millenium B.C. LC 78-63516. (Babylonian Records in the Library of J. Pierpont Morgan: No. I). reprint ed. 27.50 (*0-404-60121-9*) AMS Pr.

— Business Documents of Murashu Sons of Nippur: Dated in the Reign of Darius II (424-404 B. C.) LC 08-33650. (University of Pennsylvania, Babylonian Expedition, Series A: Cuneiform Texts: Vol. 10). 207p. reprint ed. pap. 64.20 (*0-8357-7488-0*, 205202100027) Bks Demand.

— Business Documents of Murashu Sons of Nippur Dated in the Reign of Darius II. LC 13-1107. (University of Pennsylvania, The Museum, Publications of the Babylonian Section: Vol. 2, No. 1). 180p. reprint ed. pap. 55.80 (*0-8357-7489-9*, 205201600027) Bks Demand.

— Documents from the Temple Archives of Nippur Dated in the Reigns of Cassite Rulers. LC 13-1106. (University of Pennsylvania, The Museum, Publications of the Babylonian Section: Vol. 2, No. 2). 108p. reprint ed. pap. 33.50 (*0-608-13648-4*, 205202200027) Bks Demand.

— Documents from the Temple Archives of Nippur Dated in the Reigns of Cassite Rulers (Complete Dates) LC 08-33649. (University of Pennsylvania, Babylonian Expedition, Series A: Cuneiform Texts: Vol. 14). 188p. reprint ed. pap. 58.30 (*0-608-14319-7*, 205201700027) Bks Demand.

— Empire of the Amorites. (Yale Oriental Researches Ser.: No. VI). 1919. 28.50 (*0-685-69801-7*) Elliots Bks.

— The Empire of the Amorites. LC 78-63550. (Yale Oriental Series: Researches: No. 6). reprint ed. 30.00 (*0-404-60276-2*) AMS Pr.

— Epics, Hymns, Omens & Other Texts. LC 78-63519. (Babylonian Records in the Library of J. Pierpont Morgan: 4). reprint ed. 30.00 (*0-404-60124-3*) AMS Pr.

— A Hebrew Deluge Story in Cuneiform. LC 78-63549. (Yale Oriental Series: Researches: No. 5, Pt. 3). reprint ed. 20.00 (*0-404-60275-4*) AMS Pr.

— Legal Documents from Erech, Dated in the Seleucid Era (312-65 B.C.) LC 78-63517. (Babylonian Records in the Library of J. Pierpont Morgan: 2). reprint ed. 34.50 (*0-404-60122-7*) AMS Pr.

— Letters & Transactions from Cappadocia. LC 78-63523. (Babylonian Inscriptions in the Collection of James B. Nies Ser.: 4). reprint ed. 30.00 (*0-404-60134-0*) AMS Pr.

— Miscellaneous Inscriptions in the Yale Babylonian Collection. LC 78-63530. (Yale Oriental Series: Babylonian Texts: No. 1). (Illus.). 232p. reprint ed. 42.00 (*0-404-60251-7*) AMS Pr.

— Neo-Babylonian Letters from Erech. LC 78-63532. (Yale Oriental Series: Babylonian Texts: No. 3). (Illus.). 184p. reprint ed. 35.00 (*0-404-60253-3*) AMS Pr.

— The Origin of Biblical Traditions. LC 78-63556. (Yale Oriental Series: Researches: No. 12). reprint ed. 37.50 (*0-404-60282-7*) AMS Pr.

— Personal Names from Cuneiform Inscriptions of the Cassite Period. LC 78-63543. (Yale Oriental Series: Researches: No. I). reprint ed. 37.50 (*0-404-60271-1*) AMS Pr.

Clay, Albert T., jt. auth. see Hilprecht, Hermann V.

Clay, Alvin A., III. Preparing the 1065 Return, 1992. 425p. 1992. 54.95 (*0-7811-0003-8*, Maxwell Macmillan) Macmillan.

Clay, Alvin A., III & Maule, James E. Preparing the 1065 Return, 1993. rev. ed. (Professional Tax Advisor's Guide Ser.). (Illus.). 384p. 1992. pap. text 56.00 (*0-7811-0059-3*) Res Inst Am.

Clay, Augustella. The Spirit of Beauty . . . He Holds the Reins. LC 97-101161. 40p. 1995. pap. text 6.00 (*0-8059-3730-7*) Dorrance.

Clay, Barry. The Prairie Adventures of Turk & the Gobblers. Kemnitz, Myrna, ed. 190p. (YA). (gr. 7 up). 1995. pap. 9.99 (*0-88092-324-5*) Royal Fireworks.

Clay, Brenda J. Mandak Realities: Person & Power in Central New Ireland. LC 85-22054. 327p. 1986. reprint ed. pap. 101.40 (*0-7837-5661-5*, 205908700005) Bks Demand.

— Pinikindu: Maternal Nurture, Paternal Substance. LC 76-8083. (Illus.). 1977. lib. bdg. 14.00 (*0-226-10943-7*) U Ch Pr.

Clay, Butch. Chattooga River Sourcebook: A Comprehensive Guide to the River & Its Natural & Human History. LC 95-37215. 1995. write for info. (*0-614-08624-8*) Chattooga River.

— A Guide to the Chattooga River. (Illus.). 64p. (Orig.). 1995. pap. 9.95 (*0-9647083-0-2*) Menasha Ridge.

Clay, C. H. Design of Fishways & Other Fish Facilities. 2nd ed. LC 94-17350. 256p. 1994. lib. bdg. 75.00 (*1-56670-111-2*, L1111) Lewis Pubs.

Clay, Cassius M. The Life of Cassius Marcellus Clay. (American Biography Ser.). 535p. 1991. reprint ed. lib. bdg. 99.00 (*0-7812-8072-9*) Rprt Serv.

— Writings of Cassius Marcellus Clay: Including Speeches & Addresses. Greeley, Horace, ed. LC 70-82185. (Anti-Slavery Crusade in America Ser.). 1970. reprint ed. 26.95 (*0-405-00634-9*) Ayer.

Clay, Cecil. Clay: Family of Clay of New Castle, Delaware, & Philadelphia, Pennsylvania. 51p. 1997. reprint ed. pap. 10.00 (*0-8328-7970-3*); reprint ed. lib. bdg. 20.00 (*0-8328-7969-X*) Higginson Bk Co.

Clay, Cheryl D. Schooling At-Risk Native American Children: A Journey from Reservation Head Start to Public School Kindergarten. rev. ed. LC 98-35311. (Native Americans Ser.). (Illus.). 185p. 1998. 53.00 (*0-8153-3137-1*) Garland.

Clay, Clarence. Elementary Exploration Seismology. 384p. 1989. boxed set 52.67 (*0-685-27165-X*) P-H.

Clay, Clarence S., jt. auth. see Medwin, Herman.

Clay, Clarence S., jt. auth. see Tolstoy, Ivan S.

Clay-Clopton, Virginia. A Belle of the Fifties: Memoirs of Mrs. Clay of Alabama. Sterling, Ada et al, eds. LC 99-6143. 462p. 1999. pap. 24.95 (*0-8173-0986-1*) U of Ala Pr.

— Belle Of The Fifties; Memoirs Of Mrs. Clay Of Alabama. LC 99-6143. 1999. 49.95 (*0-8173-1020-7*) U of Ala Pr.

Clay, Coleen, jt. auth. see Irish, J. A.

Clay County Homecoming '86 Historical Book Committ. The History of Clay County, Tennessee, 1870-1986. LC 86-51319. 216p. 1987. 49.95 (*0-938021-06-0*) Turner Pub KY.

Clay, Daniel. The Prophecies of His Devine Grace Daniel Clay. LC 85-876299. 305p. 1998. pap. 16.95 (*0-9667877-0-6*, 84743) Haas Pubns.

Clay, Daniel C. & Schwarzweller, Harry K., eds. Research in Rural Sociology & Development, Vol. 2: Focus on Community. 280p. 1985. 73.25 (*0-89232-558-5*) Jai Pr.

— Research in Rural Sociology & Development, Vol. 4: Rural Labor Markets. 281p. 1989. 73.25 (*0-89232-925-4*) Jai Pr.

— Research in Rural Sociology & Development, Vol. 5: Household Strategies. 263p. 1991. 73.25 (*1-55938-058-6*) Jai Pr.

— Research in Rural Sociology & Development, Vol. 6. 270p. 1995. 73.25 (*1-55938-458-1*) Jai Pr.

— Research in Rural Sociology & Development Vol. 1: Focus on Agriculture. 353p. 1984. 73.25 (*0-89232-332-9*) Jai Pr.

— Research in Rural Sociology & Development Vol. 3: Third World Contexts. 280p. 1987. 73.25 (*0-89232-586-0*) Jai Pr.

Clay, David. Information Structures: Implementing Imagination. LC 85-20321. (Illus.). 465p. (C). 1986. text 63.00 (*0-314-93163-5*) West Pub.

Clay, Dennis L., jt. auth. see Holm, Monte.

***Clay, Dexter.** Black Eye on America: A Real Story of American Life. LC 98-93142. x, 521p. 1998. 22.50 (*0-9665444-0-4*) Black Eye Wrld.

Clay, Diskin. Paradosis & Survival: Three Chapters in the History of Epicurean Philosophy. LC 98-29087. 312p. 1998. text 47.50 (*0-472-10896-4*, 10896) U of Mich Pr.

***Clay, Diskin.** Platonic Questions: Dialogues with the Silent Philosopher. LC 99-56918. 2000. write for info. (*0-271-02044-X*) Pa St U Pr.

***Clay, Diskin & Purvis, Andrea.** Four Island Utopias. (Illus.). 210p. (C). 2000. pap. text 12.95 (*1-58510-000-5*) Focus Pub-R Pullins.

Clay, Diskin, ed. see Locke, John.

Clay, Diskin, tr. see Sophocles.

Clay, E. J. & Schaffer, B. B. Room for Maneuvre. LC 84-5631. 210p. 1985. 32.50 (*0-8386-3243-2*) Fairleigh Dickinson.

Clay, E. Jefferson. Aces Wild. 1980. pap. 2.25 (*0-505-51470-2*) Dorchester Pub Co.

Clay, Edith, ed. see Ramage, Craufurd T.

***Clay, Edward & Stokke, Olav, eds.** Food Aid & Human Security. (EADI Book Ser.: No. 24). 408p. 2000. 62.50 (*0-7146-5084-6*, Pub. by F Cass Pubs); pap. 28.50 (*0-7146-8125-3*, Pub. by F Cass Pubs) Intl Spec Bk.

Clay, Edward & Stokke, Olav S., eds. Food Aid Reconsidered: Assessing the Impact on Third World Countries. LC 94-47077. (EADI Book Ser.: No. 11). (Illus.). 208p. 1995. pap. 25.00 (*0-7146-4173-1*, Pub. by F Cass Pubs) Intl Spec Bk.

Clay, Edward, jt. auth. see Benson, Charlotte.

Clay, Ele, ed. see Dean, Jennifer K.

Clay, Elizabeth. Motivation Plus. LC 83-62405. 1983. student ed., ring bd. 49.95 (*0-914607-01-4*) Master Tchr.

Clay, Elizabeth, jt. ed. see Kallio, Veikko.

Clay, G. A. The Return of Brer Rabbit. LC 96-137102. (Illus.). 30p. (Orig.). 1995. pap. 12.00 (*0-9649903-0-X*, 1) Brer Rabbit.

Clay, George R. Tolstoy's Phoenix: From Method to Meaning in War & Peace. LC 98-35288. (Studies in Russian Literature & Theory). 160p. 1998. text 59.95 (*0-8101-1621-9*); pap. text 17.95 (*0-8101-1697-9*) Northwestern U Pr.

Clay, Gertrude, ed. see Clay, Lowell T.

Clay, Grady. Close-up: How to Read the American City. LC 79-26307. (Illus.). 192p. 1980. reprint ed. pap. 17.00 (*0-226-10945-3*, P863) U Ch Pr.

— Real Places. (Illus.). 328p. 1998. pap. 23.00 (*0-226-10949-6*) U Ch Pr.

— Real Places: An Unconventional Guide to America's Generic Landscape. (Illus.). 328p. 1994. 35.00 (*0-226-10946-1*) U Ch Pr.

Clay, Gudrun. German Grammar Comparison for Lernexpress I. 2nd ed. (GER.). 234p. (C). 1998. spiral bd. 31.95 (*0-7872-5238-7*, 41523801) Kendall-Hunt.

— Geschaftsdeutsch: An Introduction to Business German. 2nd ed. LC 94-32894. (ENG & GER.). 288p. (C). 1994. pap. 44.69 (*0-07-011334-3*) McGraw.

— Lernexpress II: German Grammar Companion. 160p. (C). 1996. spiral bd. 15.95 (*0-7872-2033-7*) Kendall-Hunt.

Clay, Gwen, jt. auth. see Komarc, Marilyn.

Clay, Henry. Lord Norman. Wilkins, Mira, ed. LC 78-3906. (International Finance Ser.). (Illus.). 1979. reprint ed. lib. bdg. 47.95 (*0-405-11211-4*) Ayer.

— The Papers of Henry Clay, Vol. 2. Hopkins, James F. & Hargreaves, Mary W. M., eds. LC 59-13605. 951p. reprint ed. pap. 200.00 (*0-608-12716-7*, 202435900037) Bks Demand.

— The Papers of Henry Clay: Supplement, 1793-1852. Hay, Melba P., ed. LC 59-13605. 400p. (C). 1992. text 60.00 (*0-8131-0061-5*) U Pr of Ky.

— Private Correspondence of Henry Clay. Colton, Calvin, ed. LC 78-169756. (Select Bibliographies Reprint Ser.). 1977. reprint ed. 39.95 (*0-8369-5976-0*) Ayer.

— The Private Correspondence of Henry Clay. (American Biography Ser.). 642p. 1991. reprint ed. lib. bdg. 109.00 (*0-7812-8073-7*) Rprt Serv.

— The Works of Henry Clay. 1990. reprint ed. lib. bdg. 79.00 (*0-7812-2304-0*) Rprt Serv.

Clay, Henry & Mallory, Daniel. The Life & Speeches of the Hon. Henry Clay. 1977. 51.95 (*0-8369-6983-9*, 7861) Ayer.

Clay, Henry H. & Bassett, W. H. Clay's Handbook of Environmental Health. 18th ed. LC 98-28781. 1999. write for info. (*0-419-22960-4*, E & FN Spon) Routledge.

Clay, Horace F. & Hubbard, James C. Tropical Exotics. LC 77-7363. (Hawaii Garden Ser.: No. 1). (Illus.). 284p. 1987. reprint ed. pap. 34.95 (*0-8248-1127-5*) UH Pr.

— Tropical Shrubs. LC 77-7363. (Hawaii Garden Ser.: No. 2). (Illus.). 312p. 1987. reprint ed. pap. 34.95 (*0-8248-1128-3*) UH Pr.

***Clay, J.** The Book of Bridge. (Illus.). 1998. text 40.00 (*0-340-58979-5*, Pub. by Hodder & Stought Ltd) Trafalgar.

Clay, J. A Practical Guide to Landfill Tax. LC 98-215892. 48p. 1998. write for info. (*0-7277-2687-0*) T Telford.

Clay, J. A., jt. auth. see Sanderson, P. L.

Clay, J. E. A Motorboater's Guide to Lake Winnipesaukee: Exploring the Lake by Boat. Perlman, Heidi & Lichenstein, Carl, eds. LC 97-97173. (Illus.). 64p. 1998. pap. 8.95 (*0-9661870-0-8*) Oceanview.

Clay, Jack. Tiger Woods. (Illus.). 64p. 1997. write for info. (*1-890927-01-5*) Belden Hill.

***Clay, Jackie.** Build the Right Fencing for Horses. LC 99-88773. (Country Wisdom Bulletin Ser.). (Illus.). 1999. pap. write for info. (*1-58017-270-9*) Storey Bks.

— Renovating a Small Barn for Your Horse. LC 99-88772. (Country Wisdom Bulletin Ser.). (Illus.). 1999. pap. write for info. (*1-58017-271-7*) Storey Bks.

Clay, James H. & Krempel, Daniel. The Theatrical Image. LC 85-91268. (Illus.). 314p. 1985. reprint ed. pap. text 27.00 (*0-8191-4978-0*) U Pr of Amer.

Clay, James R. Nearrings: Geneses & Applications. LC 92-30341. (Illus.). 480p. 1992. text 105.00 (*0-19-853398-5*) OUP.

Clay, Jason W. Generating Income & Conserving Resources: 20 Lessons from the Field. LC 95-50483. 1996. pap. 12.00 (*0-89164-147-5*) World Wildlife Fund.

— Indigenous Peoples & Tropical Forests: Models of Land Use & Management from Latin America. (Cultural Survival Reports: No. 27). 116p. 1988. 19.95 (*0-939521-38-5*); pap. 8.00 (*0-939521-32-6*) Cultural Survival.

Clay, Jason W. & Holcomb, Bonnie K. Politics & the Ethiopian Famine. (Cultural Survival Reports: No. 20). 237p. 1986. 29.95 (*0-939521-34-2*); pap. 9.95 (*0-939521-25-3*) Cultural Survival.

— Politics & the Ethiopian Famine, 1984-1985. 224p. 1987. pap. 21.95 (*0-685-14275-2*) Transaction Pubs.

— Politics & the Ethiopian Famine, 1984-1985. 224p. 1987. pap. text 21.95 (*0-88738-147-2*) Transaction Pubs.

Clay, Jason W., et al. The Spoils of Famine: Ethiopian Famine Policy & Peasant Agriculture. (Cultural Survival Reports: No. 25). 303p. 1988. 29.95 (*0-939521-35-0*); pap. 15.00 (*0-939521-30-X*) Cultural Survival.

Clay, Jenny S. The Wrath of Athena: Gods & Men in the Odyssey. (Greek Studies). (C). 1996. pap. text 19.95 (*0-8226-3069-9*) Littlefield.

Clay, Jenny S., tr. see Locke, John.

Clay, Jesse. The Small One: A Good Samaritan. (Illus.). (J). 1998. 12.95 (*0-7868-3195-2*, Pub. by Disney Pr) Time Warner.

Clay, John. R.D. Laing: A Divided Self. (Illus.). 308p. 1997. pap. 13.95 (*0-340-68451-8*, Pub. by Hodder & Stought Ltd); text 29.95 (*0-340-59049-1*, Pub. by Hodder & Stought Ltd) Trafalgar.

Clay, John E. Snollygosters, Airheads & Wimps: John Clay's Dictionary of Presidential Words. 275p. (Orig.). 1995. pap. 10.00 (*0-9647638-0-X*) Logolept Pr.

***Clay, John E.** Snollygosters, Airheads, Wimps: John Clay's Dictionary of Presidential Words. Howe, Ray, ed. LC 99-68864. (Illus.). 320p. 2000. lib. bdg. 24.95 (*1-883477-42-5*) Lone Oak MN.

— Snullygosters, Airhead & Wimps: John Clay's Dictionary of Presidential Words. Huwe, Ray, ed. LC 99-68864. (Illus.). 320p. 2000. pap. 16.95 (*1-883477-41-7*) Lone Oak MN.

***Clay, John R., et al.** Guide to Compilation & Review Engagements, 4 vols. 1999. ring bd. 164.00 (*0-7646-0819-3*) Prctnrs Pub Co.

Clay, John R., et al. Guide to Compilation & Review Engagements, 4 vols. Incl. Vol. 4. Guide to Compilation & Review Engagements. 1997. ring bd. 156.00 (*0-7646-0232-2*); Vol. 1. 1997. ring bd. 156.00 (*0-7646-0229-2*); Vol. 2. 1997. ring bd. 156.00 (*0-7646-0230-6*); Vol. 3. 1997. ring bd. (*0-7646-0231-4*); 150.00 (*1-56433-984-X*) Prctnrs Pub Co.

Clay, John R., et al. Guide to Compilation & Review Engagements, 4 vols. Incl. Vol. 4. Guide to Compilation & Review Engagements. 1997. ring bd. 156.00 (*0-7646-0232-2*); Vol. 1. 1997. ring bd. 156.00 (*0-7646-0229-2*); Vol. 2. 1997. ring bd. 156.00 (*0-7646-0230-6*); Vol. 3. 1997. ring bd. (*0-7646-0231-4*); 156.00 (*0-7646-0228-4*) Prctnrs Pub Co.

Clay, John R., et al. Guide to Compilation & Review Engagements, Vol. 1. 1998. ring bd. write for info. (*0-7646-0537-2*) Prctnrs Pub Co.

***Clay, John R., et al.** Guide to Compilation & Review Engagements, Vol. 1. 1999. ring bd. write for info. (*0-7646-0820-7*) Prctnrs Pub Co.

Clay, John R., et al. Guide to Compilation & Review Engagements, Vol. 2. 1998. ring bd. write for info. (*0-7646-0538-0*) Prctnrs Pub Co.

***Clay, John R., et al.** Guide to Compilation & Review Engagements, Vol. 2. 1999. ring bd. write for info. (*0-7646-0821-5*) Prctnrs Pub Co.

Clay, John R., et al. Guide to Compilation & Review Engagements, Vol. 3. 1998. ring bd. write for info. (*0-7646-0539-9*) Prctnrs Pub Co.

***Clay, John R., et al.** Guide to Compilation & Review Engagements, Vol. 3. 1999. ring bd. write for info. (*0-7646-0822-3*) Prctnrs Pub Co.

Clay, John R., et al. Guide to Compilation & Review Engagements, Vol. 4. 1998. ring bd. write for info. (*0-7646-0540-2*) Prctnrs Pub Co.

***Clay, John R., et al.** Guide to Compilation & Review Engagements, Vol. 4. 1999. ring bd. write for info. (*0-7646-0823-1*) Prctnrs Pub Co.

Clay, John R., et al. Guide to Compilation & Review Engagements, Vols. 1-4. 1998. ring bd. 164.00 (*0-7646-0536-4*) Prctnrs Pub Co.

***Clay, John R., et al.** Guide to Personal Financial Planning, 3 vols. 1999. ring bd. 180.00 (*0-7646-0878-9*) Prctnrs Pub Co.

Clay, John R., et al. Guide to Personal Financial Planning, 3 vols. Incl. Vol. 1. 1997. ring bd. (*0-7646-0288-8*); Vol. 2. 1997. ring bd. (*0-7646-0289-6*); Vol. 3. 1997. ring bd. (*0-7646-0290-X*); 168.00 (*1-56433-989-0*); 170.00 (*0-7646-0287-X*) Prctnrs Pub Co.

— Guide to Personal Financial Planning, 3 vols., Set. 1995. ring bd. 168.00 (*1-56433-740-5*) Prctnrs Pub Co.

— Guide to Personal Financial Planning, Vol. 1. 1995. ring bd. write for info. (*1-56433-741-3*) Prctnrs Pub Co.

***Clay, John R., et al.** Guide to Personal Financial Planning, Vol. 1. 1999. ring bd. write for info. (*0-7646-0879-7*) Prctnrs Pub Co.

Clay, John R., et al. Guide to Personal Financial Planning, Vol. 2. 1995. ring bd. write for info. (*1-56433-742-1*) Prctnrs Pub Co.

C

***Clay, John R., et al.** Guide to Personal Financial Planning, Vol. 2. 1999. ring bd. write for info. (*0-7646-0880-0*) Prctnrs Pub Co.

Clay, John R., et al. Guide to Personal Financial Planning, Vol. 3. 1995. ring bd. write for info. (*1-56433-743-X*) Prctnrs Pub Co.

***Clay, John R., et al.** Guide to Personal Financial Planning, Vol. 3. 1999. ring bd. write for info. (*0-7646-0881-9*) Prctnrs Pub Co.

Clay, John R., et al. Guide to Preparing Financial Statements, 3 vols. 1992. write for info. (*1-56433-215-2*) Prctnrs Pub Co.

***Clay, John R., et al.** Guide to Preparing Financial Statements, 3 vols. 1999. ring bd. 164.00 (*0-7646-0865-7*) Prctnrs Pub Co.

Clay, John R., et al. Guide to Preparing Financial Statements, 3 vols., 1. 1992. write for info. (*1-56433-213-6*) Prctnrs Pub Co.

— Guide to Preparing Financial Statements, 3 vols., 1. 1993. ring bd. write for info. (*1-56433-337-X*) Prctnrs Pub Co.

— Guide to Preparing Financial Statements, 3 vols., 2. 1992. write for info. (*1-56433-214-4*) Prctnrs Pub Co.

— Guide to Preparing Financial Statements, 3 vols., 2. 1993. ring bd. write for info. (*1-56433-338-8*) Prctnrs Pub Co.

— Guide to Preparing Financial Statements, 3 vols., Set. 1992. ring bd. 125.00 (*1-56433-212-8*) Prctnrs Pub Co.

— Guide to Preparing Financial Statements, 3 vols., Set. 1993. ring bd. 125.00 (*1-56433-336-1*) Prctnrs Pub Co.

— Guide to Preparing Financial Statements, 3 vols., Set. 1994. ring bd. 129.00 (*1-56433-514-3*) Prctnrs Pub Co.

— Guide to Preparing Financial Statements, 3 vols., Set. 1995. ring bd. 150.00 (*1-56433-736-7*) Prctnrs Pub Co.

— Guide to Preparing Financial Statements, Vol. 1. 1995. ring bd. write for info. (*1-56433-737-5*) Prctnrs Pub Co.

***Clay, John R., et al.** Guide to Preparing Financial Statements, Vol. 1. 1999. ring bd. write for info. (*0-7646-0866-5*) Prctnrs Pub Co.

Clay, John R., et al. Guide to Preparing Financial Statements, Vol. 2. 1995. ring bd. write for info. (*1-56433-738-3*) Prctnrs Pub Co.

***Clay, John R., et al.** Guide to Preparing Financial Statements, Vol. 2. 1999. ring bd. write for info. (*0-7646-0867-3*) Prctnrs Pub Co.

Clay, John R., et al. Guide to Preparing Financial Statements, Vol. 3. 1995. ring bd. write for info. (*1-56433-739-1*) Prctnrs Pub Co.

***Clay, John R., et al.** Guide to Preparing Financial Statements, Vol. 3. 1999. ring bd. write for info. (*0-7646-0868-1*) Prctnrs Pub Co.

Clay, John R., et al. Guide to Preparing Financial Statements, 3 vols., Vol. 3: Trends Volume. 1993. ring bd. write for info. (*1-56433-339-6*) Prctnrs Pub Co.

— Guide to Texas Franchise Tax. 1997. ring bd. 150.00 (*0-7646-0108-3*) Prctnrs Pub Co.

Clay, Lowell T. Valley of the Red Hand. Clay, Gertrude, ed. 352p. 1992. pap. 11.95 (*0-9630124-0-1*) Packsaddle.

Clay, Lucius D. The Papers of General Lucius D. Clay: Germany, 1945-1949, Vol. 1. Smith, Jean E., ed. LC 73-16536. 570p. reprint ed. pap. 176.70 (*0-608-09959-7*, 205643700001) Bks Demand.

— The Papers of General Lucius D. Clay: Germany, 1945-1949, Vol. 2. Smith, Jean E., ed. LC 73-16536. 700p. reprint ed. pap. 200.00 (*0-608-09960-0*, 205643700002) Bks Demand.

Clay, Marie M. Becoming Literate: The Construction of Inner Control. LC 90-24897. 366p. (C). 1991. pap. text 30.00 (*0-435-08574-3*, 08574) Heinemann.

— By Different Paths to Common Outcomes. LC 98-15079. (Illus.). ix, 288p. 1998. pap. 22.50 (*1-57110-087-3*) Stenhse Pubs.

Clay, Marie M. Concepts about Print. 32p. pap. text, teacher ed. write for info. (*0-325-00237-1*) Heinemann.

— Follow Me, Moon. write for info. (*0-325-00235-5*) Heinemann.

— No Shoes! 24p. pap. write for info. (*0-325-00236-3*) Heinemann.

Clay, Marie M. An Observation Survey: Of Early Literacy Achievement. LC 92-46100. 120p. (C). 1993. pap. text 19.50 (*0-435-08763-0*, 08763) Heinemann.

— Observing Young Readers: Selected Papers. LC 82-12047. 242p. (C). (gr. 1). 1982. pap. text 23.00 (*0-435-08208-6*, 08208) Heinemann.

— Quadruplets & Higher Multiple Births. (Clinics in Developmental Medicine Ser.: No. 107). (Illus.). 186p. (C). 1991. text 49.95 (*0-521-41223-4*, Pub. by Mc Keith Pr) Cambridge U Pr.

— Reading Recovery: A Guidebook for Teachers in Training. LC 93-24028. 112p. (C). 1993. pap. text 17.50 (*0-435-08764-9*, 08764) Heinemann.

Clay, Marie M. Running Records for Classroom Teachers. 32p. pap. write for info. (*0-325-00299-1*) Heinemann.

Clay, Marie M. Sand: The Concepts about Print Tests. 20p. (C). 1979. pap. text 5.00 (*0-435-80237-2*, 80237) Heinemann.

— Stones: "Concepts about Print" Tests. 20p. (Orig.). (J). (ps). 1980. pap. text 5.00 (*0-435-00556-1*, 00556) Heinemann.

— What Did I Write? Beginning Writing Behaviour. LC 79-17088. (Illus.). 78p. (C). 1975. pap. text 17.00 (*0-435-01120-0*, 01120) Heinemann.

— Writing Begins at Home: Preparing Children for Writing Before They Go to School. 64p. (Orig.). (C). 1987. pap. 16.00 (*0-435-08452-6*, 08452) Heinemann.

— Writing Begins at Home: Preparing Children for Writing Before They Go to School. (Orig.). 1991. pap. 12.50 (*0-86863-277-5*) Heinemann.

Clay, Marie M., et al. Record of Oral Language & Biks & Gutches. (Illus.). 91p. (Orig.). (C). 1983. pap. text 16.00 (*0-86863-269-4*, 00571) Heinemann.

Clay, Marie M., jt. auth. see Butler, Dorothy.

Clay, Marie M., jt. auth. see Rodriguez, Irene.

Clay, Marilyn. Felicity's Folly. 256p. 1997. mass mkt. 4.99 (*0-8217-5592-7*, Zebra Kensgtn) Kensgtn Pub Corp.

***Clay, Marilyn.** Miss Darby's Debut, Vol. 1. (Zebra Regency Romance Ser.). 1999. mass mkt. 4.99 (*0-8217-6357-1*, Zebra Kensgtn) Kensgtn Pub Corp.

Clay, Marilyn. Miss Eliza's Gentleman Caller. 256p. 1998. mass mkt. 4.99 (*0-8217-6064-5*, Zebra Kensgtn) Kensgtn Pub Corp.

— The Unsuitable Suitor. 256p. 1997. mass mkt. 4.99 (*0-8217-5755-5*, Zebra Kensgtn) Kensgtn Pub Corp.

Clay, Matthew. French Alley. large type ed. 256p. 1994. pap. 18.99 (*1-85389-457-5*) Ulverscroft.

Clay, Maude Schuyler. Delta Land. LC 99-22285. 1999. write for info. (*1-57806-178-4*) U Pr of Miss.

Clay, Mel. Body Lightning. (Illus.). 67p. (Orig.). 1983. pap. text 2.50 (*1-879594-06-4*) Androgyne Bks.

— Jazz-Jail & God: Impressionistic Biography of Bob Kaufman. (Illus.). 108p. (Orig.). 1987. pap. text 8.00 (*1-879594-12-9*) Androgyne Bks.

Clay-Mendez, Deborah. The Costs & Benefits of Retail Activities at Military Bases. (Illus.). 80p. (C). 1998. pap. text 25.00 (*0-7881-4987-3*) DIANE Pub.

Clay, Mike. Cafe Racers-Rockers, Rock 'n' Roll & the Coffee Bar Cult. (Illus.). 192p. 1998. 24.95 (*0-85045-677-0*, Pub. by Ospry) Motorbooks Intl.

Clay, Rebecca. The Arts. LC 94-48996. (Native Latin American Cultures Ser.). 64p. (J). (gr. 4-8). 1995. lib. bdg. 25.27 (*0-86625-551-6*) Rourke Pubns.

— Ties That Bind: Family & Community. Steinhorn, Beth, ed. LC 94-46632. (Our Human Family Ser.). (Illus.). 80p. (YA). (gr. 7 up). 1995. lib. bdg. 22.45 (*1-56711-126-2*) Blackbirch.

Clay, Richard. Nonlinear Networks & Systems. LC 76-127660. (Illus.). 296p. reprint ed. pap. 91.80 (*0-608-10234-2*, 201017900068) Bks Demand.

Clay, Robert A. My Heart's Memory. 63p. 1998. 9.95 (*0-9662444-0-0*) R A Clay.

Clay, Robin. Backgammon: Winning Strategies. 256p. (Orig.). 1996. pap. 22.50 (*0-330-34981-3*, Pub. by Pan) Trans-Atl Phila.

— Teach Yourself Backgammon. (Illus.). 176p. 1994. pap. 8.95 (*0-8442-3907-0*, Teach Yrslf) NTC Contemp Pub Co.

***Clay, Roger.** Cosmic Bullets: High-Energy Particles in Astrophysics. 208p. 1999. pap. text 12.00 (*0-7382-0139-1*, Pub. by Perseus Pubng) HarpC.

Clay, Roger & Dawson, Bruce. Cosmic Bullets: High Energy Particles in Astrophysics. LC 97-166616. (Frontiers of Science Ser.). x, 194 p. 1997. write for info. (*1-86448-204-4*) Allen & Unwin Pty.

Clay, Russell O. From Ghost Through Bone to Man: New & Collected Poems & Plays, 1994-1996. (Illus.). 50p. (Orig.). 1997. pap. 7.00 (*0-9652706-1-0*) West End Poetry.

— Half-Life Poems. 36p. 1996. pap. 7.00 (*0-9652706-0-2*) West End Poetry.

Clay, Sampson. The Present Day Rock Garden. LC 76-1833. (Illus.). 1976. reprint ed. 25.00 (*0-913728-09-8*) Theophrastus.

Clay, Stanley B. Diva: Theater Backstage Terror. 256p. (J). 1988. mass mkt. 3.50 (*0-87067-839-6*) Holloway.

Clay, Steven & Phillips, Rodney. A Secret Location on the Lower East Side: Adventures in Writing, 1960-1980, a Sourcebook of Information. LC 98-24027. (Illus.). 342p. 1998. 44.95 (*1-887123-19-9*); pap. 27.95 (*1-887123-20-2*) Granary Bks.

Clay, Steven & Rothenberg, Jerome, eds. A Book of the Book: Some Works & Projections about the Book & Writing. (Illus.). 544p. 2000. pap. write for info. (*1-887123-28-8*, Pub. by Granary Bks) DAP Assocs.

***Clay, Steven & Rothenberg, Jerome, eds.** A Book of the Book: Some Works & Projections about the Book & Writing. (Illus.). 544p. 2000. 44.95 (*1-887123-29-6*, Pub. by Granary Bks) DAP Assocs.

Clay, Susan. No Man Knows My Story: Emotional Abuse. 195p. 1998. pap. 14.95 (*0-9660284-9-X*) Nelson Bk.

***Clay, Susan B.** Toward Better Teaching: Professional Development in 1993-94. 162p. 1998. pap. 16.00 (*0-16-063663-9*) USGPO.

Clay, Thomas. Briefe, Easie & Necessary Tables for the Valuation of Leases. LC 76-57373. (English Experience Ser.: No. 791). 1977. reprint ed. lib. bdg. 15.00 (*90-221-0791-4*) Walter J Johnson.

Clay, Vidals. Women: Menopause & Middle Age. 1977. per. 5.00 (*0-912786-37-X*) Know Inc.

Clay, Walter L. Prison Chaplain: Memoirs of the Rev. John Clay with Selections from His Reports & Correspondence & a Sketch of Prison Discipline in England. LC 69-16232. (Criminology, Law Enforcement, & Social Problems Ser.: No. 90). 1969. reprint ed. 30.00 (*0-87585-090-1*) Patterson Smith.

Clay-Warner, Jody, jt. ed. see Odem, Mary E.

Clay, Warwick. South Pacific Anchorages. (Illus.). 280p. (C). 1996. pap. 125.00 (*0-85288-362-5*, Pub. by Laurie Norie & Wilson Ltd) St Mut.

Clay, Willard, photos by. The Appalachians: West Virginia, Kentucky & Tennessee. (The Smithsonian Guides to Natural America). (Illus.). 1996. pap. 19.95 (*0-679-76474-7*, Pub. by Smithsonian Bks) Random.

Clay, Willard, et al, photos by. Grand Canyon National Park: A Photographic Natural History. (Illus.). 128p. 1995. 25.95 (*1-56313-611-2*) BrownTrout Pubs Inc.

***Clay, William L.** Just Permanent Interest. (Illus.). 524p. 1999. 24.95 (*1-56743-000-7*, Amistad) HarperTrade.

Clay, William L. Just Permanent Interests: Black Americans in Congress, 1870-1992. rev. ed. LC 92-25191. (Illus.). 432p. (Orig.). 1993. reprint ed. pap. 10.95 (*1-56743-041-4*, Amistad) HarperTrade.

***Clay, William L.** Racism in the White House: A Common Practice of Most United States Presidents. LC 99-52743. 1999. write for info. (*0-88258-206-2*) Howard U Pr.

Clay, William L., Sr. To Kill or Not to Kill: Thoughts on Capital Punishment. Burgess, Michael & Burgess, Mary A., eds. LC 87-812. (Great Issues of the Day Ser.: No. 4). 208p. 1990. pap. 23.00 (*0-89370-431-8*) Millefleurs.

Claybaugh, J. R. & Wade, C. E., eds. Hormonal Regulation of Fluid & Electrolytes: Environmental Effects. LC 89-77900. (Illus.). 254p. 1989. 79.50 (*0-306-43488-1*, Plenum Trade) Perseus Pubng.

Claybaugit, Joseph. History of Clinton County, Indiana. (Illus.). 982p. 1992. reprint ed. lib. bdg. 97.00 (*0-8328-2540-9*) Higginson Bk Co.

Clayborn, Jo C., jt. auth. see Zerwekh, JoAnn.

Clayborne, John, ed. see Peatross, Oscar F.

***Claybourn, Michael.** Infrared Reflectance Spectroscopy of Polymers; Analysis of Films, Surfaces & Interfaces. (Illus.). 250p. 1998. text 99.95 (*1-890086-03-7*) Global Pr MN.

Claybourne, A. ESP? (Paranormal Guides Ser.). (Illus.). 48p. (J). 1999. 13.95 (*1-58086-199-7*) EDC.

— How Do Bees Make Honey? (Starting Point Science Ser.). (Illus.). 24p. (J). (gr. 1 up). 1995. pap. 3.95 (*0-7460-1765-0*, Usborne); lib. bdg. 12.95 (*0-88110-727-1*, Usborne) EDC.

Claybourne, A. & Cunningham, A. Mountain Wildlife. (World Wildlife Ser.). (Illus.). 32p. (J). (gr. 3-7). 1994. lib. bdg. 14.95 (*0-88110-683-6*, Usborne) EDC.

Claybourne, A. & Cunningham, Antonia. Mountain Wildlife. (World Wildlife Ser.). (Illus.). 32p. (J). (gr. 3-7). 1994. pap. 6.95 (*0-7460-1660-3*, Usborne) EDC.

Claybourne, A. & Young, C. Treasure Hunting. 96p. (YA). (gr. 5-9). 1999. 22.95 (*1-58086-163-6*) EDC.

Claybourne, Anna. The Adventures of Ulysses. (Usborne Library of Myths & Legends). (Illus.). 112p. (YA). (gr. 5 up). 1998. pap. 10.95 (*0-7460-2731-1*, Usborne); lib. bdg. 18.95 (*0-88110-971-1*, Usborne) EDC.

— Computer Dictionary for Beginners. (Computer Guides Ser.). (Illus.). 64p. (YA). (gr. 5 up). 1996. pap. 10.95 (*0-7460-1986-6*, Usborne) EDC.

***Claybourne, Anna.** Ghosts & Hauntings. (Illus.). 96p. (gr. 3-7). 2000. 21.95 (*1-58086-268-3*) EDC.

— Read about Tornadoes. (Read about Ser.). (Illus.). 32p. (J). (gr. 2-4). 2000. 17.90 (*0-7613-1200-5*, Copper Beech Bks) Millbrook Pr.

— Read about Volcanoes. (Read about Ser.). (Illus.). 32p. (J). (gr. 2-4). 2000. lib. bdg. 17.90 (*0-7613-1173-4*, Copper Beech Bks) Millbrook Pr.

Claybourne, Anna. Starting Drawing. (First Skills Ser.). (Illus.). 32p. (J). (gr. k-3). 1997. pap. 4.95 (*0-7460-2377-4*, Usborne); lib. bdg. 12.95 (*0-88110-891-X*, Usborne) EDC.

— World Wide Web for Beginners. (Computer Guides Ser.). (Illus.). 48p. (J). (gr. 5 up). 1999. lib. bdg. 18.95 (*0-88110-788-3*, Usborne) EDC.

***Claybourne, Anna, ed.** Ghosts & Hauntings. (Illus.). 96p. (YA). (gr. 3-7). 2000. pap. 21.95 (*0-7460-3716-3*, Pub. by Usbrne Pbng UK) EDC.

Claybourne, Anna, ed. Poltergeists. (Paranormal Guides Ser.). (Illus.). 48p. (YA). (gr. 5 up). 1999. text 5.95 (*0-7460-3058-4*, Usborne) EDC.

***Claybourne, Anna, ed.** Tales of Robin Hood. (Illus.). 96p. (YA). (gr. 3-7). 2000. 19.95 (*0-7460-3791-0*, Pub. by Usbrne Pbng UK) EDC.

***Claybourne, Anna, et al, eds.** Encyclopedia of Planet Earth. (Encyclopedias Ser.). (Illus.). 160p. (YA). (gr. 4-7). 2000. 21.95 (*0-7460-3405-9*, Pub. by Usbrne Pbng UK) EDC.

Claybourne, Anna & Khanduri, Kamini, eds. Greek Myths: Ulysses & Trojan War. (Ulysses & the Trojan War Ser.). (Illus.). 160p. (YA). (gr. 5 up). 1999. 24.95 (*0-7460-3361-3*, Usborne) EDC.

***Claybourne, Anna & King, David.** Brain-Boosting Visual Logic Puzzles. Lagoon Books Staff, ed. (Brain-Boosting Ser.). (Illus.). 192p. 2000. 9.95 (*1-902813-20-0*, Pub. by Lagoon Bks) Midpt Trade.

Claybourne, Anna & Treays, Rebecca. World of Shakespeare. (Illus.). 64p. (J). (gr. 6 up). 1997. pap. 9.95 (*0-7460-2454-1*, Usborne); lib. bdg. 17.95 (*0-88110-916-9*, Usborne) EDC.

Claybourne, Anna & Young, Caroline, eds. The Usborne Book of Treasure Hunting. (Illus.). 96p. (YA). (gr. 5 up). 1999. pap. text 14.95 (*0-7460-3445-8*, Usborne) EDC.

Claybourne, Anna, et al. Drawing, Painting & Lettering. (First Skills Ser.). (Illus.). 32p. (J). (gr. k-3). 1996. pap. 12.95 (*0-7460-2381-2*, Usborne) EDC.

***Claybourne, Anna, et al.** Encyclopedia of Planet Earth. (Usborne Encyclopedia Ser.). (Illus.). 160p. (gr. 4-7). 2000. 29.95 (*1-58086-260-8*) EDC.

Claybourne, Anna, jt. ed. see Brooks, Felicity.

***Claybourne, Casey.** Cat & the Countess. 2000. mass mkt. 5.99 (*0-425-17335-6*) Berkley Pub.

Claybourne, Casey. The Devil's Darling. 208p. (Orig.). 1994. mass mkt. 4.50 (*0-515-11492-8*, Jove) Berkley Pub.

— A Ghost of a Chance. 336p. 1996. mass mkt. 5.99 (*0-515-11857-5*, Jove) Berkley Pub.

— Jaguar Eyes. 368p. 1998. mass mkt. 5.50 (*0-505-52284-5*, Love Spell) Dorchester Pub Co.

— My Lucky Lady. 224p. (Orig.). 1994. mass mkt. 4.50 (*0-515-11504-5*, Jove) Berkley Pub.

— Nick of Time. (Time Passages Romance Ser.). 304p. 1997. mass mkt. 5.99 (*0-515-12189-4*, Jove) Berkley Pub.

— A Spirited Seduction: A Prim & Proper Lady Learns the Art of Seduction--from a Ghost. 304p. 1997. mass mkt. 5.99 (*0-515-12066-9*, Jove) Berkley Pub.

***Claybourne, Casey.** Thing of Beauty. 2000. mass mkt. 6.99 (*0-425-17695-9*) Berkley Pub.

Claybourne, Casey. Tiger by the Tail. 320p. 1999. mass mkt. 5.99 (*0-425-16321-0*) Berkley Pub.

Clayburn, Barbara B. Prairie Stationmaster: The Story of One Man's Railroading Career in Nebraska 1917-1963. LC 78-78305. (Illus.). 128p. 1979. 6.50 (*0-8187-0034-3*) Harlo Press.

***Clayburn, Brenda.** Daddy's Gone. (Illus.). 40p. (J). (gr. k-4). 2000. pap. 7.50 (*1-892614-25-1*, BWP-DG1) Briarwood VA.

Claycomb, Carla. Public Schools, Private Prospects: Lessons from English School Reform. 2nd ed. 24p. 1998. pap. 9.00 (*1-58434-025-8*) NASBE.

Claycomb, Carla, et al. Issues & Trends in Statewide Assessment Systems. 2nd ed. 24p. 1997. pap. 9.00 (*1-58434-009-6*) NASBE.

— Rural Education: What's down the Road for Schools. 2nd ed. Kysilko, David, ed. 36p. 1996. pap. 10.00 (*1-58434-028-2*) NASBE.

Claycomb, Mary. Brain Research & Learning. LC TA0455.. 27p. reprint ed. pap. 30.00 (*0-8357-7377-9*, 202475400038) Bks Demand.

Claycomb, Patty. Busy Classroom. 286p. 1992. pap. 19.95 (*0-87659-159-4*) Gryphon Hse.

— Friends from Around the World: Early Learning Activities That Teach Global & Self-Awareness. (Happy World Ser.). (Illus.). (J). (ps-1). 1995. pap., teacher ed. 8.95 (*1-878279-24-6*, MM 2013) Monday Morning Bks.

— The Learning Circle: A Preschool Teachers Guide to Circle Time. Charner, Kathleen, ed. (Illus.). 224p. (Orig.). 1988. pap. 14.95 (*0-87659-115-2*) Gryphon Hse.

— Love the Earth, Exploring Environmental Activities for Young Children. 1991. pap. 12.95 (*0-933212-47-X*) Partner Pr.

Claycomb, Patty & Bittinger, Gayle. The Best of Totline Bear Hugs. Cubley, Kathleen, ed. (Best of Totline Ser.). (Illus.). 160p. (J). (ps-k). 1999. pap. 14.95 (*1-57029-238-8*, 02603) Totline Pubns.

Claycomb, Patty & McMorrow, Annalisa. Kindergarten Connections. (Ten-Minute Ser.). (Illus.). 352p. (Orig.). (J). (ps-1). 1997. pap. 26.95 (*1-57612-001-5*, MM2033) Monday Morning Bks.

Claycomb, William B. & Brummet, Ed. Pettis County, Missouri: A Pictorial History. LC 98-29022. (Illus.). 1998. 30.00 (*1-57864-043-1*) Donning Co.

Claycomb, William C. Novel Methods in Molecular & Cellular Biochemistry of Muscle. Pierce, Grant N., ed. LC 96-39968. (Developments in Molecular & Cellular Biochemistry Ser.). 304p. (C). 1997. text 289.50 (*0-7923-4387-5*) Kluwer Academic.

Claycomb, William C. & Di Nardo, Paolo, eds. Cardiac Growth & Regeneration. LC 95-2609. (Annals of the New York Academy of Sciences: No. 752). 1995. 135.00 (*0-89766-929-0*) NY Acad Sci.

— Cardiac Growth & Regeneration. LC 95-2609. (Annals of the New York Academy of Sciences: Vol. 752). 1995. pap. 135.00 (*0-89766-930-4*) NY Acad Sci.

***Clayden.** Organolithium Chemistry: A Synthetic Perspective. (Tetrahedron Organic Chemistry Ser.). 2000. 114.50 (*0-08-043262-X*, Pergamon Pr); pap. 49.50 (*0-08-043261-1*, Pergamon Pr) Elsevier.

Clayden, B. & Hewitt, A. E. Horizon Notation for New Zealand Soils. 1989. 8.00 (*0-614-07544-0*, Pub. by Manaaki Whenua) Balogh.

Clayden, B. & Webb, T. H. Criteria for Defining the Soilform: The Fourth Category of the NZ Soil Classification. 1994. 20.00 (*0-478-04523-9*, Pub. by Manaaki Whenua) Balogh.

Clayden, Dwayne E., jt. auth. see Bledsoe, Bryan E.

Clayden, Graham & Agnaarsson, Ulfur. Constipation in Childhood. (Illus.). 128p. 1991. 45.00 (*0-19-262044-4*) OUP.

Clayden, Graham, jt. auth. see Buchanan, Ann.

Clayden, Graham, jt. auth. see Lissauer, Tom.

***Clayden, Jonathan, et al.** Organic Chemistry. (Illus.). 1568p. (C). 2000. pap. text 49.95 (*0-19-850346-6*) OUP.

Claydon, Dina. The Cabin Faced West: A Study Guide. Friedland, Joyce & Kessler, Rikki, eds. (Novel-Ties Ser.). 21p. (J). (gr. 3-5). 1990. pap. text 15.95 (*0-88122-409-X*) Lrn Links.

— Maurice's Room: A Study Guide. Friedland, Joyce & Kessler, Rikki, eds. (Novel-Ties Ser.). (J). (gr. 2-4). 1991. pap. text 15.95 (*0-88122-569-X*) Lrn Links.

— Shoeshine Girl: A Study Guide. Friedland, Joyce & Kessler, Rikki, eds. (Novel-Ties Ser.). 20p. (J). (gr. 3-5). 1990. pap. text 15.95 (*0-88122-396-4*) Lrn Links.

— Stone Fox: A Study Guide. Friedland, Joyce & Kessler, Rikki, eds. (Novel-Ties Ser.). 21p. (J). (gr. 3-5). 1990. pap. text 15.95 (*0-88122-407-3*) Lrn Links.

Claydon, Graham. Time with God: How to Improve Your Daily Devotions. 48p. (Orig.). 1982. mass mkt. 1.95 (*0-310-45202-3*) Zondervan.

Claydon, Janet & Morgan, Jane. The Control & Management of Asbestos in Buildings: A System of Local Rules. 1997. pap. 150.00 (*0-948237-32-5*, Pub. by H&H Sci Cnslts) St Mut.

***Claydon, Jonathan, et al.** Organic Chemistry. (Illus.). 1408p. 2000. text 85.00 (*0-19-850347-4*) OUP.

Claydon, Tony. William III & the Godly Revolution. (Cambridge Studies in Early Modern British History). (Illus.). 288p. (C). 1996. text 64.95 (*0-521-47329-2*) Cambridge U Pr.

Claydon, Tony & McBride, Ian, eds. Protestantism & National Identity: Britain & Ireland, c. 1650-c. 1850. LC 99-211225. (Illus.). 330p. (C). 1999. text 64.95 (*0-521-62077-5*) Cambridge U Pr.

Clayes, Stanley A. Drama & Discussion. 2nd ed. (Illus.). (C). 1978. pap. text 32.20 (*0-13-219030-3*) P-H.

Clayfield, Helen & Hyatt, Robin. Designing Everyday Things: Integrated Projects for the Elementary Classroom. LC 94-8874. 97p. 1994. pap. text 17.50 (*0-435-08359-7*, 08359) Heinemann.

Clayfield, Robin. You Can Have Your Permaculture & Eat It Too. (Illus.). 254p. 1996. 34.95 (*0-646-28784-2*) RDLE INST Bkstre.

An Asterisk (*) at the beginning of an entry indicates that the title is appearing for the first time.

Claymaker, Dan. Bloodline. large type ed. (Dales Large Print Ser.). 170p. 1997. pap. 18.99 (*1-85389-699-3*) Ulverscroft.
— Border Kill. large type ed. (Linford Western Large Print Ser.). 208p. 1998. pap. 17.99 (*0-7089-5190-2*) Ulverscroft.
***Claymaker, Dan.** Go Hang the Man. large type ed. 224p. 1999. pap. 20.99 (*1-85389-945-3*, Dales) Ulverscroft.
— Gun Loose. large type ed. 216p. 2000. pap. 18.99 (*0-7089-5628-9*, Linford) Ulverscroft.
Claymaker, Dan. Hennigan's Law. large type ed. (Linford Western Library). 304p. 1996. pap. 16.99 (*0-7089-7817-7*, Linford) Ulverscroft.
— Hennigan's Reach. large type ed. (Linford Western Library). 256p. 1995. pap. 16.99 (*0-7089-7761-8*, Linford) Ulverscroft.
Clayman, Charles B., ed. The Human Body: An Illustrated Guide to Its Structure, Function, & Disorders. LC 94-37165. (Illus.). 240p. 1995. 29.95 (*1-56458-992-7*) DK Pub Inc.
Clayman, Charles B., jt. ed. see Clayman, Charles R.
Clayman, Charles R. & Clayman, Charles B., eds. American Medical Association Family Medical Guide. 3rd ed. LC 94-2116. (Illus.). 880p. 1994. 39.95 (*0-679-41290-5*) Random.
Clayman, Lewis & Kuo, Paul. Lasers in Maxillofacial Surgery & Dentisty. LC 96-36512. (Illus.). 252p. 1997. text 115.00 (*0-86577-566-4*) Thieme Med Pubs.
Clayman, Ralph V. Flexible Endoscopy of the Urinary Tract. (Illus.). 350p. 2001. pap. text 90.00 (*0-942219-98-8*) Quality Med Pub.
Clayman, Ralph V., et al, eds. Laparoscopic Urology. LC 92-48957. (Illus.). 450p. 1992. pap. 90.00 (*0-942219-41-4*) Quality Med Pub.
Clayman, Ralph V. & McDougall, Elspeth M., eds. Laparoscopic Urology. 2nd ed. 1997. 90.00 (*1-57626-025-9*, C2358) Quality Med Pub.
Claymore, David. Discovery Guide to Syria. 224p. 1995. pap. 50.00 (*1-898162-50-6*, Pub. by IMMEL Pubng) St Mut.
Claypole, Maurice, tr. see Warnecke, Hans-Jurgen & Huser, Manfred.
Claypole, Onat, tr. Sicilian Erotica. LC 96-53354. (Pueti d'Arba Sicula/Poets of Arba Sicula Ser.: Vol. V). (Illus.). 200p. 1997. pap. 20.00 (*1-881901-10-6*) LEGAS.
Claypole, William & Robottom, John. Caribbean Story, Bk. 1: Foundations. (Longman Caribbean Ser.). (Illus.). (Orig.). (C). 1989. pap. 24.60 (*0-582-76534-X*) Longman.
Claypool, et al. Kelsey: Genealogy of the Descendants of William Kelsey, Who Settled at Cambridge, MA, in 1632; at Hartford, CT in 1636; & at Killingsworth, CT, in 1663. (Illus.). 295p. 1991. reprint ed. pap. 47.00 (*0-8328-1796-1*); reprint ed. pap. 66.50 (*0-8328-1798-8*) Higginson Bk Co.
— Kelsey: Genealogy of the Descendants of William Kelsey, Who Settled at Cambridge, MA, in 1632; at Hartford, CT in 1636; & at Killingsworth, CT, in 1663, Vol. 1. (Illus.). 295p. 1991. reprint ed. lib. bdg. 57.00 (*0-8328-1795-3*) Higginson Bk Co.
— Kelsey: Genealogy of the Descendants of William Kelsey, Who Settled at Cambridge, MA, in 1632; at Hartford, CT in 1636; & at Killingsworth, CT, in 1663, Vol. 2. (Illus.). 424p. 1991. reprint ed. lib. bdg. 76.50 (*0-8328-1797-X*) Higginson Bk Co.
Claypool, Gavin, ed. see Pournelle, Jerry.
Claypool, George E., jt. ed. see Magoon, Leslie B.
Claypool, Jabe. Wise Women Don't Worry: Wise Women Don't Get the Blues. rev. ed. 225p. pap. 15.95 (*0-9643948-3-9*) Cornucopia CA.
Claypool, Jane. Saddam Hussein. LC 92-46994. (World Leaders Ser.). 112p. (YA). 1989. lib. bdg. 25.27 (*0-86625-477-3*) Rourke Pubns.
— Science of Mind Skills. 154p. 1994. pap. 14.95 (*0-9643948-0-4*) Cornucopia CA.
— Science of Mind Skills. rev. ed. 195p. Date not set. pap. 16.95 (*0-9643948-2-0*) Cornucopia CA.
— Wise Women Don't Worry: Wise Women Don't Get the Blues. 263p. 1996. pap. 11.95 (*0-9643948-1-2*) Cornucopia CA.
***Claypool, John.** Glad Reunion: Meeting Ourselves in the Lives of Bible Men & Women. rev. ed. LC 00-8193. 2000. write for info. (*0-914520-40-7*) Insight Pr.
Claypool, John. Mending the Heart. LC 99-19448. 1999. 8.95 (*1-56101-165-7*) Cowley Pubns.
— Tracks of a Fellow Struggler: How to Handle Grief. rev. ed. LC 95-6933. 1995. pap. 10.00 (*0-914520-35-0*) Insight Pr.
Claypool, John, et al. Protestant Hour Classics: The Twelve Most Requested Sermons. LC 92-12752. 112p. (Orig.). 1992. pap. 2.69 (*0-687-34377-1*) Abingdon.
Claypool, John R. God Is an Amateur. 88p. (Orig.). 1994. pap. 4.95 (*0-88028-147-2*, 1241) Forward Movement.
***Claypoole, Antoinette & Doubiago, Sharon.** Who Would Unbraid Her Hair: The Legend of Annie Mae. 320p. 1999. pap. 21.00 (*0-9673853-0-X*) Anam Cara Pr.
Claypoole, James. James Claypoole's Letter Book: London & Philadelphia, 1681-1684. Balderston, Marion, ed. LC 66-25063. 256p. 1967. 12.00 (*0-87328-027-X*) Huntington Lib.
Claypoole, Joanne. Beginner's Japanese. (Beginner's Language Ser.). (ENG & JPN.). 290p. (Orig.). 1994. pap. 11.95 (*0-7818-0234-2*) Hippocrene Bks.
Claypoole, Richard L., ed. United States Government Manual, 1996-1997. 860p. (C). 1998. pap. text 55.00 (*0-7881-7303-0*) DIANE Pub.
Claypoole, Richard L. & Ramey, Gladys Q. Guide to Record Retention Requirements in the Code of Federal Regulations. 550p. 1996. reprint ed. pap. text 45.00 (*0-7881-3648-8*) DIANE Pub.
Clayson, Alan. Beat Merchants: The Origins, History, Impact & Rock Legacy of the 1960's British Pop Groups. (Illus.). 320p. 1997. pap. 16.95 (*0-7137-2462-5*, Pub. by Blandford Pr) Sterling.
— Death Discs: An Account of Fatality in the Popular Song. (Illus.). 213p. (YA). 1997. pap. 19.95 (*1-86074-195-9*, SG00630, Pub. by Sanctuary Pubng) Music Sales.
— Hamburg: The Cradle of British Rock. 287p. 1997. pap. 14.95 (*1-86074-221-1*, SG00639, Pub. by Sanctuary Pubng) Music Sales.
— Only the Lonely: The Roy Orbison Story. 10th ed. Date not set. pap. 19.95 (*1-86074-241-6*, SGoo664) Music Sales.
— The Quiet One: George Harrison. 300p. pap. 14.95 (*1-86074-184-3*, Pub. by Sanctuary Pubng) Music Sales.
— Ringo: Straight Man or Joker? 240p. pap. 14.95 (*1-86074-189-4*, Pub. by Sanctuary Pubng) Music Sales.
***Clayson, Alan & Ryan, Jacqueline.** Rock's Wild Things: The Troggs Files. (Illus.). 2000. pap. 18.95 (*1-900924-19-6*, Pub. by Helter Skelter) Interlink Pub.
Clayson, Alan, jt. auth. see Hinton, Brian.
Clayson, D. B., jt. auth. see Krewski, D.
Clayson, Edward. Historical Narratives of Puget Sound, Hood's Canal, 1865-1885. LC 95-13416. 1998. 19.95 (*0-87770-547-X*) Ye Galleon.
Clayson, Hollis. Painted Love: Prostitution in French Art of the Impressionist Era. (Illus.). 232p. 1992. 55.00 (*0-300-04730-4*) Yale U Pr.
***Clayson, Hollis.** Paris In Despair. 1998. 60.00 (*0-226-10951-8*) U Ch Pr.
Clayton. Appleworks -- Integrated Applications. (DF - Computer Applications Ser.). 1986. mass mkt. 23.25 (*0-538-23151-3*) S-W Pub.
— Appleworks - Integrated Applications for Microcomputer. 2nd ed. (DF - Computer Applications Ser.). 1990. mass mkt. 27.95 (*0-538-60441-7*) S-W Pub.
— Appleworks Integrated Applications. 2nd ed. (DF - Computer Applications Ser.). (C). 1990. mass mkt. 30.95 (*0-538-60443-3*) S-W Pub.
— Appleworks Integrated Applications: Microcomputer. (DF - Computer Applications Ser.). 1986. 67.75 (*0-538-23152-1*) S-W Pub.
— Drums of Chaos, No. 3. 2000. text 22.95 (*0-312-86120-6*) St Martin.
***Clayton.** Economics: Principles & Practices. 1999. teacher ed. write for info. (*0-02-823560-6*) Glencoe.
Clayton. A History of Latin America. LC 98-72417. (C). 1998. pap. text 39.00 (*0-15-500253-8*, Pub. by Harcourt Coll Pubs) Harcourt.
— Line Rollering Simulation. 4th ed. (TA - Typing/Keyboarding Ser.). 1996. mass mkt. 18.95 (*0-538-65094-X*) S-W Pub.
— Math of Money. (MA - Academic Math Ser.). 1994. text, teacher ed. 107.95 (*0-538-63497-9*) S-W Pub.
— Math of Money: With Algebra. (Ma - Academic Math Ser.). 1994. pap. 93.95 (*0-538-63472-3*) S-W Pub.
— Math of Money with Algebra - Extension Activities. (MA - Academic Math Ser.). 1994. mass mkt. 11.95 (*0-538-63496-0*) S-W Pub.
— Mathematics of Money with Algebra. (MA - Academic Math Ser.). 1994. mass mkt. 51.95 (*0-538-63471-5*) S-W Pub.
— 121 Timed Writings with Selected Drills. 5th ed. (TA - Typing/Keyboarding Ser.). 1991. mass mkt. 14.25 (*0-538-60169-8*) S-W Pub.
— Supreme Court Decision Making. LC 98-20662. 1999. pap. text 19.00 (*0-226-10955-0*); lib. bdg. 55.00 (*0-226-10954-2*) U Ch Pr.
— Timed Writings about Careers. 3rd ed. (TA - Typing/Keyboarding Ser.). 1984. mass mkt. 14.25 (*0-538-20790-6*) S-W Pub.
— Timed Writings about Careers: Template D. 3rd ed. (TA - Typing/Keyboarding Ser.). 1988. 80.25 (*0-538-20795-7*) S-W Pub.
Clayton, A. C. A Key to Rev. Pope's: A Handbook of the Tamil Language. (C). 1985. reprint ed. 12.00 (*0-317-93332-9*, Pub. by Asian Educ Servs) S Asia.
Clayton, Al. Critter Cuisine. 1996. pap. 9.95 (*1-56352-356-6*) Longstreet.
Clayton, Alana. Headstrong Heart. 224p. 1999. mass mkt. 4.99 (*0-8217-6183-8*, Zebra Kensgtn) Kensgtn Pub Corp.
— Heart's Deceit. 288p. 1996. mass mkt. 4.50 (*0-8217-5322-3*) Kensgtn Pub Corp.
— Phantom Husband. (Zebra Regency Romance Ser.). 256p. 1998. mass mkt. 4.99 (*0-8217-6063-7*, Zebra Kensgtn) Kensgtn Pub Corp.
***Clayton, Alana.** Spring Kittens. 2000. mass mkt. 4.99 (*0-8217-6538-8*, Zebra Kensgtn) Kensgtn Pub Corp.
Clayton, Alana. The Willful Wife. 256p. 1998. pap. 4.99 (*0-8217-5870-5*, Zebra Kensgtn) Kensgtn Pub Corp.
Clayton, Alana, et al. Seductive & Scandalous. 288p. 1997. mass mkt. 4.99 (*0-8217-5713-X*, Zebra Kensgtn) Kensgtn Pub Corp.
Clayton, Alfred, tr. see Badura-Skoda, Paul.
Clayton, Alfred, tr. see Durr.
Clayton, Alfred S. Emergent Mind & Education: A Study of George H. Mead's Bio-Social Behaviorism from an Educational Point of View. LC 70-176694. (Columbia University. Teachers College. Contributions to Education Ser.: No. 867). reprint ed. 37.50 (*0-404-55867-4*) AMS Pr.
Clayton, Andrew & Davis, Ian. Building for Safety Compendium: An Annotated Bibliography & Information Directory for Safe Building Programs in Disaster-Prone Areas. LC 94-129122. (Building for Safety Ser.). 56p. 1994. pap. 17.50 (*1-85339-181-6*, Pub. by Intermed Tech) Stylus Pub VA.
Clayton, Andrew, jt. auth. see Fulton, Nancy.
Clayton, Ann. Martin-Leake: The First Man Ever to Be Awarded the Victoria Cross Twice. (Illus.). 256p. 1994. 31.95 (*0-85052-397-4*, Pub. by Leo Cooper) Trans-Atl Phila.
Clayton, Anne. Insight into a Career in Pharmaceutical Sales. (Illus.). 105p. 1998. pap. 29.95 (*0-9665121-0-3*) Mktg Essentials.
***Clayton, Anne.** Insight into a Career in Pharmaceutical Sales. 2nd rev. ed. (Illus.). 140p. 1999. pap. 39 90 (*0-9665121-1-1*) Mktg Essentials.
Clayton, Anthony. Communication for New Loyalties: African Soldier's Songs. LC M 1831.C6. (Papers in International Studies: Africa Ser.: No. 34). 70p. reprint ed. pap. 30.00 (*0-608-10698-4*, 200785100068) Bks Demand.
— Counter-Insurgency in Kenya: A Study of Military Operations Against Mau Mau, 1952-1960. 64p. 1984. pap. text 12.00 (*0-89745-061-2*) Sunflower U Pr.
— Forearmed: A History of the Intelligence Corps. (Illus.). 320p. 1993. 33.00 (*0-08-037701-7*, Pub. by Brasseys) Brasseys.
— Frontiersman: Warfare in Africa Since 1950. 1999. pap. text 24.95 (*1-85728-525-5*) Taylor & Francis.
— Frontiersman: Warfare in Africa Since 1950. 1999. 79.00 (*1-85728-524-7*) UCL Pr Ltd.
— The 1948 Zanzibar General Strike. (Research Report Ser.: No. 32). 66p. 1976. write for info. (*91-7106-094-4*, Pub. by Nordic Africa) Transaction Pubs.
— Three Marshals of France: Leadership after Trauma. (Illus.). 229p. 1992. 41.00 (*0-08-040707-2*, Pub. by Brasseys) Brasseys.
— The Wars of French Decolonization. LC 93-29506. (Modern Wars in Perspective Ser.). 256p. (C). 1995. pap. text 34.80 (*0-582-09801-7*) Longman.
— The Wars of French Decolonization: Modern Wars in Perspective. LC 93-29506. (Modern Wars in Perspective Ser.). (C). 1994. text 62.50 (*0-582-09802-5*) Longman.
Clayton, Anthony & Killingray, David. Khaki & Blue: Military & Police in British Colonial Africa. LC 88-34914. (Monographs in International Studies, Africa: No. 51). 347p. 1988. pap. text 20.00 (*0-89680-147-0*) Ohio U Pr.
***Clayton, Anthony & Russell, Alan, eds.** Dresden: A City Reborn. (Illus.). 256p. 2001. pap. 19.50 (*1-85973-441-3*, Pub. by Berg Pubs) NYU Pr.
— Dresden: A City Returns. (Illus.). 256p. 1999. 49.00 (*1-85973-229-1*, Pub. by Berg Pubs) NYU Pr.
Clayton, Anthony & Savage, Donald C. Government & Labour in Kenya, 1895-1963. 480p. 1974. 55.00 (*0-7146-3025-X*, Pub. by F Cass Pubs) Intl Spec Bk.
Clayton, Anthony M. & Radcliffe, Nicholas J. Sustainability: A Systems Approach. 272p. (C). 1996. pap. 32.00 (*0-8133-3185-4*, Pub. by Westview) HarpC.
***Clayton, Ashleigh Bryce.** A Gentle Spirit Devotional Journal. 384p. 2000. 19.97 (*1-57748-820-2*) Barbour Pub.
Clayton, B. E. Paediatric Chemical Pathology. 176p. 1980. pap. 24.95 (*0-632-00564-5*) Blackwell Sci.
Clayton, B. R. Mechanics of Marine Vehicles. LC 82-81291. 612p. 1982. pap. text 189.80 (*0-608-04972-7*, 206555200004) Bks Demand.
Clayton, Barbara & Whitley, Kathleen. Guide to Flemington, New Jersey. LC 87-27843. (Illus.). 192p. 1987. pap. 6.95 (*0-940001-01-2*) Clayton & Whitley.
— Guide to New Bedford. rev. ed. LC 79-54908. (Illus.). 186p. 1986. reprint ed. pap. 6.95 (*0-87106-035-3*) Clayton & Whitley.
Clayton, Barbara E. & Round, Joan M. Clinical Biochemistry & the Sick Child. 2nd ed. LC 93-38329. (Illus.). 576p. 1994. 175.00 (*0-632-03681-8*, Pub. by Blckwll Scitfc UK) Blackwell Sci.
Clayton, Bernard. Bernard Clayton's Complete Book of Small Breads. LC 97-46552. 287p. 1998. 24.50 (*0-684-82692-5*) S&S Trade.
Clayton, Bernard, Jr. Bernard Clayton's New Complete Book of Breads. (Illus.). 752p. 1987. 30.00 (*0-671-60222-5*) S&S Trade.
Clayton, Bernard. Bernard Clayton's New Complete Book of Breads. expanded rev. ed. (Illus.). 752p. 1995. per. 20.00 (*0-684-81174-X*) S&S Trade Pap.
Clayton, Bernard, Jr. The Complete Book of Soups & Stews. (Illus.). 416p. 1987. pap. 13.00 (*0-671-43864-6*, Fireside) S&S Trade Pap.
Clayton, Blondie. The Touch of the Master's Hand: A Journey into Stolen Innocence. 227p. (Orig.). 1996. pap. 10.00 (*0-9653700-0-3*) B L Pubng.
***Clayton, Brad.** The Queen of Hearts; a Transsexual Romance. Carno, Deni, ed. (Illus.). 200p. 1999. pap. 12.95 (*0-9665900-0-7*) E R Pubns.
Clayton, Bruce. Forgotten Prophet: The Life of Randolph Bourne. LC 97-46993. (Illus.). 296p. 1998. pap. 19.95 (*0-8262-1179-6*) U of Mo Pr.
— Praying for Base Hits: An American Boyhood. LC 98-21276. (Illus.). 280p. 1998. pap. 16.95 (*0-8262-1189-5*) U of Mo Pr.
— Survival Books, 1981. LC 81-80117. (Illus.). 180p. (Orig.). 1981. pap. 14.95 (*0-939216-00-0*) Media West.
— W. J. Cash: A Life. LC 90-43462. (Southern Biography Ser.). (Illus.). 256p. 1991. 24.95 (*0-8071-1647-5*) La State U Pr.
— W. J. Cash: A Life. (Illus.). 256p. 1997. pap. 13.95 (*0-8071-2215-7*) La State U Pr.
***Clayton, Bruce & Salmond, John.** Debating Southern History: Ideas & Actions in the Twentieth Century. LC 99-37014. (Debating Twentieth-Century America Ser.). 208p. 1999. text 50.00 (*0-8476-9413-5*) Rowman.
***Clayton, Bruce & Salmond, John A.** Debating Southern History: Ideas & Actions in the Twentieth Century. LC 99-37014. (Debating Twentieth-Century America Ser.). 208p. 1999. pap. 16.95 (*0-8476-9414-3*) Rowman.
Clayton, Bruce, ed. see Salmond, John A.
Clayton, Bruce D. Basic Pharmacology for Nurses. (C). text. write for info. (*981-4020-71-0*) Harcourt Coll Pubs.
— Basic Pharmacology for Nurses. 192p. (C). (gr. 13). 1996. pap. text, teacher ed. write for info. (*0-8151-2147-4*, 30758) Mosby Inc.
— Forgotten Prophet: The Life of Randolph Bourne. fac. ed. LC 84-5748. 287p. 1984. reprint ed. pap. 89.00 (*0-7837-7726-4*, 204748200007) Bks Demand.
Clayton, Bruce D. Life after Doomsday. (Illus.). 200p. 1980. 29.95 (*0-87364-175-2*) Paladin Pr.
Clayton, Bruce D. & Stock. Basic Pharmacology for Nurses. 11th ed. (Illus.). 624p. (C). (gr. 13). 1996. pap. text 37.00 (*0-8151-1512-1*, 28266) Mosby Inc.
— Basic Pharmacology for Nurses. 11th ed. 208p. (C). (gr. 13). 1996. pap. text, student ed. 14.95 (*0-8151-1508-3*, 28268) Mosby Inc.
Clayton, Bruce D. & Stock, Yvonne N. Basic Pharmacology for Nurses: Text & Student Learning Guide Package, Set. 11th ed. (Illus.). (C). 1997. text, student ed. write for info. (*0-8151-1513-X*) Mosby Inc.
Clayton, Bruce L. & Salmond, John A., eds. The South Is Another Land: Essays on the Twentieth-Century South, 124. LC 86-29625. (Contributions in American History Ser.: No. 124). 230p. 1987. 59.95 (*0-313-25556-3*, CMR/, Greenwood Pr) Greenwood.
Clayton, Bryan. High Performance Windows NT4 Optimization & Performance Tuning. 10th ed. LC 98-136329. (CTI Coriolis Ser.). 600p. (C). 1997. pap., mass mkt. 49.99 incl. cd-rom (*1-57610-164-9*) Coriolis Grp.
Clayton, C. G., ed. Nuclear Geophysics: Selected Papers on Applications of Nuclear Techniques in Minerals Exploration, Mining & Process Control. (Illus.). 479p. 1983. 55.00 (*0-08-029158-9*, 82-24570, Pergamon Pr) Elsevier.
Clayton, C. P. The Hungary One. Clayton, Michael, ed. 244p. (C). 1978. text 39.00 (*0-85088-850-6*, Pub. by Gomer Pr) St Mut.
Clayton, C. R., ed. Retaining Structures. 840p. 1993. 134.00 (*0-7844-1932-9*) Am Soc Civil Eng.
— Retaining Structures: Proceedings of the Conference Retaining Structures Organized by the Institution of Civil Engineers, Held at Robinson College, Cambridge, July 20-23, 1992. 840p. 1993. 134.00 (*0-7277-1932-7*) Am Soc Civil Eng.
Clayton, C. R., et al, eds. Advances in Coatings Technologies for Surface Engineering. LC 96-80434. (Illus.). 367p. 1997. 94.00 (*0-87339-371-6*, 3716) Minerals Metals.
Clayton, C. R. & Hashimoto, K., eds. Proceedings of the Symposium on Corrosion, Electrochemistry, & Catalysis of Metastable Metals & Intermetallics. LC 93-70061. (Proceedings Ser.: Vol. 93-30). 420p. 1994. 43.00 (*1-56677-057-2*) Electrochem Soc.
Clayton, C. R., et al. Site Investigation. 2nd ed. LC 94-44383. (Illus.). 464p. 1995. 99.95 (*0-632-02908-0*) Blackwell Sci.
Clayton, C. R. I., et al. Earth Pressure & Earth-Retaining Structures. 2nd ed. (Illus.). 408p. 1993. text 178.95 (*0-7514-0067-X*, Pub. by B Acad & Prof) Routldge.
Clayton, C. Whitney, Jr. Angels in the Snow. 256p. 1999. 23.00 (*0-8059-4741-8*) Dorrance.
Clayton-Carroll, Aline, ed. see Eichstaedt, Helen.
Clayton, Cathy. Healing for the Nation. 1998. pap. 10.00 (*1-57502-713-5*, PO2006) Morris Pubng.
Clayton, Cherry. Olive Schreiner. LC 96-36020. 1997. 32.00 (*0-8057-8287-7*, Twyne) Mac Lib Ref.
Clayton, Cheryl. Mathematics of Money. (MA - Academic Math Ser.). 1991. mass mkt. 55.95 (*0-538-61450-1*) S-W Pub.
Clayton, Christal. How to Invest Money with God. 64p. 1982. pap. 3.25 (*0-88144-093-0*) Christian Pub.
— Idea Book. 124p. 1977. pap. 10.95 (*0-88144-100-7*) Christian Pub.
Clayton, Christopher L. & Mobley, Harry L. T., eds. Helicobacter Pylori Protocols. LC 97-9080. (Methods in Molecular Medicine Ser.: Vol. 8). (Illus.). 288p. 1997. 99.50 (*0-89603-381-3*) Humana.
Clayton, Clay Worthington. Prisoners of Hope. 277p. 1998. pap. 5.95 (*1-888422-00-9*) Frost Pub.
Clayton, Clive R., ed. see Metallurgical Society of AIME Staff.
Clayton, Colin G., ed. Modern Developments in Flow Measurement: Proceedings of the International Conference Held at Harwell, September 21-23, 1971. LC 73-173002. (PPL Conference Publication Ser.: Vol. 10). (Illus.). 415p. reprint ed. pap. 128.70 (*0-608-17793-8*, 203225800079) Bks Demand.
Clayton, Cornell W. The Politics of Justice: The Attorney General & the Making of Legal Policy. LC 92-30711. (American Political Institutions & Public Policy Ser.). 296p. (gr. 13). 1992. text 75.95 (*1-56324-018-1*); pap. text 38.95 (*1-56324-019-X*) M E Sharpe.
Clayton, Cornell W., ed. Government Lawyers: The Federal Legal Bureaucracy & Presidential Politics. LC 95-6288. (Studies in Government & Public Policy). 288p. 1995. 35.00 (*0-7006-0706-4*) U Pr of KS.
Clayton, Cornell W., jt. ed. see Gillman, Howard.
Clayton, Dale H. & Moore, Janice, eds. Host-Parasite Evolution: General Principles & Avian Models. LC 96-21800. (Illus.). 486p. 1997. text 110.00 (*0-19-854893-1*); pap. text 45.00 (*0-19-854892-3*) OUP.
***Clayton, Daniel W.** Islands of Truth: The Imperial Fashioning of Vancouver Island. (Illus.). 256p. 2000. text 75.00 (*0-7748-0741-5*) UBC Pr.
— Islands of Truth: The Imperial Fashioning of Vancouver Island. (Illus.). 256p. 2000. pap. 24.95 (*0-7748-0742-3*) UBC Pr.
Clayton, David. Imperialism Revisited: Political & Economic Relations Between Britain & China, 1950-54. LC 96-49262. (Studies in Military & Strategic History Ser.). 256p. 1997. text 65.00 (*0-312-17320-2*) St Martin.

C

Clayton, David & Hills, Michael. Statistical Models in Epidemiology. (Illus.). 376p. (C). 1993. text 69.95 (*0-19-852221-5*, 7713) OUP.

Clayton, Derek. Running to the Top. LC 79-64297. (Illus.). 160p. 1980. pap. 5.95 (*0-89037-212-8*) Anderson World.

— Running to the Top. 1983. pap. 5.95 (*0-02-499740-4*, Macmillan Coll) P-H.

Clayton, Don. Motif Programming Tips & Tricks. (C). 2001. pap., pap. text 39.95 incl. cd-rom (*0-13-588212-5*) P-H.

Clayton, Donald D. Principles of Stellar Evolution & Nucleosynthesis. LC 83-5106. (Illus.). xii, 634p. 1984. reprint ed. pap. text 26.00 (*0-226-10953-4*) U Ch Pr.

Clayton, Donna. Adopted Dad: Bundles of Joy. (Romance Ser.). 2000. per. 3.50 (*0-373-19417-X*, 1-19417-4) Silhouette.

***Clayton, Donna.** Amores Robados (Stolen Loves) His Ten-Year-Old Secret. (Bianca Ser.: No. 196). (SPA.). 2000. per. 3.50 (*0-373-33546-6*, 1-33546-2) Silhouette.

Clayton, Donna. Beauty & the Bachelor Dad. (Single Daddy Club Ser.). 1997. per. 3.25 (*0-373-19223-1*, 1-19223-6) Silhouette.

— The Boss & the Beauty: Virgin Bride/Loving the Boss. (Romance Ser.). 1998. per. 3.50 (*0-373-19342-4*, 1-19342-4) Silhouette.

— Daddy down the Aisle. (Romance Ser.: No. 1162). 1996. per. 3.25 (*0-373-19162-6*, 1-19162-6) Silhouette.

***Clayton, Donna.** The Doctor's Medicine Woman. (Romance Ser.: Bk. 1483). 2000. mass mkt. 3.50 (*0-373-19483-8*, 1-19483-6) Silhouette.

Clayton, Donna. Fortune's Bride. 1995. per. 2.99 (*0-373-19118-9*, 1-19118-8) Silhouette.

— Her Dream Come True. (Romance Ser.: No. 1399). 1999. per. 3.50 (*0-373-19399-8*, 1-19399-4) Silhouette.

— His Ten - Year - Old Secret: Fabulous Fathers. (Romance Ser.: No. 1374). 1999. per. 3.50 (*0-373-19373-4*, 1-19374-7) Silhouette.

***Clayton, Donna.** His Wild Young Bride: Virgin Bride. 2000. per. 3.50 (*0-373-19441-2*) Silhouette.

Clayton, Donna. Miss Maxwell Becomes a Mom. (Romance Ser.). 1997. per. 3.25 (*0-373-19211-8*, 1-192111) Silhouette.

— Nanny & the Professor: (Fabulous Fathers) (Romance Ser.). 1995. per. 2.99 (*0-373-19066-2*, 1-19066-9) Silhouette.

— Nanny in the Nick of Time. (Single Daddy Club Ser.). 1997. per. 3.25 (*0-373-19217-7*, 1-19217-8) Silhouette.

***Clayton, Donna.** The Nanny Proposal. (Romance Ser.: Bk. 1477). 2000. mass mkt. 3.50 (*0-373-19477-3*, 1-19477-8) Silhouette.

— Une Patron Trop Serieux. (FRE.). 2000. mass mkt. 3.99 (*0-373-39541-8*) Harlequin Bks.

— Rachel & the M.D. 2001. mass mkt. 3.50 (*0-373-19489-7*) Silhouette.

Clayton, Donna. Return of the Runaway Bride. (Romance Ser.). 1994. per. 2.75 (*0-373-08999-6*, 5-08999-0) Silhouette.

— Souvenirs Enfuis. (Horizon Ser.: Bk. 493). 1999. mass mkt. 3.50 (*0-373-39493-4*, 1-39493-1) Harlequin Bks.

— The Stand-By Significant Other. 1998. per. 3.50 (*0-373-19284-3*, 1-19284-8) Silhouette.

— Who's the Father of Jenny's Baby? 1998. per. 3.50 (*0-373-19302-5*, 1-19302-8) Silhouette.

— Wife for a While. 1994. per. 2.75 (*0-373-19039-5*, 1-19039-6) Harlequin Bks.

Clayton, Dorothy J., et al, eds. Trade, Devotion & Governance: Papers in Later Medieval History. LC 94-22173. 1994. 53.95 (*0-7509-0594-8*, Pub. by Sutton Pub Ltd) Intl Pubs Mktg.

Clayton, Douglas. Floyd Dell: The Life & Times of an American Rebel. LC 94-18653. (Illus.). 352p. 1994. text 30.00 (*1-56663-059-2*) I R Dee.

Clayton, Ed. Martin Luther King: Peaceful Warrior. (J). (gr. 3 up). 1996. pap. 3.50 (*0-614-15694-7*, Archway) PB.

— Martin Luther King: The Peaceful Warrior. MacDonald, Pat, ed. (Illus.). 128p. (J). (gr. 4-6). 1991. per. 3.50 (*0-671-73242-0*, Archway) PB.

Clayton, Edward Taylor. Martin Luther King: The Peaceful Warrior. 1996. 8.35 (*0-606-03932-5*, Pub. by Turtleback) Demco.

Clayton, Elaine. The Yeoman's Daring Daughter: And the Princes in the Tower. LC 98-20573. 40p. (J). (gr. k-3). 1999. lib. bdg. 18.99 (*0-517-70985-6*) Crown Pub Group.

— The Yeoman's Daring Daughter & the Princes in the Tower. LC 98-20573. 40p. (J). (gr. k-3). 1999. 17.00 (*0-517-70984-8*) Crown Pub Group.

Clayton, Ellen. English Female Artists, 2 vols. 1976. lib. bdg. 250.00 (*0-8490-1774-2*) Gordon Pr.

Clayton, Ellen C. Queens of Song: Being Memoirs of Some of the Most Celebrated Female Vocalists. LC 77-38713. (Essay Index Reprint Ser.). 1977. reprint ed. 33.95 (*0-8369-2640-4*) Ayer.

Clayton, Elspeth. Pakistan. LC 95-26779. (Worldfocus Ser.). (J). 1998. 18.50 (*1-57572-077-9*) Heinemann Lib.

Clayton, Eve. New York's 100 Best Little Places to Shop. LC 98-35314. (Illus.). 160p. (Orig.). 1998. pap. 14.00 (*1-885492-70-7*) City & Co.

Clayton, Florence E., jt. auth. see Clayton, George D.

Clayton, Florence E., jt. ed. see Clayton, George D.

***Clayton, G. B. & Winder, Steve.** Operational Amplifiers. 4th ed. 448p. 2000. pap. 49.95 (*0-7506-4643-8*, Newnes) Buttrwrth-Heinemann.

Clayton, Gary E. A Guide to Everyday Economic Statistics. 3rd ed. LC 95-161855. (C). 1994. pap. 14.06 (*0-07-011336-X*) McGraw.

Clayton, Gary E. & Giesbrecht, Martin G. A Guide to Everyday Economic Statistics. 4th ed. 1997. pap., student ed. 14.38 (*0-07-109308-7*) McGraw.

Clayton, Gary E., jt. auth. see Giesbrecht, Martin G.

Clayton, George. Spectacle Frame Dispensing. (C). 1989. 110.00 (*0-900099-04-6*, Pub. by Assn Brit Dispen Opticians) St Mut.

Clayton, George B., jt. auth. see Newby, Bruce W.

Clayton, George D. & Clayton, Florence E. Patty's Industrial Hygiene & Toxicology Vol. 1: General Principles, Pts. A & B. 4th ed. 2199p. 1991. 435.00 (*0-471-55205-4*) Wiley.

— Patty's Industrial Hygiene & Toxicology Vol. 2, Pt. C: Toxicology, Vol. 2. 4th ed. 736p. 1994. 249.00 (*0-471-54726-3*) Wiley.

Clayton, George D. & Clayton, Florence E., eds. Patty's Industrial Hygiene & Toxicology, 3 vols. 4th ed. 9004p. 1995. 2199.00 (*0-471-13654-9*) Wiley.

— Patty's Industrial Hygiene & Toxicology, 3 vols., Vol. 3. 42p. 1996. cd-rom 2495.00 (*0-471-13530-5*) Wiley.

— Patty's Industrial Hygiene & Toxicology Vol. 1, Pt. A: General Principles, Vol. 1, Pt. A, General Principles. 4th ed. LC 90-13080. 1104p. 1991. 249.00 (*0-471-50197-2*) Wiley.

— Patty's Industrial Hygiene & Toxicology Vol. 1, Pt. B: General Principles, Vol. 1, Pt. B, General Principles. 4th ed. 1120p. 1991. 249.00 (*0-471-50196-4*) Wiley.

— Patty's Industrial Hygiene & Toxicology Vol. 2 & 6: Toxicology, Vol. 2. 4th ed. 5130p. 1994. 1295.00 (*0-471-54727-1*) Wiley.

— Patty's Industrial Hygiene & Toxicology Vol. 2, Pt. D: Toxicology, Vol. 2, Pt. D, Toxicology. 4th ed. 896p. 1994. 249.00 (*0-471-57947-5*) Wiley.

— Patty's Industrial Hygiene & Toxicology Vol. 2, Pt. A: Toxicology, Vol. 2. 4th ed. 968p. 1993. 249.00 (*0-471-54724-7*) Wiley.

— Patty's Industrial Hygiene & Toxicology Vol. 2, Pt. B: Toxicology, Vol. 2. 4th ed. 752p. 1993. 249.00 (*0-471-54725-5*) Wiley.

— Patty's Industrial Hygiene & Toxicology Vol. 2, Pt. E: Toxicology, Vol. 2. 4th ed. 1020p. 1994. 249.00 (*0-471-01282-3*) Wiley.

— Patty's Industrial Hygiene & Toxicology Vol. 2, Pt. F: Toxicology, Vol. 2. 4th ed. 760p. 1994. 249.00 (*0-471-01280-7*) Wiley.

Clayton, George T. The Site Plan for Architectural Working Drawings. (Illus.). 42p. (C). 1973. pap. text 6.80 (*0-87563-252-1*) Stipes.

Clayton, Gloria & Baj, Pamela, eds. Review of Research in Nursing Education, Vol. III. 192p. 1990. 9.95 (*0-88737-486-7*) Natl League Nurse.

Clayton, Gloria & Broome, Marion. Instruments for Use in Nursing Education Research. Moody, Linda & Shannon, Moira, eds. 64p. 1989. 8.50 (*0-88737-424-7*) Natl League Nurse.

Clayton, Gloria, jt. ed. see Baj, Pamela.

Clayton-Goldner, Susan. Just Another Heartbeat. Hageman, Georgi, ed. 282p. 1997. pap. 12.95 (*0-9658940-0-2*) Ballard Ave.

Clayton-Goldner, Susan, et al. West Wind Review. Gillette, Gillian, ed. (Illus.). 210p. (Orig.). 1997. pap. 10.00 (*0-9630694-6-2*) So Oregon.

Clayton-Harrison, Hazel. Bearers of Blackness. LC 86-83352. (Illus.). 60p. (Orig.). 1987. pap. 5.00 (*0-940248-29-8*) Guild Pr.

Clayton, Hazel, jt. auth. see Knight, Ginny.

Clayton, Hollis, jt. ed. see Sturgis, Alexander.

Clayton, Howard. The Great Swinfen Case. LC 81-141000. 211p. 1985. 50.00 (*0-7212-0630-1*) St Mut.

Clayton, J. Douglas. Chekhov Then & Now: The Reception of Chekhov in World Culture. LC 95-43863. (Middlebury Studies in Russian Languages & Literature: Vol. 7). XI, 330p. (C). 1997. 55.95 (*0-8204-3085-4*) P Lang Pubng.

— Pierrot in Petrograd: Commedia dell'Arte & Balagan in Twentieth-Century Russian Theatre & Drama. (Illus.). 400p. 1994. 65.00 (*0-7735-1136-9*, Pub. by McG-Queens Univ Pr) CUP Services.

Clayton, Jacklyn B. Your Land, My Land: Children in the Process of Acculturation. LC 95-37843. 139p. 1995. pap. text 18.50 (*0-435-08852-1*, 08852) Heinemann.

Clayton, Jade. McGraw-Hill Illustrated Telecom Dictionary. LC 98-7686. 501p. 1998. pap. 29.95 (*0-07-012063-3*) McGraw.

***Clayton, Jade.** Mcgraw-Hill Illustrated Telecom Dictionary. 2nd ed. (Illus.). 600p. 2000. pap. 29.95 (*0-07-136037-9*) McGraw-Hill Prof.

***Clayton, James A.** New World Order. 269p. 1999. pap. 19.95 (*0-9670687-0-3*) Betoi Pubg.

Clayton, James L. Does Defense Beggar Welfare: Myths vs. Realities. 71p. 1979. pap. text 19.95 (*0-87855-802-0*) Transaction Pubs.

— Fairly Fractured Fairy Tales: For Discerning Adults & Precocious Children. LC 98-91766. (Illus.). 104p. 1998. pap. 9.95 (*0-9666853-1-8*) Puttrow Bks.

***Clayton, James L.** The Global Debt Bomb. 208p. 1999. pap. text 22.95 (*0-7656-0476-0*) M E Sharpe.

Clayton, James L. The Global Debt Bomb. LC 99-22986. (Illus.). 208p. 1999. text 58.95 (*0-7656-0475-2*) M E Sharpe.

— On the Brink: Defense, Deficits & Welfare Spending. LC 83-23052. (Orig.). 1984. 8.95 (*0-915071-01-0*) Ramapo Pr.

Clayton, Jay. Romantic Vision & the Novel. LC 86-12918. 264p. 1987. text 64.95 (*0-521-32776-8*) Cambridge U Pr.

Clayton, Jay & Rothstein, Eric, eds. Influence & Intertextuality in Literary History. LC 91-11892. 360p. (Orig.). (C). 1991. pap. 19.95 (*0-299-13034-7*); lib. bdg. 49.95 (*0-299-13030-4*) U of Wis Pr.

Clayton, Jean. The Tiny Red Bathing Suit of Mr. July: Inspiration & Resources for Continuing Care Providers. 128p. Date not set. pap. 9.95 (*1-55145-246-4*, Pub. by Wood Lake Bks) Logos Prods.

— Women in Mourning: Stories of Grieving Women. LC 96-8230. 1996. 6.95 (*1-56123-094-4*, WIMC) Centering Corp.

Clayton, Jim. The RMF Job Search. 180p. (C). 1996. pap. text, spiral bd. 21.95 (*0-7872-2080-9*, 41208001) Kendall-Hunt.

***Clayton, Jim.** Who Is Going to Heaven? LC 99-66109. 224p. 2000. pap. 9.95 (*1-57921-252-2*) WinePress Pub.

Clayton, Jo. The Burning Ground. (Shadowsong Trilogy Ser.: Bk. 2). 400p. 1995. pap. 4.99 (*0-88677-663-5*, Pub. by DAW Bks) Penguin Putnam.

— Crystal Heat. (Shadowsong Ser.: Vol. 3). 368p. 1996. mass mkt. 5.99 (*0-88677-674-0*, Pub. by DAW Bks) Penguin Putnam.

— Dancer's Rise. (Dancer Trilogy Ser.: Bk. 1). 368p. (Orig.). 1993. mass mkt. 4.99 (*0-88677-567-1*, Pub. by DAW Bks) Penguin Putnam.

— Dancing Down the Stars. (Dancer Trilogy Ser.: Bk. 3). 368p. (Orig.). 1994. mass mkt. 4.99 (*0-88677-617-1*, Pub. by DAW Bks) Penguin Putnam.

— Drum Calls. (Drums of Chaos Ser.: No. 2). 1998. mass mkt. 6.99 (*0-8125-5123-0*, Pub. by Tor Bks) St Martin.

— Drum Warning. (Drums of Chaos Ser.: No. 1). 384p. 1996. 23.95 (*0-312-86177-X*) St Martin.

— Drum Warning. (Drums of Chaos Ser.: No. 1). 1996. write for info. (*0-614-10495-5*); 23.95 (*0-312-81177-2*); 22.95 (*0-614-09397-X*) Tor Bks.

— Drum Warning. (Drums of Chaos Ser.: No. 1). 1997. mass mkt. 5.99 (*0-8125-5122-2*, Pub. by Tor Bks) St Martin.

— Fire in the Sky. (Shadowsong Trilogy Ser.: Bk. 1). 352p. (Orig.). 1995. mass mkt. 4.99 (*0-88677-650-3*, Pub. by DAW Bks) Penguin Putnam.

— Serpent Waltz. (Dancer Trilogy Ser.: Bk. 2). 368p. (Orig.). 1994. mass mkt. 4.99 (*0-88677-597-3*, Pub. by DAW Bks) Penguin Putnam.

Clayton, John. Alexander Fox & the Amazing Mind Reader. LC 98-4379. (Young Readers Ser.). (Illus.). 85p. (J). 1998. pap. 12.95 (*1-57392-221-8*) Prometheus Bks.

— Faces & Places in the City. (Illus.). 217p. (Orig.). 1995. pap. 14.95 (*0-9650684-1-2*) In The City.

— In the City. (Illus.). 166p. (Orig.). 1993. pap. 11.95 (*0-9650684-0-4*) In The City.

***Clayton, John.** New Hampshire: The Way I See It. (Illus.). 172p. 1999. pap. 16.95 (*0-9650684-3-9*) In The City.

Clayton, John. Source, the. 224p. 2001. 15.99 (*1-878990-89-6*) Howard Pub LA.

— Stark Realities in the City, Vol. 1. (Illus.). 180p. 1997. pap. 14.95 (*0-9650684-2-0*) In The City.

Clayton, John, ed. Paul Tillich Main Works - Hauptwerke. (Writings in the Philosophy of Religion - Religionsphilosopbische Schriften: Vol. 4). iv, 421p. 1987. lib. bdg. 95.40 (*3-11-011543-3*) De Gruyter.

— Paul Tillich Main Works - Hauptwerke Vol. 4: Writings in the Philosophy of Religion. iv, 422p. 1987. 78.00 (*3-11-011342-2*) De Gruyter.

Clayton, John, jt. auth. see Story, Dana.

Clayton, John J. Gestures of Healing: Anxiety & the Modern Novel. LC 90-24889. 248p. (C). 1991. lib. bdg. 30.00 (*0-87023-739-X*) U of Mass Pr.

— The Heath Introduction to Fiction. 5th ed. 872p. (C). 1996. pap. text 27.96 (*0-669-35505-4*) HM Trade Div.

— The Man I Never Wanted to Be. LC 97-36395. 230p. 1998. 24.00 (*1-57962-014-0*) Permanent Pr.

***Clayton, John J.** The Man I Never Wanted to Be. 232p. 1999. pap. 16.00 (*1-57962-057-4*) Permanent Pr.

Clayton, John J. Radiance: Ten Stories. LC 97-46015. 256p. 1998. 24.95 (*0-8142-0779-0*, CLARAD); pap. 15.00 (*0-8142-0780-4*, CLARAX) Ohio St U Pr.

— Saul Bellow: In Defense of Man. 2nd ed. LC 78-19554. 346p. reprint ed. pap. 107.30 (*0-8357-6692-6*, 205687200094) Bks Demand.

Clayton, John P. The Concept of Correlation: Paul Tillich & the Possibility of a Mediating Theology. (Theologische Bibliothek Toepelmann Ser.: Vol. 37). 427p. (C). 1979. text 80.80 (*3-11-007914-3*) De Gruyter.

Clayton, John R., Jr., et al. Oil Spill Dispersants: Mechanisms of Action & Laboratory Tests. 1993. lib. bdg. 59.95 (*0-87371-946-8*, TD427) Smoley.

Clayton, Judy & Dow, Deborah. Needlepoint Gifts for All Seasons. (Illus.). 128p. 1996. 24.95 (*0-7153-0317-1*, Pub. by D & C Pub) Sterling.

Clayton, K. M., jt. ed. see Bremer, H.

Clayton, K. M., ed. see Davies, John L.

Clayton, K. Marshall. Discipline: Where Has It Gone? Do Dress Codes Equal Discipline? Bach, Jenipher & Doughty, John, eds. LC 94-93840. 180p. 1994. pap. 59.95 (*0-9644087-0-8*) Clayton & Clayton.

Clayton, LaReine W. Stories of Early Inns & Taverns of the East Tennessee Country. LC 95-70153. (Illus.). 192p. 1995. lib. bdg. 19.95 (*0-9647748-0-1*) J G Buchanan.

***Clayton, Larry.** The Evans Book: Lighters, Compacts, Perfumers & Handbags. LC 98-86379. (Illus.). 160p. 1998. pap. 29.95 (*0-7643-0641-3*) Schiffer.

Clayton, Laura E. Lollipops & Sugarplums. (Illus.). 28p. (Orig.). (J). (ps-5). 1997. pap. write for info. (*1-889732-07-9*, Key-A-Teese Prod) Word-For-Word.

Clayton, Laura E. Molly Helps Mother. (Illus.). 24p. (J). (ps-2). 1994. pap. 2.55 (*0-7399-0049-8*, 2538) Rod & Staff.

Clayton, Lawerance. Clear Fork Cowboys: Texas Ranch Life along the Clear Fork of the Brazos River. LC 97-14495. (Illus.). 144p. 1997. pap. 14.95 (*1-57168-149-3*, 149-3, Eakin Pr) Sunbelt Media.

Clayton, Lawrence. Alcohol Drug Dangers. LC 98-35776. (Drug Dangers Ser.). (Illus.). 64p. (YA). (gr. 4-10). 1999. lib. bdg. 19.95 (*0-7660-1159-3*) Enslow Pubs.

***Clayton, Lawrence.** Alcohol Drug Dangers. LC 98-35776. (Drug Dangers Ser.). (Illus.). 64p. (YA). (gr. 4-10). 1999. pap. 10.95 (*0-7660-1735-4*) Enslow Pubs.

Clayton, Lawrence. Amphetamines & Other Stimulants. (Drug Abuse Prevention Library). 64p. (YA). 1998. reprint ed. pap. 6.95 (*1-56838-210-3*) Hazelden.

— Amphetamines & Other Stimulants. rev. ed. Rosen, Ruth C., ed. (Drug Abuse Prevention Library). (Illus.). 64p. (YA). (gr. 7-12). 1997. lib. bdg. 16.95 (*0-8239-2584-6*) Rosen Group.

— Assessment & Management of the Suicidal Adolescent. 1989. pap. 5.95 (*0-929240-18-9*) EMIS.

— Barbituates & Other Depressants. (Drug Abuse Prevention Library). 64p. (YA). 1998. reprint ed. pap. 6.95 (*1-56838-211-1*) Hazelden.

— Benjamin Capps & the South Plains: A Literary Relationship. LC 89-70725. (Texas Writers Ser.: No. 2). 205p. 1990. 19.95 (*0-929398-09-2*) UNTX Pr.

— Coping with a Drug-Abusing Parent. (Coping Skills Library). 204p. (gr. 7-12). 1997. pap. 6.95 (*1-56838-178-6*, 1153 A) Hazelden.

— Coping with a Drug Abusing Parent. rev. ed. 176p. (YA). (gr. 7-12). 1995. lib. bdg. 17.95 (*0-8239-1950-1*) Rosen Group.

***Clayton, Lawrence.** Coping with a Learning Disability. 1999. pap. text 6.95 (*1-56838-291-X*) Hazelden.

Clayton, Lawrence. Designer Drugs. (Drug Abuse Prevention Library). 64p. (YA). 1998. reprint ed. pap. 6.95 (*1-56838-209-X*) Hazelden.

— Diet Pill Drug Dangers. LC 98-20514. (Drug Dangers Ser.). (Illus.). 64p. (YA). (gr. 4-10). 1999. lib. bdg. 19.95 (*0-7660-1158-5*) Enslow Pubs.

***Clayton, Lawrence.** Diet Pill Drug Dangers. LC 98-20514. (Drug Dangers Ser.). (Illus.). 64p. (YA). (gr. 4-10). 1999. pap. 10.95 (*0-7660-1737-0*) Enslow Pubs.

Clayton, Lawrence. Drugs, Drug Testing, & You. LC 97-21572. (Drug Abuse Prevention Library). (Illus.). 64p. (YA). (gr. 7-12). 1997. lib. bdg. 17.95 (*0-8239-2507-2*, D2507-2) Rosen Group.

— Elmer Kelton. LC 86-70652. (Western Writers Ser.: No. 73). (Illus.). 53p. (Orig.). 1986. pap. 4.95 (*0-88430-047-1*) Boise St U W Writ Ser.

— Everything You Need to Know about Sports Injuries. LC 94-26983. (Need to Know Library). (Illus.). 64p. (YA). (gr. 7-12). 1995. lib. bdg. 17.95 (*0-8239-1876-9*) Rosen Group.

— Historic Ranches of Texas. 2nd ed. (Illus.). 93p. 1997. pap. 16.95 (*0-292-71189-1*) U of Tex Pr.

— Horsing Around. LC 98-51158. 1998. pap. text 17.95 (*0-89672-407-7*) Tex Tech Univ Pr.

— Steroids. LC 95-1464. (Drug Abuse Prevention Library). (Illus.). 64p. (YA). (gr. 7-12). 1998. lib. bdg. 16.95 (*0-8239-2063-1*) Rosen Group.

— Tranquilizers. LC 96-26949. (Drug Library Ser.). 104p. (YA). (gr. 6 up). 1997. lib. bdg. 20.95 (*0-89490-849-9*) Enslow Pubs.

— Watkins Reynolds Matthews: A Biography. LC 93-45374. (Illus.). 144p. 1994. 16.95 (*0-89015-950-5*) Sunbelt Media.

— Working Together Against Drug Addiction, 8 vols. (Library of Social Activism). (Illus.). 64p. (YA). (gr. 7-12). 1996. lib. bdg. 16.95 (*0-8239-2263-4*) Rosen Group.

Clayton, Lawrence, ed. Horsing Around: Contemporary Cowboy Humor. LC 98-51158. 226p. 1999. pap. 17.95 (*0-89672-418-2*) Tex Tech Univ Pr.

Clayton, Lawrence & Carter, Sharon. Coping with Being Gifted. Rosen, Ruth C., ed. (Coping Ser.). (YA). (gr. 7-12). 1992. lib. bdg. 17.95 (*0-8239-1430-5*) Rosen Group.

— Coping with Depression. (Coping Skills Library). 158p. (gr. 7-12). 1997. pap. 6.95 (*1-56838-179-4*, 1154 A) Hazelden.

— Coping with Depression. rev. ed. Rosen, Ruth C., ed. (Coping Ser.). 158p. (YA). (gr. 7-12). 1995. lib. bdg. 16.95 (*0-8239-1951-X*) Rosen Group.

***Clayton, Lawrence & Farmer, Joan.** Tracks along the Clear Fork: Stories from Shackelford & Throckmorton Counties. LC 99-55764. 2000. 29.95 (*1-893114-22-8*) McWhiney Found.

Clayton, Lawrence & Morrison, Jaydene. Coping with a Learning Disability. rev. ed. Rosen, Ruth C., ed. (Coping Ser.). (YA). (gr. 7-12). 1995. lib. bdg. 17.95 (*0-8239-2212-X*) Rosen Group.

Clayton, Lawrence & Van Nostrand, Randy. Professional Alcohol & Drug Counselor Supervisor's Handbook. 2nd ed. Date not set. pap. 18.95 (*1-55691-159-9*) Learning Pubns.

Clayton, Lawrence, ed. see House, Kurt.

Clayton, Lawrence, ed. see Mullins, Reuben B.

Clayton, Lawrence A. The Bolivarian Nations. LC 84-5961. (World of Latin America Ser.). (Illus.). 102p. (C). 1984. pap. text 6.95 (*0-88273-603-5*) Forum Pr IL.

— Caulkers & Carpenters in a New World: The Shipyards of Colonial Guayaquil. LC 80-11547. (Papers in International Studies: Latin America Ser.: No. 8). 199p. (Orig.). reprint ed. pap. 61.70 (*0-7837-1331-2*, 204147900021) Bks Demand.

— Grace - W. R. Grace & Co. The Formative Years: 1850-1930. LC 85-14856. (Illus.). 416p. 1986. 22.50 (*0-915463-25-3*) Jameson Bks.

— Peru & the United States: The Condor & the Eagle. LC 98-33595. (United States & the Americas Ser.). 1999. 55.00 (*0-8203-2024-2*) U of Ga Pr.

Clayton, Lawrence A., ed. The Hispanic Experience in North America: Sources for Study in the United States. LC 91-39274. (Illus.). 199p. reprint ed. pap. 61.70 (*0-608-09662-8*, 206977700006) Bks Demand.

Clayton, Lawrence A., et al, eds. The De Soto Chronicles: The Expedition of Hernando de Soto to North America in 1539-1543, Set, 2 vols. LC 92-31504. 1216p. 1995. pap. text 50.00 (*0-8173-0824-5*) U of Ala Pr.

Clayton, Lawrence A., jt. ed. see Badger, R. Reid.

Clayton, Lawrence D., jt. auth. see Evans, Paul S.

C

An Asterisk (*) at the beginning of an entry indicates that the title is appearing for the first time.

Clayton, Lawrence R. Ranch Rodeos in West Texas. (Illus.). (Orig.). 1989. pap. text 10.00 (*0-910075-08-5*) Hardin-Simmons.

Clayton, Lawrence R., ed. see Richardson, Rupert N.

Clayton, Lawrene A. Peru & the United States: The Condor & the Eagle. LC 98-33595. (United States & the Americas Ser.). 1999. pap. 20.00 (*0-8203-2025-0*) U of Ga Pr.

***Clayton-Lea, Tony.** Elvis Costello. (Illus.). 256p. 2000. reprint ed. pap. 14.00 (*0-88064-255-6*) Fromm Intl Pub.

Clayton-Lea, Tony. Elvis Costello: A Biography. LC 99-12714. (Illus.). 243p. 1999. 23.00 (*0-88064-235-1*) Fromm Intl Pub.

Clayton, Lee. Glacial Lake Wisconsin. LC 89-27582. (Geological Society of America, Memoir Ser.: No. 173). (Illus.). 84p. 1982. reprint ed. pap. 30.00 (*0-608-00229-1*, 206073100006) Bks Demand.

Clayton, Lee, jt. ed. see Teller, James T.

Clayton, Linda A., jt. auth. see Byrd, W. Michael.

Clayton, Lisa. At the Mercy of the Sea. (Illus.). 352p. 1997. 29.95 (*0-7528-0208-9*, Pub. by Orion Pubng Grp) Trafalgar.

— At the Mercy of the Sea. LC 97-186548. (Illus.). 288p. 1997. pap. 11.95 (*0-7528-0597-5*, Pub. by Orion Pubng Grp) Trafalgar.

Clayton, Luke. Texas Hunting & Fishing. LC 97-22614. (Illus.). 176p. (Orig.). 1997. pap. 14.95 (*0-87833-967-1*) Taylor Pub.

Clayton, Lynn P. 10 Gifts Your Children Will Grow to Appreciate. LC 97-50016. 1998. pap. 10.00 (*1-57312-174-6*) Smyth & Helwys.

Clayton, Mack L. & Smyth, Charley J. Surgery for Rheumatoid Arthritis: A Comprehensive Team Approach. (Illus.). 414p. 1992. text 128.00 (*0-443-08217-0*) Church.

Clayton, Marlene & Batt, Chris. Managing Library Automation. 2nd ed. LC 92-14373. 1992. 63.95 (*1-85742-003-9*, Pub. by Gower) Ashgate Pub Co.

Clayton, Martin. Leonardo da Vinci: A Singular Vision. (Illus.). 168p. 1996. 50.00 (*0-7892-0156-9*) Abbeville Pr.

Clayton, Martin. Leonardo Da Vinci: A Singular Vision. (Illus.). 168p. 1996. 24.98 (*0-89660-101-3*, Artabras) Abbeville Pr.

Clayton, Martin. Raphael & His Circle. 224p. 1999. 60.00 (*1-85894-076-1*) Merrell Holberton.

***Clayton, Martin.** Time in Indian Music: Rhythm, Metre, & Form in North Indian Rag Performance. (Oxford Monographs on Music). (Illus.). 368p. 2000. text 74.00 (*0-19-816686-9*) OUP.

Clayton, Martin & Philo, Ron. Leonardo da Vinci: The Anatomy of Man: Drawings from the Collection of Her Majesty Queen Elizabeth II. (Illus.). 141p. 1992. 40.00 (*0-8212-1916-2*, Pub. by Bulfinch Pr) Little.

Clayton, Mary. The Apocryphal Gospels of Mary in Anglo-Saxon England. LC 98-17275. (Studies in Anglo-Saxon England: Vol. 26). 368p. (C). 1999. 69.95 (*0-521-58168-0*) Cambridge U Pr.

— Dead Men's Bones. large type ed. 455p. write for info. (*0-7505-1071-4*, Pub. by Mgna Lrg Print) Ulverscroft.

Clayton, Mary A. Dreadful Delicacies. (Illus.). 50p. 1999. reprint ed. text 16.00 (*0-7881-6466-X*) DIANE Pub.

***Clayton, Matthew.** The Ideal of Equality. 2000. text 69.95 (*0-312-23017-6*) St Martin.

Clayton, Michael, ed. see Clayton, C. P.

Clayton, Nanalee. Young Living. large type ed. 1994. 136.50 (*0-614-09812-2*, L-31472-00) Am Printing Hse.

***Clayton, Nanalee.** Young Living. 7th ed. 566p. 1999. teacher ed. 47.49 (*0-02-642817-2*) Glencoe.

Clayton, Nanci. I'm Every Woman. 96p. Date not set. 10.00 (*0-9669663-1-7*) NuB DuB.

***Clayton, Nancy L.** Strange but True Civil War Stories. LC 99-23592. (Illus.). 128p. (J). (gr. 3-6). 1999. pap. 7.95 (*0-7373-0110-4*, 01104W) NTC Contemp Pub Co.

Clayton, Nick. Early Bicycles. (Album Ser.: No. 173). (Illus.). 32p. pap. 4.75 (*0-85263-803-5*, Pub. by Shire Pubns) Parkwest Pubns.

Clayton, Nigel. Administration of Trust. 315p. 1997. pap. 120.00 (*0-85297-416-7*, Pub. by Chartered Bank) St Mut.

Clayton, Nordheim. Statistical Methods. 2002. pap. text. write for info. (*0-534-26166-3*) Thomson Learn.

— Statistical Methods abr. ed. (Statistics Ser.). 2002. pap. text. write for info. (*0-534-37126-4*) Brooks-Cole.

— Statistical Methods, 1. 2002. pap. text. write for info. (*0-534-26154-X*) Thomson Learn.

— Statistical Methods, 2. 2002. pap. text. write for info. (*0-534-26160-4*) Thomson Learn.

Clayton, Obie, Jr., ed. An American Dilemma Revisited: Race Relations in a Changing World. LC 95-47475. 384p. (C). 1996. pap. text 19.95 (*0-87154-157-2*) Russell Sage.

Clayton, P. Antony. Handbook of Electronic Connectors. 297p. 1997. pap. 276.00 (*0-901150-11-8*) St Mut.

Clayton, Pamela. Enemies & Passing Friends: Settler Ideologies in Twentieth Century Ulster. LC 95-30886. 288p. (C). 1995. text 59.95 (*0-7453-1011-7*, Pub. by Pluto GBR) Stylus Pub VA.

— Enemies & Passing Friends: Settler Ideologies in Twentieth Century Ulster. (C). 1996. pap. 21.95 (*0-7453-1010-9*, Pub. by Pluto GBR) Stylus Pub VA.

Clayton, Paol. Calling Crow Nation. 320p. (Orig.). 1997. mass mkt. 5.99 (*0-425-15604-4*) Berkley Pub.

Clayton, Patti H. Connection on the Ice: Environmental Ethics in Theory & Practice. LC 97-41265. (Environmental Ethics, Values, & Policy Ser.). (Illus.). 352p. (C). 1998. text 69.95 (*1-56639-615-8*); pap. text 24.95 (*1-56639-616-6*) Temple U Pr.

Clayton, Paul. Calling Crow. 320p. (Orig.). 1995. pap. text 4.99 (*0-425-14532-8*) Berkley Pub.

— Flight of the Crow. 304p. (Orig.). 1996. mass mkt. 5.50 (*0-515-11803-6*, Jove) Berkley Pub.

— Flight of the Crow. 2nd rev. ed. 234p. (Orig.). 1998. pap. 9.95 (*1-57502-059-9*, PO2391) Morris Pubng.

Clayton, Paul & Smith, James C., Jr. Developing the Power Within: A Guide to the Inner Self. LC 92-40740. (Orig.). 1993. pap. 10.95 (*0-86534-159-1*) Sunstone Pr.

Clayton, Paula. The Medical Basis of Psychiatry. 2nd ed. Winokur, George, ed. LC 93-22601. (Illus.). 624p. 1994. text 72.00 (*0-7216-6484-9*, W B Saunders Co) Harcrt Hlth Sci Grp.

Clayton, Paula J. & Barrett, James E., eds. Treatment of Depression: Old Controversies & New Approaches. LC 81-40379. (American Psychopathological Association Ser.). 352p. 1983. reprint ed. pap. 109.20 (*0-608-04739-2*, 206546000004) Bks Demand.

Clayton-Payne. Victorian Cottages. 1998. pap. 16.95 (*0-7538-0265-1*) Phoenix Hse.

Clayton-Payne, Andrew & Elliott, Brent. The Victorian Flower Garden. LC 94-169595. (Country Ser.). (Illus.). 160p. 1994. pap. 17.95 (*0-297-83017-1*) Trafalgar.

***Clayton, Peirce.** The Clay Lover's Guide to Making Molds. (Illus.). 2000. pap. 24.95 (*1-57990-186-7*, Pub. by Lark Books) Sterling.

Clayton, Peirce. The Clay Lover's Guide to Making Molds: Designing * Making * Using. Rich, Chris, ed. LC 97-31248. 128p. 1998. 24.95 (*1-57990-022-4*, Pub. by Lark Books) Random.

Clayton, Peter. Implementation of Organizational Innovation: Studies of Academic & Research Libraries. LC 97-1031. (Library & Information Science Ser.). (Illus.). 208p. 1997. text 59.95 (*0-12-174860-X*) Morgan Kaufmann.

***Clayton, Peter & Gammond, Peter.** The Bluffer's Guide to Jazz: Bluff Your Way in Jazz. (Bluffer's Guides Ser.). 64p. 1999. pap. 5.95 (*1-902825-10-1*) Oval Bks.

Clayton, Peter & Gammond, Peter. Fourteen Miles on a Clear Night. LC 78-5685. (Illus.). 128p. 1978. reprint ed. lib. bdg. 49.50 (*0-313-20475-6*, CLFM, Greenwood Pr) Greenwood.

Clayton, Peter & Price, Martin, eds. The Seven Wonders of the Ancient World. (Illus.). 192p. 1988. text 29.95 (*0-415-00279-6*) Routledge.

— The Seven Wonders of the Ancient World. (Illus.). 192p. (gr. 13). 1990. pap. 16.99 (*0-415-05036-7*, A4490) Routledge.

Clayton, Peter, jt. auth. see Gammond, Peter.

Clayton, Peter, jt. auth. see Gorman, G. E.

Clayton, Peter A. Chronicle of the Pharaohs. LC 94-60269. (Illus.). 224p. 1994. 29.95 (*0-500-05074-0*, Pub. by Thames Hudson) Norton.

— The Valley of the Kings. (Digging up the Past Ser.). (Illus.). 48p. (J). (gr. 4-6). 1995. lib. bdg. 24.26 (*1-56847-399-0*) Raintree Steck-V.

Clayton, Philip. Explanation from Physics to Theology: An Essay in Rationality & Religion. LC 88-39306. 256p. (C). 1989. 35.00 (*0-300-04353-8*) Yale U Pr.

***Clayton, Philip.** The Problem of God in Modern Thought. 544p. 2000. 39.00 (*0-8028-3885-5*) Eerdmans.

Clayton, Philip A., jt. ed. see LeLievre, Roger A.

Clayton, Philip D. God & Contemporary Science. LC 98-24504. (Edinburgh Studies in Constructive Theology). 279p. 1998. pap. 25.00 (*0-8028-4460-X*) Eerdmans.

Clayton, Powell. Aftermath of the Civil War, in Arkansas. LC 79-89029. 378p. 1969. reprint ed. lib. bdg. 35.00 (*0-8371-1820-4*, CLA&) Greenwood.

Clayton, R. F. Monitoring of Radioactive Contamination on Surfaces. (Technical Reports: No. 120). (Illus.). 8p. (Orig.). 1970. pap. 16.00 (*92-0-125570-5*, IDC120, Pub. by IAEA) Bernan Associates.

Clayton, R. J. & Algar, J. The GEC Research Laboratories, 1919-1984. (History of Technology Ser.: No. 10). 452p. 1989. 115.00 (*0-86341-146-0*, HT010) INSPEC Inc.

Clayton, R. J. & Algar, J., eds. A Scientist's War: The War Diary of Sir Clifford Paterson, 1939-45. (History of Technology Ser.: No. 14). 680p. 1991. 115.00 (*0-86341-218-1*, HT014) INSPEC Inc.

Clayton, R. M., et al, eds. Problems of Normal & Genetically Abnormal Retinas. 1983. text 104.00 (*0-12-176180-0*) Acad Pr.

Clayton, R. M. & Truman, D. E., eds. Coordinated Regulation of Gene Expression. LC 86-22620. 402p. 1986. 89.50 (*0-306-42410-X*, Plenum Trade) Perseus Pubng.

Clayton, Ralph. Black Baltimore, Eighteen Twenty to Eighteen Seventy. (Illus.). vii, 199p. (Orig.). 1987. pap. 12.00 (*1-55613-080-5*) Heritage Bk.

***Clayton, Ralph.** Roy Stuart, Vol. III. (Illus.). 240p. 2000. 39.99 (*3-8228-6054-9*) Taschen Amer.

Clayton, Richard. The Law of Human Rights. 700p. 2000. text 175.00 (*0-19-826223-X*) OUP.

Clayton, Richard & Tomlinson, Hugh. Judicial Review Procedure. 310p. 1997. pap. 40.00 (*1-84113-076-1*, Pub. by Hart Pub) Intl Spec Bk.

— Police Actions: A Practical Guide. 200p. 1997. pap. 36.00 (*1-84113-077-X*, Pub. by Hart Pub) Intl Spec Bk.

Clayton, Richard R., jt. auth. see Cooper, Thomas M.

Clayton, Robert. The One Minute Investor. 1998. pap. 5.95 (*1-892937-01-8*) Spec Pubns.

Clayton, Robert A. Quiet Pride: Ageless Wisdom of the American West. Hathaway, J. Bourge, ed. & frwd. by. LC 92-15228. (Earthsong Collection). (Illus.). 128p. 1992. 39.95 (*0-941831-77-9*) Beyond Words Pub.

Clayton, Robert D. & Thomas, David G. Professional Aquatic Management. 2nd ed. LC 88-8221. (Illus.). 208p. 1989. text 30.00 (*0-87322-217-2*, BCLA0217) Human Kinetics.

Clayton, Robert D., jt. auth. see Torney, John A., Jr.

Clayton, Robert D., ed. see Council for National Cooperation in Aquatics Staff.

Clayton, Robert L. Robert Russa Moton Vol. 1: Successor to Booker T. Washington & a Strong Black Presence from 1916 until 1940, "The Early Years" 50p. (Orig.). 1988. pap. 9.50 (*0-910363-05-6*) EBONICS.

— Toward an Understanding of the A. M. E. Zion Church Vol. 1: A Manual for Lay Persons, Students, & Others Who Are Interested in Learning about Zion. 60p. 1988. student ed. 11.50 (*0-910363-04-8*) EBONICS.

Clayton, Robert P. Thorns & Roses. (Orig.). 1996. pap. write for info. (*1-57553-116-X*) Watermrk Pr.

Clayton, Ronald, ed. see Otway, Thomas, et al.

Clayton, Ronnie W. Mother Wit: The Ex-Slave Narratives of the Louisiana Writers' Project. (University of Kansas Humanistic Studies). (Illus.). 263p. (C). 1990. text 59.95 (*0-8204-1240-6*) P Lang Pubng.

Clayton, Rose & Heard, Dick, eds. Elvis up Close: In the Words of Those Who Knew Him Best. (Illus.). 405p. 1998. pap. text 13.00 (*0-7881-5440-0*) DIANE Pub.

Clayton, Ross, jt. auth. see Siegel, Gilbert B.

Clayton, Rupert. Lotus Notes Release 5. LC 99-61233. (No Experience Required Ser.). (Illus.). 608p. 1999. pap. text 24.99 (*0-7821-2184-5*) Sybex.

Clayton, Sandra. The Giant. LC 93-28992. (Voyages Ser.). (Illus.). (J). 1994. 4.25 (*0-383-03745-X*) SRA McGraw.

Clayton, Sandra. Reverse Garbage Mulch. pap. 16.95 (*1-875657-40-1*, Pub. by Hyland Hse) Seven Hills Bk.

***Clayton, Sarah T.** The Angelic Sins of Jones Very. LC 97-27269. (Early American Literature & Culture Through the American Renaissance Ser.: Vol. 1). xiii, 213p. (C). 1999. text 48.95 (*0-8204-3378-0*, 33780) P Lang Pubng.

Clayton, Sheryl H. Black Men Role Models of Greater St. Louis. LC 84-81882. 1983. 16.95 (*0-9607958-2-0*); pap. 12.95 (*0-9607958-3-9*) Essai Seay Pubns.

— Black Women Models of Houston, Texas. LC 86-61778. 1986. pap. 16.00 (*0-9607958-8-X*) Essai Seay Pubns.

— Black Women Role Models of Waco, Texas. LC 86-61779. 1986. 16.95 (*0-9607958-6-3*); pap. 12.95 (*0-9607958-7-1*) Essai Seay Pubns.

Clayton, Sheryl H., ed. Black Women Role Models of Greater St. Louis. LC 81-71873. 381p. (Orig.). (YA). (gr. 6 up). 1982. 14.95 (*0-9607958-0-4*) Essai Seay Pubns.

***Clayton, Skip & Moeller, Jeff.** 50 Phabulous Phillies. (Illus.). 256p. 2000. 22.95 (*1-58261-224-2*) Sports Pub.

Clayton, Stanley G. & Newton, John R., eds. A Pocket Obstetrics & Gynecology. 11th ed. (Illus.). 392p. 1988. pap. text 25.00 (*0-443-03777-9*) Church.

Clayton, Susan, jt. auth. see Bentley, Trevor J.

Clayton, Susan D. & Crosby, Faye J. Justice, Gender, & Affirmative Action. LC 92-22871. (Critical Perspectives on Women & Gender Ser.). 168p. (C). 1992. pap. text 15.95 (*0-472-06464-9*, 06464) U of Mich Pr.

Clayton, Susan H., ed. & illus. see Hanson, Laura & Schwartz, Kathleen J.

Clayton, Thomas, ed. The Hamlet First Published (Q1, Sixteen Hundred Three) Origins, Form, Intertextualities. LC 90-50574. (Illus.). 320p. 1992. 46.50 (*0-87413-427-7*) U Delaware Pr.

Clayton, Thomas H. Close to the Land: The Way We Lived in North Carolina, 1820-1870. Nathans, Sydney. ed. LC 82-20143. (Way We Lived in North Carolina Ser.). (Illus.). viii, 98p. (YA). (gr. 8-12). 1983. pap. 12.95 (*0-8078-4103-X*) U of NC Pr.

— Close to the Land: The Way We Lived in North Carolina, 1820-1879. Nathans, Sydney, ed. LC 82-20143. (Illus.). 108p. 1983. reprint ed. pap. 33.50 (*0-608-00576-2*, 206145900009) Bks Demand.

Clayton, Tim. The English Print, 1688-1802. LC 96-43669. 240p. 1997. 75.00 (*0-300-06650-3*) Yale U Pr.

***Clayton, Tim & Craig, Philip R.** Finest Hour: The Battle of Britain. (Illus.). 352p. 2000. 27.50 (*0-684-86930-6*) Simon & Schuster.

Clayton, Tonya D., et al. Living with the Georgia Shore. LC 91-41261. (Living with the Shore Ser.). (Illus.). 296p. 1992. text 49.95 (*0-8223-1215-8*); pap. text 18.95 (*0-8223-1219-0*) Duke.

Clayton, Valerie L. Baker, see Baker Clayton, Valerie L.

Clayton, Victoria. Out of Love. LC 98-14839. 384p. 1998. text 25.95 (*0-312-18645-2*) St Martin.

***Clayton, Victoria.** Past Mischief. large type ed. 560p. 1999. 31.99 (*0-7089-9121-1*) Ulverscroft.

Clayton, Victoria V. White & Black under the Old Regime. LC 70-119928. (Select Bibliographies Reprint Ser.). 1977. 25.95 (*0-8369-5371-1*) Ayer.

***Clayton, Virginia T., ed.** The Once & Future Gardener: Garden Writing from the Golden Age of Magazines, 1900-1940. LC 99-25661. (Illus.). 352p. 1999. 45.00 (*1-56792-102-7*) Godine.

Clayton, W. D. A Revision of the Genus Hyparrhenia. (Kew Bulletin Additional Series II). (Illus.). 196p. 1969. pap. 15.00 (*0-11-240999-7*, Pub. by Royal Botnic Grdns) Balogh.

Clayton, W. D., jt. ed. see Dassanayake, M. D.

Clayton, W. G., et al. Greenberg's Guide to Early American Toy Trains: Carlisle & Finch, Hafner, Dorfan. 240p. 1993. text 59.95 (*0-89778-230-5*, 10-7215, Greenberg Books) Kalmbach.

Clayton, W. W. History of Davidson County, Tennessee. (Illus.). 499p. 1993. reprint ed. lib. bdg. 51.50 (*0-8328-2947-1*) Higginson Bk Co.

— History of Davidson County, Tennessee: With Name Index. (Illus.). 1971. reprint ed. 145.00 (*0-918450-03-9*) C Elder.

— History of Onondaga County, New York, with Illustrations & Biographical Sketches of Some of Its Prominent Men & Pioneers. (Illus.). 434p. 1997. reprint ed. lib. bdg. 47.50 (*0-8328-7146-X*) Higginson Bk Co.

— History of Onondaga County, with Illustrations & Biographical Sketches of Some of Its Prominent Men & Pioneers. (Illus.). 430p. 1996. reprint ed. lib. bdg. 52.00 (*0-8328-5463-8*) Higginson Bk Co.

— History of Steuben County, with Illustrations & Biographical Sketches of Some of Its Prominent Men & Pioneers. (Illus.). 460p. 1997. reprint ed. lib. bdg. 55.00 (*0-8328-6249-5*) Higginson Bk Co.

Clayton, W. W., ed. History of Cumberland County, Maine: With Illustrations & Biographical Sketches of Prominent Men & Pioneers. (Illus.). 456p. 1988. reprint ed. lib. bdg. 49.00 (*0-8328-0023-6*, ME0009) Higginson Bk Co.

Clayton, W. Woodford, ed. History of Union & Middlesex Co. NJ. (Illus.). 885p. 1994. reprint ed. lib. bdg. 90.00 (*0-8328-3979-5*) Higginson Bk Co.

Clayton, W. Woodford & Nelson, William, eds. History of Bergen & Passaic Counties, New Jersey, with Biographical Sketches of Many of Its Pioneers & Prominent Men. (Illus.). 577p. 1992. reprint ed. lib. bdg. 67.00 (*0-8328-2445-3*) Higginson Bk Co.

Clayton, William. An Intimate Chronicle: The Journals of William Clayton. 2nd ed. Smith, George D., ed. LC 89-27572. (Significant Mormon Diaries Ser.: No. 5). (Illus.). 678p. 1995. pap. 17.95 (*1-56085-022-1*) Signature Bks.

— Latter Day Saints' Emigrants' Guide. Kimball, Stanley B. & Franzwa, Gregory M., eds. 1983. pap. 13.95 (*0-935284-27-3*) Patrice Pr.

— The Latter-Day Saints' Emigrants Guide: Being a Table of Distances Showing All the Springs, Creeks, Hills, Mountains, Camping Places, & All Other Notable Places from Council Bluffs to the Valley of the Great Salt Lake. 24p. 1973. pap. 4.95 (*0-87770-040-0*) Ye Galleon.

— Selected Papers of William Clayton. Dobney, Frederick J., ed. LC 70-164565. 320p. reprint ed. pap. 99.20 (*0-608-11885-0*, 202309300032) Bks Demand.

— William Clayton's Journal: A Daily Record of the Journey of the Original Company of Mormon Pioneers from Nauvoo, Illinois, to the Valley of the Great Salt Lake. LC 72-9435. (Far Western Frontier Ser.). 380p. 1978. reprint ed. 29.95 (*0-405-04965-X*) Ayer.

Claytor, Constance & Potter, Joan. African Americans Who Were First. LC 97-10164. (Illus.). 128p. (J). (gr. 4). 1997. 15.99 (*0-525-65246-9*, Dutton Child) Peng Put Young Read.

Claytor, Constance, jt. auth. see Potter, Joan.

Claytor, Robert M. Made Fit for God in That Affliction. LC 96-232541. (Illus.). 155p. (Orig.). 1996. pap. 10.95 (*0-9653186-0-5*) Bedewrite Pr.

***Claywell, Gina S.** The Guide to Writing Portfolios. 128p. 2000. pap. 12.00 (*0-205-32103-8*) Allyn.

Clbement, Serge, jt. auth. see Kamena, Marina.

CLCI Staff. Be Your Own Matchmaker: You Can't Get What You Want. 128p. 1997. per. 18.95 (*0-7872-4185-7*) Kendall-Hunt.

CLCTS Staff, ed. First International Symposium on Measurement & Control in Robotics. 590p. 1990. 100.00 (*0-9627116-0-8*) Clear Lk Coun Tech Soc.

Cleaf, Aaron R. Van, see Van Cleaf, Aaron R., ed.

Cleaf, David W. Van, see Van Cleaf, David W.

Cleage, Albert B., Jr. Black Christian Nationalism: New Directions for the Black Church. 350p. 1987. reprint ed. 14.95 (*0-941205-00-2*); reprint ed. pap. 10.00 (*0-941205-01-0*) Luxor Pubs PAOCC.

— The Black Messiah. LC 88-70198. 280p. (C). 1989. reprint ed. pap. 11.95 (*0-86543-078-0*) Africa World.

Cleage, Pearl. Blues for an Alabama Sky. 1999. pap. 5.25 (*0-8222-1634-5*) Dramatists Play.

— The Brass Bed & Other Stories. 1991. pap. 8.00 (*0-88378-127-1*) Third World.

— Flyin' West. 1995. pap. 5.25 (*0-8222-1465-2*) Dramatists Play.

— Flyin' West & Other Plays. LC 99-18987. 280p. 1999. pap. 15.95 (*1-55936-168-9*, Pub. by Theatre Comm) Consort Bk Sales.

***Cleage, Pearl.** I Wish I Had a Red Dress. 2000. 24.00 (*0-380-97733-8*, Wm Morrow) Morrow Avon.

Cleage, Pearl. What Looks Like Crazy on an Ordinary Day. LC 97-17708. 256p. 1997. 20.00 (*0-380-97584-X*, Avon Bks) Morrow Avon.

***Cleage, Pearl.** What Looks Like Crazy on an Ordinary Day. 2000. mass mkt. write for info. (*0-380-81771-3*, Avon Bks) Morrow Avon.

Cleage, Pearl. What Looks Like Crazy On an Ordinary Day. LC 97-17708. 256p. 1998. pap. 13.00 (*0-380-79487-X*, Avon Bks) Morrow Avon.

— What Looks Like Crazy on an Ordinary Day: A Novel. large type ed. LC 98-49013. (Thorndike Americana Ser.). 1950. pap. 30.00 (*0-7862-1760-X*) Thorndike Pr.

— What Looks Like Crazy on an Ordinary Day: A Novel. large type ed. LC 98-49013. (Thorndike Americana Ser.). 1999. 28.95 (*0-7862-1759-6*) Thorndike Pr.

Cleal, Christopher J. & Thomas, Barry A. Plant Fossils: The History of Land Vegetation. LC 99-19437. (Fossils Illustrated Ser.). (Illus.). 288p. 1999. 110.00 (*0-85115-684-3*, Boydell Pr) Boydell & Brewer.

Cleal, D. M. & Heaton, N. O. Knowledge Based Systems: Implications for Human-Computer Interfaces. (Books in Information Technology). 256p. 1988. text 51.95 (*0-470-21082-6*) P-H.

Cleal, Rosamund & Sweeney, Ann M., eds. Grooved Ware in Great Britain & Ireland. (Oxbow Monographs). (Illus.). 200p. (Orig.). 1999. pap. 36.00 (*1-900188-77-5*, Pub. by Oxbow Bks) David Brown.

Clean Team Staff, The & Campbell, Jeff. Spring Cleaning. 208p. (Orig.). (YA). (gr. 7 up). 1989. pap. 9.95 (*0-440-50162-8*, Dell Trade Pbks) Dell.

Clean Team Staff, The, jt. auth. see Campbell, Jeff.

Cleaning Consultant Services, Inc. Staff. The Comprehensive Custodial Training Manual. 1997. pap. 118.00 (*0-9601054-1-7*) Cleaning Cons.

Cleanthes, Ted. Official Notebook. 1987. pap. 5.95 (*0-9616172-2-5*) Official Shit Co.

— Official Number Sign, Asterisk, Percent Handbook. 1987. pap. 5.95 (*0-9616172-3-3*) Official Shit Co.

— The Official Shit Notebook. Tortolini, Pete, ed. (Illus.). 128p. 1987. pap. 5.95 (*0-9616172-1-7*) Official Shit Co.

Clear. American Corrections. 5th ed. LC 99-28653. (Criminal Justice). 1999. pap. 78.95 (*0-534-52147-9*) Wadsworth Pub.

***Clear.** Clear. 1998. 16.98 (*7-474-02276-1*) Forefront.

— The Community. (Criminal Justice Ser.). 2001. 25.00 (*0-534-53409-0*) Wadsworth Pub.

Clear & Cole. American Corrections. 2nd ed. (Criminal Justice Ser.). 1990. mass mkt., teacher ed. write for info. (*0-534-12020-2*) Wadsworth Pub.

— American Corrections. 3rd ed. (Criminal Justice Ser.). 1994. teacher ed. 34.25 (*0-534-18973-3*) Wadsworth Pub.

Clear, Annette & Weideman, Linda. Dynamics of Public Relations & Journalism: A Practical Guide for Media Studies. LC 97-221134. 190p. 1997. write for info. (*0-7021-3829-0*) Juta & Co.

Clear, Caitriona. Nuns in Nineteenth-Century Ireland. LC 87-27767. (Illus.). 234p. 1988. reprint ed. pap. 72.60 (*0-7837-9108-9*, 204991000004) Bks Demand.

***Clear, Caitriona.** Women of the House: Women's Household Work in Ireland, 1922-1961: Discourses, Experiences, Memories. LC 99-88161. (Women in Irish History Ser.). 288p. 2000. pap. 26.50 (*0-7165-2717-0*, Pub. by Irish Acad Pr) Intl Spec Bk.

— Women of the House: Women's Household Work in Ireland, 1926-1961: Discourses, Experiences, Memories. LC 99-88161. (Women in Irish History Ser.). 288p. 2000. 49.50 (*0-7165-2714-6*, Pub. by Irish Acad Pr) Intl Spec Bk.

Clear, Constance. Reaching for Reality: Seven Incredible True Stories of Alien Abduction. LC 98-92297. 230p. 1999. pap. 16.95 (*0-9667053-1-9*) Consciousness.

Clear, Rebecca D. Jazz on Film & Video in the Library of Congress. 171p. (Orig.). (C). 1994. pap. text 30.00 (*0-7881-1436-0*) DIANE Pub.

Clear, T., ed. see Kervran, Joannie.

Clear, Todd & Karp, David. The Community Justice Ideal. LC 99-23202. 224p. 1999. (*0-8133-6765-4*) Westview.

***Clear, Todd & Karp, David.** The Community Justice Ideal. LC 99-23202. (Crime & Society Ser.). 224p. 1999. pap. 25.00 (*0-8133-6766-2*, Pub. by Westview) HarpC.

Clear, Todd R. Harm in American Penology: Offenders, Victims, & Their Communities. LC 94-281. (SUNY Series in New Directions in Crime & Justice Studies). 242p. (C). 1994. pap. text 24.95 (*0-7914-2174-0*) State U NY Pr.

Clear, Todd R. & Cole, George F. American Corrections. LC 85-19562. (Criminal Justice Ser.). 560p. (C). 1986. pap. 28.50 (*0-534-05688-1*) Brooks-Cole.

— American Corrections. 2nd ed. LC 89-38335. 594p. (C). 1989. pap. 50.95 (*0-534-12018-0*) Wadsworth Pub.

— American Corrections. 3rd ed. 551p. 1993. mass mkt. 48.25 (*0-534-18972-5*) Wadsworth Pub.

***Clear, Todd R. & Dammer, Harry R.** The Offender in the Community. LC 99-39956. (Illus.). 428p. 1999. pap. 57.95 (*0-534-25374-1*) Brooks-Cole.

Clear, Val. Common Cagebirds in America. LC 66-16027. 1966. pap. 4.95 (*0-672-52270-5*, Bobbs) Macmillan.

Cleare, John. Distant Mountains. 1998. 4.50 (*0-8129-3093-2*, Times Bks) Crown Pub Group.

— Distant Mountains. 1998. 35.00 (*0-679-46255-4*) Random.

— Volcanoes of the World. LC 97-26700. (Illus.). 144p. 1997. 5.99 (*1-57145-079-3*, Thunder Bay) Advantage Pubs.

Cleare, John, jt. auth. see Sale, Richard.

Clearfield, A., jt. ed. see Cocke, D. L.

Clearfield, Abraham, ed. Inorganic Ion Exchange Materials. LC 81-6109. 304p. 1982. 170.00 (*0-8493-5930-9*, QD561, CRC Reprint) Franklin.

Clearfield, Andrew M. These Fragment I Have Stored: Collage & Montage in Early Modernist Poetry. LC 84-57. (Studies in Modern Literature: No. 36). 162p. reprint ed. pap. 50.30 (*0-8357-1539-6*, 207053900001) Bks Demand.

Clearfield, Dylan. Chicagoland Ghosts. (Illus.). 124p. 1997. pap. 12.95 (*1-882376-41-2*) Thunder Bay Pr.

— Floridaland Ghosts. (Tales of the Supernatural Ser.). (Illus.). 2000. pap. 12.95 (*1-882376-70-6*) Thunder Bay Pr.

Clearfield, Elaine A. Our Colorado Immortals in Stained Glass. (Illus.). pap. 7.95 (*0-9617471-0-2*) E A Clearfield.

Clearfield, Harris R. Acid-Peptic Disorders of the Upper Gastrointestinal Tract: Diagnosis & Management. 1995. pap. 27.95 (*1-884065-04-X*) Assocs in Med.

Clearfield, William N. Celestial Stems: Five Element Diet & Exercise Program. LC 92-19423. (Illus.). 100p. (Orig.). 1992. pap. 19.95 (*0-912975-15-6*) Upshur Pr.

***Clearman, Brian.** Transportation Markings Database: Railway Signals, Signs, Marks & Markers. LC 97-25496. (Transportation Markings - A Study in Communication Monograph Ser.: Vol. III). 325p. 2000. pap. 25.95 (*0-918941-15-6*) Mt Angel Abbey.

Clearman, Deborah. The Goose's Tale. LC 94-48798. (Illus.). 32p. (J). (gr. 1-7). 1996. 15.95 (*1-879085-85-2*, Whispering Coyote) Charlesbridge Pub.

Clearwater, Bonnie. Mark Rothko: Works on Paper. LC 83-22843. (Illus.). 144p. 1984. 25.00 (*0-933920-54-7*, Pub. by Hudson Hills) Natl Bk Netwk.

Clearwater, Bonnie, ed. Ana Mendieta. limited ed. (Illus.). 76p. 1993. boxed set 75.00 (*0-9628514-5-0*) Grassfield Pr.

— Ana Mendieta: A Book of Works. LC 93-79028. (Illus.). 72p. 1993. 35.00 (*0-9628514-4-2*) Grassfield Pr.

Clearwater, Bonnie, intro. West Coast Duchamp. LC 91-70132. (Illus.). 128p. (Orig.). 1991. 65.00 (*0-9628514-0-X*) Grassfield Pr.

Clearwater, Bonnie, ed. see Lannan Museum Staff.

Clearwater, S., jt. auth. see Williams, C.

Clearwater, S., jt. auth. see Williams, Colin.

Clearwater, Scott H., ed. Market-Based Control: A Paradigm for Distributed Resource Allocation. LC 95-35276. 300p. 1996. 62.00 (*981-02-2254-8*) World Scientific Pub.

Clearwaters, Richard V. On the Upward Road. 176p. (Orig.). 1991. pap. write for info. (*0-9631570-0-0*) R V Clearwater.

Cleary. Introduction to Algebra. Date not set. pap. text, teacher ed. write for info. (*0-314-96602-1*) West Pub.

Cleary & Taylor. Northwest Indians. (Illus.). 48p. (J). (gr. 3-6). 1996. pap., teacher ed. 5.95 (*1-55799-571-0*, 557) Evan-Moor Edu Pubs.

— Southwest Indians. (Illus.). 48p. (J). (gr. 3-6). 1996. pap., teacher ed. 5.95 (*1-55799-570-2*, 556) Evan-Moor Edu Pubs.

— Woodland Indians. (Illus.). 48p. (J). (gr. 3-6). 1995. pap., teacher ed. 5.95 (*1-55799-389-0*, 541) Evan-Moor Edu Pubs.

Cleary, A. J. Adjustment of Public Liability Claims. (C). 1983. 160.00 (*0-7855-4325-2*, Pub. by Witherby & Co) St Mut.

Cleary, A. S. The Ending of Roman Britain. (Illus.). 240p. (C). 1989. lib. bdg. 62.50 (*0-389-20893-0*, N 8450) B&N Imports.

Cleary, Alan. Instrumentation for Psychology. LC 77-1250. 343p. reprint ed. pap. 106.40 (*0-608-12328-5*, 202427600035) Bks Demand.

Cleary, Alan, et al. Educational Technology: Implications for Early & Special Education. LC 75-1239. (Illus.). 201p. reprint ed. pap. 62.40 (*0-608-17695-8*, 203041700069) Bks Demand.

Cleary, Anne & Treacy, Margaret P. The Sociology of Health & Illness in Ireland. LC 97-213124. 232p. 1998. pap. 29.95 (*1-900621-11-8*, Pub. by Univ Coll Dublin Pr) Dufour.

Cleary, B. D. & Kelpsas, B. R. Five Steps to Successful Regeneration Planning. LC SD0409.. (Oregon State University, Forest Research Laboratory, Research Papers: No. 1). 33p. reprint ed. pap. 30.00 (*0-608-14969-1*, 202610700048) Bks Demand.

Cleary, Barbara A. & Duncan, Sally J. Tools & Techniques to Inspire Classroom Learning. LC 96-44602. (Illus.). 161p. 1997. 20.00 (*0-87389-411-1*, H0952) ASQ Qual Pr.

Cleary, Barbara A., jt. auth. see Langford, David P.

Cleary, Beverly. Beezus & Ramona. (Ramona Ser.). 142p. (J). (gr. 3-5). pap. 4.99 (*0-8072-1441-8*) Listening Lib.

— Beezus & Ramona. LC 55-7623. (Ramona Ser.). (Illus.). 160p. (J). (gr. 4-7). 1955. 15.89 (*0-688-31076-1*, Wm Morrow); 15.95 (*0-688-21076-7*, Wm Morrow) Morrow Avon.

Cleary, Beverly. Beezus & Ramona. (Ramona Ser.). (Illus.). 176p. (J). (gr. 3-5). 1990. mass mkt. 4.99 (*0-380-70918-X*, Avon Bks) Morrow Avon.

Cleary, Beverly. Beezus & Ramona. (Ramona Ser.). (J). (gr. 3-5). 1955. 9.60 (*0-606-03061-1*, Pub. by Turtleback) Demco.

— Beezus & Ramona. unabridged ed. (Ramona Ser.). (J). (gr. 3-5). 1990. pap. 18.00 incl. audio (*0-8072-7385-6*, TA 822 CXR) Listening Lib.

— Beezus & Ramona, Set. unabridged ed. (Ramona Ser.). (J). (gr. 3-5). 1990. pap. 21.98 incl. audio (*0-8072-7317-1*, YA 822 SP) Listening Lib.

Cleary, Beverly. The Beezus & Ramona Diary. (Illus.). 224p. (J). (gr. 3-5). 1986. pap. 11.95 (*0-688-06353-5*, Wm Morrow) Morrow Avon.

— Beverly Cleary, 4 vols. (J). (gr. 4-7). 1991. pap., boxed set 14.00 (*0-380-71719-0*, Avon Bks) Morrow Avon.

— Dear Mr. Henshaw. (Illus.). 144p. (J). (gr. k-6). 1984. pap. 3.99 (*0-440-41794-5*, YB BDD) BDD Bks Young Read.

— Dear Mr. Henshaw. (J). write for info. (*0-318-62413-3*) Dell.

— Dear Mr. Henshaw. (Illus.). (J). 1995. 9.32 (*0-395-73255-7*) HM.

— Dear Mr. Henshaw. (SPA.). (J). (gr. 4-7). 1996. pap. text 8.50 (*84-239-2766-0*) Lectorum Pubns.

— Dear Mr. Henshaw. LC 83-5372. (Illus.). 144p. (J). (gr. 4-7). 1983. 15.95 (*0-688-02405-X*, Wm Morrow) Morrow Avon.

Cleary, Beverly. Dear Mr. Henshaw. LC 83-5372. (Illus.). 144p. (J). (gr. 4-7). 1983. 15.89 (*0-688-02406-8*, Wm Morrow) Morrow Avon.

Cleary, Beverly. Dear Mr. Henshaw. 160p. (J). (gr. 3-7). 1994. pap. 4.99 (*0-380-70958-9*, Wm Morrow) Morrow Avon.

— Dear Mr. Henshaw. (J). 1996. mass mkt. 4.99 (*0-380-72798-6*, Avon Bks) Morrow Avon.

— Dear Mr. Henshaw. LC 83-5372. (J). 1983. 9.60 (*0-606-06315-3*, Pub. by Turtleback) Demco.

Cleary, Beverly. Dear Mr. Henshaw. (J). 1996. 9.60 (*0-606-09187-4*, Pub. by Turtleback) Demco.

Cleary, Beverly. Dear Mr. Henshaw. large type ed. (Illus.). 166p. (J). 1996. 41.50 (*0-614-20583-2*, L-38198-00 APHB) Am Printing Hse.

— Dear Mr. Henshaw (Spanish edition) Querido Senor Henshaw. LC 97-2997. (SPA., Illus.). 134p. (J). (gr. 3-7). 1997. 14.00 (*0-688-15465-4*, Grenwillow Bks) HarpC Child Bks.

— Dear Mr. Henshaw (Spanish edition) Querido Senor Henshaw. Bustelo, Gabriela, tr. LC 97-2997. (SPA., Illus.). 128p. (gr. 2-6). 1997. mass mkt. 5.95 (*0-688-15485-9*, Wm Morrow) Morrow Avon.

Cleary, Beverly. Ellen Tebbits. 160p. (J). (gr. 2-4). pap. 4.99 (*0-8072-1397-7*) Listening Lib.

Cleary, Beverly. Ellen Tebbits. LC 51-11430. (Illus.). 160p. (J). (gr. 4-7). 1951. 15.95 (*0-688-21264-6*, Wm Morrow) Morrow Avon.

Cleary, Beverly. Ellen Tebbits. LC 51-11430. (Illus.). 160p. (J). (gr. 4-7). 1951. 15.89 (*0-688-31264-0*, Wm Morrow) Morrow Avon.

Cleary, Beverly. Ellen Tebbits. LC 51-11430. 176p. (J). (gr. 3-7). 1990. mass mkt. 4.99 (*0-380-70913-9*, Avon Bks) Morrow Avon.

— Ellen Tebbits. (J). 1990. 9.60 (*0-606-03262-2*, Pub. by Turtleback) Demco.

Cleary, Beverly. Emily's Runaway Imagination. 221p. (J). (gr. 2-4). pap. 4.95 (*0-8072-1416-7*) Listening Lib.

— Emily's Runaway Imagination. LC 61-10939. (Illus.). 224p. (J). (gr. 4-7). 1961. 15.89 (*0-688-31267-5*, Wm Morrow) Morrow Avon.

Cleary, Beverly. Emily's Runaway Imagination. LC 61-10939. 240p. (J). (gr. 3-7). 1990. mass mkt. 4.95 (*0-380-70923-6*, Wm Morrow) Morrow Avon.

— Emily's Runaway Imagination. (J). 1990. 9.60 (*0-606-04665-8*, Pub. by Turtleback) Demco.

— Fifteen. LC 56-7509. (Illus.). 256p. (J). (gr. 6-9). 1956. 16.00 (*0-688-21285-9*, Wm Morrow) Morrow Avon.

— Fifteen. LC 56-7509. (Illus.). 256p. (J). (gr. 7 up). 1956. 16.89 (*0-688-31285-3*, Wm Morrow) Morrow Avon.

— Fifteen. 176p. (J). (gr. 4-7). 1996. pap. 4.99 (*0-380-72804-4*, Avon Bks) Morrow Avon.

— Fifteen. (J). 1956. 9.60 (*0-606-04669-0*, Pub. by Turtleback) Demco.

— Fifteen. 192p. (YA). 1991. reprint ed. mass mkt. 4.50 (*0-380-70920-1*, Avon Bks) Morrow Avon.

— A Girl from Yamhill: A Memoir. LC 87-31554. (Illus.). 320p. (J). (gr. 4-7). 1988. 19.95 (*0-688-07800-1*, Wm Morrow) Morrow Avon.

Cleary, Beverly. A Girl from Yamhill: A Memoir. 288p. (J). (gr. 4-7). 1996. pap. 10.00 (*0-380-72740-4*, Avon Bks) Morrow Avon.

— A Girl from Yamhill: A Memoir. LC 87-31554. 1996. 11.09 (*0-606-10196-9*, Pub. by Turtleback) Demco.

— The Growing up Feet. 1997. 10.15 (*0-606-12320-2*, Pub. by Turtleback) Demco.

— The Growing-Up Feet. LC 86-12585. (Illus.). 32p. (J). (ps-3). 1987. 16.00 (*0-688-06619-4*, Wm Morrow) Morrow Avon.

Cleary, Beverly. The Growing-Up Feet. LC 86-12585. (Illus.). 32p. (J). 1997. mass mkt. 4.95 (*0-688-15470-0*, Wm Morrow) Morrow Avon.

Cleary, Beverly. Henry & Beezus. (Henry Huggins Ser.). 192p. (J). (gr. 1-4). pap. 4.99 (*0-8072-1484-1*) Listening Lib.

— Henry & Beezus. LC 52-5930. (Henry Huggins Ser.). (Illus.). 192p. (J). (gr. 1-4). 1952. 15.89 (*0-688-31383-3*, Wm Morrow) Morrow Avon.

Cleary, Beverly. Henry & Beezus. LC 52-5930. (Henry Huggins Ser.). (Illus.). 192p. (J). (gr. 4-7). 1952. 16.00 (*0-688-21383-9*, Wm Morrow) Morrow Avon.

— Henry & Beezus. LC 52-5930. (Henry Huggins Ser.). 192p. (J). (gr. 4-7). 1990. pap. 4.99 (*0-380-70914-7*, Avon Bks) Morrow Avon.

Cleary, Beverly. Henry & Beezus. (Henry Huggins Ser.). (J). (gr. 1-4). 1952. 9.60 (*0-606-03441-2*, Pub. by Turtleback) Demco.

Cleary, Beverly. Henry & Ramona. 72p. (J). (gr. 1-9). 1997. pap. 5.50 (*0-87129-748-5*, H43) Dramatic Pub.

— Henry & Ribsy. LC 54-6402. (Henry Huggins Ser.). (Illus.). 192p. (J). (gr. 1-4). 1954. 15.89 (*0-688-31382-5*, Wm Morrow) Morrow Avon.

Cleary, Beverly. Henry & Ribsy. LC 54-6402. (Henry Huggins Ser.). (Illus.). 192p. (J). (gr. 1-4). 1954. 15.95 (*0-688-21382-0*, Wm Morrow) Morrow Avon.

Cleary, Beverly. Henry & Ribsy. (Henry Huggins Ser.). (Illus.). 192p. (J). (gr. 3-7). 1990. pap. 4.99 (*0-380-70917-1*, Avon Bks) Morrow Avon.

Cleary, Beverly. Henry & Ribsy. (Henry Huggins Ser.). (J). (gr. 1-4). 1954. 9.60 (*0-606-03446-3*, Pub. by Turtleback) Demco.

Cleary, Beverly. Henry & the Clubhouse. LC 62-7161. (Henry Huggins Ser.). (Illus.). (J). (gr. 4-7). 1962. 15.95 (*0-688-21381-2*, Wm Morrow) Morrow Avon.

— Henry & the Clubhouse. LC 62-7161. (Henry Huggins Ser.). 192p. (J). (gr. 4-7). 1990. pap. 4.99 (*0-380-70915-5*, Avon Bks) Morrow Avon.

Cleary, Beverly. Henry & the Clubhouse. (Henry Huggins Ser.). (J). (gr. 1-4). 1962. 9.60 (*0-606-03447-1*, Pub. by Turtleback) Demco.

Cleary, Beverly. Henry & the Paper Route. LC 57-8562. (Henry Huggins Ser.). (Illus.). 192p. (J). (gr. 1-4). 1957. 16.00 (*0-688-21380-4*, Wm Morrow) Morrow Avon.

Cleary, Beverly. Henry & the Paper Route. LC 57-8562. (Henry Huggins Ser.). (Illus.). 192p. (J). (gr. 1-4). 1957. 15.89 (*0-688-31380-9*, Wm Morrow) Morrow Avon.

Cleary, Beverly. Henry & the Paper Route. (Henry Huggins Ser.). (J). (gr. 1-4). 1990. 9.60 (*0-606-04695-X*, Pub. by Turtleback) Demco.

— Henry & the Paper Route. (Henry Huggins Ser.). 192p. (J). (gr. 1-4). 1990. reprint ed. pap. 4.99 (*0-380-70921-X*, Avon Bks) Morrow Avon.

Cleary, Beverly. Henry Huggins. LC 00-27567. (Henry Huggins Ser.). (Illus.). 160p. (J). (gr. 1-4). 1950. 15.95 (*0-688-21385-5*, Wm Morrow); 15.89 (*0-688-31385-X*, Wm Morrow) Morrow Avon.

Cleary, Beverly. Henry Huggins. Palacios, Argentina, tr. from ENG. LC 82-25889. (Henry Huggins Ser.). (SPA., Illus.). (J). (gr. 4-7). 1983. 16.00 (*0-688-02014-3*, Wm Morrow) Morrow Avon.

— Henry Huggins. (Henry Huggins Ser.). (J). (gr. 1-4). 1996. mass mkt. 4.50 (*0-380-72800-1*, Avon Bks) Morrow Avon.

— Henry Huggins. LC 82-25889. (Henry Huggins Ser.). (SPA., Illus.). 160p. (J). (gr. 4-7). 1996. mass mkt. 5.95 (*0-688-14887-5*, Wm Morrow) Morrow Avon.

— Henry Huggins. (Henry Huggins Ser.). (J). (gr. 1-4). 1978. 9.60 (*0-606-03501-X*, Pub. by Turtleback) Demco.

— Henry Huggins. (Henry Huggins Ser.). (J). (gr. 1-4). 1996. 9.60 (*0-606-09405-9*, Pub. by Turtleback); 11.05 (*0-606-10426-7*, Pub. by Turtleback) Demco.

— Henry Huggins. anniversary ed. LC 00-27567. (Henry Huggins Ser.). (Illus.). 160p. (J). (gr. 1-4). 1990. mass mkt. 4.99 (*0-380-70912-0*, Wm Morrow) Morrow Avon.

— Henry Huggins Series Boxed Set, 6 vols. (Henry Huggins Ser.). (J). (gr. 1-4). 1990. boxed set 19.50 (*0-440-36015-3*) Dell.

— Henry Huggins Series Boxed Set, 4 vols. (Henry Huggins Ser.). (J). (gr. 1-4). 1990. boxed set 14.00 (*0-380-71206-7*, Avon Bks) Morrow Avon.

— The Hullabaloo ABC. LC 97-6457. (Illus.). 40p. (J). (ps-3). 1998. 16.00 (*0-688-15182-5*, Wm Morrow) Morrow Avon.

***Cleary, Beverly.** The Hullabaloo ABC. LC 97-6457. (Illus.). 40p. (J). (ps-4). 1998. lib. bdg. 15.93 (*0-688-15183-3*, Wm Morrow) Morrow Avon.

— The Hullabaloo ABC. 2000. pap. write for info. (*0-688-17715-8*, Wm Morrow) Morrow Avon.

Cleary, Beverly. Janet's Thingamajigs. LC 86-12589. (Illus.). 32p. (J). (ps-3). 1987. 11.95 (*0-688-06617-8*, Wm Morrow) Morrow Avon.

Cleary, Beverly. Janet's Thingamajigs. LC 86-12589. (Illus.). 32p. (J). 1997. pap. 5.95 (*0-688-15278-3*, Wm Morrow) Morrow Avon.

— Janet's Thingamajigs. 1997. 10.15 (*0-606-12360-1*, Pub. by Turtleback) Demco.

— Jean & Johnny. LC 59-7806. (Illus.). 288p. (J). (gr. 6-9). 1959. 15.88 (*0-688-31740-5*, Wm Morrow) Morrow Avon.

Cleary, Beverly. Jean & Johnny. LC 59-7806. (Illus.). 288p. (J). (gr. 7 up). 1959. 15.95 (*0-688-21740-0*, Wm Morrow) Morrow Avon.

— Jean & Johnny. 240p. (YA). 1991. mass mkt. 4.50 (*0-380-70927-9*, Avon Bks) Morrow Avon.

— Jean & Johnny. 224p. (J). (gr. 5 up). 1996. mass mkt. 4.99 (*0-380-72805-2*, Avon Bks) Morrow Avon.

Cleary, Beverly. Jean & Johnny. 1996. 9.60 (*0-606-10231-0*, Pub. by Turtleback) Demco.

Cleary, Beverly. Leave It to Beaver. 18.95 (*0-88411-248-9*) Amereon Ltd.

— Leave It to Beaver. 1993. reprint ed. lib. bdg. 15.95 (*1-56849-194-8*) Buccaneer Bks.

Cleary, Beverly. The Luckiest Girl. LC 58-6667. 228p. (J). (gr. 7 up). 1970. 16.89 (*0-688-31741-3*, Wm Morrow) Morrow Avon.

Cleary, Beverly. The Luckiest Girl. 240p. (J). (gr. 4-7). 1996. pap. 4.99 (*0-380-72806-0*, Avon Bks) Morrow Avon.

— The Luckiest Girl. 1996. 9.60 (*0-606-10256-6*, Pub. by Turtleback) Demco.

— The Luckiest Girl. 224p. (J). (gr. 5-6). 1991. reprint ed. mass mkt. 4.50 (*0-380-70922-8*, Avon Bks) Morrow Avon.

— Meet Ramona Quimby. Incl. Ramona & Her Father. (J). (gr. 3-5). 1983. pap. Ramona Quimby, Age 8. (J). (gr. 3-5). 1983. pap. Ramona the Pest. (J). (gr. 3-5). 1983. pap. (J). 1983. Set boxed set 11.20 (*0-440-45548-0*) Dell.

— Meet Ramona Quimby, 5 bks., Set. Incl. Ramona & Her Family. (J). Ramona Quimby, Age 8. (J). (gr. 3-5). Ramona the Pest. (J). (gr. 3-5). (J). (gr. k-7). Set boxed set 15.50 (*0-685-19114-1*) Dell.

— Mitch & Amy. LC 67-10041. 224p. (J). (gr. 3-7). 1991. mass mkt. 4.99 (*0-380-70925-2*, Wm Morrow) Morrow Avon.

— Mitch & Amy. LC 67-10041. (Illus.). 224p. (J). (gr. 4-7). 1991. 15.00 (*0-688-10806-7*, Wm Morrow) Morrow Avon.

— Mitch & Amy. (J). 1991. 9.60 (*0-606-04747-6*, Pub. by Turtleback) Demco.

— The Mouse & the Motorcycle. 160p. (J). (gr. k-6). 1980. pap. 3.25 (*0-440-46075-1*, YB BDD) BDD Bks Young Read.

— The Mouse & the Motorcycle. (Illus.). (J). (gr. 5). 1995. 9.32 (*0-395-73250-6*) HM.

— The Mouse & the Motorcycle. LC 65-20956. (Illus.). (J). (gr. 4-7). 1965. 15.95 (*0-688-21698-6*, Wm Morrow) Morrow Avon.

Cleary, Beverly. The Mouse & the Motorcycle. LC 65-20956. (Illus.). 160p. (J). (gr. 4-7). 1965. 15.89 (*0-688-31698-0*, Wm Morrow) Morrow Avon.

Cleary, Beverly. The Mouse & the Motorcycle. (J). 1996. mass mkt. 4.50 (*0-380-72799-4*, Avon Bks) Morrow Avon.

— The Mouse & the Motorcycle. (J). 1956. 9.60 (*0-606-04754-9*, Pub. by Turtleback) Demco.

— The Mouse & the Motorcycle. (J). 1996. 8.60 (*0-606-09635-3*, Pub. by Turtleback) Demco.

— The Mouse & the Motorcycle. large type ed. (Illus.). 182p. (J). (gr. 5). 45.50 (*0-614-20606-5*, L-38189-00 APHB) Am Printing Hse.

— The Mouse & the Motorcycle. 160p. (J). (gr. 2-6). 1990. reprint ed. pap. 4.99 (*0-380-70924-4*, Wm Morrow) Morrow Avon.

— The Mouse & the Motorcycle, Set. (Illus.). (J). 1996. boxed set 15.96 (*0-380-72402-2*, Avon Bks) Morrow Avon.

— Muggie Maggie. (SPA., Illus.). (gr. 5 up). 1996. pap. text 7.50 (*84-279-3463-7*) Lectorum Pubns.

— Muggie Maggie. LC 89-38959. (Illus.). 80p. (J). (gr. 4-7). 1990. 16.00 (*0-688-08553-9*, Wm Morrow) Morrow Avon.

— Muggie Maggie. (J). 1990. 9.70 (*0-606-04980-0*, Pub. by Turtleback) Demco.

Cleary, Beverly. Muggie Maggie. (Illus.). 96p. (J). (gr. 2-7). 1990. reprint ed. mass mkt. 4.95 (*0-380-71087-0*, Wm Morrow) Morrow Avon.

C

An Asterisk (*) at the beginning of an entry indicates that the title is appearing for the first time.

Cleary, Beverly. My Own Two Feet: A Memoir. LC 95-1764. (Illus.). 288p. (YA). (gr. 8-12). 1995. 15.00 (*0-688-14267-2*, Wm Morrow) Morrow Avon.

Cleary, Beverly. My Own Two Feet: A Memoir. 272p. (J). (gr. 4-7). 1996. pap. 10.00 (*0-380-72746-3*, Avon Bks) Morrow Avon.

Cleary, Beverly. My Own Two Feet: A Memoir. LC 95-1764. 1996. 15.35 (*0-606-10264-7*) Turtleback.

— Otis Spofford. LC 53-6660. (Illus.). 192p. (J). (gr. 4-7). 1953. 16.00 (*0-688-21720-6*, Wm Morrow) Morrow Avon.

— Otis Spofford. (J). 1953. 9.60 (*0-606-04766-2*, Pub. by Turtleback) Demco.

— Otis Spofford (repackage) (Illus.). 192p. (J). (gr. 3-7). 1990. reprint ed. mass mkt. 4.99 (*0-380-70919-8*, Avon Bks) Morrow Avon.

— Pen Pals, 6 vols. (J). (gr. 4-7). 1990. boxed set 17.70 (*0-440-36028-5*) Dell.

— Petey's Bedtime Story. LC 92-6184. (Illus.). 32p. (J). (gr. k up). 1993. 15.00 (*0-688-10660-9*, Wm Morrow) Morrow Avon.

Cleary, Beverly. Petey's Bedtime Story. LC 92-6184. (Illus.). 32p. (J). (gr. k up). 1993. lib. bdg. 14.89 (*0-688-10661-7*, Wm Morrow) Morrow Avon.

Cleary, Beverly. Petey's Bedtime Story. LC 92-6184. (Illus.). 32p. (J). (ps-3). 1995. pap. 4.95 (*0-688-14390-3*, Wm Morrow) Morrow Avon.

— Petey's Bedtime Story. (J). 1995. 10.15 (*0-606-08011-2*, Pub. by Turtleback) Demco.

Cleary, Beverly. Querido Senor Henshaw.Tr. of Dear Mr. Henshaw. (J). 1997. 11.05 (*0-606-11776-8*, Pub. by Turtleback) Demco.

Cleary, Beverly. Ralph S. Mouse. LC 82-3516. (Illus.). 160p. (J). (gr. 4-7). 1982. 16.00 (*0-688-01452-6*, Wm Morrow) Morrow Avon.

Cleary, Beverly. Ralph S. Mouse. LC 82-3516. (Illus.). 160p. (J). (gr. 4-7). 1982. 15.89 (*0-688-01455-0*, Wm Morrow) Morrow Avon.

Cleary, Beverly. Ralph S. Mouse. (Illus.). 160p. (J). (gr. 4-7). 1993. pap. 4.99 (*0-380-70957-0*, Wm Morrow) Morrow Avon.

— Ralph S. Mouse. (J). 1982. 9.60 (*0-606-05984-9*, Pub. by Turtleback) Demco.

Cleary, Beverly. Ramona & Her Father. (Ramona Ser.). 186p. (J). (gr. 3-5). pap. 4.99 (*0-8072-1439-6*) Listening Lib.

Cleary, Beverly. Ramona & Her Father. LC 77-1614. (Ramona Ser.). (Illus.). 192p. (J). (gr. 4-7). 1977. 15.95 (*0-688-22114-9*, Wm Morrow) Morrow Avon.

Cleary, Beverly. Ramona & Her Father. LC 77-1614. (Ramona Ser.). (Illus.). 192p. (J). (gr. 4-7). 1977. 15.89 (*0-688-32114-3*, Wm Morrow) Morrow Avon.

Cleary, Beverly. Ramona & Her Father. LC 77-1614. (Ramona Ser.). (Illus.). 208p. (J). (gr. 3-7). 1990. mass mkt. 4.99 (*0-380-70916-3*, Avon Bks) Morrow Avon.

Cleary, Beverly. Ramona & Her Father. (Ramona Ser.). (J). (gr. 3-5). 1977. 9.60 (*0-606-04522-8*, Pub. by Turtleback) Demco.

— Ramona & Her Mother. (Ramona Ser.). (J). (gr. 3-5). 1980. pap. 4.50 (*0-440-70007-8*) BDD Bks Young Read.

Cleary, Beverly. Ramona & Her Mother. (Ramona Ser.). (J). (gr. 3-5). write for info. (*0-318-62409-5*) Dell.

— Ramona & Her Mother. (Ramona Ser.). (J). (gr. 3-5). 1983. pap. write for info. (*0-318-57245-1*) Dell.

— Ramona & Her Mother. (Ramona Ser.). (SPA.). (J). (gr. 4-7). 1996. pap. text 8.95 (*84-239-2803-9*) Lectorum Pubns.

Cleary, Beverly. Ramona & Her Mother. (Ramona Ser.). 208p. (J). (gr. 3-5). pap. 4.99 (*0-8072-1435-3*) Listening Lib.

Cleary, Beverly. Ramona & Her Mother. LC 79-10323. (Ramona Ser.). (Illus.). 208p. (J). (gr. 4-7). 1979. 17.00 (*0-688-22195-5*, Wm Morrow) Morrow Avon.

Cleary, Beverly. Ramona & Her Mother. LC 79-10323. (Ramona Ser.). (Illus.). 208p. (J). (gr. 4-7). 1979. 16.89 (*0-688-32195-X*, Wm Morrow) Morrow Avon.

— Ramona & Her Mother. (Ramona Ser.). (J). (gr. 3-5). 1979. 9.60 (*0-606-04781-6*, Pub. by Turtleback) Demco.

Cleary, Beverly. Ramona y Su Mudre. LC 97-1198. (Ramona Ser.). Orig. Title: Ramona y Su Madre. (SPA., Illus.). 208p. (J). (gr. 3-7). 1997. 15.00 (*0-688-15466-2*, Wm Morrow) Morrow Avon.

— Ramona & Her Mother. (Ramona Ser.). (Illus.). 224p. (J). (gr. 3-5). 1990. reprint ed. mass mkt. 4.99 (*0-380-70952-X*, Avon Bks) Morrow Avon.

Cleary, Beverly. Ramona & Her Mother. unabridged ed. (Ramona Ser.). (J). (gr. 3-5). 1990. pap. 21.98 incl. audio (*0-8072-7314-7*, YA 820 SP) Listening Lib.

Cleary, Beverly. Ramona & Her Mother (Spanish edition) Ramona y su madre. LC 97-1198. (SPA., Illus.). 184p. (J). 1997. mass mkt. 5.95 (*0-688-15486-7*, Wm Morrow) Morrow Avon.

— Ramona Empieza el Curso. LC 97-2998. (Ramona Ser.). Orig. Title: Ramona Quimby, Age 8. (SPA., Illus.). 192p. (J). (gr. 3-7). 1997. 15.00 (*0-688-15467-0*, Grenwillow Bks) HarpC Child Bks.

Cleary, Beverly. Ramona Empieza el Curso. Bustelo, Gabriela, tr. (Ramona Ser.). Orig. Title: Ramona Quimby, Age 8. (SPA., Illus.). 224p. (J). (gr. 3-5). 1997. mass mkt. 5.95 (*0-688-15487-5*, Wm Morrow) Morrow Avon.

— Ramona Empieza el Curso. Orig. Title: Ramona Quimby, Age 8. (J). 1997. 11.05 (*0-606-11779-2*, Pub. by Turtleback) Demco.

Cleary, Beverly. Ramona Forever. (Ramona Ser.). (J). (gr. 3-5). write for info. (*0-318-62410-9*) Dell.

— Ramona Forever. (Ramona Ser.). 192p. (J). (gr. 3-5). 1994. pap. 1.99 (*0-440-21937-X*) Dell.

— Ramona Forever. (Ramona Ser.). (SPA.). (J). (gr. 4-7). 1996. pap. text 9.75 (*84-239-7120-1*) Lectorum Pubns.

Cleary, Beverly. Ramona Forever. (Ramona Ser.). 182p. (J). (gr. 3-5). pap. 4.99 (*0-8072-1437-X*) Listening Lib.

— Ramona Forever. (Ramona Ser.). (Illus.). 192p. (J). (gr. 3-5). 1984. 15.89 (*0-688-03786-0*, Wm Morrow) Morrow Avon.

Cleary, Beverly. Ramona Forever. LC 84-704. (Ramona Ser.). (Illus.). 192p. (J). (gr. 4-7). 1984. 16.00 (*0-688-03785-2*, Wm Morrow) Morrow Avon.

— Ramona Forever. (Ramona Ser.). (J). (gr. 3-5). 1996. mass mkt. 4.50 (*0-380-72801-X*, Avon Bks) Morrow Avon.

Cleary, Beverly. Ramona Forever. (Ramona Ser.). (J). (gr. 3-5). 1995. 10.34 (*0-606-08054-6*) Turtleback.

Cleary, Beverly. Ramona Forever. (Ramona Ser.). (J). (gr. 3-5). 1996. 8.60 (*0-606-09778-3*, Pub. by Turtleback) Demco.

— Ramona Forever. LC 84-704. (Ramona Ser.). (Illus.). 192p. (J). (gr. 3-7). 1995. reprint ed. mass mkt. 4.99 (*0-380-70960-0*, Avon Bks) Morrow Avon.

— Ramona la Chince.Tr. of Ramona the Pest. 1996. 11.05 (*0-606-10495-X*, Pub. by Turtleback) Demco.

— Ramona, Mouse, 4 vols., Set. (J). (gr. 4-7). 1990. boxed set 16.47 (*0-380-71483-3*, Avon Bks) Morrow Avon.

— Ramona Quimby. (Ramona Ser.). (J). (gr. 3-5). 1994. pap. 5.50 (*0-87129-330-7*, R54) Dramatic Pub.

Cleary, Beverly. Ramona Quimby, Age 8. (Ramona Ser.). 190p. (J). (gr. 3-5). pap. 4.99 (*0-8072-1436-1*) Listening Lib.

— Ramona Quimby, Age 8. (Ramona Ser.). (Illus.). 192p. (J). (gr. 3-5). 1981. 15.89 (*0-688-00478-4*, Wm Morrow) Morrow Avon.

— Ramona Quimby, Age 8. LC 80-28425. (Ramona Ser.). (Illus.). 192p. (J). (gr. 4-7). 1981. 15.95 (*0-688-00477-6*, Wm Morrow) Morrow Avon.

Cleary, Beverly. Ramona Quimby, Age 8. LC 80-28425. (Ramona Ser.). (Illus.). 208p. (J). (gr. 2-7). 1992. mass mkt. 4.99 (*0-380-70956-2*, Avon Bks) Morrow Avon.

— Ramona Quimby, Age 8. (Ramona Ser.). 44p. (J). (gr. 3-5). 1998. 11.95 (*1-56137-708-2*, NU7082SP) Novel Units.

***Cleary, Beverly.** Ramona Quimby, Age 8. (Ramona Ser.). (J). (gr. 3-5). 1999. 9.95 (*1-56137-448-2*) Novel Units.

— Ramona Quimby, Age 8. (Ramona Ser.). (J). (gr. 3-5). 1981. 9.60 (*0-606-01002-5*, Pub. by Turtleback) Demco.

Cleary, Beverly. Ramona Quimby, Age 8. 95th ed. (Ramona Ser.). (J). (gr. 3-5). 1995. lib. bdg. 13.25 (*0-15-305205-8*, Pub. by Harcourt Coll Pubs) Harcourt.

Cleary, Beverly. Ramona Quimby Boxed Set, 4 vols., Set. (Ramona Ser.). (J). (gr. 3-5). 1993. pap., boxed set 15.96 (*0-380-72123-6*, Avon Bks) Morrow Avon.

— Ramona Quimby Boxed Set, Set. (Ramona Ser.). (Illus.). (J). (gr. 3-5). 1995. pap. 15.96 (*0-380-72654-8*, Avon Bks) Morrow Avon.

— The Ramona Quimby Diary. (Illus.). 160p. (J). (gr. 2 up). 1984. pap. 10.95 (*0-688-03883-2*, Wm Morrow) Morrow Avon.

— Ramona the Brave. (Ramona Ser.). 190p. (J). (gr. 3-5). pap. 4.99 (*0-8072-1440-X*) Listening Lib.

Cleary, Beverly. Ramona the Brave. LC 74-16494. (Ramona Ser.). (Illus.). 192p. (J). (gr. 4-7). 1975. 15.95 (*0-688-22015-0*, Wm Morrow) Morrow Avon.

Cleary, Beverly. Ramona the Brave. LC 74-16494. (Ramona Ser.). (Illus.). 192p. (J). (gr. 4-7). 1975. 15.93 (*0-688-32015-5*, Wm Morrow) Morrow Avon.

Cleary, Beverly. Ramona the Brave. LC 74-16494. (Ramona Ser.). (Illus.). 190p. (J). (gr. 2-7). 1995. mass mkt. 4.99 (*0-380-70959-7*, Avon Bks) Morrow Avon.

***Cleary, Beverly.** Ramona the Brave. (Ramona Ser.). (J). (gr. 3-5). 2000. 9.95 (*1-56137-444-X*) Novel Units.

— Ramona the Brave. (Ramona Ser.). (J). (gr. 3-5). 1995. 10.34 (*0-606-08055-4*) Turtleback.

— Ramona the Pest. (Ramona Ser.). 192p. (J). (gr. 3-5). pap. 4.99 (*0-8072-1438-8*) Listening Lib.

— Ramona the Pest. LC 68-12981. (Illus.). 192p. (J). (gr. 4-7). 1968. 15.89 (*0-688-31721-9*, Wm Morrow); 15.95 (*0-688-21721-4*, Wm Morrow) Morrow Avon.

Cleary, Beverly. Ramona the Pest. LC 68-12981. (Ramona Ser.). (Illus.). 192p. (J). (gr. 2-7). 1992. mass mkt. 4.99 (*0-380-70954-6*, Avon Bks) Morrow Avon.

Cleary, Beverly. Ramona the Pest. (Ramona Ser.). (J). (gr. 3-5). 1968. 9.60 (*0-606-00711-3*, Pub. by Turtleback) Demco.

— Ramona the Pest, Set. unabridged ed. (Ramona Ser.). (J). (gr. 3-5). 1991. pap. 21.98 incl. audio (*0-8072-7316-3*, YA 819SP) Listening Lib.

Cleary, Beverly. Ramona the Pest (Spanish edition) Ramona la chinche. Palacios, Argentina, tr. LC 83-23805. (SPA., Illus.). 192p. (J). (ps-3). 1984. 16.00 (*0-688-02783-0*, Wm Morrow) Morrow Avon.

— Ramona the Pest (Spanish edition) Ramona la chinche. LC 83-23805. (SPA., Illus.). 192p. (J). (gr. 4-7). 1996. mass mkt. 5.95 (*0-688-14888-3*, Wm Morrow) Morrow Avon.

Cleary, Beverly. Ramona y Su Madre.Tr. of Ramona & Her Mother. (J). 1997. 11.05 (*0-606-11780-6*, Pub. by Turtleback) Demco.

Cleary, Beverly. Ramona y Su Padre. LC 49-127080.Tr. of Ramona & Her Father. (SPA.). (J). (gr. 4-7). 1996. pap. text 8.95 (*84-239-2770-9*) Lectorum Pubns.

— Ramona y Su Padre.Tr. of Ramona & Her Father. (J). 1987. 14.05 (*0-606-10497-6*, Pub. by Turtleback) Demco.

Cleary, Beverly. Ramona's World. (Ramona Ser.). 208p. (J). (gr. 3-5). mass mkt. 4.95 (*0-380-73272-6*) Morrow Avon.

— Ramona's World. LC PZ7.C5792Rap 1999. (Ramona Ser.). (Illus.). 192p. (J). (gr. 3-5). 1999. 14.89 (*0-688-16818-3*, Wm Morrow) Morrow Avon.

— Ramona's World. LC 99-19038. (Ramona Ser.). (Illus.). 192p. (J). (gr. 3-7). 1999. 14.95 (*0-688-16816-7*, Wm Morrow) Morrow Avon.

Cleary, Beverly. The Real Hole. LC 85-18815. (J). (ps-3). 1996. pap. 4.95 (*0-688-14741-0*, Wm Morrow) Morrow Avon.

— The Real Hole. 1996. 10.15 (*0-606-09780-5*, Pub by Turtleback) Demco.

— Ribsy. LC 64-13263. (Henry Huggins Ser.). (Illus.). (J). (gr. 1-4). 1964. 16.00 (*0-688-21662-5*, Wm Morrow) Morrow Avon.

Cleary, Beverly. Ribsy. LC 64-13263. (Henry Huggins Ser.). (Illus.). (J). (gr. 1-4). 1964. 15.89 (*0-688-31662-X*, Wm Morrow) Morrow Avon.

Cleary, Beverly. Ribsy. (Henry Huggins Ser.). (Illus.). 192p. (J). (gr. 1-4). 1992. pap. 4.99 (*0-380-70955-4*, Avon Bks) Morrow Avon.

— Ribsy. (Henry Huggins Ser.). (J). (gr. 1-4). 1996. mass mkt. 4.50 (*0-380-72803-6*, Avon Bks) Morrow Avon.

— Ribsy. (Henry Huggins Ser.). (J). (gr. 1-4). 1964. 9.60 (*0-606-00377-0*, Pub. by Turtleback) Demco.

— Ribsy. (Henry Huggins Ser.). (J). (gr. 1-4). 1996. 9.60 (*0-606-09788-0*, Pub. by Turtleback) Demco.

Cleary, Beverly. Runaway Ralph. 175p. (J). (gr. 3-5). pap. 4.50 (*0-8072-1394-2*) Listening Lib.

Cleary, Beverly. Runaway Ralph. LC 77-95786. (Illus.). (J). (gr. 4-7). 1970. 16.00 (*0-688-21701-X*, Wm Morrow) Morrow Avon.

Cleary, Beverly. Runaway Ralph. LC 77-95786. (Illus.). 192p. (J). (gr. 4-7). 1970. 15.93 (*0-688-31701-4*, Wm Morrow) Morrow Avon.

Cleary, Beverly. Runaway Ralph. LC 77-95786. (Illus.). 176p. (J). (gr. 3-7). 1991. mass mkt. 4.95 (*0-380-70953-8*, Wm Morrow) Morrow Avon.

Cleary, Beverly. Runaway Ralph. (J). 1970. 9.60 (*0-606-00725-3*, Pub. by Turtleback) Demco.

— Sister of the Bride. LC 63-8802. (Illus.). 256p. (J). (gr. 7 up). 1963. 16.89 (*0-688-31742-1*, Wm Morrow) Morrow Avon.

Cleary, Beverly. Sister of the Bride. 240p. (J). (gr. 6). 1992. mass mkt. 4.50 (*0-380-70928-7*, Avon Bks) Morrow Avon.

— Sister of the Bride. 272p. (J). (gr. 5 up). 1996. mass mkt. 4.99 (*0-380-72807-9*, Avon Bks) Morrow Avon.

Cleary, Beverly. Socks. 156p. (J). (gr. 3-4). pap. 4.50 (*0-8072-1419-1*) Listening Lib.

Cleary, Beverly. Socks. LC 72-10298. (Illus.). 160p. (J). (gr. 4-7). 1973. 16.00 (*0-688-20067-2*, Wm Morrow) Morrow Avon.

Cleary, Beverly. Socks. LC 72-10298. (Illus.). 160p. (J). (gr. 4-7). 1973. 15.93 (*0-688-30067-7*, Wm Morrow) Morrow Avon.

Cleary, Beverly. Socks. LC 72-10298. (Illus.). 160p. (J). (gr. 3-7). 1990. mass mkt. 4.99 (*0-380-70926-0*, Wm Morrow) Morrow Avon.

— Socks. (J). 1990. 9.60 (*0-606-04800-6*, Pub. by Turtleback) Demco.

— Strider. (Illus.). (YA). (gr. 6 up). 1995. 9.28 (*0-395-73264-6*) HM.

— Strider. LC 90-6608. (Illus.). 192p. (J). (gr. 3 up). 1991. 16.00 (*0-688-09900-9*, Wm Morrow) Morrow Avon.

— Strider. LC 90-6608. (Illus.). 192p. (J). (gr. 4-7). 1991. 15.89 (*0-688-09901-7*, Wm Morrow) Morrow Avon.

— Strider. LC 90-6608. (Illus.). 176p. (J). (gr. 4-7). 1992. mass mkt. 4.99 (*0-380-71236-9*, Wm Morrow) Morrow Avon.

— Strider, 4 vols. (gr. 4-7). 1993. pap. text, boxed set 15.96 (*0-380-72125-2*, Avon Bks) Morrow Avon.

— Strider. LC 90-6608. 176p. (J). (gr. 4-7). 1996. mass mkt. 4.50 (*0-380-72802-8*, Avon Bks) Morrow Avon.

— Strider. 1991. 9.60 (*0-606-00402-5*, Pub. by Turtleback) Demco.

Cleary, Beverly. Strider. 1996. 8.60 (*0-606-09908-5*, Pub. by Turtleback) Demco.

Cleary, Beverly. Strider. large type ed. (Illus.). 182p. (YA). (gr. 6 up). 45.50 (*0-614-20623-5*, L-38202-00 APHB) Am Printing Hse.

— Troton Mi Perro.Tr. of Strider. (J). 1992. 15.05 (*0-606-10520-4*, Pub. by Turtleback) Demco.

— Two Dog Biscuits. LC 85-18816. (Illus.). 32p. (J). (ps-3). 1996. pap. 4.95 (*0-688-14735-6*, Wm Morrow) Morrow Avon.

— Two Dog Biscuits. 1996. 10.15 (*0-606-12554-X*, Pub. by Turtleback) Demco.

— Viva Ramona (Ramona Forever!) (Espasa Juvenil Ser.: Vol. 23). (SPA., Illus.). 149p. (J). (gr. 4-7). 1997 pap. text 8.95 (*84-239-8877-5*) Lectorum Pubns.

***Cleary, Beverly, et al.** It's Fun to Be Five. (Illus.). 96p. (J). (gr. k-2). 2000. pap. 4.99 (*0-439-13952-X*, Little Apple) Scholastic Inc.

— It's Great to Be Eight. (Illus.). 112p. (J). (gr. 2-5). 2000. pap. 4.99 (*0-590-37398-6*, Little Apple) Scholastic Inc.

Cleary, Bill. Centering Prayers: For Personal & Community Prayer. LC 94-60477. 144p. (Orig.). 1994. pap. 9.95 (*0-89622-608-5*) Twenty-Third.

Cleary, Bill, jt. auth. see Stern, David.

Cleary, Brendan. The Irish Card. 79p. 1994. pap. 14.95 (*1-85224-258-2*, Pub. by Bloodaxe Bks) Dufour.

— Sacrilege. LC 99-197465. 96p. 1999. pap. text 18.95 (*1-85224-460-7*) Bloodaxe Bks.

Cleary, Brian P. Give Me Bach My Schubert. LC 95-32431. (Illus.). 32p. (J). (gr. 3-6). 1996. lib. bdg. 18.60 (*0-8225-2116-4*, Lerner Publctns) Lerner Pub.

— Hairy, Scary, Ordinary: What is an Adjective? LC 98-32132. (Words are Categorical ser.). 1999. write for info. (*0-8225-2108-3*) Lerner Pub.

***Cleary, Brian P.** Hairy, Scary, Ordinary: What is an Adjective? (Words Are Categorical Ser.). 1999. pap. text 5.95 (*1-57505-419-1*) Lerner Pub.

Cleary, Brian P. Hairy, Scary, Ordinary: What Is an Adjective? LC 98-32132. (Words Are Categorical Ser.). (Illus.). 32p. (J). (gr. 2-4). 2000. 12.95 (*1-57505-401-9*, Carolrhoda) Lerner Pub.

— Mink, a Fink, a Skating Rink: What Is a Noun? 1999. write for info. (*0-8225-2109-1*) Lerner Pub.

— A Mink, a Fink, a Skating Rink: What is a Noun? LC 98-46384. (Words Are Categorical Ser.). (Illus.). 32p. (J). (gr. 2-4). 1999. 12.95 (*1-57505-402-7*, Carolrhoda); pap. text 5.95 (*1-57505-417-5*, Carolrhoda) Lerner Pub.

— To Root, to Toot, to Parachute: What is a Verb? 1999. pap. text 5.95 (*1-57505-418-3*) Lerner Pub.

— To Root, to Toot, to Parachute: What is a Verb? LC 98-49569. (Words Are Categorical Ser.). (Illus.). 32p. (J). (gr. 2-4). 2000. 12.95 (*1-57505-403-5*, Carolrhoda) Lerner Pub.

— To Root, to Toot, to Parachute: What Is a Verb? LC 98-49569. (Words Are Categorical Ser.). (Illus.). (J). 1999. write for info. (*0-8225-2110-5*, Lerner Publctns) Lerner Pub.

— You Never Sausage Love. LC 95-23530. (Illus.). 32p. (J). (gr. 3-6). 1996. lib. bdg. 18.60 (*0-8225-2115-6*) Lerner Pub.

Cleary, Chip & Schank, Roger C. Engines for Education. 1995. pap. 39.95 incl. cd-rom (*0-8058-2100-7*); cd-rom 29.95 (*1-56321-189-0*) L Erlbaum Assocs.

Cleary, Chip, jt. auth. see Schank, Roger C.

Cleary, David. Anatomy of the Amazon Gold Rush. LC 89-50857. (Illus.). 287p. (Orig.). 1990. pap. text 19.95 (*0-87745-262-8*) U of Iowa Pr.

Cleary, David & Cleary, Virginia. Retire Smart: Sound Advice to Help You Make Your Retirement Years Happy, Healthy & Active. LC 93-71917. 224p. (Orig.). 1993. pap. 12.95 (*1-880559-09-9*) Allworth Pr.

Cleary, David, et al. Brazil: The Rough Guide. 3rd ed. 736p. 1998. pap. 21.95 (*1-85828-223-3*) Viking Penguin.

Cleary, David, jt. auth. see Webb, Janette.

***Cleary, Dianne & Gorton, Jon.** In Search of Great Coffees: Fabulous Cafes Around the World. (Illus.). 120p. 1999. reprint ed. pap. text 15.00 (*0-7881-6592-5*) DIANE Pub.

Cleary, Edward J. Beyond the Burning Cross. 336p. 1995. pap. 13.00 (*0-679-74703-6*) Random.

— The ORSANCO Story: Water Quality Management in the Ohio Valley under an Interstate Compact. LC 67-16036. 351p. reprint ed. pap. 108.90 (*0-7837-3140-X*, 202308700032) Bks Demand.

Cleary, Edward L. The Struggle for Human Rights in Latin America. LC 97-5580. 192p. 1997. 57.95 (*0-275-95980-5*, Praeger Pubs); pap. 19.95 (*0-275-95981-3*, Praeger Pubs) Greenwood.

Cleary, Edward L., ed. Path from Puebla: Significant Documents of the Latin American Bishops since 1979. Berryman, Phillip, tr. 435p. (Orig.). 1989. pap. 14.95 (*1-55586-225-X*) US Catholic.

— Shaping a New World: An Orientation to Latin America. LC 78-156969. 333p. reprint ed. pap. 103.30 (*0-8357-7019-2*, 203353800086) Bks Demand.

Cleary, Edward L. & Stewart-Gambino, Hannah, eds. Power, Politics & Pentecostals in Latin America. 272p. (C). 1996. pap. 26.00 (*0-8133-2129-8*, Pub. by Westview) HarpC.

Cleary, Edward L., jt. ed. see Stewart-Gambino, Hannah W.

Cleary, Edward W., et al. Evidence, Cases & Materials. 4th ed. (American Casebook Ser.). 1060p. 1988. text 48.00 (*0-314-42672-8*) West Pub.

Cleary, J. B. & Lacombe, J. M. English Style Skill Builders: A Self-Improvement Program for Transcribers & Typists. 1980. text 17.96 (*0-07-011305-X*) McGraw.

Cleary, J. C. Zen Dawn. 1986. pap. 11.00 (*0-394-74388-1*) Random.

Cleary, J. C., ed. The Art of Worldly Wisdom: Confucian Teachings of the Ming Dynasty. LC 90-52799. (Dragon Editions Ser.). 160p. (Orig.). 1991. pap. 15.00 (*0-87773-601-4*) Shambhala Pubns.

Cleary, J. C., ed. & tr. see Hsin-Yueh.

Cleary, J. C., jt. tr. see Cleary, Thomas.

Cleary, J. C., tr. see Numata Center for Buddhist Translation & Research.

Cleary, James W. & Haberman, Frederick W. Rhetoric & Public Address: A Bibliography, 1947-1961. LC 64-7959. 506p. reprint ed. pap. 156.90 (*0-608-11107-4*, 201113200021) Bks Demand.

Cleary, James W., ed. see Robert, Henry M., et al.

Cleary, Joanna, jt. auth. see Hughes, Tim.

Cleary, Joe. The Kiss. LC 98-89507. 375p. 1998. text 25.00 (*0-7388-0225-5*); pap. text 15.00 (*0-7388-0226-3*) Xlibris Corp.

***Cleary, John, ed.** Traditions of Platonism. LC 99-72200. 450p. 1999. text 96.95 (*1-84014-684-2*, Pub. by Ashgate Pub) Ashgate Pub Co.

Cleary, John & Wians, William, eds. Proceedings of the Boston Area Colloquium in Ancient Philosophy, Vol. XI. 374p. 1996. 58.50 (*0-7618-0540-0*); pap. 38.50 (*0-7618-0541-9*) U Pr of Amer.

Cleary, John J. Aristotle & Mathematics: Aporetic Method in Cosmology & Metaphysics. LC 95-1398. (Philosophia Antiqua Ser.: Vol. 67). xxxvi, 558p. 1995. 195.50 (*90-04-10159-4*) Brill Academic Pubs.

— Aristotle on the Many Senses of Priority. LC 87-32202. (Journal of the History of Philosophy Monograph Ser.). 148p. (Orig.). (C). 1988. pap. text 17.95 (*0-8093-1465-7*) S Ill U Pr.

Cleary, John J., ed. The Perennial Tradition of Neoplatonism. (Ancient & Medieval Philosophy Ser.: No. XXIV). 614p. 1997. 117.50 (*90-6186-847-5*, Pub. by Leuven Univ) Coronet Bks.

— Proceedings of the Boston Area Colloquium in Ancient Philosophy, Vol. 3. LC 85-26323. (Illus.). 424p. (Orig.). (C). 1988. pap. text 34.50 (*0-8191-6810-6*); lib. bdg. 58.50 (*0-8191-6809-2*) U Pr of Amer.

C

— Proceedings of the Boston Area Colloquium in Ancient Philosophy, Vol. 7. 358p. (Orig.). (C). 1992. 62.00 (0-8191-8560-4); pap. 29.00 (0-8191-8561-2) U Pr of Amer.

***Cleary, John J. & Gurtler, Gary M., eds.** Proceedings of the Boston Area Colloquium in Ancient Philosophy, Vol. XIV. 296p. (Orig.). 1999. pap. 46.00 (90-04-11396-7) Brill Academic Pubs.

— Proceedings of the Boston Area Colloquium in Ancient Philosophy 1997. 312p. 1999. 71.00 (90-04-11394-0); pap. 43.00 (90-04-11393-2) Brill Academic Pubs.

— Proceedings of the Boston Area Colloquium in Ancient Philosophy, 1999. (Proceedings of the Boston Area Colloquium in Ancient Philosophy Ser.). 296p. 2000. 92.00 (90-04-11704-0) Brill Academic Pubs.

Cleary, John J. & Shartin, Daniel C., eds. Proceedings of the Boston Area Colloquium in Ancient Philosophy, Vol. IV. LC 85-26323. 392p. (Orig.). (C). 1989. pap. text 33.00 (0-8191-7336-3) U Pr of Amer.

— Proceedings of the Boston Area Colloquium in Ancient Philosophy, Vol. 5. 438p. (Orig.). (C). 1990. pap. text 38.00 (0-8191-7809-8); lib. bdg. 65.50 (0-8191-7808-X) U Pr of Amer.

— Proceedings of the Boston Area Colloquium in Ancient Philosophy, Vol. VI. 518p. (Orig.). (C). 1992. pap. text 37.50 (0-8191-8401-2); lib. bdg. 80.00 (0-8191-8400-4) U Pr of Amer.

Cleary, John J. & Wians, William, eds. Proceedings of the Boston Area Colloquium in Ancient Philosophy, Vol. IX. 320p. (Orig.). (C). 1994. pap. 29.50 (0-8191-9512-X); lib. bdg. 66.00 (0-8191-9511-1) U Pr of Amer.

— Proceedings of the Boston Area Colloquium in Ancient Philosophy, Vol. X, 1994. 310p. (Orig.). (C). 1995. pap. text 29.50 (0-8191-9982-6); lib. bdg. 66.00 (0-8191-9981-8) U Pr of Amer.

— Proceedings of the Boston Area Colloquium in Ancient Philosophy, Vol. 8: 1993. 365p. (Orig.). (C). 1994. pap. text 29.50 (0-8191-9144-2); lib. bdg. 66.00 (0-8191-9143-4) U Pr of Amer.

Cleary, John J. & Wians, William C., eds. Proceedings of the Boston Area Colloquium in Ancient Philosophy, 1996. (Illus.). 340p. 1998. pap. 29.50 (0-7618-1000-5) U Pr of Amer.

— Proceedings of the Boston Area Colloquium in Ancient Philosophy, 1996, Vol. XII. (Illus.). 340p. 1998. 65.00 (0-7618-0999-6) U Pr of Amer.

Cleary, Jon. Bleak Spring. large type ed. LC 94-9920. 416p. 1994. lib. bdg. 22.95 (0-8161-7437-7, G K Hall Lrg Type) Mac Lib Ref.

— Dark Summer. large type ed. LC 93-27026. 472p. 1993. pap. 17.95 (0-7862-0037-5) Thorndike Pr.

— Dilemma. LC 00-22428. 272p. 2000. 23.00 (0-688-17192-3, Wm Morrow) Morrow Avon.

***Cleary, Jon.** Dilemma. large type ed. LC 00-36984. (Core Ser.). 328p. 2000. 28.95 (0-7838-9069-9, G K Hall Lrg Type) Mac Lib Ref.

Cleary, Jon. Dragons at the Party. large type ed. 464p. 1988. 27.99 (0-7089-8474-6, Charnwood) Ulverscroft.

— Endpeace: A Scobie Malone Mystery. LC 97-11111. 272p. 1997. 23.00 (0-688-14710-0, Wm Morrow) Morrow Avon.

— Endpeace: A Scobie Malone Mystery. large type ed. LC 97-45558. 439p. 1998. 26.95 (0-7838-8369-2, G K Hall & Co) Mac Lib Ref.

***Cleary, Jon.** Five-Ring Circus: Suspense Down Under. LC 98-52493. 256p. 1999. 23.00 (0-688-16468-4, Wm Morrow) Morrow Avon.

Cleary, Jon. Five-Ring Circus: Suspense Down Under. large type ed. LC 99-21862. 412p. 1999. 27.95 (0-7838-8617-9, G K Hall & Co) Mac Lib Ref.

— High Road to China. 320p. 1983. mass mkt. 2.95 (0-446-31178-2, Pub. by Warner Bks) Little.

Cleary, Jon. The Sundowners. 25.95 (0-88411-467-8) Amereon Ltd.

Cleary, Jon. Winter Chill. large type ed. LC 96-16367. 1996. 24.95 (1-56895-331-3, Compass) Wheeler Pub.

Cleary, Jonathan C. Zibo: The Last Great Zen Master of China. LC 88-83532. 171p. (Orig.). reprint ed. pap. 48.80 (0-7837-5210-5, 2044941) Bks Demand.

Cleary, Kay, ed. see Hall, Jay A. & Zoros, George N.

Cleary, Kristen M., ed. Native American Wisdom. 64p. 1996. 4.98 (1-889461-00-8) DoveTail Bks.

— Native American Wisdom. (Illus.). 64p. 1996. 4.98 (0-614-29841-5) DoveTail Bks.

Cleary, Kristen M., ed. see Austen, Jane.

Cleary, Kristen Maree, ed. see Austen, Jane.

Cleary, Laura R. Security Systems in Transition. LC 98-72619. 206p. 1998. text 55.95 (1-85972-390-X, Pub. by Ashgate Pub) Ashgate Pub Co.

Cleary, Linda M. From the Other Side of the Desk: Students Speak Out About Writing. LC 91-23918. 213p. (C). 1991. pap. text 23.00 (0-86709-282-3, 0282, Pub. by Boynton Cook Pubs) Heinemann.

Cleary, Linda M., jt. auth. see Linn, Michael D.

Cleary, Linda M., jt. auth. see Peacock, Thomas D.

Cleary, M. C., tr. see Moulin, Annie.

Cleary, M. F., tr. see Moulin, Annie.

Cleary, Marie S. The Bulfinch Solution: Teaching the Ancient Classics in American Schools. LC 90-36454. (Illus.). 160p. (Orig.). (C). 1990. pap. text 19.95 (0-88143-112-5) Ayer.

Cleary, Mark. Peasants, Politicians & Producers: The Organisation of Agriculture in France since 1918. (Cambridge Studies in Historical Geography: No. 14). (Illus.). 222p. (C). 1989. text 59.95 (0-521-33347-4) Cambridge U Pr.

Cleary, Mark & Chuang Yann Wong. Oil, Economic Development, & Diversification of Brunei Darussalam. LC 93-44270. (Studies in the Economies of East & Southeast Asia). 1994. text 75.00 (0-312-12113-X) St Martin.

Cleary, Mark & Eaton, Peter. Borneo: Change & Development. (Illus.). 284p. (C). 1992. 42.00 (0-19-588587-2) OUP.

— Tradition & Reform: Land Tenure & Rural Development in South-East Asia. (South-East Asian Social Science Monographs). (Illus.). 160p. (C). 1996. text 39.95 (967-65-3108-1) OUP.

***Cleary, Mark & Goh, Kim Chuan.** Environment & Development in the Straits of Malacca. LC 99-36256. 232p. 2000. 90.00 (0-415-17243-8) Routledge.

Cleary, Melissa. And Your Little Dog, Too. 203p. 1998. mass mkt. 5.99 (0-425-16242-7, Prime Crime) Berkley Pub.

— Dead & Buried. 208p. (Orig.). 1994. mass mkt. 4.99 (0-425-14547-6, Prime Crime) Berkley Pub.

— Dog Collar Crime. (Orig.). 1993. mass mkt. 4.99 (0-425-14857-2, Prime Crime) Berkley Pub.

— First Pedigree Murder: A Dog Lover's Mystery. 208p. (Orig.). 1994. mass mkt. 4.99 (0-425-14299-X, Prime Crime) Berkley Pub.

***Cleary, Melissa.** In the Doghouse. (Dog Lover's Mystery Ser.). 256p. 2000. mass mkt. 5.99 (0-425-17311-9) Berkley Pub.

Cleary, Melissa. The Maltese Puppy. 256p. (Orig.). 1995. mass mkt. 4.99 (0-425-14721-5, Prime Crime) Berkley Pub.

— Old Dogs. 224p. 1997. mass mkt. 5.99 (0-425-15858-6, Prime Crime) Berkley Pub.

— Tail of Two Murders. 192p. (Orig.). 1993. pap. 4.99 (0-425-15809-8, Prime Crime) Berkley Pub.

Cleary, Melissa & Jove Books Publishing Staff. Hounded to Death. LC 94-116016. (Dog Lover's Mystery Ser.). 184p. 1993. 3.99 (0-515-11190-2, Jove) Berkley Pub.

Cleary, Michael. Hometown, U. S. A. Iddings, Kathleen, ed. LC 91-70957. (American Bk.). (Illus.). 79p. (Orig.). 1992. per. 10.00 (0-931289-07-6) San Diego Poet Pr.

Cleary, Michael, jt. auth. see Birch, David.

Cleary, Michael J. & Amsden, Robert T. A Data Analysis Handbook Using the SPSS System. (Illus.). (Orig.). 1979. pap. 9.95 (0-89894-015-X) Advocate Pub Group.

Cleary, Michael J., jt. auth. see Birch, David A.

Cleary, Mick. The Carling Years. (Illus.). 160p. 1997. 35.00 (0-575-06402-1, Pub. by V Gollancz) Trafalgar.

Cleary, Miriam. Performance Management: Achieving Credit Union Goals Through Employee Performance. (CUES HR Development Ser.). 54p. (Orig.). 1995. pap. 99.00 (1-889394-26-2) Credit Union Execs.

***Cleary, Patricia.** Elizabeth Murray: A Women's Pursuit of Independence in Eighteenth-Century America. 256p. 2000. 29.95 (1-55849-263-1) U of Mass Pr.

Cleary, Patrick. The Church & Usury. 1979. lib. bdg. 250.00 (0-8490-2884-1) Gordon Pr.

Cleary, Patti, ed. see Olds, Sally B.

Cleary, Rhondda. Fragrant Candles: A Practical Guide to Making Candles for the Home & Garden. LC 98-119235. (Illus.). 96p. 1997. pap. text 14.95 (1-86351-205-5, Pub. by Sally Milner) Sterling.

***Cleary, Rhondda.** Fragrant Candles: A Practical Guide to Making Candles for the Home & Garden. (Milner Craft Ser.). (Illus.). 2000. pap. 14.95 (1-86351-239-X) Sally Milner.

Cleary, Richard & McFadden, Dennis. Merchant Prince & Master Builder: Edgar J. Kaufmann & Frank Lloyd Wright. LC 98-48686. (Illus.). 200p. 1999. pap. 30.00 (0-88039-036-0) Mus Art Carnegie.

Cleary, Richard L. The Place Royale & Urban Design in the Ancien Regime. LC 98-3572. (Illus.). 320p. (C). 1999. text 90.00 (0-521-57268-1) Cambridge U Pr.

Cleary, Rita. Goldtown: A Novel of the American West. LC 95-35518. 368p. 1996. 24.95 (0-86534-241-5) Sunstone Pr.

***Cleary, Rita.** River Walk. LC 99-55129. 278p. 2000. 30.00 (0-7862-1845-2) Mac Lib Ref.

Cleary, Rita. Spies & Tories: A Novel. LC 98-7720. 384p. 1999. 26.95 (0-86534-275-X) Sunstone Pr.

Cleary, Rita M. Sorrel: A Novel. LC 92-43522. 288p. (Orig.). 1993. pap. 12.95 (0-86534-191-5) Sunstone Pr.

Cleary, Robert E., et al. Managing Public Programs: Balancing Politics, Administration, & Public Needs. LC 88-46089. (Public Administration Ser.). 312p. 1989. 39.95 (1-55542-143-1) Jossey-Bass.

Cleary, S. F., et al. Charge & Field Effects in Biosystems-Four Proceedings of the 1994 International Symposium. 544p. 1994. text 106.00 (981-02-1909-1) World Scientific Pub.

Cleary, Seamus. The Role of NGOs under Authoritarian Political Systems. LC 97-5332. (International Political Economy Ser.). 256p. 1997. text 65.00 (0-312-17464-0) St Martin.

***Cleary, Sean.** Canadian Securities Course Study Guide. 256p. 2000. pap., student ed. 29.95 (0-471-64517-6) Wiley.

Cleary, Stephen, jt. auth. see Simone, Nina.

Cleary, T., jt. auth. see Cleary, Thomas.

***Cleary, Teresa.** Front Porch Reflections. 2000. pap. 10.99 (0-570-05399-4) Concordia.

Cleary, Thomas. The Buddha Scroll. LC 99-24369. 25.00 (1-57062-513-1, Pub. by Shambhala Pubns) Random.

***Cleary, Thomas.** Classics of Strategy & Counsel: The Collected Translations of Thomas Cleary, 3 vols. Incl. Classics of Strategy & Counsel Vol. 1: The Art of War, Mastering the Art of War, The Lost Art of War, The Silver Sparrow Art of War: The Collected Translations of Thomas Cleary. 2000. 40.00 (1-57062-727-4, Pub. by Shambhala Pubns); Classics of Strategy & Counsel Vol. 2: Thunder in the Sky; The Japanese Art of War; The Book of Five Rings; Ways of Warriors, Codes of Kings: The Collected Translations of Thomas Cleary. 2000. 40.00 (1-57062-728-2, Pub. by Shambhala Pubns); Classics of Strategy & Counsel Vol. 3: The Art of Wealth, Living a Good Life, The Human Element, Back to Beginnings: The Collected Translations of Thomas Cleary. 2000. 40.00 (1-57062-729-0); 2000. 103.50 (1-57062-750-9, Pub. by Shambhala Pubns) Random.

Cleary, Thomas. Entry into the Inconceivable: An Introduction to Hua-yen Buddhism. LC 83-3613. 230p. (C). 1995. reprint ed. pap. text 17.00 (0-8248-1697-8) UH Pr.

— Essential Confucius. 1998. 7.99 (0-7858-0903-1) Bk Sales Inc.

— The Essential Confucius. rev. ed. LC 91-55282. 192p. 1993. pap. 14.00 (0-06-250215-8, Pub. by Harper SF) HarpC.

— Essential Koran. 1998. 7.99 (0-7858-0902-3) Bk Sales Inc.

— The Essential Koran: The Heart of Islam. LC 92-53926. 224p. 1994. pap. 14.00 (0-06-250198-4, Pub. by Harper SF) HarpC.

— Essential Tao. 1998. 7.99 (0-7858-0905-8) Bk Sales Inc.

— The Essential Tao: An Initiation into the Heart of Taoism Through the Authentic Tao Te Ching & the Inner Teachings of Chuang Tzu. rev. ed. LC 91-55283. 176p. 1993. pap. 13.00 (0-06-250216-6, Pub. by Harper SF) HarpC.

— Immortal Sisters: Secret Teachings of Taoist Women. 2nd ed. LC 96-22872. Orig. Title: Immortal Sisters: Secrets of Taoist Women. 130p. (Orig.). 1996. pap. 12.95 (1-55643-222-4) North Atlantic.

— Instant Zen: Waking up in the Present. LC 94-25026. 137p. 1994. pap. 14.95 (1-55643-193-7) North Atlantic.

— The Japanese Art of War: Understanding the Culture of Strategy. LC 90-52801. 136p. 1992. pap. 13.95 (0-87773-653-7, Pub. by Shambhala Pubns) Random.

— The Pocket Zen Reader. LC 98-39908. 160p. 1999. pap. text 6.95 (1-57062-447-X, Pub. by Shambhala Pubns) Random.

— Sex, Health & Long Life. 124p. 1999. pap. 10.00 (1-57062-433-X, Pub. by Shambhala Pubns) Random.

— Sleepless Nights: Verses for the Wakeful. LC 94-24048. (Illus.). 108p. (C). 1995. pap. 9.95 (1-55643-200-3) North Atlantic.

— Stopping & Seeing: A Comprehensive Course in Buddhist Meditation. LC 96-44695. 208p. 1997. pap. 12.00 (1-57062-275-2, Pub. by Shambhala Pubns) Random.

— The Taoist Classics: The Collected Translations of Thomas Cleary, Vol. 4. LC 99-27951. 485p. 1999. 39.95 (1-57062-485-2, Pub. by Shambhala Pubns) Random.

***Cleary, Thomas.** The Taoist Classics Vol. 3: The Collected Translations of Thomas Cleary. LC 99-27951. 608p. 2000. 45.00 (1-57062-487-9, Pub. by Shambhala Pubns) Random.

— The Taoist Classics Vol. 4: The Collected Translations of Thomas Cleary. LC 99-27951. 2000. 45.00 (1-57062-488-7, Pub. by Shambhala Pubns) Random.

Cleary, Thomas. Teachings of Zen. LC 97-23349. 1998. pap. 10.95 (1-57062-338-4, Pub. by Shambhala Pubns) Random.

— Understanding Reality the Inner Teachings of Taoism the Book of Balance & Harmony Practical Taoism Vol. 2: The Collected Translations of Thomas Cleary. LC 99-27951. 551p. 1999. 39.95 (1-57062-486-0, Pub. by Shambhala Pubns) Random.

— Ways of Warriors, Codes of Kings. LC 98-39906. 128p. 1999. 20.00 (1-57062-443-7, Pub. by Shambhala Pubns) Random.

— The Wisdom of the Prophet. 144p. 1996. pap. 6.00 (0-614-21097-6, 1321) Kazi Pubns.

— Zen & the Art of Insight. LC 99-34711. 128p. 1999. pap. 12.95 (1-57062-516-6, Pub. by Shambhala Pubns) Random.

— Zen Essence: The Science of Freedom. LC 94-36157. (Orig.). 1995. pap. 6.95 (1-57062-097-0, Pub. by Shambhala Pubns) Random.

Cleary, Thomas, comment. The Ecstasy of Enlightenment: Teachings of Natural Tantra Translated from the Old Bengali with Commentary. LC 97-43967. 240p. 1998. pap. 12.95 (1-57863-027-4) Weiser.

Cleary, Thomas, ed. from CHI. The Book of Balance & Harmony. LC 89-2895. 154p. 1989. pap. 13.00 (0-86547-363-3) N Point Pr.

— I Ching: The Book of Change. LC 91-53089. 155p. 1992. pap. 6.95 (0-87773-661-8, Pub. by Shambhala Pubns) Random.

— Vitality, Energy, Spirit: A Taoist Sourcebook. LC 90-53387. (Dragon Editions Ser.). 264p. (Orig.). 1991. pap. 19.00 (0-87773-519-0, Pub. by Shambhala Pubns) Random.

— Zen Antics: One Hundred Stories of Enlightenment. LC 93-12213. 128p. (Orig.). 1993. pap. 13.00 (0-87773-944-7, Pub. by Shambhala Pubns) Random.

Cleary, Thomas, tr. The Book of Leadership & Strategy: Lessons of the Chinese Masters. LC 91-53226. Orig. Title: Tao of Politics. (CHI & ENG.). 112p. 1992. pap. 11.00 (0-87773-667-7, Pub. by Shambhala Pubns) Random.

— Book of Serenity. LC 97-42454. 1998. 60.00 (1-57062-381-3, Pub. by Shambhala Pubns) Random.

— Buddhist Yoga: A Comprehensive Course. 1995. pap. 10.00 (1-57062-018-0, Pub. by Shambhala Pubns) Random.

— The Dhammapada: Sayings of Buddha. LC 94-16628. 144p. 1994. pap. 8.95 (0-553-37376-5) Bantam.

— The Essential Koran: The Heart of Islam - an Introductory Selection of Readings from the Quran. 210p. 1996. pap. 12.00 (0-614-21052-6, 264) Kazi Pubns.

— The Flower Ornament Scripture: A Translation of the Avatamsaka Sutra. LC 93-21833.Tr. of Tripitaka Sutrapitaka Buddhavatamsakamahavaipulyasutra. 1560p. 1993. 60.00 (0-87773-940-4, Pub. by Shambhala Pubns) Random.

— Kensho: The Heart of Zen. LC 96-18728. 160p. (Orig.). 1997. pap. 13.00 (1-57062-269-8, Pub. by Shambhala Pubns) Random.

— Living a Good Life. LC 96-44398. 80p. 1997. pap. 6.95 (1-57062-274-4, Pub. by Shambhala Pubns) Random.

— Minding Mind: A Course in Basic Meditation. LC 94-27845. 180p. (Orig.). 1995. pap. 11.95 (1-57062-004-0, Pub. by Shambhala Pubns) Random.

— Practical Taoism. LC 95-23894. 112p. 1996. pap. 12.95 (1-57062-200-0, Pub. by Shambhala Pubns) Random.

— Rational Zen: The Mind of Dogen Zenji. LC 92-50126. 256p. 1993. 20.00 (0-87773-689-8, Pub. by Shambhala Pubns) Random.

— The Secret of the Golden Flower. LC 90-55796. 160p. 1993. reprint ed. pap. 13.00 (0-06-250193-3, Pub. by Harper SF) HarpC.

— Sex, Health, & Long Life: Manuals of Taoist Practice. (Orig.). 1995. pap. text 48.00 (1-57062-060-1) Shambhala Pubns.

— The Taoist I Ching. LC 85-27890. 332p. 1986. pap. 18.00 (0-87773-352-X, Pub. by Shambhala Pubns) Random.

— Wen-Tzu: Understanding the Mysteries. LC 92-53700. (Dragon Editions Ser.). Orig. Title: Further Teachings of Lao-tzu. 168p. 1992. pap. 19.95 (0-87773-862-9, Pub. by Shambhala Pubns) Random.

— Zen Lessons: The Art of Leadership. LC 88-18604. 144p. (Orig.). 1989. pap. 14.00 (0-87773-446-1, Pub. by Shambhala Pubns) Random.

— Zen Lessons: The Art of Leadership. LC 92-56460. 248p. (Orig.). 1993. pap. 7.00 (0-87773-893-9, Pub. by Shambhala Pubns) Random.

— Zen Lessons: The Art of Leadership, 1, 1. abr. ed. 1990. audio 10.95 (0-87773-559-X, Z008, Pub. by Shambhala Pubns) Random.

Cleary, Thomas, tr. from SAN. Art of Wealth: Strategies for Success. LC 97-43796. 200p. 1998. pap. 11.95 (1-55874-541-6) Health Comm.

***Cleary, Thomas & Aziz, Sartaz.** Twilight Goddess: Spiritual Feminism & Feminine Spirituality. LC 00-21870. 304p. 2000. 24.95 (1-57062-499-2, Pub. by Shambhala Pubns) Random.

Cleary, Thomas & Cleary, J. C., trs. from CHI. The Blue Cliff Record. LC 91-52522. 682p. 1992. 60.00 (0-87773-622-7, Pub. by Shambhala Pubns) Random.

Cleary, Thomas & Cleary, T. The Japanese Art of War: Understanding the Culture of Strategy. abr. ed. 1991. audio 10.95 (0-87773-624-3, Z014, Pub. by Shambhala Pubns) Random.

Cleary, Thomas, ed. & tr. see Liang, Zhuge & Ji, Liu.

Cleary, Thomas, tr. see Chang Po-tuan.

Cleary, Thomas, tr. see Dogen.

Cleary, Thomas, tr. see Hui-neng.

Cleary, Thomas, tr. see Huikai, Wumen.

Cleary, Thomas, tr. see I-Ming, Liu.

Cleary, Thomas, tr. see Kaiguo, Chen & Shunchao, Zheng.

Cleary, Thomas, tr. see Liang, Zhuge, et al.

Cleary, Thomas, tr. see Liu I-Ming.

Cleary, Thomas, tr. see Musashi, Miyamoto.

Cleary, Thomas, tr. see Numata Center for Buddhist Translation & Research.

Cleary, Thomas, tr. see Tzu, Sun, 2nd.

Cleary, Thomas, tr. see Tzu, Sun.

Cleary, Thomas, tr. see Weija, Siao.

Cleary, Thomas, tr. & pref. see Tzu, Sun.

Cleary, Thomas C., jt. auth. see Greene, Richard M., Jr.

Cleary, Thomas F., tr. The Five Houses of Zen. LC 96-44399. (Dragon Editions Ser.). 208p. 1997. pap. 13.00 (1-57062-292-2, Pub. by Shambhala Pubns) Random.

Cleary, Thomas F., tr. see Daidoji, Yuzan.

Cleary, Thomas P. The Family Record. 256p. 1995. 24.95 (0-948524-13-8, Pub. by Town Hse) Roberts Rinehart.

Cleary, Timothy. Business Information Technology. (Frameworks Ser.). (Illus.). 336p. 1998. pap. 42.50 (0-273-63410-0, Pub. by Pitman Pbg) Trans-Atl Phila.

Cleary, Victoria L., et al, eds. Prehospital Care: Administrative & Clinical Management. 369p. 1987. 85.00 (0-87189-616-8, 89616) Aspen Pub.

Cleary, Virginia, jt. auth. see Cleary, David.

Cleary, William. How the Wild Things Pray. LC 99-20591. (Illus.). 111p. 1999. pap. 12.95 (0-939516-45-4) Forest Peace.

— The Lively Garden Prayer Book: Prayers of Backyard Creation from A to Z. LC 97-13947. (Illus.). 111p. 1997. pap. 11.95 (0-939516-35-7) Forest Peace.

— Prayers & Fables: Meditating on Aesop's Wisdom. LC 97-47387. (Illus.). 180p. 1997. pap. 14.95 (1-55612-960-2, LL1960) Sheed & Ward WI.

— Prayers to She Who Is. 132p. 1995. pap. 15.95 (0-8245-1527-7) Crossroad NY.

— Psalm Services for Group Prayer. LC 92-81718. 96p. (Orig.). 1993. pap. 12.95 (0-89622-526-7) Twenty-Third.

Cleasby, Adrian. What in the World Is Going On? British Television & Global Affairs. (Oxfam Research Discussion Papers). (C). 1995. pap. 7.95 (0-9525050-0-2) Humanities.

— What in the World Is Going On? British Television & Global Affairs. 1995. pap. 7.95 (0-614-11425-X, Pub. by Oxfam Pub) Stylus Pub VA.

Cleaton, Allen, jt. auth. see Cleaton, Irene.

Cleaton, Irene & Cleaton, Allen. Books & Battles: American Literature, 1920-1930. LC 73-124269. (Illus.). 1970. reprint ed. lib. bdg. 53.00 (0-8154-0339-9) Cooper Sq.

Cleator, P. E., ed. Letters from Baltimore: The Mencken-Cleator Correspondence. LC 78-75176. 280p. 1982. 38.50 (0-8386-3075-8) Fairleigh Dickinson.

***Cleave, Andrew.** Aquarium Fish. (Illus.). 72p. 1998. 10.98 (1-880908-98-0) Todtri Prods.

An Asterisk (*) at the beginning of an entry indicates that the title is appearing for the first time.

— Aquarium Fish: A Portrait of the Animal World. (Illus.). 72p. 1998. pap. 10.98 (*1-880908-79-4*) Todtri Prods.

— Bats. 1999. 10.95 (*1-57717-130-6*) Todtri Prods.

Cleave, Andrew. Big Cats: A Portrait of the Animal World, 1. 1998. pap. text 10.98 (*1-880908-27-1*) Todtri Prods.

— Curious Creatures A Portrait of the Animal World, 1. 1998. pap. text 10.98 (*1-880908-29-8*) Todtri Prods.

— Field Guide to Trees of Britain, Europe & North America. (Illus.). 320p. 1995. pap. 24.95 (*1-85223-801-1*, Pub. by Cro1wood) Trafalgar.

Cleave, Andrew. Giants of the Sea. (Illus.). 72p. 10.98 (*1-57717-076-8*) Todtri Prods.

Cleave, Andrew. Giants of the Sea: Creatures of Fascination, 1. 1998. 14.98 (*1-880908-07-7*) Todtri Prods.

***Cleave, Andrew.** Seals & Sea Lions, 1. 1998. pap. 10.98 (*1-880908-78-6*) Todtri Prods.

Cleave, Andrew. Seashells: A Portrait of the Animal World, 1. 1998. pap. text 10.98 (*1-880908-65-4*) Todtri Prods.

***Cleave, Andrew.** Sharks. 1998. pap. 10.98 (*1-880908-25-5*) Todtri Prods.

Cleave, Andrew. Snakes & Reptiles: A Portrait of the Animal World, 1. 1998. pap. text 10.98 (*1-880908-26-3*) Todtri Prods.

***Cleave, Andrew.** Whales & Dolphins. 1998. pap. 10.98 (*1-880908-20-4*) Todtri Prods.

— Wildflowers. 1998. pap. 10.98 (*1-57717-028-8*) Todtri Prods.

Cleave, Charles Van, see AEC Technical Information Center Staff & Van Cleave, Charles.

Cleave, Derek. 1st Peter. 1999. pap. text 12.99 (*1-85792-337-5*) Christian Focus.

— Know God. 1988. pap. 2.99 (*0-85234-252-7*, Pub. by Evangelical Pr) P & R Pubng.

Cleave, John P. A Study of Logics. (Oxford Logic Guides Ser.: No. 18). (Illus.). 430p. 1992. text 135.00 (*0-19-853211-3*) OUP.

Cleave, Shirley. Managing the Sport Club Program: From Theory to Practice. Zeigler, Earle F., ed. (Monograph Series on Sport & Physical Education Management). 49p. 1984. pap. text 4.80 (*0-87563-244-0*) Stipes.

Cleave, Stephen Van, see Van Cleave, Stephen.

Cleave, T. L. Saccharine Disease: Sugar & Its Role in Disease. 5.70 (*0-317-05972-6*) Hypoglycemia Foun.

Cleave, William R. Van, see Van Cleave, William R.

Cleave, William R. Van, see Gray, Colin S. & Van Cleave, William R.

Cleaveland, Agnes M. No Life for a Lady. LC 77-6825. (Illus.). xii, 356p. 1977. pap. 12.95 (*0-8032-5868-2*, Bison Books) U of Nebr Pr.

Cleaveland, Clif. Sacred Space: Stories from a Life in Medicine. LC 97-36741. 210p. 1997. text 21.95 (*0-943126-64-9*) Amer Coll Phys.

Cleaveland, John & Hutchinson, G. S. The Banking System of the State of New York. Bruchey, Stuart, ed. LC 80-1181. (Rise of Commercial Banking Ser.). 1981. reprint ed. lib. bdg. 38.95 (*0-405-13642-0*) Ayer.

Cleaveland, Parker. An Elementary Treatise on Mineralogy & Geology. Albritton, Claude C., Jr., ed. LC 77-6513. (History of Geology Ser.). (Illus.). 1978. reprint ed. lib. bdg. 58.95 (*0-405-10436-7*) Ayer.

Cleaveland, Teta, jt. auth. see Lesman, Helen.

Cleaveland, W. R., ed. CUNCUR 'Ninety-Two: International Conference on Concurrency Theory, 3rd, Stony Brook, NY, U. S. A., August 1992: Proceedings. LC 92-26385. (Lecture Notes in Computer Science Ser.: Vol. 630). x, 580p. 1992. 80.00 (*0-387-55822-5*) Spr-Verlag.

Cleaver, A. H., jt. auth. see Hatton, Thomas J.

Cleaver, Anne H. & Stann, E. Jeffrey, eds. Voyage to the Southern Ocean: The Letters of Lieutenant William Reynolds from the U. S. Exploring Expedition, 1838-1842. LC 88-10156. (Illus.). 384p. 1988. 34.95 (*0-87021-300-8*) Naval Inst Pr.

Cleaver, Arthur H., jt. auth. see Hatton, Thomas J.

Cleaver, Betty & Taylor, William. Instructional Consultant Role of the School Library Media Specialist. 88p. 1989. pap. text 15.00 (*0-8389-3377-7*) ALA.

Cleaver, Bill, jt. auth. see Cleaver, Vera.

Cleaver, Carey. The Silent Valley. large type ed. 576p. 31.50 (*0-7089-3699-7*) Ulverscroft.

Cleaver, Carole, jt. auth. see Rodman, Selden.

Cleaver, Charles G. Japanese & Americans: Cultural Parallels & Paradoxes. LC 75-18081. (Illus.). 312p. reprint ed. pap. 96.80 (*0-608-15950-6*, 203321300084) Bks Demand.

Cleaver, Dale G. Art: An Introduction. 5th ed. (Illus.). 491p. (C). 1988. pap. text 62.00 (*0-15-503434-0*, Pub. by Harcourt Coll Pubs); sl. write for info. (*0-318-64529-7*) Harcourt Coll Pubs.

Cleaver, Eldridge. Soul on Ice. 256p. 1999. pap. 11.95 (*0-385-33379-X*, Delta Trade) Dell.

Cleaver, Elizabeth. The Loon's Necklace. 24 pp.p. (J). (ps up). 1990. pap. 7.95 (*0-19-540675-3*) OUP.

Cleaver, Hedy. Parental Perspectives in Cases of Suspected Child Abuse. 230p. 1995. pap. 45.00 (*0-11-321786-2*, HM17862, Pub. by Statnry Office) Bernan Associates.

— Vulnerable Children in Schools: A Study of Catch 'em Young, a Project Helping 10 Year Olds Transfer School. 156p. 1991. pap. text 23.95 (*1-85521-211-0*, Pub. by Dartmth Pub) Ashgate Pub Co.

Cleaver, J. D. Island Immigrants. (Sauvie Island Heritage Ser.: Vol. 2). 48p. (Orig.). 1986. pap. 3.95 (*0-87595-181-3*) Oregon Hist.

— Island Life: Pioneer Homesteading. (Sauvie Island Heritage Ser.: Vol. 3). (Illus.). 48p. (Orig.). 1989. pap. 3.95 (*0-87595-182-1*) Oregon Hist.

— Island Origins. (Sauvie Island Heritage Ser.: Vol. 1). 40p. (Orig.). 1986. pap. 3.95 (*0-87595-180-5*) Oregon Hist.

Cleaver, James. History of Graphic Art. LC 73-95115. 282p. 1969. reprint ed. lib. bdg. 65.00 (*0-8371-2522-7*, CLGA, Greenwood Pr) Greenwood.

Cleaver, Joanne Y. Find & Keep Customers for Your Small Business. (CCH Business Owner's Toolkit Ser.). 1999. pap. text 16.95 (*0-8080-0354-2*) CCH INC.

Cleaver, Judith A. Sweetie Pie Cafe Cookbook. 1996. pap., spiral bd. 10.95 (*0-9650481-0-1*) Two Girls Flying.

Cleaver, Kathleen. Memories of Love & War. 1999. write for info. (*0-679-45007-6*) Random.

Cleaver, Kevin M. Rural Development Strategies for Poverty Reduction & Environmental Protection in Sub-Saharan Africa. LC 97-28449. (Directions in Development Ser.). 76p. 1997. pap. 22.00 (*0-8213-3977-X*, 13977) World Bank.

— A Strategy to Develop Agriculture in Sub-Saharah Africa & a Focus for the World Bank. LC 93-3624. (Technical Paper, Africa Department Ser.: No. 203). 153p. 1993. pap. 22.00 (*0-8213-2420-9*, 12420) World Bank.

Cleaver, Kevin M. & Donovan, W. Graeme. Agriculture, Poverty, & Policy Reform in Sub-Saharan Africa. LC 95-2574. (World Bank Discussion Papers: No. 280). 60p. 1995. pap. 22.00 (*0-8213-3189-2*, 13189) World Bank.

Cleaver, Kevin M. & Schreiber, Gotz A. Reversing the Spiral: The Population, Agriculture, & Environment Nexus in Sub-Saharan Africa. LC 94-9060. (Directions in Development Ser.). 320p. 1994. pap. 22.00 (*0-8213-2769-0*, 12769) World Bank.

Cleaver, Mary, et al. The TriBeCa Cookbook. (Illus.). 176p. 1997. pap. 16.95 (*0-89815-912-1*) Ten Speed Pr.

Cleaver, Mary L. History of the Town of Catherine, Schuyler County. (Illus.). 686p. 1997. reprint ed. lib. bdg. 68.50 (*0-8328-6110-3*) Higginson Bk Co.

***Cleaver, Pamela.** Writing a Children's Book: How to Write for Children & Get Published. 144p. 2000. pap. 14.95 (*1-85703-598-4*, Pub. by How To Bks) Midpt Trade.

Cleaver, Paul, jt. auth. see Landor, Gina.

Cleaver, Richard. Know My Name: A Gay Liberation Theology. LC 94-34207. 176p. (Orig.). 1995. pap. 18.95 (*0-664-25576-0*) Westminster John Knox.

Cleaver, Richard & Myers, Patricia, eds. A Certain Terror: Heterosexism, Militarism, Violence & Change. (Illus.). 386p. 1993. pap. 14.95 (*0-9635516-0-4*) Grt Lks Reg AFSC.

Cleaver, Richard G. New Heaven, New Earth: Practical Essays on the Catholic Worker Program. Preheim, Beth & Sprong, Michael, eds. 92p. (Orig.). 1993. pap. 5.95 (*0-9636224-0-4*) Rose Hill Bks.

Cleaver, T., jt. auth. see Wallace, M.

Cleaver, Tony. Understanding the World Economy: Global Issues Shaping the Future. LC 96-9862. 280p. (C). 1997. pap. 25.99 (*0-415-12816-1*) Routledge.

— Understanding the World Economy: Global Issues Shaping the Future. LC 96-9862. 280p. (C). 1997. 85.00 (*0-415-12815-3*) Routledge.

Cleaver, Vera. Belle Pruitt. LC 87-45879. 176p. (J). (gr. 4-7). 1988. 12.95 (*0-397-32304-2*); lib. bdg. 13.89 (*0-397-32305-0*) HarpC Child Bks.

— Belle Pruitt. LC 87-45879. (Trophy Bk.). 176p. (J). (gr. 4-7). 1990. reprint ed. pap. 3.50 (*0-06-440249-5*, HarpTrophy) HarpC Child Bks.

— Ellen Grae. LC 67-10623. (Illus.). 96p. (J). 1967. lib. bdg. 12.89 (*0-397-30938-4*) HarpC Child Bks.

— Hazel Rye. LC 85-42741. (Trophy Bk.). 192p. (J). (gr. 5-8). 1985. pap. 3.95 (*0-06-440156-1*, HarpTrophy) HarpC Child Bks.

— Sweetly Sings the Donkey. LC 85-40098. 160p. (J). (gr. 5-9). 1985. 12.95 (*0-397-32156-2*); lib. bdg. 12.89 (*0-397-32157-0*) HarpC Child Bks.

Cleaver, Vera & Cleaver, Bill. Delpha Green & Company. LC 79-172141. 144p. (J). (gr. 6 up). 1972. pap. 2.95 (*0-397-31344-6*, LSC-8) HarpC Child Bks.

— Dust of the Earth. LC 75-18939. 160p. (YA). (gr. 7 up). 1975. 13.95 (*0-397-31650-X*) HarpC Child Bks.

— Grover. LC 69-12001. (Illus.). 128p. (J). (gr. 4-7). 1970. 13.95 (*0-397-31118-4*) HarpC Child Bks.

— Hazel Rye. LC 81-48603. 160p. (J). (gr. 5-8). 1983. 12.95 (*0-397-31951-7*); lib. bdg. 13.89 (*0-397-31952-5*) HarpC Child Bks.

— Lady Ellen Grae. LC 68-10981. (Illus.). (J). (gr. 4-6). 1968. lib. bdg. 12.89 (*0-397-31012-9*) HarpC Child Bks.

— Me Too. 160p. (YA). (gr. 7-9). 1973. 13.95 (*0-397-31485-X*) HarpC Child Bks.

— Me Too. LC 85-42745. (Trophy Bk.). 160p. (J). (gr. 5-7). 1985. pap. 2.95 (*0-06-440161-8*, HarpTrophy) HarpC Child Bks.

— Mock Revolt. LC 75-151467. 160p. (J). (gr. 6 up). 1971. lib. bdg. 12.89 (*0-397-31238-5*) HarpC Child Bks.

— Queen of Hearts. LC 77-18252. 160p. (YA). (gr. 6 up). 1978. 14.00 (*0-397-31771-9*) HarpC Child Bks.

— Trial Valley. LC 76-54303. 160p. (YA). (gr. 7 up). 1987. lib. bdg. 12.89 (*0-397-32246-1*) HarpC Child Bks.

— Trial Valley. LC 76-54303. (Trophy Keypoint Bk.). 192p. (YA). (gr. 7 up). 1991. pap. 3.50 (*0-06-447076-8*, HarpTrophy) HarpC Child Bks.

— Where the Lilies Bloom. (J). 1977. 5.50 (*0-87129-546-6*, W40) Dramatic Pub.

— Where the Lilies Bloom. LC 75-82402. (Trophy Keypoint Bk.). 224p. (J). (gr. 7-12). 1989. mass mkt. 4.95 (*0-06-447005-9*, HarpTrophy) HarpC Child Bks.

— Where the Lilies Bloom. 176p. (J). 1969. 15.95 (*0-397-31111-7*, Lippnctt) Lppncott W & W.

— Where the Lilies Bloom. (J). 1989. 10.05 (*0-606-04364-0*, Pub. by Turtleback) Demco.

Cleaves. Business Math. 5th ed. LC 98-12629. 724p. 1998. pap. text 81.33 (*0-13-787763-3*, Prentice Hall) P-H.

— Business Simulations. 2nd ed. (C). 1990. pap. 14.40 (*0-13-105065-6*, Macmillan Coll) P-H.

— How to Study Business Math. 5th ed. 24p. (C). 1998. text. write for info. (*0-13-081287-0*) P-H.

Cleaves. Quick Reference Table Business Math. 4th ed. 1996. text. write for info. (*0-13-399361-2*) Allyn.

Cleaves, Cheryl & Hobbs, Margie J. Business Math. 5th ed. LC 98-12635. 544p. (C). 1998. pap. text 58.00 (*0-13-787798-6*) P-H.

Cleaves, Cheryl, et al. Business Math: Practical Applications. 3rd annot. ed. 1993. teacher ed. write for info. (*0-318-69557-X*) Prentice ESL.

— College Mathematics for Technology. 4th ed. Orig. Title: Basic Mathematics for Trades & Technologies. 1008p. (C). 1997. 80.00 (*0-13-716614-1*) P-H.

— Vocational-Technical Mathematics Simplified. (Illus.). 368p. 1987. pap. text 49.60 (*0-13-943093-8*) P-H.

***Cleaves, Cheryl S., et al.** College Algebra & Trigonometry with Applications. 4th ed. LC 97-207152. (Illus.). 1999. write for info. (*0-13-789249-7*) P-H.

Cleaves, Cheryl S., et al. College Mathematics for Technology. 4th ed. LC 97-14336. 1997. pap. text, student ed. 28.60 (*0-13-727256-1*) P-H.

***Cleaves, Cheryl S., et al.** College Mathematics for Technology. 5th ed. LC 00-31383. (Illus.). 992p. 2000. 74.67 (*0-13-086107-3*) P-H.

Cleaves, Francis W. Manual of Mongolian Astrology & Divination. 1990. pap. 7.00 (*0-674-54825-6*) HUP.

Cleaves, Francis W., ed. from MON. The Secret History of the Mongols. (Harvard-Yenching Institute Publications). 344p. 1982. 22.50 (*0-674-79670-5*) HUP.

Cleaves, Francis W., jt. ed. see Mostaert, Antoine.

Cleaves, Freeman. Meade of Gettysburg. LC 60-7735. (Illus.). 416p. 1991. pap. 16.95 (*0-8061-2298-6*) U of Okla Pr.

— Old Tippecanoe: William Henry Harrison & His Times. Speirs, Katherine E., ed. LC 90-80486. (Signature Ser.). (Illus.). 420p. 1990. reprint ed. 30.00 (*0-945707-01-0*) Amer Political.

— Rock of Chickamauga: The Life of General George H. Thomas. LC 85-40939. (Illus.). 340p. (Orig.). 1986. pap. 16.95 (*0-8061-1978-0*) U of Okla Pr.

Cleaves, Peter S. Professions & the State: The Mexican Case. LC 87-5911. (PROFMEX Ser.). 147p. 1987. 28.95 (*0-8165-1016-4*) U of Ariz Pr.

Cleaves, Peter S. & Scurrah, Martin J. Agriculture, Bureaucracy, & Military Government in Peru. LC 80-14687. 333p. reprint ed. pap. 103.30 (*0-608-08084-5*, 206904300002) Bks Demand.

Cleberg, Kathleen, ed. see Brown, Deborah.

Clebert, Jean-Paul. Dictionnaire du Symbolisme Animal. (FRE.). 455p. 1974. pap. 35.00 (*0-8288-6023-8*, M581) Fr & Eur.

— Paris Insolite. (FRE.). 1972. pap. 10.95 (*0-7859-2198-2*, 207036285X) Fr & Eur.

Clebsch, Betsy. A Book of Salvias: Sages for Every Garden. LC 96-22160. (Illus.). 269p. 1997. 29.95 (*0-88192-369-9*) Timber.

Clebsch, Ed, ed. see Kemp, Steve.

Clebsch, William A. American Religious Thought: A History. LC 73-82911. xii, 236p. 1985. reprint ed. pap. text 17.00 (*0-226-10962-3*) U Ch Pr.

Clebsch, William A. England's Earliest Protestants, 1520-1535, 11. LC 80-15226. (Yale Publications in Religion: No. 11). 358p. 1980. reprint ed. lib. bdg. 59.75 (*0-313-22420-X*, CLEE, Greenwood Pr) Greenwood.

Clebsch, William A. From Sacred to Profane America: The Role of Religion in American History. LC 81-9142. (Classics in Religious Studies: Vol. 2). 256p. reprint ed. pap. 79.40 (*0-608-08684-3*, 206920700003) Bks Demand.

Clecak, Peter. America's Quest for the Ideal Self: Dissent & Fulfillment in the 60s & 70s. 408p. 1985. pap. text 24.95 (*0-19-503544-5*) OUP.

— Radical Paradoxes: Dilemmas of the American Left, 1945-1970. LC 73-4072. 1973. 29.50 (*0-06-010819-3*) Irvington.

Cleckley, Franklin & Palmer, Louis. Introductions to the West Virginia Criminal Justice System & Its Laws. 492p. (C). 1994. pap. text, per. 57.95 (*0-8403-9797-6*) Kendall-Hunt.

Cleckley, Franklin D. Handbook of West Virginia Evidence Vol. 2: 1999 Cumulative Supplement. 3rd ed. 275p. 1999. write for info. (*0-327-01021-5*, 6086615) LEXIS Pub.

— Handbook on Evidence for West Virginia Lawyers, 2 vols., Set. 3rd ed. 1994. 160.00 (*1-55834-157-9*, MICHIE) LEXIS Pub.

— Handbook on West Virginia Criminal Procedure, 2 vols., Set. 2nd ed. 1993. 160.00 (*1-55834-107-2*, 60852-11, MICHIE) LEXIS Pub.

— Handbook on West Virginia Criminal Procedure: 1999 Cumulative Supplement, 2 vols. 2nd ed. 517p. 1999. suppl. ed. write for info. (*0-327-01280-3*, 60853-15) LEXIS Pub.

— Handbook on West Virginia Criminal Procedure Vol. 1: 1999 Cumulative Supplement. 2nd ed. 1999. suppl. ed. write for info. (*0-327-01281-1*, 6084815) LEXIS Pub.

— Handbook on West Virginia Criminal Procedure Vol. 2: 1999 Cumulative Supplement. 2nd ed. 1999. suppl. ed. write for info. (*0-327-01282-X*, 60849-15) LEXIS Pub.

— Handbook on West Virginia Evidence Vol. 1: 1999 Cumulative Supplement. 3rd ed. 275p. 1999. write for info. (*0-327-01020-7*, 6086515) LEXIS Pub.

— Handbook on West Virginia Evidence Vols. 1 & 2: 1999 Cumulative Supplement, 2 vols., Set. 3rd ed. 275p. 1999. write for info. (*0-327-01019-3*, 6086115) LEXIS Pub.

Cleckley, Hervey. The Mask of Sanity: An Attempt to Clarify Some Issues about the So-Called Psychopathic Personality. 5th ed. 471p. (C). 1988. reprint ed. text 25.00 (*0-9621519-0-4*) E S Cleckley.

Cleckley, Hervey M., jt. auth. see Thigpen, Corbett.

Cleckley, Mary, et al, eds. We Need Not Walk Alone: After the Death of a Child. 2nd ed. (Illus.). 234p. (Orig.). 1991. pap. 14.95 (*1-878615-00-9*) Compassionate Friends.

Clecvers, J. G. P. W. Application of Remote Sensing to Agricultural Field Trials. 227p. 1992. pap. 375.00 (*81-7089-122-1*, Pub. by Intl Bk Distr) St Mut.

Clede, Bill. Police Officer's Guide. 2nd rev. ed. LC 88-24987. (Illus.). 384p. (Orig.). 1995. pap. 21.95 (*0-9630016-2-0*) Lakeland Pub.

— Police Shotgun Manual: How to Survive Against All Odds. LC 86-948. 128p. 1986. reprint ed. pap. 39.70 (*0-608-00473-1*, 206129200007) Bks Demand.

— The Practical Pistol Manual: How to Use a Handgun for Self Defense. LC 98-226176. (Illus.). 176p. 1998. pap. 7.95 (*0-915463-74-1*) Jameson Bks.

— Security Officer's Manual. LC 92-85104. (Illus.). 160p. (Orig.). 1993. pap. 16.95 (*0-9630016-1-2*) Lakeland Pub.

Clediere, J. & Rocher, Daniel. Apollo Larousse French-German, German-French Dictionary: Dictionnaire Larousse Apollo Francais-Allemand-Francais. (FRE & GER.). 1120p. 1981. 24.95 (*0-8288-0339-0*, M14160) Fr & Eur.

Clediere, Jean & Rocher, Daniel. Dictionnaire Bilingue: French-German, German-French. (FRE & GER.). 560p. 1984. pap. 14.95 (*0-7859-7847-X*, 2253002801) Fr & Eur.

— Dictionnaire Francais-Allemand, Allemand-Francais. (FRE & GER.). 1987. 59.95 (*0-7859-7654-X*, 2034020537) Fr & Eur.

Clediere, Jean, et al. Dictionnaire Francais-Allemand, Deutsch-Franzosich. (FRE.). write for info. (*0-7859-7650-7*, 2034016114) Fr & Eur.

***Clee, Ken & Losonsky, Joyce.** M & M's Around the World: Collector's Guide. (Illus.). 160p. 2000. pap. 29.95 (*0-7643-1078-X*) Schiffer.

Clee, Ken, jt. auth. see Hufferd, Suzan.

Clee, Mona. Branch Point. 1996. mass mkt. 5.99 (*0-441-00291-9*) Ace Bks.

— Overshoot. 1998. mass mkt. 5.99 (*0-441-00509-8*) Ace Bks.

***Clee, Paul & Radu-Clee, Violeta.** American Dreams: Readings For Writers. 2nd rev. ed. LC 98-41960. xv, 560p. 1998. pap. text 30.95 (*0-7674-0495-5*, 0495-5) Mayfield Pub.

Cleef, A. Van, see Van Cleef, A.

Cleef, Daniel Van, see Reinhartz, Judy & Van Cleef, Daniel.

Cleeg, D. J., jt. ed. see Khera, K.

Cleek, Charles L. Doctor the Jokes on You. (Illus.). 44p. 1997. pap. write for info. (*0-9660543-2-6*) GIFTGO.

— Many Friends Many Colors. (Illus.). 44p. (gr. 3-8). 1997. pap. write for info. (*0-9660543-0-X*) GIFTGO.

— There Is a Cat for You. (Illus.). 41p. (J). (gr. 1-8). 1997. pap. write for info. (*0-9660543-1-8*) GIFTGO.

Cleek, George W. Cleek: Early Western Augusta Pioneers, Including the Families of Cleek, Gwin, Lightner & Warwick, & Related Families. (Illus.). 492p. 1997. reprint ed. pap. 74.00 (*0-8328-7972-X*); reprint ed. lib. bdg. 84.00 (*0-8328-7971-1*) Higginson Bk Co.

***Cleek, George W.** Early Western Augusta Pioneers: Including the Families of Cleek, Gwin, Lightner & Warwick & Related Families of Bratton, Campbell, Carlile, Craig, Crawford, Dyer, Gay, Givens, Graham, Harper, Henderson, Hull, Keister, Lockridge, McFarland & Moore. 492p. 1999. pap. 40.00 (*0-8063-4522-5*) Clearfield Co.

Cleek, Richard K., jt. auth. see Noble, Allen G.

***Cleeland, Hokulani.** He Leka Na Kahilina. (HAW., Illus.). 17p. (J). (gr. 1-3). 1999. pap. 6.95 incl. audio (*1-58191-051-7*) Aha Punana Leo.

— He Lumi Hou Ko Ka Hale. (HAW., Illus.). 21p. (J). (gr. 1-2). 1999. pap. 6.95 incl. audio (*1-58191-052-5*) Aha Punana Leo.

— Hele 'O Kawika Laua 'O Kamuela I Ka Pule. (HAW., Illus.). 15p. (J). (gr. k-1). 1999. pap. 6.95 incl. audio (*1-58191-055-X*) Aha Punana Leo.

— Na Hana a Ka La'i. (HAW., Illus.). 17p. (J). (gr. k). 1999. pap. 6.95 incl. audio (*1-58191-050-9*) Aha Punana Leo.

— Olelo O'iwi ke Kahua: He Puke A'o 'Olelo Hawai'i. (ENG & HAW.). xi, 439p. (YA). (gr. 10 up). 1994. text 26.95 (*1-58191-012-6*) Aha Punana Leo.

Cleeland, Hokulani, ed. see Hawaiian Lexicon Committee.

Cleeland, Hokulani, ed. see Napoleon, Kawika.

Cleeland, Sylvia A. Dalkulla Anna. 2nd ed. 288p. 1984. reprint ed. pap. 7.95 (*0-944996-03-5*) Carlsons.

Cleemput, Marcel R. Van, see Van Cleemput, Marcel R.

Cleemput, W. M. Van, see Van Cleemput, W. M.

Cleere, Henry, tr. see Audouze, Francoise & Buchsenschutz, Olivier.

Cleere, Nigel. Nightjars: A Guide to the Nightjars, Nighthawks & Their Relatives. LC 98-60961. (Illus.). 256p. 1998. 40.00 (*0-300-07457-3*) Yale U Pr.

Cleeremans, Axel. Mechanisms of Implicit Learning: A Connectionist Model of Sequence Processing. LC 92-35739. (Neural Network Modeling & Connectionism Ser.). (Illus.). 230p. 1993. 36.00 (*0-262-03205-8*, Bradford Bks) MIT Pr.

Clees, Terry. They Call It a Hardship Tour. 122p. 1997. pap. 9.99 (*1-57502-612-0*, PO1809) Morris Pubng.

***Cleese, Alyce Faye.** How to Manage Your Mother: Understanding the Most Difficult, Complicated, & Fascinating Relationship in Your Life. LC 00-20509. 272p. 2000. 24.00 (*0-06-039334-3*, ReganBks) HarperTrade.

Cleese, Armand, jt. auth. see Epps, Archie C.

***Cleese, John.** Pocket Full of Pythons, Vol. 2. (Illus.). 64p. 2000. pap. 9.99 (*0-413-74160-5*) Methn.

Cleese, John & Booth, Connie. The Complete Fawlty Towers. 1989. pap. 16.00 (*0-679-72127-4*) Pantheon.

Cleese, John & Crichton, Charles. A Fish Called Wanda. (Illus.). 112p. 1988. pap. 8.95 (*1-55783-033-9*) Applause Theatre Bk Pubs.

Cleese, John, jt. auth. see Buckman, Robert.

Cleese, John, jt. auth. see Skynner, Robin.

An Asterisk (*) at the beginning of an entry indicates that the title is appearing for the first time.

Cleeton, Claud E. Strategies for the Options Trader. LC 78-11230. 184p. reprint ed. pap. 57.10 (*0-7837-2832-8*, 205764000006) Bks Demand.

Cleeve, Emmanuel. Multinational Enterprises in Development: The Mining Industry of Sierra Leone. LC 96-79950. 160p. 1997. 55.95 (*1-85972-559-7*, Pub. by Avebry) Ashgate Pub Co.

Cleeve, Martin. Screwcutting in the Lathe. (Workshop Practice Ser.: No. 3). (Illus.). 176p. (Orig.). 1984. pap. 19.95 (*0-85242-838-3*, Pub. by Nexus Special Interests) Trans-Atl Phila.

Cleeve, Roger. The Earth. Steltenpohl, Jane, ed. (Science up Close Ser.). (Illus.). 32p. (J). (gr. 3-5). 1990. pap. 4.95 (*0-671-68629-1*, Julian Messner) Silver Burdett Pr.

— The Last Long Journey. LC 83-18172. (Phoenix Fiction Ser.). 272p. 1984. pap. 9.95 (*0-226-10990-9*) U Ch Pr.

— The Living World. Steltenpohl, Jane, ed. (Science up Close Ser.). (Illus.). 32p. (J). (gr. 3-5). 1990. pap. 4.95 (*0-671-68630-5*, Julian Messner) Silver Burdett Pr.

— Outer Space. Steltenpohl, Jane, ed. LC 89-29194. (Science up Close Ser.). (Illus.). 32p. (J). (gr. 3-5). 1990. pap. 4.95 (*0-671-68631-3*, Julian Messner); lib. bdg. 10.98 (*0-671-68628-3*, Julian Messner) Silver Burdett Pr.

Cleeves, Ann. Another Man's Poison. large type ed. 400p. 1994. 27.99 (*0-7089-3038-7*) Ulverscroft.

— Come Death & High Water. large type ed. 1989. 27.99 (*0-7089-2101-9*) Ulverscroft.

— The Healers. large type ed. LC 95-38619. (General Ser.). 385p. 1996. pap. 20.95 (*0-7862-0561-X*) Thorndike Pr.

— High Island Blues. LC 96-24211. 1997. pap. 20.00 (*0-7862-0833-3*) Thorndike Pr.

— A Lesson in Dying. large type ed. 336p. 1992. 27.99 (*0-7089-2566-9*) Ulverscroft.

— Murder in Paradise. large type ed. 1990. 27.99 (*0-7089-2200-7*) Ulverscroft.

— A Prey to Murder. large type ed. 1992. 27.99 (*0-7089-2386-0*) Ulverscroft.

Cleff, William C. & Brtis, John S. Single-Point Access to Full Life Cycle Information - The Station Basis Navigator. (ICONE 4 - Technical Papers). 1996. write for info. (*0-614-16703-5*, 96-NE-2) ASME.

Clegern, Wayne M. Origins of Liberal Dictatorship in Central America: Guatemala, 1865-1873. 192p. (C). 1994. text 34.95 (*0-87081-317-X*) Univ Pr Colo.

Clegg. Celebrating Diversity. (Teaching Methods Ser.). 1995. pap., teacher ed. 14.00 (*0-8273-6210-2*) Delmar.

— Chameleon Manager. LC 99-165857. 200p. 1998. pap. text 34.95 (*0-7506-4026-X*) Buttrwrth-Heinemann.

— Students Writing Across the Curriculum. (C). 1991. pap. text, teacher ed. 3.75 (*0-03-028763-4*) Harcourt Coll Pubs.

— You Come When I Call You. 1995. per. 5.50 (*0-671-67278-9*) PB.

Clegg, Ambrose A., Jr., jt. auth. see Banks, James A.

Clegg, Andrew W. & Nedoluha, Gerald E., eds. Astrophysical Masers: Proceedings, Arlington, Virginia, March 9-11, 1992. LC 92-46270. (Lecture Notes in Physics Ser.: Vol. 412). 1993. 104.95 (*0-387-56343-1*) Spr-Verlag.

Clegg, Averil & Woolett, Anne. Twins: From Conception to Five Years. (Illus.). 128p. 1988. pap. 11.00 (*0-345-35661-6*) Ballantine Pub Grp.

Clegg, Barbara. The Man Who Made Littlewoods: The Story of John Moores. (Illus.). 224p. 1994. 45.00 (*0-340-57479-8*, Pub. by Hodder & Stought Ltd) Trafalgar.

Clegg, Brian. Creativity & Innovation in Brief. LC 00-265228. (Illus.). 200p. 1999. pap. text 19.95 (*0-7506-4255-6*) Rector Pr.

***Clegg, Brian.** Instant Brainpower: Tune up Your Thinking Now! 192p. 1999. pap. 12.95 (*0-7494-3024-9*, Kogan Pg Educ) Stylus Pub VA.

— Instant Motivation. (Instant Ser.). 128p. 2000. pap. 12.95 (*0-7494-3101-6*, Kogan Pg Educ) Stylus Pub VA.

— Instant Stress Management. (Instant Ser.). 128p. 2000. pap. 12.95 (*0-7494-3116-4*, Kogan Pg Educ) Stylus Pub VA.

— Instant Time Management: Re-Organize Your Life & Work Now! 128p. 1999. pap. 12.95 (*0-7494-2963-1*, Kogan Pg Educ) Stylus Pub VA.

— Mining the Internet: Information Gathering & Research on the Net. 1999. pap. 16.95 (*0-7494-3025-7*) Kogan Page Ltd.

Clegg, Brian & Birch, Paul. DisOrganization: The Handbook of Creative Organizational Reformation. LC 99-219570. 256p. 1998. pap. 44.50 (*0-273-63107-1*, Pub. by Pitman Pub) Trans-Atl Phila.

***Clegg, Brian & Birch, Paul.** Instant Creativity. 128p. 1999. pap. 12.95 (*0-7494-2949-6*, Kogan Pg Educ) Stylus Pub VA.

— Instant Teamwork: Motivate & Energize Your Team Now! LC 99-234361. 128p. 1999. pap. 12.95 (*0-7494-2804-X*, Kogan Pg Educ) Stylus Pub VA.

Clegg, Brian, jt. auth. see Birch, Paul.

Clegg, Charles, jt. auth. see Beebe, Lucius.

Clegg, Chris, et al. People & Computers: How to Evaluate Your Company's New Technology. 268p. 1988. text 51.95 (*0-470-21207-1*) P-H.

Clegg, Claude Andrew, III. An Original Man: The Life & Times of Elijah Muhammad. (Illus.). 400p. 1998. pap. 14.95 (*0-312-18153-1*) St Martin.

Clegg, Cyndia S. Press Censorship in Elizabethan England. 312p. (C). 1997. text 64.95 (*0-521-57312-2*) Cambridge U Pr.

Clegg, Cyndia S., intro. The Peacable & Prosperous Regiment of Blessed Queene Elisabeth: A Facsimile from Holinshed's Chronicles (1587) (Illus.). 500p. 2000. 250.00 (*0-87328-161-6*) Huntington Lib.

Clegg, Cyndia S. & Wheeler, Michael M. Students Writing Across the Curriculum. (Illus.). 500p. (C). 1991. pap. text 32.50 (*0-03-028762-6*) Harcourt Coll Pubs.

Clegg, D. J. Tax Law Through the Cases. 957p. 1991. pap. write for info. (*0-7021-2357-9*, R160.74, Pub. by Juta & Co) Gaunt.

Clegg, D. W. & Collyer, A. A. The Structure & Properties of Polymeric Materials. 300p. 1993. 70.00 (*0-901716-39-1*, Pub. by Inst Materials) Ashgate Pub Co.

Clegg, Dai. Fast-Track Case Method. 224p. (C). 1994. 45.95 (*0-201-62432-X*) Addison-Wesley.

Clegg, David & Billington, Shirley. The Effective Primary Classroom. LC 94-219035. (Roehampton Teaching Studies). 176p. 1994. pap. 27.00 (*1-85346-271-3*, Pub. by David Fulton) Taylor & Francis.

— Making the Most of Your Inspection: Primary. LC 93-50646. 144p. 1994. write for info. (*0-7507-0246-X*, Falmer Pr) Taylor & Francis.

— Making the Most of Your Inspection: Secondary. LC 93-50131. 144p. 1994. write for info. (*0-7507-0248-6*, Falmer Pr); pap. 29.95 (*0-7507-0249-4*, Falmer Pr) Taylor & Francis.

Clegg, David & Billington, Shirly. Leading Primary Schools: The Pleasure, Pain & Principles of Leadership in the Primary School. LC 97-19357. 128p. 1998. pap. 25.95 (*0-335-19644-6*) OpUniv Pr.

Clegg, David W. & Billington, Shirley. The Primary Headteacher: The Pleasure, Pain & Principles of Leadership in the Primary School. LC 97-19357. 128p. 1998. 85.00 (*0-335-19645-4*) OpUniv Pr.

Clegg, Douglas. Dark of the Eye. 1994. mass mkt. 5.99 (*0-671-73539-X*) PB.

— Goat Dance. 1989. mass mkt. 5.99 (*0-671-66425-5*) PB.

***Clegg, Douglas.** Mischief. 368p. 2000. pap. 5.99 (*0-8439-4766-7*, Leisure Bks) Dorchester Pub Co.

Clegg, Douglas. Neverland. (Orig.). 1991. mass mkt. 4.95 (*0-671-31286-3*) PB.

***Clegg, Douglas.** The Nightmare Chronicles. 368p. 1999. mass mkt. 5.50 (*0-8439-4580-X*, Pub. by Dorchester Pub Co) CMG.

— You Come When I Call You. 448p. 2000. 40.00 (*1-881475-89-1*) Cemetery Dance.

— You Come When I Call You. 400p. 2000. pap. 5.99 (*0-8439-4695-4*, Leisure Bks) Dorchester Pub Co.

Clegg, Douglass. The Halloween Man. 368p. 1998. mass mkt. 5.50 (*0-8439-4439-0*, Leisure Bks) Dorchester Pub Co.

Clegg, Edward. Race & Politics: Partnership in the Federation of Rhodesia & Nyasaland. LC 75-3731. 280p. 1975. reprint ed. lib. bdg. 35.00 (*0-8371-8061-9*, CLRPO, Greenwood Pr) Greenwood.

Clegg, Eileen M. & Swartz, Susan F. Goodbye Good Girl: Letting Go of the Rules & Taking Back Your Self. LC 97-75475. 208p. 1998. pap. 12.95 (*1-57224-106-3*) New Harbinger.

Clegg, Eileen M., et al. Claiming Your Creative Self: True Stories from the Everyday Lives of Women. LC 98-67407. (Illus.). 192p. 1998. pap. 15.95 (*1-57224-117-9*) New Harbinger.

Clegg, Eileen M., jt. auth. see Frain, Betty.

Clegg Erickson, Gina. Hide & Seek. LC 95-15026. (Illus.). 24p. (gr. k-3). 1995. pap. 3.95 (*0-8120-9075-6*) Barron.

Clegg, Helen. Yup Finds a Friend. LC 97-26945. (Illus.). (J). 1998. write for info. (*1-56763-354-4*); pap. write for info. (*1-56763-355-2*) Ozark Pub.

Clegg, Helen & Larom, Mary. Making Wire Jewelry: 60 Easy Projects in Silver, Copper, & Brass. LC 97-17291. (Illus.). 112p. (Orig.). 1997. pap. 18.95 (*1-57990-002-X*, Pub. by Lark Books) Random.

Clegg, Holly B. The Devil's Food: A Dessert Cookbook. rev. ed. (Illus.). 192p. 1998. 19.95 (*0-9610888-2-6*) H B Clegg.

***Clegg, Holly B.** Meals on the Move: Rush Hour Recipes. LC 99-96229. (Trim & Terrific Ser.: Vol. 4). (Illus.). 256p. 2000. 19.95 (*0-9610888-6-9*, Pub. by H B Clegg) Wimmer Bk Dist.

Clegg, Holly B. Trim & Terrific American Favorites. 1996. pap. write for info. (*0-517-88739-8*) C Potter.

— Trim & Terrific American Favorites: Over 250 Easy Everyday Low-Fat Recipes. (Trim & Terrific Ser.). 224p. 1996. 18.95 (*0-517-70256-8*) C Potter.

— Trim & Terrific American Favorites: 250 Easy, Everyday Low-Fat Recipes. 1996. 18.95 (*0-614-95783-4*) C Potter.

— A Trim & Terrific Louisiana Kitchen: An Easy & Lighter Approach to Southern Cuisine. LC 92-97408. (Illus.). 240p. 1993. 18.95 (*0-9610888-3-4*) H B Clegg.

— Trim & Terrific One Dish Favorites. LC 97-157036. (Trim & Terrific Ser.). 1997. 18.95 (*0-517-70258-4*) C Potter.

Clegg, Hugh A., et al. Trade Union Officers: A Study of Full-Time Officers, Branch Secretaries & Shop Stewards in British Trade Unions. LC 61-65475. 281p. 1961. 40.00 (*0-674-89970-9*) HUP.

Clegg, Hugh G. Reparation: Restoring the Damaged Self in Child & Adult Psychotherapy. LC 95-13022. Orig. Title: The Reparative Motif in Child & Adult Therapy. 244p. 1995. reprint ed. pap. 45.00 (*1-56821-557-6*) Aronson.

Clegg, I. E., tr. see Pirenne, Henri.

Clegg, Ian. Workers' Self-Management in Algeria. (Illus.). 256p. 1972. 25.00 (*0-85345-200-8*, Pub. by Monthly Rev) NYU Pr.

Clegg, James S., jt. ed. see Welch, G. Rickey.

Clegg, Jeanette. The Eaglet That Fell to Earth. Perry, Carol J., ed. (Illus.). 28p. (Orig.). (J). (gr. k-4). 1995. pap. 4.95 (*0-9649929-0-6*) Jendi Pr.

Clegg, Jenny. Fu Manchu & the 'Yellow Peril' 72p. 1994. pap. 15.00 (*0-948080-97-3*, Trentham Bks) Stylus Pub VA.

Clegg, Jerry S. On Genius: Affirmation & Denial from Schopenhauer to Wittgenstein. LC 93-48244. (American University Studies, VI, Philosophy: Vol. 158). IX, 211p. (C). 1994. text 37.95 (*0-8204-2370-X*) P Lang Pubng.

— The Structure of Plato's Philosophy. LC 75-31467. 207p. 1978. 32.50 (*0-8387-1878-7*) Bucknell U Pr.

Clegg, John, ed. Mainstreaming ESL: Case-Studies in Integrating ESL Students into the Mainstream Curriculum. LC 96-11904. 239p. 1996. 99.00 (*1-85359-349-4*, Pub. by Multilingual Matters); pap. 34.95 (*1-85359-348-6*, Pub. by Multilingual Matters) Taylor & Francis.

Clegg, John & Dawson, Stephen. Profitable Legal Aid. 283p. 1991. 110.00 (*1-85190-124-8*, Pub. by Tolley Pubng) St Mut.

Clegg, John & Dawson, Stephen, eds. Profitable Legal Aid. 335p. 1994. 175.00 (*0-85459-950-9*, Pub. by Tolley Pubng) St Mut.

Clegg, John, jt. auth. see Stanbury, Peter.

Clegg, Ken. Thoughts on Psalm 119. 20p. (Orig.). 1997. pap. 2.50 (*1-880573-28-8*) Bible Search Pubns.

Clegg, Legrand, II & Ahmed, Karima Y. The Daughters of Isis. (Clegg Ser.: Pt. 2). 1992. pap. text 12.00 (*1-882578-77-5*) Clegg Series.

— Egypt During the Golden Age. (Clegg Ser.: Pt. 2). 50p. 1991. pap. text 10.00 (*1-882578-00-7*) Clegg Series.

Clegg, Luther B. The Empty Schoolhouse: Memories of One-Room Texas Schools. LC 96-52977. (Centennial Series of the Association of Former Students: Vol. 68). (Illus.). 240p. (C). 1997. text 24.95 (*0-89096-749-0*) Tex A&M Univ Pr.

Clegg, Luther B., et al. Celebrating Diversity: A Multicultural Resource. LC 94-6814. 288p. (C). 1994. pap. 54.95 (*0-8273-6209-9*) Delmar.

Clegg, Nigel. How to Paint Your Boat: Painting, Varnishing & Antifouling. LC 96-53260. (Illus.). 144p. 1997. pap. 19.95 (*1-57409-029-1*) Sheridan.

Clegg, Peter & Watkins, Derry. Sunspaces: New Vistas for Living & Growing. Clarkson, Sarah M., ed. LC 86-45974. (Illus.). 216p. 1987. 29.95 (*0-88266-452-2*, Garden Way Pub); pap. 16.95 (*0-88266-453-0*, Garden Way Pub) Storey Bks.

Clegg, R. E., et al, eds. Circumstellar Media in Late Stages of Stellar Evolution. (Illus.). 359p. (C). 1994. text 69.95 (*0-521-46551-6*) Cambridge U Pr.

Clegg, Roger A., ed. Protein Targeting Protocols. (Methods in Molecular Biology Ser.: Vol. 88). (Illus.). 336p. 1998. 79.50 (*0-89603-450-X*); 99.50 (*0-89603-487-9*) Humana.

Clegg, Roger A., jt. auth. see Mol, Jan A.

Clegg, Scott, ed. Advances in Heat & Mass Transfer in Biotechnology, 1997: Proceedings, ASME International Mechanical Engineering Congress & Exposition, Dallas, TX, 1997. LC 97-76719. (HTD - BED Ser.: Vols. 355 & 37). vii, 215p. 1997. pap. 100.00 (*0-7918-1844-6*, QH301) ASME Pr.

— Advances in Heat & Mass Transfer in Biotechnology, 1998: Proceedings ASME International Mechanical Engineering Congress & Exposition. 197p. 1998. 110.00 (*0-7918-1598-6*) ASME.

Clegg, Scott, jt. ed. see Hayes, Linda J.

Clegg, Stewart, et al, eds. Handbook of Organization Studies. 725p. 1996. 95.00 (*0-7619-5132-6*) Sage.

— The Politics of Management Knowledge: A Critical Perspective. LC 96-69550. 256p. 1996. 65.00 (*0-8039-7933-9*); pap. 26.95 (*0-8039-7934-7*) Sage.

Clegg, Stewart & Dunkerley, David. Organization, Class & Control. 1980. pap. 20.00 (*0-7100-0435-4*, Routledge Thoemms) Routledge.

***Clegg, Stewart, et al.** Global Management: Universal Theories & Local Realities. LC 98-61654. 308 p. 1999. 27.95 (*0-7619-5815-0*) Sage.

Clegg, Stewart, jt. auth. see Kono, Toyohiro.

Clegg, Stewart R. Frameworks of Power. 272p. (C). 1989. text 75.00 (*0-8039-8160-0*); pap. text 25.95 (*0-8039-8161-9*) Sage.

— Modern Organizations: Organization Studies in the Postmodern World. 256p. (C). 1990. 47.50 (*0-8039-8329-8*); pap. 19.95 (*0-8039-8330-1*) Sage.

Clegg, Stewart R., ed. Organization Theory & Class Analysis: New Approaches & New Issues. (Studies in Organization: No. 17). xiv, 529p. (C). 1990. lib. bdg. 74.95 (*3-11-012003-8*) De Gruyter.

***Clegg, Stewart R., et al, eds.** Global Management: Universal Theories & Local Realities. LC 98-61654. 288p. 1999. 82.00 (*0-7619-5814-2*) Sage.

— Managing Organizations: Current Issues. 288p. 1998. pap. 31.95 (*0-7619-6046-5*) Sage.

***Clegg, Stewart R. & Hardy, Cynthia, eds.** Studying Organization: Theory & Method. 484p. 1999. pap. 39.95 (*0-7619-6045-7*) Sage.

Clegg, Stewart R. & Redding, S. Gordon, eds. Capitalism in Contrasting Cultures. (Studies in Organization: No. 20). viii, 451p. (C). 1990. lib. bdg. 59.95 (*3-11-011857-2*) De Gruyter.

Clegg, Stewart R., jt. auth. see Kono, Toyohiro.

Clegg, Stuart, jt. ed. see Palmer, Gill.

Clegg, William. Crystal Structure Determination. (Oxford Chemistry Primers Ser.: No. 60). (Illus.). 96p. (C). 1998. pap. text 12.95 (*0-19-855901-1*) OUP.

Cleghorn, Andrea. Rosie's Place: Offering Women Shelter & Hope. (Illus.). 184p. Date not set. pap. write for info. (*1-889242-00-4*) VanderWyk & Burnham.

— Rosie's Place: Offering Women Shelter & Hope. LC 97-28109. (Illus.). 184p. 1997. 23.95 (*0-9641089-9-2*) VanderWyk & Burnham.

Cleghorn, Angus. Wallace Stevens Poetics: The Neglected Poems. text. write for info. (*0-312-23101-6*) St Martin.

Cleghorn, Geoffrey J., jt. ed. see Shepherd, Ross W.

Cleghorn, J. M. & Lee, B. L. Understanding & Treating Mental Illness: The Strength & Limits of Modern Psychiatry. LC 90-4429. 250p. 1991. pap. text 16.95 (*0-920887-73-2*) Hogrefe & Huber Pubs.

Cleghorn, Patricia. The Secrets of Self-Esteem: A New Approach for Everyone. 192p. 1996. pap. 10.95 (*1-85230-777-3*, Pub. by Element MA) Penguin Putnam.

Cleghorn, Sarah N. Threescore. Baxter, Annette K., ed. LC 79-8783. (Signal Lives Ser.). (Illus.). 1980. reprint ed. lib. bdg. 37.95 (*0-405-12831-2*) Ayer.

Clegy, Eric D., ed. see Russell, Lonnie D. & Ettlin, Robert A.

***Clein, Dan.** CMOS IC Layout: Concepts, Methodologies & Tools. LC 99-44934. 304p. 1999. pap. text 49.95 (*0-7506-7194-7*) Buttrwrth-Heinemann.

Clein, Wendy. Concepts of Chivalry in "Sir Gawain & the Green Knight" 151p. 1987. 29.95 (*0-937664-75-8*) Pilgrim Bks OK.

Cleir, Piaras V. De, see De Cleir, Piaras V.

Cleiren, Marc. Bereavement & Adaptation: A Comparative Study of the Aftermath of Death. LC 92-26136. 296p. 1992. 31.95 (*1-56032-279-9*) Hemisp Pub.

Clej, Alina. A Genealogy of the Modern Self: Thomas De Quincey & the Intoxication of Writing. LC 94-31754. 376p. 1995. 39.50 (*0-8047-2393-1*) Stanford U Pr.

Cleland. Learn English Through Topics about Australia. Date not set. pap. text. write for info. (*0-582-66569-8*, Pub. by Addison-Wesley) Longman.

Cleland & Evans. Learning English Thru Topics about Asia. Date not set. pap. text. write for info. (*0-582-87284-7*, Pub. by Addison-Wesley) Longman.

Cleland, Alan S. & Bruno, Albert V. The Market Value Process: Bridging Customer & Shareholder Value. LC 96-10106. (Business & Management Ser.). 244p. 1996. 39.95 (*0-7879-0275-6*) Jossey-Bass.

***Cleland, Charles E.** The Place of the Pike (Gnoozhekaaning) A History of the Bay Mills Indian Community. (Illus.). 116p. 2000. 27.95 (*0-472-09740-7*, 09740); pap. 18.95 (*0-472-06740-0*, 06740) U of Mich Pr.

Cleland, Charles E. Rites of Conquest: A History & Culture of Michigan's Native Americans. (Illus.). 360p. (C). 1992. pap. 19.95 (*0-472-06447-9*, 06447) U of Mich Pr.

Cleland, Craig J., jt. auth. see Wilson, Robert M.

Cleland, David & King, William R., eds. Project Management Handbook. 2nd ed. 1008p. 1988. 110.00 (*0-471-29384-9*, VNR) Wiley.

Cleland, David I. Automated Factory Handbook: Technology & Management. 1990. 69.95 (*0-8306-9296-7*) McGraw-Hill Prof.

— Field Guide to Project Management. LC 97-14585. 400p. (C). 1998. text 39.95 (*0-442-02345-6*, VNR) Wiley.

— The Origin & Development of a Philosophy of Long-Range Planning in American Business. LC 75-41751. (Companies & Men: Business Enterprises in America Ser.). (Illus.). 1976. 35.95 (*0-405-08068-9*) Ayer.

— Project Management: Strategic Design & Implementation. 2nd ed. 1994. 49.00 (*0-07-011351-3*) McGraw.

— Project Management: Strategic Design & Implementation. 3rd ed. LC 98-25720. (Illus.). 575p. 1998. 64.95 (*0-07-012020-X*) McGraw.

— Project Management Handbook: Proceedings of the Third International Symposium. 22nd ed. LC 87-23151. 1988. text 88.95 (*0-442-22114-2*, VNR) Wiley.

***Cleland, David I.** Project Manager's Portable Handbook. 464p. 1999. pap. 54.95 (*0-07-135263-5*) McGraw.

Cleland, David I. The Strategic Management of Teams. LC 95-35708. (Illus.). 292p. 1996. 59.95 (*0-471-12058-8*) Wiley.

Cleland, David I., ed. Field Guide to Project Management. 480p. 1997. pap. 49.95 (*0-471-29206-0*, VNR) Wiley.

Cleland, David I., et al, eds. Project Management Casebook. LC 97-3116. (Illus.). 626p. (Orig.). 1998. pap. 69.95 (*1-880410-45-1*) Proj Mgmt Inst.

***Cleland, David I. & Ireland, Lewis R.** Project Manager's Portable Handbook. LC 99-54562. 1999. write for info. (*0-07-135233-3*) McGraw-Hill Sch.

Cleland, David I. & Kerzner, Harold. Engineering Team Management. 342p. (C). 1990. reprint ed. lib. bdg. 47.50 (*0-89464-515-3*) Krieger.

Cleland, David I. & King, William R. Systems Analysis & Project Management. 3rd ed. (Illus.). 480p. (C). 1983. 88.44 (*0-07-011311-4*) McGraw.

Cleland, David I. & Vlasak, A. Yaroslav. Project Management Casebook Instructor's Manual. Busic, Karen M. & Puerzer, Richard J., eds. LC 97-10752. 196p. 1998. pap., teacher ed. 29.95 (*1-880410-18-4*) Proj Mgmt Inst.

Cleland, David J., et al. Annotated Bibliography of Project & Team Management. LC 98-30378. 600p. 1998. 89.95 (*1-880410-47-8*) Proj Mgmt Inst.

***Cleland, J. & Davis, M.** An Atlas of Heart Failure. (Encyclopedia of Visual Medicine Ser.). 2000. 85.00 (*1-85070-041-9*) Prthnon Pub.

Cleland, J. G., et al. Introduction of New Contraceptives into Family Planning Programmes: Guidelines for Social Science Research. 67p. 1990. pap. text 14.40 (*0-614-08035-5*, 1930012) World Health.

Cleland, James. The Institution of a Young Nobleman. LC 47-12445. 352p. 1979. reprint ed. 60.00 (*0-8201-1216-X*) Schol Facsimiles.

— The Institution of a Young Nobleman: 1607 Edition. (Classics in Education Ser.). 272p. 1996. reprint ed. 75.00 (*1-85506-276-3*) Bks Intl VA.

Cleland, Jane K. Collection Letters that Work: How to Get Your Letters Read & the Only 23 Collection Letters You'll Ever Need. 59p. 1991. 79.00 incl. disk (*1-877680-13-3*) Tiger Pr.

— The Telephone Collector's Fly-Up Answers: What to Do & Say No Matter What Excuse They Offer, 4 vols. 80p. 1989. 118.00 (*1-877680-00-1*) Tiger Pr.

Cleland, Janell, jt. auth. see Porter, Carol.

Cleland, Jeffery Lynn & Claik, Charles S., eds. Protein Engineering: Principles & Practice. LC 95-18093. 544p. 1996. 98.50 (*0-471-10354-3*) Wiley.

C

Cleland, Jeffrey L., ed. Protein Folding: In Vivo & in Vitro. LC 93-9740. (ACS Symposium Ser.: No. 526). (Illus.). 258p. 1993. text 59.00 (*0-8412-2640-7*, Pub. by Am Chemical) OUP.

Cleland, Jeffrey L. & Langer, Robert, eds. Formulation & Delivery of Proteins & Peptides. LC 94-3789. (Symposium Ser.: No. 567). (Illus.). 340p. 1994. text 98.00 (*0-8412-2959-7*, Pub. by Am Chemical) OUP.

Cleland, John. Fanny Hill. abr. ed. Baxter, Beth, ed. 1992. pap. 12.95 incl. audio (*1-882071-24-7*, 026) B&B Audio.

— Fanny Hill. (Twelve-Point Ser.). 245p. 2000. reprint ed. lib. bdg. 24.00 (*1-58287-120-5*) North Bks.

Cleland, John. Fanny Hill: Memoirs of a Woman of Pleasure. 300p. 1990. mass mkt. 4.95 (*0-88184-602-3*) Carroll & Graf.

— Fanny Hill: Memoirs of a Woman of Pleasure. large type ed. (Isis Clear Type Classic Ser.). 225p. 1991. 21.95 (*1-85089-454-X*, Pub. by ISIS Lrg Prnt) Transaction Pubs.

— Fanny Hill: Or, Memoirs of a Woman of Pleasure. Wagner, Peter, ed. & intro. by. (Classics Ser.). 240p. 1986. pap. 8.95 (*0-14-043249-3*, Penguin Classics) Viking Penguin.

— Memoirs of a Woman of Pleasure. LC 99-228456. (Oxford World Classics Ser.). 238p. 1999. pap. 7.95 (*0-19-283565-3*) OUP.

— Memoirs of a Woman of Pleasure (Fanny Hill) 270p. 1998. pap. text 15.00 (*0-7881-5871-6*) DIANE Pub.

Cleland, John, ed. The Clinician's Guide to Ace Inhibition. (Illus.). 224p. 1993. text 36.00 (*0-443-04855-X*) Church.

Cleland, John & Ferry, Benoit, eds. Sexual Behaviour & Knowledge about AIDS in the Developing World: Findings from a Multisite Study. LC 94-47639. (Social Aspects of AIDS Ser.). 240p. 1994. 85.00 (*0-7484-0343-4*); pap. 29.95 (*0-7484-0344-2*) Taylor & Francis.

Cleland, John, et al. The Determinants of Reproductive Change in Bangladesh: Success in a Challenging Environment. LC 94-16613. (Regional & Sectoral Studies). 200p. 1994. pap. 22.00 (*0-8213-2849-2*) World Bank.

Cleland, John G., jt. auth. see McMurray, John J.

Cleland, Lee. Quilting Makes the Quilt. Weiland, Barbara, ed. LC 94-29983. (Illus.). 128p. (Orig.). 1994. pap. 24.95 (*1-56477-075-3*, B201) Martingale & Co.

Cleland, Louise. Wife on the Farm. 86p. (Orig.). 1995. pap. write for info. (*0-9645637-1-1*) Belrock Printing.

Cleland, Marilyn. Caregiving: A Handbook for Caregivers. 145p. (Orig.). 1990. text 20.00 (*1-877592-12-9*) GSH&MC.

— Caring That Makes a Difference. 187p. (Orig.). 1990. text 45.00 (*1-877592-15-3*) GSH&MC.

— Helping You Care. (Helping Families Help Themselves Ser.). 189p. (Orig.). 1990. text 45.00 (*1-877592-11-0*) GSH&MC.

— Management of Aggressive Behavior in the Elderly. 76p. (Orig.). 1990. text 20.00 (*1-877592-13-7*) GSH&MC.

Cleland, Max. Going for the Max! 12 Principles for Living Life to the Fullest. LC 99-31464. 160p. 1999. 17.99 (*0-8054-2021-5*) Broadman.

***Cleland, Max.** Strong at the Broken Places: A Personal Story. rev. ed. LC 00-105161. 224p. 2000. 18.95 (*1-56352-633-6*) Longstreet.

Cleland, Nancy N., et al. The Archaic, Woodland & Historic Period Occupations of the Liberty Bridge Locale. Lovis, William A., ed. (Michigan Cultural Resource Investigation Ser.). 449p. 1993. pap. write for info. (*0-9623670-2-8*) MI Dept Trans.

Cleland, R. The Mexican Yearbook. 1976. lib. bdg. 59.95 (*0-8490-2240-1*) Gordon Pr.

Cleland, Robert. A History of California: The American Period. LC 75-3483. (Illus.). 512p. 1975. reprint ed. lib. bdg. 35.00 (*0-8371-8155-0*, CLHC, Greenwood Pr) Greenwood.

Cleland, Robert G. The Cattle on a Thousand Hills: Southern California, 1850-1880. (Illus.). 365p. 1990. reprint ed. 24.95 (*0-87328-006-7*); reprint ed. pap. 12.95 (*0-87328-097-0*) Huntington Lib.

— A History of California: The American Period. (BCL1 - United States Local History Ser.). 512p. 1991. reprint ed. lib. bdg. 99.00 (*0-7812-6336-0*) Rprt Serv.

— The Irvine Ranch. rev. ed. LC 62-18134. (Huntington Library Publications). (Illus.). 191p. 1984. reprint ed. pap. 59.30 (*0-608-00231-3*, 206073300006) Bks Demand.

— March of Industry. 1992. reprint ed. lib. bdg. 75.00 (*0-7812-5014-5*) Rprt Serv.

Cleland, Robert G. & Putnam, Frank B. Isaias W. Hellman & the Farmers & Merchants Bank. LC 65-12230. (Illus.). 136p. 1980. reprint ed. pap. 9.95 (*0-87328-018-0*) Huntington Lib.

***Cleland, Robert J.** Spirit Camp. LC 99-91869. 2000. 25.00 (*0-7388-1352-4*); pap. 18.00 (*0-7388-1353-2*) Xlibris Corp.

Cleland, Sheila. Pet Owner's Guide to the West Highland White Terrier. (Pet Owner's Guide Ser.). (Illus.). 80p. 1997. 8.00 (*1-86054-015-5*, Pub. by Ringpr Bks) Seven Hills Bk.

Cleland, Thom. Moses--the Making of a leader. LC 99-29559. (Victor Bible Character Ser.). 208p. 1999. 7.99 (*1-56476-716-7*, Victor Bks) Chariot Victor.

Cleland, Virginia S. The Economics of Nursing. (Illus.). 290p. (C). 1989. pap. text 39.95 (*0-8385-2036-7*, A2036-0) Appleton & Lange.

Cleland, W. Wallace. B. I. A. Plate Number Checklist: Plates Numbered 1-20,000. rev. ed. 800p. 1990. pap. text 35.00 (*0-930412-18-4*) Bureau Issues.

Clelland, Doug, ed. Berlin: An Architectural History-An Architectural Design Profile. (Illus.). 88p. 1984. pap. 14.95 (*0-312-07614-2*) St Martin.

Clelland, J. The Calcutta Journal of Natural History, 5 vols., Set. (C). 1988. text 800.00 (*0-7855-3166-1*) St Mut.

***Clelland, Mike.** Illustrated Guide to Glacier Travel & Crevasse Rescue. (Illus.). 2000. pap. 14.95 (*1-893682-06-4*) Climb Mag.

Clelland, Mike, jt. auth. see O'Bannon, Allen.

Clelland, Richard C., et al. Basic Statistics with Business Applications. LC 72-8057. (Probability & Mathematical Statistics: Applied Probability & Statistics Section Ser.). (Illus.). 703p. (C). reprint ed. pap. 200.00 (*0-8357-9843-7*, 205509900008) Bks Demand.

Clem, Alan L. Characteristics of South Dakota County Officers. 1962. 1.00 (*1-55614-025-8*) U of SD Gov Res Bur.

— Cooling the Coffee in the Saucer: Bicameralism & the Legislative Product. 1978. 1.00 (*1-55614-030-4*) U of SD Gov Res Bur.

— Election in South Dakota, 1966. 1967. 1.00 (*1-55614-037-1*) U of SD Gov Res Bur.

— Election in South Dakota, 1970. 1971. 1.00 (*1-55614-038-X*) U of SD Gov Res Bur.

— Election in South Dakota, 1974. 1975. 1.00 (*1-55614-039-8*) U of SD Gov Res Bur.

— Election in South Dakota, 1976. 1976. 1.00 (*1-55614-040-1*) U of SD Gov Res Bur.

— Election in South Dakota, 1978. 1979. 1.00 (*1-55614-041-X*) U of SD Gov Res Bur.

— Election in South Dakota, 1992. 1992. write for info. (*1-55614-135-1*) U of SD Gov Res Bur.

— The Geography of South Dakota's Presidential Vote from Hoover to Nixon: A Note on Eleven Maps. 1971. 1.00 (*1-55614-043-6*) U of SD Gov Res Bur.

— Ideology in State Legislative Decision-Making. 1974. 1.00 (*1-55614-048-7*) U of SD Gov Res Bur.

— Measuring Legislative Committee Performance. 1975. 1.00 (*1-55614-064-9*) U of SD Gov Res Bur.

— Money & Schools: Campaign Strategy in School Bond Elections. 1964. 1.00 (*1-55614-065-7*) U of SD Gov Res Bur.

— 1988 Election in South Dakota. 1989. pap. 1.00 (*1-55614-131-9*) U of SD Gov Res Bur.

— 1980 Election in South Dakota: End of an Era. 1981. 1.00 (*1-55614-069-X*) U of SD Gov Res Bur.

— 1984 Election in South Dakota. 1985. 1.00 (*1-55614-070-3*) U of SD Gov Res Bur.

— The 1986 Election in South Dakota. 1987. pap. 1.00 (*1-55614-127-0*) U of SD Gov Res Bur.

— The 1982 Election in South Dakota. 1983. 1.00 (*1-55614-071-1*) U of SD Gov Res Bur.

— The 1990 Election in South Dakota. 1991. pap. 1.00 (*1-55614-133-5*) U of SD Gov Res Bur.

— The 1964 Election: Has South Dakota Become a Two-Party State? 1965. 1.00 (*1-55614-073-8*) U of SD Gov Res Bur.

— Political Attitudes & Preferences of South Dakotans in the 1968 Presidential Election. 1972. 1.00 (*0-685-05041-6*); write for info. (*1-55614-080-0*) U of SD Gov Res Bur.

— Precinct-Level Voting Returns for Major Races in the 1972 Primary Election in South Dakota. 1972. 5.00 (*1-55614-082-7*) U of SD Gov Res Bur.

— Precinct-Level Voting Returns for Major Races in the 1974 Primary Election in South Dakota. 1975. 5.00 (*1-55614-083-5*) U of SD Gov Res Bur.

— Precinct Returns for Major Elections in South Dakota, 1968. 1969. 5.00 (*1-55614-084-3*) U of SD Gov Res Bur.

— Precinct Returns for Major Elections in South Dakota, 1972. 1973. 5.00 (*1-55614-085-1*) U of SD Gov Res Bur.

— Precinct Returns for the Nineteen Seventy-Six General Election in South Dakota. 5.00 (*1-55614-087-8*) U of SD Gov Res Bur.

— Precinct Voting. 1964. write for info. (*1-55614-088-6*) U of SD Gov Res Bur.

— El Precio Del Placer. 1975. 1.00 (*1-55614-086-X*) U of SD Gov Res Bur.

— Presidential Politics in South Dakota. 1967. 1.00 (*1-55614-090-8*) U of SD Gov Res Bur.

— Reconstruction of County Representation. 1968. 1.00 (*1-55614-104-1*) U of SD Gov Res Bur.

— Roll Call Voting Behavior in the South Dakota Legislature. 1966. 1.00 (*1-55614-110-6*) U of SD Gov Res Bur.

— South Dakota's Congressional Staffs. 1981. 1.00 (*1-55614-003-7*) U of SD Gov Res Bur.

— Spirit Mound Township in 1984: Campaign Effects in a Rural Electorate. 1985. pap. 1.00 (*1-55614-122-X*) U of SD Gov Res Bur.

— Spirit Mound Township Revisited: A Rural View of the 1972 Campaign. 1973. 1.00 (*1-55614-005-3*) U of SD Gov Res Bur.

— The Submerging Republican Majority: The 1972 Election in South Dakota. 1973. 1.00 (*1-55614-009-6*) U of SD Gov Res Bur.

— Tenure in the Courthouse. 1973. 1.00 (*1-55614-010-X*) U of SD Gov Res Bur.

— Voting Behavior in the South Dakota Legislature: An Exploratory Investigation into Divisible Roll Calls. 1966. 1.00 (*1-55614-014-2*) U of SD Gov Res Bur.

— West River Voting Patterns. 1965. 5.00 (*1-55614-016-9*) U of SD Gov Res Bur.

Clem, Alan L., ed. Contemporary Approaches to State Constitutional Revision. 1970. 7.50 (*1-55614-029-0*) U of SD Gov Res Bur.

Clem, Alan L. & Farber, William. Multi-Member Districting & Minorities. 1978. 1.00 (*1-55614-066-5*) U of SD Gov Res Bur.

Clem, Alan L. & Meyer, Kenneth. Another Look at the Effects of Divisive Party Primaries: The South Dakota Experience, 1946 to 1974. 1975. 1.00 (*1-55614-020-7*) U of SD Gov Res Bur.

Clem, Alan L. & Platt, George M. A Bibliography of South Dakota Government & Politics. 1965. 5.00 (*1-55614-023-1*) U of SD Gov Res Bur.

Clem, Dale. A Moment with God for Those Who Grieve: Prayers for Those Who Grieve. LC 99-42082. (Moment with God Ser.). 64p. 1999. pap. 5.00 (*0-687-07304-9*) Dimen for Liv.

— Winds of Fury, Circle of Grace: Life after the Palm Sunday Tornadoes. LC 97-176222. 160p. 1997. pap. 10.95 (*0-687-01795-5*) Abingdon.

Clem, Dee. Clem, Clemm & Klem, Klemm Family History, 2 vols. LC 96-60223. (Illus.). 530p. 1996. 62.50 (*1-882194-20-9*) TN Valley Pub.

***Clem, Dee.** Tracing African-American Roots. (Illus.). 232p. 2000. 29.95 (*0-9675846-0-4*); pap. 24.95 (*0-9675846-1-2*) Gator Pubng Inc.

Clem, Keith M. & Brown, Karl W. Petroleum Resources of the Paradox Basin, 1984. (Bulletin of the Utah Geological Survey Ser.: No. 119). (Illus.). 162p. (Orig.). 1984. pap. 15.00 (*1-55791-086-3*, B-119) Utah Geological Survey.

Clem, Margaret H. Elbert ein Swine No. 2: Learns Line Dancing. LC 95-78289. (Illus.). 32p. (J). (gr. k-4). 1995. pap. 9.95 (*1-878044-28-1*) Mayhaven Pub.

— Elbert Ein Swine, Genius Pig. LC 93-80378. (Illus.). 32p. (J). (gr. k-4). 1993. pap. 6.95 (*1-878044-12-5*) Mayhaven Pub.

— Little Candles: A Collection of Poems & Stories. LC 95-80768. 64p. (Orig.). 1995. pap. 4.95 (*1-878044-45-1*, Wld Rose) Mayhaven Pub.

Clem, Orlie M. Detailed Factors in Latin Prognosis. LC 78-176653. (Columbia University. Teachers College. Contributions to Education Ser.: No. 144). reprint ed. 37.50 (*0-404-55144-0*) AMS Pr.

Clem, Stephen C. Study Guide: Candide - Advanced Placement French Literature. (FRE.). 46p. (YA). (gr. 11-12). 1997. pap. text 6.67 (*1-877653-38-1*) Wayside Pub.

— Study Guide: Le Cid - Advanced Placement French Literature. (FRE.). 60p. (YA). (gr. 11-12). 1996. pap. text 6.67 (*1-877653-40-3*, 36) Wayside Pub.

— Study Guide: L'Ecole des Femmes - Advanced Placement French Literature. (FRE.). 52p. (YA). (gr. 11-12). 1996. pap. text 6.67 (*1-877653-41-1*, 37) Wayside Pub.

— Study Guide: Moderato Cantabile - Advanced Placement French Literature. (FRE.). 54p. (YA). (gr. 11-12). 1996. pap. text 6.67 (*1-877653-42-X*) Wayside Pub.

— Study Guide: Pierre et Jean - Advanced Placement French Literature. 76p. (YA). (gr. 11-12). 1996. pap. text 8.00 (*1-877653-33-0*, 33) Wayside Pub.

Clem, Stephen C. & Wilson, Z. Vance. Paths to New Curriculum. 1991. pap. 27.00 (*0-934338-73-6*) NAIS.

Clem, Stephen C., et al. Taking Measure: Perspectives on Curriculum & Change. 128p. 1998. pap. text 30.00 (*0-934338-94-9*) NAIS.

Clema, Joe K., ed. Proceedings of Summer Computer Simulation Conference, 1989: Austin, TX, 1989. 942p. 1989. 120.00 (*0-911801-57-X*, SCSC-89) Soc Computer Sim.

Cleman, John. George Washington Cable Revisited. 1996. 32.00 (*0-8057-3991-2*, Twyne) Mac Lib Ref.

Clemants, Steven E. Chenopodiaceae & Amaranthaceae of New York State. (New York State Museum Bulletin Ser.: No. 485). (Illus.). 100p. (Orig.). 1992. pap. 10.00 (*1-55557-226-X*) NYS Museum.

— Contributions to a Flora of New York State Vol. X: Juncaceae (Rush Family) of New York State. (Bulletin Ser.: No. 475). (Illus.). 67p. (Orig.). (C). 1990. pap. text 6.00 (*1-55557-191-3*) NYS Museum.

Clemen. India Software 5.25" - Making Hard Decisions. (Business Statistics Ser.). 1991. pap. 39.95 (*0-534-92688-6*) Wadsworth Pub.

Clemen, Bettine. Open Your Ears to Love. 1999. pap. 14.95 (*0-9666770-1-3*) Hovenden Pr.

Clemen, Carl. Religionsgeschichtliche Erklaerung des Neuen Testamentes: Die Abhaengigkeit des aeltesten Christentums von nichtjuedischen Religionen und philosophischen Systemen. 440p. (C). 1973. reprint ed. text 150.00 (*3-11-002412-8*) De Gruyter.

Clemen, Carl C., et al. Religions of the World. LC 69-17570. (Essay Index Reprint Ser.). 1977. 39.95 (*0-8369-0011-1*) Ayer.

Clemen, D. D. Primitive Christianity & Its Non-Jewish Sources. 1977. lib. bdg. 59.95 (*0-8490-2472-2*) Gordon Pr.

Clemen, David M. Hydro Plant Electrical Systems. 1999. 79.00 (*0-9651765-3-3*) HCI Publns.

Clemen, Otto, ed. see Luther, Martin.

Clemen, Robert T. Making Hard Decisions: An Introduction to Decision Analysis. 557p. (C). 1991. text 47.75 (*0-534-92336-4*) Wadsworth Pub.

— Making Hard Decisions: An Introduction to Decision Analysis. 2nd ed. 752p. (C). 1997. pap. 94.95 (*0-534-26034-9*) Wadsworth Pub.

***Clemen, Robert T. & Reilly, Terence.** Making Hard Decisions with Decisiontools. 2nd rev. ed. LC 00-31451. 2001. write for info. (*0-534-36597-3*) Wadsworth Pub.

Clemen-Stone, Susan, et al. Comprehensive Community Health Nursing. 5th ed. LC 97-35023. (Illus.). 888p. (C). (gr. 13). 1997. text 51.00 (*0-8151-1324-2*, 29597) Mosby Inc.

— Comprehensive Community Health Nursing: Includes Testbank. 5th ed. (Illus.). 888p. 1998. teacher ed. write for info. (*1-55664-432-9*) Mosby Inc.

Clemen, Wolfgang. Shakespeare's Soliloquies. Stokes, Charity S., tr. LC 87-1541. 211p. 1987. 45.00 (*0-416-05862-0*); pap. 13.95 (*0-416-30460-5*) Routledge.

Clemence, Alain, jt. auth. see Doise, Willem.

Clemence, Richard V., jt. ed. see Hansen, Alvin H.

Clemence, Samuel P., ed. Uplift Behavior of Anchor Foundations in Soil: Proceedings of a Session Sponsored by the Geotechnical Engineering Division. 126p. 1985. 17.00 (*0-87262-496-X*) Am Soc Civil Eng.

— Use of In Situ Tests in Geotechnical Engineering. (Conference Proceedings Ser.). 1284p. 1986. 116.00 (*0-87262-541-9*) Am Soc Civil Eng.

Clemenceau, Georges. American Reconstruction, Eighteen Sixty-Five to Eighteen Seventy. 2nd ed. LC 68-16229. (American Scene Ser.). 1969. reprint ed. 35.00 (*0-306-71010-2*) Da Capo.

Clemenceau, Georges E. Surprises of Life. Hall, Grace, tr. LC 77-132113. (Short Story Index Reprint Ser.). 1977. 20.95 (*0-8369-3670-1*) Ayer.

Clemencon, H., ed. The Species Concept in Hymenomycetes: Proceedings of a Herbett Sumposium at Lausanne, Switzerland, Aug. 16-20, 1976. (Bibliotheca Mycologica Ser.: No. 61). (Illus.). 516p. 1978. pap. text 72.00 (*3-7682-1173-8*) Lubrecht & Cramer.

Clemencon, Raymond, ed. see Kusumatmadja, Sarwond, et al.

Clemencon, Raymond G. Perceptions & Interests: Developing Countries & the International Economic System. (Illus.). XI, 309p. 1990. pap. 44.00 (*3-261-04185-4*) P Lang Pubng.

Clemens. New Perspectives on Works 4.5. 10th ed. (New Perspectives Ser.). (C). 1998. pap. 44.95 (*0-7600-7004-0*) Course Tech.

Clemens, Aurelius P. Hymns of Prudentius: The Cathemerinon; or The Daily Round by Aurelius Prudentius Clemens. Slavitt, David R., tr. from LAT. LC 95-51277. 88p. 1996. 19.95 (*0-8018-5412-1*) Johns Hopkins.

Clemens, B. M., et al, eds. Structure & Properties of Multilayered Thin Films. (Symposium Proceedings Ser.: Vol. 382). 496p. 1995. text 85.00 (*1-55899-285-5*) Materials Res.

Clemens, B. M. & Johnson, W. L., eds. Thin Film Structures & Phase Stability, Vol. 187. (Symposium Proceedings Ser.: Vol. 1). 341p. 1991. text 17.50 (*1-55899-076-3*) Materials Res.

Clemens, Barbara, jt. auth. see Beskeen, David W.

Clemens, C. H. A Scrapbook of Complex Curve Theory. LC 80-20214. (University Series in Mathematics). (Illus.). 196p. (C). 1980. text 78.00 (*0-306-40536-9*, Kluwer Plenum) Kluwer Academic.

Clemens, C. H. & Clemens, M. A. Geometry for the Classroom. (Illus.). 352p. 1997. text 34.95 (*0-387-97564-0*) Spr-Verlag.

— Geometry for the Classroom: Exercises & Solutions. (Illus.). 176p. 1995. student ed. 24.95 (*0-387-97565-9*) Spr-Verlag.

Clemens, Clara. My Father, Mark Twain. LC 74-6024. (BCL Ser.: No. I). (Illus.). reprint ed. 45.00 (*0-404-11544-6*) AMS Pr.

— My Husband Gabrilowitsch. LC 79-11316. (Music Reprint Ser.). 1979. reprint ed. 39.50 (*0-306-79563-9*) Da Capo.

Clemens, Clay. Reluctant Realists: The CDU-CSU & West German Ostpolitik. LC 88-29340. 370p. (C). 1989. text 64.95 (*0-8223-0900-9*) Duke.

Clemens, Clay & Paterson, William E., eds. The Kohl Chancellorship. LC 98-15009. 176p. 1998. 47.50 (*0-7146-4890-6*, Pub. by F Cass Pubs); pap. 19.50 (*0-7146-4441-2*, Pub. by F Cass Pubs) Intl Spec Bk.

Clemens, Cyril. Chesterton As Seen by His Contemporaries. 1973. 250.00 (*0-87968-027-X*) Gordon Pr.

— Chesterton As Seen by His Contemporaries. LC 76-92958. (English Biography Ser.: No. 31). 1969. reprint ed. lib. bdg. 75.00 (*0-8383-0968-2*) M S G Haskell Hse.

— My Cousin, Mark Twain. LC 74-16297. (American Literature Ser.: No. 49). 1974. lib. bdg. 75.00 (*0-8383-1744-8*) M S G Haskell Hse.

Clemens, Dale P. The All New Advanced Custom Rod Building. rev. ed. (Illus.). 320p. 1988. 29.95 (*0-8329-0436-8*, Winchester Pr) New Win Pub.

— Fiberglass Rod Making. (Illus.). 212p. 1974. pap. 12.95 (*0-88317-042-6*) Stoeger Pub Co.

Clemens, Daniel S. Leadership Literacy: The Solution to Our Present Crisis. (Orig.). 1992. pap. 14.95 (*0-9632640-7-9*) Lead Am.

Clemens, David A. The Cutting Edge, Vol. 2. LC 79-52420. (Steps to Maturity Ser.). 1975. teacher ed. 17.95 (*0-86508-004-6*) BCM Pubn.

— The Cutting Edge, Vol. 2. LC 79-52420. (Steps to Maturity Ser.). 1975. student ed. 15.95 (*0-86508-003-8*) BCM Pubn.

— God Encountered, Vol. 1. LC 79-52420. (Steps to Maturity Ser.). 1973. teacher ed. 17.95 (*0-86508-002-X*) BCM Pubn.

— God Encountered, Vol. 1. LC 79-52420. (Steps to Maturity Ser.). 1973. 4.95 (*0-86508-007-0*) BCM Pubn.

— God Encountered, Vol. 1. LC 79-52420. (Steps to Maturity Ser.). 1973. student ed. 15.95 (*0-86508-001-1*) BCM Pubn.

— Living!, Vol. 3. LC 79-55503. (Steps to Maturity Ser.). 1980. teacher ed. 17.95 (*0-86508-006-2*) BCM Pubn.

— Living!, Vol. 3. LC 79-55503. (Steps to Maturity Ser.). 1980. student ed. 15.95 (*0-86508-005-4*) BCM Pubn.

Clemens, Deltev, ed. & tr. see Voegelin, Eric.

Clemens, Donald F. & McAllister, Warren A. Spectrophotometric Analysis of Permanganate Ion Solutions. Neidig, H. Anthony, ed. (Modular Laboratory Program in Chemistry Ser.). 12p. (C). 1989. pap. text 1.50 (*0-87540-359-X*, ANAL 359-X) Chem Educ Res.

Clemens, Donald F., et al. Determining the Formula of an Ionic Hydrate Gravimetrically. Stanitski, Conrad L., ed. (Modular Laboratory Program in Chemistry Ser.). 8p. (C). 1996. pap. text 1.50 (*0-87540-479-0*, ANAL 479-0) Chem Educ Res.

C

Clemens, Elisabeth S. The People's Lobby: Organizational Innovation & the Rise of Interest Group Politics in the United States, 1890-1925. LC 97-1339. 1997. pap. text 19.95 (*0-226-10993-3*); lib. bdg. 58.00 (*0-226-10992-5*) U Ch Pr.

Clemens, Elisabeth S., jt. auth. see Powell, Walter W.

Clemens, Frances, et al, eds. Recreation & the Local Church. LC 57-18412. 191p. reprint ed. pap. 59.30 (*0-608-13565-8*, 202240900026) Bks Demand.

Clemens, Fred, tr. see Piekalkiewicz, Janusz.

Clemens, Frederick, tr. see Warfield, Richard S., ed.

Clemens, Gus. Christmas at Fort Concho. (Illus.). 32p. (Orig.). 1984. pap. 3.00 (*0-938036-06-8*) Mulberry Ave Bks.

— The Concho Country: A History of the Concho River Region of West Texas. LC 80-83291. (Illus.). 232p. 1981. 25.00 (*0-938036-01-7*); 100.00 (*0-938036-00-9*) Mulberry Ave Bks.

— The Concho Country: A History of the Concho River Region of West Texas. limited ed. LC 80-83291. (Illus.). 232p. 1981. 50.00 (*0-938036-03-3*) Mulberry Ave Bks.

— Legacy: The Story of the Permian Basin Region of West Texas & Southeast New Mexico. (Illus.). 256p. 1983. 25.95 (*0-938036-04-1*) Mulberry Ave Bks.

Clemens, Herbert & Kollar, Janos, eds. Current Topics in Complex Algebraic Geometry. (Mathematical Sciences Research Institute Publications: No. 28). 170p. (C). 1996. text 37.95 (*0-521-56244-9*) Cambridge U Pr.

Clemens, James. Wit'ch Fire. LC 97-48402. (Banned & the Banished Ser.: Bk.1). 448p. 1998. pap. 13.95 (*0-345-41705-4*, Del Rey) Ballantine Pub Grp.

— Wit'ch Fire. (The Banned & the Banished Ser.: Bk. 1). 1999. mass mkt. 6.99 (*0-345-41706-2*, Del Rey) Ballantine Pub Grp.

— Wit'ch Storm. LC 99-24697. (Banned & the Banished Ser.: Bk. 2). 496p. 1999. pap. 13.95 (*0-345-41707-0*, Del Rey) Ballantine Pub Grp.

***Clemens, James.** Witch Storm. (Banned & the Banished Ser.: Vol. 2). 544p. 2000. mass mkt. 6.99 (*0-345-41708-9*, Del Rey) Ballantine Pub Grp.

— Witch War. (Banned & the Banished Ser.: Bk. 3). 512p. 2000. pap. 15.00 (*0-345-41709-7*, Del Rey) Ballantine Pub Grp.

C

Clemens, James T. & Hill, Robert W., eds. X-Ray Lithography in Japan. (JTEC Panel Reports). xii, 158p. 1991. pap. write for info. (*1-883712-14-9*, JTEC) Intl Tech Res.

Clemens, Jaqueline B. Simple Gardening Fun. LC 97-62341. (Creative Kids Ser.). (Illus.). 160p. (J). 1997. pap., teacher ed. 14.95 (*1-57690-094-0*, TCM2094) Tchr Create Mat.

Clemens, John. Polls, Politics & Populism. 208p. 1983. text 82.95 (*0-566-00602-2*, Pub. by Dartmth Pub) Ashgate Pub Co.

Clemens, John, jt. auth. see Conrad, Andree.

Clemens, John K. & Albrecht, Steve. The Timeless Leader: Lessons on Leadership. 286p. 1998. text 23.00 (*0-7881-5844-9*) DIANE Pub.

Clemens, John K. & Mayer, Douglas F. The Classic Touch. LC 99-23272. 320p. 1999. pap. 14.95 (*0-8092-2797-5*, 279750, Contemporary Bks) NTC Contemp Pub Co.

Clemens, John K. & Wolff, Melora. Movies to Manage By. LC 99-26801. 240p. 1999. 22.95 (*0-8092-2798-3*, 279830, Contemporary Bks) NTC Contemp Pub Co.

***Clemens, Lillian F.** Messages from Christ to the People of Prayer. 2001. pap. 14.95 (*1-57733-053-6*) B Dolphin Pub.

Clemens, Lynda, jt. auth. see Dolph, Andrea.

Clemens, M. A., jt. auth. see Clemens, C. H.

Clemens, M. J., et al, eds. Lymphokines & Interferons: A Practical Approach. (Practical Approach Ser.: 34). 396p. 1987. 72.00 (*1-85221-036-2*); pap. 49.95 (*1-85221-035-4*) OUP.

***Clemens, Marilyn.** In His Image. 2000. write for info. (*1-58235-575-4*) Watermrk Pr.

Clemens, Martin. Alone on Guadalcanal: A Coastwatcher's Story. LC 98-34092. (Illus.). 240p. 1998. 32.95 (*1-55750-122-X*) Naval Inst Pr.

— Peter Green Founder of Fleetwood Mac: The Authorized Biography. (Illus.). 239p. 1999. pap. 19.95 (*1-86074-233-5*, SG00652, Pub. by Sanctuary Pubng) Music Sales.

Clemens, Matthew, jt. auth. see Gipple, Pat.

Clemens, Matthew V., ed. see Largent, R. Karl.

Clemens, Michael, ed. Protein Phosphorylation in Cell Regulation. 368p. 1997. text 72.00 (*90-5702-030-0*, Harwood Acad Pubs); pap. text 22.00 (*90-5702-031-9*, Harwood Acad Pubs) Gordon & Breach.

Clemens, Michael J. Biochemistry of Cellular Regulation Vol. I: Gene Expression. 288p. 1980. 157.00 (*0-8493-5454-4*, QH450, CRC Reprint) Franklin.

Clemens, Nancy. Dolphin Divination Cards. (Illus.). 108p. (Orig.). 1994. pap. 11.00 (*0-931892-79-1*) B Dolphin Pub.

— A Guide to the Dolphin Divination Cards. LC 98-48037. (Illus.). 384p. 1999. pap. 18.00 (*1-57733-017-X*) B Dolphin Pub.

Clemens, Patricia W. The Psychologist's Test File: An Illustrated Handbook of Sample Test Items. 112p. 1983. 14.00 (*0-87879-355-0*) Acad Therapy.

Clemens, Paul G. The Atlantic Economy & Colonial Maryland's Eastern Shore: From Tobacco to Grain. fac. ed. LC 79-26181. (Illus.). 253p. 1980. reprint ed. pap. 78.50 (*0-608-01012-X*, 206187000012) Bks Demand.

— The Uses of Abundance: A History of New Jersey's Economy. LC 92-38149. (New Jersey History Ser.: No. 2). 1992. 9.00 (*0-89743-078-6*) NJ Hist Com.

Clemens, Paul G., jt. auth. see Wacker, Peter O.

Clemens, Paul M., ed. see Nydahl, Ole.

Clemens, Paul M., ed. see Postlethwaite, Virgil A.

Clemens, Paul M., ed. see Underwood, Helen.

Clemens, Peter & Cohen, Shari. Wild Wings. LC 99-73114. (Illus.). 128p. (J). (gr. 3-6). 1999. pap. 8.95 (*0-7373-0312-3*, 03123W, Pub. by Lowell Hse) NTC Contemp Pub Co.

Clemens, Peter & Delgado, Jose. Super Wings: The Step-by-Step Paper Airplane Book. rev. ed. LC 98-136546. (Illus.). 64p. (J). (gr. 3-7). 1997. pap., wbk. ed. 6.95 (*1-56565-536-2*, 05362W, Pub. by Lowell Hse Juvenile) NTC Contemp Pub Co.

Clemens, Samuel L. My Debut As a Literary Person. 367p. 1998. reprint ed. lib. bdg. 79.00 (*0-7812-4780-2*) Rprt Serv.

— Punch, Brothers, Punch! 141p. 1998. reprint ed. lib. bdg. 75.00 (*0-7812-4781-0*) Rprt Serv.

Clemens, Samuel L., see Twain, Mark, pseud.

Clemens, Samuel L., creator see Twain, Mark, pseud.

Clemens, Siegfried M., tr. see Bleuler, Manfred.

Clemens, Susan L. Tokyo Pink Guide. 200p. 1993. pap. 12.95 (*0-8048-1915-7*) Tuttle Pubng.

Clemens, Sydney G. Pay Attention to the Children: Lessons for Teachers & Parents from Sylvia Ashton-Warner. LC 96-70255. 172p. 1996. pap. 14.95 (*1-883965-41-1*) Rattle OK Pubns.

Clemens, Sydney G. The Sun's Not Broken, a Cloud's Just in the Way: On Child-Centered Teaching. 137p. (Orig.). 1984. pap. 12.95 (*0-87659-109-8*) Gryphon Hse.

Clemens, Terri. American Family Farm Antiques: A Wallace-Homestead Price Guide. LC 94-13886. (Illus.). 208p. 1994. pap. 17.95 (*0-87069-690-4*, Wllce-Homestd) Krause Pubns.

Clemens, Valdine. The Return of the Repressed: Gothic Horror from The Castle of Otranto to Alien. LC 98-52055. (SUNY Series in Psychoanalysis & Culture). 320p. (C). 1999. pap. text 19.95 (*0-7914-4328-0*, Suny Pr) State U NY Pr.

— The Return of the Repressed: Gothic Horror from the Castle of Otranto to Alien. LC 98-52055. (SUNY Series in Psychoanalysis & Culture). 320p. (C). 1999. text 59.50 (*0-7914-4327-2*, Suny Pr) State U NY Pr.

Clemens, W. A., jt. ed. see Woodburne, M. O.

Clemens, Walter C., Jr. America & the World: Achievements Failtures Alternative Futures. text. write for info. (*0-312-22878-3*) St Martin.

***Clemens, Walter C.** America And The World, 1898-2025: Achievements, Failures, Alternative Futures. LC 00-40489. 2000. pap. (*0-312-23638-7*) St Martin.

Clemens, Walter C., Jr. Dynamics of International Relations: Conflict & Mutual Gain in an Age of Global Interdependence. LC 98-13242. (Illus.). 550p. (C). 1998. pap. 35.00 (*0-8476-8851-8*) Rowman.

***Clemens, William M.** After Dinner Verse: A Collection of Impulsive & Impromptu Verses Containing Repartee in Verse, Poems on Panes, Rhyming Wills, Old Tavern Signs, Envelope Poetry, Etc. LC 99-26554. 1999. lib. bdg. 40.00 (*0-7808-0300-0*) Omnigraphics Inc.

Clemens, William M. American Marriage Records Before 1699: Reprinted with a Supplement from "Genealogy Magazine," Vol. XIV, No. 4 (July 1929)-Vol. XV, No. 3 (July 1930) LC 67-30754. 259p. 1998. reprint ed. pap. 25.00 (*0-8063-0075-2*) Clearfield Co.

— Eddy: Ancestry of Mary Baker Eddy. (Illus.). 44p. 1997. reprint ed. pap. 9.00 (*0-8328-8442-1*); reprint ed. lib. bdg. 19.00 (*0-8328-8441-3*) Higginson Bk Co.

— North & South Carolina Marriage Records from the Earliest Colonial Days to the Civil War. LC 73-1942. 295p. 1995. reprint ed. 25.00 (*0-8063-0555-X*, 1025) Genealog Pub.

***Clemens, Wm. M., ed.** Mitchell Family Magazine: Genealogical, Historical & Biographical. fac. ed. 96p. 1999. reprint ed. 28.00 (*0-8328-9981-X*); reprint ed. pap. 18.00 (*0-8328-9982-8*) Higginson Bk Co.

Clemens, Wm. M., ed. Turner Family Magazine: Genealogical, Historical & Biographical, Set, Vols. 1 & 2. 95p. 1994. reprint ed. pap. 18.00 (*0-8328-4387-3*); reprint ed. lib. bdg. 28.00 (*0-8328-4386-5*) Higginson Bk Co.

***Clemens, Wm. M.** Montgomery Family Magazine: Genealogical, Historical & Biographical. fac. ed. 128p. 1999. reprint ed. 31.00 (*0-8328-9944-5*); reprint ed. pap. 21.00 (*0-8328-9945-3*) Higginson Bk Co.

Clemensen, Jessie. Study Outlines in Physics: Construction & Experimental Evaluation. LC 71-176654. (Columbia University. Teachers College. Contributions to Education Ser.: No. 553). reprint ed. 37.50 (*0-404-55553-5*) AMS Pr.

Clemenshaw, Doug. Design in Plastics. (Illus.). 256p. 1989. 49.95 (*0-935603-11-5*, 30136) Rockport Pubs.

Clemenson, Grace. Grandmother's Stories. 163p. 1991. 14.95 (*0-87770-492-9*) Ye Galleon.

Clement, A., et al, eds. Networking, Connecting Workers in & Between Organizations: Proceedings of Working Conference on Networking, Vienna, Austria, 16-18 June 1993. LC 93-45315. (IFIP Transactions A: Computer Science & Technology Ser.: Vol. A-38). 264p. 1994. 104.50 (*0-444-81720-4*, North Holland) Elsevier.

Clement, A. A. Das Blut Jesu und die Lehre von der Verschnung im Werk Johann Sebastian Bachs. 316p. pap. 53.25 (*0-444-85783-4*) Elsevier.

Clement, Alain, jt. auth. see Vatine, Olivier.

Clement, Andre. 3D Tolerancing with CAD/C. 400p. (C). 1997. pap. 29.95 (*0-201-63484-8*) Addison-Wesley.

Clement, Annie. Law in Sport & Physical Activity. 2nd ed. 254p. 1998. pap. text 40.00 (*0-9658874-1-3*) Sport & Law.

— Legal Responsibility in Aquatics. 230p. 1997. pap. text 40.00 (*0-9658874-0-5*) Sport & Law.

Clement, Annie & Hartman, Betty G. The Teaching of Physical Skills. 368p. (C). 1994. text. write for info. (*0-697-14802-5*) Brown & Benchmark.

Clement, Arthur J. Pray, Christian Pray! LC 93-84931. 123p. (Orig.). 1993. pap. 8.99 (*0-8100-0499-2*, 06N0697) Northwest Pub.

***Clement, Bonnie.** The Red Dun Filly. 99p. 2000. pap. 18.00 (*0-7388-2089-X*) Xlibris Corp.

Clement, Brian & Digeronimo, Theresa Foy. Living Foods for Optimum Health: Staying Healthy in an Unhealthy World. LC 98-28347. (Illus.). 288p. 1998. per. 15.95 (*0-7615-1448-1*) Prima Pub.

Clement, Brian R. Hippocrates Health Program: A Proven Guide to Healthful Living. Miller, Trish & Weill, Alix, eds. (Illus.). 88p. (Orig.). 1989. pap. 5.95 (*0-9622373-0-2*) Hippocrates Pubns.

— Le Programme de Sante Hippocrate: Ou Comment Vivre Sainement avec l'Alimentation Vivante. 114p. 1990. 9.95 (*2-920083-48-1*) Edns Roseau.

Clement, Brian R., jt. auth. see DiGeronimo, Theresa F.

Clement, C., jt. ed. see Colburn, T.

Clement, C. J. Religious Radicalism in England, 1535-1565. LC 94-23546. (Rutherford Studies in Historical Theology). 444p. 1995. text 109.95 (*0-7734-9121-X*) E Mellen.

— Religious Radicalism in England, 1535-1565. (Rutherford Studies in Historical Theology). xx, 425p. 1996. pap. text 45.00 (*0-946068-44-5*, Pub. by Rutherford Hse) OM Literature.

***Clement, Cari.** Terrific Tassels & Fabulous Fringe: Heirloom Accents from Modern Materials. LC 00-102688. (Illus.). 112p. 2000. pap. 19.95 (*0-87341-819-0*, TFM) Krause Pubns.

Clement, Carole. First Steps to a Vegetarian Family. 160p. 1996. pap. text 13.95 (*0-572-01977-7*, Pub. by W Foulsham) Trans-Atl Phila.

Clement, Catherine. Gandhi: The Power of Pacifism. Sharman, Ruth, tr. (Discoveries Ser.). (Illus.). 176p. 1996. pap. 12.95 (*0-8109-2803-5*, Pub. by Abrams) Time Warner.

— Growing an Indian Star: Poems. 1992. 10.00 (*0-7069-5571-4*, Pub. by Vikas) S Asia.

— Opera: The Undoing of Women. Wing, Betsy, tr.Tr. of L'Opera, ou la Defaite des Femmes. 224p. 1999. pap. 17.95 (*0-8166-3526-9*, Pub. by U of Minn Pr) Chicago Distribution Ctr.

— Syncope: The Philosophy of Rapture. O'Driscoll, Sally, tr. LC 94-7610. 1994. pap. 19.95 (*0-8166-1978-6*); text 49.95 (*0-8166-1977-8*) U of Minn Pr.

— Theo's Odyssey. Cox, Steve & Schwartz, Ros, trs. from FRE. LC 99-35735. 608p. 1999. 26.95 (*1-55970-499-3*, Pub. by Arcade Pub Inc) Time Warner.

— The Weary Sons of Freud. Ball, Nicole, tr. 115p. (C). 1987. pap. 17.00 (*0-86091-888-2*, A0639, Pub. by Verso) Norton.

Clement, Catherine, jt. auth. see Cixous, Helene.

Clement, Cathie. A Guide to Printed Sources for the History of the Kimberley Region of Western Australia. LC 97-145834. pap. 54.95 (*0-86422-465-6*, Pub. by Univ of West Aust Pr) Intl Spec Bk.

Clement, Christina, jt. auth. see Amshay, Thomas.

Clement, Christopher, et al. Anther & Pollen: From Biology to Biotechnology. LC 99-17766. 260p. 1999. 159.00 (*3-540-64986-7*) Spr-Verlag.

Clement, Clara E. Constantinople. 1977. lib. bdg. 59.95 (*0-8490-1668-1*) Gordon Pr.

— Women in the Fine Arts: From the Seventh Century B. C. to the Twentieth Century A. D. (Illus.). 395p. 1977. reprint ed. 26.95 (*0-87928-079-4*) Corner Hse.

Clement, Clare E. & Hutton, Laurence. Artists of the Nineteenth Century & Their Work. LC 70-88820. (Art Histories Collection). 1970. reprint ed. 26.95 (*0-405-02222-0*) Ayer.

Clement Clarke, Moore. 'Twas the Night Before Christmas. LC 93-37281. 32p. (J). (ps-1). 1994. write for info. (*0-689-71801-2*) Aladdin.

Clement, Claude. Gentle Little Lion. LC 93-27047. (Little Animal Adventures Ser.). (Illus.). 22p. (J). (ps-3). 1994. 5.98 (*0-89577-562-X*) RD Assn.

***Clement, D. L., ed.** From Neutralization of Leukocyte Adhesion to Leg Ulcer Healing: Session Held During the 20th European Conference on Microcirculation, Paris, August-September 1998. (Journal of Vascular Research Ser.: Vol. 36, Suppl. 1 (1999)). (Illus.). iv, 48p. 1999. pap. 25.25 (*3-8055-6933-5*) S Karger.

Clement, Daniel, ed. The Algonquins. (Mercury Ser.: CES No. 130). (Illus.). 264p. 1996. pap. 24.95 (*0-660-15961-9*, Pub. by CN Mus Civilization) U of Wash Pr.

Clement, Daniel, jt. auth. see Jauvin, Serge.

Clement-Davies, David. Trojan Horse. LC 98-53380. (Eyewitness Readers). (J). (gr. 2-4). 1999. pap. 3.95 (*0-7894-4474-7*) DK Pub Inc.

***Clement-Davies, David.** Trojan Horse. LC 98-53380. (Eyewitness Readers). (J). (gr. 2-4). 1999. pap. 12.95 (*0-7894-4475-5*) DK Pub Inc.

Clement, Diane. Clement Farm Herb Cookbook. (Illus.). 96p. 1996. reprint ed. pap. 10.00 (*0-938041-73-8*) Arc Pr AR.

— Diane Clement at the Tomato. (Illus.). 160p. 1996. pap. 11.95 (*1-895714-95-8*) Raincoast Bk.

Clement, Dieter, jt. ed. see Watkins, Wendell R.

***Clement, Doreene.** The 5 Year Journal. 272p. 1999. 29.95 (*0-9637138-0-9*, 5YJ TM1) DKC Enter Ltd.

Clement, F. A., jt. auth. see Thomason, Calvin C.

Clement, Felix & Larousse, Pierre. Dictionnaire des Operas, 2 vols., Set. LC 69-15617. (Music Reprint Ser.). (FRE.). 1969. reprint ed. 135.00 (*0-306-71197-4*) Da Capo.

Clement-Foreman, Brian, et al. Essential Guitar. (Illus.). 60p. (Orig.). 1997. pap. text 14.95 (*0-914487-04-3*) Troost Pr.

Clement, Frederic. Merchant of Marvels & the Peddler of Dreams. Cole, Emma, tr. LC 97-13104. (Illus.). 64p. 1997. 17.95 (*0-8118-1664-8*) Chronicle Bks.

Clement, Gary. The Great Poochini. (Illus.). 32p. (J). (ps-3). 1999. 15.95 (*0-88899-331-5*) Gro1undwood-Douglas.

Clement, Gary. Just Stay Put: A Chelm Story. 32p. (J). (ps-3). 1996. 14.95 (*0-88899-239-4*) Publishers Group.

Clement, Ginny & Dalrymple, Allison. How to Boil Water . . . And Other Fancy Dishes! (Illus.). 108p. 1998. spiral bd. 14.95 (*0-9660054-0-6*) Step By Step.

Clement, Grace. Care, Autonomy & Justice: Feminism & the Ethic of Care. LC 96-8449. (Feminist Theory & Politics Ser.). 144p. (C). 1996. pap. text 22.00 (*0-8133-2538-2*, Pub. by Westview) HarpC.

***Clement, Hal.** Essential Hal Clement: Music of Many Spheres, 2. Olson, Mark L. & Lewis, Anthony R., eds. 506p. 2000. 25.00 (*1-886778-07-8*, NESFA Pr) New Eng SF Assoc.

— Half Life. LC 99-22199. 252p. 1999. 23.95 (*0-312-86920-7*, Pub. by Tor Bks) St Martin.

— Half Life. 256p. 2000. mass mkt. 6.99 (*0-8125-6660-2*, Pub. by Tor Bks) St Martin.

Clement, Hal. Mission of Gravity. 1993. reprint ed. lib. bdg. 18.95 (*0-89968-336-3*, Lghtyr Pr) Buccaneer Bks.

Clement, Hutton. Artist of the Nineteenth Century. reprint ed. lib. bdg. 75.00 (*0-7812-0122-5*) Rprt Serv.

Clement, J., ed. Noble Deeds of American Women. 480p. 1975. reprint ed. 31.95 (*0-87928-061-1*) Corner Hse.

Clement, J. J., et al, eds. Materials Reliability in Microelectronics VII: Materials Research Society Symposium Proceedings, Vol. 473. 457p. 1997. text 75.00 (*1-55899-377-0*) Materials Res.

***Clement, Jane Tyson.** Jane Tyson Clement: Selected Poetry. 2000. pap. write for info. (*0-87486-900-5*) Plough.

— The Secret Flower: And Other Stories. rev. ed. Orig. Title: The Sparrow. (Illus.). 160p. 2000. pap. 12.00 (*0-87486-995-1*, Pub. by Plough) Spring Arbor Dist.

Clement, Jean-Luc, jt. ed. see Howse, P. E.

Clement, Jean-Michel. Agricultural Larousse: Larousse Agricole. (FRE.). 1207p. 1981. 195.00 (*0-8288-1174-1*, M14293) Fr & Eur.

— Dictionnaire des Industries Alimentaires. (FRE.). 361p. 1978. 85.00 (*0-8288-5184-0*, M6071) Fr & Eur.

Clement, Jerrt, et al. Manufacturing Data Structures: Building Foundations for Excellence with Bills of Materials & Process Information. LC 92-60537. 276p. 1992. 129.00 (*0-939246-27-9*) Wiley.

Clement, Jerry, et al. Manufacturing Data Structures A: Building Foundations for Excellence with Bills of Materials & Process Information, 0000. 288p. 1995. 50.00 (*0-471-13269-1*) Wiley.

Clement, Jesse, ed. Noble Deeds of American Women: With Biographical Sketches of Some of the More Prominent. LC 74-3935. (Women in America Ser.). (Illus.). 482p. 1979. reprint ed. 42.95 (*0-405-06082-3*) Ayer.

Clement, John. Sketches of the First Emigrant Settlers on Newton Township, Old Gloucester County, West New Jersey. (Illus.). 444p. 1997. reprint ed. lib. bdg. 47.50 (*0-8328-6066-2*) Higginson Bk Co.

Clement, John, jt. ed. see Lochhead, Jack.

Clement, John A. Living Messages in Sermon Outlines. unabridged ed. 139p. 1996. reprint ed. pap. 9.99 (*0-88019-349-2*) Schmul Pub Co.

Clement, John G. & Ranson, David L., eds. Craniofacial Identification in Forensic Medicine. LC 97-42826. (An Arnold Publication). (Illus.). 320p. 1998. text 169.50 (*0-340-60759-9*, Pub. by E A) OUP.

Clement, K., et al. Regional Policy & Technology Transfer: A Cross-National Perspective. 113p. 1995. pap. text 40.00 (*0-11-515357-8*, HM53578, Pub. by Statnry Office) Bernan Associates.

Clement, Ken. Understanding & Servicing CD Players. (Illus.). 256p. 1994. text 56.95 (*0-7506-0934-6*) Buttrwrth-Heinemann.

Clement, Kim. The Sound of His Voice. 180p. 1993. pap. 10.99 (*0-88419-339-X*) Creation House.

***Clement, Lesley D.** Learning to Look: A Visual Response to Mavis Gallant's Fiction. 304p. 2000. 65.00 (*0-7735-2041-4*, Pub. by McG-Queens Univ Pr) CUP Services.

Clement, Linda M. & Rickard, Scott T. Effective Leadership in Student Services: Voices from the Field. LC 92-18758. (Higher & Adult Education Ser.). 264p. 1992. text 35.45 (*1-55542-479-1*) Jossey-Bass.

Clement, M. Olivier. The Living God: A Catechism for the Christian Faith, 2 vols. Dunlap, Olga, tr. from FRE. LC 89-6291.Tr. of Dieu est Vivant. 445p. (Orig.). 1989. pap. 26.95 (*0-88141-040-3*) St Vladimirs.

***Clement, Manuel.** Friends of ED: Foundation Swift 3D. 245p. 2001. pap. 19.99 (*1-903450-05-5*) Wrox Pr Inc.

Clement, Marilene. La Fleur De Lotus. (FRE.). 304p. 1986. pap. 11.95 (*0-7859-2033-1*, 2070377318) Fr & Eur.

— Le Vent Sur la Maison. (FRE.). 212p. 1979. pap. 10.95 (*0-7859-1882-5*, 2070370615) Fr & Eur.

Clement, Marion. Schwermetallaufnahme Von Mnium Hornum Hedw. Im Hinblick Auf Seine Eignung Als Biomonitor. (Dissertationes Botanicae Ser.: Band 164). (GER., Illus.). vi, 184p. 1990. pap. 48.00 (*3-443-64076-1*, Pub. by Gebruder Borntraeger) Balogh.

Clement, Mark. The Waves That Heal. 63p. 1996. reprint ed. spiral bd. 10.00 (*0-7873-1164-2*) Hlth Research.

Clement, Mary. Bright Ideas: A Pocket Mentor for Beginning Teachers. LC 97-39905. (Checklist Ser.). 56p. (Orig.). 1997. pap. 5.95 (*0-8106-2153-3*, 2153-3) NEA.

***Clement, Mary.** How to Die without a Lawyer. LC 99-462318. 2000. pap. 15.95 (*0-312-24401-0*) St Martin.

— The Juvenile Justice System. 2nd ed. 292p. 2000. 44.95 (*0-7506-7353-2*) Buttrwrth-Heinemann.

Clement, Mary. The Juvenile Justice System: Law & Process. (Illus.). 400p. 1996. 49.95 (*0-7506-9810-1*, BH Security) Buttrwrth-Heinemann.

— Soul Soaring: New Techniques for Diagnosing & Overcoming What Separates You from Harmony Within. Martin, Stephen H., ed. 160p. 1998. pap. 11.95 (*1-892538-17-2*) Oaklea Pr.

An Asterisk (*) at the beginning of an entry indicates that the title is appearing for the first time.

Clement, Mary & Humphry, Derek. Freedom to Die: The People & Politics of the Right-to-Die Movement. LC 98-21127. 400p. 1998. text 24.95 (0-312-19415-3) St Martin.

Clement, Mary, jt. auth. see Humphry, Derek.

Clement, Mary C. Building the Best Faculty: Strategies for Hiring & Supporting New Teachers. LC 99-63649. 176p. 1999. text 36.00 (1-56676-735-0) Scarecrow.

Clement, Mary C. Put Your Oxygen Mask on First: And Other Strategies for Succeeding in Teaching! (Illus.). 118p. write for info. (1-888793-04-X) Tchrs Little Secrets.

Clement, Maud C. The History of Pittsylvania County, Virginia. LC 72-10443. (Illus.). 340p. 1999. reprint ed. pap. 29.50 (0-8063-7989-8) Clearfield Co.

Clement, Mickey. The Irish Princess. 304p. 1995. mass mkt. 6.99 (0-425-14830-0) Berkley Pub.

Clement, Nicole & Douin, Joel, eds. Interfaces & Plasticity. (Solid State Phenomena Ser.: Vols. 59-60). (Illus.). 304p. (C). 1998. text 184.00 (3-908450-30-6, Pub. by Scitec Pubns) Enfield Pubs NH.

Clement, Norris C. & M., Eduardo Zepeda, eds. San Diego-Tijuana in Transition: A Regional Analysis. 130p. (Orig.). (C). 1993. pap. text 15.00 (0-925613-10-X) SDSU Inst Reg Studies.

Clement, Norris C., et al. North American Economic Integration: Theory & Practice. LC 99-22084. 346p. 1999. 95.00 (1-84064-102-9) E Elgar.

*Clement, Norris C., et al. North American Economic Integration: Theory & Practice. 360p. 2000. text 30.00 (1-84064-412-5) E Elgar.

Clement-O'Brien & Lawler. Applying Medication Math Skills: A Dimensional Analysis Approach. LC 98-8415. 288p. 1998. text 40.95 (0-7668-0050-4) Delmar.

Clement of Alexandria. The One Who Knows God. Wilson, William, tr. from GRE. 160p. (Orig.). 1990. pap. 7.95 (0-924722-02-9) Scroll Pub.

Clement Of Alexandria. Stromateis, Bks. 1-3. Ferguson, John, tr. from LAT. LC 90-21352. (Fathers of the Church Ser.: Vol. 85). 354p. 1992. text 36.95 (0-8132-0085-7) Cath U Pr.

Clement, Oliver. Taize: A Meaning to Life. LC 97-23089. 83p. (C). 1997. pap. 10.00 (1-57999-007-X) GIA Pubns.

*Clement, Olivier. On Human Being: A Spiritual Anthropology. 176p. 2000. pap. 14.95 (1-56548-143-7) New City.

Clement, Olivier. The Roots of Christian Mysticism: Text & Commentary. 5th ed. Berkeley, Theodore, tr. from FRE. LC 94-32957. 382p. 1995. pap. 19.95 (1-56548-029-5) New City.

*Clement, Olivier. Three Prayers: Our Father, O Heavenly King, the Prayer of Saint Ephrem. LC 99-54452. 2000. write for info. (0-88141-197-3) St Vladimirs.

Clement, Ora A., ed. see O'Gara, W. H.

Clement, Page. Investigating & Making it in Art. Date not set. pap. text. write for info. (0-05-005085-0) Addison-Wesley.

Clement, Page. Knowledge & Understanding in Art. Date not set. pap. text. write for info. (0-05-005086-9) Addison-Wesley.

— Principles & Practice in Art. Date not set. pap. text. write for info. (0-05-005082-6) Addison-Wesley.

Clement, Pamelia F., jt. auth. see Bigler, Erin D.

Clement, Paul C. Petite Martinique: Traditions & Social Change. LC 99-90330. (Illus.). 160p. (C). 1999. pap. 10.95 (0-9670898-0-8) Clement Inc.

— The Quest for Economic Development in the Caribbean. 150p. 1999. pap. 10.95 (0-9670898-1-6) Clement Inc.

*Clement, Paul W. Outcomes & Incomes: How to Evaluate, Improve & Market Your Psychotherapy Practice by Measuring Outcomes. LC 99-28874. (Clinician's Toolbox Ser.). 244p. 1999. otabind 50.00 incl. cd-rom (1-57230-486-3) Guilford Pubns.

Clement, Peter. Death Rounds. 1999. mass mkt. 6.99 (0-449-00450-3) Fawcett.

— Fatal Medicine. 2000. mass mkt. write for info. (0-449-00622-0) Fawcett.

— Finches & Sparrows: An Identification Guide. LC 93-5101. (Illus.). 514p. 1994. text 49.50 (0-691-03424-9, Pub. by Princeton U Pr) Cal Prin Full Svc.

*Clement, Peter. Finches & Sparrows: An Identification Guide. 2000. pap. text 29.95 (0-691-04878-9, Pub. by Princeton U Pr) Cal Prin Full Svc.

Clement, Peter. Lethal Practice. 1997. mass mkt. 6.99 (0-345-40776-8) Ballantine Pub Grp.

— Lethal Practice. 1998. mass mkt. 6.99 (0-449-00281-0, GM) Fawcett.

— Lethal Practice. 1998. mass mkt. 6.99 (0-8041-1781-0) Ivy Books.

Clement, Philip B. & Young, Robert H. Tumors & Tumor-Like Lesions of the Uterine Corpus & Cervix. (Contemporary Issues in Surgical Pathology Ser.). (Illus.). 504p. 1993. text 121.00 (0-443-08801-2) Church.

Clement, Philippe, et al, eds. Semigroup Theory & Evolution Equations: The 2nd International Conference. (Lecture Notes in Pure & Applied Mathematics Ser.: Vol. 135). (Illus.). 544p. 1991. pap. text 215.00 (0-8247-8545-2) Dekker.

Clement, Philippe & Lumer, Gunter, eds. Evolution Equations, Control Theory, & Biomathematics. LC 93-32127. (Lecture Notes in Pure & Applied Mathematics Ser.: Vol. 155). (Illus.). 616p. 1993. pap. text 210.00 (0-8247-8885-0) Dekker.

Clement, Philippe, et al. Semigroup Theory & Applications. (Lecture Notes in Pure & Applied Mathematics Ser.: Vol. 116). (Illus.). 480p. 1989. pap. text 185.00 (0-8247-8088-4) Dekker.

Clement, Phillip B. & Young, Robert H. Atlas of Gynecologic & Peritoneal Surgical Pathology. (Illus.). 360p. Date not set. text. write for info. (0-7216-2458-8, W B Saunders Co) Harcrt Hlth Sci Grp.

*Clement, Pierre. Hypnosis & Accelerated Learning. 2nd ed. 135p. 1999. reprint ed. pap. 9.95 (0-930298-33-0) Westwood Pub Co.

Clement, Preston R. & Johnson, Walter C. Electrical Engineering Science. LC 82-14796. 602p. 1983. reprint ed. lib. bdg. 49.50 (0-89874-442-3) Krieger.

Clement, Priscilla F. Welfare & the Poor in the Nineteenth Century City: Philadelphia, 1800-1854. LC 83-49357. (Illus.). 224p. 1985. 32.50 (0-8386-3216-5) Fairleigh Dickinson.

*Clement, Priscilla F. & Reinier, Jacqueline S. Boyhood in America: An Encyclopedia, 2 Vols. 2001. lib. bdg. 150.00 (1-57607-215-0) ABC-CLIO.

Clement, Priscilla Ferguson. Growing Pains Children in the Industrial Age, 1850-1890. LC 96-41085. 1997. 33.00 (0-8057-4109-7) Macmillan.

Clement, R. Hal Leonard Guitar Blues Method, Vol. 1. 48p. 1981. pap. 6.95 (0-7935-2812-7, 00699047) H Leonard.

Clement, R. E. Emissions from Combustion Processes - Origin, Measurement, Control. (Illus.). 504p. 1990. lib. bdg. 119.00 (0-87371-172-6, L172) Lewis Pubs.

— Instrumentation for Trace Organic Monitoring. 336p. 1991. lib. bdg. 119.00 (0-87371-213-7, L213) Lewis Pubs.

Clement, R. E., jt. auth. see Karasek, Francis W.

Clement, Ray E. Gas Chromatography: Biochemical, Biomedical & Clinical Applications. LC 90-12799. (Chemical Analysis Ser.). 393p. 1990. 185.00 (0-471-01048-0) Wiley.

Clement, Ray W., et al. Reference Materials for Environmental Analysis. LC 96-22062. 288p. 1996. lib. bdg. 65.00 (1-56670-102-3) Lewis Pubs.

Clement, Richard. Homotoxicology: A Correspondence Course: Theoretical Concepts & Therapeutic Applications, 12 vols. 2nd rev. ed. Moss, Andy, ed. (Illus.). 378p. 1997. pap. text 300.00 (0-9664791-1-4) Menaco Pub.

Clement, Robert. The Art Teacher's Handbook. 2nd ed. (Illus.). 272p. 1993. pap., teacher ed. 42.50 (0-7487-1455-3, Pub. by S Thornes Pubs) Trans-Atl Phila.

Clement, Rod. Counting on Frank. LC 90-27558. (Illus.). 32p. (J). (gr. 1-3). 1991. lib. bdg. 21.27 (0-8368-0358-2) Gareth Stevens Inc.

— Frank's Great Museum Adventure. LC 98-41710. (Illus.). 32p. (J). (gr. 2-4). 1999. lib. bdg. 14.89 (0-06-027674-6) HarpC Child Bks.

— Frank's Great Museum Adventure. LC 98-41710. (Illus.). 32p. (J). (gr. 4-8). 1999. 14.95 (0-06-027673-8) HarpC Child Bks.

— Grandpa's Teeth. LC 97-14753. (Illus.). 32p. (J). (ps-3). 1998. 15.95 (0-06-027671-1) HarpC.

— Grandpa's Teeth. LC 97-14753. (Illus.). 32p. (J). (ps-3). 1999. pap. 5.95 (0-06-443557-1, HarpTrophy) HarpC Child Bks.

— Just Another Ordinary Day. LC 96-43611. (Illus.). 32p. (J). (ps-3). 1997. lib. bdg. 15.89 (0-06-027667-3) HarpC.

— Just Another Ordinary Day. LC 96-43611. (Illus.). 32p. (J). (ps-3). 1998. pap. 5.95 (0-06-443500-8) HarpC Child Bks.

Clement, Rosa, et al. Absorbing Destruction. LC 98-75407. 80p. 1999. pap. 10.00 (0-940248-52-2) Guild Pr.

Clement, Rosemary. Christopher Park. 212p. 1993. 20.00 (1-883285-00-3) Delphinium.

Clement, Russell T. Les Fauves: A Sourcebook, 17. LC 94-2848. (Art Reference Collection Ser.: No. 17). 720p. 1994. lib. bdg. 145.00 (0-313-28333-8, Greenwood Pr) Greenwood.

— Four French Symbolists: A Sourcebook on Pierre Puvis de Chavannes, Gustave Moreau, Odilon Redon, & Maurice Denis, 20. LC 96-4971. (Art Reference Collection Ser.). 600p. 1996. lib. bdg. 105.00 (0-313-29752-5, Greenwood Pr) Greenwood.

— Georges Braque: A Bio-Bibliography, 3. LC 93-45310. (Bio-Bibliographies in Art & Architecture Ser.). 256p. 1994. lib. bdg. 79.50 (0-313-29235-3, Greenwood Pr) Greenwood.

— Henri Matisse: A Bio-Bibliography, 2. LC 93-21069. (Bio-Bibliographies in Art & Architecture Ser.: Vol. 2). 416p. 1993. lib. bdg. 105.00 (0-313-28127-0, Greenwood Pr) Greenwood.

— Paul Gauguin: A Bio-Bibliography, 1. LC 91-13903. (Bio-Bibliographies in Art Ser.: No. 1). 352p. 1991. lib. bdg. 65.00 (0-313-27394-4, CPQ, Greenwood Pr) Greenwood.

Clement, Russell T., compiled by. Mormons in the Pacific: A Bibliography. 239p. (C). 1981. text 12.95 (0-939154-17-X); pap. text 7.95 (0-939154-18-8) Inst Polynesian.

*Clement, Russell T. & Houzbe, Annick. Neo-Impressionist Painters: A Sourcebook on Georges Seurat, Camille Pissarro, Paul Signac, Theo Van Rysselberghe, Henri Edmond Cross, Charles Angrand, Maximilien Luce & Albert Dubois-Pillet, 23. LC 99-36377. (Art Reference Collection Ser.). 416p. 1999. lib. bdg. 89.50 (0-313-30382-7) Greenwood.

*Clement, Russell T., et al. The Women Impressionists: A Sourcebook, 24. LC 99-59411. (Art Reference Collection Ser.: Vol. 24). 196p. 2000. lib. bdg. 75.00 (0-313-30848-9, Greenwood Pr) Greenwood.

Clement, Russell T., jt. compiled by see Craig, Robert D.

Clement, Sarah. Psychological Perspectives on Pregnancy & Childbirth. LC 97-36826. 1998. pap. text 29.50 (0-443-05760-5) Church.

Clement, Shelly, et al. Interlibrary Loan in Academic & Research Libraries: Workload & Staffing. (Occasional Papers: Vol. 15). 23p. 1989. pap. 25.00 (0-918006-60-0, OP15) ARL.

Clement, Shirley. Echoes Through the Pass. (Illus.). 44p. 1998. 20.00 (0-944551-28-9) Sundance Pr TX.

*Clement, Shirley. A Journey of Faith: Lay Witness Mission Handbook. 64p. 2000. pap. text. write for info. (0-88177-301-8, DR301) Discipleship Res.

Clement, Shirley. The Writer's Organizer: Plans, Procedures & Forms for Productivity & Profitability. 176p. 1999. pap. 14.95 (0-9637498-8-9) Toad Hall PA.

Clement, Shirley F. & Swanson, Roger K. Lay Speakers Lead in Evangelism. 16p. 1997. pap. 5.95 (0-88177-200-3, DR200) Discipleship Res.

Clement, Shirley F., jt. auth. see Swanson, Roger K.

Clement, Sledge. Orthopaedics Two Thousand & Two. 2002. 83.00 (0-8151-1555-5, 31716) Mosby Inc.

Clement, Stephanie. Consciousness & the Midheaven. 82p. 1994. 15.00 (0-86690-445-X, C3504-014) Am Fed Astrologers.

— Planets & Planet Centered Astrology. 176p. 1992. 16.00 (0-86690-426-3, C3344-014) Am Fed Astrologers.

*Clement, Stephanie J. Charting Your Career: The Horoscope Reveals Your Life Purpose. LC 99-16565. (Illus.). 208p. 1999. pap. 12.95 (1-56718-144-9) Llewellyn Pubns.

*Clement, Stephanie Jean. Dreams: Working Interactive. LC 00-34805. 2000. 24.95 (1-56718-145-7) Llewellyn Pubns.

— What Astrology Can Do for You. 192p. 2000. pap. 4.99 (1-56718-146-5) Llewellyn Pubns.

Clement, Stephen D., jt. auth. see Jaques, Elliott.

Clement, Stephen L. & Quisenberry, Sharron S. Global Plant: Genetic Resource for Insect Resistant Crops. LC 98-20377. 320p. 1998. boxed set 99.95 (0-8493-2695-8, 2695) CRC Pr.

Clement, Steven, jt. auth. see Jaques, Elliott.

Clement, Susan, jt. ed. see Donkin, Ellen.

Clement, Thomas P. The Unforgotten War: Dust of the Streets. LC 98-96721. (Illus.). 120p. 1998. pap. 11.95 (0-9667952-0-2) Truepeny Pubg Co.

Clement, Tim P., et al, eds. Logic Program Synthesis & Transformation: Proceedings of LOPSTR 91, International Workshop on Logic Program Synthesis & Transformation University of Manchester, 4-5 July 1991. (Workshops in Computing Ser.). x, 337p. 1992. 59.00 (0-387-19742-7) Spr-Verlag.

Clement, Tim P., jt. ed. see Lau, Kung-Kiu.

Clement, Vonnie V., jt. ed. see Gonzalez, Gerardo M.

Clement, W. R. Quantum Jump: A Survival Guide for the Next Renaissance. LC 99-175362. 528p. 1999. pap. 19.99 (1-895837-45-6) Insomniac.

Clement, Wallace, ed. Understanding Canada: Building on the New Canadian Political Economy. LC 98-124407. 416p. 1996. 65.00 (0-7735-1502-X, Pub. by McG-Queens Univ Pr); pap. 22.95 (0-7735-1503-8, Pub. by McG-Queens Univ Pr) CUP Services.

Clement, Wallace & Myles, John. Relations of Ruling: Class & Gender in Postindustrial Societies. LC 93-90666. 320p. (C). 1994. 65.00 (0-7735-1164-4, Pub. by McG-Queens Univ Pr); pap. text 19.95 (0-7735-1178-4, Pub. by McG-Queens Univ Pr) CUP Services.

Clement, Wallace & Williams, Glen, eds. The New Canadian Political Economy. 352p. (C). 1989. text 65.00 (0-7735-0672-1, Pub. by McG-Queens Univ Pr) CUP Services.

— The New Canadian Political Economy. 344p. (C). 1989. pap. text 24.95 (0-7735-0681-0, Pub. by McG-Queens Univ Pr) CUP Services.

Clemente, jt. auth. see Colverson.

Clemente, Adriano, jt. auth. see Norbu, Chogyal N.

Clemente, Adriano, ed. see Norbu, Namkhai.

Clemente, Alice, ed. Sweet Marmalade, Sour Oranges: Contemporary Portuguese Women's Fiction. LC 92-73209. 217p. (Orig.). 1994. pap. text 12.50 (0-943722-20-9) Gavea-Brown.

Clemente, Bill, jt. auth. see Clemente, Linda.

Clemente, Carmine D. Anatomy: A Regional Atlas of the Human Body. 1987. 49.50 (0-8121-1723-9) Lppncott W & W.

— Anatomy: A Regional Atlas of the Human Body. 3rd ed. LC 85-11157. (Illus.). 444p. (C). 1987. 52.00 (0-683-01723-3) Lppncott W & W.

— Anatomy: A Regional Atlas of the Human Body. 4th ed. LC 96-47623. (Illus.). 624p. 1997. pap. 65.00 (0-683-01733-0) Lppncott W & W.

— Clemente's Anatomy Book. 1998. 99.00 (0-683-30622-7) Lppncott W & W.

Clemente, Carmine D., ed. Gray's Anatomy of the Human Body. 30th ed. LC 84-5741. (Illus.). 1676p. 1985. 89.50 (0-8121-0644-X) Lppncott W & W.

Clemente, Francesco. Francesco Clemente: Fifty One Days at Mount Abu. (Illus.). 122p. 1999. 375.00 (0-947564-77-2) A D'Offay Gallery.

— Francesco Clemente: Anamorphosis. Foye, Raymond, ed. (Illus.). 16p. 1997. pap. 20.00 (1-880154-12-9) Gagosian Gallery.

— Francesco Clemente: India. (Illus.). 96p. 1987. 45.00 (0-942642-30-9) Twelvetrees Pr.

— Funerary Paintings. 14p. 1988. 150.00 (0-944521-16-9) Dia Ctr Arts.

Clemente, Francesco & Dorazio, Sante. Sante D'Orazio: A Private View: Photographs & Diary. LC 99-164777. (Illus.). 296p. 1998. 30.00 (0-670-88251-8) Viking Penguin.

Clemente, Frank & Lambert, Richard D., eds. The New Rural America. LC 76-27028. (Annals Ser.: No. 429). 1977. pap. 18.00 (0-87761-209-9) Am Acad Pol Soc Sci.

Clemente, Frank & Watkins, Frank, eds. Keep Hope Alive: Jesse Jackson's 1988 Presidential Campaign. 232p. (Orig.). 1989. 40.00 (0-89608-358-6); pap. 17.00 (0-89608-357-8) South End Pr.

Clemente, Gary. Cosmo Gets an Ear. LC 94-75586. (Illus.). 54p. (J). (gr. 1-6). 1994. 9.95 (0-916708-24-1) Modern Signs.

Clemente, Gerald W. & Stevens, Kevin. The Cops Are Robbers: A Convicted Cop's True Story of Police Corruption. 208p. 1989. pap. 3.95 (0-380-70626-1, Avon Bks) Morrow Avon.

Clemente, Isis. Innovationwatch Student Book. (Illus.). 160p. 1995. pap. text, student ed. 27.93 (0-13-094038-0, Prentice Hall) P-H.

*Clemente, John. Girl Groups: Fabulous Females That Rocked the World. (Illus.). 256p. 2000. pap. 19.95 (0-87341-816-6, OFD) Krause Pubns.

Clemente, Karen. The Rest of Faith. (Inter Acta Logos Ser.). (Illus.). 2p. (C). 1994. teacher ed., ring bd. write for info. (1-885702-73-6, 741-073t, Inter Acta); student ed., ring bd. 3.25 (1-885702-72-8, 741-073s, Inter Acta) WSN Pr.

Clemente, Lilia C. & Mariano, Roberto S., eds. Asian Capital Markets: Regional & Global Perspectives. LC 92-71666. (Illus.). 249p. (Orig.). 1992. pap. 29.95 (0-9633012-0-9) Asian Securit.

Clemente, Linda & Clemente, Bill. Gabrielle Roy: Creation & Memory. LC 97-141115. (Illus.). 208p. 1997. pap. 14.95 (1-55022-287-2, Pub. by ECW) Genl Dist Srvs.

Clemente, Linda M. Literary Objects d'Art: Ekphrasis in Medieval French Romance, 1150-1210. LC 90-24421. (American University Studies: Romance Languages & Literature: Ser. II, Vol. 166). 157p. (C). 1992. text 35.95 (0-8204-1506-5) P Lang Pubng.

Clemente, M. Pais. Voice Update: Proceedings of the 1st World Congress, Oporto, Portugal, April 9-13, 1995, Vol. 109. LC 96-29317. (International Congress Ser.). 428p. 1996. 206.25 (0-444-82230-5) Elsevier.

Clemente, Maribeth. Riches of France. LC 97-7064. 1997. pap. 19.95 (0-312-15640-5) St Martin.

Clemente, Mark N. The Marketing Glossary: Key Terms, Concepts, & Applications. 470p. 1992. 34.95 (0-8144-5030-X) AMACOM.

Clemente, Mark N. & Greenspan, David S. Empowering Human Resources in the Merger & Acquisition Process: Guidance for HR Professionals in the Key Areas of M&A Planning & Integration. (Illus.). 160p. 1999. pap. 75.00 (0-9671204-0-3) Clemente Greenspan.

— Winning at Mergers & Acquisitien: The Guide to Marleit - Focused Planning & Inlegrafien. LC 97-38327. 331p. 1998. 69.95 (0-471-19056-X) Wiley.

Clemente, Peter. The State of the Net: The New Frontier. LC 97-44420. (Illus.). 179p. 1998. pap. 24.95 (0-07-011979-1) McGraw.

Clemente, Rebecca & Bohlin, Roy M. Visual Literacy: A Selected Bibliography. Milheim, William D., ed. LC 90-41870. (Educational Technology Selected Bibliography Ser.: Vol. 2). 50p. 1990. pap. 24.95 (0-87778-227-X) Educ Tech Pubns.

Clemente, Steven E. For King & Kaiser! The Making of the Prussian Army Officer, 1860-1914, 123. LC 91-35235. (Contributions in Military Studies Ser.: No. 123). 304p. 1992. 59.95 (0-313-28004-5, CFK/, Greenwood Pr) Greenwood.

Clemente, Vince. This Shining Place: A Meditation. 16p. (Orig.). (C). 1992. pap. 5.00 (1-878173-25-1) Birnham Wood.

Clemente, Vincent, ed. see Marinelli, William J.

Clementi, E., et al, eds. Structure & Motion: Membranes, Nucleic Acids & Proteins. (Illus.). 582p. 1985. lib. bdg. 130.00 (0-940030-12-8) Adenine Pr.

Clementi, E. & Chin, S., eds. Structure & Dynamics of Nucleic Acids, Proteins & Membranes. LC 87-2366. 468p. 1987. 95.00 (0-306-42553-X, Plenum Trade) Perseus Pubng.

Clementi, Enrico, ed. Modern Techniques in Computational Chemistry: MOTECC, 1989. 640p. (C). 1989. text 348.00 (90-72199-05-7, Pub. by Escom Sci Pubs) Kluwer Academic.

— Modern Techniques in Computational Chemistry: MOTECC, 1990. 1188p. (C). 1990. text 260.00 (90-72199-07-3, Pub. by Escom Sci Pubs) Kluwer Academic.

— Modern Techniques in Computational Chemistry: MOTECC, 1991. 1302p. (C). 1991. text 390.00 (90-72199-10-3, Pub. by Escom Sci Pubs) Kluwer Academic.

Clementi, Enrico, et al, eds. Structure & Dynamics of Nucleic Acids & Proteins. (Illus.). 500p. (C). 1983. lib. bdg. 80.00 (0-940030-04-7) Adenine Pr.

Clementi, Enrico & Chin, S., eds. Biological & Artificial Intelligence Systems. 608p. (C). 1988. text 318.00 (90-72199-02-2, Pub. by Escom Sci Pubs) Kluwer Academic.

*Clementi, F., et al, eds. Neuronal Nicotinic Receptors: Pharmacology & Therapeutic Opportunities. (Handbook of Experimental Pharmacology Ser.: 144). xvi, 664p. 2000. (3-540-66123-9) Spr-Verlag.

*Clementi, Federica. Italian-English, English-Italian Dictionary & Phrasebook. 170p. 2000. pap. 11.95 (0-7818-0812-X) Hippocrene Bks.

Clementi, M. Six Sonatas Opus 36: Piano. 32p. 1986. pap. 4.95 (0-7935-2569-1) H Leonard.

— Twelve Sonatinas Opus 36, Opus 37, Opus 38 for the Piano. 72p. 1986. pap. 5.95 (0-7935-5173-0) H Leonard.

— Two Sonatas: 2 Pianos 4 Hands. 48p. 1986. pap. 9.95 (0-7935-5206-0, 50259880) H Leonard.

Clementi, Muzio. Collected Works, 13 vols in 5. LC 70-75299. (Music Reprint Ser.). 1973. 69.50 (0-306-77260-4); 18.50 (0-306-77267-1); 18.50 (0-306-77268-X) Da Capo.

— Gradus ad Parnassum. LC 79-18610. (Music Reprint Ser.: 1979). 1980. reprint ed. lib. bdg. 55.00 (0-306-79570-1) Da Capo.

— Piano Sonatas. 272p. 1992. pap. text 10.95 (0-486-27310-5) Dover.

C

An Asterisk (*) at the beginning of an entry indicates that the title is appearing for the first time.

— Sonata for Fortepiano, Violin & Cello, Op. 27, No. 1. Brendler, Charlene, ed. (Classical Music Ser.: Vol. 2). ii, 39p. 1999. pap. write for info. (*1-56571-157-2*, CL002) PRB Prods.

Clementini, G., jt. ed. see Cacciari, C.

Clements. Classic Board Book Snowden Raggedy Ann & Andy. (J). 1998. 5.99 (*0-689-82367-3*) S&S Childrens.

— From Cisc to Risc: Computer Architecture. (Computer Science Ser.). 2002. mass mkt. 60.95 (*0-534-95426-X*) Wadsworth Pub.

*__Clements.__ Is Manager's Guide to Implementing Internet Technology, 2000 Supplement. 2000. pap. 39.95 (*0-13-030674-6*) P-H.

Clements. Krumms Halloween Treat Real Monsters Glow in Dark Sticker Book. (Illus.). 16p. (J). (gr. k-1). 1998. pap. 3.99 (*0-689-82053-4*) S&S Childrens.

— Raggedy Andy's Christmas Shapes Snowden Board Book With Plush. (J). 1998. 4.99 (*0-689-82365-7*) S&S Childrens.

— Raggedy Anns Christmas Numbers Snowden Board Book With Plush. (J). 1998. 4.99 (*0-689-82364-9*) S&S Childrens.

— Rondo's Toy Dinosaurs. (J). 2000. 3.99 (*0-689-81305-8*) S&S Childrens.

— Snowden Raggedy Ann & Andy: Hardcover Picture Book. (J). 1998. 9.99 (*0-689-82368-1*) S&S Childrens.

— Sound Story Format Snowden Raggedy Ann & Andy. (J). 1998. 9.99 (*0-689-82369-X*) S&S Childrens.

Clements & Fields. Beginning the Search for God: Edgar Cayce's Approach. rev. ed. LC 97-12976. (Illus.). 206p. 1978. pap. 3.95 (*0-87604-101-2*, 512) ARE Pr.

Clements, jt. auth. see Gido.

Clements, jt. auth. see Shelton.

Clements, A. L., ed. John Donne's Poetry. 2nd ed. LC 90-21390. (Critical Editions Ser.). 377p. (C). 1991. pap. text 12.50 (*0-393-96062-5*) Norton.

Clements, A. N. The Biology of Mosquitoes Vol. 1; Development, Nutrition & Reproduction. (CABI Publishing Ser.). 536p. 1999. 190.00 (*0-85199-374-5*) OUP.

— The Biology of Mosquitoes Vol. 2; Sensory, Reception & Behaviour. (CABI Publishing Ser.). 756p. 1999. text 175.00 (*0-85199-313-3*) OUP.

Clements, Alan. Microprocessor Systems Design. 3rd ed. LC 96-44239. (Electrical Engineering Ser.). 992p. (C). 1997. 100.95 (*0-534-94822-7*) PWS Pubs.

— The Principles of Computer Hardware. 3rd ed. (Illus.). 816p. (C). 2000. text 82.00 (*0-19-856454-6*) OUP.

— 68000 Assembly Language. 768p. 1993. mass mkt. 67.95 (*0-534-93275-4*) PWS Pubs.

— The Voice of Hope: Aung San Suu Kyi with Alan Clements. LC 97-23640. (Illus.). 304p. 1997. 24.95 (*1-888363-50-9*) Seven Stories.

Clements, Alan & Kean, Leslie. Burma's Revolution of the Spirit: The Struggle for Democratic Freedom & Dignity. (Illus.). 104p. 1994. 53.00 (*0-89381-580-2*) Aperture.

Clements, Alan, et al. Restless Nation. (Illus.). 144p. 1996. 35.00 (*1-85158-884-1*, Pub. by Mainstream Pubng) Trafalgar.

Clements, Alan, jt. auth. see Suukyi, Aungsan.

Clements, Andrew. Allegra's Window, No. 10. LC 96-79281. (Illus.). 24p. (J). (ps-1). 1997. 3.25 (*0-689-81245-0*) S&S Childrens.

— Big Al. LC 88-15129. (Illus.). 32p. (J). (ps-2). 1997. per. 5.99 (*0-689-81722-3*) Aladdin.

— Big Al. LC 88-15129. (Illus.). 28p. (J). (ps up). 1991. 16.00 (*0-88708-075-8*, Picture Book Studio) S&S Childrens.

— Big Al. (Illus.). 32p. (J). (ps-2). 1991. pap. 3.95 (*0-590-44455-7*, Blue Ribbon Bks) Scholastic Inc.

— Big Al. 2nd ed. LC 88-15129. (Pixies Ser.). (Illus.). 32p. (J). (gr. k up). 1991. reprint ed. pap. 4.95 (*0-88708-154-1*, Picture Book Studio) S&S Childrens.

— Bright Christmas: An Angel Remembers. LC 95-20371. (Illus.). 32p. (J). (ps-3). 1996. 16.00 (*0-395-72096-6*, Clarion Bks) HM.

*__Clements, Andrew.__ Bright Christmas: An Angel Remembers. (Illus.). 32p. (J). (ps-3). 2000. pap. 5.95 (*0-618-05153-8*, Clarion Bks) HM.

Clements, Andrew. Double Trouble in Walla Walla. (Illus.). 32p. (J). (gr. k-3). 1997. lib. bdg. 21.40 (*0-7613-0306-5*) Millbrook Pr.

— Double Trouble in Walla Walla. LC 96-37746. (Illus.). 32p. (J). (ps-3). 1997. 14.95 (*0-7613-0275-1*) Millbrook Pr.

*__Clements, Andrew.__ Frindle. (2000 Kids Picks Ser.). 112p. (gr. 4-6). 2000. mass mkt. 2.99 (*0-689-83861-1*) Aladdin.

— Frindle. 105p. (J). (gr. 3-5). pap. 4.50 (*0-8072-1522-8*) Listening Lib.

Clements, Andrew. Frindle. LC 95-26671. (Illus.). 112p. (J). (gr. 4-7). 1996. 15.00 (*0-689-80669-8*) S&S Childrens.

— Frindle. 112p. (J). (gr. 3-7). 1998. per. 3.99 (*0-689-81876-9*) S&S Childrens.

— Frindle. (J). 1998. 9.09 (*0-606-12939-1*, Pub. by Turtleback) Demco.

*__Clements, Andrew.__ Frindle. large type ed. (LRS Large Print Cornerstone Ser.). (Illus.). 116p. (YA). (gr. 4-10). 2000. lib. bdg. 24.95 (*1-58118-062-4*, 23476) LRS.

Clements, Andrew. Frindle, , Set. unabridged ed. (J). (gr. 3-5). 1998. audio 16.98 (*0-8072-7993-5*, YA961CX) Listening Lib.

— Gromble's Haunted Halloween. (Real Monsters Ser.). (Illus.). 16p. (J). (ps-1). 1998. pap. 3.99 (*0-689-82052-6*) S&S Childrens.

— Hey Dad, Could I Borrow Your Hammer? LC 98-18949. (J). 1999. lib. bdg. write for info. (*0-7613-1312-5*) Millbrook Pr.

— The Janitor's Boy. LC 99-47457. 144p. (J). (gr. 4-7). 2000. per. 16.00 (*0-689-81818-1*) S&S Bks Yung.

— The Landry News. LC 98-34376. (Illus.). 128p. (J). (gr. 3-7). 1999. lib. bdg. 15.00 (*0-689-81817-3*) S&S Childrens.

— Life in the Desert. 1998. pap. 4.95 (*0-8172-7983-0*) Raintree Steck-V.

*__Clements, Andrew.__ Look Who's in the Thanksgiving Play! (Lift-the-Flap Bks.). (Illus.). (J). 1999. pap. 5.99 (*0-689-82807-1*) Litle Simon.

Clements, Andrew. Milo's Great Invention. (Ways to Communicate Ser.). 24p. (J). (gr. 1-2). 1995. 19.97 (*0-8172-5159-6*) Raintree Steck-V.

— Milo's Great Invention. LC 97-25473. (Illus.). (J). 1998. write for info. (*0-8172-7288-7*) Raintree Steck-V.

— Music Time, Any Time! (Allegra's Window 8 by 8s Ser.). (Illus.). (J). (ps-1). 1997. pap. 3.25 (*0-614-29073-2*) Aladdin.

— Noah & the Ark & the Animals. (Illus.). 40p. (J). (ps-3). 1992. pap. 4.95 (*0-590-44457-3*, Blue Ribbon Bks) Scholastic Inc.

*__Clements, Andrew.__ Norman Saves the Day! LC 99-39637. (J). 2001. per. 15.00 (*0-689-82914-0*) S&S Childrens.

Clements, Andrew. Real Monsters Go for the Mold. 16p. (J). (ps-2). 1997. 5.99 (*0-689-81609-X*) S&S Childrens.

— Real Monsters Stage Fright. (Illus.). 16p. (J). (ps-2). 1997. 5.99 (*0-689-81610-3*) S&S Childrens.

— Riff's Be Bop Book. (J). 2000. 3.99 (*0-689-81304-X*) S&S Childrens.

*__Clements, Andrew.__ Ringo Saves the Day! LC 99-39044. (J). 2001. per. 15.00 (*0-689-82915-9*) S&S Childrens.

— The Secret Fathers Day Present. (Holiday Flap Bk.). Orig. Title: Father's Day. (Illus.). 16p. (J). (ps-3). 2000. 5.99 (*0-689-83359-8*) Litle Simon.

Clements, Andrew. Temple Cat. (J). 16.00 (*0-689-80248-X*) Aladdin.

— Temple Cat. LC 94-44082. (Illus.). 32p. (J). (gr. k-3). 1996. 14.95 (*0-395-69842-1*, Clarion Bks) HM.

— Things That Go EEK on Halloween: Nickelodeon Real Monsters. LC 97-65547. (Real Monsters Ser.). (Illus.). 32p. (J). (ps-3). 1997. 5.99 (*0-689-81675-8*) S&S Childrens.

— Workshop. LC 97-48534. (Illus.). 32p. (J). (ps-3). 1999. 16.00 (*0-395-85579-9*, Clarion Bks) HM.

*__Clements, Andrew & Truesdell, Sue.__ Circus Family Dog. LC 99-52657. (Illus.). 32p. (J). (gr. k-3). 2000. 15.00 (*0-395-78648-7*, Clarion Bks) HM.

Clements, Andrew, tr. see Beaude, Pierre-Marie.

Clements, Andrew, tr. see Gantschev, Ivan.

Clements, Andrew, tr. see Pacovska, Kveta.

Clements, Andrew, tr. see Tharlet, Eve.

Clements, Andrew V., jt. auth. see Ford, Roland.

Clements, Anthony, ed. Infant & Family Health in Australia: A Textbook for Community Health Workers. 2nd ed. (Illus.). 416p. (Orig.). 1992. pap. text 48.00 (*0-443-04770-7*) Church.

Clements, Arthur L. Benedizioni Communi: Common Blessings. Bonventre, Enzo, tr. (Illus.). 80p. 1988. pap. 10.00 (*0-89304-515-2*) Cross-Cultrl NY.

— Common Blessings. LC 87-2639. 64p. (Orig.). 1987. pap. 5.95 (*0-9617589-1-0*) Lincoln Springs Pr.

Clements, Barbara E. Bolshevik Feminist: The Life of Aleksandra Kollontai. LC 78-3240. (Illus.). 378p. 1979. reprint ed. pap. 117.20 (*0-7837-1746-6*, 205728000024) Bks Demand.

— Bolshevik Women. (Illus.). 352p. (C). 1997. text 64.95 (*0-521-45403-4*); pap. text 24.95 (*0-521-59920-2*) Cambridge U Pr.

— Daughters of Revolution: A History of Women in the U. S. S. R. Eubank, Keith, ed. (European History Ser.). (Illus.). 184p. (C). 1994. pap. text 11.95 (*0-88295-908-5*) Harlan Davidson.

Clements, Barbara E., et al, eds. Russia's Women: Accommodation, Resistance, Transformation. LC 90-37203. (Illus.). 352p. 1991. 55.00 (*0-520-07023-2*, Pub. by U CA Pr); pap. 18.95 (*0-520-07024-0*, Pub. by U CA Pr) Cal Prin Full Svc.

Clements, Ben A. Seldom Remembered Now. (Illus.). 79p. (Orig.). 1989. pap. 9.95 (*0-943487-21-8*) Sevgo Pr.

Clements, Benedict J. Foreign Trade Strategies, Employment & Income Distribution in Brazil. LC 88-9718. 185p. 1988. 57.95 (*0-275-92865-9*, C2865, Praeger Pubs) Greenwood.

Clements, Bennett A., jt. auth. see Letterman, Jonathan.

Clements, Betty J. & Weeks, J. Devereux. County & Municipal Revenue Sources in Georgia. 3rd ed. LC 98-230386. 29p. 1997. pap. 5.00 (*0-89854-189-1*) U of GA Inst Govt.

Clements, Bill. Towers of Strength: Martello Towers. 1999. 36.95 (*0-85052-679-5*, Pub. by Leo Cooper) Combined Pub.

Clements, Bonnie L., compiled by. Abortion & Family Planning Bibliography for 1987. LC 72-78877. Orig. Title: Abortion Bibliography. xxii, 199p. 1990. 30.00 (*0-87875-404-0*) Whitston Pub.

— Abortion & Family Planning Bibliography for 1988. LC 72-78877. Orig. Title: Abortion Bibliography. xxii, 190p. 1991. 35.00 (*0-87875-407-5*) Whitston Pub.

— Abortion & Family Planning Bibliography for 1989-1990. 500p. 1992. 55.00 (*0-87875-420-2*) Whitston Pub.

— Abortion & Family Planning Bibliography for 1991. LC 72-78877. 263p. 1993. 35.00 (*0-87875-440-7*) Whitston Pub.

— Drug Abuse Bibliography for 1985. LC 79-116588. 689p. 1989. 68.50 (*0-87875-366-4*) Whitston Pub.

— Drug Abuse Bibliography for 1987. LC 79-116588. 695p. 1991. 75.00 (*0-87875-406-7*) Whitston Pub.

— Drug Abuse Bibliography for 1988. LC 79-116588. 791p. 1991. 85.00 (*0-87875-412-1*) Whitston Pub.

— Drug Abuse Bibliography for 1989. xxxiv, 593p. 1992. 65.00 (*0-87875-434-2*) Whitston Pub.

— Drug Abuse Bibliography for 1990. LC 79-116588. xxviii, 556p. 1993. 65.00 (*0-87875-439-3*) Whitston Pub.

— Drug Abuse Bibliography for 1986. LC 79-116588. 1240p. 1989. 120.00 (*0-87875-372-9*) Whitston Pub.

— Drug Abuse Bibliography for 1991. LC 79-116588. 601p. 1993. 65.00 (*0-87875-445-8*) Whitston Pub.

*__Clements, Brad.__ Beginning Python. 800p. 2000. pap. 39.99 (*1-86100-414-1*) Wrox Pr Inc.

Clements, Brian. Essays Against Ruin. LC 97-3167. (Southern & Southwestern Writers Breakthrough Ser.). 72p. (Orig.). 1997. pap. text 8.00 (*1-881515-09-5*) TX Review Pr.

— Flesh & Wood. 26p. (Orig.). 1992. pap. 5.00 (*0-9629248-1-4*) Mbira Pr.

*__Clements, Brian, ed.__ Best Texas Writing 2. 225p. 1999. pap. 15.00 (*0-9665754-1-5*) Firewheel Edit.

Clements, Brian, jt. ed. see Ahearn, Joe.

Clements, Bruce. Anywhere Else But Here. 1989. pap. 3.50 (*0-374-40420-8*) FS&G.

— I Tell a Lie Every So Often. LC 73-22356. (Sunburst Ser.). 160p. (J). (gr. 7 up). 1984. pap. 3.50 (*0-374-43539-1*) FS&G.

— I Tell a Lie Every So Often. (J). (gr. 5 up). 1993. 17.00 (*0-8446-6656-4*) Peter Smith.

— Tom Loves Anna Loves Tom. 176p. 1990. 15.00 (*0-374-37673-5*) FS&G.

— Tom Loves Anna Loves Tom. 176p. (YA). (gr. 7 up). 1992. reprint ed. pap. 3.95 (*0-374-47939-9*) FS&G.

Clements, C. J. When Death Calls. 140p. 1999. pap. 12.95 (*1-892745-24-0*) Petals of Life.

Clements, C. Justin. The Steward's Way: A Spirituality of Stewardship. LC 97-44521. (Pastoral Ministry Ser.). 120p. 1997. pap. 13.95 (*1-58051-011-6*, LL2011) Sheed & Ward WI.

*__Clements, C. Justin.__ Stewardship: A Parish Handbook. LC 00-30648. 304p. 2000. pap. 24.95 (*0-7648-0662-9*) Liguori Pubns.

Clements, Carole. Flavor of Normandy. 96p. 1996. 9.98 (*0-7858-0582-6*) Bk Sales Inc.

— Gourmet Soup Book. 1995. 14.98 (*0-7858-0348-3*) Bk Sales Inc.

*__Clements, Carole & Wolf-Cohen, E.__ French Country Cuisine. 96p. 1999. pap. 12.95 (*0-7548-0304-X*) Anness Pub.

Clements, Carter N. Fifty Favorite Hideaways. 48p. (Orig.). 1984. pap. 5.95 (*0-9620750-0-0*) C N Clements.

— Fifty Favorite Hideaways. rev. ed. 76p. (Orig.). 1988. reprint ed. pap. 6.95 (*0-9620750-1-9*) C N Clements.

— Gateway to California. 56p. (Orig.). 1988. pap. 5.95 (*0-9620750-2-7*) C N Clements.

Clements, Christine. The Alien King. (Illus.). 100p. (J). (gr. 6-8). 1998. pap. 4.95 (*1-57502-678-3*, PO1917) Morris Pubng.

Clements, Claire B. The Arts - Fitness Quality of Life Activities Program: Creative Ideas for Working with Older Adults in Group Settings. 1998. pap. 44.95 (*1-878812-45-9*) Hlth Prof Pr.

Clements, Clancy J. The Genesis of a Language: The Formation & Development of Korlai Portuguese. LC 96-666. (Creole Language Library: Vol. 16). xviii, 282p. 1996. lib. bdg. 79.00 (*1-55619-171-5*) J Benjamins Pubng Co.

Clements, Colin & Ryerson, Florence. Isn't Nature Wonderful? 1946. pap. 5.25 (*0-8222-0578-5*) Dramatists Play.

Clements, Colin, jt. auth. see Ryerson, Florence.

Clements, Colin C. Plays for Pagans. LC 77-94337. (One-Act Plays in Reprint Ser.). 1978. reprint ed. 20.00 (*0-8486-2035-6*) Roth Pub Inc.

Clements, Colin C., ed. Sea Plays. LC 79-50022. (One-Act Plays in Reprint Ser.). (Illus.). 1980. reprint ed. 30.00 (*0-8486-2046-1*) Roth Pub Inc.

Clements, Colleen D. Medical Genetics Casebook: A Clinical Introduction to Medical Ethics Systems Theory. LC 81-8220. (Contemporary Issues in Biomedicine, Ethics, & Society Ser.). 250p. 1982. 49.50 (*0-89603-033-4*) Humana.

Clements, Colleen D., jt. auth. see Landau-Stanton, Judith.

Clements, Cynthia & Weber, Sandra. George Burns & Gracie Allen: A Bio-Bibliography, 72. LC 96-4970. (Bio-Bibliographies in the Performing Arts Ser.). 444p. 1996. lib. bdg. 69.50 (*0-313-26883-5*, Greenwood Pr) Greenwood.

Clements, David L. An Introduction to Mathematical Models in Economic Dynamics. LC 83-23078. 175p. 1984. 18.95 (*0-936428-07-4*) Polygonal Pub.

Clements, David L. & Perez-Fournon, Ismael, eds. Quasar Hosts: Proceedings of the ESO-IAC Conference Held in Tenerife, Spain, 24-27 September 1996. LC 97-39144. (ESO Astrophysics Symposia, European Southern Observatory Ser.). xvii, 336p. 1997. 29.95 (*3-540-63793-1*) Spr-Verlag.

Clements, Doug, et al. Picturing Polygons: 2-D Geometry. Anderson, Catherine, ed. (Investigations in Number, Data, & Space Ser.). (Illus.). 206p. (J). (gr. 5-6). 1996. teacher ed. 32.95 incl. disk (*0-86651-996-3*, DS21432) Seymour Pubns.

— Picturing Polygons: 2-D Geometry. rev. ed. Anderson, Catherine et al, eds. (Investigations in Number, Data, & Space Ser.). (Illus.). 211p. (YA). (gr. 5 up). 1997. pap. text 32.95 (*1-57232-797-5*, 47044) Seymour Pubns.

Clements, Douglas H., et al. Flips, Turns, & Area: 2-D Geometry. Samii, Priscilla C. & Cory, Beverly, eds. (Investigations in Number, Data, & Space Ser.). (Illus.). 87p. (Orig.). 1994. pap., teacher ed. 32.95 (*0-86651-802-9*, DS21240) Seymour Pubns.

— Flips, Turns, & Area: 2-D Geometry. rev. ed. Sarama, Julie et al, eds. (Investigations in Number, Data, & Space Ser.). (Illus.). 82p. (Orig.). (YA). (gr. 3 up). 1997. pap. text 32.95 (*1-57232-696-4*, 43843) Seymour Pubns.

— Sunken Ships & Grid Patterns: 2-D Geometry. Samii, Priscilla C. et al, eds. (Investigations in Number, Data, & Space Ser.). (Illus.). 179p. (Orig.). 1994. pap., teacher ed. 32.95 (*0-86651-817-7*, DS21255) Seymour Pubns.

— Sunken Ships & Grid Patterns: 2-D Geometry. rev. ed. Anderson, Catherine & Cory, Beverly, eds. LC 97-207336. (Investigations in Number, Data, & Space Ser.). (Illus.). 183p. (Orig.). 1997. pap. text 32.95 (*1-57232-752-9*, 43899) Seymour Pubns.

— Turtle Paths: 2-D Geometry. Samii, Priscilla C. et al, eds. LC 96-189060. (Investigations in Number, Data, & Space Ser.). (Illus.). 171p. (Orig.). 1994. pap., teacher ed. 32.95 (*0-86651-806-1*, DS21244) Seymour Pubns.

— Turtle Paths: 2-D Geometry. rev. ed. Anderson, Catherine & Cory, Beverly, eds. (Investigations in Number, Data, & Space Ser.). (Illus.). 172p. (Orig.). (YA). (gr. 3 up). 1997. pap. text 32.95 (*1-57232-701-4*, 43848) Seymour Pubns.

Clements, Douglas H., jt. auth. see Battista, Michael T.

Clements, Douglas H., jt. auth. see Reidesel, C. Alan.

Clements, E. Introduction to the Study of Indian Music. (Illus.). xv, 104p. 1992. 11.00 (*0-685-63254-7*, Pub. by Abhishek Pubns) Nataraj Bks.

Clements, Eugene & Wright, Edward F., eds. Maryland Militia in the Revolutionary War. LC 87-81636. 280p. 1987. 20.00 (*0-940907-01-1*) Family Line Pubns.

Clements, Fiona M., jt. ed. see De Bruijn, Norbert P.

Clements, Frank. The Emergence of Arab Nationalism. LC 76-5160. 1976. 35.00 (*0-8420-2096-9*) Scholarly Res Inc.

Clements, Frank A. Arab Regional Organizations. 250p. (C). 1992. 54.95 (*1-56000-057-0*) Transaction Pubs.

— Israeli Secret Services: An Annotated Bibliography. LC 96-17331. (International Organizations Ser.: Vol. 12). 103p. (C). 1996. text 69.95 (*1-56000-228-X*) Transaction Pubs.

— Oman. 2nd rev. ed. LC 96-192673. (World Bibiographical Ser.: Vol. 29). 372p. 1994. lib. bdg. 79.00 (*1-85109-197-1*) ABC-CLIO.

— Saudi Arabia. 2nd rev. ed. LC 89-115595. (World Bibliographical Ser.: No. 5). 386p. 1988. lib. bdg. 55.00 (*1-85109-067-3*) ABC-CLIO.

— United Arab Emirates. (World Bibliographical Ser.: No. 43). 161p. 1983. lib. bdg. 45.00 (*0-903450-74-7*) ABC-CLIO.

Clements, Frank A., compiled by. Kuwait. 2nd rev. ed. LC 96-194046. (World Bibliographical Ser.: Vol. 56). 366p. 1996. lib. bdg. 97.00 (*1-85109-212-9*, TD879) ABC-CLIO.

Clements, Frank A., ed. United Arab Emirates. 2nd rev. ed. (World Bibliographical Ser.: 43). 276p. 1998. lib. bdg. 73.00 (*1-85109-274-9*) ABC-CLIO.

Clements, Frederic E., 3rd. Plant Competition: An Analysis of Community Functions. Egerton, Frank N., ed. LC 77-74209. (History of Ecology Ser.). (Illus.). 1978. reprint ed. lib. bdg. 41.95 (*0-405-10380-8*) Ayer.

Clements, Frederic E. Research Methods in Ecology. Egerton, Frank N., 3rd, ed. LC 77-74210. (History of Ecology Ser.). (Illus.). 1978. reprint ed. lib. bdg. 33.95 (*0-405-10381-6*) Ayer.

Clements, Frederic E., jt. auth. see Pound, Roscoe.

Clements, G. N. & Goldschmidt, J., eds. Autosegmental Studies in Bantu Tone. (Publications in African Languages & Linguistics). viii, 347p. 1984. pap. 83.10 (*90-70176-97-1*) Mouton.

Clements, G. R. The Law of Life & Human Health. 313p. 1998. reprint ed. pap. 26.00 (*0-7873-0177-9*) Hlth Research.

Clements, George N., jt. auth. see Halle, Morris.

Clements, George R., jt. auth. see Shelton, Herbert M.

*__Clements, Gillian.__ Into the Under World. LC 98-86855. (Illus.). 32p. (J). 1999. text 15.99 (*0-7636-0686-3*) Candlewick Pr.

Clements, Gillian. The Picture History of Great Inventors. LC 93-21705. (J). 1994. pap. 13.00 (*0-679-84787-1*, Pub. by Knopf Bks Yng Read) Random.

— The Truth about Castles. (Illus.). 40p. (J). (ps-3). 1990. pap. 6.95 (*0-87614-552-7*, Carolrhoda); lib. bdg. 14.95 (*0-87614-401-6*, Carolrhoda) Lerner Pub.

Clements, Harold M. The Mechanization of Agriculture in Brazil: A Sociological Study of Minas Gerais. LC 76-93194. (Latin American Monographs: Ser. 2, No. 7). (Illus.). 104p. reprint ed. pap. 32.30 (*0-7837-4961-9*, 204462700004) Bks Demand.

Clements, Harry F. Sugarcane Crop Logging & Crop Control: Principles & Practices. LC 79-9894. 550p. reprint ed. pap. 170.50 (*0-7837-1308-8*, 204145600020) Bks Demand.

Clements, Ian P., ed. The Electrocardiogram in Acute Myocardial Infarction. LC 97-50183. (Illus.). 272p. 1998. 65.00 (*0-87993-693-2*) Futura Pub.

Clements, J. & Zarkowska, Ewa. Problem Behavior with People with Severe Learning Disabilities. 2nd ed. 256p. 1994. text 42.50 (*1-56593-122-X*, 0447) Singular Publishing.

Clements, J. B. History of Irwin County Georgia. (Illus.). 539p. 1997. reprint ed. lib. bdg. 55.00 (*0-8328-7066-8*) Higginson Bk Co.

Clements, J. W. Clements - Spalding: Origins of Clements - Spalding & Allied Families of Maryland & Kentucky, with Appendix. xi, 87p. 1997. reprint ed. lib. bdg. 28.00 (*0-8328-7973-8*) Higginson Bk Co.

Clements, James, ed. Silent Heroes among Us: Final Flights of the Mighty 8th. (Illus.). (Orig.). 1996. pap. 24.95 (*1-884687-07-5*) N Horzns Pub.

Clements, James F. The Birds of Peru: An Annotated Checklist. 288p. 1999. 40.00 (*0-934797-18-8*) Ibis Pub CA.

*__Clements, James F.__ Birds of the World: A Checklist. (Illus.). 2000. pap. 39.95 (*0-934797-16-1*) Ibis Pub CA.

C

An Asterisk (*) at the beginning of an entry indicates that the title is appearing for the first time.

Clements, James F. & Principe, William L., Jr. English Name Index & Supplement No. 1: Birds of the World: A Check List (First Supplement to Fourth Edition) 68p. (C). 1992. pap. 9.95 (*0-934797-05-6*) Ibis Pub CA.

Clements, James F., ed. see King, Ben F.

Clements, James F., ed. see Todd, Frank S.

Clements, James F., ed. see Young, Arthur N.

Clements, Jan, jt. auth. see Windle, Jeanette.

Clements, Jehan. Alfred the Ant, An Ant Who Lives in Central Park: The First Storytelling "Flip Over" Picture Book. LC 89-61138. (Illus.). 48p. (J). (gr. k-3). 1994. 19.95 (*0-9622500-0-7*) Strytllr Co.

Clements, Jeremy. Essential Stencils: Includes 30 Ready-to-Use Stencils in Classic Designs. LC 98-40660. 1999. pap. text 24.95 (*0-8230-1623-4*) Watsn-Guptill.

Clements, John. Complete Pentax User's Guide: MZ-5-10/Z-1P/Z-70/ZX-5-10/PZ-1P/PZ-70. (Illus.). 180p. 1997. pap. 19.95 (*1-874031-97-5*, Pub. by Hove Foto) Watsn-Guptill.

***Clements, John.** Make Your Walls Tumble: How to Change Your Impossible to Difficult, Then Achieve Success. 2000. pap. 19.95 (*0-910882-16-9*) Lexngton Hse.

Clements, John. Medieval Swordsmanship: Illustrated Methods & Techniques. LC 99-188076. (Illus.). 334p. 1998. pap. 40.00 (*1-58160-004-6*) Paladin Pr.

— Nikon Pro-Guide: Nikkor AF Lenses & Their Uses. 208p. 1997. pap. text 29.95 (*1-874031-37-1*, Pub. by Hove Foto) Watsn-Guptill.

— Renaissance Swordsmanship: The Illustrated Use of Rapiers & Cut-&-Thrust Swords. (Illus.). 152p. 1997. pap. 25.00 (*0-87364-919-2*) Paladin Pr.

***Clements, John.** Stained Glass Wisdom. 2000. pap. 19.95 (*0-910882-17-7*) Lexngton Hse.

***Clements, Jonathan.** Monsters. (Unexplained Ser.). 32p. (YA). (gr. 5 up). 1999. pap. 5.95 (*0-7641-1064-0*) Barron.

— Moon in the Pines: Zen Haiku Poetry. 2000. 19.95 (*0-670-89229-7*, Viking) Viking Penguin.

Clements, Jonathan. The New Rules for Financial Success: 25 Myths You've Got to Avoid If You Want to Manage Your Money. LC 97-30430. 1998. 22.50 (*0-684-83982-2*) S&S Trade.

***Clements, Jonathan.** 25 Myths You've Got to Avoid If You Want to Manage Your Money Right You Want to Manage Your Money Right: The New Rules for Financial Success. 240p. 1999. pap. 12.00 (*0-684-85194-6*, Fireside) S&S Trade Pap.

Clements, Jonathan, jt. auth. see McCarthy, Helen.

Clements, K. W. The Theology of Ronald Gregor Smith. (Zeitschrift fur Religions- und Geistesgeschichte Ser.: No. 27). xii, 328p. 1986. pap. 89.50 (*90-04-07298-5*) Brill Academic Pubs.

Clements, Kath. Why Vegan? The Ethics of Eating & the Need for Change. rev. ed. 128p. 1995. pap. 10.95 (*0-946097-30-5*) LPC InBook.

***Clements, Keith.** Faith on the Frontier: A Life of J.H. Oldham. 608p. 1999. pap. 49.95 (*0-567-08690-9*) T&T Clark Pubs.

Clements, Keith. Henry Lamb: His Life & Works. 224p. 1984. 40.00 (*0-7855-2912-8*, Pub. by Redcliffe Pr Ltd) St Mut.

— Henry Lamb: The Artists & His Friends. 352p. (C). 1987. 54.00 (*0-905459-55-5*, Pub. by Redcliffe Pr Ltd) St Mut.

— Learning to Speak: The Church's Voice in Public Affairs. 256p. 1994. pap. 29.95 (*0-567-29266-5*, Pub. by T & T Clark) Bks Intl VA.

Clements, Keith & De Gruchy, John W., eds. Friederich Schleiermacher: Pioneer of Modern Theology. (Making of Modern Theology Ser.). 288p. (Orig.). 1991. pap. 20.00 (*0-8006-3401-2*, 1-3401, Fortress Pr) Augsburg Fortress.

***Clements, Ken.** CD Player Troubleshooting & Repair. 256p. 2000. pap. 39.95 (*0-7506-7235-8*) Buttrwrth-Heinemann.

***Clements, Kendrick A.** Hoover, Conservation & Consumerism: Engineering the Good Life. 312p. 2000. write for info. (*0-7006-1033-2*) U Pr of KS.

Clements, Kendrick A. The Presidency of Woodrow Wilson. LC 91-30591. (American Presidency Ser.). xvi, 304p. 1992. 29.95 (*0-7006-0523-1*); pap. 15.95 (*0-7006-0524-X*) U Pr of KS.

— William Jennings Bryan, Missionary Isolationist. LC 82-8342. (Illus.). 232p. reprint ed. pap. 72.00 (*0-8357-8603-X*, 203499900091) Bks Demand.

— Woodrow Wilson: World Statesman. LC 99-32040. 288p. 1999. pap. 16.95 (*1-56663-267-6*, Pub. by I R Dee) Natl Bk Netwk.

Clements, Kenneth W. & Greig, Robert A. Modeling Large Resource Development Projects in an Open Economy: The Case of Australia's North West Shelf Gas Project. (Studies in Urban & Resource Economics). (Illus.). xviii, 151p. 1994. 36.00 (*0-943893-10-0*) Blackstone.

Clements, Kenneth W. & Selvanathan, E. Anthony. Recent Developments in Applied Demand Analysis: Alcohol, Advertising & Global Consumption. LC 95-30838. (Illus.). 396p. 1995. 117.00 (*3-540-59197-4*) Spr-Verlag.

Clements, Kenneth W., jt. auth. see Theil, Henri.

Clements, Kevin & Ward, Robin, eds. Building International Community: Cooperating for Peace. 328p. 1995. pap. 19.95 (*1-86373-800-2*) Paul & Co Pubs.

Clements, Kevin P. Breaking Nuclear Ties: New Zealand's Nuclear-Free Course. 232p. (C). 2000. pap. 39.95 (*0-8133-1505-0*) Westview.

Clements, Kirby, Sr. A Philosophy of Ministry. 144p. (Orig.). 1993. pap. 8.95 (*0-917595-42-4*) Kingdom Pubs.

Clements, Kirby. The Second. 63p. 1989. mass mkt. 3.95 (*0-917595-29-7*) Kingdom Pubs.

— The Second. rev. ed. 100p. (C). pap. 7.95 (*0-917595-43-2*) Kingdom Pubs.

Clements, Kirby & Clements, Sandra. . . . And He Gave Them. . . The Biblical Design for Man & Woman Co-Laboring in Ministry & Life. Date not set. pap. text 15.00 (*0-917595-45-9*) Kingdom Pubs.

Clements, Kirby & Clements, Sandra. Discernment. 120p. (C). Date not set. pap. write for info. (*0-917595-46-7*) Kingdom Pubs.

Clements, L. M. & Fairest, P. B. Housing Law: Text, Cases & Materials. 546p. 1996. pap. 60.00 (*1-85941-222-X*, Pub. by Cavendish Pubng) Gaunt.

Clements, Len W. Inside Network Marketing: An Expert's View Into Hidden Truths. 192p. 1996. per. 14.00 (*0-7615-0672-1*) Prima Pub.

Clements, Leonard W. Beyond the Veil: A Journey into the Hidden Truths & Exploited Myths of America's Most Misunderstood Industry: Network Marketing. 156p. 1995. pap. 12.95 (*0-9646186-0-5*) Marketwave.

***Clements, Leonard W.** Inside Networking Marketing: An Expert's View into the Hidden Truths & Exploited Myths of America's Most Misunderstood Industry. 2nd rev. ed. LC 99-57314. 320p. 2000. pap. 15.00 (*0-7615-2176-3*) Prima Pub.

***Clements, Linda.** Spirit of Christmas Past: Evocative Memories of Years Gone By. (Illus.). 1998. 16.98 (*1-880908-94-8*) Todtri Prods.

Clements, Linda, jt. ed. see Paul, Eileen.

Clements, Linda, jt. ed. see Paul, Mary E.

***Clements, Luke & Young, James.** Human Rights: Changing the Culture. LC 99-32620. (Journal of Law & Society Ser.). 172p. 1999. pap. 13.99 (*0-631-21755-X*) Blackwell Publishers.

Clements, Luke, jt. ed. see Morris, Rachel.

Clements, M. A. Mathematics for the Minority: Some Historical Perspectives of School Mathematics in Victoria. 94p. (C). 1989. pap. 44.00 (*0-7300-0663-8*, ECS807, Pub. by Deakin Univ) St Mut.

Clements, M. A. & Ellerton, Nerida F. Polya, Krutetskii & the Restaurant Problem. 93p. (C). 1991. pap. 66.00 (*0-7300-1253-0*, ECT405, Pub. by Deakin Univ) St Mut.

Clements, M. A., jt. auth. see Ellerton, Nerida F.

Clements, Marcelle. The Improvised Woman: Single Women Reinventing Single Life. LC 97-38923. 352p. 1998. 26.95 (*0-393-04643-5*) Norton.

— The Improvised Woman: Single Women Reinventing Single Life. 352p. 1999. pap. 14.00 (*0-393-31953-9*) Norton.

— Single Women. Date not set. write for info. (*0-393-04025-9*) Norton.

Clements, Margaret H. Pathology: Pretest Self-Assessment & Review. 5th ed. 1988. pap. text 15.95 (*0-07-051965-X*) McGraw.

Clements, Mark A. Lorelei. 304p. 1995. pap. text, mass mkt. 4.99 (*0-8439-3867-6*) Dorchester Pub Co.

Clements, Michael & Hendry, David. Forecasting Economic Time Series. LC 97-52674. (Illus.). 390p. (C). 1998. text 69.95 (*0-521-63242-0*); pap. text 24.95 (*0-521-63480-6*) Cambridge U Pr.

Clements, Michael P. & Hendry, David F. Forecasting Non-Stationary Economic Times Series. LC 99-22998. (Zeuthen Lecture Ser.). (Illus.). 314p. 1999. 35.00 (*0-262-03272-4*) MIT Pr.

Clements, Millard, jt. auth. see Cohen, Steven.

Clements, Monica L. & Clements, Patricia R. Cameos: A Pocket Guide. LC 98-88430. (Illus.). 160p. (Orig.). 1999. pap. 19.95 (*0-7643-0737-1*) Schiffer.

— Cameos: Classical to Costume. LC 97-37937. 222p. 1998. 59.95 (*0-7643-0426-7*) Schiffer.

— Cobalt Blue Glass. LC 98-86777. (Illus.). 144p. (Orig.). 1999. pap. 24.95 (*0-7643-0685-5*) Schiffer.

— Pocket Guide to Occupied Japan. LC 98-88135. (Illus.). 160p. (Orig.). 1999. pap. 16.95 (*0-7643-0728-2*) Schiffer.

— Sarah Coventry Jewelry: An Unauthorized Guide for Collectors. LC 98-86788. (Illus.). 160p. (Orig.). 1999. pap. 29.95 (*0-7643-0686-3*) Schiffer.

Clements, Monica L., jt. auth. see Clements, Patricia.

Clements, Monica Lynn & Clements, Patricia Rosser. Avon Collectible Fashion Jewelry & Awards. 160p. 1998. pap. 29.95 (*0-7643-0523-9*) Schiffer.

— Popular Souvenir Plates. LC 98-84675. 176p. 1998. pap. 29.95 (*0-7643-0535-2*) Schiffer.

— An Unauthorized Guide to Fire King Glasswares. LC 98-83187. (Illus.). 144p. 1999. pap. 12.95 (*0-7643-0839-4*) Schiffer.

Clements, Patricia. Baudelaire & the English Tradition. LC 85-42681. 453p. 1985. reprint ed. pap. 140.50 (*0-7837-9319-7*, 206005900004) Bks Demand.

***Clements, Patricia & Clements, Monica L.** A Pocket Guide to Pink Depression Era Glass. (Illus.). 160p. 1999. pap. 16.95 (*0-7643-1009-9*) Schiffer.

Clements, Patricia R., jt. auth. see Clements, Monica L.

Clements, Patricia Rosser, jt. auth. see Clements, Monica Lynn.

***Clements, Paul.** Constructing Superior Software: Applying Proven Practices. (Software Architecture & Engineering Ser.). 350p. 1999. pap. 40.00 (*1-57870-147-3*) New Riders Pub.

Clements, Paul. Jan Morris. 125p. 1998. pap. 14.95 (*0-7083-1470-8*, Pub. by Univ Wales Pr) Paul & Co Pubs.

Clements, Paul H. Boxer Rebellion. LC 79-15870. (Columbia University. Studies in the Social Sciences: No. 160). reprint ed. 42.50 (*0-404-51160-0*) AMS Pr.

Clements, Phil. Be Positive: A Guide for Managers. (Better Management Skills Ser.). 1995. pap. 12.95 (*0-7494-1732-3*) Kogan Page Ltd.

Clements, Phil & Spinks, Tony. The Equal Opportunities Guide: How to Deal with Everyday Issues of Unfairness. 2nd ed. (Human Resource Management Ser.). 192p. 1997. pap. 25.00 (*0-7494-2103-7*, Kogan Pg Educ) Stylus Pub VA.

Clements, Phil & Spinks, Tony. Facilitating Learning. 250p. 1995. ring bd. 160.00 (*0-7494-1399-9*, Kogan Pg Educ) Stylus Pub VA.

Clements, Philip J. & Furst, Daniel E., eds. Systemic Sclerosis. LC 95-15204. (Illus.). 754p. 1996. 125.00 (*0-683-01740-3*) Lppncott W & W.

Clements, R. Songs of Experience. 10.99 (*1-85792-019-8*, Pub. by Christian Focus) Spring Arbor Dist.

Clements, R. E. Deuteronomy. (Old Testament Guides Ser.: Vol. 6). 103p. 1989. pap. 12.50 (*1-85075-214-1*, Pub. by Sheffield Acad) CUP Services.

Clements, R. R., et al. Selected Papers on the Teaching of Mathematics As a Service Subject. (CISM Ser.: Vol. 305). (Illus.). vi, 181p. 1988. 58.95 (*0-387-82056-6*) Spr-Verlag.

Clements, Rhonda, jt. auth. see Martin, Carolyn A.

Clements, Rhonda L. Games & Great Ideas: A Guide for Elementary Physical Educators & Classroom Teachers. LC 94-13200. 384p. 1995. 39.95 (*0-313-29460-7*, Greenwood Pr) Greenwood.

Clements, Rhonda L., jt. auth. see Lee, Mike.

Clements, Richard. IS Manager's Guide to Implementing & Managing Internet Technology. LC 98-50419. (Illus.). xxviii, 515 p. (C). 1999. text 69.95 (*0-13-974890-3*) P-H.

Clements, Richard & Kay, Jane. Q & A Constitutional & Administrative Law. 209p. 1997. pap. 22.00 (*1-85431-539-0*, Pub. by Blackstone Pr) Gaunt.

Clements, Richard, et al. Preparing Your Company for QS-9000: A Guide for the Automotive Industry. 2nd ed. LC 95-13759. 89p. 1996. pap. 24.00 (*0-87389-344-1*, H0928) ASQ Qual Pr.

Clements, Richard B. Quality Manager's Complete Guide to ISO 9000. 368p. (C). 1993. text 79.95 (*0-13-017534-X*) P-H.

— Quality Manager's Complete Guide to ISO 9000: 2000 Edition. (C). 1999. pap. text, suppl. ed. 39.95 (*0-13-021242-3*) P-H.

Clements, Robert D., jt. auth. see Wachowiak, Frank.

Clements, Robert J. Comparative Literature as Academic Discipline: A Statement of Principles, Praxis, Standards. LC 77-91123. 366p. reprint ed. pap. 113.50 (*0-8357-7549-6*, 203627100001) Bks Demand.

Clements, Robert J., ed. Michelangelo: A Self-Portrait. LC 68-31495. (Illus.). 237p. reprint ed. pap. 73.50 (*0-608-11187-2*, 200906200072) Bks Demand.

Clements, Robert W., jt. auth. see Tetreault, Wilfred F.

Clements, Ronald E. Ezekiel. (Westminster Bible Companion Ser.). 1996. pap. 17.00 (*0-664-25272-9*) Westminster John Knox.

Clements, Ronald E. Isaiah 1-39. (New Century Bible Ser.). 301p. 1980. pap. 24.50 (*0-551-00828-8*, Pub. by Sheffield Acad) CUP Services.

Clements, Ronald E. Jeremiah. Mays, James L. et al, eds. LC 88-9339. (Interpretation: a Bible Commentary for Preaching & Teaching Ser.). 228p. 1989. 25.00 (*0-8042-3127-3*) Westminster John Knox.

— Old Testament Prophecy: From Oracle to Canon. 288p. 1996. 32.95 (*0-664-22082-7*) Westminster John Knox.

— Wisdom for a Changing World: Wisdom in Old Testament Theology. Christensen, Duane L., ed. LC 89-62248. (Berkeley Lectures: No. 2). 80p. 1990. pap. 7.95 (*0-941037-13-4*, BIBAL Press) D & F Scott.

Clements, Roy. Faithful Living in a Faithless World. LC 98-18561. Orig. Title: Practising Faith in a Pagan World. 180p. 1998. pap. 10.99 (*0-8308-1945-2*, 1945) InterVarsity.

— The Strength of Weakness. 240p. Date not set. write for info. (*1-85792-073-2*, Pub. by Christian Focus) Spring Arbor Dist.

Clements, Sandra, jt. auth. see Clements, Kirby.

Clements, Simon, jt. ed. see Bright, Laurence.

Clements, Sue, et al. Ancient Egypt: Discovering & Building along the Nile. (Learning Packets - Social Studies Ser.). (Illus.). 68p. 1994. ring bd. 18.00 (*1-56976-010-1*, 1403-F3) Zephyr Pr AZ.

— Ancient Greece & Rome: The Continuing Influence. rev. ed. (Learning Packets - Social Studies Ser.). (Illus.). 72p. 1993. ring bd. 18.00 (*0-913705-11-X*, 1404-F3) Zephyr Pr AZ.

Clements, Susan. In the Moon When the Deer Lose Their Horns. 1993. 7.50 (*0-941608-07-7*) Chantry Pr.

Clements, Tad S. Science vs. Religion. LC 89-29812. 266p. 1990. 32.95 (*0-87975-593-8*) Prometheus Bks.

Clements, Tad S., jt. ed. see Horosz, William.

Clements, Thomas. Geological Story of Death Valley. (Illus.). 64p. 1977. 4.95 (*0-936932-03-1*) Death Valley Fortyniners.

Clements, Tom. Inside the JavaOS Operating System. LC 98-51423. (Illus.). 208p. (C). 1999. pap. text 29.95 (*0-201-18393-5*) Addison-Wesley.

Clements, Tony. African Violets. (Illus.). 192p. 1994. pap. 14.95 (*0-7153-9187-9*, Pub. by D & C Pub) Sterling.

Clements, Victoria, ed. see Sedgwick, Catharine Maria.

***Clements, W. H.** Towers of Strength: Martello Towers Worldwide. (Illus.). 2000. pap. 24.95 (*0-85052-684-1*, Pub. by Leo Cooper) Combined Pub.

Clements, William M. Care & Counseling of the Aging. LC 78-54547. (Creative Pastoral Care & Counseling Ser.). 96p. reprint ed. pap. 30.00 (*0-608-18407-1*, 203056200069) Bks Demand.

— Native American Verbal Art: Texts & Contexts. LC 96-10026. 252p. 1996. 19.95 (*0-8165-1659-6*); pap. 45.00 (*0-8165-1658-8*) U of Ariz Pr.

Clements, William M., ed. Ministry with the Aging: Designs, Challenges, Foundations. 274p. 1989. pap. text 19.95 (*0-86656-934-0*) Haworth Pr.

— Native American Folklore in Nineteenth Century Periodicals. LC 86-5409. 250p. 1985. text 29.95 (*0-8040-0872-8*) Swallow.

— Religion, Aging & Health: A Global Perspective. LC 88-16357. (Journal of Religion & Aging: Vol. 4, Nos. 3-4). (Illus.). 146p. 1989. text 39.95 (*0-86656-803-4*) Haworth Pr.

Clements, William M., jt. auth. see Ball, Larry D.

Clements, William M., jt. auth. see Malpezzi, Frances M.

Clements, William M., jt. ed. see McNeil, W. K.

Clements, William M., jt. ed. see Stone, Howard W.

Clements, Zacharie J. & Hawhes, Richard R. Mastermind: Exercises in Critical Thinking, Grades 4-6. (Illus.). 68p. (Orig.). 1985. pap. 9.95 (*0-673-16653-8*, GoodYrBooks) Addson-Wesley Educ.

Clementson, Alan & Clewett, A. J., eds. Management, Operational Research & the Micro. 96p. 1981. pap. 17.00 (*0-08-025842-5*, Pergamon Pr) Elsevier.

***Clementson, George B.** Manual Relating to Special Verdicts & Special Findings by Juriers. lxi,350p. 1999. reprint ed. 124.50 (*1-56169-450-9*) Gaunt.

Clementson, John. Happy Moose, Grumpy Goose. LC 95-80317. (Illus.). 10p. (J). (ps). 1995. pap. 4.00 (*0-15-200315-0*, Red Wagon Bks) Harcourt.

— Spots on My Shoes. LC 95-80316. (Illus.). 10p. (J). (ps). 1995. pap. 4.00 (*0-15-200313-4*, Red Wagon Bks) Harcourt.

— The Sun Rises, the Star Shines. LC 95-80315. (Illus.). 10p. (J). (ps). 1995. pap. 4.00 (*0-15-200316-9*, Red Wagon Bks) Harcourt.

Clementson, T. Strategy & Uncertainty: A Guide to Practical Systems Thinking, Vol. 17. xiv, 214p. 1988. text 148.00 (*2-88124-654-0*) Gordon & Breach.

Clementy, Jacques, jt. ed. see Aliot, Etienne.

Clementz, Kim, ed. see Young, Natalie B.

Clemenz, Bob & Clemenz, Suzanne. Focus on Sedona: All Your Favorite Scenes - with Photo Tips. (Illus.). 16p. (Orig.). pap. 3.95 (*0-9621404-2-2*) Clemenz Scenic.

— Guide to the Wonders of Sedona & the Verde Valley. (Illus.). 64p. (Orig.). 1991. pap. 7.95 (*0-9621404-1-4*) Clemenz Scenic.

Clemenz, G. Credit Markets with Asymmetric Information. (Lecture Notes in Economics & Mathematical Systems Ser.: Vol. 272). viii, 212p. 1986. 37.50 (*0-387-16778-1*) Spr-Verlag.

Clemenz, Suzanne. The Glorious Seasons of Sedona. LC 88-92363. (Illus.). 64p. (Orig.). 1989. pap. 7.95 (*0-9621404-0-6*) Clemenz Scenic.

Clemenz, Suzanne, jt. auth. see Clemenz, Bob.

Clemesha, David & Zimmerman, Andrea. My Dog Toby. LC 98-35246. (Illus.). 32p. (J). 2000. 15.00 (*0-15-202014-4*) Harcourt.

Clemesha, David & Zimmerman, Andrea G. The Cow Buzzed. LC 91-31905. (Illus.). 32p. (J). (ps-2). 1995. pap. 6.95 (*0-06-443410-9*, HarpTrophy) HarpC Child Bks.

Clemesha, David, jt. auth. see Zimmerman, Andrea G.

Clemetson, C. Alan. Vitamin C, 3 vols., Vol. 1. 336p. 1989. boxed set 169.00 (*0-8493-4841-2*, RC627) CRC Pr.

— Vitamin C, 3 vols., Vol. 2. 248p. 1989. boxed set 169.00 (*0-8493-4842-0*, RC627) CRC Pr.

— Vitamin C, 3 vols., Vol. 3. 280p. 1989. boxed set 169.00 (*0-8493-4843-9*, RC627) CRC Pr.

Clemett, Susan, jt. auth. see Vandestienne, Gena.

Clemie, C., jt. auth. see Nicholson, N.

Clemins, Vija & Close, Chuck. Vija Celmins. Bartman, William S., ed. (Illus.). 64p. (Orig.). 1992. pap. text 25.00 (*0-923183-08-6*) ART Pr NY.

Cleminshaw, Helen K. GED Fast Track to Work: Career Activity Journal. 1998. ring bd. 19.95 (*1-893679-20-9*) Int Fam.

Cleminshaw, Helen K. & Siegferth, Dee. GED Fast Track to Work: Activity Journal. 1998. ring bd. 45.00 (*1-893679-01-2*) Int Fam.

— GED Fast Track to Work: Administrator's Guide. 1998. wbk. ed. 19.99 (*1-893679-02-0*) Int Fam.

— GED Fast Track to Work: Career Administrator's Guide. 1998. wbk. ed. 9.95 (*1-893679-21-7*) Int Fam.

— GED Fast Track to Work: Comprehensive Career System. 1998. 129.95 (*1-893679-19-5*) Int Fam.

— GED Fast Track to Work: Resource Portfolio Activity Journals, 7 vols. 1998. wbk. ed. 80.44 (*1-893679-11-X*) Int Fam.

— GED Fast Track to Work: Resource Portfolio System. 1998. 999.00 (*1-893679-03-9*) Int Fam.

— GED Fast Track to Work: Resource Portfolio 1 Activity Journal Sections 1 & 2. 1998. wbk. ed. 19.95 (*1-893679-12-8*) Int Fam.

— GED Fast Track to Work: Resource Portfolio 1/Introduction & Assessment: Welcome to the Job Market: Social Studies. 1998. 190.00 (*1-893679-04-7*) Int Fam.

— GED Fast Track to Work: Resource Portfolio 2 Activity Journal Section 3. 1998. wbk. ed. 10.95 (*1-893679-13-6*) Int Fam.

— GED Fast Track to Work: Resource Portfolio 2/Choosing an Occupation: Writing. 1998. 110.00 (*1-893679-05-5*) Int Fam.

— GED Fast Track to Work: Resource Portfolio 3 Activity Journal Sections 4 & 5. 1998. wbk. ed. 19.95 (*1-893679-14-4*) Int Fam.

— GED Fast Track to Work: Resource Portfolio 3/Life Is a Balancing Act. 1998. 299.00 (*1-893679-06-3*) Int Fam.

— GED Fast Track to Work: Resource Portfolio 4 Activity Journal Section 6. 1998. wbk. ed. 10.95 (*1-893679-15-2*) Int Fam.

— GED Fast Track to Work: Resource Portfolio 4/Show That You Qualify. 1998. 90.00 (*1-893679-07-1*) Int Fam.

— GED Fast Track to Work: Resource Portfolio 5 Activity Journal Section 7. 1998. wbk. ed. 10.95 (*1-893679-16-0*) Int Fam.

— GED Fast Track to Work: Resource Portfolio 5/Achieving Total Well-Being: Science. 1998. 110.00 (*1-893679-08-X*) Int Fam.

C

— GED Fast Track to Work: Resource Portfolio 6 Activity Journal Section 8. 1998. wbk. ed. 10.95 (*1-893679-17-9*) Int Fam.

— GED Fast Track to Work: Resource Portfolio 6/Putting It All Together: Literature & the Arts. 1998. 110.00 (*1-893679-09-8*) Int Fam.

— GED Fast Track to Work: Resource Portfolio 7 Activity Journal Section 9. 1998. wbk. ed. 10.95 (*1-893679-18-7*) Int Fam.

— GED Fast Track to Work: Resource Portfolio 7/Career: Marketing & Selling Yourself. 1998. write for info. (*1-893679-10-1*) Int Fam.

— GED Fast Track to Work: Two-Kit System. 1998. 899.00 (*1-893679-00-4*) Int Fam.

***Cleminshaw, Suzanne.** The Great Ideas. 312p. 1999. write for info. (*1-85702-908-9*, Pub. by Fourth Estate) Trafalgar.

Cleminson, Ronald W., et al, eds. Guidelines & Competencies for Elementary Science Education. 93p. 1974. pap. text 12.95 (*0-8422-0446-6*) Irvington.

Clemit, Pamela. The Godwinian Novel: The Rational Fictions of Godwin, Brockden Brown, Mary Shelley. LC 92-27583. (Oxford English Monographs). 268p. 1993. text 48.00 (*0-19-811220-3*, Clarendon Pr) OUP.

Clemit, Pamela, et al, eds. Lives of the Great Romantics III: Godwin, Wollstonecraft & Mary Shelley by Their Contemporaries, 3 vols. LC 98-56142. 1050p. 1999. 360.00 (*1-85196-512-2*, Pub. by Pickering & Chatto) Ashgate Pub Co.

Clemit, Pamela, et al. Lives of the Great Romantics III: Godwin, Wollstonecraft, & Mary Shelley by Their Contemporaries. LC 98-56142. 1999. 360.00 (*1-85196-373-1*, Pub. by Pickering & Chatto) Ashgate Pub Co.

Clemit, Pamela, ed. see Shelley, Mary Wollstonecraft.

Clemm, Lisa H. Von, see Von Clemm, Lisa H.

Clemmens, Michael C. Getting Beyond Sobriety: Clinical Approaches to Long-Term Recovery. LC 96-47105. (Jossey-Bass Psychology Ser.). 1997. 34.95 (*0-7879-0840-1*) Jossey-Bass.

Clemmensen, Jane. Nonionizing Radiation: A Case for Federal Standards? (Illus.). 1984. pap. 20.00 (*0-911302-51-4*) San Francisco Pr.

Clemmer, David. Tom Sachs: Sony Outsider. LC 98-83234. (Illus.). 32p. 1999. pap. write for info. (*0-9650583-4-4*) Site Santa Fe.

Clemmer, David, ed. see Whitney, Catherine.

Clemmer, Gregg S. American Miners' Carbide Lamps: A Collector's Guide to American Carbide Mine Lighting. LC 87-50676. (Illus.). 136p. 1987. 26.95 (*0-87026-064-2*) Westernlore.

— Valor in Gray: The Recipients of the Confederate Medal of Honor. (Illus.). 528p. 1996. 29.95 (*0-9650987-0-2*) Hearthside Pub.

Clemmer, Gregg S. & Kelly, Thomas G. Valor in Gray: The Recipients of the Confederate Medal of Honor. (Illus.). 528p. 1998. pap. 19.95 (*0-9650987-1-0*) Hearthside Pub.

Clemmer, Jim. Firing on All Cylinders: The Service Quality System for High-Powered Corporate Performance. 392p. 1994. text 18.95 (*0-7863-0356-5*, Irwn Prfssnl) McGraw-Hill Prof.

***Clemmer, Jim.** Growing the Distance: Timeless Principles for Personal, Career & Family Success. 192p. 1999. pap. 17.95 (*0-9684675-0-4*) Clemmer Grp Pr.

Clemmer, Jim. Pathways to Performance: A Guide to Transforming Yourself, Your Team, & Your Organization. LC 94-47410. (Illus.). 352p. 1995. 22.95 (*0-7615-0021-9*) Prima Pub.

— Pathways to Performance: A Guide to Transforming Yourself, Your Team, & Your Organization. 352p. 1996. per. 15.00 (*0-7615-0735-3*) Prima Pub.

Clemmer, Richard O. Continuities of Hopi Culture Change. 1978. pap. 15.95 (*0-916552-15-2*) Acoma Bks.

Clemmer, Richard O., et al. Journal of California & Great Basin Anthropology. fac. ed. (Malki Museum, Journal of California & Great Basin Anthropology Ser.: Vol. 11:1). 148p. (C). 1989. reprint ed. pap. text 16.25 (*1-55567-776-2*) Coyote Press.

Clemmer, Richard O., et al. Julian Steward & the Great Basin: The Making of & Anthropologist. LC 99-13657. 376p. 1999. 45.00 (*0-87480-594-5*) U of Utah Pr.

Clemmer Steiner, Susan. God Has No Favorites: Acts 1-12. Shelley, Maynard, ed. LC 89-84827. (Faith & Life Bible Studies). 97p. (YA). (gr. 8-12). 1989. pap. 1.95 (*0-87303-134-2*) Faith & Life.

Clemmer, William M. Victims of Dementia: Services, Support, & Care. LC 91-36172. 161p. 1993. pap. 19.95 (*1-56024-265-5*) Haworth Pr.

— Victims of Dementia: Services, Support, & Care. LC 91-36172. (Illus.). 155p. 1993. lib. bdg. 39.95 (*1-56024-264-7*) Haworth Pr.

Clemmesen, J., ed. see Comparative Leukemia Research Symposium Staff.

Clemmet, Mike. Fact Finders: Electricity & Magnetism. (J). 1998. pap. 8.95 (*0-563-37308-3*, BBC-Parkwest) Parkwest Pubns.

— Factfinders: Light & Sound. (Fact Finders Ser.). (J). pap. 8.95 (*0-563-37505-1*, BBC-Parkwest) Parkwest Pubns.

Clemmet, Mike & Oxlade, Chris. Factfinders: Forces & Energy. (Fact Finders Ser.). (J). 23.95 (*0-563-37621-X*, BBC-Parkwest) Parkwest Pubns.

Clemmons, Bradley & Witwer, Julia. The Fish King's Power of Truth. LC 86-24159. (Jataka Tales Ser.). 32p. (J). (gr. k-4). 1987. lib. bdg. 16.95 (*0-89800-158-7*) Dharma Pub.

— The Fish King's Power of Truth. LC 86-24159. (Jataka Tales Ser.). 32p. (J). (ps-3). 1987. pap. 7.95 (*0-89800-144-7*) Dharma Pub.

Clemmons, David, ed. see Cicerone, Keith D.

Clemmons, David, ed. see Uomoto, Jay.

Clemmons, David, ed. see Warren, C. Gerald.

Clemmons, David, ed. see Wehman, Paul, et al.

Clemmons, David C., jt. auth. see Fraser, Robert T.

Clemmons, Ithiel. Bishop C. H. Mason & the Roots of Cogic. LC 98-126275. 1997. pap. 19.99 (*1-56229-451-2*) Pneuma Life Pub.

Clemmons, J., et al. Portfolios in the Classroom. 1993. pap. text 18.95 (*0-590-49273-X*) Scholastic Inc.

Clemmons, Janine R. & Buchholz, Richard, eds. Behavioral Approaches to Conservation in the Wild. LC 96-31559. 400p. 1997. pap. text 30.95 (*0-521-58960-6*) Cambridge U Pr.

— Behavioral Approaches to Conservation in the Wild. (Illus.). 400p. (C). 1997. text 80.00 (*0-521-58054-4*) Cambridge U Pr.

Clemmons, Joan & Laase, Lois. Mini Lessons That Teach. (Illus.). 1996. pap. 16.95 (*0-590-49643-3*) Scholastic Inc.

Clemmons, Nancy. Exploring the Religions of Our World: Student Text. 240p. (YA). (gr. 11-12). 1999. pap. text, student ed. 16.95 (*0-87793-674-9*) Ave Maria.

***Clemmons, Nancy.** Exploring the Religions of Our World: Teacher's Manual. 1999. teacher ed., spiral bd. 24.95 (*0-87793-675-7*) Ave Maria.

Clemmons, Ron. Sounds in Time: A Guide to Music Fundamentals. 224p. (C). 1998. per. 39.95 (*0-7872-5478-9*, 41547801) Kendall-Hunt.

Clemmow. Electrodynamics of Particles & Plasmas. (C). 1995. pap. 36.95 (*0-201-47986-9*) Addison-Wesley.

Clemmow, P. & Cullen, A. The Plane Wave Spectrum Representation of Electromagnetic Fields. LC 66-25066. (International Series of Monographs in Electromagnetic Waves: Vol. 12). 1966. 85.00 (*0-08-013162-X*, Pub. by Pergamon Repr) Franklin.

Clemmow, P. C. The Plane Wave Spectrum Representation of Electromagnetic Fields. (Series on Electromagnetic Wave Theory). 200p. 1996. 49.95 (*0-7803-3411-6*, PC5682) Inst Electrical.

— The Plane Wave Spectrum Representation of Electromagnetic Fields. (IREE/OUP Series on Electromagnetic Wave Theory). (Illus.). 198p. 1996. reprint ed. text 75.00 (*0-19-859225-6*) OUP.

Clemo, Jack. Approach to Murano. 63p. 1993. pap. 12.95 (*1-85224-192-6*, Pub. by Bloodaxe Bks) Dufour.

— The Bouncing Hills - Dialect Tales & Light Verse. (C). 1989. 40.00 (*0-907566-38-3*, Pub. by Dyllansow Truran) St Mut.

— The Cured Arno. 64p. 1996. pap. 16.95 (*1-85224-326-0*, Pub. by Bloodaxe Bks) Dufour.

— Selected Poems. LC 88-70228. 160p. (Orig.). 1993. pap. 15.95 (*1-85224-052-0*, Pub. by Bloodaxe Bks) Dufour.

Clemoes, Peter. Interactions of Thought & Language in Old English Poetry. (Cambridge Studies in Anglo-Saxon England: No. 12). (Illus.). 541p. (C). 1995. text 85.00 (*0-521-30711-2*) Cambridge U Pr.

Clemoes, Peter, ed. see Alfric.

Clemoes, Peter A., ed. Anglo-Saxon England. Incl. Vol. 9. LC 78-190423. 1980. 64.95 (*0-521-23449-2*); Vol. 10. LC 78-190423. 1981. 59.95 (*0-521-24177-4*); LC 78-190423. (Illus.). write for info. (*0-318-51266-1*) Cambridge U Pr.

Clemon, Heather, ed. see Burge, Weldon.

Clemon, Heather, ed. see Hart, Rhonda M.

Clemons, B. J. Wake of the Wirelessman. LC 95-80728. (Illus.). xviii, 270p. 1996. pap. 16.95 (*0-9637586-6-7*) Glencannon Pr.

Clemons, B. J., jt. auth. see Gilpatric, Guy.

Clemons, Calvin K., jt. auth. see Harris, Robert.

Clemons, Christopher L. Face-Lift (Rhytidoplasty) Index of New Information with Authors, Subjects & References. 150p. 1997. 47.50 (*0-7883-1366-5*); pap. 44.50 (*0-7883-1367-3*) ABBE Pubs Assn.

Clemons, Donna, jt. auth. see Terril, Lizabeth.

Clemons, Donnie. Greed: The Adventures of Jonas Ballender. LC 97-74744. (Jonas Ballender Ser.: Vol. 1). 145p. 1998. pap. 6.99 (*0-9657123-0-3*) Journey Bks TN.

— Quest for the Eye of Light: The First Book of Mankiah. LC 97-71118. (Mankiah Ser.: Vol. 1). (Illus.). 256p. (Orig.). 1997. pap. 12.95 (*0-9657123-2-X*) Journey Bks TN.

Clemons, E. C. People's Book of Poetry. (Illus.). 43p. 1998. pap. 15.95 (*1-890301-09-4*) M Bey.

Clemons, Hardy. Saying Goodbye to Your Grief. LC 94-13424. 96p. 1994. pap. 9.00 (*1-880837-99-4*) Smyth & Helwys.

Clemons, Linda K. Scrumptious Recipes for Sizzling Sex. 50p. 1993. ring bd., vinyl bd. 19.95 (*0-9640375-0-5*) L Clemons Promot.

Clemons, Linda M. & Fiscal Services Staff. Update: Achieving Fiscal Integrity. 29p. 1995. pap. 3.50 (*1-892075-09-1*, HRDI 002) AFL CIO.

Clemons, Michael Pinball. All Heart: The Autobiography of Michael "Pinball" Clemons. LC 98-224341. (Illus.). 272p. 1998. 21.00 (*0-00-200008-3*) HarpC.

Clemons, R. E., et al, eds. Truth of Consequence Region. (Guidebook Ser.: No. 37). (Illus.). 317p. 1986. pap. 20.00 (*1-58546-072-9*) NMex Geol Soc.

***Clemons, Randall & McBeth, Mark.** Public Policy Praxis - Theory & Pragmatism: A Case Approach. 352p. 2000. pap. 40.00 (*0-13-025882-2*, Prentice Hall) P-H.

Clemow, Brian. Employer's Guide to Connecticut Labor & Employment Laws & Regulations. 161p. 1991. pap. 67.50 (*1-882397-01-0*) CT Busn & Indus.

— Employer's Guide to Federal Labor & Employment Laws & Regulations. 244p. 1991. pap. 67.50 (*1-882397-02-9*) CT Busn & Indus.

Clempner, Jane. Here, There & Everywhere: A Find-&-Name Picture Wordbook. (Illus.). 32p. (J). (ps-1). 1993. 6.95 (*0-8249-8590-7*, Ideals Child) Hambleton-Hill.

Clemson, B. Cybernetics: A New Management Tool, Vol. 4. (Cybernetics & Systems Ser., Abacus Bks.). (Illus.). 263p. 1984. 55.00 (*0-85626-166-1*) Gordon & Breach.

— Cybernetics: A New Management Tool, Vol. 4. (Cybernetics & Systems Ser., Abacus Bks.). xiii, 263p. 1991. pap. text 118.00 (*2-88124-518-8*) Gordon & Breach.

Clemson, David & Clemson, Wendy. The Really Practical Guides: Primary Assessment. 2nd ed. (Illus.). 128p. 1999. pap. 29.50 (*0-7487-2612-8*, Pub. by S Thornes Pubs) Trans-Atl Phila.

— Times Tables. LC 95-44393. (J). 1996. write for info. (*0-7894-0472-9*) DK Pub Inc.

Clemson, David, jt. auth. see Clemson, Wendy.

Clemson, Donovan. Old Wooden Buildings. (Illus.). 96p. pap. 4.95 (*0-919654-90-8*) Hancock House.

Clemson, Josephine. United in Christ. (C). 1988. 45.00 (*0-85439-196-7*, Pub. by St Paul Pubns) St Mut.

***Clemson University Staff & Taylor, Dennis.** Rural Life in the Piedmont of South Carolina. (Images of America Ser.). (Illus.). 128p. 1999. pap. 18.99 (*0-7385-0198-0*) Arcadia Publng.

Clemson, Wendy & Clemson, David. Times Tables! (Illus.). 32p. (J). 11.99 (*0-590-24755-7*) Scholastic Inc.

Clemson, Wendy, jt. auth. see Clemson, David.

***Clench, Mary H. & Spofford, Sally H.** Beginner's Guide to Attracting Birds to Your Backyard LC 98-201132. 64p. 1998. write for info. (*0-7853-2958-7*) Pubns Intl Ltd.

Clench, W. J. Cyclophoridae & Pupinidae of Caroline, Fijian, & Samoan Islands. (BMB Ser.). 1972. reprint ed. pap. 25.00 (*0-527-02304-3*) Periodicals Srv.

Clench, William J. & Turner, Ruth D. New Names Introduced by H. A. Pilsbry in the Mollusca & Crustacea. (Special Publication: No. 4). 218p. (Orig.). 1962. pap. 7.00 (*0-910006-32-6*) Acad Nat Sci Phila.

Clendenen, Bill, jt. auth. see Orr, Dan.

Clendenen, Clarence, jt. auth. see Duignan, Peter.

Clendenen, Clarence C., jt. ed. see Smythe, Donald.

Clendenen, Gary & Kern, Julie. Fundamentals of College Math. 704p. (C). 1997. pap. text 87.00 (*0-06-501068-X*) Addson-Wesley Educ.

Clendenen, Joanne. Index: ASI Newsletter - Key Words. 26p. 1994. pap. text 15.00 (*0-936547-26-X*) Am Soc Index.

Clendenen, Phil. Sex & the Single Camel. LC 94-232623. 185p. (Orig.). 1994. pap. 13.95 (*1-879194-18-X*) GLB Pubs.

Clendenin, Bruce. The Video Book. LC 96-41803. 363p. 1997. pap. text 50.00 (*0-13-607334-4*) P-H.

Clendenin, Daniel B. Eastern Orthodox Christianity: A Western Perspective. LC 94-28158. 176p. 1994. pap. 14.99 (*0-8010-2588-5*) Baker Bks.

— Many Gods, Many Lords: Christianity Encounters World Religions. LC 95-39849. 192p. 1996. pap. 11.99 (*0-8010-2059-X*) Baker Bks.

— Theological Method in Jacques Ellul. LC 87-10506. 184p. (Orig.). (C). 1987. pap. text 19.50 (*0-8191-6428-3*) U Pr of Amer.

Clendenin, Daniel B., ed. Eastern Orthodox Theology: A Contemporary Reader. LC 95-3044. 224p. 1994. pap. 17.99 (*0-8010-2589-3*) Baker Bks.

Clendenin, Daniel B. & Buschart, W. David, eds. Scholarship, Sacraments & Service: Historical Studies in Protestant Tradition (Essays in Honor of Bard Thompson) LC 89-78415. (Texts & Studies in Religion: Vol. 49). 320p. 1990. lib. bdg. 99.95 (*0-88946-838-9*) E Mellen.

Clendenin, Denzil A. From Heaven to Earth & Return: The Words, Works & Wisdom of Jesus. 168p. (Orig.). 1988. pap. 6.50 (*0-944765-00-9*) Agape Bks.

Clendenin, Malcolm, ed. see Berkowitz, Julie S.

Clendenin, Mary J. Devotional Souvenirs. 106p. 1987. write for info. (*0-942407-02-4*) Father & Son.

— Gonzalo, Coronado's Shepherd Boy. Roberts, Melissa, ed. (Illus.). 128p. (J). (gr. 4-5). 1990. pap. 6.95 (*1-57168-007-1*) Sunbelt Media.

— The Melody Within. 152p. (Orig.). 1991. pap. 9.95 (*0-925854-04-2*) Defiant Pr.

***Clendenin, Priscilla.** No Scare Science Fair: An Extra Out of the Ordinary Guide to Doing a Science Fair Project. large type ed. LC 94-68976. Orig. Title: So You Have to Do a Science Fair Project.... (Illus.). 67p. (J). (gr. 1-8). 1998. pap. 15.95 (*0-9679713-0-6*) Ribbitt Prodns.

Clendening, A. E. Dunaway: The Dunaways of Virginia. (Illus.). 156p. 1991. reprint ed. pap. 25.00 (*0-8328-2061-X*); reprint ed. lib. bdg. 35.00 (*0-8328-2060-1*) Higginson Bk Co.

Clendening, John A., jt. auth. see Gillespie, William H.

Clendening, Logan. Source Book of Medical History. 685p. (C). 1960. pap. 15.95 (*0-486-20621-1*) Dover.

***Clendeninn, Neil J. & Appelt, Krysztof, eds.** Matrix Metalloproteinase Inhibitors in Cancer Therapy. (Cancer Drug Discovery & Development Ser.). 250p. 2000. 135.00 (*0-89603-668-5*) Humana.

Clendennen, B. H. Restaurando el Mensaje De Pentecostes. New Life Ministries International Staff et al, trs. from ENG.Tr. of Restoring the Message of Pentecost. (SPA.). 224p. (Orig.). 1991. pap. 6.95 (*1-878921-01-0*) Victory Temple.

— Restoring the Message of Pentecost. LC 90-90254. 224p. (Orig.). 1991. pap. 6.95 (*1-878921-00-2*) Victory Temple.

— The Road to Discipleship LC 99-163766. 85p. 1998. write for info. (*1-56043-215-2*) Destiny Image.

Clendenning, John. The Life & Thought of Josiah Royce. rev. expanded ed. LC 98-25325. (Library of American Philosophy). (Illus.). 432p. 1998. pap. 24.95 (*0-8265-1322-0*); lib. bdg. 49.95 (*0-8265-1312-3*) Vanderbilt U Pr.

Clendenning, P. H. & Bartlett, R. Eighteenth Century Russia: A Select Bibliography of Works Published Since 1955. (Russian Bibliography Ser.: No. 3). (Illus.). 260p. (C). 1981. 30.00 (*0-89250-110-3*) Orient Res Partners.

Clendenning, Sheila T. Emily Dickinson: A Bibliography, 1850-1966. LC 67-65585. No. 3. 175p. reprint ed. pap. 54.30 (*0-8357-5568-1*, 203519500093) Bks Demand.

***Clendenon, Donn.** Miracle in New York. (Illus.). 190p. 1999. pap. write for info. (*1-57579-167-6*) Pine Hill Pr.

***Clendinen, Dudley & Nagourney, Adam.** Out for Good: The Struggle to Build a Gay Rights Movement in America. LC 99-12523. (Illus.). 704p. 1999. 29.50 (*0-684-81091-3*) Simon & Schuster.

Clendinnen, Inga. Ambivalent Conquests: Maya & Spaniard in Yucatan, 1517-1570. (Cambridge Latin American Studies: No. 61). (Illus.). 260p. 1987. text 64.95 (*0-521-33397-0*) Cambridge U Pr.

— Ambivalent Conquests: Maya & Spaniard in Yucatan, 1517-1570. (Cambridge Latin American Studies: No. 61). (Illus.). 256p. 1989. pap. text 15.95 (*0-521-37981-4*) Cambridge U Pr.

— Aztecs: An Interpretation. (Illus.). 414p. (C). 1991. text 39.95 (*0-521-40093-7*) Cambridge U Pr.

— Aztecs: An Interpretation. (Canto Book Ser.). (Illus.). 414p. (C). 1995. pap. 13.95 (*0-521-48585-1*) Cambridge U Pr.

— Reading the Holocaust. LC 98-53636. (Illus.). 208p. (C). 1999. pap. 14.95 (*0-521-64597-2*); text 49.95 (*0-521-64174-8*) Cambridge U Pr.

Clendinning, Monte M. My Place in God's Purpose: A Commentary for Women: Galatians & Ephesians. Nelson, Becky, ed. (Illus.). 112p. 1994. pap. text 6.95 (*1-56309-100-3*, N944102, New Hope) Womans Mission Union.

Cleophas, Ton J. Human Experimentation: Methodologic Issues Fundamental to Clinical Trials. LC 99-33163. 1999. write for info. (*0-7923-5827-9*) Kluwer Academic.

***Cleophas, Ton J., et al.** Statistics Applied to Clinical Trials. 112p. 2000. pap. 35.00 (*0-7923-6184-9*) Kluwer Academic.

Cleophas, Ton M. Beta-Blockers in Hypertension & Angina Pectoris: Different Compounds, Different Strategies. LC 95-17076. 100p. (C). 1995. pap. text 44.50 (*0-7923-3516-3*) Kluwer Academic.

Clephan, R. Coltman. The Mediaeval Tournament. LC 94-47975. (Illus.). 240p. 1995. pap. text 11.95 (*0-486-28620-7*) Dover.

Clephane, Ellen J. Dance of Love: What Fifty Couples Say Makes Their Relationships Really Work. LC 95-43237. 144p. 1996. pap. 12.95 (*1-85230-802-8*, Pub. by Element MA) Penguin Putnam.

Clephane, Irene, jt. auth. see Bott, Alan.

Clepper, Henry. Professional Forestry in the United States. LC 70-171107. 349p. reprint ed. pap. 108.20 (*0-7837-3139-6*, 201573700097) Bks Demand.

Clepper, Henry, ed. Leaders of American Conservation. LC 75-155206. 365p. reprint ed. 113.20 (*0-8357-9921-2*, 201242900081) Bks Demand.

— Marine Recreational Fisheries, No. 3. 176p. (C). 1978. text 15.00 (*0-935217-06-1*) Intl Game Fish.

— Marine Recreational Fisheries, No. 4. (Illus.). 169p. (C). 1979. text 15.00 (*0-935217-07-X*) Intl Game Fish.

— Marine Recreational Fisheries, No. 5. 226p. (C). 1980. text 15.00 (*0-935217-08-8*) Intl Game Fish.

— Marine Recreational Fisheries, No. 6. 212p. (C). 1981. text 15.00 (*0-935217-09-6*) Intl Game Fish.

Clepper, Henry & Stroud, Richard H., eds. Marine Recreational Fisheries. (Illus.). 174p. (C). 1976. text 15.00 (*0-935217-04-5*) Intl Game Fish.

— Marine Recreational Fisheries, No. 2. (Illus.). 220p. (C). 1977. text 15.00 (*0-935217-05-3*) Intl Game Fish.

Clepper, Henry, jt. auth. see Randall, C.

Clepper, Henry, jt. auth. see Randall, Charles E.

Clepper, Henry, ed. see Carlton, Frank E.

Clepper, Henry, ed. see Stroud, Richard H.

Clepper, Henry, jt. ed. see Stroud, Richard H.

Clepper, Patrick M. Just for Kicks. 78p. 1975. 5.25 (*0-87129-531-8*, J14) Dramatic Pub.

Cler, Gene. Necessary Excesses. 32p. 1995. 3.00 (*0-941127-17-6*) Dacotah Terr Pr.

Clerambault, Louis-Nicolas. Louis-Nicolas Clerambault - Two Cantatas for Soprano & Chamber Ensemble. Foster, Donald H., ed. (Recent Researches in Music of the Baroque Era Ser.: Vol. B27). (Illus.). xxiv, 89p. 1979. pap. 40.00 (*0-89579-104-8*) A-R Eds.

Clerc, Albert C. Eternal Song. (Illus.). 52p. (Orig.). 1990. lib. bdg. 6.95 (*1-878149-02-4*) Counterpoint Pub.

Clerc, Charles. The Y & Other Stories. LC 96-71248. 216p. (Orig.). 1997. pap. 11.00 (*1-889883-01-8*) Provine Pr.

Clerc, Charles & Leiter, Louis H. Seven Contemporary Short Novels. 3rd ed. (C). 1997. 53.00 (*0-673-15569-2*) Addson-Wesley Educ.

***Clerc, Dean Alan.** Mindset of a Martial Artist. (Illus.). 113p. 2000. pap. text 10.85 (*1-58500-420-0*) First Bks Lib.

Clerc, G., jt. auth. see Leclant, J.

Clerc, J. M., ed. Introduction to Working Conditions & Environment. xx, 323p. (Orig.). 1990. pap. text 27.00 (*92-2-105125-0*) Intl Labour Office.

Clerc, Jean-Benoit. Homines Magici: Etude sur la Sorcellerie et la Magie dans la Societe Romaine Imperiale. (Publications Universitaires Europeennes Ser.: Series 3, Vol. 673). (FRE.). 364p. 1995. 57.95 (*3-906754-05-7*, Pub. by P Lang) P Lang Pubng.

Clerc, Jean T., jt. auth. see Pretsch, Ern.

Clerc, Jeanne M. Introduction to Clinical Laboratory Science. (Illus.). 144p. (gr. 13). 1991. text 33.95 (*0-8016-1392-2*, 01392) Mosby Inc.

Clerc, M., jt. ed. see Mackness, M.I.

Clerch, Linda B., jt. auth. see Massaro, Donald.

Clerck, F. De, see De Clerck, F., ed.

An Asterisk (*) at the beginning of an entry indicates that the title is appearing for the first time.

Clercq, Chretien Le, see Le Clercq, Chretien.
Clercq, Erik de, ed. Frontiers in Microbiology. (New Perspectives in Clinical Microbiology Ser.). 1987. text 218.00 (*0-89838-959-3*) Kluwer Academic.
Clercq, Erik De, see De Clercq, Erik, ed.
Clercq, Peter de, see De Clercq, Peter.
Clercx, Suzanne. Le Baroque et la musique: Essai d'esthetique musicale. LC 76-43910. reprint ed. 47.50 (*0-404-60153-7*) AMS Pr.
— Gretry: 1741-1813. LC 76-43911. (Music & Theatre in France in the 17th & 18th Centuries Ser.). (FRE.). reprint ed. 39.50 (*0-404-60154-5*) AMS Pr.
Clere, John R. Bryan's Sectional Maps of Oahu. enl. rev. ed. (Illus.). 212p. 1995. pap. text 12.95 (*1-878536-07-9*) EMIC Graphics.
— Bryan's Sectional Maps of Oahu. rev. ed. (Illus.). 204p. 1990. pap. 6.75 (*1-878536-00-1*) EMIC Graphics.
— Bryan's Sectional Maps of Oahu. rev. ed. (Illus.). 210p. 1991. pap. text 7.00 (*1-878536-01-X*) EMIC Graphics.
— Bryan's Sectional Maps of Oahu. rev. ed. (Illus.). 208p. 1991. pap. text 7.25 (*1-878536-02-8*) EMIC Graphics.
— Bryan's Sectional Maps of Oahu. rev. ed. (Illus.). 208p. 1992. pap. text 7.50 (*1-878536-03-6*) EMIC Graphics.
— Bryan's Sectional Maps of Oahu. rev. ed. (Illus.). 212p. 1993. pap. text 7.75 (*1-878536-04-4*) EMIC Graphics.
— Bryan's Sectional Maps of Oahu. rev. ed. (Illus.). 212p. 1994. pap. text 7.95 (*1-878536-05-2*) EMIC Graphics.
— Bryan's Sectional Maps of Oahu. rev. ed. (Illus.). 212p. 1995. pap. text 8.50 (*1-878536-06-0*) EMIC Graphics.
Clere, Jules. Hommes de la Commune: Biographie Complete de Tous ses Membres. LC 72-1005. reprint ed. 36.50 (*0-404-07119-8*) AMS Pr.
Cleres, Christian. Le Havre-New York. (Illus.). 200p. 1997. pap. 12.95 (*2-85025-563-7*) Dist Art Pubs.
— Le Havre/New York. 1997. pap. text 12.95 (*2-85025-585-8*) Hazan.
Clerget, Charles E., jt. auth. see Leconte, Emile.
Cleri, Dennis J. & Zambito, Raymond F. Immunology & Infectious Diseases of the Mouth. 425p. 1991. 49.00 (*0-685-65360-9*) Mosby Inc.
Clerici, Louisa, jt. auth. see Clerici, Rick.
Clerici, Rick & Clerici, Louisa. Sparks from the Fire of Time. 256p. 1998. pap. 14.95 (*1-56184-130-7*) New Falcon Pubns.
Clerico, Don, ed. see Miescke, Lori.
Clerico, G. F., jt. auth. see Catalani, M. S.
Clericuzio, Antonio & Rattansi, Piyo, eds. Alchemy & Chemistry in the Sixteenth & Seventeenth Centuries: Proceedings Warburg Colloquium 1989. LC 93-33464. (Archives Internationales d'Histoire des Idees (International Archives of the History of Ideas) Ser.: No. 140). 224p. (C). 1994. lib. bdg. 156.00 (*0-7923-2573-7*, Pub. by Kluwer Academic) Kluwer Academic.
Clerin, Claudette. Out on a Cloud I. 1997. pap. 56.95 (*1-57553-536-X*) Watermrk Pr.
Clerk, Christian, jt. auth. see Burt, Ben.
Clerk, Christian, jt. auth. see Nile, Richard.
Clerk, Honor & Gibson, Robin. The Twentieth Century Collection at the National Portrait Gallery. (Illus.). 64p. 1993. pap. 9.95 (*1-85514-025-X*, Pub. by Natl Port Gall) Antique Collect.
Clerk, Janet M. How to Get Admitted to College: Even If You Have Less Than Perfect High School Grades. LC 97-95373. (Illus.). 224p. 1998. pap. 12.95 (*0-9662632-0-0*) Hoops Pr.
Clerk, Jayana & Siegel, Ruth, compiled by. Modern Literature of the Non-Western World: Where the Waters Are Born. LC 94-5832. 1504p. (C). 1997. pap. 53.00 (*0-06-501269-0*) Addson-Wesley Educ.
Clerk, John. Etchings, Chiefly of Views in Scotland. LC 72-1019. (Bannatyne Club, Edinburgh. Publications: No. 8). reprint ed. 72.50 (*0-404-52719-1*) AMS Pr.
— Series of Etchings: Chiefly of Views in Scotland. Laing, David, ed. LC 72-963. (Bannatyne Club, Edinburgh. Publications: No. 98). reprint ed. 110.00 (*0-404-52854-6*) AMS Pr.
Clerk, William. An Epitome of Certaine Late Aspersions Cast at Civilians. LC 79-84095. (English Experience Ser.: No. 915). 56p. 1979. reprint ed. lib. bdg. 20.00 (*90-221-0915-1*) Walter J Johnson.
Clerk, William S. & Wheeler, Brian K., eds. A Photographic Guide to North American Raptors. (Illus.). 198p. 1995. text 32.00 (*0-12-745530-2*) Acad Pr.
Clerke, Agnes M. A Popular History of Astronomy in the Nineteenth Century. LC 70-166614. 1908. reprint ed. 79.00 (*0-403-01492-1*) Scholarly.
Clerkin, Don. Football Humor: The Game's Had Plenty of Laughs. rev. ed. Calitri, Ellen, ed. (Illus.). 104p. 1991. pap. 8.95 (*0-9627494-2-7*) D Clerkin.
— Football Humor: The Game's Had Plenty of Laughs. rev. ed. Calitri, Ellen, ed. (Illus.). 99p. 1992. pap. 5.95 (*0-9627494-3-5*) D Clerkin.
— Football Humor: The Game's Had Plenty of Laughs. 3rd rev. ed. Calitri, Ellen, ed. (Illus.). 99p. 1993. pap. 4.95 (*0-9627494-6-X*) D Clerkin.
— Overtime. 104p. 1993. 6.95 (*0-9627494-5-1*) D Clerkin.
— Recalling Great Events in Sports. (Illus.). 112p. (Orig.). 1990. pap. 12.95 (*0-9627494-1-9*) D Clerkin.
— Recalling Great Events in Sports. rev. ed. (Illus.). 112p. (Orig.). 1992. pap. 5.95 (*0-9627494-4-3*) D Clerkin.
Clerks of the Federal Courts in New York. Rules of the U. S. Courts in New York: Federal Rules of Appellate Procedure. 2nd ed. LC 65-16452. (Federal Court Rules Ser.). 1978. ring bd. 145.00 (*0-87632-070-1*) West Group.
Clermont, Kevin M. Black Letter on Civil Procedure. 4th ed. LC 95-31499. (Black Letter Ser.). 319p. (C). 1995. pap. text 24.50 (*0-314-06528-8*) West Pub.
— Civil Procedure. 3rd ed. LC 93-12068. (Black Letter Ser.). 350p. 1993. pap. text 24.50 (*0-314-01868-9*) West Pub.
***Clermont, Kevin M.** Civil Procedure. 5th ed. 1999. pap. 24.50 (*0-314-23973-1*) West Pub.
Clermont, Kevin M. Civil Procedure: Materials for a Basic Course, 1994 Supplement. 6th ed. (University Casebook Ser.). (Illus.). 108p. 1994. pap. text 7.50 (*1-56662-184-4*) Foundation Pr.
***Clermont, Kevin M.** Civil Procedure: Territorial Jurisdiction. (Paralegal). (C). 1999. pap. 9.75 (*1-56662-738-9*) Foundation Pr.
Clermont, Kevin M. Civil Procedure, 1996 Supplement to Materials for a Basic Course In. 6th ed. (University Casebook Ser.). 115p. 1996. pap. text. write for info. (*1-56662-403-7*) Foundation Pr.
— Federal Rules of Civil Procedure: And Selected Other Procedural Provisions, 1994. (Illus.). 684p. 1994. pap. text 16.95 (*1-56662-172-0*) Foundation Pr.
***Clermont, Kevin M.** Federal Rules of Civil Procedure: As Amended Through April 1st, 1999. (Paralegal). (C). 1999. pap. 15.00 (*1-56662-773-7*) Foundation Pr.
Clermont, Kevin M. Federal Rules of Civil Procedure & Selected Other Procedural Provisions. annuals 725p. 1998. pap., suppl. ed. 18.95 (*1-56662-623-4*) Foundation Pr.
— Federal Rules of Civil Procedure & Selected Other Procedural Provisions, 1996. 709p. 1996. pap. text. write for info. (*1-56662-376-6*) Foundation Pr.
— Federal Rules of Civil Procedure & Selected Other Procedural Provisions, 1997. 717p. 1997. pap. text. write for info. (*1-56662-491-6*) Foundation Pr.
***Clermont, Kevin M.** Federal Rules of Civil Procedure 2000. 2000. pap. 22.95 (*1-56662-905-5*) Foundation Pr.
***Clermont, Lisa.** The Big Yellow Coloring Book. (Illus.). 30p. (J). (gr. k-8). 1999. pap. 4.00 (*0-9656520-3-3*) B Lambers.
Clermont-Tonnerre, Alban De, see De Clermont-Tonnerre, Alban.
***Clery, E. J.** The Rise of Supernatural Fiction, 1762-1800. (Studies in Romanticism: Vol. 12). (Illus.). 235p. (C). 1999. pap. 21.95 (*0-521-66458-6*) Cambridge U Pr.
***Clery, Emma.** Gothic Documents. 2000. text 69.95 (*0-7190-4026-4*, Pub. by Manchester Univ Pr) St Martin.
— Gothic Documents: A Sourcebook 1700-1820. 2000. pap. 24.95 (*0-7190-4027-2*, Pub. by Manchester Univ Pr) St Martin.
Clery, Emma, ed. & intro. see Walpole, Horace.
***Clery, Suzanne B.** Gender Differences in Earnings Among Young Adults Entering the Labor Market. 84p. 1998. pap. 7.00 (*0-16-049503-2*) USGPO.
Clery, Suzanne B., et al. Gender Differences in Earnings among Young Adults Entering the Labor Market. (Illus.). 72p. (C). 1999. pap. text 20.00 (*0-7881-7814-8*) DIANE Pub.
***Clesceri, Lenore S.** Standard Methods for the Examination of Water & Wastewater. 20th ed. Greenberg, Arnold E. et al, eds. 1220p. 1998. 200.00 (*0-87553-235-7*) Am Pub Health.
Clessa, J. J. Math & Logic Puzzles for PC Enthusiasts. LC 96-5615. Orig. Title: Micropuzzles. 1996. reprint ed. pap. 5.95 (*0-486-29192-8*) Dover.
Clesse, Armand, ed. The Vitality of Japan: Writings on Armenia. LC 96-37768. (St. Antony's Ser.). 157p. 1997. text 59.95 (*0-312-17313-X*) St Martin.
Clesse, Armand, et al, eds. The International System After the Collapse of the East-West Order. LC 94-34813. 1994. lib. bdg. 221.00 (*0-7923-3132-X*) Kluwer Academic.
— Small States & the Security Challenge in the New Europe. (Atlantic Commentaries Ser.: No. 8). 272p. 1996. pap. 24.00 (*1-85753-153-1*, Pub. by Brasseys) Brasseys.
Clesse, Armand & Ruhl, Lothar. Beyond East-West Confrontation: Searching for a New Security Structure in Europe. 640p. 1990. 70.25 (*3-7890-2211-X*, Pub. by Nomos Verlags) Intl Bk Import.
Clesse, Armand & Schelling, Thomas C., eds. The Western Community & the Gorbachev Challenge. 408p. 1989. 63.00 (*3-7890-1789-2*, Pub. by Nomos Verlags) Intl Bk Import.
Clesse, Armand, jt. ed. see Mundell, Robert A.
Clestin, Roger & Dalmolin, Eliane, eds. Popular Culture. 200p. 1997. pap. text 23.00 (*90-5699-551-0*) Gordon & Breach.
***Cleto, Fabio, ed.** Camp: Queer Aesthetics & the Performing Subject. LC 99-47171. (Illus.). 544p. 1999. pap. 24.95 (*0-472-06722-2*, 06722) U of Mich Pr.
— Camp: Queer Aesthetics & the Performing Subject. LC 99-47171. (Illus.). 544p. (C). 1999. text 60.00 (*0-472-09722-9*, 09722) U of Mich Pr.
Cleton, F. J. & Coebergh, J. W., eds. Cancer in the Netherlands, 2 vols., Set. (C). 1988. pap. text 86.00 (*0-89838-400-1*) Kluwer Academic.
Cleton, F. J. & Simons, J. W., eds. Genetic Origins of Tumor Cells. (Developments in Oncology Ser.: Vol. 1). xv, 125p. 1980. text 88.00 (*90-247-2272-1*) Kluwer Academic.
Cletto, Arrighi. Milanese-Italian Dictionary. (ITA.). 904p. 1983. 75.00 (*0-8288-7347-X*, 8820309645) Fr & Eur.
Cleugh, James. The Marquis & the Chevalier: A Study in the Psychology of Sex As Illustrated by the Lives & Personalities of the Marquis De Sade, 1740-1814 & the Chevalier Von Sacher-Masoch, 1836-1905. LC 70-142317. (Illus.). 295p. 1972. reprint ed. lib. bdg. 65.00 (*0-8371-5920-2*, CLMC) Greenwood.
Cleugh, James, tr. see Jungk, Robert.
Cleugh, James, tr. see Wendt, Herbert.
Cleva, Gregory D. Henry Kissinger & the American Approach to Foreign Policy. LC 87-46431. 280p. 1989. 44.50 (*0-8387-5147-4*) Bucknell U Pr.
Cleve. Catalog of the Chess Collection, Including Checkers. 1981. 175.00 (*0-8161-1313-0*, G K Hall & Co) Mac Lib Ref.
Cleve, Bastian. Art of Personal Filmmaking. (Illus.). 230p. 1989. spiral bd. 49.95 incl. VHS (*0-9623848-1-X*); spiral bd. 49.95 incl. VHS (*0-9623848-2-8*); spiral bd. 24.95 (*0-9623848-0-1*) Images Intl.
— Film Production Management. (Illus.). 232p. 1994. pap. 29.95 (*0-240-80106-7*, Focal) Buttrwrth-Heinemann.
***Cleve, Bastian.** Film Production Management. 2nd ed. LC 99-30024. 240p. 1999. pap. 29.95 (*0-240-80393-0*, Focal) Buttrwrth-Heinemann.
Cleve-Euler, Astrid. Die Diatomeen Von Schweden und Finnland, 1951-1955, 5 pts. (Kungl. Sv. Vetenskapsak Handl Ser.). (GER., Illus.). 1996. 408.00 (*3-7682-0550-9*, 011859, Pub. by Koeltz Sci Bks) Lubrecht & Cramer.
Cleve, James van. Problems from Kant. LC 98-26825. 352p. 1999. text 45.00 (*0-19-508322-9*) OUP.
Cleve, James Van, see Van Cleve, James, ed.
***Cleve, Janita.** Nurse at Pinewood. large type ed. 320p. 2000. 18.99 (*1-84137-004-5*, Pub. by Mgna Lrg Print) Ulverscroft.
Cleve, Jay. Out of the Blues: Strategies That Work to Get You Through the Down Times. 368p. 1996. reprint ed. mass mkt. 6.99 (*0-425-15252-9*) Berkley Pub.
Cleve, John V. Van, see Van Cleve, John V., ed.
***Cleve, Jurgen.** Inkompatibilitat und Kumulationsverbot: Eine Untersuchung Zu C. 152 Cic/1983. XIV, 333p. 1999. 51.95 (*3-631-34020-6*) P Lang Pubng.
Cleve, K. Van, see Van Cleve, K.
Cleve, Per-Theodor & Grunow, Albert. Beitrage zur Kenntnis der Arctischen Diatomeen. (Kongl. Svenska Vetenskaps-Akademiens Handlingar Ser.: Band 17:2). (GER., Illus.). 121p. 1976. reprint ed. pap. 54.00 (*3-87429-101-4*, 000509, Pub. by Koeltz Sci Bks) Lubrecht & Cramer.
Cleve, Robert. Guide to Western Civilization. 104p. (C). 1996. pap. text 17.95 (*0-7872-2500-2*) Kendall-Hunt.
— Study Guide: History 150: Western Civilization to 1500. 2nd ed. 106p. (C). 1998. per. 28.95 (*0-7872-5336-7*, 41533601) Kendall-Hunt.
Cleveland. Simplifying Life As a Senior. LC 98-12949. 224p. 1998. pap. 13.95 (*0-312-18758-0*) St Martin.
Cleveland, Alexandra, et al. Activities Unlimited: Throughout the Day. (Illus.). 218p. (Orig.). 1994. pap. 16.95 (*0-943452-17-1*) Building Blocks.
Cleveland, Alexandra, jt. auth. see Caton, Barbara.
Cleveland, Amory. Meanwhile, Back at the Ranch. 1996. write for info. (*0-316-03766-4*) Little.
Cleveland, Ana D., jt. auth. see Cleveland, Donald B.
Cleveland, Arthur R. Women under the English Law: From the Landing of the Saxons to the Present Time. (Illus.). xvi, 315p. 1987. reprint ed. 42.50 (*0-8377-2012-5*, Rothman) W S Hein.
Cleveland Ballet Council, Cookbook Committee Staff. Light Kitchen Choreography: A Collection of Lower Fat Recipes to Benefit Cleveland Ballet. McLaughlin, Janie, ed. LC 94-71214. (Illus.). 300p. 1994. text 19.95 (*0-9609252-9-5*) Cleve Ballet Coun.
***Cleveland, Barry.** Creative Music Production: The Bold Techniques of Joe Meek. 160p. 2000. pap. 24.95 (*0-87288-754-5*) Intertec Pub.
Cleveland, Barry. Recording Industry Sourcebook. 11th ed. 1999. pap. 79.95 (*0-87288-732-4*) Intertec Pub.
Cleveland, Bernard F. Master Teaching Techniques. 4th ed. LC 83-73524. (Illus.). 248p. 1987. pap. 17.95 (*0-9608678-3-X*) Connecting Link.
Cleveland, Brad. Call Center Management on Fast Forward: Succeeding in Today's Dynamic Inbound Environment. 1997. pap. 34.95 (*0-9659093-0-1*) Call Center.
Cleveland, C. G. Clauses & Phrases. (Straight Forward Advanced English Ser.). 80p. 1993. pap., student ed. 7.95 (*0-931993-55-5*, GP-055) Garlic Pr OR.
Cleveland, C. G. & Collins, S. Harold. Mechanics. (Straight Forward Advanced English Ser.). 80p. 1993. pap., student ed. 7.95 (*0-931993-56-3*, GP-056) Garlic Pr OR.
Cleveland, Catherine. The True Story of Kaspar Hauser. 1976. lib. bdg. 59.95 (*0-8490-2774-8*) Gordon Pr.
Cleveland, Catherine C. The Great Revival in the West, 1797-1805. 1990. 16.50 (*0-8446-1117-4*) Peter Smith.
Cleveland, Ceil. Whatever Happened to Jacy Farrow? LC 97-22946. 321p. 1997. 26.50 (*1-57441-030-X*) UNTX Pr.
Cleveland, Ceil, ed. see Slack, M. E.
Cleveland, Claudette. Fly with Me. (Illus.). 96p. (Orig.). 1998. pap. 11.95 (*0-9668702-0-4*) White Star Ent.
Cleveland Clinic Foundation, Department of Nutriti & Ellis, Pat. The Cleveland Clinic Foundation Creative Cooking for Renal Diabetic Diets. LC 87-4934. 178p. (Orig.). 1987. pap. 17.95 (*0-941511-01-4*) Senay Pub.
— The Cleveland Clinic Foundation Creative Cooking for Renal Diets. LC 87-4575. 280p. (Orig.). 1987. pap. 17.95 (*0-941511-00-6*) Senay Pub.
***Cleveland Clinic Foundation Staff.** Guidelines for Antimicrobial Usage: 1999-2000 Edition. 80p. 2000. pap. text 19.95 (*1-884735-31-2*) Prof Comms.
Cleveland Clinic Foundation Staff, jt. auth. see Behrendt, Donna J.
***Cleveland Clinic Staff.** Cleveland Clinic Heart Book. (Illus.). 2000. 25.00 (*0-7868-6679-9*, Pub. by Disney Pr) Time Warner.
— Cleveland Clinic Heart Book: The Definitive Guide for the Entire Family from the Nation's Leading Heart Center. Topol, Eric J., ed. LC 99-59778. (Illus.). 400p. 2000. 25.00 (*0-7868-6495-8*, Pub. by Hyperion) Time Warner.
Cleveland Consulting Association, jt. auth. see Ernst & Young Staff.
Cleveland, Cutler. The Global Environment: An Ecological-Economic Perspective. (C). 1997. text. write for info. (*0-8053-0654-4*) Addison-Wesley.
***Cleveland, Cutler J., et al.** The Economics of Nature & the Nature of Economics. LC 00-24326. (Advances in Ecological Economics Ser.). 2000. write for info. (*1-85898-980-9*) E Elgar.
Cleveland, David. The April Rabbits. (Illus.). 32p. (J). (gr. k-3). 1986. pap. 2.95 (*0-590-42369-X*) Scholastic Inc.
— That's Life, 13 vols. (Telesis Drug Education Ser.). (Illus.). (J). (gr. k). 1990. student ed. 3.50 (*1-56117-043-7*) Telesis CA.
— That's Life, 13 vols. (Telesis Drug Education Ser.). (Illus.). (J). (ps). 1990. 35.00 (*1-56117-042-9*) Telesis CA.
— That's Life, 13 vols. (Telesis Drug Education Ser.). (Illus.). (J). (gr. k). 1994. student ed. 65.00 (*1-56117-044-5*) Telesis CA.
Cleveland, David, ed. see White, Colin & Boucke, Laurie.
***Cleveland Davis, Emily.** Ancient Americans: The Archaeological Story of Two Continents. (LC History-America-E). 311p. 1999. reprint ed. lib. bdg. 89.00 (*0-7812-4251-7*) Rprt Serv.
***Cleveland, Deb & Weiss, LeAnn.** A Woman's Faith: Sayings, Scriptures & Stories from the Bible Revealing God. (Hugs from Heaven Ser.). (Illus.). 128p. 2000. 10.99 (*1-58229-129-2*) Howard Pub LA.
Cleveland, Donald B. Cartooning for the Librarian: A How-to-Do-It Manual. (How-to-Do-It Ser.). 192p. 1992. 27.50 (*1-55570-102-7*) Neal-Schuman.
***Cleveland, Donald B. & Cleveland, Ana D.** Introduction to Indexing & Abstracting. 3rd ed. 250p. 2000. 45.00 (*1-56308-641-7*) Libs Unl.
Cleveland Foundation Staff. Criminal Justice in Cleveland. Pound, Roscoe & Frankfurter, Felix, eds. LC 68-55769. (Criminology, Law Enforcement, & Social Problems Ser.: No. 8). (Illus.). 1968. reprint ed. 35.00 (*0-87585-008-1*) Patterson Smith.
Cleveland, Frederick A. Chapters Municipal Administration & Accounting. Brief, Richard P., ed. LC 80-1479. (Dimensions of Accounting Theory & Practice Ser.). 1980. reprint ed. lib. bdg. 26.95 (*0-405-13509-2*) Ayer.
Cleveland, Frederick A. & Powell, Fred W. Railroad Promotion & Capitalization in the United States. Bruchey, Stuart, ed. LC 80-1698. (Railroads Ser.). 1981. reprint ed. lib. bdg. 38.95 (*0-405-13770-2*) Ayer.
Cleveland, Gregory C., ed. Second Annual Interim Report on the Archaeological Investigations at the Miller Site (45FR5) on Strawberry Island (1977), a Late Prehistoric Village Near Burbank, Washington. fac. ed. (Washington Archaeological Research Center Project Reports: No. 72). (Illus.). 183p. (C). 1978. reprint ed. pap. text 19.38 (*1-55567-502-6*) Coyote Press.
Cleveland, Grover. Good Citizenship. LC 96-24915. 72p. 1997. reprint ed. 9.95 (*1-55709-432-2*) Applewood.
— Letters of Grover Cleveland, 1850-1908. (American Biography Ser.). 640p. 1991. reprint ed. lib. bdg. 109.00 (*0-7812-8079-6*) Rprt Serv.
— Presidential Problems. LC 78-152978. (Select Bibliographies Reprint Ser.). 1977. reprint ed. 23.95 (*0-8369-5730-X*) Ayer.
Cleveland, Grover A., et al. PPC Tax Planning Guide - Partnerships, 3 vols. Incl. Vol. 1. PPC Tax Planning Guide - Partnerships. 1998. ring bd. (*0-7646-0474-0*); Vol. 2. PPC Tax Planning Guide - Partnerships. 1998. ring bd. 180.00 (*0-7646-0501-1*); Vol. 3. PPC Tax Planning Guide - Partnerships. 1998. 180.00 (*0-7646-0502-X*); Vol. 1. 1997. ring bd. (*0-7646-0168-7*); Vol. 2. 1997. ring bd. (*0-7646-0169-5*); Vol. 3. 1997. ring bd. (*0-7646-0170-9*); 170.00 (*0-7646-0167-9*); 180.00 (*0-7646-0473-2*) Prctnrs Pub Co.
Cleveland, H. G. Genealogy of Benjamin Cleveland, Great-Grandson of Moses Cleveland of Woburn, Mass. Native of Canterbury Windham County, Connecticut. 260p. 1993. reprint ed. pap. 28.00 (*0-8328-1361-3*); reprint ed. lib. bdg. 38.00 (*0-8328-1360-5*) Higginson Bk Co.
Cleveland, Harlan. Birth of a New World. 260p. 1993. 25.95 (*0-614-02996-1*) Amer Forum.
— The Global Commons: Policy for the Planet. 130p. (C). 1990. pap. text 19.00 (*0-8191-7836-5*) U Pr of Amer.
— The Third Try at World Order. 140p. 1977. pap. text 14.50 (*0-8191-5901-8*) U Pr of Amer.
— Toward a Strategy for the Management of Peace: U. S. Foreign Policy in the 1980's. 1983. 1.00 (*1-55614-011-8*) U of SD Gov Res Bur.
— Triple Collision of Modernization. 17p. 1979. pap. 1.50 (*0-89940-000-0*) LBJ Sch Pub Aff.
Cleveland, Harlan, ed. Hero As Statesman: Political Leadership in Military Defense. LC 87-23135. (Readings for Leaders Ser.: Vol. I). 414p. (Orig.). (C). 1988. pap. text 33.00 (*0-8191-6516-6*); lib. bdg. 56.00 (*0-8191-6515-8*) U Pr of Amer.
Cleveland, Harlan & Bloomfield, Lincoln P., eds. Prospects for Peacemaking: A Citizen's Guide to Safer Nuclear Strategy. LC 87-2622. 176p. 1987. 20.00 (*0-262-03131-0*) MIT Pr.
Cleveland, Harlan, et al. The Overseas Americans. Bruchey, Stuart, ed. LC 80-558. (Multinational Corporations Ser.). 1981. reprint ed. lib. bdg. 36.95 (*0-405-13354-5*) Ayer.
Cleveland, Harlan, jt. auth. see Association of Governing Boards of Universities &.
Cleveland, Harland. World Affairs Don't Have to Be Boring. 1960. 2.50 (*0-87060-085-0*, PUC 11) Syracuse U Cont Ed.
Cleveland, Harold Van B. & Brittain, W. Bruce. The Great Inflation: A Monetarist View. LC 76-41068. 72p. 1976. 3.50 (*0-89068-003-5*) Natl Planning.
Cleveland, Harold Van B. & Huertas, Thomas F. Citibank, 1812-1970. (Studies in Business History: No. 37). (Illus.). 512p. 1985. 25.00 (*0-674-13175-4*) HUP.
Cleveland, Hugh. Cleveland's Bottle Pricing Guide. 3rd rev. ed. (Illus.). 256p. 1996. pap. 7.95 (*0-89145-137-4*, 1128) Collector Bks.

C

Cleveland Indians Wives' Association Staff. The Tribe's Home Plates. LC 92-23879. 1992. write for info. (*0-87197-343-X*) Favorite Recipes.

Cleveland, J. C. An Introduction to Data Types. LC 85-6002. (C). 1986. text 18.36 (*0-201-11940-4*) Addison-Wesley.

Cleveland, James O., jt. auth. see Peterson, Raymond M.

Cleveland, Jeanette, jt. auth. see Murphy, Kevin R.

***Cleveland, Jeanette N., et al.** Women & Men in Organizations: Sex & Gender Issues at Work. LC 99-37807. (Volume in the Applied Psychology Ser.). 472p. 1999. 99.95 (*0-8058-1267-9*); pap. text 42.50 (*0-8058-1268-7*) L Erlbaum Assocs.

Cleveland, Jess M. The Chemistry of Plutonium. LC 78-60617. (ANS Monographs). (Illus.). 1979. reprint ed. 64.00 (*0-89448-013-8*, 300014) Am Nuclear Soc.

Cleveland, Leah, et al. Nursing Pharmacology & Clinical Management. LC 98-25822. 1114p. 1998. text 51.95 (*0-397-55244-0*) Lppncott W & W.

Cleveland, Les. Dark Laughter: War in Song & Popular Culture. LC 93-26432. 232p. 1994. 55.00 (*0-275-94764-5*, Praeger Pubs) Greenwood.

***Cleveland, Martha.** Chronic Illness & the Twelve Steps: A Practical Approach to Spiritual Resilience. LC 99-16590. 155p. 1999. pap. text 12.00 (*1-56838-347-9*) Hazelden.

***Cleveland Museum of Art, et al.** Catalogue of Egyptian Art: The Cleveland Museum of Art. LC 99-10497. (Illus.). 568p. 1999. 75.00 (*0-940717-53-0*, Pub. by Cleveland Mus Art) Hudson Hills.

Cleveland Museum of Art Staff. Catalogue of the Severence & Greta Millikin Collection. LC 90-38882. (Illus.). 112p. reprint ed. pap. 34.80 (*0-7837-7084-7*, 204689700004) Bks Demand.

— Faberge & His Contemporaries: The India Early Minshall Collection of the Cleveland Museum of Art. LC 67-28951. (Illus.). 145p. reprint ed. pap. 45.00 (*0-7837-7085-5*, 204689800004) Bks Demand.

— Indian Art from the George P. Bickford Collection. LC 74-29377. (Illus.). 132p. reprint ed. pap. 41.00 (*0-608-11280-1*, 201449700092) Bks Demand.

— The World of Ceramics: Masterpieces from the Cleveland Museum of Art. Neils, Jenifer, ed. LC 82-1308. (Illus.). 176p. reprint ed. pap. 54.60 (*0-7837-7086-3*, 204689900004) Bks Demand.

Cleveland Museum of Art Staff & Cunningham, Michael R. Masterworks of Asian Art. LC 97-45033. 1998. write for info. (*0-940717-42-5*); pap. 59.03 (*0-940717-43-3*) Cleveland Mus Art.

Cleveland Museum of Art Staff, jt. auth. see Catholic Church Clergy Staff.

Cleveland Museum of Art Staff, jt. auth. see Fliegel, Stephen N.

Cleveland Museum of Art Staff, jt. auth. see Hawley, Henry H.

Cleveland Museum of Art Staff, ed. see Cunningham, Michael R., et al.

Cleveland Music of Art Staff, jt. auth. see Fliegel, Stephen N.

Cleveland, Norman. The Healer: The Story of Francis Schlatter. LC 89-19679. (Illus.). 160p. 1989. pap. 12.95 (*0-86534-139-7*) Sunstone Pr.

Cleveland, Paul. Trail of Dreams. 176p. 1998. pap. 10.95 (*1-57532-195-5*) Press-Tige Pub.

Cleveland Public Library Staff. Index to Negro Spirituals. LC 90-2026. (CBMR Monographs: No. 3). 89p. 1991. 10.00 (*0-929911-02-4*) CCCBMR.

Cleveland, Ray L. An Ancient South Arabian Necropolis: Objects from the Second Campaign, 1951, in the Timna Cemetery. LC 65-13520. (Publications of the American Foundation for the Study of Man: Vol. 4). 329p. 1965. reprint ed. pap. 102.00 (*0-608-03646-3*, 206447200009) Bks Demand.

Cleveland, Richard & Bister, Donna. Plain & Fancy: Vermont's People & Their Quilts As a Reflection of America. LC 90-28670. (Illus.). 104p. 1991. pap. 24.95 (*0-8442-2630-0*, Quilt Dgst Pr) NTC Contemp Pub Co.

Cleveland, Rose E. George Eliot's Poetry: And Other Studies. LC 74-4275. (Essay Index Reprint Ser.). 1977. reprint ed. 19.95 (*0-518-10176-2*) Ayer.

Cleveland, Sherwood M., et al. South Carolina Corporate Practice Manual, 2 vols., I. 1989. write for info. (*0-943856-10-8*) SC Bar CLE.

— South Carolina Corporate Practice Manual, 2 vols., II. 1989. write for info. (*0-318-67279-0*) SC Bar CLE.

— South Carolina Corporate Practice Manual, 2 vols., Set. 1989. ring bd. 225.00 (*0-943856-09-4*, 419) SC Bar CLE.

Cleveland, Shirley D. Arrows of Time Spun with Gold: Native Americans. (Poems of Life Ser.: Vol. 4). Date not set. pap. 9.98 (*0-9671225-3-8*) Lyons Media.

— Poems of Life: Pet Tales Spun with Gold. 1999. pap. 5.95 (*0-9671225-1-1*) Lyons Media.

— Poems of Life: Silver Memories Spun with Gold-"Yesterdays" on the Farm. (Illus.). 2000. per. 9.98 (*0-9671225-2-X*) Lyons Media.

— Poems of Life: Silver Thoughts Spun with Gold-Love-Hope-Faith. 1999. per. 12.95 (*0-9671225-0-3*) Lyons Media.

Cleveland, Stafford C. History & Directory of Yates County, New York, Vol. 1. (Illus.). 766p. 1993. reprint ed. lib. bdg. 77.00 (*0-8328-2907-2*) Higginson Bk Co.

— History of Yates County, Vol. II. (Illus.). 407p. 1997. reprint ed. lib. bdg. 45.00 (*0-8328-6283-5*) Higginson Bk Co.

Cleveland, Theodore G., ed. see American Water Resources Association, Annual Confe.

Cleveland, Timothy. Trying Without Willing: An Essay in the Philosophy of Mind. LC 97-71455. (Series in Philosophy). 208p. 1997. text 64.95 (*1-85972-674-7*, Pub. by Avebry) Ashgate Pub Co.

Cleveland, U. S., ed. see Williams, Lindsey.

Cleveland, Will. Yo, Sacramento! And All Those Other State Capitals You Don't Know. 1994. pap. 7.95 (*0-9632778-2-0*) Goodwood Pr.

Cleveland, Will & Alvarez, Mark. Yo, Millard Fillmore! And All Those Other Presidents You Don't Know. LC 96-42098. (Illus.). 116p. (J). (gr. 5-9). 1997. 6.95 (*0-7613-0236-0*) Millbrook Pr.

— Yo, Millard Fillmore! And All Those Other Presidents You Don't Know. LC 96-42098. (Illus.). 116p. (YA). (gr. 5-9). 1997. lib. bdg. 21.40 (*0-7613-0253-0*) Millbrook Pr.

— Yo! Millard Fillmore: And All Those Other Presidents You Never Heard Of. (Fundamental Memory Book). (Illus.). 112p. (J). (gr. 5). 1992. pap. 7.95 (*0-9632778-0-4*) Goodwood Pr.

— Yo, Millard Fillmore! And All Those Other Presidents You Never Heard Of. 2nd rev. ed. (Goodwood Memory Book). (Illus.). 112p. (Orig.). (J). (gr. 5). 1993. reprint ed. pap. write for info. (*0-9632778-1-2*) Goodwood Pr.

— Yo, Sacramento! All Those Capitals You Don't Know. LC 96-42099. (Illus.). 128p. (J). (gr. 5-9). 1997. 6.95 (*0-7613-0237-9*) Millbrook Pr.

— Yo, Sacramento! And All Those Other State Capitals You Don't Know. LC 96-42099. (Illus.). 128p. (YA). (gr. 5-9). 1997. lib. bdg. 21.40 (*0-7613-0252-2*) Millbrook Pr.

Cleveland, William. Art in Other Places: Artists at Work in America's Community & Social Institutions. LC 91-44570. 320p. 1992. 45.00 (*0-275-94054-3*, C4054, Praeger Pubs) Greenwood.

— The Creative Mind. 192p. (C). 1996. pap. text, per. write for info. (*0-7872-2770-6*) Kendall-Hunt.

— Islam Against the West: Shakib Arslan & the Campaign for Islamic Nationalism. 247p. 1996. 22.50 (*0-614-21483-1*, 537) Kazi Pubns.

— Pak: The Creative Mind. 516p. 1997. pap. text 87.95 (*0-7872-3264-5*, 41326401) Kendall-Hunt.

Cleveland, William, jt. auth. see McCord, David.

Cleveland, William A., ed. Britannica Atlas. (Illus.). 560p. 1992. 99.50 (*0-85229-582-0*) Ency Brit Inc.

Cleveland, William C. & McGill, Marylyn E. Dynamic Graphics for Statistics. LC 88-26017. 455p. (C). (gr. 13). 1988. ring bd. 83.95 (*0-534-09144-X*, Chap & Hall CRC) CRC Pr.

Cleveland, William C., jt. auth. see Delivanis, Demetre J.

Cleveland, William L. History of the Modern Middle East. 528p. (C). 1993. pap. 45.00 (*0-8133-0563-2*, Pub. by Westview) HarpC.

***Cleveland, William L.** A History of the Modern Middle East. 2nd ed. LC 99-36867. 592p. 1999. pap. 32.00 (*0-8133-3489-6*) Westview.

Cleveland, William L. Islam Against the West: Shakib Arslan & the Campaign for Islamic Nationalism. LC 84-29124. (Modern Middle East Ser.: No. 10). 247p. reprint ed. pap. 76.60 (*0-608-20100-6*, 207137200011) Bks Demand.

— The Making of an Arab Nationalist: Ottomanism & Arabism in the Life & Thought of Sati Al-Husri. LC 78-155961. (Princeton Studies on the Near East). 227p. 1971. reprint ed. pap. 70.40 (*0-608-03762-1*, 206458500009) Bks Demand.

Cleveland, William S. The Elements of Graphing Data. rev. ed. LC 94-75052. (Illus.). 323p. 1994. lib. bdg. 45.00 (*0-9634884-1-4*, Chap & Hall CRC) CRC Pr.

— Elements of Graphing Data. 2nd ed. 1993. 39.95 (*0-442-01623-9*) Chapman & Hall.

— Visualizing Data. LC 92-75077. (Illus.). 360p. 1993. 45.00 (*0-9634884-0-6*) Hobart Pr.

Cleveland, William S., ed. see Tukey, John W.

Cleveland, Williams S., ed. The Collected Works of John W. Tukey: Graphics 1965-1985, Vol. 5. (Statistics-Probability Ser.). (Illus.). 646p. 1988. ring bd. 83.95 (*0-412-99261-2*, Chap & Hall CRC) CRC Pr.

***Clevely, A.** Geoff Hamilton's Year in Your Garden. 1998. text 35.00 (*0-7472-2231-2*, Pub. by Headline Bk Pub) Trafalgar.

***Clevely, Andi.** Complete Book of Herbs: The Ultimate Guide to Herbs & Their Uses. 1999. 19.98 (*1-84038-099-3*) Hermes Hse.

— Herb Identifier: Illustrated Encyclopedia. (Illus.). 129p. 1999. 9.95 (*0-7548-0002-4*) Anness Pub.

Clevely, Andi. The Kitchen Garden Month-by-Month. (Illus.). 144p. 1996. 24.95 (*0-7153-0329-5*, Pub. by D & C Pub) Sterling.

— Kitchen Garden Month by Month. (Illus.). 144p. 1998. pap. 14.95 (*0-7153-0708-8*, Pub. by D & C Pub) Sterling.

***Clevely, Andi.** The Water Garden: Month-by-Month. (Illus.). 144p. 1999. 14.95 (*0-7153-0831-9*, Pub. by D & C Pub) Sterling.

Clevely, Andi & Richmond, Katherine. The Complete Book of Herbs. (Illus.). 256p. 1994. 19.98 (*0-8317-1164-7*) Smithmark.

Clevelyd, Andi. Water Garden Month by Month. 1998. 24.95 (*0-7153-0575-1*, Pub. by D & C Pub) Sterling.

Cleven, Harry T., tr. see Ager, Waldemar.

Clevenger, Bev. Learn Together! Discovering, Organizing & Designing Cooperative Classrooms. Mitchell, Judy, ed. (Illus.). 128p. (Orig.). (J). (gr. 3-6). 1995. pap., teacher ed. 12.95 (*1-57310-035-8*) Teachng & Lrnng Co.

Clevenger, Ernest, Jr. General Bible Knowledge Bible Drill: Flash Cards Flipbook. (Bible Drill Flash Cards Flipbook Ser.). 104p. 1994. pap. 5.95 (*0-88428-017-9*) Parchment Pr.

Clevenger, Ernest. Leadership Training. (Illus.). 56p. 1992. pap. 6.00 (*0-88428-058-6*) Parchment Pr.

Clevenger, Ernest, Jr. Referecia Rapida de la Biblia. (Parchment Ready Reference Ser.). 1987. pap. 2.00 (*0-88428-054-3*) Parchment Pr.

Clevenger, Ernest. Russian-English Reference Guide for Studying the Bible. Salurien, Eugene, tr. (Parchment Ready Reference Ser.). (ENG & RUS.). 36p. 1992. pap. 2.50 (*0-88428-062-4*) Parchment Pr.

Clevenger, Ernest A., Jr. Bible Characters. (Bible Drill Flash Cards Flipbook Ser.). (J). (gr. 3 up). 1994. pap. 5.95 (*0-88428-018-7*) Parchment Pr.

— The Church. (Bible Drill Flash Cards Flipbook Ser.). 104p. (J). (gr. 3 up). 1994. pap. 5.95 (*0-88428-016-0*) Parchment Pr.

— A Pocket Bible Ready Reference for Personal Workers. 31st ed. (Parchment Ready Reference Ser.). 24p. (Orig.). 1994. pap. 2.00 (*0-88428-011-X*) Parchment Pr.

Clevenger, Ernest A., Jr. & Clevenger, Glenda W. Comprehensive Topical & Textual Lesson Commentary Index: 1922-1982. 4th ed. 114p. 1981. pap. text 8.95 (*0-88428-019-5*) Parchment Pr.

Clevenger, Glenda W., jt. auth. see Clevenger, Ernest A., Jr.

***Clevenger, L., et al, eds.** Gate Stack & Silicide Issues in Silicon Processing: Materials Research Society Symposium Proceedings, Vol. 611. 2000. text 77.00 (*1-55899-519-6*) Materials Res.

***Clevenger, Larry E.** From the Inner Self. 85p. 1999. 29.50 (*1-57529-077-4*) Kabel Pubs.

Clevenger, Lisa, et al. The Alternate Reality Romance Guide: A Reader's & Collector's Resource for the Paranormal Sub Genres. (Illus.). 175p. 1998. spiral bd. 24.95 (*0-9647291-7-2*, COL01) Blue Diamond Pubns.

Clevenger, Martha, ed. Indescribably Grand: Diaries & Letters from the 1904 World's Fair. LC 96-12981. (Illus.). 156p. 1996. 34.95 (*1-883982-14-6*); pap. 24.95 (*1-883982-09-X*) MO Hist Soc.

Clevenger, Mary A., et al, eds. Phase Equilibria Diagrams, 1996 Cumulative Indexes. 246p. (Orig.). 1996. pap. 15.00 (*1-57498-015-7*, PHIN96) Am Ceramic.

Clevenger, Patsy. The Collector's World of M&Ms: An Unauthorized Handbook & Price Guide. LC 97-80155. (Illus.). 128p. 1998. pap. 16.95 (*0-7643-0406-2*) Schiffer.

Clevenger, Shobal V. A Treatise on the Method of Government Surveying. 1978. reprint ed. pap. 12.00 (*0-686-25541-0*) CARBEN Survey.

Clevenger, Toni M. On the Bay - on the Hill: The Story of the First Baptist Church of Pensacola, Florida. Trotter, Martha P., ed. LC 86-82174. (Illus.). xiv, 338p. 1986. 19.95 (*0-9617503-0-8*) FBC Pensacola.

Clevenger, Toni Moore, ed. see Trotter, Martha Pope.

***Clevenot, Dominique.** Splendors of Islam: Architecture, Decoration, & Design. LC 00-38147. (Illus.). 224p. 2000. 70.00 (*0-86565-214-7*) Vendome.

Clevenot, Michel. Materialist Approaches to the Bible. Nottingham, William J., tr. LC 84-14711. 160p. (Orig.). 1985. reprint ed. pap. 49.60 (*0-7837-9820-2*, 206054900005) Bks Demand.

Clever. Argon. (Solubility Data Ser.). 1980. 130.00 (*0-08-023951-X*, Pergamon Pr) Elsevier.

— Helium & Neon. (Solubility Data Ser.). 1979. 130.00 (*0-08-023948-X*, Pergamon Pr) Elsevier.

— Krypton, Xenon, & Radon. (Solubility Data Ser.). 1979. 130.00 (*0-08-023949-8*, Pergamon Pr) Elsevier.

— Mercury in Liquids, Compressed Gases, Molten Salts & Other Elements. (IUPAC Solubility Data Ser.: 29). 272p. 1987. 167.00 (*0-08-035935-3*, Pergamon Pr) Elsevier.

Clever, H. L., et al. Methane. (IUPAC Solubility Data Ser.: 27). 808p. 1987. 316.50 (*0-08-029200-3*, Pergamon Pr) Elsevier.

Cleverdon, Catherine L. The Woman Suffrage Movement in Canada: The Start of Liberation. LC 73-82587. (Social History of Canada Ser.). 1974. pap. text 12.95 (*0-8020-6218-0*) U of Toronto Pr.

Cleverdon, Douglas. The Growth of Milkwood. LC 79-75384. 1969. 8.50 (*0-8112-0260-7*, Pub. by New Directions) Norton.

***Cleverdon, Mickey.** Questions of Form. (Illus.). 36p. 1999. pap. write for info. (*0-9643940-3-0*) Slow Loris Pr.

***Cleverley, James, et al.** The Spirit of a Buckeye: Brutus Buckeye's Lessons for Life. 28p. 1999. pap. write for info. (*0-9675664-0-1*) Cleverley Create.

***Cleverley, John.** In the Lap of Tigers: The Communist Labor University of Jiangxi Province. LC 99-56024. 256p. 2000. pap. 21.95 (*0-8476-9937-4*); text 60.00 (*0-8476-9936-6*) Rowman.

Cleverley, John F. & Phillips, D. C. Visions of Childhood: Influential Models from Locke to Spock. (Early Childhood Education Ser.). 176p. 1986. pap. text 18.95 (*0-8077-2800-4*) Tchrs Coll.

Cleverley, William O. Essentials of Health Care Finance. 4th ed. LC 96-29878. 592p. 1997. 49.00 (*0-8342-0736-2*, 20736) Aspen Pub.

— Handbook of Health Care Accounting & Finance, 2 vols. 2nd ed. 1043p. 1989. 270.00 (*0-8342-0056-2*) Aspen Pub.

— The 1995 Almanac of Hospital Financial & Operating Indicators. 516p. 1995. pap. 350.00 (*1-882733-04-5*) Ctr Hlthcare IPS.

— The 1994 Almanac of Hospital Financial & Operating Indicators. 516p. 1994. pap. 350.00 (*1-882733-02-9*) Ctr Hlthcare IPS.

— The 1996-97 Almanac of Hospital Financial & Operating Indicators. 520p. 1996. pap. 350.00 (*1-882733-07-X*) Ctr Hlthcare IPS.

— The 1993 Almanac of Hospital Financial & Operating Indicators. 520p. 1993. pap. 350.00 (*1-882733-01-0*) Ctr Hlthcare IPS.

Cleverley, William O. & Knott, Patrick J. The 1997-98 Physician Practice Acquisition Resource Book. 280p. 1997. pap. 295.00 (*1-882733-09-6*) Ctr Hlthcare IPS.

Cleverley, William O., et al. Physician Practice Acquisition Resource Book. (Illus.). 221p. 1995. pap. 995.00 (*1-882733-06-1*) Ctr Hlthcare IPS.

Clevers, J. G. Application of Remote Sensing to Agricultural. (C). 1981. text 460.00 (*0-89771-587-X*, Pub. by Intl Bk Distr) St Mut.

Clevers, Jan G., jt. ed. see Buiten, Henk J.

Cleves, William, tr. see Fuchs, Josef.

Clevett, Kenneth J. Process Analyzer Technology. LC 85-26302. 960p. 1986. 265.00 (*0-471-88316-6*) Wiley.

Clevinger, Mary A. & Cedeno, Christine L., eds. Phase Equilibria Diagrams Cumulative Index, 1998. (Illus.). 285p. 1998. pap. 15.00 (*1-57498-087-4*, PHIN98) Am Ceramic.

Clew, J. R. The Restoration of Vintage & Thoroughbred Motorcycles. LC 78-311857. 2-208 p. 1976. 6.95 (*0-85429-185-7*) GT Foulis.

***Clew, Jeff.** Haynes: The First 40 Years. (Illus.). 160p. 2000. 39.95 (*1-85960-418-8*, 130426AE, Pub. by Haynes Manuals) Motorbooks Intl.

Clew, Jeff. Haynes Bultaco Competition Bikes Owners Workshop Manual, No. 219: '72-'75. 1979. 23.95 (*0-85696-219-8*) Haynes Manuals.

— Haynes Honda 750 sohc Fours Owners Workshop Manual, No. 131: '69-'79. 1979. 23.95 (*0-85696-521-9*) Haynes Manuals.

— Haynes Norton Commando Owners Workshop Manual, No. 125: '68-'77. (Illus.). 1979. 23.95 (*0-85696-125-6*) Haynes Manuals.

— Haynes Triumph Pre-Unit Twins Owners Workshop Manual, No. 251: '47-'62. 1979. 23.95 (*0-85696-251-1*) Haynes Manuals.

— Haynes Vespa Scooters Owners Workshop Manual, No. 126: '59-'78. 1979. 23.95 (*0-85696-126-4*) Haynes Manuals.

— Haynes Yamaha 500 Twin Owners Workshop Manual, No. 308: '73-'76. 1980. 16.95 (*0-85696-308-9*) Haynes Manuals.

— The Restoration of Vintage & Thoroughbred Motorcycles. 2nd ed. (Illus.). 200p. 1991. 36.95 (*0-85429-853-3*, F185, Pub. by GT Foulis) Haynes Manuals.

— Veteran Motorcycles. (Album Ser.: No. 313). (Illus.). 32p. 1995. pap. 4.75 (*0-7478-0276-9*, Pub. by Shire Pubns) Parkwest Pubns.

— Vintage Motorcycles. (Album Ser.: No. 314). (Illus.). 32p. 1995. pap. 4.75 (*0-7478-0277-7*, Pub. by Shire Pubns) Parkwest Pubns.

Clew, Jeff & Rogers, Chris. Haynes Triumph 650 & 750 4-Valve Twins Owners Workshop Manual, No. 122: '63-'83. 1981. 23.95 (*0-85696-890-0*) Haynes Manuals.

Clew, Jeff & Strasman, Peter G. Haynes BSA A7 & A10 Twins Owners Workshop Manual, No. 121: '47-'62. 1979. 23.95 (*0-85696-121-3*) Haynes Manuals.

Clewell, Andre F. Guide to the Vascular Plants of the Florida Panhandle. LC 84-29126. (Illus.). 605p. 1985. pap. 39.95 (*0-8130-0896-4*) U Press Fla.

Clewell, Beatriz C. & Anderson, Bernice. Women of Color in Mathematics, Science, & Engineering: A Review of the Literature. (Educational Equity Policy Studies). 104p. (C). 1991. pap. 10.00 (*1-877966-04-5*) Ctr Women Policy.

Clewell, Beatriz C., et al. Breaking the Barriers: Helping Female & Minority Students Succeed in Mathematics & Science. LC 92-21619. (Education-Higher Education Ser.). 352p. 1992. text 38.45 (*1-55542-482-1*) Jossey-Bass.

Clewell, D. B. Bacterial Conjugation. (Illus.). 430p. (C). 1993. text 110.00 (*0-306-44376-7*, Kluwer Plenum) Kluwer Academic.

Clewell, David. The Conspiracy Quartet. 65p. 1997. pap. 12.00 (*0-9643009-2-3*) Garlic Pr MO.

***Clewell, David.** Jack Ruby's America. 50p. 2000. pap. 12.00 (*0-9643009-3-1*) Garlic Pr MO.

Clewell, David. Lost in the Fire. 32p. (Orig.). 1993. pap. 6.95 (*0-9643009-0-7*) Garlic Pr MO.

— Now We're Getting Somewhere. LC 94-10665. (Felix Pollak Prize in Poetry Ser.). 96p. 1994. pap. 11.95 (*0-299-14414-3*) U of Wis Pr.

— Room to Breathe. deluxe limited ed. LC 76-42865. 1976. 15.00 (*0-915316-30-7*) Pentagram.

Clewell, Kathleen M., ed. see Lumpkin, Libby O. & Wynn, Stephen A.

Clewer, Ann D. E. & Perkins, David. An Introduction to Health Economics: Theory & Cases. 224p. 1998. pap. 45.00 (*0-13-209461-4*) P-H.

Clewes, Quentin. Jetlag. 300p. 1995. 16.95 (*1-56886-008-0*, Eridanos Library) Marsilio Pubs.

Clewett, A. J., jt. ed. see Clementson, Alan.

Clewett, Annette. Resource Planning Using SAP R/3, Baan, & Peoplesoft. LC 98-21011. (Illus.). 416p. 1998. pap. 49.95 (*0-07-913647-8*) McGraw.

Clewley, Che'rune. Life's Trek. LC 99-475894. 32p. 1999. pap. 8.00 (*1-886094-96-9*) Chicago Spectrum.

Clewley, John. Making Out in Thai. LC 95-174525. (THA.). 104p. (Orig.). 1994. pap. 6.95 (*4-900737-01-1*) Tuttle Pubng.

Clewley, Jonathan P. Polymerase Chain Reaction (PCR) for Human Viral Diagnosis. 240p. 1994. lib. bdg. 79.95 (*0-8493-4833-1*) CRC Pr.

Clewlow, C. W., Jr., et al. Archaeological & Ethnohistoric Investigations at CA-NEV-194, Near Rough & Ready, Nevada County, California. (Archives of California Prehistory Ser.: Vol. 31). (Illus.). 104p. (Orig.). (C). 1990. pap. text 11.56 (*1-55567-071-7*) Coyote Press.

— Papers on the Archaeology of Western Great Basin. fac. ed. (Reports of the University of California Archaeological Survey: No. 73). 245p. 1968. reprint ed. pap. 25.63 (*1-55567-389-9*) Coyote Press.

Clewlow, L. & Strickland, C. Exotic Options: The State of the Art. 256p. (gr. 13). 1997. mass mkt. 129.95 (*0-412-63170-9*) Chapman & Hall.

Clewlow, Les. Option Pricing: Numerical Methods. LC 97-36998. 330p. 1998. 89.95 (*0-471-96651-7*) Wiley.

An Asterisk (*) at the beginning of an entry indicates that the title is appearing for the first time.

Clewlow, Les & Strickland, Chris. Exotic Options: The State of the Art. 232p. 1998. pap. 85.00 (*1-86152-321-1*) Thomson Learn.
Clews, Henry. Fifty Years in Wall Street. LC 73-2948. (Big Business; Economic Power in a Free Society Ser.). 1973. reprint ed. 66.95 (*0-405-05079-8*) Ayer.
— Wall Street Point of View. LC 68-28620. (Illus.). 290p. 1968. reprint ed. lib. bdg. 65.00 (*0-8371-0048-8*, CLWS, Greenwood Pr) Greenwood.
Clews, Maire. Once upon a Time at La Napoule: The Memoirs of Marie Clews. LC 98-5230. 1998. pap. 17.95 (*1-889833-03-7*) Memoirs Unltd.
Clews, R. Textbook of Insurance Broking. (C). 1987. 250.00 (*0-7855-4051-2*, Pub. by Witherby & Co) St Mut.
Clews, Roy. The Drums of War. large type ed. 560p. 1982. 27.99 (*0-7089-0866-7*) Ulverscroft.
— The Golden City. large type ed. 400p. 1983. 11.50 (*0-7089-0914-0*) Ulverscroft.
— The King's Bounty. large type ed. 686p. (Orig.). 1982. 27.99 (*0-7089-0782-2*) Ulverscroft.
— To Dream of Freedom. 1988. 25.00 (*0-904864-95-2*, Pub. by Y Lolfa) St Mut.
— The Valiant & the Damned. large type ed. Orig. Title: Young Jethro. 450p. 1982. 27.99 (*0-7089-0740-7*) Ulverscroft.
Clews, Vince, jt. auth. see Reiff, Tana.
Cleymans, J., ed. Phase Structure of Strongly Interacting Matter: Proceedings of a Summer School on Theoretical Physics Held at the University of Cape Town, South Africa January 8-19, 1990. (Illus.). 480p. 1991. 79.95 (*0-387-53138-6*) Spr-Verlag.
Cleymans, J., et al, eds. Hadrons in Dense Matter & Hadrosynthesis: Proceedings of the 11th Chris Engelbrecht Summer School, Held in Cape Town, South Africa, 4-13 February, 1998. LC 98-51427. xii, 248p. 1999. 73.00 (*3-540-65209-4*) Spr-Verlag.
Cleyre, Voltairine De, see De Cleyre, Voltairine.
Clezia, J. M. Le, see Le Clezia, J. M.
Clezio, Alexandrina Le, see Le Clezio, Alexandrina.
Clezio, Jean M. La Conquista Divina de Michoacan. (SPA.). pap. 9.99 (*968-16-1997-8*, Pub. by Fondo) Continental Bk.
Clezy, Gillian, et al. Communication Disorders: An Introduction for Community-Based Rehabilitation Workers. LC 97-143638. (Illus.). 172p. (Orig.). 1996. pap. 34.50 (*962-209-389-2*, Pub. by HK Univ Pr) Coronet Bks.
Cliacon, Kurt & Julian, Grant S. The Ultimate Fantasy Football Notebook. 175p. 1992. 19.92 (*0-9634280-0-4*) Going Deep.
Cliatt, Mary Jo Puckett. Helping Children Explore Science. (C). 1991. pap. text 22.00 (*0-675-21325-8*, Merrill Coll) P-H.
***Clibon, Esther E.** A Colorado Story: A Passion for the Prairie. Harris, Helen, ed. (Illus.). 144p. 1999. pap. write for info. (*0-9665113-2-8*, Cheyenne) Masters Page.
Cliburn, Jill K., ed. Great Lakes Regional Biomass Energy Program: Activities & Accomplishments, 1994. (Illus.). 54p. 1998. pap. text 20.00 (*0-7881-4198-8*) DIANE Pub.
Click. Administration of Schools for Young Children. 5th ed. LC 99-14793. (Early Childhood Education Ser.). 448p. (C). 1999. pap. 39.95 (*0-7668-0354-6*) Delmar.
— Caring for School Age Children. (Teaching Methods Ser.). 1992. pap., teacher ed. 14.00 (*0-8273-5412-6*) Delmar.
— Caring For School Age Children. 2nd ed. (Early Childhood Education Ser.). 1998. teacher ed. 10.50 (*0-8273-7693-6*) Delmar.
Click, Donald W. & Click, Phyllis M. Administration of Schools for Young Children. 4th ed. LC 95-4185. 416p. (C). 1995. pap. 26.25 (*0-8273-5876-8*) Delmar.
Click, E. Dale. Evangelism. LC 94-68890. 1996. 13.95 (*1-55673-958-3*, Fairway Pr) CSS OH.
— Have You Met Jesus? Eight Studies on His Life & Times. LC 96-44069. 74p. 1997. pap. 9.95 (*0-7880-1016-6*, Fairway Pr) CSS OH.
***Click, E. Dale.** The Inner Circle: Studying the Lives of 13 Apostles. LC 99-55448. 2000. pap. 7.50 (*0-7880-1590-7*) CSS OH.
Click, J. William & Baird, Russell N. Magazine Editing & Production. 6th ed. LC 91-22489. 336p. (C). 1993. text 40.50 (*0-697-13930-1*) Brown & Benchmark.
Click, Patricia C. The Spirit of the Times: Amusements in Nineteenth-Century Baltimore, Norfolk, & Richmond. LC 89-5303. (Illus.). 187p. reprint ed. pap. 58.00 (*0-608-20043-3*, 207131500011) Bks Demand.
Click, Phyllis. Administration of Schools for Young Children. (Early Childhood Education Ser.). 1996. pap., teacher ed. 10.00 (*0-8273-5877-6*) Delmar.
— Administration of Schools for Young Children. 3rd ed. (Early Childhood Education Ser.). 244p. 1990. pap., teacher ed. 10.50 (*0-8273-3658-6*); pap. text 26.00 (*0-8273-3657-8*) Delmar.
— Caring for School Age Children. 213p. 1992. pap. 21.00 (*0-8273-5411-8*) Delmar.
— Caring for School Age Children. 2nd ed. LC 97-20831. (Early Childhood Education Ser.). 288p. (C). 1997. mass mkt. 40.95 (*0-8273-7692-8*) Delmar.
Click, Phyllis M. Understanding Child Development. 3rd ed. 1992. pap., student ed. 15.95 (*0-8273-4893-2*) Delmar.
Click, Phyllis M., jt. auth. see Click, Donald W.
Click, Reid W., jt. ed. see Aliber, Robert Z.
Click, Sharon, ed. see Ray, Walter.
***Clidienst, George.** The Protege. LC 99-90156. 310p. 1999. 24.00 (*0-9670459-0-8*) Odin Pr AZ.
Clief, Ron Van, see Van Clief, Ron.
Cliff. No Telephone to Heaven. 1995. pap. 8.95 (*0-07-546059-9*) McGraw.
***Cliff, A. D., et al.** Island Epidemics. LC 99-45685. 500p. 2000. 105.00 (*0-19-828895-6*) OUP.
Cliff, Andrew, et al, eds. Diffusing Geography: Essays for Peter Haggett. (IBG Special Publications). (Illus.). 384p. (C). 1995. text 92.95 (*0-631-19534-3*) Blackwell Pubs.
Cliff, Andrew, et al. Deciphering Global Epidemics: Analytical Approaches to the Disease Records of World Cities, 1888-1912. LC 97-27050. (Cambridge Studies in Historical Geography: No. 26). (Illus.). 496p. (C). 1998. text 74.95 (*0-521-47266-0*); pap. text 29.95 (*0-521-47860-X*) Cambridge U Pr.
— Measles: A History. (Illus.). 500p. 1994. text 184.95 (*0-631-16235-6*) Blackwell Pubs.
Cliff, DAvid, et al, eds. From Animals to Animates 3: Proceedings of the Third International Conference on Simulation of Adaptive Behavior. (Bradford Series in Complex Adaptive Systems). (Illus.). 608p. 1994. pap. text 62.50 (*0-262-53122-4*, Bradford Bks) MIT Pr.
Cliff, Gerald H., jt. ed. see Allison, Bruce N.
Cliff House Staff. Dining at the Cliff House: Food That Has Delighted Guests since 1872. LC 96-220219. (Illus.). 75p. (Orig.). 1996. pap. 16.95 (*0-9653243-1-1*) Cliff Hse.
Cliff, Michelle. Abeng. 224p. 1995. pap. 11.95 (*0-452-27483-4*, Plume) Dutton Plume.
— No Telephone to Heaven. 224p. 1996. pap. 12.95 (*0-452-27569-5*, Plume) Dutton Plume.
— The Store of a Million Items. LC 97-43805. 128p. 1998. pap. 12.00 (*0-395-90129-4*, Mariner Bks) HM.
Cliff, Michelle, ed. see Smith, Lillian.
***Cliff, Norman.** A Flame of Sacred Love. 130p. 1998. reprint ed. pap. 9.99 (*1-85078-328-4*, Pub. by O M Pubng) OM Literature.
Cliff, Norman. Ordinal Methods for Behavioral Data Analysis. LC 96-22689. 224p. 1996. 45.00 (*0-8058-1333-0*) L Erlbaum Assocs.
Cliff, Roger, jt. auth. see Byman, Daniel L.
Cliff, Stafford. English Archive of Design & Decoration. LC 98-8466. (Illus.). 256p. 1998. 65.00 (*0-8109-3264-4*, Pub. by Abrams) Time Warner.
— 50 Trade Secrets of Great Design: Packing. (Trade Secrets Ser.). 224p. 1999. 50.00 (*1-56496-599-6*) Rockport Pubs.
— 50 Trade Secrets of Great Design, Retail Spaces. (Trade Secrets Ser.). 224p. 1999. 50.00 (*1-56496-600-3*) Rockport Pubs.
***Cliff, Stafford.** The French Archive of Design & Decoration. 256p. 1999. 75.00 (*0-8109-3338-1*, Pub. by Abrams) Time Warner.
— London Rooms: Portfolios from 40 European Interior Designers. (Illus.). 2000. 45.00 (*1-56496-498-1*) Rockport Pubs.
Cliff, Tony. State Capitalism in Russia. 1974. pap. text 5.95 (*0-902818-51-1*) Pluto GBR.
Cliff, Walter J. Blood Vessels. LC 74-31789. (Biological Structure & Function Ser.: No. 6). 224p. reprint ed. pap. 63.90 (*0-8357-7328-0*, 2029215) Bks Demand.
Cliffe. Radial Arm Saw Basics. 1991. pap. 12.95 (*0-8273-5385-5*) Delmar.
Cliffe, et al. Government & Rural Development in East Africa: Essays on Political Penetration. (Development of Societies Ser.: No. 2). 1977. pap. text 78.50 (*90-247-1884-8*) Kluwer Academic.
Cliffe, Albert. Let Go & Let God: Steps in Victorious Living. rev. ed. 176p. 1992. pap. 10.00 (*0-671-76396-2*) Simon & Schuster.
Cliffe, Albert, ed. Let Go & Let God. (C). 1990. pap. 30.00 (*0-85305-233-6*, Pub. by Arthur James) St Mut.
Cliffe, J. T. The World of the Country House in Seventeenth-Century England. LC 98-49211. (Illus.). 240p. 1999. 45.00 (*0-300-07643-6*) Yale U Pr.
Cliffe, Ken, et al. Chicago Chronicles: Milwaukee by Night/Ashes to Ashes/Blood Bond. (Vampire Ser.: Vol. 3). (Illus.). 150p. 1996. pap. 20.00 (*1-56504-221-2*, 2236) White Wolf.
Cliffe, Lionel & Davidson, Basil Risbridger, eds. The Long Struggle of Eritrea for Independence & Constructive Peace. LC 88-62161. 230p. (C). 1988. 29.95 (*0-932415-36-9*); pap. 9.95 (*0-932415-37-7*) Red Sea Pr.
***Cliffe, Lionel, et al.** The Politics of Lying: Implications for Democracy. LC 99-53561. 288p. 2000. text 45.00 (*0-312-23139-3*) St Martin.
Cliffe, Lionel, jt. auth. see Stoneman, Colin.
Cliffe, Roger. Shaper Project. 1998. write for info. (*0-8069-9777-X*) Sterling.
— Table Saw: Workshop Bench Reference. LC 99-12494. (Illus.). 160p. 1999. 17.95 (*0-8069-9779-6*) Sterling.
Cliffe, Roger W. Radial Arm Saw Basics. LC 91-20004. (Basics Ser.). (Illus.). 128p. 1991. pap. 10.95 (*0-8069-7218-1*) Sterling.
Cliffe, Roger W. Radial Arm Saw Techniques. LC 86-898. (Illus.). 352p. (Orig.). 1986. pap. 17.95 (*0-8069-6280-1*) Sterling.
Cliffe, Roger W. Table Saw Basics. LC 84-8676. (Basics Ser.). (Illus.). 128p. 1991. pap. 10.95 (*0-8069-7216-5*) Sterling.
Cliffe, Roger W. & Adams, Marc. Working with Plastic Laminates: A Home Craftsman's Handbook. LC 94-16845. (Illus.). 224p. 1994. pap. 19.95 (*0-8069-0570-0*) Sterling.
Cliffe, Roger W. & Holtz, Michael. Shaper Handbook. LC 90-40300. (Illus.). 256p. (Orig.). 1990. pap. 17.95 (*0-8069-6798-6*) Sterling.
Cliffes, Roger. Table Saw Techniques. rev. ed. LC 97-19321. (Illus.). 352p. 1997. 18.95 (*0-8069-4268-1*) Sterling.
Clifford. Algebras & Their Application in Mathematical Physic Saachen 1996. LC 98-13118. 1998. text 195.00 (*0-7923-5037-5*) Kluwer Academic.
Clifford. Brief History of End-Time. 1997. pap. 12.95 (*0-7459-3460-9*, Pub. by Lion Pubng) Trafalgar.
— Decision Making in Organizations. Date not set. pap. text. write for info. (*0-582-35539-7*, Pub. by Addison-Wesley) Longman.
Clifford. Environment Crime. 1998. teacher ed. 49.00 (*0-8342-1172-6*) Aspen Pub.
Clifford. Expanding Horizons. 1997. pap. 10.95 (*0-7459-3697-0*, Pub. by Lion Pubng) Trafalgar.
Clifford. Magnificent Myths. 1992. mass mkt. 10.95 (*0-8359-0207-2*) P-H.
— Organisational Decision Making: Student Book. 1992. pap. text, student ed. write for info. (*0-582-08113-1*, Pub. by Addison-Wesley) Longman.
Clifford, jt. auth. see Berg.
Clifford, A. Golden Cage. mass mkt. 6.95 (*0-7472-5146-0*, Pub. by Headline Bk Pub) Trafalgar.
— Paradise Garden. mass mkt. 6.95 (*0-7472-5069-3*, Pub. by Headline Bk Pub) Trafalgar.
— Strangers in the Night. mass mkt. 6.95 (*0-7472-5155-7*, Pub. by Headline Bk Pub) Trafalgar.
Clifford, A. H. & Preston, G. B. The Algebraic Theory of Semigroups, 2 pts., Pt. 1. LC 61-15686. (Mathematical Surveys Ser.). 224p. 1961. pap. 38.00 (*0-8218-0271-2*, SURV/7.1) Am Math.
— The Algebraic Theory of Semigroups, 2 pts., Pt. 2. LC 61-15686. (Mathematical Surveys Ser.). 352p. 1967. pap. 49.00 (*0-8218-0272-0*, SURV/7.2) Am Math.
Clifford, A. Jerome. Independence of the Federal Reserve System. LC 63-7862. 436p. 1965. 42.95 (*0-8122-7388-5*) U of Pa Pr.
Clifford, Alan C. Atonement & Justification: English Evangelical Theology, 1640-1790: An Evaluation. (Illus.). 284p. 1990. text 68.00 (*0-19-826195-0*) OUP.
Clifford, Alan N. The Fatherland Files. LC 93-45741. 288p. 1994. 22.00 (*1-56881-034-2*) AK Peters.
Clifford, Andrew J., ed. Mathematical Modeling in Experimental Nutrition: Proceedings of a Conference Held in Davis, California, August 17-20, 1997. LC 98-8315. (Advances in Experimental Medicine & Biology Ser.: Vol. 445). (Illus.). 436p. (C). 1998. text 125.00 (*0-306-46020-3*, Kluwer Plenum) Kluwer Academic.
Clifford, Angela & MacDonald, Jack. Goals 2000: Educate America ACT State Profiles. 210p. (Orig.). 1996. pap. 10.00 (*1-884037-19-4*) Coun Chief St Schl Offs.
Clifford, Ann. The Diary of Lady Ann Clifford. Barrios, Isabella, ed. 200p. 1997. pap. 9.95 (*1-888087-08-0*) Aardvark Pr CO.
Clifford, Anne. Introducing Feminist Theology. 140p. 1999. pap. 15.00 (*1-57075-238-9*) Orbis Bks.
Clifford, Anne, jt. compiled by see Katz, Bill.
Clifford, Anthony. Fundamentals of Supercritical Fluids. LC 98-19460. (Illus.). 224p. 1999. text 100.00 (*0-19-850137-4*) OUP.
Clifford, Anthony A., jt. ed. see Williams, John R.
***Clifford, Barry.** Brethren of the Sword. 2000. 27.50 (*0-06-019818-4*); pap. 14.00 (*0-06-095779-4*) HarpC.
— Expedition Whydah: The Story of the World's First Excavation of a Pirate Treasure Ship & the Man Who Found Her. 320p. 2000. pap. 15.00 (*0-06-092971-5*, Cliff Street) HarperTrade.
Clifford, Barry & Perry, Paul. Expedition Whydah: The Story of the World's First Excavation of a Pirate Treasure Ship & the Man Who Found Her. LC 99-13849. (Illus.). 320p. 1999. 27.50 (*0-06-019232-1*) HarpC.
***Clifford, Barry & Perry, Paul.** Expedition Whydah: The Story of the World's First Excavation of a Pirate Treasure Ship & the Man Who Found Her, Set. abr. ed. 1999. audio 18.00 (*0-694-52071-3*, 398998) HarperAudio.
— Expedition Wydah: The Story of the World's First Excavation of a Pirate Treasure Ship & the Man Who Found Her. large type unabridged ed. 2000. 26.95 (*0-7531-5483-8*, 154838, Pub. by ISIS Lrg Prnt) ISIS Pub.
Clifford, Brian R., et al, eds. Television & Children: Program Evaluation, Comprehension, & Impact. (LEA's Communication Ser.). 264p. 1995. text 27.50 (*0-8058-1683-6*) L Erlbaum Assocs.
Clifford, Brian R., et al. Television & Children: Program Evaluation, Comprehension, & Impact. (Communication Ser.). 264p. 1995. text 59.95 (*0-8058-1682-8*) L Erlbaum Assocs.
Clifford, Brian R., jt. ed. see Lloyd-Bostock, Sally M.
Clifford, Candace. Historic Lighthouse Preservation Handbook, 1997. 162p. 1997. ring bd. 32.00 (*0-16-049104-5*) USGPO.
Clifford, Charles B. Mastering Sybase SQL Server II. LC 96-47146. (Illus.). 320p. 1997. pap. 44.95 (*0-07-011662-8*) McGraw.
— Sybase Replication Server. LC 95-18169. 1995. 45.00 (*0-07-011515-X*) McGraw.
Clifford, Christine. Not Now . . . I'm Having a No Hair Day: Humor & Healing for People with Cancer. LC 96-10027. (Illus.). 110p. (Orig.). 1996. pap. 9.95 (*1-57025-120-7*) Pfeifer-Hamilton.
— Our Family Has Cancer, Too! LC 97-4771. (Illus.). 64p. (J). (gr. k-6). 1997. pap. 6.95 (*1-57025-144-4*) Pfeifer-Hamilton.
Clifford, Craig. The Tenure of Phil Wisdom: Dialogues. 234p. (Orig.). (C). 1995. pap. text 34.00 (*0-7618-0041-7*) U Pr of Amer.
Clifford, Craig & Feezell, Randolph M. Coaching for Character. LC 97-9534. (Illus.). 128p. (Orig.). 1997. pap. 12.95 (*0-88011-512-2*, PCLI0512) Human Kinetics.
Clifford, Craig & Pilkington, Tom, eds. Range Wars Heated Debates, Sober Reflections, & Other Assessments of Texas Writing. LC 88-42632. (Southwest Life & Letters Ser.). 208p. 1989. pap. 10.95 (*0-87074-273-6*) SMU Press.
Clifford, Craig E. In the Deep Heart's Core: Reflections on Life, Letters, & Texas. LC 85-40050. (Tarleton State University Southwestern Studies in the Humanities: No. 1). 160p. 1985. 18.95 (*0-89096-233-2*) Tex A&M Univ Pr.
Clifford, Craig E. & Pilkington, Tom, eds. Range Wars: Heated Debates, Sober Reflections, & Other Assessments of Texas Writing. LC 88-42632. (Southwest Life & Letters Ser.). 208p. 1989. 22.50 (*0-87074-282-5*) SMU Press.
Clifford, D., jt. auth. see Rogers, T.
Clifford, D. J., ed. The Diaries of Lady Anne Clifford. (Illus.). 320p. 1992. pap. 22.95 (*0-7509-0163-2*, Pub. by Sutton Pub Ltd) Intl Pubs Mktg.
Clifford, Denis. Estate Planning Basics LC 99-21018. (Quick & Legal Series). 212p. 1999. pap. 18.95 (*0-87337-535-1*) Nolo com.
— Make Your Own Living Trust. large type ed. LC 93-45047. 1994. 24.95 (*0-7862-0136-3*) Thorndike Pr.
— Make Your Own Living Trust. 3rd rev. ed. Randolph, Mary, ed. LC 97-34274. (Illus.). 336p. 1998. pap. 34.95 (*0-87337-429-0*) Nolo com.
***Clifford, Denis.** Make Your Own Living Trust. 4th ed. LC 99-45009. (Illus.). 335p. 2000. pap. 34.95 (*0-87337-556-4*) Nolo com.
Clifford, Denis. Nolo's Will Book. 3rd rev. ed. LC 97-14103. Orig. Title: Nolo's Simple Will Book. (Illus.). 336p. (Orig.). 1997. pap. 34.95 incl. disk (*0-87337-373-1*) Nolo com.
— The Quick & Legal Will Book. 2nd ed. 240p. 1999. pap. 15.95 (*0-87337-309-X*) Nolo com.
***Clifford, Denis.** The Quick & Legal Will Book. 2nd ed. LC 98-39722. 240p. 1999. 15.95 (*0-87337-505-X*) Nolo com.
— Wills. 2nd ed. (Law Form Kits Ser.). 2000. pap. 24.95 (*0-87337-602-1*) Nolo com.
Clifford, Denis & Jordan, Cora. Plan Your Estate. 3rd rev. ed. Randolph, Mary, ed. LC 94-973. (Illus.). 416p. 1997. pap. 24.95 (*0-87337-239-5*) Nolo com.
***Clifford, Denis & Jordan, Cora.** Plan Your Estate. 5th ed. LC 99-87910. 2000. write for info. (*0-87337-580-7*) Nolo com.
Clifford, Denis & Randolph, Mary. 9 Ways to Avoid Estate Taxes. LC 98-36075. (Quick & Legal Ser.). 200p. 1999. pap. 24.95 (*0-87337-466-5*) Nolo com.
Clifford, Denis & Warner, Ralph E. The Partnership Book. 5th ed. (Illus.). 304p. (Orig.). 1997. reprint ed. pap. 34.95 incl. disk (*0-87337-371-5*) Nolo com.
***Clifford, Denis & Warner, Ralph E.** The Partnership Book: How to Write a Partnership Agreement. 6th ed. LC 99-46091. 2000. write for info. (*0-87337-560-2*) Nolo com.
Clifford, Denis, jt. auth. see Elias, Steve.
Clifford, Derek. Chinese Carved Lacquer. (Illus.). 160p. 1992. 59.50 (*1-870076-20-6*, Pub. by Bamboo Pub) Antique Collect.
***Clifford, Derek.** Social Assessment Theory & Practice: A Multi-Disciplinary Framework. LC 98-22998. 289p. 1998. text 67.95 (*1-85742-429-8*) Ashgate Pub Co.
Clifford, Dermot. The Social Costs & Rewards of Caring. 261p. 1990. text 76.95 (*1-85628-074-8*, Pub. by Avebry) Ashgate Pub Co.
— Suicide. 1989. pap. 22.00 (*1-85390-166-0*, Pub. by Veritas Pubns) St Mut.
Clifford, Donald H., et al, eds. The Pit Bull Dilemma: The Gathering Storm - 1000 Annotated Abstracts from Books, Journals, Etc. LC 89-22176. 480p. 1990. text 65.00 (*0-914783-36-X*) Charles.
Clifford, E., jt. auth. see Hampton, C. W.
Clifford, Emmett. Night Whispers: A Novel of Evil. LC 98-6928. 448p. 1998. 22.95 (*1-888952-81-4*) Cumberland Hse.
Clifford, Eth. The Dastardly Murder of Dirty Pete. 001. (Illus.). 128p. (J). (gr. 2-5). 1981. 16.00 (*0-395-31671-5*) HM.
— Family for Sale. LC 94-40957. 112p. (J). (gr. 3-7). 1996. 15.00 (*0-395-73571-8*) HM.
— Flatfoot Fox & the Case of the Bashful Beaver. LC 94-14761. (Illus.). 48p. (J). (gr. 3-5). 1995. 16.00 (*0-395-70560-6*) HM.
— Flatfoot Fox & the Case of the Missing Eye. (Illus.). 48p. (J). (gr. 2-5). 1990. 16.00 (*0-395-51945-4*) HM.
— Flatfoot Fox & the Case of the Missing Schoolhouse. (Illus.). 48p. 1997. 13.95 (*0-395-81446-4*) HM.
— Flatfoot Fox & the Case of the Missing Whoooo. LC 92-21903. (Illus.). 48p. (J). 1993. 13.95 (*0-395-65364-9*) HM.
— Flatfoot Fox & the Case of the Nosy Otter. LC 91-26930. (Illus.). 48p. (J). (gr. 2-5). 1992. 15.00 (*0-395-60289-0*) HM.
— Ghost School. (J). (gr. 1-4). 1998. pap. 3.99 (*0-590-35032-3*) Scholastic Inc.
— Harvey's Horrible Snake Disaster. 001. LC 83-27299. 128p. (J). (gr. 3-6). 1984. 15.00 (*0-395-35378-5*, 5-83913) HM.
— Harvey's Marvelous Monkey Mystery. (J). (gr. 3-7). 1990. pap. 2.95 (*0-671-70927-5*) PB.
— Harvey's Mystifying Raccoon Mix-Up. LC 93-27471. 112p. (J). 1994. 14.95 (*0-395-68714-4*) HM.
— Help! I'm a Prisoner in the Library. 001. (Illus.). 112p. (J). (gr. 2-5). 1979. 16.00 (*0-395-28478-3*) HM.
— Help! I'm a Prisoner in the Library. LC 79-14447. 96p. (J). (gr. 4-7). 1991. pap. 2.95 (*0-590-44351-8*, Apple Paperbacks) Scholastic Inc.
— Help! I'm a Prisoner in the Library. LC 79-14447. (J). 1979. 9.19 (*0-606-03406-4*, Pub. by Turtleback) Demco.
— Just Tell Me When We're Dead!. 001. LC 83-10865. (Illus.). 144p. (J). (gr. 2-5). 1983. 16.00 (*0-395-33071-8*) HM.
— Just Tell Me When We're Dead! 144p. (J). (gr. 5-7). 1985. pap. 3.50 (*0-590-44010-1*, Apple Paperbacks) Scholastic Inc.
— The Remembering Box. 001. (Illus.). 64p. (J). (gr. 2-5). 1985. 16.00 (*0-395-38476-1*) HM.

C

An Asterisk (*) at the beginning of an entry indicates that the title is appearing for the first time.

— The Remembering Box. ALC Staff, ed. LC 85-10851. 64p. (J). (gr. 4-7). 1992. mass mkt. 4.95 (0-688-11777-5, Wm Morrow) Morrow Avon.
— Remembering Box. 1992. 10.15 (0-606-01385-7, Pub. by Turtleback) Demco.
— Scared Silly. 128p. (J). (gr. 3-7). 1989. pap. 2.75 (0-590-42382-7) Scholastic Inc.
Clifford, F. S. Romance of Perfume. 1977. lib. bdg. 250.00 (0-8490-2536-2) Gordon Pr.
Clifford, George F. Modern Heating & Ventilating Systems Design. 704p. (C). 1992. text 63.00 (0-13-602830-6) P-H.
Clifford, Geraldine J. Edward L. Thorndike: The Sane Positivist. LC 68-27542. 646p. reprint ed. pap. 200.00 (0-7837-0210-8, 204051800017) Bks Demand.
— Equally in View: The University of California: Its Women, & the Schools. Brentano, Carroll & Rothblatt, Sheldon, eds. LC 95-14666. (Chapters in the History of the University of California Ser.: No. 4). 103p. (Orig.). 1995. pap. 10.00 (0-87772-364-8) UCB IGS.
Clifford, Geraldine J., ed. Lone Voyagers: Academic Women in Coeducational Universities, 1870-1937. LC 89-31878. 336p. (C). 1989. 35.00 (0-935312-84-6); pap. 12.95 (0-935312-85-4) Feminist Pr.
Clifford, Geraldine J. & Guthrie, James W. Ed School: A Brief for Professional Education. 424p. 1988. 24.95 (0-226-11017-6) U Ch Pr.
— Ed School: A Brief for Professional Education. LC 87-30147. xii, 426p. 1990. pap. text 17.95 (0-226-11016-8) U Ch Pr.
Clifford, H. B. J., jt. auth. see Satchell, Stephen.
Clifford, H. J., et al. Geology of San Diego County: Legacy of the Land. Burns, Diane & Lindsay, Lowell, eds. LC 95-67499. (Natural History Bks.). (Illus.). 176p. (Orig.). 1997. pap. 14.95 (0-932653-21-9) Sunbelt Pubns.
Clifford, H. T. & Stephenson, W. An Introduction to Numerical Classification: Primarily for Biologists. 1975. text 63.00 (0-12-176750-7) Acad Pr.
Clifford, H. T., jt. auth. see Dahlgren, R. M.
Clifford, Hal. The Falling Season: Inside the Life & Death Drama of Aspen's Mountain Rescue Team. 272p. 1999. pap. 16.95 (0-89886-633-2) Mountaineers.
***Clifford, Hal.** Longstreet Highroad Guide to the Colorado Mountains. LC 99-61764. (Illus.). 352p. 1999. pap. 18.95 (1-56352-537-2) Longstreet.
Clifford, Howard. Alaska & Yukon Railroads: An Illustrated History. rev. ed. LC 99-26904. Orig. Title: Rails North. (Illus.). 240p. 1999. 42.95 (0-9647521-4-X, Pub. by Oso Pubng) Partners-West.
— Doing the White Pass. LC 82-62466. (Illus.). 96p. (Orig.). 1994. pap. 7.50 (0-911803-04-1) Sourdough.
— The Skagway Story. 2nd ed. LC 75-13918. (Illus.). 180p. 1975. reprint ed. pap. 12.95 (0-88240-330-3, Alaska NW Bks) Gr Arts Ctr Pub.
— Soapy Smith: Uncrowned King of Skagway. LC 97-185263. (Illus.). 148p. 1997. pap. 9.95 (0-911803-03-3) Sourdough.
***Clifford, Howard.** Wyatt Earp Alaska Adventures. (Illus.). 120p. 2000. 9.95 (0-911803-08-4) Sourdough.
Clifford, Howard, ed. see Jones, R. D.
Clifford, Hugh. The Gold Coast Regiment in German East Africa. (Great War Ser.: No. 40). (Illus.). 264p. 1995. reprint ed. 49.95 (0-89839-228-4) Battery Pr.
Clifford, Hugh C. Further Side of Silence. LC 79-110182. (Short Story Index Reprint Ser.). (Illus.). 1977. 26.95 (0-8369-3333-8) Ayer.
— In a Corner of Asia. LC 77-106265. (Short Story Index Reprint Ser.). 1977. 19.95 (0-8369-3302-8) Ayer.
— In Days That Are Dead. LC 77-113651. (Short Story Index Reprint Ser.). 1977. 21.95 (0-8369-3380-X) Ayer.
— Studies in Brown Humanity Being Scrawls & Smudges in Sepia, White & Yellow. 1977. text 18.95 (0-8369-9240-7, 9094) Ayer.
Clifford, J. Formal Semantics & Pragmatics for Natural Language Querying. (Cambridge Tracts in Theoretical Computer Science Ser.: No. 8). 210p. (C). 1990. text 42.95 (0-521-35433-1) Cambridge U Pr.
Clifford, J. Candace & Clifford, Mary Louise. Nineteenth-Century Lights: Historic Images of American Lighthouses. LC 99-75177. (Illus.). 304p. Date not set. 34.95 (0-9636412-2-0); pap. 24.95 (0-9636412-3-9) Cypress Communs.
Clifford, J. Candace, jt. auth. see Clifford, Mary L.
Clifford, J. Candace, jt. auth. see Delgado, James P.
Clifford, J. E., ed. Advances in Coastal Structures & Breakwaters: Proceedings of the International Conference Organized by the Institute of Civil Engineers, London, April 27-29, 1995. LC 96-228484. 338p. 1996. 96.00 (0-7277-2509-2) Am Soc Civil Eng.
Clifford, J. Garry & Spencer, Samuel R., Jr. The First Peacetime Draft. LC 86-13328. (Modern War Studies). (Illus.). xvi, 320p. 1986. 35.00 (0-7006-0305-0) U Pr of KS.
Clifford, J. Garry, et al. American Ascendant: American Foreign Relations Since 1939. 320p. (C). 1995. pap. text 28.76 (0-669-39361-4) HM Trade Div.
Clifford, J. Garry, jt. auth. see Paterson, Thomas G.
Clifford, James. Hester Lynch Piozzi. 495p. 1987. pap. text 29.00 (0-231-06389-X) Col U Pr.
— Person & Myth: Maurice Leenhardt in the Melanesian World. LC 92-14147. (Illus.). 285p. 1992. pap. text 17.95 (0-8223-1264-6) Duke.
— The Predicament of Culture: Twentieth-Century Ethnography, Literature, & Art. LC 87-24173. (Illus.). 384p. 1988. 42.50 (0-674-69842-8); pap. 22.00 (0-674-69843-6) HUP.
— Routes: Travel & Translation in the Late Twentieth Century. 1997. 39.95 (0-614-27418-4); pap. 14.95 (0-614-27419-2) HUP.
— Routes: Travel & Translation in the Late Twentieth Century. LC 96-38454. (Illus.). 416p. 1997. 43.00 (0-674-77960-6); pap. 18.95 (0-674-77961-4) HUP.
Clifford, James & Marcus, George E., eds. Writing Culture: The Poetics & Politics of Ethnography. 345p. 1986. pap. 19.95 (0-520-05729-5, Pub. by U CA Pr) Cal Prin Full Svc.
Clifford, James & Tuzhilin, Alexander, eds. Recent Advances in Temporal Databases: Proceedings of the International Workshop on Temporal Databases, Zurich, 17-18 September 1995. (Workshops in Computing Ser.). 362p. 1995. 79.00 (3-540-19945-4) Spr-Verlag.
Clifford, James F. Specifications & Tolerances for Reference Standards & Field Standard Weights & Measures. 25p. 1997. pap. 2.50 (0-16-054632-X) USGPO.
Clifford, James L. & Greene, Donald J. Samuel Johnson: A Survey & Bibliography of Critical Studies. LC 74-109940. 349p. reprint ed. pap. 108.20 (0-7837-2970-7, 205748400006) Bks Demand.
***Clifford, Jeremy.** Infant Eyes. 1999. pap. write for info. (1-58235-113-9) Watermrk Pr.
Clifford, Joan. Capability Brown. (Lifelines Ser.: No. 14). (Illus.). 48p. 1989. pap. 7.50 (0-85263-274-6, Pub. by Shire Pubns) Parkwest Pubns.
Clifford, John, ed. The Experience of Reading: Louise Rosenblatt & Reader-Response Theory. LC 90-37177. 226p. (Orig.). (C). 1990. pap. text 23.00 (0-86709-262-9, 0262, Pub. by Boynton Cook Pubs) Heinemann.
Clifford, John & DiYanni, Robert. Modern American Prose. 3rd ed. 640p. (C). 1993. pap., student ed. 37.50 (0-07-011396-3) McGraw.
Clifford, John & Schilb, John, eds. Writing Theory & Critical Theory. LC 93-50595. (Research & Scholarship in Composition Ser.: No. 3). ix, 374p. (Orig.). 1994. pap. 19.75 (0-87352-576-0, RS03P) Modern Lang.
Clifford, John & Schilb, John L., eds. Writing Theory & Critical Theory. LC 93-50595. (Research & Scholarship in Composition Ser.: No. 3). ix, 374p. (Orig.). 1994. lib. bdg. 37.50 (0-87352-575-2, RS03C) Modern Lang.
Clifford, John & Yanni, Robert. Modern American Prose: A Reader for Writers. 2nd ed. (C). 1987. pap. text. write for info. (0-318-57009-2) Random.
Clifford, John, tr. see Calderon de la Barca, Pedro.
Clifford, John, tr. see Von Weizsacker, Ernst U.
***Clifford, John D. & Rafinesque, C. S.** John D. Clifford's "Indian Antiquities" Related Material by C. S. Rafinisque. Boewe, Charles E., ed. LC 00-8890. (Illus.). 240p. (C). 2000. text 30.00 (1-57233-099-6, Pub. by U of Tenn Pr) U Ch Pr.
Clifford, John E. Tense & Tense Logic. (Janua Linguarum, Ser. Minor: No. 215). 173p. (Orig.). 1975. pap. text 35.40 (90-279-3453-3) Mouton.
Clifford, Joyce & Horvath, Kathy, eds. Advancing Professional Nursing Practice: Innovations at Boston's Beth Israel Hospital. LC 90-9463. 384p. 1990. 48.95 (0-8261-7180-X) Springer Pub.
Clifford, Karen. Becoming an Accredited Genealogist: Plus 100 Tips to Ensure Your Success. LC 97-51543. (Illus.). 234p. 1998. pap. 19.95 (0-916489-81-7) Ancestry.
Clifford, Karen, ed. & illus. see Chatham, Anne B.
***Clifford, Kathy.** Strength among Women. John Nelson Photography Staff & Johnson, Fred, trs. 168p. 1999. 12.95 (0-9676519-0-5) K Clifford.
Clifford, Linda L. Interior Design & Furnishings--Status, New & Review: Index of New Information. 150p. 1994. 47.50 (0-7883-0058-X); pap. 44.50 (0-7883-0059-8) ABBE Pubs Assn.
Clifford, Lucille, et al. Sarasota Review of Poetry, Vol. 3. Date not set. mass mkt. 9.95 (0-9662719-1-2) R B Abel.
Clifford, Lucy. Eve's Lover, & Other Stories. LC 70-128724. (Short Story Index Reprint Ser.). 1977. 19.95 (0-8369-3615-9) Ayer.
— Last Touches, & Other Stories. LC 76-150470. (Short Story Index Reprint Ser.). 1977. reprint ed. 20.95 (0-8369-3810-0) Ayer.
***Clifford, Lucy.** Mrs. Keith's Crime, Set. unabridged ed. (YA). (gr. 8 up). 1999. 41.95 incl. audio (1-55685-603-2) Audio Bk Con.
Clifford, Marcia, ed. see Hoops, Frederick K.
Clifford, Marcia, ed. see Steigmann, Robert J. & Gard, Spencer A.
Clifford, Mark L. Troubled Tiger: Businessmen, Bureaucrats & Generals in South Korea. LC 94-9867. 372p. (C). (gr. 13). 1994. 75.95 (1-56324-386-5, East Gate Bk); pap. 27.95 (1-56324-387-3, East Gate Bk) M E Sharpe.
— Troubled Tiger: Businessmen, Bureaucrats & Generals in South Korea. rev. ed. LC 97-35048. 392p. (C). (gr. 13). 1997. text 77.95 (0-7656-0140-0, East Gate Bk) M E Sharpe.
— Troubled Tiger: Businessmen, Bureaucrats & Generals in South Korea. rev. ed. LC 97-35048. (Illus.). 392p. (C). (gr. 13). 1997. pap. text 26.95 (0-7656-0141-9, East Gate Bk) M E Sharpe.
Clifford, Martin. Electrical Wiring & Repair: A Guide to Improving & Maintaining Residential Electrical Systems. (C). 1990. text 39.00 (0-13-247867-6) P-H.
— Electronic Connections: Home & Car Entertainment Systems. (Illus.). 432p. 1987. text 24.95 (0-685-14918-8) P-H.
— Master Handbook of Electronic Tables & Formulas. 4th ed. LC 84-8529. (Illus.). 392p. 1984. 24.95 (0-8306-0625-4, 1625) McGraw-Hill Prof.
— Master Handbook of Electronic Tables & Formulas. 5th ed. 576p. 1992. 39.95 (0-8306-2192-X); pap. 22.95 (0-8306-2191-1) McGraw-Hill Prof.
— Microphones. 3rd ed. (Illus.). 352p. 1986. 22.95 (0-8306-0475-8); pap. 17.95 (0-8306-2675-1, NO. 2675) McGraw-Hill Prof.
— Modern Guide to Electric Motors. 368p. (C). 1989. text 43.60 (0-13-593336-6) P-H.
Clifford, Mary. Environmental Crime: Enforcement, Policy, & Social Responsibility. LC 97-37192. 532p. 1998. pap. 51.00 (0-8342-1009-6) Aspen Pub.
***Clifford, Mary L.** From Slavery to Freetown. LC 99-21345. (Illus.). 259p. 1999. lib. bdg. 48.50 (0-7864-0615-1) McFarland & Co.
Clifford, Mary L. The Land & People of Afghanistan. LC 88-21419. (Portraits of the Nations Ser.). (Illus.). 240p. (J). (gr. 6 up). 1989. lib. bdg. 14.89 (0-397-32339-5) HarpC Child Bks.
— The Land & People of Afghanistan. LC 88-21419. (Portraits of the Nations Ser.). (Illus.). 240p. (YA). (gr. 6 up). 1989. 18.00 (0-397-32338-7) HarpC Child Bks.
— The Land & People of Sierra Leone. LC 73-20317. (Portraits of the Nations Ser.). (Illus.). 160p. (J). (gr. 5-9). 1974. 11.95 (0-397-31490-6) HarpC Child Bks.
Clifford, Mary L. & Clifford, J. Candace. Women Who Kept the Lights: An Illustrated History of Female Lighthouse Keepers. LC 93-74066. (Illus.). 192p. (Orig.). 1993. pap. 19.95 (0-9636412-0-4) Cypress Communs.
Clifford, Mary Louise. Salah of Sierra Leone. LC 75-9665. (Illus.). 224p. (J). (gr. 6 up). 1975. 9.82 (0-690-00908-9) HarpC Child Bks.
Clifford, Mary Louise, jt. auth. see Clifford, J. Candace.
***Clifford, Mathew.** Casualty of My Own Neglect. LC 99-64283. 275p. 1999. pap. 6.99 (1-893181-25-1) Le Gesse Stevens.
***Clifford, Michael.** Political Genealogy after Foucault: Savage Identities. LC 00-44632. 2001. pap. write for info. (0-415-92916-4) Routledge.
Clifford, Michael J., jt. auth. see Linzey, Donald W.
Clifford, Mike. The New Illustrated Rock Handbook. (GER.). 208p. 1992. 25.00 (3-283-00266-5) G Olms Pubs.
— Play Rock Guitar. (Illus.). 128p. 1987. pap. 17.95 (0-8256-1165-2, AM66762) Music Sales.
Clifford, N. J., et al, eds. Turbulence: Perspectives on Flow & Sediment Transport. LC 93-3142. 376p. 1993. 200.00 (0-471-93900-5) Wiley.
Clifford, Nicholas. Retreat from China: British Policy in the Far East, 1937-1941. (China in the 20th Century Ser.). 1976. reprint ed. lib. bdg. 27.50 (0-306-70757-8) Da Capo.
Clifford, Nicholas R. Spoilt Children of Empire: Westerners in Shanghai & the Chineses Revolution of the 1920s. LC 90-50904. (Illus.). 381p. Date not set. reprint ed. pap. 118.20 (0-608-20674-1, 207178100002) Bks Demand.
Clifford, Patricia H. Sitting Still: An Encounter with Christian Zen. 96p. 1995. pap. 5.95 (0-8091-3617-1) Paulist Pr.
Clifford, Paul. Historia Documental de China, Vol. 1. LC 92-107305. (SPA.). 223p. reprint ed. pap. 69.20 (0-7837-6835-4, 204666400001) Bks Demand.
Clifford, Paul, jt. auth. see Andrade, Carla-Krystin.
Clifford, Paul, jt. ed. see Williams, John F.
Clifford, Paula. Praying with Saint Augustine. (Praying With...Ser.). 1987. pap. 5.95 (0-687-86040-7) Abingdon.
Clifford, Paula, tr Praying with St. Teresa of Avila. LC 97-7859. (Praying with...Ser.). 116p. 1997. reprint ed. pap. 10.00 (0-8028-4314-X) Eerdmans.
— Praying with the Jewish Tradition. LC 97-7871. (Praying with...Ser.). 250p. 1997. reprint ed. pap. 10.00 (0-8028-4317-4) Eerdmans.
— Praying with the Orthodox Tradition. 101p. (Orig.). 1996. pap. 5.95 (0-88141-156-6) St Vladimirs.
Clifford, Peter, jt. auth. see Woollett, Mick.
***Clifford, Ralph D.** Computer & Cyber Law: Cases & Materials. LC 99-46143. 648p. 1999. boxed set 80.00 (0-89089-715-8) Carolina Acad Pr.
Clifford, Rand. Castling. LC 95-94777. 544p. (Orig.). 1996. pap. 18.95 (0-9647817-9-4) StarChief Pr.
Clifford, Richard, jt. auth. see Harms, Thelma.
Clifford, Richard C. The Wisdom Literature. LC 98-13825. (Interpreting Biblical Texts Ser.). 192p. 1996. pap. 18.95 (0-687-00846-8) Abingdon.
Clifford, Richard J. The Book of Proverbs & Our Search for Wisdom. (Pere Marquette Lectures: Vol. 26). 1995. 15.00 (0-87462-575-0) Marquette.
— The Cosmic Mountain in Canaan & the Old Testament. LC 71-188968. (Harvard Semitic Monographs: No. 4). (Illus.). 235p. 1972. reprint ed. pap. 72.90 (0-7837-1685-0, 205721500024) Bks Demand.
— Creation Accounts in the Ancient Near East & the Bible. LC 94-26565. (Catholic Biblical Quarterly Monographs: No. 26). 1994. 9.00 (0-915170-25-6) Catholic Bibl Assn.
— Proverbs: A Commentary. LC 98-50850. (Old Testament Library). 296p. 1999. 38.00 (0-664-22131-9) Westminster John Knox.
— Psalms 1-72. (Collegeville Bible Commentary - Old Testament Ser.). 80p. 1986. pap. 4.95 (0-8146-1479-5) Liturgical Pr.
— Psalms 73-150. (Collegeville Bible Commentary - Old Testament Ser.). 88p. 1986. pap. 4.95 (0-8146-1480-9) Liturgical Pr.
Clifford, Richard J., et al, eds. Creation in the Biblical Traditions. LC 92-20268. (Catholic Biblical Quarterly Monographs: No. 24). vi, 151p. 1992. pap. 7.00 (0-915170-23-X) Catholic Bibl Assn.
Clifford, Robert. On Holiday Again, Doctor? large type ed. 1991. 27.99 (0-7089-2496-4) Ulverscroft.
— What Next Doctor? large type ed. (General Ser.). 288p. 1993. 11.50 (0-7089-2874-9) Ulverscroft.
— You're Still a Doctor, Doctor! large type ed. 224p. 1992. 27.99 (0-7089-2600-2) Ulverscroft.
Clifford, Robert, jt. auth. see Wilkinson, Allen P.
Clifford, Robert C. California Automobile Insurance Law. 110.00 (0-327-13002-4) LEXIS Pub.
Clifford, Robert C. California Insurance Disputes, Revision No. 5. LC 91-62069. 272p. 1997. ring bd. 53.75 (1-55943-114-8, 80236-14) Parker Pubns.
***Clifford, Robert C.** California Uninsured Motorist Law, 2 vols. 6th ed. 1350p. 1999. ring bd. 199.00 (0-327-01378-8, 8027211) LEXIS Pub.
Clifford, Robert C. Qualifying & Attacking Expert Witnesses. 1998. ring bd. 89.98 (0-938065-39-4) James Pub Santa Ana.
Clifford, Robert C. & Sleeth, Boyd. Insurance Law Handbook: California. 134p. (Orig.). 1992. pap. 40.00 (1-55943-157-1, MICHIE) LEXIS Pub.
Clifford, Robert C., jt. auth. see Eisler, Paul A.
Clifford, Robert D. An Arrow Full of Quivers. large type ed. (Large Print Ser.). 256p. 1996. 27.99 (0-7089-3643-1) Ulverscroft.
Clifford Rose, F., ed. Methodological Problems in Migraine Trails. (Journal: Neuroepidemiology: Vol. 6, No. 4). (Illus.). iv, 80p. 1987. pap. 48.00 (3-8055-4677-7) S Karger.
— Migraine. (Illus.). xii, 280p. 1985. 152.25 (3-8055-4039-6) S Karger.
Clifford, Ross. Leading Lawyer's Case for the Resurrection. LC 97-143. 143p. 1996. reprint ed. pap. 12.50 (1-896363-02-4) CN Inst for Law.
Clifford, Sara. Making a Leap: Theatre of Empowerment: A Practical Handbook for Drama & Theatre Work with Youn. LC 99-159338. 10p. 1998. pap. text 26.95 (1-85302-632-8) Jessica Kingsley.
***Clifford, Sherry.** Opportunities in Medical Imaging Careers. rev. ed. (Opportunities in... Ser.). 160p. 2000. 14.95 (0-658-00196-5, 001965); pap. 11.95 (0-658-00197-3, 001973) NTC Contemp Pub Co.
Clifford, Simon. Play the Brazilian Way: The Secret Behind the Success of the World's Greatest Soccer Team. (Illus.). 96p. 1999. pap. 24.00 (0-7522-1347-4) Trans-Atl Phila.
Clifford, Stephen P. Beyond the Heroic "I" Reading Lawrence, Hemingway & "Masculinity" LC 98-13066. (Illus.). 352p. 1998. 48.50 (0-8387-5357-4) Bucknell U Pr.
***Clifford, Stephen P.** An Owner's Guide to Business Succession Planning. Teodosio, Alex, ed. (Illus.). 64p. 1999. pap. 14.95 (0-933522-25-8, Pub. by Kent Popular) OEOC.
Clifford, Susan B., jt. auth. see Anderson, Pauline C.
Clifford, Susannah. Village in the Hills: A History of Danville, VT, 1786-1995. LC 95-35654. (Illus.). 288p. 1995. 35.00 (0-914659-75-8) Phoenix Pub.
Clifford, Susannah, jt. auth. see King, Angela.
Clifford, Terry. Tibetan Buddhist Medicine & Psychiatry: The Diamond Healing. LC 82-61872. (Illus.). 288p. 1990. pap. 12.95 (0-87728-710-4) Weiser.
Clifford, Terry, et al, eds. The Lamp of Liberation. (Illus.). 112p. 1988. 10.00 (0-9621371-0-3) Yeshe Melong.
Clifford, Timothy, et al. The Three Graces. (Illus.). 112p. 1998. pap. 25.00 (0-903598-59-0, Pub. by Natl Galleries) Antique Collect.
Clifford, Tom N. Review of African Granulites & Related Rocks. LC 74-84196. (Geological Society of America, Special Paper: No. 156). 54p. reprint ed. pap. 30.00 (0-608-13545-3, 202547100044) Bks Demand.
Clifford, W. G. Winning Snooker. 64p. 1995. pap. 4.95 (0-572-01148-2, Pub. by Foulsham UK) Assoc Pubs Grp.
Clifford, William, jt. auth. see Freuchen, Dagmar.
Clifford, William K. Common Sense of the Exact Sciences. Pearson, Karl & Newman, James R., eds. LC 72-5510. (Biography Index Reprint Ser.). 1977. reprint ed. 21.95 (0-8369-8135-9) Ayer.
***Clifford, William K.** The Ethics of Belief & Other Essays. LC 98-52479. (Great Books in Philosophy). 140p. 1999. pap. 6.95 (1-57392-691-4) Prometheus Bks.
Clifford, William K. Mathematical Papers. LC 67-28488. 1968. reprint ed. 49.50 (0-8284-0210-8) Chelsea Pub.
Clifford, William K., et al. Geometry & Nature: A Conference on New Trends in Geometrical & Topological Methods, Vol. 203. LC 96-46141. (Contemporary Mathematics Ser.). 310p. 1996. pap. 65.00 (0-8218-0607-6, CONM/203) Am Math.
Cliffs Notes Staff. American Poets of the 20th Century. (Cliffs Notes Ser.). 300p. 2000. 12.95 (0-7645-8534-7) IDG Bks.
***Cliffs Notes Staff.** Anthem. (Cliffs Notes Ser.). 96p. 2000. pap. 4.99 (0-7645-8557-6) IDG Bks.
— Atlas Shrugged. (Cliffs Notes Ser.). 96p. 2000. pap. 4.99 (0-7645-8556-8) IDG Bks.
Cliffs Notes Staff. The Bean Trees. (Cliffs Notes Ser.). 96p. 1999. 4.95 (0-7645-8508-8) IDG Bks.
Cliffs Notes Staff. Calculus, Vol. 1. (Cliffs Studyware Ser.). 1996. write for info. (0-8220-5626-7, Cliff) IDG Bks.
Cliffs Notes Staff. The Chosen. (Cliffs Notes Ser.). 88p. 1999. 4.95 (0-7645-8509-6) IDG Bks.
***Cliffs Notes Staff.** Cliffs Notes on Cry, the Beloved Country. (Cliffs Notes Ser.). 88p. 1999. 4.95 (0-7645-8501-0) IDG Bks.
Cliffs Notes Staff. Cliff's Quick Review for U. S. History II. (Cliffs Notes Ser.). 1998. pap. 7.95 (0-8220-5361-6, Cliff) IDG Bks.
***Cliffs Notes Staff.** Contender. (Cliffs Notes Ser.). 96p. 2000. pap. 4.99 (0-7645-8553-3) IDG Bks.
Cliffs Notes Staff. Flowers for Algernon. (Cliffs Notes Ser.). 56p. 1999. 4.95 (0-7645-8502-9) IDG Bks.
***Cliffs Notes Staff.** The Giver. (Cliffs Notes Ser.). 60p. 1999. pap. 4.95 (0-7645-8510-X) IDG Bks.
— Incidents in the Life of a Slave Girl. (Cliffs Notes Ser.). 128p. 2000. pap. 4.99 (0-7645-8555-X) IDG Bks.
— Inherit the Wind. (Cliffs Notes Ser.). 96p. 2000. pap. 4.99 (0-7645-8554-1) IDG Bks.
— Killer Angels. (Cliffs Notes Ser.). 128p. 2000. pap. 4.99 (0-7645-8549-5) IDG Bks.

An Asterisk (*) at the beginning of an entry indicates that the title is appearing for the first time.

— Lesson Before Dying. (Cliffs Notes Ser.). 80p. 1999. 4.95 (*0-7645-8503-7*) IDG Bks.

Cliffs Notes Staff. The Light in the Forest. (Cliffs Notes Ser.). 64p. 1999. 4.95 (*0-7645-8504-5*) IDG Bks.

***Cliffs Notes Staff.** Much Ado about Nothing. (Cliffs Notes Ser.). 80p. 1999. pap. 4.95 (*0-7645-8505-3*) IDG Bks.

— Once & Future King. (Cliffs Notes Ser.). 112p. 2000. pap. 4.99 (*0-7645-8550-9*) IDG Bks.

— Outsiders. (Cliffs Notes Ser.). 80p. 2000. pap. 4.99 (*0-7645-8559-2*) IDG Bks.

— The Picture of Dorian Gray. (Cliffs Notes Ser.). 85p. 1999. 4.95 (*0-7645-8506-1*) IDG Bks.

Cliffs Notes Staff. Shakespeare's Comedies. (Cliffs Notes Ser.). 588p. 1999. pap. text 12.95 (*0-8220-0009-1*, Cliff) IDG Bks.

— Shakespeare's Histories, 1. (Cliffs Notes Ser.). 588p. 1999. pap. text 12.95 (*0-8220-0040-7*, Cliff) IDG Bks.

***Cliffs Notes Staff.** Shakespeare's Tragedies. (Cliffs Notes Ser.). 540p. 1999. pap. text 12.95 (*0-8220-0088-1*, Cliff) IDG Bks.

— Song of Solomon. (Cliffs Notes Ser.). 120p. 1999. pap. 4.95 (*0-7645-8507-X*) IDG Bks.

***Cliffs Notes Staff, ed.** Accounting Principles II. (Cliffs Quick Reviews Ser.). (Illus.). 80p. 2000. pap. 9.99 (*0-7645-8565-7*) IDG Bks.

Cliffs Notes Staff, ed. Algebra I. (Cliffs Studyware Ser.). 1998. pap. write for info. (*0-8220-5760-3*, Cliff) IDG Bks.

***Cliffs Notes Staff, ed.** Astronomy. (Cliffs Quick Reviews Ser.). (Illus.). 240p. 2000. pap. 9.99 (*0-7645-8564-9*) IDG Bks.

— Beowulf. (Cliffs Notes Ser.). 128p. 2000. pap. 4.99 (*0-7645-8580-0*) IDG Bks.

— Biochemistry I. (Cliffs Quick Reviews Ser.). (Illus.). 80p. 2000. pap. 9.99 (*0-7645-8563-0*) IDG Bks.

— Biochemistry II. (Cliffs Quick Reviews Ser.). (Illus.). 80p. 2000. pap. 9.99 (*0-7645-8562-2*) IDG Bks.

Cliffs Notes Staff, ed. Biology. (Cliffs Studyware Ser.). 1998. pap. write for info. (*0-8220-5761-1*, Cliff) IDG Bks.

***Cliffs Notes Staff, ed.** Brave New World. LC 00-37020. (Cliffs Notes Ser.). 80p. 2000. pap. 4.99 (*0-7645-8583-5*) IDG Bks.

Cliffs Notes Staff, ed. Calculus. (Cliffs Studyware Ser.). 1998. pap. write for info. (*0-8220-5762-X*, Cliff); pap. write for info. (*0-8220-5763-8*, Cliff) IDG Bks.

***Cliffs Notes Staff, ed.** Canterbury Tales. (Cliffs Notes Ser.). 128p. 2000. pap. 4.99 (*0-7645-8590-8*) IDG Bks.

— Catcher in the Rye. (Cliffs Notes Ser.). 128p. 2000. pap. 4.99 (*0-7645-8591-6*) IDG Bks.

— Criminal Justice. (Cliffs Quick Reviews Ser.). 80p. 2000. pap. 9.99 (*0-7645-8561-4*) IDG Bks.

— Crucible. LC 00-35108. (Cliffs Notes Ser.). 128p. 2000. pap. 4.99 (*0-7645-8588-6*) IDG Bks.

— Developmental Psychology. (Cliffs Quick Reviews Ser.). 240p. 2000. pap. 9.95 (*0-7645-8614-9*) IDG Bks.

— Frankenstein. LC 00-37036. (Cliffs Notes Ser.). 128p. 2000. pap. 4.99 (*0-7645-8593-2*) IDG Bks.

— Grapes of Wrath. (Cliffs Notes Ser.). 128p. 2000. pap. 4.99 (*0-7645-8596-7*) IDG Bks.

— Great Expectations. LC 00-35074. (Cliffs Notes Ser.). 128p. 2000. pap. 4.99 (*0-7645-8598-3*) IDG Bks.

— Great Gatsby. (Cliffs Notes Ser.). 128p. 2000. pap. 4.99 (*0-7645-8601-7*) IDG Bks.

— Hamlet. (Cliffs Complete Ser.). 240p. 2000. pap. 9.99 (*0-7645-8568-1*) IDG Bks.

— Hamlet. (Cliffs Notes Ser.). 128p. 2000. pap. 4.99 (*0-7645-8603-3*) IDG Bks.

— Heart of Darkness & the Secret Sharer. (Cliffs Notes Ser.). 128p. 2000. pap. 4.99 (*0-7645-8584-3*) IDG Bks.

— Huckleberry Finn. (Cliffs Notes Ser.). 80p. 2000. pap. 4.99 (*0-7645-8604-1*) IDG Bks.

— Iliad. (Cliffs Notes Ser.). 128p. 2000. pap. 4.99 (*0-7645-8586-X*) IDG Bks.

— Jane Eyre. (Cliffs Notes Ser.). 128p. 2000. pap. 4.99 (*0-7645-8589-4*) IDG Bks.

— Julius Caesar. (Cliffs Complete Ser.). 240p. 2000. pap. 9.99 (*0-7645-8569-X*) IDG Bks.

— Julius Caesar. (Cliffs Notes Ser.). 80p. 2000. pap. 4.99 (*0-7645-8595-9*) IDG Bks.

— King Henry IV. (Cliffs Complete Ser.: Pt. 1). 240p. 2000. pap. 9.99 (*0-7645-8570-3*) IDG Bks.

— King Lear. (Cliffs Complete Ser.). 240p. 2000. pap. 9.99 (*0-7645-8571-1*) IDG Bks.

— King Lear. (Cliffs Notes Ser.). 128p. 2000. pap. 4.99 (*0-7645-8582-7*) IDG Bks.

— Lord of the Flies. (Cliffs Notes Ser.). 80p. 2000. pap. 4.99 (*0-7645-8597-5*) IDG Bks.

— Macbeth. (Cliffs Complete Ser.). 240p. 2000. pap. 9.99 (*0-7645-8572-X*) IDG Bks.

— Macbeth. LC 00-35106. (Cliffs Notes Ser.). 128p. 2000. pap. 4.99 (*0-7645-8602-5*) IDG Bks.

— Merchant of Venice. (Cliffs Complete Ser.). 240p. 2000. pap. 9.99 (*0-7645-8575-4*) IDG Bks.

— 1984. (Cliffs Notes Ser.). 80p. 2000. pap. 4.99 (*0-7645-8585-1*) IDG Bks.

— The Odyssey. LC 00-35076. (Cliffs Notes Ser.). 96p. 2000. pap. 4.99 (*0-7645-8599-1*) IDG Bks.

— Oedipus Trilogy. (Cliffs Notes Ser.). 128p. 2000. pap. 4.99 (*0-7645-8581-9*) IDG Bks.

— Organic Chemistry II. (Cliffs Quick Reviews Ser.). (Illus.). 240p. 2000. pap. 9.99 (*0-7645-8616-5*) IDG Bks.

— Othello. (Cliffs Complete Ser.). 240p. 2000. pap. 9.99 (*0-7645-8573-8*) IDG Bks.

— Othello. (Cliffs Notes Ser.). 128p. 2000. pap. 4.99 (*0-7645-8587-8*) IDG Bks.

— Plant Biology. (Cliffs Quick Reviews Ser.). (Illus.). 80p. 2000. pap. 9.99 (*0-7645-8560-6*) IDG Bks.

— Pride & Prejudice. LC 00-38058. (Cliffs Notes Ser.). 96p. 2000. pap. 4.99 (*0-7645-8607-6*) IDG Bks.

— Rand's the Fountainhead. (Cliffs Notes Ser.). 2000. pap. 4.99 (*0-7645-8558-4*) IDG Bks.

— Red Badge of Courage. (Cliffs Notes Ser.). 128p. 2000. pap. 4.99 (*0-7645-8579-7*) IDG Bks.

— Romeo & Juliet. (Cliffs Complete Ser.). 240p. 2000. pap. 9.99 (*0-7645-8574-6*) IDG Bks.

— Romeo & Juliet. (Cliffs Notes Ser.). 80p. 2000. pap. 4.99 (*0-7645-8592-4*) IDG Bks.

— Scarlet Letter. LC 00-35105. (Cliffs Notes Ser.). 128p. 2000. pap. 4.99 (*0-7645-8605-X*) IDG Bks.

— Separate Peace. (Cliffs Notes Ser.). 128p. 2000. pap. 4.99 (*0-7645-8578-9*) IDG Bks.

— Sociology. (Cliffs Quick Reviews Ser.). (Illus.). 240p. 2000. pap. 9.95 (*0-7645-8615-7*) IDG Bks.

— Tale of Two Cities. (Cliffs Notes Ser.). 96p. 2000. pap. 4.99 (*0-7645-8606-8*) IDG Bks.

— Tempest. (Cliffs Complete Ser.). 240p. 2000. pap. 9.99 (*0-7645-8576-2*) IDG Bks.

— To Kill a Mockingbird. (Cliffs Notes Ser.). 96p. 2000. pap. 4.99 (*0-7645-8600-9*) IDG Bks.

— Twelfth Night. (Cliffs Complete Ser.). 240p. 2000. pap. 9.99 (*0-7645-8577-0*) IDG Bks.

— Wuthering Heights. LC 00-35081. (Cliffs Notes Ser.). 128p. 2000. pap. 4.99 (*0-7645-8594-0*) IDG Bks.

Cliffs Notes Staff & Knowlton, David N. Biology Quick Review. (Cliffs Quick Reviews Ser.). (Illus.). 214p. (Orig.). 1993. pap. 7.95 (*0-8220-5306-3*, Cliff) IDG Bks.

Cliffs Notes Staff, jt. auth. see Casson, Allan.

Cliffs Notes Staff, ed. see Shakespeare, William.

Clifon, Bruce. Exercise with Alcohol: The Ultimate Fitness Guide for Today's American Drinker. LC 96-24935. (Illus.). 128p. (Orig.). 1996. pap. 8.00 (*1-56980-089-8*) Barricade Bks.

Clift, A. Denis. With Presidents to the Summit. 1993. 23.95 (*0-913969-51-6*) Univ Pub Assocs.

Clift, Benedict, jt. ed. see Rowley, David I.

Clift, Charles E. Broadcast & Cable Programming: The Current Perspective. 2nd ed. 256p. 1993. per. 24.95 (*0-8403-8422-X*) Kendall-Hunt.

Clift, Dominique. Quebec Nationalism in Crisis. 164p. (C). 1982. reprint ed. pap. text 22.95 (*0-7735-0383-8*, Pub. by McG-Queens Univ Pr) CUP Services.

Clift, Dominique, jt. auth. see Arnopoulos, Sheila M.

Clift, Dominique, jt. auth. see Pernoud, R. Egine.

Clift, Dominique, tr. see Pernoud, Regine.

Clift, Elayne. Croning Tales. 160p. (Orig.). 12.95 (*0-9634827-3-4*) OGN Pubns.

— Demons Dancing in My Head: Collected Poems, 1985-1995. 110p. (Orig.). 8.95 (*0-9634827-2-6*) OGN Pubns.

— Other People, Other Lands. 72p. 1999. pap. 6.95 (*0-9634827-5-0*) OGN Pubns.

— Telling It Like It Is: Reflections of a Not So Radical Reminist. 198p. (Orig.). 1992. 14.95 (*1-879198-00-2*) Knwldg Ideas & Trnds.

— To New Jersey, with Love & Apologies. (Illus.). 140p. 1999. pap. 12.95 (*0-9634827-4-2*) OGN Pubns.

Clift, Eleanor. War Without Bloodshed. 416p. 1997. per. 14.00 (*0-684-83346-8*) S&S Trade.

***Clift, Eleanor & Brazaitis, Tom.** Madam President: Shattering the Last Glass Ceiling. LC 00-36565. (Illus.). 352p. 2000. 25.00 (*0-684-85619-0*) Scribner.

— War Without Bloodshed: The Art of Politics. (Illus.). 400p. 1999. reprint ed. text 25.00 (*0-7881-6607-7*) DIANE Pub.

Clift, G. Glenn. Remember the Raisin! Kentucky & Kentuckians in the Battles & Massacre at Frenchtown, Michigan Territory, in the War of 1812, 2 vols. 339p. 2000. pap. 29.50 (*0-8063-4520-9*) Clearfield Co.

— Second Census of Kentucky, 1800. LC 66-19191. 333p. 1993. reprint ed. 25.00 (*0-8063-0077-9*) Genealog Pub.

Clift, G. W. Mustaches & Other Stories. LC 95-43280. 92p. 1995. pap. 14.00 (*1-886157-02-2*) BkMk.

Clift, G. W., jt. auth. see Nyberg, Ben.

Clift, Garrett G. The Cornstalk Militia of Kentucky (1792-1811) 248p. 1982. reprint ed. 30.00 (*0-89308-318-6*) Southern Hist Pr.

Clift, Pamela, jt. auth. see Scavio, Michael.

Clift, Renee T., et al, eds. Encouraging Reflective Practice in Education: An Analysis of Issues & Programs. 256p. (C). 1989. pap. text 18.95 (*0-8077-2990-6*) Tchrs Coll.

Clift, Renee T., et al. Collaborative Leadership & Shared Decision Making: Teachers, Principals & University Professors. 192p. (C). 1995. text 36.00 (*0-8077-3394-6*); pap. text 17.95 (*0-8077-3393-8*) Tchrs Coll.

Clift, Russ. The Story of Cameracraftsmen, 1905-1995. (Illus.). 185p. 1998. pap. 29.95 (*0-9667688-0-9*) R Clift.

***Clift, Stephen.** Tourism & Sex: Culture, Commerce & Coercion. (Tourism, Leisure & Recreation Ser.). 2000. pap. text 28.95 (*1-85567-636-2*) Continuum.

Clift, Stephen, et al, eds. Health & the International Tourist. LC 95-17568. (Issues in Tourism Ser.). 240p. (C). (gr. 13). 1995. pap. 50.00 (*0-415-10282-0*) Thomson Learn.

Clift, Stephen & Carter, Simon. Tourism & Sex: Culture, Commerce & Coercion. LC 99-25151. (Tourism, Leisure & Recreation Ser.). 1999. 90.95 (*1-85567-549-8*) CRC Pr.

Clift, Stephen & Grabowski, Peter. Tourism & Health: Risks, Research & Responses. LC 96-39581. (Cutting Edge of Tourism Ser.). (Illus.). 256p. 1997. 90.00 (*1-85567-474-2*) Bks Intl VA.

Clift, Virgil A., jt. auth. see Low, W. Augustus.

Clift, W., jt. auth. see Baldwin, J. D.

Clift, Wallace B. Jung & Christianity: The Challenge of Reconciliation. 169p. 1990. pap. 17.95 (*0-8245-0552-2*) Crossroad NY.

Clift, William. Certain Places: Photographs by William Clift. (Illus.). 1987. 150.00 (*0-9618165-0-3*) Wm Clift Editions.

— Tim Bunker Paper: or Yankee Farming. LC 72-137727. (American Fiction Reprint Ser.). 1977. 23.95 (*0-8369-7026-8*) Ayer.

Clift, William, photos by. A Hudson Landscape: Photographs by William Clift. (Illus.). 88p. 1993. 100.00 (*0-9618165-1-1*) Wm Clift Editions.

Clift, William, jt. auth. see Baldwin, John Denison.

Clifton. Gingersnaps. (Illus.). 236p. (J). (gr. 3-6). 1998. pap. 8.70 (*0-7868-1306-7*, Pub. by Hyperion) Time Warner.

— The Lucky Stone. 1979. 12.50 (*0-440-05121-5*) Delacorte.

***Clifton.** One of the Problems of Everett Anderson. 2001. text 15.95 (*0-8050-5201-1*) St Martin.

Clifton, Barbara, ed. see Gnam, Rene.

Clifton, Barbara, ed. see Shapero, Albert.

Clifton, Beth H. And He Shall Stand. 1.00 (*0-687-50382-5*) Abingdon.

Clifton, Beth H., ed. Call to Post. 1997. 18.95 (*0-9656246-1-7*) Lex Hearing & Speech.

Clifton, C. E., et al, eds. Annual Review of Microbiology, Vol. 21. LC 49-432. 1967. text 41.00 (*0-8243-1121-3*) Annual Reviews.

— Annual Review of Microbiology, Vol. 22. LC 49-432. 1968. text 41.00 (*0-8243-1122-1*) Annual Reviews.

— Annual Review of Microbiology, Vol. 23. 1969. text 41.00 (*0-8243-1123-X*) Annual Reviews.

— Annual Review of Microbiology, Vol. 24. LC 49-432. 1970. text 41.00 (*0-8243-1124-8*) Annual Reviews.

— Annual Review of Microbiology, Vol. 26. LC 49-432. (Illus.). 1972. text 41.00 (*0-8243-1126-4*) Annual Reviews.

Clifton, Carl Stephen. What Every Engineer Should Know about Data Communications. (What Every Engineer Should Know Ser.: Vol. 19). (Illus.). 168p. 1986. text 59.75 (*0-8247-7566-X*) Dekker.

Clifton, Carr. Wild & Scenic California. (Illus.). 128p. 1995. 39.95 (*1-56313-640-6*) BrownTrout Pubs Inc.

Clifton, Carr, photos by. California Coast: Littlebook. (Illus.). 64p. 1996. 14.95 (*1-56579-136-3*) Westcliffe Pubs.

— California Reflections: Littlebook. (Illus.). 64p. 1996. 14.95 (*1-56579-135-5*) Westcliffe Pubs.

— California Wildflowers: Littlebook. (Illus.). 64p. 1996. 14.95 (*1-56579-134-7*) Westcliffe Pubs.

Clifton, Charles. Deception Detection: Winning the Polygraph Game. 152p. 1991. 20.00 (*0-87364-621-5*) Paladin Pr.

— Preemployment Integrity Testing: How to Ace the Test & Land the Job. 112p. 1993. pap. 12.00 (*0-87364-725-4*) Paladin Pr.

Clifton, Charles, et al. Perspectives on Sentence Processing. 488p. 1994. pap. 49.95 (*0-8058-1582-1*); text 89.95 (*0-8058-1581-3*) L Erlbaum Assocs.

Clifton, Charles, Jr., jt. auth. see Frazier, Lyn.

Clifton, Charles, ed. see Jones, E. J.

Clifton, Chas S. Encyclopedia of Heresies & Heretics. LC 92-29996. 156p. 1992. lib. bdg. 50.00 (*0-87436-600-3*) ABC-CLIO.

— Ghost Tales of Cripple Creek. (Illus.). 30p. 1983. pap. 3.50 (*0-936564-29-6*) Little London.

Clifton, Chas S., ed. Witchcraft Today Bk. 1: The Modern Craft Movement. LC 92-918. 208p. 1999. pap. 9.95 (*0-87542-377-9*) Llewellyn Pubns.

— Witchcraft Today Bk. 2: Modern Rites of Passage. LC 93-22967. (Witchcraft Today Ser.). 288p. 1999. pap. 9.95 (*0-87542-378-7*) Llewellyn Pubns.

— Witchcraft Today Bk. 3: Witchcraft & Shamanism. LC 94-6181. (Illus.). 288p. 1999. pap. 9.95 (*1-56718-150-3*) Llewellyn Pubns.

Clifton, Claire. A Little Book of Tropical Drinks. (Little Cookbooks Ser.). (Illus.). 1993. 6.95 (*0-8118-0362-7*) Chronicle Bks.

— A Little Book of Tropical Drinks. (Illus.). 60p. 1995. 7.95 (*0-8118-1040-2*) Chronicle Bks.

Clifton, Donald O. & Nelson, Paula. Soar with Your Strengths. 208p. 1995. reprint ed. pap. 12.95 (*0-440-50564-X*, Dial Pr) Dell.

Clifton Dozier, Gloria. Kerr County Texas Birth Records, 1877-1935. 322p. 1998. pap. 50.50 (*0-7884-0897-6*, D594) Heritage Bk.

Clifton, Fred. Darl. (Illus.). 104p. (J). (gr. 2-6). 1973. 12.00 (*0-89388-098-1*) Okpaku Communications.

Clifton, Gloria. Directory of Scientific Instrument Makers 1550-1851. (Illus.). 272p. 1994. 120.00 (*0-302-00634-6*, Pub. by P Wilson) Hoovers TX.

Clifton, Gloria C. Professionalism, Patronage & Public Service in Victorian London: Metropolitan Board of Works Staff, 1856. LC 92-10363. 192p. (C). 1992. text 80.00 (*0-485-11387-2*, Pub. by Athlone Pr) Humanities.

***Clifton, H. D. & Sutcliffe, Alistair.** Business Information Systems. 6th ed. LC 99-42791. 1999. write for info. (*0-13-082960-9*) P-H.

Clifton, H. Edward, ed. Sedimentologic Consequences of Convulsive Geologic Events. LC 88-25017. (Geological Society of America Ser.: Vol. 229). (Illus.). 163p. reprint ed. pap. 50.60 (*0-608-07754-2*, 206784200010) Bks Demand.

Clifton, Harry. Comparative Lives. 58p. 1982. pap. 11.95 (*0-904011-34-8*) Dufour.

— The Desert Route: Selected Poems, 1973-1988. 62p. 1992. pap. 12.95 (*1-85235-092-X*) Dufour.

— The Liberal Cage. 56p. 1988. pap. 12.95 (*1-85235-026-1*) Dufour.

— Night Train Through the Brenner. LC 94-151864. 70p. 1994. pap. 12.95 (*1-85235-122-5*) Dufour.

— Office of the Salt Merchant. 50p. 1979. pap. 11.95 (*0-902996-83-5*) Dufour.

— The Walls of Carthage. 46p. 1977. pap. 10.95 (*0-902996-50-9*) Dufour.

Clifton, James. The Body of Christ in the Art of Europe & New Spain, 1150-1800. (Illus.). 208p. 1998. 65.00 (*3-7913-1865-9*, Pub. by Prestel) te Neues.

Clifton, James, et al. The Body of Christ in the Art of Europe & New Spain, 1150-1800. LC 97-13416. 1997. pap. 45.00 (*0-89090-082-5*) Museum of Fine Arts.

— Five Hundred Years of French Art. Rankin, Lois, ed. LC 95-67295. (Illus.). 101p. (Orig.). 1995. pap. 14.95 (*1-883502-03-9*) San Ant Mus Art.

Clifton, James A. Being & Becoming Indian. 1988. 32.95 (*0-256-06254-4*) Dorsey.

— Being & Becoming Indian: Biographical Studies of North American Frontiers. (Illus.). 337p. (C). 1993. reprint ed. pap. text 17.95 (*0-88133-735-8*) Waveland Pr.

— Designs for the Future: The Western Washington Indian Treaties, 1854-1856: a Research Report. LC E 0095.. (Illus.). 153p. reprint ed. pap. 47.50 (*0-7837-6223-2*, AU0044300010) Bks Demand.

— Old Northwest Indian Removal, Eighteen Twenty-Five to Eighteen Fifty-Five: A Bibliography. LC 86-115302. 125p. 1988. reprint ed. pap. 38.80 (*0-608-08447-6*, AU0036500081) Bks Demand.

— The Pokagons, Sixteen Eighty-Three to Nineteen Eighty-Three: Catholic Potawatomi Indians of the St. Joseph River Valley. (Illus.). 182p. (Orig.). 1985. pap. text 23.00 (*0-8191-4283-2*) U Pr of Amer.

— The Prairie People: Continuity & Change in Potawatomi Indian Culture, 1665-1965. LC 98-24997. (Illus.). 568p. 1998. pap. text 24.95 (*0-87745-644-5*) U of Iowa Pr.

— The Saginaw Chippewa & the Isabella "Reservation" A Research Report. LC E 0095.. 223p. reprint ed. pap. 69.20 (*0-7837-6224-0*, AU0044400010) Bks Demand.

Clifton, James A., ed. The Invented Indian: Cultural Fictions & Government Policies. 388p. (C). 1994. pap. 29.95 (*1-56000-745-1*) Transaction Pubs.

Clifton, James R., ed. Cleaning Stone & Masonry. LC 86-25915. (Special Technical Publication Ser.: No. 935). (Illus.). 165p. 1986. text 29.00 (*0-8031-0932-6*, STP935) ASTM.

Clifton, Jon H. In Pursuit of Speed: A Book of Automobile Racing Trivia. (Illus.). 94p. 1998. pap. 9.95 (*1-57072-086-X*) Overmountain Pr.

***Clifton, Judith.** The Politics of Telecommunications in Mexico: Privatization & State-Labour Relations, 1982-95. LC 99-49938. (St. Antony's Ser.). 2000. text 69.95 (*0-312-23019-2*) St Martin.

Clifton, Larry. Public Speaking. 96p. (C). 1994. pap. text, per. 17.95 (*0-8403-9972-3*) Kendall-Hunt.

— The Terrible Fitzball: The Melodramatist of the Macabre. LC 92-74879. 192p. (C). 1993. 39.95 (*0-87972-608-3*); pap. 15.95 (*0-87972-609-1*) Bowling Green Univ Popular Press.

***Clifton, Larry.** Your Platform is the World! How to Celebrate Interpersonal Communication Through Vocation. 1999. pap., teacher ed. 19.95 (*1-885640-45-5*) Arrowhead Classics.

***Clifton, Lisa.** The Bunny Who Could Fly. large type ed. Begley, Melinda, ed. (Illus.). 36p. (J). (gr. k-6). 1999. 10.00 (*1-886623-07-4*) Canal Side Pubs.

***Clifton, Lucille.** Blessing the Boats: New & Selected Poems, 1988-2000. (American Poets Continuum Ser.: Vol. 59). 132p. 2000. 25.00 (*1-880238-87-X*); pap. 15.00 (*1-880238-88-8*, Pub. by BOA Edns) SPD-Small Pr Dist.

Clifton, Lucille. Book of Light. LC 92-40537. 80p. (Orig.). 1993. 21.00 (*1-55659-051-2*) Copper Canyon.

— Book of Light. LC 92-40537. 80p. (Orig.). 1998. pap. 11.00 (*1-55659-052-0*, Pub. by Copper Canyon) Consort Bk Sales.

— The Boy Who Didn't Believe in Spring. (J). (ps-3). 1992. pap. 5.99 (*0-14-054739-8*, Viking Child) Peng Put Young Read.

— Boy Who Didn't Believe in Spring. LC 72-89844. (J). 1973. 10.19 (*0-606-03738-1*, Pub. by Turtleback) Demco.

— Everett Anderson's Christmas Coming. LC 91-2041. (Illus.). 32p. (J). (ps-4). 1995. 14.95 (*0-8050-1549-3*, Bks Young Read); pap. 4.95 (*0-8050-2949-4*, Bks Young Read) H Holt & Co.

— Everett Anderson's Friend. rev. ed. LC 92-8030. (Illus.). 32p. (J). (ps-3). 1995. 14.95 (*0-8050-2246-5*, Bks Young Read) H Holt & Co.

— Everett Anderson's Goodbye. LC 82-23426. (Illus.). 32p. (J). (ps-2). 1995. pap. 5.95 (*0-8050-0800-4*, Bks Young Read) H Holt & Co.

— Everett Anderson's Goodbye. (J). 1983. 11.15 (*0-606-03779-9*, Pub. by Turtleback) Demco.

— Everett Anderson's Nine Month Long. LC 78-2402. (J). (ps-2). 1995. pap. 4.95 (*0-8050-0295-2*, Bks Young Read) H Holt & Co.

— Everett Anderson's Nine Month Long. LC 78-2402. (Illus.). 32p. (J). (ps-2). 1995. 13.95 (*0-8050-0287-1*, Bks Young Read) H Holt & Co.

— Everett Anderson's Year. rev. ed. LC 92-4683. (Illus.). 32p. (J). (ps-2). 1995. 14.95 (*0-8050-2247-3*, Bks Young Read) H Holt & Co.

— Everett Anderson's 1-2-3. rev. ed. LC 92-8031. (Illus.). 32p. (J). (ps-2). 1995. 14.95 (*0-8050-2310-0*, Bks Young Read) H Holt & Co.

— Good Woman: Poems & a Memoir, 1969-1980. (American Poets Continuum Ser.: No. 14). 276p. 1987. pap. 15.00 (*0-918526-59-0*) BOA Edns.

— The Lucky Stone. (Illus.). 64p. (J). (gr. 2-5). 1986. pap. 3.99 (*0-440-45110-8*, YB BDD) BDD Bks Young Read.

Clifton, Lucille. Lucky Stone. 1979. 8.70 (*0-606-02407-7*, Pub. by Turtleback) Demco.

Clifton, Lucille. Next: New Poems. (American Poets Continuum Ser.: No. 15). 85p. 1987. pap. 10.00 (*0-918526-61-2*) BOA Edns.

— El Nino Que No Creia en la Primavera. Ada, Alma E., tr.Tr. of Boy Who Didn't Believe in Spring. (SPA., Illus.). 32p. (J). (ps-3). 1996. pap. 4.99 (*0-14-055892-6*, PuffinBks) Peng Put Young Read.

C

Clifton, Lucille. El Nino Que No Creia En La Primavera. (SPA.). 1996. 10.19 (*0-606-09235-8*, Pub. by Turtleback) Demco.

Clifton, Lucille. Quilting: Poems, 1987-1990. LC 91-70845. (American Poets Continuum Ser.: No. 21). 89p. 1991. pap. 10.00 (*0-918526-81-7*, Pub. by BOA Edns) Consort Bk Sales.

— Some of the Days of Everett Anderson. 32p. (J). (ps-2). 1995. pap. 5.95 (*0-8050-0289-8*, Bks Young Read) H Holt & Co.

— Some of the Days of Everett Anderson. LC 78-98922. (Illus.). 32p. (J). (ps-2). 1995. 13.95 (*0-8050-0290-1*, Bks Young Read) H Holt & Co.

— The Terrible Stories. LC 96-84152. (American Poets Continuum Ser.: Vol. 38). 70p. 1996. 20.00 (*1-880238-36-5*); pap. 12.50 (*1-880238-37-3*) BOA Edns.

***Clifton, Lucille & Lewis, Earl B.** The Times They Used to Be. LC 99-42411. (J). 2000. 12.95 (*0-385-32126-0*) BDD Bks Young Read.

Clifton, Lucille, et al. Everett Anderson's Goodbye. LC 82-23426. (Illus.). 32p. (J). (ps-2). 1995. 14.95 (*0-8050-0235-9*, Bks Young Read) H Holt & Co.

Clifton, Lucille, et al. Sarasota Review of Poetry, Vol. 4. mass mkt. 10.00 (*0-9662719-2-0*, Pub. by R B Abel) SPD-Small Pr Dist.

Clifton, Marion, jt. auth. see Burton, Mary L.

Clifton, Mark & Riley, Frank. The Forever Machine. 384p. 1992. pap. 4.95 (*0-88184-842-5*) Carroll & Graf.

Clifton, Mark, tr. see Casagranda, Brigitte.

Clifton, Merritt. A Baseball Classic. 1978. pap. 5.00 (*0-686-00579-1*) Samisdat.

— Baseball in Vermont, 1887-1934. (Disorganized Baseball Ser.: Vol. II). 44p. 1991. 6.00 (*0-317-04127-4*) Samisdat.

— Baseball in Vermont, 1935-1988. (Disorganized Baseball Ser.: Vol. III). 60p. 1991. 6.00 (*0-317-04128-2*) Samisdat.

— Baseball Stories for Boys & Girls. 20p. 1982. pap. 1.50 (*0-686-37933-0*) Samisdat.

— Betrayal. 1980. 2.50 (*0-686-26981-0*) Samisdat.

— Disorganized Baseball: History of Quebec Provincial League, 1890-1976. 64p. 1991. pap. 6.00 (*0-686-89393-X*) Samisdat.

— Freedom Comes from Human Beings. 80p. (Orig.). 1980. pap. 4.00 (*0-686-28738-X*) Samisdat.

— On Small Press As Class Struggle. 1976. pap. 1.00 (*0-686-20630-4*) Samisdat.

— The Samisdat Method: A Do-It-Yourself Guide to Offset Printing. 4th ed. (Illus.). 56p. 1990. pap. 10.00 (*0-318-50051-5*) Samisdat.

— Thirty-Six Years of All-Star Rookies. 64p. 1994. pap. text 8.00 (*0-614-01212-0*) Samisdat.

Clifton, Merritt, et al, eds. Those Who Were There: Eyewitness Accounts of the War in Southeast Asia, 1956-1975, & Aftermath; Annotated Bibliography of Books, Articles, & Topic-Related Magazines, Covering Writings Both Factual & Imaginative. LC 83-25434. (American Dust Ser.: No. 15). 297p. 1984. 12.95 (*0-913218-97-9*) Dustbooks.

Clifton, Merritt & Palmer, Pete. Relative Baseball II. 80p. 1985. 5.00 (*0-317-19196-9*) Samisdat.

Clifton, Merritt & Sandman, John. A Double Play of Underground Baseball Novellas: "A Baseball Classic" & "Praying for Rain" LC 97-7466. 184p. 1997. pap. 18.50 (*0-913559-35-0*) Birch Brook Pr.

— A Double Play of Underground Baseball Novellas: "A Baseball Classic" & "Praying for Rain" deluxe limited ed. LC 97-7466. 184p. 1997. 75.00 (*0-913559-34-2*) Birch Brook Pr.

Clifton, Michael. A Victorian Convert Quintet. (Illus.). 128p. 1998. pap. 16.95 (*1-901157-03-2*) St Augustines Pr.

Clifton-Mogg, Caroline. Curtains: A Design Source Book. LC 97-12775. (Illus.). 192p. 1997. 40.00 (*1-55670-603-0*) Stewart Tabori & Chang.

***Clifton-Mogg, Caroline.** Decorating with Antiques: Confidently Combining Old & New. (Illus.). 192p. 1999. 40.00 (*0-8212-2565-0*, Pub. by Bulfinch Pr) Little.

Clifton-Mogg, Caroline. The Dollhouse Sourcebook: Classic Miniature Period Interiors. (Illus.). 208p. 1993. 39.95 (*1-55859-613-5*) Abbeville Pr.

***Clifton-Mogg, Caroline.** Textile Style. (Illus.). 192p. 2000. 35.00 (*0-8212-2684-3*) Bulfinch Pr.

Clifton-Mogg, Caroline & Paine, Melanie. The Curtain Book: A Sourcebook for Distinctive Curtains, Drapes, & Shades for Your Home. (Illus.). 180p. 1995. pap. 25.95 (*0-8212-2194-9*, Pub. by Bulfinch Pr) Little.

Clifton, N. Roy. The Figure in Film. LC 80-54539. 580p. 1983. 65.00 (*0-87413-189-8*) U Delaware Pr.

Clifton, Peter, et al. Market Research: Using Forecasting in Business. LC 93-118001. (Illus.). 280p. 1992. reprint ed. pap. 86.80 (*0-608-07428-4*, 206765500009) Bks Demand.

Clifton, Peter G., jt. ed. see Cooper, Steven J.

Clifton, R. J. & Espinosa, H. D., eds. Advances in Failure Mechanisms in Brittle Materials: Proceedings, ASME International Mechanical Engineering Congress & Exposition, 1996, Atlanta, Georgia. LC 96-79042. (MD Ser.: Vol. 75). 189p. 1996. pap. text 60.00 (*0-7918-1551-X*) ASME Pr.

***Clifton, Rita & Maughan, Esther, eds.** The Future of Brands: Twenty-Five Visions. LC 99-42581. 112p. 1999. text 35.00 (*0-8147-3766-8*) NYU Pr.

Clifton, Rob, ed. Perspectives on Quantum Reality: Non-Relativistic, Relativistic, & Field-Theoretic. LC 95-40138. (University of Western Ontario Series in Phylosophy of Science). 256p. (C). 1996. text 118.00 (*0-7923-3812-X*) Kluwer Academic.

Clifton, Robert L. & Dahms, Alan M. Grassroots Organizations: A Resource Book for Directors, Staff & Volunteers of Small, Community-Based, Nonprofit Agencies. 2nd ed. 242p. (C). 1993. pap. text 16.95 (*0-88133-726-9*) Waveland Pr.

Clifton, Robert T. Barbs, Prongs, Points, Prickers, & Stickers: Complete & Illustrated Catalogue of Antique Barbed Wire. LC 78-88140. (Illus.). 1970. pap. 19.95 (*0-8061-0876-2*) U of Okla Pr.

Clifton, Shaw. Never the Same Again: Encouragement for New & Not-So-New Christians. LC 97-66976. 192p. (Orig.). 1997. pap. 6.00 (*0-9657601-0-3*, Crest Books) SANP.

— Who Are These Salvationists? An Analysis for the 21st Century. LC 99-62151. 240p. 1999. 7.50 (*0-9657601-6-2*, Crest Books) SANP.

Clifton, Talbot, jt. auth. see O'Hamaguchi.

Clifton-Taylor, Alec. The Cathedrals of England. rev. ed. LC 79-66135. (World of Art Ser.). (Illus.). 1989. reprint ed. pap. 14.95 (*0-500-20062-9*, Pub. by Thames Hudson) Norton.

— Six English Towns. (Illus.). 176p. (Orig.). 1987. pap. 18.95 (*0-563-20490-7*, Pub. by BBC) Parkwest Pubns.

— Six More English Towns. (Illus.). 207p. (Orig.). 1987. pap. 18.95 (*0-563-20439-7*, Pub. by BBC) Parkwest Pubns.

Clifton-Taylor, Alec & Ireson, A. S. English Stone Building. LC 95-232570. (Illus.). 288p. 1995. 65.00 (*0-575-05824-2*, Pub. by V Gollancz) Trafalgar.

— English Stone Building. (Illus.). 288p. 1997. pap. 35.00 (*0-575-05846-3*, Pub. by V Gollancz) Trafalgar.

Clifton, Thomas E., ed. Central Thoughts on the Church in the 21st Century. LC 98-16755. 160p. 1998. pap. 13.00 (*1-57312-172-X*) Smyth & Helwys.

Clifton, Tony & Leroy, Catherine. God Cried. 1985. 29.95 (*0-7043-2375-3*, Pub. by Quartet) Interlink Pub.

Clifton-Wallace, Robert. Ka-Batin-Guy. Kincade-Clifton, Rena, ed. (Illus.). 336p. 1993. 20.00 (*0-9634992-0-3*) Pretani.

— Mons Graupius. Kincade-Clifton, Rena, ed. (Illus.). 600p. 1993. 24.00 (*0-9634992-1-1*) Pretani.

Clifton Waller Barrett Library Staff & Crane, Joan S. Carl Sandburg, Philip Green Wright, & the Asgard Press, 1900-1910: A Descriptive Catalogue of Early Books, Manuscripts, & Letters in the Clifton Waller Barrett Library. LC 75-6824. 158p. reprint ed. pap. 49.00 (*0-8357-2729-7*, 203983900013) Bks Demand.

— Robert Frost: A Descriptive Catalogue of Books & Manuscripts in the Clifton Waller Barrett Library, University of Virginia. LC 73-89904. 316p. reprint ed. pap. 98.00 (*0-8357-2730-0*, 203984000013) Bks Demand.

Clifton, Williams. March from "Symphonic Suite" for Orchestra: Score. LC M 1247. 159p. reprint ed. pap. 49.30 (*0-608-10799-9*, 200289300015) Bks Demand.

Clignet, Remi. The Africanization of the Labor Market: Educational & Occupational Segmentation in the Cameroun. LC 75-13145. 246p. reprint ed. pap. 76.30 (*0-8357-5243-7*, 203142800074) Bks Demand.

— Death, Deeds, & Descendants: Inheritance in Modern America. (Social Institutions & Social Change Ser.). 247p. 1992. lib. bdg. 49.95 (*0-202-30398-5*) Aldine de Gruyter.

— Many Wives, Many Powers: Authority & Power in Polygynous Families. LC 75-89821. 400p. (C). reprint ed. pap. 124.00 (*0-8357-9464-4*, 201025800068) Bks Demand.

Clinchy, Everett R., Jr. Equality of Opportunity for Latin-Americans in Texas. LC 73-14199. (Mexican American Ser.). 224p. 1979. 24.95 (*0-405-05673-7*) Ayer.

Clijsters, H., et al, eds. Biochemical & Physiological Aspects of Ethylene Production in Lower & Higher Plants. (Advances in Agricultural Biotechnology Ser.). (C). 1989. text 171.00 (*0-7923-0201-X*) Kluwer Academic.

Climaco, jt. ed. see Current.

Climaco, J., ed. Multicriteria Analysis, Vol. X. LC 97-552. (Illus.). 617p. 1997. 169.00 (*3-540-62074-5*) Spr-Verlag.

Climacus, St. John. Ljestvitsa.Tr. of Ladder. (RUS.). 266p. (Orig.). 1963. 18.00 (*0-88465-033-2*); pap. 13.00 (*0-317-38080-X*) Holy Trinity.

Climate Institute Staff. Coping with Climate Change: Proceedings of the Second North American Conference on Preparing for Climate Change: A Cooperative Approach. LC 89-62291. (Illus.). 710p. (Orig.). (C). 1989. pap. 35.00 (*0-9623610-0-3*) Climate Inst.

Climate Institute Staff, jt. auth. see Topping, John C., Jr.

***Climbing Magazine Staff.** Climbing Anthology 30 Years of Climbing. 1999. 18.95 (*1-893682-02-1*) Climb Mag.

Climenhaga, David J. A Poke in the Public Eye: Media Manipulation for Aspiring Politicians & Other Undesirables. (Illus.). 128p. (Orig.). 1995. pap. write for info. (*1-55059-110-X*) Detselig Ents.

Climenson, Emily J. A Guide to Henley-on-Thames, 1896. 156p. 1983. 35.00 (*0-905418-98-0*, Pub. by Gresham Bks); pap. 25.00 (*0-905418-97-2*, Pub. by Gresham Bks) St Mut.

Climent, Carlos E. & Burns, Barbara J. Practical Psychiatry for the Health Professional. LC 84-4926. (Illus.). 223p. 1984. text 29.50 (*0-88331-182-8*) R B Luce.

Climer, Edith L., jt. auth. see Climer, Henry J.

Climer, Henry J. & Climer, Edith L. Genesis & Science: An Introduction to Something Big That is about to Happen. LC 98-90396. 1999. pap. 10.95 (*0-533-12790-4*) Vantage.

Climer, Jerry. How to Raise a Dog When Nobody's Home. rev. ed. (Illus.). 170p. 1992. pap. 9.95 (*0-911793-03-8*) Penny Dreadful Pubs.

Climer, Ron. My Parents Are Users: Christian Living - Encouragement. Nelson, Becky, ed. 21p. (YA). (gr. 7-12). 1994. pap. text 1.95 (*1-56309-096-1*, C946105, Wrld Changers Res) Womans Mission Union.

***Climer, Steven Lee.** Demonesque. 169p. 1999. pap. 18.99 (*0-9672029-1-4*) Darktales Pubns.

Climo. Pandora's Gift. (Illus.). 64p. (J). (gr. 3-4). 14.95 (*0-06-028632-6*) HarpC.

Climo. Pandora's Gift. 64p. (J). Date not set. pap. 3.95 (*0-06-444271-3*) HarpC Child Bks.

Climo, Jacob. Distant Parents. LC 91-32605. 286p. (C). 1992. 40.00 (*0-8135-1796-6*); pap. 16.00 (*0-8135-1797-4*) Rutgers U Pr.

Climo, Jacob J., jt. ed. see Teski, Marea C.

Climo, Lindee. Chester's Barn. 1995. 11.90 (*0-606-08713-3*, Pub. by Turtleback) Demco.

— Chester's Barn. rev. ed. (Illus.). 32p. 1995. pap. 6.95 (*0-88776-351-0*) Tundra Bks.

Climo, Percy L. Haw. Genealogy of John Haw, 1821-1916. (Illus.). 47p. 1997. reprint ed. pap. 9.00 (*0-8328-9052-9*); reprint ed. lib. bdg. 19.00 (*0-8328-9051-0*) Higginson Bk Co.

Climo, S. The Little Red Ant & the Great Big Crumb. (ps-3). 1999. pap. 5.95 (*0-395-72097-4*, Clarion Bks) HM.

***Climo, Shirley.** Atalanta's Race: A Greek Myth. (Illus.). 32p. (J). (gr. 4-7). 2000. pap. 6.95 (*0-618-05154-6*, Clarion Bks) HM.

Climo, Shirley. City! San Francisco. LC 89-32912. (Illus.). 64p. (J). (gr. 3-7). 1990. lib. bdg. 16.95 (*0-02-719030-7*, Mac Bks Young Read) S&S Childrens.

— City Washington, D. C. LC 90-1785. (Illus.). 64p. (J). (gr. 3-7). 1991. lib. bdg. 16.95 (*0-02-719036-6*, Mac Bks Young Read) S&S Childrens.

— Cobweb Christmas. LC 81-43879. (Illus.). 32p. (J). (ps-3). 1982. lib. bdg. 15.89 (*0-690-04216-7*) HarpC Child Bks.

Climo, Shirley. The Cobweb Christmas. 32p. (ps-3). pap. 5.95 (*0-06-443702-7*) HarpC.

— The Cobweb Christmas. 32p. (ps-3). 2001. 15.95 (*0-06-029033-1*); lib. bdg. 15.89 (*0-06-029034-X*) HarpC Child Bks.

Climo, Shirley. The Cobweb Christmas. LC 81-43879. (Trophy Picture Bk.). (Illus.). 32p. (J). (ps-3). 1986. reprint ed. pap. 5.95 (*0-06-443110-X*, HarpTrophy) HarpC Child Bks.

— The Egyptian Cinderella. LC 88-37547. (Illus.). 32p. (J). (ps-3). 1989. 15.95 (*0-690-04822-X*) HarpC Child Bks.

— The Egyptian Cinderella. LC 88-37547. (Illus.). 32p. (J). (ps-3). 1989. lib. bdg. 15.89 (*0-690-04824-6*) HarpC Child Bks.

— The Egyptian Cinderella. LC 88-37547. (Trophy Picture Bk.). (Illus.). 32p. (J). (gr. k-3). 1992. pap. 5.95 (*0-06-443279-3*, HarpTrophy) HarpC Child Bks.

— The Egyptian Cinderella. (J). 1992. 11.15 (*0-606-00411-4*, Pub. by Turtleback) Demco.

— The Irish Cinderlad. LC 94-37545. (Illus.). 32p. (J). (ps-3). 1996. 16.95 (*0-06-024396-1*) HarpC Child Bks.

— The Irish Cinderlad. LC 94-37545. (Illus.). 32p. (J). (gr. k-4). 2000. pap. 5.95 (*0-06-443577-6*) HarpC Child Bks.

— King of the Birds. LC 87-47693. (Trophy Picture Bk.). (Illus.). 32p. (J). (ps up). 1991. pap. 5.95 (*0-06-443273-4*, HarpTrophy) HarpC Child Bks.

— The Korean Cinderella. LC 91-23268. (Illus.). 48p. (J). (gr. k-3). 1993. 15.95 (*0-06-020432-X*) HarpC Child Bks.

— The Korean Cinderella. LC 91-23268. (Illus.). 48p. (J). (ps-3). 1993. lib. bdg. 15.89 (*0-06-020433-8*) HarpC Child Bks.

— The Korean Cinderella. LC 91-23268. (Trophy Picture Bk.). (Illus.). 48p. (J). (gr. k-3). 1996. pap. 6.95 (*0-06-443397-8*, HarpTrophy) HarpC Child Bks.

— Korean Cinderella. LC 91-23268. 1993. 11.15 (*0-606-09519-5*, Pub. by Turtleback) Demco.

***Climo, Shirley.** Monkey Business. 2001. text 16.95 (*0-8050-6392-7*) St Martin.

— Pandora's Gift. 64p. (J). 2001. lib. bdg. 14.89 (*0-06-028633-4*) HarpC Child Bks.

Climo, Shirley. The Persian Cinderella. LC 98-36900. (Illus.). 32p. (J). (gr. k-4). 1999. 15.95 (*0-06-026763-1*) HarpC Child Bks.

— The Persian Cinderella. LC 98-36900. (Illus.). 32p. (J). (gr. 1-4). 1999. lib. bdg. 15.89 (*0-06-026765-8*) HarpC Child Bks.

— Piskies, Spriggans, & Other Magical Beings: Tales from the Droll-Teller. LC 79-7839. (Illus.). 128p. (J). (gr. 4-7). 1981. 11.95 (*0-690-04063-6*); lib. bdg. 11.89 (*0-690-04064-4*) HarpC Child Bks.

— A Pride of Princesses: Princess Tales from Around the World. LC 98-41740. (Trophy Chapter Bk.). (Illus.). 112p. (J). (gr. 2-5). 1999. pap. 4.25 (*0-06-442102-3*) HarpC Child Bks.

— A Serenade of Mermaids: Mermaid Tales from Around the World. LC 98-44272. (Trophy Chapter Bk.). (Illus.). 112p. (J). (gr. 2-5). 1999. mass mkt. 4.25 (*0-06-442103-1*) HarpC Child Bks.

— Stolen Thunder: A Norse Myth. LC 93-24627. (Illus.). 40p. (J). (gr. 1-5). 1994. 15.95 (*0-395-64368-6*, Clarion Bks) HM.

— T. J.'s Ghost. LC 87-42931. (Trophy Bk.). 160p. (J). (gr. 5 up). 1991. pap. 3.50 (*0-06-440396-3*, HarpTrophy) HarpC Child Bks.

— A Treasury of Mermaids: Mermaid Tales from Around the World. LC 96-29075. (Illus.). 80p. (J). (gr. 2 up). 1997. 16.95 (*0-06-023876-3*) HarpC Child Bks.

— A Treasury of Princesses: Princess Tales from Around the World. LC 95-31062. (Illus.). 80p. (J). (ps up). 1996. lib. bdg. 16.89 (*0-06-024533-6*) HarpC Child Bks.

— A Treasury of Princesses: Princess Tales from Around the World. LC 95-31062. (Illus.). 80p. (J). (ps up). 1996. 16.95 (*0-06-024532-8*) HarpC Child Bks.

Clin, Marie-Veronique, jt. auth. see Pernoud, Regine.

Clinard. Sociology of Deviant Behavior. 9th ed. (C). 1994. pap. text, teacher ed. 33.75 (*0-15-502142-7*) Harcourt Coll Pubs.

— Sociology of Deviant Behavior. 10th ed. LC 97-72383. (C). 1997. text 73.00 (*0-15-504130-4*, Pub. by Harcourt Coll Pubs) Harcourt.

Clinard, H. Gordon, et al. Steps to the Sermon: An 8 Step Plan for Preaching with Confidence. rev. ed. 240p. 1996. 24.99 (*0-8054-1238-7*, 4212-38) Broadman.

Clinard, Helen. Listen to Understand. (Illus.). 49p. (Orig.). 1995. pap. 5.00 (*0-614-14785-9*) Effect Trg Consult.

Clinard, Helen H. Winning Ways to Succeed with People. 2nd rev. ed. (Illus.). 318p. 1990. text 20.00 (*0-9623553-0-5*) Effect Trg Consult.

Clinard, Linda. Family Time Reading Fun, Vol. 3338. Thrall Cicciarelli, Joellyn, ed. LC 98-125028. (Illus.). 112p. (J). (gr. k-2). 1997. pap. 11.98 (*1-57471-292-6*) Creat Teach Pr.

Clinard, Marshall B. The Abuse of Corporate Power. LC 89-23088. 224p. 1990. 35.00 (*0-275-93485-3*, C3485, Greenwood Pr) Greenwood.

— Black Market: A Study of White Collar Crime. LC 69-16233. (Criminology, Law Enforcement, & Social Problems Ser.: No. 87). (C). 1969. reprint ed. 30.00 (*0-87585-087-1*) Patterson Smith.

— Corporate Ethics & Crime: The Role of Middle Management. LC 83-3105. 189p. 1983. reprint ed. pap. 58.60 (*0-608-01122-3*, 205942600001) Bks Demand.

Clinard, Marshall B. & Abbott, Daniel J. Crime in Developing Countries: A Comparative Perspective. LC 73-4031. 334p. reprint ed. pap. 103.60 (*0-7837-3435-2*, 205775700008) Bks Demand.

Clinard, Marshall B. & Meier, Robert F. Sociology of Deviant Behavior. 8th ed. 450p. (C). 1992. text. write for info. (*0-318-69131-0*) Harcourt Coll Pubs.

Clinard, Marshall B., et al. Criminal Behavior Systems: A Typology. 3rd rev. ed. LC 93-79362. 280p. (C). 1994. pap. 29.95 (*0-87084-180-7*) Anderson Pub Co.

Clinch, Danny. Discovery Inn: The Photographs of Danny Clinch. 1999. pap. 29.95 (*0-9664100-1-7*, Pub. by Razorfish Studios) Consort Bk Sales.

***Clinch, Danny.** Tibetan Freedom Concerts, 1996-1999: When the Iron Bird Flies. 2000. pap. 40.00 (*0-9664100-4-1*) Razorfish Studios.

Clinch, Danny & Kanarick, Craig. Discovery Inn: The Photographs of Danny Clinch. LC 98-85465. (Illus.). 128p. 1998. 60.00 (*0-9664100-0-9*) Razorfish Studios.

Clinch, J., ed. Perinatal Medicine. 1985. text 225.00 (*0-85200-908-9*) Kluwer Academic.

Clinch, Moira, ed. The Watercolor Painter's Pocket Palette. (Pocket Palette Ser.). (Illus.). 64p. 1991. 17.99 (*0-89134-401-2*, 30341, North Lght Bks) F & W Pubns Inc.

Clinch, N. On-Farm Research: An Annotated Bibliography. 127p. 1994. pap. 45.00 (*0-85954-371-4*, Pub. by Nat Res Inst) St Mut.

Clinch, P., ed. Learning Legal Research Skills. (C). 1991. 34.00 (*1-85431-191-3*, Pub. by Blackstone Pr) Gaunt.

Clinch, Richard P., jt. auth. see Northrup, Herbert R.

Clinchy. Advanced Sport Diver: Instructor's Guide. 2nd ed. 32p. 1993. pap. text 7.95 (*0-8016-9033-1*) Mosby Inc.

— Advanced Sport Diver: Workbook. 2nd ed. 35p. 1993. pap. text 6.95 (*0-8016-9032-3*) Mosby Inc.

— Open Water Sport Diver, Instructor's Guide. 5th ed. 48p. 1992. teacher ed., spiral bd. 7.95 (*0-8016-9036-6*) Mosby Inc.

— Open Water Sport Diver, Workbook. 5th ed. 51p. 1991. pap. text, wbk. ed. 7.95 (*0-8016-9037-4*) Mosby Inc.

Clinchy, Blythe & Norem, Julie K. Gender & Psychology Reader. LC 97-42572. 1998. text 75.00 (*0-8147-1546-X*) NYU Pr.

Clinchy, Blythe M. Gender & Psychology Reader. LC 97-42572. 1998. pap. text 29.50 (*0-8147-1547-8*) NYU Pr.

***Clinchy, Evans.** Creating New Schools: How Small Schools Are Changing American Education. (Illus.). 2000. pap. 23.95 (*0-8077-3876-X*) Tchrs Coll.

Clinchy, Evans. Reforming American Education from the Bottom to the Top. LC 99-33274. 224p. 1999. pap. text 24.00 (*0-325-00174-X*) Heinemann.

— Transforming Public Education: A New Course for America's Future. LC 96-3467. 224p. (C). 1996. text 43.00 (*0-8077-3569-8*); pap. text 18.95 (*0-8077-3568-X*) Tchrs Coll.

***Clinchy, Evans, ed.** Creating New Schools: How Small Schools Are Changing American Education. LC 99-48170. 240p. 2000. write for info. (*0-8077-3877-8*) Tchrs Coll.

Clinchy, Evans, jt. auth. see Young, Timothy W.

Clinchy, Richard A. Dive-First Responder. (Illus.). 160p. (C). (gr. 13). 1995. pap. text 35.95 (*0-8016-7525-1*, 21217) Mosby Inc.

Clinchy, Richard A. & Egstrom. Jeppesen's Advanced Sport Diver Manual. 2nd ed. (Illus.). 304p. (gr. 13). 1993. pap. text 25.95 (*0-8016-9031-5*, 21218) Mosby Inc.

Clinchy, Richard A., et al. Jeppesen's Open Water Sport Diver Manual. 5th ed. (Illus.). 320p. (gr. 13). 1991. pap. text 19.95 (*0-8016-9035-8*, 21219) Mosby Inc.

Cline. Jeremiah, Vol. I. 1986. write for info. (*0-88027-112-4*) Firm Foun Pub.

— John. 1989. write for info. (*0-88027-121-3*) Firm Foun Pub.

— Joshua. 1987. write for info. (*0-88027-114-0*) Firm Foun Pub.

— Just the Facts in Emergency Medicine. 320p. 2000. student ed. 39.95 (*0-07-134549-3*) McGraw-Hill Prof.

— Luke. 1988. write for info. (*0-88027-117-5*) Firm Foun Pub.

— 1998 Year Book of Medicine. (Illus.). 752p. (C). (gr. 13). 1998. text 75.00 (*0-8151-3156-9*, 26975) Mosby Inc.

An Asterisk (*) at the beginning of an entry indicates that the title is appearing for the first time.

Cline & McHaffie. The People's Guide, 1874: Directory of Henry Co., Indiana. 398p. 1979. 22.00 (*0-686-27818-6*) Bookmark.

Cline, et al. Prescriptions for Good Eating. 304p. (Orig.). 1984. pap. 11.95 (*0-9613679-0-3*) Greenville County Med.

***Cline, A. G., et al.** As I Remember It: As Told to Cindy Partington. (Illus.). x, 167p. 1999. pap. write for info. (*0-9676730-0-3*) Cline Pubng.

Cline, Ann. A Hut of One's Own: Life Outside the Circle of Architecture. LC 97-33107. (Illus.). 167p. 1998. pap. text 17.50 (*0-262-53150-X*) MIT Pr.

Cline, Barbara L. Men Who Made a New Physics: Physicists & the Quantum Theory. LC 65-18693. (Illus.). xi, 282p. (C). 1987. pap. text 19.00 (*0-226-11027-3*) U Ch Pr.

***Cline, Brenda A., et al.** Guide to Preparing Nonprofit Financial Statements. 1999. ring bd. write for info. (*0-7646-0782-0*, NFSP 99) Prctnrs Pub Co.

— Guide to Preparing Nonprofit Financial Statements, 2 vols., Set. 1999. ring bd. 164.00 (*0-7646-0781-2*, NFSP 99) Prctnrs Pub Co.

— Guide to Preparing Nonprofit Financial Statements, Vol. 2. 1999. ring bd. write for info. (*0-7646-0783-9*, NFSP 99) Prctnrs Pub Co.

Cline, C., ed. see Maheshsvari.

Cline, C. L. The Fate of Cassandra: The Newspaper War of 1821-22 & Sir Walter Scott. LC 72-5780. (Quarterly Ser.). 1971. 10.00 (*0-87959-069-6*) U of Tex H Ransom Ctr.

Cline, C. L., ed. The Letters of George Meredith, 3 vols., Set. 1786p. 1970. 75.00 (*0-87959-123-4*) U of Tex H Ransom Ctr.

Cline, Camille N. People Entertainment Almanac 1998. 1997. pap. text 9.95 (*1-883013-20-8*, People Bks) Tme Inc.

***Cline, Carol A.** Because He Lives. 1999. pap. write for info. (*1-58235-163-5*) Watermrk Pr.

Cline, Catherine, ed. & photos by see Cline, Jeff.

Cline, Catherine C. Harvest Moon Rising. unabridged ed. Cline, Jeff, ed. (Illus.). 300p. 1999. pap. 14.95 (*1-892009-03-X*) Maheshsvari Pub.

— Into the Heart of Prophesy. Cline, Jeff & Bush, Rosemary, eds. (Illus.). 153p. 1998. pap., per. 19.95 (*1-892009-02-1*) Maheshsvari Pub.

Cline, Catherine C., ed. see Cline, Jeff L.

Cline, Charles D. Boston Terriers. (Illus.). 1997. pap. 9.95 (*0-7938-2397-8*, KW-105S) TFH Pubns.

Cline, Cheryl. Women's Diaries, Journals, & Letters: An Annotated Bibliography. LC 89-1197. 754p. 1989. text 20.00 (*0-8240-6637-5*) Garland.

Cline, D. B. Exclusive B & K Decays & Novel Flavor Factories. (AIP Conference Proceeding Ser.: No. 261). 288p. 1992. 95.00 (*1-56396-055-9*) Am Inst Physics.

— Gamma Ray & Neutrino Cosmology: Proceedings of the 2nd UCLA International Conference. 356p. 1994. text 118.00 (*981-02-1234-8*) World Scientific Pub.

Cline, D. B., ed. Low Energy Antimatter: Proceedings of the Workshop on the Design of a Low Energy Antimatter Facility, Madison, Wisconsin, October 1985. 220p. 1986. text 60.00 (*9971-5-0163-5*) World Scientific Pub.

— Observational Neutrino Astronomy. 304p. (C). 1988. text 85.00 (*9971-5-0823-0*) World Scientific Pub.

Cline, D. B. & Mills, F. E., eds. The Unification of Elementary Forces & Gauge Theories: Proceedings of the Ben Lee Memorial International, Weak Neutral Currents & Gauge Theories, Held at the Fermi National Accelerator Laboratory, Oct 20-22, 1977. xx, 770p. 1980. text 306.00 (*0-906346-00-2*) Gordon & Breach.

Cline, D. B., jt. auth. see Barger, V.

Cline, D. J. Perfection, Never Less: The Vera Way Marghab Story. LC 98-61099. (Illus.). 224p. 1998. 44.95 (*0-9666544-0-4*) SD Art Museum.

Cline, Dallas. Homemade Instruments. LC 76-8073. 1976. pap. 12.95 (*0-8256-0186-X*, OK63354, Oak) Music Sales.

— How to Play Nearly Everything. LC 77-83767. (Illus.). 80p. 1998. pap. 12.95 (*0-8256-0199-1*, OK63420, Oak) Music Sales.

Cline, David, ed. Flavor-Changing Neutral Currents - Present & Future Studies. LC 97-41791. 300p. 1997. text 76.00 (*981-02-3218-7*) World Scientific Pub.

Cline, David, et al, eds. Emergency Medicine: Companion Handbook. 4th ed. (Illus.). 650p. 1996. text 38.00 (*0-07-011402-1*) McGraw-Hill HPD.

Cline, David, et al. Dictionary of Visual Science. 4th ed. LC 96-41053. 820p. 1996. text 70.00 (*0-7506-9895-0*) Buttrwrth-Heinemann.

Cline, David, jt. auth. see Barger, Vernon.

Cline, David, jt. ed. see Hubbs, Clay.

Cline, David B. Sources of Dark Matter in the Universe. 332p. 1995. text 86.00 (*981-02-2131-2*) World Scientific Pub.

Cline, David B., ed. Physical Origin of Homochirality in Life. (AIP Conference Proceedings Ser.: No. 379). 283p. 1996. 125.00 (*1-56396-507-0*, AIP Pr) Spr-Verlag.

— Physics Potential & Development of Mu-Mu Colliders: Fourth International Conference. LC 98-86574. (Conference Proceedings Ser.: Vol. 441). (Illus.). 400p. 1998. 105.00 (*1-56396-723-5*) Am Inst Physics.

Cline, David B., jt. ed. see Mann, Alfred K.

Cline, David M., et al. Emergency Medicine Companion Handbook. 5th ed. (Illus.). 1150p. 1999. pap. 39.95 (*0-07-012039-0*) McGraw-Hill HPD.

Cline, Debbie, jt. auth. see Backer, Lynn.

Cline, Debbie, jt. auth. see Backer, Lynne.

Cline, Don. Antrim & Billy. LC 90-1598. (Early West Ser.). (Illus.). 170p. (YA). 1990. 19.95 (*0-932702-48-1*) Creative Texas.

Cline, Don & Pitzer, Sara. Buying & Selling Antiques: A Dealer's Inside View. LC 85-61478. (Illus.). 112p. (Orig.). 1986. pap. 12.95 (*0-88266-406-9*) Storey Bks.

Cline, Donald. Alias Billy the Kid, the Man Behind the Legend: Another View. LC 85-26087. (Western Legacy Ser.). (Illus.). 144p. (Orig.). 1986. pap. 12.95 (*0-86534-080-3*) Sunstone Pr.

Cline, Duane A. Navigation in the Age of Discovery: An Introduction. LC 90-91870. (Illus.). 214p. (Orig.). 1990. pap. 17.50 (*0-9627213-0-1*) Montfleury.

Cline, Edward. First Prize. 1989. mass mkt. 4.95 (*0-445-40792-1*, Pub. by Warner Bks) Little.

Cline, Edward. Virtues in Verse: The Best of Berton Braley. 208p. 1991. 15.95 (*0-9626854-2-9*) Atlantean Pr.

Cline, Edward, jt. auth. see Scott, L. L.

***Cline, Eric H.** The Battles of Armageddon: Megiddo & the Jezreel Valley from the Bronze Age to the Nuclear Age. (Illus.). 200p. 2000. 27.95 (*0-472-09739-3*, 09739) U of Mich Pr.

Cline, Eric H., jt. ed. see O'Connor, David B.

Cline, Foster & Fay, Jim. Parenting Teens with Love & Logic: Preparing Adolescents for Responsible Adulthood. LC 92-64090. 272p. 1992. 18.00 (*0-89109-695-7*) Pinon Press.

Cline, Foster W. & Fay, Jim. Parenting with Love & Logic: Teaching Children Responsibility. LC 92-60546. 229p. 1990. 18.00 (*0-89109-311-7*) Pinon Press.

Cline, Foster W., jt. auth. see Fay, Jim.

Cline, Gay. Simplified Solutions for Weight Management. (Illus.). vi, 202p. (Orig.). 1996. pap. 18.00 (*0-9654762-0-0*) Simplified Solns.

Cline, George B. Human Physiology Laboratory Experiments. 1992. spiral bd. 14.65 (*0-88252-152-7*) Paladin Hse.

Cline, Gloria G. Peter Skene Ogden & the Hudson's Bay Company. LC 72-9266. (American Exploration & Travel Ser.). 311p. reprint ed. pap. 96.50 (*0-608-15451-2*, 202930200060) Bks Demand.

Cline, Greg, jt. auth. see Holmes, Edith.

Cline, Howard F. Mexico: Revolution to Evolution, 1940 to 1960. 3rd ed. LC 81-3819. (Illus.). 375p. 1981. reprint ed. lib. bdg. 65.00 (*0-313-22993-7*, CLME, Greenwood Pr) Greenwood.

Cline, Howard F., et al, eds. William Hickling Prescott: A Memorial. LC 59-16153. 189p. reprint ed. pap. 58.60 (*0-608-10396-9*, 202619200048) Bks Demand.

Cline, Howard F., tr. see De Sahagun, Fray B.

Cline, Hugh F., et al, eds. The Electronic Schoolhouse. 148p. (C). 1985. pap. 19.95 (*0-89859-795-1*) L Erlbaum Assocs.

Cline, Hugh F. & Feldmesser, Robert A. Program Evaluation in Moral Education. 1988. 10.00 (*0-317-67889-2*) Educ Testing Serv.

Cline, Hugh F., jt. auth. see Mandinach, Ellen B.

Cline, Inez E., jt. auth. see McLane, Bobbie J.

Cline, Isaac Monroe, jt. see Larson, Erik.

Cline, Isaac Monroe, jt. auth. see Larson, Erik.

***Cline, Issac Monroe.** Storms, Floods & Sunshine: Isaac Monroe Cline, an Autobiography. 3rd ed. (Illus.). 384p. 2000. 25.00 (*1-56554-766-7*) Pelican.

Cline, J. H. Standing Liberty Quarters. 3rd rev. ed. LC 98-112864. (Illus.). 192p. 1997. pap. 24.95 (*1-880731-54-1*) DLRC Pr.

Cline, James H. A Small Percentage: A Dark Tale of Alien Invasion. LC 96-61236. 542p. 1997. 21.95 (*0-965321 0-0-2*) Timberwolf Pr.

Cline, James M., ed. see Montreal--Rochester--Syracuse--Toronto Meeting (McGill University).

Cline, Janice G., ed. Adolescence: From Crisis to Coping: A Thirteen Nation Study. LC 95-25382. (International Series in Social Psychology). (Illus.). 240p. 1996. pap. 29.95 (*0-7506-2604-6*) Buttrwrth-Heinemann.

Cline, Jean D. Silencing the Voices: One Woman's Triumph over Multiple Personality Disorder. LC 97-168748. 416p. 1997. mass mkt. 6.99 (*0-425-15693-1*) Berkley Pub.

Cline, Jeff. The Ultimate Evil. Cline, Catherine, ed. & photos by by. (Illus.). 232p. 1998. pap., per. 9.95 (*1-892009-01-3*) Maheshsvari Pub.

Cline, Jeff, ed. see Cline, Catherine C.

Cline, Jeff, ed. see Maheshsvari.

Cline, Jeff L. Defender of War-Land. Cline, Catherine C., ed. 200p. 1999. pap. 9.95 (*1-892009-05-6*) Maheshsvari Pub.

— Lord of the Black Earth. Cline, Catherine C., ed. 200p. 1999. pap. 9.95 (*1-892009-04-8*) Maheshsvari Pub.

Cline, Jon, jt. auth. see Cline, Liz.

Cline, Joseph. When the Heavens Frowned: American Autobiography. 221p. 1995. lib. bdg. 79.00 (*0-7812-8485-6*) Rprt Serv.

Cline, Kyle. Chinese Massage for Infants & Children: Traditional Techniques for Alleviating Colic, Teething Pain, Earache & Other Common Childhood Conditions. LC 99-18421. (Illus.). 224p. 1999. pap. 19.95 (*0-89281-797-6*, Heal Arts VT) Inner Tradit.

***Cline, Kyle.** Chinese Pediatric Massage: A Practitioner's Guide. LC 99-49254. (Illus.). 304p. 2000. 45.00 (*0-89281-842-5*) Inner Tradit.

Cline, Linda & Hayden, Robert C. A Cultural Guide to African-American Heritage in New England: A Cultural Guide Map of African-American Heritage in New England. LC 92-90178. (Illus.). 112p. (Orig.). 1992. pap. 10.95 (*1-881224-00-7*) Cline Transport.

Cline, Lindell. Me & the Law. 504p. 1995. 24.95 (*0-9644042-0-6*) Voice Common People.

Cline, Liz & Cline, Jon. A Child's First Guide to Horses from the Horse's Mouth: Champs the Schoolmaster. LC 96-94447. (Horse of Course Ser.: Vol. 1). (Illus.). 80p. (J). (gr. 2 up). 1997. 19.95 (*0-9652995-4-6*) Heartland Educ.

Cline Love, L. J. & Eastwood, Delyle, eds. Advances in Luminescence Spectroscopy - STP 863. LC 84-71320. (Illus.). 129p. 1985. pap. text 26.00 (*0-8031-0412-X*, STP863) ASTM.

Cline Love, L. J., jt. ed. see Eastwood, DeLyle.

Cline, Lydia Sloan. Today's Military Wife: Meeting the Challenges of Service Life. 4th ed. LC 98-30431. (Illus.). 304p. 1998. pap. 16.95 (*0-8117-2941-9*) Stackpole.

Cline, Lynn. Romantic Days & Nights in Santa Fe. LC 98-36933. (Romantic Days & Nights Ser.). (Illus.). 288p. 1998. pap. 15.95 (*0-7627-0291-5*) Globe Pequot.

***Cline, Lynn.** Romantic Days & Nights in Santa Fe: Romantic Diversions in & Around the City. 2nd ed. (Illus.). 2001. pap. 15.95 (*0-7627-0840-9*) Globe Pequot.

Cline, Margaret, jt. auth. see Gonzalez, Jean.

Cline, Marjorie W., et al, eds. Scholar's Guide to Intelligence Literature: Bibliography of the Russell J. Bowen Collection. LC 83-80922. 236p. 1983. lib. bdg. 69.50 (*0-313-27048-1*, U7048, Greenwood Pr) Greenwood.

Cline, Marjorie W., ed. see Cline, Ray S.

Cline, Marshall P., et al. C++ FAQs. 2nd ed. LC 98-38674. 624p. (C). 1998. pap. text 39.95 (*0-201-30983-1*) Addison-Wesley.

Cline, Martin J. The White Cell. LC 74-25998. (Commonwealth Fund Publications). (Illus.). 616p. 1975. 50.00 (*0-674-95142-5*) HUP.

Cline, Martin J., et al, eds. 1997 Year Book of Medicine. (Illus.). 1024p. (C). (gr. 13). 1997. text 75.00 (*0-8151-3155-0*, 26974) Mosby Inc.

Cline-McCrary, Joan. Climbing the Mountain: Bible Study for Those Who "Hear" LC 96-92377. (Illus.). 448p. (Orig.). 1996. pap. 16.95 (*0-9623541-3-9*) Redite Pr.

Cline-McCrary, Joan, compiled by. Hidden Harmony. 1990. pap. 10.00 (*0-9617598-1-X*) Divine Sci Fed.

Cline, Nell & Harold, Florence. The History of Angelina County, Texas. Lufkin Historical Society Staff, ed. (Illus.). 900p. 1992. reprint ed. 75.00 (*0-88107-194-3*) Curtis Media.

Cline, Pat. Crawfordsville: A Pictorial History. (Indiana Pictorial History Ser.). (Illus.). 1988. write for info. (*0-943963-23-0*) G Bradley.

Cline, Paul. Booboo's Dream. (Illus.). 32p. (J). (ps-8). 1990. 12.95 (*0-9625261-1-8*) Medlicott Pr.

— Ginger's Moon. (Illus.). (J). (ps-8). 1990. 11.95 (*0-9625261-0-X*) Medlicott Pr.

— Grummit's Day. (J). 1991. 12.95 (*0-9625261-3-4*) Medlicott Pr.

— My Mother's Hands. (Illus.). 32p. (J). 1991. pap. 7.95 (*0-9625261-2-6*) Medlicott Pr.

Cline, Paul C. & Fleming, Daniel B., Jr. By the Good People of Virginia: Our Commonwealth's Government. 2nd ed. (Virginia Government Textbook Ser.). (Illus.). 1986. 6.00 (*0-318-01330-4*) VA Chamber Com.

Cline, Platt. They Came to the Mountain. LC 76-10424. 384p. 1976. 24.95 (*0-87358-153-9*) Northland AZ.

Cline, R. M. & Hays, J. D., eds. Investigation of Late Quaternary Paleoceanography & Paleoclimatology. LC 75-40899. (Geological Society of America, Memoir Ser.: No. 145). 482p. reprint ed. pap. 149.50 (*0-7837-1255-3*, 204139200001) Bks Demand.

Cline, Ray S. Chiang Ching-kuo Remembered: The Man & His Political Legacy. Cline, Marjorie W., ed. LC 89-51909. (Illus.). 205p. (C). 1989. pap. text 24.50 (*0-943057-01-9*) SIFT.

— The Power of Nations in the 1990s: A Strategic Assessment. 152p. 1994. 48.50 (*0-8191-9150-7*); pap. 24.50 (*0-8191-9151-5*) U Pr of Amer.

Cline, Ray S., ed. The Role of the Republic of China in the International Community. LC 91-65990. 98p. (Orig.). (C). 1991. pap. text 10.50 (*0-943057-04-3*) SIFT.

Cline, Ray S. & Carpenter, William M., eds. Secure Passage at Sea. LC 91-65338. 248p. (Orig.). (C). 1991. pap. text 12.50 (*0-943057-03-5*) SIFT.

Cline, Ray S. & Fontaine, Roger W. Foreign Policy Failures in China, Cuba & Nicaragua: A Paradigm. LC 92-85404. 256p. (Orig.). (C). 1992. pap. text 27.50 (*0-943057-05-1*) SIFT.

Cline, Rick. Escort Carrier WW II: War in the Pacific on the Aircraft Carrier U. S. S. Petrof Bay. LC 98-92696. (Illus.). 225p. 1998. pap. 19.95 (*0-9663235-0-5*) RA Cline.

***Cline, Rick.** Submarine Grayback: The Life & Death of the WW II Sub, USS Grayback. LC 99-74272. (Illus.). 252p. 1999. pap. 19.95 (*0-9663235-1-3*) RA Cline.

Cline, Rodney. Pioneer Leaders & Early Institutions in Louisiana Education. 1969. 20.00 (*0-87511-019-3*) Claitors.

Cline, Ruth H., tr. see Chretien de Troyes.

Cline, Ruth H., tr. see De Troyes, Chretien.

Cline, Ruth K. J. Focus on Families: A Reference Handbook. LC 89-17937. (Teen Issues Reference Ser.). 230p. (YA). (gr. 9-12). 1989. lib. bdg. 39.50 (*0-87436-508-2*) ABC-CLIO.

Cline, Ruth K. J., ed. The Best of Notes Plus: Practical Classroom Activities for Junior & Senior High School Students. 87p. 1989. 7.95 (*0-8141-3365-7*) NCTE.

Cline, Ruth K. J., jt. ed. see Lukens, Rebecca J.

Cline, S. L. Colonial Culhuacan, 1580-1600: A Social History of an Aztec. LC 86-7114. 276p. reprint ed. pap. 85.60 (*0-7837-5857-X*, 204557600006) Bks Demand.

Cline, S. L., ed. The Book of Tributes: Early Sixteenth-Century Nahuatl Censuses from Morelos - Museo De Antropologia E Historia, Archivo Historico, Coleccion Antigua, Vol. 549. LC 92-35264. (Latin American Studies: Vol. 81, No. 4). 1993. pap. 18.95 (*0-87903-082-8*) UCLA Lat Am Ctr.

Cline, S. L., ed. see De Sahagun, Fray B.

Cline, Sally. Couples: Scene from the Inside. LC 99-11456. 400p. 1999. text 26.95 (*0-87951-946-0*, Pub. by Overlook Pr) Penguin Putnam.

— Just Desserts: Women & Food. 262p. 1998. text 20.00 (*0-7881-5304-8*) DIANE Pub.

— Lifting the Taboo: Women, Death & Dying. LC 96-48520. 1997. text 55.00 (*0-8147-1366-1*); pap. text 19.50 (*0-8147-1406-4*) NYU Pr.

— Radclyffe Hall: A Woman Called John. LC 97-24200. (Illus.). 304p. 1998. 27.50 (*0-87951-831-6*, Pub. by Overlook Pr) Penguin Putnam.

— Radclyffe Hall: A Woman Called John. (Illus.). 432p. 1999. pap. 16.95 (*0-87951-708-5*, Pub. by Overlook Pr) Penguin Putnam.

Cline, Sibyl W. Renamo Anti-Communist Insurgents in Mozambique: The Fight Goes On. LC 89-52151. (Illus.). 68p. (C). 1989. pap. text 10.50 (*0-943057-02-7*) SIFT.

***Cline, Starr.** The Gifted Child in the Regular Classroom. LC 98-37392. 207p. (C). 1999. pap. text 31.00 (*0-13-399908-4*, Macmillan Coll) P-H.

— Giftedness Has Many Faces: Multiple Talents & Abilities in the Classroom. (Illus.). 193p. 2000. 34.95 (*1-890817-94-5*, Pub. by Winslow Pr) Publishers Group.

Cline, Ted. Searching for Real Christianity. 96p. (Orig.). 1988. pap. 2.50 (*0-933672-73-X*, C-2021) Star Bible.

Cline, Timothy R. Program Assessment. LC 98-21988. (AWL Series on Managing Human Resources). 320p. (C). 1998. pap. 47.00 (*0-201-32259-5*, Prentice Hall) P-H.

Cline, Tony. Selective Mutism in Children. 184p. (Orig.). (C). 1994. pap. text 45.00 (*1-56593-257-9*, 0546) Singular Publishing.

Cline, Tony, ed. Curriculum Related Assessment: Cummins & Bilingual Children. 160p. 1996. 69.00 (*1-85359-271-4*, Pub. by Multilingual Matters); pap. 26.95 (*1-85359-270-6*, Pub. by Multilingual Matters) Taylor & Francis.

Cline, Victor B. How to Make a Good Marriage Great. 1996. pap. 11.95 (*1-57008-255-3*) Bookcraft Inc.

Cline, Walter B. Notes on the People of Siwah & el Garah in the Libyan Desert. LC 76-44706. reprint ed. 44.50 (*0-404-15916-8*) AMS Pr.

Cline, Walter M. The Muzzle-Loading Rifle Then & Now. 1993. 32.00 (*1-879356-34-1*) Wolfe Pub Co.

Cline, Wayne. Alabama Railroads. LC 95-51241. 328p. (C). 1997. 39.95 (*0-8173-0812-1*) U of Ala Pr.

Cline, William. Policy Alternatives for a New International Economic Order. LC 79-87553. 392p. 1979. 65.00 (*0-275-90342-7*, C0342, Praeger Pubs) Greenwood.

Cline, William C. In the Nick of Time. LC 83-22231. (Illus.). 293p. 1997. pap. 20.00 (*0-7864-0471-X*) McFarland & Co.

Cline, William C. Serials-ly Speaking: Essays on Cliffhangers. LC 93-32499. (Illus.). 271p. 1994. lib. bdg. 36.50 (*0-89950-909-6*) McFarland & Co.

Cline, William C. Stroke of Fortune: The Adventures of a Motion Picture Showman. LC 95-61162. (Illus.). 260p. (Orig.). 1995. pap. 15.00 (*0-944019-18-8*) Empire NC.

Cline, William R. The Economics of Global Warming. LC 92-16111. 400p. (C). 1992. pap. 20.00 (*0-88132-132-X*) Inst Intl Eco.

— Exports of Manufactures from Developing Countries: Performance & Prospects for Market Access. LC 84-17059. 229p. 1984. 34.95 (*0-8157-1464-5*); pap. 14.95 (*0-8157-1463-7*) Brookings.

— Global Warming: The Economic Stakes. LC 92-14614. (Policy Analyses in International Economics Ser.: Vol. 36). 125p. 1992. reprint ed. pap. 38.80 (*0-608-05395-3*, 206586200006) Bks Demand.

–International Debt Reexamined. LC 93-2926. 535p. 1995. pap. 25.00 (*0-88132-083-8*) Inst Intl Eco.

The international debit crisis that erupted in 1982 threatened the world financial system & turned the 1980s into a lost decade for Latin America. But the crisis jolted governments throughout the region into adopting sweeping economic reforms. By the early 1990s inflation was lower, growth was reviving, the major debtors had reached "Brady Plan" workout agreements reducing bank debt in exchange for collateral & capital was entering the region in unprecedented magnitudes. This study tries to make sense of this historic financial episode & to derive lessons for future policy. Cline first returns to his 1983 projection models that figured importantly in the debate at that time & reruns them with the benefit of hindsight to see what went wrong (e.g., capital flight) & what went right (e.g., revival of industrial country growth). He provides a critical survey of the voluminous economics literature that emerged from the debit crisis. The study evaluates performance of the evolving international debt strategy, which eventually succeeded brilliantly in preserving international financial stability & restoring debtor access to credit markets but failed to achieve debtor country growth in the 1980s. The study reviews policy reform & Brady plan results for major Latin American countries; provides new analysis of today's debt problems in Russia & Africa; & analyzes the degree of vulnerability of Latin Americas capital market renaissance to such factors as overvalued exchange rates & a resurgence of US

C

interest rates. It concludes with suggestions for institutional change & policy guidelines to help avoid future crises. *Publisher Paid Annotation.*

Cline, William R. International Economic Policy in the 1990s. LC 94-19785. 274p. 1995. 37.50 (0-262-03221-X) MIT Pr.

Cline, William R. International Monetary Reform & the Developing Countries. LC 75-44503. 126p. 1976. 34.95 (0-8157-1476-9); pap. 14.95 (0-8157-1475-0) Brookings.

— Trade & Income Distribution. LC 96-2659. (Orig.). 1997. pap. 25.00 (0-88132-216-4) Inst Intl Eco.

Cline, William R. & Delgado, Enrique, eds. Economic Integration in Central America. LC 78-60708. 712p. 1978. 36.95 (0-8157-1470-X) Brookings.

Cline, William R. & Weintraub, Sidney, eds. Economic Stabilization in Developing Countries. LC 80-70079. 517p. 1981. pap. 17.95 (0-8157-1465-3) Brookings.

Cline, William R., et al. Trade Negotiations in the Tokyo Round: A Quantitative Assessment. LC 77-91799. 314p. 1978. 28.95 (0-8157-1472-6) Brookings.

— World Inflation & the Developing Countries. LC 80-25426. 266p. 1981. 34.95 (0-8157-1468-8); pap. 14.95 (0-8157-1467-X) Brookings.

Cline, William R., jt. auth. see Bergsten, C. Fred.

Cline, William R., jt. auth. see Berry, Albert R.

Cline, William R., ed. Trade Policy in the 1980's. LC 83-4310. 812p. 1983. pap. 200.00 (0-7837-8496-1, 204930300010) Bks Demand.

Clinebell, Howard. Anchoring Your Well Being: A Guide for Congregational Leaders. Collett, Rita, ed. 160p. 1997. pap. 9.00 (0-8358-0822-X, UR809) Upper Room Bks.

— Anchoring Your Well Being: Christian Wholeness in a Fractured World. LC 97-11005. 192p. 1997. pap. text 13.00 (0-8358-0821-1) Upper Room Bks.

— Basic Types of Pastoral Care & Counseling. LC 83-15590. 464p. write for info. (0-687-96019-3) Abingdon.

— Basic Types of Pastoral Care & Counseling. enl. rev. ed. LC 83-15590. 464p. 1984. 24.95 (0-687-02492-7) Abingdon.

— Counseling for Spiritually Empowered Wholeness: A Hope-Centered Approach. LC 94-30384. 177p. (C). 1995. lib. bdg. 39.95 (1-56024-902-1) Haworth Pr.

— Counseling for Spiritually Empowered Wholeness: A Hope-Centered Approach. LC 94-30384. 177p. 1995. pap. 14.95 (1-56024-903-X) Haworth Pr.

— Ecotherapy: Healing Ourselves, Healing the Earth. 352p. 1996. pap. 22.00 (0-8006-2769-5, 1-2769, Fortress Pr) Augsburg Fortress.

— Ecotherapy: Healing Ourselves, Healing the Earth. 293p. 1996. pap. 17.95 (0-7890-6009-4, Haworth Pastrl) Haworth Pr.

— Understanding & Counseling Persons with Alcohol, Drug, & Behavioral Addictions. LC 98-12348. 384p. 1998. pap. 36.95 (0-687-02564-8) Abingdon.

Clinebell, Howard J. Growth Counseling for Marriage Enrichment: Pre-marriage & the Early Years. LC 74-26335. (Creative Pastoral Care & Counseling Ser.). 96p. reprint ed. pap. 30.00 (0-608-15813-5, 203122100074) Bks Demand.

— Growth Counseling for Mid-Years Couples. LC 76-7863. (Creative Pastoral Care & Counseling Ser.). 96p. reprint ed. pap. 30.00 (0-608-15303-6, 202960700061) Bks Demand.

Clinefelter, Jim. A Throw of the Snore Will Surge the Potatoes: John M. Bennett Meets Stephane Mallarme. (Illus.). 12p. 1998. pap. 7.00 (1-892280-04-3) Luna Bisonte.

Cliner, Jerry. How to Raise a Cat. 1992. pap. 9.95 (0-911793-04-6) Penny Dreadful Pubs.

Clines, C. V. The Doolittle Raid: America's Daring First Strike Against Japan. rev. ed. LC 88-1822. (Illus.). 272p. 1991. reprint ed. 24.95 (0-88740-347-6) Schiffer.

Clines, D. J. I, He, We, & They: A Literay Approach to Isaiah 53. (JSOTS Ser.). 65p. 1976. pap. 11.50 (0-905774-00-0, Pub. by Sheffield Acad) CUP Services.

Clines, D. J., jt. auth. see McKay, Heather A.

Clines, D. J., jt. ed. see Davies, Philip R.

Clines, David. Job 1-20. (Biblical Commentary Ser.: Vol. 17). 29.99 (0-8499-0216-9) Word Pub.

— Job 21-42. (Biblical Commentary Ser.: Vol. 18). Date not set. 29.99 (0-8499-0217-7) Word Pub.

Clines, David J. The Bible & the Modern World. (Biblical Seminar Ser.: Vol. 51). 116p. 1997. pap. 17.95 (1-85075-841-7, Pub. by Sheffield Acad) CUP Services.

— On the Way to the Postmodern: Old Testament Essays, 1967-1998, Vol. 1. LC 99-158696. (JSOTS Ser.: No. 292). 443p. 1998. 85.00 (1-85075-901-4, Pub. by Sheffield Acad) CUP Services.

— The Sheffield Manual for Authors & Editors in Biblical Studies. (JSOT Manuals Ser.: Vol. 12). 200p. 1997. pap. 24.50 (1-85075-727-5, Pub. by Sheffield Acad) CUP Services.

— The Theme of the Pentateuch. 2nd rev. ed. (Journal for the Study of the Old Testament Supplement Ser.: Vol. 10). 176p. 1997. pap. 16.50 (1-85075-792-5, Pub. by Sheffield Acad) CUP Services.

Clines, David J., ed. The Bible & the Future of the Planet: An Ecology Reader. (Biblical Seminar Ser.: Vol. 56). 200p. 1998. pap. 19.95 (1-85075-906-5, Pub. by Sheffield Acad) CUP Services.

— The Dictionary of Classical Hebrew Vol. 4: Yodh-Lamedh. 642p. 1998. 150.00 (1-85075-681-3, Pub. by Sheffield Acad) CUP Services.

— The Poetical Books: A Sheffield Reader. (Biblical Seminar Ser.: No. 41). 370p. 1997. pap. 19.95 (1-85075-787-9, Pub. by Sheffield Acad) CUP Services.

Clines, David J. & Eskenazi, Tamara C. Telling Queen Michal's Story: An Experiment in Comparative Interpretation. (JSOT Supplement Ser.: No. 119). 301p. (C). 1991. 85.00 (1-85075-301-6, Pub. by Sheffield Acad) CUP Services.

Clines, David J., jt. ed. see Davies, Philip R.

Clines, David J., jt. ed. see Exum, J. Cheryl.

Clines, David J., jt. ed. see Sawyer, John F.

Clines, David J. A. The Esther Scroll: The Story of the Story. (JSOT Supplement Ser.: No. 30). 260p. 1984. pap. 24.95 (0-905774-67-1, Pub. by Sheffield Acad) CUP Services.

— Ezra, Nehemiah & Esther. (New Century Bible Ser.). 342p. 1984. pap. 19.95 (0-551-01118-1, Pub. by Sheffield Acad) CUP Services.

— Interested Parties: The Ideology of Writers & Readers of the Hebrew Bible. (JSOT Supplement Ser.: Vol. 205). 296p. 1995. 85.00 (1-85075-748-8, Pub. by Sheffield Acad); pap. 19.50 (1-85075-570-1, Pub. by Sheffield Acad) CUP Services.

Clines, David J. A. On the Way to the Postmodern Vol. 2: Old Testament Essays 1967-1998. LC 99-158696. (JSOT Supplement Ser.: No. 293). 450p. 1998. 85.00 (1-85075-983-9, Pub. by Sheffield Acad) CUP Services.

Clines, David J. A. What Does Eve Do to Help? And Other Readerly Questions to the Old Testament. (JSOT Supplement Ser.: No. 94). 180p. 1990. 57.50 (1-85075-248-6, Pub. by Sheffield Acad) CUP Services.

— What Does Eve Do to Help? And Other Readerly Questions to the Old Testament. 2nd ed. (JSOT Supplement Ser.: No. 94). 178p. 1994. pap. 19.95 (1-85075-734-8, Pub. by Sheffield Acad) CUP Services.

Clines, David J. A., ed. The Dictionary of Classical Hebrew Vol. 1: Aleph. 475p. 1993. 123.50 (1-85075-244-3, Pub. by Sheffield Acad) CUP Services.

— The Dictionary of Classical Hebrew Vol. 2: Beth-Waw. 660p. 1995. 123.50 (1-85075-544-2, Pub. by Sheffield Acad) CUP Services.

— The Dictionary of Classical Hebrew Vol. 3: Zayin-Tet. 424p. 1996. 123.50 (1-85075-634-1, Pub. by Sheffield Acad) CUP Services.

Clines, David J. A., et al, eds. Art & Meaning: Rhetoric in Biblical Literature. (JSOT Supplement Ser.: Vol. 19). 266p. 1982. 75.00 (0-905774-38-8, Pub. by Sheffield Acad); pap. 24.50 (0-905774-39-6, Pub. by Sheffield Acad) CUP Services.

— The Bible in Three Dimensions: Essays in Celebration of Forty Years of Biblical Studies in the University of Sheffield. (JSOT Supplement Ser.: Vol. 87). 408p. 1990. 85.00 (1-85075-227-3, Pub. by Sheffield Acad) CUP Services.

***Clines, David J. A. & Moore, Stephen D., eds.** Auguries: The Jubilee Volume of the Sheffield Department of Biblical Studies. LC 98-145442. (JSOT Supplement Ser.: Vol. 269). 336p. 1998. 85.00 (1-85075-911-1, Pub. by Sheffield Acad) CUP Services.

Clines, David J. A., jt. ed. see Exum, J. Cheryl.

Cling, B. J., jt. auth. see Wulach, James S.

***Clingan, C. Edmund.** Finance from Kaiser to Fuhrer: Budget Politics in Germany, 1912-1934, Vol. 79. (Contributions to the Study of World History Ser.: Vol. 79). 2000. write for info. (0-313-31184-6, Greenwood Pr) Greenwood.

Clingan, Donald F., jt. auth. see Gentzler, Richard H., Jr.

***Clingan, Mary.** Let's Learn Letters. (J). (ps-3). 1999. write for info. (1-929343-03-5) Peer Tutor Pr.

Clingan, T., ed. Law of the Sea: State Practice in Zones of Special Jurisdiction, 13th Annual Conference Proceedings. 550p. 1982. 14.25 (0-911189-02-5) Law Sea Inst.

Clingan, Thomas A., Jr. The Law of the Sea: Ocean Law & Policy. LC 93-3931. 638p. 1994. 95.00 (1-880921-37-5); pap. 75.00 (1-880921-28-6) Austin & Winfield.

Clingan, Thomas A., ed. The Law of the Sea: What Lies Ahead? 20th Annual Conference Proceedings. 600p. 1988. 45.00 (0-911189-18-1) Law Sea Inst.

Clingan, Thomas A., Jr. & Kolodkin, Anatoly. Moscow Symposium on the Law of the Sea: Proceedings. (Law of the Sea Institute Workshop Ser.: W10). 394p. (C). 1992. text 51.00 (0-911189-24-6) Law Sea Inst.

Clinger, C. Douglas, et al. Strategies for Success in Coaching: A Sports Medicine Paradigm. LC 91-36524. 1992. write for info. (0-87949-366-6) Ashley Bks.

Clinger, David M. The Ghosts & Glories of Monroe Park: A Sesquicentennial History. LC 99-162730. (Illus.). 52p. 1998. pap. 12.50 (0-87517-102-8) Dietz.

Clinger, Linda D., ed. see Ellenshaw, Peter.

Clinger, Marke. Internetworking with ATM: A Network's Planner's Guide. (C). 1997. text. write for info. (0-201-63380-9) Addison-Wesley.

***Clinger, Wade.** GPS Waypoints of Colorado's Fourteeners. 64p. 2000. pap. 12.95 (0-87108-914-9) Pruett.

Clingerman, Harold B. Field Man: The Chronicle of a Bank Farm Manager in the 1940's. LC 88-28406. 195p. 1989. reprint ed. pap. 60.50 (0-608-00090-6, 206085500006) Bks Demand.

Clingerman, Polly. Fast & Fabulous Hors d'Oeuvres Appetizers. Levine, Marian, ed. (Collector's Ser.: Vol. 21). 64p. 1987. per. 3.95 (0-942320-27-1) Am Cooking.

— Holiday Entertaining. Levine, Marian, ed. (Collector's Ser.: Vol. 22). 64p. 1987. pap., per. 3.95 (0-942320-28-X) Am Cooking.

— Kitchen Companion. (Illus.). 457p. 1995. pap. text 14.95 (0-942320-44-1) Am Cooking.

— A Passion for Pasta. Levine, Marian, ed. 64p. (Orig.). 1990. pap., per. 3.95 (0-942320-35-2) Am Cooking.

— Perfect Pies No. 45: From Dinner to Dessert. 64p. 1998. pap. 3.95 (0-942320-62-X) Am Cooking.

***Clingermayer, James C. & Feiock, Richard C.** Institutional Constraints & Policy Choice: An Exploration of Local Governance. (C). 2001. pap. text 17.95 (0-7914-4914-9) State U NY Pr.

— Institutional Constraints & Policy Choice: An Exploration of Local Governance. (C). 2001. text 54.50 (0-7914-4913-0) State U NY Pr.

Clingham, Greg, ed. The Cambridge Companion to Samuel Johnson. (Cambridge Companions to Literature Ser.). (Illus.). 286p. (C). 1997. text 59.95 (0-521-55411-X); pap. text 18.95 (0-521-55625-2) Cambridge U Pr.

— Making History Vol. 42, No. 1: Textuality & the Forms of Eighteenth-Century Culture (Bucknell Review) (Illus.). 160p. 1998. 24.00 (0-8387-5384-1) Bucknell U Pr.

— New Light on Boswell: Critical & Historical Essays on the Occasion of the Bicentenary of the Life of Johnson. (Illus.). 255p. (C). 1991. text 69.95 (0-521-38047-2) Cambridge U Pr.

— Questioning History: The Postmodern Turn to the Eighteenth Century. (Review Ser.: Vol. 41, No. 2). (Illus.). 200p. 1998. 24.00 (0-8387-5383-3) Bucknell U Pr.

***Clingman, Stephen.** Bram Fischer: Afrikaner Revolutionary. 512p. 2000. pap. 19.95 (1-55849-260-7) U of Mass Pr.

Clingman, Stephen. The Novels of Nadine Gordimer: History from the Inside. 296p. (C). 1986. text 39.95 (0-04-800082-5) Routledge.

— The Novels of Nadine Gordimer: History from the Inside. 2nd ed. LC 92-4691. 320p. 1992. pap. 18.95 (0-87023-802-7) U of Mass Pr.

Clingman, Stephen, ed. Regions & Repertoires: Topics in South African Politics & Culture. (South African Studies: Vol. 6). 222p. (Orig.). (C). 1992. pap. text 24.95 (0-86975-411-4, Pub. by Ravan Pr) Ohio U Pr.

Clingman, Stephen, ed. & intro. see Gordimer, Nadine.

Clinic on Library Applications of Data Processing. Artificial Intelligence & Expert Systems: Will They Change the Library? Lancaster, F. W. & Smith, Linda C., eds. LC Z 0678.93.E9. (Illus.). 297p. reprint ed. pap. 92.10 (0-7837-3410-7, 204337700008) Bks Demand.

— Professional Competencies - Technology & the Librarian. Smith, Linda C., ed. LC 84-6047. (Illus.). 144p. reprint ed. pap. 44.70 (0-7837-1176-X, 204170400022) Bks Demand.

Clinical Conference on Cancer Staff. Hodgkin's Disease & Non-Hodgkin's Lymphoma: New Perspectives in Immunopathology, Diagnosis, & Treatment. Ford, Richard J., Jr. et al, eds. LC 84-13429. (UT M. D.Anderson Clinical Conference on Cancer Ser.: No. 27). (Illus.). 496p. 1984. reprint ed. pap. 153.80 (0-608-00628-9, 206121500007) Bks Demand.

— Status of the Curability of Childhood Cancers: The University of Texas System Cancer Center, M. D. Anderson Hospital & Tumor Institute 24th Annual Clinical Conference on Cancer. Van Eys, Jan & Sullivan, Margaret P., eds. LC 79-5469. 349p. 1980. reprint ed. pap. 108.20 (0-608-03457-6, 206415800008) Bks Demand.

Clinical Neuropharmacology Staff. Clinical Neuropharmacology Vol. 15, Pt. A, 1992: Proceedings of the 18th Collegium Internationale Neuro-Psychopharmacologicum Congress, Plenary Lectures & Symposia. LC 76-644724. 746p. 1992. reprint ed. pap. 200.00 (0-608-04655-8, 204714400015) Bks Demand.

Clinical Pharmacology of Serotonin Symposium Staff. Clinical Pharmacology of Serotonin: Proceedings of the Symposium, Satellite, Helsinki, July, 1975. Sicuteri, F. & Schoenbaum, E., eds. (Monographs in Neural Sciences: Vol. 3). (Illus.). 180p. 1976. 55.75 (3-8055-2328-9) S Karger.

Clinical Pharmacology Symposium Staff. Horizons in Clinical Pharmacology. Palmer, Roger F., ed. LC 76-10118. (Modern Pharmacology-Toxicology Ser.: No. 6). (Illus.). 270p. reprint ed. pap. 83.70 (0-7837-0667-7, 204100200019) Bks Demand.

Clinical Society of London Staff. Report of a Committee to Investigate the Subject of Myxoedema. (Illus.). 250p. 1992. 19.95 (0-318-68444-6) F A Countway.

Clinite, Shelley, ed. see Hufford, Darin.

Clinkard, C. E. The Uses of Juices. 8th ed. 32p. 1993. reprint ed. spiral bd. 10.00 (0-7873-0178-7) Hlth Research.

Clinkscale, Edward. Antoine de Fevin, Opera Dubia Fragments & Intabulations. (Gesamtausgaben-Collected Works: No. XI/4). (ENG & LAT.). viii, 124p. 1996. lib. bdg. 72.00 (0-931902-41-X) Inst Mediaeval Mus.

Clinkscale, Edward, ed. Antoine de Fevin Lamentations Magnificats Motets & Chansons. (Collected Works: Vol. 3). 182p. 1994. lib. bdg. 88.00 (0-931902-89-4) Inst Mediaeval Mus.

— Les Oeuvres Completes d'Antoine de Fevin. (Gesamtausgaben - Collected Works: Vol. XI, Pt. 1). (ENG & GER.). xvi, 134p. 1980. lib. bdg. 4.00 (0-912024-68-2) Inst Mediaeval Mus.

— Oeuvres Completes d'Antoine de Fevin. (Gesamtausgaben Collected Works: Vol. XI/2). (ENG & LAT.). xxvi, 179p. 1993. lib. bdg. 108.00 (0-931902-82-7) Inst Mediaeval Mus.

— Oeuvres Completes de Robert de Fevin. (Gesamtausgaben - Collected Works: Vol. XIII). (ENG & LAT.). xx, 140p. 1993. lib. bdg. 140.00 (0-931902-77-0) Inst Mediaeval Mus.

Clinkscale, Edward & Brook, Claire, eds. A Musical Offering: Essays in Honor of Martin Bernstein. LC 76-53128. (Festschrift Ser.: No. 1). 1977. lib. bdg. 42.00 (0-918728-03-7) Pendragon NY.

***Clinkscale, Joy A.** How to Form & Operate a Crime Prevention Task Force. LC 98-60747. 54p. 1998. pap. 4.95 (0-9664897-0-5) Wisely Pubg.

Clinkscale, Lonnie. Hey Dummy! Libb, Melva, ed. (Illus.). 112p. 1991. 5.95 (0-685-51585-0) Son Rise Pubns.

Clinkscale, Lonnie J. The Cry of a Backslider: Restoration of a Saint. 296p. 1994. 15.95 (0-9640311-1-6) Clinkscale Pubns.

— Hey Dummy! A Testimony of an Overcomer. LC 94-94507. 112p. (J). (gr. 3 up). 1994. reprint ed. pap. 6.95 (0-9640311-0-8) Clinkscale Pubns.

***Clinkscale, Martha N.** Makers of the Piano, 1820-1860, Vol. 2. (Illus.). 506p. 1999. text 130.00 (0-19-816625-7) OUP.

Clinkscale, Martha N. Makers of the Piano, 1700-1820. LC 93-16320. 418p. 1993. text 85.00 (0-19-816323-1) OUP.

Clinkscales, Cynthia. Healthy at Last: Solutions to Chronic Ill Health, Allergies & Environmental Illness. LC 89-81991. (Orig.). (C). 1991. pap. 11.95 (0-9624764-1-2) CECOM Pub.

Clinkscales, John G. On the Old Plantation Reminiscences of His Childhood. LC 77-91255. 142p. 1969. reprint ed. lib. bdg. 35.00 (0-8371-2063-2, CLO&) Greenwood.

Clinloy, Peter. Real Estate Investment. 1988. lib. bdg. 150.00 (0-89838-233-5) Kluwer Academic.

Clint, J. H. Surfactant Aggregation. 320p. 1991. mass mkt. 166.95 (0-412-02481-0, A4214, Chap & Hall NY) Chapman & Hall.

Clint, John H. Surfactant Aggregation. (Illus.). 296p. (C). 1991. text 166.95 (0-216-92905-9, Pub. by B Acad & Prof) Routldge.

Clinton. Heating-&-Air Conditioning Servicer. LC 97-35226. (Careers Without College Ser.). (YA). 1998. 19.00 (1-56065-703-0) Capstone Pr.

— Tractor-Trailer-Truck Driver. LC 97-35225. (Careers Without College Ser.). (YA). 1998. 19.00 (1-56065-710-3) Capstone Pr.

Clinton & Primm, E. Russell. Correction Officer. LC 97-35240. (Careers Without College Ser.). (YA). 1998. 19.00 (1-56065-700-6) Capstone Pr.

Clinton, et al. American Indian Law: 1996 Supplement. 3rd ed. 213p. 1996. pap. text 8.00 (1-55834-189-7, 12743-11, MICHIE) LEXIS Pub.

— American Indian Law, 1991. 3rd ed. 1378p. 1991. text 52.00 (0-87473-710-9, 12742-10, MICHIE) LEXIS Pub.

Clinton, jt. auth. see Clark.

Clinton, Alan. The Post Office Worker: A Trade Union & Social History. (Illus.). 304p. 1984. text 75.00 (0-04-331086-9) Routledge.

Clinton, Allison B. Teachers for the South: Pedagogy & Educationists in the University of Tennessee, 1844-1995. LC 97-17931. (History of Schools & Schooling: Vol. 6). XIII, 295p. 1998. pap. 29.95 (0-8204-3841-3) P Lang Pubng.

Clinton-Baddeley, Vitcor. The Burlesque Tradition in the English Theatre after, 1600. LC 70-93160. 367p. 1972. 23.95 (0-405-18144-2) Ayer.

Clinton, Bill. Blair House Papers. 55p. 1997. per. 3.50 (0-16-061868-1) USGPO.

— Building The U. S. - Africa Partnership: Hand-in-Hand in the 21st Century. (Illus.). 51p. 2000. pap. text 20.00 (0-7881-8891-7) DIANE Pub.

Clinton, Bill. My Plans for a Second Term. 112p. 1995. 6.95 (0-8216-1004-X) Carol Pub Group.

— Preface to the Presidency: Selected Speeches of Bill Clinton, 1974-1992. Smith, Stephen A., ed. & intro. by. LC 96-22577. 1996. pap. 30.00 (1-55728-441-5) U of Ark Pr.

— Preface to the Presidency: Selected Speeches of Bill Clinton, 1974-1992. Smith, Stephen A., ed. & intro. by. LC 96-22577. 1996. 48.00 (1-55728-440-7) U of Ark Pr.

Clinton, Bill. Turning the Key: Unlocking Human Potential in the Family-Friendly Federal Workplace. 38p. 1997. pap. 2.00 (0-16-061874-6) USGPO.

Clinton, Bill & Gore, Al, Jr. The Blair House Papers: National Performance Review. (Illus.). 43p. 1998. pap. text 15.00 (0-7881-7120-8) DIANE Pub.

— Putting Customers First: Standards for Serving the American People. Report of the National Performance Review. 160p. (Orig.). (C). 1995. pap. text 30.00 (0-7881-2174-X) DIANE Pub.

— Reinventing Food Regulations: National Performance Review. 27p. (Orig.). 1996. pap. text 15.00 (0-7881-3685-2) DIANE Pub.

Clinton, Bill, jt. intro. see Ashley, Liza.

Clinton, Bobby. Spiritual Gifts: A Self Study or Group Study Manual. 219p. 1985. student ed., spiral bd. 12.99 (0-88965-071-3, Pub. by Horizon Books) Chr Pubns.

***Clinton, Catherine.** The Black Soldier. LC 99-48935. 2000. 17.00 (0-395-67722-X) HM.

— Civil War Stories. LC 99-54769. (Illus.). 2000. 27.95 (0-7838-8842-2, G K Hall & Co) Mac Lib Ref.

Clinton, Catherine. Civil War Stories. LC 98-15523. (Jack N. & Addie D. Averett Lecture Ser.: No. 7). 144p. 1998. pap. 14.95 (0-8203-2074-9) U of Ga Pr.

***Clinton, Catherine.** Fanny Kemble's Civil Wars: The Story of America's Most Unlikely Abolitionist. (Illus.). 320p. 2000. 26.00 (0-684-84414-1) S&S Trade.

Clinton, Catherine. I, Too, Sing America: Three Centuries of African-American Poetry. LC 97-46137. (Illus.). 128p. (YA). (gr. 5 up). 1998. 20.00 (0-395-89599-5) HM.

— Life in Civil War America. (National Park Civil War Ser.). (Illus.). 51p. 1996. pap. 4.95 (1-888213-02-7) Eastern National.

***Clinton, Catherine.** The Other Civil War: American Women in the Nineteenth Century. rev. ed. LC 98-52075. 12p. 1999. pap. 13.00 (0-8090-1622-2) Hill & Wang.

Clinton, Catherine. The Plantation Mistress: Woman's World in the Old South. 1984. pap. 13.00 (0-394-72253-1) Pantheon.

***Clinton, Catherine.** Public Women & the Confederacy. LC 99-6915. (Frank L. Klement Lecture Ser.). 1999. write for info. (0-87462-332-4) Marquette.

— Scholastic Encyclopedia of the Civil War. LC 98-45492. (Illus.). 112p. (YA). (gr. 4-9). 1999. 18.95 (*0-590-37227-0*, Pub. by Scholastic Inc) Penguin Putnam.

Clinton, Catherine. Tara Revisited: Women, War, & the Plantation Legend. LC 94-39218. (Illus.). 240p. 1996. 27.50 (*1-55859-491-4*) Abbeville Pr.

— Tara Revisited: Women, War, & the Plantation Legend. (Illus.). 240p. 1997. pap. 16.95 (*0-7892-0159-3*) Abbeville Pr.

Clinton, Catherine, ed. Half Sisters of History: Southern Women & the American Past. LC 94-7822. 256p. 1994. text 49.95 (*0-8223-1483-5*); pap. text 17.95 (*0-8223-1496-7*) Duke.

***Clinton, Catherine, ed.** Southern Families at War. (Illus.). 288p. 2000. text 35.00 (*0-19-513683-7*) OUP.

Clinton, Catherine & Gillespie, Michele, eds. The Devil's Lane: Sex & Race in the Early South. LC 96-39835. (Illus.). 304p. 1997. pap. 16.95 (*0-19-511243-1*); text 45.00 (*0-19-511242-3*) OUP.

Clinton, Catherine & Lunardini, Christine A. The Columbia Guide to American Women in the Nineteenth Century. LC 98-50373. 2000. 40.00 (*0-231-10920-2*) Col U Pr.

Clinton, Catherine & Silber, Nina. Divided Houses: Gender & the Civil War. (Illus.). 448p. 1992. pap. 17.95 (*0-19-508034-3*) OUP.

Clinton, Catherine, jt. auth. see Barker-Benfield, G. J.

Clinton, Catherine, jt. auth. see Kemble, Fanny.

Clinton, Catherine, jt. ed. see Gillespie, Michele.

Clinton, Catherine, ed. & intro. see Kemble, Fanny.

Clinton, Courtney, ed. see Heller, Steven & Fernandes, Teresa.

Clinton, Daniel J. Gomez, Tyrant of the Andes. LC 70-97833. 320p. 1970. reprint ed. lib. bdg. 55.00 (*0-8371-2698-3*, CLG, Greenwood Pr) Greenwood.

Clinton, David, ed. Presidential Transitions: The Reagan to Bush Experience, Vol. 8. 199p. (C). 1992. pap. text 24.50 (*0-8191-8710-0*, Pub. by White Miller Center); lib. bdg. 51.00 (*0-8191-8709-7*, Pub. by White Miller Center) U Pr of Amer.

Clinton, David & Lang, Daniel G., eds. What Makes a Successful Transition? (Papers on Presidential Transitions & Foreign Policy: Vol. IX). 172p. (Orig.). (C). 1993. pap. text 22.50 (*0-8191-8929-4*, Pub. by White Miller Center); lib. bdg. 48.50 (*0-8191-8928-6*, Pub. by White Miller Center) U Pr of Amer.

Clinton, Denise, ed. see Parkin, Michael.

Clinton, DeWitt, jt. auth. see Literary & Philosophical Society of New York Staff, Jr.

Clinton, Elizabeth. The Countesse of Lincolnes Nurserie. LC 74-28838. (English Experience Ser.: No. 720). 1975. reprint ed. 25.00 (*90-221-0720-5*) Walter J Johnson.

Clinton, Ellie, jt. auth. see Pearl, Diane.

Clinton, Gary. The Legend of the Little People: Brought Forth from Obscurity with Full-Hearted Devotion & in Spite of the Scoffing Protests of Non-Believers. LC 91-65736. 36p. 1991. write for info. (*1-879495-25-2*) United Design.

Clinton, Helen E., jt. auth. see Pringle, Peter K.

Clinton, Helen G., jt. ed. see Smith, Ruth B.

Clinton, Henry L. Extraordinary Cases. 403p. 1977. 24.95 (*0-8369-2940-3*) Ayer.

Clinton, Hillary Rodham. Dear Socks, Dear Buddy: Kid's Letters to the First Pets. LC 98-44149. (Illus.). 205p. (J). (gr. 1-7). 1998. 20.00 (*0-684-85778-2*) S&S Trade.

***Clinton, Hillary Rodham.** Dear Socks, Dear Buddy: Kid's Letters to the First Pets. abr. aut. ed. 1998. text 19.50 (*0-684-86417-7*) S&S Trade.

Clinton, Hillary Rodham. Dear Socks, Dear Buddy: Kid's Letters to the First Pets. unabridged ed. 1999. 17.00 incl. audio (*0-671-04368-4*, Audioworks) S&S Trade.

— Invitation to the White House. 312p. 2000. 30.00 (*0-684-85799-5*) S&S Trade.

— It Takes a Village: And Other Lessons Children Teach Us. 1996. 19.50 (*0-684-82661-5*) S&S Trade.

— It Takes a Village: And Other Lessons Children Teach Us. 336p. 1996. per. 10.00 (*0-684-82545-7*, Touchstone) S&S Trade Pap.

— It Takes a Village: And Other Lessons Children Teach Us. 318p. 1996. 20.00 (*0-684-81843-4*) Simon & Schuster.

— It Takes a Village: And Other Lessons Children Teach Us. large type ed. 1996. pap. write for info. (*0-684-81861-2*) S&S Trade.

***Clinton, Hillary Rodham.** It Takes a Village: And Other Lessons Children Teach Us. 318p. 2000. reprint ed. 20.00 (*0-7881-9332-5*) DIANE Pub.

***Clinton, Hillary Rodham, frwd.** Saving America's Treasures. 2000. 35.00 (*0-7922-7942-5*) Natl Geog.

Clinton, Hillary Rodham, et al. American Women Speak: Voices of American Women in Public Life. Earnshow, Doris & Raymond, Maria E., eds. LC 95-80502. (Women Speak Ser.: No. 2). (Illus.). xii, 140p. (Orig.). pap. 22.50 (*0-9640574-2-5*) Alta Vista Pr.

Clinton, J. Robert. The Making of a Leader: Recognizing the Stages of Leadership Development. LC 88-61777. 272p. (Orig.). 1988. pap. 11.00 (*0-89109-192-0*) NavPress.

Clinton, J. Robert & Stanley, Paul D. Connecting: Learning How to Learn from Others. LC 91-61396. 252p. (Orig.). 1992. pap. 13.00 (*0-89109-638-8*) NavPress.

Clinton, James H. What Is Fair? LC 97-18676. 64p. 1997. pap. 11.95 (*0-8071-2196-7*); text 19.95 (*0-8071-2195-9*) La State U Pr.

Clinton, James W. The Loyal Opposition: Americans in North Vietnam, 1965-1972. (Illus.). 432p. 1996. 29.95 (*0-87081-412-5*) Univ Pr Colo.

Clinton, Jeff. Big Sky Revenge. 1991. mass mkt. 3.50 (*1-55817-494-X*, Pinncle Kensgtn) Kensgtn Pub Corp.

Clinton, Jerome, tr. see Ferdowski.

Clinton, Jerome W. The Divan of Manuchihri Damghani: A Critical Study. LC 72-87873. (Studies in Middle Eastern Literatures: No. 1). 1972. pap. 15.00 (*0-88297-001-1*) Bibliotheca.

Clinton, Jerome W., tr. see Perdowsi, Abdul.

Clinton, Julie, jt. auth. see Clinton, Tim.

Clinton, Kate. Don't Get Me Started. 208p. 2000. pap. 14.00 (*0-345-43016-6*) Ballantine Pub Grp.

Clinton, Kevin. Myth & Cult: The Iconography of the Eleusinian Mysteries. (Acta Instituti Atheniensis Regni Sueciae Ser.: Series 8, XI). (Illus.). 157p. (Orig.). 1992. pap. 57.50 (*91-7916-025-5*, Pub. by P Astroms) Coronet Bks.

Clinton, Michelle T. Good Sense & the Faithless. 100p. (Orig.). 1994. pap. 9.95 (*0-931122-75-9*) West End.

Clinton, Michelle T., et al, eds. Invocation L. A. Urban Multicultural Poetry. 129p. (Orig.). 1989. pap. 8.95 (*0-931122-52-X*) West End.

Clinton, Patricia. Pediatric Nurse Practioner Certification Study Question Book. 300p. 1999. pap. text, student ed. 35.00 (*1-878028-21-9*) Hlth Lead Assoc.

Clinton, Patrick. Guide to Writing for the Business Press. LC 96-21973. (Illus.). 248p. 1997. 29.95 (*0-8442-3664-0*, NTC Business Bks) NTC Contemp Pub Co.

Clinton, Peggy A. The Collected Works of Peggy Anne Clinton. (Illus.). 40p. 1997. 10.00 (*0-8059-3953-9*) Dorrance.

Clinton, Robert. Taking Eden: Poems. LC 97-5657. 80p. 1998. 20.95 (*1-889330-09-4*); pap. 12.95 (*1-889330-10-8*) Sarabande Bks.

Clinton, Robert, et al. Federal Courts: Theory & Practice. 1553p. 1996. 60.00 (*0-316-26335-4*, 63354) Aspen Law.

Clinton, Robert L. God & Man in the Law: The Foundations of Anglo-American Constitutionalism. LC 97-11020. 304p. 1997. 35.00 (*0-7006-0841-9*) U Pr of KS.

— Marbury vs. Madison & Judicial Review. LC 89-34651. xii, 332p. 1989. pap. 19.95 (*0-7006-0517-7*) U Pr of KS.

Clinton, Roger & Moore, Jim. Growing up Clinton: The Lives, Times & Tragedies of America's Presidential Family. (Illus.). 292p. 1995. 19.95 (*1-56530-178-1*) Summit TX.

Clinton, Socks, et al. Socks & Cretin: Two Democats Helping Bill with the Presidency. LC 95-30272. (Illus.). xii, 169p. 1995. pap. 15.00 (*0-86663-212-3*) Ide Hse.

Clinton, Susan. Benjamin Harrison. LC 89-33751. (Encyclopedia of Presidents Ser.). 100p. (J). (ps up). 1989. lib. bdg. 24.00 (*0-516-01370-X*) Childrens.

— Correction Officer. (Careers Without College Ser.). (Illus.). 48p. (J). (gr. 3-7). 1998. lib. bdg. 19.00 (*0-516-21279-6*) Childrens.

— First Ladies. LC 93-36995. (Cornerstones to Freedom Ser.). (Illus.). 32p. (J). (gr. 4-7). 1994. pap. 5.95 (*0-516-46673-9*) Childrens.

— The First Ladies. LC 93-36995. (Cornerstones to Freedom Ser.). (Illus.). 32p. (J). (gr. 4-7). 1994. lib. bdg. 19.50 (*0-516-06673-0*) Childrens.

— Heating-&-Air Conditioning Servicer. (Careers Without College Ser.). (Illus.). 48p. (J). (gr. 3-7). 1998. 19.00 (*0-516-21282-6*) Childrens.

— Herbert Hoover. LC 87-35711. (Encyclopedia of Presidents Ser.). (Illus.). 100p. (J). (gr. 5-8). 1988. lib. bdg. 24.00 (*0-516-01355-6*) Childrens.

— James Madison. LC 86-13630. (Encyclopedia of Presidents Ser.). (Illus.). 100p. (J). (gr. 3 up). 1986. lib. bdg. 24.00 (*0-516-01382-3*) Childrens.

— Reading Between the Bones: The Pioneers of Dinosaur Paleontology. LC 96-36132. (Lives in Science Ser.). (J). 1997. lib. bdg. 24.00 (*0-531-11324-8*) Watts.

— Tractor-Trailer-Truck Driver. (Careers Without College Ser.). (Illus.). 48p. (J). (gr. 3-7). 1998. 19.00 (*0-516-21289-3*) Childrens.

Clinton, Susan, jt. auth. see Carruthers, Margaret W.

***Clinton, Tim & Clinton, Julie.** The Marriage You've Always Wanted: How to Grow a Stronger More Intimate Relationship. 172p. 2000. pap. 12.99 (*0-8499-3745-0*) Word Pub.

Clinton, Timothy. Before a Bad Goodbye: How to Turn Your Marriage Around, 1. LC 99-34144. 1999. pap. text 12.99 (*0-8499-3743-4*) Word Pub.

Clinton Topper Staff. History of Clinton Wisconsin. (Illus.). 357p. 1987. 60.00 (*0-88107-091-2*) Curtis Media.

Clinton, W. David. The Two Faces of National Interest. LC 93-24206. (Political Traditions in Foreign Policy Ser.). 280p. (C). 1994. text 40.00 (*0-8071-1841-9*); pap. text 19.95 (*0-8071-1895-8*) La State U Pr.

Clinton, W. David & Thompson, Kenneth W., eds. National Interest: Rhetoric, Leadership, & Policy. LC 87-29605. (Exxon Education Foundation Series on Rhetoric & Political Discourse: Vol. 13). 122p. (Orig.). (C). 1988. pap. text 17.00 (*0-8191-6734-7*); lib. bdg. 38.00 (*0-8191-6733-9*) U Pr of Amer.

***Clinton, William & Rossello, Pedro, frwds.** Puerto Rico, Hurricane Georges, September 1998: The President's Long-Term Recovery Action Plan. (Illus.). 73p. (C). 2000. pap. text 25.00 (*0-7881-8647-7*) DIANE Pub.

Clinton, William J. The Budget of the U. S. Government: Fiscal Year, 1999. (Illus.). 381p. (C). 1998. pap. text 50.00 (*0-7881-4924-5*) DIANE Pub.

— Chemical & Biological Weapons Defense: Communication from the President of the U. S. (Illus.). 86p. (C). 1999. pap. text 25.00 (*0-7881-7848-2*) DIANE Pub.

— Chemical Weapons Convention: Message from the President of the U. S. 662p. (C). 1998. pap. text 50.00 (*0-7881-4922-9*) DIANE Pub.

— Comprehensive Readiness Program for Countering Proliferation of Weapons of Mass Destruction: Message from the President of the United States. 52p. (C). 1998. pap. text 20.00 (*0-7881-4957-1*) DIANE Pub.

— Economic Report of the President, 1995. 1995. pap. 15.00 (*0-614-30795-3*, CECO95) Claitors.

— Economic Report of the President, 1996. 1996. pap. 15.00 (*0-614-30794-5*, CECONP) Claitors.

— Economic Report of the President, 1997. 1997. pap. 20.00 (*0-614-30619-1*, CEC097) Claitors.

— Economic Report of the President, 1997. 1997. pap. 20.00 (*1-57980-048-3*, CECO97) Claitors.

Clinton, William J., II. A National Security Strategy of Engagement & Enlargement, 1995-1996. (Association of the U. S. Army Book Ser.). 156p. 1995. 16.00 (*1-57488-021-7*) Brasseys.

Clinton, William J. National Security Strategy of the United States: 1994-1995 - Engagement & Enlargement. (Association of the U. S. Army Book Ser.). 136p. 1995. 15.00 (*0-02-881050-3*) Brasseys.

— Public Papers of President William Clinton, 6 vols. 1997. lib. bdg. write for info. (*0-8490-6369-8*) Gordon Pr.

Clinton, William J., ed. Constitution & Convention of the International Telecommunication Union: Message from the President of the U. S. 553p. (C). 1998. pap. text 50.00 (*0-7881-7302-2*) DIANE Pub.

Clinton, William J. & Gore, Albert J., Jr. Technology for America's Economic Growth: A New Direction to Build Economic Strength. 36p. (Orig.). (C). 1993. pap. text 25.00 (*0-7881-0129-3*) DIANE Pub.

Clinton, William J. & Yellen, Janet L. Economic Report of the President, 1998: And the Annual Report of the Council of Economic Advisors. (Illus.). 408p. 1998. pap. text 45.00 (*0-7881-7118-6*) DIANE Pub.

Clinton-Williams Corporation Staff. The Childcare Guide: A Directory to Childcare Facilities in Metropolitan Atlanta. (Illus.). 400p. (Orig.). 1989. pap. write for info. (*0-318-65308-7*) Clinton-Williams.

Clio, jt. auth. see Priceman, Marjorie.

Cliometric Society Staff. Two Pioneers of Cliometrics: Robert W. Fogel & Douglass C. North. (Illus.). 104p. (C). 1993. 17.50 (*0-9640068-0-4*) Cliometric Soc.

— Two Pioneers of Cliometrics: Robert W. Fogel & Douglass C. North. (Illus.). 104p. (C). 1993. pap. 7.50 (*0-9640068-1-2*) Cliometric Soc.

Clipp, Amy. Job Damaged People: How to Survive Worker Comp. King, Linda & Temmink, Bill, eds. 153p. 1993. pap. 20.00 (*0-9639570-0-7*) LA Injured Wrkrs.

Clipp, Katherine & Cox, Betty. Sensory Awareness & Music Focus. 60p. (C). 1994. pap. text 12.00 (*0-935273-08-5*) Chess Pub.

Clipper, Henry, jt. auth. see Randall, Charles E.

Clipper, Lawrence, ed. see Chesterton, G. K.

Clipper, Lawrence J., jt. auth. see Ackerley, Chris.

***Clippinger, David.** Body of This Life: Reading William Bronk. 2000. pap. 21.95 (*1-58498-018-4*) Talisman Hse.

Clippinger, John. The Primal Digital Soup. (C). 1998. write for info. (*0-201-40656-X*) Addison-Wesley.

***Clippinger, John H., Jr., ed.** Biology of Business: Decoding the Natural Laws of Enterprise. LC 99-6510. (Business & Management Ser.). (Illus.). 320p. 1999. 28.50 (*0-7879-4324-X*) Jossey-Bass.

Clipson-Boyles, Suzi. Drama in Primary English Teaching. 1998. pap. 25.95 (*1-85346-540-2*) Taylor & Francis.

***Clipson-Boyles, Suzi.** Putting Research into Practice in Primary Teaching & Learning. 2000. pap. 26.95 (*1-85346-642-5*) David Fulton.

Clipson-Boyles, Suzi. Supporting Language & Literacy: A Handbook for Those Who Assist in Early Years Settings. 80p. 1996. pap. 22.95 (*1-85346-438-4*, Pub. by David Fulton) Taylor & Francis.

Cliquet, R., jt. auth. see Lopez, A.

Cliquet, Robert & Thienpont, Kristiaan. Population & Development: A Message from the Cairo Conference. LC 95-39653. (European Studies of Population: No. 3). 1995. lib. bdg. 88.00 (*0-7923-3763-8*) Kluwer Academic.

Clisby, Roger D. Contemporary American Monotypes. LC 85-233859. (Illus.). 48p. (Orig.). 1985. pap. 6.50 (*0-940744-52-X*) Chrysler Museum.

Clise, M. D. Stop the Violence Please. LC 94-9168. (Illus.). 64p. (J). (gr. 5-7). 1994. pap. 9.95 (*0-295-97367-6*) U of Wash Pr.

Clise, Michele Durks. Ophelia's Bedtime Book. (Illus.). (J). 1999. pap. write for info. (*0-14-055603-6*) NAL.

***Clish, Marian L.** Don't Eat Ice Cream with Your Dirty Feet: Strange & Weird Poems for Kids. unabridged ed. (Illus.). (J). (gr. k-5). 2000. 18.95 incl. audio (*1-928632-42-4*); 22.95 incl. cd-rom (*1-928632-43-2*); 15.95 (*1-928632-41-6*); pap. 8.95 (*1-928632-39-4*); pap. 5.95 (*1-928632-38-6*); pap. 12.95 (*1-928632-40-8*) Writers Mrktpl.

— Fish Don't Swim in a Tree. (Illus.). (J). (gr. k-3). pap. 7.95 (*1-928632-12-2*) Writers Mrktpl.

Clish, Marian L. I Wonder... What Would a Fish Wish For? unabridged ed. (Illus.). 56p. (J). (gr. k-3). 1999. pap. 5.95 (*1-928632-04-1*) Writers Mrktpl.

***Clish, Marian L.** I Wonder... What Would a Fish Wish For? unabridged ed. (Illus.). (J). (gr. k-3). 1999. pap. 12.95 incl. cd-rom (*1-928632-06-8*) Writers Mrktpl.

— I Wonder... What Would Happen If I Took an Elephant to School? unabridged ed. (J). (gr. k-3). 1999. 18.95 incl. audio (*1-928632-36-X*) Writers Mrktpl.

— I Wonder... What Would Happen If I Took an Elephant to School? unabridged ed. (Illus.). (J). (gr. k-3). 1999. 15.95 (*1-928632-35-1*); 7.95 (*1-928632-32-7*); pap. 14.95 incl. cd-rom (*1-928632-34-3*); pap. 10.95 incl. audio (*1-928632-33-5*) Writers Mrktpl.

— I Wonder... What Would Happen If I Took an Elephant to School? unabridged ed. (Illus.). (J). (gr. k-3). 1999. 22.95 incl. cd-rom (*1-928632-37-8*) Writers Mrktpl.

Clish, Marian L. I Wonder...What Would a Fish Wish For. unabridged ed. (Illus.). (J). (gr. 5 up). 1999. pap. 8.95 incl. audio (*1-928632-05-X*) Writers Mrktpl.

***Clish, Marian L.** J. P. Landers - Solve a Mystery, Bk. 1. LC PZ7-L513750. (J). (gr. 2-7). 1999. 20.95 incl. cd-rom (*1-928632-27-0*) Writers Mrktpl.

Clish, Marian L. J. P. Landers - Solve a Mystery, Bk. 1. unabridged ed. LC 82-9712. (Illus.). 46p. (J). (gr. 2-5). 1999. reprint ed. 10.95 (*0-516-01991-0*) Writers Mrktpl.

— J. P. Landers - Solve a Mystery, Bk. 1. unabridged ed. LC 82-9712. (J). (gr. 3-12). 1999. pap. 8.95 incl. audio (*1-928632-02-5*); pap. 12.95 incl. cd-rom (*1-928632-03-3*) Writers Mrktpl.

***Clish, Marian L.** J. P. Landers - Solve a Mystery, Bk. 1. unabridged ed. (Illus.). (J). (gr. 2-5). 1999. 15.95 incl. audio (*1-928632-26-2*) Writers Mrktpl.

— J. P. Landers - Solve a Mystery, Bk. 2. LC PZ7-L513750. (J). (gr. 2-7). 1999. 20.95 incl. cd-rom (*1-928632-29-7*) Writers Mrktpl.

— J. P. Landers - Solve a Mystery, Bk. 2. unabridged ed. (J). (gr. 2-5). 1999. pap. 12.95 incl. cd-rom (*1-928632-11-4*) Writers Mrktpl.

— J. P. Landers - Solve a Mystery, Bk. 2. unabridged ed. (YA). (gr. 7-12). 1999. pap. 8.95 incl. audio (*1-928632-10-6*) Writers Mrktpl.

— J. P. Landers - Solve a Mystery, Bk. 2. unabridged ed. (Illus.). (J). (gr. 2-5). 1999. 15.95 incl. audio (*1-928632-28-9*) Writers Mrktpl.

— A Wolf's Tale. LC 98-90038. (J). (gr. 5-10). 1999. 22.95 incl. cd-rom (*1-928632-22-X*) Writers Mrktpl.

— A Wolf's Tale. unabridged ed. LC 98-90038. (J). pap. 14.95 incl. cd-rom (*1-928632-01-7*) Writers Mrktpl.

Clish, Marian L. A Wolf's Tale. unabridged ed. LC 98-90038. (J). 1999. pap. 10.95 incl. audio (*1-928632-00-9*) Writers Mrktpl.

***Clish, Marian L.** A Wolf's Tale. unabridged ed. LC 98-90038. (Illus.). (J). (gr. k-5). 1999. 15.95 (*1-928632-20-3*) Writers Mrktpl.

— A Wolf's Tale. unabridged ed. (Illus.). (J). (gr. k-5). 1999. 18.95 incl. audio (*1-928632-21-1*) Writers Mrktpl.

— You Choose the Way: A Book That Reads Like a Game - Mazash the Wizard. large type ed. (Illus.). 56p. (J). (gr. 3-5). 1999. pap. 5.95 (*1-928632-07-6*) Writers Mrktpl.

— You Choose the Way: A Book That Reads Like a Game: Mazash the Wizard. (J). (gr. 2-7). 1999. 22.95 incl. cd-rom (*1-928632-25-4*) Writers Mrktpl.

— You Choose the Way: A Book That Reads Like a Game: Mazash the Wizard. unabridged ed. (Illus.). (J). (gr. 2-5). 1999. 18.95 incl. audio (*1-928632-24-6*) Writers Mrktpl.

— You Choose the Way: A Book That Reads Like a Game: Mazash the Wizard. unabridged ed. (Illus.). (J). (gr. 3-5). 1999. 15.95 (*1-928632-23-8*) Writers Mrktpl.

Clissold, Augustus, tr. see Swedenborg, Emanuel.

Clissold, Augustus, tr. & intro. see Swedenborg, Emanuel.

Clissold, P. Basic Seamanship. (Illus.). (C). 1987. 50.00 (*0-85174-255-6*) St Mut.

— Yacht Master Offshore & Ocean. (C). 1987. 75.00 (*0-85174-261-0*) St Mut.

Clissold, P. & Tweddell, A. J. Brown's Nautical Star Chart. (C). 1987. pap. 30.00 (*0-85174-435-4*) St Mut.

Clissold, Stephen, compiled by. The Wisdom of St. Francis & His Companions. LC 78-27504. (Wisdom Bks.). 363p. 1979. pap. 8.95 (*0-8112-0721-8*, NDP477, Pub. by New Directions) Norton.

Clitandre, Pierre. Cathedral of the August Heat. Jones, Bridget, tr. (Readers International Ser.).Tr. of Cathedrale dumois daout. (Illus.). 161p. (C). 1987. pap. 12.95 (*0-930523-31-8*) Readers Intl.

Clitheroe, Ricky. Away from the Bombs. (C). 1989. 40.00 (*1-85022-027-1*, Pub. by Dyllansow Truran) St Mut.

Clive, Alan. State of War: Michigan in World War II. LC 79-10213. (Illus.). 318p. 1979. 34.50 (*0-472-10001-7*, 10001) U of Mich Pr.

Clive, Caroline. Paul Ferroll. (Oxford Popular Fiction Ser.). 236p. 1997. pap. 9.95 (*0-19-283247-6*) OUP.

Clive, Caroline A. Paul Ferroll: A Tale. LC 79-8256. reprint ed. 44.50 (*0-404-61821-9*) AMS Pr.

Clive, Catherine. The Case of Mrs. Clive Submitted to the Publick. LC 92-22022. (Augustan Reprints Ser.: No. 159). 1973. reprint ed. 14.50 (*0-404-70159-0*, PN2596) AMS Pr.

Clive, Geoffrey. The Romantic Enlightenment. LC 72-8238. 219p. 1973. reprint ed. lib. bdg. 59.50 (*0-8371-6544-X*, CLRE, Greenwood Pr) Greenwood.

Clive, H. P., ed. see Navarre, Marguerite de.

Clive, Jenny. Tropical Forest Expeditions. (C). 1993. 26.00 (*0-907649-63-7*, Pub. by Expedit Advisory Ctr) St Mut.

Clive, John. Macaulay: The Shaping of the Historian. LC 86-26515. 576p. 1987. pap. 21.00 (*0-674-54005-0*) Belknap Pr.

Clive, John & Head, Nicolas. The Crossing. 304p. 1988. pap. 3.95 (*0-380-70473-0*, Avon Bks) Morrow Avon.

Clive, John, ed. see Carlyle, Thomas.

Clive, John, ed. see Mittelberger, Gottlieb.

Clive, Lloyd, jt. auth. see Arnold, J. R.

Clive, Peter. Schubert & His World: A Biographical Dictionary. LC 96-24977. (Illus.). 336p. (C). 1997. text 49.95 (*0-19-816582-X*) OUP.

Clive, Williams S. & Prioh, John G., eds. Firm Foundation of God Standeth Sure. 1984. 14.94 (*0-317-16698-0*) Firm Foun Pub.

Cliver. Foodborne Infections & Intoxications. 3rd ed. 1999. 99.95 (*0-12-588365-X*) Acad Pr.

***Cliver & Riemann.** Foodborne Diseases. 2nd ed. 1999. pap. 59.95 (*0-12-176559-8*) Morgan Kaufmann.

Cliver, Dean O., ed. Foodborne Diseases. 395p. 1990. text 63.00 (*0-12-176558-X*) Acad Pr.

Cliver, Dean O. & Newman, Ruth, eds. Drinking Water Microbiology, Vol. 2. (Journal of Environmental Pathology, Toxicology & Oncology Ser.: Vol. 7, No. 5-6, 1987). 366p. 1987. 38.00 (*0-685-34724-9*) Chem-Orbital.

An Asterisk (*) at the beginning of an entry indicates that the title is appearing for the first time.

Clizbe, Kent. Xrina at Hagar Qim: The Temple Builders of Malta. (Children of Malta Ser.: Vol. 1). (Illus.). 40p. (J). (gr. k-5). 1998. pap. 12.95 (*0-9656252-1-4*, MAL001) O T S.

Clizbee, Azalea, compiled by. Catalogue of the Wymberley Jones de Renne Georgia Library. 3 vols. 1396p. 1995. reprint ed. 195.00 (*1-888262-73-7*) Martino Pubng.

Cloake. Reliability & Concurrent Engineering. (C). 2001. 65.00 (*0-13-146952-5*, Macmillan Coll) P-H.

Cloake, Dawn. Cutting & Draping Special Occasion Clothes: Designs for Eveningwear & Partywear. 1999. pap. text 17.95 (*0-7134-8332-6*) BTB Ent.

***Cloake, Dawn.** Lingerie Design on the Stand: Designs for Underwear & Nightwear. (Illus.). 96p. 2000. pap. 23.95 (*0-7134-8552-3*) B T B.

Cloar, James A., et al. Centralized Retail Management. 86p. 1990. pap. 41.95 (*0-87420-707-X*, C43) Urban Land.

Cloarec-Heiss, France. Dynamique et Equilibre d'une Syntaxe: Le Banda-Linda de Centrafrique. (Illus.). 568p. 1986. text 110.00 (*0-521-33068-8*) Cambridge U Pr.

Cloarec, Yann, ed. see Bonaparte, Napoleon.

Clochesy, John M. Advanced Technology in Critical Care Nursing. 203p. 1988. 59.00 (*0-8342-0023-6*, 20023) Aspen Pub.

— Essentials of Critical Care Nursing. 254p. 1988. 61.00 (*0-87189-884-5*, 89884) Aspen Pub.

Clochesy, John M., et al. Critical Care Nursing. 2nd ed. (Illus.). 1577p. 1996. text 103.00 (*0-7216-5674-9*, W B Saunders Co) Harcrt Hlth Sci Grp.

Clochesy, John M., jt. auth. see Welsh, Mickie D.

Clock, Herbert & Boetzel, Eric. The Light in the Sky. Reginald, R. & Melville, Douglas, eds. LC 77-84211. (Lost Race & Adult Fantasy Ser.). 1978. reprint ed. lib. bdg. 29.95 (*0-405-10966-0*) Ayer.

Clock, John R. Clockwise: Selections 1965-1967. Clock, Judith A., ed. & compiled by by. 176p. (Orig.). 1995. pap. 12.95 (*0-9648894-0-4*) Clockwise Pub.

Clock, Judith A., ed. & compiled by see Clock, John R.

Clock, Paul M. Punk Rotten & Nasty: The Saga of the Pacific Railway & Navigation Co. LC 98-93979. (Illus.). 112p. 1998. pap. write for info. (*0-9668987-0-2*) Corbett Pr.

Clocksin, W. F. Clause & Effect: Prolog Programming for the Working Programmer. LC 97-35795. 150p. 1997. pap. write for info. (*3-540-62971-8*) Spr-Verlag.

Clocksin, W. F. & Mellish, C. S. Programming in Prolog. 300p. 1993. pap. 29.00 (*0-387-17539-3*) Spr-Verlag.

— Programming in Prolog. 4th ed. LC 94-31331. 1994. 34.00 (*0-387-58350-5*) Spr-Verlag.

— Programming in Prology. 4th ed. 281p. 1994. text 34.95 (*3-540-58350-5*) Spr-Verlag.

Clodd, Alan, jt. auth. see Gascoyne, David.

Clodd, Edward. Animism: Primitive Myth & Religion. 1993. reprint ed. pap. 16.95 (*1-872736-41-6*, Pub. by Mandrake Pr) Holmes Pub.

— Animism: The Seed of Religion (1921) 100p. 1996. reprint ed. pap. 13.95 (*1-56459-908-6*) Kessinger Pub.

— The Birth & Growth of Myth & Its Survival in Folk Lore, Legend & Dogma. 26p. 1997. reprint ed. pap. 9.95 (*0-7661-0069-3*) Kessinger Pub.

— Childhood of Religions: Embracing a Simple Account of the Birth & Growth of Myths & Legends (1878) 298p. 1998. reprint ed. pap. 24.95 (*0-7661-0502-4*) Kessinger Pub.

— The Childhood of the World: A Simple Account of Man's Origin & Early History (1914) 250p. 1998. reprint ed. pap. 19.95 (*0-7661-0145-2*) Kessinger Pub.

— Magic in Names & Other Things. 246p. 1997. reprint ed. pap. 19.95 (*0-7661-0077-4*) Kessinger Pub.

— Myths & Dreams. 1993. reprint ed. pap. 23.50 (*1-55818-226-8*, Pub. by Mandrake Pr) Holmes Pub.

— Pioneers of Evolution: From Thales to Huxley; with an Intermediate Chapter on the Causes of Arrest of the Movement. LC 74-37470. (Essay Index Reprint Ser.). 1977. reprint ed. 21.95 (*0-8369-2540-8*) Ayer.

— Pioneers of Evolution from Thales to Huxley. 270p. 1997. reprint ed. pap. 19.95 (*0-7661-0086-3*) Kessinger Pub.

— Thomas Henry Huxley. LC 75-30018. reprint ed. 32.50 (*0-404-14023-8*) AMS Pr.

Clodd, Eward. The Story of the Alphabet: Ancient Languages. 2nd ed. (Illus.). 375p. 1997. reprint ed. 15.00 (*1-57179-070-5*) Intern Guild ASRS.

Clode, Drew, et al. Towards the Sensitive Bureaucracy: Consumers, Welfare & the New Pluralism. 160p. 1987. text 69.95 (*0-566-05009-9*) Ashgate Pub Co.

Clodfelter. General Fashion Test Bank. (General Business & Business Education Ser.). 1993. text 40.95 (*0-8273-5399-5*) Delmar.

Clodfelter, Mark. The Limits of Air Power: The American Bombing of North Vietnam. 297p. 1989. 32.95 (*0-02-905990-9*) Free Pr.

Clodfelter, Michael. The Dakota War: The United States Army vs. the Sioux, 1862-1865. LC 97-39147. 279p. 1998. lib. bdg. 42.50 (*0-7864-0419-1*) McFarland & Co.

— Mad Minutes & Vietnam Months. 384p. 1996. mass mkt. 5.99 (*0-7860-0337-5*, Pinncle Kensgtn) Kensgtn Pub Corp.

Clodfelter, Micheal. Mad Minutes & Vietnam Months: A Soldier's Memoir. LC 87-43170. 1989. mass mkt. 4.50 (*0-8217-2604-8*, Zebra Kensgtn) Kensgtn Pub Corp.

— Mad Minutes & Vietnam Months: A Soldier's Memoir. LC 87-43170. (Illus.). 254p. 1988. pap. 22.95 (*0-89950-326-8*) McFarland & Co.

— Vietnam in Military Statistics: A History of the Indochina Wars, 1772-1991. LC 95-15054. 336p. 1995. lib. bdg. 68.50 (*0-7864-0027-7*) McFarland & Co.

Clodfelter, Richard. Retail Buying from Staples to Fashions to Fads. LC 92-19601. 372p. 1993. mass mkt. 39.00 (*0-8273-5058-9*) Delmar.

— Retail Buying from Staples to Fashions to Fads. 106p. 1993. pap., teacher ed. 17.00 (*0-8273-5059-7*) Delmar.

Clodfelter, Richard & Dublin, Peter. Making Buying Decisions: Using the Computer as a Tool. (General Business & Business Education Ser.). (C). 1995. mass mkt. 43.95 (*0-8273-6797-X*) Delmar.

— Making Buying Decisions: Using the Computer as a Tool. (General Business & Business Education Ser.). 32p. 1996. text, teacher ed. 10.00 (*0-8273-6798-8*, VNR) Wiley.

Clodius, Jennifer, et al. Jerusalem by Night. (Vampire Ser.). (Illus.). 128p. 1999. pap. 17.95 (*1-56504-299-9*, 2821) White Wolf.

Cloe, John H. The Aleutian Warriors: A History of the 11th Air Force & Fleet Air Wing 4. LC 90-60028. (Illus.). 350p. (Orig.). 1991. pap. 19.95 (*0-929521-35-8*) Pictorial Hist.

Cloer, Eddie. The Church: The People of God's Purpose: Is the Church God's Intention or Man's Invention? 260p. 1997. 2.50 (*0-945441-26-6*) Res Pubns AR.

— The Church: The People of God's Purpose: Is the Church God's Intention or Man's Invention? 269p. 1997. pap. 6.95 (*0-945441-27-4*) Res Pubns AR.

— Le Dessein de Dieu pour "L'Eglise" Clarifiant la Nature et l'Intention de l'Eglise du Nouveau Testament. Orig. Title: God's Design for "the Church". 248p. 1999. pap. 2.50 (*0-945441-32-0*) Res Pubns AR.

Cloer, Eddie. God's Design for "The Church" 1993. 6.95 (*0-945441-19-3*) Res Pubns AR.

— God's Design for "The Church" (RUS.). 1995. 2.50 (*0-945441-22-3*) Res Pubns AR.

***Cloer, Eddie.** El modelo de Dios para "la Iglesia" Una Exposicio'n Sobre la Naturaleza y Proposito de la Iglesia. Orig. Title: God's Design for "the Church". 260p. 1999. pap. 2.50 (*0-945441-33-9*) Res Pubns AR.

— Il Piano di Dio per "La Chiesa" Uno Studio Sulla Natura e l'Intento della Chiesa del Nuovo Testamento. Orig. Title: Design of God for "the Church". 254p. 1998. pap. 2.50 (*0-945441-28-2*) Res Pubns AR.

— Que es "la Iglesia"? Identificando la Naturaleza y Diseno de la Iglesia del Nuevo Testamento. Orig. Title: What Is "the Church"?. 236p. 1998. pap. 2.50 (*0-945441-29-0*) Res Pubns AR.

— Qu'est-ce Que "L'Eglise"? Identifier la Nature et la Dessein de l'Eglise du Nouveau Testament. Orig. Title: What Is "the Church"?. 232p. 1998. pap. 2.50 (*0-945441-30-4*) Res Pubns AR.

Cloer, Eddie. What Is "The Church"? (RUS.). 1993. 2.50 (*0-945441-20-7*) Res Pubns AR.

— What Is "The Church"? 216p. 1993. pap. 6.95 (*0-945441-16-9*) Res Pubns AR.

***Cloer, Kelley E.** Rancidity in Foods. 290p. 1998. 145.00 (*0-8342-1287-0*) Aspen Pub.

Cloeren, Hermann J. Language & Thought: German Approaches to Analytical Philosophy in the 19th Centuries. (Foundations of Communication & Cognition Ser.). 267p. (C). 1988. lib. bdg. 95.40 (*3-11-011301-5*) De Gruyter.

Cloern, James E. & Nichols, Frederic H., eds. Temporal Dynamics of an Estuary: San Francisco Bay. (Developments in Hydrobiology Ser.). 1985. text 215.00 (*90-6193-538-5*) Kluwer Academic.

Cloern, Margaret, jt. ed. see Benton-Borghi, Beatrice Hope.

Cloes, Midiel, jt. auth. see Folsom, Ralph H.

Cloete, Fanie & Mokgoro, Job. Policies for Public Service Transformation. LC 95-206520. 1995. pap. 32.00 (*0-7021-3319-1*, Pub. by Juta & Co) Intl Spec Bk.

Cloete, G. Daan, jt. ed. see Van Vugt, William E.

***Cloete, Ian & Zurada, Jacek M., eds.** Knowledge-Based Neurocomputing. LC 99-41770. 1999. 55.00 (*0-262-03274-0*) MIT Pr.

Cloete, Jacobus Johannes Nicolaas. South African Public Administration & Management. 9th ed. LC 98-171957. xiv, 313p. 1998. write for info. (*0-627-02291-X*) J L Van Schaik.

Clogan, Maurice, ed. Medievalia et Humanistica, No. 15. 244p. 1988. 75.50 (*0-8476-7582-3*) Rowman.

Clogan, Paul M. Medieval Poetics. LC 75-32451. (Medievalia et Humanistica: New Ser.: No. 7). 221p. reprint ed. pap. 63.00 (*0-608-12238-6*, 2024433) Bks Demand.

Clogan, Paul M., ed. Medieval et Humanistica, Vol. 21. LC 75-32451. (Studies in Medieval & Renaissance Culture). 218p. 1994. lib. bdg. 72.00 (*0-8476-7960-8*) Rowman.

— Medieval Hagiography & Romance. LC 75-16872. (Medievalia et Humanistica: New Ser.: No. 6). 237p. reprint ed. pap. 67.60 (*0-608-17269-3*, 2029216) Bks Demand.

— Medievalia et Humanistica. LC 47-36424. (Studies in Medieval & Renaissance Culture: No. 16). 232p. 1989. lib. bdg. 68.00 (*0-8476-7608-0*) Rowman.

— Medievalia et Humanistica, Vol. 11. (New Studies in Medieval & Renaissance Culture: No. 11). 318p. (C). 1982. text 57.00 (*0-8476-7105-4*) Rowman.

— Medievalia et Humanistica, Vol. 22. (Studies in Renaissance Culture: No. 22). 352p. (C). 1995. lib. bdg. 65.00 (*0-8476-8099-1*) Rowman.

— Medievalia et Humanistica: Studies in Medieval & Renaissance Culture. (New Ser.: No. 10). 264p. 1981. 61.00 (*0-8476-6944-0*) Rowman.

— Medievalia et Humanistica: Studies in Medieval & Renaissance Culture, Vol. 17. 240p. 1991. 72.00 (*0-8476-7658-7*) Rowman.

— Medievalia et Humanistica: Studies in Medieval & Renaissance Culture, Vol. 23. 210p. 1996. lib. bdg. 71.50 (*0-8476-8272-2*) Rowman.

— Medievalia et Humanistica: Studies in Medieval & Renaissance Culture, the Columbian Quincentenary. (Medievalia et Humanistica Ser.: No. 19). 210p. (C). 1992. text 66.00 (*0-8476-7777-X*) Rowman.

— Medievalia et Humanistica No. 18: Studies in Medieval & Renaissance Culture, No. 18. 240p. (C). 1992. text 72.00 (*0-8476-7705-2*) Rowman.

— Medievalia et Humanistica Vol. 24: Studies in Medieval & Renaissance Culture. 304p. 1997. 71.50 (*0-8476-8674-4*) Rowman.

— Medievalia et Humanistica (Studies in Medieval & Renaissance Culture) (Medievalia et Humanistica Ser.: No. 42, Vo). 304p. 1998. 68.00 (*0-8476-9213-2*) Rowman.

— Studies in Medieval & Renaissance Culture. LC 75-32451. (Medievalie et Humanistica: New Ser.: No. 9). 269p. reprint ed. pap. 76.70 (*0-608-17051-8*, 2027282) Bks Demand.

— Studies in Medieval & Renaissance Culture Vol. 20: Boundaries. (Medievalia et Humanistica Ser.). 256p. (C). 1993. text 72.00 (*0-8476-7882-2*) Rowman.

***Clogan, Paul Maurice.** Civil Strife & National Identity in the Middle Ages. (Medievalia et Humanistica Ser.). 240p. 2000. text 75.00 (*0-8476-9449-6*) Rowman.

Clogg, Clifford C., ed. Sociological Methodology, 1988, Vol. 18. (C). 1988. text 40.00 (*0-912764-25-2*) Am Sociological.

Clogg, Clifford C. & Shihadeh, Edward S. Statistical Models for Ordinal Variables. (Advanced Quantitative Techniques in the Social Sciences Ser.: Vol. 4). (C). 1994. text 42.00 (*0-8039-3676-1*) Sage.

Clogg, Clifford C., jt. ed. see Von Eye, Alexander.

Clogg, Mary Jo & Clogg, Richard. Greece. Collison, Robert L., ed. (World Bibliographical Ser.: No. 17). 242p. 1981. lib. bdg. 50.00 (*0-903450-30-5*) ABC-CLIO.

Clogg, Richard. Anatolica: Studies in the Greek East in the 18th & 19th Centuries. LC 96-4770. (Collected Studies Ser.: No. CS526). 336p. 1996. 109.95 (*0-86078-543-2*, Pub. by Variorum) Ashgate Pub Co.

***Clogg, Richard.** Anglo-Greek Attitudes: Studies in History. LC 00-31116. 2000. write for info. (*0-312-23523-2*) St Martin.

Clogg, Richard. A Concise History of Greece. (Concise Histories Ser.). (Illus.). 271p. (C). 1992. text 54.95 (*0-521-37228-3*) Cambridge U Pr.

— A Concise History of Greece. (Concise Histories Ser.). (Illus.). 271p. (C). 1992. pap. 17.95 (*0-521-37830-3*) Cambridge U Pr.

— Parties & Elections in Greece: The Search for Legitimacy. LC 87-30376. xvii, 268p. (C). 1988. text 53.00 (*0-8223-0794-4*); pap. text 23.95 (*0-8223-0823-1*) Duke.

— Politics & the Academy: Arnold Toynbee & the Koraes Chair. 128p. 1986. 30.00 (*0-7146-3290-2*, Pub. by F Cass Pubs) Intl Spec Bk.

Clogg, Richard, ed. Greek Diaspora in the Twentieth Century. LC 98-55179. 1999. text 79.95 (*0-312-22189-4*) St Martin.

Clogg, Richard, jt. auth. see Clogg, Mary Jo.

Clohe, Rene. Fairyland Favorites: Town Mouse & Country Mouse. (J). 1989. 2.98 (*0-671-06188-7*) S&S Trade.

Cloherty, John P. & Stark, Ann R. Manual of Neonatal Care. 2nd ed. 688p. 1985. 25.50 (*0-316-14756-7*, Little Brwn Med Div) Lppncott W & W.

Cloherty, John P. & Stark, Ann R., eds. Manual of Neonatal Care. 4th ed. LC 97-22777. (Illus.). 688p. 1997. spiral bd. 34.95 (*0-316-14765-6*) Lppncott W & W.

Cloke, Christopher. Primary Prevention of Child Abuse. pap. text 32.00 (*0-471-97775-6*) Wiley.

Cloke, Gillian. This Female Man of God: Women & Spiritual Power in the Patristic Age, 350-450. LC 94-16028. 256p. (C). 1995. pap. 25.99 (*0-415-09470-4*, A9996) Routledge.

***Cloke, Kenneth.** Resolving Personal & Organizational Conflict: Stories of Transformation & Forgiveness. 2000. 34.95 (*0-7879-5060-2*) Jossey-Bass.

***Cloke, Kenneth & Goldsmith, Joan.** Resolving Conflicts at Work: A Complete Guide for Everyone on the Job. LC 99-50522. xiv, 251p. 2000. 25.00 (*0-7879-5059-9*) Jossey-Bass.

Cloke, Michael. A Guide to Plant Management. 94p. 1988. pap. 25.00 (*0-85295-223-6*, 9CH39) Gulf Pub.

Cloke, Paul. Introducing Human Geographies. (Illus.). 384p. 1999. pap. text 35.00 (*0-340-69193-X*) OUP.

***Cloke, Paul.** Introducing Human Geographies. (Illus.). 384p. 1999. text 85.00 (*0-340-69192-1*) OUP.

Cloke, Paul & Bell, Philip, eds. Deregulation & Transport: Market Forces in the Modern World. 244p. (C). 1990. pap. 89.95 (*0-8464-1534-8*) Beekman Pubs.

Cloke, Paul, et al. Approaching Human Geography: An Introduction to Contemporary Theoretical Debates. LC 91-2656. (Mappings Ser.). 224p. 1991. pap. text 23.95 (*0-89862-490-8*, 2490) Guilford Pubns.

Cloke, Paul J., ed. Policy & Change in Thatcher's Britain: Policy & Planning & Critical Theory. (Policy, Planning & Critical Theory Ser.). 350p. 1992. text 59.95 (*0-08-040647-5*, Prgamon Press) Buttrwrth-Heinemann.

— Rural Land-Use Planning in Developed Nations. 256p. 1992. pap. 77.95 (*0-04-711025-2*) Thomson Learn.

Cloke, Paul J. & Little, Jo. Contesting Countryside Cultures: Otherness, Marginalisation, & Rurality. LC 96-43171. (Illus.). 304p. (C). 1997. 85.00 (*0-415-14074-9*); pap. 25.99 (*0-415-14075-7*) Routledge.

— The Rural State? Limits to Planning in Rural Society. (Illus.). 304p. 1990. 75.00 (*0-19-823287-X*) OUP.

Cloke, Paul J., et al. Myth & Rural Culture. 192p. 1992. text 69.95 (*0-340-55048-1*, A9522, Pub. by E A) Routlge.

Cloke, Rene. Br'er Rabbit Stories. (J). 1988. 2.98 (*0-671-06187-9*) S&S Trade.

Cloke, Rene. Kenneth Grahame's Wind in the Willows. 1996. 9.99 (*0-614-19337-0*) Random.

Clokey, J., jt. auth. see Randolph, I.

Clokey, Joseph W. & Kirk, Hazel J. Childe Jesus: A Christmas Cantata for Mixed Voices. LC M 1530.C5. 23p. 1922. reprint ed. pap. 30.00 (*0-608-08145-0*, 201783800009) Bks Demand.

Clones, Daphne & Rist, Carl. The 1997 Development Report Card for the States: Economic Benchmarks for State & Corporate Decision-Makers, 1997. 9th ed. 114p. 1997. pap. 58.00 (*1-883187-17-6*) Corp Ent Dev.

Cloney, Tom, jt. auth. see Lopez, Gilbert T.

Clonin, Thomas N., jt. auth. see Fellow, Anthony R.

Cloninger, C. Robert, ed. Personality & Psychopathology. LC 98-30095. (American Psychopathological Association Ser.). xv, 524p. 1999. 59.95 (*0-88048-923-5*, 8923) Am Psychiatric.

Cloninger, C. Robert & Begleiter, Henri, eds. The Genetics & Biology of Alcoholism. (Banbury Reports: No. 33). (Illus.). 430p. (C). 1991. text 85.00 (*0-87969-233-2*) Cold Spring Harbor.

Cloninger, C. Robert, jt. ed. see Gershon, Elliot S.

Cloninger, C. Robert, jt. ed. see Maser, Jack D.

Cloninger, Claire. Dear Abba: Finding the Father's Heart Through Prayer. LC 97-9392. 240p. 1997. 17.99 (*0-8499-1393-4*) Word Pub.

— E-Mail from God for Teens. (Illus.). 256p. (J). 1999. 12.99 (*1-56292-810-4*) Honor Bks OK.

— Faithfully Fit. 1991. pap. 10.99 (*0-8499-3237-8*) Word Pub.

***Cloninger, Claire.** More E-Mail from God for Teens. (YA). 2000. pap. 12.99 (*1-56292-931-3*) Honor Bks.

Cloninger, Claire. A Place Called Simplicity. LC 93-7342. 1993. pap. 8.99 (*1-56507-056-9*) Harvest Hse.

— Postcards for People in Love. LC 95-2866. 128p. 1995. 12.99 (*0-8499-1208-3*) Word Pub.

— Postcards for People Who Hurt. LC 95-2867. 128p. 1995. 12.99 (*0-8499-1197-4*) Word Pub.

— Postcards from Heaven. 1997. pap. 12.99 (*0-8499-4074-5*) Word Pub.

***Cloninger, Claire.** Simple Joys: Finding Happiness in Your Own Backyard. gif. ed. (Illus.). 64p. 2000. 12.99 (*0-7369-0337-2*) Harvest Hse.

Cloninger, Curt. Drama for Worship: Contemporary Sketches for Opening Hearts to God. Caldwell, Lise, ed. LC 98-44071. (Drama Ministry Resources Ser.). 64p. 1999. 19.99 (*0-7847-0916-5*, 03393); 19.99 (*0-7847-0917-3*, 03394) Standard Pub.

Cloninger, Susan C. Personality. LC 95-48100. 608p. (C). 1996. pap. text 68.95 (*0-7167-2825-7*) W H Freeman.

— Theories of Personality: Understanding Persons. 3rd ed. LC 99-26818. 568p. 1999. 80.00 (*0-13-020989-9*) P-H.

Clonts, Howard, jt. auth. see Jolly, Curtis.

Clonts, Howard A., jt. auth. see Cerezo, German A.

Clontz, J. & Norman, I. A. Women & the Cross. LC 97-91734. (Illus.). ix, 246p. (Orig.). 1997. pap. 14.95 (*0-9658097-4-9*, 625) PFPA.

Clontz, Lucia. Microbial Limit & Bioburden Tests: Validation Approaches & Global Requirements. LC 97-41282. (Illus.). 240p. 1998. 189.00 (*1-57491-062-0*) Interpharm.

Clontz, Ralph C., Jr. Equal Credit Opportunity Manual. 4th ed. LC 87-50957. 1152p. 1988. 140.00 (*0-88712-899-8*) Warren Gorham & Lamont.

— Equal Credit Opportunity Manual, No. 1. 4th ed. LC 87-50957. 1152p. 1990. suppl. ed. 185.00 (*0-7913-0807-3*) Warren Gorham & Lamont.

— Equal Credit Opportunity Manual, No. 2. 4th ed. LC 87-50957. 1152p. 1991. suppl. ed. 82.50 (*0-7913-0929-0*) Warren Gorham & Lamont.

— Federal Fair Lending & Credit Practices Manual. 1184p. 1994. 175.00 (*0-7913-2121-5*) Warren Gorham & Lamont.

— Truth-in-Lending Manual, 2 vols. 6th rev. ed. (Illus.). 1991. pap. text 175.00 (*0-7913-0546-5*) Warren Gorham & Lamont.

Clontz, Ralph C., Jr. & Pannabecker, James H. Truth In-lending Manual: Text & Forms, 2 vols. rev. ed. LC 96-61508. 1996. write for info. (*0-7913-2958-5*) Warren Gorham & Lamont.

Cloonan. Banned ! 336p. 1996. pap. 31.95 (*1-85742-300-3*) Ashgate Pub Co.

Cloonan, Kathryn L. Sing Me a Story, Read Me a Song Bk. I: Patterns: Ideas for Making Great Books from Favorite Children's Songs. (Illus.). 56p. 10.00 (*1-879813-00-9*) Rhythm & Read.

— Sing Me a Story, Read Me a Song Bk. 2: Patterns: Ideas for Making Great Books from Favorite Children's Songs. (Illus.). 66p. 10.00 (*1-879813-04-1*) Rhythm & Read.

— Whole Language Holidays, Bk. I. (Illus.). 68p. 10.00 (*1-879813-51-3*) Rhythm & Read.

— Whole Language Holidays, Bk. II. (Illus.). 74p. 10.00 (*1-879813-53-X*) Rhythm & Read.

Cloonan, Kevin A., jt. auth. see Allen, W. B.

Cloonan, Michele. Preservation Planning Program Resource Guides: Organizing Preservation Activities. 98p. 1993. pap. 15.00 (*0-918006-66-X*) ARL.

Cloonan, Michele V. Early Bindings in Paper: A Brief History of European Handmade Paper-Covered Books with a Multilingual Glossary. (Professional Librarian Ser.). 144p. (C). 1991. 40.00 (*0-8161-1971-6*, Pub. by Macmillan) S&S Trade.

Cloonan, William. The Writing of War: French & German Fiction & World War II. LC 98-48013. 1999. 39.95 (*0-8130-1685-1*) U Press Fla.

Cloonan, William, jt. ed. see James, JoAnn.

Cloonan, William J. Racine's Theatre: The Politics of Love. LC 77-8683. (Romance Monographs: No. 28). 1978. 22.00 (*84-399-7422-1*) Romance.

Cloonen, F. Blake, jt. auth. see Hall, Robert D., Jr.

Clooney, Francis X. Hindu Wisdom for All God's Children. LC 97-49195. (Faith Meets Faith Ser.). 125p. (Orig.). 1998. pap. 18.00 (*1-57075-164-1*) Orbis Bks.

An Asterisk (*) at the beginning of an entry indicates that the title is appearing for the first time.

— Seeing Through Texts: Doing Theology among the Srivaisnavas of South India. LC 95-35858. (SUNY Series, Toward a Comparative Philosophy of Religions). 351p. (C). 1996. text 73.50 (*0-7914-2995-4*); pap. text 24.95 (*0-7914-2996-2*) State U NY Pr.

— Theology after Vedanta: An Experiment in Comparative Theology. LC 92-14007. (SUNY Series, Toward a Comparative Philosophy of Religions). 265p. (C). 1993. text 24.50 (*0-7914-1365-9*) State U NY Pr.

***Clooney, Rosemary.** Girl Singer. LC 99-36760. 1999. 24.95 (*0-375-40858-4*) Wheeler Pub.

***Clooney, Rosemary & Barthel, Joan.** Girl Singer - Rosemary Clooney: An Autobiography. LC 99-24342. (Illus.). 352p. 1999. 24.95 (*0-385-49334-7*) Doubleday.

Cloos, Ernst. Microtectonics along the Western Edge of the Blue Ridge, Maryland, & Virginia. LC 77-156828. (Johns Hopkins University Studies in Geology: No. 20). 261p. reprint ed. pap. 81.00 (*0-608-14275-1*, 201568800095) Bks Demand.

***Cloots, Andre & Sia, Santiago, eds.** Framing a Vision of the World: Essays in Philosophy, Science & Religion. 308p. 1999. 52.50 (*90-6186-986-2*, Pub. by Leuven Univ) Coronet Bks.

***Clopine, Sandra O.** Moments of Intercession. 144p. 1999. pap. 6.99 (*0-88243-727-5*, 02-0727) Gospel Pub.

Clopinel, J., jt. auth. see De Lorris, Guillaume.

***Clopper, Brian.** Graham the Gargoyle: Fear of Flying. Clopper, Michelle & Morgan, Katrina, eds. (Illus.). 108p. (J). (gr. 8-13). 2000. pap. 6.95 (*0-9700659-0-6*, Teeny Behemoth) Topsy Turvy.

Clopper, Edward N. Child Labor in City Streets. LC 77-106738. ix, 280p. 1970. write for info. (*0-512-00757-8*) Irvington.

Clopper, Edward N. Child Labor in City Streets. LC 74-22737. (Labor Movement in Fiction & Non-Fiction Ser.). ix, 280 p. 1976. reprint ed. 34.50 (*0-404-58489-6*) AMS Pr.

— Child Labor in City Streets. LC 74-1677. (Children & Youth Ser.: Vol. 2). ix, 280 p. 1974. reprint ed. 28.95 (*0-405-05956-6*) Ayer.

— Clopper. An American Family: Its Ups & Downs Through Eight Generations in New Amsterdam, N. Y., Penna., Md., Ohio & Texas, from 1650 to 1880. (Illus.). 624p. 1996. reprint ed. lib. bdg. 102.50 (*0-8328-5255-4*) Higginson Bk Co.

— Clopper. An American Family: Its Ups & Downs Through Eight Generations in New Amsterdam, N.Y., Penna., Md., Ohio & Texas, from 1650 to 1880. (Illus.). 624p. 1996. reprint ed. pap. 92.50 (*0-8328-5256-2*) Higginson Bk Co.

Clopper, Jonas. Fragments of the History of Bawlfredonia. LC 79-91076. (American Humorists Ser.). 1979. reprint ed. lib. bdg. 40.75 (*0-8398-0268-4*) Irvington.

Clopper, Lawrence M. Songs of Rechelesnesse: Langland & the Franciscans. LC 97-23685. 224p. (C). 1997. text 54.50 (*0-472-10744-5*, 10744) U of Mich Pr.

Clopper, Lawrence M., ed. Chester. LC 79-16420. (Records of Early English Drama Ser.). 1979. text 60.00 (*0-8020-5460-9*) U of Toronto Pr.

Clopper, Michele, jt. auth. see Ghikas, Patricia A.

Clopper, Michelle, ed. see Clopper, Brian.

Clopton, Beverly B. Her Honor, the Judge: The Story of Reva Beck Bosone. LC 80-12996. (Illus.). 274p. 1980. reprint ed. pap. 85.00 (*0-608-00165-1*, 206094600006) Bks Demand.

Clor, Harry M. Obscenity & Public Morality: Censorship in a Liberal Society. LC 69-16772. 1985. pap. text 16.00 (*0-226-11035-4*, Midway Reprint) U Ch Pr.

— Public Morality & Liberal Society: Essays on Decency, Law, & Pornography. LC 95-50808. 272p. (C). 1996. pap. text 17.00 (*0-268-03823-6*) U of Notre Dame Pr.

Clore, Duncan L. & American Bar Association Staff. Financial Institution Bonds. 2nd ed. LC 98-39330. 1998. write for info. (*1-57073-620-0*, ABA Tort) Amer Bar Assn.

Clore, G. M. & Gronenborn, A. M., eds. NMR of Proteins. LC 93-25445. (Topics in Molecular & Structural Biology Ser.). 1993. 110.00 (*0-8493-7771-4*) CRC Pr.

***Clore, Gerald L. & Martin, Leonard L.** Theories of Mood & Cognition: A Users Handbook. LC 00-42191. 2000. write for info. (*0-8058-2784-6*) L Erlbaum Assocs.

Clore, Jonathan. Civil Litigation. 296p. 1993. pap. write for info. (*1-874241-96-1*, Pub. by Cavendish Pubng) Gaunt.

— Civil Litigation. 2nd ed. 300p. 1996. pap. 34.00 (*1-85941-005-7*, Pub. by Cavendish Pubng) Gaunt.

***Clore, Philip.** Crossing the Street by Myself. 64p. 2000. pap. 9.95 (*1-58374-011-2*) Chicago Spectrum.

— Thank You for Not Having Sex with Me. 104p. 2000. pap. 12.95 (*1-58374-015-5*) Chicago Spectrum.

Clore, Walter J., jt. auth. see Irvine, Ronald A.

***Clores, Suzanne.** Memoirs of a Spiritual Outsider: Young Women on the Backroads of Religious Tradition. 250p. 2000. 23.95 (*1-57324-172-5*) Conari Press.

***Clorfeine, Steve.** Journey in the Valley of the Gods: An American Buddhist's Nepal Diary. (Illus.). 160p. 2000. pap. 14.95 (*1-58177-061-8*) Barrytown Ltd.

Clorfene-Casten, Liane. Breast Cancer: Poisons, Profits & Prevention. LC 96-29233. 342p. 1996. pap. 18.95 (*1-56751-094-9*); lib. bdg. 29.95 (*1-56751-095-7*) Common Courage.

Clorfene, Chaim & Rogalsky, Yakov. The Path of the Righteous Gentile: An Introduction to the 7 Laws of the Children of Noach. 142p. 1989. reprint ed. 18.95 (*0-87306-433-X*) Targum Pr.

Clorfene, Chaim, jt. auth. see Hecht, Shea.

Close. Electronic Spreadsheet Applications. (DF - Computer Applications Ser.). 1988. mass mkt. 17.95 (*0-538-10039-7*) S-W Pub.

Close, jt. auth. see Grosenick.

Close, A. University Grammar of English Workbook. 1997. pap. write for info. (*0-582-52280-3*) Addison-Wesley.

Close, Angela E., ed. The Prehistory of Arid North Africa: Essays in Honor of Fred Wendorf. LC 86-31510. (Illus.). 374p. 1987. 39.95 (*0-87074-222-1*); pap. 19.95 (*0-87074-223-X*) SMU Press.

Close, Angela E., ed. see Wendorf, Fred & Schild, Romuald.

***Close, Anthony.** Cervantes & the Comic Mind of His Age. 240p. 2000. text 70.00 (*0-19-815998-6*) OUP.

***Close, Barbara.** Well Being: Nurturing Recipes for Body & Soul. (Illus.). 168p. 2000. 18.95 (*0-8118-2593-0*) Chronicle Bks.

Close, Barbara, jt. auth. see Masline, Shelagh R.

***Close, Barbara R., ed.** California Surname Index: Biographies from Selected Histories. LC 99-76177. 325p. 2000. 39.00 (*0-9672409-1-3*) CA Genealogical.

Close, Bob. A Foot above Hell. 160p. 1997. pap. 8.95 (*1-884570-78-X*) Research Triangle.

Close, Charles M. & Frederick, Dean K. Modeling & Analysis of Dynamic Systems. 2nd ed. 704p. 1994. text 100.95 (*0-471-12517-2*) Wiley.

Close, Chuck. Vision Vol. 3: New York City. limited ed. Marioni, Tom, ed. (Illus.). 95p. 1976. pap. 20.00 (*1-891300-03-2*) Crown Point Pr.

Close, Chuck, jt. auth. see Clemins, Vija.

Close, Chuck, jt. contrib. by see Hirsh, Faye.

Close, Daryl & Meier, Nicholas. Morality in Criminal Justice: An Introduction to Ethics. LC 94-25650. 604p. 1994. 52.95 (*0-534-22116-5*) Wadsworth Pub.

Close, David. Nicaragua: Politics, Economics & Society. 220p. 1988. text 49.00 (*0-86187-434-X*, Pub. by P P Pubs); text 17.50 (*0-86187-435-8*, Pub. by P P Pubs) Cassell & Continuum.

— Nicaragua: The Chamorro Years. LC 98-27844. 244p. 1998. lib. bdg. 52.00 (*1-55587-643-9*) L Rienner.

Close, David, ed. Legislatures & the New Democracies in Latin America. LC 94-42491. 270p. 1995. pap. text 45.00 (*1-55587-475-4*) L Rienner.

Close, David H. Origins Greek Civil War. LC 94-39794. (Origins of Modern Wars Ser.). 248p. (C). 1995. pap. 72.00 (*0-582-06472-4*) Longman.

Close, David H. Origins Greek Civil War. LC 94-39794. (Origins of Modern Wars Ser.). 256p. (C). 1995. pap. text 33.53 (*0-582-06471-6*) Longman.

Close, Dick. Winning Proposals in the '90s: 546 Tips for Winning Extra Point Score & Saving Proposal Dollars. (Illus.). 230p. 1991. 89.00 (*0-9628371-0-5*) R N Close.

***Close, Elizabeth & Ramsey, Katherine D.** A Middle Mosaic: A Celebration of Reading, Writing & Reflective Practice at the Middle Level. LC 00-42378. 2000. write for info. (*0-8141-0034-1*) NCTE.

Close, Frank. The Cosmic Onion: Quarks & the Nature of the Universe. LC 86-3646. (Illus.). 182p. 1983. reprint ed. text 34.95 (*0-88318-491-5*) Spr-Verlag.

***Close, Frank.** Lucifer's Legacy: The Meaning of Asymmetry. (Illus.). 272p. 2000. 27.50 (*0-19-850380-6*) OUP.

Close, Frank. Too Hot to Handle: The Race for Cold Fusion. (Illus.). 392p. 1991. text 39.50 (*0-691-08591-9*, Pub. by Princeton U Pr) Cal Prin Full Svc.

***Close, Henry T.** The Liguus Tree Snails of South Florida. 2000. 49.95 (*0-8130-1814-5*) U Press Fla.

Close, Henry T. Metaphor in Psychotherapy: Clinical Applications of Stories & Allegories. LC 98-7500. (Practical Therapist Ser.: Vol. 4). 320p. 1998. 34.95 (*1-886230-10-2*) Impact Pubs CA.

Close, Jessie. The Warping of Al. LC 90-4058. (Charlotte Zolotow Bk.). 288p. (YA). (gr. 7 up). 1990. 15.95 (*0-06-021280-2*) HarpC Child Bks.

Close, Kenneth S. Lotus 1-2-3. (SWC-General Business). (C). 1986. mass mkt. 34.25 (*0-538-10190-3*, J19) S-W Pub.

— Spreadsheet Applications in Practice. 2nd ed. LC 92-46647. 1993. mass mkt. 27.95 (*0-538-61550-8*) S-W Pub.

Close, L. G., et al, eds. Essentials of Head & Neck Oncology. LC 97-42730. (Illus.). 400p. 1997. pap. 59.00 (*0-86577-740-3*) Thieme Med Pubs.

Close, Lanny, et al. Essentials of Head & Neck Oncology. LC 97-42730. 1998. 59.00 (*3-13-110521-6*) Thieme Med Pubs.

Close, Lanny, jt. auth. see Leach, Joseph.

Close, M. D. & William, T. A Doctor's Story. LC 96-77355. 1996. mass mkt. 5.99 (*0-8041-1468-4*) Random.

Close, Pat, ed. see Dunning, Al.

Close, Pat, ed. see Kevil, Mike.

Close, Pat, ed. see Simmons, Diane C.

Close, Pat, ed. & intro. see Shrake, Richard.

***Close, Paul.** The Legacy of Supranationalism. LC 00-36899. 2000. write for info. (*0-312-23524-0*) St Martin.

Close, Paul & Ohki-Close, Emiko. Supranationalism in the New World Order: Global Processes Reviewed. 272p. 1999. 65.00 (*0-389-21020-X*) B&N Imports.

Close, Robert. Time for Action. (Brassey Bks.). 170p. 1984. text 33.00 (*0-08-028344-6*, Pergamon Pr); pap. text 19.25 (*0-08-028345-4*, Pergamon Pr) Elsevier.

Close, Ron. Ayrshire & Arran: An Illustrated Architectural Guide. (Illus.). 216p. (C). 1992. pap. 35.00 (*1-873190-06-9*, Pub. by Rutland Pr) St Mut.

Close, Skip, jt. auth. see Colgate, Steve.

Close, Stacey K. Elderly Slaves of the Plantation South. rev. ed. LC 96-44444. (Studies in African American History & Culture). 138p. 1996. text 39.00 (*0-8153-2756-0*) Garland.

***Close up Foundation Staff.** The American Economy: Governments Role, Citizens Choice. 3rd rev. ed. Sass, Charles, ed. 62p. (YA). 2000. pap. text 9.95 (*0-932765-90-4*) Close Up Fnd.

Close up Foundation Staff. The Bill of Rights: Teacher's Guide. 3rd rev. ed. Sass, Charles, ed. 64p. 2000. pap. 13.45 (*0-614-04361-1*) Close Up Fnd.

— The First Amendment: Teacher's Resource. Sass, Charles, ed. 96p. 1994. teacher ed., ring bd. 7.95 (*0-614-07115-1*) Close Up Fnd.

— Perspectives: Teacher's Guide. 4th ed. Sass, Charles, ed. 1997. pap. text, teacher ed. 15.95 (*0-614-24121-9*, 1927-97) Close Up Fnd.

Close Up Foundation Staff. Slicing the Pie: A Federal Budget Game, 5 booklets, Set. (YA). (gr. 9-12). 1994. pap. 21.95 (*0-932765-51-3*, 1382-94) Close Up Fnd.

— U. S. Response: The Making of U. S. Foreign Policy. rev. ed. (YA). (gr. 7-12). 1990. pap. text 19.95 (*0-932765-25-4*) Close Up Fnd.

***Close up Publishing Staff.** The Breakup of the Soviet Union: U. S.-Russian Relations Ten Years Later. 35p. 1999. pap. text 6.95 (*0-932765-85-8*) Close Up Fnd.

Close, W. H. & Cole, D. J. A., eds. Nutrition of Sows & Boars. 200p. 1999. 160.00 (*1-897676-53-0*, Pub. by Nottingham Univ Pr) St Mut.

Close, William T. Ebola. 1995. mass mkt. 5.99 (*0-8041-1432-3*) Ivy Books.

Closen, Michael, jt. auth. see Rosin, Gary.

Closen, Michael L., et al. Contracts: Contemporary Cases, Comments & Problems. 843p. 1992. 59.95 (*0-87084-159-9*) Anderson Pub Co.

— Notary Law & Practice: Cases & Materials. LC 97-67209. 629p. 1997. text 68.00 (*0-933134-85-1*, 5100) Natl Notary.

***Closs, Alison.** Education of Children with Medical Conditions. 1999. pap. 34.95 (*1-85346-569-0*) David Fulton.

Closs, David J., jt. auth. see Bowersox, Donald J.

Closs, Hannah. High Are the Mountains. 352p. 1990. reprint ed. 30.00 (*0-7206-0804-X*, Pub. by P Owen Ltd) Dufour.

Closs, Michael P. Native American Mathematics. (C). 1996. pap. text 19.95 (*0-292-71185-9*) U of Tex Pr.

Closs, Peter, jt. auth. see Thole, Werner.

Closs, Sissi. Der Sol Standard. (GER.). (C). 1991. text. write for info. (*0-201-55943-9*) Addison-Wesley.

Closser, Lynne, ed. see Da Free John.

Closset, Bernard, ed. International Symposium on Production & Electrolysis of Light Metals. (Proceedings, Metallurgical Society of the Canadian Institute of Mining & Metallurgy Ser.: Vol. 16). 278p. 1989. 151.00 (*0-08-037295-3*, Pergamon Pr) Elsevier.

Closson. Computer Applications. (C). 1989. pap. text, wbk. ed. write for info. (*0-201-60192-3*) Addison-Wesley.

Closson, Bob & Closson, Mary. Abstracts of Washington County PA Willbooks (1776-1841), Bks. 1-5. LC 95-163082. 769p. 1995. 39.95 (*1-55856-196-X*, 291) Closson Pr.

— Beaver County, PA WB Index: 1800-1900. 39p. 1988. pap. text 10.00 (*1-55856-002-5*, 488) Closson Pr.

— Directory of Eighteen Fifteen: Pittsburgh, PA. & Vicinity. 29p. 1985. reprint ed. per. 6.00 (*0-933227-11-6*, 512) Closson Pr.

— Fulton County, PA: Willbook Index, 1850-1900. 19p. 1987. per. 10.00 (*0-933227-62-0*, 493) Closson Pr.

— Greene County, Pennsylvania Willbook Index: 1796-1900. 31p. 1985. per. 10.00 (*0-933227-13-2*, 494) Closson Pr.

— Register of Invalid Pensions, Revolutionary Service, 1789. 16p. 1987. reprint ed. pap. 2.50 (*0-933227-67-1*, 469) Closson Pr.

— Surname Index to Forty-Three Westmoreland County, PA. Cemeteries, Vol. 2. 127p. 1986. per. 10.00 (*0-933227-52-3*, 511) Closson Pr.

— Westmoreland County, PA Cemeteries, 7. 67p. 1979. reprint ed. per. 7.50 (*0-933227-15-9*, 476) Closson Pr.

Closson, Bob & Closson, Mary, eds. Washington County, PA WB Index, 1781-1900. 74p. 1986. per. 10.00 (*0-933227-22-1*, 500) Closson Pr.

Closson Buck, Paula. Acquiescent Villa. LC 98-27668. 64p. 1998. pap. 11.95 (*0-8071-2305-6*); text 19.95 (*0-8071-2304-8*) La State U Pr.

Closson, Ernest. History of the Piano. 1988. reprint ed. lib. bdg. 75.00 (*0-7812-0751-7*) Rprt Serv.

— History of the Piano. LC 76-181124. 168p. 1947. reprint ed. 59.00 (*0-403-01523-5*) Scholarly.

Closson, Ernest, ed. see Gretry, Andre E.

Closson, Ernest, tr. see Strauss, Richard.

Closson, Kay. Reaching in Silence. (Contemporary Poets Ser.: No. 2). 56p. (Orig.). 1983. pap. 3.95 (*0-916982-27-0*, RL227) CCR Pubns.

Closson, Mary, ed. Lancaster County, PA Cemetery Surname Index. 1988. pap. text 10.50 (*1-55856-008-4*, 235) Closson Pr.

— One Hundred Seventy-Five SW PA Marriages: Performed by Rev. Abraham Boyd 1802-1849. 7p. 1994. reprint ed. pap. 2.50 (*1-55856-164-1*, 480) Closson Pr.

Closson, Mary, jt. auth. see Closson, Bob.

Closson, Mary, jt. ed. see Closson, Bob.

Closson Press Staff, et al, eds. Eighteen Forty Census of PA Pensioners. 36p. 1978. per. 4.50 (*0-933227-59-0*, 484) Closson Pr.

Closson Press Staff, jt. auth. see Beaver County Research Center Staff.

Closson, Richard G., ed. see Pharmacists in Ophthalmic Practice, Inc. Staff.

Closter, Kathryn, et al. Fiction, Food, & Fun: The Original Recipe for the Read 'n Feed Program. LC 98-9511. (Illus.). 224p. (Orig.). 1998. pap. 24.50 (*1-56308-519-4*) Libs Unl.

Closter, Susan V. Joyce Cary & Lawrence Durrell: A Reference Guide. (Reference Guides to Literature Ser.). 1985. 60.00 (*0-8161-8627-8*, Hall Reference) Macmillan.

Closurdo, Janette S., ed. Library Management: Papers from the Management Workshops, Vol. 1. LC Z 0678.L52. 101p. reprint ed. pap. 31.40 (*0-608-11182-1*, 201728100005) Bks Demand.

Clot, Andre. Harun al-Rashid & the World of the Thousand & One Nights. Howe, John, tr. from FRE. (Illus.). 268p. (C). 1990. 21.95 (*0-941533-65-4*, NAB) I R Dee.

— Suleiman: The Magnificent. 399p. 1993. 30.00 (*1-56131-039-5*, NAB) I R Dee.

Clot, J., ed. Immunological Aspects of Rheumatoid Arthritis: Proceedings of the International Symposium, Montpellier, March, 1974. (Rheumatology Ser.: Vol. 6). 250p. 1975. 121.75 (*3-8055-2116-2*) S Karger.

Clote, Peter. Computational Biology. text. write for info. (*0-471-87251-2*) Wiley.

— Computational Biology. 2000. pap. text. write for info. (*0-471-87252-0*) Wiley.

Clote, Peter & Krajicek, Jan, eds. Arithmetic, Proof Theory, & Computational Complexity. (Oxford Logic Guides Ser.: No. 23). (Illus.). 442p. 1993. text 90.00 (*0-19-853690-9*) OUP.

Clote, Peter & Kranakis, Evangelos. Boolean Functions: Parallel Computation & Proof Systems. 350p. 1997. 34.00 (*3-540-59436-1*) Spr-Verlag.

Clote, Peter & Remmel, Jeffrey B. Feasible Mathematics II. LC 94-39297. (Progress in Computer Science & Applied Logic Ser.). viii, 447 p. 1995. write for info. (*3-7643-3675-7*) Birkhauser.

Clote, Peter & Remmel, Jeffrey B., eds. Feasible Mathematics II. LC 94-39297. (Progress in Computer Science & Applied Logic Ser.: Vol. 13). 1994. 76.50 (*0-8176-3675-7*) Birkhauser.

Clotfelter, Charles R. We Aquatus. Lamb, Patrica F., ed. LC 98-71928. 350p. 1999. 26.95 (*1-892584-14-X*, 333) Area Fifty Pubns.

Clotfelter, Caroline P., ed. On the Third Hand: Humor in the Dismal Science, an Anthology. LC 96-41214. 352p. (Orig.). 1996. pap. 20.95 (*0-472-06529-7*, 06529); text 52.50 (*0-472-09529-3*, 09529) U of Mich Pr.

Clotfelter, Charles & Ehrlich, Thomas, eds. Philanthropy & the Nonprofit Sector in a Changing America. LC 98-31856. (Illus.). 544p. 1999. text 35.00 (*0-253-33521-3*) Ind U Pr.

Clotfelter, Charles T. Buying the Best: Cost Escalation in Elite Higher Education. LC 95-26061. 272p. 1996. text 32.50 (*0-691-02642-4*, Pub. by Princeton U Pr) Cal Prin Full Svc.

— Federal Tax Policy & Charitable Giving. LC 84-16336. (National Bureau of Economic Research Monographs). 336p. 1985. lib. bdg. 47.00 (*0-226-11048-6*) U Ch Pr.

Clotfelter, Charles T., ed. Who Benefits from the Nonprofit Sector? LC 91-41221. 296p. 1992. 26.50 (*0-226-11052-4*) U Ch Pr.

— Who Benefits from the Nonprofit Sector? (Illus.). x, 296p. 1994. pap. text 13.95 (*0-226-11053-2*) U Ch Pr.

Clotfelter, Charles T. & Cook, Philip J. Selling Hope: State Lotteries in America. 336p. 1991. pap. 20.50 (*0-674-80098-2*) HUP.

Clotfelter, Charles T., et al. Economic Challenges in Higher Education. (National Bureau of Economic Research Monographs). (Illus.). 432p. 1991. 45.00 (*0-226-11050-8*) U Ch Pr.

Clotfelter, Susan. The Herb Tea Book: Blending, Brewing, & Savoring Teas for Every Mood & Occasion. LC 98-34442. 1998. pap. 12.95 (*1-883010-60-8*) Interweave.

Clothes, Esther. Women of Faith. (J). 1992. write for info. (*5-900522-81-4*, Chariot Bks) Chariot Victor.

Clothey, Fred W. The Many Faces of Murukan: The History & Meaning of a South Indian God. (Religion & Society Ser.: No. 6). 1978. text 83.85 (*90-279-7632-5*) Mouton.

— Quiescence & Passion: The Vision of Arunakiri, Tamil Mystic. LC 96-33520. (ISP Ser.). 178p. 1996. 64.95 (*1-57292-001-7*); pap. 69.95 (*1-57292-000-9*) Austin & Winfield.

Clothier, Cecil, jt. auth. see HMSO Staff.

Clothier, Galina, jt. auth. see Braun, Marina.

Clothier, Norman. Black Valour: The South African Native Labour Contingent, 1916-1918 & the Sinking of the Mendi. (Illus.). 220p. 1987. 14.95 (*0-86980-564-9*, Pub. by Univ Natal Pr) Intl Spec Bk.

Clothier, Paul. The Complete Computer Trainer. (Illus.). 299p. 1996. pap. 39.95 (*0-07-011639-3*) McGraw.

Clothier, Peter. Aspley Guise. 1970. 2.00 (*0-88031-002-2*) Invisible-Red Hill.

— David Hockney. LC 94-34739. (Modern Masters Ser.). (Illus.). 128p. 1995. pap. 14.95 (*0-7892-0036-8*) Abbeville Pr.

— David Hockney. LC 94-34739. (Modern Masters Ser.: 17). (Illus.). 128p. 1995. 35.00 (*1-55859-642-9*) Abbeville Pr.

— While I Am Not Afraid: Secrets of a Man's Heart. LC 97-39686. 1997. 19.95 (*1-56690-354-8*, InWord Pr) High Mtn.

Clothier, Richard. A Heritage of Hymns: An Exploration of Music & Religion, Music & Our Hymns, & the Stories of Hymns & Hymn Writers of the Restoration Movement. LC 96-8803. 168p. (Orig.). 1996. pap. text 15.00 (*0-8309-0737-8*) Herald Pub Hse.

***Clott, Jami & Raff, Stephen.** PeopleSoft Application Development Tools. LC 99-53269. (Tools Ser.). 512p. 1999. pap. 49.99 (*0-07-135569-3*) McGraw.

Clottes, Jean & Courtin, Jean. The Cave Beneath the Sea: Paleolithic Images at Cosquer. Garner, Marilyn, tr. from FRE. LC 95-24174. (Illus.). 200p. 1996. 60.00 (*0-8109-4033-7*, Pub. by Abrams) Time Warner.

Clottes, Jean & Lewis-Williams, J. David. The Shamans of Prehistory: Trance & Magic in the Painted Caves. Hawkes, Sophie, tr. from ENG. LC 98-4151. (Illus.). 120p. 1998. 49.50 (*0-8109-4182-1*, Pub. by Abrams) Time Warner.

Clottey, Kokomon, jt. auth. see Ababio-Clottey, Aeeshah.

Clotworthy, Willaim G. In the Footsteps of George Washington: A Guide to Places Commemorating the First President. (Guides to the American Landscape Ser.). (Illus.). 300p. 2000. pap. 19.95 (*0-939923-79-3*) M & W Pub Co.

C

Clotworthy, William G. Homes & Libraries of the Presidents. LC 94-44390. (Guides to the American Landscape Ser.). (Illus.). 356p. (Orig.). 1995. pap. 19.95 (*0-939923-32-7*) M & W Pub Co.
— Presidential Sites: A Directory of Places Associated with Presidents of the United States. LC 98-11173. (Illus.). 357p. (Orig.). 1998. pap. 18.95 (*0-939923-64-5*) M & W Pub Co.
Clouard, Henri. Petite Histoire de la Litterature Francaise. 332p. 1965. 19.95 (*0-8288-7404-2*) Fr & Eur.
Clouatre, Dallas. Anti-Fat Nutrients: Reduce Body Fat in 15 Days with Vitamins & Herbs. 3rd ed. 177p. 1997. pap. 12.95 (*0-9614914-6-9*) Pax Pub.
— Faqs All About Sam-e. 1999. mass mkt. 2.99 (*1-58333-021-6*, Avery) Penguin Putnam.
— Frequently Asked Questions All about Grape Seed Extract. (FAQs All about Health Ser.). 1998. mass mkt. 2.99 (*0-89529-907-0*, Avery) Penguin Putnam.
— Glucosamine Sulfate & Chondrotin Sulfate. (Good Health Guides Ser.). 1998. pap. 3.95 (*0-87983-874-4*, 38744K, Keats Publng) NTC Contemp Pub Co.
Clouatre, Dallas & Lewis, Alan E. Melatonin & the Biological Clock. (Good Health Guides Ser.). 48p. 1996. pap. 3.95 (*0-87983-734-9*, 37349K, Keats Publng) NTC Contemp Pub Co.
Clouche, Armelle, ed. see The Magnificent.
Cloud. Enriched Education: Teach in 2 Lang. (J). 2000. pap. text 33.95 (*0-8384-8801-3*) Heinle & Heinle.
Cloud, David W. Carrying Light in Darkness. (Illus.). 44p. (J). 1982. spiral bd. 5.00 (*1-58318-038-9*, WOL004B) Way of Life.
— Charismatic Confusion in Indianapolis. (Illus.). 50p. 1990. pap. 3.00 (*1-58318-044-3*, WOL011B) Way of Life.
— Charles Spurgeon & the Battle for Truth. 23p. 1992. pap. 2.00 (*1-58318-021-4*, WOL356B) Way of Life.
— Cremation: What Does God Think? 3rd ed. 16p. 1996. reprint ed. pap. 2.00 (*1-58318-026-5*, WOL007B) Way of Life.
— Deacons: Servants or Rulers. 2nd rev. ed. 24p. 1993. pap. 2.00 (*1-58318-031-1*, WOL008B) Way of Life.
— Dynamic Equivalency: Death Knell of Pure Scripture. 47p. Date not set. pap. 2.50 (*1-58318-040-0*, WOL059B) Way of Life.
— Evangelical Catholics. 19p. 1992. pap. 2.00 (*1-58318-047-8*, WOL404B) Way of Life.
— Evangelicals & Rome. 395p. 1999. pap. 19.95 (*1-58318-058-3*) Way of Life.
— Examining James White's, "The King James Only Controversy" 115p. 1999. pap. 4.95 (*1-58318-060-5*) Way of Life.
— For Love of the Bible: The Battle for the King James Bible & the Received Text from 1800 to Present. 3rd ed. 450p. 1998. reprint ed. 39.95 (*1-58318-004-4*, WOL476B) Way of Life.
***Cloud, David W.** Has the Southern Baptist Convention Been Rescued from Liberalism? 97p. 1999. 4.95 (*1-58318-061-3*, B-SBC) Way of Life.
Cloud, David W. Independent Baptists & Southern Baptists. 2nd enl. rev. ed. 32p. 1997. pap. 4.00 (*1-58318-024-9*, WOL473B) Way of Life.
— Is Healing in the Atonement? 3rd enl. ed. 50p. 1998. pap. 3.00 (*1-58318-033-8*, WOL333B) Way of Life.
— Is the Roman Catholic Church Changing? 3rd rev. ed. (Illus.). 41p. 1995. pap. 2.50 (*1-58318-053-2*, WOL014B) Way of Life.
— Myths about Modern Bible Versions. 248p. 1999. pap. 19.95 (*1-58318-059-1*) Way of Life.
— New Evangelicalism: Its History & Its Heart. 28p. 1995. pap. 3.00 (*1-58318-019-2*, WOL474B) Way of Life.
— The Pentecostal-Charismatic Movement Yesterday & Today. (Illus.). 49p. 1995. pap. 3.00 (*1-58318-043-5*, WOL470B) Way of Life.
— Promise Keepers Beware!, Vol. I. 44p. 1995. pap. 2.50 (*1-58318-045-1*, WOL481B) Way of Life.
— Promise Keepers Beware!, Vol. II. (Illus.). 53p. Date not set. pap. 4.00 (*1-58318-046-X*, WOL490B) Way of Life.
— The Protestant Denominations, Yesterday & Today. (Illus.). 45p. 1995. pap. 2.50 (*1-58318-023-0*, WOL471B) Way of Life.
— Proverbs: Wisdom of the Wise & Foolish. Date not set. pap. 19.95 (*1-58318-007-9*, WOL Proverbs) Way of Life.
— Repentance Is More Than a Sinner's Prayer. 156p. 1999. per. 9.95 (*1-58318-062-1*, B-MORE) Way of Life.
***Cloud, David W.** Rock Music vs. the God of the Bible. 350p. 2000. per. write for info. (*1-58318-066-4*, WOLROC) Way of Life.
Cloud, David W. Rome & the Bible: Tracing the History of the Roman Catholic Church & Its Persecution of the Bible. 2nd ed. (Illus.). 188p. 1996. pap. 19.95 (*1-58318-003-6*, WOLROME) Way of Life.
***Cloud, David W.** Testimonies of King James Bible Defenders. 64p. 2000. pap. 3.00 (*1-58318-064-8*) Way of Life.
Cloud, David W. Unholy Hands on God's Holy Book: A Report on the United Bible Societies. 2nd rev. ed. (Illus.). 84p. 1985. pap. 5.00 (*1-58318-012-5*, WOL026B) Way of Life.
— Unscriptural Presentation of the Gospel: From Azusa to Pensacola. 2nd rev. ed. 20p. 1997. pap. 2.00 (*1-58318-042-7*, WOL394B) Way of Life.
— Was Mother Teresa a True Christian? 3rd enl. rev. ed. 25p. 1998. pap. 2.00 (*1-58318-054-0*, WOL181B) Way of Life.
— Way of Life Encyclopedia of the Bible & Christianity. 2nd enl. rev. ed. 560p. 1993. 39.95 (*1-58318-005-2*, ENC) Way of Life.
— What about Ruckman? 2nd enl. rev. ed. 30p. 1997. pap. 3.00 (*1-58318-032-X*, WOL472B) Way of Life.
— Women Preachers. 15p. 1993. pap. 2.00 (*1-58318-028-1*, WOL462B) Way of Life.
— The World Council of Churches. (Illus.). 37p. 1993. pap. 2.50 (*1-58318-020-6*, WOL474B) Way of Life.
Cloud, Alvin L., tr. see Johnson, Alice, ed.
Cloud, Amy, ed. see Pavia, Tony.
Cloud, Barbara. Business of Newspapers on the Western Frontier. LC 91-47583. (Wilbur S. Shepperson Series in History & Humanities). 280p. 1992. 27.95 (*0-87417-184-9*) U of Nev Pr.
Cloud, Barbara, jt. auth. see Murphy, Tom.
Cloud, Cam. Acid Trips & Chemistry. (Illus.). 200p. 1999. pap. 16.95 (*1-57951-011-6*) Ronin Pub.
— Little Book of Acid. LC 99-219950. (Illus.). 128p. 1999. pap. 12.95 (*0-914171-88-7*) Ronin Pub.
Cloud, Dan. The Aesculapian. LC 97-36389. 368p. 1998. 24.95 (*0-913720-98-4*) Beil.
***Cloud, Dan.** The Aesculapian. LC 97-36389. 368p. 2000. pap. 19.95 (*1-929490-08-9*) Beil.
Cloud, Dana L. Control & Consolation in American Culture & Politics: The Rhetoric of Therapy. LC 97-21153. (Rhetoric & Society Ser.). 1997. 41.95 (*0-7619-0506-5*); pap. 19.95 (*0-7619-0507-3*) Sage.
Cloud, Darrah. The Stick Wife. 66p. 1996. pap. 5.60 (*0-87129-618-7*, SB1) Dramatic Pub.
Cloud, David W. Avoiding the Snare of Seventh Day Adventism. 147p. 1984. pap. 5.95 (*1-58318-036-2*, WOL035B) Way of Life.
— Call No Man Father: The Roman Catholic Church: Past, Present, Future. Date not set. pap. write for info. (*1-58318-055-9*, WOLFather) Way of Life.
***Cloud, David W.** Concise King James Bible Dictionary. 90p. 1999. per. 4.95 (*1-58318-006-0*, WOL Concise) Way of Life.
Cloud, David W. Contemporary Christian Music under the Spotlight. 452p. 1999. per. 19.95 (*1-58318-057-5*, B-CCM) Way of Life.
— Fasting. 22p. 1986. pap. 2.00 (*1-58318-029-X*, WOL028B) Way of Life.
— Flirting with Rome, 4 vols., Set. 2nd ed. 190p. 1993. pap. 10.00 (*1-58318-048-6*, WOL406B) Way of Life.
— Flirting with Rome Vol. 1: Billy Graham. 2nd ed. 49p. 1993. pap. 2.50 (*1-58318-049-4*, WOL406B) Way of Life.
— Flirting with Rome Vol. 2: Key Men & Organizations. 2nd ed. 53p. 1993. pap. 2.50 (*1-58318-050-8*, WOL407B) Way of Life.
— Flirting with Rome Vol. 3: Southern Baptist Convention. 2nd rev. ed. 34p. 1992. pap. 2.50 (*1-58318-051-6*, WOL451B) Way of Life.
— Flirting with Rome Vol. 4: The Charismatics. 2nd rev. ed. 54p. 1992. pap. 2.50 (*1-58318-052-4*, WOL452B) Way of Life.
— God's Standards for the Pastor. 57p. 1977. pap. 2.50 (*1-58318-035-4*) Way of Life.
— Grace & Authority in the Church. 22p. 1993. pap. 3.00 (*1-58318-025-7*, WOL365B) Way of Life.
— The Living Bible: Blessing or Curse. 30p. 1991. pap. 3.00 (*1-58318-011-7*, WOL321B) Way of Life.
— Modern Bible Versions. (Illus.). 48p. 1994. pap. 2.50 (*1-58318-010-9*, WOL467B) Way of Life.
— Modern Versions Founded upon Apostasy. 3rd enl. rev. ed. 76p. 1997. reprint ed. pap. 5.00 (*1-58318-009-5*, WOL482B) Way of Life.
— Mom & Dad Sleep While the Children Rock in Satan's Cradle. 2nd rev. ed. 84p. 1991. pap. 2.50 (*1-58318-034-6*) Way of Life.
— A Most Frightful Deception: The Today's English Version & Translator Robert Bratcher. 2nd rev. ed. 27p. 1986. pap. 2.00 (*1-58318-008-7*, WOL3113) Way of Life.
— Myths about the King James Bible, 5 vols., Set. 2nd rev. ed. 176p. 1993. 7.50 (*1-58318-013-3*, WOL021B) Way of Life.
— Myths about the King James Bible Vol. 1: Erasmus Was a Humanist. 2nd rev. ed. 25p. 1993. pap. 2.00 (*1-58318-014-1*, WOL021B(1)) Way of Life.
— Myths about the King James Bible Vol. 2: Reformation Editors Locked Sufficient Manuscript Evidence. 2nd rev. ed. 19p. 1993. pap. 2.00 (*1-58318-015-X*, WOL021B(2)) Way of Life.
— Myths about the King James Bible Vol. 3: No Doctrinal Differences Between Text & Versions. 2nd rev. ed. 39p. 1993. pap. 2.00 (*1-58318-016-8*, WOL021B(3)) Way of Life.
— Myths about the King James Bible Vol. 4: Inspiration Is Perfect But Preservation Is General. 2nd rev. ed. 34p. 1993. pap. 2.00 (*1-58318-017-6*, WOL021B(4)) Way of Life.
— Myths about the King James Bible Vol. 5: True Scholars Reject the Received Text. 2nd rev. ed. 37p. 1993. pap. 2.00 (*1-58318-018-4*, WOL021B(5)) Way of Life.
— Things Hard to Be Understood: A Handbook of Biblical Difficulties. 221p. 1997. pap. 19.95 (*1-58318-002-8*, WOLTHGS) Way of Life.
— A Tribute to David Otis Fuller. 45p. 1992. pap. 3.00 (*1-58318-037-0*, WOL403B) Way of Life.
Cloud, David W. Do Animals Have Rights? 18p. 1992. pap. 2.00 (*1-58318-027-3*, WOL363B) Way of Life.
— Does Salvation Make a Difference? 2nd rev. ed. 20p. 1992. pap. 2.00 (*1-58318-022-2*, WOL009B) Way of Life.
Cloud, Deborah A., ed. Let's Celebrate! A Public Relations & Special Events Guide for Nonprofit Homes & Services for the Aging. LC 88-70046. 100p. (Orig.). 1988. pap. 38.50 (*0-943774-39-X*) Am Assn Homes.
— The Volunteer Leader: Essays on the Role of Trustees of Nonprofit Facilities & Services for the Aging. LC 84-73168. 146p. 1985. pap. text 15.00 (*0-943774-24-1*) Am Assn Homes.
Cloud, Douglas, et al. Coggins Auto Supply: Practice Set One to Accompany College Accounting Procedures, Chapters 1-26. 77p. (C). 1985. pap. text 15.50 (*0-471-80892-X*) P-H.
— College Accounting Procedures: Best Sound Music Center - Practice Set 2 (Chapters 1-26) 80p. 1985. pap. text 15.50 (*0-471-80893-8*) P-H.
— Donamy Manufacturing Corporation: A Practice Set for a Manufacturing Firm to Accompany College Accounting Procedures - Chapters 1-26. 85p. 1986. pap. text 15.50 (*0-471-82226-4*) P-H.
Cloud, Enoch C. Enoch's Voyage. McLean, Elizabeth, ed. (Illus.). 240p. 1994. 24.95 (*1-55921-079-6*) Moyer Bell.
Cloud, Franklin H. Corrugator Scheduling. LC 95-51349. (Illus.). 128p. 1996. pap. 55.00 (*1-885067-04-6*) Jelmar Pub.
***Cloud, Franklin H.** Corrugator Scheduling. 2nd ed. LC 99-50193. 152p. 1999. pap. 75.00 (*1-885067-18-6*) Jelmar Pub.
Cloud, Gary L. Optical Methods of Engineering Analysis. (Illus.). 503p. (C). 1998. reprint ed. pap. text 36.95 (*0-521-63642-6*) Cambridge U Pr.
Cloud, H. Cambios Que Traen Sanidad.Tr. of Changes That Heal. (SPA.). 10.99 (*1-56063-507-X*, 490270) Editorial Unilit.
Cloud, Henry. Boundaries. 1999. pap., teacher ed. 24.99 (*0-310-22452-7*); pap., student ed. 7.99 (*0-310-22453-5*) Zondervan.
— Boundaries: When to Say Yes, When to Say No to Take Control of Your Life. 1996. pap. 10.99 (*0-310-20974-9*) Zondervan.
— Boundaries: When to Say Yes, When to Say No to Take Control of Your Life. 384p. 1997. mass mkt. 5.99 (*0-06-104347-8*) Zondervan.
***Cloud, Henry.** Boundaries in Dating: Making Dating Work. 2000. pap. 12.99 (*0-310-23330-5*) Zondervan.
Cloud, Henry. Boundaries in Marriage Workbook. 1999. pap. 9.99 (*0-310-22875-1*) Zondervan.
— Changes That Heal. 272p. 1993. pap. 12.99 (*0-310-60631-4*) Zondervan.
— Changes That Heal. 1996. mass mkt. 5.99 (*0-310-21463-7*) Zondervan.
— Changes That Heal: How to Understand Your Past to Ensure a Healthier Future. 128p. 1994. pap., wbk. ed. 8.99 (*0-310-60633-0*) Zondervan.
— Limites Para Nuestros Hijos. 1999. 9.99 (*0-8297-1689-0*) Vida Pubs.
— The Mom Factor: Discover How To: Transform the Effects of the Past - Say "No" to Your Mom Without Feeling Guilty - Build a Healthy Relationship with Your Mom, & - Improve All Your Relationships! 256p. 1998. pap. 12.99 (*0-310-22559-0*) Zondervan.
***Cloud, Henry.** Raising Great Kids. (Illus.). 2000. pap. 12.99 (*0-310-23549-9*) Zondervan.
— Raising Great Kids for Parents of Preschoolers. (Illus.). 2000. pap. 69.99 (*0-310-23238-4*) Zondervan.
Cloud, Henry & Townsend, John. Boundaries: When to Say Yes, When to Say No to Take Control of Your Life. 256p. 1992. 19.99 (*0-310-58590-2*) Zondervan.
— Boundaries: When to Say Yes, When to Say No to Take Control of Your Life. 128p. 1995. pap., wbk. ed. 9.99 (*0-310-49481-8*) Zondervan.
— Boundaries in Dating. LC 99-57936. 2000. pap. 12.99 (*0-310-20034-2*) Zondervan.
— Boundaries with Kids: When to Say Yes, When to Say No to Help Your Children Gain Control of Their Lives. LC 98-10491. (Illus.). 223p. 1998. 16.99 (*0-310-20035-0*) Zondervan.
— Boundaries with Kids Workbook: When to Say Yes, When to Say No to Help Your Children Gain Control of Their Lives. 144p. 1998. pap., wbk. ed. 9.99 (*0-310-22349-0*) Zondervan.
— The Mom Factor: Dealing with the Mother You Had, Didn't Have, or Still Contend With. 256p. 1996. 18.99 (*0-310-20036-9*) Zondervan.
— The Mom Factor Workbook: Dealing with the Mother You Had, Didn't Have, or Still Contend With. 176p. 1997. pap., wbk. ed. 9.99 (*0-310-21533-1*) Zondervan.
— Parenting with Truth: Parenting with Grace & Truth. LC 98-51434. 1999. 17.99 (*0-310-22569-8*) Zondervan.
— Safe People: How to Find Relationships That Are Good for You. 256p. 1995. 18.99 (*0-310-59560-6*); pap., wbk. ed. 8.99 (*0-310-49501-6*) Zondervan.
— Safe People: How to Find Relationships That Are Good for You & Avoid Those That Aren't. 208p. 1996. pap. 10.99 (*0-310-21084-4*) Zondervan.
— Twelve "Christian" Beliefs That Can Drive You Crazy: Relief from False Assumptions. 128p. 1995. pap. 10.99 (*0-310-49491-5*) Zondervan.
Cloud, Henry & Townsend, John S. Boundaries in Marriage. LC 99-31469. 255p. 1999. 19.99 (*0-310-22151-X*) Zondervan.
Cloud, J. G. & Thorgaard, G. H. Genetic Conservation of Salmonid Fishes. (NATO ASI Ser.: Vol. 248). (Illus.). 326p. (C). 1993. text 105.00 (*0-306-44532-8*, Kluwer Plenum) Kluwer Academic.
Cloud, Jonathan, tr. see Gorz, Andre.
Cloud, Josie H., jt. ed. see Emery, Sarah.
Cloud, Linda. Meena of Nepal. (Illus.). 37p. (J). (gr. 1-6). 1982. spiral bd. 5.00 (*1-58318-039-7*, WOL018B) Way of Life.
Cloud, Michael J. & Drachman, Byron C. Inequalities: With Applications to Engineering. LC 97-45230. (Illus.). 168p. 1998. text 39.00 (*0-387-98404-6*) Spr-Verlag.
Cloud, Nolan E. Gravity: A Force Yet Unreckoned With. LC 97-93046. (Illus.). vii, 37p. 1997. 14.95 (*0-9657391-0-4*) JB Pub GA.
***Cloud, Patrick.** Key to Five-String Banjo - Home Improvisation Workshop. 56p. 1999. pap. 19.95 incl. audio compact disk (*0-7866-3264-X*, 96926BCD) Mel Bay.
Cloud, Peter B. Clans of Many Nations: Selected Poems 1969-1994. 176p. (Orig.). 1995. pap. 14.00 (*1-877727-47-4*) White Pine.
— The Paranoid Foothills. (Illus.). (Orig.). 1981. pap. 2.50 (*0-942396-29-4*) Blackberry ME.
Cloud, Phillip A. Engineering Procedures Handbook. LC 97-26403. 394p. 1998. 109.00 (*0-8155-1410-7*) Noyes.
— How to Develop & Manage Qualification Protocols for FDA Compliance. LC 99-28537. (Illus.). 1999. 229.00 (*1-57491-098-1*) Interpharm.
— Pharmaceutical Equipment Validation: The Ultimate Qualification Guidebook. LC 98-28032. v, 443 p. 1998. 229.00 (*1-57491-079-5*) Interpharm.
***CLOUD PUB**
D STAFF, contrib. by.
D STAFF, CONTRIB. BY Arizona: Resource Binder. (J). (gr. 4-7). 2000. ring bd. 124.95 (*0-911981-62-4*) Cloud Pub.
Cloud, Robert C. Drugs in Society. LC 95-1837. (YA). 1995. write for info. (*1-56796-099-5*) WRS Group.
— Solutions for Youth Violence for Schools & Communities: A Resource Guide. LC 97-25303. 1997. write for info. (*1-56796-184-3*) WRS Group.
Cloud, Stanley & Olson, Lynne. The Murrow Boys: Pioneers on the Frontlines of Broadcast Journalism. (Illus.). 464p. 1997. pap. 15.00 (*0-395-87753-9*, Mariner Bks) HM.
Cloud, Todd & Wilsford, David. Under Construction, Round II: U.S.-Japanese Negotiations to Open Japan's Construction Markets to American Firms, 1988-1992. (Pew Case Studies in International Affairs). 50p. (C). 1993. pap. text 3.50 (*1-56927-158-5*) Geo U Inst Dplmcy.
Cloud, Townsend. Faith Step. Date not set. 19.99 (*0-310-22152-8*) HarpC.
— How People Grow. Date not set. 19.99 (*0-310-22153-6*) HarpC.
***Cloud, Townsend.** Raising Great Kids: Leader's Guide. 2000. pap. 27.99 (*0-310-23296-1*) Zondervan.
Cloud, William A., jt. auth. see Granfield, Robert.
Cloude, S. R. Introduction to Electromagnetic Wave Propagation & Antennas. 200p. 1996. 39.00 (*0-387-91501-X*) Spr-Verlag.
Clouden, Dorothy J. Here's To Life: A Collection of Poems. LC 97-90158. (Orig.). 1997. pap. 8.95 (*0-533-12312-7*) Vantage.
Clouder, Christopher & Rawson, Martyn. Waldorf Education. (Rudolf Steiner's Ideas in Practice Ser.). 144p. 1998. pap. 9.95 (*0-88010-460-0*, 3017) Anthroposophic.
Cloudsley-Thompson, J. L. Animal Twilight. (Illus.). 1967. 14.95 (*0-85429-062-1*) Dufour.
***Cloudsley-Thompson, J. L.** The Diversity of Amphibians & Reptiles: An Introduction. LC 98-45640. (Illus.). 250p. 1999. 79.95 (*3-540-65056-3*) Spr-Verlag.
Cloudsley-Thompson, J. L. Diversity of Desert Life. (C). 1993. pap. 30.00 (*81-7233-050-2*, Pub. by Scientific Pubs) St Mut.
— Evolution & Adaptation of Terrestrial Arthropods. (Illus.). 150p. 1988. 58.95 (*0-387-18188-1*) Spr-Verlag.
— Invertebrate Animals. (C). 1991. text 40.00 (*81-7233-020-0*, Pub. by Scientific Pubs) St Mut.
— Predation & Defense Amongst Reptiles. LC 95-159289. (Illus.). 138p. 1994. pap. 19.95 (*1-872688-03-9*, Pub. by R&A Pub Ltd) Serpents Tale.
Cloudsley-Thompson, J. L., ed. Biotic Interactions in Arid Lands. LC 96-10787. (Adaptations of Desert Organisms Ser.). (Illus.). 216p. 1996. 119.00 (*3-540-59261-X*) Spr-Verlag.
— Ecophysiology of Desert Arthropods & Reptiles. (Adaptations of Desert Organisms Ser.). (Illus.). 216p. 1991. 147.95 (*0-387-52057-0*) Spr-Verlag.
Cloudsley-Thompson, J. L., jt. auth. see Expert-Center for Taxonomic Identification (ETI) S.
Cloudsley-Thompson, J. L., ed. see Bothma, Jacobus du P.
Cloudsley-Thompson, J. L., ed. see Cook, William E.
Cloudsley-Thompson, J. L., ed. see Costa, Grovann.
Cloudsley-Thompson, J. L., ed. see Heatwole, Harold.
Cloudsley-Thompson, J. L., ed. see Shenbrot, Georgy Y., et al.
Cloudsley-Thompson, John. Ecology. 192p. 1999. pap. 12.95 (*0-8442-0233-9*, 02339, Natl Textbk Co) NTC Contemp Pub Co.
Clouette, Bruce & Roth, Matthew. Bristol, Connecticut: A Bicentennial History, 1785-1985. LC 84-22807. (Illus.). 336p. 1984. 22.00 (*0-914659-09-X*) Phoenix Pub.
Clough & Conley. Scales Intervals. 3rd ed. LC 99-11656. 1999. pap. text. write for info. (*0-393-97369-7*) Norton.
Clough, jt. auth. see Munsell.
Clough, Anne V., jt. ed. see Chen, Chin T.
Clough, Arthur H. Amours de Voyage; The Bothie; Dipsychus: Three Long Poems. (Twelve-Point Ser.). 1999. lib. bdg. 24.00 (*1-58287-107-8*) North Bks.
— Arthur Hugh Clough (1819-1861) Selected Poems. Chew, Shirley, ed. 1987. pap. 9.50 (*0-85635-622-0*) Carcanet Pr.
Clough, Arthur H. The Lives of the Noble Grecians & Romans, 2 vols., Vol. 1. Dryden, John, tr. LC 92-50223. 800p. 1992. 20.00 (*0-679-60008-6*) Modern Lib NY.
Clough, Arthur H. The Oxford Diaries of Arthur Hugh Clough. Kenny, Anthony, ed. (Illus.). 350p. 1990. text 95.00 (*0-19-811739-6*) OUP.
— The Poems & Prose Remains of Arthur Hugh Clough, 2 vols., Set. (BCL1-PR English Literature Ser.). 1992. reprint ed. lib. bdg. 150.00 (*0-7812-7499-0*) Rprt Serv.
— The Poems of Arthur Hugh Clough. Norrington, A. L., ed. 340p. 1986. pap. 18.95 (*0-19-812343-4*) OUP.
— The Poems of Arthur Hugh Clough. 2nd ed. Mulhauser, Frederick L., ed. (Oxford English Texts Ser.). 852p. (C). 1974. text 89.00 (*0-19-811898-8*) OUP.
Clough, Arthur H., ed. The Lives of the Noble Grecians & Romans, 2 vols., Vol. 2. Dryden, John, tr. LC 92-50223. 736p. 1992. 20.00 (*0-679-60009-4*) Modern Lib NY.

An Asterisk (*) at the beginning of an entry indicates that the title is appearing for the first time.

Clough, B. Clough's Sinhala-English Dictionary. 2nd ed. 848p. 1982. 95.00 (*0-8288-1762-6*, M14116) Fr & Eur.

Clough, Bonnie M., jt. auth. see Clough, Dick B.

***Clough, Brenda.** Doors of Death & Life. 2000. pap. write for info. (*0-312-87550-9*) St Martin.

— The Doors Of Death & Life. LC 00-23324. 272p. 2000. 22.95 (*0-312-87064-7*, Pub. by Tor Bks) St Martin.

Clough, Brenda. How Like a God. 1998. pap. 5.99 (*0-8125-7136-3*, Pub. by Tor Bks) St Martin.

Clough, Brenda W. An Impossumble Summer. 160p. (J). (gr. 3-6). 1992. 14.95 (*0-8027-8150-0*) Walker & Co.

***Clough, Brian.** Clough: The Autobiography. 2000. pap. 12.95 (*0-552-14003-1*, Pub. by Transworld Publishers Ltd) Trafalgar.

Clough, Carmen P. Spanish in the Field: Practical Spanish for Ranchers, Farmers, Vintners. LC 83-62192. 256p. 1990. pap. 24.95 (*0-932857-02-7*, Pub. by Ag Access) Fertile Ground Bks.

Clough, Carmen P., et al. Spanish in the Field Dictionary: English-Spanish - Spanish-English for Farm & Agribusiness. 160p. (C). 1990. reprint ed. pap. 7.95 (*0-932857-01-9*, 83062192, Pub. by Ag Access) Fertile Ground Bks.

Clough, Cecil H., ed. see Myers, A. R.

Clough, Charles, ed. Calaveras County Illustrated & Described, 1885. (Illus.). 112p. reprint ed. 13.45 (*0-944194-28-1*); reprint ed. pap. 8.95 (*0-944194-27-3*) Linrose Pub.

Clough, Charles, et al. Clough, Charles. (Illus.). 36p. 1983. pap. 7.50 (*0-914782-49-5*) Buffalo Fine-Albrght-Knox.

Clough, Charles W. San Juan Bautista: The Town, the Mission & the Park. LC 95-61174. (Illus.). 144p. 1995. pap. 18.95 (*1-884995-07-1*) Word Dancer.

Clough, David G. You Can Be a Philanthropist: Why Let Rich People Have All the Fun? LC 95-92684. 95p. (Orig.). 1996. 12.95 (*0-9649810-0-9*) Planned Giv Spec.

Clough, Dick B. & Clough, Bonnie M. A Handbook of Effective Techniques for Teacher Aides. (Illus.). 200p. 1978. 35.95 (*0-398-03809-0*); pap. 25.95 (*0-398-06062-2*) C C Thomas.

Clough, Donald. Decisions in Public & Private Sectors: Theories, Practices, & Processes. (Illus.). 448p. (C). 1984. text 38.00 (*0-13-198226-5*) P-H.

Clough, Dwight A. Weathering Storms: What Do You Do When There's No Way Out? Orig. Title: Weathering Storms: Healing, Help & Humor - Tonic for Tough Times. 250p. 1999. pap. 12.00 (*0-9670718-0-1*) Creative Advant.

Clough, E. The Princess' Lover. LC 92-82950. 640p. 1993. 14.95 (*1-877978-49-3*, FLF Pr) FL Lit Foundation.

Clough, Eric. Landscaping with Nature. Smith, Mike, ed. (Illus.). 96p. (Orig.). 1998. pap. 9.95 (*0-89721-341-6*, Ortho Bks) Meredith Bks.

Clough, Eric & Quarmby, Jacqueline, eds. A Public Library Service for Ethnic Minorities in Great Britain. LC 78-13622. (Illus.). 369p. 1978. 69.50 (*0-313-21201-5*, CPL, Greenwood Pr) Greenwood.

Clough, Frank C. William Allen White of Emporia. LC 73-100149. 265p. 1970. reprint ed. lib. bdg. 69.50 (*0-8371-3910-4*, CLWA, Greenwood Pr) Greenwood.

Clough, Jan, jt. auth. see Mullin, Ann.

Clough, John & Conley, Joyce. Basic Harmonic Progressions. (Orig.). (C). 1984. pap. 39.00 (*0-393-95372-6*) Norton.

Clough, John & Conley, Joyce. Scales, Intervals, Keys, Triads, Rhythm & Meter. 2nd rev. ed. (C). 1983. pap. 33.50 (*0-393-95189-8*) Norton.

Clough, John D., jt. ed. see Krakauer, Randall S.

Clough, Joy. The Characters Within: Befriending Your Deepest Emotions. 160p. (Orig.). 1997. pap. 9.95 (*0-87946-165-9*, 262) ACTA Pubns.

Clough, Judy, ed. see Cooper, Lynda S.

Clough, Judy, ed. see McCutcheon, Pam.

Clough, Katherine. Wildflowers of Prince Edward Island. (Island Pathways Ser.). (Illus.). 152p. 1992. spiral bd. 14.95 (*0-921556-27-6*, Pub. by Gynergy-Ragweed) U of Toronto Pr.

Clough, Len C., et al. Practical Guide to Planned Giving. 96th ed. Barron, Taghrid, ed. 950p. 1995. 120.00 (*0-930807-47-2*) Taft Group.

Clough, Marshall S. Mau Mau Memoirs: History, Memory, & Politics. LC 97-36869. 284p. 1997. lib. bdg. 25.00 (*1-55587-537-8*) L Rienner.

Clough, Monica. Two Houses: New Tarbat House, Easter Ross; Royston House, Edinburgh, & the Family of Mackenzie, Earls of Cromartie 1656-1784. 1990. pap. text 19.95 (*0-08-040909-1*, Pub. by Aberdeen U Pr) Macmillan.

Clough, Monica, jt. auth. see Richards, E.

Clough, Patricia T. The End(s) of Enthnography: From Realism to Social Criticism, 2nd Edition. LC 98-9854. (Counterpoints: Vol. 85). XXVII, 142p. (C). 1998. pap. 24.95 (*0-8204-4038-8*) P Lang Pubng.

— The End(s) of Ethnography: From Realism to Social Criticism. (Sociological Observations Ser.: Vol. 21). 256p. (C). 1992. text 48.00 (*0-8039-4630-9*); pap. text 21.95 (*0-8039-4631-7*) Sage.

— Feminist Thought: Desire, Power & Academic Discourse. LC 93-51072. (Contemporary Social Theory Ser.). 192p. 1994. 62.95 (*1-55786-485-3*); pap. 25.95 (*1-55786-486-1*) Blackwell Pubs.

***Clough, Patricia Ticineto.** Autoaffection: Unconscious Thought in the Age of Teletechnology. LC 99-50993. 216p. 2000. 44.95 (*0-8166-2888-2*); pap. 17.95 (*0-8166-2889-0*) U of Minn Pr.

Clough, Peter. Clay in the Classroom. (Illus.). 128p. 1996. text. write for info. (*90-5703-081-0*, Harwood Acad Pubs) Gordon & Breach.

***Clough, Peter, ed.** Managing Inclusive Education: From Policy to Experience. 224p. 1999. pap. 27.95 (*1-85396-393-3*, Pub. by P Chapman); lib. bdg. 73.95 (*1-85396-411-5*, Pub. by P Chapman) Sage.

***Clough, Peter & Barton, Len, eds.** Articulating with Difficulty: Research Voices in Inclusive Education. LC 99-210349. (BERA Dialogues Ser.). 144p. 1999. pap. 24.95 (*1-85396-410-7*, Pub. by P Chapman); lib. bdg. 73.95 (*1-85396-412-3*, Pub. by P Chapman) Sage.

Clough, Peter & Barton, Len, eds. Making Difficulties: Research & the Construction of SEN. 192p. 1995. pap. 24.95 (*1-85396-294-5*, Pub. by P Chapman) Taylor & Francis.

Clough, Peter, jt. auth. see Corbett, Jenny.

Clough, Peter W. & New Zealand Institute of Economic Research Staff. Economic Instruments & Visitor Services on the Public Estate: Full Report LC 94-151043. 34p. 1993. pap. write for info. (*0-478-04257-4*, Pub. by Manaaki Whenua) Balogh.

— Review of the Energy Efficiency & Conservation Authority: Report to Ministry of Commerce. LC 99-188636. v, 73 p. 1998. spiral bd. write for info. (*0-478-00070-7*, Pub. by Manaaki Whenua) Balogh.

Clough, R. W., jt. ed. see Serafim, J. Laginha.

Clough, Ralph N. Cooperation or Conflict in the Taiwan Strait? LC 98-39356. (Asia in World Politics Ser.: Vol. 114). 168p. 1999. 54.00 (*0-8476-9325-2*); pap. 21.95 (*0-8476-9326-0*) Rowman.

— Deterrence & Defense in Korea: The Role of U. S. Forces. LC 75-44466. (Studies in Defense Policy). 61p. 1976. pap. 7.95 (*0-8157-1481-5*) Brookings.

— East Asia & U. S. Security. LC 74-274. 248p. 1975. 32.95 (*0-8157-1480-7*); pap. 12.95 (*0-8157-1479-3*) Brookings.

— East Asia & U. S. Security. LC 74-274. 260p. 1975. reprint ed. pap. 80.60 (*0-608-01997-6*, 206265300003) Bks Demand.

***Clough, Ralph N.** Island China. 280p. 1999. 27.95 (*0-7351-0185-X*) Replica Bks.

Clough, Ralph N. Island China: A Twentieth Century Fund Study. LC 78-9483. (Twentieth Century Fund Study). 282p. 1978. 29.00 (*0-674-46875-9*) HUP.

Clough, Ralph N., et al. The United States, China & Arms Control. LC 75-15650. 165p. reprint ed. pap. 51.20 (*0-608-12167-3*, 202537000043) Bks Demand.

Clough, Ray W. & Penzien, Joseph. Dynamics of Structures. 2nd ed. LC 92-44039. (C). 1993. text 85.00 (*0-07-011394-7*) McGraw.

Clough, Richard. Mountain Madness: A Handful of Lakeland Lunacies. LC 74-181699. 32 p.p. 1974. write for info. (*0-85983-026-8*) Graham Publishing Co.

Clough, Richard H. & Sears, Glenn A. Construction Contracting. 6th ed. 600p. 1994. 99.00 (*0-471-30968-0*) Wiley.

— Construction Project Management. 3rd ed. LC 91-25488. 304p. 1991. 99.00 (*0-471-54608-9*) Wiley.

***Clough, Richard H., et al.** Construction Project Management. 4th ed. LC 99-86810. 350p. 2000. 80.00 (*0-471-32438-8*) Wiley.

Clough, Roger. The Abuse of Care in Residential Institutions. 275p. 1996. 65.00 (*1-871177-93-6*, Pub. by Whiting & Birch); pap. 29.95 (*1-871177-94-4*, Pub. by Whiting & Birch) Paul & Co Pubs.

— Old Age Homes. 1981. 60.00 (*0-7855-0583-0*, Pub. by Natl Inst Soc Work) St Mut.

— Practice, Politics & Power in Social Services: Social Work, Local Government & Politics. (Issues in Social Work Ser.). 308p. 1990. text 72.95 (*1-85628-060-8*, Pub. by Avebry) Ashgate Pub Co.

Clough, Roger, jt. auth. see Hadley, Roger.

Clough, Roger B., ed. Quantitative NDE in the Nuclear Industry: Proceedings of the Fifth International Conference on Nondestructive Evaluation in the Nuclear Industry, San Diego, CA, 10-13 May 1982--Sponsored by the American Society for Metals. LC 82-74019. 487p. reprint ed. pap. 151.00 (*0-608-16512-3*, 202704300053) Bks Demand.

Clough, Roger L., et al, eds. Polymer Durability: Degradation, Stabilization, & Lifetime Prediction. (Advances in Chemistry Ser.: Vol. 249). 728p. 1996. text 145.00 (*0-8412-3134-6*, Pub. by Am Chemical) OUP.

Clough, Roger L. & Shalaby, Shalaby W., eds. Irradiation of Polymers: Fundamentals & Technological Applications. LC 95-47865. (ACS Symposium Ser.: No. 620). (Illus.). 448p. 1996. text 115.00 (*0-8412-3377-2*, Pub. by Am Chemical) OUP.

Clough, Ronald. Japanese Business Information: An Introduction. (Information in Focus Ser.). 116p. 1995. pap. 55.00 (*0-7123-0779-6*, Pub. by SRIS) L Erlbaum Assocs.

Clough, Sandy. Heirlooms from Loving Hands: Making Memories to Cherish Forever. LC 97-46938. 64p. 1998. 15.99 (*1-56507-609-5*) Harvest Hse.

— Moments to Remember. 64p. 1999. spiral bd., boxed set 22.99 (*1-56507-915-9*) Harvest Hse.

Clough, Sandy L. And I Know He Watches Me: God's Comfort & Care for Those Who Hurt. LC 98-38534. 64p. 1999. 14.99 (*1-56507-988-4*) Harvest Hse.

— My Keepsake Recipes: A Personal Journal of Meals, Memories, & Traditions. 92p. (Orig.). 1996. 12.99 (*1-56507-494-7*) Harvest Hse.

— Woman's Journal. (Illus.). 96p. 1994. pap. 14.95 (*0-9613287-5-4*) Strawberry GA.

***Clough, Sandy Lyman.** So Rare a Treasure: Stories of God's Mercy & Abiding Love. LC 99-37262. 64p. 2000. 14.99 (*0-7369-0214-7*) Harvest Hse.

***Clough, Sandy Lynam.** Blessings among the Roses: A Journal of Faith, Hope & Love. gif. ed. (Illus.). 80p. 2000. 14.99 (*0-7369-0392-5*) Harvest Hse.

— Blessings among the Roses: Sharing the Beauty of Faith, Hope & Love. gif. ed. (Among the Roses Ser.). (Illus.). 48p. 2000. 14.99 (*0-7369-0332-1*) Harvest Hse.

***Clough, Sandy Lynam.** Time for Tea Calendar. 2000th ed. 1999. 9.99 (*0-7369-0076-4*) Harvest Hse.

Clough, Shepard B. Basic Values of Western Civilization. LC 84-27971. 132p. 1985. reprint ed. lib. bdg. 59.50 (*0-313-24735-8*, CLBV, Greenwood Pr) Greenwood.

— The Rise & Fall of Civilization: An Inquiry into the Relationship Between Economic Development & Civilization. LC 77-25973. (Illus.). 291p. 1978. reprint ed. lib. bdg. 38.50 (*0-313-20092-0*, CLRI, Greenwood Pr) Greenwood.

Clough-Smith, J. H. An Introduction to Spherical Trigonometry. (C). 1987. 44.00 (*0-85174-320-X*) St Mut.

Clough-Smith, J. H., ed. Applied Physics: Notes & Examples in SI Units for Students of Nautical Science. (C). 1987. 95.00 (*0-85174-319-6*) St Mut.

Clough, T. H. Sylloge of Coins of the British Isles Vol. 26: East Anglia. 1980. 99.00 (*0-19-725991-X*) OUP.

Clough, Virginia L., jt. auth. see Judy, Richard W.

Clough, W. R., ed. Reactive Metals: Proceedings of the 3rd Reactive Metals Conference, Buffalo, 1958. LC 59-14889. (Metallurgical Society Conference Ser.: Vol. 2). 625p. reprint ed. pap. 193.80 (*0-608-11500-2*, 200066500038) Bks Demand.

Clough, Wilson, tr. see Moraze, Charles.

Cloughen, Charles. One Minute Stewardship Sermons. LC 97-27224. 144p. 1997. pap. 12.95 (*0-8192-1720-4*) Morehouse Pub.

***Cloughen, Charles, Jr.** Sixty-Second Stewardship Sermons. LC 99-54691. 176p. 2000. pap. 14.95 (*0-8146-1219-9*) Liturgical Pr.

Clougher, Ed. HM Team. LC 98-88475. 325p. 1998. 25.00 (*0-7388-0165-8*); pap. 15.00 (*0-7388-0166-6*) Xlibris Corp.

Clougherty, Laura M., jt. auth. see Henderson, Margaret C.

***Cloughley, Brian.** A History of the Pakistan Army: Wars & Insurrections. 2nd ed. (Illus.). 444p. 2000. text 29.95 (*0-19-579374-9*) OUP.

Cloughly, Cecil, et al, eds. My Dear Mr. Bell: Letters from Dr. Jonathan Pereira to Mr. Jacob Bell, London, 1844 to 1853. 129p. (Orig.). 1987. pap. 12.00 (*0-931292-18-2*) Am Inst Hist Pharm.

Cloughton, David. Riley on Business Interruption & Consequential Loss Insurance. (C). 1985. 500.00 (*0-7855-4238-8*, Pub. by Witherby & Co) St Mut.

Clougri, Murray K. Bet Like a Chicken, Eat Like a Chicken: A Guide to Winning at the Harness Races. 266p. Date not set. mass mkt. 12.95 (*1-55197-131-3*) Picasso Publ.

Cloulas, Ivan & Bimbenet-Privat, Michele. Treasures of the French Renaissance: Architecture, Sculpture, Painting, Drawings. Goodman, John, tr. from FRE. LC 97-45860. (Illus.). 304p. 1998. 49.50 (*0-8109-3883-9*, Pub. by Abrams) Time Warner.

Clouse. Jumpstart: Workbook for Writers. 2nd ed. 2001. 31.74 (*0-07-230074-4*) McGraw.

— Patterns for a Purpose. 1994. 20.93 (*0-07-011426-9*) McGraw.

Clouse. Puzzle Maps Usa Spanish. 1993. pap., teacher ed. 4.95 (*0-8050-1846-8*) St Martin.

Clouse. Transitions: From Reading to Writing. 1993. teacher ed. 26.87 (*0-07-011428-5*) McGraw.

Clouse, Barbara F. Cornerstones: A Reader for Writers. 1994. pap. text. write for info. (*0-07-198996-X*) McGraw.

— Jumpstart! A Workbook for Writers. 496p. (C). 1995. pap. 41.25 (*0-07-011442-0*) McGraw.

— Patterns for a Purpose. LC 94-13172. 512p. (C). 1994. pap. 31.75 (*0-07-011419-6*) McGraw.

— Patterns for a Purpose: A Rhetorical Reader. 2nd ed. LC 98-2964. 752p. 1998. pap. 30.75 (*0-07-011980-5*) McGraw.

— Progressions. 4th ed. LC 98-4574. 528p. (C). 1998. pap. text 42.00 (*0-205-28157-5*) Allyn.

— The Student Writer: Editor & Critic. 3rd ed. LC 91-23061. (C). 1991. text 26.25 (*0-07-011414-5*) McGraw.

— The Student Writer: Editor & Critic. 4th ed. LC 95-14357. 512p. (C). 1995. pap. 37.56 (*0-07-011448-X*) McGraw.

— Transitions: From Reading to Writing. LC 93-28684. (C). 1994. pap. text 25.25 (*0-07-011427-7*) McGraw.

— Transitions: From Reading to Writing. 2nd ed. LC 97-5812. 576p. (C). 1997. pap. 31.25 (*0-07-011876-0*) McGraw.

— Working It Out: A Troubleshooting Guide for Writers. 2nd ed. 176p. (C). 1996. pap. 17.68 (*0-07-011619-9*) McGraw.

— Working It Out: A Troubleshooting Guide for Writers. 2nd ed. 176p. (C). 1996. pap. 13.75 (*0-07-011620-2*) McGraw.

***Clouse, Barbara Fine.** The Student Writer: Editor & Critic. 5th ed. LC 99-11790. (Illus.). 2000. write for info. (*0-07-043486-7*) McGrw-H Hghr Educ.

— Working It Out: A Troubleshooting Guide for Writers. 3rd ed. LC 00-27368. 208p. 2000. pap. 16.88 (*0-07-236748-2*) McGraw.

Clouse, Bonnidell. Teaching for Moral Growth: A Guide for the Christian Community: Teachers, Parents & Pastors. LC 93-2316. 416p. (gr. 12). 1993. pap. 16.99 (*0-8010-5746-9*, Moral Developme, Bridgept Bks) Baker Bks.

Clouse, Bonnidell & Clouse, Robert G., eds. Women in Ministry: Four Views. LC 89-1773. 252p. (Orig.). 1989. pap. 13.99 (*0-8308-1284-9*, 1284) InterVarsity.

Clouse, Jerry. Whiskey Rebellion: Southwestern Pennsylvania Frontier People Test the American Constitution. (Illus.). 79p. 1993. pap. 9.95 (*0-89271-074-8*, 0502) Pa Hist & Mus.

Clouse, Michael S. & Anderson, Kathie J. Future Choice: Why Network Marketing May Be Your Best Career Move. rev. ed. 112p. 1996. pap. 10.50 (*0-9634259-9-4*) Nexeracom.

Clouse, Nancy. Puzzle Maps U. S. A. Spanish Edition. (J). (gr. 2-6). 1995. pap. 5.95 (*0-8050-3598-2*) H Holt & Co.

Clouse, Nancy, jt. auth. see Aardema, Verna.

Clouse, Nancy L. Puzzle Maps U. S. A. (J). (gr. 2-6). 1995. pap. 5.95 (*0-8050-3597-4*) H Holt & Co.

Clouse, Robert. Biography of Bruce Lee. (Illus.). 200p. (Orig.). 1988. pap. 14.95 (*0-86568-133-3*, 144) Unique Pubns.

— The Making of Enter the Dragon. LC 87-81257. 240p. (Orig.). 1987. pap. 13.95 (*0-86568-098-1*, 145) Unique Pubns.

Clouse, Robert G. The Meaning of the Millennium. 212p. 1978. pap. 12.99 (*0-88469-099-7*) BMH Bks.

Clouse, Robert G., ed. The Meaning of the Millennium: Four Views. LC 76-55556. 223p. (Orig.). 1977. pap. 12.99 (*0-87784-794-0*, 794) InterVarsity.

— Que Es el Milenio? - Cuatro Enfoques Para una Respuesta. Sedaca, V. David, tr.Tr. of Meaning of the Millennium - Four Views. (SPA.). 208p. (Orig.). 1992. pap. 9.99 (*0-311-09136-9*) Casa Bautista.

Clouse, Robert G., et al, eds. Protest & Politics: Christianity & Contemporary Affairs. 277p. 1968. 5.95 (*0-87921-000-1*) Attic Pr.

Clouse, Robert G., et al. The New Millennium Manual: A Once & Future Guide. LC 98-48302. (Illus.). 224p. (C). 1999. pap. 12.99 (*0-8010-5848-1*, Bridgept Bks) Baker Bks.

Clouse, Robert G., jt. ed. see Clouse, Bonnidell.

Clouse, Robert G., ed. see Hoyt, Herman A., et al.

Clouse, Wendy. Painting Landscapes in Acrylics. (Leisure Arts Ser.: No. 29). (Illus.). 32p. pap. 4.95 (*0-85532-579-8*, 579-8, Pub. by Srch Pr) A Schwartz & Co.

Clouse, Wendy, jt. auth. see Monahan, Patricia.

Clouse, Woody, jt. auth. see Turner, Ed.

Clouser, K. Danner, jt. auth. see Kopelman, Loretta M.

Clouser, Lois, et al. Introduction to Microbiology Laboratory Manual: B371. 2nd ed. 120p. (C). 1996. pap. text, ring bd. 27.95 (*0-7872-1322-5*) Kendall-Hunt.

Clouser, Roy. Knowing with the Heart: Religious Experience & Belief in God. LC 98-27689. 192p. 1998. pap. 12.99 (*0-8308-1507-4*, 1507) InterVarsity.

Clouser, Roy A. The Myth of Religious Neutrality: An Essay on the Hidden Role of Religious Belief in Theories. LC 90-50928. (C). 1992. pap. text 22.00 (*0-268-01399-3*) U of Notre Dame Pr.

Clouston, A. E. The Dangerous Skies. Gilbert, James B., ed. LC 79-7240. (Flight: Its First Seventy-Five Years Ser.). (Illus.). 1980. reprint ed. lib. bdg. 19.95 (*0-405-12155-5*) Ayer.

Clouston, Andrew, jt. auth. see Kelso, Anne.

Clouston, Brian. Landscape Design with Plants. 2nd ed. 1990. 84.00 (*0-8493-7148-1*, SB) CRC Pr.

— Landscape Design with Plants. 2nd ed. (Illus.). 434p. 1994. pap. write for info. (*0-7506-1962-7*) CRC Pr.

Clouston, W A., jt. auth. see Saxby, Jessie M.

Clouston, William A. Arabian Poetry. 560p. 1986. 350.00 (*1-85077-137-5*, Pub. by Darf Pubs Ltd) St Mut.

— Flowers from a Persian Garden & Other Papers. Dorsen, Richard M., ed. LC 77-70584. (International Ser.). 1977. reprint ed. lib. bdg. 31.95 (*0-405-10088-4*) Ayer.

— Popular Tales & Fictions, Their Migrations & Transformations, 2 vols. 1968. reprint ed. 95.00 (*1-55888-211-1*) Omnigraphics Inc.

Clouston, William A., jt. ed. see Furnivall, F. J.

Clout, H. A Rural Policy for the EEC? (EEC Ser.). 227p. 1984. pap. text 12.95 (*0-416-34550-6*, 9105) Routledge.

Clout, Hugh. After the Ruins: Restoring the Countryside of France after the Great War. (Illus.). 272p. 1996. 69.95 (*0-85989-491-6*, Pub. by Univ Exeter Pr) Northwestern U Pr.

— Agriculture in France on the Eve of the Railway Age. (Illus.). 239p. 1980. 44.00 (*0-389-20017-4*, N6790) B&N Imports.

Clout, Hugh D. & Wood, Peter A., eds. London: Problems of Change. Date not set. pap. text. write for info. (*0-582-35491-9*, Pub. by Addison-Wesley) Longman.

Cloutier, David. My Grandfather's House: Tlingit Songs of Death & Sorrow. LC 80-15499. (Illus.). 40p. (Orig.). 1980. pap. 8.95 (*0-914974-26-2*) Holmgangers.

Cloutier, David, tr. Spirit Spirit: Shaman Songs. LC 89-7373. (Illus.). 100p. (C). 1980. reprint ed. pap. 8.95 (*0-914278-30-4*) Copper Beech.

Cloutier, David, tr. from CHI. By the Stream of Antique Song. 40p. (Orig.). 1988. pap. 6.00 (*0-9607756-8-4*) Singular Speech Pr.

Cloutier, David, tr. see Esteban, Claude.

Cloutier, David, tr. see Laude, Jean.

Cloutier, Douglas. The Douglas Cloutier Photography Book. 1996. 65.00 (*0-9652009-2-2*) Alluvial Ent.

Cloutier, James. The Alpine Tavern: Photographs of a Social Gathering Place. LC 77-77899. (Illus.). 1977. pap. 9.95 (*0-918966-00-0*) Image West.

— The Best of Orygun: Or, Learning How to Say Oregon So Everyone Won't Think You're from New Jersey. LC 86-62944. (Illus.). 254p. 1986. pap. 7.95 (*0-918966-10-8*) Image West.

— The Great Texas Joke Book. LC 81-84158. (Illus.). 128p. 1981. pap. 6.95 (*0-918966-08-6*) Image West.

— Letters from the Heart. LC 86-62945. 64p. 1986. pap. 5.95 (*0-918966-11-6*) Image West.

— This Day in Oregon. LC 80-83719. (Illus.). 128p. (J). 1981. pap. 6.95 (*0-918966-06-X*) Image West.

Cloutier, Kenny, jt. auth. see DeMaleissye-Melun, Judith.

Cloutier, L., jt. auth. see Gosselin, Claude.

Cloutier, Madison, jt. auth. see Howard.

Cloutier, Pierre, tr. see Ferron, Jacques.

Cloutier, Roger J., et al, eds. Medical Radionuclides: Radiation Dose & Effects, Proceedings. LC 70-606556. (AEC Symposium Ser.). 528p. 1970. pap. 21.25 (*0-87079-269-5*, CONF-691212); fiche 9.00 (*0-87079-270-9*, CONF-691212) DOE.

C

Cloutier, T. J. & McEvoy, Tom. Championship No-Limit & Pot-Limit Hold'Em: On the Road to the World Series of Poker. LC 97-67348. (Illus.). 216p. (Orig.). 1997. pap. 39.95 *(1-884466-31-1)* Poker Plus.

— Championship Omaha: Omaha High-Low, Omaha High & Pot-Limit Omaha. LC 98-67030. (Illus.). 232p. 1999. pap. 39.95 *(1-884466-27-3)* Poker Plus.

Cloutier, T. J., jt. auth. see McEvoy, Tom.

Cloutman, B. Mackay. The Law Relating to Authors & Publishers, No. 1. xvi, 145p. 1999. reprint ed. 50.00 *(1-56169-459-2)* Gaunt.

Cloux, Fokko Du, see Du Cloux, Fokko.

Clouzot, Claire. William Klein: Films. LC 98-30025. (Illus.). 120p. 1999. pap. 39.95 *(1-57687-038-3,* pwerHse Bks) pwerHse Cultrl.

Clouzot, Henri. Art Deco Decorative Ironwork. LC 97-16160. (Illus.). 112p. 1997. 11.95 *(0-486-29812-4)* Dover.

Clouzot, Henri & Morris, Frances. Painted & Printed Fabrics: The History of the Manufactory at Jouy & Other Ateliers in France, 1760-1815 by Henri Clouzot: Notes on the History of Cotton Printing Especially in England & America by Frances Morris. LC 70-168418. (Metropolitan Museum of Art Publications in Reprint). (Illus.). 222p. 1974. reprint ed. 34.95 *(0-405-02256-5)* Ayer.

***Clover.** Escape from Psychiatry: The Autobiography of Clover. 2nd ed. LC 99-74639. 396p. 1999. pap. 19.95 *(0-9671163-7-6)* Rainbow Pots.

Clover, Anne. Homeopathic First Aid: Safe & Effective Help for Accidents & Other Common Health Problems. (Illus.). 96p. 1995. pap. 8.00 *(0-614-10597-8)* Harper SF.

Clover, Carol J. The Medieval Saga. LC 81-17432. 224p. 1982. text 42.50 *(0-8014-1447-4)* Cornell U Pr.

— Men, Women, & Chain Saws: Gender in the Modern Horror Film. (Illus.). 253p. (C). 1992. pap. text 14.95 *(0-691-00620-2,* Pub. by Princeton U Pr) Cal Prin Full Svc.

Clover, Cecila W. Documenting Your Possessions: Workbook. 32p. 1994. reprint ed. 34.95 incl. 3.5 hd *(0-9639374-1-3);* reprint ed. 34.95 incl. 5.25 hd *(0-9639374-2-1)* Art Restoration.

Clover, Cecile W. Documenting Your Possessions. 32p. 1995. student ed. 89.95 incl. disk *(0-9639374-4-8)* Art Restoration.

Clover, Cecile W. & Heslich, F. T., Jr. Holsinger's Charlottesville. 2nd rev. ed. (Illus.). 116p. 1976. reprint ed. 34.95 *(0-9639374-5-6)* Art Restoration.

Clover, F. M. & Humphreys, R. S., eds. Tradition & Innovation in Late Antiquity. LC 88-40427. (Wisconsin Studies in Classics). (Illus.). 366p. reprint ed. pap. 113.50 *(0-7837-6661-0,* 204627300011) Bks Demand.

Clover, Frank M. The Late Roman West & the Vandals. LC 93-18599. (Collected Studies: No. CS401). 300p. 1993. 101.95 *(0-86078-354-5,* Pub. by Variorum) Ashgate Pub Co.

Clover, Gloria & Martin, Karen, eds. Penned from the Heart, Vol. 4. (Illus.). 1997. pap. 9.95 *(0-936369-53-1)* Son-Rise Pubns.

— Penned from the Heart Vol. 3: A Book of Devotions for Every Day. (Illus.). 196p. 1996. pap. 7.95 *(0-936369-52-3)* Son-Rise Pubns.

Clover, Helen, ed. see Lanfranc.

Clover, Joshua. Madonna Anno Domini. LC 96-45285. 64p. 1997. pap. 11.95 *(0-8071-2148-7);* text 19.95 *(0-8071-2147-9)* La State U Pr.

***Clover, Peter.** Sheltie & the Runaway. LC 99-87886. (Sheltie! Ser.: Vol. 3). (Illus.). (J). 2000. pap. 3.99 *(0-689-83576-0)* Aladdin.

— Sheltie Saves the Day! LC 99-87887. (Sheltie! Ser.: Vol. 2). (Illus.). (J). (gr. 4-6). 2000. pap. 3.99 *(0-689-83575-2)* Aladdin.

— Sheltie the Shetland Pony. LC 99-87893. (Sheltie! Ser.: Vol. 1). (Illus.). 96p. (J). (gr. 1-3). 2000. pap. 3.99 *(0-689-83574-4)* Aladdin.

Clover, R. The Festivals & Sacred Days of Yahweh. Qadesh La Yahweh Press Editors, ed. LC 98-85161. 500p. 1998. write for info. *(0-9623638-5-5)* Qadesh La Yahweh.

— The Sabbath & Jubilee Cycle Vol. I: A Historical Study. Qadesh La Yahweh Press Editors, ed. (Ancient World Chronology Ser.). 409p. (C). 1992. write for info. *(0-9623638-8-X)* Qadesh La Yahweh.

Clover, Richard. The Sacred Name. Deal, David & Runfola, Charles, eds. 315p. (Orig.). (C). 1989. lib. bdg. write for info. *(0-318-65408-3)* Qadesh La Yahweh.

— The Sacred Name, Vol. One: (Paeleo Hebrew YHWH) Qadesh La Yahweh Press Editorial Staff, ed. (Illus.). 126p. (C). 1991. pap. text. write for info. *(0-9623638-1-2);* lib. bdg. write for info. *(0-9623638-0-4)* Qadesh La Yahweh.

Cloverdale Press Staff & Passell, Peter. Where to Put Your Money. 64p. 1984. mass mkt. 3.95 *(0-446-37954-9,* Pub. by Warner Bks) Little.

Clovis, Albert L., jt. auth. see Nordstrom, Robert J.

Clovis, Donna L. Locket of Dreams: A Modern African American Fairy Tale. LC 99-72744. (Illus.). 24p. (J). (gr. 3-8). 1999. pap. text 9.95 *(1-58521-001-3)* Bks Black Chldn.

— StoryBook of Native American Wisdom. LC 97-95038. (Illus.). 56p. (J). (gr. k-12). 1997. pap. 9.95 *(1-889590-00-2)* Cherubic Pr.

— Struggles for Freedom: An Anthology of Multicultural Experiences. Blakeley, Gwendolynne A., ed. LC 94-78465. (Illus.). 144p. (Orig.). (YA). 1994. pap. 11.95 *(0-9638672-2-9)* Bryant & Dillon.

Clow, Archibald & Clow, Nan L. Chemical Revolution. (Essay Index Reprint Ser.). 1977. 46.95 *(0-8369-1909-2)* Ayer.

Clow, Archibald & Clow, Nan L. The Chemical Revolution: A Contribution to Social Technology, Vol. 8. LC 92-7259. x, 680p. 1992. pap. text 85.00 *(2-88124-549-8)* Gordon & Breach.

Clow, Barbara H. Chiron: Rainbow Bridge Between the Inner & Outer Planets. 2nd exp. rev. ed. LC 87-45244. (Modern Astrology Library). (Illus.). 336p. (Orig.). 1999. pap. 14.95 *(0-87542-094-X)* Llewellyn Pubns.

— Eye of the Centaur: A Visionary Guide into Past Lives. 2nd ed. LC 89-6929. (Mind Chronicles Ser.). (Illus.). 256p. 1990. pap. 12.95 *(0-939680-60-2)* Bear & Co.

— Heart of the Christos: Starseeding from the Pleiades. LC 89-6587. (Mind Chronicles Ser.). (Illus.). 272p. (Orig.). 1989. pap. 15.00 *(0-939680-59-9)* Bear & Co.

— Liquid Light of Sex: Kundalini Rising as Mid-Life Crisis. 1996. pap. text 15.00 *(1-879181-40-1)* Bear & Co.

— The Pleiadian Agenda: A New Cosmology for the Age of Light. (Illus.). 334p. 1995. pap. 15.00 *(1-879181-30-4)* Bear & Co.

Clow, Barbara H. Signet of Atlantis: War in Heaven Bypass. LC 92-12392. (Mind Chronicles Ser.). (Illus.). 224p. 1992. pap. 12.95 *(1-879181-02-9)* Bear & Co.

Clow, Betty J., jt. auth. see Brown, Betty J.

Clow, Deborah & Snow, Donald, eds. Northern Lights: A Selection of New Writing from the American West. 1995. 23.00 *(0-8446-6825-7)* Peter Smith.

Clow, John E., ed. Entrepreneurship Teaching Strategies. 324p. 1998. pap. 45.00 *(0-933964-52-8)* Natl Busn Ed Assoc.

Clow, Kenneth E., jt. auth. see Kurtz, David L.

Clow, Nan L., jt. auth. see Clow, Archibald.

Clow, Patricia, ed. A Place of Springs. Salisbury, Linda G., ed. LC 92-61931. (Illus.). 102p. 1992. pap. 8.95 *(0-9627974-9-9)* Tabby Hse Bks.

Clow, Simon. The International Nickel Trade. (International Trade Ser.). (Illus.). 160p. 1992. 170.00 *(1-85573-049-9,* Pub. by Woodhead Pubng) Am Educ Systs.

Clow, W. M., ed. Book of Bible Knowledge. 408p. 1994. reprint ed. pap. 8.99 *(0-529-10185-8,* BBK) World Publng.

Cloward, Richard A. Illegitimate Means, Anomie, & Deviant Behavior. (Reprint Series in Social Sciences). (C). 1993. reprint ed. pap. text 5.00 *(0-8290-3762-4,* S-44) Irvington.

Cloward, Richard A., jt. auth. see Piven, Frances F.

Cloward, Richard A., jt. auth. see Piven, Frances Fox.

Cloward, Richard A., jt. ed. see Piven, Frances F.

Clowdis, Charles W., Jr. & American Trucking Association Sales & Marketing Co. The Art of Giving Quality Service in the Motor Carrier Industry. 108p. 1984. pap. text 10.00 *(0-88711-080-0)* Am Trucking Assns.

Clower, Jerry. Stories from Home. LC 91-38118. 194p. 1993. 19.95 *(0-87805-547-9)* U Pr of Miss.

***Clower, Michael.** Champion Charlie. 1998. text 17.95 *(1-84018-122-2,* Pub. by Mainstream Pubng) Trafalgar.

Clower, Michael. Champion Charlie: The Authorised Biography of Charlie Swan. (Illus.). 224p. 1998. 35.00 *(1-85158-860-4,* Pub. by Mainstream Pubng) Trafalgar.

— Mick Kinane - Big Race King: The Authorised Biography. (Illus.). 192p. 1996. 35.00 *(1-85158-806-X,* Pub. by Mainstream Pubng) Trafalgar.

— Mick Kinane - Big Race King: The Authorised Biography. (Illus.). 224p. 1997. pap. 19.95 *(1-84018-002-1,* Pub. by Mainstream Pubng) Trafalgar.

Clower, Robert W. Economic Doctrine & Method: Selected Papers of R. W. Clower. (Economists of the Twentieth Century Ser.). 432p. 1995. 100.00 *(1-85898-004-6)* E Elgar.

Clowers, D. O. Spiritual Growth. pap. 7.95 *(0-9639956-1-8)* ISI Press.

***Clowers, George.** All That We're After. 10p. 2000. mass mkt. 3.00 *(0-9669871-1-X)* Clowers.

Clowers, George H. The Moon Is My Confessor. ii, 70p. 1999. pap. 9.40 *(0-9669871-0-1)* Clowers.

Clowers, George H., Jr. Uptown on Saturday. 11p. 2000. pap. 3.00 *(0-9669871-2-8)* Clowers.

Clowers, Michael R., jt. ed. see Stolov, Walter C.

Clowes, Brian. Call to Action: or Call to Apostacy: How Dissenters Plan to Remake the Catholic Church in Their Own Image. (Illus.). 132p. 1997. pap. 6.00 *(1-55922-046-5)* Human Life Intl.

— The Facts of Life: An Authoritative Guide to Life & Family Issues. Engler, Mike, ed. (Illus.). 404p. (Orig.). 1997. pap. text 19.95 *(1-55922-043-0)* Human Life Intl.

Clowes, Brian W. Simplified Framework Evaluation of Water Resource Project Impacts. LC 90-43713. (Environment: Problems & Solutions Ser.: Vol. 3). 486p. 1990. text 30.00 *(0-8240-0411-6)* Garland.

Clowes, Brian W., ed. Waterpower, '87, 3 vols., Set. 2622p. 1988. 15.00 *(0-87262-630-X,* 630-8) Am Soc Civil Eng.

Clowes, Carolyn. The Pandora Principle, No. 49. (Star Trek Ser.). 288p. 1990. mass mkt. 4.99 *(0-671-65815-8)* PB.

Clowes, Dan. Caricature: Nine Stories. (Illus.). 104p. 1998. 29.95 *(1-56097-329-3)* Fantagraph Bks.

— Ghost World. 80p. (YA). (gr. 1 up). 1998. pap. 9.95 *(1-56097-299-8)* Fantagraph Bks.

— Lout Rampage! 96p. 1992. per. 14.95 *(1-56097-070-7)* Fantagraph Bks.

***Clowes, Daniel.** David Boring. (Illus.). 132p. 2000. 24.95 *(0-375-40692-1)* Pantheon.

Clowes, Daniel. Ghost World. (YA). 1997. 19.95 *(1-56097-280-7)* Fantagraph Bks.

— The Official Lloyd Llewellyn Collection. (Illus.). 96p. 1989. pap. 12.95 *(0-930193-90-3)* Fantagraph Bks.

— Orgy Bound. 80p. 1996. pap. 14.95 *(1-56097-302-1)* Fantagraph Bks.

— Pussey! 64p. 1995. pap. 8.95 *(1-56097-183-5)* Fantagraph Bks.

— Pussey! 64p. 1995. 29.95 *(1-56097-186-X)* Fantagraph Bks.

Clowes, Edith W. Maksim Gorky: A Reference Guide. (Reference Bks.). 248p. 1987. 45.00 *(0-8161-8722-3,* Hall Reference) Macmillan.

— The Revolution of Moral Consciousness: Nietzsche in Russian Literature, 1890-1914. 288p. 1988. 30.00 *(0-87580-139-0)* N Ill U Pr.

— Russian Experimental Fiction: Resisting Ideology after Utopia. LC 92-46315. 200p. 1993. text 35.00 *(0-691-03222-X,* Pub. by Princeton U Pr) Cal Prin Full Svc.

Clowes, Edith W., et al, eds. Between Tsar & People: Educated Society & the Quest for Public Identity in Late Imperial Russia. 367p. 1991. pap. text 19.95 *(0-691-00851-5,* Pub. by Princeton U Pr) Cal Prin Full Svc.

Clowes, Edith W., ed. see Pasternak, Boris.

Clowes, George H. A., Jr. Trauma, Sepsis, & Shock: The Physiological Basis of Therapy. (Science & Practice of Surgery Ser.: Vol. 15). (Illus.). 616p. 1988. text 190.00 *(0-8247-7502-3)* Dekker.

Clowes, Janet. Tell Me about Heaven . . . I Think I'm Forgetting. LC 96-38764. (Illus.). 32p. (J). 1998. 14.95 *(1-57102-100-0,* Ideals Child) Hambleton-Hill.

Clowes, Jody. Drinking in Art: Mettlach Steins & Related Wares. (Illus.). 12p. 1995. pap. 7.95 *(0-944110-51-7)* Milwauk Art Mus.

Clowes, John. The Gospels: Translated from the Original Greek & Illustrated by Excerpts from the Theological Writings of Emanuel Swedenborg. 2000p. 2000. lthr. 67.50 *(1-883270-15-4)* Swedenborg Assn.

Clowes, Julie, jt. auth. see McCue, Sarah S.

Clowes, Kenneth W. The Impact of Computers on Managers. Dickson, Gary, ed. LC 82-4879. (Management Information Systems Ser.: No. 2). 206p. 1982. reprint ed. pap. 63.90 *(0-8357-1337-7,* 207005600063) Bks Demand.

***Clowes, Michael J.** The Money Flood: How Pension Funds Revolutionized Investing. LC 99-45195. (Investments Ser.). 320p. 2000. 39.95 *(0-471-38483-6)* Wiley.

Clowes, R., jt. auth. see Emerson, D.

***Clowes, W. Laird.** The Captain of the "Mary Rose" A Tale of Tomorrow. LC 99-216755. (Illus.). 1998. write for info. *(0-415-19290-0)* Routledge.

Clowes, William. A Guide to Printing, an Introduction for Print Buyers. LC 73-717. (Illus.). 134p. 1973. reprint ed. lib. bdg. 55.00 *(0-8371-6786-8,* CLGP, Greenwood Pr) Greenwood.

— A Profitable & Necessarie Booke of Observations. LC 73-171740. (English Experience Ser.: No. 366). 1971. reprint ed. 33.50 *(90-221-0366-8)* Walter J Johnson.

— A Right Fruteful Treatise for the Artificial Cure of Struma. LC 72-25835. (English Experience Ser.: No. 238). 68p. 1970. reprint ed. 15.00 *(90-221-0238-6)* Walter J Johnson.

— A Short & Profitable Treatise Touching the Cure of the Morbus Gallicus by Unctions. LC 75-38166. (English Experience Ser.: No. 443). 118p. 1972. reprint ed. 20.00 *(90-221-0443-5)* Walter J Johnson.

Clowes, William L. Black America: A Study of the Ex-Slave - His Late Master. LC 78-109322. 240p. 1970. reprint ed. lib. bdg. 38.50 *(0-8371-3588-5,* CBA&) Greenwood.

— The Royal Navy: A History from the Earliest Times to 1900, Vol. 1. LC 96-222611. (Illus.). 620p. 1996. pap. 29.95 *(1-86176-010-8)* Naval Inst Pr.

— The Royal Navy: A History from the Earliest Times to 1900, Vol. 2. LC 96-222611. (Illus.). 620p. 1996. pap. 29.95 *(1-86176-011-6)* Naval Inst Pr.

— The Royal Navy: A History from the Earliest Times to 1900, Vol. 3. LC 96-222611. (Illus.). 620p. 1996. pap. 29.95 *(1-86176-012-4)* Naval Inst Pr.

— The Royal Navy: A History from the Earliest Times to 1900, Vol. 4. (Illus.). 640p. 1997. pap. 29.95 *(1-86176-013-2)* Naval Inst Pr.

— The Royal Navy: A History from the Earliest Times to 1900, Vol. 5. (Illus.). 648p. 1997. pap. 29.95 *(1-86176-014-0)* Naval Inst Pr.

— The Royal Navy: A History from the Earliest Times to 1900, Vol. 6. (Illus.). 624p. 1997. pap. 29.95 *(1-86176-015-9)* Naval Inst Pr.

— The Royal Navy: A History from the Earliest Times to 1900, Vol. 7. (Illus.). 648p. 1997. pap. 29.95 *(1-86176-017-5)* Naval Inst Pr.

— The Royal Navy Vol. 7: A History from the Earliest Times to 1900. LC 96-222611. (Illus.). 648p. 1997. pap. 29.95 *(1-86176-016-7)* Naval Inst Pr.

Clowes, William L., ed. Royal Navy: A History from the Earliest Times, 7 vols., Set. reprint ed. 535.00 *(0-404-01640-5)* AMS Pr.

Clowney, Deborah, jt. auth. see Weininger, Jay.

Clowney, Earle D., tr. see Middlebrooks-Hutcherson, Gracie.

Clowney, Edmund P. Called to the Ministry. 1976. pap. 5.99 *(0-87552-144-4)* P & R Pubng.

— Living in Christ's Church. 1986. teacher ed. 3.95 *(0-934688-24-9);* pap. text 5.95 *(0-934688-22-2)* Great Comm Pubns.

— The Unfolding Mystery: Discovering Christ in the Old Testament. (Orig.). 1991. pap. 9.99 *(0-87552-174-6)* P & R Pubng.

Clowney, Paul & Clowney, Tessa. Exploring Churches. LC 82-210857. 94p. reprint ed. pap. 30.00 *(0-608-14487-8,* 202531700043) Bks Demand.

Clowney, Tessa, jt. auth. see Clowney, Paul.

Clowse, Barbara B. Ralph McGill: A Biography. 280p. 1998. 29.95 *(0-86554-612-6,* H461) Mercer Univ Pr.

— Women, Decision Making, & the Future. LC 85-18091. 167p. 1985. reprint ed. pap. 51.80 *(0-7837-8937-8,* 204964700002) Bks Demand.

Clowse, Barbara B., ed. Brainpower for the Cold War: The Sputnik Crisis & National Defense Education Act of 1958, 3. LC 81-1477. (Contributions to the Study of Education Ser.: No. 3). 225p. 1981. 59.95 *(0-313-22813-2,* CCW) Greenwood.

Cloy, John D. Pensive Jester: The Literary Career of W. W. Jacobs. LC 96-9816. 170p. 1996. lib. bdg. 39.50 *(0-7618-0464-1)* U Pr of Amer.

Cloyd, A. D. Cloyd: Genealogy of the Cloyd, Basye & Tapp Families in America, with Brief Sketches Referring to the Families of Ingels, Jones, Marshall & Smith. (Illus.). 297p. 1993. reprint ed. pap. 46.50 *(0-8328-3285-5);* reprint ed. lib. bdg. 56.50 *(0-8328-3284-7)* Higginson Bk Co.

Cloyd, Betty S. Children & Prayer: A Shared Pilgrimage. Williams, Karen F., ed. LC 96-46093. (Illus.). 128p. 1997. pap. 12.00 *(0-8358-0803-3,* UR803) Upper Room Bks.

***Cloyd, Betty S.** Parents & Grandparents as Spiritual Guides: Nurturing Children of the Promise. Williams, Karen, ed. 176p. 2000. pap. 13.00 *(0-8358-0923-4)* Upper Room Bks.

Cloyd, J. Timothy, jt. ed. see Elshtain, Jean B.

Cloyd, Jerald W. Drugs & Information Control: The Role of Men & Manipulation in the Control of Drug Trafficking, 23. LC 81-6675. (Contributions in Legal Studies: No. 23). 195p. 1982. 49.95 *(0-313-22178-2,* CDS/, Greenwood Pr) Greenwood.

Clozel. Automorphic Forms, Shimura Varieties, & L-Functions. 1990. 171.00 *(0-12-176653-5)* Acad Pr.

Clozel, Laurent & Milne, James S., eds. Automorphic Forms, Shimura Varieties, & L-Functions Vol. 1: Proceedings of a Conference Held at the University of Michigan, Ann Arbor, July 6-16, 1988. (Perspectives in Mathematics Ser.). 438p. 1989. text 86.00 *(0-12-176651-9)* Acad Pr.

Clozel, Laurent, jt. auth. see Arthur, James.

CLPE Staff. The Reading Book: By the Staff of the Centre for Language in Primary Education. Barrs, Myra & Thomas, Anne, eds. LC 93-22324. 116p. (YA). 1993. pap. text 19.50 *(0-435-08789-4,* 08789) Heinemann.

***CLSA Committee.** Code of Canon Law, Latin-English Edition: New Translation. 1999. 45.00 *(0-943616-79-4)* Canon Law Soc.

CLSA Committee on Procedures Staff. Protection of Rights of Persons in the Church: Revised Report of the Canon Law Society of America on the Subject of Due Process. 55p. 1991. pap. 6.50 *(0-943616-56-5)* Canon Law Soc.

CLSA Staff. CLSA Proceedings, 1983: 45th Annual Meeting. 354p. 1984. pap. 4.00 *(0-943616-22-0)* Canon Law Soc.

***CLSA Staff, ed.** CLSA Proceedings 1999: 61st Annual Meeting. 503p. 2000. pap. 24.00 *(0-943616-85-9)* Canon Law Soc.

Clu. Reference Manual. 1984. 47.95 *(0-387-91253-3)* Spr-Verlag.

Club du Sahel Staff, tr. see Elbow, Kent & Rochegude, Alain.

Club Jules Gonin Meeting Staff, et al. Limitations & Prospects for Retinal Surgery: Proceedings of the Club Jules Gonin Meeting, 8th, Miami, 1972. (Modern Problems in Ophthalmology Ser.: Vol. 12). (Illus.). 1974. 152.25 *(3-8055-1629-0)* S Karger.

Club Managers Association Staff. Job Descriptions for the Private Club Industry. (C). 1998. 45.95 *(0-7872-5187-9)* Kendall-Hunt.

Club Managers Staff. Job Descriptions for the Private Club Industry. 5th ed. 144p. 1998. per. 45.00 *(0-7872-5416-9)* Kendall-Hunt.

Club Membership Staff. The Woman's Club of Nashville Cookbook. LC 98-43869. (Illus.). 240p. 1998. spiral bd. 19.95 *(1-888608-87-0)* Cool Springs Pr.

Club Nineteen Staff, et al. Club Nineteen's Golfer's Travel & Entertainment Guide: A Savings Guide for Golfers. 192p. 1993. pap. text 49.00 *(1-880013-01-0)* Club Nineteen.

Club of Palm Beach Garden Inc. Staff. Gardens by the Sea: A Guide to Tropical Gardens & Tropical Plants. LC 99-38602. (Illus.). 1999. 34.95 *(0-8130-1729-7)* U Press Fla.

Clubb, Angela. Mad about Cheddar. (Illus.). 88p. 1998. pap. text 10.00 *(0-7881-5305-6)* DIANE Pub.

— Mad about Cheddar. (Illus.). 88p. 1983. pap. 5.95 *(0-7720-1436-1)* Genl Dist Srvs.

— Wild about Muffins. 1985. 9.95 *(0-8120-2910-0)* Barron.

Clubb, Bruce E. Foreign Trade Set. 2202p. 1991. boxed set 295.00 *(0-316-14745-1,* Aspen Law & Bus) Aspen Pub.

— Trade Vol. 2: 1994 Supplement. 1994. 75.00 *(0-316-14770-2,* Aspen Law & Bus); 75.00 *(0-316-14771-0,* Aspen Law & Bus) Aspen Pub.

— U. S. Foreign Trade, Vol. 2. 1991. 165.00 *(0-316-14766-4)* Little.

— U. S. Foreign Trade Law. 1991. 165.00 *(0-316-14748-6,* Aspen Law & Bus) Aspen Pub.

Clubb, Deborah & Ligon, Polly C., eds. Food, Hunger & Agricultural Issues. 245p. 1989. 19.50 *(0-933595-21-2)* Winrock Intl.

Clubb, Elizabeth & Knight, Jane. Fertility: Fertility Awareness & Natural Family Planning. rev. ed. (Illus.). 192p. 1996. pap. 14.95 *(0-7153-0424-0,* Pub. by D & C Pub) Sterling.

Clubb, Jerome M., jt. auth. see Austin, Erik W.

Clubb, Ken. Rifleman's Handbook: A Shooter's Guide to Rifles, Reloading & Results. 320p. (C). 1989. 21.95 *(0-9621148-2-0)* PRMDIA Spcl Intrst.

Clubb, Kevin J., et al. Psittacine Aviculture: Perspectives, Techniques & Research. 200p. (C). 1992. write for info. *(0-9631424-0-2)* Avicult Breed Res.

Clubb, O. Edmund. The Witness & I. LC 74-11385. 314p. 1974. text 57.50 *(0-231-03859-3)* Col U Pr.

Clubb, Oliver. KAL Flight 007: The Hidden Story. LC 84-62522. 174p. 1985. 22.00 *(0-932966-59-4)* Permanent Pr.

An Asterisk (*) at the beginning of an entry indicates that the title is appearing for the first time.

Clubb, Oliver E. China & Russia: The "Great Game" LC 72-155362. (Studies of the East Asian Institute, Columbia University). (Illus.). 614p. reprint ed. pap. 190.40 (*0-8357-4584-8*, 203751500008) Bks Demand.

Clubb, Pat, jt. ed. see Wyszomirski, Margaret J.

Clubb, William G., ed. & tr. see Corneille, Pierre.

Clubbe, John. Cincinnati Observed: Architecture & History. LC 91-9446. (Urban Life & Urban Landscape Ser.). (Illus.). 531p. 1992. pap. text 29.50 (*0-8142-0514-3*) Ohio St U Pr.

— Victorian Forerunner: The Later Career of Thomas Hood. LC 68-28520. 275p. reprint ed. 85.30 (*0-8357-9120-3*, 201789300010) Bks Demand.

Clubbe, John & Meckier, Jerome, eds. Victorian Perspectives. LC 88-40132. 200p. 1989. 35.00 (*0-87413-350-5*) U Delaware Pr.

Clubbe, John, ed. see Hood, Thomas.

Clube, S. V., et al, eds. Dynamics & Evolution of Minor Bodies with Galactic & Geological Implications. LC 92-23368. 1992. text 218.00 (*0-7923-1933-8*) Kluwer Academic.

Clubhouse Ministries Staff. Clubhouse Ministries Celebration & Outreach Resource Book: 32 Ways to Energize Your Clubhouse. (Illus.). 70p. (Orig.). 1993. pap., wbk. ed. 3.95 (*0-89827-122-3*, CHP01) Wesleyan Pub Hse.

— Clubhouse Ministries Champions Club: Year "A" & "B" (Illus.). 375p. (J). (gr. 5-6). 1993. ring bd. 21.95 (*0-89827-117-7*, CHD05) Wesleyan Pub Hse.

— Clubhouse Ministries Champions Club Member's Guide. (Illus.). 14p. (Orig.). (J). (gr. 5-6). 1993. pap. 1.05 (*0-89827-115-0*, CHP20) Wesleyan Pub Hse.

— Clubhouse Ministries Directors' Guide. (Illus.). 34p. (Orig.). 1993. pap. 3.25 (*0-89827-124-X*, CHW12) Wesleyan Pub Hse.

— Clubhouse Ministries Discovery Club: First Grade. (Illus.). 196p. (J). (gr. 1). 1993. ring bd. 21.95 (*0-89827-109-6*, CHD01) Wesleyan Pub Hse.

— Clubhouse Ministries Discovery Club: Fourth Grade. (Illus.). 208p. (J). (gr. 4). 1993. ring bd. 21.95 (*0-89827-112-6*, CHD04) Wesleyan Pub Hse.

— Clubhouse Ministries Discovery Club: Second Grade. (Illus.). 200p. (J). (gr. 2). 1993. ring bd. 21.95 (*0-89827-110-X*, CHD02) Wesleyan Pub Hse.

— Clubhouse Ministries Discovery Club: Third Grade. (Illus.). 200p. (J). (gr. 3). 1993. ring bd. 21.95 (*0-89827-111-8*, CHD03) Wesleyan Pub Hse.

— Clubhouse Ministries Discovery Club Chapels. (Illus.). 256p. (Orig.). (J). 1993. ring bd. 5.50 (*0-89827-120-7*, CHP24) Wesleyan Pub Hse.

— Clubhouse Ministries Discovery Club Member's Guide. (Illus.). 14p. (Orig.). (J). (gr. 1-4). 1993. pap. 1.05 (*0-89827-113-4*, CHP19) Wesleyan Pub Hse.

— Clubhouse Ministries Friendship Club: Year "A" & Year "B" (Illus.). 320p. (J). 1993. ring bd. 21.95 (*0-89827-116-9*, CHD00) Wesleyan Pub Hse.

— Clubhouse Ministries Friendship Club Member's Guide. (Illus.). 14p. (Orig.). (J). 1993. pap. 1.05 (*0-89827-114-2*, CHP18) Wesleyan Pub Hse.

— Clubhouse Ministries Staff Orientation Guide. (Illus.). 52p. (Orig.). 1993. pap., wbk. ed. 2.75 (*0-89827-125-8*, CHP00) Wesleyan Pub Hse.

— Clubhouse Ministries Summertime Resource Book. (Illus.). 34p. (Orig.). 1993. pap. 3.25 (*0-89827-121-5*, CHW05) Wesleyan Pub Hse.

Clubley, B. G., ed. Chemical Inhibitors for Corrosion Control. 142p. (C). 1990. text 93.00 (*0-85186-836-3*) CRC Pr.

Clubley, Sally. Trading in Oil Futures. 2nd ed. 144p. 1990. 42.95 (*0-89397-360-2*) Nichols Pub.

— Trading in Oil Futures & Options. 160p. 1998. 125.00 (*1-85573-387-0*, Pub. by Woodhead Pubng) Am Educ Systs.

Clucas, Humphrey. Through Time & Place to Roam: Essays on A. E. Housman. 67p. pap. write for info. (*3-7052-0435-1*, Pub. by Poetry Salzburg) Intl Spec Bk.

Clucas, Lowell, ed. The Byzantine Legacy in Eastern Europe. (East European Monographs). 1988. 59.50 (*0-88033-127-5*, Pub. by East Eur Monographs) Col U Pr.

Clucas, Richard A. Encyclopedia of American Political Reform. LC 96-26176. 346p. 1996. lib. bdg. 65.00 (*0-87436-855-3*) ABC-CLIO.

— The Speaker's Electoral Connection: Willie Brown & the California Assembly. LC 94-23863. 173p. (Orig.). (C). 1995. pap. 12.95 (*0-87772-361-3*) UCB IGS.

Cluchey, David P. & Seitzinger, Michael D. Maine Criminal Practice, 3 vols., Set. 2nd ed. 1500p. 1994. spiral bd. 185.00 (*1-56257-317-9*, 81615-10, MICHIE) LEXIS Pub.

Cluck. Microsoft Word: Tutorial & Applications. (DF - Computer Applications Ser.). 1990. mass mkt. 24.95 (*0-538-60385-2*) S-W Pub.

— Microsoft Word a Practical Approach. (DF - Computer Applications Ser.). (C). 1990. mass mkt., wbk. ed. 33.95 (*0-538-60389-5*) S-W Pub.

— Using Word for Windows. 1992. teacher ed. 39.06 (*0-07-036589-X*) McGraw.

Cluck, Bob. How to Hit/How to Pitch. (Illus.). 144p. 1995. pap. 12.95 (*0-8092-3640-0*, 364000, Contemporary Bks) NTC Contemp Pub Co.

— Play Better Baseball. 2nd ed. (Illus.). 248p. 1998. pap. 16.95 (*0-8092-2921-8*, 292180, Contemporary Bks) NTC Contemp Pub Co.

Cluck, Darrell W., et al. Facing the Music: Faith & Meaning in Popular Songs. 160p. 1998. pap. 14.99 (*0-8272-1022-1*) Chalice Pr.

Cluck, Nancy A., ed. Literature & Music: Essays on Form. LC 81-1070. viii, 258p. 1981. pap. 9.95 (*0-8425-1943-2*, Friends of the Library) Brigham.

Clue, K. Electric Power Technology: Emerging Technologies & New Applications of Old Technologies. 30p. 1994. 15.00 (*0-614-06941-6*) NARUC.

Cluet, S. & Hull, R., eds. Database Programming Languages: 6th International Workshop, DBPL-6, Estes Park, Colorado, U. S. A., August 18-20, 1997. (Lecture Notes in Computer Science Ser.: Vol. 1369). xiii, 431p. 1998. pap. 67.00 (*3-540-64823-2*) Spr-Verlag.

Cluett. Winemaking at Home. 1983. pap. 2.95 (*0-88266-289-9*) Storey Bks.

Cluett, D., et al. Croydon Airport: The Great Days, 1928-1939. 1988. pap. 35.00 (*0-9503224-8-2*, Pub. by Sutton Libs & Arts) St Mut.

Cluett, Douglas. Croydon Airport: The Australian Connection - Flights & Other Links Between Croydon Airport & Australia. (C). 1985. pap. 60.00 (*0-907335-17-9*, Pub. by Sutton Libs & Arts) St Mut.

Cluett, Douglas & Warshaw, Jack. Frank R. Dickson & Little Holland House. (C). 1985. pap. 30.00 (*0-9503224-0-7*, Pub. by Sutton Libs & Arts) St Mut.

Cluett, Douglas, et al. Croydon Airport & the Battle for Britain, 1939 to 1940, Vol. III. (C). 1985. pap. 35.00 (*0-907335-11-X*, Pub. by Sutton Libs & Arts) St Mut.

Cluett, Robert. Canadian Literary Prose: A Preliminary Stylistic Atlas. 200p. (C). 1990. text 26.00 (*1-55022-096-9*, Pub. by ECW) Genl Dist Srvs.

— Canadian Literary Prose: A Preliminary Stylistic Atlas. (Illus.). 200p. (C). 1990. pap. text 16.00 (*1-55022-098-5*, Pub. by ECW) Genl Dist Srvs.

Cluett, Robert E. George Jones Ceramics, 1861-1951. LC 97-45952. (Illus.). 288p. 1998. pap. 49.95 (*0-7643-0470-4*) Schiffer.

Cluett, William R., jt. auth. see Wang, Liuping.

Cluff, B., jt. auth. see Ashcroft, G.

Cluff, E. Dale. Microforms. Duane, James E., ed. LC 80-21457. (Instructional Media Library: Vol. 7). (Illus.). 104p. 1981. 27.95 (*0-87778-167-2*) Educ Tech Pubns.

Cluff, E. Dale, ed. Library Education & Employer Expectations. LC 89-24511. (Journal of Library Administration: Vol. 11, Nos. 3-4). (Illus.). 242p. 1990. text 49.95 (*0-86656-896-4*) Haworth Pr.

Cluff, Janet L., ed. see Cluff, Lloyd, et al.

***Cluff, Lawrence D.** Risk-Based Capital: Regulatory & Industry Approaches to Capital & Risk. (Illus.). 186p. (C). 2000. reprint ed. pap. text 30.00 (*0-7881-8670-1*) DIANE Pub.

Cluff, Leighton E., jt. ed. see Binstock, Robert H.

***Cluff, Lloyd, et al.** Lijiang, Yunnan Province, China, Earthquake, February 3, 1996: Reconnaissance Report. Cluff, Janet L., ed. (Illus.). 34p. 1998. pap. 15.00 (*0-943198-66-6*, 98-01) Earthquake Eng.

Cluff, Mike. Political Prisms. (Illus.). 46p. (Orig.). 1994. 5.95 (*1-878116-33-9*) JVC Bks.

Cluff, Russel, ed. see Rojas, Gonzalo.

Cluff, Russell M., tr. see Samperio, Guillermo.

Cluff, Sheila & Brown, Eleanor. The Ultimate Recipe for Fitness. (Illus.). 192p. 1990. pap. 14.95 (*0-9618805-3-8*); pap. 14.95 (*0-9618805-4-6*) Fitness Ojai.

Clugston, M. J. Penguin Dictionary of Science. LC 99-179482. 880p. 1998. pap. 26.99 (*0-14-051271-3*) Viking Penguin.

***Clugston-Major, Chynna.** Blue Monday: The Kids Are Alright. Rich, Jamie S., ed. (Illus.). 120p. 2000. pap. 10.95 (*1-929998-07-4*) Oni Pr Inc.

Cluisus, C. Fungorum in Pannoniis Observatorum Brevis Hist. & Codex Clusii. 1983. pap. 375.00 (*963-05-3186-0*, Pub. by Akade Kiado) St Mut.

Cluley. Structural Analysis. (C). 1999. pap. text, teacher ed. write for info. (*0-673-97644-0*) Addison-Wesley.

— Stuctural Analysis. (C). 1999. text. write for info. (*0-673-98291-2*) Addson-Wesley Educ.

Cluley, J. C. Reliability in Instrumentation & Control. LC 92-21340. (Industrial Instrumentation Ser.). (Illus.). 208p. 1993. 75.00 (*0-7506-0737-8*) Buttrwrth-Heinemann.

Clulow, C. F. To Have & to Hold: Marriage, the First Baby, & Preparing Couples for Parenthood. 168p. 1982. text 21.00 (*0-08-028470-1*, Pergamon Pr); pap. text 12.00 (*0-08-028471-X*, Pergamon Pr) Elsevier.

Clulow, Christopher, ed. Marriage: Disillusion & Hope: Papers Celebrating Forty Years of the Tavistock Institute of Marital Studies. 128p. 1990. reprint ed. pap. text 21.95 (*0-946439-93-1*, Pub. by H Karnac Bks Ltd) Brunner-Mazel.

— Partners Becoming Parents. 1997. pap. 19.95 (*0-7657-0024-7*) Aronson.

Clulow, Christopher, ed. Rethinking Marriage: Public & Private Perspectives. 157p. 1993. pap. text 25.00 (*1-85575-046-5*, Pub. by H Karnac Bks Ltd) Other Pr LLC.

Clulow, Christopher, ed. Women, Men, & Marriage: Talks from the Tavistock Marital Studies Institute. LC 96-1115. 176p. 1996. pap. 23.95 (*1-56821-819-2*) Aronson.

***Clum.** Still Acting Gay: Male Homosexuality in Modern Drama. LC 00-21499. 336p. 2000. pap. 15.95 (*0-312-22384-6*) St Martin.

Clum, Franklin D. Inebriety: Its Causes, Its Results, Its Remedy. Grob, Gerald N., ed. LC 80-1217. (Addiction in America Ser.). 1981. reprint ed. lib. bdg. 23.95 (*0-405-13573-4*) Ayer.

Clum, J. A. & Haas, Larry A., eds. Microbiological Effects on Metallurgical Processes: Proceedings of the Metallurgical Society. LC 85-28541. (Illus.). 173p. reprint ed. pap. 53.70 (*0-608-17840-3*, 203260200080) Bks Demand.

Clum, John. Escaping Kansas. (Illus.). 36p. 1995. mass mkt. 3.95 (*1-58193-008-9*) Brown Bag Prods.

Clum, John C. Acting Gay: Male Homosexuality in Modern Drama. (Illus.). 300p. 1992. 46.00 (*0-231-07510-3*) Col U Pr.

***Clum, John M.** Something For the Boys: Musical Theater & Gay Culture. LC 99-25435. (Illus.). 320p. 1999. text 26.95 (*0-312-21058-2*) St Martin.

Clum, John M., ed. Landmarks of Gay Drama. 1996. text 65.00 (*0-8133-2502-1*) Westview.

— Landmarks of Gay Drama. (C). 1996. pap. text 19.95 (*0-8133-2503-X*) Westview.

Clum, Woodworth. Apache Agent: The Story of John P. Clum. LC 77-14135. (Illus.). 313p. reprint ed. pap. 97.10 (*0-8357-5649-1*, 202791300057) Bks Demand.

Clumeck, N. & Friedland, G. Handbook of Medical Supportive Care of AIDS Patients. (Basic & Clinical Oncology Ser.). Date not set. write for info. (*0-8247-9299-8*) Dekker.

Clumpher, Bruce, ed. 1995-1996 Irvine Spectrum Business Directory. rev. ed. 184p. 1995. pap. text 39.95 (*0-9639578-1-3*) Coris Quill.

Clumpner, Bruce. 1997-1998 Irvine Spectrum Business Directory. 4th ed. 1997. pap. 39.95 (*0-9639578-3-X*, 97-001) Coris Quill.

Clumpner, Bruce, ed. 1999-2000 Irvine Spectrum Business Directory. (Illus.). 160p. Date not set. 39.95 (*0-9639578-5-6*) Coris Quill.

Clumpner, Bruce, ed. Irvine Spectrum Business. 208p. 1993. pap. text 49.95 (*0-9639578-0-5*) Coris Quill.

— 1996-1997 Irvine Spectrum Business Directory. 128p. 1996. spiral bd. 39.95 (*0-9639578-2-1*) Coris Quill.

Clumpner, Mike. The Broncbuster. 220p. (Orig.). 1980. mass mkt. 1.95 (*0-89083-671-X*, Zebra Kensgtn) Kensgtn Pub Corp.

Clunas, Craig. Art in China. (Oxford History of Art). (Illus.). 256p. 1997. pap. 16.95 (*0-19-284207-2*) OUP.

— Art in China. (Oxford History of Art Ser.). (Illus.). 256p. (C). 1997. 39.95 (*0-19-284244-7*) OUP.

— Chinese Furniture. (Illus.). 119p. 1997. 45.00 (*1-878529-23-4*) Art Media Resources.

— Fruitful Sites: Garden Culture in Ming Dynasty China. LC 95-44802. (Illus.). 240p. 1996. pap. text 19.95 (*0-8223-1795-8*) Duke.

— Fruitful Sites: Garden Culture in Ming Dynasty China. LC 95-44802. (Illus.). 240p. (C). 1996. text 49.95 (*0-8223-1800-8*) Duke.

— Pictures & Visuality in Early Modern China. LC 97-22449. 248p. 1998. text 39.50 (*0-691-05761-3*, Pub. by Princeton U Pr) Cal Prin Full Svc.

Clune, Henry W. The Genesee. text. write for info. (*0-8053-1240-4*) H Holt & Co.

Clune, Henry W. The Genesee. (Illus.). 347p. (C). 1988. reprint ed. pap. text 17.95 (*0-8156-2436-0*) Syracuse U Pr.

Clune, William, jt. ed. see Witte, John F.

Cluney, Jack. Eclipse of Intent (Deceit of Darkness) (Illus.). 128p. 1997. pap. 18.95 (*0-9661639-0-7*) Light Hse Proj.

Clunie, Gloria Bond, see Bond Clunie, Gloria.

Clunie, Gordon J. A. Textbook of Surgery. 1997. 95.00 (*0-86793-353-4*) Blackwell Sci.

Clunies-Ross, Anthony & Sudar, Petar, eds. Albania's Economy in Transition & Turmoil: Policies, Adaptations & Reactions, 1990-1997. LC 98-73406. 2p. 1998. text 63.95 (*1-84014-563-3*, Pub. by Ashgate Pub) Ashgate Pub Co.

Clunies, Sandra, ed. Laam in the Treatment of Opiate Addiction: A Treatment Improvement Protocal. 66p. (C). 1999. pap. text 20.00 (*0-7881-7592-0*) DIANE Pub.

— Planning for Alcohol & Other Drug Abuse Treatment for Adults in the Criminal Justice System. 116p. (C). 1999. pap. text 25.00 (*0-7881-7594-7*) DIANE Pub.

— Treatment Drug Courts: Integrating Substance Abuse Treatment with Legal Case Processing. 65p. (C). 1999. pap. text 20.00 (*0-7881-7593-9*) DIANE Pub.

Clunies, Sandra, jt. ed. see Barry, Kristen Lawton.

Clunies, Sandra, jt. ed. see Marsh, Anna.

Clunies, Sandra, jt. ed. see Miller, William R.

***Clunis, D. Merilee & Green, G. Dorsey.** Lesbian Couples: A Guide to Creating Healthy Relationships. 3rd ed. 288p. 2000. pap. 15.95 (*1-58005-041-7*, Pub. by Seal Pr WA) Publishers Group.

Clunis, D. Merilee & Green, G. Dorsey. The Lesbian Parenting Book: A Guide to Creating Families & Raising Children. LC 95-14905. 396p. (Orig.). 1995. pap. 16.95 (*1-878067-68-0*) Seal Pr WA.

Cluny, Claude M. Un Jeune Homme de Venise. (FRE.). 1983. pap. 11.95 (*0-7859-1972-4*, 2070374602) Fr & Eur.

Clurman, Harold. The Fervent Years: The Group Theatre & the Thirties. (Quality Paperbacks Ser.). (Illus.). 352p. 1983. reprint ed. pap. 13.95 (*0-306-80186-8*) Da Capo.

— Ibsen. (Quality Paperbacks Ser.). 238p. 1989. pap. 10.95 (*0-306-80365-8*) Da Capo.

— On Directing. LC 96-46762. 1997. per. 15.00 (*0-684-82622-4*, Fireside) S&S Trade Pap.

Clurman, Harold, ed. Nine Plays of the Modern Theater: Waiting for Godot; The Visit; Tango; The Caucasian Chalk Circle; The Balcony; Rhinoceros; American Buffalo; The Birthday Party; Rosencrantz & Guildenstein are Dead. LC 79-52121. 912p. 1981. pap. 21.00 (*0-8021-5032-2*, Grove) Grove-Atltic.

Clurman, Richard M. Beyond Malice: The Media's Years of Reckoning. 256p. 1988. 44.95 (*0-88738-234-7*) Transaction Pubs.

Clusener-Godt, M. & Sachs, I., eds. Brazilian Perspectives of Sustainable Development of the Amazon Region. LC 94-24324. (Man & the Biosphere Ser.: Vol. 15). (Illus.). 330p. (C). 1995. text 68.00 (*1-85070-576-3*) Prthnon Pub.

Clusener Godt, Miguel. Statistische Analysen Zur Beziehung Von Naehrelementen in Pflanze und Boden Am Natuerlichen Standort in Globaler Hinsicht. (Dissertationes Botanicae Ser.: Band 135). (GER., Illus.). iv, 105p. 1989. pap. 42.00 (*3-443-64047-8*, Pub. by Gebruder Borntraeger) Balogh.

Clusius, Carolus. Plant & Floral Woodcuts for Designers & Craftsmen. Menten, Theodore, ed. LC 74-77539. (Illus.). 184p. 1974. pap. 10.95 (*0-486-20722-6*) Dover.

Cluskey, William M. & Moss, Peter. The Uniform Business Rate: A Practical Guide. 250p. 1995. pap. 90.00 (*1-86012-050-4*, Pub. by Tolley Pubng) St Mut.

Cluster, Dick, jt. auth. see Institute for Policy Studies, Working Group on Hou.

Cluster, Dick, tr. see Diaz, Alejandro H.

Cluster, Dick, tr. see Ponte, Antonio Jose.

Cluster, Dick, tr. see Yanez, Mirta, ed.

Cluster, Grace. The Heart of Hiroshima. LC 97-30525. 132p. 1997. pap. 14.95 (*0-7734-2850-X*, Mellen Poetry Pr) E Mellen.

— Ups & Downs. LC 93-30581. (Lewiston Poetry Ser.: Vol. 21). 64p. 1993. pap. 14.95 (*0-7734-2791-0*, Mellen Poetry Pr) E Mellen.

Clute, J. J. Annals of Staten Island, from Its Discovery to the Present Time. LC 86-11962. (Illus.). 516p. 1986. reprint ed. lib. bdg. 35.00 (*0-932334-79-2*, NY43025) Hrt of the Lakes.

***Clute, J. J.** Old Families of Staten Island. 103p. 2000. reprint ed. pap. 16.00 (*0-8063-4768-6*, Pub. by Clearfield Co) ACCESS Pubs Network.

Clute, John. The Book of End Times: Grappling with the Millennium. LC 99-16603. (Illus.). 256p. 1999. 30.00 (*0-06-105033-4*, HarperPrism) HarpC.

— The Encyclopedia of Fantasy. LC 98-50905. 1088p. 1999. pap. 29.95 (*0-312-19869-8*) St Martin.

Clute, John. Look at the Evidence: Essays & Reviews. 465p. 1996. 30.00 (*0-934933-05-7*); pap. 15.00 (*0-934933-06-5*) Serconia Pr.

Clute, John. Strokes: Essays & Reviews, 1966-1986. 178p. 1988. 16.95 (*0-934933-03-0*) Serconia Pr.

Clute, John & Grant, John, eds. The Encyclopedia of Fantasy. LC 96-37472. 1100p. 1997. text 75.00 (*0-312-15897-1*) St Martin.

Clute, John & Nicholls, Peter. The Encyclopedia of Science Fiction. 1995. pap. 29.95 (*0-312-13486-X*, St Martin Griffin) St Martin.

Clute, John & Nicholls, Peter, eds. The Encyclopedia of Science Fiction. LC 92-47048. 1408p. 1993. text 75.00 (*0-312-09618-6*) St Martin.

Clute, John, et al. Interzone: The 1st Anthology : New Science Fiction & Fantasy Writing. LC 86-185999. (Everyman Paperbacks Ser.). ix, 210 p. 1985. 3.95 (*0-460-02294-6*) J M Dent & Sons.

Clute, John, ed. see Nodier, Charles.

Clute, Robin & Andersen, Sigrid. Carob Primer. (Illus.). 64p. 1997. pap. 3.95 (*0-685-42999-7*) Creat Arts Bk.

— Juel Andersen's Carob Primer. 56p. (Orig.). 1983. pap. 3.95 (*0-916870-60-X*) Creat Arts Bk.

Clute, Sylvia. Destiny. Charles, Rodney & Pasco, Elizabeth, eds. LC 97-66695. 275 p. 1997. 21.95 (*1-887472-21-5*) Sunstar Pubng.

Clute, Tom, jt. auth. see Fritz, Jean.

Cluts, Nancy W. Programming the Windows 95 User Interface: A Practical Insider's Guide to Coding the New UI Features. (Programming Ser.). 408p. 1995. pap. 34.95 incl. cd-rom (*1-55615-884-X*) Microsoft.

Clutter, Christopher L. Motta: Upward. (Illus.). 125p. (Orig.). 1995. mass mkt. 13.30 (*0-9644321-3-7*) Camel Dung Writ.

— Sondereinheiten: Special Purpose. (Illus.). 168p. (Orig.). 1995. mass mkt. 13.30 (*0-9644321-2-9*) Camel Dung Writ.

Clutter, Christopher L. & Bennett, Legro. 1995 Dung Annual: The Year of the Newet. 90p. 1995. mass mkt. 13.30 (*0-9644321-1-0*) Camel Dung Writ.

Clutter, Christopher L., et al. 1994 Dung Annual: Collector's Issue. (Illus.). 62p. 1994. mass mkt. 13.30 (*0-9644321-0-2*, CDWC) Camel Dung Writ.

Clutter, Jerome L., et al. Timber Management: A Quantitative Approach. LC 92-11878. 352p. (C). 1992. reprint ed. lib. bdg. 54.50 (*0-89464-747-4*) Krieger.

Clutter, Martha T. & Peterson, John C. Calculator Activities for the TI-85 to Accompany Peterson, Technical Mathematics, 2E, & Technical Mathematics with Calculus, 2E. LC 97-22205. 1997. write for info. (*0-8273-8385-1*) Delmar.

Clutter, Pat, ed. see Corona, Gyl.

Clutter, Patricia, ed. see Neely, Keith.

Clutterbuck. Art of Teaching Grammar. 1989. pap. text. write for info. (*0-582-66285-0*, Pub. by Addison-Wesley) Longman.

— The Art of Teaching Spelling. Date not set. pap. text. write for info. (*0-582-86842-4*, Pub. by Addison-Wesley) Longman.

Clutterbuck, D. & Voss, C. A. Just-in-Time Worldwide Lessons from Japan, U. S. A., Britain, & Europe. 140p. 1989. 142.50 (*0-387-51011-7*) Spr-Verlag.

***Clutterbuck, David.** Everyone Needs a Mentor: Fostering Talent at Work. 128p. 2000. pap. 32.95 (*0-8464-5052-6*) Beekman Pubs.

Clutterbuck, David. Everyone Needs a Mentor: Fostering Talent at Work. 96p. (C). 1991. pap. text 59.00 (*0-85292-461-5*, Pub. by IPM Hse) St Mut.

***Clutterbuck, David.** Learning Alliances: Tapping into Talent. 160p. 2000. pap. 56.95 (*0-8464-5103-4*) Beekman Pubs.

— Mentoring & Diversity. 224p. 2001. 47.95 (*0-7506-4836-8*) Buttrwrth-Heinemann.

Clutterbuck, David. Mentoring Executives & Directors. 167p. 1999. text 39.95 (*0-7506-3695-5*) Buttrwrth-Heinemann.

***Clutterbuck, David & Dearlove, Des.** The Interim Manager: A New Career Model for the Experienced Manager. 223p. 1999. pap. 42.50 (*0-273-63293-0*, Pub. by Pitman Pbg) Trans-Atl Phila.

C

Clutterbuck, David & Dearlove, Desmond. Raising the Profile: Marketing the HR Function. 160p. 1993. 45.00 (0-85292-526-3, Pub. by IPM Hse) St Mut.

Clutterbuck, David & Megginson, David. Mentoring in Action: A Practical Guide for Managers. LC 96-144452. 240p. 1995. 49.95 (0-7494-1390-5, Pub. by Kogan Pg) Nichols Pub.

Clutterbuck, David & Waine, Peter. The Independent Board Director: Balance on the Board - Finding, Choosing & Using Non-Executive Directors. LC 93-24571. 1993. 24.95 (0-07-707801-2) McGraw.

Clutterbuck, Ivan. Marginal Catholics. 304p. 1993. pap. 14.95 (0-85244-234-3, 947, Pub. by Gracewing) Morehouse Pub.

Clutterbuck, Mary. Animals & Birds of the Desert. (Butterfly Bks.). 32p. (J). (gr. 3-5). 1985. 9.95 (0-86685-445-2) Intl Bk Ctr.

Clutterbuck, Richard. Drugs, Crime, & Corruption: Thinking the Unthinkable. LC 95-13890. 256p. (C). 1995. text 45.00 (0-8147-1524-9); pap. text 18.50 (0-8147-1529-X) NYU Pr.

— Guerrillas & Terrorists. LC 80-83219. 125p. 1980. reprint ed. 14.95 (0-8214-0590-X) Ohio U Pr.

Clutton-Brock, Alan. Blake. LC 77-119438. (Studies in Blake: No. 3). 1970. reprint ed. lib. bdg. 75.00 (0-8383-1055-9) M S G Haskell Hse.

Clutton-Brock, Alan F., et al. Necessity of Art. LC 78-93366. (Essay Index Reprint Ser.). 1977. 19.95 (0-8369-1364-7) Ayer.

Clutton-Brock, Alan F., jt. ed. see Marvin, Francis S.

Clutton-Brock, Arthur. Essays on Art. LC 68-22906. (Essay Index Reprint Ser.). 1977. 11.95 (0-8369-0314-5) Ayer.

— Essays on Books. LC 68-29198. (Essay Index Reprint Ser.). 1977. reprint ed. 18.95 (0-8369-0316-1) Ayer.

— Essays on Life. LC 75-121455. (Essay Index Reprint Ser.). 1977. 19.95 (0-8369-1702-2) Ayer.

— Essays on Literature & Life. LC 68-54339. (Essay Index Reprint Ser.). 1977. 19.95 (0-8369-0317-X) Ayer.

— Essays on Religion. LC 79-84302. (Essay Index Reprint Ser.). 1977. 18.95 (0-8369-1078-8) Ayer.

— More Essays on Books. LC 68-57313. (Essay Index Reprint Ser.). 1977. 18.95 (0-8369-0315-3) Ayer.

— More Essays on Religion, Pt. 2. LC 76-156632. (Essay Index Reprint Ser.). 1977. reprint ed. 20.95 (0-8369-2349-9) Ayer.

— Shakespeare's Hamlet. LC 76-52923. (Studies in Shakespeare: No. 24). 1977. reprint ed. lib. bdg. 75.00 (0-8383-2133-X) M S G Haskell Hse.

— Shelley the Man & the Poet. 1977. 18.95 (0-8369-7106-X, 7940) Ayer.

Clutton-Brock, Juliet. Caballos. 1995. 18.95 (84-372-3766-1) Santillana.

***Clutton-Brock, Juliet.** Cat. (Eyewitness Books). (J). (gr. 4-7). 2000. 15.95 (0-7894-5752-0) DK Pub Inc.

Clutton-Brock, Juliet. Cats, Ancient & Modern. LC 93-19128. (Illus.). 96p. 1993. text 18.00 (0-674-10407-2) HUP.

***Clutton-Brock, Juliet.** Dog. (Eyewitness Books). (J). (gr. 4-7). 2000. 15.95 (0-7894-5774-1) DK Pub Inc.

Clutton-Brock, Juliet. Dog. LC 91-10135. (Eyewitness Books). (Illus.). 64p. (YA). (gr. 5 up). 1991. lib. bdg. 20.99 (0-679-91459-5, Pub. by Knopf Bks Yng Read) Random.

***Clutton-Brock, Juliet.** Horse. (Eyewitness Books). (J). (gr. 4-7). 2000. 15.95 (0-7894-5772-5) DK Pub Inc.

Clutton-Brock, Juliet. Horse Power: A History of the Horse & Donkey in Human Societies. (Illus.). 192p. 1992. text 29.95 (0-674-40646-X) HUP.

***Clutton-Brock, Juliet.** A Natural History of Domesticated Mammals. 2nd ed. (Illus.). 232p. (C). 1999. 90.00 (0-521-63247-1); pap. 39.95 (0-521-63495-4) Cambridge U Pr.

Clutton-Brock, Juliet. The Walking Larder: Patterns of Domestication, Pastoralism, & Predation. (One World Archaeology Ser.: No. 2). 384p. (C). 1990. text 75.00 (0-685-46017-7) Routledge.

Clutton-Brock, Juliet, jt. auth. see Hall, Stephen J.

Clutton-Brock, T. H. The Evolution of Parental Care. (Illus.). 330p. 1991. pap. text 29.95 (0-691-02516-9, Pub. by Princeton U Pr) Cal Prin Full Svc.

— Reproductive Success: Studies of Individual Variation in Contrasting Breeding Systems. (Illus.). 512p. 1988. pap. text 35.00 (0-226-11059-1); lib. bdg. 90.00 (0-226-11058-3) U Ch Pr.

Clutton-Brock, T. H., et al. Red Deer: Behavior & Ecology of 2 Sexes. LC 81-22025. (Wildlife Behavior & Ecology Ser.). (Illus.). 400p. (C). 1982. pap. text 26.00 (0-226-11057-5) U Ch Pr.

Clutton-Brock, Tim & Ball, Martim. Rhum: The Natural History of an Island. 160p. 1987. 35.00 (0-85224-513-0, Pub. by Edinburgh U Pr) Col U Pr.

Cluysenaar, Anne. Timeslips: New & Selected Poems. LC 97-216631. 144p. 1997. pap. 16.95 (1-85754-267-3, Pub. by Carcanet Pr) Paul & Co Pubs.

Cluysenaer, O. J. & Van Tongeren, J. H. Malabsorption in Coeliac Sprue. 1977. pap. text 141.50 (90-247-2000-1) Kluwer Academic.

Clyatt, Oscar W., Jr. Bulgaria's Quest for Security after the Cold War. 107p. (C). 1996. reprint ed. pap. text 25.00 (0-7881-3505-8) DIANE Pub.

Clyburn, Phyllis. It Is Finished. 180p. 1999. pap. 15.75 (0-7392-0075-5, PO2927) Morris Pubng.

Clyde, Ahmad. Cheng Ho's Voyage. LC 81-66951. (Illus.). 32p. (Orig.). (J). (gr. 3-7). 1981. pap. 2.50 (0-89259-021-1) Am Trust Pubns.

Clyde, Art, jt. auth. see Bressler, Karen W.

Clyde, Arthur, ed. The Language of the New Century Hymnal. 64p. 1995. pap. 5.00 (0-8298-1156-7) Pilgrim OH.

Clyde, Arthur G., ed. see Duck, Ruth C.

Clyde, Arthur G., jt. ed. see Throckmorton, Burton H.

Clyde, Barbara. If Giraffes Wore Necklaces. LC 98-23118. (Illus.). 32p. (J). (gr. 3-6). 1998. 9.95 (1-56492-251-0) Laredo.

Clyde C. Cone & Associates Staff. God, Why Me? Cancer. LC 88-92761. 137p. (Orig.). 1989. teacher ed. 5.95 (0-317-93541-0); pap. 7.95 (0-9621961-0-X) C C Cone.

Clyde, Craig & Hennesey, James. Wind Dancer. 135p. (J). 1997. pap. 14.95 (1-57901-003-2) Intl Promotions.

Clyde, Jean A. & Condon, Mark W. Get Real: Bringing Kids' Learning Lives into Your Classroom. LC 99-27083. 1999. 19.50 (1-57110-056-3) Stenhse Pubs.

Clyde, Jean A., jt. ed. see Mills, Heidi.

Clyde, John C. Genealogies, Necrology & Reminiscences of the "Irish Settlement" 421p. 1998. reprint ed. pap. 31.00 (0-7884-1020-2, C491) Heritage Bk.

Clyde, L. Anne. Managing Infotech in School Library Media Centers. LC 99-33116. 275p. 1999. pap. 35.00 (1-56308-724-3) Libs Unl.

Clyde, Laurel A. School Libraries & the Electronic Community: The Internet Connection. LC 97-14506. 368p. 1997. pap. 24.95 (0-8108-3193-7) Scarecrow.

Clyde, Laurel A., ed. Sustaining the Vision: A Collection of Articles & Papers on Research in School Librarianship. 331p. 1996. pap. 35.00 (0-931510-65-1) Hi Willow.

— Sustaining the Vision: A Collection of Articles & Papers on Research in School Librarianship. 331p. 1996. 35.00 (0-614-31081-4) IASL.

Clyde, Marianne. You Are One in a Million! The Art of Asking Questions That Produce Results. 144p. 1995. pap. write for info. (0-9649278-0-2) May Day Press.

Clyde, Mary. Survival Rates. pap. 13.95 (0-393-32084-7) Norton.

Clyde, Mary. Survival Rates: Stories. LC 98-19074. 1999. 24.95 (0-8203-2049-8) U of Ga Pr.

Clyde, Monica, jt. auth. see Di Donato, Robert.

Clyde, Norman. Closeups of the High Sierra. rev. ed. Benti, Wynne, ed. LC 97-46658. (Illus.). 176p. 1998. mass mkt. 14.95 (0-9647530-3-0) Spotted Dog CA.

Clyde, Paul & Beers, Burton. The Far East: A History of Western Impacts & Eastern Responses, 1830-1975. 6th ed. (Illus.). 545p. (C). 1991. reprint ed. pap. text 34.95 (0-88133-612-2) Waveland Pr.

***Clyde, Tom.** Millenial Dogs on Main Street: Another Litter. 160p. 1999. pap. 13.95 (0-9668829-1-1) Giardia Springs.

Clydesdale. Father Knows Best. 1997. pap., teacher ed. 59.95 (3-10-053673-8); pap., ring bd. 6.00 (3-10-052081-5) Word Enter.

— I Stand in Awe. 1996. pap. 7.00 (3-10-051781-4) Word Enter.

— Make Us One. 1995. pap. 6.95 (3-10-051301-0) Word Enter.

Clydesdale, Fergus S. Food Science & Nutrition: Current Issues & Answers. (Illus.). 1979. 22.95 (0-685-03860-2) P-H.

Clygout, Sanivar H. Sexology Encyclopedia Vol. 10: Homosexuality: Index & Reference Books of New Information. Bartone, John C., ed. (Illus.). 155p. 1996. pap. 39.95 (0-7883-0869-6) ABBE Pubs Assn.

— Sexology Encyclopedia Vol. 10: Homosexuality: Index & Reference Books of New Information, 25 vols., Set. Bartone, John C., ed. (Illus.). 155p. 1996. 49.95 (0-7883-0868-8) ABBE Pubs Assn.

Clyman, H. J. Jet Propulsion & Gas Turbines in Aviation. (Technical Papers: Vol. P253). (Illus.). 22p. 1946. pap. text 30.00 (1-55589-455-0) AGMA.

Clyman, Jacky, tr. see Lhote, Gilles.

Clyman, Jeff, tr. see Lhote, Gilles.

Clyman, Toby W. Russia Through Women's Eyes: Autobiographies from Tsarist Russia. (Illus.). 408p. 1999. pap. text 18.00 (0-300-06754-2) Yale U Pr.

Clyman, Toby W., ed. A Chekhov Companion. LC 84-29024. (Illus.). 347p. 1985. lib. bdg. 75.00 (0-313-23423-X, CHC/, Greenwood Pr) Greenwood.

Clyman, Toby W. & Greene, Diana. Women Writers in Russian Literature, 53. LC 93-21143. (Contributions to the Study of World Literature Ser.: No. 53). 312p. 1994. 75.00 (0-313-27521-1, Greenwood Pr) Greenwood.

Clyman, Toby W. & Greene, Diana, eds. Women Writers in Russian Literature. LC 93-21143. 312p. 1994. pap. 22.95 (0-275-94941-9, Praeger Pubs) Greenwood.

Clyman, Toby W. & Vowles, Judith, eds. Russia Through Women's Eyes: Autobiographies from Tsarist Russia. LC 96-16374. (Illus.). 352p. 1996. 35.00 (0-300-06753-4) Yale U Pr.

Clymer. Edward Kennedy: Biography. 1999. write for info. (0-201-62665-9) Addison-Wesley.

— Great Chefs of San Francisco. LC 83-45980. (Illus.). 108p. 1989. pap. 9.95 (0-929714-02-4) Great Chefs TV.

— Honda CB550 & 650, 1983-1985. (Illus.). 312p. Date not set. reprint ed. pap. 28.95 (0-89287-420-1, M345) Intertec Pub.

Clymer & Amico. Proceedings on Conference on Simulators V. (Simulation Ser.: Vol. 19, No. 4). 488p. 1988. 40.00 (0-911801-34-0, SS19-4) Soc Computer Sim.

Clymer, et al. Massachusetts Estate Planning, Will Drafting & Estate Administration Forms, 2 vols., Vol. 1 & 2. 2nd ed. 2000p. 1998. lib. bdg. 280.00 (0-327-00797-4, 8147311); lib. bdg. write for info. (0-327-00798-2, 8147311); lib. bdg. write for info. (0-327-00799-0, 8147311); lib. bdg. write for info. (0-327-00800-8, 8147311) LEXIS Pub.

***Clymer, Adam.** Edward M. Kennedy: A Biography. 720p. 2000. pap. 16.00 (0-06-095787-5, Perennial) HarperTrade.

— Edward M. Kennedy: A Biography. LC 99-39768. (Illus.). 704p. 1999. 27.50 (0-688-14285-0, Wm Morrow) Morrow Avon.

Clymer, Carolyn. Computer Shorthand: Theory Reinforcement Exercises. (Computer Shorthand Ser.). (C). 1992. text 17.99 (1-881086-12-7) Middle Wasley.

Clymer, Eleanor. My Mother Is the Smartest Woman in the World. LC 82-1685. (Illus.). 96p. (J). (gr. 4-6). 1982. 13.95 (0-689-30916-3) Atheneum Yung Read.

— Santiago's Silver. (J). 1995. pap. 3.50 (0-440-91083-8) BDD Bks Young Read.

Clymer, Emerson M. Gifts of the Spirit. 67p. (Orig.). 1976. pap. 5.00 (0-932785-74-3) Philos Pub.

— Gifts of the Spirit: The Doctor Within. 44p. 1976. pap. 2.50 (0-916285-50-2) Humanitarian.

— A Reason for Being. 116p. 1971. 6.95 (0-932785-42-5); pap. 2.95 (1-891485-00-8) Philos Pub.

Clymer, Emerson M., ed. see Randolph, Paschal B.

Clymer, Jeane, et al. Festival of Poetry Bk. 2: An Anthology from Members of Margaret Tyler's Scottsdale Library Workshop. 64p. (Orig.). 1990. pap. 9.75 (0-9622775-1-7) Tyler-Balstrode.

Clymer, John H., Jr., et al. Massachusetts Estate Planning, Will Drafting, & Estate Administration Forms, 1989-1993, 2 vols., Set. LC 92-43737. 1420p. 1994. spiral bd. 270.00 (0-8342-0061-9, 81473-10, MICHIE) LEXIS Pub.

Clymer, John J., et al. Massachusetts Estate Planning, Will Drafting, & Estate Administration Forms, 1989-1993. 224p. 1994. ring bd., suppl. ed. 85.00 (0-614-03151-6, MICHIE) LEXIS Pub.

Clymer, Kenton J. Protestant Missionaries in the Philippines, 1898-1916: An Inquiry into the American Colonial Mentality. LC 85-1278. (Illus.). 284p. 1986. text 29.95 (0-252-01210-0) U of Ill Pr.

— Quest for Freedom: The United States & India's Independence. LC 94-22120. 393p. 1995. 57.50 (0-231-10044-2); pap. text 22.00 (0-231-10045-0) Col U Pr.

— The Vietnam War: Its History, Literature & Music. LC 97-62483. 195p. 1999. pap. 15.00 (0-87404-277-1) U of Tex Pr.

Clymer, Mark & Mechoso, Carlos, eds. Mission Earth: Modeling & Simulation for a Sustainable Global System. 96p. 1997. pap. 60.00 (1-56555-106-0, ME-97) Soc Computer Sim.

Clymer Publications Staff. BMW K-Series, 1985-1995. 2nd ed. LC 94-79863. (Illus.). 744p. 1996. pap. 39.95 (0-89287-648-4, M500) Intertec Pub.

— BMW R-Series, 1970-1994. LC 94-75602. (Illus.). 792p. Date not set. reprint ed. pap. 39.95 (0-89287-624-7, M502) Intertec Pub.

***Clymer Publications Staff.** Evinrude/Johnson 2-Stroke Outboard Shop Manual 2-70 HP 1995-1998 (Includes Jet Drive Models) LC 98-75605. 784p. 1998. pap. 36.95 (0-89287-704-9) Intertec Pub.

Clymer Publications Staff. Harley-Davidson Sportsters Evolution, 1959-1985. (Illus.). 384p. Date not set. reprint ed. pap. 28.95 (0-89287-126-1, M419) Intertec Pub.

— Honda CB750 SOHC, 1969-1978: CB 750SOHC Fours, 1969-1978. 8th ed. (Illus.). 224p. Date not set. reprint ed. pap. 28.95 (0-89287-167-9, M341) Intertec Pub.

— Honda CR60R-125 Pro-Link, 1981-1988: Service Manual. (Illus.). 344p. Date not set. reprint ed. pap. 26.95 (0-89287-463-5, M442) Intertec Pub.

— Honda FL1500 Gold Wing, 1988-1992. LC 93-77122. (Illus.). 880p. 1993. pap. 49.95 (0-89287-593-3, M505) Intertec Pub.

***Clymer Publications Staff.** Honda VFR/700F-750F, 1986-1994. LC 97-75347. 576p. 1998. pap. text 28.95 (0-89287-711-1) Intertec.

Clymer Publications Staff. Honda VT500, 1983-1988. 1993. 25.95 (0-89287-589-5, M344) Clymer Pub.

— Honda XL - XR 500-600, 1979-1993: Service Manual. (Illus.). (Orig.). 1993. pap. 25.95 (0-89287-591-7, M339) Clymer Pub.

— Honda XL-XR 250-350, XR 200R, 1984-85: Service Manual. (Illus.). (Orig.). 1990. 25.95 (0-89287-524-0, M328) Clymer Pub.

— Kawasaki EX500/GPZ500S, 1987-1993. 2nd ed. LC 93-77123. (Illus.). 232p. 1994. reprint ed. pap. 28.95 (0-89287-596-8, M360) Intertec Pub.

— Mercruiser Stern Drive Shop Manual 1995-1997 Alpha One, Bravo One, Bravo Two & Bravo Three. LC 97-78083. (Illus.). 712p. 1997. 36.95 (0-89287-697-2) Intertec Pub.

— Mercury Outboard Shop Manual 3-275 HP, 1990-1993. LC 92-74933. (Illus.). 640p. 1993. pap. 36.95 (0-89287-568-2, B722) Intertec Pub.

— Mercury 3.9-135 hp Outboards, 1964-1971. pap. 34.95 (0-89287-414-7, B719) Clymer Pub.

— Mercury/Mariner Outboard Shop Manual 2.5-60 HP 1994-1997 (Includes Jet Drive Models) LC 98-72832. 712p. 1998. pap. 36.95 (0-89287-698-0) Intertec Pub.

— Mercury/Mariner 2-Stroke Outboard Shop Manual 75-275 HP 1994-1997 (Includes Jet Drive Models) LC 98-72837. (Illus.). 824p. 1998. pap. write for info. (0-89287-707-3) Intertec Pub.

— Suzuki 380-750cc, 1972-1977: 380-750cc Triples, 1972-1977 Service, Repair, Maintenance. 4th ed. (Illus.). 160p. Date not set. reprint ed. pap. 28.95 (0-89287-285-3, M368) Intertec Pub.

— Vintage Japanese Street Bikes. LC 92-74938. (Collection Series Vintage Dirt Bikes). (Illus.). 624p. 1993. pap. 29.95 (0-89287-588-7, M305) Intertec Pub.

— Yamaha 80-175 Piston-Port, 1968-1976: 80-175cc Piston Port Singles, 1968-1976. 4th ed. (Illus.). 168p. Date not set. reprint ed. pap. 26.95 (0-89287-235-7, M410) Intertec Pub.

— Yamaha PW50 Y-Zinger, PW80 Y-Zinger & BW80 Big Wheel, 1981-1998. LC 98-72833. (Illus.). 416p. 1998. pap. 26.95 (0-89287-708-1) Intertec Pub.

— Yamaha 250-400cc Piston-Port, 1968-1976. 4th ed. (Illus.). 168p. Date not set. reprint ed. pap. 26.95 (0-89287-276-4, M415) Intertec Pub.

— Yamaha 2-225hp 2-Stroke Outboards, 1984-1989. (Illus.). 480p. Date not set. reprint ed. pap. 36.95 (0-89287-498-8, B783) Intertec Pub.

— Yamaha Water Vehicles, 1987-1992. 2nd ed. (Illus.). 400p. 1994. reprint ed. pap. 36.95 (0-89287-594-1, W805) Intertec Pub.

Clymer Publications Staff, jt. auth. see Price, Brick.

Clymer, R. S. The Age of Treason: Health & Fitness. 396p. 1957. lthr. 20.00 (0-916285-43-X) Humanitarian.

— La Cultura Prenatal: Coma Crear al Hijo Perfecto por la Influencia Prenatal. Aparis, Fina, tr. (SPA.). 173p. 1950. pap. 4.95 (0-916285-46-4) Humanitarian.

— Diet: A Key to Health. xviii, 209p. 1966. 10.95 (0-916285-47-2) Humanitarian.

— Diet: A Key to Health. xviii, 209p. 1983. pap. 6.95 (0-916285-48-0) Humanitarian.

— Making Health Certain. 192p. 1921. 15.00 (0-916285-51-0) Humanitarian.

— Natura Physician. 300p. 1932. 15.00 (0-916285-52-9) Humanitarian.

— Nature's Healing Agents: The Medicines of Nature. xx, 256p. 1963. lthr. 20.00 (0-916285-54-5) Humanitarian.

— Prenatal Culture: How to Create the Perfect Baby. (Illus.). 144p. 1950. 4.95 (0-916285-56-1) Humanitarian.

Clymer, R. Swinburne. Ancient Mystic Oriental Masonry. 193p. 1996. reprint ed. spiral bd. 16.00 (0-7873-0183-3) Hlth Research.

— Ancient Mystic Oriental Masonry: Its Teachings, Rules, Laws & Present Usages Govern the Order at the Present Day (1907) 193p. 1996. reprint ed. pap. 15.95 (1-56459-725-3) Kessinger Pub.

— The Beautiful Philosophy of Life. 1998. reprint ed. pap. 22.50 (0-7873-1135-9) Hlth Research.

— Book of Rosicruciae, 3 Vols., Set. 853p. 1949. 29.50 (0-932785-61-1) Philos Pub.

— The Book of Rosicruciae, Vol. I. xxxviii, 286p. 1946. 10.95 (0-932785-03-4) Philos Pub.

— The Book of Rosicruciae, Vol. II. xxxii, 279p. 1947. 10.95 (0-932785-64-6) Philos Pub.

— The Book of Rosicruciae, Vol. II. deluxe ed. xxxii, 279p. 1947. lthr. 20.00 (0-932785-63-8) Philos Pub.

— The Book of Rosicruciae, Vol. III. xxxii, 288p. 1949. 10.95 (0-932785-66-2) Philos Pub.

— The Book of Rosicruciae, Vol. III. deluxe ed. xxxii, 288p. 1949. lthr. 20.00 (0-932785-65-4) Philos Pub.

— Christisis. x, 233p. 1945. 10.95 (0-932785-67-0) Philos Pub.

— A Compendium of Occult Laws. 311p. 1966. 10.95 (0-932785-08-5) Philos Pub.

— The Divine Law of Mastership (1922) 230p. 1998. reprint ed. pap. 17.95 (0-7661-0134-7) Kessinger Pub.

— Dr. P. B. Randolph in France. 52p. 1929. 10.00 (0-932785-72-7) Philos Pub.

— Las Ensenanzas Hermeticas. (SPA.). 48p. 1962. pap. 2.75 (0-932785-58-1) Philos Pub.

— Fraternitas Rosae Crucis. 221p. 1929. 10.95 (0-932785-11-5) Philos Pub.

— The Great Work, 4 vols., Set. Incl. Great Work: Spiritual Initiation. 270p. 1961. 8.95 (0-932785-12-3); Great Work: The Coming Masters. 280p. 1962. 8.95 (0-932785-13-1); Great Work: The Council of Three. 306p. 1963. 8.95 (0-932785-14-X); Greatwork: Its Neophytes. 285p. 1964. 8.95 (0-932785-15-8); 1141p. 1964. 34.00 (0-932785-75-1) Philos Pub.

— The Great Work Series, 4 vols. deluxe ed. 1141p. 1964. lthr. 70.00 (0-932785-76-X) Philos Pub.

— The Hidden Teachings of the Initiate Masters. 267p. 1957. 10.95 (0-932785-80-8) Philos Pub.

— The Hidden Teachings of the Initiate Masters. deluxe ed. 267p. 1957. 20.00 (0-932785-81-6) Philos Pub.

— Higher Race Development: A Course of Instructions on the Right Use of Sex (1919) 168p. 1996. reprint ed. pap. 13.95 (1-56459-665-6) Kessinger Pub.

Clymer, R. Swinburne. The Initiates & the People, 1928-1932, 5 vols. Incl. Vol. I. Initiates & the People. 204p. 1933. reprint ed. 10.00 (0-932785-18-2); Vol. II. Initiates & the People. 208p. 1933. reprint ed. 10.00 (0-932785-19-0); Vol. III. Initiates & the People. 200p. 1933. reprint ed. 10.00 (0-932785-20-4); Vol. IV. Initiates & the People. 192p. 1933. reprint ed. 9.95 (0-932785-21-2); Vol. V. Initiates & the People., s 207p. 1933. reprint ed. 9.95 (0-932785-22-0); 1928. reprint ed. 44.95 (0-932785-86-7) Philos Pub.

Clymer, R. Swinburne. The Interpretation of St. John. 266p. 1953. 10.95 (0-932785-23-9) Philos Pub.

— The Interpretation of St. John. deluxe ed. 266p. 1953. lthr. 20.00 (0-932785-87-5) Philos Pub.

Clymer, R. Swinburne. The Interpretation of St. Matthew, 2 vols. Incl. Vol. I. Interpretation of St. Matthew. 285p. 1945. 10.95 (0-932785-24-7); Vol. II. Interpretation of St. Matthew. 284p. 1945. 10.95 (0-932785-25-5); 560p. 1945. 19.95 (0-932785-88-3) Philos Pub.

Clymer, R. Swinburne. The Living Christ: The Christic Teachings. 58p. 1979. reprint ed. pap. 2.95 (0-932785-27-1) Philos Pub.

— Making Health Certain (1921) 190p. 1998. reprint ed. pap. 14.95 (0-7661-0503-2) Kessinger Pub.

— Manual of the Church of Illumination. 100p. 1952. 5.95 (0-932785-28-X) Philos Pub.

— Manual of the Church of Illumination. deluxe ed. 100p. 1952. 20.00 (0-932785-89-1) Philos Pub.

— Mastership: The Divine Law. 256p. 1949. 9.95 (0-932785-30-1) Philos Pub.

— Mastership: The Divine Law. deluxe ed. 256p. 1949. lthr. 20.00 (0-932785-92-1) Philos Pub.

— Los Misterios de Osiris: La Iniciacion del Antiguo Egipto. 2nd ed. 278p. 1978. pap. 8.95 (0-932785-57-3) Philos Pub.

— The Mysteries of Osiris: Egyptian Initiation. 287p. 1951. 10.95 (0-932785-31-X) Philos Pub.

An Asterisk (*) at the beginning of an entry indicates that the title is appearing for the first time.

C

Coad, Peter. Business Object Models. (C). 2000. text 35.00 (*0-13-396433-7*) P-H.

— Field Guide to Object Technology. (Illus.). 1996. 24.95 (*0-614-20321-X*) P-H.

— A Field Guide to Object Technology. 96p. (C). 2000. 24.95 (*0-13-456633-5*, Macmillan Coll) P-H.

***Coad, Peter.** Java Modeling Color With Uml: Enterprise Components & Process. LC 99-16018. 221p. 1999. 49.99 (*0-13-011510-X*, Prentice Hall) P-H.

Coad, Peter. Managers & Objects: Why Bother? (C). 1999. pap. 20.25 (*0-13-555103-X*) P-H.

— Object Oriented Analysis. 2nd ed. 233p. 1990. 62.00 (*0-13-629981-4*) P-H.

Coad, Peter & Mayfield, Mark. Java Design. 1997. pap. 39.95 incl. cd-rom (*0-614-28522-4*, Yourdon) P-H.

Coad, Peter & Nicola, Jill. Object-Oriented Programming: The Rest of the Story. 582p. (C). 1993. 65.00 (*0-13-032616-X*) P-H.

Coad, Peter & Yourdan, Edward. Object Oriented Design. (Yourdon Press Computing Ser.). 197p. 1991. 46.60 (*0-13-630070-7*, Yourdon) P-H.

Coad, Peter, et al. Object Models: Strategies, Patterns, & Applications. 2nd ed. LC 97-109726. (Illus.). 544p. (C). 1996. pap. 58.00 (*0-13-840117-9*) P-H.

Coade, Neil. Be Creative: The Toolkit for Business Success. LC 97-5200. (Smart Strategies Ser.). 200p. 1997. pap. 19.99 (*1-86152-087-5*) Thomson Learn.

— Managing International Business. LC 97-5330. (Self-Development for Managers Ser.). 104p. 1997. pap. 14.99 (*0-415-13919-8*) Thomson Learn.

Coady, C. A. Testimony. 336p. 1992. 59.00 (*0-19-824786-9*) OUP.

— Testimony: A Philosophical Study. 326p. 1995. pap. text 24.00 (*0-19-823551-8*) OUP.

***Coady, Chantal.** Chocolate. (Evergreens Ser.). 1998. 16.99 (*3-8228-7569-4*) Benedikt Taschen.

Coady, James & Huckin, Thomas, eds. Second Language Vocabulary Acquisition: A Rationale for Pedagogy. (Applied Linguistics Ser.). (Illus.). 309p. (C). 1996. text 59.95 (*0-521-56132-9*); pap. text 24.95 (*0-521-56764-5*) Cambridge U Pr.

Coady, Margaret & Bloch, Sidney. Codes of Ethics & the Professions. 240p. 1997. pap. 29.95 (*0-522-84701-3*, Pub. by Melbourne Univ Pr) Paul & Co Pubs.

Coady, Michael. All Souls. LC 98-138581. 128p. 1998. 26.95 (*1-85235-212-4*, Pub. by Gallery Pr); pap. 16.95 (*1-85235-211-6*, Pub. by Gallery Pr) Dufour.

— Oven Lane. 74p. 1992. pap. 12.95 (*1-85235-020-2*) Dufour.

Coady, Nick, jt. auth. see Lehmann, Peter.

***Coady, Tony, ed.** Why Universities Matter: A Conversation about Values, Means & Directions. 272p. 2000. pap. 24.95 (*1-86508-038-1*, Pub. by Allen & Unwin Pty) Paul & Co Pubs.

Coaker, J. F., et al. Wille & Millin's Mercantile Law of South Africa. 18th ed. 952p. 1984. write for info. (*0-7021-7347-9*, Pub. by Juta & Co); suppl. ed. write for info. (*0-7021-8173-0*, Pub. by Juta & Co) Gaunt.

***Coakes, Elayne, et al, eds.** The New Sociotech: Graffiti on the Long Wall. LC 99-50084. (Computer Supported Cooperative Work Ser.). 225p. 2000. pap. 69.95 (*1-85233-040-6*, Pub. by Spr-Verlag) Spr-Verlag.

Coakes, Michelle. Creative Pottery: A Step-by-Step Guide & Showcase. (Illus.). 144p. 1998. pap. 24.99 (*1-56496-315-2*, Quarry Bks) Rockport Pubs.

***Coakes, Roger L. & Sellors, Patrick Holmes.** Outline of Opthalmology. (Illus.). 192p. 2000. pap. 40.00 (*0-7506-4460-5*) Buttrwrth-Heinemann.

Coakley, jt. auth. see Wolvi.

***Coakley, C. William.** The Complete Student Planner & Teacher-Parent Communicator. 50p. 2000. wbk. ed. 25.00 (*0-9676641-1-X*) Academic Coach.

— A Smart Students Guide to Selected College Admissions: A Workbook for High Achievers. 84p. 1998. wbk. ed. 30.00 (*0-9676641-0-1*) Academic Coach.

Coakley, Carolyn G. Teaching Effective Listening: A Practical Guide for the High School Classroom. (Illus.). 1993. text 39.95 (*1-877936-01-4*) SPECTRA Inc.

— Teaching Effective Listening: A Practical Guide for the High School Classroom, Vol. 1. LC 98-96395. (Illus.). viii, 311p. 1993. ring bd. 39.95 (*0-9666249-0-4*) Coakley Comm Conn.

— Teaching Effective Listening: A Practical Guide for the High School Classroom, Vol. 2. LC 98-96395. (Illus.). viii, 353p. 1996. ring bd. 39.95 (*0-9666249-1-2*) Coakley Comm Conn.

Coakley, Carolyn G., ed. Perspectives on Listening. LC 92-42454. 306p. 1993. pap. 39.50 (*0-89391-925-X*) Ablx Pub.

Coakley, Carolyn G. & Wolvin, Andrew D., eds. Experiential Listening: Tools for Teachers & Trainers. 104p. (Orig.). 1989. pap. 18.95 (*1-877936-00-6*) SPECTRA Inc.

Coakley, Carolyn G., jt. auth. see Wolvin, Andrew D.

Coakley, Carolyn G., jt. ed. see Wolvin, Andrew D.

Coakley, Carolyn Gwynn, jt. auth. see Wolvin, Andrew.

Coakley, Davis. Oscar Wilde: The Importance of Being Irish. (Illus.). 256p. 1996. pap. 13.95 (*1-57098-083-7*) Roberts Rinehart.

Coakley, J. F. The Church of the East & the Church of England. (Illus.). 432p. 1992. text 98.00 (*0-19-826744-4*) OUP.

***Coakley, Jay J.** A Coach's Guide to Social Issues. (Illus.). 192p. (C). 1999. pap. text 25.00 (*0-7637-1078-4*) JB Pubns.

Coakley, Jay J. & Donnelly, Peter. Inside Sports: Using Sociology to Understand Athletes & Sport Experiences. LC 98-36508. 1999. 75.00 (*0-415-17088-5*); pap. 24.99 (*0-415-17089-3*) Routledge.

Coakley, John. The Social Origins of Nationalist Movements: The Contemporary West European Experience. (Modern Politics Ser.: Vol. 31). 288p. (C). 1992. text 65.00 (*0-8039-8572-X*) Sage.

— The Territorial Management of Ethnic Conflict. LC 93-10948. (Regions & Regionalism Ser.: No. 2). 230p. 1993. text 42.50 (*0-7146-3465-4*, Pub. by F Cass Pubs) Intl Spec Bk.

***Coakley, John, ed.** The Territorial Management of Ethnic Conflict. 2nd ed. 256p. 1999. 52.50 (*0-7146-4988-0*); pap. 24.50 (*0-7146-8051-6*) F Cass Pubs.

***Coakley, John & Gallagher, Michael.** Politics in Republic of Ireland. 3rd ed. LC 99-31724. 392p. (C). 1999. text. write for info. (*0-415-22193-5*) Routledge.

— Politics in the Republic of Ireland. 3rd ed. LC 99-31724. 392p. 1999. pap. 22.99 (*0-415-22194-3*) Routledge.

***Coakley, John & Galligan, Yvonne.** The Rise of the Irish Presidency. 288p. 1999. pap. 24.95 (*1-85182-407-3*, Pub. by Four Cts Pr); boxed set 55.00 (*1-85182-406-5*, Pub. by Four Cts Pr) Intl Spec Bk.

Coakley, John, jt. ed. see Matter, E. Ann.

Coakley, Lynn, ed. Army Aviation's Leaders: Who Are They? Where Are They? 300p. (C). 1993. ring bd. 175.00 (*0-9629073-1-6*) Army Aviatn.

Coakley, Robert W. The Role of Federal Military Forces in Domestic Disorders, 1789-1878. (Illus.). 372p. 1996. reprint ed. text 50.00 (*0-7881-2818-3*) DIANE Pub.

Coakley, Sarah. Christ Without Absolutes: A Study of the Christology of Ernst Troeltsch. 224p. 1995. reprint ed. pap. text 21.00 (*0-19-826374-0*) OUP.

Coakley, Sarah, ed. Religion & the Body. (Cambridge Studies in Religious Traditions: No. 8). (Illus.). 330p. 1997. text 69.95 (*0-521-36669-0*) Cambridge U Pr.

***Coakley, Sarah, ed.** Religion & the Body. (Studies in Religious Traditions: Vol. 8). (Illus.). 330p. 2000. pap. text 24.95 (*0-521-78386-0*) Cambridge U Pr.

Coakley, Sarah & Pailin, David A., eds. The Making & Remaking of Christian Theology: Essays in Honour of Maurice Wiles. LC 92-42790. (Illus.). 304p. 1993. text 49.95 (*0-19-826739-8*) OUP.

Coakley, Thomas P., ed. C3I: Issues of Command & Control. (Illus.). 408p. (Orig.). (C). 1994. pap. text 50.00 (*0-7881-1115-9*) DIANE Pub.

Coakley, William A. Handbook of Automated Analysis: Continuous Flow Technique. LC 81-1330. (Illus.). 160p. reprint ed. pap. 49.60 (*0-608-08924-9*, 206955900005) Bks Demand.

Coal Industry Advisory Board Staff, jt. auth. see OECD Int Energy Agency Staff.

Coal Mines Committee Staff. Employment & Training with Reference to Health & Safety at Coal Mines: Proceedings of the Coal Mines Committee, 11th, Session, Geneva, 1982, Report II. vi, 166p. (Orig.). 1982. pap. 11.25 (*92-2-102869-0*) Intl Labour Office.

Coaldrake, Angela K. Women's Gidayu & the Japanese Theatre Tradition. LC 96-43188. (Nissan Institute/Routledge Japanese Studies Ser.). 288p. (C). 1997. audio compact disk 85.00 (*0-415-06334-5*) Routledge.

Coaldrake, Peter. On the Brink: Australia's Universities Confronting Their Future. LC 98-199972. 234p. 1998. pap. 29.95 (*0-7022-3050-2*, Pub. by Univ Queensland Pr) Intl Spec Bk.

— Working the System: Government in Queensland. 1989. pap. 15.95 (*0-7022-2230-5*, Pub. by Univ Queensland Pr) Intl Spec Bk.

Coaldrake, William. Architecture & Authority in Japan. LC 95-25129. (Nissan Institute/Routledge Japanese Studies Ser.). (Illus.). 360p. (C). 1996. 100.00 (*0-415-05754-X*); pap. 32.99 (*0-415-10601-X*) Routledge.

Coaldrake, William H. The Way of the Carpenter: Tools & Japanese Architecture. (Illus.). 220p. 1990. 35.00 (*0-8348-0231-7*) Weatherhill.

***Coale, Ansley J.** Ansley J. Coale: An Autobiography. LC 99-87224. (Memoirs of the American Philosophical Society Ser.). 2000. write for info. (*0-87169-236-8*) Am Philos.

Coale, Ansley J. The Growth & Structure of Human Populations: A Mathematical Investigation. LC 76-166365. (Illus.). 245p. reprint ed. pap. 76.00 (*0-8357-8894-6*, 203339300085) Bks Demand.

— Rapid Population Change in China, 1952-1982. LC 84-61188. (Committee on Population & Demography Report Ser.: Vol. 27). 103p. reprint ed. pap. 32.00 (*0-7837-2415-2*, 204255200005) Bks Demand.

Coale, Ansley J. & Zelnik, Melvin. New Estimates of Fertility & Population in the United States: A Study of Annual White Births from 1855 to 1960 & of Completeness of Enumeration in the Censuses from 1880-1960. LC 63-9989. 204p. 1963. reprint ed. pap. 63.30 (*0-7837-9320-0*, 206006000004) Bks Demand.

Coale, Ansley J., et al. Aspects of the Analysis of Family Structure. LC 65-14308. 262p. reprint ed. pap. 81.30 (*0-7837-0231-0*, 204053900017) Bks Demand.

— Human Fertility in Russia since the Nineteenth Century. LC 78-70284. 312p. reprint ed. pap. 96.80 (*0-8357-2698-3*, 204023900015) Bks Demand.

Coale, Ansley J., ed. see Conference on the Princeton European Fertility Pro.

Coale, Charles B. The Life & Adventures of Wilburn Waters: The Famous Hunter & Trapper of White Top Mountain. 86p. 1994. pap. 5.95 (*1-57072-003-7*) Overmountain Pr.

Coale, Helen W. The Vulnerable Therapist: Practicing Psychotherapy in an Age of Anxiety. LC 97-37272. 272p. 1998. 49.95 (*0-7890-0179-9*); pap. 24.95 (*0-7890-0480-1*) Haworth Pr.

Coale, John. Canoeing the California Highlands: A Quiet Water Guide to Paddler's Paradise. LC 98-96050. (Illus.). 136p. 1998. pap. 19.95 (*0-9662821-0-8*, B101) Changing Sky Pubns.

Coale, Joseph M. Middling Planters of Ruxton, Maryland, 1694-1850. LC 96-47364. 1997. 24.95 (*0-938420-56-9*) MD Hist.

Coale, Phil. FSU Football: An Inside Look. Norman, Chris, ed. 112p. (Orig.). 1992. pap. text 19.95 (*0-9613040-2-2*) Talla Dem.

Coale, Samuel. Mesmerism & Hawthorne: Mediums of American Romance. LC 97-10044. 224p. 1998. text 34.95 (*0-8173-0896-2*) U of Ala Pr.

***Coale, Samuel.** Mesmerism & Hawthorne: Mediums of American Romance. 216p. 2000. pap. text 19.95 (*0-8173-1038-X*) U of Ala Pr.

— The Mystery of Mysteries: Cultural Differences & Designs. LC 99-55806. 242p. 2000. 51.95 (*0-87972-813-2*); pap. 25.95 (*0-87972-814-0*) Bowling Green Univ Popular Press.

Coale, Samuel. William Styron Revisited. (Twayne's United States Authors Ser.: No. 577). 160p. (C). 1991. 32.00 (*0-8057-7619-2*) Macmillan.

Coale, Samuel C. In Hawthorne's Shadow: American Romance from Melville to Mailer. LC 84-25792. 255p. reprint ed. pap. 79.10 (*0-7837-5820-0*, 204548700006) Bks Demand.

Coaley, J. C. Rathbone Genealogy: A Complete History of the Rathbone Family, from 1574 to Date. (Illus.). 827p. 1989. reprint ed. pap. 124.00 (*0-8328-1003-7*); reprint ed. lib. bdg. 132.00 (*0-8328-1002-9*) Higginson Bk Co.

Coalition for Child Advocacy Staff. Touching. (Illus.). 32p. (Orig.). (J). (ps). 1985. pap. 5.95 (*0-934671-00-1*) Whatcom Cty Opp.

Coalition for Social Justice Staff, jt. see Canadian Centre for Policy Alternatives Staff.

Coalition on Women & Religion Staff. The Women's Bible: Study Guide. 1975. 5.95 (*0-9603042-2-3*) Coalition Women-Relig.

Coalson, Edward B., ed. Petrogenesis & Petrophysics of Selected Sandstone Reservoirs of the Rocky Mountain Region. (Illus.). 353p. 1989. 20.00 (*0-933979-12-6*) Rocky Mtn Assoc Geol.

Coalson, Glo, jt. auth. see Nobisso, Josephine.

Coalson, J. J., jt. auth. see Bland, R. D.

Coalson, John L., jt. auth. see Houghton, Kendall L.

Coalson, Lanette. Grandma's Favorite Recipes. 318p. 1992. 15.95 (*0-942407-22-9*) Father & Son.

Coalson, R. E. Embryology. (Oklahoma Notes Ser.). (Illus.). xi, 107p. (C). 1989. pap. 12.95 (*0-387-96334-0*, 9) Spr-Verlag.

— Embryology. 2nd ed. Tomasek, J., ed. (Oklahoma Notes Ser.). (Illus.). 128p. 1992. 12.95 (*0-387-97776-7*) Spr-Verlag.

Coalson, Sheri, ed. see Ettinger, Blanche & Ettinger, Alice.

Coalter, Fred. Freedom & Constraint: The Paradoxes of Leisure. (Comedia Bk.). 240p. 1989. text 57.50 (*0-415-00649-X*) Routledge.

Coalter, Fred, et al. Recreational Welfare. 220p. 1988. text 67.95 (*0-566-05665-8*, Pub. by Avebry) Ashgate Pub Co.

Coalter, Milton J., Jr. Gilbert Tennent, Son of Thunder: A Case Study of Continental Pietism's Impact on the First Great Awakening in the Middle Colonies, 18. LC 86-9967. (Contributions to the Study of Religion Ser.: No. 18). 247p. 1986. 59.95 (*0-313-25514-8*, CGI/) Greenwood.

Coalter, Milton J., et al, eds. The Confessional Mosaic: Presbyterians & Twentieth-Century Theology. (Presbyterian Presence Ser.). 228p. (Orig.). 1990. pap. 19.95 (*0-664-25151-X*) Westminster John Knox.

— The Mainstream Protestant "Decline" The Presbyterian Pattern. (Presbyterian Presence Ser.). 168p. (Orig.). 1990. pap. 19.95 (*0-664-25150-1*) Westminster John Knox.

— The Pluralistic Vision: Presbyterians & Mainstream Protestant Education & Leadership. (Presbyterian Presence Ser.). 320p. (Orig.). 1992. pap. 24.95 (*0-664-25243-5*) Westminster John Knox.

Coalter, Milton J., Jr., et al, eds. The Presbyterian Predicament: Six Perspectives. (Presbyterian Presence Ser.). 168p. (Orig.). 1990. pap. 19.95 (*0-664-25097-1*) Westminster John Knox.

Coalter, Milton J., et al, eds. The Re-Forming Tradition Study Guide: Presbyterians & Mainstream Protestantism. LC 92-12543. (Presbyterian Presence Ser.). (Orig.). 1992. pap. 5.95 (*0-664-25411-X*) Westminster John Knox.

Coalter, Milton J. & Cruz, Virgil, eds. How Shall We Witness? Faithful Evangelism in a Reformed Tradition. LC 94-36762. 192p. (Orig.). 1995. pap. 18.95 (*0-664-25575-2*) Westminster John Knox.

Coalter, Milton J., et al. The Re-Forming Tradition: Presbyterians & Mainstream Protestantism. (Presbyterian Presence Ser.). 256p. (Orig.). 1992. pap. 24.95 (*0-664-25299-0*) Westminster John Knox.

Coan, Alphonso. Devocionario. Nolte, Gilbert, tr. 1964. 0.50 (*0-8199-0504-6*, Frncscn Herld) Franciscan Pr.

***Coan, Catherine.** Aviation. (Working Signs Ser.). 48p. 2000. 15.00 (*0-911287-39-6*) Blue Begonia.

***Coan, Dara.** Healthy Fun for Kids: Creative Kids. (Illus.). 160p. 2000. pap. 14.95 (*1-57690-599-3*) Tchr Create Mat.

Coan, Eugene, jt. auth. see Keen, A. Myra.

Coan, Eugene, jt. auth. see Keen, Angeline M.

Coan, James S. Basic BASIC: An Introduction to Computer Programming in BASIC Language. 2nd ed. LC 77-14640. (Hayden Computer Programming Ser.). 269p. 1978. write for info. (*0-8104-5106-9*) Sams.

— Basic BASIC: An Introduction to Computer Programming in BASIC Language. 2nd ed. LC 77-14640. (Illus.). 1978. reprint ed. pap. text 17.95 (*0-9618346-0-9*) Longhouse Bks.

Coan, Julie. Digging into Archaeology: Hands-On - Minds-On Unit Study. (Illus.). 120p. (YA). (gr. 5-8). 1999. pap. 16.95 (*0-89455-718-1*, MP5801) Crit Think Bks.

Coan, Peter. Taxi, the Harry Chapin Story. LC 85-9125. 1987. 22.95 (*0-87949-262-7*) Ashley Bks.

Coan, Peter M. Ellis Island Interviews: In Their Own Words. LC 97-2892. (Illus.). 464p. 1997. 29.95 (*0-8160-3414-1*) Facts on File.

— World Tennis Magazine's Guide to the Best Tennis Resorts. 208p. (Orig.). 1991. pap. 10.95 (*0-8065-1272-5*, Citadel Pr) Carol Pub Group.

Coan, Peter Morton. Ellis Island Interviews: In Their Own Words. LC 97-2892. (Illus.). 464p. 1998. pap. 16.95 (*0-8160-3548-2*) Facts on File.

Coan, Richard. Psychologists: Personal & Theoretical Pathways. LC 79-13711. 224p. (C). 1979. text 22.50 (*0-8290-0858-6*) Irvington.

Coan, Richard W. Human Consciousness & Its Evolution: A Multidimensional View, 9. LC 86-31848. (Contributions in Psychology Ser.: No. 9). 197p. 1987. 42.95 (*0-313-25619-5*, CHN/, Greenwood Pr) Greenwood.

— Psychology of Adjustment: Personal Experience & Development. LC 82-13413. (Illus.). 568p. reprint ed. pap. 176.10 (*0-7837-3498-0*, 205783100008) Bks Demand.

Coan, Sharon. Newspapers. (Illus.). 15p. 1993. pap., teacher ed. 7.95 (*1-55734-138-9*) Tchr Create Mat.

Coan, Sharon, ed. see Bauer, Larry.

Coan, Sharon, ed. see Brown, Marzella.

Coan, Sharon, ed. see Larsen, Linda J.

Coar, Ken. Apache Server for Dummies. LC 97-80876. (For Dummies Ser.). 384p. 1998. pap. 29.99 incl. cd-rom (*0-7645-0291-3*) IDG Bks.

Coase, R. H. Essays on Economics & Economists. viii, 232p. 1995. pap. text 12.95 (*0-226-11103-2*) U Ch Pr.

Coase, R. H., ed. see Kessel, Reuben A.

Coase, Ronald H. Essays on Economics & Economists. 231p. 1996. 27.95 (*0-226-11102-4*) U Ch Pr.

— The Firm, the Market & the Law. LC 87-24193. (Illus.). 232p. 1988. 29.95 (*0-226-11100-8*) U Ch Pr.

— The Firm, the Market & the Law. LC 87-24193. (Illus.). 226p. 1990. pap. text 19.00 (*0-226-11101-6*) U Ch Pr.

Coast Community College Staff. Universe: The Infinite Front. (Astronomy Ser.). 250p. 1994. pap., student ed. 20.95 (*0-534-20610-7*) Wadsworth Pub.

Coast Community College Staff & Chow, Vic. Intro Biology S. F. 3rd ed. 896p. (C). 1995. text, student ed. 83.95 (*0-7872-0347-5*) Kendall-Hunt.

Coast, Geoffrey M. & Webster, Simon G., eds. Recent Advances in Arthropod Endocrinology. LC 97-21516. (Society for Experimental Biology Seminar Ser.: No. 65). (Illus.). 424p. (C). 1998. text 110.00 (*0-521-59113-9*) Cambridge U Pr.

Coast, J. Richard, et al. Exercise Physiology Video. 208p. (C). 1994. text 30.00 (*0-697-22395-7*) Brown & Benchmark.

— Exercise Physiology Video. 208p. (C). 1994. lab manual ed. write for info. incl. VHS (*0-697-22394-9*) Brown & Benchmark.

Coast, Joanna, et al, eds. Priority Setting: The Health Care Debate. LC 95-42635. 294p. 1996. 98.95 (*0-471-96102-7*) Wiley.

Coastal Discovery Museum Staff. Hilton Head Island, South Carolina. (Images of America Ser.). (Illus.). 128p. 1999. pap. 18.99 (*0-7385-0048-8*) Arcadia Publng.

Coastal Dynamics '97 Staff & Thornton, Edward B. Coastal Dynamics '97: Conference Proceedings LC 98-176828. xii, 1063p. 1998. 139.00 (*0-7844-0321-X*) Am Soc Civil Eng.

Coastal Engineering Conference Staff. Coastal Engineering Specialty Conference, Santa Barbara, October 1965. LC 66-7562. 1017p. reprint ed. pap. 200.00 (*0-608-15121-1*, 202083500019) Bks Demand.

Coastal Engineering Research Council, jt. auth. see Kraus, Nicholas C.

Coastal New England Publications Staff. Daisy's Dairy. 1997. pap. text 2.95 (*1-886862-23-0*) Harv Hill ME.

***Coastal Resources Center Staff, prod.** Coastal Resources Management Project II, 1999 Results: Increasing Conservation & Sustainable Use of Coastal Resources. (Coastal Management Report Ser.: Vol. 2222). (Illus.). 2000. pap. write for info. (*1-885454-30-9*, CRM II) Coastal Res.

Coastes, Ken & Topham, Tony, eds. One Big Union: Founding the Transport & General Workers Union. (Birth of the Modern Labour Movement Ser.). (C). 1992. 25.00 (*1-85041-063-1*, Pub. by Univ Nottingham) St Mut.

Coastline Community College Staff. Biology Telecourse. 3rd ed. (Biology Ser.). 1996. pap., student ed. 20.25 (*0-534-50452-3*) Wadsworth Pub.

Coastline Elderly Services Staff & Standard Times Staff. Flavors from the SouthCoast. LC 97-66396. (Illus.). 160p. 1997. 14.95 (*0-9657182-0-4*) Coastline Elderly.

Coat, Tom. A Cup of Controversy: The Intrigue Behind the Strangest America's Cup Ever. (Illus.). 120p. (Orig.). (C). 1988. pap. 16.95 (*0-9621245-0-8*) T Coat.

Coate, L. Edwin. CHANGE at UCSC.EDU: Managing a Comprehensive Change Effort. LC 95-51455. 1995. 45.00 (*1-56972-002-9*) NACUBO.

Coate, M. Letter-Book of John, Viscount Mordaunt, 1658-60. (Camden Third Ser.). 35.00 (*0-86193-069-X*) David Brown.

Coate, Malcolm B. & Kleit, Andrew N., eds. The Economics of the Antitrust Process. LC 96-15511. (Topics in Regulatory Economics & Policy Ser.: Vol. 22). 272p. (C). 1996. lib. bdg. 115.00 (*0-7923-9731-2*) Kluwer Academic.

Coate, Mary. Social Life in Stuart England. LC 77-109721. (Illus.). 188p. 1971. reprint ed. lib. bdg. 35.00 (*0-8371-4211-3*, COSL, Greenwood Pr) Greenwood.

Coate, Mary Anne. Clergy Stress. 1989. pap. 11.95 (0-687-85135-1) Abingdon.

Coate, Roger. United States Policy & the Future of the United Nations. 284p. 1993. pap. 14.95 (0-87078-175-8) Century Foundation.

Coate, Roger A. Global Issue Regimes. LC 82-11269. 218p. 1982. 57.95 (0-275-90772-4, C0772, Praeger Pubs) Greenwood.

Coates. Ethics of War. LC 97-5364. 304p. 1997. text 69.95 (0-7190-4045-0) St Martin.

Coates. International Justice. 61.95 (1-84014-945-0) Ashgate Pub Co.

Coates. Webquester: Race Ethnic Relationships. 1998. 10.00 (0-07-365794-8) McGraw.

***Coates & Breeze.** Delegating with Confidence. 48p. 2000. pap. 17.95 (0-8464-5027-5) Beekman Pubs.

Coates, jt. auth. see Anderson.

Coates, A. J., ed. Comparative Studies of Magnetospheric Phenomena: Proceedings of the D1 Symposium of COSPAR Scientific Commission D Which Was Held During the 30th COSPAR Scientific Assembly, Hamburg, Germany, 11-21 July, 1994. LC 95-223566. (Advances in Space Research Ser.: Vol. 16). 220p. 1995. pap. 104.00 (0-08-042624-7, Pergamon Pr) Elsevier.

Coates, A. Marijo, et al. Canadian Trademark Practice & Procedure. Zimmerman, Colleen S., ed. 152p. 1993. pap. 50.00 (0-939190-05-2) Intl Trademark.

Coates, Alan. English Medieval Books: The Reading Abbey Collections from Foundation to Dispersal. LC 98-37085. (Oxford Historical Monographs). (Illus.). 248p. 1999. text 70.00 (0-19-820756-5) OUP.

Coates, Albert & Paul, James C. School Segregation Decision: A Report to the Governor of North Carolina on the Decision of the Supreme Court of the United States on the 17th of May 1954. (Law & Government Ser.). x, 132p. 1981. reprint ed. 30.00 (0-8377-2607-7, Rothman) W S Hein.

***Coates, Anthony G., ed.** Central America: A Natural & Cultural History. (Illus.). 296p. 1999. pap. 17.95 (0-300-08065-4) Yale U Pr.

Coates, Anthony G., ed. see Paseo Pantera Project Staff.

Coates, Austin. Quick Tidings of Hong Kong. (Illus.). 216p. 1990. text 21.00 (0-19-584024-0) OUP.

Coates, Barbara. Growing Flowers & Foliage for Cutting. (Growing Ser.). (Illus.). 96p. (Orig.). 1994. pap. 13.95 (0-86417-545-0, Pub. by Kangaroo Pr) Seven Hills Bk.

— Making Dried Flower Arrangements. (Illus.). 72p. (Orig.). 1994. pap. 15.95 (0-86417-579-5) Seven Hills Bk.

Coates, Benjamin H. Annual Discourse, Delivered Before the Historical Society of Pennsylvania, on the 28th Day of April, 1834, on the Origin of the Indian Population of America. (LC History-America-E). 83p. 1999. reprint ed. lib. bdg. 69.00 (0-7812-4318-1) Rprt Serv.

Coates, Bradley A. Divorce with Decency: The Complete How-To Handbook & Survivor's Guide to the Legal, Emotional, Economic, & Social Issues. LC 98-8626. (Illus.). 208p. 1998. pap. 16.95 (0-8248-2122-X, Latitude Twenty) UH Pr.

— Divorce with Decency: The Complete How-To Handbook & Survivor's Guide to the Legal, Emotional, Economic, & Social Issues, Hawaii State Edition. LC 98-8625. (Illus.). 208p. 1998. pap. 16.95 (0-8248-2119-X, Latitude Twenty) UH Pr.

Coates, C. Robert. The Demand for Money by Firms. LC 75-11418. (Business Economics & Finance Ser.: No. 7). 191p. reprint ed. pap. 59.30 (0-8357-6087-1, 203452500090) Bks Demand.

Coates, Carrol F., ed. Repression & Expression: Literary & Social Coding in Nineteenth-Century France. (Studies on Themes & Motifs in Literature: Vol. 22). XV, 342p. (C). 1996. text 56.95 (0-8204-2844-2) P Lang Pubng.

Coates, Carrol F., tr. see Alexis, Jacques S.

Coates, Carrol F., tr. & afterword by see Aristide, Jean-Bertrand.

Coates, Carrol F., tr. & intro. see Alexis, Jacques S.

Coates, Carrol F., tr. & intro. see Depestre, Rene.

Coates, Charles. Professional's TV News Handbook. (Illus.). 285p. 1994. 29.95 (1-56625-006-4) Bonus Books.

***Coates, Charles.** Professional's TV News Handbook. 2000. pap. 29.95 (1-56625-148-6) Bonus Books.

Coates, Charles H. & Pellegrin, Roland J. Military Sociology. 1965. pap. text 14.95 (0-686-00733-6) Md Bk Exch.

Coates, Clive. Cote d'Or: A Celebration of the Great Wines of Burgundy. LC 97-14017. (Illus.). 1008p. 1997. 55.00 (0-520-21251-7, Pub. by U CA Pr) Cal Prin Full Svc.

***Coates, Clive.** An Encyclopedia of the Wines & Domaines of France. 608p. 2000. 60.00 (0-520-22093-5) U CA Pr.

Coates, Clive. Grands Vins: The Finest Chateaux of Bordeaux & Their Wines. (Illus.). 736p. 1995. 55.00 (0-520-20220-1, Pub. by U CA Pr) Cal Prin Full Svc.

— The Wines of France. (Illus.). 416p. 39.95 (0-932664-72-5, 6585) Wine Appreciation.

— The Wines of France. 2nd rev. ed. (Illus.). 436p. 1999. 50.00 (1-891267-14-0) Wine Appreciation.

***Coates, Colin M.** The Metamorphoses of Landscape & Community in Early Quebec. (Studies on the History of Quebec). 240p. 2000. 45.00 (0-7735-1896-7) McG-Queens Univ Pr.

Coates, D. R., jt. ed. see Higgins, C. G.

Coates, Dan. Coates Piano Duets Bk. 2: 1P/4H: Piano Arrangements Mixed Folio, Bk. 2. Esposito, Tony, ed. 52p. (C). 1983. pap. 7.95 (0-7692-1578-5, PF0173) Wrner Bros.

— 100 Top Hits of the 90's. 1998. pap. text 18.95 (0-7692-1513-0) Wrner Bros.

Coates, David. Labour in Power? A Study of the Labour Government 1974-1979. LC 79-42850. 316p. reprint ed. pap. 98.00 (0-608-13096-6, 202521800043) Bks Demand.

***Coates, David.** Models of Capitalism: Growth & Stagnation in the Modern Era. LC 99-32965. 312p. 2000. text 69.95 (0-7456-2058-2, Pub. by Polity Pr); pap. text 29.95 (0-7456-2059-0, Pub. by Polity Pr) Blackwell Pubs.

— New Labour into Power. pap. write for info. (0-7190-5462-1, Pub. by Manchester Univ Pr); text. write for info. (0-7190-5461-3, Pub. by Manchester Univ Pr) St Martin.

Coates, David, ed. Economic & Industrial Performance in Europe: A Report Prepared for the Centre for Industrial Policy & Performance, University of Leeds. LC 95-5518. 272p. 1995. 100.00 (1-85278-709-0) E Elgar.

Coates, David & Hillard, John. The Economic Decline of Modern Britain: The Debate Between Left & Right. LC 86-123447. xii, 386 p. 1986. write for info. (0-7450-0107-6) Wheatsheaf Bks.

Coates, Dennis E. & Bell, Meredith M. Self-Awareness. 42p. 1995. pap. text 10.00 (1-886713-07-3) Perform Support Systs.

Coates, Donald R., ed. Geomorphology & Engineering. (Binghamton Symposia in Geomorphology: International Ser.: No. 7). (Illus.). 384p. (C). 1980. text 75.00 (0-04-551040-7) Routledge.

— Glacial Gemorphology: Binghampton Symposia in Geomorphology. (International Ser.: No. 5). (Illus.). 304p. (C). 1981. text 90.00 (0-04-551045-8) Routledge.

— Landslides. LC 79-123343. (Reviews in Engineering Geology Ser.: No. 3). (Illus.). 264p. 1977. reprint ed. pap. 81.90 (0-608-00226-7, 206072900006) Bks Demand.

Coates, Donald R., ed. see Urban Geomorphology Symposium Staff.

Coates, Donna. Stevia: Miracle of No Calorie. 1997. pap. 10.00 (0-609-80131-7) Random Hse Value.

Coates, Earl J. & Thomas, Dean S. An Introduction to Civil War Small Arms. (Illus.). 96p. (YA). 1990. pap. text 7.95 (0-939631-25-3) Thomas Publications.

Coates, Eric J. Subject Catalogues: Headings & Structure. LC Z 0695.C645. (Illus.). 192p. reprint ed. pap. 59.60 (0-608-20961-9, 207183300002) Bks Demand.

Coates, F. G. & Bell, R. S. Marie Corelli: The Writer & the Woman. 1977. lib. bdg. 59.95 (0-8490-2208-8) Gordon Pr.

***Coates, Floyd.** Our Toilets Are Not for Customers: Who Are the Customers? How to Drive Customers Away. 192p. 2000. pap. 12.95 (0-9678624-0-X) Wing & Prayer IN.

Coates, G. E. & Wade, K. Organometallic Compounds, Vol. 1, Pt. 1, Groups I-III. 4th ed. 1985. text 75.00 (0-412-23120-4, NO. 6530) Chapman & Hall.

Coates, Gary & Sanker, Joyce. Ali Baba & the Thieves. 1982. pap. 4.95 (0-686-38754-6) Eldridge Pub.

Coates, Gary M., jt. auth. see Sanker, Joyce.

Coates, Geoffrey, ed. Hypoxia: Women & Altitude. (Illus.). 350p. (Orig.). 1997. pap. 40.00 (0-614-30287-0) C S Houston.

Coates, George L. Rhythm of Life Lines. 1998. pap. write for info. (1-57553-720-6) Watermrk Pr.

Coates, Gerald. Non-Religious Christianity. LC 99-163774. 1998. pap. 10.99 (1-56043-694-8, Revival Pr) Destiny Image.

Coates, Geraldine. Classic Gin. (Classic Drinks Ser.). (Illus.). 1999. 19.95 (1-85375-334-3, Pub. by Prion) Trafalgar.

Coates, Grace, tr. see Mayfield, Karen & Whitlow, Robert, eds.

Coates, Grace, tr. see Mayfield, Karen, et al, eds.

Coates, Grace, tr. see Stenmark, Jean, ed.

Coates, Grace D., jt. auth. see Stenmark, Jean K.

Coates, Grace S., ed. see Tucker, Patrick T.

Coates, Helen R. American Festival Guide: A Handbook of More Than 200 Colonial, Homesteading, Western, Spanish, Folk, Rodeo, Sports, Cultural, & Other Annual Festivals & Celebrations. LC 97-14598. 299p. 1997. reprint ed. lib. bdg. 44.00 (0-7808-0269-1) Omnigraphics Inc.

Coates, Henry. Knowledge for the People (Philosophy) (Illus.). 200p. 1995. pap. 25.00 (0-87556-791-6) Saifer.

— Palestrina: Music Book Index. 243p. 1993. reprint ed. lib. bdg. 79.00 (0-7812-9613-7) Rprt Serv.

Coates, Henry T., ed. Children's Book of Poetry. LC 70-149101. (Granger Index Reprint Ser.). 1977. 40.95 (0-8369-6226-5) Ayer.

— Fireside Encyclopedia of Poetry: Comprising the Best Poems of the Most Famous Writers, English & American. LC 79-160903. (Granger Index Reprint Ser.). 1977. reprint ed. 52.95 (0-8369-6266-4) Ayer.

Coates, Irene. The Seed Bearers. (C). 1989. text 49.00 (1-85821-040-2, Pub. by Pentland Pr) St Mut.

***Coates, Irene.** Who's Afraid of Leonard Woolf? A Case for the Sanity of Virginia Woolf. 2000. 25.00 (1-56947-222-X) Soho Press.

Coates, J. & Taylor, M. J., eds. L-Functions in Arithmetic. (London Mathematical Society Lecture Note Ser.: No. 153). 300p. (C). 1991. pap. text 49.95 (0-521-38619-5) Cambridge U Pr.

***Coates, J., et al.** Arithmetic Theory of Elliptic Curves: Lectures Given at the 3rd Session of the Centro Internazionale Matematico Estivo (C.I.M.E.), Held in Cetraro, Italy, July 12-19, 1997. Viola, C., ed. LC 99-48773. (Lecture Notes in Mathematics Ser.: Vol. 1716). viii, 260p. 2000. pap. 52.80 (3-540-66546-3) Spr-Verlag.

Coates, J. David. Bread for the Battle: A Collection of Articles from the Illinois District News. 100p. 1997. pap. 8.95 (0-9660378-0-4) Daco Pub.

Coates, J. Dennis. A Training Intervention for Control of SBA Loan Defaults. LC 92-33006. (Studies in Entrepreneurship). 136p. 1992. text 15.00 (0-8153-0992-9) Garland.

Coates, J. F., et al. The Trireme Trials, 1988. (Oxbow Monographs in Archaeology: No. 2). (Illus.). 108p. 1990. pap. 22.00 (0-946897-21-2, Pub. by Oxbow Bks) David Brown.

Coates, James. Armed & Dangerous: The Rise of the Survivalist Right. LC 87-9278. 294p. 1995. pap. 11.00 (0-8090-0174-8) Hill & Wang.

— In Mormon Circles: Gentiles, Jack Mormons, & Latter Day Saints. 1990. 22.07 (0-201-51758-2) Addison-Wesley.

— Photographing the Invisible. LC 72-9189. (Literature of Photography Ser.). 1973. reprint ed. 34.95 (0-405-04899-8) Ayer.

Coates, James, ed. see Ireland, David.

Coates, Janet. Spiritual Traits: A Four Week Study to Help Teenagers Explore God-given Traits. Swyers, Gary et al, eds. (Bible Basics Ser.). (Illus.). 32p. (Orig.). (YA). (gr. 6-12). 1992. pap., wbk. ed. 8.95 (0-89827-094-4, BKW14) Wesleyan Pub Hse.

Coates, Jeff, et al. Control & Audit in Management Accounting. 2nd ed. 1993. pap. text 54.95 (0-7506-0995-8) Buttrwrth-Heinemann.

Coates, Jennifer. Women, Men & Language. (Studies in Language & Linguistics). 200p. 1989. pap. text 19.43 (0-582-29133-X, 71759) Longman.

— Women Talk: Conversation Between Women Friends. LC 95-49251. 288p. (C). 1996. pap. 22.95 (0-631-18253-5) Blackwell Pubs.

Coates, Jennifer, ed. Language & Gender: A Reader. LC 97-18909. (Illus.). 480p. (C). 1997. text 68.95 (0-631-19594-7); pap. text 31.95 (0-631-19595-5) Blackwell Pubs.

Coates, Jennifer & Cameron, Deborah, eds. Women in Their Speech Communities: New Perspectives on Language & Sex. (Illus.). 208p. (C). 1989. pap. text 22.54 (0-582-00969-3, 70408) Longman.

Coates, Jennifer, ed. & intro. see Madoc-Jones, Beryl.

Coates, Jerry, jt. auth. see McAulay, John D.

***Coates, John.** Bravery above Blunder: The 9th Australian Division at Finschhafen, Sattelberg & Sio. LC 99-458608. (Illus.). 336p. 1999. 45.00 (0-19-550837-8) OUP.

Coates, John. The Claims of Common Sense: Moore, Wittgenstein, Keynes & the Social Sciences. 191p. (C). 1996. text 54.95 (0-521-41256-0) Cambridge U Pr.

— The Day's Work: Kipling & the Idea of Sacrifice. LC 97-12975. 136p. 1997. 29.50 (0-8386-3754-X) Fairleigh Dickinson.

— Social Discontinuity in the Novels of Elizabeth Bowen: The Conservative Quest. LC 98-31513. (Studies in British Literature: Vol. 38). 272p. 1998. text 89.95 (0-7734-8259-8) E Mellen.

Coates, John & Yau, S. T., eds. Elliptic Curves, Modular Forms & Fermat's Last Theorem. LC 95-79521. 1995. 42.00 (1-57146-026-8, INPR/5C) Intl Pr Boston.

Coates, John, jt. auth. see Woodcock, Bruce.

Coates, John M. & Williamson, Brian J. International Consultants Manual: A Guide to Winning Consultancy Assignments Financed by the International Finance Institutions, 2 vols. Campbell, Angus L., ed. (Illus.). 1991. 242.00 (971-8763-00-7, Pub. by Aedilis) McClelland & Stewart.

Coates, Jonathan. Managing Upwards. LC 94-173. 112p. 1994. 51.95 (0-566-07485-0) Ashgate Pub Co.

Coates, Jonathan & Breeze, Claire. Delegating with Confidence. 1996. pap. 25.00 (0-85292-649-9, Pub. by IPM Hse) St Mut.

Coates, Joseph F. & Jarratt, Jennifer. What Futurists Believe. 1989. 19.50 (0-930242-40-8) World Future.

Coates, Joseph F. & Jarret, Jennifer. Managing Your Future As an Association: Thinking about Trends & Working with Their Consequences, 1993-2020. LC 94-20958. 156p. 1994. 60.00 (0-88034-084-3) Am Soc Assn Execs.

Coates, Joseph F. & Mahaffie, John B. 2025: Scenarios of U. S. & Global Society Reshaped by Science & Technology. LC 97-18378. (Illus.). 528p. 1997. 27.95 (1-886939-09-8, Pub. by OakHill Pr VA) ACCESS Pubs Network.

Coates, Judith, jt. auth. see Joseph, Jeshua B.

Coates, Julie. Enrollment Analysis. 11.95 (0-914951-09-2) LERN.

Coates, K. & Morgan, W. John. Nottinghamshire Coal Field & the British Miners Strike, 1984-85. (C). 1989. 40.00 (0-7855-6426-8, Pub. by Univ Nottingham) St Mut.

Coates, K. A., jt. ed. see Reynoldson, T. B.

Coates, Kathryn A., ed. Aquatic Oligochaete Biology VI: Proceedings of the VIth International Symposium on Aquatic Oligochaetes, Held in Stromstat, Sweden. (Developments in Hydrobiology Ser.). 296p. (C). 1997. text 239.50 (0-7923-3999-1) Kluwer Academic.

Coates, Ken. Aboriginal Land Claims in Canada. (C). 1992. pap. text 33.95 (0-7730-5196-1) Addison-Wesley.

— Beyond Wage Slavery. 170p. 1977. 42.50 (0-85124-176-X, Pub. by Spkesman) Coronet Bks.

— The Case of Nikolai Bukharin. (Illus.). 104p. (Orig.). 1978. pap. 18.95 (0-85124-241-3, Pub. by Spkesman) Coronet Bks.

— China & the Bomb. 112p. 1986. 25.00 (0-85124-444-0) Dufour.

— Culture Shock! Succeed in Business: Japan. 1999. pap. text 12.95 (1-55868-471-9) Gr Arts Ctr Pub.

— Essays on Socialist Humanism: In Honour of the Centenary of Bertrand Russell. 220p. 1983. 30.00 (0-7855-2937-3); pap. 16.25 (0-7855-2938-1) St Mut.

— Heresies: Resist Much, Obey Little. 158p. (C). 1982. 40.00 (0-85124-355-X, Pub. by Spkesman); pap. 16.95 (0-85124-356-8, Pub. by Spkesman) Dufour.

— The Most Dangerous Decade: World Militarism & the New Non-Aligned Peace Movement. (Illus.). 211p. 1984. 42.50 (0-85124-405-X, Pub. by Spkesman); pap. 24.00 (0-85124-406-8, Pub. by Spkesman) Coronet Bks.

— North to Alaska! Fifty Years on the World's Most Remarkable Highway. (Illus.). 304p. 1998. pap. text 22.00 (0-7881-5905-4) DIANE Pub.

— North to Alaska! Fifty Years on the World's Most Remarkable Highway. (Illus.). 304p. 1991. 29.95 (0-912006-55-2) U of Alaska Pr.

— The Social Democrats: Those Who Went & Those Who Stayed, the Forward March of Labour Halted? 116p. 1983. 42.50 (0-85124-357-6, Pub. by Spkesman) Coronet Bks.

***Coates, Ken.** Success Secrets to Maximize Business in Canada. (Culture Shock! Ser.). 2000. pap. 12.95 (1-55868-542-1) Gr Arts Ctr Pub.

— Success Secrets to Maximize Business in Japan. 1999. pap. 12.95 (1-55868-480-8) Gr Arts Ctr Pub.

Coates, Ken. Think Globally, Act Locally: The United Nations & the Peace Movements. 168p. 1988. 44.50 (0-85124-503-X, Pub. by Spkesman); pap. 24.00 (0-85124-504-8, Pub. by Spkesman) Coronet Bks.

— Work-Ins, Sit-Ins, & Industrial Democracy: The Implications of Factory Occupations in Great Britain in the Early Seventies. 175p. 1981. 42.50 (0-85124-278-2, Pub. by Spkesman) Coronet Bks.

Coates, Ken, ed. Democracy in the Mines: Some Documents of the Controversy on Mines Nationalisation. (Documents on Socialist History Ser.: No. 2). 129p. 1974. 32.50 (0-85124-079-8, Pub. by Spkesman) Coronet Bks.

— Detente & Socialist Democracy: A Discussion with Roy Medvedev. (European Socialist Thought Ser.: No. 6). 163p. (Orig.). 1975. pap. 24.00 (0-85124-227-8, Pub. by Spkesman) Coronet Bks.

— Eleventh Hour for Europe. 108p. 1981. 29.50 (0-85124-308-8, Pub. by Spkesman) Coronet Bks.

— Essays on Socialist Humanism: In Honour of the Centenary of Bertrand Russell. 220p. 1972. 25.00 (0-85124-047-X) Dufour.

— Essays on Socialist Humanism in Honor of the Centenary of Bertrand Russell. 1972. 14.95 (0-685-11945-9) Dufour.

— Freedom & Fairness: Empowering People at Work. 157p. 1986. 43.50 (0-85124-440-8, Pub. by Spkesman); pap. 26.50 (0-85124-450-5, Pub. by Spkesman) Coronet Bks.

— Joint Action for Jobs: A New Internationalism. 232p. (Orig.). 1986. pap. 28.50 (0-85124-428-9, Pub. by Spkesman) Coronet Bks.

— Peace Register, 1993: Drawing the Peace Dividend. (Endpapers Ser.: No. 23). 144p. (Orig.). 1993. pap. 24.50 (0-85124-548-X, Pub. by Spkesman) Coronet Bks.

— Perestroika: Global Challenge & Our Common Future. LC 88-51544. 174p. 1988. 45.00 (0-85124-501-3, Pub. by Spkesman); pap. 16.95 (0-85124-502-1, Pub. by Spkesman) Dufour.

— Socialism & the Environment. 2nd ed. 116p. (Orig.). 1979. pap. 19.95 (0-85124-242-1, Pub. by Spkesman) Coronet Bks.

— A Trade Union Strategy in the Common Market: The Programme of the Belgian Trade Unions. 149p. 1971. 33.50 (0-685-71539-6, Pub. by Spkesman) Coronet Bks.

Coates, Ken & Brown, Michael B., eds. A European Recovery Programme: Restoring Full Employment. 135p. 1993. 65.00 (0-85124-539-0, Pub. by Spkesman); pap. 28.50 (0-85124-549-8, Pub. by Spkesman) Coronet Bks.

Coates, Ken & Morrison, Bill. The Sinking of the Princess Sophia: Taking the North Down with Her. LC 90-26927. (Illus.). xviii, 220p. 1991. pap. 12.95 (0-912006-50-1) U of Alaska Pr.

Coates, Ken & Morrison, William. The Forgotten North: A History of Canada's Provincial North. 142p. 29.95 (1-55028-391-X, Pub. by J Lorimer); pap. 19.95 (1-55028-390-1, Pub. by J Lorimer) Formac Dist Ltd.

Coates, Ken & Powell, Judith. The Modern North. 168p. 29.95 (1-55028-122-4, Pub. by J Lorimer); pap. 19.95 (1-55028-120-8, Pub. by J Lorimer) Formac Dist Ltd.

Coates, Ken & Siburn, Richard. Poverty: The Forgotten Englishmen. 282p. 1988. 77.50 (0-7855-2935-7); pap. 25.00 (0-7855-2936-5) St Mut.

Coates, Ken & Topham, Tony. The Making of the Labour Movement: The Formation of the Transport & General Workers' Union, 1870-1922. LC 95-161500. (Illus.). xxxv, 909p. 1994. pap. 37.50 (0-85124-565-X, Pub. by Spkesman) Coronet Bks.

Coates, Ken, et al. Dear Commissioner: An Exchange of Letters: Will Unemployment Break Europe? 139p. (Orig.). 1996. pap. 27.50 (0-85124-592-7, Pub. by Spkesman) Coronet Bks.

Coates, Ken, jt. auth. see Holroyd, Carin.

Coates, Ken, jt. auth. see Morgan, W. John.

Coates, Ken S. Best Left as Indians: Native-White Relations in the Yukon Territory, 1840-1973. (McGill-Queen's Studies in Ethnic History). 384p. 1991. text 65.00 (0-7735-0780-9, Pub. by McG-Queens Univ Pr) CUP Services.

— Best Left as Indians: Native-White Relations in the Yukon Territory, 1840-1973. 384p. 1993. pap. 24.95 (0-7735-1100-8, Pub. by McG-Queens Univ Pr) CUP Services.

Coates, Kenneth. Canada's Colonies. 251p. mass mkt. 9.95 (0-88862-931-1, Pub. by J Lorimer) Formac Dist Ltd.

Coates, Kenneth, jt. ed. see Fisher, Robin.

Coates, Kenneth A., jt. auth. see Morrison, William R.

Coates, Kenneth S. Manitoba: The Keystone Province: An Illustrated History. 192p. (YA). (gr. 7 up). 1988. 32.95 (0-89781-257-3) Am Historical Pr.

Coates, Kevin. Geometry, Proportion & the Art of Lutherie. (Illus.). 186p. 1991. reprint ed. pap. text 55.00 (0-19-816246-4, 11990) OUP.

C

***Coates, Lawrence.** The Blossom Festival. LC 99-25314. (Western Literature Ser.). 360p. (Orig.). 1999. pap. 20.00 (*0-87417-337-X*) U of Nev Pr.

Coates, Marvin & Pederson, Donald. Thinking English. (C). 1997. text 18.33 (*0-673-39247-3*) Addson-Wesley Educ.

Coates, Mary-Margaret, ed. The Lactation Consultant's Topical Review & Bibliography of the Literature on Breastfeeding. LC 90-61943. 188p. (Orig.). 1990. pap. 12.00 (*0-912500-39-5*) La Leche.

***Coates, Nigel.** Ecstacity. (Illus.). 448p. 2000. 75.00 (*1-86154-193-7*, Pub. by Booth-Clibborn) Dist Art Pubs.

Coates, P. D. The China Consuls: British Consular Officers, 1843-1943. (Illus.). 630p. 1988. text 49.95 (*0-19-584078-X*) OUP.

***Coates, P. D., ed.** Polymer Process Engineering, 99. 200p. 1999. 80.00 (*1-86125-094-0*, Pub. by Inst Materials) Ashgate Pub Co.

Coates, Paul. The Gorgon's Gaze: German Cinema, Expressionism, & the Image of Horror. 303p. (C). 1991. text 74.95 (*0-521-38409-5*) Cambridge U Pr.

Coates, Paul & Hutto, Daniel D., eds. Current Issues in Idealism. (Idealism Ser.: No. 1). 280p. 1996. 72.00 (*1-85506-435-9*); pap. 24.00 (*1-85506-434-0*) Bks Intl VA.

Coates, Paul M. & Tanaka, Kay, eds. New Developments in Fatty Acid Oxidation: Biochemical & Molecular Aspects of Fatty Acid Oxidation, Held in Philadelphia, Pennsylvania, November 1991. (Progress in Clinical & Biological Research Ser.: No. 375). 600p. 1992. 325.00 (*0-471-56144-4*, Wiley-Interscience) Wiley.

Coates, Peter. Nature: Western Attitudes since Ancient Times. LC 99-163024. 256p. 1998. 29.95 (*0-520-21743-8*, Pub. by U CA Pr) Cal Prin Full Svc.

Coates, Peter, jt. auth. see Beinart, William.

Coates, Peter A. The Trans-Alaska Pipeline Controversy: Technology, Conservation, & the Frontier. LC 89-45420. (Illus.). 448p. 1991. 57.50 (*0-934223-10-6*) Lehigh Univ Pr.

— The Trans-Alaska Pipeline Controversy: Technology, Conservation, & the Frontier. LC 93-32931. (Illus.). vii, 447p. 1993. pap. 25.00 (*0-912006-67-6*) U of Alaska Pr.

Coates, Phil D., ed. Polymer Process Engineering 97. (Illus.). 324p. 1997. 100.00 (*1-86125-044-4*, Pub. by Inst Materials) Ashgate Pub Co.

Coates, R. & Silburn, R. Beyond the Bulldozer. (C). 1980. text 35.00 (*0-7855-3210-2*, Pub. by Univ Nottingham) St Mut.

Coates, R., jt. ed. see Pecherskaya, Natalia.

Coates, R. C., et al. Structural Analysis. 3rd ed. (Illus.). 624p. (C). (gr. 13). 1990. pap. 45.00 (*0-412-37980-5*, Chap & Hall NY) Chapman & Hall.

Coates, Richard. The Place-Names of St. Kilda: Nomina Hirtensia. LC 90-6667. (Celtic Studies: Vol. 1). (Illus.). 240p. 1990. lib. bdg. 89.95 (*0-88946-077-9*) E Mellen.

***Coates, Richard.** Word Structure. (Language Workbooks Ser.). 100p. 1999. 16.99 (*0-415-20631-6*) Routledge.

Coates, R.M., ed. see Denmark, Scott E.

Coates, Robert. Geography Workbook. 128p. (C). 1995. pap. text 27.95 (*0-7872-1234-2*) Kendall-Hunt.

— Introduction to Geography Workbook. 2nd ed. 134p. (C). 1998. spiral bd., wbk. ed. 31.95 (*0-7872-1558-9*) Kendall-Hunt.

Coates, Robert C. A Street Is Not a Home: Solving America's Homeless Dilemma. LC 90-43193. (Illus.). 356p. (Orig.). (C). 1990. pap. 19.95 (*0-87975-621-7*) Prometheus Bks.

Coates, Robert M. The Outlaw Years: The History of the Land Pirates of the Natchez Trace. LC 85-31811. (Illus.). 360p. reprint ed. pap. 111.60 (*0-608-20014-X*, 207129000010) Bks Demand.

Coates, Robert M., jt. auth. see Hood, Linda R.

Coates, Roberts, jt. auth. see Hood, Linda.

***Coates, Rodney F.** African American History 2000-2001. (Annual Editions Ser.). 240p. (C). 1999. pap. 16.56 (*0-07-233372-3*) McGrw-H Hghr Educ.

Coates, Ross B., ed. Gods among Us: American Indian Masks. 116p. 1989. pap. 15.95 (*0-934931-03-8*) SDSU Press.

Coates, Ross M. Conveyancing. 2nd ed. (Practice Notes Ser.). 108p. 1990. pap. write for info. (*0-85121-698-6*, Pub. by Cavendish Pubng) Gaunt.

— Real Property & Conveyancing. (C). 1990. 110.00 (*1-85431-089-5*, Pub. by Blackstone Pr) St Mut.

Coates, Ross M., ed. Real Property & Conveyancing. (C). 1991. text 22.00 (*1-85431-127-1*, Pub. by Blackstone Pr) Gaunt.

Coates, Ruth. Christianity in Bakhtin: God & the Exiled Author. LC 98-3715. (Studies in Russian Literature). 220p. (C). 1999. 59.95 (*0-521-57278-9*) Cambridge U Pr.

Coates, Ruth A. Waiting for the Westbound. Polese, Richard L. & Hill, Judyth, eds. LC 92-13955. 64p. 1992. per. 8.00 (*0-943734-26-6*) Ocean Tree Bks.

***Coates, Sally O'Neal.** Bed & Breakfasts in the Northwest. (Unofficial Guides Ser.). 400p. 1999. pap. 16.99 (*0-02-863277-X*) Mac Bks.

Coates, Sally O'Neal. Great Bike Rides in Eastern Washington & Oregon. LC 96-7797. (Illus.). viii, 152p. (Orig.). 1996. pap. 11.95 (*0-89997-200-4*) Wilderness Pr.

— Hot Showers, Soft Beds, & Dayhikes in the Central Cascades. LC 98-16134. (Hot Showers, Soft Beds & Dayhikes Ser.: Vol. 3). (Illus.). 208p. 1998. pap. 14.95 (*0-89997-218-7*) Wilderness Pr.

— Hot Showers, Soft Beds, & Dayhikes in the North Cascades. LC 97-250. (Illus.). 192p. (Orig.). 1997. pap. 13.95 (*0-89997-209-8*) Wilderness Pr.

***Coates, Stephen.** Computer Telephony Integration: Integrating Enterprise Communications. LC 99-40463. (Illus.). 242p. 1999. pap. 280.00 (*1-56607-076-7*) Comput Tech Res.

— Impossible Worlds. (Illus.). 192p. 2000. 65.00 (*3-7643-5317-7*) Birkhauser.

Coates, Steven L., jt. auth. see Johnson, Kurt.

Coates, Susan. Childhood Gender Identity Disorder: Etiology, Assessment, & Treatment. 2000. write for info. (*0-88163-199-X*) Analytic Pr.

Coates, T. F. & Bell, R. S. Marie Corelli: The Writer & the Woman. 352p. 1996. reprint ed. pap. 17.25 (*1-56459-693-1*) Kessinger Pub.

Coates, T. F. & Bell, Warren. Marie Corelli: The Writer & the Woman. 352p. 1996. reprint ed. spiral bd. 18.50 (*0-7873-0186-8*) Hlth Research.

Coates, Theodore. The Next Giant Leap for Mankind. 125p. 1995. 27.95 (*0-9648675-6-7*) EMC Pubng.

Coates, Tim. The Loss of the Titanic, 1912. 74p. 1998. 25.00 (*0-11-500499-8*, HM04998, Pub. by Statnry Office) Balogh.

***Coates, Tim, ed.** The Boer War: Ladysmith & Mafeking, 1900. (Uncovered Editions Ser.). 215p. 1999. pap. (*0-11-702408-2*, Pub. by Statnry Office) Balogh.

— The British Invasion of Tibet: Colonel Younghusband, 1903. (Uncovered Editions Ser.). 256p. 1999. pap. 14.00 (*0-11-702409-0*, Pub. by Statnry Office) Balogh.

— John Profumo & Christine Keeler, 1963. (Uncovered Editions Ser.). 192p. 1999. pap. (*0-11-702402-3*, Pub. by Statnry Office) Balogh.

— The Judgement of Nuremberg, 1946. (Uncovered Editions Ser.). 256p. 1999. pap. (*0-11-702406-6*, Pub. by Statnry Office) Balogh.

— The Loss of the Titanic, 1912. (Uncovered Editions Ser.). 208p. 1999. pap. 14.00 (*0-11-702403-1*, Pub. by Statnry Office) Balogh.

— Rillington Place, 1953. (Uncovered Editions Ser.). 384p. 1999. pap. (*0-11-702417-1*, Pub. by Statnry Office) Balogh.

— The R101 Airship Disaster, 1930. (Uncovered Editions Ser.). 192p. 1999. pap. (*0-11-702407-4*, Pub. by Statnry Office) Balogh.

— The Strange Story of Adolph Beck, 1908. (Uncovered Editions Ser.). 264p. 1999. pap. (*0-11-702414-7*, Pub. by Statnry Office) Balogh.

— Tragedy at Bethnal Green, 1943. (Uncovered Editions Ser.). 128p. 1999. pap. (*0-11-702404-X*, Pub. by Statnry Office) Balogh.

— War 1914: Punishing the Serbs. (Uncovered Editions Ser.). 232p. 1999. pap. (*0-11-702410-4*, Pub. by Statnry Office) Balogh.

— War 1939: Dealing with Adolph Hitler. (Uncovered Editions Ser.). 220p. 1999. pap. 14.00 (*0-11-702411-2*, Pub. by Statnry Office) Balogh.

— Wilfrid Blunt's Egyptian Garden, 1916: Fox Hunting in Cairo. (Uncovered Editions Ser.). 300p. 1999. pap. (*0-11-702416-3*, Pub. by Statnry Office) Balogh.

***Coates, Timothy T., et al.** California Government Tort Liability Practice, 2 vols. 4th ed. Waxman, Robert N., ed. 1286p. 1999. ring bd. 189.00 (*0-7626-0346-1*, TO-33130) Cont Ed Bar-CA.

Coates, Vivien. Education for Patients & Clients. LC 99-17634. 224p. (C). 1999. 75.00 (*0-415-14849-9*) Routledge.

Coates, Vivien, ed. Education for Patients & Clients. LC 99-17634. 224p. (C). 1999. pap. 24.99 (*0-415-14850-2*) Routledge.

Coates, William P. & Coates, Zelda. Soviets in Central Asia. LC 73-88983. 288p. 1969. reprint ed. lib. bdg. 65.00 (*0-8371-2091-8*, COSA, Greenwood Pr) Greenwood.

Coates, William R. History of Cuyahoga County & the City of Cleveland: Historical & Biographical, 3 vols. in 2. (Illus.). 1196p. 1997. reprint ed. lib. bdg. 125.00 (*0-8328-6210-6*) Higginson Bk Co.

Coates, Zelda, jt. auth. see Coates, William P.

***Coath, Janie.** Farm Animals. (Set & Match Ser.). 8p. (J). 2000. 8.95 (*0-7613-1339-7*, Copper Beech Bks) Millbrook Pr.

— Wild Animals. (Set & Match Ser.). (Illus.). 8p. (J). (ps-1). 2000. 8.95 (*0-7613-1340-0*) Millbrook Pr.

Coatney, Susan L., ed. see Kimerer, Neil B.

Coaton, J. R. & Marsden, A. M., eds. Lamps & Lighting. 4th ed. LC 97-118955. 1997. write for info. (*0-340-64618-7*, Pub. by E A) Routldge.

— Lamps & Lighting. 4th ed. 546p. 1996. 130.00 (*0-470-23589-6*) Wiley.

Coatrieux. The Biomedical Engineering Dictionary. (C). 1998. text. write for info. (*0-12-177375-2*) Acad Pr.

Coatrieux, J. L., jt. ed. see Roux, C.

Coats. Homoeopathic Aide Memoire. Date not set. 11.95 (*0-8464-1293-9*) Beekman Pubs.

***Coats, A. W.** The Development of Economics in Western Europe since 1945. LC 98-43368. 1999. write for info. (*0-415-20291-4*) Routledge.

Coats, A. W. On the History of Economic Thought: British & American Economic Essays, Vol. 1. LC 91-47898. (British & American Economic Essays Ser.). 512p. (C). (gr. 13). 1992. 90.00 (*0-415-06715-4*, A7548) Routledge.

— The Post-1945 Internationalization of Economics. (History of Political Economy Annual Supplement Ser.). 280p. 1996. text 40.00 (*0-8223-1876-8*) Duke.

— The Sociology & Professionalization of Economics Vol. II: British & American Economic Essays. LC 93-16563. 512p. (C). (gr. 13). 1993. 90.00 (*0-415-06716-2*, B0771) Routledge.

Coats, A. W., ed. Economists in International Agencies: An Exploratory Study. LC 85-16750. 208p. 1986. 55.00 (*0-275-92070-0*, C2010, Praeger Pubs) Greenwood.

Coats, A. W., et al, eds. Methodological Controversy in Economics Vol. 2: Historical Essays in Honor of T. W. Hutchinson. LC 83-48096. (Political Economy & Public Policy Ser.: Vol. 2). 292p. 1983. 78.50 (*0-89232-395-7*) Jai Pr.

Coats, A. W., jt. ed. see Colander, David.

Coats, Andrew J., jt. auth. see Leyva, Francisco.

Coats, Andrew J., jt. auth. see Leyva-Leon, Francisco.

Coats, Carolyn. Me, a Gourmet Cook? (Illus.). 136p. 1985. 10.00 (*1-878722-02-6*) C Coats Bestsellers.

— Things Your Dad Always Told You, but You Didn't Want to Hear. 126p. 1988. 10.00 (*1-878722-05-0*) C Coats Bestsellers.

— Things Your Mother Always Told You, but You Didn't Want to Hear. 126p. 1981. 10.00 (*1-878722-01-8*) C Coats Bestsellers.

— Things Your Mother Always Told You, but You Didn't Want to Hear. LC 93-38978. 1994. 7.99 (*0-7852-8056-1*) Nelson.

Coats, Carolyn & Smith, Pamela. Alive & Well in the Fast Lane. (Illus.). 156p. 1987. pap. 10.00 (*1-878722-03-4*) C Coats Bestsellers.

— Come Cook with Me! A Cookbook for Kids. (Illus.). 133p. (J). 1989. pap., spiral bd. 10.00 (*1-878722-06-9*) C Coats Bestsellers.

— Perfectly Pregnant! (Illus.). 174p. 1988. 10.00 (*1-878722-04-2*) C Coats Bestsellers.

Coats, Catharine R. Subverting the System: D'Aubigne & Calvinism. (Sixteenth Century Essays & Studies: Vol. 14). 214p. 1990. 40.00 (*0-940474-16-6*, SCJP) Truman St Univ.

Coats, Catherine R. Embodying the Word: Textual Resurrections in the Martyrological Narratives of Foxe, Crespin, De Beze, & D'Aubigne. LC 91-28474. (Renaissance & Baroque Studies & Texts: Vol. 4). 157p. (C). 1992. text 39.95 (*0-8204-1724-6*) P Lang Pubng.

Coats, Dan. Mending Fences: Renewing Justice between Government & Civil Society. LC 98-23846. 80p. (C). 1998. pap. 8.99 (*0-8010-5830-9*) Baker Bks.

Coats, Erik J. & Feldman, Robert S. Classic & Contemporary Readings in Social Psychology. 2nd ed. LC 97-15166. 292p. 1997. pap. text 33.40 (*0-13-743907-5*) P-H.

Coats, Erik J., et al. Critical Thinking: General Principles & Case Studies. (C). 1994. pap. text 8.75 (*0-07-020896-4*) McGraw.

Coats, George. Smart Trust Deed Investment in California. 2nd ed. LC 87-33370. (Illus.). 292p. (Orig.). 1988. pap. 23.50 (*0-934581-01-0*) Barr-Randol Pub.

— Smart Trust Deed Investor's Formsbook. LC 93-21655. 224p. (Orig.). 1993. spiral bd. 67.50 (*0-934581-02-9*) Barr-Randol Pub.

Coats, George W. Exodus 1-18. (The Forms of the Old Testament Literature Ser.). 152p. 1998. pap. 24.00 (*0-8028-0592-2*) Eerdmans.

— From Canaan to Egypt: Structural & Theological Context for the Joseph Story. Vawter, Bruce, ed. LC 75-11382. (Catholic Biblical Quarterly Monographs: No. 4). xi, 101p. 1976. pap. 4.00 (*0-915170-03-5*) Catholic Bibl Assn.

— Moses: Heroic Man, Man of God. (Journal for the Study of the Old Testament Supplement Ser.: Vol. 57). 248p. 1988. 50.00 (*1-85075-096-3*, Pub. by Sheffield Acad); pap. 23.75 (*1-85075-095-5*, Pub. by Sheffield Acad) CUP Services.

— The Moses Tradition. (Journal for the Study of the Old Testament Supplement Ser.: Vol. 161). 203p. 1993. 57.50 (*1-85075-410-1*, Pub. by Sheffield Acad) CUP Services.

Coats, George W., ed. Saga, Legend, Tale, Novella, Fable: Narrative Forms in Old Testament Literature. (JSOT Supplement Ser.: No. 35). 159p. 1986. pap. 17.95 (*0-905774-85-X*, Pub. by Sheffield Acad) CUP Services.

Coats, Glenn. Waiting for a Frog. large type ed. (Illus.). 20p. (Orig.). (J). (gr. k-2). 1997. text 4.95 (*1-879835-90-8*) Kaeden Corp.

Coats, Joel R., jt. ed. see Anderson, Todd A.

Coats, Joel R., jt. ed. see Racke, Kenneth D.

Coats, Joel R., jt. ed. see Somasundaram, L.

Coats, Larry. Then Shall the End Come. 126p. 1998. pap. 8.95 (*0-7392-0025-9*, PO2785) Morris Pubng.

Coats, Laura J. Alphabet Garden. LC 92-6235. (Illus.). 32p. (J). (ps-1). 1993. text, lib. bdg. 13.95 (*0-02-719042-0*, Mac Bks Young Read) S&S Childrens.

— Morning Window. LC 94-14515. (J). 1995. text. write for info. (*0-02-719055-2*) Macmillan.

— Ten Little Animals. LC 89-36778. (Illus.). 32p. (J). (ps-1). 1990. lib. bdg. 14.00 incl. 5.25 hd (*0-02-719054-4*, Mac Bks Young Read) S&S Childrens.

***Coats, Lucy.** Neil's Numberless World. LC 99-51676. (Share-a-Story Ser.). (Illus.). 32p. (ps-3). 2000. 5.95 (*0-7894-5616-8*) DK Pub Inc.

— Neil's Numberless World. (Illus.). 32p. (ps-3). 2000. 9.95 (*0-7894-6354-7*) DK Pub Inc.

— One Smiling Sister. (Toddlers Storybook Ser.). (Illus.). 24p. (ps-k). 2000. pap. 5.95 (*0-7894-5622-2*) DK Pub Inc.

***Coats, Lucy, et al.** A Little Princess. LC 00-24162. (Young Classics Ser.). (Illus.). (J). 2000. pap. write for info. (*0-7894-6679-1*) DK Pub Inc.

Coats, Maggie. Women's Education. LC 93-11334. (Cutting Edge Ser.). 173p. 1994. pap. 34.95 (*0-335-15734-3*) OpUniv Pr.

Coats, Peter. The Homeopathic Aide-Memoire. 106p. 1984. 8.95 (*0-85032-165-4*, Pub. by C W Daniel) Natl Bk Netwk.

— Homeopathic Aide-Memoire. 2nd ed. 96p. 11.95 (*0-8464-4227-2*) Beekman Pubs.

Coats, Susan S. Planning & Conducting Family Law (Dissolution) Discovery Pts. 1 & 2: Spring 1993, Action Guide. Johnson, Elizabeth M., ed. 155p. 1993. pap. text 52.00 (*0-88124-620-4*, FA-11321) Cont Ed Bar-CA.

***Coats, Susan S. & DeRonde, John A., Jr.** Planning & Conducting Family Law Discovery Pts. 1 & 2: Fall 1999 Action Guide. Brook, Julie H., ed. 160p. 1999. pap. text 58.00 (*0-7626-0371-2*, FA-11322) Cont Ed Bar-CA.

Coats, Victoria. Seeking Synergy: Creating a Museum Collaborative That Works. 48p. 1994. pap. text 24.95 (*0-9617645-1-1*) Oreg Mus Sci & Indus.

Coats, Warren L., Jr. In Search of a Monetary Anchor: A 'New' Monetary Standard. LC 93-33941. 1994. 9.95 (*1-55815-306-3*) ICS Pr.

Coats, Warren L. & Khatkhate, Deena R., Jr., eds. Money & Monetary Policy in Less Developed Countries: A Survey of Issues & Evidence. LC 79-42703. (Illus.). 834p. 1980. 368.00 (*0-08-024041-0*, Pub. by Pergamon Repr) Franklin.

Coats, Warren L., Jr., et al. The SDR System & the Issue of Resource Transfers. Riccardi, Margaret B., ed. LC 90-28340. (Essays in International Finance Ser.: No. 180). 30p. 1990. pap. text 10.00 (*0-88165-087-0*) Princeton U Int Finan Econ.

Coats, Wendell J., Jr. The Activity of Politics & Related Essays. LC 88-42861. 176p. 1989. 32.50 (*0-941664-95-3*) Susquehanna U Pr.

— Statesmanship: Six Modern Illustrations of a Modified Ancient Ideal. LC 95-14824. 152p. 1996. 29.50 (*0-945636-84-9*) Susquehanna U Pr.

— A Theory of Republican Character & Related Essays. LC 93-29627. 1994. 33.50 (*0-945636-58-X*) Susquehanna U Pr.

***Coats, Wendell John, Jr.** Oakeshott & His Contemporaries: St. Augustine, Hegel, Et Al. LC 99-87913. 144p. 2000. 31.50 (*1-57591-038-1*) Susquehanna U Pr.

Coatsworth, Elizabeth. The Cat Who Went to Heaven. LC 58-10917. (Illus.). 72p. (J). (gr. 4-6). 1967. lib. bdg. 16.00 (*0-02-719710-7*, Mac Bks Young Read) S&S Childrens.

Coatsworth, Elizabeth. The Cat Who Went to Heaven. 2nd rev. ed. LC 90-175. (Illus.). 74p. (J). (gr. 3-7). 1990. reprint ed. pap. 3.95 (*0-689-71433-5*) Aladdin.

Coatsworth, Elizabeth. The Enchanted. (Illus.). 156p. 1992. reprint ed. pap. 8.95 (*0-942396-65-0*) Blackberry ME.

— Fox Footprints. 1986. pap. 5.00 (*0-942396-46-4*) Blackberry ME.

— Song of the Camels: A Christmas Poem. LC 97-20944. (Illus.). 32p. (J). (gr. k-3). 1997. 15.95 (*1-55858-811-6*, Pub. by North-South Bks NYC) Chronicle Bks.

Coatsworth, Elizabeth, ed. see Beston, Henry.

Coatsworth, Elizabeth J. Cat Who Went to Heaven. (J). 1972. 9.15 (*0-606-02575-8*, Pub. by Turtleback) Demco.

— Song of the Camels: A Christmas Poem. LC 97-20944. (Illus.). 32p. (J). (gr. k-3). 1997. lib. bdg. 15.88 (*1-55858-812-4*, Pub. by North-South Bks NYC) Chronicle Bks.

Coatsworth, John H. Growth Against Development: The Economic Impact of Railroads in Porfirian Mexico. LC 80-8662. (Origins of Modern Mexico Ser.). (Illus.). 249p. 1981. 32.00 (*0-87580-075-0*) N Ill U Pr.

Coatsworth, John H. & Rico, Carlos, eds. Images of Mexico in the United States. (Dimensions of U. S.-Mexican Relations Ser.: Vol. 1). 137p. (Orig.). (C). 1989. pap. 12.50 (*0-935391-88-6*, BC-01) UCSD Ctr US-Mex.

Coatsworth, John H., et al. Latin America & the World Economy since 1800. LC 98-40390. 1998. 49.95 (*0-674-51280-4*); pap. 24.95 (*0-674-51281-2*) HUP.

Coatts, Margot. Pioneers of Modern Craft: Twelve Essays Profiling Key Figures in the History of Contemporary Crafts. LC 96-52329. (Illus.). 128p. 1997. pap. 24.95 (*0-7190-5059-6*) St Martin.

Coatts, Margot, ed. Lucie Rie - Hans Cooper: Potters in Parallel. (Illus.). 161p. 1997. 55.00 (*1-889250-07-4*) Gentle Br.

***Cobain, Bev.** When Nothing Matters Anymore: A Survival Guide for Depressed Teens. Verdick, Elizabeth, ed. LC 98-24911. (Illus.). 165p. (YA). (gr. 8 up). 1998. pap. 13.95 (*1-57542-036-8*) Free Spirit Pub.

Cobanski, Laura. The Rainbow Cupcake. LC 97-73922. (Aesop's Fables Running Start Ser.). (Illus.). 32p. (J). (ps-2). 1997. pap. 4.95 (*1-890570-44-3*) Huckleberry CT.

Cobarrubias, Juan & Fishman, Joshua A., eds. Progress in Language Planning: International Perspectives, No. xi. LC 82-22310. (Contributions to the Sociology of Language Ser.: No. 31). 383p. 1983. 93.85 (*90-279-3358-8*); pap. 41.95 (*90-279-3388-X*) Mouton.

Cobas, Jose & Duany, Jorge. Los Cubanos en Puerto Rico. (Caribbean Collection). (SPA.). 268p. 1995. pap. 13.95 (*0-8477-0220-0*) U of PR Pr.

Cobas, Jose A. & Duany, Jorge. Cubans in Puerto Rico: Ethnic Economy & Cultural Identity. LC 96-16350. (Illus.). 176p. 1997. 49.95 (*0-8130-1499-9*) U Press Fla.

Cobaugh, Barbara. Tips for TAAS Mathematics Weekly Problem Solving. 135p. (J). (gr. 5). 1997. pap. 30.00 (*0-9640524-3-1*) C & C Educ.

Cobaugh, Barbara A. Tips for TAAS Grades 1-6 Mathematics: Critical Reading, Vocabulary, & Problem Solving. 122p. (Orig.). (J). (gr. 1-6). 1995. pap. 23.00 (*0-9640524-1-5*) C & C Educ.

— Tips for TAAS Mathematics Weekly Problem Solving. 140p. (J). (gr. 4). 1997. pap. 30.00 (*0-9640524-2-3*) C & C Educ.

Cobaugh, Barbara A. & Capron, Margie L. Tips for TAAS Grade 4 Science. (Illus.). 108p. (Orig.). 1994. pap. 16.00 (*0-9640524-0-7*) C & C Educ.

Cobb. The Biology & Management of Lobsters, 2 vols. 1980. 157.00 (*0-12-177400-7*) Acad Pr.

Cobb. Don't Ask Me, I Only Work Here. 1991. 218.95 (*0-566-02885-9*) Ashgate Pub Co.

Cobb. Process & Pattern. (C). 1985. mass mkt., teacher ed. 5.00 (*0-534-03706-2*) Heinle & Heinle.

— Spiritual Challenge of Health. (C). 1998. pap. text 25.00 (*0-443-05920-9*) Church.

Cobb & Barca. Beginnings & Endings. 164p. 1993. ring bd. 131.95 (*1-85904-037-3*) Ashgate Pub Co.

Cobb & Grigsby. Stepping Beyond Eden. 256p. pap. 10.99 Multnomah Pubs.

An Asterisk (*) at the beginning of an entry indicates that the title is appearing for the first time.

Cobb, jt. auth. see Bald.

Cobb, Alice, jt. auth. see Fahs, Sophia L.

***Cobb, Allan B.** Biological & Chemical Weapons: The Debate over Modern Warfare. LC 00-8571. 2000. lib. bdg. write for info. (*0-8239-3214-1*, PowerKids) Rosen Group.

— Heroin & Your Veins: The Incredibly Disgusting Story. LC 00-24763. (Incredibly Disgusting Drugs Ser.). (Illus.). (J). 2000. 17.95 (*0-8239-3249-4*) Rosen Group.

— Scientifically Engineered Foods: The Debate over What's on Your Plate. LC 00-20583. (Focus on Science & Society Ser.). (Illus.). 2000. write for info. (*0-8239-3208-7*) Rosen Group.

— Speed & Your Brain: The Incredibly Disgusting Story. LC 99-86805. (Incredibly Disgusting Drugs Ser.). (Illus.). 2000. lib. bdg. write for info. (*0-8239-3253-2*) Rosen Group.

***Cobb, Amanda J.** Listening to Our Grandmother's Stories: The Bloomfield Academy for Chickasaw Females, 1825-1949. (North American Indian Prose Award Ser.). (Illus.). 192p. 2000. text 27.50 (*0-8032-1509-6*, Bison Books) U of Nebr Pr.

***Cobb, Andrew & Kirkwood, R. C.** Herbicides & Their Mechanisms of Action. LC 00-29765. 2000. write for info. (*0-8493-0502-0*) CRC Pr.

Cobb, Annie. B Is for Books! LC 96-11142. (Early Step into Reading Ser.). (Illus.). (J). (ps-3). 1996. pap. 3.99 (*0-679-86446-6*) Random.

— B Is for Books! LC 96-11142. (Early Step into Reading Ser.). (Illus.). (J). (ps-3). 1996. lib. bdg. 11.99 (*0-679-96446-0*) Random.

— B Is for Books! (Early Step into Reading Ser.). (J). (ps-k). 1996. 9.19 (*0-606-11064-X*, Pub. by Turtleback) Demco.

— The Fox, the Goat & Sack of Grapes. (J). 1998. pap. 3.99 (*0-679-88380-0*) Random.

***Cobb, Annie.** The Long Wait. LC 99-42682. (Math Matters Ser.). (Illus.). 32p. (J). (gr. 1-3). 2000. pap. 4.59 (*1-57565-094-0*) Kane Pr.

— Long Wait. (Math Matters Ser.). (Illus.). (J). 2000. 10.40 (*0-606-18221-7*) Turtleback.

Cobb, Annie. Wheels! (Early Step into Reading Ser.). (J). (ps-k). 1996. pap. write for info. (*0-679-88161-1*) McKay.

— Wheels! LC 94-48884. (Early Step into Reading Ser.). (Illus.). (J). (ps-k). 1996. pap. 3.99 (*0-679-86445-8*) Random.

— Wheels! LC 94-48884. (Early Step into Reading Ser.). (Illus.). (J). (ps-3). 1996. lib. bdg. 11.99 (*0-679-96445-2*) Random.

— Wheels! (Early Step into Reading Ser.). (J). (ps-k). 1996. 9.19 (*0-606-08659-5*, Pub. by Turtleback) Demco.

Cobb, Annie, jt. auth. see Hayward, Linda.

Cobb, Betsy, jt. auth. see Cobb, Hubbard.

Cobb, Bettie T. Rodgers-Hearne & Related Families. LC 97-67671. (Illus.). 313p. 1997. 29.50 (*0-9606128-6-6*) Durant Pub.

Cobb, Blanche G. Gordon Family of Maine & New Hampshire. 57p. 1997. reprint ed. pap. 11.50 (*0-8328-8793-5*); reprint ed. lib. bdg. 21.50 (*0-8328-8792-7*) Higginson Bk Co.

Cobb, Buell E., Jr. The Sacred Harp: A Tradition & Its Music. LC 77-6323. (Brown Thrasher Bks.). 272p. 1999. reprint ed. pap. 14.95 (*0-8203-1022-0*) U of Ga Pr.

Cobb, C. G. The Bad Times Primer: A Complete Guide to Survival on a Budget. LC 81-52089. (Illus.). 336p. (Orig.). 1981. pap. 14.95 (*0-9606608-0-1*) Times Pr.

Cobb, C. R., jt. auth. see Nassaney, M. S.

***Cobb, Carl W.** An Anthology of the Spanish Sonnet in English Verse Translation Vol. 1: The Golden Age. LC 99-57956. (Hispanic Literature Ser.: Vol. 52). 260p. 2000. text 89.95 (*0-7734-7863-9*) E Mellen.

— Late Sonnet Harvest, 1988-2000. LC 00-38657. 80p. 2000. pap. text 14.95 (*0-7734-1266-2*) E Mellen.

Cobb, Carl W. Roads Dreamed Clear Afternoons - An Anthology of the Poetry of Antonio Machado. LC 93-61669. 220p. (C). 1994. 40.00 (*0-938972-23-5*) Spanish Lit Pubns.

Cobb, Carl W., ed. The Bullfighter Sanchez Mejias As Elegized by Lorca, Alberti & Diego. LC 92-63042. (ENG & SPA.). 82p. 1993. 20.00 (*0-938972-19-7*) Spanish Lit Pubns.

— Poems of Love & Strife, Death & Life by Francisco de Quevedo. LC 89-64207. 290p. 1991. 37.50 (*0-938972-16-2*) Spanish Lit Pubns.

Cobb, Carl W., tr. from SPA. Songs & Sonnets of Love Still Innocent: A Representative Anthology of the Poetry of Gerardo Diego. LC 96-71333. (Romance Monographs: Vol. 51). 323p. (Orig.). 1997. pap. 40.00 (*1-889441-01-5*) Romance.

Cobb, Carl W., tr. see De Otero, Blas.

Cobb, Carl W., tr. see Gaos, Vicente.

Cobb, Carl W., tr. see Guillen, Jorge.

Cobb, Carl W., tr. see Jimenez, Juan Ramon.

Cobb, Carl W., tr. see Rivera, Jose Eustasio.

Cobb, Carl W., tr. & intro. see de Vega, Lope.

Cobb, Carroll. Advice from the Lemonade Stand: A Back to Basics Book for Business. Bremer, Joanna, ed. (Illus.). 200p. 1998. pap. 22.00 (*0-9662773-0-9*) Lafayette Pub.

Cobb, Cathy & Goldwhite, Harold. Creations of Fire: Chemistry's Lively History from Alchemy to the Atomic Age. LC 95-24804. (Illus.). 492p. (C). 1995. 28.95 (*0-306-45087-9*, Plenum Trade) Perseus Pubng.

Cobb, Charles E., Jr., jt. auth. see Moses, Robert P.

***Cobb, Charles R.** From Quarry to Cornfield: The Political Economy of Mississippian Hoe Production. 2000. pap. 29.95 (*0-8173-1050-9*) U of Ala Pr.

Cobb, Clifford W. Responsive Schools, Renewed Communities. LC 92-18357. 320p. 1992. 34.95 (*1-55815-205-9*); pap. 19.95 (*1-55815-216-4*) ICS Pr.

Cobb, Clifford W. & Cobb, John B., Jr. The Green National Product: A Proposal Index of Sustainable Economic Welfare. LC 93-23426. 352p. (Orig.). (C). 1994. text 65.00 (*0-8191-9321-6*); pap. text 26.50 (*0-8191-9322-4*) U Pr of Amer.

Cobb, David A., ed. Guide to U. S. Map Resources. 2nd ed. LC 90-1019. 495p. (C). 1990. text 65.00 (*0-8389-0547-1*, 0547-1) ALA.

Cobb, Dena. Angels Came Running: The Trauma of Hurricane Andrew. (Illus.). 208p. (Orig.). 1998. pap. 18.95 (*0-9663937-0-8*) Cobb Family.

Cobb, E. Cameron, ed. see Technical Association of the Pulp & Paper Industry.

Cobb, Edith. The Ecology of Imagination in Childhood. LC 93-9073. vii, 160p. 1993. pap. 15.00 (*0-88214-360-3*) Spring Pubns.

Cobb, G. C., jt. auth. see Murray, R. L.

Cobb, George & Cryer, Jon. Electronic Companion to Statistics. Hefto, Gunder, ed. (Electronic Companion Ser.). (Illus.). 300p. (C). 1997. pap. text, wbk. ed. write for info. (*1-888902-40-X*); pap. text, wbk. ed. 34.95 incl. cd-rom (*1-888902-42-6*) Cogito Lrning.

Cobb, George, jt. auth. see Cryer, Jon.

Cobb, George P. & Weisskopf, Carol P. Pesticide Movement in Agroecosystems. 1999. 69.95 (*0-87371-888-7*) CRC Pr.

Cobb, George W. Introduction to Design & Analysis of Experiments. LC 97-996. (Textbooks in Mathematical Sciences Ser.). 1997. write for info. (*0-387-94607-1*) Spr-Verlag.

Cobb Group Staff. Excel 4 pour Windows au Quoridien. (Illus.). 880p. 1993. pap. 150.00 (*0-7859-5649-2*, 2840820021) Fr & Eur.

— Windows pour Workgroups au Quotidien. 176p. 1993. pap. 75.00 (*0-7859-5650-6*, 2840820080) Fr & Eur.

— Windows 3.1 au Quotidien. 528p. 1993. pap. 145.00 (*0-7859-5648-4*, 2840820005) Fr & Eur.

Cobb, Harrison S. Prospecting Our Past: Gold, Silver & Tungsten Mills of Boulder County. 2nd rev. ed. Pettem, Silvia, ed. LC 99-233864. (Illus.). 160p. 1998. pap. 19.95 (*1-891274-02-3*) Book Lode.

Cobb, Hazel. Around the Keys Again. 32p. 1991. pap. text 5.95 (*0-87487-664-8*) Summy-Birchard.

Cobb, Henry N., et al. Prince of Wales Prize in Urban Design, 1990: The Urban Public Spaces of Barcelona 1981-1987. (Illus.). 47p. 1991. 10.00 (*0-614-14661-5*) Harvard Univ Graduate Schl of.

Cobb, Howell. A Scriptural Examination of the Institution of Slavery in the United States: With Its Objects & Purposes. LC 72-6455. (Black Heritage Library Collection). 1977. reprint ed. 18.95 (*0-8369-9163-X*) Ayer.

Cobb, Hubbard. American Battlefields. (Illus.). 384p. 1997. reprint ed. write for info. (*1-56852-136-7*, Konecky & Konecky) W S Konecky Assocs.

Cobb, Hubbard & Cobb, Betsy. Your Barn House. (Illus.). 256p. 1995. 35.00 (*0-8050-1151-X*) H Holt & Co.

Cobb, Hubbard & Schuler, Stanley. American Battlefields: A Complete Guide to the Historic Conflicts in Words, Maps & Photos. LC 95-19504. (Illus.). 400p. 1995. 39.95 (*0-02-860428-8*) Macmillan.

Cobb, Irvin S. The Abandoned Farmers. (Collected Works of Irvin S. Cobb). 247p. 1998. reprint ed. lib. bdg. 88.00 (*1-58201-577-5*) Classic Bks.

— Alias Ben Alibi. (Collected Works of Irvin S. Cobb). 382p. 1998. reprint ed. lib. bdg. 98.00 (*1-58201-578-3*) Classic Bks.

— Back Home: Being the Narrative of Judge Priest & His People. (Collected Works of Irvin S. Cobb). 348p. 1998. reprint ed. lib. bdg. 98.00 (*1-58201-579-1*) Classic Bks.

— Cobb's Anatomy: A Guide to Humor. (Collected Works of Irvin S. Cobb). 348p. 1998. reprint ed. lib. bdg. 98.00 (*1-58201-580-5*) Classic Bks.

— Cobb's Bill-of-Fare. (Collected Works of Irvin S. Cobb). 148p. 1998. reprint ed. lib. bdg. 88.00 (*1-58201-581-3*) Classic Bks.

— Eating in Two or Three Languages. (Collected Works of Irvin S. Cobb). 64p. 1998. reprint ed. lib. bdg. 88.00 (*1-58201-582-1*) Classic Bks.

— The Escape of Mr. Trimm: His Plight & Other Plights. (Collected Works of Irvin S. Cobb). 277p. 1998. reprint ed. lib. bdg. 88.00 (*1-58201-583-X*) Classic Bks.

— Europe Revised. (Collected Works of Irvin S. Cobb). 467p. 1998. reprint ed. lib. bdg. 108.00 (*1-58201-584-8*) Classic Bks.

— Fibble, D. D. (Collected Works of Irvin S. Cobb). 279p. 1998. reprint ed. lib. bdg. 88.00 (*1-58201-585-6*) Classic Bks.

— From Place to Place. (Collected Works of Irvin S. Cobb). 407p. 1998. reprint ed. lib. bdg. 108.00 (*1-58201-586-4*) Classic Bks.

— The Glory of the Coming: What Mine Eyes Have Seen of Americans in Action in This Year of Grace & Allied Endeaver. (Collected Works of Irvin S. Cobb). 463p. 1998. reprint ed. lib. bdg. 108.00 (*1-58201-587-2*) Classic Bks.

— Goin' on Fourteen: Being Cross-Sections Out of a Year in the Life of an Average Boy. (Collected Works of Irvin S. Cobb). 357p. 1998. reprint ed. lib. bdg. 98.00 (*1-58201-588-0*) Classic Bks.

— Here Comes the Bride & So Forth. (Collected Works of Irvin S. Cobb). 340p. 1998. reprint ed. lib. bdg. 98.00 (*1-58201-589-9*) Classic Bks.

— Indiana: Cobb's America Guyed Books. (Collected Works of Irvin S. Cobb). 52p. 1998. reprint ed. lib. bdg. 88.00 (*1-58201-590-2*) Classic Bks.

— Irvin Cobb at His Best. (Collected Works of Irvin S. Cobb). 341p. 1998. reprint ed. lib. bdg. 98.00 (*1-58201-591-0*) Classic Bks.

— J. Poindexter, Colored. (Collected Works of Irvin S. Cobb). 270p. 1998. reprint ed. lib. bdg. 98.00 (*1-58201-592-9*) Classic Bks.

— Kansas: Cobb's America Guyed Books. (Collected Works of Irvin S. Cobb). 61p. 1998. reprint ed. lib. bdg. 88.00 (*1-58201-593-7*) Classic Bks.

— Kentucky: Cobb's America Guyed Books. (Collected Works of Irvin S. Cobb). 61p. 1998. reprint ed. lib. bdg. 88.00 (*1-58201-594-5*) Classic Bks.

— Ladies & Gentlemen. LC 78-106266. (Short Story Index Reprint Ser.). 1977. 20.95 (*0-8369-3303-6*) Ayer.

— A Laugh a Day Keeps the Doctor Away. (Collected Works of Irvin S. Cobb). 246p. 1998. reprint ed. lib. bdg. 88.00 (*1-58201-595-3*) Classic Bks.

— Life of the Party. (Collected Works of Irvin S Cobb). 66p. 1998. reprint ed. lib. bdg. 88.00 (*1-58201-596-1*) Classic Bks.

— Local Color. (Collected Works of Irvin S. Cobb). 460p. 1998. reprint ed. lib. bdg. 108.00 (*1-58201-597-X*) Classic Bks.

— Lost Tribes of the Irish in South. (Collected Works of Irvin S. Cobb). 300p. 1998. reprint ed. lib. bdg. 88.00 (*1-58201-598-8*) Classic Bks.

— Maine: Cobb's America Guyed Books. (Collected Works of Irvin S. Cobb). 55p. 1998. reprint ed. lib. bdg. 88.00 (*1-58201-599-6*) Classic Bks.

— Many Laughs for Many Days. (Collected Works of Irvin S. Cobb). 243p. 1998. reprint ed. lib. bdg. 88.00 (*1-58201-600-3*) Classic Bks.

— New York: Cobb's America Guyed Books. (Collected Works of Irvin S. Cobb). 61p. 1998. reprint ed. lib. bdg. 88.00 (*1-58201-601-1*) Classic Bks.

— North Carolina: Cobb's America Guyed Books. (Collected Works of Irvin S. Cobb). 61p. 1998. reprint ed. lib. bdg. 88.00 (*1-58201-602-X*) Classic Bks.

— Old Judge Priest. (Collected Works of Irvin S Cobb). 401p. 1998. reprint ed. lib. bdg. 108.00 (*1-58201-603-8*) Classic Bks.

— One Third Off. (Collected Works of Irvin S. Cobb). 148p. 1998. reprint ed. lib. bdg. 88.00 (*1-58201-604-6*) Classic Bks.

— Paths of Glory: Impressions of War Written at & near the Front. (Collected Works of Irvin S. Cobb). 414p. 1998. reprint ed. lib. bdg. 108.00 (*1-58201-605-4*) Classic Bks.

— A Plea for Old Cap Collier. (Collected Works of Irvin S. Cobb). 56p. 1998. reprint ed. lib. bdg. 88.00 (*1-58201-606-2*) Classic Bks.

— The Red Glutton: Impressions of War Written at & near the Front. (Collected Works of Irvin S. Cobb). 414p. 1998. reprint ed. lib. bdg. 108.00 (*1-58201-607-0*) Classic Bks.

— Roughing It De Luxe. (Collected Works of Irvin S. Cobb). 219p. 1998. reprint ed. lib. bdg. 88.00 (*1-58201-608-9*) Classic Bks.

— Snake Doctor, & Other Stories. (Collected Works of Irvin S. Cobb). 343p. 1998. reprint ed. lib. bdg. 98.00 (*1-58201-609-7*) Classic Bks.

— Speaking of Operations. (Collected Works of Irvin S. Cobb). 64p. 1998. reprint ed. lib. bdg. 88.00 (*1-58201-610-0*) Classic Bks.

— Speaking of Operations. LC 71-92422. 65p. 1928. reprint ed. 39.00 (*0-403-00556-6*) Scholarly.

— Speaking of Prussians. (Collected Works of Irvin S. Cobb). 80p. 1998. reprint ed. lib. bdg. 88.00 (*1-58201-611-9*) Classic Bks.

— Stickfuls: Compositions of a Newspaper Minion. (Collected Works of Irvin S. Cobb). 355p. 1998. reprint ed. lib. bdg. 98.00 (*1-58201-612-7*) Classic Bks.

— Sundry Accounts. (Collected Works of Irvin S. Cobb). 435p. 1998. reprint ed. lib. bdg. 108.00 (*1-58201-613-5*) Classic Bks.

— Those Times & These. LC 72-5862. (Short Story Index Reprint Ser.). 1977. reprint ed. 23.95 (*0-8369-4201-9*) Ayer.

Cobb, J. C. & Cecil, C. B., eds. Modern & Ancient Coal-Forming Environments. (Special Papers: No. 286). 1994. pap. 39.38 (*0-8137-2286-1*) Geol Soc.

Cobb, J. E. Cobb's Baptist Church Manual. 1933. 1979. reprint ed. pap. 3.95 (*0-89114-056-5*) Baptist Pub Hse.

Cobb, J. Stanley & Phillips, Bruce F., eds. The Biology & Management of Lobsters Vol. 1: Physiology & Behavior. LC 79-6803. 1980. text 104.00 (*0-12-177401-5*) Acad Pr.

— The Biology & Management of Lobsters Vol. 2: Ecology & Management. LC 79-6803. 1980. text 104.00 (*0-12-177402-3*) Acad Pr.

Cobb, James, et al. Rooted in Remembering. 1989. pap. 7.60 (*1-55673-133-7*, 9858) CSS OH.

Cobb, James C. Georgia Odyssey. LC 97-15110. 168p. (Orig.). 1998. pap. 12.00 (*0-8203-1945-7*) U of Ga Pr.

— Industrialization & Southern Society, 1877-1984. LC 84-5083. (New Perspectives on the South Ser.). 200p. 1984. 24.95 (*0-8131-0304-5*) U Pr of Ky.

— The Most Southern Place on Earth: The Mississippi Delta & the Roots of Regional Identity. (Illus.). 416p. 1994. reprint ed. pap. 16.95 (*0-19-508913-8*) OUP.

— Redefining Southern Culture: Mind & Identity in the Modern South. LC 98-53758. 251p. 1999. 40.00 (*0-8203-2111-7*); pap. 17.95 (*0-8203-2139-7*) U of Ga Pr.

— The Selling of the South: The Southern Crusade for Industrial Development, 1936 - 1980. 2nd ed. LC 92-30045. 328p. (C). 1993. reprint ed. text 32.50 (*0-252-01770-6*); reprint ed. pap. text 15.95 (*0-252-06162-4*) U of Ill Pr.

Cobb, James C. & Wilson, Charles R., eds. Perspectives on the American South, Vol. 3. xiv, 298p. 1985. text 75.00 (*2-88124-108-5*) Gordon & Breach.

— Perspectives on the American South: An Annual Review of Society, Politics & Culture, Vol. 4. xvi, 218p. 1987. text 129.00 (*2-88124-157-3*) Gordon & Breach.

Cobb, James C., ed. see Cohn, David L.

***Cobb, James G.** Sermonic City Sidewalks: Sermons for Advent, Christmas, Epiphany & Holy Week. 1999. pap. 10.00 (*0-7880-1466-8*) CSS OH.

Cobb, James G. The Visit of Nicholas. (Orig.). 1988. pap. 2.50 (*1-55673-073-X*, 8870) CSS OH.

Cobb, James H. Choosers of the Slain. 352p. 1997. mass mkt. 6.99 (*0-425-16053-X*) Berkley Pub.

— Choosers of the Slain. large type ed. LC 96-29610. 1996. lib. bdg. 24.95 (*1-57490-076-5*, Beeler LP Bks) T T Beeler.

***Cobb, James H.** Sea Fighter. LC 99-51900. 368p. 2000. 24.95 (*0-399-14593-1*) Putnam Pub Group.

Cobb, James H. Sea Strike. 357p. 1999. reprint ed. mass mkt. 6.99 (*0-425-16616-3*) Berkley Pub.

— West on 66. LC 99-27251. 288p. 1999. text 23.95 (*0-312-20621-6*, Thomas Dunne) St Martin.

Cobb, Jane. I'm a Little Teapot! Presenting Preschool Storytime. LC 94-910720. (Illus.). 256p. (J). (ps). 1996. pap. 23.95 (*0-9698666-0-7*) Black Sheep WA.

Cobb, Jenna, ed. see Etpison, Mandy T.

Cobb, Jerrie. Jerrie Cobb, Solo Pilot. LC 97-92479. (Illus.). 224p. 1997. pap. 19.95 (*0-9659924-0-3*) J Cobb Found.

Cobb, Jim, jt. auth. see Elliott, Robert W.

Cobb, Jo. A Complete Introduction to Turtles & Terrapins. (Illus.). 128p. 1987. pap. 8.95 (*0-86622-280-4*, CO-026S) TFH Pubns.

Cobb, Joan C. Bound for the Promised Land. (Illus.). 567p. 1992. write for info. (*0-318-69597-9*) Anchor Pub Co.

Cobb, Jodi. Geisha: The Life, the Voices, the Art. (Illus.). 128p. 1995. 49.95 (*0-679-43774-6*) Knopf.

***Cobb, Jodi, photos by.** The Way Home: Ending Homelessness in America. LC 99-38450. (Illus.). 152p. 1999. 35.00 (*0-8109-4553-3*, Pub. by Abrams) Time Warner.

Cobb, Jodi & Buruma, Ian. Geisha: The Life, the Voices, the Art. (Illus.). 128p. 1998. pap. 25.00 (*0-375-70180-X*) Knopf.

Cobb, Joe. Carroll County & Her People. (Illus.). 149p. 1997. reprint ed. pap. 21.00 (*0-8328-6622-9*) Higginson Bk Co.

Cobb, John B., Jr. Becoming a Thinking Christian. LC 93-14951. 144p. (Orig.). 1993. pap. 9.95 (*0-687-28752-9*) Abingdon.

***Cobb, John B., Jr.** Beyond Dialogue: Toward a Mutual Transformation of Christianity & Buddhism. 172p. 1998. pap. 17.00 (*1-57910-142-9*) Wipf & Stock.

Cobb, John B., Jr. Can Christ Become Good News Again? 200p. (Orig.). 1991. pap. 15.99 (*0-8272-0456-6*) Chalice Pr.

***Cobb, John B., Jr.** Christ in a Pluralistic Age. 286p. 1999. pap. 26.00 (*1-57910-300-6*) Wipf & Stock.

Cobb, John B., Jr. Grace & Responsibility: A Wesleyan Theology for Today. LC 95-1454. 192p. (Orig.). 1995. pap. 16.95 (*0-687-00769-0*) Abingdon.

— Is It Too Late? A Theology of Ecology. rev. ed. LC 95-128252. 111p. (C). 1995. pap. 12.50 (*0-9626807-3-7*) Environ Ethics Bks.

— Lay Theology. 120p. (Orig.). 1994. pap. 10.99 (*0-8272-2122-3*) Chalice Pr.

— Matters of Life & Death. 120p. (Orig.). 1991. pap. 13.95 (*0-664-25169-2*) Westminster John Knox.

— Reclaiming the Church: Where the Mainline Church Went Wrong & What to Do about It. 120p. 1997. pap. 12.00 (*0-664-25720-8*) Westminster John Knox.

— Sustainability: Economics, Ecology, & Justice. LC 92-20552. (Ecology & Justice Ser.). 200p. 1992. pap. 18.00 (*0-88344-823-8*) Orbis Bks.

— Sustaining the Common Good: A Christian Perspective on the Global Economy. 128p. (Orig.). 1994. pap. 12.95 (*0-8298-1010-2*) Pilgrim OH.

— Transforming Christianity & the World: A Way Between Absolutism & Relativism. Knitter, Paul F., ed. & intro. by. LC 99-31694. (Faith Meets Faith Ser.). 246p. 1999. pap. 25.00 (*1-57075-271-0*) Orbis Bks.

Cobb, John B., Jr. & Gamwell, Franklin I., eds. Existence & Actuality: Conversations with Charles Hartshorne. LC 84-2476. 216p. 1984. pap. text 12.00 (*0-226-11123-7*) U Ch Pr.

— Existence & Actuality: Conversations with Charles Hartshorne. LC 84-2476. 188p. 1985. lib. bdg. 20.00 (*0-226-11122-9*) U Ch Pr.

Cobb, John B., Jr. & Griffin, David R. Process Theology: An Introductory Exposition. LC 76-10352. 192p. 1976. pap. 18.95 (*0-664-24743-1*) Westminster John Knox.

Cobb, John B., Jr. & Ives, Christopher. The Emptying God: A Buddhist-Jewish-Christian Conversation. LC 90-31442. (Faith Meets Faith Ser.). 1990. pap. 19.00 (*0-88344-670-7*) Orbis Bks.

***Cobb, John B., Jr. & Pinnock, Clark H., eds.** Searching for an Adequate God: A Dialogue Between Process & Free-Will Theists. 264p. 2000. pap. 26.00 (*0-8028-4739-0*) Eerdmans.

Cobb, John B., Jr., et al. Death or Dialogue? From the Age of Monologue to the Age of Dialogue. LC 90-31485. 160p. 1990. pap. 16.00 (*0-334-02445-5*) TPI PA.

Cobb, John B., Jr., jt. auth. see Birch, Charles.

Cobb, John B., Jr., jt. auth. see Cobb, Clifford W.

Cobb, John B., Jr., jt. auth. see Daly, Herman E.

Cobb, John B., Jr., jt. auth. see Mesle, C. Robert.

Cobb, John T. & McDonald, Olin T. Up from the Bottom. LC 95-158311. 140p. 1993. write for info. (*0-9637454-4-1*) Wrightway Prnt.

Cobb, Jonathan, jt. auth. see Sennett, Richard.

Cobb, Joshua, jt. auth. see Cobb, Vicki.

***Cobb, Joyanne.** Learning How to Learn: A Guide for Getting into College with a Learning Disability, Staying in & Staying Sane. LC 99-45582. 2000. 14.95 (*0-87868-776-9*, CWLA Pr) Child Welfare.

Cobb, Kate, jt. auth. see Barca, Michele.

An Asterisk (*) at the beginning of an entry indicates that the title is appearing for the first time.

Cobb, Katie. Happenings. 224p. (J). (gr. 7 up). 14.89 (0-06-028928-7); mass mkt. 4.95 (0-06-447232-9) HarpC.

Cobb, Kevin. Without Reservation: A Guide to America's Favorite Motels. 1995. pap. write for info. (0-316-14901-2) Little.

Cobb, Linda C. Talking Dirty with the Queen of Clean. (Illus.). 128p. 1998. pap. 8.99 (1-893048-02-0) Phoenix Magazine.

Cobb, Margaret G., ed. The Poetic Debussy: A Collection of His Song Texts & Selected Letters. Miller, Richard, tr. LC 93-21462. (Eastman Studies in Music: Vol. 1). (Illus.). 350p. (C). 1994. reprint ed. 39.95 (1-878822-33-0) Univ Rochester Pr.

Cobb, Margo. The Granite Man. LC 96-38511. 196p. (Orig.). 1996. pap. 6.95 (0-944957-64-1) Rivercross Pub.

Cobb, Mary. The Quilt-Block History of Pioneer Days: With Projects Kids Can Make. (Illus.). 64p. (J). (gr. 2-4). 1995. lib. bdg. 23.90 (1-56294-485-1) Millbrook Pr.

— The Quilt-Block History of Pioneer Days: With Projects Kids Can Make. (Illus.). 64p. (J). (gr. 2-4). 1995. pap. 8.95 (1-56294-692-7) Millbrook Pr.

Cobb, Mary. Quilt-Block History of Pioneer Days: With Projects Kids Can Make. 1995. 14.15 (0-606-09777-5, Pub. by Turtleback) Demco.

Cobb, Mary. A Sampler View of Colonial Life: With Projects Kids Can Make. LC 98-2873. (Illus.). 64p. (J). (gr. 2-4). 1999. lib. bdg. 23.90 (0-7613-0372-3, Copper Beech Bks) Millbrook Pr.

Cobb, Matthew, tr. see Gayon, Jean.

Cobb, Matthew, tr. see Morange, Michel.

Cobb, Michael, jt. auth. see Cobb, Stephen.

Cobb, Miles A. Federal Regulation of Depository Institutions: Enforcement, Powers & Procedures. LC 83-60089. (General Law Ser.). 784p. 1991. 110.00 (0-88262-911-5) Warren Gorham & Lamont.

Cobb, Nancy. In Lieu of Flowers: A Conversation for the Living. LC 99-40526. 192p. 2000. 19.95 (0-375-40341-8) Pantheon.

Cobb, Nancy, jt. auth. see Reader's Digest Editors.

Cobb, Nancy J. Adolescence: Continuity, Change & Diversity. 3rd ed. LC 97-31566. xxvi, 660p. 1997. pap. text 61.95 (1-55934-946-8) Mayfield Pub.

***Cobb, Nancy J.** Adolescence: Continuity, Change & Diversity. 4th ed. LC 00-42160. 2000. write for info. (0-7674-1687-2) Mayfield Pub.

Cobb, Nancy J. Adolescence - The Resource Book: A Teacher's Tool Kit. (C). 1995. pap. text, teacher ed. write for info. (0-7674-0005-4, 0005-4) Mayfield Pub.

Cobb, Nancy J. & Weyermann, Andrea G. Adolescence Test Bank. 169p. (C). 1998. pap. text, teacher ed. write for info. (0-7674-0006-2, 20006) Mayfield Pub.

***Cobb, Nancy P. & Grigsby, Connie.** Is There a Moose in Your Marriage? LC 99-56250. 256p. 2000. pap. 12.99 (1-57673-635-0, Pub. by Multnomah Pubs) GL Services.

Cobb, Nina, ed. The Future of Education: Perspectives on National Standards in America. (Illus.). 287p. (C). 1995. pap. 16.95 (0-87447-530-9) H Holt & Co.

Cobb, Nina K., jt. auth. see Stimpson, Catherine R.

Cobb, Noel. Archetypal Imagination: Glimpses of the Gods in Life & Art. LC 92-12751. 256p. (Orig.). 1992. pap. 16.95 (0-940262-47-9, Lindisfarne) Anthroposophic.

***Cobb, Norma & Sasser, Charles.** Arctic Homestead: One Family's Story of Survival & Courage in the Alaskan Wilds. (Illus.). 320p. 2000. 24.95 (0-312-26198-5) St Martin.

Cobb, Norman B., ed. see Feldman, Hans A.

Cobb, P. L. History of the Cobb Family, 4 pts., Set. 278p. 1993. reprint ed. pap. 41.00 (0-8328-3024-0); reprint ed. lib. bdg. 51.00 (0-8328-3023-2) Higginson Bk Co.

Cobb, Paul, ed. Learning Mathematics: Constructivist & Interactionist Theories of Mathematical Development. 196p. (C). 1994. lib. bdg. 85.50 (0-7923-2823-X) Kluwer Academic.

Cobb, Paul, et al, eds. Symbolizing & Communicating in Mathematics Classrooms: Perspectives on Discourse, Tools, & Instructional Design. LC 98-52381. 550p. 1999. write for info. (0-8058-2975-X); pap. write for info. (0-8058-2976-8) L Erlbaum Assocs.

Cobb, Paul & Bauersfeld, Heinrich, eds. The Emergence of Mathematical Meaning: Interaction in Classroom Cultures. (Studies in Mathematical Thinking & Learning Ser.). 328p. 1995. pap. 36.00 (0-8058-1729-8); text 69.95 (0-8058-1728-X) L Erlbaum Assocs.

***Cobb, Paul M.** White Banners: Contention in Abbasid Syria, 750-880. LC 00-30080. (C). 2001. pap. text 19.95 (0-7914-4880-0) State U NY Pr.

— White Banners: Contention in Abbasid Syria, 750-880. LC 00-30080. (C). 2001. text 59.50 (0-7914-4879-7) State U NY Pr.

Cobb-Poulle, L. A., jt. auth. see Larsen, M. J.

***Cobb, R.** Paris & Elsewhere. 1998. text 45.00 (0-7195-5469-1, Pub. by John Murray) Trafalgar.

Cobb, Richard. The End of the Line: A Memoir. 230p. 1998. 40.00 (0-7195-5460-8, Pub. by John Murray) Trafalgar.

— French & Germans, Germans & French: A Personal Interpretation of France under Two Occupations, 1914-1918. LC 82-40472. (Tauber Institute Ser.: Vol. 2). 222p. 1983. reprint ed. pap. 68.90 (0-608-03010-4, 206346000006) Bks Demand.

***Cobb, Richard.** Paris & Elsewhere: Selected Writings. Gilmour, David, ed. & intro. by. 288p. 1999. pap. 24.95 (0-7195-5462-4, Pub. by John Murray) Trafalgar.

Cobb, Richard. The People's Armies. Elliott, Marianne, tr. LC 87-10641. 776p. 1987. 25.00 (0-300-02728-1) Yale U Pr.

***Cobb, Richard.** Still Life. large type unabridged ed. 217p. 1999. 25.95 (0-7531-5080-8, 150808, Pub. by ISIS Lrg Prnt) ISIS Pub.

Cobb, Richard & Gilmour, David, eds. The French & Their Revolution. 471p. 1999. pap. 18.95 (1-56584-540-4, Pub. by New Press NY) Norton.

Cobb, Roger W. & Elder, Charles D. Participation in American Politics: The Dynamics of Agenda Building. 2nd ed. LC 83-48051. (Illus.). 210p. reprint ed. pap. 65.10 (0-8357-8259-X, 203414900088) Bks Demand.

Cobb, Roger W. & Ross, Marc H., eds. Cultural Strategies of Agenda Denial: Avoidance, Attack, & Redefinition. LC 97-20359. (Studies in Government & Public Policy). 240p. 1997. 35.00 (0-7006-0855-9) U Pr of KS.

— Cultural Strategies of Agenda Denial: Avoidance, Attack, & Redefinition. LC 97-20359. (Studies in Government & Public Policy). 240p. 1997. pap. 16.95 (0-7006-0856-7) U Pr of KS.

Cobb, Roger W., jt. ed. see Rochefort, David A.

Cobb, Rosalyn, jt. ed. see Maddox, Irene.

Cobb, S., jt. contrib. by see Thorburn, P.

Cobb, Sanford H. The Rise of Religious Liberty in America: A History. LC 68-27517. 541p. 1968. reprint ed. 71.00 (0-8154-0051-9) Cooper Sq.

— The Story of the Palatines: An Episode in Colonial History. 336p. 1988. reprint ed. pap. 25.50 (1-55613-144-5) Heritage Bk.

Cobb, Sarah, et al. Advanced Therapist, Vol. 34, No. 1. (Vision Therapist Ser.: Vol. 1). (Illus.). 156p. (Orig.). 1992. pap. text 18.00 (0-943599-51-2) OEPF.

— Vision Therapist Vol. 34-2: COVTT Study Guide. (Illus.). 131p. (Orig.). 1992. pap. text 18.00 (0-943599-53-9) OEPF.

Cobb, Sidney. Frequency of the Rheumatic Diseases. LC 72-158427. (Vital & Health Statistics Monographs, American Public Health Association). (Illus.). 171p. 1971. 22.00 (0-674-32325-4) HUP.

***Cobb, Sidney.** Frequency of the Rheumatic Diseases. 174p. 1999. 24.95 (0-7351-0184-1) Replica Bks.

Cobb, Stephen. Dictionary of Computer Science & Engine Technology. 1999. 89.95 (0-8493-2691-5) CRC Pr.

— The NCSA Guide to PC & LAN Security. (Illus.). 717p. 1996. 50.00 (0-07-912168-3) McGraw.

— The NCSA Guide to PC & LAN Security. (Illus.). 717p. 1999. reprint ed. pap. 30.00 incl. disk (0-7881-6537-2) DIANE Pub.

— PC Magazine Guide to 1-2-3 Release 2.3. (Guide to...Ser.). (Illus.). 640p. (Orig.). 1991. pap. 27.95 (1-56276-0.2-2, Ziff-Davis Pr) Que.

— Quattro Pro for Windows Inside & Out. 832p. 1992. pap. 27.95 (0-07-881768-4) Osborne-McGraw.

— The Stephen Cobb Complete Book of PC & LAN Security. 576p. 1992. pap. 24.95 (0-07-157559-6) McGraw.

— The Stephen Cobb Complete Book of PC & LAN Security. (Illus.). 272p. 1991. pap. 24.95 (0-8306-3280-8, Windcrest) TAB Bks.

Cobb, Stephen, ed. Firewall Buyer's Guide. 2nd ed. (Illus.). 100p. (C). 1998. pap. text 40.00 incl. disk (0-7881-7155-0, NCSA) DIANE Pub.

— Firewall Buyer's Guide, 1996. (Illus.). 325p. (C). 1998. pap. text 50.00 (0-7881-3882-0, NCSA) DIANE Pub.

Cobb, Stephen & Cobb, Michael. Implementing Set: A Guide to the Visa/MasterCard Secure Electronic Transaction Specification. (Illus.). 512p. 1997. 39.95 (0-07-012025-0) Osborne-McGraw.

Cobb, Stephen & Jost, Marty. Tops: The IBM-Macintosh Connection. (Illus.). 352p. 1989. pap. 24.95 (0-07-156830-1, OP9302, TAB-Aero) TAB Bks.

Cobb, Stephen G. The Reverend William Carwardine & the Pullman Strike of Eighteen Ninety-Four: The Christian Gospel & Social Justice. LC 92-7603. 248p. 1992. lib. bdg. 89.95 (0-7734-9508-8) E Mellen.

Cobb, Stephen H. Mist Before the Morning Wind: Rufus Crook Gates. 1997. pap. 19.95 (0-910119-46-5) SOCO Pubns.

Cobb, Steven. Quattro Pro for Windows. 1993. pap. 27.95 (0-07-881964-4) McGraw.

Cobb, Steven, jt. auth. see Appleyard, Dennis R.

Cobb-Stevens, Richard. Husserl & Analytic Philosophy. (Phaenomenologica Ser.: No. 116). 230p. (C). 1990. lib. bdg. 139.00 (0-7923-0467-5, Pub. by Kluwer Academic) Kluwer Academic.

***Cobb-Stevens, Richard, ed.** Proceedings of the Twentieth World Congress of Philosophy Vol. V: Epistemology. 250p. (C). 1999. 45.00 (1-889680-09-5) Philos Document.

Cobb, Suzanne & Blaine, Marty. Reformation: Classroom Evaluation Techniques. 3rd ed. 176p. (C). 1990. 29.60 (0-536-57893-1) Pearson Custom.

Cobb, Thomas. Crazy Heart. LC 87-395. 256p. 1988. reprint ed. 15.75 (0-00-002379-5, PL1519, Perennial) HarperTrade.

— An Inquiry into the Law of Negro Slavery in the United States of America. LC 99-22420. (Studies in the Legal History of the South). 600p. 1999. text 65.00 (0-8203-2127-3) U of Ga Pr.

Cobb, Thomas D. The Triune Connection. 165p. (Orig.). (C). 1995. pap. 6.95 (0-9650711-0-3) Sword & Vine.

***Cobb, Thomas Dorland.** Highway Signs & Wonders: Twenty-Five Years of Miracles & Ministry on the Road. LC 99-89587. 260p. 2000. pap. 10.95 (0-9650711-1-1) Sword & Vine.

Cobb, Thomas R. Historical Sketch of Slavery. LC 71-92422. 1858. 15.00 (0-403-00157-9) Scholarly.

— Historical Sketch of Slavery, from the Earliest Periods. LC 70-83943. (Black Heritage Library Collection). 1977. 26.95 (0-8369-8543-5) Ayer.

Cobb, Ty & Stump, Al. My Life in Baseball: The True Record. LC 92-35297. xiv, 315p. 1993. reprint ed. pap. 12.95 (0-8032-6359-7, Bison Books) U of Nebr Pr.

— My Life in Baseball - Ty Cobb. Date not set. lib. bdg. 27.95 (0-8488-1562-9) Amereon Ltd.

Cobb, Tyrus. The Best of Cobbwebs. (Illus.). xviii, 189p. (Orig.). 1997. pap. 15.00 (1-891033-07-7, Rainshadow Editns) Black Rock Pr.

Cobb, Tyson K., ed. Physical Diagnosis: Pretest Self-Assessment & Review. 3rd ed. LC 97-10550. (Pretest Clinical Science Ser.). (Illus.). 200p. 1997. pap. text 18.95 (0-07-052531-5) McGraw-Hill HPD.

***Cobb, Vicki.** Bangs & Twangs: Science Fun with Sound. LC 00-22116. (Illus.). 2000. lib. bdg. write for info. (0-7613-1571-3) Millbrook Pr.

— Bet You Can! Science Possibilities to Fool You. (Avon/Camelot Bks.). (J). 1983. 9.60 (0-606-02765-3, Pub. by Turtleback) Demco.

— Bet You Can't! Science Impossibilities to Fool You. (J). 1980. 9.60 (0-606-02766-1, Pub. by Turtleback) Demco.

Cobb, Vicki. Blood & Gore, Like You've Never Seen. LC 96-37971. (J). (gr. 3-7). 1997. pap. 4.99 (0-590-92665-9) Scholastic Inc.

— Brave in the Attempt. (Illus.). 128p. (Orig.). 1983. pap. 8.95 (0-914771-00-0) Pinwheel Pubs.

— Chemically Active! Experiments You Can Do at Home. LC 83-49490. (Trophy Nonfiction Bk.). (Illus.). 160p. (J). (gr. 6-8). 1990. pap. 4.95 (0-06-446101-7, HarpTrophy) HarpC Child Bks.

— Chemically Active! Experiments You Can Do at Home. LC 83-49490. (Illus.). 160p. (J). (gr. 5-8). 1985. 14.00 (0-397-32079-5); lib. bdg. 14.89 (0-397-32080-9) HarpC Child Bks.

— Dirt & Grime, Like You've Never Seen. LC 97-9336. (Illus.). (J). (gr. 3-7). 1998. 4.99 (0-590-92666-7) Scholastic Inc.

***Cobb, Vicki.** Don't Try This at Home! Science Fun for Kids on the Go. 176p. 1999. mass mkt. 4.50 (0-380-72810-9, Avon Bks) Morrow Avon.

— Don't Try This at Home! Science Fun for Kids on the Go. (Illus.). (J). 1999. 9.85 (0-606-17964-X) Turtleback.

— Feeding Yourself. LC 88-14192. (Illus.). 32p. (J). (gr. k-3). 1989. 11.95 (0-397-32324-7) HarpC Child Bks.

— Follow Your Nose: Discover Your Sense of Smell. LC 99-47872. (Five Senses Ser.). 32p. (J). (gr. 2-4). 2000. 21.90 (0-7613-1521-7) Millbrook Pr.

Cobb, Vicki. Fuzz Does It! LC 81-47758. (Illus.). (J). (gr. 1-3). 1982. 12.95 (0-397-31975-4); pap. 4.75 (0-397-31977-0); lib. bdg. 11.89 (0-397-31976-2) HarpC Child Bks.

— Getting Dressed. LC 87-26097. (Illus.). 32p. (J). (gr. k-3). 1989. 11.95 (0-397-32142-2); lib. bdg. 11.89 (0-397-32143-0) HarpC Child Bks.

— How the Doctor Knows You're Fine. LC 73-4758. (Illus.). (J). (gr. 2-3). 1973. 12.95 (0-397-31240-7) HarpC Child Bks.

***Cobb, Vicki.** How to Really Fool Yourself: Illusions for All Your Senses. LC 98-27723. 128p. (J). (gr. 3). 1999. pap. 12.95 (0-471-31592-3) Wiley.

Cobb, Vicki. Keeping Clean. LC 88-2930. (Illus.). 32p. (J). (gr. k-3). 1989. 11.95 (0-397-32312-3); lib. bdg. 11.89 (0-397-32313-1) HarpC Child Bks.

— Magic . . . Naturally! Science Entertainments & Amusements. LC 76-13179. (Illus.). (J). (gr. 5-7). 1976. 12.95 (0-397-31631-3) HarpC Child Bks.

— Magic . . . Naturally! Science Entertainments & Amusements. LC 90-21829. (Illus.). 160p. (J). (gr. 4 up). 1993. lib. bdg. 16.89 (0-06-022475-4) HarpC Child Bks.

— More Science Experiments You Can Eat. LC 78-12732. (Trophy Nonfiction Bk.). (Illus.). 128p. (J). (gr. 5-9). 1984. pap. 4.95 (0-06-446003-7, HarpTrophy) HarpC Child Bks.

— More Science Experiments You Can Eat. 1979. 10.05 (0-606-07040-0, Pub. by Turtleback) Demco.

— Science Experiments You Can Eat. 1994. 11.05 (0-606-06718-3, Pub. by Turtleback) Demco.

— Science Experiments You Can Eat: Revised Edition. LC 93-13679. (Trophy Nonfiction Bk.). (Illus.). 224p. (J). (gr. 5-9). 1984. pap. 5.95 (0-06-446002-9, Perennial) HarperTrade.

— Science Experiments You Can Eat: Revised Edition. rev. ed. LC 93-13679. (Illus.). 224p. (J). (gr. 5-9). 1994. lib. bdg. 15.89 (0-06-023551-9) HarpC Child Bks.

— The Secret Life of Cosmetics: A Science Experiment Book. LC 85-40097. (Illus.). 128p. (J). (gr. 5-9). 1985. lib. bdg. 14.89 (0-397-32122-8) HarpC Child Bks.

— The Secret Life of Hardware: A Science Experiment Book. LC 81-48607. (Illus.). 96p. (J). (gr. 5 up). 1982. 13.95 (0-397-31999-1); lib. bdg. 13.89 (0-397-32000-0) HarpC Child Bks.

— The Secret Life of School Supplies. LC 81-47108. (Illus.). 96p. (J). (gr. 5 up). 1981. lib. bdg. 13.89 (0-397-31925-8) HarpC Child Bks.

***Cobb, Vicki.** Squirts & Spurts: Science Fun with Water. LC 00-22113. (Illus.). 2000. lib. bdg. 0.00 (0-7613-1572-1) Millbrook Pr.

Cobb, Vicki. Supersuits. LC 74-19083. (Illus.). 96p. (J). (gr. 5 up). 1975. 12.95 (0-397-31559-7) HarpC Child Bks.

— This Place Is Cold. (Imagine Living Here Ser.). (Illus.). (J). (gr. 2-4). 1989. 14.95 (0-8027-6852-0); lib. bdg. 13.85 (0-8027-6853-9) Walker & Co.

— This Place Is Cold. (Imagine Living Here Ser.). (Illus.). 32p. (J). (gr. 2-5). 1990. pap. 7.95 (0-8027-7340-0) Walker & Co.

— This Place Is Crowded: Japan. 32p. (J). (gr. 2-4). 1992. 14.95 (0-8027-8145-4); lib. bdg. 15.85 (0-8027-8146-2) Walker & Co.

— This Place Is Dry. (Imagine Living Here Ser.). (J). 1989. 12.15 (0-606-05668-8, Pub. by Turtleback) Demco.

— This Place Is Dry. (Imagine Living Here Ser.). (Illus.). (J). (gr. 2-4). 1989. 12.95 (0-8027-6854-7); lib. bdg. 13.85 (0-8027-6855-5) Walker & Co.

— This Place Is Dry. (Imagine Living Here Ser.). (Illus.). 32p. (J). (gr. 2-5). 1993. pap. 6.95 (0-8027-7400-8) Walker & Co.

— This Place Is High. (Imagine Living Here Ser.). (Illus.). 32p. (J). (gr. 2-4). 1989. 12.95 (0-8027-6882-2); lib. bdg. 13.85 (0-8027-6883-0) Walker & Co.

— This Place Is Lonely: The Australian Outback. (Imagine Living Here Ser.). (Illus.). 32p. (Orig.). (J). (gr. 2-5). 1994. 13.95 (0-8027-6959-4); pap. 6.95 (0-8027-7415-6); lib. bdg. 14.85 (0-8027-6960-8) Walker & Co.

— This Place Is Wet. (Imagine Living Here Ser.). (J). 1989. 12.15 (0-606-05669-6, Pub. by Turtleback) Demco.

— This Place Is Wet. (Imagine Living Here Ser.). (Illus.). 32p. (J). (gr. 2-4). 1989. 12.95 (0-8027-6880-6); lib. bdg. 13.85 (0-8027-6881-4) Walker & Co.

— This Place Is Wet. (Imagine Living Here Ser.). (Illus.). 32p. (J). (gr. 2-5). 1993. pap. 6.95 (0-8027-7399-0) Walker & Co.

— This Place Is Wild: East Africa. LC 97-25454. (Imagine Living Here Ser.: Vol. 7). (Illus.). 33p. (J). (gr. k-3). 1998. 15.95 (0-8027-8632-4); lib. bdg. 16.85 (0-8027-8633-2) Walker & Co.

— Vicki Cobb's Papermaking Book & Kit. (Illus.). 32p. (J). (gr. 2-6). 1993. 16.95 (0-694-00467-7, HarpFestival) HarpC Child Bks.

Cobb, Vicki. Wanna Bet? Science Challenges to Fool You. 1993. 9.09 (0-606-06082-0, Pub. by Turtleback) Demco.

Cobb, Vicki. Why Can't I Live Forever? And Other Not Such Dumb Questions about Life. (Illus.). (J). (gr. 2-5). 1997. 13.99 (0-614-28850-9, Dutton Child) Peng Put Young Read.

— Why Doesn't the Earth Fall Up? And Other Not Such Dumb Questions about Motion. LC 88-11108. (Illus.). 40p. (J). (gr. 2-5). 1989. 14.99 (0-525-67253-2, Dutton Child) Peng Put Young Read.

— Writing It Down. LC 88-14191. (Illus.). 32p. (J). (gr. k-3). 1989. 11.95 (0-397-32326-3) HarpC Child Bks.

***Cobb, Vicki.** Your Tongue Can Tell: Discover Your Sense of Taste. LC 99-47873. (Five Senses Ser.). 32p. (J). (gr. 2-4). 2000. lib. bdg. 21.90 (0-7613-1473-3) Millbrook Pr.

Cobb, Vicki & Cobb, Joshua. Light Action! Amazing Experiments with Optics. LC 92-25528. (Illus.). 208p. (J). (gr. 7-11). 1993. lib. bdg. 15.89 (0-06-021437-6) HarpC Child Bks.

Cobb, Vicki & Darling, Kathy. Bet You Can! Science Possibilities to Fool You. LC 82-90530. (Illus.). 112p. (J). (gr. 4-7). 1983. mass mkt. 4.50 (0-380-82180-X, Avon Bks) Morrow Avon.

— Bet You Can't! (Illus.). 128p. (J). (gr. 4-7). 1983. mass mkt. 4.50 (0-380-54502-0, Avon Bks) Morrow Avon.

— Don't Try This at Home! Science Fun for Kids on the Go. LC 97-20481. (Illus.). 128p. (J). (gr. 3-7). 1998. 15.00 (0-688-14856-5, Wm Morrow) Morrow Avon.

— Wanna Bet! Science Challenges Bound to Fool You. LC 92-8962. 128p. (J). (gr. 4-7). 1993. 15.00 (0-688-11213-7) Lothrop.

— Wanna Bet: Science Challenges to Fool You. 160p. 1994. mass mkt. 4.50 (0-380-71722-0, Avon Bks) Morrow Avon.

***Cobb, Vicki & Darling, Kathy.** You Gotta Try This! Absolutely Irresistible Science. LC 98-29556. (Illus.). 144p. 1999. 14.95 (0-688-15740-8, Wm Morrow) Morrow Avon.

***Cobb, Vicki & Lavallee, Barbara.** This Place Is Wild: East Africa. (Imagine Living Here Ser.). (Illus.). 32p. (J). (gr. 2-5). 2000. pap. 7.95 (0-8027-7579-9) Walker & Co.

Cobb, W. History of Grays, Solicitors of York from 1695-1988. (C). 1988. 130.00 (1-85072-051-7, Pub. by W Sessions) St Mut.

Cobb, Walter J., tr. see Hugo, Victor.

Cobb, Whitney L. The Basics of Winning Horseracing. 3rd rev. ed. LC 94-70606. (Illus.). 64p. 1994. mass mkt. 4.95 (0-940685-49-3) Cardoza Pub.

Cobb, Willard. Alien Spirit Minds. 135p. (Orig.). 1991. pap. 7.95 (0-9631084-0-9) Riddlestar.

Cobb, William. Harry Reunited. LC 95-24113. 336p. 1995. 23.00 (1-881320-37-5, Black Belt) Black Belt Communs.

— Somewhere in All This Green: New & Selected Stories. 171p. 1998. 23.00 (1-57966-001-0, Black Belt) Black Belt Communs.

— A Spring of Souls. LC 99-19145. 304p. 1999. 25.95 (1-57587-137-8) Crane Hill AL.

— Spring of Souls: A Novel. LC 99-19145. 304p. 1999. pap. 15.95 (1-57587-138-6) Crane Hill AL.

— A Walk Through Fire: A Novel. 320p. 2000. pap. 16.95 (1-57587-158-0, Pub. by Crane Hill AL) Blair.

Cobb, William. A Walk Through Fire: A Novel. 464p. 1993. mass mkt. 5.50 (0-380-71832-4, Avon Bks) Morrow Avon.

Cobb, William, tr. see Merleau-Ponty, Maurice.

***Cobb, William H.** Radical Education in the Rural South: Commonwealth College, 1923-1940. LC 99-54086. 2000. 34.95 (0-8143-2773-7) Wayne St U Pr.

Cobb, William S., tr. see Plato.

Cobb, William S., tr. & intro. see Plato.

Cobb, William W., Jr. The American Foundation Myth in Vietnam: Reigning Paradigms & Raining Bombs. LC 98-28557. 232p. 1998. 48.00 (0-7618-1208-3); pap. 27.50 (0-7618-1209-1) U Pr of Amer.

Cobb, Wilton P. History of Dodge County. LC 79-11196. (Illus.). 309p. 1993. reprint ed. 30.00 (0-87152-293-4) Reprint.

Cobban, Alan B. English University Life in the Middle Ages. (Illus.). 279p. 1999. text 45.00 (0-8142-0826-6); pap. text 20.00 (0-8142-5028-9) Ohio St U Pr.

— The King's Hall Within the University of Cambridge in the Later Middle Ages. LC 69-10193. (Cambridge Studies in Medieval Life & Thought: 3rd Ser., Vol. 1). 375p. reprint ed. pap. 106.90 (0-608-12237-8, 2024432) Bks Demand.

Cobban, Alfred. The Decline of Political Theory. (Reprint Series in Social Sciences). (C). 1993. reprint ed. pap. text 5.00 (*0-8290-3248-7*, PS-43) Irvington.
— Dictatorship: Its History & Theory. LC 76-122979. (World History Ser.: No. 48). 1970. reprint ed. lib. bdg. 75.00 (*0-8383-1111-3*) M S G Haskell Hse.
— Edmund Burke & the Revolt Against the Eighteenth Century: A Study of the Political & Social Thinking of Burke, Wordsworth, Coleridge, & Southey. LC 75-28995. (BCL Ser.: No. II). reprint ed. 32.50 (*0-404-14006-8*) AMS Pr.
— The Social Interpretation of the French Revolution. 2nd ed. LC 99-11992. 228p. (C). 1999. 49.95 (*0-521-66151-X*) Cambridge U Pr.
— The Social Interpretation of the French Revolution. 2nd ed. LC 99-11992. 178p. (C). 1999. pap. 18.95 (*0-521-66767-4*) Cambridge U Pr.
***Cobban, Helena.** The Israeli-Syrian Peace Talks: 1991-96 & Beyond. LC 99-44995. (Illus.). 272p. 1999. pap. 19.95 (*1-878379-98-4*) US Inst Peace.
— The Moral Architecture of World Peace: Nobel Laureates Discuss Our Global Future. LC 99-56608. (Illus.). 288p. 2000. 24.95 (*0-8139-1987-8*) U Pr of Va.
Cobban, Helena. The Palestinian Liberation Organization: People, Power & Politics. (Cambridge Middle East Library: No. 5). (Illus.). 320p. 1985. pap. text 21.95 (*0-521-27216-5*) Cambridge U Pr.
— The Superpowers & the Syrian-Israeli Conflict: Beyond Crisis Management?, 149. LC 90-25866. (Washington Papers: No. 149). 208p. 1991. pap. 17.95 (*0-275-93945-6*, B3945, Praeger Pubs) Greenwood.
— The Superpowers & the Syrian-Israeli Conflict: Beyond Crisis Management?, 149. LC 90-25866. (Washington Papers: No. 149). 208p. 1991. 19.95 (*0-275-93944-8*, C3944, Praeger Pubs) Greenwood.
Cobbe, Frances P. Darwinism in Morals & Other Essays. 399p. 1977. 24.95 (*0-8369-2895-4*) Ayer.
Cobbe, William R. Doctor Judas: A Portrayal of the Opium Habit. Grob, Gerald N., ed. LC 80-1218. (Addiction in America Ser.). 1981. reprint ed. lib. bdg. 31.95 (*0-405-13574-2*) Ayer.
***Cobbenhagen, Jan.** Successful Innovation: Towards a New Theory for the Management of Small & Medium Sized Enterprises. LC 00-24325. (New Horizons in the Economics of Innovation Ser.). 2000. write for info. (*1-84064-388-9*) E Elgar.
Cobbett. Cobbett in Ireland. (C). 1984. pap. 19.50 (*0-85315-596-8*, Pub. by Lawrence & Wishart); text 49.95 (*0-85315-588-7*, Pub. by Lawrence & Wishart) NYU Pr.
— A Year's Residence in America. (BCL1 - U. S. History Ser.). 275p. 1991. reprint ed. lib. bdg. 79.00 (*0-7812-6011-6*) Rprt Serv.
Cobbett, Aaron. Super Eros. 1998. 39.95 (*3-86187-130-0*) B Gmunder.
— Super Eros. 1999. 29.95 (*3-86187-135-1*) B Gmunder.
Cobbett, George T., ed. A Time to Pray: Prayers, Psalms & Readings for Personal Devotion. 175p. 1981. 9.95 (*0-89869-073-0*) Church Pub Inc.
Cobbett, Thomas. Civil Magistrate's Power in Matters of Religion Modestly Debated, London, 1653. LC 74-141104. (Research Library of Colonial Americana). 1972. reprint ed. 26.95 (*0-405-03318-4*) Ayer.
Cobbett, W. Jews & the Jews in England. 1976. lib. bdg. 59.95 (*0-8490-2103-0*) Gordon Pr.
Cobbett, William. Democratic Judge Or, the Equal Liberty of the Press. LC 70-125686. (American Journalists Ser.). 1974. reprint ed. 16.95 (*0-405-01663-8*) Ayer.
— A Grammar of the English Language. LC 86-15574. (American Linguistics, 1700-1900 Ser.). 248p. 1986. reprint ed. 50.00 (*0-8201-1410-3*) Schol Facsimiles.
— A History of the Protestant Reformation in England & Ireland. LC 88-51240. 406p. 1988. reprint ed. pap. 18.00 (*0-89555-353-8*) TAN Bks Pubs.
— Peter Porcupine in America: Pamphlets on Republicanism & Revolution. LC 93-33875. (Documents in American Social History Ser.). (Illus.). 304p. 1994. text 35.00 (*0-8014-2839-4*) Cornell U Pr.
Cobbett, William, et al, eds. Parliamentary History of England from the Norman Conquest in 1066 to the Year 1803, 36 vols. LC 54-54297. reprint ed. 4140.00 (*0-404-01650-2*) AMS Pr.
Cobbett, William & Cohen, Robin, eds. Popular Struggles in South Africa. LC 88-71831. 250p. (C). 1988. 35.00 (*0-86543-114-0*); pap. 11.95 (*0-86543-115-9*) Africa World.
Cobbett, William, jt. auth. see Von Martens, George F.
***Cobbey, J. E.** Practical Treatise on the Law of Replevin. 993p. 1999. 210.00 (*1-56169-451-7*) Gaunt.
Cobbin, Ingram, ed. see Caryl, Joseph.
Cobbing, Andrew. The Japanese Discovery of Victorian Britain: Early Travel Encounters in the Far West. (Meiji Ser.: Vol. 5). 308p. 1998. text 52.00 (*1-873410-81-6*, Pub. by Curzon Pr Ltd) UH Pr.
Cobbing, Bob, et al. Light. 14p. (Orig.). 1994. pap. 3.00 (*1-57141-002-3*) Runaway Spoon.
Cobble, Dorothy S. Dishing It Out: Waitresses & Their Unions in the Twentieth Century. (Working Class in American History - Women in American History Ser.). (Illus.). 368p. 1991. text 34.95 (*0-252-01812-5*) U of Ill Pr.
— Dishing It Out: Waitresses & Their Unions in the Twentieth Century. (Working Class in American History Ser.). (Illus.). 368p. (C). 1992. pap. text 14.95 (*0-252-06186-1*) U of Ill Pr.
— Women & Unions: Forging a Partnership. 464p. 1993. text 55.00 (*0-87546-300-2*, ILR Press) Cornell U Pr.
Cobble, Dorothy S., ed. Women & Unions: Forging a Partnership. 464p. 1993. pap. text 19.95 (*0-87546-301-0*, ILR Press) Cornell U Pr.
***Cobble, James E., Jr. & Elliott, Charles M.** The Hidden Spirit: Discovering the Spirituality of Institutions. 164p. 1999. pap. 12.95 (*1-880562-37-5*) Christ Minist.
Cobble, James F., Jr. Bulletin Bloopers. 104p. (Orig.). 1995. pap. 9.95 (*1-880562-20-0*) Christ Minist.
— The Church & the Powers: A Theology of Church Structure. 180p. 1988. pap. 9.95 (*0-913573-50-7*) Hendrickson MA.
Cobble, James F., Jr. & Hammar, Richard R. The 1999 Compensation Handbook for Church Staff. 152p. 1998. pap. 19.95 (*1-880562-32-4*) Christ Minist.
***Cobble, James F., Jr. & Houts, Donald C.** Well-Being in Ministry: A Guide for Pastors, Staff Members & Congregational Leaders. 200p. 1999. pap. 12.95 (*1-880562-38-3*) Christ Minist.
Cobble, Nancy, ed. see Sawyer, Joy.
Cobbledick, Patricia, ed. Index to the South African Law Journal. 1998. 74.00 (*0-7021-3045-1*, Pub. by Juta & Co) Gaunt.
Cobblestone Publishing Staff, ed. Cobblestone's New York City Reader: A Collection from the Pages of Cobblestone & Faces Magazines. LC 99-165791. 218p. (YA). (gr. 4 up). 1997. pap. 21.95 (*0-382-40961-2*) Cobblestone Pub Co.
***Cobbold.** Guppies for Tea. (J). 2000. pap. 10.95 (*0-552-99537-1*, Pub. by Transworld Publishers Ltd) Trafalgar.
Cobbold. The World Reshaped. LC 96-16747. 200p. 1996. text 65.00 (*0-312-16221-9*) St Martin.
Cobbold, David & Hurlin, Philippe. The Great Wines & Vintages. (Illus.). 168p. 1997. 19.98 (*0-7858-0823-X*) Bk Sales Inc.
Cobbold, G. B. The Children of Romulus. 1995. pap. text. write for info. (*0-8013-1371-6*, Prentice Hall) P-H.
— Hellas: A Short History of Classical Greek Civilization & Its Predecessors. (Illus.). 216p. (YA). (gr. 9-12). 1999. pap. text 13.33 (*1-877653-64-0*) Wayside Pub.
Cobbold, Marika. Frozen Music. mass mkt. 7.50 (*0-06-109881-7*) HarpC.
***Cobbold, Marika.** Frozen Music: A Novel. LC 99-22559. 384p. 1999. 24.00 (*0-06-019449-9*) HarpC.
Cobbold, Marika. Guppies for Tea. large type ed. LC 94-61863. 360p. 1995. pap. 19.95 (*0-7862-0385-4*) Thorndike Pr.
— The Purveyor of Enchantment. LC 97-32201. 240p. 1997. text 22.95 (*0-312-18160-4*) St Martin.
***Cobbold, Marika.** The Purveyor of Enchantment. 2000. 27.95 (*0-593-04076-7*, Pub. by Transworld Publishers Ltd); pap. 12.95 (*0-552-99687-4*, Pub. by Transworld Publishers Ltd) Trafalgar.
Cobbold, Marika. The Purveyor of Enchantment. large type ed. LC 98-12007. 277p. 1998. 25.95 (*0-7838-0122-X*, G K Hall & Co) Mac Lib Ref.
***Cobbold, Marika.** A Rival Creation. 2000. 25.95 (*0-593-03593-3*, Pub. by Transworld Publishers Ltd) Trafalgar.
Cobbold, Peter H., jt. ed. see McCormack, James G.
Cobbold, Richard, ed. The World Reshaped: Fifty Years after the War in Europe. (RUSI Defence Studies). 264p. 1996. text 69.95 (*0-312-16020-8*) St Martin.
Cobbs, John L. Understanding John le Carre. LC 97-4863. (Understanding Contemporary British Literature Ser.). 300p. 1997. 29.95 (*1-57003-168-1*) U of SC Pr.
Cobbs, John L. & Barnes, Lisa T. Lure of the Phoenix: Sculpture by Doris Sams. (Illus.). 1992. 10.00 (*0-9624021-4-1*) Ursinus College.
Cobbs, Marnie. Swimming Poems. 20p. 1999. 20.00 (*0-9662146-1-7*) Uphill Hse.
— Treehouse Poems. 56p. 1998. pap. 10.00 (*0-9662146-0-9*) Uphill Hse.
Cobbs, Price M., jt. auth. see Grier, William.
Cobbs, Price M., jt. auth. see Grier, William H.
Cobden, Guy. I Saw Murder. large type ed. (Linford Mystery Library). 400p. 1993. pap. 16.99 (*0-7089-7386-8*) Ulverscroft.
— Murder for Her Birthday. large type ed. (Linford Mystery Library). 400p. 1993. pap. 16.99 (*0-7089-7381-7*, Linford) Ulverscroft.
— Murder for His Money. large type ed. (Linford Mystery Library). 1994. pap. 16.99 (*0-7089-7625-5*, Linford) Ulverscroft.
— Murder Inherited. large type ed. (Linford Mystery Library). 400p. 1993. pap. 16.99 (*0-7089-7417-1*, Linford) Ulverscroft.
— Murder Was My Neighbour. large type ed. (Linford Mystery Library). 496p. 1993. pap. 16.99 (*0-7089-7353-1*, Linford) Ulverscroft.
— Murder Was Their Medicine. large type ed. (Linford Mystery Library). 432p. 1993. pap. 16.99 (*0-7089-7390-6*, Linford) Ulverscroft.
— My Guess Was Murder. large type ed. (Linford Mystery Library). 448p. 1993. pap. 16.99 (*0-7089-7377-9*, Linford) Ulverscroft.
Cobden, John. Dachau: Reality & Myth. rev. ed. (Illus.). 49p. (Orig.). 1994. pap. 5.00 (*0-939484-49-8*, 0977, Inst Hist Rev) Legion Survival.
Cobe, Patricia, jt. auth. see Parlapiano, Ellen H.
Cobe, Patricia, jt. ed. see Plotch, Batia.
Cobean, Robert H. La Ceramica de Tula, Hidalgo. 533p. 1990. pap. 18.00 (*968-6487-37-9*, IN038) UPLAAP.
Cobeljic, Nikola & Stojanovic, Radmila. The Theory of Investment Cycles in a Socialist Economy. Karcz, Jerzy, ed. LC 68-14431. 174p. reprint ed. pap. 54.00 (*0-608-14891-1*, 202614000048) Bks Demand.
Cobelli, jt. auth. see Carson.
Cobelli, C. Carbohydrate Metabolism: Quantitative Physiology & Mathematical Modelling. Bergman, R. N., ed. LC 80-41383. 458p. pap. 142.00 (*0-608-17660-5*, 203037400069) Bks Demand.
Cobelli, C. & Mariani, L., eds. Modelling & Control in Biomedical Systems: Proceedings of the IFAC Symposium, Venice, Italy, April 6-8, 1988. (IFAC Proceedings Ser.). (Illus.). 683p. 1988. pap. 30.00 (*0-08-036609-0*, Pergamon Pr) Elsevier.
— Modelling & Control in Biomedical Systems: Proceedings of the IFAC Symposium, Venice, Italy, April 6-8, 1988. (IFAC Proceedings Ser.: 8901). (Illus.). 686p. 1989. 301.00 (*0-08-035732-6*, Pergamon Pr) Elsevier.
Cobelo, Armando F., jt. auth. see Mena, Cesar A.
Cobelo, Carolyn E. Awakening to Soul Love: Pathways to Intimacy. 96p. 2000. pap. 16.95 (*0-9670412-2-8*) Akasha Prodns.
— Handbook to Twenty-Five Power Places. 2000. 16.95 (*0-9670412-4-4*) Akasha Prodns.
— Sacred Space: Exploring Ancient Ceremonial Sites. 136p. 2000. pap. 15.95 (*0-9670412-3-6*) Akasha Prodns.
— Spring of Hope: Messages from Mary. 64p. 2000. pap. 12.95 (*0-9670412-1-X*) Akasha Prodns.
Coben, Diana. Radical Heroes: Gramsci, Freire, & the Liberal Tradition in Adult Education. LC 98-11116. (Studies in the History of Education: Vol. 6). 280p. 1998. 70.00 (*0-8153-1898-7*, SS1006) Garland.
***Coben, Diana, et al.** Perspectives on Adults Learning Mathematics: Research & Practice. LC 00-33084. (Mathematics Education Library). 2000. write for info. (*0-7923-6415-5*) Kluwer Academic.
Coben, Harlan. Back Spin: A Myron Bolitar Mystery. 368p. 1997. mass mkt. 6.50 (*0-440-22270-2*) Dell.
***Coben, Harlan.** Darkest Fear: A Myron Bolitar Novel. LC 99-89788. 304p. 2000. 23.95 (*0-385-33433-8*) Delacorte.
Coben, Harlan. Deal Breaker: A Myron Bolitar Mystery. 368p. 1995. mass mkt. 6.50 (*0-440-22044-0*) Dell.
— Dropshot. 368p. 1996. mass mkt. 6.50 (*0-440-22045-9*) Dell.
— The Final Detail. LC 98-48251. 320p. 1999. 22.95 (*0-385-32371-9*) Delacorte.
***Coben, Harlan.** The Final Detail. 384p. 2000. mass mkt. 6.50 (*0-440-22545-0*) Dell.
— One False Move: A Myron Bolitar Novel. 400p. 1999. mass mkt. 6.50 (*0-440-22544-2*) Dell.
Coben, Larry E., et al. Pennsylvania Products Liability Guide. LC 92-74117. 1998. ring bd. 69.50 (*1-887024-21-2*) Bisel Co.
Coben, Lawrence A. & Ferster, Dorothy C. Japanese Cloisonne: History, Technique & Appreciation. (Illus.). 336p. 1991. reprint ed. 75.00 (*0-8048-1666-2*) Tuttle Pubng.
Coben, Stanley. A Study in Nativism: The American Red Scare of 1919-20. (Irvington Reprint Series in American History). (C). 1991. reprint ed. pap. 2.30 (*0-8290-2611-8*, H-373) Irvington.
Cober, Harold S. Man Is Risen. (Illus.). 100p. (Orig.). (C). 1994. pap. 5.95 (*1-877633-22-4*) Luthers.
— The Rise of Man. LC 95-1101. 1995. pap. 5.99 (*1-877633-28-3*) Luthers.
— Universal Reality: Physics - Religion - Psychology. (Illus.). 96p. (Orig.). (C). 1994. pap. 5.99 (*1-877633-23-2*) Luthers.
Coberly, Lenore M., et al. Writers Have No Age: Creative Writing with Older Adults. LC 84-15715. (Activities, Adaptation & Aging Ser.: Vol. 6, No. 2). 128p. 1985. text 3.95 (*0-86656-320-2*); pap. text 19.95 (*0-86656-351-2*) Haworth Pr.
Coberly, R. L. The Wildman's Son. LC 91-77135. (Illus.). 52p. (Orig.). 1991. pap. 6.95 (*1-878149-10-5*) Counterpoint Pub.
Coberly, Rich. The No-Hit Hall of Fame: No-Hitters of the Twentieth Century. LC 85-71539. 232p. (Orig.). 1985. pap. 13.95 (*0-934289-00-X*) R Coberly.
***Cobern, William W.** Everyday Thoughts about Nature: A Worldview Investigation of Important Concepts Students Use to Make Sense of Nature with Specific Attention to Science. LC 00-30185. (Science & Technology Education Library). 2000. write for info. (*0-7923-6344-2*) Kluwer Academic.
Cobern, William W. Socio-Cultural Perspectives on Science Education: An International Dialogue. LC 98-9442. (Science & Technology Education Library). 219p. 1998. 86.00 (*0-7923-4987-3*) Kluwer Academic.
Cobern, William W., ed. Socio-Cultural Perspectives on Science Education: An International Dialogue. (Science & Technology Education Library). 228p. 1998. pap. 39.00 (*0-7923-4988-1*) Kluwer Academic.
Cobert, Robert. Dark Shadows Music Book. (Illus.). 112p. (Orig.). 1996. pap. 14.95 (*0-938817-42-6*) Pomegranate Pr.
Cobet, Carel G. Miscsellanea Critica. xv, 616p. 1981. reprint ed. 130.00 (*3-487-07127-4*) G Olms Pubs.
Cobhaim, Catherine, tr. see Al-Shaykh, Hanan.
Cobham, Catherine, tr. see Adonis, Ali Ahmed Sa'id.
Cobham, Catherine, tr. see Al-Sa'Dawi, Nawal.
Cobham, Catherine, tr. see Al-Shaykh, Hanan.
Cobham, Catherine, tr. see Idris, Yusuf.
Cobham, Catherine, tr. see Mahfouz, Naguib.
Cobham, David, ed. Markets & Dealers: The Economics of the London Financial Markets. LC 92-20208. 1992. pap. text. write for info. (*0-582-07851-2*) Longman.
Cobham, David P. Macroeconomic Analysis: An Intermediate Text. 2nd ed. LC 97-51476. 1998. pap. write for info. (*0-582-27452-4*) Longman.
***Cobham, David P., et al.** From EMS to EMU--1979 to 1999 & Beyond. LC 99-36944. 1999. text 69.95 (*0-312-22799-X*) St Martin.
Cobham, R., ed. Amenity Landscape Management: A Resources Handbook. (Illus.). 480p. 1990. text 94.95 (*0-419-11570-6*, E & FN Spon) Routledge.
Cobham, Rhonda & Collins, Merle, eds. Watchers & Seekers: Creative Writing by Black Women in Britain. pap. 13.95 (*0-7043-4024-0*, Pub. by Womens Press) Trafalgar.
Cobia, David. Cooperatives in Agriculture. 480p. 1988. 90.00 (*0-13-172461-4*) P-H.
— Cooperatives in Agriculture. 2nd ed. 512p. (C). 2001. 74.00 (*0-13-541195-5*, Macmillan Coll) P-H.
Cobin, John M. Building Regulation, Market Alternatives & Allodial Policy. 256p. 1997. text 69.95 (*1-85972-587-2*, Pub. by Avebry) Ashgate Pub Co.
Cobin, Martin. From Convincement to Conversion. LC 64-17424. (Orig.). 1964. pap. 4.00 (*0-87574-134-7*) Pendle Hill.
Cobin, R. H. & Sirota, D. K., eds. Malignant Tumors of the Thyroid: Clinical Concepts & Controversies. (Illus.). 232p. 1992. 160.00 (*0-387-97570-5*) Spr-Verlag.
Coblans. Librarianship Documentation. (C). 1977. text 12.75 (*0-233-96596-3*) Westview.
Coble. Earth Science. 1981. 19.04 (*0-13-696138-X*) P-H.
Coble, Arthur B. Algebraic Geometry & Theta Functions. LC 30-12679. (American Mathematical Society, Colloquium Publications: No. 10). 290p. reprint ed. pap. 89.90 (*0-8357-3329-7*, 203955300013) Bks Demand.
Coble, Colleen. Where Leads the Heart. 1997. pap. text 1.66 (*1-57748-312-X*) Barbour Pub.
Coble, Howard. 21st Century Patent System Improvement Act: Report to the Committee on the Judiciary, U. S. House of Representatives. 170p. (C). 1998. pap. text 30.00 (*0-7881-4958-X*) DIANE Pub.
***Coble, Howard, ed.** Attorneys' Fees & the Tobacco Settlement: Congressional Hearing. (Illus.). 183p. 2000. reprint ed. pap. text 30.00 (*0-7881-8765-1*) DIANE Pub.
Coble, Howard, ed. Federal Courts Improvement Act of 1998. 53p. (C). 1999. pap. text 20.00 (*0-7881-7846-6*) DIANE Pub.
***Coble, Howard, ed.** Internet Domain Name Trademark Protection: Congressional Hearing. 192p. (C). 2000. reprint ed. pap. text 35.00 (*0-7881-8696-5*) DIANE Pub.
Coble, Howard, et al, eds. Security & Freedom Through Encryption (SAFE) Act of 1997: Report from the Committee on the Judiciary, U. S. House of Representatives. (Illus.). 178p. (C). 1998. text 30.00 (*0-7881-7250-6*) DIANE Pub.
Coble, Larry D., jt. auth. see Brubaker, Dale L.
***Coble, Lynda.** Angel in the Road. 448p. 1999. pap. write for info. (*0-7392-0253-7*, PO3308) Morris Pubng.
Coble, Parks M. Facing Japan: Chinese Politics & Japanese Imperialism, 1931-1937. (East Asian Monographs: Vol. 135). (Illus.). 475p. (C). 1991. 32.00 (*0-674-29011-9*) HUP.
— The Shanghai Capitalists & the Nationalist Government, 1927-1937. (East Asian Monographs: No. 94). 371p. (C). 1980. 20.00 (*0-674-80535-6*) HUP.
— The Shanghai Capitalists & the Nationalist Government, 1927-1937. (East Asian Monographs: No. 94). 371p. 1986. pap. text 20.00 (*0-674-80536-4*) HUP.
Coble, Richard, jt. ed. see Dias, L. Alver.
***Coble, Richard J., et al.** Construction Safety & Health Management. LC 00-24995. 200p. 2000. pap. 60.00 (*0-13-087173-7*) P-H.
Cobleigh, Arthur M. Cobleigh: Genealogy of the Cobleigh Family & Descendants from the First John Cobleigh & His Wife Mary (Bosworth) Cobleigh at Swansea, Massachusetts, in the Plymouth Colony, 1667. 881p. 1997. reprint ed. pap. 105.00 (*0-8328-7990-8*); reprint ed. lib. bdg. 115.00 (*0-8328-7989-4*) Higginson Bk Co.
Cobleigh, Rolfe. Handy Farm Devices: And How to Make Them. LC 95-38426. (Illus.). 296p. 1996. pap. 12.95 (*1-55821-432-1*) Lyons Pr.
Coblentz. After Twelve Thousand Years. 5.00 (*0-686-00464-7*); pap. 2.00 (*0-686-00465-5*) Fantasy Pub Co.
— Planet of Youth. 1952. 3.50 (*0-686-21530-3*); pap. 1.00 (*0-686-21531-1*) Fantasy Pub Co.
Coblentz, Kathie, jt. ed. see Kapsis, Robert E.
Coblentz, Edmond E., ed. Newsmen Speak: Journalists on Their Craft. LC 68-14900. (Essay Index Reprint Ser.). 1977. 19.95 (*0-8369-0318-8*) Ayer.
Coblentz, Elizabeth. The Amish Cook Cookbook. Williams, Kevin, ed. (Illus.). 192p. 1993. pap. 15.95 (*0-9638775-1-8*) Oasis Newsfeatures.
Coblentz, J. Alex, ed. Faith of Our Fathers: Documents from the Early History of Back Creek Church, Mt. Ulla, N. C. LC 98-71384. 155p. 1998. pap. 10.00 (*1-57502-800-X*, PO2212) Morris Pubng.
***Coblentz, John.** Beauty for Ashes: Biblical Help for the Sexually Abused. 1999. pap. 5.95 (*0-87813-584-7*) Christian Light.
Coblentz, John. Christian Family Living. 1992. pap. 9.95 (*0-87813-541-3*) Christian Light.
— Courtship That Glorifies God: A Biblical Approach to Dating & Engagement. 1992. pap. 2.95 (*0-87813-545-6*) Christian Light.
— God's Will for Love in Marriage: Cultivating Marital Intimacy. 1992. pap. 4.95 (*0-87813-543-X*) Christian Light.
— God's Will for My Body: Guidance for Adolescents. 1992. pap. 2.95 (*0-87813-542-1*) Christian Light.
— Heaven at Last. 1990. pap. 3.50 (*0-87813-533-2*) Christian Light.
— Music in Biblical Perspective. 1986. pap. 1.75 (*0-87813-524-3*) Christian Light.
***Coblentz, John.** Putting Off Anger: A Biblical Study of What Anger Is & What to Do about It. 109p. 1999. 5.95 (*0-87813-579-0*) Christian Light.
Coblentz, John. Singlehood That Glorifies God: Living with Eternal Purpose. 1992. pap. 2.95 (*0-87813-546-4*) Christian Light.
— The Upward Call. 240p. (Orig.). (YA). 1997. pap. 9.95 (*0-87813-567-7*) Christian Light.
— What the Bible Says about Marriage, Divorce & Remarriage. 1992. pap. 4.95 (*0-87813-544-8*) Christian Light.

C

Coblentz, John, et al. Proclaiming God's Truth: 25 Years at Christian Light Publications, 1969-1994. 1994. pap. 7.95 (*0-87813-558-8*) Christian Light.

Coblentz, John A. The Victorious Life. 1993. pap. 2.25 (*0-87813-550-2*) Christian Light.

Coblentz, Patricia, jt. auth. see Bishop, Robert.

Coblentz, Stanlton A. Hidden World. 1976. 17.95 (*0-8488-0966-1*) Amereon Ltd.

Coblentz, Stanton A. Light Beyond: The Wonderworld of Parapsychology. LC 80-69585. (Illus.). 256p. 1982. 14.95 (*0-8453-4712-8*, Cornwall Bks) Assoc Univ Prs.

— The Literary Revolution. LC 72-94308. (BCL Ser.: No. I). reprint ed. 20.00 (*0-404-01579-4*) AMS Pr.

— The Literary Revolution. (BCL1-PR English Literature Ser.). 202p. 1992. reprint ed. lib. bdg. 79.00 (*0-685-52152-4*) Rprt Serv.

— Villains & Vigilantes. 1992. reprint ed. lib. bdg. 75.00 (*0-7812-5015-3*) Rprt Serv.

— When the Birds Fly South. Reginald, R. & Melville, Douglas, eds. LC 77-84212. (Lost Race & Adult Fantasy Ser.). 1978. reprint ed. lib. bdg. 23.95 (*0-405-10967-9*) Ayer.

Coblentz, Stanton A., ed. Modern American Lyrics: An Anthology. LC 76-167476. (Granger Index Reprint Ser.). 1977. reprint ed. 19.95 (*0-8369-6281-8*) Ayer.

— Modern British Lyrics: An Anthology. LC 70-38596. (Granger Index Reprint Ser.). 1977. reprint ed. 17.95 (*0-8369-6328-8*) Ayer.

Coblentz, Stanton A. & Elliot, Jeffrey M. Adventures of a Freelancer: The Literary Exploits & Autobiography of Stanton A. Coblentz. Burgess, Scott A., ed. LC 93-189506. (Borgo Bioviews Ser.: No. 2). 160p. 1993. pap. 19.00 (*0-89370-438-5*, 10323058) Millefleurs.

Coblenz, John. Viata Familiei Crestine (Christian Family Living) Brinzei, Daniel, ed. & tr. by. from ENG. (SPA.). 272p. (YA). pap. text. write for info. (*1-885270-02-X*) Christian Aid.

Coblenz, R. & Reeves, C. Rerating Damaged Naval Ship Propulsion Gear. (Nineteen Ninety-One Fall Technical Meeting Ser.: Vol. 91FTM9). (Illus.). 7p. 1991. pap. text 30.00 (*1-55589-606-5*) AGMA.

Cobley, jt. auth. see Briggs.

C

***Cobley, Derek, ed.** On the Tongue of a Bird: West Glamorgan Youth Theatre & Dance Company. (Illus.). 14p. 1998. pap., teacher ed. 4.95 (*0-8464-4937-4*) Beekman Pubs.

Cobley, Alan G. Class & Consciousness: The Black Petty Bourgeoisie in South Africa, 1924 to 1950, 127. LC 89-11761. (Contributions in Afro-American & African Studies: No. 127). 272p. 1990. 62.95 (*0-313-26708-1*, CPH/, Greenwood Pr) Greenwood.

— The Rules of the Game: Struggles in Black Recreation & Social Welfare Policy in South Africa, 182. LC 96-23337. (Contributions in Afro-American & African Studies: No. 182). 200p. 1997. 62.95 (*0-313-30108-5*, Greenwood Pr) Greenwood.

Cobley, Cathy. Child Abuse & the Law. Harpwood, Vivienne, ed. (Medico-Legal Practitioner Ser.). 224p. 1995. pap. 33.00 (*1-85941-011-1*, Pub. by Cavendish Pubng) Gaunt.

Cobley, Evelyn. Representing War: Form & Ideology in First World War Narratives. (Theory/Culture Ser.). 274p. 1996. pap. text 19.95 (*0-8020-7894-X*) U of Toronto Pr.

— Representing War: Form & Ideology in First World War Narratives. (Theory/Culture Ser.). 274p. (C). 1996. text 45.00 (*0-8020-0537-3*) U of Toronto Pr.

Cobley, John. The Crimes of the First Fleet Convicts. LC 70-553602. xv, 324 p. 1970. write for info. (*0-207-95192-6*, Pub. by Angus & Roberts) HarpC.

Cobley, Paul. Introducing Semiotics. LC 96-61951. 176p. 1997. pap. text 10.95 (*1-874166-55-2*, Pub. by Totem Bks) Natl Bk Netwk.

Cobley, Paul, ed. The Communication Theory Reader. LC 96-17464. 520p. (C). 1996. 85.00 (*0-415-14716-6*); pap. 24.99 (*0-415-14717-4*) Routledge.

***Coblin, W. South & Levi, Joseph Abraham, eds.** Francisco Varo's Grammar of the Mandarin Language (1703) An English Translation of 'Arte de la Lengua Mandarina' LC 99-58977. (Studies in the History of the Language Sciences: No. 93). liv, 280p. 2000. 95.00 (*1-55619-606-7*) J Benjamins Pubng.

Cobliner, W. Godfrey, jt. auth. see Spitz, Rene A.

Cobo, Bernabe. History of the Inca Empire. Hamilton, Roland, tr. from SPA. LC 79-12672. (Texas Pan American Ser.). 301p. 1979. pap. 16.95 (*0-292-73025-X*) U of Tex Pr.

— Inca Religion & Customs. Hamilton, Roland, ed. & tr. by. LC 89-37604. (Illus.). 303p. (C). 1990. pap. 15.95 (*0-292-73861-7*) U of Tex Pr.

Coborn, J. Savannah Monitors. (Illus.). 1995. pap. text 9.95 (*0-7938-0278-4*, RE113) TFH Pubns.

— White's Tree Frogs. (Illus.). 1995. pap. text 9.95 (*0-7938-0282-2*, RE114) TFH Pubns.

***Coborn, John.** Amphibians. 64p. 2000. 12.95 (*0-7938-3059-1*) TFH Pubns.

Coborn, John. Amphibians Today. (Illus.). 64p. 1997. 12.95 (*0-7938-0148-6*, WW-023) TFH Pubns.

— Atlas of Snakes. (Illus.). 591p. 1991. 129.95 (*0-86622-749-0*, TS-128) TFH Pubns.

— Boas, Pythons & Other Friendly Snakes. (Illus.). 192p. 1992. 29.95 (*0-86622-603-6*, TS154) TFH Pubns.

— Breeding & Keeping Geckos. (Illus.). 160p. 1996. 22.95 (*0-7938-0134-6*, LR109) TFH Pubns.

— Breeding & Keeping Lizards. (Illus.). 160p. 22.95 (*0-7938-0136-2*, LR-111) TFH Pubns.

— Burmese Pythons. (Illus.). 64p. 1995. pap. text 9.95 (*0-7938-0263-6*, RE112) TFH Pubns.

— Caring for Green Iguanas. (Illus.). 64p. 1995. pap. text 9.95 (*0-7938-0255-5*, RE104) TFH Pubns.

— Cockatiels As a New Pet. (Illus.). 64p. (Orig.). 1990. pap. 6.95 (*0-86622-612-5*, TU-005) TFH Pubns.

— Cockatoos As a Hobby. (Illus.). 96p. 1995. pap. text 8.95 (*0-7938-0091-9*, TT038) TFH Pubns.

— Frogs & Toads As a New Pet. (Illus.). 64p. 1991. pap. 6.95 (*0-86622-535-8*, TU024) TFH Pubns.

— Garden Ponds. (Illus.). 64p. 1996. 19.95 (*0-7938-0123-0*, WW020) TFH Pubns.

— Green Iguanas & Other Iguanids. LC 98-19049. (Basic Domestic Reptile & Amphibian Library). (Illus.). 64p. (YA). (gr. 3 up). 1999. lib. bdg. 17.95 (*0-7910-5078-5*) Chelsea Hse.

— Green Iguanas & Other Iguanids. (Illus.). 64p. 1995. pap. text 9.95 (*0-7938-0272-5*, RE105) TFH Pubns.

***Coborn, John.** Guide to Owning an Australian Python. (Illus.). 1999. pap. 9.95 (*0-7938-2057-X*) TFH Pubns.

Coborn, John. Keeping & Breeding Lizards: A Complete Authoritative Guide. (Illus.). 102p. 1998. 12.95 (*0-7938-0222-9*, WW-056) TFH Pubns.

— Keeping & Breeding Reptiles & Amphibians. (Illus.). 160p. 1998. 22.95 (*0-7938-0132-X*, LR-107) TFH Pubns.

— Lizards. LC 98-22377. (Basic Domestic Reptile & Amphibian Library). (Illus.). 90p. (YA). (gr. 3 up). 1999. lib. bdg. 17.95 (*0-7910-5084-X*) Chelsea Hse.

— Lizards: Keeping & Breeding Them in Captivity. (Illus.). 64p. 1997. pap. text 6.95 (*0-7938-2021-9*, RE165) TFH Pubns.

— Lizards As a New Pet. (Illus.). 64p. 1992. pap. 6.95 (*0-86622-536-6*, TU-025) TFH Pubns.

— Mini-Atlas of Snakes. (Illus.). 736p. 1994. 59.95 (*0-86622-601-X*, TS193) TFH Pubns.

— Prehensile-Tailed Skinks. (Illus.). 64p. 1996. pap. 9.95 (*0-7938-0279-2*, RE127) TFH Pubns.

— The Professional's Book of Conures. (Illus.). 144p. 1991. 17.95 (*0-86622-421-1*, TS-159) TFH Pubns.

— The Professional's Book of Lovebirds. (Illus.). 160p. 1991. text 17.95 (*0-86622-604-4*, TS155) TFH Pubns.

— Proper Care of Amphibians. (TW Ser.). (Illus.). 256p. 1993. text 16.95 (*0-86622-346-0*, TW116) TFH Pubns.

— Proper Care of Canaries. (Illus.). 256p. 1994. 16.95 (*0-86622-447-5*, TW114) TFH Pubns.

— The Proper Care of Reptiles. (TW Ser.). (Illus.). 256p. 1993. text 15.95 (*0-86622-345-2*, TW115) TFH Pubns.

— Proper Care of Turtles. (Illus.). 256p. 1993. 16.95 (*0-86622-534-X*, TW132) TFH Pubns.

— Salamanders & Newts As a Hobby. (Illus.). 96p. 1993. 8.95 (*0-86622-730-X*, TT020) TFH Pubns.

— Salamanders & Newts As a New Pet. (Illus.). 64p. 1994. pap. 6.95 (*0-86622-538-2*, TU023) TFH Pubns.

— Snakes. LC 98-7659. (Basic Domestic Reptile & Amphibian Library). (Illus.). 64p. (YA). (gr. 3 up). 1999. lib. bdg. 17.95 (*0-7910-5085-8*) Chelsea Hse.

— Snakes: Keeping & Breeding Them in Captivity. (Illus.). 64p. 1997. pap. 6.95 (*0-7938-2022-7*, RE-166) TFH Pubns.

— Tropical Herps. (Illus.). 160p. 22.95 (*0-7938-0135-4*, LR-110) TFH Pubns.

— Turtles. (Illus.). 64p. 1997. 6.95 (*0-7938-2023-5*, RE-167) TFH Pubns.

— Turtles Today. (Illus.). 64p. 1996. 12.95 (*0-7938-0109-5*, WW-011) TFH Pubns.

— Water Dragons, Sailfin Lizards, & Basilisks. (Illus.). 64p. 1996. pap. 9.95 (*0-7938-0281-4*, RE118) TFH Pubns.

Coborn, John & American Society for the Prevention of Cruelty to. Amphibians Today: A Complete & Up-to-Date Guide. LC 97-4188. (Basic Domestic Pet Library). 76p. (J). (gr. 3 up). 1997. 19.95 (*0-7910-4602-8*) Chelsea Hse.

— Turtles Today: A Complete & Up-to-Date Guide. LC 97-3623. (Basic Domestic Pet Library). 76p. (J). (gr. 3 up). 1997. 19.95 (*0-7910-4618-4*) Chelsea Hse.

Coborn, John & Mara, W. P. Green Iguanas. (Illus.). 64p. 1996. 12.95 (*0-7938-0101-X*, WW005) TFH Pubns.

Cobos, Ruben. Dictionary of New Mexico & Southern Colorado Spanish. (ENG & SPA.). 208p. 1983. pap. text 11.95 (*0-89013-142-2*) Museum NM Pr.

— Refranes: Southwestern Spanish Proverbs. rev. ed. (Illus.). 192p. 1985. pap. 11.95 (*0-89013-177-5*) Museum NM Pr.

Cobourn, R. Thomas. Kareem Abdul-Jabbar: Basketball Great. Huggins, Nathan I., ed. (Black Americans of Achievement Ser.). (Illus.). 124p. (YA). (gr. 5 up). 1995. lib. bdg. 19.95 (*0-7910-1860-1*) Chelsea Hse.

***Cobrera, Jane.** Panda Big, Panda Small. LC 98-28833. (Toddlers Storybook Ser.). (Illus.). 24p. (J). (ps). 2000. pap. text 5.95 (*0-7894-5747-4*, D K Ink) DK Pub Inc.

Cobun, Peter & Joiner, Melinda G. Huntsville: Where Technology Meets Tradition. LC 93-32280. 286p. 1993. text 39.00 (*0-9630029-5-3*) Community Comm.

***Coburn.** Bridges to Coll age Algebra (intermediate) (C). 2001. text 78.00 (*0-03-031319-8*) Harcourt Coll Pubs.

Coburn. Coreldraw 9: The Official Guide. 1999. pap. 49.99 (*0-07-211986-1*) McGraw.

— Visual Basic. LC 99-14607. 1999. 65.95 (*0-534-36829-8*) Brooks-Cole.

— Visual Basic 5 Made Easy. 2nd ed. (Computer Science Ser.). 800p. (C). 1998. mass mkt. 69.95 (*0-534-95044-2*) PWS Pubs.

Coburn, jt. auth. see Knowlton.

Coburn, Alan, ed. see Loring, Jewell.

Coburn, Alvin L. Alvin Langdon Coburn, Photographer: An Autobiography. Helmut & Gernsheim, Alison, eds. (Illus.). 160p. 1978. pap. 8.95 (*0-486-23685-4*) Dover.

— Jacob Boehme: Being a Cloud Wrapped Immortal. 1993. pap. 3.95 (*1-55818-230-6*, Sure Fire) Holmes Pub.

Coburn, Andrew. Birthright: A Novel. LC 97-11723. 320p. 1997. 22.50 (*0-684-81529-X*) S&S Trade.

Coburn, Andrew, et al. Gypsum Plaster: Its Manufacture & Use. 48p. 1989. pap. 15.00 (*1-85339-038-0*, Pub. by Intermed Tech) Stylus Pub VA.

— Technical Principles of Building for Safety: Technical Principles & Details of Low-Cost, Hazard-Resistant Construction. LC 94-129133. (Building for Safety Ser.). 120p. (Orig.). 1994. pap. 17.50 (*1-85339-182-4*, Pub. by Intermed Tech) Stylus Pub VA.

Coburn, Andrew, jt. auth. see Spence, Robin.

Coburn, Ann. Worm Songs. large type ed. (J). 1998. pap. 16.95 (*0-7540-6018-7*, Galaxy Child Lrg Print) Chivers N Amer.

Coburn, Broughton. AAMA in America: A Pilgrimage of the Heart. 320p. 1996. pap. 14.00 (*0-385-47418-0*, Anchor NY) Doubleday.

— Everest: Mountain Without Mercy. LC 97-10765. (Illus.). 256p. 1997. 35.00 (*0-7922-7014-2*) Natl Geog.

Coburn, Carol K. Life at Four Corners: Religion, Gender, & Education in a German-Lutheran Community, 1868-1945. LC 92-11905. (Rural America Ser.). (Illus.). 224p. 1992. 29.95 (*0-7006-0557-6*) U Pr of KS.

— Life at Four Corners: Religion, Gender, & Education in a German-Lutheran Community, 1868-1945. LC 92-11905. (Rural America Ser.). (Illus.). 224p. 1994. pap. 16.95 (*0-7006-0682-3*) U Pr of KS.

***Coburn, Carol K. & Smith, Martha.** Spirited Lives: How Nuns Shaped Catholic Culture & American Life, 1836-1920. LC 98-30828. (Illus.). 400p. 1999. lib. bdg. 49.95 (*0-8078-2473-9*) U of NC Pr.

Coburn, Carol K. & Smith, Martha. Spirited Lives: How Nuns Shaped Catholic Culture & American Life, 1836-1920. LC 98-30828. (Illus.). 328p. (C). 1999. pap. 19.95 (*0-8078-4774-7*) U of NC Pr.

Coburn, Christine, jt. auth. see Burdett, Lois.

Coburn, Christine, jt. ed. see Burdett, Lois.

Coburn, Christopher M. & Berglund, Daniel R. Partnerships: A Compendium of State & Federal Cooperative Technology Programs. LC 94-32950. 660p. 1995. pap. text 39.95 (*0-935470-78-6*) Battelle.

Coburn, Chuck. Funny You Should Say That... A Lighthearted Awakening to Psychic Awareness. 240p. (Orig.). 1995. pap. 15.95 (*0-916108-12-0*) Seed Center.

— Reality Is Just an Illusion: The World of Shamans, Ghosts & Spirit Guides. LC 99-24438. 288p. 1999. pap. 9.95 (*1-56718-155-4*) Llewellyn Pubns.

Coburn, Daniel R., jt. auth. see Knowlton, Robert E.

Coburn, David. Health & Canadian Society: Sociological Perspectives. 3rd rev. ed. LC 98-218123. 800p. 1998. text 60.00 (*0-8020-4192-2*); pap. text 34.95 (*0-8020-8052-9*) U of Toronto Pr.

Coburn, Edna. Bereavement Booklet: A Guide of Support for Those Who Are Facing the Death of a Loved One. (Illus.). 23p. 1998. pap. 5.00 (*1-880805-04-9*) Natl Org Mothers Twins.

Coburn, Edward J. Learn to Compute: Guide to Apple. 416p. 1987. pap. 31.95 (*0-8273-2931-8*) Delmar.

— Learn to Compute: Guide to Apple. 416p. 1987. pap., teacher ed. 14.00 (*0-8273-2932-6*) Delmar.

Coburn, Edward J. MASTERY APPR TO MSW 3.1 IG&DK: Instructor's Guide with Instructor's Disk, 3.5. text 69.00 (*1-56118-495-0*) EMC-Paradigm.

Coburn, Edward J. Mastery Approach to Microsoft Windows, Version 3.1. 5th ed. LC 92-36634. 1993. pap. text 27.95 (*1-56118-496-9*) Paradigm MN.

— Mastery Approach to MS - PC DOS, Version 5.0. LC 92-36635. 272p. 1993. pap. text 25.95 (*1-56118-647-3*) Paradigm MN.

— Mastery Approach to MS - PC DOS, Version 5.0. 5th ed. LC 92-36635. 272p. 1993. pap. text 25.95 (*1-56118-612-0*); pap. text, teacher ed. 69.00 (*1-56118-613-9*) Paradigm MN.

— Mastery Approach to MS-PC Dos, Version 6.2X. LC 94-20643. 300p. 1994. pap. text 27.95 (*1-56118-760-7*) Paradigm MN.

— Mastery Approach to MS-PC Dos, Version 6.2X. 25th ed. LC 94-20643. 300p. 1994. pap. text 27.95 (*1-56118-761-5*) Paradigm MN.

Coburn, Edward J. A Mastery Approach to MS/PC Dos, Version 6.2: Instructor's guide. 24.00 (*1-56118-846-8*) EMC-Paradigm.

— Microsoft Windows 98 Essentials: Instructor's Guide. 19.00 (*0-7638-0286-7*) EMC-Paradigm.

— Microsoft Windows 98 Essentials: Text with CD Rom. 480p. 1999. 29.95 (*0-7638-0283-2*) EMC-Paradigm.

Coburn, Edward J. Microsoft Windows 95. LC 96-7210. 1996. 32.95 (*1-56118-871-9*); pap. text. write for info. (*1-56118-872-7*) Paradigm MN.

Coburn, Edward J. Microsoft Windows 95: Instructor's guide. 19.00 (*1-56118-873-5*) EMC-Paradigm.

— Microsoft Windows 98: Core Concepts & Applications. LC 98-51282. 1998. write for info. (*0-7638-0282-4*) Paradigm MN.

Coburn, Edward J. Visual Basic Made Easy. LC 94-30576. 560p. 1994. pap. 56.95 (*0-534-22206-4*) PWS Pubs.

Coburn, edward J. Visual Basic Made Easy. (C). 1996. text, suppl. ed. 59.95 (*0-534-95381-6*) Brooks-Cole.

Coburn, Edward J. Windows 98: Instructor's guide. 24.00 (*0-7638-0196-8*) EMC-Paradigm.

Coburn, Edward J., et al. Business Software Applications: DOS, WordPerfect, Lotus dBASE IV. 256p. (C). 1990. teacher ed. 9.95 (*1-56118-055-6*); pap. text 24.95 (*1-56118-054-8*) Paradigm MN.

Coburn, Evelyn L. F. S. Coburn: Beyond the Landscape. LC 97-113059. 1996. 40.00 (*1-55046-159-1*, Pub. by Boston Mills) Genl Dist Srvs.

Coburn, Foster. CorelDRAW 7: The Official Guide. LC 97-156031. 1997. pap. text 34.99 (*0-07-882278-5*) Osborne-McGraw.

Coburn, Foster R., III. CorelDRAW 8: The Official Guide. LC 98-136531. 1997. pap. text 39.99 (*0-07-882447-8*) Osborne-McGraw.

Coburn, George, jt. auth. see McHale, James.

Coburn, J. Osborn. Hell on Belle Isle: Diary of a Civil War POW. Allison, Donald L., ed. LC 97-61462. (Illus.). 192p. 1997. pap. 15.95 (*0-9659201-0-0*, 00001) Faded Banner.

Coburn, J. W., jt. ed. see Massry, Shaul G.

Coburn, Janet L., ed. see Tanner, Jerre E.

Coburn, Janet L., jt. ed. see Tanner, Jerre E.

***Coburn, Jay & Bryant, Steven W., eds.** The JCAHO Survey Coordinator's Handbook. 2nd ed. LC 99-462644. (Illus.). 240p. 1999. pap. text 97.00 (*1-57839-052-4*) Opus Communs.

Coburn, Jennifer. Take Back Your Power: A Working Woman's Response to Sexual Harassment. LC 95-9548. 143p. 1995. pap. 10.00 (*0-910383-13-8*) Ism Pr.

Coburn, Jewell R. Angkat: The Cambodian Cinderella. LC 97-35686. (Illus.). 32p. (J). (gr. 1-3). 1998. 16.95 (*1-885008-09-0*) Shens Bks.

— Beyond the East Wind: Legends & Folktales of Vietnam. LC 76-50345. (Illus.). 98p. 1976. 14.95 (*0-918060-01-X*) Burn Hart.

— Encircled Kingdom: Legends & Folktales of Laos. LC 79-53838. (Illus.). 86p. 1979. 14.95 (*0-918060-03-6*) Burn Hart.

— Khmers, Tigers, & Talismans: From the History & Legends of Mysterious Cambodia. LC 77-14887. (Illus.). 98p. 1978. 14.95 (*0-918060-02-8*) Burn Hart.

— Unlocking the Stories Within You. LC 86-70472. (Illus.). 142p. (Orig.). 1986. pap. text 7.95 (*0-918060-05-2*) Burn Hart.

Coburn, Jewell R. & Lee, Tzexa C. Jouanah: A Hmong Cinderella. LC 95-36353. (Illus.). 32p. (J). (gr. 2-6). 1996. 15.95 (*1-885008-01-7*) Shens Bks.

— Jouanah: La Cenicienta Hmong. Kohen, Clarita, tr. LC 95-36353. (SPA., Illus.). 32p. (J). (gr. 3-7). 1996. 15.95 (*1-885008-02-3*) Shens Bks.

Coburn, Jewell R., et al. Ntsuag Nos: Ib Tug Cinderella Hmoob. Moua, Jean, tr. LC 95-36353. (VIE., Illus.). 32p. (J). (gr. 2-6). 1996. 15.95 (*1-885008-03-1*) Shens Bks.

Coburn, John. Ball Pythons. (Illus.). 64p. 1995. pap. text 9.95 (*0-7938-0260-1*, RE100) TFH Pubns.

Coburn, John B. Christ's Life, Our Life. LC 77-17172. 112p. 1978. pap. 4.95 (*0-8164-2616-3*) Harper SF.

— Deliver Us from Evil: The Prayer of Our Lord. 96p. 1984. 4.95 (*0-8164-2124-2*) Harper SF.

— Prayer & Personal Religion. large type ed. LC 85-10477. 160p. 1985. reprint ed. pap. 8.95 (*0-8027-2509-0*) Walker & Co.

Coburn, Judi. The Shacklands. 1999. pap. 7.95 (*1-896764-13-4*, Pub. by Sec Story Pr) LPC InBook.

Coburn, K., ed. see Coleridge, Samuel Taylor.

Coburn, Karen L. Letting Go: A Parent's Guide to Understanding the College Years. 3rd rev. ed. LC 97-5901. 384p. 1997. pap. 13.00 (*0-06-095244-X*, Perennial) HarperTrade.

Coburn, Katharine M., jt. auth. see Poirier, Laurinda.

Coburn, Katharine M., jt. auth. see Poirier, Laurinda M.

Coburn, Kathleen. Experience into Thought: Perspectives in the Coleridge Notebooks. LC 78-32099. (Alexander Lectures). 107p. reprint ed. pap. 33.20 (*0-608-16674-X*, 202638000049) Bks Demand.

— In Pursuit of Coleridge. LC 78-307705. 202p. 1977. write for info. (*0-370-30002-5*) Bodley Head.

Coburn, Kathleen & Christensen, Merton, eds. The Notebooks of Samuel Taylor Coleridge, 1819-1826: 1819-1826, Vol. 4. (Bollingen Ser.: Vol. 50, No. 4). (Illus.). 538p. (C). 1989. text 175.00 (*0-691-09906-5*, Pub. by Princeton U Pr) Cal Prin Full Svc.

Coburn, Kathleen, ed. see Coleridge, Samuel Taylor.

Coburn, Larry, jt. auth. see Gelso, Charles J.

Coburn, Laura. Desperate Call. 1999. pap. write for info. (*0-525-93933-4*) NAL.

***Coburn, Laura.** Missing Suspect. 1998. mass mkt. 6.99 (*0-451-40642-7*, Onyx) NAL.

Coburn, Lee. Runaway Father Vol. I: One Man's Odyssey from Revenge to Love. (Illus.). 347p. 1998. pap. 18.95 (*0-9664596-4-4*) Red Fox Pub.

Coburn, Lewis A. & Rieffel, Marc A. Perspectives on Quantization: Proceedings of the 1996 AMS-Siam Joint Summer Research Conference, July 7-11, 1996, Mt. Holyoke College, Vol. 214. LC 97-34607. (Contemporary Mathematics Ser.). 195p. 1997. pap. 39.00 (*0-8218-0684-X*) Am Math.

Coburn, Louise H. Skowhegan on the Kennebec (Maine), Vol. 1. (Illus.). 460p. 1993. reprint ed. lib. bdg. 46.00 (*0-8328-2954-4*) Higginson Bk Co.

— Skowhegan on the Kennebec (Maine), Vol. II. (Illus.). 590p. 1993. reprint ed. lib. bdg. 59.00 (*0-8328-2955-2*) Higginson Bk Co.

Coburn, Mathias M. Competitive Technical Intelligence: A Guide to Design, Analysis & Action. LC 98-51142. (Illus.). 14p. 1999. text 65.00 (*0-8412-3515-5*, Pub. by Am Chemical) OUP.

Coburn, Melinda. Specialized SOPs for General Surgeons. 1998. ring bd. 50.00 incl. disk (*0-910167-58-3*) Comm Unltd CA.

Coburn, Nancy C., jt. ed. see Harper, Carol J.

Coburn, O., tr. see Lasserre, Jean.

Coburn, Oliver, tr. see Schaefer, Udo.

Coburn, Peter. Practical Guide to Computers in Education. 2nd ed. 1985. text 18.30 (*0-201-10593-4*) Addison-Wesley.

Coburn, R. F. Airway Smooth Muscle in Health & Disease. (Illus.). 834p. (C). 1989. text 89.50 (*0-306-43120-3*, Kluwer Plenum) Kluwer Academic.

Coburn, Randy Sue. Remembering Jody. 336p. 1999. 22.95 (*0-7867-0566-3*) Carroll & Graf.

Coburn, Robert A., ed. Official Maine Scanner Guide. 304p. (Orig.). 1987. pap. 17.95 (*0-943809-00-2*) Offical NH Scanner.

Coburn, S., ed. Atmospheric Factors Affecting the Corrosion of Engineering Metals, STP 646. 238p. 1985. 24.50 (*0-8031-0286-0*, STP646) ASTM.

Coburn, Seymour K., ed. see American Society for Metals Staff.

Coburn, Silas R. History of Dracut, Called by the Indians Augumtoocooke & Before Incorporation, the Wilderness North of the Merrimac: First Permanent Settlement in 1669 & Incorporated As a Town in 1701. (Illus.). 434p. 1998. lib. bdg. 46.50 (*0-8328-9609-8*) Higginson Bk Co.

Coburn, Stephen P. The Chemistry & Metabolism of the Vitamin B6 Antagonist, 4' Deoxypyridoxine. 224p. 1981. 79.00 (*0-8493-5783-7*, QP772, CRC Reprint) Franklin.

Coburn, Terrence G., et al. Patterns. LC 92-44142. (Curriculum & Evaluation Standards for School Mathematics Addenda Ser.: Grades K-6). (Illus.). 53p. 1993. pap. 13.95 (*0-87353-320-8*) NCTM.

Coburn, Thomas B. Devi Mahatmya: The Crystalization of the Goddess Tradition. (C). 1989. reprint ed. 26.00 (*81-208-0557-7*, Pub. by Motilal Bnarsidass) S Asia.

— Encountering the Goddess: A Translation of the Devi-Mahatmya & a Study of Its Interpretation. LC 90-30574. (SUNY Series in Hindu Studies). (Illus.). 271p. (C). 1991. pap. text 21.95 (*0-7914-0446-3*) State U NY Pr.

Coburn, Thomas B., jt. auth. see Dehejia, Vidya.

***Coburn, Timothy C. & Yarus, Jeffrey M.** Geographic Information Systems in Petroleum Exploration & Development. LC 00-36260. 2000. write for info. (*0-89181-703-4*) AAPG.

***Coburn, Walt.** Beyond the Wild Missouri. 1999. 19.00 (*0-7540-8068-4*, Gunsmoke) Chivers N Amer.

Coburn, Walt. Buffalo Run. 1998. 17.50 (*0-7540-8028-5*, Gunsmoke) Chivers N Amer.

— Coffin Ranch. large type ed. LC 98-43339. 351 p. 1999. 30.00 (*0-7838-1709-6*, G K Hall Lrg Type) Mac Lib Ref.

— The Dark & Bloody Ground. large type ed. (Linford Western Library). 272p. 1992. pap. 16.99 (*0-7089-7257-8*) Ulverscroft.

— Law Rides the Range. large type ed. (Linford Western Library). 352p. 1992. pap. 16.99 (*0-7089-7245-4*, Linford) Ulverscroft.

— The Renegade. 1993. 17.50 (*0-7451-4577-9*, Gunsmoke) Chivers N Amer.

— The Secret of Crutcher's Cabin: A Western Quartet. Date not set. 19.95 (*0-7862-1326-4*) Thorndike Pr.

***Coburn, Walt.** The Secret of Crutcher's Cabin: A Western Trio. large type ed. LC 99-46915. 362p. 1999. 23.95 (*0-7838-8396-X*, G K Hall & Co) Mac Lib Ref.

Coburn, Walt. Stirrup High. LC 96-47112. (Illus.). iv, 190p. 1997. pap. 9.95 (*0-8032-6377-5*, Bison Books) U of Nebr Pr.

Coby, J. Patrick. Machiavelli's Romans: Liberty & Greatness in the Discourses on Livy. LC 99-19460. (Applications of Political Theory Ser.). 384p. 1999. 65.00 (*0-7391-0069-6*); pap. 23.95 (*0-7391-0070-X*) Lxngtn Bks.

Coby, Patrick. Socrates & the Sophistic Enlightenment: A Commentary on Plato's Protagoras. LC 86-47856. 216p. 1988. 35.00 (*0-8387-5109-1*) Bucknell U Pr.

Coca, Antonio & Garay, Ricardo, eds. Ionic Transport in Hypertension: New Perspectives. 352p. 1993. lib. bdg. 197.00 (*0-8493-5474-9*, RC685) CRC Pr.

Coca, Arthur F. The Pulse Test. LC 93-19656. 192p. 1993. pap. 12.00 (*0-942637-94-1*) Barricade Bks.

— The Pulse Test. 1996. mass mkt. 4.99 (*0-312-95699-1*, Pub. by Tor Bks) St Martin.

***Coca-Spofford, Diane.** Do You Love Me? (All by Myself Bks.). (Illus.). 16p. (J). 2000. 6.95 (*1-58260-020-1*) Infnty Plus One.

Cocalas, Adrienne, jt. auth. see Giese, Hugh.

Cocalis, M. W., ed. see Clabough, Jean.

Cocalis, Susan L., ed. The Defiant Muse: German Feminist Poems from the Middle Ages to the Present. LC 86-4774. (Defiant Muse Ser.). (ENG & GER.). 163p. (Orig.). 1986. text 35.00 (*0-935312-49-8*); pap. text 11.95 (*0-935312-53-6*) Feminist Pr.

Cocannouer, Joseph. Water & the Cycle of Life. 14.95 (*0-8159-7202-4*) Devin.

— Weeds: Guardians of the Soil. (Illus.). pap. 15.95 (*0-8159-7205-9*) Devin.

Cocca-Leffler, Maryann. Bus Route to Boston. LC 98-88214. (Illus.). 32p. (J). 2000. 15.95 (*1-56397-723-0*) Boyds Mills Pr.

— Clams All Year. (Illus.). 32p. (J). 1998. pap. 5.99 (*0-440-41447-4*) BDD Bks Young Read.

— Clams All Year. LC 95-79097. (Illus.). 32p. (J). (ps-2). 1996. 14.95 (*1-56397-469-X*) Boyds Mills Pr.

Cocca-Leffler, MaryAnn. Clams All Year. (J). 1998. 11.19 (*0-606-13277-5*, Pub. by Turtleback) Demco.

Cocca-Leffler, Maryann. Count the Days Till Christmas. LC 92-82915. (Illus.). 16p. (J). (ps-3). 1993. pap. 3.95 (*0-590-46929-0*, Cartwheel) Scholastic Inc.

— Daddy Hugs. (Illus.). 14p. (J). (ps-k). 1997. 5.99 (*0-689-80982-4*) S&S Bks Yung.

— Ice-Cold Birthday. (All Aboard Reading Ser.). (Illus.). 32p. (J). (ps-1). 1992. pap. 3.95 (*0-448-40380-3*, G & D) Peng Put Young Read.

Cocca-Leffler, Maryann. Ice-Cold Birthday. (All Aboard Reading Ser.). 1992. 9.15 (*0-606-12353-9*, Pub. by Turtleback) Demco.

— Jungle Halloween. LC 99-50903. (Illus.). (J). (ps-1). 2000. 14.95 (*0-8075-4056-0*) A Whitman.

Cocca-Leffler, Maryann. Lots of Hearts. LC 95-78720. (All Aboard Reading Picture Readers Ser.). (Illus.). 32p. (Orig.). (J). (ps-1). 1997. pap. 3.95 (*0-448-41304-3*, G & D) Peng Put Young Read.

***Cocca-Leffler, Maryann.** Missing: One Stuffed Rabbit. (Illus.). 32p. (J). (gr. k-3). 2000. pap. 6.95 (*0-8075-5162-7*) A Whitman.

Cocca-Leffler, Maryann. Missing One Stuffed Rabbit. LC 97-18203. (Illus.). 32p. (J). (gr. k-3). 1998. lib. bdg. 14.95 (*0-8075-5161-9*) A Whitman.

— Mr. Tanen's Ties. LC 98-33762. (Illus.). 32p. (J). (gr. k-3). 1999. lib. bdg. 14.95 (*0-8075-5301-8*) A Whitman.

— Mommy Hugs. (J). (ps-k). 1997. 5.99 (*0-614-29096-1*) Litle Simon.

— Princess for a Day. LC 98-11365. (All Aboard Reading Ser.: Level 1). (Illus.). 32p. (J). (ps-1). 1998. lib. bdg. 13.89 (*0-448-41605-0*, G & D); mass mkt. 3.99 (*0-448-41604-2*, G & D) Peng Put Young Read.

— Silly Willy. (All Aboard Reading Picture Readers Ser.). (Illus.). 32p. (J). (ps-1). 1995. pap. 3.95 (*0-448-40969-0*, G & D) Peng Put Young Read.

Cocca-Spofford, Diane. The Good-Bye Game. (All by Myself Bks.). (Illus.). 16p. (J). (ps). 1998. 6.95 (*1-58260-002-3*) Infnty Plus One.

Coccaro, Emil F., jt. auth. see Maes, Michael.

Coccheri, S., ed. Premature Vascular Disease in Homocystinaemia. (Journal: Haemostasis: Vol. 19, Suppl. 1, 1989). (Illus.). vi, 50p. 1989. pap. 77.50 (*3-8055-4998-9*) S Karger.

Coccheri, S. & Donati, Maria B., eds. International Congress on Fibrinolysis, 7th Abstracts: Venice, March 1984. (Journal: Haemostasis: Vol. 14, No. 1). 156p. 1984. pap. 45.25 (*3-8055-3882-0*) S Karger.

Cocchetto, David M. & Nardi, R. V. Managing the Clinical Drug Development Process. (Drugs & the Pharmaceutical Sciences Ser.: Vol. 51). (Illus.). 232p. 1991. text 145.00 (*0-8247-8595-9*) Dekker.

Cocchi, John. Second Feature: The Best of the "B" Films. 1990. pap. 15.95 (*0-8065-1186-9*, Citadel Pr) Carol Pub Group.

Cocchi, Renee I. Be Still & Know: Psalm 46:10. 48p. 1999. pap. write for info. (*0-7392-0299-5*, PO3416) Morris Pubng.

Cocchia, Aldo. The Hunters & the Hunted. Gwyer, M., tr. LC 79-6106. (Navies & Men Ser.). (Illus.). 1980. reprint ed. lib. bdg. 20.95 (*0-405-13035-X*) Ayer.

Cocchiareli, Joseph J. Screen Sleuths: A Filmography. LC 91-28737. (Filmographies Ser.: Vol. 3). 249p. 1992. text 20.00 (*0-8240-5427-X*, 1322) Garland.

Cocchiarella, Nino B. Logical Studies in Early Analytic Philosophy. LC 87-1584. 309p. reprint ed. pap. 95.80 (*0-608-09663-6*, 206977800006) Bks Demand.

***Cocchiola, Todd W.** Herbs in Medicine: Index of New Information. rev. ed. 139p. 1999. 47.50 (*0-7883-2150-1*); pap. 44.50 (*0-7883-2151-X*) ABBE Pubs Assn.

Coccia. Caterina di Guisa. (Italian Opera Ser., 1810-1840: Vol. 4). 1986. text 30.00 (*0-8240-6553-0*) Garland.

Cocco, D., jt. auth. see Bannister, J. V.

Cocco de Filippis, Daisy & Gutierrez, Franklin, eds. Stories from Washington Heights & Other Corners of the World - Historias de Washington Heights y Otros Rincones del Mundo. (SPA.). 204p. 1994. pap. 10.00 (*1-884912-02-8*) Latino Pr.

Cocco-Defilippis, Daisy & Rivera-Valdes, Sonia. Escritoras del Caribe Hispanohablante: Una Conversaci On. LC 98-14369. 1998. pap. write for info. (*0-8477-0344-4*) U of PR Pr.

***Cocco, Gaetano.** Motorcycle Design & Technology. (Illus.). 272p. 2000. 44.95 (*88-7911-189-2*, 129466AE, Pub. by Giorgio Nada Editore) Motorbooks Intl.

Coccossis, H. & Nijkamp, P., eds. Planning for Our Cultural Heritage. 240p. 1995. 78.95 (*1-85972-178-8*, Pub. by Avebry) Ashgate Pub Co.

Coccossis, H., jt. ed. see Nijkamp, P.

Coceani, Flavio & Olley, Peter M., eds. Prostaglandins & Perinatal Medicine. fac. ed. LC 77-17758. (Advances in Prostaglandin, Thromboxane Research Ser.: No. 4). 428p. pap. 132.70 (*0-7837-7538-5*, 204696600005) Bks Demand.

Coceani, Flavio, jt. ed. see Brazier, Mary A.

Cocetti, Robert A. & Snyder, Lee. Talk That Matters: An Introduction to Public Speaking. rev. ed. 338p. (YA). (gr. 10 up). 1992. 18.00 (*1-878276-44-1*) Educ Systs Assocs Inc.

Cochavi, Yehoyakim, jt. ed. see Cohen, Asher.

Coche, A. G., et al. Aquaculture Development & Research in Sub-Saharan Africa. (CIFA Technical Papers: No. 23). 161p. 1994. pap. 25.00 (*92-5-103511-3*, F35113, Pub. by FAO) Bernan Associates.

— Simple Methods for Aquaculture: Management for Freshwater Fish Culture Ponds. (Training Ser.: No. 21/1). 233p. 1997. pap. 45.00 (*92-5-102873-7*, F28737, Pub. by FAO) Bernan Associates.

— Simple Methods for Aquaculture: Pond Construction for Freshwater Fish Culture. (Training Ser.: No. 20-2). 224p. 1993. pap. 65.00 (*92-5-102872-9*, F28729, Pub. by FAO) Bernan Associates.

Coche, Erich, jt. auth. see Coche, Judith.

Coche, Judith & Coche, Erich. Couples Group Psychotherapy: A Clinical Practice Model. LC 90-2216. 188p. 1990. text 29.95 (*0-87630-598-2*) Brunner-Mazel.

Coche, Judith M., jt. auth. see Nevels, Lourene A.

Cochelet, C. Narrative of the Shipwreck of the Sophia. 1973. 59.95 (*0-8490-0709-7*) Gordon Pr.

Cochem, Corinne. Jewish Holiday Dances, Poems by Alfred Hayes: Music Book Index. 85p. 1993. reprint ed. lib. bdg. 69.00 (*0-7812-9651-X*) Rprt Serv.

Cochem, Martin Von, see Von Cochem, Martin.

Cocheme, Simon, jt. auth. see Bird, David.

Cochener. Elementary & Intermediate Algebra Explorations Using TI-82. (Mathematics Ser.). 1995. pap. 19.75 (*0-534-34091-1*) Brooks-Cole.

— Explorations in Beginning & Intermediate Algebra Using Ti-82: With Appendix. 2nd ed. (Mathematics Ser.). 1998. pap. 30.95 (*0-534-36149-8*) Brooks-Cole.

Cochener, Deborah J. Precalculus Explorations Using the TI-82. (Mathematics Ser.). 336p. (C). 1996. mass mkt. 26.95 (*0-534-34227-2*) Brooks-Cole.

Cochener, Deborah J. & Hodge, Bonnie M. College Algebra Explorations Using TI-82. (Mathematics Ser.). 336p. (C). 1996. mass mkt. 26.95 (*0-534-34228-0*) Brooks-Cole.

Cochener, Hodge Gustafson. Beginning & Intermediate Algebra with Graphing Calculators. LC 99-31325. (Mathematics Ser.). 1999. pap. text 81.95 (*0-534-35942-6*) Brooks-Cole.

***Cochener, Hodge Gustafson.** S.S.M. Beginning & Intermediate Algebra. 1999. pap. 18.00 (*0-534-37327-5*) Thomson Learn.

Cocheo, Steve. Distributed Computer Control Systems: Evaluation, Implementation, & Economics. LC 83-11613. (Series of Special Reports: Vol. 6). (Illus.). 164p. reprint ed. pap. 50.90 (*0-608-09005-0*, 206964000005) Bks Demand.

Cocherell, B. L. God & the Bible: Human Life & Salvation. LC 98-93970. 191p. 1998. pap. write for info. (*0-7392-0020-8*, No. PO2830) Morris Pubng.

— The Gospel. LC 98-92750. 242p. 1998. pap. write for info. (*1-57502-779-8*, P02157) Morris Pubng.

***Cocherell, B. L.** How to Become Immortal. 424p. 1999. pap. write for info. (*0-7392-0392-4*, PO3615) Morris Pubng.

Cocherell, B. L. The Resurrections: A Day of Salvation, Predestination, Immortality, the Dead, Heaven, Hell. LC 99-93291. 280p. 1999. pap. write for info. (*0-7392-0264-2*, PO3334) Morris Pubng.

***Cocherell, B. L., et al.** The Law of God. 508p. 1999. pap. write for info. (*0-7392-0418-1*, PO3681) Morris Pubng.

Cocherell, B. L., et al. Spiritual Leaders & Other Major Issues Concerning the Body of Christ. 390p. 1998. pap. write for info. (*0-7392-0030-5*, No. PO2831) Morris Pubng.

Cochern, George W., jt. auth. see Kemp, Jerrold E.

***Cochetti, Roger.** Mobile Satellite Communications Handbook. 342p. 1998. 105.00 (*0-471-29778-X*) Wiley.

Cocheu, Lincoln C. Couenhoven. The Couenhovens & Kinsfolk: Some Descendants of Wolphert Gerritse vanKouenboven & Neehtje Janse Through Their Son Jacob Wolphertson vanCouwenhoven & His First Wife Hester Jansen. (Illus.). 93p. 1997. reprint ed. pap. 18.00 (*0-8328-8076-0*); reprint ed. lib. bdg. 28.00 (*0-8328-8075-2*) Higginson Bk Co.

Cocheu, Ted. Blueprint for Quality: How Training Can Turn Strategy into Real Improvement. LC 94-16214. (Management Ser.). 1993. text 32.95 (*0-7879-0021-4*) Jossey-Bass.

Cochin, Augustin. Results of Emancipation. Booth, Mary L., tr. LC 76-83942. (Black Heritage Library Collection). 1977. 28.95 (*0-8369-8544-3*) Ayer.

— Results of Slavery. Booth, Mary L., tr. LC 73-83960. (Black Heritage Library Collection). 1977. 38.95 (*0-8369-8698-9*) Ayer.

— Results of Slavery: Work Crowned by the Institute of France. Booth, Mary L., tr. LC 70-109619. (Select Bibliographies Reprint Ser.). 1977. 38.95 (*0-8369-5228-6*) Ayer.

Cochini, Christian. Apostolic Origins of Priestly Celibacy. Marans, Nelly, tr. from FRE. LC 89-81430. 491p. (Orig.). 1990. 39.95 (*0-89870-280-1*) Ignatius Pr.

Cochise, Ciye N. The First Hundred Years of Nino Cochise. (Illus.). 420p. 1990. reprint ed. lib. bdg. 34.95 (*0-89966-735-X*) Buccaneer Bks.

Cochlin, Dennis, et al. A Text Atlas of Urogenital Ultrasound. (Illus.). 448p. 1994. text 150.00 (*0-397-51424-7*) Lppncott W & W.

Cochran. American Public Policy. 6th ed. LC 98-84986. 1998. pap. 50.95 (*0-312-17852-2*) St Martin.

— Business Environment. 1995. 65.25 (*0-07-058423-0*) McGraw.

— Hyperstudio - Mac: Quick Course. LC 94-157751. (DA - Computer Education Ser.). 1994. pap. 22.95 (*0-538-63371-9*) S-W Pub.

— Hyperstudio Apple GS: Quick Course. (DA - Computer Education Ser.). (J). (gr. k-8). 1994. pap. 22.95 (*0-538-62696-8*) S-W Pub.

— Hyperstudio Express 1.0 for Windows. LC 97-112140. (DA - K-8 Computer Education Ser.). 1997. pap. 21.95 (*0-538-66692-7*) S-W Pub.

— Making Connections '97. 4th ed. 1997. 21.50 (*0-07-292886-7*) McGraw.

— Public Policy. 2nd ed. LC 98-42232. 480p. 1998. pap. 49.69 (*0-07-290896-3*) McGraw.

— Science & Football III. (Illus.). 360p. (C). 1996. 110.00 (*0-419-22160-3*) Routledge.

Cochran, et al. American Public Policy. 5th ed. 512p. 1995. pap. 46.95 (*0-312-11616-0*) St Martin.

Cochran, A. J. Science & Golf 2: Proceedings of the World Scientific Congress of Golf. 672p. (C). 1994. 80.00 (*0-419-18790-1*, E & FN Spon) Routledge.

Cochran, Alastair & Stobbs, John. The Search for the Perfect Swing: The Proven Scientific Approach to Fundamentally Improve Your Game. (Illus.). 256p. (Orig.). 1996. pap. 22.95 (*1-57243-109-1*) Triumph Bks.

Cochran, Alastair J., jt. auth. see Farrally, Martin R.

Cochran, Alastair J., ed. Science & Golf: The Proceedings of the First World Scientific Congress of Golf. 352p. 1990. 72.50 (*0-419-15130-3*, A5019, E & FN Spon) Routledge.

Cochran, Alexander S., Jr. Gulf War Air Power Survey: Planning & Command & Control, V. 1. 713p. 1994. per. 43.00 (*0-16-042909-9*) USGPO.

Cochran, Alice L. The Saga of an Irish Immigrant Family: The Descendants of John Mullanphy. LC 76-6328. (Irish Americans Ser.). 1976. 25.95 (*0-405-09325-X*) Ayer.

Cochran, Alistair, et al. Melanocytic Tumors: A Guide to Diagnosis. LC 96-4715. (Biopsy Interpretation Ser.). 448p. 1996. text 112.00 (*0-397-51633-9*) Lppncott W & W.

Cochran, Andrew G. Tying the Knot: The Sharp Dresser's Guide to Ties & Handkerchiefs. (Illus.). 48p. (Orig.). 1996. pap. 5.95 (*0-9630152-6-5*) Five Star AZ.

Cochran, Barbara. Exploring Spokane's Past: Tours to Historical Sites. rev. ed. 76p. 1996. pap. 5.95 (*0-87770-337-X*) Ye Galleon.

Cochran, Bob. Samuel Beckett: A Study of the Short Fiction. (Twayne's Studies in Short Fiction: No. 29). 180p. (C). 1992. 29.00 (*0-8057-8320-2*, Twyne) Mac Lib Ref.

Cochran, Brian W., ed. see Higashi, Tomomitsu, et al.

Cochran, Bruce. Bass Fever. 96p. 1991. pap. 7.95 (*1-55971-127-2*, 1527, NorthWord Pr) Creat Pub Intl.

— Bass Fever. LC 91-12694. 96p. 1991. pap. 7.95 (*1-57223-000-2*, 1527) Willow Creek Pr.

— Buck Fever. (Illus.). 96p. 1990. pap. 7.95 (*1-57223-001-0*, 1532) Willow Creek Pr.

— Duck Fever: Duck Hunting Cartoons. LC 92-27586. (Illus.). 96p. 1992. reprint ed. pap. 7.95 (*1-57223-069-X*) Willow Creek Pr.

— Everything You Never Want to Know about Camping. LC 97-198773. (Illus.). 104p. (Orig.). 1995. pap. 8.95 (*1-57223-033-9*, 0339) Willow Creek Pr.

— First Birthday Bear. 10p. (J). write for info. (*1-886386-35-8*) Trisar.

— First Pony: Blue. 10p. (J). write for info. (*1-886386-34-X*) Trisar.

— First Pony: Pink. 10p. (J). write for info. (*1-886386-33-1*) Trisar.

— It's the Big 1: Blue. 10p. (J). write for info. (*1-886386-37-4*) Trisar.

— It's the Big 1: Pink. 10p. (J). write for info. (*1-886386-36-6*) Trisar.

— King of the Hill. 10p. 1995. write for info. (*1-886386-31-5*) Trisar.

***Cochran, Bruce.** Lab Fever! Living, Loving & Laughing with Labrador Retrievers. LC 00-21754. (Illus.). 91p. 2000. pap. 9.95 (*1-57223-262-5*, 2625) Willow Creek Pr.

Cochran, Bruce. The Old Fart Book. (Illus.). 10p. 1994. write for info. (*1-886386-26-9*) Trisar.

— The Old Geezer. (Illus.). 10p. 1994. write for info. (*1-886386-25-0*) Trisar.

— Queen of the Hill. 10p. 1995. write for info. (*1-886386-32-3*) Trisar.

— The Recycled Teenager. (Illus.). 10p. 1994. write for info. (*1-886386-27-7*) Trisar.

— Retired & Loving It. 10p. 1995. write for info. (*1-886386-29-3*) Trisar.

— Ribbons to Wrinkles. (Illus.). 10p. 1994. write for info. (*1-886386-28-5*) Trisar.

— Time to Retire. 10p. 1995. write for info. (*1-886386-30-7*) Trisar.

— Trout Fever: Cartoons from the Liar's Lair. LC 92-43803. (Illus.). 96p. 1993. reprint ed. 12.50 (*1-55971-148-5*, 1545) Willow Creek Pr.

— Uncle Charlie's Hunting Shack. LC 95-140988. (Illus.). 96p. 1994. 12.50 (*1-57223-018-5*, 0185) Willow Creek Pr.

Cochran, Charles L. & Malone, Eloise F. Public Policy: Perspectives & Choices. LC 94-33885. 457p. (C). 1994. 51.56 (*0-07-011528-1*) McGraw.

Cochran, Christie, jt. auth. see Greaves, Jackie.

Cochran, Chuck. Arthritis & Cetyl Myristoleate (CMO) 24p. 1997. pap. 2.95 (*0-9647080-8-6*) Healing Wisdom.

***Cochran, Chuck & Peerce, Donna.** Heart & Soul Career Tune-Up: Seven-Never-Before-Published Secrets to Capturing Heart & Soul in Your Work Life. LC 99-86522. 2000. pap. 16.95 (*0-89106-141-X*, Davies-Black Pub) Consulting Psychol.

Cochran, Chuck & Peerce, Donna. Heart & Soul Internet Job Search: 7 Never-Before-Published Secrets to Capturing Your Dream Job Using the Internet, LC 98-51049. 192p. 1999. pap. 16.95 (*0-89106-125-8*, 7811, Pub. by Consulting Psychol) Natl Bk Netwk.

— Wow! Resumes for Sales & Marketing Careers. LC 98-4969. 336p. 1998. pap. 10.95 (*0-07-012021-8*, BusinessWeek Bks) McGraw.

Cochran, Chuck, jt. auth. see Peerce, Donna.

Cochran, Dave. An Old Man's New. 55p. (Orig.). 1996. pap. 5.00 (*0-88734-360-0*) Players Pr.

***Cochran, David.** American Noir: Underground Writers & Filmmakers of the Postwar Era. LC 99-44320. 312p. 2000. 27.95 (*1-56098-813-4*) Smithsonian.

Cochran, David C. The Color of Freedom: Race & Contemporary American Liberalism. LC 98-30115. (SUNY Series in Afro-American Studies). 207p. (C). 1999. text 54.50 (*0-7914-4185-7*); pap. text 17.95 (*0-7914-4186-5*) State U NY Pr.

Cochran, David L., et al. Plaque & Calculus Removal: Considerations for the Professional. LC 94-17876. (Illus.). 109p. 1994. pap. text 32.00 (*0-86715-285-0*) Quint Pub Co.

***Cochran, David W.** Hyperstudio Express 3.1 For Windows Macintosh. LC 98-54988. (J). 1999. pap. write for info. (*0-02-654033-9*) Glencoe.

Cochran, David W. Macintosh: Quick Start. (C). 1991. mass mkt. 19.95 (*0-538-70475-6*) S-W Pub.

***Cochran, David W. & Staats, Robert A.** HyperStudio Express 3.1 for Windows/Macintosh. LC 98-54988. 2000. write for info. (*0-02-654032-0*) Glencoe.

Cochran, Debby. Fifty Squash Recipes. (Illus.). 1981. pap. 2.95 (*0-9606142-0-6*) D Cochran.

Cochran, Dewees. As If They Might Speak. LC 78-73289. (Illus.). 1979. 30.00 (*0-87833-311-8*) Paperwght Pr.

Cochran, Emily B., jt. auth. see Phelps, Stephanie J.

***Cochran, Eva.** Child Care That Works: A Parent's Guide to Finding Quality Childcare. 356p. 2000. pap. 16.95 (*0-87659-219-1*, Robins Ln Pr) Gryphon Hse.

***Cochran, Faye, ed.** The Heritage of Hale County, Alabama. (Heritage of Alabama Ser.: Vol. 33). 300p. 2000. 59.95 (*1-891647-51-2*) Herit Pub Consult.

C

An Asterisk (*) at the beginning of an entry indicates that the title is appearing for the first time.

Cochran, George M. Indian Portraits of the Pacific Northwest. 3rd ed. (Illus.). 64p. 1991. pap. 5.95 (0-8323-0488-3) Binford Mort.

Cochran, George V. A Primer of Orthopaedic Biomechanics. LC 81-38485. (Illus.). 429p. reprint ed. pap. 133.00 (0-8357-6411-7, 203577200096) Bks Demand.

***Cochran, Gerardine.** Academic Skill Keeper. 50p. (C). 2000. ring bd. 54.95 (0-7872-7280-9) Kendall-Hunt.

Cochran, Harold C., jt. auth. see Howe, Charles W.

Cochran, Holly W. Abstracts of Bath County, Virginia Will Books (1843-1875), 005. 282p. 1998. pap. 25.00 (0-9666399-0-1) Hollyhock Pr.

***Cochran, Holly W.** Snapshot Before the War: 1860 Census of Bath County Virginia with Maiden Names & Parents Added & Bath County Marriages 1853-1860. 204p. 1999. pap. 26.00 (0-9666399-1-X) Hollyhock Pr.

Cochran, J. Wesley. Time Management Handbook for Librarians. LC 91-17120. (Library Management Collection). 160p. 1991. lib. bdg. 47.95 (0-313-27842-3, CTG) Greenwood.

Cochran, J. Wesley, jt. auth. see Johnson, Nancy P.

Cochran, Jacqueline & Odlum, Floyd. The Stars at Noon. Gilbert, James B., ed. LC 79-7241. (Flight: Its First Seventy-Five Years Ser.). (Illus.). 1980. reprint ed. lib. bdg. 32.95 (0-405-12156-3) Ayer.

***Cochran, Jerry.** Mission-Critical Microsoft Exchange 2000: Building Highly Available Messaging & Knowledge Management. (Illus.). 320p. 2000. pap. 34.95 (1-55558-233-8, Digital DEC) Buttrwrth-Heinemann.

Cochran, Joan, et al, eds. Substance Abuse: Drugs. 2nd rev. ed. 132p. (Orig.). 1994. pap. text 37.00 (1-879772-03-5) Health Studies.

Cochran, John E., Jr., et al, eds. AAS/AIAA Spaceflight Mechanics Meeting, Feb. 14-16, 1994, Cocoa Beach, FL. LC 57-43769. (Advances in the Astronautical Sciences Ser.: Vol. 87). (Illus.). 1272p. 1994. 240.00 (0-87703-386-2, Am Astronaut Soc) Univelt Inc.

Cochran, John H. Dallas County, Texas, a Record of Its Pioneers & Progress, Being a Supplement to John Henry Brown's History of Dallas County (1887) . . . with Much Additional Information about Early Settlers & Their Families. (Illus.). 296p. 1997. reprint ed. lib. bdg. 34.00 (0-8328-7177-X) Higginson Bk Co.

Cochran, John P. & Glahe, Fred R. The Hayek - Keynes Debate - Lessons for Current Business Cycle Research. LC 99-26213. (Studies in Economics: Vol. 2). 240p. 1999. text 89.95 (0-7734-7970-8) E Mellen.

Cochran, Johnnie L. & Rutten, Tim. Journey to Justice. 1997. mass mkt. 6.99 (0-345-41367-9) Ballantine Pub Grp.

Cochran, Johnnie L., Jr. & Rutten, Tim. Journey to Justice. (Illus.). 383p. 1998. text 28.00 (0-7881-5856-2) DIANE Pub.

Cochran, Joseph. The Babylon Project - Game Resource Kit. (Illus.). 24p. (Orig.). 1997. 12.00 (1-887990-07-0) Chameleon Eclectic.
— The Babylon Project Rulebook. (Babylon 5 Role-Playing Game Bks.). 128p. pap. 25.00 (1-887990-05-4, WP1) Chameleon Eclectic.
— Earth Force Sourcebook. (Illus.). 177p. (Orig.). Date not set. pap. 15.00 (1-887990-06-2) Chameleon Eclectic.
— History of Mifflin County, Vol. I. (Illus.). 422p. 1997. reprint ed. lib. bdg. 46.50 (0-8328-6431-5) Higginson Bk Co.

Cochran, Joseph L. Build Your Own Beehives. 2nd rev. ed. LC 80-70051. (Illus.). iv, 128p. 1980. pap. 24.95 (0-9666150-0-X) Blue Rid.

Cochran, Judith. Archaeology: Digging Deeper to Learn about the Past. LC 99-71591. (Illus.). 144p. (J). 1999. pap. text 14.95 (0-86530-436-X) Incentive Pubns.
— Everything You Need to Know to Be a Successful Whole Language Teacher: Plan, Strategies, Techniques, & More. Britt, Leslie, ed. LC 93-77472. (Illus.). 160p. (Orig.). (J). (gr. k-6). 1993. pap. text, teacher ed. 14.95 (0-86530-236-7, 196-7) Incentive Pubns.
— Everything You Need to Know to Evaluate a Whole Language Program: Forms, Strategies, Techniques, & More. (Illus.). 160p. (Orig.). (J). (gr. k-6). 1995. pap. text 14.95 (0-86530-290-1, 271-1) Incentive Pubns.
— Incorporating Literature into the Basal Reading Program. Lewis, Sherri Y., ed. (Illus.). 160p. (Orig.). (J). (gr. k-6). 1991. pap. text 14.95 (0-86530-217-0, IP 192-5) Incentive Pubns.
— Insights to Literature: A Complete Reading Program for Middle Grades. (Illus.). 240p. (Orig.). (J). (gr. 5-8). 1990. pap. text 16.95 (0-86530-142-5, IP 190-6) Incentive Pubns.
— Insights to Literature: A Complete Reading Program for Primary Grades. (Illus.). 240p. (Orig.). (J). (gr. 1-4). 1991. pap. text 14.95 (0-86530-191-3, IP 193-5) Incentive Pubns.
— Integrating Science & Literature. Keeling, Jan, ed. (Illus.). 144p. (Orig.). (J). (gr. k-4). 1992. pap. text 12.95 (0-86530-198-0, IP194-8) Incentive Pubns.
— Using Literature to Learn about Children Around the World: A Thematic Approach to Cultural Awareness. Keeling, Jan, ed. (Illus.). 80p. (Orig.). (J). (gr. 3-6). 1993. pap. text 9.95 (0-86530-261-8, 261-8) Incentive Pubns.
— Using Literature to Learn about the First Americans: A Thematic Approach to Cultural Awareness. Keeling, Jan, ed. (Illus.). 80p. (Orig.). (J). (gr. 3-6). 1993. pap. text 9.95 (0-86530-262-6, 262-6) Incentive Pubns.
— Using Literature to Learn America's Story. Quinn, Anna, ed. (Illus.). 96p. (Orig.). (J). (gr. 1-6). 1995. pap. text 10.95 (0-86530-335-5, IP 335-5) Incentive Pubns.
— What to Do with the Gifted Child: Meeting the Needs of the Gifted Child in the Regular Classroom. (Illus.). 80p. (J). (gr. 3-8). 1992. pap. text 9.95 (0-86530-174-3, 191-0) Incentive Pubns.

Cochran, Judy, ed. from FRE. Selected Poems of Andree Chedid. LC 95-21917. (Studies in French Literature: Vol. 21). (Illus.). 224p. 1996. text 89.95 (0-7734-2908-5) E Mellen.

Cochran, Judy, jt. ed. see Linkhorn, Renee.

Cochran, Julie Lawrence, tr. see Cezanne, Paul.

Cochran, Karen, ed. see Bowen, Stella & Ford, Ford Madox.

Cochran, Kathleen R., tr. see Blagrave, Joseph.

Cochran, Kathleen R., tr. see Coley, Henry.

Cochran, Kathleen R., tr. see Ramesey, William.

Cochran, Keith. American West, a Historical Chronology. LC 91-78032. (Illus.). 464p. 1992. 35.00 (0-936259-18-3) Cochran Pub.
— American West, Vigilantes & Violence. LC 98-93521. (Illus.). 288p. 2000. 35.00 (0-936259-29-9) Cochran Pub.
— Colt Cavalry, Artillery & Militia Revolvers, 1873-1903. 2nd ed. LC 37-72969. (Illus.). 288p. 1994. reprint ed. 35.00 (0-936259-22-1) Cochran Pub.
— Colt Peacemaker - Ready Reference Handbook. 2nd rev. ed. LC 97-94605. (Illus.). 76p. 1997. pap. 17.50 (0-936259-25-6) Cochran Pub.
— Colt Peacemaker British Model. LC 88-71574. (Illus.). 160p. 1989. 35.00 (0-936259-11-6) Cochran Pub.
— Colt Peacemaker Collector - Handbook & Guide. LC 93-91059. (Illus.). 160p. 1994. 35.00 (0-936259-20-5); ring bd. 50.00 (0-936259-21-3) Cochran Pub.

Cochran, Keith. Colt Peacemaker Encyclopedia. 3rd ed. (Illus.). 434p. 1992. reprint ed. 60.00 (0-936259-19-1) Cochran Pub.

Cochran, Keith. Colt Peacemaker Encyclopedia, Vol. II. 2nd ed. LC 86-71569. (Illus.). 416p. 1998. reprint ed. 60.00 (0-936259-28-0) Cochran Pub.
— Colt Peacemaker Revolver Caliber .476 Eley. LC 97-66171. (Illus.). 55p. (Orig.). 1997. pap. 15.00 (0-936259-24-8) Cochran Pub.
— Peacemaker Evolution & Variations. 2nd rev. ed. LC 97-94604. (Illus.). 94p. 1997. pap. 17.50 (0-936259-27-2) Cochran Pub.

Cochran, Larry. Career Counseling: A Narrative Approach. LC 97-4594. 144p. (C). 1997. 45.00 (0-7619-0441-7, 04417); pap. 19.95 (0-7619-0442-5, 04425) Sage.
— Life-Shaping Decisions. LC 90-35343. (American University Studies: Psychology: Ser. VIII, Vol. 22). 178p. (C). 1991. text 33.95 (0-8204-1368-2) P Lang Pubng.
— Portrait & Story: Dramaturgical Approaches to the Study of Persons, 7. LC 85-12708. (Contributions in Psychology Ser.: No. 7). 203p. 1986. 52.95 (0-313-24966-0, CPS/, Greenwood Pr) Greenwood.
— Position & the Nature of Personhood: An Approach to the Understanding of Persons, 5. LC 84-12852. (Contributions in Psychology Ser.: No. 5). 191p. 1985. 49.95 (0-313-24633-5, CPN/, Greenwood Pr) Greenwood.
— The Sense of Vocation: A Study of Career & Life Development. LC 89-34226. 211p. (C). 1990. text 24.50 (0-7914-0245-2) State U NY Pr.

Cochran, Larry & Claspell, Emily. The Meaning of Grief: A Dramaturgical Approach to Understanding Emotion, 8. LC 86-27156. (Contributions in Psychology Ser.: No. 8). 189p. 1987. 49.95 (0-313-25607-1, CMG/, Greenwood Pr) Greenwood.

Cochran, Larry & Laub, Joan. Becoming an Agent: Patterns & Dynamics for Shaping Your Life. LC 93-9163. 186p. (C). 1993. text 20.50 (0-7914-1719-0) State U NY Pr.

Cochran, Laura J. The Old Miner & the Spider. LC 96-90708. (J). (gr. 6-8). 1998. 8.95 (0-533-12151-5) Vantage.

Cochran, Leslie E. Administrative Commitment to Teaching: Practical Research-Based Strategies to Strengthen College Teaching Effectiveness. 184p. (C). 1989. pap. 10.00 (0-9631438-0-8) Step Up Inc.
— Publish or Perish: The Wrong Issue. 180p. 1992. 22.50 (0-9631438-1-6) Step Up Inc.

Cochran, Lin. Edgar Cayce on Secrets of the Universe & How to Use Them in Your Life. Cayce, Charles T., ed. 192p. (Orig.). 1989. mass mkt. 4.99 (0-446-34984-4, Pub. by Warner Bks) Little.

Cochran, Linda. Forgiven & Set Free: A Post-Abortion Bible Study for Women. LC 97-148871. 112p. (gr. 10). 1996. pap. 7.99 (0-8010-5723-X) Baker Bks.

***Cochran, Mary E.** Dakota Cross-Bearer: The Life & World of a Native American Bishop. LC 00-23544. 272p. 2000. 29.95 (0-8032-1511-8) U of Nebr Pr.

Cochran, Michael H. Germany Not Guilty in 1914. LC 72-80274. 1972. 15.50 (0-87926-009-2); pap. 2.50 (0-87926-010-5) R Myles.

Cochran, Mickey. Mandolin Crosspicking Techniques. 128p. 1997. pap. 14.95 (0-7866-2891-X, 96613) Mel Bay.

***Cochran, Mike.** West Texas: A Portrait of Its People & Their Raw & Wondrous Land. LC 99-36542. 1999. 34.95 (0-89672-426-3) Tex Tech Univ Pr.

Cochran, Molly. The Broken Sword. LC 96-47188. 384p. 1997. text 24.95 (0-312-86283-0) St Martin.
— Normative Theory in International Relations: A Pragmatic Approach. (Cambridge Studies in International Relations: No. 68). 326p. (C). 2000. 59.95 (0-521-63050-9) Cambridge U Pr.
— Normative Theory in International Relations: A Pragmatic Approach. (Cambridge Studies in International Relations: Vol. 68). 326p. (C). 2000. pap. 22.95 (0-521-63965-4) Cambridge U Pr.
— World Without End. 1997. mass mkt. 6.99 (0-8125-3427-1, Pub. by Tor Bks) St Martin.

Cochran, Molly & Murphy, Warren. The Broken Sword. 1997. 24.95 (0-614-27872-4) Tor Bks.
— The Broken Sword. 480p. 1998. mass mkt. 6.99 (0-8125-4513-3, Pub. by Tor Bks) St Martin.
— The Forever King. 416p. 1993. mass mkt. 6.99 (0-8125-1716-4, Pub. by Tor Bks) St Martin.

Cochran, Molly, jt. auth. see Murphy, Warren.

Cochran, Mon, ed. Empowerment & Family Support. (Illus.). 212p. 1995. pap. 9.50 (1-57753-008-X, 321EFS) Corn Coop Ext.

Cochran, Moncrieff, ed. International Handbook of Child Care Policies & Programs. LC 92-25746. 712p. 1993. lib. bdg. 135.00 (0-313-26866-5, CIB, Greenwood Pr) Greenwood.

Cochran, Moncrieff, et al. Extending Families: The Social Networks of Parents & Their Children. (Illus.). 463p. (C). 1990. text 69.95 (0-521-37530-4) Cambridge U Pr.
— Extending Families: The Social Networks of Parents & Their Children. (Illus.). 456p. (C). 1993. pap. text 23.95 (0-521-44586-8) Cambridge U Pr.

Cochran, Norman A., et al. A Teacher's Guide to Elementary School Physical Education. 496p. (C). 1993. ring bd. 20.95 (0-8403-9113-7) Kendall-Hunt.

Cochran, Paul L. Polyphase Induction Motors: Analysis, Design, & Application. (Electrical Engineering & Electronics Ser.: Vol. 59). (Illus.). 704p. 1989. text 215.00 (0-8247-8043-4) Dekker.

Cochran, Peter, ed. & intro. see Byron, George Gordon.

Cochran, Philip L. & Wartick, Steven L. Corporate Governance: A Review of the Literature. LC 88-81702. (Illus.). 74p. (Orig.). 1988. pap. 20.00 (0-910586-69-1, 075-88) Finan Exec.

Cochran, Phillip E. Guide to Veterinary Medical Terminology. LC 90-85893. (Illus.). 300p. 1991. pap. text 31.95 (0-939674-31-9) Am Vet Pubns.

Cochran, R. G. & Tsoulfanidis, Nicholas. The Nuclear Fuel Cycle: Analysis & Management. 2nd ed. 392p. 1999. 58.00 (0-89448-451-6, 350015) Am Nuclear Soc.

Cochran, R. J., et al, eds. 1995 International Mechanical Engineering Congress & Exposition - Proceedings of the ASME Heat Transfer Division, Vol. 1. 488p. 110.00 (0-614-97063-6, H1032A) ASME.

Cochran, Rebecca A. Judicial Externships: The Clinic Inside the Courthouse. 2nd ed. 312p. 1998. pap. 34.00 (0-87084-440-7) Anderson Pub Co.

Cochran, Robert. Our Own Sweet Sounds: A Celebration of Popular Music in Arkansas. LC 96-30210. 1996. pap. 16.00 (1-55728-443-1) U of Ark Pr.
— Our Own Sweet Sounds: A Celebration of Popular Music in Arkansas. LC 96-30210. 120p. 1996. 30.00 (1-55728-442-3) U of Ark Pr.

***Cochran, Robert.** Singing in Zion: Music & Song in the Life of an Arkansas Family. 256p. 1999. 32.00 (1-55728-547-0) U of Ark Pr.
— Singing in Zion: Music & Song in the Life of an Arkansas Family. LC 99-10087. (Illus.). 256p. 1999. pap. 20.00 (1-55728-548-9) U of Ark Pr.

Cochran, Robert. Vance Randolph: An Ozark Life. LC 84-8647. (Illus.). 294p. 1985. text 24.95 (0-252-01164-3) U of Ill Pr.

Cochran, Robert F., Jr. & Collett, Teresa S. Cases & Materials on the Rules of the Legal Profession: American Casebook Series. LC 96-162632. (Paralegal). 375p. (C). 1996. text 24.50 (0-314-09884-4) West Pub.

Cochran, Robert F. & Collett, Teresa S. Legal Profession, Teacher's Manual to Accompany Cases & Materials on the Rules of The. (American Casebook Ser.). 148p. (C). 1996. pap. text. write for info. (0-314-22379-7) West Pub.

Cochran, Robert F., jt. auth. see Shaffer, Thomas L.

Cochran, Robert J., et al, eds. ASME Heat Transfer Division Vol. 317-1: Proceedings of the ASME International Mechanical Engineering Congress & Exposition, 1995, San Francisco, CA, 2 vols., Set. LC 95-81065. (HTD Ser.: No. 317). 477p. 1995. pap. 260.00 (0-7918-1751-2, H1032A) ASME Pr.

Cochran, Sallie B. Brave Star & the Necklace. (Illus.). 23p. (Orig.). (J). (gr. 4-7). 1991. pap. 10.95 (0-9629612-0-5) Isabels.

***Cochran, Sam V.** Men & Depression. (Illus.). 256p. 1999. 44.95 (0-12-177540-2) Acad Pr.

Cochran, Sean & House, Tom. Stronger Arms & Upper Body. LC 99-36518. (Illus.). 216p. 1999. pap. 16.95 (0-88011-977-2, PHOU0977) Human Kinetics.

Cochran, Shelley. The Pastor's Underground Guide to the Revised Common Lectionary: Year C, Year C. 184p. (Orig.). 1997. 16.99 (0-8272-2948-8) Chalice Pr.

Cochran, Shelley E. The Pastor's Underground Guide to the Revised Common Lectionary: Year A. 208p. (Orig.). 1995. pap. 18.99 (0-8272-2946-1) Chalice Pr.
— The Pastor's Underground Guide to the Revised Common Lectionary: Year B. 180p. (Orig.). 1996. pap. 16.99 (0-8272-2947-X) Chalice Pr.

Cochran, Sherman. Big Business in China: Sino-Foreign Rivalry in the Cigarette Industry, 1890-1930. LC 79-23907. (Studies in Business History: No. 33). (Illus.). 342p. 1980. 22.50 (0-674-07262-6) HUP.

***Cochran, Sherman.** Encountering Chinese Networks. LC 99-38446. (Illus.). 256p. 2000. 40.00 (0-520-21625-3, Pub. by U CA Pr) Cal Prin Full Svc.

***Cochran, Sherman, ed.** Inventing Nanjing Road Vol. 103: Commercial Culture in Shanghai, 1900-1945. (Illus.). 270p. (C). 1999. 23.80 (1-885445-63-6); pap. 14.45 (1-885445-03-2) Cornell East Asia Pgm.

Cochran-Smith, Marilyn. The Making of a Reader. Wallat, Cynthia & Green, Judith, eds. LC 83-25795. (Language & Learning for Human Service Professions Ser.: Vol. 2). 256p. 1984. pap. 39.50 (0-89391-219-0); text 73.25 (0-89391-187-9) Ablx Pub.

Cochran-Smith, Marilyn & Lytle, Susan L., eds. Inside - Outside: Teacher Research & Knowledge. LC 92-31875. (Language & Literacy Ser.). 328p. (C). 1992. pap. 22.95 (0-8077-3235-4); text 44.00 (0-8077-3236-2) Tchrs Coll.

Cochran-Smith, Marilyn, et al. Learning to Write Differently: Beginning Writers & Word Processing. Green, Judith, ed. (Language & Educational Processes Ser.: Vol. 5). 336p. (C). 1991. pap. 39.50 (0-89391-762-1); text 73.25 (0-89391-761-3) Ablx Pub.

Cochran, T. Derivatives of Links: Milnor's Concordance Invariants & Massey's Products. LC 89-18593. (Memoirs Ser.: No. 84/427). 73p. 1990. pap. 18.00 (0-8218-2489-9, MEMO/84/427) Am Math.

***Cochran, Thad, ed.** National Missile Defense & Prospects for U. S.-Russia ABM Treaty Accomodation: Congressional Hearing. 144p. (C). 1999. reprint ed. pap. text 25.00 (0-7881-8304-4) DIANE Pub.

Cochran, Thomas. Roughnecks. LC 96-43939. 256p. (J). (gr. 7). 1997. 15.00 (0-15-201433-0) Harcourt.
— Roughnecks. LC 96-43939. 256p. (YA). 1999. pap. 6.00 (0-15-202200-7) Harcourt.
— Roughnecks. 1999. pap. text 6.00 (0-15-201432-2) Harcourt.

Cochran, Thomas, et al. Nuclear Weapons Databook Vol. 3: U. S. Nuclear Warhead Facility Profiles. LC 87-14552. (Nuclear Weapons Databook Ser.). 160p. 1987. pap. 29.95 (0-88730-146-0, HarpBusn); text 39.95 (0-88730-126-6, HarpBusn) HarpInfo.

Cochran, Thomas B. The Liquid Metal Fast Breeder Reactor: An Environmental & Economic Critique. LC 73-19349. 287p. reprint ed. pap. 89.00 (0-7837-3138-8, 204284900006) Bks Demand.

Cochran, Thomas B., et al. Nuclear Weapons Databook Vol. 2: U. S. Nuclear Warhead Production. LC 82-24376. 240p. 1987. text 39.95 (0-88730-124-X, HarpBusn); pap. text 40.00 (0-88730-125-8, HarpBusn) HarpInfo.
— Nuclear Weapons Databook Vol. II: U. S. Nuclear Warhead Production. 1987. 40.00 (0-318-23279-0); pap. 25.00 (0-318-23280-4) Natl Resources Defense Coun.
— Nuclear Weapons Databook Vol. III: U. S. Nuclear Warhead Facility Profiles. 132p. 1987. 39.95 (0-318-39810-9); pap. 24.95 (0-318-39811-7) Natl Resources Defense Coun.
— Nuclear Weapons Databook Vol. 4: Soviet Nuclear Weapons. 364p. 1989. pap. text 40.00 (0-88730-049-9, HarpBusn) HarpInfo.

Cochran, Thomas C. American Business in the Twentieth Century. LC 72-78424. 269p. reprint ed. pap. 83.40 (0-8357-5355-7, 201992800015) Bks Demand.
— Business in American Life: A History. LC 78-38740. 416p. 1974. 6.95 (0-07-011520-6) McGraw-Hill Prof.
— Challenges to American Values: Society, Business & Religion. LC 84-19102. 152p. 1987. pap. text 19.95 (0-19-503535-6) OUP.
— Frontiers of Change: Early Industrialism in America. 188p. 1983. pap. text 20.95 (0-19-503284-5) OUP.
— New York in the Confederation. LC 72-77054. (Reprints of Economic Classics Ser.). (Illus.). ix, 220p. 1972. reprint ed. 35.00 (0-678-00911-2) Kelley.

Cochran, Thomas C., ed. see American Historical Association Staff.

Cochran, Vicki. My Daddy Is a Stranger. Johnson, Joy, ed. (Illus.). 24p. (Orig.). (J). (gr. 1-5). 1992. pap. 3.95 (1-56123-049-9) Centering Corp.

Cochran, W. R. History of the Town of Antrim, from Its Earliest Settlement to 1877. (Illus.). 791p. 1988. reprint ed. lib. bdg. 79.00 (0-8328-0042-2, NH0004) Higginson Bk Co.

Cochran, W. R. & Wood, George K. History of Francestown, New Hampshire, from Its Earliest Settlement, 1758 to 1891: With a Brief Genealogical Register. (Illus.). 1031p. 1988. reprint ed. lib. bdg. 95.00 (0-8328-0050-3, NH0011) Higginson Bk Co.

Cochran, William C. Student's Law Lexicon: A Dictionary of Legal Words & Phrases. LC 97-25771. vii, 332p. 1997. reprint ed. 47.50 (0-8377-2060-5, Rothman) W S Hein.
— Western Reserve & the Fugitive Slave Law: A Prelude to the Civil War. LC 71-127273. 1972. reprint ed. 29.50 (0-306-71212-1) Da Capo.

Cochran, William G. Sampling Techniques. 3rd ed. (Probability & Mathematical Statistics Ser.). 448p. 1977. text 99.95 (0-471-16240-X) Wiley.

Cochran, William G. & Cox, Gertrude M. Experimental Designs. 2nd ed. (Probability & Mathematical Statistics Ser.). 617p. 1957. text 103.95 (0-471-16203-5) Wiley.
— Experimental Designs. 2nd ed. (Classics Library). 640p. 1992. pap. 44.95 (0-471-54567-8) Wiley.

Cochran, William G., jt. auth. see Snedecor, George W.

Cochran, William R. & Speck, Gordon R., eds. Commanding Views from the Empty House: Collected Writings by the Occupants of the Empty House. (Illus.). 192p. (Orig.). 1997. pap. 18.95 (0-938501-24-0, Gasogene Bks) Wessex.

Cochrane. The Autobiography of a Seaman, Vol. 1. LC 96-162467. 425p. 1998. 35.00 (0-09-475080-7, Pub. by Constable & Co) Trafalgar.
— The Autobiography of a Seaman, Vol. 2. 488p. 1998. 35.00 (0-09-475180-3, Pub. by Constable & Co) Trafalgar.
— Color Atlas of Asthma: Current Perspectives. 2nd ed. 128p. 1996. lib. bdg. 40.95 (0-7234-2454-3) CRC Pr.
— For Better or for Worse: The Canadian Guide to Marriage Contracts & Cohabitation Agreements. 320p. 1997. pap., student ed. write for info. (0-471-64206-1) Wiley.
— On Becoming a Lawyer: The Insider'S Guide to a Legal Career in Canada. 288p. 2000. pap. write for info. (0-471-64196-0) Wiley.

Cochrane, et al, revs. History of Caroline County, from Its Beginning. (Illus.). 345p. 1997. reprint ed. lib. bdg. 42.00 (0-8328-5949-4) Higginson Bk Co.

Cochrane, Geoffrey O. Blood. LC 98-200426. 191p. 1997. write for info. (0-86473-326-7) Victoria Univ Pr.

Cochrane, Jeanett, et al. Best Practices in Mental Health Reform: Discussion Paper. LC 98-141462. vi, 39 p. 1997. write for info. (0-662-26073-2) Can7 Govern Pub.

An Asterisk (*) at the beginning of an entry indicates that the title is appearing for the first time.

C

An Asterisk (*) at the beginning of an entry indicates that the title is appearing for the first time.

Cockburn, Catharine. The Works of Mrs. Catharine Cockburn: Theological, Moral, Dramatic & Poetical (1751 Edition), 2 vols., Set. 1120p. 1996. reprint ed. 295.00 (*1-85506-124-4*) Bks Intl VA.

Cockburn, Claude. Cockburn Sums Up. 1981. 17.95 (*0-7043-2266-8*, Pub. by Quartet) Charles River Bks.

Cockburn, Cynthia. Brothers. 2nd ed. (C). 1983. pap. text 21.50 (*0-86104-384-7*) Westview.

— In the Way of Women: Men's Resistance to Sex Equality in Organizations. 264p. 1991. 45.00 (*0-87546-700-8*, ILR Press); pap. 17.95 (*0-87546-701-6*, ILR Press) Cornell U Pr.

— Machinery of Dominance: Women, Men, & Technical Know-How. (Northeastern Series in Feminist Theory). 282p. 1988. text 45.00 (*1-55553-041-9*); pap. text 16.95 (*1-55553-046-X*) NE U Pr.

— The Space Between Us: Negotiating Gender & National Identities in Conflict. LC 98-19798. 1998. text 65.00 (*1-85649-617-1*); text 25.00 (*1-85649-618-X*) Zed Books.

Cockburn, Cynthia & First-Dilic, Ruza, eds. Bringing Technology Home: Gender & Technology in a Changing Europe. LC 93-32058. 1994. pap. 34.95 (*0-335-19158-4*) OpUniv Pr.

Cockburn, Cynthia & Ormrod, Susan. Gender & Technology in the Making. LC 93-85147. (C). 1993. text 69.95 (*0-8039-8810-9*); pap. text 22.95 (*0-8039-8811-7*) Sage.

Cockburn, David. Other Times: Philosophical Perspectives on Past, Present & Future. LC 96-50077. (Studies in Philosophy). 370p. (C). 1997. text 59.95 (*0-521-59214-3*) Cambridge U Pr.

Cockburn, David, ed. Human Beings. (Royal Institute of Philosophy Supplements Ser.: No. 29). 281p. (C). 1991. pap. text 24.95 (*0-521-42245-0*) Cambridge U Pr.

Cockburn, Forrester, ed. Advances in Perinatal Medicine: The Proceedings of the XV European Congress of Perinatal Medicine. LC 97-23209. (Illus.). 420p. 1997. 110.00 (*1-85070-944-0*) Prthnon Pub.

— Fetal & Neonatal Growth. LC 87-18974. (Perinatal Practice Ser.: Vol. 5). 228p. 1988. reprint ed. pap. 70.70 (*0-608-01641-1*, 206222600002) Bks Demand.

Cockburn, Forrester, et al. Children's Medicine & Surgery. (Illus.). 544p. 1996. pap. text 75.00 (*0-340-55143-7*, Pub. by E A) OUP.

Cockburn, Gerrie L. Keeping Them at Home: A Practical Guide to Caring for the Homebound. 2nd ed. Cockburn, Ian, ed. (Homecare Ser.). (Illus.). 60p. (Orig.). 1995. pap. 5.95 (*1-887461-01-9*) Cockburn Pub.

— Why Turtles Have Shells. Cockburn, Ian, ed. (Friendship Ser.). (Illus.). 31p. (Orig.). (J). (gr. k-4). pap. 5.95 (*1-887461-00-0*) Cockburn Pub.

Cockburn, Helen. Women on Stamps, Vol. III. (Illus.). 176p. 1993. pap. 17.00 (*0-935991-19-0*) Am Topical Assn.

Cockburn, Henry. Memorials of His Time. 470p. (C). 1989. 32.00 (*0-901824-11-9*, Pub. by Mercat Pr Bks) St Mut.

Cockburn, Henry T. Life of Lord Jeffrey with a Selection from His Correspondence, 2 vols. in 1. LC 70-148763. reprint ed. 105.00 (*0-404-07297-6*) AMS Pr.

— Memorials of His Time. LC 73-148764. reprint ed. 55.00 (*0-404-07228-3*) AMS Pr.

Cockburn-Hood, T. H. The House of Cockburn of That Ilk & the Cadets Thereof. (Illus.). 394p. 1989. reprint ed. pap. 59.00 (*0-8328-0407-X*); reprint ed. lib. bdg. 67.00 (*0-8328-0406-1*) Higginson Bk Co.

Cockburn, Ian, ed. see Cockburn, Gerrie L.

Cockburn, J. & Mitchell, A. MCQ Companion to Grainger & Allison's Diagnostic Radiology, Vol. 1. Grainger, R. G. & Allison, D. V., eds. 320p. 1998. pap. write for info. (*0-443-05941-1*) Church.

Cockburn, J. S. History of English Assizes, 1558-1714. LC 85-81816. (Cambridge Studies in English Legal History). xviii, 372p. 1986. reprint ed. 91.00 (*0-912004-42-8*) Gaunt.

— Western Circuit Assize Orders, 1629-1648: A Calendar. (Camden Fourth Ser.: No. 17). 366p. 27.00 (*0-901050-29-6*) David Brown.

Cockburn, J. S., ed. Calendar of Assize Records: Kent Indictments Vol. 4: Charles II 1676-1688. LC 98-145206. 480p. 1997. 170.00 (*0-85115-709-2*) Boydell & Brewer.

— Crime in England, 1550-1800. LC 77-2867. 378p. reprint ed. pap. 117.20 (*0-8357-2773-4*, 203989800014) Bks Demand.

Cockburn, J. S. & Green, Thomas A., eds. Twelve Good Men & True: The Criminal Trial Jury in England, 1200-1800. LC 87-29118. (Illus.). 432p. reprint ed. pap. 134.00 (*0-608-06380-0*, 206674100008) Bks Demand.

Cockburn, Jack, jt. auth. see Thomas, Frank.

Cockburn, Jacqueline, tr. & compiled by see Stokes, Richard, ed.

Cockburn, Ken. Souvenirs & Homelands. LC 99-206357. 64p. 1994. pap. 21.00 (*1-898218-93-5*) St Mut.

***Cockburn, Leslie.** Looking for Trouble. 288p. 1998. 24.95 (*0-385-48319-8*) Doubleday.

Cockburn, Leslie. Looking for Trouble. 288p. 1999. pap. 12.95 (*0-385-48355-4*, Anchor NY) Doubleday.

Cockburn, Patrick, jt. auth. see Cockburn, Andrew.

Cockburn, Robert H. The Novels Of Hugh Maclennan, LC 76-109579. 165 P.p. 1970. write for info. (*0-88772-108-7*) HAR Davenport.

— The Novels of Hugh MacLennan. LC 76-109579. 165p. reprint ed. pap. 51.20 (*0-608-13578-X*, 202228800026) Bks Demand.

Cockburn, Tina & Wiseman, Leanne, eds. Disclosure Obligations in Business Relationships. 303p. 1996. 79.00 (*1-86287-235-X*, Pub. by Federation Pr) Gaunt.

Cockburn, W., jt. auth. see Street, H. E.

Cockcrof, jt. auth. see Dosman, James A.

Cockcroft, A. N. A Guide to the Collision Avoidance Rules. 5th ed. (Illus.). 256p. 1996. 56.95 (*0-7506-2690-9*) Buttrwrth-Heinemann.

Cockcroft, A. N., rev. Nicholls's Seamanship & Nautical Knowledge. rev. ed. (C). 1987. 150.00 (*0-85174-462-1*) St Mut.

***Cockcroft, Adrian.** Capacity Planning for Rapid Growth. 208p. 2001. pap. 32.00 (*0-13-089402-8*) Prntice Hall Bks.

Cockcroft, Adrian & Sunsoft Press Staff. Sun Performance & Tuning: Java & the Internet. 2nd ed. LC 98-167571. 560p. (C). 1998. pap. 54.00 (*0-13-095249-4*) P-H.

Cockcroft, B., jt. auth. see Hauxwell, Hannah.

Cockcroft, Eva, et al. Signs from the Heart: California Chicano Murals. LC 93-17526. (Illus.). 116p. 1993. pap. 25.95 (*0-8263-1448-1*) U of NM Pr.

Cockcroft, Eva S., et al. Toward a People's Art: The Contemporary Mural Movement. LC 98-19861. (Illus.). 325p. 1998. 65.00 (*0-8263-2005-8*); pap. 27.95 (*0-8263-1952-7*) U of NM Pr.

Cockcroft, James. Diego Rivera. (Hispanics of Achievement Ser.). (J). 1991. 14.05 (*0-606-05233-X*, Pub. by Turtleback) Demco.

Cockcroft, James, jt. auth. see Garza, Hedda.

Cockcroft, James, jt. ed. see Cardona, Rodolfo.

Cockcroft, James, jt. ed. see O'Brien, S.

Cockcroft, James D. Latin America: History, Politics & U. S. Policy. 2nd rev. ed. LC 94-40030. Orig. Title: Neighbors in Turmoil. 1996. pap. text 45.95 (*0-8304-1398-7*) Thomson Learn.

— Latinos in Beisbol. LC 96-11876. (Hispanic Experience in the Americas Ser.). 196p. (J). 1996. lib. bdg. 24.00 (*0-531-11284-5*) Watts.

— Latinos in Beisbol. (Hispanic Experience in the Americas Ser.). 208p. (J). 1997. pap. 9.95 (*0-531-15834-9*) Watts.

— Latinos in the Struggle for Equal Education. (Hispanic Experience in the Americas Ser.). (Illus.). 176p. (YA). (gr. 9-12). 1995. lib. bdg. 24.00 (*0-531-11226-8*) Watts.

— Mexico's Hope: An Encounter with Politics & History. LC 98-46777. 1998. 18.00 (*0-85345-925-8*, Pub. by Monthly Rev) NYU Pr.

— Mexico's Hope: An Encounter with Politics & History. LC 98-46777. 435p. 1998. 48.00 (*0-85345-926-6*, Pub. by Monthly Rev) NYU Pr.

***Cockcroft, James D. & Canning, Jane.** Latinos in Art. LC 99-89464. (Book Report Biography Ser.). 2000. 26.00 (*0-531-11312-4*) Orchard Bks Watts.

***Cockcroft, James D. & Canning, Jane Carolina, eds.** Salvador Allende Reader: Chile's Voice of Democracy. (SPA & ENG., Illus.). 300p. 2000. pap. 19.95 (*1-876175-24-9*, Pub. by Ocean Pr NJ) LPC InBook.

***Cockcroft, Lance, et al.** MCSE Windows 2000 Accelerated Exam Prep. (Exam Prep Ser.). (Illus.). 1000p. 2000. pap. 59.99 (*1-57610-690-X*) Coriolis Grp.

***Cockcroft, Shamshad, ed.** Biology of Phosphoinositides. LC 99-87330. (Frontiers in Molecular Biology Ser.: No. 27). (Illus.). 384p. 2000. text 115.00 (*0-19-963765-2*); pap. text 60.00 (*0-19-963764-4*) OUP.

Cockcroft, Susan, ed. see Bronte, Charlotte.

Cockcroft, Susan, ed. see Hawthorne, Nathaniel.

Cockcroft, T. G. Index to the Weird Fiction Magazines, 2 vols. LC 74-15955. (Science Fiction Ser.). (Illus.). 101p. 1979. 15.95 (*0-405-06322-9*) Ayer.

Cocke, Charles F. Parish Lines: Diocese of Southern Virginia. 3rd ed. (Publication Ser.: No. 22). 287p. 1996. reprint ed. pap. 15.00 (*0-88490-049-5*) Library of VA.

— Parish Lines, Diocese of Southwestern Virginia. (Publication Ser.: No. 14). 196p. 1980. reprint ed. 10.00 (*0-88490-081-9*) Library of VA.

— Parish Lines, Diocese of Virginia. LC 78-19035. (Publication Ser.: No. 28). xv, 321p. 1978. reprint ed. 10.00 (*0-88490-062-2*) Library of VA.

Cocke, Cornelia. Cracking the PRAXIS II: NTE. 2nd ed. (Princeton Review Ser.). 240p. 1997. pap., pap. text 34.95 incl. audio (*0-679-78396-2*) Villard Books.

Cocke, D. L. & Clearfield, A., eds. Design of New Materials. LC 87-3131. (Illus.). 378p. 1987. 85.00 (*0-306-42604-8*, Plenum Trade) Perseus Pubng.

Cocke, Earline & Darnell, Pam. Desktop Publishing Applications Using PageMaker 5.0. LC 93-40076. (C). 1994. mass mkt. 19.95 (*0-538-71060-8*) S-W Pub.

Cocke, Ellen M. Fox: Some Fox Trails in Old Virginia: John Fox of King Wm. Co., Ancestors, Descendants, Near Kin. (Illus.). 165p. 1997. reprint ed. pap. 25.00 (*0-8328-8642-4*); reprint ed. lib. bdg. 35.00 (*0-8328-8641-6*) Higginson Bk Co.

Cocke, Hugh. A Summary of the Principal Legal Decisions Affecting Auditors. Brief, Richard P., ed. LC 80-1480. (Dimensions of Accounting Theory & Practice Ser.). 1980. reprint ed. lib. bdg. 17.95 (*0-405-13510-6*) Ayer.

Cocke, Nancy C. Tastes & Tales of Erie, Pennsylvania. 184p. 1995. reprint ed. spiral bd. 12.95 (*0-9644737-0-4*) N C Cocke.

Cocke, Paul, ed. see Moen, Ruth R.

Cocke, Sarah J. Bypaths in Dixie: Folk Tales of the South. LC 72-6501. (Black Heritage Library Collection). 1977. reprint ed. 21.95 (*0-8369-9164-8*) Ayer.

Cocke, Thomas & Kidson, Peter. Salisbury Cathedral: Perspectives on the Architectural History. (Illus.). 200p. 1993. pap. 24.95 (*0-11-300040-5*, HM00405, Pub. by Statnry Office) Balogh.

Cocke, Thomas H. 900 Years: The Restorations of Westminster Abbey. (Illus.). 160p. 1995. text 45.00 (*1-872501-77-X*, Pub. by Harvey Miller) Gordon & Breach.

Cocke, W. J., jt. auth. see Tifft, William G.

Cocke, William. A Historical Album of Virginia. (Historical Albums Ser.). (Illus.). 64p. (J). (gr. 4-8). 1995. pap. 6.95 (*1-56294-856-3*); lib. bdg. 23.40 (*1-56294-596-3*) Millbrook Pr.

— Historical Album of Virginia. (Historical Albums Ser.). 1995. 12.15 (*0-606-07655-7*, Pub. by Turtleback) Demco.

— Historical Album of Washington. (Historical Albums Ser.). (Illus.). 64p. (J). (gr. 4-8). 1995. pap. 6.95 (*1-56294-851-2*); lib. bdg. 23.40 (*1-56294-508-4*) Millbrook Pr.

— Historical Album of Washington. (Historical Albums Ser.). 1995. 12.15 (*0-606-07656-5*, Pub. by Turtleback) Demco.

Cocke, William, et al. Astronomy: Lab Manual for Non-Scientists, 1995. 144p. (C). 1994. pap. text, spiral bd. 17.95 (*0-8403-9352-0*) Kendall-Hunt.

Cocke, William M., Jr. Breast Reconstruction Following Mastectomy for Carcinoma. 1977. text 27.50 (*0-316-14920-9*, Little Brwn Med Div) Lppncott W & W.

Cocke, William M., Jr., et al. Essentials of Plastic Surgery. 1979. 15.00 (*0-316-14921-7*, Little Brwn Med Div) Lppncott W & W.

Cocke, William M., et al. Wound Care. LC 86-21621. 132p. reprint ed. pap. 41.00 (*0-7837-1371-1*, 204152000021) Bks Demand.

***Cocke, William R.** Hanover County, VA Taxpayers: St. Paul's Parish, 1782-1815. 158p. 2000. reprint ed. pap. 17.50 (*0-8063-4952-2*) Clearfield Co.

Cockell, Jenny. Across Time & Death: The Extraordinary Search for My Past-Life Family. 160p. 1994. per. 10.00 (*0-671-88986-9*) S&S Trade Pap.

— Past Lives, Future Lives. LC 98-11094. 1998. per. 10.00 (*0-684-83216-X*, Fireside) S&S Trade Pap.

Cocker, Andrew. NYPD. 11.95 (*962-217-658-5*) China Guides.

***Cocker, Mark.** Rivers of Blood, Rivers of Gold: Europe's Conquest of Indigenous Peoples. LC 99-87927. (Illus.). 432p. 2000. 30.00 (*0-8021-1666-3*, Pub. by Grove-Atltic) Publishers Group.

Cocker, W. John. Stitches: Side-Splitting Humor from the Doctors Office, Hospital & Operating Room. 1994. pap. text 10.95 (*0-7737-5605-1*) Genl Dist Srvs.

Cockeram, Henry. The English Dictionarie. (Anglistica & Americana Ser.: No. 54). 342p. 1970. reprint ed. 95.00 (*0-685-66451-1*, 05102632) G Olms Pubs.

Cockerell, Clay J. Clinicopathologic Correlations in Dermatopathology. LC 95-3181. (Illus.). 144p. 1995. 59.50 (*0-89640-270-3*) Igaku-Shoin.

Cockerell, Douglas. Bookbinding, & the Care of Books. (Illus.). 334p. 1991. pap. 16.95 (*1-55821-104-7*, 50080) Lyons Pr.

Cockerell, Hugh. Witherby's Dictionary of Insurance. 261p. (C). 1987. 125.00 (*0-948691-21-2*, Pub. by Witherby & Co) St Mut.

— Witherby's Insurance Dictionary. 235p. 1980. 125.00 (*0-900886-50-1*, Pub. by Witherby & Co) St Mut.

Cockerell, Pete J. Using BBC BASIC. LC 83-10607. 392p. reprint ed. pap. 121.60 (*0-8357-6936-4*, 203799500009) Bks Demand.

Cockerell, Sydney C. & Plummer, John. Old Testament Miniatures: A Medieval Picture Book with 283 Paintings from the Creation to the Story of David. LC 75-82000. (Illus.). 210p. 1969. boxed set 125.00 (*0-8076-0513-1*, Pub. by Braziller) Norton.

Cockerham, Allan W. The Apostolic Succession in the Liberal Catholic Church. 2nd ed. (Illus.). 1980. pap. text 3.25 (*0-918980-09-7*) St Alban Pr.

Cockerham, Barbara & Kennedy-Jackson, Diane, eds. Sampler & Antique Needlework: A Year in Stitches, 1994. (Illus.). 144p. 1994. 24.95 (*0-932437-02-8*) Symbol Exc Pubs.

— Sampler & Antique Needlework: A Year in Stitches, 1995. (Illus.). 144p. 1995. write for info. (*0-932437-04-4*) Symbol Exc Pubs.

Cockerham, Barbara, jt. ed. see Hoffman, Phyllis.

Cockerham, Barbara, ed. see Needle's Prayse Staff & O'Steen, Darlene.

Cockerham, L. G. Radiation Toxicology. 76p. 1988. text 107.00 (*2-88124-413-0*) Gordon & Breach.

Cockerham, Lorris G. & Shane, Barbara S., eds. Basic Environmental Toxicology. 640p. 1993. boxed set 110.95 (*0-8493-8851-1*, QH545) CRC Pr.

Cockerham, Paul. Drag Racing. LC 97-28384. (Race Car Legends Ser.). (Illus.). 64p. (J). (gr. 3 up). 1997. lib. bdg. 15.95 (*0-7910-4434-3*) Chelsea Hse.

***Cockerham, Paul W.** BMW: Precision & Performance. 1998. pap. text 10.98 (*1-57717-039-3*) Todtri Prods.

Cockerham, Paul W. Ferrari: The Ultimate Dream Machine. 1998. pap. text 10.98 (*1-57717-005-9*) Todtri Prods.

***Cockerham, Paul W.** Jaguar: Spirit of the Cat. 1999. 10.95 (*1-57717-122-5*) Todtri Prods.

Cockerham, Paul W. Lamborghini: The Spirit of the Bull. 1998. pap. text 10.95 (*1-57717-006-7*) Todtri Prods.

— Mercedes-Benz, 1. 1998. pap. text 10.98 (*1-57717-084-9*) Todtri Prods.

***Cockerham, Paul W.** Porsche: Precision, Balance & Style. 1998. pap. text 10.98 (*1-57717-042-3*) Todtri Prods.

— Rolls-Royce & Bentley Classic Elegance. 1999. 10.95 (*1-57717-123-3*) Todtri Prods.

Cockerham, Stephen T. Turfgrass Sod Production. LC 88-71015. 88p. 1988. pap. 12.00 (*0-931876-85-0*, 21451) ANR Pubns CA.

Cockerham, William C. The Global Society. (C). 1995. pap., student ed. 17.19 (*0-07-011535-4*) McGraw.

— The Global Society: An Introduction to Sociology. LC 94-21197. 512p. (C). 1994. 50.94 (*0-07-011532-X*) McGraw.

— Health & Social Change in Russia & Eastern Europe. LC 98-29877. 288p. (C). 1999. pap. 22.99 (*0-415-92081-7*, D5647) Routledge.

— Health & Social Change in Russia & Eastern Europe. LC 98-29877. 288p. (C). (gr. 13). 1999. 75.00 (*0-415-92080-9*, D5643) Routledge.

— Medical Sociology. 7th ed. LC 97-6934. 395p. 1997. 57.00 (*0-13-269556-1*) P-H.

— Readings in Medical Sociology. LC 97-15095. 539p. 1997. pap. text 38.67 (*0-13-617937-1*) P-H.

***Cockerham, William C.** Sociology of Mental Disorder. 5th ed. LC 99-25838. 374p. 1999. 55.00 (*0-13-099926-1*) P-H.

Cockerham, William C. This Aging Society. 2nd ed. LC 96-41176. 275p. (C). 1996. pap. text 45.00 (*0-13-651092-2*) P-H.

***Cockerham, William C., ed.** The Blackwell Companion to Medical Sociology. 2000. 124.95 (*0-631-21703-7*) Blackwell Pubs.

Cockerham, William C., ed. The Sociology of Medicine. LC 95-24273. (International Library of Critical Writings in Sociology: No. 4). 672p. 1995. 255.00 (*1-85898-021-6*) E Elgar.

***Cockerham, William C. & Glasser, Michael.** Readings in Medical Sociology. 2nd ed. 496p. 2000. pap. 40.00 (*0-13-027453-4*) P-H.

Cockerham, William C. & Ritchey, Ferris J. Dictionary of Medical Sociology. LC 96-36575. 200p. 1997. lib. bdg. 75.00 (*0-313-29269-8*, Greenwood Pr) Greenwood.

Cockerill, Alan. Each One Must Shine: The Educational Legacy of V. A. Sukhomlinsky. LC 97-39384. (American University Studies XIV: Vol. 45). VIII, 230p. (C). 1999. text 45.95 (*0-8204-3988-6*) P Lang Pubng.

Cockerill, Charles P., jt. auth. see Daugherty, Richard F.

***Cockerill, Gareth Lee.** Hebrews: A Bible Commentary in the Wesleyan Tradition. 316p. 1999. text 24.95 (*0-89827-200-9*) Wesleyan Pub Hse.

***Cockerill, Gary, et al.** Reflecting God. 2000. pap., student ed. 12.99 (*0-8341-1866-1*) Beacon Hill.

Cockerill, T. A., jt. ed. see Pickering, J. F.

***Cockerman & Chaparian.** The Human Project. 3rd ed. 2000. pap. 75.93 (*0-13-031913-9*) P-H.

Cockett, A. T. Conferencia Internacional Sober la Hiperplasia Prostatica Benigna, Paris, June 26-27, 1991. (SPA.). 272p. 1991. pap. 36.00 (*84-7978-064-9*, Pub. by Ediciones Diaz) IBD Ltd.

Cockett, A. T. & Koshiba, Ken. Manual of Urologic Surgery. (Comprehensive Manuals of Surgical Specialties Ser.). (Illus.). 284p. 1979. 161.00 (*0-387-90423-9*) Spr-Verlag.

Cockett, Abraham T. & Koshiba, Ken. Color Atlas of Urologic Surgery. LC 96-13528. (Illus.). 434p. 1996. write for info. (*0-683-02045-5*) Lppncott W & W.

Cockett, F. B. Early Sea Painters, 1660-1730: The Group Who Worked under the Shadow of the Van De Veldes. LC 96-147443. (Illus.). 160p. 1995. 49.50 (*1-85149-230-5*) Antique Collect.

***Cockett, Frank B.** Peter Monamy. (Illus.). 98p. 2000. 49.50 (*1-85149-339-5*) Antique Collect.

Cockett, Mike, jt. ed. see Halsall, Rob.

Cockett, Richard. David Astor & the Observer. (Illus.). 320p. 1992. 39.95 (*0-233-98735-5*, Pub. by Andre Deutsch) Trafalgar.

***Cockey, Tim.** Hearse of a Different Color. 2001. 23.95 (*0-7868-6571-7*, Pub. by Hyperion) Time Warner.

Cockey, Tim. The Hearse You Came in On: A Hitchcock Sewell Mystery. 2001. mass mkt. write for info. (*0-7868-8962-4*, Pub. by Disney Pr) Little.

— The Hearse You Came in On: A Hitchcock Sewell Mystery. LC 99-22210. 320p. 2000. 22.95 (*0-7868-6570-9*, Pub. by Hyperion) Time Warner.

Cockfield. With Snow on Their Boots: The Tragic Odyssey of the Russian Expeditionary Force in France During World War I. 408p. 1999. pap. 18.95 (*0-312-22082-0*) St Martin.

Cockfield, Alfred. Forgiveness: The Key to Divine Release. 210p. (Orig.). 1995. pap. 10.99 (*1-56043-826-6*, Treasure Hse) Destiny Image.

Cockfield, Fred. Power Tools for 4, 5, & 6 String Bass. (Illus.). 80p. 1994. pap. 12.95 (*1-886714-00-2*) Acad Mus Publ.

***Cockfield, Fred & Wilton, Michael.** Power Tools for Guitar Book-CD Set. 80p. 1998. pap. 17.95 incl. cd-rom (*0-7866-3318-2*, 96913BCD) Mel Bay.

Cockfield, Jamie H. With Snow on Their Boots: The Tragic Odyssey of the Russian Expeditionary Force in France During World War I. LC 97-21440. 408p. 1997. text 35.00 (*0-312-17356-3*) St Martin.

Cockhill, Pat B., ed. see Palmer, Paul M.

Cockin, Katharine. Edith Craig (1869-1947) Dramatic Lives. LC 97-22464. 1998. 69.95 (*0-304-33645-9*); pap. 21.95 (*0-304-33644-0*) Continuum.

***Cockin, Katharine.** Women & Theatre in the Age of Suffrage: The Pioneer Players. LC 00-33341. 2000. write for info. (*0-312-23764-2*) St Martin.

Cocking, E. C., jt. ed. see Razdan, M. K.

Cocking, J. M., et al. Three Studies in Modern French Literature: Proust, Gide, & Mauriac. 1960. pap. 39.50 (*0-685-26713-X*) Elliots Bks.

Cocking, Rodney R. & Mestre, Jose P., eds. Linguistic & Cultural Influences on Learning Mathematics. (Instructional Psychology Ser.). 320p. 1988. text 65.00 (*0-89859-876-1*) L Erlbaum Assocs.

Cocking, Rodney R. & Renninger, K. Ann, eds. The Development & Meaning of Psychological Distance. 280p. 1993. text 59.95 (*0-8058-0747-0*) L Erlbaum Assocs.

Cocking, Rodney R., jt. ed. see Greenfield, Patricia M.

***Cockington, James.** Secret Sydney. 2000. pap. 18.95 (*1-86436-317-7*, Pub. by New Holland) BHB Intl.

— When the Man in the Gold Mustang Met the Girl from the Pink Pussycat. LC 97-195908. 1997. write for info. (*0-09-183389-2*) Trafalgar.

Cockle, G. R. Giants of the West. LC 81-65098. (Overland Railbook Ser.). (Illus.). 208p. 1982. pap. 23.50 (*0-916160-12-2*) G R Cockle.

C

An Asterisk (*) at the beginning of an entry indicates that the title is appearing for the first time.

— Those Bicentennials...from American Rails. LC 78-50294. (Illus.). 1986. 35.00 (*0-916160-04-1*) G R Cockle.
— Union Pacific's Snow Fighters. LC 81-65095. (Overland Railbook Ser.). (Illus.). 208p. 1984. pap. 23.50 (*0-916160-09-2*) G R Cockle.
Cockle, George R. Centennials in Action. LC 78-51541. (Overland Railbook Ser.). (Illus.). 1980. pap. 11.95 (*0-916160-05-X*) G R Cockle.
— Frisco in Transition. (Overland Railbook Ser.). (Illus.). 208p. 1985. pap. 23.50 (*0-916160-13-0*) G R Cockle.
— Union Pacific Forties . . . On the Move. LC 81-65096. (Overland Railbook Ser.). (Illus.). 208p. 1985. pap. 23.50 (*0-916160-10-6*) G R Cockle.
— Union Pacific, 1977-1980. LC 77-81546. (Illus.). 208p. 1980. pap. 18.95 (*0-916160-03-3*) G R Cockle.
Cockle, George R. & Withers, Paul K. Union Pacific, 1990. (Illus.). 208p. 1991. 42.50 (*0-9618503-8-8*) Withers Pub.
Cockley, Dave. The Homework Conspiracy: A Musical Play in 2-Acts. (Illus.). 44p. (YA). 1997. pap. 4.00 (*0-88680-442-6*) I E Clark.
— Kids' Country: A Musical Play in Two Acts. (Illus.). 68p. (Orig.). (J). (gr. 4 up). 1990. pap. 4.50 (*0-88680-331-4*) I E Clark.
Cockley, David H. Over the Falls: A Child's Guide to Chagrin Falls. (Illus.). 24p. (Orig.). (J). (gr. 1-6). 1981. pap. 2.25 (*0-940900-00-9*) Aschley Pr.
Cocklin. The Finger Print. 32p. 1992. pap. 5.95 (*0-932616-40-2*) Brick Hse Bks.
Cockman, A. W. Secrets to Successful Deer Hunting, Vol. 1. (Illus.). 90p. 1991. pap. text 10.95 (*0-9661427-0-5*) A W Cockman.
Cockman, F. G. British Railways' Steam Locomotives. (Illus.). 80p. 1999. pap. 12.50 (*0-7478-0372-2*, Pub. by Shire Pubns) Parkwest Pubns.
— Discovering Lost Railways. 1989. pap. 25.00 (*0-7478-0165-7*, Pub. by Shire Pubns) St Mut.
— Discovering Preserved Railways. 1989. pap. 25.00 (*0-7478-0073-1*, Pub. by Shire Pubns) St Mut.
— Discovering Preserved Railways. 112p. 1995. pap. 35.00 (*0-7478-0264-5*, Pub. by Shire Pubns) St Mut.
***Cockman, F. G.** Discovering Preserved Railways. (Handbook Ser.: No. 253). (Illus.). 140p. 1999. pap. 10.50 (*0-7478-0347-1*, Pub. by Shire Pubns) Parkwest Pubns.
Cockman, F. G. Railway Architecture. 1989. pap. 25.00 (*0-85263-917-1*, Pub. by Shire Pubns) St Mut.
Cockman Fowler, Mary, ed. see Cockman Kitchel, Margaret.
***Cockman Kitchel, Margaret.** The Callie King Cockman Family Cookbook: A Collection of Cockman & King Family Recipes. Kitchel Moore, Elizabeth & Cockman Fowler, Mary, eds. 132p. 1999. pap. 15.00 (*1-882194-50-0*) TN Valley Pub.
Cockman, Nelda. Is Bible Reliable? Leader's Guide. Chao, Loran Y., tr. (Basic Doctrine Ser.). (CHI.). 1986. pap. write for info. (*0-941598-34-9*) Living Spring Pubns.
Cockman, Peter, et al. Client-Centered Consulting: A Practical Guide for Internal Advisers & Trainers. LC 92-11970. (Training Ser.). 1992. write for info. (*0-07-707685-0*) McGraw.
— Client-Centered Consulting: Getting Your Expertise Used When You're Not in Charge. 203p. 1996. 29.95 (*0-07-707565-X*) McGraw.
Cockram, Gail-Maryse. Interpretation of Statutes. 3rd ed. 197p. 1987. pap. write for info. (*0-7021-1834-6*, Pub. by Juta & Co) Gaunt.
Cockram, Mary, et al. Garden in the City: Guide for Urban Gardening. (Four-H Ser.). (Illus.). 44p. (J). (gr. 7-11). 1991. pap. 4.25 (*1-57753-187-6*, 141L-7-8) Com Coop Ext.
Cockran, Deborah, ed. see Barr, Donald W.
Cockrell, Alan. Tail of the Storm. LC 94-26404. (Illus.). 248p. 1995. pap. 24.95 (*0-8173-0772-9*) U of Ala Pr.
***Cockrell, Amanda.** Children of the Horse. (Horse Catchers Trilogy Ser.: Vol. 2). 288p. 2000. mass mkt. 5.99 (*0-380-79550-7*, Avon Bks) Morrow Avon.
Cockrell, Amanda. The Deer Dancers Bk. 3: The Long Walk. (Deer Dancers Ser.: No. 3). (Orig.). 1996. mass mkt. 5.99 (*0-380-77650-2*, Avon Bks) Morrow Avon.
— The Deer Dancers Bk. One: Daughter of the Sky. 352p. (Orig.). 1995. mass mkt. 4.99 (*0-380-77648-0*, Avon Bks) Morrow Avon.
— When the Horses Came Bk. 1. LC 98-93784. (Horse Catchers Trilogy Ser.: Vol. 1). 304p. 1999. mass mkt. 5.99 (*0-380-79549-3*, Avon Bks) Morrow Avon.
— Wind Caller's Children. (Deer Dancers Ser.: No. 2). 1996. mass mkt. 5.99 (*0-380-77649-9*, Avon Bks) Morrow Avon.
Cockrell, Cathy. A Simple Fact. LC 87-8677. 1987. 15.00 (*0-914610-45-7*); pap. 8.00 (*0-914610-48-1*) Hanging Loose.
— Undershirts & Other Stories. 1982. pap. 6.00 (*0-914610-30-9*) Hanging Loose.
Cockrell, Dale. Demons of Disorder: Early Blackface Minstrels & Their World. (Studies in American Theatre & Drama: Vol. 8). (Illus.). 256p. (C). 1997. text 59.95 (*0-521-56074-8*); pap. text 18.95 (*0-521-56828-5*) Cambridge U Pr.
— Excelsior: Journals of the Hutchinson Family Singers, 1842-1846. LC 85-28398. (Sociology of Music Ser.: No. 5). (Illus.). 450p. 1989. lib. bdg. 68.00 (*0-918728-65-7*) Pendragon NY.
Cockrell, Dale, ed. Pasticcio & Temperance Plays in America: Il Pesceballo, (1862) & Ten Nights in a Bar-Room (1890) LC 94-24997. (Nineteenth-Century American Musical Theater Ser.: No. 8). (Illus.). 216p. 1994. text 88.00 (*0-8153-1380-2*) Garland.
Cockrell, Marcia W., jt. ed. see Roberts, Anne F.
Cockrell, Marcille, jt. auth. see Vestavia Elementary School Fourth Grade Class.
Cockrell, Margaret C. The Wall Came Tumbling Down. 55p. (Orig.). 1994. pap. write for info. (*0-9642017-0-4*) Armeria Pr.
Cockrell, Marian. Shadow Castle. (Illus.). 144p. 1992. reprint ed. lib. bdg. 21.95 (*0-89968-315-0*, Lghtyr Pr) Buccaneer Bks.
Cockrell, Monroe F., intro. The Lost Account of the Battle of Corinth & the Court Martial of General Van Dorn. (Illus.). 88p. 1992. reprint ed. 25.00 (*0-916107-32-9*) Broadfoot.
Cockrell, Monroe F., ed. see Poague, William T.
Cockrell, R., ed. Fadeev: The Rout (Razgrom) (Russian Texts Ser.). (RUS.). 1995. pap. 20.95 (*1-85399-418-9*, Pub. by Brist Class Pr) Focus Pub-R Pullins.
***Cockrell, Roger.** Bolshevik Ideology & Literature, 1917-1927. LC 00-40201. (Studies in Slavic Languages & Literature). 2000. write for info. (*0-7734-7709-8*) E Mellen.
Cockrell, Roger. The Exeter English - Russian Dictionary of Cultural Terms. (ENG & RUS.). 200p. 1998. 25.00 (*0-85989-504-1*, Pub. by Univ Exeter Pr) Northwestern U Pr.
Cockrell, Roger, ed. see Odoevskii, V.
Cockrell, Thomas D. & Ballard, Michael B., eds. Mississippi Rebel in the Army of Northern Virginia: The Civil War Memoirs of Private David Holt. LC 95-30226. (Illus.). 384p. (C). 1996. 34.95 (*0-8071-1981-4*) La State U Pr.
Cockren, A. Theoretical Alchemy. 1987. pap. 5.95 (*0-916411-67-2*) Holmes Pub.
Cockrill, Pauline. The Little Book of Bear Care. LC 92-53230. (Little Bear Library). (Illus.). 48p. 1992. 8.95 (*1-56458-081-4*) DK Pub Inc.
— The Little Book of Celebrity Bears. LC 92-53229. (Little Bear Library). (Illus.). 48p. 1992. 8.95 (*1-56458-082-2*) DK Pub Inc.
— Teddy Bears & Soft Toys. (Album Ser.: No. 225). (Illus.). 32p. 1989. pap. 5.25 (*0-85263-968-6*, Pub. by Shire Pubns) Parkwest Pubns.
— The Ultimate Teddy Bear Book. LC 91-60148. (Illus.). 128p. 1991. 19.95 (*1-879431-06-8*) DK Pub Inc.
— Ultimate Teddy Bear Sticker Album. 1992. pap. 6.95 (*1-56458-193-4*) DK Pub Inc.
Cockrill, W. Ross, ed. The Camelid - The All-Purpose Animal Vol. 1: Proceedings of the Khartoum Workshop on Camels, December 1979. 544p. 1984. write for info. (*91-7106-228-9*, Pub. by Nordic Africa) Transaction Pubs.
— The Carmelid - An All-Purpose Animal Vol. 2: A Bibliography. 228p. 1985. write for info. (*91-7106-246-7*, Pub. by Nordic Africa) Transaction Pubs.
Cockroft, A. N., ed. Nicholl's Seamanship & Nautical Knowledge. 27th ed. 383p. 1997. text 75.00 (*0-85174-654-3*) Sheridan.
Cockroft, James. The Hispanic Struggle for Social Justice. (Hispanic Experience in the Americas Ser.). (Illus.). 176p. (YA). (gr. 9-12). 1994. lib. bdg. 24.00 (*0-531-11185-7*) Watts.
— Mexico: Class Formation, Capital Accumulation, & the State. rev. ed. LC 81-84740. 384p. 1990. reprint ed. pap. 19.00 (*0-85345-561-9*) Monthly Rev.
Cockrum, E. Lendell. Mammals of the Southwest. LC 81-21834. (Illus.). 176p. reprint ed. pap. 54.60 (*0-7837-5044-7*, 204472200004) Bks Demand.
— Rabies, Lyme Disease, Hanta Virus: And Other Animal-Borne Human Diseases in the U. S. & Canada. LC 98-151852. (Illus.). 176p. 1997. pap. 14.95 (*1-55561-138-9*) Fisher Bks.
— The Recent Mammals of Arizona: Their Taxonomy & Distribution. LC 60-15914. (Illus.). 282p. reprint ed. pap. 87.50 (*0-608-15584-5*, 202965000062) Bks Demand.
Cockrum, E. Lendell & Petryszyn, Yar. Mammals of California & Nevada. (Illus.). 178p. 1994. pap. 9.95 (*0-918080-34-7*) Treas Chest Bks.
— Mammals of the Southwestern United States & Northwestern Mexico. rev. ed. (Illus.). 187p. 1993. reprint ed. pap. 9.95 (*0-918080-66-5*, 20988) Treas Chest Bks.
Cockrum, E. Lendell, jt. auth. see Hall, E. Raymond.
Cockrum, W. M. Pioneer History of Indiana: Including Stories, Incidents & Customs of the Early Settlers. (Illus.). 638p. 1997. reprint ed. lib. bdg. 65.00 (*0-8328-6642-3*) Higginson Bk Co.
Cockrum, William M. History of the Underground Railroad As It Was Conducted by the Anti Slavery League. LC 73-97361. (Illus.). 1969. reprint ed. lib. bdg. 69.50 (*0-8371-2406-9*, CUR&) Greenwood.
Cockrun, E. Lendell, et al. The Vertebrates of Arizona: With Major Section on Arizona Habitats. Lowe, Charles H., ed. LC 63-11981. 282p. reprint ed. pap. 87.50 (*0-8357-7788-X*, 203614900002) Bks Demand.
Cocks, A. C., ed. Mechanics of Creep Brittle Materials: Proceedings of the European Mechanics Colloquium 239 Held at Leicester University, UK, 15-17 Aug., 1988, Vol. 1. 312p. 1989. 72.00 (*1-85166-354-1*) Elsevier.
Cocks, A. C., jt. auth. see Fleck, N. A.
Cocks, C., jt. auth. see Lemay, Marc-Henry.
Cocks, Charles, tr. see Michelet, Jules.
Cocks, David & Laframboise, Larry. Compensation Planning: The Key to Profitability. Thompson, Michelle, ed. LC 95-40253. 112p. (Orig.). (C). 1995. pap. text 22.95 (*0-913652-84-9*) Realtors Natl.
***Cocks, Doug.** Future Makers, Future Takers: Life in Australia 2050. 384p. 1999. pap. 39.95 (*0-86840-473-X*, Pub. by New South Wales Univ Pr) Intl Spec Bk.
Cocks, Doug. People Policy: Australia's Population Choices. 272p. 1996. pap. 29.95 (*0-614-17757-X*, Pub. by New South Wales Univ Pr) Intl Spec Bk.
— People Policy: Australia's Population Choices. 347p. 1997. pap. 29.95 (*0-86840-247-8*, Pub. by New South Wales Univ Pr) Intl Spec Bk.
— Use with Care: Managing Australia's Natural Resources in the Twenty-First Century. (Illus.). pap. 32.95 (*0-86840-308-3*, Pub. by New South Wales Univ Pr) Intl Spec Bk.
Cocks, Elijah E. & Cocks, Josiah. Who's Who on the Moon: A Biographical Dictionary of Lunar Nomenclature. (Illus.). 599p. (C). 1995. lib. bdg. 45.00 (*0-936389-27-3*) Tudor Pubs.
Cocks, F. H., ed. see American Society for Testing & Materials Staff.
Cocks, G. W. & Cox, J., Jr. Cox: History & Genealogy of the Cock-Cocks-Cox Family, Descended from James & Sarah Cock of Killingworth upon Matinecock, in Oysterbay, Long Island, New York. (Illus.). 345p. 1993. reprint ed. pap. 51.50 (*0-8328-3289-8*); reprint ed. lib. bdg. 61.50 (*0-8328-3288-X*) Higginson Bk Co.
Cocks, G. W. & Cox, J. Cox Family in America, Including the Cock, Cocks, Cox Genealogy of Long Island. 357p. 1989. reprint ed. pap. 56.50 (*0-8328-0433-9*); reprint ed. lib. bdg. 66.50 (*0-8328-0432-0*) Higginson Bk Co.
Cocks, Geoffrey. Psychotherapy in the Third Reich. 2nd expanded rev. ed. LC 96-34060. 283p. (Orig.). 1996. pap. text 29.95 (*1-56000-904-7*) Transaction Pubs.
— Treating Mind & Body: Essays in the History of Science, Professions, & Society under Extreme Conditions. LC 97-20184. 283p. 1997. text 34.95 (*1-56000-310-3*) Transaction Pubs.
Cocks, Geoffrey, ed. The Curve of Life: The Correspondence of Heinz Kohut, 1923-1981. LC 93-40922. 460p. 1994. 39.95 (*0-226-11170-9*) U Ch Pr.
Cocks, Geoffrey & Jarausch, Konrad H., eds. German Professions, Eighteen Hundred to Nineteen Fifty. 352p. 1990. text 75.00 (*0-19-505596-9*) OUP.
Cocks, Geoffrey, jt. ed. see Berg, Manfred.
Cocks, George W. & Cox, John, Jr. Cox. History & Genealogy of the Cock-Cocks-Cox Family, Descended from James & Sarah Cock of Killingworth-upon-Matinecock in the Township of Oysterbay, Long Island. (Illus.). 415p. 1997. reprint ed. pap. 62.50 (*0-8328-8110-4*); reprint ed. lib. bdg. 72.50 (*0-8328-8109-0*) Higginson Bk Co.
Cocks, Jay, jt. auth. see Scorsese, Martin.
Cocks, Joan E. The Oppositional Imagination: Feminism, Critique & Political Theory. 288p. 1989. 42.50 (*0-415-01512-X*); pap. 13.95 (*0-415-03206-7*) Routledge.
Cocks, Josiah, jt. auth. see Cocks, Elijah E.
Cocks, L. R., et al. A Revised Correlation of Silurian Rocks in the British Isles. (Geological Society Special Reports: No. 21). 32p. (C). 1991. pap. 24.00 (*0-903317-75-3*, 268, Pub. by Geol Soc Pub Hse) AAPG.
Cocks, L. R., jt. auth. see Zhan, Ren-Bin.
Cocks, Paul, et al. The Dynamics of Soviet Politics. (Russian Research Center Studies: Vol. No. 76). 351p. 1976. 43.50 (*0-674-21881-7*) HUP.
Cocks, Richard. The Parliamentary Diary of Sir Richard Cocks 1698-1702. Hayton, D. W., ed. LC 95-49947. (Illus.). 434p. (C). 1996. text 125.00 (*0-19-822370-6*, Clarendon Pr) OUP.
***Cocks, Robert, et al.** Imaging in Trauma: How to Plan Investigations for the Injured Patient. 272p. 2000. text 75.00 (*0-19-262509-8*) OUP.
Cocks, S. W. Tales & Legends of Ancient Burma. LC 78-67697. (Folktale Ser.). reprint ed. 34.50 (*0-404-16068-9*) AMS Pr.
Cockshott. Ps-algol Implementations. 1990. pap. text 36.00 (*0-13-741190-1*, Prentice Hall) P-H.
Cockshott, Peter & Middlemiss, Howard. Clinical Radiology in the Tropics. LC 79-40190. 244p. reprint ed. pap. 75.70 (*0-8357-3379-3*, 203962500013) Bks Demand.
Cockshott, W. P., et al. Manual of Radiographic Interpretation for General Practitioners: WHO Basic Radiological System. (CHI, FRE & SPA., Illus.). 216p. 1985. pap. text 34.00 (*92-4-154177-6*, 1150231) World Health.
Cockshott, W. Paul & Cottrell, Allin. Towards a New Socialism. 234p. 1993. 72.50 (*0-85124-544-7*, Pub. by Spokesman); pap. 37.50 (*0-85124-545-5*, Pub. by Spokesman) Coronet Bks.
Cockshull, K. E. & Horticulture Research International Staff (Great B. Genetic & Environmental Manipulation of Horticultural Crops. LC 98-25881. 256p. 1998. text 85.00 (*0-85199-281-1*) OUP.
Cockshut, A. O. J. Religious Controversies of the Nineteenth Century. LC 66-18225. 271p. 1966. reprint ed. pap. 84.10 (*0-8357-3821-3*, 205703100003) Bks Demand.
Cockshut, A. O. J. & Constantine, Stephen, eds. Edward Gibbon: Memoirs of My Life & Writings. LC 93-107717. 492p. 1998. 76.00 (*1-85331-019-0*, Pub. by Edinburgh U Pr); pap. 25.00 (*1-85331-027-1*, Pub. by Edinburgh U Pr) Col U Pr.
Cocksworth, Christopher J. Evangelical Eucharistic Thought in the Church of England. 297p. (C). 1993. text 75.00 (*0-521-40441-X*) Cambridge U Pr.
Cockton, Gilbert, et al, eds. People & Computers IX: Proceedings of the HCI '94 Conference. (British Computer Society Conference Ser.). (Illus.). 440p. (C). 1995. pap. text 69.95 (*0-521-48557-6*) Cambridge U Pr.
Cockton, Peter. House of Commons Parliamentary Papers, 1801-1900: Guide to the Chadwyck-Healey Microfiche Edition. LC 99-483680. 221p. (C). 1991. lib. bdg. write for info. (*0-85964-100-7*) Chadwyck-Healey.
Cockton, Peter, compiled by. Subject Catalogue of the House of Commons Parliamentary Papers, 1801-1900, 5 vols. 4631p. 1988. lib. bdg. 2089.00 (*0-85964-133-3*) Chadwyck-Healey.
Cockwell, Lyndsey. Star Trek Interviews. 82p. 1998. pap. 12.95 (*1-901674-63-0*) Arrowhead.
Cockwill, P. Introduction to Fly Tying. 1996. 12.98 (*0-7858-0701-2*) Bk Sales Inc.
Coclanis. Confronting Southern Poverty. LC 95-80791. 208p. 1996. pap. text 15.95 (*0-312-11497-4*) St Martin.
Coclanis, Peter A. The Shadow of a Dream: Economic Life & Death in the South Carolina Low Country, 1670-1920. 384p. 1991. pap. text 22.00 (*0-19-507267-7*) OUP.
Coclanis, Peter A. & Bruchey, Stuart Weems, eds. Ideas, Ideologies, & Social Movements: The United States Experience since 1800. LC 99-6131. 256p. 1999. 29.95 (*1-57003-313-7*) U of SC Pr.
Coco, Alfred J. Finding the Law: A Workbook on Legal Research for Laypersons. xi, 272p. 1986. reprint ed. lib. bdg. 40.00 (*0-89941-472-9*, 304280) W S Hein.
Coco, Arlene. Cajun Cooking... Making It Easy. LC 98-34441. 1998. pap. 18.95 (*1-55622-649-7*, Rep of TX Pr) Wordware Pub.
***Coco De Young, C.** A Letter to Mrs. Roosevelt. 112p. (J). (gr. 3-7). 2000. pap. 4.50 (*0-440-41529-2*, Yearling) BDD Bks Young Read.
Coco, Dorothy W. & Wilson, Dede. Fourth Child Second Daughter. LC 98-66905. (Illus.). 212p. 1998. 25.00 (*0-9664811-0-0*) Pleiades LY Pr.
Coco, Eugene B. The Fiddler's Son. (Illus.). 32p. (J). 1991. pap. 5.95 (*0-88138-111-X*, Green Tiger S&S) S&S Childrens.
Coco, Gregory A. A Concise Guide to the Artillery at Gettysburg. LC 97-60260. (Illus.). 96p. 1998. pap. 10.00 (*1-57747-012-5*) Thomas Publications.
— Killed in Action. (Illus.). 128p. (C). 1992. pap. text 6.95 (*0-939631-47-4*) Thomas Publications.
— On the Bloodstained Field: 130 Fascinating Human Interest Stories of the Battle of Gettysburg. (Illus.). 56p. (C). 1989. reprint ed. pap. text 4.95 (*0-939631-12-1*) Thomas Publications.
— On the Bloodstained Field II: 132 More Human Interest Stories of the Battle of Gettysburg. LC 88-90643. (Illus.). 128p. (C). 1989. pap. text 5.95 (*0-939631-13-X*) Thomas Publications.
***Coco, Gregory A.** Rebel Humor. LC 99-70897. 128p. 2001. pap. 10.00 (*1-57747-050-8*) Thomas Publications.
Coco, Gregory A. A Strange & Blighted Land: Gettysburg: The Aftermath of a Battle. (Illus.). 448p. 1998. pap. 20.00 (*1-57747-041-9*) Thomas Publications.
— A Vast Sea of Misery: A History & Guide to the Union & Confederate Field Hospitals at Gettysburg, July 1-November 20, 1863. (Illus.). 224p. (C). 1988. pap. text 21.95 (*0-939631-88-1*) Thomas Publications.
— War Stories: A Collection of One Hundred Fifty Little Known Human Interest Stories of the Campaign & Battle of Gettysburg. (Illus.). 72p. (C). 1992. pap. text 6.95 (*0-939631-55-5*) Thomas Publications.
— Wasted Valor: The Confederate Dead at Gettysburg. (Illus.). 192p. (C). 1995. reprint ed. pap. text 11.95 (*0-939631-83-0*) Thomas Publications.
Coco, Gregory A., ed. From Ball's Bluff to Gettysburg...& Beyond: The Civil War Letters of Private Roland E. Bowen, 15th Massachusetts Infantry 1861-1864. LC 93-6064. (Illus.). 268p. (C). 1994. text 21.95 (*0-939631-72-5*) Thomas Publications.
Cocoj. The Wishing Well. (J). 1998. pap. 13.00 (*0-671-88174-4*) Litle Simon.
Cocoran, John, ed. see Han, Bong Soo.
Cocoran, John, ed. see Marchini, Ronald L. & Fong, Leo.
Cocoran, John, ed. see Norris, Chuck.
Cocores, J. A., ed. The Clinical Management of Nicotine Dependence. (Illus.). xv, 336p. 1991. 144.00 (*0-387-97464-4*) Spr-Verlag.
Cocoris, G. Michael. Seventy Years on Hope Street: A History of the Church of the Open Door 1915-1985. (Illus.). 151p. 1985. 195.95 (*0-935729-30-5*); text 25.00 (*0-935729-09-7*) Church Open Door.
Cocowitch, Victor A. & Fickenscher, Kevin M. The Turnaround Imperative: A Leader's Guide for Survival in a Turbulent Health Care Environment. LC 95-79896. 117p. (Orig.). (C). 1996. pap. text 44.00 (*0-924674-37-7*) Am Coll Phys Execs.
Cocozeella, Peter, ed. see Moner, Fray F.
Cocozzelli, Carmelo L. Social Workers' Theoretical Orientations. 206p. (Orig.). (C). 1987. pap. text 25.50 (*0-8191-5695-7*) U Pr of Amer.
Cocozzoli, Gary, jt. auth. see Keresztesi, Michael.
Cocquyt, C., et al. A Check-List of the Algal Flora of the East African Great Lakes, Vol. 8. 55p. 1993. 20.00 (*90-72619-15-3*, Pub. by Natl Botanic Grdn Belgium) Balogh.
Cocquyt, Christine. Diatoms from the Northern Basin of Lake Tanganyika. (Bibliotheca Diatomologica Ser.: Band 39). (Illus.). 276p. 1998. 110.00 (*3-443-57030-5*, Pub. by Gebruder Borntraeger) Balogh.
Cocquyt, Kathryn. Little Freddie at the Kentucky Derby. (Illus.). 128p. (J). (gr. 4-7). 1995. pap. 9.95 (*1-56554-159-6*) Pelican.
— Little Freddie's Legacy. LC 93-5558. (Illus.). 152p. (J). (gr. 3-7). 1994. 13.95 (*1-56554-000-X*) Pelican.
— A Pony for Luke. LC 97-29749. (Illus.). (J). Date not set. 14.95 (*1-56554-277-0*) Pelican.
Cocteau, Jean. L' Aigle a Deux Tetes. (FRE.). 1973. pap. 10.95 (*0-7859-1732-2*, 2070363287) Fr & Eur.
— L' Aigle a Deux Tetes. (Folio Ser.: No. 328). (FRE.). 1973. 6.95 (*2-07-036328-7*) Schoenhof.
— Antigone & les Maries de la Tour Eiffel. (Folio Ser.: No. 908). 6.95 (*2-07-036908-0*) Schoenhof.
— Antigone Suivi De les Maries De la Tour Eiffel. (FRE.). 1977. pap. 10.95 (*0-7859-1841-8*, 2070369080) Fr & Eur.

C

Cocteau, Jean. The Art of Cinema. Buss, Robin, tr. from FRE. (Illus.). 240p. 1992. 35.00 (*0-7145-2947-8*) M Boyars Pubs.

Cocteau, Jean. The Art of Cinema. Buss, Robin, tr. from FRE. (Illus.). 240p. 1993. pap. 17.95 (*0-7145-2974-5*) M Boyars Pubs.

— Beauty & the Beast: Diary of a Film. LC 77-130640. (Film Art Ser.). Orig. Title: Diary of a Film. (Illus.). 142p. 1972. reprint ed. pap. 6.95 (*0-486-22776-6*) Dover.

— Call to Order. LC 74-30365. (Studies in French Literature: No. 45). 1974. lib. bdg. 75.00 (*0-8383-2056-2*) M S G Haskell Hse.

— Le Cap de Bonne Esperance. (Poesie Ser.). (FRE.). 247p. 1967. pap. 11.95 (*2-07-030076-5*) Schoenhof.

— Le Cap de Bonne Esperance: Le Discours du Grand Sommeil. (FRE.). 1991. pap. 14.95 (*0-7859-2760-3*) Fr & Eur.

— La Corrida du 1er Mai. (FRE.). 214p. 1957. 17.95 (*0-8288-9120-6*) Fr & Eur.

— Diary of an Unknown. 234p. 1994. pap. 8.95 (*1-56924-983-0*) Marlowe & Co.

— La Difficulte d'Etre. (FRE.). 183p. 1964. 32.95 (*0-8288-9121-4*, F96471) Fr & Eur.

— The Difficulty of Being. Sprigge, Elizabeth, tr. from FRE. 156p. 1995. reprint ed. pap. 13.95 (*0-306-80633-9*) Da Capo.

— Le Discours d'Oxford. (FRE.). 64p. 1956. 10.95 (*0-8288-9122-2*, F96490) Fr & Eur.

— Drawings: One-Hundred & Twenty-Nine Drawings from "Dessins" Appelbaum, Stanley, tr. from FRE. LC 78-182100. (Illus.). 29p. 1972. reprint ed. pap. 8.95 (*0-486-20781-1*) Dover.

— Les Enfants Terribles. Lehmann, Rosamond, tr. from FRE. (Illus.). 120p. 1992. 275.00 (*0-9640399-0-7*) Elysium Pr.

— Les Enfants Terribles. 218p. 1952. 9.95 (*0-686-54524-9*); pap. 3.95 (*0-686-54525-7*) Fr & Eur.

— Les Enfants Terribles. (FRE.). 1958. 10.95 (*0-8288-9124-9*, F96501) Fr & Eur.

*__Cocteau, Jean.__ Les Enfants Terribles. Lehmann, Rosamond, tr. (Illus.). 144p. 1999. pap. 12.00 (*1-86046-688-5*, Pub. by Harvill Press) FS&G.

Cocteau, Jean. Les Enfants Terribles. (FRE.). (C). pap. 6.95 (*0-8442-1743-3*, VF1743-3) NTC Contemp Pub Co.

Cocteau, Jean. Les Enfants Terribles: B Level. text 8.95 (*0-88436-286-8*) EMC-Paradigm.

Cocteau, Jean. Erotica: Drawings. (Illus.). 110p. 1991. 45.00 (*0-7206-0822-8*) Dufour.

— Faire-Part: 91 Poemes Inedits. 128p. 1969. 14.95 (*0-686-54529-X*) Fr & Eur.

— Five Plays. 316p. 1961. pap. text 14.00 (*0-8090-0722-3*) Hill & Wang.

— The Grand Ecart. Galantiere, Lewis, tr. from FRE. LC 74-22403. 153p. 1977. reprint ed. 35.00 (*0-86527-257-3*) Fertig.

— The Hand of a Stranger. Brown, Alec, tr. LC 79-99626. (Essay Index Reprint Ser.). 1977. 20.95 (*0-8369-1401-5*) Ayer.

— Histopathologie Clinique de la Moelle Osseuse. (FRE.). 216p. 1975. 24.95 (*0-7859-1177-4*, 2243001004) Fr & Eur.

— The Holy Terrors. Lehmann, Rosamond, tr. from FRE. LC 56-13357. Orig. Title: Les Enfants Terribles. (Illus.). (C). 1966. pap. 10.95 (*0-8112-0021-3*, NDP212, Pub. by New Directions) Norton.

Cocteau, Jean. Human Voice. abr. ed. Ilyin, Maximilian, tr. LC 61-54. 1971. audio 14.00 (*0-694-50089-5*, SWC 1118, Caedmon) HarperAudio.

Cocteau, Jean. The Impostor. Williams, Dorothy, tr. from FRE. (Illus.). 1332p. 1993. pap. 19.95 (*0-7206-0843-0*, Pub. by P Owen Ltd) Dufour.

— Indiscretions. Sams, Jeremy, tr. from FRE.Tr. of Parents Terribles. 96p. 1996. pap. 12.95 (*1-85459-256-4*, I55, Pub. by N Hern Bks) Theatre Comm.

— The Infernal Machine & Other Plays. LC 63-18631. 1967. reprint ed. pap. 12.95 (*0-8112-0022-1*, NDP235, Pub. by New Directions) Norton.

— Jean Marais. (FRE., Illus.). 136p. 1975. pap. 14.95 (*0-8288-9118-4*, M702) Fr & Eur.

— Journal d'Un Inconnu. (FRE.). 240p. 1952. 16.95 (*0-8288-9119-2*) Fr & Eur.

— Lettre aux Americains. (FRE.). 102p. 1949. 14.95 (*0-8288-9127-3*) Fr & Eur.

— Le Livre Blanc: The White Book. Crosland, Margaret, tr. from FRE. LC 90-7205. 104p. 1989. pap. 5.95 (*0-87286-238-0*) City Lights.

— Maalesh: A Theatrical Tour in the Middle-East. Hoeck, Mary C., tr. LC 77-26022. (Illus.). 136p. 1978. reprint ed. lib. bdg. 49.50 (*0-313-20054-8*, COMT, Greenwood Pr) Greenwood.

— Machine Infernale: Theatre. (FRE.). 1962. 17.50 (*0-685-11299-3*, 854); pap. 10.95 (*0-8288-9128-1*, F96621) Fr & Eur.

— The Miscreant. 164p. 1975. 29.95 (*0-7206-5480-7*, Pub. by P Owen Ltd) Dufour.

— Opium. Crosland, Margaret, tr. LC 90-80804. 176p. 1996. pap. 19.95 (*0-7206-0800-7*, Pub. by P Owen Ltd) Dufour.

— Opium: Journal D'une Desintoxication. 1930. pap. 15.75 (*0-685-11469-4*) Fr & Eur.

— Orphee. (FRE.). 116p. 1961. 8.95 (*0-8288-9130-3*, M3314) Fr & Eur.

— Les Parents Terribles. (FRE.). 192p. 1972. pap. 10.95 (*0-8288-9125-7*, F96680) Fr & Eur.

— Les Parents Terribles. (Folio Ser.: No. 149). (FRE.). pap. 6.95 (*2-07-036149-7*) Schoenhof.

— The Passionate Penis: Erotic Drawings. 110p. 1993. 50.00 (*0-7206-0894-5*, Pub. by P Owen Ltd) Dufour.

— Past Tense: The Cocteau Diaries, Vol. 2. Howard, Richard, tr. (Illus.). 352p. 1988. 24.95 (*0-15-171291-3*) Harcourt.

— Poesie du Journalisme. (FRE.). 260p. 1973. 19.95 (*0-8288-9131-1*, M3309) Fr & Eur.

— Portraits Souvenir, 1900-1914. (FRE., Illus.). 216p. 1977. 16.95 (*0-8288-9132-X*, M96700) Fr & Eur.

— Positions et Fropositions, 2 vols. (FRE.). 270p. 1983. pap. 22.95 (*0-7859-4717-5*) Fr & Eur.

— Quarterly Review of Literature: The 1960s, Essay of Indirect Criticism, Vol. XII, No. 4. 1960. pap. 5.00 (*1-888545-29-1*) Quarterly Rev.

— Reines de la France. 168p. 1952. 18.95 (*0-686-54557-5*) Fr & Eur.

— Le Requiem. (FRE.). 180p. 1962. 45.00 (*0-8288-9123-0*, F96740) Fr & Eur.

*__Cocteau, Jean.__ Round the World in Eighty Days. Gilbert, Stuart, tr. 266p. 2000. pap. 11.95 (*1-86064-592-5*, Pub. by Radcliffe Pr) St Martin.

Cocteau, Jean. Souvenir Portraits. (Illus.). 173p. 1994. 17.95 (*1-56924-961-X*) Marlowe & Co.

— Tempest of Stars: Selected Poems. Reed, Jeremy, tr. from FRE. (Illus.). 137p. 1993. pap. 22.00 (*1-870612-12-4*, Pub. by Enitha Pr) Dufour.

— Thomas L'Imposteur: Roman. (FRE.). 1971. 10.95 (*0-8288-9133-8*, M3311) Fr & Eur.

— Thomas L'Imposteur: Roman. (Folio Ser.: No. 480). (FRE.). 1971. pap. 6.95 (*2-07-036480-1*) Schoenhof.

— Two Screenplays, Vol. 1. Date not set. 9.95 (*0-7145-0580-3*) St Martin.

— Two Screenplays: The Blood of a Poet, The Testament of Orpheus. Martin-Sperry, Carol, tr. from FRE. LC 63-30778. (Illus.). 144p. 1968. 16.95 (*0-910278-07-5*) Boulevard.

— Vocabulaire: Plain-Chant et Autre Poemes. (FRE.). 1983. pap. 14.95 (*0-7859-2787-5*) Fr & Eur.

— La Voix Humaine. pap. 18.95 (*0-685-37277-4*) Fr & Eur.

Cocteau, Jean & Radiquet, Raymond. Paul et Virginie. (FRE.). 128p. 1973. 7.95 (*0-8288-9134-6*, M3312) Fr & Eur.

Cocteau, Jean & Trinka, Jiri. Le Rossignol de l'Empereur de Chine. 9.95 (*0-686-54559-1*) Fr & Eur.

Cocteau, Jean, et al. Entretiens sur le Cinematographe: Andre Fraigneau, Georges Michel Bovay, Jean Domarchi, Jean-Louis Laugier. (FRE., Illus.). 203p. 1973. 12.95 (*0-8288-9136-2*) Fr & Eur.

— Psaumes: Traductions, 1918-1959. (FRE., Illus.). 200p. 1988. 39.95 (*0-7859-4718-3*) Fr & Eur.

— Venice. 68p. 1951. 27.50 (*0-686-54561-3*) Fr & Eur.

Cocteau, Jean, jt. auth. see Aragon, Louis.

Cocuzza, Ginnine, ed. see Lang, Franz.

Cocuzza, Ginnine & Cohen-Stratyner, Barbara N., eds. Performing Arts Resources Vol. 8: Stage Design: Papers from the 15th International Congress of SIBMAS. (Illus.). xix, 94p. (C). 1983. 25.00 (*0-932610-04-8*) Theatre Lib.

Cocuzza, Ginnine, ed. see Gordon, Mel.

Cocuzza, Ginnine, jt. intro. see Cohen-Stratyner, Barbara.

CODATA Staff, ed. Data in Modern Biology: Selected Papers from the 9th International CODATA Conference, Jerusalem, Israel, June 1984. (Illus.). 63p. 1985. pap. 11.00 (*0-08-032483-5*, Pergamon Pr) Elsevier.

— Evaluation of Thermophysical Property Measurement Methods & Standard Reference Materials. (CODATA Bulletin Ser.). (Illus.). 62p. 1986. pap. 15.00 (*0-08-032525-2*, Pub. by PPL) Elsevier.

— Nutrition: Cocata Directory of Data Sources for Science & Technology, Chapter Twelve. (CODATA Bulletin Ser.). 93p. 1985. pap. 11.00 (*0-08-032489-4*, Pub. by PPL) Elsevier.

— Scientific Program & Abstracts: International CODATA Conference, 10th, July 14-17, 1986, Ottawa, Canada. (CODATA Bulletin Ser.). 102p. 1986. pap. 15.00 (*0-08-032529-7*, Pergamon Pr) Elsevier.

— Thermodynamic Databases: Selected Papers from the First CODATA Symposium on Chemical Thermodynamic & Thermophysical Properties Databases, Paris, France, September 1985. (CODATA Bulletin Ser.). 1986. pap. 15.00 (*0-08-032487-8*, Pub. by PPL) Elsevier.

— Thermophysical Properties of Some Key Solids: Heat Capacity, Thermal Expansion, Electrical Resistivity, Thermal Conductivity & Absolute Thermopower. (CODATA Bulletin Ser.). (Illus.). 52p. 1986. pap. 15.00 (*0-08-032488-6*, Pub. by PPL) Elsevier.

Codd, Clara. Theosophy As the Masters See It. 1977. 7.50 (*0-8356-7177-1*, Quest) Theos Pub Hse.

Codd, Clara M. Ageless Wisdom of Life. 1993. 17.95 (*81-7059-112-0*) Theos Pub Hse.

— The Technique of the Spiritual Life. 2nd ed. 1985. 7.50 (*0-8356-7090-2*) Theos Pub Hse.

— Trust Yourself to Life. LC 75-4245. 116p. 1975. reprint ed. pap. 3.75 (*0-8356-0464-0*, Quest) Theos Pub Hse.

Codd, Clare, ed. see Blavatsky, Helena P.

Codd, E. M., tr. see Schmitt, Carl.

Codd, Edgar. TEC Course - Database Design: Relational, Distributed, & Object-Oriented Concepts. 1991. ring bd. write for info. (*0-201-41876-2*) Addison-Wesley.

Codd, Francis, jt. auth. see Redclift, M. R.

Codd, G. A., et al, eds. Detection Methods for Cyanobacterial Toxins. 191p. 1995. 89.95 (*0-85186-962-0*, R6961) CRC Pr.

Codd, Geoff A., et al, eds. Autotrophic Microbiology & One-Carbon Metabolism, Vol. 1. (Advances in Autotrophic Microbiology & One Carbon Metabolism Ser.). (C). 1990. text 151.50 (*0-7923-0656-2*) Kluwer Academic.

Codd, Geoffrey A., ed. Aspects of Microbial Metabolism & Ecology. (Social Publication Society General Microbiology Ser.: No. 11). 1984. text 157.00 (*0-12-178050-3*) Acad Pr.

Codd, Geoffrey A., jt. ed. see Herbert, R. A.

Codd, John. Knowledge & Control in Evaluation of Educational Organisation. 93p. (C). 1988. 65.00 (*0-7300-0590-9*, Pub. by Deakin Univ) St Mut.

Codd, John, ed. Philosophy: Commonsense & Action in Educational Administration. 117p. (C). 1984. 60.00 (*0-7300-0014-1*, Pub. by Deakin Univ) St Mut.

Codd, L. E. Flora of Southern Africa Series, Vol. 28, Pt. 4. (Illus.). 247p. 1985. 30.00 (*0-621-08268-6*, Pub. by Natl Botanical Inst) Balogh.

Codd, L. E., jt. auth. see Gunn, Mary.

Coddet, Christian, ed. Thermal Spray - Meeting the Challenges of the 21st Century: Proceedings of the 15th International Thermal Spray Conference, Nice, France, 25-29 May, 1998, 2 vols., Set. LC 98-70374. 1693p. 1998. 240.00 (*0-87170-659-8*) ASM.

Codding & Jerez. Empecemos. 224p. (C). 1997. 59.95 incl. audio (*0-7872-4374-4*) Kendall-Hunt.

— Espanol Segundo Nivel. 198p. (C). 1998. per. 28.95 (*0-7872-4682-4*) Kendall-Hunt.

Codding, George A., Jr. The International Telecommunication Union: An Experiment in International Cooperation. LC 72-4663. (International Propaganda & Communications Ser.). 523p. 1977. reprint ed. 30.95 (*0-405-04744-4*) Ayer.

Codding, George A. & Rutkowski, Anthony M. The International Telecommunication Union in a Changing World. LC 81-71049. (Illus.). 432p. 1982. reprint ed. pap. 134.00 (*0-608-00572-X*, 206145500009) Bks Demand.

Codding, Judy B., jt. auth. see Tucker, Marc.

Codding, Karen G. Survey of Early Childhood Abilities. 1987. pap., teacher ed. 15.00 (*0-931421-10-1*); student ed. 14.00 (*0-931421-23-3*); 8.00 (*0-931421-21-7*); 26.00 (*0-931421-24-1*); lp 22.00 (*0-931421-22-5*) Psychol Educ Pubns.

— TKFGRS Test of Kindergarten-First Grade Readiness Skills. 1987. pap. 15.00 (*0-931421-14-4*); 5.95 (*0-685-30467-1*); lp 19.50 (*0-931421-15-2*) Psychol Educ Pubns.

Codding, Karen G. & Gardner, Morrison F. Auditory-Perceptual Development Remedial Activities: Auditory Discrimination. 1988. pap. 9.95 (*0-931421-31-4*) Psychol Educ Pubns.

— Auditory-Perceptual Development Remedial Activities: Auditory Interpretation of Directions. 1988. pap. 9.95 (*0-931421-35-7*) Psychol Educ Pubns.

— Auditory-Perceptual Development Remedial Activities: Auditory Processing. 1988. pap. 9.95 (*0-931421-36-5*) Psychol Educ Pubns.

— Auditory-Perceptual Development Remedial Activities: Auditory Sentence Memory. 1988. pap. 9.95 (*0-931421-34-9*) Psychol Educ Pubns.

— Auditory-Perceptual Development Remedial Activities: Auditory Sequential Memory. 1988. pap. 9.95 (*0-931421-32-2*) Psychol Educ Pubns.

— Auditory-Perceptual Development Remedial Activities: Auditory Word Memory. 1988. pap. 9.95 (*0-931421-33-0*) Psychol Educ Pubns.

— Auditory-Perceptual Development Remedial Activities: Remedial Activities. 1988. pap. 9.95 (*0-931421-30-6*) Psychol Educ Pubns.

— Visual-Motor Development Remedial Activities. 1988. pap. 7.95 (*0-931421-16-0*); 8.95 (*0-931421-12-8*); 8.95 (*0-931421-17-9*); 8.95 (*0-931421-25-X*); 8.95 (*0-931421-26-8*); 8.95 (*0-931421-28-4*) Psychol Educ Pubns.

— Visual-Perceptual Upper Level Remedial Activities. 1993. pap. 9.95 (*0-931421-81-0*) Psychol Educ Pubns.

Codding, Karen G., jt. auth. see Gardner, Morrison F.

Codding, Penelope W. Structure-Based Drug Design: Experimental & Computational Approaches. LC 98-28192. (NATO ASI Ser.). vii, 289p. 1998. 129.00 (*0-7923-5201-7*) Kluwer Academic.

Coddington, Alan. Keynesian Economics: The Search for First Principles. 128p. 1984. pap. text 15.95 (*0-04-330341-2*) Routledge.

Coddington, Anne & Perryman, Mark, eds. The Moderniser's Dilemma: Radical Politics in the Age of Blair. 224p. 1998. pap. 19.50 (*0-85315-874-6*) Lawrence & Wishart.

Coddington, Annie H. Home School for Girls: New Hartford & Verona, N. Y. 1876-1895. LC 96-83112. (Illus.). x, 182p. (Orig.). 1996. pap. 7.95 (*0-9651178-0-4*) Chickadee Down.

Coddington, Dean, et al. Capitalizing Medical Groups: Positioning Physicians for the Future. 1998. 69.00 (*1-56829-086-1*) Med Group Mgmt.

Coddington, Dean C. & Bendrick, Barbara J. Integrated Health Care: Case Studies, 2 vols. 216p. (Orig.). 1994. pap. 33.00 (*1-56829-004-7*, 4066) Med Group Mgmt.

*__Coddington, Dean C., et al.__ Beyond Managed Care: How Consumers & Technology Are Changing the Future of Health Care. 272p. 2000. pap. 49.95 (*0-7879-5383-0*) Jossey-Bass.

Coddington, Dean C., et al. Capitalizing Medical Groups: Positioning Physicians for the Future. LC 97-48342. 1997. 75.00 (*0-07-012023-4*) McGraw.

— Integrated Health Care: Reorganizing the Physician, Hospital & Health Plan Relationship, 2 vols. 252p. 1994. 44.00 (*1-56829-003-9*, 4065) Med Group Mgmt.

— Making Integrated Health Care Work: Case Studies, 2 vols. (Health Ser.). (Illus.). 250p. (Orig.). (C). 1996. pap. 42.00 (*1-56829-011-X*, 4829) Med Group Mgmt.

— Making Integrated Health Care Work: The Analysis, 2 vols. (Health Ser.). 300p. (C). 1996. 51.00 (*1-56829-010-1*, 4828) Med Group Mgmt.

— Making Integrated Health Care Work & Making Integrated Health Care Work: Case Studies, 2 vols., Vol. 1 & 2. 1996. text 75.00 (*1-56829-014-4*) Med Group Mgmt.

Coddington, Earl A. Extension Theory of Formally Normal & Symmetric Subspaces. LC 73-7870. (Memoirs Ser.: No. 1/134). 80p. 1973. pap. 17.00 (*0-8218-1834-1*, MEMO/1/134) Am Math.

Coddington, Earl A. & Carlson, Robert. Linear Ordinary Differential Equations. LC 96-53262. (Miscellaneous Bks.: No. 57). (Illus.). xii, 341p. 1997. pap. text 59.50 (*0-89871-388-9*, OT0057) Soc Indus-Appl Math.

Coddington, Earl A. & Levinson, Norman. Theory of Ordinary Differential Equations. LC 84-4438. 444p. (C). 1984. reprint ed. lib. bdg. 51.00 (*0-89874-755-4*) Krieger.

Coddington, Edwin B. Easton Goes to War: April Eighteen Sixty-One. (Illus.). 16p. (Orig.). 1961. pap. text 4.00 (*1-877701-07-6*) NCH&GS.

— The Gettysburg Campaign. 1997. per. 24.00 (*0-684-84569-5*) S&S Trade.

— The Gettysburg Campaign: A Study in Command. (Illus.). 865p. 1984. pap. 23.95 (*0-684-18152-5*, Scribners Ref) Mac Lib Ref.

— The Role of the One Hundred & Fifty-Third Regiment, Pennsylvania Volunteers, Infantry, in the Civil War, 1862-1863. (Illus.). 37p. (Orig.). 1949. pap. text 4.00 (*1-877701-08-4*) NCH&GS.

Coddington, Edwin F. & Marshall, Oscar J. Least Squares in Engineering. LC QA0275.C64. 67p. reprint ed. pap. 30.00 (*0-608-10059-5*, 201416800096) Bks Demand.

Coddington, Herbert G. Coddington Records: Descendants of Isaac, Reuben & Uzziah Coddington of Woodbridge, NJ. (Illus.). 42p. 1997. reprint ed. pap. 9.00 (*0-8328-7996-7*); reprint ed. lib. bdg. 19.00 (*0-8328-7995-9*) Higginson Bk Co.

— Coddington Records, Descendants of William & Benjamin Coddington of Maryland, with Notes on the English & American Lines of the Coddington Family. 45p. 1997. reprint ed. pap. 9.50 (*0-8328-7998-3*) Higginson Bk Co.

— Coddington Records, Descendants of William & Benjamin Coddington of Maryland, with Notes on the English & American Lines of the Coddington Family, No. 2. 45p. 1997. reprint ed. lib. bdg. 19.50 (*0-8328-7997-5*) Higginson Bk Co.

Coddington, Jane, jt. auth. see Gonazlik, Joan.

Coddington, Mary. Seekers of the Healing Energy: Reich Cayce the Kahunas & Other Masters of the Vital Force. LC 90-24314. 191p. 1991. pap. 9.95 (*0-89281-313-X*) Inner Tradit.

Coddington, R. Dean & Wallack, Mollie M., eds. Child Psychiatry: A Primer for Those Who Work with Children. abr. ed. (Illus.). 266p. 1990. pap., teacher ed. 37.50 (*0-87527-361-0*) Green.

Coddington, R. Dean, jt. auth. see Noshpitz, Joseph D.

Coddington, Robert H. Earthbound. 1996. pap. 5.99 (*0-7860-0306-5*) Kensgtn Pub Corp.

— Earthbound. 1997. pap. 15.00 (*1-57566-170-5*) Kensgtn Pub Corp.

— Earthbound. LC 97-210047. 224p. 1997. pap. 12.00 (*1-57566-171-3*, Knsington) Kensgtn Pub Corp.

*__Coddington, Robert H.__ Earthbound: Conversations with the Ghosts. 1999. 5.99 (*0-7860-1018-5*, Pinncle Kensgtn) Kensgtn Pub Corp.

Code. Aphasia Therapy. 2nd ed. 244p. 1991. pap. 45.00 (*1-879105-14-4*, A012) Thomson Learn.

Code & Cypher School Staff. Briefing Notes Concerning Analysis of German Air-Force Low-Level Communications During World War II. 97p. 1999. pap. 26.80 (*0-89412-275-4*, C-82) Aegean Park Pr.

Code, Alan D. Aristotle. (History of Ancient & Medieval Philosophy Ser.). 224p. 1999. 65.00 (*0-8133-2464-5*); pap. 20.00 (*0-8133-2463-7*) Westview.

Code, Chris & Muller, Dave J., eds. Second International Aphasia Rehabilitation Congress: Proceedings of the Conference, Goteborg, Sweden, June 1986. (Aphasiology Special Issue Ser.: Vol. 1, No. 3, May-June 1987). 116p. 1987. pap. 25.00 (*0-85066-913-8*) Taylor & Francis.

— The Treatment of Aphasia: From Theory to Practice. 250p. (Orig.). (C). 1995. pap. text 49.95 (*1-56593-255-2*, 0430) Singular Publishing.

Code, Chris & Muller, David J. Forums in Clinical Aphasiology. (Illus.). 384p. (Orig.). 1996. pap. text 75.00 (*1-56593-139-4*, I150) Thomson Learn.

Code, Chris, jt. ed. see Ball, Martin J.

Code, Cindy, ed. see Danneberger, T. Karl.

Code, Cindy, ed. see Keesen, Larry.

Code, Grant, ed. see Murray, Joan.

Code, Joseph B. Great American Foundresses. LC 68-20291. (Essay Index Reprint Ser.). 1977. 23.95 (*0-8369-0319-6*) Ayer.

Code, Keith. The Soft Science of Roadracing Motorcycles: The Technical Procedures & Workbook for Roadracing Motorcycles. (Illus.). 166p. 1986. reprint ed. pap. 19.95 (*0-9650450-3-X*, 00455) Code Break.

— A Twist of the Wrist: The Motorcycle Roadracers Handbook. (Illus.). 144p. 1983. reprint ed. pap. 19.95 (*0-9650450-1-3*) Code Break.

— A Twist of the Wrist Vol. II: The Basics of High Performance Motorcycle Riding. (Illus.). 144p. 1993. reprint ed. pap. 19.95 (*0-9650450-2-1*, 003T2) Code Break.

Code, Keith & Gordon, David. A Gear Higher: The Bicycle Racer's Handbook of Techniques. Falcon, Su, ed. (Illus.). 130p. (Orig.). (YA). (gr. 10 up). 1997. pap. 19.95 (*0-9650450-0-5*) Code Break.

Code, Lorraine. Epistemic Responsibility. LC 86-40550. 283p. 1987. reprint ed. pap. 87.80 (*0-608-03011-2*, 206346100006) Bks Demand.

— Rhetorical Spaces: Essays on Gendered Locations. 224p. (C). 1995. pap. 19.99 (*0-415-90937-6*, B3863) Routledge.

— Rhetorical Spaces: Essays on Gendered Locations. 224p. (C). (gr. 13). 1995. 80.00 (*0-415-90936-8*, B3859) Routledge.

C

An Asterisk (*) at the beginning of an entry indicates that the title is appearing for the first time.

— What Can She Know? Feminist Theory & the Construction of Knowledge. LC 90-55755. 384p. 1991. 47.50 (*0-8014-2476-3*); pap. text 17.95 (*0-8014-9720-5*) Cornell U Pr.

Code, Lorraine, ed. Encyclopedia of Feminist Theories. LC 99-87342. 520p. 2000. text 140.00 (*0-415-13274-6*) Routledge.

Code, Lorraine, et al, eds. Feminist Perspectives: Philosophical Essays on Method & Morals. 212p. 1988. pap. 18.95 (*0-8020-6668-2*) U of Toronto Pr.

Code, Lorraine, jt. auth. see Burt, Sandra.

Code, Murray. Myths of Reason: Vagueness, Rationality, & the Lure of Logic. LC 94-41693. 260p. (C). 1995. text 60.00 (*0-391-03901-6*) Humanities.

Codee, jt. auth. see Kreyszig, Erwin.

Codel, Martin, ed. Radio & Its Future. LC 73-161135. (History of Broadcasting: Radio to Television Ser.). 1977. reprint ed. 31.95 (*0-405-03559-4*) Ayer.

***Codell, Esme Raji.** Educating Esme: Diary of a Teacher's First Year. LC 98-33333. 210p. 1999. 17.95 (*1-56512-225-9*, 72225) Algonquin Bks.

Codell, Julie F. & Sachko Macleod, Dianne, eds. Orientalism Transposed: The Impact of the Colonies on British Culture. LC 98-70163. (Illus.). 250p. 1998. text 86.95 (*1-85928-454-X*, Pub. by Ashgate Pub) Ashgate Pub Co.

Codella, Len, intro. E. F. Payne Rod Co. Corporate Record Book. 128p. 1992. pap. 17.95 (*0-9629439-9-1*) Centenn Pubns.

Codeluppi. New Dictionary of Economics & Banking. (ENG & ITA.). 1466p. 1989. 150.00 (*0-8288-4036-9*, F135525) Fr & Eur.

Codeluppi, L. Italian-English - English-Italian Dictionary of Economics & Banking. (ENG & ITA.). 1181p. 1994. 85.00 (*88-7166-152-4*) IBD Ltd.

Codeluppi, Livio, ed. Dizionario Di Economia, Banca e Borsa: English-Italian - Italian-English. 918th ed. (ENG & ITA.). 1998. 128.00 (*0-913298-90-5*) S F Vanni.

Codenoll. The Fiber Optic LAN Handbook. 1996. 17.95 (*0-614-18437-1*, B02017) Info Gatekeepers.

Codenotti, B. & Leoncini, Mauro. Parallel Complexity of Linear System Solution. 228p. 1991. text 61.00 (*981-02-0502-3*); pap. text 36.00 (*981-02-0503-1*) World Scientific Pub.

***Coder, Christopher M.** An Introduction to Grand Canyon Prehistory. Scott, Sandra, ed. (Illus.). 56p. 2000. pap. 8.95 (*0-938216-70-8*) GCA.

Coder, Kim & Wadley, Terry, eds. A Guide to the Plant Health Care Management System. 2nd ed. (Illus.). 148p. (Orig.). 1995. pap. 75.00 (*1-881956-09-1*) Int Soc Arboricult.

Coder, Leona G. The Fuzzy Wuzzy Caterpillar. (J). (ps-3). 1998. 15.95 (*1-892455-02-1*) Desk Top KS.

— Seasons & Days & Years. (Illus.). 32p. 1998. 10.00 (*1-892455-01-3*) Desk Top KS.

Coder, Maxwell S. Judas: Los Hechos de los Apostatas (Comentario Biblico Portavoz) Orig. Title: Jude: the Acts of the Apostates (Everyman's Bible Commentary. (SPA.). 136p. 1980. pap. 6.99 (*0-8254-1125-4*, Edit Portavoz) Kregel.

Coder, S. Maxwell. First Steps to Knowing God's Will. (Christian Life Application Ser.). 1995. pap. 8.99 (*1-56570-020-1*) Meridian MI.

— Jude. (Everyman's Bible Commentaries Ser.). pap. 9.99 (*0-8024-2065-6*, 498) Moody.

Codera-Martin, Jose M. Diccionario de Calculo Mercantil. 2nd ed. (SPA.). 192p. 1987. write for info. (*0-7859-4917-8*) Fr & Eur.

— Diccionario de Comercio Exterior. (SPA.). 216p. 1985. 35.00 (*0-7859-5976-9*, 8436803043) Fr & Eur.

— Diccionario de Contabilidad. 7th ed. (SPA.). 312p. 1990. 35.00 (*0-7859-5977-7*, 8436803736) Fr & Eur.

— Dictionary of Mercantile Law: Diccionario de Derecho Mercantil. 3rd ed. (ENG & SPA.). 344p. 1987. write for info. (*0-7859-4937-2*) Fr & Eur.

***Coderch de Sentmenat, Josep Antoni.** Ugalde House. 1998. pap. text 22.00 (*84-88258-18-6*) Dist Art Pubs.

Codere, Helen. Fighting with Property: A Study of Kwakiutl Potlatching & Warfare. LC 84-45519. (American Ethnological Society Monographs: No. 18). 1988. reprint ed. 30.00 (*0-404-62917-2*) AMS Pr.

***Codevilla, Angelo.** Between the Alps & a Hard Place: Switzerland in World War II. 280p. 2000. 27.50 (*0-89526-353-X*, Pub. by Regnery Pub) Natl Bk Netwk.

Codevilla, Angelo. NATO Today: Curing Self-Inflicted Sounds. (C). 1990. 35.00 (*0-907967-00-0*, Pub. by Inst Euro Def & Strat) St Mut.

Codevilla, Angelo, ed. The Cure That May Kill: Unintended Consequences of the INF Treaty. (C). 1990. 50.00 (*0-907967-93-0*, Pub. by Inst Euro Def & Strat) St Mut.

Codevilla, Angelo & Wallop, Malcolm. The Arms Control Delusion. LC 87-22562. 220p. 1987. 19.95 (*0-917616-91-X*) ICS Pr.

Codevilla, Angelo, jt. auth. see Seabury, Paul.

Codevilla, Angelo, tr. see Machiavelli, Niccolo, et al.

Codevilla, Angelo M. American Security: Back to Basics. LC 94-11095. (Essays in Public Policy Ser.: No. 51). 35p. (Orig.). 1994. pap. 5.00 (*0-8179-5562-3*) Hoover Inst Pr.

— The Character of Nations: How Politics Makes & Breaks Prosperity, Family & Civility. 352p. 1999. pap. 15.00 (*0-465-02800-4*, Pub. by Basic) HarpC.

Codex Exoniensis Staff. Exeter Book. LC 73-178532. reprint ed. 62.50 (*0-404-56598-0*) AMS Pr.

Codex Theodosianus. The Theodosian Code & Novels, & the Sirmondian Constitutions. Pharr, Clyde, tr. LC 71-91756. 643p. 1970. reprint ed. lib. bdg. 85.00 (*0-8371-2494-8*, THC, Greenwood Pr) Greenwood.

Codey, Liza. First Culprit... Lewin, Michael Z., ed. (WWL Mystery Ser.). 1994. per. 5.99 (*0-373-15275-2*, 1-15275-0) Harlequin Bks.

Codignola, Luca. The Coldest Harbour in the Land: Simon Stock & Lord Baltimore's Colony in Newfoundland, 1621-1649. 256p. 1988. 60.00 (*0-7735-0540-7*, Pub. by McG-Queens Univ Pr) CUP Services.

***Codina, Carles.** The Complete Book of Jewelry Making.Tr. of Joyeria. (Illus.). 160p. 2000. 29.95 (*1-57990-188-3*, Pub. by Lark Books) Sterling.

Codinach, Guadalupe J. The Hispanic World, 1492-1898: A Guide to Photoreproduced Manuscripts from Spain in the Collections of the United States, Guam & Puerto Rico. LC 92-23419. 1993. write for info. (*0-8444-0697-X*) Lib Congress.

Codino, Fausto. Einfuehrung in Homer. Enking, Ragna, tr. (C). 1970. reprint ed. 38.50 (*3-11-002819-0*) De Gruyter.

Codipipoy, Joseph F. Blacks - Status & Progress: Index of Modern Information. LC 90-114. 149p. 1990. 47.50 (*1-55914-148-4*); pap. 44.50 (*1-55914-149-2*) ABBE Pubs Assn.

— Blacks - Their Psychology & Behavior: Index of Modern Information. LC 90-30452. 143p. 1990. 47.50 (*1-55914-128-X*); pap. 44.50 (*1-55914-129-8*) ABBE Pubs Assn.

— Blacks & the Negroid Race: Index of Conditions & Progress. LC 90-100. 157p. 1990. 47.50 (*1-55914-192-1*); pap. 44.50 (*1-55914-193-X*) ABBE Pubs Assn.

Codkind, Melissa, jt. auth. see Magid, Renee Y.

Codling, Sylvia. Benchmarking. LC 98-5372. 156p. 1998. pap. 43.95 (*0-566-07926-7*, Pub. by Gower) Ashgate Pub Co.

— Best Practice Benchmarking. LC 96-2804. (Illus.). 178p. 1996. 39.95 (*0-88415-134-4*, 5134) Gulf Pub.

Codman, E. A. The Shoulder. (Illus.). 550p. 95.00 (*0-930405-67-6*) Norman SF.

— The Shoulder: Rupture of the Supraspinatus Tension & Other Lesions in or about the Subacronial Bursa. LC 83-25154. 495p. 1984. reprint ed. 84.50 (*0-89874-731-7*) Krieger.

Codman, Ernest A. A Study in Hospital Efficiency. Joint Commission on Accreditation of Healthcare Organizations, ed. 225p. 1996. 50.00 (*0-86688-460-2*, CQI-200) Joint Comm Hlthcare.

Codman, John T. Brook Farm: Historic & Personal Memoirs. LC 71-134371. reprint ed. 55.00 (*0-404-08419-2*) AMS Pr.

Codman, Ogden. Gravestone Inscriptions & Records of Tomb Burials in the Granary Burying Ground Boston, Massachusetts. 255p. 1998. pap. 21.00 (*0-7884-0803-8*, C515) Heritage Bk.

Codman, Ogden, et al. Hollis Street Church, Boston: Records of Admissions, Baptisms, Marriages, & Deaths, 1732-1887. LC 98-10646. 1998. 35.00 (*0-88082-075-6*) New Eng Hist.

Codman, Ogden, Jr., jt. auth. see Wharton, Edith.

Codol, J. P. & Leyens, J. P. The Cognitive Analysis of Social Behavior. 1982. lib. bdg. 141.50 (*90-247-2701-4*) Kluwer Academic.

Codor, Dick, jt. auth. see Barth, Samuel.

Codrai, Ronald. One Second in the Arab World. (Illus.). 96p. 75.00 (*1-873544-80-4*, Pub. by Motivate Pubg Ltd) Intl Bk Ctr.

Codrai, Ronald. The Seven Shaikhdoms: Life in the Trucial State Before the Federation of the United Arab Emirates. 1990. 49.95 (*0-86685-472-X*) Intl Bk Ctr.

Codrescu, Andrei. Alien Candor: Selected Poems 1970-1995. LC 96-28360. 303p. (Orig.). 1996. pap. 15.00 (*1-57423-013-1*) Black Sparrow.

— Ay Cuba! A Socio-Erotic Journey. LC 98-40545. 224p. 1999. text 25.00 (*0-312-19831-0*) St Martin.

— A Bar in Brooklyn: Novellas & Stories, 1970-1978. LC 99-22178. 250p. 1999. 25.00 (*1-57423-098-0*) Black Sparrow.

— A Bar in Brooklyn: Novellas & Stories, 1970-1978. LC 99-22178. 250p. 1999, pap. 15.00 (*1-57423-097-2*) Black Sparrow.

— Comrade Past & Mister Present: New poems & a journal. LC 86-2681. 112p. (Orig.). 1986. pap. 10.95 (*0-918273-21-8*) Coffee Hse.

***Codrescu, Andrei.** The Devil Never Sleeps: And Other Essays. LC 99-55765. (Illus.). 256p. 2000. text 27.95 (*0-312-20294-6*) St Martin.

Codrescu, Andrei. The Dog with the Chip in His Neck: Essays from NPR & Elsewhere. 1996. 22.95 (*0-614-95760-5*) St Martin.

— Hail Babylon! (Illus.). 272p. 1999. text 13.00 (*0-312-20653-4*, Picador USA) St Martin.

— Hail Babylon: In Search of the American City at the End of the Millennium. LC 97-36466. 272p. 1998. text 23.95 (*0-312-18107-8*) St Martin.

— The Hole in the Flag: A Romanian Exile's Story of Return & Revolution. 256p. 1992. pap. 11.00 (*0-380-71373-X*, Avon Bks) Morrow Avon.

— License to Carry a Gun. LC 97-76748. (Classic Contemporaries Ser.). 80p. 1997. pap. 12.95 (*0-88748-280-5*) Carnegie-Mellon.

— Messiah: A Novel. LC 98-39032. 368p. 1999. 24.50 (*0-684-80314-3*) S&S Trade.

— The Muse Is Always Half-Dressed in New Orleans & Other Essays. 208p. 1995. pap. 10.00 (*0-312-13570-X*, Picador USA) St Martin.

— Necrocorrida. (Illus.). 80p. (gr. 11 up). 1980. pap. 6.00 (*0-915572-53-2*) Panjandrum.

— Road Scholar: Coast to Coast Late in the Century. LC 92-38416. (Illus.). 224p. (J). 1993. 19.45 (*1-56282-878-9*, Pub. by Hyperion) Time Warner.

— Zombification: Stories from NPR. 1995. pap. 13.00 (*0-312-11933-X*) St Martin.

Codrescu, Andrei & Alland, Alexander. Reframing America: Alexander Alland, Otto Hagel & Hansel Mieth, John Gutmann, Lisette Model, Marion Palfi, Robert Frank. LC 95-76804. (Points of Entry Ser.). 96p. 1995. pap. 19.95 (*0-938262-27-0*) Ctr Creat Photog.

Codrescu, Andrei & Pitts, Terence, contrib. by. Reframing America: Points of Entry. (Center for Creative Photography Ser.). (Illus.). 96p. 1996. pap. 24.95 (*0-8263-1769-3*) U of NM Pr.

Codrescu, Andrei & Rosenthal, Laura, eds. American Poets Say Goodbye to the Twentieth Century. LC 96-2033. 418p. (Orig.). 1996. 35.00 (*1-56858-071-1*); pap. 18.00 (*1-56858-068-1*) FWEW.

— Thus Spake the Corpse Vol. 1: An Exquisite Corpse Reader 1988-1998 - Poetry & Essays. LC 99-32586. 424p. 1999. 30.00 (*1-57423-101-4*) Black Sparrow.

— Thus Spake the Corpse Vol. 1: An Exquisite Corpse Reader 1988-1998 - Poetry & Essays. LC 99-32586. 424p. 1999. pap. 17.95 (*1-57423-100-6*) Black Sparrow.

***Codrescu, Andrei & Rosenthal, Laura, eds.** Thus Spake the Corpse - An Exquisite Corpse Reader, 1988-1998 Vol. 2: Fictions, Travels & Translations. 450p. 2000. 30.00 (*1-57423-142-1*); pap. 17.50 (*1-57423-141-3*) Black Sparrow.

— Thus Spake the Corpse - An Exquisite Corpse Reader, 1988-1998 Vol. 2: Fictions, Travels & Translations. deluxe ed. 450p. 2000. 40.00 (*1-57423-143-X*) Black Sparrow.

Codrescu, Andrei, et al. Dog with Chip in His Neck. 304p. 1997. pap. 12.00 (*0-312-16819-5*) St Martin.

— Over America. (Wings over America Ser.). (Illus.). 128p. 1995. 35.00 (*1-887451-06-4*) Weldon Owen.

Codrescu, Andrei, jt. auth. see Pitts, Terence.

Codrington, Andrea, jt. auth. see Hall, Peter.

Codrington, H. W. Short History of Ceylon. (C). 1994. text 18.50 (*81-206-0946-8*, Pub. by Asian Educ Servs) S Asia.

Codrington, H. W., compiled by. Glossary of Native, Foreign & Anglicized Words: Commonly Used in Ceylon in Official Correspondence & Other. (C). 1996. reprint ed. 18.00 (*81-206-1202-7*, Pub. by Asian Educ Servs) S Asia.

Codrington, Humphrey W. Short History of Ceylon. LC 72-140353. (Select Bibliographies Reprint Ser.). 1977. 28.95 (*0-8369-5596-X*) Ayer.

Codrington, Robert H. The Melanesian Languages. LC 75-32811. reprint ed. 46.50 (*0-404-14115-3*) AMS Pr.

Codrington, W. S. Know Your Horse. 216p. 1990. 40.00 (*0-85131-544-5*, Pub. by J A Allen) Trafalgar.

Coduto. Geotechnical Engineering. LC 98-22191. 800p. 1998. pap. text 105.00 (*0-13-576380-0*) P-H.

Coduto, Donald P. Foundation Design. 2nd ed. 900p. (C). 2001. 90.00 (*0-13-589706-8*) P-H.

— Foundation Design: Principles & Practices. LC 93-22441. 720p. (C). 1993. 100.00 (*0-13-335381-8*) P-H.

Cody. CMA Review Manual. (Medical Assisting Ser.). 1998. teacher ed. 14.95 (*0-8273-7184-5*) Delmar.

***Cody.** Health Care Law & Ethics. (Allied Health Ser.). (C). 2000. pap. 28.00 (*0-7668-0649-9*) Delmar.

Cody. So Far Gone. LC 98-51157. 256p. 1998. pap. 13.00 (*0-312-20014-5*) St Martin.

Cody, et al. Introduction to Interpersonal Communication. 2nd ed. 1995. pap. write for info. (*0-312-13306-5*) St Martin.

Cody, jt. auth. see Canary.

Cody, A. A. Gunsong at Twilight. large type ed. (Linford Western Library). 256p. 1992. pap. 16.99 (*0-7089-7171-7*) Ulverscroft.

Cody, Aelred, et al. Oriental Orthodox-Roman Catholic Interchurch Marriages & Other Pastoral Relationships. 164p. (Orig.). 1995. pap. text 17.95 (*1-55586-097-4*) US Catholic.

Cody, Al. Return to Texas. large type ed. 1990. pap. 5.00 (*0-7451-1289-7*, Pub. by Chivers N Amer) Chivers N Amer.

Cody, Bianca. Interviewing in Action: Process & Practice. 320p. 1997. 44.00 (*0-534-35504-8*) Brooks-Cole.

Cody, Blanche & Kuttner, Stephen, eds. In Iure Veritas: Studies in Canon Law in Memory of Schafer Williams. (Illus.). 300p. 1990. 29.00 (*0-9626291-0-3*) U Cinn Law.

Cody, Bruce D., ed. Selected Papers in Illinois History, 1981. LC 85-14310. 1982. pap. 7.50 (*0-912226-14-5*) Ill St Hist Soc.

Cody, Buffalo Bill, jt. auth. see Inman, Henry.

Cody, Corine. It's OK to Learn Differently: A Program for Young Students. (Illus.). 16p. (Orig.). (J). (gr. k-3). 1993. pap. 5.95 (*1-884063-45-4*) Mar Co Prods.

Cody, Corinne. It's OK to Learn Differently: A Program for Young Students. (Illus.). 16p. 1993. 4.95 (*1-884063-88-8*) Mar Co Prods.

Cody, Denee. The Court of Love. 416p. 1996. mass mkt. 4.99 (*0-8217-5376-2*, Zebra Kensgtn) Kensgtn Pub Corp.

— The Golden Rose. 352p. 1998. pap. 4.99 (*0-8217-5908-6*) Kensgtn Pub Corp.

— Queen of the May. 416p. 1997. mass mkt. 4.99 (*0-8217-5668-0*, Zebra Kensgtn) Kensgtn Pub Corp.

Cody, F. W., ed. Neural Control of Skilled Human Movements. (Studies in Physiology: Vol. 3). (Illus.). 120p. (Orig.). (C). 1995. pap. text 37.40 (*1-85578-081-X*, Pub. by Portland Pr Ltd) Ashgate Pub Co.

Cody Fam Assoc Staff, compiled by. Cody Family in America, 1698: Descendants of Philip & Martha of Massachusetts, Biographical & Genealogical. (Illus.). 257p. 1991. reprint ed. pap. 41.00 (*0-8328-2117-9*); reprint ed. lib. bdg. 51.00 (*0-8328-2116-0*) Higginson Bk Co.

Cody, Frank & Dise, John H. Manual of Educational Risk Management. 937p. 1991. 225.00 (*0-9630262-0-8*) Educ Risk.

Cody, G. D., et al, eds. Physical Phenomena in Granular Materials, Vol. 195. (Symposium Proceedings Ser.). 679p. 1990. text 17.50 (*1-55899-084-4*) Materials Res.

***Cody, Gabrielle H.** Impossible Performances: Duras As Dramatist. LC 99-33911. (Literature & the Visual Arts Ser.: Vol. 14). 176p. (C). 2000. 44.95 (*0-8204-4485-5*) P Lang Pubng.

***Cody, H. H.** The Last Bounty. large type ed. 176p. 1999. pap. 18.99 (*0-7089-5568-1*, Linford) Ulverscroft.

Cody, H. H. Last Stop on the Trail. large type ed. (Linford Western Library Ser.). 176p. 1997. pap. 16.99 (*0-7089-5148-1*) Ulverscroft.

***Cody, H. H.** Silver Valley. large type ed. 208p. 1999. pap. 20.99 (*1-85389-950-X*, Dales) Ulverscroft.

Cody, Iron Eyes. Indian Talk: Hand Signals of the North American Indians, Vol. 1. LC 73-16246. (Illus.). 112p. (YA). 1970. pap. 7.95 (*0-911010-82-3*) Naturegraph.

Cody, J., jt. auth. see Crosby, R. W.

Cody, J. P. Delmar's Medical Assisting Exam Review: Preparation for CMA & RMA Exams. LC 97-4806. (Medical Assisting Ser.). 416p. (C). 1997. pap. 41.95 (*0-8273-7183-7*) Delmar.

Cody, James M. Return. (Illus.). 1981. pap. 5.95 (*0-916908-04-6*); lib. bdg. 25.00 (*0-916908-31-3*) Place Herons.

Cody, Jess. Gold Wagon. large type ed. (Linford Western Library). 1989. pap. 16.99 (*0-7089-6765-5*) Ulverscroft.

— Jim Steel: Die of Gold. large type ed. (Linford Western Library). 240p. 1989. pap. 16.99 (*0-7089-6712-4*, Linford) Ulverscroft.

Cody, Jim. A Book of Wonders: Dreams, Visions & Unusual Experiences. (Illus.). 1996. lib. bdg. 35.00 (*0-916908-58-5*) Place Herons.

— A Book of Wonders: Dreams, Visions & Unusual Experiences. 2nd ed. (Illus.). 1996. pap. 9.95 (*0-916908-57-7*) Place Herons.

— My Body Is a Flute. LC 92-28770. (Illus.). 80p. 1993. 35.00 (*0-916908-50-X*); pap. 9.95 (*0-916908-51-8*) Place Herons.

Cody, John. After Great Pain: The Inner Life of Emily Dickinson. LC 79-148937. 552p. reprint ed. pap. 171.20 (*0-7837-1511-0*, 204178800024) Bks Demand.

Cody, John. Atlas of Foreshortening: The Artist's Model in Deep Perspective. LC 84-3644. (Illus.). 352p. 1984. pap. 34.95 (*0-442-21595-9*, VNR) Wiley.

Cody, John. Atlas of Foreshortening: The Human Figure in Deep Perspective. 290p. 1984. pap. 44.95 (*0-471-29013-0*, VNR) Wiley.

Cody, John. Visualizing Muscles: A New Ecorche Approach to Surface Anatomy. LC 90-50112. (Illus.). xiv, 242p. 1991. pap. 25.00 (*0-7006-0426-X*) U Pr of KS.

Cody, John. Wings of Paradise: The Great Saturniid Moths. LC 95-47138. 186p. (C). 1996. 70.00 (*0-8078-2286-8*) U of NC Pr.

Cody, Liza. Bucket Nut. 224p. 1995. mass mkt. 5.50 (*0-446-40459-4*, Pub. by Warner Bks) Little.

Cody, Liza. Bucket Nut. large type ed. (Isis Large Print Ser.). 1997. 25.95 (*0-7531-5173-1*) T T Beeler.

— Dupe. 1992. mass mkt. 4.99 (*0-7704-2439-2*) Bantam.

— 2nd Culprit. Lewin, Michael Z., ed. 1995. per. 5.99 (*0-373-15280-9*, 1-15280-0) Harlequin Bks.

Cody, Liza, et al. 3rd Culprit. (Mystery Ser.). 1996. per. 5.99 (*0-373-26212-4*, Wrldwide Lib) Harlequin Bks.

***Cody, M. J. & Houck, Michael C., eds.** Wild in the City: A Guide to Portland's Natural Areas. (Illus.). 360p. 2000. pap. 18.95 (*0-87595-273-9*) Oregon Hist.

Cody, Marion R. A Guide to Colorado Rivers. 1992. pap. 11.95 (*0-9631250-0-1*) Cub Pub.

Cody, Marion R. & Walker, Doris I. On the Shoulders of a Giant. (Illus.). 180p. 1995. pap. text 9.95 (*1-57166-021-6*) Quixote Pr IA.

Cody, Martin L., ed. Habitat Selection in Birds. (Physiological Ecology Ser.). 1985. reprint ed. text 104.00 (*0-12-178080-5*) Acad Pr.

— Habitat Selection in Birds. (Physiological Ecology Ser.). 1987. reprint ed. pap. text 42.00 (*0-12-178081-3*) Acad Pr.

Cody, Martin L. & Diamond, Jared M., eds. Ecology & Evolution of Communities. LC 74-27749. (Illus.). 560p. (C). 1979. pap. 22.95 (*0-674-22446-9*) Belknap Pr.

Cody, Martin L. & Smallwood, Jeffrey A. Long-Term Studies of Vertebrate Communities. LC 96-12813. (Illus.). 597p. 1996. text 69.95 (*0-12-178075-9*) Acad Pr.

Cody, Mary L. A Personal Guide to Respite Care. (Illus.). 28p. (Orig.). 1988. pap. 3.00 (*0-685-31065-5*) Visiting Nurse Assn.

Cody, Michael J. & MacLaughlin, Margaret L., eds. The Psychology of Tactical Communication. 350p. 1989. 99.00 (*1-85359-040-1*, Pub. by Multilingual Matters); pap. 44.95 (*1-85359-039-8*, Pub. by Multilingual Matters) Taylor & Francis.

Cody, Michael J., jt. auth. see Canary, Daniel J.

Cody, Michael J., jt. ed. see Kalbfleisch, Pamela J.

Cody, Mildred M. & Keith, Mary. Food Safety for Professionals: A Reference. LC 91-29325. 1991. student ed., spiral bd. 17.00 (*0-88091-091-7*, 0181) Am Dietetic Assn.

Cody, Nancy C., jt. auth. see O'Reilly, James T.

Cody, Pat. Insurance Terminology: (For the Irreverent Underwriter) LC 89-61094. (Illus.). (Orig.). 1989. pap. 2.50 (*1-877730-00-9*) Cristal Globe.

— Kept by a Countess. (It's a Dog's Life Ser.). 368p. (Orig.). 1997. mass mkt. 5.50 (*0-505-52240-3*, Love Spell) Dorchester Pub Co.

— Why Invest in America. 50p. (Orig.). 1989. pap. write for info. (*0-318-65069-X*) Cristal Globe.

Cody, Paul. Eyes Like Mine. 252p. 1996. 20.00 (*1-880909-44-8*) Baskerville.

— So Far Gone. LC 97-33371. 240p. 1998. text 22.00 (*0-312-18180-9*) St Martin.

C

— The Stolen Child. 233p. 1995. 20.00 (1-880909-30-8) Baskerville.

Cody, Philip. God at Work. 1994. 8.95 (1-875570-25-X) Alba.

Cody, R. P. & Smith, J. K. Applied Statistics & the SAS Programming Language. 3rd ed. 424p. 1991. pap. 29.50 (0-444-01619-8) P-H.

Cody, Robin. Ricochet River. 288p. 1994. reprint ed. pap. 12.95 (0-936085-27-4) Blue Heron OR.

— Voyage of a Summer Sun: Canoeing the Columbia River. LC 96-19995. 320p. 1996. reprint ed. pap. 14.95 (1-57061-083-5) Sasquatch Bks.

Cody, Ron. Applied Statistics & the SAS Programming Language. 4th ed. LC 97-1737. 445p. (C). 1997. pap. text 46.00 (0-13-743642-4, BR55984) P-H.

— The SAS Workbook. LC 96-172012. 256p. (C). 1999. pap. 23.95 (1-55544-757-0, BR55473) SAS Publ.

— The SAS Workbook & Solutions, 2 vols. 392p. (C). 1996. pap. 40.72 (1-55544-762-7, BR55594) SAS Publ.

— The SAS Workbook Solutions. 136p. (C). 1997. pap. 19.95 (1-55544-758-9, BR55475) SAS Publ.

Cody, Ron & Pass, Ray. SAS Programming by Example. 360p. (C). 1998. pap. 32.95 (1-55544-681-7, BR55126) SAS Publ.

Cody, Sherwin. Selections from the World's Greatest Short Stories. 412p. 1977. 23.95 (0-8369-3304-4) Ayer.

Cody, Sherwin, ed. Selection from the Best English Essays, Illustrative of the History of English Prose Style. LC 68-8448. (Essay Index Reprint Ser.). 1977. 23.95 (0-8369-0320-X) Ayer.

— A Selection from the Great English Poets. LC 76-128152. (Granger Index Reprint Ser.). 1977. 35.95 (0-8369-6179-X) Ayer.

— A Selection from the Great English Poets. LC 76-128152. (Granger Index Reprint Ser.). 576p. reprint ed. lib. bdg. 20.50 (0-8290-0516-1) Irvington.

Cody, Steven. Ace: Behavoral Science. (Illus.). 192p. 1996. pap. text 30.00 incl. mac hd (0-8151-1487-7, 28955) Mosby Inc.

— Ace the Boards: Mosby's USMLE Step 1 Review for Behavioral Science. (Illus.). 192p. (C). (gr. 13). 1996. pap. text 30.00 (0-8151-1844-9, 27043) Mosby Inc.

Cody, Sue A., jt. auth. see Lowery, Roger C.

C

Cody, Thomas G. Strategy of a Megamerger: An Insider's Account of the Baxter Travenol-American Hospital Supply Combination. LC 90-8482. 328p. 1990. 65.00 (0-89930-345-5, CYS, Quorum Bks) Greenwood.

— Strategy of a Megamerger: An Insider's Account of the Baxter Travenol-American Hospital Supply Combination. LC 92-30382. 1992. pap. 23.95 (0-275-94518-9, B4518, Praeger Pubs) Greenwood.

Cody, Tod. The Cowboy's Handbook: How to Become a Hero of the Wild West. LC 95-45482. (Illus.). 36p. (J). (gr. 2-5). 1996. 12.99 (0-525-65210-8, Dutton Child) Peng Put Young Read.

— The Cowboy's Handbook: How to Become a Hero of the Wild West. (Illus.). 30p. (J). 15.99 (0-590-24896-0) Scholastic Inc.

***Cody, Tod.** The Cowboy's Handbook: How to Become a Hero of the Wild West. (Illus.). 29p. (gr. 4-7). 1999. reprint ed. text 17.00 (0-7881-6563-1) DIANE Pub.

***Cody, Tom, et al.** Security Transactions: Taxation of Your Stock & Bond Transactions for the 1999 Tax Year. 56p. 1999. pap. text 10.95 (0-8080-0438-7) CCH INC.

Cody, W. F. Buffalo Bill's Life Story. 224p. 1998. pap. 7.95 (0-486-40038-7) Dover.

Cody, W. F., jt. auth. see Inman, Henry.

Cody, W. J. & Lynn, Richardson R. Honest Government: An Ethics Guide for Public Service. LC 92-7480. 192p. 1992. 55.00 (0-275-94178-7, C4178, Praeger Pubs); pap. 15.95 (0-275-94376-3, B4376, Praeger Pubs) Greenwood.

Cody, William & Abbot, John S. Buffalo Bill - Kit Carson, 2 vols. in 1. (Real West Ser.). 336p. 1998. mass mkt. 4.99 (0-8439-4455-2, Leisure Bks) Dorchester Pub Co.

Cody, William F. Dangerous. 212p. Date not set. mass mkt. 5.99 (1-55197-074-0) Picasso Publ.

— Life & Adventures of 'Buffalo Bill' LC 74-169755. (Select Bibliographies Reprint Ser.). 1977. reprint ed. 28.95 (0-8369-5975-2) Ayer.

— Life & Adventures of Buffalo Bill: Colonel William F. Cody. (American Biography Ser.). 352p. 1991. reprint ed. lib. bdg. 79.00 (0-7812-8080-X) Rprt Serv.

***Cody, William F.** The Life of Buffalo Bill. (Illus.). 365p. 1999. reprint ed. pap. text 17.00 (0-7881-6650-6) DIANE Pub.

Cody, William F. The Life of Hon. William F. Cody. (American Biography Ser.). 365p. 1991. reprint ed. lib. bdg. 79.00 (0-7812-8081-8) Rprt Serv.

— The Life of Hon. William F. Cody, Known As Buffalo Bill, the Famous Hunter, Scout & Guide. LC 78-18732. (Illus.). xviii, 365p. 1978. pap. 11.95 (0-8032-6303-1, Bison Books) U of Nebr Pr.

— Story of the Wild West & Camp-Fire Chats: A Full & Complete History of the Renowned Pioneer Quartette, Boone, Crocket, Carson, & Buffalo Bill. LC 75-109620. (Select Bibliographies Reprint Ser.). 1977. 51.95 (0-8369-5229-4) Ayer.

Cody, William F., see Buffalo Bill, pseud.

Cody, William F., jt. auth. see Inman, Henry.

Cody, William J. Flora of the Yukon Territory. LC 96-980311. (FRE & ENG., Illus.). 600p. 1996. 99.95 (0-660-16406-X, Pub. by NRC Res Pr); pap. 62.50 (0-660-15898-1, Pub. by NRC Res Pr) Accents Pubns.

Codye, Corinn, jt. auth. see Lemaire, Jeanie.

Codye, Corinn, ed. see Lemaire, Jeanie.

Coe & Taylor. Canada. (Illus.). 48p. (J). (gr. 3-6). 1995. pap., teacher ed. 5.95 (1-55799-390-4, 542) Evan-Moor Edu Pubs.

Coe, jt. auth. see Fowler.

Coe, jt. auth. see Land.

Coe, Amanda, jt. ed. see Larson, Peter E.

***Coe, Andrew.** Cuba. 3rd ed. LC 98-51862. (Odyssey Passport Ser.). (Illus.). 314p. 1999. pap. 19.95 (962-217-610-0) Norton.

Coe, Andrew. Cuba: Pearl of the Caribbean. (Illus.). 316p. 1996. pap. 16.95 (0-8442-8950-7, Passprt Bks) NTC Contemp Pub Co.

— Latin American Guide - Cuba. 2nd ed. (Illus.). 316p. 1997. pap. text 21.95 (0-8442-4850-9, 48509, Passprt Bks) NTC Contemp Pub Co.

— Mexico: Life on the Volcano. (SPA., Illus.). 288p. 1993. pap. 15.95 (0-8442-9657-0, Passprt Bks) NTC Contemp Pub Co.

***Coe, Andrew.** Mexico City. 2nd ed. 1999. pap. 19.95 (962-217-581-3) Norton.

Coe, Andrew. Moon Handbooks: Archaeological Mexico: A Traveler's Guide to Ancient Cities & Sacred Sites. LC 99-113368. (Illus.). 420p. 1998. pap. 19.95 (1-56691-105-2, Moon Handbks) Avalon Travel.

Coe, Ben. Christian Churches at the Crossroads. LC 80-27624. 135p. (Orig.). 1981. pap. 5.95 (0-87808-178-X) William Carey Lib.

Coe, Brian & Hawarth-Booth, Mark. A Guide to Early Photographic Processes. (Illus.). 112p. (C). 1989. 125.00 (0-903696-23-1, Pub. by Hurtwood Pr Ltd) St Mut.

— A Guide to Early Photographic Processes. (Illus.). 112p. 1983. pap. 24.95 (0-905209-40-0, Pub. by V&A Ent) Antique Collect.

Coe, Bufford W. John Wesley & Marriage. LC 95-35746. 176p. 1996. 32.50 (0-934223-39-4) Lehigh Univ Pr.

Coe, Carol A. Archaeological Assessment of the Sells Vicinity, Papago Indian Reservation, Arizona. (Archaeological Ser.: No. 131). (Illus.). 147p. 1979. pap. 7.95 (1-889747-08-4) Ariz St Mus.

Coe, Charles. Picnic on the Moon: Poems by Charles Coe. LC 98-32361. 82p. 1999. pap. 12.95 (0-9654578-2-6, Pub. by Leapfrog Pr) Consort Bk Sales.

Coe, Charles H. Red Patriots: The Story of the Seminoles. A Facsimile Reproduction of the 1898 Edition with an Introduction by Charlton E. Tebeau. LC 73-5702. (Bicentennial Floridian Facsimile Ser.). 365p. reprint ed. pap. 113.20 (0-8357-6926-7, 203798500009) Bks Demand.

***Coe, Charles K.** State & Local Government Purchasing & Materials Management Handbook LC 99-186509. 1998. write for info. (1-55827-266-6) Sheshunoff.

Coe, Charles N. Shakespeare's Villains. LC 72-455. reprint ed. 14.50 (0-404-01585-9) AMS Pr.

Coe, Charles P. The Elements of Quality in Pharmaceutical Care. 350p. (Orig.). 1992. pap. write for info. (1-879907-18-6) Am Soc Hlth-Syst.

— Preparing the Pharmacy for a Joint Commission Survey. 3rd ed. LC 97-132864. 185p. 1996. pap. 40.50 (1-879907-70-4) Am Soc Hlth-Syst.

— Preparing the Pharmacy for a Joint Commission Survey. 4th rev. ed. 336p. 1998. pap. 69.00 (1-879907-86-0) Am Soc Hlth-Syst.

— Update to Joint Commission Hospital Accreditation Standards: Supplement to the Elements of Quality in Pharmaceutical Care. LC 94-218227. (Orig.). 1994. pap. text 35.00 (1-879907-45-3) Am Soc Hlth-Syst.

Coe, Christopher. I Look Divine. 128p. 1987. 12.95 (0-89919-530-X, Pub. by Ticknor & Fields) HM.

Coe, Christopher. I Look Divine. (Contemporaries Ser.). 1989. pap. 8.00 (0-394-75995-8) Vin Bks.

Coe, Christopher L., jt. auth. see Rosenblum, Leonard A.

Coe-Clough, Roth. Mosby's Biomedical Science Series: Understanding Immunology. LC 97-9892. (Illus.). 240p. (gr. 13). 1997. pap. text 23.00 (0-8151-8582-0, 28791) Mosby Inc.

Coe, David. Building Guitar Speed. 96p. 1991. pap. 11.95 (1-56222-093-4, 94399) Mel Bay.

— Weitchie: Spirit of the Redwoods. 220p. (Orig.). 1990. pap. 9.95 (0-936609-20-6) QED Ft Bragg.

Coe, David, ed. Mine Eyes Have Seen the Glory: Combat Diaries of Union Sergeant Hamlin Alexander Coe. LC 74-5896. 240p. 1975. 32.50 (0-8386-1492-2) Fairleigh Dickinson.

Coe, David B. Children of Amarid. 1998. mass mkt. 6.99 (0-8125-5254-7, Pub. by Tor Bks) St Martin.

***Coe, David B.** Eagle-Sage: The Lon Tobyn Chronicle, Bk. 3. LC 99-89861. 480p. 2000. 27.95 (0-312-86791-3, Pub. by Tor Bks) St Martin.

Coe, David B. The Outlanders. 640p. 1999. mass mkt. 6.99 (0-8125-7113-4, Pub. by Tor Bks) St Martin.

— The Outlanders: LonTobyn Chronicle. LC 98-23672. 416p. 1998. 26.95 (0-312-86447-7, Pub. by Tor Bks) St Martin.

Coe, David K. Angst & the Abyss: The Hermeneutics of Nothingness. (American Academy of Religion Academy Ser.). 234p. 1985. pap. 18.95 (0-89130-863-6) OUP.

Coe, Dorothy. Blue Bunnies in the Snow: And Other Stories. (Illus.). 58p. 1998. 10.00 (0-9661569-3-5) D Coe.

— "Never Sleep Naked" - Stories & Poems. (Illus.). 1996. pap. 10.00 (0-9661569-1-9) D Coe.

— Shadows on the Lake: A Poetry Collection. (Illus.). 68p. 1997. pap. 10.00 (0-9661569-2-7) D Coe.

Coe, Dorothy, ed. My Book: Memories & Other Stuff. (Illus.). 1994. pap. 10.00 (0-9661569-0-0) D Coe.

Coe, Edith C. Hertzler Heritage. Vandergriff, James, ed. LC 75-32001. (Illus.). 172p. 1975. 7.50 (0-686-13109-6); pap. 5.80 (0-686-13110-X) Emporia State.

Coe, Frances. Lazy Little Kitten: Includes Miniature Blanket. LC 98-44264. (Little Blanket Bks.). (Illus.). 10p. (J). 1999. bds. 3.95 (0-7641-5178-9) Barron.

***Coe, Frances.** Leap, Lamb, Leap. (Play-Along Puppet Bks.). (Illus.). 4p. (J). (ps-k). 2000. bds. 4.99 (0-448-42097-X, G & D) Peng Put Young Read.

— Playtime for Piglet. (Play-Along Puppet Bks.). (Illus.). 4p. (J). (ps-k). 2000. bds. 4.99 (0-448-42098-8, G & D) Peng Put Young Read.

Coe, Frances. Puppy Puppy, Peekaboo: Includes Miniature Blanket. LC 98-44265. (Little Blanket Bks.). (Illus.). 10p. (J). 1999. bds. 3.95 (0-7641-5179-7) Barron.

— Sleepy Little Lamb: With Soft Cloth Blanket. LC 98-31289. (Little Blanket Bks.). (Illus.). 10p. (J). 1999. bds. 3.95 (0-7641-5176-2) Barron.

***Coe, Frances.** Swim, Little Duckling. (Play-Along Puppet Bks.). (Illus.). 4p. (J). (ps-k). 2000. bds. 4.99 (0-448-42099-6, G & D) Peng Put Young Read.

— Very Hungry Mouse. (Play-Along Puppet Bks.). (Illus.). 4p. (J). (ps-k). 2000. bds. 4.99 (0-448-42096-1, G & D) Peng Put Young Read.

Coe, Frances. Who's That Bouncing? With Miniature Blanket. LC 98-44270. (Little Blanket Bks.). (Illus.). 10p. (J). 1999. bds. 3.95 (0-7641-5177-0) Barron.

Coe, Frederic L., et al, eds. Kidney Stones: Medical & Surgical Management. LC 95-416. (Illus.). 1008p. 1995. text 300.00 (0-7817-0263-1) Lppncott W & W.

Coe, Fredric L. Yearbook of Nephrology, 1991. 1991. write for info. (0-8151-5015-6) Mosby Inc.

Coe, Fredric L., ed. Nephrolithiasis. LC 80-10326. (Contemporary Issues in Nephrology Ser.: No. 5). (Illus.). 287p. reprint ed. pap. 89.00 (0-8357-6567-9, 203594100097) Bks Demand.

Coe, Fredric L. & Favus, Murray J., eds. Disorders of Bone & Mineral Metabolism. 1136p. 1991. text 215.00 (0-88167-749-3) Lppncott W & W.

Coe, George A. The Motives of Men. LC 75-3112. reprint ed. 32.50 (0-404-59108-6) AMS Pr.

— The Psychology of Religion. LC 75-3113. reprint ed. 49.50 (0-404-59109-4) AMS Pr.

— Social Theory of Religious Education. LC 78-89164. (American Education: Its Men, Institutions, & Ideas. Series 1). 1977. reprint ed. 26.95 (0-405-01402-3) Ayer.

Coe, George W. Frontier Fighter: The Autobiography of George W. Coe. (American Biography Ser.). 220p. 1991. reprint ed. lib. bdg. 69.00 (0-7812-8082-6) Rprt Serv.

Coe-Hauskins, Carole. Eddy Ant & Friends: An Unexpected Journey. 36p. (J). (gr. k-3). 1997. 17.95 (1-884187-49-8) AMICA Pub Hse.

— Eddy Ant & Friends: An Unexpected Journey. large type ed. LC 97-73468. (Illus.). 36p. (J). (gr. k-3). 1997. per. 17.95 (1-890476-00-5) Pied Piper.

Coe, Henry F. Coe. Descendants of Matthew Coe. 47p. 1997. reprint ed. pap. 9.50 (0-8328-8002-7); reprint ed. lib. bdg. 19.50 (0-8328-8001-9) Higginson Bk Co.

Coe, Jack J. International Commercial Arbitration: American Principles & Practice in a Global Context. LC 97-6429. 1997. 125.00 (1-57105-026-4) Transnatl Pubs.

Coe, Jack J., Jr., jt. auth. see Allison, Richard C.

Coe, James. Eastern Birds, a Guide Field Identification of North American Species. 1994. 19.05 (0-606-11286-3, Pub. by Turtleback) Demco.

Coe, James M. & Rogers, Donald B. Marine Debris: Sources, Impacts & Solutions. LC 96-18351. (Environmental Management Ser.). 416p. 1996. 86.95 (0-387-94759-0) Spr-Verlag.

Coe, Jeffery & Rees, Matthew. CCNA Routing & Switching Exam Cram: Exam 640-407, 1. LC 99-26452. (Exam Cram (Coriolis' Certification Insider Press) Ser.). (Illus.). 357p. 1999. pap. 29.99 (1-57610-434-6) Coriolis Grp.

***Coe, Jeffrey.** CCNA Routing & Switching Exam Cram. (Networking Ser.). (C). 1999. pap. 15.60 (0-619-01603-5) Course Tech.

***Coe, Jeffrey & Rees, Matthew.** CCNA Routing & Switching Exam Cram: Master the Fundamentals of Cisco Routers & Switches. 2nd ed. 2000. pap. text 29.99 (1-57610-628-4) Coriolis Grp.

***Coe, Jerome T.** Unlikeley Victory: How General Electric Succeeded in the Chemical Industry. LC 00-36229. 2000. write for info. (0-8169-0819-2) Am Inst Chem Eng.

***Coe, Jo Ann R. & Menon, Goutham M., eds.** Computers & Information Technology in Social Work: Education, Training & Practice. LC 99-58925. 205p. 2000. 49.95 (0-7890-0841-6); pap. 24.95 (0-7890-0952-8) Haworth Pr.

Coe, Joanna. El Autobus Magico es Devorado.Tr. of Magic School Bus Gets Eaten. (SPA.). (J). (ps-3). 1996. pap. 2.99 (0-590-73918-2) Scholastic Inc.

Coe, Joffre L. Town Creek Indian Mound: A Legacy from the Past. LC 94-17931. (Illus.). 1995. pap. 19.95 (0-8078-4490-X); text 49.95 (0-8078-2176-4) U of NC Pr.

Coe, Jonathan. The House of Sleep. 352p. 1999. pap. 13.00 (0-375-70088-9) Vin Bks.

— Jimmy Stewart: A Wonderful Life. LC 93-73979. (Illus.). 192p. 1994. 27.45 (1-55970-257-5, Pub. by Arcade Pub Inc) Time Warner.

— Jimmy Stewart: A Wonderful Life. 192p. 1995. pap. 19.45 (1-55970-325-3, Pub. by Arcade Pub Inc) Time Warner.

— The Winshaw Legacy: or What a Carve Up! 512p. 1996. pap. 15.00 (0-679-75405-9) Random.

Coe, L. E. Coe - Ward Memorial & Immigrant Ancestors. (Illus.). 136p. 1991. reprint ed. pap. 21.50 (0-8328-1751-1); reprint ed. lib. bdg. 31.50 (0-8328-1750-3) Higginson Bk Co.

Coe, Lewis. Great Days of the Heliograph. (Illus.). 70p. 1988. pap., spiral bd. 6.95 (0-9619533-0-6) L Coe.

— The Telegraph: A History of Morse's Invention & Its Predecessors in the United States. LC 92-53597. (Illus.). 192p. 1993. lib. bdg. 32.50 (0-89950-736-0) McFarland & Co.

— The Telephone & Its Several Inventors: A History. LC 95-13651. (Illus.). 240p. 1995. lib. bdg. 32.50 (0-7864-0138-9) McFarland & Co.

— Wireless Radio: A History. LC 96-25734. (Illus.). 204p. 1996. lib. bdg. 30.00 (0-7864-0259-8) McFarland & Co.

Coe, Linda & McNulty, Diane. Kids on the Go: The Houston Area Guide to Great Places to Take Kids. 2nd ed. Funcik, Christine, ed. (Illus.). 236p. (Orig.). 1997. pap. 14.95 (1-887077-06-5) Kids on the Go.

Coe, M. Human Factors for Technical Communicators. LC 95-50324. 368p. 1996. pap. 44.99 (0-471-03530-0) Wiley.

Coe, Malcolm & Beentje, Henk. A Field Guide to the Acacias of Kenya. (Illus.). 162p. 1992. 65.00 (0-19-858410-5); pap. text 35.00 (0-19-858411-3) OUP.

— Legacy. LC 92-64095. (Illus.). 373p. 1993. reprint ed. 19.95 (0-9633341-1-5) SouthLore Pr.

poet laudreate of North Carolina, says: "There are no strident pages in Marian Coe's stories, none overblown or over wrought. ..but a wonderful variety of subtitle tones, sometimes wry, sometimes dismayed, sometimes foreboding--but always openhearted. The book is comfort to have & to keep. "Says social studies professor, Dr. Allen Speer: "A feast of stories to feed the soul." *Publisher Paid Annotation.*

Coe, Mary Ann & O'Neill, Adrienne. Integrating Technology into the Curriculum. 332p. (C). 1995. text 52.00 (*0-536-59155-5*) Pearson Custom.

Coe, Mary Ann, jt. auth. see O'Neill, Adrienne.

Coe, Mary E., ed. see Aruna, Augustine S.

Coe, Michael, et al. Atlas of Ancient America. (Cultural Atlas Ser.). (Illus.). 240p. 1986. 45.00 (*0-8160-1199-0*) Facts on File.

Coe, Michael D. Breaking the Maya Code. LC 91-65312. (Illus.). 304p. 1993. pap. 14.95 (*0-500-27721-4*, Pub. by Thames Hudson) Norton.

— Breaking the Maya Code. rev. ed. LC 99-70864. (Illus.). 304p. 1999. pap. 18.95 (*0-500-28133-5*, Pub. by Thames Hudson) Norton.

— Classic Maya Pottery at Dumbarton Oaks. LC 75-1727. (Illus.). 1975. 25.00 (*0-88402-063-0*) Dumbarton Oaks.

— El Decifinamiento de los Glifos Mayas (Breaking the Maya Code) (SPA.). 333p. 1995. pap. 14.99 (*968-16-4462-X*, Pub. by Fondo) Continental Bk.

— An Early Stone Pectoral from Southeastern Mexico. LC 66-16019. (Studies in Pre-Columbian Art & Archaeology: No. 1). (Illus.). 18p. 1966. pap. 5.00 (*0-88402-013-4*) Dumbarton Oaks.

— The Maya. 5th rev. ed. LC 92-63273. (Illus.). 224p. 1993. pap. 16.95 (*0-500-27716-8*, Pub. by Thames Hudson) Norton.

— The Maya. 6th rev. expanded ed. LC 98-60191. (Illus.). 256p. 1999. pap. 18.95 (*0-500-28066-5*, Pub. by Thames Hudson) Norton.

— Mexico: From the Olmecs to the Aztecs. 4th rev. ed. LC 93-60419. (Illus.). 192p. 1994. pap. 16.95 (*0-500-27722-2*, Pub. by Thames Hudson) Norton.

Coe, Michael D. & Benson, Elizabeth P. Three Maya Relief Panels at Dumbarton Oaks. LC 66-30016. (Studies in Pre-Columbian Art & Archaeology: No. 2). (Illus.). 1966. pap. 6.00 (*0-88402-014-2*) Dumbarton Oaks.

Coe, Michael D. & Diehl, Richard A. In the Land of the Olmec, 2 vols., Set. (Illus.). 1980. 100.00 (*0-292-77549-0*) U of Tex Pr.

Coe, Michael D. & Kerr, Justin. The Art of the Maya Scribe. LC 97-25519. (Illus.). 240p. 1998. 75.00 (*0-8109-1988-5*, Pub. by Abrams) Time Warner.

Coe, Michael D., et al. The Olmec World: Ritual & Rulership. Guthrie, Jill, ed. LC 95-78295. (Illus.). 325p. (Orig.). 1996. 75.00 (*0-8109-6311-6*, Pub. by Abrams) Time Warner.

— The Olmec World: Ritual & Rulership. Guthrie, Jill, ed. LC 95-78295. (Illus.). (Orig.). 1995. pap. 45.00 (*0-943012-19-8*) Prince U Art.

Coe, Michael D., jt. auth. see Coe, Sophie D.

Coe, Mike, ed. see Stewart, David.

Coe, Montgomery. Basics of Winning Bridge. rev. ed. LC 98-74317. 64p. 1999. mass mkt. 4.95 (*1-58042-020-6*) Cardoza Pub.

Coe, Paul, pref. Wiradjuri Spirit Man: HJ Wedge. LC 97-114809. (Illus.). 120p. 1996. text 22.50 (*976-641-019-4*) Gordon & Breach.

Coe, Peter. Winning Running: Successful 800m & 1500m Racing & Training. 1996. pap. 29.95 (*1-85223-997-2*, Pub. by Crolwood) Trafalgar.

Coe, Peter N., jt. auth. see Martin, David E.

Coe, Richard M. Process, Form & Substance: A Rhetoric for Advanced Writers. 2nd ed. LC 89-29676. 448p. (C). 1990. text 36.80 (*0-13-326604-4*) P-H.

— Toward a Grammar of Passages. LC 87-9894. (Studies in Writing & Rhetoric). 142p. (Orig.). 1987. pap. text 14.95 (*0-8093-1420-7*) S Ill U Pr.

Coe, Richard N. When the Grass Was Taller: Autobiography & the Experience of Childhood. LC 84-3517. 331p. reprint ed. pap. 102.70 (*0-7837-2790-9*, 204318200006) Bks Demand.

Coe, Richard N., tr. & anno. see Stendhal, pseud.

Coe, Rodney, jt. ed. see Romeis, James C.

Coe, S. F. Hall: Memoranda Relative to the Ancestors & Family of Sophia Fidelia Hall. 231p. 1991. reprint ed. pap. 30.00 (*0-8328-1758-9*); reprint ed. lib. bdg. 40.00 (*0-8328-1757-0*) Higginson Bk Co.

Coe, Shirley, ed. see Block, Janice & Rankine, David.

***Coe, Simon.** The Dacha: A Tale of the Occult. LC 00-190704. 252p. 2000. 25.00 (*0-7388-1938-7*); pap. 18.00 (*0-7388-1939-5*) Xlibris Corp.

— The Gold Bokhara. LC 00-190567. 387'p. 2000. 25.00 (*0-7388-1834-8*); pap. 18.00 (*0-7388-1835-6*) Xlibris Corp.

Coe, Sophie, tr. see Knorozov, Yuri V.

Coe, Sophie, tr. see Knorozov, Yuri V. & Proskouriakoff, Tatiana, eds.

Coe, Sophie D. America's First Cuisines. LC 93-8836. (Illus.). 288p. (Orig.). (C). 1994. pap. 15.95 (*0-292-71159-X*) U of Tex Pr.

Coe, Sophie D. & Coe, Michael D. The True History of Chocolate. LC 95-61824. (Illus.). 288p. 1996. 27.50 (*0-500-01693-3*, Pub. by Thames Hudson) Norton.

***Coe, Sophie D. & Coe, Michael D.** The True History of Chocolate. 2nd ed. LC 95-61824. (Illus.). 280p. 2000. reprint ed. pap. 18.95 (*0-500-28229-3*, Pub. by Thames Hudson) Norton.

Coe, Stella. Ikebana: A Practical & Philosophical Guide to Flower Arrangement. Stewart, Mary L., ed. LC 83-13449. (Illus.). 1984. 39.95 (*0-87951-204-0*, Pub. by Overlook Pr) Penguin Putnam.

Coe, Sue. Dead Meat. LC 95-35536. (Illus.). 136p. 1996. 40.00 (*1-56858-050-9*); pap. 22.00 (*1-56858-041-X*) FWEW.

***Coe, Sue.** Pit's Letter. LC 00-24391. (Illus.). 48p. 2000. 22.00 (*1-56858-163-7*, Pub. by FWEW) Publishers Group.

Coe, Sue, et al. Paintings & Drawings. LC 84-27734. (Illus.). 164p. 1985. 34.50 (*0-8108-1782-9*) Scarecrow.

— Sue Coe: Police State. Zeitlin, Marilyn A., ed. (Illus.). (Orig.). 1987. pap. text 30.00 (*0-935519-07-6*) Anderson Gal.

***Coe, Susan.** The Basenji Out of Africa. Anderson, Mark, ed. (Illus.). 232p. 2000. pap. 19.95 (*0-944875-69-6*, Pub. by Doral Pub) Natl Bk Netwk.

***Coe, Teddy L., et al, eds.** API Members' Petroleum Accounting Practices: Special Supplement to the 1999 PricewaterhouseCoopers Survey of U. S. Petroleum Accounting Practices. 59p. 1999. pap. write for info. (*0-926969-06-4*) UNTIPA.

— 1999 PricewaterhouseCoopers Survey of U. S. Petroleum Accounting Practices. 261p. 1999. mass mkt. 125.00 (*0-926969-05-6*) UNTIPA.

Coe, Teddy L., et al, eds. 1997 Coopers & Lybrand L. L. P. Survey of Accounting Practices in the U. S. Oil & Gas Industry. LC 99-162739. 266p. (Orig.). 1997. pap. 125.00 (*0-926969-04-8*) UNTIPA.

***Coe, Tucker.** Kinds of Love, Kinds of Death. LC 00-30846. 2000. write for info. (*0-7862-2669-2*) Five Star.

Coe, Urling C. Frontier Doctor: Observations on Central Oregon & the Changing West. (Northwest Reprints Ser.). (Illus.). 320p. (C). 1996. pap. 15.95 (*0-87071-520-8*) Oreg St U Pr.

Coe, William R. Piedras Negras Archaeology: Artifacts, Caches, & Burials. LC 60-4422. (University Museum, University of Pennsylvania. Museum Monographs). (Illus.). 323p. reprint ed. pap. 100.20 (*0-8357-7513-5*, 203600600002) Bks Demand.

— Tikal Report No. 14: Excavations in the Great Plaza, North Terrace & North Acropolis of Tikal. (Monographs: No. 61). (Illus.). 1100p. 1990. text 395.00 (*0-934718-66-0*) U Museum Pubns.

Coe, William R., ed. see Haviland, William A.

Coe, William R., ed. see Trik, Helen W. & Kampen, Michael E.

Coebergh, J. W., jt. ed. see Cleton, F. J.

***Coecke, Bob, et al.** Current Research in Operational Quantum Logic - Algebras, Categories, Languages. 328p. 2000. 145.00 (*0-7923-6258-6*) Kluwer Academic.

Coedes, G. The Indianized States of South-East Asia. Vella, Walter F., ed. Cowing, Susan B., tr. from FRE. LC 67-29224. 424p. 1975. reprint ed. pap. text 16.00 (*0-8248-0368-X*) EW Ctr HI.

Coedes, George. Textes d'Auteurs Grecs et Latins Relatifs a l'Extreme Orient. xxxi, 187p. 1977. reprint ed. 50.00 (*3-487-06322-0*) G Olms Pubs.

Coedes, Georges. Textes d'Auteurs Grecs et Latines Relatifs a l'Extreme Orient. xxxii, 184p. 1979. reprint ed. 30.00 (*0-89005-289-1*) Ares.

Coedicion Latinoamericana Staff. Encuentrame: Fiestas Populares de America Latina. (SPA.). 24p. 1991. pap. 7.50 (*980-257-059-1*) Ediciones Huracan.

— Nino Cocinero Latinoamericano. 36p. 1996. pap. 7.50 (*968-494-063-7*) Ediciones Huracan.

— Tit. 17 Narradoras Latinoamericanas. 223p. 1996. pap. 14.95 (*0-929157-32-X*) Ediciones Huracan.

Coehlo, Elizabeth. Learning Together in the Multicultural Classroom. (Illus.). 108p. 1994. pap. text 16.50 (*0-88751-064-7*, 00771) Heinemann.

Coel, Marc & Leung, Jimmy. Atlas of Nuclear Medicine. Bralow, Lisette, ed. 720p. 1996. text 235.00 (*0-7216-3578-4*, W B Saunders Co) Harcrt Hlth Sci Grp.

Coel, Margaret. Chief Left Hand: Southern Arapaho. LC 80-5940. (Civilization of the American Indian Ser.: Vol. 159). (Illus.). 352p. 1988. pap. text 14.95 (*0-8061-2030-4*) U of Okla Pr.

— The Dream Stalker. LC 96-54797. 256p. 1997. pap. 21.95 (*0-425-15967-1*, Prime Crime) Berkley Pub.

— The Dream Stalker. 1998. reprint ed. mass mkt. 5.99 (*0-425-16533-7*, Prime Crime) Berkley Pub.

— The Eagle Catcher. (Wind River Arapaho Ser.). 1996. mass mkt. 5.99 (*0-425-15463-7*) Berkley Pub.

— The Eagle Catcher. LC 95-5383. 224p. 1995. 22.50 (*0-87081-367-6*) Univ Pr Colo.

— The Ghost Walker. 256p. 1996. pap. 21.95 (*0-425-15468-8*, Prime Crime) Berkley Pub.

— The Ghost Walker. 256p. 1997. reprint ed. mass mkt. 5.99 (*0-425-15961-2*, Prime Crime) Berkley Pub.

— Hole in the Wall. deluxe ed. (Illus.). 24p. 1998. 65.00 (*1-892011-03-4*) ASAP Pub.

— Hole in the Wall. limited ed. (Illus.). 24p. 1998. 30.00 (*1-892011-02-6*) ASAP Pub.

***Coel, Margaret.** Honor. (Illus.). 20p. 1999. 35.00 (*1-892011-12-3*) ASAP Pub.

— Honor. deluxe limited ed. (Illus.). 20p. 1999. 75.00 (*1-892011-13-1*) ASAP Pub.

— The Lost Bird. LC 99-22056. 304p. 1999. 21.95 (*0-425-17059-4*, Prime Crime) Berkley Pub.

— The Lost Bird. 304p. 2000. mass mkt. 6.50 (*0-425-17030-6*) Berkley Pub.

— The Lost Bird. large type ed. LC 99-59552. (Core Ser.). 332p. 2000. 28.95 (*0-7838-8958-5*, G K Hall Lrg Type) Mac Lib Ref.

— The Spirit Woman. LC 99-54828. 2000. 21.95 (*0-425-17597-9*) Berkley Pub.

Coel, Margaret. The Story Teller. LC 98-13765. (The/Wind River Arapaho Ser.). 256p. 1998. 21.95 (*0-425-16538-8*, Prime Crime) Berkley Pub.

— The Story Teller, 1 vol. 241p. 1999. reprint ed. mass mkt. 6.50 (*0-425-17025-X*, Prime Crime) Berkley Pub.

Coel, Margaret, jt. auth. see Speas, Sam.

Coelen, Craig, et al. Day Care Centers in the U. S. A National Profile, 1976-1977. (Illus.). 234p. 1984. reprint ed. pap. text 29.00 (*0-8191-4106-2*) U Pr of Amer.

Coelho, Alain, jt. auth. see Lhomeau, Franck.

Coelho, Christopher. A New Kind of Fool: Meditations on St. Francis & His Values. 128p. 1994. pap. 21.00 (*0-86012-184-4*, Pub. by Srch Pr) St Mut.

Coelho, Daniel H., jt. ed. see Caplan, Arthur L.

Coelho, David R. The VHDL Handbook. 416p. (C). 1989. text 132.50 (*0-7923-9031-8*) Kluwer Academic.

Coelho, David R., jt. auth. see Hill, Dwight D.

Coelho, Elizabeth. Teaching & Learning in Multicultural Schools: An Integrated Approach. LC 97-47654. (Bilingual Education & Bilingualism Ser.). 1998. pap. 24.95 (*1-85359-383-4*, Pub. by Multilingual Matters) Taylor & Francis.

— Teaching & Learning in Multicultural Schools: An Integrated Approach. LC 97-47654. (Bilingual Education & Bilingualism Ser.). 1998. 79.00 (*1-85359-384-2*, Pub. by Multilingual Matters) Taylor & Francis.

Coelho, Elizabeth, et al. All Sides of the Issue: Activities for Cooperative Jigsaw Groups. 160p. 1989. teacher ed. 19.95 (*0-13-019498-0*) Alemany Pr.

— All Sides of the Issue: Activities for Cooperative Jigsaw Groups. (Illus.). 154p. 1998. pap. text 16.95 (*1-882483-72-3*) Alta Bk Ctr.

Coelho, Helder, jt. auth. see Ibero-American Conference on Artificial Intelligence Staff.

Coelho, Paulo. The Alchemist: A Fable about Following Your Dream. LC 92-56413. 192p. 1993. 18.00 (*0-06-250217-4*, Pub. by Harper SF) HarpC.

— The Alchemist: A Fable about Following Your Dream. Clarke, Alan R., tr. LC 92-56413. 176p. 2000. pap. 13.00 (*0-06-250218-2*, Pub. by Harper SF) HarpC.

— Alquimista, El: Una Fabula Para Seguir Tus Suenos. Costa, Juan G., tr. LC 94-28948. (SPA., Illus.). 192p. 1994. pap. 11.00 (*0-06-251140-8*, Pub. by Harper SF) HarpC.

— By the River Piedra I Sat Down & Wept. 1996. 20.00 (*0-614-96774-0*); 20.00 (*0-614-96944-1*) Harper SF.

— By the River Piedra I Sat Down & Wept. Clarke, Alan R., tr. LC 95-53948. 224p. 1996. 20.00 (*0-06-251398-2*, Pub. by Harper SF) HarpC.

— By the River Piedra I Sat Down & Wept. 224p. 1997. pap. 13.00 (*0-06-097726-4*, Perennial) HarperTrade.

— The Fifth Mountain. Landers, Clifford, tr. LC 97-38387. 256p. 1999. pap. 13.00 (*0-06-093013-6*, Perennial) HarperTrade.

— The Illustrated Alchemist: A Fable About Following Your Dream. Clarke, Alan R., tr. LC 98-6950. (Illus.). 208p. 1998. 27.50 (*0-06-019250-X*) HarpC.

— A orillas del rio Piedra me sente y llore. LC 96-34273. (SPA.). 224p. 1996. pap. 11.00 (*0-06-251462-8*, Pub. by Harper SF) HarpC.

***Coelho, Paulo.** The Pilgrimage: A Contemporary Quest for Ancient Wisdom. Clarke, Alan, tr. LC 94-45312. 272p. 2000. pap. 13.00 (*0-06-251279-X*, Pub. by Harper SF) HarpC.

Coelho, Paulo. Preguntale a Paulo Coelho. 1997. pap. text 14.50 (*968-855-226-7*) J H Surovek.

— La Quinta Montana. LC 98-10477. 240p. 1998. 23.00 (*0-06-017566-4*) HarpC.

— La Quinta Montana. 240p. 1999. pap. 13.00 (*0-06-093012-8*) HarpC.

***Coelho, Paulo.** The Valkyries: An Encounter with Angels. Clarke, Alan R., tr. LC 95-5747. 256p. 2000. pap. 13.00 (*0-06-251334-6*, Pub. by Harper SF) HarpC.

— Veronika Decide Morir. 240p. 2000. 24.00 (*0-06-019665-3*) HarpC.

— Veronika Decides to Die. Costa, Margaret Jull, tr. 224p. 2000. 24.00 (*0-06-019612-2*) HarpC.

Coelho, Raquel. Monstrico (Little Monster) Matrangelo, Stella, tr. (SPA., Illus.). (J). (gr. 2). 1994. pap. 5.99 (*968-16-4573-1*, Pub. by Fondo) Continental Bk.

Coelho, Rohen & Hawash, Maher. DirectX, RDX, RSX & MMX Technology. LC 97-33102. 448p. (C). 1997. pap. text 44.95 (*0-201-30944-0*) Addison-Wesley.

Coelho, Victor. The Manuscript Sources of Seventeenth-Century Italian Lute Music. rev. ed. LC 94-36302. 736p. 1995. text 127.00 (*0-8153-1382-9*) Garland.

Coelho, Victor, ed. Music & Science in the Age of Galileo. LC 92-33288. (University of Western Ontario Ser. in Philosophy of Science: Vol. 51). 268p. (C). 1992. lib. bdg. 141.50 (*0-7923-2028-X*, Pub. by Kluwer Academic) Kluwer Academic.

Coelho, Victor A., ed. Performance on Lute, Guitar, & Vihuela: Historical Practice & Modern Interpretation. LC 96-47888. (Studies in Performance Practice: Vol. 6). (Illus.). 252p. (C). 1998. text 64.95 (*0-521-45528-6*) Cambridge U Pr.

Coelho, Z., ed. see Workshop on Dynamical Systems Staff.

Coelingh-Bennink, H. J., et al, eds. Chronic Hyperandrogenic Anovulation. (Illus.). 192p. (C). 1991. 78.00 (*1-85070-322-1*) Prthnon Pub.

Coelli, Tim, et al. An Introduction to Efficiency & Productivity Analysis. LC 97-38456. 296p. 1997. 110.00 (*0-7923-8060-6*) Kluwer Academic.

Coellnicht, Donald C., jt. ed. see Clark, David L.

Coello, Dennis. The Mountain Bike Repair Handbook. (Illus.). 176p. 1990. pap. 12.95 (*1-55821-064-4*) Lyons Pr.

— The New Complete Mountain Biker. LC 96-42439. (Illus.). 240p. 1996. pap. 18.95 (*1-55821-495-X*) Lyons Pr.

Coello, Dennis, ed. see Cameron, Ward.

Coello, Dennis, ed. see Hale, Sarah L. & Bishop, Jodi.

Coello, Dennis, ed. see Henry, Steve.

Coello, Dennis, ed. see Jones, Steve.

Coello, Dennis, ed. see Surkiewicz, Joe.

Coello, Dennis L. Living on Two Wheels: The Complete Guide to Buying, Commuting & Touring. 1982. pap. 9.95 (*0-89496-034-2*) Ross Bks.

— The Roadside Guide to Bike Repair. 112p. (Orig.). 1988. mass mkt. 3.95 (*0-446-34820-1*, Pub. by Warner Bks) Little.

Coelsch-Foisner, Sabine, et al, eds. Trends in English & American Studies: Literature & the Imagination. LC 96-44223. 468p. 1996. text 109.95 (*0-7734-8747-6*) E Mellen.

Coen, Dan. Friendly Persuasion: Dynamic Telephone Sales Training & Techniques for the 21st Century. 2nd ed. LC 97-94528. (Illus.). 200p. 1999. pap. 24.99 (*0-9660436-1-8*, Pub. by DCD Pub) ACCESS Pubs Network.

***Coen, Enrico.** The Art of Genes. (Illus.). 400p. 2000. pap. 16.95 (*0-19-286208-1*) OUP.

— The Art of Genes: How Organisms Make Themselves. LC 98-31453. (Illus.). 396p. 1999. 35.00 (*0-19-850343-1*) OUP.

Coen, Ethan. Gates of Eden. 272p. 1999. pap. 12.95 (*0-385-33438-9*) Delacorte.

— Gates of Eden: Stories. LC 98-20853. 272p. 1998. 24.00 (*0-688-15914-1*, Wm Morrow) Morrow Avon.

Coen, Ethan, jt. auth. see Coen, Joel.

Coen, Joel. Barton Fink & Miller's Crossing. (Orig.). 1991. pap. 15.95 (*0-571-16648-2*) Faber & Faber.

Coen, Joel & Coen, Ethan. Blood Simple. (Original Screenplay Ser.). (Illus.). 112p. 1989. pap. 10.95 (*0-312-02168-2*) St Martin.

— Fargo. 128p. (Orig.). 1996. pap. 13.95 (*0-571-17963-0*) Faber & Faber.

***Coen, Joel & Coen, Ethan.** O Brother, Where Art Thou? (Screenplays Ser.). (Illus.). 160p. 2000. pap. 14.00 (*0-571-20518-6*) Faber & Faber.

Coen, Joel & Coen, Ethan. Raising Arizona. 6th ed. (Original Screenplay Ser.). (Illus.). 112p. 1989. pap. 11.95 (*0-312-02270-0*) St Martin.

Coen, Larry & Crane, David. Epic Proportions. Date not set. pap. 5.95 (*0-8222-1741-4*) Dramatists Play.

Coen, Margaret, tr. see Zambonini, Franca.

Coen McCabe, Anne. English Regents: Prep for NYS Revised English Exam. Garnsey, Wayne & Stich, Paul, eds. (Illus.). 128p. (Orig.). (YA). (gr. 9-12). 1998. pap. 9.95 (*0-935487-24-7*) N & N Pub Co.

Coen, Michael, ed. Intelligent Environments: Papers from the 1998 Spring Symposium. (Technical Reports). (Illus.). 181p. 1998. spiral bd. 25.00 (*1-57735-047-2*, SS-98-02) AAAI Pr.

***Coen, Oscar Hoffman & Robeck, Mildred Coen.** Oscar: His Story. (Illus.). 152p. 1999. pap. 16.00 (*0-8059-4710-8*) Dorrance.

Coen, Patricia. Beautiful Braids. LC 97-106913. 64p. 1996. pap. 5.99 (*0-517-88617-0*) Random Hse Value.

Coen, Patricia & Milford, Bryan. Closets: Designing & Organizing the Personalized Closet. LC 87-8252. (Illus.). 128p. 1988. pap. 17.50 (*0-8021-3228-6*, Grove) Grove-Atltic.

Coen, Rena N. Elsie Palmer Payne: A Retrospective Exhibition. (Illus.). vi, 34p. (Orig.). 1987. pap. write for info. (*0-8227-2966-0*) Payne Studios.

— Elsie Palmer Payne, 1884-1971: Out of the Shadow - An American Artist Rediscovered. LC 87-62948. (Illus.). 33p. 1987. 25.00 (*0-944699-00-6*) DeRus Fine Art.

— In the Mainstream: The Art & Times of Alexis Fournier. (Illus.). 112p. 1985. 39.95 (*0-87839-041-3*) North Star.

— Minnesota Impressionists. LC 96-36446. (Illus.). 96p. 1996. 35.00 (*0-9639338-6-8*) Afton Hist Soc.

— The Paynes, Edgar & Elsie: American Artists. LC 87-63403. (Illus.). 108p. 1987. 50.00 (*0-944699-01-4*) DeRus Fine Art.

Coen, Robert & Hoogenboom, Mark C. The Web-Enabled Enterprise. LC 97-19219. (Illus.). 608p. 1997. 54.95 (*0-07-011774-8*) McGraw.

Coen, Salvatore, ed. Geometry & Complex Variables. (Lecture Notes in Pure & Applied Mathematics Ser.: Vol. 132). (Illus.). 520p. 1991. pap. text 210.00 (*0-8247-8445-6*) Dekker.

Coen, Stanley J. Between Author & Reader: A Psychoanalytic Approach to Writing & Reading. LC 93-24579. (Psychoanalysis & Culture Ser.). 210p. (C). 1994. 80.00 (*0-231-07356-9*); pap. 20.50 (*0-231-07357-7*) Col U Pr.

— The Misuse of Persons: Analyzing Pathological Dependency. 344p. 1992. text 49.95 (*0-88163-139-6*) Analytic Pr.

Coen, Sue H. Horseback Riding Made Easy & Fun. 1978. pap. 10.00 (*0-87980-194-8*) Wilshire.

Coen, Tanya L., jt. auth. see Higgins, Michael James.

Coen, V. & Holtbecker, H. Post Accident Heat Removal, Vol. 2. (European Applied Research Reports Special Topics Ser.). vi, 398p. 1979. text 607.00 (*3-7186-0025-0*) Gordon & Breach.

***Coen, Vittoria.** Alex Katz. (Illus.). 2000. pap. 45.00 (*88-7757-103-9*) Hopefulmonster Editore.

— Stephan Balkenhol. (Illus.). 2000. 34.00 (*88-7757-100-4*) Hopefulmonster Editore.

Coene, Trisha, ed. see Alexander, Tom.

Coenen, Antonius J. On Smart Dither by Absolute One-Bit Coding for Noise-Shaped PCM. (Illus.). 192p. (Orig.). 1996. pap. 57.50 (*90-407-1377-4*, Pub. by Delft U Pr) Coronet Bks.

Coenen, Dorothea. Diccionario Mitologia Griega & Romana. (SPA.). 256p. 1984. 16.95 (*0-7859-5739-1*) Fr & Eur.

Coenen, Dorothea Von, see von Coenen, Dorothea.

C

Coenen, Frans & Bench-Capon, Trevor. Maintenance of Knowledge-Based Systems: Theory, Techniques & Tools. (APIC Ser.). (Illus.). 352p. 1993. text 88.00 (*0-12-178120-8*) Acad Pr.

***Coenen, Frans H., et al.** Participation & the Quality of Environmental Decision Making. LC 98-34745. (Environment & Policy Ser.). 27p. 1998. 149.00 (*0-7923-5264-5*) Kluwer Academic.

Coenen, Frederic E. Franz Grillparzer's Portraiture of Men. LC 72-1013. (North Carolina. University. Studies in the Germanic Languages & Literatures: No. 4). reprint ed. 37.50 (*0-404-50904-5*) AMS Pr.

Coenen, George L. Basic Electronics for the Petroleum Industry: Unit I. 3rd rev. ed. Greenlaw, Martha, ed. (Illus.). 36p. (C). 1980. pap. text 15.00 (*0-88698-101-8*, 1.41130) PETEX.

— Basic Electronics for the Petroleum Industry: Unit II. 3rd rev. ed. Greenlaw, Martha, ed. (Illus.). 60p. (C). 1980. pap. text 15.00 (*0-88698-102-6*, 1.41230) PETEX.

— Basic Electronics for the Petroleum Industry: Unit III. 3rd rev. ed. Greenlaw, Martha, ed. (Illus.). 65p. (C). 1980. pap. text 15.00 (*0-88698-103-4*, 1.41330) PETEX.

— Basic Electronics for the Petroleum Industry: Unit IV. 3rd rev. ed. Greenlaw, Martha, ed. (Illus.). 53p. (C). 1980. pap. text 15.00 (*0-88698-104-2*, 1.41430) PETEX.

— Basic Electronics for the Petroleum Industry: Unit V. 3rd rev. ed. Greenlaw, Martha, ed. (Illus.). 44p. (C). 1980. pap. text 15.00 (*0-88698-105-0*, 1.41530) PETEX.

Coenen, Harry & Leisink, Peter, eds. Work & Citizenship in the New Europe. LC 93-9712. 272p. 1993. 90.00 (*1-85278-739-2*) E Elgar.

Coenen-Huther, J. & Synak, B., eds. Post-Communist Poland: From Totalitarianism to Democracy. (Illus.). 137p. (C). 1993. lib. bdg. 95.00 (*1-56072-146-4*) Nova Sci Pubs.

Coenen-Huther, Jacques, ed. Bulgaria at the Crossroads. 237p. (C). 1996. lib. bdg. 115.00 (*1-56072-305-X*) Nova Sci Pubs.

***Coenen-Mennemeier, Brigitta.** Der Schwache Held: Heroismuskritik in der Franzosischen Erzahlliteratur Des 19. und 20, Jahrhunderts. 320p. 1999. 51.95 (*3-631-34126-1*) P Lang Pubng.

Coenen, R., jt. auth. see Inzelt, Annamaria.

***Coens, Tom & Jenkins, Mary.** Abolishing Performance Appraisals: Why They Backfire & What to Do Instead. 300p. 2000. 27.95 (*1-57675-076-0*, Pub. by Berrett-Koehler) Publishers Group.

Coerne, Louis A. The Evolution of Modern Orchestration. LC 74-26035. reprint ed. 52.50 (*0-404-12881-5*) AMS Pr.

Coerper, Lois H. & Mersereau, Shirley W. The Independent School Guide: For Washington D. C. & Surrounding Area. 10th ed. 200p. 1995. 14.95 (*0-929802-01-2*) Indepnd Schl Guides.

— The Independent School Guide: For Washington, D. C. & Surrounding Area. 10th ed. 200p. 1995. 14.95 (*0-929802-11-X*) Indepnd Schl Guides.

— Independent School Guide: For Washington, D. C. & Surrounding Area. 11th rev. ed. 224p. 1998. pap. 14.95 (*0-929802-12-8*) Indepnd Schl Guides.

Coerr, Eleanor. The Bell Ringer & the Pirates. LC 82-47700. (I Can Read Bks.). (Illus.). 64p. (J). (ps-3). 1983. 9.95 (*0-06-021354-X*) HarpC Child Bks.

— The Big Balloon Race. LC 91-13606. (I Can Read Bks.). (Illus.). 64p. (J). (ps-3). 1981. lib. bdg. 15.89 (*0-06-021353-1*) HarpC Child Bks.

— The Big Balloon Race. LC 91-13607. (I Can Read Bks.). (Illus.). 64p. (J). (ps-3). 1984. pap. 3.95 (*0-06-444053-2*, HarpTrophy) HarpC Child Bks.

Coerr, Eleanor. The Big Balloon Race. (I Can Read Bks.). (J). (gr. 2-4). 1981. 8.95 (*0-606-01998-7*, Pub. by Turtleback) Demco.

Coerr, Eleanor. The Big Balloon Race. abr. ed. (I Can Read Bks.). (Illus.). (J). (gr. 2-4). 1990. 8.95 incl. audio (*1-55994-221-5*, TBC 2215) HarperAudio.

— Buffalo Bill & the Pony Express. LC 93-24261. (I Can Read Bks.). (Illus.). 64p. (J). (ps-3). 1995. 15.95 (*0-06-023372-9*); lib. bdg. 15.89 (*0-06-023373-7*) HarpC Child Bks.

— Buffalo Bill & the Pony Express. LC 93-24261. (I Can Read Bks.). (Illus.). 64p. (J). (ps-3). 1996. pap. 3.95 (*0-06-444220-9*, HarpTrophy) HarpC Child Bks.

Coerr, Eleanor. Buffalo Bill & the Pony Express. (I Can Read Bks.). (J). (gr. 2-4). 1996. 8.95 (*0-606-09115-7*, Pub. by Turtleback) Demco.

Coerr, Eleanor. Chang's Paper Pony. (I Can Read Bks.). (Illus.). 64p. (J). (gr. 2-4). 1988. lib. bdg. 15.89 (*0-06-021329-9*) HarpC Child Bks.

— Chang's Paper Pony. LC 87-45679. (I Can Read Bks.). (Illus.). 64p. (J). (ps-3). 1993. pap. 3.95 (*0-06-444163-6*, HarpTrophy) HarpC Child Bks.

— Chang's Paper Pony. (I Can Read Bks.). (J). (gr. 2-4). 1993. 8.95 (*0-606-02552-9*, Pub. by Turtleback) Demco.

— The Josefina Story Quilt. (I Can Read Bks.). (Illus.). 64p. (J). (gr. 2-4). 1986. lib. bdg. 15.89 (*0-06-021349-3*) HarpC Child Bks.

— The Josefina Story Quilt. LC 85-45260. (I Can Read Bks.). (Illus.). 64p. (J). (ps-3). 1986. 15.95 (*0-06-021348-5*) HarpC Child Bks.

— The Josefina Story Quilt. LC 85-45260. (I Can Read Bks.). (Illus.). 64p. (J). (gr. 2-4). 1989. pap. 3.95 (*0-06-444129-6*, HarpTrophy) HarpC Child Bks.

Coerr, Eleanor. The Josefina Story Quilt. (I Can Read Bks.). (J). (gr. 2-4). 1986. 8.95 (*0-606-04138-9*, Pub. by Turtleback) Demco.

Coerr, Eleanor. The Josefina Story Quilt. unabridged ed. LC 85-45260. (I Can Read Bks.). (Illus.). 64p. (J). (ps-3). 1995. 8.95 incl. audio (*0-694-70012-6*) HarperAudio.

Coerr, Eleanor. Josefina y la colcha de retazos. Marcuse, Aida E., tr. (I Can Read Bks.).Tr. of Josefina Story Quilt. (SPA., Illus.). 64p. (J). (gr. 2-4). 1995. pap. 4.95 (*0-06-444190-3*, HarpTrophy) HarpC Child Bks.

Coerr, Eleanor. Josefina y la colcha de retazos. Marcuse, Aida E., tr. from ENG. LC 94-33174. (I Can Read Bks.).Tr. of Josefina Story Quilt. (SPA., Illus.). 64p. (J). (ps-3). 1995. 13.95 (*0-06-025319-3*) HarpC Child Bks.

— Josefina y la colcha de retazos. (I Can Read Bks.).Tr. of Josefina Story Quilt. (J). (gr. 2-4). 1995. 10.15 (*0-606-07749-9*, Pub. by Turtleback) Demco.

— Mieko & the Fifth Treasure. 80p. (J). 1994. pap. 4.50 (*0-440-40947-0*) Dell.

— Mieko & the Fifth Treasure. LC 92-14660. 64p. (J). 1993. 14.95 (*0-399-22434-3*, G P Putnam) Peng Put Young Read.

Coerr, Eleanor. Mieko & the Fifth Treasure. 1993. 9.19 (*0-606-07037-0*, Pub. by Turtleback) Demco.

Coerr, Eleanor. Sadako. LC 92-41483. (Illus.). 48p. (J). (gr. 1-4). 1993. 17.95 (*0-399-21771-1*, G P Putnam) Peng Put Young Read.

— Sadako. (Illus.). 48p. (J). 1997. pap. 6.99 (*0-698-11588-0*, PapStar) Peng Put Young Read.

— Sadako. 1997. 11.15 (*0-606-12803-4*, Pub. by Turtleback) Demco.

— Sadako & the Thousand Paper Cranes. (Illus.). 64p. (J). (gr. 2-5). 1979. pap. 3.99 (*0-440-47465-5*, YB BDD) BDD Bks Young Read.

Coerr, Eleanor. Sadako & the Thousand Paper Cranes. 64p. (J). (gr. 3-5). pap. 3.99 (*0-8072-1263-6*) Listening Lib.

Coerr, Eleanor. Sadako & the Thousand Paper Cranes. LC 76-9872. (Illus.). (J). (gr. 3-5). 1977. 14.95 (*0-399-20520-9*, G P Putnam) Peng Put Young Read.

Coerr, Eleanor. Sadako & the Thousand Paper Cranes. 1977. 9.19 (*0-606-02067-5*, Pub. by Turtleback) Demco.

Coerr, Eleanor. Sadako & the Thousand Paper Cranes. unabridged ed. (Follow the Reader Ser.). (J). (gr. 3-5). 1986. pap. text 15.98 incl. audio (*0-8072-0118-9*, FTR114SP) Listening Lib.

— Sadako & the Thousand Paper Cranes Reissue Edition. (Illus.). 80p. (gr. k-3). 1999. reprint ed. pap. 4.99 (*0-698-11802-2*, PuffinBks) Peng Put Young Read.

Coerr, Eleanor. Sadako y las Mil Grullas de Papel. (Orig.). (J). (ps-3). 1996. pap. text 8.95 (*5-556-40020-2*) Lectorum Pubns.

Coerr, Eleanor. Sadako y las Mil Grullas de Papel (Sadako & the Thousand Paper Cranes) (Illus.). 64p. (J). (gr. 3-9). 1996. pap. text 8.95 (*84-241-3353-6*) Lectorum Pubns.

— Sadako y las Mil Grullas de Papel (Sadako & the Thousand Paper Cranes) 1996. 14.15 (*0-606-10499-2*, Pub. by Turtleback) Demco.

Coers, Donald V. John Steinbeck As Propagandist: "The Moon Is Down" Goes to War. LC 90-26583. 192p. (C). 1991. text 29.95 (*0-8173-0538-6*) U of Ala Pr.

Coers, Donald V., et al, eds. After The Grapes of Wrath: Essays on John Steinbeck in Honor of Tetsumaro Hayashi. 317p. (C). 1995. text 29.95 (*0-8214-1102-0*) Ohio U Pr.

Coerts, Jane, ed. see De Hoop, Helen.

Coertzen, E. J. Criminal Law Casebook: A Selection of Summaries. 246p. 1990. pap. 37.00 (*0-409-05645-6*, SA, MICHIE) LEXIS Pub.

Coertzen, E. J. & Sorgdrager, A. M. Strafregvonnisbundel - 'n Seleksie Opsommings. (AFR.). 254p. 1989. pap. write for info. (*0-409-05644-8*, MICHIE) LEXIS Pub.

Coerver, Don M. & Hall, Linda B. Tangled Destines: Latin America & the United States. LC 98-58040. 1999. 39.95 (*0-8263-2118-6*) U of NM Pr.

— Tangled Destines: Latin America & the United States. LC 98-58040. (Illus.). 224p. 1999. pap. 19.95 (*0-8263-2117-8*) U of NM Pr.

***Coerver, Don M., et al.** Mexico Today: An Encyclopedia of Contemporary History & Culture. 2001. lib. bdg. 75.00 (*1-57607-132-4*) ABC-CLIO.

Coerver, Don M., jt. auth. see Hall, Linda B.

Coerver, Wiel. Score! Soccer Tactics & Techniques for a Better Offense. LC 94-45495.Tr. of Scoren. (DUT & ENG., Illus.). 192p. 1995. pap. 16.95 (*0-8069-0976-5*) Sterling.

— Soccer Fundamentals for Players & Coaches. 192p. (C). 1985. text 29.95 (*0-13-815226-8*, Busn); pap. text 14.95 (*0-13-815218-7*, Busn) P-H.

Coes, Donald V. Macroeconomic Crises, Politics, & Growth in Brazil, 1964-90. LC 94-31420. (World Bank Comparative Macroeconomic Studies). 256p. 1995. pap. 22.00 (*0-8213-2299-0*, 12299) World Bank.

Coes, Donald V., jt. ed. see Baer, Werner.

Coes, L. Abrasives. LC 78-153451. (Applied Mineralogy Ser.: Vol. 1). (Illus.). 1971. 56.95 (*0-387-80968-6*) Spr-Verlag.

Coester, Alfred L., ed. Anthology of the Modernista Movement in Spanish America. LC 75-91347. 351p. 1970. reprint ed. 60.00 (*0-87752-023-2*) Gordian.

Coetsee, D., jt. auth. see Vorster, D. D.

Coetsem, F. Van, see Van Coetsem, F.

Coetzee, Carli, jt. ed. see Nuttall, Sarah.

Coetzee, Frans. For Party or Country: Nationalism & the Dilemmas of Popular Conservatism in Edwardian England. 240p. 1990. text 65.00 (*0-19-506238-8*) OUP.

Coetzee, Frans & Shevin-Coetzee, Marilyn, eds. Authority, Identity & the Social History of the Great War. LC 94-45335. 384p. 1995. pap. 22.95 (*1-57181-067-6*) Berghahn Bks.

Coetzee, Frans & Shevin-Coetzee, Marilyn, eds. Authority, Identity & the Social History of the Great War. LC 94-45335. 384p. (C). 1995. 59.95 (*1-57181-017-X*) Berghahn Bks.

— The First World War. (Sources in Modern History Ser.). 400p. (C). 1995. pap. text 29.16 (*0-669-33470-7*) HM Trade Div.

Coetzee, J. A. & Van Zinderen Bakker, E. M., eds. Palaeoecology of Africa Vol. 19: Proceedings of the VIIIth Biennial Conference, Bloemfontein, 20-24 March, 1987. (Illus.). 414p. (C). 1989. text 90.00 (*90-6191-834-0*, Pub. by A A Balkema) Ashgate Pub Co.

Coetzee, J. A., jt. auth. see Van Zinderen Bakker, E. M.

Coetzee, J. A., jt. ed. see Van Zinderen Bakker, E. M.

Coetzee, J. F. & Ritchie, Calvin D., eds. Solute-Solvent Interactions, Vol. 2. LC 69-12718. (Illus.). 473p. reprint ed. pap. 146.70 (*0-7837-4721-7*, 204126300002) Bks Demand.

— Solute-Solvent Interactions, 1969, Vol. 1. LC 69-12718. (Illus.). 669p. reprint ed. pap. 200.00 (*0-7837-0958-7*, 204126300019) Bks Demand.

Coetzee, J. M. Age of Iron. 208p. 1998. pap. 12.95 (*0-14-027565-7*) Viking Penguin.

— Boyhood: Scenes from Provincial Life. 176p. 1998. pap. 11.95 (*0-14-026566-X*) Viking Penguin.

***Coetzee, J. M.** Disgrace. 256p. 1999. write for info. (*0-436-20489-4*) M Secker & Warburg.

— Disgrace. 224p. 2000. pap. 13.00 (*0-14-029640-9*) Penguin Putnam.

— Disgrace. LC 99-55216. 220p. 1999. 23.95 (*0-670-88731-5*, Viking) Viking Penguin.

— Disgrace. 224p. 2000. pap. write for info. (*0-09-928952-0*) Vintage.

— Disgrace. large type ed. LC 00-20642. (General Ser.). 299p. 2000. pap. 24.95 (*0-7862-2479-7*) Thorndike Pr.

Coetzee, J. M. Doubling the Point: Essays & Interviews. Atwell, David, ed. (Illus.). 448p. 1992. 56.00 (*0-674-21517-6*); pap. 21.50 (*0-674-21518-4*) HUP.

— Dusklands. 128p. 1985. pap. 10.95 (*0-14-024177-9*) Viking Penguin.

— Foe. 160p. 1988. pap. 11.95 (*0-14-009623-X*, Penguin Bks) Viking Penguin.

— Giving Offense: Essays on Censorship. LC 95-37389. 304p. 1996. 24.95 (*0-226-11174-1*) U Ch Pr.

— Giving Offense: Essays on Censorship. xii, 290p. 1997. pap. 14.95 (*0-226-11176-8*) U Ch Pr.

— In the Heart of the Country. 144p. 1982. pap. 11.95 (*0-14-006228-9*, Penguin Bks) Viking Penguin.

— Life & Times of Michael K. LC 84-19085. 192p. 1985. pap. 11.95 (*0-14-007448-1*, Penguin Bks) Viking Penguin.

— The Master of Petersburg. 256p. 1995. pap. 12.95 (*0-14-023810-7*, Penguin Bks) Viking Penguin.

— Waiting for the Barbarians. 160p. 1982. pap. 11.95 (*0-14-006110-X*, Penguin Bks) Viking Penguin.

— Waiting for the Barbarians. (Great Books of the 20th Century Ser.). 160p. 1999. pap. 12.95 (*0-14-028335-8*, Penguin Bks) Viking Penguin.

— What Is Realism? (Chapbooks in Literature Ser.). 32p. (Orig.). 1997. pap. text 5.00 (*1-878603-09-4*) Bennington Coll.

***Coetzee, J. M. & Gutmann, Amu.** The Lives of Animals. LC 98-39591. (University Center for Human Values Ser.). 1999. 19.95 (*0-691-00443-9*, Pub. by Princeton U Pr) Cal Prin Full Svc.

***Coetzee, Karen & Bergh, Rene.** Sew-It-Yourself Home Decor: Fabric Projects for the Living Room, Bedroom & Beyond. LC 99-67517. (Illus.). 160p. 2000. pap. 21.95 (*0-87341-575-2*) Krause Pubns.

Coetzee, P. H. & Roux, A. P., eds. The African Philosophy Reader. LC 98-33970. 400p. 1998. pap. 26.99 (*0-415-18905-5*, D6003) Routledge.

Coetzer, Owen. The Anglo-Boer War: The Road to Infamy, 1899-1900. (Illus.). 294p. (C). 1998. text 25.00 (*0-7881-5451-6*) DIANE Pub.

Coeur, C. Le, see Le Coeur, C.

Coey, J. M., ed. Rare-Earth Iron Permanent Magnets. LC 95-47856. (Monographs on the Physics & Chemistry of Materials: No. 54). (Illus.). 542p. 1996. text 135.00 (*0-19-851792-0*) OUP.

Coey, J. M., jt. auth. see Moorjani, K.

Coey, Nancy. Finding Gifts in Everyday Life. Orig. Title: Bean Dip & Other Stories. (Illus.). 128p. 1995. pap. 11.95 (*0-9642515-1-5*) Login Pubs Consort.

Coey, Tim, tr. see Grigorovich, Yuri & Kamova, Sania D.

Coeymans, Juan E. & Mundlak, Yair. Sectoral Growth in Chile, 1962-82. LC 93-30465. 1993. write for info. (*0-89629-098-0*) Intl Food Policy.

Cofer, Charles N., jt. auth. see Kasschau, Richard A.

Cofer, David B. Saint-Simonism in the Radicalism of Thomas Carlyle. (English Literature Ser.: No. 33). 1970. reprint ed. pap. 39.95 (*0-8383-0017-0*) M S G Haskell Hse.

Cofer, Donna P. Judges, Bureaucrats, & the Question of Independence: A Study of the Social Security Administration Hearing Process, 130. LC 84-19771. (Contributions in Political Science Ser.: No. 130). 245p. 1985. 55.00 (*0-313-24707-2*, CJB/) Greenwood.

Cofer, E. M. Carrier on the Prairie: The Story of the U. S. Naval Air Station, Ottumwa, Iowa. LC 95-95359. (Illus.). 318p. 1996. 25.95 (*0-9649925-0-7*); pap. 16.95 (*0-9649925-1-5*) Hawley Ct Pr.

Cofer, Jennifer, ed. see Huffman, Edna K.

***Cofer, Jennifer I., ed.** Documentation & Coding Strategies for the Long-Term Care PPS. (Illus.). 112p. 1999. pap. text 79.00 (*1-57839-004-4*) Opus Communs.

Cofer, Jennifer I. & Greeley, Hugh. Continous Quality Improvement for Health Information Management. LC 98-231824. (Illus.). 250p. 1998. pap. text 67.00 (*1-57839-039-7*) Opus Communs.

— Quality Improvement Techniques for Medical Records. (Health Care Quality Improvement Ser.). 217p. 1996. pap. text 47.00 (*1-885829-04-3*) Opus Communs.

— Quality Improvement Techniques for Radiology. (Health Care Quality Improvement Ser.). 230p. 1994. pap. text 47.00 (*1-885829-06-X*) Opus Communs.

Cofer, Jennifer I., et al. Information Management: A Guide to the JCAHO Standards. 2nd ed. LC 97-126091. 144p. 1996. pap. text 67.00 (*1-885829-30-2*) Opus Communs.

Cofer, Jennifer I., jt. auth. see Greeley, Hugh.

Cofer, Jennifer L. & Greeley, Hugh. Quality Improvement Techniques for Respiratory Care. (Health Care Quality Improvement Ser.). 220p. 1993. pap. text 42.00 (*1-885829-05-1*) Opus Communs.

Cofer, Judith. An Island Like You. 176p. (J). (gr. 7). 1996. pap. 4.99 (*0-14-038068-X*) Viking Penguin.

Cofer, Judith O. An Island Like You. (YA). 1998. 18.50 (*0-8446-6967-9*) Peter Smith.

— The Latin Deli: Prose & Poetry. LC 92-44782. 172p. 1993. 22.95 (*0-8203-1556-7*) U of Ga Pr.

— The Latin Deli: Telling the Lives of Barrio Women. 182p. 1995. pap. 11.00 (*0-393-31313-1*, Norton Paperbks) Norton.

— The Line of the Sun: A Novel by Judith Ortiz Cofer. LC 88-22042. 304p. 1991. reprint ed. pap. 14.95 (*0-8203-1335-1*) U of Ga Pr.

— La Linea del Sol. 302p. 1996. pap. 12.95 (*0-8477-0249-9*) U of PR Pr.

— Peregrina. (International Poetry Chapbook Ser.). 14p. 1985. write for info. (*0-936600-06-3*) Riverstone Foothills.

— Reaching for the Mainland & Selected New Poems. LC 95-31050. 88p. (Orig.). (C). 1995. pap. 9.00 (*0-927534-55-X*) Biling Rev-Pr.

— Terms of Survival. 2nd ed. LC 87-70270. 64p. 1995. pap. 7.00 (*1-55885-079-1*) Arte Publico.

Cofer, Judith O. The Year of Our Revolution. LC 98-13097. 128p. 1998. 16.95 (*1-55885-224-7*) Arte Publico.

***Cofer, Judith O.** The Year of Our Revolution. (Illus.). 128p. (J). (gr. 4-7). 2000. pap. 5.99 (*0-14-130974-1*, PuffinBks) Peng Put Young Read.

Cofer, Judith O., jt. ed. see Kallet, Marilyn.

Cofer, Judith Ortiz. Silent Dancing: A Partial Remembrance of a Puerto Rican Childhood. 2nd ed. LC 89-77428. 168p. (YA). (gr. 9 up). 1990. pap. 12.95 (*1-55885-015-5*) Arte Publico.

***Cofer, Judith Ortiz.** Woman in Front of the Sun: On Becoming a Writer. 144p. 2000. pap. 14.95 (*0-8203-2242-3*) U of Ga Pr.

Cofer, Rebecca & McElligott, David. Good Cop - Bad Cop: A True Story of Murder & Mayhem. 1994. 22.95 (*0-88282-088-5*) New Horizon NJ.

Cofer-Shabica, Stephen V. & Magoon, Orville T., eds. Biological & Physical Aspects of Dredging, Kings Bay, Georgia. LC 91-4237. (Coastlines of the World Ser.). 159p. 1991. pap. text 24.00 (*0-87262-839-6*) Am Soc Civil Eng.

Coff, Carol. Portfolios Through the Year. (Illus.). 112p. (J). 1997. pap., teacher ed. 11.95 (*1-57690-036-3*, TCM2036) Tchr Create Mat.

Coffa, J. Alberto. The Semantic Tradition from Kant to Carnap: To the Vienna Station. Wessels, Linda, ed. 459p. (C). 1993. pap. text 23.95 (*0-521-44707-0*) Cambridge U Pr.

Coffa, S., ed. Crucial Issues in Semiconductor Materials & Processing Technologies: Proceedings of the NATO Advanced Study Institute on Semiconductor Materials & Processing Technologies, Erice, Italy, 1-13 July 1991. LC 92-33612. (NATO Advanced Science Institutes Series C: Mathematical & Physical Sciences). 556p. (C). 1992. text 332.00 (*0-7923-2003-4*) Kluwer Academic.

Coffa, S., et al, eds. Defects & Diffusion in Silicon Processing: Materials Research Society Symposium Proceedings, Vol. 469. LC 97-36151. 541p. 1997. text 75.00 (*1-55899-373-8*) Materials Res.

— Materials & Devices for Silicon-Based Optoelectronics Vol. 486: Materials Research Society Symposium Proceedings. LC 98-14958. 409p. 1998. text 68.00 (*1-55899-391-6*) Materials Res.

— Rare-Earth Doped Semiconductors II. LC 96-9886. (MRS Symposium Proceedings Ser.: Vol. 422). 366p. 1996. 70.00 (*1-55899-325-8*, 422) Materials Res.

Coffa, S., ed. see Tenth International Conference on Ion Implantation.

Coffay, Thomas P. Every Dogs Needs a Man. 1982. pap. 4.95 (*0-87193-295-4*) Dimension Bks.

— An Open Letter to Judge Reginald Stanton Vol. 5: The Champion of Legal Lunacy. 1998. pap. 4.95 (*0-87193-293-8*) Dimension Bks.

Coffee, C. Metabolism. (Integrated Medical Sciences Ser.). (C). 1997. pap. 22.95 (*1-889325-26-0*) Fence Crk Pubng.

***Coffee, Carole J.** Metabolism. 1999. pap. text 18.95 (*1-889325-39-2*) Fence Crk Pubng.

Coffee, Frank. Everything You Need to Know about Creative Home Financing: New Affordable Ways to Buy (& Sell) a Home, Condo, or Co-Op. 256p. 1983. pap. 6.95 (*0-671-44295-3*) S&S Trade.

Coffee, Frank, ed. see Waldman, Carl & Donovan, Jim.

Coffee, Hugh L. Ditch Medicine: Advanced Field Procedures for Emergencies. (Illus.). 224p. 1993. pap. 25.00 (*0-87364-717-3*) Paladin Pr.

Coffee, J. M., ed. The Atwood-Coffee Catalogue of United States & Canadian Transportation Tokens, 2 vols. 4th ed. 1348p. 1982. 55.00 (*0-318-13314-8*) Am Vecturist.

— Atwood-Coffee Catalogue of United States & Canadian Transportation Tokens, Vol. III. 946p. 1986. 50.00 (*0-318-21989-1*) Am Vecturist.

Coffee, J. M., jt. auth. see Ford, H. V.

Coffee, Jessie M. Faulkner's Un-Christlike Christians: Biblical Allusions in the Novels. LC 83-5795. (Studies in Modern Literature: No. 20). 169p. reprint ed. pap. 52.40 (*0-8357-1432-2*, 207063100011) Bks Demand.

Coffee, Jill Swedlow. Horse of the Future: The Miniature Horse. (Illus.). 180p. 1992. pap. 16.95 (*0-944963-09-9*) Glastonbury CA.

C

An Asterisk (*) at the beginning of an entry indicates that the title is appearing for the first time.

Coffee, John C., Jr., et al, eds. Knights, Raiders & Targets: The Impact of the Hostile Takeover. (Illus.). 560p. (C). 1988. pap. text 46.95 (*0-19-504404-5*) OUP.

Coffee, John C., Jr., et al. Securities Regulation, Cases & Materials. 7th ed. (University Casebook Ser.). 1992. text 48.95 (*0-88277-967-2*) Foundation Pr.

Coffee, John C., Jr., jt. auth. see Klein, William A.

Coffee, Lenore. Storyline: Recollections of a Hollywood Screenwriter. LC 74-156808. 212p. 1973. write for info. (*0-304-29245-1*) Continuum.

***Coffee, Linda.** Four Ingredient Cookbooks. (Illus.). 2000. 16.95 (*0-9677932-4-6*) Cookbook.

Coffee, Linda & Cale, Emily. The Four Ingredient Cookbook. 114p. 1991. pap. 9.95 (*0-9628550-0-6*) Coffee & Cale.

***Coffee, Linda & Cale, Emily.** The Four Ingredient Cookbooks: As Easy As: 1 2 3 4, 3 bks. in 1. 1998. 19.95 (*0-9628550-3-0*, Pub. by Coffee & Cale) Bk Marketing Plus.

Coffee, Linda & Cale, Emily. More of the Four Ingredient Cookbook. 121p. 1994. pap. 9.95 (*0-9628550-1-4*) Coffee & Cale.

Coffee, Linda, jt. auth. see Cale, Emily.

Coffee, Peter. Peter Coffee Teaches PCs. LC 98-85044. 1998. 19.99 (*0-7897-1703-4*) Que.

Coffee, Robert & Scase, Richard. Women in Charge: The Experience of Female Entrepreneurs. 180p. 1985. pap. text 15.95 (*0-04-301190-X*) Routledge.

Coffee, Russell G. The Truth about Rainforest Destruction: Facts, False Progress & Future Directions. 125p. 1996. pap. 9.95 (*0-9641721-0-0*) Better Planet.

Coffeen, J. A. The End of the Word: A Book of Bro-ken Words. unabridged ed. Coffeen, M. H., ed. (Illus.). 127p. 1999. pap. 9.50 (*0-930271-01-7*) Grounder Pub.

— Seismic Exploration Fundamentals. 2nd ed. 360p. 1986. 79.95 (*0-87814-295-9*) PennWell Bks.

Coffeen, James A. Interpreting Seismic Data. 210p. 1984. student ed. 15.00 (*0-87814-259-2*) PennWell Bks.

— Rhymes of the Orbiters, Pioneers in Space. (Illus.). 98p. (Orig.). 1984. pap. 9.95 (*0-930271-00-9*) Grounder Pub.

— Seismic on Screen: An Introduction to Interactive Interpretation. 306p. 1990. 25.00 (*0-87814-364-5*) PennWell Bks.

Coffeen, M. H., ed. see Coffeen, J. A.

Coffeen, Mary. Central Coast Wildflowers: Monterey, San Luis Obispo & Santa Barbara Counties. (Illus.). 192p. 1993. pap. 12.95 (*0-945092-21-0*) EZ Nature.

Coffel, Steve. Encyclopedia of Garbage. LC 96-4345. 320p. 1996. 60.00 (*0-8160-3135-5*) Facts on File.

Coffelt. Dogs in Space: Big Book. LC 91-29036. (Illus.). 40p. (J). 1998. pap. 23.95 (*0-15-201015-7*) Harcourt.

Coffelt, Joan W. & Coffelt, Robert. Birth of the Earth & the San Juans: Tracking Clues & Fossils. (Illus.). 64p. 1999. pap. 15.00 (*0-9629890-6-1*, 7671) Coffelt.

Coffelt, N. Good Night, Sigmund! LC 91-14708. (Illus.). 40p. (J). (ps-1). 1992. 13.95 (*0-15-200464-5*, Gulliver Bks) Harcourt.

Coffelt, Nancy. Dogs in Space. LC 91-29036. (Illus.). 32p. (J). (ps-2). 1993. 14.95 (*0-15-200440-8*, Gulliver Bks) Harcourt.

— Dogs in Space. LC 91-29036. (Illus.). 40p. (J). (ps-2). 1996. pap. 6.00 (*0-15-201004-1*, Voyager Bks) Harcourt.

— Good Night, Sigmund. 1997. pap. 6.00 (*0-15-201514-0*) Harcourt.

***Coffelt, Nancy.** The Great Space Doghouse. Eagle, Lynnea & Siegel, Joseph, eds. (Illus.). 36p. (J). 2000. pap. 9.95 (*1-883772-53-2*) Flying Rhino.

Coffelt, Nancy. Tom's Fish. LC 92-44114. (Illus.). 32p. (J). (ps-3). 1994. 13.95 (*0-15-200587-0*, Gulliver Bks) Harcourt.

Coffelt, Robert, jt. auth. see Coffelt, Joan W.

Coffelt, Robert J. & Wikman-Coffelt, Joan. Kauffelds (Coffelt) in America. (Illus.). 260p. (Orig.). 1991. pap. text 12.00 (*0-9629890-0-2*) Coffelt.

— Kauffelds in America. 260p. 1991. write for info. (*0-9629890-5-3*) Coffelt.

Coffen, David L. Organic Syntheses: An Annual Publication of Satisfactory Methods for the Preparation of Organic Chemicals, Vol. 72. 333p. 1994. 68.50 (*0-471-30727-0*) Wiley.

Coffen, Harold G. Origin by Design. LC 82-21445. (Illus.). 494p. 1983. pap. 16.99 (*0-8280-0131-6*) Review & Herald.

Coffen, Richard, ed. see Paulien, Jon.

Coffen, Richard, ed. see Slack, Juanita.

Coffen, Richard W., ed. see Vasi, Dianne.

Coffer, Walter, jt. auth. see Faulkenberry, Luces M.

Coffern, Amy J., jt. auth. see Gilley, Jerry W.

Coffey. Europe Toward 2001. 1996. pap. text 91.00 (*0-7923-3892-8*) Kluwer Academic.

Coffey, ed. Rodd's Chemistry of Carbon Compounds Vol. 4, Pt. G: Six-Membered Heterocyclic Compounds with a Single Nitrogen Atom from Group V of the Periodic Table. 506p. 1977. 357.50 (*0-444-41644-7*) Elsevier.

Coffey, Amanda & Atkinson, Paul. Making Sense of Qualitative Data: Complimentary Research Strategies. LC 95-41813. 220p. (C). 1996. 44.00 (*0-8039-7052-8*); pap. 18.50 (*0-8039-7053-6*) Sage.

— Occupational Socialization & Working Lives. LC 94-12176. (Cardiff Papers in Qualitative Research). 160p. 1994. 72.95 (*1-85628-574-X*, Pub. by Avebry) Ashgate Pub Co.

Coffey, Amanda, jt. ed. see Pilcher, Jane.

Coffey, B. R., ed. Blokes: Stories from Australian Lives. 190p. 1998. pap. 14.95 (*1-86368-234-1*, Pub. by Fremantle Arts) Intl Spec Bk.

***Coffey, B. R., ed.** Summer Days. (Illus.). 192p. 1999. pap. 16.95 (*1-86368-248-1*, Pub. by Fremantle Arts) Intl Spec Bk.

Coffey, Brian. Selected Poems. (Belacqua Ser.). 68p. 1971. pap. 14.95 (*0-906897-61-0*) Dufour.

Coffey, Brian M. Lobster Lover's Cookbook. 2nd rev. ed. 192p. (Orig.). 1996. pap. 9.95 (*0-924771-87-9*, Covered Brdge Pr) Douglas Charles Ltd.

Coffey, Brian R. Quick & Easy Guide to Bible Prophecy. LC 99-22608. 1999. pap. text 5.99 (*0-8423-3842-X*) Tyndale Hse.

Coffey, C. Edward, ed. The Clinical Science of Electroconvulsive Therapy. (Progress in Psychiatry Ser.: No. 38). 259p. 1993. text 12.95 (*0-88048-470-5*, 8470) Am Psychiatric.

Coffey, C. Edward & Brumback, Roger A. Textbook of Pediatric Neuropsychiatry. LC 97-15724. 1566p. 1998. 179.00 (*0-88048-766-6*, 8766) Am Psychiatric.

***Coffey, C. Edward & Cummings, Jeffrey L.** The American Psychiatric Press Textbook of Geriatric Neuropsychiatry. 2nd ed. LC 99-33987. 2000. 150.00 (*0-88048-841-7*) Am Psychiatric.

Coffey, Cris, ed. & illus. see Ferris, Stan.

***Coffey, D. J.** Review Questions for Clinical Neurology Board Review. (Review Questions Ser.). (Illus.). 200p. 2000. pap. 34.95 (*1-85070-054-0*) Prthnon Pub.

Coffey, D. J., jt. auth. see Henderson, G. N.

Coffey, D. S., et al, eds. Multidisciplinary Analysis of Controversies in the Management of Prostate Cancer. LC 88-18004. (Illus.). 350p. 1988. 89.50 (*0-306-42927-6*, Plenum Trade) Perseus Pubng.

Coffey, Dan. I Know More Than You Do! 1992. pap. 9.95 incl. audio (*0-942110-80-3*, Pub. by HighBridge) Penguin Putnam.

Coffey, David. Deus Trinitas: The Doctrine of the Triune God. LC 98-28134. 208p. 1999. text 35.00 (*0-19-512472-3*) OUP.

Coffey, David J., et al. Photographic Case Studies in Neurology: Diagnostic Tests for the Practitioner. (Photographic Case Studies). 96p. 1993. text. write for info. (*0-9633775-2-3*); pap. text. write for info. (*0-9633775-3-1*) Clinical Comms.

Coffey, Dennis. Guitars, Cars & Motown Superstars. Gilbert, Gordon G. G., ed. 1999. pap. write for info. (*0-9658794-3-7*) Pitbull Publ.

***Coffey, Donnis.** Hooked. LC 00-90232. 2000. pap. 7.95 (*0-533-13496-X*) Vantage.

Coffey, F. Always Home: Fifty Years of the USO-The Official Photographic History. (Illus.). 190p. 1991. 29.95 (*0-08-040576-2*) Brasseys.

Coffey, Frank. Complete Idiot's Guide to Elvis. LC 97-71189. 368p. 1997. 18.95 (*0-02-861873-4*) Macmillan Gen Ref.

— Why Do They Call It a Birdie? 1,001 Fascinating Facts about Golf. LC 97-21506. (Illus.). 160p. 1997. 14.95 (*1-55972-429-3*, Birch Ln Pr) Carol Pub Group.

***Coffey, Frank & Waldman, Carl.** Dumies Guide for Complete Idoits: The Southpaw Edition. 2000. pap. 9.95 (*1-58008-206-8*) Ten Speed Pr.

Coffey, James R., ed. Operational Costs in Acquisitions. LC 90-49254. (Acquisitions Librarian Ser.: Vol. 4). 117p. 1991. text 39.95 (*1-56024-008-3*) Haworth Pr.

Coffey, James V. Reports of Decisions in Probate (Coffey's Reports), 6 vols. LC 96-80213. 1996. reprint ed. 495.00 (*1-57588-204-3*) W S Hein.

Coffey, Jerry, ed. see Lischner, Ray.

Coffey, Jill Swedlow. The Miniature Horse: The Complete Guild to the Fascinating World of Miniatures. (Illus.). 1992. reprint ed. pap. 16.95 (*0-944963-02-1*) Glastonbury CA.

Coffey, John. Adult Connect the Dots. (Illus.). 64p. 1997. pap. 5.95 (*1-889647-19-5*) Boston Am.

— Politics, Religion & the British Revolutions: The Mind of Samuel Rutherford. (Cambridge Studies in Early Modern British History). 320p. (C). 1997. text 59.95 (*0-521-58172-9*) Cambridge U Pr.

***Coffey, John F.** Me & the Education of Johnnie Negro. LC 00-190845. 372p. 2000. 25.00 (*0-7388-2018-0*); pap. 18.00 (*0-7388-2019-9*) Xlibris Corp.

Coffey, John W., II. Finding the Forgotten: Landscape Paintings by John Beerman. (Illus.). 19p. (Orig.). 1991. pap. 6.95 (*0-88259-962-3*) NCMA.

Coffey, John W. Making Faces: Self-Portraits by Alex Katz. LC 90-60420. (Illus.). 32p. (Orig.). 1990. pap. 10.95 (*0-88259-958-5*) NCMA.

Coffey, John W., II. Moshe Kupferman: Between Oblivion & Remembrance. LC 91-62645. (Illus.). 64p. (Orig.). 1991. pap. 19.95 (*0-88259-963-1*) NCMA.

Coffey, John W. Political Realism in American Thought. 217p. 1978. 32.50 (*0-8387-1903-1*) Bucknell U Pr.

— Twilight of Arcadia: American Landscape Painters in Rome, 1830-1880. LC 87-70111. (Illus.). 89p. (Orig.). 1987. pap. 15.00 (*0-916606-14-7*) Bowdoin Coll.

Coffey, Joseph I. Arms Control & European Security: A Guide to East-West Negotiations. LC 76-29615. (Special Studies). 271p. 1977. 75.00 (*0-275-90259-5*, C0259, Praeger Pubs) Greenwood.

— The Future Role of NATO. Hoepli-Phalon, Nancy, ed. LC 97-60622. (Headline Ser.: No. 311). (Illus.). 72p. 1997. pap. 5.95 (*0-87124-175-7*) Foreign Policy.

Coffey, Judith & Rainbow Creative Concepts. Ballet, Tap & All That Jazz! The Essential Guide for Today's Young Dancer, Cheerleader, Skater. 1998. pap. 25.00 (*0-925162-22-1*) Rainbow Ed Concepts.

Coffey, Kathy. Children & Christian Initiation: A Practical Guide. 80p. 1995. pap. 14.95 (*0-8192-8000-3*) Liv Good News.

Coffey, Kathy. Children & Christian Initiation: A Practical Guide to Mystagogy. 40p. 1995. pap. 4.95 (*0-8192-8004-6*) Liv Good News.

Coffey, Kathy. Children & Christian Initiation: A Practical Guide to Purification & Enlightenment Vol. 4. Youngquist, Jo, ed. (Illus.). 40p. 1995. pap. 4.95 (*0-8192-8003-8*) Liv Good News.

— Children & Christian Initiation: A Practical Guide to the Prechatechumenate. 40p. 1995. pap. 4.95 (*0-8192-8001-1*) Liv Good News.

Coffey, Kathy. Dancing in the Margins: Meditations for People Who Struggle with Their Churches. LC 99-22091. 1999. pap. 14.95 (*0-8245-1815-2*) Crossroad NY.

— Experiencing God with Your Children. LC 96-36912. 168p. 1997. pap. 14.95 (*0-8245-1647-8*) Crossroad NY.

— God in the Moment: Making Every Day a Prayer. LC 98-52474. 200p. 1999. 16.95 (*0-8294-1174-7*, Wild Onion) Loyola Pr.

— The Hidden Women of the Gospels. 132p. 1996. pap. 14.95 (*0-8245-1561-7*) Crossroad NY.

— My Path to Easter: Initiation Journal for Children. (Children & Christian Initiation Ser.). (Illus.). 40p. (J). (gr. 1-4). 1997. 5.95 (*1-889108-35-9*) Liv Good News.

— My Path to Easter: Initiation Journal for Youth. (Children & Christian Initiation Ser.). (Illus.). 40p. (J). (gr. 5-9). 1997. 5.95 (*1-889108-36-7*) Liv Good News.

***Coffey, Kathy.** Preparing for Baptism & Nurturing Your Child's Spirituality: Parent Guide. (Baptism & Beyond Ser.: Vol. 2). (Illus.). 160p. 2000. pap. 10.95 (*1-889108-72-3*) Liv Good News.

— Sessions for Parents: Leader's Guide. (Baptism & Beyond Ser.: Vol. 1). 40p. 2000. pap., teacher ed. 9.95 (*1-889108-71-5*) Liv Good News.

Coffey, Kathy. Thresholds to Prayer, Vol. 1. 144p. 1998. pap. 9.95 (*0-86716-295-3*, B2953) St Anthony Mess Pr.

Coffey, Kathy & Youngquist, Jo. Children & Christian Initiation: A Practical Guide to the Catecheumenate. 40p. 1995. pap. 4.95 (*0-8192-8002-X*) Liv Good News.

Coffey, Kathy, jt. auth. see Morris, Thomas H.

Coffey, Kathy, ed. see Figlino, Mary A., et al.

Coffey, Kathy, ed. see McGovern, Kathy.

Coffey, Kathy, ed. see Pike, Maggie, et al.

Coffey, Kathy, ed. see Pramuk, Christopher.

Coffey, Kathy, ed. see Reese, Mary A.

Coffey, Kathy, ed. see Rockers, Colleen.

Coffey, Kendall. Florida Foreclosures: Remedies, Defenses, & Lender Liability, 2 vols., Set. LC 92-20556. 1000p. Date not set. ring bd. 180.00 (*0-409-27217-5*, 80656-10, MICHIE) LEXIS Pub.

— Florida Foreclosures, Remedies, Defenses & Lender Liability, 2 vols. 1995. ring bd. 180.00 (*0-327-03907-8*, 80656-10, MICHIE) LEXIS Pub.

Coffey, Kenneth J. Strategic Implications of the All-Volunteer Force: The Conventional Defense of Central Europe. LC 79-19110. (Studies on Armed Forces & Society). 220p. reprint ed. pap. 68.20 (*0-8357-4405-1*, 203722500008) Bks Demand.

Coffey-Lewis, Lou. Be Restored to Health. 1984. mass mkt. 2.95 (*0-345-31645-2*) Ballantine Pub Grp.

Coffey, Lonny, jt. auth. see Boyd, Patricia.

Coffey, M. Roman Satire. 2nd ed. (Bristol Classical Paperbacks Ser.). 312p. 1989. pap. 29.95 (*1-85399-046-9*, Pub. by Brist Class Pr) Focus Pub-R Pullins.

Coffey, Margaret P. Communication Through Writing. (Illus.). 208p. 1987. pap. text 36.33 (*0-13-152984-6*) P-H.

— Fitting In: A Functional-National Test for Learners of English. (Illus.). 224p. 1983. pap. text 13.50 (*0-13-320820-6*) P-H.

Coffey, Margaret P. & Grace, Susan. Intercultural Advising in English-Language Programs. LC 97-37904. 1997. pap. write for info. (*0-912207-76-0*) NAFSA Washington.

Coffey, Maria. A Boat in Our Baggage. 1995. pap. text 13.95 (*0-07-015547-X*) McGraw.

— A Cat in a Kayak. (Illus.). 32p. (J). (ps-4). 1998. pap. 6.95 (*1-55037-508-3*, Pub. by Annick); lib. bdg. 16.95 (*1-55037-509-1*, Pub. by Annick) Firefly Bks Ltd.

***Coffey, Maria.** Fragile Edge: A Personal Portrait of Loss on Everest. LC 00-9289. (Illus.). 192p. 2000. pap. 16.95 (*0-89886-737-1*) Mountaineers.

— Fragile Edge: Living with Loss on Everest. rev. ed. (Illus.). 192p. 1999. pap. 16.95 (*1-55017-218-2*) Harbour Pub Co.

Coffey, Maria. Sailing Back in Time: A Nostalgic Voyage on Canada's West Coast. (Illus.). 168p. 1996. 34.95 (*1-55110-487-3*) Gr Arts Ctr Pub.

— A Seal in the Family. (Illus.). 32p. (J). (gr. k-3). 1999. pap. 6.95 (*1-55037-580-6*, Pub. by Annick Pr) Firefly Bks Ltd.

***Coffey, Maria.** A Seal in the Family. (Illus.). 32p. (J). (gr. k-3). 1999. lib. bdg. 17.95 (*1-55037-581-4*, Pub. by Annick Pr) Firefly Bks Ltd.

***Coffey, Maria & Pearson, Debora.** Jungle Islands: My South Sea Adventure. (Adventure Ser.). (Illus.). 88p. (YA). (gr. 3). 2000. lib. bdg. 26.95 (*1-55037-597-0*, Pub. by Annick Pr) Firefly Bks Ltd.

— Jungle Islands: My South Sea Adventure. (Adventure Ser.). (Illus.). 88p. (YA). (gr. 3 up). 2000. pap. 14.95 (*1-55037-596-2*, Pub. by Annick Pr) Firefly Bks Ltd.

Coffey, Marilyn. Great Plains Patchwork: A Memoir. LC 89-34091. 199p. 1989. reprint ed. pap. 61.70 (*0-608-00038-8*, 206080400006) Bks Demand.

Coffey, Marilyn & Bogan, Kathleen. Prairie Hearts: Women View the Midwest. Scott, Whitney, ed. (Illus.). 208p. (Orig.). 1996. pap. 14.95 (*0-9621039-3-4*) Outrider Pr.

Coffey, Mary A. & Moss, Murphy. Deliverance of a Treasure: The Cupola House Association & It's Mission. LC 95-71888. 84p. (Orig.). 1995. pap. 10.00 (*1-884570-41-0*) Research Triangle.

Coffey, Michael. Days of Infamy: Great Military Blunders of the 20th Century. LC 99-30839. 320p. 1999. 24.95 (*0-7868-6556-3*, Pub. by Hyperion) Time Warner.

***Coffey, Michael.** 87 North: Poems. LC 98-56290. 104p. 1999. pap. 13.95 (*1-56689-085-3*, Pub. by Coffee Hse) SPD-Small Pr Dist.

Coffey, Michael. Elemenopy. (New American Poetry Ser.: No. 22). 100p. 1995. pap. 10.95 (*1-55713-240-2*) Sun & Moon CA.

— Great Blunders of the 20th Century. 2001. mass mkt. write for info. (*0-7868-8958-6*, Pub. by Disney Pr) Little.

***Coffey, Michael.** The Irish in America. 288p. 2000. pap. 19.95 (*0-7868-8543-2*, Pub. by Disney Pr) Time Warner.

Coffey, Michael. Military Blunders. 320p. 2000. pap. 15.95 (*0-7868-8470-3*, Pub. by Hyperion) Time Warner.

Coffey, Michael, ed. The Irish in America. LC 97-21907. (Illus.). 256p. (J). 1997. 40.00 (*0-7868-6344-7*, Pub. by Hyperion) Time Warner.

Coffey, Michael, jt. auth. see Chaloner, Chris.

***Coffey, November.** Tortured Eves, Contemporary Monologues for Women, One. 43p. 1999. reprint ed. pap. 12.00 (*0-9677176-0-4*, 701) Quiet Scream Pub.

Coffey, Osa & Carter, Dianne. Improving Corrections Education: Two Perspectives for Vocational Education. 38p. 1986. 4.25 (*0-318-21256-0*, OC111); VHS 125.00 (*0-317-01378-5*, VS108VHS, VS108UM) Ctr Educ Trng Employ.

***Coffey, Osa D.** Choosing Life Skills: A Guide for Selecting Life Skills Programs for Adult & Juvenile Offenders. 88p. 1998. pap. 8.50 (*0-16-049467-2*) USGPO.

***Coffey, Osa D. & Knoll, John F.** Choosing Life Skills: A Guide for Selecting Life Skills Programs for Adult & Juvenile Offenders. (Illus.). 76p. (C). 2000. reprint ed. pap. text 20.00 (*0-7881-8481-4*) DIANE Pub.

Coffey, Osa D., et al. Correctional Education: Perspective on Programs for Adult Offenders. Wolford, Bruce I., ed. (Eric Information Analysis Ser.). 53p. 1986. 7.00 (*0-318-22356-2*, IN 310) Ctr Educ Trng Employ.

Coffey, Paul, jt. auth. see Bartley, Richard.

***Coffey, Peter.** Europe: Toward the Next Enlargement. LC 00-37074. 2000. write for info. (*0-7923-7847-4*) Kluwer Academic.

Coffey, Peter. Europe-Toward 2001. (International Studies in Economics & Econometrics). 392p. (C). 1996. lib. bdg. 195.00 (*0-7923-3891-X*) Kluwer Academic.

— European Monetary System. 1986. lib. bdg. 84.00 (*90-247-3446-0*, Pub. by M Nijhoff) Kluwer Academic.

— The Future of Europe. LC 93-49829. 224p. 1995. 85.00 (*1-85278-586-1*); pap. 25.00 (*1-85278-587-X*) E Elgar.

— Latin America - Mercosur. LC 98-15004. (International Handbooks on Economic Integration). 263p. 1998. 150.00 (*0-7923-8152-1*); pap. 59.95 (*0-7923-8153-X*) Kluwer Academic.

— Main Economic Policy Areas of the EEC. 1983. lib. bdg. 94.00 (*90-247-2793-6*) Kluwer Academic.

***Coffey, Peter.** Nafta-Past, Present & Future LC 99-13099. (International Handbooks on Economic Integration). xxiv, 187p. 1999. write for info. (*0-7923-8482-2*) Kluwer Academic.

Coffey, Peter. Ontology. 1990. 16.50 (*0-8446-1119-0*) Peter Smith.

Coffey, Peter, ed. Main Economic Policy Areas of the EC after 1992. 4th ed. LC 93-24818. (International Studies in Economics & Econometrics: Vol. 30). 1993. lib. bdg. 138.50 (*0-7923-2375-0*) Kluwer Academic.

— Main Economic Policy Areas of the EEC - Toward 1992: The Challenge to the Community's Economic Policies When the "Real" Common Market Is Created by the End of 1992. 3rd rev. ed. (C). 1990. lib. bdg. 120.00 (*0-7923-0810-7*) Kluwer Academic.

Coffey, Peter & Correa Do Lago, Luiz, eds. The EEC & Brazil: Trade, Capital Investment, & the Debt Problem. 280p. 1992. 52.50 (*0-86187-969-4*, Pub. by P P Pubs) Cassell & Continuum.

Coffey, Peter, jt. auth. see Angarita, Ciro.

***Coffey, Phil.** Martin Brodeur: Picture Perfect. (SuperStar Ser.: Vol. 6). (Illus.). 96p. 1999. pap. 4.95 (*1-58261-157-2*, Pub. by Sprts Pubng) Partners-West.

Coffey, Rebecca. Unspeakable Truths & Happy Endings: Human Cruelty & the New Trauma Therapy. LC 97-30737. 248p. (Orig.). 1998. pap. 19.95 (*1-886968-05-5*) Sidran Pr.

Coffey, Richard. Virtual Health Systems: A Guide to Assessing Organizational Readiness & Strategic Partners. LC 97-39788. 1997. 36.95 (*0-7879-1078-3*) Jossey-Bass.

Coffey, Richard J., jt. auth. see Gaucher, Ellen M.

Coffey, Richard J., jt. auth. see Marszalek-Gaucher, Ellen.

Coffey, Richard T. New Horizons: An AOCS CSMA Detergent Industry Conference. LC 96-49995. 1996. 60.00 (*0-935315-78-0*) Am Oil Chemists.

Coffey, Robert & Cook, Curtis. Management & Organizational Behavior. (C). 1994. text 66.25 (*0-256-18239-6*, Irwn McGrw-H) McGrw-H Hghr Educ.

Coffey, Robert, et al. Management & Organizational Behavior. 168p. (C). 1994. text, student ed. 26.87 (*0-256-16655-2*, Irwn McGrw-H) McGrw-H Hghr Educ.

Coffey, Robert E., et al. Management & Organizational Behavior. LC 93-36578. 672p. (C). 1993. text 68.95 (*0-256-11685-7*, Irwn Prfssnl) McGraw-Hill Prof.

Coffey, Robert J. Neuroimaging Atlas of Radiosurgery. LC 97-10983. 224p. 1997. text 99.00 (*0-397-51766-1*) Lppncott W & W.

Coffey, Ronald G., ed. Granulocyte Responses to Cytokines: Basic & Clinical Research. LC 92-18487. (Immunology Ser.: Vol. 57). (Illus.). 736p. 1992. text 245.00 (*0-8247-8655-6*) Dekker.

Coffey, Rosalie L. & Glenn, John S. Completing the Promise. (Religious Awards for Boy Scouts Ser.). 1984. pap. 4.95 (*0-938758-17-9*) MTM Pub Co.

Coffey, Rosemary K. & Howard, Elizabeth F. America As Story: Historical Fiction for Middle & Secondary Schools. 2nd ed. LC 96-43453. 240p. 1997. 25.00 (*0-8389-0702-4*) ALA.

Coffey, S. Rodd's Chemistry of Carbon Compounds Vol. 4, Pt. A: Three, Four & Five-Membered Heterocyclic Compounds. 650p. 1973. 407.50 (*0-444-41093-7*) Elsevier.

C

An Asterisk (*) at the beginning of an entry indicates that the title is appearing for the first time.

— Rodd's Chemistry of Carbon Compounds Vol. 4, Pt. E: Heterocyclic Compounds; Six-Membered Monoeterocyclic Compounds. 522p. 1977. 357.50 (*0-444-41363-4*) Elsevier.

— Rodd's Chemistry of Carbon Compounds Vol. 4, Pt. J: Proteins. 1989. 460.75 (*0-685-84873-6*) Elsevier.

— Rodd's Chemistry of Carbon Compounds Vol. 4, Pt. K: Six Membered Heterocyclic Compounds with Two or More Hetero-Atoms. 552p. 1979. 357.50 (*0-444-41647-1*) Elsevier.

Coffey, S., ed. Rodd's Chemistry of Carbon Compounds Vol. 4, Pt. L: Heterocyclic Compounds, Fused-Ring Heterocycles with Three or More N Atoms. 506p. 1980. 322.00 (*0-444-40664-6*) Elsevier.

— Rodd's Chemistry of Carbon Compounds Vol. 4, Pt. L: Heterocyclic Compunds, Fused-Ring Heterocycles with Three or More N Atoms. 506p. 1980. 357.50 (*0-444-41768-0*) Elsevier.

— Rodd's Chemistry of Carbon Compounds Vol. 4, Pt. H: Heterocyclic Compounds. 2nd ed. 536p. 1978. 357.50 (*0-444-41575-0*) Elsevier.

Coffey, S. & Ansell, M. F., eds. Rodd's Chemistry of Carbon Compounds Vol. 4, Pt. C: Heterocyclic Compounds; Five-Membered Heterocyclic Compounds with Two Hetero-Atoms in the Ring from Groups V or VI of the Periodic Table. 2nd ed. 594p. 1986. 562.50 (*0-444-42555-1*) Elsevier.

— Rodd's Chemistry of Carbon Compounds Heterocyclic Compounds, Vol. 4, Pt. D: Five Membered Heterocyclic Compunds with More Than Two Hetero-Atoms in the Ring. 274p. 1986. 281.00 (*0-444-42556-X*) Elsevier.

Coffey, Thomas F., Jr. Only in Savannah: Stories & Insights on Georgia's Mother City. LC 93-37722. 1993. 22.00 (*0-913720-84-4*) Beil.

Coffey, Thomas F. & McGovern, Terrence J., eds. A Middle French Translation of Bernard Gui's Shorter Historical Works by Jean Golein. LC 93-15104. 660p. 1993. text 129.95 (*0-7734-9263-1*) E Mellen.

Coffey, Thomas H., jt. auth. see Kramer, Stanley.

Coffey, Thomas M. Iron Eagle: The Turbulent Life of General Curtis LeMay. xvi, 496p. 1988. mass mkt. 4.95 (*0-380-70480-3*, Avon Bks) Morrow Avon.

Coffey, Thomas M., jt. auth. see Kramer, Stanley.

***Coffey, Thomas P.** A Boy Descending into Black Hell: The Adventures of Tom in Coal Country. unabridged ed. 112p. 2000. pap. 8.95 (*0-87193-318-7*) Dimension Bks.

Coffey, Thomas P. A Candle in the Wind: My Thirty Years in Book Publishing. 222p. 1984. pap. 5.95 (*0-87193-212-1*) Dimension Bks.

— The Morristown Courthouse Atrocity, Vol. 1. (Studies in Judicial Perversion). 96p. 1995. pap. 6.95 (*0-87193-300-4*) Dimension Bks.

— The Morristown Courthouse Atrocity, Vol. 2. (Studies in Judicial Perversion). 1995. pap. 4.95 (*0-87193-301-2*) Dimension Bks.

— The Morristown Courthouse Atrocity, Vol. 3. (Studies in Judicial Perversion). 96p. (J). 1997. pap. 4.95 (*0-87193-302-0*) Dimension Bks.

— The Morristown Courthouse Atrocity, Vol. 4. (Studies in Judicial Perversion). 1997. pap. 4.95 (*0-87193-303-9*) Dimension Bks.

— One Man Said No: Fighting Judicial Corruption in New Jersey. 144p. 1998. pap. 9.95 (*0-87193-317-9*) Dimension Bks.

— There Is a Singing Underneath: Meditations in Central Park. 120p. 1984. pap. 4.95 (*0-87193-217-2*) Dimension Bks.

— Windows on the Night: My Dreams & Their Meaning. 112p. 1998. pap. 14.95 (*0-87193-290-3*) Dimension Bks.

Coffey, Timothy. History & Folklore of North American Wildflowers. 378p. 1994. pap. 16.00 (*0-395-51593-9*) HM.

Coffey, Tom. The Serpent Club. LC 99-26938. 322p. 1999. 23.00 (*0-671-02827-8*, PB Hardcover) PB.

***Coffey, Tom.** The Serpent Club. 416p. 2000. reprint ed. per. 6.99 (*0-671-02828-6*) PB.

Coffey, Tony. Once a Catholic. LC 92-45212. 166p. 1993. pap. 8.99 (*1-56507-045-3*) Harvest Hse.

— Una Vez Fui Catolico: Lo Que Necesita Saber Sobre el Catolicismo Romano. (SPA.). 176p. 1994. pap. 7.99 (*0-8254-1124-6*, Edit Portavoz) Kregel.

Coffey, Vincent J. The Battle of Gettysburg. LC 84-40834. (Turning Points in American History Ser.). (Illus.). 64p. (J). (gr. 5 up). 1985. lib. bdg. 14.95 (*0-382-06830-0*) Silver Burdett Pr.

— The Battle of Gettysburg. LC 84-40834. (Turning Points in American History Ser.). (Illus.). 64p. (YA). (gr. 5 up). 1985. pap. 7.95 (*0-382-09911-7*) Silver Burdett Pr.

Coffey, W. t. & Kalmykov, Yu P. The Langevin Equation & Its Applications to Stochastic Problems in Physics, Chemistry. (Contemporary Chemical Physics Ser.). 500p. 1996. text 99.00 (*981-02-1651-3*) World Scientific Pub.

Coffey, Walt. A Bartender's View of Life: 101 Things You Sure Didn't Learn in School. LC 97-72779. (Illus.). 78p. (Orig.). 1997. pap. 12.95 (*1-890622-02-8*) Leathers Pub.

Coffey, Wayne. Jim Thorpe: Athlete of the Century. LC 92-21230. (Olympic Gold! Ser.). (Illus.). 64p. (J). (gr. 5-7). 1993. lib. bdg. 12.25 (*1-56711-001-0*) Blackbirch.

— The Kobe Bryant Story. LC 99-204991. (Fast Breaks Ser.). (Illus.). 64p. (J). (gr. 2-5). 1999. pap. 4.99 (*0-590-05234-9*) Scholastic Inc.

***Coffey, Wayne.** Meet the Women of American Soccer: An Inside Look at America's Team. LC 99-232061. (Illus.). 48p. (gr. 2-7). 1999. pap. text 5.99 (*0-439-08654-X*) Scholastic Inc.

— Wilma Rudolph: Beating the Odds. LC 92-41292. (Olympic Gold! Ser.). (Illus.). 64p. (J). (gr. 5-7). 1993. lib. bdg. 12.25 (*1-56711-004-5*) Blackbirch.

Coffey, Wayne, jt. auth. see Miller, Faye Y.

Coffey, William, ed. Relaxation Phenomena in Condensed Matter. (Advances in Chemical Physics Ser.: Vol. 87). 784p. 1994. 249.00 (*0-471-30312-7*) Wiley.

Coffey, William E. & Riddel, Frank S. American Government: The U. S. A. & West Virginia. Buckalew, Marshall, ed. (Illus.). 304p. (J). (gr. 8). 1990. 25.00 (*0-914498-08-8*) WV Hist Ed Found.

Coffey, William E., et al. West Virginia Government. Buckalew, Marshall & Thoenen, Eugenia G., eds. (Illus.). 112p. (Orig.). (J). (gr. 8). 1984. pap. 10.00 (*0-914498-05-3*) WV Hist Ed Found.

Coffey, William J. Evolution of Canada's Metropolitan Economies. 1168p. 1994. pap. 15.95 (*0-88645-155-8*, Pub. by Inst Res Pub) Ashgate Pub Co.

Coffey, William J. & McRae, James J. Service Industries in Regional Development. 166p. 1990. pap. text 29.95 (*0-88645-103-5*, Pub. by Inst Res Pub) Ashgate Pub Co.

Coffield, Caroline. A Rococo Adventure, Discovering the Art of Belgian Bobbin Lace. (Illus.). 100p. 1988. 14.95 (*0-915113-05-8*) Bizarre Butterfly.

Coffield, F. Repositioning H E. LC 96-47781. 1997. 124.00 (*0-335-19715-9*); pap. 37.95 (*0-335-19716-7*) OpUniv Pr.

Coffield, Frank & Goodings, Richard, eds. Sacred Cows in Education. 214p. 1984. pap. 25.00 (*0-85224-484-3*, Pub. by Edinburgh U Pr) Col U Pr.

Coffield, Frank, jt. auth. see MacDonald, Robert.

Coffield, Patrick C., text. Pages of Italian Photography, 1900-1998. (Illus.). 216p. 1999. pap. 35.00 (*88-8158-177-9*, Pub. by Charta) Dist Art Pubs.

Coffield, Patrick C., jt. ed. see Shi, Hongchi.

Coffield, Tom. The Badlands Coloring Book. (Illus.). 48p. (Orig.). (J). (gr. 1-5). 1996. pap. 3.95 (*0-9646577-1-6*) Chicken Hse.

— A Brown Bear Coloring Book. (Illus.). 48p. (J). (gr. 1-5). 1995. pap. 3.95 (*0-9646577-0-8*) Chicken Hse.

Coffin. Algebra & Pre-Calculus on the HP 48G/GX. 330p. 1994. pap. 19.95 (*0-931011-43-4*) Grapevine Pubns.

Coffin. The HP 48G/GX Pocket Guide. 80p. 1996. pap. 9.95 (*0-931011-45-0*) Grapevine Pubns.

Coffin & Cohen. Folklore of American Holidays. 3rd ed. LC 98-37035. 608p. 1998. 105.00 (*0-8103-8864-2*, 008502) Gale.

Coffin, Alex. Brookshire & Belk, Businessmen in City Hall. LC 94-27729. 1994. 19.95 (*0-945344-01-5*) UNC Charlotte Urban Inst.

Coffin, Arthur B. The Questions of Tragedy. LC 91-45037. 340p. 1992. lib. bdg. 34.95 (*0-7734-9903-2*) E Mellen.

— Robinson Jeffers: Poet of Inhumanism. LC 74-121767. 324p. 1971. 32.50 (*0-299-05840-9*) U of Wis Pr.

— Robinson Jeffers: Poet of Inhumanism. LC 74-121767. 324p. reprint ed. pap. 100.50 (*0-7837-7022-7*, 204683700004) Bks Demand.

Coffin, Becca, jt. auth. see Stamford, Bryant A.

Coffin, Berton. Coffin's Overtones of Bel Canto: Phonetic Basis of Artistic Singing with One Hundred Chromatic Vowel-Chart Exercises. LC 80-21958. 254p. (C). 1980. text 52.00 (*0-8108-1370-X*); 10.00 (*0-8108-2028-5*) Scarecrow.

— Coffin's Sounds of Singing: Principles & Applications of Vocal Techniques Chromatic Vowel Chart. 2nd ed. LC 86-15491. (Illus.). 314p. 1987. 45.00 (*0-8108-1933-3*) Scarecrow.

— Historical Vocal Pedagogy Classics. LC 89-6258. (Illus.). 319p. 1989. 37.00 (*0-8108-2199-0*) Scarecrow.

— The Singer's Repertoire, 4 vols. 2nd ed. Incl. Vol. 1. Coloratura, Lyric & Dramatic Soprano. LC 60-7265. 1960. text 45.00 (*0-8108-0188-4*); Vol. 2. Mezzo Soprano & Contralto. LC 60-7265. 1960. text 39.50 (*0-8108-0189-2*); Vol. 3. Lyric & Dramatic Tenor. LC 60-7265. 1960. text 39.50 (*0-8108-0190-6*); Vol. 4. Baritone & Bass. LC 60-7265. 1960. text 39.50 (*0-8108-0191-4*); LC 60-7265. 1960. 145.00 (*0-8108-2023-4*) Scarecrow.

Coffin, Berton & Singer, Werner. Program Notes for the Singer's Repertoire. LC 60-7265. 230p. 1962. 32.00 (*0-8108-0169-8*) Scarecrow.

Coffin, Berton, et al. Phonetic Readings of Songs & Arias: With Revised German Transcriptions. 2nd ed. LC 82-874. 400p. (C). 1982. pap. text 38.50 (*0-8108-1533-8*) Scarecrow.

— Word-by-Word Translations of Songs & Arias Pt. 1: German & French. LC 66-13746. 620p. 1966. 55.00 (*0-8108-0149-3*) Scarecrow.

Coffin, Bill. Overmind. (Illus.). (Orig.). (YA). (gr. 10 up). 1995. pap. 9.99 (*0-88092-141-2*); lib. bdg. 23.00 (*0-88092-142-0*) Royal Fireworks.

— Prime Mover. Kemnitz, Myrna, ed. (Illus.). 465p. (Orig.). (YA). (gr. 7 up). 1996. pap. 10.00 (*0-88092-349-0*) Royal Fireworks.

***Coffin, Bill & Siembieda, Kevin.** Baalgor Wastelands. Marciniszyn, Alex et al, eds. (Palladium Sourcebook Ser.: Vol. 9). (Illus.). 216p. (YA). (gr. 8 up). 1999. pap. 20.95 (*1-57457-022-6*, 463) Palladium Bks.

— Century Station. 2nd ed. (Heroes Unlimited Ser.). (Illus.). 224p. (YA). (gr. 8). 2000. pap. 20.95 (*1-57457-040-4*, 517) Palladium Bks.

— Mount Nimro. Marciniszyn, Alex et al, eds. (Palladium Sourcebook Ser.: Vol. 10). (Illus.). 160p. (YA). (gr. 8 up). 1999. pap. 16.95 (*1-57457-028-5*, 464) Palladium Bks.

— Systems Failure. Marciniszyn, Alex et al, eds. (Illus.). 144p. (YA). (gr. 8 up). 1999. pap. 12.95 (*1-57457-038-2*) Palladium Bks.

Coffin, Bill & Siembieda, Kevin. Western Empire. Marciniszyn, Alex et al, eds. (Sourcebook Ser.: Vol. 8). (Illus.). 224p. (YA). (gr. 8 up). 1998. pap. 20.95 (*1-57457-015-3*, 462) Palladium Bks.

Coffin, Carlyn. Noel & His Friends. (Illus.). 130p. (J). (ps up). 1987. pap., bds. 10.95 (*0-931474-30-2*) TBW Bks.

Coffin, Carrie L. Waiting for the Tears to Dry. (Illus.). 180p. Date not set. pap. 16.95 (*1-884540-44-9*) Haleys.

***Coffin, Charles.** Boys of '76, 6 vols., Vol. 3 (Illus.). 400p. 2000. reprint ed. 18.00 (*1-889128-64-3*) Mantle Ministries.

— Building the Nation, 6 vols., Vol. 4. (Illus.). 486p. 2000. reprint ed. write for info. (*1-889128-69-4*) Mantle Ministries.

— Drumbeat of the Nation, 6 vols., Vol. 5. (Illus.). 478p. 2000. write for info. (*1-889128-70-8*) Mantle Ministries.

— Marching to Victory, 6 vols., Vol. 6. 496p. 2000. write for info. (*1-889128-71-6*) Mantle Ministries.

— Old Times in the Colonies. (Illus.). 460p. 2000. write for info. (*1-889128-68-6*) Mantle Ministries.

— The Story of Liberty. (Illus.). 432p. 2000. write for info. (*1-889128-67-8*) Mantle Ministries.

Coffin, Charles C. Boscawen & Webster, 1733-1878. (Illus.). 666p. 1992. reprint ed. lib. bdg. 67.00 (*0-8328-2503-4*) Higginson Bk Co.

— The Boys of '76. 398p. (Orig.). 1998. pap. 16.95 (*0-938558-82-X*) Maranatha.

— Caleb Krinkle. LC 79-83932. (Black Heritage Library Collection). 1977. 36.95 (*0-8369-8545-1*) Ayer.

— Eyewitness to Gettysburg. LC 97-28001. (Illus.). 131p. 1997. 19.95 (*1-57249-065-9*, Burd St Pr) White Mane Pub.

— Four Years of Fighting. LC 74-125687. (American Journalists Ser.). 1977. reprint ed. 35.95 (*0-405-01664-6*) Ayer.

***Coffin, Charles Carleton & Schildt, John W.** Eyewitness to Gettysburg: The Story of Gettysburg as Told by the Leading Correspondent of His Day. LC 00-39632. 2000. pap. write for info. (*0-7838-9088-5*, G K Hall & Co) Mac Lib Ref.

Coffin, Cheryl M., et al. Pediatric Soft Tissue Tumors: A Clinical, Pathological, & Therapeutic Approach. LC 96-27565. (Illus.). 428p. 1997. 99.00 (*0-683-02047-1*) Lppncott W & W.

Coffin, Chris, et al. An Easy Course in Using & Programming the HP48 G/GX. 300p. 1993. pap. 19.95 (*0-931011-41-8*) Grapevine Pubns.

Coffin, Chris, jt. auth. see Coffin, Dan.

Coffin, Chris, jt. auth. see Pearson, Olen.

Coffin, Chris, jt. auth. see Wadman, Ted.

Coffin, Dan & Coffin, Chris. The Answers You Need for the HP-95LX Palmtop PC. 160p. 1991. 9.95 (*0-931011-35-3*) Grapevine Pubns.

— An Easy Course in Using the HP-42S. 384p. 1989. 19.95 (*0-931011-26-4*) Grapevine Pubns.

Coffin, David. Shirtmaking: Developing Skills for Fine Sewing. LC 92-27291. (Illus.). 192p. 1993. 29.95 (*1-56158-015-5*, 070156) Taunton.

Coffin, David P. Shirtmaking: Developing Skills for Fine Sewing. (Illus.). 192p. 1998. pap. 19.95 (*1-56158-264-6*) Taunton.

Coffin, David R. The English Garden: Meditation & Memorial. 288p. 1994. text 37.50 (*0-691-03432-X*, Pub. by Princeton U Pr) Cal Prin Full Svc.

— Gardens & Gardening in Papal Rome. LC 90-37355. 285p. 1991. text 75.00 (*0-691-04089-3*, Pub. by Princeton U Pr) Cal Prin Full Svc.

— Gardens & Gardening in Papal Rome. LC 90-37355. (Illus.). 299p. reprint ed. pap. 92.70 (*0-608-09109-X*, 206974100005) Bks Demand.

— The Villa in the Life of Renaissance Rome. (Monographs in Art & Archaeology: No. XLII). (Illus.). 408p. 1979. reprint ed. pap. text 35.00 (*0-691-00279-7*, Pub. by Princeton U Pr) Cal Prin Full Svc.

Coffin, E. B., jt. auth. see Pagel, David.

Coffin, Edna A. Encounters in Modern Hebrew, Level 1. (Illus.). 280p. (C). 1992. pap. text 21.95 (*0-472-08221-3*, 08221) U of Mich Pr.

Coffin, Edna A. Encounters in Modern Hebrew, Level 1. 280p. 1993. pap. 50.00 incl. audio (*0-472-08233-7*, 08233) U of Mich Pr.

Coffin, Edna A. Encounters in Modern Hebrew: Level Two. (Illus.). 320p. (C). 1993. pap. text 21.95 (*0-472-06490-8*, 06490) U of Mich Pr.

Coffin, Edna A. Encounters in Modern Hebrew: Level Two. 320p. 1994. pap. 35.00 (*0-472-08234-5*, 08234) U of Mich Pr.

— Encounters in Modern Hebrew: Level 1. LC 90-72019. (Illus.). 280p. (C). 1993. audio 34.50 (*0-472-00251-1*, 00251) U of Mich Pr.

Coffin, Edna A. Encounters in Modern Hebrew: Level 1, Level 1. (Illus.). 280p. (C). 1992. text 42.50 (*0-472-10124-2*, 10124) U of Mich Pr.

Coffin, Edna A. Encounters In Modern Hebrew: Level 2. LC 90-72019. (Illus.). 320p. (C). 1994. audio 21.95 (*0-472-00252-X*, 00252) U of Mich Pr.

Coffin, Edna A. Encounters in Modern Hebrew: Level 3. LC 97-217882. 416p. (Orig.). 1997. pap. text 21.95 (*0-472-06540-8*, 06540) U of Mich Pr.

Coffin, Edna A. Encounters in Modern Hebrew Level 3. (Illus.). 416p. (C). write for info. (*0-472-08235-3*) U of Mich Pr.

Coffin, Edna A. Lessons in Modern Hebrew, 2 vols., I. LC 76-49149. 544p. 1977. pap. text 21.95 (*0-472-08225-6*, 08225) U of Mich Pr.

— Lessons in Modern Hebrew, 2 vols., II. LC 76-49149. 496p. 1978. pap. text 21.95 (*0-472-08226-4*, 08226) U of Mich Pr.

Coffin, Frank. On Appeal: Courts, Lawyering & Judging. (C). 1995. pap. text 12.50 (*0-393-96731-X*, Norton Paperbks) Norton.

Coffin, George. Endplays in Bridge: Eliminations, Squeezes, & Coups. 6th ed. 224p. 1982. reprint ed. pap. 5.95 (*0-486-24230-7*) Dover.

Coffin, George, ed. see Lavinthal, Hy.

Coffin, Henry S. In a Day of Social Rebuilding: Lectures on the Ministry of the Church. 1919. 49.50 (*0-686-51402-5*) Elliots Bks.

— The Public Worship of God: A Source Book. 1977. 18.95 (*0-8369-7272-4*, 8071) Ayer.

— Religion Yesterday & Today. LC 75-117769. (Essay Index Reprint Ser.). 1977. 20.95 (*0-8369-1790-1*) Ayer.

— Some Christian Convictions: A Practical Restatement in Terms of Present-Day Thinking. LC 79-167328. (Essay Index Reprint Ser.). 1977. reprint ed. 19.95 (*0-8369-2763-X*) Ayer.

— What Men Are Asking. LC 70-117770. (Essay Index Reprint Ser.). 1977. 15.95 (*0-8369-1791-X*) Ayer.

Coffin, Howard. Full Duty: Vermonters in the Civil War. LC 93-32417. (Illus.). 376p. 1995. pap. 21.00 (*0-88150-349-5*, Pub. by Countryman) Norton.

— Nine Months to Gettysburg: Stannard's Vermonters & the Repulse of Pickett's Charge. LC 97-20031. (Illus.). 340p. 1997. 29.95 (*0-88150-400-9*, Pub. by Countryman) Norton.

Coffin, John M., et al, eds. Retroviruses. LC 97-32263. (Illus.). 900p. (C). 1997. text 185.00 (*0-87969-497-1*) Cold Spring Harbor.

***Coffin, John M., et al, eds.** Retroviruses. (Illus.). 843p. (C). 1999. pap. 95.00 (*0-87969-571-4*) Cold Spring Harbor.

Coffin, Judith G. The Politics of Women's Work: The Paris Garment Trades, 1750-1915. LC 95-25915. (Illus.). 240p. 1996. text 37.50 (*0-691-03447-8*, Pub. by Princeton U Pr) Cal Prin Full Svc.

***Coffin, Julie.** Dangerous Involvement. large type ed. 155p. 2000. pap. 20.95 (*0-7838-8998-4*) Mac Lib Ref.

— Shadows of Regret. large type ed. LC 00-39532. (Nightingale Ser.). 2000. write for info. (*0-7838-9095-8*, G K Hall & Co) Mac Lib Ref.

Coffin, Julie. Summer of Enchantment. LC 99-19634. 1999. 19.95 (*0-7838-8574-1*, G K Hall & Co) Mac Lib Ref.

Coffin, Levi. Reminiscences of Levi Coffin. Richmond, Ben, ed. 1997. pap. text 16.00 (*0-944350-20-8*) Friends United.

— Reminiscences of Levi Coffin. (American Biography Ser.). 732p. 1991. reprint ed. lib. bdg. 119.00 (*0-7812-8083-4*) Rprt Serv.

— Reminiscences of Levi Coffin. 1993. reprint ed. lib. bdg. 89.00 (*0-7812-5351-9*) Rprt Serv.

— Reminiscences of Levi Coffin, the Reputed President of the Underground Railroad. LC 68-28991. (American Negro: His History & Literature. Series 1). 1968. reprint ed. 51.95 (*0-405-01810-X*) Ayer.

Coffin, Louis, ed. The Coffin Family. LC 62-18214. 576p. 1962. 20.00 (*0-317-47143-0*) Nantucket Hist Assn.

— Coffin Family. (Illus.). 579p. 1996. reprint ed. pap. 59.50 (*0-8328-5605-3*); reprint ed. lib. bdg. 69.50 (*0-8328-5604-5*) Higginson Bk Co.

Coffin, Lyn. Crystals of the Unforseen: A Book of Women's Voices. LC 97-69877. (Illus.). 128p. 1999. pap. 14.95 (*0-911051-64-3*) Plain View.

— The Poetry of Wickedness & Other Poems. LC 81-20085. 65p. (Orig.). 1981. pap. 4.00 (*0-87886-116-5*, Greenfld Rev Pr) Greenfld Rev Lit.

Coffin, Lyn, tr. see Akhmatova, Anna Andreevena.

Coffin, M. T. Billy Baker's Dog Won't Stay Buried. LC 94-96282. (Spinetinglers Ser.: No. 2). 160p. (Orig.). (J). (gr. 4-7). 1995. pap. 3.50 (*0-380-77742-8*, Avon Bks) Morrow Avon.

— Blood Red Eightball. (Spinetinglers Ser.: No. 14). 160p. (Orig.). (J). (gr. 4-7). 1996. pap. 3.50 (*0-380-78539-0*, Avon Bks) Morrow Avon.

— Boogey's Back for Blood, Vol. 19. (Spinetinglers Ser.: No. 19). 144p. (Orig.). (J). 1997. pap. 3.99 (*0-380-72772-2*, Avon Bks) Morrow Avon.

— Camp Crocodile. (Spinetinglers Ser.: No. 21). 128p. (Orig.). (J). 1997. pap. 3.99 (*0-380-78826-8*, Avon Bks) Morrow Avon.

— Check It Out - & Die. (Spinetinglers Ser.: No. 5). 160p. (Orig.). (J). (gr. 6-8). 1995. pap. 3.50 (*0-380-78116-6*, Avon Bks) Morrow Avon.

— Curse of the Cheerleaders, Vol. 25. (Spinetinglers Ser.). (J). 1997. pap. 3.99 (*0-380-78926-4*, Avon Bks) Morrow Avon.

— Don't Go to the Principal's Office. (Spinetinglers Ser.: No. 8). 144p. (J). 1996. pap. 3.50 (*0-380-78313-4*, Avon Bks) Morrow Avon.

— Don't Go to the Principal's Office. (Spinetinglers Ser.). 1996. 8.60 (*0-606-09202-1*, Pub. by Turtleback) Demco.

— Escape from the Haunted Museum. (Spinetinglers Ser.: No. 15). 144p. (Orig.). (J). 1996. pap. 3.50 (*0-380-78461-0*, Avon Bks) Morrow Avon.

— Escape from the Haunted Museum. (Spinetinglers Ser.). (Orig.). 1996. 8.60 (*0-606-10176-4*, Pub. by Turtleback) Demco.

— Fly by Night. (Spinetinglers Ser.). 1996. 8.60 (*0-606-09287-0*, Pub. by Turtleback) Demco.

— Killer Computer. (Spinetinglers Ser.: No. 12). 144p. (J). 1996. pap. 3.50 (*0-380-78312-6*, Avon Bks) Morrow Avon.

— Killer Computer. (Spinetinglers Ser.). 1996. 8.60 (*0-606-09516-0*, Pub. by Turtleback) Demco.

— Lights, Camera, Die! (Spinetinglers Ser.: Vol. 20). 128p. (J). 1997. pap. 3.99 (*0-380-78805-5*, Avon Bks) Morrow Avon.

— Lizard People. (Spinetinglers Ser.: No. 27). 128p. (J). (gr. 3-7). 1997. pap. 3.99 (*0-380-79162-5*, Avon Bks) Morrow Avon.

— Lizard People. (Spinetinglers Ser.). 1997. 9.09 (*0-606-12759-3*, Pub. by Turtleback) Demco.

— Mirror, Mirror. (Spinetinglers Ser.). 1997. 9.09 (*0-606-10878-5*, Pub. by Turtleback) Demco.

— Mirror, Mirror, Vol. 18. (Spinetinglers Ser.). (J). 1997. pap. 3.99 (*0-380-78611-7*, Avon Bks) Morrow Avon.

— Monster Channel. (Spinetinglers Ser.). 1997. 8.60 (*0-606-10880-7*, Pub. by Turtleback) Demco.

— Monster Channel, Vol. 17. (Spinetinglers Ser.). (J). 1997. pap. 3.50 (*0-380-78610-9*, Avon Bks) Morrow Avon.

An Asterisk (*) at the beginning of an entry indicates that the title is appearing for the first time.

— My Dentist Is a Vampire. LC 97-93867. (Spinetinglers Ser.: No. 29). 128p. (J). (gr. 3-7). 1998. pap. 3.99 (*0-380-79163-3*, Avon Bks) Morrow Avon.
— My Teacher's a Bug. (Spinetinglers Ser.: No. 3). 160p. (Orig.). (J). (gr. 3-6). 1995. pap. 3.50 (*0-380-77785-1*, Avon Bks) Morrow Avon.
— My Teacher's a Bug. (Spinetinglers Ser.). (Orig.). (J). 1995. 8.60 (*0-606-07911-4*) Turtleback.
— Pet Store. (Spinetinglers Ser.: No. 13). 144p. (Orig.). (J). (gr. 4-7). 1996. pap. 3.50 (*0-380-78460-2*, Avon Bks) Morrow Avon.
— Pet Store. (Spinetinglers Ser.). (Orig.). 1996. 8.60 (*0-606-09744-9*, Pub. by Turtleback) Demco.
— Saber-Toothed Tiger. (Spinetinglers Ser.: No. 30). 128p. 1998. pap. 3.99 (*0-380-79606-6*, Avon Bks) Morrow Avon.
— Simon Says, "Croak!" (Spinetinglers Ser.: No. 6). 144p. (J). 1995. pap. 3.50 (*0-380-78232-4*, Avon Bks) Morrow Avon.
— Simon Says, "Croak!" (Spinetinglers Ser.). 1995. 8.60 (*0-606-08605-6*, Pub. by Turtleback) Demco.
Coffin, M. T. Spinetinglers: Circus F.R.E.A.K.S., Bk. 28. (Spinetinglers Ser.: No. 28). 128p. (J). (gr. 3-7). 1997. mass mkt. 3.99 (*0-380-79445-4*, Avon Bks) Morrow Avon.
— Spinetinglers: Your Turn--to Scream!, Vol. 24. (Spinetinglers Ser.). 128p. (J). 1997. mass mkt. 3.99 (*0-380-78927-2*, Avon Bks) Morrow Avon.
— Spinetinglers: Gimme Back My Brain. 23rd ed. LC 96-95264. (Spinetinglers Ser.: No. 23). 128p. (J). (gr. 3-7). 1997. mass mkt. 3.99 (*0-380-78919-1*, Avon Bks) Morrow Avon.
Coffin, M. T. Student Exchange. (Spinetinglers Ser.: No. 22). 144p. (J). (gr. 3-7). 1997. pap. 3.99 (*0-380-78804-7*, Avon Bks) Morrow Avon.
— The Substitute Creature. (Spinetinglers Ser.: No. 1). 128p. (Orig.). (J). (gr. 3-6). 1995. pap. 3.50 (*0-380-77829-7*, Avon Bks) Morrow Avon.
— Substitute Creature. (Spinetinglers Ser.). (J). 1995. 8.60 (*0-606-08213-1*) Turtleback.
— We Wish You a Scary Christmas. (Spinetinglers Ser.: No. 16). 144p. (Orig.). (J). 1996. pap. 3.50 (*0-380-78996-5*, Avon Bks) Morrow Avon.
— Wear & Scare. (Spinetinglers Ser.: No. 26). 128p. 1997. pap. 3.99 (*0-380-78928-0*, Avon Bks) Morrow Avon.
— Where Have All the Parents Gone? (Spinetinglers Ser.: No. 4). 160p. (J). (gr. 4-5). 1995. pap. 3.50 (*0-380-78117-4*, Avon Bks) Morrow Avon.
— Where Have All the Parents Gone? (Spinetinglers Ser.). 1995. 8.60 (*0-606-08375-8*, Pub. by Turtleback) Demco.
Coffin, M T. Blood Red Eightball. (Spinetinglers Ser.). 1996. 8.60 (*0-606-10141-1*, Pub. by Turtleback) Demco.
— Boogey's Back for Blood. (Spinetinglers Ser.). 1997. 9.09 (*0-606-11156-5*, Pub. by Turtleback) Demco.
— Camp Crocodile. (Spinetinglers Ser.). 1997. 9.09 (*0-606-11184-0*, Pub. by Turtleback) Demco.
— Circus F. R. E. A. K. S. (Spinetinglers Ser.). (J). 1997. 9.09 (*0-606-12659-7*, Pub. by Turtleback) Demco.
— Curse of the Cheerleaders, 1. (Spinetinglers Ser.). (J). 1997. 9.09 (*0-606-11228-6*, Pub. by Turtleback) Demco.
— Gimmie Back My Brain. (Spinetinglers Ser.). 1997. 9.09 (*0-606-11387-8*, Pub. by Turtleback) Demco.
Coffin, M T. Lights, Camera, Die! (Spinetinglers Ser.). (J). 1997. 9.09 (*0-606-11560-9*, Pub. by Turtleback) Demco.
Coffin, M T. Wear & Scare, 26. (Spinetinglers Ser.). (J). 1997. 9.09 (*0-606-12843-3*, Pub. by Turtleback) Demco.
— Your Turn-To Scream! (Spinetinglers Ser.). (J). 1997. 9.09 (*0-606-12127-7*, Pub. by Turtleback) Demco.
Coffin, Margaret. Borders & Scrolls: American Brush-Stroke Wall Painting, 1790-1820. (Illus.). 80p. (Orig.). 1987. pap. 14.95 (*0-939072-08-4*) Albany Hist & Art.
Coffin, Marilyn F. Team Science: Organizing Classroom Experiments That Develop Group Skills, Grades 4-8. LC 95-47823. 1995. pap. 25.00 (*1-56976-013-6*) Zephyr Pr AZ.
Coffin, Michael H. Parallel Programming: A New Approach. 300p. (Orig.). 1992. 29.95 (*0-929306-13-9*) Silicon Pr.
Coffin, Michael J. Direct Digital Control for Building HVAC Systems. LC 90-40592. (gr. 13). 1992. mass mkt. 63.95 (*0-412-07001-4*) Chapman & Hall.
Coffin, Millard F. & Rabinowitz, Philip D. Evolution of the Conjugate East African - Madagascan Margins & the Western Somali Basin. LC 88-24588. (Geological Society of America Ser.: Vol. 226). (Illus.). 86p. 1988. reprint ed. pap. 30.00 (*0-608-07751-8*, 206783900010) Bks Demand.
Coffin, Millard F., jt. ed. see Mahoney, John J.
Coffin, M.T. Billy Baker's Dog Won't Stay Buried. (Spinetinglers Ser.). 1995. 8.60 (*0-606-07289-6*, Pub. by Turtleback) Demco.
— Check It Out, & Die! (Spinetinglers Ser.). (YA). 1995. 8.60 (*0-606-07360-4*, Pub. by Turtleback) Demco.
— Dead Kid Did It. (Spinetinglers Ser.). 1996. 8.60 (*0-606-09185-8*, Pub. by Turtleback) Demco.
— Step on a Crack. (Spinetinglers Ser.). 1996. 8.60 (*0-606-09899-2*, Pub. by Turtleback) Demco.
— Student Exchange. (Spinetinglers Ser.). (J). 1997. 9.09 (*0-606-11934-5*, Pub. by Turtleback) Demco.
Coffin, Peggy, jt. auth. see Ruff, Jack J.
Coffin, Phillip O., ed. Heroin Overdose: Research & Interventions. (Illus.). 48p. write for info. (*1-930517-00-9*) Lindesmith Ctr.
Coffin, Robert P. Lost Paradise. 1988. reprint ed. lib. bdg. 79.00 (*0-7812-0366-X*) Rprt Serv.
— Lost Paradise: A Boyhood on a Maine Coast Farm. LC 78-144951. 1971. reprint ed. 49.00 (*0-403-00904-9*) Scholarly.
Coffin, Robert P. & Coffin, Ruth P. Maine Cooking - Old Time Secrets: Mainstays of Maine. (Illus.). 159p. 1991. reprint ed. pap. 8.95 (*0-9621570-6-6*) North Lights.
Coffin, Royce A. The Negotiator: A Manual for Winners. LC 73-75768. 174p. reprint ed. pap. 54.00 (*0-608-11093-0*, 202261800028) Bks Demand.
Coffin, Ruth P., jt. auth. see Coffin, Robert P.
***Coffin, Sarah & Hofstetter, Bodo.** Gilbert Collection: Portrait Miniatures in Enamel. (Illus.). 128p. 2000. 47.50 (*0-85667-513-X*, Pub. by P Wilson) Antique Collect.
Coffin, Stephen. UNIX System V Release 4: The Complete Reference. 905p. 1990. pap. 34.95 (*0-07-881653-X*) Osborne-McGraw.
Coffin, Tammis E., ed. The Rusticator's Journal: Essays about Mount Desert Island & Acadia National Park. (Illus.). 104p. (Orig.). 1993. pap. 14.95 (*0-9637694-0-5*) Frnds of Acadia.
Coffin, Tristram. The Lost Gold Mine of the Hudson. 64p. pap. 5.95 (*0-941567-30-3*) J C & A L Fawcett.
Coffin, Tristram P., jt. auth. see Cohen, Hennig.
Coffin, Tristram P., jt. intro. see Chambers, Robert.
Coffin, Victor. The Province of Quebec & the Early American Revolution: A Study in English-American Colonial History. 566p. 1995. reprint ed. pap. text 21.00 (*0-7884-0154-8*) Heritage Bk.
***Coffin, William S.** The Heart Is a Little to the Left: Essays on Public Morality. LC 99-34297. 93p. 1999. 15.95 (*0-87451-958-6*) U Pr of New Eng.
Coffin, William S. A Passion for the Possible: A Message to U. S. Churches. LC 93-8022. 96p. (Orig.). 1993. pap. 13.95 (*0-664-25428-4*) Westminster John Knox.
Coffinberry, A. S., ed. see World Metallurgical Congress Staff.
***Coffing, Courtney.** Guide & Checklist of World Notgeld, 1914-1947: And Other Local Issue Emergency Monies. 2nd rev. ed. LC 90-63918. (Illus.). 400p. 2000. pap. 29.95 (*0-87341-810-7*, WN02) Krause Pubns.
Coffland, David A., jt. auth. see Coffland, Jack.
Coffland, Jack & Coffland, David A. BasketballMath: Slam-Dunk Activities & Projects for Grades 4-8. 112p. (Orig.). 1995. pap. 9.95 (*0-673-36223-X*, GoodYrBooks) Addson-Wesley Educ.
— FootballMath: Touchdown Activities & Projects for Grades 4-8. (Illus.). 100p. (Orig.). 1994. pap. 9.95 (*0-673-36174-8*, GoodYrBooks) Addson-Wesley Educ.
Coffland, Jack A. & Cuevas, Gilbert J. Primary Problem Solving in Math. (Illus.). 200p. (Orig.). (J). (gr. k-3). 1992. pap. 13.95 (*0-673-38745-3*, GoodYrBooks) Addson-Wesley Educ.
***Coffland, Robert T.** Contemporary Japanese Bamboo Arts. (Illus.). 136p. 2000. 50.00 (*1-878529-66-8*); pap. 35.00 (*1-878529-67-6*) Art Media Resources.
Coffler, Gail H. Melville's Classical Allusions: A Comprehensive Index & Glossary, 2. LC 84-22513. 153p. 1985. lib. bdg. 55.00 (*0-313-24626-2*, CMV/, Greenwood Pr) Greenwood.
Coffman. Advanced Accounting. 4th ed. 1994. teacher ed. 55.31 (*0-07-032669-X*) McGraw.
— Emergence of a Global Army. 1996. 30.00 (*0-02-905915-1*) Free Pr.
— Emergence of a Global Army. 2000. 30.00 (*0-684-82778-6*) Free Pr.
***Coffman.** Untitled Romance. 1999. mass mkt. write for info. (*0-312-97035-8*) St Martin.
Coffman, Carlos. Jumping Rope the Second Time Around. LC 98-94927. (Illus.). 96p. 1998. pap. 16.00 (*0-9665897-0-X*) Coffman MD.
Coffman, Carl. Unto a Perfect Man. 4th ed. 212p. 1982. pap. 13.99 (*0-943872-83-9*) Andrews Univ Pr.
Coffman, Carrie S. Bored Readers Don't Pray Much: Three Simple Steps to Writing Newsletters That Recruit Prayer. 104p. 1991. pap. 12.00 (*0-9633283-1-X*) Apples of Gold.
— Bored Readers Don't Pray Much: Three Simple Steps to Writing Newsletters That Recruit Prayer. 2nd ed. 112p. 1992. pap. 15.00 (*0-9633283-0-1*) Apples of Gold.
— Weary Warriors: Lessons from Christian Workers Who Burned Out. Coffman, King, ed. (Illus.). 248p. (Orig.). 1997. pap. 12.95 (*0-9633283-2-8*) Apples of Gold.
Coffman, Charlotte W. The Fabric/Flight Connection. Pohl, Susan, ed. (Illus.). 207p. 1997. ring bd. 36.00 (*1-57753-221-X*, 329LM1) Corn Coop Ext.
Coffman, Curt, jt. auth. see Buckingham, Marcus.
Coffman, Dewitt. Marketing for a Full House. (Illus.). 1984. pap. 10.00 (*0-937056-03-0*, M1) Cornell U Sch Hotel.
Coffman, Don, ed. Complete Guide for the Guitar: Bass Guitar Edition. 2nd rev. ed. 260p. 1998. spiral bd. 36.95 (*1-879542-02-1*) Ellis Family Mus.
Coffman, Don, et al. The Advancing Jazz-Rock-Pop Guitarist. (Complete Guide for the Guitar Ser.: Vol. 1). (Illus.). 277p. 1995. teacher ed., wbk. ed. 39.95 (*1-879542-42-0*, EFM 5001T); student ed., wbk. ed. 36.95 (*1-879542-41-2*, EFM 5001S) Ellis Family Mus.
Coffman, E. G., Jr., et al, eds. Computing. LC 92-16696. (Handbooks in Operations Research & Management Science Ser.: Vol. 3). 682p. 1992. 165.00 (*0-444-88097-6*, North Holland) Elsevier.
Coffman, Edward M. The Hilt of the Sword: The Career of Peyton C. March. LC 66-10493. 370p. 1966. reprint ed. pap. 114.70 (*0-608-07001-7*, 206720900009) Bks Demand.
— The Old Army: A Portrait of the American Army in Peacetime, 1784-1898. 536p. (C). 1988. reprint ed. pap. text 27.95 (*0-19-504555-6*) OUP.
— The War to End All Wars: The American Military Experience in World War I. LC 98-15563. 1998. 35.00 (*0-8131-2096-9*); pap. 19.00 (*0-8131-0955-8*) U Pr of Ky.
Coffman, Edward N., jt. auth. see Burns, Thomas J.
Coffman, Elaine. Angel in Marble. 1998. mass mkt. 6.50 (*0-449-15055-0*, GM) Fawcett.
— Angel in Marble. large type ed. LC 98-25651. 1998. 27.95 (*0-7862-1553-4*) Thorndike Pr.
— The Bride of Black Angus. 1999. mass mkt. 5.99 (*0-449-15007-0*, GM) Fawcett.
***Coffman, Elaine.** The Bride of Black Douglas. 2000. mass mkt. 6.99 (*1-55166-596-4*, 1-66596-7, Mira Bks) Harlequin Bks.
Coffman, Elaine. Escape Not My Love. 1997. mass mkt. 5.99 (*0-449-15057-7*, GM) Fawcett.
— Escape Not My Love. large type ed. LC 97-32443. (Large Print Book Ser.). 1997. 25.95 (*1-56895-509-X*) Wheeler Pub.
— For All the Right Reasons. 1998. mass mkt. 6.50 (*0-449-15053-4*, GM) Fawcett.
— For All the Right Reasons. LC 99-10598. 1999. 25.95 (*1-56895-637-1*) Wheeler Pub.
— Heaven Knows. 404p. (Orig.). 1994. reprint ed. mass mkt. 5.99 (*0-449-14861-0*, GM) Fawcett.
— Heaven Knows. 404p. (Orig.). 1995. reprint ed. pap. 8.95 (*0-449-91049-0*) Fawcett.
— If My Love Could Hold You. 1998. mass mkt. 6.50 (*0-449-15056-9*, GM) Fawcett.
***Coffman, Elaine.** If My Love Could Hold You. LC 98-46752. (Large Print Book Ser.). 1998. 22.95 (*1-56895-689-4*) Wheeler Pub.
Coffman, Elaine. If My Love Could Hold You. 392p. 1993. reprint ed. lib. bdg. 22.00 (*0-7278-4428-8*, 44288) Severn Hse.
— If You Love Me. 1997. mass mkt. 5.99 (*0-449-15005-4*, GM) Fawcett.
— If You Love Me. large type ed. LC 97-1887. (Core Ser.). 443p. 1997. 26.95 (*0-7838-8122-3*, G K Hall Lrg Type) Mac Lib Ref.
— So This Is Love. (Orig.). 1993. reprint ed. mass mkt. 5.99 (*0-449-14860-2*, GM) Fawcett.
— Someone Like You. 1998. mass mkt. 5.99 (*0-449-15006-2*, GM) Fawcett.
— Someone Like You. large type ed. LC 98-14661. 1998. pap. 23.95 (*1-56895-543-X*, Wheeler) Wheeler Pub.
— Somewhere along the Way. 1999. mass mkt. 6.50 (*0-449-15054-2*, GM) Fawcett.
***Coffman, Elaine.** Somewhere along the Way. LC 99-31380. 1999. 26.95 (*1-56895-745-9*) Wheeler Pub.
Coffman, Elaine. When Love Comes Along. 358p. (Orig.). 1995. mass mkt. 6.50 (*0-446-60212-4*, Warner Vision) Warner Bks.
— When Love Comes Along. 368p. (Orig.). 1998. mass mkt. 3.99 (*0-446-60687-1*) Warner Bks.
Coffman, Elaine & Langan, Ruth. Outlaw Brides. 1996. per. 5.99 (*0-373-83315-6*, 1-83315-1) Harlequin Bks.
Coffman, Elaine, et al. Seeing Fireworks, Vol. 1. 1997. mass mkt. 5.99 (*0-312-96258-4*) St Martin.
Coffman, Elaine, jt. auth. see Sutcliffe, Katherine.
Coffman, Elizabeth T., jt. auth. see Palmer, Mary S.
Coffman, Floyd W. The Conrad Clan: Family of John Stephen Conrad, Sr., & Allied Lines. (Illus.). 355p. 1993. reprint ed. pap. 52.50 (*0-8328-3106-9*); reprint ed. lib. bdg. 62.50 (*0-8328-3105-0*) Higginson Bk Co.
Coffman, Gayle. SQL Server 7: The Complete Reference. LC 99-174968. (SQL Server Professional Library). 1008p. 1998. pap. 49.99 (*0-07-882494-X*) Osborne-McGraw.
Coffman, Gina. If You Print This, Please Don't Use My Name: Questions from Teens & Their Parents about Things That Matter. LC 91-36306. 256p. (Orig.). (YA). (gr. 7-12). 1992. pap. 8.95 (*0-944176-03-8*) Terra Nova.
Coffman, Gratton E. Fires of Time. 180p. 1997. pap. 7.95 (*0-9655206-0-9*) Caster Ent.
Coffman, Gratton E. The Next World. 222p. 1996. pap. 8.95 (*0-9655206-1-7*) Caster Ent.
Coffman, Howard. Coffman's Comparative Reference Guide to Dog Food. rev. ed. LC 97-76244. 412p. 1998. pap. 119.95 (*0-9645009-7-3*, PDP09) PigDog Pr.
Coffman, Howard D. The Cat Food Reference. LC 96-92751. 426p. 1996. spiral bd. 39.95 (*0-9645009-3-0*, PDP04) PigDog Pr.
— Coffman's Mini-Label Reference to Dog Food. LC 97-76245. 646p. 1998. pap. 49.95 (*0-9645009-8-1*, PDP10) PigDog Pr.
Coffman, Howard D., ed. see Zezula, Jerilee A.
***Coffman, J. B.** The Right Move. LC 98-94014. 1999. 21.95 (*0-533-12945-1*) Vantage.
Coffman, J. L., jt. auth. see Stover, C. W.
Coffman, James B. Commentary on Acts. 546p. 1984. 18.95 (*0-915547-07-4*) Abilene Christ U.
— Commentary on Daniel, Vol. 4. LC 88-71656. (Coffman Commentaries Ser.). 320p. 1989. 19.95 (*0-89112-078-5*) Abilene Christ U.
— Commentary on Deuteronomy. LC 87-72300. 413p. 1988. 19.95 (*0-915547-76-7*) Abilene Christ U.
— Commentary on Ecclesiastes, Song of Solomon, Lamentations, Vol. 3: The Wisdom Literature. 1993. 19.95 (*0-89112-065-3*) Abilene Christ U.
— Commentary on Exodus. 1984. 19.95 (*0-915547-49-X*) Abilene Christ U.
— Commentary on Ezekiel. LC 90-83132. 431p. 1991. 29.95 (*0-89112-077-7*) Abilene Christ U.
— Commentary on Ezra, Nehemiah, Esther, Vol. 8: The Historical Books. 1993. 19.95 (*0-89112-088-2*) Abilene Christ U.
— Commentary on First & Second Chronicles. LC 93-70445. 385p. 1993. 19.95 (*0-89112-087-4*) Abilene Christ U.
— Commentary on First & Second Corinthians. 1984. 18.95 (*0-915547-02-3*) Abilene Christ U.
— Commentary on First Kings. LC 92-73842. 317p. 1993. 19.95 (*0-89112-085-8*) Abilene Christ U.
— Commentary on First Samuel, Vol. 3. LC 92-72090. 381p. 1993. 19.95 (*0-89112-082-3*) Abilene Christ U.
— Commentary on Galatians, Ephesians, Philippians, Colossians. 1984. 18.95 (*0-915547-10-4*) Abilene Christ U.
— Commentary on Genesis. 1984. 19.95 (*0-915547-48-1*) Abilene Christ U.
— Commentary on Hebrews. 1984. 18.95 (*0-915547-12-0*) Abilene Christ U.
— Commentary on Isaiah. LC 89-81143. 647p. 1990. 29.95 (*0-89112-075-0*) Abilene Christ U.
— Commentary on James, First & Second Peter, First, Second & Third John, Jude. 1984. 18.95 (*0-915547-13-9*) Abilene Christ U.
— Commentary on Jeremiah. LC 90-81193. 571p. 1990. write for info. (*0-89112-076-9*) Abilene Christ U.
— Commentary on John, Vol. 4. 1984. 18.95 (*0-915547-06-6*) Abilene Christ U.
— Commentary on Joshua. LC 88-71026. 550p. 1988. 17.95 (*0-915547-78-3*) Abilene Christ U.
— Commentary on Judges & Ruth, Vol. 2. LC 91-78067. 380p. 1992. write for info. (*0-89112-081-5*) Abilene Christ U.
— Commentary on Leviticus & Numbers. 580p. 1987. 19.95 (*0-915547-75-9*) Abilene Christ U.
— Commentary on Luke, Vol. 3. 1984. 18.95 (*0-915547-05-8*) Abilene Christ U.
— Commentary on Mark, Vol. 2. 1984. 18.95 (*0-915547-04-X*) Abilene Christ U.
— Commentary on Matthew. 1984. 18.95 (*0-915547-03-1*) Abilene Christ U.
— Commentary on Minor Prophets: Hosea, Obadiah & Micah, Vol. II. 1984. 13.95 (*0-915547-45-7*) Abilene Christ U.
— Commentary on Minor Prophets: Nahum, Habakkuk, Zephaniah & Haggai, Vol. III. 1984. 13.95 (*0-915547-46-5*) Abilene Christ U.
— Commentary on Minor Prophets: Zechariah & Malachi, Vol. IV. 1984. 13.95 (*0-915547-47-3*) Abilene Christ U.
— Commentary on Minor Prophets Vol. 1: Joel, Amos & Jonah. 1984. 13.95 (*0-915547-44-9*) Abilene Christ U.
— Commentary on Proverbs Vol. 2: The Wisdom Literature. 1993. 19.95 (*0-89112-064-5*) Abilene Christ U.
— Commentary on Psalms, Vol. 1, Chapters 1-72. LC 91-73451. 650p. 1992. 29.95 (*0-89112-079-3*) Abilene Christ U.
— Commentary on Revelation. 1984. 18.95 (*0-915547-14-7*) Abilene Christ U.
— Commentary on Romans. 1984. 18.95 (*0-915547-08-2*) Abilene Christ U.
— Commentary on Second Kings. LC 92-75210. 351p. 1993. 19.95 (*0-89112-086-6*) Abilene Christ U.
— Commentary on Second Samuel. LC 92-73036. 350p. 1993. 19.95 (*0-89112-083-1*) Abilene Christ U.
— Commentary on the Book of Job, Vol. 1: The Wisdom Literature. 1993. 19.95 (*0-89112-063-7*) Abilene Christ U.
— Commentary on Thessalonians - Philemon. 364p. 1993. 18.95 (*0-915547-11-2*) Abilene Christ U.
— The Ten Commandments Yesterday & Today. 1982. pap. 4.50 (*0-88027-094-2*) Firm Foun Pub.
Coffman, James Burton. Commentary on Psalms 73-150, Vol. 2. LC 91-92970. 1992. 29.95 (*0-89112-080-7*) Abilene Christ U.
Coffman, Janet, jt. auth. see O'Neil, Edward H.
Coffman, Jay D. Raynaud's Phenomenon. (Illus.). 200p. 1989. text 39.95 (*0-19-505756-2*) OUP.
Coffman, Jean & Horton, Bruce. Effective Written Expression: Writing for ESL Students. 116p. (C). 1989. pap. text 13.95 (*0-89641-175-3*) American Pr.
***Coffman, Judythe.** A New Owner's Guide to Weimaraners. LC 99-205925. (New Owner's Guide to Ser.). (Illus.). 160p. 1998. 12.95 (*0-7938-2805-6*) TFH Pubns.
***Coffman, Ken.** Practical FPGA: Designer's Guide to VHDL & Verilog. 320p. 2001. 79.00 incl. cd-rom (*0-13-028026-7*) P-H.
— Real World Verilog. LC 99-46369. 320p. 1999. 70.00 incl. cd-rom (*0-13-099851-6*) Prntice Hall Bks.
Coffman, King, ed. see Coffman, Carrie S.
Coffman, Lisa. Likely. LC 96-11211. (Wick Poetry First Bks.: No. 2). 60p. 1996. 17.00 (*0-87338-554-3*); pap. 9.50 (*0-87338-555-1*) Kent St U Pr.
Coffman, Marion. Versatile Vizsla. LC 91-40141. (Illus.). 272p. 1992. 39.95 (*0-931866-54-5*) Alpine Pubns.
Coffman, Mary S. Barbour Co. West Virginia: Book of Deaths 1853-1919 & Will Books 1 & 1 1/2 1839-1889. LC 95-139396. 281p. (Orig.). 1995. pap. text 22.00 (*0-7884-0111-4*) Heritage Bk.
Coffman, Michael S. Environmentalism! The Dawn of Aquarius or the Twilight of a New Dark Age. 200p. 1992. pap. 9.95 (*0-9632373-0-6*) Environ Perspect.
— Saviors of the Earth? The Politics & Religion of the Enviromental Movement. (Orig.). 1994. pap. 11.99 (*1-881273-27-X*) Northfield Pub.
— Saviors of the Earth? The Politics & Religion of the Environmental Movement. LC 94-172445. pap. 12.99 (*0-8024-7327-X*) Moody.
Coffman, R. L., ed. Regulation & Functional Significance of T-Cell Subsets. (Chemical Immunology Ser.: Vol. 54). (Illus.). x, 218p. 1992. 182.75 (*3-8055-5577-6*) S Karger.
Coffman, R. L. & Romagnani, S., eds. Redirection of Th1 & Th2 Responses. (Illus.). 170p. 1999. 109.00 (*3-540-65048-2*) Spr-Verlag.
Coffman, Ralph J. Coleridge's Library: A Bibliography of Books Owned or Read by Samuel Taylor. 260p. 1987. 85.00 (*0-8161-8101-2*, Hall Reference) Macmillan.
Coffman, Robert L., jt. auth. see Narula, Satwant K.
Coffman, Rodney E., jt. auth. see Barker, Wayne G.
Coffman, S. F., ed. Church Hymnal. 560p. 1927. 14.99 (*0-8361-1106-0*) Herald Pr.
Coffman, Sara J. How to Survive at College. 6th ed. 1984. pap. text 15.95 (*0-89917-511-2*) Tichenor Pub.
Coffman, Stephen & Wiedensohler, Pat, eds. The FISCAL Directory of Fee-Based Information Services in Libraries. 3rd ed. 1990. ring bd. 29.00 (*0-9627818-0-0*) Cnty of Los Angeles Public Library.

C

An Asterisk (*) at the beginning of an entry indicates that the title is appearing for the first time.

Coffman, Steve. FISCAL Directory of Fee-Based Researched & Document Supply Services. 4th ed. 445p. 1993. pap. text 75.00 (0-8389-2161-2) ALA.

Coffman, Steve, et al, eds. Internet-Plus Directory of Express Library Services: Research & Document Delivery for Hire. LC 97-24820. 200p. 1997. 55.00 (0-8389-0688-5) ALA.

Coffman, Steven. How to Walk a Pig & Other Lessons in Country Living. (Illus.). 208p. 1996. pap. 12.95 (1-55821-488-7) Lyons Pr.

Coffman, Sue, ed. see Cottrell, David.

***Coffman, Suzanne E.** Williamsburg-Three Hundred Years: Freedom's Journey. LC 99-28789. 112p. 1999. 12.95 (0-87935-192-6) Colonial Williamsburg.

Coffman, Taylor. The Cambria Forest: Reflections on Its Native Pines & Its Eventful Past. Porter, John, ed. LC 95-69476. (Illus.). 96p. (Orig.). 1995. pap. 12.00 (0-9647195-0-9) Coast Herit Pr.

— Hearst's Dream: The Evolution of the Enchanted Hill, from Camp to Castle, & a History of the San Simeon Area. (Illus.). 96p. (Orig.). (C). 1989. pap. 8.95 (0-945092-07-5) EZ Nature.

Coffman, Ted. How to Be up No Matter What's Going Down: The How-to Book on Success & Happiness. 150p. 1987. 19.95 (0-939975-02-5) Exec Pr NC.

Coffman, Tom. Catch a Wave: A Case Study of Hawaii's New Politics. 2nd ed. LC 72-98011. 232p. 1973. reprint ed. pap. 66.20 (0-608-00532-0, 2061411) Bks Demand.

— Nation Within: The Story of America's Annexation of the Nation of Hawaii. LC 98-71420. 345p. 1998. pap. 20.00 (1-892122-00-6, 1) Epicenter.

Coffman, Virginia. Black Heather. 1980. mass mkt. 1.95 (0-451-09468-9, J9468, Sig) NAL.

— The Candidate's Wife. 1991. 19.00 (0-7278-4114-9) Severn Hse.

— The Candidate's Wife. large type ed. LC 91-29409. 295p. 1992. reprint ed. lib. bdg. 18.95 (1-56054-255-1) Thorndike Pr.

— The Cliffs of Dread. large type ed. 1983. 15.95 (0-7089-0944-2) Ulverscroft.

— Curse of the Island Pool. 1980. mass mkt. 1.95 (0-451-09126-4, J9126, Sig) NAL.

— Dangerous Loyalties. large type ed. LC 93-13196. 479p. 1993. lib. bdg. 21.95 (1-56054-332-9) Thorndike Pr.

— Dark Desire. 384p. 1987. mass mkt. 3.95 (0-445-20221-1, Pub. by Warner Bks) Little.

— Emerald Flame. (Jewels Ser.: Bk. 1). 320p. 1996. 24.00 (0-7278-4890-9) Severn Hse.

— Of Love & Intrigue. 1980. mass mkt. 1.95 (0-451-09313-5, J9313, Sig) NAL.

— The Orchid Tree. large type ed. 592p. 1987. 27.99 (0-7089-1638-4) Ulverscroft.

— Return To Moura. 1999. 26.00 (0-7278-5461-5, Pub. by Severn Hse) Chivers N Amer.

***Coffman, Virginia.** Return to Moura. large type ed. LC 99-48478. 2000. 30.00 (0-7838-8838-4, G K Hall Lrg Type) Mac Lib Ref.

Coffman, Virginia. The Royles IV: Heir to a Throne. (Royles Ser.: Bk. 4). 320p. 1995. 22.00 (0-7278-4825-9) Severn Hse.

— The Royles III: The Princes Royal. 1994. 22.00 (0-7278-4608-6) Severn Hse.

***Coffman, Virginia.** A Splash of Rubies LC 99-10929. 299p. 1999. write for info. (0-7540-1290-5) Chivers N Amer.

— A Splash of Rubies. 320p. 1999. 26.00 (0-7278-2240-3, Pub. by Severn Hse) Chivers N Amer.

Coffman, Virginia. A Splash of Rubies large type ed. LC 99-10929. 332p. 1999. 26.95 (0-7838-8589-X, G K Hall & Co) Mac Lib Ref.

— Tiger's Eye. 256p. 1998. 24.00 (0-7278-5313-9) Severn Hse.

— Tiger's Eye. large type ed. LC 98-24629. (G. K. Hall Romance (Large Print) Ser.). 1998. 25.95 (0-7838-0306-0, G K Hall Lrg Type) Mac Lib Ref.

— The Vampyre of Moura, Vol. 2. 224p. 24.00 (0-7278-5236-1) Severn Hse.

— The Wine-Dark Opal, Vol. 2. (Jewels Ser.). 320p. 1996. 24.00 (0-7278-5139-X) Severn Hse.

Coffman, W. Thomas. Oklahoma Estate Planning, Will Drafting & Estate Administration Forms. 970p. 1993. spiral bd. 240.00 (0-87189-977-9, 82238-10, MICHIE) LEXIS Pub.

***Coffman, Warren.** I Never Intended to Be a Soldier: The Life Story of Warren Coffman, Col., U. S. Army (Ret.) (Illus.). 222p. 2000. pap. 12.95 (1-58320-012-6) Lifestyles.

Coffrey, Kathleen, jt. auth. see Gruen, Andrew.

Coffron. Z80 Applications. 1983. pap. 13.95 (0-89599-094-6) Smithsonian Bks.

Coffron, James W. Practical Troubleshooting for Microprocessors. (Illus.). 256p. 1981. text 47.00 (0-13-694273-3) P-H.

— Understanding & Troubleshooting the Microprocessors. 1980. text 47.00 (0-13-936625-3) P-H.

— Your First Microprocessor: Organizing, Construction, Debugging. LC 83-62032. (Illus.). 352p. 1984. 17.95 (0-13-978446-2) P-H.

Cofield, Lisa & Dongerson, Debbie. Mrs. Aesop's Fables. Caton, Patrick, ed. 168p. (Orig.). 1996. pap. 5.95 (1-56245-227-4) Great Quotations.

Cofield, Lisa, et al. Mrs. Murphy's Laws: If Anything Can Go Wrong It Will . . . And It's Usually a Man's Fault. 168p. (Orig.). 1995. pap. 5.95 (1-56245-222-3) Great Quotations.

— Mrs. Webster's Daily Dictionary. 366p. (Orig.). 1994. pap., spiral bd. 8.95 (1-56245-166-9) Great Quotations.

— Mrs. Webster's Dictionary. 168p. (Orig.). 1994. pap. 5.95 (1-56245-090-5) Great Quotations.

— Working Woman's World: www.help.com. Caton, Patrick, ed. LC 96-78979. 168p. 1997. pap. 5.95 (1-56245-277-0) Great Quotations.

Cofield, Rogers E., Jr. Design Manual for High Temperature Hot Water Steam Systems. 364p. 1988. 50.00 (0-471-89363-3) Krieger.

Cofman, Judita. What to Solve? Problems & Suggestions for Young Mathematicians. (Illus.). 264p. 1990. pap. text 35.00 (0-19-853294-6) OUP.

Cofone, Charles J., ed. Elizabeth Rogers, Hir Virginall Booke. LC 73-94344. 125p. (Orig.). 1975. pap. 10.95 (0-486-23138-0) Dover.

— Favorite Christmas Carols. (Illus.). 79p. 1975. pap. 4.95 (0-486-20445-6) Dover.

Cofone, Joseph N. A Guide to Determining Occupant Seating Positions from Physical Evidence & Injury Patterns LC 98-208747. 59p. 1997. write for info. (1-884566-29-4) Inst Police Tech.

— The Investigation of Automobile Collisions with Wooden Utility Poles & Trees. LC 97-124916. (Illus.). 60p. 1996. pap. text 15.95 (1-884566-19-7) Inst Police Tech.

Cofrancesco, Jan. Cat Bones in the Tree. LC 98-70399. 72p. 1998. per. 10.00 (0-9643477-4-1) Hale Mary Pr.

***Cofrancesco, Joan.** Riding on Dragons. LC 99-69001. 88p. 2000. pap. 13.00 (0-9643477-7-6) Hale Mary Pr.

Cofrancesco, Joan. Walpurgis Night. Iddings, Kathleen, ed. LC 93-84138. 80p. (Orig.). 1993. per. 10.00 (0-931289-13-0) San Diego Poet Pr.

Cogan. European Bedford Series 96. 1995. text 13.00 (0-312-14848-8) St Martin.

— Meaning of Gaulism. 243p. 1995. pap. 15.95 (0-312-10790-0) St Martin.

Cogan Akmon, Nancy. Our Photograph Album. (Illus.). 22p. 1998. 19.95 (1-884807-36-4) Blushing Rose.

***Cogan Akmon, Nancy.** Love: A Giftbook with Envelope. Akmon, Roni, tr. & des. by. (Giftbook Ser.). (Illus.). 48p. 1999. 6.95 (1-884807-40-2, EC 708) Blushing Rose.

Cogan Akmon, Nancy. Remember When Photograph Album. (Illus.). 22p. 1998. 19.95 (1-884807-34-8) Blushing Rose.

— Special Occasions Photograph Album. (Illus.). 22p. 1998. 19.95 (1-884807-35-6) Blushing Rose.

Cogan, Carolyn, ed. see Knox, Carol R.

Cogan, Charles G. Charles de Gaulle: A Brief History with Documents. (Bedford Series in History & Culture). 256p. 1995. text 45.00 (0-312-12804-5) St Martin.

— Forced to Choose: France, the Atlantic Alliance & NATO, Then & Now. LC 96-45330. 176p. 1997. 55.00 (0-275-95704-7, Praeger Pubs) Greenwood.

— Oldest Allies, Guarded Friends: The United States & France since 1940. LC 94-1150. 256p. 1994. 69.50 (0-275-94868-4, Praeger Pubs); pap. 21.95 (0-275-95116-2, Praeger Pubs) Greenwood.

Cogan, David G. David Glendenning Cogan, M. D. The Howe Laboratory of Ophthalmology at Harvard Medical School, the Massachusetts Eye & Ear Infirmary, & the National Eye Institute. (Ophthalmology Oral History Ser.). (Illus.). xxvii, 284p. 1990. pap. 45.00 (0-926886-05-3) FAAO.

— History of the Howe Laboratory. LC 93-12361. 1993. 55.00 (0-86542-337-7) Blackwell Sci.

Cogan, Donard de, see De Cogan, Donard.

Cogan, Doug, ed. see Jordan, Christopher & Wilson, Amy.

Cogan, Douglas G. The Greenhouse Effect: Investment Implications & Opportunities. 158p. 1990. pap. 20.00 (0-931035-42-2) IRRC Inc DC.

— The Greenhouse Gambit: Industry Response to Climate Change. 506p. 1992. pap. 20.00 (0-931035-86-4) IRRC Inc DC.

Cogan, Douglas G., ed. see MacKerron, Conrad B.

***Cogan, Elaine.** Successful Public Meetings: A Practical Guide for Managers in Government. 2nd ed. LC 99-75581. (Illus.). 152p. 2000. pap. 22.95 (1-884829-38-4, Planners Press) Am Plan Assn.

Cogan, Frances B. All-American Girl: The Ideal of Real Womanhood in Mid-Nineteenth Century America. LC 88-8590. (Illus.). 312p. (C). 1989. text 40.00 (0-8203-1062-X) U of Ga Pr.

— Captured: The Japanese Internment of American Civilians in the Philippines, 1941-1945. LC 99-30959. (Illus.). 400p. 2000. 39.95 (0-8203-2117-6) U of Ga Pr.

***Cogan, Jeanine & Erickson, Joanie, eds.** Lesbians, Levis & Lipstick: The Meaning of Beauty in Our Lives. LC 99-31178. (Journal of Lesbian Studies: Vol. 3, No. 4). 154p. (C). 1999. 39.95 (0-7890-0661-8, Harrington Park); pap. 14.95 (1-56023-121-1) Haworth Pr.

***Cogan, John & Derricott, Ray.** Citizenship for the 21st Century: An International Perspective on Education. 224p. 2000. pap. 32.50 (0-7494-3201-2, Kogan Pg Educ) Stylus Pub VA.

Cogan, John & Derricott, Ray, eds. Citizenship for the 21st Century: An International Perspective on Education. 224p. 1998. 59.95 (0-7494-2512-1, Kogan Pg Educ) Stylus Pub VA.

Cogan, John F. The Congressional Response to Social Security Surpluses, 1935-1994. LC 98-12390. (Essays in Public Policy Ser.: No. 92). 23p. 1998. pap. 5.00 (0-8179-5972-6) Hoover Inst Pr.

— Federal Budget Deficits: What's Wrong with the Congressional Budget Process. LC 92-35203. (Essays in Public Policy Ser.: No. 36). 17p. 1992. pap. 5.00 (0-8179-5412-0) Hoover Inst Pr.

Cogan, John F., et al. The Budget Puzzle: Understanding Federal Spending. 176p. (C). 1993. 35.00 (0-8047-2091-6); pap. 12.95 (0-8047-2092-4) Stanford U Pr.

— The Budget Puzzle: Understanding Federal Spending. LC 93-31627. 1994. 30.00 (0-8047-2322-2); pap. 12.95 (0-8047-2323-0) Stanford U Pr.

***Cogan, Karen.** Mi Hermanito Ben. Romo, Alberto, tr. (Books for Young Learners).Tr. of My Little Brother Ben. (SPA., Illus.). 12p. (J). (gr. k-2). 1999. pap. text 5.00 (1-57274-343-3, A2878) R Owen Pubs.

Cogan, Karen. My Little Brother Ben. (Books for Young Learners). (Illus.). 12p. (J). (gr. k-2). 1999. pap. text 5.00 (1-57274-142-2) R Owen Pubs.

***Cogan, Karen.** When Animals Sleep. (Illus.). 8p. 1999. pap. 3.75i (1-880612-98-4) Seedling Pubns.

Cogan, Lee. Negroes for Medicine. LC 68-31769. (Josiah Macy Foundation Ser.). 85p. reprint ed. 30.00 (0-8357-9280-3, 201568900095) Bks Demand.

Cogan, Lee, jt. ed. see Kreuzer, James R.

***Cogan, Marc.** The Design in the Wax: The Structure of the Divine Comedy & Its Meaning. LC 98-54915. (William & Katherine Devers Series in Dante Studies). 432p. 1999. pap. 35.00 (0-268-00887-6, Pub. by U of Notre Dame Pr) Chicago Distribution Ctr.

Cogan, Marc. The Human Thing: The Speeches & Principles of Thucydides' History. LC 80-24226. (Chicago Original Paperback Ser.). 248p. (C). 1981. pap. text 24.00 (0-226-11194-6) U Ch Pr.

— The Human Thing: The Speeches & Principles of Thucydides' History. LC 80-24226. 327p. reprint ed. pap. 101.40 (0-608-09285-1, 205415900004) Bks Demand.

Cogan, Martin G. & Garovoy, Marvin R., eds. Introduction to Dialysis. LC 84-17513. 317p. reprint ed. pap. 98.30 (0-7837-1378-9, 204152600021) Bks Demand.

Cogan, Martin G. & Schoenfeld, Patricia, eds. Introduction to Dialysis. 2nd ed. (Illus.). 384p. 1991. text 83.00 (0-443-08720-2) Church.

Cogan, Mary De Paul. Sisters of Maryknoll: Through Troubled Waters. LC 72-167329. (Essay Index Reprint Ser.). 1977. reprint ed. 20.95 (0-8369-2764-8) Ayer.

Cogan, Mordechai. Second Kings, Vol. 11. 408p. 1988. 20.00 (0-385-02388-X) Doubleday.

Cogan, Mordechai & Ep'hal, Israel, eds. Ah, Assyria...Studies in Assyrian History & Ancient Near Eastern Historiography: Presented to Hayim Tadmor. (Scripta Hiersolymitana Ser.: No. 33). 347p. 1991. 33.00 (0-685-53241-0, Pub. by Magnes Pr) Eisenbrauns.

Cogan, Mordechai & Paul, Shalom M., eds. Joel, Amos: Introduction & Commentary. (HEB.). 162p. 1994. text 12.00 (965-13-0974-1, Pub. by Magnes Pr) Eisenbrauns.

Cogan, Mordechai & Simon, Uriel, eds. Obadiah, Jonah: Introduction & Commentary. (HEB.). 96p. 1992. text 12.00 (965-13-0834-6, Pub. by Magnes Pr) Eisenbrauns.

Cogan, Nancy. My Grandchild: Photo Album & Journal. (Illus.). 1998. 13.95 (1-884807-29-1, EC724) Blushing Rose.

Cogan, Nancy & Akmon, Roni. Baby's Book of Days. 84p. 1993. 8.95 (0-926684-10-8) Eclectic Oregon.

— Baby's Notebook. 84p. 1993. 7.95 (0-926684-11-6) Eclectic Oregon.

— Bride's Notebook. (Wedding Album Ser.). 84p. 1994. 7.95 (1-884807-03-8, EC716) Blushing Rose.

— Guest Book. 84p. 13.95 (1-884807-06-2, EC7141) Blushing Rose.

— Wedding Diary. (Wedding Album Ser.). 120p. 1994. 8.95 (1-884807-01-1) Blushing Rose.

Cogan, Neil H., ed. The Complete Bill of Rights: The Drafts, Debates, Sources, & Origins. LC 96-46588. 708p. 1997. text 110.00 (0-19-510322-X) OUP.

— The Complete Reconstruction Bill of Rights Volume 1: Amendment XIII & the Civil Rights Act: The Drafts, Debates, Sources, & Origins. 900p. 2000. text 125.00 (0-19-513444-3) OUP.

Cogan, Patrick J., ed. CLSA Advisory Opinions 1984-1993. LC 95-161414. 505p. 1995. 30.00 (0-943616-67-0) Canon Law Soc.

— Selected Issues in Religious Law. ii, 168p. 1997. pap. 18.00 (0-943616-74-3) Canon Law Soc.

***Cogan, Priscilla.** Compass of the Heart: A Novel of Discovery. LC 99-38019. 352p. 1999. pap. 12.95 (0-385-49671-0, Anchor NY) Doubleday.

— Compass of the Heart: A Novel of Discovery. LC 98-24117. 352p. 1998. 23.00 (0-684-84764-7) S&S Trade.

— Crack at Dusk: Crook of Dawn: A Novel of Discovery. 356p. 2000. 25.95 (1-929590-05-9, Pub. by Two Canoes) Partners Pubs Grp.

Cogan, Priscilla. Winona's Web. large type ed. 1998. 24.95 (0-7862-1322-1) Thorndike Pr.

— Winona's Web: A Novel of Discovery. 288p. 1997. pap. 12.95 (0-385-49048-8, Main St Bks) Doubleday.

Cogan, Robert. Critical Thinking: Step by Step. LC 98-5370. 392p. (C). 1998. pap. 39.50 (0-7618-1067-6) U Pr of Amer.

***Cogan, Robert.** Music Seen, Music Heard: A Picture Book of Musical Design. (Illus.). 127p. 1998. pap. 35.00 (0-9634500-3-4) Pubn Contact Intl.

Cogan, Robert. New Images of Musical Sound. (Illus.). 224p. 1984. 36.50 (0-674-61585-9) HUP.

— New Images of Musical Sound. (Illus.). 177p. 1998. reprint ed. pap. 28.00 (0-9634500-2-6) Pubn Contact Intl.

***Cogan, Robert.** The Sound of Song: A Picture Book of Music for Voice. (Illus.). 149p. 1999. pap. 35.00 (0-9634500-4-2) Pubn Contact Intl.

Cogan, Robert & Escot, Pozzi. Sonic Design: Practice & Problems. 2nd ed. (Illus.). 191p. (C). 1986. reprint ed. pap. text, student ed. 25.00 (0-9634500-1-8) Pubn Contact Intl.

— Sonic Design: The Nature of Sound & Music. 4th ed. (Illus.). 350p. (C). 1985. reprint ed. pap. 35.00 (0-9634500-0-X) Pubn Contact Intl.

Cogan, Sara. The Jews of San Francisco & the Greater Bay Area, 1849-1919: Bibliography. (Western Jewish Americana Ser.: No. 2). 127p. 1972. 22.00 (0-943376-03-3) Magnes Mus.

Cogan, Sara, compiled by. The Jews of Los Angeles, 1849-1945, No. 3. 237p. 1980. pap. 14.95 (0-943376-11-4) Magnes Mus.

Cogan, Sara G. Pioneer Jews of the California Mother Lode, 1849-1880: An Annotated Bibliography. (Western Jewish Americana Ser.: No. 1). 1968. 7.50 (0-943376-01-7) Magnes Mus.

Cogan, Thomas, tr. The Tale of the Soga Brothers. (JPN.). 310p. 1987. 39.50 (0-86008-411-6, Pub. by U of Tokyo) Col U Pr.

Cogan, Timothy M. & Accolas, Jean-Pierre, eds. Dairy Starter Cultures. 290p. 1995. 165.00 (0-471-18584-1) Wiley.

Cogan, Timothy M. & Accolas, Jean-Pierre, eds. Dairy Starter Cultures. LC 95-14986. (Food Science & Technology Ser.). (Illus.). xii, 278p. 1995. 125.00 (1-56081-628-7, Wiley-VCH) Wiley.

Cogan, William J. A Brief Catechism for Adults: A Complete Handbook on How to Be a Good Catholic. rev. ed. LC 93-60780. 176p. 1993. reprint ed. pap. 9.00 (0-89555-492-5) TAN Bks Pubs.

Cogancherry, Helen, jt. auth. see Sanders, Scott R.

Cogar, William, jt. auth. see Bruce, Anthony.

Cogar, William B. Dictionary of Admirals of the U. S. Navy Vol. 1: 1862-1900. (Illus.). 256p. 1989. 47.50 (0-87021-431-4) Naval Inst Pr.

— Dictionary of Admirals of the U. S. Navy Vol. II: 1901-1918, Vol. 2. LC 89-3339. (Illus.). 416p. 1991. 47.50 (0-87021-195-1) Naval Inst Pr.

Cogar, William B., ed. Naval History: The 7th Symposium of the U. S. Naval Academy. LC 88-11691. 336p. 1988. 65.00 (0-8420-2299-6) Scholarly Res Inc.

— New Interpretations in Naval History: Selected Papers from the Twelfth Naval History Symposium. LC 97-25160. (Illus.). 400p. 1997. 37.50 (1-55750-624-8) Naval Inst Pr.

Cogar, William B., jt. auth. see Bruce, Anthony.

Cogburn, Debra. Bobby Bumblebee Learns to Fly. LC 94-92457. (Illus.). 32p. (Orig.). (J). (ps-4). 1998. pap. write for info. (0-9644825-0-9) Cogburn Enter.

Cogburn, Derrick L., et al. Information & Communications for Development: Nationalism, Regionalism, & Globalism in Building the Global Information Society: GIIC Report on the Global Information Society & Development Forum, Midrand, South Africa, 14 May 1996. LC 96-34288. 1996. pap. 25.00 (0-89206-341-6) CSIS.

Cogburn, Keith L. Like the Book of Acts: The Baptist Convention of New York Story. LC 96-70444. 256p. (Orig.). 1996. pap. 14.95 (1-881576-80-9) Providence Hse.

Cogburn, Nan, ed. see Daddy, S. Kwaku.

Cogdell. Foundations of Electric Power. LC 98-44923. 362p. 1998. pap. 38.40 (0-13-907767-7) P-H.

— Foundatns of Electronics. LC 98-44924. 415p. 1998. pap. 38.40 (0-13-907759-6) P-H.

Cogdell, Evelyn D. Auntie Eve's Favorite Dishes. 29p. 1998. pap. 8.00 (0-9664898-0-2) Green Apple Pubns.

Cogdell, J. R. Foundations of Electrical Engineering. 2nd ed. LC 95-30313. 944p. 1995. 100.00 (0-13-092701-5) P-H.

***Cogdell, James, et al, eds.** Selected Works of Ilya Piatetski-Shapiro. (CWORKS Ser.: Vol. 15). 856p. 2000. 136.00 (0-8218-0930-X) Am Math.

Cogdill, J. J., jt. auth. see Cogdill, John L., Jr.

***Cogdill, John L., Jr. & Cogdill, J. J.** The American Dream/The American Nightmare: The Authoritative Guide to Building Your Custom Home. Bowman, Kelly A., ed. (Illus.). 324p. 2000. 17.95 (0-9678684-3-2) Keystone Pubng FLA.

Cogdill, Ron. Slow Dust Rising. LC 99-34257. 2000. 22.95 (1-58151-019-5, Pub. by BookPartners) Midpt Trade.

Cogelow, Fred. Sculptor in Wood: The Collected Woodcarvings of Fred Cogelow. 1991. 24.95 (0-9622663-4-5) Heart Prairie Pr.

Cogen, V. Boosting the Adolescent Underachiever: How Parents Can Change a "C" Student into an "A" Student. (Illus.). 292p. (C). 1992. 24.95 (0-306-44328-7, Plenum Trade) Perseus Pubng.

Coger, Greta M. New Perspectives on Margaret Laurence: Poetic Narrative, Multiculturalism & Feminism, 154. LC 95-35711. (Contributions in Women's Studies: No. 154). 264p. 1996. 65.00 (0-313-29042-3, Greenwood Pr) Greenwood.

Coger, Greta M., compiled by. Index of Subjects, Proverbs, & Themes in the Writings of Wole Soyinka, 21. LC 88-160. (Bibliographies & Indexes in Afro-American & African Studies: No. 21). 333p. 1988. lib. bdg. 85.00 (0-313-25712-4, CXS/, Greenwood Pr) Greenwood.

Coggan, D., et al. Epidemiology for the Uninitiated. 4th ed. 80p. 1997. pap. text 18.00 (0-7279-1102-3, Pub. by BMJ Pub) Login Brothers Bk Co.

Coggan, D. A., ed. Industrial Instrumentation Technician Assessment: Study Guide to Certification, Level II. 2nd ed. 270p. 1992. pap. 76.00 (1-55617-218-4) ISA.

Coggan, D. A. & Albert, C. L., eds. Fundamentals of Industrial Control. 800p. 1992. 145.00 (1-55617-335-0) ISA.

Coggan, David, ed. Statistics in Clinical Practice. 120p. (Orig.). 1995. pap. text 19.00 (0-7279-0907-X, Pub. by BMJ Pub) Login Brothers Bk Co.

Coggan, Donald. The Servant-Son: Jesus Then & Now. 128p. 1995. pap. 5.95 (0-687-86162-4) Abingdon.

Coggan, Donald, ed. see Scott, Douglas G.

Coggan, Donald A. Preparing for Instrumentation Technician Evaluation: Self-Study System. LC 90-24340. 307p. reprint ed. pap. 95.20 (0-7837-5144-3, 204487200004) Bks Demand.

***Coggan, Paul.** Mustang: A Gathering of Legends. (Illus.). 160p. 2000. 34.95 (1-57427-094-X) Howell Pr VA.

Coggan, Paul. Warbirds Worldwide, No. 27. 58p. 1994. pap. 10.95 (1-870601-36-X, Pub. by Warbirds Worldwide) Motorbooks Intl.

— Warbirds Worldwide, No. 30. (Illus.). 60p. 1994. pap. 10.95 (1-870601-39-4, Pub. by Warbirds Worldwide) Motorbooks Intl.

C

— Warbirds Worldwide, No. 31. (Illus.). 50p. 1995. pap. 10.95 (*1-870601-41-6*, Pub. by Warbirds Worldwide) Motorbooks Intl.

— Warbirds Worldwide, No. 32. (Illus.). 50p. 1995. pap. 10.95 (*1-870601-43-2*, Pub. by Warbirds Worldwide) Motorbooks Intl.

— Warbirds Worldwide, No. 33. (Illus.). 50p. 1995. pap. 10.95 (*1-870601-44-0*, Pub. by Warbirds Worldwide) Motorbooks Intl.

Coggan, Philip. Money Machine. 224p. 1995. pap. 15.95 (*0-14-023399-7*, Pub. by Pnguin Bks Ltd) Trafalgar.

Coggans, Niall, et al. Adolescent Drinking & Disorder. Gillham, Bill, ed. (Facts About Ser.). 96p. 1995. 80.00 (*0-304-32664-X*) Continuum.

Cogger, H. G. & Cameron, E. E., eds. Arid Australia. 338p. (C). 1989. text 85.00 (*0-7305-0222-8*, Pub. by Surrey Beatty & Sons) St Mut.

Cogger, Harold C. & Zweifel, Richard G., eds. Encyclopedia of Reptiles & Amphibians. 2nd ed. LC 98-88226. (Illus.). 240p. (C). 1998. text 39.95 (*0-12-178560-2*) Acad Pr.

***Cogger, Harold G.** Reptiles & Amphibians. LC 99-39355. (Little Guides Ser.). 320p. 1999. pap. 14.95 (*1-875137-58-0*) Weldon Owen.

Cogger, Harold G. Reptiles & Amphibians of Australia. 5th ed. LC 91-34103. (Illus.). 704p. 1992. text 105.00 (*0-8014-2739-8*) Cornell U Pr.

***Cogger, Harold G.** Reptiles & Amphibians of Australia: Sixth Edition. 6th rev. ed. LC 99-76016. (Illus.). 808p. 2000. 110.00 (*0-88359-048-4*) Chelsea Green Pub.

Cogger, Susan K. Fitting Contact Lenses. LC 84-42727. 136p. 1985. reprint ed. pap. 42.20 (*0-608-03396-0*, 206409300008) Bks Demand.

Cogger, Virginia, ed. see Saloom, Barbara B.

***Coggeshall, Ina.** Too Many Suspects. LC 99-90721. 192p. 1999. 18.95 (*0-8034-9378-9*, Avalon Bks) Bouregy.

Coggeshall, John M. Carolina Piedmont Country. LC 95-49438. (Folklife in the South Ser.). (Illus.). 256p. 1996. 45.00 (*0-87805-766-8*); pap. 16.95 (*0-87805-767-6*) U Pr of Miss.

— Like Salt & Sugar: German-American Ethnicity in Southwestern Illinois. LC 91-9091. (Immigrant Communities & Ethnic Minorities in the U. S. & Canada Ser.: No. 78). 1991. 69.50 (*0-404-19488-5*) AMS Pr.

Coggeshall, John M. & Nast, Jo A. Vernacular Architecture in Southern Illinois: The Ethnic Heritage. LC 87-26448. (Shawnee Bks.). (Illus.). 218p. 1988. pap. 16.95 (*0-8093-1463-0*) S Ill U Pr.

Coggeshall, John M., jt. ed. see Frese, Pamela R.

Coggeshall, Robert W. Ancestors & Kin. LC 88-11647. 602p. 1988. 30.00 (*0-87152-427-9*) Reprint.

***Coggeshall, Rosanne.** Fire or Fire. 72p. 2000. 22.50 (*0-8071-2627-6*); pap. 14.95 (*0-8071-2628-4*) La State U Pr.

Coggeshall, William T. The Poets & Poetry of the West: With Biographical & Critical Notices. LC 75-92. (Mid-American Frontier Ser.). 1975. reprint ed. 57.95 (*0-405-06859-X*) Ayer.

Coggeshau, Tim, ed. see Jeffrey, Kevin.

Coggin, D. Epidemiology for the Uninitiated. 3rd ed. Rose, Geoffrey & Barker, D. J., eds. (Illus.). 80p. 1993. pap. text 14.00 (*0-7279-0770-0*, Pub. by BMJ Pub) Login Brothers Bk Co.

Coggin, H. Mason & Coggin, Janice, compiled by. Cowboy Poetry: Classic Rhymes by Bruce Kiskaddon. (Illus.). 208p. 1998. 14.95 (*0-9662091-0-9*) Cowboy Miner.

Coggin, H. Mason & Coggin, Janice, eds. Cowboy Poetry: Classic Rhymes by S. Omar Barker (1894-1985) LC 98-88574. (Illus.). 208p. 1998. 19.95 (*0-9662091-9-2*) Cowboy Miner.

Coggin, H. Mason & Coggin, Janice M., eds. Cowboy Poetry Classic Rhymes by Henry Herbert Knibb. (Illus.). 208p. 1999. 19.95 (*0-9662091-1-7*) Cowboy Miner.

Coggin, H. Mason, ed. see Davis, Duke.

Coggin, Janice, jt. compiled by see Coggin, H. Mason.

Coggin, Janice, jt. ed. see Coggin, H. Mason.

Coggin, Janice, ed. see Davis, Duke.

Coggin, Janice, ed. see McWhorter, Larry.

Coggin, Janice M., jt. ed. see Coggin, H. Mason.

Coggin, T. Daniel, et al, eds. Handbook of Equity Style Management. 2nd rev. ed. (Illus.). 325p. (Orig.). 1997. 65.00 (*1-883249-18-X*) F J Fabozzi.

Coggin, T. Daniel & Fabozzi, Frank J., eds. Applied Equity Valuation. (Illus.). 1999. 65.00 (*1-883249-51-1*) F J Fabozzi.

Coggin, William & Porter, Lynnette R. Research Strategies in Technical Communication. LC 96-194031. 369p. 1995. pap. 34.95 (*0-471-11994-6*) Wiley.

***Coggins, Allen R.** Place Names of the Smokies. Kemp, Steve & Cave, Kent, eds. (Cultural History Handbooks Ser.). (Illus.). 168p. 1999. pap. 9.95 (*0-937207-23-3*) GSMNH.

Coggins, Bruce. Does Financial Deregulation Work? A Critique of Free Market Approaches. LC 97-30627. (New Directions in Modern Economics Ser.). 240p. (C). 1998. 85.00 (*1-85898-638-9*) E Elgar.

Coggins, Cecil H., ed. Annual Review of Medicine, Vol. 45. LC 51-1659. (Illus.). 1994. text 47.00 (*0-8243-0545-0*) Annual Reviews.

— Annual Review of Medicine, Vol. 46 (1996) (Illus.). 590p. 1995. text 47.00 (*0-8243-0546-9*) Annual Reviews.

— Annual Review of Medicine, Vol. 49. LC 51-1659. 1998. text 60.00 (*0-8243-0549-3*) Annual Reviews.

Coggins, Cecil H., et al, eds. Annual Review of Medicine, Vol. 47. LC 51-1659. (Illus.). 1996. text 52.00 (*0-8243-0547-7*) Annual Reviews.

— Annual Review of Medicine Vol. 50: Selected Topics in the Clinical Sciences 1999. 581p. 1999. 120.00 (*0-8243-0550-7*) Annual Reviews.

Coggins, Clemency. El Cenote de los Sacrificios. (SPA.). 38.99 (*968-16-3074-2*, Pub. by Fondo) Continental Bk.

Coggins, Clemency C. The Stucco Decoration & Architectural Assemblage of Structure 1-Sub Dzibilchaltun, Yucatan, Mexico. LC 83-61021. (Publications: No. 49). 70p. 1983. pap. 20.00 (*0-939238-78-0*) Tulane MARI.

Coggins, Clemency C., ed. Artifacts from the Cenote of Sacrifice, Chichen Itza, Yucatan: Textiles, Basketry, Stone, Bone, Shell, Ceramics, Wood, Copal, Rubber & Other Organic Materials. LC 90-63182. (Memoirs of the Peabody Museum Ser.: Vol. 10, No. 3). (Illus.). 406p. (C). 1992. pap. 65.00 (*0-87365-694-6*, MR10-3) Peabody Harvard.

Coggins, Dana, jt. auth. see Bohnen, Michael J.

Coggins, Dana C. & Bohnen, Michael J. Massachusetts Corporate Forms, Issue 11. 100p. 1999. ring bd. 87.00 (*0-327-01301-X*, 8145516); ring bd. 85.00 incl. disk (*0-327-01302-8*, 8145516) LEXIS Pub.

Coggins, Frank W. All about Lamps: Construction, Repair & Restoration. (Illus.). 256p. 1986. 24.95 (*0-8306-0258-5*, 2658) McGraw-Hill Prof.

Coggins, George C. Public Natural Resources Law, 2 vols. LC 89-27186. (Environmental Law Ser.). 1990. ring bd. 250.00 (*0-87632-689-0*) West Group.

Coggins, George C. & Wilkinson, Charles F. Federal Public Land & Resources Law. 2nd ed. (University Casebook Ser.). 1066p. (C). 1991. reprint ed. text 36.95 (*0-88277-345-3*) Foundation Pr.

— Federal Public Land & Resources Law: Statutory Supplement. 2nd ed. (University Casebook Ser.). 510p. 1990. pap. text 19.50 (*0-88277-806-4*) Foundation Pr.

— Federal Public Lands & Resources Law. 3rd ed. Leshy, John D., ed. (University Casebook Ser.). xlix, 1092p. (C). 1992. text 43.95 (*1-56662-011-2*) Foundation Pr.

Coggins, George C., et al. Federal Public Land & Resources Law, Statutory Supplement To. 3rd ed. (University Casebook Ser.). 528p. 1997. pap. text. write for info. (*1-56662-558-0*) Foundation Pr.

— Federal Public Land & Resources Law, 1996 Case Supplement To. 3rd ed. (University Casebook Ser.). 200p. 1996. pap. text. write for info. (*1-56662-401-0*) Foundation Pr.

Coggins, George C., jt. auth. see Glicksman, Robert L.

Coggins, Jack. Horseman's Bible. rev. ed. LC 83-16500. (Illus.). 192p. 1984. pap. 12.95 (*0-385-18343-7*) Doubleday.

Coggins, James R. John Smyth's Congregation: English Separatism, Mennonite Influence & the Elect Nation. 2nd ed. (Studies in Anabaptist & Mennonite History). 240p. 1991. pap. 19.99 (*0-8361-3121-5*) Herald Pr.

Coggins, K. P. The Recovery Medicine Wheel. 2nd ed. (Illus.). 64p. 1999. pap. 22.50 (*1-892380-04-8*) Ventajas.

***Coggins, Mark.** The Immortal Game. LC 99-56642. (Illus.). 310p. 1999. 25.00 (*0-918395-17-8*, Pub. by Poltroon Pr) SPD-Small Pr Dist.

Coggins, R. J. Haggai, Zechariah, Malachi. (Old Testament Guides Ser.: No. 30). 88p. 1996. pap. 12.50 (*1-85075-025-4*, Pub. by Sheffield Acad) CUP Services.

Coggins, R. J. Introducing the Old Testament. (Oxford Bible Ser.). 176p. 1990. pap. text 18.95 (*0-19-213255-5*) OUP.

Coggins, R. J. & Houlden, J. L., eds. A Dictionary of Biblical Interpretation. LC 89-28178. 768p. 1990. 50.00 (*0-334-00294-X*) TPI PA.

Coggins, Richard J. Sirach. (Guides to the Apocrypha & Pseudepigrapha Ser.: Vol. 6). 112p. 1998. pap. 14.95 (*1-85075-765-8*, Pub. by Sheffield Acad) CUP Services.

Coggins, Timothy L. National Conference on Legal Information Issues: Selected Essays. LC 96-14889. (AALL Publications Ser.: No. 51). xxvi, 288p. 1996. 57.50 (*0-8377-0148-1*, Rothman) W S Hein.

Coggins, William N. Basic Technique: A System of Body Mechanics. LC 98-84869. (C). 1998. mass mkt., per. 21.95 (*1-889131-25-3*) CasAnanda.

Coggle, Paul. German Complete Course. (GER.). 334p. 1995. pap. 17.95 incl. audio (*0-8442-3862-7*, Teach Yrslf) NTC Contemp Pub Co.

— Teach Yourself Further German. (GER., Illus.). 368p. 1995. pap. 14.95 (*0-8442-3885-6*, Teach Yrslf) NTC Contemp Pub Co.

— Teach Yourself Further German, 2 cass., Set. (Teach Yourself Ser.). (GER.). 368p. 1995. pap. 19.95 incl. audio (*0-8442-3982-8*, Teach Yrslf) NTC Contemp Pub Co.

— Teach Yourself German. (Teach Yourself Ser.). 1992. 14.95 (*0-8288-8336-X*); 37.95 incl. audio (*0-8288-8338-6*) Fr & Eur.

— Teach Yourself German. (ENG & GER.). 1993. pap. 39.95 incl. cd-rom (*0-7859-1066-2*, 0-340-586699) Fr & Eur.

— Teach Yourself German: A Complete Course for Beginners. (ENG & GER., Illus.). 334p. 1994. pap. 8.95 (*0-8442-3779-5*, Teach Yrslf) NTC Contemp Pub Co.

***Coggle, Paul.** Teach Yourself German Extra! (Teach Yourself... Extra! Ser.). (Illus.). 224p. 2000. pap. 10.95 (*0-658-00496-4*, 004964) NTC Contemp Pub Co.

Coggle, Paul. Teach Yourself German, Further. (ENG & GER.). 1993. pap. 29.95 (*0-7859-1064-6*, 0-340-585420) Fr & Eur.

Coggle, Paul & Schenke, Heiner. German Complete Course. 2nd ed. (Teach Yourself Ser.). (GER.). 320p. 1998. pap. 9.95 (*0-8442-0219-3*, 02193, Teach Yrslf) NTC Contemp Pub Co.

Coggle, Paul & Schenke, Heiner. German Complete Course, Set. 2nd ed. (GER.). 320p. 1999. pap. 19.95 incl. audio (*0-8442-0222-3*, 02223) NTC Contemp Pub Co.

Coggle, Paul, jt. auth. see Graham, Gaelle.

Coggle, Paul, jt. auth. see Kattan-Ibarra, Juan.

Cogher, Lesley, et al, eds. Cerebral Palsy. (Management of Disability Ser.: No. 1). (Illus.). 240p. 1992. text 49.00 (*0-412-30900-9*, Pub. by E A) OUP.

Coghill, Elstan. Prints of a Priest: Writings by Father Elstan. Orsen, Susan M., ed. & photos by by. LC 96-68734. (Illus.). 150p. (Orig.). 1996. pap. 16.95 (*0-9652263-0-1*) S M Orsen.

Coghill, George E. Early Embryonic Somatic Movements in Birds & Mammals Other Than Man. (SRCD M Ser.: Vol. 5, No. 2). 1940. pap. 25.00 (*0-527-01514-8*) Periodicals Srv.

Coghill, Hamish. Discovering the Water of Leith. (Discovering Ser.). 168p. (C). 1996. pap. 22.50 (*0-85976-227-0*, Pub. by J Donald) St Mut.

Coghill, Harry. Mrs. Oliphant: The Autobiography & Letters of Mrs. M. O. W. Oliphant. 510p. (C). 1989. 95.00 (*0-907839-44-4*, Pub. by Brynmill Pr Ltd) St Mut.

Coghill, Jesse. Voices Are Calling: Poetry for the Common Man. LC 97-69815. 1997. audio 15.00 (*0-9652263-1-X*) S M Orsen.

Coghill, Nevill. Shakespeare's Professional Skills. 240p. reprint ed. pap. 68.40 (*0-608-17029-1*, 2027277) Bks Demand.

Coghill, Nevill & Bradbrook, M. C. British Writers & Their Work No. 1: Geoffrey Chaucer & Sir Thomas Malory. LC 63-63096. 115p. reprint ed. pap. 35.70 (*0-8357-7436-8*, 202320700001) Bks Demand.

Coghill, Nevill, tr. see Chaucer, Geoffrey.

***Coghill, Roger.** The Book of Magnet Healing: A Holistic Approach to Pain Relief. LC 00-32196. 2000. write for info. (*0-684-86967-5*) Simon & Schuster.

— The Healing Energies of Light. 2000. pap. 17.95 (*1-58290-012-4*, Pub. by Jrny Editions) Tuttle Pubng.

Coghill, Roger & Oldfield, Harry. The Dark Side of the Brain: Major Discoveries in the Use of Kirlion Photography & Electrosrystal Therapy. (Illus.). 208p. 1993. pap. 16.95 (*1-85230-025-6*, Pub. by Element MA) Penguin Putnam.

***Coghill, Sheila & Tammaro, Thom, eds.** Visiting Emily: Poems Inspired by the Life & Work of Emily Dickinson. 156p. 2001. pap. 14.95 (*0-87745-739-5*); text 34.95 (*0-87745-734-4*) U of Iowa Pr.

Coghill, William H. Coghill. Family of Coghill, Continued: Supplement to & Continuation of "The Family of Coghill (1879)" & Setting Forth the Genealogy of the Coghill Family, with Particular Emphasis upon the Virginia Descent of Frederick Coghill & the Illinois Descent of Benjamin Coleman Coghill, & Family Trees. (Illus.). 292p. 1997. reprint ed. pap. 45.00 (*0-8328-8006-X*); reprint ed. lib. bdg. 55.00 (*0-8328-8005-1*) Higginson Bk Co.

Coghlan, David. Review of Canadian Securities: Quarterly. 1995. 4.85 (*1-888279-00-1*) Re Can Sec.

Coghlan, David, jt. auth. see Rashford, Nicholas.

Coghlan, David A. Automotive Chassis Systems. 2nd ed. (Automotive Technology Ser.). 1985. pap. 37.95 (*0-8273-3865-1*) Delmar.

Coghlan, E. L. As in the Days. 130p. 1991. 8.95 (*1-880495-01-5*) Rhenaria.

— To Rule & Reign. 250p. 1992. 8.95 (*1-880495-02-3*) Rhenaria.

Coghlan, Frank J. They Still Call Me Junior: Autobiography of a Child Star; with a Filmography. LC 92-50432. (Illus.). 383p. 1992. lib. bdg. 37.50 (*0-89950-762-X*) McFarland & Co.

Coghlan, John F. Sport & British Politics since 1960. 240p. 1990. pap. 34.95 (*1-85000-810-8*, Falmer Pr) Taylor & Francis.

Coghlan, Lin. Waking. (Nick Hern Bks.). 96p. 1997. pap. 14.95 (*1-85459-392-7*, Pub. by N Hern Bks) Theatre Comm.

Coghlan, Margaret. Memoirs of Mrs. Coghlan, Daughter of the Late Major Moncrieffe. LC 75-140859. (Eyewitness Accounts of the American Revolution Ser.). 1978. reprint ed. 18.95 (*0-405-01213-6*) Ayer.

Coghlan, Margaret M. Memoirs of Mrs. Coghlan. (American Biography Ser.). 158p. 1991. reprint ed. lib. bdg. 59.00 (*0-7812-8085-0*) Rprt Serv.

Coghlan, Peg. Irish Names for Children. 95p. 1998. pap. 7.95 (*1-85635-214-5*) Irish Bks Media.

Coghlan, Richard. Strategic Cycle Investing: The Investor's Survival Guide for All Markets. LC 93-16272. 440p. 1993. 34.95 (*0-07-707596-X*) McGraw.

Coghlan, Ronan. The Encyclopedia of Arthurian Legends. 256p. 1991. pap. 18.95 (*1-85230-199-6*, Pub. by Element MA) Penguin Putnam.

— The Encyclopedia of Arthurian Legends. (Illus.). 256p. 1992. pap. 12.95 (*1-85230-373-5*, Pub. by Element MA) Penguin Putnam.

— Handbook of Fairies. 1997. pap. 21.95 (*1-898307-91-1*, Pub. by Capall Bann Pubng) Holmes Pub.

— Illustrated Encyclopedia of Arthurian Legends. 256p. 1995. pap. 24.95 (*1-85230-647-5*, Pub. by Element MA) Penguin Putnam.

— The Illustrated Encyclopedia of Arthurian Legends. (Illus.). 224p. 1993. pap. 29.95 (*1-85230-428-6*, Pub. by Element MA) Penguin Putnam.

— Irish First Names. (Pocket Guide Ser.). 72p. (Orig.). 1985. pap. 7.95 (*0-86281-153-8*, Pub. by Appletree Pr) Irish Bks Media.

Cogill, Burgess. A Simpler Life: Memories of Childhood at Sea, 1902-1910. (Illus.). 1990. 17.95 (*0-393-02716-3*) Norton.

***Coglas, Monica.** Miracles of the Heart. LC 99-68311. 240p. 2000. pap. 12.99 (*1-57921-264-6*) WinePress Pub.

Cogley. History of Seventh Indiana Cavalry. 1976. 31.95 (*0-8488-0216-0*, J M C & Co) Amereon Ltd.

Cogley, David R., jt. auth. see Butler, James N.

Cogley, John. Catholic America. rev. ed. Van Allen, Rodger, ed. LC 85-63356. 270p. 1986. reprint ed. pap. 12.95 (*0-934134-78-2*) Sheed & Ward WI.

— Report on Blacklisting: Part One, the Movies. LC 79-169349. (Arno Press Cinema Program Ser.). 326p. 1979. reprint ed. 26.95 (*0-405-03915-8*) Ayer.

Cogley, John, jt. auth. see Miller, Merle.

Cogley, Michele, jt. auth. see Haas-Foletta, Karen.

Cogley, Thomas. History of the Seventh Indiana Cavalry. 312p. 1991. reprint ed. 24.95 (*0-89029-543-3*) Morningside Bkshop.

Cogley, Thomas S. Law of Strikes, Lockouts & Labor Organizations. xiv, 377p. 1981. reprint ed. 45.00 (*0-8377-0435-9*, Rothman) W S Hein.

Cogliano, Francis D. No King, No Popery: Anti-Catholicism in Revolutionary New England, 164. LC 95-19322. (Contributions in American History Ser.: Vol. 164). 192p. 1996. 55.00 (*0-313-29729-0*, Greenwood Pr) Greenwood.

***Cogliano, Francis D.** Revolutionary America, 1763-1815: Political History. LC 99-27130. 224p. (C). 1999. text. write for info. (*0-415-18057-0*) Routledge.

— Revolutionary America, 1763-1815: Political History. LC 99-27130. 1999. pap. write for info. (*0-415-18058-9*) Routledge.

***Cogliano, Vincent J., et al.** Perspectives on Biologically Based Cancer Risk Assessment. LC 99-30081. (NATO - Challenges of Modern Society Ser.). 319p. 1999. write for info. (*0-306-46108-0*, Kluwer Plenum) Kluwer Academic.

Cogly, Richard W. John Eliot's Mission to the Indians Before King Philip's War. LC 98-45386. 1999. 45.00 (*0-674-47537-2*) HUP.

***Cogman, Genevieve R.** In Nomine: You Are Here: Around the World 666 Days. (Illus.). 1999. pap. 19.95 (*1-55634-395-7*) S Jackson Games.

Cognac, Camille D. Quilt Restoration: A Practical Guide. LC 94-35126. (Illus.). 128p. 1994. pap. 29.95 (*0-939009-83-8*, EPM) Howell Pr VA.

Cognard, Jacques. Alignment of Nematic Liquid Crystals & Their Mixtures. (Molecular Crystals & Liquid Crystals Ser.). vi, 78p. 1982. pap. text 112.00 (*0-677-05905-1*) Gordon & Breach.

Cognazzo, M. T., jt. auth. see Bussi, L.

Cognets, Anna R. Des, see Des Cognets, Anna R.

Cognets, Louis Des, see Des Cognets, Anna R. & Des Cognets, Louis, Jr.

Cogniat, Raymond. Picasso: Figures. (Rhythem & Color One Ser.). 1970. 9.95 (*0-8288-9502-3*) Fr & Eur.

Cogniaux, Alfred. Orchidees Dictionnaire Iconographique, 2 vols. (FRE.). 1990. 995.00 (*0-7859-8241-8*, 2908041049) Fr & Eur.

C

Cognition & Technology Group at Vandenberg University Staff, jt. auth. see Cooper, James M.

Cognition & Technology Group at Vanderbilt Staff. The Jasper Project: Lessons in Curriculum, Instruction, Assessment & Professional Development. LC 96-51912. 200p. 1997. pap. write for info. (*0-8058-2593-2*) L Erlbaum Assocs.

— The Jasper Project: Lessons in Curriculum, Instruction, Assessment & Professional Development. LC 96-51912. 200p. 1997. 59.95 (*0-8058-2592-4*) L Erlbaum Assocs.

Cognitive Science Society Staff. Proceedings of the Eighteenth Annual Conference of the Cognitive Science Society. 904p. 1996. pap. 150.00 (*0-8058-2541-X*) L Erlbaum Assocs.

— Proceedings of the Fourteenth Annual Conference of the Cognitive Science Society. 1300p. 1992. pap. 150.00 (*0-8058-1291-1*) L Erlbaum Assocs.

— Proceedings of the Nineteenth Annual Conference of the Cognitive Science Society. 1128p. 1997. pap. 150.00 (*0-8058-2941-5*) L Erlbaum Assocs.

— Proceedings of the Seventeenth Annual Conference of the Cognitive Science Society. 1995. cd-rom. write for info. (*1-56321-191-2*) L Erlbaum Assocs.

— Proceedings of the Seventeenth Annual Conference of the Cognitive Science Society. Lehman, Jill F. & Moore, Johanna D., eds. 824p. 1995. pap. 150.00 (*0-8058-2159-7*) L Erlbaum Assocs.

— Proceedings of the Twelfth Annual Conference of the Cognitive Science Society. 1112p. 1990. pap. 150.00 (*0-8058-0938-4*) L Erlbaum Assocs.

— Proceedings of the Twentieth Annual Conference of the Cognitive Science Society. 1280p. 1998. pap. 180.00 (*0-8058-3231-9*) L Erlbaum Assocs.

Cognito. Agency & Intermediaries. 48p. 1998. 24.00 incl. cd-rom (*0-13-082571-9*) P-H.

— Deceptive Trade Practices ACT & Rules of the Commission. 48p. 1998. pap. text 24.00 (*0-13-082572-7*) P-H.

— Real Estate & the Environment. 48p. 1998. pap. text 24.00 (*0-13-099848-6*) P-H.

— Residential Sales Contracts. 40p. 1998. 24.00 incl. cd-rom (*0-13-099846-X*) P-H.

— Tex Mandatory Continue Education. 31p. 1998. 96.00 incl. cd-rom (*0-13-636424-1*) P-H.

Cognito Inc. Staff, ed. Contracts & Real Estate. 48p. 1998. 24.00 incl. cd-rom (*0-13-082591-3*) S&S Trade.

Cognos Associates Staff, jt. ed. see InfoChem GmbH Staff.

Cogny, Denise, ed. see Huysmans, J. K.

Cogny, Pierre. Naturalisme. 126p. 1968. 9.95 (*0-8288-7414-X*) Fr & Eur.

Cogny, Pierre, jt. auth. see Maupassant, Guy de.

Cogny, Pierre, ed. see Huysmans, J. K.

Cogny, Pierre, ed. see Huysmans, J. K.

Cogo, Annalisa, jt. ed. see Allegra, Luigi.

Cogoli, A., et al, eds. Life Sciences & Space Research XXV (1) Gravitational Biology: Proceedings of the Topical Meeting of the COSPAR Interdisciplinary Scientific Commission F (Meeting F1) of the COSPAR 29th Plenary Meeting Held in Washington, D. C., U. S. A. 28 August-5 September, 1992. (Advances in Space Research Ser.: Vol. 14). (Illus.). 472p. 1994. pap. 176.00 (*0-08-042485-6*) Elsevier.

Cogoli, Augusto, jt. ed. see Bonting, Sjoerd L.

Cogoli, John E. Photo Offset Fundamentals. 5th ed. 1986. pap. 32.97 (*0-02-675590-4*) Macmillan.

— Photo-Offset Fundamentals: Teacher's Resource Guide. 5th ed. (Illus.). 80p. 1999. teacher ed. 13.82 (*0-02-675610-2*) Glencoe.

Cogordan, J. A., et al, eds. Ceramic Superconductors. (Progress in High Temperature Superconductivity Ser.: Vol. 26). 208p. (C). 1991. text 74.00 (*981-02-0212-1*) World Scientific Pub.

Cogswell, Betty E. & Sussman, Marvin B., eds. Family Medicine: A New Approach to Health Care. LC 81-6980. (Marriage & Family Review Ser.: Vol. 4, Nos. 1-2). 187p. 1982. text 39.95 (*0-917724-25-9*) Haworth Pr.

Cogswell, Carol J., et al, eds. Three-Dimensional & Multidimensional Microscopy: Image Acquisition & Processing V. LC 98-233145. (Proceedings of SPIE Ser.: Vol. 3261). 346p. 1998. 89.00 (*0-8194-2700-4*) SPIE.

— Three-Dimensional Microscopy Vol. 2984: Image Acquisition & Processing IV. LC 97-175344. 284p. 1997. 69.00 (*0-8194-2395-5*) SPIE.

Cogswell, David. Chomsky for Beginners. (For Beginners Ser.). (Illus.). 176p. 11.95 (*0-86316-233-9*) Writers & Readers.

Cogswell, E. C. History of Nottingham, Deerfield & Northwood, Nottingham & Rockingham Counties with Genealogical Sketches. (Illus.). 790p. 1988. reprint ed. lib. bdg. 79.00 (*0-8328-0068-6*, NH0017) Higginson Bk Co.

Cogswell, Elliott C. History of New Boston, NH. (Illus.). 469p. 1993. reprint ed. lib. bdg. 49.00 (*0-8328-3203-0*) Higginson Bk Co.

Cogswell, F. N. Polymer Melt Rheology: A Guide for Industrial Practice. 190p. 1995. 135.00 (*1-85573-198-3*, Pub. by Woodhead Pubng) Am Educ Systs.

— Thermoplastic Aromatic Polymer Composites: A Study of the Structure, Processing & Properties of Carbon Fibre Reinforced Polyetheretherketone & Related Materials. (Illus.). 289p. 1992. 110.95 (*0-7506-1086-7*, Pub. by Woodhead Pubng) Technomic.

Cogswell, Fred. Charles Mair & His Works. 42p. (C). 1988. pap. text 9.95 (*0-920763-70-7*, Pub. by ECW) Genl Dist Srvs.

Cogswell, Fred, ed. Doors of the Morning. LC 97-24454. 122p. 1997. pap. 12.00 (*1-884206-03-4*) Unfinish Monumnt.

— The Poetry of Modern Quebec: An Anthology. LC 77-362075. (French Writers of Canada Ser.). 206p. reprint ed. pap. 63.90 (*0-608-13918-1*, 202375000033) Bks Demand.

Cogswell, Fred & Elder, Jo-Anne, eds. Unfinished Dreams: Contemporary Poetry of Acadie. 172p. 1990. pap. 16.95 (*0-86492-132-2*, Pub. by Goose Ln Edits) Genl Dist Srvs.

Cogswell, James A. No Place Left Called Home. LC 82-24215. (Illus.). 139p. 1983. reprint ed. pap. 43.10 (*0-608-01655-1*, 206230700002) Bks Demand.

Cogswell, Jeff. Java Database Programming with Latte. 1997. pap. 39.95 (*1-55851-512-7*, M&T Bks) IDG Bks.

— Learn Delphi Today! 528p. 1996. pap. 34.99 (*1-56884-835-8*) IDG Bks.

Cogswell, John. Voice of the Plains: Selected Radio Commentaries. (Illus.). (Orig.). 1987. pap. 9.95 (*0-944720-01-3*) Greenridge Pr.

Cogswell, Leander W. History of the Town of Henniker, New Hampshire, from the Date of the Canada Grant by the Province of Mass. in 1735 to 1880: With a Genealogical Register. 807p. 1988. reprint ed. lib. bdg. 81.00 (*0-8328-0054-6*, NH0038) Higginson Bk Co.

Cogswell, Margaret, ed. see Breitenbach, Edgar.

Cogswell, Philip, Jr. Capitol Names: Individuals Woven into Oregon's History. LC 76-56657. (Illus.). 133p. 1977. pap. 2.95 (*0-87595-054-X*) Oregon Hist.

Cogswell, Robert E. Copyright Law for Unpublished Manuscripts & Archival Collections. Mersky, Roy M., ed. (Law Library Information Reports: Vol. 14). 150p. 1992. pap. text 50.00 (*0-87802-091-8*) Glanville.

Cogswell, Theodore, ed. PITFCS: The Proceedings of the Institute for Twenty-First Century Studies. (Illus.). x, 374p. 1993. 40.00 (*0-911682-30-9*) Advent.

Cogswell, Thomas. Home Divisions: Aristocracy, the State, & Provincial Conflict. LC 97-62463. (Illus.). 368p. 1998. 55.00 (*0-8047-3386-4*) Stanford U Pr.

Cogswell, Fred. Selected Poems. 64p. pap. 5.00 (*0-919349-21-8*) Guernica Editions.

***Cohadon, F., et al, eds.** Adavances & Technical Standards in Neurosurgery, Vol. 26. (Illus.). 350p. 2000. 110.00 (*3-211-83424-9*) Spr-Verlag.

Cohadon, F., et al, eds. Advances & Technical Standards in Neurosurgery, Vol. 23. (Illus.). 330p. 1997. 169.00 (*3-211-82827-3*) Spr-Verlag.

— Advances & Technical Standards in Neurosurgery, Vol. 24. (Illus.). 300p. 1998. 159.00 (*3-211-83064-2*) Spr-Verlag.

— Advances & Technical Standards in Neurosurgery, Vol. 25. 300p. 1999. 139.00 (*3-211-83217-3*) Spr-Verlag.

— Traumatic Brain Edema. (FIDIA Research Ser.). 195p. 1987. 90.00 (*0-387-96507-6*) Spr-Verlag.

Cohadon, F. & Antunes, J. Lobo, eds. Recovery of Function in the Nervous System. (FIDIA Research Ser.: Vol. 13). xii, 191p. 1988. 90.00 (*0-387-96785-0*) Spr-Verlag.

Cohagan, Jerry. Relatively Speaking: Three One-Acts & a Monologue about the Family. 63p. 1988. pap. 8.99 (*0-8341-9730-8*, MP-642) Nazarene.

— The Worship Drama Library Vol. 11: 12 Sketches for Enhancing Worship. 1994. 19.99 (*0-8341-9268-3*, MP-711) Lillenas.

Cohagan, Jerry & Cohagan, Lynda. Gone with the Mortgage: And Other Heir-Raising Stories. 96p. (Orig.). 1996. pap. 8.99 (*0-8341-1624-3*) Beacon Hill.

— Honey?..."Yes, Dear?" 70p. 1989. 15.99 (*0-8341-9244-6*, MP-651) Lillenas.

Cohagan, Jerry, et al. Youth Enclosed- Handle with Care: Three One-Act Plays for Teens. LC 99-216313. 1998. pap. 8.99 (*0-8341-9785-5*) Nazarene.

Cohagan, Jerry, jt. auth. see Hicks, Stephen.

Cohagan, Jery. The Carpenter's Tools. 1994. pap. text 8.99 (*0-00-501719-X*) Lillenas.

Cohagan, Lynda, jt. auth. see Cohagan, Jerry.

Cohagn. He's Got My Number. 1991. pap. 8.99 (*0-00-528655-7*) Lillenas.

Cohalan, Florence D. A Popular History of the Archdiocese of New York. LC 82-84246. (Monographs: Vol. 37). (Illus.). xviii, 354p. 1983. 15.00 (*0-930060-17-2*) US Cath Hist.

Cohall, Alwyn T., jt. auth. see Isler, Charlotte.

Cohan. Multimedia Transport & Fate of Pollutants. 372p. (C). 2001. boxed set 64.00 (*0-13-605734-9*) P-H.

Cohan, Andrey, et al. Sexual Harassment & Sexual Abuse: A Handbook for Teachers & Administrators. 112p. 1996. 43.95 (*0-8039-6440-4*); pap. 18.95 (*0-8039-6441-2*) Corwin Pr.

Cohan, Avery B. Yields on Corporate Debt Directly Placed. (General Ser.: No. 84). 202p. 1967. reprint ed. 52.60 (*0-87014-472-3*) Natl Bur Econ Res.

Cohan, Beatty & Cohan, Elliot. For Better, for Worse, Forever: 10 Steps for Building a Lasting Relationship with the Man You Love. LC 98-74422. 256p. 1999. 19.95 (*1-886284-22-9*, Pub. by Chandler Hse) Natl Bk Netwk.

Cohan, Carol, et al. Coping with Heart Surgery & Bypassing Depression: A Family's Guide to the Medical, Emotional, & Practical Issues. LC 97-21699. (Illus.). 280p. 1997. pap. 27.95 (*1-887841-07-5*, 60609, Psychosocial) Intl Univs Pr.

Cohan, Carol, jt. auth. see Diethrich, Edward B.

Cohan, Elliot, jt. auth. see Cohan, Beatty.

Cohan, G. George M! 72p. 1984. pap. 8.95 (*0-7935-3339-2*, 8203) H Leonard.

Cohan, George M. 45 Minutes from Broadway: Musical. 79p. (YA). (gr. 10 up). 1978. pap. 5.95 (*0-87129-872-4*, F06) Dramatic Pub.

— Twenty Years on Broadway, & the Years It Took to Get There. (American Biography Ser.). 264p. 1991. reprint ed. lib. bdg. 69.00 (*0-7812-8086-9*) Rprt Serv.

Cohan, James H. & Greenberg, Arthur M. Exploring Joseph Cornell's Visual Poetry. LC 82-50470. 24p. 1982. pap. 2.50 (*0-936316-03-9*) Wash U Gallery.

Cohan, John R., et al. Drafting California Irrevocable Trusts, 2 vols. 3rd ed. Tom, Janette, ed. LC 97-66099. 1308p. 1997. ring bd. 199.00 (*0-7626-0064-0*, ES-32710) Cont Ed Bar-CA.

Cohan, Jon. The Drummer's Almanac: Tips & Tales from the Pros. 80p. 1998. per. 12.95 (*0-7935-6696-7*, 00330237) H Leonard.

— Star Sets: Vintage & Custom Drum Kits of the Great Drummers. (Illus.). 160p. (Orig.). 1995. per. 22.95 (*0-7935-3489-5*, HL00330113) H Leonard.

— Zildjian: The History of the Legendary Cymbal Makers. 1999. per. 19.95 (*0-7935-9154-6*) H Leonard.

— Zildjian: The History of the Legendary Cymbal Makers. (Illus.). 128p. 1999. per. 29.95 (*0-7935-9155-4*) H Leonard.

Cohan, Leo M. The Hebrew Alphabet: From Generation to Generation. (Jewish History Ser.). (Illus.). 21p. (Orig.). (J). (gr. 4). 1989. pap. 5.95 (*0-9636415-0-6*) Kol Yisrael Pub.

Cohan, Malcolm, jt. auth. see Hayward, Susan.

***Cohan, Peter S.** E-Profit: High-Payoff Strategies for Capturing the E-Commerce Edge. LC 99-59361. (Illus.). 288p. 2000. 27.95 (*0-8144-0544-4*) AMACOM.

Cohan, Peter S. Net Profit: How to Invest & Compete in the Real World of Internet Business. LC 99-6217. 1999. 28.00 (*0-7879-4476-9*) Jossey-Bass.

— The Technology Leaders: How America's Most Profitable High-Tech Companies Innovate Their Way to Success. LC 97-11674. (Business & Management Ser.). 1998. 27.95 (*0-7879-1072-4*) Jossey-Bass.

Cohan, Robert P. Choreographers - Composers - Collaboration. 98p. 1992. pap. text 15.00 (*3-7186-5183-1*, Harwood Acad Pubs) Gordon & Breach.

Cohan, Steven. Masked Men: Masculinity & the Movies in the Fifties. LC 96-29965. (Arts & Politics of the Everyday Ser.). (Illus.). 448p. 1997. pap. 18.95 (*0-253-21127-1*) Ind U Pr.

— Violation & Repair in the English Novel: The Paradigm of Experience from Richardson to Woolf. LC 86-1297. 253p. reprint ed. pap. 78.50 (*0-608-10625-9*, 207124700009) Bks Demand.

Cohan, Steven & Hark, Ina M. The Road Movie Book. LC 97-8924. (Illus.). 400p. 1997. pap. 22.99 (*0-415-14937-1*) Routledge.

Cohan, Steven & Hark, Ina M., eds. Screening the Male: Exploring Masculinities in the Hollywood Cinema. LC 92-5815. 224p. (C). (gr. 13). 1993. pap. 21.99 (*0-415-07759-1*, A7262); text 59.95 (*0-415-07758-3*) Routledge.

Cohan, Steven & Hark, Ina R. The Road Movie Book. LC 97-8924. (Illus.). 400p. (C). 1997. 75.00 (*0-415-14936-3*) Routledge.

Cohan, Steven & Shires, Linda M. Telling Stories: A Theoretical Analysis of Narrative Fiction. (New Accents Ser.). 224p. 1988. text 55.00 (*0-415-01386-0*) Routledge.

— Telling Stories: A Theoretical Analysis of Narrative Fiction. (New Accents Ser.). 208p. (C). 1988. pap. 22.99 (*0-415-01387-9*) Routledge.

Cohan, Tony. Canary. LC 80-2045. 336p. 1981. 13.95 (*0-385-17086-6*) Acrobat.

— The Flame: Notes on the Writer's Art. LC 82-73826. 63p. 1983. pap. 9.00 (*0-918226-10-4*) Acrobat.

— Nine Ships: A Book of Tales. (Illus.). 1975. 12.00 (*0-918226-02-3*); pap. 9.95 (*0-918226-00-7*) Acrobat.

***Cohan, Tony.** On Mexican Time. 2000. reprint ed. pap. 13.00 (*0-7679-0319-6*) Broadway BDD.

Cohan, Tony. On Mexican Time: A New Life in San Miguel. LC 99-29296. 288p. 2000. 25.00 (*0-7679-0318-8*) Broadway BDD.

— Opium. large type ed. 736p. 1986. 27.99 (*0-7089-8363-4*, Charnwood) Ulverscroft.

Cohan, Tony & Beam, Gordon, eds. Outlaw Visions. LC 77-80089. (Illus.). 1977. 11.00 (*0-918226-05-8*); pap. 9.95 (*0-918226-04-X*) Acrobat.

Cohane, John P. White Papers of an Outraged Conservative. LC 72-190112. 1972. 10.00 (*0-672-51280-7*, Bobbs) Macmillan.

Cohassey, John F., jt. auth. see Wilson, Sunnie.

Cohat, Elisabeth, ed. The Seashore. LC 94-25896. (First Discovery Book). (Illus.). 24p. (J). (gr. 4-7). 1995. 11.95 (*0-590-20303-7*, Cartwheel) Scholastic Inc.

Cohat, Yves. The Vikings: Lords of the Seas. (Discoveries Ser.). (Illus.). 176p. 1992. pap. 12.95 (*0-8109-2865-5*, Pub. by Abrams) Time Warner.

Cohausen, Johann H. Hermippus Redivivus. Kastenbaum, Robert J., ed. LC 78-22194. (Aging & Old Age Ser.). 1979. reprint ed. lib. bdg. 21.95 (*0-405-11811-2*) Ayer.

Cohe, J. M., tr. see Rabelais, Francois.

Cohee, Gail. The Feminist Teacher Anthology: Pedagogies & Classroom Strategy. LC 98-4870. 1998. 70.00 (*0-8077-6296-2*); pap. 24.95 (*0-8077-6295-4*) Tchrs Coll.

Cohee, Marcia, jt. auth. see Cohee, Pat.

Cohee, Marcia L. Bonefire. limited ed. (Illus.). 90p. 1996. pap. write for info. (*0-9624205-9-X*) Inevitable Pr.

— Languna Canyon Was Once a River. (Illus.). 81p. (Orig.). 1991. pap. 7.50 (*0-9624205-2-2*) Inevitable Pr.

***Cohee, Pat & Cohee, Marcia.** Coheesion: Poems. (Illus.). 32p. 1999. pap. 5.00 (*0-9670175-1-8*) Valley Contemp.

Cohelan, Timothy D. Cohelan on California Class Actions. LC 97-60489. (The Expert Ser.). 1997. pap. 60.00 (*0-314-22196-4*) West Pub.

Cohen. Applications in High School Math. 1991. text, teacher ed. 78.04 (*0-395-59126-0*); text, student ed. 60.28 (*0-395-59125-2*) HM.

— Applied Mathematics. 1989. pap., teacher ed. 139.92 (*0-395-51470-3*) HM.

— Art Through the Ages. 9th ed. (C). 1991. pap. text, teacher ed. 34.25 (*0-15-503774-9*) Harcourt Coll Pubs.

— Bankruptcy Law Digest, No. 2. 592p. 1992. suppl. ed. 60.00 (*0-7913-1037-X*) Warren Gorham & Lamont.

— Bankruptcy Law Digest, No. 2739. 592p. 1989. boxed set, suppl. ed. 125.00 (*0-7913-0382-9*) Warren Gorham & Lamont.

— Bankruptcy Law Digest, No. 2739. 592p. 1992. suppl. ed. 54.50 (*0-7913-1181-3*) Warren Gorham & Lamont.

— Because They're Men: Reader on Men & Masculinity. (Sociology Ser.). 2000. pap. 28.00 (*0-534-53658-1*) Brooks-Cole.

— Broken Bonds. 1998. 24.00 (*0-8133-3329-6*) Westview.

— Contemporary Economic Issues: Trade, Payments & Debt, Vol. 122. LC 97-4526. 209p. 1997. text 69.95 (*0-312-17760-7*) St Martin.

— Creating & Coping with Change in Human Services. (Counseling Ser.). 320p. 1999. 33.95 (*0-534-34862-9*) Brooks-Cole.

— Developing Africa's Working Class. Date not set. pap. text. write for info. (*0-582-64180-2*, Pub. by Addison-Wesley) Longman.

Cohen. Essentials High School Mathematics, 001. (YA). 1989. pap., suppl. ed. 35.52 (*0-395-39362-0*) HM.

— Essentials of Mathematics, 001. 1988. pap., suppl. ed. 11.12 (*0-395-39366-3*) HM.

Cohen. Federal Income Tax. Date not set. pap. text, teacher ed. write for info. (*0-88277-725-4*) Foundation Pr.

— Fundamentals of Algebra & Trigonometry. Date not set. text. write for info. (*0-314-48118-4*) West Pub.

— A Guide to Networking. 112p. (C). 1990. pap. 10.00 (*0-87835-554-5*) Course Tech.

— Introduction to the Quantum Theory of Semiconductors. 2nd ed. 1998. pap. write for info. (*0-201-32829-1*) Addison-Wesley.

— Legal Research & Writing. (C). 2000. pap. 26.50 (*0-314-12578-7*) Thomson Learn.

— Medical Terminology. 592p. 1993. 27.50 (*0-685-74492-2*) Lppncott W & W.

— Medical Terminology: An Illustrated Guide. (Illus.). 396p. 1989. text 26.00 (*0-397-54716-1*) Lppncott W & W.

— Medical Terminology Medical Tapes. 1993. 24.95 (*0-397-55135-5*) Lppncott W & W.

— Metabolic & Molecular Bases of Disease, 2 vols. (Illus.). 2248p. 1990. text 375.00 (*0-7020-1493-1*, W B Saunders Co) Harcrt Hlth Sci Grp.

— Neuroendoscopy. Date not set. text. write for info. (*0-7216-7442-9*, W B Saunders Co) Harcrt Hlth Sci Grp.

— Oligonucleotides As Inhibitors of Gene Expression. 1990. 104.00 (*0-8493-7118-X*, QH) CRC Pr.

— Philosophers at Work. 1997. 41.00 (*0-15-504453-2*, Pub. by Harcourt Coll Pubs) Harcourt.

— Philosophers at Work. 2nd ed. (C). 1999. text 45.00 (*0-15-505599-2*, Pub. by Harcourt Coll Pubs) Harcourt.

— Post-Colonial Middle Ages. 1999. text 45.00 (*0-312-21929-6*) St Martin.

— Precalc High School. 2nd ed. (Math). 1987. mass mkt. 51.75 (*0-314-26211-3*) West Pub.

— Precalculus. 2nd ed. Date not set. pap. text, student ed. 21.95 (*0-314-60651-3*) West Pub.

— Precalculus. 4th ed. Date not set. pap. text, teacher ed. write for info. (*0-314-02298-8*) West Pub.

— Precalculus. 4th ed. 1993. mass mkt., student ed. 18.75 (*0-314-02299-6*) West Pub.

— Precalculus: A Problem Oriented Approach. 5th ed. (Mathematics Ser.). 1996. student ed. 25.00 (*0-314-20385-0*) Brooks-Cole.

— Precalculus with Unit Circle Trigonometry. 3rd ed. (Mathematics Ser.). 1998. student ed. 21.00 (*0-534-35277-4*) Brooks-Cole.

***Cohen.** The Reader Presidency. 2002. 22.00 (*0-07-239041-7*) McGraw.

Cohen. Rosty. 1998. 22.95 (*0-02-874099-8*) Free Pr.

— Systems Engineering Design. 2000. text. write for info. (*0-13-462359-2*) P-H.

— Tourist Guides. (Annals of Tourism Research Ser.). 1985. pap. 19.75 (*0-08-032397-9*, Pergamon Pr) Elsevier.

— The VirtuousTherapist: Ethical Practice of Counseling & Psychotherapy. LC 98-37866. (Counseling Ser.). 1998. pap. 24.95 (*0-534-34408-9*) Brooks-Cole.

Cohen. Workbook Constats. 162p. 1997. pap. text 30.67 (*0-13-522848-4*) P-H.

Cohen & Bushnell. The Basic Writing Notebook. 3rd ed. 162p. (C). 1997. ring bd. 24.95 (*0-7872-3940-2*) Kendall-Hunt.

Cohen & DeBack, Vivien. The Outcomes Mandate: Case Management in Healthcare Today. LC 98-37881. 432p. 1998. text 42.95 (*0-323-00277-3*) Mosby Inc.

Cohen & Hall. Criminal Prosecution: Post Investigative Cases & Materials, 1996 Supplement. 60p. 1996. pap. text, suppl. ed. 48.00 (*1-55834-391-1*, 10893-10, MICHIE) LEXIS Pub.

— Criminal Prosecution: Post Investigative Process, 1997 Supplement. 144p. 1997. pap. text, suppl. ed. 8.00 (*1-55834-654-6*, 10893-11, MICHIE) LEXIS Pub.

Cohen & Kraus. Thermal Management of Electronic Systems. 650p. 1997. write for info. (*0-12-078155-7*) Acad Pr.

Cohen & Lederer. Basic ACOL. 6th ed. 1993. 9.95 (*0-00-218440-0*, Pub. by HarpC) Trafalgar.

Cohen & Osterloh, Karl-Heinz. Herzlich Willkommen! (Advanced Course in Hotel & Restaurant Ser.). 102p. wbk. ed. 10.50 incl. audio (*3-468-49424-6*); 17.50 incl. audio (*3-468-49423-8*); 8.95 (*3-468-49425-4*) Langenscheidt.

***Cohen & Reddick.** Market Your Small Business Made E-Z. 224p. 2000. pap. 17.95 (*1-56382-454-X*) E-Z Legal.

Cohen & Sivit. Atlas of Pediatric & Fetal Ultrasound. LC 99-88758. (Illus.). 400p. 2000. 155.00 (*0-8385-8864-6*) McGraw.

Cohen, jt. auth. see Coffin.

Cohen, jt. auth. see Lilo.

Cohen, jt. auth. see Neft, David S.

Cohen, jt. auth. see Warr, Gregory W.

Cohen, David Bennett. David Bennett Cohen Teaches Blues Piano: A Hands-On Course in Traditional Blues Piano, Level 3. 2nd ed. (Listen & Learn Ser.). 40p. 1998. pap. 19.95 incl. audio compact disk (*0-7935-8857-X*) H Leonard.

Cohen, Evan. I Was a Murder Junkie: The Last Days of G. G. Allin. REC # 53. 153p. Date not set. pap. 15.99 (*0-9670170-0-9*) Recess Rcrds.

Cohen, Marie, ed. see Lott, Deborah A.

Cohen, Marie, jt. ed. see Lott, Deborah A.

Cohen, Mark L., jt. ed. see Prayson, Richard A.

Cohen, A. Algorithms in Algebra. (London Mathematical Society Student Texts Ser.: Vol. 30). (Illus.). 250p. (C). 1998. write for info. (*0-521-43046-1*); pap. write for info. (*0-521-43630-3*) Cambridge U Pr.

— Belle de Seigneur. (FRE.). 1986. 110.00 (*0-8288-3464-4*, F73582) Fr & Eur.

— Buffalo Nickel. (Illus.). 1979. pap. 13.00 (*0-932106-11-0*) S J Durst.

— Proverbs. rev. ed. 217p. 1985. 16.95 (*0-900689-33-1*) Soncino Pr.

— The Psalms: Hebrew Text, English Translation & Commentary Digest. rev. ed. 495p. 1992. 14.95 (*1-871055-65-2*) Soncino Pr.

— The Soncino Chumash. rev. ed. 1203p. 1993. 30.00 (*0-900689-24-2*) Soncino Pr.

Cohen, A., comment. The Twelve Prophets: Hebrew Text & English Translation. LC 93-23901. (Books of the Bible Ser.). 368p. 1994. 16.95 (*1-871055-80-6*) Soncino Pr.

Cohen, A., ed. Chronicles I & II. (HEB.). 360p. 1985. 16.95 (*0-900689-37-4*) Soncino Pr.

— Joshua & Judges. rev. ed. 332p. 1996. reprint ed. 16.95 (*0-900689-20-X*) Soncino Pr.

— Samuel One & Two. 361p. 1987. reprint ed. 16.95 (*0-900689-26-9*) Soncino Pr.

Cohen, A., et al, eds. Extrachromosomal Inheritance in Bacteria. (Contributions to Microbiology & Immunology Ser.: Vol. 6). 1980. pap. 92.25 (*3-8055-2943-0*) S Karger.

Cohen, A., tr. Ezekiel. 366p. 1985. 16.95 (*0-900689-30-7*) Soncino Pr.

— The Five Megilloth. rev. ed. (HEB.). 192p. 1990. 16.95 (*0-900689-85-4*) Soncino Pr.

— Isaiah: Hebrew Text, English Translation & Commentary Digest. rev. ed. (HEB.). 330p. 1987. 16.95 (*0-900689-28-5*) Soncino Pr.

— Jeremiah: Hebrew Text, English Translation & Commentary Digest. rev. ed. (HEB.). 361p. 1985. 16.95 (*0-900689-29-3*) Soncino Pr.

— Job. rev. ed. 226p. 1993. 16.95 (*0-900689-34-X*) Soncino Pr.

Cohen, A. & Van den Broecke, M. P., eds. The Tenth International Congress of Phonetic Sciences: Proceedings. (Netherlands Phonetic Archives Ser.). xviii, 819p. 1984. 229.25 (*90-70176-91-2*) Mouton.

Cohen, A. Clifford. Truncated & Censored Samples: Theory & Applications. (Statistics: Textbooks & Monographs: Vol. 119). (Illus.). 328p. 1991. text 165.00 (*0-8247-8447-2*) Dekker.

Cohen, A. Clifford & Whitten, Jones. Parameter Estimation in Reliability & Life Span Models. (Statistics: Textbooks & Monographs: Vol. 96). (Illus.). 312p. 1988. text 135.00 (*0-8247-7980-0*) Dekker.

C

Cohen, A. K. Delinquent Boys: The Culture of the Gang. LC 55-7337. 1971. pap. 14.95 (*0-02-905770-1*) Free Pr.

Cohen, A. M. Algebra Interactive. 1999. pap. text 39.95 (*3-540-14755-1*) Spr-Verlag.

Cohen, A. M., et al, eds. Algebraic Groups: Lecture Notes in Mathematics, Vol. 1271. 284p. 1987. 43.95 (*0-387-18234-9*) Spr-Verlag.

— Some Tapas of Computer Algebra. LC 98-51740. (Algorithms & Computation in Mathematics Ser.: Vol. 4). 350p. 1998. 49.95 (*3-540-63480-0*) Spr-Verlag.

Cohen, A. M. & Rosenmann, E., eds. The Cohen Diabetic Rat. (Illus.). xii, 200p. 1991. pap. 58.50 (*3-8055-5025-1*) S Karger.

Cohen, A. M., et al. Learning Algebra Was Never More Exciting! Algebra Interactive! LC 99-40882. 80p. 1999. 39.95 incl. cd-rom (*3-540-65368-6*) Spr-Verlag.

Cohen, A. S., et al. Capillary Electrophretic Separations of Drugs, Vol. 735. LC 96-33181. 458p. 1996. 258.50 (*0-444-82519-3*) Elsevier.

Cohen, Aaron & Woodring, Mike. Win32 Multithreaded Programming: Building Efficient High Performance Win32 Applications. Petrusha, Ronald, ed. (Nutshell: Windows 95/NT Ser.). (Illus.). 724p. (Orig.). 1997. pap. 39.95 (*1-56592-296-4*) OReilly & Assocs.

Cohen, Aaron I. International Encyclopedia of Women Composers, 2 vols. 2nd rev. ed. LC 86-72857. 1151p. 1987. 130.00 (*0-9617485-2-4*) Bks Music USA.

Cohen, Abner. Custom & Politics in Urban Africa: A Study of Hausa Migrants in Yoruba Towns. LC 68-55743. 264p. reprint ed. pap. 81.90 (*0-608-17919-1*, 202904100058) Bks Demand.

— Masquerade Politics: Explorations in the Structure of Urban Cultural Movements. LC 92-26339. 1993. 40.00 (*0-520-07838-1*, Pub. by U CA Pr) Cal Prin Full Svc.

— Two-Dimensional Man: An Essay on the Anthropology of Power & Symbolism in Complex Society. LC 72-93525. 1974. pap. 15.95 (*0-520-03241-1*, Pub. by U CA Pr) Cal Prin Full Svc.

Cohen, Abraham. Everyman's Talmud: The Major Teachings of the Rabbinic Sages. 1995. pap. 18.00 (*0-8052-1032-6*) Schocken.

Cohen, Ada. The Alexander Mosaic: Stories of Victory & Defeat. (Cambridge Studies in Classical Art & Iconography). (Illus.). 295p. (C). 1997. text 64.95 (*0-521-56339-9*) Cambridge U Pr.

***Cohen, Ada.** The Alexander Mosaic: Stories of Victory & Defeat. (Studies in Classical Art & Iconography). 295p. (C). 2000. pap. 29.95 (*0-521-77543-4*) Cambridge U Pr.

Cohen-Adad, R. Computer Assisted Calculation. text. write for info. (*0-471-48983-2*) Wiley.

Cohen, Adam & Posner, John, eds. A Guide to Clinical Drug Research. LC 95-8825. 212p. (C). 1996. text 99.50 (*0-7923-3508-2*) Kluwer Academic.

Cohen, Adam, jt. auth. see Taylor, Elizabeth.

***Cohen, Adam S.** The Uta Codex: Art, Philosophy & Reform. LC 99-40189. (Illus.). 2000. 65.00 (*0-271-01959-X*) Pa St U Pr.

Cohen-Addad, J. P., ed. Physical Properties of Polymeric Gels. 324p. 1996. 235.00 (*0-471-93971-4*) Wiley.

Cohen, Adele. Diary of an Exhibition. (Illus.). 36p. 1983. pap. 3.75 (*0-89822-032-7*) Visual Studies.

Cohen, Adir. The Educational Philosophy of Martin Buber. LC 81-68074. 350p. 1983. 40.00 (*0-8386-3098-7*) Fairleigh Dickinson.

— The Gate of Light: Janusz Korczak, the Educator & Writer Who Overcame the Holocaust. LC 92-55108. 1995. 46.50 (*0-8386-3523-7*) Fairleigh Dickinson.

— Love & Hope: Fromm & Education. Evans, Roy, ed. (Special Aspects of Education Ser.: Vol. 10). xiv, 114p. 1990. pap. text 69.00 (*2-88124-294-4*) Gordon & Breach.

Cohen, Akiba A. The Television News Interview. LC 87-13025. (Sage Context Ser.: No. 18). 160p. reprint ed. pap. 49.60 (*0-7837-6716-1*, 204634300011) Bks Demand.

Cohen, Akiba A. & Wolfsfeld, Gadi, eds. Framing the Intifada: People & Media. LC 92-42664. 248p. 1994. 73.25 (*0-89391-899-7*); pap. 39.50 (*0-89391-958-6*) Ablx Pub.

Cohen, Akiba A., et al. Social Conflict & Television News. LC 90-38951. (Sage Library of Social Research: Vol. 183). 258p. 1990. reprint ed. pap. 80.00 (*0-608-03372-3*, 205963600008) Bks Demand.

Cohen, Alain J., jt. auth. see Zakian, Michael.

Cohen, Alan. Are You As Happy As Your Dog? Sure Fire Ways to Wake Up with a Smile As Big As Your Pooch's. (Illus.). 96p. (Orig.). 1995. pap. 6.95 (*0-910367-29-9*) A Cohen.

— Companions of the Heart. (Illus.). 887p. 1987. 19.95 (*0-910367-38-8*) A Cohen.

— Dare to Be Yourself. 416p. 1994. reprint ed. pap. 12.50 (*0-449-90839-9*, Columbine) Fawcett.

— A Deep Breath of Life: Daily Inspiration for Heart-Centered Living. LC 96-22747. 384p. (Orig.). 1996. pap. 12.00 (*1-56170-337-0*, 198) Hay House.

— The Dragon Doesn't Live Here Anymore: Living Fully, Loving Freely. 416p. 1993. pap. 12.50 (*0-449-90840-2*, Columbine) Fawcett.

— Handle with Prayer: Harnessing the Power to Make Your Dreams Come Through. LC 97-38449. 208p. 1998. 12.95 (*1-56170-467-9*, 858) Hay House.

— Handle with Prayer: Harnessing the Power to Make Your Dreams Come Through. 208p. 1999. reprint ed. pap. 8.95 (*1-56170-616-7*, 858T) Hay House.

— Happily Even after: Can You Be Friends after Lovers? LC 99-27904. 224p. 1999. pap. 12.95 (*1-56170-629-9*) Hay House.

— Have You Hugged a Monster Today? (Illus.). 64p. (Orig.). 1984. pap. 3.95 (*0-910367-32-9*) A Cohen.

— Have You Hugged a Monster Today? 2nd ed. (Illus.). 64p. (Orig.). 1983. reprint ed. pap. 5.00 (*0-942494-73-3*) Coleman Pub.

— I Had It All the Time: When Self-Improvement Gives Way to Ecstasy. 348p. (Orig.). 1994. pap. 12.50 (*0-910367-53-1*) A Cohen.

— If We Only Have Love. (Illus.). (Orig.). 1984. pap. 2.00 (*0-942494-86-5*) Coleman Pub.

— Joy Is My Compass: Taking the Risk to Follow Your Bliss. LC 96-38824. 240p. 1996. reprint ed. pap. 11.95 (*1-56170-341-9*, 848) Hay House.

— Lifestyles of the Rich in Spirit: Living in a Win-Win World. LC 96-30689. 352p. 1996. pap. 12.95 (*1-56170-339-7*, 849) Hay House.

***Cohen, Alan.** Now. 2000. 40.00 (*0-226-11294-2*) U Ch Pr.

Cohen, Alan. The Peace That You Seek. (Illus.). 193p. (Orig.). 1985. 13.95 (*0-910367-35-3*, 157) A Cohen.

— Rising in Love: Opening Your Heart in All Your Relationships. LC 96-24369. 160p. 1996. reprint ed. pap. 10.95 (*1-56170-340-0*) Hay House.

— Setting the Seen: Creative Visualization for Healing. (Illus.). 27p. (Orig.). (C). 1982. pap. 2.95 (*0-910367-33-7*) A Cohen.

— Structure, Logic & Program Design. LC 83-10207. (Illus.). 301p. reprint ed. pap. 93.40 (*0-8357-4610-0*, 203754300008) Bks Demand.

— Time to Awaken: Collected Art & Writings of Ali Miner. 1997. pap. text 16.95 (*0-9655890-2-1*) Markowitz Pub.

— Visual Education Medical Terminology. 1991. pap. 10.95 (*1-55637-020-2*) Visual Educ.

Cohen, Alan M. A Guide to Networking. 2nd ed. LC 94-40235. 128p. 1995. pap. 25.95 (*0-87709-986-3*) Course Tech.

Cohen, Alan R. Surgical Disorders of the Fourth Ventricle. 512p. 1995. 235.00 (*0-86542-360-1*) Blackwell Sci.

Cohen, Alan R., ed. Cooley's Anemia: 7th Symposium. LC 98-17791. (Annals of the New York Academy of Sciences Ser.: No. 850). 527p. 1998. pap. 140.00 (*1-57331-122-7*) NY Acad Sci.

— Cooley's Anemia Vol. 850: 7th Symposium, Vol. 850. LC 98-17791. (Annals of the New York Academy of Sciences Ser.: No. 853). 527p. 1998. 140.00 (*1-57331-121-9*) NY Acad Sci.

Cohen, Alan R., jt. auth. see Haines, Stephen J.

Cohen, Alan S., ed. Laboratory Diagnostic Procedures in the Rheumatic Diseases. 3rd rev. ed. (Illus.). 416p. 1985. text 99.00 (*0-8089-1737-4*, 790879, Grune & Strat) Harcrt Hlth Sci Grp.

Cohen, Alan Y. Acid-Base Balance. (Illus.). 127p. 1990. pap. text 16.95 (*0-910271-01-1*) Critical Care Pr.

Cohen, Albert. Belle du Seigneur. (Gallimard Ser.). (FRE.). 1968. pap. 44.95 (*2-07-026917-5*) Schoenhof.

— Belle du Seigneur. Coward, David, tr. & intro. by. (SPA.). xviii, 974p. 1998. pap. 15.95 (*0-14-018871-1*) Viking Penguin.

— The Book of My Mother. Cohen, Bella, tr. from FRE. 124p. 1998. 32.95 (*0-7206-1024-9*, Pub. by P Owen Ltd) Dufour.

— Livre de Ma Mere. (Folio Ser.: No. 561). (FRE.). pap. 6.95 (*2-07-036561-1*) Schoenhof.

— Le Livre de Ma Mere. (FRE.). 192p. 1954. pap. 10.95 (*0-7859-1908-2*, 2070365611) Fr & Eur.

— Mangeclous. (Solal Et les Solal Ser.: Vol. II). (FRE.). 448p. 1983. pap. 13.95 (*0-7859-1909-0*, 2070371700) Fr & Eur.

— Mangeclous. (Folio Ser.: No. 1170). (FRE.). pap. 13.95 (*2-07-037170-0*) Schoenhof.

— Music in the French Royal Academy of Sciences: A Study in the Evolution of Musical Thought. LC 81-47118. 169p. 1981. reprint ed. pap. 52.40 (*0-7837-9321-9*, 206006100004) Bks Demand.

— O Vous, Freres Humaines. (FRE.). 213p. 1988. pap. 10.95 (*0-7859-2084-6*, 2070379159) Fr & Eur.

— Solal. (FRE.). 1981. pap. 11.95 (*0-7859-1933-3*, 2070372693) Fr & Eur.

— Solal. (Folio Ser.: No. 1269). (FRE.). pap. 10.95 (*2-07-037269-3*) Schoenhof.

— Les Valeureux. (FRE.). 344p. 1986. pap. 11.95 (*0-7859-2035-8*, 2070377407) Fr & Eur.

***Cohen, Albert, et al, eds.** Curve & Surface Fitting: Saint-Malo 1999. LC 99-86093. (Innovations in Applied Mathematics Ser.). (Illus.). 520p. 2000. 60.00 (*0-8265-1357-3*, Pub. by Vanderbilt U Pr) U of Okla Pr.

Cohen, Albert, ed. see Loulie.

Cohen, Alexander L. Elements of Ergonomics Programs: A Primer Based on Workplace Evaluations of Musculoskeletal Disorders. (Illus.). 133p. (C). 1998. pap. text 35.00 (*0-7881-7095-3*) DIANE Pub.

Cohen, Alfred M. & Winawer, Sidney J., eds. Cancer of the Colon, Rectum & Anus. (Illus.). 1154p. 1994. text 135.00 (*0-07-011601-6*) McGraw-Hill HPD.

Cohen, Alfred S. Tekhelet: The Renaissance of a Mitzvah. LC 96-41810. 1996. 17.95 (*0-88125-577-7*) Yeshiva Univ Pr.

Cohen, Alfred S., ed. Halacha & Contemporary Society. LC 84-741. 1985. pap. 12.95 (*0-88125-043-0*) Ktav.

Cohen, Alice Eve. The Tale of the Souvenir Shop. (Are You Afraid of the Dark? Ser.: No. 16). 144p. (YA). (gr. 3-6). 1997. pap. 3.99 (*0-671-00909-5*) PB.

Cohen, Allan R. Effective Behavior in Organizations: Cases, Concepts, & Student Experiences. 6th ed. LC 94-29530. 702p. (C). 1994. text 67.95 (*0-256-13164-3*, Irwn McGrw-H) McGrw-H Hghr Educ.

— The Portable MBA in Management. LC 92-41917. 392p. 1993. 29.95 (*0-471-57379-5*) Wiley.

— The Portable MBA in Management. LC 92-41917. 400p. 1995. pap. 19.95 (*0-471-12723-X*) Wiley.

Cohen, Allan R. & Bradford, David F. Influence Without Authority. 336p. 1991. pap. 19.95 (*0-471-54894-4*) Wiley.

***Cohen, Allan R. & Fink, Stephen L.** Effective Behavior in Organizations: Cases, Concepts & Student Experiences. 7th ed. LC 00-37002. 2001. write for info. (*0-07-239670-9*) McGraw-Hill Prof.

Cohen, Allan R. & Gadon, Herman. Alternative Work Schedules: Integrating Individual & Organizational Needs. LC 78-52506. 1978. pap. text. write for info. (*0-201-01052-6*) Addison-Wesley.

Cohen, Allan R., jt. auth. see Bradford, David L.

Cohen, Allen. John Huston: A Guide to Reference & Resources. LC 97-26286. 1997. 85.00 (*0-8161-1619-9*, G K Hall & Co) Mac Lib Ref.

— Reagan Poems. 31p. (Orig.). 1984. pap. text 3.50 (*1-879594-11-0*) Androgyne Bks.

Cohen, Allen, intro. The San Francisco Oracle Facsimile Edition. deluxe ed. (Illus.). 420p. 1990. reprint ed. 700.00 (*0-916147-12-6*) Regent Pr.

— The San Francisco Oracle Facsimile Edition. (Illus.). 420p. 1990. reprint ed. lib. bdg. 175.00 (*0-916147-11-8*) Regent Pr.

Cohen, Allen C. Beyond Basic Textiles. (Illus.). 323p. (C). 1982. pap. 40.00 (*0-87005-407-4*) Fairchild.

Cohen-Almagor, Raphael. The Boundaries of Liberty & Tolerance: The Struggle Against Kahanism in Israel. LC 93-33425. 352p. (C). 1994. 49.95 (*0-8130-1258-9*) U Press Fla.

***Cohen-Almagor, Raphael.** Liberal Democracy & the Limits of Tolerance: Essays in Honor & Memory of Yitzhak Rabin. 320p. (C). 2000. text 54.50 (*0-472-11016-0*, 11016) U of Mich Pr.

— Medical Ethics at the Dawn of the 21st Century. LC 00-40186. (Annals of the New York Academy of Sciences Ser.). 2000. pap. write for info. (*1-57331-300-9*) NY Acad Sci.

— Speech, Media & Ethics, the Limits of Free Expression: Critical Studies on Freedom of Expression, Freedom of the Press & the Public's Right to Know. LC 00-33301. 2000. write for info. (*0-312-23607-7*) St Martin.

***Cohen-Almagor, Raphael, ed.** Challenges to Democracy: Essays in Honour & Memory of Isaiah Berlin. LC 99-55687. 298p. 2000. text 87.95 (*0-7546-2095-6*, Pub. by Ashgate Pub) Ashgate Pub Co.

Cohen, Amanda. Two's Company. 1999. pap. 4.99 (*0-14-054901-3*) NAL.

Cohen, Amnon. A World Within: Jewish Life As Reflected in Muslim Court Documents from the Sijill of Jerusalem (XVIth Century), 2 vols., Set. LC 94-43469. 587p. 1995. pap., suppl. ed. 50.00 (*0-9602686-8-5*) Center Judaic Studies.

Cohen, Amnon & Lewis, Bernard. Population & Revenue in the Towns of Palestine in the Sixteenth Century. LC 78-51160. 228p. 1978. reprint ed. pap. 70.70 (*0-7837-9322-7*, 206006200004) Bks Demand.

***Cohen, Amy & Muskat, Hedda.** Dating: A Singles Guide to a Fun, Flirtatious & Possibly Meaningful Relationship. LC 99-16914. 176p. 1999. pap. 12.95 (*1-57071-478-9*) Sourcebks.

Cohen, Andrea. The Cartographer's Vacation. 84p. 1999. pap. 12.00 (*0-937669-63-6*) Owl Creek Pr.

Cohen, Andrea M. & Weiner, William J. The Comprehensive Management of Parkinson's Disease. LC 94-26984. (Comprehension Neurologic Rehabilitation Ser.: 8). 288p. 1994. text 74.95 (*0-939957-74-4*) Demos Medical.

Cohen, Andrew. Absolute Relationship to Life: A Talk on Enlightenment & the Human Condition. LC 98-122185. 60p. 1997. pap. text 6.00 (*1-883929-19-9*) Moksha Pr.

— Autobiography of an Awakening. 152p. 1992. pap. 10.95 (*0-9622678-4-8*) Moksha Pr.

***Cohen, Andrew.** The Battle for Freedom, Set. 2000. 17.95 incl. audio (*1-883929-31-8*) Moksha Pr.

Cohen, Andrew. British Policy in Changing Africa. LC 59-6733. (Northwestern University, Evanston, Ill. African Studies: No. 2). 126p. reprint ed. pap. 39.10 (*0-8357-7427-9*, 200694200060) Bks Demand.

— Challenge of Enlightenment: A Voyage into the Multidimensional Integrity of Nonduality. 60p. 1996. pap. text 6.00 (*1-883929-14-8*) Moksha Pr.

***Cohen, Andrew.** Embracing Heaven & Earth: The Liberation Teachings of Andrew Cohen. 150p. 2000. pap. 14.95 (*1-883929-29-6*, Pub. by Moksha Pr) New Leaf Dist.

Cohen, Andrew. Enlightenment Is a Secret: Teachings of Liberation. 2nd ed. LC 95-79669. 276p. 1995. pap. 14.95 (*1-883929-08-3*) Moksha Pr.

— Freedom Has No History: A Call to Awaken. LC 96-77414. 130p. 1997. pap. text 10.95 (*1-883929-17-2*) Moksha Pr.

— In Defense of the Guru Principle. 1999. pap. 5.95 (*1-883929-27-X*) Moksha Pr.

— My Master Is My Self: The Birth of a Spiritual Teacher. 2nd ed. LC 95-75484. 103p. 1995. pap. 10.95 (*1-883929-07-5*) Moksha Pr.

— Promise of Perfection. 1998. pap. 6.00 (*1-883929-21-0*) Moksha Pr.

Cohen, Andrew. An Unconditional Relationship to Life. LC 94-73672. 155p. 1995. pap. 10.95 (*1-883929-04-0*) Moksha Pr.

— What Is Enlightenment?, Set. 2000. 34.95 incl. audio (*1-883929-28-8*) Moksha Pr.

— Who Am I? & How Shall I Live? 1998. pap. 6.00 (*1-883929-24-5*) Moksha Pr.

***Cohen, Andrew.** Who Am I? & How Shall I Live? 1998. 10.95 incl. audio (*1-883929-26-1*) Moksha Pr.

***Cohen, Andrew & Granatstein, Jack L.** Trudeau's Shadow: The Life & Legacy of Pierre Elliott Trudeau. 408p. 1999. pap. 0.00 (*0-679-31006-1*) Random.

Cohen, Andrew, jt. auth. see Brown, Don.

Cohen, Andrew, ed. see Andrew Cohen Students.

Cohen, Andrew D. Assessing Language Ability in the Classroom. 2nd ed. LC 93-41932. (J). 1994. text 27.95 (*0-8384-4262-5*) Heinle & Heinle.

— Language Learning: Insights of Learning. (J). 1990. mass mkt., teacher ed. 27.95 (*0-8384-2676-X*) Heinle & Heinle.

— Strategies in Learning & Using a Second Language. LC 97-33360. (Annotated English Poets Ser.). 1998. pap. text 26.08 (*0-582-30588-8*) Addison-Wesley.

Cohen, Andrew D., jt. ed. see Bachman, Lyle F.

Cohen, Andrew M. New York State & Federal Criminal Practice & Procedure. LC 96-14376. 1996. write for info. (*1-57588-079-2*, 310460) W S Hein.

Cohen, Andrew N. Gateway to the Inland Coast: The Story of the Carquinez Strait. unabridged ed. (Illus.). 162p. 1996. 35.00 (*0-9660534-0-0*); pap. 21.95 (*0-9660534-1-9*) CA St Lands.

Cohen, Annabelle. Handbook of Cellular Chemistry. 304p. (C). 1995. pap. text, per. 29.95 (*0-7872-0484-6*) Kendall-Hunt.

Cohen, Annabelle & Hayman, Linda. Traditions: America's Thanksgiving Parade Cookbook. LC 98-235597. ii, 100 p. write for info. (*0-9660885-0-6*) Parade Co.

Cohen, Anne. Practical Administrative Law Paralegals. LC 95-37729. (Paralegal). 450p. (C). 1996. mass mkt. 87.95 (*0-314-06505-9*) West Pub.

Cohen, Anne B. Poor Pearl, Poor Girl! The Murdered Girl Stereotype in Ballad & Newspaper. LC 73-7919. (Publications of the American Folklore Society, Bibliographical & Special Ser.: No. 58). 149p. reprint ed. pap. 46.20 (*0-7837-0089-X*, 204036400016) Bks Demand.

Cohen, Annette R. & Druley, Ray M. The Buffalo Nickel. (Illus.). 130p. (Orig.). 1979. pap. 7.50 (*0-939836-00-9*) Potomac Ent.

***Cohen, Anthea.** Angel Dust. large type ed. 336p. 1999. pap. 20.99 (*1-85389-928-3*, Dales) Ulverscroft.

— Angel of Vengeance. large type ed. 336p. 2000. 20.99 (*1-84137-013-4*) Mgna Lrg Print.

Cohen, Anthea. The Green Girl. 1978. pap. 1.25 (*0-590-05371-X*) Scholastic Inc.

***Cohen, Anthea.** Ministering Angels. large type ed. 336p. 1999. pap. 20.99 (*1-85389-929-1*, Dales) Ulverscroft.

Cohen, Anthony. Underground Railroad in Montgomery County, Maryland: A History & Driving Guide. rev. ed. 38p. 1995. pap. text 7.00 (*0-9601094-0-4*) Montgomery Co Hist.

Cohen, Anthony P. Self Consciousness: An Alternative Anthropology of Identity. LC 94-344. 244p. (C). 1997. pap. 24.99 (*0-415-08324-9*, B4363) Routledge.

***Cohen, Anthony P.** Signifying Identities: Anthropological Perspectives on Boundaries & Contested Values LC 99-30607. 1999. pap. write for info. (*0-415-19238-2*) Routledge.

Cohen, Anthony P. Symbolic Construction of Community. (Key Ideas Ser.). 150p. (C). 1985. pap. 17.99 (*0-415-04616-5*) Routledge.

— Symbolic Construction of Community. (Key Ideas Ser.). 150p. 1985. pap. 8.95 (*0-85312-855-3*, 9583, Pub. by Tavistock-E Horwood) Routldge.

***Cohen, Anthony P., ed.** Signifying Identities: Anthropological Perspectives on Boundaries & Contested Values. LC 99-30607. 208p. (C). 1999. text. write for info. (*0-415-19237-4*) Routledge.

Cohen, Anthony P., ed. Whalsay: Symbol, Segment & Boundary in the Shetland Community. LC 87-34004. 248p. 1989. text 59.95 (*0-7190-2340-8*) Manchester Univ Pr.

Cohen, Anthony P. & Fukui, Katsuyoshi, eds. Humanizing the City: Social Contexts of Urban Life at the Turn of the Millennium. (Illus.). 240p. 1993. 68.00 (*0-7486-0388-3*, Pub. by Edinburgh U Pr) Col U Pr.

Cohen, Anthony P. & Rapport, Nigel, eds. Questions of Consciousness. LC 95-15785. (ASA Monographs Ser.: Vol. 33). 256p. (C). 1995. pap. 27.99 (*0-415-12396-8*) Routledge.

Cohen-Apte. Manufacturing Automation. LC 96-29709. 352p. 1997. 75.00 (*0-256-14606-3*) McGraw.

Cohen, Ariel. Russian Imperialism: Development & Crisis. LC 95-43730. 200p. 1996. 59.95 (*0-275-95337-8*, Praeger Pubs) Greenwood.

— Russian Imperialism: Development & Crisis. LC 95-43730. 200p. 1998. pap. 19.95 (*0-275-96481-7*, Praeger Pubs) Greenwood.

— Think Generic! The Meaning & Use of Generic Sentences. LC 99-13301. (Dissertations in Linguistics Ser.). 224p. 1999. 64.95 (*1-57586-207-7*, Pub. by CSLI); pap. 22.95 (*1-57586-208-5*, Pub. by CSLI) Cambridge U Pr.

Cohen, Arlene, ed. PIALA '98: Libraries, Archives & Museums - What's in Them for Us? LC 99-462607. 1999. pap. text 25.00 (*1-892485-05-2*) Pacfc Islds Assn.

— Piala '95: Preservation of Culture Through Archives & Libraries. vii, 125p. 1996. pap. text 20.00 (*1-892485-02-8*) Pacfc Islds Assn.

— Piala '94 - Pacific Information Liberation: The Wave of the Future. vi, 114p. 1995. pap. text 13.50 (*1-892485-01-X*) Pacfc Islds Assn.

— Piala '97 Wasahn Kamarain: Place of Enlightenment. LC 99-179475. 1998. pap. text 25.00 (*1-892485-04-4*) Pacfc Islds Assn.

— Piala '96: Jaketo Jaketak Kobban Alele Eo: Identifying, Using & Sharing Local Resources. vii, 125p. 1997. pap. text 25.00 (*1-892485-03-6*) Pacfc Islds Assn.

Cohen, Armond. Poletown, Detroit: A Case Study in Public Use & Reindustrialization. LC KF9922.C6. (Lincoln Institute Monograph: No. 82-5). 53p. reprint ed. pap. 30.00 (*0-7837-2161-7*, 204246600004) Bks Demand.

Cohen, Arnold. Introduction to Jewish Civil Law. 23.95 (*0-87306-537-9*) Feldheim.

C

Cohen, Arnold B. Guide to Secured Lending Transactions. 1988. text 115.00 (*0-685-69623-5*, TGSL) Warren Gorham & Lamont.

Cohen, Arnold B. & Miller, Mitchell W. Consumer Bankruptcy Manual. 2nd ed. (Bankruptcy Law Ser.). 1186p. 1991. 145.00 (*0-7913-0895-2*) Warren Gorham & Lamont.

— Consumer Bankruptcy Manual, No. 1. 2nd ed. (Bankruptcy Law Ser.). 1186p. 1992. suppl. ed. 57.00 (*0-7913-1238-0*) Warren Gorham & Lamont.

Cohen, Arnon. Biomedical Signal Processing. 2nd ed. 1994. 125.00 (*0-8493-4238-4*) CRC Pr.

— Biomedical Signal Processing, Vol. I: Time & Frequency Domains Analysis. 176p. 1986. 105.00 (*0-8493-5933-3*, R857, CRC Reprint) Franklin.

— Biomedical Signal Processing, Vol. II: Compression & Automatic Recognition. 192p. 1986. 120.00 (*0-8493-5934-1*, CRC Reprint) Franklin.

Cohen, Arthur. Become Streetwise! A Woman's Guide to Personal Safety. (Illus.). 132p. 1993. pap. 11.95 (*0-922759-01-4*) Target Consult Intl.

Cohen, Arthur A. Acts of Theft. (Phoenix Fiction Ser.). viii, 312p. 1987. pap. 11.95 (*0-226-11250-0*) U Ch Pr.

— An Admirable Woman. LC 82-49342. 240p. 1998. pap. 10.95 (*0-87923-705-8*) Godine.

— Artists & Enemies. LC 86-45535. 256p. 1987. 16.95 (*0-87923-650-7*) Godine.

— The Communism of Mao Tse-Tung. LC 64-23420. 210p. reprint ed. pap. 65.10 (*0-608-09286-X*, 205416000004) Bks Demand.

— Herbert Bayer: The Complete Work. (Illus.). 448p. 1984. pap. text 38.50 (*0-262-53075-9*) MIT Pr.

— A Hero in His Time. (Phoenix Fiction Ser.). 280p. 1987. pap. 11.95 (*0-226-11252-7*) U Ch Pr.

— In the Days of Simon Stern. (Phoenix Fiction Ser.). vi, 466p. 1987. pap. 12.95 (*0-226-11254-3*) U Ch Pr.

— The Tremendum: A Theological Interpretation of the Holocaust. 120p. 1993. reprint ed. pap. 10.95 (*0-8264-0634-3*) Continuum.

Cohen, Arthur A., et al, eds. Humanistic Education & Western Civilization: Essays for Robert M. Hutchins. LC 72-13226. (Essay Index Reprint Ser.). 1977. reprint ed. 18.95 (*0-8369-8150-2*) Ayer.

C

Cohen, Arthur A. & Mendes-Flohr, Paul R. Contemporary Jewish Religious Thought. 1184p. 1988. per. 27.95 (*0-02-906040-0*) Free Pr.

Cohen, Arthur A., et al. An Arthur A. Cohen Reader: Selected Fiction & Writings on Judaism, Theology, Literature & Culture. LC 97-23839. 1998. pap. 29.95 (*0-8143-2282-4*) Wayne St U Pr.

Cohen, Arthur M. College Responses to Community Demands. LC 74-27912. (Jossey-Bass Higher Education Ser.). 208p. reprint ed. pap. 64.50 (*0-608-14790-7*, 202565200045) Bks Demand.

— The Shaping of American Higher Education: Emergence & Growth of the Contemporary System. LC 98-11854. (Health & Psychology Ser.). 512p. 1998. 39.95 (*0-7879-1029-5*) Jossey-Bass.

Cohen, Arthur M., ed. Relating Curriculum & Transfer. LC 85-644753. (New Directions for Community Colleges Ser.: No. CC86). 110p. (Orig.). 1994. pap. 22.00 (*0-7879-9958-X*) Jossey-Bass.

Cohen, Arthur M. & Brawer, Florence B. The American Community College. LC 81-19319. (Jossey-Bass Series in Higher Education). 475p. reprint ed. pap. 147.30 (*0-8357-4874-X*, 203780600009) Bks Demand.

— The American Community College. 3rd rev. ed. (Higher & Adult Education Ser.). 524p. 1996. 40.00 (*0-7879-0189-X*) Jossey-Bass.

Cohen, Arthur M., et al. Managing Community Colleges: A Handbook for Effective Practice. LC 93-43162. (Higher & Adult Education Ser.). 522p. 1994. 48.00 (*1-55542-620-4*) Jossey-Bass.

Cohen, Arthur M., jt. auth. see Epperly, Robert W.

Cohen, Aryeh & Magid, Shaul. Reading a Beginning, Beginning a Reading: Toward a Hermeneutic of Jewish Texts. (Illus.). 2000. pap. text 25.95 (*1-889119-23-7*) Seven Bridges.

Cohen, Asher. The Halutz Resistance in Hungary, 1942-1944. (East European Monographs: No. 206). 277p. 1986. text 55.50 (*0-88033-103-8*, Pub. by East Eur Monographs) Col U Pr.

Cohen, Asher, ed. Dapim: Studies on the Shoah, Vol. 1. Alpert, Carl, tr. from HEB. LC 91-31432. 450p. 1992. 65.95 (*0-8204-1663-0*) P Lang Pubng.

Cohen, Asher, et al, eds. Comprehending the Holocaust: Historical & Literary Research. 372p. 1988. 57.00 (*3-631-40428-X*) P Lang Pubng.

— Dapim: Studies on the Shoah. (American University Studies: History: Ser. IX, Vol. 73). (Illus.). 278p. (C). 1991. text 46.95 (*0-8204-0960-X*) P Lang Pubng.

Cohen, Asher & Cochavi, Yehoyakim, eds. Tenu' ot ha-no' ar ha-Tsiyoniyot ba-Sho ah (eng.) Zionist Youth Movements During the Shoah. 4. Gorelick, Ted, tr. from HEB. LC 94-27841. (Studies on the Shoah: Vol. 4). 346p. (C). 1995. pap. text 40.95 (*0-8204-2586-9*) P Lang Pubng.

***Cohen, Asher & Susser, Bernard.** Israel & the Politics of Jewish Identity: The Secular-Religious Impasse. LC 99-89238. 2000. 36.00 (*0-8018-6345-7*) Johns Hopkins.

Cohen, Avis H., et al. Neural Control of Rhythmic Movements in Vertebrates. LC 87-21573. (Neurobiology Ser.). 500p. 1988. 325.00 (*0-471-81968-9*) Wiley.

Cohen, Avner. Israel & the Bomb. LC 98-3402. 432p. 1998. 27.50 (*0-231-10482-0*) Col U Pr.

— Israel & the Bomb. 478p. 1999. pap. 17.95 (*0-231-10483-9*) Col U Pr.

Cohen, Avner & Dascal, Marcelo, eds. The Institution of Philosophy: A Discipline in Crisis? 350p. 1989. 46.95 (*0-8126-9093-1*) Open Court.

— The Institution of Philosophy: A Discipline in Crisis? 350p. 1989. pap. 22.95 (*0-8126-9094-X*) Open Court.

Cohen, Avner & Lee, Steven, eds. Nuclear Weapons & the Future of Humanity: The Fundamental Questions. LC 84-18362. (Philosophy & Society Ser.). (Illus.). 512p. (C). 1986. pap. 31.00 (*0-8476-7258-1*) Rowman.

Cohen, B. Developing Sociological Knowledge: Theory & Method. 1980. pap. 22.95 (*0-685-03828-9*) P-H.

Cohen, B., et al. The Specification of Complex Systems. 160p. (C). 1986. text. write for info. (*0-201-14400-X*) Addison-Wesley.

Cohen, B. Bernard, ed. The Recognition of Nathaniel Hawthorne: Selected Criticism since 1828. LC 70-83454. 320p. reprint ed. pap. 99.20 (*0-608-13969-6*, 205560900029) Bks Demand.

Cohen, Barbara. The Carp in the Bathtub. LC 87-80446. (Illus.). 32p. (J). (gr. k-5). 1987. pap. 5.95 (*0-930494-67-9*) Kar-Ben.

Cohen, Barbara. The Carp in the Bathtub. 48p. (J). (gr. 2-4). pap. 5.95 (*0-8072-1332-2*) Listening Lib.

Cohen, Barbara. The Carp in the Bathtub. (J). 1972. 11.15 (*0-606-03993-7*, Pub. by Turtleback) Demco.

— The Chocolate Wolf. LC 91-46434. (Illus.). 32p. (J). (ps-3). 1996. 15.95 (*0-399-21961-7*, Philomel) Peng Put Young Read.

— David, a Biography. (Illus.). 128p. (J). (gr. 4-7). 1995. 15.95 (*0-395-58702-6*, Clarion Bks) HM.

— First Fast. (Illus.). 32p. (J). (gr. 4-6). 1987. 7.95 (*0-8074-0354-7*, 101066) UAHC.

— Here Come the Purim Players! LC 97-52632. (Illus.). (J). (gr. k-3). 1998. 12.95 (*0-8074-0645-7*, 101251) UAHC.

— Make a Wish, Molly. (J). 1994. pap. 4.50 (*0-440-91018-8*) BDD Bks Young Read.

— Make a Wish, Molly. 48p. (J). (gr. 4-7). 1995. pap. 3.50 (*0-440-41058-4*) Dell.

— Make a Wish, Molly. (J). 1995. 8.95 (*0-606-07831-2*) Turtleback.

— Molly y los Peregrinos (Molly's Pilgrims) Fiol, Maria A., tr. (Illus.). 32p. (YA). (gr. 5 up). 1995. 12.95 (*1-880507-17-X*) Lectorum Pubns.

— Molly y los Peregrinos (Molly's Pilgrims) Fiol, Maria A., tr. (Illus.). 32p. (YA). (gr. 5 up). 1997. pap. 6.95 (*1-880507-34-X*) Lectorum Pubns.

— Molly's Pilgrim. 48p. (J). (gr. 4-7). 1990. pap. 3.50 (*0-440-41057-6*) Dell.

— Molly's Pilgrim. (Bantam First Skylark Bks.). (J). 1990. 8.70 (*0-606-04748-4*, Pub. by Turtleback) Demco.

— Molly's Pilgrim. rev. ed. LC 98-9227. (Illus.). 32p. (J). (gr. 1 up). 1998. mass mkt. 3.99 (*0-688-16280-0*, Wm Morrow) Morrow Avon.

— Molly's Pilgrim. rev. ed. LC 98-9227. (Illus.). 32p. (J). (gr. 1 up). 1998. 15.00 (*0-688-16279-7*, Wm Morrow) Morrow Avon.

— Robin Hood & Little John. 1998. 11.19 (*0-606-13744-0*, Pub. by Turtleback) Demco.

— The Secret Grove. LC 85-51146. (Illus.). 32p. (J). (gr. 5-7). 1985. 7.95 (*0-8074-0301-6*, 101065) UAHC.

— The Secret Grove. large type ed. (Illus.). 1993. 9.50 (*0-614-09854-8*, L-34125-00) Am Printing Hse.

Cohen, Barbara. Seven Daughters & Seven Sons. 1994. 10.05 (*0-606-06727-2*, Pub. by Turtleback) Demco.

— A Stranger Came Ashore, Set. unabridged ed. (J). (gr. 5). 1997. pap. 38.75 incl. audio Recorded Bks.

Cohen, Barbara. Thank You, Jackie Robinson. LC 87-29341. (Illus.). 128p. 1997. mass mkt. 4.95 (*0-688-15293-7*, Wm Morrow) Morrow Avon.

— Thank You, Jackie Robinson. 128p. (J). (gr. 3-7). 1989. pap. 3.99 (*0-590-42378-9*) Scholastic Inc.

— Two Hundred & Thirteen Valentines. 1993. 10.15 (*0-606-12555-8*, Pub. by Turtleback) Demco.

— Two Hundred Thirteen Valentines. LC 91-7151. (Redfeather Fiction Ser.). (Illus.). 64p. (J). (gr. 2-4). 1995. 13.95 (*0-8050-1536-1*, Redfeather BYR); pap. 4.95 (*0-8050-2627-4*, Redfeather BYR) H Holt & Co.

— Woman's Best Friend: A Celebration of Dogs & Their Women. 128p. (gr. 8). 1996. 16.95 (*0-316-15054-1*) Little.

Cohen, Barbara & Lovejoy, Bahija. Seven Daughters & Seven Sons. 1995. 18.75 (*0-8446-6806-0*) Peter Smith.

— Seven Daughters & Seven Sons. Cohn, Amy, ed. LC 94-80. 128p. (YA). (gr. 7 up). 1994. reprint ed. mass mkt. 4.95 (*0-688-13563-3*, Wm Morrow) Morrow Avon.

Cohen, Barbara & Taylor, Louise. Cats & Their Women. (Illus.). 117p. 1992. pap. 12.95 (*0-316-15046-0*) Little.

— Dogs & Their Women. (Illus.). 116p. (Orig.). 1989. pap. 12.95 (*0-316-15036-3*) Little.

— Horses & Their Women. LC 92-26924. 117p. 1993. pap. 12.95 (*0-316-15051-7*) Little.

— Woman's Best Friend. 1996. 15.95 (*0-614-96842-9*); 15.95 (*0-614-96965-4*) Little.

Cohen, Barbara & Tornberg, Robert E. First Fast. (Illus.). 32p. (J). (gr. 4-6). 1988. pap., teacher ed. 5.00 (*0-8074-0411-X*, 201445) UAHC.

Cohen, Barbara, jt. auth. see Duff, Carolyn.

Cohen, Barbara E. Dog in the Dunes. LC 99-176148. (Illus.). 32p. 1998. 8.95 (*0-8362-6920-9*) Andrews & McMeel.

Cohen, Barbara E., jt. auth. see Burt, Martha R.

Cohen, Barbara E., ed. see Fowler, Melvin L.

Cohen, Barbara Janson. Medical Terminology: An Illustrated Guide. 3rd ed. LC 97-4344. 544p. 1997. spiral bd. 32.00 (*0-7817-1411-7*) Lppncott W & W.

Cohen, Barbara Janson & Wood, Dena Lin. Memmler's Structure & Function of the Human Body. 7th ed. 416p. pap. text 34.95 (*0-7817-2438-4*) Lppncott W & W.

— Memmler's Structure of Function of the Human Body. 8th ed. LC 99-37062. 384p. 2000. text. write for info. (*0-7817-2113-X*) Lppncott W & W.

— Memmler's Study Guide for Structure & Function of the Human Body. 7th ed. 320p. pap. text 18.95 (*0-7817-2115-6*) Lppncott W & W.

— Memmler's Study Guide for the Human Body in Health & Disease. 9th ed. 320p. pap. text 18.95 (*0-7817-2111-3*) Lppncott W & W.

— Memmler's the Human Body in Health & Disease. 9th ed. 544p. text 39.95 (*0-7817-2439-2*) Lppncott W & W.

Cohen, Barend, jt. auth. see Physicians for Human Rights Staff.

Cohen, Barney, ed. see Committee on Population, National Research Council.

Cohen, Barney, ed. see National Research Council Staff.

***Cohen, Barry.** Let the Storm Burst. LC 99-96860. 2000. pap. 12.95 (*0-533-13363-7*) Vantage.

Cohen, Barry & Quirin, Jim. Rock One Hundred: An Authoritative Ranking of the Most Popular Songs for Each Year, 1954 Through 1991. 5th deluxe ed. 280p. 1993. pap. 12.95 (*0-917190-21-1*) Chartmasters.

Cohen, Barry, jt. auth. see Quinn, Jim.

***Cohen, Barry H.** Explaining Psychological Statistics. 2nd ed. 830p. 2000. 65.00 (*0-471-34582-2*) Wiley.

Cohen, Barry M. W. O. W. 2000: How to Turn Employees into Owners, How to Create a Profitable Concept, How to Find the W. O. W. Niche, How to Change. Scurlock, James D., ed. (Illus.). 205p. (Orig.). 1997. pap. 15.00 (*0-9657602-0-0*) Savannah Corp.

Cohen, Barry M., et al, eds. Multiple Personality Disorder from the Inside Out. LC 91-60530. (Illus.). xxii, 245p. (Orig.). 1991. pap. 16.95 (*0-9629164-0-4*) Sidran Pr.

Cohen, Barry M. & Cox, Carol T. Telling Without Talking: Art As a Window into the World of Multiple Personality. (Illus.). 320p. (C). 1995. 45.00 (*0-393-70196-4*) Norton.

Cohen, Barry M., et al. Managing Traumatic Stress Through Art: Drawing from the Center. LC 95-68155. xviii, 174p. (Orig.). 1995. pap. 19.95 (*0-9629164-7-1*) Sidran Pr.

Cohen, Barry M., jt. auth. see Scurlock, James D.

Cohen, Barry S., et al. Traffic Law & Practice in Wisconsin, 2 vols. 2nd ed. LC 94-24027. 1050p. 1995. ring bd. 149.00 (*0-945574-65-7*) State Bar WI.

Cohen, Basuk & Cohen, Waye. Practical Flexible Sigmoidoscopy. (Illus.). 192p. 1995. 54.95 (*0-89640-272-X*) Igaku-Shoin.

Cohen, Becky, jt. auth. see Oliveros, Pauline.

Cohen, Bella, tr. see Cohen, Albert.

Cohen, Ben. Ben & Jerry's Double Dip. 304p. 1998. per. 13.00 (*0-684-83855-9*, Fireside) S&S Trade Pap.

— VHDL Answers to Frequently Asked Questions. LC 96-43190. 320p. (C). 1996. text 121.00 (*0-7923-9791-6*) Kluwer Academic.

— VHDL Answers to Frequently Asked Questions. 2nd ed. LC 97-47346. 416p. 1998. lib. bdg. 120.00 (*0-7923-8115-7*) Kluwer Academic.

— VHDL Coding Styles & Methodologies. LC 95-30425. 365p. (C). 1995. text 114.00 (*0-7923-9598-0*) Kluwer Academic.

— VHDL Coding Styles & Methodologies. 2nd ed. LC 99-17750. xviii, 453p. 1999. write for info. (*0-7923-8474-1*) Kluwer Academic.

Cohen, Ben, et al. Ben & Jerry's Homemade Ice Cream & Dessert Book. LC 86-40543. (Illus.). 128p. (Orig.). 1987. pap. 8.95 (*0-89480-312-3*, 1312) Workman Pub.

Cohen, Benjamin, ed. Banks & the Balance of Payments: Private Lending in the International Adjustment Process. LC 81-1805. 256p. 1981. 53.00 (*0-86598-038-1*) Rowman.

Cohen, Benjamin I. Multinational Firms & Asian Exports. LC 74-17551. (Publication of the Economic Growth Center, Yale University Ser.). 189p. reprint ed. pap. 58.60 (*0-8357-8741-9*, 203369400087) Bks Demand.

Cohen, Benjamin J. Developing-Country Debt: A Middle Way. LC 89-7511. (Essays in International Finance Ser.: No. 173). 42p. 1989. pap. 10.00 (*0-88165-080-3*) Princeton U Int Finan Econ.

— The Financial Support Fund of the OECD: A Failed Initiative. LC 97-17544. (Essays in International Finance Ser.: Vol. 204). 36p. 1997. pap. 10.00 (*0-88165-111-7*) Princeton U Int Finan Econ.

— The Geography of Money. LC 97-32860. 1998. pap. 17.95 (*0-8014-8513-4*) Cornell U Pr.

— The Geography of Money. LC 97-32860. (Illus.). 272p. 1998. text 25.00 (*0-8014-3513-7*) Cornell U Pr.

Cohen, Benjamin J., ed. The International Political Economy of Monetary Relations. (Library of International Political Economy: Vol. 3). 680p. 1993. 255.00 (*1-85278-575-6*) E Elgar.

— International Trade & Finance: New Frontiers for Research. LC 96-49927. (Illus.). 412p. (C). 1997. text 54.95 (*0-521-58086-2*) Cambridge U Pr.

Cohen, Benjamin J. & Lipson, Charles, eds. Issues & Agents in International Political Economy: An International Organization Reader. LC 98-50262. (IO Reader Ser.). (Illus.). 384p. 1999. 50.00 (*0-262-03267-8*); pap. 25.00 (*0-262-53160-7*) MIT Pr.

Cohen, Benjamin J., jt. ed. see Lipson, Charles.

Cohen, Benjamin V. The United Nations: Constitutional Developments, Growth & Possibilities. LC 61-16691. (Oliver Wendell Holmes Lectures: 1961). 116p. 1961. 20.00 (*0-674-92265-4*) HUP.

***Cohen, Benjamin V.** The United Nations: Constitutional Developments, Growth & Possibilities. 118p. 1999. 22.95 (*0-7351-0183-3*) Replica Bks.

Cohen, Bentsi & Kellner, Maya G., eds. Haggadah from Four Corners of the Earth. (HEB, RUS, SPA, FRE & ENG., Illus.). 112p. 1999. reprint ed. text 20.00 (*0-7881-6427-9*) DIANE Pub.

Cohen, Benyamin. Torah from Dixie. 1997. 17.95 (*0-87306-907-2*) Feldheim.

Cohen, Bernard. Interactions: Some Contacts Between the Natural Sciences & the Social Sciences. LC 94-11074. 224p. 1994. 38.50 (*0-262-03223-6*) MIT Pr.

— Radon: A Homeowner's Guide to Detection & Control. 1989. pap. 3.95 (*0-380-70782-9*, Avon Bks) Morrow Avon.

— Science & Founding Fathers: Science in the Political Thought of Thomas Jefferson, Benjamin Franklin, John Adams, & James Madison. 368p. 1997. pap. 15.95 (*0-393-31510-X*) Norton.

— Sociocultural Changes in American Jewish Life As Reflected in Selected Jewish Literature. LC 75-146162. 282p. 1975. 36.50 (*0-8386-7848-3*) Fairleigh Dickinson.

Cohen, Bernard & Hess, Bernhard J. M. Otolith Function in Spatial Orientation & Movement. LC 99-24766. (Annals of the New York Academy of Science Ser.). 1999. write for info. (*1-57331-218-5*) NY Acad Sci.

Cohen, Bernard, jt. auth. see David.

Cohen, Bernard, jt. auth. see Rosenzweig, Luc.

Cohen, Bernard C. Democracies & Foreign Policy: Public Participation in the United States & the Netherlands. LC 94-38501. 208p. (Orig.). (C). 1995. pap. text 19.95 (*0-299-14644-8*); lib. bdg. 55.00 (*0-299-14640-5*) U of Wis Pr.

— Political Process & Foreign Policy: The Making of the Japanese Peace Settlement. LC 80-19832. 293p. 1980. reprint ed. lib. bdg. 75.00 (*0-313-22715-2*, COPF, Greenwood Pr) Greenwood.

— The Press & Foreign Policy. LC 83-12989. 288p. 1993. reprint ed. pap. 14.95 (*0-87772-346-X*) UCB IGS.

Cohen, Bernard L. Before It's Too Late: A Scientist's Case for Nuclear Energy. LC 83-11083. (Illus.). 308p. (C). 1983. 18.95 (*0-306-41425-2*, Kluwer Plenum) Kluwer Academic.

— Law Without Order: Capital Punishment & the Liberals. LC 82-45661. reprint ed. 30.00 (*0-404-62410-3*) AMS Pr.

Cohen, Bernice. The Edge of Chaos: Financial Booms, Bubbles, Crashes & Chaos. LC 96-34241. 1997. pap. text 32.00 (*0-471-96907-9*) Wiley.

— The Edge of Chaos: Financial Booms, Bubbles, Crashes & Chaos. LC 96-34241. 412p. 1997. 60.50 (*0-471-97237-1*) Wiley.

Cohen, Berthe. They Called Me Gigi: A True Story. LC 98-90691. 1999. 17.95 (*0-533-12890-0*) Vantage.

Cohen, Bertram, et al, eds. Group Psychotherapy & Political Reality: A Two-Way Mirror. 300p. 2000. 41.50 (*0-8236-2228-2*, 02228) Intl Univs Pr.

Cohen, Beth, ed. The Distaff Side: Representing the Female in Homer's Odyssey. (Illus.). 288p. 1995. pap. text 19.95 (*0-19-508683-X*) OUP.

***Cohen, Beth, ed.** Not the Classical Ideal: Athens & the Construction of the Other in Greek Art. (Illus.). 560p. 2000. 87.00 (*90-04-11618-4*); 48.00 (*90-04-11712-1*) Brill Academic Pubs.

Cohen, Betty, ed. Poets at Work: Contemporary Poets-Lives, Poems, Process. 309p. (Orig.). (YA). (gr. 7-12). 1995. pap. 15.00 (*0-9647047-0-6*) Just Buffalo.

Cohen, Betty, jt. auth. see Fish, Dorothy.

***Cohen, Bill.** Life Mapping: Finding Your Vision for the Future. LC 97-38812. 176p. 1998. pap. 12.95 (*0-688-15573-1*, Wm Morrow) Morrow Avon.

Cohen, Bill, ed. Stories & Images of What the Horse Has Done for Us: An Illustrated History of Okanagan Ranching & Rodeo. (Illus.). 146p. 1998. pap. 18.95 (*0-919441-72-6*, Pub. by Theytus Bks) Orca Bk Pubs.

Cohen, Boaz. Jewish & Roman Law, 2 Vols, Set. 1966. 15.00 (*0-8381-4100-5*) USCJE.

— Law & Tradition in Judaism. 1959. 17.50 (*0-87068-023-4*) Ktav.

Cohen, Boaz & Katz, Steven, eds. Saadia Anniversary Volume. LC 79-7168. (Jewish Philosophy, Mysticism & History of Ideas Ser.). 1980. reprint ed. lib. bdg. 31.95 (*0-405-12244-6*) Ayer.

Cohen, Bob. Encyclopedia of Auto Sales Vol. 1: Selling Skills. 3rd rev. ed. Bailey, Bob, ed. 191p. 1998. ring bd. 99.00 (*1-893850-00-5*) B Cohen Ent.

— Encyclopedia of Auto Sales Vol. 2: Closing. 2nd rev. ed. Bailey, Bob, ed. 149p. 1998. ring bd. 99.00 (*1-893850-01-3*) B Cohen Ent.

— Encyclopedia of Auto Sales Vol. 3; Professional Sales Management. 3rd rev. ed. Bailey, Bob, ed. 210p. 1997. ring bd. 99.00 (*1-893850-02-1*) B Cohen Ent.

Cohen, Bonnie B. Sensing Feeling & Action: The Experiential Anatomy of Body-Mind Centering. (Illus.). 171p. (Orig.). 1993. pap. 25.00 (*0-937645-03-6*) Contact Edit.

Cohen, Brenda H., jt. auth. see Cohen, Paul S.

Cohen, Brian M. Management of Infertility: A Clinician's Manual. 2nd ed. 172p. 1991. pap. 12.95 (*0-929240-33-2*) EMIS.

Cohen, Bruce J. & Orbuch, Terri L. Introduction to Sociology. (College Core Bks.). (C). 1989. pap. text 13.95 (*0-07-011602-4*) McGraw.

Cohen, Bruce P., et al. Georgia Real Estate Forms, Issue 12. MacNeil Hesmer, Elizabeth, ed. 200p. 1998. ring bd. write for info. (*0-327-00548-3*, 8095914) LEXIS Pub.

Cohen-Bunim, Simcha. The Radiance of Shabbos. (ArtScroll Halachah Ser.). (Illus.). 200p. 1986. 18.99 (*0-89906-212-1*); pap. 15.99 (*0-89906-213-X*) Mesorah Pubns.

Cohen, Burton. The Great American Cheese Sandwich. 1983. pap. 3.25 (*0-8222-0479-7*) Dramatists Play.

— Jackie Lantern's Hallowe'en Revenge. 1986. pap. 5.25 (*0-8222-0587-4*) Dramatists Play.

— Wedding of the Siamese Twins. 1989. pap. 5.25 (*0-8222-1228-5*) Dramatists Play.

Cohen, Burton I. Case Studies in Jewish School Management: Applying Educational Theory to School Practice. LC 92-27303. 1992. 17.95 (*0-87441-542-X*) Behrman.

Cohen, Burton J. Cost-Effective Information Systems. LC 78-152375. 71p. reprint ed. pap. 30.00 (*0-608-11399-9*, 205038900078) Bks Demand.

An Asterisk (*) at the beginning of an entry indicates that the title is appearing for the first time.

Cohen, C. & Sivan, D. The Ugaritic Hippiatric Texts: A Critical Edition. (American Oriental Ser.: No. 9). x, 72p. 1983. pap. 12.50 (*0-940490-99-4*) Am Orient Soc.

Cohen, C. D. British Economic Policy, 1960-1969. LC 74-867818. (Studies in Theoretical & Applied Economics). 281p. 1971. write for info. (*0-408-70187-0*) Buttrwrth-Heinemann.

Cohen, Cafi. And What about College? How Homeschooling Can Lead to Admissions to the Best Colleges & Universities. 252p. (Orig.). 1996. pap. write for info. (*0-945097-29-8*) Home Educ Pr.

— "And What about College?" How Homeschooling Leads to Admissions to the Best Colleges & Universities. Farenga, Patrick, ed. & intro. by. LC 00-29589. 168p. 2000. pap. 18.95 (*0-913677-11-6*) Holt Assocs.

***Cohen, Cafi.** Homeschooler's College Admissions Annual. 8th ed. 2000. pap. 16.00 (*0-7615-2754-0*) Prima Pub.

— Homeschooling: The Teen Years: Your Guide to Successfully Homeschooling the 13 to 18 Year Old. LC 00-26151. (Prima's Home Learning Library Ser.). 288p. 2000. pap. 16.95 (*0-7615-2093-7*) Prima Pub.

Cohen, Cambria. Fifty Nifty Crafts to Make with Things Around the House. (Illus.). 64p. (J). 1992. pap. 4.95 (*0-929923-88-X*) Lowell Hse.

— 50 Nifty Super Crafts to Make with Things Around the House. LC 98-75608. (50 Nifty Ser.). (Illus.). 80p. (J). (gr. 2). 1999. pap. 6.95 (*0-7373-0157-0*, 01570W) NTC Contemp Pub Co.

***Cohen, Cambria.** 150 Nifty Super Crafts. (Illus.). (J). 2000. pap. 9.95 (*0-7373-0514-2*) Lowell Hse Juvenile.

Cohen, Carl. Communism, Fascism, & Democracy: The Theoretical Foundations. 3rd ed. LC 96-21812. 512p. (C). 1996. pap. 40.63 (*0-07-011609-1*) McGraw.

— Democracy. 318p. (C). 1996. 17.95 (*1-57074-230-8*) Greyden Pr.

— Four Systems. 256p. (C). 1982. pap. text 27.25 (*0-07-554305-2*) McGraw.

— Naked Racial Preference: The Case Against Affirmative Action. 240p. (C). 1995. 21.95 (*1-56833-053-7*) Madison Bks UPA.

Cohen, Carl, jt. auth. see Copi, Irving M.

Cohen, Carol. The Oregon Trail. 39.00 (*1-56696-145-9*) Jackdaw.

Cohen, Carol J., jt. ed. see Stein, Terry.

Cohen, Caron L. Crookjaw. LC 96-44214. (Illus.). 40p. (J). (ps-2). 1997. 15.95 (*0-8050-5300-X*) H Holt & Co.

— How Many Fish? LC PZ8.3.C66Ho 1998. (My First I Can Read Bks.). (Illus.). 32p. (J). (ps-k). 1998. pap. 12.95 (*0-06-027713-0*); lib. bdg. 12.89 (*0-06-027714-9*) HarpC.

— How Many Fish? (My First I Can Read Bks.). (Illus.). 32p. (J). (ps-k). 2000. pap. 3.95 (*0-06-444273-X*) HarpC Child Bks.

— The Mud Pony. LC 87-23451. 32p. (J). (ps-3). 1989. pap. 4.99 (*0-590-41526-3*) Scholastic Inc.

— The Mud Pony. 32p. (J). (ps-3). 1993. 19.95 (*0-590-72838-5*) Scholastic Inc.

— Three Yellow Dogs. LC 85-24823. (Illus.). 32p. 1997. mass mkt. 3.95 (*0-688-15286-4*, Wm Morrow) Morrow Avon.

— Where's the Fly. LC 95-962. (Illus.). 32p. (J). (ps-3). 1996. 15.00 (*0-688-14044-0*, Grenwillow Bks) HarpC Child Bks.

***Cohen, Caron Lee.** Digger Pig & the Turnip. (Green Light Readers Ser.). (Illus.). 20p. (J). (gr. 1-3). 2000. 10.95 (*0-15-202524-3*) Harcourt.

— Digger Pig & the Turnip. (Illus.). (J). 2000. 9.40 (*0-606-18171-7*) Turtleback.

— How Many Fish? (Illus.). (J). 2000. 9.40 (*0-606-18695-6*) Turtleback.

Cohen, Caron Lee. The Mud Pony, a Traditional Skidi Pawnee Tale. (J). 1988. 10.15 (*0-606-07897-5*, Pub. by Turtleback) Demco.

***Cohen, Caron Lee & Denise, Christopher.** Digger Pig & the Turnip. LC 99-6802. (Green Light Readers Ser.). 20p. (J). (gr. 1-3). 2000. pap. 3.95 (*0-15-202530-8*) Harcourt.

***Cohen, Caron Lee & Litzinger, Rosanne.** Happy to You! LC 99-39433. (J). 2001. write for info. (*0-689-82421-1*) S&S Childrens.

Cohen, Cary. Effective Contract Administration: The Complete Handbook & Guide. LC 96-43144. 304p. 1996. 95.00 (*0-8144-0129-5*) AMACOM.

***Cohen, Cathi.** Raise Your Child's Social IQ: Stepping Stones to People Skills for Kids. LC 99-39733. 2000. write for info. (*0-9660366-8-9*) Advantage Books.

Cohen, Cathy. The Boundaries of Blackness: AIDS & the Breakdown of Black Politics. 1999. lib. bdg. 57.00 (*0-226-11288-8*) U Ch Pr.

— The Boundaries of Blackness: AIDS & the Breakdown of Black Politics. LC 98-31088. (Illus.). 390p. 1999. pap. 18.00 (*0-226-11289-6*) U Ch Pr.

Cohen, Cathy J., et al, eds. Women Transforming Politics: An Alternative Reader. LC 97-19645. 1997. text 75.00 (*0-8147-1557-5*); pap. text 23.00 (*0-8147-1558-3*) NYU Pr.

Cohen, Chapman. Essays in Freethinking, 2 vols., Set. 2nd ed. 1987. pap. 20.00 (*0-910309-32-9*, 5060) Am Atheist.

— Essays in Freethinking, 2 vols., Vol. I. 2nd ed. 229p. 1987. pap. 10.00 (*0-910309-33-7*, 5052) Am Atheist.

— Essays in Freethinking, 2 vols., Vol. II. 2nd ed. 240p. 1987. pap. 10.00 (*0-910309-34-5*, 5056) Am Atheist.

— Materialism Revisited. 190p. 1998. reprint ed. 20.00 (*0-936128-88-7*) De Young Pr.

— Primitive Survivals in Modern Thought. LC 74-169207. (Atheist Viewpoint Ser.). 142p. 1976. reprint ed. 16.95 (*0-405-03807-0*) Ayer.

— Religion & Sex. LC 72-9631. reprint ed. 47.50 (*0-404-57430-0*) AMS Pr.

Cohen, Charles & Sherwood, Vance R. Becoming a Constant Object in Psychotherapy with the Borderline Patient. LC 90-14556. 336p. 1991. 65.00 (*0-87668-613-7*) Aronson.

Cohen, Charles E. The Art of Giovanni Antonio da Pordenone: Between Dialect & Language, 2 vols. LC 94-26236. (Cambridge Studies in the History of Art). (Illus.). 524p. (C). 1996. text 295.00 (*0-521-30630-2*) Cambridge U Pr.

Cohen, Charlotte S. It Pays to Know: Making Money in Stocks & Bonds. (Illus.). 136p. (Orig.). 1994. pap. text 10.00 (*0-9642709-0-0*) C S Cohen.

Cohen, Chester G. Shtetl Finder Gazetteer: Jewish Communities in the 19th & Early 20th Centuries in the Pale of Settlement of Russia & Poland, & in Lithuania, Latvia, Galicia, & Bukovina, with Names of Residents. 154p. (Orig.). 1989. pap. 18.50 (*1-55613-248-4*) Heritage Bk.

Cohen, Christina M., ed. Orr White Hitchcock, 1796-1863. (Illus.). 16p. 1992. pap. 8.00 (*0-9632800-0-7*) Deerfield Acad.

Cohen, Cindy K. & Heiney, John T. Daddy's Promise. large type ed. LC 96-93084. (Illus.). 32p. (Orig.). (J). (ps up). 1997. pap. 12.95 (*0-9656498-0-6*) Promise Pubns.

— My Daddy's Cancer. (Illus.). 32p. (J). (ps-6). 1999. pap. 7.95 (*0-9656498-1-4*) Promise Pubns.

***Cohen, Cindy Klein & Heiney, John T.** My Mommy's Cancer. Baseman, Sharon R., ed. (Illus.). 32p. (J). 1999. pap. 7.95 (*0-9656498-2-2*) Promise Pubns.

Cohen, Clarita, tr. see Bang, Molly.

***Cohen, Claudine.** Fate of the Mammoth. 1998. lib. bdg. 27.50 (*0-226-11292-6*) U Ch Pr.

Cohen, Colin. House of Kidz. Steele, Hope, ed. LC 98-96250. 319p. 1999. 21.95 (*0-9664724-2-X*) CC Six Hund.

Cohen, Colleen B., et al, eds. Beauty Queens on the Global Stage: Gender, Contests, & Power. LC 95-8994. (Illus.). 250p. (C). 1995. pap. 22.99 (*0-415-91153-2*) Routledge.

Cohen-Cruz, Jan. Playing Boal: Theatre, Therapy, Activism. Schutzman, Mady, ed. LC 93-12884. 256p. (C). (gr. 13). 1993. pap. 24.99 (*0-415-08608-6*) Routledge.

Cohen-Cruz, Jan, ed. Radical Street Performance: An International Anthology. LC 97-38986. (Illus.). 328p. (C). 1998. 75.00 (*0-415-15230-5*); pap. 22.99 (*0-415-15231-3*) Routledge.

Cohen, Cynthia B., ed. Casebook on the Termination of Life-Sustaining Treatment & the Care of the Dying. LC 88-45101. (Medical Ethics Ser.). 176p. (Orig.). 1988. 25.00 (*0-253-31321-X*); pap. 4.25 (*0-253-21207-3*) Ind U Pr.

— New Ways of Making Babies: The Case of Egg Donation. LC 95-51471. (Medical Ethics Ser.). (Illus.). 352p. (C). 1996. 39.95 (*0-253-33058-0*) Ind U Pr.

Cohen, D. Crucial Ten Per Cent That Really Counts for Trial Victories. 1974. 59.50 (*0-685-03818-1*) P-H.

— Dictionnaire Racines Semitiques, Attestees dans Langues Semitiques. (FRE.). 1998. 75.00 (*0-320-00270-5*) Fr & Eur.

— Simchas Yaavetz Haggadah. 1993. 18.99 (*0-89906-073-0*); pap. 14.99 (*0-89906-074-9*) Mesorah Pubns.

Cohen, D. B., jt. auth. see Willerman, L.

Cohen, D. Bernard, ed. see Bond, William C.

Cohen, D. W. An Introduction to Hilbert Space & Quantum Logic. (Problem Books in Mathematics). (Illus.). xii, 149p. 1989. 59.95 (*0-387-96870-9*) Spr-Verlag.

Cohen, D. Walter, et al. Educating the Dentist of the Future: The Pennsylvania Experiment. LC 84-19602. 224p. 1985. text 36.50 (*0-8122-7947-6*) U of Pa Pr.

Cohen, D. Walter, jt. auth. see Genco, Robert J.

Cohen, D. Walter, ed. see Isaacson, George.

Cohen, D. Walter, ed. see Seibert, J. S.

Cohen, Dale C. & Cohen, Korene C. Museums & Other Attractions of Arizona's Smaller Communities, Bk. 2. (Illus.). 61p. (Orig.). 1993. 4.95 (*0-9637255-1-3*) Dancing Unicorn.

Cohen, Dale C., jt. auth. see Cohen, Korene C.

Cohen, Dan. Wrestling Renegades: An in Depth Look at Todays Superstars of Pro Wrestling. (J). 1999. per. 4.99 (*0-671-03674-2*) PB.

Cohen, Dana S. Tropical Sins LC 98-194371. 315p. 1992. write for info. (*976-625-037-5*) Kingston Pub.

Cohen, Daniel. The Alaska Purchase. LC 95-14180. (Spotlight on American History Ser.). (Illus.). 64p. (J). (gr. 4-6). 1996. lib. bdg. 21.90 (*1-56294-528-9*) Millbrook Pr.

— Animal Rights: A Handbook for Young Adults. LC 92-40875. (Illus.). 128p. (YA). (gr. 7 up). 1993. lib. bdg. 22.40 (*1-56294-219-0*) Millbrook Pr.

***Cohen, Daniel.** Apatosaurus. LC 00-21735. (Discovering Dinosaurs Ser.). (Illus.). 24p. (J). (ps-3). 2000. lib. bdg. 15.93 (*0-7368-0616-4*, Bridgestone Bks) Capstone Pr.

Cohen, Daniel. Are You Ready? The Best & Worst Predictions for the Millennium. (YA). 1999. mass mkt. 3.99 (*0-671-02587-2*, Archway) PB.

— The Beheaded Freshman & Other Nasty Rumors. 128p. (Orig.). 1993. pap. 3.50 (*0-380-77020-2*, Avon Bks) Morrow Avon.

***Cohen, Daniel.** Civil War Ghosts. 128p. (gr. 3-7). 1999. pap. 4.50 (*0-439-05387-0*) Scholastic Inc.

— Civil War Ghosts. (Illus.). (J). 1999. 9.85 (*0-606-18532-1*) Turtleback.

Cohen, Daniel. Cloning. LC 98-7015. (Illus.). 128p. (YA). (gr. 7 up). 1998. 22.90 (*0-7613-0356-1*, Copper Beech Bks) Millbrook Pr.

— Conspiracy. (Alien Files Ser.: No. 2). (J). (gr. 3-7). 1998. pap. 3.99 (*0-590-76342-3*) Scholastic Inc.

***Cohen, Daniel.** Conspiracy. (Illus.). (J). 1999. 9.44 (*0-606-15858-8*) Turtleback.

Cohen, Daniel. Contact. (Alien Files Ser.: No. 1). (J). (gr. 3-7). 1998. pap. 3.99 (*0-590-76341-5*) Scholastic Inc.

***Cohen, Daniel.** Contact. (Illus.). (J). 1999. 9.34 (*0-606-15857-X*) Turtleback.

Cohen, Daniel. Cults. LC 94-966. (Illus.). 128p. (YA). (gr. 7 up). 1994. lib. bdg. 22.40 (*1-56294-324-3*) Millbrook Pr.

— Curses, Hexes, & Spells. LC 74-6425. (Weird & Horrible Library). (Illus.). 128p. (J). (gr. 6 up). 1974. lib. bdg. 12.89 (*0-397-31493-0*) HarpC Child Bks.

— Dangerous Ghosts. LC 95-45439. 96p. (J). (gr. 5-9). 1996. 14.95 (*0-399-22913-2*, G P Putnam) Peng Put Young Read.

— Dinosaur Discovery. (J). 1994. 22.99 (*0-525-65171-3*) NAL.

— Dinosaur Discovery: Facts, Fossils & Fun! (Picture Puffin Ser.). 32p. (J). 1998. pap. 5.99 (*0-14-056413-6*, PuffinBks) Peng Put Young Read.

— Dinosaurs of North America, 4 bks. Incl. Allosaurus & Other Jurassic Meat-Eaters. (Illus.). 48p. (J). (gr. 3-4). 1995. lib. bdg. 19.00 (*1-56065-286-1*, Cpstone High Low); Stegosaurus & Other Jurassic Plant-Eaters. (Illus.). 48p. (J). (gr. 3-4). 1996. lib. bdg. 19.00 (*1-56065-287-X*, Cpstone High Low); Triceratops & Other Cretaceous Plant-Eaters. (Illus.). 48p. (J). (gr. 3-4). 1996. lib. bdg. 19.00 (*1-56065-289-6*, Cpstone High Low); Tyrannosaurus Rex & Other Cretaceous Meat-Eaters. (Illus.). 48p. (J). (gr. 3-4). 1996. lib. bdg. 19.00 (*1-56065-288-8*, Cpstone High Low); 76.00 (*1-56065-641-7*, Cpstone High Low) Capstone Pr.

— The Encyclopedia of Ghosts. 304p. 1991. mass mkt. 4.99 (*0-380-71484-1*, Avon Bks) Morrow Avon.

— The Encyclopedia of Monsters. 272p. 1991. mass mkt. 4.99 (*0-380-71485-X*, Avon Bks) Morrow Avon.

— Encyclopedia of the Strange. 272p. 1987. mass mkt. 4.50 (*0-380-70268-1*, Avon Bks) Morrow Avon.

— The Female Marine in an Era of Good Feelings: Cross Dressing & the "Genius" of Nathaniel Coverly, Jr. (Illus.). 33p. (Orig.). 1994. reprint ed. pap. 6.50 (*0-944026-51-6*) Am Antiquarian.

***Cohen, Daniel.** George W. Bush: The Family Business. LC 99-54082. (Gateway Biographies Ser.). (Illus.). 48p. (J). (gr. k-3). 2000. 21.90 (*0-7613-1851-8*) Millbrook Pr.

Cohen, Daniel. Ghost in the House. (J). 1995. 8.44 (*0-606-07562-3*) Turtleback.

— Ghost of Elvis & Other Celebrity Spirits. 112p. (J). 1997. per. 3.99 (*0-671-53513-7*) PB.

— Ghost of Elvis & Other Celebrity Spirits. 1997. 9.09 (*0-606-11373-8*, Pub. by Turtleback) Demco.

— Ghostly Tales of Love & Revenge. MacDonald, Pat, ed. 112p. (J). (gr. 3-7). 1995. pap. 3.50 (*0-671-79523-6*, Minstrel Bks) PB.

Cohen, Daniel. Ghostly Tales of Love & Revenge. 1995. 8.60 (*0-606-07565-8*, Pub. by Turtleback) Demco.

Cohen, Daniel. Ghosts of the Deep. LC 92-34669. 112p. (J). (gr. 5-9). 1993. 14.95 (*0-399-22435-1*, G P Putnam) Peng Put Young Read.

— Ghosts of the Deep. (J). (gr. 3-6). 1996. pap. 3.50 (*0-671-89840-X*) S&S Trade.

— Ghosts of the Deep. LC 92-34669. 1996. 8.60 (*0-606-09323-0*, Pub. by Turtleback) Demco.

— The Ghosts of War. 96p. (J). (gr. 5-8). 1990. 13.95 (*0-399-22200-6*, G P Putnam) Peng Put Young Read.

Cohen, Daniel. Ghosts of War. (J). 1990. 8.09 (*0-606-02651-7*, Pub. by Turtleback) Demco.

Cohen, Daniel. Ghosts of War. MacDonald, Pat, ed. 96p. (J). (gr. 3-7). 1993. reprint ed. pap. 2.99 (*0-671-74086-5*, Minstrel Bks) PB.

— Great Conspiracies & Elaborate Cover Ups. LC 96-36483. (Illus.). 128p. (YA). (gr. 7 up). 1997. lib. bdg. 22.40 (*0-7613-0010-4*) Millbrook Pr.

— Great Ghosts. LC 90-34333. (Illus.). (J). (gr. 4-7). 1990. 14.99 (*0-525-65039-3*, Dutton Child) Peng Put Young Read.

— Great Ghosts. 48p. (J). (gr. 4-7). 1992. pap. 1.95 (*0-590-45734-9*, Apple Paperbacks) Scholastic Inc.

— Great Ghosts. (J). 1990. 7.15 (*0-606-01847-6*, Pub. by Turtleback) Demco.

— Gus the Bear, The Flying Cat & The Lovesick Moose. (J). (gr. 3-6). 1995. pap. 3.50 (*0-671-53624-9*) PB.

— Gus the Bear, the Flying Cat & the Lovesick Moose: Twenty Real Life Animal Stories. 1995. 8.60 (*0-606-09373-7*, Pub. by Turtleback) Demco.

— Hollywood Dinosaur. (J). 1997. per. 3.99 (*0-671-01681-4*) PB.

— Impeachment of William Jefferson Clinton. LC 99-56179. 112p. (J). (gr. 7). 1999. 23.90 (*0-7613-1711-2*) TFC Bks NY.

— Into the Darkness: Nineteen Tales to Tell after Midnight. 96p. (YA). 1994. pap. 3.50 (*0-380-72230-5*, Avon Bks) Morrow Avon.

— Introduction to Computer Theory. 2nd ed. LC 97-133565. 648p. 1996. text 92.95 (*0-471-13772-3*) Wiley.

— Joseph McCarthy: The Misuse of Political Power. LC 95-48314. (Illus.). 128p. (YA). (gr. 7 up). 1996. lib. bdg. 23.90 (*1-56294-917-9*) Millbrook Pr.

— The Manhattan Project. 144p. (YA). (gr. 7 up). 1999. 21.90 (*0-7613-1309-5*, Copper Beech Bks) Millbrook Pr.

— Manhattan Project. LC 98-44499. (Illus.). 128p. 1999. lib. bdg. 22.95 (*0-7613-0359-6*) TFC Bks NY.

— The Millennium. (YA). 1999. mass mkt. 3.99 (*0-671-01562-1*) PB.

— The Misfortunes of Prosperity: An Introduction to Modern Political Economy. Lindenfeld, Jacqueline, tr. LC 94-47022.Tr. of Infortunes de la Prosperite. (ENG & FRE.). 186p. 1995. 26.50 (*0-262-03230-9*) MIT Pr.

— The Modern Ark: Saving Endangered Species. LC 94-34007. (Illus.). 120p. (J). (gr. 5-9). 1995. 15.95 (*0-399-22442-4*, G P Putnam) Peng Put Young Read.

— Monster Dinosaur. LC 82-48460. 192p. (J). (gr. 3-6). 1983. 11.95 (*0-397-31953-3*) HarpC Child Bks.

— The Mummy's Curse: One Hundred One of the World's Strangest Mysteries. LC 94-4378. 224p. (Orig.). (J). 1994. pap. 3.99 (*0-380-77093-8*, Avon Bks) Morrow Avon.

— Phantom Animals. (J). 1991. 8.09 (*0-606-05541-X*, Pub. by Turtleback) Demco.

— Phantom Animals. Ashby, Ruth, ed. 112p. (J). (gr. 4-7). 1993. reprint ed. pap. 2.99 (*0-671-75930-2*, Minstrel Bks) PB.

— Phone Call from a Ghost: Strange Tales from Modern America. MacDonald, Patricia, ed. (Illus.). 112p. (J). (gr. 5-7). 1990. pap. 3.50 (*0-671-68242-3*, Minstrel Bks) PB.

— Phone Call from a Ghost: Strange Tales from Modern America. (J). 1988. 8.60 (*0-606-04769-7*, Pub. by Turtleback) Demco.

— Private Lending to Sovereign States: A Theoretical Autopsy. (Illus.). 196p. 1991. 27.50 (*0-262-03172-8*) MIT Pr.

— Prohibition: America Makes Alcohol Illegal. LC 94-37756. (Spotlight on American History Ser.). (Illus.). 64p. (J). (gr. 4-6). 1995. lib. bdg. 21.90 (*1-56294-529-7*) Millbrook Pr.

— Prophets of Doom: Millennium Edition. LC 98-38462. 144p. (YA). (gr. 7 up). 1999. 20.90 (*0-7613-1317-6*, Copper Beech Bks) Millbrook Pr.

***Cohen, Daniel.** Pteranodon. (Discovering Dinosaurs Ser.). 24p. (J). (ps-3). 2000. lib. bdg. 15.93 (*0-7368-0617-2*, Bridgestone Bks) Capstone Pr.

Cohen, Daniel. Railway Ghosts & Highway Horrors. (J). 1991. 8.05 (*0-606-05562-2*, Pub. by Turtleback) Demco.

— Railway Ghosts & Railway Horrors. 112p. (J). (gr. 3-7). 1993. pap. 2.95 (*0-590-45423-4*, Apple Paperbacks) Scholastic Inc.

— Real Ghosts. MacDonald, Pat, ed. 128p. (J). (gr. 3-6). 1992. pap. 3.50 (*0-671-78622-9*, Minstrel Bks) PB.

— Real Ghosts. 1977. 8.60 (*0-606-02093-4*, Pub. by Turtleback) Demco.

Cohen, Daniel. Real Vampires. (J). (gr. 3-7). 1996. pap. text 3.50 (*0-590-64542-0*) Scholastic Inc.

Cohen, Daniel. The Restless Dead: Ghostly Tales from Around the World. (J). (gr. 3-6). 1996. pap. 3.50 (*0-671-53512-9*, Minstrel Bks) PB.

— The Restless Dead: Ghostly Tales from Around the World. 1996. 9.09 (*0-606-09784-8*, Pub. by Turtleback) Demco.

— The Riddle of the Stones: And Other Unsolved Mysteries. LC 94-41802. (Illus.). 64p. (J). (gr. 2-7). 1995. pap. 3.95 (*1-85697-571-1*) LKC.

***Cohen, Daniel.** Riqueza Del Mundo, Pobreza de las Naciones. 142p. 1999. pap. 9.99 (*950-557-255-7*) Fondo CA.

Cohen, Daniel. Southern Fried Rat & Other Gruesome Tales. 128p. (YA). (gr. 5 up). 1989. pap. 3.50 (*0-380-70655-5*, Avon Bks) Morrow Avon.

***Cohen, Daniel.** Stegosaurus. LC 00-21737. (Discovering Dinosaurs Ser.). (Illus.). 24p. (J). (ps-3). 2000. lib. bdg. 15.93 (*0-7368-0618-0*, Bridgestone Bks) Capstone Pr.

Cohen, Daniel. There's a Ghost in the House. (Illus.). 64p. (J). (gr. 4-7). 1995. pap. 2.99 (*0-590-54333-4*) Scholastic Inc.

***Cohen, Daniel.** Triceratops. LC 00-21738. (Discovering Dinosaurs Ser.). (Illus.). 24p. (J). (ps-3). 2000. lib. bdg. 15.93 (*0-7368-0619-9*, Bridgestone Bks) Capstone Pr.

— Tyrannosaurus Rex. LC 00-21736. (Discovering Dinosaurs Ser.). (Illus.). 24p. (J). (ps-3). 2000. lib. bdg. 15.93 (*0-7368-0620-2*, Bridgestone Bks) Capstone Pr.

Cohen, Daniel. UFO's, the Third Wave. LC 88-16558. 172p. (YA). (gr. 7 up). 1988. 12.95 (*0-87131-541-6*) M Evans.

***Cohen, Daniel.** Velociraptor. LC 00-21948. (Discovering Dinosaurs Ser.). 24p. (J). (ps-3). 2000. lib. bdg. 15.93 (*0-7368-0621-0*, Bridgestone Bks) Capstone Pr.

Cohen, Daniel. Watergate: Deception in the White House. LC 97-26881. (Spotlight on American History Ser.). (Illus.). 64p. (J). (gr. 4-6). 1998. lib. bdg. 21.90 (*0-7613-0271-9*) Millbrook Pr.

— The Wealth of the World & the Poverty of Nations. LC 97-38755. (Illus.). 148p. 1998. 27.50 (*0-262-03253-8*) MIT Pr.

— Werewolves. 128p. (YA). (gr. 5-12). 1996. 14.99 (*0-525-65207-8*, Dutton Child) Peng Put Young Read.

— The World's Most Famous Ghosts. (Illus.). 112p. (J). (gr. 3-6). 1989. pap. 2.99 (*0-671-69145-7*, Minstrel Bks) PB.

***Cohen, Daniel.** Yellow Journalism: The Shocking Story of Sensationalism in the Media. LC 99-48934. 128p. (J). (gr. 7). 2000. 22.90 (*0-7613-1502-0*) TFC Bks NY.

Cohen, Daniel. Young Ghosts. (J). (gr. 4-7). 1995. pap. 3.50 (*0-590-62429-6*) Scholastic Inc.

Cohen, Daniel & Cohen, Susan. Teenage Stress: Understanding the Tensions You Feel at Home, at School & among Your Friends. LC 83-16477. 160p. (J). (gr. 5 up). 1984. 13.95 (*0-87131-423-1*) M Evans.

Cohen, Daniel & Lennox, Elsie. The Phantom Hitchhiker: And Other Ghost Stories. LC 94-42549. (Illus.). 64p. (J). (gr. 2-7). 1995. pap. 3.95 (*1-85697-572-X*) LKC.

Cohen, Daniel, et al. Marbling on Fabric. LC 89-78121. (Illus.). 94p. (Orig.). 1990. pap. 12.95 (*0-934026-54-8*) Interweave.

Cohen, Daniel, jt. auth. see Cohen, Susan.

Cohen, Daniel A., ed. "The Female Marine" & Related Works: Narratives of Cross-Dressing & Urban Vice in America's Early Republic. LC 97-20655. (Illus.). 216p. 1998. 40.00 (*1-55849-123-6*); pap. 16.95 (*1-55849-124-4*) U of Mass Pr.

Cohen, Daniel E. Computability & Logic. (Mathematics & Its Applications Ser.). 268p. 1987. text 69.95 (*0-470-20847-3*) P-H.

Cohen, Daniel J. The Body Snatchers. LC 74-32115. (Weird & Horrible Library). (J). (gr. 6 up). 1975. 10.95 (*0-397-31560-0*) HarpC Child Bks.

Cohen, Daphne M. In Search of the Seven Wonders of Noah. (Illus.). 64p. (J). (gr. 1-6). 1998. pap. 9.95 (*0-9668892-0-7*) Treas Gard.

An Asterisk (*) at the beginning of an entry indicates that the title is appearing for the first time.

*__Cohen, Daphne M.__ Resource Manual for in Search of the Seven Wonders of Noah. (Illus.). 28p. 1999. spiral bd. 12.95 (0-9668892-1-5) Treas Gard.

Cohen, Daphne M. & Hofer, M. Ultrasound Teaching Manual. (Illus.). 80p. 1999. pap. 16.95 (0-86577-725-X) Thieme Med Pubs.

Cohen, Darlene. Arthritis: Stop Suffering, Start Moving. (Illus.). 160p. 1995. 22.95 (0-8027-1308-4); pap. 14.95 (0-8027-7466-0) Walker & Co.

*__Cohen, Darlene.__ Finding a Joyful Light in the Heart of Pain. LC 99-53191. 256p. 2000. 22.00 (1-57062-467-4, Pub. by Shambhala Pubns) Random.

Cohen, David. African Americans. 1993. pap. 45.00 (0-670-77295-X); pap. 45.00 (0-670-77296-8); pap. 45.00 (0-670-77297-6) Viking Penguin.

— Cohencidents: Cartoons by David Cohen. (Illus.). 64p. 1987. pap. 3.95 (0-9619739-0-0) D Cohen.

Cohen, David. Conversational Calculus, Vol. 1. 246p. (C). 1997. pap. text 35.66 (0-201-19913-0) Addison-Wesley.

— Conversational Calculus, Vol. 2. (Illus.). 272p. (C). 1997. pap. text 35.66 (0-201-19917-3) Addison-Wesley.

Cohen, David. David Cohen Teaches Blues Piano: A Hands-on Beginner's Course in Traditional Blues. (Listen & Learn Ser.). 24p. 1998. pap. 19.95 incl. audio compact disk (0-7935-6257-0) H Leonard.

Cohen, David. A Day in the Life of Israel: Photographed by over 50 of the World's Leading Journalists on One Day, May 5, 1994. Liberman, Lee, ed. LC 94-28746. (Illus.). 244p. 1994. 29.95 (0-00-255119-5) Collins SF.

Cohen, David. The Development of Play. 192p. (C). 1989. pap. text 19.50 (0-8147-1429-3) NYU Pr.

— The Development of Play. 2nd ed. LC 93-32142. (Concepts in Developmental Psychology Ser.). 256p. (C). 1993. pap. 25.99 (0-415-09488-7); text 69.95 (0-415-09487-9) Routledge.

— Etudes De Linguistique Semitique Et Arabe. (Janua Linguarum, Ser. Practica: No. 81). (Orig.). 1970. text 55.40 (90-279-0732-3) Mouton.

— Law, Sexuality, & Society: The Enforcement of Morals in Classical Athens. 271p. (C). 1994. pap. text 24.95 (0-521-46642-3) Cambridge U Pr.

— Law, Violence, & Community in Classical Athens. (Key Themes in Ancient History Ser.). 226p. (C). 1995. pap. text 19.95 (0-521-38837-6) Cambridge U Pr.

— Le Parler Arabe des Juifs de Tunis Tome 2: Etude Linguistique. LC 72-94452. (Janua Linguarum, Ser. Practica: No. 161). (FRE.). 318p. 1975. 85.40 (90-279-3296-4) Mouton.

— The Political Process. (Task Force on the Eighties Ser.). 34p. 1981. pap. 2.50 (0-87495-040-6) Am Jewish Comm.

— Precalculus: A Problems-Oriented Approach. 5th ed. LC 95-47495. 750p. (C). 1996. 88.95 (0-314-06921-6) West Pub.

*__Cohen, David.__ Precalculus with Unit-Circle Trigonometry. 3rd ed. LC 97-27630. 1998. mass mkt. 86.95 (0-534-35275-8) Brooks-Cole.

Cohen, David. The Secret Language of the Mind: A Visual Inquiry into the Mysteries of Consciousness. LC 96-10435. (Illus.). 192p. 1996. 29.95 (0-8118-1407-6); pap. 19.95 (0-8118-1431-9) Chronicle Bks.

*__Cohen, David, compiled by.__ Phil Ochs: A Bio-bibliography, 74. LC 99-31634. Vol. 74. 336p. 1999. lib. bdg. 65.00 (0-313-31029-7) Greenwood.

Cohen, David, ed. America Then-Now. LC 91-76080. (Illus.). 168p. (Orig.). 1992. pap. 19.95 (0-9630960-0-1) CPI.

— Challenging the Therapeutic State: Critical Perspectives on Psychiatry & the Mental Health System. 350p. 1990. pap. 25.00 (0-930195-05-1) Inst Mind Behavior.

— Challenging the Therapeutic State Pt. 2: Further Disquisitions on the Mental Health System. LC 82-642121. (Special Issue of the Journal of Mind & Behavior Ser.). 212p. 1994. pap. text 20.00 (0-930195-07-8) Inst Mind Behavior.

— Melanges Marcel Cohen: Etudes de Linguistique, Ethnographie et Sciences Connexes Offertes par Ses Amis et Ses Eleves a lL'Occasion dDe Son 80eme Anniversaire. (Janua Linguarum, Series Major: No. 27). 1970. 173.10 (90-279-0720-X) Mouton.

Cohen, David, ed. Requiem for the Heartland. LC 95-22055. (Illus.). 124p. 1995. pap. 19.95 (0-00-649203-7) Collins SF.

Cohen, David, et al, eds. Teaching for Understanding: Challenges for Policy & Practice. LC 92-35498. (Education-Higher Education Ser.). 312p. 1993. text 36.45 (1-55542-515-1) Jossey-Bass.

Cohen, David, text. Moore in the Bagatelle Gardens, Paris. (Illus.). 128p. 1994. 60.00 (0-87951-526-0, Pub. by Overlook Pr) Penguin Putnam.

Cohen, David & Collins, Charles, eds. The African Americans. LC 93-1574. (Illus.). 240p. 1993. 45.00 (0-670-84982-0, Viking Studio) Studio Bks.

Cohen, David, jt. auth. see Breggin, Peter R.

Cohen, David, jt. auth. see Willcox, Scott.

Cohen, David, jt. ed. see Smolan, Rick.

Cohen, David, ed. see Wels, Susan.

Cohen, David B. Out of the Blue: Depression & Human Nature. 368p. 1995. pap. 13.95 (0-393-31299-2, Norton Paperbks) Norton.

— Stranger in the Nest: Do Parents Really Shape Their Child's Personality, Intelligence, or Character? LC 98-31371. (Illus.). 312p. 1999. 27.95 (0-471-31922-8) Wiley.

Cohen, David C. Algebra & Trigonometry. 3rd ed. Marshall, ed. LC 92-11099. 725p. (C). 1993. text 63.75 (0-314-93363-8) West Pub.

— College Algebra. (Illus.). 475p. (C). 1986. text 40.75 (0-314-93164-3) West Pub.

— College Algebra. 3rd ed. Marshall, ed. (Math). 592p. (C). 1992. mass mkt. 47.50 (0-314-93362-X) West Pub.

— College Algebra. 4th ed. (Mathematics Ser.). 1996. student ed. 17.50 (0-314-21464-X) Brooks-Cole.

— College Algebra. 4th ed. LC 95-31199. 700p. (C). 1996. mass mkt. 81.95 (0-314-06117-7) West Pub.

*__Cohen, David C.__ College Algebra. 5th ed. 2000. pap. 17.00 (0-534-36899-9) Brooks-Cole.

— College Algebra. 5th ed. (Mathematics Ser.). (C). 2000. text 12.00 (0-534-37819-6) Brooks-Cole.

Cohen, David C. College Algebra: Graph Manual. 4th ed. Date not set. write for info. (0-314-09440-7) West Pub.

— College Algebra & Trigonometry. (Illus.). 475p. (C). 1989. reprint ed. text 40.75 (0-314-93165-1) West Pub.

— College Algebra & Trigonometry. 4th ed. LC 96-26004. (C). 1996. 95.95 (0-314-06922-4) West Pub.

— College Algebra with Unit-Circle Trigonometry. Marshall, ed. LC 92-16241. 725p. (C). 1993. mass mkt. 51.25 (0-314-93361-1) West Pub.

— Dictionnaire des Racines Semitiques, 2 vols. (FRE.). 76p. 1976. pap. 79.95 (0-8288-5646-X, M6640) Fr & Eur.

— How to Win Criminal Cases by Establishing a Reasonable Doubt. 1970. 29.50 (0-685-01589-0) Exec Reports.

— Precalculus. 2nd ed. (Illus.). 725p. (C). 1987. pap. text, teacher ed. 13.00 (0-314-34724-0) West Pub.

— Precalculus, a Problems-Oriented Approach. 4th ed. Marshall, ed. LC 92-41652. 725p. (C). 1993. text 62.50 (0-314-01255-9) West Pub.

— Precalculus W/unit-circle Trigonometry. 2nd ed. Marshall, ed. LC 93-2612. (Math). 725p. (C). 1994. mass mkt. 53.50 (0-314-01254-0) West Pub.

Cohen, David C. & Smolan, Rick. A Day in the Life of Spain. (Illus.). 224p. 1988. 45.00 (0-318-33330-9) Collins SF.

*__Cohen, David E.__ One Year Off: Leaving It All Behind for a Round-the-World Journey with Our Children. LC 99-21760. (Illus.). 320p. 1999. 24.00 (0-684-83601-7) Simon & Schuster.

Cohen, David H. & Hess, Catherine. Looking at European Ceramics: A Guide to Technical Terms. LC 92-79943. (Looking at . . . Ser.). (Illus.). 92p. (Orig.). 1993. pap. 12.95 (0-89236-216-2) OUP.

Cohen, David M. Baby Grand. 88p. 1996. pap. 5.50 (0-87129-643-8, B81) Dramatic Pub.

Cohen, David S. The Dutch-American Farm. (American Social Experience Ser.: No. 15). (Illus.). 256p. (C). 1993. pap. text 17.50 (0-8147-1500-1) NYU Pr.

— Folk Legacies Revisited. LC 94-16185. 150p. (C). 1994. text 35.00 (0-8135-2138-6); pap. text 17.00 (0-8135-2139-4) Rutgers U Pr.

— The Folklore & Folklife of New Jersey. 223p. 1983. pap. 22.00 (0-8135-0989-0); text 40.00 (0-8135-0964-5) Rutgers U Pr.

Cohen, David S., ed. America the Dream of My Life: Selections from the Federal Writers' Project's New Jersey Ethnic Survey. LC 89-37770. (Illus.). 250p. (Orig.). (C). 1990. pap. 15.95 (0-8135-1515-7); text 40.00 (0-8135-1514-9) Rutgers U Pr.

Cohen, David W. The Combing of History. LC 93-34883. (Illus.). 290p. 1994. pap. text 17.95 (0-226-11278-0); lib. bdg. 47.95 (0-226-11277-2) U Ch Pr.

— The Historical Tradition of Busoga: Mukama & Kintu. (Oxford Studies in African Affairs). (Illus.). 234p. 1972. text 12.75 (0-19-821673-4) OUP.

— Womunafu's Bunafu: A Study of Authority in a Nineteenth-Century African Community. LC 77-71976. (Illus.). 227p. reprint ed. pap. 70.40 (0-8357-7931-9, 205233100002) Bks Demand.

Cohen, David W. & Atieno Odhiambo, E. S. Burying SM: The Politics of Knowledge & the Sociology of Power in Africa. LC 91-28283. (Social History of Africa Ser.). 159p. (C). 1992. pap. 19.95 (0-435-08063-6, 08063) Heinemann.

Cohen, David W. & Odhiambo, E. S. Siaya: The Historical Anthropology of an African Landscape. LC 88-15182. 160p. (Orig.). 1988. pap. 16.95 (0-8214-0902-6) Ohio U Pr.

*__Cohen, Deborah A. & Gelfand, Robert M.__ Just Get Me Through This: The Practical Guide to Breast Cancer. 272p. 2000. pap. 13.00 (1-57566-551-4, Knsington) Kensgtn Pub Corp.

*__Cohen, Debra Nussbaum.__ Celebrating Your New Jewish Daughter: Creating Jewish Ways to Welcome Baby Girls into the Covenant - New & Traditional Ceremonies. 2000. pap. 16.95 (1-58023-090-3) Jewish Lights.

*__Cohen, Denis.__ The International Protection of Designs. 176p. 2000. pap. 79.50 (90-411-9783-4) Kluwer Law Intl.

*__Cohen, Dennis.__ The Big Book of Space Discovery: A Fun-Filled Adventure into the Planets, Stars & Space Exploration. large type ed. Fry, Sharon, ed. (Illus.). 12p. (J). (gr. k-7). 1999. mass mkt. 12.00 (0-9674289-0-4) Schmidt-Cannon.

*__Cohen, Dennis J.__ Project Manager's MBA: How to Translate Project Decisions Into Business Success. 2000. 34.95 (0-7879-5256-7) Jossey-Bass.

Cohen, Dennis L. & Daniel, John, eds. Political Economy of Africa: Selected Readings. LC 82-101006. 295p. reprint ed. pap. 91.50 (0-8357-6269-6, 203449800090) Bks Demand.

Cohen, Derek. The Appropriation of Shakespeare: Post-Renaissance Reconstructions of the Works & the Myth. Marsden, Jean I. & Bloom, Clive, eds. LC 91-29982. (Insights Ser.). 230p. 1992. text 45.00 (0-312-07198-1) St Martin.

— The Politics of Shakespeare. LC 93-8141. 1993. text 55.00 (0-312-10187-2) St Martin.

Cohen, Derek & Heller, Deborah, eds. Jewish Presences in English Literature. 152p. (C). 1990. text 65.00 (0-7735-0781-7, Pub. by McG-Queens Univ Pr) CUP Services.

*__Cohen, Dian.__ The New Retirement. 320p. 1999. pap. 12.95 (0-385-25786-4, Pub. by Doubleday) Random House.

— The New Retirement: Financial Strategies for Life after Work. 320p. 1999. 23.50 (0-385-25746-5, Pub. by Doubleday) Random House.

— The State, the Wire & Taxes. 24.95 (0-385-25747-3, Pub. by Doubleday) Random House.

Cohen, Diana. Somewhere: Poems & Drawings. 1986. 5.95 (0-913152-19-6) Folder Edns.

Cohen, Don. An Introduction to Cranialsacral Therapy: Anatomy, Function & Treatment. (Illus.). 114p. (Orig.). (C). 1996. pap. 18.95 (1-55643-183-X) North Atlantic.

*__Cohen, Don & Prusak, Laurence.__ In Good Company: How Social Capital Makes Organizations Work. 2001. 27.50 (0-87584-913-X) Harvard Busn.

Cohen, Donald. Calculus by & for Young People (Ages 7, Yes 7 & Up) rev. ed. (Illus.). 177p. (Orig.). (J). (gr. 1 up). 1989. spiral bd. 13.95 (0-9621674-1-X) D Cohen Mathman.

— Calculus by & for Young People-Worksheets. (Illus.). 319p. (Orig.). (J). (gr. 1 up). 1989. pap. 22.95 (0-9621674-5-2) D Cohen Mathman.

— Changing Shapes with Matrices. (Illus.). (Orig.). (J). (gr. 3 up). 1995. pap., student ed. 9.95 (0-9621674-3-6) D Cohen Mathman.

— Getting Ready for Calculus, 3 bks., 2 videotapes, Includes map. rev. ed. (Orig.). (J). (gr. 1 up). 1989. student ed. 124.90 incl. VHS (0-9621674-9-5) D Cohen Mathman.

Cohen, Donald J. & Volkmar, Fred R. Handbook of Autism & Pervasive Developmental Disorders. 2nd ed. LC 96-34955. 1120p. 1997. 125.00 (0-471-53242-8) Wiley.

Cohen, Donald J., et al. Yale Child Guide to Your Child's Behavior & Development. 704p. 2001. 40.00 (0-316-95432-2) Little.

Cohen, Donald J., jt. ed. see Cicchetti, Dante.

Cohen, Donald J., jt. ed. see Leckman, James F.

Cohen, Donald N. Knowledge Based Theorem Proving & Learning. LC 81-7494. (Computer Science: Artificial Intelligence Ser.: No. 4). 212p. reprint ed. pap. 65.80 (0-8357-1202-8, 207037000088) Bks Demand.

Cohen, Donald S., ed. Mathematical Aspects of Chemical & Biochemical Problems & Quantum Chemistry: Proceedings of the SIAM-AMS Seminar, New York, 1974. LC 74-26990. (SIAM-AMS Proceedings Ser.: Vol. 8). 153p. 1974. text 45.00 (0-8218-1328-5, SIAMS-8) Am Math.

Cohen, Donna. Caring for Your Aging Parents: A Planning & Action Guide. 1995. pap. 13.95 (0-87477-799-2, Tarcher Putnam) Putnam Pub Group.

Cohen, Donna. Loss of Self. 2nd ed. 27.95 (0-393-05016-5) Norton.

Cohen, Donna & Eisdorfer, Carl. Caring for Your Aging Parents: A Planning & Action Guide. 1995. pap. 10.95 (0-399-07992-0) Pub Group.

— The Loss of Self: A Family Resource for the Care of Alzheimer's Disease & Related Disorders. LC 85-15515. 1986. 19.95 (0-393-02263-3) Norton.

— The Loss of Self: A Resource for the Care of Alzheimer's Disease & Related Disorders. large type ed. (Illus.). 574p. 1987. reprint ed. lib. bdg. 20.95 (1-55736-005-7) BDD LT Grp.

Cohen, Doris, jt. auth. see Jones, Robert T.

Cohen, Dorothy, et al. Observing & Recording the Behavior of Young Children. 4th ed. LC 96-35584. 264p. (C). 1996. pap. text 19.95 (0-8077-3575-2) Tchrs Coll.

Cohen, Dov, jt. auth. see Kagan, Jack.

Cohen, Dov, jt. auth. see Nisbett, Richard E.

Cohen, E. Meteoritenkunde, Set, Teile I-III. (Chronostratigraphie und Neostratotypen Ser.). (DUT.). 158.00 (3-510-99015-3, Pub. by E Schweizerbartsche) Balogh.

— Net Assessment & Strategic Analysis. 1994. 23.99 (0-02-926911-3) S&S Trade.

— Programming in the 1990s: An Introduction to the Calculation of Programs. Gries, David, ed. (Texts & Monographs in Computer Science). 288p. 1990. 48.95 (0-387-97382-6) Spr-Verlag.

Cohen, E. & Guthoff, E., eds. Modern Coating & Drying Technology. 336p. 1992. 119.00 (0-471-18806-9) Wiley.

Cohen, E. G., ed. Statistical Mechanics at the Turn of the Decade. LC 70-134789. (Illus.). 245p. reprint ed. pap. 76.00 (0-7837-0762-2, 204107600019) Bks Demand.

Cohen, E. Richard. Physics Quick Reference Guide. 209p. 1995. pap. 30.00 (1-56396-143-1) Spr-Verlag.

*__Cohen, E. Richard, et al, contrib. by.__ Physicist's Desk Reference. 3rd ed. LC 99-59693. 400p. 2000. 59.95 (0-387-98973-0, AIP Pr) Spr-Verlag.

Cohen, Ed. Talk on the Wilde Side. 224p. (C). 1992. pap. 20.99 (0-415-90230-4, A4046) Routledge.

Cohen, Ed, jt. auth. see Cohen, Susan.

*__Cohen, Edie L.__ West Coast Rooms: Portfolios of 40 North American Interior Designers, 2000. 45.00 (1-56496-626-7) Rockport Pubs.

Cohen, Edie L., jt. auth. see Emery, Sherman R.

Cohen, Edmund. The Practice of Thoracic Anesthesia: Principles in Clinical Practice. 608p. 1995. text 72.50 (0-397-51078-0) Lppncott W & W.

Cohen, Edmund D. The Mind of the Bible-Believer. rev. ed. LC 86-42574. 438p. 1988. pap. 22.95 (0-87975-495-8) Prometheus Bks.

Cohen, Edward. Athenian Economy & Society: A Banking Perspective. LC 92-5685. 288p. 1992. text 45.00 (0-691-03609-8, Pub. by Princeton U Pr) Cal Prin Full Svc.

*__Cohen, Edward.__ Athenian Nation. LC 99-54905. 240p. 2000. 39.50 (0-691-04842-8, Pub. by Princeton U Pr) Cal Prin Full Svc.

Cohen, Edward. The Peddler's Grandson: Growing up Jewish in Mississippi. LC 99-10146. (Illus.). 193p. 1999. 25.00 (1-57806-167-9) U Pr of Miss.

Cohen, Edward & Gutoff, Edgar B., eds. Modern Coating & Drying Technology: Center for Interfacial Engineering. (Illus.). 310p. 1992. 85.00 (1-56081-097-1, Wiley-VCH) Wiley.

Cohen, Edward A. & Goldfarb, Lewis. The Cohen/Goldfarb Collection. LC 96-132921. 1995. 32.50 (0-7884-0997-2) Heritage Bk.

— Jewish Cemeteries of Hartford, CT Vol. 1: The Cohen/Goldfarb Collection. LC 96-132921. 209p. (Orig.). 1995. pap. 30.50 (0-7884-0368-0, C531) Heritage Bk.

Cohen, Edward D., jt. auth. see Gutoff, Edgar B.

Cohen, Edward E. Athenian Economy & Society: A Banking Perspective. 306p. 1992. pap. text 16.95 (0-691-01592-9, Pub. by Princeton U Pr) Cal Prin Full Svc.

Cohen, Edward H. Works & Criticism of Gerard Manley Hopkins: A Comprehensive Bibliography. LC 68-31683. reprint ed. pap. 58.50 (0-608-17266-9, 2029517) Bks Demand.

Cohen, Edward M. Working on a New Play: A Play Development Handbook for Actors, Directors, Designers & Playwrights. LC 94-42986. 216p. 1995. pap. 13.95 (0-87910-190-3) Limelight Edns.

Cohen, Edward M., ed. New Jewish Voices: Plays Produced by the Jewish Repertory Theatre. LC 84-8799. (SUNY Series in Modern Jewish Literature & Culture). 260p. (C). 1985. pap. text 21.95 (0-87395-997-3) State U NY Pr.

Cohen, Edward S. Atlas of Cosmetic & Reconstructive Periodontal Surgery. 2nd ed. (Illus.). 424p. 1994. text 95.00 (0-8121-1518-X) Lppncott W & W.

Cohen, Edward S. Atlas of Plastic & Reconstructive Periodontal Surgery. 3rd ed. 480p. 99.95 (0-683-30573-5) Lppncott W & W.

Cohen, Edwin, jt. auth. see Eaton, R. J.

Cohen, Edwin S. A Lawyer's Life: Deep in the Heart of Taxes. LC 95-108708. 718p. 1994. pap. 34.95 (0-918255-24-4) Tax Analysts.

Cohen, Elaine L., ed. Nurse Case Management in the 21st Century. LC 95-41096. (Illus.). 288p. (C). (gr. 13). 1995. text 43.95 (0-8151-1518-0, 25106) Mosby Inc.

Cohen, Elaine L. & Cesta, Toni G. Nursing Case Management: From Concept to Evaluation. 2nd ed. (Illus.). 368p. (C). (gr. 13). 1996. text 41.95 (0-8151-1906-2, 28201) Mosby Inc.

Cohen, Elaine L., jt. auth. see Lupton, Ellen.

Cohen, Elaine P. & Gainer, Ruth S. Art, Another Language for Learning. 3rd ed. LC 95-8328. (Illus.). 273p. 1995. pap. text 26.00 (0-435-08847-5, 08847) Heinemann.

Cohen, Eleanor, ed. Expanding the Environmental Responsibility of Local Government: Claremont's Environmental Task Force & Its Recommendations. LC 72-83451. (Environmental Studies: No. 3). 172p. 1972. pap. 10.00 (0-912102-07-1) Cal Inst Public.

Cohen, Eleanor M., ed. How Can Land Be Saved for Agriculture? Proceedings of a Working Conference to Find Solutions for California. LC 83-10107. (Illus.). 70p. (Orig.). 1983. pap. 15.00 (0-912102-65-9) Cal Inst Public.

— Local Farmlands Protection in California: Studies of Problems, Programs, & Politics in Seven Counties. (California Farmlands Project Working Papers: No. 2). 56p. (Orig.). 1983. pap. 10.00 (0-912102-63-2) Cal Inst Public.

Cohen, Eli, jt. auth. see Tichy, Noel M.

Cohen, Eli B., jt. auth. see Tichy, Noel M.

Cohen, Elie A. Human Behavior in the Concentration Camp. LC 84-544. 295p. 1984. reprint ed. lib. bdg. 38.50 (0-313-24417-0, CHBE/, Greenwood Pr) Greenwood.

Cohen, Eliot, et al. The Baseball Annual, 1990. 256p. (Orig.). 1990. mass mkt. 12.95 (0-446-38577-8, Pub. by Warner Bks) Little.

Cohen, Eliot A. Citizens & Soldiers: The Dilemmas of Military Service. LC 84-14266. (Cornell Studies in Security Affairs). 227p. 1990. reprint ed. pap. text 16.95 (0-8014-9719-1) Cornell U Pr.

— Commandos & Politicians: Elite Military Units in Modern Democracies. 136p. 1984. reprint ed. pap. text 16.00 (0-8191-4061-9); reprint ed. lib. bdg. 36.00 (0-8191-4060-0) U Pr of Amer.

— Commandos & Politicians Elite. (Studies in International Affairs). 1978. pap. text 4.75 (0-87674-041-7) Harvard U Intl Aff.

Cohen, Eliot A. & Gooch, John. Military Misfortunes: The Anatomy of Failure in War. 1990. 29.95 (0-02-906060-5) Free Pr.

— Military Misfortunes: The Anatomy of Failure in War. LC 90-50491. 320p. 1991. pap. 13.00 (0-679-73296-9) Vin Bks.

Cohen, Eliot A., et al. Knives, Tanks, & Missiles: Israel's Security Revolution. LC 98-10302. 154p. 1998. pap. 19.95 (0-944029-72-8) Wash Inst NEP.

Cohen, Eliot A., jt. auth. see Keaney, Thomas A.

Cohen, Elizabeth, et al. Business Law & Practice. 250p. 1996. pap. write for info. (1-874241-95-3, Pub. by Cavendish Pubng) Gaunt.

Cohen, Elizabeth G. Designing Groupwork: Strategies for the Heterogeneous Classroom. 2nd ed. LC 93-40799. 296p. (C). 1994. pap. text 18.95 (0-8077-3331-8) Tchrs Coll.

Cohen, Elizabeth G. & Lotan, Rachel A., eds. Working for Equity in Heterogeneous Classrooms: Sociological Theory in Practice. LC 97-20465. 516p. (Orig.). 1997. text 68.00 (0-8077-3644-9); pap. text 19.95 (0-8077-3643-0) Tchrs Coll.

Cohen, Elizabeth K. Cave Drawings. (Chapbook Series I: No. 1). 16p. 1980. pap. 2.00 (1-880649-01-2) Writ Ctr Pr.

Cohen, Elizabeth S., jt. auth. see Cohen, Thomas V.

Cohen, Elizabeth W. Cookie Book. 128p. 1994. 12.98 (0-7858-0164-2) Bk Sales Inc.

C

— Encyclopedia of Cooking Techniques. 144p. 1997. 14.98 (*0-7858-0613-X*) Bk Sales Inc.

— New Jewish Cuisine. 128p. 1993. 12.98 (*1-55521-926-8*) Bk Sales Inc.

— Simple Tarts. (Illus.). 80p. 1997. 9.98 (*0-7858-0746-2*) Bk Sales Inc.

Cohen, Elizabeth Wolf. Colossal Cookie Cookbook. 1999. 19.99 (*0-7858-1052-8*) Bk Sales Inc.

Cohen, Elliot D. Caution: Faulty Thinking Can be Harmful to Your Happiness: Everyday Logic for Stress Reduction, Assertiveness, Effective Decision Making & Improved Interpersonal Relations, Self Help Edition. 160p. (C). 1992. pap. 9.95 (*1-880454-01-7*); disk 58.95 (*1-880454-06-8*); disk 49.95 (*1-880454-03-3*) Trace-Wilco.

— Journalism Ethics: Contemporary Ethical Issues. LC 97-26874. (Contemporary Ethical Issues Ser.). (Illus.). 196p. 1997. lib. bdg. 55.00 (*0-87436-873-1*) ABC-CLIO.

— Making Value Judgements: Principles of Sound Reasoning. LC 84-28874. 180p. (C). 1985. pap. text 9.50 (*0-89874-802-X*) Krieger.

— Philosophical Issues in Journalism. 288p. (C). 1992. pap. text 23.95 (*0-19-506898-X*) OUP.

Cohen, Elliot D. & Davis, Michael, eds. AIDS: Crisis in Professional Ethics. 320p. (C). 1994. pap. 22.95 (*1-56639-165-2*); text 69.95 (*1-56639-164-4*) Temple U Pr.

Cohen, Elliot P., ed. Philosophers at Work: An Introduction to the Issues & Practical Uses of Philosophy. LC 88-22984. 480p. (C). 1989. pap. text 26.75 (*0-03-013234-7*) Harcourt Coll Pubs.

Cohen, Elwood. Alzheimer's Disease. LC 99-13014. 272p. 1999. pap. 16.95 (*0-87983-964-3*, 39643K, Keats Publng) NTC Contemp Pub Co.

Cohen, Emily C. American Jewish Year Book Index. 1968. 45.00 (*0-87068-040-4*) Ktav.

Cohen, Emma. It's Mine! His. (Nuk Bks.). (Illus.). 8p. (J). 1998. 6.95 (*0-7641-7232-8*) Barron.

Cohen, Emmeline. Growth of the British Civil Service, 1780-1939. 221p. 1965. reprint ed. 27.50 (*0-7146-1293-6*, BHA-01293, Pub. by F Cass Pubs) Intl Spec Bk.

Cohen, Enya, et al. A New Dictionary of Sign Language: Employing the Eshkol-Wachmann Movement Notation System. (Approaches to Semiotics Ser.: No. 50). 1977. text 113.85 (*90-279-3334-0*) Mouton.

Cohen, Eric & Sterling, Gregory. You Owe Me: The Emotional Debts That Cripple Relationships. LC 98-68325. 209p. 1999. pap. 14.95 (*0-88282-178-4*) New Horizon NJ.

***Cohen, Eric E.** Accountant's Guide to the Internet. 2nd ed. LC 99-40253. 364p. 2000. pap. 44.95 (*0-471-35834-7*) Wiley.

***Cohen, Erik.** The Commercialized Crafts of Thailand: Hill Tribes & Lowland Villages. LC 99-40080. (Consumasian Ser.). (Illus.). 288p. 2000. text 39.00 (*0-8248-2296-X*); pap. text 19.95 (*0-8248-2297-8*) UH Pr.

Cohen, Esther. The Crossroads of Justice: Law & Culture in Late Medieval France. LC 92-570. (Brill's Studies in Intellectual History: Vol. 36). 1992. 86.00 (*90-04-09569-1*) Brill Academic Pubs.

Cohen, Evelina G. Family Facts & Fairy Tales. 2nd rev. ed. (Illus.). 192p. 1988. text 25.00 (*0-932727-21-2*) Hope Pub Hse.

Cohen, Evelyn, jt. auth. see Pynoos, Jon.

Cohen, F., jt. auth. see Benson, D.

Cohen, F. R. The Homology of Iterated Loop Spaces. (Lecture Notes in Mathematics Ser.: Vol. 533). 1976. 36.95 (*0-387-07984-X*) Spr-Verlag.

Cohen, Felissa & Durham, Jerry, eds. Tuberculosis: A Sourcebook for Nursing Practice. LC 94-35452. (Illus.). 312p. 1995. 49.95 (*0-8261-8720-X*) Springer Pub.

Cohen, Felissa L. & Durham, Jerry D., eds. Women, Children, & HIV - AIDS. LC 92-48971. 328p. 1993. 39.95 (*0-8261-7880-4*) Springer Pub.

Cohen, Felix. Ethical Systems & Legal Ideals: An Essay on the Foundations of Legal Criticism. LC 75-40440. 303p. 1976. reprint ed. lib. bdg. 59.75 (*0-8371-8643-9*, COETS, Greenwood Pr) Greenwood.

Cohen, Felix S. Handbook of Federal Indian Law with Reference Tables & Index. xxiv, 662p. 1988. reprint ed. 95.00 (*0-89941-671-3*, 201910) W S Hein.

Cohen, Florence. Sea of Stones. 1993. 25.00 (*0-916366-88-X*, Pub. by Pushcart Pr) Norton.

Cohen, Frank J. The Y2K Compliance Manual for the Medical Office. LC 99-25759. 1999. write for info. (*1-57066-145-6*) Practice Mgmt Info.

Cohen, Fred. The Law of Deprivation of Liberty. LC 91-73517. 856p. 1991. lib. bdg. 60.00 (*0-89089-463-9*) Carolina Acad Pr.

— The Mentally Disordered Inmate & the Law. rev. ed. LC 98-72903. Orig. Title: Legal Rights of the Mentally Disordered Prison Inmate. 585p. 1998. 98.95 (*1-887554-06-8*) Civic Res Inst.

Cohen, Fred & Rahmberg-Walsh, Elizabeth. Sex Offender Registration & Community Notification: A 'Megan's Law' Sourcebook. LC 98-72462. 952p. 1998. ring bd. 179.90 (*1-887554-05-X*, MEG) Civic Res Inst.

Cohen, Fred, jt. auth. see Schlank, Anita.

***Cohen, Frederick B.** Protection & Security on the Information Highway. 301p. 1999. reprint ed. pap. text 20.00 (*0-7881-6550-X*) DIANE Pub.

Cohen, Frederick B. A Short Course on Computer Viruses. 2nd ed. 288p. 1994. pap., pap. text 44.95 incl. disk (*0-471-00769-2*); disk 10.00 (*0-471-00770-6*) Wiley.

— A Short Course on Computer Viruses. 2nd ed. 288p. 1994. pap. 34.95 (*0-471-00768-4*) Wiley.

Cohen, Fredrick B. Protection & Security on the Information Superhighway. LC 94-40488. 320p. 1995. pap. 24.95 (*0-471-11389-1*) Wiley.

Cohen, Fritz G. The Poetry of Christian Hofmann von Hofmannswaldau: A New Reading. LC 85-72042. (GERM Ser.: Vol. 22). (Illus.). 195p. 1986. 35.00 (*0-938100-38-6*) Camden Hse.

Cohen, Frumi. Try a Little Shakespeare. LC 93-32493. (J). 1993. pap. 10.00 (*0-88734-519-0*) Players Pr.

— Try a Little Shakespeare: Music & Lyrics. LC 93-32493. (J). 1993. pap. 15.00 (*0-88734-029-6*) Players Pr.

Cohen, G. Oseas & Amos. (SPA.). 208p. 1997. pap. 7.99 (*0-8254-1128-9*) Kregel.

Cohen, G., et al, eds. Algebraic Coding: First French-Israeli Workshop, Paris, France, July 1993. LC 94-8268. (Lecture Notes in Computer Science Ser.: Vol. 781). xii, 326p. 1994. 50.95 (*0-387-57843-9*) Spr-Verlag.

— Eurocode '90: International Symposium on Coding Theory & Applications, Udine, Italy, November 5-9, 1990 Proceedings. (Lecture Notes in Computer Science Ser.: Vol. 514). xi, 392p. 1991. 44.95 (*0-387-54303-1*) Spr-Verlag.

Cohen, G. & Godlewski, P., eds. Coding Theory & Applications. (Lecture Notes in Computer Science Ser.: Vol. 311). 196p. 1988. 33.00 (*0-387-19368-5*) Spr-Verlag.

Cohen, G. & Wolfmann, J., eds. Coding Theory & Applications. (Lecture Notes in Computer Science Ser.: Vol. 388). ix, 329p. 1989. 40.00 (*0-387-51643-3*, 3542) Spr-Verlag.

Cohen, G., et al. Covering Codes. LC 97-2461. (North-Holland Mathematical Library: 54). 564p. 1997. 169.50 (*0-444-82511-8*) Elsevier.

***Cohen, G. A.** If You're an Egalitarian, How Come You're So Rich? LC 99-86974. 256p. 2000. text 35.00 (*0-674-00218-0*) HUP.

— Karl Marx's Theory of History: A Defense. 2000. pap. 24.95 (*0-691-07068-7*) Princeton U Pr.

Cohen, G. A. Self-Ownership, Freedom, & Equality. (Studies in Marxism & Social Theory). 287p. (C). 1995. pap. text 19.95 (*0-521-47751-4*) Cambridge U Pr.

— Self-Ownership, Freedom, & Equality. (Studies in Marxism & Social Theory). 287p. (C). 1995. text 59.95 (*0-521-47174-5*) Cambridge U Pr.

Cohen, G. A., ed. History, Labour, & Freedom: Themes from Marx. 336p. 1989. pap. 27.00 (*0-19-824816-4*); text 68.00 (*0-19-824779-6*) OUP.

Cohen, G. J. The Nature of Management. 300p. 1985. pap. text 36.00 (*0-86010-565-2*); lib. bdg. 50.00 (*0-86010-582-2*) G & T Inc.

— The Nature of Management. 300p. 1985. pap. text, student ed. 25.00 (*0-86010-590-3*) G & T Inc.

— The Nature of Management. 2nd ed. 300p. 1988. pap. text 36.00 (*1-85333-030-2*) G & T Inc.

Cohen, Gail & Dumelle, Grace. Nativity Stories: Featuring the Art of Fontanini. (Illus.). 80p. 1996. text 22.50 (*0-937739-30-8*) Roman IL.

***Cohen-Gallet, Bonnie.** NYS Felony Sentencing Guidelines. 24p. 2000. 8.95 (*1-889031-33-X*) Looseleaf Law.

Cohen, Garnett K. Lost Women, Banished Souls. 168p. (C). 1996. pap. 17.95 (*0-8262-1073-2*) U of Mo Pr.

Cohen, Garry W., jt. auth. see Bloom, Barbara L.

Cohen, Gary, et al, eds. Third International Conference on Mathematical & Numerical Aspects of Wave Propagation. LC 95-2390. (Proceedings in Applied Mathematics Ser.: Vol. 77). xiii, 808p. 1995. pap. 106.00 (*0-89871-350-1*) Soc Indus-Appl Math.

Cohen, Gary & Kirban, Salem. Israel, Land of Promise, Land of Peace. LC 74-77252. (Illus.). 1974. pap. 5.95 (*0-912582-16-2*) Second Comng Inc.

Cohen, Gary & O'Connor, John, eds. Fighting Toxics: A Manual for Protecting Your Family, Community & Workplace. LC 90-4064. 346p. 1990. pap. 24.00 (*1-55963-012-4*); text 45.00 (*1-55963-013-2*) Island Pr.

Cohen, Gary, jt. auth. see Kirban, Salem.

Cohen, Gary B. Education & Middle-Class Society in Imperial Austria, 1848-1918. LC 95-51646. 400p. (C). 1996. 42.95 (*1-55753-087-4*) Purdue U Pr.

Cohen, Gaynor. Social Change & the Life Course. 300p. (C). (gr. 13). 1987. pap. text 29.99 (*0-422-79940-8*, Pub. by Tavistock) Routledge.

Cohen, Gene D. The Brain in Human Aging. (Adulthood & Aging Ser.). 272p. (C). 1988. 37.95 (*0-8261-5830-7*) Springer Pub.

***Cohen, Gene D.** The Creative Age: Awakening Human Potential in the Second Half of Life. LC 99-58721. (Illus.). 432p. 2000. 25.00 (*0-380-97684-6*, Avon Bks) Morrow Avon.

Cohen, Gene D., jt. ed. see Miller, Nancy E.

Cohen, George D. & Gladstone, William. How to Test & Improve Your Own Mental Health. LC 94-27376. 240p. 1994. pap. 9.95 (*1-55958-555-2*) Prima Pub.

Cohen, George J., ed. see American Academy of Pediatrics Staff.

Cohen, Georges N. Biosyntheses. LC 94-30699. 1994. write for info. (*0-412-99551-4*) Chapman & Hall.

Cohen, Gerald. Effective Management in Financial Services. (Banking & Finance Ser.). 336p. 1990. pap. text 41.50 (*1-85333-456-1*, Pub. by Graham & Trotman) Kluwer Academic.

Cohen, Gerald A. Karl Marx's Theory of History: A Defence. LC 78-51206. 385p. 1978. reprint ed. pap. 119.40 (*0-608-07660-0*, 205998100010) Bks Demand.

Cohen, Gerald L. Studies in Slang, Pt. V. (Forum Anglicum Ser.: Bd. 22). (Illus.). vii, 182p. 1997. pap. 42.95 (*3-631-31383-7*) P Lang Pubng.

— Studies in Slang, Pt. V. (Forum Anglicum Ser.: Bd. 22). (Illus.). VII, 182p. 1997. pap. 42.95 (*0-8204-3248-2*) P Lang Pubng.

***Cohen, Gerald Leonard & Popik, Barry A.** Studies in Slang. (Forum Anglicum Ser.: Vol. 24, Pt. VI). x, 132p. 1999. pap. text 26.95 (*0-8204-4377-8*) P Lang Pubng.

— Studies in Slang: Part VI. (Forum Anglicum Ser.). (Illus.). x, 132p. 1999. pap. 26.95 (*3-631-35435-5*) P Lang Pubng.

Cohen, Gerald M. Target Organ Toxicity, 2 vols. 1986. 339.90 (*0-8493-5769-1*, RA1211) CRC Pr.

— Target Organ Toxicity, 2 vols., Vol. I. 272p. 1986. lib. bdg. 206.00 (*0-8493-5775-6*) CRC Pr.

— Target Organ Toxicity, 2 vols., Vol. 2. 288p. 1986. lib. bdg. 206.00 (*0-8493-5776-4*) CRC Pr.

Cohen, Gerard, et al, eds. AAECC-10: Applied Algebra, Algebraic Algorithms, & Error-Correcting Codes - 10th International Symposium, San Juan de Puerto Rico, Puerto Rico, May 10-14, 1993 - Proceedings. LC 93-15375. (Lecture Notes in Computer Science Ser.: Vol. 673). 1993. 55.95 (*0-387-56686-4*) Spr-Verlag.

— Applied Algebra, Algebraic Algorithms, & Error-Correcting Codes: 11th International Symposium, AAECC-11, Paris, France, July 1995: Proceedings. (Lecture Notes in Computer Science Ser.: Vol. 948). 1995. 75.00 (*3-540-60114-7*) Spr-Verlag.

Cohen, Gered, tr. see Hattab, Jocelyn Y.

Cohen, Gerson D. Jewish History & Jewish Destiny. LC 96-49373. (Moreshet Ser.). 1997. write for info. (*0-87334-074-4*) Jewish Sem.

Cohen, Getzel M. The Hellenistic Settlements in Europe, the Islands, & Asia Minor. LC 93-44342. (Hellenistic Culture & Society Ser.: Vol. 17). 1995. 70.00 (*0-520-08329-6*, Pub. by U CA Pr) Cal Prin Full Svc.

Cohen, Gillian. Psychology of Cognition. 2nd ed. 1983. pap. text 44.95 (*0-12-178762-1*) Acad Pr.

Cohen, Gillian, et al. Memory: A Cognitive Approach. 2nd ed. LC 92-40621. (Open Guides to Psychology Ser.). 1993. pap. 25.00 (*0-335-19079-0*) OUP.

Cohen, Greta L., ed. Women in Sport: Issues & Controversies. (Illus.). 336p. (C). 1993. text 59.95 (*0-8039-4979-0*); pap. text 28.95 (*0-8039-4980-4*) Sage.

Cohen Grossman, Grace, ed. see Kirschner, Robert, et al.

Cohen, Gustav, tr. see Hanslick, Eduard.

Cohen, Gustav, tr. see Hanslick, Edward.

Cohen, Gustave, ed. Recueil de Farces Francaises Inedites du XVe Siecle. (Medieval Academy Bks.: No. 47). 1949. 30.00 (*0-910956-21-9*) Medieval Acad.

Cohen, H. & Green, J. Apprehending & Prosecuting the Drunk Driver: A Manual for Police & Prosecution. 1992. ring bd. 165.00 (*0-8205-1197-8*) Bender.

Cohen, H. & Muncaster, R. G. The Theory of Pseudo-Rigid Bodies. (Tracts in Natural Philosophy Ser.: Vol. 33). (Illus.). 210p. 1988. 89.95 (*0-387-96635-8*) Spr-Verlag.

Cohen, H., et al. Gas Turbine Theory. 4th ed. 450p. (C). 1996. 105.00 (*0-582-23632-0*) Addison-Wesley.

Cohen, H. F. Quantifying Music. 328p. 1984. lib. bdg. 203.00 (*90-277-1637-4*, D Reidel) Kluwer Academic.

Cohen, H. Floris. The Scientific Revolution: A Historiographical Inquiry. LC 93-41784. 680p. 1994. pap. text 26.95 (*0-226-11280-2*) U Ch Pr.

— The Scientific Revolution: A Historiographical Inquiry. LC 93-41784. 680p. 2000. lib. bdg. 75.00 (*0-226-11279-9*) U Ch Pr.

Cohen, H. L. The Ballad. 1972. 59.95 (*0-87968-696-0*) Gordon Pr.

Cohen, H. Robert. The Original Staging Manuals for Ten Parisian Operatic Premieres. (Musical Life in Nineteenth Century France Ser.: No. 6). 1998. 55.00 (*0-945193-61-0*) Pendragon NY.

Cohen, H. Robert, ed. Allgemeine Musikalische Zeitung, mit Besonderer Rucksich auf den Osterreichischen Kaiserstaat 1817-1824, 2 vols., Set. (Repertoire International de la Presse Musicale Ser.). (GER.). 1992. lib. bdg. 240.00 (*0-8357-2218-X*) Univ Microfilms.

Cohen, H. Robert, ed. Allgemeine Musikalische Zeitung 1863-1882, 7 vols. Incl. Vol. 1. Allgemeine Musikalische Zeitung 1863-1882. (GER.). 1995. lib. bdg. 145.00 (*0-8357-2378-X*); Vol. 2. Allgemeine Musikalische Zeitung 1863-1882. (GER.). 1995. lib. bdg. 145.00 (*0-8357-2379-8*); Vol. 3. Allgemeine Musikalische Zeitung 1863-1882. (GER.). 1995. lib. bdg. 145.00 (*0-8357-2380-1*); Vol. 4. Allgemeine Musikalische Zeitung 1863-1882. (GER.). 1995. lib. bdg. 145.00 (*0-8357-2381-X*); Vol. 5. Allgemeine Musikalische Zeitung 1863-1882. (GER.). 1995. lib. bdg. 145.00 (*0-8357-2382-8*); Vol. 6. Allgemeine Musikalische Zeitung 1863-1882. (GER.). 1995. lib. bdg. 145.00 (*0-8357-2383-6*); Vol. 7. Allgemeine Musikalische Zeitung 1863-1882. (GER.). 1995. lib. bdg. 145.00 (*0-8357-2384-4*); (Repertoire International de la Presse Musicale Ser.). (GER.). 1995. Set lib. bdg. 1000.00 (*0-8357-2377-1*) UMI.

Cohen, H. Robert, ed. Allgemeine Wiener Musik-Zeitung, 4 vols. (Repertoire International de la Presse Musicale Ser.). (GER.). 1990. 480.00 (*0-8357-0892-6*) Univ Microfilms.

Cohen, H. Robert, ed. Archivio Musicale 1882-1884. (Repertoire International de la Presse Musicale Ser.). (ITA.). 251p. 1996. lib. bdg. 145.00 (*0-8357-2419-0*) UMI.

Cohen, H. Robert, ed. L' Armonia, 1856-1859. (Repertoire International de la Presse Musicale Ser.). (ITA.). 367p. 1989. 120.00 (*0-8357-0889-6*) Univ Microfilms.

— L' Art Musical, 5 vols. (Repertoire International de la Presse Musicale Ser.). (FRE.). 1988. 600.00 (*0-685-46005-3*) Univ Microfilms.

Cohen, H. Robert, ed. A Arte Musical 1873-1875; 1890-1891. (Repertoire International de la Presse Musicale Ser.). (POR.). 191p. 1996. lib. bdg. 145.00 (*0-8357-2418-2*) UMI.

— Berliner Allgemeine Musikalische Zeitung 1824-1830, Vols. 1 & 2. (Repertoire International de la Presse Musicale Ser.). (GER.). 536p. 1994. lib. bdg. 285.00 (*0-8357-2306-2*) UMI.

— Berliner Musikalische Zeitung 1844-1847. (Repertoire International de la Presse Musicale Ser.). (GER.). 253p. 1994. lib. bdg. 145.00 (*0-8357-2310-0*) UMI.

Cohen, H. Robert, ed. Berlinische Musikalische Zeitung. (Repertoire International de la Presse Musicale Ser.). 1990. 120.00 (*0-8357-0934-5*) Univ Microfilms.

Cohen, H. Robert, ed. Cacilia 1824-1837, 1839, 1842-1848, Vols. 1 & 2. (Repertoire International de la Presse Musicale Ser.). (GER.). 565p. 1994. lib. bdg. 285.00 (*0-8357-2305-4*) UMI.

Cohen, H. Robert, ed. La Chronique Musicale, 1873-1876. (Repertoire International de la Presse Musicale Ser.). (FRE.). 217p. 1988. 120.00 (*0-685-46004-5*) Univ Microfilms.

Cohen, H. Robert, ed. Deutsche Musik-Zeitung 1860-1862. (Repertoire International de la Presse Musicale Ser.). (GER.). 332p. 1994. lib. bdg. 145.00 (*0-8357-2307-0*) UMI.

Cohen, H. Robert, ed. Dwight's Journal of Music 1852-1881, 6 vols., Set. (Repertoire International de la Presse Musicale Ser.). 1991. lib. bdg. 720.00 (*0-8357-2084-5*) Univ Microfilms.

— Eutonia. (Repertoire International de la Presse Musicale Ser.). (GER.). 1990. 120.00 (*0-8357-0935-3*) Univ Microfilms.

— I Teatri, 1827-1831, 2 vols., Set. (Repertoire International de la Presse Musicale Ser.). (ITA.). 1992. lib. bdg. 240.00 (*0-8357-2209-0*) Univ Microfilms.

— Gazetta Musicale di Firenze, 1853-1855. (Repertoire International de la Presse Musicale Ser.). (ITA.). 314p. 1989. 120.00 (*0-8357-0874-8*) Univ Microfilms.

— The Harmonicon, 4 vols., Set. (Repertoire International de la Presse Musicale Ser.). 1989. 480.00 (*0-8357-0828-4*) Univ Microfilms.

Cohen, H. Robert, ed. Het Muziekcollege 1913-1917. (Repertoire International de la Presse Musicale Ser.). (DUT.). 194p. 1993. lib. bdg. 145.00 (*0-8357-2268-6*) UMI.

Cohen, H. Robert, ed. L' Italia Musicale, 1847-1859, 5 vols., Set. (Repertoire International de la Presse Musicale Ser.). (ITA.). 1992. lib. bdg. 600.00 (*0-8357-2179-5*) Univ Microfilms.

Cohen, H. Robert, ed. Monatschrift fur Theater und Musik 1855-1865, 3 vols. (Repertoire International de la Presse Musicale Ser.). (GER.). 1993. lib. bdg. 430.00 (*0-8357-2267-8*) UMI.

Cohen, H. Robert, ed. La Musica, 1855, 1857-1859. (Repertoire International de la Presse Musicale Ser.). (ITA.). 282p. 1989. 120.00 (*0-8357-0873-X*); 120.00 (*0-8357-0872-1*) Univ Microfilms.

Cohen, H. Robert, ed. La Musica Ilustrada Hispano-Americana 1898-1902. (Repertoire International de la Presse Musicale Ser.). (SPA.). 286p. 1997. lib. bdg. 145.00 (*0-608-06502-1*) UMI.

Cohen, H. Robert, ed. The Musical Standard, 1862-1871 (First Series), 3 vols., Set. (Repertoire International de la Presse Musicale Ser.). 1991. lib. bdg. 360.00 (*0-8357-2123-X*) Univ Microfilms.

Cohen, H. Robert, ed. Musical Times 1844-1900, 9 vols. (Repertoire International de la Presse Musicale Ser.). 1995. lib. bdg. 1285.00 (*0-8357-2330-5*) UMI.

— The Musical World 1836-1865, 11 vols. Incl. Vol. 1. Musical World 1836-1865. 1996. lib. bdg. 145.00 (*0-8357-2431-X*); Vol. 2. Musical World 1836-1865. 1996. lib. bdg. 145.00 (*0-8357-2432-8*); Vol. 3. Musical World 1836-1865. 1996. lib. bdg. 145.00 (*0-8357-2433-6*); Vol. 4. Musical World 1836-1865. 1996. lib. bdg. 145.00 (*0-8357-2434-4*); Vol. 5. Musical World 1836-1865. 1996. lib. bdg. 145.00 (*0-8357-2435-2*); Vol. 6. Musical World 1836-1865. 1997. lib. bdg. 145.00 (*0-8357-2436-0*); Vol. 7. Musical World 1836-1865. 1997. lib. bdg. 145.00 (*0-8357-2437-9*); Vol. 8. Musical World 1836-1865. 1997. lib. bdg. 145.00 (*0-8357-2438-7*); Vol. 9. Musical World 1836-1865. 1997. lib. bdg. 145.00 (*0-8357-2439-5*); Vol. 10. Musical World 1836-1865. 1997. lib. bdg. 145.00 (*0-8357-2440-9*); Vol. 11. Musical World 1836-1865. 1997. lib. bdg. 145.00 (*0-8357-2441-7*); (Repertoire International de la Presse Musicale Ser.). Set lib. bdg. 1570.00 (*0-8357-2430-1*) UMI.

Cohen, H. Robert, ed. Musik-Welt, 1880-1882. (Repertoire International de la Presse Musicale Ser.). (GER.). 229p. 1992. lib. bdg. 120.00 (*0-8357-2210-4*) Univ Microfilms.

Cohen, H. Robert, ed. Nederlandsch Muzikaal Tijdschrift 1839-1848. (Repertoire International de la Presse Musicale Ser.). (DUT.). 284p. 1994. lib. bdg. 145.00 (*0-8357-2329-1*) UMI.

— The New York Musical World 1852-1860, 4 vols. (Repertoire International de la Presse Musicale Ser.). 1993. lib. bdg. 570.00 (*0-8357-2255-4*) UMI.

Cohen, H. Robert, ed. Niederrheinische Musik-Zeitung, 3 vols. (Repertoire International de la Presse Musicale Ser.). (GER.). 1990. 360.00 (*0-8357-0936-1*) Univ Microfilms.

Cohen, H. Robert, ed. Nordisk Musik-Tidende 1880-1892; Orkestertidende 1892-1894. (Repertoire International de la Presse Musicale Ser.). (NOR.). 352p. (gr. 1). 1996. lib. bdg. 145.00 (*0-8357-2420-4*) UMI.

— Paganini 1887-1891. (Repertoire International de la Presse Musicale Ser.). (ITA.). 310p. 1993. lib. bdg. 145.00 (*0-8357-2260-0*) UMI.

Cohen, H. Robert, ed. Quarterly Musical Magazine & Review, 1818-1828, 2 vols., Vols. 1 & 2. (Repertoire International de la Presse Musicale Ser.). 1989. 240.00 (*0-8357-0807-1*) Univ Microfilms.

— Revue Musicale, 1827-1835, 2 vols., Set. (Repertoire International de la Presse Musicale Ser.). (FRE.). 1991. lib. bdg. 240.00 (*0-8357-2147-7*) Univ Microfilms.

Cohen, H. Robert, ed. Ruch Muzyczny 1857-1862, 2 vols. Incl. Vol. 1. Ruch Muzyczny 1857-1862. (POL.). 209p. 1997. lib. bdg. (*0-608-06500-5*); Vol. 2. Ruch Muzyczny 1857-1862. (POL.). 312p. 1997. lib. bdg. (*0-608-06501-3*); (Repertoire International de la Presse Musicale Ser.). (POL.). 521p. 1997. Set lib. bdg. 285.00 (*0-608-06505-6*) UMI.

— Stockholms Musik-Tidning 1843-1844; Ny Tidning for Musik 1853-1857. (Repertoire International de la Presse Musicale Ser.). (SWE.). 261p. 1997. lib. bdg. 145.00 (*0-608-06503-X*) UMI.

Cohen, H. Robert, ed. Strenna Teatrale Europea. (Repertoire International de la Presse Musicale Ser.). (ITA.). 182p. 1989. 120.00 (*0-8357-0871-3*) Univ Microfilms.

Cohen, H. Robert, ed. Il Teatro Illustrato 1880-1892, 4 vols. (Repertoire International de la Presse Musicale Ser.). (ITA.). 1993. lib. bdg. 570.00 (*0-8357-2246-5*) UMI.

— Tidsskrift for Musik 1857-1859; Nordisk Tidsskrift for Musik 1871-1873; Musikbladet 1884-1895; Skandinaviske Signaler 1894-1895. (Repertoire International de la Presse Musicale Ser.). (DAN.). 404p. 1997. lib. bdg. 145.00 (*0-608-06504-8*) UMI.

— Zeneszeti Kozlony 1882; Zenevilag 1890-1891; Zeneirodalmi Szemle-Muveszeti Lapok 1894-1896. (Repertoire International de la Presse Musicale Ser.). (HUN.). 297p. 1996. lib. bdg. 145.00 (*0-8357-2421-2*) UMI.

Cohen, H. Robert & Gigou, Marie O. One Hundred Years of Operatic in France (ca. 1830-1930) A Descriptive Catalogue of Staging Manuals. LC 86-1449. (Musical Life in 19th-Century France Ser.: Vol. 2).Tr. of Cent ans de Mise en Scene Lyrique en France (env. 1830-1930). (FRE & ENG., Illus.). 334p. (C). 1987. text 55.00 (*0-918728-69-X*) Pendragon NY.

Cohen, H. Rodgin. Financial Institutions: Successful Techniques for Cross-industry Expansion in the New Era. LC 99-161564. (Corporate Law & Practice Course Handbook Ser.). 672p. 1998. write for info. (*0-87224-549-7*) PLI.

Cohen, H. Rodgin, et al. Financial Institutions Mergers & Acquisitions: The New Era. LC 97-136404. (Corporate Law & Practice Course Handbook Ser.). 960 p. 1997. 129.00 (*0-87224-305-2*) PLI.

Cohen, H. Rodgin, jt. auth. see Vartanian, Thomas P.

Cohen, Haim H. Human Rights in the Bible & Talmud. 118p. 1989. pap. 12.00 (*965-05-0563-6*, Pub. by Israel Ministry Def) Gefen Bks.

***Cohen, Harlan.** Campus Life Exposed: Advice from the Inside. 247p. (C). 2000. pap. text 14.95 (*0-7689-0498-6*) Petersons.

Cohen, Harlan. Fade Away. 368p. 1996. mass mkt. 6.50 (*0-440-22268-0*) Dell.

Cohen, Harold L. & Filipczak, James. A New Learning Environment. LC 70-151108. (Jossey-Bass Behavioral Science Ser.). 220p. reprint ed. pap. 68.20 (*0-608-14901-2*, 202566800045) Bks Demand.

— A New Learning Environment: A Case for Learning. LC 70-151108. (Illus.). xxviii, 192p. reprint ed. pap. 19.95 (*0-9623311-3-9*) Authors Coop.

Cohen, Harold R. Biblical Hapax Legomena in the Light of Akkadian & Ugaritic: Society of Biblical Literature. LC 77-13422. (Dissertation Ser.: No. 37). 201p. reprint ed. pap. 62.40 (*0-8357-9565-9*, 201752800007) Bks Demand.

Cohen, Harris L., jt. auth. see Berman, Mimi C.

Cohen, Harry, ed. see Kimchi, David B.

Cohen, Harvey, jt. auth. see Webb, Frank.

Cohen, Harvey Jay. Taking Care after 50: A Self-Care Guide for Seniors. (Illus.). 352p. 2000. pap. 17.00 (*0-8129-3174-2*, Three Riv Pr) Crown Pub Group.

Cohen, Haskel & Weil, Geraldine R. Tasks of Emotional Development. LC 75-42572. 359p. reprint ed. 35.00 (*0-916598-02-0*); reprint ed. pap., teacher ed. 12.00 (*0-317-00903-6*); reprint ed. 25.00 (*0-317-00904-4*) T E D Assocs.

Cohen, Helaine, ed. see Hewitt, Sally.

Cohen, Helaine, ed. see Janes, Susan N.

Cohen, Helaine, ed. see Llewellyn, Claire.

Cohen, Helaine, ed. see Robson, Pam.

Cohen, Helen. Neuroscience for Rehabilitation. 2nd ed. LC 98-24809. 544p. 1998. text 41.95 (*0-397-55465-6*) Lppncott W & W.

Cohen, Helen, ed. Neuroscience for Rehabilitation. LC 92-49041. (Illus.). 480p. 1993. pap. text 42.00 (*0-397-54930-X*) Lppncott W & W.

Cohen, Helen A. The Nurse's Quest for a Professional Identity. 1981. pap. write for info. (*0-201-01157-3*) Addison-Wesley.

Cohen, Hennig & Coffin, Tristram P. America Celebrates! A Patchwork of Weird & Wonderful Holiday Lore. (Illus.). 355p. 1998. pap. text 15.00 (*0-7881-5273-4*) DIANE Pub.

Cohen, Hennig & Dillingham, William B. Humor of the Old Southwest. rev. ed. LC 93-11281. 528p. 1994. 50.00 (*0-8203-1604-0*); pap. 25.00 (*0-8203-1605-9*) U of Ga Pr.

Cohen, Hennig & Yannella, Donald, eds. Herman Melville's Malcolm Letter: "Man's Final Lore" LC 91-28140. (Illus.). xii, 258p. 1993. 30.00 (*0-8232-1184-3*) Fordham.

Cohen, Hennig, jt. compiled by see Levernier, James A.

Cohen, Hennig, ed. see Melville, Herman.

Cohen, Henning. America Celebrates! A Patchwork of Weird & Wonderful Holiday Lore. (Illus.). 384p. 1991. 14.95 (*0-8103-9407-3*) Visible Ink Pr.

Cohen, Henri. Advanced Topics in Computational Number Theory. LC 99-20756. 570p. 1999. 59.95 (*0-387-98727-4*) Spr-Verlag.

— Algorithmic Number Theory: Second International Symposium, ANTS-II, Talence, France, May 18-23, 1996: Proceedings. LC 96-27489. (Lecture Notes in Computer Science Ser.: Vol. 1122). 405p. 1996. 68.00 (*3-540-61581-4*) Spr-Verlag.

Cohen, Henry. Brutal Justice: The Ordeal of an American City. LC 79-26797. 248p. 1980. lib. bdg. 10.00 (*0-89444-027-6*) John Jay Pr.

— Business & Politics in America from the Age of Jackson to the Civil War: The Career Biography of W. W. Corcoran, 4. LC 79-98708. (Illus.). 409p. 1971. 39.95 (*0-8371-3300-9*, CBP/, Greenwood Pr) Greenwood.

— A Course in Computational Algebraic Number Theory. LC 93-3701. (Graduate Texts in Mathematics Ser.: Vol. 138). (Illus.). xxii, 525p. 1996. 49.95 (*0-387-55640-0*) Spr-Verlag.

Cohen, Henry, ed. Criminal Justice History Vol. I: An International Annual, 1980, 1. 304p. 1980. lib. bdg. 79.50 (*0-313-28058-4*, CJ80, Greenwood Pr) Greenwood.

— Criminal Justice History Vol. II: An International Annual, 1981, 2. 208p. 1981. lib. bdg. 79.50 (*0-313-28059-2*, CJ81, Greenwood Pr) Greenwood.

— Criminal Justice History Vol. III: An International Annual, 1982, 3. 200p. 1983. lib. bdg. 79.50 (*0-313-28060-6*, CJ82, Greenwood Pr) Greenwood.

— Criminal Justice History Vol. IV: An International Annual, 1983, 4. 168p. 1984. lib. bdg. 79.50 (*0-313-28061-4*, CJ83, Greenwood Pr) Greenwood.

— The Public Enemy. LC 80-52292. (Warner Bros. Screenplay Ser.). (Illus.). 190p. (Orig.). 1981. pap. 9.95 (*0-299-08464-7*) U of Wis Pr.

Cohen, Henry & De Ricci, Seymour. Guide de l'Amateur de Livres a Gravures du XVIII e Siecle. 66p. 1997. 90.00 (*1-57898-047-X*) Martino Pubng.

Cohen, Henry & Karger, Arthur. Powers of the New York Court of Appeals. LC 92-81351. 1026p. 1992. reprint ed. 125.00 (*0-89941-790-6*, 307510) W S Hein.

Cohen, Henry E., ed. see Proudhon, P. J.

Cohen, Herb. Negotiating the Game Vol. 1: New Perspectives on Negotiating. unabridged ed. 1993. audio 11.00 (*1-55994-711-X*, CPN 1956) HarperAudio.

Cohen, Herb. You Can Negotiate Anything. 256p. 1982. mass mkt. 6.99 (*0-553-28109-7*) Bantam.

— You Can Negotiate Anything. 1980. 12.95 (*0-8184-0305-5*) Carol Pub Group.

— You Can Negotiate Anything. 264p. (C). 1995. reprint ed. pap. 10.95 (*0-8065-0847-7*, Citadel Pr) Carol Pub Group.

Cohen, Herb, ed. A Book of Proverbs: Inspirational Thoughts for Every Day. 144p. 1998. 12.95 (*1-55836-195-2*) Chain Sales Mktg.

— A Book of Psalms: Inspirational Thoughts for Every Day. 160p. 1998. 12.95 (*1-55836-196-0*) Chain Sales Mktg.

Cohen, Herbert & Whitin, Nancy R. Snap Out of It! 6 Steps to Banish Bad Habits, Addictions & Negative Thoughts. LC 99-46777. 192p. 1999. 17.95 (*0-87131-896-2*, Pub. by M Evans) Natl Bk Netwk.

Cohen, Herbert G. A Book of Readings for Science Education. 272p. (C). 1994. pap. text, spiral bd. 31.95 (*0-8403-9111-0*) Kendall-Hunt.

Cohen, Herbert J. Page One: Major Events, 1922-1980 as Presented in the New York Times. 1980. 19.95 (*0-405-13698-6*) Ayer.

— Page One: Major Events As Presented in the New York Times, 1920-1981. 19.95 (*0-405-14350-8*, 19818) Ayer.

Cohen, Herbert J., et al. Health Care Financing for Severe Developmental Disabilities. 1990. pap. 18.00 (*0-940898-24-1*) Am Assn Mental.

Cohen, Herbert J., jt. auth. see Birenbaum, Arnold.

Cohen, Herman. The History of Speech Communication: The Emergence of a Discipline, 1914-1945. 370p. (Orig.). (C). 1994. pap. text 40.00 (*0-944811-14-0*) Natl Comm Assn.

— The Spirit Of Our Laws. LC 97-74797. xi, 299p. 1997. reprint ed. 94.00 (*1-56169-334-0*) Gaunt.

***Cohen, Herman J.** Intervening in Africa: Superpower Peacemaking in a Troubled Continent. LC 99-87453. 288p. 2000. text 65.00 (*0-312-23221-7*) St Martin.

Cohen, Hermann. Hermann Cohen's Judische Schriften, 3 vols. Katz, Steven, ed. LC 79-7128. (Jewish Philosophy, Mysticism & History of Ideas Ser.). 1980. reprint ed. lib. bdg. 113.95 (*0-405-12245-4*) Ayer.

— Hermann Cohen's Philosophy of Religion. Moses, Stephane & Wiedebach, Hartwig, eds. LC 98-126655. (Philosophische Texte und Studien: Bd. 44). viii, 294p. 1997. write for info. (*3-487-10509-8*) G Olms Pubs.

— Kleinere Schriften V, 1913-1915, Bd. 16. (GER.). xxxv, 671p. 1997. reprint ed. write for info. (*3-487-10566-7*) G Olms Pubs.

— System der Philosophie Bd. 6: Erster Teil: Logik der Reinen Erkenntnis. (GER.). xxviii, 722p. 1997. reprint ed. write for info. (*3-487-06396-4*) G Olms Pubs.

— Werke, Bd. 1.1. (GER.). 890p. 1987. reprint ed. write for info. (*3-487-07876-7*) G Olms Pubs.

— Werke, Bd. 1.2. (GER.). 255p. 1987. reprint ed. write for info. (*3-487-07877-5*) G Olms Pubs.

— Werke, Bd. 1.3. (GER.). viii, 271p. 1987. reprint ed. write for info. (*3-487-07878-3*) G Olms Pubs.

— Werke, Bd. 4. 2nd ed. (GER.). xxiii, 256p. 1989. reprint ed. write for info. (*3-487-07881-3*) G Olms Pubs.

— Werke, Bd. 5. (GER.). vii, 370p. 1984. reprint ed. write for info. (*3-487-06395-6*) G Olms Pubs.

— Werke, Bd. 7. (GER.). xxiii, 707p. 1981. reprint ed. write for info. (*3-487-06397-2*) G Olms Pubs.

— Werke, Bd. 8. (GER.). xxv, 401p. 1982. reprint ed. write for info. (*3-487-06398-0*); reprint ed. write for info. (*3-487-06399-9*) G Olms Pubs.

Cohen, Hermann & Strauss, Bruno. Judische Schriften, Vol. 1. 1980. 37.95 (*0-405-12298-5*) Ayer.

— Judische Schriften, Vol. 2. 1980. 37.95 (*0-405-12299-3*) Ayer.

— Judische Schriften, Vol. 3. 1980. 37.95 (*0-405-12303-5*) Ayer.

Cohen, Hilary H. & Gummerman, Doug. Organizing Corporations in California: May, 1992 Update. 2nd ed. Giacomini, Edward D. et al, eds. LC 82-74145. 615p. 1992. ring bd. 60.00 (*0-88124-502-X*, BU-37767) Cont Ed Bar-CA.

— Organizing Corporations in California: May, 1994 Update. 2nd ed. Briggs, Donald R., ed. LC 82-74145. 184p. 1994. 49.00 (*0-88124-759-6*, BU-37768) Cont Ed Bar-CA.

Cohen, Howard S. & Feldberg, Michael. Power & Restraint: The Moral Dimension of Police Work. LC 90-28100. 184p. 1991. 49.95 (*0-275-93856-5*, C3856, Praeger Pubs); pap. 18.95 (*0-275-93857-3*, B3857, Praeger Pubs) Greenwood.

Cohen, Hubert I. Ingmar Bergman: The Art of Confession. LC 93-9506. (Filmmakers Ser.). 544p. 1993. 28.95 (*0-8057-9312-7*) Macmillan.

Cohen, I. Alan. Minyan Miracle: A Jewish Tradition - A Daily Blessing. 1993. pap. 9.95 (*1-55673-585-5*) CSS OH.

Cohen, I. Bernard. Album of Science: From Leonardo to Lavoisier, 1450-1800. LC 80-15542. (Illus.). 320p. 1998. 90.00 (*0-684-15377-7*, Scribners Ref) Mac Lib Ref.

— Benjamin Franklin: Scientist & Statesman. LC 75-7595. (DSB Editions Ser.). 1975. pap. 2.65 (*0-684-14252-X*, SL 588, Scribners Ref) Mac Lib Ref.

— Benjamin Franklin's Science. (Illus.). 288p. 1990. 46.95 (*0-674-06658-8*) HUP.

— Benjamin Franklin's Science. (Illus.). 288p. 1996. pap. 17.95 (*0-674-06659-6*) HUP.

— The Birth of a New Physics. rev. ed. LC 84-25582. (Illus.). 224p. 1985. reprint ed. 19.95 (*0-393-01994-2*) Norton.

— The Birth of a New Physics. rev. ed. LC 84-25582. (Illus.). 224p. 1985. reprint ed. pap. 13.95 (*0-393-30045-5*) Norton.

— Cotton Mather & American Science & Medicine: With Studies & Documents Concerning the Introduction of Inoculation or Variolation, Vol. 1. 1980. 41.95 (*0-405-12520-8*) Ayer.

— Cotton Mather & American Science & Medicine: With Studies & Documents Concerning the Introduction of Inoculation or Variolation, Vol. 2. 1980. 41.95 (*0-405-12521-6*) Ayer.

— Howard Aiken: Portrait of a Computer Pioneer. LC 98-43965. (Illus.). 412p. 1999. 34.95 (*0-262-03262-7*) MIT Pr.

***Cohen, I. Bernard.** Howard Aiken: Portrait of a Computer Pioneer. (History of Computing Ser.). (Illus.). 412p. (C). 2000. reprint ed. pap. 19.95 (*0-262-53179-8*) MIT Pr.

Cohen, I. Bernard. Interactions: Some Contacts Between the Natural Sciences & the Social Sciences. LC 94-11074. 224p. 1994. pap. text 18.50 (*0-262-53124-0*) MIT Pr.

— Introduction to Isacc Newton's Principia. LC 76-28770. (Illus.). 410p. 1976. pap. 18.95 (*0-674-46193-2*) HUP.

— The Leibniz-Clarke Correspondence. LC 80-2100. (Development of Science Ser.). (Illus.). 1981. lib. bdg. 55.95 (*0-405-13865-2*) Ayer.

— The Life & Scientific & Medical Career of Benjamin Waterhouse: With Some Account of the Introduction of Vaccination in America, Vol. 1. 1980. 37.95 (*0-405-12522-4*) Ayer.

— The Life & Scientific & Medical Career of Benjamin Waterhouse: With Some Account of the Introduction of Vaccination in America, Vol. 2. 1980. 37.95 (*0-405-12523-2*) Ayer.

— Revolution in Science. (Illus.). 704p. 1985. 47.95 (*0-674-76777-2*) Belknap Pr.

— Revolution in Science. LC 84-12916. (Illus.). 704p. 1987. pap. text 18.50 (*0-674-76778-0*) Belknap Pr.

— Science & the Founding Fathers: Science in the Political Thought of Thomas Jefferson, Benjamin Franklin, John Adams, & James Madison. 256p. 1995. 25.00 (*0-393-03501-8*) Norton.

Cohen, I. Bernard, ed. Album of Science, 5 vols., Set. 1989. text 395.00 (*0-684-19074-5*, Scribners Ref) Mac Lib Ref.

— Andrew N. Meldrum. LC 80-2096. (Development of Science Ser.). (Illus.). 1981. lib. bdg. 49.95 (*0-405-13861-X*) Ayer.

— Aspects of Astronomy in America in the Nineteenth Century: An Original Anthology. LC 79-7948. (Three Centuries of Science in America Ser.). (Illus.). 1980. lib. bdg. 48.95 (*0-405-12529-1*) Ayer.

— Benjamin Peirce: Father of Pure Mathematics in America. An Original Anthology. LC 79-7981. (Three Centuries of Science in America Ser.). (Illus.). 1980. lib. bdg. 35.95 (*0-405-12563-1*) Ayer.

— The Conservation of Energy & the Principle of Least Action. LC 80-2097. (Development of Science Ser.). (Illus.). 1981. lib. bdg. 49.95 (*0-405-13862-8*) Ayer.

— Cotton Mather & American Science & Medicine: With Studies & Documents Concerning the Introduction of Inoculation or Variolation, 2 vols. LC 79-7974. (Three Centuries of Science in America Ser.). (Illus.). 1980. lib. bdg. 82.95 (*0-405-12556-9*) Ayer.

— The Development of Science Series, 63 vols., Set. 1981. lib. bdg. 2004.00 (*0-405-13850-4*) Ayer.

— Electro-Magnetism. LC 80-2098. (Development of Science Ser.). (Illus.). 1981. lib. bdg. 35.95 (*0-405-13863-6*) Ayer.

— Gravitation, Heat & X-Rays. LC 80-2104. (Development of Science Ser.). (Illus.). 1981. lib. bdg. 38.95 (*0-405-13869-5*) Ayer.

— Laws of Gases. LC 80-2099. (Development of Science Ser.). (Illus.). 1981. lib. bdg. 38.95 (*0-405-13864-4*) Ayer.

— The Life & Scientific Work of Othniel Charles Marsh: An Original Anthology. LC 79-7973. (Three Centuries of Science in America Ser.). (Illus.). 1980. lib. bdg. 63.95 (*0-405-12555-0*) Ayer.

— The Life & the Scientific & Medical Career of Benjamin Waterhouse: With Some Account of the Introduction of Vaccination in America, An Original Anthology, 2 vols., Set. LC 79-8004. (Three Centuries of Science in America Ser.). (Illus.). 1980. lib. bdg. 75.95 (*0-405-12591-7*) Ayer.

— The Natural Sciences & the Social Sciences: Some Critical & Historical Perspectives. LC 93-3226. (Boston Studies in the Philosophy of Science: Vol. 150). 448p. 1993. lib. bdg. 214.50 (*0-7923-2223-1*, Pub. by Kluwer Academic) Kluwer Academic.

— Puritanism & the Rise of Modern Science: The Merton Thesis. 360p. (Orig.). (C). 1990. text 45.00 (*0-8135-1529-7*); pap. text 19.00 (*0-8135-1530-0*) Rutgers U Pr.

— Research & Technology. LC 79-7982. (Three Centuries of Science in America Ser.). (Illus.). 1980. lib. bdg. 25.95 (*0-405-12564-X*) Ayer.

— Studies on William Harvey. LC 80-2101. (Development of Science Ser.). (Illus.). 1981. lib. bdg. 71.95 (*0-405-13866-0*) Ayer.

— Theory of Solutions & Stereo-Chemistry. LC 80-2103. (Development of Science Ser.). (Illus.). 1981. lib. bdg. 38.95 (*0-405-13868-7*) Ayer.

— Thomas Jefferson & the Sciences: An Original Anthology. LC 79-7970. (Three Centuries of Science in America Ser.). (Illus.). 1980. 63.95 (*0-405-12552-6*) Ayer.

— Three Centuries of Science in America Series, 66 bks. (Illus.). 1980. lib. bdg. 2939.00 (*0-405-12525-9*) Ayer.

— The Wave Theory of Light & Spectra. LC 80-2102. (Development of Science Ser.). (Illus.). 1981. lib. bdg. 38.95 (*0-405-13867-9*) Ayer.

Cohen, I. Bernard & Welch, Gregory W., eds. Makin' Numbers: Howard Aiken & the Computer. LC 98-43964. (Illus.). 320p. 1999. 40.00 (*0-262-03263-5*) MIT Pr.

Cohen, I. Bernard, ed. see Ackerknecht, Erwin H.

Cohen, I. Bernard, ed. see Adams, John Q.

Cohen, I. Bernard, jt. ed. see Airy, George B.

Cohen, I. Bernard, jt. ed. see Anderson, David L.

Cohen, I. Bernard, ed. see Archibald, Raymond C.

Cohen, I. Bernard, ed. see Beaumont, William.

Cohen, I. Bernard, ed. see Beer, John B.

Cohen, I. Bernard, ed. see Borell, Merriley.

Cohen, I. Bernard, ed. see Bowditch, Henry P.

Cohen, I. Bernard, ed. see Bridgman, Percy Williams.

Cohen, I. Bernard, jt. ed. see Brown, Theodore L.

Cohen, I. Bernard, jt. ed. see Buchwald, Jed Z.

Cohen, I. Bernard, ed. see Bush, Vannevar.

Cohen, I. Bernard, ed. see Cajori, Florian.

Cohen, I. Bernard, ed. see Cheyne, Charles H.

Cohen, I. Bernard, jt. ed. see Coleman, William.

Cohen, I. Bernard, ed. see Cooper, Thomas.

Cohen, I. Bernard, ed. see Dalton, John C.

Cohen, I. Bernard, ed. see Darton, Nelson H.

Cohen, I. Bernard, ed. see De Candolle, Alphonse.

Cohen, I. Bernard, jt. ed. see Domson, Charles.

Cohen, I. Bernard, jt. ed. see Donahue, William H.

Cohen, I. Bernard, ed. see Dupree, A. Hunter.

Cohen, I. Bernard, ed. see Ellicott, Andrew.

Cohen, I. Bernard, jt. ed. see Farrell, Maureen.

Cohen, I. Bernard, ed. see Fulton, John F.

Cohen, I. Bernard, ed. see Gardner, Walter M.

Cohen, I. Bernard, ed. see Getman, Frederick H.

Cohen, I. Bernard, ed. see Gingerich, Owen.

Cohen, I. Bernard, ed. see Godfray, Hugh.

Cohen, I. Bernard, ed. see Goode, George B.

Cohen, I. Bernard, ed. see Graetzerk, Hans G. & Anderson, David L.

Cohen, I. Bernard, ed. see Grimaux, Edouard.

Cohen, I. Bernard, ed. see Hale, George E.

Cohen, I. Bernard, ed. see Hall, Diana L.

Cohen, I. Bernard, jt. ed. see Hall, Marie B.

Cohen, I. Bernard, ed. see Hannequin, Arthur.

Cohen, I. Bernard, ed. see Harding, T. Swann.

Cohen, I. Bernard, ed. see Harvey-Gibson, Robert J.

Cohen, I. Bernard, jt. ed. see Heibron, John L.

Cohen, I. Bernard, ed. see Heidel, William A.

Cohen, I. Bernard, jt. ed. see Herschel, John F.

Cohen, I. Bernard, ed. see Hiebert, Erwin N.

Cohen, I. Bernard, jt. ed. see Hilts, Victor L.

Cohen, I. Bernard, ed. see Hindle, Brooke.

Cohen, I. Bernard, jt. ed. see Hindle, Brooke.

Cohen, I. Bernard, ed. see Holden, Edward S.

Cohen, I. Bernard, ed. see Home, Roderick W.

Cohen, I. Bernard, ed. see Howard, Leland O.

Cohen, I. Bernard, ed. see Jaffe, Bernard.

Cohen, I. Bernard, ed. see Karpinski, Louis C.

Cohen, I. Bernard, ed. see Loomis, Elias.

Cohen, I. Bernard, ed. see Maeir, Clifford L.

Cohen, I. Bernard, ed. see Merill, Elmer D.

Cohen, I. Bernard, ed. see Meyer, Kirstine B.

Cohen, I. Bernard, ed. see Millikan, Robert Andrews.

Cohen, I. Bernard, ed. see Milne-Edwards, Henri.

Cohen, I. Bernard, ed. see Mitchel, Ormsby M.

Cohen, I. Bernard, ed. see Mouy, Paul.

Cohen, I. Bernard, ed. see Newton, Sir Isaac.

Cohen, I. Bernard, ed. see OECD Staff.

Cohen, I. Bernard, ed. see Olmsted, J. M.

Cohen, I. Bernard, ed. see Packard, Alpheus S.

Cohen, I. Bernard, ed. see Partington, James R. & McKie, Douglas.

Cohen, I. Bernard, ed. see President's Scientific Research Board Staff & Steelman, John R.

An Asterisk (*) at the beginning of an entry indicates that the title is appearing for the first time.

Cohen, I. Bernard, ed. see Priestley, Joseph.
Cohen, I. Bernard, ed. see Pupin, Michael.
Cohen, I. Bernard, ed. see Quetelet, Adolphe J.
Cohen, I. Bernard, ed. see Rhees, William J.
Cohen, I. Bernard, jt. ed. see Roe, Shirley A.
Cohen, I. Bernard, ed. see Sayili, Aydin.
Cohen, I. Bernard, ed. see Schofield, Christine J.
Cohen, I. Bernard, ed. see Scott, William B.
Cohen, I. Bernard, ed. see Shirley, John W.
Cohen, I. Bernard, ed. see Shryock, Richard H.
Cohen, I. Bernard, ed. see Shute, Michael.
Cohen, I. Bernard, ed. see Silliman, Benjamin, Jr.
Cohen, I. Bernard, ed. see Smith, David E. & Ginsberg, Jekuthiel.
Cohen, I. Bernard, ed. see Smith, Edgar F.
Cohen, I. Bernard, ed. see Sopka, Katherine.
Cohen, I. Bernard, ed. see Stewart, Irvin.
Cohen, I. Bernard, jt. ed. see Stigler, Stephen M.
Cohen, I. Bernard, ed. see Trowbridge, John T.
Cohen, I. Bernard, ed. see True, Alfred C.
Cohen, I. Bernard, jt. ed. see True, Frederick W.
Cohen, I. Bernard, ed. see Turner, Dorothy M.
Cohen, I. Bernard, ed. see Tyndall, John.
Cohen, I. Bernard, ed. see U. S. House of Representatives Staff.
Cohen, I. Bernard, ed. see U. S. National Resources Committee Staff.
Cohen, I. Bernard, ed. see U. S. Senate Joint Commission, 49th Congress, 1st.
Cohen, I. Bernard, ed. see Wilhelm, Friedrich G.
Cohen, I. Bernard, ed. see Wool, Harry.
Cohen, I. Bernard, ed. see Wurtz, Adolf.
Cohen, I. Bernard, ed. see Youmans, Edward L.
Cohen, I. Bernard, ed. see Zloczower, A.
Cohen, I. Bernard, tr. see Newton, Sir Isaac.
Cohen, I. Kelman, frwd. A Brief History of Wound Care. (Illus.). 52p. 1997. text. write for info. (0-9660389-0-8) OCC.
Cohen, I. R., jt. ed. see Atlan, H.
***Cohen, Ian, et al.** Men Love Football/Women Love Foreplay: And Other Crazy Comparisons. (Illus.). 96p. 2000. pap. text 6.99 (1-57644-114-8) CCC Pubns.
Cohen, Ira. On Feet of Gold. (Illus.). 148p. 1986. pap. 7.95 (0-907791-10-7) Synerg CA.
Cohen, Ira J., jt. auth. see Weber, Max.
Cohen, Irun, jt. auth. see Rosenberg, Eugene.
***Cohen, Irun R.** Tending Adam's Garden: Evolving the Cognitive Immune Self. 288p. 1999. 49.95 (0-12-178355-3) Acad Pr.
— Tending Adam's Garden: Evolving the Cognitive Immune Self. 288p. 2000. pap. 24.95 (0-12-178356-1) Acad Pr.
Cohen, Irun R., ed. Perspectives on Autoimmunity. 272p. 1987. 136.00 (0-8493-6431-0, RC600, CRC Reprint) Franklin.
Cohen, Irvin, Jr. Lessons from an Ever-Evolving Therapist. LC 96-26290. 192p. (Orig.). 1996. pap. 28.95 (1-56887-021-3, EETBP, Prof Resc Pr) Pro Resource.
Cohen, Irving. Addiction: The High-Low Trap. 1995. pap. 13.95 (0-929173-10-4) Health Press.
Cohen, Isaac. American Management & British Labor: A Comparative Study of the Cotton Spinning Industry, 109. LC 90-2753. (Contributions in Economics & Economic History Ser.: No. 109). 256p. 1990. 65.00 (0-313-26780-4, CMB/, Greenwood Pr) Greenwood.
Cohen, Izhar. ABC Discovery! An Alphabet Book of Picture Puzzles. LC 97-39646. (Illus.). 64p. (J). (gr. 1-7). 1998. 17.99 (0-8037-2321-0, Dial Yng Read) Peng Put Young Read.
Cohen, J., et al, eds. Random Matrices & Their Applications. LC 85-30842. (Contemporary Mathematics Ser.: Vol. 50). 358p. 1986. reprint ed. pap. 43.00 (0-8218-5044-X, CONM/50) Am Math.
Cohen, J., jt. auth. see Marshall, J.
Cohen, J., jt. ed. see Bekkers, Y.
Cohen, J. B. & Hilliard, J. E., eds. Local Atomic Arrangements Studied by X-ray Diffraction, Chicago, Illionis, Feruary 15, 1965. LC 66-28062. (Metallurgical Society Conference Ser.: Vol. 36). 393p. reprint ed. pap. 121.90 (0-608-11325-5, 200152500079) Bks Demand.
Cohen, J. B., jt. auth. see Noyan, I. C.
Cohen, J. B., jt. auth. see Schwartz, L. H.
Cohen, J. E., et al. Community Food Webs: Data & Theory. Levin, S. A. et al, eds. (Biomathematics Ser.: Vol. 20). 312p. 1990. 97.95 (0-387-51129-6) Spr-Verlag.
Cohen, J. J., et al, eds. Nephrology Forum. (Illus.). 376p. 1982. 117.00 (0-387-90764-5) Spr-Verlag.
Cohen, J. L. Mies Van Der Rohe. (Illus.). 144p. 1995. pap. 29.99 (0-419-20330-3, E & FN Spon) Routledge.
Cohen, J. L., et al, eds. Logic, Methodology & Philosophy of Science, Vol. 6. (Studies in Logic & the Foundations of Mathematics: Vol. 104). 104p. 1983. 246.50 (0-444-85423-1, North Holland) Elsevier.
Cohen, J. M. & Cohen, M. J. The Penguin Dictionary of Twentieth-Century Quotations. 640p. 1996. pap. 14.95 (0-14-051165-2) Viking Penguin.
Cohen, J. M., tr. see Columbus, Christopher.
Cohen, J. M., tr. see Diaz, Bernal.
Cohen, J. M., tr. see Eliade, Mircea.
Cohen, J. M., tr. see Rabelais, Francois.
Cohen, J. M., tr. & intro. see Rousseau, Jean-Jacques.
Cohen, J. Simcha. How Does Jewish Law Work? Vol. 1: A Rabbi Analyzes 95 Contemporary Halachic Questions. LC 93-19756. 328p. 1994. 40.00 (0-87668-155-0) Aronson.
— How Does Jewish Law Work Vol. 2: A Rabbi Analyzes 119 More Contemporary Halachic Questions. 368p. 2000. 35.00 (0-7657-6090-8) Aronson.
— The 613th Commandment: An Analysis of the Mitzvah to Write a Sefer Torah. LC 94-9226. 172p. 1996. pap. 30.00 (1-56821-249-6) Aronson.
— Timely Jewish Questions, Timeless Rabbinic Answers. LC 90-33511. 376p. 1991. 40.00 (0-87668-784-2) Aronson.
Cohen, J. W. The Single Server Queue. 2nd rev. ed. (North-Holland Series in Applied Mathematics & Mechanics: Vol. 8). xiv,694p. 1982. pap. 89.50 (0-444-89482-9, North Holland) Elsevier.
***Cohen, Jack.** Guides for an Age of Confusion: Studies in the Thinking of Avraham Y. Kook & Mordecai M. Kaplan. LC 99-16639. 352p. 1999. pap. 19.95 (0-8232-2003-6) Fordham.
Cohen, Jack. The Reunion of Isaac & Ishmael. 169p. 1987. pap. 12.95 (0-88962-395-3) Mosaic.
— The Reunion of Isaac & Ishmael. 180p. 1988. pap. 12.95 (0-88962-396-1) Mosaic.
Cohen, Jack & Stewart, Ian. The Collapse of Chaos: Discovering Simplicity in a Complex World. (Illus.). 512p. 1995. pap. 14.95 (0-14-017874-0, Penguin Bks) Viking Penguin.
Cohen, Jack, et al. Nuclear Magnetic Resonance in Biology & Medicine: A Special Issue of the Journal Life Chemistry Reports, Vol. 1, Part 4. (Life Chemistry Reports: Vol. 1, No. 4). ii, 176p. 1983. pap. text 171.00 (3-7186-0170-2) Gordon & Breach.
***Cohen, Jack, et al.** Stop Working, Start Thinking. (Illus.). 128p. 2000. (0-7487-4334-0) S Thornes Pubs.
Cohen, Jack, jt. auth. see Stewart, Ian.
Cohen, Jack, tr. see Marx, Karl.
Cohen, Jack J. Major Philosophers of Jewish Prayer in the Twentieth Century. LC 99-49432. 227p. 2000. pap. 19.95 (0-8232-1957-7, Pub. by Fordham) BookMasters.
Cohen, Jack K. Calculus with Texas Instrument Graphing Calculator. 104p. (C). 1996. pap. text 20.40 (0-13-518978-0) P-H.
Cohen, Jack K., jt. auth. see Hagin, Frank G.
Cohen, Jack L. Guides for an Age of Confusion: Studies in the Thinking of Avraham Y. Kook & Mordecai Kaplan. LC 99-49432. 352p. 1999. 37.50 (0-8232-1956-9, Pub. by Fordham) BookMasters.
Cohen, Jack S. Intermarriage & Conversion: A Halakhic Solution. 19.95 (0-88125-124-0); pap. 14.95 (0-88125-125-9) Ktav.
Cohen, Jacob. Statistical Power Analysis for the Behavioral Sciences. 2nd ed. 567p. (C). 1988. 89.95 (0-8058-0283-5) L Erlbaum Assocs.
Cohen, Jacob & Cohen, Patricia. Applied Multiple Regression/Correlation Analysis for the Behavioral Sciences. 2nd ed. 545p. 1983. text 39.95 (0-89859-268-2) L Erlbaum Assocs.
Cohen, Jacob, jt. auth. see Borenstein, Michael.
Cohen, Jacob, jt. auth. see Cohen, Patricia.
Cohen, Jacob W., ed. Analysis of Random Walks. LC 92-52688. 382p. (gr. 12). 1992. 98.00 (90-5199-086-3, Pub. by IOS Pr) IOS Press.
Cohen, Jacques, et al. Micromanipulation of Human Gametes & Embryos. 336p. 1991. text 98.00 (0-88167-835-X) Lppncott W & W.
Cohen, James. Through a Lens Darkly. 256p. 1993. mass mkt. 4.99 (0-446-36340-5, Pub. by Warner Bks) Little.
Cohen, James & Wilkin, Graham, eds. Neural Cell Culture: A Practical Approach. (Practical Approach Ser.: Vol. 165). (Illus.). 268p. (C). 1996. pap. text 55.00 (0-19-963484-X) OUP.
Cohen, James, jt. auth. see Hickey, Elizabeth.
Cohen, James A., tr. see Mattelart, Armand.
Cohen, James A., tr. see Mattelart, Armand & Mattelart, Michele.
Cohen, James S. & Stieglitz, Maria N. Career Education For Physically Disabled Students: Classroom Business Ventures. LC 79-91614. (Illus.). 50p. 1980. 2.00 (0-686-38798-8) Human Res Ctr.
— Career Education For Physically Disabled Students: Speaker's Bureau. LC 79-93340. (Illus.). 62p. 1980. 2.00 (0-686-38801-1) Human Res Ctr.
Cohen, James S., jt. auth. see Stieglitz, Maria N.
Cohen, Jane G. & Wannamaker, Marilyn. Expressive Arts for the Very Disabled & Handicapped for All Ages. 2nd ed. LC 96-23680. (Illus.). 236p. 1996. pap., spiral bd. 42.95 (0-398-06704-X) C C Thomas.
Cohen, Janie. Vision & Revision: Recent Art from the Netherlands. LC 89-85769. (Illus.). 50p. (Orig.). 1989. 12.00 (1-878248-00-6) Danforth Mus.
Cohen, Janie, et al. Picasso: Inside the Image: Prints from the Ludwig Museum, Cologne. (Illus.). 136p. (Orig.). 1995. pap. 19.95 (0-934658-06-4) R H Flem Mus.
Cohen, Jason & Krugman, Michael. Generation Ecch. 176p. 1994. pap. 11.00 (0-671-88694-0, Fireside) S&S Trade Pap.
Cohen, Jay S. Make Your Medicine Safe: How to Prevent Side Effects from the Drugs You Take. LC 98-92458. 1998. mass mkt. 7.50 (0-380-79075-0, Avon Bks) Morrow Avon.
Cohen, Jayne. The Gefilte Variations: A Food Lover's Improvisations on Jewish Themes. 416p. 2000. 34.50 (0-684-82719-0) S&S Trade.
Cohen, Jean, ed. Oral Contraceptives & Cardiovascular Disease: An Analysis of the Recent Discussions on the Safety of the Pill. LC 96-39337. (Illus.). 88p. 1997. text 32.00 (1-85070-787-1) Prthnon Pub.
Cohen, Jean, et al. Dictionnaire de la Vie Affective et Sexuelle. (FRE.). 272p. 1974. 29.95 (0-8288-6016-5, M6605) Fr & Eur.
— Encyclopedie de la Vie Sexuelle, 3: De la Physiologie a la Psychologie, 14-16 Ans. (FRE.). 160p. 1973. 22.95 (0-8288-6281-8, M-6074) Fr & Eur.
— Encyclopedie de la Vie Sexuelle, 4: De la Physiologie a la Psychologie, 17-18 Ans. (FRE.). 48p. 1973. 26.50 (0-7859-0737-8, M-6075) Fr & Eur.
— Encyclopedie de la Vie Sexuelle, 5: De la Physiologie a la Psychologie, Adultes. (FRE.). 48p. 1973. 32.95 (0-8288-6283-4, M-6076) Fr & Eur.
Cohen, Jean L. Class & Civil Society: The Limits of Marxian Critical Theory. LC 82-11104. 276p. 1983. lib. bdg. 32.50 (0-87023-380-7) U of Mass Pr.
Cohen, Jean L. & Arato, Andrew. Civil Society & Political Theory. (Studies in Contemporary German Social Thought). (Illus.). 793p. 1994. pap. text 35.00 (0-262-53121-6) MIT Pr.
Cohen, Jean-Louis. Le Corbusier & the Mystique of the U. S. S. R. Theories & Projects for Moscow, 1928-1936. (Illus.). 300p. 1991. text 57.50 (0-691-04076-1, Pub. by Princeton U Pr) Cal Prin Full Svc.
— Le Corbusier & the Mystique of the U. S. S. R. Theories & Projects for Moscow, 1928-1936. Hylton, Kenneth, tr. from RUS. LC 90-25235. (Illus.). 270p. 1992. reprint ed. pap. 83.70 (0-608-02583-6, 206322900004) Bks Demand.
— Scenes of the World to Come: European Architecture & the American Challenge 1893-1960. LC 97-202089. (Illus.). 224p. 1995. 45.00 (2-08-013576-7, Pub. by Flammarion) Abbeville Pr.
Cohen, Jeff & Solomon, Norman. Adventures in Medialand: Behind the News, Beyond the Pundits. 1993. lib. bdg. 29.95 (1-56751-015-9) Common Courage.
— Adventures in Medialand: Behind the News, Beyond the Pundits. 1993. pap. 11.95 (1-56751-014-0) Common Courage.
Cohen, Jeff, jt. auth. see Solomon, Norman.
***Cohen, Jeffery Jerome.** Of Giants: Sex, Monsters & the Middle Ages, 17. LC 98-53479. Vol. 17. (Illus.). 240p. 1999. pap. text 18.95 (0-8166-3217-0) U of Minn Pr.
Cohen, Jeffrey, tr. see Hoffe, Otfried.
Cohen, Jeffrey A. & Brownell, Charles E. The Architectural Drawings of Benjamin Henry Latrobe. Vol. 2. (Illus.). write for info. (0-318-72581-9) Yale U Pr.
— Papers of Benjamin Henry Latrobe: Series 2: The Architectural & Engineering Drawings; Vol. 2: The Architectural Drawings of Benjamin Henry Latrobe, Pts. 1 & 2. (Illus.). 992p. 1995. 130.00 (0-300-06100-5) Yale U Pr.
Cohen, Jeffrey C., tr. see Kriegel, Blandine.
Cohen, Jeffrey E. Politics & Economic Policy in the United States. 384p. (C). 1997. pap. text 33.56 (0-395-74603-5) HM.
— The Politics of Telecommunications Regulation: The States & the Divestiture of AT&T. LC 92-9815. (Bureaucracies, Public Administration & Public Policy Ser.). 202p. (gr. 13). 1992. text 66.95 (1-56324-050-5) M E Sharpe.
— Presidential Responsiveness & Public Policy-Making: The Public & the Policies That Presidents Choose. LC 97-4690. 304p. (C). 1997. text 54.50 (0-472-10812-3, 10812) U of Mich Pr.
***Cohen, Jeffrey E.** Presidential Responsiveness & Public Policy-Making: The Public & the Policies That Presidents Choose. 304p. (C). 1999. pap. text 19.95 (0-472-08630-8, 08630) U of Mich Pr.
Cohen, Jeffrey H. The Challenge of Grassroots Development: Society, Economy, & Change in Southern Mexico. Cuffel, Victoria, ed. (Occasional Papers). 67p. (Orig.). 1994. pap. 4.00 (1-881157-28-8) In Ctr Global.
***Cohen, Jeffrey H.** Cooperation & Community: Economy & Society in Oaxaca. LC 99-24836. 232p. 1999. pap. 17.95 (0-292-71221-9) U of Tex Pr.
— Cooperation & Community: Economy & Society in Oaxaca. LC 99-24836. 232p. 2000. 40.00 (0-292-71220-0) U of Tex Pr.
***Cohen, Jeffrey J.** Of Giants: Sex, Monsters & the Middle Ages. LC 98-53479. (Medieval Cultures Ser.). 1999. write for info. (0-8166-3216-2) U of Minn Pr.
Cohen, Jeffrey J., ed. Monster Theory: Reading Culture. 288p. (C). 1996. pap. 21.95 (0-8166-2855-6); text 54.95 (0-8166-2854-8) U of Minn Pr.
Cohen, Jeffrey J. & Fish, Marian C. Handbook of School-Based Interventions: Resolving Student Problems & Promoting Healthy Educational Environments. LC 93-3619. (Social & Behavioral Sciences Ser.). 542p. 1993. text 50.00 (1-55542-549-6) Jossey-Bass.
Cohen, Jeffrey J. & Wheeler, Bonnie, eds. Becoming Male in the Middle Ages. LC 97-1520. (New Middle Ages Ser.: Vol. 4). (Illus.). 408p. 1997. text 68.00 (0-8153-2836-2, H2066) Garland.
***Cohen, Jeffrey L., ed.** K-Line Collector's Guide, Pocket Edition: Trains: 1985-2000. 152p. 2000. pap. 14.95 (0-934580-24-3) MDK Inc.
Cohen, Jeffrey M. Blessed Are You: A Comprehensive Guide to Jewish Prayer. LC 92-21456. 344p. 1993. 30.00 (0-87668-465-7) Aronson.
— Blessed Are You: A Comprehensive Guide to Jewish Prayer. LC 92-21456. 344p. 1997. pap. 30.00 (0-7657-5974-8) Aronson.
— Moments of Insight: Biblical & Contemporary Themes. 216p. 1989. text 22.50 (0-85303-233-5, Pub. by M Vallentine & Co) Intl Spec Bk.
— 1001 Questions & Answers on Pesach. LC 95-22903. 384p. 1996. 50.00 (1-56821-523-1) Aronson.
— 1,001 Questions & Answers on Rosh Hashanah & Yom Kippur. LC 97-13022. 1997. 50.00 (0-7657-9973-1) Aronson.
— Prayer & Penitence: A Commentary on the High Holy Day Machzor. LC 94-3077. 336p. 1994. 40.00 (1-56821-046-9) Aronson.
Cohen, Jefrey. Dear Chief Rabbi: From the Correspondence of the Chief Rabbi Immanuel Jakobovitz on Matters of Jewish Law, Ethics & Contemporary Issues, 1980-1990. LC 95-6166. 1995. 29.50 (0-88125-471-1) Ktav.
Cohen, Jennie & Spencer, Cat. The Broadway Cafe. 48p. 1997. pap. 5.00 (0-87440-054-6) Bakers Plays.
Cohen, Jennifer & Christian, Kent, eds. Hart's Oil & Gas Finance Sourcebook. 7th rev. ed. 650p. 1996. pap. 545.00 (0-912553-61-8) Hart Pubns.
Cohen, Jennifer L. When the Wind Is Blue. (Illus.). 24p. 1995. 15.00 (0-9650549-0-X) Barking at the Moon.
Cohen, Jeremy. Be Fertile & Increase, Fill the Earth & Master It: The Ancient & Medieval Career of a Biblical Text. LC 89-7149. 392p. 1989. 57.50 (0-8014-2307-4) Cornell U Pr.
— Be Fertile & Increase, Fill the Earth & Master It: The Ancient & Medieval Career of a Biblical Text. LC 89-7149. 392p. 1992. pap. text 19.95 (0-8014-8053-1) Cornell U Pr.
— Congress Shall Make No Law: Oliver Wendell Holmes, the First Amendment, & Judicial Decision Making. LC 88-12793. 164p. reprint ed. pap. 50.90 (0-608-06848-9, 206705400009) Bks Demand.
— Living Letters of the Law: Ideas of the Jew in Medieval Christianity. LC 99-20634. 461p. 1999. 60.00 (0-520-21680-6, Pub. by U CA Pr) Cal Prin Full Svc.
***Cohen, Jeremy.** Living Letters of the Law: Ideas of the Jews in Medieval Christianity. LC 99-20634. 461p. 1999. pap. text 24.95 (0-520-21870-1, Pub. by U CA Pr) Cal Prin Full Svc.
Cohen, Jeremy, ed. Essential Papers on Judaism & Christianity in Conflict. 528p. (C). 1991. text 75.00 (0-8147-1442-0); pap. text 27.50 (0-8147-1443-9) NYU Pr.
Cohen, Jeremy & Gleason, Timothy, eds. Social Research in Communication & Law. (CommText Ser.: Vol. 23). 160p. (C). 1990. 42.00 (0-8039-3266-9); pap. 18.95 (0-8039-3267-7) Sage.
Cohen, Jeremy, jt. auth. see Pember, Donald R.
Cohen, Jerome, et al, eds. Psychosocial Aspects of Cancer. LC 80-5057. Orig. Title: Research Issues in Psychological Dimensions of Cancer. 336p. 1982. reprint ed. pap. 104.20 (0-608-03397-9, 206409400008) Bks Demand.
Cohen, Jerome, et al. Investment Analysis & Portfolio Management. 5th ed. (C). 1993. 20.94 (0-256-16368-5, Irwn McGrw-H) McGrw-H Hghr Educ.
Cohen, Jerome A., ed. China's Practice of International Law: Some Case Studies. LC 72-80656. (Studies in East Asian Law: No. 6). (Illus.). 429p. 1972. 46.50 (0-674-11975-4) HUP.
— Criminal Process in the People's Republic of China, 1949-1963: An Introduction. LC 68-14252. (Studies in East Asian Law: No. 2). (Illus.). 722p. 1968. 62.95 (0-674-17650-2) HUP.
— The Dynamics of China's Foreign Relations. LC 78-133219. (East Asian Monographs: No. 39). 139p. 1970. 20.00 (0-674-21875-2) HUP.
Cohen, Jerome A., et al, eds. Contemporary Chinese Law: Research Problems & Perspectives. LC 74-106957. (Studies in East Asian Law: No. 4). 394p. 1970. 37.00 (0-674-16675-2) HUP.
— Essays on China's Legal Tradition. LC 79-3197. (Studies in East Asian Law). 450p. 1980. reprint ed. pap. 139.50 (0-608-03362-6, 206407400008) Bks Demand.
Cohen, Jerome A. & Chiu, Hungdah. People's China & International Law Vol. 1: A Documentary Study. LC 73-2475. (Studies in East Asian Law). 950p. 1974. reprint ed. pap. 200.00 (0-608-02921-1, 206398600001) Bks Demand.
***Cohen, Jerome B.** Japan's Economy in War & Reconstruction. LC 00-25575. (Japanese Economic History Ser.). 2000. write for info. (0-415-21817-9) Routledge.
Cohen, Jerome B. Personal Finance. 3rd ed. (Plaid Ser.). 1981. pap. 12.00 (0-256-02126-0, Irwn Prfssnl) McGraw-Hill Prof.
Cohen, Jerome B., et al. Investment Analysis & Portfolio Management. 5th ed. 752p. (C). 1986. text 70.95 (0-256-03624-1, Irwn McGrw-H) McGrw-H Hghr Educ.
Cohen, Jerome L. The Gravestone Accord. LC 98-93904. 448p. 1998. pap. 12.95 (0-9667643-0-7) T Von Taus & Co.
***Cohen, Jerry.** Trademarks & Related Unfair Competition Law. 3rd ed. (Corporate Practice Ser.: Vol. 18). 2000. pap. 95.00 (1-55871-424-3) BNA.
Cohen, Jerry, jt. auth. see Campbell, Francis W.
Cohen, Jerry, jt. auth. see Gutterman, Alan S.
Cohen, Jessie, jt. auth. see Galvin, Laura Gates.
Cohen, Joan & Hantover, Jeff. Art of Shan-Shan Sheng. (Illus.). 96p. (Orig.). 1992. 28.00 (0-9634729-3-3); pap. 16.00 (0-9634729-6-8) East West Art.
Cohen, Joan L. Yunnan School: A Renaissance in Chinese Painting. LC 87-83744. (Illus.). 160p. 1988. 75.00 (0-9619771-0-8) Fingerhut Group.
Cohen, Joan S. Helping Your Grandchildren Through Their Parents Divorce. 256p. (Orig.). 1994. 22.95 (0-8027-1298-3); pap. 12.95 (0-8027-7433-4) Walker & Co.
***Cohen, Joan Schrager.** Helping Your Grandchildren Through Their Parents' Divorce. (Illus.). 177p. 2000. reprint ed. 23.00 (0-7881-9373-2) DIANE Pub.
Cohen, Joanna. Baseball Superstars: Today's Best Baseball Players. Thomas, Stephen, ed. LC 98-112194. 32p. (J). (gr. 5-6). 1996. pap. 3.95 (1-886749-20-5) SI For Kids.
Cohen, Jocelyn H., et al, eds. Women in Social Protest: The U. S. since 1915: A Photographic Postcard Series. (Illus.). 22p. (Orig.). (C). 1989. pap. text. write for info. (0-318-65535-7) Helaine Victoria.
Cohen, Jocelyn H., et al. Women in Social Protest: The U. S. since 1915. (Photographic Postcard Ser.). (Illus.). 22p. (C). 1989. pap. text 8.95 (0-9623911-0-7, WSP-07) Helaine Victoria.
Cohen, Jodi R. Introduction to Communication Criticism: Developing Your Critical Powers. LC 97-45334. (Rhetoric & Society Ser.). 1998. 48.00 (0-7619-0629-0); pap. 22.95 (0-7619-0630-4) Sage.

C

***Cohen, Joe.** Oakland Glimmer (a Novella) & Tales of the Want Ads (Stories) 231p. 2000. pap. 14.95 (*1-889059-83-8*) Regent Pr.

***Cohen, Joel.** Breast Cancer Survival Rates & Health Plan Services. 23p. 2000. pap. write for info. (*1-58703-118-3*, CRB-00-001) CA St Libry.

— Focus Groups: A Valuable Tool for Public Policy. 9p. 2000. pap. write for info. (*1-58703-119-1*, CRB Note 7) CA St Libry.

— Odd Moments in Baseball. (Odd Sports Stories Ser.: Vol. 1). (Illus.). 96p. (J). (gr. 3-6). 2000. mass mkt. 4.50 (*0-590-37066-9*) Scholastic Inc.

— Odd Moments in Sports, Vol. 2. (Odd Sports Stories Ser.: Vol. 2). (Illus.). 96p. (YA). (gr. 4-7). 2000. pap. text 4.50 (*0-590-37067-7*) Scholastic Inc.

— School Facility Financing: A History of the Role of the State Allocation Board & Options for the Distribution of Proposition 1A Funds. 43p. 1999. pap. write for info. (*1-58703-098-5*, CRB-99-001) CA St Libry.

Cohen, Joel, jt. auth. see Mizerak, Steve.

Cohen, Joel E. How Many People Can the Earth Support? 544p. 1996. pap. 16.95 (*0-393-31495-2*) Norton.

— A Model of Simple Competition. LC 66-23470. (Annals of the Computation Laboratory of Harvard University Ser.: No. 41). 150p. 1966. reprint ed. pap. 46.50 (*0-7837-2237-0*, 205732700004) Bks Demand.

Cohen, Joel E., et al. Comparisons of Stochastic Matrices: With Applications in Information Theory, Statistics, Economics & Population. LC 98-16659. 1998. 59.95 (*3-7643-4082-7*) Birkhauser.

— Comparisons of Stochastic Matrices: With Applications in Information Theory, Statistics, Economics & Population. LC 98-16659. 220p. 1998. 59.95 (*0-8176-4082-7*) Spr-Verlag.

Cohen, Joel H. Norman Rockwell: America's Best-Loved Illustrator. LC 96-35103. (First Bks.). (J). 1997. lib. bdg. 22.00 (*0-531-20266-6*) Watts.

— Norman Rockwell: America's Best-Loved Illustrator. (First Books-Biographies Ser.). (J). 1997. pap. text 6.95 (*0-531-15840-3*) Watts.

***Cohen, Joel H.** R. L. Stine. LC 99-50764. (People in the News Ser.). (Illus.). 144p. (YA). (gr. 6-9). 2000. lib. bdg. 18.96 (*1-56006-608-3*) Lucent Bks.

Cohen, Joel H. Superstars of Women's Gymnastics. LC 96-321555. (Female Sports Stars Ser.). 64p. (J). (gr. 3 up). 1997. lib. bdg. 15.95 (*0-7910-4391-6*) Chelsea Hse.

***Cohen, Joel I.** Managing Agricultural Biotechnology: Addressing Research Program Needs & Policy Implications. LC 99-57155. (Biotechnology in Agriculture Ser.). 350p. 2000. 85.00 (*0-85199-400-8*) OUP.

Cohen, Joel M. Complete Guide to OSHA Compliance. 416p. 1995. lib. bdg. 75.00 (*0-87371-681-7*, L681) Lewis Pubs.

***Cohen, Joel M. & Peterson, Robert D.** The Cal/OSHA Source 2000. rev. ed. 500p. 2000. pap. 70.00 (*0-9663378-1-6*) CA Safety.

Cohen, John & Seger, Mike, eds. Old-Time String Band Songbook. (Illus.). 240p. 1976. pap. 17.95 (*0-8256-0179-7*, OK63255, Oak) Music Sales.

Cohen, John, jt. ed. see Gupta, Sudhir.

Cohen, John I. & Travers, Robert M., eds. Education for Democracy. LC 72-128222. (Essay Index Reprint Ser.). 1977. 30.95 (*0-8369-1944-0*) Ayer.

Cohen, John M. Integrated Rural Development: The Ethiopian Experience & the Debate. 267p. 1987. text 55.00 (*91-7106-267-X*, Pub. by Nordisk Afrikainstitutet) Coronet Bks.

Cohen, John M., ed. The Penguin Book of Spanish Verse. 640p. 1988. pap. 16.95 (*0-14-058570-2*, Penguin Bks) Viking Penguin.

Cohen, John M., intro. The Life of Saint Teresa of Avila by Herself. 320p. 1988. pap. 10.95 (*0-14-044073-9*, Penguin Classics) Viking Penguin.

***Cohen, John M. & Peterson, Stephen B.** Administrative Decentralization: Strategies for Developing Countries. LC 99-14051. 207p. 1999. pap. 24.95 (*1-56549-096-7*) Kumarian Pr.

Cohen, John M. & Peterson, Stephen B. Administrative Decentralization: Strategies for Developing Countries. LC 99-14051. 256p. 1999. 60.00 (*1-56549-097-5*) Kumarian Pr.

Cohen, John M. & Uphoff, John M. Rural Development Participation: Concepts & Measures for Project Design, Implementation & Evaluation. (Monograph: No. 2). 317p. (Orig.). (C). 1977. pap. text 14.25 (*0-86731-001-4*) Cornell CIS RDC.

Cohen, John M., et al. Revolution & Land Reform in Ethiopia: Peasant Associations, Local Government & Rural Development. (Occasional Paper Ser.: No. 6). 127p. (Orig.). (C). 1976. pap. text 4.80 (*0-86731-019-7*) Cornell CIS RDC.

Cohen, John M., tr. see De Cervantes Saavedra, Miguel.

Cohen, Jon. The Man in the Window. 256p. 1993. mass mkt. 5.99 (*0-446-36402-9*, Pub. by Warner Bks) Little.

— Max Lakeman & the Beautiful Stranger. large type ed. 323p. 1990. reprint ed. 17.95 (*1-56054-028-1*) Thorndike Pr.

Cohen, Jon. Shots in the Dark. 27.95 (*0-393-05027-0*) Norton.

Cohen, Jon S. Finance & Industrialization in Italy, 1894-1914. Bruchey, Stuart, ed. LC 77-81825. (Dissertations in European Economic History Ser.). (Illus.). 1978. lib. bdg. 26.95 (*0-405-10777-3*) Ayer.

Cohen, Jonathan. BMW M-Series & Performance Specials. LC 96-9392. (Sports Car Color History Ser.). (Illus.). 128p. 1996. pap. 21.95 (*0-7603-0171-9*) MBI Pubg.

***Cohen, Jonathan.** Communication & Design with the Internet: A Guide for Architects Planners & Building Professionals. LC 99-86574. (Illus.). 304p. 1999. 52.50 (*0-393-73043-3*) Norton.

Cohen, Jonathan. Educating Minds & Hearts: Social Emotional Learning & the Passage into Adolescence: A Guide for Educators. LC 98-50479. 1999. 21.95 (*0-8077-3838-7*) Tchrs Coll.

— The Sephardi Haggadah & the Laws of Pesach & the Seder. 1988. 18.95 (*0-87306-460-7*); pap. 12.95 (*0-317-66554-5*) Feldheim.

Cohen, Jonathan, ed. Educating Minds & Hearts: Social Emotional Learning & the Passage into Adolescence. LC 98-50749. (Series on Social Emotional Learning). 202p. 1999. pap. 21.95 (*0-87120-348-0*, 199001) ASCD.

— Educating Minds & Hearts: Social Emotional Learning & the Passage into Adolescence: A Guide for Educators. LC 98-50479. 1. 216p. 1999. 45.00 (*0-8077-3839-5*) Tchrs Coll.

***Cohen, Jonathan, ed.** Psychoanalytical Study of Lives over Time: Clinical & Reserch Perspectives on Children Who Return to Treatment in Adulthood. 320p. (C). 1999. pap. text 49.95 (*0-12-178410-X*) Acad Pr.

Cohen, Jonathan & Bonfiglio, Michael. Orthopedic Pathophysiology in Diagnosis & Treatment. LC 89-22215. (Illus.). 538p. reprint ed. pap. 166.80 (*0-7837-8849-5*, 204949400012) Bks Demand.

Cohen, Jonathan & Peach, Andrew. IDDS Almanac 1994: World Combat Aircraft Holdings, Production & Trade. 140p. 1994. 30.00 (*0-614-04671-8*) Inst Def & Dis.

Cohen, Jonathan, et al. Orthopedic Pathophysiology in Diagnosis & Treatment. (Illus.). 526p. 1989. text 140.00 (*0-443-08070-4*) Church.

Cohen, Jonathan, jt. ed. see Keylin, Arleen.

Cohen, Jonathan, tr. see Dalton, Roque.

Cohen, Jonathan, tr. see Lihn, Enrique.

Cohen, Jonathan D. & Schooler, Jonathan W., eds. Scientific Approaches to Consciousness. (Carnegie Mellon Symposia on Cognition Ser.). 300p. 1996. text 119.00 (*0-8058-1471-X*); pap. text 45.00 (*0-8058-1472-8*) L Erlbaum Assocs.

Cohen, Jordan. Netwise Investor: Free Investment Resources on the Internet. LC 97-70478. 1997. pap. 14.95 (*0-9657299-5-8*) Joralis Grp.

Cohen, Jordan J. & Kassirer, Jerome P. Acid-Base. 1982. 79.95 (*0-316-15011-8*, Little Brwn Med Div) Lppncott W & W.

Cohen, Josef, tr. see Hadakov, Mordechai I.

Cohen, Joseph. A Good Friend. LC 85-40901. (Illus.). 96p. 1986. pap. 5.95 (*0-89480-035-3*, 1035) Workman Pub.

— How to Make Money with Baseball Cards: A Hobby Worth Millions. LC 90-93468. (Orig.). 1991. pap. 7.95 (*0-9628663-6-9*) Sportsayama.

— The Jewish Anarchist Movement in the United States. 1977. lib. bdg. 59.95 (*0-685-74872-3*) Gordon Pr.

— Voices of Israel: Essays on & Interviews with Yehuda Amichai, A. B. Yehoshua, T. Carmi, Aharon Appelfeld, & Amos Oz. LC 89-11512. (SUNY Series in Modern Jewish Literature & Culture). 231p. (C). 1990. text 21.50 (*0-7914-0243-6*) State U NY Pr.

— You Know You're Gay When . . . LC 95-515. (Illus.). 112p. 1995. bds. 12.00 (*0-8092-3320-7*, 332070, Contemporary Bks) NTC Contemp Pub Co.

Cohen, Joseph & Solomon, Debra. I Love You Because... 112p. 1994. pap. 7.95 (*0-671-88229-5*, Fireside) S&S Trade Pap.

Cohen, Joseph E. Anarchism & Libertarian Socialism in Israel: A Study of Anti-Statist Movements. 1979. lib. bdg. 42.95 (*0-686-24784-1*) M Buber Pr.

Cohen, Joseph J. In Quest of Heaven: The Story of the Sunrise Cooperative Farm Community. LC 74-26760. (American Utopian Adventure Ser.). (Illus.). xvi, 255p. 1975. reprint ed. lib. bdg. 37.50 (*0-87991-023-2*) Porcupine Pr.

Cohen, Joshua & Fung, Archon, eds. Constitution, Democracy & State Power: Institutions of Justice, 4 vols., Set. LC 96-605. (Schools of Thought in Politics Ser.: No. 7). 2144p. 1996. 720.00 (*1-85278-342-7*) E Elgar.

Cohen, Joshua & Rogers, Joel. Inequity & Intervention: The Federal Budget & Central America. LC 86-3755. (PACCA Domestic Roots Ser.: No. 1). 66p. 1986. pap. 5.00 (*0-89608-325-X*) South End Pr.

Cohen, Joshua, ed. see Nussbaum, Martha C., et al.

Cohen, Joshua, ed. see Schor, Juliet.

Cohen, Joy, jt. auth. see Pranis, Eve.

Cohen, Joyce S. & Westhues, Anne. Well-Functioning Families for Adoptive & Foster Children: A Handbook for Child Welfare Workers. 176p. 1990. pap. text 18.95 (*0-8020-6754-9*) U of Toronto Pr.

***Cohen, Jozef.** Visual Color & Color Mixture: The Fundamental Color Space. LC 99-47681. (Illus.). 2000. write for info. (*0-252-02549-0*) U of Ill Pr.

Cohen, Judith & Cohen, Michael. Dinah's Enormous Diaper. large type unabridged ed. (Potti Pets Ser.). (Illus.). 15p. (J). (ps). 1997. pap. 2.99 (*0-9664396-2-7*) PPP Enterp.

— Dinah's Enormous Diaper: Incl. Chart. large type unabridged ed. (Potti Pets Ser.). (Illus.). 15p. (J). (ps). 1997. pap. 19.99 incl. audio (*0-9664396-3-5*) PPP Enterp.

— No More Diapers for Elvis! large type unabridged ed. (Potti Pets Ser.). (Illus.). 15p. (J). (ps). 1997. pap. 2.99 (*0-9664396-0-0*) PPP Enterp.

— No More Diapers for Elvis! Incl. Chart. large type unabridged ed. (Potti Pets Ser.). (Illus.). 15p. (J). (ps). 1997. pap. write for info. incl. audio (*0-9664396-1-9*) PPP Enterp.

Cohen, Judith, jt. auth. see Bryan, Betsy M.

Cohen, Judith, jt. auth. see Dixon, Tamecka.

Cohen, Judith, jt. auth. see Franks, Sharon.

Cohen, Judith, jt. auth. see Gabriel, Diane.

Cohen, Judith, jt. auth. see Gordon, Sol.

Cohen, Judith, ed. see Quagliati, Paolo.

Cohen, Judith, ed. see Schlank, Carol H. & Metzger, Barbara.

Cohen, Judith B. Seasons. LC 83-63240. 224p. 1984. 22.00 (*0-932966-38-1*) Permanent Pr.

Cohen, Judith H., jt. auth. see Wiener, Roberta B.

Cohen, Judith L. Homework Troubleshooter: Whose Problem Is It & What to Do about It. 75p. 1994. pap. 12.95 (*0-9642237-0-8*) Parent Pro Pubns.

— Tu Puedes Ser una Ingeniera. Yanez, Juan, tr. from ENG.Tr. of You Can Be a Woman Engineer. (SPA., Illus.). 40p. (Orig.). (J). (gr. 4-7). 1992. pap. 7.00 (*1-880599-03-1*) Cascade Pass.

— You Can Be a Woman Engineer. LC 95-35232. 40p. (J). (gr. 3-7). 1991. pap. 6.00 (*1-880599-01-5*); audio 4.00 (*1-880599-02-3*) Cascade Pass.

— You Can Be a Woman Engineer. (Illus.). 40p. (J). (gr. 3-6). 1996. pap. 20.00 incl. cd-rom (*1-880599-19-8*) Cascade Pass.

***Cohen, Judith L.** You Can Be a Woman Engineer. rev. ed. Wheeler, Janice, ed. (Illus.). 40p. (J). (gr. 3-6). 2000. 13.95 (*1-880599-51-1*, Pub. by Cascade Pass); pap. 7.00 (*1-880599-50-3*, Pub. by Cascade Pass) Follett Library.

Cohen, Judith L. & Ghez, Andrea M. You Can Be a Woman Astronomer. (Illus.). 40p. (J). (gr. 1-6). 1998. 19.95 incl. cd-rom (*1-880599-27-9*) Cascade Pass.

Cohen, Judith L. & Katz, David A. You Can Be . . . Science Career Books - Activities: Learn, Have Fun, Earn Badges & Tryits. 80p. 1997. wbk. ed. 12.99 (*1-880599-26-0*) Cascade Pass.

Cohen, Judith L. & Siegel, Margot. Tu Puedes Ser una Arquitecta. Yanez, Juan, tr. from ENG.Tr. of You Can Be a Woman Architect. (SPA., Illus.). 40p. (Orig.). (J). (gr. 4-7). 1992. pap. 7.00 (*1-880599-05-8*) Cascade Pass.

— You Can Be a Woman Architect. Yanez, Juan, tr. (Illus.). 40p. (J). (gr. k-6). 1998. 19.95 incl. cd-rom (*1-880599-28-7*) Cascade Pass.

— You Can Be a Woman Architect. rev. ed. LC 99-47613. (Illus.). 40p. (J). 1999. pap. 7.00 (*1-880599-04-X*) Cascade Pass.

Cohen, Judith L. & Thompson, Valerie. Tu Puedes Ser una Zoologa. Yanez, Juan, tr. (SPA., Illus.). 40p. (J). (gr. 4-7). 1993. pap. 7.00 (*1-880599-09-0*) Cascade Pass.

— You Can Be a Woman Zoologist. LC 93-1092. (Illus.). 40p. (Orig.). (J). (gr. 3-7). 1992. pap. 6.00 (*1-880599-08-2*) Cascade Pass.

Cohen, Judith L., jt. auth. see Bozak, Kristin.

Cohen, Judith L., jt. auth. see Dixon, Tamecka.

Cohen, Judith L., jt. auth. see McAlary, Florence.

Cohen, Judith L., jt. auth. see Redborg, Rita.

Cohen, Judith Love, jt. auth. see Bryan, Betsy M.

Cohen, Judith Love, jt. auth. see Douty, Sheila Cornell.

Cohen, Judith Love, jt. auth. see Gabriel, Diane L.

Cohen, Judith Love, jt. auth. see Siegel, Margot.

Cohen, Judith Love, jt. auth. see Venturini, Tisha.

Cohen, Judith R. The Mayflower Hotel: Grande Dame of Washington, D. C. (Illus.). 160p. 1987. 29.95 (*0-940577-00-3*, Balance Hse Ltd) Intl Archive Art.

Cohen, Julian. Sex Matters. (Illus.). 62p. 1996. write for info. (*0-237-51509-1*) EVN1 UK.

Cohen, Julius, et al. Parental Authority: The Community & the Law. LC 80-153. (Illus.). 301p. 1980. reprint ed. lib. bdg. 38.50 (*0-313-22351-3*, COPR, Greenwood Pr) Greenwood.

Cohen, Julius H. The Law: Business or Profession? 1980. lib. bdg. 79.95 (*0-8490-3133-8*) Gordon Pr.

— They Builded Better Than They Knew. LC 70-156633. (Essay Index Reprint Ser.). 1977. reprint ed. 23.95 (*0-8369-2350-2*) Ayer.

Cohen, Kalman J. & Cyert, Richard M. Theory of the Firm: Resource Allocation in a Market Economy. 2nd ed. (Illus.). 640p. 1975. text 26.95 (*0-13-913798-X*) P-H.

Cohen, Karen C., ed. Internet Links for Science Education: Student - Scientist Partnerships. LC 97-5780. (Innovations in Science Education & Technology Ser.). 280p. (C). 1997. pap. 27.50 (*0-306-45558-7*, Plenum Trade) Perseus Pubng.

Cohen, Karen C., ed. see Dyer, D., et al.

Cohen, Karen C., ed. see Shinskey, F. Greg.

Cohen, Karl F. Forbidden Animation: Censored Cartoons & Blacklisted Animators in America. LC 97-23882. (Illus.). 238p. 1997. lib. bdg. 35.00 (*0-7864-0395-0*) McFarland & Co.

Cohen, Kate. The Neppi Modona Diaries: Reading Jewish Survival Through My Italian Family. LC 96-24968. (Illus.). 284p. 1997. 24.95 (*0-87451-783-4*) U Pr of New Eng.

Cohen, Katherine E., jt. auth. see Rossuck, Virginia P.

Cohen, Kathryn K. Independence Mine & the Willow Creek Mining District. LC 82-620015. (History & Archaeology Ser.: No. 32). (Illus.). 170p. (Orig.). 1996. pap. 20.00 (*0-943712-22-X*) Alaska Hist.

Cohen, Keith. Film & Fiction: The Dynamics of Exchange. LC 79-64073. (Illus.). 228p. reprint ed. pap. 70.70 (*0-8357-3744-6*, 203647000003) Bks Demand.

Cohen, Keith, ed. Writing in a Film Age: Essays by Contemporary Novelists. 208p. (C). 1991. pap. 19.95 (*0-87081-180-0*); text 29.95 (*0-87081-183-5*) Univ Pr Colo.

Cohen, Keith, tr. see Cixous, Helene.

***Cohen, Ken.** Enterprise Development with JDBC: A4, Version 3.07. McKenna, Jill, ed. (CIW Enterprise Developer Track A4 Ser.). (Illus.). 1999. pap. write for info. (*1-58143-079-5*) Prosoft I-net.

— Enterprise Development with JDBC: Version 3.07. McKenna, Jill, ed. (Illus.). 1999. pap. write for info. (*1-58143-043-4*) Prosoft I-net.

***Cohen, Ken & Frosti, Gregg.** Java Programming Fundamentals. Lane, Susan M., ed. (Illus.). 298p. (C). 1999. pap. write for info. (*0-7423-0300-4*) ComputerPREP.

— Java Programming Fundamentals: Version 4.07. Lane, Susan M., ed. (CIW Enterprise Developer Track Ser.). (Illus.). 1999. pap. write for info. (*1-58143-046-9*) Prosoft I-net.

***Cohen, Ken, et al.** Fundamentals of CGI Using Perl: A4, Version 2.07. McKenna, Jill, ed. (CIW Application Developer Track A4 Ser.). (Illus.). 1999. pap. write for info. (*1-58143-073-6*) Prosoft I-net.

— Fundamentals of CGI Using Perl: Version 2.07. McKenna, Jill, ed. (CIW Application Developer Track Ser.). (Illus.). 1999. pap. write for info. (*1-58143-037-X*) Prosoft I-net.

— Java Programming Fundamentals: A4, Version 4.07. Lane, Susan M., ed. (CIW Enterprise Developer Track A4 Ser.). (Illus.). 1999. pap. write for info. (*1-58143-082-5*) Prosoft I-net.

Cohen, Ken, jt. auth. see Pease, Lisa.

Cohen, Kenneth K. Imagine That! A Child's Guide to Yoga. (Illus.). 48p. 1983. pap. 12.95 (*0-932040-40-3*) Integral Yoga Pubns.

Cohen, Kenneth M., jt. ed. see Savin-Williams, Ritch C.

Cohen, Kenneth S. The Way of Qigong: The Art & Science of Chinese Energy Healing. 1999. pap. 14.95 (*0-345-42109-4*) Ballantine Pub Grp.

Cohen, Keri, ed. see Mazzola, Toni & Guten, Mimi.

Cohen-Kiener, Andrea, tr. see Shapira, Kalonymus K.

Cohen, Korene C. & Cohen, Dale C. Museums & Other Attractions of Arizona's Smaller Communities, Bk. 1. (Illus.). 50p. (Orig.). 1992. 4.95 (*0-9637255-0-5*) Dancing Unicorn.

Cohen, Korene C., jt. auth. see Cohen, Dale C.

Cohen, L., jt. auth. see Class, C. M.

Cohen, L. Jonathan. The Dialogue of Reason: An Analysis of Analytical Philosophy. 248p. 1989. pap. text 29.95 (*0-19-824865-2*) OUP.

— An Essay on Belief & Acceptance. 174p. 1995. reprint ed. pap. text 19.95 (*0-19-823604-2*) OUP.

Cohen, L. Jonathon. The Probable & Provable. (Modern Revivals in Philosophy Ser.). 380p. 1992. 63.95 (*0-7512-0011-5*, Pub. by Gregg Revivals) Ashgate Pub Co.

Cohen, Larry. Following the Law: The Total Tricks Sequel. (Illus.). 248p. 1994. pap. 12.95 (*0-9634715-4-6*) L Cohen NJ.

— To Bid or Not to Bid: The Law of Total Tricks. 2nd ed. McCallum, Karen T., ed. (Illus.). 272p. 1992. reprint ed. pap. 12.95 (*0-9634715-0-3*) L Cohen NJ.

Cohen, Larry & Davis, Liz. Bridge below the Belt. LC 97-91842. 240p. (Orig.). 1997. pap. 12.95 (*0-9634715-5-4*) L Cohen NJ.

Cohen, Larry, ed. see Hall, Burt & Rose-Hall, Lynn.

Cohen, Laura A., et al. One Family under the Same Sky. (Illus.). 88p. (J). 1997. pap. 13.95 (*1-882801-04-0*) Feelings Factory.

Cohen, Laura B., ed. Reference Services for Archives & Manuscripts. LC 96-51733. (Reference Librarian Monograph Ser.: Vol. 26, No. 56). 215p. (C). 1997. 49.95 (*0-7890-0042-3*) Haworth Pr.

— Reference Services for Archives & Manuscripts. LC 96-51733. (Reference Librarian Monograph Ser.: Vol. 26, No. 56). 215p. (C). 1997. pap. text 24.95 (*0-7890-0048-2*) Haworth Pr.

Cohen, Lawrence. Chalk Dust: Five Tales Out of School. (Illus.). 72p. (Orig.). (J). (gr. 4). 1995. pap. 7.95 (*1-56474-114-1*) Fithian Pr.

— No Aging in India: Alzheimer's, Bad Families, & Other Modern Things. LC 97-38659. 400p. 1998. 45.00 (*0-520-08396-2*, Pub. by U CA Pr) Cal Prin Full Svc.

***Cohen, Lawrence.** No Aging in India: Alzheimer's, the Bad Family & Other Modern Things. LC 97-38659. (Illus.). 400p. 2000. pap. 18.95 (*0-520-22462-0*) U CA Pr.

Cohen, Lawrence, et al, eds. Crisis Intervention. 2nd ed. (Community Psychology Ser.: Vol. IV). (Illus.). 222p. 1982. 38.95 (*0-89885-107-6*, Kluwer Acad Hman Sci); pap. 20.95 (*0-89885-108-4*, Kluwer Acad Hman Sci) Kluwer Academic.

Cohen, Lawrence H. Life Events & Psychological Functioning: Theoretical & Methodological Issues. (Focus Editions Ser.: Vol. 90). 310p. 1988. text 59.95 (*0-8039-2821-1*); pap. text 26.00 (*0-8039-2822-X*) Sage.

Cohen, Lawrence H., ed. Life Events & Psychological Functioning: Theoretical & Methodological Issues. LC 87-28889. (Sage Focus Editions Ser.: No. 90). (Illus.). 280p. reprint ed. pap. 86.80 (*0-7837-4572-9*, 204410100003) Bks Demand.

Cohen, Leah Hager. Glass, Paper, Beans: Revelations on the Nature & Value of Ordinary Things. 320p. 1998. pap. 12.95 (*0-385-49257-X*) Doubleday.

— Heat Lightning. LC 96-47656. 326p. 1997. mass mkt. 22.00 (*0-380-97468-1*, Avon Bks) Morrow Avon.

— Train Go Sorry: Inside a Deaf World. 316p. 1999. 28.95 (*0-7351-0142-6*) Replica Bks.

Cohen, Leah Hager. Train Go Sorry: Inside a Deaf World. LC 94-23501. 320p. 1995. pap. 14.00 (*0-679-76165-9*) Vin Bks.

Cohen, Lee & Kenedy, Roger, intros. Art of Clay: Timeless Pottery of the Southwest. LC 91-58828. (Illus.). 144p. 1993. 39.95 (*0-940666-19-7*) Clear Light.

Cohen, Lenard, et al. The Vision & the Game: Making the Canadian Constitution. 197p. (Orig.). (C). 1987. pap. text 14.95 (*0-920490-67-0*) Temeron Bks.

Cohen, Lenard J. The Socialist Pyramid: Elites & Power in Yugoslavia. 300p. 1996. 29.95 (*0-88962-386-4*); pap. 19.95 (*0-88962-385-6*) Mosaic.

Cohen, Leo J. Creating & Planning the Corporate Data Base System Project. LC 80-85044. (Illus.). 400p. (C). 1981. 34.95 (*0-939274-00-0*) Mntn Hse Pub.

Cohen, Leon. Time Frequency Analysis: Theory & Applications. 320p. 1994. 75.00 (*0-13-594532-1*) P-H.

Cohen, Leon & Loughlin, Patrick. Recent Developments in Time-Frequency Analysis. LC 98-41653. 1998. 105.00 (*0-7923-8314-1*) Kluwer Academic.

C

An Asterisk (*) at the beginning of an entry indicates that the title is appearing for the first time.

Cohen, Leon J. Say It in French. (Orig.). 1950. pap. 2.95 (*0-486-20803-6*) Dover.

Cohen, Leon J. & Rogers, A. C. Digalo en Ingles, (Say It in English for Spanish-Speaking People) (Orig.). 1953. pap. 3.50 (*0-486-20802-8*) Dover.

— Say It in Spanish. (Orig.). 1954. pap. 2.95 (*0-486-20811-7*) Dover.

Cohen, Leon J., tr. see Dover Staff.

Cohen, Leonard. Beautiful Losers. LC 93-10916. 1993. pap. 12.00 (*0-679-74825-3*) Vin Bks.

— Book of Mercy. 114p. 1994. pap. 10.95 (*0-7710-2182-8*) McCland & Stewart.

— Dance Me to the End of Love. Sunshine, Linda, ed. LC 94-44504. (Illus.). 32p. 1995. 17.95 (*1-55670-406-2*) Stewart Tabori & Chang.

— Dance Me to the End of Love. (Illus.). 1998. 17.95 (*0-941807-29-0*) Stewart Tabori & Chang.

Cohen, Leonard. Favorite Game. 240p. 1997. pap. text 6.95 (*0-7710-9954-1*) NCanadian Lib.

Cohen, Leonard. Leonard Cohen: Anthology. (Illus.). 208p. pap. 24.95 (*0-8256-1238-1*, AM 80060) Omnibus NY.

— Stranger Music: Selected Poems & Songs. 415p. 1994. pap. write for info. (*0-7710-2232-8*) McCland & Stewart.

— Stranger Music: Selected Poems & Songs. 1994. pap. 15.00 (*0-679-75541-1*) Random.

Cohen, Leonard A., jt. ed. see Reddy, Bandaru S.

***Cohen, Leonard J.** Serpent in the Bosom: The Rise & Fall of Slobodan Milosevic. 2000. pap. 25.00 (*0-8133-2902-7*, Pub. by Westview) HarpC.

Cohen, LeoNora & Frydenburg, Erica. Coping for Capable Kids: Strategies for Students, Parents, & Teachers. 350p. 1996. pap. 27.95 (*1-882664-23-X*) Prufrock Pr.

Cohen, Leslie. Nourishing a Happy Affair: Nutrition Alternatives for Individual & Family Needs. LC 82-16226. (Illus.). 150p. (Orig.). 1983. pap. 5.95 (*0-943914-02-7*) Larson Pubns.

Cohen, Leslie & Falco, Antoinette. Cracking the TASP. Salazar, Yolanda L. & Cullen, Emily A., eds. (Illus.). 198p. 1992. per. 11.95 (*1-877709-21-2*) ADAPT Pub Co.

Cohen, Lester H., ed. see Warren, Mercy O.

Cohen, Libby G. Before Their Time: Fetuses & Infants at Risk. 1990. pap. 18.00 (*0-940898-26-8*) Am Assn Mental.

— Children with Exceptional Needs in Regular Classrooms. 208p. 1992. pap. 11.95 (*0-8106-3009-5*) NEA.

— What Socrates Began: An Examination of the Intellect, Vol. 1. (Orig.). (C). 1988. pap. write for info. (*0-939561-01-8*) Univ South ME.

— What Socrates Began: An Examination of the Intellect, Vol. 2. (Orig.). 1989. write for info. (*0-939561-04-2*) Univ South ME.

Cohen, Libby G. & Spenciner, Loraine J. Assessment of Infants & Young Children. LC 92-35208. 528p. (C). 1995. teacher ed. write for info. (*0-8013-1248-5*, 79879) Longman.

Cohen, Lila Beldock. The King Who Loved His Lollipops. 30p. 1973. pap. 3.25 (*0-87129-976-3*, K15) Dramatic Pub.

Cohen, Lilly & Young, Dennis R. Careers for Dreamers & Doers: A Guide to Management Careers in the Nonprofit Sector. LC 89-38376. (Orig.). 1989. pap. 24.95 (*0-87954-294-2*) Foundation Ctr.

Cohen, Lily & Oppedisano-Reich, Marie. Funding in Aging: Public, Private & Voluntary. 1979. pap. 18.80 (*0-88461-006-3*) Adelphi Univ.

Cohen, Lily Y. Lost Spirituals. LC 74-39081. (Black Heritage Library Collection). (Illus.). 1977. reprint ed. 23.95 (*0-8369-9019-6*) Ayer.

Cohen, Linda R. & Noll, Roger G., eds. The Technology Pork Barrel. 400p. 1991. 44.95 (*0-8157-1508-0*); pap. 19.95 (*0-8157-1507-2*) Brookings.

Cohen, Linda R., et al. Challenges to Research Universities. LC 97-21084. 217p. 1997. text 38.95 (*0-8157-1510-2*); pap. text 16.95 (*0-8157-1509-9*) Brookings.

Cohen, Lionel, ed. Biophysical Models in Radiation Oncology. 192p. 1982. 110.00 (*0-8493-6055-2*, RC271, CRC Reprint) Franklin.

Cohen, Liora A. Cooking in English & Spanish. (ENG & SPA., Illus.). 340p. (Orig.). 1990. pap. 14.95 (*0-9623559-1-7*) Housekeepers Bible.

— The Housekeeper's Bible - La Biblia de la Empleada de Casa: How to Communicate with Your Spanish Speaking Help & Friends. (ENG & SPA.). 220p. (Orig.). 1989. pap. 12.95 (*0-9623559-0-9*) Housekeepers Bible.

Cohen, Lisa A. & Flaxington, Beverly. Wealthbuilding: A Consumer's Guide to Making Profitable & Comfortable Investment Decisions. LC 98-13581. 224p. 1998. pap. 19.95 (*0-7931-2837-4*) Dearborn.

Cohen, Lizabeth. Making a New Deal: Industrial Workers in Chicago, 1919-1939. (Illus.). 544p. (C). 1991. pap. text 17.95 (*0-521-42838-6*) Cambridge U Pr.

Cohen, Lloyd R. Increasing the Supply of Transplant Organs: The Virtue of an Options Market. LC 95-18622. (Medical Intelligence Unit Ser.). 154p. 1995. 79.00 (*1-57059-259-4*) Landes Bioscience.

Cohen, Lois, ed. see MacHovec, et al.

Cohen, Lois Sciarratta. Who Wants to Know? The Story of the Chiarenza & Sciarratta Families. LC 98-142617. 196p. 1998. 25.00 (*0-379-21390-7*) Oceana.

Cohen, Lorraine. Scenes for Young Actors. 384p. (J). (gr. 6 up). 1990. mass mkt. 5.99 (*0-380-00997-8*, Avon Bks) Morrow Avon.

Cohen, Lorraine, ed. Monologues for Young Act. 192p. 1994. mass mkt. 5.99 (*0-380-76187-4*, Avon Bks) Morrow Avon.

Cohen, Lorraine & Imundo, Richard A. Scenes for Mature Actors. LC 98-93308. 576p. 1999. mass mkt. 6.99 (*0-380-79287-7*, Avon Bks) Morrow Avon.

Cohen, Lottie & Arkin, Lois. Cooperative Housing Compendium: Resources for Collaborative Living. (Illus.). 188p. (Orig.). (C). 1993. pap. 15.00 (*1-885641-03-6*, B3) U CA Ctr Cooperatives.

Cohen, Lou, jt. auth. see Fowler, Jim.

Cohen, Louis. Quality Function Deployment: How to Make It Work. 368p. (C). 1995. 52.00 (*0-201-63330-2*) Addison-Wesley.

Cohen, Louis & Holliday, Mike. Practical Statistics for Students. LC 96-226109. 408p. 1996. pap. text 26.95 (*1-85396-329-1*; Pub. by P Chapman) Taylor & Francis.

Cohen, Louis & Manion, Lawrence. A Guide to Teaching Practice. 3rd ed. 320p. 1989. pap. 18.95 (*0-415-00913-8*, A3661) Routledge.

— Research Methods in Education. 2nd ed. LC 85-362. 383p. 1985. pap. 19.95 (*0-7099-3438-6*, Pub. by C Helm) Routldge.

— Research Methods in Education. 4th ed. LC 93-34390. 416p. (C). 1994. pap. 25.99 (*0-415-10235-9*) Routledge.

Cohen, Louis, et al. A Guide to Teaching Practice. 4th ed. 512p. (C). 1996. pap. 24.99 (*0-415-14221-0*) Routledge.

***Cohen, Louis, et al.** Research Methods in Education. 5th ed. LC 99-88211. (Illus.). 2000. pap. write for info. (*0-415-19541-1*) Routledge.

Cohen, Louis H. The Cultural-Political Traditions & Development of the Soviet Cinema: 1917-1972. LC 74-2077. (Dissertations on Film Ser.: Vol. 1). 724p. 1977. 51.95 (*0-405-04876-9*) Ayer.

Cohen, Louise G., ed. see Gomez, Antonio E.

Cohen, Luanne. Imaging Essentials. Impress Group Staff & Prentice Hall Japan Staff, trs. LC 93-80007. (JPN., Illus.). 144p. (Orig.). 1993. pap. text 39.95 (*4-8443-5414-0*, Adobe) Hayden.

Cohen, Luanne S. Quilt Design Masters. Gideon, Joan, ed. (Illus.). 146p. (Orig.). (YA). (gr. 3-10). 1995. pap. 12.95 (*0-86651-941-6*, 21401) Seymour Pubns.

Cohen, Luanne Seymour & Wendling, Tanya. Design Essentials. 2nd ed. LC 94-76914. (Illus.). 103p. 1994. 40.00 (*1-56830-093-X*) Adobe Pr.

Cohen, Luanne Seymour, jt. auth. see Adobe Creative Team Staff.

Cohen, Lucy M., jt. auth. see Weber, George H.

Cohen, Lynn. Lynn Cohen: Lost & Found. (Illus.). 108p. 1993. pap. 30.00 (*2-908257-08-4*, Pub. by F R A C) Dist Art Pubs.

Cohen, Lynne. Occupied Territory. (Illus.). 112p. 1988. 37.95 (*0-89381-313-3*) Aperture.

Cohen, M. & Baum, B., eds. Studies in Stomatology & Craniofacial Biology. LC 96-77470. 500p. (gr. 12). 1997. 125.00 (*90-5199-283-1*, 283-1) IOS Press.

Cohen, M., et al. Plays from the New York Shakespeare Festival. 400p. (Orig.). 1986. pap. 14.95 (*0-88145-036-7*) Broadway Play.

Cohen, M. E. & Hudson, D. L., eds. Comparative Approaches in Medical Reasoning. LC 94-48854. (Advances in Fuzzy Systems Ser.: Vol. 3). 328p. 1995. text 86.00 (*981-02-2162-2*) World Scientific Pub.

— Computers & Their Applications (CATA-96), 11th International Conference, March 7-9, 1996, San Francisco, California, U.S.A. (Conference Proceedings Ser.). 300p. (C). 1996. write for info. (*1-880843-15-3*) Int Soc Comp App.

***Cohen, M. J.** Penguin Thesaurus of Quotations. 672p. 2000. pap. 13.95 (*0-14-051440-6*, Penguin Bks) Viking Penguin.

Cohen, M. J., jt. auth. see Cohen, J. M.

Cohen, M. L. & Chelikowsky, J. R. Electronic Structure & Optical Properties of Semiconductors. (Solid-State Sciences Ser.: Vol. 75). (Illus.). 270p. 1988. 59.00 (*0-387-18818-5*) Spr-Verlag.

— Electronic Structure & Optical Properties of Semiconductors. 2nd ed. (Solid-State Sciences Ser.: Vol. 75). (Illus.). xii, 264p. 1989. 49.95 (*0-387-51391-4*, 3267) Spr-Verlag.

Cohen, M. M. Admiralty: Jurisdiction, Law, & Practice - With an Appendix Containing Rules, Statutes, & Forms. xxxvii, 505p. 1993. reprint ed. 57.50 (*0-8377-2023-0*, Rothman) W S Hein.

Cohen, M. M., et al, eds. Biochemistry, Ultrastructure & Physiology of Cerebral Anoxia, Hypoxia & Ischaemia. (Monographs in Neural Sciences: Vol. 1). (Illus.). 1972. 42.75 (*3-8055-1420-4*) S Karger.

Cohen, M. Michael, Jr. The Child with Multiple Birth Defects. 2nd ed. (Oxford Monographs on Medical Genetics: No. 31). (Illus.). 288p. 1996. text 72.50 (*0-19-509926-5*) OUP.

***Cohen, M. Michael & MacLean, Ruth E., eds.** Craniosynostosis: Diagnosis, Evaluation & Management. 2nd ed. LC 99-32749. 480p. 2000. 199.00 (*0-19-511843-X*) OUP.

Cohen, M. Michael, Jr., ed. see Jirasek, Jan E.

Cohen, M. P. Diabetes & Protein Glycosylation. (Illus.). 170p. 1986. 61.00 (*0-387-96297-2*) Spr-Verlag.

— The Polyol Paradigm & Complications of Diabetes. (Illus.). xii, 143p. 1986. 99.00 (*0-387-96418-5*) Spr-Verlag.

Cohen, M. P. & Foa, Piero P., eds. The Brain As an Endocrine Organ. (Endocrinology & Metabolism Ser.: Vol. 3). (Illus.). 225p. 1988. 175.00 (*0-387-96644-7*) Spr-Verlag.

Cohen, M. P., jt. ed. see Foa, Piero P.

Cohen, Malcolm S. Labor Shortages: Myth or Reality? LC 94-36244. 200p. 1995. text 49.50 (*0-472-10353-9*, 10353) U of Mich Pr.

— On the Feasibility of a Labor Market Information System, 3 vols., Set. 1974. pap. 10.95 (*0-87736-331-5*) U of Mich Inst Labor.

Cohen-Mansfield, Jiska, et al, eds. Satisfaction Surveys in Long-Term Care. LC 99-15736. (Illus.). 360p. 1999. text 42.95 (*0-8261-1284-6*) Springer Pub.

Cohen, Marc. Mecox Road. LC 96-78066. 88p. (Orig.). 1997. pap. 12.00 (*1-877593-02-8*) GP Hudson NY.

Cohen, Marc, jt. auth. see Rechtschaffen, Stephan.

Cohen, Marc J., ed. Hunger, 1993: Uprooted People. (Annual Reports on the State of World Hunger). (Illus.). 204p. (Orig.). 1990. 4.95 (*0-9628058-6-6*) Bread for the World.

— Hunger 1994: Transforming the Politics of Hunger. (Annual Reports on the State of World Hunger). 189p. (YA). (gr. 6 up). 1993. 8.95 (*0-9628058-9-0*) Bread for the World.

— Hunger 1995: Causes of Hunger. (Annual Reports on the State of World Hunger). 141p. (YA). (gr. 6 up). 1994. 17.95 (*1-884361-50-1*) Bread for the World.

Cohen, Marc J., et al, eds. Putting Children First: A Report on the Effectiveness of U. S. Agency for International Development Child Survival Programs in Fiscal Year 1991. (Hunger Policy Occasional Papers: No. 3). (C). 1995. pap. text 5.00 (*1-884361-00-5*) Bread for the World.

***Cohen, Marc J. & Reeves, Don, eds.** Hunger in a Global Economy: Hunger 1998: Eighth Annual Report on the State of World Hunger. (Illus.). 130p. (C). 1999. pap. text 30.00 (*0-7881-8348-6*) DIANE Pub.

Cohen, Marc J., jt. ed. see Biro, Lajos.

Cohen, Marcel. Language: Its Structure & Evolution. Muller, Leonard, tr. from FRE. 157p. (C). 1970. pap. 14.95 (*0-8464-1156-3*) Beekman Pubs.

— Mirrors, Vol. 144. Weiss, Jason, tr. (Green Integer Ser.: No. 7). 224p. 1998. pap. 12.95 (*1-55713-313-1*) Green Integer.

— The Peacock Emperor Moth: Short Fictions. Corman, Cid, tr. from FRE. (Serie d'Ecriture: No. 9). 112p. (Orig.). 1995. pap. 8.00 (*1-886224-07-2*) Burning Deck.

Cohen, Marcel, ed. see Jabes, Edmond.

Cohen, Marcelo. El Instrumento Mas Caro de la Tierra. (SPA.). 168p. 1981. pap. 7.00 (*84-85859-24-3*, 2003) Ediciones Norte.

Cohen, Marcia. The History of Feminism. 1988. 19.95 (*0-317-64419-X*) S&S Trade.

Cohen, Marcie, ed. see Knapp, William.

Cohen, Marcus, et al. Student Research Projects in Calculus. LC 91-62052. (Spectrum Ser.). 232p. (C). 1992. pap. text 29.95 (*0-88385-503-8*, SRPC) Math Assn.

Cohen, Margaret. Profane Illumination: Walter Benjamin & the Paris of Surreal Revolution. LC 92-36861. (Weimar & Now Ser.: Vol. 5). 1993. 45.00 (*0-520-08023-8*, Pub. by U CA Pr) Cal Prin Full Svc.

— Profane Illumination: Walter Benjamin & the Paris of Surrealist Revolution. (Weimar & Now: German Cultural Criticism Ser.: Vol. 5). (Illus.). 271p. 1995. pap. 15.95 (*0-520-20150-7*, Pub. by U CA Pr) Cal Prin Full Svc.

***Cohen, Margaret & Hahn, Alberto, eds.** Exploring the Work of Donald Meltzer: A Festschrift. 256p. 2000. pap. 32.00 (*1-85575-240-9*, Pub. by H Karnac Bks Ltd) Other Pr LLC.

Cohen, Margaret & Prendergast, Christopher. Spectacles of Realism: Gender, Body, Genre. (Cultural Politics Ser.: Vol. 10). 1995. pap. 21.95 (*0-8166-2521-2*) U of Minn Pr.

Cohen, Margo P. Diabetes & Protein Glycation: Clinical & Pathophysiologic Relevance. (Illus.). x, 275p. (Orig.). 1996. pap. 35.00 (*0-9654654-0-3*) J C Press.

Cohen, Marilyn. Linen, Family & Community in Tullylish, County Down, 1690-1914. LC 98-113382. 320p. 1997. boxed set 60.00 (*1-85182-312-3*, Pub. by Four Cts Pr) Intl Spec Bk.

— The Warp of Ulster's Past: Interdisciplinary Perspectives on the Irish Linen Industry. LC 96-28130. 304p. 1996. text 49.95 (*0-312-12907-6*) St Martin.

Cohen, Marilyn, ed. Reclaiming Gender: Transgressive Identies in Modern Ireland. LC 99-23512. 320p. 1999. text 49.95 (*0-312-21337-9*) St Martin.

Cohen, Marilyn & Prior, Karen Swallow. Common Ground on Abortion Clinic Activism. 1998. pap. 7.50 (*0-9668493-0-2*) Syracuse Univ-PARC.

Cohen, Marilyn & Watson, Nick. The Bond Bible: Whatever Your Age, Income or Total Assets, Bonds Belong in Your Portfolio. 224p. 2000. text 24.00 (*0-7352-0138-2*) PH Pr.

Cohen, Marion. She Was Born, She Died: A Collection of Poems. rev. ed. LC 95-26731. (Illus.). 24p. 1996. pap. 3.25 (*1-56123-044-8*, SWBC) Centering Corp.

Cohen, Marion, jt. ed. see Burr, Gillian.

Cohen, Marion D. Counting to Zero: Poems on Repeated Miscarriage. LC 88-72229. 102p. 1988. pap. 9.95 (*0-930194-18-7*) Ctr Thanatology.

— Dirty Details: The Days & Nights of a Well Spouse. LC 95-42473. (Illus.). 165p. (C). 1996. pap. 18.95 (*1-56639-426-0*) Temple U Pr.

— Dirty Details: The Days & Nights of a Well Spouse. LC 95-42473. (Illus.). 165p. (C). 1996. lib. bdg. 49.95 (*1-56639-425-2*) Temple U Pr.

***Cohen, Marion Deutsche.** Dear Aunt X & Uncle Y: How to Ask for Help. rev. ed. LC 96-8472. 60p. 2000. reprint ed. 6.95 (*0-930194-61-6*) Ctr Thanatology.

Cohen, Marion Deutsche. Epsilon Country. LC 92-7438. (Orig.). 1995. pap. 9.95 (*0-930194-50-0*, FBPD) Ctr Thanatology.

Cohen, Marion Deutsche, compiled by. Limits of Miracles: Poems about the Loss of Babies. LC 84-16813. 52p. 1984. 16.95 (*0-89789-066-3*, Bergin & Garvey) Greenwood.

Cohen, Marjorie G. Women's Work, Markets, & Economic Development in Nineteenth-Century Ontario. 286p. 1988. text 40.00 (*0-8020-2651-6*) U of Toronto Pr.

— Women's Work, Markets & Economic Development in Nineteenth-Century Ontario. 286p. 1988. pap. 19.95 (*0-8020-6677-1*) U of Toronto Pr.

Cohen, Marjorie G., jt. auth. see Pierson, Ruth R.

Cohen, Mark. Close Combat 3: Russian Front Official Strategies. LC 98-83184. 336p. 1999. pap. 19.99 (*0-7821-2526-3*) Sybex.

***Cohen, Mark.** Ridge Racer 64: Prima's Official Strategy Guide. LC 00-100737. (Official Strategy Guides Ser.). (Illus.). 94p. (YA). 2000. pap. 14.99 (*0-7615-2837-7*, Prima Games) Prima Pub.

— Starcraft 64: Prima's Official Strategy Guide. (Official Strategy Guides Ser.). (Illus.). 128p. (YA). 2000. pap. 14.99 (*0-7615-2720-6*) Prima Pub.

— Tomb Raider: Game Boy. (Official Strategy Guides Ser.). (Illus.). 112p. 2000. pap. 9.99 (*0-7615-2859-8*) Prima Pub.

Cohen, Mark & Commoner, Barry. How Government Purchase Programs Can Get Electric Vehicles on the Road (June-1993) (Electric Vehicle Information Ser.: Vol. 13). (Illus.). 55p. 1996. pap. 45.00 (*0-89934-265-5*, BT040); lib. bdg. 95.00 (*0-89934-266-3*, BT940) Bus Tech Bks.

Cohen, Mark, jt. auth. see Prima Staff.

Cohen, Mark A., et al. Chinese Intellectual Property: Law & Practice. LC 99-32099. 1999. 135.00 (*90-411-9372-3*) Kluwer Law Intl.

— Environmental & Financial Performance: Are They Related? 27p. (Orig.). 1995. pap. 40.00 (*1-879775-26-3*) IRRC Inc DC.

Cohen, Mark A., tr. see Weil, Eric.

Cohen, Mark E. The Cultic Calendars of the Ancient Near East. LC 93-6751. 1993. 37.50 (*1-883053-00-5*) CDL Pr.

Cohen, Mark E., et al, eds. The Tablet & the Scroll: Near Eastern Studies in Honor of William W. Hallo. LC 92-42780. 1993. 58.00 (*0-9620013-9-2*) CDL Pr.

Cohen, Mark H. New Media for Kids, Vol. 1. Byrne, Christopher, ed. 144p. (Orig.). 1997. pap. 24.95 (*0-9655999-0-6*) Market Focus.

Cohen, Mark L. The Settlers No. III: Prima's Official Strategy Guide. LC 98-68119. 240p. 1998. pap. 19.99 (*0-7615-1979-3*) Prima Pub.

***Cohen, Mark N.** Culture of Intolerance: Chauvinism, Class & Racism in the United States. LC 97-17951. 344p. 1998. 35.00 (*0-300-07072-1*) Yale U Pr.

Cohen, Mark N. The Food Crisis in Prehistory: Over Population & Origins of Agriculture. LC 76-41858. 1979. pap. 20.00 (*0-300-02351-0*) Yale U Pr.

— Health & the Rise of Civilization. 295p. (C). 1991. reprint ed. pap. 17.00 (*0-300-05023-2*) Yale U Pr.

Cohen, Mark N. & Katz, Joan. Win Your Weight-Loss War . . . Sensationally. unabridged ed. (Illus.). 200p. 1998. pap. 9.95 (*0-9662966-0-5*) Best-Sellers Pub.

Cohen, Mark N., jt. auth. see Hogan, Kevin L.

***Cohen, Mark Nathan.** Culture of Intolerance: Chauvinism, Class & Racism in the United States. 344p. 1999. pap. 14.95 (*0-300-08066-2*) Yale U Pr.

Cohen, Mark R. Jewish Self-Government in Medieval Egypt: The Origins of the Office of the Head of Jews, CA 1065-1126. LC 80-7514. (Princeton Studies on the Near East). 408p. 1980. reprint ed. pap. 126.50 (*0-608-03315-4*, 206402700008) Bks Demand.

— Under Crescent & Cross: The Jews in the Middle Ages. LC 93-42865. 304p. 1994. text 39.50 (*0-691-03378-1*, Pub. by Princeton U Pr) Cal Prin Full Svc.

— Under Crescent & Cross: The Jews in the Middle Ages. 304p. (C). 1994. pap. text 15.95 (*0-691-01082-X*, Pub. by Princeton U Pr) Cal Prin Full Svc.

Cohen, Mark R. & Udovitch, Abraham L., eds. Jews among Arabs: Contacts & Boundaries. LC 89-23563. 140p. 1989. 14.95 (*0-87850-068-5*) Darwin Pr.

Cohen, Mark R., jt. auth. see Schafer, Peter.

***Cohen, Marlene Zichi, et al.** Hermeneutic Phenomenological Research: A Practical Guide for Nurse Researchers. LC 00-9007. (Methods in Nursing Research Ser.). 2000. pap. write for info. (*0-7619-1720-9*) Sage.

Cohen, Marsha P., jt. auth. see Alford, Marcus R.

Cohen, Marshall, ed. Ronald Dworkin & Contemporary Jurisprudence. LC 83-11091. (Philosophy & Society Ser.). 316p. (C). 1984. text 59.50 (*0-8476-7124-0*) Rowman.

Cohen, Marshall, et al, eds. Marx, Justice & History. LC 79-5478. (Philosophy & Public Affairs Reader Ser.). 325p. 1980. reprint ed. pap. 100.80 (*0-7837-9278-6*, 206001700004) Bks Demand.

— Medicine & Moral Philosophy. LC 81-47986. 320p. reprint ed. pap. 99.20 (*0-7837-0100-4*, 204037800016) Bks Demand.

Cohen, Marshall, jt. auth. see Braudy, Leo.

Cohen, Marshall, jt. auth. see Copeland, Roger.

Cohen, Marshall, jt. ed. see Copeland, Roger.

Cohen, Marshall, ed. see Goodin, Robert E.

Cohen, Marshall, ed. see Kleinig, John.

Cohen, Marshall, ed. see Norton, Bryan G.

Cohen, Marshall, ed. see Thiele, Leslie P.

Cohen, Marshall, ed. see Wertheimer, Alan.

***Cohen, Martin.** 101 Philosophy Problems. LC 98-31117. 1999. 60.00 (*0-415-19126-2*); pap. 14.99 (*0-415-19127-0*) Routledge.

Cohen, Martin A. & Croner, Helga, eds. Christian Mission - Jewish Mission. LC 82-60856. 1982. pap. 7.95 (*0-8091-2475-0*) Paulist Pr.

Cohen, Martin A. & Peck, Abraham J., eds. Sephardim in the Americas: Studies in Culture & History. LC 93-20083. (Judaic Studies). 510p. 1993. reprint ed. pap. 158.10 (*0-608-03803-2*, 206465400009) Bks Demand.

Cohen, Martin B., ed. see George Mason Lectures Staff.

Cohen, Martin S. Light from Dead Stars. 368p. (Orig.). 1997. pap. 10.95 (*1-55050-102-X*, Pub. by Coteau) Genl Dist Srvs.

— The Shiur Qomah: Texts & Recensions. 250p. 1985. lib. bdg. 74.50 (*3-16-144907-X*, Pub. by JCB Mohr) Coronet Bks.

— The Sword of Goliath: A Co(s)mic Mystery. 340p. 1998. mass mkt. 8.95 (1-55050-116-X, Pub. by Coteau) Genl Dist Srvs.
— The Truth about Marvin Kalish: A Mystery. LC 92-71041. 280p. 1992. pap. 13.95 (0-914539-05-1) Ben-Simon.
Cohen, Marty. A Traveller's Alphabet. Gale, Vi, ed. LC 79-84509. (First Bk.). (Illus.). 1979. pap. 5.00 (0-915986-16-7) Prescott St Pr.
— A Traveller's Alphabet. limited ed. Gale, Vi, ed. LC 79-84509. (First Bk.). (Illus.). 1979. 20.00 (0-915986-15-9) Prescott St Pr.
Cohen, Marty, jt. auth. see Aloff, Mindy.
Cohen, Marvin. Baseball the Beautiful. 1974. 15.00 (0-8256-3030-4); pap. 7.50 (0-8256-3034-7) Ultramarine Pub.
— The Monday Rhetoric of the Love Club & Other Parables. LC 72-93979. 128p. 1973. pap. 3.75 (0-8112-0475-8, NDP352, Pub. by New Directions) Norton.
— The Monday Rhetoric of the Love Club & Other Parables. LC 72-93979. 128p. 1973. 15.00 (0-89366-250-X) Ultramarine Pub.
— Objection: A Tennis Novel. 256p. (Orig.). 1996. pap. 14.95 (0-9647940-8-X) Adventura Pubng.
— Others, Including Morstive Sternbump: A Novel. LC 76-11615. 247p. 1976. 15.00 (0-672-52145-8) Ultramarine Pub.
— You the Man. 320p. 1996. pap. 14.95 (0-942963-72-5) Distinctive Pub.
Cohen, Marvin A. Astrology & Your Cat. (Illus.). 68p. (Orig.). 1996. pap. 10.00 (1-57502-298-2, P1019) Morris Pubng.
***Cohen, Marvin M.** Conquering Investment Risk in the Wall Street Garden of Eden. LC 99-88372. 2000. pap. write for info. (1-886388-20-2) Flower Valley Pr.
Cohen, Marvin M. Introduction to the Quantum Theory of Semiconductors. LC 79-123485. (Illus.). x, 300p. 1972. text 274.00 (0-677-02980-2) Gordon & Breach.
— Introduction to the Quantum Theory of Semiconductors. 312p. 1998. pap. text 30.00 (90-5699-641-X, ECU44, Harwood Acad Pubs) Gordon & Breach.
Cohen, Mary, ed. see Denton, Betty.
Cohen, Mary, ed. see Hopper, Beebe.
Cohen, Mary, ed. see Jenkins, Kathwren.
Cohen, Mary A. French Toast for Breakfast: Declaring Peace with Emotional Eating. 272p. (Orig.). 1995. pap. 12.95 (0-936077-22-0) Gurze Bks.
Cohen, Marylin. Reginald Marsh's New York: Paintings, Drawings, Prints & Photographs. LC 83-6465. (Fine Art Ser.). (Illus.). 128p. (Orig.). 1983. pap. 9.95 (0-486-24594-2) Dover.
Cohen, Matt. The Colours of War. 216p. 1993. pap. 14.95 (1-55082-070-2, Pub. by Quarry Pr) LPC InBook.
— The Disinherited. 254p. 1993. pap. 14.95 (1-55082-069-9, Pub. by Quarry Pr) LPC InBook.
***Cohen, Matt.** Elizabeth & After. 384p. 2000. text 25.00 (0-312-26151-9, Picador USA) St Martin.
Cohen, Matt. Emotional Arithmetic. 208p. 1995. 19.95 (0-312-13064-3) St Martin.
— Flowers of Darkness. 216p. 1993. pap. 14.95 (1-55082-072-9, Pub. by Quarry Pr) LPC InBook.
— Freud: The Paris Notebooks. 144p. 1991. pap. 12.95 (1-55082-004-4, Pub. by Quarry Pr) LPC InBook.
— Lives on the Mind Slaves. LC 95-109993. 192p. 1994. pap. write for info. (0-88984-139-X) Porcup Quill.
— The Sweet Second Summer of Kitty Malone. 232p. 1993. pap. 14.95 (1-55082-071-0, Pub. by Quarry Pr) LPC InBook.
***Cohen, Matt.** Typing: A Life in Twenty-Six Keys. (Illus.). 2000. write for info. (0-679-31050-9) Random.
Cohen, Matt & Carpentier, Andre, eds. Parallel Voices. 249p. 1993. pap. 18.95 (1-55082-065-6, Pub. by Quarry Pr) LPC InBook.
Cohen, Mattew M., et al. Anticipatory Guidance Sheets for Parents: Who Have a High School Reading Level. LC 94-68363. 72p. 1994. pap. 22.50 (0-924381-21-3) Sunbelt Med Pubs.
Cohen, Matthew M. Instructions for Parents. 2nd rev. ed. (Illus.). 432p. 1992. pap. write for info. (0-924381-08-6) Sunbelt Med Pubs.
Cohen, Matthew M. & Lanigan, Anni. Ambulatory Family Practice Protocols. 264p. 1994. pap. 55.00 (0-924381-18-3); ring bd. 85.00 (0-924381-20-5); 3.5 hd. write for info. (0-924381-19-1) Sunbelt Med Pubs.
— Nurse Practitioner Protocols. rev. ed. 264p. 1991. disk. write for info. (0-924381-14-0) Sunbelt Med Pubs.
— Nurse Practitioner Protocols. 2nd rev. ed. 264p. 1995. pap. 55.00 (0-924381-24-8); ring bd. 85.00 (0-924381-23-X) Sunbelt Med Pubs.
— Physician Assistant Protocols. 264p. 1994. pap. 55.00 (0-924381-15-9); ring bd. 85.00 (0-924381-17-5); disk. write for info. (0-924381-16-7) Sunbelt Med Pubs.
Cohen, Matthew M., et al. Anticipatory Guidance Sheets for Parents: Who Have a Middle School Reading Level. LC 94-68362. 72p. 1994. pap. 22.50 (0-924381-22-1) Sunbelt Med Pubs.
Cohen, Maurice E., jt. auth. see Hudson, Donna L.
Cohen, Maurice S. Does There Have to Be an Occasion? A Harvest of Pulpit Reflections. LC 92-34025. 1992. 20.00 (0-88125-433-9) Ktav.
Cohen, Max M. Biological Protection with Prostaglandins, Vol. II. 272p. 1986. 152.00 (0-8493-5963-5, QP801, CRC Reprint) Franklin.
Cohen, Max M., ed. Biological Protection with Prostaglandins, Vol. I. 288p. 1985. 162.00 (0-8493-5962-7, QP801, CRC Reprint) Franklin.
Cohen, Maxwell T. The Police Card Discord. LC 93-4173. (Studies in Jazz: No. 15). (Illus.). 194p. 1993. 26.50 (0-8108-2638-0) Scarecrow.
Cohen, Maynard M. A Stand Against Tyranny: Norway's Physicians & the Nazis. LC 96-14957. (Illus.). 380p. 1996. 39.95 (0-8143-2603-X) Wayne St U Pr.
***Cohen, Maynard M.** A Stand Against Tyranny: Norway's Physicians & the Nazis. (Illus.). 380p. 2000. pap. 19.95 (0-8143-2934-9) Wayne St U Pr.
Cohen, Mel. The Secret of the Pros: How to Become a Baseball Card Dealer. 176p. (Orig.). (YA). (gr. 8 up). 1991. pap. 12.95 (0-9631104-1-1) M Cohen.
Cohen, Melvin J., jt. ed. see Gordon, Solon A.
***Cohen, Menasui, et al, eds.** The Sidney Diamond Symposium: Materials Science of Concrete Special Volume. (Materials Science of Concrete Ser.). (Illus.). 579p. 1998. 95.00 (1-57498-072-6, MSCDIA) Am Ceramic.
Cohen, Mervyn D. Pediatric Magnetic Resonance Imaging. (Illus.). 162p. 1986. text 86.00 (0-7216-1396-9, W B Saunders Co) Harcrt Hlth Sci Grp.
Cohen, Michael. A Garden of Bristlecones: Tales of Change in the Great Basin. LC 97-23933. (Illus.). 334p. 1998. pap. 34.95 (0-87417-296-9) U of Nev Pr.
— Melatonin: From Contraception to Breast Cancer Prevention. (Illus.). 180p. (Orig.). (C). 1995. pap. 75.00 (1-880613-10-7) Sheba Pr.
***Cohen, Michael.** Murder Most Fair: The Appeal of Murder Mystery. LC 00-37120. 2000. write for info. (0-8386-3851-1) Fairleigh Dickinson.
— 1 Sure Way to Relax: Mike Cohen's Journey to Tranquility. 16p. 1999. pap. 16.98 incl. cd-rom (0-9675050-0-3) Audio Educ.
Cohen, Michael. Restructuring the Education System: Agenda for the 1990s. 40p. 1988. pap. text 7.50 (1-55877-006-2) Natl Governor.
— Sisters: Relation & Rescue in Nineteenth-Century British Novels & Paintings. LC 94-14414. 1995. 60.00 (0-8386-3555-5) Fairleigh Dickinson.
Cohen, Michael & Golembiewski, Robert T., eds. Public Personnel Update. LC 84-19892. (Public Administration & Public Policy Ser.: No. 27). 277p. 1984. reprint ed. pap. 85.90 (0-608-01362-5, 206210100002) Bks Demand.
Cohen, Michael, jt. auth. see Cohen, Judith.
Cohen, Michael, jt. auth. see David, Jane L.
Cohen, Michael, jt. ed. see Serageldin, Ismail.
Cohen, Michael A. Urban Policy & Political Conflict in Africa: A Study of the Ivory Coast. LC 73-90942. 262p. 1974. lib. bdg. 18.00 (0-226-11223-3) U Ch Pr.
Cohen, Michael A., et al, eds. Preparing for the Urban Future: Global Pressures & Local Forces. (Woodrow Wilson Center Press Ser.). 448p. (C). 1996. text 55.00 (0-943875-78-1); pap. text 19.95 (0-943875-79-X) Johns Hopkins.
Cohen, Michael D. & March, James G. Leadership & Ambiguity. 2nd ed. 1986. text 27.50 (0-07-103223-1) McGraw.
Cohen, Michael D. & Sproull, Lee S., eds. Organizational Learning. LC 95-35478. (Organizational Science Ser.: Vol. 2). (Illus.). 432p. 1995. 69.95 (0-8039-7088-9); pap. 32.95 (0-8039-7089-7) Sage.
Cohen, Michael D., jt. auth. see Axelrod, Robert.
Cohen, Michael E. & Duffner, Patricia K. Brain Tumors in Children: Principles of Diagnosis & Treatment. 2nd ed. LC 93-34357. (International Review of Child Neurology Ser.). 512p. 1993. text 104.00 (0-7817-0064-7) Lppncott W & W.
Cohen, Michael F. & Wallace, John R. Radiosity & Realistic Image Synthesis. (Illus.). 381p. 1993. text 56.00 (0-12-178270-0) Morgan Kaufmann.
***Cohen, Michael H.** Beyond Complementary Medicine: Legal & Ethical Perspectives on Health Care & Human Evolution. LC 99-50870. 200p. 2000. text 39.50 (0-472-11135-3, 11135) U of Mich Pr.
Cohen, Michael H. Complementary & Alternative Medicine: Legal Boundaries & Regulatory Perspectives. LC 97-21874. 176p. 1998. pap. text 16.95 (0-8018-5689-2) Johns Hopkins.
— Complementary & Alternative Medicine: Legal Boundaries & Regulatory Perspectives. LC 97-21874. 176p. 1999. text 45.00 (0-8018-5687-6) Johns Hopkins.
— Creative Writing for Lawyers. 1991. pap. 7.95 (0-8065-1213-X, Citadel Pr) Carol Pub Group.
— On the Job Survival. 94p. (Orig.). (C). 1984. pap. 6.95 (0-9613768-0-5) Canoe Press.
— The Power of Self-Management: Achieving Success in Your Healthcare Career. (Illus.). 196p. (Orig.). 1992. pap. 7.95 (0-9613768-1-3) Canoe Press.
Cohen, Michael J. Across the Running Tide. (Illus.). 1979. pap. 10.00 (0-89166-010-0) Cobblesmith.
— Churchill & the Jews. (Illus.). 408p. 1985. 49.50 (0-7146-3254-6, Pub. by F Cass Pubs) Intl Spec Bk.
— Fighting World War Three from the Middle East: Allied Contingency Plans, 1945-1954. LC 96-44697. 368p. (C). 1997. 57.50 (0-7146-4720-9, Pub. by F Cass Pubs); pap. 24.50 (0-7146-4269-X, Pub. by F Cass Pubs) Intl Spec Bk.
— The Origins & Evolution of the Arab-Zionist Conflict. 1987. pap. 13.95 (0-520-06598-0, Pub. by U CA Pr) Cal Prin Full Svc.
— Our Classroom Is Wild America. LC 74-76019. (Illus.). 1978. pap. 10.00 (0-89166-011-9) Cobblesmith.
— Palestine & the Great Powers, 1945-1948. LC 82-3858. 432p. reprint ed. pap. 134.00 (0-8357-3428-5, 203968600013) Bks Demand.
— Palestine to Israel: From Mandate to Independence. 1987. 49.50 (0-7146-3312-7, Pub. by F Cass Pubs) Intl Spec Bk.
— Prejudice Against Nature. (Illus.). 1983. pap. 10.00 (0-89166-016-X) Cobblesmith.
— Reconnecting with Nature: Finding Wellness through Restoring Your Bond with the Earth. 2nd ed. LC 96-29597. 230p. 1997. pap. 14.95 (0-9639705-2-6) Ecopress.
Cohen, Michael J., ed. How Nature Works. 265p. 1988. 10.95 (0-939169-06-1) Inst Glbl Educ.
Cohen, Michael J. & Kolinsky, Martin, eds. Britain & the Middle East in the 1930s: Security Problems 1935-39. LC 91-32524. 256p. 1992. text 45.00 (0-312-07211-2) St Martin.
— Demise of the British Empire in the Middle East: Britain's Responses to Nationalist Movements, 1943-55. LC 98-14415. xv, 255 p. 1998. 59.50 (0-7146-4804-3, Pub. by F Cass Pubs); pap. 24.50 (0-7146-4477-3, Pub. by F Cass Pubs) Intl Spec Bk.
***Cohen, Michael L. & King, Benjamin F.** Designing the 2010 Census: First Interim Report. 50p. 2000. pap. 12.00 (0-309-06944-0) Natl Acad Pr.
Cohen, Michael L., jt. ed. see Citro, Constance F.
Cohen, Michael L., ed. see National Research Council Staff.
Cohen, Michael P. The Pathless Way: John Muir & American Wilderness. LC 83-40260. 500p. 1986. pap. 19.95 (0-299-09724-2) U of Wis Pr.
Cohen, Michael R., ed. Medication Errors. LC 99-31972. (Illus.). 380p. 1999. text 70.00 (0-917330-89-7) Am Pharm Assn.
Cohen, Michael V. Myocardial Ischemia & Reperfusion. LC 98-7849. (Developments in Molecular & Cellular Biochemistry Ser.). 1998. write for info. (0-7923-8173-4) Kluwer Academic.
Cohen, Michael W. The Attention Zone: A Parent's Guide to Attention Deficit/Hyperactivity Disorder. LC 97-22972. 234p. 1997. 22.95 (0-87630-860-4) Brunner-Mazel.
Cohen, Michele. Fashioning Masculinity: National Identify & Language in the Eighteenth Century. LC 96-7553. 192p. (C). 1996. 65.00 (0-415-10736-9) Routledge.
Cohen, Michele, jt. ed. see Hitchcock, Tim.
Cohen, Milton. Ilana & the Monsters. (Illus.). 40p. (Orig.). (J). (ps). 1985. pap. 4.00 (0-9616076-0-2) Jomilt Pubns.
Cohen, Mimis, ed. Mastery of Plastic & Reconstructive Surgery. LC 93-33838. 2736p. 1994. text 357.00 (0-316-15003-7) Lppncott W & W.
Cohen, Miriam. Backpack Baby. LC 99-70742. (Illus.). 12p. (J). (gr. k). 1999. bds. 6.95 (1-887734-58-9) Star Brght Bks.
— Bee My Valentine! (Illus.). 32p. (J). (gr. k-3). 1996. pap. 5.99 (0-440-41121-1, Yearling) BDD Bks Young Read.
Cohen, Miriam. Bee My Valentine! LC 77-21950. 1996. 9.94 (0-606-09062-2, Pub. by Turtleback) Demco.
Cohen, Miriam. Best Friends. LC 70-146620. (Illus.). 32p. (J). (ps-1). 1971. lib. bdg. 15.00 (0-02-722800-2, Mac Bks Young Read) S&S Childrens.
— Best Friends. (J). 1989. 10.15 (0-606-04170-2, Pub. by Turtleback) Demco.
— Best Friends. LC 89-31266. (Illus.). 32p. (J). (ps-1). 1989. reprint ed. mass mkt. 4.95 (0-689-71334-7) Aladdin.
Cohen, Miriam. Don't Eat Too Much Turkey! LC 86-25660. (J). 1996. 10.19 (0-606-11269-3, Pub. by Turtleback) Demco.
Cohen, Miriam. Don't Eat too Much Turkey! LC 86-25660. (Illus.). 32p. (J). (ps-3). 1987. 16.00 (0-688-07141-4, Grenwillow Bks) HarpC Child Bks.
***Cohen, Miriam.** Down in the Subway. LC 97-43603. (Illus.). 32p. (J). (ps-2). 1998. 15.95 (0-7894-2510-6) DK Pub Inc.
Cohen, Miriam. Eddy's Dream. large type ed. LC 99-38636. (Illus.). 40p. (J). (gr. 1-6). 2000. 15.95 (1-887734-57-0) Star Brght Bks.
— First Grade Takes a Test. (J). 1995. 10.19 (0-606-07518-6) Turtleback.
— It's George! Welcome to First Grade! (Illus.). 32p. (J). (ps-4). 1998. pap. 4.99 (0-440-41164-5) BDD Bks Young Read.
***Cohen, Miriam.** It's George! Welcome to First Grade! 1998. 10.19 (0-606-13530-8, Pub. by Turtleback) Demco.
— Jim Meets the Thing: Welcome to the First Grade! (Dell Picture Yearling Ser.). 1997. 10.19 (0-606-13538-3, Pub. by Turtleback) Demco.
Cohen, Miriam. Jim's Dog Muffins. LC 83-14090. 1996. 10.19 (0-606-09492-X, Pub. by Turtleback) Demco.
— Liar, Liar, Pants on Fire! (J). 1995. 10.19 (0-606-07785-5) Turtleback.
— Lost in the Museum. 1995. 10.19 (0-606-07808-8, Pub. by Turtleback) Demco.
— Mimmy & Sophie. LC 97-15683. (Illus.). 40p. (YA). (gr. k up). 1999. 16.00 (0-374-34988-6) FS&G.
— Mine: A Backpack Baby Story. LC 99-70750. (Illus.). 12p. (J). 1999. bds. 6.95 (1-887734-59-7) Star Brght Bks.
Cohen, Miriam. No Good in Art. LC 79-16566. (Illus.). 32p. (J). (gr. k-3). 1980. 16.93 (0-688-84234-8, Grenwillow Bks) HarpC Child Bks.
Cohen, Miriam. No Good in Art. (J). 1996. 10.19 (0-606-09689-2, Pub. by Turtleback) Demco.
— Real-Skin Rubber Monster Mask. (J). 1995. 10.44 (0-606-08061-9) Turtleback.
— Robert & Dawn Marie 4Ever. LC 85-45269. 160p. (YA). (gr. 7 up). 1986. 11.95 (0-06-021396-5) HarpC Child Bks.
***Cohen, Miriam.** Say Hi Backpack Baby. large type ed. LC 00-100230. (Backpack Baby Story Ser.). (Illus.). 12p. (J). (ps). 2000. bds. 6.95 (1-887734-82-1) Star Brght Bks.
Cohen, Miriam. Second Grade --Friends Again! (J). 1994. 8.70 (0-606-06723-X, Pub. by Turtleback) Demco.
— Second Grade Friends. (J). 1993. pap. 2.99 (0-590-47463-4) Scholastic Inc.
Cohen, Miriam. Second-Grade Friends. (J). 1993. 8.19 (0-606-05585-1, Pub. by Turtleback) Demco.
Cohen, Miriam. Second Grade Friends . . . Again! (J). (ps-3). 1994. pap. 2.95 (0-590-45906-6) Scholastic Inc.
— See You in Second Grade! 1996. 10.19 (0-606-09840-2, Pub. by Turtleback) Demco.
— See You Tomorrow, Charles. (Illus.). 32p. 1997. pap. 4.99 (0-440-41151-3) Dell.
— See You Tomorrow, Charles. 1997. pap. 4.99 (0-440-91192-3) Dell.
— So What? (Welcome to the First Grade Ser.). 1998. 10.19 (0-606-13783-1, Pub. by Turtleback) Demco.
— So What? (Welcome to the First Grade! Ser.). (Illus.). 32p. (J). (ps-3). 1998. reprint ed. pap. 4.99 (0-440-41148-3, Yearling) BDD Bks Young Read.
Cohen, Miriam. Starring First Grade. 1996. 10.19 (0-606-09895-X, Pub. by Turtleback) Demco.
Cohen, Miriam. Starring First Grade: Welcome to First Grade! (Illus.). 32p. (J). (gr. k-3). 1996. pap. 4.99 (0-440-41154-8, Yearling) BDD Bks Young Read.
Cohen, Miriam. Starring First Grade: Welcome to First Grade! LC 84-5929. (Illus.). 32p. (J). (ps-k). 1985. 17.89 (0-688-04030-6, Grenwillow Bks) HarpC Child Bks.
— Wah! Wah! large type ed. LC 00-100536. (Backpack Baby Story Ser.). (Illus.). 12p. (J). (ps). 2000. bds. 6.95 (1-887734-81-3) Star Brght Bks.
Cohen, Miriam. When Will I Read? (J). 1996. mass mkt. 6.99 (0-440-91170-2) BDD Bks Young Read.
Cohen, Miriam. When Will I Read. LC 76-28320. (Illus.). 32p. (J). (ps-3). 1977. 16.93 (0-688-84073-6, Grenwillow Bks) HarpC Child Bks.
— When Will I Read? Welcome to First Grade! (Dell Picture Yearling Ser.). (J). 1996. 10.19 (0-606-12083-1, Pub. by Turtleback) Demco.
Cohen, Miriam. Will I Have a Friend? LC 67-10127. (Illus.). 32p. (J). (ps-1). 1967. mass mkt. 15.00 (0-02-722790-1, Mac Bks Young Read) S&S Childrens.
Cohen, Miriam. Will I Have a Friend? 2nd ed. (J). 1989. 9.15 (0-606-03955-4, Pub. by Turtleback) Demco.
— Will I Have a Friend? 2nd ed. LC 89-31340. (Illus.). 32p. (J). (ps-1). 1989. reprint ed. mass mkt. 4.99 (0-689-71333-9) Aladdin.
Cohen, Miriam. Workshop to Office: Two Generations of Italian Women in New York City, 1900-1950. LC 92-52746. (Illus.). 256p. 1993. text 45.00 (0-8014-2722-3); pap. text 17.95 (0-8014-8005-1) Cornell U Pr.
Cohen, Misha. The HIV Wellness Sourcebook. LC 97-31830. 224p. 1998. pap. 14.95 (0-8050-5117-1) H Holt & Co.
Cohen, Misha R. & Doner, Kalia. The Chinese Way to Healing. 272p. 1996. pap. 15.00 (0-399-52232-8, Perigee Bks) Berkley Pub.
Cohen, Mitch, tr. see Munzberg, Olav.
Cohen, Mitch, tr. see Steinberg, Rolf.
Cohen, Mitchell. The Wager of Lucien Goldmann: Tragedy, Dialectics, & a Hidden God. LC 93-40394. 368p. 1994. text 45.00 (0-691-03420-6, Pub. by Princeton U Pr) Cal Prin Full Svc.
— Zion & State: Nation, Class & the Shaping of Modern Israel. 336p. 1992. text 57.50 (0-231-07940-0); pap. text 20.00 (0-231-07941-9) Col U Pr.
Cohen, Mitchell, et al, eds. Sexual Interactions & HIV Risk: New Conceptual Perspectives in European Research. LC 95-17936. (Social Aspects of AIDS Ser.). 266p. 1995. 79.00 (0-7484-0345-0, Pub. by Tay Francis Ltd) Taylor & Francis.
Cohen, Mitchell & Fermon, Nicole, eds. Princeton Readings in Political Thought: Essential Texts since Plato. LC 95-23990. 600p. 1996. pap. text 19.95 (0-691-03689-6, Pub. by Princeton U Pr) Cal Prin Full Svc.
Cohen, Mitchell, ed. see Borochov, Ber.
Cohen, Mitchell J. & Campbell, James N., eds. Pain Treatment Centers at a Crossroads: A Practical & Conceptual Reappraisal. LC 96-12622. (Progress in Pain Research & Management Ser.: Vol. 7). (Illus.). 352p. 1996. 39.00 (0-931092-14-0) Intl Assn Study Pain.
Cohen, Monica F. Professional Domesticity in the Victorian Novel: Women, Work & Home. LC 97-11305. (Studies in Nineteenth-Century Literature & Culture: No. 14). 230p. (C). 1998. text 54.95 (0-521-59141-4) Cambridge U Pr.
***Cohen, Monique.** Counseling Addicted Women. LC 99-50415. 2000. write for info. (0-7619-0910-9) Sage.
Cohen, Monroe D., ed. see McCune, Shirley D., et al.
Cohen-Mor, Dalya. An Arabian Mosaic: Short Stories by Arab Women Writers. (C). 1993. 24.95 (1-880613-08-5); pap. 15.95 (1-880613-06-9) Sheba Pr.
***Cohen-Mor, Dalya.** A Matter of Fate: The Concept of Fate in the Arab World As Reflected in Modern Arabic Literature. LC 99-30401. 288p. 2000. write for info. (0-19-513398-6) OUP.
Cohen-Mor, Dalya. Yusuf Idris: Changing Visions. (C). 1992. 39.95 (1-880613-00-X) Sheba Pr.
— Yusuf Idris: The Piper Dies & Other Stories. (C). 1992. pap. 15.95 (1-880613-03-4) Sheba Pr.
Cohen-Mor, Dalya, ed. The Emigrants: An Anthology of Arab-American Writers. (ARA & HEB.). 150p. 1998. pap. text 15.95 (1-880613-12-3) Sheba Pr.
— Voices of Their Own: An Anthology of Arab Women Writers. (ARA & HEB.). 250p. 1998. pap. text 15.95 (1-880613-11-5) Sheba Pr.
Cohen, Morrel H., ed. Superconductivity in Science & Technology. LC 67-25534. 171p. reprint ed. pap. 53.10 (0-608-30633-9, 202004700016) Bks Demand.
Cohen, Morris. Bench & Bar. 1997. 35.00 (0-88363-497-X) H L Levin.
— Introduccion a la Logica. (Breviarios Ser.). (SPA.). pap. 8.99 (968-16-0866-6, Pub. by Fondo) Continental Bk.
— Martensite: A Tribute to Morris Cohen. Olson, G. B. & Owen, W. S., eds. LC 91-76275. (Illus.). 345p. 1992. reprint ed. pap. 107.00 (0-608-02644-1, 206330300004) Bks Demand.
Cohen, Morris & Hynd, George W. Dyslexia: Neuropsychological Theory, Research, & Clinical Differentiation. (C). 1989. pap. text 81.95 (0-205-10117-8) Allyn.

Cohen, Morris L. Bibliography of Early American Law (BEAL), 6 vols. LC 97-40260. 1998. 1695.00 (*1-57588-233-7*, 310470) W S Hein.
— The Lawyers' Book of Days. (Illus.). 128p. 1991. 10.95 (*0-88363-291-8*) H L Levin.
Cohen, Morris L. & O'Connor, Sharon H. Guide to the Early Reports of the Supreme Court of the United States. LC 95-7547. xii, 237p. 1995. 45.00 (*0-8377-0468-5*, Rothman) W S Hein.
Cohen, Morris L. & Olson, Kent C. Legal Research in a Nutshell. (Nutshell Ser.). 361p. (C). 1996. pap. text 22.50 (*0-314-09589-6*) West Pub.
Cohen, Morris L. & Olson, Kent C. Legal Research in a Nutshell. 5th ed. LC 92-15829. (Nutshell Ser.). 500p. (C). 1992. pap. text 17.00 (*0-314-00783-0*) West Pub.
Cohen, Morris L., et al. How to Find the Law. 9th ed. (American Casebook Ser.). 716p. (C). 1989. reprint ed. 39.50 (*0-314-53318-4*) West Pub.
Cohen, Morris M. An Introduction to the Study of Constitution: A Study Showing the Play of Physical & Social Factors in the Creation of Institutional Law. LC 78-64255. (Johns Hopkins University. Studies in the Social Sciences. Thirtieth Ser. 1912: 11). reprint ed. 37.50 (*0-404-61359-4*) AMS Pr.
Cohen, Morris R. A Dreamer's Journey: The Autobiography of Morris Raphael Cohen. LC 74-27972. (Modern Jewish Experience Ser.). (Illus.). 1975. reprint ed. 33.95 (*0-405-06702-X*) Ayer.
— The Faith of a Liberal. LC 76-111820. (Essay Index Reprint Ser.). 1977. 28.95 (*0-8369-1598-4*) Ayer.
— The Faith of a Liberal. 497p. (C). 1992. pap. text 29.95 (*1-56000-616-1*) Transaction Pubs.
— Law & the Social Order: Essays in Legal Philosophy. LC 94-75665. xii, 404p. 1994. reprint ed. 105.00 (*1-56169-093-7*) Gaunt.
— Law & the Social Order: Essays in Legal Philosophy. Supplemented by Cohen's "Moral Aspects of Criminal Law" LC 81-4394. (Social & Moral Thought Ser.). 520p. (Orig.). 1982. pap. 29.95 (*0-87855-876-4*) Transaction Pubs.
Cohen, Morris R. & Drabkin, I. E. A Source Book in Greek Science. LC 58-12979. (Source Books in the History of the Sciences). (Illus.). 602p. reprint ed. pap. 186.70 (*0-7837-4457-9*, 205798700012) Bks Demand.
Cohen, Morris R. & Nagel, Ernest. An Introduction to Logic. 2nd ed. LC 93-6067. 288p. (C). 1993. pap. text 16.95 (*0-87220-144-9*); lib. bdg. 34.95 (*0-87220-145-7*) Hackett Pub.
Cohen, Morris R., ed. see De Tourtoulon, Pierre.
Cohen, Morris R., ed. & intro. see Peirce, Charles Sanders.
Cohen, Morton, ed. see Kipling, Rudyard.
Cohen, Morton N. Lewis Carroll. 1996. pap. 17.00 (*0-679-74562-9*) Knopf.
— Lewis Carroll: A Biography. 12.95 (*0-614-28402-3*) Vin Bks.
— Reflections in a Looking Glass: A Centennial Celebration of Lewis Carroll, Photographer. LC 98-85808. (Illus.). 145p. 1998. 50.00 (*0-89381-796-1*) Aperture.
Cohen, Morton N., ed. Lewis Carroll & the Kitchins. limited ed. (Illus.). 64p. 1980. 37.50 (*0-317-64759-8*) Argosy.
Cohen, Morton N., tr. see Carroll, Lewis, pseud.
Cohen, Murray. The Chance Factor. (Star Trek Voyager Ser.: Vol. 2). (J). 1984. per. 1.95 (*0-671-00732-7*, Archway) PB.
— Sensible Words: Linguistic Practice in England, 1640-1785. LC 77-1856. (Illus.). 219p. reprint ed. pap. 67.90 (*0-608-06697-4*, 206689400009) Bks Demand.
Cohen, Myron. Myron Cohen's Big Joke Book. 410p. 1983. reprint ed. pap. 5.95 (*0-8065-0853-1*, Citadel Pr) Carol Pub Group.
Cohen, Myron L. House United, House Divided: A Chinese Family in Taiwan. LC 75-28473. (Studies of the East Asian Institute). (Illus.). 272p. 1976. text 57.50 (*0-231-03849-6*) Col U Pr.
Cohen, Myron L., ed. Asia: Case Studies in the Social Sciences: A Guide for Teaching. LC 92-31585. (Columbia Project on Asia in the Core Curriculum Ser.). 656p. (C). (gr. 13). 1992. text 91.95 (*1-56324-156-0*, East Gate Bk); pap. text 34.95 (*1-56324-157-9*, East Gate Bk) M E Sharpe.
Cohen, Myron S., jt. auth. see Henderson, Gail E.
Cohen, N. Claude, ed. Guidebook on Molecular Modeling in Drug Design. LC 95-21396. (Illus.). 361p. 1996. text 59.95 (*0-12-178245-X*) Acad Pr.
Cohen, Nachman. Bar-Bat Mitzvah & Beyond. 1988. 19.95 (*0-87306-212-4*) Feldheim.
— Tractate Berakhos: Commentary & Study Guide. 600p. (C). 1989. write for info. (*1-877650-00-5*) Torah Lishmah.
Cohen, Nahoum. Urban Conservation. LC 98-43963. (Illus.). 380p. 1999. 100.00 (*0-262-03268-6*); pap. text 49.95 (*0-262-53161-5*) MIT Pr.
Cohen, Nancy E. Doing a Good Business: 100 Years at the Bon-Ton. LC 98-86813. (Illus.). 112p. 1998. 19.95 (*0-944641-33-4*) Greenwich Pub Group.
Cohen, Nancy E., jt. auth. see Kagan, Sharon L.
***Cohen, Nancy J.** Permed to Death. 304p. 1999. 20.00 (*1-57566-482-8*, Knsington) Kensgtn Pub Corp.
Cohen, Nancy W. Open Season: A Survival Guide for Natural Childbirth in the 1990s. LC 91-10569. 464p. 1991. pap. 16.95 (*0-89789-272-0*, G272, Bergin & Garvey) Greenwood.
— Open Season: A Survival Guide for Natural Childbirth in the 1990s. LC 91-10569. 464p. 1991. 29.95 (*0-89789-252-6*, H252, Bergin & Garvey) Greenwood.
Cohen, Nancy W. & Estner, Lois J. Silent Knife: Cesarean Prevention & Vaginal Birth after Cesarean. LC 82-24276. (Illus.). 456p. 1983. pap. 24.95 (*0-89789-027-2*, Bergin & Garvey) Greenwood.
— Silent Knife: Vaginal Birth After Cesarean (VBAC) & Cesarean Prevention. 464p. 1983. 13.46 (*0-318-17499-5*) C Sec.
Cohen, Naomi. American Jews & the Zionist Idea. pap. 11.95 (*0-87068-272-5*) Ktav.
— Feminism & Marxism in the Nineties: A Revolutionary Women's Agenda. 26p. 1993. pap. 2.50 (*0-89567-119-0*) World View Forum.
Cohen, Naomi, et al. Capitalism's War on Women. 27p. 1995. pap. 2.50 (*0-89567-125-5*) World View Forum.
Cohen, Naomi C. Philo Judaeus: His Universe of Discourse. LC 95-173093. 381p. 1995. 57.95 (*3-8204-1650-1*) P Lang Pubng.
***Cohen, Naomi W.** Jacob H. Schiff: A Study in American Jewish Leadership. LC 99-30392. (Brandeis Series in American Jewish History, Culture, & Life). 336p. 1999. 35.00 (*0-87451-948-9*) U Pr of New Eng.
Cohen, Naomi W. The Year after the Riots: American Responses to the Palestinian Crisis of 1929-30. LC 87-32538. 212p. 1988. 29.95 (*0-8143-1914-9*) Wayne St U Pr.
Cohen, Naomi W., ed. Essential Papers on Jewish-Christian Relations in the United States. 400p. (C). 1991. text 75.00 (*0-8147-1445-5*); pap. text 27.50 (*0-8147-1446-3*) NYU Pr.
Cohen, Nate. Home Maintenance for Residential Service Providers. (High Tide Disability Ser.: Vol. 2). 40p. 1997. spiral bd. 10.95 (*0-9653744-6-7*) High Tide Pr.
Cohen, Nathan M. Library Science Dissertations, 1925-1960: An Annotated Bibliography of Doctoral Studies. (Library Science Ser.). 1980. lib. bdg. 55.00 (*0-8490-3167-2*) Gordon Pr.
Cohen, Neal H. Miller's Clinical Case Companion. 1994. pap. 49.95 (*0-443-08961-2*) Church.
Cohen, Neal J. & Eichenbaum, Howard. Memory, Amnesia, & the Hippocampal System. (Illus.). 344p. 1995. reprint ed. pap. text 27.00 (*0-262-53132-1*, Bradford Bks) MIT Pr.
Cohen, Neal L., ed. Psychiatry Takes to the Streets: Outreach & Crisis Intervention for the Mentally Ill. LC 89-23741. 306p. 1990. lib. bdg. 42.00 (*0-89862-426-6*) Guilford Pubns.
Cohen, Neil. Everything You Want to Know about Sports Encyclopedia. (Illus.). 416p. (J). (gr. 4-7). 1994. pap. 9.99 (*0-553-48166-5*) Bantam.
Cohen, Neil. Everything You Wanted to Know About Sports Encyclopedia. (Sports Illustrated for Kids Ser.). (J). 1994. 14.09 (*0-606-06975-5*, Pub. by Turtleback) Demco.
Cohen, Neil. Magic Johnson. (J). 1992. pap. write for info. (*0-316-15050-9*) Little.
— Shaquille O'Neal. (J). 1996. pap. 4.99 (*0-553-54243-5*) BDD Bks Young Read.
***Cohen, Neil.** The Super Super Bowl Trivia Book. rev. ed. 48p. (J). (gr. 3-8). 2000. pap. 2.99 (*1-930623-01-1*) SI For Kids.
***Cohen, Neil A.** Child Welfare. 2nd ed. LC 99-26271. 278p. 1999. pap. text 37.00 (*0-205-29890-7*, Longwood Div) Allyn.
Cohen, Neil B., jt. auth. see McLaughlin, Gerald T.
Cohen, Neil P. & Hall, Donald J. Criminal Procedure: The Post-investigative Process : Cases & Materials LC 95-75142. (Contemporary Legal Eudcation Ser.). xxxi, 805 p. 1995. (*1-55834-216-8*, MICHIE) LEXIS Pub.
— Criminal Procedure: The Post-Investigative Process, Cases & Materials, 1999 Supplement. 200p. 1999. pap. write for info. (*0-327-01314-1*, 1089313) LEXIS Pub.
Cohen, Neil P., et al. Tennessee Law of Evidence. 3rd ed. LC 95-81088. 766p. 1995. 95.00 (*1-55834-288-5*, 65803-11, MICHIE) LEXIS Pub.
Cohen, Neil P., jt. auth. see Gobert, James J.
Cohen, Neil P., jt. auth. see Hall, Donald J.
Cohen, Nicholas & Sigel, Michael, eds. The Reticuloendothelial System Vol. 3: A Comprehensive Treatise: Phylogeny & Ontogeny. LC 79-25933. 790p. 1982. 135.00 (*0-306-40928-3*, Plenum Trade) Perseus Pubng.
***Cohen, Nick.** Cruel Britannia: Reports of the Sinister & Preposterous. 248p. 1999. 25.00 (*1-85984-720-X*, Pub. by Verso) Norton.
— Cruel Britannia: Reports on the Sinister & the Preposterous. 260p. 2000. pap. 15.00 (*1-85984-288-7*, Pub. by Verso) Norton.
***Cohen, Nick & Maguire, Kevin.** Blair's Babylon. 160p. 2000. pap. 20.00 (*1-85984-306-9*, Pub. by Verso) Norton.
Cohen, Norm. Long Steel Rail: The Railroad in American Folksong. LC 80-14874. (Music in American Life Ser.). (Illus.). 736p. 1981. pap. 18.95 (*0-252-01145-7*) U of Ill Pr.
***Cohen, Norm.** Long Steel Rail: The Railroad in American Folksong. 2nd ed. (Illus.). 744p. 2000. pap. 32.95 (*0-252-06881-5*) U of Ill Pr.
Cohen, Norm. Traditional Anglo-American Folk Music: An Annotated Discography of Published Sound Recordings. LC 93-26934. (Library of Music Ethnology: Vol. 2). 543p. 1993. text 30.00 (*0-8153-0377-7*, H1469) Garland.
Cohen, Norman. ADA as a Second Language. 2nd ed. LC 96-134097. 1133p. (C). 1995. pap. 79.38 (*0-07-011607-5*) McGraw.
Cohen, Norman, ed. see Horn, Arthur D. & Horn, Lynette M.
Cohen, Norman H. Mentoring Adult Learners: A Guide for Educators & Trainers. LC 94-36430. (Illus.). 224p. (C). 1995. 27.50 (*0-89464-850-0*) Krieger.
Cohen, Norman J. Self, Struggle & Change: Family Conflict Stories in Genesis & Their Healing Insights for Our Lives. LC 94-39880. 224p. 1995. 21.95 (*1-879045-19-2*) Jewish Lights.
— Self, Struggle & Change: Family Conflict Stories in Genesis & Their Healing Insights for Our Lives. LC 94-39880. 244p. 1996. pap. 16.95 (*1-879045-66-4*) Jewish Lights.
— Voices from Genesis: Guiding Us through the Stages of Life. LC 98-35476. 192p. 1998. 21.95 (*1-879045-75-3*) Jewish Lights.
***Cohen, Norman J.** The Way Into Torah. LC 00-23563. (Way Into... Ser.). 160p. 2000. 21.95 (*1-58023-028-8*) Jewish Lights.
Cohen, Norman J., ed. The Fundamentalist Phenomenon: A View from Within: a Response from Without. fac. ed. LC 90-31018. (Starkoff Institute Studies in Ethics & Contemporary Moral Problems). 280p. 1990. reprint ed. pap. 86.80 (*0-7837-7950-X*, 204770600008) Bks Demand.
Cohen, Norman J., jt. ed. see Seltzer, Robert M.
Cohen, Norman M. Jewish Bible Personages in the New Testament. 176p. (C). 1989. lib. bdg. 34.00 (*0-8191-7252-9*) U Pr of Amer.
Cohen, Norman S. The American Presidents. (Magill Bibliographies Ser.). 175p. 1989. 42.00 (*0-8108-2815-4*) Scarecrow.
Cohen, Octavus R. Bigger & Blacker. LC 78-106268. (Short Story Index Reprint Ser.). 1977. 27.95 (*0-8369-3305-2*) Ayer.
— Black & Blue. LC 71-106269. (Short Story Index Reprint Ser.). 1977. 28.95 (*0-8369-3306-0*) Ayer.
— Florian Slappey Goes Abroad. LC 70-130054. (Short Story Index Reprint Ser.). 1977. 18.95 (*0-8369-3570-5*) Ayer.
— Polished Ebony. LC 74-128725. (Short Story Index Reprint Ser.). (Illus.). 1977. 18.95 (*0-8369-3616-7*) Ayer.
Cohen, Oded, jt. auth. see Lepore, Domenico.
Cohen, P. Advances in Intelligent Data Analysis - Reasoning about Data: Proceedings, Second International Symposium, IDA-97, London, U. K., August 4-6, 1997. Liu, X. & Berthold, M., eds. LC 97-27840. (Lecture Notes in Computer Science Ser.: Vol. 1280). xii, 621p. pap. write for info. (*3-540-63346-4*) Spr-Verlag.
Cohen, P. I., et al, eds. Advances in Surface & Thin Film Diffraction Vol. 208: Materials Research Society Symposium Proceedings. 367p. 1991. text 50.00 (*1-55899-100-X*) Materials Res.
Cohen, P. T. & Volberding, Paul A. The AIDS Knowledge Base: A Textbook on HIV Disease from the University of California, San Francisco, & the San Francisco General Hospital. 2nd ed. Sande, Merle A., ed. LC 94-10498. (Illus.). 1552p. 1994. text 125.00 (*0-316-77067-1*) Lppncott W & W.
Cohen, P. T., et al. The AIDS Knowledge Base: A Textbook on HIV Disease from the University of California, San Francisco School of Medicine, & San Francisco General Hospital. 3rd ed. LC 98-38890. 1999. write for info. (*0-316-14903-9*, Little Brwn Med Div) Lppncott W & W.
Cohen, Pamela & Antoniotti, Walter. Mathematics Review. (Quick Notes Learning System Ser.). (Illus.). 20p. (Orig.). (YA). (gr. 4-12). 1998. pap. text 4.95 (*0-9632772-7-8*) Twen Frst Cent Lrn.
— Test-Prep Mathematics. rev. ed. (Quick Notes Learning System Ser.). (Illus.). 252p. (YA). (gr. 4-12). 1998. pap. text 14.95 (*0-9632772-6-X*) Twen Frst Cent Lrn.
Cohen, Patricia. The Best of Marco Island. (Illus.). 144p. (Orig.). 1996. pap. 6.95 (*1-879685-01-9*) Best of Bks Pubng.
— The Best of Sanibel & Captiva Islands. (Illus.). 144p. (Orig.). 1996. pap. 6.95 (*1-879685-00-0*) Best of Bks Pubng.
Cohen, Patricia, et al, eds. Historical & Geographical Influences on Psychopathology. LC 98-7194. 408p. 1998. 99.95 (*0-8058-2426-X*); pap. 45.00 (*0-8058-2427-8*) L Erlbaum Assocs.
Cohen, Patricia & Cohen, Jacob. Life Values & Adolescent Mental Health. (Research Monographs in Adolescence). 192p. 1995. text 45.00 (*0-8058-1774-3*) L Erlbaum Assocs.
Cohen, Patricia, jt. auth. see Cohen, Jacob.
Cohen, Patricia C. A Calculating People: The Spread of Numeracy in Early America. LC 82-7089. (Illus.). x, 276p. (C). 1983. lib. bdg. 22.50 (*0-226-11283-7*) U Ch Pr.
— A Calculating People: The Spread of Numeracy in Early America. LC 82-7089. (Illus.). x, 276p. (C). 1985. pap. 9.95 (*0-226-11284-5*) U Ch Pr.
***Cohen, Patricia C.** A Calculating People: The Spread of Numeracy in Early America LC 99-35030. 1999. pap. 17.99 (*0-415-92578-9*) Routledge.
Cohen, Patricia C. A Calculating People: The Spread of Numeracy in Early America. LC 82-7089. 281p. reprint ed. pap. 87.20 (*0-608-09287-8*, 205416100004) Bks Demand.
Cohen, Patricia C., et al. Serendipity & Synergy: Collection Development, Access & Research Opportunities at the American Antiquarian Society in the McCorison Era. 61p. 1993. pap. 9.50 (*0-944026-40-0*) Am Antiquarian.
Cohen, Patricia C., ed. see Roark, James L.
Cohen, Patricia Cline. The Murder of Helen Jewett: Life & Death of a Prostitute in 19th Century New York. LC 98-14561. (Illus.). 433p. 1998. 27.50 (*0-679-41291-3*) Random.
— The Murder of Helen Jewett: Life & Death of a Prostitute in 19th Century New York. (Vintage Ser.). (Illus.). 512p. 1999. pap. 14.00 (*0-679-74075-9*) Vin Bks.
Cohen, Patricia F., ed. see Bandy, Marcia & Bandy, Maurice.
Cohen, Patsy & Somerville, Margaret. Ingeleba & the Five Black Matriachs. (Illus.). 192p. (C). 1990. pap. text 17.95 (*0-04-442147-8*) Routledge.
Cohen, Paul. Discovering History in China: American Historical Writing on the Recent Chinese Past. LC 83-20868. 264p. 1985. pap. text 19.50 (*0-231-05811-X*) Col U Pr.
— History in Three Keys: The Boxers as Event, Experience, & Myth. LC 96-27118. (Illus.). 428p. 1998. pap. 19.50 (*0-231-10651-3*) Col U Pr.
— Water Coolant Technology of Power Reactors. LC 79-57306. (Monographs). 440p. 1980. reprint ed. 37.00 (*0-89448-020-0*, 300016) Am Nuclear Soc.
***Cohen, Paul & Shayler, Julie.** The Direct Marketing Industry Online: E-Commerce Practices for Direct Marketers, Publishers & Business Suppliers. unabridged ed. Gurney, Margaret, ed. (Illus.). 150p. 1999. 1295.00 (*1-58637-012-X*) ActivMedia.
Cohen, Paul, jt. ed. see Hesselbein, Frances.
Cohen, Paul A. Between Tradition & Modernity: Wang T'ao & Reform in Late Ch'ing China. LC 87-13606. (East Asian Monographs: No. 133). 347p. 1987. reprint ed. pap. 20.00 (*0-674-06876-9*) HUP.
— China & Christianity: The Missionary Movement & the Growth of Chinese Anti-Foreignism, 1860-1870. LC 63-19135. (Harvard East Asian Ser.: No. 11). (Illus.). 420p. 1963. reprint ed. pap. 130.20 (*0-7837-6070-1*, 205911600007) Bks Demand.
— History in Three Keys: The Boxers as Event, Experience, & Myth. LC 96-27118. 400p. 1997. 37.00 (*0-231-10650-5*) Col U Pr.
Cohen, Paul A. & Goldman, Merle R., eds. Ideas Across Cultures: Essays on Chinese Thought in Honor of Benjamin I. Schwartz. (East Asian Monographs: No. 150). 385p. 1990. 30.00 (*0-674-44225-3*) HUP.
Cohen, Paul A. & Schrecker, John E., eds. Reform in Nineteenth-Century China. (East Asian Monographs: No. 72). 349p. 1976. 20.00 (*0-674-75281-3*) HUP.
Cohen, Paul E. & Augustyn, Robert T. Manhattan in Maps, 1556-1990. LC 97-19200. (Illus.). 176p. 1997. 50.00 (*0-8478-2052-1*, Pub. by Rizzoli Intl) St Martin.
Cohen, Paul M. Freedom's Moment: An Essay on the French Idea of Liberty from Rousseau to Foucault. LC 96-17928. 1997. pap. text 13.95 (*0-226-11286-1*); lib. bdg. 39.95 (*0-226-11285-3*) U Ch Pr.
Cohen, Paul M., jt. ed. see Hesselbein, Frances.
Cohen, Paul R. Empirical Methods for Artificial Intelligence. 560p. 1995. 60.00 (*0-262-03225-2*, Bradford Bks) MIT Pr.
Cohen, Paul S. Growth of Scientific Ideas: Laboratory Manual. 120p. 1993. ring bd., lab manual ed. 33.95 (*0-8403-8980-9*) Kendall-Hunt.
Cohen, Paul S. & Cohen, Brenda H. America's Scientific Treasures: A Travel Companion. LC 97-51948. (An American Chemical Society Publication). (Illus.). 464p. 1998. pap. text 24.95 (*0-8412-3444-2*) OUP.
Cohen, Paula, et al. Long Island: The Golden Isle. LC 96-42432. 1996. pap. write for info. (*1-885352-51-4*) Community Comm.
Cohen, Paula M. Alfred Hitchcock: The Legacy of Victorianism. LC 95-2325. (Illus.). 208p. 1995. 34.95 (*0-8131-1930-8*); pap. 17.00 (*0-8131-0850-0*) U Pr of Ky.
— The Daughters As Reader: Encounters Between Literature & Life. LC 95-40044. 176p. (C). 1996. text 34.50 (*0-472-10693-7*, 10693) U of Mich Pr.
Cohen, Payl, jt. auth. see Cohen, Shari.
Cohen, Percy S., jt. ed. see Shack, William A.
***Cohen, Pete & Verity, Judith.** Doing It with Pete: The Lighten up Slimming Fun Book. 280p. 1998. pap. 19.95 (*1-899836-19-5*, Pub. by Crown Hse) LPC Group.
— Feeling Good for No Good Reason. (Essentials Ser.). (Illus.). 64p. 2000. pap. 9.95 (*1-85703-528-3*, Pub. by How To Bks) Midpt Trade.
Cohen, Pete & Verity, Judith. Slimming with Pete: Taking the Weight off Body & Mind. 280p. 1999. reprint ed. pap. 14.95 (*1-899836-13-6*, Pub. by Crown Hse) LPC Group.
Cohen, Peter F. Love & Anger: Essays on AIDS, Activism, & Politics. LC 97-51814. 194p. 1998. 39.95 (*0-7890-0455-0*, Harrington Park); pap. 16.95 (*1-56023-930-1*, Harrington Park) Haworth Pr.
Cohen, Peter J., jt. ed. see Healy, Thomas E. J.
Cohen, Peter R. Helping Your Chemically Dependent Teenager Recover: A Guide for Parents & Other Concerned Adults. 1991. pap. 12.00 (*1-56246-015-3*, 3178, HazeldenJohnson Inst) Hazelden.
Cohen, Phil. Children of the Revolution. LC 98-101443. (C). 1997. pap. 19.50 (*0-85315-841-X*, Pub. by Lawrence & Wishart) NYU Pr.
***Cohen, Phil.** New Ethnicities, Old Racisms. 2000. text 65.00 (*1-85649-651-1*) St Martin.
— New Ethnicities, Old Racisms. 1999. pap. text 22.50 (*1-85649-652-X*) Zed Books.
Cohen, Phil. Rethinking the Youth Question: Education, Labour, & Cultural Studies. LC 97-52379. 1998. write for info. (*0-8223-2136-X*); pap. 18.95 (*0-8223-2270-6*) Duke.
Cohen, Phil, ed. It Ain't Half Racist, Mum: Fighting Racism in the Media. 1982. 36.00 (*0-906890-31-4*); pap. 25.00 (*0-906890-30-6*) St Mut.
Cohen, Phil, jt. ed. see Schwarz, Bill.
Cohen, Philip. Control of Enzyme Activity. 2nd ed. (Outline Studies in Biology). 1983. pap. 8.50 (*0-412-25560-X*, 6870) Chapman & Hall.
— That They All May Be One: Relating to Different Backgrounds in the Church. 80p. 1997. pap. text 6.00 (*0-9656046-1-6*) Lghthse Pub TN.
Cohen, Philip, ed. Devils & Angels: Textual Editing & Literary Theory. xviii, 212p. (C). 1991. text 35.00 (*0-8139-1315-2*) U Pr of Va.
Cohen, Philip, ed. see American Water Resources Association Staff.
Cohen, Philip A., jt. auth. see Hess, Laura A.

C

An Asterisk (*) at the beginning of an entry indicates that the title is appearing for the first time.

Cohen, Philip G. Texts & Textuality: Textual Instability, Theory & Interpretation. LC 96-23047. (Wellesley Studies in Critical Theory, Literary History & Culture). 360p. 1997. text 80.00 (*0-8153-1956-8*) Garland.

Cohen, Philip J. Serbia's Secret War: Propaganda & the Deceit of History. LC 95-46662. (Eastern European Studies: Vol. 2). (Illus.). 264p. (C). 1997. pap. 15.95 (*0-89096-760-1*) Tex A&M Univ Pr.

Cohen, Philip K. The Moral Vision of Oscar Wilde. LC 76-50283. (Illus.). 287p. 1978. 38.50 (*0-8386-2052-3*) Fairleigh Dickinson.

Cohen, Philip R., et al, eds. Intentions in Communications. (System Development Foundation, Benchmark Ser.). 520p. 1990. 65.00 (*0-262-03150-7*) MIT Pr.

Cohen, Phillip. Weeping May Endure for a Night. (Illus.). 111p. (Orig.). 1996. pap. 6.00 (*0-9656046-0-8*) Lghthse Pub TN.

Cohen, Phillip M. Bathymetric Navigation & Charting. LC 79-6107. (Navies & Men Ser.). (Illus.). 1980. reprint ed. lib. bdg. 17.95 (*0-405-13036-8*) Ayer.

Cohen, Phyllis, ed. see Experience Las Vegas Staff.

Cohen, Phyllis, jt. ed. see Hammer, Hy.

Cohen-Posey, Kate. Brief Therapy Client Handouts. LC 99-40382. 256p. 2000. pap. 49.95 incl. disk (*0-471-32846-4*) Wiley.

— How to Handle Bullies, Teasers, & Other Meanies: A Book That Takes the Nuisance Out of Name Calling & Other Nonsense. LC 95-9191. (Illus.). 96p. (Orig.). (J). (gr. 4-7). 1995. pap. 8.95 (*1-56825-029-0*) Rainbow Books.

— Trans-Formation in Everyday Life: A Short Cut to Relaxation & Problem Solving. LC 94-78440. 102p. (Orig.). 1994. pap. 9.95 (*1-885961-00-6*) Leightons Sales.

***Cohen, Preston Scott.** Contested Symmetries: And Other Predicaments in Architecture. (Illus.). 176p. 2001. pap. 35.00 (*1-56898-250-X*) Princeton Arch.

Cohen, R. U. S. Half Cents. LC 81-53032. (Illus.). 1982. lib. bdg. 35.00 (*0-932106-12-9*) S J Durst.

Cohen, R., jt. ed. see Pilkey, W. D.

Cohen, R. A. The Neuropsychology of Attention. (Critical Issues in Neuropsychology Ser.). (Illus.). 566p. (C). 1993. text 85.00 (*0-306-43953-0*, Kluwer Plenum) Kluwer Academic.

Cohen, R. A., et al, eds. Trends in the Health of Older Americans: U. S., 1994. LC 94-44483. (Vital & Health Statistics, Series 3, Analytical & Epidemiological Studies: No. 30). 328p. 1995. 21.00 (*0-8406-0504-8*) Natl Ctr Health Stats.

Cohen, R. A. & Van Nostrand, J. F. Trends in the Health of Older Americans: U. S., 1994. (Illus.). 326p. 1996. pap. text 45.00 (*0-7881-2796-9*) DIANE Pub.

Cohen, R. L. House Officer: Becoming a Medical Specialist. LC 88-17930. (Illus.). 272p. (C). 1988. text 36.50 (*0-306-42942-X*, Kluwer Plenum) Kluwer Academic.

Cohen, R. L. Justice: Views from the Social Sciences. LC 86-20503. (Critical Issues in Social Justice Ser.). (Illus.). 296p. (C). 1986. 52.50 (*0-306-42256-5*, Plenum Trade) Perseus Pubng.

Cohen, R. L. Psychiatric Consultation in Childbirth Settings: Parent- & Child-Oriented Approaches. LC 88-6005. (Illus.). 298p. (C). 1988. text 57.50 (*0-306-42758-3*, Kluwer Plenum) Kluwer Academic.

Cohen, R. S., et al, eds. Boston Studies in the Philosophy of Science, Vol. 15: Scientific, Historical & Political Essays in Honor of Dirk J. Struik. LC 73-83556. (Synthese Library: No. 61). 679p. 1974. pap. text 148.50 (*90-277-0379-5*, D Reidel); lib. bdg. 194.00 (*90-277-0393-0*, D Reidel) Kluwer Academic.

— Essays in Memory of Imre Lakatos. LC 76-16770. (Synthese Library: No. 99). 778p. 1976. pap. text 148.50 (*90-277-0655-7*, D Reidel); lib. bdg. 216.50 (*90-277-0654-9*, D Reidel) Kluwer Academic.

Cohen, R. S. & Seeger, R. J., eds. Boston Studies in the Philosophy of Science: Ernst Mach, Physicist & Philosopher, Vol. 6. (Synthese Library: No. 27). 303p. 1975. text 94.00 (*90-277-0016-8*, D Reidel) Kluwer Academic.

Cohen, R. S. & Stachel, J. J., eds. Leon Rosenfeld: Selected Papers. (Synthese Library: No. 100). 963p. 1978. pap. text 115.50 (*90-277-0652-2*, D Reidel); lib. bdg. 245.50 (*90-277-0651-4*, D Reidel) Kluwer Academic.

Cohen, R. S., et al. Potentiality, Entanglement & Passion-at-a-Distance, Vol. 2. LC 97-189206. 1997. lib. bdg. 136.00 (*0-7923-4453-7*) Kluwer Academic.

Cohen, R. S., ed. see American Association for the Advancement of Science Staff.

Cohen, R. S., ed. see Colloquium for the Philosophy of Science Staff.

Cohen, R. S., ed. see Mittelstaedt, Peter.

Cohen, R. S., jt. ed. see Neurath, Maria.

Cohen, R. S., ed. see Philosophy of Science Association Staff.

Cohen, R. S., ed. & tr. see Helmholtz, Hermann.

Cohen, Ralph. New Directions in Literary History. LC 73-8115. (Illus.). 277p. reprint ed. pap. 85.90 (*0-8357-6743-4*, 203539800095) Bks Demand.

— The Unfolding of the Seasons. LC 70-82867. 350p. reprint ed. pap. 108.50 (*0-608-11889-3*, 202308800032) Bks Demand.

Cohen, Ralph, ed. The Future of Literary Theory. 600p. 1988. text 59.50 (*0-415-90077-8*) Routledge.

— Studies in Historical Change. LC 91-36668. 335p. reprint ed. pap. 103.90 (*0-608-10478-7*, 207109600008) Bks Demand.

Cohen, Ralph, et al, eds. Algebraic Topology & Its Applications. LC 93-5264. 1993. 79.95 (*0-387-94098-7*) Spr-Verlag.

Cohen, Ralph & Peck, Jeffrey M., eds. New Literary History International Bibliography of Literary Theory & Criticism (1984-85) LC 88-3016. xix, 188p. 1989. text 32.00 (*0-8018-3687-5*) Johns Hopkins.

Cohen, Ralph & Roth, Michael S., eds. History &... Histories Within the Human Sciences. 448p. (C). 1995. pap. text 22.50 (*0-8139-1499-X*) U Pr of Va.

Cohen, Ralph L. Odd Primary Infinite Families in Stable Homotopy Theory. LC 80-28537. (Memoirs Ser.: No. 30/242). 92p. 1981. pap. 16.00 (*0-8218-2242-X*, MEMO/30/242) Am Math.

Cohen, Randy, ed. United Arts Fundraising, 1997. (Illus.). 20p. 1997. spiral bd. 32.50 (*1-879903-04-0*) Am for the Arts.

Cohen, Raquel E. & Ahearn, Frederick L., Jr. Handbook for Mental Health Care of Disaster Victims. LC 80-81426. 144p. 1980. reprint ed. pap. 44.70 (*0-608-05934-X*, 206627000008) Bks Demand.

Cohen, Raymond. Amarna Diplomacy: The Beginnings of International Relations. LC 99-30915. 312p. 1999. 48.00 (*0-8018-6199-3*) Johns Hopkins.

— Culture & Conflict in Egyptian-Israeli Relations: A Dialogue of the Deaf. LC 89-45478. 206p. 1990. 29.95 (*0-253-31379-1*) Ind U Pr.

— International Politics: The Rules of the Game. LC 80-41594. 192p. reprint ed. pap. 59.60 (*0-7837-1593-5*, 204188500024) Bks Demand.

— Negotiating Across Cultures: International Communication in an Interdependent World. rev. ed. LC 97-45198. 1997. pap. 19.95 (*1-878379-72-0*) US Inst Peace.

— Theatre of Power: The Art of Diplomatic Signalling. LC 86-15300. 239p. (Orig.). reprint ed. pap. 74.10 (*0-7837-1586-2*, 204187800024) Bks Demand.

— Threat Perception in International Crisis. LC 79-3964. 239p. 1979. reprint ed. pap. 74.10 (*0-608-01944-5*, 206259900003) Bks Demand.

Cohen, Renae, ed. see Smith, Tom W.

Cohen, Rhoda, jt. auth. see Caiserman-Roth, Ghitta.

Cohen, Ricardo, et al, eds. Tropical Surgery. LC 96-27741. (Vademecum Series Book). (Illus.). xx, 338p. 1997. 98.00 (*3-8055-6497-X*) S Karger.

Cohen, Ricardo V. & Aun, Frederico. Tropical Disease. LC 96-27741. (On Call In...Ser.). 362p. 1997. write for info. (*1-57059-356-6*) Landes Bioscience.

***Cohen, Rich.** The Avengers. LC 00-21062. 2000. pap. write for info. (*0-375-70529-5*) Knopf.

— The Avengers: A Jewish War Story. LC 00-21062. (Illus.). 272p. 2000. 25.00 (*0-375-40546-1*) Knopf.

Cohen, Rich. Tough Jews: Fathers, Sons & Gangster Dreams in Jewish America. LC 98-41410. 1999. pap. 13.00 (*0-375-70547-3*) Knopf.

— Tough Jews: Fathers, Sons & Gangster Dreams in Jewish America. LC 97-39282. 288p. 1998. 25.00 (*0-684-83115-5*) S&S Trade.

Cohen, Richard. Housing Trust Funds in New Jersey. 100p. 1987. 10.95 (*0-89788-103-6*) CPA Washington.

***Cohen, Richard.** Pronoun Music. 260p. 2000. pap. write for info. (*1-929355-03-3*) Pleasure Boat.

Cohen, Richard. Say You Want Me. LC 88-4492. 268p. 1988. 17.95 (*0-939149-12-5*) Soho Press.

— The School Mediator's Field Guide: Prejudice, Sexual Harassment, Large Groups & Other Daily Challenges. 256p. 1999. pap. 24.95 (*0-9664408-0-3*) School Mediation.

— Students Resolving Conflict: Peer Mediation in Schools. 400p. (Orig.). 1995. pap. text 14.95 (*0-673-36096-2*, GoodYrBooks) Addson-Wesley Educ.

— Writer's Mind: Crafting Fiction. (Illus.). 288p. 1994. 19.95 (*0-8442-5819-9*, 58199, Passprt Bks) NTC Contemp Pub Co.

— Writer's Mind: Crafting Fiction. LC 94-66706. (Illus.). 288p. 1996. pap. 12.95 (*0-8442-5864-4*, 58644) NTC Contemp Pub Co.

Cohen, Richard, et al. Snail Trails & Tadpole Tails: Nature Education for Young Children. LC 93-5850. (Illus.). 96p. (Orig.). 1993. pap. text 13.95 (*0-934140-78-2*, 4570) Redleaf Pr.

Cohen, Richard, jt. auth. see Bailey, Norman A.

Cohen, Richard, tr. see Levinas, Emmanuel.

Cohen, Richard A. Alfie's Home. LC 93-78368. (Illus.). 30p. (J). (gr. 3-12). 1993. 14.95 (*0-9637058-0-6*) Intl Healing.

***Cohen, Richard A.** Coming Out Straight: Understanding & Healing Homosexuality. LC 00-21844. (Illus.). 312p. 2000. 27.95 (*1-886939-41-1*, Pub. by OakHill Pr VA) ACCESS Pubs Network.

Cohen, Richard A. Elevations: The Height of the Good in Rosenzweig & Levinas. LC 94-1165. (Chicago Studies in the History of Judaism). 364p. 1994. lib. bdg. 44.00 (*0-226-11274-8*) U Ch Pr.

— Elevations: The Height of the Good in Rosenzweig & Levinas. LC 94-1165. (Chicago Studies in the History of Judaism). 364p. 1994. pap. text 17.95 (*0-226-11275-6*) U Ch Pr.

Cohen, Richard A., ed. see Rosenzweig, Franz.

Cohen, Richard A., tr. see Levinas, Emmanuel.

Cohen, Richard A., tr. & intro. see Levinas, Emmanuel.

***Cohen, Richard E.** Physics Quick Reference Guide. 2nd ed. (Illus.). 2000. pap. text 29.95 (*0-387-98986-2*) Spr-Verlag.

Cohen, Richard E. Rostenkowski: The Pursuit of Power & the End of the Old Politics. LC 99-25239. (Illus.). 320p. 1999. 27.50 (*1-56663-254-4*, Pub. by I R Dee) Natl Bk Netwk.

***Cohen, Richard E.** Rostenkowski: The Pursuit of Power & the End of the Old Politics. (Illus.). 320p. 2000. reprint ed. pap. 15.95 (*1-56663-310-9*, Pub. by I R Dee) Natl Bk Netwk.

Cohen, Richard E. Washington at Work. 2nd ed. LC 94-26095. 256p. 1994. pap. text 32.46 (*0-02-323200-5*, Macmillan Coll) P-H.

Cohen, Richard E., jt. auth. see Hagin, Frank G.

Cohen, Richard I. The Burden of Conscience: French Jewish Leadership during the Holocaust. LC 85-45991. (Modern Jewish Experience Ser.). (Illus.). 252p. 1987. 35.00 (*0-253-31263-9*) Ind U Pr.

— Jewish Icons: Art & Society in Modern Europe. LC 96-45375. 382p. 1998. 50.00 (*0-520-20545-6*, Pub. by U CA Pr) Cal Prin Full Svc.

Cohen, Richard I., jt. auth. see Mann, Vivian B.

Cohen, Richard I., jt. ed. see Mendelsohn, Ezra.

Cohen, Richard M. World Series, No. 2. 3rd ed. 1986. pap. 22.50 (*0-02-526980-1*) Macmillan.

— World Trade & Payments Cycles: The Advance & Retreat of the Postwar Order. LC 89-3856. 322p. 1989. 65.00 (*0-275-93251-6*, C3251, Praeger Pubs) Greenwood.

Cohen, Richard M. & Neft, David S. The World Series. 448p. 1990. pap. 16.95 (*0-685-28832-3*) St Martin.

Cohen, Richard M. & Wilson, Peter A. Superpowers in Economic Decline. (Illus.). 350p. (C). 1990. text 49.50 (*0-685-32668-3*, Crane Russak); pap. text 27.00 (*0-685-32669-1*, Crane Russak) Taylor & Francis.

Cohen, Richard M., jt. auth. see Neft, David S.

Cohen, Richard S. The Love Drug: Marching to the Beat of Ecstasy. LC 97-39231. 166p. 1998. 39.95 (*0-7890-0453-4*, Hawrth Medical); pap. 19.95 (*0-7890-0454-2*, Hawrth Medical) Haworth Pr.

***Cohen, Ricky.** Attracting Your Extraordinary Love: Thoughts for Living. xiiii, 94p. 2000. pap. 19.95 (*1-893077-96-9*) Hues Blue.

— From Me to My Children: Bubbles of Thought Trilogy. (Illus.). v, 35p. 1999. pap. 35.00 (*1-893077-99-3*) Hues Blue.

Cohen, Rip. Thirty-Two Cantigas d'Amigo of Dom Diniz: Typology of a Portuguese Renunciation. (Portuguese Ser.: No. 1). 1987. 12.50 (*0-942260-55-4*) Hispanic Seminary.

Cohen, Rob, ed. Scream When You Burn: A Pound of Seared Flesh from the Lap of Coffee Culture. 200p. (Orig.). 1996. pap. 14.00 (*1-888277-00-9*) Incommcdo San Diego.

Cohen, Robbin G., ed. Minimally Invasive Cardiac Surgery. LC 99-10903. 359p. 1999. 245.00 (*0-942219-79-1*) Quality Med Pub.

Cohen, Robert. Acting in Shakespeare. LC 90-36912. 230p. (C). 1991. text 48.95 (*0-87484-951-9*, 951) Mayfield Pub.

— Acting One. 3rd rev. ed. LC 97-14556. 242p. (C). 1997. text 40.95 (*1-55934-940-9*, 1940) Mayfield Pub.

— Acting Power. LC 77-89918. 266p. (C). 1978. text 44.95 (*0-87484-408-8*, 408) Mayfield Pub.

— Acting Professionally: Raw Facts about Careers in Acting. 5th rev. ed. LC 97-14559. (Illus.). 177p. (C). 1997. pap. text 17.95 (*1-55934-941-7*, 1941) Mayfield Pub.

— The Development of Spatial Cognition. 416p. 1985. 89.95 (*0-89859-543-6*) L Erlbaum Assocs.

— Eight Plays for Theatre. LC 87-31437. 275p. 1988. pap. text 26.95 (*0-87484-850-4*, 850) Mayfield Pub.

— Focus on Reading & Writing: Advanced Level. LC 97-41539. 288p. 1997. pap. text 23.10 (*0-201-69421-2*) Addison-Wesley.

— Giraudoux: Three Faces of Destiny. LC 68-29058. 1970. pap. text 2.45 (*0-226-11248-9*, P371) U Ch Pr.

— The Here & Now. 1997. per. 11.00 (*0-684-83141-4*, Scribner Pap Fic) S&S Trade Pap.

***Cohen, Robert.** Inspired Sleep. 2001. 25.00 (*0-684-85079-6*) Scribner.

Cohen, Robert. Jews in Another Environment: Surinam in the Second Half of the Eighteenth Century. LC 91-14402. (Jewish Studies: No. 1). xv, 350p. 1991. 119.00 (*90-04-09373-7*) Brill Academic Pubs.

— Majorski's Ghost: A Marty Fenton Novel. LC 95-12322. 1995. pap. 14.95 (*0-925168-39-4*) North Country.

— Milk: The Deadly Poison. unabridged ed. LC 97-94585. (Illus.). 317p. 1998. 24.95 (*0-9659196-0-9*) Argus Pub.

— New Careers Grow Older: A Perspective on the Paraprofessional Experience, 1965-1975. LC 76-26036. (Policy Studies in Employment & Welfare: No. 26). 144p. reprint ed. pap. 44.70 (*0-608-11888-5*, 202308900032) Bks Demand.

***Cohen, Robert.** The Theatre. 5th ed. LC 98-53678. 1999. pap. text 46.95 (*0-7674-0493-9*) Mayfield Pub.

Cohen, Robert. Theatre: Brief Version. 5th ed. LC 98-52451. 1999. pap. text 40.95 (*0-7674-0494-7*) Mayfield Pub.

— Understanding Peter Weiss. LC 93-17439. (Understanding Modern European & Latin American Literature Ser.). 225p. 1993. text 29.95 (*0-87249-898-0*) U of SC Pr.

— Versuche Ueber Weiss' Astheetik des Widerstands. (New York University Ottendorfer Series: Neue Folge: Vol. 33). 256p. (C). 1989. text 39.00 (*3-261-03974-4*) P Lang Pubng.

— When the Old Left Was Young: Student Radicals & America's First Mass Student Movement, 1929-1941. (Illus.). 456p. 1997. reprint ed. pap. 24.95 (*0-19-511136-2*) OUP.

Cohen, Robert, ed. Twelve Plays for the Theatre. LC 93-2608. 628p. 1993. pap. text 37.95 (*1-55934-144-0*, 1144) Mayfield Pub.

Cohen, Robert & Donow, Kenneth. Telecommunications Policy, High Definition Television, & U. S. Competitiveness. LC 89-80758. 50p. 1989. 12.00 (*0-944826-10-5*) Economic Policy Inst.

Cohen, Robert & Siegel, Alexander, eds. Context & Development. 336p. (C). 1991. text 69.95 (*0-8058-0481-1*) L Erlbaum Assocs.

Cohen, Robert, ed. see Ickowicz, Charles.

Cohen, Robert, ed. see Liberson, Wladimir T.

Cohen, Robert, ed. see Weiss, Peter.

Cohen, Robert, tr. see Moliere.

Cohen, Robert S. Acting Professionally: Raw Facts about Careers in Acting. 3rd ed. 1982. pap. 7.95 (*0-06-463453-1*, EH 570) HarpC.

— Experimental Metaphysics. LC 97-2399. 1997. lib. bdg. 130.00 (*0-7923-4452-9*) Kluwer Academic.

Cohen, Robert S., ed. Herbert Feigl: Inquiries & Provocations, Selected Writings. 1929 to 1974. (Vienna Circle Collection: No. 14). 466p. 1980. lib. bdg. 123.50 (*90-277-1101-1*, D Reidel) Kluwer Academic.

— Herbert Feigl: Inquiries & Provocations, Selected Writings. 1929 to 1974. (Vienna Circle Collection: No. 14). 466p. 1980. pap. text 78.00 (*90-277-1102-X*, D Reidel) Kluwer Academic.

— Realism & Anti-Realism in the Philosophy of Science: Beijing International Conference, 1992. LC 94-39752. (Boston Studies in the Philosophy of Science: Vol. 169). 510p. (C). 1996. lib. bdg. 207.50 (*0-7923-3233-4*, Pub. by Kluwer Academic) Kluwer Academic.

Cohen, Robert S., et al, eds. Experimental Metaphysics. LC 97-2399. (Boston Studies in the Philosophy of Science). 1997. text 239.00 (*0-7923-4454-5*) Kluwer Academic.

— Progress & Rationality in Science. (Boston Studies in the Philosophy of Science: No. 58). 426p. 1978. lib. bdg. 117.50 (*90-277-0921-1*) Kluwer Academic.

Cohen, Robert S. & Harrop, John. Creative Play Direction. 2nd ed. (Illus.). 352p. 1983. 83.00 (*0-13-190926-6*) P-H.

Cohen, Robert S. & Schnelle, Thomas, eds. Cognition & Fact: Materials on Ludwik Fleck. 480p. 1986. text 201.00 (*90-277-1902-0*, D Reidel) Kluwer Academic.

Cohen, Robert S. & Tauber, Alfred I., eds. Philosophies of Nature: The Human Dimension. LC 97-16262. (Boston College Studies in Philosophy of Science 95). 352p. 1998. 140.00 (*0-7923-4579-7*) Kluwer Academic.

Cohen, Robert S. & Wartofsky, Marx W. Epistemology, Methodology, & the Social Sciences. 271p. 1983. text 160.00 (*90-277-1454-1*, D Reidel) Kluwer Academic.

— Hegel & the Sciences. 383p. 1984. text 206.50 (*90-277-0726-X*, D Reidel) Kluwer Academic.

— Language, Logic & Method. 484p. 1982. text 234.00 (*90-277-0725-1*, D Reidel) Kluwer Academic.

— Physical Sciences & the History of Physics. 272p. 1983. text 148.50 (*90-277-1615-3*, D Reidel) Kluwer Academic.

Cohen, Robert S. & Wartofsky, Marx W., eds. Methodology, Metaphysics & the History of Science: In Memory of Benjamin Nelson. (Boston Studies in the Philosophy of Science: No. 84). 384p. 1984. text 206.50 (*90-277-1711-7*) Kluwer Academic.

— A Portrait of Twenty-Five Years. 336p. 1985. pap. text 53.50 (*90-277-1971-3*, D Reidel) Kluwer Academic.

Cohen, Robert S., et al. Physics, Philosophy & Psychoanalysis. 356p. 1983. text 191.50 (*90-277-1533-5*, D Reidel) Kluwer Academic.

Cohen, Robert S., jt. ed. see Agassi, Joseph.

Cohen, Robert S., jt. ed. see Dainian, Fan.

Cohen, Robert S., jt. ed. see Ginev, Dimitri.

Cohen, Robert S., jt. ed. see Gould, Carol C.

Cohen, Robert S., ed. see Kaila, Eiono.

Cohen, Robert S., jt. ed. see Kucuradi, Ioanna.

Cohen, Robert S., jt. ed. see Marion, Mathieu.

Cohen, Robert S., ed. see Neurath, Otto.

Cohen, Robert S., jt. ed. see Ramirez, Santiago.

Cohen, Robert S., ed. see Reichenbach, H.

Cohen, Robert S., ed. see Tamas, Gyorgy.

Cohen, Robert S., jt. ed. see Woodward, William R.

Cohen, Robert S., ed. & tr. see Frank, Philipp.

Cohen, Robert S., tr. see Canguilhem, Georges.

Cohen, Roberta. People's Republic of China: The Human Rights Exception, No. 3. 103p. 1988. 5.00 (*0-942182-89-8*, 86) Occasional Papers.

Cohen, Roberta & Deng, Francis M. Masses in Flight: The Global Crisis of Internal Displacement. LC 98-8939. 414p. 1998. text 52.95 (*0-8157-1512-9*); pap. text 22.95 (*0-8157-1511-0*) Brookings.

Cohen, Roberta & Deng, Francis M., eds. The Forsaken People: Case Studies of the Internally Displaced. LC 98-8942. 420p. 1998. pap. 22.95 (*0-8157-1513-7*); text 52.95 (*0-8157-1514-5*) Brookings.

Cohen, Roberta G., jt. auth. see Lipkin, Gladys B.

Cohen, Robin. Contested Domains: Debates in International Labour Studies. 208p. (C). 1991. text 22.50 (*1-85649-013-0*, Pub. by Zed Books) St Martin.

— Endgame in South Africa? The Changing Structures & Ideology of Apartheid. LC 88-70604. 120p. (C). 1988. reprint ed. 24.95 (*0-86543-090-X*); reprint ed. pap. 7.95 (*0-86543-091-8*) Africa World.

— Frontiers of Identity: The British & Others. LC 94-11852. (Longman Sociology Ser.). 1994. text. write for info. (*0-582-24577-X*, Pub. by Addison-Wesley) Longman.

— Frontiers of Identity: The British & the Others. LC 94-11852. (Longman Sociology Ser.). 264p. (C). 1995. pap. 34.60 (*0-582-24576-1*, 77017) Longman.

— Global Diasporas Vol. 1: An Introduction. 224p. 1997. 50.00 (*0-295-97619-5*); pap. 19.95 (*0-295-97620-9*) U of Wash Pr.

— The New Helots: Migrants in the International Division of Labour. 250p. 1987. text 78.95 (*0-566-00932-3*, Pub. by Avebry) Ashgate Pub Co.

Cohen, Robin, ed. African Islands & Enclaves. LC 83-2997. (Sage Series on African Modernization & Development: No. 7). 279p. 1983. reprint ed. pap. 86.50 (*0-608-01084-7*, 205939300001) Bks Demand.

— The Cambridge Survey of World Migration. (Illus.). 592p. (C). 1995. text 135.00 (*0-521-44405-5*) Cambridge U Pr.

— The Sociology of Migration. LC 96-12607. (International Library of Studies on Migration: Vol. 3). 576p. (C). 1996. text 215.00 (*1-85898-000-3*) E Elgar.

— Theories of Migration. LC 96-14469. (International Library of Studies on Migration: Vol. 1). 544p. (C). 1996. text 200.00 (*1-85898-001-1*) E Elgar.

Cohen, Robin, et al, eds. Peasants & Proletarians: The Struggles of Third World Workers. fac. ed. LC 79-10020. 505p. pap. 156.60 (*0-7837-7548-2*, 204680800005) Bks Demand.

C

An Asterisk (*) at the beginning of an entry indicates that the title is appearing for the first time.

— Repression & Resistance: Insiders' Account of Apartheid. (African Discourse Ser.: Vol. 2). 320p. 1990. 65.00 (*0-905450-86-8*, Pub. by H Zell Pubs) Seven Hills Bk.

***Cohen, Robin & Kennedy, Paul M.** Global Sociology. LC 00-21548. 2000. pap. write for info. (*0-8147-1610-5*) NYU Pr.

Cohen, Robin & Layton-Henry, Zig, eds. The Politics of Migration. LC 97-22599. (International Library of Studies on Migration: No. 5). 360p. 1997. 135.00 (*1-85898-014-3*) E Elgar.

***Cohen, Robin & Rai, Shirin.** Global Social Movements. LC 99-87577. 2000. pap. write for info. (*0-485-00615-4*, Pub. by Athlone Pr) Humanities.

Cohen, Robin, jt. ed. see Cobbett, William.

Cohen, Robin, jt. ed. see Johy, Daniele.

Cohen, Robin, jt. ed. see Sandbrook, Richard.

Cohen, Robin, jt. ed. see Vertovec, Steven.

Cohen, Robin A. Access to Health Care: Older Adults, Vol. 3. 36p. 1997. pap. 4.00 (*0-16-049120-7*) USGPO.

Cohen, Robin A., et al, eds. Chartbook on Health Data on Older Americans: United States, 1992. LC 92-48231. (Vital & Health Statistics Ser.: Series 3, No. 29). (Illus.). 1992. write for info. (*0-8406-0475-0*) Natl Ctr Health Stats.

Cohen, Robyn & Rousso, Robyn. The Yiddish Are Coming. LC 94-77583. (Illus.). 56p. 1994. pap. 8.95 (*1-56352-169-5*) Longstreet.

Cohen, Robyn L., jt. auth. see Langan, Patrick A.

***Cohen, Rodney T.** The Black Colleges of Atlanta. (College History Ser.). (Illus.). 128p. 2000. pap. 19.99 (*0-7385-0554-4*, Pub. by Tempus Pubng) Arcadia Publng.

Cohen, Roger. Hearts Grown Brutal: Sagas of Sarajevo. LC 99-204500. 400p. 1998. 29.95 (*0-679-45243-5*) Random.

Cohen, Roger & Gatti, Claudio. In the Eye of the Storm: The Life of General H. Norman Schwarzkopf. large type ed. (General Ser.). 478p. 1992. lib. bdg. 21.95 (*0-8161-5359-0*, G K Hall Lrg Type) Mac Lib Ref.

Cohen, Ronald, ed. Satisfying Africa's Food Needs: Food Production & Commercialization in African Agriculture. LC 88-3164. 244p. 1988. lib. bdg. 35.00 (*1-55587-083-X*) L Rienner.

Cohen, Ronald, et al, eds. Human Rights & Governance in Africa. LC 93-14893. (Carter Lecture Series, Center for African Studies). 312p. 1993. 49.95 (*0-8130-1220-1*) U Press Fla.

Cohen, Ronald, ed. see Carpenter, Allan & Balow, Tom.

Cohen, Ronald C., ed. see Reuss, Richard A. & Reuss, JoAnne C.

Cohen, Ronald D. Children of the Mill: Schooling & Society in Gary, Indiana, 1906-1960. LC 89-45477. (Midwestern History & Culture Ser.). 296p. 1990. 13.95 (*0-253-31377-5*) Ind U Pr.

— Children of the Mill: Schooling & Society in Gary, Indiana 1906-1960. LC 89-45477. (Midwestern History & Culture Ser.). (Illus.). 294p. Date not set. reprint ed. pap. 91.20 (*0-608-20535-4*, 205444900002) Bks Demand.

Cohen, Ronald D., ed. Wasn't That a Time! Firsthand Accounts of the Folk Music Revival. LC 94-24902. (American Folk Music & Musicians Ser.: No. 1). (Illus.). 258p. 1995. 34.50 (*0-8108-2955-X*) Scarecrow.

Cohen, Ronald D., ed. see Chicago, South Shore & South Bend Railroad Staff, et al.

Cohen, Ronald D., ed. see Cunningham, Agnes & Friesen, Gordon.

Cohen, Ronald E., ed. First-Principles Calculations for Ferroelectrics: Fifth Williamsburg Workshop. LC 98-71901. (Conference Proceedings Ser.: Vol. 436). (Illus.). 302p. 1998. 95.00 (*1-56396-730-8*) Spr-Verlag.

Cohen, Ronald J. & Demore, Paula M. Powerful Witness Preparation. 223p. 1995. pap. 185.00 incl. audio (*0-943380-97-9*) PEG MN.

— Preparing for & Conducting a Winning Deposition. 265p. 1995. pap. 185.00 incl. audio (*0-943380-99-5*) PEG MN.

***Cohen, Ronald J., et al.** Exercises in Psychological Testing & Assessment: An Introduction to Tests & Measurement. 4th ed. 1999. pap. text, student ed. 20.95 (*0-7674-0510-2*) Mayfield Pub.

Cohen, Ronald J., et al. Psychological Testing & Assessment: An Introduction to Tests & Measurement. 4th ed. LC 98-20417. xxvii, 769p. 1998. text 71.95 (*0-7674-0509-9*, 0509-9) Mayfield Pub.

Cohen, Ronald J., jt. auth. see Santoro, Joseph.

Cohen, Ronnie A. & Curtis, Jennifer. Agricultural Solutions: Improving Water Quality in California Through Water Conservation & Pesticide Reduction. (Illus.). 68p. 1998. pap. 7.50 (*1-893340-10-4*) Natl Resources Defense Coun.

Cohen, Ronny. Colunga. (Illus.). 24p. 1990. 20.00 (*0-925941-02-6*) Dorsky Gallery.

Cohen, Rose. Out of the Shadow: A Russian Jewish Girlhood on the Lower East Side. (Documents in American Social History Ser.). (Illus.). 336p. 1995. text 39.95 (*0-8014-3156-5*); pap. text 15.95 (*0-8014-8268-2*) Cornell U Pr.

Cohen, Rose N. The Financial Control of Education in the Consolidated City of New York. LC 79-176700. (Columbia University. Teachers College. Contributions to Education Ser.: No. 943). reprint ed. 37.50 (*0-404-55943-3*) AMS Pr.

***Cohen, Rosemary H.** Korban: The Sacrifice Of Liana, 1. LC 98-94076. 285p. 1998. 24.95 (*0-9667361-0-9*) LICO Publ.

Cohen-Rosenthal, Edward. Unions, Management, & Quality: Opportunities for Innovation & Excellence. 275p. 35.00 (*0-614-04832-X*, DJ21H) Assn Qual & Part.

Cohen-Rosenthal, Edward & Burton, Cynthia E. Mutual Gains: A Guide to Union-Management Cooperation. LC 86-25249. 302p. 1986. 57.95 (*0-275-92204-9*, C2204, Praeger Pubs) Greenwood.

— Mutual Gains: A Guide to Union-Management Cooperation. 2nd rev. ed. LC 93-11918. 360p. 1993. pap. text 26.95 (*0-87546-312-6*, ILR Press) Cornell U Pr.

Cohen, Rosetta M. Domestic Scenes. 1982. pap. 4.00 (*0-936600-02-0*) Riverstone Foothills.

— A Lifetime of Teaching: Portraits of Five Veteran High School Teachers. 136p. (C). 1991. text 33.00 (*0-8077-3096-3*); pap. text 16.95 (*0-8077-3095-5*) Tchrs Coll.

— Understanding How School Change Really Happens: Reform at Brookville High. LC 95-22652. 168p. 1995. 51.95 (*0-8039-6254-1*); pap. 22.95 (*0-8039-6255-X*) Corwin Pr.

Cohen, Rosetta M. & Scheer, Samuel, eds. The Work of Teachers in America: A Social History Through Stories. 352p. 1997. 79.95 (*0-8058-2690-4*) L Erlbaum Assocs.

— The Work of Teachers in America: A Social History Through Stories. LC 96-43350. 304p. 1997. pap. text 32.50 (*0-8058-2250-X*) L Erlbaum Assocs.

Cohen, Roy. Obsessive Compulsive Disorder: A Survival Guide for Family & Friends. LC 93-83800. 90p. 1993. pap. 9.95 (*0-9628066-1-7*) OCA.

Cohen, Ruth. Elements of Play in Bridge. (Ideal Student Textbooks Ser.). 80p. (Orig.). 1961. pap. 4.95 (*0-87643-007-8*) Barclay Bridge.

— Whose File Is It Anyway? (C). 1988. 40.00 (*0-901108-97-9*, Pub. by NCCL) St Mut.

Cohen, Ruth, et al. Quest: Academic Skills Program. 293p. (C). 1973. pap. text, teacher ed. 2.50 (*0-15-574611-1*) Harcourt Coll Pubs.

Cohen, Ruth, jt. auth. see Michaels, Charles.

Cohen, Ruth L. Neighborhood Network Conversations on Nutrition. 150p. (Orig.). 1992. pap. 11.50 (*0-9633720-0-9*) Environ Comms.

Cohen, S. Eric Owen Moss: The Box. LC 94-66961. 128p. 1996. pap. 24.95 (*1-56898-033-7*) Princeton Arch.

Cohen, S., et al. Behavior, Health, & Environmental Stress. (Illus.). 294p. (C). 1986. 49.50 (*0-306-42138-0*, Plenum Trade) Perseus Pubng.

Cohen, S., ed. see International Convocation in Immunology Staff.

Cohen, S. B. Children in Halachah. 1993. 18.99 (*0-89906-611-9*); 15.99 (*0-89906-612-7*) Mesorah Pubns.

— Sanctity of Shabbos. (ArtScroll Halachah Ser.). 1992. 18.99 (*0-89906-880-4*); pap. 15.99 (*0-89906-881-2*) Mesorah Pubns.

— Shabbos Kitchen. 1992. 18.99 (*0-89906-882-0*); pap. 15.99 (*0-89906-883-9*) Mesorah Pubns.

Cohen, S. H., et al. Atomic Force Microscopy & Scanning Tunneling Microscopy: Proceedings of the First U. S. Army Natik Research, Development, & Engineering Center (AFM-STM) Symposium, Held in Natick, Massachusetts, June 8-10, 1993, Vol. 1. LC 94-48894. (Illus.). 464p. 1995. 135.00 (*0-306-44890-4*, Kluwer Plenum) Kluwer Academic.

Cohen, S. I. Human Resource Development & Utilization: Economic Analysis for Policy Making. 244p. 1994. 72.95 (*1-85972-009-9*, Pub. by Avebry) Ashgate Pub Co.

***Cohen, S. I.** Microeconomic Policy. LC 00-30607. 2000. pap. write for info. (*0-415-23601-0*) Routledge.

Cohen, S. I., ed. Patterns of Economic Restructuring for Eastern Europe. LC 93-19256. 219p. 1993. 72.95 (*1-85628-516-2*, Pub. by Avebry) Ashgate Pub Co.

Cohen, S. J., ed. see Smith, Morton.

Cohen, S. M., et al, eds. Readings in Ancient Greek Philosophy: From Thales to Aristotle. LC 94-44162. 800p. (C). 1995. text 49.95 (*0-87220-313-1*); pap. text 29.95 (*0-87220-312-3*) Hackett Pub.

Cohen, S. Malkah, ed. see Housman, Mordechai.

Cohen, S. Malkah, ed. see Welcher, Sharon H.

Cohen, S. Marc, tr. see Ammonius.

Cohen, S. T. The Neutron Bomb: Political, Technological & Military Issues. LC 78-63388. (Special Report Ser.). 95p. 1978. 11.95 (*0-89549-009-9*) Inst Foreign Policy Anal.

— Shame: Confessions of the Father of the Neutron Bomb. LC 98-2576. 1998. write for info. (*981-02-3431-7*) World Scientific Pub.

Cohen, S. T., jt. auth. see Van Cleave, William R.

Cohen, S. V. & Vantcek, P., eds. Slow Deformation & Transmission of Stress in the Earth, IUGG 4. (Geophysical Monograph Ser.: Vol. 49). 148p. 1989. 25.00 (*0-87590-453-X*) Am Geophysical.

***Cohen, Sacha.** Inspirations: Stencilling. 2000. pap. 12.95 (*1-84215-050-2*) Anness Pub.

— Paint Recipes & Paint Effects. (Practical Encyclopedia of ... Ser.). 1999. 35.00 (*0-7548-0199-3*, Lorenz Bks) Anness Pub.

Cohen, Sacha. Simple Stamps & Stencils Style, 7 vols. (Simple Style Ser.). (Illus.). 150p. 1998. 24.95 (*0-8230-4807-1*) Watsn-Guptill.

Cohen, Sacha & Stanley, Isabel. Cushions. (Inspirations Ser.). (Illus.). 96p. 1997. 12.95 (*1-85967-430-5*, Lorenz Bks) Anness Pub.

— Stenciling. (The Inspirations Ser.). (Illus.). 96p. 1997. 12.95 (*1-85967-429-1*, Lorenz Bks) Anness Pub.

Cohen, Sally, jt. auth. see Rohe, Terry.

Cohen, Sam, ed. & selected by see Brunton, Paul.

Cohen, Samuel H. & Lightbody, Marcia, eds. Atomic Force Microscopy/Scanning Tunneling Microscopy Vol. 2: Proceedings of the Second Symposium Held in Natick, Massachusetts, June 7-9, 1994. LC 97-9548. (Illus.). 260p. (C). 1997. text 85.00 (*0-306-45596-X*, Kluwer Plenum) Kluwer Academic.

***Cohen, Samuel H. & Lightbody, Marcia L.** Atomic Force Microscopy/Scanning Tunneling Microscopy 3. LC 99-52124. 1999. write for info. (*0-306-46297-4*, Kluwer Plenum) Kluwer Academic.

Cohen, Samuel M., jt. ed. see Bryan, George T.

Cohen, Sande. Academia & the Luster of Capital. LC 92-35102. 210p. (C). 1993. pap. 16.95 (*0-8166-2231-0*); text 42.95 (*0-8166-2230-2*) U of Minn Pr.

***Cohen, Sande.** Passive Nihilism: Cultural Historiography & the Rhetorics of Scholarship. 1999. pap. 18.95 (*0-312-22747-7*) St Martin.

***Cohen, Sandee.** Fireworks for Windows & MacIntosh: Visual QuickStart Guide. Baer, Marjorie, ed. LC 98-216558. 280p. (C). 1998. pap. text 18.95 (*0-201-35361-X*) Peachpit Pr.

— Fireworks 3 for Windows & Macintosh: Visual QuickStart Guide. (Visual QuickStart Guides Ser.). (Illus.). 304p. 2000. pap. 18.99 (*0-201-70452-8*) Peachpit Pr.

Cohen, Sandee. Fireworks 2 for Windows & Macintosh: Visual Quickstart Guide. 2nd ed. LC 99-462642. 304p. (C). 1999. pap. text 18.99 (*0-201-35458-6*) Addison-Wesley.

— FreeHand 8 for Windows & Macintosh: Visual QuickStart Guide. LC 98-172785. 304p. (C). 1998. pap. text 18.95 (*0-201-69697-5*) Peachpit Pr.

— FreeHand 5.5 for Macintosh: Visual QuickStart Guide. (Illus.). 312p. (C). 1996. pap. text 18.95 (*0-201-88447-X*) Peachpit Pr.

***Cohen, Sandee.** FreeHand 9 for Windows & Macintosh: Visual QuickStart Guide. (Visual QuickStart Guide Ser.). (Illus.). 304p. 2000. pap. text 19.99 (*0-201-35489-6*) Peachpit Pr.

Cohen, Sandee. FreeHand 7 for Macintosh: Visual QuickStart Guide. LC 97-162065. (Visual QuickStart Guide Ser.). 320p. (C). 1996. pap. text 18.95 (*0-201-68828-X*) Peachpit Pr.

— InDesign for Macintosh & Windows: Visual QuickStart Guide. 304p. (C). 1999. pap. text 17.99 (*0-201-35447-0*) Peachpit Pr.

***Cohen, Sandee.** InDesign 1.0/1.5 for Macintosh & Windows: Visual QuickStart Guide. (Visual QuickStart Guide Ser.). 304p. 2000. pap. 17.99 (*0-201-71036-6*) Peachpit Pr.

Cohen, Sandee. Kai's Power Tools 3 for Macintosh: Visual QuickStart Guide. 192p. (C). 1997. pap. 17.95 (*0-201-68816-6*) Peachpit Pr.

— Kai's Power Tools 3 for Windows: Visual QuickStart Guide. LC 98-104894. 192p. (C). 1997. pap. text 17.95 (*0-201-69668-1*) Peachpit Pr.

Cohen, Sandee, jt. auth. see McClelland, Deke.

***Cohen, Sandi.** Poems from the Heart...& the Funny Bone. 1999. pap. write for info. (*1-58235-316-6*) Watermrk Pr.

Cohen-Sandler, Roni & Silver, Michelle. "I'm Not Mad, I Just Hate You!" A New Understanding of Mother-Daughter Conflict. LC 98-39724. 280p. 1999. 22.95 (*0-670-88343-3*) Viking Penguin.

***Cohen-Sandler, Roni & Silver, Michelle.** "I'm Not Mad, I Just Hate You!" A New Understanding of Mother-Daughter Conflict. 288p. 2000. pap. 12.95 (*0-14-028600-4*, Penguin Bks) Viking Penguin.

Cohen, Sandy, jt. auth. see Williams, Robin C.

Cohen, Sara. Rock Culture in Liverpool: Popular Music in the Making. (Illus.). 256p. 1991. text 49.95 (*0-19-816178-6*, 11969) OUP.

Cohen, Sara & Shafferman, Avigdor, eds. Novel Strategies in the Design & Production of Vaccines: Proceedings of the 39th OHOLO Conference Held in Eilat, Israel, May 7-11, 1995. (Illus.). 214p. 1996. 85.00 (*0-306-45211-1*, Kluwer Plenum) Kluwer Academic.

Cohen, Sarabel K. Contemporary Social Issues: Authentic Readings for the ESL Learner. LC 96-61012. 160p. (Orig.). 1997. pap. text 16.95 (*0-472-08389-9*, 08389) U of Mich Pr.

Cohen, Sarah. How to Raise a Happy & Creative Child. LC 80-80725. 1980. 7.95 (*0-87212-143-7*) Libra.

Cohen, Sarah B. Cynthia Ozick's Comic Art: From Levity to Liturgy. LC 93-13994. 212p. 1994. 25.00 (*0-253-31398-8*) Ind U Pr.

Cohen, Sarah B., ed. Comic Relief: Humor in Contemporary American Literature. LC 78-16510. 339p. 1978. text 29.95 (*0-252-00576-7*) U of Ill Pr.

— Comic Relief: Humor in Contemporary American Literature. LC 91-15723. (Humor in Life & Letters Ser.). 370p. 1992. pap. 19.95 (*0-8143-1915-7*) Wayne St U Pr.

Cohen, Sarah B., ed. Making a Scene: The Contemporary Drama of Jewish-American Women. LC 96-21140. 436p. 1996. 45.00 (*0-8156-2713-0*, COMS); pap. 19.95 (*0-8156-0404-1*, COMSP) Syracuse U Pr.

Cohen, Sarah B., intro. Jewish Wry: Essays on Jewish Humor. (Humor in Life & Letters Ser.). 256p. 1990. pap. 18.95 (*0-8143-2366-9*) Wayne St U Pr.

***Cohen, Sarah R.** Art, Dance & the Body in the French Court of the "Ancien Regime" (Illus.). 368p. (C). 2000. 75.00 (*0-521-64046-6*) Cambridge U Pr.

Cohen, Sascha B., jt. auth. see Caspi, Mishael.

Cohen, Sascha B., jt. auth. see Caspi, Mishael M.

Cohen, Saul. The Columbia Gazetteer of the World, 3 vols. LC 98-71262. 3578p. 1998. 750.00 (*0-231-11040-5*) Col U Pr.

***Cohen, Saul & Powell, Lawrence Clark.** Southwest Writer Harvey Fergusson: A Collector's View & Checklist. limited ed. Smith, Pamela, ed. (Illus.). 68p. 2000. write for info. (*0-9701348-0-0*) Press Palace.

Cohen, Saul B. Jerusalem: A Geopolitical Perspective. 1977. 10.00 (*0-930832-54-X*) Herzl Pr.

— Jerusalem Undivided. 1980. pap. 3.00 (*0-930832-58-2*) Herzl Pr.

***Cohen, Saul B., ed.** The Columbia Gazetteer of North America. (Illus.). 2000. 250.00 (*0-231-11990-9*) Col U Pr.

***Cohen, Scott.** Blood Treachery. 2000. pap. 14.95 (*1-56504-409-6*) White Wolf.

Cohen, Scott. Yakety-Yak: The Midnight Confessions & Revelation of Thirty-Seven Rock Stars & Legends. 192p. 1994. pap. 12.50 (*0-671-88092-6*, Fireside) S&S Trade Pap.

Cohen, Selma J. International Encyclopedia of Dance, 6 vols. LC 97-36562. (Illus.). 4048p. (C). 1998. text 1250.00 (*0-19-509462-X*) OUP.

Cohen, Selma J., ed. Dance As a Theatre Art: Source Readings in Dance History from 1581 to the Present. 271st ed. LC 92-116094. (Illus.). 288p. (C). 1991. pap. 19.95 (*0-87127-173-7*, Dance Horizons) Princeton Bk Co.

— Next Week, Swan Lake: Reflections on Dance & Dances. LC 82-2614. (Illus.). 207p. 1982. pap. 17.95 (*0-8195-6110-X*, Wesleyan Univ Pr) U Pr of New Eng.

Cohen, Selma J., ed. The Modern Dance: Seven Statements of Belief. LC 66-14663. (Illus.). 112p. 1966. pap. 15.95 (*0-8195-6003-0*, Wesleyan Univ Pr) U Pr of New Eng.

Cohen, Selma J., jt. auth. see Humphrey, Doris.

Cohen, Seymour. Affirming Life. 350p. 1987. 20.00 (*0-88125-112-7*) Ktav.

— The Holy Letter: A Study in Jewish Sexual Morality. LC 93-22582.Tr. of Ihgeret Ha-Kodesh. 192p. 1994. 30.00 (*1-56821-086-8*) Aronson.

Cohen, Seymour J., ed. from HEB. The Holy Letter: A Study in Jewish Sexual Morality. 187p. 1998. text 20.00 (*0-7881-5261-0*) DIANE Pub.

Cohen, Seymour J., jt. auth. see Sherwin, Byron L.

Cohen, Seymour S. A Guide to the Polyamines. LC 96-27561. (Illus.). 624p. 1998. text 160.00 (*0-19-511064-1*) OUP.

***Cohen, Shara, et al.** Cord Blood Characteristics: Role in Stem Cell Transplantation. (Illus.). 296p. 2000. 99.95 (*1-85317-794-6*, Pub. by Martin Dunitz) Blackwell Sci.

Cohen, Shari. Draw Fantasy: Dragons, Centaurs & Other Mythological Characters. LC 97-21763. (Illus.). 64p. (J). 1997. pap. 7.95 (*1-56565-770-5*, 07705W, Pub. by Lowell Hse) NTC Contemp Pub Co.

— Future Wings: The Step-by-Step Paper Spacecraft Book. LC 98-137445. (Illus.). 64p. (J). (gr. 3-7). 1997. pap. 7.95 (*1-56565-653-9*, 06539W, Pub. by Lowell Hse) NTC Contemp Pub Co.

Cohen, Shari & Cohen, Payl. Careers in Law Enforcement & Security. rev. ed. Rosen, Ruth C., ed. (Careers Ser.). (Illus.). (YA). (gr. 7-12). 1994. lib. bdg. 16.95 (*0-8239-1878-5*) Rosen Group.

Cohen, Shari, jt. auth. see Clemens, Peter.

Cohen, Shari J. Politics Without a Past: The Absence of History in Post-Communist Nationalism. LC 99-28322. 304p. 1999. pap. 18.95 (*0-8223-2399-0*) Duke.

***Cohen, Shari J.** Politics Without a Past: The Absence of History in Postcommunist Nationalism. LC 99-28322. 304p. 1999. 54.95 (*0-8223-2378-8*) Duke.

Cohen, Sharleen C. Lives of Value. 576p. 1993. mass mkt. 5.99 (*0-446-36389-8*, Pub. by Warner Bks) Little.

Cohen, Sharon, jt. auth. see Ellis, Garry.

Cohen, Sharron. The Mysteries of Research. 2nd ed. LC 95-43103. 135p. 1996. pap. 16.95 (*0-917846-76-1*, Alleyside) Highsmith Pr.

Cohen, Shaul E. The Politics of Planting: Israeli-Palestinian Competition for Control of Land in the Jerusalem Periphery. (Geography Research Papers: Vol. 236). (Illus.). 222p. (C). 1993. lib. bdg. 19.00 (*0-226-11276-4*) U Ch Pr.

Cohen, Shaye J. D. The Beginnings of Jewishness: Boundaries, Varieties, Uncertainties. LC 98-39899. (S. Mark Taper Foundation Imprint in Jewish Studies). 458p. 1999. 45.00 (*0-520-21141-3*, Pub. by U CA Pr) Cal Prin Full Svc.

— From the Maccabees to the Mishnah. Meeks, Wayne A., ed. LC 86-28077. (Library of Early Christianity: Vol. 7). 252p. 1987. pap. 24.95 (*0-664-25017-3*) Westminster John Knox.

Cohen, Shaye J. D. & Greenstein, Edward L., eds. The State of Jewish Studies. LC 89-39860. 280p. (C). 1990. pap. text 19.95 (*0-8143-2195-X*) Wayne St U Pr.

— The State of Jewish Studies. LC 89-39860. 279p. reprint ed. pap. 86.50 (*0-608-10615-1*, 207123700009) Bks Demand.

Cohen, Shaye J. D., ed. see Smith, Morton.

Cohen, Sheldon, et al, eds. Measuring Stress: A Guide for Health & Social Scientists. LC 94-13307. (Illus.). 256p. 1995. text 60.00 (*0-19-508641-4*) OUP.

— Measuring Stress: A Guide for Health & Social Scientists. (Illus.). 256p. 1997. reprint ed. pap. text 29.50 (*0-19-512120-1*) OUP.

***Cohen, Sheldon, et al, eds.** Social Support Measurement & Intervention: A Guide for Health & Social Scientists. LC 99-43200. 352p. 2000. 45.00 (*0-19-512670-X*) OUP.

Cohen, Sheldon & Burgiel, Stanley W., eds. Exploring Biodiversity Indicators & Targets under the Convention on Biological Diversity: A Synthesis Report of the Sixth Session of the Global Biodiversity Forum : U. N. Headquarters, New York, 3-4 April 1997. LC 98-228932. 1998. write for info. (*2-8317-0452-9*) IUCN.

Cohen, Sheldon & Samter, Max, eds. Excerpts from Classics in Allergy (& Immunology) 224p. 1992. 69.50 (*0-88372-006-X*) OceanSide Pubns.

Cohen, Sheldon M. Aristotle on Nature & Incomplete Substance. 199p. (C). 1996. text 57.95 (*0-521-56081-0*) Cambridge U Pr.

— The Military. (Contemporary Ethical Issues Ser.). 1997. lib. bdg. 39.50 (*0-87436-880-4*) ABC-CLIO.

Cohen, Sheldon S. Yankee Sailors in British Gaols: Prisoners of War at Forton & Mill, 1777-1783. LC 95-2448. 280p. 1996. 42.50 (*0-87413-564-8*) U Delaware Pr.

Cohen, Shelia E., jt. auth. see Riley, Edward T.

Cohen, Shemy S. Looking for the Other Side. 1998. mass mkt. 6.99 (*0-425-16307-5*) Berkley Pub.

Cohen, Sherman. The Year of the Persian Lamb. 60p. 1995. 6.95 (*0-9657286-0-9*) Sherman Cohen.

Cohen, Sherrill & Taub, Nadine, eds. Reproductive Laws for the 1990s. LC 88-25867. (Contemporary Issues in Biomedicine, Ethics, & Society Ser.). 482p. 1988. 49.50 (*0-89603-157-8*); pap. 29.50 (*0-89603-175-6*) Humana.

Cohen, Sherry, jt. auth. see Crumb, Dana.

Cohen, Sherry, jt. auth. see Wood, Merle.

Cohen, Sherry, jt. auth. see Wood, Merle W.

Cohen, Sherry S. Secrets of a Very Good Marriage: Lessons from the Sea. 160p. 1994. pap. 9.95 (*0-14-023877-8*, Penguin Bks) Viking Penguin.

— Tough Gazoobies on That! Young, Billie, ed. LC 73-83476. 1974. 17.95 (*0-87949-016-0*) Ashley Bks.

Cohen, Sherry S., jt. auth. see Roppatte, Vincent.

Cohen, Shirley. Targeting Autism: What We Know, Don't Know & Can Do to Help Young Children with Autism. LC 97-28090. 228p. 1998. pap. text 14.95 (*0-520-21309-2*, Pub. by U CA Pr) Cal Prin Full Svc.

— Targeting Autism: What We Know, Don't Know, & Can Do to Help Young Children with Autism & Related Disorders. LC 97-28090. 217p. 1998. 40.00 (*0-520-21011-5*, Pub. by U CA Pr) Cal Prin Full Svc.

Cohen, Shy. Professional Java Fundamentals. LC 96-60892. 500p. 1996. pap. 35.00 (*1-86100-038-3*) Wrox Pr Inc.

Cohen, Sidney. The Alcoholism Problems: Selected Issues. LC 83-179. 193p. 1983. text 6.95 (*0-86656-209-5*); pap. text 3.95 (*0-86656-179-X*) Haworth Pr.

— The Drug Dilemma. 2nd ed. (Health Education Paperback Ser.). 144p. 1975. 17.95 (*0-07-011587-7*); pap. text. write for info. (*0-07-011588-5*) McGraw.

— The Substance Abuse Problems. LC 80-21280. 392p. 1981. text 6.95 (*0-917724-18-6*); pap. text 24.95 (*0-917724-22-4*) Haworth Pr.

— The Substance Abuse Problems Vol. 2: New Issues for the 1980s, Vol. 2. LC 80-21280. 323p. 1985. text 6.95 (*0-86656-368-7*); pap. text 24.95 (*0-86656-369-5*) Haworth Pr.

Cohen, Sidney, ed. Clinical Gastroenterology: A Problem-Oriented Approach. fac. ed. LC 82-10926. (Wiley Medical Publication). (Illus.). 478p. 1983. reprint ed. pap. 148.20 (*0-7837-7879-1*, 204763600007) Bks Demand.

— Drug Abuse & Alcoholism: Current Critical Issues. LC 79-25648. 62p. 1981. pap. text 9.95 (*0-917724-10-0*) Haworth Pr.

Cohen, Sidney & Callahan, James F., eds. The Diagnosis & Treatment of Drug & Alcohol Abuse. LC 85-24833. 305p. 1986. text 69.95 (*0-86656-479-9*) Haworth Pr.

Cohen, Sidney & Soloway, Roger D., eds. Chronic Active Liver Disease. LC 82-12923. (Contemporary Issues in Gastroenterology Ser.: No. 2). (Illus.). 282p. reprint ed. pap. 87.50 (*0-7837-2565-5*, 204272400006) Bks Demand.

— Diseases of the Esophagus. LC 82-17681. (Contemporary Issues in Gastroenterology Ser.: No. 1). (Illus.). 317p. reprint ed. pap. 98.30 (*0-7837-2569-8*, 204272800006) Bks Demand.

— Functional Disorders of the Gastrointestinal Tract. fac. ed. LC 87-20950. (Contemporary Issues in Gastroenterology Ser.: No. 6). (Illus.). 231p. 1987. reprint ed. pap. 71.70 (*0-7837-7900-3*, 204765600008) Bks Demand.

Cohen, Simcha B. The Shabbos Home. pap. 15.99 (*0-89906-335-7*, HO1P) Mesorah Pubns.

— The Shabbos Home, Vol. 1. 18.99 (*0-89906-334-9*, HO1H) Mesorah Pubns.

Cohen, Simon L. Whose Life Is It Anyway? The Doctors Dilemma in Intensive Care. (Illus.). 206p. 1995. 27.95 (*0-86051-806-X*, Robson-Parkwest) Parkwest Pubns.

Cohen, Simon S. Practical Statistics. (Illus.). 224p. (Orig.). 1988. pap. text 17.95 (*0-7131-3648-0*, Pub. by E A) Routldge.

Cohen, Skip, jt. auth. see Blair, Don.

Cohen, Skip, jt. auth. see Cantrell, Bambi.

Cohen, Smadar & Bernstein, Howard. Microparticulate Systems for the Delivery of Proteins & Vaccines. LC 96-25983. (Drugs & the Pharmaceutical Sciences Ser.: Vol. 77). (Illus.). 552p. 1996. text 180.00 (*0-8247-9753-1*) Dekker.

***Cohen, Sol.** Challenging Orthodoxies: Toward a New Cultural History of Education. LC 97-38331. (Counterpoints Ser.: Vol. 76). XXIV, 326p. (C). 1999. pap. 29.95 (*0-8204-3940-1*) P Lang Pubng.

Cohen, Sol & Solomon, Lewis C., eds. From the Campus: Perspectives on the School Reform Movement. LC 89-33960. 245p. 1989. 59.95 (*0-275-93263-X*, C3262, Greenwood Pr) Greenwood.

Cohen-Solal, Annie. Sartre, 1905-1980. (Folio Essais Ser.). (FRE.). pap. 19.95 (*2-07-032508-3*) Schoenhof.

***Cohen, Sonia.** With Love from Your Mother. 2000. 10.95 (*0-533-13434-X*) Vantage.

Cohen, Stan. Alaska's Flying Expedition: The Black Wolf Squadron. (Illus.). 120p. 1998. pap. 12.95 (*1-57510-041-X*) Pictorial Hist.

— Alcan & Canol: A Pictorial History of Two Great WWII Construction Projects. LC 92-80910. 1992. pap. 19.95 (*0-929521-50-1*) Pictorial Hist.

— Beyond Hell. (Steam Press Ser.). (Illus.). 104p. 1992. pap. 16.00 (*0-9627440-5-0*) LAD Publishing.

— Beyond Hell. limited ed. (Steam Press Ser.). (Illus.). 104p. 1992. 790.00 (*0-9627440-4-2*) LAD Publishing.

***Cohen, Stan.** The Civil War in West Virginia: A Pictorial History. LC 82-80964. (Illus.). 170p. 1999. pap. 14.95 (*1-891852-03-5*) Quarrier Pr.

Cohen, Stan. 8.6: The Great Alaska Earthquake March 27, 1964. LC 95-67027. (Illus.). 120p. 1995. pap. 12.95 (*0-929521-96-X*) Pictorial Hist.

— The Eisenhowers: Gettysburg's First Family. (Illus.). 48p. 1983. 4.95 (*0-933126-25-5*) Pictorial Hist.

— The First Lady of Waikiki: A Pictorial History of the Sheraton Moana Surfrider. LC 95-71786. (Illus.). 96p. 1996. pap. 9.95 (*1-57510-008-8*) Pictorial Hist.

— The Games of '36: A Pictorial History of the 1936 Olympics in Germany. Van Valkenburg, Carol, ed. LC 96-67534. (Illus.). 248p. (Orig.). 1996. pap. 19.95 (*1-57510-009-6*) Pictorial Hist.

— Highway on the Sea: A Pictorial History of the Alaska Marine Highway System. LC 94-66360. (Illus.). 54p. 1994. pap. text 7.95 (*0-929521-87-0*) Pictorial Hist.

— Images of the Spanish-American War: April-August 1898 - A Pictorial History. LC 97-66760. 1997. pap. text 29.95 (*1-57510-031-2*) Pictorial Hist.

***Cohen, Stan.** John Brown: "The Thundering Voice of Jehovah" LC 98-68738. (Illus.). 208p. 1999. pap. 14.95 (*1-57510-055-X*) Pictorial Hist.

Cohen, Stan. King Coal: A Pictorial Heritage of West Virginia Coal Mining. (Illus.). 146p. 1999. pap. 12.95 (*1-891852-06-X*) Quarrier Pr.

— Seeping into - out of the Well. (Steam Press Ser.). (Illus.). 72p. 1991. pap. 16.00 (*0-9627440-3-4*) LAD Publishing.

— Seeping into - out of the Well. limited ed. (Steam Press Ser.). (Illus.). 72p. 1991. 725.00 (*0-9627440-2-6*) LAD Publishing.

— The Western Montana Fair: A Pictorial Heritage. LC 95-70125. (Illus.). 68p. (Orig.). 1995. pap. 7.95 (*1-57510-002-9*) Pictorial Hist.

Cohen, Stan & Bogle, James G. The General & The Texas: A Pictorial History of the Andrews Raid, April 12, 1862. LC 99-70473. (Illus.). 160p. (Orig.). 1999. pap. 17.95 (*1-57510-060-6*, Pub. by Pictorial Hist) Motorbooks Intl.

Cohen, Stan, jt. auth. see Glines, Carroll V.

Cohen, Stan, jt. auth. see Parker, Robert B.

Cohen, Stan B. The Civil War in West Virginia: A Pictorial History. rev. ed. LC 82-80964. (Illus.). 160p. (Orig.). 1982. pap. text 14.95 (*0-933126-17-4*) Pictorial Hist.

— Destination Tokyo: A Pictorial History of Doolittle's Tokyo Raid, April 18, 1942. rev. ed. LC 83-60014. (Illus.). 136p. 1992. pap. 12.95 (*0-929521-52-8*) Pictorial Hist.

— East Wind Rain: A Pictorial History of the Pearl Harbor Attack. 50th anniversary ed. (Illus.). 308p. (Orig.). 1981. pap. 14.95 (*0-933126-15-8*) Pictorial Hist.

— Enemy on Island-Issue in Doubt: The Capture of Wake Island. LC 83-62543. (Illus.). 106p. 1983. pap. 9.95 (*0-933126-39-5*) Pictorial Hist.

— The Forgotten War Vol. 1: A Pictorial History of WWII in Alaska & Northwestern Canada. LC 81-80570. (Illus.). 272p. 1981. pap. 16.95 (*0-933126-13-1*) Pictorial Hist.

— The Forgotten War Vol. 2: A Pictorial History of WWII in Alaska & NW Canada. LC 81-80570. (Illus.). 264p. (C). 1988. pap. text 16.95 (*0-933126-70-0*) Pictorial Hist.

— The Forgotten War Vol. 3: A Pictorial History of W. W. II in Alaska & Northwestern Canada. LC 88-80570. (Illus.). 264p. 1992. pap. 16.95 (*0-929521-30-7*) Pictorial Hist.

— The Forgotten War Vol. 4: A Pictorial History of W. W. II in Alaska & Northwestern Canada. LC 81-80570. (Illus.). 1993. pap. text 16.95 (*0-929521-64-1*) Pictorial Hist.

— Gold Rush Gateway: Skagway & Dyea, Alaska. LC 86-60127. (Illus.). 142p. (Orig.). 1986. pap. text 9.95 (*0-933126-48-4*) Pictorial Hist.

— The Great Alaska Pipeline. Vaughan, Bill, ed. LC 88-60470. (Illus.). 142p. 1988. pap. text 9.95 (*0-933126-71-9*) Pictorial Hist.

— Hands Across the Wall: The 50th & 75th Reunions of the Gettysburg Battle. rev. ed. LC 82-80962. (Illus.). 76p. 1982. pap. 7.95 (*0-933126-18-2*) Pictorial Hist.

— Hawaiian Airlines: Pictorial History of the Pioneer Carrier in the Pacific. Smith, Steve, ed. LC 86-62549. (Illus.). 116p. 1986. pap. 12.95 (*0-933126-81-6*) Pictorial Hist.

— Historic Springs of the Virginias: A Pictorial History. LC 81-80698. (Illus.). 216p. 1981. pap. 14.95 (*0-933126-14-X*) Pictorial Hist.

— The Homestead & Warm Springs Valley Virginia: A Pictorial Heritage. LC 84-60467. (Illus.). 96p. 1984. pap. 12.95 (*0-933126-45-X*) Pictorial Hist.

— Klondike Centennial Scrapbook: The Great Klondike Gold Rush. LC 96-67479. (Illus.). 184p. (Orig.). 1997. pap. 19.95 (*1-57510-014-2*) Pictorial Hist.

— A Pictorial Guide to West Virginia's Civil War Sites & Related Information. LC 90-60031. (Illus.). 124p. (Orig.). 1990. pap. text 9.95 (*0-929521-34-X*) Pictorial Hist.

— A Pictorial History of Smoke Jumping. LC 83-62751. (Illus.). 180p. 1983. pap. 12.95 (*0-933126-40-9*) Pictorial Hist.

— The Pink Palace: The Royal Hawaiian Hotel, a Sheraton Hotel in Hawaii. Smith, Steve, ed. LC 86-62548. (Illus.). 100p. 1986. pap. 9.95 (*0-933126-82-4*) Pictorial Hist.

— Queen City of the North: Dawson City, Yukon a Pictorial History. 136p. 1990. pap. 9.95 (*0-929521-31-5*) Pictorial Hist.

— Rails Across the Tundra: A Historical Album of the Alaska Railroad. LC 84-60465. (Illus.). 152p. 1984. pap. 9.95 (*0-933126-43-3*) Pictorial Hist.

— The Streets Were Paved with Gold: A Pictorial History of the Klondike Gold Rush 1896-99. LC 77-80011. (Illus.). 192p. 1977. pap. 12.95 (*0-933126-03-4*) Pictorial Hist.

— The Trail of '42: A Pictorial History of the Alaska Highway. rev. ed. (Illus.). 1988. pap. 7.95 (*0-933126-06-9*) Pictorial Hist.

— The Tree Army: A Pictorial History of the Civilian Conservation Corps 1933-1943. LC 80-81071. 172p. 1980. 12.95 (*0-933126-11-5*) Pictorial Hist.

— The White Pass & Yukon Route: A Pictorial History. LC 79-90884. (Illus.). 120p. 1980. pap. text 9.95 (*0-933126-08-5*) Pictorial Hist.

— Wings to the Orient: Pan American Clipper Planes, 1935-1945. LC 85-60319. (Illus.). 214p. 1985. pap. 14.95 (*0-933126-61-1*) Pictorial Hist.

— Yukon River Steamboats: A Pictorial History. LC 82-81717. (Illus.). 128p. (Orig.). 1982. pap. text 9.95 (*0-933126-19-0*) Pictorial Hist.

Cohen, Stan B. & Andre, Richard. Capitols of West Virginia: A Pictorial History. LC 89-50354. (Illus.). 112p. (Orig.). 1989. pap. 9.95 (*0-929521-18-8*) Pictorial Hist.

Cohen, Stan B. & Miller, Don C. The University of Montana: A Pictorial History. LC 80-53616. (Illus.). 96p. 1980. pap. 5.95 (*0-933126-12-3*) Pictorial Hist.

Cohen, Stan B. & Miller, Donald C. Big Burn: The Northwest's Forest Fire of 1910. LC 78-51507. (Illus.). 96p. 1978. pap. 9.95 (*0-933126-04-2*) Pictorial Hist.

Cohen, Stan B. & Pervical, Mary B. King Coal: A Pictorial Heritage of West Virginia Coal Mining. LC 84-61934. (Illus.). 152p. (Orig.). 1984. pap. 12.95 (*0-933126-53-0*) Pictorial Hist.

Cohen, Stan B., jt. auth. see Guth, A. Richard.

Cohen, Stanley. Against Criminology. 352p. 1988. 44.95 (*0-88738-153-7*); pap. 24.95 (*0-88738-689-X*) Transaction Pubs.

— Dodgers: The First One Hundred Years. 1990. 19.95 (*1-55972-030-1*, Birch Ln Pr) Carol Pub Group.

— Dodgers! The First One Hundred Years. (Illus.). 256p. 1992. pap. 4.50 (*0-8216-2508-X*, Carol Paperbacks) Carol Pub Group.

— A Magic Summer. (Illus.). 319p. 1989. pap. 8.95 (*0-15-655117-9*) Harcourt.

— Police Law Problems & Solutions. 249p. 1995. text 24.95 (*0-685-29114-6*) PA PCLB.

***Cohen, Stanley.** States of Denial. 2001. 59.95 (*0-7456-1657-7*, Pub. by Polity Pr); pap. 27.95 (*0-7456-2392-1*, Pub. by Polity Pr) Blackwell Pubs.

Cohen, Stanley. Visions of Social Control: Crime, Punishment & Classification. 336p. 1985. pap. 28.95 (*0-7456-0021-2*) Blackwell Pubs.

Cohen, Stanley, ed. Lymphokines & the Immune Response. 304p. 1989. lib. bdg. 230.00 (*0-8493-6427-2*, QR185) CRC Pr.

— Pediatric Emergency Management: Guidelines for Rapid Diagnosis. (Illus.). 416p. (C). 1982. text 32.95 (*0-87619-924-4*) P-H.

Cohen, Stanley, photos by. A Magic Summer: The '69 Mets. LC 87-33362. (Illus.). 352p. 1988. 16.95 (*0-15-155096-4*) Harcourt.

Cohen, Stanley & Taylor, Laurie. Escape Attempts: The Struggle of Resistance in Everyday Life. 2nd ed. LC 92-5431. 272p. (C). 1992. pap. 22.99 (*0-415-06500-3*, A6973) Routledge.

Cohen, Stanley & Young, Jock, eds. The Manufacture of News: Deviance, Social Problems & the Mass Media. rev. ed. LC 81-50585. (Communication & Society Ser.). 506p. 1981. reprint ed. pap. 156.90 (*0-608-02796-0*, 206386300007) Bks Demand.

Cohen, Stanley, jt. auth. see Garbus, Martin W.

Cohen, Stanley, jt. ed. see Blomberg, Thomas G.

Cohen, Stanley, jt. ed. see Green, Ira.

Cohen, Stanley B., jt. ed. see Ziff, Morris.

Cohen, Stanley N. Managing Stroke. (Illus.). 624p. 1999. 89.00 (*0-07-012045-5*) McGraw-Hill HPD.

Cohen, Stephan S., et al. The Tunnel at the End of the Light: Privatization, Business Networks & Economic Transformation in Russia. LC 98-34006. (Research Ser.). x, 149p. 1998. pap. text 11.50 (*0-87725-000-6*) U of Cal IAS.

***Cohen, Stephen.** Catch-It. 1999. pap. write for info. (*1-58235-352-2*) Watermrk Pr.

Cohen, Stephen. Commonplace Moraliser: Insights & Outrages. LC 92-41784. 1993. 38.50 (*0-8191-9007-1*); pap. 17.50 (*0-8191-9008-X*) U Pr of Amer.

— The Language of Power, the Power of Language: The Effects of Ambiguity on Sociopolitical Structures in Shakespeare's Plays. LC 87-72452. (LeBaron Russell Briggs Prize Honors Essays in English Ser.: 1987). 152p. (Orig.). 1988. pap. 6.30 (*0-674-51056-9*) HUP.

Cohen, Stephen & Burns, Richard C. Pathways of the Pulp. 7th ed. LC 98-184459. (Illus.). 912p. (C). (gr. 13). 1997. text 89.00 (*0-8151-8613-4*, 30606) Mosby Inc.

Cohen, Stephen, et al. Economic Implications of Electric Utility Restructuring in California. (Illus.). 20p. 1997. pap. 10.00 (*0-918714-52-4*) Intl Res Ctr Energy.

Cohen, Stephen, jt. auth. see Grace, Damien.

Cohen, Stephen B. Federal Income Taxation: A Conceptual Approach. (University Casebook Ser.). 938p. 1989. text 43.00 (*0-88277-707-6*) Foundation Pr.

Cohen, Stephen D. Cowboys & Samurais: Why the U.S. Is Losing the Battle with the Japanese & Why It Matters. 352p. 1991. 29.95 (*0-88730-416-8*, HarpBusn) HarpInfo.

— The Making of United States International Economic Policy
 Principles, Problems & Proposals for Reform. 5th ed. LC 99-34427. 328p. 2000. 69.50 (*0-275-96503-1*) Greenwood.

— The Making of United States International Economic Policy
 Principles, Problems & Proposals of Reform. 5th ed. LC 99-34427. 328p. 2000. pap. 29.95 (*0-275-96504-X*) Greenwood.

— An Ocean Apart: Explaining Three Decades of U. S.-Japanese Trade Frictions. LC 97-22802. 272p. 1998. 65.00 (*0-275-95686-5*, Praeger Pubs) Greenwood.

— Uneasy Partnership: Competition & Conflict in U. S.-Japanese Trade Relations. LC 84-16924. 248p. 1986. pap. 16.95 (*0-88730-123-1*, HarpBusn) HarpInfo.

Cohen, Stephen D. & Niederreiter, Harald, eds. Finite Fields & Applications. (London Mathematical Society Lecture Note Ser.: No. 233). (Illus.). 421p. (C). 1996. pap. text 49.95 (*0-521-56736-X*) Cambridge U Pr.

Cohen, Stephen D., et al. Fundamentals of U. S. Foreign Trade Policy: Economics, Politics, Law & Issues. 336p. (C). 1996. pap. 75.00 (*0-8133-1746-0*, Pub. by Westview) HarpC.

— Fundamentals of U. S. Foreign Trade Policy: Economics, Politics, Laws & Issues. 336p. (C). 1996. pap. 29.00 (*0-8133-1747-9*, Pub. by Westview) HarpC.

Cohen, Stephen F. Bukharin & the Bolshevik Revolution: A Political Biography, 1888-1938. (Illus.). 560p. 1980. reprint ed. pap. text 17.95 (*0-19-502697-7*) OUP.

***Cohen, Stephen F.** Failed Crusade: America & the Tragedy of Post-Communist Russia. 160p. 2000. 21.95 (*0-393-04964-7*) Norton.

Cohen, Stephen F. Rethinking the Soviet Experience: Politics & History since 1917. 235p. 1986. reprint ed. pap. text 8.95 (*0-19-504016-3*) OUP.

— Rethinking the Soviet Experience: Politics & History Since 1917. 2nd ed. 288p. Date not set. text 29.95 (*0-19-506635-9*) OUP.

— Rethinking the Soviet Experience: Politics & History Since 1917. 2nd ed. 288p. 2000. pap. 8.95 (*0-19-505714-7*) OUP.

— Voices of Glasnost. 1991. pap. 12.95 (*0-393-30735-2*) Norton.

Cohen, Stephen F., et al, eds. The Soviet Union since Stalin. LC 79-3092. 350p. 1980. reprint ed. pap. 108.50 (*0-608-01055-3*, 205936300001) Bks Demand.

Cohen, Stephen M., ed. Operative Laparoscopy & Hysteroscopy. 320p. 1996. text 149.00 (*0-443-08950-7*) Church.

Cohen, Stephen P. Heartless. 224p. 1989. pap. 3.50 (*0-380-70799-3*, Avon Bks) Morrow Avon.

— The Indian Army: Its Contribution to the Development of a Nation. 2nd ed. 268p. (C). 1991. reprint ed. 16.95 (*0-19-562757-1*) OUP.

— Island of Steel. 256p. 1989. pap. 3.50 (*0-380-70805-1*, Avon Bks) Morrow Avon.

***Cohen, Stephen P.** The Pakistan Army 1998. annuals 2nd ed. LC 98-930868. (Oxford Pakistan Paperbacks Ser.). (Illus.). 210p. 1999. pap. text 12.95 (*0-19-577948-7*) OUP.

Cohen, Stephen P., ed. The Security of South Asia: American & Asian Perspectives. LC 87-10772. 304p. 1987. text 29.95 (*0-252-01394-8*) U of Ill Pr.

Cohen, Stephen P., jt. auth. see Garn, Jake.

***Cohen, Stephen S. & Boyd, Gavin.** Corporate Governance & Globalization: Long Range Planning Issues. LC 00-28844. (New Horizons in International Business Ser.). 2000. write for info. (*1-84064-179-7*) E Elgar.

Cohen, Steve. Adventure Guide to the High Southwest: Travel in the Four Corners Region. 2nd ed. LC 98-138306. (Adventure Guide Ser.). (Illus.). 380p. (Orig.). 1996. pap. 15.95 (*1-55650-723-2*) Hunter NJ.

— Disowned: A Twentieth-Century Jew & His Experience with Jesus. 27p. 1995. pap. 3.00 (*1-881022-20-X*, BK063) Purple Pomegranate.

— Learn-to-Read Treasure Hunts. LC 97-185334. (Illus.). 464p. (J). (gr. k-2). 1997. pap. 8.95 (*0-7611-0330-9*, 10338) Workman Pub.

Cohen, Steven. Tools for Innovators: Creative Strategies for Strengthening Public Sector Organizations. LC 97-51284. 1998. 26.95 (*0-7879-0953-X*) Jossey-Bass.

Cohen, Steven & Brand, Ronald. Total Quality Management in Government: A Practical Guide for the Real World. LC 92-42281. (Public Administration Ser.). 252p. 1993. 29.95 (*1-55542-539-9*) Jossey-Bass.

Cohen, Steven & Clements, Millard. Was the Vietnam War Legal? rev. ed. Starr, Jerold M., ed. (Lessons of the Vietnam War Ser.). (Illus.). 32p. (C). 1991. pap. text 5.00 (*0-945919-03-4*) Ctr Social Studies.

Cohen, Steven & Micke, William E. The New Effective Public Manager: Achieving Success in a Changing Government. LC 94-44963. (Public Administration Ser.). 307p. 1995. 26.95 (*0-7879-0087-7*) Jossey-Bass.

Cohen, Steven, jt. auth. see Cox, Brneda G.

Cohen, Steven A. & Cole. The Medical Interview: A Functional & Operational Approach. (Illus.). 224p. (C). (gr. 13). 1990. pap. text 32.95 (*0-8016-0345-5*, 00345) Mosby Inc.

***Cohen, Steven L.** Lazy Man's Guide to Purchasing a Digital Piano. (Illus.). 42p. 1999. pap. 12.95 (*0-9677606-1-5*) S L Cohen.

— The Lazy Man's Guide to Purchasing an Acoustic Piano. (Illus.). 42p. 1999. pap. 12.95 (*0-9677606-0-7*) S L Cohen.

Cohen, Steven M. American Assimilation or Jewish Revival? LC 87-45374. (Jewish Political & Social Studies). 152p. 1988. pap. 47.20 (*0-608-05011-3*, 205967200004) Bks Demand.

— American Modernity & Jewish Identity. 250p. 1983. pap. 14.95 (*0-422-77750-1*, NO.3495) Routledge.

— Becker's Ring. 432p. 1997. mass mkt. 6.50 (*0-446-60443-7*, Pub. by Warner Bks) Little.

— Interethnic Marriage & Friendship. Zuckerman, Harriet & Merton, Robert K., eds. LC 79-8985. (Dissertations on Sociology Ser.). 1980. lib. bdg. 31.95 (*0-405-12958-0*) Ayer.

— The National Survey of American Jews, 1984: Political & Social Outlooks. iv, 60p. (Orig.). 1985. pap. 4.00 (*0-87495-069-4*) Am Jewish Comm.

— Seven Shades of Black. 400p. (Orig.). 1995. mass mkt. 5.99 (*0-446-60104-7*, Pub. by Warner Bks) Little.

— Ties & Tensions: The 1986 Survey of American Jewish Attitudes Toward Israel & Israelis. LC 87-70839. 114p. (Orig.). 1987. pap. 7.50 (*0-87495-088-0*) Am Jewish Comm.

Cohen, Steven M. & Eisen, Arnold. In Search of Jewish Meaning in America. (C). (gr. 13). 1999. 25.00 (*0-415-91484-1*) Routledge.

Cohen, Steven M. & Horenczyk, Gabriel, eds. National Variations in Jewish Identity: Implications for Jewish Education. LC 99-19029. 288p. (C). 1999. text 65.50 (*0-7914-4371-X*, Suny Pr); pap. text 21.95 (*0-7914-4372-8*, Suny Pr) State U NY Pr.

Cohen, Steven M. & Liebman, Charles S. The Quality of American Jewish Life: Two Views. LC 87-72930. (Jewish Sociology Papers). 55p. (Orig.). 1987. pap. 3.50 (*0-87495-095-3*) Am Jewish Comm.

An Asterisk (*) at the beginning of an entry indicates that the title is appearing for the first time.

Cohen, Steven M., jt. auth. see Eisen, Arnold M.

Cohen, Steven M., jt. auth. see Heilman, Samuel C.

Cohen, Steven M., jt. auth. see Liebman, Charles S.

Cohen, Stewart C. The Twins Book. Bohanan, Ana, ed. & des. by. (Illus.). 32p. (Orig.). 1997. pap. write for info. (*1-888457-01-5*) Photo Do Not Bend.

Cohen, Stewart J., et al. Mackenzie Basin Impact Study (MBIS) Final Report. LC 98-141416. vii, 372 p. 1997. write for info. (*0-660-16973-8*, Pub. by Can7 Govern Pub) Intl Spec Bk.

Cohen-Stratyner, Barbara, ed. Popular Music, 1900-1919. 656p. 1992. 104.00 (*0-8103-2595-0*, 006514-99584) Gale.

Cohen-Stratyner, Barbara, intro. Performing Arts Resources Vol. 12: Topical Bibliographies of the American Theatre. LC 75-646287. (Performing Arts Resources Ser.). 195p. 1987. 25.00 (*0-932610-09-9*) Theatre Lib.

— Performing Arts Resources Vol. 13: The Drews & the Barrymores, a Dynasty of Actors. LC 75-646287. (Illus.). 161p. 1988. 25.00 (*0-932610-10-2*) Theatre Lib.

— Performing Arts Resources Vol. 14: Performances in Periodicals. LC 75-646287. (Illus.). 142p. 1989. 25.00 (*0-932610-11-0*) Theatre Lib.

— Performing Arts Resources Vol. 15: Arts & Access: Management Issues for Performing Arts Collections. LC 75-646287. 102p. 1990. 25.00 (*0-932610-12-9*, Z6935.P46) Theatre Lib.

— Performing Arts Resources Vol. 16: Taking the Pledge & Other Public Amusements. LC 75-646287. (Illus.). 129p. 1991. 25.00 (*0-932610-13-7*) Theatre Lib.

Cohen-Stratyner, Barbara & Cocuzza, Ginnine, intros. Performing Arts Resources, Vol. 10. LC 75-646287. (Illus.). 85p. 1985. 25.00 (*0-932610-07-2*) Theatre Lib.

Cohen-Stratyner, Barbara & Kueppers, Brigitte, eds. Preserving America's Performing Arts. LC 85-20975. (Illus.). 170p. (Orig.). 1986. pap. 25.00 (*0-932610-05-6*) Theatre Lib.

Cohen-Stratyner, Barbara, et al. After the Dance: Documents of Ruth St. Denis & Ted Shawn. Brady, Susan, ed. LC 75-646287. (Performing Arts Resources Ser.: Vol. 20). (Illus.). 141p. 1997. 25.00 (*0-932610-17-X*) Theatre Lib.

Cohen-Stratyner, Barbara, ed. see Fabris, Jacopo & Boullet, Cityoen.

Cohen-Stratyner, Barbara N., jt. ed. see Cocuzza, Ginnine.

Cohen-Stratyner, Barbara N., ed. see Gordon, Mel.

Cohen-Stratyner, Barbarba N., ed. see Lang, Franz.

Cohen, Stuart. Book of Rumor. 2000. 25.00 (*0-06-039228-2*) HarpC.

— The Book of Rumors. Date not set. 13.00 (*0-06-098742-1*) HarpC.

— Photographer's Resource: The Watson-Guptill Guide to Workshops, Conferences, Artists' Colonies. LC 97-60100. (Getting Your Act Together Ser.). (Illus.). 224p. 1997. pap. text 19.95 (*0-8230-7654-7*) Watsn-Guptill.

***Cohen, Stuart A.** Democratic Societies & Their Armed Forces: Israel in Comparative Context. LC 99-59809. (BESA Studies in International Security). 320p. 2000. 62.50 (*0-7146-5038-2*, Pub. by F Cass Pubs); pap. 26.50 (*0-7146-8092-3*, Pub. by F Cass Pubs) Intl Spec Bk.

Cohen, Stuart A. The Sword or the Scroll? Dilemmas of Religion & Military Service in Israel. (Sherman Lectures: Vol. 3). 112p. 1997. text 14.00 (*90-5702-083-1*, Harwood Acad Pubs) Gordon & Breach.

— The Three Crowns: Structures of Communal Politics in Early Rabbinic Jewry. 306p. (C). 1990. text 80.00 (*0-521-37290-9*) Cambridge U Pr.

Cohen, Stuart A., jt. auth. see Elazar, Daniel J.

Cohen, Suleiman. Agrarian Structures & Agrarian Reform. (Studies in Development & Planning: Vol. 8). 1978. lib. bdg. 72.50 (*90-207-0764-7*) Kluwer Academic.

***Cohen, Susan.** Pan Am 103: The Bombing, the Betrayals & a Bereaved Family's Search for Justice. 2000. 21.95 (*0-451-20165-5*, Sig) NAL.

Cohen, Susan, ed. Antisemitism: An Annotated Bibliography, Vol. II: 1986-87. LC 87-11842. 592p. 1991. text 83.00 (*0-8240-5846-1*, 462) Garland.

Cohen, Susan & Cohen, Daniel. Teenage Competition: A Survival Guide. LC 86-24307. 144p. (J). (gr. 7 up). 1986. 13.95 (*0-87131-487-8*) M Evans.

Cohen, Susan & Cohen, Ed. Mothers Who Drive Their Daughters Crazy: The 10 Types of "Impossible" Moms & How to Deal with Them. LC 97-19769. 240p. 1997. boxed set 20.00 (*0-7615-0985-2*) Prima Pub.

Cohen, Susan, jt. auth. see Cohen, Daniel.

Cohen, Susan D. Women & Discourse in the Fiction of Marguerite Duras: Love, Legends, Language. LC 92-13945. 256p. (C). 1993. 37.50 (*0-87023-827-2*); pap. 17.95 (*0-87023-828-0*) U of Mass Pr.

Cohen, Susan E., ed. Time after Time, the Photographs of Alice Wells. (Illus.). 60p. 1990. pap. 10.00 (*0-89822-065-3*) Visual Studies.

Cohen, Susan G. Bridging the Gap: Student to Professional Actor. (Classroom to the Stage & Screen Ser.: No. 1). (Illus.). 36p. (YA). (gr. 11 up). 1994. pap. 6.95 (*0-9641831-0-2*) Stage Coach.

Cohen, Susan S., ed. Antisemitism: An Annotated Bibliography, 1984-1985, Vol. 1. xxix, 392p. 1987. write for info. (*3-598-23697-2*) K G Saur Verlag.

— Antisemitism: An Annotated Bibliography, 1986-1987, Vol. 2. xxxiv, 559p. 1991. write for info. (*3-598-23698-0*) K G Saur Verlag.

— Antisemitism: An Annotated Bibliography, 1987-1988, Vol. 3. xxxiv, 544p. 1994. write for info. (*3-598-23699-9*) K G Saur Verlag.

Cohen, Susan S., ed. Antisemitism: An Annotated Bibliography 1988-1990, Vol. 4-6. 1997. write for info. (*3-598-23703-0*) K G Saur Verlag.

Cohen, Susan S., ed. Antisemitism: An Annotated Bibliography, 1991, Vol. 7. 500p. 1997. write for info. (*3-598-23704-9*) K G Saur Verlag.

— Antisemitism: An Annotated Bibliography 1991-1993, Vol. 7-9. 1997. write for info. (*3-598-23710-3*) K G Saur Verlag.

— Antisemitism: An Annotated Bibliography, 1992, Vol. 8. 500p. 1997. write for info. (*3-598-23705-7*) K G Saur Verlag.

— Antisemitism: An Annotated Bibliography, 1993, Vol. 9. 500p. 1997. write for info. (*3-598-23706-5*) K G Saur Verlag.

— Antisemitism: An Annotated Bibliography 1994-1995, Vol. 10-11. 1999. write for info. (*3-598-23707-3*) K G Saur Verlag.

— Antisemitism: An Annotated Bibliography 1996, Vol. 12. 450p. 2000. write for info. (*3-598-23709-X*) K G Saur Verlag.

— Antisemitism: An Annotated Bibliography 1997, Vol. 13. 450p. 2000. write for info. (*3-598-23712-X*) K G Saur Verlag.

Cohen, Sylvan. Your First Aquarium. (Illus.). 32p. 1992. pap. 2.29 (*0-86622-057-7*, YF100) TFH Pubns.

Cohen, Sylvan H., jt. auth. see Gabriel, Richard A.

***Cohen-Tannoudji.** Atom - Photon Interactions: Basic Processes & Applications. 680p. 1998. pap. 49.95 (*0-471-29336-9*) Wiley.

Cohen-Tannoudji, C. Atoms in Electromagnetic Fields. 684p. 1994. text 124.00 (*981-02-1242-9*); pap. text 61.00 (*981-02-1243-7*) World Scientific Pub.

Cohen-Tannoudji, Claude, et al. Atom Photon Interactions: Basic Processes & Applications. LC 91-40587. 680p. 1992. 129.00 (*0-471-62556-6*) Wiley.

— Photons & Atoms: Introduction to Quantum Electrodynamics. LC 88-37845. 468p. 1989. 135.00 (*0-471-84526-4*) Wiley.

— Photons & Atoms: Introduction to Quantum Electrodynamics. LC 88-37845. 496p. 1997. pap. 59.95 (*0-471-18433-0*, Wiley-Interscience) Wiley.

— Quantenmechanik 1 + 2, Vol. 1. 756p. 1997. text 61.00 (*3-11-013592-2*) De Gruyter.

— Quantenmechanik 1 + 2, Vol. 2. 676p. 1997. text 61.00 (*3-11-015859-0*) De Gruyter.

— Quantum Mechanics, 2 vols., 2 Vol. 1524p. 1992. pap. 175.00 (*0-471-56952-6*) Wiley.

— Quantum Mechanics, 2 vols., Vol. 1. Vol. 1. 898p. 1978. pap. 98.50 (*0-471-16433-X*) Wiley.

— Quantum Mechanics, 2 vols., Vol. 2. LC 76-5874. 626p. 1978. pap. 98.50 (*0-471-16435-6*) Wiley.

Cohen, Ted. Jokes: Philosophical Thoughts on Joking Matters. LC 99-12810. 1999. 15.00 (*0-226-11230-6*) U Ch Pr.

Cohen, Ted, et al, eds. Pursuits of Reason: Essays in Honor of Stanley Cavel. (Philosophical Inquiries Ser.: No. 2). 412p. (C). 1992. text 45.00 (*0-89672-266-X*) Tex Tech Univ Pr.

Cohen, Ted & Guyer, Paul. Essays in Kant's Aesthetics. LC 81-13091. (C). 1982. lib. bdg. 25.00 (*0-226-11226-8*) U Ch Pr.

— Essays in Kant's Aesthetics. LC 81-13091. (C). 1985. pap. text 14.50 (*0-226-11227-6*) U Ch Pr.

Cohen, Ted, et al. Nine Decades: The Northern California Craft Movement 1907-Present. 32p. (Orig.). 1993. pap. write for info. (*1-877742-03-1*) SF Craft & Folk.

Cohen, Theodore B., et al, eds. The Vulnerable Child, Vol. 1. (Vulnerable Child Monographs). 300p. 1993. 45.00 (*0-8236-6755-3*) Intl Univs Pr.

— The Vulnerable Child, Vol. 2. (Vulnerable Child Monographs). 231p. 1995. 37.50 (*0-8236-6756-1*) Intl Univs Pr.

— The Vulnerable Child, Vol. III. 1998. 52.50 (*0-8236-6757-X*, BN06757) Intl Univs Pr.

Cohen, Thomas. The Fire of Tongues: Antonio Vieira & the Missionary Church in Brazil & Portugal. LC 97-47357. 280p. 1998. 49.50 (*0-8047-2907-7*) Stanford U Pr.

Cohen, Thomas V. & Cohen, Elizabeth S. Words & Deeds in Renaissance Rome: Trials Before the Papal Magistrates. (Illus.). 304p. 1993. text 50.00 (*0-8020-2825-X*); pap. text 19.95 (*0-8020-7699-8*) U of Toronto Pr.

Cohen, Tim. The AntiChrist & a Cup of Tea. LC 98-84509. (Illus.). 448p. 1998. pap. 19.95 (*0-9662793-0-1*) Prophecy Hse.

— Messiah, History, & the Tribulation Period. 2000. write for info. (*0-9662793-1-X*, BK-02, Pub. by Prophecy Hse) Spring Arbor Dist.

***Cohen, Todd R.** Ultimate Conquest: Games for a New Generation. Flaig, Donald W., ed. LC 98-93624. (Illus.). 260p. (YA). (gr. 7-12). 1998. pap. text 39.95 (*0-9667921-1-4*) Tribute Pub.

Cohen, Tom. Anti-Mimesis from Plato to Hitchcock. LC 93-43559. (Literature, Culture, Theory Ser.: No. 10). 280p. (C). 1994. text 59.95 (*0-521-46013-1*); pap. text 18.95 (*0-521-46584-2*) Cambridge U Pr.

— Ideology & Inscription: Cultural Studies after Benjamin, de Man, & Bakhtin. LC 97-44526. (Literature, Culture, Theory Ser.: No. 27). 250p. (C). 1998. 59.95 (*0-521-59048-5*); pap. 17.95 (*0-521-59967-9*) Cambridge U Pr.

Cohen, Ulrike & Osterloh, Karl-Heinz. Zimmer Frei. Incl. Zimmer Frei. (GER.). 89p. text 17.50 incl. audio (*3-468-49420-3*); Zimmer Frei. (GER.). 57p. wbk. ed. 10.50 incl. audio (*3-468-49421-1*); Zimmer Frei. (GER.). 32p. teacher ed. 7.95 (*3-468-49422-X*); write for info. (*0-318-56964-7*) Langenscheidt.

Cohen, Uriel & Day, Kristen. Contemporary Environments for People with Dementia. LC 92-49834. (Illus.). 200p. 1993. pap. text 45.00 (*0-8018-4489-4*) Johns Hopkins.

Cohen, Uriel & McMurtry, Ruth. Museums & Children: A Design Guide. (Publications in Architecture & Urban Planning: No. R89-2). (Illus.). vi, 138p. (C). 1989. per. 15.00 (*0-938744-62-3*) U of Wis Ctr Arch-Urban.

Cohen, Uriel & Weisman, Gerald D. Holding on to Home: Designing Environments for People with Dementia. LC 90-4785. (Series in Contemporary Medicine & Public Health). (Illus.). 208p. (Orig.). 1991. pap. text 45.00 (*0-8018-4069-4*) Johns Hopkins.

Cohen, Uriel, et al. Case Studies of Child Play Areas & Child Support Facilities. (Publications in Architecture & Urban Planning: No. R78-2). (Illus.). v, 405p. 1992. reprint ed. per. 25.00 (*0-938744-03-8*) U of Wis Ctr Arch-Urban.

— Mainstreaming the Handicapped: A Design Guide. (Publications in Architecture & Urban Planning: No. R79-5). (Illus.). vi, 64p. 1992. reprint ed. per. 11.00 (*0-938744-05-4*) U of Wis Ctr Arch-Urban.

— Recommendations for Child Play Areas. (Publications in Architecture & Urban Planning: No. R79-1). (Illus.). vi, 380p. 1992. reprint ed. 25.00 (*0-938744-07-0*) U of Wis Ctr Arch-Urban.

Cohen, Uriel, ed. see Popox, Lubomir.

Cohen, Varda, et al. Yesh Lanu Llama, Level 1. (J). 1995. pap. 5.95 (*0-87441-492-X*); pap., wbk. ed. 4.95 (*0-87441-503-9*) Behrman.

— Yesh Lanu Llama, Level 2. (J). 1995. pap. 5.95 (*0-87441-569-1*) Behrman.

***Cohen, Victor.** From the Wellsprings of Chasidut. 2000. write for info. (*0-7657-6141-6*) Aronson.

Cohen, Von U., et al. Zimmer Frei. (GER.). pap. 23.95 incl. audio (*3-468-84440-9*) Langenscheidt.

Cohen, Walter. Drama of a Nation: Public Theater in Renaissance England & Spain. LC 85-2633. 416p. (C). 1985. pap. text 19.95 (*0-8014-9494-X*) Cornell U Pr.

Cohen, Warren. Ethics in Thought & Action: Social & Political Perspectives. (Illus.). 318p. (C). 1995. pap. text 35.95 (*1-880157-14-4*) Ardsley.

Cohen, Warren I. The American Revisionists: The Lessons of Intervention in World War I. LC 66-20594. 266p. reprint ed. pap. 82.50 (*0-8357-5397-2*, 202004600016) Bks Demand.

— America's Response to China: A History of Sino-American Relations. 3rd ed. 256p. 1989. text 22.00 (*0-231-06804-2*) Col U Pr.

***Cohen, Warren I.** America's Response to China: A History of Sino-American Relations. 4th ed. LC 89-17431. 270p. 2000. 45.00 (*0-231-11928-3*); pap. text 17.50 (*0-231-11929-1*) Col U Pr.

Cohen, Warren I. The Cambridge History of American Foreign Relations, 4 vols., Set. (C). 1993. 115.00 (*0-521-44988-X*) Cambridge U Pr.

— The Cambridge History of American Foreign Relations Vol. 4: America in the Age of Soviet Power, 1945-1991. (Illus.). 299p. (C). 1993. 44.95 (*0-521-38193-2*) Cambridge U Pr.

— The Cambridge History of American Foreign Relations Vol. 4: America in the Age of Soviet Power, 1945-1991. (Illus.). 299p. (C). 1995. pap. text 17.95 (*0-521-48381-6*) Cambridge U Pr.

***Cohen, Warren I.** East Asia as the Center: Four Thousand Years of Engagement with the World. 2001. 35.00 (*0-231-10108-2*) Col U Pr.

— East Asia at the Center: 4000 Years of Engagement with the World. LC 00-31615. 2000. write for info. (*0-231-10109-0*) Col U Pr.

Cohen, Warren I. East Asian Art & American Culture. (Illus.). 252p. 1992. text 40.50 (*0-231-07644-4*) Col U Pr.

Cohen, Warren I., ed. Pacific Passage: The Study of American-East Asian Relations on the Eve of the Twenty-First Century. LC 95-44851. 352p. 1996. 44.50 (*0-231-10406-5*) Col U Pr.

— Pacific Passage: The Study of American-East Asian Relations on the Eve of the Twenty First Century. LC 95-44851. 352p. 1996. pap. 20.00 (*0-231-10407-3*) Col U Pr.

Cohen, Warren I. & Iriye, Akira. The Great Powers in East Asia. (United States & Pacific Asia: Studies in Social, Economic & Political Interaction). 350p. 1990. text 57.50 (*0-231-07174-4*) Col U Pr.

Cohen, Warren I. & Tucker, Nancy B., eds. Lyndon Johnson Confronts the World: American Foreign Policy, 1963-1968. 352p. (C). 1995. text 54.95 (*0-521-41428-8*); pap. text 19.95 (*0-521-42479-8*) Cambridge U Pr.

Cohen, Warren I. & Zhao, Li, eds. Hong Kong under Chinese Rule: The Economic & Political Implications of Reversion. (Modern China Ser.). 263p. (C). 1997. text 59.95 (*0-521-62158-5*); pap. text 19.95 (*0-521-62761-3*) Cambridge U Pr.

Cohen, Warren I., et al. The China Connection. LC 77-18101. (Studies of the East Asian Institute). 322p. 1978. text 57.50 (*0-231-04444-5*) Col U Pr.

Cohen, Warren I., jt. ed. see Iriye, Akira.

Cohen, Waye, jt. auth. see Cohen, Basuk.

Cohen, Wayne R., et al. Cherry & Merkatz's Complications of Pregnancy. 5th ed. LC 98-32438. 1999. write for info. (*0-683-01673-3*) Lppncott W & W.

Cohen, Wilbur J. The New Deal 50 Years After: A Historical Assessment. LC 84-82347. (Symposia Ser.). 178p. 1984. pap. 10.50 (*0-89940-415-4*) LBJ Sch Pub Aff.

Cohen, Wilbur J. & Heffernan, W. Joseph. Welfare Reform: State & Federal Roles. (Policy Research Project Report: No. 59). 163p. 1984. pap. 9.95 (*0-89940-661-0*) LBJ Sch Pub Aff.

Cohen, William. At Freedom's Edge: Black Mobility & the Southern White Quest for Racial Control, 1861-1915. LC 90-44493. 340p. 1991. text 47.50 (*0-8071-1621-1*); pap. text 19.95 (*0-8071-1652-1*) La State U Pr.

— Constitutional Law Civil Liberty & Individual Rights: 1997 Supplement. 4th ed. (University Casebook Ser.). 71p. (C). 1997. pap. text. write for info. (*1-56662-574-2*) Foundation Pr.

— 1996 Supplement to Constitutional Law, Civil Liberty & Individual Rights. 3rd ed. 179p. 1996. pap. text, suppl. ed. write for info. (*1-56662-372-3*) Foundation Pr.

Cohen, William, ed. European Empire Building. LC 79-57459. (Problems in Civilization Ser.). 112p. (Orig.). 1980. pap. text 8.95 (*0-88273-410-5*) Forum Pr IL.

Cohen, William & Danelski, David J. Constitutional Law, Civil Liberty & Individual Rights. 3rd ed. LC 93-32111. 1138p. 1994. text 46.50 (*1-56662-089-9*) Foundation Pr.

— Constitutional Law, Civil Liberty & Individual Rights: Civil Liberty & Individual Rights. 4th ed. LC 97-5441. 1211p. 1997. text 42.75 (*1-56662-534-3*) Foundation Pr.

— 1998 Supplement to Constitutional Law, Civil Liberty & Individual Rights. 4th ed. (Pamphlet Ser.). 75p. 1998. pap. text, suppl. ed. 6.50 (*1-56662-664-1*) Foundation Pr.

— 1995 Supplement to Constitutional Law, Civil LIberty, & Individual Rights. 3rd ed. 70p. 1995. pap. text 5.50 (*1-56662-325-1*) Foundation Pr.

Cohen, William & Varat, Jonathan D. Constitutional Law, Cases & Materials: Cases & Materials. 10th ed. LC 97-5442. (University Casebook Ser.). 1718p. 1997. text 45.00 (*1-56662-529-7*) Foundation Pr.

— Constitutional Law, Cases & Materials: 1997 Supplement. 10th ed. (University Casebook Ser.). 154p. (C). 1997. pap. text. write for info. (*1-56662-498-3*) Foundation Pr.

— Constitutional Law, 1994: Cases & Materials. 9th ed. (University Casebook Ser.). 150p. 1994. suppl. ed. 7.95 (*1-56662-217-4*) Foundation Pr.

— 1998 Supplement to Constitutional Law, Cases & Materials. 10th ed. (University Casebook Ser.). 229p. 1998. pap. text, suppl. ed. 9.95 (*1-56662-663-3*) Foundation Pr.

Cohen, William, jt. auth. see Varat, Jonathan D.

Cohen, William, ed. see Facun, Anolia O.

Cohen, William A. The Art of the Leader. 215p. (C). 1991. pap. text 12.95 (*0-13-048471-7*, Busn) P-H.

— Building a Mail Order Business: A Complete Manual for Success. 4th ed. LC 95-23344. 592p. 1996. 42.95 (*0-471-10946-0*) Wiley.

— Constitutional Law, Cases & Materials. 9th ed. Varat, Jonathan D., ed. (University Casebook Ser.). (C). 1993. text. write for info. (*1-56662-058-9*) Foundation Pr.

— Developing a Winning Marketing Plan. LC 86-32402. (Business Strategy Ser.). 336p. 1987. 42.50 (*0-471-84529-9*) Wiley.

— Direct Response Marketing: An Entrepreneurial Approach. LC 83-19825. (Illus.). 510p. reprint ed. pap. 158.10 (*0-7837-3504-9*, 205783700008) Bks Demand.

— The Entrepreneur & Small Business Marketing Problem Solver. LC 91-13562. 288p. 1991. pap. 14.95 (*0-471-53133-2*) Wiley.

— The Entrepreneur & Small Business Problem Solver. 2nd ed. LC 89-32064. 565p. 1990. 168.95 (*0-471-50123-9*) Wiley.

— Entrepreneur & Sml Bus Prob So. 2nd ed. LC 89-32064. 592p. 1990. pap. 44.95 (*0-471-50124-7*) Wiley.

— The Executive's Guide to Finding a Superior Job. LC 78-7370. 176p. reprint ed. pap. 54.60 (*0-608-12904-6*, 202354300033) Bks Demand.

— How to Make It Big As a Consultant. 2nd ed. 320p. 1993. pap. 17.95 (*0-8144-7860-3*) AMACOM.

***Cohen, William A.** How to Make It Big as a Consultant. 3rd ed. 2001. pap. 17.95 (*0-8144-7073-4*) AMACOM.

— The Marketing Plan. 2nd ed. LC 97-12926. 352p. 1997. pap. 48.95 (*0-471-18033-5*) Wiley.

Cohen, William A. Model Business Plans for Product Businesses. 352p. 1995. 89.95 (*0-471-03030-9*); pap. 22.95 (*0-471-03028-7*) Wiley.

— Model Business Plans for Service Businesses. LC 94-41827. 352p. 1995. 75.00 (*0-471-03037-6*) Wiley.

***Cohen, William A.** The New Art of the Leader. 2000. 23.00 (*0-7352-0166-8*) PH Pr.

Cohen, William A. Principles of Technical Management. LC 79-54829. 234p. reprint ed. pap. 72.60 (*0-608-12697-7*, 202351500033) Bks Demand.

— Sex Scandal: The Private Parts of Victorian Fiction. LC 96-7641. (Series Q). 272p. 1996. text 49.95 (*0-8223-1856-3*); pap. text 16.95 (*0-8223-1848-2*) Duke.

— The Stuff of Heroes: The Eight Universal Laws of Leadership. LC 98-66359. 272p. 1998. 24.00 (*1-56352-524-0*) Longstreet.

***Cohen, William A.** The Wisdom of the Generals. LC 00-38551. 2001. 23.00 (*0-7352-0167-6*) P-H.

Cohen, William A. & Reddick, Marshall E. Successful Marketing for Small Business. LC 80-69699. 288p. reprint ed. pap. 89.30 (*0-608-11866-4*, 202307700031) Bks Demand.

Cohen, William B. The French Encounter with Africans: White Response to Blacks, 1530-1880. LC 79-84260. (Illus.). 384p. 1980. reprint ed. pap. 119.10 (*0-7837-9646-3*, 205927900005) Bks Demand.

— The Transformation of Modern France. 256p. (C). 1996. pap. text 26.76 (*0-669-41678-9*) HM Trade Div.

— Urban Governments & the Rise of the City: Five Munivipalities in the Nineteenth Century France. LC 97-32955. 350p. 1998. text 49.95 (*0-312-17695-3*) St Martin.

Cohen, William S. Report of the Quadrennial Defense Review. (Illus.). 69p. (C). 1997. pap. text 25.00 (*0-7881-4545-2*) DIANE Pub.

Cohen, William S., ed. Social Security Reform Options: Preparing for the 21st Century Hearing Before the Special Committee on Aging, U. S. Senate. 140p. (C). 1998. pap. text 25.00 (*0-7881-7295-6*) DIANE Pub.

C

— Suicide & the Elderly: A Population at Risk: Hearing Before the Special Committee on Aging, U. S. Senate. (Illus.). 143p. 1998. pap. text 30.00 (*0-7881-4316-6*) DIANE Pub.

— The United States Security Strategy for the East Asia-Pacific Region. (Illus.). 68p. (C). 1999. pap. text 20.00 (*0-7881-4356-5*) DIANE Pub.

Cohen, William S. & Allen, Thomas B. Murder in the Senate. large type ed. LC 93-13140. 533p. 1993. lib. bdg. 18.95 (*1-56054-752-9*) Thorndike Pr.

Cohen, William S. & Hart, Gary. The Double Man. 352p. 1986. pap. 3.95 (*0-380-70122-7*, Avon Bks) Morrow Avon.

Cohen, William S. & Lasson, Kenneth. Getting the Most Out of Washington. LC 81-12573. 236p. reprint ed. pap. 73.20 (*0-608-18301-6*, 203155900075) Bks Demand.

Cohen, William S., et al. U. S. Strategic Airlift Choices. LC 86-21425. (National Security Papers: No. 8). 1986. 7.50 (*0-89549-079-X*) Inst Foreign Policy Anal.

Cohen, William W. & Hirsh, Haym, eds. Machine Learning: Proceedings of the Eleventh International Conference. LC 94-21011. 381p. (C). 1998. pap. text 49.95 (*1-55860-335-2*) Rutgers U Pr.

Cohen, Y. & Peters, R. W., eds. Novel Adsorbents & Their Environmental Applications. 82p. 1995. 75.00 (*0-8169-0689-0*, S-309) Am Inst Chem Eng.

Cohen, Yehoshua. The Laws of Meat & Milk: Hebrew Text, English Translation & Commentary Digest.Tr. of Chochmas Adam: Hilchos Basur V'Cholov. 288p. 1991. pap. 16.95 (*1-880582-42-2*) Judaica Pr.

Cohen, Yehoshua, tr. from HEB. The Laws of Meat & Milk: Hebrew Text, English Translation & Commentary Digest.Tr. of Chochmas Adam: Hilchos Basur V'Cholov. 288p. 1990. 19.95 (*0-910818-91-6*) Judaica Pr.

Cohen, Yehoshua, jt. auth. see Danzig, Abraham ben Jehiel Michal.

Cohen, Yehoshua S. Diffusion of an Innovation in an Urban System: The Spread of Planned Regional Shopping Centers in the United States, 1949-1968. LC 72-76011. (University of Chicago, Department of Geography, Research Paper Ser.: No. 140). 148p. 1972. reprint ed. pap. 45.90 (*0-608-02240-3*, 206288100004) Bks Demand.

C

***Cohen, Yehoshua S.** The Experience of Immigration: A Literary Perspective on Immigration to Israel. LC 98-162979. 163 p. :p. 1998. write for info. (*965-223-996-8*) Magnes Pr.

Cohen, Yehoshua S. & Berry, Brian J. L. Spatial Components of Manufacturing Change, 1950-1960. LC 75-33654. (University of Chicago, Department of Geography, Research Paper Ser.: No. 172). 272p. 1975. reprint ed. pap. 84.40 (*0-608-02273-X*, 206291400004) Bks Demand.

Cohen, Yehoshua S. & Shinar, Amnon. Neighborhoods & Friendship Networks: A Study of 3 Residential Neighborhoods in Jerusalem. LC 85-21020. (University of Chicago, Department of Geography, Research Paper Ser.: No. 215). 154p. 1985. reprint ed. pap. 47.80 (*0-608-02261-6*, 206290200004) Bks Demand.

Cohen, Yehuda & Rosenberg, Eugene, eds. Microbial Mats: Physiological Ecology of Benthic Microbial Communities. LC 88-34241. (Illus.). 512p. reprint ed. pap. 158.80 (*0-608-08634-7*, 206915700003) Bks Demand.

Cohen, Yehudi A. Man in Adaptation Vol. 2: Cultural Present. 2nd ed. 615p. 1974. pap. text 34.95 (*0-202-01110-0*) Aldine de Gruyter.

Cohen, Yehudis, ed. see Shollar, Leah P.

Cohen, Yoel. Media Diplomacy: The Foreign Office in the Mass Communications Age. 224p. 1986. 37.50 (*0-7146-3269-4*, Pub. by F Cass Pubs) Intl Spec Bk.

***Cohen, Yoel.** The Whistle-Blower of Dimona: Israel, Vanunu, & the Bomb. 352p. 2000. pap. 20.00 (*0-8419-1409-5*) Holmes & Meier.

Cohen, Yolande, ed. Women & Counter-Power. 230p. 1989. 48.99 (*0-921689-11-X*, Pub. by Black Rose); pap. 19.99 (*0-921689-10-1*, Pub. by Black Rose) Consort Bk Sales.

Cohen, Yoram, ed. Pollutants in a Multimedia Environment. LC 86-22704. 340p. 1986. 79.50 (*0-306-42405-3*, Plenum Trade) Perseus Pubng.

Cohen, Yosef. JavaScript Cookbook. LC 97-1559. 683p. 1997. pap. 49.99 incl. cd-rom (*0-471-18145-5*) Wiley.

Cohen, Youseff, et al. Representation & Development in Brazil, 1972-1973. 2nd ed. LC 80-84095. 1980. write for info. (*0-89138-950-4*) ICPSR.

Cohen, Youssef. The Manipulation of Consent: The State & Working-Class Consciousness in Brazil. LC 89-5403. (Latin American Ser.). 194p. 1989. pap. 15.95 (*0-8229-5806-6*) U of Pittsburgh Pr.

— Radicals, Reformers, & Reactionaries: The Prisoner's Dilemma & the Collapse of Democracy in Latin America. LC 93-43274. 196p. 1994. pap. text 19.00 (*0-226-11272-1*); lib. bdg. 34.95 (*0-226-11271-3*) U Ch Pr.

Cohen, Ziv. Chemicals from Microalgae. 1999. 185.00 (*0-7484-0515-1*) Taylor & Francis.

Cohendet, Patrick. The Economics of Networks: Interaction & Behaviours. Llerena, P. et al, eds. LC 98-39222. (Illus.). xiv, 339p. 1998. 96.00 (*3-540-64699-X*) Spr-Verlag.

Cohick, Lynn, jt. ed. see Kee, Howard C.

***Cohill, Andrew M. & Kavanaugh, Andrea L.** Community Networks: Lessons from Blacksburg, Virginia. 2nd ed. LC 99-41777. 424p. 1999. 47.00 (*1-58053-030-3*) Artech Hse.

Cohl, Barbara. Bad Dog, Good Question! LC 98-46325. (Illus.). 192p. 1999. pap. text 12.95 (*0-87605-198-0*) Howell Bks.

Cohl, H. Aaron. The Book of Mosts. LC 97-6274. 304p. 1997. 22.95 (*0-312-15482-8*, Thomas Dunne) St Martin.

Cohl, H. Aaron, ed. see King, Alan.

Cohle, Stephen D., jt. auth. see Byard, Roger W.

Cohlene, Terri. Clamshell Boy. (Native American Legends Ser.). (Illus.). 48p. (J). (gr. 4-8). 1990. lib. bdg. 16.95 (*0-86593-001-5*) Rourke Corp.

— Clamshell Boy: A Makah Legend. (Illus.). 48p. (J). (gr. 4-7). 1990. pap. 4.95 (*0-8167-2361-3*) Troll Communs.

— Dancing Drum. (Native American Legends Ser.). (Illus.). 48p. (J). (gr. 4-8). 1990. lib. bdg. 16.95 (*0-86593-007-4*) Rourke Corp.

— Dancing Drum: A Cherokee Legend. (Illus.). 48p. (J). (gr. 4-7). 1990. pap. 4.95 (*0-8167-2362-1*) Troll Communs.

— Dancing Drum: A Cherokee Legend. (Native American Legends Ser.). (J). 1990. 10.15 (*0-606-04899-5*, Pub. by Turtleback) Demco.

— Ka-ha-si & the Loon. (Native American Legends Ser.). (Illus.). 48p. (J). (gr. 4-8). 1990. lib. bdg. 16.95 (*0-86593-002-3*) Rourke Corp.

— Ka-Ha-Si & the Loon: An Eskimo Legend. (Illus.). 48p. (J). (gr. 4-7). 1997. pap. 4.95 (*0-8167-2359-1*) Troll Communs.

— Little Firefly. (Native American Legends Ser.). (Illus.). 48p. (J). (gr. 4-8). 1990. lib. bdg. 16.95 (*0-86593-005-8*) Rourke Corp.

— Little Firefly: An Algonquian Legend. (Illus.). 48p. (J). (gr. 4-7). 1996. pap. 4.95 (*0-8167-2363-X*) Troll Communs.

— Native American Legends, 6 bks., Set. (Illus.). 288p. (J). (gr. 4-8). 1990. lib. bdg. 119.58 (*0-86593-000-7*); lib. bdg. 89.70 (*0-685-46445-8*) Rourke Corp.

— Quillworker: A Cheyenne Legend. (Native American Legends Ser.). (Illus.). 48p. (J). (gr. 4-8). 1990. lib. bdg. 16.95 (*0-86593-004-X*); lib. bdg. 14.95 (*0-685-36334-1*) Rourke Corp.

— Quillworker: A Cheyenne Legend. (Illus.). 48p. (J). (gr. 4-7). 1996. pap. 4.95 (*0-8167-2358-3*) Troll Communs.

— Quillworker: A Cheyenne Legend. (Native American Legends Ser.). Date not set. 10.15 (*0-606-05004-3*, Pub. by Turtleback) Demco.

— Turqoise Boy. (Native American Legends Ser.). (Illus.). 48p. (J). (gr. 4-8). 1990. lib. bdg. 16.95 (*0-86593-003-1*) Rourke Corp.

— Turquoise Boy: A Navajo Legend. (Legends Of The World Ser.). (Illus.). 48p. (J). (gr. 4-7). 1996. pap. 4.95 (*0-8167-2360-5*) Troll Communs.

— Turquoise Boy: A Navajo Legend. (Native American Legends Ser.). 1990. 9.15 (*0-606-05038-8*, Pub. by Turtleback) Demco.

Cohler, Anne M., ed. see De Montesquieu, Charles.

***Cohler, Bertram J.** Course of Gay & Lesbian Lives: Social & Psychoanalytic Perspectives. LC 99-87700. (Worlds of Desire Ser.). 1998. 50.00 (*0-226-11303-5*) U Ch Pr.

Cohler, Bertram J., jt. auth. see Galatzer-Levy, Robert M.

Cohler, Bertram J., jt. ed. see Anthony, E. James.

Cohler, Bertram J., jt. ed. see Tolan, Patrick H.

Cohler, David K. Broadcast Journalism: A Guide for the Presentation of Radio & Television News. 2nd ed. LC 93-17586. 1993. pap. text 41.00 (*0-13-088659-9*) Prntice Hall Bks.

Cohlmia, Kenneth, jt. auth. see Aurthur, Robert.

Cohn. Atlas of Jewish History. (Illus.). 232p. (C). 1996. pap. 29.99 (*0-415-08800-3*) Routledge.

— Mallarme's Masterwork. (Coll. De Proprietatibus Litterarum, Series Practica). 22.50 (*0-685-34939-X*, F67500) Fr & Eur.

Cohn, ed. International Political Economy: Global & Regional. LC 99-29540. 448p. (C). 1999. pap. text 52.00 (*0-321-01165-1*) Addson-Wesley Educ.

***Cohn, et al.** Religions of the World Series: Judaism. (Religions of the World Ser.). 128p. (C). 1998. pap. text 17.33 (*0-13-266271-X*) P-H.

Cohn, A. G., ed. see European Conference on Artificial Intelligence Sta.

***Cohn, Alan.** Sage Guide to Mutual Funds: Superior Investment Wisdom from the #1 Online Fund Gurus. LC 99-38442. 272p. 2000. 26.00 (*0-06-662007-4*) HarpC.

Cohn, Alan M. & Collins, K. K., compiled by. The Cumulated Dickens Checklist, 1970-1979. LC 81-52807. vi, 391p. 1982. 49.50 (*0-87875-230-7*) Whitston Pub.

***Cohn, Alayna.** HTML User's Interactive Workbook. 366p. 1999. pap. text 39.99 (*0-13-017004-6*) P-H.

Cohn, Albert. Shakespeare in Germany in the Sixteenth & Seventeenth Centuries. LC 75-166208. (Studies in Shakespeare: No. 24). 1971. reprint ed. lib. bdg. 75.00 (*0-8383-1330-2*) M S G Haskell Hse.

Cohn, Albert & Knopf, Barry. Professional Negligence: Malpractice Law in New Jersey. 3rd ed. 547p. 1991. 75.00 (*0-685-65977-1*) NJ Inst CLE.

Cohn, Albert & Miller, Leta E. Music in the Paris Academy of Sciences: 1666-1793. LC 78-70025. (Detroit Studies in Music Bibliography: No. 43). 69p. 1979. 16.00 (*0-911772-96-0*) Harmonie Park Pr.

Cohn, Albert M. George Cruikshank: A Catalogue Raisonne of the Work Executed During the Years 1806-1877. (Illus.). 391p. 1996. reprint ed. 75.00 (*1-888262-08-7*) Martino Pubng.

Cohn, Alfred & Chisholm, Joe. Take the Witness! 328p. 1996. reprint ed. 85.00 (*1-56169-211-5*) Gaunt.

Cohn, Alfred E. Medicine, Science & Art. LC 72-86742. (Essay Index Reprint Ser.). 1977. 18.95 (*0-8369-1126-1*) Ayer.

— Medicine, Science & Art. (Essay Index Reprint Ser.). 1982. reprint ed. lib. bdg. 15.50 (*0-8290-0840-3*) Irvington.

Cohn, Alvin & Crim, D. Correctional Supervision II Correspondence Course - Final Test. rev. ed. Geiman, Diane & Flannery, Denise, eds. 12p. 1994. pap. 40.00 (*1-56991-030-8*) Am Correctional.

Cohn, Alvin W., ed. Corrections: State of the Art: Critical Issues, Developments & Concerns. 94p. (Orig.). (C). 1993. pap. text 30.00 (*1-56806-351-2*) DIANE Pub.

— The Future of Policing. LC 77-92833. (Sage Criminal Justice System Annuals Ser.: No. 9). 303p. reprint ed. pap. 94.00 (*0-8357-4776-X*, 203771300009) Bks Demand.

Cohn, Amy & Schmidt, Suzy. Lincoln. LC 96-48709. (J). 1999. write for info. (*0-590-93566-6*) Scholastic Inc.

Cohn, Amy, ed. see Beatty, Patricia.

Cohn, Amy, ed. see Caseley, Judith.

Cohn, Amy, ed. see Child, Lydia Maria.

Cohn, Amy, ed. see Cohen, Barbara & Lovejoy, Bahija.

Cohn, Amy, ed. see Cole, Joanna & Calmenson, Stephanie.

Cohn, Amy, ed. see Dexter, Catherine.

Cohn, Amy, ed. see Giganti, Paul, Jr.

Cohn, Amy, ed. see Haviland, Virginia.

Cohn, Amy, ed. see Hayes, Sarah.

Cohn, Amy, ed. see Heide, Florence P. & Gilliland, Judith H.

Cohn, Amy, ed. see Hutchins, Pat.

Cohn, Amy, ed. see Jones, Diana Wynne.

Cohn, Amy, ed. see Kalan, Robert.

Cohn, Amy, ed. see Kellogg, Steven.

Cohn, Amy, ed. see Merriam, Eve.

Cohn, Amy, ed. see Morris, Ann.

Cohn, Amy, ed. see Prelutsky, Jack.

Cohn, Amy, ed. see Reiser, Lynn W.

Cohn, Amy, ed. see Roop, Peter & Roop, Connie.

Cohn, Amy, ed. see Ryder, Joanne.

Cohn, Amy, ed. see Schwartz, David M.

Cohn, Amy, ed. see Skurzynski, Gloria.

Cohn, Amy, ed. see Smee, Nicola.

Cohn, Amy, ed. see Williams, Vera B.

Cohn, Anthony G., et al, eds. Proceedings of the 1st-6th International Conferences on Principles of Knowledge Representation & Reasoning (KR) 672p. (C). 1998. pap. text 95.00 (*1-55860-554-1*) Morgan Kaufmann.

Cohn, Arlan. Kill As Few Patients As Possible & Fifty-Six Other Essays on How to Be the World's Best Doctor. 102p. 1987. pap. 9.95 (*0-89815-197-X*) Ten Speed Pr.

Cohn, Arlen. Friends of a Feather: An Eyeball Animation Adventure. LC 98-12608. (Eyeball Animation Ser.). (Illus.). 32p. (J). 1998. pap. 15.95 (*0-939251-96-5*) Accord CO.

— Lacey O'Neal: A Shoelace Book. LC 99-41980. (Books-in-Motion Ser.). (Illus.). 32p. (J). 1998. 15.95 (*0-939251-99-X*) Accord CO.

— Solar System SOS. LC 98-19491. (Illus.). 32p. (J). 1998. 15.95 (*0-939251-98-1*) Accord CO.

Cohn, Arthur. The Collector's Twentieth-Century Music in the Western Hemisphere. LC 74-167848. (Music Ser.). 1972. reprint ed. 35.00 (*0-306-70404-8*) Da Capo.

— Literature of Chamber Music. 3075p. 1998. 275.00 (*0-937276-16-2*) Hinshaw Mus.

— Musical Mind Benders. (Musical Quizzical II Ser.). 192p. (Orig.). 1992. pap. 13.95 (*0-911318-16-X*) E C Schirmer.

— Musical Quizzical. 96p. 1985. pap. 5.95 (*0-7935-0015-X*, HL00123471) H Leonard.

Cohn, Arthur B., jt. auth. see Crisman, Kevin J.

Cohn, Arthur B., jt. auth. see Lundeberg, Philip K.

Cohn-Bendit, Daniel. Petit Dictionnaire de L'Euro. (FRE., Illus.). 1998. 39.95 (*0-320-00282-9*) Fr & Eur.

Cohn, Benjamin & Osborne, W. Larry. Group Counseling: A Practical Self-Concept Approach for the Helping Professional. (Illus.). 147p. (Orig.). 1992. pap. text 15.00 (*0-9639116-0-0*) LS Communs.

Cohn, Bernard S. An Anthropologist among the Historians & Other Essays. 700p. 1988. 49.95 (*0-19-561875-0*) OUP.

— An Anthropologist among the Historians & Other Essays. (Oxford India Paperbacks Ser.). (Illus.). 706p. 1991. pap. text 19.95 (*0-19-562616-8*) OUP.

— Colonialism & Its Forms of Knowledge: The British in India. LC 96-6448. (Princeton Studies in Culture, Power & History). 200p. 1996. text 49.50 (*0-691-03293-9*, Pub. by Princeton U Pr); pap. text 16.95 (*0-691-00043-3*, Pub. by Princeton U Pr) Cal Prin Full Svc.

Cohn, Bernard S. & Singer, Milton B., eds. Structure & Change in Indian Society. LC 67-17609. (Viking Fund Publications in Anthropology: No. 47). 523p. reprint ed. pap. 162.20 (*0-608-12406-0*, 205213700040) Bks Demand.

Cohn, Bert M. An Illustrated Guide to Electrical Safety. 3rd ed. LC 97-20498. 235p. 1997. 37.95 (*1-885581-07-6*) ASSE.

Cohn, Beverly. What a Year It Was! - 1955. 1997. per. 22.50 (*0-922658-01-3*) MMS Pub.

— What a Year It Was! - 1945. 1997. per. 22.50 (*0-922658-02-1*) MMS Pub.

— What a Year It Was! - 1947. 1997. per. 22.50 (*0-922658-05-6*) MMS Pub.

— What a Year It Was! - 1948. 175p. 1997. per. 22.50 (*0-922658-11-0*) MMS Pub.

— What a Year It Was! - 1949. 175p. 1998. per. 22.50 (*0-922658-13-7*) MMS Pub.

— What a Year It Was! - 1950. (Illus.). 175p. 1999. per. 22.50 (*0-922658-15-3*) MMS Pub.

— What a Year It Was! - 1958. 175p. 1997. per. 22.50 (*0-922658-12-9*) MMS Pub.

— What a Year It Was! - 1959. 175p. 1998. per. 22.50 (*0-922658-14-5*) MMS Pub.

— What a Year It Was! - 1960. (Illus.). 175p. 1999. per. 22.50 (*0-922658-16-1*) MMS Pub.

***Cohn, Beverly.** What a Year It Was! 1951. (Illus.). 175p. 2000. per. 22.50 (*0-922658-17-X*) MMS Pub.

— What a Year It Was! 1961. (Illus.). 175p. 2000. per. 22.50 (*0-922658-18-8*) MMS Pub.

Cohn, Beverly & Nadel, Jack. Aging. (Nit-Wits Ser.). 80p. 1997. pap. 4.95 (*0-922658-09-9*) MMS Pub.

— Matrimony. (Nit-Wits Ser.). 80p. (Orig.). 1997. pap. 4.95 (*0-922658-08-0*) MMS Pub.

— Money. (Nit-Wits Ser.). 80p. 1997. pap. 4.95 (*0-922658-10-2*) MMS Pub.

— Sex. (Nit-Wits Ser.). 80p. 1997. pap. 4.95 (*0-922658-07-2*) MMS Pub.

Cohn, Bruce M. & Azzara, Alan J. Legal Aspects of Emergency Medical Services. LC 98-9780. (Illus.). 208p. (C). 1998. pap. text 18.00 (*0-7216-7014-8*, W B Saunders Co) Harcrt Hlth Sci Grp.

Cohn, Daniel & Kost, Joseph, eds. Biomedical Polymers: Molecular Design to Clinical Applications. LC 93-27080. vi,177p. 1993. pap. 250.00 (*1-85861-043-5*, Pergamon Pr) Elsevier.

Cohn, David. Aix Companion (Book) 496p. 1994. pap. text 63.00 incl. disk (*0-13-291220-1*) P-H.

— AutoCAD Release 14 CD-ROM Encyclopedia. (C). 1998. cd-rom 62.50 (*0-201-33152-7*) Addison-Wesley.

Cohn, David, jt. auth. see Higgins, Justin.

Cohn, David L. The Good Old Days. LC 75-22809. (America in Two Centuries Ser.). (Illus.). 1976. reprint ed. 50.95 (*0-405-07680-0*) Ayer.

— Mississippi Delta & the World: The Memoirs of David L. Cohn. Cobb, James C., ed. LC 94-24290. (Library of Southern Civilization). (Illus.). 312p. 1995. 24.95 (*0-8071-1991-1*) La State U Pr.

— Where I Was Born & Raised. (History - United States Ser.). 380p. 1993. reprint ed. lib. bdg. 89.00 (*0-7812-4834-5*) Rprt Serv.

— Workplace. (C). 2000. pap. text 40.00 (*0-13-459058-9*) P-H.

Cohn, David S. AutoCAD. (Expert Advisor Ser.). 1988. pap. text 26.95 (*0-201-05954-1*) Addison-Wesley.

— AutoCAD 14: The Complete Reference. LC 99-177276. (Complete Reference Ser.). 1089p. 1999. 49.99 incl. cd-rom (*0-07-882530-X*) Osborne-McGraw.

— AutoCAD LT: The Complete Guide. 640p. (C). 1994. pap. text 32.95 (*0-201-40908-9*) Addison-Wesley.

***Cohn, David S.** AutoCAD 2000: The Complete Reference. Cuthbertson, Joanne, ed. (Complete Reference Ser.). (Illus.). 1275p. 2000. pap. 49.99 (*0-07-212241-2*) McGrw-H Intl.

Cohn, David S. David Cohn's Autocad R14 Essentials: A Concise Reference. LC 98-27211. 480p. (C). 1998. pap. 40.00 (*0-201-45731-8*, Prentice Hall) P-H.

Cohn, David S., jt. auth. see Higgins, Justin.

Cohn, Deborah N. History & Memory in the Two Souths: Recent Southern & Spanish American Fiction. LC 98-58119. 256p. 1999. 39.95 (*0-8265-1332-8*); pap. 19.95 (*0-8265-1337-9*) Vanderbilt U Pr.

Cohn, Don. Beijingwalks: Six Intimate Walking Tours. (Illus.). 280p. 1995. pap. 15.95 (*0-8050-2105-1*, Owl) H Holt & Co.

***Cohn, Don, ed.** Virtue by Design: Illustragted Chinese Children's Books from the Cotsen Children's Library. (Illus.). 2000. pap. write for info. (*0-9666084-3-7*) Cotsen Occas Pr.

Cohn, Don, tr. from CHI. The Ugly Chinaman & the Crisis of Chinese Culture. 224p. reprint ed. pap. 19.95 (*1-86373-116-4*, Pub. by Allen & Unwin Pty) Paul & Co Pubs.

***Cohn, Dona E., et al.** California Automobile Collision Handbook. LC 00-42912. 2000. write for info. (*0-8205-4396-9*) Bender.

Cohn, Donald. Measure Theory. 276p. 1997. 49.50 (*0-8176-3003-1*) Birkhauser.

Cohn, Dorrit. The Distinction of Fiction. LC 98-6733. 232p. 1998. 42.00 (*0-8018-5942-5*) Johns Hopkins.

***Cohn, Dorrit.** Distinction of Fiction. 208p. 2000. pap. 15.95 (*0-8018-6522-0*) Johns Hopkins.

Cohn, Douglas. Jackson's Vil Campaign with Maps of the Civil War. 120p. 1986. 6.95 (*0-317-67959-7*) American Pub VA.

Cohn, E. R., jt. auth. see Skolnick, M. Leon.

Cohn, E. S. & White, S. O. Legal Socialization: A Study of Norms & Rules. 200p. 1990. 89.95 (*0-387-97213-7*) Spr-Verlag.

Cohn, Edward, et al. Genetics of Hearing Loss & Genetic Counseling: What the Practicing Audiologist Needs to Know. 44p. 1998. 48.00 incl. audio (*1-58041-025-1*, 0112146) Am Speech Lang Hearing.

Cohn, Einar. Danmark under Den Store Krig: En Okonomisk Oversigt. (Verdenskrigens Okonomiske Og Sociale Historie (Skandinavisk Serie)). (GER.). 1928. 100.00 (*0-317-27428-7*) Elliots Bks.

Cohn, Elchanan. Market Approaches to Education: Vouchers & School Choice. LC 96-41664. 600p. 1996. 96.00 (*0-08-042567-4*, Pergamon Pr) Elsevier.

Cohn, Elchanan, ed. Federal Block Grants to Education. 123p. 1986. 24.50 (*0-08-032691-9*, Pub. by PPL) Elsevier.

Cohn, Elchanan & Johnes, Geraint, eds. Recent Developments in the Economics of Education. (International Library of Critical Writings in Economics: Vol. 40). 680p. 1994. 265.00 (*1-85278-828-3*) E Elgar.

Cohn, Elizabeth C. & Gilroy-Doohan, Mary. Flip & See ECG. (Illus.). 120p. 1995. pap. text 21.95 (*0-7216-5834-2*, W B Saunders Co) Harcrt Hlth Sci Grp.

Cohn, Ellen G., et al. Evaluating Criminology & Criminal Justice, 51. LC 97-37969. (Contributions in Criminology & Penology Ser.: Vol. 51). 160p. 1998. 55.00 (*0-313-30153-0*, Greenwood Pr) Greenwood.

Cohn, Emil B. This Immortal People: A Short History of the Jewish People. LC 84-62563. 180p. (Orig.). 1985. pap. 5.95 (*0-8091-2693-1*) Paulist Pr.

Cohn, Franklin M., jt. auth. see Garay, Paul N.

***Cohn, Frederick G.** With All Five Senses. Hamburger, Michael, tr. 64p. 1999. pap. 12.95 (*1-874320-21-7*, Pub. by Menard Pr) SPD-Small Pr Dist.

Cohn, Gabriel H. & Fisch, Harold, eds. Prayer in Judaism: Continuity & Change. LC 95-51821. 272p. 1996. pap. 35.00 (*1-56821-501-0*) Aronson.

An Asterisk (*) at the beginning of an entry indicates that the title is appearing for the first time.

*Cohn, Gary. Michael J. Fox. (Overcoming Adversity Ser.). (Illus.). 128p. 1999. 19.95 (0-7910-5425-X) Chelsea Hse.

Cohn, Gerald E., ed. Systems & Technologies for Clinical Diagnostics & Drug Discovery, Vol. 3259. 254p. 1998. 69.00 (0-8194-2698-9) SPIE.

*Cohn, Gerald E. & Owicki, Jack C., eds. Systems & Technologies for Clinical Diagnostics & Drug Discovery II. 336p. 1999. pap. text 84.00 (0-8194-3073-0) SPIE.

Cohn, Gerald E. & Spoer, Steven A., eds. Ultrasensitive Biochemical Diagnostics II, Vol. 2985. LC 97-193041. 306p. 1997. 80.00 (0-8194-2396-3) SPIE.

Cohn, Haim. A Classical Invitation to Algebraic Numbers & Class Fields. LC 78-13785. (Illus.). 1995. 49.95 (0-387-90345-3) Spr-Verlag.

— The Trial & Death of Jesus. 1977. pap. 22.95 (0-87068-432-9) Ktav.

Cohn, Haim H. Human Rights in Jewish Law. LC 83-14846. 266p. 1984. 25.00 (0-88125-036-8) Ktav.

Cohn, Harry, ed. Doeblin & Modern Probability. LC 93-17268. (Contemporary Mathematics Ser.: Vol. 149). 347p. 1993. pap. 49.00 (0-8218-5149-7, CONM/149) Am Math.

Cohn, Harvey. Advanced Number Theory. (Illus.). 288p. 1998. reprint ed. pap. 8.95 (0-486-64023-X) Dover.

— Conformal Mapping on Riemann Surfaces. (Illus.). 352p. 1980. pap. text 11.95 (0-486-64025-6) Dover.

— Introduction to the Construction of Class Fields. unabridged ed. (Illus.). 224p. 1995. pap. text 7.95 (0-486-68346-X) Dover.

Cohn, Henry & Bollier, David. The Great Hartford Circus Fire: Creative Settlement of Mass Disasters. (Illus.). 224p. 1992. 42.00 (0-300-05012-7) Yale U Pr.

Cohn, Henry J. The Government of the Rhine Palatinate in the Fifteenth Century. (Modern Revivals in History Ser.). 300p. 1992. 72.95 (0-7512-0005-0, Pub. by Gregg Revivals) Ashgate Pub Co.

Cohn, Howard & Miller, Bill, eds. Moving Ahead in Your Career. 256p. (Orig.). 1987. pap. text 6.95 (0-07-606981-8) McGraw.

Cohn, Ilene, jt. auth. see Goodwin-Gill, Guy S.

Cohn, J. A., jt. auth. see Biegeleisen, Jacob I.

Cohn, Jan. Creating America: George Horace Lorimer & The Saturday Evening Post. LC 88-28083. (Illus.). 368p. 1990. pap. 15.95 (0-8229-5438-9) U of Pittsburgh Pr.

— Improbable Fiction: The Life of Mary Roberts Rinehart. LC 79-3997. (Illus.). 309p. 1980. reprint ed. pap. 95.80 (0-608-00902-4, 206169600010) Bks Demand.

— Romance & the Erotics of Property: Mass Market Fiction for Women. LC 87-27401. vii, 181p. (C). 1988. text 38.95 (0-8223-0799-5) Duke.

Cohn, Janice. The Christmas Menorahs: How a Town Fought Hate. LC 95-2053. (Albert Whitman Concept Bks.). (Illus.). 40p. (J). (gr. 2-6). 1995. lib. bdg. 16.95 (0-8075-1152-8) A Whitman.

*Cohn, Janice. The Christmas Menorahs: How a Town Fought Hate. (Illus.). 40p. (J). (gr. 2-6). 2000. pap. 6.95 (0-8075-1153-6) A Whitman.

Cohn, Janice. Molly's Rosebush. Tucker, Kathy, ed. LC 93-50612. (Illus.). 32p. (J). (ps-2). 1994. lib. bdg. 14.95 (0-8075-5213-5) A Whitman.

— Raising Compassionate, Courageous Children in a Violent World. LC 95-82234. 1996. pap. 15.95 (1-56352-276-4) Longstreet.

Cohn, Jay & Kubo, Spencer. Management of Heart Failure. 1990. pap. 12.95 (0-929240-17-0) EMIS.

Cohn, Jay B. Dementia: Annotated Bibliography of the Dementia Associated Diseases & Diagnostic Tests. 437p. (Orig.). 1992. pap. text 40.00 (0-935645-03-9) AJFP.

Cohn, Jay N., jt. auth. see Willerson, James T.

Cohn, Jay N., jt. ed. see Willerson, James T.

Cohn, Jim. The Dance of Yellow Lightning over the Ridge: Poems, 1993-1997. LC 98-172987. 160p. 1998. pap. 12.00 (0-9618487-4-X) Writers & Bks.

— Prairie Falcon. 96p. (Orig.). 1989. pap. 7.95 (1-55643-058-2) North Atlantic.

*Cohn, Jim. Sign Mind: Studies in ASL Poetics. 104p. 1999. pap. 21.95 (0-9671217-0-1) Mus Am Poetic Pubns.

Cohn, Joan, jt. auth. see Cohn, Peter.

Cohn, Joel R. Studies in the Comic Spirit in Modern Japanese Fiction. LC 97-30523. (Harvard-Yenching Institute Monograph Ser.: No. 41). 250p. 1998. 40.00 (0-674-84711-3) HUP.

Cohn, John, jt. auth. see Stephenson, Rex.

Cohn, John M., et al. Analog Device-Level Layout Automation. LC 93-42917. (International Series in Engineering & Computer Science, VLSI, Computer Architecture, & Digital Screen Processing). 304p. (C). 1994. text 125.00 (0-7923-9431-3) Kluwer Academic.

— Planning for Automation: A How-to-Do-It Manual for Librarians. 2nd ed. LC 97-27284. (How-to-Do-It Manuals for Libraries Ser.). 148p. 1997. 55.00 (1-55570-313-5) Neal-Schuman.

*Cohn, John M., et al. Writing & Updating Technology Plans: A Guidebook with Sample Policies on CD-ROM. LC 99-48200. 100p. 1999. pap. 99.95 incl. cd-rom (1-55570-365-8) Neal-Schuman.

Cohn, Jonas. Geschichte des Unendlichkeitsproblems im Abendlandischen Denken bis Kant. xi, 261p. 1983. reprint ed. 65.00 (3-487-00060-1) G Olms Pubs.

Cohn, Jordan. The Pro Basketball Bible: Formerly Rick Barry's Pro Basketball Scouting Report. (Illus.). 400p. 1993. pap. 16.95 (0-9636385-0-5) Basketball Bks.

Cohn, Jordan, jt. auth. see Barry, Rick.

Cohn, Joseph, Jr., ed. see Parker Hannifin Corporation Staff.

Cohn, Joseph H. I Have Loved Jacob. 109p. (Orig.). 1984. pap. 4.95 (1-882675-01-0) Chosen People.

Cohn, Jules. The Conscience of the Corporations: Business & Urban Affairs, 1967-1970. LC 77-135533. (Policy Studies in Employment & Welfare: No. 6). 136p. reprint ed. pap. 42.20 (0-608-11887-7, 202309000032) Bks Demand.

Cohn, Laura. The Door to a Secret Room: A Portrait of Wells Coates. (Illus.). 240p. 1999. text 43.95 (1-84014-695-8, Pub. by Ashgate Pub) Ashgate Pub Co.

Cohn, Laurence S. Effective Use of ANS COBOL Computer Programming Language: A Supplemental Text for Programmers Working with IBM's OS & DOS Systems. LC 75-5584. (Business Data Processing, a Wiley Ser.). 192p. reprint ed. pap. 59.60 (0-8357-9877-1, 201783100009) Bks Demand.

Cohn, Lawrence. Nothing but the Blues The Music & the Musicians. 1999. pap. text 35.00 (0-7892-0607-2) Abbeville Pr.

Cohn, Lawrence, ed. Nothing But the Blues: The Music & the Musicians. LC 93-2791. (Illus.). 432p. 1993. 45.00 (1-55859-271-7) Abbeville Pr.

— Nothing But the Blues: The Music & the Musicians. limited deluxe ed. (Illus.). 432p. 1995. 100.00 incl. cd-rom (1-55859-698-4) Abbeville Pr.

Cohn, Leigh, jt. auth. see Hall, Lindsey.

Cohn, Leigh, jt. auth. see Lemberg, Raymond.

Cohn, Leigh, jt. ed. see Schwartz, Mark F.

Cohn, Leopold, ed. see Alexandrinus, Philo.

Cohn, Leslie. The Dimension of Spaces of Automorphic Forms on a Certain Two-Dimensional Complex Domain. (Memoirs Ser.: No. 2/158). 96p. 1975. pap. 18.00 (0-8218-1858-9, MEMO/2/158) Am Math.

Cohn, Leslie, tr. see Shreider, Yu A.

Cohn, Linkie S. & Anderson, Donny. Winners for Life: A Teenager's Guide to Success Using the Proven Power of Goal Setting. 4th unabridged ed. (Illus.). 86p. 1996. per. 9.25 (0-9650545-0-0) Winners for Life.

Cohn, Louis. A Bibliography of the Writings of Ernest Hemingway. LC 73-2635. (American Literature Ser.: No. 49). 1973. reprint ed. lib. bdg. 75.00 (0-8383-1694-8) M S G Haskell Hse.

Cohn, Louis F., ed. Computing in Civil & Building Engineering: Proceedings of the Fifth International Conference (V-ICCCBE) Sponsored by the Technical Council on Computer Practices of the American Society of Civil Engineers, Anaheim, California, June 7-9, 1993. LC 93-17524. 1904p. 1993. 167.00 (0-87262-915-5) Am Soc Civil Eng.

— Computing in Civil Engineering & Symposium on Data Bases. LC 91-12813. 952p. 1991. pap. text 11.00 (0-87262-803-5) Am Soc Civil Eng.

Cohn, Lynne M. Driving off the Horizon: Poems by Lynne Meredith Cohn. (Illus.). 80p. (Orig.). 1997. pap. 7.00 (0-9654651-2-8) IM Press.

Cohn, Lynne M., ed. My First Time at a Swim Meet: Poetry from Summer Camp. 52p. (YA). 1998. pap. text 20.00 (1-56439-100-0, Pub. by Ridgeway) Partners Pubs Grp.

Cohn, M. Woerterbuch des Juedischen Rechts. (GER., Illus.). xii, 196p. 1981. 85.25 (3-8055-2062-X) S Karger.

Cohn, M. A., jt. auth. see Biegeleisen, Jacob I.

Cohn, M. Z. Limit Design for Reinforced Concrete Structures: An Annotated Bibliography. LC 77-12859. (American Concrete Institute Bibliography Ser.: No. 8). 90p. reprint ed. pap. 30.00 (0-608-15535-7, 202971500063) Bks Demand.

Cohn, M. Z., ed. Partial Prestressing, from Theory to Practice: Proceedings of NATO Advanced Research Workshop on Partial Prestressing, from Theory to Practice, 2 vols., Vol. I: Survey Reports. 1987. text 440.00 (90-247-3372-3) Kluwer Academic.

Cohn, Marc M. Dictionnaire Francais-Hebreu. rev. ed. (FRE & HEB.). 760p. 1988. 79.95 (0-7859-4813-9) Fr & Eur.

— Nouveau Dictionnaire Hebreu-Francais. rev. ed. (FRE & HEB.). 266p. 1934. pap. 12.95 (0-7859-4714-0) Fr & Eur.

Cohn, Margaret, et al. The ABCs of Behavior Change: Skills for Working with Behavior Problems in Nursing Homes. LC 94-61218. 246p. 1994. spiral bd. 29.95 (0-910251-69-X, ABC72) Venture Pub PA.

Cohn, Maria, jt. auth. see Raichur, Pratima.

Cohn, Marilyn M. & Kottkamp, Robert B. Teachers: The Missing Voice in Education. LC 92-14008. (SUNY Series, Teacher Preparation & Development). 358p. (C). 1992. text 24.50 (0-7914-1341-1) State U NY Pr.

Cohn, Marjorie & Dow, David. Cameras in the Courtroom: Television & the Pursuit of Justice. LC 98-16132. (Illus.). 203p. 1998. lib. bdg. 32.50 (0-7864-0502-3) McFarland & Co.

Cohn, Marjorie B. Francis Calley Gray & Art Collecting for America. (Illus.). 354p. 1986. 7.95 (0-916724-60-3, 4603) Harvard Art Mus.

— A Noble Collection: The Spencer Albums of Old Master Prints. (Illus.). 368p. 1992. pap. 19.95 (0-916724-80-8, 480-8) Harvard Art Mus.

Cohn, Marjorie B. & Becker, David P. Collecting for a College: Gifts from David P. Becker. LC 95-755252. (Illus.). 64p. 1995. pap. 15.00 (0-916606-28-7) Bowdoin Coll.

Cohn, Marjorie B. & Rogan, Clare I. Touchstone: 200 Years of Artists' Lithographs. LC 98-35410. (Illus.). 1998. pap. 15.00 (0-916724-99-9) Harvard Art Mus.

Cohn, Marjorie B., et al. Mark Rothko's Harvard Murals. (Illus.). 62p. 1988. pap. 12.95 (0-916724-69-7) Harvard Art Mus.

Cohn, Martin, jt. auth. see O'Higgins, Paul.

Cohn, Martin, jt. ed. see Storer, James A.

Cohn, Meryl. Do What I Say: Ms. Behavior's Guide to Gay & Lesbian Etiquette. 224p. 1995. pap. 11.95 (0-395-74538-1) HM.

Cohn, Michael. Jewish Bridges: East to West. LC 96-15386. 160p. 1996. 47.95 (0-275-95463-3, Praeger Pubs) Greenwood.

— The Jews in Germany, 1945-1993: The Building of a Minority. LC 94-12045. 144p. 1994. 49.95 (0-275-94878-1, Praeger Pubs) Greenwood.

— Technoshock: Combatting Stress at Work & Home in the 90's & Beyond. 124p. 1996. pap. text, per. 15.00 (0-7872-2807-9) Kendall-Hunt.

Cohn, Michael & Walters, Michael. Database Developer's Guide to Borland C++ 5. 1996. 49.99 (0-614-14446-9) Macmillan.

Cohn, Mike. Java Developer's Reference. 1996. 69.99 incl. cd-rom (0-614-20293-0, SamsNet Software) MCP SW Interactive.

— Java Developer's Reference. LC 96-68243. 1296p. 1996. 59.99 (1-57521-129-7) Sams.

— Sams Teach Yourself Visual Cafe 2 in 21 Days. LC 97-65451. 849p. 1997. pap. 39.99 (1-57521-303-6) Sams.

Cohn, Mike & Jory, James. Web Programming with Visual J++ LC 97-69400. 652p. 1997. pap. text 39.99 incl. cd-rom (1-57521-174-2) Sams.

*Cohn, Mike & Pearl, Jayne. Keep Or Sell Your Business: How to Make the Decision That Every Private Company Faces. 2000. pap. 22.95 (1-57410-139-0) Dearborn.

Cohn, Morris M. Essay on the Growth of Law. ix, 181p. 1983. reprint ed. 35.00 (0-8377-0444-8, Rothman) W S Hein.

*Cohn, Morris M. An Introduction to the Study of the Constitution: A Study Showing the Play of Physical & Social Factors in the Creation of Institutional Law, 1892. LC 99-38730. 2000. 50.00 (1-58477-032-5) Lawbk Exchange.

Cohn, N. & Peellaert, G. Twentieth Century Dreams. 1999. write for info. (0-375-40046-X) Vin Bks.

Cohn, Nik. Awopbopaloobop Alopbamboom: The Golden Age of Rock. rev. ed. (Illus.). 267p. 1996. pap. 13.95 (0-306-80709-2) Da Capo.

— The Heart of the World. LC 92-56357. 1993. pap. 12.00 (0-679-74437-1) Vin Bks.

— Yes We Have No: Adventures in the Other England. LC 99-15607. 327p. 1999. 22.00 (0-394-56870-2) Knopf.

Cohn, Nik, jt. auth. see Peelaert, Guy.

Cohn, Norman. Cosmos, Chaos, & the World to Come. 1995. pap. 17.00 (0-300-06551-5) Yale U Pr.

— Cosmos, Chaos, & the World to Come: The Ancient Roots of Apocalyptic Faith. LC 93-1294. 320p. 1993. 40.00 (0-300-05598-6) Yale U Pr.

— Noah's Flood: The Genesis Story in Western Thought. LC 96-18500. (Illus.). 166p. 1996. 35.00 (0-300-06823-9) Yale U Pr.

*Cohn, Norman. Noah's Flood: The Genesis Story in Western Thought. (Illus.). 166p. 1999. pap. 16.00 (0-300-07648-7) Yale U Pr.

Cohn, Norman. Pursuit of the Millennium. rev. ed. (Illus.). 412p. 1970. pap. text 16.95 (0-19-500456-6) OUP.

— Warrant for Genocide: The Myth of the Jewish World Conspiracy & the Protocols of the Elders of Zion. (Illus.). 320p. 1998. pap. 19.95 (1-897959-25-7, Pub. by Serif) IPG Chicago.

*Cohn, Norman Rufus Colin. Europe's Inner Demons: The Demonization of Christians in Medieval Christendom. rev. ed. LC 00-41169. 2000. write for info. (0-226-11307-8) U Ch Pr.

*Cohn, P. M. Classic Algebra. 3rd ed. LC 00-33014. (Illus.). 2000. pap. write for info. (0-471-87732-8) Wiley.

Cohn, P. M. Elements of Linear Algebra. 240p. 1994. per. 36.95 (0-412-55280-9, Chap & Hall CRC) CRC Pr.

*Cohn, P. M. Introduction to Ring Theory. LC 99-41609. (Undergraduate Mathematics Ser.). (Illus.). 225p. 2000. pap. 29.95 (1-85233-206-9, Pub. by Spr-Verlag) Spr-Verlag.

Cohn, P. M. Skew Fields: Theory of General Division Rings. (Encyclopedia of Mathematics & Its Applications Ser.: No. 57). 516p. (C). 1995. text 99.95 (0-521-43217-0) Cambridge U Pr.

Cohn, P. M., tr. see Carter, R. W., et al.

Cohn, Patrick J. The Mental Art of Putting: Using Your Mind to Putt Your Best. LC 95-22030. (Illus.). 140p. 1995. 19.95 (0-912083-87-5) Diamond Communications.

— The Mental Game of Golf: A Guide to Peak Performance. LC 93-34172. 1993. 19.95 (0-912083-65-4) Diamond Communications.

*Cohn, Patrick J. Peak Performance Golf: How Good Golfers Become Great Ones. LC 99-40995. 224p. 2000. pap. 16.95 (0-8092-2432-1, 243210, Contemporary Bks) NTC Contemp Pub Co.

Cohn, Paul D. Shelee & Me: Journeys of Intimate Discovery. 392p. 1996. pap. 11.95 (0-9645876-3-7) Burns-Cole Pub.

Cohn, Paul M. Algebra, Vol. 2. LC 73-2780. 497p. reprint ed. pap. 154.10 (0-8357-5305-0, 202668700002) Bks Demand.

— Algebra, Vol. 2. 2nd ed. LC 81-21932. 444p. 1989. reprint ed. pap. 137.70 (0-608-04598-5, 206536800002) Bks Demand.

Cohn, Paul V., tr. see Nietzsche, Friedrich Wilhelm.

Cohn, Pauline & Griffith, Dotty. Cooking with Days of Our Lives. LC 97-41552. (Illus.). 192p. 1997. 19.95 (1-55853-553-5) Rutledge Hill Pr.

Cohn, Pete F. Silent Myocardial Ischemia & Infarction. 3rd ed. LC 92-48488. (Fundamental & Clinical Cardiology Ser.: Vol. 13). (Illus.). 288p. 1993. text 115.00 (0-8247-9054-5) Dekker.

Cohn, Peter & Cohn, Joan. Fighting the Silent Killer: How Men & Women Can Prevent & Cope with Heart Disease Today. LC 93-31115. (Illus.). 240p. 1993. pap. 24.00 (1-56881-021-0) AK Peters.

*Cohn, Peter F. Silent Myocardial Ischemia & Infarction. 4th ed. LC 00-22916. (Fundamental & Clinical Cardiology Ser.). (Illus.). 327p. 2000. 125.00 (0-8247-0354-5) Dekker.

Cohn, Peter F., ed. Diagnosis & Therapy of Coronary Artery Disease. 1985. text 186.00 (0-89838-693-4) Kluwer Academic.

Cohn, Priscilla, ed. Ethics & Wildlife. LC 99-24443. (Animal Rights Library: Vol. 2). 276p. 1999. 89.95 (0-7734-8712-3) E Mellen.

Cohn, Priscilla N., et al, eds. Contraception in Wildlife, Bk. 1. LC 96-15830. 368p. 1996. text 99.95 (0-7734-8827-8) E Mellen.

Cohn, R. J. Baker's Gold. 226p. 1998. pap. 12.95 (0-9656811-8-1) Four Seasons.

Cohn, Robby. The Other Side of the Table. Kearns, Debrah L., ed. 144p. 1996. 13.95 (1-877804-12-6) Chandler White.

Cohn, Robert. Aphasia: A Pathophysiological Key to Memory & Volitional Naming. 137p. 1995. lib. bdg. 125.00 (1-56072-234-7) Nova Sci Pubs.

Cohn, Robert G. A Critical Work III: Illustrations. LC 94-70643. (Stanford French & Italian Studies: No. 81). 176p. 1994. pap. 56.50 (0-915838-97-4) Anma Libri.

— Mallarme's Divagations: A Guide & Commentary. LC 89-13832. (American University Studies: Romance Languages & Literature: Ser. II, Vol. 144). X, 411p. (C). 1991. text 55.95 (0-8204-1313-5) P Lang Pubng.

Cohn, Robert G., Jr. Mallarme's Masterpiece: New Findings. (De Proprietatibus Litterarum, Ser. Practica: No. 1). 1966. pap. text 24.65 (90-279-0089-2) Mouton.

Cohn, Robert G. Mallarme's un Coup de Des: An Exegesis. LC 77-10256. reprint ed. 34.50 (0-404-16311-4) AMS Pr.

— Modes of Art No. 1: A Critical Work. (Stanford French & Italian Studies: No. 1). 217p. 1976. pap. 56.50 (0-915838-29-X) Anma Libri.

— Toward the Poems of Mallarme. 1965. pap. 12.95 (0-520-03846-0, Pub. by U CA Pr) Cal Prin Full Svc.

— Ways of Art: Literature, Music, Painting in France: A Critical Work, II. (Stanford French & Italian Studies: Vol. 40). 384p. 1986. pap. 56.50 (0-915838-52-4) Anma Libri.

Cohn, Robert G. & Gillespie, Gerald E., eds. Mallarme in the Twentieth Century. LC 98-2933. 304p. 1998. 43.50 (0-8386-3795-7) Fairleigh Dickinson.

*Cohn, Robert Greer. Poetry of Rimbaud. 460p. 1999. pap. 29.95 (1-57003-332-3) U of SC Pr.

Cohn, Robert L. The Shape of Sacred Space: Four Biblical Studies. LC 80-11086. (American Academy of Religion Studies in Religion: Vol. 23). 87p. 1981. reprint ed. pap. 30.00 (0-608-08858-7, 206949700004) Bks Demand.

— They Called it Pilot Error: True Stories Behind General Aviation Accidents. LC 93-8267. 1993. 26.95 (0-8306-4464-4); pap. 16.60 (0-8306-4463-6) McGraw-Hill Prof.

— They Called It Pilot Error: True Stories Behind General Aviation Accidents. 330p. 1994. pap. 19.95 (0-07-011606-7) McGraw.

*Cohn, Robert L., et al. 2 Kings. LC 99-49660. (Berit Olam Ser.). 216p. 2000. 34.95 (0-8146-5054-6) Liturgical Pr.

Cohn, Robert L., jt. ed. see Silberstein, Laurence J.

Cohn, Robert M. & Roth, Karl S. Biochemistry & Disease: Bridging Basic Science & Clinical Practice. LC 96-24383. (Illus.). 587p. 1996. pap. 39.95 (0-683-02049-8) Lppncott W & W.

*Cohn, Robin. The P. R. Crisis Bible: How to Take Charge of the Media When All Hell Breaks Loose. LC 00-40232. 2000. write for info. (0-312-25230-7) St Martin.

Cohn, Rosanne & Monson, Suzanne. Discover Washington with Kids. 2nd ed. LC 98-38472. 1998. pap. 16.95 (1-881409-22-8) Jhnstn Assocs.

Cohn, Roy & Zion, Sidney. The Autobiography of Roy Cohn. (Illus.). 304p. 1988. 18.95 (0-8184-0471-X) Carol Pub Group.

Cohn, Roy M. How to Stand up for Your Rights & Win! 326p. 1981. 18.95 (0-8159-5723-8) Devin.

Cohn, Ruby. Anglo-American Interplay in Recent Drama. (Illus.). 202p. (C). 1995. text 49.95 (0-521-47267-9) Cambridge U Pr.

— Dialogue in American Drama. LC 76-154898. 348p. reprint ed. 107.90 (0-8357-9202-1, 201761300007) Bks Demand.

— Just Plays: Beckett's Theater. LC 79-83981. (Illus.). 328p. reprint ed. pap. 101.70 (0-8357-7557-7, 205232100097) Bks Demand.

— Samuel Beckett: The Comic Gamut. LC 62-13761. 348p. reprint ed. pap. 107.90 (0-8357-7943-2, 205701600002) Bks Demand.

Cohn, Ruby, ed. see Beckett, Samuel.

Cohn, Ruby, tr. see Aslan, Odette.

Cohn, S. When Strikes Make Sense - And Why? Lessons from Third Republic French Coal Miners. LC 93-28082. (Studies in Work & Industry). (Illus.). 290p. (C). 1993. 53.00 (0-306-44445-3, Plenum Trade) Perseus Pubng.

Cohn, S. H., ed. Non-Invasive Measurements of Bone Mass & Their Clinical Application. 240p. 1981. 138.00 (0-8493-5789-6, RC930, CRC Reprint) Franklin.

Cohn, Samuel. Race, Gender, & Discrimination at Work. LC 99-46078. (Foundations of Social Inquiry Ser.). 208p. 1999. text 59.00 (0-8133-3201-X); pap. text 22.00 (0-8133-3202-8) Westview.

*Cohn, Samuel K., Jr. Creating the Florentine State: Peasants & Rebellion, 1348-1434. (Illus.). 322p. 2000. 49.95 (0-521-66337-7) Cambridge U Pr.

Cohn, Samuel K., Jr. The Cult of Remembrance & the Black Death: Six Renaissance Cities in Central Italy. (Illus.). 429p. 1997. reprint ed. pap. text 18.95 (0-8018-5606-X) Johns Hopkins.

— Death & Property in Siena, Twelve Hundred Five-Eighteen Hundred: Strategies for the Afterlife. LC 88-35249. (Studies in Historical & Political Science: 10th Series, No. 2 (1988)). 352p. 1988. text 49.50 (0-8018-3594-1) Johns Hopkins.

C

— Women in the Streets: Essays on Sex & Power in Renaissance Italy. LC 96-11611. 1996. pap. text 15.95 (*0-8018-5309-5*) Johns Hopkins.

— Women in the Streets: Essays on Sex & Power in Renaissance Italy. LC 96-11611. (Illus.). 208p. 1996. text 45.00 (*0-8018-5308-7*) Johns Hopkins.

Cohn, Samuel K., Jr. & Epstein, Stephen A. Portraits of Medieval & Renaissance Living: Essays in Memory of David Herlihy. LC 96-5360. (Illus.). 480p. (C). 1996. text 64.00 (*0-472-10671-6*, 10671) U of Mich Pr.

Cohn, Samuel K., Jr., ed. & intro. see Herlihy, David.

Cohn, Sara D. Malpractice & Liability in Clinical Obstetrical Nursing. LC 89-18588. (Aspen Ser. in Obstetrical & Gynecological Nursing). 244p. 1990. pap. 72.00 (*0-8342-0141-0*, 20141) Aspen Pub.

Cohn-Sherbok, Dan. Fifty Key Jewish Thinkers. 152p. 1997. pap. 17.99 (*0-415-12628-2*) Routledge.

— Fifty Key Jewish Thinkers. LC 96-7554. 152p. (C). 1997. 65.00 (*0-415-12627-4*) Routledge.

— The Future of Judaism. 240p. 1994. pap. text 24.95 (*0-567-29267-3*, Pub. by T & T Clark) Bks Intl VA.

— God & the Holocaust. 140p. 1997. pap. 14.95 (*0-85244-341-2*, 1987, Pub. by Gracewing) Morehouse Pub.

— Understanding The Holocaust: An Introduction. LC 99-11715. (Issues in Contemporary Religion Ser.). 288p. (Orig.). 1999. pap. 24.50 (*0-304-70443-1*) Continuum.

— Islam in a World of Diverse Faiths. 240p. 1997. pap. 19.95 (*0-312-16597-8*) St Martin.

— Israel: The History of an Idea. 1992. pap. 22.95 (*0-687-85561-6*) Abingdon.

— The Jewish Messiah. 224p. 1997. pap. 24.95 (*0-567-08586-4*, Pub. by T & T Clark) Bks Intl VA.

— Jewish Mysticism: An Anthology. LC 96-148263. 210p. 1995. pap. 12.95 (*1-85168-104-3*, Pub. by Onewrld Pubns) Penguin Putnam.

***Cohn-Sherbok, Dan.** Jews, Christians & Religious Pluralism. LC 99-16931. (Toronto Studies in Theology: Vol. 79). 352p. 1999. text 99.95 (*0-7734-7920-1*) E Mellen.

Cohn-Sherbok, Dan. Medieval Jewish Philosophy: An Introduction. (Jewish Philosophy Ser.). 220p. pap. 14.95 (*0-7007-0453-1*, Pub. by Curzon Pr Ltd) Paul & Co Pubs.

***Cohn-Sherbok, Dan.** Messianic Judaism. LC 99-50300. 2000. 29.95 (*0-304-70730-9*) Continuum.

Cohn-Sherbok, Dan. On Earth As It Is in Heaven: Jews, Christians, & Liberation Theology. LC 86-23509. 144p. (Orig.). reprint ed. pap. 44.70 (*0-7837-5507-4*, 204527700005) Bks Demand.

Cohn-Sherbok, Dan. A Short History of Judaism. 160p. 1995. pap. 10.95 (*1-85168-206-6*, Pub. by Onewrld Pubns) Penguin Putnam.

Cohn-Sherbok, Dan. A Traditional Quest: Essays in Honour of Louis Jacobs. (JSOTS Ser.: Vol. 114). 233p. 1991. 70.00 (*1-85075-279-6*, Pub. by Sheffield Acad) CUP Services.

— Understanding the Holocaust: An Introduction. (Issues in Contemporary Religion Ser.). 288p. 1999. 19.95 (*0-304-70442-3*) Continuum.

Cohn-Sherbok, Dan, ed. Divine Intervention & Miracles in Jewish Theology. LC 95-18806. (Jewish Studies: Vol. 6). 220p. 1996. text 89.95 (*0-7734-9093-0*) E Mellen.

***Cohn-Sherbok, Dan, ed.** The Future of Jewish-Christian Dialogue. (Toronto Studies in Theology: Vol. 80). 291p. 1999. 89.95 (*0-7734-7923-6*) E Mellen.

Cohn-Sherbok, Dan, ed. Problems in Contemporary Jewish Theology. LC 91-38782. 292p. 1992. lib. bdg. 89.95 (*0-7734-9645-9*) E Mellen.

— The Saying Of Moses. LC 98-20015. 64p. 1998. reprint ed. pap. 5.95 (*0-88001-637-X*) HarpC.

— Theodicy. LC 97-3725. (Jewish Studies: Vol. 18). 104p. 1997. text 59.95 (*0-7734-8690-9*) E Mellen.

— Torah & Revelation. LC 92-34722. 256p. 1992. text 89.95 (*0-7734-9165-1*) E Mellen.

— World Religions & Human Liberation. LC 91-47696. (Faith Meets Faith Ser.). 151p. reprint ed. pap. 46.90 (*0-608-20255-X*, 207151400012) Bks Demand.

Cohn-Sherbok, Dan & Cohn-Sherbok, Lavinia. Jewish & Christian Mysticism. 192p. (C). 1994. 22.50 (*0-8264-0695-5*) Continuum.

Cohn-Sherbok, Dan & Lewis, Christopher, eds. Beyond Death: Theological & Philosphical Reflections on Life After Death. LC 94-34880. 232p. 1995. text 45.00 (*0-312-12482-1*) St Martin.

Cohn-Sherbok, Dan, jt. auth. see Cohn-Sherbok, Lavinia.

Cohn-Sherbok, Dan, jt. auth. see Linzey, Andrew.

Cohn-Sherbok, Dan, jt. ed. see Leahy, Michael.

Cohn-Sherbok, Daniel. Atlas of Jewish History. LC 93-15018. (Illus.). 224p. (C). 1994. 75.00 (*0-415-08684-1*) Routledge.

— Holocaust Theology. 144p. 1991. reprint ed. 10.95 (*0-551-01829-1*) Harper SF.

— Jewish Petitionary Prayer: A Theological Exploration. LC 88-9256. (Toronto Studies in Theology: Vol. 35). 150p. 1989. lib. bdg. 69.95 (*0-88946-781-1*) E Mellen.

— Judaism. 288p. 1998. pap. text 14.95 (*1-85168-176-0*, Pub. by Onewrld Pubns) Penguin Putnam.

— Judaism & Other Faiths. LC 93-26260. 1994. text 59.95 (*0-312-10384-0*) St Martin.

— Rabbinic Perspectives on the New Testament. LC 90-21375. (Studies in the Bible & Early Christianity: Vol. 28). 140p. 1990. lib. bdg. 69.95 (*0-88946-689-0*) E Mellen.

***Cohn-Sherbok, Daniel.** Wisdom of Judaism. 2000. 15.95 (*1-85168-228-7*, Pub. by Onewrld Pubns) Penguin Putnam.

Cohn-Sherbok, Daniel. World Religions & Human Liberation. (Faith Meets Faith Ser.). 1992. 40.00 (*0-88344-796-7*); pap. 17.00 (*0-88344-795-9*) Orbis Bks.

Cohn-Sherbok, Daniel, ed. The Salman Rushdie Controversy in Inter-Religious Perspective. LC 90-6186. (Symposium Ser.: Vol. 27). 164p. 1990. lib. bdg. 79.95 (*0-88946-719-6*) E Mellen.

Cohn-Sherbok, Daniel & McLellan, David, eds. Religion in Public Life. LC 91-32830. 135p. 1992. text 59.95 (*0-312-07279-1*) St Martin.

Cohn-Sherbok, Lavinia. A History of Jewish Civilization. (Illus.). 192p. 1997. 17.98 (*0-7858-0798-5*) Bk Sales Inc.

Cohn-Sherbok, Lavinia. A Short Introduction to Judaism. 192p. 1997. pap. 13.95 (*1-85168-207-4*, Pub. by Onewrld Pubns) Penguin Putnam.

Cohn-Sherbok, Lavinia. Who's Who in Christianity. LC 97-22310. 384p. 1997. pap. 19.99 (*0-415-13583-4*) Routledge.

— Who's Who in Christianity. LC 97-22310. 384p. (C). 1997. 75.00 (*0-415-13582-6*) Routledge.

Cohn-Sherbok, Lavinia & Cohn-Sherbok, Dan. A Popular Dictionary of Judaism. LC 95-229166. 216p. (C). 1995. 45.00 (*0-7007-0366-7*); pap. 19.95 (*0-7007-0357-8*, Pub. by Curzon Pr Ltd) Paul & Co Pubs.

— A Popular Dictionary of Judaism. LC 97-21950. (Illus.). 208p. 1997. pap. 14.95 (*0-8442-0423-4*, 04234) NTC Contemp Pub Co.

— Short Reader in Judaism. LC 96-185610. 191p. 1996. pap. 14.95 (*1-85168-112-4*, 573, Pub. by Onewrld Pubns) Penguin Putnam.

Cohn-Sherbok, Lavinia, jt. auth. see Cohn-Sherbok, Dan.

Cohn, Sherrye. Arthur Dove: Nature as Symbol. LC 85-5848. (Studies in the Fine Arts: The Avant-Garde: No. 49). 254p. reprint ed. pap. 78.80 (*0-8357-2018-7*, 207065800015) Bks Demand.

Cohn, Stephen, tr. see Rilke, Rainer Maria.

Cohn, Steven M. California Law & Ethics for Therapists. Robbins, Judd, ed. (In Your Face Flash Card Study Sets Ser.). 206p. (Orig.). 1996. pap. 24.99 (*1-961493-72-1*) Present Dynam.

— DSM-IV Flash Card Set, Vol. 1. Robbins, Judd, ed. (In Your Face Flash Card Sets Ser.). 412p. (Orig.). (C). 1995. pap. 34.99 (*0-9614937-1-2*) Present Dynam.

— Too Cheap to Meter: An Economic & Philosophical Analysis of the Nuclear Dream. LC 96-41499. (SUNY Series in Radical, Social & Political Theory). 476p. (C). 1997. text 65.50 (*0-7914-3389-7*); pap. text 21.95 (*0-7914-3390-0*) State U NY Pr.

Cohn, Stuart R. Securities Counseling for New & Developing Companies, 1 vol. (Corporate Law Ser.). 1993. 130.00 (*0-685-68840-2*) West Group.

Cohn, Stuart R. & Ames, Stuart D. Florida Business Laws Annotated 1997 Edition: With Commentary, Cases & Forms. LC 96-77289. 720p. 1996. pap. text. write for info. (*0-7620-0080-5*) West Group.

***Cohn, Stuart R. & Zake, Fred.** Capital Market Development in Uganda. 456p. 1999. pap. 45.00 (*0-935328-88-2*) Intl Law Inst.

Cohn, Susan. Do It One-Handed: A Manual of Daily Living Skills for Stroke Rehabilitation. Kurtis, Arlene, ed. LC 93-79093. (Illus.). vi, 51p. 1997. spiral bd. 11.50 (*0-9657693-0-5*) Lenox Hse.

— Green at Work: Finding a Business Career That Works for the Environment. expanded rev. ed. LC 94-47939. 400p. 1995. pap. 19.95 (*1-55963-334-4*) Island Pr.

***Cohn, Susan & Hudson, Don.** Finding Your Way with an MBA: Insights from Those Landing Their Ideal Jobs. LC 99-89690. 320p. 2000. pap. 16.95 (*0-471-38378-3*) Wiley.

Cohn, Susan L., jt. ed. see Walterhouse, David O.

Cohn, Terri. Diego Rivera: Selected Works, 1918-1949. (Illus.). 10p. (Orig.). 1984. pap. 10.00 (*0-9605194-4-0*) Mexican Museum.

Cohn, Theodore & Anderson, Robert, eds. Innovation Systems in a Global Context: The North American Experience. pap. 22.95 (*0-7735-1809-6*) McG-Queens Univ Pr.

Cohn, Theodore & Lindberg, Roy A. Survival & Growth: Management Strategies for the Small Firm. LC 73-92163. 240p. reprint ed. pap. 74.40 (*0-608-14416-9*, 205170000002) Bks Demand.

Cohn, Theodore E., ed. Visual Detection: Collected Works in Optics, Vol. 3. 470p. (Orig.). 1993. pap. 74.00 (*1-55752-265-0*) Optical Soc.

***Cohn, Theodore H., et al.** Power in the Global Era: Grounding Globalization. LC 00-33300. 2000. write for info. (*0-312-23562-3*) St Martin.

Cohn, Victor. News & Numbers: A Guide to Reporting Statistical Claims & Controversies in Health & Other Fields. 190p. (C). 1988. pap. text 16.95 (*0-8138-1437-5*) Iowa St U Pr.

Cohn-Vossen, S., jt. auth. see Hilbert, David.

Cohn-Vossen, Stephan, jt. auth. see Hilbert, David.

Cohn, Waldo E. & Moldave, Divie, eds. Progress of Nucleic Acid Research & Molecular Biology, Vol. 56. (Illus.). 391p. (C). 1997. text 89.00 (*0-12-540056-X*) Morgan Kaufmann.

Cohn, Waldo E. & Moldave, Kivie, eds. Progress in Nucleic Acid Research & Molecular Biology, Vol. 5. (Illus.). 345p. (C). 1995. text 90.00 (*0-12-540050-0*) Acad Pr.

— Progress in Nucleic Acid Research & Molecular Biology, Vol. 27. (Illus.). 408p. (C). 1994. text 104.00 (*0-12-540047-0*) Acad Pr.

— Progress in Nucleic Acid Research & Molecular Biology, Vol. 33. (Illus.). 401p. (C). 1996. text 85.00 (*0-12-540053-5*) Acad Pr.

— Progress in Nucleic Acid Research & Molecular Biology, Vol. 48. (Illus.). 379p. (C). 1994. text. write for info. (*0-12-540048-9*) Acad Pr.

— Progress in Nucleic Acid Research & Molecular Biology, Vol. 51. (Illus.). 369p. (C). 1995. text 90.00 (*0-12-540051-9*) Acad Pr.

— Progress in Nucleic Acid Research & Molecular Biology, Vol. 52. (Illus.). 370p. (C). 1996. text 85.00 (*0-12-540052-7*) Acad Pr.

— Progress in Nucleic Acid Research & Molecular Biology, Vol. 54. (Illus.). 387p. (C). 1996. text 85.00 (*0-12-540054-3*) Acad Pr.

— Progress in Nucleic Acid Research & Molecular Biology, Vol. 55. (Illus.). 291p. (C). 1996. text 85.00 (*0-12-540055-1*) Acad Pr.

— Progress with Nucleic Acid Research & Molecular Biology, Vol. 49. (Illus.). 394p. (C). 1994. text 100.00 (*0-12-540049-7*) Acad Pr.

Cohn, Werner. Partners in Hate: Noam Chomsky & the Holocaust Deniers. (Illus.). 164p. (Orig.). 1995. pap. 9.95 (*0-9645897-0-2*) Avukah Pubns.

Cohn, Y., ed. Application of Control Theory in Ecology: Lecture Notes in Biomathematics, Vol. 73. vii, 101p. 1987. pap. 33.00 (*0-387-18104-0*) Spr-Verlag.

Cohn, Zanvil A., ed. see Abraham, Edward P., et al.

***Coho, Donald E.** Design Project Tutorial Using SolidWorks 99. (Illus.). 1999. pap. 49.95 (*1-58503-018-X*, SDC Pubns) Schroff Dev Corp.

Cohodas. When the Band Plays Dixie. 1997. 23.00 (*0-02-874011-4*) Free Pr.

Cohodas, Marvin. Basket Weavers for the California Curio Trade: Elizabeth & Louise Hickoc. LC 97-4814. (Illus.). 464p. (C). 1997. text 39.95 (*0-8165-1518-2*) U of Ariz Pr.

Cohodas, Marvin, et al. The Arts of the North American Indian: Native Traditions in Evolution. Wade, Edwin L., ed. LC 85-21932. (Illus.). 320p. 1986. 50.00 (*0-933920-55-5*) Hudson Hills.

— The Arts of the North American Indian: Native Traditions in Evolution. Wade, Edwin L., ed. LC 85-21932. (Illus.). 320p. 1986. reprint ed. 35.00 (*0-933920-56-3*) Hudson Hills.

Cohodas, Nadine. The Band Played Dixie: Race & the Liberal Conscience at Ole Miss. LC 97-3685. (Illus.). 309p. 1997. 25.50 (*0-684-82721-2*) S&S Trade.

***Cohodas, Nadine.** Spinning Blues into Gold: The Chess Brothers & the Legendary Chess Records. LC 00-25480. (Illus.). 368p. 2000. text 25.95 (*0-312-26133-0*) St Martin.

Cohodas, Nadine. Strom Thurmond: And the Politics of Southern Change. LC 94-15867. 1994. 18.95 (*0-86554-446-8*, MUP/P108) Mercer Univ Pr.

— Strom Thurmond: And the Politics of Southern Change. (Illus.). 608p. 1993. 27.50 (*0-671-68935-5*) S&S Trade.

Cohodes, Donald R. & Kinkead, Brian M. Hospital Capital Formation in the 1980s. LC 83-49192. (Johns Hopkins Studies in Health Care Finance & Administration: No. 1). (Illus.). 157p. 1984. reprint ed. pap. 48.70 (*0-608-05935-8*, 206627100008) Bks Demand.

***Cohon.** Hume - Moral & Political Philosophy. 500p. 2000. 165.00 (*1-84014-721-0*) Ashgate Pub Co.

Cohon, George & Macfarlane, David. To Russia with Fries. (Illus.). 352p. 1999. 21.95 (*0-7710-2198-4*) McCland & Stewart.

Cohon, Helen S., jt. auth. see Cohon, Mary E.

Cohon, Mary E. & Cohon, Helen S. Mud Bud & Poxie: Their Very First Adventure. LC 98-91218. (Illus.). 30p. (J). (ps-k). 1998. pap. 5.99 (*0-9663116-0-4*) Little Idea.

Cohoon. C++Programming Design. 1997. lab manual ed. 16.00 (*0-256-24092-2*) McGraw.

Cohoon, J. W., tr. Discourses, 5 vols., 1. (Loeb Classical Library: No. 257, 339, 358, 376, 385). 586p. 1932. 18.95 (*0-674-99283-0*) HUP.

Cohoon, James & Davidson, Jack. C++ Program Design: An Introduction to Programming & Object Oriented Design. 2nd ed. 840p. (C). Date not set. pap. 45.00 (*0-07-228235-5*) McGraw.

Cohoon, James P. Algorithms for Some Design Automation Problems. LC 84-24101. (Computer Science: Computer Architecture & Design Ser.: No. 3). (Illus.). 114p. reprint ed. pap. 35.40 (*0-8357-1615-5*, 207037200088) Bks Demand.

Cohoon, James P. & Davidson, Jack W. C++ Program Design: An Introduction to Programming & Object-Oriented Design. 704p. (C). 1996. text 47.00 (*0-256-19744-X*, Irwn McGrw-H) McGrw-H Hghr Educ.

Cohorst, Lois. High Mileage. LC 95-81513. (Illus.). 172p. 1996. pap. 9.95 (*1-882420-27-6*) Hearth KS.

Cohoughlcyn-Burroughs, Charles E. Bristol Masonic Ritual: The Oldest & Most Unique Craft Ritual Used in England. 76p. 1996. reprint ed. pap. 24.95 (*1-56459-984-1*) Kessinger Pub.

Cohr, Amy, ed. see Neitzel, Shirley.

Cohrs, I. Lifelong: A Personal Health & Medical Journal. 160p. 1997. ring bd. write for info. (*0-9659954-8-8*) LIHNC Co.

Cohrs, Timothy. Michael Chernishov - Aggressive Symbols. (Illus.). 20p. (Orig.). 1987. pap. 10.00 (*0-913263-15-X*) Exit Art.

Cohrssen, John J. & Covello, Vincent T. Risk Analysis: A Guide to Principles & Methods for Analyzing Health & Environmental Risks. 407p. (C). 1999. reprint ed. pap. text 50.00 (*0-7881-4998-9*) DIANE Pub.

Coia, Denise A., jt. auth. see Atkinson, Jacqueline M.

Coia, Lawrence R. & Moylan, David J. Introduction to Clinical Radiation Oncology. 3rd ed. LC 96-9113. (Illus.). 580p. 1998. pap. text 48.95 (*0-944838-70-7*) Med Physics Pub.

Coiera, E. Clinician's Guide to Medical Informatics, the Internet & Telemedicine: The Internet, Communication & Information Technologies in Healthcare. LC 97-199098. 384p. 1997. pap. text 29.99 (*0-412-75710-9*, Pub. by E A) OUP.

***Coifman, Ronald, ed.** Topics in Analysis & Its Applications. 470p. 2000. 78.00 (*981-02-4093-7*); pap. 38.00 (*981-02-4094-5*) World Scientific Pub.

Coifman, Ronald & Weiss, Guido. Transference Methods in Analysis. LC 77-24098. (CBMS Regional Conference Series in Mathematics: No. 31). 59p. 1977. pap. 21.00 (*0-8218-1681-0*, CBMS/31) Am Math.

Coifman, Ronald, jt. auth. see Meyer, Yves.

Coifman, Ronald R., jt. ed. see Zeevi, Yehoshua Y.

Coignard, Sophie. Nouveau Dictionnaire des Girouettes. (FRE.). 245p. 1993. pap. 45.00 (*0-7859-7812-7*, 2221074793) Fr & Eur.

Coignet, Jean-Roch. The Notebooks of Captain Coignet: Soldier of the Empire, 1799-1816. (Illus.). 292p. 1998. pap. 18.95 (*1-85367-313-7*, Pub. by Greenhill Bks) Stackpole.

Coigney, Rodolphe L. Izaak Walton a New Bibliography, 1653-1987. 434p. 1989. 250.00 (*1-882860-01-2*) J Cummins Bksell.

Coil, Carolyn. Australia. (Questivities Ser.: Set 2). 1995. pap. 6.95 (*1-880505-63-0*, CLC0174) Pieces of Lrning.

— Becoming an Achiever: A Student Guide. (Illus.). 96p. 1993. pap. 11.95 (*1-880505-07-X*, CLC0162) Pieces of Lrning.

— Celebrations. (Illus.). 48p. 1998. pap. 7.95 (*1-880505-28-2*, GGA2001) Pieces of Lrning.

***Coil, Carolyn.** Encouraging Achievement. (Illus.). 160p. 1999. pap. 18.95 (*1-880505-49-5*, CLC233) Pieces of Lrning.

Coil, Carolyn. Japan. (Questivities Ser.: Set 7). 1995. pap. 6.95 (*1-880505-68-1*, CLC0180) Pieces of Lrning.

— Motivating Underachievers. 1992. pap. 11.95 (*1-880505-04-5*, CLC0195) Pieces of Lrning.

— Teaching Tools for the 21st Century. (Illus.). 184p. 1997. pap. 18.95 (*1-880505-55-X*, CLC0200) Pieces of Lrning.

Coil, Henry W. Coil's Masonic Encyclopedia. rev. ed. LC 60-53289. (Illus.). 749p. 1996. lib. bdg. 69.50 (*0-88053-054-5*, M 316) Macoy Pub.

— A Comprehensive View of Freemasonry. (Illus.). xiv, 256p. 1985. reprint ed. text 21.00 (*0-88053-053-7*, M 314) Macoy Pub.

Coil, James H. The New Supervisor's EEO Handbook: A Guide to Federal Antidiscrimination Laws & Regulations. 5th ed. 64p. 1994. pap. 32.95 (*0-471-11282-8*) Wiley.

Coil, Suzanne M. The Civil Rights Movement. (Liberty & Justice For All Ser.). (Illus.). 64p. (J). (gr. 5-8). 1995. lib. bdg. 15.98 (*0-8050-2987-7*) TFC Bks NY.

— Harriet Beecher Stowe. LC 93-13710. (Impact Biographies Ser.). (Illus.). 112p. (YA). (gr. 7-12). 1993. lib. bdg. 24.00 (*0-531-13006-1*) Watts.

— Jazz & Blues. (Illus.). 160p. 1998. 19.95 (*0-8160-3559-8*) Facts on File.

— Mabel. LC 94-9791. (Illus.). 32p. (J). (ps-3). 1994. 15.95 (*0-87905-602-9*) Gibbs Smith Pub.

— Poisonous Plants. (First Bks.). (Illus.). 64p. (J). (gr. 5-8). 1992. pap. 6.95 (*0-531-15647-8*) Watts.

— Robert Hutchings Goddard: Pioneer of Rocketry & Space Flight. (Makers of Modern Science Ser.). (Illus.). 144p. (YA). (gr. 7-12). 1992. lib. bdg. 19.95 (*0-8160-2591-6*) Facts on File.

— Struggle for Child Labor Laws. (Liberty & Justice For All Ser.). (Illus.). 64p. (J). (gr. 5-8). 1995. lib. bdg. 15.98 (*0-8050-2986-9*) TFC Bks NY.

Coile, B. W. Roscoe Pucannon at Lodge Vol. 3: First Two Blurred: How I Spent All My Life up till Now Trying to Survive Being Born. LC 90-86217. (Illus.). 128p. (Orig.). 1991. pap. 8.95 (*0-9628749-0-6*) B W Coile.

Coile, Caroline D. American Eskimo Dogs: Everything about Purchase, Care, Nutrition, Breeding, Behavior, & Training. LC 95-7319. (Complete Pet Owner's Manual Ser.). (Illus.). 1995. pap. 6.95 (*0-8120-9198-1*) Barron.

***Coile, Caroline D.** Australian Shepherds. LC 98-33445. (Complete Pet Owner's Manual Ser.). (Illus.). 104p. 1999. pap. 6.95 (*0-7641-0558-2*) Barron.

Coile, Caroline D. Encyclopedia of Dog Breeds. LC 98-20368. (Illus.). 320p. 1998. 25.00 (*0-7641-5097-9*) Barron.

***Coile, Caroline D.** Golden Retriever Handbook. 144p. 2000. pap. 9.95 (*0-7641-1237-6*) Barron.

Coile, D. Caroline. Cavalier King Charles Spaniels. LC 97-22429. (Barron's Complete Pet Owner's Manuals). (Illus.). 1998. pap. 6.95 (*0-7641-0227-3*) Barron.

***Coile, D. Caroline.** Chihuahua Handbook. (Pet Handbks.). (Illus.). 2000. pap. text 9.95 (*0-7641-1521-9*) Barron.

Coile, D. Caroline. Chihuahuas: Everything about Purchase, Care, Nutrition, Diseases, Behavior & Breeding. LC 95-15009. (Complete Pet Owner's Manual Ser.). (Illus.). 102 p. 1995. pap. 6.95 (*0-8120-9345-3*) Barron.

— German Shepherd Dogs. LC 99-19609. (Complete Idiot's Guides (Lifestyle) Ser.). (Illus.). 298p. 1999. pap. 14.95 (*1-58245-047-1*) Macmillan Gen Ref.

***Coile, D. Caroline.** German Shepherds for Dummies. (For Dummies (Lifestyles) Ser.). (Illus.). 334p. 2000. pap. 15.99 (*0-7645-5280-5*) IDG Bks.

Coile, D. Caroline. Greyhounds. LC 95-49004. (Complete Pet Owner's Manual Ser.). 1996. pap. 6.95 (*0-8120-9314-3*) Barron.

***Coile, D. Caroline.** The Jack Russell Terrier Handbook. LC 00-22523. (Illus.). 2000. 9.95 (*0-7641-1411-5*) Barron.

Coile, D. Caroline. Jack Russell Terriers. (Complete Pet Owner's Manual Ser.). (Illus.). 1996. pap. text 6.95 (*0-8120-9677-0*) Barron.

— Miniature Pinschers: Everything about Purchase, Care, Nutrition, Breeding, Behavior, & Training with Color Photos. (Complete Pet Owner's Manual Ser.). 1996. pap. 6.95 (*0-8120-9346-1*) Barron.

— Pekingese: Everything about Adoption, Purchase, Care, Nutrition, Behavior, & Training. LC 96-1967. (Illus.). 112p. 1996. pap. 6.95 (*0-8120-9676-2*) Barron.

***Coile, D. Caroline.** Pit Bulls Terriers. 1999. pap. 14.95 (*1-58245-146-X*) Howell Bks.

Coile, D. Caroline. Show Me! LC 96-3193. 1997. pap. 9.95 (*0-8120-9710-6*) Barron.

An Asterisk (*) at the beginning of an entry indicates that the title is appearing for the first time.

— Whippets. LC 97-46536. (Barron's Complete Pet Owner's Manuals). (Illus.). 1998. pap. 6.95 (*0-7641-0312-1*) Barron.

Coile, D. Carolyn. Afghan Hounds. LC 97-13645. (Barron's Complete Pet Owner's Manuals). (Illus.). 120p. 1997. pap. text 6.95 (*0-7641-0225-7*) Barron.

Coile, Russell. The Five Stages of Managed Care: Strategies for Providers, HMOs, & Suppliers. LC 96-44119. (Orig.). 1997. pap. 48.00 (*1-56793-050-6*) Health Admin Pr.

Coile, Russell C. Millennium Management: "Better, Faster, Cheaper" Strategies for Managing 21st Century Healthcare Organizations. LC 98-19872. 215p. 1998. 49.00 (*1-56793-084-0*) Health Admin Pr.

***Coile, Russell C.** New Century Healthcare: Strategies for Providers, Purchasers & Plans. LC 00-25719. 2000. write for info. (*1-56793-123-5*) Health Admin Pr.

Coile, Russell C., Jr. The New Governance: Strategies for an Era of Health Reform. LC 93-44914. 241p. 1994. text 22.00 (*1-56793-007-7*, 0940) Health Admin Pr.

— The New Hospital: Future Strategies for a Changing Industry. 220p. 1986. 85.00 (*0-87189-363-0*) Aspen Pub.

— The New Medicine: Reshaping Medical Practice & Health Care Management. (Health Care Administration Ser.). 420p. 1990. 73.00 (*0-8342-0103-8*) Aspen Pub.

Coile, Russell C., Jr., jt. auth. see Reeves, Philip N.

Coile, T. S., jt. auth. see Schumacher, Francis X.

Coile, Theodore S. Soil Changes Associated with Loblolly Pine Succession on Abandoned Agricultural Land of the Piedmont Plateau. LC SD0397.P58C5. (Duke University, School of Forestry Bulletin Ser.: No. 5). (Illus.). 85p. reprint ed. pap. 30.00 (*0-7837-6051-5*, 204586400008) Bks Demand.

Coile, Theodore S. & Schumacher, F. X. Soil-Site Relations, Stand Structure, & Yields of Slash & Loblolly Pine Plantations in the Southern United States. LC 82-170983. (Illus.). 310p. reprint ed. pap. 96.10 (*0-7837-6225-9*, 204593900010) Bks Demand.

Coile, Theodore S., jt. auth. see Korstian, Clarence F.

***Coiley, John.** Train. (Eyewitness Books). (Illus.). (J). (gr. 4-7). 2000. 19.99 (*0-7894-6588-4*) DK Pub Inc.

— Train. (Eyewitness Books). (J). (gr. 4-7). 2000. 15.95 (*0-7894-5756-3*) DK Pub Inc.

Coillard, Francois. On the Threshold of Central Africa: Record of Twenty Years Pioneering among the Barotsi of the Upper Zambesi. (Illus.). 664p. 1971. reprint ed. 47.50 (*0-7146-1865-9*, Pub. by F Cass Pubs) Intl Spec Bk.

Coin Educational Products Staff. Career Targets Implementation Guide. 4th rev. ed. (Illus.). 69p. 1994. pap., teacher ed. 13.95 (*1-892312-18-2*) Coin Eductnl.

— Coin Clue Teacher's Guide: Using Coin Clue in the Classroom. (Illus.). 50p. 1996. pap., teacher ed. 5.95 (*1-892312-17-4*) Coin Eductnl.

Coin World Magazine Editors. The Comprehensive Catalog & Encyclopedia of U. S. Coins. (The Confident Collector Ser.). (Illus.). 576p. (Orig.). 1995. pap. 18.00 (*0-380-78187-5*, Avon Bks) Morrow Avon.

Coin World Staff. Coin World Guide, 1997. 1996. mass mkt. 5.99 (*0-451-19305-9*, Sig) NAL.

— Ledger of U. S. Coins. 3rd rev. ed. Rattkay, Suellen, ed. (Illus.). 1998. pap. 9.95 (*0-944945-28-7*) Amos Ohio.

Coinage of the America's Conference Staff. America's Copper Coinage, 1783-1857. LC 85-195862. (Coinage of the America's Conference, Proceedings Ser.: Vol. 1). 196p. 1985. reprint ed. pap. 60.80 (*0-608-00466-9*, 206128500007) Bks Demand.

Coinage of the Americas Conference Staff. Money of Pre-Federal America. LC 92-246906. (Proceedings/ Coinage of the Americas Conference Ser.: No. 7). (Illus.). 266p. 1992. pap. 82.50 (*0-608-05184-5*, 206572100001) Bks Demand.

Coiner. Global Economy. 2nd ed. 400p. 1998. pap. text 65.00 (*0-536-01681-X*) Pearson Custom.

Coiner & Adams, Alayne B. Tennessee Tort Case Finder: 1991 Supplement. 81p. 1996. pap. text 25.00 (*0-87473-904-7*, 60974-10, MICHIE) LEXIS Pub.

Coiner, Constance. Better Red: The Writing & Resistance of Tillieolsen & Meridellesueur. LC 97-39933. 312p. Date not set. pap. text 19.95 (*0-252-06695-2*) U of Ill Pr.

Coiner, Constance & George, Diana H. The Family Track: Keeping Your Faculties While You Mentor, Nurture, Teach & Serve. LC 97-33786. 376p. 1998. 19.95 (*0-252-06694-4*); text 49.95 (*0-252-02291-2*) U of Ill Pr.

Coiner, Mayo L. Tennessee Law of Damages: 1989 Supplement. 1989. write for info. (*0-87473-589-0*, 60981-10, MICHIE) LEXIS Pub.

Coiner, Mayo L. & Adams, Alayne B. Tennessee Torts Case Finder. 458p. 1989. 70.00 (*0-87473-522-X*, 60973-10, MICHIE) LEXIS Pub.

Coing, J. P. Bank & Stock Exchange Lexicon. (ENG, FRE & GER.). 64p. 1988. pap. 19.95 (*0-8288-4037-7*, F135590) Fr & Eur.

Coinman, Nancy R., ed. see Clark, Geoffrey A., et al.

Coint Reports Staff. Books vs. CD-ROM. LC 85-641403. (COINT Reports: Vol. 6, No. 6). 22p. (Orig.). 1986. pap. 3.50 (*0-939670-12-7*) Info Digest.

— CD-ROM: Revolution Maker. (COINT Reports: Vol. 6, No. 5). 22p. (Orig.). 1986. pap. 3.50 (*0-939670-13-5*) Info Digest.

Coint Reports Staff. Information Resources Management & Libraries. (COINT Reports: Vol. 7, No. 1). 26p. 1988. pap. 3.95 (*0-939670-16-X*) Info Digest.

Coint Reports Staff. Online Catalog. (COINT Reports: Vol. 6, No. 4). 28p. (Orig.). 1986. pap. 3.50 (*0-939670-11-9*) Info Digest.

Cointe, P. ECOOP '96 - Object-Oriented Programming: 10th European Conference, Linz, Austria, July 1996 - Proceedings, Vol. 1098. LC 96-26229. (Lecture Notes in Computer Science Ser.). 502p. 1996. pap. 81.00 (*3-540-61439-7*) Spr-Verlag.

***Cointe, Pierre, ed.** Meta-Level Architectures & Reflection: Proceedings, 2nd International Conference, Reflection '99, Saint Malo, France, July 19-21, 1999. LC 99-39040. (Lecture Notes in Computer Science Ser.: Vol. 1616). xi, 273p. 1999. pap. 52.00 (*3-540-66280-4*) Spr-Verlag.

Cointreau, Andre, intro. Le Cordon Bleu at Home. (Illus.). 592p. 1991. 40.00 (*0-688-09750-2*, Hearst) Hearst Commns.

Cointreau-Levine, Sandra. Private Sector Participation in Municipal Solid Waste Services in Developing Countries, Vol. 1: The Formal Sector. (Urban Management Program Ser.: Paper 13). 64p. 1994. pap. 22.00 (*0-8213-2825-5*, 12825) World Bank.

Coirault, Yves, ed. see Saint-Simon.

Coirier, Pierre, jt. ed. see Andriessen, Jerry.

Coiro, Ann B. Robert Herrick's Hesperides & the Epigram Book Tradition. LC 87-22827. 280p. 1988. text 44.00 (*0-8018-3571-2*) Johns Hopkins.

— Robert Herrick's Hesperides & the Epigram Book Tradition. LC 87-22827. (Illus.). 280p. reprint ed. pap. 86.80 (*0-608-08809-9*, 206944800004) Bks Demand.

Coiro, Mary J. Health of Our Nation's Children: United States, 1988. LC 94-33533. (Vital & Health Statistics. Series 10, Data from the National Health Survey: No. 191). 1994. 4.75 (*0-8406-0500-5*) Natl Ctr Health Stats.

Coit. Great Entertainers. 1991. 12.95 (*0-931618-15-0*) Buffalo Bill Hist Ctr.

Coit, Daniel W. Digging for Gold Without a Shovel: Letters of Daniel Wadsworth Coit from Mexico & California. limited ed. Hammond, George P., ed. (Illus.). 1967. 35.00 (*0-912094-11-7*) Old West.

Coit, Laura, et al. Michigan Gardener's Guide: The What, Where, When, How & Why of Gardening in Michigan. LC 97-181167. (Illus.). 424p. (Orig.). 1997. pap. 19.95 (*1-888608-29-3*) Cool Springs Pr.

Coit, Lee. Accepting: How to Increase Your Awareness of Perfection. LC 96-38823. 128p. 1996. reprint ed. pap. 8.95 (*1-56170-401-6*, 851) Hay House.

— Being: How to Increase Your Awareness of Oneness. LC 96-36546. 128p. 1997. pap. 7.95 (*1-56170-405-9*) Hay House.

— Listening: How to Increase Awareness of Your Inner Guide. 80p. 1994. pap. 6.95 (*0-936475-00-5*, 654) Las Brisas.

— Listening: How to Increase Awareness of Your Inner Guide. rev. ed. LC 96-8984. 100p. 1996. pap. 7.95 (*1-56170-400-8*, 654) Hay House.

— Listening . . . Still: How to Increase Your Acceptance of Perfection. 130p. 1985. pap. 8.95 (*0-936475-04-8*, 655) Las Brisas.

Coit, Margaret L. John C. Calhoun: American Portrait. LC 90-45589. (Illus.). 602p. 1990. reprint ed. 39.95 (*0-87797-185-4*) Cherokee.

***Coit, Margaret L.** Mr. Baruch. LC 00-40404. 2000. pap. write for info. (*1-58798-021-5*) Beard Bks.

Coit, Margaret L., ed. John C. Calhoun. (Great Lives Observed Ser.). 1970. pap. 1.95 (*0-13-112391-2*, Spectrum IN) Macmillan Gen Ref.

Coit, Stanton. Neighbourhood Guilds: An Instrument of Social Reform. LC 73-11917. (Metropolitan America Ser.). 164p. 1974. reprint ed. 17.95 (*0-405-05391-6*) Ayer.

***Coito, Albert & Coito, Shelly.** Elsie the Cow & Borden's Collectibles. (Illus.). 160p. 2000. pap. 29.95 (*0-7643-1072-0*) Schiffer.

Coito, Shelly, jt. auth. see Coito, Albert.

Coj, P. O., tr. see Solomon, Joel A.

Cok, Jerry O. Worship Resources for Youth. 133p. (Orig.). 1983. pap. 12.00 (*0-914527-25-8*) C-Four Res.

Cok, P., et al. Synoptic Food Composition Tables. 444p. 1987. pap. text 40.00 (*1-57235-046-6*) Piccin Nuova.

Cokain, Aston. The Dramatic Works of Sir Aston Cokain. Maidment, James & Logan, W. H., eds. LC 67-18423. 319p. 1972. reprint ed. 24.95 (*0-405-08365-3*, Pub. by Blom Pubns) Ayer.

Cokas, William. UNC-ology: The Man from UNCle, 1984-1988. (Illus.). 168p. 1998. pap. 11.95 (*1-880849-09-7*) Chapel Hill NC.

Cokayne, G. E., jt. ed. see Fry, Edward A.

***Coke, Al.** How to Create a Successful Business Plan: A Manager's Step-by-Step Guide. 304p. 1999. 75.00 (*0-8144-0482-0*) AMACOM.

Coke, Allison H., jt. ed. see Ahtone, Heather.

Coke, Andrea, ed. see Allen, Minerva & Allen, Kirkland.

Coke, Daniel P. Royal Commission on the Losses & Services of the American Loyalists 1783-1785. Egerton, Hugh E., ed. LC 79-90166. (Mass Violence in America Ser.). 1969. reprint ed. 27.95 (*0-405-01308-6*) Ayer.

Coke, David, ed. Hans Feibusch: The Heat of Vision. (Illus.). 88p. 1995. pap. 25.00 (*0-85331-670-8*, Pub. by Lund Humphries) Antique Collect.

Coke, Edward. Coke on Magna Carta: The Common Law. 1979. lib. bdg. 300.00 (*0-8490-2885-X*) Gordon Pr.

***Coke, Edward.** The First Part of the Institutes of the Laws of England: or A Commentary upon Littleton: Not the Name of the Author Only, but of the Law Itself. 18th ed. LC 99-41675. 2000. 195.00 (*1-58477-033-3*) Lawbk Exchange.

Coke, Edwardo. Second Part of the Institutes of the Laws on England, 4 vols. Reams, Bernard D., Jr., ed. LC 86-62937. (Historical Writings in Law & Jurisprudence Ser.: No. 5B). 1992. reprint ed. 250.00 (*0-89941-520-2*, 304560) W S Hein.

Coke-Enguidanos, Mervyn. Word & Work in the Poetry of Juan Ramon Jimenez. (Monagrafias A Ser.: Vol. LXXXVIII). 157p. (C). 1982. 51.00 (*0-7293-0139-7*, Pub. by Tamesis Bks Ltd) Boydell & Brewer.

Coke, Fletch. Hermitage Landscape: Before & after the 1998 Tornado, 1. 1999. pap. text 14.95 (*1-57736-140-7*, Hillsboro Pr) Providence Hse.

Coke, James G., jt. ed. see Gargan, John J.

Coke, Marguerite M. & Twaite, James A. The Black Elderly: Satisfaction & Quality of Later Life. LC 94-33089. 131p. (C). 1995. lib. bdg. 39.95 (*1-56024-914-5*) Haworth Pr.

Coke, Roger. Discourse of Trade. LC 78-141121. (Research Library of Colonial Americana). 1972. reprint ed. 20.95 (*0-405-03332-X*) Ayer.

Coke, Thomas. History of the West Indies, 3 Vols. LC 70-89418. (Black Heritage Library Collection). reprint ed. lib. bdg. 96.00 (*0-8290-0851-9*) Irvington.

— History of the West Indies, 3 Vols, Set. LC 70-89418. (Black Heritage Library Collection). 1977. 108.95 (*0-8369-8546-X*) Ayer.

Coke, Van D. Helmuth Naumer, Old New Mexico. (Illus.). 64p. (Orig.). 1996. pap. 15.00 (*0-935037-96-9*) G Peters Gallery.

— Secular & Sacred: Photographs of Mexico. LC 92-15219. (Illus.). 181p. 1992. reprint ed. pap. 56.20 (*0-608-04141-6*, 206487400011) Bks Demand.

Coke, Van D. & Barrow, Thomas. Light & Substance. (Illus.). 63p. 1974. pap. 4.00 (*0-942006-48-8*) U of CA Art.

Coke, Van Deren, ed. One Hundred Years of Photographic History: Essays in Honor of Beaumont Newhall. LC 74-83381. 190p. reprint ed. pap. 58.90 (*0-608-12944-5*, 202467900038) Bks Demand.

Coke, Van Deren & Greene, Jonathan. The Robert C. May Photography Collection. LC 95-60170. (Illus.). 114p. 1995. pap. 12.00 (*1-882007-09-3*) Univ KY Art Mus.

Cokely, Dennis. Interpretation: A Sociolinguistic Model. (Sign Language Dissertation Ser.). 199p. (C). 1992. pap. text 19.95 (*0-932130-10-0*, LP301) Linstok Pr.

Cokely, Dennis & Baker-Shenk, Charlotte. American Sign Language: A Teacher's Resource Text on Curriculum, Methods & Evaluation. (Green Bks.). (Illus.). 212p. 1980. pap. text, teacher ed. 24.95 (*0-930323-85-8*, Clerc Bks) Gallaudet Univ Pr.

— American Sign Language: A Teacher's Resource Text on Grammar & Culture. (Green Bks.). (Illus.). 488p. 1980. pap. text, teacher ed. 29.95 (*0-930323-84-X*, Clerc Bks) Gallaudet Univ Pr.

— American Sign Language Units 1-9: A Student Text. (Green Bks.). 202p. 1980. pap. text, student ed. 19.95 (*0-930323-86-6*, Clerc Bks) Gallaudet Univ Pr.

— American Sign Language Units 10-18: A Student Text. (Green Bks.). (Illus.). 196p. 1981. pap. text, student ed. 19.95 (*0-930323-87-4*, Clerc Bks) Gallaudet Univ Pr.

— American Sign Language Units 19-27: A Student Text. (Green Bks.). (Illus.). 196p. 1981. pap. text, student ed. 19.95 (*0-930323-88-2*, Clerc Bks) Gallaudet Univ Pr.

Cokendolpher, James & Francke, Oscar F. The Ants (Hymenoptera, Formicidea) of Western Texas, Parts II & III: Subfamilies Ecitoninae, Ponerine, Psuedomyrmecinae, Dolichoderinae, & Formicinae, Additions & Corrections. (Special Publications: Nos. 30 & 31). (C). 1990. pap. 14.00 (*0-89672-175-2*) Tex Tech Univ Pr.

Coker, A. Valuing the Environment. 183p. 1992. pap. 300.00 (*81-7089-180-9*, Pub. by Intl Bk Distr) St Mut.

Coker, Alec, jt. auth. see Johnson, Doris.

Coker, Annabel, ed. Valuing the Environment: Economic Approaches to Environmental Evaluation. (Illus.). 192p. 1992. text 49.00 (*1-85293-212-0*) St Martin.

Coker, Annabel & Richards, Cathy, eds. Valuing the Environment: Economic Approaches to Environmental Evaluation. 198p. 1995. pap. 54.95 (*0-471-96112-4*, ES21) Wiley.

Coker, Caleb, ed. The News from Brownsville: Helen Chapman's Letters from the Texas Military Frontier, 1848-1852. (Barker Texas History Center Ser.: No. 2). (Illus.). 452p. 1992. 29.95 (*0-87611-115-0*) Tex St Hist Assn.

— The News from Brownsville: Helen Chapman's Letters from the Texas Military Frontier, 1848-1852. limited ed. (Illus.). 452p. 1992. boxed set 85.00 (*0-87611-114-2*) Tex St Hist Assn.

Coker, Carolyn. Appearance of Evil. LC 95-2317. 250p. 1995. per. 3.99 (*0-373-26185-3*, 1-26185-8, Wrldwide Lib) Harlequin Bks.

Coker, Christopher. Less Important Than Opulence the Conservatives & Dence. (C). 1990. 55.00 (*0-907967-92-2*, Pub. by Inst Euro Def & Strat) St Mut.

— South Africa's Security Dilemmas, 126. LC 87-2437. (Washington Papers: No. 126). 125p. 1987. 45.00 (*0-275-92771-7*, C2771, Praeger Pubs); pap. 12.95 (*0-275-92772-5*, B2772, Praeger Pubs) Greenwood.

— Twilight of the West. LC 97-31015. 216p. 1997. 30.00 (*0-8133-3368-7*, Pub. by Westview) HarpC.

— War & the Illiberal Conscience. LC 98-153063. 272p. 1998. text 45.00 (*0-8133-3369-5*, Pub. by Westview) HarpC.

Coker, Christopher, ed. A Farewell to Arms Control, the Irrelevance of CFE. (C). 1990. 50.00 (*0-907967-23-X*, Pub. by Inst Euro Def & Strat) St Mut.

— Who Only England Know: Conservatives & Foreign Policy. (C). 1990. 35.00 (*0-907967-18-3*, Pub. by Inst Euro Def & Strat) St Mut.

Coker, Daniel P. Mastering Microcaps: Strategies, Trends & Stock Selection. LC 98-46111. (Professional Library). (Illus.). 282p. 1999. 55.00 (*1-57660-062-9*, Pub. by Bloomberg NJ) Norton.

***Coker, Darlene, et al.** High Performance Sales Organizations: Creating Competitive Advantage in the Global Marketplace. 2nd ed. LC 99-37629. 224p. 1999. 29.95 (*0-07-135160-4*) McGraw.

Coker, Deborah C. Aunt Mattie's Present. LC 95-52365. (Illus.). (J). 1998. write for info. (*0-316-23498-2*) Little.

Coker, Don W. Loan Officer Complete Handbook. (C). 1992. pap. 69.95 (*0-13-554288-X*) P-H.

Coker, Donald W. Complete Guide to Income Property Financing & Loan Packaging. LC 83-22574. 408p. 1984. text 99.50 (*0-87624-099-6*, Inst Busn Plan) P-H.

Coker, Doug, jt. auth. see Smith, Mark.

Coker, G., jt. auth. see Van Der Meer, B. W.

Coker Group Staff. Practice Success! The Physician's Guide to Survival & Success in the Medical Practice. 3rd ed. Stanley, Kay B., ed. 500p. 1997. 195.00 (*0-9655304-0-X*) Coker Publishing.

***Coker Group Staff, ed.** Assessing & Improving Billing & Collections. (Assessing & Improving Practice Operations Ser.). 2000. pap. 34.00 (*1-57947-078-5*) AMA.

— Assessing & Improving Staffing & Organization. (Assessing & Improving Practice Operations Ser.). 2000. pap. 34.00 (*1-57947-080-7*) AMA.

— Assessing & Improving the Patient Encounter Process. (Assessing & Improving Practice Operations Ser.). 2000. pap. 34.00 (*1-57947-079-3*) AMA.

— Beyond Disengagement 2000. 2000. pap. 40.00 (*1-57947-076-9*) AMA.

Coker Group Staff, jt. auth. see Landholt, Thomas.

Coker, Gylbert & Jennings, Corrine. The Harmon & Harriet Kelley Collection of African American Art. LC 94-65015. (Illus.). 80p. (Orig.). 1994. pap. 19.95 (*1-883502-01-2*) San Ant Mus Art.

Coker, Jerry. Improvising Jazz. (Illus.). 114p. 1986. pap. 11.00 (*0-671-62829-1*, Touchstone) S&S Trade Pap.

Coker, Joan, jt. auth. see Berry, Bertice.

Coker, Kayode A. FORTRAN: Programs for Chemical Process Design, Analysis & Simulation. LC 94-25401. (Illus.). 854p. 1995. 125.00 (*0-88415-280-4*, 5280) Gulf Pub.

Coker, Lawrence T. & Gaddis, Robert S., eds. Maintenance Painting Program for Maximum Return on Investment. (Press Reports). 58p. 1982. 15.00 (*0-89852-395-8*, 0101R095) TAPPI.

Coker, Newton. Atlas of Otologic Surgery. 540p. 1999. text 175.00 (*0-7216-2216-X*, W B Saunders Co) Harcrt Hlth Sci Grp.

Coker, P. C., III. Charleston's Maritime Heritage, 1670-1865. (Illus.). 314p. 1987. 50.00 (*0-914432-03-6*) Coker Craft Pr.

Coker, P. D. How to Deal with Disk Disasters. 2nd ed. 1996. pap. 39.95 (*1-898307-65-2*, Pub. by Capall Bann Pubng) Holmes Pub.

Coker, Paddy, jt. auth. see Kent, Martin.

Coker, Paul, jt. auth. see Hart, Stan.

Coker, Paul, jt. auth. see Hart, Stan, Jr.

Coker, Paul J. Keeper of the Game Bk. 1: Visions from Ephraim. (Illus.). 135p. (Orig.). 1996. pap. 7.00 (*0-9653684-0-8*) Boston Gray Bks.

Coker, R. Mycotoxins & Their Control: Constraints & Opportunities. 73p. 1997. pap. 60.00 (*0-85954-478-8*, Pub. by Nat Res Inst) St Mut.

Coker, Richard J. From Chaos to Coersion: Detention & the Control of Tuberculosis. LC 99-30119. 261p. 2000. text 27.95 (*0-312-22250-5*) St Martin.

Coker, W. C. The Clavarias of the United States & Canada. 1932. reprint ed. pap. 80.00 (*3-7682-0913-X*) Lubrecht & Cramer.

— The Saprolegniaceae with Notes on Other Water Molds. (Illus.). 1969. reprint ed. pap. 50.00 (*3-7682-0620-3*) Lubrecht & Cramer.

Coker, W. C. & Couch, J. N. The Gastromycetes of the Eastern U. S. & Canada. 1969. reprint ed. pap. 64.00 (*3-7682-0602-5*) Lubrecht & Cramer.

Coker, William C. The Club & Coral Mushrooms (Clavarias) of the United States & Canada. (Illus.). 1990. 16.00 (*0-8446-5171-0*) Peter Smith.

— The Club & Coral Mushrooms (Clavarias) of the United States & Canada. LC 74-82202. (Illus.). 320p. 1974. reprint ed. pap. 7.95 (*0-486-23101-1*) Dover.

Coker, William C., ed. Studies in Science. LC 77-39098. (Essay Index Reprint Ser.). 1977. reprint ed. 44.95 (*0-8369-2683-8*) Ayer.

Coker, William C. & Beers, Alma. The Boleti of North Carolina. (Illus.). 163p. 1974. reprint ed. pap. 6.95 (*0-486-20377-8*) Dover.

Coker, William C. & Beers, Alma H. The Boleti of North Carolina. (Illus.). 1990. 13.00 (*0-8446-5016-1*) Peter Smith.

Coker, William C. & Couch, John N. The Gasteromycetes of Eastern United States & Canada (Includes Gasteromycetes of Ohio) (Illus.). 1996. 15.50 (*0-8446-5017-X*) Peter Smith.

Coker, William C. & Couch, John N. The Gasteromycetes of the Eastern United States & Canada. LC 73-91490. (Illus.). 447p. 1974. reprint ed. pap. 9.95 (*0-486-23033-3*) Dover.

Coker, William S. The Papers of Panton, Leslie & Company: A Guide to the Microfilm Collection. 764p. 1987. lib. bdg. 425.00 (*0-89235-117-9*) Primary Srce Media.

Coker, William S., ed. The Mobile Cadets, 1845 to 1945: A Century of Honor & Fidelity, Anonymous Manuscript. LC 92-42668. 1992. 30.00 (*1-882695-04-6*) Patagonia Pr.

Coker, William S. & Rea, Rober R., eds. Anglo-Spanish Confrontation on the Gulf Coast During the American Revolution: Proceedings of the Gulf Coast History & Humanities Conference, Vol IX. 1983. pap. 10.00 (*0-940836-17-3*) U of S AL.

Coker, William S. & Shofner, Jerrell H. Florida: From the Beginning to Nineteen Ninety-Two: A Columbus Jubilee Commemorative. 216p. 1992. 25.00 (*1-881547-12-4*) Pioneer Pubns.

Coker, William S. & Watson, Thomas D. Indian Traders of the Southeastern Spanish Borderlands: Panton, Leslie & Company & John Forbes & Company, 1783 to 1847. LC 84-25806. (Illus.). 448p. 1986. 49.95 (*0-8130-0801-8*) U Press Fla.

C

An Asterisk (*) at the beginning of an entry indicates that the title is appearing for the first time.

Coker, William S., ed. see Mandrell, Regina M.

***Cokinos, Christopher.** Hope is the Thing with Feathers: A Personal Chronicle of Vanished Birds. (Illus.). 368p. 2000. 24.95 (*1-58542-006-9*, Tarcher Putnam) Putnam Pub Group.

Cokinos, Christopher. Killing Seasons. Coop, Mahlon, ed. 72p. (Orig.). 1993. pap. 7.00 (*0-939391-19-8*) B Woodley Pr.

Cokins, Gary. ABC Manager's Primer: Straight Talk on Activity Based Costing. 1993. pap. 20.00 (*0-86641-220-4*, 93282) Inst Mgmt Account.

— Activity-Based Cost Management Making It Work: A Manager's Guide to Implementing & Sustaining an Effective ABC System. LC 95-48434. 226p. 1996. text 32.50 (*0-7863-0740-4*, Irwn Prfssnl) McGraw-Hill Prof.

Cokins, Gary, et al. An ABC Manager's Primer: Straight Talk on Activity-Based Costing. 1993. pap. 15.00 (*0-07-413133-8*) McGraw-Hill Prof.

***Cokorinos, Lee.** Antifeminist Organizations: Institutionalizing the Backlash. 36p. 2000. pap. 15.00 (*0-9679106-1-7*) Inst for Democracy.

***Cokorinos, Lee & Kane, Gillian.** The Global Assault on Reproductive Rights: A Crucial Turning Point. 35p. 2000. pap. 15.00 (*0-9679106-2-5*) Inst for Democracy.

Col. Sleepytown Days. 1986. 19.95 (*0-02-621560-8*) Macmillan.

Col, Andrea Del, see Del Col, Andrea.

Col, Ivar Da, see Da Col, Ivar.

Col Legi d'Advocats Staff. Diccionari Juridic Catala. (CAT.). 480p. 1986. 55.00 (*0-7859-6340-5*, 8485194799) Fr & Eur.

Col, Nananda F. A Woman Doctor's Guide to Hormone Therapy: How to Choose What's Right for You. LC 97-60743. 175p. 1997. 24.95 (*1-886284-03-2*, Tatnuck) Chandler Hse.

Cola, Lee De, see Balzani, Vincenzo & De Cola, Lee.

Colacello, Bob. Andy Warhol. (Illus.). 80p. 1997. text 18.95 (*0-7893-0086-9*) St Martin.

***Colacello, Bob.** Holy Terror: Andy Warhol Close Up. LC 99-39872. (Illus.). 560p. 1999. pap. 17.95 (*0-8154-1008-5*) Cooper Sq.

Colaco, Camilo. The Glycation Hypothesis of Atherosclerosis. (Mecical Intelligence Unit Ser.). 224p. 1997. 99.00 (*1-57059-444-9*) Landes Bioscience.

Colacurcio, Michael J. Doctrine & Difference: Essays in the Literature of New England. 320p. (C). 1996. 75.00 (*0-415-91238-5*); pap. 22.99 (*0-415-91239-3*) Routledge.

— The Province of Piety: Moral History in Hawthorne's Early Tales. LC 94-42365. 680p. 1995. pap. text 21.95 (*0-8223-1572-6*) Duke.

— The Province of Piety: Moral History in Hawthorne's Early Tales. LC 83-26586. 680p. 1984. 45.00 (*0-674-71957-3*) HUP.

Colagrande, John, jt. auth. see Felder, Larry.

***Colahan.** Equine Medicine & Surgery & Manual Package. 96p. 1999. pap. text 259.00 (*0-8151-1736-1*) Mosby Inc.

Colahan, et al. Pocket Companion to Equine Medicine & Surgery. LC 98-35658. (Illus.). 800p. (C). (gr. 13). 1999. pap. text 39.95 (*0-8151-1741-8*, 28581) Mosby Inc.

Colahan, jt. auth. see Mayhew, Edgar D.

Colahan, Clark. The Visions of Sor Maria de Agreda: Writing Knowledge & Power. LC 94-9569. 194p. 1994. 36.00 (*0-8165-1419-4*) U of Ariz Pr.

Colahan, P., et al. Equine Medicine & Surgery, 2 vols. 4th ed. LC 90-81427. (Illus.). 1878p. 1991. text 189.95 (*0-939674-27-0*) Am Vet Pubns.

Colaiacovo, Juan Luis, et al. U. S.-Latin American Trade Relations: Issues & Concerns. Czinkota, Michael R., ed. LC 83-2311. 297p. 1983. 55.00 (*0-275-90966-2*, C0966, Praeger Pubs) Greenwood.

Colaianni, James F. Pulpit Humor. 320p. (Orig.). pap. 14.95 (*0-941685-05-5*) Voicings Pubns.

Colaianni, Louis. The Joy of Phonetics & Accents. 192p. 1994. pap. 22.50 (*0-89676-134-7*, Drama Pubs) QSMG Ltd.

— Shakespeare's Names: A New Pronouncing Dictionary. 265p. 1998. pap. 22.50 (*0-89676-215-7*, Drama Pubs) QSMG Ltd.

Colaizzi, Giulia, tr. see Talens, Jenaro.

Colaizzi, Giuliana. Heart of Ashes. Ramos-Garcia, Luis A., ed. 1988. 9.95 (*0-934840-10-5*) Studia Hispanica.

Colaizzi, Giuliana, tr. see Talens, Jenaro.

Colakis, Marianthe. The Classics in the American Theater of the Nineteen Sixties & Early Nineteen Seventies. 96p. (C). 1993. lib. bdg. 37.50 (*0-8191-8972-3*) U Pr of Amer.

Colakovic, Branko A. Yugoslav Migrations to America. LC 73-76007. (Illus.). 1973. pap. 15.00 (*0-88247-209-7*) Ragusan Pr.

Colalillo-Katz, Isabella. Tasting Fire. (Essential Poets Ser.: No. 92). 96p. 1999. pap. 10.00 (*1-55071-090-7*, Pub. by Guernica Editions) SPD-Small Pr Dist.

Colalucci, Gianluigi, jt. auth. see De Vecchi, Pierluigi.

***Colamery, S. N.** Medicare: Issues & Options. LC 99-29242. 1999. 49.00 (*1-56072-694-6*) Nova Sci Pubs.

Colamery, S. N., ed. Affirmative Action: Catalyst or Albatross? LC 98-138844. 331p. 1998. 59.00 (*1-56072-552-4*) Nova Sci Pubs.

***Colamery, S. N., ed.** Literacy: Background & Bibliography. 227p. 2000. lib. bdg. 49.00 (*1-56072-833-7*) Nova Sci Pubs.

Colamery, S. N., jt. ed. see Shohov, Tatiana.

Colamos, jt. auth. see Wolman.

Colander. Economics. 3rd ed. 1997. pap. 23.44 (*0-256-17280-3*) McGraw.

— Economics. 3rd ed. 1997. pap. 23.44 (*0-07-109295-1*) McGraw.

— Economics. 4th ed. 2001. 67.50 (*0-07-231793-0*) McGraw.

— Economics Classic Readings. 3rd ed. 1997. 7.74 (*0-256-17285-4*) McGraw.

— Economics WSJ Edition. 3rd ed. 968p. 1997. pap. 100.94 (*0-256-26610-7*) McGraw.

— Intermediate Macroeconomics. 2000. pap., student ed. 13.50 (*0-07-290376-7*) McGraw.

— Macroeconomic Wall Street Journal. 3rd ed. 560p. 1997. pap. 74.06 (*0-256-26612-3*) McGraw.

— Macroeconomics. 3rd ed. 1997. pap. 20.31 (*0-07-109300-1*) McGraw.

— Macroeconomics. 4th ed. 2000. 47.74 (*0-07-231795-7*) McGraw.

— Macroeconomics: Custom Edition. 1994. 34.00 (*0-256-18680-4*) McGraw.

— Microeconmics: Drill & Review. 2nd ed. 1996. 47.74 (*0-256-22871-X*) McGraw.

— Microeconomics. 3rd ed. 1997. pap. 20.31 (*0-07-109304-4*) McGraw.

— Microeconomics. 4th ed. 2001. 47.74 (*0-07-231794-9*) McGraw.

— Microeconomics WSJ Edition. 3rd ed. 560p. 1997. pap. 76.88 (*0-256-26614-X*) McGraw.

Colander, jt. auth. see Hunt.

Colander, David. Economics: With Macro Interactive Software 3.50. 2nd ed. (C). 1996. text, pap. text 79.50 incl. 3.5 hd (*0-256-24679-3*, Irwn McGrw-H) McGrw-H Hghr Educ.

— Economics Honors Companion. 2nd ed. (C). 1995. text, student ed. 26.25 (*0-256-16813-X*, Irwn McGrw-H) McGrw-H Hghr Educ.

— Macroeconomics Drill & Review. 2nd ed. (C). 1995. text, student ed. 21.25 (*0-256-22261-4*, Irwn McGrw-H) McGrw-H Hghr Educ.

— Microeconomics. 344p. (C). 1993. text, student ed. 21.25 (*0-256-12690-9*, Irwn McGrw-H) McGrw-H Hghr Educ.

— Microeconomics Drill & Review. 2nd ed. (C). 1995. text, student ed. 21.25 (*0-256-22262-2*, Irwn McGrw-H) McGrw-H Hghr Educ.

Colander, David, ed. Beyond Microfoundations: Post-Walrasian Macroeconomics. (Illus.). 280p. (C). 1996. text 52.95 (*0-521-55237-0*) Cambridge U Pr.

Colander, David & Coats, A. W., eds. The Spread of Economic Ideas. (Illus.). 288p. (C). 1989. text 59.95 (*0-521-36233-4*) Cambridge U Pr.

— The Spread of Economic Ideas. (Illus.). 278p. (C). 1993. pap. text 19.95 (*0-521-44650-3*) Cambridge U Pr.

Colander, David & Copeland, Douglas. Macroeconomics Student Workbook. 2nd ed. 304p. (C). 1995. text, student ed., wbk. ed. 18.12 (*0-256-18628-6*, Irwn McGrw-H) McGrw-H Hghr Educ.

— Microeconomics Student Workbook. 2nd ed. 336p. (C). 1995. text, wbk. ed. 18.12 (*0-256-18631-6*, Irwn McGrw-H) McGrw-H Hghr Educ.

Colander, David & Gamber, Jenifer. Case Studies in Macroeconomics: Selections From The Wall Street Journal. 2nd ed. (C). 1995. text 16.25 (*0-256-21875-7*, Irwn McGrw-H) McGrw-H Hghr Educ.

— Case Studies in Microeconomics: Selections From The Wall Street Journal Journal. 2nd ed. (C). 1995. text 16.25 (*0-256-21876-5*, Irwn McGrw-H) McGrw-H Hghr Educ.

Colander, David & Landreth, Harry H. Economics Class Readings. 2nd ed. (C). 1995. text 8.50 (*0-256-16816-4*, Irwn McGrw-H) McGrw-H Hghr Educ.

Colander, David & Sephton, Peter. Macroeconomics (Canadian) LC 95-78245. 528p. (C). 1996. per. 39.95 (*0-256-17572-1*, Irwn McGrw-H) McGrw-H Hghr Educ.

— Microeconomics (Canadian) 480p. (C). 1996. per. 39.95 (*0-256-17575-6*, Irwn McGrw-H) McGrw-H Hghr Educ.

Colander, David, jt. auth. see Copeland, Douglas.

Colander, David, jt. auth. see Ortman, Andres.

Colander, David C. Contents Macroeconomics. 2nd ed. 528p. (C). 1994. text 46.75 (*0-256-13812-5*, Irwn McGrw-H) McGrw-H Hghr Educ.

— Economics. 2nd ed. LC 94-35112. (Economics Ser.). 928p. (C). 1994. text 67.00 (*0-256-13799-4*, Irwn McGrw-H) McGrw-H Hghr Educ.

— Economics. 3rd ed. LC 97-25681. 968p. 1997. 86.25 (*0-256-17217-X*) McGraw.

— Macroeconomics. 2nd ed. LC 94-32398. (Series in Economics). 1994. write for info. (*0-256-16820-2*, Irwn McGrw-H) McGrw-H Hghr Educ.

— Macroeconomics. 3rd ed. LC 97-25686. 1997. write for info. (*0-07-115226-1*) McGraw.

— Macroeconomics. 3rd ed. LC 97-25681. 560p. 1997. pap. 60.94 (*0-256-17266-8*) McGraw.

— Macroeconomics: Theory & Policy. LC 85-27863. (Illus.). 580p. reprint ed. pap. 179.80 (*0-7837-4742-X*, 204455100004) Bks Demand.

— Microeconomics. 2nd ed. LC 94-32399. (Series in Economics). 1994. teacher ed. write for info. (*0-256-16821-0*, Irwn McGrw-H) McGrw-H Hghr Educ.

— Microeconomics. 2nd ed. LC 94-32399. (Series in Economics). 560p. (C). 1994. text 46.75 (*0-256-13825-7*, Irwn McGrw-H) McGrw-H Hghr Educ.

— Microeconomics. 3rd ed. 560p. 1997. pap. 60.94 (*0-256-17273-0*) McGraw.

— Why Aren't Economists As Important As Garbagemen? Essays on the State of Economics. LC 90-8841. 200p. (gr. 13). 1991. text 61.95 (*0-87332-776-4*); pap. text 32.95 (*0-87332-777-2*) M E Sharpe.

Colander, David C., ed. Incentive-Based Incomes Policies: Advances in TIP & MAP. LC 85-20090. 320p. 1986. text 34.95 (*0-88730-082-0*, HarpBusn) HarpInfo.

— Neoclassical Political Economy: The Analysis of Rent-Seeking & DUP Activities. LC 84-11124. 288p. 1984. text 34.95 (*0-88410-999-2*, HarpBusn) HarpInfo.

Colander, David C. & Daane, Dewey, eds. The Art of Monetary Policy. LC 93-45869. 232p. (gr. 13). 1994. text 74.95 (*1-56324-346-6*); pap. text 35.95 (*1-56324-347-4*) M E Sharpe.

Colander, David C. & Landreth, Harry H., eds. The Coming of Keynesianism to America: Conversations with the Founders of Keynesian Economics. LC 95-19493. 256p. (Orig.). 1996. 90.00 (*1-85898-087-9*) E Elgar.

— The Coming of Keynesianism to America: Conversations with the Founders of Keynesian Economics. LC 95-19493. 256p. (Orig.). 1997. pap. 25.00 (*1-85898-602-8*) E Elgar.

Colander, David C., jt. auth. see Hung, Elgin F.

Colander-Estens. Economics. 2nd rev. ed. 1996. 21.25 (*0-256-26271-3*, WCB McGr Hill) McGrw-H Hghr Educ.

Colander, Valerie N. Neena Gathering. 1988. 2.95 (*0-517-00643-X*) Random Hse Value.

Colaneri, John & Luciani, Vincent. 501 Italian Verbs: Fully Conjugated in All the Tenses. (ITA & ENG.). 600p. (C). 1992. pap. text 13.95 (*0-8120-4757-5*) Barron.

Colaneri, John, jt. auth. see Lipton, Gladys C.

Colaneri, John, jt. auth. see Luciani, Vincent.

Colaneri, Patricio, et al, eds. Control Theory & Design: RH2 & RH00 Viewpoint. LC 96-49595. (Illus.). 378p. 1997. text 65.00 (*0-12-179190-4*) Morgan Kaufmann.

Colangelo. Sea Analysis of Metallurgical Failures. 2nd ed. 368p. 1995. pap. 147.00 (*0-471-15475-X*) Wiley.

Colangelo, Cheryl, et al. A Normal Baby: The Sensorimotor Processes of the First Year. 2nd rev. ed. (Illus.). (C). 1986. pap. text. write for info. (*0-911681-03-5*) Valhalla Rehab.

Colangelo, Jerry & Sherman, Len. How You Play the Game: Lessons for Life from the Billion-Dollar Business of Sports. LC 98-56068. (Illus.). 256p. 1999. 24.95 (*0-8144-0488-X*) AMACOM.

Colangelo, Nancy, et al. Talent Development: Symposium Proceedings, August, 1991. 432p. 1992. pap. 20.00 (*0-89824-538-9*) Trillium Pr.

Colangelo, Nicholas, et al, eds. Talent Development II: Proceedings of the Henry B. & Jocelyn Wallace National Research Symposium on Talent Development. LC 94-35336. (Illus.). 524p. 1994. pap. 28.00 (*0-910707-23-5*) Gifted Psych Pr.

Colangelo, Nicholas & Assouline, Susan, eds. Talent Development III: Proceedings from the 1995 Henry B. & Jocelyn Wallace National Research Symposium on Talent Development. (Illus.). 540p. 1998. pap. 30.00 (*0-910707-28-6*) Gifted Psych Pr.

Colangelo, Nicolas & Davis, Gary A. Handbook of Gifted Education. 2nd ed. LC 96-19246. 608p. 1996. 83.00 (*0-205-26085-3*) Allyn.

Colangelo, Paul G., ed. see Carlin, Christopher J.

Colangelo, Robert & Miller, Ronald. Environmental Site Assessment. 1995. 44.00 (*0-922154-19-8*) Appraisal Inst.

Colangelo, Shelton, jt. auth. see Rand.

Colangelo, Vito J. & Heiser, F. A. Analysis of Metallurgical Failures. 2nd ed. LC 86-22406. 368p. 1987. 150.00 (*0-471-89168-1*) Wiley.

Colangelo, Vito J. & Thornton, Peter A. Engineering Aspects of Product Liability. LC 80-27704. (Illus.). 352p. reprint ed. pap. 109.20 (*0-608-15942-5*, 203305600083) Bks Demand.

Colantonio, Ernest S. Microcomputers & Applications. LC 88-83917. (Laboratory Ser.). 750p. (C). 1989. student ed. 17.00 incl. disk (*0-318-42521-1*) HM Trade Div.

— Using dBase III Plus. 118p. (C). 1989. disk. write for info. (*0-318-70085-9*) HM Trade Div.

— Using PC-Calc Plus. 128p. (C). 1989. disk. write for info. (*0-318-70082-4*) HM Trade Div.

— Using PC-File Plus. 110p. (C). 1989. disk. write for info. (*0-318-70084-0*) HM Trade Div.

— Using PC-Type Plus. 106p. (C). 1989. disk. write for info. (*0-318-70081-6*) HM Trade Div.

— Using VP-Expert. 116p. (C). 1989. disk. write for info. (*0-318-70086-7*) HM Trade Div.

— Using WordPerfect 5.0. 148p. (C). 1989. disk. write for info. (*0-318-70083-2*) HM Trade Div.

Colantuono, Anthony. Guido Reni's Abduction of Helen: The Politics & Rhetoric of Painting in Seventeenth-Century Europe. LC 96-26650. (Illus.). 326p. (C). 1997. text 80.00 (*0-521-56397-6*) Cambridge U Pr.

***Colantuono, Susan L.** Make Room for Joy: Finding Magical Moments in Your Everyday Life. Brooks, Nancy, ed. 142p. 2000. pap. 14.95 (*0-9673129-0-6*) Interlude Prodns.

Colao, Flora & Hosansky, Tamar. Your Children Should Know: Teach Your Children the Strategies That Will Keep Them Safe from Assault & Crime. LC 83-5981. (Illus.). 192p. 1983. 16.95 (*0-672-52777-4*) Macmillan.

Colapietro, S. J., ed. see Potter, Vincent G., et al.

Colapietro, Vincent, ed. & intro. see Potter, Vincent G.

Colapietro, Vincent M. Glossary of Semiotics. LC 92-32621. (Glossary for Research, Reading, & Writing Ser.). 192p. 1993. 12.95 (*1-55778-564-3*); pap. 8.95 (*1-55778-502-3*) Paragon Hse.

Colapietro, Vincent M., ed. Reason, Experience, & God: John E. Smith in Dialogue. LC 97-8014. (American Philosophy Ser.: Vol. 7). xx, 158p. (C). 1996. text 28.00 (*0-8232-1706-X*); pap. text 18.00 (*0-8232-1707-8*) Fordham.

Colapietro, Vincent M. & Olshewsky, Thomas M., eds. Pierce's Doctrine of Signs: Theory, Applications, & Connections. LC 95-37229. (Approaches to Semiotics Ser.: No. 123). xi, 463p. (C). 1995. lib. bdg. 190.80 (*3-11-014252-X*) Mouton.

Colapinto, John. About the Author. Date not set. 25.00 (*0-06-019417-0*); 13.00 (*0-06-093217-1*) HarpC.

***Colapinto, John.** As Nature Made Him: The Boy Who Was Raised a Girl. LC 99-40167. 304p. 2000. 26.00 (*0-06-019211-9*) HarpC.

Colares, A. G., jt. auth. see Barbosa, J. L.

Colarulli, Paul F., et al. Conducting Internal Investigations in the Academic & Research Setting. (Monograph Ser.: No. 61). 25p. 1998. pap. 12.00 (*1-56534-073-6*) Ed Law Assn.

Colarusso, C. A., jt. auth. see Nemiroff, R. A.

Colarusso, Calvin A. Child & Adult Development: A Psychoanalytic Introduction for Clinicians. (Critical Issues in Psychiatry Ser.). (Illus.). 240p. (C). 1992. 45.00 (*0-306-44285-X*, Plenum Trade) Perseus Pubng.

Colarusso, Calvin A. & Nemiroff, Robert A. Adult Development: A New Dimension in Psychodynamic Theory & Practice. LC 80-20250. (Critical Issues in Psychiatry Ser.). (Illus.). 320p. (C). 1981. 49.50 (*0-306-40619-5*, Plenum Trade) Perseus Pubng.

Colarusso, Ron, jt. auth. see O'Rourke, Colleen M.

Colarusso, Ron, jt. auth. see Schultz, Karen.

Colarusso, Ronald P. & Hammill, Donald D. Motor-Free Visual Perception Test (MVPT-R) rev. ed. Martin, Nancy, ed. 32p. 1995. pap. 27.00 (*0-87879-042-X*, 042-1-A) Acad Therapy.

Colas, Dominique. Civil Society & Fanaticism: Conjoined Histories. Jacobs, Amy, tr. from FRE. LC 96-50098. (Espaces M Etisses Ser.). 1997. write for info. (*0-8047-2734-1*); pap. 22.95 (*0-8047-2736-8*) Stanford U Pr.

Colas, Emily. Just Checking: Scenes from the Life of an Obsessive-Compulsive. LC 98-15001. 176p. 1998. 22.00 (*0-671-02437-X*, PB Hardcover) PB.

— Just Checking: Scenes from the Life of an Obsessive-Compulsive. 165p. 1999. pap. 10.00 (*0-671-02438-8*, WSP) PB.

***Colas, Rafael, et al, eds.** 1st International Automotive Heat Treating Conference Proceedings: Puerto Vallarta, Mexico, 13-15 July 1998. LC 98-74786. 450p. 1999. 128.00 (*0-87170-625-3*, 06660G) ASM.

Colas, Rene. Bibliographie Generale du Costume ed de la Mode. (FRE.). 812p. 1994. reprint ed. 90.00 (*1-888262-42-7*) Martino Pubng.

Colas, Santiago. Postmodernity in Latin America: The Argentine Paradigm. LC 94-11348. (Post-Contemporary Interventions Ser.). 240p. 1994. text 49.95 (*0-8223-1508-4*); pap. text 17.95 (*0-8223-1520-3*) Duke.

Colasante, John. UNIX Companion. 1995. ring bd. 89.00 (*0-929321-16-2*) WEKA Pub.

Colasanti, G., ed. Advances in Nephrology & Dialysis. (Contributions to Nephrology Ser.: Vol. 77). (Illus.). vi, 202p. 1990. 155.75 (*3-8055-5064-2*) S Karger.

Colasanti, G. & D'Amico, G., eds. Clinical Nephrology: Immunologic Considerations, Invasive Techniques & Dialytic Strategies. (Contributions to Nephrology Ser.: Vol. 69). (Illus.). 1989. 29.75 (*3-8055-4857-5*) S Karger.

— New Perspectives in Diagnosis & Treatment of Kidney Disease. (Contributions to Nephrology Ser.: Vol. 55). (Illus.). vi, 258p. 1987. 29.75 (*3-8055-4393-X*) S Karger.

Colasanti, G., jt. ed. see D'Amico, G.

Colasanti, Robert. How to Be a Black Belt. Corcoran, John, ed. (Illus.). 160p. (Orig.). 1998. pap. 14.95 (*0-9655539-1-4*) Graden Media Grp.

Colasse. Lexique de Comptabilite et de Gestion. (FRE.). 1979. pap. 29.95 (*0-8288-5928-0*, M6079) Fr & Eur.

Colasurdo, Christine. Return to Spirit Lake: Journey Through a Lost Landscape. LC 97-16044. 288p. (Orig.). 1997. pap. 16.95 (*1-57061-081-9*) Sasquatch Bks.

Colatosti, Camille & Karg, Elissa. Stopping Sexual Harassment: A Handbook. 112p. (Orig.). 1992. pap. text 9.00 (*0-914093-06-1*) Labor Notes.

Colatrella, Carol & Alkana, Joseph, eds. Cohesion & Dissent in America. LC 92-45265. (SUNY Series in American Literature). 252p. (C). 1993. text 64.50 (*0-7914-1717-4*); pap. text 21.95 (*0-7914-1718-2*) State U NY Pr.

Colatsky, Thomas J. Potassium Channels: Basic Function & Therapeutic Aspects. (Progress in Clinical & Biological Research Ser.). 362p. 1990. 275.00 (*0-471-56714-0*) Wiley.

Colau, J. C., ed. Meeting the Patients' Needs in the Climacteric: The Proceedings of a Symposium Held at the 15th World Congress on Fertility & Sterility, Montpellier, France, September 1995. LC 96-33684. (Illus.). 84p. 1996. pap. 25.00 (*1-85070-761-8*) Prthnon Pub.

Colavito, Maria M. The Heresy of Oedipus & the Mind - Mind Split: A Study of the Biocultural Origins of Civilization. LC 95-39715. 1995. 89.95 (*0-7734-8854-5*) E Mellen.

— The New Theogony: Mythology for the Real World. LC 91-22107. 163p. (C). 1992. text 19.50 (*0-7914-1067-6*) State U NY Pr.

— The Pythagorean Intertext in Ovid's Metamorphoses: A New Interpretation. LC 89-13155. (Studies in Comparative Literature: Vol. 5). 168p. 1989. lib. bdg. 79.95 (*0-88946-398-0*) E Mellen.

Colavito, William A., jt. auth. see Colletti, Paul J.

Colb, jt. auth. see Desberg.

Colb, Valerie H., jt. auth. see Goldstein, Susan T.

***Colbary, Richard.** Customer Service in the Printing Industry. 300p. (C). 2000. 75.00 (*0-88362-247-5*) GATFPress.

Colbath, Arnold. Two Plays. 1980. pap. text 5.95 (*0-913006-17-3*) Puckerbrush.

Colbaugh, Nancy L., jt. auth. see Ashton, Bob B.

Colbeck, I. & MacKenzie, A. R. Air Pollution by Photochemical Oxidants. LC 94-16255. (Air Quality Monographs: Vol. 1). 388p. 1994. 190.00 (*0-444-88542-0*) Elsevier.

Colbeck, Julian. Keyfax Omnibus. LC 96-79301. 208p. 1997. pap. 24.95 (*0-918371-08-2*, MixBooks) Intertec Pub.

Colbere, Hope. The Scars Within. large type ed. 1991. pap. 16.99 (*0-7089-6971-2*) Ulverscroft.

An Asterisk (*) at the beginning of an entry indicates that the title is appearing for the first time.

Colberg, Janet O. Red Light, Green Light, Preventing Teen Pregnancy. LC 96-70009. (Illus.). 138p. (Orig.). 1997. pap. 14.50 (*0-9653647-0-4*) Summer Kitchen Press.

***Colberg, Janet Ollila.** Montana Bed & Breakfast Guide & Cookbook. 2nd rev. ed. (Illus.). 288p. 2001. pap. 14.95 (*0-9653647-3-9*) Summer Kitchen Press.

Colberg, Marshall, et al. CPS Business Economics: Principles & Cases Select Chapters. 6th ed. 396p. (C). 1995. text 35.95 (*0-256-21136-1*, Irwn McGrw-H) McGrw-H Hghr Educ.

***Colberg, Sheri.** The Diabetic Athlete. LC 00-31907. (Illus.). 280p. 2000. pap. 17.95 (*0-7360-3271-1*) Human Kinetics.

Colberg, Thomas P., et al. EDI Handbook. LC 94-36693. 320p. 1995. 165.00 (*0-471-10753-0*) Wiley.

— EDI Handbook 97S. 135p. 1997. pap., suppl. ed. 57.00 (*0-471-14039-2*) Wiley.

Colbert. An Integrated Approach to Health Science. (Health Occupations Ser.). 144p. (C). 1996. text, wbk. ed. 20.50 (*0-8273-6083-5*) Delmar.

— An Integrated Approach to Health Science. (Allied Health Ser.: I). 72p. 1996. text, teacher ed. 15.95 (*0-8273-6084-3*) Delmar.

— An Integrated Approach to Health Sciences. 288p. 1996. teacher ed., ring bd. 59.95 (*0-8273-7688-X*) Delmar.

— An Integrated Approach to Health Sciences. 1996. disk 71.95 (*0-8273-7689-8*) Delmar.

— Workplace Readiness: Health Occupations. (Health Occupations Ser.). 1998. teacher ed. 13.95 (*0-8273-7783-5*); 55.00 (*0-8273-7782-7*); 19.95 (*0-8273-7784-3*) Delmar.

— Workplace Readiness for Health Occupations. LC 98-22220. (Health Occupations Ser.). 240p. 1998. text 25.95 (*0-8273-7781-9*) Delmar.

Colbert, Agatha P., jt. auth. see Schock, Nancy C.

***Colbert, Bob.** Last Call. LC 99-65326. 192p. 2000. pap. 11.95 (*1-56315-259-2*, Pub. by SterlingHse) Natl Bk Netwk.

Colbert, Bruce J., et al. An Integrated Approach to Health Sciences: Anatomy & Physiology, Math, Physics, & Chemistry. rev. ed. LC 95-15277. 496p. (C). 1995. mass mkt. 52.95 (*0-8273-6082-7*) Delmar.

***Colbert, Carol.** Easy French Cooking. (Illus.). 144p. 2000. pap. 14.95 (*1-58091-062-9*, Pub. by Crossing Pr) Publishers Group.

Colbert, Charles. Idea: The Shaping Force. LC 87-91998. (Illus.). 152p. (C). 1988. 60.00 (*0-944853-01-3*) Pendaya Pubns.

— A Measure of Perfection: Phrenology & the Fine Arts in America. LC 97-8449. (Cultural Studies of the United States). 464p. 1998. pap. 27.50 (*0-8078-4673-2*); lib. bdg. 59.95 (*0-8078-2370-8*) U of NC Pr.

— Seeing What I Like & Liking What I See. LC 91-90374. (Illus.). 204p. 1991. 49.50 (*0-944853-04-8*) Pendaya Pubns.

Colbert, Cynthia & Taunton, Martha. Discover Art - Kindergarten. (Illus.). (J). (gr. k). 1990. pap. text 234.00 (*0-87192-219-3*) Davis Mass.

— The National Visual Arts Standards. 36p. (Orig.). 1994. pap. 14.00 (*0-937652-65-2*, 216) Natl Art Ed.

Colbert, David. The Birth of the Ballad: The Scandinavia Midieval Genre. 244p. (Orig.). 1989. pap. 65.00 (*91-85374-21-0*) Coronet Bks.

***Colbert, David.** Eyewitness to Wall Street. 2000. 30.00 (*0-7679-0660-8*) Broadway BDD.

Colbert, David, ed. Eyewitness to America: 500 Years of America in the Words of Those Who Saw It Happen. LC 96-24150. 1997. 30.00 (*0-679-44224-3*) Random.

— Eyewitness to America: 500 Years of America in the Words of Those Who Saw It Happen. LC E173.E9 1997. 752p. 1998. pap. 16.00 (*0-679-76724-X*) Vin Bks.

***Colbert, David, ed.** Eyewitness to the American West: 500 Years of History. 496p. 1999. pap. 14.95 (*0-14-028054-5*, Penguin Bks) Viking Penguin.

Colbert, David W., tr. see Rossel, Sven Hakon & Elbrond-Bek, Bo, eds.

Colbert, Dom. MCQs in Basic & Clinical Physiology. 350p. 1996. pap. text 29.95 (*0-19-262736-8*) OUP.

***Colbert, Don.** Allergies: Ancient Truths, Natural Remedies & the Latest Findings for Your Health Today. (Bible Cure Ser.). 2000. pap. 5.99 (*0-88419-685-2*) Creation House.

Colbert, Don. Bible Cure for Anxiety & Depression. (Bible Cure Ser.). 1999. pap. 5.99 (*0-88419-650-X*) Creation House.

— Bible Cure for Arthritis. (Bible Cure Ser.). 1999. pap. 5.99 (*0-88419-649-6*) Creation House.

***Colbert, Don.** The Bible Cure for Cancer. (Bible Cure Ser.). 1999. pap. 5.99 (*0-88419-625-9*) Creation House.

Colbert, Don. Bible Cure for Diabetes. (Bible Cure Ser.). 1999. pap. 5.99 (*0-88419-648-8*) Creation House.

— Bible Cure for Heart Disease. LC 99-35432. (Bible Cure Ser.). 1999. pap. 5.99 (*0-88419-647-X*) Creation House.

— Bible Cure for Heartburn & Ulcers. (Bible Cure Ser.). 1999. pap. 5.99 (*0-88419-651-8*) Creation House.

***Colbert, Don.** Colon Cancer: Ancient Truths, Natural Remedies & the Latest Findings for Your Health Today. (Bible Cure Ser.). 2000. pap. 5.99 (*0-88419-683-6*) Creation House.

— Lung Cancer: Ancient Truths, Natural Remedies & the Latest Findings for Your Health Today. (Bible Cure Ser.). 2000. pap. 5.99 (*0-88419-680-1*) Creation House.

— Osteoporosis: Ancient Truths, Natural Remedies & the Latest Findings for Your Health Today. (Bible Cure Ser.). 2000. pap. 5.99 (*0-88419-681-X*) Creation House.

— Stroke & Circulatory Health: Ancient Truths, Natural Remedies & the Latest Findings for Your Health Today. (Bible Cure Ser.). 2000. pap. 5.99 (*0-88419-682-8*) Creation House.

— Weight Loss: Ancient Truths, Natural Remedies & the Latest Findings for Your Health Today. (Bible Cure Ser.). 2000. pap. 5.99 (*0-88419-684-4*) Creation House.

— What You Don't Know May Be Killing You. 224p. 2000. 18.99 (*0-88419-627-5*) Creation House.

Colbert, Edouard C. & Chinard, Gilbert. Voyage dans l'Interieur des Etats-Unis et au Canada. 1979. 17.95 (*0-405-10596-7*) Ayer.

Colbert, Edwin H. The Age of Reptiles. unabridged ed. (Illus.). 256p. 1997. reprint ed. pap. text 9.95 (*0-486-29377-7*) Dover.

— The Great Dinosaur Hunters & Their Discoveries. LC 84-4204. 384p. 1984. reprint ed. pap. 9.95 (*0-486-24701-5*) Dover.

— The Triassic Dinosaur Coelophysis. (Bulletin Ser.). 174p. 1989. pap. 14.95 (*0-89734-097-3*, BS-57) Mus Northern Ariz.

— Wandering Lands & Animals: The Story of Continental Drift & Animal Populations. (Illus.). 352p. 1985. reprint ed. pap. 9.95 (*0-486-24918-2*) Dover.

— William Diller Matthew, Paleontologist: The Splendid Drama Observed. LC 92-14027. (Illus.). 272p. 1992. text 52.50 (*0-231-07964-8*) Col U Pr.

Colbert, Edwin H. & Morales, Michael. Evolution of the Vertebrates: A History of Backboned Animals Through Time. 4th ed. LC 90-40025. 488p. 1991. 245.00 (*0-471-85074-8*) Wiley.

Colbert, Edwin H., et al. Fossils of Arizona: Proceedings of the 3rd Annual Fossils of Arizona Symposium. Tegowski, B. J. et al, eds. (Illus.). 111p. 1995. pap. 16.95 (*0-935810-61-7*) R H Pub.

Colbert, Edwin H., jt. auth. see Kay, Marshall.

Colbert, J. M. Super Bowl Trivia: 75 A to Z Quizzes. LC 96-90692. 160p. (Orig.). 1996. pap. 14.95 (*0-9653182-1-4*) Tuff Turtle.

Colbert, J. M., jt. auth. see Leache, Allen.

***Colbert, Jaimee W.** Climbing the God Tree: A Novel in 24 Stories. LC 98-40365. (Winner of the 1997 Willa Cather Fiction Prize Ser.). 208p. 1998. pap. 12.95 (*1-884235-25-5*) Helicon Nine Eds.

Colbert, Jamal R., jt. auth. see Colbert, Norman.

Colbert, James. God Bless the Child: A Story of Child Abuse, Professional Gamblers, Government Corruption - & One Woman's Efforts to Make Things Right. (Illus.). 256p. 1993. text 22.00 (*0-689-12167-9*, Pub. by Ctrl Bur voor Schimmel) Macmillan.

— Skinny Man. 224p. 1991. text 18.95 (*0-689-12098-2*) Atheneum Yung Read.

***Colbert, James, ed.** Countering the Missile Threat: International Military Strategies. 258p. 1999. pap. 15.00 (*0-9644523-7-5*) Jewish Inst Nat Secur.

Colbert, James, ed. A Palestinian State: Implications for Security & American Policy. 68p. 1999. pap. 10.00 (*0-9644523-6-7*) Jewish Inst Nat Secur.

Colbert, James, ed. see Berman, Ilan.

Colbert, James, ed. see Blank, Stephen.

Colbert, James G., tr. see Pellicani, Luciano.

***Colbert, Jan.** Dear Dr. King. LC 97-32031. (Illus.). 64p. (J). (gr. 4-7). 2000. pap. 6.99 (*0-7868-1462-4*, Pub. by Hyprn Child) Time Warner.

— Dear Dr. King: Letters from Today's Children to Dr. Martin Luther King, Jr. (Illus.). (J). 2000. 12.34 (*0-606-18256-X*) Turtleback.

Colbert, Jan & Harms, Ann M. Dear Dr. King: Today's Children Write to Dr. Martin Luther King, Jr. LC 97-32031. (Illus.). 63p. (J). (gr. 4-7). 1998. 14.95 (*0-7868-0417-3*, Pub. by Hyprn Child) Time Warner.

Colbert, Jean B. Lettres, Instructions et Memoires de Colbert, 8 vols. (FRE.). 1969. reprint ed. pap. 1080.00 (*0-8115-3817-6*) Periodicals Srv.

***Colbert, Jeffrey M.** Vital Readings in American Politics. 160p. (C). 2000. per. 35.95 (*0-7872-7284-1*) Kendall-Hunt.

Colbert, Joanna P., ed. The Sage Woman Calendar for 1998: The Goddess of the Zodiac. (Illus.). 1997. pap. 8.95 (*0-9630360-7-6*) Blessed Bee Inc.

Colbert, Joel & Desberg, Peter. The Case for Education: Contemporary Approaches for Using Case Methods. LC 96-187956. 256p. (C). 1995. 48.00 (*0-205-17394-2*) Allyn.

Colbert, Joel A., jt. ed. see Shulman, Judith H.

Colbert, Judy. Country Towns of Maryland & Delaware. LC 96-48167. (Country Towns Ser.). (Illus.). 152p. 1996. pap. 10.95 (*1-56626-167-8*, Cntry Rds Pr) NTC Contemp Pub Co.

***Colbert, Judy.** Country Towns of Maryland & Delaware: Charming Small Towns & Villages to Explore. 2nd ed. LC 98-54642. (Country Towns of... Ser.). 160p. 1999. pap. 12.95 (*0-658-00178-7*, 001787, Cntry Rds Pr) NTC Contemp Pub Co.

Colbert, Judy. Divorce: Common Sense Handbook: 180+ Things to Do & 8+ Things Not to Do. 80p. (Orig.). 1999. pap. 9.95 (*0-9653182-0-6*) Tuff Turtle.

— Fun Places to Go with Children in Colorado. 2nd ed. LC 99-160623. (Fun Places to Go with Children Ser.). 224p. 1998. pap. 11.95 (*0-8118-1915-9*) Chronicle Bks.

— Fun Places to Go with Children in Washington, D. C. 3rd ed. LC 99-166684. (Fun Places to Go with Children Ser.). 176p. 1998. pap. 11.95 (*0-8118-1940-X*) Chronicle Bks.

— Maryland & Delaware: Off the Beaten Path: A Guide to Unique Places. 4th ed. LC 99-28880. (Off the Beaten Ser.). (Illus.). 225p. 1999. pap. text 12.95 (*0-7627-0458-6*) Globe Pequot.

***Colbert, Judy.** Virginia: A Guide to Unique Places. 6th ed. (Off the Beaten Path Ser.). (Illus.). 2000. pap. 12.95 (*0-7627-0797-6*) Globe Pequot.

Colbert, Judy. Virginia: Off the Beaten Path: A Guide to Unique Places. 5th ed. LC 98-7144. (Off the Beaten Path Ser.). (Illus.). 256p. 1998. pap. 12.95 (*0-7627-0219-2*) Globe Pequot.

Colbert, Karen K., jt. auth. see Martin, Carole A.

Colbert, Larry L. 33 Truths You Should Know about Jesus & the Cross. 64p. 1997. pap. 4.95 (*1-887399-04-6*) Colbert Hse.

***Colbert, Nancy A.** The Firing on Fort Sumter: A Splintered Nation Goes to War. 112p. (YA). (gr. 5 up). 2000. lib. bdg. 19.95 (*1-883846-51-X*) M Reynolds.

Colbert, Nancy A. Lou Henry Hoover: The Duty to Serve. LC 97-33329. (Notable Americans Ser.). (Illus.). 112p. (YA). (gr. 5 up). 1998. lib. bdg. 18.95 (*1-883846-22-6*) M Reynolds.

Colbert, Norman & Colbert, Jamal R. Streets of Death Inside the Black Community. 48p. 1999. pap. 8.00 (*0-8059-4613-6*) Dorrance.

Colbert, Patrick J., jt. ed. see McLuckie, Craig W.

Colbert, Roman. Brief French Reference Grammar. (C). 1972. mass mkt. 35.95 (*0-442-21615-7*) Heinle & Heinle.

— Colbert's Medico English - Spanish Instant Communication for the Medical Profession. 322p. 1991. pap. write for info. (*0-9630253-0-9*) R Colbert.

Colbert, Sharon K. Stand with Angels: Conversations with God from the Eye of the Storm. LC 99-94665. (Illus.). 144p. 1999. pap. 15.98 (*0-9670192-9-X*) Angel Writ.

Colbert, Teddy. The Living Wreath. (Illus.). 128p. 1996. pap. 19.95 (*0-87905-700-9*) Gibbs Smith Pub.

Colbert, Ty. Broken Brains or Wounded Hearts: What Causes Mental Illness? LC 96-76762. (Illus.). 316p. 1996. 23.95 (*0-9643635-4-2*) Kevco Pubg.

Colbert, Ty C. Depression & Mania: Friends Or Foes. LC 94-79289. (Illus.). 221p. (Orig.). 1995. pap. 13.95 (*0-9643635-5-0*) Kevco Pubg.

— The Four False Pillars of Biopsychiatry. (Illus.). 50p. (Orig.). 1997. pap. 9.95 (*0-9643635-6-9*) Kevco Pubg.

Colbert, W. Who Wrote That Song? Popular Songs in America & Their Composers. 1974. lib. bdg. 250.00 (*0-87700-216-9*) Revisionist Pr.

Colbey, Richard. Residential Tenancies. 2nd ed. (Practice Notes Ser.). 104p. 1990. pap. write for info. (*0-85121-694-3*, Pub. by Cavendish Pubng) Gaunt.

— Residential Tenancies. 3rd ed. (Cavendish Practice Notes Ser.). 1996. pap. 32.00 (*1-85941-293-9*, Pub. by Cavendish Pubng) Gaunt.

Colbey, Richard, et al. Landlord & Tenant in Practice. 217p. 1998. pap. 48.00 (*1-85431-720-2*, Pub. by Blackstone Pr) Gaunt.

— Landlord & Tenant in Practice. 2nd ed. 219p. 1999. pap. 50.00 (*1-85431-904-3*, Pub. by Blackstone Pr) Gaunt.

***Colbey, Richard, et al.** Landlord & Tenant in Practice. 3rd ed. (Inns of Court School of Law Ser.). 219p. 2000. pap. 46.00 (*1-84174-007-1*, Pub. by Blackstone Pr) Gaunt.

Colbi, Saul P. A History of the Christian Presence in the Holy Land. LC 88-14829. (Illus.). 392p. (C). 1988. lib. bdg. 55.00 (*0-8191-7036-4*) U Pr of Amer.

Colbin, Annemarie. The Book of Whole Meals: A Seasonal Guide to Assembling Balanced Vegetarian Breakfasts, Lunches & Dinners. 240p. (Orig.). 1985. pap. 12.00 (*0-345-33274-1*) Ballantine Pub Grp.

— Food & Healing. LC 96-129391. 368p. (Orig.). 1986. pap. 12.95 (*0-345-30385-7*) Ballantine Pub Grp.

— Food & Our Bones: The Natural Way to Prevent Osteoporosis. LC 97-53118. 352p. 1998. pap. 13.95 (*0-452-27806-6*, Plume) Dutton Plume.

— The Natural Gourmet: Delicious Recipes for Healthy, Balanced Eating. 336p. 1991. pap. 12.50 (*0-345-37028-7*) Ballantine Pub Grp.

— Osteoporosis. 256p. 1999. pap. 23.95 (*0-525-94286-6*) NAL.

Colbin, Kaila, jt. auth. see LaVan, Ken.

Colbo, M. H., jt. auth. see Matthysee, J. G.

Colborn, Candace. What Do Children Read Next? 700p. 1994. 55.00 (*0-8103-8886-3*, 022180) Gale.

Colborn, Candace & Spencer, Pamela G. What Do Children & Young Adults Read Next?, 2 Vols., Vol. 2. 1994. 110.00 (*0-8103-8885-5*, 022155) Gale.

Colborn, D. Promotion of Continence in Adult Nursing. 192p. 1994. 32.99 (*1-56593-192-0*, 0507) Singular Publishing.

Colborn, Francis. Living As a Catholic Today. (Catholic Home Library). 128p. 1989. 4.95 (*1-55944-003-1*) Franciscan Comns.

Colborn, Gene L. & Lause, David B. Musculoskeletal Anatomy: A Text & Guide to Dissection for Students in the Allied Health Sciences. LC 93-13736. (Illus.). 247p. (C). 1993. pap. 19.95 (*1-85070-523-2*) Prthnon Pub.

Colborn, Gene L. & Skandalakis, John E., eds. Clinical Gross Anatomy: A Guide for Dissection, Study, & Review. LC 93-11127. (Illus.). 581p. (C). 1993. pap. text 29.95 (*1-85070-522-4*) Prthnon Pub.

Colborn, J. G. The Thermal Structure of the Indian Ocean. LC 75-17812. (International Indian Ocean Expedition. Oceanographic Monographs: No. 2). 181p. reprint ed. pap. 56.20 (*0-7837-3986-9*, 204381600011) Bks Demand.

Colborn, Mark, et al. Maximum Metal. (Cyberpunk Ser.). (Illus.). 104p. (Orig.). 1993. pap. 12.00 (*0-937279-34-X*, CP3191) Talsorian.

***Colborn, Nigel.** Container Garden. (Illus.). 2000. pap. 19.95 (*1-85029-798-3*) Conran Octopus.

Colborn, Nigel. Container Garden. 1990. 29.95 (*0-316-15045-2*) Little.

***Colborn, Nigel.** The Garden Floor: From Gravel Gardens to Chamomile Lawns. (Illus.). 2000. 29.95 (*1-57076-166-3*, Trafalgar Sq Pub) Trafalgar.

Colborn, Nigel. Plant by Numbers: A Step-by-Step Planting Guide. (Illus.). 160p. 1998. 30.00 (*1-57959-032-2*, SOMA) BB&T Inc.

— Shortcuts to Great Gardens. 144p. 1993. pap. 24.95 (*0-316-15052-5*) Little.

Colborn, Theo, et al, eds. Advances in Modern Environmental Toxicology Vol. 24: Environmental Endocrine-Disrupting Chemicals; Neural Endocrine & Behavioral Effects. unabridged ed. LC 98-970762. (Illus.). 365p. 1998. 75.00 (*0-911131-56-6*) Specialist Journals.

Colborne, Desmond & Dos Santos, Solvi. South Africa: Private Worlds. (Illus.). 208p. 1999. 39.95 (*1-84091-047-X*, Pub. by Conran Octopus) BHB Intl.

Colborne, Robert. Visual Merchandising. (SV-Fashion Merchandising). 64p. 1995. teacher ed. 10.00 (*0-8273-5760-5*) Delmar.

— Visual Merchandising: The Business of Merchandise Presentation. LC 95-10179. 352p. (C). 1996. mass mkt. 50.95 (*0-8273-5759-1*) Delmar.

Colbough, Nancy, jt. auth. see Ashton, Bob.

Colbourn, C. J., ed. see Harms, Darl D.

Colbourn, Charles J. & Dinitz, Jeffrey H., eds. CRC Handbook of Combinatorial Designs. (Discrete Mathematics & Its Applications Ser.). 784p. 1996. boxed set 109.95 (*0-8493-8948-8*) CRC Pr.

Colbourn, Charles J. & Rosa, Alex. Triple Systems. LC 98-53085. (Oxford Mathematical Monographs). (Illus.). 576p. 1999. text 140.00 (*0-19-853576-7*) OUP.

Colbourn, E. A., ed. Computer Simluation of Polymers. LC 93-36416. 1996. (*0-582-08374-5*) Addison-Wesley.

Colbourn, Trevor. The Lamp of Experience: Whig History & the Intellectual Origins of the American Revolution. 2nd ed. LC 97-3351. 1998. 12.00 (*0-86597-158-7*); pap. 5.00 (*0-86597-159-5*) Liberty Fund.

Colbourn, Trevor, jt. auth. see Adair, Douglass.

Colbourne, J. R. The Geometry of Involute Gears. (Illus.). 545p. 1987. 73.00 (*0-387-96522-X*) Spr-Verlag.

Colbourne, John R. Contact Stresses in Gear Teeth. (1990 Fall Technical Meeting). 1990. pap. text 30.00 (*1-55589-553-0*) AGMA.

— Effect of Oblique Loading on the Fillet Stress in Helical Gears. (Nineteen Eighty-Six Fall Technical Meeting Ser.: Vol. 86FTM6). (Illus.). 13p. 1986. pap., pap. text 30.00 incl. audio compact disk (*1-55589-470-4*, 86FTM6) AGMA.

— Efficiency of High Contact Ratio Planetary Gear Trains. (Technical Papers: Vol. 95FTM10). (Illus.). 8p. 1995. pap. text 30.00 (*1-55589-659-6*) AGMA.

— The Geometric Design of Internal Gear Pairs. (Nineteen Eighty-Seven Fall Technical Meeting Ser.: Vol. 87FTM2). (Illus.). 13p. 1987. pap. text 30.00 (*1-55589-478-X*) AGMA.

— Optimum Number of Teeth for Span Measurement. (1985 Fall Technical Meeting Ser.: Vol. 85FTM9). (Illus.). 9p. 1985. pap. text 30.00 (*1-55589-102-0*) AGMA.

— Undercutting in Worms & Worm-Gears. (Nineteen Ninety-Three Fall Technical Meeting Ser.: Vol. 93FTM1). (Illus.). 10p. 1993. pap. text 30.00 (*1-55589-594-8*) AGMA.

— The Use of Oversize Hobs to Cut Worm Gears. (Nineteen Eighty-Nine Fall Technical Meeting Ser.: Vol. 89FTM8). (Illus.). 16p. 1989. pap. text 30.00 (*1-55589-534-4*) AGMA.

Col'Braikh, E., jt. auth. see Ryabchikov, D.

Colburn, Alan. Constructivism & Science Teaching. (Fastback Ser.: No. 435). 44p. 1998. pap. 3.00 (*0-87367-635-1*, FB435) Phi Delta Kappa.

Colburn, Betsy & Tyning, Tom. Pond Watchers Guide to Ponds & Vernal Pools of Eastern North America. Leahy, Christopher, ed. (Habitat Ser.). (Illus.). 8p. 1995. 3.95 (*0-932691-14-5*) MA Audubon Soc.

Colburn, Bolton. Across the Street: Self-Help Graphics & Chicano Art in Los Angeles. LC 94-46424. 1995. write for info. (*0-940872-21-8*) Laguna Beach.

Colburn, Charles J., ed. Combinatorics Advances. (Mathematics & Its Applications Ser.). 340p. (C). 1995. text 176.50 (*0-7923-3574-0*) Kluwer Academic.

Colburn, David R. Racial Change & Community Crisis: St. Augustine, Florida, 1877-1980. (Florida Sand Dollar Bk.). 280p. (C). 1991. reprint ed. pap. 19.95 (*0-8130-1066-7*) U Press Fla.

Colburn, David R. & deHaven-Smith, Lance. Government in the Sunshine State: Florida since Statehood. LC 98-36030. (Florida History & Culture Ser.). (Illus.). 1999. 20.00 (*0-8130-1652-5*) U Press Fla.

Colburn, David R. & Landers, Jane L., eds. The African American Heritage of Florida. LC 94-40977. (Illus.). 402p. 1995. pap. 19.95 (*0-8130-1412-3*) U Press Fla.

Colburn, David R. & Pozzetta, George E., eds. Reform & Reformers in the Progressive Era, 101. LC 82-6140. (Contributions in American History Ser.: No. 101). (Illus.). 196p. 1982. 52.95 (*0-313-22907-4*, CRP/, Greenwood Pr) Greenwood.

Colburn, David R. & Scher, Richard K. Florida's Gubernatorial Politics in the Twentieth Century. LC 80-10277. (Illus.). viii, 342p. 1981. 49.95 (*0-8130-0644-9*) U Press Fla.

Colburn, Forrest D. My Car in Managua. (Illus.). 148p. 1991. pap. 10.95 (*0-292-75124-9*); text 17.95 (*0-292-75123-0*) U of Tex Pr.

— Paraprofesionales en Salud Rural en Guatemala. (Special Series on Paraprofesionals: No. 8). (SPA.). 55p. 1981. pap. text 6.45 (*0-86731-058-8*) Cornell CIS RDC.

— The Vogue of Revolution in Poor Countries. LC 94-10318. 152p. 1994. text 24.95 (*0-691-03676-4*, Pub. by Princeton U Pr) Cal Prin Full Svc.

Colburn, Forrest D., ed. Everyday Forms of Peasant Resistance. LC 89-10143. 256p. (gr. 13). 1990. text 70.95 (*0-87332-575-3*); pap. text 34.95 (*0-87332-622-9*) M E Sharpe.

Colburn, Harvey C. The Story of Ypsilanti. (Illus.). 327p. 1995. reprint ed. lib. bdg. 39.00 (*0-8328-5047-0*) Higginson Bk Co.

C

An Asterisk (*) at the beginning of an entry indicates that the title is appearing for the first time.

Colburn, I. P. & Ramirez, P. C., eds. The Paleocene Stratigraphic Successions in the Northern Peninsular Ranges, Orange & Riverside Counties, California. 74p. 1995. 9.00 (*1-878861-72-7*) Pac Section SEPM.

Colburn, Ivan P., et al, eds. Conglomerates in Basin Analysis: A Symposium Dedicated to A. O. Woodford. (Illus.). 312p. (Orig.). 1989. pap. 17.00 (*1-878861-07-7*) Pac Section SEPM.

Colburn, James T. Trading in Options on Futures. 310p. (C). 1990. text 45.00 (*0-13-638552-4*) NY Inst Finance.

Colburn, Joel C., jt. ed. see Grossman, Paul D.

Colburn, John, et al, eds. A Definitive Guide to the Twin Cities: In Poetry & Prose. 104p. 1997. pap. 7.95 (*0-9659443-0-1*) Spout Pr.

Colburn, Marta, ed. see Buringa, Joke.

***Colburn, Mary A.** Rainy Day Slug. LC 99-47253. (Illus.). 32p. (J). (ps-1). 2000. 15.95 (*1-57061-238-2*) Sasquatch Bks.

Colburn, Mona L., et al. Coles Creek & Mississippi Period Forages in the Felsenthal Region of the Lower Mississippi Valley: Evidence from the Bangs Slough Site, Southeast Arkansas. Schambach, Frank F., ed. (Research Ser.). (Illus.). 137p. (Orig.). 1990. pap. text 12.00 (*1-56349-069-2*, RS39) AR Archaeol.

Colburn, Nancy H. Genes & Signal Transduction in Multistage Carcinogenesis. (Illus.). 480p. 1988. text 189.00 (*0-8247-7996-7*) Dekker.

Colburn, Nigel. A Flower for Every Day. LC 96-68266. (Illus.). 144p. 1996. 32.50 (*1-55670-505-0*) Stewart Tabori & Chang.

Colburn, Patricia, et al. Oekoaktiv - Buchlein. (GER., Illus.). 40p. 1997. spiral bd. 17.00 incl. vdisk (*0-942017-48-X*, 04-64647) Amer Assn Teach German.

***Colburn, Rafe.** Sams Teach Yourself CGI in 24 Hours. (Illus.). 512p. 2000. 24.99 (*0-672-31880-6*) Sams.

— Using SQL. (Special Edition Using... Que Ser.). 900p. 1999. 34.99 (*0-7897-1974-6*) Que.

Colburn, Rafe, jt. auth. see Tatters, Wes.

Colburn, Rhonda. The Story of Elijah. (Story of...Ser.). (Illus.). 24p. (J). (ps-2). 1990. pap. 3.95 (*0-8249-8419-6*, Ideals Child) Hambleton-Hill.

Colburn, Steven E., ed. Anne Sexton: Telling the Tale. 496p. 1988. text 47.50 (*0-472-09379-7*, 09379) U of Mich Pr.

Colburn, Steven E., ed. see Sexton, Anne.

Colburn, T. & Clement, C., eds. Chemically Induced Alterations in Sexual & Functional Development: The Wildlife-Human Connection, Vol. 8, No. 4. (Advances in Modern Environmental Toxicology Ser.: Vol. 21). (Illus.). 403p. (Orig.). 1992. 68.00 (*0-911131-35-3*) Specialist Journals.

Colburn, Theo, et al. Our Stolen Future. LC 97-159794. 1997. pap. 13.95 (*0-452-27414-1*, Plume) Dutton Plume.

Colburn, Timothy R. Philosophy & Computer Science. LC 99-28936. (Explorations in Philosophy Ser.). 256p. 1999. text 58.95 (*1-56324-990-1*); pap. text 22.95 (*1-56324-991-X*) M E Sharpe.

Colburn, Timothy R., et al, eds. Program Verification: Fundamental Issues in Computer Science. LC 92-26748. (Studies in Cognitive Systems: Vol. 14). 471p. (C). 1993. lib. bdg. 289.50 (*0-7923-1965-6*, Pub. by Kluwer Academic) Kluwer Academic.

Colby. Heart to Give. 1997. pap. 4.95 (*3-512-60055-7*) Vineyard Music.

Colby, et al. Tumors of the Lower Respiratory Tract. (AFIP Atlas of Tumor Pathology Ser.: Vol. 13). (Illus.). 554p. 1995. pap. text 69.00 (*1-881041-17-4*) Am Registry Path.

Colby, Anita, ed. Thesaurus of Linguistic Indexing Terms. LC 92-62352. 97p. (C). 1992. 65.00 (*0-930710-10-X*) Soc Abstracts.

Colby, Anne. Daily Meditations for Dieters: How to Think Thin 365 Days a Year. LC 94-17784. 192p. 1997. pap. 7.95 (*0-8065-1580-5*, Citadel Pr) Carol Pub Group.

Colby, Anne, et al, eds. Competence & Character Through. LC 97-35198. 248p. 1998. 25.00 (*0-226-11316-7*) U Ch Pr.

Colby, Anne & Damon, William. Some Do Care: Contemporary Lives of Moral Commitment. 1994. pap. 14.95 (*0-02-906356-6*) Free Pr.

Colby, Barbara. Color & Light: Influences & Impact. (Illus.). 100p. (Orig.). 1990. pap. 14.50 (*0-9628138-0-X*) Chroma Prods.

Colby, Barnard L. Whaling Captains of New London County, Connecticut: For Oil & Buggy Whips. (Illus.). 256p. 1990. pap. 17.95 (*0-913372-54-4*) Mystic Seaport.

Colby, Benjamin. A Guide to Health. enl. rev. ed. 1985. 9.95 (*0-913923-53-2*) Woodland UT.

Colby, Benjamin N. & Colby, Lore M. The Daykeeper: The Life & Discourse of As Ixtil Dviner. (Illus.). 345p. (C). 1981. 46.50 (*0-674-19409-8*) HUP.

Colby, C. B. World's Best "True" Ghost Stories. LC 88-11703. (Illus.). 128p. (J). (gr. 4 up). 1989. pap. 4.95 (*0-8069-6898-2*) Sterling.

Colby, Charles C., ed. Geographic Aspects of International Relations. LC 76-99687. (Essay Index Reprint Ser.). 1977. 33.95 (*0-8369-1402-3*) Ayer.

Colby, Charles W. Canadian Types of the Old Regime, 1608-1698. (Illus.). 382p. 1997. reprint ed. pap. 30.95 (*1-886560-46-3*, 097004) Quintin Pub RI.

Colby, Constance T. Skunk in the House. 1976. 18.95 (*0-8488-0967-X*) Amereon Ltd.

Colby, David P. Fishing California - Freshwater: A Travel Guide to Proven Spots & Proven Methods. (Illus.). 189p. (Orig.). 1994. pap. 14.95 (*0-9628688-3-3*) Sabertooth Pub.

— Fishing California - Saltwater: A Travel Guide to Proven Spots & Proven Methods. (Illus.). 192p. (Orig.). 1994. pap. 14.95 (*0-9628688-2-5*) Sabertooth Pub.

Colby, Douglas. As the Curtain Rises: On Contemporary British Drama 1966-1976. LC 77-92566. 103p. 1979. 15.00 (*0-8386-2194-5*) Fairleigh Dickinson.

Colby, Elbridge. English Catholic Poets, Chaucer to Dryden. LC 67-28733. (Essay Index Reprint Ser.). 1977. 20.95 (*0-8369-0321-8*) Ayer.

— The First Army in Europe, 1943-1945. (Combat Arms Ser.: No. 23). (Illus.). 200p. 1993. reprint ed. 29.95 (*0-89839-189-X*) Battery Pr.

— The National Guard of the United States: A Half Century of Progress. 369p. 1977. pap. text 46.95 (*0-89126-037-4*) MA-AH Pub.

Colby, Elbridge, ed. see Holcroft, Thomas.

Colby, Frank M. Constrained Attitudes. LC 68-8449. (Essay Index Reprint Ser.). 1977. reprint ed. 19.95 (*0-8369-0322-6*) Ayer.

— Imaginary Obligations. LC 76-128223. (Essay Index Reprint Ser.). 1977. 21.95 (*0-8369-1870-3*) Ayer.

Colby, Gail. The Kingdom & the Power. 384p. 1998. 25.00 (*0-06-016907-9*) HarperTrade.

***Colby, Gail.** Angels Walking on Earth. 102p. 1999. pap. 7.50 (*0-7392-0355-X*, PO3428) Morris Pubng.

Colby, H. A Genealogy of the Descendants of Abraham Colby & Elizabeth Blaisdell, His Wife, Who Settled in Bow in 1768, by One of Them. (Illus.). 152p. 1993. reprint ed. pap. 22.50 (*0-8328-1365-6*); reprint ed. lib. bdg. 32.50 (*0-8328-1364-8*) Higginson Bk Co.

Colby, Helen. Where the River Flows: Tales of Love & Romance in the Glorious Steamboat Era. (Illus.). 130p. (Orig.). 1993. pap. write for info. (*0-9639817-0-6*) H C Swiers.

Colby, Howard D., et al. Atlas of Pulmonary Surgical Pathology. (Illus.). 400p. 1990. text 205.00 (*0-7216-2893-1*, W B Saunders Co) Harcrt Hlth Sci Grp.

Colby, Howard D., jt. auth. see Thomas, J. A.

***Colby, Ira C. & Dziegielewski, Sophia F.** Introduction to Social Work: The People's Profession. (Illus.). 448p. (C). 2000. pap. text 49.95 (*0-925065-33-1*) Lyceum IL.

Colby, J., ed. see Brabb, E.

Colby, J., ed. see Clark, Liz.

Colby, J., ed. see Drzewucki, Vincent, Jr.

Colby, J., ed. see Edwards, Bernard.

Colby, J., ed. see Kaufman, Sheilah.

Colby, J., ed. & pref. see Cusack, James S.

Colby, J. W. Colby. History of the Colby Family, with Genealogical Tables. 119p. 1995. reprint ed. pap. 22.00 (*0-8328-4758-5*); reprint ed. lib. bdg. 32.00 (*0-8328-4757-7*) Higginson Bk Co.

Colby, Jenna, jt. auth. see Bland, John.

Colby, Joan. The Atrocity Book. LC 84-17078. 69p. 1986. pap. 8.00 (*0-89924-045-3*) Lynx Hse.

— How the Sky Begins to Fall. 64p. 1982. pap. 4.50 (*0-933180-32-2*) Spoon Riv Poetry.

***Colby, John H.** The Law & Practice Regulating the Disposition of Surplus Moneys Arising from the Sale of Lands upon Mortgage Foreclosures: With an Appendix of Precedents Including the Practice upon Orders of Reference & the Review Thereof, upon Expections, as Applied to Such Cases. iv, 116p. 1999. reprint ed. 40.00 (*1-56169-555-6*) Gaunt.

Colby, John H., ed. Littleton: Crossroads of Northern New Hampshire. LC 84-4941. 702p. 1984. 34.95 (*0-914659-03-0*) Phoenix Pub.

Colby, John K. Latin Word Lists. (C). 1978. pap. text 3.95 (*0-88334-097-6*) Longman.

Colby, Kate, ed. see Hornbeak, Sam L.

Colby, Kenneth M. & Stoller, R. J. Cognitive Science & Psychoanalysis. 176p. 1988. 39.95 (*0-8058-0177-4*) L Erlbaum Assocs.

Colby, Kimberlee W., ed. A Guide to the Equal Access Act. rev. ed. LC 93-72012. 47p. (Orig.). 1993. pap. text 25.00 (*0-944561-22-5*) Chr Legal.

Colby, Lee. Post Merger Management. 1989. pap. 19.95 (*0-88057-909-9*) Exec Ent Pubns.

Colby, Lore M., jt. auth. see Colby, Benjamin N.

Colby, Louis B. Colby's Book of the American Pit Bull Terrier. (Illus.). 192p. 1997. 39.95 (*0-7938-2091-X*, TS-246) TFH Pubns.

Colby, Lynn A., jt. auth. see Kisner, Carolyn.

Colby, Marilyn. Motor Learning Applied to Sports. 4th ed. (Illus.). 208p. (C). 2000. pap. text 27.95 (*0-89641-290-3*) American Pr.

Colby, Mark A. & Birt, Michael P. Negotiating the Gray Maze: The Business of Medicine in Japan. 176p. 1998. 24.95 (*1-891640-00-3*) Float World.

Colby, Marvelle S. & Alkon, Selig. Introduction to Business. LC 90-56017. (HarperCollins College Outline Ser.). (Illus.). 352p. (Orig.). 1991. pap. 13.00 (*0-06-467104-6*, Harper Ref) HarpC.

Colby, Paul L., jt. auth. see Klonoff, Robert H.

Colby, Peter W., jt. auth. see Riley, Susan L.

Colby, Robert. A Piece of the Cake. (Midnight Reading Ser.). 1997. pap. 4.20 (*1-55855-691-5*) Raintree Steck-V.

— Seajack. (Midnight Reading Ser.). 1997. pap. 4.20 (*1-55855-696-6*) Raintree Steck-V.

Colby, Robert & Drummond, Robert. AFDCS Handbook of U. S., 1909 Commemoratives on First Day Covers. 2nd rev. ed. (Illus.). 148p. 1997. pap. 14.95 (*1-879390-23-X*) AFDCS.

Colby, Robert & Sharp, C. A Run for the Money. (Midnight Reading Ser.). 1997. pap. 4.20 (*1-55855-686-9*) Raintree Steck-V.

Colby, Robert A., jt. auth. see Colby, Vineta.

Colby, Robert W. & Meyers, Thomas A. The Encyclopedia of Technical Market Indicators. 581p. 1988. text 70.00 (*1-55623-049-4*, Irwn Prfssnl) McGraw-Hill Prof.

Colby, Robin B. Some Appointed Work to Do: Women & Vocation in the Fiction of Elizabeth Gaskell, 150. LC 94-46946. (Contributions in Women's Studies: No. 150). 136p. 1995. 55.00 (*0-313-29373-2*, Greenwood Pr) Greenwood.

Colby, Sas & Shirkus, Lorraine. The Pocket Book: A Child's Activity Book. (Illus.). 10p. (J). (ps). 1988. 39.95 (*0-922656-00-2*) Design Matters Inc.

Colby, Thomas E., 3rd, ed. see Hesse, Hermann.

Colby, Todd. Cush. 108p. 1995. pap. 8.00 (*1-887128-14-X*) Soft Skull Pr.

***Colby, Todd.** Heights of the Marvelous. LC 00-22339. 224p. 2000. pap. 13.95 (*0-312-26335-X*) St Martin.

Colby, Todd. Riot in the Charm Factory. 125p. 1999. pap. 13.00 (*1-887128-38-7*, Pub. by Soft Skull Pr) SPD-Small Pr Dist.

— Ripsnort. 76p. 1994. pap. 10.00 (*1-887128-05-0*) Soft Skull Pr.

Colby, Ursula S., jt. auth. see Chapman, Sara S.

Colby, Vineta, ed. World Authors, 1985-1990. (Wilson Authors Ser.). 970p. 1995. 85.00 (*0-8242-0875-7*) Wilson.

— World Authors, 1980-1985: Authoritative Biographies of 320 Contemporary Writers. (Wilson Authors Ser.). 938p. 1991. 85.00 (*0-8242-0797-1*) Wilson.

— World Authors, 1975-1980. LC 85-10045. 829p. 1985. 85.00 (*0-8242-0715-7*) Wilson.

Colby, Vineta & Colby, Robert A. Equivocal Virtue: Mrs. Oliphant & the Victorian Literary Marketplace. LC 66-12770. 295p. reprint ed. 91.50 (*0-8357-9582-9*, 201541300093) Bks Demand.

Colby, Vineta, jt. ed. see Kunitz, Stanley J.

Colby, W. H. A Century of Transportation in Shasta County, 1821-1920. (ANCRR Occasional Publications: No. 7). 105p. 1982. 7.00 (*0-686-38931-X*) Assn NC Records.

Colcal Marketing Staff. How to Inspect a Used Car, Vol. 1. (Illus.). 13p. (Orig.). Date not set. pap. 1.95 (*0-9649053-0-2*) Gem Mktg.

Colchester. Computer Architecture. (ITCP-UK Computer Science Ser.). 1999. mass mkt. 25.95 (*1-85032-225-2*, VNR) Wiley.

Colchester, A. C., et al, eds. Information Processing in Medical Imaging: Proceedings of the International Conference, IPMI, Wye, U. K., 12th, July 7-12, 1991. (Lecture Notes in Computer Science Ser.: Vol. 511). xi, 512p. 1991. 93.95 (*0-387-54246-9*) Spr-Verlag.

Colchester, Chloe. The New Textiles: Trends & Traditions. LC 96-61511. (Illus.). 192p. (Orig.). 1997. pap. 24.95 (*0-500-27737-0*, Pub. by Thames Hudson) Norton.

Colchester, Marcus. Forest Politics in Suriname. 96p. (Orig.). 1996. pap. 17.50 (*90-6224-975-2*, Pub. by Uitgeverij Arkel) LPC InBook.

— Guyana: Fragile Frontier. LC 96-214905. (Illus.). 200p. (Orig.). (C). 1996. pap. text 19.00 (*0-85345-971-1*, Pub. by Lat Am Bur) Monthly Rev.

Colchester, Marcus & Lohmann, Larry, eds. The Struggle for Land & the Fate of the Forests. 208p. (C). 1995. text 25.00 (*1-85649-140-4*, Pub. by Zed Books) St Martin.

— The Struggle for Land & the Fate of the Forests. 208p. (C). 1996. text 59.95 (*1-85649-139-0*, Pub. by Zed Books) St Martin.

Colchester, Marcus. Salvaging Nature: Indigenous Peoples, Protected Areas & Biodiversity Conservation. (Illus.). 76p. (C). 1998. reprint ed. pap. text 25.00 (*0-7881-7194-1*) DIANE Pub.

Colchie, Thomas. Jorge Amado: Biography. 1999. pap. 9.95 (*0-14-010825-4*) Viking Penguin.

Colchie, Thomas, ed. A Hammock Beneath the Mangoes: Stories from Latin America. LC 92-53571. 448p. 1992. pap. 14.95 (*0-452-26866-4*, Plume) Dutton Plume.

Colchie, Thomas, tr. see Puig, Manuel.

Colclaser, Judith. Double Exposures: Integrated Art & Writing Activities. (Illus.). 152p. 1987. pap. 12.95 (*0-915817-16-0*) ISS Pubns.

Colclaser, R. A. & Nagle, S. D. Materials & Devices for Electrical Engineers & Physicists. 284p. (C). 1984. 97.50 (*0-07-011693-8*) McGraw.

Colclaser, Roy A. Microelectronics: Process & Device Design. LC 79-29727. 84p. 1980. pap. text 8.50 (*0-471-08709-2*) Wiley.

Colclazer, Susan. In Pictures Bryce Canyon: The Continuing Story. LC 89-45016. (Illus.). 48p. (Orig.). 1989. pap. 7.95 (*0-88714-032-7*) KC Pubns.

— In Pictures Bryce Canyon: The Continuing Story. (GER., Illus.). 48p. (Orig.). 1989. pap. 8.95 (*0-88714-704-6*) KC Pubns.

— In Pictures Bryce Canyon: The Continuing Story. Le Bras, Yvon, tr. (FRE., Illus.). 48p. (Orig.). 1989. pap. 8.95 (*0-88714-705-4*) KC Pubns.

— In Pictures Bryce Canyon: The Continuing Story. Petzinger, Saori, tr. (JPN., Illus.). 48p. (Orig.). 1991. pap. 8.95 (*0-88714-706-2*) KC Pubns.

— In Pictures Bryce Canyon: The Continuing Story. Lee, Frances Y., tr. (CHI., Illus.). 48p. (Orig.). 1993. pap. 8.95 (*0-88714-707-0*) KC Pubns.

— In Pictures Bryce Canyon: The Continuing Story. Comollo, Adriano, tr. (ITA., Illus.). 48p. (Orig.). 1994. pap. 8.95 (*0-88714-784-4*) KC Pubns.

***Colclough.** Effective Way to Stop Drinking. 256p. 1998. pap. 11.95 (*0-14-026664-X*, Pub. by Pnguin Bks Ltd) Trafalgar.

Colclough, Beauchamp. Tomorrow I'll Be Different. 240p. 1995. pap. 11.95 (*0-87951-629-1*, Pub. by Overlook Pr) Penguin Putnam.

— Tomorrow I'll Be Different: The Effective Way to Stop Drinking. 242p. 1994. 21.95 (*0-87951-565-1*, Pub. by Overlook Pr) Penguin Putnam.

Colclough, Chrisopher. Public Sector Pay & Adjustment: Lessons from Five Countries. LC 96-22701. 176p. (C). 1997. 80.00 (*0-415-15338-7*) Routledge.

Colclough, Christopher. Marketizing Education & Health in Developing Countries: Miracle or Mirage? (IDS Development Studies). (Illus.). 388p. 1998. text 95.00 (*0-19-829255-4*) OUP.

Colclough, Christopher & Lewin, Keith M. Educating All the Children. LC 92-32445. 344p. 1993. 58.00 (*0-19-828747-X*, Clarendon Pr); pap. 23.00 (*0-19-828746-1*, Clarendon Pr) OUP.

Colclough, Christopher & Manor, James, eds. States or Markets? Neo-Liberalism & the Development Policy Debate. (IDS Development Studies Ser.). (Illus.). 370p. (C). 1993. reprint ed. pap. text 21.00 (*0-19-828811-5*, 5133) OUP.

Colclough, Christopher & McCarthy, Stephen. The Politocal Economy of Botswana: A Study of Growth & Distribution. (Illus.). 1980. 45.00 (*0-19-877136-3*) OUP.

Colclough, Glenna & Tolbert, Charles M., II. Work in the Fast Lane: Flexibility, Divisions of Labor, & Inequality in High-Tech Industries. LC 90-20851. (SUNY Series, the New Inequalities). 160p. (C). 1992. text 24.50 (*0-7914-0783-7*) State U NY Pr.

***Colclough, John.** Mould Making. (Illus.). 128p. 1999. text. write for info. (*90-5703-891-9*, Pub. by Craftsman House) Gordon & Breach.

Colclough, Len. Lessons from the Fish: An Anthology of Fishing Experiences. (Illus.). 192p. 1997. 35.95 (*1-85310-818-9*, Pub. by Swan Hill Pr) Voyageur Pr.

Colcolough, Lisa, ed. see Junior League of Memphis Staff.

Colcord, Ann, tr. see Spina, Michele.

Colcord, Anna. A Friend in the Kitchen. fac. ed. LC 93-61510. (Illus.). 112p. 1997. reprint ed. per. 8.95 (*0-945383-51-7*) Teach Servs.

Colcord, D. B. Descendants of Edward Colcord of New Hampshire, 1630 to 1908. (Illus.). 166p. 1993. reprint ed. pap. 24.00 (*0-8328-1367-2*); reprint ed. lib. bdg. 34.00 (*0-8328-1366-4*) Higginson Bk Co.

Colcord, Esther B., jt. auth. see Board, Prudy T.

Colcord, Joanna C. Sea Language Comes Ashore. Dorsen, Richard M., ed. (International Folklore Ser.). 1977. reprint ed. lib. bdg. 19.95 (*0-405-10089-2*) Ayer.

Colcord, Lincoln. Game of Life & Death. LC 76-106270. (Short Story Index Reprint Ser.). 1977. 20.95 (*0-8369-3307-9*) Ayer.

— An Instrument of the Gods: And Other Stories of the Sea, Vol. 1. LC 72-5863. (Short Story Index Reprint Ser.). 1977. reprint ed. 25.95 (*0-8369-4202-7*) Ayer.

— Sea Stories from Searsport to Singapore: Selected Works of Lincoln Colcord. Mortland, Donald, ed. LC 87-5643. (Illus.). 217p. 1987. 17.95 (*0-89621-104-5*); pap. 8.95 (*0-945980-29-9*) Nrth Country Pr.

Colcord, Willard Allen, jt. auth. see Blakely, William Addison.

Cold, G. E. Cerebral Blood Flow in Acute Head Injury: The Regulation of Cerebral Blood Flow & Metabolism During the Acute Phase of Head Injury, & Its Significance for Therapy. (Acta Neurochirugica - Supplementum Ser.: Supplementum No. 49). (Illus.). 100p. 1990. 79.95 (*0-387-82224-0*) Spr-Verlag.

Cold, G. E., jt. auth. see Madsen, J. B.

***Cold Mountain Staff.** The Collected Songs of Cold Mountain. rev. ed. Pine, Red, tr. (CHI & ENG.). 272p. 2000. reprint ed. pap. 17.00 (*1-55659-140-3*) Copper Canyon.

Cold Regions Hydrology Symposium Staff. Cold Regions Hydrology: Proceedings of the Symposium. Kane, Douglas L., ed. LC 86-70416. (American Water Resources Association Technical Publication Ser.: No. TPS-86-1). 624p. reprint ed. pap. 193.50 (*0-8357-3171-5*, 203943400012) Bks Demand.

Cold Spring Harbor Lab. Staff. Chromosome Structure & Function: Cold Spring Harbor Symposia on Quantitative Biology, 38th, 1974. LC 34-8174. (Cold Spring Harbor Symposia on Quantitative Biology Ser.: No. 38). (Illus.). 1032p. 1974. reprint ed. pap. 200.00 (*0-608-04091-6*, 206482300038) Bks Demand.

Cold Spring Harbor Laboratory Staff. Hybridoma Techniques: EMBO, SKMB Course 1980, Basel. LC QR0185.8.H9H. 72p. reprint ed. pap. 30.00 (*0-8357-2757-2*, 203987300013) Bks Demand.

— Safety Sense. LC 98-39532. 1998. write for info. (*0-87969-555-2*) Cold Spring Harbor.

Cold Spring Harbor Staff, contrib. by. Mechanisms of Transcription. (Cold Spring Harbor Symposia on Quantitative Biology Ser.: Vol. LXIII). (Illus.). 600p. (C). 1999. text 258.00 (*0-87969-550-1*); pap. text 110.00 (*0-87969-552-8*) Cold Spring Harbor.

Cold Spring Harbor Symposia on Quantitative Biolog. Amino Acids & Proteins. LC 34-8174. (Cold Spring Harbor Symposia on Quantitative Biology Ser.: Vol. 14). (Illus.). 247p. 1950. pap. 76.60 (*0-7837-8972-6*, 204975300003) Bks Demand.

— Antibodies. LC 34-8174. (Cold Spring Harbor Symposia on Quantitative Biology Ser.: No. 32). 639p. reprint ed. pap. 198.10 (*0-7837-2015-7*, 204229000002) Bks Demand.

— Basic Mechanisms in Animal Virus Biology. LC 34-8174. (Cold Spring Harbor Symposia on Quantitative Biology Ser.: No. 27). (Illus.). 551p. 1963. reprint ed. pap. 170.90 (*0-608-04163-7*, 206489600027) Bks Demand.

— Biological Applications of Tracer Elements. LC 34-8174. (Cold Spring Harbor Symposia on Quantitative Biology Ser.: Vol. 13). (Illus.). 240p. pap. 74.40 (*0-7837-8971-8*, 204975200003) Bks Demand.

— Biological Clocks. LC 34-8174. (Cold Spring Harbor Symposia on Quantitative Biology Ser.: Vol. 25). (Illus.). 538p. 1960. pap. 166.80 (*0-7837-8978-5*, 204975900003) Bks Demand.

— Cellular Regulatory Mechanisms. LC 34-8174. (Cold Spring Harbor Symposia on Quantitative Biology Ser.: No. 26). 424p. reprint ed. pap. 131.50 (*0-7837-2014-9*, 204228900002) Bks Demand.

— Cold Spring Harbor Symposia on Quantitative Biology, Vol. 1: 1933. LC 34-8174. (Illus.). 251p. 1933. reprint ed. pap. 77.90 (*0-608-04156-4*, 206488900001) Bks Demand.

— Cold Spring Harbor Symposia on Quantitative Biology, Vol. 2: 1934. LC 34-8174. (Illus.). 296p. 1934. reprint ed. pap. 91.80 (*0-608-04157-2*, 206489000002) Bks Demand.

An Asterisk (*) at the beginning of an entry indicates that the title is appearing for the first time.

— Cold Spring Harbor Symposia on Quantitative Biology, Vol. 3: 1935. LC 34-8174. (Illus.). 375p. 1935. reprint ed. pap. 116.30 (0-608-04158-0, 206489100003) Bks Demand.
— Cold Spring Harbor Symposia on Quantitative Biology, Vol. 4: 1936. LC 34-8174. (Illus.). 388p. 1936. reprint ed. pap. 120.30 (0-608-04159-9, 206489200004) Bks Demand.
— Cold Spring Harbor Symposia on Quantitative Biology, Vol. 5: 1937. LC 34-8174. (Illus.). 449p. 1937. reprint ed. pap. 139.20 (0-608-04160-2, 206489300005) Bks Demand.
— Cold Spring Harbor Symposia on Quantitative Biology, Vol. 6: 1938. LC 34-8174. (Illus.). 409p. 1938. reprint ed. pap. 126.80 (0-608-04161-0, 206489400006) Bks Demand.
— Cold Spring Harbor Symposia on Quantitative Biology: Chromatin, Vol. 42. (Illus.). 1260p. 1978. 139.00 (0-87969-041-0) Cold Spring Harbor.
— Cold Spring Harbor Symposia on Quantitative Biology: Exchange of Genetic Material, Vol. 23. (Illus.). 449p. 1959. 38.00 (0-87969-022-4) Cold Spring Harbor.
— Cold Spring Harbor Symposia on Quantitative Biology: Origins of Lymphocyte Diversity, 2 bks., Set, Vol. 41. (Illus.). 1024p. 1977. 107.50 (0-87969-040-2) Cold Spring Harbor.
— Cold Spring Harbor Symposia on Quantitative Biology: Sensory Receptors, Vol. 30. (Illus.). 663p. 1966. 38.00 (0-87969-029-1) Cold Spring Harbor.
— Cold Spring Harbor Symposia on Quantitative Biology: The Synapse, Vol. 40. (Illus.). 694p. 1976. 88.50 (0-87969-039-9) Cold Spring Harbor.
— Cold Spring Harbor Symposia on Quantitative Biology: Tumor Viruses, 2 bks., Set., Vol. 39. (Illus.). 1258p. 1975. 120.00 (0-87969-038-0) Cold Spring Harbor.
— Cold Spring Harbor Symposia on Quantitative Biology: Viral Oncogenes, 2 bks., Set. (Illus.). 1322p. 1980. 164.50 (0-87969-043-7) Cold Spring Harbor.
— The Evolution of Catalytic Function. (Symposia on Quantitative Biology Ser.: Vol. 52). (Illus.). 956p. 1988. text 150.00 (0-87969-054-2) Cold Spring Harbor.
— Genes & Chromosomes: Structure & Organization. LC 34-8174. (Cold Spring Harbor Symposia on Quantitative Biology Ser.: Vol. 9). (Illus.). 345p. 1941. pap. 107.00 (0-7837-8970-X, 204975100003) Bks Demand.
— Genes & Mutations. LC 34-8174. (Cold Spring Harbor Symposia on Quantitative Biology Ser.: No. 16). (Illus.). 537p. 1952. reprint ed. pap. 166.50 (0-608-04162-9, 206489500016) Bks Demand.
— The Genetic Code. LC 34-8174. (Cold Spring Harbor Symposia on Quantitative Biology Ser.: No. 31). (Illus.). 784p. 1967. reprint ed. pap. 200.00 (0-608-04164-5, 206489700031) Bks Demand.
— Genetic Mechanisms: Structure & Function. LC 34-8174. (Cold Spring Harbor Symposia on Quantitative Biology Ser.: No. 21). 410p. reprint ed. pap. 127.10 (0-7837-2013-0, 204228800002) Bks Demand.
— Genetics & Twentieth Century Darwinism. LC 34-8174. (Cold Spring Harbor Symposia on Quantitative Biology Ser.: Vol. 24). (Illus.). 335p. 1959. pap. 103.90 (0-7837-8977-7, 204975800003) Bks Demand.
— The Mammalian Fetus: Physiological Aspects of Development. LC 34-8174. (Cold Spring Harbor Symposia on Quantitative Biology Ser.: Vol. 19). (Illus.). 238p. 1954. pap. 73.80 (0-7837-8975-0, 204975600003) Bks Demand.
— The Mechanism of Protein Synthesis. LC 34-8174. (Cold Spring Harbor Symposia on Quantitative Biology Ser.: No. 34). 879p. 1969. reprint ed. pap. 200.00 (0-7837-2029-7, 204229100002) Bks Demand.
— Molecular Biology of Homo Sapiens. LC 34-8174. (Cold Spring Harbor Symposia on Quantitative Biology Ser.: No. 51, Pt. 1). 728p. reprint ed. pap. 200.00 (0-7837-6445-6, 204644500001) Bks Demand.
— Molecular Biology of Homo Sapiens. LC 34-8174. (Cold Spring Harbor Symposia on Quantitative Biology Ser.: No. 51, Pt. 2). 543p. reprint ed. pap. 168.40 (0-7837-6446-4, 204644500002) Bks Demand.
— Molecular Biology of Signal Transduction. (Cold Spring Harbor Symposia on Quantitative Biology Ser.: Vol. 53). (Illus.). 1200p. 1989. 180.00 (0-87969-055-0) Cold Spring Harbor.
— Molecular Neurobiology. LC 34-8174. (Cold Spring Harbor Symposia on Quantitative Biology Ser.: No. 48). 943p. reprint ed. pap. 200.00 (0-7837-6448-0, 204644700012) Bks Demand.
— Movable Genetic Elements, 2 pts., Pt. 1. LC 34-8174. (Cold Spring Harbor Symposia on Quantitative Biology Ser.: No. 45). 467p. reprint ed. pap. 144.80 (0-7837-2016-5, 204229200001) Bks Demand.
— Movable Genetic Elements, 2 pts., Pt. 2. LC 34-8174. (Cold Spring Harbor Symposia on Quantitative Biology Ser.: No. 45). 594p. reprint ed. pap. 184.20 (0-7837-2017-3, 204229200002) Bks Demand.
— The Neuron. LC 34-8174. (Cold Spring Harbor Symposia on Quantitative Biology Ser.: Vol. 17). (Illus.). 337p. 1985. pap. 104.50 (0-7837-8974-2, 204975500003) Bks Demand.
— Organization of the Cytoplasm, Pt. 1. LC 34-8174. (Cold Spring Harbor Symposia on Quantitative Biology Ser.: Vol. 46). (Illus.). 513p. 1982. pap. 159.10 (0-7837-8984-X, 204976400001) Bks Demand.
— Organization of the Cytoplasm, Pt. 2. LC 34-8174. (Cold Spring Harbor Symposia on Quantitative Biology Ser.: Vol. 46). (Illus.). 566p. 1982. pap. 175.50 (0-7837-8985-8, 204976400002) Bks Demand.
— Origin & Evolution of Man. LC 34-8174. (Cold Spring Harbor Symposia on Quantitative Biology Ser.: Vol. 15). (Illus.). 439p. 1951. pap. 136.10 (0-7837-8973-4, 204975400003) Bks Demand.
— Population Genetics: The Nature & Causes of Genetic Variability in Populations. LC 34-8174. (Cold Spring Harbor Symposia on Quantitative Biology Ser.: Vol. 20). (Illus.). 362p. 1955. pap. 112.30 (0-7837-8976-9, 204975700003) Bks Demand.
— Recombination at the DNA Level. LC 34-8174. (Cold Spring Harbor Symposia on Quantitative Biology Ser.: Vol. 49). (Illus.). 880p. 1984. pap. 200.00 (0-7837-8988-2, 204976600003) Bks Demand.
— Replication of DNA in Micro-Organisms. LC 34-8174. (Cold Spring Harbor Symposia on Quantitative Biology Ser.: Vol. 33). (Illus.). 906p. 1968. pap. 200.00 (0-7837-8980-7, 204976100003) Bks Demand.
— Structures of DNA, Pt. 1. LC 34-8174. (Cold Spring Harbor Symposia on Quantitative Biology Ser.: Vol. 47). (Illus.). 599p. 1983. pap. 185.70 (0-7837-8986-6, 204976500001) Bks Demand.
— Structures of DNA, Pt. 2. LC 34-8174. (Cold Spring Harbor Symposia on Quantitative Biology Ser.: Vol. 47). (Illus.). 675p. 1983. pap. 200.00 (0-7837-8987-4, 204976500002) Bks Demand.
— Synthesis & Structure of Macromolecules. LC 34-8174. (Cold Spring Harbor Symposia on Quantitative Biology Ser.: Vol. 28). (Illus.). 630p. 1963. pap. 195.30 (0-7837-8979-3, 204976000003) Bks Demand.
— Transcription of Genetic Material. LC 34-8174. (Cold Spring Harbor Symposia on Quantitative Biology Ser.). (Illus.). 910p. 1971. reprint ed. pap. 200.00 (0-608-04165-3, 206489800035) Bks Demand.
— Viruses. LC QR0355.. (Cold Spring Harbor Symposia on Quantitative Biology Ser.: Vol. 18). 317p. 1953. reprint ed. pap. 98.30 (0-608-00716-1, 206149000009) Bks Demand.

Cold Spring Harbor Symposium on Quantitative Biolo. The Molecular Genetics of Cancer. LC 34-8174. (Cold Spring Harbor Symposia on Quantitative Biology Ser.: No. 59). (Illus.). 767p. 1994. reprint ed. pap. 200.00 (0-608-07906-5, 206788700011) Bks Demand.

Colden, Cadwallader. An Explication of the First Causes of Action in Matter. (Works of Cadwallader Colden). 1990. reprint ed. lib. bdg. 90.00 (0-7812-2308-3) Rprt Serv.
— The History of the Five Indian Nations. 205p. 1958. pap. text 9.95 (0-8014-9086-3) Cornell U Pr.
— The History of the Five Indian Nations of Canada Which Are Dependent on the Province of New York. (Works of Cadwallader Colden). 1990. reprint ed. lib. bdg. 79.00 (0-7812-2307-5) Rprt Serv.
— The History of the Five Indian Nations of Canada Which Are Dependent on the Province of New York, & Are a Barrier Between the English & the French, 2 vols. LC 72-2827. (American Explorers Ser.). reprint ed. 79.50 (0-404-54908-X) AMS Pr.
— Letters & Papers of Cadwallader Colden. (Works of Cadwallader Colden). 1990. reprint ed. lib. bdg. 79.00 (0-7812-2310-5) Rprt Serv.
— Letters & Papers of Cadwallader Colden, 1711-1775, 9 vols., Set. LC 72-996. reprint ed. 795.00 (0-404-01690-1) AMS Pr.
— Letters on Smith's History of New York. (Works of Cadwallader Colden). 1990. reprint ed. lib. bdg. 79.00 (0-7812-2309-1) Rprt Serv.
— The Works of Cadwallader Colden. 1990. reprint ed. lib. bdg. 79.00 (0-685-27667-8) Rprt Serv.

Colden, J. Botanic Manuscript. Rickett, Harold W. & Hall, E. C., eds. (Illus.). 1963. 30.00 (0-934454-15-9) Lubrecht & Cramer.

Colden United Methodist Women Staff. Colden Country Cookbook. 4th ed. 360p. 1985. write for info. (0-9615568-0-3) Colden UMW.

Coldewey, John C., ed. Early English Drama: An Anthology. LC 92-7686. 392p. 1993. text 30.00 (0-8240-4699-4, H313); pap. 24.95 (0-8240-5465-2) Garland.

Coldewey, John C. & Streitberger, W. R. Drama: Classical to Contemporary. LC 96-30972. 1382p. (C). 1998. pap. text 57.00 (0-13-359647-8) P-H.

Coldewey, John C., jt. ed. see Briscoe, Marianne G.

Coldfelter. Strategic Bombing. 1997. 22.95 (0-02-905585-7) Free Pr.

Coldham, Margaret, jt. auth. see Cyriax, James.

Coldham, Peter W. American Loyalist Claims, No. 45. LC 80-8609. 615p. 1980. 21.50 (0-915156-45-8) Natl Genealogical.

***Coldham, Peter W.** American Migrations, 1765-1799: The Lives, Times & Families of Colonial Americans Who Remained Loyal to the British Crown Before, During & After the Revolutionary. 948p. 2000. 75.00 (0-8063-1618-7) Genealog Pub.

Coldham, Peter W. American Wills & Administrations: In the Prerogative Court of Canterbury, 1610-1857. xii, 416p. 1989. 30.00 (0-8063-1235-1, 1108) Genealog Pub.
— American Wills Proved in London, 1611-1775. 350p. 1992. 30.00 (0-8063-1363-3, 1116) Genealog Pub.
— The Bristol Registers of Servants Sent to Foreign Plantations, 1654-1686. 491p. 1988. 22.50 (0-8063-1223-8, 1096) Genealog Pub.
— Child Apprentices in America from Christ's Hospital, London, 1617-1778. 164p. 1990. 15.00 (0-8063-1270-X, 1114) Genealog Pub.
— The Complete Book of Emigrants in Bondage, 1614-1775. 920p. 1988. 45.00 (0-8063-1221-1, 1098) Genealog Pub.
— The Complete Book of Emigrants, 1607-1660. LC 87-80832. 600p. 1998. reprint ed. 34.95 (0-8063-1192-4) Genealog Pub.
— Emigrants from England to the American Colonies, 1773-1776. 182p. 1988. 15.00 (0-8063-1231-9, 1099) Genealog Pub.
— Emigrants in Chains: A Social History of Forced Emigration to the Americas of Felons, Destitute Children, Political & Religious Non-Conformists, Vagabonds, Beggars & Other Undesirables, 1607-1776. LC 91-67630. 196p. 1994. 21.95 (0-8063-1329-3) Genealog Pub.
— English Adventurers & Emigrants, 1609-1660: Abstracts of Examinations in the High Court of Admiralty with Reference to Colonial America. LC 84-80790. 219p. 1991. reprint ed. 22.50 (0-8063-1082-0) Clearfield Co.
— Lord Mayor's Court of London: Depositions Relating to Americans, 1641-1736. LC 80-80349. 119p. 1980. pap. 10.00 (0-686-27217-X); lib. bdg. 12.00 (0-915156-23-7, SP 44) Natl Genealogical.
— Supplement to the Complete Book of Emigrants in Bondage, 1614-1775. 86p. 1992. pap. 9.00 (0-8063-1345-5, 1115) Genealog Pub.

Coldham, Peter Wilson. Settlers of Maryland, 1751-1765. 367p. 1996. 32.50 (0-8063-1514-8) Genealog Pub.
— Settlers of Maryland, 1766-1783. 204p. 1996. text 25.00 (0-8063-1519-9) Genealog Pub.

***Colding, Tobias H.** Minimal Surfaces LC 99-72225. (Lecture Notes in Mathematics 4 Ser.). 124p. 1999. write for info. (0-9658703-3-2) NYU Courant.

Coldiron, A. E. Canon, Period, & the Poetry of Charles of Orleans: Found in Translation. (Illus.). 230p. (C). text 44.50 (0-472-11146-9, 11146) U of Mich Pr.

Coldiron, Nita G., jt. auth. see Shanley, Michael P.

Colditz. Cancer Culture. 1995. 24.95 (0-226-11321-3) U Ch Pr.

Colditz, I., jt. ed. see Morley, John.

Colditz, Judy C., ed. see Coppard, Brenda M. & Lohman, Helene.

Colditz, Karl. Lehr-, Ubungs- und Testbuch der Schachkombinationen. (GER.). 184p. 1992. 20.00 (3-283-00302-5) G Olms Pubs.

Coldman, A. J., jt. auth. see Goldie, J. H.

Coldren, J. David, jt. pref. see Thompson, James.

Coldren, Jeffrey T. & Colombo, John. The Nature & Processes of Preverbal Learning: Implications from Nine Month-Old Infants' Discrimination Problem-Solving. (Monographs of the Society for Research in Child Development: No. 1). 104p. 1994. pap. text 15.00 (0-226-11327-2) U Ch Pr.

***Coldren, Larry A.** Problem Solutions for Diode Lasers & Photonic in Tegrated Circuits. 204p. 1998. pap. 27.50 (0-471-17865-9) Wiley.

Coldren, Larry A. & Corzine, S. W. Diode Lasers & Photonic Integrated Circuits. LC 94-39383. (Microwave & Optical Engineering Ser.). 624p. 1995. 105.00 (0-471-11875-3) Wiley.

Coldrey, Christopher. Courses for Horses: A Complete Guide to Construction Show Jumping Courses. 128p. 1990. 60.00 (0-85131-541-0, Pub. by J A Allen) Trafalgar.

Coldrey, Christopher & Coldrey, Victoria. Breaking & Training Young Horses. (Illus.). 144p. 1995. 34.95 (1-85223-286-2, Pub. by Crolwood) Trafalgar.
— Buying & Re-Schooling Ex-Racehorses. (Illus.). 160p. 1997. 35.00 (1-86126-088-1, Pub. by Crolwood) Trafalgar.
— Training Your Horse with Lunge & Long Reins. (Illus.). 160p. 1996. 24.95 (1-85223-944-1, Pub. by Crolwood) Trafalgar.

Coldrey, Jennifer. Strawberry. (Stopwatch Ser.). (Illus.). 25p. (J). (gr. k-4). 1950. pap. 3.95 (0-382-24340-4, Silver Pr NJ) Silver Burdett Pr.
— Strawberry. (Stopwatch Ser.). (Illus.). 25p. (J). (gr. k-4). 1990. lib. bdg. 9.95 (0-382-09801-3, Silver Pr NJ) Silver Burdett Pr.

Coldrey, Jennifer & Bernard, George. Mosquito. LC 96-22648. (Stopwatch Ser.). (J). 1997. pap. 4.95 (0-382-39763-0); lib. bdg. 11.95 (0-382-39758-4) Silver Burdett Pr.

Coldrey, Victoria, jt. auth. see Coldrey, Christopher.

***Coldrum, Stan.** Girlfriend Dada. 24p. 2000. pap. 3.95 (0-9676660-4-X, Pick Pocket Pr) Phony Lid Pubns.

Coldsmith, Dan. Walks in the Sun, No. 20. 256p. 1993. mass mkt. 5.50 (0-553-56364-5) Bantam.

Coldsmith, Don. The Changing Wind. (Spanish Bit Saga Super Ser.: No. 1). 320p. 1990. mass mkt. 5.99 (0-553-28334-0) Bantam.
— Child Dead. 272p. 1995. mass mkt. 4.99 (0-553-29469-5) Bantam.
— Daughter of the Eagle. LC 83-45564. 1984. 11.95 (0-385-18092-6) Doubleday.
— Follow the Wind. LC 82-45391. 1983. 11.95 (0-385-17502-7) Doubleday.
— Medicine Hat. (Spanish Bit Ser.: No. 25). 272p. 1998. mass mkt. 4.99 (0-553-29475-X) Bantam.
— Medicine Hat: A Novel. LC 97-15335. vi, 266p. 1997. 21.95 (0-8061-2959-X) U of Okla Pr.
— Moon of Thunder. LC 84-13516. 1985. 11.95 (0-385-18923-0) Doubleday.
— Pale Star. LC 85-16032. 1986. 12.95 (0-385-23227-6) Doubleday.

Coldsmith, Don. Runestone. 608p. 1995. reprint ed. pap., mass mkt. 6.50 (0-553-57280-6) Bantam.

Coldsmith, Don. The Sacred Hills. LC 84-28710. 1985. 12.95 (0-385-18924-9) Doubleday.
— Song of the Rock, No. 15. (Spanish Bit Saga Ser.: Bk. 15). 224p. (J). 1991. mass mkt. 5.50 (0-553-29123-8) Bantam.
— South Wind. 1999. mass mkt. 6.50 (0-553-57779-4) Bantam.
— Spanish Bit No. 24: Bearer of the Pipe. 272p. 1996. reprint ed. mass mkt. 5.50 (0-553-29470-9) Bantam.
— Tallgrass. 576p. 1998. reprint ed. mass mkt. 6.50 (0-553-57776-X) Bantam.
— Track of the Bear, No. 22. 240p. 1997. mass mkt. 5.50 (0-553-56362-9) Bantam.
— Trail of the Spanish Bit, No. 1. 224p. 1987. mass mkt. 5.50 (0-553-26397-8) Bantam.
— The Traveler. (Spanish Bit Saga Ser.: No. 2). 336p. 1991. mass mkt. 5.50 (0-553-28868-7) Bantam.

Coldstream, Nicola. The Decorated Style: Architecture & Ornament, 1240-1360. (Illus.). 210p. 1995. text 50.00 (0-8020-0700-7) U of Toronto Pr.
— Masons & Sculptors. (Medieval Craftsmen Ser.). (Illus.). 72p. 1991. pap. text 19.95 (0-8020-6916-9) U of Toronto Pr.

Coldwell, C. T. William Coaldwell, Caldwell or Coldwell; & a Record of His Descendants. (Illus.). 82p. 1989. reprint ed. pap. 16.00 (0-8328-1299-4); reprint ed. lib. bdg. 24.00 (0-8328-1298-6) Higginson Bk Co.

Coldwell, Douglas M. Embolotherapy. LC 96-29621. (Radiologic Interventions Ser.). 1997. write for info. (4-260-14328-X) Igaku-Shoin.
— Embolotherapy. LC 96-29621. (Radiologic Interventions Ser.). (Illus.). 256p. 1997. write for info. (0-89640-328-9) Igaku-Shoin.
— Embolotherapy. LC 96-29621. (Radiologic Interventions Ser.). 185p. 1997. 59.00 (0-683-30268-X) Lppncott W & W.

Coldwell, E. Calendar Girl. 1997. mass mkt. 6.95 (0-7472-5648-9, Pub. by Headline Bk Pub) Trafalgar.

Coldwell, Frederic L. Selling the All-American Wonder: The World II Consumer Advertising of Willys-Overland Motors, Inc. (Illus.). 104p. 1997. pap. 30.00 (0-910667-25-X) Victory WW Two.

Coldwell, Joan, ed. The Tightrope Walker: Autobiographical Writings of Anne Wilkinson. 288p. 1992. text 35.00 (0-8020-5745-4) U of Toronto Pr.

Coldwell, Lynn & Robinson, Marilyn, eds. Flood Nineteen Eighty-Three: What Happened & Why. (Illus.). 64p. 1983. pap. 7.95 (0-910141-09-6) Kino Pubns.

Coldwell, Mark, tr. see Lipp, Markus D., et al.

Coldwell, R. L. & Bamford, G. J. The Theory & Operation of Spectral Analysis Using ROBFIT. 350p. 1991. 89.95 (0-88318-929-1); pap. 49.95 (0-88318-941-0) Spr-Verlag.

Cole. After Great Pain a New Self Emerges. 1994. 19.18 (0-02-906461-9) S&S Trade.
— American System Criminal Justice. 6th ed. (Criminal Justice Ser.). 1992. mass mkt., teacher ed. write for info. (0-534-14703-8) Wadsworth Pub.
— The American System of Criminal Justice. (Adaptable Courseware-Softside Ser.). Date not set. pap. 50.00 (0-534-16069-7) Wadsworth Pub.
— American System of Criminal Justice. 2nd ed. (Criminal Justice Ser.). 1979. pap., teacher ed. write for info. (0-534-02605-2) Wadsworth Pub.
— American System of Criminal Justice. 7th ed. (Criminal Justice Ser.). 1995. pap. 21.95 (0-534-24049-6) Wadsworth Pub.
— American System of Criminal Justice: Criminal Justice Series. 8th ed. (Criminal Justice). (C). 1997. student ed. 19.00 (0-534-52535-0) Wadsworth Pub.
— Annual Editions: Macroeconomics. 12th ed. 1997. pap. text 11.10 (0-697-39301-1) McGraw.
— Annual Editions: Microeconomics. 4th ed. 1997. pap. text 11.10 (0-697-39300-3) McGraw.
— Chocolate Conspiracy. (Cooking Companion Ser.). 1996. pap. text 7.95 (1-56426-842-X) Cole Group.
— College Algebra: A Graphing Approach. (Mathematics Ser.). 1997. text 63.95 (0-534-94938-X) PWS Pubs.
— Cpsq Rdgs Mktg Info Analysis. 1998. pap. text 58.25 (0-07-234139-4) McGraw.
— Criminal Justice Reader. (Criminal Justice Ser.). 2000. mass mkt. 19.95 (0-534-52711-6) Wadsworth Pub.
— Criminal Justice System. (Adaptable Courseware-Softside Ser.). Date not set. pap. 16.00 (0-534-15875-7) Wadsworth Pub.
— The Development of Children. (C). 1993. 16.80 (0-7167-2474-X) W H Freeman.
— The Development of Children. 1994. student ed. 47.20 (0-7167-2602-5) W H Freeman.
— The Development of Children. 2nd ed. 1994. 48.00 (0-7167-2586-X) W H Freeman.
— The Development of Children. 3rd ed. (C). 1996. pap. text, student ed. 22.95 (0-7167-2807-9) W H Freeman.
— Development of Children. 3rd ed. 1996. pap. 12.80 (0-7167-2796-X) W H Freeman.
— The Development of Children Text & Study Guide. (C). 1991. student ed. 48.80 (0-7167-2264-X) W H Freeman.
— Economics. 24th ed. 1995. 12.74 (1-56134-352-8) McGraw.
— Economics. 29th ed. 240p. 1999. pap. 16.56 (0-07-236513-7) McGraw.
— Economics 1999-2000 Edition. 28th ed. 1999. pap., student ed. 16.56 (0-07-041322-3) McGraw.
— The Emergence of Net-Centric Computing: Network Computers, Internet Appliances & Connected PC's. LC 98-34641. 352p. 1998. 49.99 (0-13-897869-7) P-H.
— Fishheads. 7.95 (0-910791-90-2, 0546) Devyn Pr.
— Handbook of Fungal Metabolites. 750p. 1997. write for info. (0-12-179261-7) Acad Pr.
— The Hole in the Universe: How Scientists Peered over the Edge of Emptiness & Found Everything. 240p. 2000. 24.00 (0-15-100398-X) Harcourt.
— An Introduction to Political Inquiry. 347p. 1995. pap. text 44.95 (0-312-07192-2) St Martin.
— Introduction to Political Inquiry: Mistakes. 2000. pap. text 38.25 (0-312-13773-7) St Martin.

***Cole.** Introduction to Voice & Data Communication. LC 99-45770. 592p. 2000. 98.00 (0-13-927161-9) P-H.

Cole. The Life of Mind: Introduction to Philosophy. (Philosophy Ser.). 2000. pap. 36.00 (0-534-55851-8) Wadsworth Pub.
— Mac Testbank Development of Children. (C). 1993. 48.00 (0-7167-2473-1) W H Freeman.
— The Medical Interview: The Three-Function Approach. 2nd ed. (Illus.). 225p. (C). 1999. pap. text 25.95 (0-8151-1992-5, 30377) Mosby Inc.

***Cole.** Michelangelo Bramante & Raphael. 2000. 35.00 (0-8133-3787-9, Pub. by Westview); pap. 25.00 (0-8133-3788-7, Pub. by Westview) HarpC.

Cole. MSB Fun Sound. (J). 1994. 7.98 (1-57042-137-4) Warner Bks.

C

An Asterisk (*) at the beginning of an entry indicates that the title is appearing for the first time.

— MSB Habitat. 1995. pap. 7.98 (1-57042-228-1) Warner Bks.

***Cole.** My Big Boy Potty Book. 2000. lib. bdg. 5.89 (0-06-029223-7) HarpC.

— My Big Girl Potty Book. 2000. lib. bdg. 5.89 (0-06-029222-9) HarpC.

Cole. Partial Solutions Manual T-A Precalculus. 5th ed. 232p. (C). 1987. mass mkt., teacher ed. 15.50 (0-87150-147-3) PWS Pubs.

— Pornography & the Sex Crisis. 184p. 1994. pap. 14.95 (0-929005-46-5, Pub. by Sec Story Pr) LPC InBook.

— Safe from the Start. 1991. pap. 4.50 (0-312-92455-0, Pub. by Tor Bks) St Martin.

— So You Want to Take Physics. (C). 1993. pap. text, teacher ed. 32.00 (0-03-096021-5) Harcourt Coll Pubs.

— So You Want to Take Physics. (C). 1994. pap. text, teacher ed. 33.75 (0-03-097216-7) Harcourt Coll Pubs.

— State & Local Politics. 2nd ed. Date not set. pap. text. write for info. (0-312-17084-X) St Martin.

— Stephen Hawking. LC 96-18931. (Innovative Minds Ser.). 112p. (J). (gr. 7-8). 1996. lib. bdg. 27.11 (0-8172-4401-8) Raintree Steck-V.

***Cole.** Telecommunications. LC 98-4274. 571p. 1998. 101.00 (0-13-612129-2) P-H.

Cole. Understanding Economics. LC 95-3092. 198p. (C). pap. 28.95 (0-7453-0893-7, Pub. by Pluto GBR) Stylus Pub VA.

Cole & Gertz. Crime Victims & the Criminal Justice System. (Adaptable Courseware-Softside Ser.). 1998. pap. 28.75 (0-534-15868-4) Wadsworth Pub.

Cole & Havlena, June. Children. 2nd ed. (C). 1993. pap. text, teacher ed. 16.80 (0-7167-2346-8) W H Freeman.

Cole & Semb. Psychology Journal. 5th ed. 1995. pap. text, student ed. 26.00 (0-13-563578-0) P-H.

Cole & Visona. A Survey of the History of African Art. 544p. (C). 2000. 40.00 (0-13-442187-6) P-H.

***Cole, et al.** Lifespan Development. 2002. pap. text. write for info. (0-7167-5108-9) W H Freeman.

Cole, jt. auth. see Clear.

Cole, jt. auth. see Cohen, Steven A.

Cole, jt. auth. see Swokowski.

Cole, M. A., jt. auth. see Stevenson, F. J.

Cole, A. & Bunch, Chris. Vortex. 1992. mass mkt. 4.99 (0-345-37151-8) Ballantine Pub Grp.

***Cole, A. J.** From Evaporation to Vapourisation: A Study of Satistical Models for the Decay of Highly Excited. (Fundamental & Applied Nuclear Physics Ser.). 1999. 160.00 (0-7503-0512-6) IOP Pub.

Cole, A. Thomas, tr. see Gentili, Bruno.

***Cole, Adam.** Ballet Music for the Dance Accompanist. LC 98-68545. 111p. 1999. pap. 19.95 (0-9668502-0-3) Nuncici Pr.

— The Myth of Magic. LC 99-91485. 1999. 25.00 (0-7388-0824-5); pap. 18.00 (0-7388-0825-3) Xlibris Corp.

Cole, Adeline P., ed. Notes on Wenham History, 1643-1943. (Illus.). 155p. 1993. reprint ed. lib. bdg. 25.00 (0-8328-3135-2) Higginson Bk Co.

Cole, Adrian. Blood Red Angel. 384p. (Orig.). 1993. mass mkt. 4.99 (0-380-76889-5, Avon Bks) Morrow Avon.

— The Gods in Anger: The Omaran Saga, Bk. 4. 384p. 1991. mass mkt. 4.50 (0-380-75842-3, Avon Bks) Morrow Avon.

— King of Light & Shadows: The Omaran Saga, Bk. 3. 1990. mass mkt. 4.50 (0-380-75841-5, Avon Bks) Morrow Avon.

— A Place among the Fallen. 384p. 1990. mass mkt. 4.99 (0-380-70556-7, Avon Bks) Morrow Avon.

— Star Requiem No. 1: Mother of Storms. 384p. (Orig.). 1992. mass mkt. 4.99 (0-380-76767-8, Avon Bks) Morrow Avon.

— Star Requiem No. 2: Thief of Dreams. 384p. (Orig.). 1993. mass mkt. 4.99 (0-380-76768-6, Avon Bks) Morrow Avon.

— Star Requiem No. 3: Warlord of Heaven. 368p. (Orig.). 1993. mass mkt. 4.99 (0-380-76769-4, Avon Bks) Morrow Avon.

— Star Requiem No. 4: Labyrinth of Worlds. 352p. (Orig.). 1993. mass mkt. 4.99 (0-380-76770-8, Avon Bks) Morrow Avon.

— Throne of Fools: The Omaran Saga, Bk. 2. 384p. 1990. pap. 3.95 (0-380-75840-7, Avon Bks) Morrow Avon.

Cole, Alastair. French Political Parties In Transition. 226p. 1990. text 72.95 (1-85521-012-6, Pub. by Dartmth Pub) Ashgate Pub Co.

Cole, Alfred & Whitman, Charles F. A History of Buckfield, Oxford County, Maine. (Illus.). 758p. 1994. reprint ed. lib. bdg. 75.00 (0-8328-4360-1) Higginson Bk Co.

Cole, Alison. Virtue & Magnificence. 192p. (C). 1995. pap. text 16.40 (0-13-433673-9) P-H.

— Virtue & Magnificence: Art of the Italian Renaissance Courts. LC 94-34268. (The Perspectives Ser.). (Illus.). 176p. 1995. 16.95 (0-8109-2733-0, Pub. by Abrams) Time Warner.

Cole, Alistair. Franco-German Relations. (C). 1998. pap. text 17.95 (0-582-31997-8) Addison-Wesley.

— Francois Mitterrand: Study in Political Leadership. 2nd ed. 240p. (C). 1997. pap. 25.99 (0-415-16336-6) Routledge.

— French Politics & Society. 336p. 1998. pap. 38.00 (0-13-433954-1) P-H.

Cole, Alistair & Campbell, Peter. French Electoral Systems & Elections since 1789. 3rd ed. 202p. 1989. text 72.95 (0-566-05696-8, Pub. by Dartmth Pub) Ashgate Pub Co.

Cole, Allan. The Gods Awakened: Timura Tril. 1999. mass mkt. 6.99 (0-345-40181-6) Ballantine Pub Grp.

Cole, Allan. Sten. 1982. mass mkt. 2.50 (0-345-28503-4) Ballantine Pub Grp.

Cole, Allan. The Warrior Returns. 1997. mass mkt. 6.99 (0-345-41312-1, Del Rey) Ballantine Pub Grp.

— When the Gods Slept LC 98-234325. (Timura Trilogy Ser.). 470 p. 1997. 17.99 (0-340-68191-8) St Martin.

— Wizard of the Winds. LC 96-41577. 416p. 1997. pap. 12.95 (0-345-40176-X) Ballantine Pub Grp.

— Wizard of the Winds: The Timura Trilogy Book. 1998. mass mkt. 6.99 (0-345-40177-8) Ballantine Pub Grp.

— Wolves of the Gods: Timura Trilogy, Vol.2. 1999. mass mkt. 6.99 (0-345-42319-4, Del Rey) Ballantine Pub Grp.

Cole, Allan & Bunch, Chris. The Court of a Thousand Suns. 288p. (Orig.). 1986. mass mkt. 4.99 (0-345-31681-9, Ballantine) Ballantine Pub Grp.

— Empires End, No. 8. 1993. mass mkt. 5.99 (0-345-37696-X, Del Rey) Ballantine Pub Grp.

— Fleet of the Damned. LC 87-91377. 352p. 1988. mass mkt. 0.04 (0-345-33172-9, Del Rey) Ballantine Pub Grp.

— Kingdoms of the Night. 1996. mass mkt. 5.99 (0-345-38732-5, Del Rey) Ballantine Pub Grp.

— The Return of the Emperor. (Sten Adventure Ser.: No. 6). 1990. mass mkt. 5.99 (0-345-36130-X, Del Rey) Ballantine Pub Grp.

— Revenge of the Damned. 1989. mass mkt. 5.99 (0-345-33173-7, Del Rey) Ballantine Pub Grp.

— Sten. (Military Science Fiction Promotion Ser.). 1984. mass mkt. 5.99 (0-345-32460-9, Del Rey) Ballantine Pub Grp.

— The Warrior's Tale. (The Wizards of Fantasy Promotion). 1995. mass mkt. 5.99 (0-345-38734-1, Del Rey) Ballantine Pub Grp.

— The Wolf Worlds. 304p. 1984. mass mkt. 5.99 (0-345-31229-5, Ballantine) Ballantine Pub Grp.

Cole, Allan B. Conflict in Indo-China & International Repercussions: A Documentary History, 1945-1955. LC 56-14338. (Fletcher School Studies in International Affairs). 295p. reprint ed. pap. 91.50 (0-608-30467-0, 200057000030) Bks Demand.

Cole, Allan B. & Totten, George O. Socialist Parties in Postwar Japan. LC 66-21511. (Illus.). 508p. reprint ed. 157.50 (0-608-30698-3, 202198900024) Bks Demand.

Cole, Almus D., ed. see Cole, Bernedette K.

Cole, Alonzo D. The Witch's Tale: Stories of Gothic Horror from the Golden Age of Radio. Siegel, David S., ed. LC 98-71725. 256p. 1998. pap. 19.95 (1-891379-01-1, Dunwich Pr) Book Hunter Pr.

Cole, Alphaeus P. & Cole, Margaret W. Timothy Cole, Wood-Engraver: Illustrated with Nineteen of Timothy Cole's Finest Wood-Engravings. LC 92-24170. (Illus.). 1992. reprint ed. pap. 18.50 (0-87233-106-7) Bauhan.

Cole, Anastasia. Paint Your Feelings Starting Today: Anastasia's Basic of Painting I. LC 89-80074. (Illus.). 116p. (C). 1989. student ed. 15.95 (0-9622944-0-3) Anastasias Art.

Cole, Andrew. Neck Care. (Illus.). 24p. 1999. pap. 1.42 (0-934230-47-1) Medic Pub.

Cole, Andrew J. & Herring, Stanley, eds. The Low Back Pain Handbook: A Practical Guide for the Primary Care Clinician. LC 96-20355. 500p. (Orig.). 1996. pap. text 46.00 (1-56053-152-5) Hanley & Belfus.

Cole, Andrew J., jt. ed. see Becker, Bruce E.

Cole, Ann, et al. I Saw a Purple Cow & 100 Other Recipes for Learning. (Illus.). 96p. (J). (gr. k-3). 1972. pap. 10.95 (0-316-15175-0) Little.

Cole, Anthony R. The Securing of ISO Containers: Theory & Practice. 95p. (C). 1981. 220.00 (0-906297-19-2, Pub. by ICHCA) St Mut.

***Cole, Ardra L.** Researching Teaching: Exploring Teacher Development Through Reflexive Inquiry. LC 99-17833. 220p. (C). 1999. pap. text 37.00 (0-205-18076-0, Macmillan Coll) P-H.

Cole, Ardra L., et al. The Heart of the Matter: Teacher Educators & Teacher Education Reform. LC 98-26765. 1998. 39.95 (1-880192-28-4) Caddo Gap Pr.

Cole, Arthur, ed. Theoretical & Experimental Biophysics, 1. LC 66-29484. 409p. 1967. reprint ed. pap. 126.80 (0-608-08473-5, 202712400001) Bks Demand.

— Theoretical & Experimental Biophysics, 2. LC 66-29484. 357p. 1969. reprint ed. pap. 110.70 (0-608-08474-3, 202712400002) Bks Demand.

Cole, Arthur C. The Era of the Civil War, 1848-1870. LC 72-148875. (Select Bibliographies Reprint Ser.). 1977. reprint ed. 41.95 (0-8369-5646-X) Ayer.

— The Era of the Civil War, 1848-1870. LC 86-19253. (Sesquicentennial History of Illinois Ser.). (Illus.). 522p. 1987. reprint ed. text 29.95 (0-252-01339-5) U of Ill Pr.

— The Irrepressible Conflict, 1850-1865. (History - United States Ser.). 468p. 1993. reprint ed. lib. bdg. 99.00 (0-7812-4808-6) Rprt Serv.

— The Irrepressible Conflict, 1850-1865. LC 71-144952. (Illus.). 1971. reprint ed. 89.00 (0-403-00930-8) Scholarly.

Cole, Arthur H. Business Enterprise in Its Social Setting. LC 59-7649. 299p. 1959. 33.00 (0-674-08751-8) HUP.

***Cole, Arthur H.** Business Enterprise in Its Social Setting. 304p. 1999. 27.95 (0-7351-0182-5) Replica Bks.

Cole, Arthur H. The Great Mirror of Folly: Het Groote Tafereel der Dwasheid. (Kress Library of Business & Economics Publication: No. 6). 40p. 1949. pap. 9.95 (0-678-09901-4) Kelley.

Cole, Arthur H. & Watts, George B. The Handicrafts of France As Recorded in the Description Des Arts et Metiers, 1761-1788. (Kress Library of Business & Economics Publication: No. 8). (Illus.). 43p. 1952. pap. 9.95 (0-678-09903-0) Kelley.

Cole, Babette. Babette Cole's Cats. (Illus.). 5p. (J). 1995. 4.95 (0-446-91067-8, Pub. by Warner Bks) Little.

— Babette Cole's Dogs. (Illus.). 5p. (J). 1995. 4.95 (0-446-91068-6, Pub. by Warner Bks) Little.

— Babette Cole's Fish. (Illus.). 5p. (J). 1995. 4.95 (0-446-91069-4, Pub. by Warner Bks) Little.

— Babette Cole's Ponies. (Illus.). 5p. (J). 1995. 4.95 (0-446-91071-6, Pub. by Warner Bks) Little.

— Bad Habits! The Taming of Lucretzia Crum. Sherry, Toby, ed. LC 98-29247. (Illus.). 32p. (J). (ps-3). 1999. 14.99 (0-8037-2432-2, Dial Yng Read) Peng Put Young Read.

— Dr. Dog. (J). 1997. pap. 6.99 (0-679-88548-X) Knopf.

***Cole, Babette.** Hair in Funny Places: A Book about Puberty. LC 99-48448. (Illus.). 32p. (J). (gr. 2-5). 2000. 15.99 (0-7868-0590-0, Pub. by Hyprn Child) Time Warner.

Cole, Babette. Hurray for Ethelyn. (Illus.). (J). (ps-3). 1991. 14.95 (0-316-15189-0) Little.

— El Libro Apestoso (The Smelly Book) Segovia, Francisco, tr. (SPA., Illus.). 32p. (J). (gr. 1-3). 1994. 12.99 (968-16-4559-6, Pub. by Fondo) Continental Bk.

— Mommy Laid an Egg: or Where Do Babies Come From? (Illus.). 40p. (J). (ps-3). 1993. 13.95 (0-8118-0350-3) Chronicle Bks.

— Mommy Laid an Egg: or Where Do Babies Come From? (Illus.). 40p. (J). (ps-3). 1996. pap. 6.95 (0-8118-1319-3) Chronicle Bks.

— Prince Cinders. (CHI & ENG.). (J). write for info. (1-85430-308-2, 93437, Pub. by MAGI1 UK); write for info. (1-85430-309-0, 93438, Pub. by MAGI1 UK) Midpt Trade.

— Prince Cinders. (BEN.). (J). 1995. write for info. (1-85430-306-6, Pub. by MAGI1 UK); write for info. (1-85430-307-4, Pub. by MAGI1 UK) Midpt Trade.

— Prince Cinders. (Illus.). 32p. (J). (ps-3). 1997. pap. 5.99 (0-698-11554-6, PapStar) Peng Put Young Read.

— Princess Smartypants. (ENG & SPA.). (J). write for info. (1-85430-297-3, 93436, Pub. by MAGI1 UK) Midpt Trade.

— Princess Smartypants. (J). 1996. write for info. (1-85430-296-5, Pub. by MAGI1 UK); write for info. (1-85430-298-1, Pub. by MAGI1 UK); write for info. (1-85430-299-X, Pub. by MAGI1 UK) Midpt Trade.

— Princess Smartypants. (BEN., Illus.). 32p. (J). 1996. write for info. (1-85430-295-7, Pub. by MAGI1 UK) Midpt Trade.

— Princess Smartypants. LC 86-12381. (Illus.). 32p. (J). (ps-3). 1997. pap. 5.99 (0-698-11555-4, PapStar) Peng Put Young Read.

— The Trouble with Mom. (Illus.). 32p. (J). (ps-3). 1997. pap. 5.95 (0-698-11593-7, PapStar) Peng Put Young Read.

— Winni Allfours. LC 93-28447. (Illus.). 32p. (J). (gr. k-4). 1996. 13.95 (0-8167-3308-2) BrdgeWater.

— Winni Allfours. (J). 1993. 9.15 (0-606-08389-8, Pub. by Turtleback) Demco.

Cole, Babette. The Un-Wedding. LC 97-13854. 32p. (J). 1998. 17.00 (0-679-88898-5, Pub. by Knopf Bks Yng Read) Random.

Cole, Barbara. Little Wives. 35p. 1998. 7.00 (0-937013-82-X) Potes Poets.

— Postcards. 24p. 1998. write for info. (0-9667655-1-6) Beautifulswimmer.

Cole, Barbara & Winter, Sydney. Alex the Great. 1989. lib. bdg. 12.95 (0-8239-0941-7) Rosen Group.

***Cole, Barbara S.** The Gifts of Sobriety: When the Promises of Recovery Come True. LC 99-86013. 140p. 2000. pap. 12.00 (1-56838-354-1) Hazelden.

Cole, Barry. After the Breakup: Assessing the New Post-AT&T Divestiture Era. 1991. text 69.50 (0-231-07322-4) Col U Pr.

Cole, Barry L. A Visual Aid to Electronics. pap. 1.25 (0-89741-011-4) Gila River.

Cole, Basil. Music & Morals: A Theological Appraisal of the Moral & Psychological Effects of Music. LC 92-36135. 172p. 1993. pap. 8.95 (0-8189-0660-X) Alba.

Cole, Basil & Conner, Paul M. Christian Totality: Theology of the Consecrated Life. LC 97-14223. 360p. (Orig.). 1997. pap. 18.95 (0-8189-0798-3) Alba.

Cole, Bernard D. Gunboats & Marines: The United States Navy in China, Nineteen Twenty-Five to Nineteen Twenty-Eight. LC 81-72063. (Illus.). 232p. 1983. 32.50 (0-87413-203-7) U Delaware Pr.

Cole, Bernedette K. The Voice of the Turtle & Other Poems. Cole, Almus D., ed. Cushing, Jean, tr. LC 89-85217. 104p. 1989. 12.95 (0-9623488-0-5) Hse Kim Pub.

Cole, Bets. Fantastic Folded Forms: Patterns for Boxes, Envelopes & Unusual Forms. (Illus.). 62p. (Orig.). 1994. pap. 13.95 (0-9640373-0-0) Letterlines.

Cole, Betsy. Green Creatures Ten to One. LC 88-71429. (Illus.). 32p. (Orig.). (J). (gr. k-3). 1988. pap. 4.95 (0-9620606-0-7) Adventure VA.

— Is Aetosaur a Dinosaur? (Illus.). 64p. (Orig.). (J). (gr. k-3). 1992. pap. 11.95 (0-9625801-4-7) VA Mus Natl Hist.

Cole, Beverly. Cleaning Closets: A Mother's Story. 152p. (Orig.). 1995. pap. 13.99 (0-8272-0464-7) Chalice Pr.

***Cole, Beverly & Durack, Richard.** Railway Posters, 1923-1947. (Illus.). 160p. 2000. pap. text 29.95 (1-85669-014-8) L King Pubng.

Cole, Bill. John Coltrane. (Illus.). 278p. 1993. reprint ed. pap. 13.95 (0-306-80530-8) Da Capo.

— Law in a Business Context. 264p. 1990. pap. 29.95 (0-412-37520-6) Thomson Learn.

— Miles Davis: The Early Years. LC 93-36391. 256p. 1994. reprint ed. pap. 13.95 (0-306-80554-5) Da Capo.

Cole, Brenda, ed. Shade Gardens: A Harrowsmith's Gardener's Guide. (Illus.). 96p. 1993. pap. 12.95 (0-921820-63-1) Firefly Bks Ltd.

Cole, Brock. Alpha & the Dirty Baby. LC 90-55383. (Illus.). 32p. (J). (ps-3). 1995. pap. 5.95 (0-374-40357-0) FS&G.

Cole, Brock. Alpha & the Dirty Baby. LC 90-55383. 1995. 11.15 (0-606-08981-0, Pub. by Turtleback) Demco.

— Buttons. LC 99-27162. (Illus.). 32p. (YA). (ps-3). 2000. 16.00 (0-374-31001-7) FS&G.

Cole, Brock. Celine. 224p. (YA). (gr. 7 up). 1991. pap. 3.95 (0-374-41082-8) FS&G.

— Celine. 224p. (YA). (gr. 7 up). 1993. pap. 3.95 (0-374-41083-6) FS&G.

— Celine. Barbadillo, Pedro, tr. (SPA.). 172p. (YA). (gr. 9-12). 1992. pap. write for info. (84-204-4711-0) Santillana.

— Celine. (J). 1991. 9.05 (0-606-00340-1, Pub. by Turtleback) Demco.

— The Facts Speak for Themselves. LC 97-4250. 192p. (YA). (gr. 7 up). 1997. 16.95 (1-886910-14-6) Front Str.

***Cole, Brock.** The Facts Speak for Themselves. LC 99-27766. (Illus.). (J). 2000. pap. 5.99 (0-14-130696-3) Peng Put Young Read.

— Facts Speak for Themselves. (Illus.). (J). 2000. 11.34 (0-606-18403-1) Turtleback.

Cole, Brock. The Giant's Toe. (Sunburst Ser.). (Illus.). 32p. (J). (ps-3). 1988. pap. 3.95 (0-374-42557-4) FS&G.

— The Goats. 192p. 1987. 15.00 (0-374-32678-9) FS&G.

— The Goats. LC 87-45362. 192p. (J). (gr. 4-7). 1990. pap. 4.95 (0-374-42575-2) FS&G.

— The Goats. 1987. 9.05 (0-606-03389-0, Pub. by Turtleback) Demco.

— The Goats. 192p. (YA). (gr. 7 up). 1992. reprint ed. pap. 3.95 (0-374-42576-0) FS&G.

Cole, Brock. Lost above the Timberline. text. write for info. (0-374-34660-7) FS&G.

Cole, Brock. Nothing but a Pig. 32p. 1990. pap. 3.95 (0-374-45541-4) FS&G.

— The Winter Wren. LC 84-1583. (Illus.). 32p. (J). (gr. 2 up). 1984. 15.00 (0-374-38454-1) FS&G.

— The Winter Wren. LC 84-1583. (Illus.). 32p. (J). (ps-3). 1988. pap. 4.95 (0-374-48408-2) FS&G.

Cole, Bruce. Giotto: The Scrovegni Chapel, Padua. LC 93-6993. (Great Fresco Cycles of the Renaissance Ser.). (Illus.). 120p. 1993. 25.00 (0-8076-1310-X) Braziller.

— The Informed Eye: Understanding Masterpieces of Western Art. LC 99-39154. (Illus.). 256p. 1999. 30.00 (1-56663-255-2, Pub. by I R Dee) Natl Bk Netwk.

***Cole, Bruce.** The Informed Eye: Understanding Masterpieces of Western Art. LC 99-39154. (Illus.). 256p. 2000. reprint ed. pap. 16.95 (1-56663-278-1, Pub. by I R Dee) Natl Bk Netwk.

— ITALIAN ART 1250-1550. 320p. 1987. pap. 33.00 (0-06-430162-1) HarpC.

Cole, Bruce. Italian Art, 1250-1550: The Relation of Art to Life & Society. LC 86-45087. (Illus.). 352p. 1987. pap. 15.95 (0-685-18120-0, IN-162, Icon Edns) HarpC.

— Major Monuments of Western Art: An Introduction to the Visual Arts. 176p. 2000. 30.00 (0-06-430907-X, Icon Edns) HarpC.

— The Pumpkinville Mystery. LC 87-2533. (Illus.). 32p. (J). (ps-3). 1991. pap. 3.95 (0-671-74199-3) Litle Simon.

Cole, Bruce. Rena Artist at Work. LC 82-48102. (Icon Editions Ser.). (Illus.). 208p. 1984. pap. 22.00 (0-06-430129-X, IN-129, Icon Edns) HarpC.

Cole, Bruce. Sienese Painting in the Age of the Renaissance. LC 84-48246. (Illus.). 216p. 1985. 39.95 (0-253-18130-5) Ind U Pr.

— Titian & Venetian Painting, 1450-1590. 1998. pap. write for info. (0-06-430193-1, Icon Edns) HarpC.

— Titian & Venetian Painting, 1450-1590. LC 98-21705. (Illus.). 272p. 2000. 35.00 (0-06-430905-3, Icon Edns) HarpC.

Cole, Bruce & Gealt, Adelheid M. Art of the Western World: From Ancient Greece to Post-Modernism. (Illus.). 368p. 1991. per. 22.00 (0-671-74728-2, Touchstone) S&S Trade Pap.

Cole, Bruce & Warholа, James. The Pumpkinville Mystery. (Illus.). 32p. (J). (gr. 1-4). 1988. pap. 6.95 incl. audio (0-671-67147-2) S&S Trade.

Cole, Bruce K. How to Build Your Information Services with Information Technology. 1994. pap. 16.95 (0-9632631-1-0) Diaspora Pr.

Cole, Bruce K., ed. Business Information Services: Building Your Organization with Interactive Technology. Met, Philippe, tr. 200p. (Orig.). (C). 1992. pap. text 21.95 (0-9632631-0-2) Diaspora Pr.

Cole, Burt. The Quick. 304p. 1991. mass mkt. 3.99 (0-380-71178-8, Avon Bks) Morrow Avon.

Cole, Byron K. The Language of Medicine: A General Guide to Medical Care. 365p. (Orig.). 1997. pap. 19.95 (0-9656764-0-4) Medical Info Assocs.

***Cole, C. Bard.** Briefly Told Lives. LC 00-29119. 224p. 2000. text 22.95 (0-312-25351-6) St Martin.

Cole, C. Donald. All You Need to Believe. (Foundations of the Faith: The Apostles Creed Ser.). (Orig.). 1998. pap. 8.99 (0-8024-3053-8) Moody.

— How to Know You're Saved. pap. 5.99 (0-8024-3634-X, 171) Moody.

***Cole Cady, Annie.** The American Continent & Its Inhabitants Before Its Discovery by Columbus: A Unique History, 2 vols. (LC History-America-E). 1999. reprint ed. lib. bdg. 180.00 (0-7812-4315-7) Rprt Serv.

***Cole, Candace Y.** Daughter, There Is More to You Than Meets the Eye..., Vol. 1. 2000. pap. 15.00 (0-9678779-1-1) Dare to Dream Schola.

Cole, Candia L. Not Milk...Nut Milks! 40 of the Most Original Dairy-Free Recipes Ever! LC 97-41706. (Illus.). 128p. 1997. pap. 9.95 (0-88007-218-0) Woodbridge Pr.

— Super Smoothies! Taste the Nectar of Life. 2nd rev. ed. LC 96-7197. (Illus.). 192p. (Orig.). 1996. pap. 12.95 (0-88007-214-8) Woodbridge Pr.

Cole, Carlene. Slotplay: Build Your Own Jackpot! Messer, Keith, ed. (Illus.). 204p. 1999. pap. 9.95 (0-9672140-0-9) Diamond Pr CA.

Cole, Carol J. No Longer a Victim. (Illus.). 196p. (Orig.). 1996. pap. 19.95 (1-890961-02-7) C Communs.

— Practical Guide to DSM-IV Diagnosis & Treatment. 2nd ed. 173p. 1998. 39.95 (1-890961-03-5) C Communs.

Cole, Carol S., ed. see Redenbach, Sandi.

Cole, Carole O. Camp: North of 55. (Illus.). 193p. (Orig.). 1996. pap. 16.95 (0-945767-02-1) Write Place.

An Asterisk (*) at the beginning of an entry indicates that the title is appearing for the first time.

— Lidge & the Pahana Legend. (Illus.). 137p. (Orig.). 1996. pap. 13.95 (*0-945767-03-X*) Write Place.
— Who Are You? (Illus.). 24p. (J). (gr. k-2). 1997. pap. 11.95 (*0-945767-09-9*) Write Place.
Cole, Carole O., ed. 1998 League of Utah Writers Anthology. 100p. 1999. pap. 15.00 (*0-945767-04-8*) Write Place.
Cole, Carolyn. Shades of L A: Creating a Family Album. (Illus.). 112p. (Orig.). 1996. pap. 20.00 (*1-56584-313-4*, Pub. by New Press NY) Norton.
Cole, Catherine, jt. auth. see Palmer, Adrian.
Cole, Charles A., ed. Memorials of Henry V, King of England. (Rolls Ser.: No. 11). 1974. reprint ed. 70.00 (*0-8115-1014-X*) Periodicals Srv.
Cole, Charles B. Tool Design: Fundamental Principles of Design as Applied to Tooling for Production. LC 41-19998. (Illus.). 595p. reprint ed. pap. 184.50 (*0-608-11616-5*, 200457400043) Bks Demand.
***Cole, Charles C., Jr.** A Fragile Capital: Identity & the Early Years of Columbus, Ohio. 320p. 2001. 45.00 (*0-8142-0853-3*) Ohio St U Pr.
Cole, Charles C., Jr. Lion of the Forest: James B. Finley, Frontier Reformer. LC 93-47932. (Ohio River Valley Ser.). 288p. (C). 1994. 34.95 (*0-8131-1863-8*) U Pr of Ky.
Cole, Charles E., ed. Something More Than Human: Biographies of Leaders in American Methodist Higher Education. LC 85-51267. (Illus.). 256p. 1986. 7.95 (*0-938162-04-7*) United Meth Educ.
Cole, Charles E., jt. ed. see Trotter, F. Thomas.
Cole, Charles F. Korea Remembered: Enough of a War! The USS Ozbourn's First Tour, 1950-1951. LC 95-60802. (Illus.). 320p. (Orig.). 1995. pap. 17.95 (*1-881325-13-X*) Yucca Tree Pr.
***Cole, Charlotte.** Between You & Me. 1999. pap. 11.95 (*0-7043-4955-8*, Pub. by Womens Press) Trafalgar.
— The Female Odyssey: Visions for the 21st Century. 1999. pap. 14.95 (*0-7043-4613-3*, Pub. by Womens Press) Trafalgar.
Cole, Cheryl L., jt. ed. see Birrell, Susan.
Cole-Christensen, Darryl. A Place in the Rainforest: Settling the Costa Rican Frontier. LC 96-32321. 216p. 1997. 35.00 (*0-292-71190-5*); pap. 14.95 (*0-292-71191-3*) U of Tex Pr.
Cole, Christine L., jt. auth. see Shapiro, Edward S.
Cole, Christopher. Wordplay A Curious Dictionary of Language Oddities. LC 99-22459. 1999. pap. text 14.95 (*0-8069-1797-0*) Sterling.
Cole, Claire G. Nurturing a Teacher Advisory Program. 54p. (C). 1992. pap. text 10.00 (*1-56090-064-4*) Natl Middle Schl.
Cole, Claire G., jt. auth. see Hutchins, David E.
Cole, Corey & Cole, Lori. Shannara: The Official Strategy Guide. 1995. pap. 19.95 (*0-7615-0295-5*) Prima Pub.
Cole, Cyrenus, et al. Souvenir History of Pella, 1857-1922. (Illus.). 344p. 1997. reprint ed. lib. bdg. 39.50 (*0-8328-6698-9*) Higginson Bk Co.
Cole, D. Isaac Kool (Cool or Cole) & Catherine Serven, Married 1764 at Tappan, New York: Their Descendants Complete to 1876, Also Their American Ancestry from the Settlement of N. Y. City. (Illus.). 269p. 1993. reprint ed. pap. 40.00 (*0-8328-1369-9*); reprint ed. lib. bdg. 50.00 (*0-8328-1368-0*) Higginson Bk Co.
Cole, D. & Vogenberg, F. Managed Care Concepts. (Orig.). 1996. pap. text 49.46 (*1-56870-226-4*) RonJon Pub.
***Cole, D. J.** Geoffrey Prime: The Imperfect Spy. 256p. 1999. 29.95 (*0-7090-6060-2*, Pub. by R Hale Ltd) Seven Hills Bk.
Cole, D. J. & Brander, George C., eds. Bioindustrial Ecosystems. (Ecosystems of the World Ser.: No. 21). xii,296p. 1986. 178.00 (*0-444-42421-0*) Elsevier.
Cole, D. J., jt. auth. see Ewing, W. N.
Cole, D. J., ed. see Easter School in Agricultural Science (21st: 1974:.
Cole, D. J., ed. see International Symposium on Protein Metabolism & Nu.
Cole, D. J. A., et al, eds. Principles of Pig Science. 472p. 1999. 200.00 (*1-897676-22-0*, Pub. by Nottingham Univ Pr) St Mut.
— Recent Developments in Pig Nutrition, Vol. 2. 375p. 1999. pap. 120.00 (*1-897676-41-7*, Pub. by Nottingham Univ Pr) St Mut.
Cole, D. J. A., jt. ed. see Close, W. H.
Cole, D. J. A., jt. ed. see Garnsworthy, P. C.
Cole, D. J. A., jt. ed. see Lyons, T. P.
Cole-Dai, Phyllis, jt. auth. see Miller, Paul E.
Cole, Dale, jt. auth. see Cole, S.
Cole, Dale W. & Gessel, Stanley P., eds. Forest Site Evaluation & Long-Term Productivity. (Illus.). 200p. 1988. 40.00 (*0-295-96683-1*) U of Wash Pr.
Cole, Dan, ed. Archaeology & the Bible: The Best of BAR Series, 2 vols., Set. (Illus.). (C). 1990. reprint ed. pap. 29.95 (*0-9613089-3-1*, 7H8S) Biblical Arch Soc.
— Archaeology & the Bible: The Best of BAR Series, 2 vols., Vol. I: Early Israel. (Illus.). 324p. (C). 1990. reprint ed. pap. 18.95 (*0-9613089-5-8*, 7H80) Biblical Arch Soc.
— Archaeology & the Bible: The Best of BAR Series, 2 vols., Vol. II: Archaeology in the World of Herod, Jesus. (Illus.). 293p. (C). 1990. reprint ed. pap. 18.95 (*0-9613089-6-6*, 7H81) Biblical Arch Soc.
Cole, Dan P. Archaeology & Religion: With Slides. Shanks, Hershel, ed. 55p. (Orig.). 1991. pap. text 99.50 (*1-880317-31-1*, 5094) Biblical Arch Soc.
— Biblical Archaeology. Shanks, Hershel, ed. 32p. (Orig.). 1981. pap. text 99.50 incl. sl. (*1-880317-32-X*, 5071) Biblical Arch Soc.
— Dead Sea Scrolls: With Slides. Shanks, Hershel, ed. 40p. (Orig.). 1993. pap. text 119.50 (*1-880317-33-8*, 5096) Biblical Arch Soc.
— New Testament Archaeology. Shanks, Hershel, ed. 48p. (Orig.). 1986. pap. text 159.50 (*1-880317-38-9*, 5091) Biblical Arch Soc.
— Shechem I: The Middle Bronze IIB Pottery. LC 84-3004. (Excavation Reports of the American Schools of Oriental Research). (Illus.). xiv, 203p. 1984. text 50.00 (*0-89757-206-8*) Am Sch Orient Res.
— Supplemental New Testament Archaeology. Shanks, Hershel, ed. 48p. (Orig.). (C). 1995. pap. text 99.50 incl. sl. (*1-880317-42-7*, 5097) Biblical Arch Soc.
Cole, Dan P. & Bahat, Dan. Jerusalem Archaeology: With Slides. Shanks, Hershel, ed. 36p. (Orig.). 1983. pap. text 119.50 (*1-880317-36-2*, 5081) Biblical Arch Soc.
Cole, Daniel H. Instituting Environmental Protection in Poland: From Red to Green in Poland. LC 97-22904. 343p. 1998. text 69.95 (*0-312-17721-6*) St Martin.
Cole, Daniel H., jt. ed. see Clark, John.
Cole, David. Butterfly Lost. 384p. 2000. mass mkt. 5.99 (*0-06-101394-3*) HarpC.
— The Complete Guide to Book Marketing. LC 98-74530. 288p. 1999. pap. 19.95 (*1-58115-028-8*) Allworth Pr.
***Cole, David.** Dreamweaver. 160p. 2000. pap. 9.95 (*0-595-09089-3*, Writers Club Pr) iUniversecom.
Cole, David. First Record Book of the "Old Dutch Church of Sleepy Hollow" Organized in 1697 & Now the First Reformed Church of Tarrytown, NY. 252p. 1986. reprint ed. lib. bdg. 25.00 (*1-56012-078-9*, 77) Kinship Rhinebeck.
— No Equal Justice: Race & Class in the American Criminal Justice System. (Illus.). 224p. 1999. 25.00 (*1-56584-473-4*, Pub. by New Press NY) Norton.
— No Equal Justice: Race & Class in the American Criminal Justice System. 224p. 2000. pap. text 14.95 (*1-56584-566-8*, Pub. by New Press NY) Norton.
— The Work of Sir Gilbert Scott. (Illus.). 256p. 1980. 60.00 (*0-85139-723-9*) Eastview.
Cole, David, ed. History of Rockland County, New York. LC 86-27133. (Illus.). 558p. 1986. reprint ed. 45.00 (*0-911183-24-8*) Rockland County Hist.
Cole, David & Cole, Elaine. Greeting Card Book. (Illus.). 40p. 1994. pap. 4.50 (*1-883426-05-7*) Chldrns Outrch.
— How to Lead a Child to the Lord. 16p. 1994. pap. 1.00 (*1-883426-01-4*) Chldrns Outrch.
— Professional People Puppets. (Illus.). 32p. (Orig.). 1994. pap. 12.95 (*1-883426-08-1*) Chldrns Outrch.
— Puppet Director's Survival Kit. (Illus.). 36p. 1994. 14.00 (*1-883426-04-9*) Chldrns Outrch.
— Puppeteer Training Manual. (Illus.). 32p. (J). (gr. 4-12). 1994. pap. 4.00 (*1-883426-03-0*) Chldrns Outrch.
— A Trip Through the Old Testament. 56p. (Orig.). (J). (gr. 1-6). 1994. pap. 15.95 incl. audio (*1-883426-06-5*) Chldrns Outrch.
***Cole, David & Slade, Betty F.** Building a Modern Financial System: The Indonesian Experience. (Trade & Development Ser.). 379p. (C). 1999. pap. 24.95 (*0-521-65088-7*) Cambridge U Pr.
Cole, David, et al. Three Places in New Inkland. LC 77-72826. 1977. pap. 5.95 (*0-9605610-1-3*) P Zelevansky.
Cole, David, jt. auth. see Cole, Elaine.
Cole, David, jt. auth. see Dempsey, James X.
Cole, David, jt. auth. see Hampton, Bruce.
Cole, David, jt. auth. see Mooney, Jonathan.
Cole, David C. & Huntington, Richard. Between a Swamp & a Hard Place: Developmental Challenges in Remote Rural Africa. LC 97-12483. (Harvard Institute for International Development Ser.). (Illus.). 320p. 1997. 33.95 (*0-674-06860-2*); pap. 17.95 (*0-674-06861-0*) HUP.
Cole, David C. & Lyman, Princeton N. Korean Development: The Interplay of Politics & Economics. LC 75-131468. 336p. reprint ed. pap. 104.20 (*0-7837-2238-9*, 205732800004) Bks Demand.
Cole, David C. & Park, Yung C. Financial Development in Korea, 1945-1978. (East Asian Monographs: No. 106). (Illus.). 340p. 1983. 30.00 (*0-674-30147-1*) HUP.
Cole, David C. & Slade, Betty F. Building a Modern Financial System: The Indonesian Experience. (Trade & Development Ser.). 406p. (C). 1996. text 59.95 (*0-521-57092-1*) Cambridge U Pr.
Cole, David C., et al. Asian Money Markets. (Illus.). 488p. 1995. text 80.00 (*0-19-507429-7*) OUP.
— The Korean Economy: Issues of Development. LC 79-620015. (Korean Research Monograph: No. 1). 90p. reprint ed. pap. 30.00 (*0-608-13136-9*, 201946600011) Bks Demand.
Cole, David J., et al, eds. Philosophy, Mind, & Cognitive Inquiry: Resources for Understanding Mental Processes. (Studies in Cognitive Systems). 462p. (C). 1990. lib. bdg. 186.00 (*0-7923-0427-6*, Pub. by Kluwer Academic) Kluwer Academic.
Cole, David L. The Quest for Industrial Peace. LC 77-26873. (Meyer Kestnbaum Lectures). 164p. 1978. reprint ed. lib. bdg. 55.00 (*0-313-20072-6*, COQI, Greenwood Pr) Greenwood.
Cole, David N., jt. auth. see Hammitt, William E.
Cole, David N., jt. ed. see McCool, Stephen F.
Cole, David P., jt. ed. see Roberts, Julian V.
Cole, Debbie L. Sign Language & the Health Care Professional. LC 89-20083. 92p. (C). 1990. pap. 12.50 (*0-89464-417-3*) Krieger.
Cole, Deborah & Demoss, Daniel. Precious Memories. Norris, Charles E., ed. 135p. (Orig.). 1995. pap. 10.95 (*0-9647602-0-7*) Heartworks.
— Precious Memories, Vol. 1. rev. ed. Norris, Charles E., ed. 140p. (Orig.). 1995. reprint ed. pap. 10.95 (*0-9647602-1-5*) Heartworks.
Cole, Deborah D. & Duran, Maureen Gallagher. Sex & Character. Dembski, William, ed. LC 98-72932. (Pandas Publications: A Series about Central Questions). (Illus.). 210p. (YA). (gr. 8-10). 1998. text 27.50 (*0-914513-50-8*) Haughton.
***Cole, Dennis R.** Numbers. (New American Commentary Ser.: Vol. 3B). 2000. 27.99 (*0-8054-9503-7*) Broadman.
Cole, Dermot. Amazing Pipeline Stories: How Building the Trans-Alaska Pipeline Transformed Life in America's Last Frontier. LC 97-60785. (Illus.). 160p. (Orig.). (C). 1997. pap. 14.95 (*0-945397-46-1*) Epicenter Pr.
— Fairbanks: The Gold Rush Town That Beat the Odds. (City History Ser.: Vol. 2). (Illus.). 224p. 1999. pap. 14.95 (*0-945397-73-9*) Epicenter Pr.
— Frank Barr: Bush Pilot in Alaska & the Yukon. (Caribou Classics Ser.). (Illus.). 115p. 1999. pap. 8.95 (*0-88240-525-X*, Alaska NW Bks) Gr Arts Ctr Pub.
Cole, Desmond T. & Mokaila, Dingaan M. A Course in Tswana. LC 70-278557. 146p. reprint ed. pap. 45.30 (*0-7837-6311-5*, 204602600010) Bks Demand.
Cole, Desmond T., et al. Lithops. LC 68-22957. (Illus.). 114p. 1975. 85.00 (*0-8386-6902-6*) Fairleigh Dickinson.
Cole, Diane, jt. auth. see Wetzler, Scott.
Cole, Don. Annual Editions: Economics 97-98. 26th ed. 256p. (C). 1997. text. write for info. (*0-697-37246-4*) Brown & Benchmark.
— Annual Editions: Macroeconomics, 96-97. 11th ed. 256p. (C). 1995. per. write for info. (*1-56134-431-1*) Brown & Benchmark.
— Annual Editions: Microeconomics, 96-97. 3rd ed. 256p. (C). 1995. per. write for info. (*1-56134-432-X*) Brown & Benchmark.
— Economics, 98-99. 27th ed. (Annual Ser.). (Illus.). 240p. 1998. pap. text 12.25 (*0-697-41794-8*, Dshkn McG-Hill) McGrw-H Hghr Educ.
— Economics, 1996-1997. annuals 25th ed. 256p. (C). 1996. text. write for info. (*0-697-31532-0*) Brown & Benchmark.
— Encyclopedic Dictionary of Economics. 4th ed. (C). 1991. text. write for info. (*1-56134-042-1*, Dshkn McG-Hill) McGrw-H Hghr Educ.
Cole, Donald, jt. auth. see Altorki, Soraya.
Cole, Donald B. Handbook of American History. 1998. pap. text 12.95 (*0-15-504513-X*) Harcourt.
— Jacksonian Democracy in New Hampshire, 1800-1851. LC 79-127878. (Illus.). 295p. 1970. 29.00 (*0-674-46990-9*) HUP.
***Cole, Donald B.** Jacksonian Democracy in New Hampshire, 1800-1851. 298p. 1999. 27.95 (*0-7351-0181-7*) Replica Bks.
Cole, Donald B. Martin Van Buren & the American Political System. LC 84-3402. 492p. reprint ed. pap. 152.60 (*0-7837-0099-7*, 204037700016) Bks Demand.
— The Presidency of Andrew Jackson. LC 92-43377. (American Presidency Ser.). 352p. 1999. 29.95 (*0-7006-0600-9*); pap. 15.95 (*0-7006-0961-X*) U Pr of KS.
Cole, Donald B. & Cornell, Robert H., eds. Respecting the Pupil, Essays on Teaching Able Students by Members of the Faculty of Phillips Exeter Academy. 2nd ed. LC 81-81104. (Illus.). 132p. 1981. pap. 13.95 (*0-939618-01-X*) Phillips Exeter.
Cole, Donald B., ed. see French, Benjamin B.
Cole, Donna. Lightland. 190p. 1996. pap. 13.00 (*1-883721-19-9*) Silver Mtn Pr.
— Liturgical Ministry: A Practical Guide to Spirituality. LC 96-8153. 96p. (Orig.). 1996. pap. 8.95 (*0-89390-372-8*) Resource Pubns.
Cole, Donna J., et al. Portfolios Across the Curriculum & Beyond. Herman, Janice L. & Hernam, Jerry J., eds. LC 95-22649. (Illus.). 104p. 1995. pap. 17.95 (*0-8039-6303-3*) Corwin Pr.
— Portfolios Across the Curriculum & Beyond. LC 95-22649. (Illus.). 104p. 1995. 41.95 (*0-8039-6403-X*) Corwin Pr.
***Cole, Donna J., et al.** Portfolios Across the Curriculum & Beyond. 2nd ed. LC 99-6842. 104p. (C). 1999. pap. 18.95 (*0-7619-7534-9*); lib. bdg. 43.95 (*0-7619-7533-0*) Corwin Pr.
Cole, Dora J. & Wichman, Juliet R. Early Kauai Hospitality: A Family Cookbook of Receipts, 1820-1920. 1977. 12.00 (*0-686-86235-X*) Kauai Museum.
Cole Dore', Susan, ed. see Bienvenu, Marcelle.
Cole, Doris. Eleanor Raymond, Architect. LC 80-67474. (Illus.). 160p. 1981. 40.00 (*0-87982-036-5*) Art Alliance.
— From Tipi to Skyscraper: A History of Women in Architecture. 1978. pap. text 12.00 (*0-262-53033-3*) MIT Pr.
Cole, Doris & Taylor, Karen C. The Lady Architects: Howe, Manning & Almy. LC 89-63768. (Illus.). 160p. (Orig.). 1990. pap. text 11.50 (*1-877675-01-6*) Midmarch Arts.
Cole, Douglas. Captured Heritage: The Scramble for the Northwest Coast Artifacts. LC 95-35735. (Illus.). 392p. 1995. pap. 16.95 (*0-8061-2777-5*) U of Okla Pr.
— Christopher Marlowe & the Renaissance of Tragedy. LC 95-23019. 200p. 1995. pap. 18.95 (*0-275-93673-2*, Praeger Pubs) Greenwood.
— Christopher Marlowe & the Renaissance of Tragedy, 63. LC 95-23019. (Contributions in Drama & Theatre Studies: Vol. 63). 200p. 1995. 59.95 (*0-313-27516-5*, Greenwood Pr) Greenwood.
— Franz Boas The Early Years, 1858-1906. LC 99-42589. (Illus.). 484p. 1999. 50.00 (*0-295-97903-8*) U of Wash Pr.
Cole, Douglas & Chaikin, Ira. An Iron Hand upon the People: The Law Against the Potlatch on the Northwest Coast. LC 90-44889. (Illus.). 248p. 1995. pap. 14.95 (*0-295-97449-4*) U of Wash Pr.
Cole, Duane. Conquest of Lines & Symmetry: Aerobatics. (Illus.). 127p. 1970. pap. 14.95 (*0-911721-41-X*) Aviation.
— Planes, Pilots & Progress. 140p. 1993. pap. 14.95 (*0-916413-25-X*) Aviation.
— Roll Around a Point: Aerobatics. (Illus.). 101p. 1976. pap. 14.95 (*0-911721-28-2*) Aviation.
Cole, E. Hombria Al Maximo.Tr. of Maximized Manhood. (SPA.). 192p. 1989. pap. 5.99 (*0-8297-0931-2*) Vida Pubs.
Cole, E. B. The Descendants of James Cole of Plymouth, 1633: Record of the Families of Lt. Thomas Burnham, Ipswich, 1635, Lt. Edward Winship, Cambridge, 1634, Simon Huntington; Norwich, England, 1635. (Illus.). 449p. 1989. reprint ed. pap. 55.00 (*0-8328-0415-0*); reprint ed. lib. bdg. 65.00 (*0-8328-0414-2*) Higginson Bk Co.
Cole, Earline R. Led by a Child. 1990. pap. 10.95 (*0-938645-34-X*) In His Steps.
Cole, Ed. Manhood 101. LC 96-122342. 1996. pap. 6.99 (*1-56292-051-0*, HB-051) Honor Bks OK.
Cole, Eddie C. Now Techniques for Today's Poets. 76p. 1977. pap. 10.95 (*0-317-17453-3*) World Poetry Pr.
Cole, Eddie L. The Family Treasury of Great Poems. 256p. 1982. 39.95 (*0-317-17452-5*) World Poetry Pr.
Cole, Eddie-Lou, ed. Best-Loved Contemporary Poems. 39.95 (*0-317-29086-X*) World Poetry Pr.
— Great Contemporary Poems. 25.00 (*0-317-29078-9*) World Poetry Pr.
— Great Poems of the Western World. 39.95 (*0-317-29093-2*) World Poetry Pr.
— The Great Treasury of World Poems. 39.95 (*0-317-29097-5*) World Poetry Pr.
— Today's Best Poems. 39.95 (*0-317-29091-6*) World Poetry Pr.
— World Treasury of Great Poems. 39.95 (*0-317-29095-9*) World Poetry Pr.
— The World's Great Contemporary Poems. 39.95 (*0-317-29100-9*) World Poetry Pr.
Cole, Edwin. Absolute Answers to Prodigal Problems: Break Through Life's Barriers Forever. LC 98-7201. 224p. 1998. pap. 10.99 (*0-7852-7348-4*) Nelson.
— Hombre de Verdad. (SPA.). 1992. pap. 10.99 (*0-88113-140-7*) Caribe Betania.
— Real Man. 1993. pap. 10.99 (*0-8407-6974-1*) Nelson.
Cole, Edwin L. Communication, Sex & Money: The Three Most Common Obstacles That Challenge Relationships Between Men & Women. 176p. (Orig.). 1997. pap. 8.99 (*1-57778-081-7*, AP-081, Pub. by Albury Pub) Appalach Bk Dist.
— Courage: Building the Character of a Champion. 176p. 1997. pap. 5.99 (*1-57778-046-9*, Pub. by Albury Pub) Appalach Bk Dist.
— Entering & Leaving Crisis: A Step-by-Step Guide for Times of Transition, 10 Vols. 32p. 1997. pap. 9.90 (*1-57778-082-5*, Pub. by Albury Pub) Appalach Bk Dist.
— Hombres Fuertes en Tiempos Dificiles.Tr. of Strong Men in Tough Times. (SPA.). 224p. 1994. 9.99 (*0-88113-264-0*, B007-2640) Caribe Betania.
— Man Power: The Call for the Spiritual Revival of Men in America. LC 96-46548. 1997. pap. 10.99 (*0-7852-7347-6*) Nelson.
— Maximized Manhood: A Guide To Family Survival. 176p. 1982. mass mkt. 5.99 (*0-88368-107-2*) Whitaker Hse.
— Sexual Integrity: A Sexual Revolution Called Purity. 128p. 1998. pap. 6.99 (*1-57778-031-0*, AP-031, Pub. by Albury Pub) Appalach Bk Dist.
— Strong Men in Tough Times: Developing Strong Character in an Age of Compromise. 1994. pap. 11.99 (*0-88419-376-4*) Creation House.
— The Substance of Great Achievement. 1996. pap. 9.99 (*0-88419-366-7*) Word Pub.
— Winners Are Not Those Who Never Fail: But Those Who Never Quit. 128p. 1997. pap. 7.99 (*1-57778-079-5*, AP-079, Pub. by Albury Pub) Appalach Bk Dist.
Cole, Edwin L. & Cole, Nancy C. The Unique Woman: Insight & Wisdom to Maximize Your Life. 176p. 1997. pap. 8.99 (*1-57778-080-9*, AP-080, Pub. by Albury Pub) Appalach Bk Dist.
Cole, Edwin Louis. Profiles in Courageous Manhood. 224p. 1998. pap. 11.99 (*1-57778-087-6*, Pub. by Albury Pub) Appalach Bk Dist.
Cole, Elaine. Bible Verse Coloring Book. 32p. (J). (gr. 1-6). 1994. pap. 2.80 (*1-883426-00-6*) Chldrns Outrch.
— My Alphabet & Bible Verse Coloring Book. 28p. (J). (ps). 1994. pap. 2.50 (*1-883426-02-2*) Chldrns Outrch.
Cole, Elaine & Cole, David. Animal Puppet Patterns, Bk. 1. (Illus.). 32p. (Orig.). 1994. pap. 12.95 (*1-883426-09-X*) Chldrns Outrch.
— Animal Puppet Patterns, Bk. 2. (Illus.). 32p. (Orig.). 1994. pap. 12.95 (*1-883426-10-3*) Chldrns Outrch.
— Animal Puppet Patterns, Bk. 3. (Illus.). 32p. (Orig.). 1994. pap. 12.95 (*1-883426-11-1*) Chldrns Outrch.
— Animal Puppet Plays. 32p. (Orig.). (J). (gr. 1-6). 1994. pap. 4.50 (*1-883426-17-0*) Chldrns Outrch.
— Animal Puppets on Stage, Bk. 1. 16p. (Orig.). (J). (gr. 1-6). 1994. pap. 9.95 incl. audio (*1-883426-15-4*) Chldrns Outrch.
— Animal Puppets on Stage, Bk. 2. 16p. (Orig.). (J). (gr. 1-6). 1994. pap. 9.95 incl. audio (*1-883426-16-2*) Chldrns Outrch.
— Bird Puppet Patterns, Bk. 4. (Illus.). 32p. (Orig.). 1994. pap. 12.95 (*1-883426-12-X*) Chldrns Outrch.
— Creative Paper Plate Puppetry. (Illus.). 32p. (Orig.). (J). (gr. 1-12). 1995. pap. 5.00 (*1-883426-18-9*) Chldrns Outrch.
— Gospel Draw & Tell, Bk. 1. (Illus.). 32p. (Orig.). (J). 1995. pap. 5.00 (*1-883426-21-9*) Chldrns Outrch.
— Gospel Draw & Tell, Bk. 2. (Illus.). 32p. (Orig.). (J). (gr. 1-5). 1995. pap. 5.00 (*1-883426-22-7*) Chldrns Outrch.

C

An Asterisk (*) at the beginning of an entry indicates that the title is appearing for the first time.

— Gospel Draw & Tell, Bk. 3. (Illus.). 32p. (Orig.). (YA). (gr. 6-12). 1995. pap. 5.00 (*1-883426-23-5*) Chldrns Outrch.

— Let's Talk about Salvation. 36p. (Orig.). (J). (gr. 1-6). 1994. pap. 11.95 incl. audio (*1-883426-14-6*) Chldrns Outrch.

— Take Anywhere Puppets. (Illus.). 16p. (Orig.). 1994. pap. 8.95 (*1-883426-13-8*) Chldrns Outrch.

— A Trip Through the New Testament. 56p. (Orig.). (J). (gr. 1-6). 1994. pap. 15.95 incl. audio (*1-883426-07-3*) Chldrns Outrch.

Cole, Elaine, jt. auth. see Cole, David.

Cole, Elizabeth & Duva, Joy. Family Preservation: An Orientation for Administrators & Practitioners. 1990. pap. 7.50 (*0-87868-404-2*) Child Welfare.

Cole, Elizabeth & Gregory, Hilda, eds. Auditory Learning. LC HV2430.A83. 127p. reprint ed. pap. 39.40 (*0-7837-1252-9*, 204138900020) Bks Demand.

Cole, Elizabeth, jt. auth. see Press, Andrea L.

Cole, Elizabeth B. Listening & Talking: A Guide to Promoting Spoken Language in Hearing-Impaired Children. 201p. (Orig.). (C). 1992. pap. text 25.95 (*0-88200-172-8*) Alexander Graham.

Cole, Ellen, et al, eds. Refugee Women & Their Mental Health: Shattered Societies, Shattered Lives. LC 92-24548. (Women & Therapy Ser.: Vol. 13, Nos. 1-2 & Vol. 13, No. 3, 1992). (Illus.). 376p. 1992. 49.95 (*1-56024-372-4*) Haworth Pr.

— Refugee Women & Their Mental Health: Shattered Societies, Shattered Lives. LC 92-24548. (Women & Therapy Ser.: Vol. 13, Nos. 1-2 & Vol. 13, No. 3, 1992). (Illus.). 376p. 1993. pap. 19.95 (*1-56023-030-4*, Harrington Park) Haworth Pr.

— Wilderness Therapy for Women: The Power of Adventure. LC 94-17240. 262p. 1994. 49.95 (*1-56024-682-0*) Haworth Pr.

Cole, Ellen, et al, eds. Wilderness Therapy for Women: The Power of Adventure. LC 94-17240. 1994. pap. 19.95 (*1-56023-058-4*, Harrington Park) Haworth Pr.

Cole, Ellen & Rothblum, Esther D., eds. Faces of Women & Aging. LC 93-6593. (Women & Therapy Ser.: Vol. 14, Nos. 1-2). (Illus.). 225p. 1993. pap. 19.95 (*1-56023-042-8*, Harrington Park); lib. bdg. 49.95 (*1-56024-435-6*) Haworth Pr.

— Women & Sex Therapy. LC 88-11068. (Women & Therapy Ser.: Vol. 7, Nos. 2-3). (Illus.). 300p. 1989. text 49.95 (*0-86656-808-5*) Haworth Pr.

Cole, Ellen, jt. auth. see Rothblum, Esther D.

Cole, Ellen, jt. ed. see Knowles, Jane P.

Cole, Ellen, jt. ed. see Ochshorn, Judith.

Cole, Ellen, jt. ed. see Rothblum, Esther D.

Cole, Ellen, jt. ed. see Siegel, Rachel J.

Cole, Emma, tr. see Clement, Frederic.

Cole, Emma A. I Do, I Do: Etiquette from Colonial Days to the 1920s. LC 98-38349. 228p. 1998. 19.95 (*0-7818-0650-X*) Hippocrene Bks.

Cole, Eugene E. & Shea, Gail H., eds. Costa Rica Earthquake of April 22, 1991, Reconnaissance Report. (Illus.). 170p. 1991. pap. 15.00 (*0-943198-72-0*, 91-02) Earthquake Eng.

Cole, Eve B. Philosophy & Feminist Criticism. LC 92-10720. (Issues in Philosophy Ser.). 144p. 1993. pap. 16.95 (*1-55778-457-4*) Paragon Hse.

Cole, Eve B. & Coultrap-McQuin, Susan, eds. Explorations in Feminist Ethics: Theory & Practice. LC 91-21235. 224p. 1992. text 37.50 (*0-253-31384-8*); pap. text 14.95 (*0-253-20697-9*, MB-697) Ind U Pr.

Cole, F. C. Chinese Pottery in the Philippines: The Wild Tribes of Davao District, Mindanao. (Chicago Field Museum of Natural History Fieldiana Anthropology Ser.: Vol. 12). 1913. 30.00 (*0-527-01872-4*) Periodicals Srv.

— Traditions of the Tinguian, a Study in Philippine Folk-Lore: The Tinguian Social Religious & Economic Life of a Philippine Tribe. (Chicago Field Museum of Natural History Fieldiana Anthropology Ser.: Vol. 14). 1974. reprint ed. 60.00 (*0-527-01874-0*) Periodicals Srv.

Cole, F. Russell, jt. auth. see Wilson, Don E.

Cole, F. T. The Early Genealogies of the Cole Family in America: (Including Coles & Cowles) 340p. 1989. reprint ed. pap. 44.50 (*0-8328-0413-4*); reprint ed. lib. bdg. 54.50 (*0-8328-0412-6*) Higginson Bk Co.

Cole, Fay C. Traditions of the Tinguian. LC 78-67698. (Folktale Ser.). reprint ed. 22.50 (*0-404-16069-7*) AMS Pr.

Cole, Fay-Cooper. Traditions of the Tinguian: A Study in Philippine Folklore. The R. F. Cummings Philippine Expedition. LC 15-8602. (Field Museum of Natural History Anthropological Ser.: Vol. 14, No. 1). 226p. 1915. reprint ed. pap. 70.10 (*0-608-02707-3*, 206337200004) Bks Demand.

— The Wild Tribes of Davao District, Mindanao. The R. F. Cummings Philippine Expedition. LC 13-24658. (Field Museum of Natural History Anthropological Ser.: Vol. 12, No. 2). (Illus.). 347p. 1913. reprint ed. pap. 107.60 (*0-608-02710-3*, 206337500004) Bks Demand.

Cole, Fay-Cooper & Deuel, Thorne. Rediscovering Illinois: Archaeological Explorations in & Around Fulton County. (Midway Reprint Ser.). (Illus.). xvi, 296p. (C). 1975. reprint ed. pap. text 12.50 (*0-226-11336-1*) U Ch Pr.

Cole, Fran & Hanson, Debra. Christopher, Go in the Corner. (Illus.). 50p. (Orig.). (J). 1996. pap. 6.95 (*1-57502-229-X*, P0893) Morris Pubng.

Cole, Francis, jt. auth. see Cole, John.

Cole, Franklyn W. Introduction to Meteorology. 3rd ed. LC 79-1212. (Illus.). 525p. 1980. reprint ed. pap. 162.80 (*0-7837-3494-8*, 205782700008) Bks Demand.

Cole, G. A. Organisational Behaviour. 300p. 1995. pap. 59.95 (*1-85805-135-5*, Pub. by DP Publns) St Mut.

— Strategic Management. 284p. 1994. pap. 59.95 (*1-85805-099-5*, Pub. by DP Publns) St Mut.

Cole, G. D. Guild Socialism Restated. (Social Science Classics Ser.). 224p. 1980. reprint ed. text 39.95 (*0-87855-386-X*); reprint ed. pap. text 24.95 (*0-87855-817-9*) Transaction Pubs.

— Labour in the Coal-Mining Industry, 1914-1921. (Economic & Social History of the World War Ser.). 1923. 100.00 (*0-317-27503-8*) Elliots Bks.

Cole, G. D. & Philip, Andre, eds. A Report on the UNESCO La Breviere Seminar on Workers. (UNESCO Education Studies & Documents: No. 1). 1974. reprint ed. pap. 25.00 (*0-8115-1325-4*) Periodicals Srv.

Cole, G. D. & Postgate, Raymond. The Common People: Seventeen Forty-Six to Nineteen Forty-Six. 4th ed. 1961. pap. 17.95 (*0-416-31360-4*, NO.2149) Routledge.

Cole, G. D., ed. see Morris, William.

Cole, G. D., tr. see Rousseau, Jean-Jacques.

Cole, G. H. The Structure of Planets. (Wykeham Science Ser.: No. 45). 232p. 1977. 32.00 (*0-85109-610-7*); pap. 18.00 (*0-85109-600-X*) Taylor & Francis.

— Thermodynamics in Engineering & Physical Science: Heat-Power Conversion by Gas & Vapour Cycles. LC 97-117440. 144p. 1997. pap. text 29.95 (*1-898563-22-5*, Pub. by Horwood Pub) Paul & Co Pubs.

Cole, G. H. A. Thermal Power Cycles. (Mechanical Engineering Ser.). 1993. pap. 40.95 (*0-340-54522-4*, VNR) Wiley.

Cole, G. Mattney. Remediation of Petroleum Contaminated Soils. 384p. 1994. lib. bdg. 75.00 (*0-87371-824-0*, L824) Lewis Pubs.

— Underground Storage Tank Installation Practices. 192p. 1991. lib. bdg. 79.95 (*0-87371-596-9*, L596) Lewis Pubs.

Cole, G. T. & Hoch, H. C. The Fungal Spore & Disease Initiation in Plants & Animals. (Illus.). 578p. (C). 1991. text 135.00 (*0-306-43454-7*, Kluwer Plenum) Kluwer Academic.

Cole, G. W. Early Library Development in New York State. 19p. 1993. reprint ed. lib. bdg. 69.00 (*0-7812-5318-7*) Rprt Serv.

Cole, Garold L. Travels in America: From the Voyages of Discovery to the Present: An Annotated Bibliography of Travel Articles in Periodicals, 1955-1980. LC 84-40273. 344p. 1985. 65.00 (*0-8061-1791-5*) U of Okla Pr.

Cole, Geert, jt. auth. see Logan, Leanne.

Cole, Geert, jt. contrib. by see Logan, Leanne.

Cole, George. Water Boundaries. (Riparian Boundaries Ser.: No. 1). (Illus.). 1997. 55.00 (*0-910845-13-1*, 645) Wiley.

Cole, George D. The British Co-operative Movement in a Socialist Society. LC 76-22523. 168p. 1976. reprint ed. lib. bdg. 65.00 (*0-8371-9002-9*, COBCM, Greenwood Pr) Greenwood.

— Chartist Portraits. LC 74-22738. reprint ed. 39.50 (*0-404-58490-X*) AMS Pr.

— Labour in the Commonwealth: Book for the Younger Generation. LC 75-157330. (Select Bibliographies Reprint Ser.). 1977. reprint ed. 18.95 (*0-8369-5790-3*) Ayer.

— Persons & Periods: Studies. LC 67-26726. (Essay Index Reprint Ser.). 1977. 20.95 (*0-8369-0323-4*) Ayer.

— Persons & Periods: Studies by G. D. H. Cole. LC 73-75412. vii, 332p. 1969. reprint ed. 39.50 (*0-678-00495-1*) Kelley.

— Self-Government in Industry. LC 71-152979. (Select Bibliographies Reprint Ser.). 1977. reprint ed. 23.95 (*0-8369-5731-8*) Ayer.

— Studies in Class Structure. LC 76-2503. 195p. 1976. reprint ed. lib. bdg. 35.00 (*0-8371-8779-6*, COSS, Greenwood Pr) Greenwood.

— Studies in World Economics. LC 67-23195. (Essay Index Reprint Ser.). 1977. 20.95 (*0-8369-0324-2*) Ayer.

— What Marx Really Meant. LC 79-00489. 309p. 1971. reprint ed. lib. bdg. 65.00 (*0-8371-3082-4*, COWM, Greenwood Pr) Greenwood.

Cole, George F. The American System of Criminal Justice. 4th ed. LC 85-15169. (Criminal Justice Ser.). 576p. (C). 1985. pap. 28.00 (*0-534-05226-6*) Brooks-Cole.

— The American System of Criminal Justice. 5th ed. LC 88-26263. 706p. (C). 1988. pap. 44.95 (*0-534-09288-8*) Brooks-Cole.

— The American System of Criminal Justice. 6th ed. LC 91-18701. 752p. (C). 1991. pap. 53.95 (*0-534-14700-3*) Wadsworth Pub.

— The American System of Criminal Justice. 6th ed. LC 91-18701. 743p. (C). 1992. pap., student ed. 17.95 (*0-534-14702-X*) Wadsworth Pub.

— The American System of Criminal Justice. 7th ed. LC 94-11411. 686p. 1994. mass mkt. 62.95 (*0-534-24048-8*) Wadsworth Pub.

— Criminal Justice: Law & Politics. 4th ed. LC 83-7501. (C). 1984. mass mkt. 14.75 (*0-534-02767-9*) Brooks-Cole.

— Criminal Justice: Law & Politics. 5th ed. LC 87-21806. 516p. (C). 1987. mass mkt. 22.50 (*0-534-08382-X*) Wadsworth Pub.

— Criminal Justice in America. (Criminal Justice Ser.). 1995. pap., student ed. 19.50 (*0-534-24422-X*) Wadsworth Pub.

— Criminal Justice in America. 2nd ed. LC 98-33542. (Criminal Justice Ser.). 1998. pap. 57.95 (*0-534-54666-8*) Wadsworth Pub.

— Criminal Justice in America. 2nd ed. (Criminal Justice Ser.). 1998. ring bd. 35.50 (*0-534-54674-9*) Wadsworth Pub.

— Criminal Justice in America "In a Box" 2nd ed. (Criminal Justice). 1998. pap. 46.75 (*0-534-54673-0*) Wadsworth Pub.

Cole, George F., et al, eds. Major Criminal Justice Systems: A Comparative Survey. 2nd ed. LC 87-23232. (Sage Focus Editions Ser.: Vol. 32). 288p. 1987. reprint ed. pap. 89.30 (*0-608-03565-3*, 205965000009) Bks Demand.

Cole, George F. & Frankowski, Stanislaw. Abortion & Protection of the Human Fetus: Legal Problems in a Cross-Cultural Perspective. LC 86-23626. (Current Legal Issues in International & Comparative Law Ser.). 352p. 1987. lib. bdg. 138.00 (*0-89838-922-4*) Kluwer Academic.

Cole, George F. & Gertz, Marc G. The Criminal Justice System: Politics & Policies. 7th ed. LC 97-22775. (C). 1997. pap. 35.95 (*0-534-52708-6*) Wadsworth Pub.

Cole, George F. & Smith, Christopher E. The American System of Criminal Justice. 8th ed. LC 97-18074. (Criminal Justice Ser.). (C). 1997. 80.95 (*0-534-52533-4*) Wadsworth Pub.

— Criminal Justice In America. LC 95-12626. (Criminal Justice). 1995. pap. 36.75 (*0-534-24420-3*) Wadsworth Pub.

— S.G. Criminal Justice in America. 2nd ed. (Criminal Justice). 1998. pap., student ed. 19.50 (*0-534-54668-4*) Wadsworth Pub.

Cole, George F., jt. auth. see Clear, Todd R.

Cole, George M. Land Surveyor-in-Training Sample Examination. LC 98-119612. 70p. 1998. pap. 25.95 (*0-912045-66-3*, LSSE) Prof Pubns CA.

— Water Boundaries. LC 96-44730. 208p. 1997. 75.00 (*0-471-17929-9*) Wiley.

Cole, George W. Graphs & Their Application to Speculation. Mack, Donald, ed. (Traders Masterclass Ser.). (Illus.). 278p. 1998. 45.00 (*0-273-63738-X*) F T P-H.

Cole, George W., compiled by. The E. D. Church Library: A Catalogue of Books Relating to the Discovery & Early History of North & South America, 5 vols. (Illus.). 2635p. 1995. reprint ed. 250.00 (*1-57898-022-4*) Martino Pubng.

Cole, Gerald A. Textbook of Limnology. 4th rev. ed. (Illus.). 412p. (C). 1994. text 41.50 (*0-88133-800-1*) Waveland Pr.

Cole, Gloria H. & Chandler, Carla E. Network Analysis. (C). 1989. pap. text 12.00 (*0-13-613191-3*, Macmillan Coll) P-H.

Cole, Gordon. Drive & Survive. 180p. (Orig.). 1990. pap. 15.95 (*0-8464-1372-8*) Beekman Pubs.

Cole, Grace. Bill the Bull. (Illus.). 18p. (J). (ps-1). 1998. pap. 4.99 (*1-893181-07-3*, Simon & Northrop) Le Gesse Stevens.

— The Donkey's Thanksgiving. (Illus.). 16p. (J). 1998. pap. 4.99 (*1-893181-06-5*, Simon & Northrop) Le Gesse Stevens.

Cole, Grace. Fundamental Nursing Concepts & Skills. 2nd ed. (Illus.). 912p. 1996. teacher ed. write for info. (*0-8151-1816-3*) Mosby Inc.

— Fundamental Nursing Concepts & Skills, Set. 2nd ed. (Illus.). 912p. (C). 1996. text. write for info. (*0-8151-1926-7*) Mosby Inc.

Cole, Grace. School of Fish. (Illus.). 15p. (J). (ps-1). 1998. pap. 4.99 (*1-893181-05-7*, Simon & Northrop) Le Gesse Stevens.

Cole, Grace, ed. Basic Nursing Skills & Concepts Two. 2nd ed. (Illus.). 912p. (C). (gr. 13). 1995. text 41.95 (*0-8016-7884-6*, 07884) Mosby Inc.

Cole, Graham C. Pharmaceutical Production Facilities: Design & Applications. 2nd ed. LC 98-130223. 334p. 1998. 165.00 (*0-7484-0438-4*, Pub. by Tay Francis Ltd) Taylor & Francis.

Cole, Gregory. Passport Indonesia: Your Pocket Guide to Indonesian Business, Culture & Etiquette. Szerlip, Barbara, ed. LC 97-12973. (Passport to the World Ser.). (Illus.). 96p. (Orig.). 1996. pap. 6.95 (*1-885073-37-2*) Thomson Learn.

Cole, Gregory K. Pausal Sighs. 64p. 2000. pap. 9.95 (*1-56315-209-6*, Pub. by SterlingHse) Natl Bk Netwk.

***Cole, Gregory K.** Spanish Women Poets of the Generation of 1927. LC 99-36634. (Hispanic Literature Ser.: Vol. 48). 200p. 1999. text 79.95 (*0-7734-7944-9*) E Mellen.

Cole Group Editors. Tortilla International. LC 94-45540. (Cole's Cooking Companion Ser.). 96p. (Orig.). 1995. pap. 7.95 (*1-56426-803-9*) Cole Group.

Cole Group Editors Staff. Appetizing Hors D'Oeuvres. (Cole's Cooking Companion Ser.). (Illus.). 96p. (Orig.). 1995. pap. 7.95 (*1-56426-808-X*) Cole Group.

— Chocolate Conspiracy. (Cole's Cooking Companion Ser.). (Illus.). 96p. 1995. pap. 7.95 (*1-56426-815-2*) Cole Pub Co Inc.

— Glorious Garlic. (Cole's Cooking Companion Ser.). (Illus.). 96p. 1995. pap. 7.95 (*1-56426-809-8*) Cole Pub Co Inc.

— Low-Fat Italian. (Cole's Cooking Companion Ser.). (Illus.). 96p. 1996. pap. 7.95 (*1-56426-814-4*) Cole Group.

— Mexican Low-Fat Cooking. LC 95-45067. (Cole's Cooking Companion Ser.). (Illus.). 96p. 1996. pap. 7.95 (*1-56426-816-0*) Cole Group.

— Muffins & Other Quick Breads. (Cole's Cooking Companion Ser.). (Illus.). 96p. (Orig.). 1995. pap. 7.95 (*1-56426-811-X*) Cole Group.

Cole Group Editors Staff. Pasta Perfect. (Cooking Companion Ser.). 96p. (Orig.). 1995. pap. 47.70 (*1-56426-835-7*) Cole Group.

Cole Group Editors Staff. Pasta Perfect. LC 94-40117. (Cole's Cooking Companion Ser.). (Illus.). 96p. (Orig.). 1995. pap. 7.95 (*1-56426-802-0*) Cole Group.

— Pizza Primer. (Cole's Cooking Companion Ser.). 96p. 1995. pap. 7.95 (*1-56426-806-3*) Cole Group.

Cole Group Editors Staff. Red Hot Gourmet. (Cooking Companion Ser.). 96p. 1995. pap. 47.70 (*1-56426-836-5*) Cole Group.

Cole Group Editors Staff. Red Hot Gourmet. (Cole's Cooking Companion Ser.). 96p. 1995. pap. 7.95 (*1-56426-800-4*) Cole Group.

— The Rice Cooker. (Cole's Cooking Companion Ser.). (Illus.). 96p. (Orig.). 1995. pap. 7.95 (*1-56426-810-1*) Cole Group.

Cole Group Editors Staff. Sizzle: Barbecuing & Grilling. (Cooking Companion Ser.). 96p. (Orig.). 1995. pap. 47.70 (*1-56426-831-4*) Cole Group.

Cole Group Editors Staff. Sizzle: Barbecuing & Grilling. (Cole's Cooking Companion Ser.). 96p. (Orig.). 1995. pap. 7.95 (*1-56426-801-2*) Cole Group.

— Sweet Scoop: Low-Fat Frozen Desserts. LC 95-45658. (Cooking Companion Ser.). (Illus.). 96p. 1996. pap. 7.95 (*1-56426-818-7*) Cole Group.

— Vegetarian Gourmet. (Cole's Cooking Companion Ser.). 96p. (Orig.). 1995. pap. 7.95 (*1-56426-807-1*) Cole Group.

Cole Group Staff, jt. auth. see Gooch, Annette.

Cole, Gwen, ed. see Anderson Publishing Company Staff.

Cole, H. A. Understanding Nuclear Power. 300p. 1987. text 76.95 (*0-291-39704-2*, Pub. by Gower) Ashgate Pub Co.

Cole, H. S., jt. ed. see Camerini-Davalos, R. A.

Cole-Hamilton, D. J. & Williams, J. O., eds. Mechanisms of Reactions of Organometallic Compounds with Surfaces. (Illus.). 312p. 1989. 89.50 (*0-306-43205-6*, Plenum Trade) Perseus Pubng.

Cole, Harriette. How to Be: A Guide to Contemporary Living for African-Americans. 528p. 2000. per. 15.00 (*0-684-86308-1*) S&S Trade.

— How To Be: Contemporary Etiquette for African Americans. LC 98-48335. (Illus.). 528p. 1999. 24.50 (*0-684-82645-3*) Simon & Schuster.

— Jumping the Broom: The African-American Wedding Planner. 1995. pap. 26.95 (*0-8050-2142-6*) H Holt & Co.

— Jumping the Broom: The African-American Wedding Planner. (Illus.). 208p. 1995. 27.50 (*0-8050-2143-4*) H Holt & Co.

— Jumping the Broom Wedding Workbook: A Step-by-Step Write-in-Guide for Planning the Perfect Wedding. 1995. pap. 16.95 (*0-8050-4212-1*) H Holt & Co.

Cole, Harry. Billie's Bunch. 386p. 1996. pap. 11.95 (*0-7472-4830-3*, Pub. by Headline Bk Pub) Trafalgar.

— Understanding Radar. 2nd ed. (Illus.). 300p. 1992. text 65.00 (*0-632-03124-7*) Blackwell Sci.

Cole, Harry A. Helpmates: Support in Times of Critical Illness. 144p. 1991. pap. 12.00 (*0-664-25141-2*) Westminster John Knox.

— One in a Million. 352p. 1993. mass mkt. 4.50 (*1-55817-708-6*, Pinncle Kensgtn) Kensgtn Pub Corp.

Cole, Harry E. Stagecoach & Tavern Tales of the Old Northwest. Kellogg, Louise P., ed. LC 96-51161. (Shawnee Classics Ser.). (Illus.). 382p. 1997. pap. 12.95 (*0-8093-2125-4*) S Ill U Pr.

Cole, Heidi B., jt. auth. see Quigley, Thomas M.

Cole, Henderson, ed. Instrumentation for Tomorrow's Crystallography. (Transactions of the American Crystallographic Association Ser.: Vol. 12). 146p. 1976. pap. 25.00 (*0-686-60382-6*) Polycrystal Bk Serv.

Cole, Henri. The Look of Things: Poems. LC 94-23297. 71p. 1995. 20.00 (*0-679-43352-X*) Knopf.

— The Look of Things: Poems. 1996. pap. 13.00 (*0-679-76593-X*) Knopf.

— The Visible Man: Poems. LC 98-27443. 80p. 1998. 22.00 (*0-375-40396-5*) Knopf.

***Cole, Henri.** The Visible Man: Poems. 80p. 2000. pap. 15.00 (*0-375-70366-7*) Knopf.

Cole, Henry. Jack's Garden. LC 94-6249. (Illus.). 32p. (J). (ps-3). 1995. 16.00 (*0-688-13501-3*, Grenwillow Bks) HarpC Child Bks.

Cole, Henry. Jack's Garden. LC 94-6249. (Illus.). 24p. 1997. mass mkt. 5.95 (*0-688-15283-X*, Wm Morrow) Morrow Avon.

Cole, Henry. Jack's Garden. (J). 1997. 10.15 (*0-606-11514-5*, Pub. by Turtleback) Demco.

***Cole, Henry.** On the Way to the Beach. (J). 2001. 15.95 (*0-688-17515-5*, Grenwillow Bks) HarpC Child Bks.

Cole, Henry. I Took a Walk. LC 97-6692. 28p. (J). (ps-3). 1998. 15.00 (*0-688-15115-9*, Grenwillow Bks) HarpC Child Bks.

Cole, Henry, tr. see Calvin, John.

Cole, Henry P. Process Education: The New Direction for Elementary-Secondary Schools. LC 79-178843. 288p. 1972. 37.95 (*0-87778-030-7*) Educ Tech Pubns.

Cole, Henry S. & Stevens, Mark A. Learning from Success: Health Agency Effort to Improve Community Involvement in Communities Affected by Hazardous Waste Sites. (Illus.). 219p. (C). 1998. pap. text 40.00 (*0-7881-4850-8*) DIANE Pub.

Cole, Herbert. Heraldry & Floral Forms As Used in Decoration. LC 92-11091. 1992. reprint ed. 46.00 (*1-55888-550-1*) Omnigraphics Inc.

***Cole, Herbert & Turner, Jane, eds.** Encyclopedia of African Art. (Library of World Art). (Illus.). 900p. 2001. lib. bdg. 175.00 (*1-884446-08-6*) Groves Dictionaries.

Cole, Herbert M. & Aniakor, Chike C. Igbo Arts: Community & Cosmos. LC 84-51463. (Illus.). 256p. 1984. text 60.00 (*0-930741-00-5*) UCLA Fowler Mus.

Cole, Herbert M., jt. ed. see Fraser, Douglas.

Cole, Hillis R. & Haag, Judith H. The Complete Guide to Standard Script Formats Pt. 1: The Screenplay. 7th ed. 173p. (C). 1995. pap. text 18.95 (*0-929583-00-0*) CMC Pub CA.

Cole, Howard C. The All's Well Story from Boccaccio to Shakespeare. fac. ed. LC 81-2474. 159p. 1994. pap. 49.30 (*0-7837-7615-2*, 204736700007) Bks Demand.

— Quest of Inquirie: Some Contexts of Tudor Literature. LC 73-91621. 1973. 42.50 (*0-672-53583-1*) Irvington.

An Asterisk (*) at the beginning of an entry indicates that the title is appearing for the first time.

Cole, Howard N. Coronation & Royal Commemorative Medals, 1887-1977. (Illus.). 68p. (C). 1987. 35.00 (*0-7855-2219-0*, Pub. by Picton) St Mut.

Cole, Hubert. The War of the Roses. LC 74-157059. (The British at War Ser.). 208p. 1973. write for info. (*0-246-10618-2*) Grfton HrprCllns.

Cole, Hugh M. United States Army in World War 2, European Theater of Operations, the Ardennes, the Battle of the Bulge. 720p. 1994. pap. 47.00 (*0-16-061315-9*) USGPO.

Cole, J. Monday Philosophy. Jacquline, P. & Waido, L., eds. (Illus.). 76p. (Orig.). 1992. pap. 6.95 (*0-9632204-0-3*) J Alfieri.

Cole, J. A. Astrological Geomancy in Africa. Sichen, Kali, ed. (Illus.). 61p. 1990. pap. 9.95 (*0-916299-12-0*) North Scale Co.

Cole, J. A., et al, eds. Prokaryotic Structure & Function: A New Perspective. (Society for General Microbiology Symposium Ser.: No. 47). (Illus.). 452p. (C). 1992. text 125.00 (*0-521-41570-5*) Cambridge U Pr.

Cole, J. D. & Cook, L. P. Transonic Aerodynamics. (North-Holland Series in Applied Mathematics & Mechanics: Vol. 30). viii, 474p. 1986. 142.00 (*0-444-87958-7*, North Holland) Elsevier.

Cole, J. D., jt. auth. see Kevorkian, J.

Cole, J. David, jt. auth. see Watson, Virginia D.

Cole, J. M., jt. auth. see Berthelot, Jean M.

Cole, J. M., tr. see Hladik, J.

Cole, J. R. History of Greenbrier County: With Biographical Sketches. (Illus.). 347p. 1997. reprint ed. lib. bdg. 39.50 (*0-8328-6944-9*) Higginson Bk Co.

— History of Washington & Kent Counties, Rhode Island. (Illus.). 1344p. 1993. reprint ed. lib. bdg. 125.00 (*0-8328-3536-6*) Higginson Bk Co.

— Roots of North Indian Shi'ism in Iran & Iraq: Religion & State in Awadh, 1722-1859. (Comparative Studies on Muslim Societies: No. 6). 352p. (C). 1988. 55.00 (*0-520-05641-8*, Pub. by U CA Pr) Cal Prin Full Svc.

Cole, J. R., jt. auth. see Morton, Oren F.

Cole, Jack. California Angels. LC 96-23778. (America's Game Ser.). (Illus.). 32p. (J). (gr. 3-8). 1997. lib. bdg. 16.48 (*1-56239-676-5*) ABDO Pub Co.

— Plastic Man Archives. (Illus.). 224p. 1998. 49.95 (*1-56389-468-8*, Pub. by DC Comics) Time Warner.

— Wandering Voices: A Collection of Verse. LC 99-31009. 72p. 1999. pap. text 14.95 (*0-7734-3125-X*) E Mellen.

Cole, Jack T., jt. auth. see Cole, Martha L.

Cole, Jackie. Osborne & Little Style: Decorating Themes & Combinations. LC 97-72787. (Illus.). 176p. 1997. 40.00 (*0-8212-2385-2*, Pub. by Bulfinch Pr) Little.

Cole, Jackie, jt. auth. see Willis, Michelle.

***Cole, Jackson.** The Death Riders. LC 98-48522. 167 p. 1999. write for info. (*0-7540-3651-0*) Chivers N Amer.

Cole, Jackson. The Death Riders. LC 98-48522. Date not set. 30.00 (*0-7838-0445-8*, G K Hall Lrg Type) Mac Lib Ref.

— The Devil's Legion. large type ed. (Nightingale Ser.). 1996. pap. 17.95 (*0-7838-1617-0*, G K Hall Lrg Type) Mac Lib Ref.

***Cole, Jackson.** Guns of Mist River: A Texas Ranger Novel. large type ed. LC 99-29287. 1999. pap. 19.95 (*0-7838-8648-9*, G K Hall & Co) Mac Lib Ref.

Cole, Jackson. Land Grab. LC 99-19636. 1999. 19.95 (*0-7838-8577-6*, G K Hall & Co) Mac Lib Ref.

— The Land Pirates. large type ed. 1981. 12.00 (*0-7089-0729-6*) Ulverscroft.

— Texas Fury. large type ed. LC 97-13073. (Nightingale Ser.). 181p. 1997. pap. 18.95 (*0-7838-8203-3*, G K Hall Lrg Type) Mac Lib Ref.

— Thunder Range: A Jim Hatfield Texas Ranger Western. large type ed. LC 98-21236. 188p. 1998. 18.95 (*0-7838-0244-7*, G K Hall & Co) Mac Lib Ref.

***Cole, Jackson.** Two-Gun Devil. large type ed. LC 99-54773. (G. K. Hall Nightingale Ser.). 208p. 2000. 20.95 (*0-7838-8847-3*, G K Hall & Co) Mac Lib Ref.

***Cole, Jackson A.** Killer Country. LC 99-35749. 1999. pap. 21.95 (*0-7838-8719-1*, G K Hall Lrg Type) Mac Lib Ref.

Cole, Jackson A. Texas Trigger. large type ed. (Linford Western Library). 272p. 1992. pap. 16.99 (*0-7089-7250-0*, Linford) Ulverscroft.

Cole, James. A Brave Passenger. LC 94-28271. 64p. (Orig.). 1995. pap. 10.00 (*1-881119-43-2*) Pyncheon Hse.

***Cole, James, III.** A Squirrel on My Roof. 1999. pap. write for info. (*1-58235-111-2*) Watermrk Pr.

Cole, James H. The People vs. the Taipings: Bao Lisheng's "Righteous Army of Dongan" LC 81-80965. (China Research Monographs: No. 21). 83p. 1981. pap. 7.00 (*0-912966-39-4*) IEAS.

— Shaohsing: Competition & Cooperation in Nineteenth-Century China. LC 86-30825. (Monographs: No. 44). xvi, 315p. 1986. 21.00 (*0-8165-0994-8*) Assn Asian Studies.

— Twentieth Century China: An Annotated Bibliography of Reference Works in Chinese & Japanese, 2 vols. (Illus.). 1500p. 2000. 225.00 (*0-7656-0395-0*, East Gate Bk) M E Sharpe.

— Updating Wilkinson: An Annotated Bibliography of Reference Works on Imperial China Published Since 1973. LC 91-91848. viii, 111p. (Orig.). (C). 1991. pap. text 12.00 (*0-9629122-0-4*) J H Cole.

Cole, James K., ed. see Nebraska Symposium on Motivation Staff.

Cole, James L., jt. auth. see Baldus, David C.

Cole, James M. Cancellations & Killers of the Banknote Era, 1870-1894. (Illus.). 345p. 1995. 49.50 (*0-9603548-5-9*) US Phil Classics.

Cole, Jameson. A Killing in Quail County. 1997. per. 4.99 (*0-373-26251-5*, 1-26251-8, Wrldwide Lib) Harlequin Bks.

Cole, Janis & Dale, Holly. Calling the Shots: Profiles of Women Filmmakers. 288p. 1994. pap. 16.95 (*1-55082-085-0*, Pub. by Quarry Pr) LPC InBook.

Cole, Jas. E. Cole. Genealogy of the Family of Cole of the Co. of Devon, & of Those of Its Branches Which Settled in Suffolk, Hampshire, Surrey, Lincolnshire & Ireland. 66p. 1997. reprint ed. pap. 13.00 (*0-8328-8008-6*); reprint ed. lib. bdg. 23.00 (*0-8328-8007-8*) Higginson Bk Co.

Cole, Jeff. Eyeball Animation Drawing Pad & Hand Book. 1997. 15.95 (*0-939251-92-2*) Accord CO.

Cole, Jefferey, jt. auth. see Swokowski, Earl W.

Cole, Jeffery A., jt. auth. see Swokowski, Earl W.

Cole, Jeffrey. The New Racism in Europe: A Sicilian Ethnography. LC 97-4075. (Studies in Social & Cultural Anthropology: Vol. 107). (Illus.). 170p. (C). 1998. text 54.95 (*0-521-58493-0*) Cambridge U Pr.

Cole, Jeffrey A. The Potosi Mita, 1573-1700: Compulsory Indian Labor in the Andes. LC 84-40331. (Illus.). 224p. 1985. 39.50 (*0-8047-1256-5*) Stanford U Pr.

Cole, Jeffrey A., jt. auth. see Swokowski, Earl W.

Cole, Jennifer & Kisserberth, Charles, eds. Perspectives in Phonology. LC 94-30497. (CSLI Lecture Notes Ser.: Vol. 51). 328p. 1995. pap. 19.95 (*1-881526-54-2*) CSLI.

Cole, Jennifer Elin, jt. auth. see Hirschman, Jessica Elin.

Cole, Jennifer S. Planar Phonology & Morphology. (Linguistics Ser.). 219p. 1991. text 15.00 (*0-8153-0165-0*) Garland.

Cole, Jeremiah, ed. Invitation to Change 1991 Winners. (Better Government Competition Ser.). 84p. (Orig.). 1991. pap. 10.00 (*0-929930-07-X*) Pioneer Inst.

***Cole, Jerry R.** Bless This Mind: Back to School Celebrations. (Illus.). 1999. pap. 10.00 (*0-7880-1442-0*) CSS OH.

Cole, Jerryne, jt. auth. see Potter, Louise.

Cole, Jesse A. & Plantz, Scott H., eds. Emergency Medicine: Pretest Self-Assessment & Review. (Pretest Specialty Level Ser.). (Illus.). 356p. 1990. pap. text 45.00 (*0-07-050323-0*) McGraw-Hill HPD.

Cole, Jim. The Controllers: A View of Our Responsibility. (Illus.). (C). 1971. pap. 6.95 (*0-88310-004-5*) Publishers Consult.

— The Controllers: A View of Our Responsibility. 2nd ed. (Illus.). 100p. 1989. reprint ed. pap. 4.95 (*0-9601200-0-9*) Growing Images.

— The Facade: A View of Our Behavior. (Illus.). 64p. (C). 1970. pap. 5.95 (*0-88310-003-7*) Publishers Consult.

— The Facade-A View of Ourselves. (C). 1970. pap. 2.75 (*0-9601200-1-7*) Growing Images.

— Facing Our Future: Moving from Denial into Action. (Illus.). 290p. (Orig.). 1990. pap. 14.95 (*0-9601200-7-6*) Growing Images.

— Fifty More Programs in BASIC for the Home, School & Office. 96p. (Orig.). 1981. pap. 9.95 (*0-86668-003-9*) ARCsoft.

— Fifty Programs in BASIC for the Home, School & Office. 2nd ed. (Illus.). 96p. 1981. pap. 9.95 (*0-86668-502-2*) ARCsoft.

— Filtering People: A View of Our Prejudices. (Illus.). 200p. (Orig.). 1987. pap. 9.95 (*0-317-55016-0*) Growing Images.

— Forty-four Programs for the TRS-80 Model 100 Portable Computer. 96p. 1983. 8.95 (*0-86668-034-9*) ARCsoft.

— The Helpers: A View of Our Helpfulness. (C). 1973. pap. 6.95 (*0-9601200-3-3*) Growing Images.

— The Helpers: A View of Our Helpfulness. (Illus.). (C). 1973. pap. 6.95 (*0-88310-005-3*) Publishers Consult.

— Holder: A View of Our Relationships. (Illus.). (C). 1973. pap. 5.95 (*0-88310-006-1*) Publishers Consult.

— The Holder-A View of Our Relationships. (C). 1975. pap. 6.95 (*0-9601200-4-1*) Growing Images.

— Murder in the Mansion & Other Computer Adventures. 2nd ed. (Illus.). 96p. 1981. pap. 6.95 (*0-86668-501-4*) ARCsoft.

— Ninety-Nine Tips & Tricks for the New Pocket Computers. 128p. (Orig.). 1982. pap. 7.95 (*0-86668-019-5*) ARCsoft.

— One Hundred One Pocket Computer Programming Tips & Tricks. (Illus.). 128p. (Orig.). 1982. pap. 7.95 (*0-86668-004-7*) ARCsoft.

— Pocket Computer Programming Made Easy. (Illus.). 128p. (Orig.). 1982. pap. 8.95 (*0-86668-009-8*) ARCsoft.

— Practical PC-2-PC-1500 Pocket Computer Programs. 96p. 1983. 7.95 (*0-86668-028-4*) ARCsoft.

— Thwarting Anger: A View of Anger. 1985. pap. 5.50 (*0-9601200-5-X*) Growing Images.

— Thwarting Anger: A View of How We Keep Anger Alive. (Illus.). 1985. pap. 5.50 (*0-88310-007-X*) Publishers Consult.

— Utah Wildlife Viewing Guide. LC 90-80041. (Watchable Wildlife Ser.). (Illus.). 88p. 1990. pap. 8.95 (*1-56044-023-6*) Falcon Pub Inc.

Cole, Jim E. & Williams, James W., eds. Serials Cataloging No. II: Modern Perspectives & International Developments. LC 92-18492. (Serials Librarian Ser.: Vol. 22, Nos. 1-4). (Illus.). 415p. 1993. lib. bdg. 89.95 (*1-56024-281-7*) Haworth Pr.

— Serials Management in the Electronic Era: Papers in Honor of Peter Gellatly, Founding Editor of The Serials Librarian. LC 96-38911. (Serials Librarian Ser.: Vol. 29, Nos. 3 & 4). 234p. (C). 1997. 39.95 (*0-7890-0021-0*) Haworth Pr.

Cole, Jim E. & Zajanc, Jackie, eds. Serials Cataloging: The State of the Art. LC 87-2877. (Serials Librarian Ser.: Vol. 12, Nos. 1-2). 184p. 1987. text 49.95 (*0-86656-619-8*) Haworth Pr.

Cole, Joan H., et al. Muscles in Action: An Approach to Manual Muscle Testing. (Illus.). 184p. 1988. pap. 29.00 (*0-443-03613-6*) Church.

Cole, Joan S., jt. auth. see Cole, Kenneth J.

Cole, Joan S., ed. see Cole, Kenneth J.

Cole, Joanna. Anna Banana: One Hundred One Jump-Rope Rhymes. LC 88-29108. (Illus.). 64p. (J). (gr. 3-7). 1989. 16.00 (*0-688-07788-9*, Wm Morrow); mass mkt. 7.95 (*0-688-08809-0*, Wm Morrow) Morrow Avon.

— Asking about Sex & Growing Up: A Question-&-Answer Book for Boys & Girls. LC 87-26140. (Illus.). 96p. (J). (gr. 3-7). 1988. 16.00 (*0-688-06927-4*, Wm Morrow) Morrow Avon.

— Asking about Sex & Growing Up: A Question-&-Answer Book for Boys & Girls. LC 87-26140. (Illus.). 96p. (J). (gr. 4-7). 1988. mass mkt. 4.95 (*0-688-06928-2*, Wm Morrow) Morrow Avon.

— El Autobus Magico Conoce al Escuadron de la Discomposicion. (SPA.). 32p. (J). (ps-3). 1995. pap. 2.50 (*0-590-62236-6*, Cartwheel) Scholastic Inc.

— El Autobus Magico Dentro De Un Huracan. LC 49-233270. (Magic School Bus Ser.).Tr. of Magic School Bus Inside a Hurricane. (SPA., Illus.). 56p. (J). (gr. 4-7). 1996. pap. text 4.95 (*0-590-94365-0*) Scholastic Inc.

Cole, Joanna. El Autobus Magico Dentro De Un Huracan.Tr. of Magic School Bus Inside a Hurricane. (SPA.). (J). 1996. 10.15 (*0-606-09232-3*, Pub. by Turtleback) Demco.

Cole, Joanna. El Autobus Magico en el Artico: Un Libro Sobre el Calor. (Magic School Bus Ser.).Tr. of Magic School Bus in the Arctic: A Book about Heat. (Illus.). (J). (gr. k-2). 1998. pap. text 3.50 (*0-590-38664-6*) Scholastic Inc.

***Cole, Joanna.** El Autobus Magico en el Artico: Un Libro Sobre el Calor.Tr. of Magic School Bus in the Arctic: A Book about Heat. (Illus.). (J). 1999. 8.95 (*0-606-15520-1*, Pub. by Turtleback) Demco.

Cole, Joanna. El Autobus Magico En El Cuerpo De Ralphie: Un Libro Sobre Germenes. (J). 1995. 7.70 (*0-606-07469-4*, Pub. by Turtleback) Demco.

— El Autobus Magico en el Cuerpo Humano. (Autobus Magico Ser.). (SPA.). (J). 1991. 10.15 (*0-606-05820-6*, Pub. by Turtleback) Demco.

— El Autobus Magico en el Cuerpo Humano-Spanish. (SPA., Illus.). 56p. (J). (gr. 4-7). 1994. pap. 4.95 (*0-590-46428-0*) Scholastic Inc.

— El Autobus Magico en el Interior de la Tierra. Cordoba, Maria & Cortes, Jose L., trs. from ENG. (SPA., Illus.). 56p. (J). (gr. 1-4). 1993. pap. 4.95 (*0-590-46342-X*) Scholastic Inc.

— El Autobus Magico en el Interior de la Tierra. (Autobus Magico Ser.). (SPA.). (J). 1991. 10.15 (*0-606-02621-5*, Pub. by Turtleback) Demco.

Cole, Joanna. El Autobus Magico En El Sistema Solar. (Magic School Bus Ser.).Tr. of Magic School Bus in the Solar System. (J). (gr. 1-4). 1991. 10.15 (*0-606-06354-4*, Pub. by Turtleback) Demco.

Cole, Joanna. El Autobus Magico En Tiempos De Los Dinosaurios. 1995. 10.15 (*0-606-09015-0*, Pub. by Turtleback) Demco.

— El Autobus Magico en Tiempos de los Dinosauros. (Magic School Bus Ser.).Tr. of Magic School Bus in the Time of the Dinosaurs. (SPA., Illus.). 56p. (J). (gr. 1-4). 1996. mass mkt. 4.95 (*0-590-67702-0*) Scholastic Inc.

Cole, Joanna. El Autobus Magico es Devorado. (Autobus Magico Ser.). 1996. 8.19 (*0-606-13354-2*, Pub. by Turtleback) Demco.

Cole, Joanna. El Autobus Magico Explota.Tr. of Magic School Bus Blows Its Top. (SPA.). (J). (ps-3). 1996. pap. 2.99 (*0-590-73920-4*) Scholastic Inc.

Cole, Joanna. El Autobus Magico Explota. (Autobus Magico Ser.).Tr. of Magic School Bus Blows Its Top. 1996. 8.19 (*0-606-13355-0*, Pub. by Turtleback) Demco.

Cole, Joanna. El Autobus Magico Hace Un Arco Iris: Un Libro Sobre Color. (SPA.). (J). (gr. k-2). 1997. pap. 2.99 (*0-590-39099-6*) Scholastic Inc.

Cole, Joanna. El Autobus Magico Hace Un Arco Iris: Un Libro Sobre Color. 1997. 8.44 (*0-606-12691-0*) Turtleback.

Cole, Joanna. El Autobus Magico Juega a la Pelota: Un Libro Sobre Fuerzas. (Autobus Magico Ser.). (SPA., Illus.). 32p. (J). (gr. k-2). 1998. pap. 2.99 (*0-590-76128-5*, Blue Sky Press) Scholastic Inc.

— El Autobus Magico Juega a la Pelota: Un Libro Sobre Fuerzas. (Autobus Magico Ser.). (SPA.). 1998. 8.19 (*0-606-13356-9*, Pub. by Turtleback) Demco.

— El Autobus Magico Planta una Semilla. LC 94-40027. (SPA., Illus.). 32p. (J). (ps-3). 1995. pap. 2.99 (*0-590-22851-X*) Scholastic Inc.

— El Autobus Magico Salta Hasta Llegar a Casa: Un Libro Sobre Los Habitats de Los Animales. LC 94-40024. (SPA., Illus.). 32p. (J). (ps-3). 1995. pap. 2.50 (*0-590-20548-X*) Scholastic Inc.

***Cole, Joanna.** El Autobus Magico se Descompone.Tr. of Magic School Bus in a Pickle. (SPA.). (gr. k-2). 1998. pap. 3.50 (*0-590-76126-9*) Scholastic Bk Fairs.

Cole, Joanna. El Autobus Magico Se Reseca. (Magic School Bus Ser.).Tr. of Magic School Bus All Dried Up. (SPA.). (J). (ps-3). 1996. pap. 2.99 (*0-590-73921-2*) Scholastic Inc.

— El Autobus Magico Se Zambulle: Un Libro Sobre los Arrecifes de Coral. (Magic School Bus Ser.).Tr. of Magic School Bus Takes a Dive: A Book about Coral Reefs. (Illus.). (J). (gr. k-2). 1998. pap. text 3.50 (*0-590-51040-1*) Scholastic Inc.

— El Autobus Magico Siente un Inquietante Hormigueo.Tr. of Magic School Bis Gets Ants in Its Pants. (SPA.). (J). (ps-3). 1996. pap. 2.99 (*0-590-73919-0*) Scholastic Inc.

— El Autobus Magico Sube Y Baja: Un Libro Sobre Como Flotar Y Hundirse. (Magic School Bus Ser.).Tr. of Magic School Bus Ups & Downs. (SPA.). (J). (gr. k-2). 1997. pap. 2.99 (*0-614-29033-3*) Scholastic Inc.

— El Autobus Magico Ve las Estrella. (Magic School Bus Ser.).Tr. of Magic School Bus Out of This World. (SPA.). (J). (ps-3). 1996. pap. text 2.99 (*0-590-94520-3*) Scholastic Inc.

— Autobus Magico Vevastra: A Book about Stars. (SPA.). 32p. (ps-3). 1999. mass mkt. 3.50 (*0-439-05613-6*) Scholastic Inc.

— El Autobus Magico Viaja por el Agua. Cano, Isabel & Cortes, Jose L., trs. from ENG. (SPA., Illus.). 56p. (J). (gr. 1-4). 1993. pap. 4.95 (*0-590-46427-2*) Scholastic Inc.

— El Autobus Magico Viaja por el Agua. (Autobus Magico Ser.). (SPA.). (J). 1991. 11.15 (*0-606-05252-6*, Pub. by Turtleback) Demco.

— El Autobus Magico Vuelo Nocturno. (Magic School Bus Ser.).Tr. of Magic School Bus Going Batty. (SPA., Illus.). (J). (ps-3). 1996. pap. text 2.99 (*0-590-94519-X*) Scholastic Inc.

— El Autobus Magico y la Excursion al Campo Electrico. (Autobus Magico Ser.). (SPA., Illus.). (J). (gr. 1-4). 1999. pap. 4.99 (*0-590-00637-1*) Scholastic Inc.

— Best Loved Folktales of the World. 1982. 15.95 (*0-385-18520-0*) Doubleday.

— Bony-Legs. LC 85-5070. (Illus.). 48p. (J). (ps-3). 1984. text, lib. bdg. 16.00 (*0-02-722970-X*, Four Winds Pr) S&S Childrens.

— Bony-Legs. LC 85-5070. (Illus.). 48p. (J). (ps-3). 1986. pap. 3.99 (*0-590-40516-0*) Scholastic Inc.

— Bony-Legs. (J). 1983. 9.19 (*0-606-00565-X*, Pub. by Turtleback) Demco.

— Bully Trouble. LC 89-3757. (Step into Reading Ser.: A Step 2 Book). (Illus.). 48p. (J). (ps-3). 1989. pap. 3.99 (*0-394-84949-3*, Pub. by Random Bks Yng Read) Random.

Cole, Joanna. Bully Trouble. (Step into Reading Ser.: A Step 2 Book). (J). (gr. 1-3). 1989. 9.19 (*0-606-12206-0*, Pub. by Turtleback) Demco.

— Card Games. 2000. write for info. (*0-688-17729-8*, Wm Morrow) Morrow Avon.

— Crazy Eights & Other Card Games. LC 93-5427. 1994. 12.15 (*0-606-06293-9*, Pub. by Turtleback) Demco.

— Dentro de una Colmena. (SPA.). (gr. 4-7). 1998. pap. text 4.95 (*0-590-25745-5*) Scholastic Inc.

Cole, Joanna. Doctor Change. LC 86-881. (Illus.). 32p. (J). (ps-3). 1986. lib. bdg. 12.88 (*0-688-06136-2*, Wm Morrow) Morrow Avon.

— Don't Tell the Whole World. LC 89-29283. (Illus.). 32p. (J). (gr. k-3). 1990. 13.95 (*0-690-04809-2*); lib. bdg. 13.89 (*0-690-04811-4*) HarpC Child Bks.

— Don't Tell the Whole World! 1992. 11.15 (*0-606-01043-2*, Pub. by Turtleback) Demco.

Cole, Joanna. A Fish Hatches. LC 78-13445. (Illus.). 40p. (J). (gr. k-3). 1978. 14.89 (*0-688-32153-4*, Wm Morrow) Morrow Avon.

Cole, Joanna. Fun on the Run: Travel Games & Songs. 128p. 1999. mass mkt. 6.95 (*0-688-14662-7*, Wm Morrow) Morrow Avon.

***Cole, Joanna.** The Gator Girls: Get Well, Gators!, Vol. 4. (J). (gr. 1-3). 1998. 15.89 (*0-688-14787-9*, Wm Morrow) Morrow Avon.

Cole, Joanna. The Gator Girls: Get Well, Gators!, Vol. 4. Vol. 3. (Illus.). 64p. (J). (gr. 1-4). 1998. 16.00 (*0-688-14786-0*, Wm Morrow) Morrow Avon.

***Cole, Joanna.** Gator Halloween. 2000. pap. 5.95 (*0-688-17725-5*, Wm Morrow) Morrow Avon.

— Get Well, Gators. (gr. 1-4). 2000. pap. 4.95 (*0-688-17641-0*, Wm Morrow) Morrow Avon.

Cole, Joanna. Give a Dog a Bone: Stories, Poems, Jokes & Riddles about Dogs. (Illus.). 96p. (gr. 2-5). 1999. pap. 7.99 (*0-439-08708-2*) Scholastic Inc.

***Cole, Joanna.** Hopscotch & Sidewalk Game. 2000. write for info. (*0-688-17709-3*, Wm Morrow) Morrow Avon.

Cole, Joanna. How I Was Adopted: Samantha's Story. LC 94-42969. (Illus.). 48p. (J). (gr. k up). 1995. 16.00 (*0-688-11929-8*, Wm Morrow) Morrow Avon.

— How You Were Born. rev. ed. LC 92-23970. (Illus.). 48p. (J). (ps-3). 1994. reprint ed. mass mkt. 5.95 (*0-688-12061-X*, Wm Morrow) Morrow Avon.

— How You Were Born: Illustrated with Photographs. rev. ed. LC 92-23970. (Illus.). 48p. (J). (ps-3). 1993. 14.95 (*0-688-12059-8*, Wm Morrow) Morrow Avon.

— Hungry, Hungry Sharks. LC 85-2218. (Step into Reading Ser.: A Step 2 Book). (Illus.). 48p. (J). (gr. 1-3). 1986. pap. 3.99 (*0-394-87471-4*, Pub. by Random Bks Yng Read) Random.

Cole, Joanna. Hungry, Hungry Sharks. (Step into Reading Ser.: A Step 2 Book). (J). (gr. 1-3). 1986. 9.19 (*0-606-12347-4*, Pub. by Turtleback) Demco.

Cole, Joanna. I'm a Big Brother. LC 96-14850. (Illus.). 32p. (J). (ps up). 1997. 5.95 (*0-688-14507-8*, Wm Morrow) Morrow Avon.

— I'm a Big Sister Now. LC 96-14837. (Illus.). 32p. (J). 1997. 5.95 (*0-688-14509-4*, Wm Morrow) Morrow Avon.

***Cole, Joanna.** Jump Rope Rhymes. 2000. write for info. (*0-688-17708-5*, Wm Morrow) Morrow Avon.

Cole, Joanna. Liz Busca un Hogar. (Magic School Bus:). Orig. Title: Liz Looks for a Home. (SPA., Illus.). 24p. (J). (ps-1). 1999. pap. 3.50 (*0-590-68935-5*) Scholastic Inc.

— Liz Looks for a Home. LC PZ7.W51937Li 1998. (Magic School Bus:). (Illus.). 24p. (J). (ps-1). 1998. pap. 2.99 (*0-590-81839-2*, Pub. by Scholastic Inc) Penguin Putnam.

— Liz Pone Orden. (Magic School Bus:).Tr. of Liz Sorts It Out. (SPA.). (J). (ps-1). 1999. pap. 3.50 (*0-439-05869-4*) Scholastic Inc.

— Liz Sorts It Out. LC QA248.W47 1998. (Magic School Bus:). (Illus.). 24p. (J). (ps-1). 1998. pap. 2.99 (*0-590-81838-4*, Pub. by Scholastic Inc) Penguin Putnam.

— The Magic School Bus: Hello Out There. 24p. (J). (gr. k-2). 1995. pap. 3.50 (*0-590-52792-4*) Scholastic Inc.

C

An Asterisk (*) at the beginning of an entry indicates that the title is appearing for the first time.

— The Magic School Bus All Dried Up: A Book about Deserts. (Magic School Bus Ser.). (J). (ps-3). 1996. pap. 2.99 (*0-590-50831-8*) Scholastic Inc.

— The Magic School Bus Answers Questions: A Book of Questions & Answers. (Magic School Bus Ser.). (Illus.). 32p. (J). (gr. k-2). 1999. mass mkt. 3.50 (*0-439-04332-8*) Scholastic Inc.

— The Magic School Bus Ant Farm Package. (Illus.). (J). (ps-3). 1996. pap. 9.99 (*0-590-56621-0*) Scholastic Inc.

— The Magic School Bus at the Waterworks. (Magic School Bus Ser.). (FRE., Illus.). (J). (gr. 1-4). pap. 6.99 (*0-590-71792-8*); pap. 13.99 incl. audio (*0-590-73932-8*) Scholastic Inc.

— The Magic School Bus at the Waterworks. (Magic School Bus Ser.). (Illus.). 56p. (J). (ps-3). 1986. 14.95 (*0-590-43739-9*, Scholastic Hardcover) Scholastic Inc.

— The Magic School Bus at the Waterworks. LC 86-6672. (Magic School Bus Ser.). (Illus.). 40p. (J). (gr. 1-4). 1988. pap. 4.95 (*0-590-40360-5*, Scholastic Hardcover) Scholastic Inc.

— The Magic School Bus at the Waterworks. (Magic School Bus Ser.). (Illus.). (J). (gr. 1-4). 1995. 14.95 (*0-614-03341-1*) Scholastic Inc.

Cole, Joanna. The Magic School Bus at the Waterworks. (Magic School Bus Ser.). (J). (gr. 1-4). 1986. 10.15 (*0-606-03611-3*, Pub. by Turtleback) Demco.

Cole, Joanna. The Magic School Bus at the Waterworks. large type ed. (Magic School Bus Ser.). (J). (ps-3). 1989. 19.95 (*0-590-72488-6*) Scholastic Inc.

— The Magic School Bus at the Waterworks, Big Bk. large type ed. (Magic School Bus Ser.). (FRE., Illus.). (J). (gr. 1-4). 35.99 (*0-590-73528-4*) Scholastic Inc.

— The Magic School Bus Beehive Activity. 1996. pap. write for info. (*0-590-94832-6*, Scholastic Hardcover) Scholastic Inc.

— The Magic School Bus Briefcase, 5 bks., Set. (Magic School Bus Ser.). (Illus.). (J). (ps-3). 1995. pap. 24.75 (*0-590-22300-3*) Scholastic Inc.

— The Magic School Bus Explores the Senses. LC 98-18662. (Magic School Bus Ser.). (Illus.). 47p. (J). (gr. 1-4). 1999. 15.95 (*0-590-44697-5*); 159.50 (*0-439-05987-9*) Scholastic Inc.

— The Magic School Bus Gets Planted: A Book about Photosynthesis, Incl. planting pkg. (Magic School Bus Ser.). (Illus.). (J). (gr. k-2). 1997. pap. text 9.99 (*0-590-33117-5*) Scholastic Inc.

— The Magic School Bus Hello Out There: A Sticker Book about the Solar System. LC 96-143571. 16p. (J). (ps-3). 1995. pap. 3.50 (*0-590-88129-9*, Scholastic Hardcover) Scholastic Inc.

— The Magic School Bus in the Arctic: A Book about Heat. LC QC256.S32 1998. (Magic School Bus Ser.). (Illus.). 32p. (J). (gr. k-2). 1998. pap. 2.99 (*0-590-18724-4*, Pub. by Scholastic Inc) Penguin Putnam.

— The Magic School Bus in the Rain Forest: A Book about Rainforest Ecology. LC 99-158336. (Magic School Bus Ser.). (Illus.). 32p. (J). (gr. k-2). 1998. pap. 8.95 (*0-590-81837-6*, Pub. by Scholastic Inc) Penguin Putnam.

— The Magic School Bus Inside a Beehive. (Magic School Bus Ser.). (SPA., Illus.). 56p. (J). (gr. 1-4). pap. 4.95 (*0-590-37042-1*); pap. 4.95 (*0-590-44685-1*) Scholastic Inc.

— The Magic School Bus Inside a Beehive. LC 95-38288. (Magic School Bus Ser.). (Illus.). 56p. (J). (ps-3). 1996. 15.95 (*0-590-44684-3*) Scholastic Inc.

— The Magic School Bus Inside a Beehive. (Magic School Bus Ser.). (Illus.). (J). (ps-3). 1998. pap. text 4.95 (*0-590-25721-8*) Scholastic Inc.

— The Magic School Bus Inside a Beehive. (Magic School Bus Ser.). (Illus.). (J). (gr. 1-4). 1997. 10.15 (*0-606-12881-6*, Pub. by Turtleback) Demco.

— The Magic School Bus Inside a Beehive. (Magic School Bus Ser.). (Illus.). (J). (gr. 1-4). 1998. 10.15 (*0-606-12989-8*, Pub. by Turtleback) Demco.

— The Magic School Bus Inside a Hurricane. LC 94-34703. (Magic School Bus Ser.). (Illus.). 48p. (J). (gr. 1-4). 1996. pap. 4.95 (*0-590-44687-8*) Scholastic Inc.

Cole, Joanna. The Magic School Bus Inside a Hurricane. (Magic School Bus Ser.). (J). (gr. 1-4). 1995. 10.15 (*0-606-09588-8*, Pub. by Turtleback) Demco.

Cole, Joanna. The Magic School Bus Inside the Earth. LC 87-4563. (Magic School Bus Ser.). (Illus.). 56p. (J). (ps-3). 1987. 15.95 (*0-590-40759-7*, Scholastic Hardcover) Scholastic Inc.

— The Magic School Bus Inside the Earth. (Magic School Bus Ser.). (Illus.). 56p. (J). (gr. 1-4). 1989. pap. 4.95 (*0-590-40760-0*, Scholastic Hardcover) Scholastic Inc.

— The Magic School Bus Inside the Earth. (Magic School Bus Ser.). (Illus.). (J). (gr. 1-4). 1989. 9.90 (*0-606-04012-9*, Pub. by Turtleback) Demco.

— The Magic School Bus Inside the Human Body. LC 88-3070. (Magic School Bus Ser.). (Illus.). 56p. (J). (gr. 1-4). 1990. pap. 4.95 (*0-590-41427-5*, Scholastic Hardcover) Scholastic Inc.

— The Magic School Bus Inside the Human Body. (Magic School Bus Ser.). (Illus.). (J). (gr. 1-4). 1992. pap. 3.95 (*0-685-53602-5*) Scholastic Inc.

— The Magic School Bus Inside the Human Body. (Magic School Bus Ser.). (J). (ps-3). 1993. 19.95 (*0-590-72633-1*) Scholastic Inc.

— The Magic School Bus Inside the Human Body. (Magic School Bus Ser.). (Illus.). (J). (gr. 1-4). 1990. 9.90 (*0-606-04736-0*, Pub. by Turtleback) Demco.

— The Magic School Bus Lost in the Solar System. LC 89-10185. (Magic School Bus Ser.). (Illus.). 56p. (J). (ps-3). 1990. 15.95 (*0-590-41428-3*, Scholastic Hardcover) Scholastic Inc.

— The Magic School Bus Lost in the Solar System. LC 89-10185. (Magic School Bus Ser.). (Illus.). 40p. (J). (gr. 1-4). 1992. pap. 4.95 (*0-590-41429-1*, Scholastic Hardcover) Scholastic Inc.

— The Magic School Bus Lost in the Solar System. (Magic School Bus Ser.). (J). (ps-3). 1993. 19.95 (*0-590-72599-8*) Scholastic Inc.

— The Magic School Bus Lost in the Solar System. (Magic School Bus Ser.). (SPA., Illus.). 56p. (J). (gr. 1-4). 1994. pap. 4.95 (*0-590-46429-9*) Scholastic Inc.

— The Magic School Bus Lost in the Solar System. (Magic School Bus Ser.). (Illus.). (J). (gr. 1-4). 1990. 10.15 (*0-606-00583-8*, Pub. by Turtleback) Demco.

— The Magic School Bus Makes a Rainbow: A Book about Color. (Magic School Bus Ser.). (Illus.). 32p. (J). (gr. k-2). 1997. pap. text 2.99 (*0-590-92251-3*) Scholastic Inc.

Cole, Joanna. The Magic School Bus Makes a Rainbow: A Book about Color. (Magic School Bus Ser.). (Illus.). (J). (gr. k-2). 1997. 8.95 (*0-606-12763-1*) Turtleback.

Cole, Joanna. The Magic School Bus on the Ocean Floor. (Magic School Bus Ser.). (FRE., Illus.). (J). (gr. 1-4). pap. 6.99 (*0-590-24318-7*) Scholastic Inc.

— The Magic School Bus on the Ocean Floor. LC 91-17695. (Magic School Bus Ser.). (Illus.). 56p. (J). (ps-3). 1992. 15.95 (*0-590-41430-5*, 003, Scholastic Hardcover) Scholastic Inc.

— The Magic School Bus on the Ocean Floor. (Magic School Bus Ser.). (Illus.). (J). (ps-3). 1993. 19.95 (*0-590-72836-9*) Scholastic Inc.

— The Magic School Bus on the Ocean Floor. LC 91-17695. (Magic School Bus Ser.). (Illus.). 56p. (J). (gr. 1-4). 1994. pap. 4.95 (*0-590-41431-3*) Scholastic Inc.

— The Magic School Bus on the Ocean Floor. (Magic School Bus Ser.). (SPA., Illus.). 56p. (J). (ps-3). 1994. pap. 4.95 (*0-590-47506-1*) Scholastic Inc.

— The Magic School Bus on the Ocean Floor. (Magic School Bus Ser.). (Illus.). (J). (gr. 1-4). 1994. 9.90 (*0-606-06552-0*, Pub. by Turtleback) Demco.

— The Magic School Bus Plays Ball: A Book about Forces. (Magic School Bus Ser.). (Illus.). 32p. (J). (gr. k-2). 1998. pap. 2.99 (*0-590-92240-8*) Scholastic Inc.

— The Magic School Bus Plays Ball: A Book about Forces. (Magic School Bus Ser.). (Illus.). (J). (gr. k-2). 1998. 8.19 (*0-606-13591-X*, Pub. by Turtleback) Demco.

— The Magic School Bus Sees Stars: A Book About Stars. (Magic School Bus Ser.). (Illus.). (J). (gr. k-2). 1999. pap. 3.50 (*0-590-52102-0*) Scholastic Inc.

— The Magic School Bus Sees Stars: A Book About Stars. (Magic School Bus Ser.). (Illus.). (J). (ps-3). 1999. pap. text 3.50 (*0-590-18732-5*) Scholastic Inc.

— The Magic School Bus Spins a Web: A Book about Spiders. (Magic School Bus Ser.). (Illus.). 32p. (J). (gr. k-2). 1997. pap. text 2.99 (*0-590-92234-3*) Scholastic Inc.

— The Magic School Bus Spins a Web: A Book about Spiders. (Magic School Bus Ser.). (Illus.). (J). (gr. k-2). 1997. 8.95 (*0-606-12764-X*) Turtleback.

— The Magic School Bus Takes a Dive: A Book about Coral Reefs. LC QH541.5.C7W48 1998. (Magic School Bus Ser.). (Illus.). 32p. (J). (gr. k-2). 1998. pap. 2.99 (*0-590-18723-6*, Pub. by Scholastic Inc) Penguin Putnam.

***Cole, Joanna.** The Magic School Bus Takes Flight: A Book about Flight. (Magic School Bus Ser.). (Illus.). (J). (ps-3). 1999. pap. 10.55 (*0-613-03342-6*) Econo-Clad Bks.

Cole, Joanna. The Magic School Bus Takes Flight: A Book about Flight. (Magic School Bus Ser.). (J). (gr. k-2). 1997. pap. text 2.99 (*0-590-73871-2*) Scholastic Inc.

Cole, Joanna. The Magic School Bus Takes Flight: A Book about Flight. (Magic School Bus Ser.). (Illus.). (J). (gr. k-2). 1997. 8.95 (*0-606-11592-7*) Turtleback.

Cole, Joanna. Marbles: 101 Ways to Play. (Illus.). 128p. (J). (gr. k-3). 1998. mass mkt. 8.95 (*0-688-12207-8*, Wm Morrow) Morrow Avon.

— Marbles: 101 Ways to Play. LC 97-36251. (Illus.). 127p. (J). 1998. 16.00 (*0-688-12205-1*, Wm Morrow) Morrow Avon.

— The Missing Tooth. LC 88-1903. (Step into Reading Ser.: A Step 2 Book). (Illus.). 48p. (J). (ps-3). 1988. pap. 3.99 (*0-394-89279-8*, Pub. by Random Bks Yng Read) Random.

Cole, Joanna. The Missing Tooth. (Step into Reading Ser.: A Step 2 Book). (J). (gr. 1-3). 1988. 9.19 (*0-606-03860-4*, Pub. by Turtleback) Demco.

Cole, Joanna. Monster Manners. (Hello Reader! Ser.). (Illus.). 56p. (J). (gr. 1-2). 1995. pap. 3.50 (*0-590-53951-5*, Cartwheel) Scholastic Inc.

— Monster Manners. (Hello, Reader! Ser.). (J). 1995. 9.19 (*0-606-07881-9*, Pub. by Turtleback) Demco.

— MSB Inside Earth. (Illus.). (J). (ps-3). 1993. 19.95 (*0-590-72782-6*) Scholastic Inc.

***Cole, Joanna.** My Big Boy Potty. LC 99-50286. (Illus.). 32p. (J). (ps up). 2000. 5.95 (*0-688-17042-0*, Wm Morrow) Morrow Avon.

— My Big Girl Potty. LC 99-50287. (Illus.). 32p. (J). (ps up). 2000. 5.95 (*0-688-17041-2*, Wm Morrow) Morrow Avon.

Cole, Joanna. My New Kitten. LC 94-20295. (Illus.). 40p. (J). (ps up). 1995. 15.00 (*0-688-12901-3*, Wm Morrow) Morrow Avon.

Cole, Joanna. My New Kitten. LC 94-20295. (Illus.). 40p. (J). (ps up). 1995. 14.93 (*0-688-12902-1*, Wm Morrow) Morrow Avon.

Cole, Joanna. My Puppy Is Born. (J). 1991. 10.15 (*0-606-04983-5*, Pub. by Turtleback) Demco.

— My Puppy Is Born. rev. ed. LC 90-42011. (Illus.). 48p. (J). (ps-3). 1991. mass mkt. 5.95 (*0-688-10198-4*, Wm Morrow) Morrow Avon.

— The New Baby at Your House. LC 85-10653. (Illus.). 48p. (J). (ps-3). 1987. mass mkt. 5.95 (*0-688-07418-9*, Wm Morrow) Morrow Avon.

***Cole, Joanna.** The New Baby at Your House. LC 97-29267. (Illus.). 48p. (J). (ps-2). 1998. 15.95 (*0-688-13897-7*, Wm Morrow) Morrow Avon.

— The New Baby at Your House. rev. ed. LC 97-29267. (Illus.). 48p. (J). (ps-3). 1998. 15.93 (*0-688-13898-5*, Wm Morrow) Morrow Avon.

Cole, Joanna. The New Baby at Your House. rev. ed. 48p. (J). 1999. mass mkt. 5.95 (*0-688-16698-9*, Wm Morrow) Morrow Avon.

— Norma Jean, Jumping Bean. LC 86-15588. (Step into Reading Ser.: A Step 2 Book). (Illus.). 48p. (J). (ps-3). 1987. pap. 3.99 (*0-394-88668-2*, Pub. by Random Bks Yng Read) Random.

Cole, Joanna. Norma Jean, Jumping Bean. (Step into Reading Ser.: A Step 2 Book). (J). (gr. 1-3). 1987. 9.19 (*0-606-03055-7*, Pub. by Turtleback) Demco.

— Parents Book of Toilet Teaching. 126p. 1999. mass mkt. 5.98 (*0-345-43641-5*, Ballantine Epiphany) Ballantine Pub Grp.

Cole, Joanna. A Pocketful of Laughs: Stories, Poems, Jokes & Riddles. (J). 1995. 9.95 (*0-385-32154-6*) Doubleday.

— Riding Silver Star. (Illus.). (J). (gr. k-4). 1996. 15.00 (*0-688-13895-0*, Wm Morrow) Morrow Avon.

Cole, Joanna. Riding Silver Star. (Illus.). (J). (gr. k-4). 1996. 14.93 (*0-688-13896-9*, Wm Morrow) Morrow Avon.

Cole, Joanna. Riding the Magic School Bus with Joanna Cole & Bruce Degen. (J). 1993. pap. 39.95 (*0-590-45904-X*) Scholastic Inc.

— Scary Book. 1994. 10.05 (*0-606-06715-9*, Pub. by Turtleback) Demco.

— Six Sick Sheep. LC 92-5715. (Illus.). 64p. (J). (gr. k up). 1993. mass mkt. 6.95 (*0-688-11068-1*, Wm Morrow) Morrow Avon.

— Six Sick Sheep: 101 Tongue Twisters. (J). 1993. 12.15 (*0-606-05604-1*, Pub. by Turtleback) Demco.

— Spider's Lunch. LC 94-22490. (All Aboard Reading Ser.). (Illus.). 32p. (J). (ps-1). 1995. pap. 3.99 (*0-448-40223-8*, G & D) Peng Put Young Read.

— Spider's Lunch: All about Garden Spiders. (All Aboard Reading Ser.). (J). 1995. 9.44 (*0-606-08192-5*) Turtleback.

***Cole, Joanna.** Street Rhymes. 2000. write for info. (*0-688-17730-1*, Wm Morrow) Morrow Avon.

Cole, Joanna. This Is the Place for Me. (Illus.). 32p. (Orig.). (J). (gr. k-3). 1986. pap. 2.99 (*0-590-33996-6*) Scholastic Inc.

— This Place for Me. large type ed. (J). (ps-2). 1993. 19.95 (*0-590-71917-3*) Scholastic Inc.

***Cole, Joanna.** When You Were Inside Mommy. LC 00-40890. (Illus.). (J). 2001. write for info. (*0-688-17043-9*) HarpC.

Cole, Joanna. Who Put the Pepper in the Pot? (Illus.). (J). (gr. 3). 1995. 8.60 (*0-395-73232-8*) HM.

— Who Put the Pepper in the Pot? large type ed. (Illus.). 62p. (J). (gr. 3). 15.50 (*0-614-20628-6*, L-38217-00 APHB) Am Printing Hse.

Cole, Joanna. Why Did the Chicken Cross the Road? And Other Riddles, Old & New. 1994. 12.15 (*0-606-06878-3*, Pub. by Turtleback) Demco.

Cole, Joanna. You Can't Smell a Flower with Your Ear! All about Your 5 Senses. LC 93-27264. (All Aboard Reading Ser.). (Illus.). 48p. (J). (gr. 1-3). 1994. pap. 3.95 (*0-448-40469-9*, G & D) Peng Put Young Read.

Cole, Joanna. You Can't Smell a Flower With Your Ear! All About Your 5 Senses. (All Aboard Reading Ser.). (J). 1994. 9.15 (*0-606-06895-3*, Pub. by Turtleback) Demco.

Cole, Joanna. Your Insides. (Illus.). 40p. (J). (ps-3). 1998. pap. 9.99 (*0-698-11675-5*, PapStar) Peng Put Young Read.

— Your New Potty. LC 88-39862. (Illus.). 40p. (J). (ps). 1989. mass mkt. 5.95 (*0-688-08966-6*, Wm Morrow) Morrow Avon.

Cole, Joanna. Yours 'Till Banana Splits 201 Autograph Rhymes. (J). 1995. 12.15 (*0-606-08412-6*, Pub. by Turtleback) Demco.

Cole, Joanna, ed. Best Loved Folktales of the World. LC 81-43288. (Anchor Folktale Library). 816p. 1983. pap. 17.00 (*0-385-18949-4*, Anchor NY) Doubleday.

Cole, Joanna & Beech, Linda. El Autobus Magico en el Museo Encantado. LC 94-40025. (SPA.). 32p. (J). (ps-3). 1995. pap. 2.50 (*0-590-20549-8*) Scholastic Inc.

Cole, Joanna & Berenstain, Stan. El Autobus Magico Muestra Y Cuenta: Un Libro Sobre Arqueologia.Tr. of Magic School Bus Shows & Tells: A Book about Archaeology. (SPA.). (J). (gr. k-2). 1997. pap. 2.99 (*0-590-13478-7*) Scholastic Inc.

Cole, Joanna & Calmenson, Stephanie. Bug in a Rug. LC 95-35355. (Illus.). (J). 1996. 16.00 (*0-688-12208-6*, Wm Morrow) Morrow Avon.

— Bug in a Rug: Reading Fun. LC 95-35355. (Illus.). 48p. (J). 1996. mass mkt. 7.95 (*0-688-12210-8*, Wm Morrow) Morrow Avon.

— Crazy Eights: And Other Card Games. LC 93-5427. (Illus.). 80p. (J). (gr. 2 up). 1994. 16.00 (*0-688-12199-3*, Wm Morrow); pap. 6.95 (*0-688-12201-9*, Wm Morrow) Morrow Avon.

Cole, Joanna & Calmenson, Stephanie. Crazy Eights: And Other Card Games. LC 93-5427. (Illus.). 80p. (J). (gr. 4-7). 1994. 15.93 (*0-688-12200-0*, Wm Morrow) Morrow Avon.

Cole, Joanna & Calmenson, Stephanie. The Eentsy, Weentsy Spider: Fingerplays & Action Rhymes. LC 90-44594. (Illus.). 64p. (J). (ps up). 1991. mass mkt. 6.95 (*0-688-10805-9*, Wm Morrow) Morrow Avon.

— Fun on the Run: Travel Games & Songs. LC 98-42245. (Illus.). 144p. (J). (gr. k-3). 1999. 17.00 (*0-688-14660-0*, Wm Morrow) Morrow Avon.

— The Gator Girls. LC 94-20110. (Illus.). 64p. (J). (gr. 1-4). 1995. lib. bdg. 14.93 (*0-688-12121-7*, Wm Morrow) Morrow Avon.

— The Gator Girls. LC 94-20110. Vol. 1. (Illus.). 64p. (J). (gr. 1-4). 1995. 15.00 (*0-688-12120-9*, Wm Morrow) Morrow Avon.

— Miss Mary Mack: And Other Children's Street Rhymes. LC 89-37266. (Illus.). 64p. (J). (ps-3). 1990. mass mkt. 7.95 (*0-688-09749-9*, Wm Morrow) Morrow Avon.

Cole, Joanna & Calmenson, Stephanie. Miss Mary Mack: And Other Children's Street Rhymes. LC 89-37266. (Illus.). 64p. (J). (ps-3). 1990. 11.89 (*0-688-08330-7*, Wm Morrow) Morrow Avon.

Cole, Joanna & Calmenson, Stephanie. Pat a Cake: And Other Play Phymes. LC 91-32264. (Illus.). 48p. (J). (ps). 1992. 14.00 (*0-688-11038-X*, Wm Morrow) Morrow Avon.

— Pin the Tail on the Donkey & Other Party Games. LC 92-29786. (Illus.). 48p. (J). (ps up). 1993. pap. 6.95 (*0-688-12521-2*, Wm Morrow); lib. bdg. 14.93 (*0-688-11892-5*, Wm Morrow) Morrow Avon.

— Rain or Shine Activity Book. (Illus.). (J). 1997. pap. 9.95 (*0-614-29271-9*, Wm Morrow) Morrow Avon.

Cole, Joanna & Calmenson, Stephanie. The Rain or Shine Activity Book. LC 96-37756. (Illus.). 192p. (J). 1997. pap. 9.95 (*0-688-12133-0*, Wm Morrow) Morrow Avon.

Cole, Joanna & Calmenson, Stephanie. Rain or Shine Activity Book: Fun Things to Make & Do. LC 96-37756. (Illus.). 192p. (J). 1997. student ed. 20.00 (*0-688-12131-4*, Wm Morrow) Morrow Avon.

— Rockin' Reptiles. (Illus.). (J). (gr. 1-4). 1997. 15.00 (*0-614-28867-3*, Wm Morrow) Morrow Avon.

— Six Sick Sheep: One Hundred One Tongue Twisters. LC 92-5715. (Illus.). 64p. (J). (gr. 3 up). 1993. reprint ed. lib. bdg. 14.93 (*0-688-11140-8*, Wm Morrow) Morrow Avon.

— Why Did the Chicken Cross the Road? And Other Riddles, Old & New. LC 94-2582. (Illus.). 64p. (J). (gr. 2 up). 1994. lib. bdg. 14.93 (*0-688-12203-5*, Wm Morrow) Morrow Avon.

— Why Did the Chicken Cross the Road? And Other Riddles, Old & New. Cohn, Amy, ed. LC 94-2582. (Illus.). 64p. (J). (gr. 2 up). 1994. reprint ed. mass mkt. 6.95 (*0-688-12204-3*, Wm Morrow) Morrow Avon.

— Yours 'til Banana Splits. LC 94-10654. (Illus.). 64p. (J). (gr. 2 up). 1995. pap. 6.95 (*0-688-14019-X*, Wm Morrow) Morrow Avon.

Cole, Joanna & Calmenson, Stephenia. The Gator Girls: Gator Halloween. LC 97-15756. (Gator Girls Ser.: Vol. 3). (Illus.). 64p. (J). (gr. 1-4). 1999. 15.00 (*0-688-14784-4*, Wm Morrow) Morrow Avon.

***Cole, Joanna & Calmenson, Stephenia.** The Gator Girls: Gator Halloween. LC 97-15756. (Gator Girls Ser.: Vol. 3). (Illus.). 64p. (J). (gr. 1-4). 1999. 14.89 (*0-688-14785-2*, Wm Morrow) Morrow Avon.

***Cole, Joanna & Chambliss, Maxie.** How I Was Adopted: Samantha's Story. 48p. (J). 1999. mass mkt. 5.95 (*0-688-17055-2*, Grenwillow Bks) HarpC Child Bks.

Cole, Joanna & Degen, Bruce. The Magic School Bus Inside the Human Body. LC 88-3070. (Magic School Bus Ser.). (Illus.). 56p. (J). (ps-3). 1989. 14.95 (*0-590-41426-7*, Scholastic Hardcover) Scholastic Inc.

***Cole, Joanna & Degen, Bruce.** Ms. Frizzle's Adventures in Egypt. LC 99-18374. 2000. write for info. (*0-590-44680-0*) Scholastic Inc.

Cole, Joanna & Degen, Bruce, creators. El Autobus Magico Dentro De Un Pastel: Un Libro Sobre Cocina. LC 94-40026. (SPA.). (J). (ps-3). 1995. pap. 2.50 (*0-590-22850-1*) Scholastic Inc.

Cole, Joanna & Saul, Wendy. On the Bus with Joanna Cole. LC 95-40133. (Creative Sparks Ser.). 36p. (J). 1996. 16.95 (*0-435-08131-4*, 08131) Heinemann.

Cole, Joanna & Van Horn, William. Ca C'est Chez Moi.Tr. of This is the Place for Me. (FRE.). (Orig.). (J). mass mkt. 6.99 (*0-590-71919-X*) Scholastic Inc.

— This Is the Place for Me. (FRE.). (Orig.). (J). pap. 13.99 incl. audio (*0-614-28373-6*) Scholastic Inc.

Cole, Joanna, et al. Pat-a-Cake. LC 91-32264. (Illus.). 48p. (J). (ps up). 1992. mass mkt. 6.95 (*0-688-11533-0*, Wm Morrow) Morrow Avon.

— Ready! Set! Read! 144p. (J). 1990. 17.95 (*0-385-41416-1*) Doubleday.

— Yours Till Banana Splits. LC 94-10654. (Illus.). 64p. (J). (gr. 4-7). 1995. 15.00 (*0-688-13185-9*, Wm Morrow) Morrow Avon.

Cole, Joanna, et al. Yours 'Till Banana Splits: 201 Autograph Rhymes. LC 94-10654. (Illus.). 64p. (J). (gr. 2 up). 1995. lib. bdg. 14.93 (*0-688-13186-7*, Wm Morrow) Morrow Avon.

Cole, Joanna, jt. auth. see Calmenson, Stephanie.

Cole, Joanna, jt. auth. see Krulik, Nancy.

Cole, Joanna, jt. auth. see Relf, Patricia.

Cole, Joe. Planet Joe. (Illus.). 140p. (Orig.). 1992. pap. 9.00 (*1-880985-09-8*) Two Thirteen Sixty-one.

Cole, John. Development & Underdevelopment: A Profile of the Third World. 160p. 1987. pap. text 9.95 (*0-416-92080-2*, 1205) Routledge.

— Global 2050: A Basis for Speculation. 355p. 1999. pap. 76.00 (*1-897676-65-4*, Pub. by Nottingham Univ Pr) St Mut.

— Maine Trivia. LC 98-2977. 192p. 1998. pap. 6.95 (*1-55853-603-5*) Rutledge Hill Pr.

— Striper: A Story of Fish & Man. 272p. 1989. pap. 18.95 (*1-55821-040-7*) Lyons Pr.

Cole, John & Cole, Francis. Geography of the European Union. 2nd ed. LC 98-218322. (Illus.). 424p. (C). 1997. pap. 29.99 (*0-415-14311-X*) Routledge.

— Geography of the European Union. 2nd ed. LC 98-218322. (Illus.). 424p. (C). 1997. 85.00 (*0-415-14310-1*) Routledge.

Cole, John & Pollard, Hawk, eds. West of Key West. LC 95-52458. (Illus.). 224p. 1996. 50.00 (*0-8117-1881-6*) Stackpole.

An Asterisk (*) at the beginning of an entry indicates that the title is appearing for the first time.

Cole, John & Reed, Henrey H., eds. The Library of Congress: Its Construction, Architecture & Decoration. LC 97-42115. (Illus.). 320p. 1998. 60.00 (*0-393-04563-3*) Norton.

Cole, John, ed. see Fournier, Paul A.

***Cole, John L.** A Post Card History of Kenyon, Minnesota: From the Post Card Collection of John L. Cole. (Illus.). x, 110p. 1999. pap. 16.95 (*0-9676652-0-5*) J L Cole MN.

Cole, John N. Away All Boats. 304p. 1995. write for info. (*0-8050-2706-8*) H Holt & Co.

— Fish of My Years. (Illus.). 134p. 1995. 50.00 (*1-886967-01-6*) Meadow Run Pr.

— Fishing Came First. 224p. 1991. reprint ed. pap. 7.95 (*0-380-71223-7*, Avon Bks) Morrow Avon.

— Fishing Came First: A Memoir. 224p. 1997. reprint ed. pap. 16.95 (*1-55821-619-7*) Lyons Pr.

— Introduction to the Natural World. 1995. 25.00 (*0-8050-4492-2*); pap. 12.95 (*0-8050-4493-0*) H Holt & Co.

— Life List: Remembering the Birds of My Years. LC 97-26445. (Illus.). 208p. 1997. 21.95 (*0-89272-415-3*) Down East.

— Tarpon Quest. 128p. 1997. reprint ed. pap. 14.95 (*1-55821-622-7*) Lyons Pr.

***Cole, John N. & Burns, Bradford E.** Fly Fishing for Saltwater's Finest: How to Catch the 10 Best Sport Fish at Premier Inshore Sites. LC 99-53766. (Illus.). 200p. 2000. pap. 21.95 (*0-7360-0130-1*) Human Kinetics.

Cole, John P. Geography of the World's Major Regions. LC 94-46987. (Illus.). 512p. (C). 1996. pap. 34.99 (*0-415-11743-7*) Routledge.

— Geography of the World's Major Regions. LC 94-46987. (Illus.). 512p. (C). (gr. 13). 1996. 100.00 (*0-415-11742-9*) Routledge.

Cole, John R. The Olympian Dreams & Youthful Rebellion of Rene Descartes. 312p. 1992. text 34.95 (*0-252-01870-2*) U of Ill Pr.

— Pascal: The Man & His Two Loves. 304p. (C). 1995. text 45.00 (*0-8147-1510-9*) NYU Pr.

Cole, John R., Jr. Politics, Barbecue, & Balderdash. (Illus.). 120p. 1995. pap. text 7.95 (*0-9648472-0-5*) Durham Herald.

Cole, John R., Jr., jt. ed. see Carter, Gary R.

***Cole, John W. & Wolf, Eric R.** The Hidden Frontier. LC 99-27499. 348p. 1999. 16.95 (*0-520-21681-4*, Pub. by U CA Pr) Cal Prin Full Svc.

Cole, John W., tr. see Guizot, Francois P., ed.

Cole, John Y. Book Collectors of Stanford: An Eclectic Eight Who Shaped the Stanford University Libraries. 96p. 1991. pap. text 15.00 (*0-929722-46-9*) CA State Library Fndtn.

— Capital Libraries & Librarians: A Brief History of the District of Columbia Library Association. LC 94-12277. 1994. write for info. (*0-8444-0837-9*) Lib Congress.

— Jefferson's Legacy: A Brief History of the Library of Congress. (Illus.). 103p. 1997. pap. text 30.00 (*0-7881-3895-2*) DIANE Pub.

— Jefferson's Legacy: A Brief History of the Library of Congress. LC 92-30311. (Illus.). 103p. 1992. pap. 9.50 (*0-8444-0764-X*) Lib Congress.

— On These Walls: Inscriptions & Quotations in the Buildings of the Library of Congress. (Illus.). 106p. 1995. pap. 8.50 (*0-8444-0845-X*) Lib Congress.

Cole, John Y., ed. Books Change Lives: 1993-1994 Reading Promotion Campaign. LC 95-39994. 1995. write for info. (*0-8444-0899-9*) Lib Congress.

— Books in Our Future: Perspectives & Proposals. LC 87-600047. 399p. 1987. 16.00 (*0-8444-0554-X*, 030-000-00188-5) Lib Congress.

— The Community of the Book: A Directory of Selected Organizations & Programs. 1987. 34.95 (*0-88738-145-6*) Transaction Pubs.

— The Republic of Letters: Librarian of Congress Daniel J. Boorstin on Books, Reading, & Libraries, 1975-1987. LC 88-600451. 128p. 1989. 17.50 (*0-8444-0629-5*) Lib Congress.

— Responsibilities of the American Book Community. LC 81-607006. 88p. 1981. 7.95 (*0-8444-0328-8*) Lib Congress.

Cole, John Y., jt. ed. see Dain, Phyllis.

Cole, John Y., ed. see Thompson, Michael.

Cole, Johnetta B. Dream the Boldest Dreams: And Other Lessons of Life. LC 97-71932. (Illus.). 90p. 1997. 9.95 (*1-56352-424-4*) Longstreet.

Cole, Johnnetta B. All American Women: Lines That Divide, Ties That Bind. 448p. 1986. pap. 19.95 (*0-02-906460-0*) Free Pr.

Cole, Johnnetta B., ed. Anthropology for the Nineties: Introductory Readings. 592p. 1988. pap. 19.95 (*0-02-906441-4*) Free Pr.

Cole, Jonathan. About Face. LC 97-2099. (Illus.). 244p. 1997. 27.50 (*0-262-03246-5*, Bradford Bks) MIT Pr.

— About Face. (Illus.). 1999. pap. text 17.50 (*0-262-53163-1*) MIT Pr.

— Pride & a Daily Marathon. LC 95-13650. 214p. 1995. pap. text 15.00 (*0-262-53136-4*, Bradford Bks) MIT Pr.

Cole, Jonathan, jt. ed. see Engler, Gordon.

Cole, Jonathan O., jt. auth. see Schatzberg, Alan F.

Cole, Jonathan O., ed. see American Psychopathological Association Staff.

Cole, Jonathan R. Fair Science: Women in the Scientific Community. (Morningside Bk.). (Illus.). 336p. 1987. reprint ed. pap. text 22.00 (*0-231-06629-5*) Col U Pr.

Cole, Jonathan R., et al, eds. The Research University in a Time of Discontent. LC 94-19837. 320p. 1994. text 45.00 (*0-8018-4957-8*); pap. text 17.95 (*0-8018-4958-6*) Johns Hopkins.

Cole, Jonathan R., jt. auth. see Kingston, Paul W.

Cole, Jonathon R. Fair Science: Women in the Scientific Community. LC 79-7341. (Illus.). 1979. 32.95 (*0-02-906360-4*) Free Pr.

Cole, Joseph O. Cole: The Descendants of Elisha Cole, Who Came from Cape Cod to What Is Now Putnam County, N.Y., about 1745. (Illus.). 237p. 1994. reprint ed. pap. 37.00 (*0-8328-4071-8*); reprint ed. lib. bdg. 47.00 (*0-8328-4070-X*) Higginson Bk Co.

***Cole, Joshua.** The Power of Large Numbers: Population, Politics & Gender in Nineteenth-Century France. LC 99-46229. 2000. 39.95 (*0-8014-3701-6*) Cornell U Pr.

Cole, Joy, et al. Health Units for Nonreaders. (Illus.). 143p. 1995. spiral bd. 24.00 (*1-884135-17-X*) Mayer-Johnson.

Cole Jr., Olen. The African-American Experience in the Civilian Conservation Corps. LC 98-43058. (Illus.). 1999. 49.95 (*0-8130-1660-6*) U Press Fla.

***Cole, Juan.** Modernity & the Millennium: The Genesis of the Baha'i Faith in the Nineteenth-Century Middle East. LC 97-45661. (Illus.). 400p. 1998. 50.00 (*0-231-11080-4*) Col U Pr.

— Modernity & the Millennium: The Genesis of the Baha'i Faith in the Nineteenth-Century Middle East. LC 97-45661. (Illus.). 400p. 1998. pap. 20.50 (*0-231-11081-2*) Col U Pr.

Cole, Juan, tr. see Gibran, Kahlil.

Cole, Juan R. Colonialism & Revolution in the Middle East: Social & Cultural Origins of Egypt's Urabi Movement. LC 92-11115. (Studies in the Near East). (Illus.). 416p. (C). 1993. text 62.50 (*0-691-05683-8*, Pub. by Princeton U Pr) Cal Prin Full Svc.

Cole, Juan R. & Momen, Moojan, eds. Studies in Babi & Baha'i History Vol. 2: From Iran East & West. (Illus.). 205p. (C). 1984. 32.50 (*0-933770-40-5*) Kalimat.

Cole, Juan R., tr. see Abu'l-Fadl, Mirza.

Cole, Juan R., tr. see Gibran, Kahlil.

Cole, Juan R., tr. & intro. see Gibran, Kahlil.

Cole, Judd. Arrow Keeper/Death Chant. (Cheyenne Ser.: Nos. 1 & 2). 352p. 1997. mass mkt. 4.99 (*0-8439-4280-0*, Leisure Bks) Dorchester Pub Co.

***Cole, Judd.** Black Hills Hellhole. (Wild Bill Ser.: Vol. 6). 176p. 2000. pap. 3.99 (*0-8439-4770-5*, Leisure Bks) Dorchester Pub Co.

Cole, Judd. Bleeding Kansas. (Wild Bill Ser.: Vol. 3). 176p. 1999. mass mkt. 3.99 (*0-8439-4584-2*, Pub. by Dorchester Pub Co) CMG.

***Cole, Judd.** Blood on the Arrows. (Cheyenne Ser.). 368p. 2000. mass mkt. 5.50 (*0-8439-4734-9*, Leisure Bks) Dorchester Pub Co.

Cole, Judd. Blood on the Plains. (Cheyenne Ser.: No. 5). 176p. (Orig.). 1993. pap. text, mass mkt. 3.50 (*0-8439-3441-7*) Dorchester Pub Co.

— Blood on the Plains - Comanche Raid. (Cheyenne Ser.: No. 5 & 6). 352p. 1998. mass mkt. 4.99 (*0-8439-4348-3*, Leisure Bks) Dorchester Pub Co.

***Cole, Judd.** Bloody Bones Canyon & Renegade Seige, 2 in 1. 336p. 1999. mass mkt. 4.99 (*0-8439-4586-9*, Pub. by Dorchester Pub Co) CMG.

Cole, Judd. Buffalo Hiders. (Cheyenne Ser.: No. 10). 176p. (Orig.). 1994. pap. text, mass mkt. 3.99 (*0-8439-3623-1*) Dorchester Pub Co.

— Comancheros/War Party, 2 vols. in 1. (Cheyenne Ser.). 352p. 1998. mass mkt. 4.99 (*0-8439-4382-3*, Leisure Bks) Dorchester Pub Co.

***Cole, Judd.** Dead Man's Hand. (Wild Bill Ser.). 176p. 1999. mass mkt. 3.99 (*0-8439-4487-0*, Leisure Bks) Dorchester Pub Co.

Cole, Judd. Death Camp. (Cheyenne Ser.: No. 14). 176p. (Orig.). 1995. pap. text, mass mkt. 3.99 (*0-8439-3800-5*) Dorchester Pub Co.

— Death Chant. (Cheyenne Ser.: No. 2). 176p. (Orig.). 1992. pap. text, mass mkt. 3.50 (*0-8439-3337-2*) Dorchester Pub Co.

***Cole, Judd.** The Kinkaid County War. (Wild Bill Ser.: Vol. 2). 176p. 1999. mass mkt. 3.99 (*0-8439-4529-X*, Leisure Bks) Dorchester Pub Co.

Cole, Judd. Ophan Train. (Cheyenne Ser.: No. 16). 176p. (Orig.). 1996. pap. text, mass mkt. 3.99 (*0-8439-3909-5*) Dorchester Pub Co.

— Pathfinder & Buffalo Hiders, 2 vols. in 1. (Cheyenne Ser.: Vols. 9 & 10). 352p. 1998. mass mkt. 4.99 (*0-8439-4413-7*, Leisure Bks) Dorchester Pub Co.

— Renegade Justice. (Cheyenne Ser.: No. 3). 176p. (Orig.). 1993. pap. text, mass mkt. 3.50 (*0-8439-3385-2*) Dorchester Pub Co.

— Renegade Justice: Vision Quest, 2 vols. in 1. (Cheyenne Ser.: Nos. 3 & 4). 352p. 1997. mass mkt. 4.99 (*0-8439-4309-2*, Leisure Bks) Dorchester Pub Co.

— Renegade Nation/Orphan Train. (Cheyenne Ser.: Vols. 15 & 16). 352p. 1999. mass mkt. 4.99 (*0-8439-4511-7*) Dorchester Pub Co.

Cole, Judd. Renegade Siege. (Cheyenne Ser.: No. 20). 176p. (Orig.). 1996. mass mkt. 3.99 (*0-8439-4123-5*) Dorchester Pub Co.

Cole, Judd. River of Death. (Cheyenne Ser.: Vol. 21). 176p. (Orig.). 1997. mass mkt. 3.99 (*0-8439-4206-1*) Dorchester Pub Co.

***Cole, Judd.** River of Death - Desert Manhunt, 2 bks. in 1. (Cheyenne Ser.). 352p. 2000. pap. 4.99 (*0-8439-4676-8*, Leisure Bks) Dorchester Pub Co.

— Santa Fe Death Trap. (Wild Bill Ser.: Vol. 5). 176p. 2000. mass mkt. 3.99 (*0-8439-4720-9*, Leisure Bks) Dorchester Pub Co.

Cole, Judd. Spirit Killer: Mankiller. (Cheyenne Ser.: Vols. 11 & 12). 352p. 1998. mass mkt. 4.99 (*0-8439-4445-5*, Leisure Bks) Dorchester Pub Co.

— The Spirit Path. (Cheyenne Ser.: No. 11). 176p. (Orig.). 1994. pap. text, mass mkt. 3.99 (*0-8439-3656-8*) Dorchester Pub Co.

***Cole, Judd.** Vengeance Quest: Warrior Fury, 2 vols. (Cheyenne Ser.: Vols. 17 & 18). 352p. 1999. mass mkt. 4.99 (*0-8439-4531-1*, Leisure Bks) Dorchester Pub Co.

Cole, Judd. Vision Quest. (Cheyenne Ser.: No. 4). 176p. (Orig.). 1993. pap. text, mass mkt. 3.50 (*0-8439-3411-5*) Dorchester Pub Co.

***Cole, Judd.** Wendigo Mountain - Death Camp, 2 vols. in 1. (Cheyenne Ser.: Nos. 13 & 14). 352p. 1999. mass mkt. 4.99 (*0-8439-4479-X*, Leisure Bks) Dorchester Pub Co.

— Yuma Bustout. (Wild Bill Ser.: Vol. 4). 176p. (Orig.). 2000. pap. 3.99 (*0-8439-4674-1*, Leisure Bks) Dorchester Pub Co.

Cole, Julia. My Parents' Divorce. LC 98-16956. (How Do I Feel About... Ser.). (Illus.). 24p. (J). (gr. k). 1998. lib. bdg. 19.90 (*0-7613-0869-5*, Copper Beech Bks) Millbrook Pr.

Cole, Julio H. Latin American Inflation: Theoretical Interpretations & Empirical Results. LC 87-15156. 104p. 1987. 49.95 (*0-275-92809-8*, C2809, Praeger Pubs) Greenwood.

Cole, K. C. First You Build a Cloud: And Other Reflections on Physics As a Way of Life. LC 98-47050. 224p. (C). 1999. pap. 13.00 (*0-15-600646-4*, Harvest Bks) Harcourt.

— The Universe & the Teacup: The Mathematics of Truth & Beauty. LC 97-22338. 232p. 1998. 22.00 (*0-15-100323-8*) Harcourt.

***Cole, K. C.** The Universe & the Teacup: The Mathematics of Truth & Beauty. 224p. 1999. pap. 13.00 (*0-15-600656-1*, Harvest Bks) Harcourt.

Cole, Karen. The Low Fat Times: Delicious Recipes 20Fat & Less. 277p. (Orig.). 1995. pap. 13.95 (*0-9644225-0-6*) Karon Assocs.

Cole, Kate. Addition & Subtraction, No. 2. (Step Ahead Plus Workbks.). (Illus.). 64p. (J). (gr. 1-2). 1986. pap., wbk. ed. 3.49 (*0-307-03652-9*, 03652) Gldn Bks Pub Co.

— Multiplication & Division. (Step Ahead Plus Ser.). (Illus.). 64p. (J). (gr. 3-4). 1986. pap., wbk. ed. 3.49 (*0-307-03656-1*, 03656, Goldn Books) Gldn Bks Pub Co.

— Phonics. (Step Ahead Plus Workbks.). (Illus.). 64p. (J). (gr. k-2). 1986. pap., wbk. ed. 3.49 (*0-307-03650-2*, 03650) Gldn Bks Pub Co.

— Word Skills. (Step Ahead Plus Workbks.). (Illus.). (J). (gr. k-1). 1986. pap. 3.49 (*0-307-03651-0*, 03651) Gldn Bks Pub Co.

Cole, Kathleen. Encyclopedia of Lady Head Vases. LC 95-39663. 208p. 1996. pap. 29.95 (*0-88740-928-8*) Schiffer.

— Head Vases Identification. (Illus.). 142p. 1996. pap. 14.95 (*0-89145-378-4*, 1917) Collector Bks.

Cole, Kathleen A. Preschool Skills. (Illus.). 64p. (YA). 1993. pap. 3.49 (*0-307-03667-7*, 03667) Gldn Bks Pub Co.

Cole, Kathleen M. & Sheath, Robert G., eds. Biology of the Red Algae. (Illus.). 525p. (C). 1990. text 130.00 (*0-521-34301-1*) Cambridge U Pr.

Cole, Kathleen M., jt. auth. see Fisher, James C.

Cole, Kathryn. Double Take. 256p. 1996. 19.95 (*0-7737-2905-4*) Stoddart Publ.

— Double Take: A Single Woman's Journey to Motherhood. 256p. 1997. pap. 13.95 (*0-7737-5875-5*) Stoddart Publ.

Cole, Ken. Cuba: From Revolution to Development. LC 97-30478. 224p. 1998. 75.00 (*1-85567-502-1*); pap. 24.95 (*1-85567-554-4*) Bks Intl VA.

Cole, Ken. Economy-Environment-Development-Knowledge. LC 99-28165. 304p. 1999. pap. 29.99 (*0-415-16259-9*) Routledge.

***Cole, Ken.** Economy-Environment-Development-Knowledge. LC 99-28165. 304p. (C). 1999. text. write for info. (*0-415-16258-0*) Routledge.

Cole, Ken, ed. Sustainable Development for a Democratic South Africa. LC 94-7199. 1994. text 49.95 (*0-312-12205-5*) St Martin.

Cole, Ken, et al. Why Economists Disagree: The Political Economy of Economics. 2nd ed. LC 90-13461. 1991. pap. text. write for info. (*0-582-06400-7*) Longman.

Cole, Kenneth J. The Executive Search Research Directory: Researchers, Resources, Services. 6th ed. LC 91-202121. xvii, 203 p. 1991. write for info. (*1-878451-16-2*) Recruiting & Search.

Cole, Kenneth J. The Recruiter's Technique Book: Best of RSR. Cole, Joan S., ed. 108p. 1983. 79.50 (*1-878451-00-6*) Recruiting & Search.

Cole, Kenneth J. & Cole, Joan S. Executive Search Research Directory. 5th rev. ed. 175p. 1994. 88.00 (*1-878451-17-0*) Recruiting & Search.

Cole, Kevin N., et al, eds. Advances in Assessment of Communication & Language. LC 96-20950. (Communication & Language Intervention Ser.: Vol. 6). 432p. 1996. text 39.00 (*1-55766-193-6*, 1936) P H Brookes.

***Cole, Lance.** Giant Airliners. (Illus.). 112p. 2000. pap. 24.95 (*0-7603-0945-0*, 130681AP, Pub. by MBI Pubg) Motorbooks Intl.

— New Illustrated Encyclopedia of Aircraft: Military & Civil Aviation from the Beginnings to the Present. (Illus.). 2000. 24.99 (*0-7858-1164-8*) Bk Sales Inc.

— Vickers VC10. (Illus.). 200p. 2000. 52.95 (*1-86126-231-0*, 130052AE, Pub. by Cro1wood) Motorbooks Intl.

***Cole, Larry.** Communication Is the Key to Successful Grower Relations: A Blueprint to Design, Implement, & Measure the Grower-Relations Culture. LC 99-58465. (Illus.). 280p. 2000. 39.95 (*0-8138-2736-1*) Iowa St U Pr.

Cole, Larry. Frustration Is Your Organization's Best Friend: Measuring Corporate Culture Change. (Illus.). 128p. (Orig.). 1996. pap. 12.95 (*1-888134-00-3*) LifeSkills Pub.

Cole, Lawrence T. The Basis of Early Christian Theism. 1972. lib. bdg. 59.95 (*0-8490-1478-6*) Gordon Pr.

Cole, Lee S. The Investigation of Motor Vehicle Fires. 3rd ed. (Illus.). 192p. 1992. pap. 29.95 (*0-685-55356-6*) Lee Bks.

— Motorcycle Identification. 159p. (Orig.). 1986. pap. 9.00 (*0-939818-11-6*) Lee Bks.

— Okie Mafioso. 231p. (Orig.). 1986. pap. 12.95 (*0-939818-14-0*) Lee Bks.

— Truck-Tractor Identification. 2nd ed. 96p. (Orig.). 1995. reprint ed. pap. 14.95 (*0-939818-25-6*) Lee Bks.

— Vehicle Identification, 1983. (Illus.). 80p. (Orig.). 1983. pap. 6.50 (*0-939818-06-X*) Lee Bks.

— Vehicle Identification, 1986-1987. 184p. (Orig.). 1986. pap. 15.00 (*0-939818-12-4*) Lee Bks.

— Vehicle Identification, 1988-1989. 183p. (Orig.). 1988. pap. 18.00 (*0-939818-18-3*) Lee Bks.

— Vehicle Identification, 1984-1985. 164p. (Orig.). 1984. pap. 15.00 (*0-939818-09-4*) Lee Bks.

— Vehicle Indentification, 1938-1968. 75p. 1980. pap. 5.00 (*0-939818-03-5*) Lee Bks.

— Vehicle Identification, 1969-1982. 136p. (Orig.). 1982. pap. 6.00 (*0-939818-05-1*) Lee Bks.

Cole, Lee S. & Boyer, Gerald D. Vehicle Identification, 1990-1991. 160p. (Orig.). 1991. pap. 18.00 (*0-939818-22-1*) Lee Bks.

Cole, Lee S., jt. auth. see Boyer, Gerald D.

Cole, Leonard A. Clouds of Secrecy: The Army's Germ Warfare Tests over Populated Areas. LC 87-12777. 188p. (C). 1988. pap. 14.95 (*0-8226-3001-X*) Littlefield.

— Clouds of Secrecy: The Army's Germ Warfare Tests over Populated Areas. LC 87-12777. 188p. 1988. 44.50 (*0-8476-7579-3*) Rowman.

— Element of Risk: The Politics of Radon. (Illus.). 256p. 1994. pap. 11.95 (*0-19-509367-4*) OUP.

— The Eleventh Plague: The Politics of Biological & Chemical Warfare. 250p. 1996. pap. text 22.95 (*0-7167-2950-4*) W H Freeman.

— The Eleventh Plague: The Politics of Biological & Chemical Warfare. 1998. pap. 14.95 (*0-7167-3301-3*) W H Freeman.

— Politics & the Restraint of Science. LC 83-2992. (Illus.). 200p. 1983. 29.50 (*0-86598-125-6*) Rowman.

Cole, Leonard P. Cost Accounting for Financial Institutions: The Complete Desktop Reference Guide. 2nd rev. ed. 1994. text 60.00 (*1-55738-739-7*, Irwn Prfssnl) McGraw-Hill Prof.

— Management Accounting for Financial Institutions: The Complete Desktop Reference. 2nd rev. ed. (C). 1994. text 60.00 (*1-55738-738-9*, Irwn Prfssnl) McGraw-Hill Prof.

Cole, Leone. Sentenced to Life: Fifty Years of Missionary Life in Japan. 288p. 1987. pap. write for info. (*0-9618026-1-8*) Natl Design Assocs.

Cole, Leslie. Waste Management in the States. LC 82-147343. 30p. reprint ed. pap. 30.00 (*0-608-11405-7*, 202042700017) Bks Demand.

Cole, Leslie D. California Gold Country in a Nutshell. (In a Nutshell Ser.). (Illus.). (Orig.). 1996. pap. 5.95 (*1-884497-05-5*) Nutshell TourMaps.

— Central Oregon in a Nutshell. 2nd ed. (In a Nutshell Guides Ser.). (Illus.). 2p. (Orig.). 1999. reprint ed. pap. 5.95 (*1-884497-06-3*) Nutshell TourMaps.

— Lake Tahoe & High Sierra in a Nutshell. (In a Nutshell Ser.). (Illus.). 1995. pap. 5.95 (*1-884497-03-9*) Nutshell TourMaps.

— Nutshell California Gift Set, 3 vols., Set. (Illus.). 1996. pap. 17.49 (*0-614-17781-2*) Nutshell TourMaps.

— Nutshell Oregon Gift Set. (In a Nutshell Tourmaps Ser.). (Illus.). 6p. 1994. pap. 17.49 (*1-884497-99-3*) Nutshell TourMaps.

— Oregon's South Coast in a Nutshell. (In a Nutshell Ser.). (Illus.). 1994. pap. 5.95 (*1-884497-02-0*) Nutshell TourMaps.

— Yosemite & Eastern Sierra in a Nutshell. (In a Nutshell Ser.). (Illus.). 1995. pap. 5.95 (*1-884497-04-7*) Nutshell TourMaps.

Cole, Letha B., jt. ed. see Winkler, Mary G.

Cole, Linda L. Catalog of Type Specimens in the International Protozoan Type Collection. fac. ed. LC 94-9547. (Smithsonian Contributions to Zoology Ser.: No. 561). 34p. 1994. reprint ed. pap. 30.00 (*0-7837-8262-4*, 204904300009) Bks Demand.

Cole, Lisa A., jt. auth. see Harrell, Rhett D.

Cole, Lo. The Friendship Notebook: A Personal Journal. 96p. 1995. pap. 5.95 (*1-56138-631-6*) Running Pr.

Cole, Lori, jt. auth. see Cole, Corey.

Cole, Lorraine, jt. ed. see Hewson, Margaret.

Cole, Louis M. Processed Words. 36p. 1998. pap. 7.95 (*0-9663293-5-X*) Main St Rag.

Cole, Luane, ed. Patterns & Pieces. rev. ed. (Illus.). 392p. 1999. write for info. (*0-9672297-1-5*); pap. write for info. (*0-9672297-0-7*) Lyme Historians.

***Cole, Luke & Foster, Sheila.** From the Ground Up: Environmental Racism & the Rise of the Environmental Justice Movement. 2000. 45.00 (*0-8147-1537-0*) NYU Pr.

Cole, Luke W., intro. Stanford Environmental Law Journal, Vol. 14, No. 1. 211p. (Orig.). 1995. pap. text 15.00 (*0-942007-39-5*) Stanford Enviro.

***Cole, M.** Runaway. 1998. mass mkt. 13.95 (*0-7472-5539-3*, Pub. by Headline Bk Pub) Trafalgar.

Cole, M., tr. see Berger, M.

Cole, M., tr. see Parent, D. P.

Cole, M. C., jt. auth. see Cross, J. N.

Cole, M. M. Publishing Company Editorial Staff. One Thousand Fiddle Tunes: Authentic Country Fiddle Playing--The Fiddler's Bible. 128p. 1992. spiral bd. 30.00 (*0-8471-0450-8*) M M Cole.

Cole, M. R., tr. Pastores. (AFS Memoirs Ser.: Vol. 9). (SPA., Illus.). 1974. reprint ed. 30.00 (*0-527-01061-8*) Periodicals Srv.

Cole, Mabel. Philippine Folk Tales. LC 78-67699. (Folktale Ser.). (Illus.). reprint ed. 37.50 (*0-404-16073-5*) AMS Pr.

Cole, Maija J., et al, eds. Commons Debates, 1628: Introduction & Reference Materials, Vol. 1. 136p. 1977. 125.00 (*1-58046-006-2*) Univ Rochester Pr.

C

— Commons Debates, 1628 Volume 2: 17/3 - 19/4, Vol. 2. 584p. 1977. 125.00 (*1-58046-007-0*) Univ Rochester Pr.
— Commons Debates, 1628, Volume 3: 21/4 - 27/5, Vol. 3. 641p. 1977. 125.00 (*1-58046-008-9*) Univ Rochester Pr.
— Commons Debates, 1628, Volume 4: 28/5 - 26/6, Vol. 4. 512p. 1978. 125.00 (*1-58046-009-7*) Univ Rochester Pr.
— Proceedings in Parliament, 1628: Appendices & Indices, Vol. 6. 616p. 1983. 125.00 (*1-58046-011-9*) Univ Rochester Pr.
Cole, Maija J. & Bidwell, William B., eds. Proceedings in Parliament, 1626, Volume 2: House of Commons, Vol. 2. 447p. 1992. 125.00 (*1-58046-003-8*) Univ Rochester Pr.
— Proceedings in Parliament, 1626: Appendices & Indices, Vol. 3. 461p. 1992. 125.00 (*1-58046-004-6*) Univ Rochester Pr.
— Proceedings in Parliament, 1626: Appendices & Indices, Vol. 4. 537p. 1996. 125.00 (*1-58046-005-4*) Univ Rochester Pr.
Cole, Maija Jansson, see Jansson Cole, Maija.
Cole, Malcolm S. & Barclay, Barbara. Armseelchen: The Life & Music of Eric Zeisl, 6. LC 84-520. (Contributions to the Study of Music & Dance Ser.: No. 6). 441p. 1984. 59.95 (*0-313-23800-6*, CAR/, Greenwood Pr) Greenwood.
Cole, Margaret. The Murder at Crome House. 1976. lib. bdg. 13.95 (*0-89968-167-0*, Lghtyr Pr) Buccaneer Bks.
— Never Too Old for God. 125p. 1987. pap. 3.95 (*0-310-55272-9*, 19027P) Zondervan.
— The Story of Fabian Socialism. LC 61-16949. (Illus.). xv, 366p. 1961. reprint ed. pap. 18.95 (*0-8047-0092-3*) Stanford U Pr.
Cole, Margaret I. Marriage: Past & Present. LC 72-9632. reprint ed. 41.50 (*0-404-57431-9*) AMS Pr.
— Robert Owen of New Lanark. LC 75-77254. vii, 231p. 1969. reprint ed. 35.00 (*0-678-00565-6*) Kelley.
— Women of To-Day. LC 68-16920. (Essay Index Reprint Ser.). 1977. 23.95 (*0-8369-0325-0*) Ayer.
Cole, Margaret I., ed. The Webbs & Their Work. LC 84-22459. (Illus.). 304p. 1985. reprint ed. lib. bdg. 65.00 (*0-313-24677-7*, COWW, Greenwood Pr) Greenwood.
Cole, Margaret I. & Smith, Charles, eds. Democratic Sweden. LC 70-128224. (Essay Index Reprint Ser.). 1977. 21.95 (*0-8369-1871-1*) Ayer.
Cole, Margaret W., jt. auth. see Cole, Alphaeus P.
Cole, Marie. Welcome the Seasons. (Illus.). 44p. 1997. 8.99 (*1-58050-015-3*, 40-6142) Provo Craft.
Cole, Mariette, jt. auth. see Hale, Mason E., Jr.
Cole, Marilyn B. Group Dynamics in Occupational Therapy: Instructor's Manual. (Illus.). 80p. 1998. pap., teacher ed. Price not set. (*1-55642-410-8*, 34108) SLACK Inc.
— Group Dynamics in Occupational Therapy: The Theoretical Basis & Practice Application of Group Treatment. 2nd ed. LC 98-16670. (Illus.). 408p. 1998. pap. text 33.00 (*1-55642-382-9*, 33829) SLACK Inc.
***Cole, Marlise A.** When I Was a Kid..., Vol. I. (Illus.). 1999. pap. 10.00 (*0-9677636-0-6*) Imagework.
Cole, Martha L. & Cole, Jack T. Effective Intervention with the Language Impaired Child. 2nd ed. LC 88-19003. 301p. (C). 1989. 65.00 (*0-87189-798-9*) Aspen Pub.
***Cole, Martin.** Millennium Blitzkrieg. LC 99-93990. 279p. 2000. pap. 13.95 (*0-533-13213-4*) Vantage.
Cole, Martin & Dryden, Wendy. Sex Therapy in Britain. (Psychotherapy in Britain Ser.). 320p. 1988. 123.00 (*0-335-09838-X*); pap. 41.95 (*0-335-09828-2*) OpUniv Pr.
Cole, Martin & Walker, Stephen, eds. Teaching & Stress. 224p. 1989. 123.00 (*0-335-09548-8*); pap. 34.99 (*0-335-09547-X*) OpUniv Pr.
Cole, Mary H. The Portable Queen: Elizabeth I & the Politics of Ceremony. LC 99-27676. (Studies in Early Modern Culture). 288p. 2000. text 35.00 (*1-55849-214-3*) U of Mass Pr.
Cole, Mary I. Cooperation Between the Faculty of the Campus Elementary Training School & the Other Departments of Teachers Colleges & Normal Schools. LC 76-176658. (Columbia University. Teachers College. Contributions to Education Ser.: No. 746). reprint ed. 37.50 (*0-404-55746-5*) AMS Pr.
Cole, Mary L. Pattern-Free Fashions. LC 94-23897. (Illus.). 96p. 1995. pap. 15.95 (*0-8019-8497-1*) Krause Pubns.
Cole, Mary N. Eggs Before Breakfast: One Woman's Collection of Recipes & Recollections. (Illus.). 192p. (Orig.). 1985. pap. write for info. (*0-931515-03-3*) Triumph Pr.
Cole, Mary V., jt. auth. see Norstrom, Barbara.
Cole, Mason, ed. see Caroselli, Marlene.
***Cole, Matthew A.** Trade Liberalisation, Economic Growth & the Environment. LC 99-87154. (New Horizons in Environmental Economics Ser.). 160p. 2000. 75.00 (*1-84064-176-2*) E Elgar.
Cole, Melanie. Celine Dion. LC 98-30686. (Real-Life Reader Biographies Ser.). (Illus.). 32p. (J). (gr. 3-8). 1998. lib. bdg. 15.95 (*1-883845-76-9*) M Lane Pubs.
— Chuck Norris. LC 98-38129. (Real Life Reader Biography Ser.). (Illus.). 32p. (J). (gr. 3-8). 1998. lib. bdg. 15.95 (*1-883845-91-2*) M Lane Pubs.
— Jimmy Smits. LC 97-43445. (Real-Life Reader Biographies Ser.). (Illus.). 32p. (J). (gr. 3-8). 1998. lib. bdg. 15.95 (*1-883845-59-9*) M Lane Pubs.
— Mariah Carey. large type ed. LC 97-21843. (Real Life Reader Biographies Ser.). (Illus.). 32p. (J). (gr. 3-8). 1997. lib. bdg. 15.95 (*1-883845-51-3*) M Lane Pubs.
— Mary Joe Fernandez. LC 97-43510. (Real-Life Reader Biographies Ser.). (Illus.). 32p. (J). (gr. 3-8). 1998. lib. bdg. 15.95 (*1-883845-63-7*) M Lane Pubs.
— Sinbad. LC 98-38128. (Real-Life Reader Biographies Ser.). (Illus.). 32p. (J). (gr. 3-8). 1998. lib. bdg. 15.95 (*1-883845-73-4*) M Lane Pubs.
Cole, Merle T. Cradle of Invasion: A History of the U. S. Naval Amphibious Training Base, Solomons, Maryland, 1942-1945. LC 85-179786. (Illus.). 37p. (Orig.). 1984. reprint ed. pap. 3.95 (*0-941647-03-X*) Calvert MM Pr.
— Solomon Mines: A History of the U. S. Naval Mine Warfare Test Station, Solomons, Maryland. (Illus.). 46p. 1999. pap. 6.95 (*0-941647-08-0*) Calvert MM Pr.
Cole, Merrilee D., jt. auth. see Willhite, Robert G.
Cole, Michael. Cultural Psychology: A Once & Future Discipline. LC 96-8234. (Illus.). 432p. 1996. 29.95 (*0-674-17951-X*) Belknap Pr.
— Cultural Psychology: An Once & Future Discipline. 432p. 1998. pap. text 18.95 (*0-674-17956-0*) HUP.
— Manna for Winter. 30p. 1994. pap. 7.00 (*0-937669-52-0*) Owl Creek Pr.
— The Pianoforte in the Classical Era. (Illus.). 412p. 1998. text 75.00 (*0-19-816634-6*) OUP.
— Soviet Developmental Psychology: An Anthology. LC 77-85709. 644p. reprint ed. pap. 199.70 (*0-608-30670-3*, 202185400024) Bks Demand.
Cole, Michael, et al, eds. Mind, Culture & Activity: Seminal Papers from the Laboratory of Comparative Human Cognition. (Illus.). 516p. (C). 1997. text 59.95 (*0-521-55238-9*); pap. text 21.95 (*0-521-55823-9*) Cambridge U Pr.
Cole, Michael & Means, Barbara. Comparative Studies of How People Think: An Introduction. (Illus.). 222p. 1986. pap. 15.00 (*0-674-15261-1*) HUP.
Cole, Michael, jt. auth. see Gauvain, Mary.
Cole, Michael, jt. auth. see Scribner, Sylvia.
Cole, Michael, ed. see Luria, Aleksandr R.
Cole, Michael, ed. see Vygotsky, L. S.
Cole, Michael, tr. see Ljapin, E. S. & Evseev, A. E.
Cole, Michael C. & Jurey, Mark E. Dr. Dither's Digital Basics. (Illus.). vi, 120p. 1998. pap. text 24.00 (*0-9662258-0-5*) Vis tech Pubg.
Cole, Michael D. Apollo 13: Space Emergency. LC 94-41179. (Countdown to Space Ser.). (Illus.). 48p. (J). (gr. 4-10). 1995. lib. bdg. 18.95 (*0-89490-542-2*) Enslow Pubs.
— Astronauts: Training for Space. LC 98-3299. (Countdown to Space Ser.). 48p. (J). (gr. 4-10). 1999. lib. bdg. 18.95 (*0-7660-1116-X*) Enslow Pubs.
— Bill Clinton: United States President. LC 93-37411. (People to Know Ser.). (Illus.). 112p. (YA). (gr. 6 up). 1994. lib. bdg. 20.95 (*0-89490-437-X*) Enslow Pubs.
— Challenger: America's Space Tragedy. LC 94-41177. (Countdown to Space Ser.). (Illus.). 48p. (J). (gr. 4-10). 1995. lib. bdg. 18.95 (*0-89490-544-9*) Enslow Pubs.
— Columbia: First Flight of the Space Shuttle. LC 94-41181. (Countdown to Space Ser.). (Illus.). 48p. (J). (gr. 4-10). 1995. lib. bdg. 18.95 (*0-89490-543-0*) Enslow Pubs.
***Cole, Michael D.** Earth - The Third Planet. LC 00-9188. (Countdown to Space Ser.). (Illus.). 2001. write for info. (*0-7660-1507-6*) Enslow Pubs.
Cole, Michael D. Friendship 7: First American in Orbit. LC 94-29433. (Countdown to Space Ser.). (Illus.). 48p. (J). (gr. 4-10). 1995. lib. bdg. 18.95 (*0-89490-540-6*) Enslow Pubs.
— Galileo Spacecraft: Mission to Jupiter. LC 98-3627. (Countdown to Space Ser.). 48p. (J). (gr. 4-10). 1999. lib. bdg. 18.95 (*0-7660-1119-4*) Enslow Pubs.
— Hubble Space Telescope: Exploring the Universe. LC 98-3298. (Countdown to Space Ser.). 48p. (J). (gr. 4-10). 1999. lib. bdg. 18.95 (*0-7660-1120-8*) Enslow Pubs.
— International Space Station: A Space Mission. LC 98-18781. (Countdown to Space Ser.). 48p. (J). (gr. 4-10). 1999. lib. bdg. 18.95 (*0-7660-1117-8*) Enslow Pubs.
— John F. Kennedy: President of the New Frontier. LC 95-23481. (People to Know Ser.). (Illus.). 128p. (YA). (gr. 6 up). 1996. lib. bdg. 20.95 (*0-89490-693-3*) Enslow Pubs.
***Cole, Michael D.** Jupiter - The Fifth Planet. LC 00-9262. (Countdown to Space Ser.). (Illus.). 2001. write for info. (*0-7660-1511-4*) Enslow Pubs.
Cole, Michael D. The L. A. Riots: Rage in the City of Angels. LC 98-30263. (American Disasters Ser.). 48p. (YA). (gr. 4-10). 1999. lib. bdg. 18.95 (*0-7660-1219-0*) Enslow Pubs.
— Living on Mars: Mission to the Red Planet. LC 98-13125. (Countdown to Space Ser.). 48p. (J). (gr. 4-10). 1999. lib. bdg. 18.95 (*0-7660-1121-6*) Enslow Pubs.
— Moon Base: First Colony in Space. LC 98-13126. (Countdown to Space Ser.). 48p. (J). (gr. 4-10). 1999. lib. bdg. 18.95 (*0-7660-1118-6*) Enslow Pubs.
***Cole, Michael D.** NASA Space Vehicles: Capsules, Shuttles & Space Stations. LC 99-35533. (Countdown to Space Ser.). (Illus.). 48p. (gr. 4-10). 2000. lib. bdg. 18.95 (*0-7660-1308-1*) Enslow Pubs.
Cole, Michael D. The Siege at Waco: Deadly Inferno. LC 98-35033. (American Disasters Ser.). 48p. (J). (gr. 4-10). 1999. lib. bdg. 18.95 (*0-7660-1218-2*) Enslow Pubs.
***Cole, Michael D.** Space Emergency: Astronauts in Danger. LC 99-26855. (Countdown to Space Ser.). (Illus.). 48p. (gr. 4-10). 2000. lib. bdg. 18.95 (*0-7660-1307-3*) Enslow Pubs.
— Space Launch Disaster: When Liftoff Goes Wrong. LC 99-32179. (Countdown to Space Ser.). (Illus.). 48p. (gr. 4-10). 2000. lib. bdg. 18.95 (*0-7660-1309-X*) Enslow Pubs.
— The Sun: The Center of the Solar System. LC 00-8729. (Countdown to Space Ser.). (Illus.). (YA). 2001. write for info. (*0-7660-1508-4*) Enslow Pubs.
Cole, Michael D. TWA Flight 800: Explosion in Midair. LC 98-30265. (American Disasters Ser.). 48p. (YA). (gr. 4-10). 1999. lib. bdg. 18.95 (*0-7660-1217-4*) Enslow Pubs.
***Cole, Michael D.** Venus: The Second Planet. LC 00-8730. (Countdown to Space Ser.). (Illus.). (YA). 2001. write for info. (*0-7660-1509-2*) Enslow Pubs.
Cole, Michael D. Vostok 1: First Human in Space. LC 94-41180. (Countdown to Space Ser.). (Illus.). 48p. (J). (gr. 4-10). 1995. lib. bdg. 18.95 (*0-89490-541-4*) Enslow Pubs.
— Walt Disney: Creator of Mickey Mouse. LC 95-31202. (People to Know Ser.). (Illus.). 112p. (YA). (gr. 6 up). 1996. lib. bdg. 20.95 (*0-89490-694-1*) Enslow Pubs.
Cole, Mike. Education for Equality: Some Guidelines for Good Practice. 208p. (C). 1988. lib. bdg. 49.95 (*0-415-00546-9*) Routledge.
Cole, Mike & Hill, Dave. Promoting Equality in Primary Schools. LC 97-142331. (Introduction to Education Ser.). (Illus.). 160p. 1996. pap. 35.00 (*0-304-33308-5*); text 79.50 (*0-304-33307-7*) Continuum.
Cole-Misch, Sally, et al. Sourcebook for Watershed Education. 216p. 1996. pap. text, per. 29.95 (*0-7872-2372-7*) Kendall-Hunt.
Cole, Monica. The Savannas: Biogeography & Geobotany. 1986. text 167.00 (*0-12-179520-9*) Acad Pr.
Cole, Muriel. There Is a Child Hidden in This Picture. LC 91-8812. 160p. (Orig.). 1991. pap. 7.95 (*0-934678-35-9*) New Victoria Pubs.
Cole, Murray I. Algorithmic Skeletons: Structural Management of Parallel Computation. (Research Monographs in Parallel & Distributed Computing). 224p. 1989. pap. text 30.00 (*0-262-53086-4*) MIT Pr.
Cole, Nancy. Assessment & Teacher Education: Sharing the Bull's-Eye. (Charles W. Hunt Memorial Lecture Ser.). 16p. 1999. pap. 11.95 (*0-89333-175-9*) AACTE.
Cole, Nancy & Skerrett, P. J. Renewables Are Ready: People Creating Renewable Energy Solutions. (Real Goods Independent Living Ser.). (Illus.). 239p. 1995. pap. 19.95 (*0-930031-73-3*) Chelsea Green Pub.
Cole, Nancy C., jt. auth. see Cole, Edwin L.
Cole, Nancy S., jt. ed. see Willingham, Warren W.
***Cole, Natalie & Diehl, Digby.** Angel on My Shoulder: An Autobiography. (Illus.). 304p. 2000. 25.95 (*0-446-52746-7*) Warner Bks.
Cole, Nathan. The Road to Hunting Island, South Carolina. LC 97-191443. (Images of America Ser.). (Illus.). 128p. 1997. pap. 16.99 (*0-7524-0823-2*) Arcadia Publng.
Cole, Neil. Cultivating a Life for God: Multiplying Disciples Through Life Transformation Groups. 128p. (Orig.). 1999. pap. 10.00 (*1-889638-06-4*) ChurchSmart.
Cole, Neil, jt. auth. see Logan, Robert E.
Cole, Nick. Off-Road Recovery Techniques: A Practical Handbook. (Illus.). 72p. 1996. pap. 21.95 (*1-899870-13-X*, Pub. by Motor Racing) Motorbooks Intl.
Cole, Norma. And the Tide Shall Cover the Earth. (YA). 1994. 6.00 (*0-87602-328-6*) Anchorage.
Cole, Norma. Blast Off! A Space Counting Book. LC 93-28794. 1994. 12.15 (*0-606-06237-8*, Pub. by Turtleback) Demco.
Cole, Norma. Blast Off! A Space Counting Book. LC 93-28794. (Illus.). 32p. (J). (ps-3). 1994. 15.95 (*0-88106-499-8*); pap. 6.95 (*0-88106-498-X*) Charlesbridge Pub.
— Contrafact. 92p. (Orig.). 1996. pap. 11.00 (*0-937013-54-4*) Potes Poets.
— The Final Tide. LC 90-6072. 160p. (YA). (gr. 5 up). 1990. 14.95 (*0-689-50510-8*) McElderry Bks.
— Mars. LC 93-80298. (Poetry Ser.: No. 1). 128p. 1994. pap. text 10.00 (*0-9639321-0-1*) Listening Chamber.
— Metamorphopsia. 99p. (Orig.). (C). 1988. pap. 8.50 (*0-937013-23-4*) Potes Poets.
— Moira. 1996. 9.00 (*1-882022-28-9*) O Bks.
— My Bird Book. (Littoral Bks.). 112p. 1991. pap. 9.95 (*1-55713-090-6*) Sun & Moon CA.
***Cole, Norma, ed. from FRE.** Crosscut Universe: Writing on Writing from France. (Serie D'Ecriture: Vol. 13-14). (Illus.). 160p. 2000. pap. 15.00 (*1-886224-39-0*, 10, Pub. by Burning Deck) SPD-Small Pr Dist.
Cole, Norma & Doris, Stacy, eds. Raddle Moon 16: Modern French Poetry in Translation. (Illus.). 194p. 1997. pap. 8.00 (*0-921331-25-8*, Pub. by Tsunami Edits) Barnholden.
Cole, Norma & Elliott, Naneki. Just Desserts. 40p. Date not set. pap. 3.60 (*1-58342-018-5*, J37) Dramatic Pub.
Cole, Norma, tr. see Collobert, Danielle.
Cole, Orest. Dummy with Desire. LC 98-50195. (Illus.). 128p. 1999. 17.95 (*1-58141-027-1*) Rivercross Pub.
Cole, Owen. Teach Yourself Sikhism. (Illus.). 192p. 1995. pap. 11.95 (*0-8442-3747-7*, Teach Yrslf) NTC Contemp Pub Co.
Cole, Owen & Kanitkar, Hemant. Hinduism. (Illus.). 224p. 1995. pap. 12.95 (*0-8442-3682-9*, Teach Yrslf) NTC Contemp Pub Co.
Cole, P. Imbabura Quechua. (Descriptive Grammars Ser.). 250p. 1986. 72.50 (*0-7099-3444-0*, Pub. by C Helm) Routldge.
Cole, Pat & McNichol, Janet. Tools for a Successful Job Search. 1997. pap. 24.00 (*1-58041-012-X*, 0112013) Am Speech Lang Hearing.
Cole, Patricia A., et al. Funding Sources: A Guide for Future Audiologists, Speech-Language Pathologists, & Speech, Language, & Hearing Scientists. LC 98-116508. 1996. pap. 20.00 (*0-910329-85-0*, 0112018) Am Speech Lang Hearing.
Cole, Paul M. Global Wireless Competitiveness Study: Final Report. (Illus.). 150p. (C). 1999. pap. text 35.00 (*0-7881-4121-X*) DIANE Pub.
— POW - MIA Issues, Vol. I: The Korean War, 1. LC 93-40829. 1994. pap. 15.00 (*0-8330-1482-X*, MR-351/1-USDP) Rand Corp.
Cole, Paul M., jt. auth. see Wayland, Robert E.
Cole, Penny J. The Preaching of the Crusades to the Holy Land, 1095-1270. LC 89-63251. (Medieval Academy Bks.: No. 98). xiv, 281p. 1991. 35.00 (*0-915651-03-3*) Medieval Acad.
Cole, Percival R. Herbart & Froebel: An Attempt at Synthesis. LC 70-176659. (Columbia University. Teachers College. Contributions to Education Ser.: No. 14). reprint ed. 37.50 (*0-404-55014-2*) AMS Pr.
— A History of Educational Thought. LC 74-138214. 316p. (C). 1972. reprint ed. lib. bdg. 35.00 (*0-8371-5569-X*, COET, Greenwood Pr) Greenwood.
Cole, Peter. Hymns & Qualms. LC 97-39309. 109p. 1998. pap. 12.95 (*1-878818-64-3*, Pub. by Sheep Meadow) U Pr of New Eng.
***Cole, Peter.** Long Distance Reflexives, Vol. 33. (Syntax & Semantics Ser.). 350p. 2000. 120.00 (*0-12-613533-9*) Acad Pr.
Cole, Peter. Rift. 93p. 1997. pap. text 9.95 (*1-886449-62-7*) Barrytown Ltd.
— Selected Poems of Shmuel HaNagid. 312p. (C). 1996. pap. 14.95 (*0-691-01120-6*, Pub. by Princeton U Pr) Cal Prin Full Svc.
Cole, Peter, ed. Radical Pragmatics. 1981. text 74.95 (*0-12-179660-4*) Acad Pr.
Cole, Peter, tr. Selected Poems of Shmuel HaNagid. (Lockert Library of Poetry in Translation). 312p. 1996. text 39.95 (*0-691-01121-4*, Pub. by Princeton U Pr) Cal Prin Full Svc.
Cole, Peter & Jonath, Leslie. Snowmen: Creatures, Crafts, & Other Winter Projects. LC 99-20145. (Illus.). 80p. 1999. 14.95 (*0-8118-2554-X*) Chronicle Bks.
Cole, Peter, jt. auth. see Owen, Deborah.
Cole, Peter, tr. see Shabtai, Aharon.
Cole, Peter S. How to Write a Statement of Work. 4th rev. ed. LC 99-229015. 241p. 1999. pap. 68.00 (*1-56726-082-9*); lib. bdg. 98.00 (*1-56726-081-0*) Mgmt Concepts.
— Technical Evaluations in Government Contracting: A Complete Guide. 254p. (Orig.). 1995. pap. 99.00 (*1-56726-032-2*, B568) Mgmt Concepts.
Cole, Phil, ed. see Anderson Publishing Company Staff.
Cole, Philip. The Free, the Unfree & the Excluded: A Treatise on the Conditions of Liberty. LC 98-71968. (Avebury Series in Philosophy). 234p. 1998. text 63.95 (*1-85628-954-0*, Pub. by Ashgate Pub) Ashgate Pub Co.
Cole, Phyllis. The American Writer & the Condition of England, 1815-1860. (Harvard Dissertations in American & English Literature Ser.). 543p. 1987. lib. bdg. 15.00 (*0-8240-0056-0*) Garland.
— Mary Moody Emerson & the Origins of Transcentalism: A Family History. LC 97-1413. (Illus.). 400p. (C). 1998. 45.00 (*0-19-503949-1*) OUP.
Cole, Phyllis & Tilson, Everett. Litanies & Other Prayers for the Revised Common Lectionary: Year B. LC 92-47126. (Orig.). 1993. pap. 13.95 (*0-687-22120-X*) Abingdon.
— Litanies & Other Prayers for the Revised Common Lectionary: Year C. LC 93-42153. (Orig.). 1994. pap. 13.95 (*0-687-22122-6*) Abingdon.
— Prayers for One Voice: Two Hundred Prayers Based on the Revised Common Lectionary. LC 92-42141. 176p. 1993. pap. 12.95 (*0-687-30339-7*) Abingdon.
Cole, Phyllis, jt. auth. see Tilson, Everet.
Cole, R. Computer Communications. 2nd ed. 1987. 52.84 (*0-387-91306-8*) Spr-Verlag.
Cole, R. Alan. Exodus. LC 72-97952. (Tyndale Old Testament Commentary Ser.: Vol. 20). 239p. 1973. pap. 12.99 (*0-87784-252-3*, 252) InterVarsity.
— Mark. rev. ed. Morris, Leon, ed. (Tyndale New Testament Commentaries Ser.). 340p. 1989. pap. 14.00 (*0-8028-0481-0*) Eerdmans.
— Mothers & Sons in Chinese Buddhism. LC 97-46028. x, 303p. 1998. 39.50 (*0-8047-3152-7*) Stanford U Pr.
Cole, R. E. A Glossary of Words Used in South-West Lincolnshire: Wapentake of Graffoe. (English Dialect Society Publications: No. 52). 1969. reprint ed. pap. 25.00 (*0-8115-0474-3*) Periodicals Srv.
Cole, Randall W. Encyclopedia of Landscaping & Patio Design: Over 325 Ideas for Landscaping & Patio Design. 1996. pap. text 19.95 (*0-9653287-0-8*) R C Publishing.
Cole, Ray, jt. auth. see Woo, Dennis.
Cole, Raymond & Bhaerman, Steve. Exercising Your Wellpower for Optimal Physical Health. (Illus.). 233p. (Orig.). 1984. pap. 9.95 (*0-917073-00-2*) Wellpower.
Cole, Raymond C., Jr., jt. auth. see Hales, H. Lee.
Cole, Raymond E. Choices? The Whole-Person Health Profile. 2nd ed. LC 86-50257. 52p. 1986. reprint ed. pap. 4.95 (*0-917073-02-9*) Wellpower.
***Cole, Raymond E.** Osteoporosis: Unmask a Silent Thief. Kehoe, Donna, ed. (Illus.). 240p. 2000. 19.95 (*0-917073-03-7*) Wellpower.
Cole, Rebecca. Paradise Found. LC 99-24767. 2000. 35.00 (*0-609-60415-5*) C Potter.
— Potted Gardens. LC 97-11235. 1997. 27.50 (*0-517-70457-9*) Crown Pub Group.
Cole, Rex D., et al. The Prairie Canyon Member, a New Unit of the Upper Cretaceous Mancos Shale, West-Central Colorado & East-Central Utah. (Miscellaneous Publication of the Utah Geological Survey Ser.: Vol. 97-4). (Illus.). 23p. 1997. pap. 3.00 (*1-55791-603-9*, MP-97-4) Utah Geological Survey.
Cole, Rex V. Artistic Anatomy of Trees. 2nd ed. (Illus.). 347p. 1965. pap. 8.95 (*0-486-21475-3*) Dover.
— Perspective for Artists. LC 77-15743. (Illus.). 279p. 1976. reprint ed. pap. 7.95 (*0-486-22487-2*) Dover.
Cole, Richard. The Glass Children. LC 86-4330. (Contemporary Poetry Ser.). 64p. 1986. pap. 15.95 (*0-8203-0873-0*) U of Ga Pr.
— Success Stories: Poems & Essays. 104p. 1998. pap. 11.95 (*0-9663248-0-3*) Limestone Bks.

C

Cole, Richard B. Corporate Personnel Protection: Developing & Executing an Effective Program Within a Business Corporation. LC 96-23680. (Illus.). 372p. (Orig.). 1997. text 74.95 (*0-398-06705-8*); pap. text 54.95 (*0-398-06706-6*) C C Thomas.

— Management of Internal Business Investigations: A Survival Guide. LC 96-9152. (Illus.). 178p. 1996. text 49.95 (*0-398-06702-3*); pap. text 33.95 (*0-398-06703-1*) C C Thomas.

Cole, Richard B., ed. Electrospray Ionization Mass Spectrometry: Fundamentals, Instrumentation & Applications. LC 96-36522. 600p. 1997. 94.95 (*0-471-14564-5*) Wiley.

Cole, Richard C. Thomas Mante Writer, Soldier, Adventurer. LC 93-25230. (American University Studies: Vol. 148). XVII, 214p. (C). 1994. text 39.95 (*0-8204-2259-2*) P Lang Pubng.

Cole, Richard C., et al, eds. The General Correspondence of James Boswell, 1766-1769, Vol. 2: 1768-1769. 268p. 1998. 75.00 (*0-300-07403-4*) Yale U Pr.

Cole, Richard J. & Cox, Richard H., eds. Handbook of Toxic Fungal Metabolites. LC 81-4082. 1981. text 188.00 (*0-12-179760-0*) Acad Pr.

Cole, Richard L. & Taebel, Delbert A. Texas: Politics & Public Policy. 411p. (C). 1987. teacher ed. write for info. (*0-318-61980-6*) Harcourt Coll Pubs.

Cole, Richard R., ed. Communication in Latin America: Journalism, Mass Media, & Society. LC 95-43170. (Jaguar Books on Latin America: No. 14). 256p. (C). 1996. 55.00 (*0-8420-2558-8*); pap. 18.95 (*0-8420-2559-6*) Scholarly Res Inc.

Cole, Richard W., jt. auth. see Carbo, Marie.

Cole, Robert. A. J. P. Taylor: The Traitor Within the Gates. LC 93-13506. 1993. text 45.00 (*0-312-10066-3*) St Martin.

— The Basenji Stacked & Moving. 188p. 1992. 21.95 (*0-920939-00-7*) Doral Pub.

— Getting Started in Unit & Investment Trusts. LC 96-39898. 256p. 1997. pap. 60.50 (*0-471-96844-7*) Wiley.

— The Moral Life of Children. (Illus.). 324p. 1991. pap. 14.00 (*0-395-59921-0*) HM.

— Propaganda in Twentieth Century War & Politics: An Annotated Bibliography. LC 96-27825. (Magill Bibliographies Ser.). 416p. 1996. 48.50 (*0-8108-3196-1*) Scarecrow.

— The Spiritual Life of Children. (Illus.). 384p. 1991. pap. 13.00 (*0-395-59923-7*) HM.

— A Traveller's History of France. 5th ed. (Traveller's History Ser.). 1998. pap. text 14.95 (*1-56656-280-5*) Interlink Pub.

— A Traveller's History of Paris. 2nd ed. (Traveller's History Ser.). (Illus.). 304p. 1998. pap. 14.95 (*1-56656-228-7*) Interlink Pub.

***Cole, Robert.** Wide-Area Data Network Performance Engineering. (Illus.). 1999. 89.00 (*0-89006-569-1*) Artech Hse.

Cole, Robert, ed. The Encyclopedia of Propaganda, 3 vols., Set. LC 97-18036. (Illus.). 1024p. (C). (gr. 13). 1997. text 249.00 (*0-7656-8009-2*, Sharpe Ref) M E Sharpe.

Cole, Robert & Reiss, David, eds. How Do Families Cope with Chronic Illness? (Advances in Family Research Ser.). 240p. 1993. text 49.95 (*0-8058-1111-7*) L Erlbaum Assocs.

Cole, Robert & Vaillant, Janet, eds. Activities for Teaching Russian & Soviet Studies in the High School. (Illus.). 212p. (Orig.). 1993. pap. 22.50 (*0-89994-328-4*) Soc Sci Ed.

Cole, Robert, jt. auth. see Carter, Randolph.

***Cole, Robert A.** Issues in Web-based Pedagogy: A Critical Primer. LC 99-49046. (The Greenwood Educators' Reference Collection). 432p. 2000. lib. bdg. 95.00 (*0-313-31226-5*, Greenwood Pr) Greenwood.

Cole, Robert B. Drug Treatment of Respiratory Disease. LC 81-10055. (Monographs in Clinical Pharmacology: No. 5). (Illus.). 346p. reprint ed. pap. 107.30 (*0-8357-6562-8*, 203593300097) Bks Demand.

Cole, Robert E. Managing Quality Fads: How American Business Learned to Play the Quality Game. (Illus.). 304p. 1999. 30.00 (*0-19-512260-7*) OUP.

— Strategies for Learning: Small-Group Activities in American, Japanese, & Swedish Industry. (Illus.). 364p. 1991. pap. 16.95 (*0-520-07398-3*, Pub. by U CA Pr) Cal Prin Full Svc.

Cole, Robert E., ed. Automobiles & the Future: Competition, Cooperation, & Change. LC 83-14345. (Michigan Papers in Japanese Studies: No. 10). x, 106p. 1983. pap. 9.00 (*0-939512-14-9*) U MI Japan.

— The Death & Life of the American Quality Movement. (Illus.). 256p. 1995. 30.00 (*0-19-509206-6*) OUP.

— Industry at the Crossroads. (Michigan Papers in Japanese Studies: No. 7). vii, 108p. 1982. pap. 9.00 (*0-939512-12-2*) U MI Japan.

— The Japanese Automobile Industry: Model & Challenge for the Future? LC 81-6185. (Michigan Papers in Japanese Studies: No. 3). ix, 147p. 1981. pap. 7.00 (*0-939512-08-4*) U MI Japan.

Cole, Robert F. Shattered Lives: The Path to Recovery. 135p. 1997. 11.95 (*1-880451-27-1*) Rainbows End.

Cole, Robert H. & Mishler, Lon. Consumer & Business Credit Management. 11th ed. LC 97-10347. 1997. write for info. (*0-256-18704-5*, Irwn Prfssnl) McGraw-Hill Prof.

Cole, Robert H. & Mishler, Lon L. Consumer & Business Credit Management. 10th ed. LC 94-1346. (Marketing Ser.). 468p. (C). 1994. text 68.95 (*0-256-13948-2*, Irwn McGrw-H) McGrw-H Hghr Educ.

***Cole, Robert L.** The Shape & Message of Book III (Psalms 73-89) (Journal for the Study of the Old Testament Supplement Ser.: No. 307). 300p. 2000. 85.00 (*1-84127-100-4*, Pub. by Sheffield Acad) CUP Services.

Cole, Robert W., ed. see ASCD Improving Student Achievement Research Panel.

***Cole, Robin.** Born Again Texan! LC 99-48505. 1999. pap. text 16.95 (*1-55622-730-2*) Wordware Pub.

Cole, Rodney. Physics for Scientists & Engineers. 1216p. (C). 2000. text 76.00 (*0-03-097362-7*) SCP.

— So You Want to Take Physics: A Preparatory Course. LC 92-25836. (C). 1993. text 40.00 (*0-03-096020-7*, Pub. by SCP) Harcourt.

— So You Want to Take Physics: A Preparatory Course with Algebra & Trigonometry. LC 92-41426. (C). 1993. text 40.00 (*0-03-097215-9*, Pub. by SCP) Harcourt.

Cole, Roger W., ed. see University of South Florida, Linguistic Institute.

Cole, Ron. Bats! Weidenman, Lauren, ed. (Ranger Rick Science Spectacular Ser.). 16p. (J). (gr. 2-4). 1996. pap. 16.95 (*1-56784-222-4*) Newbridge Educ.

— Bats! Student Book. Weidenman, Lauren, ed. (Ranger Rick Science Spectacular Ser.). (Illus.). 16p. (Orig.). (J). (gr. 2-4). 1996. pap. 3.95 (*1-56784-247-X*) Newbridge Educ.

— Bats! Theme Pack. Weidenman, Lauren, ed. (Ranger Rick Science Spectacular Ser.). (Illus.). 16p. (J). (gr. 2-4). 1996. pap. 36.90 (*1-56784-283-6*) Newbridge Educ.

— Remarkable Rocks. Weidenman, Lauren, ed. (Ranger Rick Science Spectacular Ser.). 16p. (J). (gr. 2-4). 1996. pap. 16.95 (*1-56784-221-6*) Newbridge Educ.

— Remarkable Rocks: Student Book. Weidenman, Lauren, ed. (Ranger Rick Science Spectacular Ser.). (Illus.). 16p. (Orig.). (J). (gr. 2-4). 1996. pap. 3.95 (*1-56784-246-1*) Newbridge Educ.

— Remarkable Rocks Theme Pack. Weidenman, Lauren, ed. (Ranger Rick Science Spectacular Ser.). (Illus.). 16p. (J). (gr. 2-5). 1996. pap. 36.90 (*1-56784-282-8*) Newbridge Educ.

— The World of Matter: Big Book. Weidenman, Lauren, ed. (Ranger Rick Science Spectacular Ser.). 16p. (J). (gr. 2-4). 1997. pap. text 16.95 (*1-56784-451-0*) Newbridge Educ.

— The World of Matter: Mini-Book. Weidenman, Lauren, ed. (Ranger Rick Science Spectacular Ser.). 16p. (J). (gr. 2-4). 1997. pap. text 19.95 (*1-56784-476-6*) Newbridge Educ.

Cole, Ron & Murawski, Darlyne. Secrets of Nature Set. Schaffer, Donna et al, eds. (Ranger Rick Science Spectacular Ser.). (Illus.). 16p. (J). (gr. 2-4). 1996. pap. write for info. (*1-56784-287-9*) Newbridge Educ.

Cole, Ron, et al. Secrets of Nature: Big Book Collection. Schaffer, Donna & Weidenman, Lauren, eds. (Ranger Rick Science Spectacular Ser.). (Illus.). 16p. (J). (gr. 2-4). 1996. pap. write for info. (*1-56784-288-7*) Newbridge Educ.

Cole, Ronald A., ed. Perception & Production of Fluent Speech. LC 79-25481. (Illus.). 576p. 1980. text 99.95 (*0-89859-019-1*) L Erlbaum Assocs.

Cole, Ronald H. Chairmanship of the Joint Chiefs of Staff. 239p. 1996. boxed set 39.00 (*0-16-048726-9*) USGPO.

— Operation Just Cause: The Planning & Execution of Joint Operations in Panama, February 1988-January 1990. 88p. (C). 1996. reprint ed. pap. text 25.00 (*0-7881-3557-0*) DIANE Pub.

Cole, Ronald H., et al. The History of the Unified Command Plan 1946-1993. 145p. (Orig.). (C). 1996. pap. text 35.00 (*0-7881-2827-2*) DIANE Pub.

Cole, Ronald H., jt. auth. see Laurie, Clayton D.

Cole, Ronald L. The Gentle Greeting: A Caring Obstetrician's Guide to Planning a Loving Pregnancy & Birth Experience. LC 98-10357. 192p. 1998. pap. 11.95 (*1-57071-325-1*) Sourcebks.

Cole, Ronnie M., et al. Handling Traffic Cases in South Carolina. LC 97-122189. 528p. (Orig.). 1996. pap. 50.00 (*0-943856-48-5*) SC Bar CLE.

Cole, Ronny M. Zany Knock Knocks. LC 92-43068. (Illus.). 96p. (J). (gr. 2-7). 1993. pap. 4.95 (*0-8069-8589-5*) Sterling.

Cole, Rosanne. Errors in Provisional Estimates of Gross National Product. (Studies in Business Cycles: No. 21). 123p. 1970. reprint ed. 32.00 (*0-87014-207-0*) Natl Bur Econ Res.

Cole, Roy. Functional Assessment of Low Vision. Rosenthal, Bruce P., ed. (Illus.). 192p. (C). (gr. 13). 1995. pap. text 37.95 (*0-8151-7347-4*, 24266) Mosby Inc.

— Measuring Drought & Drought Impacts in Red Sea Province, Sudan: Oxfam Research Discussion Papers. (Oxfam Research Discussion Papers). 304p. (C). 1989. 15.95 (*0-85598-168-7*, Pub. by Oxfam Pub) Stylus Pub VA.

Cole, Roy G. & Rosenthal, Bruce P., eds. Functional Assessment of Low Vision. (Mosby's Optometric Problem-Solving Ser.). 164p. 1996. pap. 29.95 (*1-888504-11-0*, P240) Lighthouse NYC.

— Problems in Optometry, Vol. 3, No. 3. 1991. write for info. (*1-888504-13-7*) Lighthouse NYC.

— Remediation & Management of Low Vision. (Mosby's Optometric Problem-Solving Ser.). 296p. 1996. pap. 31.95 (*1-888504-14-5*, P241) Lighthouse NYC.

— Remediation & Management of Low Vision. LC 95-39180. (Mosby's Optometric Problem Solving Ser.). (Illus.). 320p. (C). (gr. 13). 1995. pap. text 39.95 (*0-8151-5204-3*, 26454) Mosby Inc.

Cole, S. & Cole, Dale. The European Union & Migrant Labor. 1999. 65.00 (*1-85973-960-1*, Pub. by Berg Pubs); pap. 19.50 (*1-85973-965-2*, Pub. by Berg Pubs) NYU Pr.

Cole, S. G., et al. Applications of Interactionist Psychology: Essays in Honor of Saul B. Sells. 322p. 1988. 69.95 (*0-8058-0188-X*) L Erlbaum Assocs.

Cole, S. W. Nippur Vol. 4: The Early Neo-Babylonian Governor's Archive from Nippur. LC 96-67507. (Publications: Vol. 114). (Illus.). xliv, 458p. 1996. text 65.00 (*1-885923-03-1*) Orient Inst.

Cole, Sally. Women of the Praia: Work & Lives in a Portuguese Coastal Community. (Illus.). 181p. 1991. text 45.00 (*0-691-09464-0*, Pub. by Princeton U Pr); pap. text 15.95 (*0-691-02862-1*, Pub. by Princeton U Pr) Cal Prin Full Svc.

Cole, Sally J. Legacy on Stone: Rock Art of the Colorado Plateau & Four Corners Region. LC 90-45715. (Illus.). 280p. (Orig.). 1990. pap. 15.95 (*1-55566-074-5*) Johnson Bks.

Cole, Sam & Miles, Ian. Worlds Apart: Technology & North-South Relations in the Global Economy. LC 84-125439. 256p. (C). 1984. 38.50 (*0-8476-7374-X*) Rowman.

Cole, Sandra S., jt. auth. see Baker, Dianne I.

Cole, Scott C. Thirty-Fourth Battalion Virginia Cavalry. (Virginia Regimental Histories Ser.). 183p. 1993. 19.95 (*1-56190-054-0*) H E Howard.

Cole, Scott C. Thirty-Fourth Battalion Virginia Cavalry. (Virginia Regimental Histories Ser.). (Illus.). 183p. 1993. 19.95 (*0-685-74824-3*) H E Howard.

Cole, Shari. Plaited Patchwork. 128p. 1995. 19.95 (*0-89145-831-X*, 4513, Am Quilters Soc) Collector Bks.

Cole, Sharon A. The Emperor's New Clothes: A Comedy for All Ages. (Illus.). 30p. (J). (ps up). 1976. pap. 3.50 (*0-88680-045-5*) I E Clark.

***Cole, Shaun.** Don We Now Our Gay Apparel: Gay Men's Dress in the Twentieth Century. (Dress, Body, Culture Ser.). (Illus.). 224p. 2000. 65.00 (*1-85973-415-4*, Pub. by Berg Pubs); pap. 22.50 (*1-85973-420-0*, Pub. by Berg Pubs) NYU Pr.

Cole, Sheila. A Desirable Residence. large type ed. (Dales General Fiction Ser.). 367p. 1993. pap. 18.99 (*1-85389-426-5*, Dales) Ulverscroft.

— Growing up in America: The Different Lives of Boys & Girls. 2002. write for info. (*0-316-15196-3*) Little.

— What Kind of Love. 144p. (YA). (gr. 7 up). 1995. mass mkt. 4.50 (*0-380-72575-4*, Avon Bks) Morrow Avon.

— What Kind of Love? The Diary of a Pregnant Teenager. LC 94-78938. (Illus.). 192p. (YA). (gr. 5 up). 1995. 15.00 (*0-688-12848-3*) Lothrop.

— What Kind of Love? The Diary of a Pregnant Teenager. LC 94-78938. 1996. 9.60 (*0-606-10052-0*, Pub. by Turtleback) Demco.

— When the Tide Is Low. LC 84-10023. (Illus.). 32p. (J). (ps-1). 1985. 16.00 (*0-688-04066-7*) Lothrop.

Cole, Sheila, ed. see Luria, Aleksandr R.

Cole, Sherwood O. Not in Our Family! Helping Teenagers Cope with the Drug Scene. 224p. (Orig.). 1998. pap. 12.95 (*0-939497-49-2*) Promise Pub.

Cole, Sonia M. Early Man in East Africa. 3rd ed. LC 70-575763. 96 p. 1970. write for info. (*0-333-06001-6*) Macmillan.

Cole, Stephanie, jt. auth. see Parker, Alison M.

Cole, Stephen. Making Science: Between Nature & Society. (Illus.). 304p. (Orig.). 1992. text 49.95 (*0-674-54347-5*) HUP.

— Making Science: Between Nature & Society. (Illus.). 304p. (Orig.). (C). 1995. pap. text 16.95 (*0-614-07250-6*) HUP.

— Noel Coward: A Bio-Bibliography, 44. LC 93-28704. (Bio-Bibliographies in the Performing Arts Ser.: No. 44). 344p. 1993. lib. bdg. 69.50 (*0-313-28599-3*, Greenwood Pr) Greenwood.

— That Book about That Girl. (Illus.). 224p. 1999. pap. 16.95 (*1-58063-076-6*, Pub. by Renaissance) St Martin.

***Cole, Stephen.** 3-D Dinosaurs: Walking with Dinosaurs. (Illus.). 24p. (J). (gr. 4-7). 2000. pap. 9.95 (*0-7894-5207-3*, D K Ink) DK Pub Inc.

Cole, Stephen. The Unionization of Teachers: A Case Study of the UFT. Zuckerman, Harriet & Merton, Robert K., eds. LC 79-8986. (Dissertations on Sociology Ser.). 1980. reprint ed. lib. bdg. 25.95 (*0-405-12959-9*) Ayer.

***Cole, Stephen.** What's Wrong with Sociology? 2000. 39.95 (*0-7658-0039-X*) Transaction Pubs.

Cole, Stephen & Gardner, Louise. Alien Olympics. (Alien Pop-Ups Ser.). (Illus.). 12p. (J). 1998. 4.95 (*1-899607-65-X*) Sterling.

Cole, Stephen & Gardner, Lousie. Cars on Mars. (Alien Pop-Ups Ser.). (Illus.). 12p. (J). 1998. 4.95 (*1-899607-63-3*) Sterling.

— Mucky Martians. (Alien Pop-Ups Ser.). (Illus.). 12p. (J). 1998. 4.95 (*1-899607-62-5*) Sterling.

— School on Saturn. (Alien Pop-Ups Ser.). (Illus.). 12p. (J). 1998. 4.95 (*1-899607-64-1*) Sterling.

Cole, Stephen & Gordon, Linda. Making Science: Between Nature & Society. (Illus.). 304p. (Orig.). (C). 1995. pap. text 18.50 (*0-674-54344-0*) HUP.

Cole, Stephen, jt. auth. see Dallaire, Natalie.

Cole, Stephen A., jt. auth. see Rouverol, Alicia J.

***Cole, Steven Roger.** How Big is a Dinosaur? (J). 2000. pap. 4.95 (*0-7894-5209-X*) DK Pub Inc.

***Cole, Steven Rogers.** Walking with Dinosaurs Photo Journal. LC 99-42514. 48p. (J). (gr. 3-6). 2000. pap. 6.95 (*0-7894-5210-3*, D K Ink) DK Pub Inc.

Cole, Steven W. Nippur in Late Assyrian Times, c. 755-612 B. C. (State Archives of Assyria Ser.: Vol. 4). x, 116p. (Orig.). 1996. pap. text 29.50 (*951-45-7286-6*, Pub. by Neo-Assyrian Text) Eisenbrauns.

***Cole, Steven W. & Machinist, Peter, eds.** Letters from Priests to the Kings Esarhaddon & Assurbanipal. xxx, 221p. 1999. text 50.00 (*951-570-437-5*); pap. text 44.00 (*951-570-436-7*) Eisenbrauns.

Cole, Susan. Directors in Rehearsal: A Hidden World. 1992. pap. 15.95 (*0-685-59368-1*, Thtre Arts Bks) Routledge.

— Directors in Rehearsal: A Hidden World. (Illus.). 352p. (C). (gr. 13). 1992. pap. 20.99 (*0-87830-019-8*, Thtre Arts Bks) Routledge.

— Passion for Apocalypse. (Illus.). 36p. (Orig.). 1997. pap. 5.00 (*0-9637704-7-0*) Red Dragon VA.

— Preservation Guide No. 1: Family Papers. LC 84-106237. (Illus.). ii, 14p. 1983. pap. 3.95 (*0-917860-16-0*) Historic New Orleans.

Cole, Susan, jt. auth. see Porter, Douglas R.

Cole, Susan G. & Gail, Susan G. Power Surge: Sex, Violence & Pornography. 253p. 1995. pap. 14.95 (*0-929005-78-3*) Africa World.

Cole, Susan L. The Absent One: Mourning Ritual, Tragedy & the Performance of Ambivalence. LC 84-43063. 179p. 1985. 28.50 (*0-271-00391-X*) Pa St U Pr.

— The Absent One: Mourning Ritual, Tragedy, & the Performance of Ambivalence. 192p. 1991. pap. 16.95 (*0-271-00785-0*) Pa St U Pr.

— Playwrights in Rehearsal. (Illus.). 256p. (C). (gr. 13). 1999. 65.00 (*0-415-91969-X*, Thtre Arts Bks) Routledge.

Cole, SuzAnne C. To Our Heart's Content. LC 96-44117. 384p. 1997. pap. 12.95 (*0-8092-3146-8*, 314680, Contemporary Bks) NTC Contemp Pub Co.

Cole, SuzAnne C. & Lindemann, Jeff W. Reading & Responding to Literature. 328p. (C). 1989. pap. text 31.00 (*0-15-575501-3*) Harcourt Coll Pubs.

Cole, Sylvan, Jr. Grant Wood: The Lithographs: A Catalogue Raisonne. 48p. 1984. pap. 25.00 (*1-55660-122-0*) A Wofsy Fine Arts.

— John Steuart Curry - The Lithograph: A Catalogue Raisonne. 967p. 1976. pap. 30.00 (*1-55660-119-0*) A Wofsy Fine Arts.

— Raphael Soyer: Fifty Years of Printmaking, 1917-1967. LC 67-29917. (Graphic Art Ser.). 1983. 39.50 (*0-306-70986-4*) Da Capo.

Cole, Sylvan Jr. Kleinholz (Frank) Graphics, 1940-1975: Catalogue Raisonne. deluxe limited ed. (Illus.). 128p. 1975. 75.00 (*1-55660-160-3*) A Wofsy Fine Arts.

***Cole, Sylvia.** Facts on File Dictionary of Cultural & Historical Allusions. (Illus.). 560p. 2000. 35.00 (*0-8160-4057-5*) Facts on File.

***Cole, T.** Dictionary of Biology. (GER & ENG.). 774p. 1998. 195.00 (*0-320-01934-9*) Fr & Eur.

Cole, T. J., jt. ed. see Davies, Peter S.W.

Cole, Taylor. Canadian Bureaucracy & Federalism, Nineteen Forty-Seven to Sixty-Five. (Monograph Series in World Affairs: Vol. 3, 1965-66, Bk. 3). (Orig.). pap. 3.95 (*0-87940-009-9*) Monograph Series.

Cole, Taylor, ed. see Callaway, Archibald, et al.

Cole, Ted. Apart or A Part: Integration & the Growth of British Education. 160p. 1989. 113.00 (*0-335-09226-8*); pap. 33.95 (*0-335-09225-X*) OpUniv Pr.

***Cole, Ted.** Effective Schooling for Pupils with Emotional & Behavioural Difficulties. LC 98-203748. 1998. pap. text 29.95 (*1-85346-544-5*) Taylor & Francis.

Cole, Terence F., jt. auth. see Rohl, John C.

Cole, Terence F., tr. see Rohl, John C.

Cole, Terrence. The Cornerstone on College Hill: An Illustrated History of the University of Alaska, Fairbanks. LC 93-40545. (Illus.). xii, 394p. 1994. 35.00 (*0-912006-57-9*) U of Alaska Pr.

— Crooked Past: The History of a Frontier Mining Camp: Fairbanks, Alaska. LC 91-4024. (Illus.). ix, 164p. 1991. pap. 8.95 (*0-912006-53-6*) U of Alaska Pr.

— Ghosts of the Goldrush: A Walking Tour of Fairbanks. Haigh, Jane G. & Nielson, Jon, eds. (Illus.). 44p. 1987. pap. 3.95 (*0-940457-40-7*) Tanana Yukon Hist Soc.

Cole, Terrence, ed. see Rassmussen, Knud.

Cole, Terrence, ed. & frwd. see Harkey, Ira.

Cole, Terrence, ed. & pref. see Haskell, William B.

Cole, Thacker. Clipart Book of Owls in Action. LC 73-94337. 64p. 1974. pap. 10.95 (*0-87874-011-2*) Galloway.

Cole, Theodor. Pocket Dictionary of Botany: English-German, German-English. (ENG & GER.). 156p. 1994. 59.95 (*0-7859-9975-2*) Fr & Eur.

— Pocket Dictionary of Zoology: English-German, German-English. (ENG & GER.). 200p. 1995. 69.95 (*0-7859-9974-4*) Fr & Eur.

***Cole, Thomas.** The Article Book: Practice Toward Mastering a, an & The. (Illus.). 128p. (C). 2000. pap. text 16.95 (*0-472-08639-1*, 08639) U of Mich Pr.

Cole, Thomas. Democritus & the Sources of Greek Anthropology. (APA Philological Monographs). 238p. 1990. pap. 21.95 (*1-55540-514-2*) OUP.

— Epiploke: Rhythmical Continuity & Poetic Structure in Greek Lyric. LC 87-30467. (Loeb Classical Monographs). 288p. 1988. 35.00 (*0-674-25822-3*) HUP.

Cole, Thomas. Fish Trek: An Adventure in Articles. (Illus.). (C). audio compact disk 29.95 (*0-472-00299-6*, 00299) U of Mich Pr.

Cole, Thomas. The Origins of Rhetoric in Ancient Greece. LC 90-36983. (Ancient Society & History Ser.). 208p. 1995. pap. text 16.95 (*0-8018-5118-1*) Johns Hopkins.

— Thomas Cole's Poetry: The Collected Poems of America's Foremost Painter of the Hudson River School, Reflecting His Feelings for Nature & the Romantic Spirit of the 19th Century. Tymn, Marshall B., ed. LC 72-7843. (Illus.). 1972. boxed set 25.00 (*0-87387-057-3*) Shumway.

Cole, Thomas G., et al. Vegetation Survey & Forest Inventory, American Samoa. (Illus.). 20p. 1998. reprint ed. pap. 3.00 (*0-89904-903-6*, Ecosytems Resrch) Crumb Elbow Pub.

— Vegetation Survey of the Republic of Palau. (Illus.). 24p. 1998. reprint ed. pap. 3.50 (*0-89904-949-4*, Ecosytems Resrch) Crumb Elbow Pub.

Cole, Thomas R. The Journey of Life: A Cultural History of Aging in America. (Canto Book Ser.). (Illus.). 298p. (C). 1997. pap. 12.95 (*0-521-59579-7*) Cambridge U Pr.

— No Color Is My Kind: The Life of Eldrewey Stearns & the Integration of Houston. LC 96-44105. (Illus.). 272p. 1997. 40.00 (*0-292-71197-2*); pap. 17.95 (*0-292-71198-0*) U of Tex Pr.

C

Cole, Thomas R., et al, eds. Handbook of Humanities & Aging. 2nd ed. LC 99-41209. 472p. 1999. text 58.95 (*0-8261-6241-X*) Springer Pub.
— Handbook of the Humanities & Aging. LC 91-21954. 512p. 1992. 58.95 (*0-8261-6240-1*) Springer Pub.
— Voices & Visions of Aging: Toward a Critical Gerontology. LC 92-10680. 368p. 1992. 41.95 (*0-8261-8020-5*) Springer Pub.
Cole, Thomas R. & Gadow, Sally A., eds. What Does It Mean to Grow Old: Reflections from the Humanities. LC 85-27406. (Illus.). xiv, 302p. 1986. text 59.95 (*0-8223-0545-3*); pap. text 21.95 (*0-8223-0817-7*) Duke.
Cole, Thomas R. & Winkler, Mary C. The Oxford Book of Aging: Reflections on the Journey of Life. 432p. 1994. 30.00 (*0-19-507369-X*) OUP.
Cole, Tim. Selling the Holocaust: From Auschwitz to Schindler, How History Is Bought, Packaged & Sold. LC 99-16916. 224p. 1999. 22.95 (*0-415-92581-9*) Routledge.
***Cole, Tim.** Selling the Holocaust: From Auschwitz to Schindler, How History Is Bought, Packaged & Sold. 240p. 2000. pap. text 17.95 (*0-415-92813-3*) Routledge.
Cole, Tipton. Mastering SAP's ABAP-4. 1998. pap. text. write for info. (*0-7821-2253-1*) Sybex.
Cole, Toby. Acting: A Handbook. 1995. pap. 12.00 (*0-517-88477-1*) Random Hse Value.
— Actors on Acting. 1995. pap. 17.00 (*0-517-88478-X*) Random Hse Value.
Cole, Toby & Chinoy, Helen K. Directors on Directing: A Sourcebook of the Modern Theatre. 440p. (C). 1963. pap. text 62.00 (*0-02-323300-1*, Macmillan Coll) P-H.
Cole, Tom. About Time. 1991. pap. 5.25 (*0-8222-0002-3*) Dramatists Play.
— Hell West & Crooked. (Illus.). 304p. 1998. pap. 13.95 (*0-207-18984-6*) HarpC.
— Hell West & Crooked. large type ed. (Illus.). 1990. 27.99 (*0-7089-2166-3*) Ulverscroft.
— A Short History of San Francisco. LC 81-2588. (Illus.). 144p. (Orig.). 1981. pap. 12.95 (*0-938530-00-3*, 00-3) Lexikos.
Cole, Tom, ed. see Allen, Dorothy S.
Cole, Tom, ed. see Rosen, Robert N.
Cole, Trafford R. Italian Genealogical Records: How to Use Italian Civil, Ecclesiastical, & Other Records in Family History Research. LC 95-2042. 265p. 1995. 34.95 (*0-916489-58-2*) Ancestry.
Cole, Trevor. Gardening with Trees & Shrubs: In Canada & the Northern U. S. (Illus.). 240p. 1996. pap. text 19.95 (*1-55110-400-8*) Whitecap Bks.
Cole, Trisha. Who's That Whale? (Illus.). 15p. (J). (ps-3). 1995. 4.95 (*1-56550-026-1*) Vis Bks Intl.
Cole, Troy. Figure Eight Animals. 96p. teacher ed. 11.99 (*0-86653-721-X*, GA1439) Good Apple.
Cole, Troy, jt. auth. see Jackman, Tom.
Cole, Troy W. Minding Minutes with Minute Minders: More Than 150 Activities to Stimulate Creative Thinking. (Illus.). 96p. (J). (gr. k-9). 1994. 11.99 (*0-86653-795-3*, GA1489) Good Apple.
Cole-Turner, Ron, ed. Human Cloning - Religious Responses. LC 97-30287. 1997. pap. 15.00 (*0-664-25771-2*) Westminster John Knox.
Cole-Turner, Ronald. The New Genesis: Theology & the Genetic Revolution. LC 92-26564. 144p. (Orig.). 1993. pap. 15.95 (*0-664-25406-3*) Westminster John Knox.
***Cole-Turner, Ronald, ed.** Beyond Cloning: Religion & the Remaking of Humanity. 144p. 2000. pap. 17.00 (*1-56338-317-9*) TPI PA.
Cole-Turner, Ronald & Waters, Brent. Pastoral Genetics: Theology & Care at the Beginning of Life. LC 95-50981. 192p. (Orig.). 1996. pap. 15.95 (*0-8298-1077-3*) Pilgrim OH.
Cole, Vicki, ed. see Bialek, Kathy, et al.
Cole, Vicki, ed. see Dunnavant, Sandra, et al.
Cole, Vicki, ed. see Genet, Donna, et al.
Cole, Vicki, ed. see Lewellyn, Angie, et al.
Cole, Vicki, ed. see Payne, Claudine, et al.
Cole, Vicki, ed. see Trawick, Cynthia, et al.
Cole, Vicki L., ed. see Payne, Claudine, et al.
Cole, Victor, ed. see DiMaria, Ernie.
Cole, Victoria. Mind Reader. (Intimate Moments Ser.). 1993. per. 3.50 (*0-373-07510-3*, 5-07510-6) Silhouette.
Cole, W. Sex: Most Fun You Can Without Laughing. 1997. 5.98 (*0-7858-0807-8*) Bk Sales Inc.
Cole, W., et al. Law in a Business Context. (Business in Context Ser.). 300p. 1990. pap. text 29.95 (*0-412-02731-3*, A4469, Chap & Hall NY) Chapman & Hall.
Cole, W. A., jt. auth. see Deane, Phyllis.
Cole, W. G., jt. ed. see Williams, P. F.
Cole, W. Owen. Christianity. 124p. 1989. pap. 16.95 (*1-871402-08-5*) Dufour.
— Five Religions in the 20th Century. LC 81-68724. (Illus.). 256p. 1981. pap. 13.95 (*0-8023-1272-1*) Dufour.
— The Sikhs: Their Religious Beliefs. 1985. pap. 9.00 (*0-7100-8843-4*, Routledge Thoemms) Routledge.
Cole, W. Owen & Morgan, Peggy. Six Religions in the Twentieth Century. 320p. (Orig.). (C). 1993. pap. 27.50 (*0-7175-1290-8*, Pub. by S Thornes Pubs) Trans-Atl Phila.
***Cole, W. Owen & Morgan, Peggy.** Six Religions in the Twentieth Century. rev. ed. (Illus.). 352p. (Orig.). (YA). 2000. pap. 39.50 (*0-7487-5167-X*, Pub. by S Thornes Pubs) Trans-Atl Phila.
Cole, W. Owen & Sambhi, Piara S. The Sikhs. (Library of Religious Beliefs & Practices). 210p. (C). 1986. pap. text 13.95 (*0-415-04028-0*, 8843-4) Routledge.
— The Sikhs: Their Religious Beliefs & Practices. 220p. pap. 24.95 (*0-614-21935-3*, Pub. by Sussex Acad Pr) Intl Spec Bk.
— The Sikhs: Their Religious Beliefs & Practices. 2nd rev. ed. LC 96-126999. 1995. pap. 19.95 (*1-898723-13-3*, Pub. by Sussex Acad Pr) Intl Spec Bk.
Cole, W. Owen, ed. see Connolly, Holly & Connolly, Peter.
Cole, W. R. A Checklist of Science-Fiction Anthologies. LC 74-15956. (Science Fiction Ser.). (Illus.). 390p. 1977. reprint ed. 30.95 (*0-405-06323-7*) Ayer.
Cole, W. Roger, ed. see Lebeda, Guy & Neibaur, Alexander.
Cole, W. S. & Applin, E. A. Bulletins of American Paleontology Vol. 58, Issue 258: Analysis of Some American Upper Cretaceious Larger Forminifera. 46p. 1970. 2.00 (*0-87710-196-5*) Paleo Res.
Cole, Walter. Rough Seas & Fruit Trees: My Life in the 20th Century. (Illus.). 306p. 1997. pap. 10.00 (*1-887188-03-7*) Silesia Cos.
Cole, Wanda G., contrib. by. Grass Roots Art: Wisconsin. LC 78-65315. (Illus.). 48p. 1978. pap. 8.50 (*0-614-04928-8*) Kohler Arts.
Cole, Warren H., ed. Chemotherapy of Cancer. LC 74-85838. (Illus.). 359p. 1970. reprint ed. pap. 111.30 (*0-608-08143-4*, 201453500093) Bks Demand.
Cole, Wayne S. Determinism & American Foreign Relations During the Franklin D. Roosevelt Era. LC 94-32939. 1995. 33.50 (*0-8191-9739-4*) U Pr of Amer.
— Norway & the United States, 1905-1955: Two Democracies in Peace & War. LC 89-1860. (Illus.). 233p. 1989. reprint ed. pap. 72.30 (*0-608-00045-0*, 206081100006) Bks Demand.
— Roosevelt & the Isolationists, 1932-1945. LC 82-8624. 710p. reprint ed. pap. 200.00 (*0-7837-4654-7*, 204437800002) Bks Demand.
Cole, Wendell. Kyoto in the Momoyama Period. LC 67-15586. (Centers of Civilization Ser.: Vol. 12). 180p. reprint ed. pap. 55.80 (*0-608-12443-5*, 205214600042) Bks Demand.
Cole, Wendy. A Guide to Starting a Business in Las Vegas. 3rd ed. Kuhlmann, Mary E., ed. 155p. 1996. spiral bd. 24.95 (*0-9630890-0-5*) Abacus & Quill.
— Whoremaster: A Biography. 206p. 1997. pap. 13.95 (*0-9630890-1-3*) Abacus & Quill.
Cole, Wendy M. Vietnam: Major World nations. LC 97-21880. (Major World Nations Ser.). (Illus.). 144p. (YA). (gr. 5 up). 1999. lib. bdg. 19.95 (*0-7910-4751-2*) Chelsea Hse.
Cole-Whittaker, Terry. What You Think of Me Is None of My Business. (Orig.). 1988. mass mkt. 5.99 (*0-515-09479-X*, Jove) Berkley Pub.
Cole, William. Have I Got Dogs! LC 93-12464. 1996. 10.19 (*0-606-09396-6*, Pub. by Turtleback) Demco.
— Monster Knock Knocks. (Orig.). (J). (gr. 3-6). 1990. mass mkt. 2.75 (*0-671-70653-5*) PB.
— Oh What Nonsense. 80p. 1997. pap. 3.99 (*0-14-038554-1*) Penguin Putnam.
— Poem Stew. (J). 1983. 10.15 (*0-606-02564-2*, Pub. by Turtleback) Demco.
— When You Consider the Alternative. 144p. 1996. pap. 8.95 (*0-312-14445-8*) St Martin.
— A Zooful of Animals. LC 91-21885. (Illus.). 96p. (J). 1996. pap. 8.95 (*0-395-77873-5*, Sandpiper) HM.
— A Zooful of Animals. LC 91-21885. (J). 1992. 14.15 (*0-606-10108-X*, Pub. by Turtleback) Demco.
Cole, William, ed. New York: A Literary Companion. 1992. 13.95 (*0-916366-59-6*, Pub. by Pushcart Pr) Norton.
— Poem Stew. (Illus.). (J). (gr. 3-6). 1981. 7.66 (*0-397-31963-0*, 229850) Lppncott W & W.
Cole, William & Phillips, Louis. Sex: Even More Fun Without Laughing. (Illus.). 150p. 1997. 5.98 (*0-7858-0808-6*) Bk Sales Inc.
Cole, William C., jt. ed. see Sperelakis, Nicholas.
Cole, William E. Arkful of Animals. 88p. (J). (gr. 4-7). 1992. pap. 4.95 (*0-395-61618-2*) HM.
— Corpus Vitrearum Medii Aevi: Great Britain, Summary Catalogue 1. (Corpus Vitraearum Medii Aevi: Great Britain Summary Catalogue 1 British Academy Ser.). (Illus.). 368p. 1993. text 135.00 (*0-19-726116-7*) OUP.
Cole, William E., ed. Quotable New York: A Literary Companion. LC 92-44784. (Illus.). 96p. 1993. pap. 9.95 (*0-14-017631-4*, Penguin Bks) Viking Penguin.
Cole, William E., et al. Technology, Innovation, & Industrial Economics: Institutionalist Perspectives: Essays in Honor of William E. Cole. LC 98-19017. 1998. 89.95 (*0-7923-8191-2*) Kluwer Academic.
Cole, William E., ed. & intro. see Street, James H., et al.
Cole, William H., ed. Some Aspects of Amino Acid Supplementation. LC TX0553.A5S64. 97p. reprint ed. pap. 30.10 (*0-608-10063-3*, 205049200083) Bks Demand.
***Cole, William J., et al.** Guide to Physicians & Other Health Care Professionals, 3 vols. 1999. ring bd. 155.00 (*0-7646-0874-6*) Prctnrs Pub Co.
— Guide to Physicians & Other Health Care Professionals, Vol. 1. 1999. ring bd. write for info. (*0-7646-0875-4*) Prctnrs Pub Co.
— Guide to Physicians & Other Health Care Professionals, Vol. 2. 1999. ring bd. write for info. (*0-7646-0876-2*) Prctnrs Pub Co.
— Guide to Physicians & Other Health Care Professionals, Vol. 3. 1999. ring bd. write for info. (*0-7646-0877-0*) Prctnrs Pub Co.
Cole, William M. Accounts: Their Construction & Interpretation for Business Men & Students of Affairs. LC 75-18462. (History of Accounting Ser.). 1976. 36.95 (*0-405-07546-4*) Ayer.
Cole, William M. & Geddes, Anne E. The Fundamentals of Accounting: With a List of Best Books in Accounting. Brief, Richard P., ed. LC 77-87265. (Development of Contemporary Accounting Thought Ser.). 1978. reprint ed. lib. bdg. 37.95 (*0-405-10894-X*) Ayer.
Cole, Willis S., Jr. The Last Flight of "The Lady Jeannette" LC 99-167483. viii, 288p. 1998. 25.00 (*0-9662728-0-3*) BCWSCMM.
Colean, M. L. Housing for Defense: A Review of the Role of Housing in Relation to America's Defense & a Program for Actions. LC 77-74932. (American Federalism-the Urban Dimension Ser.). (Illus.). 1978. reprint ed. lib. bdg. 23.95 (*0-405-10480-4*) Ayer.
Colean, Miles L. The Impact of Government on Real Estate Finance in the United States. (Financial Research Program IV: Studies in Urban Mortgage Financing: No. 2). 189p. 1950. reprint ed. 49.20 (*0-87014-140-6*) Natl Bur Econ Res.
Colebatch. Market, Bureaucracy & Com: A Student's Guide to Organisation. LC 93-33091. 144p. (C). 44.95 (*0-7453-0762-0*, Pub. by Pluto GBR); pap. 15.95 (*0-7453-0763-9*, Pub. by Pluto GBR) Stylus Pub VA.
Colebatch, H. K. Policy. LC 97-36034. (Concepts in Social Thought Ser.). 1998. 37.95 (*0-8166-3137-9*); pap. 14.95 (*0-8166-3138-7*) U of Minn Pr.
Colebourn, R. Latin Sentence & Idiom: A Composition Course. 292p. 1987. reprint ed. 25.95 (*0-86292-265-8*, Pub. by Brist Class Pr) Focus Pub-R Pullins.
Colebrook. New Literary Histories: New Historicism & Contemporary Criticism. LC 97-11953. 208p. 1997. pap. 27.95 (*0-7190-4987-3*, Pub. by Manchester Univ Pr) St Martin.
— New Literary Histories: New Historicism & Contemporary Criticism. LC 97-11953. 208p. 1998. 59.95 (*0-7190-4986-5*, Pub. by Manchester Univ Pr) St Martin.
Colebrook, Binda. Winter Gardening in the Maritime Northwest: Cool Season Crops for the Year-Round Gardener. 2nd rev. ed. (Illus.). 170p. 1984. pap. 10.95 (*0-916239-00-4*) Maritime Pubns.
— Winter Gardening in the Maritime Northwest: Cool Season Crops for the Year-Round Gardener. 3rd ed. LC 98-26952. (Illus.). 164p. 1998. pap. 15.95 (*1-57061-162-9*) Sasquatch Bks.
***Colebrook, Claire.** Ethics & Representation: From Kant to Poststructuralism. 2000. 65.00 (*0-7486-1101-0*, Pub. by Edinburgh U Pr) Col U Pr.
Colebrook, Claire, jt. ed. see Buchanan, Ian.
Colecchia, Francesca & Matas, Julio, trs. Selected Latin American One-Act Plays. LC 72-92696. 224p. 1973. pap. 69.50 (*0-608-05090-3*, 206564400005) Bks Demand.
Colecchia, Francesca, ed. & tr. see Solorzano, Carlos.
Colecchia, Francesca M., jt. ed. see Gonzalez-Cruz, Luis F.
Colectivo de Medicina Natural. La Curacion Natural del Asma y las Alergias.Tr. of Natural Cure for Asthma & Alergies. 25.50 (*84-7927-200-7*) Robinbook.
Colegate, S. M. & Dorling, P. R., eds. Plant-Associated Toxins: Agricultural, Phytochemical & Ecological Aspects. (Illus.). 596p. 1994. text 150.00 (*0-85198-909-8*) OUP.
Colegate, Steven M. Bioactive Natural Products: Detection - Isolation - Etc. 544p. 1993. boxed set 225.95 (*0-8493-4372-0*, QD415) CRC Pr.
Colegrave, Sukie. By Way of Pain: A Passage into Self. 1988. pap. 9.95 (*0-89281-241-9*, Park St Pr) Inner Tradit.
***Colegrove, Charles.** Charlie Goes West. Headrick, Richard, ed. (Illus.). 302p. 2000. pap. 9.95 (*0-9768882-7-1*) MBrio Bks.
Colegrove, James W. Vacation Dreams. (Illus.). 66p. (Orig.). 1984. pap. 10.00 (*0-918855-01-2*) Aldin Pub.
Colehour, Julie, jt. auth. see Frause, Bob.
Coleiro, E. Tematica e Structtura Dell'Eneide Di Virgilio. (ITA.). 148p. (Orig.). 1983. pap. 24.00 (*90-6032-245-2*, Pub. by B R Gruner) Humanities.
Colella, A. Dictionary of Electrical Science & Technology. (ENG & ITA.). 759p. 1988. 195.00 (*0-8288-4038-5*, F135870) Fr & Eur.
— Italian-English - English-Italian Dictionary of Science & Electronic Technology. 759p. 1988. 132.00 (*0-88431-073-6*) IBD Ltd.
— Nuovo Dizionario di Elettrotecnic e di Elettronica: Italiano-Inglese, Inglese-Italiano. (ENG & ITA.). 541p. 1977. 125.00 (*0-8288-5505-6*, M9296) Fr & Eur.
Colella, C. Paul. C. I. Lewis & the Social Theory of Conceptualistic Pragmatism: The Individual & the Good Social Order. LC 92-1107. 232p. 1992. lib. bdg. 89.95 (*0-7734-9800-1*) E Mellen.
Colella, David. Commutative Harmonic Analysis. LC 89-7039. 305p. 1989. pap. 43.00 (*0-8218-5097-0*, CONM/91) Am Math.
Colella, Rick. Fear Society Twist: Poems & Stories, 1989-1990. Iddings, Kathleen, ed. LC 91-62375. 95p. (Orig.). 1992. per. 10.00 (*0-931289-08-4*) San Diego Poet Pr.
Coleman. Choppers, Vol. 1. 1998. 6.99 (*0-312-96635-0*, Pub. by Tor Bks) St Martin.
Coleman. Couples. (Focus Ser.). 1994. pap. 5.95 (*1-883419-28-X*) Serendipty Hse.
Coleman. Ghosts of the Trianon. 1988. 12.95 (*0-85030-774-0*, Pub. by Aqrn Pr) Harper SF.
— Hospital Transport Ship Diary. (J). 1995. 15.00 (*0-671-87156-0*) S&S Bks Yung.
— Intimate Relationships in Marriage. 2nd ed. 1988. pap. text, student ed. 20.00 (*0-02-323440-7*, Macmillan Coll) P-H.
— Management Ready Notes, \. 1998. 14.74 (*0-07-428372-3*) McGraw.
— Mastering Basics: Ephesians. 1994. pap. 5.95 (*1-883419-30-1*) Serendipty Hse.
— Mastering Basics: Ephesians. large type ed. 1994. pap. 15.00 (*1-883419-40-9*) Serendipty Hse.
— Mastering Basics: I & II Timothy. large type ed. 1994. pap. 15.00 (*1-883419-42-5*) Serendipty Hse.
— Mastering Basics: I Corinthian. large type ed. 1994. pap. 15.00 (*1-883419-39-5*) Serendipty Hse.
Coleman. Mastering Basics: I Corinthians. 1994. pap. 5.95 (*1-883419-29-8*) Serendipty Hse.
Coleman. Mastering Basics: I John. 1994. pap. 5.95 (*1-883419-35-2*) Serendipty Hse.
— Mastering Basics: I Peter. 1994. pap. 5.95 (*1-883419-34-4*); pap. 15.00 (*1-883419-44-1*) Serendipty Hse.
— Mastering Basics: James. 1994. pap. 5.95 (*1-883419-33-6*); pap. 15.00 (*1-883419-43-3*) Serendipty Hse.
— Mastering Basics: Philippians. large type ed. 1994. pap. text 15.00 (*1-883419-41-7*) Serendipty Hse.
— Mastering Basics: Romans. 1995. pap. 5.95 (*1-883419-27-1*) Serendipty Hse.
— Mastering Basics: Romans. large type ed. 1994. pap. 15.00 (*1-883419-38-7*) Serendipty Hse.
Coleman. Mastering Basics: 1 & 2 Timothy. 1994. pap. 5.95 (*1-883419-32-8*) Serendipty Hse.
— The Okeefe Empire. LC 98-42373. Date not set. 19.95 (*0-7862-1324-8*) Thorndike Pr.
Coleman. The Practice & Procedure of the Commercial Court. 4th ed. (Lloyd's Commercial Law Library). 300p. 1995. 175.00 (*1-85044-859-0*) LLP.
— Redesigning American Education. 192p. 2000. pap. text 24.00 (*0-8133-9102-4*, Pub. by Westview) HarpC.
— Social Problems. 7th ed. LC 98-38657. 576p. (C). 1998. 69.00 (*0-321-01848-6*, Prentice Hall) P-H.
***Coleman.** Spin Cycle. 2000. mass mkt. 18.00 (*0-306-80984-2*, Pub. by Da Capo) HarpC.
Coleman. Strategies for College Writing: A Rhetorical Reader. LC 99-14777. 584p. (C). 1999. pap. 36.80 (*0-13-081224-2*) P-H.
***Coleman.** Televised Election Debates. LC 99-32868. 211p. 1999. text 65.00 (*0-312-22561-X*) St Martin.
Coleman, et al, eds. The Popular Carol Book: Music Edition, Words Edition. (Illus.). 1998. pap. 9.50 (*0-264-67480-4*, Pub. by A R Mowbray) Cassell & Continuum.
Coleman & Calvi. Texas Government. 254p. 1995. pap. text 37.40 (*0-13-912932-4*) P-H.
Coleman, et al. American Pie, Myth Representation. (Illus.). 16p. 1992. pap. 3.00 (*0-939784-22-X*) CEPA Gall.
— Package Design & Brand Identity: 38 Case Studies of Strategic Imagery for the Marketplace. LC 94-230304. (Illus.). 160p. 1993. 34.95 (*1-56496-041-2*, 30533) Rockport Pubs.
Coleman, jt. auth. see Claris.
Coleman, ed. see Cassell Publishing Staff.
Coleman, ed. see La Peruse.
***Coleman, Jane Candia.** Doc Holliday's Gone: A Western Duo. LC 99-41705. 261p. 1999. 19.95 (*0-7862-1841-X*) Mac Lib Ref.
Coleman, Jane Candia. Moving On: Stories of the West, 1. (Love Spell Ser.). 320p. 1999. mass mkt. 4.99 (*0-8439-4545-1*) Dorchester Pub Co.
— Moving On: Stories of the West. large type ed. LC 96-43960. (Five Star Ser.). 310p. 1997. 17.95 (*0-7862-0732-9*) Five Star.
— Moving On: Stories of the West. large type ed. LC 97-45642. (G. K. Hall Western Ser.). 1998. 23.95 (*0-7838-8383-8*, G K Hall Lrg Type) Mac Lib Ref.
— Moving On: Stories of the West. large type ed. 1999. 20.00 (*0-7862-0755-8*) Thorndike Pr.
Coleman, Rita M., ed. see Andersen Consulting Staff.
Coleman, A. Flaubert's Literary Development in the Light of His Memories D'un Fou Novembre, & Education Sentimentale. (Elliott Monographs: Vol. 1). 1914. 25.00 (*0-527-02605-0*) Periodicals Srv.
— Sources & Structure of Flaubert's Salammbo. (Elliott Monographs: Vol. 2). 1914. pap. 25.00 (*0-527-02606-9*) Periodicals Srv.
Coleman, A. D. Critical Focus. 172p. 1996. pap. text 24.95 (*3-923922-26-4*, Pub. by Nazraeli Pr) Dist Art Pubs.
— Depth of Field: Essays on Photographs, Mass Media, & Lens Culture. LC 98-6965. (Illus.). 216p. 1998. pap. 19.95 (*0-8263-1816-9*); lib. bdg. 45.00 (*0-8263-1815-0*) U of NM Pr.
— The Digital Evolution: Photography in the Electronic Age. (Illus.). 200p. 1998. pap. 24.95 (*3-923922-52-3*, 810571, Pub. by Nazraeli Pr) Dist Art Pubs.
— Manuel Alvarez Bravo. 2nd ed. (Masters of Photography Ser.). (Illus.). 96p. 1997. reprint ed. 18.95 (*0-89381-742-2*) Aperture.
— Robert Stivers: Photographs. 112p. 1997. 65.00 (*0-9657280-0-5*) Dist Art Pubs.
— Tarnished Silver - After the Photo Boom: Essays on Photography & Related Matters 1979-1989. LC 95-80903. (Illus.). 224p. (Orig.). 1996. pap. 20.00 (*1-877675-20-2*) Midmarch Arts.
Coleman, A. D., intro. Brad Cole: The Last Dream. (Lux Ser.: Vol. V). (Illus.). 60p. 1998. 50.00 (*0-9630393-7-7*) Ctr for Photo.
Coleman, A. D. & Auer, Anna, contrib. by. Exodus from Austria: Emigration of Austrian Photographers, 1920-1940. (GER & ENG., Illus.). 278p. 1998. 60.00 (*3-908161-27-4*) Abbeville Pr.
Coleman, A. D., et al. Photography A-V Program Directory. LC 80-83469. (Illus.). 224p. 1980. 28.00 (*0-936524-00-6*) PMI Inc.
***Coleman, A. Eugene.** 52-Week Baseball Training. (Illus.). 296p. 2000. pap. 19.95 (*0-7360-0322-3*) Human Kinetics.
***Coleman, A. John & Yukalov, V. I., eds.** Reduced Density Matrices: Coulson's Challenge. LC 00-28022. (Lecture Notes in Chemistry Ser.). (Illus.). xii, 282p. 2000. pap. 69.80 (*3-540-67148-X*) Spr-Verlag.
***Coleman, A. Michael.** Collection Management Handbook: The Art of Getting Paid. 2nd ed. LC 98-17814. 300p. 1998. 99.00 (*0-471-25414-2*) Wiley.

C

Coleman, A. Michael. A Passion for Trains: A Rail Aficionado's Diary. Ziel, Ron, ed. & illus. by. 238p. 1989. 59.00 (*0-685-26484-X*) A M Coleman.

Coleman, Alexander, ed. Cinco Maestros. (SPA.). 328p. (C). 1969. pap. text 42.00 (*0-15-507551-9*) Harcourt Coll Pubs.

Coleman, Alexander & Simmons, Charles. All There Is To Know: From Abracadabra to Emile Zola...Here is the Highest Monument to Victorian Culture-Readings from the Illustrious 11th Edition of the Encyclopaedia Britannica. 432p. 1995. pap. 15.00 (*0-671-50005-8*, Touchstone) S&S Trade Pap.

Coleman, Alexander, tr. see Padilla, Heberto.

Coleman, Alexis I., tr. see Maeterlinck, Maurice.

Coleman, Allan D. Confirmation. 2nd ed. (Illus.). 48p. 1982. pap. 4.00 (*0-9608870-0-8*) ADCO Enterp.

Coleman, Amy. The Best of Home Cooking with Amy Coleman. LC 98-20860. (Illus.). 192p. 1999. pap. 19.95 (*0-8118-2256-7*) Chronicle Bks.

Coleman, Andrew, ed. see Borges, Jorge Luis.

Coleman, Ann. A Marriage Made in Heaven. LC 97-65640. 192p. (Orig.). 1997. pap. 13.95 (*1-57736-032-X*) Providence Hse.

***Coleman, Ann M.** On Your Own: A Resource Manual for Starting a Successful Private Practice as a Solo Practitioner in Speech-Language Pathology. LC 00-27971. 2000. write for info. (*0-89079-853-2*) PRO-ED.

Coleman, Anna M. We Would Lie on the Air. (Illus.). 32p. (Orig.). 1987. pap. 10.00 (*0-944290-00-0*) Light Speed.

Coleman, Anne. Creative Embroidery: A Practical Guide. (Illus.). 120p. 1987. 15.95 (*0-900873-85-X*, Pub. by Bishopsgte Pr); pap. 11.95 (*0-900873-86-8*, Pub. by Bishopsgte Pr) Intl Spec Bk.

— Fabrics & Yarns. (Craft Projects Ser.). (Illus.). 32p. (J). (gr. 2-6). 1990. lib. bdg. 22.60 (*0-86592-483-X*) Rourke Enter.

— A Family Affair. LC 99-41965. 1999. 24.95 (*0-7862-2138-0*, Five Star MI) Mac Lib Ref.

***Coleman, Anne.** Riotous Roscommon: Social Unrest in the 1840s. LC 99-31101. (Maynooth Studies in Local History). 64p. 1999. 10.95 (*0-7165-2671-9*, Pub. by Irish Acad Pr) Intl Spec Bk.

Coleman, Annette W., jt. auth. see International Symposium on Inclusion Phenomena & Molecular Recognition Staff.

Coleman, Anthony. The Practice & Procedure of the Commercial Court. 3rd enl. ed. 252p. 1990. 105.00 (*1-85044-287-8*) LLP.

Coleman, Antoinette A. Child Abuse Reporting: An Urban Profile. rev. ed. LC 95-38866. (Children of Poverty Ser.). (Illus.). 184p. 1995. text 55.00 (*0-8153-2194-5*) Garland.

Coleman, Arica L. Poetic Praise, Vol. I. 50p. (Orig.). 1993. pap. 10.00 (*1-883435-01-3*) Insight Pubns.

***Coleman, Arry.** Blue Eyes. LC 99-91533. 2000. 25.00 (*0-7388-0852-0*); pap. 18.00 (*0-7388-0853-9*) Xlibris Corp.

Coleman, Arthur D. Keeping Christmas Christian. LC 99-28069. 1999. lib. bdg. write for info. (*1-55888-826-8*) Omnigraphics Inc.

Coleman, Arthur P. Humor in the Russian Comedy from Catherine to Gogol. LC 25-11187. reprint ed. 20.00 (*0-404-01589-1*) AMS Pr.

— The Last Million Years: A History of the Pleistocene in North America. LC 75-41062. (BCL Ser.: Ii). reprint ed. 49.50 (*0-404-14656-2*) AMS Pr.

Coleman, Arthur P., tr. see Slowacki, Juliusz.

Coleman, B. I. Conservatism & the Conservative Party in 19th-Century Britain. 192p. (C). 1988. pap. text 13.95 (*0-7131-6496-4*, Pub. by E A) Routldge.

Coleman, Barbara J. Primer on ERISA. 4th ed. LC 92-35173. 214p. 1993. text 45.00 (*0-87179-781-X*, 0781) BNA Books.

Coleman, Barbara T. The Parkinson Predicament & a Spoonful of Sugar: My Life with Parkinson's Disease/A Prescription for Living with Parkinson's Disease. Green, Barry, ed. (Illus.). 112p. 1997. pap. text 24.95 (*0-9642109-2-4*) Parkinsonian.

Coleman, Bernadene H. Mama Rose: A Novel. 292p. 1998. pap. 12.95 (*1-881524-35-3*) Milligan Bks.

Coleman, Bernard H. Diseases of the Nose, Throat & Ear. 14th ed. (Illus.). 304p. (Orig.). 1992. pap. text 35.00 (*0-443-04563-1*) Church.

Coleman, Bernice. Cooking Creole, Cajun, & Southern Chicago Style. (Orig.). 1988. pap. 12.00 (*0-9645268-0-8*) B Coleman.

Coleman, Bill & Coleman, Patty. God's Own Child, Parents' Book. rev. ed. LC 95-60062. 64p. 1995. pap. 4.95 (*0-89622-652-2*) Twenty-Third.

— My Confirmation Journal. rev. ed. 112p. (J). (gr. 6-9). 1991. pap. 4.95 (*0-89622-483-X*, B67) Twenty-Third.

— Only Love Can Make It Easy, 2 vols. rev. ed. LC 80-53335. 160p. 1997. pap., teacher ed. 9.95 (*0-89622-132-6*); pap., student ed. 4.95 (*0-89622-131-8*) Twenty-Third.

— Only Love Can Make It Easy: Episcopal Edition. LC 88-50890. 80p. 1997. pap. 4.95 (*0-89622-383-3*); pap., teacher ed. 9.95 (*0-89622-382-5*) Twenty-Third.

Coleman, Bob. The Great American Idea Book. 336p. 1995. pap. 13.00 (*0-393-31211-9*) Norton.

Coleman, Bob & Neville, Deborah. The Great American Idea Book -- Make Money from Your Ideas: Movies, Music, Books, Inventions, Businesses, & Almost Anything Else! 334p. 1998. text 23.00 (*0-7881-5747-7*) DIANE Pub.

Coleman, Bob, ed. see Slutsky, Jeff.

Coleman Brawer, Catherine & Wu, Geri. Trade Winds: The Lure of the China Trade 16th-19th Centuries. (Illus.). 24p. 1985. 6.00 (*0-915171-01-5*) Katonah Gal.

***Coleman, Brooke.** The Colony of Georgia. LC 98-32371. (Library of the Thirteen Colonies & the Lost Colony). (Illus.). 24p. (J). (gr. 3). 2000. 19.33 (*0-8239-5474-9*, PowerKids) Rosen Group.

Coleman, Bruce R. True Stars of the Major Leagues. LC 97-92532. (Illus.). 512p. 1998. 39.95 (*0-9659796-2-8*) Circuit Clout.

Coleman, C. Understanding Crime Data: Haunted by the Dark Figure. (Crime & Justice Ser.). 160p. 1996. pap. 29.95 (*0-335-19518-0*) OpUniv Pr.

Coleman, C. & Hart, G. Income Tax Analysis: Cases, Questions & Commercial Applications. 600p. 1994. pap. 97.00 (*0-409-30494-8*, Austral, MICHIE) LEXIS Pub.

Coleman, C., jt. auth. see Gisolfi, Anthony M.

Coleman, C., jt. auth. see Lehmann, G.

Coleman, C. B., ed. Three French Comedies. Magruder, James, tr. & intro. by. 1996. 32.50 (*0-300-06275-3*); pap. 16.00 (*0-300-06276-1*) Yale U Pr.

Coleman, Candy. Santa Claus in My Kitchen. (Illus.). 48p. (Orig.). 1979. pap. text 3.00 (*0-943768-01-2*) C Coleman.

— Super Menus for Football Fans. (Illus.). 48p. (Orig.). 1981. pap. text 3.00 (*0-943768-04-7*) C Coleman.

— Tailgate Picnics for the Southwest Conference. (Illus.). 48p. (Orig.). 1981. pap. text 4.00 (*0-943768-05-5*) C Coleman.

— A Taste & Tour of Dallas. (Illus.). 112p. (Orig.). 1986. spiral bd. 7.95 (*0-943768-08-X*) C Coleman.

— There's a One-Armed Bandit in My Kitchen. (Illus.). 48p. (Orig.). 1980. pap. text 3.00 (*0-943768-03-9*) C Coleman.

— The Way to a Man's Heart. (Illus.). 32p. (Orig.). 1979. pap. text 3.00 (*0-943768-02-0*) C Coleman.

Coleman, Candy, ed. see Hickey, Dave.

Coleman, Candy, ed. see Myers, Terry R.

Coleman, Carol & Smith, Steve. Life As a Peace Corps Volunteer in the Federated States of Micronesia. (Illus.). 28p. 1986. pap. text 6.95 (*0-936731-04-4*) Devel Self Rel.

— Life As a Peace Corps Volunteer in the Republic of the Marshall Islands. (Illus.). 28p. 1986. pap. text 6.95 (*0-936731-05-2*) Devel Self Rel.

Coleman, Carol, jt. auth. see Packer, Lester.

Coleman, Carol, jt. auth. see Smith, Steven C.

Coleman, Carol, ed. see Garcia, Oz.

Coleman, Carter. The Volunteer. LC 97-46659. 288p. 1998. 24.00 (*0-446-52203-1*, Pub. by Warner Bks) Little.

— The Volunteer. 1999. pap. write for info. (*0-446-67473-7*) Warner Bks.

Coleman, Catherine. The Cape Cod Collection: Stories & Poems for Children. (Illus.). 55p. (J). (gr. k-8). 1998. pap. 15.00 (*1-891331-10-8*) Nebbadoon Pr.

Coleman, Catherine N., ed. see Taylor, Martin D.

Coleman, Charles. Mayday! Mayday! Mayday! This Is the Haleakala. LC 92-27856. 264p. 1997. 24.95 (*0-9634022-1-8*); pap. 17.95 (*0-9634022-0-X*) Word Prof.

— Mythology of the Hindus. (C). 1995. reprint ed. 88.00 (*81-206-0971-9*, Pub. by Asian Educ Servs) S Asia.

Coleman, Charles C. Early Records of the First Presbyterian Church at Goshen, 1767-1885. (Illus.). 215p. 1997. reprint ed. pap. 25.00 (*0-8328-6149-9*) Higginson Bk Co.

Coleman, Charles D. Heartful's Educational Coloring Book. (J). (gr. 1-3). 1998. pap. 7.95 (*0-533-12802-1*) Vantage.

Coleman, Charles G. The Shining Sword. LC 96-33537. (Illus.). 1998. pap. 9.99 (*0-87213-084-3*) Loizeaux.

— That Voice Behind You: God's Guidance in Daily Decisions. LC 77-6796. 175p. 1991. pap., student ed. 8.99 (*0-87213-087-8*) Loizeaux.

Coleman, Charles J., et al, eds. Labor Arbitration: An Annotated Bibliography. LC 94-18840. (Cornell Industrial & Labor Relations Bibliography Ser.: No. 17). 352p. 1994. text 37.50 (*0-87546-322-3*, ILR Press) Cornell U Pr.

— Labor Arbitration: An Annotated Bibliography, 1991-1996. LC 97-30643. (ILR Bibliography Ser.: No. 18). (Illus.). 112p. 1997. text 25.00 (*0-8014-3440-8*) Cornell U Pr.

***Coleman, Charles J. & Haynes, Theodora T., eds.** Labor Arbitration (to 1993) An Annotated Bibliography. annot. ed. 269p. 2000. text 25.00 (*0-7881-9002-4*) DIANE Pub.

Coleman, Charles J., jt. ed. see Bognanno, Mario F.

***Coleman, Cheryl.** The Easy Spoon Cookie Caterer: A Timeless Collection of Cherished Cookie Recipes. LC 99-63220. (Illus.). 96p. 2000. pap. 15.95 (*0-9672280-0-X*) Gindele Hse.

Coleman, Chrisena. Just Between Girlfriends: African-American Women Celebrate Friendship. LC 98-3201. (Illus.). 160p. 1998. 17.95 (*0-684-84676-4*) S&S Trade.

Coleman, Christopher. Ghosts & Haunts of the Civil War. LC 99-23798. 1999. pap. 12.95 (*1-55853-785-6*) Rutledge Hill Pr.

Coleman, Christopher, et al, compiled by. Yugoslavia - Peoples, States & Society: Guide to the Microfilm Collection. LC 96-43395. ix, 191p. 1996. lib. bdg. 75.00 (*0-88354-228-5*) N Ross.

Coleman, Christopher & Starkey, David R., eds. Revolution Reassessed: Revisions in the History of Tudor Government & Administration. 228p. 1986. pap. 19.95 (*0-19-873063-2*) OUP.

Coleman, Christopher B. Coleman. Memoirs of Louis Harrison Coleman, with Genealogical Notes. 62p. 1997. reprint ed. pap. 12.50 (*0-8328-8014-0*); reprint ed. lib. bdg. 22.50 (*0-8328-8013-2*) Higginson Bk Co.

— Constantine the Great & Christianity. LC 70-155636. (Columbia University. Studies in the Social Sciences: No. 146). reprint ed. 37.50 (*0-404-51146-5*) AMS Pr.

— The Treatise of Lorenzo Valla on the Donation of Constantine: Text & Translation into English. (Renaissance Society of America Reprint Text Ser.). (LAT & ENG.). 188p. 1993. pap. text 16.95 (*0-8020-7734-X*) U of Toronto Pr.

Coleman, Christopher D., compiled by. Preservation Education. 7th ed. 69p. 1995. spiral bd. 8.50 (*0-8389-7767-7*) ALA.

Coleman, Christopher K. Strange Tales of the Dark & Bloody Ground. LC 98-34829. 1998. pap. 9.95 (*1-55853-661-2*) Rutledge Hill Pr.

Coleman, Clare. Child of the Dawn. 336p. (Orig.). 1994. mass mkt. 4.99 (*0-515-11334-4*, Jove) Berkley Pub.

Coleman, Clive & Moynihan, Jenny. Understanding Crime Data: Haunted by the Dark Figure. (Crime & Justice Ser.). 160p. 1996. 91.95 (*0-335-19519-9*) OpUniv Pr.

Coleman, Courtney S., jt. auth. see Borrelli, Robert L.

Coleman, Craig S. American Images of Korea. LC 97-77667. 304p. 1998. pap. 20.00 (*1-56591-089-3*, Pub. by Hollym Bks) Weatherhill.

— American Images of Korea. 298p. 1997. write for info. (*1-56591-088-5*) Hollym Intl.

— Social Studies Guide on Korea for High School Teachers. Matthieu, Carol Y., ed. (Illus.). 100p. (Orig.). 1994. pap. 11.95 (*0-9637888-1-7*) Korea Soc LA.

Coleman, Craig S. & Matthieu, Carol Y., eds. A Guide to Korean Studies in the United States: 1993 Edition. 463p. (Orig.). 1993. pap. 30.00 (*0-9637888-0-9*) Korea Soc LA.

Coleman, Cynthia, jt. auth. see Lehmann, Geoffrey.

Coleman, D. Directory of Capillary Electrophoresis. LC 96-38115. (TRAC Supplement Ser.). 198p. 1996. 91.50 (*0-444-82600-9*) Elsevier.

— TrAC - Trends in Analytical Chemistry. (TrAC Compendium Ser.: Vol. 14). 540p. 1995. 568.50 (*0-444-82388-3*) Elsevier.

— TrAC - Trends in Analytical Chemistry: Reference Edition. (TrAC Compendium Ser.: Vol. 12). (Illus.). 510p. 1994. 447.00 (*0-444-81805-7*) Elsevier.

— TrAC - Trends in Analytical Chemistry: Reference Edition. (TRAC Compendium Ser.: Vol. 15). 878p. 1997. 573.50 (*0-444-82662-9*) Elsevier.

Coleman, D., ed. TrAC - Trends in Analytical Chemistry: Reference Edition. (TrAC Compendium Ser.: Vol. 16). 646p. 1998. 647.00 (*0-444-82939-3*) Elsevier.

***Coleman, D., ed.** TRAC - Trends in Analytical Chemistry: Reference Edition. (TRAC Compendium Ser.). 740p. 1999. 800.00 (*0-444-50408-7*) Elsevier.

Coleman, D. & Doyle, M. R. Date Smart! A Program to Help You Stop Revolving & Start Evolving. LC 99-48743. 1999. pap. 14.00 (*0-7615-2173-9*) Prima Pub.

Coleman, D. C. Courtaulds Vol. III: An Economic & Social History:Crisis & Change 1940-65. (Illus.). 1980. 49.95 (*0-19-920111-0*) OUP.

— Myth, History & the Industrial Revolution. 225p. 1992. 55.00 (*1-85285-074-4*) Hambledon Press.

Coleman, D. G. & Jondorf, G. Words or Power: Essays in Honour of Alison Fairlie, 1917-1993. 1993. 95.00 (*0-85261-209-5*, Pub. by Univ of Glasgow) St Mut.

Coleman, D. M. Dusk at Dawn. 100p. (Orig.). 1993. pap. 9.95 (*0-9639355-0-X*) D M Coleman.

Coleman, Daniel. Masculine Migrations: Reading the Postcolonial Male in New Canadian Narratives. LC 98-220236. (Theory/Culture Ser.). 216p. 1998. text 40.00 (*0-8020-4264-3*); pap. text 16.95 (*0-8020-8102-9*) U of Toronto Pr.

Coleman, Daniel A. Eco-Politics: Building a Green Society. LC 93-6029. 240p. (C). 1994. pap. 15.95 (*0-8135-2055-X*); text 37.00 (*0-8135-2054-1*) Rutgers U Pr.

Coleman, Daniel R. Credit Repair: The Process. 40p. 1996. pap. 10.95 (*0-8059-3991-1*) Dorrance.

Coleman, David. For the Long Term. LC 78-59906. 1979. 12.95 (*0-930726-05-7*); pap. 8.95 (*0-930726-04-9*) Concept Pub.

— The Game of Society. LC 79-52348. 12.95 (*0-930726-07-3*); pap. 8.95 (*0-930726-06-5*) Concept Pub.

— Groupeware 93: Proceedings of the Second Conference. 1998. pap. text 49.95 (*1-55860-311-5*) Morgan Kaufmann.

— Management of the Firm. LC 77-86276. 1979. 13.95 (*0-930726-03-0*); pap. 9.95 (*0-930726-02-2*) Concept Pub.

— Starting a Business in New York State. 4th ed. LC 92-74156. (For the Proprietor Ser.). 110p. 1995. pap. 20.00 (*0-930726-12-X*) Concept Pub.

— Tax Tricks. 4th ed. LC 90-86067. (For the Proprietor Ser.). 1995. pap. 20.00 (*0-930726-10-3*) Concept Pub.

Coleman, David, ed. Advances in Molecular & Cell Biology Vol. 16: Adhesion Molecules. 248p. 1997. 128.50 (*0-7623-0143-0*) Jai Pr.

Coleman, David, ed. Europe's Population in the 1990s. (Illus.). 382p. 1996. pap. text 27.00 (*0-19-828894-8*) OUP.

Coleman, David, ed. GroupWare '92. LC 92-25700. 1998. pap. text 39.95 (*1-55860-261-5*) Morgan Kaufmann.

Coleman, David & Salt, John. The British Population: Patterns, Trends, & Processes. (Illus.). 706p. 1992. pap. text 45.00 (*0-19-874098-0*) OUP.

***Coleman, David & Wadensjo, Eskil.** Immigration to Denmark: International & National Perspectives. 348p. 1999. 24.95 (*87-7288-775-3*, Pub. by Aarhus Univ Pr) David Brown.

Coleman, David, jt. auth. see Caesar, Bishop.

Coleman, David, jt. auth. see Fox, Phyllis W.

Coleman, David, jt. ed. see Macura, Miroslav.

Coleman, David, jt. ed. see Sors, Andrew I.

Coleman, David C. & Crossley, D. A., Jr. Fundamentals of Soil Ecology. LC 95-31375. (Illus.). 196p. 1996. text 41.00 (*0-12-179725-2*) Acad Pr.

Coleman, David C. & Fry, Brian, eds. Carbon Isotope Techniques. (Isotopic Techniques in Plant, Soil, & Aquatic Biology Ser.: Vol. 1). (Illus.). 274p. 1991. pap. 52.00 (*0-12-179731-7*) Acad Pr.

***Coleman, David C. & Hendrix, Paul F.** Invertebrates as Webmasters in Ecosystems LC 99-41246. 350p. 2000. 100.00 (*0-85199-394-X*) OUP.

Coleman, David C., et al. Soil Biota & Nutrient Cycling Farming Systems. 336p. 1993. lib. bdg. 99.95 (*0-87371-919-0*, L919) Lewis Pubs.

Coleman, David C., jt. auth. see Haynes, Ken A.

Coleman, David D. & Coleman, Diane J. 101 Great Dates. LC 94-35288. 144p. (Orig.). 1995. pap. 9.95 (*0-687-00775-5*) Abingdon.

Coleman, David L., et al. BLR Encyclopedia of Workers' Compensation. rev. ed. LC 96-156304. 1995. ring bd. 199.95 (*1-55645-025-7*, 315569) Busn Legal Reports.

Coleman, Debra, et al, eds. Architecture & Feminism: Yale Publications on Architecture. LC 96-34510. (Illus.). 368p. (Orig.). 1997. pap. 19.95 (*1-56898-043-4*) Princeton Arch.

Coleman, Deidre. Maiden Voyages & Infant Colonies: Two Women's Travel Narratives of the 1790s. (Literature of Travel, Exploration & Empire Ser.). (Illus.). 224p. 1998. 75.00 (*0-7185-0149-7*, Pub. by Leicester U Pr) Cassell & Continuum.

Coleman, Deirdre. Coleridge & the Friend (1809-1810) (Oxford English Monographs). 248p. 1989. 70.00 (*0-19-812957-2*) OUP.

Coleman, Deirdre. Maiden Voyages & Infant Colonies: Two Women's Travel Narratives of the 1790s. (Literature of Travel, Exploration & Empire Ser.). (Illus.). 224p. 1998. pap. 24.95 (*0-7185-0150-0*) Bks Intl VA.

Coleman, Deirdre & Otto, Peter, eds. Imagining Romanticism: Essays on English & Australian Romanticisms. LC 91-36509. (Locust Hill Literary Studies: No. 10). (Illus.). 301p. (C). 1992. lib. bdg. 35.00 (*0-933951-42-6*) Locust Hill Pr.

Coleman, Denis R., jt. auth. see Edge, Alfred G.

Coleman, Derek, et al. Object-Oriented Development: The Fusion Method. LC 93-2015. (Object-Oriented Ser.). 350p. (C). 1993. 70.00 (*0-13-338823-9*) P-H.

Coleman, Diane & Monger, Joyce. Economics & the Zoo. (J). (gr. 4-12). 1992. pap. text 8.97 (*0-937659-58-4*) GCT.

Coleman, Diane J., jt. auth. see Coleman, David D.

Coleman, Donald C. The British Paper Industry, Fourteen Ninety-Five to Eighteen Sixty: A Study in Industrial Growth. LC 75-74. (Illus.). 367p. 1975. reprint ed. lib. bdg. 69.50 (*0-8371-8015-5*, COBP, Greenwood Pr) Greenwood.

Coleman, Donald G. Woodworking Factbook: Basic Information on Wood for Wood Carvers, Home Woodshop Craftsmen, Tradesmen & Instructors. (Illus.). 1966. 22.50 (*0-8315-0024-7*) Speller.

Coleman, Dorothy. Montaigne's Essais. (Unwin Critical Library). 192p. (C). 1987. text 49.95 (*0-04-800072-8*) Routledge.

Coleman, Dulcie V. Biopsy Pathology & Cytology of the Cervix. 2nd ed. LC 99-201835. (Illus.). 456p. 1999. text 110.00 (*0-340-74087-6*, Pub. by E A) OUP.

Coleman, E. C. The Royal Navy in Lincolnshire. 82p. (C). 1989. text 65.00 (*0-902662-99-6*, Pub. by R K Pubns) St Mut.

Coleman, Earle J. Creativity & Spirituality: Bonds Between Art & Religion. LC 97-19143. 237p. (C). 1998. pap. text 21.95 (*0-7914-3700-0*) State U NY Pr.

— Creativity & Spirituality: Bonds Between Art & Religion. LC 97-19143. 237p. (C). 1998. text 65.50 (*0-7914-3699-3*) State U NY Pr.

— Magic: A Reference Guide. LC 86-29611. (American Popular Culture Ser.). 214p. 1987. lib. bdg. 47.95 (*0-313-23397-7*, CMA/) Greenwood.

— Philosophy of Painting by Shih-T'ao. (Studies in Philosophy: No. 19). 1978. pap. text 40.80 (*90-279-7756-9*) Mouton.

Coleman, Edmund. Psychology. 272p. (C). 1994. pap. text, spiral bd., wbk. ed. 19.95 (*0-8403-9565-5*) Kendall-Hunt.

Coleman, Edmund C., tr. see Bray, Edmund C. & Colman, Martha, eds.

Coleman, Edmund T. Mountaineering on the Pacific in 1868. Jones, William R., ed. (Illus.). 24p. 1977. reprint ed. pap. 2.00 (*0-89646-014-2*) Vistabooks.

Coleman, Edward D. Bible in English Drama: An Annotated Bibliography. rev. ed. 1969. 35.00 (*0-87068-034-X*) Ktav.

— Plays of Jewish Interest on the American Stage. 1972. 59.95 (*0-8490-0842-5*) Gordon Pr.

Coleman, Edwin J. & Morse, Ronald A. Data: Where It Is & How to Get It: The 1993 Directory of Business, Environment & Energy Data Sources. 272p. (Orig.). 1992. pap. text 30.00 (*0-941375-56-0*) DIANE Pub.

Coleman, Eli. Human Sexuality & the Family Physician: A Special Journal Issue of Family Practice Research. 66p. 1988. pap. 14.95 (*0-89885-426-1*, Kluwer Acad Hman Sci) Kluwer Academic.

Coleman, Eli, ed. Gender Dysphoria: Interdisciplinary Approaches in Clinical Management. LC 93-20482. (Journal of Psychology & Human Sexuality: Vol. 5, No. 4). (Illus.). 174p. 1993. lib. bdg. 39.95 (*1-56024-459-3*) Haworth Pr.

— Gender Dysphoria: Interdisciplinary Approaches in Clinical Management. LC 93-20482. (Journal of Psychology & Human Sexuality: Vol. 5, No. 4). (Illus.). 174p. 1993. pap. text 19.95 (*1-56024-473-9*) Haworth Pr.

— John Money: A Tribute. LC 91-21841. (Journal of Psychology & Human Sexuality). (Illus.). 212p. 1991. lib. bdg. 6.95 (*1-56024-190-X*) Haworth Pr.

C

— Psychotherapy with Homosexual Men & Women: Integrated Identity Approaches for Clinical Practice. 343p. 1987. 49.95 (*0-86656-638-4*) Haworth Pr.

Coleman, Eli, ed. Chemical Dependency & Intimacy Dysfunction. LC 87-26173. (Journal of Chemical Dependency Treatment: Vol. 1, No. 1). 268p. 1988. pap. text 24.95 (*0-86656-826-3*) Haworth Pr.

— Chemical Dependency & Intimacy Dysfunction. LC 87-26173. (Journal of Chemical Dependency Treatment: Vol. 1, No. 1). 268p. 1988. text 49.95 (*0-86656-640-6*) Haworth Pr.

Coleman, Eli, et al, eds. Sex Offender Treatment: Biological Dysfunction, Intrapsychic Conflict, Interpersonal Violence. LC 96-20107. (Offender Rehabilitation Monographs: Vol. 23, Nos. 3/4). 177p. 1996. 39.95 (*1-56024-834-3*) Haworth Pr.

— Sex Offender Treatment: Psychological & Medical Approaches. LC 92-48795. (Journal of Offender Rehabilitation: Vol. 18, Nos. 3/4). (Illus.). 233p. 1992. 39.95 (*1-56024-438-0*) Haworth Pr.

— Sex Offender Treatment: Psychological & Medical Approaches. LC 92-48795. (Journal of Offender Rehabilitation: Vol. 18, Nos. 3/4). 233p. 1996. pap. 19.95 (*0-7890-0069-5*) Haworth Pr.

***Coleman, Eli & Miner, Michael.** Sexual Offender Treatment: Biopsychosocial Perspective. 102p. (C). 2000. 39.95 (*0-7890-1017-8*) Haworth Pr.

— Sexual Offender Treatment: Biopsychosocial Perspectives. 102p. (C). 2000. pap. text 14.95 (*0-7890-1018-6*) Haworth Pr.

Coleman, Eli, jt. auth. see DeCecco, John.

Coleman, Eliot. Four-Season Harvest: How to Harvest Fresh, Organic Vegetables from Your Home Garden All Year Long. rev. expanded ed. LC 99-13209. 272p. 1999. pap. text 24.95 (*1-890132-27-6*) Chelsea Green Pub.

— The New Organic Grower: A Master's Manual of Tools & Techniques for the Home & Market Gardener. 2nd expanded rev. ed. (Illus.). 304p. 1995. pap. 24.95 (*0-930031-75-X*) Chelsea Green Pub.

Coleman, Eliot & Terre Vivante. Keeping Food Fresh: Old World Techniques & Recipes. LC 99-35132. 186p. 1999. pap. 16.95 (*1-890132-10-1*) Chelsea Green Pub.

Coleman, Elizabeth. Hot Water, Please. large type ed. (General Ser.). 640p. 1993. 27.99 (*0-7089-2875-7*) Ulverscroft.

— The Tangled Garden. large type ed. 320p. 1989. 27.99 (*0-7089-1991-X*) Ulverscroft.

— The Tangled Garden: Memories of My Girlhood. 192p. 1989. 24.95 (*0-575-04187-0*, Pub. by V Gollancz) Trafalgar.

Coleman, Elizabeth, jt. auth. see McDonnell, Jullian B.

Coleman, Ellen. Eating for Endurance. 3rd ed. LC 96-50205. (Illus.). 164p. 1997. pap. text 14.95 (*0-923521-38-0*) Bull Pub.

***Coleman, Ellen.** Ultimate Sports Nutrition. 2nd ed. (Illus.). 2000. pap. 15.95 (*0-923521-56-9*) Bull Pub.

Coleman, Ellen & Steen, Suzanne N. The Ultimate Sports Nutrition Handbook. (Illus.). 240p. (Orig.). 1996. pap. 14.95 (*0-923521-34-8*) Bull Pub.

Coleman, Elliot, tr. see Poulet, Georges.

Coleman, Elliott, tr. see Poulet, Georges.

Coleman, Emily H. The Shutter of Snow. LC 96-51794. 245p. 1997. reprint ed. pap. 12.95 (*1-56478-147-X*) Dalkey Arch.

Coleman, Emma L. New England Captives Carried to Canada Between 1677 & 1760 During the French & Indian Wars. 1977. 48.95 (*0-8369-6970-7*, 7851) Ayer.

Coleman, Evelyn. Bloody Waters. 2001. pap. write for info. (*0-684-83176-7*) S&S Trade.

— Cymbals. LC 93-8690. (Illus.). (J). 1995. text 15.95 (*0-02-722817-7*) Macmillan.

— The Foot Warmer & the Black Crow. LC 92-38352. (Illus.). 32p. (J). (gr. 1 up). 1994. mass mkt. 14.95 (*0-02-722816-9*, Mac Bks Young Read) S&S Childrens.

— The Glass Bottle Tree. LC 94-45921. (Illus.). 32p. (J). (ps-2). 1996. 15.95 (*0-531-09467-7*); lib. bdg. 16.99 (*0-531-08767-0*) Orchard Bks Watts.

— The Riches of Oseola McCarty. LC 98-11570. (Illus.). 48p. (J). (gr. 2-5). 1998. lib. bdg. 14.95 (*0-8075-6961-5*) A Whitman.

— To Be a Drum. LC 96-54068. (Illus.). 32p. (YA). (gr. k up). 1998. lib. bdg. 16.95 (*0-8075-8006-6*) A Whitman.

***Coleman, Evelyn.** To Be a Drum. (Illus.). 32p. (YA). (gr. k up). 2000. lib. bdg. 6.95 (*0-8075-8007-4*) A Whitman.

Coleman, Evelyn. What a Woman's Gotta Do. 400p. 1999. mass mkt. 6.50 (*0-440-23500-6*) Dell.

— What a Woman's Gotta Do. LC 97-40257. 320p. 1998. 22.50 (*0-684-83175-9*) S&S Trade.

— White Socks Only. LC 95-38324. (Illus.). (J). (gr. k-4). 1996. lib. bdg. 15.95 (*0-8075-8955-1*) A Whitman.

— White Socks Only. (Prairie Paperback Bks.). (Illus.). 32p. (J). (gr. k-4). 1999. pap. 6.95 (*0-8075-8956-X*) A Whitman.

Coleman, Evelyn J. Collector's Book Doll Clothes, Vol. I. 1976. 132.95 (*0-8488-1533-5*) Amereon Ltd.

— Collectors Book Doll Clothes, Patterns. 1976. 42.95 (*0-8488-1534-3*) Amereon Ltd.

Coleman, Feay S. Nostrums for Fashionable Entertainments: Dining in Georgia, 1800-1850. LC 85-50257. 1992. pap. 19.95 (*0-933075-00-6*) Telfair Mus.

Coleman, Floyd & Day, Holliday T. Felrath Hines. (Illus.). 30p. (Orig.). (C). 1995. pap. text 9.95 (*0-936260-63-7*) Ind Mus Art.

Coleman, Francis L. The Northern Rhodesia Copperbelt, 1899-1962: Technological Development up to the End of the Central African Federation. LC 72-149805. (Illus.). xx, 206p. 1971. lib. bdg. 35.00 (*0-678-06784-8*) Kelley.

Coleman, Francis T. Conducting Lawful Terminations. 64p. (Orig.). (C). 1995. pap. 20.00 (*0-939900-67-X*) Soc Human Resc Mgmt.

Coleman, Francis T. & Rosenfeld, Douglas E. Handling Personnel Issues in the Law Office. LC 96-80097. 124p. 1997. pap. 69.95 (*1-57073-386-4*, 511-0381) Amer Bar Assn.

Coleman, Francis X. The Harmony of Reason: A Study in Kant's Aesthetics. LC 74-4520. 237p. reprint ed. pap. 73.50 (*0-7837-2149-8*, 204243500004) Bks Demand.

Coleman, Francis X. J. Neither Angel nor Beast. 1986. pap. 24.95 (*0-7102-0693-3*, Routledge Thoemms) Routledge.

***Coleman, Frank R.** To Russia for Love: The American Man's Best Option. (Illus.). 200p. 2000. pap. 17.95 (*1-929757-07-7*) Red Star.

Coleman, Fred. Decline & Fall of Soviet Empire. 2nd ed. (Illus.). 480p. 1997. pap. 19.95 (*0-312-16816-0*) St Martin.

Coleman, G. S., jt. auth. see Williams, A. G.

Coleman, Gail S. Kevin & Ben. LC 99-167947. (Illus.). 16p. (J). (ps-k). 1998. pap. 5.95 (*0-9655442-8-1*) Busn Word.

Coleman, Gary J. A Look at Mormonism. pap. 4.95 (*0-89036-142-8*) Liahona Pub Trust.

Coleman, George. Into the Storm: A Vietnam Odyssey. Morales, Alejandro & Boies, Bob, eds. LC 88-64124. 112p. (Orig.). (C). 1989. pap. 10.95 (*0-944870-01-5*) Pacific Writers Pr.

Coleman, George, et al. Exploring IBM S/390: See Why IBM's Re-Designed S/390 Computer Family Is More Popular Than Ever! 6th ed. LC 99-6021. (Exploring IBM Ser.). (Illus.). 400p. 1999. pap. 39.95 (*1-885068-30-1*) Maximum Pr.

Coleman, George, ed. see Cunningham, Ronald M.

Coleman, Gerald D. Homosexuality: Catholic Teaching & Pastoral Practice. LC 95-45756. 224p. (Orig.). 1996. pap. 14.95 (*0-8091-3605-8*) Paulist Pr.

— Human Sexuality: An All-Embracing Gift. LC 92-20661. (Illus.). 460p. 1992. pap. 18.95 (*0-8189-0643-X*) Alba.

Coleman, Gerald D. & Pettingill, David M. Following in the Footsteps of Jesus. LC 98-35620. 1999. 5.95 (*0-8091-3841-7*) Paulist Pr.

Coleman, Geraldine. African-American Stories of Triumph Over Adversity: Joy Cometh in the Morning. LC 96-906. 208p. 1996. 55.00 (*0-89789-505-3*, Bergin & Garvey) Greenwood.

— Issues in Education: View from the Other Side of the Room. LC 98-38308. 216p. 2000. 55.00 (*0-89789-634-3*, H634, Bergin & Garvey) Greenwood.

— Joy Cometh in the Morning: African-American Stories of Triumph over Adversity. LC 96-906. 1996. text. write for info. (*0-275-95554-0*, Praeger Pubs) Greenwood.

Coleman, Glen. The Man Who Fenced the West. Schoonover, Shirley, ed. (Illus.). 104p. 1984. 20.00 (*0-9614346-0-0*) Osthoff-Thalden.

Coleman, Glenn, jt. auth. see Crown, Judith.

Coleman, Graham. Countdown to Dinosaur Doom! LC 95-3826. (Illus.). 32p. (J). (gr. 2-4). 1995. pap. 5.95 (*0-8120-9415-8*) Barron.

***Coleman, Graham.** Tibetan Book of the Dead. 272p. 1999. 24.95 (*0-670-85886-2*, Viking) Viking Penguin.

Coleman, Grahame J., jt. auth. see Hemsworth, Paul H.

Coleman, Gregory D. We're Heaven Bound! Portrait of a Black Sacred Drama. LC 94-15273. (Illus.). 200p. 1994. 24.95 (*0-8203-1684-9*) U of Ga Pr.

— We're Heaven Bound! Portrait of a Black Sacred Drama. LC 94-15273. (Illus.). 216p. 1999. pap. 16.00 (*0-8203-2112-5*) U of Ga Pr.

Coleman, Gregory S., ed. see O'Connor, Michol.

Coleman, Hal B. The Other Side of Justice: A Novel. LC 92-32567. 288p. (Orig.). 1993. pap. 14.95 (*0-86534-183-4*) Sunstone Pr.

Coleman, Hardin L., jt. ed. see Pope-Davis, Don.

Coleman, Harry, jt. auth. see Rogers, Paul T.

Coleman, Harvey. Empowering Yourself. 1996. 24.95 (*0-7872-1386-1*) Kendall-Hunt.

Coleman, Heath & Coleman, Susan E. Southbound: Advice for Northerners Moving South. large type ed. LC 96-9614. (Illus.). 96p. 1996. mass mkt. 6.95 (*0-9652350-0-9*) Doberdor Pub.

Coleman, Henry. Church Organist. 2nd ed. 1968. 13.95 (*0-19-322100-4*) OUP.

Coleman, Horace. In the Grass. 80p. pap. write for info. (*1-885215-14-2*, Viet Nam Gnrtn) Burning Cities Pr.

Coleman, Howard & Swenson, Eric. DNA in the Courtroom: A Trial Watcher's Guide. LC 94-73363. (Illus.). 150p. (Orig.). 1994. pap. 12.95 (*0-9644507-0-4*) Genelex.

Coleman, Hubert A., jt. auth. see Link, Mae M.

Coleman, Hugh & Steele, W. G. Experimentation & Uncertainty Analysis for Engineers. 2nd ed. LC 98-22956. 296p. 1999. 69.95 (*0-471-12146-0*, Wiley-Interscience) Wiley.

Coleman, Hugh W. Experimentation & Uncertainty Analysis for Engineers. LC 89-5550. 205p. 1989. 110.00 (*0-471-63517-0*) Wiley.

Coleman, Hywel. Society & the Language Classroom. (Cambridge Language Teaching Library). (Illus.). 249p. (C). 1997. text 54.95 (*0-521-49616-0*); pap. text 20.95 (*0-521-49949-6*) Cambridge U Pr.

Coleman, Hywel, ed. Working with Language: A Multidisciplinary Consideration of Language Use in Work Contexts. (Contributions to the Sociology of Language Ser.: No. 52). xii, 617p. (C). 1989. lib. bdg. 176.95 (*0-89925-466-7*) Mouton.

Coleman, Hywel & Cameron, Lynne, eds. Change & Language: Papers from the Annual Meeting of the British Association for Applied Linguistics Held at the University of Leeds, September 1994. LC 95-53300. (British Studies in Applied Linguistics: Vol. 10). 182p. 1996. pap. 39.95 (*1-85359-359-1*, Pub. by Multilingual Matters) Taylor & Francis.

Coleman, Ike D. Love Is a Derivative of Attracted Differences Between a Man & a Woman. LC 98-90074. 1998. pap. 12.95 (*0-533-12702-5*) Vantage.

Coleman, Irene S., jt. auth. see Coleman, James C.

***Coleman, Ivy L.** God, a Keeper. 25p. 2000. 15.00 (*0-9672580-4-9*) BBI Pubng.

Coleman, Ivy L. God Is... 19p. 2000. spiral bd. 10.00 (*0-9672580-0-6*) BBI Pubng.

***Coleman, Ivy L.** Renewed in Spirit & Mind. LC 99-98087. 50p. 2000. pap. 15.00 (*0-9672580-2-2*) BBI Pubng.

— Should We Fear God. 18p. 2000. pap. 10.00 (*0-9672580-1-4*) BBI Pubng.

— Written in the Book of Life, 1. 18p. (YA). 2000. 10.00 (*0-9672580-3-0*) BBI Pubng.

Coleman, J. & Jimack, C., eds. Rabelais in Glasgow: Proceedings of the 1993 Colloquium. 1993. 40.00 (*0-9509831-0-1*, Pub. by Univ of Glasgow) St Mut.

Coleman, J. C. Genealogy of William Coleman of Gloucester. (Illus.). 240p. 1993. reprint ed. pap. 40.00 (*0-8328-1371-0*); reprint ed. lib. bdg. 50.00 (*0-8328-1370-2*) Higginson Bk Co.

Coleman, J. D. Incursion: From America's Choke Hold on the NVA Lifelines to the Sacking of the Cambodian, Vol. 1. 1992. mass mkt. 5.99 (*0-312-92776-2*) St Martin.

***Coleman, J. D.** Wonju: The Gettysburg of the Korean War. 2000. 24.95 (*1-57488-212-0*) Brasseys.

Coleman, J. Walter. The Molly Maguire Riots. 1993. reprint ed. lib. bdg. 89.00 (*0-7812-5442-6*) Rprt Serv.

Coleman, J. Winston, Jr. Six Sketches of Kentucky: From the Pamphlets of J. Winston Coleman, Jr. Houlihan, Edward T., ed. & intro. by. (Bluegrass Bookshelf Ser.: Vol. 1). (Illus.). 128p. 1996. 12.95 (*0-87642-014-5*) Henry Clay.

— Stage-Coach Days in the Bluegrass. LC 95-21201. (Illus.). 304p. 1995. 27.50 (*0-8131-1914-6*) U Pr of Ky.

— Stage-Coach Days in the Bluegrass. (Illus.). 226p. 1989. reprint ed. 12.50 (*0-935680-25-X*) Kentucke Imprints.

Coleman, James & Doyle, Mark. The Life & Work of James Coleman. Eaton, Angela, ed. LC 95-92276. (Illus.). 168p. 1995. 39.95 (*0-9646447-0-3*) J Coleman.

Coleman, James & Willis, Don. SGML As a Framework for Digital Preservation & Access. 47p. 1997. pap. 20.00 (*1-887334-54-8*) Coun Lib & Info.

Coleman, James, et al. James Coleman: Selected Works. LC 98-219024. 55p. 1985. write for info. (*0-905263-70-7*) ICA.

***Coleman, James A.** Relativity for the Layman. 2nd ed. (Illus.). 140p. 1999. reprint ed. pap. 12.00 (*0-9671061-0-9*) J A Coleman.

Coleman, James A. & Rollet, Brigitte. Television in Europe. LC 98-123218. (European Studies). 123 p. 1997. write for info. (*1-871516-92-7*) Intellect.

Coleman, James C. Fort McRee: A Castle Built on Sand. (Illus.). 124p. 1986. pap. 7.95 (*0-939566-06-0*) Pensacola Hist.

Coleman, James C. & Coleman, Irene S. Pensacola Fortifications, 1698-1980: Guardians of the Gulf. (Illus.). 120p. 1983. pap. 7.95 (*0-939566-02-8*) Pensacola Hist.

Coleman, James C., jt. auth. see Morris, Charles.

Coleman, James J., Jr., ed. Semiconductor Diode Lasers. 350p. 1992. 65.00 (*0-8194-0892-1*); pap. 50.00 (*0-8194-0893-X*) SPIE.

Coleman, James K. State Administration in South Carolina. LC 70-76647. (Columbia University. Studies in the Social Sciences: No. 406). reprint ed. 29.50 (*0-404-51406-5*) AMS Pr.

Coleman, James M. Aesculapius on the Colorado. 1971. 17.50 (*0-88426-028-3*) Encino Pr.

— Art Price Trends, Nineteenth & Early Twentieth Century American Paintings Vol. 1: Overall Market, Regions & Styles. 315p. (Orig.). 1995. pap. 39.95 (*0-9631671-1-1*) Connemara-Coleman.

— Art Price Trends, Nineteenth & Early Twentieth Century American Paintings Vol. 2: The Artists. 450p. Date not set. pap. 44.95 (*0-9631671-2-X*) Connemara-Coleman.

Coleman, James M., ed. Art Auction Trends: Major Nineteenth Century American Artists. 342p. 1992. pap. 31.95 (*0-9631671-0-3*) Connemara-Coleman.

Coleman, James M. & Prior, David B. Deltaic Sand Bodies: A 1980 Short Course. LC QE0026.2.A43. (Education Course Note Ser.: Vol. 15). (Illus.). 175p. reprint ed. pap. 54.30 (*0-608-08729-7*, 206936800004) Bks Demand.

Coleman, James R. & Dugan, Robert E. The Public Administration Desk Book. 175p. (Orig.). 1990. pap. text 35.00 (*0-931684-12-9*) Gov Res Pubns.

Coleman, James S. The Asymmetric Society. LC 81-23255. (Frank W. Abrams Lectures). 1p. 1982. pap. 19.95 (*0-8156-0174-3*) Syracuse U Pr.

— The Asymmetric Society. LC 81-23255. (Frank W. Abrams Lectures). 203p. reprint ed. pap. 63.00 (*0-608-07602-3*, 205991700010) Bks Demand.

— Foundations of Social Theory. (Illus.). 1016p. 1994. pap. text 31.50 (*0-674-31226-0*, COLFOX) Belknap Pr.

— Foundations of Social Theory. (Illus.). 1024p. 1990. 59.50 (*0-674-31225-2*) HUP.

— Nationalism & Development in Africa: Selected Essays. Sklar, Richard L., ed. LC 93-25774. (C). 1994. 60.00 (*0-520-08374-1*, Pub. by U CA Pr); pap. 20.00 (*0-520-08376-8*, Pub. by U CA Pr) Cal Prin Full Svc.

— Parents, Their Children & Schools. Schneider, Barbara, ed. (C). 1996. pap. 27.00 (*0-8133-3077-7*, Pub. by Westview) HarpC.

— Rational Choice Theory: Advocacy & Critique. (Key Issues in Sociological Theory Ser.: Vol. 7). 240p. (C). 1992. text 56.00 (*0-8039-4761-5*); pap. text 26.00 (*0-8039-4762-3*) Sage.

— Redesigning American Education. LC 97-21628. (C). 1997. pap. 69.00 (*0-8133-2495-5*, Pub. by Westview) HarpC.

Coleman, James S., et al, eds. Approaches to Social Theory. LC 85-62806. 450p. (C). 1986. text 45.00 (*0-87154-205-6*) Russell Sage.

Coleman, James S. & Court, David. University Development in the Third World: The Rockefeller Foundation Experience. LC 93-14907. 350p. 1993. 89.95 (*0-08-041936-4*, Pergamon Press) Buttrwrth-Heinemann.

Coleman, James S. & Court, David. University Development in the Third World: The Rockefeller Foundation Experience. LC 93-14907. 437p. 1993. reprint ed. pap. 135.50 (*0-608-07479-9*, 206770100009) Bks Demand.

Coleman, James S. & Karweit, Nancy L. Information Systems & Performance Measures in Schools. LC 72-79547. 152p. 1972. 32.95 (*0-87778-038-2*) Educ Tech Pubns.

Coleman, James S., et al. The Adolescent Society: The Social Life of the Teenager & Its Impact on Education. LC 81-1737. (Illus.). 368p. 1981. reprint ed. lib. bdg. 65.00 (*0-313-22934-1*, COADS, Greenwood Pr) Greenwood.

— Youth: Transition to Adulthood. LC 73-92757. viii, 202p. 1986. reprint ed. pap. text 16.00 (*0-226-11343-4*, Midway Reprint) U Ch Pr.

Coleman, James S., jt. auth. see United States Office of Education , Equal Opportun.

Coleman, James S., jt. ed. see Almond, Gabriel Abraham.

Coleman, James W. Blackness & Modernism: The Literary Career of John Edgar Wideman. LC 88-36906. 177p. reprint ed. pap. 54.90 (*0-608-08718-1*, 206928600004) Bks Demand.

— Social Problems Study Guide. 7th ed. (C). 1999. pap. text, student ed. 13.13 (*0-321-04049-X*) Addson-Wesley Educ.

Coleman, James W. & Cressey, Donald R. Social Problems. 5th ed. LC 92-24775. (C). 1997. pap. 53.00 (*0-06-500144-3*) Addson-Wesley Educ.

***Coleman, James William.** The New Buddhism: The Western Transformation of an Ancient Tradition. 256p. 2000. 25.00 (*0-19-513162-2*) OUP.

Coleman, James William, ed. Social Problems: A Brief Introduction. LC 97-23113. 480p. (C). 1997. pap. text 61.33 (*0-321-01249-6*, Prentice Hall) P-H.

Coleman, Jane C. Deep in His Heart J. R. Is Laughing at Us. 28p. (Orig.). 1991. pap. 7.00 (*0-938566-49-0*) Adastra Pr.

— Discovering Eve: Short Stories. LC 92-37638. 136p. 1993. 24.95 (*0-8040-0964-3*) Swallow.

— Doc Holliday's Woman. 82p. 1995. 19.95 (*0-446-51825-5*) Warner Bks.

— Doc Holliday's Woman. 288p. 1996. mass mkt. 6.50 (*0-446-60344-9*, Pub. by Warner Bks) Little.

***Coleman, Jane C.** I, Pearl Hart: A Western Story. large type ed. LC 98-48518. (Thorndike Western Ser.). 1999. 19.95 (*0-7862-1026-5*) Thorndike Pr.

Coleman, Jane C. No Roof but Sky: Poetry of the American West. LC 90-84811. 74p. (Orig.). 1990. pap. 9.95 (*0-931271-13-4*) Hi Plains Pr.

— The Red Drum: Poetry of the American West. 72p. (Orig.). 1994. pap. 9.95 (*0-931271-28-2*) Hi Plains Pr.

— Stories from Mesa Country. LC 91-4174. 160p. 1991. 24.95 (*0-8040-0949-X*) Swallow.

— Stories from Mesa Country. LC 91-4174. 160p. 1992. reprint ed. pap. 10.95 (*0-8040-0957-0*) Swallow.

Coleman, Janet. Ancient & Medieval Memories. (Studies in the Reconstruction of the Past). 666p. (C). 1992. text 95.00 (*0-521-41144-0*) Cambridge U Pr.

— The Compass: The Improvisational Theatre That Revolutionized American Comedy. (Illus.). 362p. 1991. pap. 17.50 (*0-226-11345-0*) U Ch Pr.

***Coleman, Janet.** A History of Political Thought: From the Middle Ages to the Renaissance. 320p. 1999. pap. text 27.95 (*0-631-18653-0*) Blackwell Pubs.

— A History of Political Thought: From the Middle Ages to the Renaissance. Vol. 2. 320p. 1999. 62.95 (*0-631-18652-2*) Blackwell Pubs.

— A History of Political Thought Vol. 1: From Ancient Greece to Early Christianity. 320p. 1999. 62.95 (*0-631-21821-1*); pap. text 27.95 (*0-631-21822-X*) Blackwell Pubs.

Coleman, Janet, ed. The Individual in Political Theory & Practice. LC 96-33693. (The Origins of the Modern State in Europe Ser.: No. 6). (Illus.). 422p. 1996. text 98.00 (*0-19-820549-X*, Clarendon Pr) OUP.

Coleman, Janet. Scholastics, Enlightenments & Philosophic Radicals. Date not set. 29.95 (*0-907845-35-5*) Philos Document.

Coleman, Janet & Young, Al. Mingus - Mingus: Two Memoirs. LC 88-38524. 160p. 1989. 14.95 (*0-88739-067-6*) Creat Arts Bk.

— Mingus - Mingus: Two Memoirs. LC 91-23247. (Illus.). 164p. 1991. reprint ed. pap. 10.95 (*0-87910-149-0*) Limelight Edns.

Coleman, Janet A. Ehwa Study Tour for Speed Management & Enforcement Technology. (Illus.). 83p. 1998. reprint ed. pap. text 25.00 (*0-7881-4263-1*) DIANE Pub.

Coleman, Janet R. & Wolf, Elizabeth E. Advanced Sign Language Vocabulary: A Resource Text for Educators, Interpreters, Parents & Sign Language Instructors. (Illus.). 202p. (C). 1991. pap. text 46.95 (*0-398-05722-2*) C C Thomas.

Coleman, Janet W. Fast Eddie. LC 92-31243. (Illus.). 128p. (J). (gr. 3-5). 1993. lib. bdg. 13.95 (*0-02-722815-0*, Four Winds Pr) S&S Childrens.

Coleman, Jason. Meddling with the Past: An Historical & Archaeological Analysis of Metal Artifacts from San Leandro Reservoir. (MA in Anthropology, UC Hayward Ser.). (Illus.). 142p. (C). 1996. pap. text 15.63 (*1-55567-796-7*) Coyote Press.

Coleman, Jeanine G. The Early Intervention Dictionary: A Multidisciplinary Guide to Terminology. 2nd ed. LC 99-29729. 410p. 1999. pap. 16.95 (*1-890627-05-4*) Woodbine House.

An Asterisk (*) at the beginning of an entry indicates that the title is appearing for the first time.

Coleman, Jill. WaterYoga: Water Assisted Postures & Stretches for Flexibility & Wellbeing. (Illus.). 214p. 1998. pap. 17.95 (*0-9662970-0-8*) Eglantine Pr.

Coleman, Jim. The Rittenhouse Cookbook: A Year of Heart-Healthy Recipes. LC 97-15249. (Illus.). 234p. 1997. 29.95 (*0-89815-864-8*) Ten Speed Pr.

Coleman, Jim, et al. Flavors of America. LC 99-12319. (Illus.). 192p. 1999. pap. 16.95 (*0-940159-52-X*) Camino Bks.

Coleman, Joan. Forever Friends: Resolving Grief after the Loss of a Beloved Animal. LC 92-84033. 128p. 1993. pap. text 14.95 (*1-883018-03-X*) J C Tara Ent.

Coleman, Joe. Cosmic Retribution: The Infernal Art of Joe Coleman. 220p. 1991. pap. 22.95 (*0-922915-06-7*) Feral Hse.

— The Man of Sorrows. limited ed. (Illus.). 32p. 1993. 40.00 (*0-9638129-0-4*) Gates of Heck.

— Muzzlers, Guzzlers,& Good Yeggs. 1998. pap. 12.95 (*0-87816-636-X*) Kitchen Sink.

Coleman, Joe, et al. Original Sin: The Visionary Art of Joe Coleman. LC 96-77596. (Illus.). 144p. 1997. 45.00 (*0-9638129-9-8*); pap. 29.95 (*0-9638129-6-3*, 620231) Heck Editions.

Coleman, John. Committee of 300. 3rd ed. 1994. pap. 20.00 (*0-9634019-2-0*) J Holding.

— The Conspirators' Hierarchy: The Committee of Three Hundred. (Illus.). 267p. (C). 1992. pap. text 16.95 (*0-922356-57-2*) Amer West Pubs.

— The Conspirators' Hierarchy: The Committee of Three Hundred. 2nd ed. 304p. 1992. pap. 20.00 (*0-9634019-0-4*) J Holding.

Coleman, John. The Conspirators' Hierarchy: The Committee of Three Hundred. 4th ed. (Illus.). 1997. pap. 20.00 (*0-9634019-4-7*) J Holding.

— Conspirators' Hierarchy: The Story of the Committee of (300) unabridged ed. 296p. 1992. reprint ed. pap. 17.00 (*0-945001-43-6*) GSG & Assocs.

Coleman, John. Inside America's Electronic Gulags. 1999. pap. 25.00 (*0-9634019-6-3*) J Holding.

— One World Order: Socialist Dictatorship. LC 98-43399. ii, 229p. 1998. 16.95 (*0-9640104-9-6*) Bridger Hse.

— Phonological Representations: Their Names, Forms & Powers. LC 97-1847. (Studies in Linguistics: No. 85). (Illus.). 364p. (C). 1998. text 74.95 (*0-521-47208-3*) Cambridge U Pr.

— Questions from Your Cosmic Dance. LC 96-39580. 400p. pap. 12.00 (*1-56838-143-3*) Hazelden.

— What You Don't Know about the U. S. Constitution. 258p. 1998. pap. 22.00 (*0-9634019-5-5*) J Holding.

*__Coleman, John.__ What You Should Know about the U. S. Constitution & the Bill of Rights. 328p. 1998. pap. 20.00 (*1-893157-03-2*) Bridger Hse.

Coleman, John. Working with Troubled Adolescents. 1987. text 70.00 (*0-12-179720-1*) Acad Pr.

— Your Book of Veteran & Edwardian Cars. (J). (gr. 7 up). 1972. 7.95 (*0-571-09375-2*) Transatl Arts.

— Your Book of Vintage Cars. (Illus.). (J). (gr. 7 up). 1969. 7.95 (*0-571-08276-9*) Transatl Arts.

Coleman, John, ed. The School Years. 2nd ed. LC 91-28498. (Illus.). 208p. (C). 1992. pap. 24.99 (*0-415-06170-9*, A7784) Routledge.

Coleman, John & Hendry, Leo. The Nature of Adolescence. 2nd ed. 272p. (C). 1990. pap. 22.99 (*0-415-01485-9*) Routledge.

Coleman, John & Roker, Debi. Teenage Sexuality: Health, Risk & Education. 216p. 1998. text 41.00 (*90-5702-307-5*, ECU28); pap. text 20.00 (*90-5702-308-3*, ECU15) Gordon & Breach.

Coleman, John & Tomka, Miklos, eds. Mass Media. (Concilium Ser.). 1993. 15.00 (*0-88344-874-2*) Orbis Bks.

— Religion & Nationalism. 150p. (Orig.). 1995. pap. 15.00 (*0-88344-887-4*) Orbis Bks.

Coleman, John, jt. auth. see Liell, Peter.

Coleman, John, jt. ed. see Baum, Gregory B.

Coleman, John A. An American Strategic Theology. 1985. pap. 10.95 (*0-8091-2469-6*) Paulist Pr.

— View from Ground Level. (Illus.). 64p. 1996. pap. 8.95 (*1-891210-91-2*, VFGL010) Bartlett Pub.

Coleman, John A., jt. ed. see Sanks, T. Howland.

*__Coleman, John C. & Hendry, Leo B.__ Nature of Adolescence. 3rd ed. LC 99-21503. (Adolescence & Society Ser.). 1999. pap. write for info. (*0-415-19898-4*) Routledge.

— Nature of Adolescence. 3rd ed. LC 99-21503. (Adolescence & Society Ser.). 232p. (C). 1999. text. write for info. (*0-415-19897-6*) Routledge.

Coleman, John E. Excavations at Pylos in Elis. LC 86-20562. (Hesperia Supplement Ser.: No. 21). (Illus.). xvi, 176p. 1986. pap. 25.00 (*0-87661-521-3*) Am Sch Athens.

— Kephala: A Late Neolithic Settlement & Cemetery. LC 76-13187. (Keos Ser.: Vol. 1). (Illus.). xxvi, 170p. 1977. pap. 35.00 (*0-87661-701-1*) Am Sch Athens.

Coleman, John E. & Walz, Clark A., eds. Greeks & Barbarians: Essays on the Interactions Between Greeks & Non-Greeks in Antiquity & the Consequences for Eurocentrism. LC 97-40631. (Occasional Publications of the Department of Near Eastern Studies & the Program of Jewish Studies, Cornell U.: Vol. 4). 329p. 1997. 42.00 (*1-883053-44-7*) CDL Pr.

Coleman, John E., et al. Alambra: A Middle Bronze Age Settlement in Cyprus; Archaeological I Investigations by Cornell University. (Studies in Mediterranean Archaeology: Vol. CXVIII). (Illus.). 545p. (Orig.). 1996. pap. 195.00 (*91-7081-156-3*, Pub. by P Astroms) Coronet Bks.

Coleman, John F. The Disruption of the Pennsylvania Democracy, 1848-1860. LC 75-623874. (Illus.). 184p. 1975. 7.95 (*0-911124-82-9*) Pa Hist & Mus.

— Incident Management for the Street-Smart Fire Officer. LC 96-46764. (Illus.). 49.50 (*0-912212-60-8*) Fire Eng.

Coleman, John H. Written Composition Interests of Junior & Senior High School Pupils. LC 71-176662. (Columbia University. Teachers College. Contributions to Education Ser.: No. 494). reprint ed. 37.50 (*0-404-55494-6*) AMS Pr.

Coleman, John J. Disability Discrimination in Employment. LC 91-22911. 1991. ring bd. 125.00 (*0-87632-818-4*) West Group.

Coleman, John J., III. Employment Discrimination in Alabama. 1991. 79.95 (*0-87651-946-X*) Southern U Pr.

Coleman, John J. Listening to the Law: English Listening Comprehension Cassettes for Lawyers & Other Legal Professionals. (Illus.). (C). pap. text. write for info. (*0-472-08425-9*) U of Mich Pr.

Coleman, John J. Party Decline in America: Policy, Politics, & the Fiscal State. LC 96-6801. (Princeton Studies in American Politics). 288p. 1996. text 39.95 (*0-691-02731-5*, Pub. by Princeton U Pr) Cal Prin Full Svc.

Coleman, John J., III. Supplement to Employment Discrimination in Alabama, 1992. 39.95 (*0-685-61683-5*) Southern U Pr.

Coleman, John J., III, et al. Aesthetic Surgery of the Craniofacial Skeleton. LC 96-13192. (Illus.). 174p. 1996. 125.00 (*0-387-94757-4*) Spr-Verlag.

Coleman, John L. Operational Mid-Level Management for Police. 2nd ed. LC 94-45755. (Illus.). 410p. (C). 1995. text 90.95 (*0-398-05981-0*); pap. text 55.95 (*0-398-05982-9*) C C Thomas.

— Police Assessment Testing: An Assessment Center Handbook for Law Enforcement Personnel. 2nd ed. (Illus.). 182p. 1992. pap. 26.95 (*0-398-06065-7*) C C Thomas.

— Police Assessment Testing: An Assessment Center Handbook for Law Enforcement Personnel. 2nd ed. (Illus.). 182p. (C). 1992. text 41.95 (*0-398-05809-1*) C C Thomas.

— Practical Knowledge for a Private Security Officer. 2nd ed. LC 93-11147. (Illus.). 258p. 1993. pap. 32.95 (*0-398-06066-5*) C C Thomas.

— Practical Knowledge for a Private Security Officer. 2nd ed. LC 93-11147. (Illus.). 258p. (C). 1993. text 51.95 (*0-398-05875-X*) C C Thomas.

— Practical Legal Guidelines for the Private Security Officer: The Essential Consequences of the Laws Regarding Private Security & the Affective Social Trends of Today. 324p. 1990. pap. 40.95 (*0-398-06067-3*) C C Thomas.

— Practical Legal Guidelines for the Private Security Officer: The Essential Consequences of the Laws Regarding Private Security & the Affective Social Trends of Today. 324p. (C). 1990. text 59.95 (*0-398-05694-3*) C C Thomas.

Coleman, John M. Thomas McKean. LC 74-19952. 1975. 16.95 (*0-912834-07-2*) Am Faculty Pr.

Coleman, John W. A Bibliography of Kentucky History. LC 49-11965. 534p. reprint ed. pap. 165.60 (*0-8357-7195-4*, 200146800079) Bks Demand.

Coleman, Jonathan. Long Way to Go: Black & White in America. 1997. 27.50 (*0-517-59087-5*, Crown) Crown Pub Group.

*__Coleman, Jonathan.__ Long Way to Go: Black & White in America. 480p. 1998. reprint ed. pap. 15.00 (*0-87113-723-2*, Atlntc Mnthly) Grove-Atltic.

Coleman, Jonathan R., jt. auth. see Faruqee, Rashid.

Coleman, Joseph S. The Sholari Pack. Sellers, Janice, ed. (Skyrealms of Jorune Ser.). (Illus.). 112p. (Orig.). 1994. pap. text 18.00 (*1-883240-02-6*) Chessex.

Coleman, Joseph S. & Leker, Andrew. The Sobayid Atlas. Sellers, Janice, ed. (Skyrealms of Jorune Ser.). (Illus.). 64p. (Orig.). 1994. pap. text 16.00 (*1-883240-03-4*) Chessex.

Coleman, Joyce. Public Reading & the Reading Public in Late Medieval England & France. LC 95-37984. (Studies in Medieval Literature: No. 26). (Illus.). 264p. (C). 1996. text 69.95 (*0-521-55391-1*) Cambridge U Pr.

Coleman, Jules. Law & Economics, Vol. 1. (C). 1992. lib. bdg. 125.00 (*0-8147-1462-5*) NYU Pr.

— Law & Economics, Vol. 2. (C). 1992. lib. bdg. 125.00 (*0-8147-1463-3*) NYU Pr.

*__Coleman, Jules.__ The Practice of Principle: Defence of the Pragmatic Approach to Legal Theory. (Clarendon Law Lectures). 280p. 2000. 39.95 (*0-19-829814-5*) OUP.

Coleman, Jules & Lange, Jeffrey, eds. Law & Economics, Set, Vols. I & II. (International Library of Essays in Law & Legal Theory). 1100p. (C). 1992. lib. bdg. 250.00 (*0-8147-1464-1*) NYU Pr.

*__Coleman, Jules L.__ Readings in the Philosophy of Law. LC 99-57180. 1999. pap. 29.95 (*0-8153-3718-3*) Garland.

Coleman, Jules L. Risks & Wrongs. (Cambridge Studies in Philosophy & Law). 528p. (C). 1992. text 74.95 (*0-521-32950-7*) Cambridge U Pr.

Coleman, Jules L., ed. Crimes & Punishments. LC 93-35605. (Philosophy of Law Ser.: Vol. 4). 576p. 1994. text 97.00 (*0-8153-1400-0*) Garland.

— Private Law Theory. LC 93-32673. (Philosophy of Law Ser.: Vol. 5). 648p. 1994. text 105.00 (*0-8153-1401-9*) Garland.

— Rights & Their Foundations. LC 93-33074. (Philosophy of Law Ser.: Vol. 2). 448p. 1994. text 77.00 (*0-8153-1398-5*) Garland.

Coleman, Jules L. & Buchanan, Allen, eds. In Harm's Way: Essays in Honor of Joel Feinberg. (Cambridge Studies in Philosophy & Law). 371p. (C). 1994. text 85.00 (*0-521-45410-7*) Cambridge U Pr.

Coleman, Jules L. & Morris, Christopher W., eds. Rational Commitment & Social Justice: Essays for Gregory Kavka. LC 98-20681. (Illus.). 272p. (C). 1998. text 54.95 (*0-521-63179-3*) Cambridge U Pr.

Coleman, Jules L. & Sebok, Anthony, eds. Constitutional Law & Its Interpretation. LC 93-32690. (Philosophy of Law Ser.: Vol. 3). 592p. 1994. text 99.00 (*0-8153-1399-3*) Garland.

— Philosophy of Law: Anthology of Scholarly Articles, 5 vols. LC 93-32672. 2856p. 1995. 403.00 (*0-8153-1396-9*) Garland.

Coleman, Jules L., jt. auth. see Murphy, Jeffrie G.

Coleman, Julia. Faith That Works. 60p. 1997. pap. write for info. (*1-57502-540-X*, PO1586) Morris Pubng.

*__Coleman, Julie & Kay, Christian J., eds.__ Lexicology, Semantics & Lexicography: Selected Papers from the Fourth G. L. Brook Symposium, Manchester, August 1998. LC 99-88593. (Current Issues in Linguistic Theory Ser.: Vol. 194). xi, 240p. 2000. 75.00 (*1-55619-972-4*) J Benjamins Pubng Co.

Coleman, Kathleen. Guide to French Poetry Explication. LC 92-22129. (G. K. Hall Reference Ser.). 200p. 1993. 65.00 (*0-8161-9075-5*, G K Hall & Co) Mac Lib Ref.

Coleman, Keith. Nationalisation Beyond the Slogans. 191p. (Orig.). (C). 1992. pap. text 19.95 (*0-86975-413-0*, Pub. by Ravan Pr) Ohio U Pr.

Coleman, Ken & Valenti, Dan. Diary of a Sportscaster. LC 82-82096. 176p. (Orig.). 1982. pap. 6.95 (*0-943514-03-7*) Literations.

*__Coleman, Ken & Valenti, Dan.__ Talking on Air: A Broadcaster's Life in Sports. (Illus.). 288p. 2000. 22.95 (*1-58382-062-0*) Sports Pub.

Coleman, Ken, ed. see Haynes, Charles.

Coleman, Kenneth. America's Endangered Banks: Check the Safety of Your Savings. rev. ed. 36p. 1986. pap. 14.95 (*0-942632-02-8*) Seraphim Pr.

— Georgia History in Outline. rev. ed. LC 78-14087. 136p. (C). 1979. pap. 12.00 (*0-8203-0467-0*) U of Ga Pr.

— The Misdirection Conspiracy: or Who Really Killed the American Dream? (Exposed by Reality Investing) LC 82-50091. (Illus.). 216p. 1983. pap. 12.95 (*0-942632-00-1*) Seraphim Pr.

— U. S. Financial Institutions in Crisis: Overview of the 50 Largest Banks & 50 Largest S&Ls. 4th ed. Chambers, Catherine & Lewis, David, eds. 24p. 1986. pap. 14.95 (*0-942632-01-X*) Seraphim Pr.

Coleman, Kenneth, ed. Athens 1861-1865: As Seen Through Letters in the University of Georgia Libraries. LC 70-104399. 132p. 1969. pap. 12.50 (*0-8203-0253-8*) U of Ga Pr.

— A History of Georgia. 2nd ed. LC 90-41759. (Illus.). 464p. 1991. pap. 24.00 (*0-8203-1269-X*) U of Ga Pr.

Coleman, Kenneth M. & Herring, George C., eds. The Central American Crisis: Sources of Conflict & the Failure of U. S. Policy. LC 84-27624. 240p. 1985. 35.00 (*0-8420-2238-4*); pap. text 12.95 (*0-8420-2240-6*) Scholarly Res Inc.

— Understanding the Central American Crisis: Sources of Conflict, U. S. Policy, & Options for Peace. LC 91-2974. (Latin American Silhouettes Ser.). 240p. 1991. 45.00 (*0-8420-2382-8*) Scholarly Res Inc.

Coleman, Kevin, et al. Reengineering MIS: Aligning Information Technology with Business Operations. 458p. (C). 1996. text 59.95 (*1-878289-30-6*) Idea Group Pub.

Coleman, L. Genealogy of the Lyman Family in Great Britain & America: The Ancestors & Descendants of Richard Lyman, from High Ongar in England, 1631. (Illus.). 549p. 1989. reprint ed. pap. 82.00 (*0-8328-0794-X*); reprint ed. lib. bdg. 90.00 (*0-8328-0793-1*) Higginson Bk Co.

Coleman, L. F. Aspects of Indian Civilization As Revealed in Representative Mexican Novels. 1971. 59.95 (*0-87968-670-7*) Gordon Pr.

Coleman, L. H. Give & It Shall Be Given Unto You... 1994. pap. 6.95 (*1-56794-077-3*) Star Bible.

Coleman, Larry. Up from the Eagle's Nest: A Collection of Stories. LC 96-33350. (Storytellers Ser.). (Illus.). (J). 1996. write for info. (*0-929978-88-9*) Sights Prods.

Coleman, Larry G. Up from the Eagles' Nest. (Illus.). 44p. (J). 1996. 12.95 (*0-9629978-8-9*) Sights Prods.

*__Coleman, Laurence J. & Cross, Tracy L.__ Being Gited in School: An Introduction to Development, Guidance & Teaching. 516p. (C). 2000. text 49.95 (*1-882664-59-0*) Prufrock Pr.

*__Coleman, Lee & Clancy, Patrick E.__ Has a Child Been Molested? The Disturbing Facts about Current Methods of Investigating. Yates, Joanne, ed. 174p. 1999. pap. 29.95 (*0-9677418-0-7*) Berkeley Creek.

Coleman, Leon. Carl Van Vechten & the Harlem Renaissance: A Critical Assessment. LC 98-21097. (Studies in African American History & Culture). 198p. 1998. 48.00 (*0-8153-3126-6*) Garland.

Coleman, Leonard R. The Chronicles of DerLec. LC 97-65323. (Orig.). Date not set. pap. 12.95 (*1-884570-63-1*) Research Triangle.

Coleman, Leslie L., ed. Coal Data: 1992 Edition. rev. ed. 100p. 1992. pap. 75.00 (*0-9658257-0-1*) Natl Mining.

— Coal Data: 1993 Edition. 2nd ed. 100p. 1993. pap. 75.00 (*0-9658257-1-X*) Natl Mining.

— Coal Data: 1994 Edition. rev. ed. 100p. 1994. pap. 75.00 (*0-9658257-2-8*) Natl Mining.

— Coal Data: 1995 Edition. 100p. 1995. pap. 75.00 (*0-9658257-3-6*) Natl Mining.

— Coal Data: 1996 Edition. rev. ed. 100p. 1996. pap. 75.00 (*0-9658257-4-4*) Natl Mining.

— Coal Data: 1997 Edition. rev. ed. 100p. 1997. pap. 75.00 (*0-9658257-5-2*) Natl Mining.

— Coal Data: 1998 Edition. 100p. 1998. pap. 75.00 (*0-9658257-6-0*) Natl Mining.

Coleman, Lester, jt. auth. see Goddard, Donald.

Coleman, Linda. Seeking Out Harry. 310p. 1998. pap. 6.99 (*1-57532-194-7*) Press-Tige Pub.

*__Coleman, Linda K.__ Randy Manhatten. 310p. 2001. pap. write for info. (*1-57532-235-8*) Press-Tige Pub.

Coleman, Linda S., ed. Women's Life-Writing: Finding Voice/Building Community. LC 97-12724. 1997. 49.95 (*0-87972-747-0*); pap. 25.95 (*0-87972-748-9*) Bowling Green Univ Popular Press.

Coleman, Lisa. Million Dollar Salespeople: Success Stories of Top Sales Performers. 2nd ed. 152p. 1996. reprint ed. pap. 14.95 (*0-9660493-0-6*) Scrivo Inc.

Coleman, Loren. BattleTech. (Battletech Ser.: No. 32). 1997. mass mkt. 5.99 (*0-451-45597-5*, ROC) NAL.

— Battletech #32. 1997. mass mkt. 5.99 (*0-451-45633-5*, ROC) NAL.

— Battletech #32. (Battletech Ser.: No. 32). 288p. 1997. mass mkt. 5.99 (*0-451-45604-1*, ROC) NAL.

— Bloodlines. (Magic the Gathering Ser.). 1999. pap. 5.99 (*0-7869-1380-0*, Pub. by TSR Inc) Random.

Coleman, Loren, et al, eds. Working with Older Adoptees. 1989. reprint ed. pap. write for info. (*0-939561-05-0*) Univ South ME.

Coleman, Loren & Buxton, Kathryn. Elder Fire Safety for the Nineties. (Orig.). 1991. pap. write for info. (*0-939561-11-5*) Univ South ME.

Coleman, Loren & Clark, Jerome. Cryptozoology A to Z: The Encyclopedia of Loch Monsters, Sasquatch, Chupacabras & Other Authentic Mysteries of Nature. LC 99-31023. (Illus.). 272p. 1999. pap. 12.00 (*0-684-85602-6*, Fireside) S&S Trade Pap.

Coleman, Loren & Huyghe, Patrick. The Field Guide To Bigfoot, Yeti And Other Mystery Primates Worlwide. LC 99-11792. (Illus.). 224p. 1999. pap. 12.50 (*0-380-80263-5*, Avon Bks) Morrow Avon.

Coleman, Loren & Porter, Dan. Mattering: A Journey with Rural Youth. 1992. 25.00 incl. VHS (*0-939561-13-1*) Univ South ME.

Coleman, Loren & Porter, Dan, eds. Working with Rural Youth. 250p. (Orig.). (C). 1994. pap. text 15.00 (*0-939561-19-0*) Univ South ME.

Coleman, Loren & Sahonchik, Kris. Child Maltreatment & Abuse Investigation for Law Enforcement Officers. 100p. (Orig.). 1995. pap. text 15.00 (*0-939561-25-5*) Univ South ME.

*__Coleman, Loren L.__ Illusions of Victory. (Battletech Ser.: No. 47). 274p. 2000. mass mkt. 5.99 (*0-451-45790-0*, ROC) NAL.

— Rogue Flyer. 2000. pap. 6.95 (*1-55560-406-4*) FASA Corp.

— Threads of Ambition. (Battletech Ser.: 44). 288p. 1999. mass mkt. 5.99 (*0-451-45744-7*, ROC) NAL.

— VOR: Into the Maelstrom. 336p. 1999. mass mkt. 6.50 (*0-446-60488-7*, Pub. by Warner Bks) Little.

*__Coleman, Loretta.__ There is Hope. (Illus.). 69p. 1999. pap. 11.95 (*0-9643374-1-X*) PBLSH.

Coleman, Lori. Fundamental Soccer. LC 94-11907. (Fundamental Sports Ser.). (Illus.). 64p. (J). (gr. 5-9). 1995. lib. bdg. 21.27 (*0-8225-3451-7*, Lerner Publctns) Lerner Pub.

— My Pet Fish. LC 97-10861. (All about Pets Ser.). (Illus.). 64p. (J). (gr. 3-6). 1997. lib. bdg. 22.60 (*0-8225-2262-4*) Lerner Pub.

*__Coleman, Lori.__ Soccer. LC 99-47670. (Play-by-Play Ser.). (Illus.). 80p. (YA). (gr. 6-9). 2000. pap. 7.95 (*0-8225-9876-0*, First Ave Edns) Lerner Pub.

Coleman, Lori & Savage, Jeff. Beginning Strength Training. LC 97-51712. (Beginning Sports). (Illus.). 80p. (J). (gr. 3-5). 1998. 15.95 (*0-8225-3511-4*) Lerner Pub.

Coleman, Lori, jt. auth. see Jensen, Julie.

Coleman, Louise C., ed. More Gardening in New Orleans. (Orig.). 1989. pap. write for info. (*0-944681-03-4*) Celestial Pub.

Coleman, Louise C., ed. see Seidenberg, Charlotte.

Coleman, Louise C., ed. see Thibodaux Service League Members Staff.

Coleman, Lucien E., Jr. Comprendamos al Adulto de Hoy: Understanding Today's Adults. Quezada, Victor A., tr. (SPA.). 144p. (Orig.). 1992. text 6.50 (*0-311-11904-2*) Casa Bautista.

*__Coleman, Lucien E.__ How to Teach the Bible. 1999. pap. text 14.99 (*0-8054-2011-8*) Broadman.

Coleman, Lucile. Hunter of Time: Gnomic Verses. Eng, Steve, ed. (Blue Meadow Poetry Ser.: No. 1). 20p. (Orig.). 1984. pap. 3.50 (*0-910151-02-4*) Nashville Hse.

Coleman, Lyman. Interactive Bible Studies: 45 Guided Questionaires for Group Building. 1998. pap. text 7.99 (*1-57494-046-5*) Serendipty Hse.

— Serendipity Encyclopedia. 1997. pap. text 29.95 (*1-57494-049-X*) Serendipty Hse.

— Youth Crowd Breakers: Crowd Breakers, Games & Warm-ups for Youth Groups. 1998. pap. text 7.99 (*1-57494-034-1*) Serendipty Hse.

Coleman, Lyman, et al, eds. The Serendipity Group Study Book. 496p. 1986. pap. 9.95 (*0-310-25081-1*, 12032P) Zondervan.

Coleman, M., ed. see Damiecki, P.

Coleman, M. J., ed. Annual Meeting of the American Solar Energy Society, 1988: SOLAR 88. (Illus.). 583p. (Orig.). (C). 1988. pap., per. 50.00 (*0-89553-161-5*) Am Solar Energy.

— Thirteenth National Passive Solar Conference Proceedings, 1988: Solar 88. (Illus.). 523p. (Orig.). (C). 1988. per. 50.00 (*0-89553-204-2*) Am Solar Energy.

Coleman, M. J., jt. ed. see Burley, M. A.

Coleman, M. L., et al, eds. Quantifying Sedimentary Geochemical Processes: Royal Society Discussion Meeting. (Illus.). 194p. 1994. text 70.00 (*0-19-854831-1*) OUP.

Coleman, M. P. & Domaret, E. Cancer Registration in the European Economic Community. (IARC Technical Report Ser.: No. 3). 172p. 1988. text 30.00 (*92-832-1414-5*) World Health.

Coleman, Mac. Once upon a Little Town. 228p. mass mkt. 4.99 (*1-55197-065-1*) Picasso Publ.

C

Coleman, Maggie, ed. see Nussbaum, Nancy & Bigler, Erin D.

Coleman, Maggie, ed. see Toth, Michele.

Coleman, Margaret, ed. & illus. see Richardson, Eric.

Coleman, Margaret C. Emotional & Behavioral Disorders: Theory & Practice, Test Bank. 3rd ed. (C). 1995. pap. write for info. (*0-205-18386-7*, H8386-8) Allyn.

— Emotional Behavioral Disorders: Theory & Practice. 3rd ed. LC 95-5505. 416p. 1995. 75.00 (*0-205-16632-6*) Allyn.

Coleman, Margaret M. & Rothrock, Gail C., eds. Circling Historic Landscapes: Bicycling, Canoeing, Walking & Rail T Rails Near Sugarloaf Mountain, MD. 2nd rev. ed. (Illus.). 91p. 1999. reprint ed. pap. 19.95 (*0-9670682-0-7*) Sugarloaf Reg.

***Coleman, Marie.** County Longford & the Irish Revolution, 1910-1923. (New Directions in Irish History Ser.). (Illus.). 224p. 2000. 52.50 (*0-7165-2703-0*, Pub. by Irish Acad Pr) Intl Spec Bk.

Coleman, Marigold, compiled by. Indians of North America. 39.00 (*1-56696-120-3*) Jackdaw.

Coleman, Marilyn, jt. auth. see Ganong, Lawrence H.

Coleman, Marion M., tr. see Slowacki, Juliusz.

Coleman, Marion T., jt. ed. see Rodriguez, Reymundo.

Coleman, Mark J., et al. Sales & Leases in California Commercial Law Practice: 7/97 Update, 2 vols. Peyerwold, David L., ed. LC 93-70675. 464p. 1997. ring bd. 38.00 (*0-7626-0136-1*, BU-32073) Cont Ed Bar-CA.

Coleman, Marlene. Healthful Travel: Travel the Globe with Peace of Mind. 128p. 1995. pap. 9.95 (*0-9641050-0-4*) Intl Challenge.

Coleman, Martin. Communing with the Spirits. LC 97-27089. xi, 240p. 1997. 25.00 (*1-57863-019-3*) Weiser.

***Coleman, Martin & Grenfell, Michael.** The Competition Act 1998: Law & Practice. LC 99-32962. 744p. 1999. text 165.00 (*0-19-826874-2*) OUP.

— The Competition Act 1998: Law & Practice. 160p. 2000. pap. text 72.00 (*0-19-829956-7*) OUP.

Coleman, Mary. Picking Your Perfect Partner: A Guide to Compatibility in Relationships. LC 96-34671. (Illus.). 224p. (Orig.). 1996. pap. 12.00 (*0-916360-61-X*) CRCS Pubns CA.

Coleman, Mary & Gillberg, Christopher. The Schizophrenias: A Biological Approach to the Schizophrenia Spectrum Disorders. (Series on Psychiatry). (Illus.). 288p. 1996. 46.95 (*0-8261-9290-4*) Springer Pub.

Coleman, Mary, jt. auth. see Gillberg, Christopher.

Coleman, Mary A. The Dreams of Hummingbirds: Poems from Nature. Mathews, Judith, ed. LC 92-28169. (Illus.). 32p. (J). (gr. 3-7). 1993. lib. bdg. 14.95 (*0-8075-1720-8*) A Whitman.

Coleman, Mary D. Legislators, Law, & Public Policy: Political Change in Mississippi & the South, 267. LC 90-38422. (Contributions in Political Science Ser.: No. 267). 200p. 1993. 52.95 (*0-313-27271-9*, CPJ, Greenwood Pr) Greenwood.

***Coleman, Mary Sullivan & Krueger, Laura.** Play & Learn: A Motor-Based Preschool Curriculum for Children of All Abilities. Curran, Theresa L, ed. (Illus.). 314p. 1999. pap. 59.00 (*0-9666667-2-0*) AbleNet Inc.

Coleman, Mary T. Impact Zone: The Coleman Report to the President & Senate on Freedom of Religion. 90p. (Orig.). 1997. pap. write for info. (*0-9646569-1-4*) Dharma Inst.

— Monastic: An Ordained Tibetan Buddhist Speaks on Behalf of Full Ordination for Women. (Illus.). 117p. (Orig.). 1995. pap. write for info. (*0-9646569-0-6*) Dharma Inst.

Coleman, Matt. Trains, Tracks & Tall Timber: The History, Making & Modeling of Lumber & Paper. (Illus.). 144p. 1997. text 49.98 (*0-941952-49-5*) W K Walthers.

Coleman, Matt, ed. Fibers & Forming for Nonwovens: A TAPPI Press Anthology of Published Papers, 1985-1991. (Illus.). 489p. (Orig.). 1992. pap. 83.00 (*0-89852-261-7*, 0101R197) TAPPI.

Coleman, Matthew, ed. Energy Engineering & Management in the Pulp & Paper Industry: A TAPPI Anthology of Published Papers, 1986-1990. 706p. 1991. 30.00 (*0-89852-509-8*, 0101R182) TAPPI.

— Recycling Paper: From Fiber to Finished Product, 2 vols., Vol. 1. LC 90-19531. 446p. reprint ed. pap. 138.30 (*0-8357-3002-6*, 203927100001) Bks Demand.

— Recycling Paper: From Fiber to Finished Product, 2 vols., Vol. 2. LC 90-19531. 391p. reprint ed. pap. 121.30 (*0-8357-3003-4*, 203927100002) Bks Demand.

Coleman, McAlister. Men & Coal. LC 71-89725. (American Labor, from Conspiracy to Collective Bargaining Ser., No. 1). 350p. 1972. reprint ed. 23.95 (*0-405-02111-9*) Ayer.

— Pioneers of Freedom. LC 68-20292. (Essay Index Reprint Ser.). 1977. reprint ed. 19.95 (*0-8369-0326-9*) Ayer.

— Red Neck. LC 74-22772. (Labor Movement in Fiction & Non-Fiction Ser.). reprint ed. 42.50 (*0-404-58412-8*) AMS Pr.

Coleman, Melba F., et al. Children Grieve, Too: Developing, Understanding & Interventions for the Grief & Loss Process. (Illus.). 75p. (Orig.). 1994. pap. 79.95 (*0-9642578-0-7*) Caring About.

Coleman, Michael. Bible Stories. (Illus.). 192p. (gr. 6-12). 1999. pap. text 4.50 (*0-439-07801-6*) Scholastic Inc.

— Ciberdominio. 1990. pap. text 7.95 (*84-406-7380-9*) Lectorum Pubns.

— Cyber Feud. (Internet Detectives Ser.: No. 4). 128p. (J). (gr. 3-7). 1998. pap. 3.99 (*0-553-48643-8*, Skylark BDD) BDD Bks Young Read.

***Coleman, Michael.** Cyber Feud. (Internet Detectives Ser.). 1998. 9.09 (*0-606-13522-7*, Pub. by Turtleback) Demco.

Coleman, Michael. Escape Key. (Internet Detectives Ser.). 128p. (J). (gr. 2-6). 1997. pap. 3.99 (*0-553-48621-7*) Bantam.

Coleman, Michael. Escape Key. (Internet Detectives Ser.). 1997. 9.09 (*0-606-12739-9*, Pub. by Turtleback) Demco.

Coleman, Michael. Grounds for Suspicion. LC 94-79394. (Ten-Minute Mysteries Ser.). 32p. (YA). (gr. 6-12). 1994. pap. 2.95 (*0-7854-0842-8*, 40757) Am Guidance.

— Grounds for Suspicion Readalong. LC 94-79394. (Ten-Minute Mysteries Ser.). 32p. 1994. pap. 12.95 incl. audio (*0-7854-1051-1*, 40759) Am Guidance.

— Hank the Clank. LC 96-31081. (Illus.). 32p. (J). (ps up). 1996. lib. bdg. 21.27 (*0-8368-1625-0*) Gareth Stevens Inc.

— Hank the Clank. (Illus.). 32p. (J). Date not set. write for info. (*0-19-279959-2*) OUP.

— Los Bandidos De Internet. 1990. pap. text 7.95 (*84-406-7287-X*) Lectorum Pubns.

— The Much Better Story Book: Stories, Poems & Illustrations from Children & Bestselling Authors & Artists. (Illus.). 192p. (J). (gr. 3-5). 1994. pap. 7.95 (*0-09-911531-X*, Pub. by Hutchnson) Trafalgar.

— Net Bandits. (Internet Detectives Ser.). 128p. (J). (gr. 2-6). 1997. pap. 3.99 (*0-553-48620-9*) Bantam.

Coleman, Michael. Net Bandits, 1. (Internet Detectives Ser.). 1997. 9.09 (*0-606-12738-0*, Pub. by Turtleback) Demco.

Coleman, Michael. One, Two, Three, Oops! LC 98-6476. (Illus.). 32p. (J). (gr. k-2). 1999. 14.95 (*1-888444-45-2*) Little Tiger.

— Race Against Time. LC 94-79399. (Ten-Minute Mysteries Ser.). 32p. (YA). (gr. 6-12). 1994. pap. 2.95 (*0-7854-0847-9*, 40772) Am Guidance.

— Race Against Time Readalong. LC 94-79399. (Ten-Minute Mysteries Ser.). 32p. (YA). (gr. 6-12). 1994. pap. 12.95 incl. audio (*0-7854-1056-2*, 40774) Am Guidance.

— Speed Surf. (Internet Detectives Ser.: No. 3). 128p. (J). (gr. 3-7). 1997. pap. 3.99 (*0-553-48622-5*) BDD Bks Young Read.

Coleman, Michael. Speed Surf, 3. (Internet Detectives Ser.). 1997. 9.09 (*0-606-12740-2*, Pub. by Turtleback) Demco.

Coleman, Michael. Surf En La Red. 1990. pap. text 7.95 (*84-406-7316-7*) Lectorum Pubns.

— System Crash. (Internet Detectives Ser.: No. 5). (J). (gr. 3-7). 1998. pap. 3.99 (*0-553-48654-3*, Skylark BDD) BDD Bks Young Read.

***Coleman, Michael.** System Crash. 1998. 9.09 (*0-606-13523-5*, Pub. by Turtleback) Demco.

Coleman, Michael. Tecla De Escape. 1990. pap. text 7.95 (*84-406-7317-5*) Lectorum Pubns.

— Weirdo's War. LC 98-10482. 192p. (J). (gr. 4-8). 1998. 16.95 (*0-531-30103-6*) Orchard Bks Watts.

Coleman, Michael C. American Indian Children at School, 1850-1930. LC 92-37760. 240p. 1993. text 39.50 (*0-87805-616-5*) U Pr of Miss.

— Presbyterian Missionary Attitudes Toward American Indians, 1837-1893. LC 85-7496. (Illus.). 222p. 1985. text 32.00 (*0-87805-278-X*) U Pr of Miss.

***Coleman, Michael G. & Austin, Sandra B.** Manage for the Long Term Present: A Framework for Sustainable Growth. (Illus.). 320p. 1999. 29.95 (*1-929733-04-6*) MicroPress.

Coleman, Michael M., et al. Specific Interactions & the Miscibility of Polymer Blends. LC 91-65261. 520p. 1991. 49.95 (*0-87762-823-8*) Technomic.

Coleman, Michael M., jt. auth. see Painter, Paul C.

Coleman, Michel P., ed. Cancer Risk after Medical Treatment. (Illus.). 200p. 1991. 45.00 (*0-19-261781-8*) OUP.

***Coleman, Michel P. & Great Britain Office for National Statistics Staff.** Cancer Survival Trends in England & Wales, 1971-1995: Deprivation & NHS Region. xii, 695p. 1999. 338.25 incl. audio compact disk (*0-11-621243-8*, Pub. by Statnry Office) Balogh.

Coleman, Michel P., jt. auth. see Office for National Statistics Staff.

Coleman, Mildred H. Frances Virginia Tea Room Cookbook. 2nd ed. Orig. Title: The Frances Virginia Tea Room Cookbook. (Illus.). 190p. reprint ed. 14.95 (*0-9653416-0-7*) M H Coleman.

Coleman, Morocco. Coming Full Circle. 1998. pap. 19.99 (*0-9640122-3-5*) Pen & Pr United.

Coleman, Moses. Captain Moses Rich Colman: Master Mariner: American Autobiography. 119p. 1995. lib. bdg. 69.00 (*0-7812-8486-4*) Rprt Serv.

Coleman, Nancy L. Step-by-Step Narratives: Illustrated Lessons for Telling & Writing Stories. LC 97-8516. 1997. 37.00 (*1-888222-04-2*) Thinking Pubns.

Coleman, Neil F. Honeycomb. LC 99-26536. 176p. 1999. 18.95 (*1-58141-010-7*) Rivercross Pub.

Coleman, Neville. Dive Sites of the Great Barrier Reef. (Illus.). 176p. 1997. pap. 24.95 (*0-8442-4860-6*, 48606) NTC Contemp Pub Co.

Coleman, Norman C. Understanding Cancer: A Patient's Guide to Diagnosis, Prognosis & Treatment. LC 98-18732. 144p. 1998. pap. 13.95 (*0-8018-6020-2*) Johns Hopkins.

— Understanding Cancer: A Patient's Guide to Diagnosis, Prognosis & Treatment. LC 98-18732. 144p. 1998. 32.50 (*0-8018-6019-9*) Johns Hopkins.

Coleman-Norton, Paul R., ed. Studies in Roman Economic & Social History in Honor of Allan Chester Johnson. LC 70-80384. (Essay Index Reprint Ser.). 1977. 35.95 (*0-8369-1027-3*) Ayer.

Coleman, Pat, jt. auth. see Dyson, Peter.

Coleman, Pat, jt. auth. see Nelson, Stephen L.

Coleman, Patricia, jt. auth. see Coleman, William.

Coleman, Patricia B. Practical Sampling Techniques for Infrared Analysis. 320p. 1993. boxed set 136.95 (*0-8493-4203-1*, QD96) CRC Pr.

Coleman, Patrick. The Limits of Sympathy: Gabrielle Roy's The Tin Flute. (Canadian Fiction Studies: No. 26). 120p. (C). 1993. pap. text 14.95 (*1-55022-135-3*, Pub. by ECW) Genl Dist Srvs.

***Coleman, Patrick, et al, eds.** Representations of the Self from the Renaissance to Romanticism. (Illus.). 296p. (C). 2000. text 59.95 (*0-521-66146-3*) Cambridge U Pr.

Coleman, Patrick, ed. see Rousseau, Jean-Jacques.

Coleman, Patrick K. & Lamb, Charles R. The Nonpartisan League, 1915-1922: An Annotated Bibliography. LC 85-21480. xiii, 86p. (Orig.). 1985. pap. 12.95 (*0-87351-189-1*) Minn Hist.

Coleman, Patty, jt. auth. see Coleman, Bill.

***Coleman, Paul.** How to Say It To Your Kids: The Right Words to Solve Problems, Soothe Feelings, & Teach Values. 2000. 36.00 (*0-13-030884-6*) P-H.

— How to Say It To Your Kids: The Right Words to Solve Problems, Soothe Feelings, & Teach Values. 2000. pap. 14.00 (*0-7352-0177-3*) PH Pr.

Coleman, Paul. The Thirty Secrets of Happily Married Couples. 240p. (Orig.). 1992. pap. 7.95 (*1-55850-166-5*) Adams Media.

— Where the Balloons Go: Saying Goodbye. LC 95-26335. (Illus.). 56p. (J). 1995. pap. 8.95 (*1-56123-089-8*) Centering Corp.

Coleman, Paul, ed. Positron Beams & Their Applications. LC 99-89198. 300p. 1998. 68.00 (*981-02-3394-9*) World Scientific Pub.

Coleman, Paul D., ed. Neurobiology of Aging: Research on Age-Related Phenomena, Neurodegeneration & Neuropathology. 1989. 65.00 (*0-685-26770-9*, Pergamon Pr) Elsevier.

Coleman, Paul W. Second Peter & Jude: Staying Power for Today's Christian. (Deeper Life Pulpit Commentary Ser.). 167p. 1999. pap. 12.99 (*0-87509-823-1*) Chr Pubns.

***Coleman, Penny.** Village Elders. (Illus.). 168p. 2000. 24.95 (*0-252-02552-0*) U of Ill Pr.

Coleman, Peter. The Liberal Conspiracy: The Congress for Cultural Freedom & the Struggle for the Mind of Postwar Europe. 350p. 1989. 29.95 (*0-02-906481-3*) Free Pr.

— Power of Three: Parent, Student & Teacher Collaboration. LC 98-234102. 1998. pap. 29.95 (*1-85396-399-2*, Pub. by P Chapman) P H Brookes.

— The Real Barry Humphries. (Illus.). 191p. 1992. pap. 8.95 (*0-340-55907-1*, Pub. by Hodder & Stought Ltd) Trafalgar.

— The Real Barry Humphries. 246p. 1991. 24.95 (*1-85089-541-4*, Pub. by ISIS Lrg Prnt); pap. 16.95 (*1-85089-337-3*, Pub. by ISIS Lrg Prnt) Transaction Pubs.

Coleman, Peter, et al, eds. Struggling to Be 'Good Enough' Administrative Practices & School District Ethos. 240p. 1990. pap. 34.95 (*1-85000-861-2*, Falmer Pr) Taylor & Francis.

Coleman, Peter, jt. ed. see Bond, John.

Coleman, Peter, jt. ed. see Deutsch, Morton.

Coleman, Peter J. Debtors & Creditors in America: Insolvency, Imprisonment for Debt, & Bankruptcy 1607-1900. LC 74-502. 375p. 1974. 17.50 (*0-87020-141-7*) State Hist Soc Wis.

— Progressivism & the World of Reform: New Zealand & the Origins of the American Welfare State. LC 87-6187. xiv, 248p. 1987. 29.95 (*0-7006-0321-2*) U Pr of KS.

— The Transformation of Rhode Island, 1790-1860. LC 84-27932. 314p. 1985. reprint ed. lib. bdg. 75.00 (*0-313-24796-X*, COTR, Greenwood Pr) Greenwood.

Coleman, Phil, et al. Shades of Sun at Pigeon Creek. 52p. (Orig.). 1996. pap. 6.00 (*1-889729-00-0*) Pigeon Crk Poets.

Coleman, Phyllis. Florida Family Law: Statutes, Treaties & Materials. LC 97-35253. 456p. 1998. pap. 39.95 (*0-89089-712-3*) Carolina Acad Pr.

***Coleman, Phyllis.** Florida Family Law: Text & Commentary - 2000 Edition. 684p. 2000. pap. 49.95 (*0-89089-714-X*) Carolina Acad Pr.

Coleman, R. E. El Plan Maestro de la Evangelizacion.Tr. of Master Plan of Evangelism. (SPA.). 8.99 (*0-7899-0357-1*, 498612) Editorial Unilit.

Coleman, R. E. Positron Emission Tomography: Research & Clinical Applications. Date not set. write for info. (*0-8247-9486-9*) Dekker.

Coleman, R. Edward, et al. Diagnostic Nuclear Medicine, 2 vols. 3rd ed. Sandler, Martin P., ed. LC 94-32470. (Illus.). 1600p. 1996. 279.00 (*0-683-07503-9*) Lppncott W & W.

Coleman, R. G. & Juvigne, E. H., eds. Proceedings of the 29th International Geological Congress Pt. B: Reconstruction of the Paleo-Asian Ocean; Quarternary Environmental Changes. 326p. 1994. 140.00 (*90-6764-174-X*, Pub. by VSP) Coronet Bks.

Coleman, Ralph S. A Skiff of Snow: Poems. 32p. 1997. pap. 6.00 (*1-885912-16-1*) Sows Ear Pr.

Coleman, Ray. Clapton! 368p. (Orig.). 1988. mass mkt. 14.95 (*0-446-38630-8*, Pub. by Warner Bks) Little.

— Lennon: The Definitive Biography. LC 92-52621. 784p. 1992. pap. 20.00 (*0-06-098608-5*, Perennial) HarperTrade.

— McCartney: Yesterday . . . And Today. (Illus.). 194p. 1998. pap. text 17.00 (*0-7881-5935-6*) DIANE Pub.

— McCartney: Yesterday & Today, 2 cass. abr. ed. (Illus.). 1996. audio. write for info. (*0-7871-1003-5*, Dove Audio) NewStar Media.

— Phil Collins: The Definitive Biography. (Illus.). 288p. 1999. 23.50 (*0-684-86830-X*) S&S Trade.

Coleman, Ray, jt. auth. see Wyman, Bill.

Coleman, Rebecca, ed. see Superior Quality Foods, Inc. Staff.

Coleman, Reed F. Life Goes Sleeping. LC 90-53325. 271p. 1991. 22.00 (*1-877946-05-2*) Permanent Pr.

— Little Easter. LC 92-34305. 221p. 1993. 22.00 (*1-877946-23-0*) Permanent Pr.

— They Don't Play Stickball in Milwaukee. 208p. 1997. 24.00 (*1-877946-95-8*) Permanent Pr.

Coleman, Richard. Is Your Prescription Killing You? Richards, Carolyn, ed. LC 79-28294. 1981. 21.95 (*0-87949-164-7*) Ashley Bks.

Coleman, Richard J. Issues of Theological Conflict: Evangelicals & Liberals. rev. ed. LC 79-19494. 296p. reprint ed. pap. 91.80 (*0-608-11857-5*, 202320900032) Bks Demand.

Coleman, Richard M. The 24-Hour Business: Maximizing Productivity Through Round-the-Clock Operations. LC 95-5703. 208p. 1995. 24.95 (*0-8144-0240-2*) AMACOM.

Coleman, Richard P. & Neugarten, Bernice L. Social Status in the City. LC 70-132820. (Jossey-Bass Behavioral Science Ser.). 338p. reprint ed. 104.80 (*0-8357-9348-6*, 201378200087) Bks Demand.

Coleman, Rita. The Stations of the Cross for Children. 24p. 1992. pap. 2.95 (*0-8146-2062-0*) Liturgical Pr.

Coleman, Rita, ed. see Maltz, Arnold.

Coleman, Rita, ed. see Napolitano, Maida.

Coleman, Rita M., ed. see Warehousing Research Center Staff.

Coleman, Robert. The Development of Informal Geometry. LC 78-176696. (Columbia University. Teachers College. Contributions to Education Ser.: No. 865). reprint ed. 37.50 (*0-404-55865-8*) AMS Pr.

Coleman, Robert, ed. New Studies in Latin Linguistics: Proceedings from the 4th International Colloquium on Latin Linguistics, Cambridge, April 1987. LC 91-8624. (Studies in Language Companion: Vol. 21). x, 480p. 1991. 148.00 (*90-272-3024-2*) J Benjamins Pubng Co.

Coleman, Robert, ed. see Virgil.

Coleman, Robert E. The Coming World Revival. rev. ed. LC 94-45708. 176p. 1995. 13.99 (*0-89107-840-1*) Crossway Bks.

— The Great Commission Lifestyle: Conforming Your Life to Kingdom Priorities. LC 92-9487. 128p. (Orig.). (gr. 11). 1992. pap. 7.99 (*0-8007-5450-6*) Revell.

— The Master Plan of Discipleship. 160p. 1998. mass mkt. 4.99 (*0-8007-8655-6*) Revell.

— The Master Plan of Evangelism. 2nd abr. ed. LC 93-6792. 144p. 1994. mass mkt. 4.99 (*0-8007-8624-6*, Spire) Revell.

— The Master Plan of Evangelism: 30th Anniversary Edition. 2nd anniversary ed. LC 93-6792. 204p. (YA). (gr. 10). 1992. pap. 9.99 (*0-8007-5467-0*) Revell.

— The Master's Way of Personal Evangelism: A Companion to "The Master Plan of Evangelism" LC 96-41251. 192p. 1997. pap. 10.99 (*0-89107-912-2*) Crossway Bks.

— Nothing to Do but to Save Souls: John Wesley's Charge to His Preachers. LC 93-50723. 107p. 1994. reprint ed. pap. 8.00 (*0-915143-05-4*) Evangel Indiana.

— Nothing to Do but to Save Souls...John Wesley: John Wesley's Charge to His Preachers. 112p. 1990. 9.95 (*0-310-75480-1*); pap. 7.99 (*0-310-75481-X*) Zondervan.

— Plan Supremo de Evangelizacion.Tr. of Master Plan of Evangelism. (SPA.). 1972. 4.99 (*0-311-13816-0*) Casa Bautista.

— Singing with the Angels. LC 98-21486. 160p. (C). 1998. pap. 7.99 (*0-8007-5673-8*) Revell.

Coleman, Robert E., et al, eds. Disciplemaking: Self-Study Course in Understanding & Applying Jesus' Command to "Make Disciples" (Illus.). 231p. 1994. pap. 41.95 incl. audio (*1-879089-12-2*); student ed. 10.95 (*1-879089-13-0*) B Graham Ctr.

Coleman, Robert E. & Tunstall, Frank G. The Master Plan of Evangelism: Leader's Guide. 1990. pap. 9.95 (*0-911866-24-8*) LifeSprings Res.

Coleman, Robert E., ed. see Lawrence.

Coleman, Robert E., ed. & intro. see Wesley, John.

Coleman, Robert G. Geologic Evolution of the Red Sea. (Oxford Monographs on Geology & Geophysics: No. 24). (Illus.). 200p. (C). 1993. text 100.00 (*0-19-507048-8*) OUP.

Coleman, Robert G. & Wang, Xiaomin, eds. Ultrahigh Pressure Metamorphism. (Cambridge Topics in Petrology Ser.: No. 1). (Illus.). 540p. (C). 1995. text 90.00 (*0-521-43214-6*) Cambridge U Pr.

Coleman, Robert M., et al. Fundamental Immunology. 2nd ed. 624p. (C). 1992. text. write for info. (*0-697-11310-8*, WCB McGr Hill); text, student ed. 24.37 (*0-697-16329-6*, WCB McGr Hill) McGrw-H Hghr Educ.

Coleman, Roberta, et al. Gestion y Majora de la Calidad del Proceso Directrices. 2nd rev. ed. Annitto, Susan, ed. (AT&T Quality Library). (Illus.). 131p. (Orig.). 1988. pap. 24.95 (*0-932764-44-4*) AT&T Customer Info.

Coleman, Robin R. Means, see Means Coleman, Robin R.

Coleman, Roger. New Light & Truth: The Making of the Revised English Bible. (Illus.). 96p. 1989. 5.00 (*0-19-101441-9*) OUP.

Coleman, Roger. Ways of Drawing Eyes: A Guide to Expanding Your Visual Self-Awareness. 64p. 1998. text 13.00 (*0-7881-5556-3*) DIANE Pub.

Coleman, Ron. Car Smart: Save Hundreds on Car Repairs & Avoid Ripoffs. (Illus.). 256p. 1998. pap. 14.95 (*0-9663627-4-8*) Autowise.

— The Princeton Review: Prelaw School Companion. LC 97-189221. 1996. pap. 15.00 (*0-679-77372-X*) Villard Books.

Coleman, Ron & Barrie, Giles. 525 Ways to Be a Better Manager. 2nd rev. ed. LC 98-24977. 160p. 1998. 56.95 (*0-566-07969-0*, Pub. by Gower) Ashgate Pub Co.

— Five Hundred Twenty-five Ways to be a Better Manager. (Illus.). 133p. 1990. text 49.95 (*0-566-02820-4*, Pub. by Gower) Ashgate Pub Co.

An Asterisk (*) at the beginning of an entry indicates that the title is appearing for the first time.

Coleman, Ron J. Opportunities in Fire Protection Services. (Opportunities In . . . Ser.). (Illus.). 160p. pap. 12.95 (0-8442-8624-9, 297OIFPS, VGM Career) NTC Contemp Pub Co.

— Opportunities in Fire Protection Services. (Illus.). 160p. 1992. 14.95 (0-8442-8623-0, VGM Career) NTC Contemp Pub Co.

Coleman, Rona. Encyclopedia of Flower Arranging: Decorating with Fresh, Dried & Pressed Flowers. 1989. 22.98 (1-55521-333-2) Bk Sales Inc.

Coleman, Ronald. Hazardous Materials Dictionary. LC 87-71934. 180p. 1987. 44.95 (0-87762-539-5) Technomic.

Coleman, Ronald A. The Wild Orchids of California. (Comstock Bk.). (Illus.). 264p. 1995. text 47.50 (0-8014-3012-7) Cornell U Pr.

Coleman, Ronny. Going for Gold: Pursuing & Assuming the Job of Fire Chief. LC 98-38802. 288p. 1998. text 34.95 (0-7668-0868-8) Delmar.

Coleman, Ronny J. Hazardous Materials Dictionary. 2nd rev. ed. LC 94-60735. 212p. 1994. 79.95 (1-56676-160-3) Technomic.

— Opportunities in Fire Protection Services. LC 96-52404. (Opportunities in... Ser.). (Illus.). 160p. 1997. 14.95 (0-8442-4680-8, 46808, Natl Textbk Co); pap. 11.95 (0-8442-4681-6, 46816, Natl Textbk Co) NTC Contemp Pub Co.

Coleman, Ronny J. & Granito, John A., eds. Managing Fire Services. 2nd ed. (Municipal Management Ser.). 506p. 1988. text 39.95 (0-87326-078-3) Intl City-Cnty Mgt.

Coleman, Ronny J. & Russell, Raymond M. Fire Truck Toys for Men & Boys. (Catalogue of Toy Fire Apparatus Ser.: Vol. I). (Illus.). 168p. 1981. pap. 9.95 (0-910105-00-6) Phenix Pub.

— Fire Truck Toys for Men & Boys. (Catalogue of Toy Fire Apparatus Ser.: Vol. II). (Illus.). 168p. 1982. pap. 10.95 (0-910105-01-4) Phenix Pub.

Coleman, Ruby. Heritage Lines, the First Ten Years. 192p. (Orig.). 1993. pap. 20.00 (0-9639433-0-8) R Coleman.

Coleman, Ruth, jt. auth. see Shakespeare, William.

Coleman, Ruth, jt. auth. see Steinbeck, John.

Coleman, Sally. Seasons of the Spirit: Daily Mediations for Adults in Mid-Life & Beyond. 1992. pap. 10.00 (1-56838-060-7) Hazelden.

Coleman, Sally & Anderson, David S., eds. Charting Your Course: A Life-Long Guide to Health & Compassion. LC 98-3010. 400p. (YA). 1998. pap. 16.00 (0-268-00827-2) U of Notre Dame Pr.

Coleman, Sally & Hull-Mast, Nancy. Can't Buy Me Love: Freedom from Compulsive Spending & Money Obsession. LC 92-37139. 240p. (Orig.). 1995. pap. text 12.95 (0-925190-46-2) Fairview Press.

Coleman, Samuel, jt. auth. see Hall, Clifton.

***Coleman, Samuel J.** Japanese Science: From the Inside. LC 99-27363. (Studies in the Growth Economies of Asia Ser.). 1999. text. write for info. (0-415-20169-1) Routledge.

Coleman, Samuel S., jt. auth. see Hall, Clifton D.

Coleman, Sandra B., ed. Failures in Family Therapy. LC 84-19325. (Family Therapy Ser.). 401p. 1985. lib. bdg. 47.50 (0-89862-048-1) Guilford Pubns.

Coleman, Sandy & Hull-Mast, Nancy. Our Best Days. LC 90-61371. (Meditation Ser.). 400p. pap. 10.00 (1-56838-114-X, 7813 A) Hazelden.

Coleman, Satis N. Bells, Their History, Legends, Making, & Uses. LC 70-109722. (Illus.). 462p. 1971. reprint ed. lib. bdg. 38.50 (0-8371-4212-1, COBE, Greenwood Pr) Greenwood.

— Bells, Their History, Legends, Making & Uses. 462p. 1990. reprint ed. lib. bdg. 89.00 (0-7812-9112-7) Rprt Serv.

Coleman, Satis N. & Bregman, Adolph, eds. Songs of American Folks. LC 68-57060. (Granger Index Reprint Ser.). 1977. 16.95 (0-8369-6011-4) Ayer.

Coleman-Selden, Sally. The Promise of Representative Bureaucracy: Diversity & Responsiveness in a Government Agency. LC 97-12695. (Bureaucracies, Public Administration, & Public Policy Ser.). 172p. (C). (gr. 13). 1998. pap. text 29.95 (0-7656-0056-0) M E Sharpe.

Coleman, Sherman S. Complex Foot Deformities in Children. LC 82-15249. 313p. reprint ed. pap. 97.10 (0-7837-2695-3, 204307300006) Bks Demand.

Coleman, Shirley, et al. The Pocket Statistician: A Practical Guide to Quality Improvement. (An Arnold Publication). 260p. 1996. pap. text 29.95 (0-340-67721-X, Pub. by E A) OUP.

Coleman, Sidney, et al, eds. Quantum Cosmology & Baby Universes: Proceedings of the Seventh Jerusalem Winter School. 300p. (C). 1991. text 68.00 (981-02-0345-4); pap. text 40.00 (981-02-0346-2) World Scientific Pub.

Coleman, Silas B. Coleman Family: Descendants of Thos. Coleman of Nantucket, in Line of the Oldest Son, Ten Generations, 1602 to 1898. 36p. 1997. reprint ed. pap. 7.50 (0-8328-8012-4); reprint ed. lib. bdg. 17.50 (0-8328-8011-6) Higginson Bk Co.

***Coleman, Simon.** The Globalisation of Charismatic Christianity: Spreading the Gospel of Prosperity. (Cambridge Studies in Ideology & Religion: Vol. 12). (Illus.). 276p. (C). 2000. text Price not set. (0-521-66072-6) Cambridge U Pr.

Coleman, Simon & Elsner, John. Pilgrimage: Past & Present in the World Religions. (Illus.). 240p. (C). 1995. 29.95 (0-674-66765-4) HUP.

— Pilgrimage: Past & Present in the World Religions. (Illus.). 240p. 1997. reprint ed. pap. 20.50 (0-674-66766-2) HUP.

Coleman, Simon, jt. ed. see Bell, Sandra.

Coleman, Skeets, et al. Convair XFY-1 Pogo. (Naval Fighters Ser.: No. 27). (Illus.). 34p. (Orig.). 1994. pap. text 7.95 (0-942612-27-2) Naval Fighters.

Coleman, Stephanie C. & Minnich, Joseph L. Understanding Limited Appraisals & Appraisal Reporting Options. LC 96-31829. 1996. 27.50 (0-922154-31-7) Appraisal Inst.

Coleman, Stephen. Measurement & Analysis of Political Systems: A Science of Social Behavior. LC 75-8704. (Comparative Studies in Behavioral Science). (Illus.). 231p. reprint ed. pap. 71.70 (0-608-20295-9, AU0050700002) Bks Demand.

Coleman, Stephen & O'Sullivan, Paddy, eds. William Morris & News from Nowhere: A Vision for Our Time. 224p. 1996. pap. 14.95 (1-870098-37-4, Pub. by Green Bks) Chelsea Green Pub.

***Coleman, Stephen, et al.** Parliament in the Age of the Internet. (Hansard Society Series in Government & Politics). 217p. 2000. pap. text 24.95 (0-19-922422-6) OUP.

Coleman, Stephen E., jt. auth. see Melville, Bruce W.

Coleman, Steven, Sr. Judge Clarence W. Allgood: His Brothers' Keeper. (Illus.). 64p. (Orig.). 1991. pap. 12.95 (0-943994-18-7) Birmingham Hist Soc.

Coleman, Steven J., ed. see Fein, Mark.

Coleman, Susan E., et al. Texas Government. LC 95-14145. 1995. pap. write for info. (0-614-07804-0) P-H.

Coleman, Susan E., jt. auth. see Calvi, James V.

Coleman, Susan E., jt. auth. see Coleman, Heath.

Coleman, Susan E., jt. auth. see Smith, Franci.

***Coleman, Sydney R.** Structural Fat Grafting. (Illus.). 400p. 2000. text 250.00 (1-57626-133-6) Quality Med Pub.

Coleman, T. & Van Loan, Charles F. Handbook for Matrix Computations. LC 88-61637. (Frontiers in Applied Mathematics Ser.: No. 4). vii, 264p. (C). 1988. pap. text 34.00 (0-89871-227-0) Soc Indus-Appl Math.

Coleman, Ted P. Florida Summary Claims Handbook. 1994. ring bd., suppl. ed. 45.00 (0-685-11441-4, MICHIE) LEXIS Pub.

***Coleman, Teresa.** Dragons & Silk. 1999. 14.95 (962-217-602-X) Norton.

Coleman, Teresa. Dragons & Silk. 2nd ed. (Illus.). 32p. 1999. pap. 9.95 (962-217-489-2) Norton.

Coleman, Terry. Fantasy General. 1996. pap. text 19.99 (0-7615-0635-7) Prima Pub.

— Going to America. (Illus.). 317p. 1998. reprint ed. pap. 19.95 (0-8063-1189-4, 1125) Genealog Pub.

Coleman, Terry, jt. auth. see Wilson, Johnny L.

Coleman, Terry Lee, jt. auth. see Wilson, Johnny L.

Coleman, Terry S. Legal Aspects of Medicare & Medicaid Reimbursement: Payment for Hospital & Physician Services. Chambers, Susan K., ed. LC 90-61619. (NHLA Focus Ser.). 216p. 1990. pap. 45.00 (0-918945-06-2) Am Hlth Lawyers.

Coleman, Terry S., ed. Legal Aspects of Medicare & Medicaid Reimbursement: Payment for Hospital & Physician Services. 199p. 1990. 35.00 (0-918945-05-4) Am Hlth Lawyers.

— Legal Aspects of Medicare & Medicaid Reimbursement: Payment for Hospital & Physician Services; Supplement RBRVS & the New Medicare Physician Fee Schedule. 44p. 1990. 35.00 (0-918945-13-5) Am Hlth Lawyers.

***Coleman, Thalia J.** Assessment & Intervention Comm. LC 99-34179. 344p. 1999. pap. text 42.00 (0-205-26724-6) Allyn.

Coleman, Thomas. Computer Estimating for Home Builders. LC 97-50146. 1998. 52.50 (0-86718-439-6) Builderburg Grp.

— Computer Estimating for Home Builders. LC 97-50146. (Illus.). 87p. 1998. pap. 27.50 (0-86718-440-X) Home Builder.

***Coleman, Thomas.** Uniform Laws & Regulations in the Areas of Legal Metrology & Engine Fuel Quality: As Adopted by the 83d National Conference on Weights & Measures, 1998. 233p. 1998. per. 19.00 (0-16-060886-4) USGPO.

— Uniform Laws & Regulations in the Areas of Legal Metrology & Engine Fuel Quality: As Adopted by the 84th National Conference On Weights & Measures, 1999. 238p. 2000. per. 22.00 (0-16-050262-4) USGPO.

Coleman, Thomas F. & Li, Yuying, eds. Large Scale Numerical Optimization. LC 90-23912. (Proceedings in Applied Mathematics Ser.: No. 46). 255p. 1990. pap. 40.75 (0-89871-268-8) Soc Indus-Appl Math.

***Coleman, Thomas H., et al.** Advising & Defending Corporate Directors & Officers, 9/99 Update. Peyerwold, David, ed. 276p. 1999. ring bd. 52.00 (0-7626-0314-3, BU-32721) Cont Ed Bar-CA.

Coleman, Thomas J. & Curtsinger, George. Brain, Body & Breath. 64p. (Orig.). 1996. pap. 5.00 (0-941179-43-5) Latitudes Pr.

Coleman, Thomas S., et al. Historical U. S. Treasury Yield Curves, 1993 Edition. 1993. 90.00 (1-882864-02-6) Ibbotson Assocs.

Coleman, Tim. Fishable Wrecks & Rockpiles. (Illus.). 196p. (Orig.). 1989. pap. write for info. (0-318-63674-3) MT Pubns.

— Fishing Connecticut Waters. rev. ed. (Illus.). 148p. 1988. reprint ed. pap. 7.95 (0-317-91186-4) MT Pubns.

— To Catch a Bass. (Illus.). 160p. (Orig.). 1992. pap. text. write for info. (0-929775-04-X) MT Pubns.

Coleman, Timothy. Learn PAL 4.5 in a Day: Versions 4.0 & 4.5. (Popular Applications Ser.). 192p. 1994. pap. 15.95 incl. disk (1-55622-368-4) Wordware Pub.

Coleman, Val. Beverly & Marigold. LC 96-3096. (Illus.). 240p. 1996. 23.95 (0-312-14549-7) St Martin.

Coleman, Vanessa D., ed. see Burruss, Pricellious J.

Coleman, Verna. Adela Pankhurst: The Wayward Suffragette, 1885-1961. (Illus.). 192p. 1996. pap. 19.95 (0-522-84728-5, Pub. by Melbourne Univ Pr) Paul & Co Pubs.

Coleman, Vernon. The Bilbury Chronicles. large type ed. 480p. 1995. 27.99 (0-7089-3424-2) Ulverscroft.

— Bilbury Grange. large type ed. 512p. 1996. 27.99 (0-7089-3602-4) Ulverscroft.

— The Bilbury Revels. large type ed. 576p. 1996. 27.99 (0-7089-3532-X) Ulverscroft.

— Bodypower. 128p. 1989. reprint ed. pap. 8.95 (1-878290-00-2) Intl Hlth MD.

— Know Yourself. 224p. 1989. mass mkt. 5.99 (0-449-21778-7, Crest) Fawcett.

— Stress Control. 214p. 1979. 20.00 (0-85117-167-2) Transatl Arts.

— The Village Cricket Tour. (C). 1992. pap. 50.00 (0-9503527-3-X, Pub. by Chilton Designs) St Mut.

— Why Animal Experiments Must Stop: And How You Can Stop Them. 107p. (Orig.). 1997. reprint ed. pap. text 10.00 (0-7881-5049-9) DIANE Pub.

Coleman, Victor. Lapsed W. A. S. P. Poems, 1978-89. LC 95-102393. 128p. 1994. pap. 12.00 (1-55022-221-X, Pub. by ECW) Genl Dist Srvs.

Coleman, W. Bevel Gear Rating Using the New Standard - AGMA 2003-A86 (formerly known as AGMA 219) Pts. I & II: General Gearing; Vehicle Gearing. (1985 Fall Technical Meeting Ser.: Vol. 85FTM2). 32p. 1985. pap. text 30.00 (1-55589-095-4) AGMA.

— A New Perspective on the Strength of Bevel Gear Teeth. (Technical Papers: Vol. P229.13). (Illus.). 18p. 1969. pap. text 30.00 (1-55589-280-9) AGMA.

— Pitting Resistance of Bevel & Hypoid Gear Teeth. (Technical Papers: Vol. P229.05). (Illus.). 35p. 1960. pap. text 30.00 (1-55589-273-6) AGMA.

— Progress Report of Gear Rating Coordinating Committee Pt. II: Propsed Practice for Beam Strength of Bevel Gears. (Technical Papers: Vol. 229.01A). (Illus.). 49p. 1951. pap. text 30.00 (1-55589-140-3) AGMA.

— Vehicle Axle Drive: Gear Design in the 70s. (Technical Papers: Vol. P109.25). (Illus.). 24p. 1971. pap. text 30.00 (1-55589-196-9) AGMA.

Coleman, Walter. The Molly Maguire Riots: Industrial Conflict in the Pennsylvania Coal Region. Stein, Leon & Taft, Philip, eds. LC 78-89726. (American Labor, from Conspiracy to Collective Bargaining Ser., No. 1). 189p. 1997. reprint ed. pap. 23.95 (0-405-02112-7) Ayer.

Coleman, Wanda. African Sleeping Sickness: Stories & Poems. LC 90-1294. 332p. 1993. reprint ed. pap. 14.00 (0-87685-812-4) Black Sparrow.

— American Sonnets. (Light & Dust Bks.). 62p. (Orig.). 1994. pap. 6.00 (0-87924-069-5) Membrane Pr.

— Bathwater Wine. LC 98-17689. 288p. 1998. pap. 15.00 (1-57423-064-6); pap. 27.50 (1-57423-065-4) Black Sparrow.

— Hand Dance. LC 92-45125. 271p. (Orig.). 1993. 25.00 (0-87685-897-3); pap. 13.00 (0-87685-896-5) Black Sparrow.

— Hand Dance, signed ed. deluxe ed. LC 92-45125. 271p. (Orig.). 1993. 30.00 (0-87685-898-1) Black Sparrow.

— Heavy Daughter Blues: Poems & Stories, 1968-1986. LC 87-12177. 224p. (C). 1991. reprint ed. pap. 14.00 (0-87685-701-2) Black Sparrow.

— Imagoes. LC 83-11949. 174p. 1991. reprint ed. 20.00 (0-87685-510-9); reprint ed. pap. 12.00 (0-87685-509-5) Black Sparrow.

— Imagoes, signed ed. LC 83-11949. 174p. 1991. reprint ed. 30.00 (0-87685-511-7) Black Sparrow.

— Mambo Hips & Make Believe: A Novel. LC 99-43143. 403p. 1999. 25.00 (1-57423-095-6); pap. 16.00 (1-57423-094-8) Black Sparrow.

— Native in a Strange Land: Trials & Tremors. LC 96-32027. 292p. (Orig.). 1996. pap. 15.00 (1-57423-022-0) Black Sparrow.

— A War of Eyes & Other Stories. LC 88-14714. 246p. 1989. pap. 14.00 (0-87685-735-7) Black Sparrow.

Coleman, Wanda, ed. Women for All Seasons: Poetry & Prose about the Transitions in Women's Lives. 76p. (Orig.). 1988. pap. 8.00 (0-944587-00-3) Womans Bldg.

Coleman-Wells, Shirley & Wells, Anna B. Fortress of the Heart...: The Story of Anna. unabridged ed. LC 98-36397. 250p. 1998. pap. 20.00 (0-9617223-2-0, No. 10) Hughes Henshaw Pubs.

Coleman, Wendy S. Attention, Behavior & Learning Disorders in Children: Forms & Information Materials for Educators & Health Professionals. 85p. 1996. spiral bd. 40.00 (0-9620187-4-0) Calliope Bks.

— Attention Deficit Disorders, Hyperactivity & Associated Disorders: A Handbook for Parents & Professionals. 6th rev. ed. 104p. 1993. pap. 12.95 (0-9620187-2-4) Calliope Bks.

***Coleman, Will.** Tribal Talk: Black Theology, Hermeneutics, & African-American Ways of "Telling the Story" LC 99-10387. 2000. write for info. (0-271-01944-1) Pa St U Pr.

Coleman, William. Before I Give You Away. 16p. 1995. text 11.99 (1-55661-487-X) Bethany Hse.

— Being a Christian at School. 48p. (Orig.). (YA). 1994. pap., student ed. 3.50 (1-56476-291-2, 6-3291, Victor Bks) Chariot Victor.

— Death Is a Social Disease: Public Health & Political Economy in Early Industrial France. LC 81-69817. (Wisconsin Publications in the History of Science & Medicine: Vol. 1). 345p. reprint ed. pap. 107.00 (0-608-09900-7, 206923800003) Bks Demand.

— Earning Your Wings. LC 84-6299. 144p. (YA). (gr. 7 up). 1984. pap. 6.99 (0-87123-311-8) Bethany Hse.

— Friends Forever. LC 87-700. 144p. (Orig.). (YA). (gr. 8-12). 1987. pap. 6.99 (0-87123-959-0) Bethany Hse.

— If I Could Raise My Kids Again. 176p. 1996. pap. 8.99 (1-55661-657-0) Bethany Hse.

— Life in a Teenage Jungle. LC 94-5741. 160p. (Orig.). (YA). (gr. 9-12). 1994. pap. 6.99 (0-8007-5525-1) Revell.

***Coleman, William.** A Light In The Shadows: Emerging from the Darkness of Depression. LC 00-23352. 194p. 2000. pap. 10.99 (1-56955-151-0, Vine Bks) Servant.

Coleman, William. A Measured Pace. LC 86-11750. 144p. (Orig.). 1986. pap. 6.99 (0-87123-671-0) Bethany Hse.

— The Newlywed Book. LC 85-1345. 144p. (Orig.). 1985. pap. 6.99 (0-87123-799-7) Bethany Hse.

— Tribal Talk: Black Theology, Hermeneutics, & African/american Ways of "telling the Story" LC 99-10387. 346p. 2000. pap. text 18.95 (0-271-01945-X) Pa St U Pr.

— What Makes Your Teen Tick? 16p. (Orig.). 1993. pap. 7.99 (1-55661-322-9) Bethany Hse.

— Yellow Fever in the North: The Methods of Early Epidemiology. LC 86-40456. (Wisconsin Publications in the History of Science & Medicine: No. 6). 224p. 1987. text 34.95 (0-299-11110-5) U of Wis Pr.

— Yellow Fever in the North: The Methods of Early Epidemiology. LC 86-40456. (Wisconsin Publications in the History of Science & Medicine: Vol. 6). (Illus.). 219p. 1987. reprint ed. pap. 67.90 (0-608-07464-0, 206769100009) Bks Demand.

Coleman, William, et al, eds. A Casebook of Grant Proposals in the Humanities. LC 81-18859. 248p. 1982. 45.00 (0-918212-45-6) Neal-Schuman.

Coleman, William & Cohen, I. Bernard, eds. French Views of German Science. LC 80-2106. (Development of Science Ser.). (Illus.). 1981. lib. bdg. 49.95 (0-405-13871-7) Ayer.

— Physiological Programmatics of the Nineteenth Century. LC 80-2107. (Development of Science Ser.). (Illus.). 1981. lib. bdg. 55.95 (0-405-13872-5) Ayer.

Coleman, William & Coleman, Patricia. Because of Love: Celebrations of the Heart. 1998. 6.97 (1-56955-110-3) Servant.

— Because We're Friends: 100 Things I Love about You. LC 97-37875. 134p. 1997. reprint ed. 12.99 (1-56955-038-7, Vine Bks) Servant.

— Before Your Baby Comes: Parent's Thoughts on Motherhood. LC 95-20774. 16p. 1995. text 11.99 (1-55661-564-7) Bethany Hse.

***Coleman, William & Coleman, Patricia.** Every Morning Brings Promise: A Celebration of Hope. LC 99-51892. 1999. 12.99 (1-56955-164-2, Vine Bks) Servant.

Coleman, William & Limoges, Camille, eds. Studies in History of Biology, Vol. 1, 1977. LC 78-647138. (Illus.). 229p. 1977. reprint ed. pap. 71.00 (0-608-04063-0, 206479900001) Bks Demand.

— Studies in History of Biology, Vol. 2, 1978. LC 78-647138. (Illus.). 217p. 1978. reprint ed. pap. 67.30 (0-608-04064-9, 206479900002) Bks Demand.

— Studies in History of Biology, Vol. 5, 1981. LC 78-647138. (Illus.). 213p. 1981. reprint ed. pap. 66.10 (0-608-04065-7, 206479900005) Bks Demand.

— Studies in History of Biology, Vol. 6, 1983. LC 78-647138. (Illus.). 227p. 1983. reprint ed. pap. 70.40 (0-608-04066-5, 206479900006) Bks Demand.

— Studies in History of Biology, Vol. 7, 1984. LC 78-647138. (Illus.). 155p. 1984. reprint ed. pap. 48.10 (0-608-04067-3, 206479900007) Bks Demand.

Coleman, William, jt. auth. see Von Baer, Carl E.

Coleman, William, ed. see Hamilton, Alexander.

Coleman, William B. & Tsongalis, Gregory, eds. Molecular Basis of Human Cancer: Genomic Instability & Molecular Mutation in Neoplastic Transformation. 600p. 2000. 125.00 (0-89603-634-0) Humana.

Coleman, William B. & Tsonjalis, Gregory J., eds. Molecular Diagnostics: For the Clinical Laboratorian. LC 96-37505. (Pathology & Laboratory Medicine Ser.). (Illus.). 400p. 1996. 79.50 (0-89603-373-2) Humana.

Coleman, William D. Business & Politics: A Study of Collective Action. 352p. 1988. 65.00 (0-7735-0648-9, Pub. by McG-Queens Univ Pr); pap. 27.95 (0-7735-0664-0, Pub. by McG-Queens Univ Pr) CUP Services.

— The Independence Movement in Quebec 1945-1980. (Studies in the Structure of Power: No. 11). 288p. 1984. pap. text 18.95 (0-8020-6542-2) U of Toronto Pr.

Coleman, William D. & Jacek, Henry J., eds. Regionalism, Business Interests & Public Policy. (Studies in Neo-Corporatism). 256p. (C). 1989. text 49.95 (0-8039-8227-5) Sage.

Coleman, William D. & Jacek, Henry J., eds. Regionalism, Business Interests & Public Policy. (Studies in Neo-Corporatism). 256p. (C). 1989. pap. text 19.95 (0-8039-8272-0) Sage.

Coleman, William D. & Underhill, Geoffrey R., eds. Regionalism & Global Economic Integration: Europe, Asia & the Americas. LC 98-167564. 264p. (C). 1998. 85.00 (0-415-16247-5); pap. 27.99 (0-415-16248-3) Routledge.

Coleman, William E. On the Discrimination of Gothicisms. rev. ed. Varma, Devendra P., ed. LC 79-8447. (Gothic Studies & Dissertations). 1980. lib. bdg. 31.95 (0-405-12651-4) Ayer.

Coleman, William E., Jr. & Coleman, William E., Sr. A Rhetoric of the People: The German Greens & the New Politics. LC 92-28477. 168p. 1993. 47.95 (0-275-94083-7, C4083, Praeger Pubs) Greenwood.

Coleman, William E., Sr., jt. auth. see Coleman, William E., Jr.

Coleman, William H. Historical Sketch Book & Guide to New Orleans & Environs. (Illus.). 1977. text 23.95 (0-8369-9238-5, 9092) Ayer.

Coleman, William L. Before the Ring: Questions Worth Asking. expanded rev. ed. LC 98-11309. (Illus.). 176p. 1998. pap. 9.99 (1-57293-036-5) Discovery Hse Pubs.

— Diez Cosas Que Su Hijo le Agradecera un Dia.Tr. of Ten Things Your Teen Will Thank You for Someday. (SPA.). 192p. 1994. 8.99 (0-88113-146-6, B052-1466) Caribe Betania.

— Eight Things Not to Say to Your Teen: Ways to Talk with Teens That Really Work. LC 94-6776. 16p. 1994. pap. 8.99 (1-55661-404-7) Bethany Hse.

C

— Entering the Teen Zone: Devotions to Guide You. LC 90-43092. 112p. (Orig.). (J). (gr. 7-10). 1991. pap. 6.99 (0-8066-2499-X, 9-2499, Augsburg) Augsburg Fortress.

— From Full House to Empty Nest: Learning to Enjoy Life Again Now That Your Children Are Grown. LC 94-33944. 160p. 1994. pap. 9.99 (0-929239-82-2) Discovery Hse Pubs.

— God Doesn't Play Favorites: Gutsy Devotions for Teens. LC 91-33317. 176p. (YA). (gr. 9-12). 1992. pap. 7.99 (0-8007-5430-1) Revell.

— How to Go Home Without Feeling Like a Child: Resolving Difficult Relationships Between Adult Children & Their Parents. LC 98-46479. 224p. (J). 1999. pap. 10.99 (1-57293-046-2) Discovery Hse Pubs.

— Listen to the Animals. LC 79-11312. 128p. (J). (ps-6). 1979. pap. 6.99 (0-87123-341-X) Bethany Hse.

— Teen Stress: Stories to Guide You. LC 94-33427. 112p. (J). (gr. 4-7). 1994. pap. 6.99 (0-8066-2732-8, 9-2732, Augsburg) Augsburg Fortress.

— What Children Need to Know When Parents Get Divorced. 128p. (J). 1998. pap. 7.99 (0-7642-2051-9) Bethany Hse.

— When Someone You Love Dies. (Grubstake Adventure Ser.). 128p. (J). (gr. 4-7). 1994. pap. 6.99 (0-8066-2670-4, 9-2670, Augsburg) Augsburg Fortress.

Coleman, William Macon. Epitome of Fearne on Contingent Remainders & Executory Devises: Intended Principally for the Use of Students. xxiv, 101p. 1981. reprint ed. 27.50 (0-8377-0431-6, Rothman) W S Hein.

Coleman, William O. Rationalism & Anti-Rationalism in the Origins of Economics: The Philosophical Roots of 18th Century Economic Thought. 192p. 1995. 90.00 (1-85278-995-6) E Elgar.

Coleman, William P., 3rd & Hanke, C. William. Cosmetic Surgery of the Skin. 2nd ed. LC 96-52513. (Illus.). 512p. (C). (gr. 13). 1997. text 169.00 (0-8151-1460-5, 29156) Mosby Inc.

Coleman, William P., III & Lawrence, Naomi. Skin Resurfacing. LC 97-48638. (Illus.). 400p. 1998. 139.00 (0-683-30165-9) Lppncott W & W.

Coleman, William P., III, et al. Body Contouring: The New Art of Liposculture. LC 96-71746. (Illus.). 120p. (Orig.). 1997. 16.00 (1-884125-64-6) Cooper Pubng.

C

Coleman, William R. & Limoges, Camille, eds. Studies in History of Biology, Vol. 3. LC 76-47139. (Illus.). 297p. reprint ed. pap. 92.10 (0-608-18337-7, 203301400082); reprint ed. pap. 67.60 (0-608-10342-X, 200521500051) Bks Demand.

— Studies in History of Biology, Vol. 4. LC 76-47139. 206p. 1980. reprint ed. pap. 63.90 (0-8357-8337-5, 203413300088) Bks Demand.

***Coleman, William S., ed.** Voices of Wounded Knee. LC 99-87377. (Illus.). 512p. 2000. 35.00 (0-8032-1506-1) U of Nebr Pr.

Coleman-Willis, Linda. Loving Yourself First: A Woman's Guide to Personal Power. abr. ed. (Illus.). 250p. 1997. pap. 12.95 (1-890368-00-8, WLW Pub) L Coleman-Willis.

Coleman, Wim. The Mexican War. (Perspectives on History Ser.: Pt. III). 1998. pap. 6.95 (1-57960-044-1) Disc Enter Ltd.

Coleman, Wim, ed. The Age of Broadcasting: Radio. LC 96-86663. (Perspectives on History Ser.: Pt. II). (Illus.). 68p. 1997. pap. 6.95 (1-878668-85-4) Disc Enter Ltd.

— The Age of Broadcasting: Television. LC 97-69408. (Perspectives on History Ser.: Pt. II). (Illus.). 64p. 1997. pap. 6.95 (1-57960-006-9) Disc Enter Ltd.

— American Quakers. LC 97-68486. (Perspectives on History Ser.: Pt. II). (Illus.). 6p. 1997. pap. 6.95 (1-57960-029-8) Disc Enter Ltd.

— The Declaration of Independence. LC 97-68485. (Perspectives on History Ser.: Pt. III). (Illus.). 64p. 1997. pap. 6.95 (1-57960-024-7) Disc Enter Ltd.

— The Shakers. LC 97-67539. (Perspectives on History Ser.: Pt. II). (Illus.). 68p. 1997. pap. 6.95 (1-57960-005-0) Disc Enter Ltd.

***Coleman, Wim & Perrin, Pat.** Sister Anna: A Story of Shaker Life. LC 00-100398. 232p. (J). (gr. 5-12). 2000. pap. 10.95 (1-57960-059-X) Disc Enter Ltd.

Coleman, Wim & Perrin, Pat, eds. Aviation: Early Flight in America. LC 99-61092. (Perspectives on History Ser.: Vol. 75). (Illus.). 64p. 1999. pap. 6.95 (1-57960-050-6) Disc Enter Ltd.

Coleman, Wim, et al. Retold Classic Chillers LC 98-165482. 142 p. (J). 1997. (0-7807-6576-1) Perfection Learn.

Coleman, Winifred, jt. auth. see Feinen, Cynthia.

Colemann, R. Flower Arranging. 1996. 6.98 (0-7858-0677-6) Bk Sales Inc.

Colemon, Johnnie. Open Your Mind & Be Healed. LC 97-67757. 96p. 1997. 12.95 (0-87516-709-8) DeVorss.

Colemont, Patrick, et al, eds. Creativity & Innovation: Towards a European Network. (C). 1988. lib. bdg. 162.50 (90-247-3797-4) Kluwer Academic.

Colen, Harold. HVAC Systems Evaluation: Maintenance, Operation, & Retrofit. (Illus.). 300p. 1990. 84.95 (0-87629-182-5, 67281) R S Means.

Colen, Kimberly. Kids Can Care about Mammals & Learn about Responsibility! Grades K-3. Mitchell, Judy, ed. (Illus.). 112p. 1994. pap., teacher ed. 9.95 (1-57310-004-8) Teachng & Lrning Co.

— My Hanukkah Book: Questions, Answers, Activities. (Illus.). 24p. (Orig.). (J). (gr. 4-6). 1987. pap. 3.95 (0-590-40965-4) Scholastic Inc.

— A Note from Your Teacher: More Than 450 Ready-Made Notes for Communication & Personalizing Report Cards. Mitchell, Judy, ed. (Illus.). 240p. (Orig.). (J). (gr. k-6). 1995. pap., teacher ed. 19.95 (1-57310-033-1) Teachng & Lrning Co.

— The Only Baby-Sitting Book You'll Ever Need: A Guide for Parents. Mitchell, Judy, ed. (Illus.). 112p. 1997. pap. 10.95 (1-57310-104-4) Teachng & Lrning Co.

— Peas & Honey: Recipes for Kids (with a Pinch of Poetry) LC 91-68052. (Illus.). 64p. (J). (gr. 4-6). 1995. 15.95 (1-56397-062-7, Wordsong) Boyds Mills Pr.

Colen, Kimberly & Boyko, Carrie, compiled by. Graduation Day: A Collection of Commencement Speeches. LC 95-36057. 1996. write for info. (0-614-08621-3) Scholastic Inc.

Colen, Shellee, jt. ed. see Sanjek, Roger.

***Colenbrander, Bernard.** Dutchtown: A City Center Design. (Illus.). 2000. pap. 29.95 (90-5662-140-8) NAi Uitgevers.

Colenso, Frances E. My Chief & I. Daymond, Margaret, ed. 250p. 1994. pap. 22.00 (0-86980-886-9, Pub. by Univ Natal Pr) Intl Spec Bk.

Colenso, Harriette. Cases of Six Usutu Punished for Having Taken Part in the Disturbances of 1888. 52p. 1997. pap. 13.95 (0-86980-927-X, Pub. by Univ Natal Pr) Intl Spec Bk.

Colenso, John W. Bringing Forth Light: Five Tracts on Bishop Colenso's Zulu Mission. Edgecombe, Ruth, ed. No. 4. (Illus.). 298p. 1982. 14.95 (0-86980-283-6, Pub. by Univ Natal Pr) Intl Spec Bk.

Colenso, Michael. High Performance Teams. LC 97-180574. 160p. 1997. pap. text 29.95 (0-7506-3354-9) Buttrwrth-Heinemann.

***Colenso, Michael.** Kaizen Strategies for Improving Team Performance: How to Accelerate Team Development & Enhance Team Productivity. (Illus.). 222p. 2000. 29.95 (0-273-63986-2, Pub. by F T P-H) Trans-Atl Phila.

— Kaizen Strategies for Successful Organizational Change: Enabling Evolution & Revolution Within the Organization. (Illus.). 192p. 2000. 29.95 (0-273-63985-4) F T P H.

Colenso, Michael. Strategic Skills for Team Leaders & Line Managers. LC 99-169786. 192p. 1998. pap. text 19.95 (0-7506-3982-2) Buttrwrth-Heinemann.

Colenso, Michael, tr. see Vainshtein, Sevian I.

Colentuono, Frank, jt. ed. see Kamenir, Mel.

Coler, Christfried. Diccionario por Fechas de Historia Universal. 3rd ed. (SPA.). 480p. 1985. 75.00 (0-7859-5067-2) Fr & Eur.

Coler, Marga S. & Vincent, Karen G. Psychiatric-Mental Health Nursing. LC 94-29976. 288p. (C). 1995. pap. 28.00 (0-8273-6102-5) Delmar.

Coler, Mark, ed. The Discount Brokerage Survey: Stocks. 1994. pap. write for info. (1-877638-25-0) Mercer Inc.

Coleridge, E. P., tr. see Euripides.

Colerick, George. Fron the Italian Girl to Cabaret. 160p. 1999. pap. 14.95 (0-9524964-3-7) Parkwest Pubns.

— Romanticism & Melody. LC 97-69440. (Illus.). 160p. 1997. pap. 12.95 (0-9524964-2-9) Parkwest Pubns.

Coleridge, E. H., ed. see Coleridge, Samuel Taylor.

Coleridge, E. P., tr. see Euripides.

Coleridge, Hartley. Essays & Marginalia. 2 Vols., Set. LC 72-13289. (Essay Index Reprint Ser.). 1977. reprint ed. 45.95 (0-8369-8151-0) Ayer.

— Letters of Hartley Coleridge. Griggs, Grace E. & Griggs, Earl L., eds. LC 75-41063. reprint ed. 30.00 (0-404-14524-8) AMS Pr.

Coleridge, Henry N. Six Months in the West Indies in 1825. LC 72-100284. 1970. reprint ed. 49.50 (0-8371-2948-6, CSM&, Greenwood Pr) Greenwood.

Coleridge, Henry N., ed. see Coleridge, Samuel Taylor.

Coleridge, John T. A Memoir of the Rev. John Keble, 2 vols. in 1. 2nd rev. ed. LC 75-30019. reprint ed. 67.50 (0-404-14024-6) AMS Pr.

Coleridge, K. A. A Descriptive Catalogue of the Milton Collection in the Alexander Turnbull Library, Wellington, New Zealand. (Illus.). 1980. 108.00 (0-19-920110-2) OUP.

Coleridge, M. The Birth of the Lukan Narrative: Narrative as Christology in Luke 1-2. (JSNTS Ser.: Vol. 88). 261p. 1993. 75.00 (1-85075-447-0, Pub. by Sheffield Acad) CUP Services.

Coleridge, Mary E. Gathered Leaves from the Prose of Mary E. Coleridge: With a Memoir by Edith Sichel. LC 70-169545. (Short Story Index Reprint Ser.). 1977. reprint ed. 23.95 (0-8369-4006-7) Ayer.

— The King with Two Faces: An Historical Romance. LC 79-8255. reprint ed. 44.50 (0-404-61831-6) AMS Pr.

Coleridge, Nicholas. Paper Tigers: The Latest, Greatest Newspaper Tycoons & How They Won the World. LC 93-45736. 1994. 24.95 (1-55972-215-0, Birch Ln Pr) Carol Pub Group.

— Streetsmart. 416p. 2000. 26.95 (0-312-19960-0) St Martin.

— With Friends Like These. LC 97-16646. 384p. 1997. text 24.95 (0-312-17066-1) St Martin.

Coleridge, Peter. Disability, Liberation & Development. (Illus.). 252p. (C). 1993. 39.95 (0-85598-194-6, Pub. by Oxfam Pub); pap. 12.95 (0-85598-195-4, Pub. by Oxfam Pub) Stylus Pub VA.

Coleridge, Samuel Taylor. Christabel. LC 91-30898. (Revolution & Romanticism Ser.). 82p. 1991. reprint ed. 35.00 (1-85477-063-2) Continuum.

— Coleridge: The Complete Poems of Samuel Taylor Coleridge. Keach, William, ed. LC 97-208514. 640p. 1997. pap. 15.95 (0-14-042353-2) Viking Penguin.

— Coleridge: The Early Family Letters. Engell, James, ed. (Illus.). 132p. 1995. text 59.00 (0-19-818244-9) OUP.

— Coleridge's Ancient Mariner: An Experimental Edition of Texts & Revisions. 176p. 1997. pap. text 16.95 (1-886449-47-3) Barrytown Ltd.

— Coleridge's Ancient Mariner: An Experimental Edition of Texts & Revisions, 1798-1828. Wallen, Martin, ed. & comment by. LC 92-37977. (Clinamen Studies). 1993. 34.95 (0-88268-123-0) Station Hill Pr.

— Coleridge's Dejection: The Earliest Manuscripts & the Earliest Printings. Parrish, Stephen M., ed. LC 87-24393. (Illus.). 184p. 1988. text 42.50 (0-8014-1255-2) Cornell U Pr.

— Collected Works of Samuel T. Coleridge, Vol. 1. Coburn, K. & Winer, B., eds. LC 68-10210. (Bollingen Ser.). 512p. 1970. text 80.00 (0-691-09861-1, Pub. by Princeton U Pr) Cal Prin Full Svc.

— Collected Works of Samuel T. Coleridge, Vols. 1-4 & 6. Coburn, K. & Winer, B., eds. Incl. Set, Vol. 4. Friend., 2 vols. Rooke, B., ed. LC 68-10210. 1260p. 1969. text 175.00 (0-691-09854-9, Pub. by Princeton U Pr); Vol. 2. Watchman. Patton, Lewis, ed. LC 68-10210. 490p. 1970. text 75.00 (0-691-09719-4, Pub. by Princeton U Pr); Vol. 3. Essays on His Time., 3 vols. Erdman, David V., ed. LC 68-10210. 1451p. 1975. text 210.00 (0-691-09871-9, Pub. by Princeton U Pr); Vol. 6. Lay Sermons. White, R. J., ed. LC 68-10210. 341p. 1972. text 55.00 (0-691-09873-5, Pub. by Princeton U Pr); Vol. 7. Biographia Literaria: Biographical sketches of my literary life & opinions. LC 68-10210. 866p. 1982. text 125.00 (0-691-09874-3, Pub. by Princeton U Pr); Vol. 7. Biographia Literaria: Biographical sketches of my literary life & opinions. LC 68-10210. 859p. 1982. pap. text 35.00 (0-691-01861-8, Pub. by Princeton U Pr); LC 68-10210. (Bollingen Ser.: Vol. 75). write for info. (0-318-55351-1) Princeton U Pr.

— The Collected Works of Samuel Taylor Coleridge: Logic, Vol. 13. Jackson, J. R., ed. LC 68-10201. (Bollingen Ser.: No. LXXV). 487p. 1981. text 80.00 (0-691-09880-8, Pub. by Princeton U Pr) Cal Prin Full Svc.

— The Collected Works of Samuel Taylor Coleridge Vol. 5: Lectures On Literature,1808-1819, 2 Vols. Coburn, Kathleen et al. eds. LC 85-43198. (Bollingen Ser.: No. 75). 1175p. 1986. text 150.00 (0-691-09872-7, Pub. by Princeton U Pr) Cal Prin Full Svc.

— The Collected Works of Samuel Taylor Coleridge Vol. 10: On the Constitution of the Church & State. Colmer, J. & Winer, B., eds. (Bollingen Ser.: No. 75). (Illus.). 245p. 1975. text 55.00 (0-691-09877-8, Pub. by Princeton U Pr) Cal Prin Full Svc.

— The Collected Works of Samuel Taylor Coleridge Vol. 12: Marginalia. Whalley, George, ed. LC 68-10201. 1152p. 1980. text 150.00 (0-691-09879-4, Pub. by Princeton U Pr) Cal Prin Full Svc.

— The Collected Works of Samuel Taylor Coleridge Vol. 12: Marginalia. Coburn, Kathleen et al, eds. LC 68-10201. (Bollingen Ser.: Vol. 75). (Illus.). 1280p. 1985. text 150.00 (0-691-09889-1, Pub. by Princeton U Pr) Cal Prin Full Svc.

— The Collected Works of Samuel Taylor Coleridge Vol. 12: Marginalia III. Jackson, H. J. & Whalley, George, eds. LC 87-104402. (Bollingen Ser.: LXXV). (Illus.). 1300p. 1992. text 150.00 (0-691-09954-5, Pub. by Princeton U Pr) Cal Prin Full Svc.

***Coleridge, Samuel Taylor.** The Collected Works of Samuel Taylor Coleridge Vol. 12: Marginalia IV (Pamphlets to Shakespeare) Jackson, H. J. & Whalley, George, eds. (Bollingen Ser.: No. LXXV). (Illus.). 1200p. 1998. text 150.00 (0-691-09957-X, Pub. by Princeton U Pr) Cal Prin Full Svc.

Coleridge, Samuel Taylor. Conciones Ad Populum, 1795. (Revolution & Romanticism Ser.). 84p. 1992. reprint ed. 35.00 (1-85477-116-7) Continuum.

— Essays on His Own Times, 3 vols. Coleridge, Sara, ed. LC 72-113579. reprint ed. 215.00 (0-404-01700-2) AMS Pr.

— The Friend: A series of essays, to aid in the formation of fixed principles in politics, morals & religion, with literary amusements interspersed. LC 75-154146. (Select Bibliographies Reprint Ser.). 1977. reprint ed. 25.95 (0-8369-5762-8) Ayer.

— Inquiring Spirit: A New Presentation of Coleridge from His Published & Unpublished Writings. rev. ed. Coburn, Kathleen, ed. LC 80-501775. 454p. reprint ed. pap. 140.80 (0-608-17979-5, 202645100049) Bks Demand.

— Lectures & Notes on Shakespeare & Other English Poets: Now First Collected by T. Ashe. LC 70-38347. (Select Bibliographies Reprint Ser.). 1977. reprint ed. 27.95 (0-8369-6764-X) Ayer.

— Literary Remains of Samuel Taylor Coleridge, 4 vols. Coleridge, Henry N., ed. reprint ed. 400.00 (0-404-01710-X) AMS Pr.

***Coleridge, Samuel Taylor.** Lyrical Romantic. (Illus.). 1999. 19.95 (1-86019-313-7) Chelsea Hse.

Coleridge, Samuel Taylor. Notebooks. Coburn, Kathleen, ed. Incl. Vol. 1. Notebooks of Samuel Taylor Coleridge, 1794-1804. LC 56-13196. 1161p. 1957. text 175.00 (0-691-09802-6, Pub. by Princeton U Pr); Vol. 2. Notebooks of Samuel Taylor Coleridge, 1804-1808., 2 pts. LC 56-13196. 1026p. 1981. text 165.00 (0-691-09803-4, Pub. by Princeton U Pr); Vol. 3. Notebooks of Samuel Taylor Coleridge, 1808-1819. LC 56-13196. 1652p. 1974. text 210.00 (0-691-09804-2, Pub. by Princeton U Pr); LC 56-13196. (Bollingen Ser.: Vol. 50). (Illus.). write for info. (0-318-55361-9) Princeton U Pr.

— The Notebooks of Samuel Taylor Coleridge, Vol. 5. Vol. 5. 1989. 100.00 (0-691-09907-3, Pub. by Princeton U Pr) Cal Prin Full Svc.

— Poems. 400p. 1991. 17.00 (0-679-40669-7) Everymns Lib.

— Poems. Beer, John B., ed. 412p. 1993. pap. 7.95 (0-460-87316-4, Everyman's Classic Lib) Tuttle Pubng.

— Poems, 1833. LC 90-12670. (Revolution & Romanticism Ser.). 176p. 1990. reprint ed. 48.00 (1-85477-043-8) Continuum.

— Poems of Samuel Taylor Coleridge. LC 98-125159. 256p. 1997. 12.50 (0-375-40072-9) Everymns Lib.

— Poetical works [of] Coleridge, including poems & versions of poems herein. Coleridge, E. H., ed. (Oxford Standard Authors Ser.). 638p. 1961. pap. 21.00 (0-19-281051-0) OUP.

— The Portable Coleridge. Richards, Ivor A., ed. (Portable Library: No. 48). (J). (gr. 10 up). 1977. pap. 16.95 (0-14-015048-X, P48, Penguin Bks) Viking Penguin.

— The Rime of the Ancient Mariner. Dorbe, Gustave, ed. 1979. 19.95 (0-405-11896-1) Ayer.

— The Rime of the Ancient Mariner. (Chatto Pocket Library). (Illus.). 44p. 1994. 13.95 (0-7011-6051-9, Pub. by Chatto & Windus) Trafalgar.

— The Rime of the Ancient Mariner. Motter, Dean, ed. (Classics Illustrated Ser.). (Illus.). 52p. (YA). pap. 4.95 (1-57209-024-3) Classics Int Ent.

— The Rime of the Ancient Mariner. (Illus.). 1991. pap. 3.95 (0-425-12763-X) First Classics.

— The Rime of the Ancient Mariner. (Illus.). 88p. 1995. 19.95 (1-879582-10-4) Platinum Pr.

— Rime of the Ancient Mariner. LC 98-87524. 320p. 1999. text 39.95 (0-312-21917-2) St Martin.

— The Rime of the Ancient Mariner: The Three Great Nineteenth Century Folios. 2nd ed. (Illus.). 112p. 1996. pap. 14.95 (0-9631135-4-2) MCE Publ Co.

— The Rime of the Ancient Mariner & Other Poems. 80p. 1992. reprint ed. pap. text 1.00 (0-486-27266-4) Dover.

— Samuel Taylor Coleridge. (Poets Ser.). 146p. 1993. 5.95 (0-7117-0441-4, Pub. by JARR UK) Seven Hills Bk.

— Samuel Taylor Coleridge: A Selection. Jackson, H. J., ed. (Oxford Authors Ser.). 750p. (C). 1986. pap. text 24.95 (0-19-281383-8) OUP.

***Coleridge, Samuel Taylor.** Samuel Taylor Coleridge: The Major Works. Jackson, H. J., ed. (Oxford World's Classics Ser.). 734p. 2000. pap. 15.95 (0-19-284043-6) OUP.

Coleridge, Samuel Taylor. Selected Letters. Jackson, H. J., ed. LC 86-18150. 336p. 1987. 60.00 (0-19-818540-5) OUP.

— Selected Poems. LC 94-13081. 1994. text 9.95 (0-312-11250-5) St Martin.

— Selected Poetry. (Oxford World's Classics Ser.). 220p. 1999. pap. 9.95 (0-19-283932-2) OUP.

— Selected Poetry & Prose. Stauffer, Donald, ed. (Modern Library College Editions). 608p. (C). 1951. 8.44 (0-07-553638-2, T52) McGraw.

***Coleridge, Samuel Taylor.** Selected Poetry of Samuel T. Coleridge. (Penguin Classics Ser.). 400p. 2000. pap. 12.00 (0-14-042429-6, Penguin Bks) Viking Penguin.

Coleridge, Samuel Taylor. Seven Lectures on Shakespeare & Milton. Collier, John P., ed. LC 72-962. reprint ed. 37.50 (0-404-01617-0) AMS Pr.

— Shorter Works & Fragments Vol. 11: The Collected Works of Samuel Taylor Coleridge. LC 95-214098. Vol. 11. 1760p. (C). 1995. text 150.00 (0-691-09878-6, Pub. by Princeton U Pr) Cal Prin Full Svc.

— Sibylline Leaves. LC 90-31895. (Revolution & Romanticism Ser.). 328p. 1990. reprint ed. 55.00 (1-85477-042-X) Continuum.

— Table Talk Vol. 14. Woodring, Carl, ed. (Bollingen Ser.: Vol. 75, No. 14). (Illus.). 744p. (C). 1989. text 150.00 (0-691-09881-6, Pub. by Princeton U Pr) Cal Prin Full Svc.

— The Watchman. LC 97-28613. (Revolution & Romanticism Ser.). 324p. 1998. 70.00 (1-85477-198-1) Continuum.

***Coleridge, Samuel Taylor & Jackson, J. R.** Lectures 1818-1819 on the History of Philosophy, 2 vols. LC 99-30471. (Collected Works of Samuel Taylor Colerid Ser.: Vol. 8). (Illus.). 1328p. 1999. text 150.00 (0-691-09875-1, Pub. by Princeton U Pr) Cal Prin Full Svc.

***Coleridge, Samuel Taylor & Mays, J. C.** Poetical Works. LC 00-21206. (Bollinger Ser.). 2001. write for info. (0-691-09883-2) Princeton U Pr.

Coleridge, Samuel Taylor & Southey. The Fall of Robespierre. LC 91-16917. (Revolution & Romanticism Ser.). 48p. 1991. reprint ed. 35.00 (1-85477-064-0) Continuum.

Coleridge, Samuel Taylor, et al. Poems, 1797. LC 96-35546. (Revolution & Romanticism Ser.). 1997. 75.00 (1-85477-197-3) Continuum.

Coleridge, Samuel Taylor, jt. auth. see Southey, Robert.

Coleridge, Samuel Taylor, jt. auth. see Wordsworth, William.

Coleridge, Sara. Memoir & Letters of Sara Coleridge. LC 76-37677. reprint ed. 55.00 (0-404-56736-3) AMS Pr.

— Minnow among Tritons: Mrs. S. T. Coleridge's Letters to Thomas Poole, 1799-1834. Potter, Stephen, ed. LC 75-38028. reprint ed. 34.50 (0-404-56737-1) AMS Pr.

— Phantasmion. LC 93-46493. (Revolution & Romanticism, 1789-1834 Ser.). 1994. 65.00 (1-85477-166-3) Continuum.

Coleridge, Sara, ed. see Coleridge, Samuel Taylor.

Coleridge, Sarah J. Painting Flowers in Watercolour. (Leisure Arts Ser.: No. 6). (Illus.). 32p. pap. 4.95 (0-85532-405-8, 405-8, Pub. by Srch Pr) A Schwartz & Co.

Coleridge Smith, P. D. Microcirculation in Venous Disease. 2nd ed. LC 97-49120. (Medical Intelligence Unit Ser.). 1998. 99.00 (1-57059-476-7) Landes Bioscience.

Coles. Cosmology. 2nd ed. text. write for info. (0-471-48909-3) Wiley.

Coles. Old & On Their Own. (Illus.). 192p. 1999. pap. 19.95 (0-393-31912-1) Norton.

— Practical Electronics Microprocessor Handbook. 1988. 32.00 (0-408-01583-7) CRC Pr.

— Three Years Behind Barbed Wire: The Diary of a British Internee in Schloss Wurzach Germany 1942-1945. (Jersey Heritage Editions Ser.). 1991. 40.00 (0-86120-008-X, Pub. by Aris & Phillips) David Brown.

— The Youngest Parents. 192p. 2000. pap. 19.99 (0-393-31996-2, Norton Paperbks) Norton.

Coles & Naoum Staff. Dissertation Writing & Research for Construction Students. LC 98-11013. 224p. 1997. pap. text 32.95 (0-7506-2988-6) Buttrwrth-Heinemann.

***Coles, Alex.** Optic of Walter Benjamin: De-, Dis-, Ex-, 3. (Illus.). 240p. 1999. pap. 21.95 (1-901033-41-4, Pub. by Black Dog Pubg) RAM Publications.

An Asterisk (*) at the beginning of an entry indicates that the title is appearing for the first time.

***Coles, Alex, ed.** The Anxiety of Interdisciplinarity, 2. (Illus.). 208p. 1998. pap. 15.95 (*1-901033-75-9*, Pub. by Black Dog Pubg) RAM Publications.

Coles, Alex, jt. ed. see Bentley, Richard.

Coles, Ann, ed. see Electrical Apparatus Magazine Editors.

Coles, B. H. Avian Medicine & Surgery. 2nd ed. (Illus.). 416p. 1998. pap. text 57.95 (*0-632-03356-8*, Pub. by Blckwell Science) Iowa St U Pr.

Coles, B. R., jt. auth. see Hume-Rothery, W.

Coles, Blanche. Shakespeare's Four Giants. 1957. 10.95 (*0-87233-809-6*) Bauhan.

Coles, Bryony, jt. auth. see Coles, John.

Coles, Carol, jt. auth. see Mitchell, Donald.

Coles, Caroline & Field, Richard. Business Planning for Special Schools: A Practical Guide. LC 98-104073. 112p. 1997. pap. 25.95 (*1-85346-471-6*, Pub. by David Fulton) Taylor & Francis.

Coles, Caroline, jt. auth. see Barnes, David.

Coles, Catherine M. & Entwisle, Barbara. Nigerian Women in Development: A Research Bibliography. 170p. 1986. pap. 25.00 (*0-918456-58-4*, Crossroads) African Studies Assn.

Coles, Clarence, jt. auth. see Coles, Joan.

Coles, Clarence W. Marine Jet Drive, 1961-1996. (Marine Tune-Up & Repair Manuals). (C). 1998. pap. text 34.95 (*0-89330-029-2*, Pub. by Seloc) Natl Bk Netwk.

Coles, Clarence W. & Young, Howard U. Johnson-Evinrude Outboard, 1956-70 Vol. I: 1.5 HP Thru 40 HP. (Marine Tune-Up & Repair Manuals). (Illus.). 430p. (C). 1998. pap. 34.95 (*0-89330-007-1*, Pub. by Seloc) Natl Bk Netwk.

— Johnson-Evinrude Outboard, 1971-89 Vol. II: 2.0 HP Thru 60 HP. LC 98-159838. (Marine Tune-Up & Repair Manuals). (Illus.). 600p. (C). 1998. pap. 34.95 (*0-89330-008-X*, Pub. by Seloc) Natl Bk Netwk.

— Johnson/Evinrude Outboard, 1958-72 Vol. III: 50 HP Thru 125 HP. (Marine Tune-Up & Repair Manuals). (Illus.). 530p. (C). 1998. pap. 34.95 (*0-89330-009-8*, Pub. by Seloc) Natl Bk Netwk.

— Johnson/Evinrude Outboard, 1973-91 Vol. IV: 65 HP Thru 235 HP. LC 99-475072. (Marine Tune-Up & Repair Manuals: Vol. IV). (Illus.). 392p. (C). 1998. pap. 34.95 (*0-89330-010-1*, Pub. by Seloc) Natl Bk Netwk.

— Mercruiser Stern Drive, 1964-1992. LC 99-475069. (Marine Tune-Up & Repair Manuals). (Illus.). 600p. (C). 1998. pap. 34.95 (*0-89330-005-5*, Pub. by Seloc) Natl Bk Netwk.

— OMC Stern Drive, 1964-1986. (Marine Tune-Up & Repair Manuals). (Illus.). 580p. (C). 1998. pap. 34.95 (*0-89330-004-7*, Pub. by Seloc) Natl Bk Netwk.

Coles, Clarence W., jt. auth. see Coles, Joan.

Coles, Colin & Holm, Hans A., eds. Learning in Medicine. (Illus.). 212p. (C). 1994. 25.00 (*82-00-21811-2*) Scandnvan Univ Pr.

Coles, Colin, jt. auth. see Fish, Della.

Coles, D., ed. Perspectives in Fluid Mechanics. (Lecture Notes in Physics Ser.: Vol. 320). vii, 207p. 1989. 45.95 (*0-387-50644-6*) Spr-Verlag.

***Coles, David.** Numeracy & Mathematics Across the Primary Curriculum: Building Confidence & Understanding. 2000. pap. 26.95 (*1-85346-640-9*) David Fulton.

Coles, David, jt. compiled by see Hartman, David W.

Coles, Don. Forests of the Medieval World. 64p. 1993. pap. write for info. (*0-88984-158-6*) Porcup Quill.

Coles, Don, ed. see Glickman, Susan.

Coles, Edward W. These Were My Days: A Welsh Boyhood in Portland, 1900-1919. 95p. (Orig.). 1990. pap. 7.95 (*1-880222-03-5*) Red Apple Pub.

Coles, Elisha. An English Dictionary. (Anglistica & Americana Ser.: No. 76). 326p. 1973. reprint ed. 95.00 (*3-487-04748-9*) G Olms Pubs.

Coles, Embert H. Veterinary Clinical Pathology. 4th ed. (Illus.). 486p. 1986. text 67.00 (*0-7216-1828-6*, W B Saunders Co) Harcrt Hlth Sci Grp.

Coles, G. A. A Manual of Peritoneal Dialysis. (C). 1988. pap. text 72.50 (*0-7462-0081-1*) Kluwer Academic.

Coles, G. A., et al, eds. Continuous Ambulatory Peritoneal Dialysis: Host Defense, Nutrition & Ultrafiltration. (Contributions to Nephrology Ser.: Vol. 85). (Illus.). viii, 172p. 1990. 29.75 (*3-8055-5215-7*) S Karger.

Coles, Gerald. Misreading Reading: The Bad Science That Hurts Children. LC 99-55573. 144p. pap. text 15.00 (*0-325-00060-3*) Heinemann.

Coles, Gerald. Reading Lessons: The Debate over Literacy. LC 97-35066. 212p. 1998. 25.00 (*0-8090-6490-1*) Hill & Wang.

***Coles, Gerald.** Reading Lessons: The Debate over Literacy. 224p. 1999. pap. 12.00 (*0-8090-8038-9*) Hill & Wang.

Coles, Gerald S., ed. Learning Disabilities & Social Activity. 1985. 49.95 (*0-915340-15-1*) PJD Pubns.

Coles, Gladys M. Mary Webb. 160p. 1990. pap. 17.95 (*1-85411-035-7*) Dufour.

— Mary Webb. 160p. 1990. 27.00 (*1-85411-034-9*, Pub. by Seren Bks) Dufour.

Coles, Harry L. A History of the Administration of Federal Land Policies & Land Tenure in Louisiana, 1803-1860. Bruchey, Stuart, ed. LC 78-56718. (Management in Public Lands in the U. S. Ser.). (Illus.). 1979. lib. bdg. 31.95 (*0-405-11327-7*) Ayer.

— The War of 1812. 22. LC 65-17283. (Illus.). 312p. 1966. pap. text 16.95 (*0-226-11350-7*) U Ch Pr.

***Cole's Home Library Edition Staff.** The Essential Microwave Cookbook. 120p. 2000. pap. 11.95 (*1-56426-162-X*, Pub. by Cole Group) ACCESS Pubs Network.

— Pasta Cookbook. 120p. 2000. pap. 11.95 (*1-56426-161-1*, Pub. by Cole Group) ACCESS Pubs Network.

— Salads: Simple Fast & Fresh. 120p. 2000. pap. 11.95 (*1-56426-163-8*, Pub. by Cole Group) ACCESS Pubs Network.

— The Seasoned Wok. 120p. 2000. pap. 11.95 (*1-56426-160-3*, Pub. by Cole Group) ACCESS Pubs Network.

Coles, J. M. Archaeology by Experiment LC 73-177700. 182 p. 1973. write for info. (*0-09-116870-8*) Hutchinson.

— Archaeology by Experiment LC 74-3668. 182 p. 1974. 8.95 (*0-684-13818-2*) S&S Trade.

— World Prehistory: Studies in Memory of Grahame Clark. (British Academy Ser.). (Illus.). 272p. 1999. text 52.00 (*0-19-726196-5*) OUP.

Coles, James S., ed. Technological Innovation in the '80s. LC 84-2072. 1984. 12.95 (*0-13-902123-X*); pap. 6.95 (*0-13-902115-9*) Am Assembly.

Coles, Jane, ed. see Shakespeare, William.

Coles, Janet. Beads: An Exploration of Bead Traditions around the World. LC 97-34005. (Illus.). 160p. 1997. 24.50 (*0-684-83462-6*) Simon & Schuster.

— Fun with Beads - Ancient Egypt: From the Metropolitan Museum of Art. (Illus.). 64p. (YA). (gr. 7 up). 1995. text 29.95 (*0-670-85865-X*, Viking Child) Peng Put Young Read.

Coles, Janet & Bigham, Elizabeth. African Beads. LC 99-24315. 60p. 1999. 24.50 (*0-684-86784-2*) S&S Trade.

Coles, Janet & Budwig, Robert. Book of Beads: A Practical & Inspirational Guide to Beads & Jewelry Making. (Illus.). 150p. 1990. 22.95 (*0-671-70525-3*) S&S Trade.

Coles, Janet & Foster, Sandra. Three Shot Golf for Women: A Revolutionary Approach to Lower Scores in Less Time. LC 98-52417. (Illus.). 160p. (Orig.). 1999. pap. 14.95 (*1-58080-032-7*) Burford Bks.

Coles, Janis. Counterfeit Countess. large type ed. 272p. 1996. 27.99 (*0-7089-3481-1*) Ulverscroft.

— The Craigdarroch Girl. large type ed. (Ulverscroft). 336p. 1994. 27.99 (*0-7089-3017-4*) Ulverscroft.

— Lucy Grey. large type ed. 288p. 1994. 27.99 (*0-7089-3090-5*) Ulverscroft.

— The Major's Jacobite. large type ed. 1995. 27.99 (*0-7089-3290-8*) Ulverscroft.

— Mistress Cavalier. large type ed. 336p. 1996. 27.99 (*0-7089-3533-8*) Ulverscroft.

— Ravensmount. large type ed. 1994. 27.99 (*0-7089-3199-5*) Ulverscroft.

— Winter at Winslade. large type ed. 256p. 1994. 27.99 (*0-7089-3130-8*) Ulverscroft.

Coles, Jessie V. The Consumer-Buyer & the Market. Assael, Henry, ed. LC 78-265. (Century of Marketing Ser.). (Illus.). 1979. lib. bdg. 51.95 (*0-405-11168-1*) Ayer.

Coles, Joan & Coles, Clarence. Johnson/Evinrude Outboard, 1992-96 Vol. V: 4, 6 & 8 Cylinder. LC 98-159760. (Marine Tune-Up & Repair Manuals: Vol. V). (Illus.). 320p. (C). 1998. pap. 34.95 (*0-89330-040-3*, Pub. by Seloc) Natl Bk Netwk.

— Johnson/Evinrude Outboard, 1990-95 Vol. IIA: 1 & 2 Cylinder. LC 98-159761. (Marine Tune-Up & Repair Manuals: Vol. IIA). (Illus.). 500p. (C). 1998. pap. 34.95 (*0-89330-026-8*, Pub. by Seloc) Natl Bk Netwk.

— Mercruiser Stern Drive, Alpha Generation II, 1992-96, Vol. II. (Marine Tune-Up & Repair Manuals: Vol. II). (Illus.). 512p. (C). 1998. pap. 34.95 (*0-89330-039-X*, Pub. by Seloc) Natl Bk Netwk.

— Mercruiser Stern Drive, Bravo 1, Bravo 2 & Bravo 3, 1992-96, Vol. III. (Marine Tune-Up & Repair Manuals: Vol. III). (Illus.). 360p. (C). 1998. pap. 34.95 (*0-89330-046-2*, Pub. by Seloc) Natl Bk Netwk.

— Mercury/Mariner, 1990- 1994, Vol. I. (Marine Tune-Up & Repair Manuals: Vol. I). (Illus.). 350p. (C). 1998. pap. 34.95 (*0-89330-035-7*, Pub. by Seloc) Natl Bk Netwk.

— Mercury/Mariner Outboards, 1990-1994 Vol. II: 3 & 4 Cylinder. LC 96-104373. (Marine Tune-Up & Repair Manuals). (Illus.). 430p. (C). 1998. pap. 34.95 (*0-89330-036-5*, Pub. by Seloc) Natl Bk Netwk.

— Mercury/Mariner, 1990-94 Vol. III: V-6 Powerhead Outboard. (Marine Tune-Up & Repair Manuals). (Illus.). 400p. (C). 1998. pap. 34.95 (*0-89330-037-3*, Pub. by Seloc) Natl Bk Netwk.

— Volvo Penta Stern Drive OHC & DOHC, 1992-93, Vol. II. LC 98-203557. (Marine Tune-Up & Repair Manuals: Vol. II). (Illus.). 320p. (C). 1998. pap. 34.95 (*0-89330-038-1*, Pub. by Seloc) Natl Bk Netwk.

— Volvo Penta Stern Drive, Including "SX" Cobra, 1992-95, Vol. III. LC 98-203557. (Marine Tune-Up & Repair Manuals: Vol. III). (Illus.). 630p. (C). 1998. pap. 34.95 (*0-89330-041-1*, Pub. by Seloc) Natl Bk Netwk.

Coles, Joan & Coles, Clarence W. Chrysler Outboard 1962-1984: Tune-Up & Repair Manual, All Models. LC 95-119313. (Marine Tune-Up & Repair Manuals). (Illus.). 550p. (C). 1998. pap. 34.95 (*0-89330-018-7*, Pub. by Seloc) Natl Bk Netwk.

— Force Outboard 1984-1996. (Marine Tune-Up & Repair Manuals). (Illus.). 544p. (C). 1998. pap. write for info. (*0-89330-024-1*, Pub. by Seloc) Natl Bk Netwk.

— Mariner Outboard Vol. 2: Tune-Up & Repair Manual, 3, 4 & 6 Cylinder In-Line, V-6 with EFI. (Marine Tune-Up & Repair Manuals: Vol. 2). (Illus.). 616p. (C). 1998. pap. 34.95 (*0-89330-016-0*, Pub. by Seloc) Natl Bk Netwk.

— Mariner Outboard 1977-1989 Vol. 1: Tune-Up & Repair Manual, 1 & 2 Cylinder. LC 95-118717. (Marine Tune-Up & Repair Manuals: Vol. 1). (Illus.). 456p. (C). 1998. pap. 34.95 (*0-89330-015-2*, Pub. by Seloc) Natl Bk Netwk.

— Mercury Outboard, 1965-1991 Vol. I: 1 & 2 Cylinder Models. LC 86-218766. (Marine Tune-Up & Repair Manuals: Vol. I). (Illus.). 528p. (C). 1998. pap. 34.95 (*0-89330-012-8*, Pub. by Seloc) Natl Bk Netwk.

— Mercury Outboard, 1965-92 Vol. II: 3 & 4 Cylinder Models. LC 99-475070. (Marine Tune-Up & Repair Manuals). (Illus.). 575p. (C). 1998. pap. 34.95 (*0-89330-013-6*, Pub. by Seloc) Natl Bk Netwk.

— Mercury Outboards, 1965-1991 Vol. III: 6-in-Line & V6 Models. LC 91-195390. (Marine Tune-Up & Repair Manuals: Vol. III). (Illus.). 640p. (C). 1998. pap. 34.95 (*0-89330-014-4*, Pub. by Seloc) Natl Bk Netwk.

— OMC Cobra Stern Drive, 1985-95. LC 91-201997. (Marine Tune-Up & Repair Manuals). (Illus.). 660p. (C). 1998. pap. 34.95 (*0-89330-025-X*, Pub. by Seloc) Natl Bk Netwk.

— Volvo Penta Stern Drive, 1968-91. (Marine Tune-Up & Repair Manuals). (Illus.). 535p. (C). 1998. pap. 34.95 (*0-89330-011-X*, Pub. by Seloc) Natl Bk Netwk.

— Yamaha Outboard, 1984-91 Vol. I: 1 & 2 Cylinder. LC 99-475071. (Marine Tune-Up & Repair Manuals). (Illus.). 380p. (C). 1998. pap. 34.95 (*0-89330-021-7*, Pub. by Seloc) Natl Bk Netwk.

— Yamaha Outboard, 1984-91 Vol. II: 3-Cylinder. (Marine Tune-Up & Repair Manuals). (Illus.). 368p. (C). 1998. pap. 34.95 (*0-89330-022-5*, Pub. by Seloc) Natl Bk Netwk.

— Yamaha Outboard, 1984-91 Vol. III: 4 & 6 Cylinder. LC 99-475073. (Marine Tune-Up & Repair Manuals: Vol. III). (Illus.). 352p. (C). 1998. pap. 34.95 (*0-89330-023-3*, Pub. by Seloc) Natl Bk Netwk.

Coles, Joan M., jt. auth. see Post, Elizabeth L.

***Coles, Joanna.** Three of Us: A New Life in New York. 2000. 22.95 (*0-312-26667-7*) St Martin.

Coles, John. Experimental Archaeology. LC 79-41520. 1980. text 110.00 (*0-12-179750-3*) Acad Pr.

Coles, John & Coles, Bryony. Enlarging the Past: The Contribution of Wetland Archaeology. (Wetland Archaeological Research Project, Monograph Ser.: Vol. 11). (Illus.). 292p. 1996. pap. 38.00 (*0-903903-11-3*, Pub. by Society of Antiquaries) David Brown.

Coles, John M. & Lawson, Andrew J. European Wetlands in Prehistory. (Illus.). 320p. 1987. 115.00 (*0-19-813406-1*) OUP.

Coles, K. Adlard. Heavy Weather Sailing. 3rd rev. ed. 1987. 10.95 (*0-07-156209-5*) McGraw.

— Heavy Weather Sailing. 4th ed. (Illus.). 432p. 1996. pap. 27.95 (*0-07-011732-2*) Intl Marine.

***Coles, K. Adlard.** North Biscay: Quessant to the Gironde Estuary. 260p. 1999. 125.00 (*0-85288-416-8*, Pub. by Laurie Norie & Wilson Ltd) St Mut.

Coles, K. Adlard. North Biscay: Quessant to the Gironde Estuary. 6th rev. ed. (Illus.). 224p. 1994. 125.00 (*0-85288-245-9*, Pub. by Laurie Norie & Wilson Ltd) St Mut.

— North Brittany: St. Malo to Quessant. 6th rev. ed. (Illus.). 256p. (C). 1992. 125.00 (*0-85288-162-2*, Pub. by Laurie Norie & Wilson Ltd) St Mut.

Coles, K. Adlard & Black, A. N. North Biscay Pilot. 1979. 49.95 (*0-8464-0072-3*) Beekman Pubs.

Coles, Katharine. A History of the Garden: Poems. LC 96-47670. (Western Literature Ser.). 80p. (Orig.). 1997. pap. 10.00 (*0-87417-298-5*) U of Nev Pr.

— The Measurable World: A Novel. LC 95-17114. (Western Literature Ser.). 320p. 1995. 23.00 (*0-87417-273-X*) U of Nev Pr.

— The One Right Touch. 2nd ed. Boyer, Dale K., ed. LC 92-81877. (Ahsahta Press Modern & Contemporary Poets of the West Ser.). 60p. (Orig.). 1992. pap. 6.95 (*0-916272-54-0*) Ahsahta Pr.

Coles, Kim. I'm Free, but It'll Cost You: The Single Life According to Kim Coles. LC 96-51867. 256p. (J). 1997. 18.45 (*0-7868-6272-6*, Pub. by Hyperion) Time Warner.

— I'm Free, but It'll Cost You: The Single Life According to Kim Coles. 256p. (J). 1998. reprint ed. pap. 10.50 (*0-7868-8322-7*, Pub. by Hyperion) Time Warner.

Coles Kitchen Arts Staff. Fire & Smoke: The Complete Grill Guide. (Illus.). 240p. 1998. pap. 19.95 (*1-56426-081-X*) Cole Group.

Coles, L. Stephen & Steinman, David W. The IP-6 with Inositol Question & Answer Book: Nature's Ultimate Anti-Cancer Pill. unabridged ed. 96p. 1999. pap. 8.95 (*1-893910-00-8*, Pub. by Freedom Pr Inc) Nutri-Books Corp.

Coles, Lee. Metaphor: The Season Reflected in What You See. LC 99-34767. (Illus.). 80p. 1999. pap. 12.95 (*1-882897-39-0*) Lost Coast.

***Coles, Madeline.** Jewelry: Two Books in One, 2 bks. in 1. LC 98-47135. 128p. 1999. spiral bd. 24.95 (*0-8069-4822-1*) Sterling.

***Coles, Manning.** Brief Candles. Schantz, Tom & Schantz, Enid, eds. 154p. 2000. reprint ed. pap. 14.00 (*0-915230-24-0*) Rue Morgue.

Coles, Manning. Fifth Man. Date not set. lib. bdg. 22.95 (*0-8488-1965-9*) Amereon Ltd.

***Coles, Manning.** Happy Returns. 156p. 2000. pap. 14.00 (*0-915230-31-3*) Rue Morgue.

Coles, Manning. Toast to Tomorrow. (Spies & Intrigues Ser.: No. 3). 320p. 1984. pap. 5.95 (*0-918172-15-2*) Leetes Isl.

— Without Lawful Authority. (Spies & Intrigues Ser.: No. 4). 246p. 1984. pap. 5.95 (*0-918172-16-0*) Leetes Isl.

Coles, Martin & Hall, Christine. Children's Reading Choices. LC 98-36491. 1999. pap. write for info. (*0-415-18387-1*) Routledge.

Coles, Martin, jt. ed. see Harrison, Colin.

Coles, Matthew A. Kids, Try This at Home! A Do-It-Yourself-Guide to Instituting Lesbian & Gay Civil Rights Policy. (ACLU Handbook Ser.). 352p. 1996. pap. 14.95 (*1-56584-309-6*, Pub. by New Press NY) Norton.

Coles, Michael G., jt. ed. see Jennings, J. Richard.

Coles, Michael G., jt. ed. see Rugg, Michael D.

Coles-Mogford, Anne, jt. auth. see Drummond, Archie.

Coles-Mogford, Anne M., jt. auth. see Drummond, Archie.

Coles, Nicholas. For a Living: The Poetry of Work. 432p. 1994. 18.95 (*0-252-06410-0*) U of Ill Pr.

Coles, Nicholas & Oresick, Peter, eds. For a Living: The Poetry of Work. LC 94-4377. 432p. 1994. reprint ed. text 44.95 (*0-252-02122-3*) U of Ill Pr.

Coles, Nicholas, jt. ed. see Oresick, Peter.

Coles, Norman A. John Ashton's Case for James II As Rightful King of England: Rebellion or Revolution. LC 98-40427. (Studies in British History: Vol. 50). 164p. 1998. text 79.95 (*0-7734-8276-8*) E Mellen.

Coles, P. A. Comparative Radiator Testing: Plus Supplement. (C). 1983. 65.00 (*0-86022-091-5*, Pub. by Build Servs Info Assn) St Mut.

Coles, Peter. Einstein & the Total Eclipse. 64p. 1999. pap. 7.95 (*1-84046-089-X*) Icon Bks.

— Routledge Critical Dictionary of the New Cosmology. LC 98-52552. 416p. 1999. pap. 22.99 (*0-415-92354-9*) Routledge.

***Coles, Peter.** Stephen Hawking & the Mind of God. 80p. 2000. pap. 7.95 (*1-84046-124-1*, Pub. by Icon Bks) Natl Bk Netwk.

Coles, Peter, et al, eds. Mapping, Measuring & Modelling the Universe. (ASP Conference Series Proceedings: Vol. 94). 383p. 1996. 34.00 (*1-886733-15-5*) Astron Soc Pacific.

Coles, Peter & Ellis, George F. Is the Universe Open or Closed? The Density of Matter in the Universe. LC 96-41205. (Cambridge Lecture Notes in Physics Ser.: No. 7). (Illus.). 251p. (C). 1997. pap. text 33.95 (*0-521-56689-4*) Cambridge U Pr.

Coles, Peter & Lucchin, Francesco. Cosmology: The Origin & Evolution of Cosmic Structure. LC 94-46441. 470p. 1995. 84.95 (*0-471-95473-X*) Wiley.

Coles, R. N., et al. Epic Battles of the Chessboard. unabridged ed. LC 96-32394. (Illus.). 176p. 1996. reprint ed. pap. text 7.95 (*0-486-29355-6*) Dover.

Coles, R. T. From Huntsville to Appomattox: R. T. Cole's History of the 4th Regiment, Alabama Volunteer Infantry, C. S. A., Army of Northern Virginia. Stocker, Jeffrey D., ed. LC 95-32487. (Voices of the Civil War Ser.). (Illus.). 336p. 1996. 32.95 (*0-87049-924-6*) U of Tenn Pr.

Coles, Richard N. Dynamic Chess: The Modern Style of Aggressive Play. enl. rev. ed. (Illus.). 195p. 1966. pap. 5.95 (*0-486-21676-4*) Dover.

Coles, Robert. Adolescence. 1996. write for info. (*0-201-19898-3*) Addison-Wesley.

— Adolescents & Moral Development. write for info. (*0-318-65156-4*) Addison-Wesley.

— Anna Freud: The Dream of Psychoanalysis. 1993. pap. 10.95 (*0-201-62232-7*) Addison-Wesley.

— Black Writers Abroad: A Study of Black American Writers in Europe & Africa. rev. ed. LC 96-36741. (Studies in African American History & Culture). 176p. 1999. 48.00 (*0-8153-2751-X*) Garland.

— The Call of Service. 384p. 1994. pap. 13.00 (*0-395-71084-7*) HM.

— The Call of Service: A Witness to Idealism. large type ed. LC 94-10670. 482p. 1994. lib. bdg. 22.95 (*0-8161-7404-0*, G K Hall Lrg Type) Mac Lib Ref.

— The Call of Stories: Stories & the Moral Imagination. 256p. 1990. pap. 14.00 (*0-395-52815-1*) HM.

— Children of Crisis Vol. 2: Migrants, Sharecroppers, Mountaineers. (Children of Crisis Ser.). (Illus.). 1973. pap. 24.95 (*0-316-15176-9*) Little.

— Children of Crisis Vol. 5: Privileged Ones: The Well-off & Rich in America. LC 73-10825. (Children of Crisis Ser.). (Illus.). 1980. pap. 12.95 (*0-685-03065-2*) Little.

***Coles, Robert.** The Children of Crisis Reader. 640p. 2000. pap. 22.95 (*0-316-15102-5*) Little.

Coles, Robert. Conversations with Robert Coles. Woodruff, Jay & Woodruff, Sarah C., eds. LC 91-36584. (Literary Conversations Ser.). 272p. 1992. pap. 15.95 (*0-87805-553-3*); text 39.50 (*0-87805-552-5*) U Pr of Miss.

— Doing Documentary Work. LC 97-292. (New York Public Library Lectures in Humanities). (Illus.). 288p. (C). 1997. 25.00 (*0-19-511629-1*) OUP.

— Doing Documentary Work. (New York Public Library Lectures in Humanities). (Illus.). 288p. 1998. reprint ed. pap. 14.95 (*0-19-512495-2*) OUP.

— Dorothy Day: A Radical Devotion. (Radcliffe Biography Ser.). 224p. 1989. pap. 16.50 (*0-201-07974-7*) Addison-Wesley.

— Erik H. Erikson: The Growth of His Work. (Quality Paperbacks Ser.). 462p. 1987. pap. 12.95 (*0-306-80291-0*) Da Capo.

— A Festering Sweetness: Poems of American People. LC 77-15736. (Poetry Ser.). 72p. (C). 1978. pap. 10.95 (*0-8229-5290-4*) U of Pittsburgh Pr.

— Flannery O'Connor's South. LC 92-41956. (Brown Thrasher Bks.). 208p. 1993. reprint ed. pap. 15.95 (*0-8203-1536-2*) U of Ga Pr.

— Harvard Diary: Reflections on the Sacred & the Secular. 216p. 1990. reprint ed. pap. 13.95 (*0-8245-1034-8*) Crossroad NY.

— Harvard Diary II: Reflections on Values in Life & Literature. 228p. 1997. 19.95 (*0-8245-1649-4*) Crossroad NY.

— Irony in the Mind's Life: Essays on Novels by James Agee, Elizabeth Bowen, & George Eliot. LC 74-5260. 222p. reprint ed. pap. 68.90 (*0-7837-4359-9*, 204406900012) Bks Demand.

***Coles, Robert.** Lives of Moral Leadership. 272p. 2000. 23.95 (*0-375-50108-8*) Random.

Coles, Robert. The Mind's Fate. 1996. pap. 14.95 (*0-614-20826-2*) Little.

— The Moral Intelligence of Children: How to Raise a Moral Child. LC 97-41475. 240p. (C). 1998. pap. 12.95 (*0-452-27937-2*) Dutton Plume.

***Coles, Robert.** Moral Life of Children. 320p. 2000. pap. 13.50 (*0-87113-770-4*, Atlntc Mnthly) Grove-Atltic.

C

Coles, Robert. Old & on Their Own. LC 97-36922. (Illus.). 192p. 1998. 27.50 (*0-393-04606-0*) Norton.

***Coles, Robert.** Political Life of Children. 352p. 2000. pap. 13.50 (*0-87113-771-2*, Atlntc Mnthly) Grove-Atltic.

Coles, Robert. Robert Coles: An Intimate Biographical Interview. Baird-Middleton, Bruce, ed. (C). 1988. pap. text 59.95 incl. VHS (*0-674-77525-2*) HUP.

— A Robert Coles Omnibus. LC 92-38346. 782p. (Orig.). 1993. pap. 25.95 (*0-87745-411-6*) U of Iowa Pr.

— Rumors of Separate Worlds. LC 89-32838. (Illus.). 90p. 1989. text 19.95 (*0-87745-258-X*); pap. text 11.95 (*0-87745-260-1*) U of Iowa Pr.

— School. LC 97-78282. (Illus.). 176p. (gr. 8). 1998. 35.00 (*0-8212-2501-4*) Little.

— The Secular Mind. LC 98-39388. 189p. 1999. 19.95 (*0-691-05805-9*, Pub. by Princeton U Pr) Cal Prin Full Svc.

— The Spiritual Life of Children. 360p. 1990. reprint ed. pap. 19.95 (*0-00-599310-5*, Pub. by T & T Clark) Bks Intl VA.

— The Story of Ruby Bridges. LC 92-33674. (Illus.). 32p. (J). (gr. k-4). 1995. 13.95 (*0-590-43967-7*) Scholastic Inc.

— The Story of Ruby Bridges. LC 92-33674. (Illus.). (ps-3). 1995. 13.95 (*0-590-57281-4*) Scholastic Inc.

— The Students Themselves: Assembly on University Goals & Governance. 320p. 1974. text 18.95 (*0-87073-432-6*) Schenkman Bks Inc.

— That Red Wheelbarrow: Selected Literary Essays. LC 88-14281. 368p. 1988. text 28.95 (*0-87745-208-3*) U of Iowa Pr.

— Times of Surrender: Selected Essays. LC 87-30221. 292p. 1988. text 28.95 (*0-87745-188-5*) U of Iowa Pr.

— William Carlos Williams: The Knack of Survival in America. LC 75-6560. (Mason Welch Gross Lectureship Ser.). 207p. 1975. reprint ed. pap. 64.20 (*0-7837-5664-X*, 205909000005) Bks Demand.

— Women of Crisis II: Lives of Work & Dreams, Vol. II. 1990. pap. 9.95 (*0-201-51811-2*) Addison-Wesley.

— The Youngest Parents: Teenage pregnancy as it shapes lives. LC 96-47258. (Illus.). 192p. (YA). 1997. 27.50 (*0-393-04082-8*) Norton.

Coles, Robert, ed. Dietrich Bonhoeffer: Writings Selected with an Introduction by Robert Coles. LC 98-26303. (Modern Spiritual Masters Ser.). 128p. 1998. pap. 13.00 (*1-57075-194-3*) Orbis Bks.

***Coles, Robert, et al, eds.** Growing Up Poor. 2001. 23.95 (*1-56584-623-0*, Pub. by New Press NY) Norton.

Coles, Robert & Lancaster, Bill, eds. Geordies: Roots & Regionalism. (Illus.). 192p. 1993. pap. 25.00 (*0-7486-0394-8*, Pub. by Edinburgh U Pr) Col U Pr.

Coles, Robert & Nixon, Nicholas. School. 1998. pap. write for info. (*0-8212-2545-6*) Little.

Coles, Robert, et al. The Ongoing Journey: Awakening Spiritual Life in At Risk Youth. 225p. 1994. pap. 14.95 (*0-938510-48-7*, 32-001) Boys Town Pr.

Coles, Robert, jt. auth. see Erikson, Erik.

Coles, Robert, ed. see Williams, William Carlos.

Coles, Romand. Rethinking Generosity: Critical Theory & the Politics of Caritas. LC 97-18760. (Contestations Ser.). 272p. 1997. text 39.95 (*0-8014-3341-X*); pap. text 16.95 (*0-8014-8487-1*) Cornell U Pr.

— Self - Power - Other: Political Theory & Dialogical Ethics. LC 91-55546. 224p. 1992. text 39.95 (*0-8014-2609-X*) Cornell U Pr.

***Coles, Ryan T.** Western National Forests: A Cohesive Strategy Is Needed to Address Catastrophic Wildfire Threats. (Illus.). 60p. (C). 2000. pap. text 20.00 (*0-7881-8617-5*) DIANE Pub.

Coles, Stuart. Alanis Morissette: Death of Cinderella. 1997. pap. text 15.95 (*0-85965-258-0*, Pub. by Plexus) Publishers Group.

— Garbage: An Illustrated Biography. (Illus.). 48p. 1997. pap. 12.95 (*0-7119-6580-3*, OP48009) Omnibus NY.

— Primal Scream: An Illustrated Biography. (Illus.). 73p. (YA). 1998. pap. 14.95 (*0-7119-6807-1*, OP48047) Omnibus NY.

— Prodigy: An Illustrated Biography. (Illus.). 1998. pap. text 12.95 (*0-7119-6718-0*) Omnibus NY.

— Punks: Street Revolution. (Illus.). 128p. 1999. pap. 15.95 (*0-85965-251-3*) Publishers Group.

Coles-Thorburn, Carolyn. Mastery of Conversational Spanish: Workbook. 304p. (C). 1994. per. 32.95 (*0-8403-9542-6*) Kendall-Hunt.

Coles, Tim. Isolation Technology: A Practical Guide. LC 97-46339. (Illus.). 322p. 1998. 191.00 (*1-57491-059-0*) Interpharm.

Coles, Tim, jt. auth. see Shaw, Gareth.

Coles, W. The Art of Simpling. 114p. 1986. spiral bd. 15.00 (*0-7873-0189-2*) Hlth Research.

Coles, W. B. Coles Family of Virginia: Its Numerous Connections from Emigration to America to 1915. (Illus.). 885p. 1991. reprint ed. pap. 125.00 (*0-8328-1900-X*); reprint ed. lib. bdg. 135.00 (*0-8328-1899-2*) Higginson Bk Co.

Coles, Waltraud & Dodd, Bill. Reading German: A Course Book & Reference Grammar. 388p. 1998. text 95.00 (*0-19-870004-0*); pap. text 38.00 (*0-19-870020-2*) OUP.

Coles, Waltraud & Koreik, Uwe. Simple Guide to Germany: Customs & Etiquette. 3rd rev. ed. (Simple Guides Ser.: Series 1). 80p. 1999. pap. 8.95 (*1-86034-031-8*, Pub. by Global Bks) Midpt Trade.

— Very Simple German. (Illus.). 64p. 1991. pap. 8.95 (*1-873411-15-4*, Pub. by A & C Blk) Talman.

Coles, William. Alfred Stevens. (Illus.). 152p. 1977. pap. 12.50 (*0-912303-12-3*) Michigan Mus.

Coles, William A. East Meets West: American Impressionism. Fleischer, Donna H. & Verplank, Kathy, eds. (Illus.). 79p. (Orig.). 1996. pap. 15.00 (*0-614-30184-X*) FFCA Pub.

— East Meets West: American Impressionism. Fleischer, Donna H. et al, eds. (Illus.). 79p. (Orig.). 1996. 30.00 (*0-9617882-6-7*) FFCA Pub.

Coles, William A. & Reed, Henry H., Jr., eds. Architecture in America: A Battle of Styles. LC 61-5653. (Illus.). (Orig.). 1961. pap. text 17.95 (*0-89197-029-0*) Irvington.

Coles, William A., ed. see Van Brunt, Henry.

Coles, William C., Jr. The Postal Markings of New Jersey Stampless Covers. LC 83-72780. (Illus.). 287p. 1983. 35.00 (*0-318-41003-6*) Collectors Club IL.

Coles, William E., Jr. Another Kind of Monday. 240p. (J). (gr. 7 up). 1996. 17.00 (*0-689-80254-4*) Atheneum Yung Read.

— Another Kind of Monday. LC 95-33395. 256p. (YA). (gr. 7-12). 1999. mass mkt. 6.99 (*0-380-73133-9*, Avon Bks) Morrow Avon.

— Composing: Writing As a Self-Creating Process. LC 74-10987. 120p. (Orig.). 1983. pap. text 17.50 (*0-86709-119-3*, 0119, Pub. by Boynton Cook Pubs) Heinemann.

— The Plural I - & After. 298p. (Orig.). (C). 1988. pap. text 23.00 (*0-86709-217-3*, 0217, Pub. by Boynton Cook Pubs) Heinemann.

Coles, William E., Jr. & Vopat, James. What Makes Writing Good: A Multiperspective. LC 84-80295. 360p. (C). 1985. pap. text 38.76 (*0-669-06614-1*) HM Trade Div.

Coles, William H. Ophthalmology: A Diagnostic Text. (Illus.). 424p. 1989. pap. text 35.00 (*0-683-02056-0*) Lppncott W & W.

Coles, William H., jt. auth. see Haik, George M.

Colescott, Warrington & Hove, Arthur. Progressive Printmakers: Wisconsin Artists & the Print Renaissance. LC 98-51818. 1999. 39.95 (*0-299-16110-2*) U of Wis Pr.

Coleson, Joseph & Mathews, Victor, eds. Go to the Land I Will Show You: Studies in Honor of Dwight W. Young. 1996. text 42.50 (*0-931464-91-9*) Eisenbrauns.

Colestock, P. L., jt. ed. see Granatstein, V. L.

***Colesworthy, Robert & Reher, David.** Lower Engine Assembly: Reher-Morrison Racing Engines. Barfield, James, ed. & photos by by. (Illus.). 150p. 1999. pap. 79.95 (*0-9669002-2-7*) Educ Tech Consul.

— Upper Engine Assembly: Reher-Morrison Racing Engines. Barfield, James, ed. & photos by by. (Illus.). 150p. 1999. pap. 49.95 (*0-9669002-3-5*) Educ Tech Consul.

Colet, John. Cambodia Handbook. LC 96-72525. (Illus.). 240p. 1997. 16.95 (*0-8442-4922-X*) NTC Contemp Pub Co.

Colet, John. Cambodia Handbook. 2nd ed. (Footprint Handbooks Ser.). 240p. Date not set. pap. text 15.95 (*0-658-00067-5*, 000675, NTC Business Bks) NTC Contemp Pub Co.

Colet, John. Vietnam Handbook. (Illus.). 352p. 1997. 16.95 (*0-8442-4920-3*) NTC Contemp Pub Co.

— Vietnam Handbook. 4th ed. (Footprint Handbooks Ser.). 384p. 1999. pap. 16.95 (*0-8442-2193-7*, 21937) NTC Contemp Pub Co.

Colet, Roger, tr. see Maupassant, Guy de.

Colett, Simone. Ecstasy. 20.95 (*0-8488-0075-3*) Amereon Ltd.

Coletta. Physics. 1995. pap., student ed. 26.88 (*0-8151-9165-0*) McGraw.

— Physics. 1996. 294.68 (*0-8151-1940-2*) Mosby Inc.

— Physics Quick Reference. 1995. (*0-8151-1909-7*) Mosby Inc.

Coletta, Anthony. Childhood Stress Checklist. (Illus.). 40p. 1992. pap. text 6.00 (*0-935493-79-4*) Modern Learn Pr.

— Coping with Parent Burnout. 40p. (Orig.). 1992. pap. text 6.00 (*0-935493-86-7*) Modern Learn Pr.

— How to Teach a Child to Learn. 40p. (Orig.). 1992. pap. text 6.00 (*0-935493-89-1*) Modern Learn Pr.

— Love & Limits. 40p. (Orig.). 1992. pap. text 6.00 (*0-935493-93-X*) Modern Learn Pr.

Coletta, Anthony J. What's Best for Kids? A Guide to Developmentally Appropriate Practices for Teachers & Parents. 1992. pap. 14.95 (*0-935493-43-3*) Modern Learn Pr.

Coletta, Anthony J. & Coletta, Cathleen. Year 'Round Activities for Four-Year-Old Children. LC 85-30934. 272p. 1986. pap. text 19.95 (*0-87628-983-9*) Ctr Appl Res.

— Year 'Round Activities for Three-Year-Old Children. LC 85-26998. 272p. 1986. pap. text 19.95 (*0-87628-982-0*) Ctr Appl Res.

— Year 'Round Activities for Two-Year-Old Children. LC 85-24264. 272p. 1986. pap. text 19.95 (*0-87628-981-2*) Ctr Appl Res.

Coletta, Bernarr B., jt. auth. see Coletta, Paolo E.

Coletta, Cathleen, jt. auth. see Coletta, Anthony J.

Coletta, Cristina Della, see Della Coletta, Cristina.

Coletta, Gerard C., jt. ed. see Barker, Roger L.

***Coletta, Maggie.** In Remembrance Vol. II: Abstracts of Marriage & Death Notices 1882 Brooklyn Daily Eagle Newspaper Brooklyn, New York. 445p. 1999. 31.00 (*0-7884-1400-3*, C540) Heritage Bk.

Coletta, Maggie. Remembrance Abstracts of Marriage & Death Notices: 1881 Brooklyn Daily Eagle Newspaper Brooklyn, New York. LC 99-198150. 368p. 1999. 30.50 (*0-7884-1100-4*, C543) Heritage Bk.

Coletta, Paolo E. Admiral Marc A. Mitscher & U. S. Naval Aviation: Bald Eagle. LC 97-5008. (Studies in American History: Vol. 12). (Illus.). 508p. 1997. text 109.95 (*0-7734-8676-3*) E Mellen.

— Allied & American Naval Operations in the European Theater, World War I. LC 95-46440. (Studies in American History: Vol. 7). (Illus.). 604p. 1996. text 129.95 (*0-7734-8883-9*) E Mellen.

— The American Naval Heritage. 4th ed. LC 97-21321. (Illus.). 540p. (C). 1997. text 64.00 (*0-7618-0806-X*); pap. text 44.50 (*0-7618-0807-8*) U Pr of Amer.

— The American Naval Heritage in Brief. 3rd ed. 654p. (C). 1987. text 66.50 (*0-8191-5596-9*) U Pr of Amer.

— American Naval History: A Guide. 3rd ed. LC 98-5955. 936p. 1999. 125.00 (*0-8108-3302-6*) Scarecrow.

— Patrick N. L. Bellinger & U. S. Naval Aviation. (Illus.). 478p. (Orig.). (C). 1987. lib. bdg. 62.00 (*0-8191-6534-4*) U Pr of Amer.

— The Presidency of William Howard Taft. LC 97-50019. (American Presidency Ser.). xii, 308p. 1973. 29.95 (*0-7006-0096-5*) U Pr of KS.

— A Survey of U. S. Naval Affairs, 1865-1917. LC 87-10394. (Illus.). 272p. (Orig.). (C). 1987. lib. bdg. 50.50 (*0-8191-6397-X*) U Pr of Amer.

— A Survey of U. S. Naval Affairs, 1865-1917. LC 87-10394. (Illus.). 272p. (Orig.). (C). 1987. pap. text 26.00 (*0-8191-6398-8*) U Pr of Amer.

— The United States Navy & Defense Unification, 1947-1953. LC 77-74410. (Illus.). 550p. 1981. 55.00 (*0-87413-126-X*) U Delaware Pr.

— William Howard Taft: A Bibliography. 26. LC 89-3388. (Bibliographies of the Presidents of the United States Ser.: No. 26). 312p. 1989. lib. bdg. 72.95 (*0-313-28184-X*, AP26, Greenwood Pr) Greenwood.

Coletta, Paolo E., compiled by. A Selected & Annotated Bibliography of American Naval History. 548p. (C). 1988. lib. bdg. 66.50 (*0-8191-7111-5*) U Pr of Amer.

Coletta, Paolo E. & Bauer, K. Jack, eds. United States Navy & Marine Corps Bases, Domestic. LC 84-4468. 740p. 1985. lib. bdg. 135.00 (*0-313-23133-8*, CUN/, Greenwood Pr) Greenwood.

— United States Navy & Marine Corps Bases, Overseas. LC 84-4470. 459p. 1985. lib. bdg. 115.00 (*0-313-24504-5*, COU/, Greenwood Pr) Greenwood.

Coletta, Paolo E. & Coletta, Bernarr B. Admiral William A. Moffet & U. S. Naval Aviation. LC 97-29426. (Studies in American History: Vol. 13). (Illus.). 255p. 1997. text 89.95 (*0-7734-8595-3*) E Mellen.

Coletta, Vincent P. College Physics: Student Study Guide. 240p. 1993. 18.95 (*0-8016-7723-8*) Mosby Inc.

— Quick Reference Guide to College Physics. 112p. (C). 1995. text. write for info. (*0-8151-1939-9*, WCB McGr Hill) McGrw-H Hghr Educ.

Colette, Chatte. Gigi & the Cat: Novels. LC 95-214662. (Twentieth-Century Classics Ser.). 160p. 1995. pap. 10.95 (*0-14-018319-1*, Penguin Classics) Viking Penguin.

Colette, John & Quinn, Meredith, eds. The Business of Electronic Publishing. LC 99-161278. (Illus.). 220p. 1998. pap. 35.00 (*0-642-27093-7*, Pub. by Allen & Unwin Pty) Paul & Co Pubs.

Colette, Martine. A Tiger in My Salad. Date not set. 12.50 (*0-06-093064-0*) HarpC.

Colette, Martine & Nickles, Liz. Wildlife Waystation: True Animal Rescue Stories from an Animal Refuge Center. (Illus.). 224p. 1999. 24.00 (*0-06-019128-7*) HarpC.

Colette, Sidonie-Gabrielle. Bella-Vista. 1996. 1.99 (*0-679-77097-6*) Modern Lib NY.

— Bella Vista: Avec: Trois, Six, Neuf. (FRE.). 1974. pap. 11.95 (*0-8288-9137-0*, M3321) Fr & Eur.

— Le Ble en Herbe. Pichois, ed. (Coll. GF). (FRE.). pap. 10.95 (*0-8288-9161-3*, F97001) Fr & Eur.

— Chambre d'Hotel. (FRE.). 1964. pap. 11.95 (*0-8288-9153-2*, F85830) Fr & Eur.

— Chats. (FRE., Illus.). 1950. pap. 10.95 (*0-8288-9138-9*, F97031) Fr & Eur.

— La Chatte. (FRE.). 212p. 1950. 24.95 (*0-8288-9146-X*, F97030) Fr & Eur.

— La Chatte. (FRE.). 1955. pap. 10.95 (*0-8288-9155-9*, F97031) Fr & Eur.

— Cheri. (FRE.). 1958. pap. 10.95 (*0-8288-9154-0*, F97041) Fr & Eur.

— Les Claudine. 256p. 1969. pap. 8.95 (*0-7859-0691-6*) Fr & Eur.

— Claudine a l'Ecole. (FRE.). 1956. pap. 11.95 (*0-8288-9165-6*, F97061) Fr & Eur.

— Claudine a Paris. (FRE.). 1957. pap. 10.95 (*0-8288-9156-7*, F97071) Fr & Eur.

— Claudine et Menage. (FRE.). 256p. 1973. pap. 10.95 (*0-8288-9139-7*, M3323) Fr & Eur.

— Claudine s'en Va. (FRE.). 1957. pap. 10.95 (*0-8288-9157-5*) Fr & Eur.

— Colette Par Colette: La Jeunesse de Claudine. (FRE.). 1976. 59.95 (*0-7859-4770-1*) Fr & Eur.

Colette, Sidonie-Gabrielle. Contes des Milles et un Matins. (FRE.). 248p. 1970. pap. 24.95 (*0-8288-9141-9*, F97000) Fr & Eur.

Colette, Sidonie-Gabrielle. Dialogue de Betes. (Folio Ser.: No. 701). (FRE.). 160p. 1974. 6.95 (*2-07-036701-0*) Schoenhof.

— Dialogues de Betes. (FRE.). 1975. pap. 10.95 (*0-7859-1811-6*, 2070367010) Fr & Eur.

— Duo. Incl. Toutounier. (FRE.). Set pap. 10.95 (*0-8288-9158-3*, F97100) Fr & Eur.

— Duo & le Toutounier. 1974. 30.00 (*0-7206-0273-4*, Pub. by P Owen Ltd) Dufour.

***Colette, Sidonie-Gabrielle.** Duo & le Toutounier. 214p. 2000. pap. 19.95 (*0-7206-1069-9*, Pub. by P Owen Ltd) Dufour.

Colette, Sidonie-Gabrielle. L' Enfants et les Sortileges. (FRE., Illus.). 40p. 1981. pap. 29.95 (*0-7859-4719-1*) Fr & Eur.

— L' Entrave. (FRE.). pap. 10.95 (*0-8288-9160-5*, F97121) Fr & Eur.

— The Evening Star. Le Vey, David, tr. from FRE. LC 73-11793. 144p. 1974. 5.95 (*0-672-51876-7*, Bobbs) Macmillan.

Colette, Sidonie-Gabrielle. The Evening Star: Recollections. LC 73-161804. 144p. 1973. write for info. (*0-7206-0212-2*) P Owen Ltd.

Colette, Sidonie-Gabrielle. Le Fanal Bleu. (FRE.). 160p. 1975. pap. 10.95 (*0-8288-9148-6*) Fr & Eur.

— La Femme Cachee. (FRE.). 192p. 1974. pap. 10.95 (*0-7859-2208-3*, 207036612X) Fr & Eur.

— La Femme Cachee. (Folio Ser.: No. 612). (FRE.). pap. 6.95 (*2-07-036612-X*) Schoenhof.

— La Fin de Cher. (FRE.). 1983. pap. 10.95 (*0-7859-2982-7*) Fr & Eur.

— Gigi. (FRE.). 1959. 12.50 (*0-685-11214-4*, F97151); pap. 10.95 (*0-8288-9159-1*) Fr & Eur.

— Gigi & Julie De Carneilhan. 18.95 (*0-88411-298-5*) Amereon Ltd.

— Histoires pour Bel Gazou. 7th ed. (FRE.). 121p. 1992. pap. 10.95 (*0-7859-4720-5*) Fr & Eur.

— L' Ingenue Libertine. 256p. 1973. 10.95 (*0-8288-9144-3*, F97171); pap. 3.95 (*0-686-54578-8*) Fr & Eur.

Colette, Sidonie-Gabrielle. Journey for Myself: Selfish Memories. LC 77-859343. 156p. 1971. write for info. (*0-7206-0430-3*) P Owen Ltd.

Colette, Sidonie-Gabrielle. Julie de Carneilhan. (FRE.). 1982. pap. 10.95 (*0-7859-1947-3*, 2070373444) Fr & Eur.

— Julie de Carneilhan. (Folio Ser.: No. 1344). (FRE.). pap. 8.95 (*2-07-037344-4*) Schoenhof.

— Le Kepi. (FRE.). 1987. pap. 10.95 (*0-7859-3420-0*) Fr & Eur.

— Lettres a Sa Fille. (FRE.). 1984. pap. 46.95 (*0-7859-3303-4*, 2721002643) Fr & Eur.

— Lettres a Ses Pairs: Correspondances Inedite de Colette a Marcel Proust, Alfred Jarry, Paul Leautaud. (FRE.). 456p. 1973. 41.95 (*0-8288-9150-8*, M3330) Fr & Eur.

— Lettres au Petit Corsaire. 153p. 1963. 19.95 (*0-8288-7465-4*) Fr & Eur.

— Ma mere et les Betes. (POR.). 24.95 incl. audio (*0-685-21216-5*) Fr & Eur.

— La Maison de Claudine. (FRE.). 158p. 1990. pap. 10.95 (*0-7859-4721-3*) Fr & Eur.

— Mitsou ou Comment l'Esprit Vient aux Filles. (FRE.). 1987. pap. 10.95 (*0-7859-3139-2*) Fr & Eur.

— My Mother's House & Sido. Troubridge, Una V. & McLeod, Enid, trs. from FRE. 219p. 1975. pap. 10.00 (*0-374-51218-3*) FS&G.

— La Naissance du Jour. (POR.). 24.95 incl. audio (*0-685-21218-1*); pap. 8.95 (*0-685-37283-9*) Fr & Eur.

— L' Oeuvre Romanesque, 3 vols., Vol. 1: 1900-1919. (FRE.). 1989. pap. 60.00 (*0-7859-3027-2*) Fr & Eur.

— L' Oeuvre Romanesque, 3 vols., Vol. 2: 1920-1940. (FRE.). 1989. pap. 60.00 (*0-7859-3028-0*) Fr & Eur.

— L' Oeuvre Romanesque, 3 vols., Vol. 3: 1941-1949. (FRE.). 1989. pap. 60.00 (*0-7859-3029-9*) Fr & Eur.

— Oeuvres, Tome 1. deluxe ed. (Pleiade Ser.). (FRE.). 89.95 (*2-07-011079-6*) Schoenhof.

— Oeuvres, Tome 2. deluxe ed. (Pleiade Ser.). (FRE.). 1794p. 1986. 99.95 (*2-07-011101-6*) Schoenhof.

— Oeuvres, Tome 3. deluxe ed. (Pleiade Ser.). (FRE.). 119.95 (*2-07-011215-2*) Schoenhof.

— Oeuvres, Vol. 1. Pichois, Claude, ed. (FRE.). 1984. lib. bdg. 135.00 (*0-7859-3955-5*) Fr & Eur.

— Oeuvres, Vol. 2. Pichois, Claude, ed. (FRE.). 1986. lib. bdg. 140.00 (*0-7859-3872-9*) Fr & Eur.

— Oeuvres, Vol. 3. Pichois, Claude, ed. (FRE.). 1986. lib. bdg. 195.00 (*0-7859-3898-2*) Fr & Eur.

— Oeuvres Completes, 16 vols., Set. (FRE.). 1973. 995.00 (*0-7859-1164-2*, 2080606832) Fr & Eur.

— Oeuvres Completes: Belles Saisons, Nudite, le Fanal Bleu, Vol. 11. 1974. 150.00 (*0-686-54594-X*) Fr & Eur.

— Oeuvres Completes: Chambre d'Hotel, la Lune de Pluie, Julie de Carneilhan, Vol. 9. 1974. 150.00 (*0-686-54592-3*) Fr & Eur.

— Oeuvres Completes: Claudine a l'Ecole, Claudine a Paris, Claudine en Menage, Vol. 1. (Illus.). 1973. 150.00 (*0-686-54584-2*) Fr & Eur.

— Oeuvres Completes: Claudine s'en va, la Retraite Sentimentale, L'Ingenue Libertine, Vol. 2. 1973. 150.00 (*0-686-54585-0*) Fr & Eur.

— Oeuvres Completes: De ma Fenetre, Trois, Six, Neuf, Gigi, Vol. 10. 1974. 150.00 (*0-686-54593-1*) Fr & Eur.

— Oeuvres Completes: Duo, Le Toutounier, Mes Apprentissages, Vol. 8. 1974. 150.00 (*0-686-54591-5*) Fr & Eur.

— Oeuvres Completes: La Chambre Eclairee, Cheri, la Fin de Cheri, Vol. 5. 1974. 150.00 (*0-686-54588-5*) Fr & Eur.

— Oeuvres Completes: La Jumelle Noire, Vol. 12. 1975. 150.00 (*0-686-54595-8*) Fr & Eur.

— Oeuvres Completes: La Maison de Claudine, Sido Noces, Vol. 6. 1974. 150.00 (*0-686-54589-3*) Fr & Eur.

— Oeuvres Completes: La Seconde, Prisons et Paradis, le Pur et l'Impur, Vol. 7. 1974. 150.00 (*0-686-54590-7*) Fr & Eur.

— Oeuvres Completes: L'Entrave, l'Envers du Musichall, la Paix chez les Betes, Vol. 4. 1974. 150.00 (*0-686-54587-7*) Fr & Eur.

— Oeuvres Completes: Les Vrilles de la Vigne, Douze Dialogues de Betes, Autres Betes, Vol. 3. 1973. 150.00 (*0-686-54586-9*) Fr & Eur.

— Oeuvres Completes: Lettres au Petit Corsaire, Lettres a ses Pairs, Vol. 16. 1976. 150.00 (*0-686-54599-0*) Fr & Eur.

— Oeuvres Completes: Lettres de Vagabonde, Lettres a Helene Picard, Vol. 15. 1976. 150.00 (*0-686-54598-2*) Fr & Eur.

— Oeuvres Completes: Melanges, Derniers Ecrits, Discours de Reception, Vol. 14. 1975. 150.00 (*0-686-54597-4*) Fr & Eur.

— Oeuvres Completes: Theatre: Cheri, la Vagabonde, l'Enfant et les Sortileges, Vol. 13. 1975. 150.00 (*0-686-54596-6*) Fr & Eur.

— The Other One. Tait, Elizabeth & Senhouse, Roger, trs. LC 70-178783. 160p. 1972. reprint ed. lib. bdg. 55.00 (*0-8371-6295-5*, COTO, Greenwood Pr) Greenwood.

An Asterisk (*) at the beginning of an entry indicates that the title is appearing for the first time.

— The Other Woman. LC 79-173201. Orig. Title: Mon Ami Valentine. 1972. write for info. (*0-672-51651-9*) Macmillan.

— La Paix Chez les Betes. 1984. pap. 28.95 (*0-7859-5237-3*) Fr & Eur.

— Prison et Paradis. (FRE.). 1986. pap. 31.95 (*0-8288-9151-6*, M3331) Fr & Eur.

— Le Pur et l'Impur. (FRE.). 191p. 1971. pap. 11.95 (*0-8288-9149-4*, F97400) Fr & Eur.

*__Colette, Sidonie-Gabrielle.__ The Pure & the Impure. (Classics Ser.). 200p. 2000. pap. 12.95 (*0-940322-48-X*, Pub. by NY Rev Bks) Midpt Trade.

Colette, Sidonie-Gabrielle. La Retraite Sentimentale. (FRE.). 256p. 1972. pap. 10.95 (*0-7859-1702-0*, 2070361357) Fr & Eur.

— La Retraite Sentimentale. (Folio Ser.: No. 135). (FRE.). pap. 8.95 (*2-07-036135-7*) Schoenhof.

— Retreat from Love. Crosland, Margaret, tr. LC 79-19831. 240p. 1980. reprint ed. pap. 10.00 (*0-15-676588-8*, Harvest Bks) Harcourt.

— The Ripening Seed. 128p. 1996. pap. 11.95 (*0-14-018321-3*, Penguin Classics) Viking Penguin.

— Seconde. (FRE.). 1955. pap. 10.95 (*0-8288-9162-1*, F97311) Fr & Eur.

— Sido. (FRE.). 1958. pap. 10.95 (*0-8288-9163-X*, F97320) Fr & Eur.

— La Vagabonde. (FRE.). 256p. 1958. pap. write for info. (*0-7859-4722-1*) Fr & Eur.

— Le Voyage Egoiste: Quatre Saisons. (FRE.). 1989. pap. 10.95 (*0-7859-3124-4*) Fr & Eur.

Coletti, A. Italian-Singala - Singala-Italian Lexicon: Lessico Italiano-Singalese e Singalese-Italiano. 1981. 39.95 (*0-8288-1763-4*, F58050) Fr & Eur.

Coletti, G., et al. Mathematical Models for Handling Partial Knowledge in Artificial Intelligence: Proceedings of the International School of Mathematics "G Stampacchia" 18th Workshop Held in Erice, Italy, June 19-25, 1994. LC 95-34723. (Illus.). 318p. (C). 1995. text 110.00 (*0-306-45076-3*, Kluwer Plenum) Kluwer Academic.

Colewsworthy, Robert & Bickel, Jerry. Jerry Bickel's Complete Guide to Chassis Performance. Barfield, James, ed. (Illus.). 150p. 1998. spiral bd. 129.00 (*0-9669002-1-9*) Educ Tech Consul.

Coley, A., et al, eds. General Relativity & Relativistic Astrophysics: Proceedings of the 2nd Canadian Conference on General Relativity & Relativistic Astrophysics, Toronto, Canada 14-16 May 1987. 428p. 1988. text 99.00 (*9971-5-0431-6*, ZA0480PP) World Scientific Pub.

— General Relativity & Relativistic Astrophysics: Proceedings of the 3rd Canadian Conference. 392p. (C). 1990. text 89.00 (*981-02-0175-3*) World Scientific Pub.

Coley, Andrew J. & Kay, Nicholas J. ENT Practice for the GP's Surgery. (Illus.). 98p. (Orig.). 1992. pap. text. write for info. (*0-443-04813-4*) Church.

Coley, Betty A., jt. ed. see Kelley, Philip.

Coley, David A. Introduction to Genetic Algorithms for Scientists & Engineers. 1998. 28.00 (*981-02-3602-6*) World Scientific Pub.

Coley, Henry. Clavis Astrologie Elimata: Key to the Whole Art of Astrology, 3 vols. Wiggers, Carol A., ed. Cochran, Kathleen R., tr. Incl. Vol. 1. large type ed.Tr. of Key to the Whole Art of Astrology. (Illus.). 134p. 1996. pap. 15.00 (*1-878935-26-7*); Vol. 2. large type ed.Tr. of Key to the Whole Art of Astrology. (Illus.). 220p. 1996. pap. 20.00 (*1-878935-27-5*); Vol. 3. large type ed.Tr. of Key to the Whole Art of Astrology. (Illus.). 441p. 1996. pap. 30.00 (*1-878935-28-3*); 75.00 (*1-878935-29-1*) JustUs & Assocs.

Coley, Henry, jt. auth. see Lilly, William.

Coley, Henry, tr. see Bonatus, Guido.

Coley, Henry, jt. tr. see Bonatus, Guido.

Coley, Janis, jt. auth. see Allen, Anne.

Coley, Noel George. Darwin to Einstein. Date not set. pap. text. write for info. (*0-582-49159-2*, Pub. by Addison-Wesley) Longman.

Coley, Robert S., jt. auth. see Auriemma, Michael J.

Coley, Soraya M. Proposal Writing. (Human Services Guides Ser.: Vol. 63). 160p. (C). 1990. pap. text 18.95 (*0-8039-3232-4*) Sage.

Coley, Trevor, jt. auth. see Owen, Keith.

Coley, W. B., ed. see Fielding, Henry.

Colf. Dictionary of Water: Dictionnaire de l'Eau. (ENG & FRE.). 545p. 1981. pap. 59.95 (*0-8288-1484-8*, F38100) Fr & Eur.

Colf, Mary K. & Oszustowicz, Len. 301 Random Acts of Kindness: A User's Guide to a Giving Life. LC 94-13555. 128p. (Orig.). 1994. pap. 7.95 (*1-56530-135-8*) Summit TX.

Colfax, David & Colfax, Micki. Hard Times in Paradise: An American Family's Struggle to Carve Out a Homestead in California's Redwood Mountains. (Illus.). 1997. 19.95 (*0-939665-06-9*) Mountain Hse Pr.

— Homeschooling for Excellence. 150p. (Orig.). 1988. pap. 11.99 (*0-939665-00-X*) Mountain Hse Pr.

— Homeschooling for Excellence. 128p. (Orig.). 1988. mass mkt. 12.99 (*0-446-38986-2*, Pub. by Warner Bks) Little.

Colfax, David, ed. see Crepin, Joseph.

Colfax, Micki, jt. auth. see Colfax, David.

Colfax, Micki, ed. see Crepin, Joseph.

Colfelter, Charles T. & Rothschild, Michael, eds. Studies of Supply & Demand in Higher Education. LC 92-37932. (National Bureau of Economic Research Project Report Ser.). (Illus.). 304p. (C). 1993. 45.00 (*0-226-11054-0*) U Ch Pr.

*__Colfen, H., ed.__ Analytical Ultracentrifugation V. (Progress in Colloid & Polymer Science Ser.: Vol. 113). 260p. 1999. 159.00 (*3-540-66175-1*) Spr-Verlag.

*__Colfen, Hermann.__ Werbeweltbilder im Wandel: Eine Linguistische Untersuchung Deutscher Werbeanzeigen im Zeitvergleich, 1960-1990. 226p. 1999. 51.95 (*3-631-35087-2*) P Lang Pubng.

Colfer, Carol J., et al. Beyond Slash & Burn: Building on Indigenous Management of Borneo's Tropical Rain Forests. LC 97-17675. (Advances in Economic Botany Ser.: Vol. 11). xi, 236p. 1997. pap. 28.00 (*0-89327-405-4*) NY Botanical.

Colfer, George & Gibbons, Emma. Total Fitness for the Physical Educator: A Programmed Approach for Assessment. 138p. (C). 1990. pap. text 9.80 (*0-87563-412-5*) Stipes.

Colfer, George R. Aerobic Running: Help Yourself to Fitness & Fun. 144p. (C). 1993. per. 12.95 (*0-8403-8906-X*) Kendall-Hunt.

Colfer, Michael A. Morality, Kindred, & Ethnic Boundary: A Study of the Oregon Old Believers. LC 83-45351. (Immigrant Communities & Ethnic Minorities in the U. S. & Canada Ser.: No. 3). (Illus.). 1985. 37.50 (*0-404-19404-4*) AMS Pr.

Colflesh, Linda. Making Friends: Training Your Dog Positively. (Illus.). 224p. 1990. 19.95 (*0-87605-687-7*) Howell Bks.

Colford, Paul. The King of All Media. 1996. 23.95 (*0-614-95713-3*) St Martin.

Colford, Paul D. Howard Stern: King of All Media. 1997. mass mkt. 6.99 (*0-312-96221-5*) St Martin.

*__Colford, Paul D.__ Howard Stern: King of All Media - The Unauthorized Biography of Howard Stern. (Illus.). 271p. 1999. reprint ed. 24.00 (*0-7881-6336-1*) DIANE Pub.

Colford, Paul D. North Dakota Criminal & Traffic Law Manual, 1993 Edition. 25.00 (*0-614-05933-X*, MICHIE) LEXIS Pub.

Colford, William E., tr. see de Vega, Lope.

Colgan, Becky & Youngberg, Barbara J. Nursing & Malpractice Risks: Understanding the Law. 3rd ed. 160p. (C). 1996. pap. text 49.95 (*1-878025-91-0*) Western Schls.

Colgan, Becky, ed. see Gustafson, Nancy.

Colgan, Becky, ed. see Huber, J.

Colgan, Becky, ed. see Severance, Tom.

Colgan, Becky, ed. see York, Gloria.

Colgan, Bill. World War II Fighter Bomber Pilot. 2nd ed. (Illus.). 209p. 1996. pap. 16.95 (*0-89745-105-8*) Sunflower U Pr.

Colgan, Bryan, ed. The New Best of Sheryl Crow. (Orig.). Date not set. pap. 12.95 (*0-7692-0072-9*, 0067B) Wrner Bros.

Colgan, Charles S. Places Left Behind: Regional Development Policies in the United States & Canada, 1930-1990. 328p. 1996. text 50.00 (*0-8020-0433-4*); pap. text 21.95 (*0-8020-7223-2*) U of Toronto Pr.

Colgan, Charles S., ed. Sustaining Coastal Resources: Economics & the Natural Sciences. (Orig.). 1995. pap. 11.95 (*0-939561-23-9*) Univ South ME.

Colgan, Charles S. & Slavet, Joseph S., eds. The Fiscal Crisis in the States: Lessons from the Northeast. 232p. (Orig.). 1993. pap. 11.95 (*0-939561-16-6*) Univ South ME.

Colgan, Helen H., et al. Eight Writers Seeking Readers. Evans, Robert L., ed. LC 85-90996. (Illus.). 1985. pap. 10.00 (*0-9606698-2-5*) R L Evans.

*__Colgan, Jenny.__ Amanda's Wedding. 288p. 2001. 23.95 (*0-446-52647-9*) Warner Bks.

Colgan, Karina. You Have to Scream with Your Mouth Shut: Violence in the Home. 190p. 1996. pap. 16.95 (*1-86023-018-0*) Dufour.

Colgan, M. Flavonoid Revolution: Grape Seed Extract & Other Flavonoids Against Disease. 1997. pap. text 3.99 (*1-896817-05-X*) ApPubng.

— Prevent Cancer Now! Arm Yourself with Powerful Weapons Against Cancer. 2000. pap. text 12.95 (*1-896817-07-6*) ApPubng.

Colgan, Michael. Antioxidants: The Real Story. 1999. pap. 4.99 (*1-896817-11-4*) ApPubng.

*__Colgan, Michael.__ Beat Arthritis: New Protocols for the Treatment of Arthritis. 1999. pap. 14.95 (*1-896817-15-7*) ApPubng.

— Best Arthritis: The World Renowned Colgan Institute Reveals Its Programs for Nutritional Treatment. 2000. pap. 14.95 (*1-896817-23-8*) ApPubng.

Colgan, Michael. The New Nutrition: Medicine for the Millennium. (Your Personal Guide to Health Ser.). (Illus.). 261p. 1995. 24.95 (*0-9624840-6-7*); pap. 14.95 (*0-9624840-7-5*) Colgan Inst.

— La Nueva Nutricion: Una Medicina para el Proximo Milenio. 1998. pap. text 17.95 (*84-7808-197-6*) Sirio Editorial.

— Optimum Sports Nutrition: Your Competitive Edge - A Nutritional Guide for Optimizing Athletic Performance. 562p. 1993. pap. 24.95 (*0-9624840-5-9*) Advanced Research Pr.

— Prevent Cancer Now: Your Guide to Self Protection. 2nd Edition. (Illus.). 140p. 1992. 19.50 (*0-9624840-2-4*) Colgan Inst.

*__Colgan, Michael.__ Protect Your Prostate: The World-Renowned Colgan Institute Reveals Its Program for a Healthy Prostate. 2000. pap. 12.95 (*1-896817-17-3*) ApPubng.

— Right Protein for Muscle & Strength. (Illus.). 1999. pap. 4.99 (*1-896817-09-2*) ApPubng.

Colgan, Michael. Win the War Against Arthritis. 1999. pap. 4.99 (*1-896817-20-3*) ApPubng.

— Yr Prsnl Vitamin Pfl. LC 82-12560. 1982. pap. 10.00 (*0-688-01506-9*, Quil) HarperTrade.

Colgan, Micheal. Prevent Cancer Now. 2nd ed. (Illus.). 140p. 1992. pap. text 9.95 (*0-9624840-3-2*, C I Pubns CA) Colgan Inst.

Colgan, Patrick. Animal Motivation. (Chapman & Hall Animal Behavior Ser.). (Illus.). 160p. 1989. pap. 19.95 (*0-412-31860-1*) Chapman & Hall.

Colgan, Susan. Pieces of Me. 1999. pap. 11.95 (*0-9656748-4-3*) Winter Again.

*__Colgan, Timothy.__ Rory Stays Safe. (Staying Safe Stories Ser.). (Illus.). 35p. 1999. pap. 19.95 (*0-9675587-0-0*) T J S Security.

Colgan, Tobias. Gentle Shepherd Choral Book. 88p. 1997. pap. 9.95 (*0-915531-58-5*) OR Catholic.

Colgate. A Roar from the Valley. 1990. write for info. (*0-316-99900-8*) Little.

*__Colgate, Doris.__ Sailing. LC 98-37840. 174p. 1999. pap. 14.95 (*0-07-006720-1*, Ragged Mntain) McGraw-Hill Prof.

*__Colgate, Isabel.__ Winter Journey. 2001. 24.00 (*1-58243-122-1*) Counterpt DC.

Colgate, Stephen. Fundamentals of Sailing, Cruising & Racing. 2nd expanded rev. ed. (Illus.). 380p. 1996. 35.00 (*0-393-03811-4*) Norton.

— Steve Colgate on Sailing. Wiley, Marcia, ed. (Illus.). 1991. 29.95 (*0-393-02903-4*) Norton.

Colgate, Steve. Colgate's Basic Sailing. (Illus.). 1991. pap. 9.95 (*0-914747-02-9*) Offshore Sail Schl.

— Fundamentals of Sailing, Cruising, & Racing. 1996. text 35.00 (*0-07-006112-2*) McGraw.

— Performance Sailing. (Illus.). 1993. pap. 9.95 (*0-914747-03-7*) Offshore Sail Schl.

— Steve Colgate on Cruising. (Illus.). (Orig.). 1990. pap. 12.95 (*0-914747-01-0*) Offshore Sail Schl.

Colgate, Steve & Close, Skip. U. S. Sailing Official Logbook of Sailing. rev. ed. 1993. pap. text 8.95 (*1-882502-31-0*) US Sail Assn.

Colgate, Steve, ed. see Kantor, John.

Colgate, Terry & Diggle, Martin. Riding a Dressage Test. 120p. 1990. pap. 30.00 (*0-85131-464-3*, Pub. by J A Allen) St Mut.

Colgin, Mary L. One Potato, Two Potato, Three Potato, Four! 165 Chants for Children. Orig. Title: Chants for Children. 77p. 1988. reprint ed. pap. 9.95 (*0-87659-116-0*) Gryphon Hse.

Colgin, Mary L. & Van der Ven, Thea S. It's Your Story - Pass It On. LC 86-70785. (Illus.). 96p. (Orig.). 1986. pap. 9.95 (*0-9604582-2-0*) Colgin Pub.

Colglazier, R. Scott. Circling the Divine: Spiritual Reflections on the Journey. LC 98-17313. 168p. 1998. pap. 14.99 (*0-8272-0473-6*) Chalice Pr.

— Finding a Faith That Makes Sense. 144p. (Orig.). 1996. pap. 14.99 (*0-8272-1020-5*) Chalice Pr.

— Touchstones: Spiritual Awakenings in Everyday Life. LC 99-38237. 1999. pap. 15.99 (*0-8272-3636-0*) Chalice Pr.

*__Colglazier, R. Scott, ed.__ Yes to Peace: Sermons on the Shalom of God. 2001. pap. 18.99 (*0-8272-4409-6*) Chalice Pr.

*__Colgrass, Michael.__ My Lessons with Kumi: How I Learned to Perform with Confidence in Life & Work. LC 99-88119. (Illus.). 440p. 2000. pap. 18.50 (*0-911226-40-0*) Real People.

Colgrave, Bertram, ed. Two Lives of Saint Cuthbert. LC 69-13862. 375p. 1968. reprint ed. lib. bdg. 70.00 (*0-8371-0355-X*, COST, Greenwood Pr) Greenwood.

Colgrave, Bertram, ed. & tr. see Bede.

Colgrove, Marianne M., jt. auth. see Crandall, Richard E.

Colgrove, Melba, et al. How to Survive the Loss of a Love. 212p. 1991. 10.00 (*0-931580-45-5*) Prelude Press.

— How to Survive the Loss of a Love. 212p. 1993. pap. 5.95 (*0-931580-43-9*) Prelude Press.

— Surviving, Healing & Growing: The How to Survive the Loss of a Love Workbook. 198p. 1991. pap. 11.95 (*0-931580-46-3*) Prelude Press.

Colhocker, Lawrence, ed. see Arnandez, Richard, et al.

Colhoon, J. W., tr. Discourses, 5 vols., 2. (Loeb Classical Library: No. 257, 339, 358, 376, 385). 448p. 1939. 18.95 (*0-674-99374-8*) HUP.

Colhour, Olive M. Creating Lapidary Art: Working with Gemstones. (Illus.). 200p. 1998. pap. 44.95 (*0-9662121-0-X*) CAT Graphics.

Coli, Waltraud B. & Lobban, Richard A. The Cape Verdeans in Rhode Island: A Brief History. (Rhode Island Ethnic Heritage Pamphlet Ser.). (Illus.). 52p. (Orig.). 1990. pap. 6.75 (*0-917012-94-1*) RI Pubns Soc.

Colianni, John. From Danny Boy to Black Hole Sun. 64p. (YA). 1995. pap. 14.95 (*0-89524-994-4*) Cherry Lane.

Colicchio, Joseph. High Gate Health & Beauty. LC 98-83259. 361p. 2000. pap. 14.95 (*0-88739-251-2*) Creat Arts Bk.

*__Colicchio, Tom, et al.__ Think Like a Chef. LC 00-22983. (Illus.). 288p. 2000. 37.50 (*0-609-60485-6*) C Potter.

Colie, Christopher W. Naked to Love: Letters from a Young American in Panama, 1952-54. LC 99-24688. 232p. 1999. 19.95 (*1-57178-082-3*, Pub. by Coun Oak Bks) SPD-Small Pr Dist.

Colie, Rosalie L. Light & Enlightenment: A Study of the Cambridge Platonists & the Dutch Arminans. 176p. reprint ed. pap. 50.20 (*0-608-31001-8*, 2050767) Bks Demand.

Colie, Rosalie L. & Flahiff, F. T., eds. Some Facets of King Lear: Essays in Prismatic Criticism. LC 73-81755. 256p. reprint ed. pap. 79.40 (*0-608-12901-1*, 202361600033) Bks Demand.

Coligan, John E. Current Protocols in Immunology. 1994. 635.00 incl. cd-rom (*0-471-30660-6*) Wiley.

Coligan, John E., et al, eds. Current Protocols in Immunology. LC 90-15726. 920p. 1991. pap. text 635.00 (*0-471-52276-7*) Wiley.

— Current Protocols in Protein Science Vol. 1. 1995. cd-rom 495.00 (*0-471-14098-8*) Wiley.

Coligan, G. Jan & Littell, Marcia S., eds. Confronting the Holocaust: A Mandate for the 21st Century. LC 97-7205. (Studies in the Shoah (STS): Vol. XIX). 200p. 1997. 37.50 (*0-7618-0726-8*) U Pr of Amer.

Colignon, Richard A. Power Plays: Critical Events in the Institutionalization of the Tennessee Valley Authority. LC 95-39702. (SUNY Series in the Sociology of Work). 367p. (C). 1996. pap. text 24.95 (*0-7914-3012-X*) State U NY Pr.

— Power Plays: Critical Events in the Institutionalization of the Tennessee Valley Authority. LC 95-39702. (SUNY Series in the Sociology of Work). 367p. (C). 1997. text 74.50 (*0-7914-3011-1*) State U NY Pr.

Colijn, G. Jan & Littell, Marcia S., eds. The Netherlands & Nazi Genocide: Papers of the 21st Annual Scholars' Conference. LC 92-8011. (Symposium Ser.: Vol. 32). (Illus.). 560p. 1992. lib. bdg. 119.95 (*0-7734-9516-9*) E Mellen.

Colijn, Helen. Song of Survival: Women Interned. 224p. 1995. 22.95 (*1-883991-10-2*) Whte Cloud Pr.

— Song of Survival: Women Interned. (Illus.). 224p. 1997. pap. 13.95 (*1-883991-14-5*) Whte Cloud Pr.

Colijn, Hendrik. Weighing & Proportioning of Bulk Solids. 2nd ed. LC 74-77792. (Bulk Materials Handling Ser.: Vol. 3). (Illus.). 362p. (C). 1983. 60.00 (*0-87849-047-7*, Pub. by Trans T Pub) Enfield Pubs NH.

Colilli. Angels Corpse. LC 99-23106. 1999. text 45.00 (*0-312-22150-9*) St Martin.

Colilli, Paul. The Idea of a Living Spirit: Poetic Logic as a Contemporary Theory. LC 98-143699. (Toronto Studies in Semiotics). 240p. 1997. text 45.00 (*0-8020-4100-0*) U of Toronto Pr.

— Poliziano's Science of Tropes. (American University Studies: Romance Languages & Literature: Ser. 2, Vol. 98). XIV, 189p. 1988. 31.95 (*0-8204-0788-7*) P Lang Pubng.

Colimon, L. Doyle. Towards the Spiritualization of Kwanzaa. (Illus.). 25p. (Orig.). 1996. pap. write for info. (*0-9651363-2-9*) L D Colimon.

*__Colimore, Edward.__ The Philadelphia Inquirer's Guide to Historic Philadelphia. (Illus.). 220p. 2000. pap. 14.95 (*0-940159-67-8*) Camino Bks.

Colimore, Vincent J., ed. Selected Readings in Scholasticism & Education. 115p. (C). 1971. pap. text 12.95 (*0-8422-0142-4*) Irvington.

Colin & Fleur. The Resort Timeshare Industry in the Caribbean. (Regional Studies). 108p. 1994. 45.00 (*0-614-04635-1*) ARDA.

Colin, jt. auth. see Lankshear.

Colin, ed. see Townsley, David & Bjork, Russell.

Colin, A. B., ed. see Daley, C. R.

Colin, Amy D., ed. Argumentum e Silentio: International Paul Celan Symposium. xii, 452p. (C). 1986. lib. bdg. 165.40 (*0-89925-314-8*); lib. bdg. 165.40 (*3-11-010555-1*) De Gruyter.

Colin, Andrew J. Programming & Problem-Solving in ALGOL 68. LC 78-306642. (Computer Science Ser.). 251p. 1977. write for info. (*0-333-21716-0*) Macmillan.

Colin, Ann. Willie: Raising & Loving a Child with Attention Deficit Disorder. 1996. 22.95 (*0-614-19892-5*) Viking Penguin.

Colin, Christine. Philippe Starck. (Illus.). 128p. 1997. pap. 23.50 (*2-906571-63-6*) Dist Art Pubs.

Colin, Christine & Vedrenne, Elisabeth. Garouste & Bonetti. (Illus.). 128p. 1998. pap. 23.50 (*2-906571-72-5*, Pub. by Editions Dis Voir) Dist Art Pubs.

*__Colin, Cowie.__ Weddings. LC 97-14916. (Illus.). 256p. (gr. 8). 1998. 65.00 (*0-316-24661-1*) Little.

Colin, Darch. Tanzania. 2nd rev. ed. (World Bibliographical Ser.). 414p. 1996. lib. bdg. 105.00 (*1-85109-219-6*) ABC-CLIO.

Colin, Eric & Morin, Beatrice. Lexique de Droit Civil: Contrats, Responsabilite. 160p. 1993. pap. 32.95 (*0-7859-5577-1*, 2010200985) Fr & Eur.

Colin, F. & Quevauviller, P. Monitoring of Water Quality: The Contribution of Advanced Technologies. LC 98-24452. 1998. 122.50 (*0-08-043340-5*); pap. 60.50 (*0-08-043203-4*) Elsevier.

*__Colin, G. B.__ The Facial Workout: A Great Body Concept. LC 99-93379. (Illus.). 65p. 2000. 19.95 (*0-9674168-9-2*) Mercury Pubg Co.

Colin, Henri, et al. A Guide to the HPLC Literature, Vol. 1. LC 84-11967. 947p. 1984. reprint ed. pap. 200.00 (*0-7837-3533-2*, 205785600001) Bks Demand.

— A Guide to the HPLC Literature, 3 vols., Vol. 2. LC 84-11967. 973p. 1984. reprint ed. pap. 200.00 (*0-7837-3534-0*, 203433400089) Bks Demand.

Colin, J. Robert Dictionnaire des Difficultes du Francais. (FRE.). 623p. 1997. 69.95 (*0-320-00493-7*) Fr & Eur.

Colin, Jean-Paul. Dictionnaire des Difficultes du Francais. (FRE.). 640p. 1990. 95.00 (*0-7859-9218-9*) Fr & Eur.

— Dictionnaire des Difficultes du Francais. (FRE.). 676p. 1994. 34.95 (*0-7859-9199-9*) Fr & Eur.

— Larousse Dictionnaire de l'Argot. (FRE.). 763p. 1990. 79.95 (*0-7859-7646-9*, 2033403238) Fr & Eur.

*__Colin, Jean Phillipe & Crawford, Eric W.__ Research on Agricultural Systems Accomplishments Perspectives & Issues. 190p. 2000. lib. bdg. 69.00 (*1-56072-826-4*) Nova Sci Pubs.

Colin, Lady. The Real Diana. 1998. text 24.95 (*0-312-19349-1*) St Martin.

Colin, Leopoldo G. Liquidos Exoticos. (Cienciapara Todos Ser.). (SPA.). pap. 6.99 (*968-16-3580-9*, Pub. by Fondo) Continental Bk.

Colin, Patrick L. Marine Invertebrates & Plants of the Living Reef. (Illus.). 512p. (YA). (gr. 7 up). 1988. 35.95 (*0-86622-875-6*, H-971) TFH Pubns.

Colin, Patrick L. & Arneson, Charles. Tropical Pacific Invertebrates: A Field Guide to Marine Invertebrates Occurring on Tropical Pacific Ocean Coral Reefs, Seagrass Beds, & Mangroves. (Illus.). 304p. (Orig.). 1995. pap. text 59.95 (*0-9645625-0-2*) Coral Reef CA.

Colin, Paul, et al. Josephine Baker & La Revue Negre: Paul Colin's Lithographs of le Tumulte Noir in Paris, 1927. LC 98-10072. (Illus.). 64p. 1998. pap. 24.95 (*0-8109-2772-1*, Pub. by Abrams) Time Warner.

C

An Asterisk (*) at the beginning of an entry indicates that the title is appearing for the first time.

Colin, Paul, jt. auth. see Lippman, Deborah.

Colin, Scipio A., 3rd, jt. ed. see Hayes, Elisabeth R.

Colin, Thomas D., jt. auth. see George, Cynnthia.

Colin, Thomas D., jt. auth. see George, Cynthia C.

Colin, Virginia L. Human Attachment. (Series in Developmental Psychology). 448p. (C). 1995. pap. 25.63 (*0-07-011839-6*) McGraw.

— Human Attachment. 448p. (C). 1996. lib. bdg. 69.95 (*1-56639-459-7*) Temple U Pr.

Colina, Jose De La, see De la Colina, Jose.

Coling, Jerome F., jt. auth. see Doerr, Arthur.

Coling, Marcia C. Activity-Based Intervention Guide: With More Than 250 Multisensory Play Ideas. (Illus.). 332p. 1998. pap. text 58.00 (*0-12-784553-4*) Acad Pr.

— Developing Integrated Programs: A Transdisciplinary Approach for Early Intervention. (Illus.). 138p. 1991. pap. text 48.00 (*0-7616-4188-2*) Commun Skill.

COLING Staff, ed. ACL Proceedings: COLING: The 1994 International Conference on Computational Linguistics. 1998. pap. text 170.00 (*1-55860-367-0*) Morgan Kaufmann.

— ACL Proceedings: COLING: The 1996 International Conference on Computational Linguistics. (C). 1998. pap. text 150.00 (*1-55860-473-1*) Morgan Kaufmann.

Colinge, J. P., ed. Physical & Technical Problems of SOI Structures & Devices: Proceedings of the NATO Advanced Research Workshop, Gurzuf, Ukraine, November 1-4, 1994. (NATO ASI - Partnership Sub-Series 3). 300p. (C). 1995. text 166.00 (*0-7923-3600-3*) Kluwer Academic.

Colinge, Jean-Pierre. Silicon-on-Insulator Technology: Materials to VLSI. (C). 1991. text 98.00 (*0-7923-9150-0*) Kluwer Academic.

— Silicon-on-Insulator Technology: Materials to VLSI. 2nd ed. LC 97-35777. 288p. 1997. text 126.50 (*0-7923-8007-X*) Kluwer Academic.

Colinin, Maurice. Guide des Monasteres, France, Belgique, Luxembourg, Suisse. 14th ed. (FRE.). 392p. 1998. pap. 59.95 (*0-7859-9673-7*) Fr & Eur.

***Colins, Andrew.** Gateway to Atlantis: The Search for the Source of a Lost Civilization. (Illus.). 448p. 2000. 26.00 (*0-7867-0810-7*, Pub. by Carroll & Graf) Publishers Group.

C

Colins, Leopoldo G. De la Maquina de Vapor Al Cero Absoluto. (Ciencia para Todos Ser.). (SPA.). pap. 6.99 (*968-16-2392-4*, Pub. by Fondo) Continental Bk.

Colinvaux, P A., ed. The Environment of Crowded Men. 1970. pap. text 10.95 (*0-8422-0086-X*) Irvington.

Colinvaux, Paul. Why Big Fierce Animals Are Rare: An Ecologist's Perspective. LC 77-71977. 264p. 1978. pap. text 13.95 (*0-691-02364-6*, Pub. by Princeton U Pr) Cal Prin Full Svc.

Colinvaux, Paul A. Ecology. 2nd ed. 704p. 1993. text 86.95 (*0-471-55860-5*) Wiley.

***Colinvaux, Paul A., et al.** Amazon Pollen Manual & Atlas. 344p. 1999. text 90.00 (*90-5702-587-6*, Harwood Acad Pubs) Gordon & Breach.

Colinvaux, R. Law of Insurance. 5th ed. (C). 1984. 600.00 (*0-7855-4105-5*, Pub. by Witherby & Co) St Mut.

Colip, Carol, intro. Olephia Leafy King: Dust & Desire, Laughter & Tears: Recollections of a Nevada Pioneer Cowgirl & Poet. 281p. 1980. lib. bdg. 46.50 (*1-56475-197-X*); fiche. write for info. (*1-56475-198-8*) U NV Oral Hist.

Colip, Lynn. Colorado's Gold Cone: Cripple Creek-Victor Gold Camp: A Hundred Year Beehive. LC 97-138024. (Illus.). 50p. (Orig.). 1996. pap. 5.00 (*0-9652382-0-2*) L Colip.

Colish, Chana. The Great Mitzvah Fair. (Illus.). 13p. (J). 1982. reprint ed. spiral bd. 11.00 (*0-8266-0356-4*, Merkos LInyonei Chinuch) Kehot Pubn Soc.

Colish, Chanah, ed. see Leiberman, Sara.

Colish, Marcia. Medieval Foundations of the Western Intellectual Tradition, 400-1400. LC 97-24370. (Illus.). 448p. 1997. 40.00 (*0-300-07142-6*) Yale U Pr.

— Medieval Foundations of the Western Intellectual Tradition, 400-1400. (Illus.). 400p. 1999. pap. text 18.00 (*0-300-07852-8*) Yale U Pr.

Colish, Marcia L. The Mirror of Language: A Study in the Medieval Theory of Knowledge. rev. ed. LC 83-3599. 356p. 1983. reprint ed. pap. 110.40 (*0-608-02688-3*, 206334100004) Bks Demand.

— The Stoic Tradition from Antiquity to the Early Middle Ages Vol. 1: Stoicism in Classical Latin Literature. 2nd ed. LC 90-46844. xii, 459p. 1990. reprint ed. pap. 71.00 (*90-04-09327-3*) Brill Academic Pubs.

— The Stoic Tradition from Antiquity to the Early Middle Ages Vol. 2: Stoicism in Christian Latin Thought Through the Sixth Century. 2nd ed. LC 90-46844. 1990. reprint ed. pap. 127.00 (*90-04-09330-3*) Brill Academic Pubs.

— The Stoic Tradition from Antiquity to the Early Middle Ages Vol. 2: Stoicism in Christian Latin Thought Through the Sixth Century. 2nd ed. LC 90-46844. xii, 342p. 1990. reprint ed. pap. 56.00 (*90-04-09328-1*) Brill Academic Pubs.

***Colitt, Leslie R.** Spy Master: The Real-Life Karla, His Moles, & the East German Secret Police. (Illus.). 302p. 2000. reprint ed. text 25.00 (*0-7881-6281-0*) DIANE Pub.

Colitt, Leslie R. Spymaster: The Real-Life Karla, His Moles & the East German Secret Police. LC 95-25065. 304p. 1995. 23.00 (*0-201-40738-8*, Pub. by Perseus Pubng) Addison-Wesley.

Coliver, Sandra, ed. The Right to Know: Human Rights & Access to Reproductive Health Information. (Pennsylvania Studies in Human Rights). 416p. (Orig.). 1996. pap. text 26.95 (*0-8122-1588-5*) U of Pa Pr.

Colker. The Law of Disability Discrimination, 2 vols., set. 58.95 (*0-87084-242-0*) Anderson Pub Co.

***Colker, Carlon.** The Greenwich Diet: Lose Fat While Gaining Health & Wellness. (Illus.). 200p. 2000. 21.95 (*1-889462-10-1*, Pub. by Advanced Research Pr) Midpt Trade.

Colker, Carlon M. Sex Pills A to Z: From Adrostenedione to Zinc, What Works & What Doesn't. (Illus.). 140p. 1999. pap. 14.95 (*1-889462-07-1*) Advanced Research Pr.

Colker, Jay & Niswonger, Dennis. What Do I Do If . . . ? Practical Solutions to Common Parenting Problems. LC 97-72073. (Illus.). 120p. 1997. pap. 15.95 (*0-9657549-0-1*) InfoTele.

— What Do I Do If . . . ? (Site Licensed Version) Practical Solutions to Common Parenting Problems. (Illus.). 134p. 1997. spiral bd. 89.95 (*0-9657549-2-8*) InfoTele.

Colker, Laura, et al. Drug-Free Schools & Children: A Primer for School Policymakers. 140p. 1990. 25.00 (*0-942348-24-9*) Am Council Drug Ed.

Colker, Laura J., jt. auth. see Dodge, Diane T.

Colker, Marvin L., ed. Analecta Dublinensia: Three Mediaeval Latin Texts in the Library of Trinity College Dublin. LC 75-1954. (Medieval Academy Bks.: No. 82). 1975. 30.00 (*0-910956-56-1*) Medieval Acad.

Colker, Rachel. Pittsburgh Zoo: A 100 Year History. 1998. write for info. (*1-57864-055-5*); pap. write for info. (*1-57864-076-8*) Donning Co.

Colker, Ruth. Abortion & Dialogue: Pro-Choice, Pro-Life, & American Law. LC 91-46603. 200p. 1992. pap. 16.95 (*0-253-20738-X*, MB-738) Ind U Pr.

— American Law in the Age of Hypercapitalism: The Worker, the Family, & the State. LC 97-33959. (Critical America Ser.). 1998. text 50.00 (*0-8147-1562-1*); pap. text 18.50 (*0-8147-1563-X*) NYU Pr.

— Hybrid: Bisexuals, Multiracials, & Other Misfits under American Law. LC 95-50157. (Critical America Ser.). 300p. (C). 1996. text 50.00 (*0-8147-1520-6*); pap. text 19.50 (*0-8147-1538-9*) NYU Pr.

— Pregnant Men: Practice, Theory, & Law. LC 94-3922. 1994. 29.95 (*0-253-31371-6*) Ind U Pr.

***Colker, Ruth & Poitras Tucker, Bonnie.** The Law of Disability Discrimination Handbook: Statutes & Regulatory Guidance. 2nd rev. ed. 488p. 1998. pap. 19.95 (*0-87084-332-X*) Anderson Pub Co.

Colker, Ruth & Tucker, Bonnie P. The Law of Disability Discrimination. 2nd ed. 734p. (C). 1998. 51.95 (*0-87084-240-4*) Anderson Pub Co.

Colkmire, Lance. Children's Church Programmer, Vol. II. LC 87-62383. 1988. 21.99 (*0-87148-188-X*) Pathway Pr.

— Kid Konnection, Vol. 1. (Illus.). (J). (gr. 1-6). 1995. 69.95 (*0-87148-480-3*) Pathway Pr.

— Kid Konnection, Vol. 2. (Illus.). (J). (gr. 1-6). 1996. 69.95 (*0-87148-481-1*) Pathway Pr.

— Welcome to the Family Vol. 3: A Church Membership Manual for Preteens. LC 93-87393. (Illus.). 78p. 1994. pap. 5.99 (*0-87148-202-9*) Pathway Pr.

Colkmire, Lance, jt. ed. see Vining, John K.

Colky, Michael, et al. Managing & Developing People in the Virtual Organization. Date not set. write for info. (*1-57524-080-7*) Krieger.

Coll, Alberto R. Should the Reagan Administration Have Signed the U. N. Convention on the Law of the Sea? (Pew Case Studies in International Affairs). 50p. (C). 1994. pap. text 3.50 (*1-56927-403-7*) Geo U Inst Dplmcy.

— The Wisdom of Statecraft: Sir Herbert Butterfield & the Philosophy of International Politics. LC 85-1535. xvii, 173p. (C). 1985. 31.95 (*0-8223-0607-7*) Duke.

Coll, Blanche D. Safety Net: Welfare & Social Security, 1929-1979. LC 94-32737. 400p. (C). 1995. text 47.00 (*0-8135-2159-9*) Rutgers U Pr.

Coll, C. G., jt. ed. see Lamberty, G.

Coll, Cynthia G. & Mattei, Marie D., eds. The Psychosocial Development of Puerto Rican Women. LC 88-26047. (Illus.). 290p. 1989. 55.00 (*0-275-92345-2*, C2345, Praeger Pubs) Greenwood.

Coll, Edna. Altiplano, Vol. V. (Indice Informativo de la Novela Hispano Americana Ser.: Tomo V). (SPA.). 550p. 1992. 30.00 (*0-8477-2012-8*) U of PR Pr.

— Cayetano Coll y Toste: Sintensis de Estimulos Humanos. (SPA.). 146p. 1985. 3.40 (*0-8477-3114-6*) U of PR Pr.

— Indice Informativo de la Novela Hispano Americana: Centroamerica, Vol. 2. LC 74-235886. 343p. 1976. 8.50 (*0-8477-2003-9*) U of PR Pr.

— Indice Informativo de la Novela Hispano-Americana, Vol. 1: Las Antillas. LC 74-235886. 418p. (C). 1974. 8.50 (*0-8477-2001-2*) U of PR Pr.

— Indice Informativo de la Novela Hispanoamericana, Vol. V. 550p. 1992. 30.00 (*0-8477-2005-5*) U of PR Pr.

— Indice Informativo de la Novela Hispanoamericana: Venezuela, Tomo III. LC 74-235886. 346p. 1977. 8.50 (*0-8477-2004-7*) U of PR Pr.

— Indice Informativo de la Novela Hispanoamericana, Vol. IV: Colombia. LC 74-235886. (SPA.). 587p. 1974. 8.50 (*0-8477-2008-X*) U of PR Pr.

Coll, Gary. Mass Communication Law in Wisconsin. 92p. 1996. pap. 12.95 (*0-913507-77-6*) New Forums.

Coll, Juan C., jt. auth. see Hirshleifer, Jack.

Coll, M. & Ruberson, J. R. Predatory Heteroptera: Their Ecology & Use in Biological Control. (Thomas Say Publications in Entomology). 1997. pap. 35.00 (*0-938522-62-0*, ESATSP12) Entomol Soc.

Coll, Regina. Christianity & Feminism in Conversation. LC 93-79451. 208p. (Orig.). 1994. pap. 14.95 (*0-89622-579-8*) Twenty-Third.

— How to Understand Church & Ministry in the United States. (Adult Christian Formation Program Ser.). (Illus.). 128p. (Orig.). 1995. pap. 16.95 (*0-8245-1468-8*) Crossroad NY.

— Supervision of Ministry Students. 120p. (Orig.). 1992. pap. 11.95 (*0-8146-2040-X*) Liturgical Pr.

Coll, Steve, jt. auth. see Vise, David A.

Coll, Susan. Karlmarx.com: A Love Story. 2000. write for info. (*0-316-15060-6*) Little.

Coll, Victoria. These United States. 1140p. 1999. pap. text 49.50 (*0-536-02397-2*) Pearson Custom.

Coll, William E. Use of Public Attitude Assessment in the Development of Emergency Service Policy for the City of Austin, Texas. 218p. 1989. pap. 10.00 (*0-89940-865-6*) LBJ Sch Pub Aff.

Coll Y Cuchi, Cayetano. Historias Que Parecen Cuentos. (UPREX, Ensayo Ser.: No. 11). 215p. (C). 1972. pap. 1.50 (*0-8477-0011-9*) U of PR Pr.

Coll Y Toste, Cayetano. Cofresm: The Pirate. Ramirez-Rivera, Jose, tr. (Puerto Rico a Crayola Ser.: No. 1). (Illus.). 20p. (J). 1978. reprint ed. pap. 3.95 (*0-9601700-4-9*) Editl Libero.

— Leyendas Puertorriquenas. rev. ed. Ramirez-Rivera, Jose, tr. LC 78-73076. (SPA., Illus.). 120p. 1979. reprint ed. pap. 9.95 (*0-9601700-2-2*) Editl Libero.

— Puerto Rican Tales: Legends of Spanish Colonial Times. 4th ed. Ramirez-Rivera, Jose, tr. LC 78-108190. (Illus.). 111p. 1977. reprint ed. pap. 9.95 (*0-9601700-3-0*) Editl Libero.

Colla, E. L., jt. ed. see Setter, N.

Collaci, Dorothy. The Contender: A Study Guide. (Novel-Ties Ser.). (J). (gr. 6-8). 1989. pap. text, teacher ed., student ed. 15.95 (*0-88122-059-0*) Lrn Links.

Collacott, Raoph A. Structural Integrity Monitoring. 450p. 1986. text 69.95 (*0-412-21920-4*, 9640) Chapman & Hall.

Colladay, Morrison. Introducing Nikola Tesla Throughout Some of His Achievements: or Prodigal Genius. 80p. 1996. reprint ed. spiral bd. 12.00 (*0-7873-0190-6*) Hlth Research.

Colladay, Morrison & O'Neill, John J. Nikola Tesla: Incredible Scientist & Prodigal Genius the Life of Nikola Tesla. 76p. 1996. reprint ed. pap. 12.95 (*1-56459-738-5*) Kessinger Pub.

Colladi, Carlo. The Adventures of Pinocchio: The Ultimate Illustrated Edition. (Illus.). 160p. (J). (ps up). write for info. (*0-318-62823-6*) Bantam.

Collado-Vides, Julio, et al, eds. Integrative Approaches to Molecular Biology. (Illus.). 352p. (C). 1996. 55.00 (*0-262-03239-2*) MIT Pr.

Collados, M., et al, eds. Observational & Physical Cosmology: Second Canary Islands Winter School of Astrophysics. (Illus.). 352p. (C). 1992. text 80.00 (*0-521-41996-4*) Cambridge U Pr.

Collander, Carl E., Sr. Excursion to Europe. Collander, Lloyd, ed. LC 83-91463. (Illus.). 100p. 1985. pap. 5.95 (*0-9613100-0-6*, 100A) Three Crowns Indus.

Collander, Don. Geomancer. 272p. (Orig.). 1994. mass mkt. 5.50 (*0-441-28036-6*) Ace Bks.

Collander, Lloyd, ed. see Collander, Carl E., Sr.

Collantes, Mark. The Academy. LC 98-83256. 208p. 2000. pap. 13.95 (*0-88739-248-2*) Creat Arts Bk.

Collar, A. R. & Simpson, A. Matrix Methods & Engineering Dynamics. (Engineering Science Ser.). 513p. 1987. text 179.00 (*0-470-20271-8*) P-H.

Collar Anson, Nellie. Shattered Dreams: A Nightmare in a Nursing Home. LC 87-80849. 240p. (Orig.). Date not set. 19.95 (*0-89896-328-1*); pap. 11.95 (*0-89896-324-9*) Larksdale.

Collar, Charles S. Barnstorming to Air Safety. LC 98-75482. (Illus.). 177p. 1998. pap. 11.95 (*0-9667784-0-5*) Lysmata Publ.

Collar, Hugh. Captive in Shanghai: A Story of Internment in World War II. abr. ed. (Illus.). 256p. (C). 1991. 27.00 (*0-19-585004-1*) OUP.

Collar, N. J. & Stuart, S. N. Threatened Birds of Africa & Related Islands: The ICBP/IUCN Red Data Book, Pt. 1. (Illus.). 761p. 1993. text 50.00 (*1-56098-266-7*) Smithsonian.

Collar, N. J., et al. Birds to Watch 2: The World List of Threatened Birds. LC 96-114696. (Birdlife Conservation Ser.). 320p. 1995. pap. text 45.00 (*1-56098-528-3*) Smithsonian.

— Threatened Birds of the Americas: The ICBP/IUCN Red Data Book, Pt. 2. 3rd ed. 1150p. (C). 1993. text 75.00 (*1-56098-267-5*) Smithsonian.

Collard, ed. Euripidis: Supplices. (GRE.). 1984. 19.95 (*3-322-00149-0*, T1338, Pub. by B G Teubner) U of Mich Pr.

Collard, Andree & Contrucci, Joyce. Rape of the Wild: Man's Violence Against Animals & the Earth. LC 88-32042. 208p. 1989. 27.50 (*0-253-31514-X*); pap. 10.95 (*0-253-20519-0*, MB-519) Ind U Pr.

Collard, B., ed. see Euripides.

Collard, C., ed. see Euripides.

Collard, Christopher, compiled by. Composite Index to the 'Clarendon' Commentaries on Euripides 1938-1971. 82p. (Orig.). 1981. pap. 21.00 (*90-6088-074-9*, Pub. by Boumas Boekhuis) Gen Pub ON.

Collard, Christopher, ed. see Euripides.

Collard, Clyde & O'Brien, Paul. Family: Past, Present & Future. 292p. (C). 1995. text 52.00 (*0-536-58969-0*) Pearson Custom.

Collard, Cyril. Savage Nights. Rodarmor, William, tr. LC 93-31881. 240p. 1994. 18.95 (*0-87951-534-1*, Pub. by Overlook Pr) Penguin Putnam.

— Savage Nights. LC 93-31881. 223p. 1995. pap. 11.95 (*0-87951-580-5*, Pub. by Overlook Pr) Penguin Putnam.

Collard, D. A., et al, eds. Economic Theory & Hicksian Themes. 1985. pap. 14.95 (*0-19-828493-4*) OUP.

Collard, David. Fiscal Policy: Essays in Honour of Cedric Sandford. (Illus.). 224p. 1989. text 91.95 (*0-566-05498-1*, Pub. by Avebry) Ashgate Pub Co.

Collard, David & Deutsch, Howard. Molecular Modeling Using Chem Office. 64p. 1998. pap. 7.50 (*0-7637-0742-2*) Jones & Bartlett.

Collard, Elizabeth. Nineteenth-Century Pottery & Porcelain in Canada. 2nd rev. ed. (Illus.). 497p. 1984. 60.00 (*0-7735-0392-7*, Pub. by McG-Queens Univ Pr) CUP Services.

— The Potters' View of Canada: Canadian Scenes on Nineteenth-Century Earthenware. (Illus.). 196p. 1983. 55.00 (*0-7735-0421-4*, Pub. by McG-Queens Univ Pr) CUP Services.

Collard, Frances. Regency Furniture. (Illus.). 348p. 1996. 89.50 (*0-907462-51-0*) Antique Collect.

Collard, Jared. Sepulcher. LC 98-92312. (Illus.). 224p. 1999. pap. 9.95 (*0-9668963-0-0*) Ostaris Publ.

Collard, M. Lothian, Historical Guide. LC 99-488179. 1998. pap. 14.95 (*1-874744-45-9*, Pub. by Birlinn Ltd) Dufour.

Collard, Patrick. The Development of Microbiology. LC 81-11669. 255p. reprint ed. pap. 79.10 (*0-608-08655-X*, 206917800003) Bks Demand.

Collard, Paul M. Cambodge et Cambodgiens: Metamorphose du Royaume Khmer par une Methode Francaise de Protectorat. LC 77-87068. reprint ed. 37.50 (*0-404-16806-X*) AMS Pr.

Collard, Ron. Total Quality: Success Through People. 224p. (C). 1989. 95.00 (*0-85292-423-2*, Pub. by IPM Hse) St Mut.

— Total Quality: Success Through People. 216p. (C). 1993. 51.00 (*0-85292-511-5*, Pub. by IPM Hse) St Mut.

Collard, Sneed B., III. Acting for Nature: What Young People Around the World Have Done to Protect the Environment. LC 99-39670. (Illus.). 104p. (J). 1999. pap. 8.95 (*1-890771-24-4*, Pub. by Heyday Bks) SPD-Small Pr Dist.

— Alien Invaders: The Continuing Threat of Exotic Species. LC 96-13552. (Venture Bks.). 128p. 1996. lib. bdg. 24.00 (*0-531-11298-5*) Watts.

— Animal Dads. LC 96-22171. (Illus.). 32p. (J). 1997. 15.95 (*0-395-83621-2*) HM.

***Collard, Sneed B., III.** Animal Dads. (Illus.). 32p. (J). 2000. pap. 5.95 (*0-618-03299-1*) HM.

— Animal Dads. (Illus.). (J). 2000. 11.40 (*0-606-18207-1*) Turtleback.

Collard, Sneed B., III. Animal Dazzlers. LC 97-26725. (First Book Ser.). (J). 1998. 22.50 (*0-531-20362-X*) Watts.

— Animal Dazzlers: The Role of Brilliant Colors in Nature. (Illus.). 64p. (J). (gr. 4-6). 1999. pap. text 6.95 (*0-531-15918-3*) Watts.

— Birds of Prey: A Look at Daytime Raptors. LC 98-38196. (Watts Library: Animals). (J). (gr. 5-7). 1999. 24.00 (*0-531-20363-8*) Watts.

***Collard, Sneed B., III.** Birds of Prey: A Look at Daytime Raptors. (Watts Library). (Illus.). (J). 2000. pap. 8.95 (*0-531-16419-5*) Watts.

Collard, Sneed B., III. Creepy Creatures. (J). 1997. 12.15 (*0-606-05235-6*, Pub. by Turtleback) Demco.

— Creepy Creatures. rev. ed. LC 97-16389. (Illus.). 32p. (J). (ps-3). 1997. 15.95 (*0-88106-837-3*); pap. 6.95 (*0-88106-836-5*) Charlesbridge Pub.

— Criaturas Espeluznantes (Creepy Creatures) LC 93-41497. (SPA., Illus.). 32p. (J). (ps-3). 1993. pap. 6.95 (*0-88106-423-8*) Charlesbridge Pub.

— Criaturas Espeluznantes (Creepy Creatures) LC 93-41497. (SPA., Illus.). 32p. (J). (ps-4). 1993. lib. bdg. 15.88 (*0-88106-643-5*) Charlesbridge Pub.

***Collard, Sneed B., III.** A Firefly Biologist at Work. LC 00-29622. (Illus.). 2001. write for info. (*0-531-11798-7*) Watts.

Collard, Sneed B., III. Forest in the Clouds. LC 98-6150. (Illus.). 32p. (J). (gr. k-5). 2000. 16.95 (*0-88106-985-X*) Charlesbridge Pub.

— Forest in the Clouds. LC 98-6150. (Illus.). 32p. (J). (ps-5). 2000. pap. 6.95 (*0-88106-986-8*) Charlesbridge Pub.

— Green Giants. LC 93-15936. (J). (gr. 1-5). 1994. 9.95 (*1-55971-222-8*, NorthWord Pr) Creat Pub Intl.

— Monteverde: Science & Scientists in a Costa Rican Cloud Forest. LC 96-49515. (Venture Books-Science). 144p. (J). 1997. lib. bdg. 24.00 (*0-531-11369-8*) Watts.

— Monteverde: Science & Scientists in a Costa Rican Cloud Forest. (Venture Books-Science). (Illus.). (YA). (gr. 7 up). 1998. pap. 9.95 (*0-531-15901-9*) Watts.

— 1000 Years Ago on Planet Earth. LC 98-43243. (Illus.). 32p. 1999. 15.00 (*0-395-90866-3*) HM.

— Our Natural Homes: Exploring Terrestrial Biomes of North & South America. LC 95-23978. (Illus.). 32p. (J). (gr. k-5). 1996. pap. 6.95 (*0-88106-928-0*) Charlesbridge Pub.

— Our Natural Homes: Exploring Terrestrial Biomes of North & South America. LC 95-23978. (Illus.). 32p. (J). (ps-3). 1996. 16.95 (*0-88106-929-9*) Charlesbridge Pub.

— Our Wet World. LC 97-11873. (Illus.). 32p. (J). (ps-3). 1998. pap. 6.95 (*0-88106-268-5*) Charlesbridge Pub.

— Our Wet World. LC 97-11873. (Illus.). 32p. (J). (gr. 8-12). 1998. 16.95 (*0-88106-267-7*) Charlesbridge Pub.

— Sea Snakes. LC 91-77604. (Illus.). 32p. (J). (gr. 2 up). 1997. pap. 7.95 (*1-56397-690-0*) Boyds Mills Pr.

— Smart Survivors. LC 93-19650. (J). (gr. 1-5). 1994. 9.95 (*1-55971-224-4*, NorthWord Pr) Creat Pub Intl.

***Collard, Sneed B., III.** Smart Survivors. (Illus.). 2000. pap. 7.95 (*1-55971-750-5*) Creat Pub Intl.

Collard, Sneed B., III. Te Asustan? Criaturas Espeluznantes. 1994. 12.15 (*0-606-08271-9*, Pub. by Turtleback) Demco.

***Collard, Sneed B., III.** Tough Terminators. (Illus.). 2000. pap. 7.95 (*1-55971-633-9*) Creat Pub Intl.

— A Whale Biologist at Work. LC 99-40941. (J). 2000. 22.50 (*0-531-11786-3*) Watts.

***Collard, Sneed B., III & Jenkins, Steve.** Making Animal Babies. LC 99-35797. 32p. (J). 2000. 16.00 (*0-395-95317-0*) HM.

Collas, Sara F., jt. auth. see Neal, Arthur G.

Collato, Richard, ed. see Lewis, Myron.

Collaton, Elizabeth, jt. auth. see Bartsch, Charles.

An Asterisk (*) at the beginning of an entry indicates that the title is appearing for the first time.

Collatz. Differential Equations. text 103.00 (0-471-99860-5) Wiley.

Collatz, K. G, ed. see Sohal, R. S.

Collatz, Lothar, ed. Numerical Treatment of Eigenvalue Problems. (International Series of Numerical Mathematics: No. 83, Vol. 4). 264p. 1987. 84.00 (0-8176-1856-2) Birkhauser.

Collatz, Lothar, et al, eds. Numerical Methods of Approximation Theory. (International Series of Numerical Mathematics: No. 81). 264p. 1987. 84.00 (0-8176-1855-4) Birkhauser.

— Numerical Methods of Approximation Theory, Vol. 7. (International Series of Numerical Mathematics: Vol. 67). (ENG & GER.). 148p. 1984. 42.50 (3-7643-1580-6) Birkhauser.

— Numerische Methoden bei Optimierungsaufgaben, 3 vols., Vol. 2. (International Series of Numerical Mathematics: Nos. 17, 23 & 36). (GER., Illus.). 166p. 1980. 32.95 (0-8176-0732-3) Birkhauser.

Collatz, Lothar & Meinardus, Gunter, eds. Numerische Methoden der Approximationstheorie, 4 vols., Vol. 3. (International Series of Numerical Mathematics: Nos. 16, 26, 30 & 42). (GER., Illus.). 334p. 1980. 54.00 (0-8176-0824-9) Birkhauser.

Collatz, Lothar & Wetterling, W. Optimization Problems. Hadsack, P. R., tr. from GER. (Applied Mathematical Sciences Ser.: Vol. 17). (Illus.). 370p. (Orig.). 1975. 72.95 (0-387-90143-4) Spr-Verlag.

Collatz, Lothar, ed. see Albrecht, Julius.

Collatz, Lothar, jt. ed. see Albrecht, Julius.

Collay, Casey, jt. auth. see Antonini, Orlando.

Collay, Michelle, et al. Learning Circles: Creating Conditions for Professional Development. LC 98-9058. (1-Off Ser.). (Illus.). 168p. 1998. 51.95 (0-8039-6675-X, 82113); pap. 22.95 (0-8039-6676-8, 82114) Corwin Pr.

Collay, Ryan & Dubrow, Joanne. Stuartship. (Illus.). 40p. (J). (gr. k-3). 1998. pap. 9.95 (0-9667394-0-X) Flowerpr Bks.

Collazo, J. L. Spanish-English, Spanish Encyclopedic Dictionary of Technical Terms, 3 vols. (ENG & SPA.). 2216p. 1980. 295.00 (0-8288-0665-9, S32369) Fr & Eur.

Collazo, Javier L. English-Spanish Spanish-English Encyclopedic Dictionary of Technical Terms, 3 vols., Set. LC 79-16074. (ENG & SPA.). 1979. 215.00 (0-07-079162-7); text 215.00 (0-07-079172-4) McGraw.

Collazo, Wayne R., jt. auth. see Garcia, Irma S.

Collazos, Oscar. La Ballena Varada.Tr. of Beached Whale. (SPA., Illus.). 103p. (J). (gr. 5-7). 1994. pap. 8.95 (958-24-0160-5, Pub. by Santillana) T R Bks.

Collcutt, Martin. Five Mountains: The Rinzai Zen Monastic Institution in Medieval Japan. (East Asian Monographs: No. 85). (Illus.). 420p. (Orig.). 1981. 25.00 (0-674-30497-7) HUP.

— Five Mountains: The Rinzai Zen Monastic Institution in Medieval Japan. (Harvard East Asian Monographs: No. 85). 399p. (Orig.). (C). 1995. pap. text 19.00 (0-674-30498-5) HUP.

Collcutt, Martin, et al. Cultural Atlas of Japan. (Cultural Atlas Ser.). (Illus.). 240p. 1988. 45.00 (0-8160-1927-4) Facts on File.

Colldeweih, Jack & Goldstein, Kalman. Graphic Opinions: Editorial Cartoonists & Their Art. LC 97-52131. 1998. 45.95 (0-87972-757-8); pap. 24.95 (0-87972-758-6) Bowling Green Univ Popular Press.

Colle, Gisela. The Star Tree. Lanning, Rosemary, tr. LC 97-7542. (Illus.). 32p. (J). (gr. k-3). 1997. 15.95 (1-55858-741-1, Pub. by North-South Bks NYC); lib. bdg. 15.88 (1-55858-742-X, Pub. by North-South Bks NYC) Chronicle Bks.

Colle, M. P. & Rivera, Guadalupe. Las Fiestas de Frida. (SPA.). 1994. 35.00 (0-517-70044-1, Crown) Crown Pub Group.

Colle, Marie-Pierre. Houses of Puebla. LC 97-28293. 1998. text 50.00 (0-86565-966-4) Vendome.

— Mexico: Casas del Pacifico. Loera, Gabriel, ed. LC 94-71534. (SPA., Illus.). 224p. 1994. 55.00 (1-883051-02-9) ALTI Pub.

— Mexico: Houses of the Pacific. Loera, Gabriel, ed. LC 94-71535. (Illus.). 224p. 1994. 55.00 (1-883051-01-0) ALTI Pub.

Colle, Marie-Pierre, jt. auth. see Rivera, Guadalupe.

Colle, Marie-Pierre, jt. text see Ashton, Dore.

Colle, Ralph Del, see Del Colle, Ralph.

Colle, Royal, et al. Superfortress over Japan: Twenty-Four Hours with a B-29. (Illus.). 96p. 1996. pap. 9.98 (0-87938-976-1) MBI Pubg.

Collecium of Cuban Economists Staff. La Economia de Cuba: Pasado, Presente y Futuro: The Cuban Economy: Past, Present & Future. LC 98-73272. (Illus.). v, 195p. 1998. pap. 30.00 (0-9668189-0-3, Colegio De Economistas) Collegium Cuban.

Collecott. Denise Levertov, Revisited. 1997. 21.95 (0-8057-4503-3, Twyne) Mac Lib Ref.

Collecott, Nan, ed. Peggles & Primroses. 136p. 1994. pap. 24.00 (0-86138-066-5, Pub. by T Dalton) St Mut.

Collecters Antique Staff. Kwan Architects, 1. 1997. pap. text 19.95 (1-875498-83-4) Images Aust AT.

Collecting Consort Staff, contrib. by. Celebrating Our Spiritual Heritage: Traditional Folk Melodies. 1997. audio 9.95 (0-87793-885-7, A885COSH) Ave Maria.

Collection Development & Bibliography Committee St. Women's Studies Collection Development Policies. 122p. (Orig.). 1992. pap. text 35.95 (0-8389-7596-8) ALA.

Collective Bargaining Negotiations & Contracts Sta, ed. Basic Patterns in Union Contracts. 14th ed. 135p. 1995. pap. 35.00 (0-87179-895-6) BNA Books.

Collective Bargaining Negotiations & Contracts Staff. 10 Relatos de Qencia Ficcion. 1995. pap. text 14.95 (84-01-54001-1) Plaza.

— 10 Relatos de Suspense. 1996. pap. text 14.95 (84-01-54000-3) Plaza.

Collective Group Researchers in Colorado Staff. Adult Cyberguide: A Must Have Guide for Anyone Who Wants to Explore the Steamier Side of the Internet. xvi, 592p. 1997. pap. 29.95 (0-9660413-0-5) Cyberplex.

***Collector Books Staff, et al.** Schroeder's Antiques Price Guide: Identification & Values of over 50,000 Antiques & Collectibles. 19th ed. (Illus.). 608p. 2000. pap. 14.95 (1-57432-204-4) Collector Bks.

Collector, Stephen. Law of the Range: Portraits of Old-Time Brand Inspectors. LC 91-73462. (Illus.). 132p. 1991. 45.00 (0-944439-45-4) Clark City Pr.

Collectors Books Ltd. Staff. The Little Ships of Dunkirk. (C). 1989. 110.00 (0-7855-4940-4, Pub. by Fuel Metallurgical Jrnl) St Mut.

Collectors Classic Antiques Staff. Michael Graves. 1999. 59.95 (1-875498-73-7) Images Aust AT.

Collectors Club. Blue Sky Architecture & Planning, Inc., 1. 1999. pap. text 35.00 (1-86470-028-9) Images.

— House & House Architects, 1. 1999. pap. text 35.00 (1-86470-029-7) Images.

— International Architecture Yearbook, 1. 1999. pap. text 99.50 (1-86470-017-3) Images.

— Ken Woolley, 1. LC 99-495114. 1999. 59.95 (1-86470-024-6) Images.

Collectors Club Library Staff. Philately: The Catalog of the Collectors Club Library. 1974. 160.00 (0-8161-1538-9, G K Hall & Co) Mac Lib Ref.

— UnDivided: The Projects of Moore Ruble Yudell In Berlin, 1980-2000, 1. 1999. pap. text 29.95 (1-86470-026-2) Images.

***Collectors' Guide Publishers Staff.** Glam. (20th Century Rock & Roll Ser.). 2000. pap. 13.95 (1-896522-26-2) CN06.

— Last Wacks. 1996. pap. 24.95 (0-9698080-3-8) Hot Wacks.

— Punk. (20th Century Rock & Roll Ser.). 2000. pap. 13.95 (1-896522-27-0) CN06.

— Women in Rock. (20th Century Rock & Roll Ser.). 2000. pap. 13.95 (1-896522-29-7) CN06.

Collectors' Guide Publishing Staff. Hot Wacks. 1997. pap. 17.95 (0-9698080-8-9) Hot Wacks.

***Collectors' Guide Publishing Staff, ed.** Heavy Metal. (20th Century Rock & Roll Ser.). 2000. pap. 13.95 (1-896522-47-5) CN06.

***Collectors' Information Bureau Staff.** Collectibles Market Guide & Price Index: Today's Most Comprehensive Guide to Collectibles. 18th rev. ed. (Illus.). 560p. 2000. pap. 24.95 (0-87341-943-X, CIB18) Krause Pubns.

Collectors' Information Bureau Staff. Collectibles Price Guide & Directory to Secondary Market Retailers 1999. 9th ed. (Illus.). 248p. 1999. per. 14.95 (0-87341-747-X, Pub. by Collectors Info) Krause Pubns.

Collectors' Information Bureau Staff, ed. Collectibles Market Guide & Price Index: Today's Most Comprehensive Guide to Limited Edition. 14th rev. ed. LC 95-71406. (Illus.). 561p. 1996. pap. 23.95 (0-930785-22-3, CIB) Collectors Info.

— Collectibles Market Guide & Price Index: Today's Most Comprehensive Guide to Limited Edition. 16th rev. ed. LC 95-71406. (Illus.). 648p. 1998. pap. 23.95 (0-930785-26-6, CIB) Collectors Info.

— Collectibles Price Guide: Directory to Secondary Market Dealers. 7th rev. ed. 245p. (Orig.). 1997. pap. 14.95 (0-930785-48-7, CIB) Collectors Info.

Collectors Informations Bureau Staff. Collectibles Market Guide & Price Index. 17th ed. LC 93-660552. (Illus.). 640p. 1999. pap. 23.95 (0-87341-762-3) Krause Pubns.

Collectors Press Staff. Maxfield Parrish. (Edison Mazda Collection). (Illus.). 40p. 1995. pap. 17.50 (0-9635202-3-7, 20237) Collectors Pr.

Collectors Publishing Co. Staff. Ty Beanie Babies: Collector's Value Guide, Summer 1998 Edition. 1998. pap. write for info. (1-888914-29-7) CheckerBee.

— Ty Beanie Babies Collector's Pocket Planner, 1. 1999. pap. text 2.95 (1-888914-58-0) CheckerBee.

— Ty Beanie Babies Summer Value Guide: 1999 Edition. 1999. pap. text 9.95 (1-888914-57-2) CheckerBee.

Collectors' Publishing Company, Inc. Staff. Ty's Beanie Babies Winter 1999 Value Guide. (Illus.). 160p. 1998. pap. 9.95 (1-888914-37-8) CheckerBee.

— Ty's Stuffed Animals: The Complete Story & Value Guide. (Illus.). 170p. 1998. pap. 14.95 (1-888914-35-1) CheckerBee.

Collectors' Publishing Company, Inc. Staff, ed. Hallmark Value Collectors' Guide. Date not set. pap. 19.95 (1-888914-06-8) CheckerBee.

— Pufkins. (Illus.). (Orig.). Date not set. pap. 7.95 (1-888914-45-9) CheckerBee.

***Colledge, Anne.** Northern Lights. 94p. (YA). (gr. 3 up). 2000. 12.00 (1-902628-75-6) Pipers Ash.

Colledge, Edmund, ed. The Latin Poems of Richard Ledrede, OFM, Bishop of Ossory, 1317-1360. 164p. text 29.14 (0-88844-030-8) Brill Academic Pubs.

Colledge, Edmund, et al, eds. Julian of Norwich, "Showings" LC 77-90953. (Classics of Western Spirituality Ser.). 384p. 1978. pap. 19.95 (0-8091-2091-7) Paulist Pr.

Colledge, Edmund & McGinn, Bernard, trs. Everything As Divine: The Wisdom of Meister Eckhart. LC 96-13803. (Spiritual Samplers Ser.). 96p. (Orig.). 1996. pap. 1.95 (0-8091-3675-9) Paulist Pr.

— Meister Eckhart: The Essential Sermons, Commentaries, Treatises & Defense. (Classics of Western Spirituality Ser.). 1987. pap. 22.95 (0-8091-2370-3) Paulist Pr.

Colledge, Edmund & Walsh, James, trs. The Life of the Soul: The Wisdom of Julian of Norwich. LC 96-14803. (Spiritual Samplers Ser.). 96p. (Orig.). 1996. pap. 1.95 (0-8091-3673-2) Paulist Pr.

Colledge, Edmund, ed. see Julian of Norwich.

Colledge, Edmund, tr. see Suso, Henry.

Colledge, Eric, tr. see Tauler, John.

Colledge, M. Migration & Health: Towards an Understanding of the Health Care Needs of Ethnic Minorities. 210p. 1987. pap. text 17.00 (92-890-1045-2, 1340032) World Health.

Colledge, M. A. The Parthian Period. (Iconography of Religions Ser.: Vol. XIV-3). (Illus.). xiv, 47p. 1986. pap. 66.50 (90-04-07115-6) Brill Academic Pubs.

Colledge, Tony. Pascal's Triangle. (Illus.). 28p. (Orig.). 1992. pap., teacher ed. 10.95 (0-906212-84-7, Pub. by Tarquin Pubns) Parkwest Pubns.

Collee. Practical Medical Microbiology. 14th ed. (C). 1997. text 127.00 (0-443-04721-9, W B Saunders Co) Harcrt Hlth Sci Grp.

Collee, et al. Mackie & McCartney's Medical Microbiology, Vol. 2. 13th ed. (Illus.). 928p. 1989. text 59.00 (0-443-02332-8) Church.

Collee, J. G. Applied Medical Microbiology. 2nd ed. (Illus.). 158p. 1981. pap. text 21.00 (0-632-00853-9) Blackwell Sci.

College. Nursing Book. 1984. 6.95 (0-316-15182-3, Little Brwn Med Div) Lppncott W & W.

College, ed. Poster Brochure Little. 6th ed. 1997. pap. text 11.00 (0-673-54296-3) P-H.

College & University Personnel Assoc. Staff, ed. National Faculty Salary Survey by Discipline & Rank in Private Colleges & Universities. 1995. 40.00 (1-878240-45-5) Coll & U Personnel.

— National Faculty Salary Survey by Discipline & Rank in Private Colleges & Universities, 1994-95. 1995. 40.00 (1-878240-44-7) Coll & U Personnel.

College Art Association of America Staff, et al. The Index of Twentieth Century Artists: October 1933 to April 1937, Vol. 7. 42.50 (0-685-11367-1, 19511) Ayer.

College Board Colloquium on College Affordability & Enrollment Challenges Staff. A Report on the College Board Colloquium on College Affordability & Enrollment Challenges. LC 99-174849. ix, 66 p. 1998. write for info. (0-87447-609-7) College Bd.

***College Board Staff.** CLEP Official Study Guide 2001. 12th ed. 528p. 2000. pap. 18.00 (0-87447-643-7) College Bd.

College Board Staff. The CLEP Official Study Guide 2000. 500p. 1999. pap. text 18.00 (0-87447-631-3) College Bd.

— The College Board College Cost & Financial Aid Handbook 2000. LC 63-660134. 665p. 1999. pap. text 21.95 (0-87447-628-3) College Bd.

— The College Board College Handbook 2000 with College Explorer CD-Rom. 37th ed. LC 41-12971. 1623p. 1999. pap. text 25.95 incl. cd-rom (0-87447-625-9, 006259) College Bd.

— College Board Guide to High Schools. 2nd ed. 1779p. (C). 1994. pap. 79.00 (0-87447-466-3) College Bd.

— College Board Guide To 150 Popular College Majors, 2nd Ed. 1999. pap. text 18.95 (0-87447-637-2) College Bd.

— The College Board Index of Majors & Graduate Degrees 2000. 22nd ed. 699p. 1999. pap. text 21.95 (0-87447-629-1) College Bd.

— The College Board International Student Handbook of U. S. Colleges 2000. 358p. 1999. pap. text 25.95 incl. cd-rom (0-87447-630-5) College Bd.

— The College Board Scholarship Handbook 2000. 812p. 1999. pap. text 24.95 incl. cd-rom (0-87447-627-5) College Bd.

***College Board Staff.** College Cost & Financial Aid Handbook 2001. annuals 21st ed. 712p. 2000. pap. 21.95 (0-87447-646-1) College Bd.

College Board Staff. College Costs & Financial Aid Handbook, 1997. 320p. (C). 1996. pap. 16.95 (0-87447-544-9, Owl) H Holt & Co.

— The College Handbook for Transfer Students, 1997. 552p. (C). 1996. pap. 17.95 (0-87447-546-5) H Holt & Co.

— The College Handbook Foreign Student Supplement, 1997: Foreign Student Supplement, 1997. 288p. (C). 1996. pap. 16.95 (0-87447-545-7) H Holt & Co.

— The College Handbook, 1997. 1700p. (C). 1995. pap. 21.95 (0-87447-542-2) H Holt & Co.

***College Board Staff.** College Handbook 2001. 38th ed. 1888p. 2000. pap. 25.95 (0-87447-644-5) College Bd.

College Board Staff. Index of Majors & Graduate Degrees: 1997 Edition. 688p. (C). 1996. pap. 17.95 (0-87447-543-0) H Holt & Co.

***College Board Staff.** Index of Majors & Graduate Degrees 2001. annuals 23rd ed. 696p. 2000. pap. 21.95 (0-87447-645-3) College Bd.

— International Student Handbook 2001. annuals 14th ed. 368p. 2000. pap. 25.95 (0-87447-649-6) College Bd.

College Board Staff. Meeting College Costs: A Workbook for Families 2000. 1999. pap. text, wbk. ed. 13.95 (0-87447-636-4) College Bd.

— Real SAT II: Subject Tests. 2nd ed. LC 97-77029. (Illus.). 807p. 1998. pap. 17.95 (0-87447-599-6) College Bd.

***College Board Staff.** Regents College Examinations Official Study Guide 2001. annuals 2rd ed. 2000. pap. 18.95 (0-87447-651-8) College Bd.

— Scholarship Handbook 2001. annuals 4th ed. 592p. 2000. pap. 24.95 (0-87447-648-8) College Bd.

College Board Staff. 10 Real SATs. LC 97-67530. 600p. 1997. pap. 17.95 (0-87447-567-8) College Bd.

College Board Staff & Policy Studies in Education Staff. Training by Contract: Models of Success Between Colleges & Employers. 150p. 1995. pap. 20.00 (0-87447-523-6, 5236) College Bd.

College Board Staff, jt. auth. see Educational Testing Service Staff.

College Division Staff. Cuyas Dictionary Special Education. 1985. per. 4.50 (0-13-472820-3) P-H.

College of American Pathologists Committee on Nomenclature& Classification of Disease, jt. auth. see Wagner, Loyd R.

College of American Pathologists Staff, jt. auth. see Ccotbe, Roger A.

***College of Animal Welfare Staff.** Physiology & Applied Anatomy for Veterinary Nurses. (Illus.). 500p. 2001. pap. 49.50 (0-7506-4802-3) Buttrwrth-Heinemann.

— 300 MCQS in Anatomy & Physiology for VNS. (Veterinary Nursing Ser.). (Illus.). 80p. 2000. pap. text 18.00 (0-7506-4695-0) Buttrwrth-Heinemann.

— Veterinary Nursing 300 Questions & Answers in Radiography & Fluid Therapy. (Veterinary Nursing Ser.). 80p. 2000. pap. text 18.00 (0-7506-4794-9) Buttrwrth-Heinemann.

***College of Animal Welfare Staff, ed.** MCQS in Veterinary Nursing, Pt. 1. 2nd ed. 128p. 2000. pap. 18.00 (0-7506-4699-3) Buttrwrth-Heinemann.

— MCQS in Veterinary Nursing, Pt. 2. 2nd ed. 128p. 2000. pap. 18.00 (0-7506-4700-0) Buttrwrth-Heinemann.

— Portfolio Guidance for Veterinary Nurses. 112p. 2000. pap. text 24.50 (0-7506-4809-0) Buttrwrth-Heinemann.

— 300 MCQS in Exotics & Wildlife for VNS. 128p. 2000. pap. text 18.00 (0-7506-4696-9) Buttrwrth-Heinemann.

— 300 MCQS in Medical & General Nursing for VNS. 128p. 2000. pap. text 18.00 (0-7506-4697-7) Buttrwrth-Heinemann.

— 300 MCQS in Theatre Practice & Anaesthesia for VNS. (Veterinary Nursing Ser.). 128p. 2000. pap. text 18.00 (0-7506-4698-5) Buttrwrth-Heinemann.

College of Animal Welfare, U. K. Staff. Veterinary Nursing: A Guide to Surgical Instruments. 128p. 1997. pap. text 20.00 (0-7506-3613-0) Buttrwrth-Heinemann.

College of Oceaneering Staff, jt. ed. see Best Publishing Co. Staff.

College of the Redwoods, Del Norte Staff. First Annual Aleutian Goose Festival Winner & Finalists. Letko, Ken, ed. 1999. pap. write for info. (0-9646865-5-4) Col of Redwoods.

— The Kerf: May 1995. Letko, Ken, ed. (Orig.). 1995. pap. 5.00 (0-9646865-0-3) Col of Redwoods.

— The Kerf: May, 1996. Letko, Ken, ed. (Orig.). 1996. pap. 5.00 (0-9646865-1-1) Col of Redwoods.

— The Kerf: May, 1997. Letko, Ken, ed. 1997. pap. 5.00 (0-9646865-2-X) Col of Redwoods.

— The Kerf: May, 1999. Letko, Ken, ed. 1999. pap. write for info. (0-9646865-4-6) Col of Redwoods.

College of the University of Chicago Staff. The Idea & Practice of General Education: An Account of the College of the University of Chicago. LC 91-40878. (Centennial Publication Ser.). 350p. 1992. pap. text 15.00 (0-226-10079-0) U Ch Pr.

College of Wooster Art Museum Staff. Prints from Solo Impression, Inc., New York, New York. Gouma-Peterson, Thalia, ed. LC 94-72324. (Illus.). 52p. (C). 1994. 25.00 (0-9604658-8-X) Coll Wooster.

College of Wooster Art Museum Staff, et al. Emma Amos Paintings & Prints, 1982-92. Zurko, Kathleen M., ed. LC 93-72059. (Illus.). 88p. (C). 1993. 25.00 (0-9604658-7-1) Coll Wooster.

— We, the Human Beings: Twenty-Seven Contemporary Native American Artists. 2nd ed. Zurko, Kathleen M., ed. LC 93-72134. (Illus.). 52p. (C). 1993. 20.00 (0-9604658-6-3) Coll Wooster.

College Placement Council, Inc. Staff. CPC Minority Recruitment Sourcebook. 1990. 89.95 (0-913936-24-3) Coll Placement.

College Placement Council Staff. 1990 College Relations & Recruitment Survey. LC 91-131725. 127p. 1990. write for info. (0-913936-25-1) Coll Placement.

College Research Group of Concord, Mass. Staff. The Right College. 6th ed. (Illus.). 1184p. 1992. pap. 22.00 (0-13-781758-4, Arco) Macmillan Gen Ref.

College Research Group of Concord, Mass. Staff, ed. The Right College. 7th ed. 1216p. 1994. per. 22.00 (0-671-89030-1, Arco) Macmillan Gen Ref.

College Student Editors, jt. auth. see MasterCard International Staff.

Collegium Hyperboreum Group Staff, ed. Acta Hyperborea: East & West Cultural Relations in the Ancient World. (Danish Studies in Classical Archaeology: No. 1). (Illus.). 168p. (Orig.). 1988. pap. 76.50 (87-7289-061-4) Coronet Bks.

Collegium Internationale Allergologicum Staff. Cellular & Molecular Mechanisms of Cell-Mediated Allergic Reactions, Chemistry of Allergens & Transactions: Proceedings of the Collegium Internationale Allergologicum, 8th Symposium, Montreux, 1970. Kallos, P. et al, eds. (International Archives of Allergy & Applied Immunology Ser.: Vol. 41, No. 1). 1971. pap. 47.00 (3-8055-1191-4) S Karger.

— New Approaches to the Management of Allergic Diseases: Proceedings of the Collegium Internationale Allergologicum, 12th, New Orleans, LA, Sept. 1978. Lichtenstein, Lawrence M. & Gleich, G. J., eds. (Monographs in Allergy: Vol. 14). (Illus.). 1979. pap. 126.25 (3-8055-3039-0) S Karger.

— The Theoretical & Practical Aspects of Allergic Disorders: Proceedings of the Collegium Internationale Allergologicum, 9th, London, Sept. 1972. Parker, D. et al, eds. (International Archives of Allergy & Applied Immunology Ser.: Vol. 45, Nos. 1-2). (Illus.). 1973. reprint ed. pap. 68.00 (3-8055-1605-3) S Karger.

Collegium Internationale Allergologicum Symposium. Mediators of the Immediate Type Inflammatory Reaction: Proceedings of the Collegium Internationale Allergologicum Symposium, 11th, Heidelberg, May 1976. Rother, K. O., ed. (Monographs in Allergy: Vol. 12). (Illus.). 1977. 85.25 (3-8055-2660-1) S Karger.

— Molecular & Cellular Aspects of Allergy: Proceedings of the Collegium Internationale Allergologicum Symposium, 10th, Copenhagen, 1974. Diamant, B. et al, eds. (International Archives of Allergy & Applied Immunology Ser.: Vol. 49, No. 1-2). (Illus.). 250p. 1975. pap. 88.75 (3-8055-2166-9) S Karger.

C

An Asterisk (*) at the beginning of an entry indicates that the title is appearing for the first time.

Collegium Internationale Neuro-Psychopharmacologic. Collegium Internationale Neuro-Psychopharmacologicum: Proceedings of the 15th Congress, Puerto Rico, 1986. Bunney, William E., Jr. et al, eds. LC 86-29716. 620p. 1986. reprint ed. pap. 192.20 (0-608-00324-7, 206104100007) Bks Demand.

— Monoamine Oxidase Inhibitors: Proceedings of the Collegium Internationale Neuro-Psychopharnacologicum,12th Congress, Gothenberg, 1980. Youdim, M. B. & Paykel, E. S., eds. LC 80-41258. (Wiley-Interscience Publications). 232p. reprint ed. pap. 72.00 (0-608-13105-9, 205210100033) Bks Demand.

— Proceedings of the 14th Collegium Internationale Neuro-Psychopharmacologium Congress, Florence, Italy, 1984. Racagni, Giorgio et al, eds. LC RM0315.. (Clinical Neuropharmacology Ser.: Vol. 7, Supplement 1). 1008p. 1984. reprint ed. pap. 200.00 (0-608-00439-1, 206115400007) Bks Demand.

Collelo, Thomas, ed. Chad: A Country Study. 2nd ed. LC 89-600373. (Area Handbook Ser.). (Illus.). 278p. 1990. boxed set 20.00 (0-16-024770-5, S/N 008-020-01220-3) USGPO.

— Lebanon: A Country Study. 3rd ed. LC 88-600488. (Area Handbook Ser.). (Illus.). 308p. 1989. text 20.00 (0-16-001731-9, S/N 008-020-011) USGPO.

Collen, Arne. Friends & Fiends. (Illus.). 72p. (Orig.). (YA). (gr. 7 up). 1989. pap. write for info. (0-318-64430-4) Eagleye Bks Intl.

Collen, Arne & Gasparski, Wojciech W., eds. Design & Systems: General Applications of Methodology. LC 93-6404. (Praxiology Ser.: Vol. 3). 1994. 54.95 (1-56000-140-2) Transaction Pubs.

— Design & Systems: General Applications of Methodology. LC 93-6404. (Praxiology: International Annual of Practical Philosophy & Methodology Ser.: Vol. 3). 480p. (C). 1994. 54.95 (1-56000-187-9) Transaction Pubs.

Collen, Arne, jt. auth. see Minati, Gianfranco.

Collen, John. Buying & Selling Real Estate in Bankruptcy. LC 97-61761. 1997. write for info. (0-8366-1168-3) West Group.

Collen, Libby. What Makes You Feel Like Shouting? 1987. 3.45 (0-89741-026-2) Gila River.

Collen, Lindsey. The Rape of Sita. (African Writers Ser.). 256p. 1995. pap. 10.95 (0-435-90958-4, 90958) Heinemann.

Collen, M. J. & Benjamin, S. B., eds. Pharmacology of Peptic Ulcer Disease: With Contributions by Numerous Experts. (Handbook of Experimental Pharmacology Ser.: Vol. 99). xxii, 464p. 1991. 357.00 (0-387-52840-7) Spr-Verlag.

Collen, Morris F. A History of Medical Informatics in the United States: 1950 to 1990. LC 95-34109. 489p. 1995. 40.00 (0-9647743-0-5) Am Med Info Assn.

Collen, Robert. Burning World. (Illus.). 100p. (Orig.). 1996. pap. 9.95 (1-884540-21-X) Haleys.

— A Few Pianos. LC 77-83731. 27p. 1978. pap. 4.00 (0-89924-016-X) Lynx Hse.

— The Town & the River. rev. ed. LC 93-79010. (Illus.). 8p. (Orig.). 1994. pap. 1.50 (1-884540-03-1) Haleys.

Collenberg, H., jt. auth. see Joachim, Franz J.

Collenberg, H. F., jt. auth. see Winter, Hans.

***Collender, Stanley E.** Guide to the Federal Budget. 1999. 22.95 (0-87078-434-X) Century Foundation.

Collender, Stanley E. The Guide to the Federal Budget: Fiscal 1997. (C). 1996. pap. text 22.95 (0-8476-8225-0); lib. bdg. 56.00 (0-8476-8224-2) Rowman.

— The Guide to the Federal Budget: Fiscal 1998. 200p. 1997. 56.00 (0-8476-8403-2); pap. 22.95 (0-8476-8404-0) Rowman.

Collenette, Eric. The Secret of the Kara Sea. 1987. 16.95 (0-8027-0990-7) Walker & Co.

Collens, T. Wharton. Eden of Labor, or, the Christian Utopia. LC 79-154435. (Utopian Literature Ser.). (Illus.). 1976. reprint ed. 23.95 (0-405-03518-7) Ayer.

Collentro, William V. Pharmaceutical Water: System Design, Operation, & Validation. (Illus.). 682p. 1997. 229.00 (1-57491-027-2) Interpharm.

Colleott, Diana. H. D. & Sapphic Modernism. LC 98-38426. (Illus.). 290p. (C). 1999. text 59.95 (0-521-55078-5) Cambridge U Pr.

***Coller, Barbara.** Millennium Messages. Welker, Janie M., ed. 24p. 1999. pap. text. write for info. (1-879195-10-0) Heckscher Mus.

Coller, Barbara G. & Kuspit, Donald. The Edge of Childhood. (Illus.). 48p. (Orig.). 1992. pap. text 9.00 (1-879195-07-0) Heckscher Mus.

Coller, Barry S. Pipejacking & Microtunnelling. 1991. text 99.95 (0-442-31332-2, VNR) Wiley.

— Progress in Hemostasis & Thrombosis, Vol. 10. (Illus.). 368p. 1990. text 180.00 (0-7216-3445-1, W B Saunders Co) Harcrt Hlth Sci Grp.

Coller, Derek. Jess Stacy: The Quiet Man of Jazz. Martyn, Barry, ed. (Illus.). 298p. Date not set. pap. 39.95 (0-9638890-4-4, Jazzology Pr) GHB Jazz Fnd.

Colleran, Jeanne & Spencer, Jenny S., eds. Staging Resistance: Essays on Political Theater. LC 98-8958. (Theater--Theory/Text/Performance Ser.). (Illus.). 320p. (C). 1998. text 49.50 (0-472-09671-0, 09671); pap. text 21.95 (0-472-06671-4, 06671) U of Mich Pr.

Colleran, Joseph M., tr. see Augustine, Saint.

Colleran, P. K., ed. Walking with Contemplation: A Walker's Guide. rev. ed. (Illus.). 230p. (Orig.). 1998. pap. 15.95 (0-9609102-0-4) CAFH Found Inc.

Colleran, Patricia, ed. & tr. see Waxemberg, Jorge.

Collerson, John. English Grammar: A Functional Approach. 160p. 1998. pap. text 19.50 (1-875622-11-X, 62211X, Pub. by Primary English) Calendar Islands.

Collerson, John, ed. Writing for Life. (Illus.). 122p. (Orig.). (C). 1988. pap. text 16.50 (0-909955-81-6, 00625) Heinemann.

***Collert, Jay.** Environmental, Health & Safety CFR Training Requirements. 4th ed. 425p. 2000. pap. 89.00 (0-86587-673-8) Gov Insts.

Collert, Jay, ed. Environmental Health & Safety CFR Training Requirements. 3rd rev. ed. 422p. 1997. pap. text 89.00 (0-86587-587-1, 587) Gov Insts.

***Colles, Christ.** Functional Anatomy. (Threshold Picture Guides Ser.: Vol. 43). (Illus.). 24p. 2000. pap. 12.00 (1-872119-19-0, Pub. by Kenilworth Pr) Half Halt Pr.

***Colles, Christopher M., et al.** Clinical Radiology of the Horse. 2nd ed. Butler, Janet A., ed. LC 99-38331. (Illus.). 610p. 2000. text 214.95 (0-632-05268-6, Pub. by Blckwell Science) Iowa St U Pr.

Colles, Henry C. Brahms. LC 74-24060. (Music of the Masters Ser.). reprint ed. 32.50 (0-404-12883-1) AMS Pr.

— Essays & Lectures. LC 73-128225. (Essay Index Reprint Ser.). 1977. 21.95 (0-8369-1910-6) Ayer.

Colles, Lisa. Fat: Exploding the Myths, 1. 224p. 1999. pap. 12.95 (1-56649-337-4) Welcome Rain.

Collester, Colette, ed. see Hosmer, Charles B., Jr.

Collester, Jeanne C. Rudolph Ganz: A Musical Pioneer. LC 94-9688. 1994. 31.00 (0-8108-2883-9) Scarecrow.

***Collet, Anne.** Swimming with Giants: My Encounters with Whales, Dolphins & Seals. Wurst, Gayle, tr. 228p. 2000. 22.00 (1-57131-244-7) Milkweed Ed.

Collet, Carey & Komarinski, Mark F. Linux System Administration Handbook. LC 97-52143. 416p. (C). 1998. pap. text 39.95 (0-13-680596-5) P-H.

Collet, Georges-Paul, ed. see Mauriac, Francois & Blanche, Jacques-Emile.

Collet, Iris W., jt. auth. see Greenspan, A. J.

Collet, Pierre & Eckman, Jean-Pierre. Iterated Maps on the Interval As Dynamical Systems. (Progress in Physics Ser.: No. 1). 227p. 1997. text 54.50 (0-8176-3026-0) Birkhauser.

Collet, Pierre & Eckmann, J. P. Iterated Maps on the Interval As Dynamical Systems. (Progress in Physics Ser.: Vol. 1). 256p. 1990. reprint ed. pap. 49.00 (0-8176-3510-6) Birkhauser.

Collet, Pierre & Eckmann, Jean-Pierre. Instabilities & Fronts in Extended Systems. 216p. 1990. text 55.00 (0-691-08568-4, Pub. by Princeton U Pr) Cal Prin Full Svc.

Collet, Rita, ed. see Standish, N. Graham.

Collete, jt. auth. see Bowers.

Collets. English-Polish Business Dictionary. 878p. (C). 1991. 195.00 (0-89771-894-1, Pub. by Collets) St Mut.

— New Great English-Russian Dictionary, 3 vols., Set. (C). 1992. 1035.00 (0-89771-853-4, Pub. by Collets) St Mut.

— Russian Samovar. 223p. (C). 1991. 150.00 (0-89771-891-7, Pub. by Collets) St Mut.

— The Tears of the Heliads. 169p. 1991. 150.00 (0-89771-892-5, Pub. by Collets) St Mut.

Collet's Holdings Limited Staff, ed. Civilization, Science & Philosophy. 268p. 1983. 40.00 (0-7855-0796-5) St Mut.

Collets Holdings, Ltd. Staff. Bratislava City Map. (ENG, GER & RUS., Illus.). (C). 1990. pap. 40.00 (0-569-09230-2, Pub. by Collets) St Mut.

— Budapest City Plan. (ENG, GER, HUN & RUS., Illus.). (C). 1990. pap. 45.00 (0-7855-5217-0, Pub. by Collets) St Mut.

— Budapest Guide & Atlas. (Illus.). 119p. (C). 1990. 60.00 (0-7855-5223-5, Pub. by Collets) St Mut.

Collet's Holdings, Ltd. Staff. The Budapest Museum of Fine Arts. 128p. 1981. pap. 50.00 (0-7855-1515-1, Pub. by Collets) St Mut.

Collets Holdings, Ltd. Staff. The Comparison of Law: Selected Essays for the International Congress of Comparative Law, 9th. 324p. 1974. 23.00 (0-569-08167-X) St Mut.

— Czechoslovakia Road Map. (Illus.). (C). 1990. pap. 50.00 (0-569-09229-9, Pub. by Collets) St Mut.

Collet's Holdings, Ltd. Staff. John Heartfield. (ENG & GER.). 1985. 192.00 (0-7855-1532-1) St Mut.

— Karl Friedrich Schinkler. 1985. 390.00 (0-7855-1563-1) St Mut.

— Landscapes of S. Bohemia in the 19th Century. (CZE, ENG, FRE & GER., Illus.). 1987. 50.00 (0-7855-1554-2) St Mut.

Collet's Holdings, Ltd. Staff. Monuments of Russian Architecture & Monumental Art. 280p. 1983. 45.00 (0-7855-7572-3) St Mut.

Collet's Holdings, Ltd. Staff. Recent Developments in the Nuclear Many-Body Problem. 1986. 60.00 (0-7855-1214-4, Pub. by Collets) St Mut.

— The State Hermitage: Proceedings, Vol. 22. 1982. 50.00 (0-7855-1619-0) St Mut.

— Zagorsk Museum of History & Art: A Guide. (RUS.). 1983. 40.00 (0-7855-1589-5) St Mut.

Collet's Holdings, Ltd. Staff, ed. Aram Khachaturyan. Kournokoff, Nicholas & Bobrov, Vladimi, trs. LC 85-18265. (Illus.). 286p. 1985. 40.00 (0-943071-00-3) Sphinx Pr.

— The Armenian Alphabet. 1983. 50.00 (0-7855-0953-4) St Mut.

— The Azerbaijan Soviet Encyclopedia. 608p. 1982. 130.00 (0-7855-0789-2) St Mut.

— Barskii, Iu. P. NA 100 Kletkakh. (RUS.). 160p. 1985. 29.00 (0-7855-0928-3) St Mut.

— Belorussian Painting XII - XVIII Centuries. 316p. 1985. 110.00 (0-7855-0791-4) St Mut.

— Belourussian SSSR: Facts & Figures. 64p. 1984. 45.00 (0-7855-0932-1) St Mut.

— Capitalism, Socialism & Scientific Technical Revolution. (Library of Political Knowledge: No. 9). 182p. 1983. 30.00 (0-7855-0794-9) St Mut.

Collets Holdings, Ltd. Staff, ed. Concise Russian-English & English-Russian Phraseological Dictionary. 400p. (C). 1978. 25.00 (0-7855-4231-0, Pub. by Collets) St Mut.

Collet's Holdings, Ltd. Staff, ed. Constronic 1984. 405p. 1984. 280.00 (0-7855-1174-1) St Mut.

Collet's Holdings, Ltd. Staff, ed. Constructive Theory of Functions. 940p. 1984. 105.00 (0-7855-7560-X) St Mut.

Collet's Holdings, Ltd. Staff, ed. Developed Socialism: Theory & Practice. 264p. 1980. 30.00 (0-7855-0800-7) St Mut.

— Dictionary of the Middle Ages, Vol. 9. LC 82-5904. 1987. 115.00 (0-684-18275-0, Scribners Ref) Mac Lib Ref.

— Early Russian Painting 11th to Early 13th Centuries: Mosaics, Frescoes & Icons. 308p. 1982. 125.00 (0-7855-0802-3) St Mut.

— Economic Development of the Newly Free Countries. (Developing Countries Problems & Perspectives Ser.: No. 3). 192p. 1985. 23.00 (0-7855-0803-1) St Mut.

— Folk Art of the Russian Federation from the Ethnographical Museum of the People's of the U. S. S. R. 1985. 150.00 (0-7855-0804-X) St Mut.

— Graphs & Other Combinatorial Topics. 1982. 91.00 (0-7855-1178-4, Pub. by Collets) St Mut.

— Multiobjective & Stochastic Optimization Based on Parametric Optimization. 1986. 49.00 (0-7855-1181-4, Pub. by Collets) St Mut.

— The Nationalities Question: Lenin's Approach. (Library of Political Knowledge). 190p. 1983. 25.00 (0-317-39517-3) St Mut.

— Numerical Analysis of Selected Semilinear Differential Equations. 1986. 63.00 (0-7855-1182-2, Pub. by Collets) St Mut.

— Peterburg V. Russkom Ocherke XIX Veka. 376p. 1984. 49.00 (0-7855-0902-X) St Mut.

— Proceedings of the Third Symposium on Technical Diagnostics, Moscow, October 3-5, 1983. 512p. 1984. pap. 410.00 (0-7855-1184-9) St Mut.

— Recent Developments in the Chemistry of Natural Carbon Compounds, Vol. 6. 198p. 1975. 60.00 (0-569-08195-5, Pub. by Collets) St Mut.

— Recent Developments in the Chemistry of Natural Carbon Compounds, Vol. 9. 420p. 1979. 150.00 (0-569-08590-X, Pub. by Collets) St Mut.

— Soviet Ukraine. 1984. 45.00 (0-7855-0971-2) St Mut.

— The Systematic Dictionary of English Adverbs, Vol. 3. 296p. 1983. 50.00 (0-7855-0973-9) St Mut.

Collet's Holdings, Ltd. Staff & Rumiantsev, A., eds. A Dictionary of Scientific Communism. 288p. 1984. 39.00 (0-7855-0937-2) St Mut.

Collet's Holdings, Ltd. Staff, ed. see Chekhov, Anton.

Collets Holdings, Ltd.Staff. Brest, Minsk, Smolensk, Moscow. (Illus.). 151p. (C). 1982. 40.00 (0-7855-5206-5, Pub. by Collets) St Mut.

Collet's Holdings Staff, ed. Dictionary of Technical Information: Power Electronics, Vols. 54-55. 584p. 1985. 110.00 (0-7855-0985-2) St Mut.

Collet's Publishing UK Staff. Azerbaijan Carpet, 2 vols., Vol. 2. (RUS.). 304p. 1983. 245.00 (0-7855-1573-9, Pub. by Collets) St Mut.

— Azerbaijan Carpet, 2 vols., Vols. 2-3. (RUS.). 1983. write for info. (0-7855-2563-7, Pub. by Collets) St Mut.

Collets Staff. From Hungary to the United States, 1880-1914. (Studia Historica Academiae Scientiarum Hungaricae Ser.: No. 184). 226p. 1982. 90.00 (0-7855-1237-3) St Mut.

— The Great Patriotic War in Fine Art: Velikaia Otechestvennaia Voina V Izobrazitel'nom Iskusstve. 1982. pap. 29.00 (0-7855-1634-4) St Mut.

— Guide to the Silk Road. (C). 1991. 100.00 (0-569-09296-5, Pub. by Collets) St Mut.

— Tallinn in 19th Century Engravings. 1983. 165.00 (0-7855-1674-3) St Mut.

Collett, Anne, et al, eds. Teaching Post-Colonialism & Post-Colonial Literatures. LC 98-107120. (Dolphin Ser.: Vol. 27). 200p. 1997. pap. 19.95 (87-7288-378-2, Pub. by Aarhus Univ Pr) David Brown.

***Collett, Barry.** Frulovisi's de Republica of 1433: A Critical Edition. 224p. 1999. 55.00 (1-85182-505-3, Pub. by Four Cts Pr) Intl Spec Bk.

Collett, Barry. Italian Benedictine Scholars & the Reformation: The Congregation of Santa Giustina of Padua. (Oxford Historical Monographs). 300p. 1986. 59.00 (0-19-822934-8) OUP.

Collett, Bill & Taylor, Gary. River Rock: A Climber's Guide to Mississippi Palisades State Park. (Illus.). (Orig.). 1991. pap. text 9.25 (0-9619571-2-3) Granite WI.

Collett, C. V. & Hope, A. D. Engineering Measurements. 2nd ed. LC 87-4939. (Illus.). 399p. reprint ed. pap. 123.70 (0-7837-5183-4, 204491300004) Bks Demand.

Collett, Camilla. The District Governor's Daughters. Seaver, Kirsten, tr. from NOR. (Norvik Press Series B: No. 10). 310p. (Orig.). 1992. pap. 25.00 (1-870041-17-8, Pub. by Norvik Pr) Dufour.

Collett, Casey, jt. auth. see Melum, Mara M.

Collett, D. Modelling Binary Data. 384p. (gr. 13). 1991. per. 52.95 (0-412-38800-6, A6276, Chap & Hall CRC) CRC Pr.

— Modelling Survival Data. LC 99-26358. (Illus.). 350p. (gr. 13). 1994. text 63.95 (0-412-44880-7) Chapman & Hall.

— Modelling Survival Data in Medical Research. (Illus.). 368p. (gr. 13). 1993. per. 47.95 (0-412-44890-4, Chap & Hall CRC) CRC Pr.

Collett, D., jt. auth. see Collett, John P.

Collett, Dennis, jt. auth. see McCloskey, Larry.

Collett, H. Flora Simlensis. 652p. (C). 1976. text 250.00 (0-89771-588-8, Pub. by Intl Bk Distr) St Mut.

— Flora Simlensis. 652p. 1971. reprint ed. 150.00 (0-7855-6737-2, Pub. by Intl Bk Distr) St Mut.

Collett, Iris W. Accosting the Golden Spire. LC 88-82327. 1988. pap. text 10.95 (0-913878-43-X) T Horton & Dghts.

— Ultimate Rip-Off: A Taxing Tale. rev. ed. LC 87-83032. 1998. pap. text 10.95 (0-913878-59-6) T Horton & Dghts.

Collett, Iris W. & Forgione, Dana. Costly Reflections in a Midas Mirror. 2nd ed. LC 94-77805. 182p. (Orig.). (C). 1999. pap. text 10.95 (0-913878-54-5) T Horton & Dghts.

Collett, Iris W., jt. auth. see Smith, Lawrence M.

Collett, John P., ed. Making Sense of Space: The History of Norwegian Space Activities. 1995. 48.00 (82-00-22692-1) Scandnvan Univ Pr.

Collett, John P. & Collett, D. Black & White Landscape Photography. 128p. 1999. pap. text 29.95 (1-58428-004-2, Pub. by Amherst Media) IPG Chicago.

Collett, Jonathan & Karakashian, Stephen, eds. Greening the College Curriculum: A Guide to Environmental Teaching in the Liberal Arts. LC 95-39225. 320p. 1995. pap. 24.00 (1-55963-422-7) Island Pr.

Collett, Lorna S. Psychology of Temperament: Index of New Information with Authors, Subjects & References. rev. ed. 150p. 1998. 47.50 (0-7883-1944-2); pap. 44.50 (0-7883-1945-0) ABBE Pubs Assn.

Collett, Merrill. At Home with Dying: A Zen Hospice Approach. LC 99-24856. 256p. 1999. pap. 15.00 (1-57062-515-8, Pub. by Shambhala Pubns) Random.

— The Cocaine Connection: Drug Trafficking & Inter-American Relations. LC 89-85130. (Headline Ser.: No. 290). 72p. 1989. pap. 5.95 (0-87124-128-5) Foreign Policy.

— Stay Close & Do Nothing: A Spiritual & Practical Guide to Caring for the Dying at Home. 256p. 1998. pap. 9.95 (0-8362-6940-3) Andrews & McMeel.

Collett, Michael. House Mice. (Contemporary Literature for Children Ser.: No. 1). (Illus.). 34p. (Orig.). (J). (ps-8). 1986. pap. 5.95 (0-916843-09-2, 106) Order of Legion.

Collett, Nicholas & Schell, Charles. Corporate Credit Analysis. 2nd ed. 296p. 1996. pap. 170.00 (1-85564-303-0, Pub. by Euromoney) Am Educ Systs.

Collett, Nick & Schell, Charles. Analysing Corporate Credit: Self-Study Workbook. 2nd ed. 1993. pap. 295.00 (1-85564-323-5, Pub. by Euromoney) Am Educ Systs.

Collett, Rita, ed. A Book of Personal Prayer. LC 97-17257. 160p. 1997. pap. 13.00 (0-8358-0812-2, UR824) Upper Room Bks.

— The Upper Room Disciplines, 1999. 392p. 1998. pap. 9.00 (0-8358-0825-4, UR825) Upper Room Bks.

— The Upper Room Disciplines, 2000: A Book of Daily Devotions. 392p. 1999. pap. 9.00 (0-8358-0863-7) Upper Room Bks.

***Collett, Rita, ed.** The Upper Room Disciplines, 2001. large type ed. 504p. 2000. pap. 14.00 (0-8358-0928-5) Upper Room Bks.

— The Upper Room Disciplines, 2001: A Book of Daily Devotions. 392p. 2000. pap. 10.00 (0-8358-0878-5) Upper Room Bks.

Collett, Rita, ed. see Brown-Oden, Marilyn.

Collett, Rita, ed. see Canham, Elizabeth.

Collett, Rita, ed. see Clinebell, Howard.

Collett, Rita, ed. see DelBene, Ron, et al.

Collett, Rita, ed. see Gregg-Schroeder, Susan.

Collett, Rita, ed. see Howell, James C.

Collett, Rita, ed. see Indermark, John.

Collett, Rita, ed. see Johnson, Ben C.

Collett, Rita, ed. see Rice, Howard.

Collett, Rita, ed. see Stickney, Sandy.

Collett, Rita, ed. see Thompson, Marjorie J.

Collett, Rita, ed. see Vest, Norvene.

Collett, Ritter. Sports in Dayton: A Bicentennial Celebration of the Dayton Area. LC 96-75102. (Bicentennial Bookshelf Ser.: Vol. 3). (Illus.). 376p. 1996. 34.95 (0-913428-78-7) Landfall Pr.

Collett, Teresa S., jt. auth. see Cochran, Robert F., Jr.

Collett, Teresa S., jt. auth. see Cochran, Robert F.

Colletta, John P. Finding Italian Roots: The Complete Guide for Americans. rev. ed. LC 96-129480. (Illus.). 130p. 1995. pap. 11.95 (0-8063-1393-5, 1127) Genealog Pub.

— They Came in Ships: A Guide to Finding Your Immigrant Ancestor's Arrival Record. rev. ed. LC 93-26835. (Illus.). 108p. 1993. pap. 9.95 (0-916489-42-6) Ancestry.

Colletta, Nat J. & Reinhold, Amy J. Review of Early Childhood Development Policy & Programs in Sub-Saharan Africa. (World Bank Technical Papers: No. 367). 104p. 1997. pap. 22.00 (0-8213-3968-0, 13968) World Bank.

Colletta, Nat J., et al. Case Studies of War-to-Peace Transition: The Demobilization & Reintegration of Ex-Combatants in Ethiopia, Namibia & Uganda. LC 96-8989. (World Bank Discussion Papers, Africa Technical Department Ser.). 372p. 1996. pap. 23.00 (0-8213-3674-6) World Bank.

— The Condition of Young Children in Sub-Saharan Africa: The Convergence of Health, Nutrition, & Early Education. LC 96-25649. (World Bank Technical Papers: No. 326). 64p. 1996. pap. 22.00 (0-8213-3677-0, 13677) World Bank.

— The Transition from War to Peace in Sub-Saharan Africa. LC 96-10245. (Directions in Development Ser.). 96p. 1996. pap. 22.00 (0-8213-3581-2, 13581) World Bank.

Collette, Alfred T., jt. auth. see Chiappetta, Eugene L.

***Collette, Buddy & Isoardi, Stephen.** Jazz Generation: A Life in American Music & Society. 192p. 2000. 49.95 (0-8264-4720-1); pap. 19.95 (0-8264-4721-X) Continuum.

Collette, Carolyn P. Species, Phantasms & Images: Vision & Medieval Psychology in the Canterbury Tales. (Illus.). 208p. (C). text 44.50 (0-472-11161-2, 11161) U of Mich Pr.

Collette, Christine. The International Faith: Labour's Attitudes to European Socialism, 1918-39. (Studies in Labour History). (Illus.). 211p. 1998. 56.95 (1-85928-385-3, HD6475.A1C53, Pub. by Ashgate Pub) Ashgate Pub Co.

Collette, Christine, jt. ed. see Montgomery, Fiona.

An Asterisk (*) at the beginning of an entry indicates that the title is appearing for the first time.

Collette, Jean Y. The Death of Andre Breton, Vol. 1. 96p. pap. write for info. (*0-919349-39-0*) Guernica Editions.

Collette, Paul & Wright, Robert. Huddles: Playscript. LC 91-51081. (Orig.). (J). (gr. 3-12). 1985. pap. 6.00 (*0-88734-512-3*) Players Pr.

***Collette, Tony.** The Volunteer Workforce: How Your Business Can Thrive in a Tight Labor Market by Hiring Volunteers. 2000. pap. 15.00 (*0-615-11515-2*) Direct Access Tech.

Colletti, Al, ed. see Lott, Bob.

Colletti, Deborah L., et al. Effective Bank Product Management: How to Be Profitable in a Competitive Environment. 1987. per. 37.50 (*1-55520-043-5*, Irwn Prfssnl) McGraw-Hill Prof.

Colletti, Dominic J. Class A Foam - Best Practice for Structure Firefighters. Davis, Larry, ed. LC 98-196607. (Illus.). 285p. 1998. text 39.99 (*0-9663468-0-7*, 71860) Lyons Publ.

Colletti, Jerome A. Compensating New Sales Roles: How to Design Rewards That Work in Today's Selling Environment. LC 98-41831. 300p. 1998. 85.95 (*0-8144-0436-7*) AMACOM.

Colletti, Jerome A. & Cichelli, David J. Designing Sales Compensation Plans: An Approach to Developing & Implementing Incentive Plans for Salespeople. (Building Blocks Ser.: Vol. 13). (Illus.). 24p. (Orig.). 1994. pap. 24.95 (*1-57963-016-2*, A0033) Am Compensation.

Colletti, Jerome A. & Fiss, Mary S. Designing Incentive Plans for Customer Teams. (Innovations Ser.: Vol. 1). (Illus.). 20p. (Orig.). 1995. pap. 24.95 (*1-57963-003-0*, A0101) Am Compensation.

Colletti, John B., pref. IPC Proceedings, 1991: Integrating People & Technology for Competitive Manufacturing. (Illus.). 1010p. 1991. 95.00 (*1-56378-000-3*) ESD.

Colletti, Joseph F. A Field Guide to Focused Planning: Hoshin Kanri-American Style. 2nd rev. ed. (Illus.). 238p. 1996. pap. 59.95 (*0-9650718-1-2*) Woodledge Grp.

***Colletti, Joseph F.** From the Heart: A Father's Journey of Grief. 64p. 1999. pap. 9.95 (*0-9650718-2-0*) Woodledge Grp.

Colletti, L. De Rousseau a Lenine. 318p. 1972. pap. text 92.00 (*0-677-50645-7*) Gordon & Breach.

Colletti, Lucio. From Parlor to Prison: From Rousseau to Lenin: Studies in Ideology & Society. Merringer, John, tr. LC 72-92035. 240p. 1985. pap. 15.00 (*0-85345-350-0*, Pub. by Monthly Rev) NYU Pr.

Colletti, Ned. You Gotta Have Heart: Dallas Green's Rebuilding of the Cubs. LC 85-4405. (Illus.). 272p. 1985. 15.95 (*0-912083-11-5*) Diamond Communications.

Colletti, Paul J. & Colavito, William A. Guide to New York Real Estate Salespersons. 4th ed. (C). 1989. text 43.51 (*0-13-370743-1*) P-H.

Colletti, V. & Stephens, S. D., eds. Disorders with Defective Hearing. (Advances in Audiology Ser.: Vol. 3). (Illus.). viii, 216p. 1985. 142.75 (*3-8055-3965-7*) S Karger.

Colley. Reforming Energy: Sustainable Energy Futures. 1997. 49.95 (*0-7453-1266-7*, Pub. by Pluto GBR); pap. 16.95 (*0-7453-1261-6*, Pub. by Pluto GBR) Stylus Pub VA.

Colley, Allan, jt. auth. see Largan, Mark.

Colley, Ann C. Edward Lear & the Critics. LC 93-25216. (LCENG Ser.). xiv, 120p. 1994. 50.00 (*1-879751-80-1*) Camden Hse.

Colley, Ann M. & Beech, John R., eds. Acquisition & Performance of Cognitive Skills. LC 88-34579. (Wiley Series, Human Performance & Cognition). (Illus.). 366p. 1989. pap. 113.50 (*0-608-05255-8*, 206579300001) Bks Demand.

Colley, Barbara. Practical Manual of Land Development. 3rd ed. LC 98-34765. (Illus.). 352p. 1998. 59.95 (*0-07-011967-8*) McGraw-Hill Prof.

Colley, Bernadette A., et al. Minds Alive: Teachers as Scholars. (Illus.). 80p. 1999. pap. 12.00 (*0-931989-12-4*, J W Boarman) Coun Basic Educ.

Colley, Betty B., jt. auth. see Monday, Jane C.

Colley, Charles C., jt. ed. see Reinhartz, Dennis.

Colley, Craig W. You Can Make Money in Mu$ic: Everything a Musician Needs to Know to Become Steadily Employed as a Live Performer. 88p. 1991. pap. 14.95 (*1-56516-000-2*) H Leonard.

Colley, David P. The Road to Victory: The Untold Story of the Red Ball Express. LC 99-48012. (Illus.). 288p. 2000. 17.95 (*1-57488-173-6*) Brasseys.

Colley, Iain. Dos Passos & the Fiction of Despair LC 79-305201. 170p. 1978. write for info. (*0-333-23212-7*) Macmillan.

Colley, John L., Jr. Case Studies in Service Operations. 567p. (C). 1995. mass mkt. 88.95 (*0-534-51126-0*) Wadsworth Pub.

Colley, Linda. Britons: Forging the Nation, 1707-1837. LC 92-13256. (Illus.). 432p. (C). 1992. 45.00 (*0-300-05737-7*) Yale U Pr.

— Britons: Forging the Nation 1707-1837. (Illus.). 432p. (C). 1994. pap. 17.00 (*0-300-05925-6*) Yale U Pr.

***Colley, Linda.** Contradictions Of, Vol. 8. (History of Britain Ser.). 320p. 1999. 0.00 (*0-7139-9070-8*, Viking) Viking Penguin.

Colley, Linda, contrib. by. Crown Pictorial: Art & the British Monarchy. LC 90-71832. (Illus.). 45p. 1990. pap. 9.95 (*0-930606-64-7*) Yale Ctr Brit Art.

Colley, Macey. Fifty Is Fun & Funny. (Illus.). 64p. (Orig.). 1992. pap. 7.95 (*0-89896-435-0*) Larksdale.

Colley, Michael F. & Roscoe Pound-American Trial Lawyers Assn. Staff. Product Safety in America. LC 85-60392. (Annual Chief Justice Earl Warren Conference on Advocacy in the U.S. Ser.). 127p. (Orig.). 1985. pap. 25.00 (*0-933067-00-3*) Roscoe Pound Inst.

Colley, P. H. Quincunx. 258p. 1994. pap. 10.95 (*0-9643685-1-X*); lib. bdg. 15.95 (*0-9643685-0-1*) Chiron Rising.

Colley, Relan. Oregon's Swimming Holes. LC 94-28360. 320p. (Orig.). 1994. pap. 14.95 (*0-89997-169-5*) Wilderness Pr.

Colley, Russell. Dagmar Defining Advertising Goals for Measured Advertising Results. 2nd rev. ed. (Illus.). 144p. 1995. 34.95 (*0-8442-3422-2*, NTC Business Bks) NTC Contemp Pub Co.

Colley, Scott. Richard's Himself Again: A Stage History of "Richard III", 46. LC 91-36834. (Contributions in Drama & Theatre Studies: No. 46). 304p. 1992. 59.95 (*0-313-26293-4*, COR/, Greenwood Pr) Greenwood.

Colley, Susan Jane. Vector Calculus. LC 97-1738. 532p. 1997. 89.33 (*0-13-149204-7*) P-H.

Colli, C. & Montinari, Mazzino, eds. Nietzsche-Briefwechsel: Briefe an Nietzsche, 1869-1872, Vol. 2, Section 2. (C). 1977. 213.85 (*3-11-006635-1*) De Gruyter.

Colli, G. & Montinari, Mazzino, eds. Nietzsche - Werke: Kritische Gesamtausgabe, Vol. 1, Sect. 7. (C). 1976. 160.00 (*3-11-004979-1*) De Gruyter.

— Nietzsche-Briefwechsel: Briefe April, 1869-1872, Vol. 2, Section 1. (C). 1977. 113.85 (*3-11-006633-5*) De Gruyter.

Colli, Giorgio, ed. see Nietzsche, Friedrich Wilhelm.

Colli, J. C., jt. auth. see Bernard, Y.

Colli, Jean-Claude, jt. auth. see Bernard, Yves.

Colli, Monica. Twins. LC 91-36606. (Illus.). 24p. (J). 1992. 4.99 (*0-85953-394-8*) Childs Play.

Colliandor, Tito, ed. The Way of the Ascetics: The Ancient Tradition of Discipline & Inner Growth. Ferre, Katharine, tr. from SWE. LC 85-83900. 110p. 1985. pap. 7.95 (*0-88141-049-7*) St Vladimirs.

Collias, Dimitris I., jt. auth. see Baird, Donald G.

Collias, Elsie C., jt. auth. see Collias, Nicholas E.

Collias, Joe G. Search for Steam. (Illus.). 360p. 1998. pap. 27.95 (*0-911581-44-8*) Heimburger Hse Pub.

Collias, Joe G. The Last of Steam. LC 60-14067. (Illus.). 269p. 1994. 39.95 (*0-911581-32-4*); pap. 26.95 (*0-911581-34-0*) Heimburger Hse Pub.

***Collias, Karen.** A Report on STEP & Its Pilot Project in Georgia. 35p. 2000. write for info. (*0-931989-14-0*) Coun Basic Educ.

Collias, Nicholas E. & Collias, Elsie C. Nest Building & Bird Behavior. LC 84-42585. 357p. reprint ed. pap. 110.70 (*0-8357-3435-8*, 203969200013) Bks Demand.

Colliau, Russ, jt. auth. see Robinson, James W.

Collicott. Mildred & Sam. 40p. (J). (ps-2). lib. bdg. 14.89 (*0-06-026682-1*) HarpC Child Bks.

Collicott, Howard E., jt. ed. see Bauer, Paul E.

Collicott, Purnel L. Down the Path. 1998. pap. write for info. (*1-57553-824-5*) Watermrk Pr.

— Through the Open Door. (Orig.). 1997. pap. write for info. (*1-57553-459-2*) Watermrk Pr.

Collicott, Sharleen. Toestomper & the Caterpillars. LC 98-23268. (Illus.). 32p. (J). (gr. k-3). 1999. 15.00 (*0-395-91168-0*) HM.

***Collicutt, Paul.** This Plane. LC 99-26693. 2000. 15.00 (*0-374-37494-5*) FS&G.

Collicutt, Paul. This Train. LC 97-35342. 32p. (J). (ps-2). 1999. 15.00 (*0-374-37493-7*) FS&G.

Collidge, Daniel S., jt. auth. see Jimmerson, J. Michael.

Collidge, Joseph, tr. see MacDiarmid, Jim.

Collidge, Susan. What Katy Did. (Children's Library). (J). 1998. pap. 3.95 (*1-85326-131-9*, 1319WW, Pub. by Wrdsworth Edits) NTC Contemp Pub Co.

— What Katy Did at School. (Children's Library). 192p. (J). 1998. pap. 3.95 (*1-85326-142-4*, 1424WW, Pub. by Wrdsworth Edits) NTC Contemp Pub Co.

— What Katy Did Next. 192p. (J). 1998. pap. 3.95 (*1-85326-150-5*, 1505WW, Pub. by Wrdsworth Edits) NTC Contemp Pub Co.

Collie. English Library. 7th ed. 25.95 (*1-85928-012-9*) Ashgate Pub Co.

***Collie, Ashley.** The World of Soccer. Rolfe, John, ed. (Sports Illustrated for Kids Bks.). 96p. (J). (gr. 4-8). 2000. pap. 3.99 (*1-886749-87-6*) SI For Kids.

Collie, C. H. Kinetic Theory & Entropy. LC 81-8332. (Illus.). 403p. reprint ed. pap. 125.00 (*0-8357-6179-7*, 203450500090) Bks Demand.

Collie Club of America Staff. The New Collie. LC 82-19049. (Complete Breed Bk.). (Illus.). 304p. 1982. pap. 25.95 (*0-87605-130-1*) Howell Bks.

— The New Collie. 4th ed. (Illus.). 288p. 1996. 25.95 (*0-87605-127-1*) Howell Bks.

Collie-Cooper, Mary. Brazos County Texas, 1820 Census. 243p. (Orig.). 1987. pap., spiral bd. 10.00 (*0-943553-04-0*) Collie-Cooper Ent.

— Bryan City Cemetery Brazos County Texas Books 1, 2, 3, & 4. 193p. (Orig.). 1987. pap. 10.00 (*0-943553-03-2*) Collie-Cooper Ent.

— Letters from Two Brothers, 1870-1873: William Anderson Patrick & Beverly Prior Patrick. LC 88-70358. (Illus.). 155p. (Orig.). 1988. pap. 12.50 (*0-943553-05-9*) Collie-Cooper Ent.

— Robertson County, Texas 1860 Census. 72p. (Orig.). 1985. spiral bd. 6.50 (*0-943553-02-4*) Collie-Cooper Ent.

Collie-Cooper, Mary & Whitley, Allie. Brazos County Texas, 1860 Census, (Also 1842 Tax Roll & Surnames on 1850 Census) 59p. (Orig.). 1983. pap. 6.25 (*0-943553-01-6*) Collie-Cooper Ent.

Collie-Cooper, Mary, jt. auth. see Whitley, Allie M.

Collie, David, ed. see Ssu Shu.

Collie, Joanne & Ladousse, Gillian P. Paths into Poetry. (Illus.). 64p. 1993. pap. text 11.95 (*0-19-421716-7*) OUP.

Collie, Joanne & Slater, Stephen. Literature in the Language Classroom: A Resource Book of Ideas & Activities. (Cambridge Handbooks for Language Teachers Ser.). 272p. 1988. pap. text 20.95 (*0-521-31224-8*) Cambridge U Pr.

Collie, Keith. Spirit of the Wind: The Horse in Saudi Arabia. 112p. (C). 1995. 90.00 (*0-907151-01-9*, Pub. by IMMEL Pubng) St Mut.

Collie, Margaret. Games of Patience. 64p. 1987. pap. 60.00 (*0-85937-153-0*, Pub. by K Mason Pubns Ltd) St Mut.

Collie, Michael. George Gissing: A Bibliography. LC 75-22129. 143p. reprint ed. pap. 44.40 (*0-608-12845-7*, 202360300033) Bks Demand.

Collie, Michael & Bennett, Susan. George Gordon: An Annotated Catalogue of His Scientific Correspondence. 328p. 1996. 113.95 (*1-85928-070-6*, Pub. by Scolar Pr) Ashgate Pub Co.

Collie, Michael & Diemer, John. Murchison in Moray: A Geologist on Home Ground with the Correspondence of Roderick Impey Murchison & the Reverend Dr. George Gordon of Birnie. LC 94-78514. (Transactions Ser.: Vol. 85, Pt. 3). (Illus.). 263p. (C). 1995. pap. 20.00 (*0-87169-853-6*, T853-com) Am Philos.

Collie, Robert M. The Obsessive-Compulsive Disorder: Pastoral Care for the Road to Change. LC 99-23094. 267p. 1999. pap. 19.95 (*0-7890-0862-9*, Haworth Pastrl) Haworth Pr.

***Collie, Robert M.** The Obsessive-Compulsive Disorder: Pastoral Care for the Road to Change. LC 99-23094. 267p. 1999. 49.95 (*0-7890-0707-X*, Haworth Pastrl) Haworth Pr.

Collier. Authors & Artists for Young Adults, Vol. 12. 250p. 1994. text 82.00 (*0-8103-8565-1*, 003492) Gale.

— Authors & Artists for Young Adults, Vol. 13. 250p. 1994. text 82.00 (*0-8103-8566-X*, 003493) Gale.

Collier. Campaigns & Elections. (C). 2001. pap. 18.67 (*0-205-26904-4*, Macmillan Coll) P-H.

***Collier.** Construction Contracts. 3rd ed. 400p. 2000. 77.33 (*0-13-755927-5*) P-H.

— Engineering Economic & Analysis. 3rd ed. 216p. (C). 1998. pap. text, teacher ed. 93.66 (*0-673-97771-4*) Addison-Wesley.

Collier. Engineering Economic & Cost Analysis. 3rd ed. LC 98-15681. 712p. (C). 1998. 92.00 (*0-673-98394-3*, Prentice Hall) P-H.

***Collier.** Harlem Is... 32p. 1998. 15.95 (*0-8050-5721-8*) H Holt & Co.

Collier. The King's Giraffe. (J). 1996. 14.00 (*0-671-88133-7*) S&S Bks Yung.

— Science & Technology Year Book, 1992. 1992. 45.00 (*0-02-527175-X*) Mac Lib Ref.

— Socialist Reasoning: An Inquiry into the Political Philosophy of Socialist China. 1995. 63.00 (*0-7453-0364-1*) Pluto GBR.

Collier, et al. Collier Bankruptcy Manual, 3 vols. 3rd ed. LC 98-115071. 1979. ring bd. 485.00 (*0-8205-1224-9*) Bender.

Collier, A. M. A Handbook of Textiles. 3rd ed. 1980. pap. text 7.80 (*0-08-024974-4*, Pergamon Pr) Elsevier.

Collier, Albert, jt. auth. see Warr, Diana.

Collier, Amy. Long Highway Home. LC 97-61415. 112p. 1998. pap. 8.95 (*1-57921-044-9*) WinePress Pub.

***Collier, Andrew.** Being & Worth. LC 98-43369. 1999. write for info. (*0-415-20735-5*); pap. write for info. (*0-415-20736-3*) Routledge.

Collier, Andrew. Critical Realism: An Introduction to Roy Bhaskar's Philosophy. LC 93-39601. 240p. (C). 1994. pap. 20.00 (*0-86091-602-2*, Pub. by Verso) Norton.

Collier, B., jt. ed. see Cuello, A. C.

Collier, B. David, Jr., et al, eds. Skeletal Nuclear Medicine. (Illus.). 512p. (C). (gr. 13). 1996. text 195.00 (*0-8151-3273-5*, 23963) Mosby Inc.

Collier, Basil. Defense of the United Kingdom. (Official Ser.: No. 11). (Illus.). 688p. 1995. reprint ed. 54.95 (*0-89839-212-8*) Battery Pr.

Collier, Berna. Romalpa Clauses: Reservation of Title in Sale of Goods Transactions. xxxiv, 192p. 1989. 44.50 (*0-455-20833-6*, Pub. by LawBk Co) Gaunt.

Collier, Billie J. & Epps, Helen H. Textile Testing & Analysis. LC 97-43883. 374p. 1998. 69.00 (*0-13-488214-8*, Merrill Coll) P-H.

Collier, Billie J., jt. auth. see Tortora, Phyllis G.

***Collier, Bo.** The Truth about Christmas. (Illus.). 150p. 2000. pap. 9.95 (*1-891929-44-5*) Four Seasons.

Collier Books Staff. Sesame Street Songbook: Sixty-Four Favorite Songs. (J). 1994. pap. 20.00 (*0-02-019201-0*) Macmillan.

Collier, Brian, jt. ed. see Cuello, A. Claudio.

Collier, Bruce & MacLachlan, James. Charles Babbage: And the Engines of Perfection. Gingerich, Owen, ed. LC 98-17054. (Oxford Portraits in Science Ser.). (Illus.). 128p. (YA). (gr. 7 up). 1999. 22.00 (*0-19-508997-9*) OUP.

***Collier, Bruce & MacLachlan, James.** Charles Babbage: And the Engines of Perfection. (Oxford Portraits in Science Ser.). (Illus.). 144p. (YA). 2000. pap. 11.95 (*0-19-514287-X*) OUP.

***Collier, Bryan.** To All My Sisters. 2001. text 15.95 (*0-8050-6463-X*) H Holt & Co.

***Collier, C. & Collier, J. L.** A Century of Immigration, 1820-1920. LC 98-33858. (Drama of American History Ser.: Group 3). (Illus.). 96p. (YA). (gr. 5-9). 1999. lib. bdg. 29.93 (*0-7614-0821-5*, Benchmark NY) Marshall Cavendish.

— The Civil War, 1860-1866. LC 97-49178. (Drama of American History Ser.: Group 3). (Illus.). 96p. (YA). (gr. 5-9). 1999. lib. bdg. 29.93 (*0-7614-0818-5*, Benchmark NY) Marshall Cavendish.

— The Reconstruction Era, 1864-1896. LC 98-8821. (Drama of American History Ser.: Group 3). (Illus.). 96p. (YA). (gr. 5-9). 1999. lib. bdg. 29.93 (*0-7614-0819-3*, Benchmark NY) Marshall Cavendish.

— The Rise of Industry, 1860-1900. LC 98-38528. (Drama of American History Ser.: Group 3). (Illus.). 96p. (YA). (gr. 5-9). 1999. lib. bdg. 29.93 (*0-7614-0820-7*, Benchmark NY) Marshall Cavendish.

Collier, C. & Collier, J. L. The Road to the Civil War, 1831-1861. LC 98-2620. (Drama of American History Ser.: Group 3). (Illus.). 96p. (YA). (gr. 5-9). 1998. lib. bdg. 29.93 (*0-7614-0817-7*, Benchmark NY) Marshall Cavendish.

Collier, C. G. Applications of Weather Radar Systems: A Guide to Uses of Radar Data in Meteorology. 1989. text 99.95 (*0-470-21449-X*) P-H.

Collier, C. G., ed. International Weather Radar Networking: Final Seminar of the COST Project 73. 344p. (C). 1992. text 179.50 (*0-7923-1706-8*) Kluwer Academic.

Collier, C. G. & Chapuis, M., eds. Weather Radar Networking: Seminar on COST Project 73. (C). 1990. text 248.50 (*0-7923-0672-4*) Kluwer Academic.

Collier, C. Patrick. Geometry for Teachers. 3rd rev. ed. (Illus.). 316p. (C). 1994. pap. text 26.95 (*0-88133-757-9*) Waveland Pr.

Collier, Calvin L. War Child's Children: A Story of the Third Arkansas Cavalry. (Illus.). 139p. 1965. 19.95 (*0-939130-05-X*) J W Bell.

Collier, Carlie. Passages of Light, Vol. I. 210p. 1991. pap. 16.95 (*0-9636489-0-X*) Celest Pr.

Collier, Carole. The Three-Bead Brick Stitch: Necklace Expressions. Krist, Rosemarie T., ed. (Illus.). 64p. 1998. pap. 19.99 (*0-9667689-0-6*) C Collier.

Collier, Catherine & Hoover, John J. Cognitive Learning Strategies for Minority Handicapped Students. LC 87-81734. 81p. 1987. pap. text 8.50 (*0-940059-02-9*) Hamilton Pubns.

Collier, Catherine, jt. auth. see Hoover, John J.

Collier, Catrin. All That Glitters. 432p. 1995. 26.00 (*0-7126-5850-5*, Pub. by CEN3) Trafalgar.

— Hearts of Gold. 464p. 1992. 24.95 (*0-7126-4606-X*, Pub. by CEN3) Trafalgar.

— One Blue Moon. large type ed. 584p. 1995. 27.99 (*0-7505-0712-8*, Pub. by Mgna Lrg Print) Ulverscroft.

***Collier, Catrin.** Past Remembering. 1999. pap. 11.00 (*0-09-953871-7*, Pub. by Arrow Bks) Trafalgar.

— Past Remembering. (*0-7126-7513-2*) Random House.

***Collier, Charles W.** Basic Themes in Law & Jurisprudence. LC 99-87576. (C). 2000. pap. 45.95 (*1-58360-763-3*) Anderson Pub Co.

Collier, Christopher. Drama of American History, 5 vols. 2000. boxed set 149.65 (*0-7614-0816-9*, Benchmark NY) Marshall Cavendish.

***Collier, Christopher.** Drama of American History, No. 4. (Illus.). (J). 2000. 119.72 (*0-7614-1050-3*, Benchmark NY) Marshall Cavendish.

Collier, Christopher. Outside Chicago: Richardsons' Trail Traveler. Johnson, John, ed. (Illus.). 50p. (Orig.). (C). 1996. spiral bd. 15.95 (*0-932647-17-0*) Rchrdsns Pubng.

***Collier, Christopher.** The Progressivism, the Great Depression & the New Deal 1901-1941. (Drama of American History Ser.). (Illus.). (J). 2000. 29.93 (*0-7614-1054-6*, Benchmark NY) Marshall Cavendish.

Collier, Christopher. Roger Sherman's Connecticut: Yankee Politics & the American Revolution. LC 78-153104. 423p. reprint ed. pap. 131.20 (*0-608-17887-X*, 205665900080) Bks Demand.

— Short Bike Rides in & Around Chicago. LC 99-18235. (Short Bike Rides Ser.). (Illus.). 224p. 1999. pap. text 11.95 (*0-7627-0410-1*) Globe Pequot.

***Collier, Christopher.** The U. S. Enters the World Stage, 1867-1919. (Drama of American History Ser.). (Illus.). (J). 2000. 29.93 (*0-7614-1053-8*, Benchmark NY) Marshall Cavendish.

Collier, Christopher & Collier, James L. Brother Sam & All That: A Teacher's Guide to the Historical Novels of James & Christopher Collier. (Illus.). 230p. 1999. teacher ed., per. 19.95 (*0-9667657-0-2*, 001) Clearwater Pr.

— Decision in Philadelphia: The Constitutional Convention, 1787. 448p. 1987. mass mkt. 6.99 (*0-345-34652-1*) Ballantine Pub Grp.

***Collier, Christopher & Collier, James L.** The Drama of American History: Group 1, 5 bks. Incl. American Revolution, 1763-1783. LC 96-45440. (Illus.). 96p. (YA). (gr. 4-7). 1997. lib. bdg. 29.93 (*0-7614-0440-6*, Benchmark NY); Clash of Cultures, Prehistory-1638. LC 96-31859. (Illus.). 96p. (YA). (gr. 5-7). 1997. lib. bdg. 29.93 (*0-7614-0436-8*, Benchmark NY); French & Indian War: 1660-1763. LC 96-44063. (Illus.). 96p. (YA). (gr. 4-7). 1997. lib. bdg. 28.50 (*0-7614-0439-2*, Benchmark NY); Paradox of Jamestown, 1585-1700. LC 96-34998. (Illus.). 96p. (YA). (gr. 4-7). 1997. lib. bdg. 29.93 (*0-7614-0437-6*, Benchmark NY); Pilgrims & Puritans, 1620-1676. LC 96-49382. (Illus.). 96p. (YA). (gr. 5 up). 1997. lib. bdg. 29.93 (*0-7614-0438-4*, Benchmark NY); (YA). (gr. 4-7). 1998. Set lib. bdg. 149.65 (*0-7614-0408-2*, Benchmark NY) Marshall Cavendish.

— The Rise of the Cities. LC 99-38409. (Drama of American History Ser.). 2000. 29.93 (*0-7614-1051-1*) Marshall Cavendish.

***Collier, Christopher & Collier, James Lincoln.** Indians, Cowboys & Farmers & the Battle for The Great Plains, 1865-1910. LC 00-21103. (Illus.). (J). 2000. 29.93 (*0-7614-1052-X*, Benchmark NY) Marshall Cavendish.

Collier, Christopher & Wells, Margaret. Outside Wisconsin: Richardsons' Trail Traveler, 2 vols. LC 97-219120. (Illus.). (Orig.). 1997. pap., spiral bd. 15.95 (*0-932647-18-9*) Rchrdsns Pubng.

Collier, Christopher, jt. auth. see Collier, James L.

Collier, Christopher, jt. auth. see Wells, Margaret.

Collier, Christopher, ed. see Wells, Margaret.

Collier, Clive. An Atlas of Epidurograms: Epidural Blocks Investigated. 100p. 1998. text 41.00 (*90-5702-323-7*) Gordon & Breach.

Collier, Courtland & Ledbetter, William B. Engineering Economics & Cost Analysis. 2nd ed. 635p. (C). 1997. pap. 93.67 (*0-06-041333-6*) Addson-Wesley Educ.

C

Collier, Courtland A. & Halperin, Don A. Construction Funding. 2nd ed. LC 83-21753. (Practical Construction Guides Ser.: 1-344). 304p. 1984. 90.00 (0-471-89065-0) Wiley.

Collier, David. Chinese-English Dictionary of Colloquial Terms Used in Modern Chinese Literature. 1979. 19.95 (0-88710-016-3) Yale Far Eastern Pubns.

— Just the Facts: A Decade of Comic Strip Essays. 1999. pap. text 11.95 (1-896597-25-4) LPC InBook.

— Squatters & Oligarchs: Authoritarian Rule & Policy Change in Peru. LC 75-34112. 200p. reprint ed. pap. 62.00 (0-7837-1617-6, 204191000024) Bks Demand.

Collier, David, et al, eds. The New Authoritarianism in Latin America. LC 79-83982. (Illus.). 467p. reprint ed. pap. 144.80 (0-608-06356-8, 206671700008) Bks Demand.

Collier, David, jt. auth. see Collier, Ruth B.

Collier, David, jt. auth. see Wagner, Laurie.

Collier, David A. The Service-Quality Solution: Using Service Management to Gain Competitive Advantage. LC 93-41421. 324p. 1994. text 40.00 (1-55623-753-7, Irwn Prfssnl) McGraw-Hill Prof.

Collier, Diana G. The Invisible Women of Washington. LC 86-72862. 186p. (Orig.). 1987. pap. 15.00 (0-932863-02-7) Clarity Pr.

Collier, Diane M., jt. ed. see Sawyer, Deborah.

Collier, Donald. Cultural Chronology & Change as Reflected in the Ceramics of the Viru Valley, Peru. LC 56-1086. (Field Museum of Natural History Anthropological Ser.: Vol. 43). (Illus.). 228p. 1955. reprint ed. pap. 70.70 (0-608-02726-X, 206339100004) Bks Demand.

Collier, Donald & Murra, John V. Survey & Excavations in Southern Ecuador. LC 43-11409. (Field Museum of Natural History Anthropological Ser.: Vol. 35, May 15, 1943). (Illus.). 227p. 1943. reprint ed. pap. 70.40 (0-608-02701-4, 206336600004) Bks Demand.

Collier, Donald, jt. auth. see Kroeber, Alfred L.

Collier, Edward A. A History of Old Kinderhook, New York. (Illus.). 572p. 1994. reprint ed. lib. bdg. 57.50 (0-8328-3913-2) Higginson Bk Co.

Collier, Elsie, jt. auth. see Collier, John.

Collier, Eric. Three Against the Wilderness. large type ed. 559p. 1969. 27.99 (0-85456-560-4) Ulverscroft.

Collier, Eugenia. Breeder & Other Stories. LC 91-74133. 200p. 1994. reprint ed. pap. 11.95 (0-933121-79-2) Black Classic.

Collier, Eugenia W., jt. ed. see Long, Richard A.

Collier, Everett. Boatowner's Guide to Corrosion: Find It, Stop It, Fix It. (Illus.). 176p. 1999. pap. 27.95 (0-07-155019-4) McGraw.

Collier, G. K. The Golden Web. large type ed. (Large Print Ser.). 560p. 1997. 27.99 (0-7089-3682-2) Ulverscroft.

Collier, Gary. Emotional Expression. 264p. 1985. text 49.95 (0-89859-505-3) L Erlbaum Assocs.

— Social Origins of Mental Ability. LC 93-3625. (Series on Personality Processes). 300p. 1993. 115.00 (0-471-30407-7) Wiley.

Collier, Gary, et al. Currents of Thought in American Social Psychology. (Illus.). 352p. 1991. text 65.00 (0-19-506129-2) OUP.

***Collier, Gaydell, et al.** Flint-Edge Refrains. Siebken, Lee Ann, ed. 36p. 2000. pap. 6.00 (0-917557-06-9, WYOPoets) Wyo Writers.

Collier, Gaydell M., jt. auth. see Prince, Eleanor F.

Collier, Gaydell M., jt. auth. see Steinkraus, William C.

Collier, George A. Socialists of Rural Andalusia: Unacknowledged Revolutionaries of the Second Republic. LC 87-9929. (Illus.). 264p. 1987. 37.50 (0-8047-1411-8) Stanford U Pr.

***Collier, George A. & Quaratiello, Elizabeth L.** Basta! Land & the Zapatista Rebellion in Chiapas. (C). 1999. pap. text 14.95 (0-935028-79-X) Inst Food & Develop.

Collier, Graham & Collier, Patricia. Antarctic Odyssey: In the Footsteps of the South Polar Explorers. 208p. 1999. 35.00 (0-7867-0653-8) Carroll & Graf.

***Collier, Grant.** Colorado: Yesterday & Today. (Illus.). (YA). (gr. 7 up). 2000. write for info. (1-890437-48-4) Western Reflections.

Collier, H., ed. Further Advances in Chemical Information. 192p. 1994. 94.00 (0-85186-545-3, R6545) CRC Pr.

— Recent Advances in Chemical Information 2. 322p. 1989. 22.95 (0-85186-235-7) CRC Pr.

Collier, H. R., ed. Chemical Information. (Illus.). 320p. 1990. 112.95 (0-387-51804-5, 3720) Spr-Verlag.

— Chemical Information No. 2: Information in Chemistry, Pharmacology & Patents: 2nd Proceedings of the International Conference Montreux, Switzerland, September 1990. (Illus.). viii, 232p. 1991. pap. 89.00 (0-387-53199-8) Spr-Verlag.

Collier, Helen H. Get Next to Yourself. 45p. pap. 4.50 (0-87516-393-9) DeVorss.

Collier, Helen V. Counseling Women: A Guide for Therapists. (Illus.). 352p. 1982. 35.00 (0-02-905840-6) Free Pr.

Collier, Herbert L. The Psychology of Twins: A Practical Handbook for Parents of Multiples. 3rd rev. ed. LC 96-79634. (Orig.). 1996. pap. 13.95 (0-9655442-0-6) Busn Word.

Collier, Howard. Why Some Get Snared in Sexual Traps. 32p. 1995. pap. 5.00 (1-887939-00-8) VisionQuest Media.

Collier, Howard E. Experiment with a Life. (Orig.). 1953. pap. 4.00 (0-87574-069-3) Pendle Hill.

— The Quaker Meeting. (C). 1944. pap. 4.00 (0-87574-026-X) Pendle Hill.

***Collier, Irwin L.** Welfare States in Transition: East & West LC 98-47081. (Studies in Economic Transition). xvi, 206 p. 1999. write for info. (0-333-73845-4, Pub. by S1 & J) Trafalgar.

Collier, Irwin L., ed. Welfare States in Transition: East & West. LC 98-47081. (Studies in Economic Transition Ser.). (Illus.). 256p. 1999. text 65.00 (0-312-21911-3) St Martin.

Collier, J. A., et al. Oxford Handbook of Clinical Specialties. 5th ed. (Illus.). 864p. 1999. pap. 32.50 (0-19-262943-3) OUP.

Collier, J. L., jt. auth. see Collier, C.

Collier, J. Payne. Bibliographical & Critical Account of the Rarest Books in the English Language, 4 vols. reprint ed. 345.00 (0-404-01720-7) AMS Pr.

— Farther Particulars Regarding Shakespeare & His Works. LC 70-113581. reprint ed. 29.50 (0-404-01607-3) AMS Pr.

— History of English Dramatic Poetry to the Time of Shakespeare, & the Annals of the Stage to the Restoration, 3 vols., Set. LC 74-113582. reprint ed. 225.00 (0-404-01730-4) AMS Pr.

— Memoirs of the Principal Actors in the Plays of Shakespeare. LC 77-113580. reprint ed. 55.00 (0-404-01599-9) AMS Pr.

— New Facts Regarding the Life of Shakespeare. LC 78-113583. (BCL Ser.: I). 1978. reprint ed. 18.00 (0-404-01609-X) AMS Pr.

— New Particulars Regarding the Works of Shakespeare. LC 71-113584. reprint ed. 21.50 (0-404-01614-6) AMS Pr.

— Old Man's Diary Forty Years Ago, 1823-33, 4 vols. in 1. reprint ed. 49.50 (0-404-07289-5) AMS Pr.

— Reasons for a New Edition of Shakespeare's Works. LC 79-113586. reprint ed. 39.50 (0-404-01616-2) AMS Pr.

Collier, J. Payne, ed. see Bale, John.

Collier, J. Payne, ed. see Dowdall, John.

Collier, J. Payne, ed. see Egerton, Francis.

Collier, J. W. Wood Finishing. 1967. 147.00 (0-08-011242-0, Pub. by Pergamon Repr) Franklin.

***Collier, James.** Corn Raid: A Story of the Jamestown Settlement. (Jamestown's American Portraits Ser.). 144p. (J). 2000. pap. 5.95 (0-8092-0619-6, 06196E, Jamestwn Pub) NTC Contemp Pub Co.

Collier, James. Jump Ship to Freedom. (J). 1996. pap. 5.99 (0-440-91158-3) BDD Bks Young Read.

***Collier, James.** Worst of Times: A Story of Texas Liberation. (Jamestown's American Portraits Ser.). 144p. 2000. pap. 5.95 (0-8092-0621-8, 06128E, Jamestwn Pub) NTC Contemp Pub Co.

Collier, James H., ed. Scientific & Technical Communication: Theory, Practice & Policy. LC 96-2537. 420p. 1996. 58.00 (0-7619-0320-8); pap. 26.95 (0-7619-0321-6) Sage.

***Collier, James L.** Biblical Challenges for Christian Singles. 1998. 8.93 (0-910683-09-3) Townsnd-Pr.

Collier, James L. Clock. 176p. (J). (gr. 4-7). 1994. pap. 4.99 (0-440-40999-3) Dell.

— Clock. 1995. 9.60 (0-606-07380-9, Pub. by Turtleback) Demco.

— Duke Ellington. large type ed. 1995. 37.50 (0-614-09572-7, L-81918-00) Am Printing Hse.

— Jazz: An American Saga. LC 97-3004. 98p. (J). (gr. 5-9). 1995. 16.95 (0-8050-4121-4) H Holt & Co.

Collier, James L. Jump Ship to Freedom. (Arabus Family Saga Ser.). (J). 1987. 9.60 (0-606-02265-1, Pub. by Turtleback) Demco.

Collier, James L. My Crooked Family. LC 90-27747. 288p. (YA). (gr. 5-9). 1991. pap. 15.00 (0-671-74224-8) S&S Bks Yung.

— Outside Looking In. 144p. 1990. pap. 2.95 (0-380-70961-9, Avon Bks) Morrow Avon.

— The Reception of Jazz in America: A New View. LC 88-80503. (I.S.A.M. Monographs: No. 27). 104p. (Orig.). 1988. pap. 12.00 (0-914678-30-2) Inst Am Music.

— The Rise of Selfishness in America. 320p. 1991. text 30.00 (0-19-505277-3) OUP.

— War Comes to Willy Freeman. LC 82-70317. 1983. 12.95 (0-440-09642-1) Dell.

— War Comes to Willy Freeman. (Arabus Family Saga Ser.). (J). 1987. 10.09 (0-606-03076-X, Pub. by Turtleback) Demco.

— The Winchesters. 176p. (J). (gr. 4). 1989. mass mkt. 2.95 (0-380-70808-6, Avon Bks) Morrow Avon.

Collier, James L. & Collier, Christopher. The Bloody Country. 192p. (YA). (gr. 4-7). 1985. pap. 4.50 (0-590-43126-9) Scholastic Inc.

— Jump Ship to Freedom. 208p. (J). (gr. k-6). 1987. pap. 4.99 (0-440-44323-7, YB BDD) BDD Bks Young Read.

— My Brother Sam Is Dead. LC 84-28787. 224p. (YA). (gr. 7 up). 1984. lib. bdg. 17.00 (0-02-722980-7, Four Winds Pr) S&S Childrens.

— My Brother Sam Is Dead. LC 84-28787. (Illus.). 224p. (YA). (gr. 5-9). 1985. pap. 4.50 (0-590-42792-X) Scholastic Inc.

— My Brother Sam Is Dead. (Scholastic Literature Guide Ser.). 16p. (J). 1997. pap. text 3.95 (0-590-37362-5) Scholastic Inc.

— My Brother Sam Is Dead. (J). 1974. 9.60 (0-606-00962-0, Pub. by Turtleback) Demco.

— War Comes to Willy Freeman. 192p. (J). (gr. k-6). 1987. pap. 4.99 (0-440-49504-0, YB BDD) BDD Bks Young Read.

— Who Is Carrie? 176p. (J). (gr. k-6). 1987. pap. 4.99 (0-440-49536-9, YB BDD) BDD Bks Young Read.

— The Winter Hero. 132p. (YA). (gr. 9 up). 1985. pap. 3.50 (0-590-42604-4) Scholastic Inc.

— With Every Drop of Blood: A Novel of the Civil War. 256p. (YA). (gr. 5 up). 1996. mass mkt. 4.99 (0-440-21983-3) Dell.

Collier, James L., jt. auth. see Collier, Christopher.

Collier, James Lincoln. Bloody Country. (Point Ser.). 1976. 8.35 (0-606-02448-4, Pub. by Turtleback) Demco.

— The Jazz Kid. 216p. (YA). (gr. 6 up). 1995. 15.95 (0-8050-2821-8) H Holt & Co.

— The Jazz Kid. LC 95-46366. (YA). (gr. 6 up). 1996. 10.09 (0-606-09485-7, Pub. by Turtleback) Demco.

— Who is Carrie? (Arabus Family Saga Ser.). (J). 1987. 9.60 (0-606-03505-2, Pub. by Turtleback) Demco.

— With Every Drop of Blood. LC 93-37655. (J). 1997. 10.09 (0-606-12108-0, Pub. by Turtleback) Demco.

Collier, James Lincoln, jt. auth. see Collier, Christopher.

Collier, James M. & Collier, Kenneth F. Votescam: The Stealing of America. 2nd ed. Vernick, Phyllis J., ed. 250p. (Orig.). 1993. pap. 9.95 (0-9634163-0-8) Victoria House.

Collier, James R. Yachting Signal Book. LC 84-45262. (Illus.). 128p. reprint ed. pap. 39.70 (0-608-20039-5, 207131100010) Bks Demand.

Collier, Jan, ed. see Bhakta, Ragini J.

Collier, Jane. The Art of Ingeniously Tormenting: 1757 Edition. Roberts, Marie M., ed. (Subversive Women Ser.). 256p. 1996. reprint ed. pap. 29.95 (1-85506-246-1) Bks Intl VA.

— Deadly Feast. large type ed. (Dales Large Print Ser.). 292p. 1997. pap. 18.99 (1-85389-720-5) Ulverscroft.

Collier, Jane & Esteban, Rafael. From Complicity to Encounter: The Church & the Culture of Economism. (CMMC Ser.). 128p. 1998. pap. 11.00 (1-56338-260-1) TPI PA.

Collier, Jane & Maurer, Bill, eds. Sanctioned Identities. 188p. 1995. pap. text 20.00 (2-88449-222-4) Gordon & Breach.

Collier, Jane F. From Duty to Desire: Remaking Families in a Spanish Village. LC 97-10672. (Studies in Culture - Power - History). 304p. 1997. pap. text 17.95 (0-691-01664-X, Pub. by Princeton U Pr) Cal Prin Full Svc.

— Marriage & Inequality in Classless Societies. LC 87-19132. xx, 290p. 1988. 42.50 (0-8047-1365-0) Stanford U Pr.

Collier, Jane F. & Yanagisako, Sylvia J., eds. Gender & Kinship: Essays Toward a Unified Analysis. LC 87-9951. 392p. 1987. 49.50 (0-8047-1366-9); pap. 17.95 (0-8047-1819-9) Stanford U Pr.

Collier, Jane F., jt. ed. see Starr, June.

Collier, Jane Fishburne. Marriage & Inequality in Classless Societies. xx, 290p. 1993. pap. 17.95 (0-8047-2177-7) Stanford U Pr.

Collier, Jeremy. Essays upon Several Moral Subjects, 3 vols., Set. (Anglistica & Americana Ser.: No. 35). 1969. reprint ed. 320.00 (0-685-66452-X, 05102385) G Olms Pubs.

— A Short View of the Immorality & Profaneness of the English Stage. 3rd ed. LC 74-3401. reprint ed. 21.50 (0-404-01619-7) AMS Pr.

— A Short View of the Profaneness & Immorality of the English Stage, Etc. (Anglistica & Americana Ser.: No. 46). x, 437p. 1969. reprint ed. 110.00 (0-685-66453-8, 05102589) G Olms Pubs.

Collier, Jess. Gypsy Summer. (Rainbow Romances Ser.). 160p. 1993. 14.95 (0-7090-4920-X) Parkwest Pubns.

Collier, Jo Leslie. From Wagner to Murnau: The Transposition of Romanticism from Stage to Screen. Kirkpatrick, Diane, ed. LC 87-28944. (Studies in Cinema: No. 45). 180p. reprint ed. pap. 55.80 (0-8357-1843-3, 207070600004) Bks Demand.

Collier, Joanne. A Horse Called Poppyseed. LC 97-37442. (YA). 1997. pap. 7.99 (0-8280-1307-1) Review & Herald.

Collier, John. Fancies & Goodnights. 1993. reprint ed. lib. bdg. 18.95 (0-89968-393-2, Lghtyr Pr) Buccaneer Bks.

— His Monkey Wife. 1993. reprint ed. lib. bdg. 18.95 (0-89968-394-0, Lghtyr Pr) Buccaneer Bks.

***Collier, John.** His Monkey Wife: Or Married to a Chimp. LC 99-58283. xvi, 224p. 2000. reprint ed. pap. 14.95 (0-9664913-3-5, Pub. by Paul Dry Bks) IPG Chicago.

— The Indians of the Americas. (LC History-America-E). 326p. 1999. reprint ed. lib. bdg. 89.00 (0-7812-4249-5) Rprt Serv.

Collier, John & Collier, Elsie. China's Socialist Revolution. LC 74-7782. 286p. 1976. pap. 10.00 (0-85345-368-3, Pub. by Monthly Rev) NYU Pr.

Collier, John, Jr. & Collier, Malcolm. Visual Anthropology: Photography As a Research Method. enl. rev. ed. LC 86-6926. (Illus.). 248p. 1986. pap. 24.95 (0-8263-0899-6) U of NM Pr.

***Collier, John & Lowe, Vaughan.** The Settlement of Disputes in International Law: Institutions & Procedures. LC 99-16148. 424p. 1999. text 135.00 (0-19-825669-8) OUP.

— The Settlement of Disputes in International Law: Institutions & Procedures. 424p. 2000. pap. text 49.95 (0-19-829927-3) OUP.

Collier, John, jt. auth. see Moskowitz, Ira.

Collier, John G. & Hewitt, G. F. Introduction to Nuclear Power. 2nd ed. LC 97-13559. 256p. 1997. 69.95 (1-56032-454-6) Hemisp Pub.

Collier, John G. & Thome, John R. Convective Boiling & Condensation. 3rd ed. (Oxford Engineering Science Ser.: Vol. 38). (Illus.). 640p. 1996. reprint ed. pap. text 75.00 (0-19-856296-9) OUP.

Collier, John P. New Facts Regarding the Life of Shakespeare. (BCL1-PR English Literature Ser.). 55p. 1992. reprint ed. lib. bdg. 59.00 (0-7812-7280-7) Rprt Serv.

Collier, John P., ed. Illustrations of Early English Popular Literature, 2 vols., Set. LC 65-16234. 860p. 1972. reprint ed. 44.95 (0-405-08366-1, Pub. by Blom Pubns) Ayer.

— Illustrations of Early English Popular Literature, 2 vols., Vol. 1. LC 65-16234. 1972. reprint ed. 23.95 (0-405-08367-X, Pub. by Blom Pubns) Ayer.

— Illustrations of Early English Popular Literature, 2 vols., Vol. 2. LC 65-16234. (Illus.). 1972. reprint ed. 24.95 (0-405-08368-8, Pub. by Blom Pubns) Ayer.

— Illustrations of Old English Literature, 3 vols., 3. LC 65-16233. (Illus.). 1972. reprint ed. 24.95 (0-405-08372-6, Pub. by Blom Pubns) Ayer.

— Illustrations of Old English Literature, 3 vols., Set. LC 65-16233. (Illus.). 1202p. 1972. reprint ed. 72.95 (0-405-08369-6, Pub. by Blom Pubns) Ayer.

— Illustrations of Old English Literature, 3 vols., Vol. 1. LC 65-16233. (Illus.). 1972. reprint ed. 24.95 (0-405-08370-X, Pub. by Blom Pubns) Ayer.

— Illustrations of Old English Literature, 3 vols., Vol. 2. LC 65-16233. (Illus.). 1972. reprint ed. 24.95 (0-405-08371-8, Pub. by Blom Pubns) Ayer.

Collier, John P., ed. see Coleridge, Samuel Taylor.

Collier, John P., ed. see Gosson, Stephen.

Collier, John P., ed. see Shakespeare, William.

Collier, Keith. Managing Construction: The Contractual Viewpoint. LC 93-3778. 432p. 1993. pap. 54.50 (0-8273-5700-1) Delmar.

— Managing Construction - The Contractual Viewpoint: Instructor's Guide. 75p. 1994. 16.95 (0-8273-5702-8) Delmar.

Collier, Ken. After the Welfare State. LC 98-114129. 200p. 1997. pap. 16.00 (0-921586-42-6, Pub. by New Star Bks) Genl Dist Srvs.

Collier, Ken. Social Work with Rural Peoples. 2nd rev. ed. 118p. 1993. pap. 9.95 (0-921586-29-9, Pub. by New Star Bks) Genl Dist Srvs.

Collier, Kenneth. Between the Branches: The White House Office of Legislative Affairs. LC 96-51293. (Policy & Institutional Studies). 330p. 1997. text 50.00 (0-8229-3978-9) U of Pittsburgh Pr.

— Between the Branches: The White House Office of Legislative Affairs. LC 96-51293. (Policy & Institutional Studies). (Illus.). 330p. 1997. pap. 22.95 (0-8229-5629-2) U of Pittsburgh Pr.

— C for Engineers. 224p. 1995. pap. text 34.67 (0-8053-6477-3) Benjamin-Cummings.

Collier, Kenneth F., jt. auth. see Collier, James M.

Collier, Kenneth W. Our Seven Principles in Story & Verse: A Collection for Children & Adults. LC 97-161440. 120p. 1997. pap. 12.00 (1-55896-353-7, Skinner Hse Bks) Unitarian Univ.

Collier, L. D. Teach Yourself Spanish, Everyday. (Teach Yourself Ser.). 1992. 10.95 (0-8288-8398-X) Fr & Eur.

Collier, Larry. How to Fly Helicopters. (Modern Aviation Ser.). (Illus.). 1979. pap. 10.95 (0-8306-2264-0, 2264) McGraw-Hill Prof.

— How to Fly Helicopters. 2nd ed. (Illus.). 226p. 1986. 15.95 (0-8306-0286-0, 2386); pap. 15.95 (0-8306-2386-8) McGraw-Hill Prof.

Collier, Laurie. Authors & Artists for Young Adults, Vol. 7. 250p. 1991. text 82.00 (0-8103-5056-4) Gale.

Collier, Laurie, ed. Authors & Artists for Young Adults, Vol. 9. (Illus.). 250p. 1992. text 82.00 (0-8103-7584-2, 003421) Gale.

Collier, Laurie & Nakamura, Joyce, eds. Major Authors & Illustrators for Children & Young Adults: A Selection of Sketches from Something about the Author, 6 vols., Set. LC 92-73849. (Illus.). 2609p. 1992. 299.00 (0-8103-7702-0, 007290-M94800) Gale.

Collier, Leslie. Topley & Wilson's Microbiology & Microbial Infections Vol. 1: Virology. 9th ed. (Illus.). 750p. 1998. text 195.00 (0-340-66316-2, Pub. by E A) OUP.

— Virology for Medical & Dental Students. Oxford, John S., ed. (Illus.). 416p. 1993. pap. text 39.95 (0-19-261662-5) OUP.

Collier, Leslie, et al, eds. Topley & Wilson's Microbiology & Microbial Infections, 6 vols. 9th ed. LC 98-137864. (Arnold Publication). 4500p. 1998. text 995.00 (0-340-61470-6, Pub. by E A) OUP.

— Topley & Wilson's Microbiology & Microbial Infections, 6 vols. 9th ed. (Arnold Publication). (Illus.). 1998. text 1250.00 incl. cd-rom (0-340-70069-6) OUP.

— Topley & Wilson's Microbiology & Microbial Infections Vol. 3: Bacterial Infections. 9th ed. 750p. 1998. text 195.00 (0-340-66318-9, Pub. by E A) OUP.

***Collier, Leslie & Oxford, John S.** Human Virology. 2nd ed. LC 99-42842. (Illus.). 304p. 2000. pap. text 37.95 (0-19-262820-8) OUP.

Collier, Leslie H. Topley & Wilson's Principles of Bacteriology, Virology & Immunity. 8th ed. 736p. text. write for info. (0-7131-4592-7, Pub. by E A) Routldge.

Collier, Lindsay. Get Out of Your Thinking Box: 365 Ways to Brighten Your Life & Enhance Your Creativity. Jacobs, Pamela D., ed. LC 94-17657. (Illus.). 125p. 1994. pap. 7.95 (1-885003-01-3) R D Reed Pubs.

Collier, Louise W. Pilgrimage: A Tale of Old Natchez. LC 94-27835. 480p. 1994. 6.95 (1-56554-064-6) Pelican.

Collier, M. Geology of Denali NP. (Illus.). 48p. 1995. pap. 7.95 (0-930931-04-1) Alaska Natural.

Collier, Malcolm, jt. auth. see Collier, John, Jr.

Collier, Margaret. Border Collies. rev. ed. (Illus.). 1996. pap. 9.95 (0-7938-2305-6, KW-192S) TFH Pubns.

Collier, Marjorie. Siamese Cats. (Complete Pet Owner's Manual Ser.). (Illus.). 64p. 1992. pap. 6.95 (0-8120-4764-8) Barron.

Collier, Mark. How to Read Egyptian Hieroglyphs: A Step-by-Step Guide to Teach Yourself. 192p. 1998. pap. 18.95 (0-520-21597-4, Pub. by U CA Pr) Cal Prin Full Svc.

— How to Read Egyptian Hieroglyphs: A Step-by-Step Guide to Teach Yourself. LC 98-167197. ix, 179p. 1998. write for info. (0-7141-1910-5) BRI5.

Collier, Mary. The Narnia Paper Dolls: The Lion, the Witch & the Wardrobe Collection. (World of Narnia Ser.). 24p. (J). (ps-3). 1998. 7.95 (0-694-01078-2) HarpC Child Bks.

— The World of Narnia Advent Calendar: Adapted from C. S. Lewis's The Chronicles of Narnia. (J). 1998. 12.95 (0-694-00984-9) HarpC Child Bks.

An Asterisk (*) at the beginning of an entry indicates that the title is appearing for the first time.

Collier, Mary B. La Carmen Essentialle et sa Realisation au Spectacle. LC 93-2215. (Currents in Comparative Romance Languages & Literatures Ser.: Vol. 14). (FRE.). X, 194p. (C). 1994. text 46.95 (*0-8204-2045-X*) P Lang Pubng.

Collier, Mary E. & Thalman, Sylvia B., eds. Interviews with Tom Smith & Maria Copa: Isabel Kelly's Ethnographic Notes on the Coast Miwok Indians of Marin & Southern Sonoma Counties, California. (Mapom Occasional Papers: No. 6). (Illus.). 580p. (Orig.). 1991. pap. 50.00 (*0-9629718-0-4*) Miwok Archaeol Preserve.

***Collier, Mary J.** Constituting Cultural Difference Through Discourse. LC 00-9516. 2000. write for info. (*0-7619-2230-X*) Sage Pub.

Collier, Mary J., et al. Kids' Stuff Kindergarten-Nursery School: Language Arts, Science, Social Studies, Math, Art & Music. rev. ed. LC 78-70904. (Kids' Stuff Set Ser.). (Illus.). 264p. (J). (ps-k). 1981. pap. 16.95 (*0-913916-61-7*, IP005) Incentive Pubns.

Collier, Mary Jo, jt. auth. see Collier, Peter.

***Collier, Maxie D.** The IFILM Digial Video Filmmaker's Handbook. 325p. 2000. pap. 24.95 incl. cd-rom (*1-58065-031-7*, Pub. by Lone Eagle Pub) Natl Bk Netwk.

Collier, Mel. Microcomputer Software for Information Management. 150p. 1986. text 54.95 (*0-566-03555-3*) Ashgate Pub Co.

Collier, Michael. The Folded Heart. LC 88-28090. (Wesleyan Poetry Ser.). 63p. 1989. pap. 12.95 (*0-8195-1171-4*, Wesleyan Univ Pr) U Pr of New Eng.

— An Introduction to the Geology of Death Valley. LC 90-81612. (Illus.). 60p. (Orig.). (C). 1990. pap. 7.95 (*1-878900-13-7*) DVNH Assn.

***Collier, Michael.** A Land in Motion: California's San Andreas Fault. 128p. 1999. pap. 19.95 (*0-520-21897-3*, Pub. by U CA Pr) Cal Prin Full Svc.

— The Ledge. LC 99-85997. 96p. 2000. 22.00 (*0-618-05014-0*) HM.

Collier, Michael. Longest Day. (Doctor Who Ser.). 1998. pap. 5.95 (*0-563-40581-3*) BBC.

— The Neighbor. (Phoenix Poets Ser.). 74p. 1994. pap. 10.00 (*0-226-11359-0*) U Ch Pr.

— The Neighbor. (Phoenix Poets Ser.). 74p. 1995. lib. bdg. 20.00 (*0-226-11358-2*) U Ch Pr.

— Taint. 1999. mass mkt. 5.95 (*0-563-55568-8*) BBC Bks.

***Collier, Michael, ed.** The New American Poets: A Bread Loaf Anthology. LC 99-56171. (Bread Loaf Anthology Ser.). (Illus.). 302p. 2000. pap. 19.95 (*0-87451-964-0*); text 50.00 (*0-87451-963-2*) U Pr of New Eng.

Collier, Michael, ed. The Wesleyan Tradition: Four Decades of American Poetry. LC 93-17846. (Wesleyan Poetry Ser.). 316p. 1993. pap. 17.95 (*0-8195-1229-X*, Wesleyan Univ Pr) U Pr of New Eng.

— The Wesleyan Tradition: Four Decades of American Poetry. LC 93-17846. (Wesleyan Poetry Ser.). 316p. 1993. text 35.00 (*0-8195-2210-4*, Wesleyan Univ Pr) U Pr of New Eng.

Collier, Michael & Plumly, Stanley, eds. The New Bread Loaf Anthology of Contemporary American Poetry. LC 99-20942. (Bread Loaf Anthology Ser.). 381p. 1999. pap. 19.95 (*0-87451-950-0*); text 45.00 (*0-87451-949-7*) U Pr of New Eng.

Collier, Michael, et al. Dams & Rivers: Primer on the Downstream Effects of Dams. (Illus.). 94p. (C). 1998. pap. text 30.00 (*0-7881-2698-9*) DIANE Pub.

***Collier, Michael, et al.** Water, Earth, & Sky: The Colorado River Basin. LC 98-41925. (Illus.). 128p. 1999. 29.95 (*0-87480-598-8*) U of Utah Pr.

Collier, Michael, jt. auth. see Houk, Rose.

Collier, Millard, ed. see Virgil, James.

Collier-Morales, Roberta. The Lord's Prayer: Forgive Us Our Trespasses, Wall Chart. (Basic Bible Charts Ser.). (Illus.). (J). (gr. 2-8). 1997. pap. 12.95 (*0-9655082-5-0*, 509L) Rose Publshg.

Collier-Morales, Roberta. Dancers. (Costumes for Coloring Ser.). 64p. (Orig.). (J). (gr. 2 up). 1996. pap. 3.95 (*0-448-41477-5*, G & D) Peng Put Young Read.

Collier-Morales, Roberta, jt. auth. see Colon-Vila, Lillian.

Collier Newfield Inc. Staff. Young Students Learning Library. LC 97-209688. 23 p. 1997. write for info. (*1-57161-122-3*) Atlas Editions.

Collier, Oscar & Leighton, Frances S. How to Write & Sell Your First Nonfiction Book. 288p. 1994. pap. 9.95 (*0-312-11001-4*) St Martin.

— How to Write & Sell Your First Novel. rev. ed. LC 97-19374. 256p. 1997. pap. 16.99 (*0-89879-770-5*, Wrtrs Digest Bks) F & W Pubns Inc.

Collier, P., jt. auth. see Beeby, W.

Collier, Patricia. The Thatched Kitchen: Harvest & Holiday Cookbook. LC 72-87655. 1972. 5.95 (*0-88351-008-1*) Test Recipe.

Collier, Patricia, jt. auth. see Collier, Graham.

Collier, Pattillo. Investment & Risk in Africa. LC 99-32994. 1999. text 85.00 (*0-312-22604-7*) St Martin.

Collier, Paul. Living Down the Past: How Europe Can Help Africa Grow. (Studies in Trade & Development: Vol. 2). 39p. 1998. pap. 13.95 (*0-255-36466-0*) Inst Economic Affairs.

— Petril Wava. (Illus.). 26p. (Orig.). 1993. pap. 5.00 (*0-926935-79-8*) Runaway Spoon.

Collier, Paul & Gunning, Jan W. Trade Shocks: Consequences & Policy Responses Theory & Evidence from Africa, Asia & Latin America. LC 94-15540. (Occasional Papers: No. 51). 1994. pap. 9.95 (*1-55815-326-8*) ICS Pr.

— Trade Shocks in Developing Countries: Asia & Latin America, Vol. 2. (Illus.). 370p. 2000. text 85.00 (*0-19-829463-8*) OUP.

— Trade Shocks in Developing Countries Vol. 1: Africa. (Illus.). 502p. 2000. text 98.00 (*0-19-829338-0*) OUP.

Collier, Paul & Lal, Deepak. Labour & Poverty in Kenya, 1900-80. (Illus.). 240p. 1986. 69.00 (*0-19-828505-1*) OUP.

Collier, Paul, et al. Labour & Poverty in Rural Tanzania: Ujamaa & Rural Development in the United Republic of Tanzania. (Illus.). 160p. 1991. pap. 22.00 (*0-19-828315-6*) OUP.

Collier, Peggy, jt. auth. see Jones, Valarie.

Collier, Peter. Les Kennedy: Une Dynastie Americaine. 1985. 29.95 (*2-920083-15-5*) Edns Roseau.

— Proust & Venice: "Swann's Way" (Landmarks of World Literature Ser.). (Illus.). 196p. (C). 1989. text 59.95 (*0-521-36206-7*) Cambridge U Pr.

Collier, Peter & Collier, Mary Jo. The King's Giraffe. LC 95-22417. (Illus.). 40p. (J). (gr. k-5). 1996. 16.00 (*0-689-80679-5*) S&S Bks Yung.

Collier, Peter & Geyer-Ryan, Helga, eds. Literary Theory Today. LC 90-55166. 280p. 1990. pap. 17.95 (*0-8014-9761-2*) Cornell U Pr.

Collier, Peter & Horowitz, David. Deconstructing the Left: From Vietnam to the Persian Gulf. 212p. (Orig.). 1991. pap. 14.95 (*0-8191-8315-6*) Madison Bks UPA.

— Destructive Generation. LC 96-222466. 400p. 1996. per. 14.00 (*0-684-82641-0*) Free Pr.

— The Kennedys: An American Drama. 736p. 1994. mass mkt. 6.99 (*0-446-35383-3*) Warner Bks.

— The Race Card: White Guilt, Black Resentment. LC 96-52393. 256p. 1997. boxed set 24.00 (*0-7615-0942-9*) Prima Pub.

— The Roosevelts: An American Saga. 544p. 1995. per. 15.00 (*0-684-80140-X*) S&S Trade Pap.

— Second Thoughts: Former Radicals Look Back at the Sixties. LC 88-13427. 288p. 1989. 22.95 (*0-8191-7147-6*) Madison Bks UPA.

— Surviving the PC University: The Best of Heterodoxy. 368p. 1996. pap. 9.95 (*1-886442-06-1*) Ctr Study Popular.

Collier, Peter & Horowitz, David, eds. Second Thoughts about Race in America. 175p. 1991. 17.95 (*0-8191-8243-5*) Madison Bks UPA.

Collier, Peter & Lethbridge, Robert, eds. Artistic Relations: Literature & the Visual Arts in Nineteenth-Century France. LC 94-4503. (Illus.). 368p. 1994. 45.00 (*0-300-06009-2*) Yale U Pr.

Collier, Peter, jt. auth. see Chace, William M.

Collier, Peter, jt. ed. see Best, Victoria.

Collier, Peter, ed. see Cooper, Sarah.

Collier, Peter, jt. ed. see Horowitz, David.

Collier, Peter, tr. see Bourdieu, Pierre.

Collier, Peter, tr. see Zola, Emile.

Collier, Philip E. It Seems to Me. 1982. 4.95 (*0-86544-019-0*) Salv Army Suppl South.

Collier, Phylis, ed. see Kensington, Olivia, et al.

Collier, Price. America & the Americans from a French Point of View. 1977. text 18.95 (*0-8369-9215-6*, 9071) Ayer.

Collier, R. Equal Opportunities in Service. LC 98-9786. 1998. pap. 29.95 (*0-335-19729-9*); pap. 85.00 (*0-335-19730-2*) OpUniv Pr.

Collier, R. B. Pleneurethic: A New Approach to Life & Health. Myers, Iris, ed. (Illus.). 1974. text 4.50 (*0-533-01143-4*) Pleneurethic Intl.

— Pleneurethic & the Brain. LC 65-81608. 2.50 (*0-686-17437-2*) Pleneurethic Intl.

Collier, R. S. The Economics of Machinery Replacement. (Technical Papers: Vol. P990.07). (Illus.). 13p. 1952. pap. text 30.00 (*1-55589-459-3*) AGMA.

Collier, Ras M., et al. Rodney King & the L. A. Rebellion: Analysis & Commentary by 13 Independent Black Writers. 144p. (Orig.). 1992. pap. 10.00 (*1-56411-036-2*) Untd Bros & Sis.

Collier, Raymond O., Jr. & Hummel, Thomas J., eds. Experimental Design & Interpretation. LC 76-18039. (Readings in Educational Research Ser.). 1977. 46.00 (*0-8211-0225-7*) McCutchan.

***Collier, Richard.** D-Day: 06-06-1944. (Illus.). 224p. 2000. pap. 24.95 (*1-84188-031-0*) Seven Dials.

— Masculinities, Crime & Criminology: Men, Heterosexuality & the Criminalized Other LC 98-60954. xiv, 205 p. 1998. write for info. (*0-8039-7997-5*) Sage.

Collier, Richard. Masculinity, Law, & the Family. LC 94-5591. 352p. (C). 1995. pap. 24.99 (*0-415-09195-0*, B2217) Routledge.

— The Years of Attrition, 1940-1941. 685p. 1995. pap. text. write for info. (*0-7490-0236-0*) Allison & Busby.

— The Years of Victory, 1944-1945. (Illus.). 464p. 1995. pap. write for info. (*0-7490-0251-4*) Allison & Busby.

Collier, Richard, jt. auth. see Webb, Hugh B.

Collier, Richard A. Profitable Product Management: Powerful Techniques for Improving Products & Performance for Maximizing Profits. (Marketing Ser.). (Illus.). 304p. 1995. pap. text 39.95 (*0-7506-1888-4*) Buttrwrth-Heinemann.

Collier, Richard B. Pleneurethics: A New Concept of Healing, Vol. 1. 2nd ed. Terrey, John N., ed. xlvii, 292p. (C). 1992. 17.95 (*1-882152-08-5*); pap. 11.95 (*1-882152-09-3*) R B Collier Pleneurethics.

— Pleneurethics: A New Concept of Healing, Vol. 2. 2nd ed. xxvi, 288p. 1993. 17.95 (*1-882152-10-7*); pap. 11.95 (*1-882152-11-5*) R B Collier Pleneurethics.

— Pleneurethics: A Philosophical System Uniting Body, Brain & Mind. 2nd ed. Terrey, John N., ed. xxiv, 436p. (C). 17.95 (*1-882152-06-9*); pap. 11.95 (*1-882152-07-7*) R B Collier Pleneurethics.

Collier, Robert. The Amazing Secrets of the Masters of the Far East. 1991. pap. 10.95 (*0-912576-02-2*) R Collier.

— Be Rich. 1985. pap. 4.95 (*0-912576-05-7*) R Collier.

— Be Rich! 46p. 1996. reprint ed. pap. 10.00 (*0-7873-1078-6*) Hlth Research.

— Prayer Works! 1985. pap. 6.95 (*0-912576-01-4*) R Collier.

— Riches Within Your Reach. 1984. 19.95 (*0-912576-14-6*); pap. 12.50 (*0-912576-13-8*) R Collier.

— Secret of the Ages. rev. ed. 1984. 18.95 (*0-912576-12-X*); pap. 12.50 (*0-912576-11-1*) R Collier.

Collier, Roberta. Little Animal Follow-the-Dots Coloring Book. 80th ed. (Illus.). (J). (gr. k-3). 1991. pap. 1.00 (*0-486-26666-4*) Dover.

Collier, Roberta. Little Zoo Animals Coloring Book. (Illus.). (J). 1990. pap. text 1.00 (*0-486-26403-3*) Dover.

Collier, Rohan. Combatting Sexual Harrasment in the Workplace. LC 94-26386. 160p. 1995. pap. 33.95 (*0-335-19082-0*) OpUniv Pr.

Collier, Ron & Wilkinson, Roni. Dark Peak Aircraft Wrecks No. 2: Stories Behind the Crash Sites in the Dark Peak National Park. rev. ed. (Illus.). 192p. (C). 1995. reprint ed. pap. 16.95 (*0-85052-336-2*, Pub. by Leo Cooper) Trans-Atl Phila.

Collier, Ruth B. The Contradictory Alliance: State-Labor Relations & Regime Change in Mexico. LC 91-46976. (Research Ser.: No. 83). x, 188p. (Orig.). (C). 1992. pap. text 18.50 (*0-87725-183-5*) U of Cal IAS.

— Paths Toward Democracy: The Working Class & Elites in Western Europe & South America. LC 99-12564. (Cambridge Studies in Comparative Politics). (Illus.). 232p. (C). 1999. 49.95 (*0-521-64369-4*); pap. 17.95 (*0-521-64382-1*) Cambridge U Pr.

Collier, Ruth B. & Collier, David. Shaping the Political Arena: Critical Junctures, the Labor Movement, & Regime Dynamics in Latin America. (Illus.). 845p. 1991. text 95.00 (*0-691-07830-0*, Pub. by Princeton U Pr); pap. text 27.95 (*0-691-02313-1*, Pub. by Princeton U Pr) Cal Prin Full Svc.

Collier, S. L., ed. see Petroleum Mechanical Engineering Conference & Work.

Collier, Samuel L. Mud Pump Handbook. LC 82-20743. (Illus.). 256p. 1983. pap. 79.40 (*0-608-04973-5*, 206555300004) Bks Demand.

***Collier, Sandra.** Bible Story Skitlets Too! 1999. pap. 8.99 (*0-570-05374-9*) Concordia.

Collier, Sandra. Wake up to Your Dreams. 120p. (YA). pap. 5.99 (*0-590-24761-1*) Scholastic Inc.

Collier, Sargent F. Mount Desert Island & Acadia National Park: An Informal History. Helfrich, G. W., ed. (Illus.). 146p. 1978. pap. 12.95 (*0-89272-044-1*) Down East.

Collier, Simon. Ideas & Politics of Chilean Independence 1808-1833. LC 67-15395. (Cambridge Latin American Studies: No. 1). 414p. reprint ed. pap. 118.00 (*0-608-15707-4*, 2031634) Bks Demand.

— The Life, Music & Times of Carlos Gardel. LC 86-4029. (Pitt Latin American Ser.). 358p. 1986. pap. 111.00 (*0-608-05082-2*, 206563600005) Bks Demand.

Collier, Simon, et al, eds. The Cambridge Encyclopedia of Latin America & the Caribbean. 2nd ed. (Illus.). 480p. (C). 1992. 69.95 (*0-521-41322-2*) Cambridge U Pr.

Collier, Simon & Sater, William F. A History of Chile, 1808-1994. (Latin American Studies: No. 82). (Illus.). 448p. (C). 1996. text 59.95 (*0-521-56075-6*); pap. text 18.95 (*0-521-56827-7*) Cambridge U Pr.

Collier, Simon, et al. Tango. LC 95-60478. (Illus.). 208p. 1995. 40.00 (*0-500-01671-2*, Pub. by Thames Hudson) Norton.

— Tango! The Dance, the Song, the Story. LC 95-6078. (Illus.). 208p. 1997. pap. 29.95 (*0-500-27979-9*, Pub. by Thames Hudson) Norton.

Collier, Simon, jt. auth. see Azzi, Maria Susana.

Collier, Simon, jt. auth. see Mayo, John.

Collier-Slone, Kay. Single in the Church: New Ways to Minister with 52 Percent of God's People. LC 92-72459. (Orig.). 1992. pap. 15.95 (*1-56699-058-0*, AL137) Alban Inst.

Collier Staff. Collier Encyclopedia, 1996, 24 vols. 1996. 950.00 (*0-02-864841-2*) Mac Lib Ref.

— Collier's Encyclopedia, 1980, Vol. 1. 1980. 25.00 (*0-02-940910-1*) Mac Lib Ref.

— Collier's Encyclopedia, 1980, Vol. 2. 1980. 25.00 (*0-02-940920-9*) Mac Lib Ref.

— Collier's Encyclopedia, 1980, Vol. 3. 1980. 25.00 (*0-02-940930-6*) Mac Lib Ref.

— Collier's Encyclopedia, 1980, Vol. 4. 1980. 25.00 (*0-02-940940-3*) Mac Lib Ref.

— Collier's Encyclopedia, 1980, Vol. 5. 1980. 25.00 (*0-02-940950-0*) Mac Lib Ref.

— Collier's Encyclopedia, 1980, Vol. 6. 1980. 25.00 (*0-02-940960-8*) Mac Lib Ref.

— Collier's Encyclopedia, 1989, 24 vols., Vol. 19. 1989. 40.00 (*0-02-942918-8*) Mac Lib Ref.

— Collier's Encyclopedia, 1996. 1996. 1199.00 incl. cd-rom (*0-02-864664-9*) Colliers En.

— Collier's Encyclopedia, 1996, Vol. 15. 1996. 45.00 (*0-02-864700-9*) Mac Lib Ref.

— Collier's Encyclopedia, 1996, Vol. 16. 1996. 45.00 (*0-02-864701-7*) Mac Lib Ref.

— Collier's Encyclopedia, 1996, Vol. 17. 1996. 45.00 (*0-02-864702-5*) Mac Lib Ref.

— Collier's Encyclopedia, 1996, Vol. 18. 1996. 45.00 (*0-02-864704-1*) Mac Lib Ref.

— Collier's Encyclopedia 1996, Vol. 19. 1996. 45.00 (*0-02-864705-X*) Mac Lib Ref.

— Collier's Encyclopedia, 1996, Vol. 20. 1996. 45.00 (*0-02-864706-8*) Mac Lib Ref.

— Collier's Encyclopedia, 1996, Vol. 21. 1996. 45.00 (*0-02-864707-6*) Mac Lib Ref.

— Collier's Encyclopedia, 1996, Vol. 22. 1996. 45.00 (*0-02-864708-4*) Mac Lib Ref.

— Collier's Encyclopedia, 1996, Vol. 23. 1996. 45.00 (*0-02-864709-2*) Mac Lib Ref.

— Collier's Encyclopedia, 1996, Vol. 24. 1996. 45.00 (*0-02-864710-6*) Mac Lib Ref.

— Collier's Encyclopedia 1997, 24 vols. 1997. 499.00 incl. cd-rom (*0-02-864874-9*) Mac Lib Ref.

— Collier's Encyclopedia 1997. 1997. 50.00 (*0-02-864820-X*); 50.00 (*0-02-864831-5*); 50.00 (*0-02-864817-X*) S&S Trade.

— Collier's Encyclopedia 1997. 1998. 50.00 (*0-02-864825-0*) S&S Trade.

— Collier's Encyclopedia 1997, 1. 1998. 50.00 (*0-02-864816-1*) S&S Trade.

— Collier's Encyclopedia 1997, 3. 1998. 50.00 (*0-02-864818-8*) S&S Trade.

— Collier's Encyclopedia 1997, 4. 1998. 50.00 (*0-02-864819-6*) S&S Trade.

— Collier's Encyclopedia 1997, 6. 1997. 50.00 (*0-02-864821-8*) S&S Trade.

— Collier's Encyclopedia 1997, 7. 1997. 50.00 (*0-02-864822-6*) S&S Trade.

— Collier's Encyclopedia 1997, 8. 1997. 50.00 (*0-02-864823-4*) S&S Trade.

— Collier's Encyclopedia 1997, 9. 1997. 50.00 (*0-02-864824-2*) S&S Trade.

— Collier's Encyclopedia 1997, 11. 1997. 50.00 (*0-02-864826-9*) S&S Trade.

— Collier's Encyclopedia 1997, 12. 1998. 50.00 (*0-02-864827-7*) S&S Trade.

— Collier's Encyclopedia 1997, 13. 1998. 50.00 (*0-02-864828-5*) S&S Trade.

— Collier's Encyclopedia 1997, 14. 1997. 50.00 (*0-02-864829-3*) S&S Trade.

— Collier's Encyclopedia 1997, 15. 1998. 50.00 (*0-02-864830-7*) S&S Trade.

— Collier's Encyclopedia 1997, 17. 1998. 50.00 (*0-02-864832-3*) S&S Trade.

— Collier's Encyclopedia 1997, 18. 1997. 50.00 (*0-02-864833-1*) S&S Trade.

— Collier's Encyclopedia 1997, 19. 1997. 50.00 (*0-02-864834-X*) S&S Trade.

— Collier's Encyclopedia 1997, 20. 1997. 50.00 (*0-02-864835-8*) S&S Trade.

— Collier's Encyclopedia 1997, 21. 1998. 50.00 (*0-02-864836-6*) S&S Trade.

— Collier's Encyclopedia 1997, 22. 1997. 50.00 (*0-02-864837-4*) S&S Trade.

— Collier's Encyclopedia 1997, 23. 1997. 50.00 (*0-02-864838-2*) S&S Trade.

— Collier's Encyclopedia 1997, 24. 1997. 50.00 (*0-02-864839-0*) S&S Trade.

Collier Staff, ed. Collier Dictionary, 2 vols. 1981. 29.95 (*0-02-942270-1*) Mac Lib Ref.

— Collier Encyclopedia, 1980, 24 vols., Vol. 7. 1980. 25.00 (*0-02-940970-5*) Mac Lib Ref.

— Collier Encyclopedia, 1980, 24 vols., Vol. 8. 1980. 25.00 (*0-02-940980-2*) Mac Lib Ref.

— Collier Encyclopedia, 1980, 24 vols., Vol. 9. 1980. 25.00 (*0-02-940990-X*) Mac Lib Ref.

— Collier Encyclopedia, 1980, 24 vols., Vol. 10. 1980. 25.00 (*0-02-941000-2*) Mac Lib Ref.

— Collier Encyclopedia, 1980, 24 vols., Vol. 11. 1980. 25.00 (*0-02-941010-X*) Mac Lib Ref.

— Collier Encyclopedia, 1980, 24 vols., Vol. 12. 1980. 25.00 (*0-02-941020-7*) Mac Lib Ref.

— Collier Encyclopedia, 1980, 24 vols., Vol. 14. 1980. 25.00 (*0-02-941040-1*) Mac Lib Ref.

— Collier Encyclopedia, 1980, 24 vols., Vol. 15. 1980. 25.00 (*0-02-941050-9*) Mac Lib Ref.

— Collier Encyclopedia, 1980, 24 vols., Vol. 16. 1980. 25.00 (*0-02-941060-6*) Mac Lib Ref.

— Collier Encyclopedia, 1980, 24 vols., Vol. 17. 1980. 25.00 (*0-02-941070-3*) Mac Lib Ref.

— Collier Encyclopedia, 1980, 24 vols., Vol. 19. 1980. 25.00 (*0-02-941090-8*) Mac Lib Ref.

— Collier Encyclopedia, 1980, 24 vols., Vol. 20. 1980. 25.00 (*0-02-941100-9*) Mac Lib Ref.

— Collier Encyclopedia, 1980, 24 vols., Vol. 21. 1980. 25.00 (*0-02-941110-6*) Mac Lib Ref.

— Collier Encyclopedia, 1980, 24 vols., Vol. 22. 1980. 25.00 (*0-02-941120-3*) Mac Lib Ref.

— Collier Encyclopedia, 1980, 24 vols., Vol. 24. 1980. 467.00 (*0-02-941730-9*) Mac Lib Ref.

— Collier Encyclopedia, 1985, Vol. 8. 1985. 30.00 (*0-02-941660-4*) Mac Lib Ref.

— Collier Encyclopedia, 1985, Vol. 9. 1985. 30.00 (*0-02-941670-1*) Mac Lib Ref.

— Collier's Encyclopedia, 24 vols., Vol. 19. 1988. 38.00 (*0-02-940491-6*) Mac Lib Ref.

— Collier's Encyclopedia, 1982, 24 vols., Vol. 1. 1982. 25.00 (*0-02-941360-5*) Mac Lib Ref.

— Collier's Encyclopedia, 1982, 24 vols., Vol. 3. 1982. 25.00 (*0-02-941380-X*) Mac Lib Ref.

— Collier's Encyclopedia, 1982, 24 vols., Vol. 4. 1982. 25.00 (*0-02-941390-7*) Mac Lib Ref.

— Collier's Encyclopedia, 1982, 24 vols., Vol. 5. 1982. 25.00 (*0-02-941400-8*) Mac Lib Ref.

— Collier's Encyclopedia, 1982, 24 vols., Vol. 6. 1982. 25.00 (*0-02-941410-5*) Mac Lib Ref.

— Collier's Encyclopedia, 1982, 24 vols., Vol. 7. 1982. 25.00 (*0-02-941420-2*) Mac Lib Ref.

— Collier's Encyclopedia, 1982, 24 vols., Vol. 8. 1982. 25.00 (*0-02-941430-X*) Mac Lib Ref.

— Collier's Encyclopedia, 1982, 24 vols., Vol. 9. 1982. 25.00 (*0-02-941440-7*) Mac Lib Ref.

— Collier's Encyclopedia, 1982, 24 vols., Vol. 10. 1982. 25.00 (*0-02-941450-4*) Mac Lib Ref.

— Collier's Encyclopedia, 1982, 24 vols., Vol. 11. 1982. 25.00 (*0-02-941460-1*) Mac Lib Ref.

— Collier's Encyclopedia, 1982, 24 vols., Vol. 12. 1982. 25.00 (*0-02-941470-9*) Mac Lib Ref.

— Collier's Encyclopedia, 1982, 24 vols., Vol. 13. 1982. 25.00 (*0-02-941480-6*) Mac Lib Ref.

— Collier's Encyclopedia, 1982, 24 vols., Vol. 14. 1982. 25.00 (*0-02-941490-3*) Mac Lib Ref.

— Collier's Encyclopedia, 1982, 24 vols., Vol. 15. 1982. 25.00 (*0-02-941500-4*) Mac Lib Ref.
— Collier's Encyclopedia, 1982, 24 vols., Vol. 16. 1982. 25.00 (*0-02-941510-1*) Mac Lib Ref.
— Collier's Encyclopedia, 1982, 24 vols., Vol. 17. 1982. 25.00 (*0-02-941520-9*) Mac Lib Ref.
— Collier's Encyclopedia, 1982, 24 vols., Vol. 18. 1982. 25.00 (*0-02-941560-8*) Mac Lib Ref.
— Collier's Encyclopedia, 1982, 24 vols., Vol. 19. 1982. 25.00 (*0-02-941570-5*) Mac Lib Ref.
— Collier's Encyclopedia, 1982, 24 vols., Vol. 20. 1982. 25.00 (*0-02-941600-0*) Mac Lib Ref.
— Collier's Encyclopedia, 1982, 24 vols., Vol. 21. 1982. 25.00 (*0-02-941610-8*) Mac Lib Ref.
— Collier's Encyclopedia, 1982, 24 vols., Vol. 22. 1982. 25.00 (*0-02-941620-5*) Mac Lib Ref.
— Collier's Encyclopedia, 1982, 24 vols., Vol. 23. 1982. 25.00 (*0-02-941630-2*) Mac Lib Ref.
— Collier's Encyclopedia, 1982, 24 vols., Vol. 24. 1982. 25.00 (*0-02-941640-X*) Mac Lib Ref.
— Collier's Encyclopedia, 1984, 24 vols., Vol. 10. 1984. 28.00 (*0-02-940650-1*) Mac Lib Ref.
— Collier's Encyclopedia, 1984, 24 vols., Vol. 11. 1984. 28.00 (*0-02-940660-9*) Mac Lib Ref.
— Collier's Encyclopedia, 1984, 24 vols., Vol. 12. 1984. 28.00 (*0-02-940670-6*) Mac Lib Ref.
— Collier's Encyclopedia, 1984, 24 vols., Vol. 13. 1984. 28.00 (*0-02-940680-3*) Mac Lib Ref.
— Collier's Encyclopedia, 1984, 24 vols., Vol. 14. 1984. 28.00 (*0-02-940690-0*) Mac Lib Ref.
— Collier's Encyclopedia, 1984, 24 vols., Vol. 15. 1984. 28.00 (*0-02-940700-1*) Mac Lib Ref.
— Collier's Encyclopedia, 1984, 24 vols., Vol. 16. 1984. 28.00 (*0-02-940710-9*) Mac Lib Ref.
— Collier's Encyclopedia, 1984, 24 vols., Vol. 17. 1984. 28.00 (*0-02-940720-6*) Mac Lib Ref.
— Collier's Encyclopedia, 1984, 24 vols., Vol. 18. 1984. 28.00 (*0-02-940730-3*) Mac Lib Ref.
— Collier's Encyclopedia, 1984, 24 vols., Vol. 19. 1984. 28.00 (*0-02-940740-0*) Mac Lib Ref.
— Collier's Encyclopedia, 1984, 24 vols., Vol. 20. 1984. 28.00 (*0-02-940750-8*) Mac Lib Ref.
— Collier's Encyclopedia, 1984, 24 vols., Vol. 21. 1984. 28.00 (*0-02-940760-5*) Mac Lib Ref.
— Collier's Encyclopedia, 1984, 24 vols., Vol. 22. 1984. 28.00 (*0-02-940770-2*) Mac Lib Ref.
— Collier's Encyclopedia, 1984, 24 vols., Vol. 23. 1984. 28.00 (*0-02-940780-X*) Mac Lib Ref.
— Collier's Encyclopedia, 1984, 24 vols., Vol. 24. 1984. 28.00 (*0-02-940790-7*) Mac Lib Ref.
— Collier's Encyclopedia, 1986, 24 vols., Vol. 1. 1986. 35.00 (*0-02-942510-7*) Mac Lib Ref.
— Collier's Encyclopedia, 1986, 24 vols., Vol. 2. 1986. 35.00 (*0-02-942520-4*) Mac Lib Ref.
— Collier's Encyclopedia, 1986, 24 vols., Vol. 3. 1986. 35.00 (*0-02-942530-1*) Mac Lib Ref.
— Collier's Encyclopedia, 1986, 24 vols., Vol. 4. 1986. 35.00 (*0-02-942540-9*) Mac Lib Ref.
— Collier's Encyclopedia, 1986, 24 vols., Vol. 5. 1986. 35.00 (*0-02-942550-6*) Mac Lib Ref.
— Collier's Encyclopedia, 1986, 24 vols., Vol. 6. 1986. 35.00 (*0-02-942560-3*) Mac Lib Ref.
— Collier's Encyclopedia, 1986, 24 vols., Vol. 7. 1986. 35.00 (*0-02-942570-0*) Mac Lib Ref.
— Collier's Encyclopedia, 1986, 24 vols., Vol. 8. 1986. 35.00 (*0-02-942580-8*) Mac Lib Ref.
— Collier's Encyclopedia, 1986, 24 vols., Vol. 9. 1986. 35.00 (*0-02-942590-5*) Mac Lib Ref.
— Collier's Encyclopedia, 1986, 24 vols., Vol. 10. 1986. 35.00 (*0-02-942600-6*) Mac Lib Ref.
— Collier's Encyclopedia, 1986, 24 vols., Vol. 11. 1986. 35.00 (*0-02-942610-3*) Mac Lib Ref.
— Collier's Encyclopedia, 1986, 24 vols., Vol. 12. 1986. 35.00 (*0-02-942620-0*) Mac Lib Ref.
— Collier's Encyclopedia, 1986, 24 vols., Vol. 13. 1986. 35.00 (*0-02-942630-8*) Mac Lib Ref.
— Collier's Encyclopedia, 1986, 24 vols., Vol. 14. 1986. 35.00 (*0-02-942640-5*) Mac Lib Ref.
— Collier's Encyclopedia, 1986, 24 vols., Vol. 15. 1986. 35.00 (*0-02-942650-2*) Mac Lib Ref.
— Collier's Encyclopedia, 1986, 24 vols., Vol. 16. 1986. 35.00 (*0-02-942660-X*) Mac Lib Ref.
— Collier's Encyclopedia, 1986, 24 vols., Vol. 17. 1986. 35.00 (*0-02-942670-7*) Mac Lib Ref.
— Collier's Encyclopedia, 1986, 24 vols., Vol. 18. 1986. 35.00 (*0-02-942680-4*) Mac Lib Ref.
— Collier's Encyclopedia, 1986, 24 vols., Vol. 19. 1986. 35.00 (*0-02-942690-1*) Mac Lib Ref.
— Collier's Encyclopedia, 1986, 24 vols., Vol. 20. 1986. 35.00 (*0-02-942700-2*) Mac Lib Ref.
— Collier's Encyclopedia, 1986, 24 vols., Vol. 21. 1986. 35.00 (*0-02-942710-X*) Mac Lib Ref.
— Collier's Encyclopedia, 1986, 24 vols., Vol. 22. 1986. 35.00 (*0-02-942720-7*) Mac Lib Ref.
— Collier's Encyclopedia, 1986, 24 vols., Vol. 23. 1986. 35.00 (*0-02-942730-4*) Mac Lib Ref.
— Collier's Encyclopedia, 1986, 24 vols., Vol. 24. 1986. 35.00 (*0-02-942740-1*) Mac Lib Ref.
— Collier's Encyclopedia, 1987, 24 vols., Vol. 1. 1987. 35.00 (*0-02-942801-7*) Mac Lib Ref.
— Collier's Encyclopedia, 1987, 24 vols., Vol. 2. 1987. 35.00 (*0-02-942802-5*) Mac Lib Ref.
— Collier's Encyclopedia, 1987, 24 vols., Vol. 3. 1987. 35.00 (*0-02-942803-3*) Mac Lib Ref.
— Collier's Encyclopedia, 1987, 24 vols., Vol. 4. 1987. 35.00 (*0-02-942804-1*) Mac Lib Ref.
— Collier's Encyclopedia, 1987, 24 vols., Vol. 5. 1987. 35.00 (*0-02-942805-X*) Mac Lib Ref.
— Collier's Encyclopedia, 1987, 24 vols., Vol. 6. 1987. 35.00 (*0-02-942806-8*) Mac Lib Ref.
— Collier's Encyclopedia, 1987, 24 vols., Vol. 7. 1987. 35.00 (*0-02-942807-6*) Mac Lib Ref.
— Collier's Encyclopedia, 1987, 24 vols., Vol. 8. 1987. 35.00 (*0-02-942808-4*) Mac Lib Ref.
— Collier's Encyclopedia, 1987, 24 vols., Vol. 9. 1987. 35.00 (*0-02-942809-2*) Mac Lib Ref.
— Collier's Encyclopedia, 1987, 24 vols., Vol. 10. 1987. 35.00 (*0-02-942810-6*) Mac Lib Ref.
— Collier's Encyclopedia, 1987, 24 vols., Vol. 11. 1987. 35.00 (*0-02-942811-4*) Mac Lib Ref.
— Collier's Encyclopedia, 1987, 24 vols., Vol. 12. 1987. 35.00 (*0-02-942812-2*) Mac Lib Ref.
— Collier's Encyclopedia, 1987, 24 vols., Vol. 13. 1987. 35.00 (*0-02-942813-0*) Mac Lib Ref.
— Collier's Encyclopedia, 1987, 24 vols., Vol. 14. 1987. 35.00 (*0-02-942814-9*) Mac Lib Ref.
— Collier's Encyclopedia, 1987, 24 vols., Vol. 15. 1987. 35.00 (*0-02-942815-7*) Mac Lib Ref.
— Collier's Encyclopedia, 1987, 24 vols., Vol. 16. 1987. 35.00 (*0-02-942816-5*) Mac Lib Ref.
— Collier's Encyclopedia, 1987, 24 vols., Vol. 17. 1987. 35.00 (*0-02-942817-3*) Mac Lib Ref.
— Collier's Encyclopedia, 1987, 24 vols., Vol. 18. 1987. 35.00 (*0-02-942818-1*) Mac Lib Ref.
— Collier's Encyclopedia, 1987, 24 vols., Vol. 19. 1987. 35.00 (*0-02-942819-X*) Mac Lib Ref.
— Collier's Encyclopedia, 1987, 24 vols., Vol. 20. 1987. 35.00 (*0-02-942820-3*) Mac Lib Ref.
— Collier's Encyclopedia, 1987, 24 vols., Vol. 21. 1987. 35.00 (*0-02-942821-1*) Mac Lib Ref.
— Collier's Encyclopedia, 1987, 24 vols., Vol. 22. 1987. 35.00 (*0-02-942822-X*) Mac Lib Ref.
— Collier's Encyclopedia, 1987, 24 vols., Vol. 23. 1987. 35.00 (*0-02-942823-8*) Mac Lib Ref.
— Collier's Encyclopedia, 1987, 24 vols., Vol. 24. 1987. 35.00 (*0-02-942824-6*) Mac Lib Ref.
— Collier's Encyclopedia, 1988, 24 vols., Vol. 1. 1988. 38.00 (*0-02-940311-1*) Mac Lib Ref.
— Collier's Encyclopedia, 1988, 24 vols., Vol. 2. 1988. 38.00 (*0-02-940321-9*) Mac Lib Ref.
— Collier's Encyclopedia, 1988, 24 vols., Vol. 3. 1988. 38.00 (*0-02-940331-6*) Mac Lib Ref.
— Collier's Encyclopedia, 1988, 24 vols., Vol. 4. 1988. 38.00 (*0-02-940341-3*) Mac Lib Ref.
— Collier's Encyclopedia, 1988, 24 vols., Vol. 5. 1988. 38.00 (*0-02-940351-0*) Mac Lib Ref.
— Collier's Encyclopedia, 1988, 24 vols., Vol. 6. 1988. 38.00 (*0-02-940361-8*) Mac Lib Ref.
— Collier's Encyclopedia, 1988, 24 vols., Vol. 7. 1988. 38.00 (*0-02-940371-5*) Mac Lib Ref.
— Collier's Encyclopedia, 1988, 24 vols., Vol. 8. 1988. 38.00 (*0-02-940381-2*) Mac Lib Ref.
— Collier's Encyclopedia, 1988, 24 vols., Vol. 9. 1988. 38.00 (*0-02-940391-X*) Mac Lib Ref.
— Collier's Encyclopedia, 1988, 24 vols., Vol. 10. 1988. 38.00 (*0-02-940401-0*) Mac Lib Ref.
— Collier's Encyclopedia, 1988, 24 vols., Vol. 11. 1988. 38.00 (*0-02-940411-8*) Mac Lib Ref.
— Collier's Encyclopedia, 1988, 24 vols., Vol. 12. 1988. 38.00 (*0-02-940421-5*) Mac Lib Ref.
— Collier's Encyclopedia, 1988, 24 vols., Vol. 13. 1988. 38.00 (*0-02-940431-2*) Mac Lib Ref.
— Collier's Encyclopedia, 1988, 24 vols., Vol. 14. 1988. 38.00 (*0-02-940441-X*) Mac Lib Ref.
— Collier's Encyclopedia, 1988, 24 vols., Vol. 15. 1988. 38.00 (*0-02-940451-7*) Mac Lib Ref.
— Collier's Encyclopedia, 1988, 24 vols., Vol. 16. 1988. 38.00 (*0-02-940461-4*) Mac Lib Ref.
— Collier's Encyclopedia, 1988, 24 vols., Vol. 17. 1988. 38.00 (*0-02-940471-1*) Mac Lib Ref.
— Collier's Encyclopedia, 1988, 24 vols., Vol. 18. 1988. 38.00 (*0-02-940481-9*) Mac Lib Ref.
— Collier's Encyclopedia, 1988, 24 vols., Vol. 20. 1988. 38.00 (*0-02-940501-7*) Mac Lib Ref.
— Collier's Encyclopedia, 1988, 24 vols., Vol. 21. 1988. 38.00 (*0-02-940511-4*) Mac Lib Ref.
— Collier's Encyclopedia, 1988, 24 vols., Vol. 22. 1988. 38.00 (*0-02-940521-1*) Mac Lib Ref.
— Collier's Encyclopedia, 1988, 24 vols., Vol. 23. 1988. 38.00 (*0-02-940531-9*) Mac Lib Ref.
— Collier's Encyclopedia, 1988, 24 vols., Vol. 24. 1988. 38.00 (*0-02-940541-6*) Mac Lib Ref.
— Collier's Encyclopedia, 1989, 24 vols., Vol. 1. 1989. 40.00 (*0-02-942900-5*) Mac Lib Ref.
— Collier's Encyclopedia, 1989, 24 vols., Vol. 2. 1989. 40.00 (*0-02-942901-3*) Mac Lib Ref.
— Collier's Encyclopedia, 1989, 24 vols., Vol. 3. 1989. 40.00 (*0-02-942902-1*) Mac Lib Ref.
— Collier's Encyclopedia, 1989, 24 vols., Vol. 4. 1989. 40.00 (*0-02-942903-X*) Mac Lib Ref.
— Collier's Encyclopedia, 1989, 24 vols., Vol. 5. 1989. 40.00 (*0-02-942904-8*) Mac Lib Ref.
— Collier's Encyclopedia, 1989, 24 vols., Vol. 6. 1989. 40.00 (*0-02-942905-6*) Mac Lib Ref.
— Collier's Encyclopedia, 1989, 24 vols., Vol. 7. 1989. 40.00 (*0-02-942906-4*) Mac Lib Ref.
— Collier's Encyclopedia, 1989, 24 vols., Vol. 8. 1989. 40.00 (*0-02-942907-2*) Mac Lib Ref.
— Collier's Encyclopedia, 1989, 24 vols., Vol. 9. 1989. 40.00 (*0-02-942908-0*) Mac Lib Ref.
— Collier's Encyclopedia, 1989, 24 vols., Vol. 10. 1989. 40.00 (*0-02-942909-9*) Mac Lib Ref.
— Collier's Encyclopedia, 1989, 24 vols., Vol. 11. 1989. 40.00 (*0-02-942910-2*) Mac Lib Ref.
— Collier's Encyclopedia, 1989, 24 vols., Vol. 12. 1989. 40.00 (*0-02-942911-0*) Mac Lib Ref.
— Collier's Encyclopedia, 1989, 24 vols., Vol. 13. 1989. 40.00 (*0-02-942912-9*) Mac Lib Ref.
— Collier's Encyclopedia, 1989, 24 vols., Vol. 14. 1989. 40.00 (*0-02-942913-7*) Mac Lib Ref.
— Collier's Encyclopedia, 1989, 24 vols., Vol. 15. 1989. 40.00 (*0-02-942914-5*) Mac Lib Ref.
— Collier's Encyclopedia, 1989, 24 vols., Vol. 16. 1989. 40.00 (*0-02-942915-3*) Mac Lib Ref.
— Collier's Encyclopedia, 1989, 24 vols., Vol. 17. 1989. 40.00 (*0-02-942916-1*) Mac Lib Ref.
— Collier's Encyclopedia, 1989, 24 vols., Vol. 18. 1989. 40.00 (*0-02-942917-X*) Mac Lib Ref.
— Colliers Encyclopedia 1989, 24 vols., Vol. 20. 1989. 40.00 (*0-02-942919-6*) Mac Lib Ref.
— Collier's Encyclopedia, 1989, 24 vols., Vol. 21. 1989. 40.00 (*0-02-942920-X*) Mac Lib Ref.
— Collier's Encyclopedia, 1989, 24 vols., Vol. 22. 1989. 40.00 (*0-02-942921-8*) Mac Lib Ref.
— Collier's Encyclopedia, 1989, 24 vols., Vol. 23. 1989. 40.00 (*0-02-942922-6*) Mac Lib Ref.
— Collier's Encyclopedia, 1989, 24 vols., Vol. 24. 1989. 40.00 (*0-02-942923-4*) Mac Lib Ref.
— Collier's Encyclopedia, 1990, 24 vols., Vol. 1. 1990. 40.00 (*0-02-943100-X*) Mac Lib Ref.
— Collier's Encyclopedia, 1990, 24 vols., Vol. 2. 1990. 40.00 (*0-02-943101-8*) Mac Lib Ref.
— Collier's Encyclopedia, 1990, 24 vols., Vol. 3. 1990. 40.00 (*0-02-943102-6*) Mac Lib Ref.
— Collier's Encyclopedia, 1990, 24 vols., Vol. 4. 1990. 40.00 (*0-02-943103-4*) Mac Lib Ref.
— Collier's Encyclopedia, 1990, 24 vols., Vol. 5. 1990. 40.00 (*0-02-943104-2*) Mac Lib Ref.
— Collier's Encyclopedia, 1990, 24 vols., Vol. 6. 1990. 40.00 (*0-02-943105-0*) Mac Lib Ref.
— Collier's Encyclopedia, 1990, 24 vols., Vol. 7. 1990. 40.00 (*0-02-943106-9*) Mac Lib Ref.
— Collier's Encyclopedia, 1990, 24 vols., Vol. 8. 1990. 40.00 (*0-02-943107-7*) Mac Lib Ref.
— Collier's Encyclopedia, 1990, 24 vols., Vol. 9. 1990. 40.00 (*0-02-943108-5*) Mac Lib Ref.
— Collier's Encyclopedia, 1990, 24 vols., Vol. 10. 1990. 40.00 (*0-02-943109-3*) Mac Lib Ref.
— Collier's Encyclopedia, 1990, 24 vols., Vol. 11. 1990. 40.00 (*0-02-943110-7*) Mac Lib Ref.
— Collier's Encyclopedia, 1990, 24 vols., Vol. 12. 1990. 40.00 (*0-02-943111-5*) Mac Lib Ref.
— Collier's Encyclopedia, 1990, 24 vols., Vol. 13. 1990. 40.00 (*0-02-943112-3*) Mac Lib Ref.
— Collier's Encyclopedia, 1990, 24 vols., Vol. 14. 1990. 40.00 (*0-02-943113-1*) Mac Lib Ref.
— Collier's Encyclopedia, 1990, 24 vols., Vol. 16. 1990. 40.00 (*0-02-943115-8*) Mac Lib Ref.
— Collier's Encyclopedia, 1990, 24 vols., Vol. 17. 1990. 40.00 (*0-02-943116-6*) Mac Lib Ref.
— Collier's Encyclopedia, 1990, 24 vols., Vol. 18. 1990. 40.00 (*0-02-943117-4*) Mac Lib Ref.
— Collier's Encyclopedia, 1990, 24 vols., Vol. 19. 1990. 40.00 (*0-02-943118-2*) Mac Lib Ref.
— Collier's Encyclopedia, 1990, 24 vols., Vol. 20. 1990. 40.00 (*0-02-943119-0*) Mac Lib Ref.
— Collier's Encyclopedia, 1990, 24 vols., Vol. 21. 1990. 40.00 (*0-02-943120-4*) Mac Lib Ref.
— Collier's Encyclopedia, 1990, 24 vols., Vol. 22. 1990. 40.00 (*0-02-943121-2*) Mac Lib Ref.
— Collier's Encyclopedia, 1990, 24 vols., Vol. 23. 1990. 40.00 (*0-02-943122-0*) Mac Lib Ref.
— Collier's Encyclopedia, 1990, 24 vols., Vol. 24. 1990. 40.00 (*0-02-943123-9*) Mac Lib Ref.
— Collier's Encyclopedia, 1991, 24 vols., Vol. 1. 1991. 45.00 (*0-02-942491-7*) Mac Lib Ref.
— Collier's Encyclopedia, 1991, 24 vols., Vol. 2. 1991. 45.00 (*0-02-942492-5*) Mac Lib Ref.
— Collier's Encyclopedia, 1991, 24 vols., Vol. 3. 1991. 45.00 (*0-02-942493-3*) Mac Lib Ref.
— Collier's Encyclopedia, 1991, 24 vols., Vol. 4. 1991. 45.00 (*0-02-942494-1*) Mac Lib Ref.
— Collier's Encyclopedia, 1991, 24 vols., Vol. 5. 1991. 45.00 (*0-02-942495-X*) Mac Lib Ref.
— Collier's Encyclopedia, 1991, 24 vols., Vol. 6. 1991. 45.00 (*0-02-942496-8*) Mac Lib Ref.
— Collier's Encyclopedia, 1991, 24 vols., Vol. 7. 1991. 45.00 (*0-02-942497-6*) Mac Lib Ref.
— Collier's Encyclopedia, 1991, 24 vols., Vol. 8. 1991. 45.00 (*0-02-942498-4*) Mac Lib Ref.
— Collier's Encyclopedia, 1991, 24 vols., Vol. 9. 1991. 45.00 (*0-02-942499-2*) Mac Lib Ref.
— Collier's Encyclopedia, 1991, 24 vols., Vol. 10. 1991. 45.00 (*0-02-942501-8*) Mac Lib Ref.
— Collier's Encyclopedia, 1991, 24 vols., Vol. 11. 1991. 45.00 (*0-02-942502-6*) Mac Lib Ref.
— Collier's Encyclopedia, 1991, 24 vols., Vol. 12. 1991. 45.00 (*0-02-942503-4*) Mac Lib Ref.
— Collier's Encyclopedia, 1991, 24 vols., Vol. 13. 1991. 45.00 (*0-02-942504-2*) Mac Lib Ref.
— Collier's Encyclopedia, 1991, 24 vols., Vol. 14. 1991. 45.00 (*0-02-942505-0*) Mac Lib Ref.
— Collier's Encyclopedia, 1991, 24 vols., Vol. 15. 1991. 45.00 (*0-02-942506-9*) Mac Lib Ref.
— Collier's Encyclopedia, 1991, 24 vols., Vol. 16. 1991. 45.00 (*0-02-942507-7*) Mac Lib Ref.
— Collier's Encyclopedia, 1991, 24 vols., Vol. 17. 1991. 45.00 (*0-02-942508-5*) Mac Lib Ref.
— Collier's Encyclopedia, 1991, 24 vols., Vol. 18. 1991. 45.00 (*0-02-942509-3*) Mac Lib Ref.
— Collier's Encyclopedia, 1991, 24 vols., Vol. 19. 1991. 45.00 (*0-02-942511-5*) Mac Lib Ref.
— Collier's Encyclopedia, 1991, 24 vols., Vol. 20. 1991. 45.00 (*0-02-942512-3*) Mac Lib Ref.
— Collier's Encyclopedia, 1991, 24 vols., Vol. 21. 1991. 45.00 (*0-02-942513-1*) Mac Lib Ref.
— Collier's Encyclopedia, 1991, 24 vols., Vol. 22. 1991. 45.00 (*0-02-942514-X*) Mac Lib Ref.
— Collier's Encyclopedia, 1991, 24 vols., Vol. 23. 1991. 45.00 (*0-02-942515-8*) Mac Lib Ref.
— Collier's Encyclopedia, 1991, 24 vols., Vol. 24. 1991. 45.00 (*0-02-942516-6*) Mac Lib Ref.
— Collier's Yearbook 1983. 1983. 10.95 (*0-02-940550-5*) Mac Lib Ref.
— Science Horizons Year Book, 1993. 1993. 45.00 (*0-02-942579-4*) Mac Lib Ref.

Collier Staff & King, Lawrence P. Collier Forms Manual, 2 vols. 3rd ed. 1979. ring bd. 370.00 (*0-8205-1215-X*) Bender.

Collier Staff & Sulmeyer, Irving. Collier Handbook for Trustees & Debtors in Possession. LC 82-72098. (Illus.). 1985. ring bd. write for info. (*0-8205-1149-8*) Bender.

Collier Staff, et al. Collier Bankruptcy Practice Guide, 6 vols. 1981. ring bd. 1180.00 (*0-8205-1200-1*) Bender.
— Collier on Bankruptcy, 16 vols. 15th ed. 1979. ring bd. write for info. (*0-8205-1219-2*) Bender.

Collier, Stephen F. Raising the Rafters: How to Assemble Your Team of Architects, Contractors, Interior Designers, Subcontractors, Suppliers, Engineers & Bankers to Get Your Dream House Built. 160p. 1994. reprint ed. pap. 12.95 (*0-87951-557-0*, Pub. by Overlook Pr) Penguin Putnam.
— Raising the Rafters: How to Work with Architects, Contractors, Interior Designers...to Get Your Dream House Built. 160p. 1993. 19.95 (*0-87951-490-6*, Pub. by Overlook Pr) Penguin Putnam.

Collier-Stone, Kay, jt. auth. see Bohmer, Whitney.

***Collier, Susan.** Time Heals. 400p. 2000. mass mkt. 4.99 (*0-505-52157-1*, Love Spell) Dorchester Pub Co.

Collier, T. Design, Technology & the Development Process in the Built Environment. (Built Environment Series of Textbooks). (Illus.). 232p. (Orig.). (C). 1995. pap. 27.99 (*0-419-19550-5*, E & FN Spon) Routledge.

Collier, T. O., Jr. Supervisor's Guide to Labor Relations. Date not set. pap. 17.95 (*0-939900-83-1*) Soc Human Resc Mgmt.

***Collier-Thomas.** Africa American in Perfect Arts: Encyclopedia. 1999. text 50.00 (*0-8050-5124-4*) St Martin.

Collier-Thomas. Chronology of the Civil Rights. 1996. pap. 14.95 (*0-8050-4770-0*) St Martin.
— Over the Footlights. 1996. pap. 14.95 (*0-8050-4406-X*); text 25.00 (*0-8050-4405-1*) St Martin.

***Collier-Thomas.** Treasury of African-american Christmas Stories. 1998. pap. 11.00 (*0-8050-5123-6*) St Martin.

Collier-Thomas, Betty. Daughters of Thunder: Black Women Preachers & Their Sermons. LC 97-4850. (Religion in Practice Ser.). (Illus.). 304p. 1997. 24.50 (*0-7879-0918-1*) Jossey-Bass.

Collier-Thomas, Bettye. My Soul Is a Witness: A Chronology of the Civil Rights Era in the United States, 1954-1965. Franklin, V. P., ed. LC 99-27987. 256p. 2000. text 30.00 (*0-8050-4769-7*) St Martin.
— A Treasury of African-American Christmas Stories. 224p. 1999. 22.00 (*0-8050-6045-6*) H Holt & Co.

***Collier-Thomas, Bettye & Franklin, V. P., eds.** Sisters in the Struggle: African-American Women in the Civil Rights & Black Power Movements. 2001. 55.00 (*0-8147-1603-2*) NYU Pr.

Collier-Thomas, Bettye, jt. auth. see King-Hammond, Leslie.

Collier, Tom. History of Jazz. 178p. (C). 1997. pap. text, spiral bd. 28.95 (*0-7872-3318-8*, 41331801) Kendall-Hunt.

Collier, Ute. Energy & Environment in the European Union: The Challenge of Integration. LC 94-37849. (Studies in Green Research). 288p. 1994. 82.95 (*1-85972-007-2*, Pub. by Avebry) Ashgate Pub Co.

Collier, Ute, ed. Deregulation in the European Union. LC 98-119228. (Routledge/EUI Environmental Policy Ser.). (Illus.). 240p. (C). 1997. 85.00 (*0-415-15694-7*) Routledge.

Collier-Vanhimbeeck, Sonja. A Guide to the Optometric Training of Myopia Control. LC 97-37728. (Illus.). 54p. 1997. 20.00 (*0-943599-94-6*) OEPF.

Collier, Virginia, jt. auth. see Ovando, Carlos.

Collier, Virginia P. Promoting Academic Success for E. S. C. Students: Understanding Second Language Acquisition for Schools. 52p. (C). 1998. pap. text 12.95 (*1-883514-00-2*) Bastos Bk.

Collier, Virginia P., jt. auth. see Ovando, Carlos J.

Collier, William W. Reasoning about Parallel Architectures. LC 91-22202. (Illus.). 256p. 1992. reprint ed. pap. 79.40 (*0-608-05711-8*, AU0049000007) Bks Demand.

Colliers. Health & Medical Year Book, 1993. 1993. 45.00 (*0-02-942578-6*) Free Pr.

Collier's Staff. Collier's Encyclopedia: 1997 Edition, 24 vols. 1997. 499.00 (*0-02-864840-4*) Macmillan Gen Ref.

Colliers Staff, ed. Collier's Encyclopedia, 1984, 24 vols., Vol. 2. 1984. 28.00 (*0-02-940570-X*) Mac Lib Ref.
— Collier's Encyclopedia, 1984, 24 vols., Vol. 3. 1984. 28.00 (*0-02-940580-7*) Mac Lib Ref.
— Collier's Encyclopedia, 1984, 24 vols., Vol. 4. 1984. 28.00 (*0-02-940590-4*) Mac Lib Ref.
— Collier's Encyclopedia, 1984, 24 vols., Vol. 5. 1984. 28.00 (*0-02-940600-5*) Mac Lib Ref.
— Collier's Encyclopedia, 1984, 24 vols., Vol. 6. 1984. 28.00 (*0-02-940610-2*) Mac Lib Ref.
— Collier's Encyclopedia, 1984, 24 vols., Vol. 7. 1984. 28.00 (*0-02-940620-X*) Mac Lib Ref.
— Collier's Encyclopedia, 1984, 24 vols., Vol. 8. 1984. 28.00 (*0-02-940630-7*) Mac Lib Ref.
— Collier's Encyclopedia, 1984, 24 vols., Vol. 9. 1984. 28.00 (*0-02-940640-4*) Mac Lib Ref.
— Collier's Encyclopedia, 1990, 24 vols., Vol 15. 1990. 40.00 (*0-02-943114-X*) Mac Lib Ref.

Colligan, John, et al. Calling Disciples. 54p. (Orig.). 1984. 1.95 (*0-911905-22-7*) Past & Mat Rene Ctr.
— Calling Disciples, Mentality. LC 84-60459. (Calling Disciples Ser.: Bk. 2). 67p. (Orig.). 1984. pap. text 2.95 (*0-911905-21-9*) Past & Mat Rene Ctr.

C

An Asterisk (*) at the beginning of an entry indicates that the title is appearing for the first time.

Colligan, John B. The Juan Paez Hurtado Expedition of 1695: Fraud in Recruiting Colonists for New Mexico. LC 94-48676. 175p. reprint ed. pap. 54.30 (*0-608-20973-2*, 207184500002) Bks Demand.

Colligan, John J. & Colligan, Kathleen A. Day-by-Day: A Program of Preparation for Christian Marriage. 112p. (Orig.). 1994. pap. 12.95 (*0-8091-3457-8*) Paulist Pr.

— Day-by-Day: Reflection Guide for the Engaged & Newly Married. LC 93-31032. 112p. (Orig.). 1994. pap. 8.95 (*0-8091-3458-6*) Paulist Pr.

Colligan, Kathleen A., jt. auth. see Colligan, John J.

Colligan, Louise. One Thousand & One Things to Do When There's Nothing to Do. 128p. (J). (gr. 4-7). 1994. pap. 2.50 (*0-590-46359-4*) Scholastic Inc.

Colligan, Michael J., et al, eds. Mass Psychogenic Illness: A Social Psychological Analysis. 288p. 1982. 49.95 (*0-89859-160-0*) L Erlbaum Assocs.

Colligan, Robert C. & Offord, Kenneth P. The MMPI: A Contemporary Normative Study of Adolescents. Caddy, Glenn R., ed. (Developments in Clinical Psychology Ser.). 640p. (C). 1992. pap. 49.50 (*0-89391-985-3*); text 125.00 (*0-89391-872-5*) Ablx Pub.

Colligan-Taylor, Karen, tr. see Hoshino, Michio.

Colligan-Taylor, Karen, tr. see Yamazaki, Tomoko.

Collignon Hoff, Juan, et al. Under Ephemeral Light: Vignettes de Lumiere. LC 96-96244. (Illus.). 110p. 1997. 49.95 incl. cd-rom (*0-9651824-7-9*) Calif Pubng.

Collignon, Jeff. Her Monster. LC 91-44363. 212p. 1993. pap. 10.00 (*1-56947-001-4*) Soho Press.

Collignon, M. Manual of Mythology in Relation to Greek Art. Harrison, J. Ellen, tr. xxi, 335p. (C). 1982. reprint ed. lib. bdg. 55.00 (*0-89241-141-4*) Caratzas.

Collignon, Rick. Journal of Antinio Monta. 224p. 1997. pap. 10.00 (*0-380-73056-1*, Avon Bks) Morrow Avon.

— The Journal of Antonio Montoya. LC 95-52618. 217p. 1996. 17.00 (*1-878448-69-2*) MacMurray & Beck.

— Perdido. LC 96-53857. 224p. 1997. 19.50 (*1-878448-76-5*) MacMurray & Beck.

— Perdido. LC 96-53857. 224p. 1999. pap. 10.00 (*0-380-73220-3*, Avon Bks) Morrow Avon.

Collignon, Stefan, ed. European Monetary Policy. LC 96-43601. 224p. 1997. 85.00 (*1-85567-457-2*) Bks Intl VA.

Collignon, Stefan, et al. Europe's Monetary Future. LC 94-12181. 224p. 1994. 38.50 (*0-8386-3606-3*) Fairleigh Dickinson.

— Exchange Rate Policies in Emerging Asian Countries. LC 98-5915. (Illus.). 328p. (C). 1999. 110.00 (*0-415-17852-5*) Routledge.

Collignon, Stefan, jt. auth. see Johnson, Christopher.

Colligon, J. S., ed. Directory of Manufacturers of Vacuum Plant, Components & Associated Equipment in the U. K., 1982. 56p. 1982. pap. 14.50 (*0-08-029323-9*, C145, A145, Pergamon Pr) Elsevier.

Collin. Foundations of Microwave Engineering. 2nd ed. 1992. 15.31 (*0-07-011812-4*) McGraw.

— Larousse Business Dictionary: English-French, French-English. (ENG & FRE.). 704p. 1990. pap. 85.00 (*0-7859-7658-2*, 2034040015) Fr & Eur.

***Collin & Janssen.** Legal Dictionary: German/English - English/German. (ENG & GER.). 471p. 1998. 99.00 (*0-320-02134-3*) Fr & Eur.

***Collin, Audrey & Young, Richard A., eds.** The Future of Career. LC 99-57076. 306p. (C). 2000. text. write for info. (*0-521-64021-0*); pap. text. write for info. (*0-521-64965-X*) Cambridge U Pr.

Collin, Audrey, jt. ed. see Young, Richard.

Collin, F., et al. Harrap's French & English Business Dictionary. (ENG & FRE.). 508p. 1981. 75.00 (*0-8288-0081-2*, M9452) Fr & Eur.

Collin, Finn. Social Reality. LC 96-48387. (Problems of Philosophy Series: Their Past & Present). 272p. (C). 1997. 70.00 (*0-415-14796-4*); pap. 22.99 (*0-415-14797-2*) Routledge.

Collin, Francesca. The Arts & Entertainment in London. (Illus.). 192p. 1998. pap. 17.95 (*0-7063-7513-0*) Sterling.

— Kids' London: The Best of the Capital's Activities for Children. (Illus.). 160p. 1997. pap. 19.95 (*0-7063-7514-9*, Pub. by WrLock) Sterling.

Collin, H. A., jt. auth. see Edwards, S.

Collin, Henry P. Twentieth Century History & Biographical Record of Branch County. (Illus.). 879p. 1997. reprint ed. lib. bdg. 89.50 (*0-8328-6750-0*) Higginson Bk Co.

Collin, J. R. Manual of Sytematic Eyelid Surgery. 2nd ed. (Illus.). 166p. 1989. text 54.95 (*0-443-04009-5*) Church.

Collin, J. R., jt. auth. see Tyers, A. G.

Collin, J. R., jt. ed. see Tyers, A. G.

***Collin, J. R. O.** Manual of Systematic Eyelid Surgery. 2nd ed. 166p. 1999. 80.00 (*0-7506-4572-5*) Buttrwrth-Heinemann.

— Manual of Systematic Eyelid Surgery. 3rd ed. (Illus.). 192p. 2000. pap. 65.00 (*0-7506-4550-4*) Buttrwrth-Heinemann.

Collin, John F. History of Hillsdale, Columbia County a Memorabilia of Persons & Things of Interest, Passes & Passing. Johnson, H. S., ed. (Illus.). 195p. 1995. reprint ed. lib. bdg. 29.50 (*0-614-07055-4*) Higginson Bk Co.

Collin, Matthew. Altered State: The Story of Ecstasy Culture & Acid House. LC 96-70952. 288p. 1997. pap. 16.99 (*1-85242-377-3*) Serpents Tail.

— Altered State: The Story of Ecstasy Culture & Acid House. 1998. pap. 11.99 (*1-85242-604-7*) Serpents Tail.

Collin, P. Business Spanish Dictionary Spanish-English/English-Spanish. (ENG & SPA.). 632p. 1997. 39.95 (*0-948549-90-4*, Pub. by Peter Collin) IBD Ltd.

— English-German Dictionary of Business. (ENG & GER.). 455p. 1990. 49.95 (*0-8288-7244-9*, 948549173) Fr & Eur.

— English-German Dictionary of Ecology. (ENG & GER.). 294p. 1991. 49.95 (*0-8288-7235-X*, 948549211); 49.95 (*0-8288-7236-8*, 3125179408) Fr & Eur.

— English-German Dictionary of Printing & Publishing. (ENG & GER.). 364p. 1991. 49.95 (*0-8288-7237-6*, 094854919X) Fr & Eur.

— English-German, German-English Dictionary of Ecology. (ENG & GER.). 294p. 1991. 95.00 (*0-8288-7567-7*, 3125179408) Fr & Eur.

— English-German Law Dictionary. (ENG & GER.). 325p. 1990. 49.95 (*0-8288-7245-7*, 948549181) Fr & Eur.

— English-Swedish Business Dictionary. (ENG & SWE.). 407p. 1990. 59.95 (*0-8288-7246-5*, 948549149) Fr & Eur.

— English-Swedish Computing Dictionary. (ENG & SWE.). 342p. 1990. 59.95 (*0-8288-7247-3*, 948549165) Fr & Eur.

— English-Swedish Law Dictionary. (ENG & SWE.). 340p. 1990. 59.95 (*0-8288-7248-1*, 948549157) Fr & Eur.

— English to French Dictionary of Computing, Information Technology. (ENG & FRE.). 500p. 1996. 95.00 (*0-320-00524-0*) Fr & Eur.

— French-English, English-French Dictionary of Computer Science. (ENG & FRE.). 600p. 1991. 40.95 (*0-8288-7240-6*, 948549246) Fr & Eur.

— Pons English-German, German-English Business Dictionary. (ENG & GER.). 370p. 1990. 95.00 (*0-8288-7568-5*, 3125179300) Fr & Eur.

— Pons English-German, German-English Law Dictionary. (ENG & GER.). 340p. 1990. 95.00 (*0-8288-7566-9*, 3125179505) Fr & Eur.

— Pons German-English, English-German Dictionary of Marketing. (ENG & GER.). 269p. 1991. 95.00 (*0-8288-7565-0*, 3125179807) Fr & Eur.

— Pons German/English/German Law Dictionary. (ENG & GER.). 340p. 1997. 95.00 (*0-320-00463-5*) Fr & Eur.

Collin, P. & Stephens, Alan. Pons English-German, German-English Dictionary of Agriculture. (ENG & GER.). 383p. 1992. 95.00 (*0-8288-7569-3*, 3125178509) Fr & Eur.

Collin, P., jt. auth. see Klett, S.

Collin, P. H. American Business Dictionary. 302p. 1991. reprint ed. pap. text 15.95 (*0-948549-11-4*, Pub. by Peter Collin) IBD Ltd.

— Beginner's Dictionary of American English Usage. LC 97-43675. (Illus.). 288p. 1995. pap. 5.95 (*0-8442-0439-0*, 04390) NTC Contemp Pub Co.

— Business Spanish Dictionary. 2nd ed. 1999. pap. text 19.95 (*1-901659-23-2*) IPG Chicago.

— Dictionary of American Business. 2nd ed. 340p. 1999. pap. text 15.95 (*1-901659-22-4*) IPG Chicago.

— Dictionary of Banking & Finance. 260p. 1991. pap. text 15.95 (*0-948549-12-2*, Pub. by Peter Collin) IBD Ltd.

— Dictionary of Business. 334p. 1995. reprint ed. pap. text 15.95 (*0-948549-51-3*, Pub. by Peter Collin) IBD Ltd.

***Collin, P. H.** Dictionary of Business. 3rd ed. 400p. 2000. pap. 15.95 (*1-901659-50-X*, Pub. by P Collin) IPG Chicago.

Collin, P. H. Dictionary of Law. 2nd ed. 400p. 1999. 55.00 (*1-57958-155-2*) Fitzroy Dearborn.

— Dictionary of Printing & Publishing. 1989. pap. text 15.95 (*0-948549-09-2*, Pub. by Peter Collin) IBD Ltd.

— English-German Dictionary of Ecology with German-English Glossary. 294p. 1991. text 49.95 (*0-948549-21-1*, Pub. by Peter Collin) IBD Ltd.

— English-German Dictionary of Law with German-English Glossary. 440p. 1993. text 49.95 (*0-948549-18-1*, Pub. by Peter Collin) IBD Ltd.

— English-German Dictionary of Printing & Publishing with German-English Glossary. 364p. 1991. text 49.95 (*0-948549-19-X*, Pub. by Peter Collin) IBD Ltd.

— English-German Medical Dictionaries. (ENG & GER.). 620p. 1992. 62.50 (*0-8288-7563-4*, 3125179904) Fr & Eur.

— English Medical Dictionary. 2nd ed. 385p. 1993. pap. text 15.95 (*0-948549-36-X*, Pub. by Peter Collin) IBD Ltd.

— English-Swedish - Swedish-English Dictionary of Medicine. 684p. 1992. 25.94 (*0-7859-8714-2*) Fr & Eur.

— English-Swedish Dictionary of Business. (ENG & SWE.). write for info. (*0-8288-7659-2*) Fr & Eur.

— English-Swedish Dictionary of Business with Swedish-English Glossary. 407p. 1990. text 49.95 (*0-948549-14-9*, Pub. by Peter Collin) IBD Ltd.

— English-Swedish Dictionary of Law with Swedish-English Glossary. 340p. 1990. text 49.95 (*0-948549-15-7*, Pub. by Peter Collin) IBD Ltd.

— English-Swedish Dictionary of Medicine: With Swedish-English Glossary. (ENG & SWE.). 697p. 1993. 68.00 (*0-7859-8772-X*) Fr & Eur.

— French-English, English-French Dictionary of Business. 704p. 1990. text 39.95 (*0-948549-64-5*, Pub. by Peter Collin) IBD Ltd.

***Collin, P. H.** Pons Fachwhorterbuch Recht: Englisch-Deutsch, Deutsch-Englisch. 2nd ed. LC 99-194397. 499p. 1998. 53.00 (*3-12-517951-3*) Intl Bk Import.

***Collin, P. H.** Spanish Law Dictionary. 1999. 49.95 (*1-901659-09-7*, Pub. by P Collin) IPG Chicago.

Collin, P. H., ed. Dictionary of Business. 2nd rev. ed. 345p. 1999. lib. bdg. 45.00 (*1-57958-077-7*) Fitzroy Dearborn.

— Dictionary of Ecology & the Environment. 3rd rev. ed. 288p. 1998. lib. bdg. 45.00 (*1-57958-075-0*) Fitzroy Dearborn.

— Law Dictionary. (C). 1990. reprint ed. 75.00 (*0-89771-133-5*) St Mut.

Collin, P. H., et al, eds. Phase I Environmental Site Assessments: The State of the Practice. 288p. 25.00 (*0-614-05192-4*, PIESAO4943.5M) ASFE.

— Preacquisition Assessments: Recommended Management Procedures for Consulting Engineering Firms. 288p. 25.00 (*0-614-05191-6*, GC10895MPPRP) ASFE.

Collin, P. H. & Howe, Beata, eds. Business Glossary: English-Polish/Polish-English. LC 98-161079. 180 p. 1997. write for info. (*0-948549-46-7*) Peter Collin.

Collin, P. H. & Myrman, M. B. English-Swedish Dictionary of Medicine: With Swedish-English Glossary. (ENG & SWE.). 697p. 1993. 49.95 (*0-948549-23-8*, Pub. by Peter Collin) IBD Ltd.

Collin, P. H., et al. Beginner's Dictionary of American English Usage. (Illus.). 288p. 1995. text 9.95 (*0-8325-0440-8*, Natl Textbk Co) NTC Contemp Pub Co.

— Beginner's Dictionary of American English Usage. (Illus.). 288p. 1995. pap. 5.95 (*0-8325-0439-4*, Natl Textbk Co) NTC Contemp Pub Co.

— Beginner's Dictionary of American English Usage: A Basic Dictionary with Examples Accompanying Each Definition. (Illus.). 288p. 1986. pap. 9.95 (*0-8442-0440-4*, 04404) NTC Contemp Pub Co.

— Business German Dictionary: English-German - German-English. 2nd ed. 645p. 1994. 49.95 (*0-948549-50-5*, Pub. by Peter Collin) IBD Ltd.

— Chinese Business Dictionary Eng-Chin. (CHI.). 534p. 1995. 49.95 (*0-948549-63-7*, Pub. by Peter Collin) IBD Ltd.

— Dictionary of Hotels, Tourism, & Catering Management English-German with an German-English Glossary. (ENG & GER.). 387p. 1997. 49.95 (*0-948549-85-8*, Pub. by Peter Collin) IBD Ltd.

Collin, P. H., jt. auth. see Ivanovic, A.

Collin, P. Von, see Von Collin, P.

Collin, Peter. Gran Diccionario de Negocios, Ingles-Espanol/Espanol-Ingles. (SPA.). 728p. 1995. 95.00 (*0-7859-9879-9*) Fr & Eur.

— Larousse Informatique: English-French. (ENG & FRE.). 321p. 1991. pap. 79.95 (*0-7859-7659-0*, 2034040023) Fr & Eur.

***Collin, Peter, ed.** Dictionary of Wine. 240p. 1999. 45.00 (*1-57958-197-8*) Fitzroy Dearborn.

Collin, Peter, ed. Harrap's French Dictionary. 1991. pap. 27.95 (*0-13-387861-9*) P-H.

Collin, Peter & Peter Collin Publishing Staff. Dictionary of Accounting. 260p. 1992. pap. 15.95 (*0-948549-27-0*, Pub. by Peter Collin) IBD Ltd.

Collin, Peter & Schuwer, Martine. Larousse French & English Dictionary of the Environment & Ecology. (ENG & FRE., Illus.). 386p. 1992. pap. 75.00 (*0-8288-6975-8*, 2034040031) Fr & Eur.

Collin, Peter, et al. Harrap - Dictionnaire de 2,000 Mots Anglais-Francais. (ENG & FRE.). 305p. 1982. pap. 9.95 (*0-8288-1213-6*, M14519) Fr & Eur.

— Harrap's French Dictionary: French-English, English-French. rev. ed. (ENG & FRE.). 1844p. 1991. 39.95 (*0-8288-0780-9*, 781) Fr & Eur.

Collin, Peter H. Dictionnaire Anglais Elementaire. (FRE.). 1991. write for info. (*0-7859-8585-9*, 0-245-50152-5) Fr & Eur.

Collin, Peter H. Webster's Concise English Dictionary. LC 93-135330. 1992. pap. 5.95 (*0-88029-773-5*) Dorset Pr MA.

Collin, P.H., ed. Dictionary of Government & Politics. 2nd ed. 350p. 1998. lib. bdg. 45.00 (*1-57958-072-6*) Fitzroy Dearborn.

— Dictionary of Medicine. 2nd rev. ed. 393p. 1998. lib. bdg. 55.00 (*1-57958-074-2*) Fitzroy Dearborn.

Collin, R. E. Field Theory of Guided Waves. 2nd ed. LC 90-42254. 864p. 1990. 79.95 (*0-87942-237-8*, PC02568) Inst Electrical.

Collin, Richard, jt. auth. see Collin, Rima.

Collin, Richard E., ed. see Innis, Ben.

Collin, Richard H. Theodore Roosevelt's Caribbean: The Panama Canal, the Monroe Doctrine, & the Latin American Context. LC 89-28161. 520p. 1990. text 67.50 (*0-8071-1507-X*) La State U Pr.

Collin, Rima & Collin, Richard. The New Orleans Cookbook. 1987. pap. 17.00 (*0-394-75275-9*) Knopf.

Collin, Robert E. Antennas & Radiowave Propagation. LC 84-17108. 508p. (C). 1985. 104.06 (*0-07-011808-6*) McGraw.

— Field Theory of Guided Waves. 2nd ed. (IEEE/OUP Series on Electromagnetic Wave Theory). (Illus.). 864p. (C). 1996. text 135.00 (*0-19-859213-2*) OUP.

Collin, Rodney. The Christian Mystery. 1984. pap. 5.95 (*0-916411-26-5*, Sure Fire) Holmes Pub.

— The Herald of Harmony. 1984. pap. 5.95 (*0-916411-27-3*, Sure Fire) Holmes Pub.

— Lessons in Religion for a Skeptical World. 1991. pap. 7.95 (*1-55818-178-4*) Holmes Pub.

— The Mysteries of the Seed. 1987. pap. 7.95 (*1-55818-100-8*, Sure Fire) Holmes Pub.

— The Theory of Celestial Influence. 1997. pap. 13.95 (*0-14-019365-0*, Arkana) Viking Penguin.

— The Theory of Celestial Influence: Man, the Universe, & Cosmic Mystery. (Orig.). 1984. pap. 10.95 (*0-394-72391-0*) Random.

Collin, S. Dictionary of Personal Computing & the Internet. LC 97-217936. (Illus.). 205p. 1997. pap. 17.95 (*0-948549-93-9*, Pub. by Peter Collin) IBD Ltd.

— Michaelis Dicionario Pratico de Informatica, Ingles-Portugues Portugues-Ingles. (ENG & POR.). 452p. 1993. 95.00 (*0-7859-9797-0*) Fr & Eur.

— Pons German/English/German Dictionary of Data Processing. (ENG & GER.). 500p. 1997. 95.00 (*0-320-00451-1*) Fr & Eur.

Collin, S. M. Dictionary of Personal Computing & the Internet. 2nd ed. (Illus.). 234p. 1999. pap. 17.95 (*1-901659-12-7*) IPG Chicago.

— English-Swedish Dictionary of Computing. (ENG & SWE.). write for info. (*0-8288-7660-6*) Fr & Eur.

— English-Swedish Dictionary of Computing with Swedish-English Glossary. 342p. 1990. text 49.95 (*0-948549-16-5*, Pub. by Peter Collin) IBD Ltd.

— Pons, English-German, German-English Dictionary of Data Processing. (ENG & GER.). 410p. 1991. 95.00 (*0-8288-7564-2*, 3125179602) Fr & Eur.

Collin, S. M. H. Bradford's Crossword Key Dictionary. 760p. 2000. pap. 17.95 (*1-901659-40-2*, Pub. by P Collin) IPG Chicago.

— Dictionary of Wine Terms. 2000. pap. 17.95 (*1-901659-41-0*, Pub. by P Collin) IPG Chicago.

— Menu Reader's Dictionary: A Guide to International Menu Terms. (FRE, ENG, GER, ITA & SPA.). 260p. 2000. pap. 9.95 (*0-948549-86-6*, Pub. by P Collin) IPG Chicago.

Collin, Simon. A Complete Guide to Lotus Notes 4.5. LC 97-148990. 336p. 1997. pap. 34.95 (*1-55558-175-7*, Digital DEC) Buttrwrth-Heinemann.

***Collin, Simon.** Dictionary of Multimedia. 3rd ed. (Illus.). 350p. 2000. pap. 12.95 (*1-901659-51-8*, Pub. by P Collin) IPG Chicago.

— Dictionary of Personal Computing & the Internet. 3rd ed. (Illus.). 350p. 2000. pap. 12.95 (*1-901659-52-6*, Pub. by P Collin) IPG Chicago.

Collin, Simon. Doing Business on the Internet. (Business & Management Ser.). 1997. 19.95 (*0-7494-2128-2*) Kogan Page Ltd.

— The Essential LAN Source Book. LC 94-30166. 1994. write for info. (*0-07-707881-0*) McGraw.

— Integrating E-Mail: From the Intranet to the Internet. LC 98-40472. 146p. 1998. pap. text 29.95 (*1-55558-198-6*) DEC.

— Networking Windows 95. LC 96-209056. 350p. 1996. pap. 41.95 (*0-7506-2418-3*) Buttrwrth-Heinemann.

— Setting up a Web Server. LC 97-18157. 273p. 1997. pap. text 34.95 (*1-55558-174-9*, Digital DEC) Buttrwrth-Heinemann.

— Visual Basic for Network Applications. LC 98-122589. 200p. 1997. pap. 29.95 (*1-55558-173-0*, Digital DEC) Buttrwrth-Heinemann.

***Collin, Simon, ed.** Dictionary of Art. 240p. 1999. 45.00 (*1-57958-198-6*) Fitzroy Dearborn.

Collin, Simon, ed. Dictionary of Personal Computing & the Internet. 250p. 1997. lib. bdg. 35.00 (*1-57958-016-5*) Fitzroy Dearborn.

***Collin, Simon, ed.** Dictionary of Science & Technology. 300p. 1999. 45.00 (*1-57958-193-5*) Fitzroy Dearborn.

Collin, Wilkie. Law & the Lady. LC 99-236047. 432p. 1999. pap. 10.95 (*0-14-043607-3*, PuffinBks) Peng Put Young Read.

Collin, William E. The White Savannahs. LC 73-92516. (Literature of Canada, Poetry & Prose in Reprint Ser.: No. 15). 383p. reprint ed. pap. 118.80 (*0-608-12844-9*, 202360400033) Bks Demand.

Collinet. Le Monde Litteraire de la Fontaine. 59.40 (*0-685-34231-X*) Fr & Eur.

Collinet, Jean-Pierre, ed. see La Fontaine, Jean de.

Colling, David A. & Vasilos, Thomas. Industrial Materials, Vol. 1. LC 94-10077. 352p. (C). 1994. pap. text 37.60 (*0-02-323560-8*, Macmillan Coll) P-H.

— Industrial Materials: Polymers, Ceramics & Composites, Vol. 2. LC 94-10077. 256p. 1995. pap. text 37.60 (*0-02-323553-5*, Macmillan Coll) P-H.

Colling, James K. Medieval Decorative Ornament. 160p. 1995. pap. 9.95 (*0-486-28740-8*) Dover.

***Colling, John.** Family Prayers for Mealtime Grace. 2nd ed. 1999. pap. 5.95 (*1-929338-00-7*) Verrius.

Colling, Lynn, jt. auth. see Bluestein, Jane.

***Colling, Russell L.** Hospital & Healthcare Security. 4th ed. 416p. 2000. 54.95 (*0-7506-9892-6*) Buttrwrth-Heinemann.

Colling, Russell L. Hospital Security. 3rd ed. 345p. 1992. 59.95 (*0-7506-9027-5*) Buttrwrth-Heinemann.

Colling, Russell L. & Joint Commission on Accreditation of Healthcare Organizations. Security: Keeping the Health Care Environment Safe. (Illus.). 143p. 1996. pap. 35.00 (*0-86688-469-6*, EC-503) Joint Comm Hlthcare.

Colling, Terry. Beyond Mateship: Understanding Australian Men LC 92-250208. xii, 164p. 1992. (*0-7318-0264-0*) Simon & Schuster.

Collingbourne, L., ed. ADA: Towards Maturity. LC 93-6113. (Studies in Computer & Communications Systems: Vol. 6). 250p. (gr. 12). 1993. pap. 75.00 (*90-5199-142-8*, Pub. by IOS Pr) IOS Press.

Collinge, jt. auth. see Ayers, Ronald M.

Collinge, John. The Law Relating to Restrictive Trade Practices & Monopolies, Mergers & Take-overs in New Zealand. 2nd ed. 518p. 1982. boxed set 99.00 (*0-409-60125-X*, NZ, MICHIE) LEXIS Pub.

Collinge, John & Clarke, Bruce. Law of Marketing in Australia & New Zealand. 2nd ed. 531p. 1989. pap. 65.00 (*0-409-49548-4*, Austral, MICHIE) LEXIS Pub.

Collinge, John & Palmer, Mark, eds. Prion Diseases. LC 96-30984. (Illus.). 212p. 1997. text 59.50 (*0-19-854789-7*) OUP.

Collinge, N. E. Collectanea Linguistica: Essays in General & Genetic Linguistics. LC 76-129298. (Janua Linguarum, Ser. Minor: No. 21). (Orig.). 1971. pap. text 52.30 (*90-279-1544-X*) Mouton.

Collinge, N. E., ed. The Laws of Indo-European. LC 85-9192. (Current Issues in Linguistic Theory Ser.: No. 35). xviii, 273p. 1985. pap. 23.00 (*0-915027-75-5*) J Benjamins Pubng Co.

Collinge, Nancy E. Introduction to Primate Behavior. 256p. (C). 1995. per. 29.95 (*0-8403-8569-2*) Kendall-Hunt.

Collinge, Robert A. & Ayers, Ronald M. Economics by Design. LC 96-32847. 1996. pap. text 58.00 (*0-13-373788-8*) P-H.

Collinge, William. The American Holistic Health Association Complete Guide to Alternative Medicine. 384p. 1997. mass mkt. 15.95 (*0-446-67258-0*, Pub. by Warner Bks) Little.

— Cancer: A Guide to Alternative Self-Healing Techniques,

C

unabridged ed. (Mind-Body Medicine Library: Vol. 1). 1998. pap. 16.95 incl. audio (*1-55927-497-2*, 395766, Pub. by Audio Renaissance) Lndmrk Audiobks.
— Courting the Spirit: The Book of Subtle Energy. 1997. write for info. (*0-614-13861-2*) Warner Bks.
— Recovering from Chronic Fatigue Syndrome: A Guide to Self Empowerment. LC 92-35606. 224p. (Orig.). 1993. pap. 13.95 (*0-399-51807-X*, Body Pr-Perigee) Berkley Pub.

***Collinge, William.** Stress Reduction: A Guide to Alternative Self-Healing Techniques. unabridged ed. (Mind-Body Medicine Library: Vol. 3 3). 1998. pap. 16.95 incl. audio (*1-55927-498-0*) Audio Renaissance.

Collinge, William. Subtle Energy: Awakening to the Unseen Forces in Our Lives. LC 97-6221. 352p. 1998. 24.00 (*0-446-52017-9*, Pub. by Warner Bks) Little.
— Subtle Energy: Awakening to the Unseen Forces in Our Lives. 1999. pap. write for info. (*0-446-67474-5*) Warner Bks.

Collinge, William J. Historical Dictionary of Catholicism. LC 96-30421. (Religions, Philosophies & Movements Ser.: No. 12). 576p. 1997. 60.00 (*0-8108-3233-X*) Scarecrow.

Collinge, William J., tr. see Augustine, Saint.

Collingham, H. A. July Monarchy: France 1830. (FRE.). 468p. (C). 1988. pap. text 32.95 (*0-582-01334-8*, 70412) Longman.

Collingridge, David. Criticism: Its Philosophical Structure. LC 87-2089. 178p. (Orig.). 1988. pap. text 19.00 (*0-8191-6282-5*) U Pr of Amer.
— The Management of Scale. 224p. (C). 1992. mass mkt. 26.95 (*0-415-07857-1*, A9705) Routledge.

Collingridge, Graham L. & Watkins, Jeffrey C., eds. The NMDA Receptor. 2nd ed. (Illus.). 522p. 1995. 115.00 (*0-19-262371-0*) OUP.
— The NMDA Receptor. 2nd ed. (Illus.). 516p. 1995. pap. text 54.50 (*0-19-262502-0*) OUP.

Collingridge, Graham L., jt. ed. see Fazeli, Sam.

Collings. Classic Victorian & Edwardian Ghost Stories. (Classics Library). 1998. pap. 3.95 (*1-85326-186-6*, Pub. by Wrdsworth Edits) NTC Contemp Pub Co.

Collings, A. J. & Luxon, S. G. Safe Use of Solvents. 1982. text 139.00 (*0-12-181250-2*) Acad Pr.

Collings, Beth & Jamerson, Anna. Connections: Unraveling Our Alien Abduction Mystery. LC 95-49150. (Illus.). 360p. 1996. per. 13.00 (*0-926524-35-6*) Granite Pub.

Collings, Betty & Kuspit, Donald. Thomas Macaulay: Sculptural Views on Perceptual Ambiguity, 1968-1986. LC 86-61901. 71p. (Orig.). 1986. pap. text 14.95 (*0-937809-00-4*) Dayton Art.

Collings, Chik. Language, Ideology & Social Consciousness: Developing a Sociohistorical Approach. LC 98-74510. 16p. 1999. text 69.95 (*1-84014-842-X*) Ashgate Pub Co.

Collings, David. Wordsworthian Errancies: The Poetics of Cultural Dismemberment. LC 94-6204. 1994. text 39.95 (*0-8018-4848-2*) Johns Hopkins.

Collings, Deirdre, ed. Peace for Lebanon? From War to Reconstruction. LC 93-39746. 342p. 1994. pap. text 22.00 (*1-55587-501-7*); lib. bdg. 46.00 (*1-55587-367-7*) L Rienner.

Collings, E. W. Applied Superconductivity, Metallurgy & Physics of Titanium Alloys, Vol. 1: Fundamentals. LC 85-12063. (International Cryogenics Monographs). (Illus.). 854p. (C). 1986. text 222.00 (*0-306-41690-5*, Kluwer Plenum) Kluwer Academic.
— Applied Superconductivity, Metallurgy & Physics of Titanium Alloys, Vol. 2: Applications. LC 85-12063. (International Cryogenics Monographs). (Illus.). 726p. (C). 1986. text 198.00 (*0-306-41691-3*, Kluwer Plenum) Kluwer Academic.
— A Sourcebook of Titanium Alloy Superconductivity. 550p. 1983. 125.00 (*0-306-41344-2*, Plenum Trade) Perseus Pubng.

Collings, E. W., et al, eds. Materials Properties Handbook: Titanium Alloys. 1169p. 1994. 290.00 (*0-87170-481-1*, 6005) ASM.

Collings, E. W., ed. see Hume-Rothery Memorial Symposium Staff.

Collings, E. W., ed. see Metallurgical Society of AIME Staff.

Collings, Ellsworth & England, Alma M. The One Hundred One Ranch. LC 73-167774. (Illus.). 286p. 1986. pap. 15.95 (*0-8061-1047-3*) U of Okla Pr.

Collings, Francis d'A. The Discovery of the Chesapeake Bay: An Account of the Explorations of Captain John Smith in the year 1608. LC 88-23703. (Illus.). (Orig.). 1988. pap. 10.95 (*0-922249-00-8*) Ches Bay Mus.

Collings, George. Circular Work in Carpentry & Joinery. Shumaker, Karl, ed. LC 92-9358. (Illus.). 126p. 1992. reprint ed. pap. 21.95 (*0-941936-48-1*) Linden Pub Fresno.

Collings, Jillie. Principles of Colonic Irrigation: The Only Introduction You'll Ever Need. 160p. 1996. pap. 11.00 (*0-7225-3029-3*) Harper SF.

***Collings, Julie & Elton, Candice.** Beadlings: How to Make Beaded Creatures & Creations. (Illus.). 90p. (J). (gr. 4-7). 2000. 16.95 (*1-57054-476-X*) Klutz.

Collings, Matthew. Blimey! From Bohemia to Britpop: The London Artworld from Francis Bacon to Damien Hirst. (Illus.). pap. 29.95 (*1-901785-00-9*, Pub. by Twenty-One) Dist Art Pubs.

Collings, Matthew. New York Art from Warhol to Now. 1998. pap. text 29.95 (*1-901785-03-3*) Twenty-One.

***Collings, Matthew.** This is Modern Art. (Illus.). 272p. 2000. pap. write for info. (*0-8230-5362-8*) Watsn-Guptill.

Collings, Michael R. All Calm, All Bright: Christmas Meditations. 2nd ed. 100p. Date not set. pap. 15.00 (*1-886405-57-3*) White Crow Pr.
— All Calm, All Bright: Christmas Offerings. LC 95-65159. 120p. (Orig.). 1995. pap. text 14.00 (*1-886405-50-6*) White Crow Pr.
— The Art & Craft of Poetry: Twenty Exercises Toward Mastery. 100p. (Orig.). Date not set. pap. 13.00 (*1-886405-58-1*, BuckThorne) White Crow Pr.
— Brian Aldiss. Schlobin, Roger C., ed. LC 85-17224. (Starmont Reader's Guide Ser.: Vol. 28). (Illus.). iv, 115p. 1986. pap. 17.00 (*0-916732-74-6*) Millefleurs.
— Compositae: Chapbooks & Poems. LC 99-71316. 108p. 1999. 15.00 (*1-886405-65-4*, Zarahemla Motets) White Crow Pr.

***Collings, Michael R.** Elementals: Auto-Reductive Sonets in Major & Minor Modes. xv, 62p. 1999. 15.00 (*1-886405-67-0*, Zarahemla Motets) White Crow Pr.

Collings, Michael R. Epyllion in Anamnesis: Two Cycles of Poems. 75p. (Orig.). Date not set. pap. 15.00 (*1-886405-53-0*, Zarahemla Motets) White Crow Pr.
— Filamental Emblems. (Illus.). 80p. (C). 1998. 35.00 (*1-886405-62-X*, Zarahemla Motets) White Crow Pr.

***Collings, Michael R.** For Judi: Selected Poems. LC 99-71315. 60p. 1999. 15.00 (*1-886405-66-2*, Zarahemla Motets) White Crow Pr.

Collings, Michael R. The House Beyond the Hill. LC 96-80404. 218p. (Orig.). (C). 1997. pap. 20.00 (*1-886405-60-3*) White Crow Pr.
— In the Image of God: Theme, Characterization & Landscape in the Fiction of Orson Scott Card, 42. LC 89-26031. (Contributions to the Study of Science Fiction & Fantasy Ser.: No. 42). 208p. 1990. 55.00 (*0-313-26404-X*, CIE/, Greenwood Pr) Greenwood.
— The Many Facets of Stephen King. LC 85-12598. (Starmont Studies in Literary Criticism: No. 11). (Illus.). vi, 190p. 1985. pap. 21.00 (*0-930261-14-3*) Millefleurs.
— Milton in Context: The Seventeenth Century: Annotated Chronology, Genealogical Tables, & Selected Bibliographies. 400p. (C). 1998. 50.00 (*1-886405-61-1*, Zarahemla Motets) White Crow Pr.

***Collings, Michael R.** The Nephiad: An Epic in Twelve Books. 175p. 1999. 30.00 (*1-886405-68-9*, Zarahemla Motets) White Crow Pr.

Collings, Michael R. The Nephiad: An Epic Poem in 12 Books. LC 96-61331. 180p. (Orig.). Date not set. pap. 20.00 (*1-886405-52-2*, Zarahemla Motets) White Crow Pr.
— Nestlings of a Dark God: Poems: Science Fiction, Fantasy, Myth & Horror - Millennial Collection, 1974-1999. 2nd rev. ed. LC 99-71315. 350p. (C). 1999. 35.00 (*1-886405-64-6*, Zarahemla Motets) White Crow Pr.
— Nestlings of a Dark God: Poems, 1974-1996 - Science Fiction, Fantasy, Horror, Myth. LC 96-90726. xii, 302p. (Orig.). 1996. reprint ed. pap. 30.00 (*1-886405-56-5*, Zarahemla Motets) White Crow Pr.
— Piers Anthony. Schlobin, Roger C., ed. LC 83-2466. (Starmont Reader's Guide Ser.: Vol. 20). 96p. 1983. pap. 17.00 (*0-916732-52-5*) Millefleurs.
— Potpourri: A Medley of Poems. 54p. (Orig.). Date not set. pap. 6.00 (*1-886405-59-X*, Zarahemla Motets) White Crow Pr.
— Som Certaine Sonets. LC 98-91046. 85 p. 1998. write for info. (*1-886405-63-8*) White Crow Pr.
— Stephen King As Richard Bachman. LC 85-2832. (Starmont Studies in Literary Criticism: No. 10). (Illus.). vi, 168p. 1985. pap. 21.00 (*0-930261-00-3*) Millefleurs.
— Still Secrecies of Love: Poems L. D. S. & Other. 130p. (Orig.). pap. 15.00 (*1-886405-54-9*, Zarahemla Motets) White Crow Pr.
— Tales Through Time. 2nd rev. ed. 100p. Date not set. pap. 15.00 (*1-886405-55-7*, Zarahemla Motets) White Crow Pr.

Collings, Michael R., ed. Reflections on the Fantastic: Selected Essays from the 4th International Conference on the Fantastic in the Arts, 24. LC 86-12123. (Contributions to the Study of Science Fiction & Fantasy Ser.: No. 24). 124p. 1986. 47.95 (*0-313-25555-5*, CRF/) Greenwood.

Collings, Michael R. & Engebretson, David. The Shorter Works of Stephen King. LC 85-2822. (Starmont Studies in Literary Criticism: No. 9). (Illus.). vi, 202p. 1985. pap. 23.00 (*0-930261-02-X*) Millefleurs.

***Collings, Michael R. & Straub, Peter.** Hauntings: The Official Peter Straub Bibliography. (Illus.). 240p. 2000. 45.00 (*1-892950-15-4*, Biblio); pap. 25.00 (*1-892950-16-2*, Biblio) Overlook Connect.

Collings, Nick & Pirault, J. P. Lean Burn Engines. (Cambridge Engine Technology Ser.). 170p. 1995. write for info. (*0-521-33018-1*) Cambridge U Pr.

Collings, Peter & Hird, Mike. An Introduction to Liquid Crystals: Chemistry & Physics. LC 97-198772. (Liquid Crystals Book Ser.). 300p. 1997. 89.00 (*0-7484-0643-3*, Pub. by Tay Francis Ltd); pap. 27.95 (*0-7484-0483-X*, Pub. by Tay Francis Ltd) Taylor & Francis.

Collings, Peter J. Liquid Crystals: Nature's Delicate Phase of Matter. (Science Library). (Illus.). 252p. 1991. pap. 15.95 (*0-691-02429-4*, Pub. by Princeton U Pr); text 49.50 (*0-691-08509-9*, Pub. by Princeton U Pr) Cal Prin Full Svc.

Collings, Peter J. & Patel, Jay S., eds. Handbook of Liquid Crystal Research. (Illus.). 624p. 1997. text 195.00 (*0-19-508442-X*) OUP.

Collings, Robert B., et al, eds. Federal Civil Litigation in the First Circuit, 1998 Supplement: 1997 Supplement. LC 94-77711. 1998. ring bd. 59.50 (*1-57589-089-5*, 97-05.60-SP) Mass CLE.

Collings, Robert B., et al. Federal Civil Litigation in the First Circuit. LC 94-77711. 764p. 1995. ring bd. 125.00 (*0-944490-67-0*) Mass CLE.

Collings, Timothy. The New Villeneuve: The Life of Jacques Villeneuve. LC 97-10909. (Illus.). 200p. 1997. 24.95 (*0-7603-0411-4*) MBI Pubg.

Collings, Timothy, ed. Stevenage, 1946-1986: Images of the First New Town. 170p. (C). 1986. 85.00 (*0-907590-18-7*) St Mut.

Collingswood, R. G. & Wright, R. P. The Roman Inscriptions of Britain, Vol. II, Fascicule 4. Frere, S. S. & Tomlin, R. S., eds. (Illus.). 256p. 1992. 62.95 (*0-7509-0086-5*, Pub. by Sutton Pub Ltd) Intl Pubs Mktg.

Collingsworth, J. B. 10-Minute Devotions for Youth Groups: 52 Quick Devotions to Involve Teenagers. (Illus.). 90p. 1989. pap. 14.99 (*0-931529-85-9*) Group Pub.

***Collington, Peter.** Clever Cat. LC 99-40373. (Illus.). 32p. (J). (ps-3). 2000. 15.95 (*0-375-80477-3*, Pub. by Knopf Bks Yng Read); lib. bdg. 17.99 (*0-375-90477-8*, Pub. by Knopf Bks Yng Read) Random.

Collington, Peter. A Small Miracle. LC 96-53916. (Illus.). 32p. (J). (ps up). 1997. 18.00 (*0-679-88725-3*, Pub. by Random Bks Yng Read) Random.

Collington, Stephen, tr. see Kawamoto, Koju.

Collingwood. Precalculus. (C). 1998. text 40.00 (*0-03-024754-3*) Harcourt Coll Pubs.
— Precalculus. (C). 1999. pap. text 29.50 (*0-03-023512-X*, Pub. by Harcourt Coll Pubs); pap. text 19.50 (*0-03-023513-8*) Harcourt Coll Pubs.

Collingwood, Christopher. The Divine Dance of Love: Sharing in the Mystery of Christ. 176p. 1997. pap. 15.95 (*1-85311-146-5*, 826, Pub. by Canterbury Press Norwich) Morehouse Pub.

Collingwood, D. H. Representations of Rank One Lie Groups 2: N-Cohomology. LC 88-10415. (Memoirs Ser.: No. 74/387). 101p. 1988. pap. 18.00 (*0-8218-2450-3*, MEMO/74/387) Am Math.

Collingwood, David H. & McGovern, William M. Nilpotent Orbits in Semisimple Lie Algebras. LC 92-30461. 192p. (gr. 13). 1993. ring bd. 94.95 (*0-534-18834-6*, Chap & Hall CRC) CRC Pr.

Collingwood, David H., jt. auth. see Boe, Brian D.

Collingwood, Donald. Captain-Class Frigates in the Second World War. LC 98-68549. 1999. 34.95 (*1-55750-195-5*) Naval Inst Pr.

Collingwood, Edward F. & Lohwater, A. J. The Theory of Cluster Sets. LC 66-18115. (Cambridge Tracts in Mathematics & Mathematical Physics Ser.: No. 56). reprint ed. pap. 55.80 (*0-608-30913-3*, 2013053) Bks Demand.
— The Theory of Cluster Sets. LC 66-18115. (Cambridge Tracts in Mathematics & Mathematical Physics Ser.: No. 56). 223p. 1966. reprint ed. pap. 69.20 (*0-608-10352-7*, 2013271) Bks Demand.

Collingwood, Fred. How to Be Invisible: The Complete Guide to Privacy in Today's High-Tech World. (Orig.). 1995. pap. 24.95 (*0-9646578-0-5*) F Collingwood.

Collingwood, G. H. & Brush, Warren D. Knowing Your Trees. rev. ed. Butcher, Devercuy, ed. LC 78-52994. (Illus.). 392p. 1984. 9.50 (*0-685-54100-2*) Am Forests.

Collingwood, Guillermo. Las Dos Naturalezas del Creyente. 2nd ed. Bennett, Gordon H., ed. Bautista, Sara, tr. from ENG. (Serie Diamante).Tr. of Believer's Two Natures. (SPA., Illus.). 52p. 1982. pap. 0.85 (*0-942504-03-8*) Overcomer Pr.

***Collingwood, Herbert.** Andersonville Violets: A Story of Northern & Southern Life. 2000. pap. 19.95 (*0-8173-1061-4*) U of Ala Pr.

Collingwood, Lucy. Helpmates. 80p. (Orig.). 1989. teacher ed. 10.00 (*0-87879-628-2*) Acad Therapy.
— Postcards from Europe Workbook. Kratoville, Betty Lou, ed. 64p. (Orig.). (J). (gr. 4 up). 1995. pap., student ed. 14.00 (*0-87879-995-8*) High Noon Bks.
— Second Chance in Centerville. 64p. 1991. pap. text 12.00 (*0-87879-909-5*) High Noon Bks.

Collingwood, Peter. Rug Weaving Techniques: Beyond the Basics. (Illus.). 160p. 1991. pap. 29.95 (*0-934026-62-9*) Interweave.

***Collingwood, Peter.** Techniques of Plysplit Braiding. 1998. 60.00 (*0-9625586-9-9*) Unicorn Bks & Crafts.

Collingwood, Peter. The Techniques of Rug Weaving. LC 68-24486. (Illus.). 480p. 1987. 60.00 (*0-8230-5200-1*) Watsn-Guptill.

***Collingwood, Peter.** Techniques of Sprang: Plaiting of Stretched Threads. (Illus.). 1999. pap. 35.00 (*1-55821-967-6*) Lyons Pr.

Collingwood, Peter. The Techniques of Sprang: Plaiting on Stretched Threads LC 99-12336. 1999. write for info. (*1-55821-930-7*) Lyons Pr.
— The Techniques of Tablet Weaving. 2nd rev. ed. 1996. reprint ed. pap. 36.00 (*1-56659-055-8*) Robin & Russ.

Collingwood, R. C., tr. see De Ruggiero, Guido.

Collingwood, R. G. The Archaeology of Roman Britain. (Illus.). 293p. 1998. reprint ed. pap. text 17.00 (*0-7881-5408-7*) DIANE Pub.
— An Essay on Metaphysics: New Edition with Introduction & Additional Material. 2nd ed. Martin, Rex, ed. & intro. by. LC 98-15538. 546p. 1998. text 85.00 (*0-19-823561-5*) OUP.
— An Essay on Philosophical Method: 1933 Edition. (Key Texts Ser.). 240p. 1996. reprint ed. pap. 22.00 (*1-85506-392-1*) Bks Intl VA.
— Essays in Political Philosophy. Boucher, David, ed. & intro. by. 246p. 1995. reprint ed. pap. text 19.95 (*0-19-823566-6*) OUP.
— The First Mate's Log: 1940 Edition. 196p. 1996. reprint ed. 58.00 (*1-85506-328-X*) Bks Intl VA.
— Human Nature & Human History. (Studies in Philosophy: No. 40). (C). 1972. reprint ed. lib. bdg. 59.95 (*0-8383-0132-0*) M S G Haskell Hse.

Collingwood, R. G. The Idea of History with Lectures 1926-1928. 2nd rev. ed. Van Der Dussen, Jan, ed. & intro. by. 564p. 1994. reprint ed. pap. text 15.95 (*0-19-285306-6*) OUP.

Collingwood, R. G. The New Leviathan: Or Man, Society, Civilization & Barbarism. 2nd rev. ed. Boucher, David, ed. 584p. 1999. pap. text 29.95 (*0-19-823880-0*) OUP.

Collingwood, R. G. Outlines of a Philosophy of Art, 1925. (Key Texts Ser.). 110p. 1996. reprint ed. pap. 15.00 (*1-85506-316-6*) Bks Intl VA.

Collingwood, R. G. The Principles of History: And Other Writings in Philosophy of History. Dray, Williams H. & Dussen, W., eds. LC 98-49637. (Illus.). 382p. 1999. text 75.00 (*0-19-823703-0*) OUP.
— Religion & Philosophy: 1916 Edition. 238p. 1996. reprint ed. pap. 20.00 (*1-85506-317-4*) Bks Intl VA.

Collingwood, R. G. & Myres, John N. Roman Britain & the English Settlements. 515p. 1936. pap. 30.00 (*0-8196-1160-3*) Biblo.

Collingwood, R. G. & Wright, R. P. The Roman Inscriptions of Britain, Vol. II, Fascicule 5. (C). 1993. text 62.95 (*0-7509-0319-8*, Pub. by Sutton Pub Ltd) Intl Pubs Mktg.

Collingwood, Robin George. Autobiography. 192p. 1983. pap. text 26.00 (*0-19-824694-3*) OUP.
— Idea of Nature. 192p. 1960. pap. text 11.95 (*0-19-500217-2*) OUP.
— The Idea of Nature. LC 86-4642. 191p. 1986. reprint ed. lib. bdg. 65.00 (*0-313-25166-5*, COID, Greenwood Pr) Greenwood.
— The New Leviathan: Man, Society, Civilization & Barbarism. LC 84-19284. 387p. 1984. reprint ed. lib. bdg. 55.50 (*0-313-24621-1*, CONL, Greenwood Pr) Greenwood.
— The New Leviathan: or Man, Society, Civilization & Barbarism. LC 83-45423. reprint ed. 40.00 (*0-404-20066-4*) AMS Pr.
— The New Leviathan: or Man, Society, Civilization & Barbarism. 2nd rev. ed. LC 92-17771. 586p. 1993. text 95.00 (*0-19-823981-5*, Clarendon Pr) OUP.
— Outlines of a Philosophy of Art. 1988. reprint ed. lib. bdg. 49.00 (*0-7812-0127-6*) Rprt Serv.
— Outlines of a Philosophy of Art. LC 25-26891. 104p. 1925. reprint ed. 39.00 (*0-403-07231-X*) Somerset Pub.
— Principles of Art. 360p. 1958. pap. text 14.95 (*0-19-500209-1*) OUP.
— Speculum Mentis: The Map of Knowledge. LC 82-15552. 327p. 1982. reprint ed. lib. bdg. 41.50 (*0-313-23701-8*, COSM, Greenwood Pr) Greenwood.

Collingwood, Robin George, tr. see Croce, Benedetto.

Collingwood, Sharon L. Market Pledge & Gender Bargain: Commercial Relations in French Farce, 1450-1550. LC 95-33323. (Studies in the Humanities: Vol. 23). XII, 209p. (C). 1997. text 44.95 (*0-8204-2869-8*) P Lang Pubng.

Collingwood, Stuart D. The Life & Letters of Lewis Carroll. (BCL1-PR English Literature Ser.). 448p. 1992. reprint ed. lib. bdg. 99.00 (*0-7812-7518-0*) Rprt Serv.

Collingwood, Thomas R., jt. auth. see Hoffman, Robert.

Collingwood, Tom. Helping At-Risk Youth Through Physical Fitness Programming. LC 96-53063. (Illus.). 216p. (Orig.). 1997. pap. text 24.00 (*0-88011-549-1*, BCOL0549) Human Kinetics.

Collingwood, W. G. & Steffanson, Jon, trs. Life & Death of Cormac the Skald. LC 76-43948. (Viking Society for Northern Research: Translation Ser.: Vol. 1). (Illus.). 416p. reprint ed. 39.50 (*0-404-60011-5*) AMS Pr.

Collini, Emanuela, jt. auth. see Padoan, Gianni.

Collini, Stefan. English Pasts: Essays in History & Culture. LC 98-47247. 358p. 1999. pap. 24.95 (*0-19-820780-8*); text 70.00 (*0-19-820779-4*) OUP.
— Public Moralists: Political Thought & Intellectual Life in Britain, 1850-1930. -90p. 1993. reprint ed. pap. text 35.00 (*0-19-820422-1*) OUP.

***Collini, Stefan, et al, eds.** Economy, Polity & Society: British Intellectual History 1750-1950. LC 99-42116. 288p. (C). 2000. 59.95 (*0-521-63018-5*); pap. 22.95 (*0-521-63978-6*) Cambridge U Pr.
— History, Religion & Culture: British Intellectual History 1750-1950. LC 99-42115. 288p. (C). 2000. 59.95 (*0-521-62638-2*); pap. 22.95 (*0-521-62639-0*) Cambridge U Pr.

Collini, Stefan, ed. see Arnold, Matthew.

Collini, Stefan, ed. see Eco, Umberto.

Collini, Stefan, ed. see Mill, John Stuart.

***Collini, Susan J.** Two Girlfriends Get Real about Cosmetic Surgery: A Woman-to-Woman Guide to Today's Most Popular Cosmetic Surgeries. LC 99-49561. (Illus.). 304p. 2000. pap. 19.95 (*1-58063-127-4*) Renaissance.

***Collins.** Caring for Your Child with Severe Food Allergies: Emotional Support & Practical Advice From a Parent Who's Been There. LC 99-15192. 116p. 1999. pap. 10.95 (*0-471-34785-X*) Wiley.
— Gamma World Campaign Setting. (Alternity Ser.). 192p. 2000. 24.95 (*0-7869-1629-X*) TSR Inc.
— Gem Canadian English Dictionary. 2000. pap. 6.75 (*0-00-638668-7*) HarpCollins.

Collins. How to Recognize Emotional Unavailability & Make Healthier Relationships. 304p. 1999. 7.98 (*1-56731-344-2*, MJF Bks) Fine Comms.

***Collins.** Pad. 402p. 2000. 120.00 (*0-471-87736-0*) Wiley.
— Running. 1993. boxed set 12.95 (*1-56530-076-9*) Summit TX.
— Seurat to Picasso. 2000. 45.00 (*0-8133-3594-9*, Pub. by Westview) HarpC.
— Strategic Human Resourses. 148.95 (*1-85521-939-5*) Ashgate Pub Co.
— Van Gogh & Gauguin. 2000. 35.00 (*0-8133-3595-7*, Pub. by Westview) HarpC.
— Ya Veras! Gold, Vol. 2. 1998. pap., wbk. ed. 12.50 (*0-8384-0905-9*) Heinle & Heinle.
— Ya Veras! Gold, Vol. 3. 1998. pap., wbk. ed. 12.50 (*0-8384-0914-8*) Heinle & Heinle.

Collins & Davies. Modern Medical Language Act Cards. (Medical Terminology). (C). 1996. 21.75 (*0-314-08925-X*) Brooks-Cole.

***Collins, et al.** Algebra 1, Vol. 1. 1998. student ed. 31.34 (*0-02-825333-7*) Glencoe.
— Algebra 1, Vol. 2. 1998. student ed. 31.34 (*0-02-825334-5*) Glencoe.

An Asterisk (*) at the beginning of an entry indicates that the title is appearing for the first time.

C

— Algebra 1, Vols. 1 & 2. 1998. wbk. ed. 5.99 (*0-02-824858-9*) Glencoe.

— Algebra 1: Integration - Applications - Connections: Teacher's Wraparound Edition. 1999. teacher ed. 62.70 (*0-02-825328-0*) Glencoe.

— Algebra 1 Vols. 1 & 2: Teacher's Wraparound Edition & Teacher's Edition, Chapters A & B. 1998. teacher ed. 72.62 (*0-02-825419-8*) Glencoe.

— Algebra 2. 1998. student ed. 46.99 (*0-02-825178-4*) Glencoe.

— Mathematics Course 1, Teacher's Wraparound Edition: Applications & Connections. 1999. teacher ed. 62.69 (*0-02-833053-6*) Glencoe.

— Mathematics Course 2, Teacher's Wraparound: Applications & Connections. 1999. teacher ed. 62.69 (*0-02-833054-4*) Glencoe.

— Mathematics Course 3, Teacher's Wraparound Edition: Applications & Connections. 1999. teacher ed. 62.69 (*0-02-833055-2*) Glencoe.

— Thomas A. Edison & Modern America. 2001. pap. text. write for info. (*0-312-24734-6*) St Martin.

Collins, jt. auth. see Diaz.

Collins, jt. auth. see Keleher.

Collins, Lori & Koski, Mary. Impatient Pamela Says: Learn How to Call 9-1-1: Reproducible. (Illus.). (J). (gr. k-2). 1999. teacher ed., ring bd. 8.95 (*0-9663281-5-9*) Trellis Pubg Inc.

Collins, Lori & Koski, Mary B. Impatient Pamela Says: "Learn How to Call 9-1-1!" (Illus.). 16p. (J). (gr. k-2). 1999. pap., wbk. ed. 4.95 (*0-9663281-1-6*) Trellis Pubg Inc.

Collins, Mary B. Pride & Prejudice: A Unit Plan. 174p. 1994. teacher ed., ring bd. 26.95 (*1-58337-115-X*) Teachers Pet Pubns.

Collins, Mary B. Black Boy: A Unit Plan. 168p. 1994. teacher ed., ring bd. 26.95 (*1-58337-024-2*) Teachers Pet Pubns.

— Call of the Wild: A Unit Plan. 1994. teacher ed., ring bd. 26.95 (*1-58337-061-7*) Teachers Pet Pubns.

— The Canterbury Tales: A Unit Plan. 262p. 1994. teacher ed., ring bd. 26.95 (*1-58337-073-0*) Teachers Pet Pubns.

— The Catcher in the Rye: A Unit Plan. 152p. 1994. teacher ed., ring bd. 26.95 (*1-58337-023-4*) Teachers Pet Pubns.

— Cheaper by the Dozen: A Unit Plan. 80p. 1992. teacher ed., ring bd. 16.95 (*1-58337-067-6*) Teachers Pet Pubns.

— The Contender: A Unit Plan. 154p. 1994. teacher ed., ring bd. 26.95 (*1-58337-019-6*) Teachers Pet Pubns.

— The Crucible: A Unit Plan. 160p. 1994. teacher ed., ring bd. 26.95 (*1-58337-004-8*) Teachers Pet Pubns.

— Cry, the Beloved Country: A Unit Plan. 158p. 1994. teacher ed., ring bd. 26.95 (*1-58337-120-6*) Teachers Pet Pubns.

— Death of a Salesman: A Unit Plan. 154p. 1994. teacher ed., ring bd. 26.95 (*1-58337-008-0*) Teachers Pet Pubns.

— Dicey's Song: A Unit Plan. 150p. 1994. teacher ed., ring bd. 26.95 (*1-58337-054-4*) Teachers Pet Pubns.

— A Doll's House: A Unit Plan. 138p. 1994. ring bd. 26.95 (*1-58337-123-0*) Teachers Pet Pubns.

— E. A. Poe Stories: A Unit Plan. 198p. 1994. teacher ed., ring bd. 26.95 (*1-58337-013-7*) Teachers Pet Pubns.

— Fahrenheit 451: A Unit Plan. 144p. 1994. teacher ed., ring bd. 26.95 (*1-58337-060-9*) Teachers Pet Pubns.

— A Farewell to Arms: A Unit Plan. 87p. 1990. teacher ed., ring bd. 16.95 (*1-58337-016-1*) Teachers Pet Pubns.

— The Glass Menagerie: A Unit Plan. 150p. 1994. teacher ed., ring bd. 26.95 (*1-58337-014-5*) Teachers Pet Pubns.

— Great Expectations: A Unit Plan. 200p. 1994. teacher ed., ring bd. 26.95 (*1-58337-100-1*) Teachers Pet Pubns.

— The Great Gatsby: A Unit Plan. 166p. 1994. teacher ed., ring bd. 26.95 (*1-58337-007-2*) Teachers Pet Pubns.

— Hamlet: A Unit Plan. 172p. 1994. teacher ed., ring bd. 26.95 (*1-58337-074-9*) Teachers Pet Pubns.

— Hiroshima: A Unit Plan. 150p. 1995. teacher ed., ring bd. 26.95 (*1-58337-021-8*) Teachers Pet Pubns.

— The Hound of the Baskervilles: A Unit Plan. 162p. 1995. teacher ed., ring bd. 26.95 (*1-58337-117-6*) Teachers Pet Pubns.

— Huckleberry Finn: A Unit Plan. 172p. 1994. teacher ed., ring bd. 26.95 (*1-58337-001-3*) Teachers Pet Pubns.

— I Heard the Owl Call My Name: A Unit Plan. 154p. 1995. teacher ed., ring bd. 26.95 (*1-58337-057-9*) Teachers Pet Pubns.

— Inherit the Wind: A Unit Plan. 148p. 1994. teacher ed., ring bd. 26.95 (*1-58337-055-2*) Teachers Pet Pubns.

— Julie of the Wolves: A Unit Plan. 154p. 1994. teacher ed., ring bd. 26.95 (*1-58337-056-0*) Teachers Pet Pubns.

— Julius Caesar: A Unit Plan. 164p. 1994. teacher ed., ring bd. 26.95 (*1-58337-102-8*) Teachers Pet Pubns.

— The Learning Tree: A Unit Plan. 98p. 1992. teacher ed., ring bd. 16.95 (*1-58337-071-4*) Teachers Pet Pubns.

— Macbeth: A Unit Plan. 172p. 1994. teacher ed., ring bd. 26.95 (*1-58337-072-2*) Teachers Pet Pubns.

— A Man for All Seasons: A Unit Plan. 70p. 1992. teacher ed., ring bd. 16.95 (*1-58337-119-2*) Teachers Pet Pubns.

— Mayor of Casterbridge: A Unit Plan. 75p. 1990. teacher ed., ring bd. 16.95 (*1-58337-112-5*) Teachers Pet Pubns.

— A Midsummer Night's Dream: A Unit Plan. 158p. 1994. teacher ed., ring bd. 26.95 (*1-58337-114-1*) Teachers Pet Pubns.

— My Antonia: A Unit Plan. 180p. 1994. teacher ed., ring bd. 26.95 (*1-58337-124-9*) Teachers Pet Pubns.

— Native Son: A Unit Plan. 158p. 1994. teacher ed., ring bd. 26.95 (*1-58337-050-1*) Teachers Pet Pubns.

— Of Mice & Men: A Unit Plan. 150p. 1994. teacher ed., ring bd. 26.95 (*1-58337-002-1*) Teachers Pet Pubns.

— The Old Man & the Sea: A Unit Plan. 146p. 1994. teacher ed., ring bd. 26.95 (*1-58337-009-9*) Teachers Pet Pubns.

— One Day in the Life of Ivan Denisovich: A Unit Plan. 144p. 1994. teacher ed., ring bd. 26.95 (*1-58337-121-4*) Teachers Pet Pubns.

— Our Town: A Unit Plan. 146p. 1994. teacher ed., ring bd. 26.95 (*1-58337-010-2*) Teachers Pet Pubns.

— The Outsiders: A Unit Plan. 152p. 1994. teacher ed., ring bd. 26.95 (*1-58337-020-X*) Teachers Pet Pubns.

— The Pearl: A Unit Plan. 140p. 1994. teacher ed., ring bd. 26.95 (*1-58337-006-4*) Teachers Pet Pubns.

— The Pigman: A Unit Plan. 154p. 1994. teacher ed., ring bd. 26.95 (*1-58337-015-3*) Teachers Pet Pubns.

— A Raisin in the Sun: A Unit Plan. 148p. 1994. teacher ed., ring bd. 26.95 (*1-58337-017-X*) Teachers Pet Pubns.

— The Red Badge of Courage: A Unit Plan. 152p. 1994. teacher ed., ring bd. 26.95 (*1-58337-005-6*) Teachers Pet Pubns.

— The Red Pony: A Unit Plan. 142p. 1994. teacher ed., ring bd. 26.95 (*1-58337-011-0*) Teachers Pet Pubns.

— Return of the Native: A Unit Plan. 93p. 1992. teacher ed., ring bd. 16.95 (*1-58337-116-8*) Teachers Pet Pubns.

— Roll of Thunder, Hear My Cry: A Unit Plan. 162p. 1994. teacher ed., ring bd. 26.95 (*1-58337-066-8*) Teachers Pet Pubns.

— Romeo & Juliet: A Unit Plan. 156p. 1994. teacher ed., ring bd. 26.95 (*1-58337-103-6*) Teachers Pet Pubns.

— The Scarlet Letter: A Unit Plan. 156p. 1994. teacher ed., ring bd. 26.95 (*1-58337-003-X*) Teachers Pet Pubns.

— A Separate Peace: A Unit Plan. 162p. 1994. teacher ed., ring bd. 26.95 (*1-58337-018-8*) Teachers Pet Pubns.

— Sister Carrie: A Unit Plan. 78p. 1990. teacher ed., ring bd. 16.95 (*1-58337-052-8*) Teachers Pet Pubns.

— Sounder: A Unit Plan. 140p. 1994. teacher ed., ring bd. 26.95 (*1-58337-064-1*) Teachers Pet Pubns.

— Summer of My German Soldier: A Unit Plan. 172p. 1994. teacher ed., ring bd. 26.95 (*1-58337-059-5*) Teachers Pet Pubns.

— To Kill a Mockingbird: A Unit Plan. 138p. 1994. teacher ed., ring bd. 26.95 (*1-58337-000-5*) Teachers Pet Pubns.

— Tom Sawyer: A Unit Plan. 162p. 1994. teacher ed., ring bd. 26.95 (*1-58337-058-7*) Teachers Pet Pubns.

— Travels with Charley: A Unit Plan. 95p. 1992. teacher ed., ring bd. 16.95 (*1-58337-063-3*) Teachers Pet Pubns.

— Treasure Island: A Unit Plan. 162p. 1994. teacher ed., ring bd. 26.95 (*1-58337-113-3*) Teachers Pet Pubns.

— Twelfth Night: A Unit Plan. 72p. 1992. teacher ed., ring bd. 16.95 (*1-58337-118-4*) Teachers Pet Pubns.

— When the Legends Die: A Unit Plan. 160p. 1995. teacher ed., ring bd. 26.95 (*1-58337-070-6*) Teachers Pet Pubns.

— White Fang: A Unit Plan. 156p. 1994. teacher ed., ring bd. 26.95 (*1-58337-062-5*) Teachers Pet Pubns.

— The Witch of Blackbird Pond: A Unit Plan. 160p. 1994. teacher ed., ring bd. 26.95 (*1-58337-065-X*) Teachers Pet Pubns.

— A Wrinkle in Time: A Unit Plan. 158p. 1995. teacher ed., ring bd. 26.95 (*1-58337-053-6*) Teachers Pet Pubns.

— Wuthering Heights: A Unit Plan. 170p. 1994. teacher ed., ring bd. 26.95 (*1-58337-105-2*) Teachers Pet Pubns.

Collins & Milazzo Staff, ed. see Kuspit, Donald.

Collins, A. & Rodin, Judith, eds. Women & New Reproductive Technologies: Medical, Psychosocial, Legal & Ethical Dilemmas. 176p. (C). 1991. text 36.00 (*0-8058-0919-8*) L Erlbaum Assocs.

Collins, A. G. & Johnson, A. I., eds. Ground - Water Contamination: Field Methods, STP 963. LC 88-10303. (Special Technical Publication (STP) Ser.). (Illus.). 481p. 1988. text 59.00 (*0-8031-0968-7*, STP963) ASTM.

Collins, A. J., jt. auth. see Chatfield, Christopher.

***Collins, A. N., et al, eds.** Chirality in Industry: The Commercial Manufacture & Applications of Optically Active Compounds & Chirality in Industry II. 844p. 1998. pap. 175.00 (*0-471-98417-5*) Wiley.

Collins, A. S. The Profession of Letters: A Study of the Relation of Author to Patron Publisher, & Public 1780-1832. LC 77-134832. 279p. 1973. reprint ed. lib. bdg. 39.50 (*0-678-00789-6*) Kelley.

Collins, A. S., ed. Treasury of English Verse: New & Old. LC 79-168778. (Granger Index Reprint Ser.). 1977. reprint ed. 24.95 (*0-8369-6298-2*) Ayer.

Collins, Ace. All about the Dixie Chicks. 2nd ed. (Illus.). 192p. (Orig.). 1999. pap. 9.99 (*0-312-24705-2*, St Martins Paperbacks) St Martin.

— Bryan White: An Unauthorized Biography of the Hot Young Country Music Sensation. 208p. 1999. pap. 15.95 (*1-58063-096-0*) Renaissance.

— Country Music Book of List. LC 98-12195. 192p. 1998. pap. 12.95 (*0-312-18709-2*) St Martin.

— Disco Duck & Other Adventures in Music. LC 98-165248. 304p. 1998. pap. 12.00 (*0-425-16358-X*) Blvd Books.

— Evel Knievel: An American Hero. LC 99-17000. 222p. 1999. text 23.95 (*0-312-24390-1*) St Martin.

— Lassie's Guide to a Family's Best Friend: Raising the Family Dog. unabridged ed. LC 98-14972. (Illus.). 176p. 1998. pap. 11.95 (*0-307-44074-5*, Whitman Coin) St Martin.

— Pam Tillis. LC 97-222716. 1997. mass mkt. 5.99 (*0-312-96404-8*, St Martins Paperbacks) St Martin.

— Stars of Country Music: Ranking the 50 Greatest. (Illus.). 224p. 1998. pap. text 14.95 (*0-8065-1992-4*, Citadel Pr) Carol Pub Group.

— The Stories Behind Country Music's All Time Greatest 100 Songs. 224p. (Orig.). 1996. pap. 12.00 (*1-57297-072-3*) Blvd Books.

— Tanya Tucker Story. 1995. mass mkt. 4.99 (*0-312-95614-2*, Pub. by Tor Bks) St Martin.

Collins, Ace & Hillman, John. Blackball Superstars: Legendary Players of the Negro Baseball Leagues. LC 99-19370. (Young Adult Ser.). (Illus.). 144p. (YA). (gr. 6-12). 1999. lib. bdg. 19.95 (*1-888105-38-0*) Avisson Pr.

Collins, Adela Y. The Apocalypse. (New Testament Message Ser.: No. 22). 155p. (Orig.). 1979. pap. text 14.95 (*0-8146-5145-3*, M Glazier) Liturgical Pr.

— The Beginning of the Gospel: Probings of Mark in Context. LC 92-32115. 160p. 1992. pap. 17.00 (*0-8006-2622-2*, 1-2622) Augsburg Fortress.

— Cosmology & Eschatology in Jewish & Christian Apocalypticism. LC 96-24190. (Supplements to the Journal for the Study of Judaism Ser.). 250p. 1996. 93.50 (*90-04-10587-5*) Brill Academic Pubs.

— Is Mark's Gospel a Life of Jesus? The Question of Genre. LC 89-64322. (Pere Marquette Lectures). 1990. 15.00 (*0-87462-545-9*) Marquette.

Collins, Adela Y., ed. Ancient & Modern Perspectives on the Bible & Culture: Essays in Honor of Hans Dieter Betz. LC 98-47964. (Homage Ser.). 452p. 1999. 59.95 (*0-7885-0521-1*) Duke.

Collins, Adela Y., ed. see Betz, Hans D.

Collins, Adrian. The Use & Abuse of History: Nietzsche. 88p. (C). 1957. pap. text 8.60 (*0-02-323730-9*, Macmillan Coll) P-H.

Collins, Adrian, tr. see De Gobineau, Arthur.

Collins, Aileen S., ed. see Aspinwall, John.

Collins, Alan. Joshua. (YA). 1995. pap. 12.95 (*0-7022-2809-5*, Pub. by Univ Queensland Pr) Intl Spec Bk.

***Collins, Alan.** The Security Dilemmas of Southeast Asia. LC 00-31120. 2000. write for info. (*0-312-23525-9*) St Martin.

Collins, Alan & Smith, Edward, eds. Readings in Cognitive Science: A Perspective from Psychology & Artificial Intelligence. 630p. (C). 1998. pap. text 46.95 (*1-55860-013-2*) Morgan Kaufmann.

Collins, Alfred. Fatherson: A Self Psychology of the Archetypal Masculine. LC 93-26635. 168p. (Orig.). 1994. pap. 4.95 (*0-933029-75-6*) Chiron Pubns.

— Planning for Information as a Corporate Resource. 118p. 83.50 (*0-08-037270-8*, Pergamon Pr) Elsevier.

— Planning for Information as a Corporate Resource. (Best of Long Range Planning Ser.). 118p. 1990. pap. text 42.00 (*0-08-037409-3*, Pergamon Pr) Elsevier.

Collins, Alice H. & Pancoast, Diane L. Natural Helping Networks: A Strategy for Prevention. LC 76-10027. 144p. reprint ed. pap. 44.70 (*0-7837-6541-X*, 204567800007) Bks Demand.

Collins, Amy. Hair Style. 2000. pap. 35.00 (*0-06-273468-7*) HarpC.

Collins, Amy F., jt. auth. see Goldsmith, Olivia.

Collins, Andrea, ed. see Tenney, Tabitha G.

Collins, Andrew. Billy Bragg: Still Suitable for Miners. (Illus.). 1998. pap. 17.95 (*0-7535-0232-1*, Pub. by Virgin Bks) London Brdge.

— Fodor's Gay Guide to Amsterdam. LC 98-138968. 144p. 1998. pap. 12.00 (*0-679-03379-3*) Fodors Travel.

— Fodor's Gay Guide to New York City: With Fire Island & New Hope, P. A. 208p. 1997. pap. 12.00 (*0-679-03378-5*) Fodors Travel.

— Fodor's Gay Guide to South Florida: With South Beach & Key West. 176p. 1997. pap. 11.00 (*0-679-03382-3*) Fodors Travel.

— Gay Guide to Montreal & Toronto, 1998. pap. 11.00 (*0-679-03380-7*) Fodors Travel.

— Gay U. S. A. 1996. pap. 19.50 (*0-614-97927-7*) Fodors Travel.

***Collins, Andrew.** Moon Handbooks: Connecticut. (Illus.). 400p. 2000. pap. 17.95 (*1-56691-181-8*, Moon Handbks) Avalon Travel.

Collins, Andrew E. Environment, Health & Population Displacement: Development & Change in Mozambique's Diarrhoeal Disease Ecology. LC 97-77896. (Making of Modern Africa Ser.). (Illus.). 315p. 1998. text 72.95 (*1-84014-329-0*, Pub. by Ashgate Pub) Ashgate Pub Co.

***Collins, Ann.** Protecting Jennie. (Historical Ser.). 2000. mass mkt. 4.99 (*0-373-29142-6*, 1291426) Harlequin Bks.

Collins, Ann & Aber, J. Lawrence. State Welfare Waiver Evaluations: Will They Increase Our Understanding of the Impact of Welfare Reform on Children? 37p. 1996. pap. 10.00 (*0-926582-16-X*) NCCP.

Collins, Ann & Clary, Linda. Sing & Play--Preschool Piano, Bk. 1. (Illus.). 60p. (J). (ps). 1987. spiral bd. 5.00 (*0-87563-307-2*) Stipes.

Collins, Ann, et al. Children & Welfare Reform: Highlights from Recent Research. 64p. 1996. pap. 10.00 (*0-926582-17-8*) NCCP.

Collins, Anna & Sullivan, Elliot. Women Are from Bras, Men Are from Penus: A Survival Guide for Bypassing Communication & Getting Even In Your Relationships. (Illus.). 128p. 1997. pap. 11.95 (*1-890410-10-1*, Ship Of Fools Bks) Sullivan & Foster.

Collins, Anne. In the Sleep Room: The Story of the CIA Brainwashing Experiments in Canada. 288p. 1998. pap. 14.95 (*1-55013-932-0*, Pub. by Key Porter) Firefly Bks Ltd.

Collins, Anthony. A Discourse Concerning Ridicule & Irony in Writing, in a Letter to the Reverend Dr. Nathanael Marshall. LC 92-23095. (Augustan Reprints Ser.: No. 142). 1970. reprint ed. 14.50 (*0-404-70142-6*, PN6149) AMS Pr.

Collins, Anthony E., jt. ed. see Campbell, Dennis.

Collins, April, jt. ed. see Abosh, Beverley.

Collins, Ardis B. The Secular Is Sacred: Platonism & Thomism in Marsilio Ficino's Platonic Theology. 1974. lib. bdg. 99.50 (*90-247-1588-1*, Pub. by M Nijhoff) Kluwer Academic.

Collins, Ardis B., ed. Hegel on the Modern World. LC 94-36783. 248p. (C). 1995. text 22.50 (*0-7914-2403-0*) State U NY Pr.

***Collins, Art.** Market Rep: The Odyssey of a Still-Struggling Commodity Trader. 230p. 2000. 24.95 (*0-934380-61-9*) Traders Pr.

Collins, Arthur. Collins' Peerage of England, 9 vols. LC 70-115003. reprint ed. 720.00 (*0-404-01740-1*) AMS Pr.

— Letters & Memorials of State, in the Reigns of Queen Mary, Queen Elizabeth, King James, King Charles the First, Part of the Reign of King Charles the Second, & Oliver's Usurpation, 2 vols. LC 72-997. reprint ed. lib. bdg. 185.00 (*0-404-01631-6*) AMS Pr.

Collins, Arthur S., Jr. Common Sense Training: A Working Philosphy for Leaders. 256p. 1998. pap. 14.95 (*0-89141-676-5*, Pub. by Presidio Pr) Natl Bk Netwk.

Collins, Arthur W. Possible Experience: Understanding Kant's Critique of Pure Reason. LC 98-33670. 219p. 1999. 40.00 (*0-520-21498-6*, Pub. by U CA Pr); pap. 15.95 (*0-520-21499-4*, Pub. by U CA Pr) Cal Prin Full Svc.

Collins, B. W., ed. see Showalter, Dennis E.

Collins, Barbara. Guide to Sheepdog Trials in Britain & Ireland. (Illus.). 400p. 1994. pap. text 29.95 (*0-85236-277-3*, Pub. by Farming Pr) Diamond Farm Bk.

Collins, Barbara & Giles, Floyd. Landscaping Herbs. (Illus.). 234p. 1998. pap. text 27.80 (*0-87563-796-5*) Stipes.

Collins, Barbara, jt. auth. see Allan, Max.

Collins, Barbara, jt. auth. see Collins, Hale.

Collins, Barbara, jt. auth. see Joner, H. Glyn.

Collins, Barbara J. Keys to Coastal & Chaparral Flowering Plants of Southern California. 2nd ed. LC 87-80519. 336p. 1996. per. 31.95 (*0-8403-4329-9*) Kendall-Hunt.

Collins, Barbara L., ed. A New Concordance to the Doctrine & Covenants. rev. ed. 455p. 1992. pap. text 15.00 (*0-8309-0623-1*) Herald Pub Hse.

Collins, Barry E., jt. auth. see Gross, Alan E.

Collins, Barry E., jt. ed. see Brewer, Marilynn B.

Collins, Beryl R. & Anderson, Karl H. Plant Communities of New Jersey: A Study in Landscape Diversity. rev. ed. LC 93-36695. Orig. Title: Vegetation of New Jersey. (Illus.). 280p. (C). 1994. text 47.00 (*0-8135-2070-3*); pap. text 20.00 (*0-8135-2071-1*) Rutgers U Pr.

Collins, Beryl R. & Russell, Emily W., eds. Protecting the New Jersey Pinelands: A New Direction in Land-Use Management. (Illus.). 234p. 1988. pap. 18.95 (*0-8135-1275-1*); text 45.00 (*0-8135-1267-0*) Rutgers U Pr.

Collins, Betty. The Copper Crucible. 232p. 1996. pap. 16.95 (*0-7022-2777-3*, Pub. by Univ Queensland Pr) Intl Spec Bk.

Collins, Betty & Collins, Ken. Kaleidoscope of Living Thoughts. 112p. (C). 1988. 45.00 (*0-7212-0715-4*, Pub. by Regency Pr GBR) St Mut.

Collins, Betty, jt. auth. see Collins, Kevin.

Collins, Beverley & Mees, Inger. The Real Professor Higgins: The Life & Career of Daniel Jones. LC 98-37959. 1998. 160.00 (*3-11-015124-3*) De Gruyter.

— Working with the Sounds of English & Dutch. 3rd enl. rev. ed. (Illus.). 80p. 1994. reprint ed. pap. text, per. 20.50 (*90-04-09313-3*) Brill Academic Pubs.

Collins, Beverly & Mees, Inger. The Phonetics of English & Dutch. LC 96-11518. (DUT & ENG.). 380p. 1996. pap. 32.50 (*90-04-10340-6*) Brill Academic Pubs.

— Working with the Phonetics of English & Dutch. 81p. 1997. pap. 23.00 (*90-04-10910-2*) Brill Academic Pubs.

Collins, Bill, ed. see Steele, Lisa J.

Collins, Billie J. The Representation of Wild Animals in Hittite Texts. pap. text. write for info. (*0-614-03992-4*, Pub. by Netherlands Inst) Eisenbrauns.

Collins, Billy. The Art of Drowning. LC 95-3297. (Poetry Ser.). 95p. 1995. pap. 10.95 (*0-8229-5567-9*) U of Pittsburgh Pr.

Collins, Billy. Daddy's Little Boy. 32p. (ps-3). 1994. 14.95 (*0-06-029003-X*); pap. 5.95 (*0-06-443687-X*) HarpC.

Collins, Billy. Picnic, Lightning. LC 97-33955. (Pitt Poetry Ser.). 103p. 1998. pap. 12.95 (*0-8229-5670-5*) U of Pittsburgh Pr.

— Picnic, Lightning. LC 97-33955. (Pitt Poetry Ser.). 104p. 1998. text 25.00 (*0-8229-4066-3*) U of Pittsburgh Pr.

— Questions about Angels: Poems. LC 98-45376. (Pitt Poetry Ser.). 88p. 1999. pap. 12.95 (*0-8229-5698-5*) U of Pittsburgh Pr.

***Collins, Billy.** Sailing Alone Around the Room: New & Selected Poems. LC 99-52861. 2001. 22.00 (*0-375-50380-3*) Random.

Collins, Billy, jt. auth. see Webb, Jack.

Collins, Blackie. Knife Throwing: Sport . . . Survival . . . Defense. (Illus.). 31p. (Orig.). 1978. pap. 3.95 (*0-940362-03-1*) Knife World.

Collins, Blackie & Collins, Michael. How to Scrimshaw & Carve Ivory. LC 81-162210. (Illus.). 45p. 1978. reprint ed. pap. 6.95 (*0-940362-01-5*) Knife World.

***Collins, Block Cathy.** Teaching Language Arts: Expanding Thinking. 3rd ed. 580p. 2000. pap. 53.00 (*0-205-30924-0*) Allyn.

Collins-Block, Cathy. Teaching the Language Arts: Expanding Thinking Through Student-Centered Instruction. 2nd ed. LC 96-43559. 580p. 1997. pap. 58.00 (*0-205-26080-2*) Allyn.

Collins, Bob. Building Leaders for the New Business Arena: How to Cultivate Strong Leadership for the New Corporate Environment. LC 88-50555. 179p. 1988. 17.95 (*0-9620580-0-9*) Vision Pubs.

Collins, Bonnie J. & Marsh, Kathryn. Structured Exercises in Healing for Adult Survivors of Childhood Sexual Abuse: A 12-Session Program. LC 98-8937. 1998. 24.95 (*1-57025-165-7*) Whole Person.

***Collins, Boyd, et al.** Building a Scholarly Communications Center: Modeling the Rutgers Experience. LC 99-29859. 272p. 1999. pap. 48.00 (*0-8389-0765-2*) ALA.

***Collins, Brad, ed.** Gwathmey Siegel: Buildings & Projects, 1965-2000. (Illus.). 240p. 2000. pap. 25.00 (*0-7893-0401-5*) Universe.

Collins, Brad & Robbins, Juliette. Antoine Predock, Architect. (Illus.). 224p. 1994. 60.00 (*0-8478-1697-4*, Pub. by Rizzoli Intl); pap. 35.00 (*0-8478-1698-2*, Pub. by Rizzoli Intl) St Martin.

C

An Asterisk (*) at the beginning of an entry indicates that the title is appearing for the first time.

Collins, Brad, ed. see Gwathmey, Charles & Siegel, Robert.

Collins, Bradford R., ed. 12 Views of Manet's Bar. LC 95-38924. (Series in Nineteenth-Century Art, Culture, & Society). 384p. 1996. text 55.00 (*0-691-03690-X*, Pub. by Princeton U Pr); pap. text 21.95 (*0-691-03691-8*, Pub. by Princeton U Pr) Cal Prin Full Svc.

***Collins, Bradford R., et al.** The Abridged Walmsley: Selections from the Career of William Aubrey Walmsley. (Illus.). 64p. 1999. pap. 17.50 (*1-889282-06-5*) FSU Mus Fine Arts.

Collins, Bradley. Leonardo, Psychoanalysis, & Art History. LC 97-3215. 1997. 30.00 (*0-8101-1419-4*) Northwestern U Pr.

Collins, Brandilyn. Question of Innocence. 440p. (Orig.). 1995. mass mkt. 5.99 (*0-380-77849-1*, Avon Bks) Morrow Avon.

Collins, Brian. Peter Warlock, the Composer. 370p. 1996. 83.95 (*1-85928-216-4*, Pub. by Scolar Pr) Ashgate Pub Co.

Collins, Brian & Powell, Terry. Old Crumlin to Pontymister in Photographs, Vol. 2. (C). 1989. 59.00 (*0-900807-53-9*, Pub. by D Brown & Sons Ltd) St Mut.

Collins, Brian C. Cedar Falls. LC 98-87703. (Images of America Ser.). 1998. write for info. (*0-7524-1358-9*) Arcadia Publng.

Collins, Brian C., jt. auth. see Swietochowski, Tadeusz.

Collins, Bruce. Origins of America's Civil War. LC 81-81340. 165p. (C). 1981. 29.50 (*0-8419-0714-5*) Holmes & Meier.

— White Society Antebellum. (Studies in Modern History). 216p. (C). 1985. pap. text 18.95 (*0-582-49194-0*, 73519) Longman.

Collins, Bruce, jt. ed. see Jeffreys-Jones, Rhodri.

Collins, Bruce M. Current Patent Interference Practice. 538p. 1987. 95.00 (*0-13-288184-5*) Aspen Law.

Collins, Bruce M. & Fabozzi, Frank J. Derivatives & Equity Portfolio Management. (Illus.). 219p. 1999. 58.00 (*1-883249-60-0*) F J Fabozzi.

Collins, Bryn C. Emotional Unavailability. 304p. 1998. pap. 14.95 (*0-8092-2914-5*, 291450, Contemporary Bks) NTC Contemp Pub Co.

Collins, Bud. Bud Collins Tennis Encyclopedia. 3rd ed. Hollander, Zander, ed. LC 97-13215. (Illus.). 700p. 1997. 19.95 (*1-57859-000-0*, 00156895) Visible Ink Pr.

Collins, Bud & Hollander, Zander. Bud Collins' Modern Encyclopedia of Tennis. 2nd ed. (Illus.). 696p. 1993. pap. 14.95 (*0-8103-9443-X*, 089154) Visible Ink Pr.

Collins, C. Edward & Bosley, Deborah S. Technical Communication at Work. LC 93-80815. (Illus.). 380p. (Orig.). (C). 1994. pap. text 51.50 (*0-15-500853-6*) Harcourt Coll Pubs.

Collins, C. Edward & Davies, Juanita J. Modern Medical Language. 750p. (C). 1996. mass mkt. 63.95 (*0-314-06702-7*) West Pub.

Collins, C. H. Laboratory-Acquired Infections: History, Incidence, Causes, & Prevention. 3rd ed. LC 92-45169. (Illus.). 274p. 1993. pap. 70.00 (*0-7506-0642-8*) Buttrwrth-Heinemann.

Collins, C. H., et al, eds. Disinfectants: Their Use & Evaluation of Effectiveness. (Society for Applied Bacteriology Technical Ser.: No. 16). 1981. text 142.00 (*0-12-181380-0*) Acad Pr.

Collins, C. H. & Kennedy, D. A., eds. Prevention of Occupationally-Acquired Blood-Borne Infections. (A CAB International Publication). 320p. 1998. text 100.00 (*0-85199-167-X*) OUP.

Collins, C. H., et al. Microbial Diseases of Occupations, Sports, & Recreations. LC 96-38862. 192p. 1996. pap. text 52.50 (*0-7506-2183-4*) Buttrwrth-Heinemann.

— Tuberculosis Bacteriology: Organization & Practice. 2nd ed. LC 97-3038. 160p. 1997. text 57.50 (*0-7506-2458-2*) Buttrwrth-Heinemann.

***Collins, C. John.** The God of Miracles: An Exegetical Examination of God's Action in the World. LC 99-53546. 176p. 2000. pap. 15.99 (*1-58134-141-5*) Crossway Bks.

Collins, Camille, tr. see Irigaray, Luce.

Collins, Carol. With This Ring. large type ed. (Linford Romance Library). 304p. 1994. pap. 16.99 (*0-7089-7552-6*) Ulverscroft.

Collins, Carol C., ed. Nuclear Energy: Salvation or Suicide? LC 84-5943. (Editorials on File Bk.). (Illus.). 255p. reprint ed. pap. 79.10 (*0-7837-5331-4*, 204507100005) Bks Demand.

— Our Aging Population: The Social Security Crisis. LC 83-1413. (Illus.). 224p. reprint ed. pap. 69.50 (*0-8357-4241-5*, 203702900007) Bks Demand.

— United States Defense Spending: How Much Is Enough? LC 83-20603. (Illus.). 256p. reprint ed. pap. 79.40 (*0-7837-5330-6*, 204507000005) Bks Demand.

Collins, Carol C. & Dewart, Tracey, eds. America's Schools: Passing the Test of the '80s? LC 85-20412. (Editorials on File Bk.). (Illus.). 239p. reprint ed. pap. 74.10 (*0-8357-4240-7*, 203702800007) Bks Demand.

Collins, Carol C. & Trager, Oliver C., eds. Abortion: The Continuing Controversy. LC 85-27601. (Editorials on File Bk.). 191p. reprint ed. pap. 59.30 (*0-7837-2670-8*, 204303600006) Bks Demand.

Collins, Caroline, jt. auth. see Guilds, John C.

***Collins, Carolyn Strom.** Inside Laura's Little House: The Little House on the Prairie Treasury. LC 99-26797. (Illus.). 112p. (J). (gr. 3-7). 2000. lib. bdg. 24.89 (*0-06-029015-3*) HarpC Child Bks.

***Collins, Carolyn Strom & Eriksson, Christina Wyss.** Inside Laura's Little House: The Little House on the Prairie Treasury. LC 99-26797. (Illus.). 112p. (J). (gr. 3-7). 2000. 24.95 (*0-06-027827-7*) HarpC Child Bks.

— My Little House Crafts Book: 18 Projects from Laura Ingalls Wilder's Little House Stories. LC TT160.C643 1998. (Illus.). 64p. (J). (gr. 3 up). 1998. pap. 9.95 (*0-06-446204-8*, HarpTrophy) HarpC Child Bks.

Collins, Carolyn Strom, et al. My Little House Christmas Crafts Book. LC TT900.C4M93 1997. (Illus.). 48p. (J). (gr. 3 up). 1997. 9.95 (*0-694-01016-2*, HarpFestival) HarpC Child Bks.

Collins, Carolyn Strom, jt. auth. see Eriksson, Christina Wyss.

Collins, Carvel, ed. see Norris, Frank.

Collins, Catherine, jt. auth. see Frantz, Douglas.

Collins, Catherine F., ed. African American Women's Health & Social Issues. LC 96-10376. 248p. 1996. 59.95 (*0-86569-250-5*, Auburn Hse) Greenwood.

Collins, Catherine Fisher. The Imprisonment of African American Women: Causes, Conditions & Future Implications. LC 96-39937. 166p. 1997. lib. bdg. 29.95 (*0-7864-0263-6*) McFarland & Co.

Collins, Catherine L. The Golden Years: A Resource Guide for Caregivers of Aging Adults. Ward, Janice, ed. 180p. (Orig.). 1990. pap. write for info. (*0-923109-02-1*); pap. text. write for info. (*0-923109-01-3*) Hlth Care Creat.

Collins, Catherine L., ed. see Health Care Creative Services Staff.

Collins, Cathy. One Hundred Twenty-Six Strategies to Build Language Art Abilities: A Month-by-Month Resource. LC 91-6672. 320p. (C). 1991. pap. text 57.00 (*0-205-13025-9*) Allyn.

Collins, Cathy, jt. ed. see Mangieri, John N.

Collins, Cecil. The Vision of the Fool & Other Writings. Keeble, Brian, ed. & intro. by. LC 95-131489. (Illus.). 192p. (Orig.). 1994. pap. 32.95 (*0-903880-64-4*, Pub. by Golgonooza Pr) S Perennis.

Collins Celtic Staff. Burns Anthology. (Collins Gem Ser.). 1998. pap. 6.95 (*0-00-470500-9*) Collins SF.

— Castles of Scotland. (Collins Gem Ser.). (Illus.). 240p. 1998. pap. 6.95 (*0-00-470499-1*) Collins SF.

— Clans & Tartans. (Collins Gem Ser.). 1998. pap. 6.95 (*0-00-458958-0*) Collins SF.

— Classic Malts. (Scottish Collections). 1998. pap. 8.95 (*0-00-472068-7*) Collins SF.

— Cycling in Scotland. (Collins Pocket Reference Ser.). 1998. pap. 16.95 (*0-00-471010-X*) Collins SF.

— Famous Irish Lives. (Collins Gem Ser.). 1998. pap. 6.95 (*0-00-470940-3*) Collins SF.

— Famous Scots. (Collins Gem Ser.). (Illus.). 286p. 1998. pap. 6.95 (*0-00-470809-1*) Collins SF.

— Homelands of the Clans. (Scottish Collections). 1998. 8.95 (*0-00-472165-9*) Collins SF.

— Irish Family Names. (Collins Pocket Reference Ser.). 1998. pap. 12.95 (*0-00-472070-9*) Collins SF.

— Scots Dictionary. (Collins Gem Ser.). 1998. pap. 6.95 (*0-00-470486-X*) Collins SF.

***Collins Celtic Staff.** Scots Kith & Kin: A Guide to the Clans & Surnames of Scotland. (Collins Pocket Guides). 1998. pap. 8.95 (*0-00-435665-9*) Collins SF.

Collins Celtic Staff. Scottish Country Dancing. (Collins Pocket Reference Ser.). 1998. pap. 9.95 (*0-00-470987-X*) Collins SF.

— Scottish Myths & Customs. (Collins Pocket Reference Ser.). 1998. pap. 9.95 (*0-00-472114-4*) Collins SF.

— Scottish Recipes. (Scottish Collections). 1998. 8.95 (*0-00-472167-5*) Collins SF.

— Scottish Surnames. (Collins Pocket Reference Ser.). 1998. pap. 9.95 (*0-00-470463-0*) Collins SF.

— Tracing Irish Ancestors. (Collins Pocket Reference Ser.). 1998. pap. 9.95 (*0-00-472095-4*) Collins SF.

— Whisky. 3rd ed. (Collins Gem Ser.). 1998. pap. 6.95 (*0-00-472120-9*) Collins SF.

— Wilde Anthology. (Collins Gem Ser.). 1998. pap. 6.95 (*0-00-472063-6*) Collins SF.

Collins, Charles. A B C's of Life. 2nd ed. (Illus.). 1974. pap. 8.00 (*0-615-00360-5*) Do IT.

Collins, Charles. An Apache Nightmare: The Battle at Cibecue Creek LC 98-31383. (Civilization of the American Indian Ser.). 1999. 27.95 (*0-8061-3114-4*) U of Okla Pr.

— The Great Escape: The Apache Outbreak of 1881. (Great West & Indian Ser.: 62). (Illus.). 1994. 26.95 (*0-87026-089-8*) Westernlore.

Collins, Charles, jt. ed. see Cohen, David.

Collins, Charles A. Strathcairn: A Novel, 2 vols., 1 bk. LC 79-8257. reprint ed. 44.50 (*0-404-61832-4*) AMS Pr.

Collins, Charles D. The Iconography & Ritual of Siva at Elephanta. LC 87-27975. (Illus.). 331p. (C). 1988. pap. text 24.95 (*0-88706-774-3*) State U NY Pr.

Collins, Charles H. Public Administration in Hong Kong. LC 70-179180. reprint ed. 37.50 (*0-404-54810-5*) AMS Pr.

Collins, Charles W. The Acadians of Madawaska, Maine. 68p. 1997. reprint ed. pap. 10.00 (*1-886560-99-4*, 097609) Quintin Pub RI.

— The Fourteenth Amendment & the States. LC 74-5437. (American Constitutional & Legal History Ser). 1974. reprint ed. lib. bdg. 27.50 (*0-306-70638-5*) Da Capo.

— Sins of Saint Anthony: Tales of the Theatre. LC 72-116948. (Short Story Index Reprint Ser.). 1977. 20.95 (*0-8369-3450-4*) Ayer.

Collins, Chase. Tell Me a Story: Creating Bedtime Stories Your Children Will Dream On. 160p. 1992. pap. 8.95 (*0-395-61211-X*) HM.

Collins-Chobanian, Shari, jt. auth. see May, Larry.

Collins, Chris. The Care & Conservation of Palaeontological Material. LC 95-20182. (Conservation & Museology Ser.). (Illus.). 168p. 1995. 115.00 (*0-7506-1742-X*) Buttrwrth-Heinemann.

— Local Economy. LC 96-8711. (Linguistic Inquiry Monographs: No. 29). (Illus.). 160p. 1996. pap. text 17.50 (*0-262-53144-5*) MIT Pr.

***Collins, Chris, et al.** Pigment Compendium: Optical Microscopy of Historical Pigments. 288p. 2000. 250.00 (*0-7506-4553-9*) Buttrwrth-Heinemann.

Collins, Chris, jt. ed. see Baltin, Mark.

Collins, Christopher. Authority Figures: Metaphors of Mastery from the Iliad to the Apocalypse. (Illus.). 196p. 1996. lib. bdg. 55.50 (*0-8476-8238-2*); lib. bdg. 24.95 (*0-8476-8239-0*) Rowman.

— The Poetics of the Mind's Eye: Literature & the Psychology of Imagination. LC 91-20561. (Illus.). 224p. (Orig.). (C). 1991. text 35.00 (*0-8122-3133-3*); pap. text 15.95 (*0-8122-1360-2*) U of Pa Pr.

— Reading the Written Image: Verbal Play, Interpretation, & the Roots of Iconophobia. 224p. 1991. 35.00 (*0-271-00763-X*) Pa St U Pr.

***Collins, Chuck.** Robin Hood Was Right: A Guide to Giving Your Money for Social Change. 304p. 2000. pap. 17.95 (*0-393-32085-5*) Norton.

***Collins, Chuck, et al.** Economic Apartheid in America: A Primer on Economic Inequality & Insecurity. (Illus.). 288p. 2000. pap. 16.95 (*1-56584-594-3*, Pub. by New Press NY) Norton.

— Robin Hood was Right. 224p. 2000. text 28.95 (*0-393-04827-6*) Norton.

Collins, Chuck, et al. Shifting Fortunes: The Perils of the Growing American Wealth Gap. (Illus.). 94p. 1999. pap. 6.95 (*0-9659249-2-0*) United Fair Econo.

Collins, Cindy, jt. auth. see Weiss, Thomas G.

Collins, Claire, jt. auth. see O'Donnell, Francis.

Collins, Clarence G. Fingerprint Science: How to Roll, Classify, File & Use Fingerprints. 2nd ed. LC 84-73191. (Illus.). 178p. (C). 1998. pap. 19.95 (*0-942728-18-1*) Copperhouse.

Collins, Claudia C., jt. auth. see Gottdiener, Mark.

Collins, Colleen. Right Chapel, Wrong Couple. (Love & Laughter Ser.: Vol. 54). 1998. per. 3.50 (*0-373-44054-5*, 1-44054-4) Harlequin Bks.

— Right Chest, Wrong Name. (Love & Laughter Ser: No. 26). 1997. per. 3.50 (*0-373-44026-X*) Silhouette.

Collins, Colleen, jt. auth. see Kistler, Julie.

Collins, Colleen, jt. auth. see Roszel, Renee.

***Collins, Corbin.** The Little Palm Book: A Gentle Guide to Palm III, IIIx, V & VII Devices. (Little Book Ser.). (Illus.). 288p. 1999. pap. text 17.99 (*0-201-69954-0*) Peachpit Pr.

Collins, Corbin, ed. see Cataudella, Joe, et al.

Collins, Corbin, ed. see Davis, Fred & Crosby, Kip.

Collins, Corbin, ed. see Sagman, Steve.

Collins, Corbin, ed. see Towers, J. Tarin.

Collins, Corbin, ed. see Wagstaff, Sean.

Collins, Corbin, ed. see Weinmann, Elaine.

Collins, Craig, et al. Visitors. (Buffy the Vampire Slayer Ser.: No. 9). (YA). (gr. 7 up). 1999. per. 4.99 (*0-671-02628-3*) S&S Trade.

Collins, Crystal. The Ballerina. (Little Activity Bks.). (Illus.). (J). 1994. pap. 1.00 (*0-486-28178-7*) Dover.

Collins, Crystal. Teddy Bear Paper Dolls. (J). 1983. pap. 4.95 (*0-486-24550-0*) Dover.

***Collins, D.** Rock Island. (Images of America Ser.). 1999. pap. 18.99 (*0-7385-0157-3*) Arcadia Publng.

Collins, D. A. Practical Rules for the Management & Medical Treatment of Negro Slaves, in the Sugar Colonies. LC 70-153484. (Black Heritage Library Collection). 1977. 24.95 (*0-8369-8773-X*) Ayer.

Collins, D. J., et al. Combinational Group Theory & Applications to Geometry: Foundations of the Classical Theory. Kostrikin, A. I. et al, eds. LC 98-150706. (Illus.). 240p. 1998. reprint ed. pap. 49.95 (*3-540-63704-4*) Spr-Verlag.

Collins, D. Ray & Oxton, John R. Golf: Playing It Straight. 2nd ed. 96p. 1996. per. 18.95 (*0-7872-2109-0*, 41210901) Kendall-Hunt.

Collins, D. Ray, et al. The Art & Science of Racquetball. 4th rev. ed. (Illus.). 1996. pap. text 14.19 (*0-89917-942-8*) Tichenor Pub.

Collins, Dan, jt. auth. see Falvey, Pat.

Collins, Dan, jt. auth. see Mills, Richard.

Collins, Dan S., jt. ed. see Kinney, Arthur F.

Collins, Dana & Canner, Mark, eds. The Second Berkshire Authology, 2 vols., Set. LC 74-78475. (Illus.). 230p. 1975. pap. 20.00 (*0-912846-10-0*) Bookstore Pr.

Collins, D'Andre. Bail Enforcement Agent Course: An Introduction for the Bounty Hunter. (Illus.). (Orig.). 1996. pap. text 89.95 (*0-9636273-2-5*) ICR Pub.

— Bounty Hunter & Boundaries. (Illus.). 185p. 1998. pap. text 30.00 (*0-9636273-6-8*) ICR Pub.

— Security One Information & "How To" Personal Pocket Manual. Maricella, tr. (SPA.). 75p. (Orig.). 1993. pap. text. write for info. (*0-9636273-1-7*) ICR Pub.

Collins, D'Andre & Johnson, Samuel. Bounty Hunter 2000: The Complete Book on Audio Tape. (Illus.). 1997. 89.95 incl. audio (*0-9636273-3-3*) ICR Pub.

***Collins, Daniel.** Carrier Class Voice Over IP. 2000. pap. 59.95 (*0-07-136326-2*) McGraw.

Collins, Daniel, jt. auth. see Seldon, Anthony.

Collins, Daniel A. Postmortem Administration. 476p. 1997. ring bd. 795.00 (*0-922943-06-0*) Esperti Petrsn.

Collins, Daniel G., jt. ed. see Estreicher, Samuel.

Collins, Danny R. South Carolina Evidence. 1995. pap. 34.95 (*0-943856-53-1*, 570) SC Bar CLE.

Collins, Darrell L. Forty-Sixth Virginia Infantry. (Virginia Regimental Histories Ser.). (Illus.). 156p. 1992. 19.95 (*1-56190-035-4*) H E Howard.

— General William Averell's Salem Raid: Breaking the Knoxville Supply Line. LC 98-39878. (Illus.). 184p. 1999. 24.95 (*1-57249-111-6*) White Mane Pub.

— Jackson's Valley Campaign: The Battles of Cross Keys & Port Republic June 8-9, 1862. (Virginia Civil War Battles & Leaders Ser.). (Illus.). 212p. 19.95 (*1-56190-056-7*) H E Howard.

Collins, Dave. Designing Object-Oriented User Interfaces. (C). 1994. text 48.50 (*0-8053-1270-6*) Benjamin-Cummings.

— Designing Object-Oriented User Interfaces. LC 94-24586. 608p. (C). 1994. pap. 55.95 (*0-8053-5350-X*) Benjamin-Cummings.

Collins, David. Clara Barton. (Young Reader's Christian Library). (Illus.). 224p. (J). (gr. 3-7). 1999. pap. 1.39 (*1-57748-601-3*) Barbour Pub.

— Elsie & Darcy Go to Bible School. (Illus.). 45p. (Orig.). Date not set. pap. 3.95 (*0-9657352-1-4*) Elsie & Darcy.

— Eng & Chang: The Original Siamese Twins. (People in Focus Ser.). 112p. (J). (gr. 5). 1994. pap. 7.95 (*0-382-24719-1*, Dillon Silver Burdett) Silver Burdett Pr.

— Florence Nightingale: God's Servant at the Battlefield. (Sower Ser.). (Illus.). 160p. (J). (gr. 5-9). 1985. pap. 7.99 (*0-88062-126-5*) Mott Media.

— Francis Scott Key: God's Courageous Composer. (Sower Ser.). (Illus.). 113p. (YA). (gr. 5-9). 1982. pap. 7.99 (*0-915134-91-8*) Mott Media.

— George Washington Carver: Man's Slave Becomes God's Scientist. (Sower Ser.). (Illus.). 131p. (J). (gr. 5-9). 1981. pap. 7.99 (*0-915134-90-X*) Mott Media.

— Get Ready for Squash: A Complete Training Programme. (Illus.). 128p. 1991. pap. 22.95 (*1-85223-389-3*, Pub. by Cro1wood) Trafalgar.

— Johnny Appleseed: John Chapman - God's Faithful Planter. LC 84-60315. (Sower Ser.). (Illus.). 160p. (J). (gr. 5-9). 1985. pap. 7.99 (*0-88062-134-6*) Mott Media.

— Managing Truancy in Schools. LC 99-167631. 224p. 1999. 75.00 (*0-304-70300-1*); pap. 26.50 (*0-304-70301-X*) Continuum.

***Collins, David.** Mumbai (Bombay) (Illus.). 224p. 1999. pap. 14.95 (*0-86442-702-6*) Lonely Planet.

Collins, David. Noah Webster: Master of Words. (Sower Ser.). (Illus.). 146p. (YA). (gr. 5-9). 1989. pap. 7.99 (*0-88062-158-3*) Mott Media.

***Collins, David.** Number Eight. (Numberlies Ser.). 24p. (J). 2000. pap. text 3.25 (*0-7894-5304-5*, D K Ink) DK Pub Inc.

— Number Five. (Numberlies Ser.). 24p. (J). 2000. pap. text 3.25 (*0-7894-5326-6*, D K Ink) DK Pub Inc.

— Number Four. (Numberlies Ser.). 24p. (J). 2000. pap. text 3.25 (*0-7894-5325-8*, D K Ink) DK Pub Inc.

— Number Nine. (Numberlies Ser.). 24p. (J). 2000. pap. text 3.25 (*0-7894-5305-3*, D K Ink) DK Pub Inc.

— Number One. (Numberlies Ser.). 24p. (J). 2000. pap. text 3.25 (*0-7894-5322-3*, D K Ink) DK Pub Inc.

— Number Seven. (Numberlies Ser.). 24p. (J). 2000. pap. text 3.25 (*0-7894-5303-7*, D K Ink) DK Pub Inc.

— Number Six. (Numberlies Ser.). 24p. (J). 2000. pap. text 3.25 (*0-7894-5302-9*, D K Ink) DK Pub Inc.

— Number Ten. (Numberlies Ser.). 24p. (J). 2000. pap. text 3.25 (*0-7894-5332-0*, D K Ink) DK Pub Inc.

— Number Three. (Numberlies Ser.). 24p. (J). 2000. pap. text 3.25 (*0-7894-5324-X*, D K Ink) DK Pub Inc.

— Number Two. (Numberlies Ser.). 24p. (J). 2000. pap. text 3.25 (*0-7894-5323-1*, D K Ink) DK Pub Inc.

Collins, David. Organisational Change: Sociological Perspectives. LC 97-42959. 256p. (C). 1998. pap. 25.99 (*0-415-17156-3*) Routledge.

— Organisational Change: Sociological Perspectives. LC 97-42959. 232p. (C). 1998. 85.00 (*0-415-17155-5*) Routledge.

— Rotator Cuff Repair: A Guide for Patients. (Ortho Ser.). 32p. 1997. pap. text 2.95 (*1-885274-52-1*) Health InfoNet Inc.

***Collins, David.** A Small Town for Its Size. 484p. 2000. pap. 22.95 (*0-595-09016-8*, Writers Showcase) iUniversecom.

Collins, David, et al. Concise Guide to Customs of Minority Ethnic Religions. 84p. 1993. pap. 9.95 (*1-85742-120-5*, Pub. by Arena) Ashgate Pub Co.

— Moline: City of Mills. LC 98-85881. (Images of America Ser.). (Illus.). 128p. 1998. pap. 16.99 (*0-7524-1283-3*) Arcadia Publng.

Collins, David E., jt. ed. see Benz, George W.

Collins, David J. & Whipple, Nancy N. Using Bar Code: Why It's Taking Over. 2nd ed. (Illus.). 328p. (C). 1994. reprint ed. pap. 34.95 (*0-9627406-1-6*) Data Capture Pr.

Collins, David N. M. A. Czaplicka Collected Works, 4 vols. 1998. 600.00 (*0-7007-1001-9*, Pub. by Curzon Pr Ltd) Paul & Co Pubs.

— Siberia & the Soviet Far East. LC 92-122990. (World Bibliographical Ser.). 244p. 1991. lib. bdg. 75.00 (*1-85109-157-2*) ABC-CLIO.

Collins, David R. Abraham Lincoln: God's Leader for a Nation. LC 76-2456. (Sower Ser.). (Illus.). 150p. (YA). (gr. 5-9). 1976. pap. 7.99 (*0-915134-93-4*) Mott Media.

— Ara's Amazing Spinning Wheel. (Illus.). (J). (ps-2). 1991. pap. 5.10 (*0-8136-5681-8*); lib. bdg. 7.95 (*0-8136-5181-6*) Modern Curr.

— Arthur Ashe: Against the Wind. (People in Focus Ser.). 112-160p. (J). (gr. 5). 1994. pap. 7.95 (*0-382-24718-3*, Dillon Silver Burdett); lib. bdg. 13.95 (*0-87518-647-5*, Dillon Silver Burdett) Silver Burdett Pr.

— Beyond the Clouds: The Story of Christa McAuliffe. LC 96-6881. (Weaver Bks.). (Illus.). 64p. (Orig.). (YA). (gr. 5-9). 1996. pap. 2.95 (*0-8198-1140-8*) Pauline Bks.

— Bix Beiderbecke: Jazz Age Genius. LC 98-19824. (Notable Americans Ser.). (Illus.). 112p. (YA). (gr. 5 up). 1998. lib. bdg. 18.95 (*1-883846-36-6*) M Reynolds.

— Casimir Pulaski: Soldier on Horseback. LC 95-34383. (Illus.). 96p. (J). (gr. 4-7). 1995. 14.95 (*1-56554-082-4*) Pelican.

— Ceb's Amazing Tail. (Illus.). (J). (ps-2). 1987. pap. 5.10 (*0-8136-5685-0*); lib. bdg. 7.95 (*0-8136-5185-9*) Modern Curr.

— The Country Artist: A Story about Beatrix Potter. (Illus.). 56p. (J). (gr. 3-6). 1989. pap. 5.95 (*0-87614-509-8*, Carolrhoda); lib. bdg. 19.93 (*0-87614-344-3*, Carolrhoda) Lerner Pub.

— The Country Artist: A Story about Beatrix Potter. large type ed. (Illus.). 1993. 15.50 (*0-614-09819-X*, L-34100-00) Am Printing Hse.

An Asterisk (*) at the beginning of an entry indicates that the title is appearing for the first time.

*Collins, David R. Dr. Shinichi Suzuki: Teaching Music from the Heart. (Masters of Music Ser.). (Illus.). 112p. (YA). (gr. 5 up). 2000. lib. bdg. 19.95 (*1-883846-49-8*) M Reynolds.

Collins, David R. Farmworker's Friend: The Story of Cesar Chavez. LC 95-42759. (Trailblazers Ser.). (Illus.). (J). 1996. lib. bdg. 22.60 (*0-87614-982-4*, Carolrhoda) Lerner Pub.

— Farmworker's Friend: The Story of Cesar Chavez. (Trailblazers Ser.). (Illus.). 80p. (J). (gr. 4-7). 1996. pap. 6.95 (*1-57505-031-5*, First Ave Edns) Lerner Pub.

— Got a Penny? The Story of Dorothy Day. LC 96-6895. (Weaver Bks.). 64p. (Orig.). (YA). (gr. 6-9). 1996. pap. 2.95 (*0-8198-3082-8*) Pauline Bks.

— The Greatest Life Ever Lived. LC 90-36949. (Illus.). 82p. (Orig.). 1991. reprint ed. pap. 30.00 (*0-608-04169-6*, 206490300011) Bks Demand.

— Grover Cleveland: 22nd & 24th President of the United States. Young, Richard G., ed. LC 87-35794. (Presidents of the United States Ser.). (Illus.). (J). (gr. 5-9). 1988. lib. bdg. 21.27 (*0-944483-01-1*) Garrett Ed Corp.

— Hali's Amazing Wings. (Illus.). (J). (ps-2). 1987. pap. 5.10 (*0-8136-5683-4*); lib. bdg. 7.95 (*0-8136-5183-2*) Modern Curr.

— Harry S. Truman: 33rd President of the United States. Young, Richard G., ed. LC 87-32750. (Presidents of the United States Ser.). (Illus.). (J). (gr. 5-9). 1988. lib. bdg. 21.27 (*0-944483-00-3*) Garrett Ed Corp.

— Hero on Horseback: The Story of Casimir Pulaski. LC 96-54009. (Illus.). 32p. (J). Date not set. 14.95 (*1-56554-266-5*) Pelican.

— J. R. R. Tolkien: Master of Fantasy. (Biographies Ser.). (Illus.). 144p. (YA). (gr. 5 up). 1992. lib. bdg. 23.93 (*0-8225-4906-9*, Lerner Publctns) Lerner Pub.

— James Buchanan: Fifteenth President of the United States. Young, Richard G., ed. LC 89-39948. (Presidents of the United States Ser.). (Illus.). 128p. (J). (gr. 5-9). 1990. lib. bdg. 21.27 (*0-944483-62-3*) Garrett Ed Corp.

— Lee Iacocca: Chrysler's Good Fortune. Young, Richard G., ed. LC 91-31989. (Wizards of Business Ser.). (Illus.). 64p. (J). (gr. 4-8). 1992. lib. bdg. 17.26 (*1-56074-017-5*) Garrett Ed Corp.

— Leo's Amazing Paws & Jaws. (Illus.). (J). (ps-2). 1987. pap. 5.10 (*0-8136-5682-6*); lib. bdg. 7.95 (*0-8136-5182-4*) Modern Curr.

— Magnificent Failure: The Story of Father Solanus Casey. LC 99-19049. 66p. (YA). (gr. 6-9). 1999. pap. 3.95 (*0-8198-4800-X*) Pauline Bks.

— Malcolm X: Black Rage. LC 91-39951. (People in Focus Ser.). (Illus.). 104p. (YA). (gr. 5 up). 1992. lib. bdg. 13.95 (*0-87518-498-7*, Dillon Silver Burdett) Silver Burdett Pr.

— Mark T-W-A-I-N! A Story about Samuel Clemens. LC 93-15164. (Creative Minds Ser.). (Illus.). (J). (gr. 3-6). 1993. lib. bdg. 19.95 (*0-87614-801-1*, Carolrhoda) Lerner Pub.

— Mark T-W-A-I-N! A Story about Samuel Clemens. (Illus.). 56p. (J). (gr. 3-6). 1994. pap. 5.95 (*0-87614-640-X*, Carolrhoda) Lerner Pub.

— Pioneer Plowmaker: A Story about John Deere. (Creative Minds Ser.). (Illus.). 64p. (J). (gr. 3-6). 1990. lib. bdg. 19.95 (*0-87614-424-5*, Carolrhoda) Lerner Pub.

— Probo's Amazing Trunk. (Illus.). (J). (ps-2). 1987. pap. 5.10 (*0-8136-5684-2*); lib. bdg. 7.95 (*0-8136-5184-0*) Modern Curr.

***Collins, David R.** Servant to the Slaves: The Story of Henriette Delille. LC 00-8108. (Weaver Bks.). 72p. (YA). (gr. 7-9). 2000. pap. 3.95 (*0-8198-7039-0*) Pauline Bks.

Collins, David R. Shattered Dreams: The Story of Mary Todd Lincoln. LC 93-44792. (Notable Americans Ser.). 128p. (YA). (gr. 5 up). 1994. lib. bdg. 17.95 (*1-883846-07-2*) M Reynolds.

— Tad Lincoln: White House Wildcat. (Illus.). 48p. (J). (gr. 1-4). 1995. pap. 7.95 (*1-878668-40-4*); lib. bdg. 14.95 (*1-878668-33-1*) Disc Enter Ltd.

— Tales for Hard Times: A Story about Charles Dickens. (Creative Minds Ser.). (Illus.). 64p. (J). (gr. 3-6). 1990. lib. bdg. 14.95 (*0-87614-433-4*, Carolrhoda) Lerner Pub.

— Tiger Woods: Golf Superstar. LC 97-30574. (Illus.). 32p. (J). (gr. k-3). 1998. text 14.95 (*1-56554-321-1*) Pelican.

— To the Point: A Story about E. B. White. (Illus.). 56p. (J). (gr. 3-6). 1989. pap. 5.95 (*0-87614-508-X*, Carolrhoda); lib. bdg. 14.95 (*0-87614-345-1*, Carolrhoda) Lerner Pub.

— Ursi's Amazing Fur Coat. (Illus.). (J). (ps-2). 1987. pap. 5.10 (*0-8136-5686-9*); lib. bdg. 7.95 (*0-8136-5186-7*) Modern Curr.

***Collins, David R.** Washington Irving: Storyteller for a New Nation. LC 99-48295. (World Writers Ser.). (Illus.). 112p. (YA). (gr. 5 up). 2000. lib. bdg. 19.95 (*1-883846-50-1*) M Reynolds.

Collins, David R. William Jefferson Clinton: 42nd President of the United States. Stefoff, Rebecca, ed. LC 95-852. (Presidents of the United States Ser.). (Illus.). 128p. (YA). (gr. 5-9). 1995. lib. bdg. 21.27 (*1-56074-056-6*) Garrett Ed Corp.

— William McKinley: Twenty-Fifth President of the United States. Young, Richard G., ed. LC 89-39954. (Presidents of the United States Ser.). (Illus.). 128p. (J). (gr. 5-9). 1990. lib. bdg. 21.27 (*0-944483-55-0*) Garrett Ed Corp.

— Woodrow Wilson: Twenty-Eighth President of the United States. Young, Richard G., ed. LC 88-24563. (Presidents of the United States Ser.). (J). (gr. 5-9). 1989. lib. bdg. 21.27 (*0-944483-18-6*) Garrett Ed Corp.

— Write a Book for Me: The Story of Marguerite Henry. LC 99-11667. (World Writers Ser.). 112p. (YA). (gr. 5 up). 1999. lib. bdg. 18.95 (*1-883846-39-0*) M Reynolds.

— You're Never Alone: The Story of Thomas Merton. LC 96-6880. (Weaver Bks.). 64p. (YA). (gr. 6-9). 1996. pap. 2.95 (*0-8198-8708-0*) Pauline Bks.

— Zachary Taylor: Twelfth President of the United States. Young, Richard G., ed. LC 88-24539. (Presidents of the United States Ser.). (Illus.). (J). (gr. 5-9). 1989. lib. bdg. 21.27 (*0-944483-17-8*) Garrett Ed Corp.

***Collins, David R. & Bergren, Kris.** Ishi: The Last of His People. (Notable Americans Ser.). (Illus.). 96p. (YA). (gr. 5 up). 2000. lib. bdg. 19.95 (*1-883846-54-4*) M Reynolds.

Collins, Dean, jt. auth. see Kowalski, Judith.

Collins, Dean T., jt. ed. see Allen, Jon G.

***Collins, Deborah A.** Science & Technology Pocket Data Book (1996) (Illus.). 57p. (C). 1999. reprint ed. pap. text 20.00 (*0-7881-8346-X*) DIANE Pub.

Collins, Deborah A., ed. Science & Technology: Pocket Data Book (1994) (Illus.). 57p. (Orig.). (C). 1995. pap. text 25.00 (*0-7881-1745-9*) DIANE Pub.

Collins Deming, Margaret. Friendship Ahoy. 1998. pap. write for info. (*1-57553-831-8*) Watermrk Pr.

Collins, Denis. Gainsharing & Power: Lessons from Six Scanlon Plans. LC 97-39573. (Illus.). 272p. 1998. text 39.95 (*0-8014-3490-4*, ILR Press) Cornell U Pr.

Collins, Denis & Lane, Eamonn. Programmable Controllers. LC 95-9892. 1995. write for info. (*0-07-709017-9*) McGraw.

Collins, Denis & O'Rourke, Thomas. Ethical Dilemmas in Business. LC 93-36210. (C). 1993. mass mkt. 15.95 (*0-538-83512-5*) S-W Pub.

***Collins, Denise A.** Kaleidoscope: A Retrospective: Poems. LC 99-94603. 70 p. 1999. write for info. (*1-887213-23-6*) Blck Oak Pr.

Collins, Denise A., ed. see DelVecchio, et al.

Collins, Dennis. Indians Last Fight or the Dull Knife Raid. LC 72-1004. reprint ed. 37.50 (*0-404-07122-8*) AMS Pr.

Collins, Dennis & Cormier, Steve. The Car Opening Business: A Manual for Operating Your Own Lockout Service Business. Graphics West Staff, ed. (Illus.). 153p. 1997. write for info. (*0-9669082-2-8*); pap. write for info. (*0-9669082-1-X*); spiral bd. write for info. (*0-9669082-0-1*) Bdgt Lock & Key.

Collins, Derek. Immortal Armor: The Concept of Alke in Archaic Greek Poetry. LC 97-39944. (Greek Studies). 152p. 1997. 56.00 (*0-8476-8820-8*); pap. 23.95 (*0-8476-8821-6*) Rowman.

Collins, Derek, tr. see Calame, Claude.

Collins, Desmond. The Origins of Europe: Four New Studies in Archaeology & History. LC 75-313261. 347p. 1975. 6.95 (*0-04-940045-2*) Allen & Unwn AT.

Collins, Diana. Partners in Protest: Life with Canon Collins. (Illus.). 288p. 1993. 55.00 (*0-575-04823-9*, Pub. by V Gollancz) Trafalgar.

— Partners in Protest: Life with Canon Collins. 384p. 1995. pap. 27.50 (*0-575-05753-X*, Pub. by V Gollancz) Trafalgar.

Collins, Diane, jt. auth. see Kaura, Sita R.

Collins, Don. Cookbook of the Year. LC 96-78299. 370p. (Orig.). 1997. pap. 23.95 (*1-883697-35-2*) Hara Pub.

Collins, Donald, et al. An Introduction to Family Social Work. LC 98-68668. 286p. 1999. pap. text 40.00 (*0-87581-424-7*) F E Peacock Pubs.

Collins, Donald, jt. auth. see White, William C.

Collins, Donald B. Libraries & Research: A Practical Approach. 3rd ed. 260p. 1996. per. 23.95 (*0-8403-8480-7*) Kendall-Hunt.

Collins, Donald E. Native American Aliens: Disloyalty & the Renunciation of Citizenship by Japanese Americans During World War II, 32. LC 84-25239. (Contributions in Legal Studies: No. 32). (Illus.). 218p. 1985. 62.95 (*0-313-24711-0*, CNA/) Greenwood.

— When the Church Bell Rang Racist: The Methodist Church & the Civil Rights Movement in Alabama. 170p. 1998. text 29.95 (*0-86554-605-3*, H456) Mercer Univ Pr.

Collins, Donald N., jt. auth. see White, William C.

Collins, Donald P., jt. auth. see Keleher, Terry R. J.

Collins, Donna B. Colorado Traveler: A Guide to Colorado Scenic Tours. (American Traveler Ser.: Vol. 44). (Illus.). 48p. 1999. pap. 6.95 (*1-55838-090-6*) R H Pub.

Collins, Donna Bishop. Colorado Traveler: Natural Sites: A Guide to Colorado's Natural Wonders. (American Traveler Ser.: Vol. 41). (Illus.). 48p. 1987. pap. 3.95 (*0-939650-77-0*) R H Pub.

Collins, Donna M. Ethnic Identification: The Greek Americans of Houston, Texas. (Immigrant Communities & Ethnic Minorities in the U. S. & Canada Ser.: No. 68). 1991. 72.50 (*0-404-19478-8*) AMS Pr.

Collins, Donna R. On the Wings of Love: Michael's Story. LC 96-80498. (Illus.). 171p. 1997. 24.95 (*1-878044-52-4*) Mayhaven Pub.

Collins, Doris. Fun Times Growing Up. (Illus.). 24p. (Orig.). (J). (gr. k-3). 1988. pap. 7.95 (*0-9621650-0-X*) Periwinkle MA.

Collins, Doris L., jt. auth. see Joel, Lucille A.

Collins, Dorothy, ed. see Chesterton, G. K.

Collins, Douglas. Olympic Dreams: 100 Years of Excellence. (Illus.). 272p. 1996. pap. 25.00 (*0-7893-0030-3*, Pub. by Universe) St Martin.

— Sartre As Biographer. LC 79-25863. 230p. 1980. reprint ed. pap. 71.30 (*0-7837-4458-7*, 205798800012) Bks Demand.

— Seeing the Unseen: Dr. Harold E. Edgerton & the Wonders of Strobe Alley. (Illus.). 106p. 1994. spiral bd. 35.00 (*0-935398-21-X*) G Eastman Hse.

Collins, Douglas & Bedi, Joyce. Seeing the Unseen: Dr. Harold E. Edgerton & the Wonders of Strobe Alley. Bruce, Roger R., ed. LC 94-66131. (Illus.). 100p. 1994. 42.50 (*0-262-02387-3*) MIT Pr.

Collins, Dyrel W. Marriage Is God's Plan. 3rd ed. 28p. 1996. pap. 2.95 (*1-56794-152-4*, C2465) Star Bible.

Collins, E. Dale, jt. ed. see Martin, David S.

Collins, E. J. Irish Family Research Made Simple. rev. ed. (Illus.). 73p. 1985. pap. 10.00 (*1-878311-18-2*, Heritge House) Ye Olde Genealogie Shoppe.

***Collins, E. J. T., ed.** The Agrarian History of England & Wales, 1850-1914, Vol. 7. (Agrarian History of England & Wales Ser.). (Illus.). 2000p. (C). 2000. 290.00 (*0-521-66214-1*) Cambridge U Pr.

Collins, Eamon. Killing Rage. LC 98-191263. 372p. 1998. 23.95 (*1-86207-008-3*, Pub. by Granta) Midpt Trade.

— Killing Rage. 373p. 1999. pap. 14.95 (*1-86207-047-4*, Pub. by Granta) Midpt Trade.

Collins, Earl A., jt. auth. see Snider, Felix E.

Collins, Edward M. Myth, Manifesto, Meltdown: Communist Strategy, 1848-1991. LC 97-22806. 256p. 1998. 59.95 (*0-275-95938-4*, Praeger Pubs) Greenwood.

Collins, Edward M., tr. see Von Clausewitz, Karl.

Collins, Eileen L., jt. ed. see Hoenack, Stephen A.

Collins, Elaine, ed. see Mehta, Mira.

***Collins, Eldridge, Jr., et al.** Poultry Waste Management Handbook. LC 99-31153. (NRAES Ser.: Vol. 132). (Illus.). 64p. 1999. pap. text 16.00 (*0-935817-42-5*) NRAES.

Collins, Eliza G. & Devanna, Mary A. New Portable MBA. 2nd ed. 441p. 1994. 27.95 (*0-471-08004-7*) Wiley.

Collins, Elizabeth. The Living Ocean. LC 93-26205. (Earth at Risk Ser.). (Illus.). 128p. (YA). (gr. 5 up). 1994. lib. bdg. 19.95 (*0-7910-1586-6*) Chelsea Hse.

Collins, Elizabeth, jt. auth. see Berkoff, Nancy.

Collins, Elizabeth A. Honesty the Best Policy. (Illus.). 96p. (Orig.). 1996. pap. 5.95 (*1-57502-321-0*, P01086) Morris Pubng.

Collins, Elizabeth F. Pierced by Murugan's Lance: Ritual, Power & Moral Redemption among Malaysian Hindus. LC 96-52671. (Illus.). 230p. 1997. pap. text 22.50 (*0-87580-574-4*); lib. bdg. 35.00 (*0-87580-223-0*) N Ill U Pr.

Collins, Ellen M. Catechesis for Infant Baptism. LC 97-148984. 80p. (Orig.). 1996. pap. 8.95 (*1-55612-953-X*, LL1953) Sheed & Ward WI.

Collins, Ellwyn. Unprepared! A Husband's Story of Coping with His Wife's Stroke. 208p. 1992. pap. 9.95 (*0-925190-50-0*) Fairview Press.

Collins, Emerson & Jordan, John W., eds. Genealogical & Personal History of Lycoming County, 2 vols. (Illus.). 1073p. 1997. reprint ed. lib. bdg. 110.00 (*0-8328-6426-9*) Higginson Bk Co.

Collins, Eoin, jt. ed. see O'Carroll, Ide.

Collins, Ernestine A. Down Mare Creek Road. Sohn, Mark F. & Sohn, Kathy, eds. 148p. 1993. 11.00 (*0-9616911-9-0*) M F Sohn Pubns.

Collins, F. S. The Green Algae of North America & Supplements 1-2. 1970. 144.00 (*3-7682-0680-7*) Lubrecht & Cramer.

Collins, Fletcher, Jr., ed. Medieval Church Music-Dramas: A Repertory of Complete Plays. LC 75-33896. 514p. reprint ed. 159.40 (*0-8357-9809-7*, 201318000085) Bks Demand.

Collins, Floyd. The Forecast. (Paper Moon Bks.), 57p. (C). 1993. pap. text 7.95 (*1-884438-04-0*) Epiphany AR.

***Collins, Frank.** Baptism of Fire. 2000. 29.95 (*0-385-40916-8*, Pub. by Transworld Publishers Ltd) Trafalgar.

Collins, Frank, jt. ed. see Perron, Paul.

Collins, Frank, tr. see Greimas, Algirdas J. & Fontanille, Jacques.

Collins, Frank, tr. see Ubersfeld, Anne.

Collins, Frederick W. Answers to Iridiagnosis Questions. 12p. 1993. reprint ed. spiral bd. write for info. (*0-7873-1180-4*) Hlth Research.

— Osteopathy (Original Osteopathic Moves As Taught by Still) 9th ed. 11p. 1997. reprint ed. spiral bd. 8.00 (*0-7873-0191-4*) Hlth Research.

Collins, G. B., et al, eds. Weak Interactions As Probes of Unification: Virginia Polytechnic Institute 1980. (AIP Conference Proceedings Ser.: No. 72). 689p. 1981. lib. bdg. 39.50 (*0-88318-171-1*) Am Inst Physics.

Collins, G. E., ed. see Wang, D.

Collins, G. M., et al, eds. Procurement, Preservation & Allocation of Vascularized Organs. LC 96-38863. 384p. 1997. lib. bdg. 275.00 (*0-7923-4299-2*) Kluwer Academic.

Collins, G. W., II, ed. see Heller, Michael.

Collins, Gail. Scorpion Tongues: Gossip, Politics, & Celebrity in America. LC 97-40795. 320p. 1998. 25.00 (*0-688-14914-6*, Wm Morrow) Morrow Avon.

***Collins, Gail.** Scorpion Tongues: The Irresistible History of Gossip in American Politics. LC 99-31817. 352p. 1999. pap. 14.00 (*0-15-600650-2*, Harvest Bks) Harcourt.

Collins, Galen & Malik, Tarun. Hospitality Information Technology. LC 98-149726. 448p. (C). 1997. pap. text, per. 49.95 (*0-7872-3260-2*) Kendall-Hunt.

***Collins, Galen & Malik, Tarun.** Hospitality Information Technology: Learning How to Use It. 4th ed. 460p. (C). 1999. pap. text 52.95 (*0-7872-6292-7*) Kendall-Hunt.

Collins, Garry. Computer Operations. 192p. (C). 1998. pap. text 24.00 (*1-58076-127-5*) Que Educ & Trng.

Collins, Gary. The Biblical Basis of Christian Counseling for People Helpers: Relating the Basic Teachings of Scripture to People's Problems. LC 93-6435. 288p. 1993. 20.00 (*0-89109-753-8*) NavPress.

— Case Studies in Christian Counseling. (Resources for Christian Counseling Ser.: Vol. 29). 18.99 (*0-8499-0885-X*) Word Pub.

— Christian Counseling. rev. ed. 711p. 1988. pap. 18.99 (*0-8499-3124-X*) Word Pub.

— Consejeria Cristiana Efectiva.Tr. of Effective Christian Counseling. (SPA.). 208p. 1992. pap. 8.99 (*0-8254-1126-2*, Edit Portavoz) Kregel.

— Excellence & Ethics in Counseling. (Resources for Christian Counseling Ser.: Vol. 30). 18.99 (*0-8499-0696-2*) Word Pub.

— Innovative Approaches to Counseling. (Resources for Christian Counseling Ser.: Vol. 1). 224p. 18.99 (*0-8499-0510-9*) Word Pub.

Collins, Gary & Chilton. Baby Boomer Blues. (Contemporary Christian Counseling Ser.: Vol. 1). 18.99 (*0-8499-0909-0*) Word Pub.

Collins, Gary B. & Kalinsky, Robert G. Studies on Ohio Diatoms: Diatoms of the Scioto River Basin & Referenced Checklist from Ohio Exclusive of Lake Erie & the Ohio River. (Bulletin New Ser.: Vol. 5, No. 3). 1977. pap. text 7.00 (*0-86727-080-2*) Ohio Bio Survey.

Collins, Gary M., jt. auth. see Paul, Stephen C.

Collins, Gary R. The Biblical Basis of Christian Counseling for People Helpers: Relating the Basic Teachings of Scripture to People's Problems. 1997. pap. 15.00 (*1-57683-081-0*) NavPress.

— Breathless: Transform Your Time-Starved Days into a Life Well Lived. LC 98-24159. 1998. 10.99 (*0-8423-0196-8*) Tyndale Hse.

Collins, Gary R. La Busqueda del Alma (The Soul Search) (What You Need to Know about ... in 12 Lessons Ser.). (Illus.). 220p. (YA). 10.99 (*0-88113-499-6*) Caribe Betania.

Collins, Gary R. How to Be a People Helper. LC 94-34388. 208p. 1995. pap. 9.99 (*0-8423-1385-0*) Tyndale Hse.

— Usted Puede Hacer la Diferencia.Tr. of You Can Make a Difference. (SPA.). 295p. write for info. (*1-56063-506-1*) Editorial Unilit.

— You Can Make a Difference. 1993. 4.99 (*0-310-96255-2*) Zondervan.

— You Can Make a Difference: Fourteen Ways to Change Your World. 240p. 1992. 15.99 (*0-310-57380-7*) Pyranee.

Collins, Geneva & Editors of Washington Consumers' Checkbook Magazin. Guide to Washington Area Restaurants. rev. ed. LC 97-117767. 128p. 1998. pap. 7.95 (*1-888124-03-2*) Ctr Study Serv.

Collins, Geneva, jt. auth. see Consumers' Checkbook Magazine Editors.

Collins, George, tr. see Derrida, Jacques.

Collins, George, tr. see Stiegler, Bernard.

Collins, George, tr. see Virilio, Paul & Parent, Claude.

***Collins, George J. & Alexander, Kathy.** Chessie Racing: The Story of Maryland's Entry in the 1997-1998 Whitbread Round the World Race. LC 00-8232. 2001. write for info. (*0-8018-6413-5*) Johns Hopkins.

Collins, George K. Memoirs of the 149th Regiment New York Infantry: 3rd Brigade, 2nd Division, 12th & 20th A. C. LC 95-3707. (Illus.). 443p. 1995. reprint ed. 35.95 (*0-9622393-7-2*) Edmonston Publ.

— Town of Spafford, Onondaga County, New York. 280p. 1993. reprint ed. lib. bdg. 33.00 (*0-8328-2968-4*) Higginson Bk Co.

Collins, George R. & Nonell, Juan B. The Designs & Drawings of Antonio Gaudi. LC 81-8596. (Illus.). 173p. 1983. reprint ed. pap. 53.70 (*0-608-07794-1*, 2059861) Bks Demand.

Collins, George W., II. Foundations of Celestial Mechanics. (Astronomy & Astrophysics Ser.: Vol. 16). (Illus.). 145p. (C). 1989. pap. 27.00 (*0-88126-009-6*) Pachart Pub Hse.

— The Virial Theorem in Stellar Astrophysics. (Astronomy & Astrophysics Ser.: Vol. 7). 143p. 1978. pap. text 19.00 (*0-912918-13-6*, 0013) Pachart Pub Hse.

Collins, Georgia & Sandell, Renee, eds. Gender Issues in Art Education: Content, Contexts & Strategies. 164p. (Orig.). 1996. pap. text 22.00 (*0-937652-85-7*, 239) Natl Art Ed.

***Collins, Gerald W.** Fundamentals of Digital Television Transmission. 320p. 2000. 69.95 (*0-471-39199-9*) Wiley.

Collins, Geralyn M., jt. ed. see Sandler, Merton.

Collins, Glenn B. & Petolino, Joseph G., eds. Applications of Genetic Engineering to Crop Improvement. (Advances in Agricultural Biotechnology Ser.). 1984. text 256.50 (*90-247-3084-8*) Kluwer Academic.

Collins, Glenn B. & Shepherd, Robert J., eds. Engineering Plants for Commercial Products & Applications. LC 96-15813. (Annals of the New York Academy of Sciences Ser.: Vol. 792). 1996. pap. 100.00 (*1-57331-047-6*) NY Acad Sci.

— Engineering Plants for Commercial Products & Applications. LC 96-43704. (Annals of the New York Academy of Sciences Ser.: Vol. 792). 1996. write for info. (*1-57331-046-8*) NY Acad Sci.

Collins, Gloria L. Homage to Basilicata: Life in Southern Italy. (Poetry Chapbook Ser.: Vol. 1). 32p. 1998. 5.00 (*0-9659832-1-8*) ByLine Pr.

Collins, Grace. A Trumpet for His People: Leopold Sedar Senghor of Senegal. LC 95-7602. (Illus.). 32p. (J). 1996. 16.95 (*0-9629978-0-3*) Sights Prods.

— A Trumpet for His People: Leopold Sedar Senghor of Senegal. LC 95-7602. (Illus.). (J). 1996. pap. 8.95 (*1-886366-04-7*) Sights Prods.

Collins, Gregg C., jt. ed. see Birnbaum, Lawrence A.

Collins, Gretchen. English Grammar Flipper: A Guide to Correct English Usage. 49p. (J). (gr. 5 up). 1989. reprint ed. 6.95 (*1-878383-01-9*) C Lee Pubns.

Collins, H. When You Were Little & I Was Big. (Illus.). 32p. (J). (ps-8). 1984. pap. 4.95 (*0-920236-71-5*, Pub. by Annick) Firefly Bks Ltd.

Collins, H. Elizabeth. To Sleep with the Angels. LC 98-43247. (Illus.). 32p. (J). (gr. 3 up). 1999. 15.95 (*0-935699-16-3*) Illum Arts.

A young girl meets angels of many races & spends her nights flying on magical adventures. This warm & gentle book reassures children at bedtime & encourages them to communicate with their special angels. Sure to become a night time classic. "Wrap

C

your child in a blanket of peace & love as you share the warmth & gentle spirit of To Sleep with the Angels." Connie Bowen, Author. ***Publisher Paid Annotation.***

Collins, H. P. John Cowper Powys: Old Earth Man. 1967. 10.50 (*0-8079-0070-2*) October.
Collins, H. Thomas. Destination: Cameroon, Study Guide. 58p. 1995. pap. 4.25 (*0-16-042652-9*) USGPO.
Collins, H. Thomas & Majeske, Christopher. Destination Cameroon. 3rd ed. (Illus.). 58p. 1996. reprint ed. pap. text, student ed. 20.00 (*0-7881-2791-8*) DIANE Pub.
Collins, Hale & Collins, Barbara. A New Concordance to the Book of Mormon. rev. ed. 1995. pap. text 25.00 (*0-8309-0637-1*) Herald Pub Hse.
Collins, Harold E. Rich & Judgment Proof. 264p. (Orig.). 1995. pap. 20.00 (*1-886094-22-5*) Chicago Spectrum.
Collins, Harold P., et al, eds. The Significance & Regulation of Soil Biodiversity. LC 95-14925. (Developments in Plant & Soil Sciences Ser.: Vol. 63). 1995. lib. bdg. 170.00 (*0-7923-3138-9*) Kluwer Academic.
Collins, Harry. 101 American English Proverbs: Teacher's Manual & Resource Book. 1992. teacher ed. 21.15 (*0-8442-0595-8*) NTC Contemp Pub Co.
Collins, Harry & Kusch, Martin. The Shape of Actions: What Humans & Machines Can Do. LC 98-36125. (Illus.). 240p. 1999. 25.00 (*0-262-03257-0*) MIT Pr.
Collins, Harry & Pinch, Trevor. The Golem: What You Should Know about Science. 2nd rev. ed. LC 99-161543. (Canto Book Ser.). (Illus.). 180p. (C). 1998. pap. 12.95 (*0-521-64550-6*) Cambridge U Pr.
Collins, Harry M. Changing Order: Replication & Induction in Scientific Practice. 212p. (Orig.). 1992. pap. text 15.00 (*0-226-11376-0*) U Ch Pr.
Collins, Harry M. & Pinch, Trevor. The Golem at Large: What You Should Know about Technology. LC 98-29501. (Illus.). 180p. (C). 1998. 19.95 (*0-521-55141-2*) Cambridge U Pr.
Collins, Heather. Eensy Weensy Spider. unabridged ed. (Illus.). 12p. (J). 1997. bds. 4.95 (*1-55074-406-2*, Pub. by Kids Can Pr) Genl Dist Srvs.
— Hickory Dickory Dock. unabridged ed. (Illus.). 12p. (J). 1997. bds. 4.95 (*1-55074-408-9*, Pub. by Kids Can Pr) Genl Dist Srvs.
— One, Two, Buckle My Shoe. unabridged ed. (Illus.). 12p. (J). 1997. bds. 4.95 (*1-55074-410-0*, Pub. by Kids Can Pr) Genl Dist Srvs.
— This Little Piggy. unabridged ed. (Illus.). 12p. (J). 1997. bds. 4.95 (*1-55074-404-6*, Pub. by Kids Can Pr) Genl Dist Srvs.
***Collins, Heather.** Rock-a-Bye Baby. 12p. (J). (ps). 2000. bds. 4.95 (*1-55074-572-7*, Pub. by Kids Can Pr) Genl Dist Srvs.
— Row, Row, Row Your Boat. 12p. (J). 2000. bds. 4.95 (*1-55074-570-0*, Pub. by Kids Can Pr) Genl Dist Srvs.
— Twinkle, Twinkle Little Star. 12p. (J). (ps). 2000. bds. 4.95 (*1-55074-566-2*, Pub. by Kids Can Pr) Genl Dist Srvs.
— Wee Willie Winkie. 12p. (J). (ps). 2000. bds. 4.95 (*1-55074-568-9*, Pub. by Kids Can Pr) Genl Dist Srvs.
Collins, Heather, jt. auth. see Aldis, Dorothy.
Collins, Heather, jt. auth. see Hickman, Pamela.
***Collins, Heidi.** Corporate Portals: Revolutionizing Information Access to Increase Productivity & Drive the Bottom Line. 2000. 29.95 (*0-8144-0593-2*) AMACOM.
Collins, Helen. Equality in the Workplace: An Equal Opportunities Handbook for Trainers. (Human Resource Management in Action Ser.). (Illus.). 220p. (Orig.). 1995. pap. 43.95 (*0-631-19393-6*) Blackwell Pubs.
— Equality Matters: Equal Opportunities in the '90s Background & Current Issues. LC 92-42248. 135p. Date not set. reprint ed. pap. 41.90 (*0-608-20725-X*, 207182300002) Bks Demand.
— Mutagenesis. 320p. 1994. mass mkt. 4.99 (*0-8125-2163-3*) Tor Bks.
Collins, Henry H. Collins Gem French Grammar. 2nd ed. (FRE.). 256p. 1994. pap. 6.95 (*0-00-470999-3*, Pub. by Harper SF) HarpC.
Collins, Henry H. HarCo Sansoni Italian Dict. 3rd unabridged ed. (ITA.). 2300p. 1993. 55.00 (*0-06-275516-1*, Harper Ref) HarpC.
Collins, Henry H., Jr. What Bird Is This? (Illus.). 1965. pap. 3.95 (*0-486-21490-7*) Dover.
Collins, Herbert M., et al, eds. Pesticide Formulations & Application Systems, Vol. 15. (STP Ser.: No. 1268). (Illus.). 215p. 1996. 59.00 (*0-8031-2007-9*, STP1268) ASTM.
Collins, Herbert R. The First U. S. Postal Museum. (Illus.). 50p. (Orig.). 1991. pap. 9.95 (*1-878770-01-2*) Paragon OK.
***Collins, Herbert Ridgeway.** Caroline County, Virginia, Bureau of Vital Statistics: Death Records, 1853-1896. 203p. 1999. pap. 33.00 (*0-7884-1291-4*, C546) Heritage Bk.
Collins, Hubert E. Storm & Stampede on the Chisholm. LC 97-32941. (Illus.). 296p. 1998. pap. 14.95 (*0-8032-6386-4*, Bison Books) U of Nebr Pr.
Collins, Hubert E., et al, eds. Warpath & Cattle Trail. LC 97-48704. (Illus.). 296p. 1998. 34.95 (*0-87081-492-3*); pap. 17.50 (*0-87081-468-0*) Univ Pr Colo.
Collins, Hugh. Justice in Dismissal: The Law of Termination of Employment. (Oxford Monographs on Labour Law). 304p. 1992. 65.00 (*0-19-825435-0*) OUP.
— The Law of Contract. 2nd ed. LC 95-211352. (Law in Context Ser.). 428p. (C). 1994. pap. text 37.95 (*0-406-03147-9*) Northwestern U Pr.
— Marxism & Law. LC 84-7199. (Marxist Introductions Ser.). (Illus.). 176p. 1996. pap. text 16.95 (*0-19-285144-6*) OUP.
— Regulating Contracts. LC 99-27430. 408p. 1999. text 75.00 (*0-19-829817-X*) OUP.
***Collins, Hugh E. L.** The Order of the Garter, 1348-1461: Chivalry & Politics in Late Medieval England. LC 99-57223. 336p. 2000. write for info. (*0-19-820817-0*) OUP.
Collins, Ian, jt. auth. see Cameron, Samuel.
Collins, Ina. The New 5-Week Formula for Winning Fabulous Sweepstakes Prizes! How to Win More . . . Mailing Fewer Than 20 Entries. 2nd rev. ed. (Illus.). 1996. pap. 10.95 (*0-9620910-1-4*) CollinsBooks.
Collins, Irene. Jane Austen & the Clergy. LC 94-2050. 256p. 1994. 40.00 (*1-85285-114-7*) Hambledon Press.
— Jane Austen, The Parson's Daughter. LC 98-35350. 1998. 45.00 (*1-85285-172-4*) Hambledon Press.
Collins, Irma & Music Educators National Conference Staff. Why Teach? Why Music? Why Me? 8p. 1992. pap. 9.50 (*1-56545-070-1*, 4007) MENC.
Collins, Ivan L. Horse Power Days: Popular Vehicles of Nineteenth Century America. LC 52-12857. (Illus.). 102p. reprint ed. pap. 31.70 (*0-608-11485-5*, 205108600075) Bks Demand.
Collins, J., et al. Reminiscence of Isaac & Rachel (Budd) Collins, with Accounts of Some Descendants & History of a Reunion Held at Philadelphia, 1892. (Illus.). 164p. 1993. reprint ed. pap. 24.50 (*0-8328-1373-7*); reprint ed. lib. bdg. 34.50 (*0-8328-1372-9*) Higginson Bk Co.
Collins, J., tr. see Schwenk, Theodor.
Collins, J. A. Failure of Materials in Mechanical Design: Analysis, Prediction, Prevention. 2nd ed. LC 92-35907. 672p. 1993. 125.00 (*0-471-55891-5*) Wiley.
Collins, J. C. The Matrix of Life. (Illus.). 104p. (Orig.). 1992. pap. 14.95 (*0-9629719-0-1*) Molecular Present.
Collins, J. Churton. Critical Essays & Literary Fragments. LC 64-16745. (Arber's an English Garner Ser.). 1964. reprint ed. 60.00 (*0-8154-0052-7*) Cooper Sq.
— Greek Influence on English Poetry. LC 72-3186. (English Literature Ser.: No. 33). 1972. reprint ed. lib. bdg. 75.00 (*0-8383-1498-8*) M S G Haskell Hse.
Collins, J. Churton, ed. see Greene, Robert.
Collins, J. K. The Sex We Want: Straight Talking from 90s Women. 228p. 1996. pap. 16.50 (*0-04-440973-7*, Pub. by Rivers Oram) NYU Pr.
***Collins, J. Robert & VanLinder, George.** Student Athlete College Scholarships System Set, Incls. Video: Written by College Coaches, Specifically, to Help Players Get to College, 3 bks. deluxe ed. 560p. 1999. pap. text 97.00 (*0-9673579-0-X*, P7) Student Athlete.
Collins, J. W. Fearful Experience of a Gloucester Halibut Fisherman. 2nd ed. (Illus.). 24p. 1987. reprint ed. pap. 4.00 (*0-938459-02-3*) Ten Pound Isl Bk.
Collins, J. Wesley & Culp, Christine P. From the Crest of the Wood Pile. (Illus.). (Orig.). 1989. pap. 19.95 (*0-317-93864-9*) Prairie Sales.
Collins, Jackie. American Star. 1998. per. 7.99 (*0-671-02349-7*, Pocket Books) PB.
— American Star. large type ed. 1993. 27.95 (*1-56895-025-X*) Wheeler Pub.
— American Star. Rubenstein, Julie, ed. 752p. 1993. reprint ed. mass mkt. 7.50 (*0-671-87311-3*) PB.
— The Bitch. 272p. 1997. mass mkt. 4.99 (*0-06-101252-1*, Harp PBks) HarpC.
— The Bitch. 256p. 1990. mass mkt. 5.99 (*0-671-73785-6*) PB.
— Chances. 816p. 1991. reprint ed. mass mkt. 7.99 (*0-446-35717-0*, Pub. by Warner Bks) Little.
— Dangerous Kiss: A Lucky Santangelo Novel. LC 99-27091. 559p. 1999. 24.50 (*0-684-85030-3*) S&S Trade.
***Collins, Jackie.** Dangerous Kiss: A Lucky Santangelo Novel. large type ed. LC 99-41392. (G. K. Hall Core Ser.). 704p. 1999. 30.95 (*0-7838-8747-7*, G K Hall Lrg Type) Mac Lib Ref.
— Dangerous Kiss: A Lucky Santangelo Novel. large type ed. LC 99-41392. (G. K. Hall Core Ser.). 2000. pap. 28.95 (*0-7838-8748-5*, G K Hall Lrg Type) Mac Lib Ref.
— Dangerous Kiss: A Lucky Santangelo Novel. 592p. 2000. reprint ed. per. 7.99 (*0-671-02095-1*, Pocket Books) PB.
Collins, Jackie. Hollywood Husbands. 1990. mass mkt. 6.99 (*0-671-72451-7*) PB.
— Hollywood Husbands. 1997. pap. 14.00 (*0-671-01935-X*) PB.
— Hollywood Husbands. 1999. per. 7.99 (*0-671-02354-3*) PB.
— Hollywood Kids. 1995. pap. 6.50 (*0-671-89856-6*) PB.
— Hollywood Kids. 1995. mass mkt. 6.99 (*0-671-89849-3*) PB.
— Hollywood Kids. 1999. per. 7.99 (*0-671-02356-X*) PB.
— Hollywood Kids. 624p. 1994. 23.50 (*0-671-66627-4*) S&S Trade.
— Hollywood Kids. large type ed. LC 94-44322. 850p. 1995. 25.95 (*0-7838-1211-6*, G K Hall Lrg Type) Mac Lib Ref.
— Hollywood Wives. 560p. 1987. per. 6.99 (*0-671-70459-1*) PB.
— Hollywood Wives. 1999. per. 7.99 (*0-671-02355-1*) PB.
— Jackie Collins. 1987. boxed set 14.85 (*0-671-91548-7*) PB.
— Jackie Collins, 3 vols. 1989. boxed set 14.40 (*0-671-92229-7*) PB.
— Jackie Collins, 3 vols. 1990. boxed set 17.85 (*0-671-96365-1*) S&S Trade.
***Collins, Jackie.** Lady Boss. 640p. 1998. per. 7.99 (*0-671-02347-0*, Pocket Books) PB.
Collins, Jackie. Lady Boss. 1990. 21.95 (*0-671-94826-1*) S&S Trade.
— Lady Boss. Grose, Bill, ed. 640p. 1991. reprint ed. mass mkt. 6.99 (*0-671-74418-6*, Pocket Star Bks) PB.
***Collins, Jackie.** Lethal Seduction. 480p. 2000. 25.50 (*0-684-85031-1*) Simon & Schuster.
— Lethal Seduction. large type ed. 720p. 2000. 26.00 (*0-7432-0425-5*) S&S Trade.
Collins, Jackie. The Love Killers. Orig. Title: Love Head. 1991. per. 5.99 (*0-671-73786-4*) PB.
— Lovers & Gamblers. 592p. 1991. reprint ed. mass mkt. 7.99 (*0-446-35660-3*, Pub. by Warner Bks) Little.
— Lucky. 1987. pap. 4.95 (*0-317-59662-4*, Sig) NAL.
— Lucky. 1987. pap. 6.99 (*0-671-70419-2*) PB.
***Collins, Jackie.** Lucky. 624p. 1998. per. 7.99 (*0-671-02348-9*, Pocket Books) PB.
— Mujeres de Hollywood. (SPA.). 16.95 (*950-04-0395-1*) Emece.
Collins, Jackie. Murder. 1998. mass mkt. 3.99 (*0-671-02460-4*) S&S Trade.
— Obsession. 114p. 1998. mass mkt. 3.99 (*0-671-02459-0*) S&S Trade.
— Rock Star. 1990. mass mkt. 6.99 (*0-671-70880-5*) PB.
— Sinners. 1991. mass mkt. 5.99 (*0-671-73787-2*) PB.
— Sinners: Sinners. 336p. 1997. mass mkt. 4.99 (*0-06-101253-X*, Harp PBks) HarpC.
— Thrill. 1999. mass mkt. 7.99 (*0-671-02094-3*, Pocket Star Bks) PB.
— Thrill. LC 98-9342. 528p. 1998. 24.50 (*0-684-85029-X*) Simon & Schuster.
— Thrill! LC 98-9342. 479 p. 1998. 25.00 (*0-684-85396-5*) S&S Trade.
— Thrill. large type ed. LC 98-26430. (Large Print Book Ser.). 1998. 26.95 (*1-56895-601-0*) Wheeler Pub.
— Vendetta: Lucky's Revenge. LC 96-43458. 544p. 1997. 25.00 (*0-06-039209-6*, ReganBks) HarperTrade.
— Vendetta: Lucky's Revenge. 1998. 5.98 (*0-7651-0824-0*) Smithmark.
— Vendetta: Lucky's Revenge. large type ed. LC 97-2922. (Large Print Book Ser.). 1997. 27.95 (*1-56895-435-2*) Wheeler Pub.
— The World Is Full of Divorced Women. 416p. 1991. reprint ed. mass mkt. 7.99 (*0-446-35719-7*, Pub. by Warner Bks) Little.
— The World Is Full of Married Men. 1993. mass mkt. 5.99 (*0-671-73788-0*) PB.
Collins, Jackson. The Himmler Plaque. 320p. 1987. pap. 3.95 (*0-380-70324-6*, Avon Bks) Morrow Avon.
— The Votan Treasure. 288p. (Orig.). 1989. mass mkt. 3.95 (*0-380-75509-2*, Avon Bks) Morrow Avon.
Collins, Jacquelin, ed. Documents in British History, Vol. 2. 2nd rev. ed. LC 92-31437. 288p. (C). 1993. 30.31 (*0-07-005702-8*) McGraw.
Collins, Jacquelin, jt. auth. see Blakely, Brian.
***Collins, James.** Seattle Then & Now. McNulty, Elizabeth, ed. LC 00-26906. (Then & Now Ser.). (Illus.). 144p. 2000. 17.98 (*1-57145-244-3*) Advantage Pubs.
Collins, James. Understanding Tolowa Histories: Western Hegemonies & Native American Responses. LC 96-46667. 240p. (C). 1997. pap. 23.99 (*0-415-91208-3*) Routledge.
— Your Eyes: An Owner's Guide. 242p. (C). 1995. pap. text 12.95 (*0-13-182379-5*) P-H.
Collins, James A. Contemporary Theater in Puerto Rico: The Decade of the Seventies. LC 81-12946. (Illus.). xxiii, 265p. (Orig.). 1982. pap. 20.00 (*0-8477-3174-X*) U of PR Pr.
Collins, James B. The State in Early Modern France. (New Approaches to European History Ser.: Vol. 5). (Illus.). 314p. (C). 1995. text 54.95 (*0-521-38284-X*); pap. text 16.95 (*0-521-38724-8*) Cambridge U Pr.
Collins, James C. Accident Reconstruction. (Illus.). 308p. 1979. pap. 38.95 (*0-398-06069-X*) C C Thomas.
— Accident Reconstruction. fac. ed. (Illus.). 308p. 1979. 52.95 (*0-398-03907-0*) C C Thomas.
— Beyond Entrepreneurship: Turning Your Business into an Enduring Great Company. 246p. (C). 1995. pap. text 13.95 (*0-13-381526-9*) P-H.
Collins, James C. & Lazier, William C. Managing the Small to Mid-Sized Company: Concepts & Cases. LC 94-30044. 688p. (C). 1994. text 68.95 (*0-256-14280-7*, Irwn McGrw-H) McGrw-H Hghr Educ.
Collins, James C. & Morris, Joe L. Highway Collision Analysis. (Illus.). 304p. 1974. pap. 35.95 (*0-398-06070-3*) C C Thomas.
Collins, James C. & Morris, Joe L. Highway Collision Analysis. fac. ed. (Illus.). 304p. 1974. 49.95 (*0-398-03042-1*) C C Thomas.
Collins, James C. & Porras, Jerry. Built to Last: Successful Habits of Visionary CompaniesCollins,&James C. abr. ed. 1994. audio 18.00 (*0-694-51479-9*) HarperAudio.
Collins, James C. & Porras, Jerry I. Built to Last: Successful Habits of Visionary Companies. LC 94-20571. (Illus.). 256p. 1994. 25.00 (*0-88730-671-3*, HarpBusn) HarpInfo.
— Built to Last: Successful Habits of Visionary Companies. 336p. 1996. pap. 16.00 (*0-88730-739-6*, HarpBusn) HarpInfo.
Collins, James D. God in Modern Philosophy. LC 77-25963. 476p. 1978. reprint ed. lib. bdg. 85.00 (*0-313-20079-3*, COGM, Greenwood Pr) Greenwood.
— Interpreting Modern Philosophy. LC 70-160259. 475p. 1972. reprint ed. pap. 147.30 (*0-8357-8925-X*, 203337900085) Bks Demand.
— Lure of Wisdom. LC 62-13514. (Aquinas Lectures). 1962. 15.00 (*0-87462-127-5*) Marquette.
Collins, James F. Your Eyes: An Owner's Manual. (Illus.). 224p. (Orig.). 1989. pap. write for info. (*0-9621975-0-5*) Infinity NY.
Collins, James F., et al, eds. The Ophthalmic Desk Reference. LC 91-14969. (Illus.). 702p. 1991. reprint ed. pap. 200.00 (*0-608-07265-6*, 206749300009) Bks Demand.
Collins, James J. Dante: Layman, Prophet, Mystic. LC 89-38909. 331p. (Orig.). 1989. pap. 14.95 (*0-8189-0564-6*) Alba.
***Collins, James J.** Law Enforcement Policies & Practices Regarding Missing Children & Homeless Youth: Final Report (1993) (Illus.). 210p. (C). 1999. reprint ed. pap. text 30.00 (*0-7881-8639-6*) DIANE Pub.
— Praying with Dante. LC 00-8145. (Companions for the Journey Ser.). (Illus.). 120p. (C). 2000. pap. 8.95 (*0-88489-674-9*) St Marys.
Collins, James J., Jr., ed. Drinking & Crime: Perspectives on the Relationships Between Alcohol Consumption & Criminal Behavior. LC 80-28046. (Guilford Alcohol Studies). 378p. 1981. reprint ed. pap. 117.20 (*0-608-07574-4*, 205988800010) Bks Demand.
Collins, James L. John Brown & the Fight Against Slavery. (Gateway Civil Rights Ser.). (Illus.). 32p. (J). (gr. 2-4). 1991. pap. 4.95 (*1-878841-72-6*); lib. bdg. 20.90 (*1-56294-043-0*) Millbrook Pr.
— Strategies for Struggling Writers. LC 97-31435. 244p. 1997. lib. bdg. 44.95 (*1-57230-299-2*, C0299) Guilford Pubns.
Collins, James L. Strategies for Struggling Writers. LC 97-31435. 244p. 1997. pap. text 24.95 (*1-57230-300-X*, C0300) Guilford Pubns.
Collins, James L., ed. Teaching All the Children to Write. 100p. 1983. pap. text 7.00 (*0-930348-10-9*) NY St Eng Coun.
— Vital Signs 1: Bringing Together Reading & Writing. 170p. (Orig.). (C). 1989. pap. text 21.50 (*0-86709-253-X*, 0253, Pub. by Boynton Cook Pubs) Heinemann.
— Vital Signs 3: Restructuring the English Classroom. 197p. (C). 1992. pap. text 22.50 (*0-86709-297-1*, 0297, Pub. by Boynton Cook Pubs) Heinemann.
— Vital Signs 2: Teaching & Learning Language Collaboratively. 149p. (C). 1990. pap. text 21.50 (*0-86709-269-6*, 0269, Pub. by Boynton Cook Pubs) Heinemann.
Collins, James L. & Collins, Kathleen M. Handbook of Strategic Writing Lessons. 2nd ed. (Special Studies in Teacher Education: Vol. 8). 56p. (C). 1998. reprint ed. pap. 10.00 (*0-924197-18-8*) SUNYB Coun Intl Studies.
Collins, James M. The Archaeology of the Cahokia Mounds, ICT-Two: Site Structure. Emerson, Thomas E. & Taylor, Evelyn, eds. (Illinois Cultural Resources Study: No. 10). (Illus.). 260p. (Orig.). 1990. pap. 14.00 (*0-942579-10-0*) IHPA.
Collins, James M. & Ruefli, Timothy W. Strategic Risk: A State-Defined Approach. LC 95-44243. 240p. (C). 1995. lib. bdg. 100.00 (*0-7923-9661-8*) Kluwer Academic.
Collins, James P. Autobiography of a Revolutionary Soldier. Kohn, Richard H., ed. LC 78-22378. (American Military Experience Ser.). 1980. reprint ed. lib. bdg. 25.95 (*0-405-11855-4*) Ayer.
Collins, James T. & Kozub, Robert M. State & Local Taxation Answer Book. LC 97-134782. 784p. 1997. boxed set 118.00 (*1-56706-374-8*, 63748) Panel Pubs.
Collins, James T., ed. see Echols, John M. & Shadily, Hassan.
Collins, Jan M. & McCarthy, Joseph E. Nature Walks in Southern Maine: An AMC Nature Walks Book - Nature Rich Walks along the Maine Coast & Interior Foothills. LC 95-44595. (AMC Nature Walks Guides Ser.). (Illus.). 336p. (Orig.). 1996. pap. 12.95 (*1-878239-46-5*) AMC Books.
Collins, Jane. Jane's Gem Warships of World War II. LC 96-204915. 256p. 1996. pap. 8.00 (*0-00-470872-5*, Harper Ref) HarpC.
— 10 Minutes to Better Health: Fast, Effective Ways to a Fitter, More Radiant You. LC 98-30639. (Illus.). 128p. 1999. 19.95 (*0-7621-0039-7*, Pub. by RD Assn) Penguin Putnam.
Collins, Jane E., jt. auth. see Garrod, David R.
Collins, Jane L. & Gimenez, Martha E., eds. Work Without Wages: Comparative Studies of Domestic Labor & Self-Employment. LC 88-37031. (SUNY Series on Women & Work). 264p. (C). 1990. text 65.50 (*0-7914-0106-5*); pap. text 21.95 (*0-7914-0107-3*) State U NY Pr.
Collins, Jane L., jt. auth. see Lutz, Catherine A.
Collins, Jane S. Free at Last. LC 71-37586. (Black Heritage Library Collection). 1977. reprint ed. 25.95 (*0-8369-8962-7*) Ayer.
Collins, Janet. Pass Me a Poem. LC 99-93540. (Illus.). ix, 87p. (J). (gr. 1-7). 13.95 (*0-9674824-0-2*); pap. 7.50 (*0-9674824-1-0*) J Collins.
Collins, Janet. The Quiet Child. (Issues in Education Ser.). (Illus.). 144p. 1996. pap. 29.95 (*0-304-33473-1*); text 90.00 (*0-304-33472-3*) Continuum.
Collins, Janet M. & Messick, Samuel, eds. Intelligence & Personality: Bridging the Gap in Theory & Measurement. LC 99-58492. 350p. 2000. write for info. (*0-8058-3166-5*) L Erlbaum Assocs.
Collins, Jannette & Stern, Eric J. Chest Radiology: The Essentials. LC 99-31263. 284p. 2000. text 79.00 (*0-7817-1582-2*) Lppncott W & W.
***Collins, Jeff.** Heidegger & the Nazis. 80p. 2000. pap. 7.95 (*1-84046-130-6*, Pub. by Icon Bks) Natl Bk Netwk.
Collins, Jeff. Introducing Derrida. LC 96-61109. 1997. pap. 10.95 (*1-874166-38-2*, Pub. by Totem Bks) Natl Bk Netwk.
— Introducing Heidegger. (Illus.). 176p. 1999. pap. 10.95 (*1-84046-003-2*, Pub. by Totem Bks) Natl Bk Netwk.
Collins, Jeffery D. A Finite Element-Boundary Integral Method for Electromagnetic Scattering. LC QC0794.6. (University of Michigan Reports: No. 025921-31-T). 174p. reprint ed. pap. 54.00 (*0-7837-3209-0*, 204321100007) Bks Demand.
Collins, Jerry M., ed. see Chabner, Bruce A.
Collins, Jim. Architecture of Excess: Cultural Life in the Information Age. 256p. (C). (gr. 13). 1994. 80.00 (*0-415-90705-5*, A9776); pap. 21.99 (*0-415-90706-3*, A9780) Routledge.

C

An Asterisk (*) at the beginning of an entry indicates that the title is appearing for the first time.

— The Mountain Men. LC 95-49301. (First Bks.). (Illus.). 64p. (J). (gr. 5-8). 1996. lib. bdg. 22.00 (*0-531-20229-1*) Watts.

— Uncommon Cultures: Popular Culture & Post-Modernism. 224p. 1989. 35.00 (*0-415-90016-6*) Routledge.

— Uncommon Cultures: Popular Culture & Post-Modernism. 176p. (C). 1989. pap. 18.99 (*0-415-90137-5*) Routledge.

Collins, Jim, jt. auth. see McCabe, J. L.

Collins, Joan. Infamous. 1995. 22.95 (*0-614-96246-3*, Dutt) Dutton Plume.

— Infamous. 368p. 1997. mass mkt. 6.99 (*0-451-18805-5*, Sig) NAL.

— Love & Desire & Hate. Rubenstein, Julie, ed. 480p. 1991. reprint ed. mass mkt. 5.99 (*0-671-66581-2*) PB.

— Memories from Mother. Wightman, Kimberly J. & Wightman, Teresa E., eds. 70p. 1998. pap. 9.95 (*1-888911-09-3*) Benson Smythe.

***Collins, Joan.** My Friends' Secrets. (Illus.). 144p. 2000. 24.95 (*0-233-99494-7*, Pub. by Andre Deutsch) Trafalgar.

Collins, Joan. Prime Time. 1989. mass mkt. 5.99 (*0-671-67962-7*) PB.

— Second Act. LC 97-2547. 368p. 1997. text 24.95 (*0-312-16997-3*) St Martin.

— Second Act. large type ed. LC 97-42240. 572p. 1997. 27.95 (*0-7838-8355-2*, G K Hall Lrg Type) Mac Lib Ref.

Collins, John. Caldwell & West Caldwell. LC 98-88302. (Images of America Ser.). (Illus.). 128p. 1998. pap. 16.99 (*0-7524-1312-0*) Arcadia Publng.

— The Complete Guide to the Music of Frank Sinatra. (Illus.). 143p. 1998. pap. text 8.95 (*0-7119-6624-9*, OP48014) Omnibus NY.

— Musicmakers of West Africa. LC 81-51651. (Illus.). 177p. 1985. 25.00 (*0-89410-075-0*, Three Contnts) L Rienner.

— Perfect Presentations. LC 98-53806. (Self-Development for Success Ser.: Vol. 8). (Illus.). 96p. 1999. pap. 12.95 (*0-8144-7040-8*) AMACOM.

— The Two Forgers: A Biography of Harry Buxton Forman & Thomas James Wise. (Illus.). 330p. 1992. 55.00 (*0-938768-29-8*) Oak Knoll.

— West African Pop Roots. 350p. (C). 1992. pap. 22.95 (*0-87722-916-3*) Temple U Pr.

— West African Pop Roots. 350p. (C). 1992. 69.95 (*0-87722-793-4*) Temple U Pr.

Collins, John, et al, eds. Polarized Collider Workshop. LC 91-71303. (AIP Conference Proceedings Ser.: No. 223, 42). (Illus.). 400p. 1991. lib. bdg. 95.00 (*0-88318-826-0*) Am Inst Physics.

Collins, John, jt. auth. see Barker, Nicolas.

Collins, John, ed. see Carter, John & Pollard, Graham.

Collins, John, jt. ed. see Fisher, Kevin.

Collins, John A., jt. auth. see Taylor, Patrick J.

Collins, John C. Illustrations of Tennyson. LC 77-148765. reprint ed. 27.50 (*0-404-08738-8*) AMS Pr.

— Renormalization: An Introduction to Renormalization, the Renormalization Group, & the Operator-Product Expansion. (Cambridge Monographs on Mathematical Physics). (Illus.). 380p. 1986. pap. text 44.95 (*0-521-31177-2*) Cambridge U Pr.

— Studies in Shakespeare. LC 72-944. reprint ed. 34.50 (*0-404-01637-5*) AMS Pr.

Collins, John C., ed. see Greene, Robert.

Collins, John D. Tested Positive. 116p. 1994. pap. 15.00 (*0-938245-13-9*) Inverted-A.

Collins, John E. Mysticism & New Paradigm Psychology. 282p. (C). 1991. lib. bdg. 49.50 (*0-8476-7669-2*) Rowman.

Collins, John E., jt. ed. see Wood, Ralph C.

Collins, John F. Einhard Vita Karoli Magni. (Latin Commentaries Ser.). 95p. (Orig.). (C). 1984. pap. text 6.00 (*0-929524-39-X*) Bryn Mawr Commentaries.

— Erasmus: Stultitiae Laus. 1991. pap. text 8.00 (*0-929524-71-3*) Bryn Mawr Commentaries.

— A Primer of Ecclesiastical Latin. LC 84-22957. 451p. (C). 1985. pap. 17.95 (*0-8132-0667-7*) Cath U Pr.

Collins, John F. & Adleman, Marvin. Livable Landscape Design. (Information Bulletin Ser.). (Illus.). 64p. (Orig.). 1988. pap. 14.00 (*1-57753-029-2*, 1411B211) Corn Coop Ext.

Collins, John G. Prevalence of Selected Chronic Conditions: United States, 1990-1992. LC 96-50061. (Vital & Health Statistics Ser.: Series 10, No. 194). 1996. write for info. (*0-8406-0522-6*) Natl Ctr Health Stats.

Collins, John Gary. Health & Selected Socioeconomic Characteristics of the Family: United States, 1988-90. 91p. 1997. per. 12.00 (*0-16-061451-1*) USGPO.

— Prevalence of Selected Chronic Conditions: United States, 1990-92. 94p. 1997. per. 12.00 (*0-16-061455-4*) USGPO.

Collins, John J. The Apocalyptic Imagination: An Introduction to Jewish Apocalyptic Literature. 2nd rev. ed. LC 97-49578. 331p. 1998. pap. 30.00 (*0-8028-4371-9*) Eerdmans.

— Apocalypticism in the Dead Sea Scrolls. LC 97-214134. (Dead Sea Scrolls Ser.). 208p. (C). 1997. 65.00 (*0-415-14636-4*); pap. 20.99 (*0-415-14637-2*) Routledge.

***Collins, John J.** Between Athens & Jerusalem: Jewish Identity In the Hellenistic Diaspora. 2nd rev. ed. (Biblical Resource Ser.). 384p. 1999. pap. 32.00 (*0-8028-4372-7*) Eerdmans.

Collins, John J. The Cult Experience: An Overview of Cults, Their Traditions & Why People Join Them. 142p. 1991. pap. 24.95 (*0-398-06071-1*) C C Thomas.

Collins, John J. The Cult Experience: An Overview of Cults, Their Traditions & Why People Join Them. 142p. (C). 1991. text 36.95 (*0-398-05721-4*) C C Thomas.

Collins, John J. Daniel. Cross, Frank M., ed. LC 93-14731. (Hermeneia: A Critical & Historical Commentary on the Bible Ser.). 528p. 1994. 50.00 (*0-8006-6040-4*, 1-6060, Fortress Pr) Augsburg Fortress.

— Daniel: With an Introduction to Apocalyptic Literature. Knierim, Rolf P. et al, eds. (Forms of the Old Testament Literature Ser.: Vol. XX). 160p. (Orig.). (C). 1984. pap. 15.00 (*0-8028-0020-3*) Eerdmans.

— Isaiah. (Collegeville Bible Commentary - Old Testament Ser.). 144p. 1986. pap. 4.95 (*0-8146-1420-5*) Liturgical Pr.

— Jewish Wisdom in the Hellenistic Age. LC 97-20102. (The Old Testament Library). 1997. 35.00 (*0-664-22109-2*) Westminster John Knox.

— Native American Religions: A Geographical Survey. LC 90-33942. (Native American Studies: Vol. 1). 394p. 1991. lib. bdg. 99.95 (*0-88946-483-9*) E Mellen.

— Never Off Pay: The Story of the Independent Tanker Union, 1937-1962. LC 63-16395. 351p. reprint ed. pap. 108.90 (*0-7837-0440-2*, 204076300018) Bks Demand.

— The Scepter & the Star: Jewish Messianism in Light of the Dead Sea Scrolls. LC 94-16886. (Bible Reference Library Ser.). 228p. 1995. 30.00 (*0-385-47457-1*, Anchor NY) Doubleday.

— Sibyls, Seers & Sages in Hellenistic-Roman Judaism. LC 97-183215. 248p. 1997. text 123.50 (*90-04-10752-5*) Brill Academic Pubs.

***Collins, John J., ed.** Origins of Apocalypticism in Judaism & Christianity. (Encyclopedia of Apocalypticism Ser. : Vol. 1). 520p. 2000. pap. text 39.95 (*0-8264-1253-X*) Continuum.

Collins, John J., et al, eds. Families in Ancient Israel. LC 96-41778. (Family, Religion, & Culture Ser.). 272p. 1997. pap. 20.00 (*0-664-25567-1*) Westminster John Knox.

Collins, John J. & Charlesworth, James H., eds. Mysteries & Revelations: Apocalyptic Studies since the Uppsala Colloquium. (Journal for the Study of the Pseudepigrapha Supplement Ser.: No. 9). 172p. (C). 1991. 52.50 (*1-85075-299-0*, Pub. by Sheffield Acad) CUP Services.

Collins, John J. & Fishbane, Michael, eds. Death, Ecstasy, & Other Worldly Journeys. LC 94-13469. 423p. (C). 1995. text 74.50 (*0-7914-2345-X*); pap. text 24.95 (*0-7914-2346-8*) State U NY Pr.

***Collins, John J. & Sterling, Gregory E., eds.** Hellenism in the Land of Isreal. (Christianity & Judaism in Antiquity Ser.: Vol. 13). 272p. 2001. pap. 18.95 (*0-268-03052-9*, Pub. by U of Notre Dame Pr); lib. bdg. 45.00 (*0-268-03051-0*, Pub. by U of Notre Dame Pr) Chicago Distribution Ctr.

***Collins, John Joseph & Kugler, Robert A., eds.** Religion in the Dead Sea Scrolls. LC 00-35470. (Studies in the Dead Sea Scrolls & Related Literature). 2000. pap. 18.00 (*0-8028-4743-9*) Eerdmans.

Collins, John M. American & Soviet Military Trends since the Cuban Missile Crisis. 496p. 1978. boxed set 44.95 (*0-89206-003-4*) Transaction Pubs.

— Gliding Flight. (Illus.). 160p. (YA). (gr. 5 up). 1989. pap. 13.95 (*0-89815-313-1*) Ten Speed Pr.

— Military Geography: For Professionals & the Public. LC 98-24963. (Association of the U. S. Army Book Ser.). (Illus.). 460p. 1998. pap. 32.95 (*1-57488-180-9*) Brasseys.

— Military Geography: For Professionals & the Public. LC 97-34721. 1997. write for info. (*1-57906-002-1*) Natl Defense.

— Military Geography for Professionals & the Public. 459p. 1998. per. 39.00 (*0-16-049405-2*) USGPO.

— Military Space Forces: The Next 50 Years. (Illus.). 236p. (C). 1997. reprint ed. text 25.00 (*0-7881-5091-X*) DIANE Pub.

— Special Operations Forces: An Assessment. (Illus.). 189p. (Orig.). (C). 1994. pap. text 30.00 (*0-7881-1361-5*) DIANE Pub.

Collins, John N. Are All Christians Ministers? 176p. (Orig.). 1992. pap. text 11.95 (*0-8146-2168-6*) Liturgical Pr.

Collins, John P. & Saukin, Walter, eds. The Hazardous Waste Dilemma: Issues & Solutions. LC 81-65627. 334p. 1981. pap. 5.00 (*0-87262-266-5*) Am Soc Civil Eng.

Collins, John W., III & DiBona, Leslie. Harvard Graduate School of Education: A Bibliography of Doctoral Dissertations, 1918-1987. LC 89-12276. 560p. 1989. lib. bdg. 115.00 (*0-313-28086-X*, CBN/, Greenwood Pr) Greenwood.

Collins, Jonathan. Insights from the CoffeeHouse: Miracles, Mysteries & Epiphanies from Everyday Life. 224p. 2000. 15.95 (*1-86204-725-1*, Pub. by Element MA) Penguin Putnam.

Collins, Joseph. Idling in Italy. LC 77-128226. (Essay Index Reprint Ser.). 1977. 21.95 (*0-8369-1824-X*) Ayer.

— What's Your Menopause Type. LC 99-15127. 288p. 1999. 22.95 (*0-7615-1815-0*) Prima Pub.

Collins, Joseph & Bowdoin, Gabrielle D. Beyond Unilateral Economic Sanctions: Better Alternatives for U. S. Foreign Policy. LC 99-13181. (Report Ser.). 56p. (C). 1999. pap. text 16.95 (*0-89206-351-3*) CSIS.

Collins, Joseph & Lear, John. Chile's Free-Market Miracle: A Second Look. 336p. (Orig.). 1994. pap. 16.95 (*0-935028-63-3*) Inst Food & Develop.

Collins, Joseph D. Galaxy Seven. 380p. 1996. pap. 15.95 (*0-9654285-4-0*) Caezar.

Collins, Joseph T. Amphibians & Reptiles in Kansas. rev. ed. LC 93-18564. (PE Ser.: No. 13). (Illus.). 432p. 1993. pap. text 19.95 (*0-89338-043-1*) U Pr of KS.

— Amphibians & Reptiles in Kansas. 2nd ed. (Public Education Ser.: No. 8). (Illus.). 356p. 1982. 17.95 (*0-89338-013-X*) U KS Nat Hist Mus.

— Amphibians & Reptiles in Kansas. 3rd ed. (Public Education Ser.: No. 8). (Illus.). 397p. 1993. pap. 19.95 (*0-89338-012-1*) U KS Nat Hist Mus.

— Amphibians & Reptiles in Kansas. 3rd rev. ed. LC 93-18564. (PE Ser.: No. 13). (Illus.). 397p. 1993. text 29.95 (*0-89338-044-X*) U Pr of KS.

Collins, Joseph T., ed. Natural Kansas. LC 85-7542. (Illus.). xiv, 290p. 1985. 25.00 (*0-7006-0258-5*) U Pr of KS.

Collins, Joseph T., et al, photos by. Kansas Wildlife. LC 91-18859. (Illus.). 128p. 1991. 19.95 (*0-7006-0503-7*) U Pr of KS.

Collins, Joseph T., et al. An Illustrated Guide to Endangered or Threatened Species in Kansas. LC 95-19590. (Illus.). 152p. (C). 1995. pap. 12.95 (*0-7006-0726-9*) U Pr of KS.

— Kansas Wetlands: A Wildlife Treasury. LC 94-18368. (Illus.). 128p. 1994. 24.95 (*0-7006-0635-1*) U Pr of KS.

Collins, Joseph T., jt. auth. see Cross, Frank B.

Collins, Joseph T., jt. auth. see Potts, George D.

Collins, Joseph T., ed. see Armstrong, Barry L. & Murphy, James B.

Collins, Joseph T., ed. see Bee, James W., et al.

Collins, Joseph T., ed. see Clark, Tim W. & Stromberg, Mark R.

Collins, Joseph T., ed. see Low, Denise.

Collins, Joseph T., jt. ed. see Seigel, Richard A.

Collins, Joseph T., ed. see Wilson, Larry D. & Porras, Louis.

Collins, Jude. Booing the Bishop: And Other Stories. LC 95-229070. 144p. 1996. pap. 14.95 (*0-85640-567-1*, Pub. by Blackstaff Pr) Dufour.

— Only Human & Other Stories. 144p. 1998. pap. 14.95 (*0-85640-622-8*, Pub. by Blackstaff Pr) Dufour.

Collins, Judith. Eric Gill: Sculpture. (Illus.). 128p. (C). 1992. pap. 35.00 (*0-85331-629-5*, Pub. by Lund Humphries) Antique Collect.

— Eric Gill: The Sculpture: A Catalog Raisonne. LC 97-31270. (Illus.). 240p. 1998. text 65.00 (*0-87951-830-8*, Pub. by Overlook Pr) Penguin Putnam.

Collins, Judith & Bell, Quentin, frwds. The Omega Workshops. LC 83-18285. (Illus.). x, 310p. (C). 1984. 25.00 (*0-226-11374-4*) U Ch Pr.

— The Omega Workshops. LC 83-18285. (Illus.). x, 320p. (C). 1985. pap. 21.00 (*0-226-11375-2*) U Ch Pr.

Collins, Judith, et al. Techniques of the Modern Artists. 192p. 1997. 19.98 (*0-7858-0841-8*) Bk Sales Inc.

Collins, Judith, jt. auth. see Atroshenko, V. I.

Collins, Judy. Baby's Bedtime. (J). 1993. pap. 9.98 incl. audio (*1-879496-07-0*) Lightyear Entrtnmnt.

— My Father. (Illus.). 32p. (J). (gr. k-3). 1997. pap. 4.95 (*0-316-15238-2*) Little.

— My Father. 1997. 10.15 (*0-606-13630-4*, Pub. by Turtleback) Demco.

— Shameless: A Novel. 352p. 1996. per. 6.50 (*0-671-89234-7*) S&S Trade.

— Singing Lessons: A Memoir of Love, Loss, Hope & Healing. LC 98-221221. (Illus.). 400p. 1998. 25.00 (*0-671-02745-X*, PB Hardcover) PB.

— Singing Lessons: A Memoir of Love, Loss, Hope & Healing. 368p. 1999. pap. 14.95 incl. audio compact disk (*0-671-00398-4*, PB Trade Paper) PB.

— Singing Lessons: A Memoir of Love, Loss, Hope & Healing. 368p. 1999. pap. 14.95 (*0-671-03976-8*, PB Trade Paper) PB.

— Singing Lessons: A Memoir of Love, Loss, Hope & Healing With CD. LC 98-221221. (Illus.). 346p. 1998. 25.00 incl. audio compact disk (*0-671-00397-6*, PB Hardcover) PB.

— Voices. 1995. 25.00 incl. cd-rom (*0-614-15424-3*) C Potter.

Collins, Judy, frwd. The Way Home: A Collective Memoir of the Hazelden Experience. LC 97-28093. 260p. 24.95 (*1-56838-159-X*, 5673 A) Hazelden.

Collins, Judy, jt. auth. see Griffin, Ricky.

Collins, Julie. Art Nouveau. (Stencil Collection). (Illus.). 32p. 1999. pap. 14.95 (*1-85391-737-0*) Sterling.

— Classic Borders. (Stencil Collection). (Illus.). 32p. 1999. pap. 14.95 (*1-85391-696-X*) Sterling.

***Collins, Julie.** Painted Pieces in a Weekend. 2000. pap. 14.95 (*1-58290-022-1*, Pub. by Jrny Editions) Tuttle Pubng.

Collins, Julie, jt. auth. see Collins, Miki.

Collins, June M., jt. auth. see Collins, Orvis.

Collins, K. Go & Learn: The International Story of Jews & Medicine in Scotland. (Illus.). 240p. 1988. 29.95 (*0-08-036408-X*, Pub. by Aberdeen U Pr) Macmillan.

Collins, K. J. & Roberts, D. F., eds. The Capacity for Work in the Tropics. (Society for the Study of Human Biology Symposium Ser.: No. 26). (Illus.). 310p. 1988. text 74.95 (*0-521-30935-2*) Cambridge U Pr.

Collins, K. J., ed. see Youle, A.

Collins, K. K., jt. compiled by see Cohn, Alan M.

Collins, Karen S., jt. ed. see Falik, Marilyn M.

Collins, Kathleen, tr. see Mars, Louis B.

Collins, Kathleen C., et al. Getting Started: An Overview of School Development Practices. LC 97-204549. (Illus.). 87p. 1997. pap. 12.00 (*1-55833-183-2*) Natl Cath Educ.

Collins, Kathleen C., jt. auth. see Kealey, Robert J.

Collins, Kathleen K. Washingtoniana: Photographs; Collections in the Prints & Photographs Division of the Library of Congress. LC 87-600421. (Illus.). 310p. 1989. 25.00 (*0-8444-0588-4*, 030-000-00210-5) Lib Congress.

Collins, Kathleen M., jt. auth. see Collins, James L.

***Collins, Kaye C., et al, eds.** Foxfire Vol. 11: Wild Plant Uses, Gardening Wit & Wisdom, Beekeeping, Tool Making, Fishing & More Affairs of Plain Living. LC 99-27305. Vol. 11. 336p. 1999. pap. 15.95 (*0-385-49461-0*, Anchor NY) Doubleday.

Collins, Keith. From Coach to First Class: Developing the Spirit of Excellence. 132p. (Orig.). 1997. pap. 9.99 (*1-889389-08-0*) End-Time Wave.

Collins, Ken, jt. auth. see Collins, Betty.

Collins, Kenneth J. A Faithful Witness: John Wesley's Homiletical Theology. LC 93-19294. 1993. write for info. (*0-915143-04-6*) F A Society.

— A Real Christian: The Life of John Wesley. LC 99-10346. 1999. 20.00 (*0-687-08246-3*) Abingdon.

— The Scripture Way of Salvation: The Heart of John Wesley's Theology. LC 97-16419. 256p. 1997. pap. 18.95 (*0-687-00962-6*) Abingdon.

— Wesley on Salvation: Studies in the Standard Sermons. 144p. 1989. pap. 7.95 (*0-310-75421-6*) Zondervan.

***Collins, Kenneth J., ed.** Exploring Christian Spirituality: An Ecumenical Reader. LC 00-23079. 352p. (gr. 13). 2000. pap. 26.99 (*0-8010-2233-9*) Baker Bks.

***Collins, Kenneth M., Sr.** The Tithing Message: Deceptions Exposed. Guest, Dean, ed. 75p. (C). 2000. pap. 5.95 (*1-879667-15-0*) Dove Pr TX.

Collins, Kevin & Collins, Betty. Experimenting with Science Photography. LC 93-31074. (Experimental Science Ser.). (Illus.). 144p. (YA). (gr. 9-12). 1994. lib. bdg. 24.00 (*0-531-11166-0*) Watts.

Collins, Kevin R., jt. auth. see Nowak, Andrzej S.

Collins, L. Newsmakers, 1996 Subscription. 96th ed. 1996. 129.00 (*0-8103-9320-4*) Gale.

Collins, L. J. Gearing - For Steel Mill Auxiliaries & Cranes. (Technical Papers: Vol. P329.01). (Illus.). 11p. 1947. pap. text 30.00 (*1-55589-391-0*) AGMA.

— Gears, Their Applications, Design & Manufacture. (Technical Papers: Vol. P109.01). (Illus.). 25p. 1947. pap. text 30.00 (*1-55589-193-4*) AGMA.

Collins, L. J., jt. auth. see Davidson, R. S.

Collins, Lane. Financial Accounting Standards Practice Updated Series. (Illus.). 640p. 1982. text 230.00 (*0-07-044641-5*) McGraw.

***Collins, Larry.** Is Paris Burning? (Illus.). 376p. 2000. 9.99 (*0-7858-1246-6*) Bk Sales Inc.

Collins, Larry & La Pierre, Dominique. The Fifth Horseman. 496p. 1982. mass mkt. 4.95 (*0-380-54734-1*, Avon Bks) Morrow Avon.

Collins, Larry & Lapierre, Dominique. The Fifth Horseman. large type ed. 768p. 1983. 27.99 (*0-7089-8138-0*) Ulverscroft.

— Freedom at Midnight. 608p. 1976. mass mkt. 5.95 (*0-380-00693-6*, Avon Bks) Morrow Avon.

Collins, Larry & LaPierre, Dominique. Is Paris Burning? 1991. mass mkt. 12.99 (*0-446-39225-1*, Pub. by Warner Bks) Little.

Collins, Larry & Lapierre, Dominique. Is Paris Burning? 398p. 1993. reprint ed. lib. bdg. 37.95 (*0-89968-319-3*, Lghtyr Pr) Buccaneer Bks.

— O Jerusalem! 704p. 1988. pap. 16.00 (*0-671-66241-4*, Touchstone) S&S Trade Pap.

***Collins, Larry R.** Physical Hazards of the Workplace. (Occupational Safety & Health Guide Ser.). 290p. 1999. 59.95 (*1-56670-339-5*) Lewis Pubs.

Collins, Latrice. My Child's PHJ: Personal Health Journal. 112p. 1996. spiral bd. 14.95 (*0-9660451-0-6*) Empower Press.

***Collins, Latrice.** PHJ: Personal Health Journal. 112p. 1999. 14.95 (*0-9660451-1-4*) Empower Press.

Collins, Laura R. English Country Life in the Barsetshire Novels of Angela Thirkell, 57. LC 94-29831. (Contributions to the Study of World Literature Ser.: Vol. 57). 168p. 1994. 55.00 (*0-313-28494-6*, Greenwood Pr) Greenwood.

Collins, Laurel. Dream Weaver. 400p. 1995. mass mkt. 4.99 (*0-8217-4903-X*) NAL.

— The Firebrand. 384p. 1997. mass mkt. 4.99 (*0-8217-5667-2*, Zebra Kensgtn) Kensgtn Pub Corp.

— Patchwork Angel. 320p. 1998. pap. 4.99 (*0-8217-5881-0*, Zebra Kensgtn) Kensgtn Pub Corp.

Collins, Lauren F., jt. auth. see Mitchell, Charlie R.

Collins, Laurence W., et al, eds. Nonferrous Wire Handbook Vol. 1: Nonferrous Wire Rod. 2nd ed. (Illus.). 417p. 1979. 50.00 (*0-685-26881-0*) Wire Assn Intl.

— Nonferrous Wire Handbooks, 2 vols. 2nd ed. (Illus.). 1981. 80.00 (*0-685-26882-9*) Wire Assn Intl.

Collins, Lawrence. Essays in International Litigation & the Conflict of Laws. LC 93-15682. 518p. 1994. text 85.00 (*0-19-825732-5*, Clarendon Pr) OUP.

— Essays in International Litigation & the Conflict of Laws. 518p. 1997. reprint ed. pap. text 39.95 (*0-19-826566-2*) OUP.

— European Community Law in the United Kingdom. 4th ed. 270p. 1990. 74.00 (*0-406-59200-4*, UK, MICHIE); pap. 42.00 (*0-406-59201-2*, U.K., MICHIE) LEXIS Pub.

Collins, Lawrence D. The Fifty-Sixth Evac Hospital: Letters of a WWII Army Doctor. LC 94-45516. (War & the Southwest Ser.: No. 4). (Illus.). 304p. 1995. 29.95 (*0-929398-83-1*) UNTX Pr.

Collins, Leighton. Takeoffs & Landings. 1982. text 19.95 (*0-02-527240-3*) Macmillan.

Collins, Lester. Innisfree: An American Garden. LC 93-44041. 1994. 35.00 (*0-89831-045-8*) Sagapr.

Collins, Lewis. Collins' Historical Sketches of Kentucky: Embracing Prehistoric Annals for 331 Years...; Incidents of Pioneer Life; & Nearly Five Hundred Biographical Sketches of Distinguished Pioneers, Etc., 2 vols. Collins, Richard H., ed. & rev. by. (Illus.). 1487p. 1997. reprint ed. lib. bdg. 155.00 (*0-8328-6726-8*) Higginson Bk Co.

— Historical Sketches of Kentucky Embracing Its History, Antiquities, & Natural Curiosities, Geographical, Statistical, & Geological Description. LC 77-146385. (First American Frontier Ser.). (Illus.). 1971. reprint ed. 36.95 (*0-405-02836-9*) Ayer.

— History of Kentucky, 2 vols., Set. enl. rev. ed. (Illus.). 1487p. 1995. reprint ed. lib. bdg. 145.00 (*0-8328-5032-2*) Higginson Bk Co.

Collins, Lewis & Collins, Richard H. A History of Kentucky, Set. 1979. 125.00 (*0-89308-168-X*) Southern Hist Pr.

— A History of Kentucky, Vol. 1. 683p. 1979. write for info. (*0-89308-166-3*) Southern Hist Pr.

— A History of Kentucky, Vol. 2. 804p. 1979. write for info. (*0-89308-167-1*) Southern Hist Pr.

C

Collins, Linda B. Recall: Activities for Word Retrieval. 1991. 45.00 (*0-937857-20-3*, 1591) Speech Bin.

Collins, Linda B. & Chadwell, Sandra S. ACQUIRE: Answer - Comprehend - Question - Interpret - Reason - Express. (Illus.). 160p. 1990. pap. text 34.95 (*0-937857-14-9*, 1572) Speech Bin.

Collins, Linda B. & Spangler, Carol S. The Communication Curriculum: A Practical Guide for Speech & Language. 200p. (Orig.). (gr. k-12). 1988. teacher ed. 39.95 (*0-937857-06-8*, 1558) Speech Bin.

— The Communication Program Planning Book: A Plan Book for Speech-Language Pathologists. 200p. (J). (gr. k-12). 1989. 19.95 (*0-937857-10-6*, 1567) Speech Bin.

***Collins, Linda M., ed.** Innovative Methods for Prevention Research: A Special Issue of Multivariate Behavioral Research. 165p. 1999. pap. 34.50 (*0-8058-9788-7*) L Erlbaum Assocs.

Collins, Linda M. & Horn, John L., eds. Best Methods for the Analysis of Change: Recent Advances, Unanswered Questions, Future Directions. 355p. (Orig.). (C). 1991. pap. 19.95 (*1-55798-310-0*) Am Psychol.

Collins, Lloyd R., jt. ed. see Aschenbrenner, Joyce.

Collins, Loel. Kayaking. LC 95-17937. (Know the Sport Ser.). (Illus.). 48p. 1996. pap. 5.95 (*0-8117-2825-0*) Stackpole.

Collins-Longman Publishing Staff. Collins Longman Atlas for Secondary Schools. 1994. text. write for info. (*0-582-09496-8*, Pub. by Addison-Wesley); pap. text. write for info. (*0-582-09247-7*, Pub. by Addison-Wesley) Longman.

Collins Longman Staff. Collins Longman Atlas Two. 1995. pap. text. write for info. (*0-582-23759-9*, Pub. by Addison-Wesley) Longman.

— Collins Longman Atlas 1. 1994. pap. text. write for info. (*0-582-23768-8*, Pub. by Addison-Wesley) Longman.

Collins-Lowry, Sharon M. Black Corporate Executives: The Making & Breaking of a Black Middle Class. LC 96-10735. (Labor & Social Change Ser.). 208p. (C). 1996. 69.95 (*1-56639-473-2*); pap. 22.95 (*1-56639-474-0*) Temple U Pr.

Collins, Lyndhurst & Walker, David F., eds. Locational Dynamics of Manufacturing Activity. LC 73-21939. 412p. reprint ed. pap. 127.80 (*0-608-15627-2*, 203175600076) Bks Demand.

Collins, Lynn, jt. auth. see Bluestein, Jane.

Collins, Lynn H., et al. Career Strategies for Women in Academia: Arming Athena. LC 98-19761. 333p. 1998. write for info. (*0-7619-0989-3*); pap. write for info. (*0-7619-0990-7*) Sage.

Collins, Lynn M., jt. ed. see Robinson, James K.

Collins, Lynn M., ed. see Wade, Michael D. & Strom, Jennifer J.

***Collins, Lynne.** Convalescent Heart. large type ed. 336p. 1999. pap. 18.99 (*0-7089-5508-8*, Linford) Ulverscroft.

— Dream of a Doctor. large type ed. 304p. 1998. pap. 18.99 (*0-7089-5407-3*) Ulverscroft.

Collins, Lynne. The Golden Key. large type ed. 1990. 27.99 (*0-7089-2215-5*) Ulverscroft.

***Collins, Lynne.** Heart in Crisis. large type ed. 332p. 2000. 20.99 (*1-84137-024-X*, Pub. by Mgna Lrg Print) Ulverscroft.

— Heart in Waiting. 320p. 2000. 18.99 (*0-7089-5701-3*) Ulverscroft.

Collins, Lynne. Hospital Magic. large type ed. (Linford Romance Library). 352p. 1997. pap. 16.99 (*0-7089-5118-X*, Linford) Ulverscroft.

— Need for a Nurse. large type ed. (Linford Romance Library). 304p. 1997. pap. 16.99 (*0-7089-5077-9*, Linford) Ulverscroft.

***Collins, Lynne.** Never Say Goodbye. large type ed. LC 99-49382. (General Ser.). 2000. pap. 22.95 (*0-7862-2307-3*) Thorndike Pr.

Collins, Lynne. No Other Love. large type ed. 1991. 27.99 (*0-7089-2427-1*) Ulverscroft.

— Out of Practice. large type ed. 304p. 1998. pap. 17.99 (*0-7089-5358-1*, Linford) Ulverscroft.

— Proud Surgeon. large type ed. (Linford Romance Library). 224p. 1997. pap. 16.99 (*0-7089-5034-5*) Ulverscroft.

— The Sister & the Surgeon. large type ed. (Linford Romance Library). 336p. 1993. pap. 16.99 (*0-7089-7406-6*, Linford) Ulverscroft.

— Sister of Serenity Ward. large type ed. (Linford Romance Library). 1995. pap. 16.99 (*0-7089-7779-0*, Linford) Ulverscroft.

— A Tangle of Nurses. large type ed. LC 97-29673. 1997. 21.95 (*0-7862-1226-8*) Thorndike Pr.

— To Be Loved. large type ed. 1990. 27.99 (*0-7089-2292-9*) Ulverscroft.

Collins, Lynne A. Dream in My Heart. large type ed. 304p. 1992. 27.99 (*0-7089-2658-4*) Ulverscroft.

— Tread Softly, Nurse. large type ed. (Linford Romance Library). 304p. 1992. pap. 16.99 (*0-7089-7273-X*, Linford) Ulverscroft.

Collins, Lynne D., jt. auth. see Chatton, Barbara.

Collins, M. Money & Banking in Britain: A History. 656p. 1988. lib. bdg. 99.95 (*0-7099-0760-5*, Pub. by C Helm) Routldge.

Collins, M., et al. Managing Finance & Financial Information. (In-Charge Ser.). 240p. (Orig.). (C). 1993. pap. text 36.95 (*0-631-19009-0*) Blackwell Pubs.

— Managing People. (In-Charge Ser.). 272p. (Orig.). (C). 1993. pap. text 36.95 (*0-631-19012-0*) Blackwell Pubs.

Collins, M. F. & Cooper, I. S., eds. Leisure Management: Issues & Applications. LC 97-22231. (A CAB International Publication). 336p. (C). 1998. 75.00 (*0-85199-215-3*) OUP.

Collins, M. G. Introduction to Insurance: Insurance Learner. 3rd ed. (C). 1988. 85.00 (*0-7855-4116-0*, Pub. by Witherby & Co) St Mut.

Collins, M. J. Representations & Characters of Finite Groups. (Cambridge Studies in Advanced Mathematics: No. 22). 254p. (C). 1990. text 80.00 (*0-521-23440-9*) Cambridge U Pr.

***Collins, M. P. & Mitchell, D.** Reinforced & Prestressed Concrete Structures. 2nd ed. (Illus.). 784p. (C). (gr. 13). 2000. text 90.00 (*0-419-24920-6*, E & FN Spon) Routledge.

Collins, M. W., ed. Nanoscale Physiology. (Advances in Computational Bioengineering Ser.). 250p. 2001. 129.00 (*1-85312-670-5*, 6705, Pub. by WIT Pr) Computational Mech MA.

***Collins, M. W. & Atherton, M. A., eds.** The World of Science & Nature Vol. 1: The Laws of Design. (Design in Nature Ser.). 500p. 2000. 239.00 (*1-85312-852-X*, Pub. by WIT Pr) Computational Mech MA.

— The World of Science & Nature Vol. 2: The Information Revolution. (Design in Nature Ser.). 500p. 2000. 239.00 (*1-85312-853-8*, Pub. by WIT Pr) Computational Mech MA.

Collins, M. W. & Xu, X. Y., eds. Haemodynamics of Arterial Organs: Comparison of Computational Predictions with in Vitro & in Vivo Data. (Advances in Computational Bioengineering Ser.: Vol. 1). (Illus.). 288p. 1999. 136.00 (*1-85312-509-1*, 5091) Computational Mech MA.

Collins, Mabel. The Blossom & the Fruit. 332p. 1974. reprint ed. spiral bd. 20.00 (*0-7873-1136-7*) Hlth Research.

— The Blossom & the Fruit: A True Story of a Black Magician (1890) 332p. 1996. reprint ed. pap. 19.95 (*1-56459-703-2*) Kessinger Pub.

— Crucible. 126p. 1998. reprint ed. pap. 14.95 (*0-7661-0473-7*) Kessinger Pub.

— Illusions. 72p. 1996. reprint ed. spiral bd. 10.00 (*0-7873-1186-3*) Hlth Research.

— Illusions (1905) 72p. 1996. reprint ed. pap. 9.95 (*1-56459-909-4*) Kessinger Pub.

— Light on the Path. 1986. 5.95 (*81-7059-011-6*, 7183, Quest) Theos Pub Hse.

— Light on the Path. 46p. 1997. reprint ed. pap. 9.95 (*0-7661-0068-5*) Kessinger Pub.

— Light on the Path. 4th ed. 28p. 1993. reprint ed. spiral bd. 8.00 (*0-7873-0193-0*) Hlth Research.

— Light on the Path: And an Essay on Karma. 1999. 2.95 (*81-7059-194-5*) Theos Pub Hse.

— Light on the Path & Through the Gates of Gold, 2 vols. in 1. 1976. 16.95 (*0-911500-37-5*) Theos U Pr.

— Light on the Path & Through the Gates of Gold, 2 vols. in 1. 1977. pap. 10.95 (*0-911500-38-3*) Theos U Pr.

— Our Glorious Future: The Interpretation of "Light on the Path" 115p. 1995. reprint ed. pap. 15.95 (*1-56459-503-X*) Kessinger Pub.

— Through the Gates of Gold: A Fragment of Thought. 151p. 1996. reprint ed. spiral bd. 12.00 (*0-7873-1229-0*) Hlth Research.

— Through the Gates of Gold (1888) 110p. 1998. reprint ed. pap. 10.95 (*0-7661-0269-6*) Kessinger Pub.

— The Transparent Jewel. 142p. 1913. reprint ed. pap. 15.50 (*0-7873-1231-2*) Hlth Research.

— The Transparent Jewel, (1913) 142p. 1996. reprint ed. pap. 13.95 (*1-56459-914-0*) Kessinger Pub.

— When the Sun Moves Northward, Being a Treatise on the Six Sacred Months (1912) 180p. 1998. reprint ed. pap. 19.95 (*0-7661-0268-8*) Kessinger Pub.

Collins, Mabel C. Light on the Path. reprint ed. pap. 5.00 (*0-911662-13-8*) Yoga.

Collins-Magnus, Bab, jt. auth. see Magnus, Ralph A.

Collins, Malcolm F. Magnetic Critical Scattering. (Oxford Series on Neutron Scattering in Condensed Matter). (Illus.). 200p. 1989. text 65.00 (*0-19-504600-5*) OUP.

Collins, Marcia & Land, Norman E. Early Books on Art, 1500 to 1800. (Illus.). 74p. (Orig.). 1977. pap. 4.00 (*0-910501-04-1*) U of Missouri Mus Art Arch.

Collins, Marcia R. & Anderson, Linda. Libraries for Small Museums. 3rd ed. Feldman, Lawrence, ed. LC 78-620740. (Miscellaneous Publications in Anthropology Ser.: No. 4). iii, 48p. 1977. pap. text 2.50 (*0-913134-90-2*) Mus Anthro MO.

Collins, Marie, jt. auth. see Berge, Zane.

Collins, Marie C., tr. see Hernández, Ramon.

***Collins, Marilyn, et al.** Beaufort's Old Burying Ground, North Carolina. (Images of America Ser.). (Illus.). 128p. 1999. pap. 16.99 (*0-7385-0018-6*) Arcadia Publng.

Collins, Marion S. Baby Makes Three. 1996. per. 3.99 (*0-373-07747-5*, 1-07747-8) Silhouette.

— Every Night at Eight. (Romance Ser.: No. 849). 1992. per. 2.59 (*0-373-08849-3*, 5-08849-7) Silhouette.

— Fire on the Mountain. (Intimate Moments Ser.). 1993. per. 3.50 (*0-373-07514-6*, 5-07514-8) Silhouette.

— Surrogate Dad. (Intimate Moments Ser.). 1994. per. 3.50 (*0-373-07610-X*, 1-07610-8) Silhouette.

Collins, Marion S. & Palmer, Diana. Royal Weddings. 1996. per. 5.99 (*0-373-20129-X*, 1-20129-2) Harlequin Bks.

Collins, Marita R. The Light Body... A Transformation Cooking Guide to Health-Supportive Eating. LC 96-61615. (Illus.). 240p. 1997. pap. 19.95 (*0-9654751-0-7*) Traveling Gourmet.

Collins, Mark. Married White Male in Search Of . . . An Offbeat Look at Family Life, Faith Life & Mid-Life. LC 97-52263. 176p. 1998. pap. 11.00 (*0-7648-0179-1*, Liguori Triumph) Liguori Pubns.

Collins, Mark & Kimmel, Margaret M., eds. Mister Rogers' Neighborhood: Children, Television, & Fred Rogers. (Illus.). 249p. 1996. pap. 16.95 (*0-8229-5652-7*) U of Pittsburgh Pr.

— Mister Rogers' Neighborhood: Children, Television, & Fred Rogers. LC 95-48461. (Illus.). 249p. (C). 1996. text 27.95 (*0-8229-3921-5*) U of Pittsburgh Pr.

Collins, Marsha S. Pio Baroja's Memorias de un Humbre de Acion & the Ironic Mode: The Search for Order & Meaning. 1986. 69.00 (*0-7293-0252-0*, Pub. by Tamesis Bks Ltd) Boydell & Brewer.

Collins, Martha. Some Things Words Can Do: Poems (Includes a History of Small Life on a Windy Planet) LC 98-42844. 131p. 1998. pap. 12.95 (*1-878818-74-0*, Pub. by Sheep Meadow) U Pr of New Eng.

Collins, Martha & Chung, Nguyen B., eds. The Women Carry River Water: Poems. Thieu, Nguyen Q. et al, trs. from VIE. LC 96-48658. xii, 125p. 1997. pap. 14.95 (*1-55849-087-6*); text 27.50 (*1-55849-086-8*) U of Mass Pr.

Collins, Martha D. & Moss, Barbara G., eds. Literacy Assessment for Today's Schools. (Monograph Series of the College Reading Association). 234p. (Orig.). (C). 1996. pap. 15.00 (*1-883604-25-7*) Coll Read Assn.

Collins, Martha D., et al. Diagnostic-Prescriptive Reading Instruction: A Guide. 4th ed. 512p. (C). 1994. text. write for info. (*0-697-25751-7*) Brown & Benchmark.

Collins, Martha S. Buckhouse. LC 98-84052. 68p. 1998. pap. 5.95 (*1-56167-408-7*) Am Literary Pr.

Collins, Martin. France: Normandy. (Visitor's Guides Ser.). (Illus.). 224p. (Orig.). 1993. pap. 13.95 (*1-55650-575-2*) Hunter NJ.

Collins, Martin J. & Division of Space History, National Air & Space Museum, The Smithsonian Institution Staff. Space Race: The U. S. - U. S. S. R. Competition to Reach the Moon. LC 98-47057. (Illus.). 1999. pap. 25.00 (*0-7649-0905-3*) Pomegranate Calif.

Collins, Martin J. & Fries, Sylvia D., eds. A Spacefaring Nation: Perspectives on American Space History & Policy. LC 90-9762. xx, 245 p. (C). 1991. text 39.00 (*0-87474-907-7*) Smithsonian.

Collins, Marva. Ordinary Children, Extraordinary Teachers. 264p. 1992. pap. 12.95 (*1-878901-41-9*) Hampton Roads Pub Co.

— Values: Lighting the Candle of Excellence, Set. abr. ed. 1996. audio. write for info. (*0-7871-1007-8*, 394461, Pub. by NewStar Media) Lndmrk Audiobks.

Collins, Marva & Tamarkin, Civia. Marva Collins' Way: Returning to Excellence in Education. rev. ed. LC 82-10516. 256p. 1990. pap. 10.95 (*0-87477-572-8*, Tarcher Putnam) Putnam Pub Group.

Collins, Mary. Contemplative Participation: Sacrosanctum Concilium - Twenty-Five Years Later. 96p. 1990. pap. text 5.95 (*0-8146-1922-3*) Liturgical Pr.

***Collins, Mary.** The Franklin Delano Roosevelt Memorial. LC 99-52352. (Cornerstones to Freedom Ser.). (J). 2000. 20.50 (*0-516-21598-1*) Childrens.

— Industrial Revolution. (Cornerstones to Freedom Ser.). (Illus.). 32p. (J). (gr. 4-7). 2000. pap. 5.95 (*0-516-27036-2*) Childrens.

Collins, Mary. Mount Vernon. LC 97-26584. (Cornerstones to Freedom Ser.). (Illus.). 32p. (J). (gr. 4-6). 1998. 19.50 (*0-516-20939-6*) Childrens.

— Mount Vernon. (Cornerstones to Freedom Ser.). (Illus.). 32p. (J). (gr. 4-6). 1999. pap. text 5.95 (*0-516-26343-9*) Childrens.

— National Public Radio: The Cast of Characters. LC 92-34825. (Illus.). 150p. 1993. text 19.95 (*0-929765-19-2*) Seven Locks Pr.

— Renewal to Practice. (Worship Ser.). 295p. 1987. 14.95 (*0-912405-32-5*, Pastoral Press) OR Catholic.

— Revelation, Rites, & Remembering: A Liturgy Text. 160p. (Orig.). Date not set. pap. text 9.95 (*0-8146-6127-0*) Liturgical Pr.

— The Smithsonian Institution. LC 98-31225. (Cornerstones to Freedom Ser.). 32p. (J). (gr. 4-6). 1999. 20.00 (*0-516-21168-4*) Childrens.

***Collins, Mary.** Smithsonian Institution. LC 98-31225. (Cornerstones to Freedom Ser.). 32p. (J). (gr. 4-6). 2000. pap. text 5.95 (*0-516-26518-0*) Childrens.

Collins, Mary. The Spanish-American War. LC 97-10964. (Cornerstones to Freedom Ser.). (Illus.). 32p. (J). (gr. 4-6). 1998. lib. bdg. 19.50 (*0-516-20759-8*) Childrens.

— The Spanish-American War. DeCapua, Sarah, ed. (Cornerstones to Freedom Ser.). (Illus.). 32p. (J). (gr. 4-6). 1998. pap. 5.95 (*0-516-26337-4*) Childrens.

— Women at Prayer. (Madeleva Lectures, 1987). 56p. 1988. pap. 3.95 (*0-8091-2949-3*) Paulist Pr.

Collins, Mary, ed. Canada, 1995: An International Regulatory & Strategy Report. 312p. 1994. pap. 275.00 (*1-882615-09-3*) Parexel Intl.

Collins, Mary, et al, eds. The New Dictionary of Theology. LC 87-82327. (Illus.). 1120p. (C). 1987. text 69.95 (*0-8146-5609-9*) Liturgical Pr.

Collins, Mary & Power, David, eds. A Creative Tradition. (Concilium Ser.: Vol. 162). 128p. (Orig.). 1983. 6.95 (*0-8164-2442-X*) Harper SF.

Collins, Mary, jt. auth. see Cappi, Paul.

Collins, Mary, ed. see Grizzle, Anne.

Collins, Mary, jt. ed. see Komonchak, Joseph A.

Collins, Mary, jt. ed. see Power, David.

Collins, Mary A. Early Childhood Program Participation Data File User's Manual. 434p. 1996. pap. 35.00 (*0-16-048898-2*) USGPO.

— National Household Education Survey: A Guide to Using Data from the National Household Education Survey (NHES) 69p. (Orig.). 1997. pap. 5.00 (*0-16-049200-9*) USGPO.

— National Household Education Survey: NHES. 97p. 1997. pap. 10.00 (*0-16-049202-5*) USGPO.

— National Household Education Survey of 1996: Data File User's Manual. 160p. 1997. pap. 14.00 (*0-16-049195-9*) USGPO.

— National Household Education Survey of 1996: Data File User's Manual, Vol. 4. 98p. 1997. pap. 10.00 (*0-16-049198-3*) USGPO.

— National Household Education Survey of 1996: Data File User's Manual, Household & Library Data File, Vol. 2. 174p. 1997. pap. 15.00 (*0-16-049196-7*) USGPO.

— National Household Education Survey of 1996: Data File User's Manual, Parent & Family Involvement in Education & Civic Involvement, Parent Data File, Vol. 3. 188p. 1997. pap. 15.00 (*0-16-049197-5*) USGPO.

— National Household Education Survey of 1996: Data Files User's Manual. 68p. 1997. pap. 5.00 (*0-16-049199-1*) USGPO.

Collins, Mary B. Across Five Aprils: A Unit Plan. 170p. 1994. teacher ed. 26.95 incl. lp (*1-58337-069-2*) Teachers Pet Pubns.

— Animal Farm: A Unit Plan. 146p. 1994. teacher ed., ring bd. 26.95 (*1-58337-012-9*) Teachers Pet Pubns.

— Anne Frank Diary: A Unit Plan. 152p. 1994. teacher ed., ring bd. 26.95 (*1-58337-122-2*) Teachers Pet Pubns.

— Brave New World: A Unit Plan. 152p. 1994. teacher ed., ring bd. 26.95 (*1-58337-106-0*) Teachers Pet Pubns.

— Gulliver's Travels: A Unit Plan. 186p. 1995. teacher ed., ring bd. 26.95 (*1-58337-108-7*) Teachers Pet Pubns.

— Jane Eyre: A Unit Plan. 178p. 1995. teacher ed., ring bd. 26.95 (*1-58337-104-4*) Teachers Pet Pubns.

— Lord of the Flies: A Unit Plan. 154p. 1994. teacher ed., ring bd. 26.95 (*1-58337-109-5*) Teachers Pet Pubns.

— Othello: A Unit Plan. 170p. 1994. teacher ed., ring bd. 26.95 (*1-58337-111-7*) Teachers Pet Pubns.

— Pygmalion: A Unit Plan. 140p. 1994. teacher ed., ring bd. 26.95 (*1-58337-107-9*) Teachers Pet Pubns.

— A Tale of Two Cities: A Unit Plan. 176p. 1994. teacher ed., ring bd. 26.95 (*1-58337-101-X*) Teachers Pet Pubns.

— The Tempest: A Unit Plan. 152p. 1994. teacher ed., ring bd. 26.95 (*1-58337-110-9*) Teachers Pet Pubns.

— A Tree Grows in Brooklyn: A Unit Plan. 110p. 1992. teacher ed., ring bd. 16.95 (*1-58337-068-4*) Teachers Pet Pubns.

Collins, Mary B. & Kitwood, Tom. Dementia Reconsidered: The Person Comes First. LC 96-52125. (Rethinking Aging Ser.). 1997. 98.00 (*0-335-19856-2*) OpUniv Pr.

Collins, Mary B. The Good Earth: A Unit Plan. 172p. 1994. teacher ed., ring bd. 26.95 (*1-58337-051-X*) Teachers Pet Pubns.

— The Grapes of Wrath: A Unit Plan. 170p. 1994. teacher ed., ring bd. 26.95 (*1-58337-022-6*) Teachers Pet Pubns.

Collins, Mary C. How to Make Money Writing Corporate Communications. LC 94-3627. 208p. (Orig.). 1995. pap. 12.00 (*0-399-51894-0*, Perigee Bks) Berkley Pub.

Collins, Mary E., compiled by. Education Journals & Serials: An Analytical Guide, 12. LC 87-31442. (Annotated Bibliographies of Serials: A Subject Approach Ser.: No. 12). 378p. 1988. lib. bdg. 75.00 (*0-313-24514-2*, KEE/, Greenwood Pr) Greenwood.

Collins, Mary E., ed. Pedological Perspectives in Archaeological Research: Proceedings of 2 Symposia Sponsored. LC 96-6912. (SSSA Special Publications: No. 44). (Illus.). 157p. 1995. 30.00 (*0-89118-820-7*) Soil Sci Soc Am.

Collins, Mary K., ed. Practical Molecular Virology. LC 91-7049. (Methods in Molecular Biology Ser.: Vol. 8). (Illus.). 340p. 1991. 54.50 (*0-89603-191-8*); pap. 59.50 (*0-89603-299-X*) Humana.

Collins, Mary R. The Aerial Photo Sourcebook. LC 98-30428. (Illus.). 224p. 1998. 45.00 (*0-8108-3519-3*) Scarecrow.

Collins, Mary R. & Stouffer, Cindy. One Soldier's Legacy: The National Homestead at Gettysburg. (Illus.). 128p. (C). 1993. pap. 6.95 (*0-939631-67-9*) Thomas Publications.

Collins, Mary S., jt. auth. see Baker, John A.

Collins, Matthew. If I Die on the Jersey Front. 287p. 1995. pap. 5.99 (*0-9645726-0-5*) Orchard Pr.

Collins, Mauri, jt. auth. see Berge, Zane.

Collins, Mauri L., jt. ed. see Berge, Zane.

Collins, Max A. Blood & Thunder. abr. ed. Landt, Fran, ed. 1995. 16.95 incl. audio (*1-882071-57-3*) B&B Audio.

— Blood & Thunder. 320p. 1999. reprint ed. text 22.00 (*0-7881-6601-8*) DIANE Pub.

— Carnal Hours: A Nathan Heller Novel. abr. ed. 1996. 16.95 incl. audio (*1-882071-71-9*) B&B Audio.

Collins, Max A. Elvgren Girls I. LC 99-28119. (Artist Archives Ser.). (Illus.). 32p. 1999. pap. 11.95 (*1-888054-33-6*, Pub. by Collectors Pr) Universe.

— Elvgren Girls II. LC 99-29640. (Artist Archives Ser.). (Illus.). 32p. 1999. pap. 11.95 (*1-888054-34-4*, Pub. by Collectors Pr) Universe.

— Exotic Ladies. LC 99-29641. (Artist Archives Ser.). (Illus.). 32p. 1999. pap. 11.95 (*1-888054-36-0*) Collectors Pr.

***Collins, Max A.** Majic Man. large type ed. (Basic Ser.). 512p. 2000. 28.95 (*0-7862-2529-7*) Thorndike Pr.

Collins, Max A. Majic Man: A Nathan Heller Novel. LC 99-13679. 304p. 1999. 23.95 (*0-525-94515-6*) NAL.

Collins, Max A. Mommy. 1996. 16.95 incl. audio (*1-882071-87-5*) B&B Audio.

— Mourn the Living. LC 99-45469. 157p. 1999. 20.95 (*0-7862-2211-5*) Five Star.

Collins, Max A. The Mummy: A Novel. 256p. 1999. mass mkt. 5.99 (*0-425-16948-0*) Blvd Books.

— Swimsuit Sweeties. (Artist Archives Ser.). (Illus.). 32p. 1999. pap. 11.95 (*1-888054-35-2*, Pub. by Collectors Pr) Universe.

— The Titanic Murders. 272p. (Orig.). 1999. mass mkt. 5.99 (*0-425-16810-7*, Prime Crime) Berkley Pub.

— Varga Girls I. LC 99-28117. (Artist Archives Ser.). (Illus.). 32p. 1999. pap. 11.95 (*1-888054-31-X*, Pub. by Collectors Pr) Universe.

— Varga Girls II. LC 99-28118. (Artist Archives Ser.). (Illus.). 32p. 1999. pap. 11.95 (*1-888054-32-8*, Pub. by Collectors Pr) Universe.

Collins, Max Allan. Air Force One Has Landed. 1997. mass mkt. 5.99 (*0-345-41975-8*) Ballantine Pub Grp.

An Asterisk (*) at the beginning of an entry indicates that the title is appearing for the first time.

— Butcher's Dozen. 1998. 19.95 (*0-7862-1662-X*, Five Star MI) Mac Lib Ref.

— Damned in Paradise: A Nathan Heller Novel. 320p. 1998. mass mkt. 5.99 (*0-451-19104-8*, Sig) NAL.

— Daylight. 208p. 1996. mass mkt. 5.99 (*1-57297-155-X*) Blvd Books.

— Dick Tracy: Tracy's Wartime Memories. (U. S. Classics Ser.). (Illus.). 64p. 1986. pap. 5.95 (*0-912277-32-7*) K Pierce Bks.

— Dick Tracy & Nightmare Machine. (Illus.). 124p. 1991. pap. 3.50 (*0-8125-1344-4*, Pub. by Tor Bks) St Martin.

— Earl MacPherson: The Sketchbook Pin-Ups. Manchur, Gail, ed. (Illus.). 64p. 1997. 9.95 (*1-888054-10-7*, 54107) Collectors Pr.

— Flying Blind. LC 98-4901. 352p. 1998. 24.95 (*0-525-94311-0*) NAL.

— Flying Blind. 368p. 1999. mass mkt. 5.99 (*0-451-19262-1*) NAL.

***Collins, Max Allan.** For the Boys! The Racy Pin-Ups of WWII. Bennett, Ann Granning, ed. LC 99-55701. (Illus.). 144p. 2000. 39.95 (*1-888054-39-5*, 54395, Pub. by Collectors Pr) Universe.

Collins, Max Allan. Gil Elvgren Vol. I: The Wartime Pin-Ups. Manchur, Gail, ed. (Illus.). 64p. 1997. 9.95 (*1-888054-08-5*, 54085) Collectors Pr.

***Collins, Max Allan.** The Hindenburg Murders. 272p. 2000. mass mkt. 6.50 (*0-425-17409-3*, Prime Crime) Berkley Pub.

— Majic Man. (Nathan Heller Novels Ser.). 2000. mass mkt. 8.99 (*0-451-19945-6*, Pub. by Signet) Penguin Books.

Collins, Max Allan. Mommy. 272p. (Orig.). 1997. mass mkt. 4.99 (*0-8439-4322-X*, Leisure Bks) Dorchester Pub Co.

— Mommy's Day. 272p. 1998. mass mkt. 4.99 (*0-8439-4386-6*, Leisure Bks) Dorchester Pub Co.

***Collins, Max Allan.** Mommy's Day. 272p. 1999. reprint ed. mass mkt. 4.99 (*0-8439-4640-7*, Pub. by Dorchester Pub Co) CMG.

— Murder by the Numbers, Set. 1994. 19.95 incl. audio (*1-882071-47-6*) B&B Audio.

Collins, Max Allan. Nice Weekend for a Murder. 208p. 1994. mass mkt. 3.99 (*0-8125-0138-1*, Pub. by Tor Bks) St Martin.

— NYPD Blue Pt. 1: Blue Beginning. 48p. 1998. pap. 7.00 (*0-14-081644-5*) Viking Penguin.

***Collins, Max Allan.** NYPD Blue Pt. 1: Blue Beginning. rev. ed. (Penguin Readers : Level 3). 1p. (YA). 1999. pap. text 7.00 (*0-582-40170-4*) Longman.

Collins, Max Allan. Pin-Up Poster Book: The Billy DeVorss Collection. LC 97-66771. (Illus.). 48p. 1997. pap. 17.95 (*1-888054-11-5*, 54115) Collectors Pr.

— Road to Perdition. Heifer, Andrew, ed. (Illus.). 304p. 1998. pap. 13.95 (*1-56389-449-1*) DC Comics.

— Road to Perdition. (Illus.). 304p. 1984. per. 1.50 (*0-671-00921-4*) PB.

— Saving Private Ryan. 1998. mass mkt. 6.50 (*0-451-19727-5*, Sig) NAL.

***Collins, Max Allan.** U-571. 256p. 2000. mass mkt. 6.50 (*0-380-81290-8*, Avon Bks) Morrow Avon.

Collins, Max Allan. U. S. Marshals. 1998. mass mkt. 5.99 (*0-425-16438-1*) Berkley Pub.

— Waterworld. 1995. mass mkt. 5.99 (*1-57297-001-4*); mass mkt. 5.99 (*1-57297-002-2*) Blvd Books.

Collins, Max Allan & Elvgren, Drake. Elvgren: His Life & Art. Bennett, Ann G., ed. LC 97-51938. (Illus.). 202p. 1998. 39.95 (*1-888054-05-0*, 54050) Collectors Pr.

— Elvgren: His Life & Art. limited ed. Bennett, Ann G., ed. LC 97-51938. (Illus.). 202p. 1998. 69.95 (*1-888054-17-4*, 54174) Collectors Pr.

Collins, Max Allan & Hagenauer, George. True Crime: G-Men & Gangsters - From Slum Gangs to the Mafia. (Illus.). 61p. 1998. pap. text 5.00 (*0-7881-5561-X*) DIANE Pub.

Collins, Max Allan & Locher, Dick, compiled by. Dick Tracy Casebook. (Illus.). 224p. (Orig.). 1990. pap. 15.96 (*0-685-33413-9*) St Martin.

Collins, Max Allan & Traylor, James L. One Lonely Knight: Mickey Spillane's Mike Hammer. LC 84-71256. 186p. 1984. 20.95 (*0-87972-301-7*); pap. 11.95 (*0-87972-302-5*) Bowling Green Univ Popular Press.

Collins, Max Allan, ed. see Capp, Al.

Collins, Max Allan, ed. see Gotto, Ray.

Collins, Max Allan, ed. see Spillane, Mickey, pseud.

***Collins, Melanie M.** The Directory of Stained Glass Books & Patterns, Vol. 6. 59p. 1998. pap. 19.95 (*0-936459-42-5*) Stained Glass.

Collins, Melvin, Jr. Common Knowledge - Discipline: Children Don't Come with Instructions. Cullen, Emily A. & Salazar, Yolanda L., eds. (Life Skills Ser.). 1991. 2.25 (*1-877709-15-8*) ADAPT Pub Co.

Collins, Melvin, Jr., jt. auth. see Salazar, Yolanda L.

Collins, Merle. Angel. 2nd ed. 304p. 1998. pap. 12.95 (*1-58005-014-X*) Seal Pr WA.

— Lady in a Boat: Poems. 1999. pap. text 12.95 (*1-885214-22-7*) Azul Edits.

Collins, Merle, jt. ed. see Cobham, Rhonda.

***Collins, Michael.** Alessi. 1999. 14.95 (*1-85868-737-3*, Pub. by Carlton Bks Ltd) Natl Bk Netwk.

Collins, Michael. Banks & Industrial Finance in Britain, 1800-1939. (New Studies in Economic & Social History: Vol. 12). 118p. (C). 1995. text 34.95 (*0-521-55271-0*); pap. text 10.95 (*0-521-55782-8*) Cambridge U Pr.

— Carrying the Fire. rev. ed. LC 98-72579. (Adventure Library Ser.: Vol. 15). (Illus.). 412p. 1998. reprint ed. 35.00 (*1-885283-14-8*) Advent Library.

— Chasing Eights. 400p. 1992. reprint ed. pap. text, mass mkt. 4.99 (*0-8439-3274-0*) Dorchester Pub Co.

— Critical Crosscurrents in Education. LC 97-52360. 214p. 1998. 26.50 (*0-89464-755-5*) Krieger.

— Diagnosis & Treatment of Global Aphasia. (Illus.). 194p. (Orig.). (C). 1991. reprint ed. pap. text 45.00 (*1-879105-23-3*, A013) Singular Publishing.

— Flying to the Moon: An Astronaut's Story. 2nd rev. ed. LC 93-42001. (Illus.). 172p. (J). (gr. 5 up). 1994. pap. 4.50 (*0-374-42356-3*) FS&G.

— The Network Toolkit Vol. II: Business Opportunity Networks. 77p. (Orig.). (C). 1997. pap. 40.00 (*0-9636927-6-3*) Reg Tech Strat.

— The Path to Freedom: Articles & Speeches. LC 95-72790. 160p. 1996. pap. 10.95 (*1-57098-064-0*) Roberts Rinehart.

— Red Rosa. 304p. 1989. reprint ed. mass mkt. 3.95 (*0-373-97099-4*) Harlequin Bks.

Collins, Michael, ed. Central Banking in History, 3 vols., Set. (International Library of Macroeconomic & Financial History: Vol. 10). 1264p. 1993. 465.00 (*1-85278-569-1*) E Elgar.

Collins, Michael & Price, Matthew. Story of Christianity: A Celebration of 2,000 Years of Faith. LC 99-23294. 240p. 1999. 29.95 (*0-7894-4605-7*) DK Pub Inc.

Collins, Michael, et al. Ethics of Change: Humanistic Values vs. Technological Imperatives. LC 88-83425. (Proceedings of the February Forums Ser.: Vol. 2). (Illus.). 222p. (Orig.). 1989. pap. text 15.00 (*1-882070-03-8*) Atlantic Ctr Arts.

— Show Me the Money: Business Opportunity Networks. Broun, Daniel, ed. 59p. (Orig.). (C). 1997. pap. 20.00 (*0-9636927-5-5*) Reg Tech Strat.

Collins, Michael, jt. auth. see Collins, Blackie.

Collins, Michael, jt. ed. see Moore, Kenneth.

Collins, Michael, ed. see Rossini, Gioachino.

Collins, Michael, ed. see Scarlatti, Alessandro.

Collins, Michael B. Clovis Blade Technology. LC 98-47835. 232p. 1999. 40.00 (*0-292-71215-4*) U of Tex Pr.

Collins, Michael F. & Pharoah, Timothy M. Transport Organisation in a Great City: The Case of London. LC 74-77339. 660p. reprint ed. pap. 200.00 (*0-608-14201-8*, 202187700026) Bks Demand.

Collins, Michael G. Buying or Selling an Insurance Broker. (C). 1986. 250.00 (*0-7855-4310-4*, Pub. by Witherby & Co) St Mut.

— Insurance of the Person. 100p. (C). 1990. 69.00 (*0-948691-87-5*, Pub. by Witherby & Co) St Mut.

— Insurances of the Person. 120p. (C). 1987. pap. 75.00 (*0-948691-72-7*, Pub. by Witherby & Co) St Mut.

— Introduction to Insurance. 121p. (C). 1990. 95.00 (*1-85609-004-3*, Pub. by Witherby & Co) St Mut.

— Introduction to Insurance. 3rd ed. 116p. (C). 1988. pap. 65.00 (*0-948691-73-5*, Pub. by Witherby & Co) St Mut.

— Litigation in a Nutshell - Section 1983. LC 97-30637. (Paralegal). 351p. (C). 1997. pap. text 15.00 (*0-314-21190-X*) West Pub.

— Motor Insurance. 120p. (C). 1989. 75.00 (*0-948691-74-3*, Pub. by Witherby & Co) St Mut.

Collins, Michael J. Shakespeare's Sweet Thunder: Essays on the Early Comedies. LC 96-5747. (Illus.). 256p. 1997. 40.50 (*0-87413-582-6*, 96-5747) U Delaware Pr.

— Western European Integration: Implications for U. S. Policy & Strategy. LC 91-26376. 160p. 1992. 47.95 (*0-275-94170-1*, C4170, Praeger Pubs) Greenwood.

Collins, Michael L. That Damned Cowboy: Theodore Roosevelt & the American West, 1883-1898. (Recent American History Ser.: Vol. 2). 229p. (C). 1989. text 58.95 (*0-8204-1004-7*) P Lang Pubng.

Collins, Michael L., jt. auth. see Porter, Elias H.

Collins, Michael M. Genetics & Ecology of a Hybrid Zone in Hyalophora: Lepidoptera: Saturniidae. LC 83-18019. (University of California Publications in Entomology: No. 104, March 1984). 107p. 1984. pap. 33.20 (*0-7837-7475-3*, 204919700010) Bks Demand.

Collins, Michael P. Manufacturer's Guide to Business Marketing: How Small & Mid-Size Companies Can Increase Profits with Limited Resources. LC 94-11216. 240p. 1994. text 45.00 (*1-55623-837-1*, Irwn Prfssnl) McGraw-Hill Prof.

Collins, Michael T., jt. ed. see Manning, Elizabeth J. B.

Collins, Micheal. Minnesota Strip. 1988. pap. 3.95 (*0-373-97093-5*) Harlequin Bks.

Collins, Mike. Windows NT Infrastructure Design. LC 97-38048. 623p. 1998. pap. text 49.95 (*1-55558-170-6*, Digital DEC) Buttrwrth-Heinemann.

Collins, Mike, ed. see Matthews, David L., 3rd.

Collins, Miki & Collins, Julie. Dog Driver: A Guide for the Serious Musher. LC 90-523. (Illus.). 396p. 1991. 32.95 (*0-931866-48-0*) Alpine Pubns.

— Riding the Wild Side of Denali: Alaska Adventures with Horses & Huskies. Ummel, Christine, ed. LC 97-78446. (Illus.). 224p. 1998. pap. 14.95 (*0-945397-64-X*) Epicenter Pr.

***Collins, Minta.** Medieval Herbals: The Illustrative Traditions. (Illus.). 256p. 1999. pap. text 34.95 (*0-8020-8313-7*) U of Toronto Pr.

Collins, Mitchell. Assessment Manual for Health & Physical Fitness: Fitness for Living. 96p. (C). 1996. pap. text, spiral bd. 19.95 (*0-8403-8772-5*) Kendall-Hunt.

Collins, Monty, jt. auth. see Ullman, Elwood.

Collins, Myrtle T. & Benjamin, Susan J. Survival Kit for Teachers & Parents. 2nd ed. LC 92-43037. 1993. 12.95 (*0-673-36035-0*, GoodYrBooks) Addson-Wesley Educ.

Collins, N. M., jt. auth. see New, Tim R.

Collins, N. Mark & Morris, Michael G. Threatened Swallowtail Butterflies of the World. (IUCN Red Data Bks.). (Illus.). 401p. 1985. 30.00 (*2-88032-603-6*, Pub. by IUCN) Island Pr.

***Collins, Nancy.** Darkest Heart. (Borealis Legends Ser.). 2000. pap. 11.99 (*1-56504-845-8*) White Wolf.

Collins, Nancy. A Dozen Black Roses. 1996. 21.99 (*0-614-20660-X*, Wrld of Darkness) White Wolf.

— A Dozen Black Roses. 1997. reprint ed. pap. 11.99 (*1-56504-873-3*, 11019, Wrld of Darkness) White Wolf.

***Collins, Nancy.** Sunglasses after Dark. anniversary ed. (Borealis Ser.). 2000. pap. text 11.99 (*1-56504-849-0*) White Wolf.

Collins, Nancy A. Angels on Fire. 1998. pap. 11.99 (*1-56504-909-8*, 12999, Borealis) White Wolf.

— Dark Love. 1996. mass mkt. 5.99 (*0-451-45550-9*, ROC) NAL.

— Dhampire: Stillborn. Stathis, L., ed. (Illus.). 64p. 1996. pap. 5.95 (*1-56389-256-1*, Pub. by DC Comics) Time Warner.

— A Dozen Black Roses. (Illus.). 1996. 21.99 (*1-56504-872-5*, Wrld of Darkness) White Wolf.

— Fantastic Four: To Free Atlantis. 320p. (Orig.). 1995. mass mkt. 5.99 (*1-57297-054-5*) Blvd Books.

— Midnight Blue: The Sonja Blue Collection. LC 95-215664. (Illus.). 1995. pap. 14.99 (*1-56504-900-4*, 13000, Borealis) White Wolf.

— Nameless Sins. limited ed. (Classics Revisited Ser.). 1994. boxed set 60.00 (*0-9629659-7-9*) Gauntlet.

— Walking Wolf. 1995. 25.00 (*0-929480-42-2*) Mark Ziesing.

Collins, Nancy A., et al, eds. Forbidden Acts. 400p. (Orig.). 1995. mass mkt. 5.99 (*0-380-77915-3*, Avon Bks) Morrow Avon.

Collins, Nancy A., et al. Dark Destiny: Proprietors of Fate. Kramer, Edward E., ed. (Illus.). 1996. pap. 5.99 (*1-56504-816-4*, 11811, Wrld of Darkness) White Wolf.

— Elric: Tales of the White Wolf. Kramer, Edward E., ed. (Illus.). 1996. pap. 5.99 (*1-56504-174-7*, 12502, Borealis) White Wolf.

Collins, Nancy A., jt. auth. see Kramer, Edward E.

Collins, Nancy W. In the Shadow of Gray Tower. LC 99-94602. iv, 200p. 1999. pap. 13.00 (*0-9669515-0-6*) N W Collins.

Collins, Nate. Matters of the Heart. LC 96-90791. (Orig.). 1997. pap. 10.95 (*0-533-12177-9*) Vantage.

Collins, Neil. Irish Politics Today. 2nd ed. (Politics Today Ser.). 128p. 1992. 49.95 (*0-685-52914-2*, Pub. by Manchester Univ Pr) St Martin.

— Political Issues in Ireland Today. 2nd ed. LC 99-41937. 210p. 1999. 69.95 (*0-7190-5403-6*, Pub. by Manchester Univ Pr) St Martin.

— Political Issues in Ireland Today, 2nd Ed. 2nd ed. LC 99-41937. 1999. pap. text 24.95 (*0-7190-5404-4*, Pub. by Manchester Univ Pr) St Martin.

— Politics & Elections in 19th Century Liverpool. (Nineteenth Century Ser.). (Illus.). 256p. 1994. 86.95 (*1-85928-076-5*, Pub. by Scolar Pr) Ashgate Pub Co.

Collins, Neil & Cradden, Terry. Irish Politics Today. 3rd ed. LC 96-40139. 1997. 69.95 (*0-7190-5135-5*, Pub. by Manchester Univ Pr) St Martin.

***Collins, Nigel, et al, eds.** Seasons of Life: A Poetic Anthology. LC 99-46312. (Literary Classics). 235p. 1999. pap. 14.95 (*1-57392-771-6*) Prometheus Bks.

***Collins, Nina L.** Library in Alexandria & the Bible in Greek. 176p. 2000. 53.00 (*90-04-11866-7*) Brill Academic Pubs.

Collins, Norma, ed. see Ruberry, Mary.

Collins, Norman. Facts of Fiction. LC 70-111821. (Essay Index Reprint Ser.). 1977. 20.95 (*0-8369-1599-2*) Ayer.

Collins, Orvis & Collins, June M. Interaction & Social Structure. (Approaches to Semiotics Ser.: No. 32). 1973. text 44.65 (*3-11-000031-8*) Mouton.

***Collins, Owen.** Wisdom of Jesus. 1999. pap. 5.95 (*0-00-628131-1*, Pub. by HarpC) Trafalgar.

Collins, Owen, ed. The Classic Bible Commentary: An Essential Collection of HIstory's Finest Commentaries in One Volume. LC 99-31863. 1584p. 1999. 39.99 (*1-58134-124-5*) Crossway Bks.

***Collins, Owen, ed.** The Daily Book of Common Prayer: Readings & Prayers Through the Year. LC 99-88804. 372p. 2000. pap. 15.00 (*0-8028-4711-0*) Eerdmans.

— 2000 Years of Classic Christian Prayers: A Collection for Public & Personal Use. 342p. 2000. reprint ed. pap. 20.00 (*1-57075-306-7*) Orbis Bks.

Collins, Owen, ed. see Backhouse, Robert.

Collins, P. & Beale, C. The Cardioprotective Role of HRT: A Clinical Update. (Illus.). 60p. (C). 1996. pap. text 24.95 (*1-85070-740-5*) Prthnon Pub.

Collins, P., jt. auth. see Lyusternik, L.

Collins, P. A., ed. see International Symposium on Aboveground Storage Tan.

Collins, P. D. & Martin, A. D. Hadron Interactions. (Graduate Student Series in Physics). (Illus.). 180p. (C). 1984. pap. 49.00 (*0-85274-768-3*) IOP Pub.

Collins, P. D. & Squires, E. J. Regge Poles in Particle Physics. (Tracts in Modern Physics Ser.: Vol. 45). 1968. 73.95 (*0-387-04339-X*) Spr-Verlag.

Collins, P. D., et al. Particle Physics & Cosmology. LC 88-33938. 512p. 1989. 186.95 (*0-471-60088-1*) Wiley.

Collins, P. E., ed. see James, Paul.

Collins, P. Elizabeth. Secrets Unbecoming. LC 99-90487. 365p. 1999. 25.00 (*0-7388-0420-7*); pap. 15.00 (*0-7388-0421-5*) Xlibris Corp.

Collins, Pamela, jt. ed. see Morton, Brian.

Collins, Pamela C., jt. auth. see Blessington, Thomas M.

Collins, Pat. Finding Faith in Troubled Times. 208p. (Orig.). 1993. pap. 9.95 (*1-85607-066-2*) Twenty-Third.

— Unveiling the Heart: How to Overcome Evil. LC 95-133025. 130p. 1996. pap. text 12.95 (*1-85390-239-X*) Ignatius Pr.

Collins, Pat L. I Am an Artist. (Illus.). 32p. (J). (gr. k-3). 1994. pap. 8.95 (*1-56294-729-X*) Millbrook Pr.

— The Quiet Woman Wakes up Shouting. 40p. 1998. pap. 8.95 (*0-9649463-7-8*) Folly Cove.

— Waiting for Baby Joe. Tucker, Kathy, ed. LC 89-21457. (Albert Whitman Concept Bks.). (Illus.). 48p. (J). (ps-2). 1990. lib. bdg. 13.95 (*0-8075-8625-0*) A Whitman.

***Collins, Pat Lowery.** Signs & Wonders. LC 99-10647. 192p. (YA). (gr. 5-9). 1999. 15.00 (*0-395-97119-5*) HM.

Collins, Patricia, ed. see Marsicano, Ed.

Collins, Patricia H. Fighting Words: Black Women & the Search for Justice. LC 98-17051. (Contradictions of Modernity Ser.: Vol. 7). 304p. 1998. 47.95 (*0-8166-2376-7*); pap. 18.95 (*0-8166-2377-5*) U of Minn Pr.

Collins, Patricia H., jt. auth. see Andersen, Margaret L.

***Collins, Patricia Hill.** Black Feminist Thought: Knowledge, Consciousness & Politics of Empowerment. 2nd ed. LC 99-29144. 320p. 2000. text 80.00 (*0-415-92483-9*) Routledge.

— Black Feminist Thought: Knowledge, Consciousness & the Politics of Empowerment. 2nd ed. LC 99-29144. 320p. 2000. pap. 19.95 (*0-415-92484-7*) Routledge.

Collins, Patricia Hill, jt. auth. see Andersen, Margaret L.

Collins, Patricia L. Holy Week in San Miguel: A Story of Faithfulness. LC 96-125649. (Illus.). 110p. (Orig.). 1994. pap. 12.50 (*0-9640461-0-5*) P L Collins.

Collins, Patricia W. Cambria County, Pa Willbook Index: 1804-1900. 1983. per. 10.00 (*1-55856-039-4*, 491) Closson Pr.

Collins, Patricia W. Marriages & Deaths from the Cambria Tribune, Vol. 4. 242p. 1985. per. 18.00 (*0-933227-42-6*, 307) Closson Pr.

Collins, Patricia W., ed. Cambria Tribune Marriages & Deaths, Vol. 5. 302p. 1986. pap. text 23.00 (*0-933227-58-2*, 308) Closson Pr.

— Marriages & Deaths from the Cambria Tribune, Vol. 1. 32p. 1981. per. 7.00 (*0-933227-18-3*, 304) Closson Pr.

— Marriages & Deaths from the Cambria Tribune, Vol. 2. 61p. 1982. per. 8.00 (*0-933227-23-X*, 305) Closson Pr.

Collins, Patrick. Living in Troubled Lands: Beating the Terrorist Threat Overseas. 192p. 1991. 20.00 (*0-87364-198-1*) Paladin Pr.

— Say It with Power & Confidence. LC 97-29006. 352p. (C). 1997. pap. text 16.95 (*0-13-614280-X*) P-H.

Collins, Patrick D. & Jackson, A. Applied Mechanics. LC 75-301190. (Illus.). 341p. reprint ed. pap. 105.80 (*0-8357-5680-7*, 203035200068) Bks Demand.

Collins, Paul. British Motorcycles since 1900. 128p. 1998. 24.95 (*0-7110-2490-1*, Pub. by Ian Allan) Motorbooks Intl.

***Collins, Paul.** Oracle 8 DBA; Database Administration Exam Cram. LC 00-22938. (Oracle Certified Professional Ser.). (Illus.). 404p. 2000. pap. text 29.99 (*1-57610-603-9*) Coriolis Grp.

Collins, Paul. Small Garden Design. LC 99-195852. (Illus.). 128p. 1998. pap. 14.95 (*0-8069-3787-4*) Sterling.

***Collins, Paul.** Tricksters LC 99-191650. (Supa Doopers Ser.). 56p. 1999. write for info. (*0-7608-3287-0*) Sundance Pub.

— Upon This Rock: The Popes & Their Changing Role. 350p. 2000. 24.95 (*0-522-84849-4*, Pub. by Melbourne Univ Pr) Paul & Co Pubs.

Collins, Paul, ed. Administration for Development in Nigeria: Introduction & Readings. 337p. (Orig.). 1981. pap. text 24.95 (*978-2308-00-5*) Transaction Pubs.

Collins, Paula, jt. auth. see Bergwall Productions Staff.

Collins, Paula, jt. auth. see Huang, Han-Uei.

Collins, Paula, jt. auth. see Intellipro Staff.

Collins, Penny. Freshwater Fish Identification. Boye, Amelia, ed. & illus. by. (Freshwater Fish Identification-Slide Ser.). 68p. (Orig.). (C). 1995. pap. text 17.95 (*1-56502-008-1*, 4040N) Ohio Agri Educ.

Collins-Perry, Bobbie, ed. North Carolina's Literary Resource Guide. 5th ed. 92p. 1999. pap. 10.00 (*1-883314-10-0*) NC Writers Network.

Collins-Perry, Bobbie, ed. see Hobson, Linda, et al.

Collins, Peter. Changing Ideals in Modern Architecture. (Illus.). 312p. 1965. pap. 22.95 (*0-7735-0048-0*, Pub. by McG-Queens Univ Pr) CUP Services.

— Changing Ideals in Modern Architecture. 2nd ed. (Illus.). 416p. 1998. pap. 22.95 (*0-7735-1775-8*, Pub. by McG-Queens Univ Pr); text 65.00 (*0-7735-1704-9*, Pub. by McG-Queens Univ Pr) CUP Services.

— Pathways to Ulster's Past: Sources for Local Studies. LC 99-165840. (Illus.). 150p. 1998. pap. 13.95 (*0-85389-693-3*, Pub. by Inst Irish Studies) Irish Bks Media.

Collins, Peter, ed. Nationalism & Unionism: Conflict in Ireland, 1885-1921. 2nd ed. LC 94-193877. (Illus.). 206p. 1996. reprint ed. pap. 19.95 (*0-85389-495-7*, Pub. by Inst Irish Studies) Irish Bks Media.

Collins, Peter & Blair, David, eds. Australian English: The Language of a New Society. 300p. (Orig.). 1989. pap. text 39.95 (*0-7022-2110-4*, Pub. by Univ Queensland Pr) Intl Spec Bk.

Collins, Peter & Lee, David, eds. The Clause in English: In Honor of Rodney Huddleston. LC 98-39788. (Studies in Language Companion Ser.: Vol. 45). xv, 342p. 1999. 89.00 (*1-55619-931-7*) J Benjamins Pubng Co.

Collins, Peter C. Cleft & Pseudo-Cleft Constructions in English. (Theoretical Linguistics Ser.). 248p. (C). (gr. 13). 1991. 85.00 (*0-415-06328-0*, A6156) Routledge.

Collins, Peter H. Ideology After the Fall of Communism. LC 92-40391. (Briefings Ser.). 1993. pap. 14.95 (*0-7145-2970-2*) M Boyars Pubs.

Collins, Peter M. & Ferrier, Robert J. Monosaccharides: Their Chemistry & Their Roles in Natural Products. LC 94-26989. 594p. 1995. pap. 69.95 (*0-471-95343-1*) Wiley.

Collins, Phil, jt. auth. see Stevens, R. Paul.

Collins, Philip. The Art of the Cocktail: One Hundred Classic Cocktail Recipes. (Illus.). 120p. 1992. pap. 12.95 (*0-8118-0154-3*) Chronicle Bks.

— Charles Dickens. (Critical Heritage Ser.). 602p. 1987. 69.50 (*0-7100-2942-X*, 69073, Routledge Thoemms) Routledge.

— Dickens & Crime. 3rd ed. LC 94-25477. 1995. pap. 19.95 (*0-312-12327-2*) St Martin.

C

***Collins, Philip.** Pastime: Telling Time from 1879 to 1969. (Illus.). 95p. 1999. text 17.00 (*0-7881-6007-9*) DIANE Pub.

Collins, Philip. Radios: The Golden Age. (Illus.). 128p. 1987. 29.95 (*0-87701-477-9*); pap. 17.95 (*0-87701-419-1*) Chronicle Bks.

Collins, Philip. Radios: The Golden Age. LC 96-37591. (Illus.). 120p. 1997. reprint ed. 12.98 (*1-884822-66-5*) Blck Dog & Leventhal.

Collins, Philip, intro. Hard Times. 294p. 1994. 4.95 (*0-460-87450-0*, Everyman's Classic Lib) Tuttle Pubng.

Collins, Philip, ed. see Dickens, Charles.

***Collins, Philip R.** Aneroid Barometers & their Restoration. (Illus.). 212p. 1998. 35.00 (*0-948382-11-2*, Pub. by Baros Bks) Antique Collect.

Collins, Philip R. Care & Restoration of Barometers. (Illus.). 128p. 1997. pap. 14.95 (*0-948382-05-8*, Pub. by Baros Bks) Antique Collect.

Collins Publishers. Britain. 1999. 12.95 (*0-00-448825-3*) Collins SF.

— Ireland. 1999. 12.95 (*0-00-448827-X*) Collins SF.

***Collins Publishers Staff.** Australia. (Illus.). 2000. pap. text 12.95 (*0-00-448900-4*) Collins.

— Indian Subcontinent: India, Pakistan, Bangladesh, Sri Lanka. 2000. pap. text 12.95 (*0-00-448764-8*) Collins.

Collins Publishers Staff. The International Garlic Cookbook. 2nd ed. LC 95-16656. (Illus.). 96p. 1995. 12.95 (*0-00-225056-X*) Collins SF.

— Scotland. 1999. 12.95 (*0-00-448826-1*) Collins SF.

***Collins-Queen, Niki.** Earth, the Forgotten Temple: A Woman's Spirit Quest in the Wilderness. 210p. 1999. pap. 12.95 (*0-9672112-0-4*) Impala Pr.

Collins, R. New Orleans Jazz - A Revised History: The Development of American Music from the Origin to the Big Bands. LC 95-90004. (Illus.). 290p. 1996. 21.95 (*0-533-11427-6*) Vantage.

Collins, R., et al, eds. Nondestructive Testing of Materials. LC 95-7902. (Studies in Applied Electromagnetics & Mechanics: Vol. 8). 362p. (YA). (gr. 12). 1996. 121.00 (*90-5199-239-4*, 239-4) IOS Press.

Collins, R. Douglas. Algorithmic Approach to Treatment. LC 96-49629. 600p. 1997. write for info. (*0-89640-336-X*); pap. text. write for info. (*0-89640-291-6*) Igaku-Shoin.

— Algorithmic Approach to Treatment. LC 96-49629. 528p. 1997. pap. 35.00 (*0-683-30303-1*) Lppncott W & W.

— Algorithmic Diagnosis of Symptoms & Signs: Cost Effective Approach. LC 95-1040. 616p. 1995. pap. 35.00 (*0-89640-283-5*) Igaku-Shoin.

— Algorithmic Selection & Interpretation of Diagnostic Tests. LC 97-31730. 1997. write for info. (*0-683-30426-7*) Lppncott W & W.

— Differential Diagnosis in Primary Care. 2nd ed. LC 65-9814. (Illus.). 560p. 1987. text 49.95 (*0-397-50816-6*, Lippnctt) Lppncott W & W.

Collins, R. L. & Buchsbaum, Herbert J., eds. Ovulation Induction. (Clinical Perspectives in Obstetrics & Gynecology Ser.). (Illus.). 184p. 1990. 89.00 (*0-387-97351-6*) Spr-Verlag.

Collins, R. Lorraine, et al, eds. Alcohol & the Family: Research & Clinical Perspectives. LC 89-37204. (Substance Abuse Ser.). 386p. 1990. lib. bdg. 45.00 (*0-89862-169-0*) Guilford Pubns.

Collins, R. T., et al, eds. Silicon-Based Optoelectronic Materials. (Symposium Proceedings Ser.: Vol. 298). 461p. 1993. text 65.00 (*1-55899-194-8*) Materials Res.

***Collins, R. W., et al, eds.** Amorphous & Heterogeneous Silicon Thin Films -- 2000: Materials Research Society Symposium Proceedings, Vol. 609. 2000. text 82.00 (*1-55899-517-X*) Materials Res.

Collins Radio Company Staff. Amateur Single Sideband. LC 77-71665. (Illus.). 1977. reprint ed. pap. text 4.95 (*0-918232-05-8*, HR-SSB) Comm Tech.

Collins-Ranadive, Gail. Writing Re-Creatively: A Spiritual Quest for Women. 104p. 1994. pap. 10.00 (*1-55896-276-X*, Skinner Hse Bks) Unitarian Univ.

Collins, Randall. Four Sociological Traditions. expanded rev. ed. 336p. (C). 1994. pap. text 22.95 (*0-19-508208-7*) OUP.

***Collins, Randall.** Macrohistory: Essays in Sociology of the Long Run. LC 99-31771. 312p. 1999. 65.00 (*0-8047-3523-9*) Stanford U Pr.

— Macrohistory: Essays in The Sociology of Then Long Run. LC 99-31771. 1999. pap. text 18.95 (*0-8047-3600-6*) Stanford U Pr.

Collins, Randall. Sociological Insight: An Introduction to Non-Obvious Sociology. 2nd ed. 224p. (C). 1992. pap. text 19.95 (*0-19-507442-4*) OUP.

— The Sociology of Philosophies: A Global Theory of Intellectual Change. LC 97-18446. 1998. 51.95 (*0-674-81647-1*) Belknap Pr.

***Collins, Randall.** Sociology of Philosophies: A Global Theory of Intellectual Change. 2000. pap. text 24.95 (*0-674-00187-7*) HUP.

Collins, Randall. Theoretical Sociology. 565p. (C). 1988. text 57.00 (*0-15-591474-X*, Pub. by Harcourt Coll Pubs) Harcourt.

Collins, Randall, ed. Four Sociological Traditions: Selected Readings. LC 93-23445. (Illus.). 368p. 1994. pap. text 22.95 (*0-19-508702-X*) OUP.

— Sociological Theory, 1984. LC HM0024.S5573. (Jossey-Bass Social & Behavioral Science Ser.). 452p. pap. 140.20 (*0-7837-0164-0*, 204046100017) Bks Demand.

— Sociological Theory, 1983. LC 83-187481. (Jossey-Bass Social & Behavioral Science Ser.). (Illus.). 381p. reprint ed. pap. 118.20 (*0-8357-4875-8*, 203780700009) Bks Demand.

***Collins, Randall & Coltrane, Scott.** Sociology of Marriage & Family: Gender, Love & Property. 5th ed. 2000. pap. 39.50 (*0-534-57960-4*) Thomson Learn.

Collins, Randall & Coltrane, Scott. Sociology of Marriage & the Family: Gender, Love & Property. 4th ed. LC 94-15709. (Sociology - Intro Level). 500p. 1995. text 57.95 (*0-8304-1392-8*) Thomson Learn.

Collins, Randall & Makowsky, Michael. The Discovery of Society. 6th ed. LC 97-11606. 368p. 1997. pap., student ed. 27.50 (*0-07-011883-3*) McGraw.

Collins, Raymond. Divorce in the New Testament. (Good News Studies: Vol. 38). 405p. (Orig.). 1992. pap. text 19.95 (*0-8146-5691-9*, M Glazier) Liturgical Pr.

— First Corinthians. LC 98-51063. (Sacra Pagina Ser.). 652p. 1999. 39.95 (*0-8146-5809-1*) Liturgical Pr.

Collins, Raymond F. The Birth of the New Testament: The Origin & Development of the First Christian Generation. 324p. 1993. 29.95 (*0-8245-1276-6*) Crossroad NY.

— Preaching the Epistles. LC 95-44476. 160p. (Orig.). 1996. pap. 9.95 (*0-8091-3625-2*) Paulist Pr.

— Sexual Ethics & the New Testament: Behavior & Belief. LC 99-53598. 216p. 2000. pap. text 17.95 (*0-8245-1801-2*, Pub. by Crossroad NY) Natl Bk Netwk.

— These Things Have Been Written: Studies on the Fourth Gospel. (Louvain Theological & Pastoral Monographs). 270p. (Orig.). 1991. pap. 20.00 (*0-8028-0561-2*) Eerdmans.

Collins, Raymond F., et al. The Living Light, Vol. 32, No. 1. 88p. (Orig.). 1995. pap. 8.95 (*1-55586-062-1*) US Catholic.

Collins, Reba, ed. Will Rogers: Courtship & Correspondence, 1900-1915. (Illus.). 224p. 1992. 24.95 (*0-9632882-0-2*) Neigh & Quaid.

— Will Rogers Says. (Illus.). 86p. 1993. 11.95 (*0-9632882-1-0*) Neigh & Quaid.

Collins, Rhonda. From Patient to Payment: Insurance Procedures for the Medical Office. 240p. 1993. write for info. (*0-02-800053-6*) Glencoe.

— From Patient to Payment: Insurance Procedures for the Medical Office. 2nd ed. LC 97-28931. 1997. pap. write for info. (*0-02-801988-1*) Glencoe.

Collins, Richard. Culture, Communication, & National Identity: The Case of Canadian Television. 368p. 1990. text 55.00 (*0-8020-2733-4*); pap. text 21.95 (*0-8020-6772-7*) U of Toronto Pr.

— From Satellite to Single Market: New Communication Technology & European Public Service Television. LC 98-6977. (Research in Cultural & Media Studies). 272p. (C). 1998. 90.00 (*0-415-17970-X*) Routledge.

— John Fante: A Literary Portrait. (Essay Ser.: No. 39). 302p. 2000. pap. 18.00 (*1-55071-071-0*, , Pub. by Guernica Editions) Paul & Co Pubs.

Collins, Richard, ed. Mandeville's Used Book Price Guide: Five Year, 1989 Edition. 604p. 1988. 89.00 (*0-911182-88-8*) Price Guide.

Collins, Richard & Murroni, Cristina. New Media New Policies: Media & Communication Strategy for the Future. LC 96-33130. 233p. (Orig.). 1996. pap. text 25.95 (*0-7456-1786-7*) Blackwell Pubs.

— New Media New Policies: Media & Communication Strategy for the Future. LC 96-33130. 233p. (Orig.). 1996. text 72.95 (*0-7456-1785-9*) Blackwell Pubs.

Collins, Richard, et al. The Economics of Television: The UK Case. (Media, Culture & Society Ser.: Vol. 2). 160p. (C). 1988. text 29.95 (*0-8039-8112-0*) Sage.

Collins, Richard, jt. ed. see Alvarado, Manuel.

Collins, Richard, ed. see Collins, Richard L., et al.

Collins, Richard B., et al. Indian Water, 1985: Collected Essays. 137p. (Orig.). (C). 1986. pap. text 6.00 (*0-939890-06-2*) Am Indian LTP.

Collins, Richard C., et al. America's Downtowns: Growth, Politics & Preservation. LC 95-45752. (Illus.). 160p. (Orig.). 1995. pap. 14.95 (*0-471-14499-1*) Wiley.

Collins, Richard E. The Cooking Cardiologist. 2nd rev. ed. (Illus.). 224p. 1999. spiral bd. 21.95 (*1-889462-05-5*) Advanced Research Pr.

Collins, Richard H., jt. auth. see Collins, Lewis.

Collins, Richard H., ed. & rev. see Collins, Lewis.

Collins, Richard J., ed. see Danson, Gia E. & Danson, Julianna A.

Collins, Richard L. Air Crashes: What Went Wrong, Why & What Can Be Done about It. rev. ed. LC 91-46944. (Aviation Library). 236p. 1992. 24.95 (*1-56566-006-4*, Pub. by Thomasson-Grant) ASA Inc.

— Flying IFR. 3rd ed. LC 93-19594. 244p. 1993. 29.95 (*1-56566-043-9*) Thomasson-Grant.

***Collins, Richard L.** Flying IFR: The Practical Information You Need to Fly Actual IFR Flights. 4th rev. ed. LC 93-19594. 226p. 2000. pap. 19.95 (*1-56027-385-2*) ASA Inc.

Collins, Richard L. Flying the Weather Map. LC 91-46945. (Illus.). 244p. 1992. 29.95 (*1-56566-003-X*) Thomasson-Grant.

***Collins, Richard L.** Flying the Weather Map. 2nd rev. ed. LC 91-46945. (Illus.). 234p. 1999. pap. 19.95 (*1-56027-319-4*) ASA Inc.

Collins, Richard L. Mastering the Systems: Air Traffic Control & Weather. 256p. 1991. 24.95 (*0-02-527245-4*, Aude IN) IDG Bks.

— The Perfect Flight. 1988. text 19.95 (*0-02-527161-X*) Macmillan.

— The Perfect Flight: The Pilot's Greatest Challenge - The Search for Excellence. rev. ed. LC 93-48566. (Aviation Library). 215p. 1994. 29.95 (*1-56566-055-2*, Pub. by Thomasson-Grant) ASA Inc.

— Tips to Fly By. Friede, Eleanor, ed. LC 92-34460. 304p. 1993. 24.95 (*1-56566-035-8*) Thomasson-Grant.

***Collins, Richard L.** Tips to Fly By: Thousands of PIC Hours' Worth of Tips & Tricks of the Trade. 2nd rev. ed. LC 92-34460. 224p. 1999. pap. 19.95 (*1-56027-338-0*) ASA Inc.

Collins, Richard L., ed. Mandeville's Used Book Price Guide: Five Year, 1994 Edition. 604p. 1993. text 90.00 (*0-911182-94-2*) Price Guide.

Collins, Richard L. & Bradley, Patrick E. Instrument Flying Refresher. Friede, Eleanor, ed. LC 92-14751. 294p. 1992. 24.95 (*1-56566-023-4*) Thomasson-Grant.

***Collins, Richard L. & Bradley, Patrick E.** Instrument Flying Refresher: A Practical Way to Stay Sharp on the Fine Points of Judgment. 2nd rev. ed. LC 92-14751. 236p. 1999. pap. 19.95 (*1-56027-335-6*) ASA Inc.

Collins, Richard L., et al. The Screen Education Reader: Cinema, Television, Culture. Buscombe, Edward & Collins, Richard, eds. LC 92-25729. (Communications & Culture Ser.). 320p. (C). 1993. pap. 22.00 (*0-231-08111-1*); text 49.50 (*0-231-08110-3*) Col U Pr.

Collins, Richard L. E.D.T. Mandevilles Used Book Price Guide. 1998. 93.00 (*0-911182-12-8*) Price Guide.

***Collins, Richard S.** Piano Playing: A Handbook for the Advanced Student. Orig. Title: Piano Playing: A Positive Approach. (Illus.). 70p. 2000. pap. 22.50 (*0-9678421-0-7*) R S Collins.

Collins, Rives & Cooper, Pamela J. The Power of Story: Teaching Through Storytelling. 2nd ed. 182p. (C). 1996. reprint ed. pap. text 23.00 (*0-13-776709-9*) Allyn.

***Collins, Rives & Shannon, Julie.** Let's Fill up the House with Stories & Songs. unabridged ed. (J). (gr. k-6). 1999. audio 10.00 (*1-888019-03-4*) L M Alleycat Mus.

Collins, Rob, jt. auth. see Hammond, Merryl.

Collins, Robert. Arkansas Valley Interurban: The Electric Way. (Illus.). 60p. 1999. pap. 17.95 (*0-942035-50-X*) South Platte.

— Ghost Railroads of Kansas. 2nd ed. (Illus.). 80p. 1998. reprint ed. pap. 19.95 (*0-942035-47-X*) South Platte.

— The Glass Blower. 18p. 1997. pap. 7.95 (*0-944754-45-7*) Pudding Hse Pubns.

— Japan-Think, Ameri-Think. 1999. text 18.95 (*0-670-83815-2*, Viking) Viking Penguin.

— Kansas Pacific: An Illustrated History. (Illus.). 60p. 1998. pap. 18.95 (*0-942035-46-1*) South Platte.

Collins, Robert. You Had to Be There: An Intimate Portrait of the Generation That Survived a Depression, Won the War & Re-Invented Canada. LC 98-118585. (Illus.). 309p. 1998. text 32.50 (*0-7710-2255-7*) McCland & Stewart.

***Collins, Robert.** You Had to Be There: An Intimate Portrait of the Generation That Survived a Depression, Won the War & Re-Invented Canada. (Illus.). 320p. 2000. pap. 19.99 (*0-7710-2256-5*) McClelland & Stewart.

Collins, Robert & Peterson, Alan H. The New Aviation Identification Manual for Police Officers: An Aid for Investigating Aviation-Related Crime. rev. ed. (Illus.). 100p. 1992. pap. text 75.00 (*1-877858-07-2*, NAIDINVMPO) Amer Focus Pub.

Collins, Robert, ed. see Guenter, Abraham.

Collins, Robert A. Webster's New World French Dictionary. (ENG & FRE.). 536p. 1981. 19.95 (*0-8288-1211-X*, S60720) Fr & Eur.

Collins, Robert A. & Latham, Robert. Science Fiction & Fantasy Book Review Annual, 1990. 728p. 1991. lib. bdg. 85.00 (*0-313-28150-5*, SF90, Greenwood Pr) Greenwood.

— Science Fiction & Fantasy Book Review Annual, 1991. 896p. 1993. lib. bdg. 115.00 (*0-313-28326-5*, Greenwood Pr) Greenwood.

Collins, Robert A. & Latham, Robert, eds. Science Fiction & Fantasy Book Review Annual, 1988. 496p. 1988. lib. bdg. 75.00 (*0-313-28069-X*, SF88, Greenwood Pr) Greenwood.

— Science Fiction & Fantasy Book Review Annual, 1989. 625p. 1990. lib. bdg. 75.00 (*0-313-28070-3*, SF89, Greenwood Pr) Greenwood.

Collins, Robert A. & Pearce, Howard D., eds. The Scope of the Fantastic-Culture, Biography, Themes, Children's Literature: Selected Essays from the First International Conference on the Fantastic in Literature & Film, 11. LC 84-530. (Contributions to the Study of Science Fiction & Fantasy Ser.: No. 11). (Illus.). 284p. 1985. 62.95 (*0-313-23448-5*, COF/02) Greenwood.

— The Scope of the Fantastic-Theory, Technique, Major Authors: Selected Essays from the First International Conference on the Fantastic in Literature & Film, 10. LC 84-538. (Contributions to the Study of Science Fiction & Fantasy Ser.: No. 10). (Illus.). 295p. 1985. 59.95 (*0-313-23447-7*, COF/01) Greenwood.

Collins, Robert A., jt. auth. see Latham, Robert A.

Collins, Robert C. Neurology. Schmitt, William, ed. LC 96-48724. 224p. 1997. pap. text 36.95 (*0-7216-5992-6*, W B Saunders Co) Harcrt Hlth Sci Grp.

Collins, Robert C., jt. auth. see Francis, William H.

Collins, Robert C., jt. ed. see Pearlman, Alan L.

Collins, Robert F. America at Its Best: Opportunities in the National Guard. Rosen, Ruth C., ed. (Military Missions Ser.). (YA). (gr. 7-12). 1989. lib. bdg. 15.95 (*0-8239-1024-5*) Rosen Group.

— Basic Training: What to Expect & How to Prepare. Rosen, Ruth C., ed. (Military Missions Ser.). 196p. (YA). (gr. 7-12). 1988. lib. bdg. 15.95 (*0-8239-0833-X*) Rosen Group.

— Qualifying for Admission to the Service Academies: A Student's Guide. rev. ed. Rosen, Ruth C., ed. (Military Opportunities Ser.). (Illus.). 154p. (YA). (gr. 7-12). 1990. lib. bdg. 15.95 (*0-8239-1187-X*) Rosen Group.

— Reserve Officer Training Corps: Campus Paths to Service Commissions. (Military Opportunities Ser.). (Illus.). 148p. (YA). (gr. 7-12). 1986. lib. bdg. 15.95 (*0-8239-0695-7*) Rosen Group.

Collins, Robert G. E. J. Pratt. (World Authors Ser.). 232p. 1988. 32.95 (*0-8057-8231-1*, 342) Macmillan.

Collins, Robert G., comment. The Hand of the Arch-Sinner: Two Angrian Chronicles of Branwell Bronte, a Reader's Edition. LC 92-25034. (Illus.). 308p. (C). 1993. text 49.95 (*0-19-812258-6*, Clarendon Pr) OUP.

Collins, Robert J. Japan-Think, Ameri-Think: An Irreverent Guide to Understanding the Cultural Differences Between Us. 288p. (Orig.). 1992. pap. 12.95 (*0-14-014860-4*, Penguin Bks) Viking Penguin.

— Max Danger: The Adventures of an Expat in Tokyo. LC 87-51178. 206p. 1987. pap. 9.95 (*0-8048-1531-3*) Tuttle Pubng.

— More Max Danger: The Continuing Adventures of an Expat in Tokyo. LC 88-51066. 180p. 1988. pap. 9.95 (*0-8048-1570-4*) Tuttle Pubng.

— Murder at the Tokyo Lawn Tennis Club. 200p. (Orig.). 1994. pap. 9.95 (*0-8048-1934-3*) Tuttle Pubng.

— Murder at Tokyo American Club. 1991. pap. 9.95 (*0-8048-1673-5*) Tuttle Pubng.

***Collins, Robert M.** More: The Politics of Economic Growth in Postwar America. LC 99-22524. 304p. 2000. 35.00 (*0-19-504646-3*) OUP.

Collins, Robert O. African History in Documents - Text & Readings Vol. I: Western Africa. LC 89-70619. (Topics in World History Ser.). (Illus.). 220p. (Orig.). (C). 1990. pap. text 16.95 (*1-55876-015-6*) Wiener Pubs Inc.

— African History in Documents - Text & Readings Vol. II: Eastern Africa. LC 89-70615. (Topics in World History Ser.). 260p. (Orig.). (C). 1991. 16.95 (*1-55876-016-4*) Wiener Pubs Inc.

— African History in Documents - Text & Readings Vol. III: Central & South Africa. LC 89-70617. (Topics in World History Ser.). 289p. 1990. pap. text 16.95 (*1-55876-017-2*) Wiener Pubs Inc.

— King Leopold, England & the Upper Nile, 1899-1909. LC 68-27750. (Illus.). 364p. reprint ed. 112.90 (*0-8357-9376-1*, 201109500074) Bks Demand.

— The Waters of the Nile: An Annotated Bibliography. 343p. 1991. lib. bdg. 100.00 (*0-905450-84-1*, Pub. by H Zell Pubs) Seven Hills Bk.

— The Waters of the Nile: Hydropolitics & the Jonglei Canal, 1900-1988. (Oxford Studies in African Affairs). (Illus.). 464p. 1990. 85.00 (*0-19-821784-6*) OUP.

— The Waters of the Nile: Hydropolitics & the Jonglei Canal 1900-1988. LC 94-39649. 468p. (C). 1996. reprint ed. pap. text 24.95 (*1-55876-099-7*) Wiener Pubs Inc.

Collins, Robert O., ed. Historical Problems of Imperial Africa. rev. ed. 320p. (C). 1994. pap. text 19.95 (*1-55876-060-1*) Wiener Pubs Inc.

Collins, Robert O., et al, eds. Problems in the History of Modern Africa. (Problems in African History Ser.: Vol. III). (Illus.). 320p. (Orig.). (C). 1997. pap. text 19.95 (*1-55876-124-1*) Wiener Pubs Inc.

Collins, Robert O., intro. Problems in African History: Precolonial Centuries, Vol. 1. (Illus.). 328p. (C). 1992. pap. text 19.95 (*1-55876-059-8*) Wiener Pubs Inc.

Collins, Robert O., jt. auth. see Burr, J. Millard.

Collins, Robert W., et al, eds. Microcrystalline & Nanocrystalline Semiconductors. (MRS Symposium Proceedings Ser.: Vol. 358). 1059p. 1995. 88.00 (*1-55899-259-6*) Materials Res.

Collins, Robin, jt. auth. see Graham, N. J.

Collins, Rodnell P. & Bailey, A. Peter. Seventh Child: A Family Memoir of Malcolm X. LC 98-22141. (Illus.). 230p. 1998. 21.95 (*1-55972-491-9*, Birch Ln Pr) Carol Pub Group.

Collins, Roger. Arab Conquest of Spain: 710-797. 1995. pap. 27.95 (*0-631-19405-3*) Blackwell Pubs.

— Charlemagne. LC 98-229698. 292p. 1998. text 55.00 (*0-8020-4416-6*); pap. text 19.95 (*0-8020-8218-1*) U of Toronto Pr.

— Early Medieval Europe, 300-1000. 2nd ed. LC 98-38110. (History of Europe Ser.). 560p. 1999. pap. 20.95 (*0-312-21886-9*) St Martin.

— Early Medieval Spain: Unity in Diversity, 400-1000. 2nd ed. LC 95-4155. (New Studies in Medieval History). 1995. pap. 19.95 (*0-312-12662-X*) St Martin.

— Law, Culture & Regionalism in Early Medieval Spain. (Collected Studies: No. CS356). 336p. 1992. text 109.95 (*0-86078-308-1*, Pub. by Variorum) Ashgate Pub Co.

— Spain: An Oxford Archaeological Guide. LC 97-30251. (Oxford Archaeological Guides Ser.). (Illus.). 344p. 1998. pap. 18.95 (*0-19-285300-7*) OUP.

Collins, Roger, jt. auth. see Straw, Carole.

Collins, Ronald K., jt. auth. see Hacker, George A.

Collins, Ronald K., ed. see Gilmore, Grant.

Collins, Ross, jt. auth. see Wallace, Karen.

Collins, Rowland L., ed. see Beowulf.

Collins, Roy E. Collins. Ancestors & Descendants of James Harrah Collins & Jane Hill Collins, of Batavia Iowa, Monte Vista Colorado, & Del Norte Colorado. 82p. 1997. reprint ed. pap. 16.00 (*0-8328-8020-5*); reprint ed. lib. bdg. 26.00 (*0-8328-8019-1*) Higginson Bk Co.

Collins, Royal E. Mathematical Methods for Physicists & Engineers. 2nd unabridged ed. LC 98-28913. 15p. 1998. pap. 14.95 (*0-486-40229-0*) Dover.

Collins, Russell. The Spot. 160p. 1996. pap. 12.95 (*0-684-83421-9*) S&S Trade.

Collins, S. H. Advanced Addition. (Straight Forward Math Ser.). (Illus.). 32p. (J). (gr. 1-6). 1987. pap. 3.95 (*0-931993-15-6*, GP-015) Garlic Pr OR.

— An Alphabet of Animal Signs. (Beginning Sign Language Ser.). (Illus.). 15p. (J). (ps-k). 1994. pap. text 3.95 (*0-931993-65-2*, GP-065) Garlic Pr OR.

Collins, S. H. Basic Equations. (Applied Math Ser.). 56p. (Orig.). (YA). (gr. 7 up). 1997. pap., wbk. ed. 7.95 (*0-931993-84-9*, GP-084) Garlic Pr OR.

Collins, S. H. Emigrant's Guide to the United States of America, Containing All Things Necessary to Be Known by Every Class of Persons Emigrating to That Continent. LC 70-145476. (American Immigration Library). vi, 144p. 1971. reprint ed. lib. bdg. 24.95 (*0-89198-008-3*) Ozer.

***Collins, S. H.** Percent. (Straight Forward Math Ser.). 39p. (J). (gr. 4-8). 2000. pap., wbk. ed. 3.95 (*0-931993-25-3*, GP-025) Garlic Pr OR.

An Asterisk (*) at the beginning of an entry indicates that the title is appearing for the first time.

Collins, S. Harold. Addition. (Straight Forward Math Ser.). (Illus.). 31p. (J). (gr. 1-6). 1986. pap. 3.95 (*0-931993-06-7*, GP-006) Garlic Pr OR.

Collins, S. Harold. Adjectives & Adverbs. (Straight Forward English Ser.). 34p. (Orig.). (J). (gr. 4-8). 1990. pap., wbk. ed. 3.95 (*0-931993-35-0*, GP-035) Garlic Pr OR.

— Advanced Decimals. (Straight Forward Math Ser.). (Illus.). 36p. (J). (gr. 4-8). 1988. wbk. ed. 3.95 (*0-931993-20-2*, GP-020) Garlic Pr OR.

— Advanced Division. (Straight Forward Math Ser.). (Illus.). 34p. (J). (gr. 4-8). 1987. pap., wbk. ed. 3.95 (*0-931993-18-0*, GP-018) Garlic Pr OR.

— Advanced Fractions. (Straight Forward Math Ser.). (Illus.). 34p. (J). (gr. 4-8). 1988. pap., wbk. ed. 3.95 (*0-931993-21-0*, GP-021) Garlic Pr OR.

— Advanced Multiplication. (Straight Forward Math Ser.). (Illus.). 32p. (J). (gr. 4-6). 1987. pap., wbk. ed. 3.95 (*0-931993-17-2*, GP-017) Garlic Pr OR.

— Advanced Subtraction. (Straight Forward Math Ser.). (Illus.). 34p. (J). (gr. 1-6). 1987. pap., wbk. ed. 3.95 (*0-931993-16-4*, GP-016) Garlic Pr OR.

— Braille for the Sighted. (Illus.). 32p. 1998. pap., wbk. ed. 4.95 (*0-931993-95-4*, GP-095) Garlic Pr OR.

— Can I Help? Helping the Hearing Impaired in Emergency Situations. (Beginning Sign Language Ser.). (Illus.). 32p. (J). (gr. 1-8). 1993. pap. 3.95 (*0-931993-57-1*, GP-057) Garlic Pr OR.

— Capitalization & Punctuation. (Straight Forward English Ser.). (Illus.). 35p. (Orig.). (J). (gr. 4-6). 1990. pap. 3.95 (*0-931993-32-6*, GP-032) Garlic Pr OR.

— Caring for Young Children: Signing for Day Care Providers & Sitters. (Beginning Sign Language Ser.). (Illus.). 32p. (gr. 1-8). 1993. pap. 3.95 (*0-931993-58-X*, GP-058) Garlic Pr OR.

— Classroom Management for Substitute Teachers. (Substitute Teaching Ser.). (Illus.). 45p. (Orig.). 1982. pap. 7.95 (*0-931993-03-2*, GP-003) Garlic Pr OR.

— Coyote & Bobcat. (Sign Language Literature Ser.). (Illus.). 32p. (Orig.). (J). (gr. 2 up). 1996. pap. text 4.95 (*0-931993-81-4*, GP-081) Garlic Pr OR.

— Division. (Straight Forward Math Ser.). (Illus.). 32p. (J). (gr. 4-6). 1986. pap. 3.95 (*0-931993-13-X*, GP-013) Garlic Pr OR.

— Expanded Songs in Sign. (Beginning Sign Language Ser.). (Illus.). 31p. (J). (ps up). 1998. pap. 4.95 (*0-931993-05-9*, GP-005) Garlic Pr OR.

— The Finger Alphabet Book. (Beginning Sign Language Ser.). (Illus.). 32p. (J). (gr. 1-6). 1992. pap. 3.95 (*0-931993-46-6*, GP-046) Garlic Pr OR.

— Fractions. (Straight Forward Math Ser.). (Illus.). 33p. (J). (gr. 4-6). 1991. pap. 3.95 (*0-931993-39-3*, GP-039) Garlic Pr OR.

— Mastering the Art of Substitute Teaching. (Substitute Teaching Ser.). (Illus.). 69p. 1979. pap. 8.95 (*0-931993-02-4*, GP-002) Garlic Pr OR.

— Mastery Tests. (Straight Forward Math Ser.). (Illus.). 35p. (J). (gr. 3-6). 1992. pap. 3.95 (*0-931993-44-X*, GP-044) Garlic Pr OR.

— Mother Goose in Sign. (Beginning Sign Language Ser.). (Illus.). 15p. (J). (ps). 1994. pap. 3.95 (*0-931993-66-0*, GP-066) Garlic Pr OR.

Collins, S. Harold. Multiplication. (Straight Forward Math Ser.). (Illus.). 34p. (J). (gr. 4-6). 1986. pap. 3.95 (*0-931993-07-5*, GP-007) Garlic Pr OR.

Collins, S. Harold. Nouns & Pronouns. (Straight Forward English Ser.). (Illus.). 35p. (Orig.). (J). (gr. 4-6). 1990. pap. 3.95 (*0-931993-33-4*, GP-033) Garlic Pr OR.

— Number & Letter Games. (Beginning Sign Language Ser.). (Illus.). 29p. (J). 1995. pap. 3.95 (*0-931993-72-5*, GP-072) Garlic Pr OR.

— Pre-Algebra, Bk. 1. (Straight Forward Math Ser.). (Illus.). 34p. (YA). (gr. 6-12). 1989. pap. 3.95 (*0-931993-28-8*, GP-028) Garlic Pr OR.

— Pre-Algebra, Bk. 2. (Straight Forward Math Ser.). (Illus.). 34p. (YA). (gr. 6-12). 1989. pap. 3.95 (*0-931993-29-6*, GP-029) Garlic Pr OR.

— Pre-Geometry, Bk. 1. (Straight Forward Math Ser.). (Illus.). 29p. (YA). (gr. 6-12). 1990. pap. 3.95 (*0-931993-30-X*, GP-030) Garlic Pr OR.

— Pre-Geometry, Bk. 2. (Straight Forward Math Ser.). (Illus.). 33p. (YA). (gr. 8-12). 1990. pap. 3.95 (*0-931993-31-8*, GP-031) Garlic Pr OR.

— Prepositions, Conjunctions & Interjections. (Straight Forward English Ser.). (Illus.). 32p. (Orig.). (J). (gr. 4-8). 1992. pap. 3.95 (*0-931993-43-1*, GP-043) Garlic Pr OR.

— Raven & Water Monster. (Sign Language Literature Ser.). (Illus.). 32p. (Orig.). (J). (gr. 2 up). 1996. pap. text 4.95 (*0-931993-82-2*, GP-082) Garlic Pr OR.

— Sentences. (Straight Forward English Ser.). 34p. (Orig.). (J). (gr. 4-6). 1991. pap. 3.95 (*0-931993-41-5*, GP-041) Garlic Pr OR.

— Signing at Church. (Beginning Sign Language Ser.). (Illus.). 31p. 1998. pap. text 4.95 (*0-931993-98-9*, GP-098) Garlic Pr OR.

— Signing at School. (Beginning Sign Language Ser.). (Illus.). 32p. (J). (gr. 1-6). 1992. pap. 3.95 (*0-931993-47-4*, GP-047) Garlic Pr OR.

— Signing at Sunday School. (Beginning Sign Language Ser.). (Illus.). 31p. 1998. pap. text 4.95 (*0-931993-99-7*, GP-099) Garlic Pr OR.

Collins, S. Harold. Songs in Sign. (Beginning Sign Language Ser.). (Illus.). 16p. (J). 1995. pap. 3.95 (*0-931993-71-7*, GP-071) Garlic Pr OR.

— Sound Hearing or Hearing What You Miss. 12p. 1988. pap. 8.95 incl. reel tape (*0-931993-26-1*, GP-026) Garlic Pr OR.

Collins, S. Harold. Substitute Ingredients. rev. ed. (Substitute Teaching Ser.). 98p. 1989. pap. 8.95 (*0-931993-01-6*, GP-001) Garlic Pr OR.

— Subtraction. (Straight Forward Math Ser.). (Illus.). 34p. (J). (gr. 1-6). 1986. pap. 3.95 (*0-931993-12-1*, GP-012) Garlic Pr OR.

— Verbs. (Straight Forward English Ser.). 36p. (Orig.). (J). (gr. 4-6). 1990. pap. 3.95 (*0-931993-34-2*, GP-034) Garlic Pr OR.

Collins, S. Harold, jt. auth. see Cleveland, C. G.

Collins, S. Harold, jt. auth. see Kitterman, Jane.

Collins, S. P., jt. auth. see Lovesey, Steven W.

Collins, Sally. Small Scale Quiltmaking: Precision, Proportion & Detail. Lytle, Joyce E. & Roberts, Diana, eds. LC 95-46104. (Illus.). 112p. (Orig.). 1996. pap. 24.95 (*1-57120-009-6*) C & T Pub.

Collins, Scott L. & Wallace, Linda L., eds. Fire in North American Tallgrass Prairies. LC 90-12044. (Illus.). 192p. 1990. pap. 17.95 (*0-8061-2315-X*) U of Okla Pr.

Collins, Selwyn D. & Tibbitts, Clark. Research Memorandum on Social Aspects of Health in the Depression. LC 72-162846. (Studies in the Social Aspects of the Depression). 1974. reprint ed. 19.95 (*0-405-00849-X*) Ayer.

Collins SF Staff. Collins Gem Span Ver. 3rd ed. 256p. 1995. pap. 6.95 (*0-00-471001-0*) Collins SF.

Collins, Sharon. Lonely Planet Diving & Snorkeling Guide to Roatan & Honduras' Bay Islands. LC 93-17943. (Diving & Snorkeling Guides Ser.). 96p. 1993. pap. 14.95 (*1-55992-074-2*, Pisces Books) Lonely Planet.

— Lonely Planet Diving & Snorkeling Guide to Roatan & Honduras' Bay Islands. 2nd ed. LC 93-17943. (Pisces Diving & Snorkeling Guides Ser.). 96p. 1997. pap. 14.95 (*1-55992-093-9*, 2093, Pisces Books) Lonely Planet.

Collins, Shawn. Computing @ SIS: A Guide to Tools & Techniques. unabridged ed. Davis, Amy I., ed. 80p. (C). 1998. pap. text 12.00 (*1-893260-04-6*) Harrison Pubg.

Collins, Sheila. Half a Winter to Go. LC 76-12003. (Sunburst Originals Ser.: No. 4). 52p. (Orig.). 1976. pap. 2.25 (*0-934648-04-2*) Sunburst Pr.

Collins, Sheila D. Let Them Eat Ketchup! The Politics of Poverty & Inequality. (Cornerstone Ser.). (Illus.). 144p. 1995. text 26.00 (*0-85345-904-5*, Pub. by Monthly Rev); pap. text 13.00 (*0-85345-905-3*, Pub. by Monthly Rev) NYU Pr.

— The Rainbow Challenge: The Jackson Campaign & the Future of U. S. Politics. LC 86-21778. 384p. 1986. reprint ed. pap. 119.10 (*0-7837-9604-8*, 206036100005) Bks Demand.

Collins, Sheila D. & Goldberg, Gertrude S. Washington's New Poor Law: Welfare Reform & the Jobs Illusion. 320p. 2000. 43.50 (*0-945257-84-8*); pap. 21.50 (*0-945257-83-X*) Apex Pr.

Collins, Sheila H. Cendrillon: A Cajun Cinderella. LC 98-19955. (Illus.). 32p. (J). (ps-3). 1998. 14.95 (*1-56554-326-2*) Pelican.

— Petite Rouge: A Cajun Twist to an Old Tale. LC 97-21250. (Illus.). 32p. (J). (gr. 4-7). 1997. 14.95 (*1-56554-310-6*) Pelican.

***Collins, Sheila H.** Les Trois Cochons: A Cajun Twist to an Old Tale. LC 99-25569.Tr. of Three Little Pigs. (FRE., Illus.). 32p. (J). (gr. k-3). 1999. 14.95 (*1-56554-325-4*) Pelican.

Collins, Sheila Hebert. Jolie Blonde & the Three Heberts: A Cajun Twist to an Old Tale. LC 98-46397. 32p. (J). (gr. k-3). 1999. 14.95 (*1-56554-324-6*) Pelican.

Collins, Sheila K. Stillpoint: The Dance of Selfcaring, Selfhealing: A Playbook for People Who Do Caring Work. LC 91-68151. (Illus.). (Orig.). 1992. pap. 14.95 (*0-9631856-0-8*) TLC Prods.

Collins, Sheldan. How to Photograph Works of Art. (Illus.). 204p. 1992. reprint ed. pap. 24.95 (*0-8174-4019-4*, Amphoto) Watsn-Guptill.

Collins, Sherri, ed. see Sigmon, Cheryl M.

Collins, Sherri, ed. see Van Hise, Carol L.

Collins, Simon. Making Your Money Work for You: How to Use Simple Investment Principles to Increase Your Wealth. (Personal Finance Ser.). (Illus.). 144p. 1999. pap. 19.95 (*1-85703-462-7*, Pub. by How To Bks) Trans-Atl Phila.

Collins, Simon. Pons German / English - English / German Dictionary of Data Processing. (ENG & GER.). 1997. 95.00 (*0-320-03706-1*) Fr & Eur.

Collins, Sophie, ed. see Opie, James.

Collins Staff. Cobuild English Language Dictionary: Helping Learners with Real English. 2nd ed. 1728p. 1996. 55.00 (*0-00-375029-9*, Harper Ref) HarpC.

Collins Staff. Collins French-English, English-French. 448p. 1991. mass mkt. 5.99 (*0-06-100244-5*, Harper Ref) HarpC.

***Collins Staff.** Collins Gem French Dictionary: French-English, English-French. 5th ed. 640p. 2000. pap. 6.95 (*0-00-470766-4*, HarpRes) HarpInfo.

Collins Staff. Collins German-English, English-German. 448p. 1991. mass mkt. 5.99 (*0-06-100243-7*, Harper Ref) HarpC.

— Collins Italian-English, English-Italian. 448p. 1991. mass mkt. 5.99 (*0-06-100246-1*, Harper Ref) HarpC.

— Collins Spanish-English, English-Spanish. 448p. 1991. mass mkt. 5.99 (*0-06-100245-3*, Harper Ref) HarpC.

— Diccionario Collins Espanol-Aleman, Deutsche-Spanisch "Pocket" (GER & SPA.). 416p. 1990. pap. 24.95 (*0-7859-6453-3*) Fr & Eur.

— Jane's Gem Modern Civil Aircraft. 256p. 1996. pap. 8.00 (*0-00-470943-8*, Harper Ref) HarpC.

— Robert & Collins Senior: Dictionnaire Francais-Anglais, Anglais-Francais. (ENG & FRE.). 2016p. 1993. 95.00 (*0-7859-8061-X*, 2850362271) Fr & Eur.

Collins Staff, jt. ed. see Eriksson.

Collins, Stanley H. Ananse the Spider: Why Spiders Stay on the Ceiling. (Sign Language Literature Ser.). (Illus.). 28p. (Orig.). (J). (gr. 2 up). 1997. pap. 4.95 (*0-931993-85-7*, GP-085) Garlic Pr OR.

— Family & Community. (Beginning Sign Language Ser.). (Illus.). 30p. 1999. pap. 4.95 (*0-931993-73-3*, GP-073) Garlic Pr OR.

— Foods. (Beginning Sign Language Ser.). (Illus.). 15p. (J). (ps up). 1997. pap. 3.95 (*0-931993-87-3*, GP-087) Garlic Pr OR.

— Fountain of Youth. (Sign Language Literature Ser.). (Illus.). (Orig.). (J). (gr. 2 up). 1997. pap. 4.95 (*0-931993-86-5*, GP-086) Garlic Pr OR.

— Fruits & Vegetables. (Beginning Sign Language Ser.). (Illus.). 13p. (J). (ps up). 1997. pap. 3.95 (*0-931993-88-1*, GP-088) Garlic Pr OR.

Collins, Stanley H. Pets, Animals & Creatures. (Beginning Sign Language Ser.). (Illus.). 29p. (J). (ps up). 1997. pap. 4.95 (*0-931993-89-X*, GP-089) Garlic Pr OR.

***Collins, Stanley H., et al.** Holidays & Celebrations. (Beginning Sign Language Ser.). (Illus.). 31p. (J). 1999. pap. 4.95 (*0-931993-10-5*) Garlic Pr OR.

Collins, Stephanie. Living the Days of Advent & the Christmas Season 1998. LC 98-218010. (Illus.). 48p. 1998. pap. text 3.95 (*0-8091-3825-5*) Paulist Pr.

***Collins, Stephanie.** Living the Days of Advent & the Christmas Season 2000. 48p. 2000. pap. 3.95 (*0-8091-3969-3*) Paulist Pr.

Collins, Stephanie. Living the Days of Advent & the Christmas Season,1999. (Illus.). 48p. 1999. pap. 3.95 (*0-8091-3884-0*) Paulist Pr.

Collins, Stephen. Classical Music. LC 96-72378. (Illus.). 224p. 1998. pap. 9.95 (*0-8442-0025-5*, 00255, Teach Yrslf) NTC Contemp Pub Co.

— Double Exposure. LC 97-42983. 310p. 1999. mass mkt. 6.99 (*0-380-73232-7*, Avon Bks) Morrow Avon.

— Double Exposure: A Novel. LC 97-42983. 256p. 1998. 24.00 (*0-688-15893-5*, Wm Morrow) Morrow Avon.

***Collins, Stephen & Solomon, David, eds.** Managing the General Ledger, 2000 Yearbook. annuals (Illus.). 200p. 2000. pap. 199.00 (*1-58673-020-7*) IOMA.

Collins, Stephen H. Controller's Business Adviser. 1008p. 1994. 125.00 (*0-7913-2070-7*) Warren Gorham & Lamont.

Collins, Sterling C. Doll-Victorian Mouse Paper Dolls in Full Color. (J). 1986. pap. 4.95 (*0-486-25045-8*) Dover.

Collins-Sterling, Crystal. Bunny Rabbit-Sticker Paper Doll. (Illus.). (J). 1991. pap. text 1.00 (*0-486-26615-X*) Dover.

— Country Duckling. (Little Activity Bks.). (Illus.). (J). 1995. pap. 1.00 (*0-486-26990-6*) Dover.

— The Cowboy Teddy Bear. (Little Activity Bks.). (Illus.). (J). 1996. pap. 1.00 (*0-486-29243-6*) Dover.

Collins-Sterling, Crystal. Make Your Own Christmas Sticker Postcards: Eight Blank Cards & 73 Colorful Stickers. (Illus.). (J). (gr. k-3). 1993. pap. 4.95 (*0-486-27538-8*) Dover.

Collins-Sterling, Crystal. Make Your Own Valentine Sticker Postcard. (Illus.). 1996. pap. text 4.95 (*0-486-28814-5*) Dover.

Collins-Sterling, Crystal. Panda-Paper Dolls. (J). 1989. pap. 2.95 (*0-486-25929-3*) Dover.

Collins-Sterling Crystal Staff. Turtle. (Little Activity Bks.). (Illus.). (J). 1991. pap. 1.00 (*0-486-26835-7*) Dover.

Collins, Steve & Howard, Paul. Celtic Warrior. (Illus.). 214p. 1997. pap. 10.95 (*0-86278-439-5*, Pub. by OBrien Pr) Irish Amer Bk.

Collins, Steven. Christian Discipleship: Foundations for Maximum Spiritual Growth. (Illus.). 304p. 1988. reprint ed. pap. 18.99 (*1-56322-022-9*) Hensley Pub.

Collins, Steven. Nirvana & Other Buddhist Felicities. (Studies in Religious Traditions: Vol. 12). 708p. (C). 1998. text 85.00 (*0-521-57054-9*) Cambridge U Pr.

— Selfless Persons: Imagery & Thought in Theravada Buddhism. 333p. (C). 1990. pap. text 27.95 (*0-521-39726-X*) Cambridge U Pr.

Collins, Steven, tr. see Wijayaratna, Mohan.

Collins, Steven C. Pluckin' Corn on the Sabbath. (Illus.). 72p. 1997. pap. 9.00 (*1-877603-47-3*) Pecan Grove.

Collins, Steven M. The "Lost" Ten Tribes of Israel... Found! 2nd rev. ed. 439p. 1992. pap. 16.00 (*0-944379-11-7*, 900-292) CPA Bk Pub.

Collins, Susan. The Me Book: An Illustrated Manual for Being Human. LC 84-60763. (Illus.). 226p. 1986. pap. 9.95 (*0-915677-24-5*) Roundtable Pub.

***Collins, Susan.** Quotation Marks: Teaching the Basics about Quotation Marks. (Teaching the Boring Stuff Ser.). (Illus.). 47p. (YA). (gr. 5-9). 1999. pap. 12.95 (*1-877673-37-4*) Cottonwood Pr.

***Collins, Susan, ed.** Oversight Review of the Treasury Department's Inspector General: Congressional Hearings. 1736p. (C). 2000. reprint ed. pap. text 95.00 (*0-7881-8683-3*) DIANE Pub.

Collins, Susan D. & Stauffer, Devin. Empire & the Ends of Politics: Plato's 'Menexenus' & Pericles' Funeral Oration. (Focus Philosophical Library). 80p. 1999. pap. text 6.95 (*0-941051-70-6*) Focus Pub-R Pullins.

Collins, Susan D., jt. ed. see Bartlett, Robert C.

***Collins, Susan M.** Brookings Trade Forum 1999 1999. pap. 24.95 (*0-8157-1525-0*) Brookings.

***Collins, Susan M., ed.** Cramming: An Emerging Telephone Billing Fraud: Congressional Hearing. (Illus.). 164p. (C). 2000. reprint ed. pap. text 25.00 (*0-7881-8688-4*) DIANE Pub.

Collins, Susan M., ed. Imports, Exports, & the American Worker. LC 97-45315. 557p. (C). 1997. 59.95 (*0-8157-1520-X*); pap. 26.95 (*0-8157-1519-6*) Brookings.

***Collins, Susan M., ed.** Medicare at Risk: Emerging Fraud in Medicare Programs: Congressional Hearing. 326p. (C). 2000. reprint ed. pap. text 40.00 (*0-7881-8773-2*) DIANE Pub.

Collins, Susan M. & Bosworth, Barry P., eds. The New GATT: Implications for the U. S. (Integrating National Economies: Promise & Pitfalls Ser.). 128p. (C). 1995. pap. 14.95 (*0-8157-1029-1*) Brookings.

Collins, Susan M. & Rodrik, Dani. Eastern Europe & the Soviet Union in the World Economy. LC 91-15968. (Policy Analysis in International Economics Ser.: No. 32). (Illus.). 116p. 1991. reprint ed. pap. 36.00 (*0-7837-9167-4*, 204986800003) Bks Demand.

Collins, Susan M., jt. ed. see Sachs, Jeffrey D.

Collins, Suzanne. Fire Proof. (Mystery Files of Shelby Woo Ser.: No. 11). 144p. (J). (gr. 4-7). 1999. pap. 3.99 (*0-671-02695-X*, Pocket Books) PB.

Collins, Suzanne, jt. auth. see Carr, Janet H.

Collins, Suzanne, ed. see Flynn, Julia L.

Collins, T. H. Analog Electronic Handbook. 320p. 1989. reprint ed. text, boxed set 48.00 (*0-318-37807-8*) P-H.

Collins, Tammy S. The Pet Sitter's Career Guide. 80p. (Orig.). pap. 11.95 (*0-9633885-0-9*) Pet Indulgence HPCS.

Collins, Terah K. Home Design with Feng Shui A-Z. LC 98-36480. (Hay House Lifestyles Ser.). (Illus.). 145p. 1999. text 19.95 (*1-56170-572-1*, L439) Hay House.

— The Western Guide to Feng Shui: Creating Balance, Harmony, & Prosperity in Your Environment. LC 95-47274. (Illus.). 224p. (Orig.). 1996. pap. 12.95 (*1-56170-324-9*, 194) Hay House.

— The Western Guide to Feng Shui: Room by Room. LC 99-11957. (Illus.). 250p. 1999. text 13.95 (*1-56170-568-3*, 573) Hay House.

***Collins, Terah Kathryn.** Feng Shui "Heaven on Earth" Cards. (Illus.). 2001. pap. 18.95 (*1-56170-787-2*, Hay Hse Lifestyles) Hay House.

— Home Design with Feng Shui A-Z. (Illus.). 156p. 2001. pap. 11.95 (*1-56170-788-0*, L474) Hay House.

Collins, Terence. The Mantle of Elijah: The Redaction Criticism of the Prophetical Books. (Biblical Seminar Ser.: Vol. 20). 197p. 1993. pap. 23.00 (*1-85075-425-X*, Pub. by Sheffield Acad) CUP Services.

Collins, Terence, jt. auth. see Kassner, Linda A.

Collins, Teresa. Reiki at Hand. LC 99-181908. (Illus.). 186p. 1998. pap. 19.95 (*1-898256-40-3*, Pub. by Collins Press) Dufour.

Collins, Teresa R. Low Fat & Happy: Flavorful Family-Style Recipes That Will Leave You Feeling Satisfied Not Deprived. LC 97-94333. 223p. 1997. pap. 11.95 (*0-9660238-7-0*) Aspire Pub.

Collins, Terry. The Andy Griffith Story: An Illustrated Biography. LC 95-90187. (Illus.). 192p. 1995. 23.95 (*1-887138-00-5*); pap. 12.95 (*1-887138-01-3*) Explorer Pr.

Collins, Terry & Kong, Emilie. The Perfect Bone. (Catdog Chapter Bks.: No. 3). (Illus.). 64p. (J). (gr. 2-5). 1999. pap. 3.99 (*0-689-83010-6*, Simon Spot) Litle Simon.

Collins, Tess. The Law of the Dead. 1999. mass mkt. 6.99 (*0-8041-1795-0*) Ivy Books.

Collins, Theresa. The Law of Revenge. 1997. mass mkt. 6.99 (*0-449-22534-8*) Fawcett.

— The Law of Revenge. LC 96-30585. 1997. write for info. (*0-449-91075-X*) Fawcett.

— The Law of Revenge. large type ed. (Niagara Large Print Ser.). 416p. 1997. 29.50 (*0-7089-5888-5*) Ulverscroft.

Collins, Thomas. Comprehensive Health Care for Everyone: A Guide for Body, Mind & Spirit. LC 95-18693. (Illus.). 418p. (Orig.). 1995. pap. 19.95 (*0-931892-97-X*) B Dolphin Pub.

***Collins, Thomas & Rundle, Vivienne, eds.** The Anthology of Victorian Poetry & Poetic Theory. (Anthologies of English Literature Ser.). 1460p. 1999. pap. 37.95 (*1-55111-100-4*) Broadview Pr.

Collins, Thomas J., ed. A Concordance to the Poems & Plays of Robert Browning, 7 vols. LC 93-4051. (AMS Studies in the Nineteenth Century: No. 14). 1993. 1728.00 (*0-404-61494-9*) AMS Pr.

Collins, Thomas J. & American Bar Association Staff. Punitive Damages & Business Torts: A Practitioner's Handbook. LC 98-87811. (Antitrust Practice Guide Ser.). xi, 206p. 1998. 89.00 (*1-57073-617-0*) Amer Bar Assn.

Collins, Thomas L., jt. auth. see Rapp, Stan.

***Collins, Thomas W. & Wingard, John D., eds.** Communities & Capital: Local Struggles Against Corporate Power & Privatization. LC 99-29098. (Southern Anthropological Society Proceedings Ser.: Vol. 33). 160p. 1999. 40.00 (*0-8203-2172-9*) U of Ga Pr.

— Communities & Capital: Local Struggles Against Corporate Power & Privatization. LC 99-29098. (Southern Anthropological Society Proceedings Ser.: Vol. 33). 160p. 2000. pap. text 20.00 (*0-8203-2173-7*) U of Ga Pr.

Collins, Tim & Lehr, Jane. Spend on Your Future: Investing & Money Management Made Easy. LC 94-2863. (Illus.). 187p. (Orig.). 1994. pap. 13.95 (*0-9639889-3-X*) Orca Bks.

Collins, Timothy J., jt. auth. see Wilson, David M.

Collins, Tom. The Centre Cannot Hold: Britain's Failure in Northern Ireland. (Illus.). 190p. 1985. pap. 10.95 (*0-946968-00-4*) Devin.

— The Lost Child: Hope for Kids Without Hope. 128p. 1992. pap. 9.95 (*0-925190-52-7*) Fairview Press.

— A Poet's Ink. 85p. (Orig.). 1995. pap. 6.95 (*0-9649165-0-9*) Marion Prods.

— Steven Spielberg: Creator of E. T. LC 83-21068. (Taking Part Ser.). (Illus.). 64p. (J). (gr. 3 up). 1983. lib. bdg. 13.95 (*0-87518-249-6*, Dillon Silver Burdett) Silver Burdett Pr.

Collins, Tom, ed. & intro. see Lovecraft, H. P.

Collins, Toni. The Almost-Perfect Proposal. (Yours Truly Ser.). 1997. per. 3.50 (*0-373-52041-7*, 1-52041-0) Silhouette.

— Miracle Dad. 1997. per. 42.00 (*0-373-91008-8*) Silhouette.

— Miss Scrooge: Under the Mistletoe. (Romance Ser.). 1994. per. 2.75 (*0-373-19050-6*, 1-19050-3) Silhouette.

— Something Old. (Romance Ser.). 1993. per. 2.75 (*0-373-08941-4*, 5-08941-2) Silhouette.

— Unhappily Unwed. 1995. per. 3.50 (*0-373-52006-9*, 1-52006-3) Silhouette.
— Willfully Wed. (Romance Ser.). 1996. per. 3.25 (*0-373-19159-6*, 1-19159-2) Silhouette.
Collins, Tony. Rock Mr. Blues: The Life & Music of Wynonie Harris. 180p. 1995. pap. 25.00 (*0-936433-19-1*) Big Nickel.
— Rugby's Great Split: Class, Culture & the Origins of Rugby League Football. LC 97-43920. (Sport in the Global Society Ser.). 273p. (C). 1998. 49.50 (*0-7146-4867-1*, Pub. by Woburn Pr); pap. 22.50 (*0-7146-4424-2*, Pub. by Woburn Pr) Intl Spec Bk.
Collins, Tony & Bicknell, David L. Crash: Ten Easy Ways to Avoid a Computer Disaster. 432p. 1999. per. 15.00 (*0-684-86835-0*) S&S Trade.
Collins, Tricia & Milazzo, Richard. A Deer Manger, a Dress Patter, Farthest Sea Water, & a Signature: Carrino, Etkin, Scarpitta, Webster. (Illus.). 4p. (Orig.). (C). 1988. pap. text. write for info. (*0-945295-01-4*) T Collins.
— Media Post Media: Twenty Women Artists. 54p. (Orig.). (C). 1988. pap. text. write for info. (*0-945295-00-6*) T Collins.
Collins, Tricia, et al. Hybrid Neutral: Modes of Abstraction & the Social. 64p. 1988. pap. 12.00 (*0-916365-27-1*) Ind Curators.
Collins, Trish & Prince, Anthony. Catoons: The Ultimate Cat Dictionary. 128p. 1992. pap. 6.95 (*1-56755-012-6*) Silverlake.
Collins, Una, jt. ed. see McNiff, Jean.
Collins, V. H., ed. see Byron, George Gordon.
Collins, V. H., pseud. A Book of English Idioms with Explanations. LC 85-12617. 258p. 1985. reprint ed. lib. bdg. 59.75 (*0-8371-8152-6*, COEI, Greenwood Pr) Greenwood.
Collins, Valerie. Recreation & the Law. 2nd ed. LC 93-17601. (Illus.). 200p. (C). 1994. pap. 37.99 (*0-419-18240-3*, E & FN Spon) Routledge.
Collins, Valerie G. Job-Hunting: The Basics. LC 96-90307. 54p. (Orig.). 1997. pap. 12.50 (*0-9619210-2-1*) VGC Commns.
Collins, Varnum L. President Witherspoon. LC 78-83416. (Religion in America, Ser. 1). 1980. reprint ed. 33.95 (*0-405-00242-4*) Ayer.
Collins, Varnum L., ed. Brief Narrative of the Ravages of the British & Hessians at Princeton in 1776-1777. LC 67-29024. (Eyewitness Accounts of the American Revolution Ser.). 1975. reprint ed. 16.95 (*0-405-01110-5*) Ayer.
Collins, Varnum L., ed. see Witherspoon, John.
Collins, Vere H., ed. Three Centuries of English Essays: From Francis Bacon to Max Beerbohm. LC 67-26727. (Essay Index Reprint Ser.). 1977. 13.95 (*0-8369-0327-7*) Ayer.
Collins, Verite R. About the Border Terrier: AKC Rank #88. (Illus.). 224p. 1997. 35.95 (*1-85279-022-9*, GB-009) TFH Pubns.
— Becoming a Tour Guide. (Illus.). 160p. 2000. pap. 18.95 (*0-304-70740-6*) Continuum.
— Becoming a Tour Guide: The Principles of Guiding & Site Interpretation. 2000. pap. 18.95 (*0-8264-4788-0*) Continuum.
Collins, Verite R. Working in Tourism: The U. K., Europe & Beyond. 320p. (Orig.). 1997. pap. 17.95 (*1-85458-133-3*, Pub. by Vac Wrk Pubns) Seven Hills Bk.
Collins, Vicky, ed. see Dalton, Robb E.
***Collins, Victoria.** Invest Beyond.Com. LC 00-22740. 2000. pap. 18.95 (*0-7931-3817-5*) Dearborn.
Collins, Victoria. Your Next Fifty Years: A Completely New Way to Look at How, When & If You Should Retire. LC 96-40390. 240p. 1995. pap. 14.95 (*0-8050-4568-6*) H Holt & Co.
Collins, Victoria F. & Blair, Suzanne. Couples & Money: A Couples' Guide, Updated for the New Millennium. LC 97-77884. Orig. Title: Couples & Money, a Financial Guide for Surviving & Thriving in the 80's. 224p. 1998. pap. 13.95 (*1-891689-98-3*) Gabriel Pubns.
Collins, Vincent J. Principles of Anesthesiology: General & Regional Anesthesia. 3rd ed. LC 91-7038. (Illus.). 850p. 1992. 198.50 (*0-8121-1322-5*) Lppncott W & W.
Collins, Vincent J., ed. Physiologic & Pharmacologic Bases of Anesthesia. LC 95-14786. (Illus.). 890p. 1996. 89.00 (*0-683-02011-0*) Lppncott W & W.
Collins, Vincent P. Acceptance. 1960. pap. 18.75 (*0-87029-072-X*) Abbey.
Collins, Violet, ed. see Gallagher, Steve.
Collins, Virgil D. World Marketing. Assael, Henry, ed. LC 78-271. (Century of Marketing Ser.). 1979. reprint ed. lib. bdg. 29.95 (*0-405-11186-X*) Ayer.
Collins, W. Cathedral Cities of Spain. 1976. lib. bdg. 59.95 (*0-8490-1585-5*) Gordon Pr.
— An Ecological Theory of Democracy: Steps Toward a Non-Equilibrium View of Politics. (Illus.). viii, 260p. 1989. 66.00 (*0-387-91354-8*) Spr-Verlag.
Collins, W., jt. auth. see Leyden, D.
Collins, W. A., ed. Minnesota Symposia on Child Psychology, Vol. 11. 286p. 1978. 59.95 (*0-89859-113-9*) L Erlbaum Assocs.
Collins, W. Andrew, ed. Aspects of the Development of Competence Vol. 14: The Minnesota Symposium on Child Psychology. LC 80-20568. 288p. 1981. 59.95 (*0-89859-070-1*) L Erlbaum Assocs.
— Children's Language & Communication Vol. 12: The Minnesota Symposium on Child Psychology. LC 79-364. (Illus.). 256p. 1979. text 49.95 (*0-89859-000-0*) L Erlbaum Assocs.
— The Concept of Development Vol. 15: The Minnesota Symposium on Child Psychology. 192p. 1982. 49.95 (*0-89859-159-7*) L Erlbaum Assocs.
— Development of Cognition, Affect, & Social Relations Vol. 13: The Minnesota Symposium on Child Psychology. LC 79-27560. (Illus.). 320p. 1980. text 49.95 (*0-89859-023-X*) L Erlbaum Assocs.
Collins, W. Andrew & Laursen, Brett, eds. Relationships As Developmental Contexts: The Minnesota Symposia on Child Psychology, Vol. 30. LC 98-45394. (Minnesota Symposia on Child Psychology Ser.). 384p. 1998. 79.95 (*0-8058-2616-5*) L Erlbaum Assocs.
Collins, W. Andrew, jt. ed. see Gunnar, Megan R.
Collins, W. Andrew, ed. see National Research Council (U. S.), Panel on Altern.
Collins, W. Andrew, jt. ed. see Shulman, Shmuel.
Collins, W. E., et al, eds. Analytical Techniques for Material Characterization: Proceedings of the Int'l Workshop on Analytical Techniques for Material Characterization. 428p. (C). 1987. pap. 60.00 (*9971-5-0512-6*); text 127.00 (*9971-5-0511-8*) World Scientific Pub.
***Collins, W. J.** A Handbook for Dental Hygienists. 4th ed. LC 99-198085. 284p. 1999. 47.50 (*0-7236-1740-6*, Pub. by John Wright) Buttrwrth-Heinemann.
Collins, W. J. & Walsh, T. W. A Handbook for Dental Hygienists. 3rd ed. (Illus.). 336p. 1992. pap. text 60.00 (*0-7236-0980-2*) Buttrwrth-Heinemann.
Collins, W. T., jt. ed. see Leyden, D. E.
Collins, Wallace. Blood & Wine. (Orig.). 1997. pap. 6.95 (*0-533-12152-3*) Vantage.
Collins, Wanda, jt. ed. see Serageldin, Ismail.
Collins, Wanda L. Becoming Important to You. (Orig.). 1994. pap. text 7.95 (*0-9640943-0-4*) WanCol Pubns.
Collins, Wanda Williams & Qualset, Calvin O. Biodiversity in Agroecosystems. LC 98-13056. (Advances in Agroecology Ser.). 352p. 1999. lib. bdg. 59.95 (*1-56670-290-9*) Lewis Pubs.
Collins, Ward T., jt. ed. see Leyden, Donald E.
Collins, Warwick. Computer One. LC 97-16768. 288p. 1997. 24.95 (*0-7145-3033-6*) M Boyars Pubs.
— Computer One: A Novel. LC 97-16768. 1997. pap. write for info. (*0-7145-3034-4*) M Boyars Pubs.
— Gents: A Novel. LC 96-49832. 128p. 1997. 19.95 (*0-7145-3028-X*) M Boyars Pubs.
— The Rationalist. 256p. 1995. pap. 11.00 (*0-345-39185-3*) Ballantine Pub Grp.
Collins, Wilkie. After Dark & Other Stories. 536p. 1977. 29.95 (*0-8369-4204-3*) Ayer.
— Armadale. Peters, Catharine, ed. (Oxford World Classics Ser.). 865p. 1999. pap. 12.95 (*0-19-283467-3*) OUP.
— Armadale. Sutherland, John, ed. & intro. by. 752p. 1995. pap. 11.95 (*0-14-043411-9*, Penguin Classics) Viking Penguin.
— Armadale, 2 vols., Set. 1988. reprint ed. lib. bdg. 150.00 (*0-7812-0752-5*) Rprt Serv.
— Armadale, 2 vols., Set. LC 70-107168. (Illus.). 1972. reprint ed. 69.00 (*0-403-00433-0*) Scholarly.
***Collins, Wilkie.** Basil. Goldman, Dorothy, ed. (Oxford World's Classics Ser.). 400p. 2000. pap. 11.95 (*0-19-283548-3*) OUP.
Collins, Wilkie. The Black Robe. (Pocket Classics Ser.). 272p. 1994. pap. 8.95 (*0-7509-0654-5*, Pub. by Sutton Pub Ltd) Intl Pubs Mktg.
— Blind Love. (Illus.). 312p. 1986. reprint ed. pap. 8.95 (*0-486-25189-6*) Dover.
***Collins, Wilkie.** Classic Crimes of Passion, Set. 1998. 16.95 incl. audio (*1-896552-25-0*) Tangled Web.
Collins, Wilkie. The Dead Secret. (Oxford World's Classics Ser.). 402p. 1999. pap. 12.95 (*0-19-283841-5*) OUP.
Collins, Wilkie. The Dead Secret. LC 78-74113. (Illus.). 384p. 1979. reprint ed. pap. 9.95 (*0-486-23775-3*) Dover.
Collins, Wilkie. The Frozen Deep & Mr. Wray's Cash-Box. LC 97-158680. (Pocket Classics Ser.). 144p. 1996. pap. 10.95 (*0-7509-1206-5*, Pub. by Sutton Pub Ltd) Intl Pubs Mktg.
— The Guilty River. (Paperback Classics Ser.). 1991. reprint ed. pap. text 12.95 (*0-7509-0010-5*, Pub. by Sutton Pub Ltd) Intl Pubs Mktg.
— The Haunted Hotel. (Mystery Ser.). 127p. 1982. reprint ed. pap. 4.95 (*0-486-24333-8*) Dover.
— Hide & Seek. (Oxford World Classics Ser.). 472p. 1999. pap. 10.95 (*0-19-283659-5*) OUP.
***Collins, Wilkie.** Hide & Seek, Set. unabridged ed. (YA). (gr. 10 up). 1998. 65.95 incl. audio (*1-55685-578-8*) Audio Bk Con.
Collins, Wilkie. Hide & Seek: The Mystery of Mary Grice. (Illus.). 384p. 1982. reprint ed. pap. 8.95 (*0-486-24211-0*) Dover.
— "I Say No" or the Love-Letter Answered & Other Stories. 233p. 1972. 26.95 (*0-8369-4205-1*) Ayer.
***Collins, Wilkie.** Iolani, or Tahiti As It Was. 216p. 1999. 24.95 (*0-691-03446-X*, Pub. by Princeton U Pr) Cal Prin Full Svc.
— The Law & the Lady. Taylor, Jenny B., ed. & intro. by. (Oxford World's Classics Ser.). 462p. 1999. pap. 11.95 (*0-19-283679-X*) OUP.
Collins, Wilkie. Mad Monkton & Other Stories. Page, Norman, ed. & intro. by. (Oxford World's Classics). 432p. 1999. pap. 10.95 (*0-19-283772-9*) OUP.
— Mad Monkton & Other Stories. reprint ed. lib. bdg. 19.95 (*0-89190-247-3*, Rivercity Pr) Amereon Ltd.
— Man & Wife. Page, Norman, ed. & intro. by. (Oxford World's Classics Ser.). 688p. 1999. pap. 13.95 (*0-19-283696-X*) OUP.
— Miss Bertha & the Yankee & Other Stories. reprint ed. lib. bdg. 18.95 (*0-89190-248-1*, Rivercity Pr) Amereon Ltd.
— Miss or Mrs?; The Haunted Hotel; The Guilty River. Page, Norman & Sasaki, Toru, eds. LC 98-22118. (Oxford World's Classics Ser.). 400p. 1999. pap. 10.95 (*0-19-283307-3*) OUP.
***Collins, Wilkie.** The Moonstone. Farmer, Steve, ed. 720p. 1999. pap. 9.95 (*1-55111-243-4*) Broadview Pr.
Collins, Wilkie. The Moonstone. LC 92-52918. 480p. 1992. 17.00 (*0-679-41722-2*) Everymns Lib.
— The Moonstone. 496p. 1984. mass mkt. 6.95 (*0-451-52394-6*, Sig Classics) NAL.
— The Moonstone. LC 99-461888. (Oxford World's Classics Hardcovers Ser.). 576p. 1999. 16.50 (*0-19-210028-9*) OUP.
— The Moonstone. 576p. 1999. pap. 6.95 (*0-14-043408-9*, PuffinBks) Peng Put Young Read.
— The Moonstone. 1984. 12.05 (*0-606-01905-7*, Pub. by Turtleback) Demco.
— The Moonstone. (Classics Library). 1997. pap. 3.95 (*1-85326-044-4*, 0444WW, Pub. by Wrdsworth Edits) NTC Contemp Pub Co.
— The Moonstone. large type ed. (Isis Clear Type Classic Ser.). 605p. 1992. 25.95 (*1-85089-543-0*, Pub. by ISIS Lrg Prnt) Transaction Pubs.
— The Moonstone. 1976. reprint ed. lib. bdg. 29.95 (*0-89190-241-4*, Rivercity Pr) Amereon Ltd.
— The Moonstone. 1990. reprint ed. lib. bdg. 25.95 (*0-89968-498-X*) Buccaneer Bks.
— The Moonstone. 570p. 1998. reprint ed. lib. bdg. 25.00 (*1-58287-094-2*) North Bks.
— The Moonstone. 2nd ed. Sutherland, John, ed. (Oxford World's Classics Ser.). 560p. 2000. pap. 6.95 (*0-19-283338-3*) OUP.
Collins, Wilkie. Moonstone: Masters of Literature. 1996. pap. 5.00 (*81-207-1887-9*, Pub. by Sterling Pubs) S Asia.
Collins, Wilkie. The New Magdalen. LC 93-26285. (Pocket Classics Ser.). 1993. pap. 8.95 (*0-7509-0455-0*, Pub. by Sutton Pub Ltd) Intl Pubs Mktg.
— No Name. Blain, Virginia, ed. & intro. by. (Oxford World's Classics Ser.). (Illus.). 780p. 1998. pap. 10.95 (*0-19-283388-X*) OUP.
— No Name. (Classics Ser.). 640p. 1995. pap. 12.95 (*0-14-043397-X*, Penguin Classics) Viking Penguin.
— No Name, a Novel. (BCL1-PR English Literature Ser.). 609p. 1992. reprint ed. lib. bdg. 109.00 (*0-7812-7503-2*) Rprt Serv.
— Poor Miss Finch. Peters, Catherine, ed. (The World's Classics Ser.). 480p. 1995. pap. 11.95 (*0-19-282322-1*) OUP.
— Poor Miss Finch. (Oxford World Classics Ser.). 480p. 2000. pap. 12.95 (*0-19-283699-4*) OUP.
— Poor Miss Finch. (Pocket Classics Ser.). 384p. 1994. pap. 10.95 (*0-7509-0655-3*, Pub. by Sutton Pub Ltd) Intl Pubs Mktg.
— Poor Miss Finch: A Novel. LC 77-131672. (Literature Ser.). (Illus.). 454p. 1972. reprint ed. 69.00 (*0-403-00559-0*) Scholarly.
— The Queen of Hearts. LC 75-32740. (Literature of Mystery & Detection Ser.). 1976. reprint ed. 39.95 (*0-405-07868-4*) Ayer.
— Tales of Terror & the Supernatural. Van Thal, Herbert, ed. & intro. by. LC 75-189974. 294p. (Orig.). 1972. pap. 8.95 (*0-486-20307-7*) Dover.
— Three Great Novels: The Woman in White - The Moonstone - The Law & the Lady. LC 93-37406. 1,168p. 1994. pap. 16.95 (*0-19-282333-7*) OUP.
***Collins, Wilkie.** The Traveller's Tale of a Terrible Bed. (Short Stories Ser.). 22p. 2000. pap. 3.95 (*1-86092-042-X*, Pub. by Travelman Pub) IPG Chicago.
Collins, Wilkie. The Woman in White. 576p. 1985. mass mkt. 5.95 (*0-553-21263-X*, Bantam Classics) Bantam.
— The Woman in White. 608p. 1991. 20.00 (*0-679-40563-1*) Everymns Lib.
— The Woman in White. Sutherland, John, ed. & intro. by. (Oxford World's Classics Ser.). 734p. 1998. pap. 6.95 (*0-19-283429-0*) OUP.
— The Woman in White. Symons, Julian, ed. (English Library). 654p. 1975. pap. 7.95 (*0-14-043096-2*, Penguin Classics) Viking Penguin.
— The Woman in White. (Classics Library). 1998. pap. 3.95 (*1-85326-077-0*, 0770WW, Pub. by Wrdsworth Edits) NTC Contemp Pub Co.
***Collins, Wilkie.** The Woman in White. (Penguin Classics Ser.). 2000. pap. 7.95 (*0-14-043731-2*) Viking Penguin.
Collins, Wilkie. The Woman in White. 1976. reprint ed. lib. bdg. 35.95 (*0-89190-242-2*, Rivercity Pr) Amereon Ltd.
— The Woman in White. 1990. reprint ed. lib. bdg. 30.95 (*0-89968-499-8*) Buccaneer Bks.
— The Woman in White. (Works of Wilkie Collins: Vol. 1). 575p. 1998. reprint ed. lib. bdg. 90.00 (*0-7812-7716-7*) Rprt Serv.
— Works of Wilkie Collins, 30 vols. reprint ed. 2790.00 (*0-404-01750-9*) AMS Pr.
Collins, Wilkie. Works of Wilkie Collins, 30 vols. Incl. After Dark. 544p. 1999. reprint ed. lib. bdg. 98.00 (*1-58201-040-4*); Antonina: or The Fall of Rome. 656p. 1999. reprint ed. lib. bdg. 98.00 (*1-58201-038-2*); Basil & Little Novels: Mrs. Zant & the Ghost; Miss Morris & the Stranger; Mr. Lismore & the Widow. 576p. 1999. reprint ed. lib. bdg. 98.00 (*1-58201-031-5*); Black Robe. 448p. 1999. reprint ed. lib. bdg. 98.00 (*1-58201-044-7*); Blind Love. 544p. 1999. reprint ed. lib. bdg. 98.00 (*1-58201-049-8*); Dead Secret, a Novel: Incl. the Little Novel: Miss Bertha & the Yankee. 590p. 1999. reprint ed. lib. bdg. 98.00 (*1-58201-037-4*); Evil Genius: A Domestic Story. 464p. 1999. reprint ed. lib. bdg. 98.00 (*1-58201-045-5*); Fallen Leaves. 525p. 1999. reprint ed. lib. bdg. 98.00 (*1-58201-042-0*); Haunted Hotel - A Mystery of Modern Venice & My Lady's Money. 477p. 1999. reprint ed. lib. bdg. 98.00 (*1-58201-043-9*); Heart & Science: A Story of the Present Time. 539p. 1999. reprint ed. lib. bdg. 98.00 (*1-58201-046-3*); Hide & Seek. 624p. 1999. reprint ed. lib. bdg. 98.00 (*1-58201-032-3*); "I Say No": or The Love-Letter Answered & Other Stories. 512p. 1999. reprint ed. lib. bdg. 98.00 (*1-58201-050-1*); Jezebel's Daughter. 416p. 1999. reprint ed. lib. bdg. 98.00 (*1-58201-048-X*); Law & the Lady: A Novel. 560p. 1999. reprint ed. lib. bdg. 98.00 (*1-58201-026-9*); Legacy of Cain: A Novel. 480p. 1999. reprint ed. lib. bdg. 98.00 (*1-58201-047-1*); Man & Wife, Pt. 2: Incl. the Short Stories: Miss or Mrs.?; The Frozen Deep. 615p. 1999. reprint ed. lib. bdg. 98.00 (*1-58201-025-0*); Moonstone Pt. 2: Incl. The New Magdalen. 602p. 1999. reprint ed. lib. bdg. 98.00 (*1-58201-028-5*); My Miscellanies. 540p. 1999. reprint ed. lib. bdg. 98.00 (*1-58201-041-2*); No Name, Pt. 2: Incl. the Little Novels: Mr. Cosway & the Landlady; Miss Mina & the Groom. reprint ed. lib. bdg. 98.00 (*1-58201-034-X*); Poor Miss Finch: A Domestic Story. 656p. 1999. reprint ed. lib. bdg. 98.00 (*1-58201-036-6*); Queen of Hearts: Incl. the Little Novel: Mr. Lepel & the Housekeeper. 608p. 1999. reprint ed. lib. bdg. 98.00 (*1-58201-035-8*); Rogue's Life - From His Birth to His Marriage: Little Novels: Miss Dulane & My Lord; Mr. Policeman & the Cook. 320p. 1999. reprint ed. lib. bdg. 98.00 (*1-58201-051-X*); Two Destinies, a Novel: Incl. the Little Novels: Mr. Medhurst & the Princess; Miss Jeromette & the Clergyman; Mr. Captain & the Nymph; Mr. Marmaduke & the Minister; Mr. Percy & the Prophet. 576p. 1999. reprint ed. lib. bdg. 98.00 (*1-58201-039-0*); Woman in White, Pt. 2: Incl. the Short Stories: The Dead Alive; The Fatal Cradle; Fatal Fortune; Blow up with the Brig! 556p. 1999. reprint ed. lib. bdg. 98.00 (*1-58201-023-4*); Pt. 1. Armadale. 579p. 1999. reprint ed. lib. bdg. 98.00 (*1-58201-029-3*); Pt. 1. Man & Wife: A Novel. 574p. 1999. reprint ed. lib. bdg. 98.00 (*1-58201-024-2*); Pt. 1. Moonstone. 580p. 1999. reprint ed. lib. bdg. 98.00 (*1-58201-027-7*); Pt. 1. No Name. 576p. 1999. reprint ed. lib. bdg. 98.00 (*1-58201-033-1*); Pt. 1. Woman in White. 575p. 1999. reprint ed. lib. bdg. 98.00 (*1-58201-022-6*); Pt. 2. Armadale. 575p. 1999. reprint ed. lib. bdg. 98.00 (*1-58201-030-7*); reprint ed. Set lib. bdg. 2940.00 (*1-58201-021-8*) Classic Bks.
Collins, Wilkie & Farmer, Steve. Heart & Science: A Story of the Present Time. 380p. 1997. pap. 12.95 (*1-55111-124-1*) Broadview Pr.
***Collins, William A. & Land- en Volkenkunde (Netherlands)Koninklijk Instituut voor Taal-.** The Guritan of Radin Suane: A Study of the Besemah: Oral Epic from South Sumatra. LC 98-192396. (Bibliotheca Indonesica Ser.: Vol. 28). 548 p. 1998. pap. 65.00 (*90-6718-115-3*, Pub. by KITLV Pr) Book Bin.
Collins, William A., jt. auth. see Gleim, Irvin N.
Collins, William C. Correctional Law for the Correctional Officer. 2nd ed. LC 97-12501. 157p. 1997. pap. 19.95 (*1-56991-066-9*) Am Correctional.
— A Practical Guide to Inmate Discipline. 2nd ed. 120p. 1997. ring bd. 97.50 (*1-887554-04-1*) Civic Res Inst.
Collins, William C., jt. auth. see Drapkin, Martin.
Collins, William C., jt. auth. see Sechrest, Dale K.
Collins, William F., jt. ed. see Tindall, George T.
Collins, William J. An Introduction to Programming & Pascal LC 83-14950. xi, 388 p. 1984. write for info. (*0-02-323780-5*) Macmillan.
Collins, William J. & McMillan, Thomas C. Data Structures: An Object-Oriented Approach. (Illus.). 500p. (C). 1992. text 45.00 (*0-201-56953-1*) Addison-Wesley.
Collins, William P., compiled by. Bibliography of English Language Works on the Babi & Baha'i Faiths 1844-1985. 550p. 1991. 65.00 (*0-85398-315-1*) G Ronald Pub.
Collins, Winifred Q. & Levine, Herbert M. More Than a Uniform: A Navy Woman in a Navy Man's World. LC 96-29497. (Illus.). 224p. (Orig.). 1997. pap. 16.95 (*1-57441-022-9*) UNTX Pr.
***Collins, Yvonne & Rideout, Sandy.** Totally Me: The Teenage Girl's Survival Guide. 240p. (YA). 2000. pap. 10.95 (*1-58062-410-3*) Adams Media.
Collins, Zipporah W., ed. Selected Reprints from Museums, Adults & the Humanities: A Guide for Educational Programming. 178p. 1993. spiral bd. 15.00 (*0-931201-07-1*) Am Assn Mus.
Collinson. Europe & International Migration Handbook. 1995. 55.00 (*1-85567-296-0*) St Martin.
— Particle Mechanics. (Plastics Ser.). 1997. pap. 15.95 (*0-340-61046-8*, VNR) Wiley.
Collinson, A. S. Introduction to World Vegetation. (C). 1988. pap. text 14.95 (*0-04-581013-3*) Routledge.
— Introduction to World Vegetation. 2nd ed. (Illus.). 336p. (C). 1988. pap. 39.95 (*0-04-581031-1*) Thomson Learn.
Collinson, Alan. Grasslands. LC 92-4021. (Ecology Watch Ser.). (Illus.). 48p. (J). (gr. 5 up). 1992. text 13.95 (*0-87518-492-8*, Dillon Silver Burdett) Silver Burdett Pr.
— Pollution. LC 91-24081. (Repairing the Damage Ser.). (Illus.). 48p. (J). (gr. 4-6). 1992. lib. bdg. 21.00 (*0-02-722995-5*, Mac Bks Young Read) S&S Childrens.
Collinson, Allan. Mountains. LC 91-34171. (Ecology Watch Ser.). (Illus.). 48p. (YA). (gr. 5 up). 1992. lib. bdg. 13.95 (*0-87518-493-6*, Dillon Silver Burdett) Silver Burdett Pr.
***Collinson, C. Peter.** All Churches Great & Small. 190p. 1998. reprint ed. mass mkt. 9.99 (*1-85078-311-X*, Pub. by O M Pubng) OM Literature.
Collinson, D. W., ed. Methods in Rock Magnetism & Palaeomagnetism: Techniques & Instrumentation. (Illus.). 528p. 1983. text 171.50 (*0-412-22980-3*, NO. 6752) Chapman & Hall.
Collinson, David C. & Hearn, Jeff, eds. Men As Managers, Managers As Men: Critical Perspectives on Men, Masculinities & Management. 288p. 1996. 75.00 (*0-8039-8928-8*) Sage.
— Men As Managers, Managers As Men: Critical Perspectives on Men, Masculinities & Management. LC 96-70153. 1996. pap. text 26.95 (*0-8039-8929-6*) Sage.
Collinson, David L. Managing the Shop-Floor: Subjectivity, Masculinity & Workplace Culture. (Studies in Organization: No. 36). (Illus.). xii, 255p. (C). 1992. lib. bdg. 54.95 (*3-11-012257-X*, 41-92) De Gruyter.
***Collinson, Diana & Plant, Kathryn.** Fifty Eastern Thinkers. 448p. (C). 2000. text 65.00 (*0-415-20283-3*) Routledge.

C

An Asterisk (*) at the beginning of an entry indicates that the title is appearing for the first time.

*Collinson, Diana, et al. Fifty Key Eastern Thinkers. 256p. 1999. pap. 18.99 (0-415-20284-1) Routledge.
Collinson, Diane. Fifty Major Philosophers: A Reference Guide. 176p. 1987. pap. text 12.95 (0-7099-4871-9, Pub. by C Helm) Routldge.
Collinson, Diane, ed. Biographical Dictionary of Twentieth-Century Philosophers. LC 97-185841. 968p. (C). (gr. 13 up). 1995. 180.00 (0-415-06043-5) Routledge.
Collinson, Diane, et al. Plain English. 2nd ed. 128p. 1992. pap. 21.95 (0-335-15675-4) OpUniv Pr.
Collinson, Diane, jt. auth. see Campbell, Robert.
Collinson, F., et al. Financial Products: A Survival Guide. 230p. 1996. 125.00 (1-85564-413-4, Pub. by Euromoney) Am Educ Systs.
Collinson, Francis, jt. ed. see Campbell, John L.
Collinson, Frank. Life in the Saddle. Clarke, Mary W., ed. LC 96-44366. (Western Frontier Library: Vol. 21). (Illus.). 256p. 1997. pap. 14.95 (0-8061-2923-9) U of Okla Pr.
Collinson, Helen. Green Guerrillas: Environmental Conflicts & Intiatives in Latin America & the Caribbean. 249p. 1997. 52.99 (1-55164-067-8, Pub. by Black Rose) Consort Bk Sales.
Collinson, Helen, ed. Green Guerrillas: Environmental Conflicts in Latin America - A Reader. 244p. 1997. pap. 19.00 (0-85345-980-0, Pub. by Monthly Rev) NYU Pr.
— Women & Revolution in Nicaragua. LC 90-38982. (Illus.). 224p. (C). 1990. pap. 15.00 (0-86232-935-3, Pub. by Zed Books); text 49.95 (0-86232-934-5, Pub. by Zed Books) St Martin.
Collinson, Howard C. Documenting Design: Works on Paper in the European Collection of the Royal Ontario Museum. LC 93-93488. 120p. 1993. pap. 35.00 (0-8020-7454-5); text 65.00 (0-8020-0557-8) U of Toronto Pr.
Collinson, J. D. & Thompson, D. B. Sedimentary Structures. 2nd ed. (Illus.). 240p. 1987. text 80.00 (0-04-445171-7); pap. text 29.95 (0-04-445172-5) Routledge.
Collinson, John, ed. Correlation in Hydrocarbon Exploration. (C). 1990. lib. bdg. 378.00 (1-85333-284-4, Pub. by Graham & Trotman) Kluwer Academic.
*Collinson, M. P. A History of Farming Systems Research LC 99-42827. 480p. 2000. 120.00 (0-85199-405-9) OUP.
Collinson, Patrick. Elizabethan Essays. LC 94-2051. 256p. 1994. 60.00 (1-85285-092-2) Hambledon Press.
— The Elizabethan Puritan Movement. 528p. 1990. pap. text 32.00 (0-19-822298-X) OUP.
— Godly People: Essays on English Protestantism & Puritanism. 634p. (C). 1983. 75.00 (0-907628-15-X) Hambledon Press.
— The Religion of Protestants: The Church in English Society 1559-1625. 310p. 1984. pap. text 26.00 (0-19-820053-6) OUP.
Collinson, Patrick, et al, eds. A History of Canterbury Cathedral. (Illus.). 708p. 1995. 45.00 (0-19-820051-X) OUP.
Collinson, Patrick & Craig, John. The Reformation in English Towns, 1500-1640. LC 98-4783. (Themes in Focus Ser.). 1998. text 59.95 (0-312-21425-1) St Martin.
Collinson, R. P. G. Introduction to Avionics. 480p. 1997. 59.95 (0-7803-3433-7) Inst Electrical.
Collinson, Richard. Journal of H. M. S. Enterprise on the Expedition in Search of Sir John Franklin's Ships by Behring Strait, 1850-55. LC 74-5830. 1976. reprint ed. 82.50 (0-404-11636-1) AMS Pr.
Collinson, Robert W., jt. ed. see Houlton, John E.
Collinson, Rufus. Turning the Stones. (Chapbook Ser.: No. 5). 40p. (Orig.). 1997. pap. 8.95 (0-9649463-4-3) Folly Cove.
Collinson, Sarah. Beyond Borders: West European Migration Policy Towards the 21st Century. 115p. (C). 1994. pap. 14.95 (0-905031-71-7) Brookings.
— Europe & International Migration. LC 93-15208. 189p. 1993. 57.50 (1-85567-049-6) St Martin.
— Europe & International Migration, Vol. 1. 2nd ed. 1995. pap. 20.00 (1-85567-297-9) St Martin.
— Shore to Shore: The Politics of Migration in Euro-Maghreb Relations. 117p. 1996. pap. 16.95 (1-86203-010-3, Pub. by Royal Inst Intl Affairs) Brookings.
Collinson, Simon. Small & Successful in Japan: A Study of 30 British Firms in the World's Most Competitive Market. LC 96-83831. 160p. 1996. 63.95 (1-85628-921-4, Pub. by Avebry) Ashgate Pub Co.
Collinson, Vivienne. Teachers as Learners: Exemplary Teachers' Perception of Personal & Professional Development. LC 94-3924. 175p. 1994. 64.95 (1-880921-79-0); pap. 44.95 (1-880921-78-2) Austin & Winfield.
Collinson, William E. & Morris, A. V. Indication: A Study of Demonstratives, Articles & Other Indicaters. (LM Ser.: Vol. 17). 1937. pap. 25.00 (0-527-00821-4) Periodicals Srv.
*Collinsworth, Joseph & Collinsworth, Shannon. Arousing Chats. 328p. 2000. pap. 13.95 (0-9700492-9-3) Steel Pr Pubng.
Collinsworth, Shannon, jt. auth. see Collinsworth, Joseph.
Collinsworth, Van K. Red Earth: Agrarian Reform in Revolutionary Nicaragua. LC 88-81879. (Illus.). 200p. (Orig.). 1988. pap. 10.95 (0-929797-00-0) Earth Review Pr.
Collins1. Algebraic Structures. (C). 1994. pap. text, teacher ed. write for info. (0-03-051087-2) Harcourt Coll Pubs.
— Chirality in Industry. 418p. 1998. pap. 95.00 (0-471-98284-9) Wiley.
— Chirality in Industry: The Commercial Manufacture & Applications of Optically Active Compounds. 426p. (C). 1995. pap. 110.00 (0-471-96313-5) Wiley.
— Collaborative Field Education. 208p. (C). 1998. pap. text 18.00 (0-536-01313-6) Pearson Custom.
— Collins Bible Handbook. LC 88-45700. (Illus.). 528p. 1989. 14.95 (0-06-061528-1) Harper SF.
— Collins Gem Five Thousand German Words. (ENG & GER.). 256p. 1980. 8.95 (0-8288-1432-5, M14284) Fr & Eur.
— Collins Italian English-English Italian Dictionary. 49.95 (0-8288-8430-7) Fr & Eur.
— Collins Italian-English, English-Italian Dictionary. (ENG & ITA.). write for info. (0-8288-7662-2) Fr & Eur.
— La Connections. 1999. per. 6.99 (0-671-03664-5) S&S Trade.
— The Cork Diary 1998. 128p. 1997. pap. 21.00 (1-898256-09-8) Dufour.
— Daylight. large type ed. Date not set. 30.00 (0-7862-1725-1) Thorndike Pr.
— Deadlock. 1999. text. write for info. (0-312-93087-9) St Martin.
— Dictionary of Carbohydrates, 1 vol. 1997. ring bd. 695.00 (0-412-38670-4) CRC Pr.
— Ethical Dilemmas in Accounting. (GC - Principles of Management Ser.). (C). 1994. mass mkt. 10.95 (0-538-83695-4) S-W Pub.
— Flying IFR. 1983. pap. 11.95 (0-02-527210-1) Macmillan.
— Guide to Evening Classes in Cork City & County. Date not set. pap. 6.95 (1-898256-10-1) Dufour.
— Intelligent Machines. Date not set. pap. 18.00 (0-465-03338-5) Basic.
— Irish Politics Today. 3rd ed. LC 96-40139. 1997. pap. 19.95 (0-7190-5136-3, Pub. by Manchester Univ Pr) St Martin.
— Island for Sale. 1992. pap. text. write for info. (0-582-07482-7, Pub. by Addison-Wesley) Longman.
— Lorrie Morgan, Vol. 1. LC 98-158128. 1998. 5.99 (0-312-96608-3, Pub. by Tor Bks) St Martin.
— Malayalam Dictionary. 3rd ed. (MAL.). 544p. 1918. 75.00 (0-7859-9817-9) Fr & Eur.
— Map of Historical Scotland. 1997. pap. 11.95 (0-00-448687-0, 0-8437-6646-8) Hammond World.
— Medical Language. Date not set. teacher ed. write for info. (0-314-06959-3) West Pub.
— Multimedia for Windows 95 Made Simple. 160p. Date not set. pap. text. write for info. (0-7506-3397-2) Buttrwrth-Heinemann.
— Turn Your Radio On: The Stories Behind Gospel Musics All-Time Greatest Songs. LC 99-24350. 256p. 1999. pap. 12.99 (0-310-21153-0) Zondervan.
— Power. 1998. mass mkt. 3.99 (0-671-02458-2) S&S Trade.
— Revenge. 135p. 1998. per. write for info. (0-671-02461-2) S&S Trade.
— Security Dilemma & End of Cold. 256p. 1997. text 59.95 (0-312-17672-4) St Martin.
— See Dangerous Kiss. Date not set. 25.00 (0-684-85996-3) S&S Trade.
— Standard Common & Scientific Names. 1990. pap. write for info. (0-916984-21-4) SSAR.
— Stud. 1999. mass mkt. 7.99 (0-671-02824-3) PB.
— Teaching Choral Music. 2nd ed. 509p. (C). 1999. 55.00 (0-13-081356-7) P-H.
— Technical Communication at Work. (C). 1994. pap. text, teacher ed. 33.75 (0-15-500854-4) Harcourt Coll Pubs.
Collins1. Turkish Phrase Finder. (ENG & TUR.). 1997. 12.00 incl. audio (0-00-472049-0, Pub. by HarpC) Trafalgar.
Collins1. Weddings. 1997. pap. 8.00 (0-00-472062-8) Collins.
— Working with Children with Special Needs: ECE 103 Course. 250p. (C). 1992. ring bd. write for info. (0-933195-44-3) CA College Health Sci.
Collins1 & Broughton. The Child, Family & Community: ECE 110 Course. 212p. (C). 1992. ring bd. write for info. (0-933195-42-7) CA College Health Sci.
— Fundamentals of Child Development: ECE 100 Course. 150p. (C). 1992. ring bd. write for info. (0-933195-43-5) CA College Health Sci.
Collins1 & Cheek. Diagnostic Pressure Reading. 5th ed. 1999. 30.74 (0-697-24140-8, WCB McGr Hill) McGrw-H Hghr Educ.
Collins1 & Kennedy. Laboratory Acquired Infection. LC 98-32458. 336p. 1999. text 105.00 (0-7506-4023-5) Buttrwrth-Heinemann.
Collins1 & Nycz. Chemistry 1046L. 2nd ed. 132p. (C). 1997. per., lab manual ed. 19.95 (0-7872-4412-0) Kendall-Hunt.
Collins1, jt. auth. see Murray, Colin.
Collins1, jt. auth. see Simon.
Collinwood, Dean. Global Studies: Japan & the Pacific Rim. 4th ed. 224p. (C). 1997. text. write for info. (0-697-37423-8) Brown & Benchmark.
*Collinwood, Dean. Japan & the Pacific Rim. 5th ed. (Global Studies). (C). 1999. pap., student ed. 18.75 (0-07-024948-2) McGrw-H Hghr Educ.
Collinwood, Dean W. The Bahamas Between Worlds. 120p. (Orig.). 1989. pap. 8.95 (0-932265-15-4) White Sound.
— Global Studies in Japan. 3rd ed. 1995. pap. 18.56 (1-56134-380-3, Dshkn McG-Hill) McGrw-H Hghr Educ.
Collinwood, Dean W., et al. Samurais in Salt Lake. Matsui-Haag, Kazue, tr. from JPN. (Illus.). 72p. (Orig.). 1996. pap. 5.00 (0-9651163-9-5) Harkness Pubng.
Colliot-Thelene, J. L., et al. Arithmetic Algebraic Geometry. Ballico, E., ed. LC 93-28781. (Lecture Notes in Mathematics Ser.: Vol. 1553). 1994. 43.95 (0-387-57110-8) Spr-Verlag.
— Arithmetic Algebraic Geometry: Lectures Given at the 2nd Session of the Centro Internazionale Matematico Estivo Held in Trento, Italy, June 24-July 2, 1991. (Lecture Notes in Mathematics Ser.: Vol. 1553). vii, 223p. 1993. pap. write for info. (3-540-57110-8) Spr-Verlag.
Collip, Bruce G. Buoyancy, Stability & Trim. (Rotary Drilling Ser.: Unit V, Lesson 3). (Illus.). 30p. (Orig.). 1976. pap. text 15.00 (0-88698-071-2, 2.50310) PETEX.
Collis, Betty & Davies, Gordon. Innovative Adult Learning with Innovative Technologies: Results of the Joint Meeting of the IFIP WG3.2 & WG3.6, Nantes, France, 27-30 October, 1994. LC 95-30420. (IFIP Transactions A: Computer Science & Technology Ser.: No. A-61). (Illus.). 220p. 1995. 73.00 (0-444-82246-1) Elsevier.
Collis, Betty A., et al. Children & Computers in School. LC 96-18083. 250p. 1996. pap. 17.00 (0-8058-2074-4); text 34.50 (0-8058-2073-6) L Erlbaum Assocs.
Collis, David J. Corporate Strategy. 2nd ed. 2001. 33.25 (0-07-231286-6) McGraw.
Collis, David J. & Montgomery, Cynthia A. Corporate Strategy: A Resource-Based Approach. LC 97-24230. 240p. 1997. 42.50 (0-07-289543-8) McGraw.
— Corporate Strategy: Resources & the Scope of the Firm. LC 95-36380. 734p. (C). 1997. text 53.60 (0-256-17894-1, Irwn McGrw-H) McGrw-H Hghr Educ.
Collis, Edgar L. & Greenwood, Major. The Health of the Industrial Worker. Stein, Leon, ed. LC 77-70489. (Illus.). 1977. reprint ed. lib. bdg. 42.95 (0-405-10161-9) Ayer.
Collis, Eirene, tr. see Sand, George.
*Collis, Harry. 101 American English Customs: Understanding Language & Culture Through Common Practices. LC 99-29186. 128p. 1999. pap. 7.95 (0-8442-2407-3, 24073) NTC Contemp Pub Co.
Collis, Harry. 101 American English Idioms. (Illus.). 128p. 1995. pap. 7.95 (0-8442-5446-0, 54460, Passprt Bks) NTC Contemp Pub Co.
— 101 American English Proverbs. (Illus.). 144p. pap. 29.95 incl. audio (0-8442-0594-X, 0594X, Passprt Bks) NTC Contemp Pub Co.
— 101 American English Proverbs. LC 91-60823. (Illus.). 144p. 1994. pap. 6.95 (0-8442-5412-6, 54126, Passprt Bks) NTC Contemp Pub Co.
— 101 American English Riddles. Nolan, John, ed. (Illus.). 128p. (Orig.). 1995. pap. 6.95 (0-8442-5606-4, 56064, Natl Textbk Co) NTC Contemp Pub Co.
— 101 American English Superstitions. LC 98-140548. (Illus.). 144p. 1997. pap. 7.95 (0-8442-5599-8, 55998, Natl Textbk Co) NTC Contemp Pub Co.
Collis, Harry & Risso, Mario. 101 American English Idioms. (Illus.). 128p. 1995. pap. 29.95 incl. audio (0-8442-5424-X, 5424X, Passprt Bks) NTC Contemp Pub Co.
Collis, Hubert. I'm Walking to the End of the World. LC 87-51372. (Illus.). 54p. (Orig.). 1987. pap. write for info. (0-945126-00-X) Undiscovd Worlds Pr.
Collis, J., tr. see Swassjan, Karen.
Collis, J., tr. see Van Manen, Hans P.
Collis, J., tr. see Wolff, Otto.
Collis, J. R., jt. ed. see Champion, Timothy C.
Collis, Johanna, tr. see Grosse, Rudolf.
Collis, Johanna, tr. see Steiner, Rudolf.
Collis, Johanna, tr. see Thomas, Nick.
Collis, John. Educational Malpractice: Liability Educators, 1990 Edition. 1990. text 55.00 (0-87473-638-2, 60985-10, MICHIE) LEXIS Pub.
— European Iron Age. (Illus.). 192p. (C). 1997. pap. 32.99 (0-415-15139-2) Routledge.
*Collis, John. John Denver: Mother Nature's Son. (Illus.). 208p. 2000. 24.95 (1-84018-124-9) Mainstream Pubng.
Collis, John. Mexico. (Blue Guide Ser.). Date not set. 27.50 (0-393-01665-X) Norton.
— Mexico. LC 96-32289. (Blue Guide Ser.). 960p. 1996. pap. 25.00 (0-393-30072-2, Norton Paperbks) Norton.
— The 7 Fatal Management Sins: Understanding & Avoiding Managerial Malpractice. (Illus.). 288p. (Orig.). 1997. per. 34.95 (1-57444-015-2) St Lucie Pr.
— The Story of Chess Records. 192p. 1998. 24.95 (1-58234-005-6) Bloomsbury Pubg.
— Van Morrison: Inarticulate Speech of the Heart. LC 97-204062. (Illus.). 272p. (Orig.). 1997. pap. 14.95 (0-306-80811-0) Da Capo.
Collis, Joyce. Show Border Collie. (Illus.). 144p. 1993. 24.95 (0-948955-35-X, Pub. by Ringpr Bks) Seven Hills Bk.
Collis, Joyce & Jones, Pat. The Complete Bearded Collie. (Book of the Breed). (Illus.). 160p. 1995. 24.95 (0-948955-37-6, Pub. by Ringpr Bks) Seven Hills Bk.
Collis, L., jt. ed. see Smith, M. R.
Collis, Len. Card Games for Children. (Illus.). 96p. (J). (gr. 3 up). 1989. pap. 6.95 (0-8120-4290-5) Barron.
— Magic Tricks for Children. (Illus.). 96p. (J). (gr. 3 up). 1989. pap. 6.95 (0-8120-4289-1) Barron.
Collis, Len. Magic Tricks for Children. (J). 1989. 12.05 (0-606-04472-8, Pub. by Turtleback) Demco.
Collis, Louise. Memoirs of a Medieval Woman. LC 82-48226. (Illus.). 288p. 1991. pap. 13.50 (0-06-090992-7, CN 992, Perennial) HarperTrade.
Collis, Mark & Dalton, Joan. Becoming Responsible Learners: Strategies for Positive Classroom Management. LC 90-49851. 68p. (C). 1990. pap. text 18.50 (0-435-08568-9, 08568) Heinemann.
Collis, Mark & Lacey, Penny. Interactive Approaches to Teaching: A Framework for INSET. LC 96-212678. 112p. 1996. pap. text 24.95 (1-85346-366-3, Pub. by David Fulton) Taylor & Francis.
Collis, Maurice. Great Within. LC 72-128876. (Select Bibliographies Reprint Ser.). 1977. 25.95 (0-8369-5496-3) Ayer.
— Hurling Time. 323p. 1958. 69.50 (0-614-00064-5) Elliots Bks.
— The Land of the Great Image. LC 85-13438. (New Directions Classics Ser.). (Illus.). 256p. (Orig.). 1985. reprint ed. pap. 9.95 (0-8112-0972-5, NDP612, Pub. by New Directions) Norton.
— Lords of the Sunset: A Tour in the Shan States. LC 77-87074. reprint ed. 42.50 (0-404-16807-8) AMS Pr.
— She Was a Queen. LC 90-21153. (New Directions Classics Ser.). (Illus.). 304p. 1991. reprint ed. pap. 12.95 (0-8112-1169-X, NDP716, Pub. by New Directions) Norton.
— Trials in Burma. LC 74-179181. reprint ed. 32.50 (0-404-54812-1) AMS Pr.
Collis, Maurice, ed. Cortes & Montezuma. LC 99-15278. (Classic Ser.). 256p. 1999. pap. 12.95 (0-8112-1423-0, Pub. by New Directions) Norton.
Collis-Montgome. Corporate Strategy. 1997. 42.18 (0-256-25659-4) McGraw.
Collis, Roger. Survivor's Guide to Business Travel. 2000. pap. 19.95 (0-7494-3074-5) Kogan Page Ltd.
*Collis, Rose. K. D. Lang. 1999. pap. text 9.95 (1-899791-47-7) Theatre Comm.
Collis, Rose. Portraits to the Wall: Historic Lesbian Lives Unveiled. (Women on Women Ser.). 224p. 1994. 69.95 (0-304-32853-7, Pub. by Cassell); pap. 19.95 (0-304-32851-0, Pub. by Cassell) LPC InBook.
— A Trouser-Wearing Character: The Life & Times of Nancy Spain. (Sexual Politics Ser.). (Illus.). 256p. 1997. 39.95 (0-304-32879-0) Continuum.
*Collis, Rose. A Trouser-Wearing Character: The Life & Times of Nancy Spain. 1999. pap. 21.95 (0-304-70624-8) Continuum.
*Collis, Rose, ed. The Mammoth Book of Lesbian Erotica. 512p. 2000. pap. 11.95 (0-7867-0726-7, Pub. by Carroll & Graf) Publishers Group.
*Collis, S. The 7 Fatal Management Sins. 1998. pap. 298.00 (81-86982-40-X, Pub. by Business Pubns) St Mut.
*Collischan, Judy. Welded Sculpture of the 20th Century. LC 99-53999. (Illus.). 140p. 2000. 50.00 (1-55595-167-8) Hudson Hills.
Collischan, Judy, ed. Judy Moonelis: Sculpture, December 3, 1993 Thru January 28, 1994. LC 94-13697. 1994. write for info. (0-933699-32-8) Hillwood Art.
— Shari Urquhart Fiber: December 3, 1993 Thru January 28, 1994. LC 94-16141. 1994. 10.00 (0-933699-31-X) Hillwood Art.
Collischan Van Wagner, Judy K. Transformations into Color: The Art of Stan Brodsky. LC 90-85139. (Illus.). 32p. (Orig.). 1991. pap. text 8.00 (1-879195-06-2) Heckscher Mus.
Collision, Catherine W. Why Is a Barn Red? The Little Book of BIG Questions. 128p. (J). (gr. 1-8). 1993. pap. 6.95 (0-937247-58-8) Detroit Pr.
Collison-Black, R. D., ed. see Jevons, William S.
Collison, Brooke B. & Garfield, Nancy J., eds. Careers in Counseling & Human Services. 2nd ed. 153p. 1995. pap. 19.95 (1-56032-415-5) Hemisp Pub.
Collison, Brooke B. & House, Reese M. Social & Cultural Foundations in the Helping Professions. (C). 2001. 44.00 (0-205-17447-7, Macmillan Coll) P-H.
*Collison, Catherine Wilde, et al, eds. Yaklennium: A Kid's Guide to the Future. (Illus.). 64p. (J). (gr. 1-8). 1999. pap. 9.95 (0-937247-30-8) Detroit Pr.
Collison, D., jt. auth. see Mabbs, F. E.
Collison, David, jt. auth. see Mabey, David.
Collison, Gary L. Shadrach Minkins: From Fugitive Slave to Citizen. LC 96-35555. (Illus.). 304p. 1997. 27.95 (0-674-80298-5) HUP.
— Shadrach Minkins: From Fugitive Slave to Citizen. (Illus.). 304p. 1998. pap. 15.95 (0-674-80299-3) HUP.
Collison, Jill, jt. auth. see Edwards, Anne.
Collison, Jim, ed. The Complete Employee Handbook Made Easy. 2nd ed. 300p. 1997. ring bd. 239.00 (0-9624320-7-5) Sunburst IA.
Collison, Joanne, ed. see Timothy, Kevin.
Collison, Linda & Russell, Bob. Colorado Kids: A Statewide Family Outdoor Adventure Guide. LC 97-6771. (Illus.). 302p. 1997. pap. 18.50 (0-87108-862-2) Pruett.
Collison, Linda & Russell, Bob. Rocky Mountain Wineries: A Travel Guide to the Wayside Vineyards: Colorado, New Mexico, Idaho, Arizona, Utah & Montana. LC 94-18957. (Illus.). 165p. 1994. pap. 16.95 (0-87108-848-7) Pruett.
Collison, Mary, jt. auth. see Collison, Robert L.
Collison, Mike. Police, Drugs & Community. 275p. (C). 1995. 55.00 (1-85343-318-7, Pub. by Free Assoc Bks) NYU Pr.
— Police, Drugs & Community. (C). 1995. pap. 25.00 (1-85343-319-5, Pub. by Free Assoc Bks) NYU Pr.
Collison, Mike, jt ed. see Carlen, Pat.
Collison-Morley, Lacy. Shakespeare in Italy. LC 67-23862. 1972. reprint ed. 18.95 (0-405-08373-4, Pub. by Blom Pubns) Ayer.
Collison, Robert L. Kenya. (World Bibliographical Ser.: No. 25). 157p. 1982. lib. bdg. 45.00 (0-903450-34-8) ABC-CLIO.
Collison, Robert L., ed. Dictionary of Dates. LC 77-95116. 428p. 1969. reprint ed. lib. bdg. 79.50 (0-8371-2495-6, CODD, Greenwood Pr) Greenwood.
— Luxembourg. (World Bibliographical Ser.: No. 23). 184p. 1981. lib. bdg. 45.00 (0-903450-37-2) ABC-CLIO.
Collison, Robert L. & Collison, Mary. Dictionary of Foreign Quotations. LC 81-124080. 415p. reprint ed. pap. 128.70 (0-608-12112-6, 202515100042) Bks Demand.
Collison, Robert L., ed. see Clogg, Mary Jo & Clogg, Richard.
Collison, Robert L., ed. see Findlay, Allan M., et al.
Collison, Vivienne. Reaching Students: Teachers' Ways of Knowing. LC 95-50186. (Illus.). 136p. 1996. pap. 19.95 (0-8039-6228-2) Corwin Pr.
— Reaching Students: Teachers' Ways of Knowing. LC 95-50186. (Illus.). 136p. 1996. 45.95 (0-8039-6227-4) Corwin Pr.
Collister, Laurie, ed. see Kononenko, Yuri.

C

***Collister, Linda.** Country Breads of the World: 88 of the World's Best Recipes for Baking Bread. 2000. 35.00 (*1-58574-112-4*) Lyon Press.

— Morning Bakes. LC 99-40075. 64p. (J). (gr. 11). 2000. write for info. (*0-7370-2033-4*) Time-Life Educ.

Collister, Linda. Sensational Sauces. LC 97-31688. (Illus.). 144p. 1998. 24.95 (*0-7621-0059-1*, Pub. by RD Assn) Penguin Putnam.

***Collister, Linda & Blake, Anthony.** The Bread Book. (Illus.). 224p. 2000. 35.00 (*1-58574-057-8*) Lyons Pr.

Collister, Peter. Bhutan & the British. 1996. reprint ed. 33.00 (*81-7476-143-8*, Pub. by UBS Pubs Dist) S Asia.

Collister, Rob. Lightweight Expeditions. (Illus.). 144p. 1989. 24.95 (*0-938567-15-2*) Mountaineers.

Collitt, Josephine F. Johnny Reb & the Molasses Cookies. (Illus.). 12p. (Orig.). (J). (gr. 4-10). 1994. pap. 5.00 (*0-9648441-0-9*) J F Collitt.

Collitt, Josephine F. The Last of the Good Old Days. (Illus.). 80p. 1998. pap. 11.95 (*0-9648441-4-1*) J F Collitt.

***Collitt, Josephine F.** Mechanicsburg Reflections, 1900-2000. (Illus.). 1999. pap. 10.00 (*0-9648441-6-8*) J F Collitt.

Collitt, Josephine F. My Mechanicsburg in the Thirties. 34p. (Orig.). 1995. pap. 6.00 (*0-9648441-1-7*) J F Collitt.

— Sycamores & More. (Illus.). 70p. 1995. pap. 7.50 (*0-9648441-2-5*) J F Collitt.

— Today the Lord Said to Me. 46p. 1997. pap. 5.00 (*0-9648441-5-X*) J F Collitt.

Collitz, K. H. Verbs of Motion in Their Semantic Divergence. (LM Ser.: Vol. 8). 1931. pap. 25.00 (*0-527-00812-5*) Periodicals Srv.

Colliver, David J. Compound Semiconductor Technology. LC 75-31377. (Illus.). 301p. reprint ed. pap. 93.40 (*0-8357-4183-4*, 203696100006) Bks Demand.

Colliver, Douglas & Proctor, Charles, eds. Norton Rose: Cross Border Security. 1997. write for info. (*0-406-05463-0*, NRCB, MICHIE) LEXIS Pub.

Colliver, James, et al. Substance Abuse among Women & Parents. (Illus.). 62p. (Orig.). (C). 1996. pap. text 20.00 (*0-7881-2746-2*) DIANE Pub.

Collman, Barbara J. Kid's Book to Welcome a New Baby: Fun for a Big Brother or Big Sister. 3rd rev. ed. 120p. 1999. pap. 12.95 (*1-892147-00-9*, Pub. by Marlor Pr) IPG Chicago.

Collman, Charles A. Our Mysterious Panics, 1830-1930: A Story of Events & the Men Involved. LC 68-28621. 310p. 1968. reprint ed. lib. bdg. 69.50 (*0-8371-0050-X*, COMP, Greenwood Pr) Greenwood.

Collman, Gwen, jt. ed. see Dearry, Allen.

Collman, James P., et al. Principles & Applications of Organotransition Metal Chemistry. 2nd ed. (Illus.). 989p. (C). 1987. text 65.00 (*0-935702-51-2*) Univ Sci Bks.

Collman, Russ, ed. Trails among the Columbine, 1993/1994: 93/94. (Illus.). 192p. 1994. 37.00 (*0-913582-59-X*, 0251) Sundance.

Collman, Russ, et al. The RGS Story Vol. 3: Over the Bridges, Vance Junction to Ophir. LC 90-232248. (Illus.). 496p. 1993. 72.00 (*0-913582-50-6*, 0250) Sundance.

— The RGS Story Vol. 4: Over the Bridges, Ophir to Rico. LC 90-232248. (Illus.). 496p. 1994. 72.00 (*0-913582-58-1*, 0252) Sundance.

— The RGS Story Vol. 5: Rico & the Mines. (RGS Story Ser.: Vol. 5). (Illus.). 496p. 1996. 72.00 (*0-913582-61-1*, 0254) Sundance.

Collman, Russ, jt. auth. see McCoy, Dell A.

Collman, Russ, ed. see Dixon, Dick.

Collman, Russ, ed. see McCoy, Dell A. & Cook, W. George.

Collman, Russ, ed. see Polley, Rodger.

Collman, Russ, ed. see Sundance Publications, Ltd. Staff.

Collman, Russ, ed. see Sundance Staff.

Collmann, Jeff. Fringe Dwellers & Welfare: The Aboriginal Response to Bureaucracy. LC 86-27216. 276p. (Orig.). (C). 1988. pap. text 29.95 (*0-7022-2067-1*, Pub. by Univ Queensland Pr) Intl Spec Bk.

***Collmann, Jeff, ed.** CPRI Toolkit: Managing Information Security in Health Care. (Illus.). 1999. 250.00 (*0-9649285-4-X*) Comp-based Patient Rec.

***Collmann, Lilliam Oliva.** Jesus Diaz: El Ejercicio de los Limites de la Expresion Revolucionaria en Cuba. (Caribbean Studies: Vol. 2). 181p. (C). 1999. text 48.00 (*0-8204-4279-8*) P Lang Pubng.

Collmann, Robin D. The Psychogalvanic Reactions of Exceptional & Normal School Children. LC 79-176664. (Columbia University. Teachers College. Contributions to Education Ser.: No. 469). reprint ed. 37.50 (*0-404-55469-5*) AMS Pr.

Collmer, H., ed. & tr. see Huygens, L., et al.

Collmer, Robert G., ed. Bunyan in Our Time. LC 89-33452. 251p. 1990. 26.00 (*0-87338-391-5*) Kent St U Pr.

Collmer, Robert G. & Herring, Jack W., eds. American Bypaths: Essays in Honor of E. Hudson Long. LC 80-82061. 250p. 1980. 19.50 (*0-918954-22-3*) Baylor Univ Pr.

Collobert, Danielle. It Then. Cole, Norma, tr. LC 88-90555. 128p. 1989. 9.00 (*1-882022-02-5*) O Bks.

Collocott, E. E. V. Tales & Poems of Tonga. (BMB Ser.: No. 46). 1974. reprint ed. 25.00 (*0-527-02152-0*) Periodicals Srv.

Collocott, T. C. Diccionario Cientifico y Tecnologico Chambers, 2 vols., Set. 3rd ed. (SPA.). 2812p. 1979. 495.00 (*0-7859-5854-1*, 8428205310) Fr & Eur.

Collodi, Carlo. The Adventure of Pinocchio. Lucas, Ann L., tr. & intro. by. (The World's Classics Ser.). (Illus.). 248p. 1996. pap. 8.95 (*0-19-282340-X*) OUP.

— The Adventures of Pinocchio. 256p. 1984. lib. bdg. 25.95 (*0-89968-257-X*, Lghtyr Pr) Buccaneer Bks.

— The Adventures of Pinocchio. LC 96-6297. (Illustrated Junior Library). (Illus.). 272p. (YA). 1996. 15.95 (*0-448-41479-1*, G & D) Peng Put Young Read.

— The Adventures of Pinocchio: Le Avventure di Pinocchio. Perella, Nicolas J., tr. & intro. by. 1997. reprint ed. pap. 18.95 (*0-520-07782-2*, Pub. by U CA Pr) Cal Prin Full Svc.

Collodi, Carlo. Le Aventure di Pinocchio Level B. text 7.95 (*0-88436-050-4*) EMC-Paradigm.

Collodi, Carlo. The Commedia Pinocchio. (Commedia Plays Ser.). 31p. (Orig.). (J). (gr. 1-9). 1989. pap. 3.00 (*1-57514-213-9*, 1030) Encore Perform Pub.

Collodi, Carlo. Pinocchio. 22.95 (*0-88411-249-7*) Amereon Ltd.

Collodi, Carlo. Pinocchio. LC 97-52928. (Illus.). (J). 1998. pap. 1.00 (*0-486-40090-5*) Dover.

— Pinocchio. (FRE., Illus.). (J). (gr. 3-8). 5.95 (*0-685-11495-3*, S16273) Fr & Eur.

— Pinocchio. 1986. pap. 2.50 (*0-451-51986-8*, Sig Classics) NAL.

— Pinocchio. (Illus.). 272p. (YA). (gr. 5 up). 1996. pap. 4.99 (*0-14-036708-X*, PuffinBks) Peng Put Young Read.

— Pinocchio. LC 95-10127. (Illus.). 48p. (J). (ps-3). 1996. 18.95 (*0-399-22941-8*, Philomel) Peng Put Young Read.

— Pinocchio. (Folio - Junior Ser.: No. 283). (FRE., Illus.). 235p. (J). (gr. 5-10). 1985. pap. 10.95 (*2-07-033283-7*) Schoenhof.

— Pinocchio. (J). (gr. 4-7). 1996. mass mkt. 2.99 (*0-8125-6702-1*, Pub. by Tor Bks) St Martin.

Collodi, Carlo. Pinocchio. 1996. 8.09 (*0-606-11750-4*, Pub. by Turtleback) Demco.

Collodi, Carlo. Pinocchio. (Children's Library). (J). (gr. 4-7). 1998. pap. 3.95 (*1-85326-160-2*, 1602WW, Pub. by Wrdsworth Edits) NTC Contemp Pub Co.

— Pinocchio: Storia di un Burattino. (ITA.). 70p. 1997. pap. text 19.50 (*1-58085-003-0*) Interlingua VA.

— Pinocchio: Storia di un Burattino. Gibson, Dick, tr. (ENG & ITA.). 140p. 1997. pap. text 29.50 (*1-58085-004-9*) Interlingua VA.

— Pinocchio Coloring Book. (Illus.). (J). (gr. k-3). 1994. pap. 2.95 (*0-486-28003-9*) Dover.

— Pinoccio. (Fairy Tales Ser.). 1998. 12.95 (*2-215-06193-6*) CE75.

— Pinocho (Pinocchio) La Historia de un Muneco (Story of a Puppet) (ENG & SPA.). 220p. (J). 1998. 29.50 (*1-58085-015-4*); pap. 19.50 (*1-58085-014-6*) Interlingua VA.

Collodi, Carlo & Ajhar, Brian. Pinocchio. unabridged ed. LC 95-8578. (Illus.). 40p. (J). (ps-3). 1996. per. 19.95 incl. audio (*0-689-80230-7*, Rabbit Ears) Litle Simon.

Collodi, Carlo & Blaisdell, Bob. The Adventures of Pinocchio. unabridged ed. (Children's Thrift Classics Ser.). (Illus.). 96p. (J). 1995. reprint ed. pap. text 1.00 (*0-486-28840-4*) Dover.

Collodi, Carlo, et al. Pinocchio. LC 97-214344. (Pair-It Bks.). 32 p. 1998. write for info. (*0-8172-7290-9*) Raintree Steck-V.

Colloff, M. J. & Halliday, B. Oribatid Mites: A Catalogue of Australian Genera & Species. (Monographs on Invertebrate Taxonomy: Vol. 6). 224p. 120.00 (*0-643-06371-4*, Pub. by CSIRO) Accents Pubns.

Collom, Jack. Arguing with Something Plato Said (a Few Environs Poems) 64p. 1990. pap. 7.50 (*0-9614378-3-9*) Rocky Ledge.

— Dog Sonnets. 32p. 1998. pap. 4.00 (*1-893032-05-1*) Jensen Daniels.

— Eight-Ball. LC 92-81818. (Illus.). 60p. 1992. pap. 7.95 (*1-880743-00-0*) Dead Metaphor.

— Entering the City. Kosmicki, Greg, ed. 86p. (Orig.). 1997. pap. 12.00 (*1-57502-472-1*, P01412) Morris Pubng.

— Moving Windows: Evaluating the Poetry Children Write. LC 85-9803. 225p. (Orig.). 1985. pap. 14.95 (*0-915924-55-2*) Tchrs & Writers Coll.

— The Task. (Illus.). 53p. 1996. 7.00 (*1-887997-06-7*) Baksun Bks.

— What a Strange Way of Being Dead. (Illus.). 65p. (Orig.). 1995. pap. 10.00 (*1-887289-09-7*) Rodent Pr.

Collom, Jack, ed. Sound Is My Number: Handbook for the Outreach Writing Program at Naropa. 85p. (C). 1995. pap. text 10.00 (*1-887997-03-2*) Baksun Bks.

Collom, Jack & Bernstein, Ken. Callusses of Poetry. pap. 17.50 incl. audio compact disk (*0-9651878-0-2*) TreeHse Pr.

Collom, Jack & Noethe, Sheryl. Poetry Everywhere: Teaching Poetry Writing in School & in the Community. LC 93-32351. 280p. 1994. pap. 17.95 (*0-915924-98-6*) Tchrs & Writers Coll.

Collom, Jack, jt. auth. see Hejinian, Lyn.

Collomb, Michel, ed. see Morand, Paul.

***Collombet, Francois.** The Flammarion Guide to World Wines. 2000. 30.00 (*2-08-013685-2*, Pub. by Flammarion) Abbeville Pr.

Colloms, Martin. High Performance Loudspeakers. 5th ed. 494p. 1997. 160.00 (*0-471-97091-3*, EE00); pap. 79.95 (*0-471-97089-1*) Wiley.

Collon, Dominique. First Impressions: Cylinder Seals in the Ancient Near East. LC 87-19117. (Illus.). 208p. 1993. 29.95 (*0-226-11388-4*) U Ch Pr.

— First Impressions: Cylinder Seals in the Ancient Near East. 208p. 1998. pap. text 21.95 (*0-226-11389-2*) U Ch Pr.

— Near Eastern Seals. (Interpreting the Past Ser.). (Illus.). 64p. 1991. pap. 13.95 (*0-520-07308-8*, Pub. by U CA Pr) Cal Prin Full Svc.

— Seal Impressions from Tell Atchana/Alalakh. (Alter Orient und Altes Testament Ser.: Vol. 27). xii, 217p. 1975. text 34.50 (*3-7887-0496-9*) NeukirchenerV.

Collon, Domonique. Ancient Near Eastern Art. LC 95-10205. (Illus.). 240p. 1995. pap. 29.95 (*0-520-20307-0*, Pub. by U CA Pr) Cal Prin Full Svc.

Collonson, Diane. Fifty Major Philosophers. 176p. 1987. pap. 17.99 (*0-415-03135-4*) Routledge.

Collop, John. The Poems of John Collop. Hilberry, Conrad, ed. LC 61-5905. 239p. 1962. reprint ed. pap. 74.10 (*0-608-01981-X*, 206263600003) Bks Demand.

Collopy. Assembler Language. (C). 1994. text. write for info. (*0-318-70352-1*, BF0980) S-W Pub.

— Introduction to Cobol Programming. LC 99-34019. (Illus.). 568p. 1999. pap. text 78.00 incl. cd-rom, audio compact disk (*0-13-909060-6*) P-H.

Collopy, David M. An Introduction to C Programming. LC 96-17983. 625p. (C). 1996. pap. text 86.00 (*0-13-190174-5*) P-H.

— Introduction to C++ Programming: A Modular Approach. LC 98-4594. 614p. (C). 1998. pap. 87.00 (*0-13-888801-9*) P-H.

Collopy, George. Extraordinary Banners for Ordinary Times. LC 92-347. (Illus.). 240p. (Orig.). 1992. pap. 11.95 (*0-89390-225-X*) Resource Pubns.

Collopy, George F. Clip Art for Bulletins & Beyond. LC 88-4624. (Illus.). 144p. (C). 1988. pap. 17.95 (*0-89390-124-5*) Resource Pubns.

***Collopy, Michael.** Architects of Peace: Visions of Hope in Words & Images. (Illus.). 180p. 2000. 45.00 (*1-57731-081-0*, Pub. by New Wrld Lib) Publishers Group.

Collopy, Michael. Works of Love Are Works of Peace: Mother Teresa & the Missionaraies of Charity. LC 96-76027. 224p. 1996. 34.95 (*0-89870-561-4*) Ignatius Pr.

Colloque du Club Jules Gonin Staff & Assemblee de la Societe Suisse d'Ophthalmologie St. Secondary Detachment of the Retina: Proceedings of the Collogue du Club Jules Gonin, 7th & the Assemblee de la Societe Suisse d'Ophthalmologie, 63rd, Lausanne, 1970. Dufour, R., ed. (Modern Problems in Ophthalmology Ser.: Vol. 10). (Illus.). 1972. 139.25 (*3-8055-1300-3*) S Karger.

Colloquium for the Philosophy of Science Staff. Boston Studies in the Philosophy of Science: Proceedings of the Colloquium for the Philosophy of Science, Boston, 1966-69, Vol. 4. Cohen, R. S. & Wartofsky, Marx W., eds. (Synthese Library: No. 18). 545p. 1969. text 148.50 (*90-277-0014-1*, D Reidel) Kluwer Academic.

— Boston Studies in the Philosophy of Science: Proceedings of the Colloquium for the Philosophy of Science, Boston, 1966-69, Vol. 5. Cohen, R. S. & Wartofsky, Marx W., eds. (Synthese Library: No. 19). 490p. 1969. text 222.50 (*90-277-0015-X*, D Reidel) Kluwer Academic.

— Boston Studies in the Philosophy of Science Vol. 13: Proceedings of the Colloquium for the Philosophy of Science, Boston, 1969-1972. Cohen, R. S. & Wartofsky, Marx W., eds. LC 73-83557. 462p. 1973. pap. text 89.00 (*90-277-0377-9*); lib. bdg. 141.50 (*90-277-0391-4*) Kluwer Academic.

— Boston Studies in the Philosophy of Science, Vol. 1: Proceedings of the Colloquium for the Philosophy of Science, Boston, 1961-1962. Wartofsky, Marx W., ed. (Synthese Library: No. 6). 220p. 1970. text 78.50 (*90-277-0021-4*, D Reidel) Kluwer Academic.

— Boston Studies in the Philosophy of Science, Vol. 14: Proceedings of the Colloquium for the Philosophy of Science, Boston, 1969-1972. Cohen, R. S. & Wartofsky, Marx W., eds. LC 73-83558. (Synthese Library: No.60). 413p. 1974. pap. text 84.00 (*90-277-0378-7*, D Reidel); lib. bdg. 129.50 (*90-277-0392-2*, D Reidel) Kluwer Academic.

Colloquium in the Philosophy of Science Staff. Induction, Physics, & Ethics: Proceedings of the Colloquium in the Philosophy of Science, Salzburg, 1969. Weingartner, Paul & Zecha, G., eds. LC 78-118137. (Synthese Library: No. 31). 392p. 1970. text 208.00 (*90-277-0158-X*, D Reidel) Kluwer Academic.

Colloquium, International Union of History & Philo. The Concept & the Role of the Model in Mathematics & Natural & Social Sciences: Proceedings of the Colloquium on the International Union of History & Philosophy of Science, Utrecht, 1960. Freudenthal, H., ed. (Synthese Library: No. 3). 200p. 1961. text 132.50 (*90-277-0017-6*, D Reidel) Kluwer Academic.

Colloquium on Drought Management & Its Impact on P. Drought Management & Its Impact on Public Water Systems: Report on a Colloquium Sponsored by the Water Science & Technology Board, September 5, 1985. LC TD0388.A1.D7. 135p. reprint ed. pap. 41.90 (*0-7837-1266-9*, 204140500020) Bks Demand.

Colloquium on Electronic Transition Lasers Staff. High-Power Lasers & Applications: Proceedings of the Colloquium on Electronic Transition Lasers, Munich, June 20-22, 1977. Kompa, K. L. & Walter, H., eds. (Optical Sciences Ser.: Vol. 9). (Illus.). 1979. 44.95 (*0-387-08641-2*) Spr-Verlag.

Colloquium on Hispanic & Luso-Brazilian Linguistic. Colloquium on Spanish & Luso-Brazilian Linguistics. Lantolf, James P. et al, eds. LC 79-18824. 167p. reprint ed. pap. 51.80 (*0-7837-6332-8*, 204604500010) Bks Demand.

Colloquium on Hispanic Linguistics Staff. Colloquium on Hispanic Linguistics, 1975. Aid, Frances M. et al, eds. LC 76-53729. 163p. reprint ed. pap. 50.60 (*0-7837-6759-5*, 205915800011) Bks Demand.

Colloquium on Mathematics & Cybernetics in the Eco. Pseudo-Boolean Programming & Applications. Ivanescu, P. L., ed. (Lecture Notes in Mathematics Ser.: Vol. 9). 1965. 32.95 (*0-387-03352-1*) Spr-Verlag.

Colloquium on Public Policy & Family Support Staff. Helping Families Grow Strong: New Directions in Public Policy. 246p. 1990. pap. 30.00 (*1-885429-01-0*) Family Resource.

Colloquium on Spanish & Portuguese Linguistics Sta. Colloquium on Spanish & Portuguese Linguistics, 1974. LC 75-28427. 154p. reprint ed. pap. 47.80 (*0-7837-6333-6*, 204604600010) Bks Demand.

Colloquium on Spanish, Portuguese, & Catalan Lingu. On Spanish, Portuguese, & Catalan Linguistics. fac. ed. Staczek, John J., ed. LC 88-4282. (Romance Languages & Linguistics Ser.). (Illus.). 245p. 1988. reprint ed. pap. 76.00 (*0-7837-7785-X*, 204754000007) Bks Demand.

Colloquium on the Age of the Universe Staff. Colloquium on the Age of the Universe, Dark Matter & Structure Formation. LC 98-196884. vii, 84 p. 1998. write for info. (*0-309-06026-5*) Natl Acad Sci.

Colloquium on the Law of Outer Space 13th, Constan. Proceedings. Schwartz, Mortimer D., ed. iii, 381p. (Orig.). 1971. pap. text 27.50 (*0-685-04973-6*) U of Cal Sch Law.

Colloquium on the Law of Outer Space, 15th, Vienna. Proceedings. Schwartz, Mortimer D., ed. iv, 284p. (Orig.). 1973. pap. text 27.50 (*0-685-04974-4*) U of Cal Sch Law.

Colloquium Spectroscopicum Internationale Staff. Atomic Spectroscopy: XXI Colloquium Spectroscopicum Internationale, 8th International Conference on Atomic Spectroscopy, Cambridge, July 1-6, 1979: Keynote Lectures. LC 81-197242. 285p. reprint ed. pap. 88.40 (*0-8357-5858-3*, 202400000035) Bks Demand.

***Colloquy on Legal Data Processing in Europe Staff & Council of Europe Staff.** Computerised Registers in the Public Sector: (In Civil, Penal, & Administrative Law): Proceedings [of the] 12th Colloquy on Legal Processing in Europe Lubania (Slovenia), 2-4 October 1995. LC 98-181010. 28 p. 1998. write for info. (*92-871-3596-7*) Council of Europe.

Collorafi, John, tr. see Tangari, Katharina.

Colloredo-Mansfield. Weavers TV. LC 99-28259. 240p. 1999. pap. text 18.00 (*0-226-11395-7*); lib. bdg. 45.00 (*0-226-11394-9*) U Ch Pr.

Collos, Alana, ed. see Smith, Artemis, pseud.

Collot, Georges H. Journey in North America, 3 vols. LC 72-1001. reprint ed. 345.00 (*0-404-01790-8*) AMS Pr.

Collotti, Enzo. Hitler & Nazism. LC 98-12354. (Illustrated Histories Ser.). (Illus.). 160p. 1999. pap. 15.00 (*1-56656-238-4*, Interlink Bks) Interlink Pub.

Colls, J. Air Pollution. LC 96-70574. (Illus.). 256p. 1996. pap. 31.95 (*0-419-20650-7*) Chapman & Hall.

Collu, Robert, et al, eds. Central Nervous System Effects of Hypothalamic Hormones & Other Peptides. fac. ed. LC 77-94310. (Illus.). 453p. pap. 140.50 (*0-7837-7515-6*, 204699000005) Bks Demand.

— Pediatric Endocrinology. LC 85-43385. (Comprehensive Endocrinology Ser.). 704p. 1989. reprint ed. pap. 200.00 (*0-608-03398-7*, 206409500008) Bks Demand.

Collum, Danny D., ed. African Americans in the Spanish Civil War: This Ain't Ethiopia, but It'll Do. 256p. 1992. 45.00 (*0-8161-7378-8*, Hall Reference) Macmillan.

Collum, Lyn, et al. Dangerous & Dashing. 288p. 1998. pap. 4.99 (*0-8217-5933-7*) Kensgtn Pub Corp.

Collum, Lynn. All Dressed in White. 256p. 1999. mass mkt. 4.99 (*0-8217-6216-8*) Kensgtn Pub Corp.

— Elizabeth & the Major. 224p. 1997. mass mkt. 4.99 (*0-8217-5712-1*, Zebra Kensgtn) Kensgtn Pub Corp.

— A Game of Chance. 224p. 1996. mass mkt. 4.50 (*0-8217-5383-5*, Zebra Kensgtn) Kensgtn Pub Corp.

— Lady Miranda's Masquerade. 224p. 1999. mass mkt. 4.99 (*0-8217-6208-7*) Kensgtn Pub Corp.

— Spy's Bride. 224p. 1999. mass mkt. 4.99 (*0-8217-6105-6*) Kensgtn Pub Corp.

***Collum, Lynn.** Sweet Temptations. (Regency Romance Ser.). 2000. mass mkt. 4.99 (*0-8217-6656-2*, Zebra Kensgtn) Kensgtn Pub Corp.

— The Unlikely Father. (Zebra Regency Romance Ser.). 224p. 1999. mass mkt. 4.99 (*0-8217-6418-7*, Zebra Kensgtn) Kensgtn Pub Corp.

Collum, Lynn, et al. Christmas Kittens. 1997. pap. 4.99 (*0-8217-5792-X*) Kensgtn Pub Corp.

— A Winter Kiss. 352p. 1997. mass mkt. 4.99 (*0-8217-5546-3*, Zebra Kensgtn) Kensgtn Pub Corp.

Collura, Jennie O., ed. see Golde, Muriel C.

Collura, Mario A. & Mac, Viccie. Tri Timeshare Vaction Ownership Resort Directory, 1995-1996. 81p. (Orig.). 1995. pap. 12.95 (*1-888176-10-5*) TRI Pubng.

Collura, Mary E. Sunny. 160p. (YA). (gr. 7-11). 1991. reprint ed. pap. 4.95 (*0-7736-7289-3*) Stoddart Publ.

Collver, J. J. The Campaign in German South West Africa, 1914-1915. (Great War Ser.: No. 64). (Illus.). 212p. 1997. reprint ed. 34.95 (*0-89839-273-X*) Battery Pr.

Collver, Michael & Dickey, Bruce. A Catalog of Music for the Cornett. LC 94-44769. (Publications of the Early Music Institute). 1995. pap. 18.95 (*0-253-20974-9*) Ind U Pr.

Collwtte, Patricia & Jones, Mark. Realizing Our Dream: How to Become the You You Really Want to Be. 2nd ed. 105p. (Orig.). 1992. reprint ed. pap., mass mkt. 7.95 (*0-614-13236-3*) Evolvement.

Collyer, A. A. A Practical Guide to the Selection of High-Temperature Engineering Thermoplastics. viii, 104p. 1990. 105.00 (*0-946395-87-X*, Pub. by Elsvr Adv Tech) Elsevier.

Collyer, A. A., jt. auth. see Clegg, D. W.

Collyer, Charles E., jt. ed. see Rosenbaum, David A.

Collyer, Gary, ed. see International Chamber of Commerce Staff.

Collyer, Glenn, jt. auth. see Lindstrom, Robert L.

Collyer, Graham. The Surrey Village Book. 168p. 1987. 50.00 (*0-905392-32-9*) St Mut.

Collyer, Jaime. People on the Prowl. Miller, Yvette E., ed. De Tagle, Lilian L., tr. from SPA. LC 95-21099. (Discoveries Ser.). 144p. 1996. pap. 13.95 (*0-935480-73-0*) Lat Am Lit Rev Pr.

Collyer, Moses W., jt. auth. see Verplanck, William E.

Collyer, Robert. Augustus Conant: Geneva's Pioneer Abolitionist Preacher. (Illus.). vi, 98p. 1991. reprint ed. 22.00 (*0-9625624-1-6*) Grant Hse Pr.

Collymore, Frank. The Man Who Loved Attending Funerals. (Caribbean Writers Ser.). 192p. 1993. pap. 9.95 (*0-435-98931-6*, 98931) Heinemann.

Collyns, Charles. Alternatives to the Central Bank in the Developing World. (Occasional Papers: No. 20). 23p. 1983. pap. 5.00 (*1-55775-057-2*) Intl Monetary.

Collyns, Charles & International Monetary Fund Staff. Private Market Financing for Developing Countries. LC 95-153399. (World Economic & Financial Surveys Ser.). vii, 81 p. 1995. write for info. (*1-55775-456-X*) Intl Monetary.

Collyns, Charles, jt. auth. see Bayoumi, Tamim A.

Colman. New England. (Discover America Ser.). 1985. 6.99 (*0-8442-7473-9*) NTC Contemp Pub Co.

Colman, A. Game Theory & Experimental Games: The Study of Strategic Interaction. (International Series in Experimental Social Psychology: Vol. 4). 300p. 1982. 142.00 (*0-08-026070-5*, Pub. by Pergamon Repr) Franklin.

Colman, Alfredo, jt. ed. see Casey, William.

Colman, Andrew M. Game Theory & Its Applications: Strategic Interaction in the Social & Biological Sciences. 2nd ed. (International Series in Experimental Social Psychology: Vol. 30). 320p. 1995. write for info. (*0-08-041037-5*, Pergamon Pr); pap. write for info. (*0-08-041944-5*, Pergamon Pr) Elsevier.

— What Is Psychology? 3rd ed. LC 98-31960. 1999. 50.00 (*0-415-16901-1*) Routledge.

— What Is Psychology? The Inside Story. 2nd ed. 196p. 1989. pap. 14.95 (*0-09-172989-0*) Routledge.

— What Is Psychology? The Inside Story. 3rd ed. LC 98-31960. 1999. pap. 16.99 (*0-415-16902-X*) Routledge.

Colman, Andrew M., ed. Companion Encyclopedia of Psychology, 2 vols., Set. LC 94-177554. (Companion Encyclopedia Ser.). 1356p. (C). 1994. 305.00 (*0-415-06446-5*) Routledge.

— Psyc Resrch Methd Stats. LC 95-18117. (Essential Psychology Ser.). 123p. (C). 1995. pap. text 14.06 (*0-582-27801-5*, Pub. by Addison-Wesley) Longman.

Colman, Andrew M., jt. ed. see Argyle, Michael.

Colman, Andrew M., jt. ed. see French, Christopher C.

Colman, Andrew M., jt. ed. see Gregory, Richard L.

Colman, Andrew M., jt. ed. see Hampson, Sarah E.

Colman, Andrew M., jt. ed. see Kimble, Daniel.

Colman, Andrew M., jt. ed. see Lazarus, Arnold A.

Colman, Andrew M., jt. ed. see Parkinson, Brian.

Colman, Andrew S. Game Theory & Its Applications in the Social & Biological Sciences. 2nd ed. 320p. 1995. pap. 31.95 (*0-7506-2369-1*) Buttrwrth-Heinemann.

Colman, Anthony, ed. Encyclopedia of International Commercial Litigation. 725p. 1991. 299.00 (*1-85333-572-X*, Pub. by Graham & Trotman) Kluwer Academic.

— Encyclopedia of International Commercial Litigation, Suppl. 2, 1992. 92p. (C). 1993. ring bd. 75.00 (*1-85333-824-9*) Kluwer Academic.

— Encyclopedia of International Commercial Litigation: Basic Work, 1995. 950p. 1995. ring bd. 408.00 (*1-85333-822-2*, Pub. by Graham & Trotman) Kluwer Academic.

— Encyclopedia of International Commercial Litigation, Supplement 2, 1992. 92p. 1993. ring bd. 75.00 (*1-85333-772-2*, Pub. by Graham & Trotman) Kluwer Academic.

Colman, Arthur & Colman, Libby. Earth Father-Sky Father: The Changing Concept of Fathering. (Illus.). 206p. 1981. pap. 5.95 (*0-13-223024-0*) P-H.

— The Father. 256p. 1993. mass mkt. 5.99 (*0-380-71916-9*, Avon Bks) Morrow Avon.

Colman, Arthur D. Up from Scapegoating: Awakening Consciousness in Groups. LC 95-14098. 160p. (Orig.). 1995. pap. 19.95 (*0-933029-95-0*) Chiron Pubns.

Colman, Arthur D. & Bexton, Harold W., eds. Group Relations Reader 1. LC 75-24569. 1975. 28.50 (*0-916050-02-5*) Rice Inst.

Colman, Arthur D. & Geller, Marvin H., eds. Group Relations Reader 2. LC 75-24569. (A. K. Rice Institute Ser.: No. 2). 450p. (C). 1985. text 28.50 (*0-9615099-0-2*) Rice Inst.

Colman, B. H. & Pfaltz, C. R., eds. Modern Perspectives in Otology. (Advances in OtoRhinoLaryngology Ser.: Vol. 31). (Illus.). xii, 252p. 1983. 172.25 (*3-8055-3641-0*) S Karger.

Colman, Beverly, ed. see Dickson, Robert.

Colman, Carol & Schwartz, Erika. Natural Energy: From Tired to Terrific in Ten Days. LC 98-38124. 256p. 1999. 22.95 (*0-399-14461-7*) Putnam Pub Group.

Colman, Carol, jt. auth. see Dibner, Robin.

Colman, Carol, jt. auth. see Eagle, Carol J.

Colman, Carol, jt. auth. see Legato, Marianne.

Colman, Carol, jt. auth. see Legato, Marianne J.

Colman, Carol, jt. auth. see Roundtree, Robert Collins.

Colman, Carol, jt. auth. see Schwartz, Erika.

Colman, Carol, jt. auth. see Scott, W. Norman.

Colman, Carol, jt. auth. see Semchyshyn, Stefan.

Colman, Carol, jt. auth. see Whitaker, Julian.

***Colman, Charles, et al.** Songs with Theorbo (ca. 1650-1663) Oxford, Bodleian Library, Broxbourne 84.9, London, Lambeth... Callon, Gordon J., ed. (Recent Researches in the Music of the Baroque Era Ser.: Vol. B105). (Illus.). 2000. 55.00 (*0-89579-461-6*) A-R Eds.

Colman, David, jt. auth. see Nixson, Frederick I.

Colman, David, jt. ed. see Rayner, A. J.

Colman, Ernest A. The Dramatic Use of Bawdy in Shakespeare. LC 73-86132. 240p. reprint ed. pap. 74.40 (*0-608-13097-4*, 202522000043) Bks Demand.

Colman, Fran. Money Talks: Reconstructing Old English. LC 91-34452. (Trends in Linguistics, Studies & Monographs: No. 56). viii, 391p. 1991. lib. bdg. 129.25 (*3-11-012741-5*) Mouton.

Colman, G. Cross-Examination. 168p. 1970. 27.50 (*0-7021-0305-5*, Pub. by Juta & Co) Gaunt.

— 22 Quaint Cases in South African Law. 114p. 1980. pap. 15.00 (*0-7021-1085-X*, Pub. by Juta & Co) Gaunt.

Colman, George. Broad Grins: Comprising, with New Additional Tales in Verse, Those Formerly Published Under the Title of "My Nightgown & Slippers", Repr. of 1802 Ed. LC 75-31180. (Romantic Context: Poetry 1789-1830 Ser.: Vol. 33). 1977. lib. bdg. 57.00 (*0-8240-2132-0*) Garland.

— Critical Edition of "The Jealous Wife" & "Polly Honeycombe" by George Colman the Elder (1732-1794) Price, Thomas, ed. LC 97-12461. (Studies in British Literature: Vol. 30). 304p. 1997. text 99.95 (*0-7734-8626-7*) E Mellen.

— The Dramatick Works, 4 vols. in 2, Set. (Anglistica & Americana Ser.: No. 172). 1976. reprint ed. 270.00 (*3-487-05961-4*) Lubrecht & Cramer.

— New Brooms & the Manager in Distress. LC 80-14205. 80p. 1980. 50.00 (*0-8201-1353-0*) Schol Facsimiles.

— Poetical Vagaries, Repr. of 1812 Ed. LC 75-31182. (Romantic Context: Poetry 1789-1830 Ser.: Vol. 34). 1976. lib. bdg. 52.00 (*0-8240-2133-9*) Garland.

Colman, George, jt. auth. see Garrick, David.

Colman, Hila. Diary of a Frantic Kid Sister. (J). (gr. 4-7). 1985. pap. 2.95 (*0-671-61926-8*, Archway) PB.

— Diary of a Frantic Kid Sister. (J). 1973. 8.05 (*0-606-03060-3*, Pub. by Turtleback) Demco.

— That's the Way It Is, Amigo. LC 74-30398. (Illus.). 96p. (J). (gr. 6 up). 1975. 11.95 (*0-690-00750-7*) HarpC Child Bks.

Colman, Hila, jt. auth. see Morris, Richard.

Colman, Lee. Advanced Activities for English Language Learners. (Activities for English Language Learners Ser.). (Illus.). 160p. 1992. pap. 22.54 (*0-8442-7406-2*) NTC Contemp Pub Co.

— Beginning Activities for English Language Learners. (Activities for English Language Learners Ser.). (Illus.). 160p. 1992. pap. 22.54 (*0-8442-7404-6*) NTC Contemp Pub Co.

— Intermediate Activities for English Language Learners. (Activities for English Language Learners Ser.). (Illus.). 160p. 1992. pap. 22.54 (*0-8442-7405-4*) NTC Contemp Pub Co.

Colman, Libby, jt. auth. see Colman, Arthur.

Colman, Louis. Lumber. LC 74-22773. (Labor Movement in Fiction & Non-Fiction Ser.). reprint ed. 36.50 (*0-404-58413-6*) AMS Pr.

Colman, Martha, jt. ed. see Bray, Edmund C.

Colman, Penny. Corpses, Coffins & Crypts: A History of Burial. LC 97-7842. (YA). (gr. 6 up). 1997. 17.95 (*0-8050-5066-3*, Bks Young Read) H Holt & Co.

— Dark Closets & Noises in the Night. (J). 1991. pap. 3.95 (*0-8091-6600-3*) Paulist Pr.

— Fannie Lou Hamer & the Fight for the Vote. LC 92-21380. (Gateway Civil Rights Ser.). (Illus.). 32p. (J). (gr. 2-4). 1993. pap. 4.95 (*1-56294-789-3*); lib. bdg. 20.90 (*1-56294-323-5*) Millbrook Pr.

***Colman, Penny.** Girls: The History of Growing up Female in America. LC 99-28150. (Illus.). 192p. (YA). (gr. 3-7). 2000. 18.95 (*0-590-37129-0*, Scholastic Ref) Scholastic Inc.

Colman, Penny. Madam C. J. Walker: Building a Business Empire. LC 93-13824. (Gateway Biographies Ser.). (Illus.). 48p. (J). (gr. 2-4). 1994. lib. bdg. 21.90 (*1-56294-338-3*) Millbrook Pr.

— One Hundred One Ways to Do Better in School. LC 93-30872. (Illus.). (J). 1996. pap. 2.95 (*0-8167-3285-X*) Troll Communs.

— Rosie the Riveter: Women Working on the Home Front in World War II. LC 94-3614. 128p. (J). 1995. lib. bdg. 20.99 (*0-517-59791-8*, Pub. by Crown Bks Yng Read) Random.

— Rosie the Riveter: Women Working on the Homefront in World War II. 1998. pap. 10.99 (*0-517-88567-0*) Crown Pub Group.

***Colman, Penny.** Rosie the Riveter, Women Working on the Home Front in World War II. 1998. 15.19 (*0-606-13026-8*, Pub. by Turtleback) Demco.

Colman, Penny. Strike! The Bitter Struggle of American Workers from Colonial Times to the Present. LC 94-29706. (Illus.). 80p. (J). (gr. 4-6). 1995. lib. bdg. 23.40 (*1-56294-459-2*) Millbrook Pr.

Colman, Penny, photos by. Toilets, Bathtubs, Sinks, & Sewers: A History of the Bathroom. LC 93-48413. (Illus.). 96p. (J). (gr. 5-9). 1994. 16.00 (*0-689-31894-4*) Atheneum Yung Read.

Colman, Robert. Modern Business Financing. LC 85-20490. 281p. 1985. 59.95 (*0-13-589060-8*, Busn) P-H.

Colman, Robert W., et al. Hemostasis & Thrombosis: Basic Principles & Clinical Practice. 3rd ed. LC 93-24077. 1,748p. 1993. text 254.00 (*0-397-51059-4*) Lppncott W & W.

***Colman, Sam.** This Life. 320p. 1998. pap. 11.95 (*0-14-027431-6*, Pub. by Pnguin Bks Ltd) Trafalgar.

Colman, Samuel. Nature's Harmonic Unity: A Treatise on Its Relation to Proportional Form. LC 78-177520. (Illus.). 1972. reprint ed. 27.95 (*0-405-08374-2*) Ayer.

Colman, Steven M. & Dethier, David P., eds. Rates of Chemical Weathering of Rocks & Minerals. LC 85-13328. 1986. text 174.00 (*0-12-181490-4*) Acad Pr.

Colman, W. On Call: The Work of Telephone Helplines for Child Abusers. 104p. 1989. pap. text 18.00 (*0-08-037958-3*, Pergamon Pr) Elsevier.

Colman, William G. Cities, Suburbs & States: Governing & Financing Urban America. LC 75-2810. (Illus.). 1975. 27.95 (*0-02-906490-2*) Free Pr.

— State & Local Government & Public-Private Partnerships: A Policy Issues Handbook. LC 88-24627. (Illus.). 451p. 1989. lib. bdg. 105.00 (*0-313-26206-3*, CLL, Greenwood Pr) Greenwood.

Colman, William G., jt. auth. see Stenberg, Carl W.

Colmbaro, Pasqualino, tr. see Ferrarotti, Franco.

Colmenero, J. Quasielastic Neutron Scattering: Proceeding of the Conference. 324p. 1994. text 121.00 (*981-02-1604-1*) World Scientific Pub.

Colmenero, J. & Alegria, A., eds. Basic Features of the Glassy State. 596p. (C). 1990. text 151.00 (*981-02-0031-5*) World Scientific Pub.

Colmer, David, tr. see Moeyaert, Bart.

Colmer, Francis. Shakespeare in Time of War. LC 76-30691. (Studies in Shakespeare: No. 24). 1977. lib. bdg. 75.00 (*0-8383-2165-8*) M S G Haskell Hse.

Colmer, J., ed. see Coleridge, Samuel Taylor.

Colmer, John. Australian Autobiography: The Personal Quest. 182p. 1990. pap. text 24.95 (*0-19-554881-7*) OUP.

Colmer, Malcolm R., ed. Moroney's Surgery for Nurses. 16th ed. LC 85-26938. (Illus.). 624p. 1987. text 39.95 (*0-443-03355-2*) Church.

Colmer, Rebecca S. Gems: Everyday Tips for Building Your Business. 336p. 1996. 9.95 (*0-9651672-2-4*) Eklektika Pr.

Colmerauer, Alan, jt. ed. see Benhamou, Frederic.

***Colmers, John M., et al, frwds.** Pediatric Dental Care in CHIP & Medicaid: Paying for What Kids Need, Getting Value for State Payments. 36p. 1999. pap. write for info. (*1-887748-28-8*) Milbank Memorial.

Colmers, John M., et al, frwds. Public-Private Collaboration in Health Information Policy. 32p. 1999. pap. write for info. (*1-887748-29-6*) Milbank Memorial.

***Colmers, John M. & Fox, Daniel M., frwds.** Tracking State Oversight of Managed Care. (Illus.). 44p. 1999. pap. write for info. (*1-887748-32-6*) Milbank Memorial.

Colmers, William F. & Wahlestedt, Claes, eds. The Biology of Neuropeptide Y & Related Peptides. LC 92-28742. (Contemporary Neuroscience Ser.). (Illus.). 579p. 1993. 125.00 (*0-89603-241-8*) Humana.

***Colmont, Marie.** Michka. (SPA.). 2000. 12.95 (*84-241-3345-5*) Everest SP.

Colmore, Perry. Living with Breast Cancer: 39 Women & One Man Speak Candidly about Surviving Breast Cancer. (Illus.). 84p. (Orig.). 1997. pap. 24.95 (*0-9655817-0-5*) Andover Townsman.

Colo, Papo, ed. Dirty Pictures. (Illus.). 20p. (Orig.). 1982. pap. 5.00 (*0-913263-04-4*) Exit Art.

Colo, Papo, et al. Films with a Purpose: A Puerto Rican Experiment in Social Films. (Illus.). 48p. (Orig.). 1987. pap. 25.00 (*0-913263-16-8*) Exit Art.

Colo, Papo, jt. auth. see Ingberman, Jeanette.

Colo, Papo, jt. auth. see Sims, Lowry S.

Colo, Papo, jt. ed. see Ingberman, Jeanette.

Colo, Papo, ed. see Lippard, Lucy, et al.

Colo, Papo, ed. see Tupitsyn, Margarita, et al.

Coloane, Francisco. Cape Horn & Other Stories from the End of the World. Petreman, David A., tr. from SPA. LC 90-19924. (Discoveries Ser.). 192p. 1991. pap. 14.95 (*0-935480-50-1*) Lat Am Lit Rev Pr.

Colodey, A. G., jt. ed. see Hall, E. R.

Colodny, Robert G., ed. Mind & Cosmos: Essays in Contemporary Science & Philosophy. LC 83-21662. (CPS Publications in Philosophy of Science). (Illus.). 380p. (C). 1984. pap. text 31.00 (*0-8191-3650-6*); lib. bdg. 57.00 (*0-8191-3649-2*) U Pr of Amer.

— Paradigms & Paradoxes: The Philosophical Challenge of the Quantum Domain. LC 79-158189. (University of Pittsburgh Series in the Philosophy of Science: No. 5). 466p. reprint ed. pap. 144.50 (*0-608-15648-5*, 203190100077) Bks Demand.

Colodny, Robert G. & Savage, Leonard J., eds. Logic, Laws & Life: Some Philosophical Complications. LC 76-50886. (University of Pittsburgh Series in the Philosophy of Science: No. 6). (Illus.). 272p. reprint ed. pap. 84.40 (*0-8357-8211-5*, 203395600087) Bks Demand.

Colodny, Robert G., et al. Frontiers of Science & Philosophy. LC 61-9401. (University of Pittsburgh Series in the Philosophy of Science: No. 1). 296p. reprint ed. pap. 91.80 (*0-608-15677-9*, 203199300077) Bks Demand.

Colodny, Robert G., ed. see Maxwell, Grover, et al.

Colodzin, Benjamin. How to Survive Trauma: A Program for War Veterans & Survivors of Rape, Assault, Abuse, or Emotional Disorders. 128p. 1996. pap. text 9.95 (*1-886449-29-5*) Barrytown Ltd.

Cologne-Brookes, Gavin. Novels of William Styron: From Harmony to History. LC 94-19731. (Southern Literary Studies). 288p. (C). 1995. text 40.00 (*0-8071-1900-8*) La State U Pr.

Cologne-Brookes, Gavin, et al. Writing America Crosscurrents. LC 95-49355. (Crosscurrents Ser.). (C). 1996. pap. text 21.45 (*0-582-21417-3*) Addison-Wesley.

Cologne-Brookes, Gavin, ed. see Sammells, Neil, et al.

Cologne Mani Codex, English & Greek Staff. The Cologne Mani Codex (P. Colon, Inv. Nr. 4780) Concerning the Origin of His Body. Cameron, Ron & Dewey, Arthur J., trs. LC 79-14743. (Texts & Translations Ser.: No. 15). 87p. reprint ed. pap. 30.00 (*0-7837-5423-X*, 204518700005) Bks Demand.

Cologne Museum Ludwig Staff. Art in the 20th Century. (Klotz Ser.). (Illus.). 756p. 1996. pap. 29.99 (*3-8228-8647-5*) Taschen Amer.

— Photography in the Twentieth Century. (Illus.). 756p. 1996. pap. 29.99 (*3-8228-8648-3*) Taschen Amer.

Cologni, Franco & Flechon, Dominique. Cartier, The Tank Watch: Design for Our Time. LC 98-11749. (Illus.). 264p. 1998. 75.00 (*2-08-013633-X*, Pub. by Flammarion) Abbeville Pr.

Cologni, Franco & Mocchetti, Ettore. Made by Cartier: One Hundred Fifty Years of Tradition & Innovation. (Illus.). 256p. 1993. 75.00 (*1-55859-599-6*) Abbeville Pr.

Cologni, Franco & Nussbaum, Eric. Platinum by Cartier: Triumphs of the Jewelers' Art. (Illus.). 280p. 1996. 85.00 (*0-8109-3738-7*, Pub. by Abrams) Time Warner.

Cologni, Franco, et al. Piaget: Watches & Wonders since 1874. (Illus.). 264p. 1996. 85.00 (*0-7892-0078-3*); 39.98 (*0-89660-097-1*, Artabras) Abbeville Pr.

Colojoara, I. & Folias, C. Theory of Generalized Spectral Operators, Vol. 9. LC 68-24488. (Mathematics & Its Applications Ser.). xvi, 232p. 1968. text 348.00 (*0-677-01480-5*) Gordon & Breach.

Colokathis, Jane. Comprehensive Index to CPL Exchange Bibliographies, No. 1-1565: A Numerical Index. (CPL Bibliographies Ser.: No. 3). 89p. 1979. pap. 9.00 (*0-86602-003-9*, Sage Prdcls Pr) Sage.

— Comprehensive Index to CPL Exchange Bibliographies, No. 1-1565: A Subject Index. (CPL Bibliographies Ser.: No. 1). 119p. 1979. pap. 12.00 (*0-317-00021-7*, Z5942, Sage Prdcls Pr) Sage.

— Comprehensive Index to CPL Exchange Bibliographies, No. 1-1565: An Author Index. (CPL Bibliographies Ser.: No. 2). 100p. 1979. pap. 10.00 (*0-86602-002-0*, Sage Prdcls Pr) Sage.

Colom, Connie, jt. ed. see Klee, Lois.

Colom, Vicente, jt. auth. see Van Bolhuis, Herman E.

Coloma, Jose M. Lexico de Politica. 6th ed. (SPA.). 200p. 1976. pap. 14.95 (*0-8288-5727-X*, S50039) Fr & Eur.

Colomb, A. La Tribu de Wagap (Nouvelle-Caledonie) LC 75-32812. reprint ed. 44.50 (*0-404-14116-1*) AMS Pr.

Colomb, F. R., jt. auth. see Bajada, E.

Colomb, Gregory G. Designs on Truth: The Poetics of the Augustan Mock-Epic. 288p. 1992. text 35.00 (*0-271-00805-9*) Pa St U Pr.

Colomb, P., et al. The Great War of 189- A Forecast. LC 74-16390. (Science Fiction Ser.). (Illus.). 320p. 1975. reprint ed. 29.95 (*0-405-06282-6*) Ayer.

***Colomb, P. H. & Tatsumi, Takayuki.** The Great War of 189- A Forecast. LC 99-216809. (Illus.). 1998. write for info. (*0-415-19289-7*) Routledge.

Colomb, Philip. Naval Warfare: It's Ruling Principles & Practice Historically Treated, 2 vols. Hattendorf, John B. & Hughes, Wayne P., eds. LC 89-13389. (Classics of Sea Power Ser.). (Illus.). 487p. 1990. 69.90 (*0-87021-777-1*) Naval Inst Pr.

Colomban, Philippe, ed. Proton Conductors: Solids, Membranes & Gels; Materials & Devices. (Chemistry of Solid State Materials Ser.: No. 3). (Illus.). 613p. (C). 1992. text 140.00 (*0-521-38317-X*) Cambridge U Pr.

Colombari, Bari, ed. see Rendler, Elaine.

Colombari, V. Reliability Data Collection & Use in Risk & Availability Assessment. (Illus.). x, 898p. 1989. 170.00 (*0-387-50834-1*) Spr-Verlag.

Colombas, Garcia M. Reading God: Lectio Divina. Lauer, Alphonse M., ed. Roettger, Gregory J., tr. from SPA. (Schuyler Spiritual Ser.: No. 9). 144p. (Orig.). (C). 1993. pap. 5.50 (*1-56788-010-X*, 10-009) BMH Pubns.

Colombat, Andre. Deleuze et la Litterature. LC 89-13966. (American University Studies: Romance Languages & Literature: Ser. II, Vol. 132). (FRE.). XVI, 348p. (C). 1990. text 62.95 (*0-8204-1189-2*) P Lang Pubng.

Colombat, Andre P. The Holocaust in French Film. LC 93-17016. (Filmmakers Ser.: No. 33). (Illus.). 459p. 1993. 52.00 (*0-8108-2668-2*) Scarecrow.

Colombatti, Alfonso & Doliana, Roberto. The Superfamily with Von Willebrand Factor Va Domains. LC 96-28891. (Molecular Biology Intelligence Unit Ser.). 200p. 1996. 99.00 (*1-57059-387-6*) Landes Bioscience.

Colombe, Paul D. Grapho-Therapeutics Vol. 1437: Handwriting Therapy. (Illus.). 340p. (YA). 1996. pap. 15.00 (*0-9654514-0-2*) R L Toomey.

Colombeau, Jean F. Multiplication of Distributions: A Tool in Mathematics, Numerical Engineering, & Theoretical Physics. LC 92-39265. 1993. write for info. (*3-540-56288-5*); 36.95 (*0-387-56288-5*) Spr-Verlag.

Colombet, Pierre, et al, eds. Nuclear Magnetic Resonance Spectroscopy of Cement-Based Materials. LC 97-43419. (Illus.). 300p. 1997. 129.00 (*3-540-63134-8*) Spr-Verlag.

Colombet, Pierre & Grimmer, Arnd-Rudiger. Applications of NMR to Cement Science. 400p. 1995. text 198.00 (*2-88124-965-5*) Gordon & Breach.

Colombetti, Giuliano & Lenci, Francesco, eds. Membranes & Sensory Transduction. LC 84-3373. 396p. 1984. 95.00 (*0-306-41439-2*, Plenum Trade) Perseus Pubng.

Colombetti, L. Biological Transport of Radiotracers, I. 447p. 1982. pap. 191.00 (*0-8493-6017-X*, QP519, CRC Reprint) Franklin.

Colombetti, L., jt. auth. see Anghileri, Leopold J.

Colombetti, Marco, jt. auth. see Dorigo, Marco.

Colombi, David. The Probation Service & Information Technology. (CEDR Ser.). 225p. 1994. 72.95 (*1-85628-953-2*, Pub. by Avebry) Ashgate Pub Co.

Colombi, David, jt. auth. see Steyaert, Jan.

Colombi, M. Cecelia & Alarcon, Francisco X., eds. La Ensenanza del Espanol a Hispanohablantes: Praxis y Teoria. (Heath Series on Foreign Language Acquisition Research & Instruction: Vol. 4). (SPA.). 368p. (C). 1996. pap. text 35.96 (*0-669-39844-6*) HM Trade Div.

Colombi, M. Cecilia. Los Refranes en el "Quijote" Texto y Contexto. 1990. 40.50 (*0-916379-66-3*) Scripta.

Colombi-Monguio, Alicia de. Petrarquismo Peruano: Diego Davalos y Figuera y la Poesia de la Miscelanea Austral. (Monagrafias A Ser.: Vol. XCIX). (SPA.). 217p. 1985. 58.00 (*0-7293-0207-5*, Pub. by Tamesis Bks Ltd) Boydell & Brewer.

Colombian Cultural Concil Colcuc. Staff, ed. Con el Perdon de los Pajaros. (Poesia Ser.: Vol. 3). (SPA.). 83p. 1996. pap. 7.00 (*1-889111-02-3*) Colombian Cultural.

Colombian Cultural Concil Staff, ed. La Palabra del Sol. (Poesia Ser.: Vol. 3). (SPA.). 75p. 1996. pap. 7.00 (*1-889111-00-7*) Colombian Cultural.

C

An Asterisk (*) at the beginning of an entry indicates that the title is appearing for the first time.

— Presagio/Omen. (Poesia Ser.: Vol. 3). 81p. 1996. pap. 7.00 (*88-911106-0-4*) Colombian Cultural.

Colombiere, Claude De La, see Saint-Jure, Jean B. & De La Colombiere, Claude.

Colombies, Pierre Du, see Du Colombies, Pierre.

Colombini, et al. Partial Differential Equations & the Calculus of Variations, 2 vols., Set. (Progress in Nonlinear Differential Equations & Their Applications Ser.: Nos. 1 & 2). 900p. 1989. 120.50 (*0-8176-3426-6*) Birkhauser.

— Partial Differential Equations & the Calculus of Variations, 2 vols., Vol. 1. (Progress in Nonlinear Differential Equations & Their Applications Ser.: Nos. 1 & 2). 519p. 1989. 75.50 (*0-8176-3424-X*) Birkhauser.

— Partial Differential Equations & the Calculus of Variations, 2 vols., Vol. 2. (Progress in Nonlinear Differential Equations & Their Applications Ser.: Nos. 1 & 2). 498p. 1989. 75.50 (*0-8176-3425-8*) Birkhauser.

Colombini, F. & Lerner, Nicolas, eds. Geometrical Optics & Related Topics. LC 97-1244. (Progress in Nonlinear Differential Equations & Their Applications Ser.). 340p. 1997. 79.50 (*0-8176-3958-6*) Birkhauser.

Colombini, Marco, jt. ed. see Forte, Michael.

Colombo. The Little Blue Book of UFOs. 96p. 1995. per. 4.95 (*0-88978-256-3*, Pub. by Arsenal Pulp) LPC InBook.

— Reclaim Our Stories. LC 96-86767. 520p. 1997. pap. 39.95 (*0-312-10334-4*) St Martin.

Colombo, A. G., ed. Environmental Impact Assessment: Proceedings of the Eurocourse Held at the Joint Research Centre, Ispra, Italy, September 30-October 4, 1991. LC 92-26376. 352p. 1992. text 181.00 (*0-7923-1589-8*) Kluwer Academic.

Colombo, A. G. & Keller, A. Z. Reliability Modelling & Applications. (C). 1987. text 201.00 (*90-277-2566-7*) Kluwer Academic.

Colombo, Allan B. The Best of Kinks & Hints. LC 97-36247. 200p. 1998. pap. 22.95 (*0-7506-9890-X*, BH Security) Buttrwrth-Heinemann.

Colombo, Anthony. Understanding the Mentally Disordered Offenders: A Multi-Agency Perspective. LC 97-72079. (Welfare & Society Ser.). (Illus.). 240p. 1997. text 69.95 (*1-85972-689-5*, Pub. by Avebry) Ashgate Pub Co.

Colombo, Bernardo, et al, eds. Resources & Population: Natural, Institutional, & Demographic Dimsensions of Development. LC 95-38883. (Pointficiae Academiae Scientiarum Scripta Varia Ser.: Vol. 20). (Illus.). 362p. 1996. text 70.00 (*0-19-828918-9*, Clarendon Pr) OUP.

C

***Colombo, Corey, et al.** Candle in the Window. unabridged ed. Stolz, Claudia M., ed. 64p. (J). (gr. 3-6). 1999. 5.00 (*0-918761-08-5*); pap. 2.50 (*0-918761-07-7*) Miami U Pubns.

Colombo, Ellen. Windows 95 Essentials: Level II, 2. LC 95-71643. (Essentials Ser.). (Illus.). 160p. 1997. pap. 22.99 (*1-57576-255-2*) Que Educ & Trng.

Colombo, Furio. God in America: Religion & Politics in the United States. Jarrat, Kristin, tr. from ITA. LC 84-4278. 208p. 1984. text 40.50 (*0-231-05972-8*) Col U Pr.

***Colombo, Gary.** Rereading America: Cultural Contexts for Critical Thinking & Writing. 5th ed. 2001. pap. text, teacher ed. write for info. (*0-312-25743-0*) St Martin.

Colombo, Gary, et al, eds. Rereading America: Cultural Contexts for Critical Thinking & Writing. 4th ed. LC 97-74958. 768p. 1998. pap. 35.95 (*0-312-14837-2*) St Martin.

Colombo, Gary, et al. Rereading America: Cultural Contexts for Critical Thinking & Writing. 2nd ed. 784p. (C). 1992. teacher ed. write for info. (*0-318-68816-6*) St Martin.

— Rereading America: Cultural Contexts for Critical Thinking & Writing. 3rd ed. 1995. pap. text, teacher ed. 5.00 (*0-312-10341-7*) St Martin.

***Colombo, George.** Capturing Customers.com: Radical Strategies for Selling & Marketing in the Wired World. 224p. 2001. 22.99 (*1-56414-507-7*) Career Pr Inc.

Colombo, George W. Sales Force Automation: Using the Latest Technology to Make Your Sales Force More Competitive. 224p. 1994. 27.95 (*0-07-011840-X*) McGraw.

Colombo, J. P., jt. auth. see Richterich, Roland.

Colombo, J. P., ed. see Eastham, R. C.

Colombo, Jean-Pierre & Richterich, Roland, eds. Klinische Chemie - Theorie, Praxis, Interpretation, 4: Vollstaendig neu Bearbeitete Auflage. (Illus.). 1978. 71.50 (*3-8055-2796-9*) S Karger.

Colombo, John. Infant Cognition: Predicting Later Intellectual Functioning. LC 93-16099. (Individual Differences & Development Ser.: Vol. 5). 1993. 48.00 (*0-8039-4959-6*); pap. 21.50 (*0-8039-4960-X*) Sage.

— 999 Questions. 1989. mass mkt. 14.95 (*0-385-25207-2*) Doubleday.

Colombo, John, ed. The Dictionary of Canadian Quotations. 671p. 1991. 29.95 (*0-7737-2515-6*) Genl Dist Srvs.

Colombo, John & Fagen, Jeffrey W., eds. Individual Differences in Infancy: Reliability, Stability, & Prediction. 480p. (C). 1990. text 125.00 (*0-8058-0369-6*) L Erlbaum Assocs.

Colombo, John, jt. auth. see Coldren, Jeffrey T.

Colombo, John, jt. ed. see Horowitz, Frances D.

Colombo, John A. Ask Trapper John Again. Date not set. pap. text 13.95 (*1-884687-08-3*) N Horzns Pub.

Colombo, John R. Colombo's All-Time Great Canadian Quotations. 272p. 1995. pap. text 14.95 (*0-7737-5639-6*) Stoddart Publ.

Colombo, John Robert. New Direction in Canadian Poetry. LC 70-865600. (Aspects of English Ser.). 87p. 1971. write for info. (*0-03-923345-6*) Holt R&W.

— Other Canadas: An Anthology of Science Fiction & Fantasy. LC 80-487461. 360 p. 1979. write for info. (*0-07-082952-7*) McGraw.

— Rhymes & Reasons: Nine Canadian Poets Discuss their Work. LC 73-150243. (Aspects of English Ser.). 117p. 1971. write for info. (*0-03-923386-3*) Holt R&W.

Colombo, Joleen. Writers Northwest Handbook. (Illus.). 1995. pap. 19.95 (*0-9647212-0-1*) Media Weavers.

***Colombo, Luann.** Buzz Off! Build Your Own Electronic Doorbell. (Illus.). 16p. (J). (gr. 3-9). 2000. pap. 7.95 (*0-8167-6196-5*) Troll Communs.

Colombo, Luann. Enter If You Dare. (Illus.). 16p. (J). (gr. 3-7). 1998. pap. 9.95 (*0-8167-4465-3*) Troll Communs.

— Gross but True Creatures with Slug. (Illus.). 32p. (J). (gr. 1-7). 1997. 8.99 (*0-689-81494-1*) Atheneum Yung Read.

— Gross but True Germs with Toy. (Illus.). 32p. (J). (gr. 1-7). 1997. 8.99 (*0-689-81495-X*) Atheneum Yung Read.

— The Human Body. (Book & See-Through Model Ser.). (Illus.). 64p. (J). (gr. 3 up). 1997. pap. 19.95 (*0-8362-3262-3*) Andrews & McMeel.

— Sleepover Madness! Party Pack. (Illus.). 8p. (J). (gr. 3-7). 1999. pap. 6.95 (*0-8167-4940-X*) Troll Communs.

— Truth or Dare LC 99-183267. 1998. write for info. (*0-8167-4948-5*) Troll Communs.

Colombo, Luann & McQuinn, Conn. Fun with Electronics, Jr. Another Idea from Becker & Mayer. (Illus.). 32p. 1995. pap. 19.95 (*0-8362-0597-9*) Andrews & McMeel.

Colombo, Marcella. American Southwest. (Places & History Ser.). 1998. 24.95 (*1-55670-690-1*) Stewart Tabori & Chang.

***Colombo, Mario.** 80 Years of Moto Guzzi Motorcycles. (Illus.). 452p. 2000. pap. 39.95 (*88-7911-219-8*, 130513AE, Pub. by Giorgio Nada Editore) Motorbooks Intl.

Colombo, Mario & Patrignani, Roberto. Moto MV Agusta. (Illus.). 248p. 1991. 60.00 (*88-7911-060-8*, Pub. by Giorgio Nada Editore) Howell Pr VA.

***Colombo, Mario & Patrignani, Roberto.** Moto MV Agusta. (Illus.). 278p. 2000. 44.95 (*88-7911-180-9*, 117733AE, Pub. by Giorgio Nada Editore) Motorbooks Intl.

Colombo, Massimo, ed. Changing Boundaries of the Firm: Explaining Evolving Interfirm Relations. LC 97-42868. (Studies in Business Organization & Networks Ser.). 256p. (C). 1998. 85.00 (*0-415-15470-7*) Routledge.

Colombo, Oscar & Mueller, I. I., eds. From Mars to Greenland: Charting Gravity with Space & Airborne Instruments: Fields, Tides, Methods, Results. LC 92-14148. (International Association of Geodesy Symposia Ser.: Vol. 110). 368p. 1992. 96.95 (*0-387-97857-7*) Spr-Verlag.

Colombo, Peter, et al. Innovative Site Remediation Technology Vol. 4: Stabilization - Solidification. Anderson, William C., ed. LC 93-20786. (Illus.). 166p. 1994. 79.95 (*1-883767-04-0*) Am Acad Environ.

Colombo, U. & Galli, R. Planning Research & Development. 1995. write for info. (*81-224-0708-0*, Pub. by Wiley Estrn) Franklin.

Colombo, Umberto, ed. see International Conference on Materials Science Staf.

Colombo, Umberto, jt. ed. see Parker, Earl R.

Colombrari, Geraldine C. & Billings, Diane M. NurseNotes: Pediatric Nursing. LC 96-20788. 256p. 1997. pap. text 29.95 (*0-7817-1129-0*) Lppncott W & W.

Colombraro, Geraldine C. & Lagerquist, Sally L. Little, Brown's Pediatric Nursing Review. LC 96-20788. 1997. pap. text 22.95 (*0-316-15137-8*) Lppncott W & W.

Colome. Microbiology Laboratory Exercises. Date not set. pap. text, teacher ed. write for info. (*0-314-91279-7*) West Pub.

Colome, Jaime S., et al. Laboratory Exercises in Microbiology. (Illus.). 283p. (C). 1986. 32.50 (*0-314-87262-0*) West Pub.

Colome, Steve, et al, eds. Total Exposure & Assessment Methodology (TEAM) Toxic Substances & Chemicals, an International Symposium, Pt. I. (Journal of Exposure Analysis & Environmental Epidemiology Ser.: Vol. 1, No. 1). (Illus.). 1991. pap. text 60.00 (*0-911131-30-2*) Specialist Journals.

Colomeda, Lorelei A. Lambert, see Lambert Colomeda, Lorelei A.

Colomeda, Lorelei Anne Lambert. Through the Northern Looking Glass: Breast Cancer Stories of Northern Native Women. LC 96-18865. 200p. 1996. pap. 17.95 (*0-88737-682-7*) Natl League Nurse.

Colomer, Gilbert. French-Arabic Lexicon: Lexique Francais-Arabe; Le Parler Maghrebin. (ARA & FRE.). 440p. 1983. 69.95 (*0-8288-0996-8*, F362) Fr & Eur.

Colomer, J. New English-Catalan, Catalan-English Dictionary: Nou Diccionari Angles-Catala-Angles. 4th ed. (CAT & ENG.). 770p. 1987. 59.95 (*0-8288-0554-7*, S31734) Fr & Eur.

Colomer, Josep, ed. Political Institutions in Europe. 304p. (C). 1996. pap. 25.99 (*0-415-10820-9*) Routledge.

Colomer, Josep M. Game Theory & the Transition to Democracy: The Spanish Model. LC 94-45020. 160p. 1995. 80.00 (*1-85898-201-4*) E Elgar.

***Colomer, Josep Maria.** Strategic Transitions: Game Theory & Democratization. LC 99-53307. (Illus.). 192p. 2000. 34.95 (*0-8018-6384-8*) Johns Hopkins.

Colomina, Beatriz. Privacy & Publicity: Modern Architecture As Mass Media. LC 93-36205. (Illus.). 401p. 1994. 52.50 (*0-262-03214-7*) MIT Pr.

— Privacy & Publicity: Modern Architecture As Mass Media. (Illus.). 408p. 1996. reprint ed. pap. text 25.00 (*0-262-53139-9*) MIT Pr.

Colomina, Beatriz, ed. Sexuality & Space. LC 91-40146. (Princeton Papers on Architecture: No. 1). (Illus.). 288p. (Orig.). 1992. pap. 19.95 (*1-878271-08-3*) Princeton Arch.

Colomina, Beatriz, et al. Robert Lehman Lectures on Contemporary Art, Vol. 2. Kelly, Karen & Cooke, Lynne, eds. 206p. 2000. pap. text 16.95 (*0-944521-76-2*, Pub. by Dia Ctr Arts) Dist Art Pubs.

Colomy, Paul. The Dynamics of Social Systems. (International Sociology Ser.: Vol. 42). (Illus.). 272p. (C). 1992. 69.95 (*0-8039-8759-5*); pap. 25.95 (*0-8039-8760-9*) Sage.

— Macro/Micro Divide. (Key Ideas Ser.). 200p. (C). 2000. pap. write for info. (*0-415-08187-4*) Routledge.

Colomy, Paul, ed. Functionalist Sociology: Classic Statements. (Schools of Thought in Sociology Ser.: Vol. 3). 427p. 1990. text 200.00 (*1-85278-172-6*) E Elgar.

— Neofunctionalist Sociology: Contemporary Statements. (Schools of Thought in Sociology Ser.: Vol. 4). 396p. 1990. text 190.00 (*1-85278-195-5*) E Elgar.

Colomy, Paul, jt. auth. see Alexander, Jeffrey C.

***Colon, A. R. & Colon, P. A.** A History of Children: A Socio-Cultural Survey Across Millennia. 2001. lib. bdg. write for info. (*0-313-31574-4*) Greenwood.

Colon, A. R. & Colon, P. A. Nurturing Children: A History of Pediatrics. LC 99-25000. 344p. 1999. lib. bdg. 69.50 (*0-313-31080-7*, GR1080, Greenwood Pr) Greenwood.

Colon Aponte, Olimpia. Los Amigos del Nino Jesus. (SPA.). 48p. 1997. pap. write for info. (*1-881713-11-3*) Pubns Puertorriquenas.

Colon Cora, Rafael. The Professor's Attitude & Performance. LC 78-12813. 161p. 1981. pap. 5.00 (*0-8477-2450-6*) U of PR Pr.

Colon, Cristobal. Amigos de la Plaza. (SPA.). 108p. 1996. pap. write for info. (*0-929441-29-X*) Pubns Puertorriquenas.

Colon De Zalduondo, Baltazara. The Growing Puerto Rican Economy: Saving & Consumption Variables. 1976. lib. bdg. 250.00 (*0-8490-1357-7*) Gordon Pr.

Colon, Doris E. & Rivera, Illeana. Genetica: Manual de Laboratorio. 163p. (C). 1991. pap. text, teacher ed. 24.95 (*1-881375-05-6*) Libreria Univ.

Colon, E. J., et al, eds. Evoked Potential Manual. 1983. text 199.50 (*0-89838-614-4*) Kluwer Academic.

Colon, E. J. & Visser, S. L., eds. Evoked Potential Manual: A Practical Guide to Clinical Applications. 2nd rev. ed. (C). 1990. text 257.50 (*0-7923-0791-7*) Kluwer Academic.

Colon, Eliseo. Publicidad, Modernidad, Hegemonia. (SPA.). 1996. pap. 9.95 (*0-8477-0235-9*) U of PR Pr.

Colon, Eliseo, contrib. by. Antologia de la Literatura del Caribe: Puerto Rico, Cuba y Republica Dominicana. (SPA.). 424p. (C). 1997. pap. text 13.95 (*1-56328-081-7*) Edit Plaza Mayor.

Colon, Ernesto M. Keep Your Car on the Road: And Your Money in the Bank. LC 93-74666. (Illus.). 118p. (Orig.). 1994. pap. 11.95 (*0-918751-39-X*, 39) Delta Pr.

Colon, Fernando. The Life of Admiral Christopher Columbus by His Son Ferdinand. Keen, Benjamin, tr. from ITA. LC 77-27400. (Illus.). 316p. 1978. reprint ed. lib. bdg. 35.00 (*0-313-20175-7*, COAC, Greenwood Pr) Greenwood.

Colon, Gilbert, ed. see Hionas, Peter A.

Colon, Hernando. Vida Del Almirante Don Cristobal. (Fondo 2000 Ser.). (SPA.). pap. 2.99 (*968-16-5046-8*, Pub. by Fondo) Continental Bk.

Colon, Jesus. A Puerto Rican in New York & Other Sketches. LC 74-14229. (Puerto Rican Experience Ser.). 206p. 1979. reprint ed. 20.95 (*0-405-06218-4*) Ayer.

— A Puerto Rican in New York & Other Sketches. LC 82-6100. (Illus.). 204p. 1992. reprint ed. pap. 6.95 (*0-7178-0589-1*) Intl Pubs Co.

— The Way It Was & Other Writings. Acosta-Belen, Edna & Korrol, Virginia A., eds. LC 92-42443. 128p. 1993. pap. 12.00 (*1-55885-057-0*) Arte Publico.

Colon, Luis D. La Retranca Del Ela. 1996. pap. text. write for info. (*1-56758-044-0*) Edit Cultl.

Colon, Matilde, et al. Antologia de Literatura Hispanica: Hacia una Nueva Conciencia (1960-1995) (SPA.). 696p. (C). 1995. pap. text 18.95 (*1-56328-101-5*) Edit Plaza Mayor.

— Antologia de Literatura Hispanica Contemporanea: Espanol 3101-3102, 2 vols. LC 84-20849. (SPA.). 362p. (C). 1994. write for info. (*0-8477-3515-X*) U of PR Pr.

— Antologia de Literatura Hispanica Contemporanea: Espanol 3101-3102, 2 vols., 2. LC 84-20849. (SPA.). 362p. (C). 1993. pap. 9.95 (*0-8477-3514-1*) U of PR Pr.

— Antologia de Literatura Hispanica Contemporanea: Espanol 3101-3102, 2 vols., Vol. 1. LC 84-20849. (SPA.). 240p. (C). 1994. pap. 5.75 (*0-8477-3511-7*) U of PR Pr.

— El Estilo en la Redaccion Comercial. 2nd ed. (SPA.). 200p. (C). 1992. pap. text 12.95 (*1-56328-023-X*) Edit Plaza Mayor.

Colon, P. A., jt. auth. see Colon, A. R.

Colon, Rafael. Journey to Success: 8 Steps to Avoid the Career Dormido Virus. Lightbourne, Aleaa, ed. (Illus.). iv, 59p. 1998. pap. 10.00 (*0-9665785-0-3*) Voices Internacional.

Colon, Rafael H. Manual de Derecho Procesal Civil. 2nd rev. ed. 450p. 1981. pap. 25.00 (*0-88063-499-5*, MICHIE) LEXIS Pub.

Colon, Robert, jt. auth. see Tedeschi, Frank P.

Colon, V. Franklin, jt. auth. see Schumann, Gilbert B.

Colon, Victor, jt. auth. see Osborne, David.

Colon-Vila, Lillian & Collier-Morales, Roberta. Salsa. LC 97-23305. (J). 1998. 14.95 (*1-55885-220-4*, Pinata Bks) Arte Publico.

Colon, Wanda N., ed. see Stein, David.

***Colona, Sharon.** For Men Only. 192p. 2000. pap. 14.95 (*0-88391-020-9*) F Fell Pubs Inc.

Colonell, J. M. & Stockholm, H. K., eds. Port Valdez, Alaska: Environmental Studies, Nineteen Seventy-Six to Nineteen Seventy-Nine. (Occasional Publications: No. 5). (Illus.). 373p. 1980. 20.00 (*0-685-04965-5*) U of AK Inst Marine.

Colonero, Jerri. With You & Your Baby All the Way: The Complete Guide to Pregnancy, Childbirth, Recovery, & Baby Care. LC 98-41647. (Illus.). 448p. 1998. pap. 16.95 (*0-923521-43-7*, 437) Bull Pub.

Colonial Dames of America, Chapter 1, Baltimore St. Ancestral Records & Portraits, 2 vols. LC 68-57950. (Illus.). 835p. 1997. reprint ed. pap. 75.00 (*0-8063-0078-7*) Clearfield Co.

Colonial Dames of America Ser. Herbs & Herb Lore of Colonial America. LC 94-48527. Orig. Title: Simples, Superstitions & Solace. (Illus.). 80p. 1995. pap. text 3.95 (*0-486-28529-4*) Dover.

Colonial Dames of America Staff. Ancestral Records & Portraits: A Compilation from the Archives of Chapter I, The Colonial Dames of America. (Illus.). 835p. 1994. reprint ed. pap. text 55.00 (*1-55613-941-1*) Heritage Bk.

Colonial Society of Massachusetts Staff. Music in Colonial Massachusetts, 1630-1820: A Conference Held by the Colonial Society of Massachusetts, May 17 & 18, 1973, Vol. 1: Music in Public Places. LC 80-66188. (Publications of the Colonial Society of Massachusetts: Nos. 53-54). 451p. reprint ed. pap. 139.90 (*0-7837-3739-4*, 204342200001) Bks Demand.

— Music in Colonial Massachusetts, 1630-1820: A Conference Held by the Colonial Society of Massachusetts, May 17 & 18, 1973, Vol. 2: Music in Homes & in Churches. LC 80-66188. (Publications of the Colonial Society of Massachusetts: Nos. 53-54). 840p. reprint ed. pap. 200.00 (*0-7837-3740-8*, 204342200002) Bks Demand.

***Colonial Society of Pennsylvania Staff.** Records of the Court of New Castle on Delaware, 1676-1699, 2 vols., Set. 797p. 2000. reprint ed. pap. 59.95 (*0-8063-4980-8*, Pub. by Clearfield Co) ACCESS Pubs Network.

Colonial Williamsburg Foundation Staff. Animals at Colonial Williamsburg. (Illus.). 8p. (J). (ps). 1993. bds. 3.95 (*0-87935-092-X*) Colonial Williamsburg.

— Apothecary in Eighteenth-Century Williamsburg. (Historic Trades Ser.). (Illus.). 37p. (Orig.). 1965. pap. 2.95 (*0-910412-16-2*) Colonial Williamsburg.

— Bookbinder in Eighteenth-Century Williamsburg. (Historic Trades Ser.). (Illus.). 32p. (Orig.). 1959. pap. 2.95 (*0-910412-15-4*) Colonial Williamsburg.

— Christmas Decorations from Williamsburg's Folk Art Collection: Step-by-Step Illustrated Instructions for Christmas Ornaments You Can Make at Home. LC 76-41253. (Illus.). 80p. (Orig.). 1976. pap. 10.95 (*0-87935-040-7*) Colonial Williamsburg.

— Colonial Colors. (Illus.). 8p. (J). (ps). 1993. bds. 3.95 (*0-87935-094-6*) Colonial Williamsburg.

— Count with the Cooper. (Illus.). 8p. (J). (ps). 1993. bds. 3.95 (*0-87935-093-8*) Colonial Williamsburg.

— The Folk Art Coloring Book. (Illus.). 24p. 1996. pap. 3.95 (*0-87935-155-1*) Colonial Williamsburg.

— Leatherworker in Eighteenth-Century Williamsburg. (Historic Trades Ser.). (Illus.). 36p. (Orig.). 1967. pap. 2.95 (*0-910412-18-9*) Colonial Williamsburg.

— Miller in Eighteenth-Century Virginia. (Historic Trades Ser.). (Illus.). 32p. (Orig.). 1958. pap. 2.95 (*0-910412-19-7*) Colonial Williamsburg.

— Printer in Eighteenth-Century Williamsburg. rev. ed. (Historic Trades Ser.). (Illus.). 34p. (Orig.). 1958. pap. 2.95 (*0-910412-20-0*) Colonial Williamsburg.

— Recipes from the Raleigh Tavern Bake Shop. (Illus.). 29p. 1984. pap. 4.07 (*0-87935-106-3*) Colonial Williamsburg.

— Silversmith in Eighteenth-Century Williamsburg. rev. ed. (Historic Trades Ser.). (Illus.). 37p. (Orig.). 1972. pap. 2.95 (*0-910412-21-9*) Colonial Williamsburg.

***Colonial Williamsburg Foundation Staff.** When Virginia Was the Wild West: A Williamsburg Comic Book. (Illus.). 37p. 1999. pap. 2.95 (*0-87935-210-8*) Colonial Williamsburg.

Colonial Williamsburg Foundation Staff. Wigmaker in Eighteenth-Century Williamsburg. (Historic Trades Ser.). (Illus.). 36p. (Orig.). 1959. pap. 2.95 (*0-910412-22-7*) Colonial Williamsburg.

— Williamsburg: Decorating with Style. LC 97-42917. (Illus.). 176p. 1998. 30.00 (*0-609-60049-4*) C Potter.

Colonial Williamsburg Foundation Staff & Watson, Amy Z. The Folk Art Counting Book: From the Abby Aldrich Rockefeller Folk Art Center. (Illus.). 40p. (J). (ps). 1999. 9.95 (*0-87935-084-9*) Colonial Williamsburg.

Colonial Williamsburg Foundation Staff, jt. auth. see Desamper, Hugh.

Colonial Williamsburg Foundation Staff, jt. auth. see Gaynor, James M.

Colonial Williamsburg Staff. Colonial Williamsburg Cookbook. 1999. write for info. (*0-609-60286-1*) C Potter.

— The Colonial Williamsburg Historic Trades Annual, Vol. I. (Illus.). 77p. 1988. pap. 7.95 (*0-87935-179-9*) Colonial Williamsburg.

Colonius, F. Optimal Periodic Control. (Lecture Notes in Mathematics Ser.: Vol. 1313). vi, 177p. 1988. 35.95 (*0-387-19249-2*) Spr-Verlag.

Colonius, Fritz & Kliemann, W. H. The Dynamics of Control. LC 99-16920. (Systems & Control Ser.). 592p. 1999. 79.95 (*0-8176-3683-8*, Pub. by Birkhauser) Spr-Verlag.

***Colonius, Fritz & Wirth, F. Harold, eds.** Advances in Mathematical Systems Theory: A Volume in Honor of D. Hinrichsen. (Systems & Control: Foundations & Applications Ser.). (Illus.). 321p. 2000. 89.95 (*0-8176-4162-9*, Pub. by Birkhauser) Spr-Verlag.

Colonna, Bob. The Addiction Process: A Systemic Cultural Condition. unabridged ed. 78p. 1998. pap. 10.95 (*1-892896-61-3*) Buy Books.

Colonna, Francesco. Hypnerotomachia: The Strife of Love in a Dreame (1592). Dallington, Robert, tr. from LAT. LC 73-16223. 208p. 1973. reprint ed. lib. bdg. 50.00 (*0-8201-1124-4*) Schol Facsimiles.

An Asterisk (*) at the beginning of an entry indicates that the title is appearing for the first time.

— Hypnerotomachia Poliphili: "The Strife of Love in a Dream" Godwin, Joscelyn, tr. LC 99-70844. (Illus.). 474p. 1999. 70.00 (*0-500-01942-8*, Pub. by Thames Hudson) Norton.

Colonna, Giovanni P. Giovanni Paolo Colonna: Messe a Nove Voci Concertata con Stromenti. Schnoebelen, Anne, ed. (Recent Researches in Music of the Baroque Era Ser.: Vol. RRB17). (Illus.). xiv, 109p. 1974. pap. 40.00 (*0-89579-054-8*, RRB17) A-R Eds.

Colonna, M., et al, eds. Capitalism, Socialism & Knowledge Vol. 2: The Economics of F. A. Hayek. LC 93-42575. 256p. 1994. text 100.00 (*1-85898-012-7*) E Elgar.

Colonna, M. & Hagemann, Harald, eds. Money & Business Cycles Vol. 1: The Economics of F. A. Hayek. LC 93-42575. 256p. 1994. text 100.00 (*1-85898-011-9*) E Elgar.

Colonna, M., jt. ed. see Karre, K.

Colonna, Marco, jt. ed. see Campbell, Kerry S.

Colonna-Romano, Sergio, et al. Differential-Display Reverse Transcription-PCR. LC 97-31477. (Springer Lab Manual Ser.). (Illus.). 200p. 1998. pap. text 64.95 (*3-540-63297-2*) Spr-Verlag.

Colonomos, Betty & Bienvenu, MJ. Group Norms Workbook. (Introduction to American Deaf Culture Ser.: Vol. 4). 64p. (C). 1993. pap. text 8.95 (*1-881133-03-6*, 405-W) Sign Media.

— Identity. (Introduction to American Deaf Culture Ser.). 54p. (C). 1993. pap. text 8.95 (*1-881133-04-4*, 406-W) Sign Media.

— Language & Traditions. (Introduction to American Deaf Culture Ser.: Vol. 3). 54p. (C). 1993. pap. text 8.95 (*1-881133-02-8*, 404-W) Sign Media.

Colonomos, Betty, jt. auth. see Bienvenu, MJ.

Colony, Horatio. Collected Works: Drama, Verse, Novels, 2 vols., Set. 1500p. 1982. 60.95 (*0-8283-1741-0*) Branden Bks.

Colophonius, Antimachus. Reliquiae. lxxii, 106p. 1974. write for info. (*3-296-10410-0*) G Olms Pubs.

Color Resource Staff. Complete Color Glossary. 230p. 1994. pap. 19.95 (*1-56830-096-4*) Hayden.

***Colorado.** Colorado Related Regulations. LC 99-70448. 1999. write for info. (*0-89246-518-2*) NILS Pub.

Colorado, Antonio J., tr. see Mathews, Thomas.

Colorado Assoc. of Legal Secretaries Staff. Colorado Law Office Handbook, No. 3. Pritchard, Donna L., ed. 1993. ring bd., suppl. ed. 42.50 (*0-685-74404-3*, MICHIE) LEXIS Pub.

Colorado Assoc. of Legal Secretaries Staff & Pritchard, Donna L. Colorado Law Office Handbook. 420p. 1994. ring bd. 75.00 (*1-55943-129-6*, MICHIE) LEXIS Pub.

Colorado Chautauqua Cottagers Staff. Chautauqua Porches: A Centennial Cookbook, 1898-1998. (Illus.). 380p. 1998. pap. 24.95 (*0-9663523-0-0*) CO Chautauqua.

Colorado Council on High School-College Relations. Handbook: A Publication of the Colorado Council on High School-College Relations. rev. ed. (Illus.). 172p. 1988. 6.00 (*0-318-35422-5*) CCHSCR.

Colorado Dietetic Association, Staff. Simply Colorado: Nutritious Recipes for Busy People. Massey, Kay P., ed. 200p. (Orig.). 1990. 9.95 (*0-9626337-0-4*) CO Dietetic Assn.

Colorado Dietetic Association Staff. Simply Colorado: Nutritious Recipes for Busy People. rev. ed. Massey, Kay P., ed. 260p. 1992. 14.95 (*0-9626337-1-2*) CO Dietetic Assn.

***Colorado Dietetic Association Staff.** Simply Colorado Too: More Nutritious Recipes for Busy People. (Illus.). 1999. 19.95 (*0-9626337-2-0*) CO Dietetic Assn.

Colorado Dude & Guest Ranch Association Staff, et al. Mountain Magic Cuisine: Secret Recipes of the Dude & Guest Ranches of Colorado. unabridged ed. LC 98-65071. (Illus.). 420p. 1998. pap. 23.95 (*1-889120-11-1*) StarsEnd Creations.

Colorado Geological Survey Staff. Highway Rockfall Research Report. (Special Publications: No. 37). (Illus.). 27p. (Orig.). 1992. pap. 5.00 (*1-884216-49-8*) Colo Geol Survey.

Colorado Historical Society Staff. Bent's Old Fort. 1992. pap. 14.95 (*0-87081-637-3*) Univ Pr Colo.

— The Santa Fe Trail: New Perspectives. LC 92-30677. 1992. pap. 14.95 (*0-87081-278-5*) Univ Pr Colo.

Colorado Mountain Club Staff & Ormes, Robert M. Guide to the Colorado Mountains. 9th rev. ed. Jacobs, Randy, ed. LC 96-53136. (Illus.). 336p. 1997. pap. 17.50 (*1-55566-194-7*) Johnson Bks.

Colorado Native Plant Society Staff. Rare Plants of Colorado. 2nd ed. LC 96-51430. (Illus.). 124p. 1997. pap. 16.95 (*1-56044-529-7*) Falcon Pub Inc.

Colorado Outdoor Education Center Staff. Colorado Outdoor Education Center Teacher's Field Guide. (Illus.). 280p. 1985. reprint ed. pap. 20.00 (*0-910715-06-8*) Search Public.

Colorado Publishing Company Staff. Discover the Rockies: 1992-1993 Travel & Recreation Guide. 320p. 1992. pap. text 14.95 (*0-9632304-0-9*) CO Pub Co.

***Colorado Rail Road Museum Staff.** Official Roster of the D&RGW&RGS (1923) 160p. 1998. pap. 19.95 (*0-918654-56-4*) CO RR Mus.

Colorado State Grange Staff. The Flavor of Colorado. LC 92-11892. 1992. write for info. (*0-87197-335-9*) Favorite Recipes.

Colorado State Society of the National Society Dau. Colorado DAR Member & Ancestor Index. 775p. Date not set. write for info. (*0-9654355-3-9*) Fmly History.

Colorado State University Staff. Mathematics Placement Examination Review. 2nd ed. Davies Group Staff, ed. & illus. by. 96p. (C). 1997. pap. 4.25 (*1-888570-07-5*) Davies Grp.

Colorado State University Staff, ed. see MacTurk, Robert H. & Morgan, George A.

Colorado Supreme Court Staff, et al. Civil Rules Annotated. write for info. (*0-318-59330-0*) West Pub.

***Colorado Trail Foundation Staff.** Colorado Trail: The Official Guidebook. 5th ed. (Illus.). 2000. pap. 22.95 (*0-9671466-2-3*) Colorado Mt.

Colored Pencil Society of America Staff. The Best of Colored Pencil. (Illus.). 160p. 1993. 24.95 (*1-56496-049-8*, 30503) Rockport Pubs.

Colored Pencil Society of America Staff. The Best of Colored Pencil, Vol. 4. (Illus.). 144p. 1997. bds. 27.99 (*1-56496-389-6*, Quarry Bks) Rockport Pubs.

— The Best of Colored Pencil 2. (Illus.). 160p. 1994. 24.95 (*1-56496-108-7*) Rockport Pubs.

Colorexpert Staff. Colorcourse/Illustration. (Graphic Communications Ser.). (C). 1995. 39.95 (*0-8273-7213-2*) Delmar.

— Colorcourse/Image Setting. (Graphic Communications Ser.). (C). 1995. 39.95 (*0-8273-7214-0*) Delmar.

— Colorcourse/Photography. (Graphic Communications Ser.). (C). 1995. 39.95 (*0-8273-7212-4*) Delmar.

— Colorexpert Tutorial. (Graphic Communications Ser.). (C). 1995. 79.95 (*0-8273-7211-6*) Delmar.

Colorni, Evelina. Singer's Italian: A Manual of Diction & Phonetics. LC 71-113927. 192p. 1970. 13.50 (*0-02-870620-X*, Schirmer Books) Mac Lib Ref.

Coloroso, Barbara. Kids Are Worth It! Giving Your Child the Gift of Inner Discipline. 256p. 1998. write for info. (*0-921051-74-3*) Somerville Hse.

***Coloroso, Barbara.** Kids Are Worth It! Giving Your Child the Gift of Inner Discipline. 256p. 1998. pap. write for info. (*1-895897-57-2*) Somerville Hse.

— Kids Are Worth It Co. 256p. 1995. reprint ed. pap. 12.50 (*0-380-71954-1*, Avon Bks) Morrow Avon.

— Parenting Through Crisis: Helping Kids in Times of Loss, Grief & Change. 288p. 2000. 24.00 (*0-06-019856-7*, HarpRes) HarpInfo.

— A Pocket Guide to Kids Are Worth It! Giving Your Child the Gift of Inner Discipline. 216p. 1998. write for info. (*1-894042-08-5*) Somerville Hse.

Colorprint Staff. Solar System. 1989. pap. 4.95 (*0-8416-9572-5*) Am Map.

— Star Chart. 1988. pap. 4.95 (*0-8416-9574-1*, 695741) Am Map.

***Colorsport Staff, photos by.** The Spirit of Rugby: A Photographic Portrait of Rugby Union. (Illus.). 144p. 2000. 24.95 (*1-871349-79-6*, Pub. by Kensington West) Midpt Trade.

Colosi, Thomas R. On & off the Record: Colosi on Negotiation. 1993. write for info. (*0-943001-27-7*) Am Arbitration.

Colosi, Thomas R. & Berkeley, Arthur E. Collective Bargaining: How It Works & Why: A Manual of Theory & Practice. 2nd ed. LC 85-72636. 219p. 1992. pap. 19.95 (*0-685-65037-5*) Am Arbitration.

Colosi, Thomas R., jt. auth. see Miller, Jeffrey G.

Colours, Lahore. Lahore Colours. (Illus.). 130p. 1998. text 85.00 (*0-19-577822-7*) OUP.

Colovich, Dana M., ed. see DeJournette, Richard F. & DeJournette, Daun T.

Colowick. Affinity Labeling. (Methods in Enzymology Ser.: Vol. 46). 1977. text 199.00 (*0-12-181946-9*) Acad Pr.

— Amyloids, Prions & Other Protein Aggregates. (Methods in Enzymology Ser.: Vol. 309). 589p. 1999. 99.95 (*0-12-182210-9*) Acad Pr.

— Confocal Microscopy. 602p. 1999. 105.00 (*0-12-182208-7*) Acad Pr.

— Enzyme Kinetics & Mechanisms, Part E. (Methods in Enzymology Ser.: Vol. 308). 404p. 1999. 99.95 (*0-12-182209-5*) Acad Pr.

— Expression of Recombinant Genes in Eukaryotic Systems. (Methods in Enzymology Ser.: Vol. 306). 394p. 1999. 99.95 (*0-12-182207-9*) Acad Pr.

— Methods in Enzymology, Vol. 303. 608p. 1999. text 105.00 (*0-12-182204-4*) Acad Pr.

— Methods in Enzymology, Vol. 305. 640p. 1999. 99.00 (*0-12-182206-0*) Acad Pr.

— Methods in Enzymology, Vol. 310. 582p. 1999. 99.95 (*0-12-182211-7*) Acad Pr.

— Methods in Enzymology, Vol. 311. 585p. 1999. 110.00 (*0-12-182212-5*) Acad Pr.

— Methods in Enzymology, Vol. 312. 540p. 2000. write for info. (*0-12-182213-3*) Acad Pr.

— Methods in Enzymology, Vol. 313. 279p. 1999. 105.00 (*0-12-182214-1*) Acad Pr.

— Methods in Enzymology, Vol. 314. 515p. 1999. 105.00 (*0-12-182215-X*) Acad Pr.

— Methods in Enzymology, Vol. 315. Vol. 315. 774p. 1997. 115.00 (*0-12-182216-8*) Acad Pr.

— Methods in Enzymology, Vol. 316. Vol. 316. 657p. 1997. 129.95 (*0-12-182217-6*) Acad Pr.

— Methods in Enzymology, Vol. 317. Vol. 317. 466p. 1997. 90.00 (*0-12-182218-4*) Acad Pr.

— Methods in Enzymology, Vol. 318. Vol. 318. (Illus.). 431p. 1997. 90.00 (*0-12-182219-2*) Acad Pr.

— Methods in Enzymology, Vol. 319. Vol. 319. (Illus.). 626p. 2000. 119.95 (*0-12-182220-6*) Acad Pr.

— Methods in Enzymology, Vol. 321. 1997. write for info. (*0-12-182222-2*) Acad Pr.

— Methods in Enzymology, Vol. 322. Vol. 322. 650p. 1997. 119.95 (*0-12-182223-0*) Acad Pr.

— Methods in Enzymology: ABC Transporters: Biochemical, Cellular, & Molecular Aspects, Suppl. 292. (Illus.). 853p. (C). 1998. text 115.00 (*0-12-182193-5*) Acad Pr.

— Methods in Enzymology: Cumulative Subject Index Volumes 290-319. Vol. 320. 450p. 2000. 129.95 (*0-12-182221-4*) Acad Pr.

— Methods in Enzymology Vol. 300: Oxidants & Antioxidants. Abelson, John N. et al, eds. (Illus.). 530p. (C). 1998. boxed set 99.95 (*0-12-182201-X*) Acad Pr.

— Methods in Enzymology Vol. 301, Pt. C: Nitric Oxide. Abelson, John N. et al, eds. (Illus.). 589p. (C). 1998. boxed set 99.95 (*0-12-182202-8*) Acad Pr.

— Methods in Enzymology Vol. 302: Green Flourescent Proteins. Abelson, John N. & Simon, Melvin I., eds. (Illus.). 528p. 1999. 99.95 (*0-12-182203-6*) Acad Pr.

— Proteolytic Enzymes, Pt. B. (Methods in Enzymology Ser.: Vol. 45). 1976. text 199.00 (*0-12-181945-0*) Acad Pr.

— Recombinant DNA, Pt. D. (Methods in Enzymology Ser.: Vol. 153). 1987. text 157.00 (*0-12-182054-8*) Acad Pr.

Colowick & Kaplan, Anthan O., eds. Cumulative Subject Index, Vols. 61-74, 76-80. (Methods in Enzymology Ser.: Vol. 95). 1986. text 179.00 (*0-12-181995-7*) Acad Pr.

— Glutamate, Glutamine, Glutathione, & Related Compounds, Vol. 113. (Methods in Enzymology Ser.). 1985. text 179.00 (*0-12-182013-0*) Acad Pr.

Colowick, Kaplan, ed. Diffraction Methods for Biological Macromolecules, Pt. B. (Methods in Enzymology Ser.: Vol. 115). 1985. text 188.00 (*0-12-182015-7*) Acad Pr.

Colowick, Sidney P. Methods in Enzymology. (C). 1998. text. write for info. (*0-12-182197-8*) Acad Pr.

— Methods in Enzymology: Caged Compounds, Vol. 291. Marriott, Gerard, ed. (Illus.). 529p. (C). 1998. text. write for info. (*0-12-182192-7*) Acad Pr.

— Methods in Enzymology: Ion Channels, Vol. 293. (Illus.). 805p. (C). 1998. text 110.00 (*0-12-182194-3*) Acad Pr.

— Methods in Enzymology Vol. 298: Molecular Motors & the Cytoskeleton. Vallee, Richard B., ed. (Illus.). 636p. (C). 1998. boxed set 110.00 (*0-12-182199-4*) Acad Pr.

Colowick, Sidney P., et al, eds. Bioluminescence & Chemiluminescence, Pt. B. (Methods in Enzymology Ser.: Vol. 133). 603p. 1986. text 167.00 (*0-12-182033-5*) Acad Pr.

— Enzyme Kinetics & Mechanism, Pt. B. LC 54-9110. (Methods in Enzymology Ser.: Vol. 64). 1980. text 188.00 (*0-12-181964-7*) Acad Pr.

— Enzyme Structure, Vol. 130, Pt. K. (Methods in Enzymology Ser.: Vol. 130). 1986. text 167.00 (*0-12-182030-0*) Acad Pr.

— Enzyme Structure, Vol. 131, Pt. L. (Methods in Enzymology Ser.: Vol. 131). 587p. 1986. text 167.00 (*0-12-182031-9*) Acad Pr.

— Guide to Molecular Cloning Techniques. (Methods in Enzymology Ser.: Vol. 152). 812p. 1987. text 157.00 (*0-12-182053-X*) Acad Pr.

— Guide to Molecular Cloning Techniques. (Methods in Enzymology Ser.: Vol. 152). 812p. 1987. spiral bd. 53.00 (*0-12-181775-X*) Acad Pr.

— Immobilized Enzymes & Cells, Pt. C. (Methods in Enzymology Ser.: Vol. 136). 584p. 1987. text 159.00 (*0-12-182036-X*) Acad Pr.

— Immunochemical Techniques, Pt. A. (Methods in Enzymology Ser.: Vol. 70). 1980. text 188.00 (*0-12-181970-1*) Acad Pr.

— Immunochemical Techniques, Pt. B. (Methods in Enzymology Ser.: Vol. 73). 1981. text 188.00 (*0-12-181973-6*) Acad Pr.

— Immunochemical Techniques Pt. J: Phagocytosis & Cell-Mediated Cytotoxicity. (Methods in Enzymology Ser.: Vol. 132). 658p. 1986. text 167.00 (*0-12-182032-7*) Acad Pr.

— Lipids, Pt. C. (Methods in Enzymology Ser.: Vol. 71). 1981. text 188.00 (*0-12-181971-X*) Acad Pr.

— Lipids, Pt. D. (Methods in Enzymology Ser.: Vol. 72). 1981. text 188.00 (*0-12-181972-8*) Acad Pr.

— Nucleic Acids, Vol. 65, Pt. I. LC 54-9110. (Methods in Enzymology Ser.). 1980. text 179.00 (*0-12-181965-5*) Acad Pr.

— Peptide Growth Factors, Pt. A. (Methods in Enzymology Ser.: Vol. 146). 452p. 1987. text 157.00 (*0-12-182046-7*) Acad Pr.

— Peptide Growth Factors, Pt. B. (Methods in Enzymology Ser.: Vol. 147). 487p. 1987. text 157.00 (*0-12-182047-5*) Acad Pr.

— Plant Cell Membranes. (Methods in Enzymology Ser.: Vol. 148). 762p. 1987. text 157.00 (*0-12-182048-3*) Acad Pr.

— Plant Molecular Biology. (Methods in Enzymology Ser.: Vol. 118). 856p. 1986. text 188.00 (*0-12-182018-1*) Acad Pr.

— Plasma Lipoproteins, Pt. A. (Methods in Enzymology Ser.: Vol. 128). 992p. 1986. text 178.00 (*0-12-182028-9*) Acad Pr.

— Recombinant DNA. LC 54-9110. (Methods in Enzymology Ser.: Vol. 68). 1980. text 188.00 (*0-12-181968-X*) Acad Pr.

— Structural & Contractile Proteins Pt. C: The Contractile Apparatus & the Cytoskeleton. (Methods in Enzymology Ser.: Vol. 134). 705p. 1986. text 167.00 (*0-12-182034-3*) Acad Pr.

— Vitamins & Coenzymes, Pt. F. (Methods in Enzymology Ser.: Vol. 67). 1980. text 188.00 (*0-12-181967-1*) Acad Pr.

Colowick, Sidney P. & Antonini, Eraldo, eds. Hemoglobins. (Methods in Enzymology Ser.: Vol. 76). 1981. text 188.00 (*0-12-181976-0*) Acad Pr.

Colowick, Sidney P. & Cunningham, Leon W., eds. Structural & Contractile Proteins Pt. A: Extracellular Matrix. (Methods in Enzymology Ser.: Vol. 82). 1982. text 188.00 (*0-12-181982-5*) Acad Pr.

Colowick, Sidney P. & Dennis, Martha, eds. Cumulative Subject Index: Volumes 31, 32, 34-60. (Methods in Enzymology Ser.: Vol. 75). 1982. text 188.00 (*0-12-181975-2*) Acad Pr.

Colowick, Sidney P. & Frederiksen, D. W., eds. Structural & Contractile Proteins Pt. B: The Contractile Apparatus & the Cytoskeleton. (Methods in Enzymology Ser.: Vol. 85). 774p. 1982. text 188.00 (*0-12-181985-X*) Acad Pr.

Colowick, Sidney P. & Ginsburg, Victor, eds. Complex Carbohydrates, Pt. D. (Methods in Enzymology Ser.: Vol. 83). 1982. text 188.00 (*0-12-181983-3*) Acad Pr.

Colowick, Sidney P. & Jakoby, William B., eds. Detoxication & Drug Metabolism: Conjugation & Related Systems. (Methods in Enzymology Ser.: Vol. 77). 1981. text 188.00 (*0-12-181977-9*) Acad Pr.

Colowick, Sidney P. & Kaplan, Nathan O. Cumulative Subject Index, Vols. 102-119, 121-134. (Methods in Enzymology Ser.: Vol. 140). 288p. 1988. text 157.00 (*0-12-182040-8*) Acad Pr.

— Enzyme Purification & Related Techniques, Pt. C. (Methods in Enzymology Ser.: Vol. 104). 1984. text 188.00 (*0-12-182004-1*) Acad Pr.

— Oxygen Radicals in Biological Systems. (Methods in Enzymology Ser.: Vol. 105). 1984. text 188.00 (*0-12-182005-X*) Acad Pr.

— Posttranslational Modifications, Vol. 107, Pt. B. (Methods in Enzymology Ser.). 1984. text 179.00 (*0-12-182007-6*) Acad Pr.

— Vitamins & Coenzymes, Pt. H. (Methods in Enzymology Ser.: Vol. 123). 1986. text 178.00 (*0-12-182023-8*) Acad Pr.

Colowick, Sidney P. & Kaplan, Nathan O., eds. Biomembranes Pt. M: Transport in Bacteria, Mitochondria, & Chloroplasts: General Approaches & Transport Systems. (Methods in Enzymology Ser.: Vol. 125). 1986. text 178.00 (*0-12-182025-4*) Acad Pr.

— Biomembranes Pt. N: Transport in Bacteria, Mitochondria, & Chloroplasts: Protonmotive Force. (Methods in Enzymology Ser.: Vol. 126). 1986. text 178.00 (*0-12-182026-2*) Acad Pr.

— Biomembranes Pt. Q: Protons & Water: Structure & Translocation. (Methods in Enzymology Ser.: Vol. 127). 1986. text 178.00 (*0-12-182027-0*) Acad Pr.

— Cellular Regulators, Pt. A. (Methods in Enzymology Ser.: Vol. 139). 1987. text 167.00 (*0-12-182039-4*) Acad Pr.

— Complex Carbohydrates, Pt. E. (Methods in Enzymology Ser.: Vol. 138). 1987. text 167.00 (*0-12-182038-6*) Acad Pr.

— Cumulative Subject Index, Vols. 81-95, 96-101. (Methods in Enzymology Ser.: Vol. 120). 250p. 1986. text 188.00 (*0-12-182020-3*) Acad Pr.

— Diffraction Methods for Biological Macromolecules, Pt. A. (Methods in Enzymology Ser.: Vol. 114). 1985. text 188.00 (*0-12-182014-9*) Acad Pr.

— Drug & Enzyme Targeting, Pt. A. (Methods in Enzymology Ser.: Vol. 112). 1985. text 188.00 (*0-12-182012-2*) Acad Pr.

— Enzyme Kinetics & Mechanism, Pt. C. (Methods in Enzymology Ser.: Vol. 87). 752p. 1982. text 188.00 (*0-12-181987-6*) Acad Pr.

— Enzyme Kinetics & Mechanism, Pt. A. LC 54-9110. (Methods in Enzymology Ser.: Vol. 63). 1979. text 188.00 (*0-12-181963-9*) Acad Pr.

— Enzyme Structure, Vol. 91, Pt. I. (Methods in Enzymology Ser.: Vol. 91). 1983. text 188.00 (*0-12-181991-4*) Acad Pr.

— Enzyme Structure, Vol. 117, Pt. J. (Methods in Enzymology Ser.: Vol. 117). 1985. text 188.00 (*0-12-182017-3*) Acad Pr.

— Hormone Action Pt. I: Peptide Hormones. (Methods in Enzymology Ser.: Vol. 109). 1985. text 188.00 (*0-12-182009-2*) Acad Pr.

— Hormone Action Pt. J: Neuroendocrine Peptides. (Methods in Enzymology Ser.: Vol. 124). 1986. text 178.00 (*0-12-182024-6*) Acad Pr.

— Immunochemical Techniques Pt. E: Monoclonal Antibodies & General Immunoassay Methods. (Methods in Enzymology Ser.: Vol. 92). 1983. text 188.00 (*0-12-181992-2*) Acad Pr.

— Immunochemical Techniques Pt. F: Conventional Antibodies, Fc Receptors, & Cytotoxicity. (Methods in Enzymology Ser.: Vol. 93). 393p. 1983. text 188.00 (*0-12-181993-0*) Acad Pr.

— Immunochemical Techniques Pt. H: Effectors & Mediators of Lymphoid Cell Functions. (Methods in Enzymology Ser.: Vol. 116). 1985. text 188.00 (*0-12-182016-5*) Acad Pr.

— Immunochemical Techniques Vol. 121, Pt. I: Hybridoma Technology & Monoclonal Antibodies. (Methods in Enzymology Ser.). 1986. text 179.00 (*0-12-182021-1*) Acad Pr.

— Interferons, Pt. C. (Methods in Enzymology Ser.: Vol. 119). 1986. text 188.00 (*0-12-182019-X*) Acad Pr.

— Pholosynthesis & Nitrogen Fixation, Pt. C. LC 54-9110. (Methods in Enzymology Ser.: Vol. 69). 1980. text 188.00 (*0-12-181969-8*) Acad Pr.

— Plasma Lipoproteins, Pt. B. (Methods in Enzymology Ser.: Vol. 129). 960p. 1986. text 178.00 (*0-12-182029-7*) Acad Pr.

— Posttranslational Modifications, Pt. A. (Methods in Enzymology Ser.: Vol. 106). 1984. text 188.00 (*0-12-182006-8*) Acad Pr.

— Recombinant DNA, Pt. C. LC 79-26584. (Methods in Enzymology Ser.: Vol. 101). 1983. text 188.00 (*0-12-182001-7*) Acad Pr.

— Recombinant DNA, Pt. B. LC 79-26584. (Methods in Enzymology Ser.: Vol. 100). 1983. text 188.00 (*0-12-182000-9*) Acad Pr.

— Steroids & Isoprenoids, Pt. A. (Methods in Enzymology Ser.: Vol. 110). 1985. text 188.00 (*0-12-182010-6*) Acad Pr.

— Steroids & Isoprenoids, Pt. B. (Methods in Enzymology Ser.: Vol. 111). 1985. text 188.00 (*0-12-182011-4*) Acad Pr.

— Vitamins & Coenzymes, Pt. E. LC 54-9110. (Methods in Enzymology Ser.: Vol. 66). 1980. text 188.00 (*0-12-181966-3*) Acad Pr.

C

Colowick, Sidney P. & Lands, William E., eds. Prostaglandins & Arachidonate Metabolites. LC 82-6791. (Methods in Enzymology Ser.: Vol. 86). 1982. text 188.00 (*0-12-181986-8*) Acad Pr.

Colowick, Sidney P. & Langone, John J., eds. Immunochemical Techniques Pt. D: Selected Immunoassays. LC 82-1678. (Methods in Enzymology Ser.: Vol. 84). 736p. 1982. text 188.00 (*0-12-181984-1*) Acad Pr.

Colowick, Sidney P. & Lorand, Laszlo, eds. Proteolytic Enzymes, Pt. C. (Methods in Enzymology Ser.: Vol. 80). 1982. text 188.00 (*0-12-181980-9*) Acad Pr.

Colowick, Sidney P. & Packer, Lester, eds. Biomembranes: Visual Pigments & Purple Membranes, I, Pt. H. LC 82-1736. (Methods in Enzymology Ser.: Vol. 81). 1982. text 188.00 (*0-12-181981-7*) Acad Pr.

— Biomembranes: Visual Pigments & Purple Membranes, II, Pt. I. (Methods in Enzymology Ser.: Vol. 88). 750p. 1982. text 188.00 (*0-12-181988-4*) Acad Pr.

Colowick, Sidney P. & Pestka, Sidney, eds. Interferons, Pt. A. (Methods in Enzymology Ser.: Vol. 78). 1981. text 188.00 (*0-12-181978-7*) Acad Pr.

— Interferons, Pt. B. (Methods in Enzymology Ser.: Vol. 79). 1981. text 188.00 (*0-12-181979-5*) Acad Pr.

Colowick, Sidney P. & Wood, Willis A., eds. Carbohydrate Metabolism, Pt. D. (Methods in Enzymology Ser.: Vol. 89). 656p. 1982. text 188.00 (*0-12-181989-2*) Acad Pr.

— Carbohydrate Metabolism, Pt. E. (Methods in Enzymology Ser.: Vol. 90). 559p. 1982. text 188.00 (*0-12-181990-6*) Acad Pr.

Colowick, Sidney P., ed. see Kaplan, Nathan O.

Colozona Research Corporation Staff. How to Be Happy & Stop Flubbing It. LC 87-13141. 1988. 13.95 (*0-87949-251-1*) Ashley Bks.

— Job Jitters: How to Beat the Competition. LC 87-31930. 1988. 13.95 (*0-87949-277-5*) Ashley Bks.

Colozzi, John. The Apple & the Snake: A Spiritual Memoir. LC 98-93332. 250p. 1998. pap. 12.95 (*0-9666154-0-9*) J Colozzi.

Colozzi, Phil. Budget My Money, Are You Nuts? (Illus.). 120p. 1999. pap. text 20.00 (*0-9670530-0-5*) PMC Ent.

Colozzo, Paola, tr. see Charbonneau, Hubert, et al.

Colp, Harry D. Strangest Story Ever Told. (ENG.). 30p. 1953. pap. text 6.00 (*1-57833-082-3*) Todd Commns.

Colp, Norman B. Stories Your Mother Never Told You. (Illus.). 8p. 1982. 10.00 (*0-685-70931-0*) Gal Assn NY.

Colp, Ralph, Jr. To Be an Invalid: The Illness of Charles Darwin. LC 76-17698. 1977. 30.00 (*0-226-11401-5*) U Ch Pr.

Colpaert, F. Noradrenergic Mechanisms in Parkinson's Disease. 288p. 1993. lib. bdg. 159.00 (*0-8493-8391-9*) CRC Pr.

Colpe, Carsten. Weltdeutungen im Widerstreit. 400p. 1997. text 124.00 (*3-11-015712-8*) De Gruyter.

Colpi, G. M. & Balerna, M., eds. Treating Male Infertility: New Possibilities. (Progress in Reproductive Biology & Medicine Ser.: Vol. 16). (Illus.). xx, 314p. 1994. 259.25 (*3-8055-5892-9*) S Karger.

Colpi, Giovanni M. & Pozza, D., eds. Diagnosing Male Infertility: New Possibilities & Limits. (Progress in Reproductive Biology & Medicine Ser.: Vol. 15). (Illus.). x, 250p. 1992. 214.00 (*3-8055-5443-5*) S Karger.

Colpi, Terri. The Italian Factor: The Italian Community of Great Britain. (Illus.). 300p. 1992. 34.95 (*1-85158-334-3*, Pub. by Mainstream Pubng) Trafalgar.

— Italians Forward: A Visual History of the Italian Community in Great Britain. (Illus.). 190p. 1992. 34.95 (*1-85158-349-1*, Pub. by Mainstream Pubng) Trafalgar.

Colpitt, F. Minimal Art: Critical Perspectives. LC 92-23902. (Illus.). 284p. 1993. reprint ed. pap. 16.95 (*0-295-97236-X*) U of Wash Pr.

Colpitt, Frances. Chromaform: Color in Sculpture. (Illus.). 56p. 1998. 20.00 (*0-9640911-1-9*) U TX San Antonio.

— Mapping. 40p. 1994. pap. 18.00 (*0-9640911-0-0*) U TX San Antonio.

Colpitt, Frances & Plous, Phyllis. Abstract Options. (Illus.). 68p. 1989. 18.00 (*0-942006-17-8*) U of CA Art.

Colpitt, Frances, jt. auth. see Plous, Phyllis.

Colpron, Gilles. Anglicisms of Quebec. (FRE.). 247p. 1979. 59.95 (*0-8288-9167-2*, M6080) Fr & Eur.

Colquett, Mary. Some Sweet Chance. 284p. 1997. 20.00 (*0-9648890-2-1*) Southern Ink.

Colquett, Mary S. Broadhorn. 279p. 1996. 18.00 (*0-9648890-0-5*) Southern Ink.

— The Uninvited Tenant. 286p. 1997. 18.00 (*0-9648890-1-3*) Southern Ink.

Colquhoun. Contemporary Parish Prayers. text 34.95 (*0-340-19622-X*, Pub. by Hodder & Stought Ltd) Trafalgar.

— Health Research in Practice: Political, Ethical & Methodological Issues. 160p. 1993. pap. 47.75 (*1-56593-143-2*, 0455) Singular Publishing.

— New Parish Prayers. text 34.95 (*0-340-27237-6*, Pub. by Hodder & Stought Ltd) Trafalgar.

***Colquhoun.** Riba Book of 20th Century British Housing. 358p. 1999. pap. text 59.95 (*0-7506-3074-4*) Buttrwrth-Heinemann.

Colquhoun & Fauset. Housing Design in Practice. 1991. text. write for info. (*0-582-06360-4*, Pub. by Addison-Wesley) Longman.

Colquhoun, Alan. Essays in Architectural Criticism: Modern Architecture & Historical Change. (Oppositions Bks.). (Illus.). 224p. 1985. pap. text 20.95 (*0-262-53063-5*) MIT Pr.

Colquhoun, Archibald, tr. see Calvino, Italo.

Colquhoun, Archibald, tr. see Rigoni Stern, Mario.

Colquhoun, Archibald, tr. see Tomasi Di Lampedusa, Giuseppe.

Colquhoun, Archibald R. Mastery of the Pacific. LC 70-111750. (American Imperialism: Viewpoints of United States Foreign Policy, 1898-1941 Ser.). 1970. reprint ed. 29.95 (*0-405-02009-0*) Ayer.

Colquhoun, D. & Kellehear, Allan, eds. Health Research in Practice Vol. 2: Personal Experiences, Public Issues, 2. 224p. (Orig.). 1995. pap. 42.95 (*1-56593-608-6*, 1262) Singular Publishing.

Colquhoun, H. M., et al. Carbonylation: Direct Synthesis of Carbonyl Compounds. LC 91-10817. (Illus.). 308p. (C). 1991. text 79.50 (*0-306-43747-3*, Kluwer Plenum) Kluwer Academic.

— New Pathways for Organic Synthesis: Practical Applications of Transition Metals. LC 83-16085. (Illus.). 468p. (C). 1984. text 135.00 (*0-306-41318-3*, Kluwer Plenum) Kluwer Academic.

Colquhoun, J. C., jt. auth. see French Royal Academy of Sciences, Medical Section.

Colquhoun, John. The Chefs of Hilton Head: A Selection of Island Recipes. 150p. 1996. 13.95 (*0-9655662-0-X*) Southern Island.

— Spiritual Comfort. rev. ed. Kistler, Don, ed. 400p. 1998. reprint ed. 29.95 (*1-57358-075-9*) Soli Deo Gloria.

— A Treatise on the Law & the Gospel. 320p. 1999. 24.95 (*1-57358-083-X*) Soli Deo Gloria.

Colquhoun, M. C. & Handley, A. J., eds. ABC of Resuscitation. 3rd ed. (Illus.). 95p. 1995. pap. text 24.00 (*0-7279-0839-1*, Pub. by BMJ Pub) Login Brothers Bk Co.

Colquhoun, Marcus. The Leisure Environment. 208p. (Orig.). 1993. pap. 41.50 (*0-273-03752-8*, Pub. by Pitman Pub) Trans-Atl Phila.

***Colquhoun, Michael & Jevon, Philip.** Resuscitation in Primary Care. (Illus.). 192p. 2000. pap. text 34.00 (*0-7506-4249-1*) Buttrwrth-Heinemann.

Colquhoun, Patrick. Treatise on the Commerce & Police of the River Thames. LC 69-14917. (Criminology, Law Enforcement, & Social Problems Ser.: No. 41). 1969. reprint ed. 35.00 (*0-87585-041-3*) Patterson Smith.

— Treatise on the Police of the Metropolis. 7th ed. LC 69-14918. (Criminology, Law Enforcement, & Social Problems Ser.: No. 42). 1969. reprint ed. 35.00 (*0-87585-042-1*) Patterson Smith.

Colquhoun, W. Peter, et al, eds. Shiftwork: Problems & Solutions. LC 96-166333. (Arbeitswissenschaft in der Betrieblichen Praxis Ser.: Bd. 7). (GER.). 224p. 1996. pap. 42.95 (*3-631-49133-6*) P Lang Pubng.

— Shiftwork: Problems & Solutions. LC 96-166333. (Arbeitswissenschaft in der Betrieblichen Praxis Ser.: Bd. 7). (GER., Illus.). 224p. 1996. pap. 42.95 (*0-8204-3151-6*) P Lang Pubng.

Colquhuon, John. Hadrian & the Girl. (C). 1989. pap. text 39.00 (*1-85821-004-6*, Pub. by Pentland Pr) St Mut.

Colquichagagua, Diana & Franco, Eduardo. Fruta Confitada. 35p. 1994. pap. 9.00 (*1-85339-165-4*, Pub. by Intermed Tech) Stylus Pub VA.

Colquitt, Clare, et al. A Forward Glance: New Essays on Edith Wharton. LC 98-42688. (Illus.). 248p. 1999. 41.50 (*0-87413-667-9*) U Delaware Pr.

Colquitt, Betsy. Eve: From the Autobiography & Other Poems. LC 97-10118. 260p. 1997. 22.50 (*0-87565-174-7*) Tex Christian.

Colquitt, Betsy, ed. see Barney, William D.

Colquitt, James E., ed. Alabama Bound: Contemporary Stories of a State. LC 95-76058. 224p. 1994. pap. 13.95 (*0-942979-26-5*); text 24.95 (*0-942979-25-7*) Livingston U Pr.

Colquitt, Joseph. Alabama Law of Evidence: 1991 Supplement. 126p. 1991. pap. text. write for info. (*0-87473-835-0*, 60991-10, MICHIE) LEXIS Pub.

— Alabama Law of Evidence: 1992 Supplement. 190p. 1992. write for info. (*0-87473-984-5*, 60992-10, MICHIE) LEXIS Pub.

Colquitt, Joseph A. Alabama Law of Evidence. 813p. 1994. suppl. ed. 85.00 (*0-87473-645-5*, 60990-10, MICHIE) LEXIS Pub.

Colquttoun, Margaret & Ewald, Alex. New Eyes for Plants: A Workbook for Plant Observation & Drawing. (Social Ecology Ser.). (Illus.). 208p. (Orig.). 1996. pap. 24.95 (*1-869890-85-X*, Pub. by Hawthorn Press) Anthroposophic.

Colrick, Patricia. Hoboken. (Images of America Ser.). 1998. pap. 16.99 (*0-7524-0898-4*) Arcadia Publng.

— Spring Lake. (Images of America Ser.). 1997. pap. 16.99 (*0-7524-0583-7*) Arcadia Publng.

***Colsman, Edla.** Furniture: Guide to Art Noveau: The Collection in the Museum Fur Angewandte Kunst Koln. (Illus.). 2000. 125.00 (*3-925369-08-2*) Arnoldsche Art Pubs.

Colsn, Rafael Hernandez. Practica Jurmdica De Puerto Rico -- Derecho Procesal Civil. 89.00 (*0-327-12499-7*) LEXIS Pub.

***Colson.** Burden of Truth: Defending the Truth in an Age of Unbelief. 1998. pap. 11.99 (*0-8423-0190-9*) Tyndale Hse.

Colson, Adrien-Joseph. Lettres d'un Bourgeois de Paris a un Ami de Province. (FRE.). 200p. 1995. pap. 69.95 (*2-86808-079-0*) Intl Scholars.

Colson, Brett, jt. auth. see Black, Geoff.

Colson, C. Fe en Practica.Tr. of Faith on the Line. (SPA.). 112p. 1995. pap. 5.99 (*0-8297-1827-3*) Vida Pubs.

***Colson, Charles.** Answers to Your Kids Questions. 2000. pap. 10.99 (*0-8423-1817-8*) Tyndale Hse.

Colson, Charles. Collected Works of Charles Colson: A Collection Consisting of Loving God & Kingdoms In... 656p. 1995. 15.98 (*0-88486-121-X*) Galahad Bks.

— El Cuerpo.Tr. of Body. (SPA.). 464p. 1994. 11.99 (*0-88113-194-6*, B008-1946) Caribe Betania.

— The Enduring Revolution. LC 97-155111. 64p. 1997. 5.97 (*1-55748-936-X*) Barbour Pub.

— How Now Shall We Live? LC 99-22149. 500p. 1999. 19.97 (*0-8423-1808-9*) Tyndale Hse.

***Colson, Charles.** How Now Shall We Live? 1999. pap. text 5.99 (*0-8423-3607-9*) Tyndale Hse.

Colson, Charles. Inspirational Writings of Charles Colson. 1992. 16.98 (*0-88486-064-7*) Arrowood Pr.

— Kingdoms in Conflict. 368p. 1987. 15.95 (*0-310-39770-7*, 11308) Zondervan.

— Kingdoms in Conflict. 2000. 6.99 (*0-310-21481-5*) Zondervan.

— Loving God. 1997. mass mkt. 5.99 (*0-310-21439-4*) Zondervan.

— Loving God. 320p. 1997. pap. 12.99 (*0-310-21914-0*) Zondervan.

— Reclaiming the Soul of America. Date not set. write for info. (*0-345-40709-1*, Moorings) Ballantine Pub Grp.

Colson, Charles & Pearcey, Nancy R. A Dangerous Grace: Daily Readings. 1994. 19.99 (*0-8499-1171-0*) Word Pub.

Colson, Charles & Vaughn, Ellen S. The Body: Being Light in Darkness. 320p. 1994. pap. 13.99 (*0-8499-3579-2*) Word Pub.

— Gideon's Torch: A Novel. 544p. 1995. 21.99 (*0-8499-1146-X*) Word Pub.

— Gideon's Torch: A Novel. 544p. 1996. pap. 12.99 (*0-8499-3977-1*) Word Pub.

Colson, Charles, et al. Christ in Easter: A Family Celebration of Holy Week. LC 90-60399. 80p. (Orig.). 1990. pap. 8.00 (*0-89109-309-5*) NavPress.

Colson, Charles, jt. auth. see Neuhaus, Richard J.

Colson, Charles M. Loving God. large type ed. 1987. pap. 16.95 (*0-8027-2594-5*) Walker & Co.

Colson, Charles W. Against the Night: Living in the New Dark Ages. LC 99-26124. 224p. 1999. pap. 10.99 (*1-56955-144-8*, Vine Bks) Servant.

— Born Again: Twentieth Anniversary Edition. 2nd anniversary ed. LC 96-134093. 352p. (gr. 11). 1995. mass mkt. 5.99 (*0-8007-8633-5*, Spire) Revell.

— Life Sentence. 320p. 1999. mass mkt. 6.99 (*0-8007-8668-8*, Spire) Revell.

***Colson, Charles W.** Nici de Nuevo. (SPA.). 1999. pap. 7.99 (*0-7899-0778-X*) Spanish Hse Distributors.

— Y Ahora...Como Viviremos. (SPA.). 1999. pap. 13.99 (*0-7899-0714-3*) Spanish Hse Distributors.

Colson, Chuck. A Dance with Deception. 1995. mass mkt. 5.99 (*0-8499-3882-1*) Word Pub.

Colson, Constance. Chase the Dream. 454p. 1996. pap. 11.99 (*0-88070-928-6*, Multnomah Bks) Multnomah Pubs.

Colson, Dennis C. Idaho's Constitution: The Tie That Binds. LC 90-49454. (Illus.). 304p. (C). 1991. lib. bdg. 14.95 (*0-89301-132-0*) U of Idaho Pr.

Colson, Donald B., ed. see Horwitz, Leonard, et al.

Colson, Elise, ed. see Stanley, Charles A.

Colson, Elizabeth. The Makah Indians. LC 73-15051. (Illus.). 308p. 1974. reprint ed. lib. bdg. 35.00 (*0-8371-7153-9*, COMI, Greenwood Pr) Greenwood.

— Tradition & Contract: The Problem of Order. LC 74-82603. 152p. (C). 1974. lib. bdg. 23.95 (*0-202-01131-3*) Aldine de Gruyter.

Colson, Elizabeth, jt. ed. see Morgan, Scott M.

Colson, F. H., ed. Cicero: Pro Milone. (Bristol Latin Texts Ser.). (LAT.). 180p. 1980. pap. 20.95 (*0-906515-50-5*, Pub. by Brist Class Pr) Focus Pub-R Pullins.

Colson, Francis H. The Week. LC 73-7697. 126p. 1974. reprint ed. lib. bdg. 38.50 (*0-8371-6940-2*, CTHW, Greenwood Pr) Greenwood.

Colson, Francis H., ed. see Quintilianus.

Colson, H. P. & Dean, R. Galatas Vol. 9: Libertad en Cristo.Tr. of Galatians Freedom in Christ. (SPA.). 160p. 1972. pap. 7.99 (*0-311-04337-2*) Casa Bautista.

Colson, Helen A. Philanthropy at Independent Schools. 1996. pap. 30.00 (*0-934338-83-3*) NAIS.

Colson, J. B., jt. auth. see Davis, John T.

Colson, Jean. Dictionnaire des Monuments de Paris. (FRE.). 920p. 1992. 450.00 (*0-7859-8213-2*, 2903118663) Fr & Eur.

***Colson, John.** A Bend in the Willows. 2000. pap. 13.00 (*0-8059-5000-1*) Dorrance.

Colson, Joseph S., intro. Proceedings of the National Communications Forum, 1991, Vol. XXXXV. (Illus.). 771p. 1991. 139.00 (*0-933217-07-2*) Prof Educ Intl.

Colson, Lucy W., jt. auth. see Colson, Robert E.

Colson, Percy. Their Ruling Passions. LC 70-136645. (Biography Index Reprint Ser.). 1977. 23.95 (*0-8369-8040-9*) Ayer.

— Victorian Portraits. LC 68-16921. (Essay Index Reprint Ser.). 1977. 18.95 (*0-8369-0328-5*) Ayer.

Colson, Rene, et al, eds. Memories Originaus Des Createurs de la Photographic. LC 76-23043. (Sources of Modern Photography Ser.). (FRE.). 1979. reprint ed. lib. bdg. 15.95 (*0-405-09605-4*) Ayer.

Colson, Robert E. & Colson, Lucy W. Monroe & Conecuh Counties, Alabama, Marriages, 1833-1880. 172p. 1983. 20.00 (*0-89308-335-6*) Southern Hist Pr.

Colson, S. Darnbrook. The Hanging Man. (Illus.). 64p. 1997. pap. 5.00 (*1-886988-03-X*) Jasmine Sail.

Colson, Thomas. Molecular Radiations. 190p. 1996. reprint ed. spiral bd. 14.50 (*0-7873-0194-9*) Hlth Research.

Colson, W. B., et al. Laser Handbook Vol. 6: Free Electron Lasers. x, 528p. 1990. 231.00 (*0-444-86953-0*, North Holland) Elsevier.

Colst, Sheldon. Finding Love in a Cold World. 230p. (Orig.). 1991. pap. 14.95 (*0-931174-09-0*) Beau Rivage.

Colston, Chris. Rare Birds: A Look at the Baltimore Orioles from A to Z. LC 98-15954. (Illus.). 96p. 1998. pap. 8.95 (*1-886110-42-5*) Addax Pubng.

Colston, Lowell G. Pastoral Care with Handicapped Persons. LC 77-15229. (Creative Pastoral Care & Counseling Ser.). 94p. (Orig.). reprint ed. pap. 30.00 (*0-608-15814-3*, 203124100074) Bks Demand.

Colt, Anna N., jt. auth. see Erickson, Theodore A.

***Colt, Cassandra.** Secret Library Vol. 2: A Brush with Passion. 2000. pap. 8.95 (*1-58571-011-3*, Pub. by Genesis Press) BookWorld.

Colt, Clem. Quick-Trigger Country. large type ed. (Linford Western Library). 272p. 1985. pap. 16.99 (*0-7089-6087-1*) Ulverscroft.

Colt, David E., ed. Current Issues in Athletic Training. 129p. 1995. 27.95 (*0-9633819-6-2*) Prescott Pub.

Colt, Henri & Mathur, Praveen N. Manual of Pleural Procedures. 22p. 1998. pap. text 34.95 (*0-7817-1476-1*) Lppncott W & W.

Colt, J. Computation of Dissolved Gas Concentrations in Water As Functions of Temperature, Salinity, & Pressure. LC 83-72886. (Special Publication Ser.: No. 14). 154p. 1984. pap. 26.00 (*0-913235-02-4*, 510.10P) Am Fisheries Soc.

Colt, J. & White, R. J., eds. Fisheries Bioengineering Symposium. LC 91-71561. (Symposium Ser.: No. 10). 556p. 1991. text 91.00 (*0-913235-72-5*, 540.10) Am Fisheries Soc.

Colt, John. The Guide: The Essential Resource Book for Picking up Women. 114p. 1998. mass mkt. 5.95 (*0-9663940-0-3*) First Choice Pr.

Colt, Margaretta Barton. Defend the Valley: A Shenandoah Family in the Civil War. LC 99-11769. (Illus.). 442p. 1999. pap. 17.95 (*0-19-513237-8*) OUP.

Colt, Stockton B., ed. The Sales Compensation Handbook. 2nd ed. LC 98-13160. 336p. 1998. 75.00 (*0-8144-0411-1*) AMACOM.

Colt, Thomas C., jt. auth. see Bedford, Henry F.

Coltan, Mary J., ed. see Friends of the Maitland Public Library Staff.

Coltart, Nina. The Baby & the Bathwater. 192p. 1996. pap. 31.00 (*1-85575-134-8*, Pub. by H Karnac Bks Ltd) Other Pr LLC.

— The Baby & the Bathwater. LC 96-28318. 1996. 35.00 (*0-8236-0535-3*) Intl Univs Pr.

— Slouching Toward Bethlehem. 200p. 1998. reprint ed. 35.00 (*1-892746-07-7*, 46077) Other Pr LLC.

***Coltart, Nina.** Slouching Towards Bethlehem. LC 00-39191. 2000. pap. 27.00 (*1-892746-55-7*) Other Pr LLC.

Coltart, Nina E. How to Survive As a Psychotherapist. LC 93-30192. 128p. pap. 25.00 (*1-56821-064-7*) Aronson.

Coltart, W. D., jt. auth. see Burrows, H. Jackson.

Coltelli, Laura. Winged Words: American Indian Writers Speak. LC 89-39323. (American Indian Lives Ser.). (Illus.). x, 211p. 1990. reprint ed. pap. 9.95 (*0-8032-6351-1*, Bison Books) U of Nebr Pr.

Coltelli, Laura, ed. see Harjo, Joy.

Colten, Carig E. & Skinner, Peter N. The Road to Love Canal: Managing Industrial Waste before EPA. LC 95-15399. (Illus.). 240p. (Orig.). 1996. text 35.00 (*0-292-71182-4*) U of Tex Pr.

***Colten, Craig.** Transforming New Orleans & Its Environs: Centuries of Change. (Illus.). 210p. 2001. 45.00 (*0-8229-4134-1*) U of Pittsburgh Pr.

***Colten, Craig, ed.** Transforming New Orleans & Its Environs: Centuries of Change. (Illus.). 210p. 2001. pap. 19.95 (*0-8229-5740-X*) U of Pittsburgh Pr.

Colten, Craig E. & Skinner, Peter N. The Road to Love Canal: Managing Industrial Waste before EPA. LC 95-15399. (Orig.). 1996. pap. 14.95 (*0-292-71183-2*) U of Tex Pr.

Colten, Mary E. & Gore, Susan, eds. Adolescent Stress. (Social Institutions & Social Change Ser.). 342p. 1991. pap. text 26.95 (*0-202-30421-3*); lib. bdg. 51.95 (*0-202-30420-5*) Aldine de Gruyter.

Colten, Roger H. Intrasite Variability in Early & Middle Period Subsistence Remains from CA-SBA-143, Goleta, Santa Barbara County, California. Breschini, Gary S. & Haversat, Trudy, eds. (Archives of California Prehistory Ser.: No. 13). (Illus.). 98p. (Orig.). 1987. pap. 11.56 (*1-55567-046-6*) Coyote Press.

***Colter, Cara.** A Babe in the Woods. (Silhouette Romance Ser.: No. 1424). 2000. per. 3.50 (*0-373-19424-2*, 1-19424-0) Harlequin Bks.

Colter, Cara. Baby in Blue. (Romance Ser.). 1996. per. 3.25 (*0-373-19161-8*, 1-19161-8) Silhouette.

— A Bride Worth Waiting For. (Romance Ser.: No. 1388). 1999. per. 3.50 (*0-373-19388-2*, 1-19388-7) Silhouette.

— The Cowboy, the Baby & the Bride-to-Be. (Romance Ser.). 1998. per. 3.50 (*0-373-19319-X*, 1-19319-2) Silhouette.

***Colter, Cara.** First Time, Forever. (Romance Ser.). 2000. mass mkt. 3.50 (*0-373-19464-1*, 1-19464-6) Silhouette.

Colter, Cara. Husband in Red. 1997. per. 3.25 (*0-373-19243-6*, 1-19243-4) Silhouette.

— Un Papa au Grand Coeur. (Horizon Ser.: No. 524). (FRE.). 1999. mass mkt. 3.99 (*0-373-39524-8*, 1-39524-3) Harlequin Bks.

***Colter, Cara.** Un Papa Merveilleux. (Horizon Ser.: No. 540). (FRE.). 2000. mass mkt. 3.99 (*0-373-39540-X*, 1-39540-9, Harlequin French) Harlequin Bks.

— A Royal Marriage: Royally Wed. 2000. per. 3.50 (*0-373-19440-4*) Harlequin Bks.

Colter, Cara. Truly Daddy. 1999. per. 3.50 (*0-373-19363-7*, 1-19363-0) Silhouette.

— Weddings Do Come True. (Romance Ser.: No. 1406). 1999. per. 3.50 (*0-373-19406-4*, 1-19406-7) Silhouette.

Colter, Cyrus. The Beach Umbrella & Other Stories. 283p. 1996. pap. 14.95 (*0-8101-5050-6*) Northwestern U Pr.

— A Chocolate Soldier. 278p. 1995. pap. 14.95 (*0-8101-5038-7*) Northwestern U Pr.

— City of Light: A Novel. LC 97-47303. 432p. 1998. 17.95 (*0-8101-5080-8*, TriQuart) Northwestern U Pr.

— The Hippodrome: A Novel. LC 94-17022. 224p. 1994. reprint ed. pap. 13.95 (*0-8101-5036-0*, TriQuart) Northwestern U Pr.

An Asterisk (*) at the beginning of an entry indicates that the title is appearing for the first time.

— Night Studies: A Novelistic Investigation of Race Relations in America. LC 97-16024. 1997. pap. text 19.95 (*0-8101-5065-4*, TriQuart) Northwestern U Pr.

— The Rivers of Eros. (Prairie State Bks.). 248p. 1990. reprint ed. 12.95 (*0-252-06089-X*) U of Ill Pr.

Colter, Ephen G., et al, eds. Policing Public Sex: Queer Politics & the Future of AIDS Activism. LC 96-12714. (Illus.). 416p. 1996. 40.00 (*0-89608-550-3*); pap. 20.00 (*0-89608-549-X*) South End Pr.

Colter, Gordon. Artist's Proof. 1999. per. 4.99 (*0-373-26300-7*) Harlequin Bks.

Colter, James F. Colter. Family Records of the Colters & Culbertsons, with Biographical Sketches. (Illus.). 141p. 1997. reprint ed. pap. 22.00 (*0-8328-8022-1*); reprint ed. lib. bdg. 32.00 (*0-8328-8021-3*) Higginson Bk Co.

Coltharp, Barbara. Colonel Neverfail's Christmas. Sandifer, Shannon & Woolfolk, Doug, eds. (Illus.). (Orig.). (J). (gr. 1-3). 1981. 7.95 (*0-86518-019-9*) Moran Pub Corp.

Coltheart, Max, ed. Pure Alexia (Letter-by-Letter Reading) LC 99-168807. 240p. 1998. 59.95 (*0-86377-999-9*) Minerals Metals.

Coltheart, Max, et al, eds. Deep Dyslexis. (International Library of Psychology). 472p. (C). 1988. pap. text 27.50 (*0-7102-1235-6*, Routledge Thoemms) Routledge.

***Coltheart, Max & Davies, Martin, eds.** Pathologies of Belief. (Readings in Mind & Language Ser.). 112p. 2000. pap. 24.95 (*0-631-22136-0*) Blackwell Pubs.

Coltheart, Max, jt. auth. see Harris, Margaret.

Coltheart, Veronika, ed. Fleeting Memories: Cognition of Brief Visual Stimuli. LC 98-36547. (Cognitive Psychology Ser.). (Illus.). 300p. 1999. 35.00 (*0-262-03261-9*, Bradford Bks) MIT Pr.

Colthup, Norman B., et al. Introduction to Infrared & Raman Spectoscopy. 3rd ed. 547p. 1990. text 81.00 (*0-12-182554-X*) Acad Pr.

Coltman. Hospitality Accounting. 7th ed. 2001. pap. text, teacher ed. 0.01 (*0-471-36929-2*) Wiley.

***Coltman.** Hospitality Management Accounting. 7th ed. 700p. 2001. 49.99 (*0-471-34884-8*) Wiley.

Coltman, Debbie. Alpha-Capers & Characters: Student Practice Book. Mammen, Sarah N., ed. (Illus.). 80p. (J). (ps-1). 1998. student ed. 12.95 (*1-57022-182-0*, ECS1820) ECS Lrn Systs.

— Alpha-Capers & Characters: Teacher Resource Book. Mammen, Sarah N., ed. (Illus.). 144p. 1998. pap., teacher ed. 20.95 (*1-57022-181-2*, ECS1812) ECS Lrn Systs.

Coltman, Derek, tr. see Belmont, Nicole.

Coltman, Derek, tr. see Doubrovsky, Serge.

Coltman, Derek, tr. see Dumezil, Georges.

Coltman, Derek, tr. see Duroselle, Jean B.

Coltman, Derek, tr. see Eliade, Mircea.

Coltman, Derek, tr. see Leduc, Violette.

Coltman, Derek, tr. see Leites, Nathan C.

Coltman, Derek, tr. see Piaget, Jean.

Coltman, Derek, tr. see Piaget, Jean, et al.

Coltman, Derek, tr. see Pierrot, Jean.

Coltman, Derek, tr. see Touraine, Alain.

Coltman, Derek, tr. see Varenne, Jean.

Coltman, Edward & Metzenbaum, Shelley. Investing in Ourselves: Strategies for Massachusetts. 85p. 1980. 5.95 (*0-89788-028-5*) CPA Washington.

Coltman, Michael. Introduction to Travel & Tourism: An International Approach. 384p. 1989. 54.95 (*0-471-28862-4*, VNR) Wiley.

Coltman, Michael M. Beverage Management Instructor's Manual. 1989. text 20.95 (*0-442-23540-2*, VNR) Wiley.

— Cost Control for the Hospitality Industry. 2nd ed. 372p. 1989. text 48.95 (*0-442-20591-0*, VNR) Wiley.

Coltman, Michael M. Cost Control for the Hospitality Industry. 2nd ed. 400p. 1989. 54.95 (*0-471-28859-4*, VNR) Wiley.

Coltman, Michael M. Financial Control for Your Hotel. 288p. 1991. pap. 49.95 (*0-471-29036-X*, VNR) Wiley.

— Franchising in Canada: Pros & Cons. 4th ed. LC 96-910581. (Business Ser.). (Illus.). 176p. 1997. pap. 8.95 (*1-55180-094-2*) Self-Counsel Pr.

— Franchising in the U. S. Pros & Cons. 2nd ed. (Business Ser.). 160p. 1988. pap. 6.95 (*0-88908-923-X*, 9504) Self-Counsel Pr.

— Hospitality Management Accounting. 5th ed. (Illus.). 536p. 1993. text 50.95 (*0-442-01655-7*, VNR) Wiley.

— Hospitality Management Accounting. 6th ed. (Hospitality, Travel & Tourism Ser.). 1997. pap. 19.95 (*0-442-02579-3*, VNR) Wiley.

— Hospitality Management Accounting. 6th ed. 160p. 1997. pap., wbk. ed. 24.95 (*0-471-28840-3*, VNR) Wiley.

— Hospitality Management Accounting. 6th ed. 608p. 1997. 54.95 (*0-471-28799-7*, VNR) Wiley.

— Hospitality Management Accounting. 6th ed. LC 97-6825. (Miscellaneous/Catalogs Ser.). (Illus.). 608p. 1997. text 44.95 (*0-442-02382-0*, VNR) Wiley.

***Coltman, Michael M.** Hospitality Management Accounting. 6th ed. 763p. 1998. student ed., wbk. ed. 67.95 (*0-471-32248-2*) Wiley.

Coltman, Michael M. Introduction to Travel & Tourism. 370p. 1989. text 48.95 (*0-442-20652-6*, VNR) Wiley.

— Understanding & Managing Financial Information: The Non-Financial Manager's Guide. (Business Ser.). 232p. 1993. pap. 9.95 (*0-88908-297-9*) Self-Counsel Pr.

Coltman, Robert. Chinese. LC 72-4164. (Select Bibliographies Reprint Ser.). 1977. reprint ed. 25.95 (*0-8369-6874-3*) Ayer.

Coltman, Rodney R. The Language of Hermeneutics: Gadamer & Heidegger in Dialogue. LC 97-42842. (Series in Contemporary Continental Philosophy). 160p. (C). 1998. pap. text 19.95 (*0-7914-3900-3*) State U NY Pr.

— The Language of Hermeneutics: Gadamer & Heidegger in Dialogue. LC 97-42842. (Series in Contemporary Continental Philosophy). 187p. (C). 1998. text 59.50 (*0-7914-3899-6*) State U NY Pr.

Coltman, Virginia, jt. auth. see Rich, Jacqueline.

Coltoff, Philip. Community Schools: Education Reform & Partnership with Out Nation's Social Service Agencies - An Issue Brief. LC 99-163575. 36p. 1998. pap. 6.95 (*0-87868-700-9*, 7009, CWLA Pr) Child Welfare.

***Colton.** Boris Yeltsin & the Transformation. 2000. 30.00 (*0-465-01271-X*, Pub. by Basic); pap. 16.00 (*0-465-01272-8*) Basic.

Colton. Politics & the Media. (Political Science Ser.). 2000. pap. 24.00 (*0-534-55827-5*) Wadsworth Pub.

— Procedures in Scanning Probe Microscopies, 1 vol. 672p. 1998. 550.00 (*0-471-95912-X*) Wiley.

***Colton, Aaron Alexander.** Prisoners & Luminaries. 16p. 1999. pap. 4.00 (*1-930714-03-3*) Good SAMAR.

Colton, Ann R. Draughts of Remembrance. 177p. 1959. 9.95 (*0-917187-09-1*); pap. 9.95 (*0-917189-20-5*) A R Colton Fnd.

— Ethical ESP. LC 78-149600. 367p. 1971. 11.50 (*0-917187-03-2*) A R Colton Fnd.

— The Human Spirit. LC 67-66332. 289p. 1966. 12.95 (*0-917187-05-9*) A R Colton Fnd.

— Islands of Light. 203p. 1953. 12.95 (*0-917187-14-8*) A R Colton Fnd.

— The Jesus Story. 396p. 1969. 15.95 (*0-917187-04-0*) A R Colton Fnd.

— The Jesus Story. 2nd expanded ed. LC 98-92688. 309p. 1998. pap. 15.95 (*0-917189-24-8*) A R Colton Fnd.

— The King. 72p. 1968. 8.50 (*0-917187-08-3*) A R Colton Fnd.

— Kundalini West. LC 79-100659. (Illus.). 403p. 1978. 17.95 (*0-917187-01-6*) A R Colton Fnd.

— The Lively Oracles. LC 67-9752. 151p. 1962. 12.95 (*0-917187-13-X*) A R Colton Fnd.

— Men in White Apparel: Revelations about Death & the Life after Death. LC 68-58. 202p. 1961. 12.95 (*0-917187-10-5*) A R Colton Fnd.

— My Son, Ikhnaton. LC 91-76904. (Illus.). 172p. 1992. 15.95 (*0-917189-09-4*) A R Colton Fnd.

— Precepts for the Young. LC 68-335. 66p. (J). (gr. 1-8). 1959. pap. 2.50 (*0-917187-15-6*) A R Colton Fnd.

— The Soul & the Ethic. LC 67-31989. 262p. 1965. 12.95 (*0-917187-07-5*) A R Colton Fnd.

— The Third Music. LC 83-102627. (Illus.). 432p. 1982. 15.95 (*0-917187-00-8*) A R Colton Fnd.

— The Third Music. 2nd ed. LC 97-91581. (Illus.). 415p. 1999. reprint ed. pap. 15.95 (*0-917189-21-3*) A R Colton Fnd.

— The Venerable One. LC 67-66241. 166p. 1963. 9.95 (*0-917187-11-3*) A R Colton Fnd.

— Vision for the Future. LC 96-83732. 124p. 1960. pap. 9.95 (*0-917189-17-5*) A R Colton Fnd.

— Watch Your Dreams. LC 96-83735. 339p. 1973. pap. 15.95 (*0-917189-18-3*) A R Colton Fnd.

Colton, Ann R. & Murro, Jonathan. Galaxy Gate I & II, 2 vols., Set. Incl. Galaxy Gate I: The Holy Universe. LC 84-70851. (Illus.). 285p. 1984. 16.95 (*0-917189-02-7*); . Galaxy Gate II: The Angel Kingdom. LC 84-70850. (Illus.). 351p. 1984. 16.95 (*0-917189-03-5*); LC 84-70851. (Illus.). 636p. 1984. 33.90 (*0-917189-01-9*) A R Colton Fnd.

— Owe No Man: Scriptural Principles of Good Stewardship & Divine Providence. LC 86-70153. (Illus.). 374p. 1986. 21.95 (*0-917189-05-1*) A R Colton Fnd.

— The Pelican & the Chela: The Teacher-Student Relationship in the Spiritual Life. LC 85-70766. (Illus.). 420p. 1985. 21.95 (*0-917189-04-3*) A R Colton Fnd.

— Prophet for the Archangels. LC 64-6257. (Illus.). 257p. 1964. pap. 9.95 (*0-917187-06-7*) A R Colton Fnd.

Colton, Ann Ree. The Archetypal Kingdom. LC 88-70974. (Illus.). 454p. 1988. 21.95 (*0-917189-07-8*) A R Colton Fnd.

***Colton, Ann Ree.** Kundalini West. LC 99-94819. (Illus.). 300p. 2000. pap. 17.95 (*0-917189-26-4*) A R Colton Fnd.

Colton, Ann Ree & Murro, Jonathan. The Anointed: Sacred Keys to Healing, Exorcism & the Divine Marriage. LC 87-70497. (Illus.). 444p. 1987. 21.95 (*0-917189-06-X*) A R Colton Fnd.

Colton, Arthur W. Delectable Mountains. LC 71-86139. (Short Story Index Reprint Ser.). 1977. 19.95 (*0-8369-3043-6*) Ayer.

Colton Bk Staff. New Tagalog English Dictionary Including Everyday Tagalog. 1994. pap. 5.50 (*971-686-041-2*) Colton Bk.

Colton, C., jt. auth. see Texhammar, R.

Colton, C. A., jt. auth. see Gilbert, D. L.

***Colton, C. E.** A Twenty First Century New Testament Church: A Study of the Polity & Problems of a New Testament Church. 156p. (Orig.). 1999. pap. 12.95 (*0-9646448-1-9*) Colton Bks.

Colton, C. E. What's Next? A Perceptive Study of the End Times & Christ's Second Coming. 138p. (Orig.). 1995. pap. 7.95 (*0-9646448-0-0*) Colton Bks.

Colton, C. E., et al, eds. Respiratory Protection: A Manual & Guideline. 2nd ed. 146p. 1991. 50.00 (*0-932627-45-5*) Am Indus Hygiene.

Colton, Calvin. Abolition a Sedition. LC 72-1054. reprint ed. 32.50 (*0-404-00017-7*) AMS Pr.

— Abolition a Sedition, by a Northern Man. LC 73-133152. (Black Heritage Library Collection). 1977. 21.95 (*0-8369-8707-1*) Ayer.

— Manual for Emigrants to America. LC 69-18767. (American Immigration Collection. Series 1). 1969. reprint ed. 12.95 (*0-405-00515-6*) Ayer.

— Public Economy for the United States. 2nd ed. LC 68-30517. (Reprints of Economic Classics Ser.). xvi, 536p. 1969. reprint ed. 57.50 (*0-678-00513-3*) Kelley.

Colton, Calvin, ed. see Clay, Henry.

***Colton, D. L., et al, eds.** Surveys on Solution Methods for Inverse Problems. 270p. 2000. pap. 52.00 (*3-211-83470-2*) Spr-Verlag.

Colton, Dale. A Little Book of Relaxation Techniques. (Illus.). 48p. spiral bd. 18.00 (*0-9640043-0-5*) Mat Possessions.

***Colton, David.** Mensa Covert Puzzles. 1999. pap. 7.99 (*0-7858-1156-7*) Book Sales.

Colton, David & Kress, Rainer. Integral Equation Methods in Scattering Theory. LC 91-21132. (Pure & Applied Mathematics Ser.). 286p. (C). 1992. reprint ed. text 65.00 (*0-89464-636-2*) Krieger.

— Inverse Acoustic & Electromagnetic Scattering Theory. LC 92-16437. (Applied Mathematical Sciences Ser.: Vol. 93). 1992. 64.95 (*0-387-55518-8*) Spr-Verlag.

— Inverse Acoustic & Electromagnetic Scattering Theory. 2nd ed. LC 97-45046. (Applied Mathematical Sciences Ser.: Vol. 93). (Illus.). 334p. 1998. 69.95 (*3-540-62838-X*) Spr-Verlag.

Colton, David M. Colton's Book of Short Stories. Thomson-Shore Inc. Printers Staff, ed. 339p. write for info. (*0-318-63111-3*) D M Colton.

— Harbor Lights. 411p. (Orig.). pap. 10.00 (*0-318-22528-X*) D M Colton.

Colton, Douglas J. Antitrust Law. (Hospital Law in North Carolina Ser.: Chap. 12). 63p. (C). 1988. ring bd. 10.50 (*1-56011-084-8*, 85.03L) Institute Government.

Colton, Elizabeth O., jt. auth. see Bergmann, Elizabeth.

Colton, Ellie, jt. auth. see Elkins, Stephen.

Colton, Ethan T. Four Patterns of Revolution. LC 79-121456. (Essay Index Reprint Ser.). 1977. 21.95 (*0-8369-1747-2*) Ayer.

Colton, H. S., jt. auth. see Colton, M. R.

Colton, Harold S. Black Sand: Prehistory in Northern Arizona. LC 73-13453. (Illus.). 132p. 1973. reprint ed. lib. bdg. 35.00 (*0-8371-7137-7*, COBS, Greenwood Pr) Greenwood.

— Hopi Kachina Dolls. rev. ed. LC 82-8413. (Illus.). 159p. 1970. reprint ed. pap. 13.95 (*0-8263-0180-0*) U of NM Pr.

— A Survey of Prehistoric Sites in the Region of Flagstaff, Arizona. (Bureau of American Ethnology Bulletins Ser.). 69p. 1995. lib. bdg. 79.00 (*0-7812-4104-9*) Rprt Serv.

— A Survey of Prehistoric Sites in the Region of Flagstaff, Arizona. reprint ed. 59.00 (*0-403-03702-6*) Scholarly.

Colton, Harold S. & Hargrave, Lyndon L. Handbook of Northern Arizona Pottery Wares. LC 76-43677. (Museum of Northern Arizona Bulletin Ser.: No. 11). reprint ed. 32.50 (*0-404-15511-1*) AMS Pr.

Colton, Helen. The Gift of Touch. 272p. 1995. pap. 12.00 (*1-57566-012-1*) Kensgtn Pub Corp.

— The Gift of Touch. 320p. 1995. pap. 12.00 (*0-8217-4884-X*) NAL.

— Touch Therapy. Orig. Title: The Gift of Touch. 320p. 1988. mass mkt. 4.95 (*0-8217-2361-8*, Zebra Kensgtn) Kensgtn Pub Corp.

— Touch Therapy. Orig. Title: The Gift of Touch. 1989. pap. 4.95 (*0-8217-2774-5*) NAL.

Colton, James. The Outward Side. 1995. mass mkt. 6.95 (*1-56333-304-X*, Hard Candy) Masquerade.

— Todd. 1995. mass mkt. 6.95 (*1-56333-312-0*, Hard Candy) Masquerade.

Colton, James & Colton, Sheelagh. Iridology: Health Analysis & Treatments from the Iris of the Eye. LC 96-43198. (Health Essentials Ser.). 128p. 1996. pap. 9.95 (*1-85230-880-X*, Pub. by Element MA) Penguin Putnam.

Colton, Joel. A History of the Modern World, Vol. 3. 8th ed. LC 94-14758. 1259p. (C). 1994. 70.31 (*0-07-040826-2*) McGraw.

— A History of the Modern World, Vol. 3. 8th ed. (C). 1994. pap., student ed. 15.63 (*0-07-040828-9*) McGraw.

— A History of the Modern World Vol. 1: To 1815. 8th ed. LC 94-26364. (C). 1994. pap. 44.69 (*0-07-040829-7*) McGraw.

— A History of the Modern World Vol. 1: To 1815, Vol. 2. 7th ed. (C). 1992. text 35.00 (*0-07-048564-X*) McGraw.

— A History of the Modern World Vol. 2: Since 1815, Vol. 2. 8th ed. LC 94-26364. (C). 1994. pap. 44.69 (*0-07-040830-0*) McGraw.

— Leon Blum: Humanist in Politics. LC 73-21892. (Illus.). xxv, 523p. 1987. pap. text 24.95 (*0-8223-0762-6*) Duke.

Colton, Joel & Bruchey, Stuart, eds. Technology, the Economy, & Society: The American Experience. LC 86-24475. 304p. 1987. text 64.50 (*0-231-05964-7*) Col U Pr.

Colton, Judith. The Parnasse Francois: Titon du Tillet & the Origins of the Monument to Genius. LC 78-9878. (Yale Publications in the History of Art: No. 27). 323p. reprint ed. pap. 100.20 (*0-8357-8745-1*, 203369500087) Bks Demand.

Colton, Judith, et al. A Taste for Angels: Neapolitan Painting in North America, 1650-1750. Kenney, Elise K., ed. LC 87-50866. (Illus.). 355p. (Orig.). 1987. pap. 25.00 (*0-89467-046-8*) Yale Art Gallery.

Colton, Katherine. Smart Guide to Getting Thin & Healthy. LC 98-33832. (Smart Guides Ser.). 192p. 1998. pap. 10.95 (*0-471-29634-1*) Wiley.

Colton, Kent W. & Kraemer, Kenneth L., eds. Computers & Banking: Electroinc Funds Transfer Systems & Public Policy. LC 79-9307. (Applications of Modern Technology in Business Ser.: Vol. 1). (Illus.). 325p. 1980. reprint ed. pap. 100.80 (*0-608-05463-1*, 206593200006) Bks Demand.

***Colton, Larry.** Counting Coup: A True Story of Basketball & Honor On the Little Big Horn. (Illus.). 432p. 2000. 24.95 (*0-446-52683-5*) Warner Bks.

Colton, Linda. Flutter & Fly. (Illus.). 40p. 1994. pap. text 7.95 (*1-884329-02-0*) Teach It Pubns.

— Frogmania. (Theme Ser.). (Illus.). 44p. 1994. pap. text 7.95 (*1-884329-00-4*) Teach It Pubns.

Colton, M. J. Dimensions of Substitute Child Care: A Comparative Study of Foster & Residential Care Practice. 301p. 1988. text 67.95 (*0-566-05612-7*, Pub. by Avebry) Ashgate Pub Co.

Colton, M. J. & Hellinckx, W. Child Care in the EC: A Country-Specific Guide to Foster & Residential Care. 272p. 1993. 64.95 (*1-85742-178-7*, Pub. by Arena); pap. 36.95 (*1-85742-179-5*, Pub. by Arena) Ashgate Pub Co.

Colton, M. J. & Williams, Margret. World of Foster Care: An International Sourcebook on Foster Family Care System. LC 97-19599. 500p. 1997. text 69.95 (*1-85742-339-9*, Pub. by Arena) Ashgate Pub Co.

Colton, M. R. & Colton, H. S. Little-Known Small House Ruins in the Coconino Forest. LC 19-15014. (American Anthropological Association Memoirs Ser.: No. 24). 1918. pap. 25.00 (*0-527-00523-1*) Periodicals Srv.

Colton, Matthew, et al, eds. The Art & Science of Child Care: Research, Policy & Practice in European Union. 288p. 1995. 69.95 (*1-85742-285-6*, Pub. by Arena) Ashgate Pub Co.

Colton, Matthew & Vanstone, Maurice. Betrayal of Trust: Professionals Who Sexually Abuse Children. 200p. (C). 1997. 45.00 (*1-85343-356-X*, Pub. by Free Assoc Bks); pap. 19.95 (*1-85343-357-8*, Pub. by Free Assoc Bks) NYU Pr.

Colton, Matthew, et al. Children in Need: Family Support under the Children Act 1989. 256p. 1995. text 66.95 (*1-85628-932-X*, Pub. by Avebry) Ashgate Pub Co.

— Stigma & Social Welfare: An International Comparative Study. LC HV41.S798 1997. (Welfare & Society Ser.). 174p. 1997. text 65.95 (*1-85972-525-2*, Pub. by Avebry) Ashgate Pub Co.

Colton, Mike, jt. auth. see Kenson, Steve.

Colton, Molly. Sojourn. 328p. Date not set. mass mkt. 4.99 (*1-55197-169-0*) Picasso Publ.

***Colton, Paul.** Developing JAVA Server Pages. 500p. 2000. pap. 39.99 (*0-672-31939-X*) Sams.

Colton, Paul. JavaScript Unleashed. LC 96-68239. 912p. 1996. pap. text 49.99 incl. cd-rom (*1-57521-118-1*) Sams.

Colton, R. J., et al, eds. Secondary Ion Mass Spectrometry: SIMS V. (Chemical Physics Ser.: Vol. 44). (Illus.). 590p. 1986. 87.00 (*0-387-16263-1*) Spr-Verlag.

Colton, Ray C. The Civil War in the Western Territories: Arizonia, Colorado, New Mexico, & Utah. LC 59-7964. (Illus.). 240p. 1984. pap. 15.95 (*0-8061-1902-0*) U of Okla Pr.

Colton, Raymond, et al. Understanding Voice Problems. (Illus.). 376p. 1989. pap. 43.00 (*0-683-02058-7*) Lppncott W & W.

Colton, Raymond H. & Casper, Janina K. Understanding Voice Problems: A Physiological Perspective for Diagnosis & Treatment. 2nd ed. LC 95-33492. (Illus.). 432p. 1996. 46.95 (*0-683-02059-5*) Lppncott W & W.

Colton, Raymond H., jt. auth. see Casper, Janina K.

Colton, Robert E. Juvenal & Boileau: A Study of Literary Influence. (Studien Zur Vergleichenden Literaturwissenschaft Ser.: Vol. 1). 108p. 1987. 25.00 (*3-487-07850-3*) G Olms Pubs.

— Studies of Classical Influence on Boileau & la Fontaine. LC 97-103105. 1996. write for info. (*3-487-10219-6*) G Olms Pubs.

— Studies of Imitation in Some Latin Authors. xii, 396p. 1995. pap. 80.00 (*90-256-1005-6*, Pub. by AM Hakkert) BookLink Distributors.

Colton, Sheelagh, jt. auth. see Colton, James.

Colton, Ted, jt. auth. see Hall, Betty L.

Colton, Ted, jt. ed. see Armitage, Peter.

Colton, Theodore. Statistics in Medicine. LC 73-1413. 400p. 1975. pap. text 45.00 (*0-316-15250-1*) Lppncott W & W.

Colton, Timothy J. Big Daddy: Frederick G. Gardiner & the Building of Metropolitan Toronto. LC 81-126092. (Illus.). 240p. reprint ed. pap. 74.40 (*0-8357-8044-9*, 203397500088) Bks Demand.

— Commissars, Commanders, & Civilian Authority: The Structure of Soviet Military Politics. LC 78-23342. (Russian Research Center Studies: No. 79). (Illus.). 373p. 1979. 44.50 (*0-674-14535-6*) HUP.

— Moscow: Governing the Socialist Metropolis. LC 95-14662. (Russian Research Center Studies: Vol. 88). (Illus.). 896p. (C). 1996. 45.00 (*0-674-58741-3*) Belknap Pr.

— Moscow: Governing the Socialist Metropolis. (Russian Research Center Studies). (Illus.). 960p. 1998. pap. 24.95 (*0-674-58749-9*) HUP.

***Colton, Timothy J.** Transitional Citizens: Voters & What Influences Them in the New Russia. 2000. text 65.00 (*0-674-00277-6*); pap. text 24.95 (*0-674-00153-2*) HUP.

Colton, Timothy J. & Hough, Jerry F., eds. Growing Pains: Russian Democracy & the Election of 1993. LC 97-45314. 745p. 1998. 59.95 (*0-8157-1522-6*) Brookings.

— Growing Pains: Russian Democracy & the Election of 1993. LC 97-45314. (Illus.). 745p. 1998. pap. 26.95 (*0-8157-1521-8*) Brookings.

Colton, Timothy J. & Legvold, Robert H., eds. After the Soviet Union: From Empire to Nations. (American Assembly Book Ser.). 240p. (C). 1992. pap. text 16.00 (*0-393-96359-4*) Norton.

Colton, Virginia, ed. see Reader's Digest Editors.

Colton, Walter. Three Years in California. Cortes, Carlos E., ed. LC 76-1221. (Chicano Heritage Ser.). (Illus.). 1977. reprint ed. 39.95 (*0-405-09496-5*) Ayer.

— Three Years in California. 1992. reprint ed. lib. bdg. 75.00 (*0-7812-5016-1*) Rprt Serv.

***Coltrane, James.** Good Day to Die: A Novel. LC 98-46970. 160p. 1999. text 21.95 (*0-393-04766-0*) Norton.

— Good Day to Die; A Novel of Cuba after Castro. 2000. pap. 11.00 (*0-385-49898-5*, Anchor NY) Doubleday.

Coltrane, John. John Coltrane Plays Giant Steps. 72p. 1996. per. 19.95 (*0-7935-6345-3*) H Leonard.

C

— The Music of John Coltrane: Over One Hundred Compositions by Jazz Saxophone Great John Coltrane. (Jazz Giants Ser.). 128p. (Orig.). 1991. spiral bd. 22.95 (*0-7935-0409-0*, 00660165) H Leonard.

*Coltrane, John & Theolonius Monk.** Jazz Heroes. (Illus.). 160p. 1999. 27.95 (*1-57500-042-3*) TV Bks.

Coltrane, Robbie. Coltrane's Planes & Automobiles: Engines That Turned the World LC 99-204603. 189 p. 1997. write for info. (*0-684-81957-0*) S&S Trade.

Coltrane, Robert, ed. see Dreiser, Theodore.

Coltrane, Scott. Family Man: Fatherhood, Housework & Gender Equality. 304p. 1997. reprint ed. pap. 14.95 (*0-19-511909-6*) OUP.

— Family Man: Fatherhood, Housework & Gender Equity. 304p. 1996. 30.00 (*0-19-508216-8*) OUP.

— Gender & Families. LC 97-4878. (Gender Lens Ser.). 240p. (Orig.). (C). 1997. pap. text 18.95 (*0-8039-9036-7*) Pine Forge.

Coltrane, Scott, jt. auth. see Collins, Randall.

Coltrera, Joseph T., ed. Lives, Events & Other Players: Studies in Psychobiography. LC 79-51911. (Downstate Psychoanalytic Institute Twenty-Fifth Anniversary Ser.: Vol. IV). 1979. 40.00 (*0-87668-369-3*) Aronson.

Coltrin, Charles W. Castle: Genealogical Notes on the Ancestry & Descendants of Lester Delos Castle & Lucy Angelia (Taylor) Castle of Barrington Cook County, Illinois, 1613-1923. (Illus.). 125p. 1997. reprint ed. pap. 21.00 (*0-8328-7892-8*); reprint ed. lib. bdg. 31.00 (*0-8328-7891-X*) Higginson Bk Co.

Colucci, Wilson. Heart Failure: Cardiac Function & Dysfunction. LC 94-41113. (Atlas of Heart Diseases Ser.: No. 4). (Illus.). 272p. 1995. text 134.00 (*1-878132-27-X*) Current Med.

***Colucci, Wilson S. & Braunwald, Eugene, eds.** Atlas of Heart Failure: Cardiac Function & Dysfunction. 2nd ed. LC 98-26627. (Atlas of Heart Diseases Ser.). (Illus.). 1998. 75.00 (*0-632-04381-4*) Blackwell Sci.

Coluccio, Vincent M., ed. see ATC Environmental Inc. Staff.

Colum, Padraic. The Boy Apprenticed to an Enchanter. (Illus.). (J). (gr. 3-7). 1991. 20.50 (*0-8446-6482-0*) Peter Smith.

— The Children's Homer. 1992. pap. 20.00 (*0-8196-1278-2*) Biblo.

— The Children's Homer: The Adventures of Odysseus & the Tale of Troy. LC 82-12643. (Illus.). 256p. (YA). (gr. 5 up). 1982. mass mkt. 9.95 (*0-02-042520-1*, Pub. by Macmillan) S&S Trade.

— The Golden Fleece: And the Heroes Who Lived Before Achilles. LC 82-21667. (Illus.). 320p. (YA). (gr. 5 up). 1983. mass mkt. 9.95 (*0-02-042260-1*, Pub. by Macmillan) S&S Trade.

— The Golden Fleece: And the Heroes Who Lived Before Achilles. LC 82-21667. (Illus.). 320p. (YA). (gr. 5 up). 1967. lib. bdg. 17.00 (*0-02-723620-X*, Mac Bks Young Read) S&S Childrens.

— Golden Fleece & the Heroes Who Lived Before. (J). 1983. 15.05 (*0-606-01674-0*, Pub. by Turtleback) Demco.

— Half-Day's Ride. LC 77-90625. (Essay Index Reprint Ser.). 1977. 20.95 (*0-8369-1282-9*) Ayer.

— Kate Mary Ellen & the Fairies. LC 95-3784. (Illus.). (J). 1999. lib. bdg. write for info. (*0-7868-2149-3*) Hyperion.

— The King of Ireland's Son. (Illus.). 320p. (J). 1997. reprint ed. pap. text 8.95 (*0-486-29722-5*) Dover.

— Nordic Gods & Heroes: Padraic Column. unabridged ed. LC 95-22396. (Illus.). 304p. (Orig.). 1996. reprint ed. pap. text 8.95 (*0-486-28912-5*) Dover.

— Orpheus: Myths of the World. 1996. pap. text 21.95 (*0-86315-519-7*, Pub. by Floris Bks) Anthroposophic.

— Selected Plays of Padraic Colum. Sternlicht, Sanford, ed. (Irish Studies). (Illus.). 128p. 1986. text 26.95 (*0-8156-2386-0*) Syracuse U Pr.

— Selected Poems of Padraic Colum. Sternlicht, Sanford, ed. (Irish Studies). (Illus.). 120p. 1989. text 26.95 (*0-8156-2458-1*) Syracuse U Pr.

— The Trojan War & the Adventures of Odysseus. LC 96-34415. (Books of Wonder). (Illus.). 192p. (J). 1997. 22.00 (*0-688-14588-4*, Wm Morrow); 22.00 (*0-614-29270-0*, Wm Morrow) Morrow Avon.

***Colum, Robert M.** Deductive Databases & Their Applications. LC 98-151074. 1998. 79.95 (*0-7484-0796-0*) Taylor & Francis.

Columba, Stewart. Prayer & Community: The Benedictine Tradition. LC 98-21362. (Traditions of Christian Spirituality Ser.). 128p. 1998. pap. 13.00 (*1-57075-219-2*) Orbis Bks.

Columbano, A., et al, eds. Chemical Carcinogenesis 2: Modulating Factors. (Illus.). 666p. (C). 1991. text 186.00 (*0-306-43896-8*, Kluwer Plenum) Kluwer Academic.

Columbaro, Barbara, tr. see Ferrarotti, Franco.

Columbaro, Pasqualino, tr. see Ferrarotti, Franco.

Columbetti, Lelio G., ed. Principles of Radiopharmacology, 3 vols., Vol. 1. 304p. 1979. 165.00 (*0-8493-5465-X*, RM858, CRC Reprint) Franklin.

— Principles of Radiopharmacology, 3 vols., Vol. 2. 288p. 1979. 158.00 (*0-8493-5466-8*, CRC Reprint) Franklin.

— Principles of Radiopharmacology, 3 vols., Vol. 3. 352p. 1979. 194.00 (*0-8493-5467-6*, CRC Reprint) Franklin.

***Columbia Books Staff.** National Directory of Corporate Public Affairs, 2000. 18th ed. Steele, J. Valerie, ed. 1277p. 2000. pap. 109.00 (*1-880873-38-9*) Columbia Bks.

— Washington Representatives. 2000. 109.00 (*1-880873-40-0*) Columbia Bks.

***Columbia Books Staff, ed.** Washington 2000. (Illus.). 2000. 89.00 (*1-880873-41-9*) Columbia Bks.

***Columbia Books Staff & Downs, Buck, eds.** National Trade & Professional Associations, 2000. 35th ed. 959p. 2000. pap. 99.00 (*1-880873-37-0*) Columbia Bks.

— State & Regional Associations of the U. S., 2000. 12th ed. 719p. 2000. pap. 79.00 (*1-880873-39-7*) Columbia Bks.

Columbia Business School Staff. Introductory Management Science. 224p. (C). 1994. text 35.20 (*0-536-58748-5*) Pearson Custom.

Columbia College Contemporary Civilization Staff. Introduction to Contemporary Civilization in the West, 2 vols., Vol. 1. 3rd ed. LC 60-16650. 1960. text 55.50 (*0-231-02423-1*) Col U Pr.

— Introduction to Contemporary Civilization in the West, 2 vols., Vol. 2. 3rd ed. LC 60-16650. 1961. text 80.50 (*0-231-02477-0*) Col U Pr.

Columbia Daily Tribune. Beyond the Norm: A Salute to Missouri's Norm Stewart. 96p. 1999. pap. 12.95 (*1-58261-133-5*) Sprts Pubng.

Columbia Human Rights Law Review Staff. World Population Control: Rights & Restrictions. LC 75-27963. (Symposia of the Columbia Human Rights Law Review Ser.). 575p. reprint ed. pap. 178.30 (*0-608-18321-0*, 203159400075) Bks Demand.

Columbia Law Review Staff. Essays on Jurisprudence from the Columbia Law Review. LC 77-10131. 413p. 1977. reprint ed. lib. bdg. 75.00 (*0-8371-9776-7*, CLEJ, Greenwood Pr) Greenwood.

Columbia Pacific University Faculty Staff & Crews, Richard L. Clear Thinking. 115p. (C). 1989. student ed. write for info. (*0-945864-26-4*); pap. text. write for info. (*0-945864-25-6*) Columbia Pacific U Pr.

— Cogitat Ergo Erst: An Introductory Course in Computer Literacy. 45p. (C). 1989. pap. text. write for info. (*0-945864-21-3*) Columbia Pacific U Pr.

— Columbia Pacific University Faculty Manual. 44p. (C). 1989. pap. text. write for info. (*0-945864-24-8*) Columbia Pacific U Pr.

— Course Equivalency Catalog. 59p. (C). 1989. pap. text. write for info. (*0-945864-23-X*) Columbia Pacific U Pr.

— A Course on Writing. 29p. (C). 1989. student ed. write for info. (*0-945864-17-5*); pap. text. write for info. (*0-945864-16-7*) Columbia Pacific U Pr.

— Essential Statistics. 35p. (C). 1989. pap. text. write for info. (*0-945864-18-3*); write for info. (*0-945864-19-1*) Columbia Pacific U Pr.

Columbia University , School of Social Work Staff. Counseling in Abortion Services: Physician-Nurse-Social Worker. 1974. 3.00 (*0-686-09562-6*) Univ Bk Serv.

Columbia University Ancient Near East Society Staf. Journal, Set, Vols. 1-13. reprint ed. write for info. (*0-404-19569-5*) AMS Pr.

Columbia University, Avery Architectural & Fine Ar. The Art of Architecture: Address Book. (Illus.). 19.95 (*0-87654-593-2*, A562) Pomegranate Calif.

Columbia University, Bureau of Applied Social Rese. The People Look at Radio. LC 75-22803. (America in Two Centuries Ser.). 1976. reprint ed. 18.95 (*0-405-07675-4*) Ayer.

Columbia University, Department of Classical Philo. Greek Literature. LC 69-18922. (Essay Index Reprint Ser.). 1977. 21.95 (*0-8369-0038-3*) Ayer.

Columbia University, Department of Philosophy Staff, ed. Studies in the History of Ideas, 3 vols. LC 79-130993. reprint ed. 120.00 (*0-404-19510-5*) AMS Pr.

Columbia University Editors. Dictionary Catalogue of the Library of the School of Library Service, 7 Vols, Set. 1970. 795.00 (*0-8161-0634-7*, G K Hall & Co) Mac Lib Ref.

— Dictionary Catalogue of the Library of the School of Library Service, First Supplement, 4 vols, Set. 1976. 555.00 (*0-8161-1166-9*, G K Hall & Co) Mac Lib Ref.

— Dictionary Catalogue of the Teachers College Library, 36 vols., Set. 1979. 4910.00 (*0-8161-0855-2*, G K Hall & Co) Mac Lib Ref.

Columbia University, English Institute Annual Publ. English Institute Annual Publications, 33 vols., Set. Kirk, Rudolf, ed. 19.50 (*0-404-52200-9*) AMS Pr.

Columbia University Law Library Staff. Dictionary Catalog of the Columbia University Law Library. 1970. 3270.00 (*0-8161-1495-1*, G K Hall & Co) Mac Lib Ref.

— Dictionary Catalog of the Columbia University Law Library, Supplement 1. 1978. suppl. ed. 1185.00 (*0-8161-1501-X*, G K Hall & Co) Mac Lib Ref.

— Dictionary Catalog of the Columbia University Law Library, Supplement 2. 1980. suppl. ed. 630.00 (*0-8161-1272-X*, G K Hall & Co) Mac Lib Ref.

Columbia University, National Project on Asian in, compiled by. National Review of Asia in American Textbooks in 1993-Secondary Level: World History, World Cultures, World Geography. LC 93-27198. 139p. (Orig.). 1993. pap. 15.00 (*0-924304-16-2*) Assn Asian Studies.

Columbia University, New York Staff, compiled by. Cumulative Author Index to Psychological Index, 1894 to 1935, & Psychological Abstracts, 1927 to 1958, 5 vols. 1970. 160.00 (*0-8161-0598-7*, G K Hall & Co) Mac Lib Ref.

Columbia University Press. Columbia Encyclopedia. 5th ed. 3072p. 1993. 59.95 (*0-395-62438-X*) HM.

Columbia University Press Editors. The Concise Columbia Encyclopedia. (Illus.). 960p. 1983. pap. 14.95 (*0-380-63396-5*, Avon Bks) Morrow Avon.

***Columbia University Press Staff, ed.** Mothers & Daughters in the 20th Century: A Literary Anthology. 2000. 19.95 (*0-7486-1175-4*, Pub. by Edinburgh U Pr) Col U Pr.

Columbia University Press Staff & Lagasse, Paul, eds. The Concise Columbia Encyclopedia. 3rd ed. (Illus.). 992p. 1995. pap. 19.95 (*0-395-75184-5*) HM.

Columbia University Staff. Author Index to Psychological Abstracts, 1964 to 1968. 1982. 370.00 (*0-8161-1355-6*, G K Hall & Co) Mac Lib Ref.

— Avery Index to Architectural Periodicals. 2nd ed. 1987. 1875.00 (*0-8161-1735-7*, G K Hall & Co) Mac Lib Ref.

— Avery Index to Architectural Periodicals. 2nd ed. 1990. 2005.00 (*0-8161-1736-5*, G K Hall & Co) Mac Lib Ref.

— Avery Index to Architectural Periodicals. 2nd ed. 1991. suppl. ed. 455.00 (*0-8161-1574-5*, G K Hall & Co) Mac Lib Ref.

— Avery Index to Architectural Periodicals, Supplement 1. 1988. suppl. ed. 185.00 (*0-8161-1737-3*, G K Hall & Co) Mac Lib Ref.

— Avery Index to Architectural Periodicals, Supplement 2. 2nd ed. 1980. suppl. ed. 185.00 (*0-8161-1291-6*, G K Hall & Co) Mac Lib Ref.

— Avery Index to Architectural Periodicals, Supplement 3. 2nd ed. 1983. suppl. ed. 185.00 (*0-8161-1292-4*, G K Hall & Co) Mac Lib Ref.

— Avery Index to Architectural Periodicals, Supplement 4. 2nd ed. 1990. suppl. ed. 375.00 (*0-8161-1777-2*, G K Hall & Co) Mac Lib Ref.

— Avery Index to Architectural Periodicals, Supplement 5. 2nd ed. 1982. suppl. ed. 645.00 (*0-8161-1483-8*, G K Hall & Co) Mac Lib Ref.

— Avery Index to Architectural Periodicals, Supplement 5. 2nd ed. 1988. suppl. ed. 470.00 (*0-8161-1543-5*, G K Hall & Co) Mac Lib Ref.

— Avery Index to Architectural Periodicals, Supplement 7. 2nd ed. 1988. suppl. ed. 470.00 (*0-8161-1545-1*, G K Hall & Co) Mac Lib Ref.

— Avery Index to Architectural Periodicals, Supplement 8. 2nd ed. 1990. suppl. ed. 470.00 (*0-8161-1567-2*, G K Hall & Co) Mac Lib Ref.

— Avery Index to Architectural Periodicals, Supplement 9. 2nd ed. 1991. suppl. ed. 470.00 (*0-8161-1573-7*, G K Hall & Co) Mac Lib Ref.

— Avery Obituary Index of Architects. 2nd expanded ed. 1970. 160.00 (*0-8161-1425-0*, G K Hall & Co) Mac Lib Ref.

— Catalog of the Avery Memorial Architectural Library, Supplement 1. 2nd enl. ed. 1990. suppl. ed. 560.00 (*0-8161-1772-1*, G K Hall & Co) Mac Lib Ref.

— Catalog of the Avery Memorial Architectural Library, Supplement 2. 2nd enl. ed. 1990. suppl. ed. 560.00 (*0-8161-1773-X*, G K Hall & Co) Mac Lib Ref.

— Catalog of the Avery Memorial Architectural Library, Supplement 3. 2nd enl. ed. 1990. suppl. ed. 420.00 (*0-8161-1774-8*, G K Hall & Co) Mac Lib Ref.

— Catalog of the Avery Memorial Architectural Library, Supplement 4. 2nd enl. ed. 1989. suppl. ed. 435.00 (*0-8161-1775-6*, G K Hall & Co) Mac Lib Ref.

— Catalog of the Avery Memorial Architectural Library, Supplement 5. 2nd enl. ed. 1988. 650.00 (*0-8161-1546-X*, G K Hall & Co) Mac Lib Ref.

— Catalog of the Roman Law Collection of the Columbia Law School Library. 1992. 190.00 (*0-7838-1009-1*, G K Hall & Co) Mac Lib Ref.

— Dictionary Catalog of the Teachers' College Library, Supplement 2. 1983. suppl. ed. 345.00 (*0-8161-1376-9*, G K Hall & Co) Mac Lib Ref.

— Dictionary Catalog of the Whitney M. Young, Jr., Memorial Library of Social Work. 1994. 1675.00 (*0-7838-2293-6*, G K Hall & Co) Mac Lib Ref.

— Guide to the Manuscript Collections in the Rare Book & Manuscript Library of Columbia University. 500p. 1992. 170.00 (*0-8161-0516-2*, G K Hall & Co) Mac Lib Ref.

— Index to Learned Chinese Periodicals. 1970. 160.00 (*0-8161-1407-2*, G K Hall & Co) Mac Lib Ref.

— Japanese Building Practice: From Ancient Times to the Meiji Period. LC 97-825. (Architecture Ser.). 1997. text 34.95 (*0-442-02031-7*, VNR) Wiley.

— Lectures on Literature. LC 67-22059. (Essay Index Reprint Ser.). 1977. 23.95 (*0-8369-0329-3*) Ayer.

— Quarter Century of Learning, 1904-1929. LC 68-58780. (Essay Index Reprint Ser.). 1977. 23.95 (*0-8369-1028-1*) Ayer.

— Russia in the 20th Century: Catalog of the Bakhmeteff Archives. 1992. 125.00 (*0-8161-1796-9*, G K Hall & Co) Mac Lib Ref.

— Thermodynamic Properties of Aqueous Inorganic Copper Systems. 132p. 1977. write for info. (*0-318-60399-3*) Intl Copper.

Columbia University Staff & Heiman, L. Corporate Financial Reporting in a Competitive Economy. (Accounting Ser.). 220p. 1986. text 15.00 (*0-8240-7875-6*) Garland.

Columbia University Staff, jt. auth. see Raeff, Marc.

Columbia University Teachers College OCLC Tapes St & New York Public Library Staff. Bibliographic Guide to Education: 1990. (Bibliographic Guides Ser.). 625p. (C). 1991. 300.00 (*0-8161-7138-6*, G K Hall & Co) Mac Lib Ref.

Columbia university's Health Education Program Staf. The "Go Ask Alice" Book of Answers: A Guide to Good Physical, Sexual & Emotional Health. LC 98-3318. (Illus.). 368p. 1998. pap. 15.95 (*0-8050-5570-3*, Owl) H Holt & Co.

Columbia Unversity Staff. Avery Index to Architectural Periodicals, Supplement 6. 2nd ed. 1988. suppl. ed. 470.00 (*0-8161-1544-3*, G K Hall & Co) Mac Lib Ref.

Columbo, Luann. How to Have Sex in the Woods. LC 99-24834. 1999. pap. 10.00 (*0-609-80402-2*, Three Riv Pr) Crown Pub Group.

— Make Your Own Incredible Jewelry with Friendly Plastic: A Book & Kit. (Illus.). 32p. (Orig.). (J). 1996. pap. 9.95 (*0-8362-2228-8*) Andrews & McMeel.

Columbo, Luann & McQuinn, Conn. Fun with Computer Electronics. LC 97-119189. (Illus.). 72p. (Orig.). (J). 1996. pap. 21.95 (*0-8362-2306-3*) Andrews & McMeel.

Columbo, Robert J. Guide on Evaluation & Abatement of Traffic Noise. (Planning & Environment Ser.). 48p. (C). 1993. pap. text 8.00 (*0-614-06468-6*, GTN-3) AASHTO.

Columbu, Franco & Fragomeni, Lydia. The Bodybuilder's Nutrition Book. LC 85-13317. (Illus.). 176p. (Orig.). 1985. pap. 14.95 (*0-8092-5457-3*, 545730, Contemporary Bks) NTC Contemp Pub Co.

Columbus-America Discovery Group, Inc. Staff. Story of an American Tragedy: Survivors' Accounts of the Sinking of the Steamship Central America. Conrad, Judy, ed. (Illus.). 77p. 1988. pap. write for info. (*0-9621091-0-X*) Columbus-America.

Columbus, Christopher. Christopher Columbus. (J). (gr. 1-9). 1992. pap. 2.95 (*0-88388-156-X*) Bellerophon Bks.

— The Diario of Christopher Columbus' First Voyage to America, 1492-1493. Kelley, James E., Jr., ed. LC 87-40551. (American Exploration & Travel Ser.: Vol. 70). (Illus.). 504p. 1989. 60.00 (*0-8061-2101-7*) U of Okla Pr.

— The Diario of Christopher Columbus's First Voyage to America, 1492-1493. Dunn, Oliver & Kelley, James E., Jr., trs. from SPA. LC 87-40551. (American Exploration & Travel Ser.: Vol. 70). (Illus.). 504p. 1991. pap. 26.95 (*0-8061-2384-2*) U of Okla Pr.

— First Voyage to America: From the Log of the "Santa Maria" Orig. Title: The Log of Christopher Columbus' First Voyage to America in the Year 1492 as Copied Out in Brief by Bartholomew Las Casas One of His Companions. (Illus.). 96p. 1991. reprint ed. pap. 6.95 (*0-486-26844-6*) Dover.

— The Four Voyages. Cohen, J. M., tr. 320p. 1992. pap. 10.95 (*0-14-044217-0*, Penguin Classics) Viking Penguin.

— Four Voyages to the New World. Major, Richard H., ed. & tr. by. 1990. 23.00 (*0-8446-1883-7*) Peter Smith.

— I, Columbus: My Journal 1492-1493. Roop, Peter & Roop, Connie, eds. (Illus.). 64p. (J). (gr. 5). 1991. reprint ed. mass mkt. 5.99 (*0-380-71545-7*, Avon Bks) Morrow Avon.

— Journal of First Voyage to America. LC 77-150177. (Select Bibliographies Reprint Ser.). 1980. reprint ed. 18.95 (*0-8369-5690-7*) Ayer.

— The Journal of the First Journey: Diario del Primer Viaje. Ife, B. W., ed. & tr. by. from SPA. (Hispanic Classics Ser.). 288p. (C). 1991. 59.95 (*0-85668-350-7*, Pub. by Aris & Phillips); pap. 25.00 (*0-85668-351-5*, Pub. by Aris & Phillips) David Brown.

— The Letter of Columbus on His Discovery of the New World. Morison, Samuel Eliot, tr. LC 88-21730. (Illus.). 51p. 1989. 320.00 (*0-944585-01-9*) Bieler.

Columbus, Christopher & Pigafetta, Antonio. To America & Around the World: The First Logs of Columbus & Magellan. (Illus.). 340p. 1990. 19.95 (*0-8283-1992-8*) Branden Bks.

Columbus, F. Cancer Immunoembryotherapy: A New Weapon Against Cancer. 72p. (Orig.). 1994. pap. 35.00 (*1-56072-107-3*) Nova Sci Pubs.

***Columbus, Frank.** Kosovo - Serbia: A Just War? 173p. 1999. lib. bdg. 34.00 (*1-56072-724-1*) Nova Sci Pubs.

***Columbus, Frank, ed.** Advances in Psychology Research I. 267p. 2000. lib. bdg. 49.00 (*1-56072-774-8*) Nova Sci Pubs.

Columbus, Frank, ed. Asian Economic & Political Issues. 226p. 69.00 (*1-56072-598-2*) Nova Sci Pubs.

***Columbus, Frank, ed.** Asian Economic & Political Issues, Vol. II. 223p. 1999. lib. bdg. 59.00 (*1-56072-688-1*) Nova Sci Pubs.

— Asian Economic & Political Issues, Vol. III. Vol. III. 226p. 2000. lib. bdg. 59.00 (*1-56072-773-X*) Nova Sci Pubs.

— European Economic & Political Issues, No. I. 157p. (C). 1999. lib. bdg. 59.00 (*1-56072-686-5*) Nova Sci Pubs.

— European Economic & Political Issues, No. II. 202p. 2000. lib. bdg. 59.00 (*1-56072-793-4*) Nova Sci Pubs.

— Kosovo - Serbia: A Just War? 173p. 1999. pap. 18.95 (*1-56072-722-5*, Nova Kroshka Bks) Nova Sci Pubs.

Columbus, Frank H. Central & Eastern Europe in Transition. LC 98-40665. 1998. 59.00 (*1-56072-596-6*); 59.00 (*1-56072-597-4*) Nova Sci Pubs.

***Columbus, Frank H.** Russia Upside Down, Inside Out. LC 99-24708. 2000. 19.95 (*1-56072-672-5*) Nova Sci Pubs.

***Columbus, Frank H., ed.** Central & Eastern Europe in Transition, No. III. 293p. 1999. lib. bdg. 59.00 (*1-56072-687-3*) Nova Sci Pubs.

Columbus Health Department Staff. 1992 Columbus & Franklin County Cancer Incidence: Assessment & Mapping 5 Leading Cancer Sites. (Columbus Community Health Assessment Ser.: Vol. 8). (Illus.). iii, 93p. 1998. pap. write for info. (*1-888492-54-6*) Columbus Hlth.

Columbus Health Department Staff & Franklin County Board of Health Staff. City of Columbus & Franklin County, Ohio, 1995-96 Community Health Risk Assessment. (Columbus Community Health Assessment Ser.: Vol. 6). (Illus.). vii, 102p. 1997. pap. write for info. (*1-888492-52-X*) Columbus Hlth.

***Columbus, Louis.** Administrator's Guide to E-Commerce: A Hands-On Guide to Setting Up Systems & Websites. LC 99-62442. 368p. 1999. pap. 34.95 (*0-7906-1187-2*) Prompt Publns.

Columbus, Louis. Deploying Electronic Commerce Solutions with Microsoft BackOffice. 512p. 49.99 incl. cd-rom (*1-57231-823-6*) Microsoft.

***Columbus, Louis.** Exploring the World of S. C. S. I. 2000. pap. 34.95 (*0-7906-1208-9*) Prompt Publns.

— Exploring the World of SCSI. LC 00-101403. 352p. 2000. 34.95 (*0-7906-1210-0*) Prompt Publns.

Columbus, Louis. HP LaserJet Handbook. (Popular Applications Ser.). 152p. (Orig.). 1995. pap. 15.95 (*1-55622-454-0*) Wordware Pub.

— Learn Computers in a Day. LC 96-38404. (Popular Applications Ser.). (Illus.). 232p. (Orig.). (C). 1997. pap. 19.95 incl. disk (*1-55622-525-3*) Wordware Pub.

— Learn Microsoft Windows NT 4.0 Administration. LC QA76. (Illus.). 450p. (Orig.). (C). 1997. pap. 29.95 (*1-55622-513-X*) Wordware Pub.

An Asterisk (*) at the beginning of an entry indicates that the title is appearing for the first time.

— Learn Microsoft Windows NT 4.0 Networking. 2nd rev. ed. 350p. (Orig.). (C). 1997. pap. 39.95 incl. audio compact disk (*1-55622-515-6*) Wordware Pub.

***Columbus, Louis.** The Microsoft 2000 Windows Professional Handbook. (Illus.). 400p. 2000. pap. 41.95 (*1-58450-009-3*) Chrles River Media.

Columbus, Louis. Networking with Windows NT. (Advanced Computer Book Ser.). 280p. (Orig.). 1994. pap. 24.95 incl. disk (*1-55622-421-4*) Wordware Pub.

***Columbus, Louis.** Site Server 324 Seven: Commerce Edition. 2000. pap. 34.99 (*0-7821-2677-4*) Sybex.

Columbus, Louis & Simpson, Nik. Windows NT for the Technical Professional, 3. (Illus.). 368p. (C). 1995. pap. 44.95 (*1-56690-064-6*) Thomson Learn.

Columbus, Marge, ed. see Chan, Janis F.

Columbus, Marge, ed. see De Lone, Susan T.

Columbus, Marge, ed. see Johnson, Nancy C.

Columbus, Marge, ed. see Murch, Muriel.

Columbus, Marge, ed. see Poth, Dee.

***Columbus, Maria.** Elvis in Print. (Illus.). 400p. 2001. 55.00 (*1-56075-049-9*) Popular Culture.

Columbus, Megan, jt. ed. see Allen, John P.

Columbus Museum of Art Staff. Art of Glass: Selections from Columbus Collections. (Illus.). 96p. (Orig.). 1981. pap. 6.50 (*0-918881-09-9*) Columbus Mus Art.

— Catalogue of the Collection. LC 78-74705. (Illus.). 249p. (Orig.). 1978. pap. 7.50 (*0-918881-02-1*) Columbus Mus Art.

— Elijah Pierce, Woodcarver. Roberts, Norma J., ed. LC 91-78320. (Illus.). 272p. (Orig.). 1992. pap. 35.00 (*0-918881-30-7*) Columbus Mus Art.

— The Frederick W. Schumacher Collection. LC 76-28630. (Illus.). 280p. (Orig.). 1976. 15.00 (*0-918881-00-5*); pap. 5.00 (*0-918881-01-3*) Columbus Mus Art.

— Shadow of the Dragon: Chinese Domestic & Trade Ceramics. (Illus.). 100p. (Orig.). 1982. pap. 10.00 (*0-918881-10-2*) Columbus Mus Art.

— Two Hundred Selections from the Permanent Collection. LC 78-74706. (Illus.). 130p. (Orig.). 1978. pap. 2.50 (*0-918881-03-X*) Columbus Mus Art.

Columbus Museum of Art Staff & Bishop, Budd H., intros. Oriental Images. (Illus.). 20p. (Orig.). 1985. pap. 3.50 (*0-918881-13-7*) Columbus Mus Art.

Colussi, G. Finnish-Italian Dictionary. (FIN & ITA.). 302p. 1978. 24.95 (*0-8288-5243-X*, M9650) Fr & Eur.

— Finnish-Italian-Finnish Dictionary. (FIN & ITA.). 532p. 1981. pap. 59.95 (*0-8288-4655-3*, M9640) Fr & Eur.

— Italian/Finnish/Italian Dictionary. 8th ed. (FIN & ITA.). 531p. 1997. 59.95 (*0-320-00073-7*) Fr & Eur.

Colussi, G., ed. Dizionario Italiano-Finlandes, Finlandes-Italiano. deluxe ed. (FIN & ITA.). 9.95 (*0-686-92443-6*, M-9170) Fr & Eur.

Colussi, Luciana. Universality of Tagore: Souvenir of a Symposium. (C). 1991. 19.50 (*0-8364-2754-8*, Pub. by Firma KLM) S Asia.

Coluzzi, Robert, tr. see Spriet, Alain & Dupin-Spriet, Therese.

Colver, Anne. Thomas Jefferson: Author of Independence. LC 91-22493. (Discovery Biographies Ser.). (Illus.). 80p. (J). (gr. 2-6). 1992. reprint ed. lib. bdg. 12.95 (*0-7910-1443-6*) Chelsea Hse.

Colver, F. L. Colver - Culver Genealogy, Descendants of Edward Colver of Boston, Dedham & Roxbury, Mass., & New London & Mystic, Connecticut, 1635-1909. 271p. 1993. reprint ed. pap. 40.50 (*0-8328-1375-3*); reprint ed. lib. bdg. 50.50 (*0-8328-1374-5*) Higginson Bk Co.

Colver, Jay. The Colver Trading Method for Winning the Commodity Game. 1983. pap. 50.00 (*0-930233-23-9*) Windsor.

Colver, Marylou, ed. see Association for Library Collections & Technical Services, American Library Association.

Colverd, Edward C. Equipment & Adapted Methodologies for Teaching in a Fully Modified Van. LC 81-80996. (Driver Education for the Severely Physically Disabled Ser.). 101p. (Orig.). 1983. pap. 7.95 (*0-318-23896-9*) Human Res Ctr.

Colverd, Edward C., et al. Teaching Driver Education to the Physically Disabled: A Sample Course. LC 78-62053. (Driver Education Ser.). (Illus.). 54p. (C). 1978. 5.00 (*0-686-38805-4*) Human Res Ctr.

Colverson & Clemente. Environmental Science Lab Manual. 2nd ed. 144p. (C). 1998. spiral bd. 20.95 (*0-7872-5327-8*, 41532701) Kendall-Hunt.

Colverson, jt. auth. see Gillespie.

Colvert, DeLynn C. Play Winning Cribbage. 2nd ed. LC 80-67576. (Illus.). 154p. 1979. write for info. (*0-9612548-1-5*) Starr Studios.

— Play Winning Cribbage. 3rd ed. 1997. pap. 10.95 (*0-614-29365-0*) ISBN Agency.

Colvert, DeLynn C. Play Winning Cribbage. 3rd ed. LC 80-67576. (Illus.). 154p. 1997. pap. 10.95 (*0-9612548-0-7*) Starr Studios.

Colvig, Ray, jt. auth. see Seaborg, Glenn Theodore.

Colvile, Georgiana M., ed. Contemporary Women Writing in Canada & Quebec. LC 94-49046. (Contemporary Women Writing in the Other Americas Ser.: Vol. III). Orig. Title: Women's Voices from the Other Americas: Expanding the Feminist Problematics. 180p. 1996. text 59.95 (*0-7734-8810-3*) E Mellen.

— Contemporary Women Writing in Latin America: Expanding the Feminist Problematics. LC 94-49046. (Contemporary Women Writing in the Other Americas Ser.: Vol. I). Orig. Title: Women's Voices from the Other Americas: Expanding the Feminist Problematics. (Illus.). 184p. 1996. text 59.95 (*0-7734-9005-1*) E Mellen.

— Contemporary Women Writing in the Caribbean. LC 94-49046. (Contemporary Women Writing in the Other Americas Ser.: Vol. II). Orig. Title: Women's Voices from the Other Americas: Expanding the Feminist Problematics. 152p. 1996. text 59.95 (*0-7734-8808-1*) E Mellen.

Colvile, Henry. History of the Sudan Campaign. (Victorian War Ser.: No. 4). (Illus.). 648p. 1996. reprint ed. 69.95 (*0-89839-246-2*) Battery Pr.

Colvile, Kenneth N. Fame's Twilight. LC 73-117771. (Essay Index Reprint Ser.). 1977. 21.95 (*0-8369-1703-0*) Ayer.

Colvill, Robert. Atalanta (Seventeen Seventy-Seven) & Savannah (Seventeen Eighty) LC 87-4553. 1987. 50.00 (*0-8201-1421-9*) Schol Facsimiles.

Colville, Berres, ed. Library Service to Isolated Schools & Communities: IASL Occasional Paper. (Occasional Paper Ser.). 51p. 1981. pap. 25.00 (*0-9598398-7-9*) IASL.

Colville, James & Amde, Amde M., eds. Innovative Technologies for Site Remediation & Hazardous Waste Management: Proceedings of the National Conference, Pittsburgh, Pennsylvania, July 23-26, 1995. LC 95-219. 748p. 1995. 72.00 (*0-7844-0094-6*) Am Soc Civil Eng.

***Colville, Jim.** Avarice & the Avaricious. 214p. 1999. 110.00 (*0-7103-0645-8*, Pub. by Kegan Paul Intl) Col U Pr.

***Colville, Jim, tr.** Two Andalusian Philosophers: Avveroes & Ibn Tufayl. 107p. 1999. 110.00 (*0-7103-0643-1*, Pub. by Kegan Paul Intl) Col U Pr.

Colville, Jim, tr. see Al-Jahiz, Abu Uthman Amir Ibn Bahir.

Colville, Jim, tr. see Al-Nafzawi, Muhammad.

Colville, John. Historie & Life of King James the Sext. LC 72-1010. (Bannatyne Club, Edinburgh. Publications: No. 13). reprint ed. 57.50 (*0-404-52713-2*) AMS Pr.

— Original Letters. Laing, David, ed. LC 72-976. (Bannatyne Club, Edinburgh. Publications: No. 104). reprint ed. 62.50 (*0-404-52859-7*) AMS Pr.

Colville, Penelope O. The Multiversa Strategy. LC 99-13. 430p. 1999. 64.35 (*1-55212-244-1*) Trafford Pub.

Colville, Ruth M. MT Lookout "Where You Can See for Two Days" LC 97-70484. (Illus.). 226p. (Orig.). 1997. pap. 14.95 (*0-614-30312-5*) Benson Enterp.

— La Vereda: A Trail Through Time. (Illus.). 400p. 1996. 24.95 (*0-9650560-3-1*); pap. 14.95 (*0-9650560-4-X*) S Luis Vly Hist Soc.

Colville, Thomas P. Review Questions & Answers for Veterinary Technicians. 2nd ed. 368p. (C). (gr. 13). 1995. pap. text 34.95 (*0-8151-1850-3*, 27466) Mosby Inc.

Colville, W. J. Ancient Mysteries & Modern Revelations. 366p. 1993. reprint ed. pap. 24.95 (*1-56459-400-9*) Kessinger Pub.

— Ancient Mystery & Modern Revelation. 366p. 1994. pap. 30.00 (*0-89540-122-3*, SB-122) Sun Pub.

— Dashed Against the Rock, 1894-1985. 310p. 1986. 25.00 (*0-87556-349-X*) Saifer.

— The Human Aura & the Significance of Color. 70p. 1996. reprint ed. spiral bd. 10.00 (*0-7873-0195-7*) Hlth Research.

— The Human Aura & the Significance of Color. 70p. 1996. reprint ed. pap. 9.95 (*1-56459-852-7*) Kessinger Pub.

— Kabbalah the Harmony of Opposites: A Treatise Elucidating Bible Allegories & the Significance of Numbers. 189p. 1995. reprint ed. pap. 17.95 (*1-56459-495-5*) Kessinger Pub.

— Significance of Birthdays. 161p. 1996. reprint ed. spiral bd. 10.00 (*0-7873-1230-4*) Hlth Research.

— Significance of Birthdays (1911) 161p. 1996. reprint ed. pap. 9.95 (*1-56459-706-7*) Kessinger Pub.

— Studies in Theosophy - Historical & Practical: A Manual for the People (1890) 503p. 1996. reprint ed. pap. 33.00 (*1-56459-644-3*) Kessinger Pub.

Colvim, E. W. Silicon Reagents. 147p. 1988. text 93.00 (*0-12-182560-4*) Acad Pr.

Colvin. Milling Metal Made Easy. (Illus.). 140p. 1991. reprint ed. pap. 16.00 (*1-877767-34-4*) Univ Publng Hse.

— Penitentiaries Reform Chain. 2000. pap. 18.95 (*0-312-22128-2*) St Martin.

Colvin, jt. auth. see Hamilton.

Colvin, Adele B. The Donkeys' Tales. LC 97-30495. (Illus.). 32p. (J). 1998. pap. 9.95 (*1-57587-073-8*) Crane Hill AL.

Colvin, Alan L. Chevrolet by the Numbers 1970-75: The Essential Chevrolet Parts Reference. (Illus.). 312p. 1994. pap. 29.95 (*0-8376-0927-5*) Bentley Pubs.

— Chevrolet by the Numbers 1955-1959: The Essential Chevrolet Parts Reference, 1955-1959. (Illus.). 240p. 1996. pap. 29.95 (*0-8376-0875-9*) Bentley Pubs.

— Chevrolet by the Numbers 1960-1964: The Essential Chevrolet Parts Reference, 1960-1964. LC 95-40934. (Illus.). 300p. 1995. 29.95 (*0-8376-0936-4*) Bentley Pubs.

— Chevrolet by the Numbers 1965-69: The Essential Chevrolet Parts Reference. (Illus.). 352p. 1994. pap. 29.95 (*0-8376-0956-9*) Bentley Pubs.

Colvin, Andy, et al. How about Them Claymores? The Murrayfield Miracle. (Illus.). 128p. 1997. 29.95 (*1-85158-925-2*, Pub. by Mainstream Pubng) Trafalgar.

Colvin, Ann D. Ever-Growing, Ever-Green. (Illus.). 88p. (Orig.). 1991. pap. 9.00 (*0-9621498-6-1*, Robin Hood) R Hood Little.

Colvin, Christina, ed. see Edgeworth, Maria.

Colvin, Claire, jt. auth. see Bush, Karen.

***Colvin, Clare.** Masque of the Gonzagas. 2000. pap. 13.99 (*1-900850-25-7*) Arcadia Bks.

Colvin, David. Aubrey Beardsley: A Slave to Beauty. (Illus.). 112p. 1998. pap. 22.95 (*1-56649-013-8*) Welcome Rain.

Colvin, David & Hunter, Leslie, eds. Middle East Organizations in Washington, D. C. 104p. 1998. 12.00 (*0-916808-40-8*) Mid East Inst.

Colvin, David, jt. auth. see Calloway, Stephen.

Colvin, Fred. Sixty Years with Men & Machines: American Autobiography. 297p. 1995. lib. bdg. 79.00 (*0-7812-8487-2*) Rprt Serv.

Colvin, Fred H. Metal Lathes - How to Run Them. (Illus.). 117p. 1991. reprint ed. pap. 12.00 (*1-877767-20-4*) Univ Publng Hse.

— Sixty Years with Men & Machines. 298p. reprint ed. pap. 14.95 (*0-917914-86-4*) Lindsay Pubns.

Colvin, Geoffrey. Managing Acting-Out Behavior. 26p. 1992. pap. 169.00 incl. VHS (*1-57035-261-5*, 51KIT) Sopris.

Colvin, Geoffrey. Managing Acting-Out Behavior: A Staff Development Program to Prevent & Manage Acting-Out Behavior. (C). 1992. ring bd. write for info. incl. VHS (*0-9631777-0-2*) Behav Assocs.

— Managing Problem Behavior: Basic Skills for Paraprofessionals & Beginning Teachers. (C). 1993. ring bd. write for info. incl. VHS (*0-9631777-2-9*) Behav Assocs.

Colvin, Geoffrey & Lazar, Mike. The Effective Elementary Classroom: Managing for Success. LC 98-117879. 132p. (Orig.). 1997. pap. text 17.50 (*1-57035-044-2*, C94ELEM) Sopris.

Colvin, Gregory L. Fiscal Sponsorship: Six Ways to Do It Right. 96p. 1993. 14.95 (*0-936434-65-1*) SF Study Ctr.

Colvin, Howard. Architecture & the After-Life. (Illus.). 432p. (C). 1992. 75.00 (*0-300-05098-4*) Yale U Pr.

— A Biographical Dictionary of British Architects, 1600-1840. 3rd ed. LC 94-39135. 1264p. 1995. 85.00 (*0-300-06091-2*) Yale U Pr.

— Biographical Dictionary of British Architects, 1600-1840. 3rd ed. 1264p. 1997. pap. text 40.00 (*0-300-07207-4*) Yale U Pr.

— The Canterbury Quadrangle, St. John's College, Oxford. (Illus.). 144p. 1988. text 65.00 (*0-19-920159-5*) OUP.

— Unbuilt Oxford. LC 83-42870. (Illus.). 208p. 1983. pap. 27.50 (*0-300-03126-2*, Y-481) Yale U Pr.

Colvin, Howard & Simmons, J. S. All Souls: An Oxford College & Its Buildings (Chichele Lectures 1986) (Illus.). 108p. 1989. text 39.95 (*0-19-920161-7*) OUP.

Colvin, Howard, ed. see North, Roger & Newman, John Henry.

Colvin, Howard M. A Biographical Dictionary of English Architects 1660-1840. LC 94-23143. 1995. reprint ed. lib. bdg. 48.00 (*0-7808-0042-7*) Omnigraphics Inc.

***Colvin, Howard M.** Essays in English Architectural History. LC 98-50532. (Illus.). 320p. 1999. 60.00 (*0-300-07034-9*) Yale U Pr.

Colvin, Ian D., ed. Cape of Adventure. LC 76-94309. (Illus.). 1969. reprint ed. 57.50 (*0-404-01638-3*) AMS Pr.

Colvin, Irene. A Princess Who Could Never Be: The Untold Story of Mary Vetsera. LC 94-68856. (Illus.). 320p. (Orig.). 1995. pap. 12.99 (*0-9628093-0-6*) NuDawn Pub.

Colvin, J. Norman. Colvin's Clinic: Bonanza - DeBonair-Baron Maintenance Simplified. LC 84-60672. (Illus.). 130p. 1984. write for info. (*0-911978-02-X*) McCormick-Armstrong.

— Colvin's Clinic: Bonanza-DeBonair-Baron-Travelair Maintenance Simplified. 2nd rev. ed. LC 92-61832. (Illus.). 256p. 1992. write for info. (*0-911978-06-2*) McCormick-Armstrong.

Colvin, Joan. The Nature of Design: A Quilt Artist's Personal Journal. LC 96-3199. (Illus.). 128p. (Orig.). 1996. pap. 29.95 (*1-56477-131-8*, B247, Fiber Studio Pr) Martingale & Co.

— Quilts from Nature. Weiland, Barbara, ed. LC 92-41488. (Illus.). 112p. (Orig.). 1993. pap. 24.95 (*1-56477-026-5*, B154, That Patchwrk Pl) Martingale & Co.

Colvin, John. Giap - Volcano under Snow: The Genius General of Vietnam. LC 95-26280. 336p. 1996. 25.00 (*1-56947-053-7*) Soho Press.

***Colvin, John.** Nomonhan. 2000. pap. 25.00 (*0-7043-7112-X*, Pub. by Quartet) Interlink Pub.

Colvin, John. Not Ordinary Men: The Story of the Battle of Kohima. (Illus.). 256p. 1995. pap. 16.95 (*0-85052-477-6*, Pub. by Leo Cooper) Trans-Atl Phila.

Colvin, L. & Irving, N. Essential French. (Essential Guides Ser.). (Illus.). 64p. (YA). (gr. 7-12). 1990. pap. 6.95 (*0-7460-0316-1*) EDC.

— Essential French. (Essential Guides Ser.). (Illus.). 64p. (YA). 1999. lib. bdg. 14.95 (*0-88110-420-5*) EDC.

— Essential German. (Essential Guides Ser.). (Illus.). 64p. (YA). (gr. 7-12). 1990. pap. 6.95 (*0-7460-0318-8*) EDC.

— Essential German. (Essential Guides Ser.). (Illus.). 64p. (YA). 1999. lib. bdg. 14.95 (*0-88110-419-1*) EDC.

— Essential Spanish. (Essential Guides Ser.). (Illus.). 64p. (YA). (gr. 7-12). 1990. pap. 6.95 (*0-7460-0320-X*) EDC.

— Essential Spanish. (Essential Guides Ser.). (Illus.). 64p. (YA). 1999. lib. bdg. 14.95 (*0-88110-421-3*) EDC.

Colvin, Leslie. The Living World Encyclopedia. 128p. (gr. 4-7). 1999. 22.95 (*1-58086-171-7*) EDC.

Colvin, Leslie & Speare, Emma, eds. Living World Encyclopedia. (Encyclopedias Ser.). (Illus.). 128p. (J). (gr. 3-7). 1999. pap. 14.95 (*0-7460-3051-7*, Usborne) EDC.

Colvin, Leslie & Stockley, Corinne. Living World Encyclopedia. (Encyclopedias Ser.). (Illus.). 128p. (J). (gr. 5-7). 1992. lib. bdg. 22.95 (*0-88110-434-5*, Usborne) EDC.

Colvin, Lucie G., et al. The Uprooted of the Western Sahel: Migrants' Quest for Cash in the Senegambia. LC 81-5005. 385p. 1981. 75.00 (*0-275-90597-7*, C0597, Praeger Pubs) Greenwood.

Colvin, M. P., jt. auth. see Dunnill, R. P.

***Colvin, Maggie.** Decorating Projects: Tricks to Transform Your Home. (Illus.). 2000. pap. 17.95 (*0-600-60109-9*) P HM.

Colvin, Maggie. Decorating Tricks: Touches of Style: Over 40 Quick-to-Do Projects, from an Hour to a Weekend. (Illus.). 144p. 1999. pap. 17.95 (*0-600-59948-5*, Pub. by Hamlyn Publishing Group Ltd) Sterling.

***Colvin, Maggie.** Maggie Colvin's Fabulous Fakes. (Illus.). 2000. 27.95 (*0-7153-0920-X*, Pub. by D & C Pub) Sterling.

Colvin, Mark. Crime & Coercion. text. write for info. (*0-312-23389-2*) St Martin.

Colvin, Mark. Penitentiaries, Reformatories & Chain Gangs: Social Theory & the History of Punishment in Nineteenth Century America. LC 97-12045. 254p. 1997. text 45.00 (*0-312-17327-X*) St Martin.

— The Penitentiary in Crisis: From Accommodation to Riot in New Mexico. LC 91-3407. (SUNY Series in Deviance & Social Control). 257p. (C). 1992. text 67.50 (*0-7914-0929-5*); pap. text 24.95 (*0-7914-0930-9*) State U NY Pr.

Colvin, Mary N., ed. see Guilelmus.

Colvin, Raymond J. The Guidebook to Successful Safety Programming. 320p. 1991. lib. bdg. 99.95 (*0-87371-481-4*, L481) Lewis Pubs.

Colvin, Robert B., et al, eds. Diagnostic Immunopathology. 2nd ed. LC 93-41659. 848p. 1994. text 256.00 (*0-7817-0020-5*) Lppncott W & W.

***Colvin, Rod.** Evil Harvest: The True Story of Cult Murder in the American Heartland. LC 99-39530. (Illus.). 364p. 1999. pap. 15.95 (*1-886039-42-9*) Addicus Bks.

Colvin, Rod. First Heroes: The POWs Left Behind in Vietnam. (Illus.). 365p. 1987. 19.95 (*0-8290-2008-X*) Irvington.

— Prescription Drug Abuse: The Hidden Epidemic; A Guide to Coping & Understanding. 196p. (Orig.). 1995. pap. 14.95 (*1-886039-22-4*) Addicus Bks.

Colvin, Rod, ed. see Adams, Susan L.

Colvin, Rod, ed. see Craighead, Joni.

Colvin, Rod, ed. see Cram, David L.

Colvin, Rod, ed. see Kosares, Michael J.

Colvin, Rod, ed. see Press, Margaret & Pinkham, Joan.

Colvin, Ruth J. Great Traveling after Fifty-Five. (Illus.). 200p. 1989. 14.95 (*0-685-27178-1*) Nivloc Pr.

— I Speak English. 103p. 1986. pap. 9.00 (*0-930713-28-1*) Lit Vol Am.

— A Way with Words: The Story of Literacy Volunteers of America. 52p. 1987. pap. text 4.00 (*0-930713-38-9*) Lit Vol Am.

Colvin, Ruth J. & Root, Jane. Tutor. 6th ed. Lawson, V. K., ed. 106p. 1987. pap. text 9.50 (*0-318-41220-9*) Lit Vol Am.

Colvin, Ruth J. & Root, Jane H., eds. Read Test: Reading Evaluation Adult Diagnosis Test. rev. ed. 55p. 1982. pap. text 6.00 (*0-930713-23-0*) Lit Vol Am.

Colvin, Sarah. The Rhetorical Feminine: Gender & Orient on the German Stage, 1647-1742. (Oxford Modern Languages & Literature Monographs). 344p. 1999. text 85.00 (*0-19-818636-3*) OUP.

Colvin, Sidney, ed. see Finiguerra, Maso.

Colvin, Stephen. Dialect in Aristophanes: The Politics of Language in Ancient Greek Literature. (Oxford Classical Monographs). 360p. 1999. text 75.00 (*0-19-815249-3*) OUP.

Colvin, Stephen S., ed. see Burrow, N. Trigant.

Colvin, Thomas E. Steel Boatbuilding. 1996. pap. 34.95 (*1-888671-02-5*) Tiller.

— Steel Boatbuilding: From Plans to Launching. 1996. pap. text 34.95 (*0-07-012121-4*) McGraw.

Colvin, Tom. Christmas Carols for Friends & Families: Saddle Stitch Binding. Tindall, Adrienne, ed. & tr. by. from GER. Vajda, Jaroslav J. et al, trs. from GER. 90p. 1995. pap., student ed. 5.95 (*1-889079-02-2*) Darcey Pr.

Colvin, Verplanck. Adirondack Explorations: Nature Writings of Verplanck Colvin. Schaefer, Paul, ed. & compiled by by. LC 96-43781. (Illus.). 272p. 1997. text 34.95 (*0-8156-2732-7*) Syracuse U Pr.

— Report of the Superintendent of the State Land Survey of the State of New York, 1898. (Illus.). 350p. 1989. 60.00 (*0-685-29368-8*) Assn Protect Adirondacks.

Colvin, Vonnie, et al. Teaching the Nuts & Bolts of Physical Activity: Building Basic Movement Skills. LC 99-38507. (Illus.). 288p. 1999. pap. 23.00 (*0-88011-883-0*, YMCA USA) Human Kinetics.

Colwell. Children of the Isles. (British Island Heritage Editions Ser.). 1991. pap. 40.00 (*0-86120-024-1*, Pub. by Aris & Phillips) David Brown.

Colwell, Anne. Inscrutable Houses: Metaphors of the Body in the Poems of Elizabeth Bishop. LC 96-39167. 264p. 1997. text 39.95 (*0-8173-0808-3*); pap. text 19.95 (*0-8173-0890-3*) U of Ala Pr.

Colwell, David. The Bitter Fruits: The Civil War Comes to a Small Town in Pennsylvania. Tritt, Richard, ed. (Illus.). 215p. 1998. 39.95 (*0-9638923-6-3*) Cumberlnd Cnty Hist.

Colwell, David, jt. auth. see Colwell, Max.

***Colwell, Eileen.** Cats in a Basket. (Illus.). 128p. (J). (gr. 3). 1998. pap. 6.95 (*0-14-034660-0*, Pub. by Pnguin Bks Ltd) Trafalgar.

Colwell, Ernest C. The Study of the Bible. rev. ed. LC 64-23411. (Midway Reprint Ser.). 218p. reprint ed. pap. 67.60 (*0-608-16535-2*, 202676900052) Bks Demand.

Colwell, Frederic S. Rivermen: A Romantic Iconography of the River & the Source. 232p. (C). 1989. text 65.00 (*0-7735-0711-6*, Pub. by McG-Queens Univ Pr) CUP Services.

Colwell, Gary. You Won't Believe This, But . . . Responding to Student Complaints & Excuses. 96p. (Orig.). (C). 1996. pap. text. write for info. (*1-55059-137-1*) Detselig Ents.

Colwell, Guy. Central Body: The Art of Guy Colwell. (Illus.). 96p. 1991. pap. 16.95 (*0-89620-116-3*) Rip Off.

— Doll. (Illus.). 108p. (Orig.). pap. 9.95 (*0-89620-114-7*) Rip Off.

— The Further Adventures of Doll. (Illus.). 136p. 1994. pap. 15.95 (*0-87816-264-X*) Kitchen Sink.

Colwell, Guy, ed. see Shelton, Gilbert & Sheridan, Dave.

Colwell, J. D. Estimating Fertilizer Requirements: A Quantitative Approach. LC 95-161876. (Illus.). 272p. 1994. text 80.00 (*0-85198-905-5*) OUP.

Colwell, John E. Actuality & Provisionality: Eternity & Election in the Theology of Karl Barth. LC 92-5142. (Rutherford Studies in Contemporary Theology). 470p. 1992. reprint ed. 109.95 (*0-7734-1639-0*) E Mellen.

***Colwell, Linda.** When the Lilacs Bloom. Schulte, Colleen, ed. 277p. 2000. mass mkt. 6.50 (*1-929613-09-1*) Avid MI.

Colwell, Lynn, ed. see Milionis, Steve.

Colwell, Mary A. Private Foundations & Public Policy: The Political Role of Philanthropy. LC 92-29719. (Non-profit Institutions in America Ser.). 296p. 1993. text 10.00 (*0-8153-0904-X*) Garland.

Colwell, Mary H., jt. auth. see Bell, Edmund H.

Colwell, Max. The Carroll Inheritance. 174p. (C). 1989. 29.00 (*0-7270-1344-0*, Pub. by M Colwell Pubns) St Mut.

— Full Days & Pressed Pants. 160p. (C). 1989. 20.00 (*0-9594393-2-3*, Pub. by M Colwell Pubns) St Mut.

— Glorious Days & Khaki Pants. 146p. (C). 1989. 20.00 (*0-9594393-7-4*, Pub. by M Colwell Pubns) St Mut.

Colwell, Max & Colwell, David. Australia's Timeless Land: Alice Springs, Ayers Rock, The Olgas. 64p. (C). 1989. 50.00 (*0-9594393-5-8*, Pub. by M Colwell Pubns) St Mut.

— Heritage Preserved with the National Trust of South Australia. (Illus.). 160p. (C). 1989. 59.00 (*0-9594393-6-6*, Pub. by M Colwell Pubns) St Mut.

— Light's Vision: The City of Adelaide & Surrounding Districts. (Illus.). 88p. (C). 1989. 80.00 (*0-9594393-4-X*, Pub. by M Colwell Pubns) St Mut.

Colwell, Miriam. Young. 2nd ed. 183p. 1998. pap. 9.95 (*0-913006-66-1*) Puckerbrush.

Colwell, Peter. Solving Kepler's Equation over Three Centuries. LC 93-6379. 1993. 24.95 (*0-943396-40-9*) Willmann-Bell.

Colwell, R. J. & Davis, E. P. Output, Productivity & Externalities: The Case of Banking. LC 93-5002. (Bank of England, Economics Division: Vol. 3). (Illus.). 38p. 1992. reprint ed. pap. 30.00 (*0-608-07934-0*, 206790700012) Bks Demand.

C

Colwell, R. R., et al, eds. Microbial Diversity in Time & Space. LC 96-13455. (Illus.). 180p. 1996. 75.00 (*0-306-45194-8*, Kluwer Plenum) Kluwer Academic.

Colwell, R. R. & Grigorova, R., eds. Methods in Microbiology, Vol. 19. 518p. 1988. text 136.00 (*0-12-521519-3*) Acad Pr.

Colwell, R. R., jt. ed. see Costerton, J. W.

Colwell, Richard, ed. Symposium in Music Education: A Festschrift for Charles Leonhard. LC 81-71592. 329p. 1982. 15.00 (*0-686-38473-3*) U IL Sch Music.

Colwell, Richard J., ed. Basic Concepts in Music Education II. 1991. 39.95 (*0-87081-228-9*) Univ Pr Colo.

Colwell, Richard J. & Colwell, Ruth. Concepts for a Musical Foundation. LC 73-4749. (Illus.). 320p. (C). 1974. pap. text 23.95 (*0-685-03800-9*) P-H.

Colwell, Richard J. & Goolsby, Thomas. The Teaching of Instrumental Music. 2nd ed. 432p. 1991. 77.00 (*0-13-892688-3*, 650801) P-H.

***Colwell, Rita & Grimes, D. Jay, eds.** Nonculturable Organisms in the Environment. (Illus.). 360p. 2000. 89.95 (*1-55581-196-5*) ASM Pr.

Colwell, Rita R., et al, eds. Microbial Hazards of Diving in Polluted Waters. 1981. 3.00 (*0-943676-08-8*) MD Sea Grant Col.

Colwell, Rita R., pref. Forum Proceedings: Global Change & the Human Prospect: Issues in Population, Science, Technology, & Equity. (Orig.). 1992. pap. 18.50 (*0-914446-03-7*) Sigma Xi.

Colwell, Rita R. & Foster, J., eds. Aquatic Microbial Ecology: Proceedings of the ASM Conference. 1983. pap. 4.95 (*0-943676-07-X*) MD Sea Grant Col.

Colwell, Robert K. Biota: The Biodiversity Database Manager: BiotaApp for Macintosh 68030 or 68040 (Quadra) 1996. pap. 125.00 incl. disk (*0-87893-125-2*) Sinauer Assocs.

— Biota: The Biodiversity Database Manager: BiotaApp for PowerPC. 1996. pap. 125.00 incl. disk (*0-87893-123-6*) Sinauer Assocs.

— Biota: The Biodiversity Database Manager: BiotaApp for Windows 95 or Windows NT (Pentium) 1996. pap. 125.00 incl. disk (*0-87893-141-4*) Sinauer Assocs.

— Biota: The Biodiversity Database Manager: BiotaApp for Windows 95 or Windows NT (386/486) 1996. pap. 125.00 incl. disk (*0-87893-139-2*) Sinauer Assocs.

— Biota: The Biodiversity Database Manager: Biota4D Multiplatform for Mac OS. 1996. pap. 175.00 incl. disk (*0-87893-146-5*) Sinauer Assocs.

— Biota: The Biodiversity Database Manager: Biota4D Multiplatform for Windows 95 or Windows NT (Pentium) 1996. pap. 175.00 incl. disk (*0-87893-145-7*) Sinauer Assocs.

— Biota User's Manual. (C). 1996. pap. text 40.00 (*0-87893-128-7*) Sinauer Assocs.

Colwell, Robert K., jt. auth. see Naskrecki, Piotr.

Colwell, Ruth, jt. auth. see Colwell, Richard J.

Colwell, Stella. Family History. LC 95-71309. (Teach Yourself Ser.). (Illus.). 224p. 1996. pap. 9.95 (*0-8442-3790-6*, Teach Yrslf) NTC Contemp Pub Co.

— Family History: A Guide & Troubleshooter. (Illus.). 224p. 1998. pap. 24.95 (*0-7509-1187-5*, Pub. by Sutton Pub Ltd) Intl Pubs Mktg.

Colwell, Stephen. New Themes for the Protestant Clergy. LC 71-83417. (Religion in America, Ser. 1). 1975. reprint ed. 35.95 (*0-405-00243-2*) Ayer.

— The Position of Christianity in the United States, in Its Relations with Our Political Institutions, & Specially with Reference to Religious Instruction in the Public Schools. LC 78-38444. (Religion in America, Ser. 2). 180p. 1972. reprint ed. 19.95 (*0-405-04063-6*) Ayer.

— Trouble-Free Travel: What to Do When Things Go Wrong. 2nd ed. LC 98-13690. 352p. 1998. pap. 14.95 (*0-87337-478-9*) Nolo com.

— The Ways & Means of Payment: A Full Analysis of the Credit System, with Its Various Modes of Adjustment. LC 65-23212. (Reprints of Economic Classics Ser.). xii, 644p. 1965. reprint ed. 57.50 (*0-678-00110-3*) Kelley.

Colwell, W., et al, compiled by. Waldoboro Vital Records, 1773 to 1891. 249p. 1997. reprint ed. pap. 25.00 (*0-8328-5922-2*) Higginson Bk Co.

Colwill. War Crimes International Relations & the Law. 65.95 (*1-85521-720-1*) Ashgate Pub Co.

Colwill & Birchall. Practical Management. 1992. pap. text. write for info. (*0-582-86980-3*, Pub. by Addison-Wesley) Longman.

Colwill, Nina L., jt. auth. see Vinnicombe, Susan.

Colwill, Stiles T., jt. auth. see Klots, Alfred P.

Colwin, Cecil. Swimming Dynamics: Winning Techniques & Strategies. LC 98-34051. (Illus.). 384p. 1999. pap. 19.95 (*1-57028-206-4*, 82064H, Mstrs Pr) NTC Contemp Pub Co.

Colwin, Cecil M. Swimming into the Twenty-First Century. LC 90-28869. 272p. (Orig.). 1993. pap. 19.95 (*0-87322-456-6*, PCOL0456) Human Kinetics.

Colwin, Laurie. Another Marvelous Thing. LC 94-32224. 144p. 1994. pap. 11.00 (*0-06-097650-0*) HarperTrade.

— A Big Storm Knocked It Over. LC 92-56219. 272p. 2000. pap. 12.00 (*0-06-092546-9*, Perennial) HarperTrade.

***Colwin, Laurie.** Big Storm Knocked It Over. 2000. pap. 13.00 (*0-06-095898-7*) HarpC.

Colwin, Laurie. A Big Storm Knocked It Over. large type ed. LC 93-44178. 1994. lib. bdg. 22.95 (*0-7862-0155-X*) Thorndike Pr.

***Colwin, Laurie.** Family Happiness. 2000. pap. 13.00 (*0-06-095897-9*) HarpC.

— Family Happiness. LC 89-45641. 272p. 1993. reprint ed. pap. 13.00 (*0-06-097272-6*, Perennial) HarperTrade.

— Goodbye Without Leaving. 256p. 2000. pap. 12.00 (*0-06-095533-3*, Perennial) HarperTrade.

Colwin, Laurie. Goodbye Without Leaving: A Novel. LC 90-56102. 256p. 1993. pap. 12.50 (*0-06-097392-7*, Perennial) HarperTrade.

***Colwin, Laurie.** Happy All the Time. 224p. 2000. pap. 12.00 (*0-06-095532-5*, Perennial) HarperTrade.

Colwin, Laurie. Happy All the Time. LC 92-56267. 224p. 1993. reprint ed. pap. 12.00 (*0-06-097564-4*, Perennial) HarperTrade.

— Home Cooking. LC 92-53385. (Illus.). 208p. 1993. pap. 12.00 (*0-06-097522-9*, Perennial) HarperTrade.

***Colwin, Laurie.** Home Cooking: A Writer in the Kitchen. (Illus.). 208p. 2000. pap. 12.00 (*0-06-095530-9*, Perennial) HarperTrade.

Colwin, Laurie. The Lone Pilgrim: A Book of Short Stories. LC 89-45642. 224p. 1990. reprint ed. pap. 11.00 (*0-06-097270-X*, Perennial) HarperTrade.

— More Home Cooking. 240p. 1995. pap. 12.00 (*0-06-092578-7*) HarperTrade.

***Colwin, Laurie.** More Home Cooking: A Writer Returns to the Kitchen. (Illus.). 240p. 2000. pap. 12.00 (*0-06-095531-7*, Perennial) HarperTrade.

Colwin, Laurie. Passion & Affect. LC 94-24623. 192p. 1994. pap. 12.00 (*0-06-097633-0*) HarperTrade.

— Shine on, Bright & Dangerous Object. LC 94-24622. 192p. 1994. pap. 12.00 (*0-06-097632-2*) HarperTrade.

Coly. Campbell Comparative Law Yearbook. 1982. lib. bdg. 181.00 (*90-247-2697-2*) Kluwer Academic.

— Campbell Comparative Law Yearbook. 1983. lib. bdg. 146.50 (*90-247-2839-8*) Kluwer Academic.

— Campbell Comparative Law Yearbook. 1984. lib. bdg. 131.50 (*90-247-2966-1*) Kluwer Academic.

— Campbell Comparative Law Yearbook. 1986. lib. bdg. 130.50 (*90-247-3350-2*, Pub. by M Nijhoff) Kluwer Academic.

— Campbell Comparative Law Yearbook. 1988. lib. bdg. 126.50 (*90-247-3541-6*, Pub. by M Nijhoff) Kluwer Academic.

Coly, Lisette & McMahon, Joanne D., eds. PSI & Clinical Practice: Proceedings, International Conference, London, England, Oct. 28-29, 1989. LC 93-85463. 1993. 20.00 (*0-912328-44-4*) Parapsych Foun.

— PSI Research Methodology: A Re-Examination: Proceedings, International Conference, Chapel Hill, N. C., Oct. 29-30, 1988. LC 93-85453. 1993. 20.00 (*0-912328-43-6*) Parapsych Foun.

Coly, Lisette & White, Rhea A., eds. Women & Parapsychology: Proceedings, International Conference, Dublin, Ireland, Sept. 21-22, 1991. LC 94-66458. 1994. 20.00 (*0-912328-45-2*) Parapsych Foun.

Coly, Lisette, ed. see International Conference, Montreal Canada Staff.

Coly, Lisette, ed. see International Conference, New York Staff.

Coly, Lisette, ed. see International Conference, Paris Staff.

Coly, Lisette, jt. ed. see Shapin, Betty.

Colyar, Margaret R. & Ehrhardt, Cynthia. Ambulatory Care Procedures for the Nurse Practitioner. LC 98-42191. (Illus.). 472p. (C). 1998. pap. text 39.95 (*0-8036-0364-9*) Davis Co.

Colyer, jt. auth. see Ebisawa.

Colyer, Elmer M., ed. Evangelical Theology in Transition: Theologians in Dialogue with Donald Bloesch. LC 99-21811. 264p. 1999. pap. 19.99 (*0-8308-1594-5*, 1594) InterVarsity.

Colyer, Carlton. The Art of Acting: From Basic Exercises to Multi-Dimensional Performances. Zapel, Arthur L., ed. LC 89-27928. (Illus.). 224p. (Orig.). (YA). (gr. 9 up). 1989. pap. 15.95 (*0-916260-62-3*, B171) Meriwether Pub.

***Colyer, Dale, et al, eds.** Competition in Agriculture: The United States in the World Market. LC 99-462142. 360p. (C). 2000. 69.95 (*1-56022-892-X*, Food Products); pap. text 39.95 (*1-56022-893-8*, Food Products) Haworth Pr.

Colyer, Martin. How to Find & Work with an Illustrator to Get the Results You Want. (Illus.). 144p. 1998. reprint ed. text 25.00 (*0-7881-5873-2*) DIANE Pub.

Colyer, Richard J. The Teifi: Scenery & Antiquities of a Welsh River. 94p. (C). 1987. text 30.00 (*0-86383-435-3*, Pub. by Gomer Pr) St Mut.

Colyer, Richard J., ed. A Land of Pure Delight: Selections from the Letters of Thomas Johnes of Hafod, 1748-1816. 314p. 1992. 47.95 (*0-8464-4702-9*) Beekman Pubs.

Colyer, Vincent. Peace with the Apaches of New Mexico & Arizona. LC 70-165622. (Select Bibliographies Reprint Ser.). 1977. reprint ed. 15.95 (*0-8369-5929-9*) Ayer.

Colz, Hans-Georg. Staring at Variations: The Concept of 'Self' in Breyten Breytenbach's Mouroir. LC 95-40803. (Aachen British & American Studies: Vol. 5). 103p. 1995. 29.95 (*0-8204-2910-4*) P Lang Pubng.

Coma, Javier. Diccionario del Cine Negro. 3rd ed. (SPA.). 264p. 1991. 125.00 (*0-7859-5685-9*, 8401604893) Fr & Eur.

Coma, Miguel A. Diccionario Enciclopedico Ilustrado Argos Vergara Vol. 7: Lazaro-Carreter. 2nd ed. (CAT.). 1046p. 1987. 29.95 (*0-7859-6196-8*, 8472111571) Fr & Eur.

— Diccionario Enciclopedico Ilustrado Argos Vergara Vol. 8: Monoclamidea-Parpado. 12th ed. (CAT.). 304p. 1983. pap. 10.95 (*0-7859-6195-X*, S50050) Fr & Eur.

— Diccionario Enciclopedico Ilustrado Argos Vergara Vol. 9: Parpallo-Redoute. 2nd ed. (CAT.). 310p. 1987. pap. 15.95 (*0-7859-6487-8*, 847211158X) Fr & Eur.

Comac, Linda, jt. auth. see Lane, I. William.

Comac, Linda, jt. auth. see Price, Ira Marc.

Comacchio, Cynthia R. Nations Are Built of Babies: Saving Ontario's Mothers & Children, 1900-1940. (Illus.). 360p. 1993. 60.00 (*0-7735-0991-7*, Pub. by McG-Queens Univ Pr) CUP Services.

— "Nations Are Built of Babies" Saving Ontario's Mothers & Children, 1900-1940. (Illus.). 352p. 1998. pap. text 22.95 (*0-7735-1770-7*, Pub. by McG-Queens Univ Pr) CUP Services.

Comacho, Laura, jt. auth. see Roraff, Susan.

Comain, Micheal O. The Poolbeg Book of Irish Heraldry. (Illus.). 173p. 1991. pap. 12.95 (*1-85371-126-8*, Pub. by Poolbeg Pr) Dufour.

Comair-Obeid, Nayla. The Law of Business Contracts in the Arab Middle East. LC 96-17767. (Arab & Islamic Law Ser.). 1996. 175.00 (*90-411-0216-7*) Kluwer Law Intl.

Comair, Y. G., jt. auth. see Tamraz, J. C.

Comair, Youssef G., jt. auth. see L[0001]ders, Hans Otto.

Coman, Carolyn. Bee & Jacky. LC 98-13370. 101p. (J). (gr. 7-12). 1998. 14.95 (*1-886910-33-2*) Front Str.

***Coman, Carolyn.** Bee & Jacky. LC 99-21469. (Illus.). 108p. (YA). (gr. 7-12). 1999. reprint ed. pap. 4.99 (*0-14-130637-8*, PuffinBks) Peng Put Young Read.

— Many Stones. 2000. 15.95 (*1-886910-55-3*, Front Street) Front Str.

Coman, Carolyn. Tell Me Everything. 160p. (YA). 1993. 15.00 (*0-374-37390-6*) FS&G.

— Tell Me Everything. LC 98-16343. 160p. (J). (gr. 5-9). 1998. pap. 4.99 (*0-14-038791-9*, PuffinBks) Peng Put Young Read.

— Tell Me Everything. 1995. 9.05 (*0-606-09955-7*, Pub. by Turtleback) Demco.

— What Jamie Saw. LC 95-23545. 112p. (YA). (gr. 5 up). 1995. 13.95 (*1-886910-02-2*) Front Str.

— What Jamie Saw. (YA). (gr. 5 up). 1998. 18.50 (*0-8446-6968-7*) Peter Smith.

Coman, Carolyn. What Jamie Saw. LC 96-34911. (J). 1997. 9.09 (*0-606-12072-6*, Pub. by Turtleback) Demco.

Coman, Carolyn. What Jamie Saw. LC 96-34911. (Illus.). 128p. (J). 1997. pap. 4.99 (*0-14-038335-2*) Viking Penguin.

Coman, Cory. Interview & Career Booster Manual: ICBM. 192p. (Orig.). 1994. pap. 23.45 (*1-883895-01-4*) Expert Staff.

Coman, Dan. Book of Poems & Petals. (Illus.). 49p. 1997. pap. 25.00 (*0-9653899-7-9*) Digi Print.

— Compassion. LC 98-85976. 325p. 1998. 25.00 (*0-7388-0012-0*); pap. 15.00 (*0-7388-0030-9*) Xlibris Corp.

***Coman, Florence.** Treasures of Impressionism & Post-Impressionism. 1999. 11.95 (*0-7892-0491-6*) Abbeville Pr.

Coman, Florence. Treasures of Impressionism & Post-Impressionism from the National Gallery of Art. LC 93-10768. (Tiny Folios Ser.). (Illus.). 320p. 1996. pap. 11.95 (*1-55859-561-9*) Abbeville Pr.

Coman, Jana. My Two Worlds. 256p. (Orig.). 1997. mass mkt. 9.95 (*0-89914-048-3*) Third Party Pub.

Coman, Katharine. Economic Beginnings of the Far West: How We Won the Land Beyond the Mississippi, 2 vols., Set. LC 67-29510. (Library of Early American Business & Industry). 1969. reprint ed. 95.00 (*0-678-00422-6*) Kelley.

— The Industrial History of the United States. LC 73-1999. (Big Business; Economic Power in a Free Society Ser.). 1973. reprint ed. 36.95 (*0-405-05080-1*) Ayer.

Coman, Katharine, jt. ed. see Bates, Katharine L.

Coman, Katharine & Lind, Andrew W. The History of Contract Labor in the Hawaiian Islands & Hawaii's Japanese, 2 vols. Daniels, Roger, ed. LC 78-54813. (Asian Experience in North America Ser.). (Illus.). 1979. reprint ed. lib. bdg. 28.95 (*0-405-11269-6*) Ayer.

Coman, Katharine, jt. ed. see Bates, Katharine L.

Coman, Marcia J. How To Improve Your Study Skills. 208p. 1994. pap. 9.95 (*0-8442-5653-6*, VGM Career) NTC Contemp Pub Co.

Coman, Marcia J. & Heavers, Kathy. What You Need to Know about Reading Comprehension & Speed, Skimming & Scanning, Reading for Pleasure. (NTC's Skill Builders Ser.). (Illus.). 96p. 1994. pap. 6.95 (*0-8442-5176-3*, Natl Textbk Co) NTC Contemp Pub Co.

Coman, Marcia J. & Heavers, Kathy L. El GED Esencial. LC 98-86545. (SPA.). 496p. 1998. pap. 12.95 (*0-8092-2892-0*, 289200, Contemporary Bks) NTC Contemp Pub Co.

— How to Improve Your Study Skills. 208p. Date not set. pap., teacher ed. 7.95 (*0-8442-5654-4*, VGM Career) NTC Contemp Pub Co.

Coman, Marcia J. & Heavers, Kathy L. How to Improve Your Study Skills. 2nd ed. LC 97-16138. (Illus.). 208p. 1997. pap. 14.94 (*0-8442-5886-5*, 58865) NTC Contemp Pub Co.

Coman, Marcia J. & Heavers, Kathy L. Improve Your Study Skills. LC 99-13608. (Here's How Ser.). 232p. 1999. pap. 12.95 (*0-8442-2073-6*, 20736, Natl Textbk Co) NTC Contemp Pub Co.

Coman, Marcia J. & Heavers, Kathy L. What You Need to Know about Developing Study Skills, Taking Notes & Tests, Using Dictionaries & Libraries. 2nd ed. LC 98-132815. (Illus.). 96p. 1997. pap. 11.19 (*0-8442-5888-1*, 58881) NTC Contemp Pub Co.

— What You Need to Know about Reading Comprehension & Speed, Skimming & Scanning, Reading for Pleasure. 2nd ed. (Illus.). 112p. 1997. pap. 11.19 (*0-8442-5887-3*, 58873) NTC Contemp Pub Co.

Coman, Peter. Catholics & the Welfare State. LC 76-49523. 128p. reprint ed. pap. 39.70 (*0-608-30465-4*, 201128800075) Bks Demand.

Coman, Stuart, ed. see Herakovich, Douglas.

Coman, Susan, ed. see Jobe, C. C.

Coman, Susan, ed. see Wayne, Joseph E.

Comandari, John. The Million Dollar Secret: Create the Business of Your Dreams!! Take Action!! large type ed. Comandari, Lisa, ed. 70p. 1997. pap. 8.95 (*0-9666913-0-X*) Diamond Enterprises.

Comandari, John C. & Comandari, Lisa V. How to Keep Your Wife in Love with You Forever: Secrets That Will Keep That Magical Spark & Make It Last Forever. 120p. Date not set. pap. 8.95 (*0-9666913-1-8*) Diamond Enterprises.

Comandari, Lisa, ed. see Comandari, John.

Comandari, Lisa V., jt. auth. see Comandari, John C.

***Comanescu, Sorin & Balaban, Gheorghe.** The Life of the Holy Hierarch & Confessor Glicherie of Romania. LC 99-61475. 1999. write for info. (*0-911165-38-X*) Ctr Trad Orthodox.

Comanor, Pauline. The Story of Chunky Monkey. (Illus.). 52p. (J). 1983. pap. write for info. (*0-9675175-0-8*) Chunky Monkey.

Comanor, William. Competition Policy in Europe & North America: Economic Issues & Institutions, Vol. 43. LC 96-3666. (Fundamentals of Pure & Applied Economics Ser.). viii, 260p. 1990. pap. text 97.00 (*3-7186-5059-2*, Harwood Acad Pubs) Gordon & Breach.

Comanor, William S. & Wilson, Thomas A. Advertising & Market Power. LC 73-90849. (Economic Studies: No. 144). (Illus.). xvi, 257p. 1974. 17.50 (*0-674-00580-5*) HUP.

Comans, Michael, tr. Extracting the Essence of the Sru: The Srutisarasanuddharanan of Totakacarya. (C). 1997. 11.00 (*81-208-1410-X*, Pub. by Motilal Bnarsidass) S Asia.

Comap. For All Practical Purposes. 4th ed. LC 96-4941. 800p. (C). 1996. pap. text 69.95 (*0-7167-2841-9*) W H Freeman.

***Comap.** For all Practical Purposes. 5th ed. 1999. pap. text 70.95 (*0-7167-3817-1*) W H Freeman.

— For all Practical Purposes. 5th ed. 1999. pap. text, student ed. 20.95 (*0-7167-3699-3*) W H Freeman.

— For all Practical Purposes Telecourse. 5th ed. 1999. pap. text, student ed. 20.95 (*0-7167-3703-5*) W H Freeman.

Comap. For All Practice Purposes & logic. 4th ed. 1997. 56.00 (*0-7167-3309-9*) W H Freeman.

— Introduction to Modeling. (Mathematics Ser.). 2001. pap. 55.00 (*0-534-36604-X*) Brooks-Cole.

Comap. Mathematics: Modeling Our World. 1997. pap. 43.75 (*0-538-68210-8*) Thomson Learn.

— Mathematics: Modeling Our World. 1998. pap. 43.75 (*0-538-68224-8*) Thomson Learn.

— Mathematics: Modeling Our Worldarise Crs 2. 1998. pap. 43.75 (*0-538-68218-3*) Thomson Learn.

Comap. Telecourse Guide. 3rd ed. 1994. 18.95 (*0-7167-2530-4*) W H Freeman.

***COMAP Inc. Staff.** Mathematics: Modeling Our World Course. 2000. pap. text; teacher ed. write for info. (*0-7167-4114-8*, Pub. by W H Freeman) VHPS.

***COMAP, Inc. Staff.** Mathematics: Modeling Our World Course. 2000. pap. text, student ed. write for info. (*0-7167-4115-6*, Pub. by W H Freeman) VHPS.

COMAP, Inc. Staff. UMAP Modules: Tools for Teaching, 1986. Campbell, Paul J., ed. (Illus.). 350p. 1987. pap. text 35.00 (*0-912843-11-X*) COMAP Inc.

— UMAP Modules: Tools for Teaching, 1987. Campbell, Paul J., ed. (Illus.). 320p. (Orig.). 1988. pap. text 35.00 (*0-912843-12-8*) COMAP Inc.

— UMAP Modules: Tools for Teaching, 1988. Campbell, Paul J., ed. (Illus.). 314p. (Orig.). 1989. pap. text 35.00 (*0-912843-14-4*) COMAP Inc.

— UMAP Modules: Tools for Teaching, 1989. Campbell, Paul J., ed. (Illus.). 250p. (Orig.). (C). 1990. pap. text 35.00 (*0-912843-18-7*) COMAP Inc.

COMAP Inc. Staff. UMAP Modules: Tools for Teaching, 1991. Campbell, Paul J., ed. (Illus.). 208p. 1992. pap. text 35.00 (*0-912843-22-5*) COMAP Inc.

COMAP, Inc. Staff, ed. UMAP Modules: Tools for Teaching, 1982. 544p. (Orig.). 1983. pap. 35.00 (*0-912843-03-9*) COMAP Inc.

Comaq, jt. auth. see Witherspoon, Coletta.

Comar, C. L. & Bronner, Felix, eds. Mineral Metabolism: An Advanced Treatise, 3 vols. Incl. Vol. 1, Pt. A. Principles, Processes & Systems. 1960. 72.00 (*0-12-183201-5*); Vol. 1, Pt. B. Principles, Processes & Systems. 1961. 84.00 (*0-12-183241-4*); Vol. 2, Pt. A. Elements. 1964. 94.00 (*0-12-183202-3*); Vol. 2, Pt. B. Elements. 1962. 88.00 (*0-12-183242-2*); Vol. 3. Supplementary Volume. 1969. 84.00 (*0-12-183250-3*); 342.00 (*0-685-00058-3*) Acad Pr.

Comar, D., ed. Pet for Drug Development & Evaluation. LC 95-24830. (Developments in Nuclear Medicine Ser.: Vol. 26). 384p. (C). 1995. text 144.00 (*0-7923-3716-6*) Kluwer Academic.

Comar, Mildred C., ed. see Cornell Laboratory of Ornithology Staff.

***Comar, Philippe.** Images of the Body. LC 99-11000. (Discoveries Ser.). 160p. 1999. pap. 12.95 (*0-8109-2858-2*, Pub. by Abrams) Time Warner.

Comaraswamy, Amanda K. Spiritual Authority & Temporal Power in the Indian Theory of Government. Comaraswamy, Rama P. & Iengar, Keshavram N., eds. (Illus.). 226p. 1994. text 24.00 (*0-19-563253-2*) OUP.

Comaraswamy, Rama P., ed. see Comaraswamy, Amanda K.

Comaroff. Of Revelation & Revolution, Vol. 2. 560p. 1997. lib. bdg. 70.00 (*0-226-11443-0*) U Ch Pr.

Comaroff, Jean. Body of Power, Spirit of Resistance: The Culture & History of a South African People. LC 84-24012. (Illus.). 308p. 1985. pap. text 17.95 (*0-226-11423-6*); lib. bdg. 32.00 (*0-226-11422-8*) U Ch Pr.

***Comaroff, Jean, ed.** Millennial Capitalism & the Culture of Neoliberalism. 320p. 2000. pap. 12.00 (*0-8223-6480-8*) Duke.

Comaroff, Jean & Comaroff, John L. Of Revelation & Revolution Vol. 1: Christianity, Colonialism, & Consciousness in South Africa. LC 90-46753. (Illus.). 434p. 1991. pap. text 21.95 (*0-226-11442-2*) U Ch Pr.

— Of Revelation & Revolution Vol. 1: Christianity, Colonialism, & Consciousness in South Africa. annuals LC 90-46753. Vol. 1. (Illus.). 434p. 1991. lib. bdg. 72.00 (*0-226-11441-4*) U Ch Pr.

Comaroff, Jean & Comaroff, John L., eds. Modernity & Its Malcontents: Ritual & Power in Postcolonial Africa. LC 93-17. (Illus.). 272p. 1993. pap. text 17.95 (*0-226-11440-6*) U Ch Pr.

— Modernity & Its Malcontents: Ritual & Power in Postcolonial Africa. LC 93-17. (Illus.). 272p. 1993. lib. bdg. 46.95 (*0-226-11439-2*) U Ch Pr.

Comaroff, Jean, jt. auth. see Comaroff, John.

Comaroff, Jean, jt. auth. see Comaroff, John L.

Comaroff, John & Comaroff, Jean. Ethnography & the Historical Imagination. 352p. (C). 1992. pap. 32.00 (*0-8133-1305-8*, Pub. by Westview) HarpC.

Comaroff, John, ed. see Plaatje, Solomon T.

Comaroff, John L. Civil Society & the Political Imagination in Africa: Critical Perspectives. LC 99-23280. 344p. 2000. pap. text 19.00 (*0-226-11414-7*); lib. bdg. 50.00 (*0-226-11413-9*) U Ch Pr.

Comaroff, John L. & Comaroff, Jean. Of Revelation & Revolution, Vol. 2. 560p. 1997. pap. text 24.95 (*0-226-11444-9*) U Ch Pr.

Comaroff, John L. & Roberts, Simon. Rules & Processes: The Cultural Logic of Dispute in An African Context. LC 80-26640. (Illus.). 304p. (C). 1981. 27.50 (*0-226-11424-4*) U Ch Pr.

— Rules & Processes: The Cultural Logic of Dispute in An African Context. LC 80-26640. (Illus.). 304p. (C). 1986. pap. text 16.95 (*0-226-11425-2*) U Ch Pr.

— Rules & Processes: The Cultural Logic of Dispute in an African Context. LC 80-26640. 303p. reprint ed. pap. 94.00 (*0-608-08819-6*, 206945800004) Bks Demand.

Comaroff, John L. & Stern, Paul, eds. New Perspectives on Nationalism & War. (International Studies in Global Change). 336p. 1995. text 75.00 (*2-88449-165-1*); pap. text 32.00 (*2-88449-166-X*) Gordon & Breach.

Comaroff, John L., jt. auth. see Comaroff, Jean.

Comaroff, John L., jt. ed. see Comaroff, Jean.

Comaroff, John L., jt. ed. see Krige, Eileen L.

Comaromi, John P. The Eighteen Editions of the Dewey Decimal Classification. LC 76-10604. 678p. 1976. 20.00 (*0-910608-17-2*) OCLC Forest Pr.

Comarow, Donna D. & Chescheir, Martha W. Talking about Therapy. LC 98-20127. 240p. 1999. 26.95 (*0-89789-537-1*, Bergin & Garvey) Greenwood.

Comartin, Craig D., ed. The Guam Earthquake of August 8, 1993, Reconnaissance Report. (Illus.). 175p. 1995. pap. 15.00 (*0-943198-76-3*, 95-02) Earthquake Eng.

Comartin, Craig D., et al, eds. The Hyogo-ken Nanbu Earthquake, January 17, 1995: Preliminary Reconnaissance Report. (Illus.). 116p. 1995. pap. 15.00 (*0-943198-47-X*, 95-04) Earthquake Eng.

Comas. A Tapestry of Language & Culture. (C). 1999. pap. text 52.00 (*0-15-501441-2*, Pub. by Harcourt Coll Pubs) Harcourt.

Comas-Diaz, Lillian & Greene, Beverly, eds. Women of Color: Integrating Ethnic & Gender Identities in Psychotherapy. LC 94-10840. 518p. 1994. lib. bdg. 52.00 (*0-89862-371-5*, C2371) Guilford Pubns.

Comas, Juan. Racial Myths. LC 76-5909. (Race Question in Modern Science Ser.). 51p. 1976. reprint ed. lib. bdg. 35.00 (*0-8371-8801-6*, CORM, Greenwood Pr) Greenwood.

***Comay, Aribe & Tsur, Naomi.** NTC's Hebrew & English Dictionary. LC 99-27862. 1280p. 1999. 39.95 (*0-658-00065-9*, 000659) NTC Contemp Pub Co.

Comay, Joan. Who's Who in Jewish History. 2nd rev. ed. (Illus.). 448p. (gr. 13). 1995. pap. 24.99 (*0-415-11887-5*, B4893) Routledge.

— Who's Who in Jewish History. 2nd rev. ed. (Illus.). 448p. (C). (gr. 13). 1995. 75.00 (*0-415-12583-9*, B4953) Routledge.

— Who's Who in the Old Testament. (Who's Who Ser.). 432p. (C). 1993. pap. 16.95 (*0-19-521029-8*, 3778) OUP.

Comay, Joan, jt. auth. see Brownrigg, Ronald.

Comay, Rebecca & McCumber, John, eds. Endings: Questions of Memories in Hegel. LC 98-49938. (SPEP Studies in Historical Ser.). 276p. 1999. 79.95 (*0-8101-1506-9*); pap. text 29.95 (*0-8101-1507-7*) Northwestern U Pr.

Comba, Emilio. History of the Waldenses of Italy: From Their Origin to the Reformation. LC 77-84713. reprint ed. 57.50 (*0-404-16119-7*) AMS Pr.

Comba, Peter & Hambley, Trevor W. Molecular Modeling of Inorganic Compounds. LC 95-24487. 207p. 1995. 175.00 (*3-527-29076-1*, Wiley-VCH) Wiley.

Comba, Peter, jt. ed. see Banci, Lucia.

Combahee River Collective Staff. The Combahee River Collective Statement: Black Feminist Organizing in the Seventies & Eighties. (Freedom Organizing Pamphlet Ser.). 28p. (Orig.). 1986. pap. 3.95 (*0-913175-05-6*) Kitchen Table.

Combe. Employee Benefits Answer Book, 1997: Supplement. 1996. 79.00 (*1-56706-319-5*) Panel Pubs.

Combe, Andrew. Observations on Mental Derangement: Being an Application of the Principles of Phrenology to the Elucidation of the Causes, Symptoms, Nature, Treatment of Insanity. LC 72-161928. (History of Psychology Ser.). 352p. 1972. reprint ed. 50.00 (*0-8201-1089-2*) Schol Facsimiles.

Combe, Carter K. Employment Disputes: Law & Strategy for Representing the Employer. 570p. 1994. ring bd., suppl. ed. 47.00 (*0-685-74337-3*, MICHIE) LEXIS Pub.

Combe, Cynthia & Dankner, Harold. Retiree Medical Liabilities, FAS 106, & Cost Containment: New Approaches to Redesign, Prefunding, & Disclosure. (Tax Law & Estate Planning Course Handbook Ser.). 247p. 1992. pap. 17.50 (*0-685-69487-9*); audio 40.00 (*0-685-69488-7*) PLI.

***Combe, Cynthia M.** Employee Benefits Answer Book, 1. 6th ed. 1272p. 1999. text 136.00 (*0-7355-0462-8*) Panel Pubs.

Combe, Cynthia M. & Talbot, Gerald J. Employee Benefits Answer Book. annuals 4th ed. 1000p. 1995. 118.00 (*1-56706-100-1*, S67) Panel Pubs.

Combe, Cynthia M. & Talbot, Gerard J. Employee Benefits Answer Book. (Answer Book Ser.). 400p. 1989. 74.00 (*0-916592-88-X*) Panel Pubs.

— Employee Benefits Answer Book. 2nd ed. Kaiser, Laura B., ed. 1990. 79.00 (*1-878375-21-0*) Panel Pubs.

Combe, Cynthia M., et al. Employee Benefits Answer Book, 1992: Supplement. 250p. 1991. pap. text 49.00 (*1-878375-53-9*) Panel Pubs.

Combe, Cynthia M., jt. auth. see Golub, Ira M.

Combe, David A., tr. see Seruzier, C.

Combe, Dom P. Justine Ward & Solesmes. 410p. 1987. 30.00 (*0-8132-0200-0*) Cath U Pr.

***Combe, E. C., et al.** Dental Biomaterials LC 99-27913. 1999. write for info. (*0-7923-8531-4*) Kluwer Academic.

Combe, G. A. A Tibetan on Tibet. (C). 1994. reprint ed. text 28.50 (*81-7305-036-8*, Pub. by Aryan Bks Intl) S Asia.

— A Tibetan on Tibet. 2nd ed. LC 88-23854. (Illus.). 238p. 1989. reprint ed. pap. 12.95 (*0-943389-02-X*) Snow Lion-SLG Bks.

Combe, George. The Constitution of Man Considered in Relation to External Objects. 2nd ed. LC 74-16109. (History of Psychology Ser.). 313p. 1974. reprint ed. 50.00 (*0-8201-1136-8*) Schol Facsimiles.

— Notes on the United States of North America During a Phrenological Visit in 1838-1940, 2 vols. LC 73-13125. (Foreign Travelers in America, 1810-1935 Ser.). 780p. 1974. reprint ed. 58.95 (*0-405-05448-3*) Ayer.

Combe, Iris. Border Collies: An Owners Companion. (Illus.). 224p. 1993. 39.95 (*1-85223-617-5*, Pub. by Crolwood) Trafalgar.

— Rough Collie Records. 1999. 23.95 (*1-85279-062-8*) TFH Pubns.

Combe, Kirk. A Martyr for Sin: Rochester's Critique of Polity, Sexuality, & Society. LC 97-40382. 192p. 1998. 35.00 (*0-87413-647-4*) U Delaware Pr.

***Combe, Louis.** Watching the Watcher. LC 00-103874. 2000. pap. 12.95 (*1-880849-24-0*) Chapel Hill NC.

Combe, P. Neuronal Information Processing: From Biological Data to Modelling & Application Cargese. (Series in Mathematical Biology & Medicine). 400p. 1999. 88.00 (*981-02-3826-6*) World Scientific Pub.

Combe, Pierre. Histoire de la Restauration du Chant Gregorien: D'Apres des Documents Inedits. (FRE., Illus.). 488p. 1969. pap. 34.95 (*1-55725-154-1*, 4041, Pub. by Abbey St Peter Solesmes) Paraclete MA.

Combe, Thomas. Theater of Fine Devices. (Illus.). 240p. 1990. text 67.95 (*0-85967-769-9*, Pub. by Scolar Pr) Ashgate Pub Co.

— Theatre of Fine Devices: Containing an Hundred Morall Emblems. (Illus.). 120p. 1983. pap. 3.00 (*0-87328-075-X*) Huntington Lib.

Combellack, Frederick M., tr. & intro. see Quintus, Smyrnaeus.

Combellack, Muyrna. Playing Place. (C). 1989. 50.00 (*1-85022-041-7*, Pub. by Dyllansow Truran) St Mut.

Combellack, Myrna. The Camborne Play: A Verse Translation of Beunans Meriasek. (C). 1989. text 70.00 (*1-85022-039-5*, Pub. by Dyllansow Truran) St Mut.

Combelles-Siegel, Pascale. Target Bosnia: Integrating Information Activities in Peace Operations: NATO-Led Operations in Bosnia-Herzegovina, December 1995-1997. LC 98-13326. 1998. write for info. (*1-57906-008-0*) Natl Defense.

***Comber, Barbara & Simpson, Anne, eds.** Negotiating Critical Literacies in the Classroom. 400p. 2000. pap. write for info. (*0-8058-3794-9*) L Erlbaum Assocs.

— Negotiting Critical Literacies in the Classroom. 400p. 2000. write for info. (*0-8058-3793-0*) L Erlbaum Assocs.

Comber, Chris, jt. auth. see Paris, Mike.

***Comber, Geoffrey, et al, eds.** Touchpebbles Vol. A: Textos para la Discusion. unabridged ed. Gonzalo Villasenor Maldonado, Juan, tr. (SPA., Illus.). 88p. (J). (gr. 3-5). 1999. pap. text 8.00 (*1-878461-47-8*) CZM Pr.

Comber, Geoffrey, et al, eds. Touchpebbles Vol. A: Texts for Discussion. 2nd rev. ed. (Illus.). 72p. (J). (gr. 2-5). 1997. pap. text 8.00 (*1-878461-43-5*) CZM Pr.

— Touchstones, Vol. C. (Touchstones - Middle Schools Ser.). 162p. 1998. pap. text, teacher ed. 24.00 (*1-878461-37-0*) CZM Pr.

— Touchstones: Readings in Social Studies. 163p. (Orig.). 1991. pap. text 20.00 (*1-878461-07-9*) CZM Pr.

— Touchstones Vol. III: Texts for Discussion. 182p. (Orig.). 1986. pap. text 14.00 (*1-878461-24-9*) CZM Pr.

— Touchstones Vol. IV: Texts for Discussion. 178p. (Orig.). 1994. pap. text 14.00 (*1-878461-25-7*) CZM Pr.

— Touchstones Vol. C: Texts for Discussion. (Touchstones - Middle Schools Ser.). 85p. (J). (gr. 6-8). 1998. pap. text 9.50 (*1-878461-36-2*) CZM Pr.

***Comber, Geoffrey, et al, eds.** Touchstones Vol. A: Textos para la Discusion. 2nd rev. ed. Gonzalo Villasenor Maldonado, Juan, tr. (Touchstones for Middle Schools Ser.). (SPA.). 105p. (YA). (gr. 6-8). 1998. pap. text 9.50 (*1-878461-48-6*) CZM Pr.

Comber, Geoffrey, et al, eds. Touchstones Vol. A: Texts for Discussion. rev. ed. (Touchstones - Middle Schools Ser.). 90p. (J). (gr. 6-8). 1998. pap. text 9.50 (*1-878461-45-1*) CZM Pr.

***Comber, Geoffrey, et al, eds.** Touchstones Vol. B: Texts for Discussion. 2nd ed. (Touchstones for Middle Schools Ser.). 116p. (YA). (gr. 6-8). 1999. pap. text 9.50 (*1-878461-51-6*) CZM Pr.

Comber, Geoffrey & Zeiderman, Howard, eds. Touchstones Vol. I: Texts for Discussion. 3rd ed. Maistrellis, Nicholas, tr. & intro. by. 160p. (YA). (gr. 9-12). 1995. pap. text 11.00 (*1-878461-34-6*) CZM Pr.

Comber, Geoffrey, et al. Courage to Care, Strength to Serve: Reflections on Community Service. 161p. (Orig.), 1989. pap. 11.00 (*1-878461-19-2*) CZM Pr.

— Guide & Workpad Vol. III. (Touchstones Ser.). 32p. 1986. 4.50 (*1-878461-31-1*) CZM Pr.

— SAT Preparation for Critical Reading: The Touchstones Method. 128p. (YA). (gr. 11-12). 1995. pap., teacher ed. 12.95 (*1-878461-32-X*) CZM Pr.

— Touchpebbles, Vol. A. (Touchpebbles Ser.). 219p. 1994. teacher ed. 24.00 (*1-878461-27-3*) CZM Pr.

— Touchstones Vol. II: Texts for Discussion. (Touchstones Ser.: No. 2). 167p. (Orig.). 1988. pap. 12.00 (*1-878461-23-0*) CZM Pr.

***Comber, Geoffrey, et al.** Touchstones - Teacher's Edition Vol. A: Texts for Discussion. 2nd rev. ed. (Touchstones for Middle Schools Ser.). 235p. 1998. pap. text 24.00 (*1-878461-46-X*) CZM Pr.

— Touchstones - Teacher's Edition Vol. B: Texts for Discussions. 2nd rev. ed. (Touchstones for Middle Schools Ser.). 200p. 1999. pap. text 24.00 (*1-878461-52-4*) CZM Pr.

Comber, J. B. Orchids of Java. (Illus.). vi, 407p. 1990. 60.00 (*0-947643-21-4*, Pub. by Royal Botnic Grdns) Balogh.

Comber, Leon. Chinese Magic & Superstitions in Malaya. LC 77-87023. (Illus.). 104p. reprint ed. 27.50 (*0-404-16808-6*) AMS Pr.

— More Oriental Stories for Young & Old. (Illus.). 128p. 1988. reprint ed. pap. 5.95 (*9971-4-9088-9*) Heian Intl.

Comberiati, C. P. & Steel, M. C. Music from the Middle Ages Through the Twentieth Century: A Seventieth Birthday Tribute to Gwynn S. McPeek. xiv, 394p. 1988. text 86.00 (*2-88124-216-2*) Gordon & Breach.

Comberiati, Carmelo P. Late Renaissance Music at the Habsburg Court. (Monographs on Musicology: Vol. 4). xx, 242p. 1987. text 46.00 (*2-88124-192-1*) Gordon & Breach.

***Combes, Cecile.** Scintillation Properties of 6Li-Based Materials for Thermal-Neutron Detection. 126p. 1999. pap. 39.50 (*90-407-1815-6*, Pub. by Delft U Pr) Coronet Bks.

Combes, Chantel, tr. see Hooks, Bell.

***Combes, Claude.** Interactions Durables. 1998. 55.00 (*0-226-11445-7*) U Ch Pr.

Combes, F. & Casoli, F., eds. Dynamics of Galaxies & Their Molecular Cloud Distributions. (C). 1991. pap. text 73.00 (*0-7923-1097-7*); lib. bdg. 161.00 (*0-7923-1096-9*) Kluwer Academic.

Combes, F., et al. Galaxies & Cosmology. Seymour, M., tr. (Astronomy & Astrophysics Library). 1995. 69.95 (*3-540-58933-3*) Spr-Verlag.

Combes, Francoise. Galaxies & Cosmology. (Illus.). 440p. 1995. 69.00 (*0-387-58933-3*) Spr-Verlag.

***Combes, Francoise & Pineau des Forets, Guillaume, eds.** Molecular Hydrogen in Space. (Cambridge Contemporary Astrophysics Ser.). (Illus.). 420p. 2000. write for info. (*0-521-78224-4*) Cambridge U Pr.

Combes, I. A. The Metaphor of Slavery in the Writings of the Early Church: From the New Testament to the Beginning of the Fifth Century. (JSNTS Ser.: Vol. 156). 216p. 1998. 57.50 (*1-85075-846-8*, Pub. by Sheffield Acad) CUP Services.

Combes, J. M., et al, eds. Wavelets. (Illus.). ix, 315p. 1989. pap. 88.10 (*0-387-51159-8*) Spr-Verlag.

— Wavelets: Time-Frequency Methods & Phase Space: Proceedings of the International Conference, Marseille, France, December 14-18, 1987. Inverse Problems & Theoretical Imaging. 2nd enl. rev. ed. (Illus.). 352p. 1992. 59.00 (*0-387-53014-2*) Spr-Verlag.

Combes, J. M., jt. auth. see Langford, R. P.

Combes, John D. The Excavation of Squirt Cave 45WW25. (Washington State University, Laboratory of Archaeology & History Ser.). 53p. (C). 1969. reprint ed. pap. text 6.56 (*1-55567-607-3*) Coyote Press.

Combes, Paul F. Microwave Transmission for Telecommunications. LC 90-38435. (Illus.). 331p. 1991. reprint ed. pap. 102.70 (*0-608-05277-9*, 206581500001) Bks Demand.

***Combes, Richard.** Sugar Free Love. (Pocket Oracle Ser.). (Illus.). 64p. 2000. mass mkt. 5.99 (*1-903222-18-4*, Pub. by Wimbledon Publishing Co) Anthem.

— The Tao of Modern Living. (Pocket Oracle Ser.). (Illus.). 64p. 2000. mass mkt. 5.99 (*1-903222-17-6*, Pub. by Wimbledon Publishing Co) Anthem.

Combes, Simon. Great Cats: Stories & Art from a World Traveller. LC 98-16870. (Illus.). 168p. 1998. 35.00 (*0-86713-048-2*, 85129) Greenwich Wrkshop.

Combest, Larry, jt. auth. see Moynihan, Daniel P.

Combie, William M. Cattle & Cattle Breeders. 3rd rev. ed. 164p. 1983. 5.00 (*0-87012-628-8*) McClain.

Combined Books Editors. The Civil War Book of Lists. 240p. 1994. pap. 14.95 (*0-938289-43-8*, 289438) Combined Pub.

***Combined Publishing Staff.** La Ligne Maginot et l'Infanterie de Fortresse. (FRE.). 1999. 39.95 (*2-908182-97-1*) Histoire.

Combley, Margaret, jt. auth. see Broomfield, Hilary.

Comblin, Jose. Being Human: A Christian Anthropology. 272p. 1994. pap. 35.00 (*0-86012-168-2*, Pub. by Srch Pr) St Mut.

— Called for Freedom: The Changing Context of Liberation Theology. Berryman, Phillip, tr. from POR. LC 97-48999.Tr. of Cristaos Rumo Ao Seculo XXI: Nova Caminada de Libertacao. 240p. 1998. reprint ed. pap. 25.00 (*1-57075-173-0*) Orbis Bks.

— The Holy Spirit & Liberation.Tr. of O Espirito Santo e a Libertacao. 232p. 1994. pap. 27.00 (*0-86012-163-1*, Pub. by Srch Pr) St Mut.

— Jesus of Nazareth: Meditations on His Humanity. LC 75-29580. Orig. Title: Jesus De Nazare. 167 p. 1976. write for info. (*0-88344-231-0*) Orbis Bks.

Comblin, Joseph. The Church & the National Security State. LC 79-10881. 254p. (Orig.). reprint ed. pap. 78.80 (*0-7837-6415-4*, 204639500012) Bks Demand.

— Cry of the Oppressed, Cry of Jesus: Meditations on Scripture & Contemporary Struggle. Barr, Robert, tr. from POR. LC 87-24029. 96p. 1988. reprint ed. pap. 30.00 (*0-7837-9866-0*, 206059200005) Bks Demand.

— The Holy Spirit & Liberation. Burns, Paul, tr. from POR. LC 89-135476. (Theology & Liberation Ser.).Tr. of O Espirito Santo e a Libertacao. 231p. reprint ed. pap. 71.70 (*0-7837-6973-3*, 204678400004) Bks Demand.

— Jesus of Nazareth: Meditations on His Humanity. Kabat, Carl, tr. LC 75-29580. Orig. Title: Jesus De Nazare. 173p. (Orig.). reprint ed. pap. 53.70 (*0-8357-4063-3*, 203675300005) Bks Demand.

— Retrieving the Human: A Christian Anthropology. Barr, Robert R., tr. from POR. LC 89-78416. (Theology & Liberation Ser.). 271p. 1990. reprint ed. pap. 84.10 (*0-7837-9845-8*, 206057400005) Bks Demand.

— Sent from the Father: Meditations on the Fourth Gospel. Kabat, Carl, tr. LC 78-16750. Orig. Title: O Enviado do Pai. 128p. (Orig.). reprint ed. pap. 39.70 (*0-8357-4071-4*, 203676100005) Bks Demand.

Combo, Luann. Creatures. (Gross But True Ser.). (Illus.). (J). (gr. 1-7). 1997. 8.99 (*0-614-29112-7*) Litle Simon.

— Germs. (Gross But True Ser.). (Illus.). (J). (gr. 1-7). 1997. 8.99 (*0-614-29113-5*) Litle Simon.

— Gross But True Food. (Gross But True Ser.). (Illus.). 32p. (J). (gr. 1-7). 1997. 8.99 (*0-689-81502-6*) Litle Simon.

— Gross But True Smells. (Gross But True Ser.). (Illus.). 32p. (J). (gr. 1-7). 1997. 8.99 (*0-689-81496-8*) Litle Simon.

Combrinck-Graham, Lee. Children in Families at Risk: Maintaining the Connections. LC 95-8793. 429p. 1995. lib. bdg. 46.00 (*0-89862-852-0*) Guilford Pubns.

Combrinck-Graham, Lee, ed. Children in Family Contexts: Perspectives on Treatment. LC 88-5108. 537p. 1988. lib. bdg. 52.00 (*0-89862-732-X*) Guilford Pubns.

Combs. Electrician Draft Workbook Fundamentals. 1997. pap. text 15.45 (*0-13-758566-7*) P-H.

— The Vitamins. 2nd ed. LC 98-84424. 618p. (C). 1998. text 59.95 (*0-12-183492-1*) Acad Pr.

***Combs & Zirbel.** Electonics Drafting: Fundamentals of Autocad - Using Autocad 2000. 192p. 2000. pap. write for info. (*0-13-087056-0*) P-H.

Combs, A., jt. ed. see Sulis, W. H.

Combs, Allan. The Radiance of Being: Complexity, Chaos & the Evolution of Consciousness Introduced by Herbert Guenther. LC 96-41972. 350p. 1996. pap. 18.95 (*1-55778-755-7*) Paragon Hse.

Combs, Allan, ed. Cooperation: Beyond the Age of Competition, Vol. 4. (World Futures General Evolution Studies). xv, 248p. 1992. text 82.00 (*2-88124-537-4*) Gordon & Breach.

Combs, Allan & Holland, Mark. Synchronicity: Science, Myth & the Trickster. 2nd ed. 200p. (Orig.). (C). 1995. pap. 12.95 (*1-56924-845-1*) Marlowe & Co.

Combs, Allan, jt. ed. see Robertson, Robin.

Combs, Arthur W. Being & Becoming: A Field Approach to Psychology. LC 98-54240. 240p. 1999. 39.95 (*0-8261-1257-9*) Springer Pub.

— A Theory of Therapy: Guidelines for Counseling Practice. LC 89-4295. 180p. reprint ed. pap. 55.80 (*0-7837-6585-1*, 204615000011) Bks Demand.

Combs, Arthur W. & Gonzalez, David M. Helping Relationships: Basic Concepts for the Helping Professions. 4th ed. LC 93-9852. 256p. 1993. pap. text 45.00 (*0-205-15022-5*) Allyn.

Combs, Arthur W., et al. On Becoming a School Leader: A Person-Centered Challenge. LC 98-58054. 231p. 1999. pap. 22.95 (*0-87120-336-7*, 199024) ASCD.

C

Combs, Cindy C. Terrorism in the 21st Centry. 2nd ed. LC 99-21272. 240p. 1999. pap. 28.00 (*0-13-020887-6*, Pub. by P-H) S&S Trade.

Combs, Clint & Bradshaw, Larry. Retiring First Class. 144p. 1993. 9.98 (*0-88290-470-1*, 2050) Horizon Utah.

Combs, Colleen J. Women in the Short Stories of Pedro Antonio de Alarcon. LC 97-37564. (Hispanic Literature Ser.: Vol. 42). 152p. 1997. text 69.95 (*0-7734-8424-8*) E Mellen.

Combs, Diana W. Early Gravestone Art in Georgia & South Carolina. LC 85-1129. (Illus.). 260p. 1986. reprint ed. pap. 80.60 (*0-7837-9754-0*, 206048200005) Bks Demand.

Combs, Eugene. Runpoem. LC 92-21595. 68p. 1992. pap. 14.95 (*0-7734-9523-1*, Mellen Poetry Pr) E Mellen.

Combs, Eugene & Post, Kenneth H. The Foundations of Political Order in Genesis & the Chandogya Upanishad. LC 87-10995. (Studies in Comparative Religion: Vol. 1). 824p. 1987. lib. bdg. 149.95 (*0-88946-501-0*) E Mellen.

Combs, F. Michael. Percussion Manual. 160p. (C). 1977. pap. 20.25 (*0-534-00504-7*) Wadsworth Pub.

***Combs, F. Michael.** Percussion Manual. 2nd ed. (Illus.). 167p. (C). 2000. pap. 21.95 (*1-57766-106-0*) Waveland Pr.

Combs, Gary B., jt. auth. see Cassity, Brad.

Combs, Gene & Freedman, Jill. Symbol, Story, & Ceremony: Using Metaphor in Individual & Family Therapy. (C). 1990. 29.95 (*0-393-70092-5*) Norton.

Combs, Gene, jt. auth. see Freedman, Jill.

Combs, Gerald. Brief U. S. Foreign Policy. (C). 1986. text 37.74 (*0-07-554643-4*) McGraw.

Combs, Gerald F., Jr. The Vitamins: Fundamental Aspects in Nutrition & Health. (Illus.). 528p. 1991. text 69.00 (*0-12-183490-5*) Acad Pr.

Combs, H. C. & Sullens, Z. R. Concordance to the English Poems of John Donne. LC 74-92960. (Studies in Poetry: No. 38). 1970. reprint ed. lib. bdg. 75.00 (*0-8383-0969-0*) M S G Haskell Hse.

Combs, Harry. Brules. 720p. 1995. mass mkt. 5.99 (*0-440-21728-8*) Dell.

— Brules: A Novel. 1992. 19.95 (*0-89141-455-X*) TernStyle Pr.

— Kill Devil Hill: Discovering the Secret of the Wright Brothers. 6th ed. (Illus.). 389p. (C). 1989. reprint ed. 24.95 (*0-940053-01-2*); reprint ed. pap. 16.95 (*0-940053-02-0*) TernStyle Pr.

— Legend of Crazy Horse. 320p. 1997. mass mkt. 6.50 (*0-440-21732-6*) Dell.

— The Legend of the Painted Horse. 1997. mass mkt. write for info. (*0-614-27735-3*) Dell.

— The Legend of the Painted Horse. large type ed. LC 96-50222. 1997. pap. 22.95 (*1-56895-402-6*) Wheeler Pub.

— The Scout. 736p. 1996. mass mkt. 6.50 (*0-440-21729-6*) Dell.

— Where Was Custer? At the Battle of the Little Big Horn. (Illus.). 120p. 1999. 19.95 (*0-940053-03-9*) TernStyle Pr.

Combs, James. Phony Culture: Confidence & Malaise in Contemporary America. 201p. (C). 1994. 39.95 (*0-87972-667-9*); pap. 18.95 (*0-87972-668-7*) Bowling Green Univ Popular Press.

— Polpop: Politics & Popular Culture in America. LC 83-73574. 1984. 25.95 (*0-87972-276-2*) Bowling Green Univ Popular Press.

— Polpop 2: Politics & Popular Culture in America Today. LC 83-73574. 200p. (C). 1991. 39.95 (*0-87972-541-9*); pap. 19.95 (*0-87972-542-7*) Bowling Green Univ Popular Press.

— The Reagan Range: The Nostalgic Myth in American Politics. LC 92-73977. 151p. 1993. 29.95 (*0-87972-565-6*) Bowling Green Univ Popular Press.

Combs, James, ed. Movies & Politics: The Dynamic Relationship. LC 92-23456. (Illus.). 320p. 1993. text 25.00 (*0-8153-0043-3*) Garland.

***Combs, James E.** Play World: The Emergence of the New Ludenic Age. LC 00-22344. 208p. 2000. 53.00 (*0-275-96838-3*, C6838, Praeger Pubs) Greenwood.

Combs, James E., jt. auth. see Nimmo, Dan.

***Combs, James L.** Bradleyville Basketball, a True Story of "The Hicks from the Sticks" LC 99-96383. (Illus.). 272p. 1999. 29.95 (*0-9674853-0-4*) Beav Creek.

Combs, Jane H. No Kidding! A Primer for Teachers-Tutors New to Adult Education. Shaffer, Sandra, ed. 49p. (Orig.). 1990. pap. text, teacher ed. 5.56 (*0-9625440-0-0*) Longmuir Jones Pub.

Combs, Jane H., ed. see Gerstner-Horvath, Marilyn.

Combs, Jane H., ed. see Hogenson, Mary L.

Combs, Jerald A. The History of American Foregn Policy, Vol. 2. 2nd ed. LC 96-20940. 256p. (C). 1996. pap. 27.81 (*0-07-553401-0*) McGraw.

— The History of American Foregn Policy, Vol. 3. 2nd ed. LC 96-20940. 384p. (C). 1996. pap. 32.81 (*0-07-553402-9*) McGraw.

— The History of American Foregn Policy: Combined Edition, Vol. 1. 2nd ed. LC 96-20940. 576p. (C). 1996. pap. 51.56 (*0-07-553400-2*) McGraw.

Combs, Jim. Mysteries of the Book of Daniel. (Illus.). 176p. (Orig.). (C). 1994. pap. 9.95 (*1-884764-01-0*) Baptist Bible.

— Rainbows from Revelation: How to Understand the Apocalypse. 252p. (Orig.). (C). 1994. pap. 19.95 (*1-884764-02-9*) Baptist Bible.

Combs, Jim, ed. see Jeffrey, Grant, et al.

Combs, Jo, et al. Microchemistry, Vol. II. (Illus.). 20p. 1995. pap. text 20.00 (*1-877960-19-5*) Kemtec Educ.

Combs, Joe. Thy Gentle Call. 140p. (Orig.). 1996. pap. 6.00 (*1-57502-195-1*, P0823) Morris Pubng.

Combs, Judy. Tricks We Played in Iowa. (Illus.). 186p. (Orig.). 1990. pap. 9.95 (*1-878488-56-2*) Quixote Pr IA.

Combs, Karen. Optical Illusions for Quilters. LC 97-30330. (Illus.). 144p. 1997. pap. 22.95 (*0-89145-892-1*, 4831, Am Quilters Soc) Collector Bks.

Combs, Linda. A Long Goodbye & Beyond: Coping with Alzheimers. LC 97-77070. 160p. 1998. pap. 12.95 (*1-885221-83-5*) BookPartners.

Combs, Linda M. Long Goodbye: Reflections on Dealing with Alzheimers. 200p. 1994. write for info. (*0-9640312-0-5*) Combs Pubng.

***Combs, Lisa M.** Dozer to the Rescue. (Illus.). 32p. (J). (ps-2). 2000. pap. 2.95 (*0-8167-6358-5*) Troll Communs.

— Dozer's Wild Adventure. (Illus.). 32p. (J). (ps-2). 2000. pap. 2.95 (*0-8167-6962-1*) Troll Communs.

— Rocket to the Moon: The Incredible Story of the First Lunar Landing. LC 99-24917. (Illus.). 32p. (J). (gr. k-6). 1999. 17.95 (*0-8167-6331-3*) BrdgeWater.

***Combs, Lisa M.** Rocket to the Moon: The Incredible Story of the First Lunar Landing. (Illus.). 32p. (J). (gr. k-6). 2000. pap. 5.95 (*0-8167-6332-1*) Troll Communs.

Combs, Loula L. My Revelation. abr. ed. LC 91-65172. (Illus.). 351p. 1991. reprint ed. 25.95 (*0-9625511-2-0*) Storm Ridge Pr.

Combs, Martha. Developing Competent Readers & Writers for Middle Grades. LC 96-39205. 406p. (C). 1997. pap. text 63.00 (*0-13-376435-4*) P-H.

— Developing Competent Readers & Writers in the Primary Grades. LC 95-44369. 555p. (C). 1996. pap. text 66.00 (*0-13-324922-0*, Merrill Pub Co) Macmillan.

Combs, Maxine. Handbook of the Strange. (Tidewater Fiction Ser.). 326p. 18.00 (*0-930095-18-9*); pap. 14.00 (*0-930095-19-7*) Signal Bks.

— The Inner Life of Objects. LC 99-36783. 240p. 1999. 28.95 (*0-934971-73-0*, Pub. by Calyx Bks); pap. 14.95 (*0-934971-72-2*, Pub. by Calyx Bks) Consort Bk Sales.

— Swimming Out of the Collective Unconscious. pap. 4.95 (*0-9612158-3-6*) Signal Bks.

***Combs-Moore, Wanda & Queenan, Charles F.** Never, Never, Give Up! xi, 120p. 1998. pap. 12.95 (*0-9675119-0-9*) W L Moore Assocs.

Combs-Orme, Terri. Social Work Practice in Maternal & Child Health. LC 89-26218. (Social Work Ser.: Vol. 15). 336p. 1990. 41.95 (*0-8261-6370-X*) Springer Pub.

***Combs, Patrick.** Major in Success: Make College Easier, Beat the System & Get a Very Cool Job. 3rd ed. 2000. pap. 11.95 (*1-58008-209-2*) Ten Speed Pr.

Combs, Phil G., jt. ed. see Espey, William H., Jr.

Combs-Ramirez, Ginger. The Gringo's Investment Guide: Every Legal Thing You Need to Know about Buying Real Estate in Mexico. Slovensky, Cathryn, ed. 144p. (Orig.). 1994. pap. 24.95 (*0-9642234-0-6*) Monmex Pubng.

Combs, Ray. The Universal Life Insurance Ripoff: Money down the Drain. LC 95-68227. 72p. (Orig.). 1995. pap. 9.95 (*1-884570-26-7*) Research Triangle.

Combs, Richard & Gillen, Stephen E. Canoeing & Kayaking Ohio's Streams: An Access Guide for Paddlers & Anglers. LC 93-45778. (Illus.). 208p. 1994. pap. 17.00 (*0-88150-252-9*, Pub. by Countryman) Norton.

Combs, Richard E. & Moorhead, John D. The Competitive Intelligence Handbook. LC 92-32740. (Illus.). 197p. 1992. 30.00 (*0-8108-2606-2*) Scarecrow.

Combs, Richard E. & Owen, Nancy R. Authors: Critical & Biographical References. 2nd ed. LC 93-774. 477p. 1993. 60.00 (*0-8108-2679-8*) Scarecrow.

Combs, Rodney. Dietrich Bonhoeffer's the Cost of Discipleship. LC 98-21266. (Shepherd's Notes Ser.). 1999. 5.95 (*0-8054-9198-8*) Broadman.

— First, Second, & Third John. LC 98-15307. (Shepherd's Notes Ser.). 1998. 5.95 (*0-8054-9214-3*) Broadman.

Combs, Roger. Crossbows. LC 86-72619. (Illus.). 192p. 1987. pap. 15.95 (*0-87349-007-X*, CROSS, DBI Bks) Krause Pubns.

Combs, Roger, ed. Archer's Digest. 6th ed. LC 77-148722. (Illus.). 256p. (Orig.). 1995. pap. 18.95 (*0-87349-167-X*, AD6, DBI Bks) Krause Pubns.

Combs, Roger, jt. auth. see Lewis, Jack.

Combs, Ron. Office Design Ideas. 1995. 49.95 (*0-87814-451-X*) PennWell Bks.

Combs-Schilling, M. E. Sacred Performances: Islam, Sexuality, & Sacrifice. (Illus.). 390p. 1990. pap. text 20.00 (*0-231-06975-8*) Col U Pr.

Combs, Stephen. Using AutoCAD 14: Special Edition. 1100p. 1999. 39.99 (*0-7897-1470-1*) Que.

Combs, Steven & Zurbek, Hat. Using AutoCAD 14. 1997. 49.99 (*0-7897-1476-0*) Que.

Combs, Steven B. Illustrated 3D Studio Quick Reference, Version 4. (CAD/CAM Ser.). (Illus.). 750p. 1996. pap. 27.95 (*0-8273-7731-2*) Delmar.

Combs, Steven B. & Zirbel, Jay H. Fundamentals of AutoCAD. LC 97-27756. 494p. 1997. pap. text 66.00 incl. disk (*0-13-256439-4*) P-H.

— Fundamentals of AutoCAD: Using AutoCAD 2000. LC 99-46375. 2000. write for info. (*0-13-016818-1*) P-H.

Combs, Steven B. & Zirbel, Jay H. Fundamentals of AutoCAD Using Release 14. LC 98-33447. 544p. 1998. pap. text 60.00 (*0-13-011302-6*) P-H.

Combs, Steven B., jt. auth. see Zirbel, Jay H.

Combs, Terri T. Guide to Life-Span Development for Future Nurses. 6th ed. LC 96-196864. 96p. (C). 1996. text. write for info. (*0-697-35557-8*) Brown & Benchmark.

Combs, Tram. Saint Thomas, Poems. LC 65-14050. (Wesleyan Poetry Program Ser.). 84p. reprint ed. pap. 30.00 (*0-608-09074-3*, 206970800005) Bks Demand.

Combs, Trey. Alaska Fly Fishing: The Call of the River. (Fly Fishing Alaska Ser.). (Illus.). 252p. (Orig.). 1995. pap. 14.95 (*0-614-13438-2*) D Heiners Fish.

— Bluewater Fly Fishing. (Illus.). 336p. 1996. 60.00 (*1-55821-331-7*) Lyons Pr.

— Steelhead Fly Fishing. (Illus.). 512p. 1991. 45.00 (*1-55821-119-5*) Lyons Pr.

— Steelhead Fly Fishing. 494p. 1999. pap. text 29.95 (*1-55821-903-X*) Lyons Pr.

— Steelhead Fly Fishing & Flies. (Illus.). 118p. (Orig.). 1976. pap. 19.95 (*0-936608-03-X*) F Amato Pubns.

— The Steelhead Trout. (Illus.). 187p. 1988. reprint ed. pap. 9.95 (*0-936608-77-3*) F Amato Pubns.

Combs, W. V. Second Federal Issue, 1801-1802: U. S. Embossed Revenue Stamped Paper. (Illus.). xvi, 142p. 1989. 20.00 (*0-945735-00-6*) Amer Revenue Assn.

— Third Federal Issue 1814 - 1817 & Other U. S. Embossed Revenue Stamped Paper 1791 - 1869. (Illus.). xvi, 224p. 1993. 27.50 (*0-945735-01-4*) Amer Revenue Assn.

Comby, Jean. How to Read Church History, Vol. 1. (Adult Christian Formation Program Ser.: Vol. 1). 1985. pap. 17.95 (*0-8245-0722-3*, Pub. by Crossroad NY) Natl Bk Netwk.

— How to Read Church History Vol. 2: From Reformation to Present Day. (Adult Christian Formation Program Ser.: Vol. 2). (Illus.). 208p. 1989. pap. 18.95 (*0-8245-0908-0*, Pub. by Crossroad NY) Natl Bk Netwk.

Comden. Bells Are Ringing. 32p. 1988. pap. 8.95 (*0-7935-2660-4*, 00312031) H Leonard.

Comden, Betty. Off Stage. LC 96-2779. (Illus.). 216p. 1996. reprint ed. pap. 16.95 (*0-87910-084-2*) Limelight Edns.

— Off Stage: My Non-Show Business Life. LC 94-39115. 1995. 23.00 (*0-671-70579-2*) S&S Trade.

***Comden, Betty & Green, Adolph.** The New York Musicals of Comden & Green. (Illus.). 328p. 1998. pap. 19.95 (*1-55783-360-5*) Applause Theatre Bk Pubs.

Comden, Betty & Green, Adolph. The New York Musicals of Comden & Green: On the Town, Wonderful Town & Bells Are Ringing. (Illus.). 328p. 1996. 35.00 (*1-55783-242-0*) Applause Theatre Bk Pubs.

Come, Arnold B. Kierkegaard as Humanist: Discovering My Self. LC 96-128118. (Illus.). 512p. 1995. 55.00 (*0-7735-1019-2*, Pub. by McG-Queens Univ Pr) CUP Services.

— Kierkegaard as Theologian: Recovering My Self. 408p. 1997. text 55.00 (*0-7735-1023-0*, Pub. by McG-Queens Univ Pr) CUP Services.

Come, B. & Chapman, Neil A., eds. Natural Analogues in Radioactive Waste Disposal. (C). 1988. lib. bdg. 287.50 (*1-85333-105-8*, Pub. by Graham & Trotman) Kluwer Academic.

Come, B., et al. Design & Instrumentation of In-Situ Experiments in Underground Laboratories for Radioactive Waste Disposal: Proceedings of a Joint CEC-NEA Workshop, Brussels, 15-17 May 1984. Johnston, P. & Muller, E., eds. 500p. (C). 1984. text 207.00 (*90-6191-594-5*, Pub. by A A Balkema) Ashgate Pub Co.

Come, Michele B., jt. ed. see Arnould, Marcel.

Come-packt Furniture Company Staff. Illustrated Mission Furniture Catalog, 1912-1913. (Illus.). 80p. 1991. pap. 8.95 (*0-486-26529-3*) Dover.

Comeau. Ensemble: Grammaire. 5th ed. (C). 1994. pap. text, wbk. ed. 28.00 (*0-15-500643-6*) Harcourt Coll Pubs.

— Ensemble Culture et Societe. 6th ed. LC 98-87999. (C). 1998. text 36.50 (*0-03-022246-X*, Pub. by Harcourt Coll Pubs) Harcourt.

— Ensemble Grammaire. 6th ed. (C). 1998. text 51.50 (*0-03-021369-X*, Pub. by Harcourt Coll Pubs) Harcourt.

— Ensemble Literature. 6th ed. (C). 1998. pap. text 37.00 (*0-03-022248-6*, Pub. by Harcourt Coll Pubs) Harcourt.

Comeau, Alexander De, see De Comeau, Alexander.

Comeau, Cecile, jt. auth. see Dupuis, Henriette.

***Comeau, Gilles.** 10 Teachers' Viewpoints on Suzuki Piano. 164p. 1998. pap. text 24.95 (*2-89442-552-X*, Pub. by Frnco-Ontarien Pedagog) Wrner Bros.

Comeau, Gilles & Covert, Rosemary. An Illustrated History of Music for Young Musicians: Baroque Period. 76p. 1997. pap. text 14.95 (*2-89442-522-8*, Pub. by Frnco-Ontarien Pedagog) Wrner Bros.

— An Illustrated History of Music for Young Musicians: Classical Period. 92p. 1998. pap. text 14.95 (*2-89442-758-1*, Pub. by Frnco-Ontarien Pedagog) Wrner Bros.

— An Illustrated History of Music for Young Musicians: Romantic Period. 96p. 1999. pap. text 14.95 (*2-89442-791-3*, Pub. by Frnco-Ontarien Pedagog) Wrner Bros.

Comeau-Grasso, Lois, ed. see Kravitz, Judith.

Comeau, Paul R. & Klein, Mark S. The New York Residency Audit Handbook. 1993. pap. 39.95 (*0-9639171-0-2*) Guaranty NY.

— The New York Residency Audit Handbook, 1995-1996. 2nd ed. 200p. 1995. 59.95 (*0-9639171-2-9*) Guaranty NY.

— The New York Residency Audit Handbook, 1995-1996. 2nd ed. 200p. 1996. pap. 19.95 (*0-9639171-1-0*) Guaranty NY.

— Understanding New York's Nonresident Income Allocation Rules: A Guidebook Specially Designed to Assist Taxpayers & Tax Advisors in Understanding & Interpreting New York's Complex Income Sourcing Rules. Kelly, Sharon M., ed. 87p. (Orig.). 1996. pap. 10.95 (*0-9639171-3-7*) Guaranty NY.

Comeau, Paul R. & Rosen, Arthur R. New York Tax Cases, 48 vols., Set. 1988. ring bd. 3995.00 (*0-89941-640-3*, 305590) W S Hein.

Comeau, Paul T. Workbook for Wheelock's Latin. 3rd ed. 352p. 1997. pap., wbk. ed. 15.00 (*0-06-273471-7*, Harper Ref) HarpC.

***Comeau, Paul T. & LaFleur, Richard.** Workbook for Wheelock's Latin. 3rd ed. 352p. 2000. pap., wbk. ed. 17.00 (*0-06-095642-9*, HarpRes) HarpInfo.

Comeau, Pauline & Santin, Aldo. The First Canadians. 2nd rev. ed. LC 95-231601. 219p. pap. 19.95 (*1-55028-478-9*, Pub. by J Lorimer) Formac Dist Ltd.

Comeau, Raymond & Lamoureux, Normand J. CAMERA 1(FRENCH)VID CASS 1&2+ 4th ed. (ENG & FRE.). 240p. (C). 1990. 31.00 (*0-03-034588-X*) Harcourt Coll Pubs.

— Ensemble: Grammaire. 4th ed. (ENG & FRE.). 240p. (C). 1990. write for info. (*0-318-69152-3*) Harcourt Coll Pubs.

***Comeau, Raymond F.** Ensemble Literature. 6th ed. 1998. pap. text 37.00 (*0-03-026059-0*) Dryden Pr.

Comeau, Raymond F. Ensemble Literature. 6th ed. (C). 1999. pap. text 18.00 (*0-03-022249-4*) Harcourt.

— Tout Ensemble. (ENG & FRE.). (C). 1996. pap. text, lab manual ed. 34.00 (*0-03-009599-9*) Harcourt Coll Pubs.

Comeau, Raymond F. & Bunting, Marie-France. Classiques pour Debutants. (FRE.). 140p. (C). 1992. pap. text 23.96 (*0-395-61555-0*) HM.

Comeau, Raymond F. & Lamoureux, Normand J. Ensemble: Culture et Societe. 4th ed. (FRE.). 368p. (C). 1990. write for info. (*0-03-051073-2*); VHS. write for info. (*0-318-69157-4*) Harcourt Coll Pubs.

— Ensemble: Grammaire. 5th ed. LC 93-77002. (FRE., Illus.). 280p. (C). 1994. pap. text 50.00 (*0-15-500642-8*, Pub. by Harcourt Coll Pubs) Harcourt.

— Ensemble: Litterature. 4th ed. (FRE.). 240p. (C). 1990. student ed. write for info. (*0-318-69153-1*); write for info. (*0-318-69155-8*); VHS. write for info. (*0-318-69154-X*) Harcourt Coll Pubs.

— Ensemble: Litterature. 5th ed. (FRE., Illus.). 280p. (C). 1993. pap. text 36.50 (*0-15-500660-6*, Pub. by Harcourt Coll Pubs) Harcourt.

Comeau, Raymond F. & Lamoureux, Normand J. Tout Ensemble. LC 95-38460. (ENG & FRE.). (C). 1996. pap. text 56.00 (*0-03-009598-0*) Holt R&W.

Comeau, Raymond F., et al. Ensemble: Histoire. (ENG & FRE.). 240p. (C). 1992. pap. text 36.50 (*0-03-020834-3*) Harcourt Coll Pubs.

Comeau, Rosalin U. Kamehameha V: Lot Kapuaiwa. (Kamehameha Schools Intermediate Reading Program Ser.). (Illus.). 127p. (Orig.). (J). (gr. 3-7). 1995. pap. 7.95 (*0-87336-039-7*) Kamehameha Schools.

— O Kamehameha V: Lot Kapuaiwa. Pau, Hana, ed. Wong, Ipo, tr. (HAW., Illus.). 127p. (Orig.). (YA). (gr. 7-12). 1996. pap. 7.95 (*0-87336-036-2*) Kamehameha Schools.

Comeaux, Dolores. Angelle & the Comet. 20p. 1994. 8.95 (*0-9642936-9-2*) Clothes For You.

Comeaux, Joya. Ave Maria: Angels Sing a Journey of Remembrance. LC 98-96424. (Illus.). 272p. 1998. per. 16.95 (*0-9666201-0-0*) Family of Light.

***Comeaux, Kimberley, et al.** The Heart of a Child. 352p. 2000. pap. 4.97 (*1-57748-646-3*) Barbour Pub.

Comeaux, Kimberly. One More Chance. 1987. mass mkt. 1.99 (*1-57748-427-4*) Barbour Pub.

Comeaux, Patricia. Workbook for Public Speaking. 2nd ed. 400p. (C). 1995. text. write for info. (*0-697-24656-6*) Brown & Benchmark.

Comeaux, Paul E. & Kinsella, N. Stephan. Digest of Commercial Laws of the World. LC 65-22163. 1998. ring bd. 295.00 (*0-379-01000-3*) Oceana.

— Protecting Foreign Investment under International Law: Legal Aspects of Political Risk. LC 96-41023. 448p. 1997. text 105.00 (*0-379-21371-0*) Oceana.

Comedy Central staff. Comedy Central's Web Sightings: A Collection of Web Sites We'd Like to See. LC 96-208606. 80p. 1996. per. 10.00 (*0-671-00299-6*) PB.

— Daily Show's Five Questions from Comedy Central. LC 97-48737. 1998. pap. text 9.95 (*0-8362-5325-6*) Andrews & McMeel.

***Comegys, Benjamin B., ed.** Ethics: An Early American Handbook. Orig. Title: A Primer of Ethics. 127p. (YA). (gr. 5 up). 1999. reprint ed. pap. 7.95 (*0-925279-72-2*, Pub. by Wallbuilders) Spring Arbor Dist.

Comegys, Cornelius. Summer Sojourn among the Inns of Court. (10) 131p. 1960. 35.00 (*0-89941-596-2*, 500280) W S Hein.

Comegys, Walker B. Antitrust Compliance Manual: A Guide for Counsel & Executives of Businesses & Professions. 2nd ed. 435p. 1993. 95.00 (*0-685-69380-5*, B1-1342) PLI.

Comel, M., ed. see Symposia Angiologica Santoriana Staff.

Comella, Frank R. Produce Facts: What Your Mother Maybe Didn't Tell You. LC 95-92209. 207p. 1995. spiral bd. 12.95 (*0-9646221-0-6*) Comella Pr.

Comella, M. Angels. Acuarelas/Watercolors, Spanish ed. LC 96-33015. (Creative Painting & Drawing Ser.). 1997. pap. text 10.00 (*0-382-39854-8*) Silver Burdett Pr.

— Creyones/Wax Crayons, Spanish ed. LC 96-32915. (Creative Painting & Drawing Ser.). 1997. pap. text 10.00 (*0-382-39855-6*) Silver Burdett Pr.

Comella, M. Angels. Poster Paints. LC 96-33018. (Painting & Drawing Ser.). (J). 1997. pap. 6.95 (*0-382-39849-1*, Silver Pr NJ); lib. bdg. 15.95 (*0-382-39850-5*, Silver Pr NJ) Silver Burdett Pr.

Comella, M. Angels. Temperas/Poster Paints, Spanish ed. LC 96-33106. (Creative Painting & Drawing Ser.). 1997. pap. text 10.00 (*0-382-39853-X*) Silver Burdett Pr.

Comella, M. Angels. Watercolors. LC 96-33017. (Painting & Drawing Ser.). (J). 1997. pap. 6.95 (*0-382-39847-5*, Silver Pr NJ); lib. bdg. 15.95 (*0-382-39852-1*, Silver Pr NJ) Silver Burdett Pr.

— Wax Crayons. LC 96-32334. (Painting & Drawing Ser.). (J). 1997. pap. 6.95 (*0-382-39848-3*, Silver Pr NJ); lib. bdg. 15.95 (*0-382-39851-3*, Silver Pr NJ) Silver Burdett Pr.

Comella, Patricia A., et al, eds. The Emotional Side of Organizations: Applications of Bowen Theory. (Illus.). 216p. (Orig.). 1996. pap. 28.00 (*0-9658540-1-9*) Georgetwn Fmly.

Comellini, Carla. D.H. Lawrence: A Study on Mutual & Cross References & Interferences. 156p. 1996. pap. 14.00 (*88-8091-159-7*) Paul & Co Pubs.

An Asterisk (*) at the beginning of an entry indicates that the title is appearing for the first time.

Comely, Peter & Meyer, Salome. Botswana. LC 94-80157. (Regional Guides of Africa Ser.). (Illus.). 192p. 1995. pap. text 19.95 (*0-8442-8960-4*, 89604, Passprt Bks) NTC Contemp Pub Co.

Comenius, Johann A. Ausgewahlte Werke Band I: Padagogik. Schaller, Klaus & Tschizewskij, Dmitrij, eds. (GER.). xviii, 322p. 1973. reprint ed. write for info. (*3-487-04779-9*) G Olms Pubs.

— Ausgewahlte Werke Band II: Biographisches, Trostschriften, Theologie und Predigtkunst, No. 1. Schaller, Klaus & Tschizewskij, Dmitrij, eds. (GER.). 1976. reprint ed. write for info. (*3-487-04780-2*) G Olms Pubs.

— Ausgewahlte Werke Band II: Biographisches, Trostschriften, Theologie und Predigtkunst, No. 2. Schaller, Klaus & Tschizewskij, Dmitrij, eds. (GER.). 1976. reprint ed. write for info. (*3-487-04781-0*) G Olms Pubs.

— Ausgewahlte Werke Band III: Das Programm der "Emendatio Rerum Humanarum" Schaller, Klaus & Tschizewskij, Dmitrij, eds. (GER., Illus.). xxviii, 404p. 1977. reprint ed. write for info. (*3-487-06353-0*) G Olms Pubs.

— Ausgewahlte Werke Band IV: Antisozinianische Schriften, No. 1. Schaller, Klaus et al, eds. (GER.). 1983. reprint ed. write for info. (*3-487-07410-9*) G Olms Pubs.

— Ausgewahlte Werke Band IV: Antisozinianische Schriften, No. 2. Schaller, Klaus et al, eds. (GER.). 1983. reprint ed. write for info. (*3-487-07411-7*) G Olms Pubs.

Comenius, John A. The Labyrinth of the World & the Paradise of the Heart. 170p. 1992. reprint ed. pap. 16.95 (*1-56459-293-6*) Kessinger Pub.

— Orbis Pictus (1887) 236p. 1999. reprint ed. pap. 24.95 (*0-7661-0825-2*) Kessinger Pub.

Comens, Bruce. Apocalypse & After: Modern Strategy & Postmodern Tactics in Pound, Williams, & Zukofsky. LC 94-5843. 232p. 1995. pap. text 24.95 (*0-8173-0732-X*) U of Ala Pr.

Comensoli, Viviana. Discontinuities: New Essays on Renaissance Literature & Criticism. LC 99-217362. 280p. 1998. text 65.00 (*0-8020-0436-9*); pap. text 21.95 (*0-8020-7225-9*) U of Toronto Pr.

Comensoli, Viviana. Household Business: Domestic Plays of Early Modern England. LC 97-130072. (Mental & Cultural World of Tudor & Stuart England Ser.). 238p. 1996. text 50.00 (*0-8020-0733-3*) U of Toronto Pr.

***Comensoli, Viviana.** Household Business: Domestic Plays of Early Modern England. 238p. 1999. pap. text 22.95 (*0-8020-8297-1*) U of Toronto Pr.

Comensoli, Viviana & Russell, Anne, eds. Enacting Gender on the English Renaissance Stage. LC 98-8991. 288p. 1998. text 49.95 (*0-252-02423-0*); text 19.95 (*0-252-06730-4*) U of Ill Pr.

***Comer.** Abnormal Psychology. 4th ed. 2000. pap. text. write for info. (*0-7167-3852-X*); pap. text, student ed. write for info. (*0-7167-3853-8*) Worth.

— Abnormal Psychology: Case Studies. 4th ed. 2000. pap. text. write for info. (*0-7167-3854-6*) Worth.

Comer. Abnormal Psychology Preview Sampler. pap. text. write for info. (*0-7167-2696-3*) W H Freeman.

— Digital Logic & State Machine Design. 3rd ed. (Illus.). 168p. 1995. suppl. ed. write for info. (*0-19-510410-2*) OUP.

— Fundamental of Abnormal Psychology. 2nd ed. 1998. pap. text 48.00 (*0-7167-3343-9*) W H Freeman.

— Fundamental of Abnormal Psychology. 2nd ed. 2000. pap. 24.00 (*0-7167-3341-2*) W H Freeman.

— Fundamental of Abnormal Psycology. 2000. wbk. ed. 47.40 (*0-7167-3060-X*) W H Freeman.

— Fundamentals of Abnormal Psychology. (C). Date not set. pap., teacher ed. 16.00 (*0-7167-2963-6*) W H Freeman.

— Fundamentals of Abnormal Psychology. 2nd ed. 1998. teacher ed. 24.00 (*0-7167-3345-5*); pap. text, student ed., wbk. ed. 19.95 (*0-7167-3348-X*) W H Freeman.

— Fundamentals of Abnormal Psychology. 2nd ed. 1998. 48.00 (*0-7167-3342-0*) W H Freeman.

***Comer.** Fundamentals of Abnormal Psychology. 2nd ed. 1999. pap. text. write for info. (*0-7167-3722-1*) Worth.

— Fundamentals of Abnormal Psychology. 3rd ed. 2002. pap. text, student ed. write for info. (*0-7167-5117-8*) W H Freeman.

Comer. IBM Test Bank Abnormal Psychology. 2nd ed. (C). 1995. 12.80 (*0-7167-2692-0*) W H Freeman.

— Mac Test Bank Abnormal Psychology. 2nd ed. 1995. 48.00 (*0-7167-2693-9*) W H Freeman.

Comer, jt. auth. see Sawyer.

Comer, Brooke. The Secret Caribbean: Affordable Hideaways of the Rich & Famous. (Illus.). 360p. 1998. pap. 16.95 (*1-55650-851-4*) Hunter NJ.

Comer, Cornelia A. Book of Martyrs. LC 77-94711. (Short Story Index Reprint Ser.). 1977. 18.95 (*0-8369-3090-8*) Ayer.

— Preliminaries, & Other Stories. LC 78-128726. (Short Story Index Reprint Ser.). 1977. 17.95 (*0-8369-3617-5*) Ayer.

Comer, David J. Digital Logic & State Machine Design. 2nd ed. 514p. (C). 1990. write for info. (*0-03-031039-3*) SCP.

— Digital Logic & State Machine Design. 3rd ed. (Oxford Series in Electrical & Computer Engineering). (Illus.). 592p. 1994. text 84.95 (*0-19-510723-3*) OUP.

— Electronic Design & Integration: A Solution Manual. LC 80-23365. (Electrical Engineering Ser.). (Illus.). 416p. (C). 1981. pap. text, teacher ed. 1.25 (*0-201-03932-X*) Addison-Wesley.

— Microprocessor-Based System Design. (Oxford Series in Electrical & Computer Engineering). (Illus.). 400p. (C). 1995. text 79.95 (*0-03-063781-3*) OUP.

— Microprocessor-Based System Design. 390p. (C). 1986. student ed. write for info. (*0-03-063782-1*) SCP.

Comer, David J., jt. auth. see Miner, Gayle F.

Comer, Diana E. Developing Safety Skills with the Young Child. LC 86-11438. 192p. (C). 1987. teacher ed. 10.00 (*0-8273-2669-6*); pap. 20.25 (*0-8273-2668-8*) Delmar.

Comer, Diana E. & Sawyer, Walter E. Growing up with Literature. 1991. teacher ed. 10.50 (*0-8273-3441-9*); pap. 26.50 (*0-8273-3440-0*) Delmar.

Comer, Diana E., jt. auth. see Sawyer, Walter E.

Comer, Donald T. Introduction to Mixed Signal VLSI. 480p. (C). 1994. 65.00 (*0-9638049-0-1*) Array Pubng.

— Mixed Signal VLSI: A Management Overview. (C). 1994. pap. text 19.99 (*0-9638049-1-X*) Array Pubng.

Comer, Douglas. Computer Networks & Internets. 2nd ed. LC 98-47110. 590p. 1998. pap. 82.00 (*0-13-083617-6*) P-H.

***Comer, Douglas.** Internetworking with TCP/IP, Vol. I. 4th ed. LC 00-27439. Vol. 1. 755p. 2000. 67.00 (*0-13-018380-6*) P-H.

Comer, Douglas C. Ritual Ground: Bent's Old Fort, World Formation, & the Annexation of the Southwest. (Illus.). 328p. 1996. 45.00 (*0-520-20429-8*, Pub. by U CA Pr); pap. 17.95 (*0-520-20774-2*, Pub. by U CA Pr) Cal Prin Full Svc.

Comer, Douglas E. Design, Implementation, & Internals: ANSI C Version, Vol. 2. 3rd ed. LC 90-7829. (Internetworking with TCP/IP Ser.: Vol. 2). (Illus.). 660p. 1998. 68.00 (*0-13-973843-6*) P-H.

— The Internet Book. 2nd ed. LC 97-8261. 350p. (C). 1997. pap. 32.20 (*0-13-890161-9*, Pub. by P-H) S&S Trade.

***Comer, Douglas E.** The Internet Book: Everything You Need to Know about Computer Networking & How the Internet Works. 3rd ed. 351p. 2000. pap. 32.00 (*0-13-030852-8*, Prentice Hall) P-H.

Comer, Douglas E. Internetworking with TCP/IP: Principles, Protocols, & Architecture, Vol. 1. 3rd ed. LC 95-1830. (C). 1999. text 65.00 (*0-13-216987-8*) P-H.

Comer, Douglas E. Operating System Design: The Xinu Approach. (Software Ser.). (Illus.). 496p. (C). 1983. 61.00 (*0-13-637539-1*) P-H.

Comer, Douglas E. Operating System Design: The Xinu Design, Vol. 1. LC 88-2543. 528p. 1988. 55.60 (*0-13-638180-4*) P-H.

Comer, Douglas E. Operating System Design-Internetworking with XINU, Vol. II. (Illus.). 640p. 1987. 57.00 (*0-13-637414-X*) P-H.

Comer, Douglas E. & Stevens, David. Internetworking for Windows Sockets Vol. 3: Client/Server Programming & Applications for the Windows Socket, Vol. 3. LC 97-16393. Vol. 3. 512p. 1997. 64.00 (*0-13-848714-6*) P-H.

Comer, Douglas E. & Stevens, David L. Internetworking with TCP/IP Vol. 3: Client/Server Programming & Applications for . . ., Vol. 3. 2nd ed. LC 96-207037. Vol. 3. 552p. 1996. 68.00 (*0-13-260969-X*) P-H.

Comer, Fred R. Coming of Age: Teachers in Iowa 1954 to 1993. LC 93-78742. (Illus.). 240p. (YA). 1993. 20.00 (*0-9637413-0-6*) Iowa St Educ.

Comer, George. An Arctic Whaling Diary: The Journal of Captain George Comer in Hudson Bay, 1903-1905. Ross, W. Gillies, ed. LC 84-217794. (Illus.). 303p. reprint ed. pap. 94.00 (*0-8357-3649-0*, 203637700003) Bks Demand.

Comer, James. Father Figures. 65p. (Orig.). (J). (gr. 5-12). 1996. pap. 6.95 (*0-9650690-1-X*) Lyndel Publns.

Comer, James E. Katie of Oak Point. 142p. (YA). (gr. 5-12). 1998. pap. 11.00 (*0-9650690-2-8*) Lyndel Publns.

— My Picture of Jenny. 123p. (Orig.). (J). (gr. 7-12). 1997. pap. 10.00 (*0-9650690-3-6*) Lyndel Publns.

— The Rare Editions. 134p. (YA). (gr. 5-12). 1998. pap. 11.00 (*0-9650690-4-4*) Lyndel Publns.

Comer, James M. Sales Management: People & Profit. 750p. 1991. text. write for info. incl. disk (*0-318-68010-6*, H25976); boxed set. write for info. (*0-318-68009-2*, H25968); disk 54.00 (*0-685-47330-9*, H25984) P-H.

Comer, James P. Child by Child: The Comer Process for Change in Education. LC 99-21584. 1999. pap. 19.95 (*0-8077-3868-9*) Tchrs Coll.

— Maggie's American Dream: The Life & Times of a Black Family. (Illus.). 352p. 1989. pap. 13.95 (*0-452-26318-2*, Dutt) Dutton Plume.

— Rallying the Whole Village: The Comer Process for Reforming Education. Haynes, Norris et al, eds. LC 96-2130. 208p. (C). 1996. pap. 21.95 (*0-8077-3539-6*) Tchrs Coll.

— School Power: Implications of an Intervention Project. 336p. 1995. pap. 17.95 (*0-02-874053-X*) Free Pr.

— Waiting for a Miracle: Why Schools Can't Solve Our Problems & How We Can. 272p. (C). 1999. pap. 13.95 (*0-452-27646-2*) Dutton Plume.

Comer, James P. & Poussaint, Alvin F. Raising Black Children: Questions & Answers for Parents & Teachers. LC 92-53563. 400p. (Orig.). 1992. pap. 14.95 (*0-452-26839-7*, Plume) Dutton Plume.

***Comer, James P., et al.** Child by Child: The Comer Process for Change in Education. 336p. 1999. text 44.00 (*0-8077-3869-7*) Tchrs Coll.

Comer, James P., et al. Rallying the Whole Village: The Comer Process for Reforming Education. Haynes, Norris et al, eds. LC 96-2130. 208p. (C). 1996. text 45.00 (*0-8077-3540-X*) Tchrs Coll.

Comer, James P., jt. auth. see Schorr, Alvin L.

***Comer, James Ray.** Mokole. (Werewolf Ser.). (Illus.). 144p. 1999. pap. 19.95 (*1-56504-306-5*, 3081) White Wolf.

Comer, Jeanette. Poems by Bonnie Paques, the Poet Pooch. LC 91-78093. (Illus.). 1993. 8.95 (*0-8158-0482-2*) Chris Mass.

Comer, John, jt. auth. see Welch, Susan.

Comer, John, ed. see Petralia, Joseph F.

Comer, Krista. Landscapes of the New West: Gender & Geography in Contemporary Women's Writing. LC 98-47516. (Cultural Studies of the United States). 288p. 1999. pap. 18.95 (*0-8078-4813-1*); lib. bdg. 45.00 (*0-8078-2485-2*) U of NC Pr.

Comer, Lauren. Between the Lines. unabridged ed. Grommett, Gary & Normile, Christine, eds. LC 97-72273. 80p. (Orig.). 1997. pap. 12.95 (*0-9657925-0-1*) Art Review.

Comer, Michael J. Corporate Fraud. 2nd ed. LC 85-11686. 416p. 1985. 31.95 (*0-07-084791-6*) McGraw.

— Corporate Fraud. 3rd ed. LC 96-41787. 400p. 1997. text 113.95 (*0-566-07810-4*, Pub. by Gower) Ashgate Pub Co.

Comer, Michael J., et al. Bad Lies in Business: The Commonsense Guide to Detecting Deceit in Negotiations, Interviews & Investigations. 256p. 1988. text 26.95 (*0-07-707073-9*) McGraw.

Comer, Michael J., jt. auth. see Ardis, Patrick M.

Comer, O. B. Chile & Co. Mrs. Fable's Ghost & the Kidnappers. LC 97-81255. 105p. (J). (gr. 4-6). 1998. pap. 4.95 (*0-9662064-9-5*) Paige Publ.

— Chile & Company: The Mysterious Bank Robbers. LC 99-90337. (Mysterious Bank Robbers Ser.: Vol. 2). 117p. (J). 1999. pap. 4.95 (*0-9662064-8-7*) Paige Publ.

Comer, Patrick. Consumer's Survival Guide - Florida Edition. LC 94-41814. (Orig.). 1995. pap. 12.95 (*1-56164-067-0*) Pineapple Pr.

Comer, Ronald. Computerized Testbank Abnormal Psychology Version B. (C). 1993. 48.00 (*0-7167-2454-5*) W H Freeman.

— Mac Computerized Testbank Abnormal Psychology Version B. (C). 1993. 48.00 (*0-7167-2455-3*) W H Freeman.

— Printed Testbank Abnormal Psychology Version B. (C). 1992. 16.80 (*0-7167-2453-7*) W H Freeman.

Comer, Ronald J. Abnormal Psychology. (C). 1992. text 46.40 (*0-7167-2057-4*); pap. text, teacher ed. 16.00 (*0-7167-2299-2*) W H Freeman.

— Abnormal Psychology. (C). 1992. pap. text, student ed. 14.40 (*0-7167-2298-4*) W H Freeman.

— Abnormal Psychology. 2nd ed. 816p. (C). 1994. text. write for info. (*0-7167-2494-4*) McGraw.

— Abnormal Psychology. 2nd ed. 1995. pap. text 16.00 (*0-7167-2690-4*) W H Freeman.

— Abnormal Psychology. 3rd ed. LC 97-25100. 896p. 1997. pap. text 77.95 (*0-7167-3089-8*) W H Freeman.

— Abnormal Psychology. 3rd ed. 1997. pap. text, student ed. 22.95 (*0-7167-3205-X*) W H Freeman.

— Abnormal Psychology. 3rd ed. 1998. student ed. 68.60 (*0-7167-3322-6*) W H Freeman.

— Abnormal Psychology, Vol. 1. 3rd ed. 1997. teacher ed. 24.00 (*0-7167-3202-5*) W H Freeman.

***Comer, Ronald J.** Fundamentals of Abnormal Psychology 2nd ed. LC 98-55694. 1999. write for info. (*0-7167-3314-5*) Worth.

Comer, S. D., ed. Universal Algebra & Lattice Theory. (Lecture Notes in Mathematics Ser.: Vol. 1149). vi, 282p. 1985. pap. 38.40 (*0-387-15691-7*) Spr-Verlag.

Comer, Sheree. Critical Care Nursing Care Plans. 420p. (C). 1998. per. 39.95 (*1-56930-035-6*) Skidmore Roth Pub.

Comer, Sheree R. The I. C. U. Quick Reference. 2nd rev. ed. 435p. (C). 1998. per. 42.95 (*1-56930-071-2*) Skidmore Roth Pub.

Comer, Suzanne, ed. Common Bonds: Stories by & about Modern Texas Women. LC 88-43251. (Southwest Life & Letters Ser.). 320p. 1990. pap. 10.95 (*0-87074-288-4*); text 22.50 (*0-87074-287-6*) SMU Press.

Comer, Virginia L. Angels Flight: A History of Bunker Hill's Incline Railway. LC 96-77452. 158p. (Orig.). (C). 1996. pap. 17.50 (*0-914421-18-2*) Hist Soc So CA.

***Comer, Virginia L.** Fountains. LC 00-131711. (Urban Details Los Angeles Ser.: Vol. 3). (Illus.). 64p. 2000. 14.95 (*1-890449-11-3*, Pub. by Balcony Pr) Princeton Arch.

Comer, Virginia L. In Victorian Los Angeles, Witmers of Crown Hill. 107p. (C). 1988. 24.95 (*0-9617800-2-9*); pap. 15.95 (*0-9617800-3-7*) Talbot Pr.

— Los Angeles, a View from Crown Hill. LC 86-51391. (Illus.). 107p. (C). 1986. 24.95 (*0-9617800-0-2*); pap. 15.95 (*0-9617800-1-0*) Talbot Pr.

***Comer, Virginia L.** Stairways. LC 00-131709. (Urban Details Los Angeles Ser.: Vol. 2). (Illus.). 64p. 2000. 14.95 (*1-890449-09-1*, Pub. by Balcony Pr) Princeton Arch.

— Streetlights. LC 00-131708. (Urban Details Los Angeles Ser.: Vol. 1). (Illus.). 64p. 2000. 14.95 (*1-890449-10-5*, Pub. by Balcony Pr) Princeton Arch.

Comer, William L., et al. Freedom, Asset Protection & You: The Complete Encyclopedia of Asset Protection & Estate Preservation. 460p. 1992. per. 69.95 (*0-942360-01-X*) Finan Freedom.

Comerchero, Victor, ed. Values in Conflict: Christianity, Marxism, Psychoanalysis & Existentialism. LC 74-111099. 986p. (Orig.). (C). 1970. pap. text 22.95 (*0-89197-463-6*) Irvington.

Comerford, Anthony, compiled by. The Easter Rising: Dublin, 1916. 39.00 (*1-56696-076-2*) Jackdaw.

Comerford, Dan, jt. auth. see Baird, Ron.

Comerford, Kieran A. How to Find & License New Products. (Illus.). 100p. 1990. text 56.95 (*0-566-02848-4*, Pub. by Gower) Ashgate Pub Co.

Comerford, Patrick. Desmond Tutu: Black Africa's Man of Destiny. 1989. pap. 25.00 (*1-85390-005-2*, Pub. by Veritas Pubns) St Mut.

Comerford, R. V. The Fenians in Context: Irish Politics & Society 1848-82. (Illus.). 272p. 1998. pap. 24.95 (*0-86327-627-X*, Pub. by Wolfhound Press) Irish Amer Bk.

Comerford, Robert A. Marina & Boatyard Industry Financial Performance. (Illus.). 66p. (Orig.). 1988. pap. 20.00 (*0-929803-01-9*) Intl Marina Inst.

Comerio, Mary C. Disaster Hits Home: New Policy for Urban Housing Recovery. LC 98-6245. (Illus.). 326p. 1998. 39.95 (*0-520-20780-7*, Pub. by U CA Pr) Cal Prin Full Svc.

Comerota, Anthony J., ed. Thrombolytic Therapy in Vascular Disease. (Illus.). 400p. 1994. text 89.50 (*0-397-51343-7*) Lppncott W & W.

Comerota, Anthony J., jt. ed. see Katz, Mira L.

Comes, James H., III, jt. auth. see White, Joseph L.

Comes, Juan Baptista, Juan Bautista Comes Pt. 1: Masses for One or Two Choirs, 2 vols. Olson, Greta J., ed. (Recent Researches in Music of the Baroque Era Ser.: Vol. RRB95). (Illus.). 1999. pap. 70.00 (*0-89579-427-6*) A-R Eds.

— Juan Bautista Comes Pt. 2: Masses for Three Choirs, 2 vols. Olson, Greta J., ed. (Illus.). 1999. pap. 75.00 (*0-89579-428-4*) A-R Eds.

Comes, Lisa. Overcoming Opposition: How to Succeed in Doing the Will of God. 28p. 1990. mass mkt. 1.50 (*0-912631-40-6*) J O Pubns.

— Seis Mentiras que Usa el Diablo para Destruir Matrimonios.Tr. of Six Lies the Devil Uses to Destroy Marriages. (SPA.). 48p. 1988. mass mkt. 2.00 (*0-912631-68-6*) J O Pubns.

— Venciendo la Oposicion: Como Triunfar para Hacer la Voluntad de Dios.Tr. of Overcoming Opposition: How to Succeed in Doing the Will of God. (SPA.). 32p. 1990. mass mkt. 1.50 (*0-912631-43-0*) J O Pubns.

Comesky, Robert. The Quality Professor: Implementing TQM in the Classroom. 209p. 1993. pap. text 22.95 (*1-891859-15-3*) Atwood Pub LLC.

Comesky, Robert, et al. Implementing Total Quality Management in Higher Education. 133p. 1992. pap. text 31.95 (*1-891859-14-5*) Atwood Pub LLC.

Comet, Renee, jt. auth. see Cherkasky, Lisa.

Cometti, Elizabeth, ed. see Dal Verme, Francesco.

Comex Systems Editorial Staff. Review for the SAT & PSAT. 1997. pap. text, student ed. 15.95 (*1-56030-118-X*) Comex Systs.

Comey, Arthur C. Transition Zoning. LC 73-2903. (Metropolitan America Ser.). (Illus.). 184p. 1974. reprint ed. 12.95 (*0-405-05392-4*) Ayer.

Comey, David, ed. & tr. see Zinoviev, A. A., et al.

Comey, Dennis J. The Waterfront Peacemaker. LC 82-60025. 202p. 1983. pap. 5.95 (*0-916101-03-7*) St Joseph.

Comford, Charles F., frwd. The Controversial Century: 1850 to 1950: Paintings from the Collection of Walter P. Chrysler, Jr. (Illus.). 200p. 1962. pap. 10.00 (*0-940744-02-3*) Chrysler Museum.

Comfort, jt. auth. see Terrass, Joyce J.

Comfort, A., et al. Aging in Cold Blooded Animals, Vol. 2. 236p. 1974. text 24.50 (*0-8422-7209-7*) Irvington.

Comfort, Alex. Barbarism & Sexual Freedom. LC 76-30586. (Anarchy & Anarchism Ser.: No. 99). 1977. lib. bdg. 75.00 (*0-8383-2147-X*) M S G Haskell Hse.

Comfort, Alex. Guia Ilustrada del Amor. 1997. pap. text 14.98 (*970-05-0777-7*) Grijalbo Edit.

Comfort, Alex. More Joy of Sex. rev. ed. 1991. pap. 20.00 (*0-671-74076-8*) PB.

— The New Joy of Sex: A Gourmet Guide to Lovemaking for the Nineties. rev. ed. Rubenstein, Julie, ed. 256p. 1992. per. 20.00 (*0-671-77859-5*) PB.

— The New Joy of Sex: The Gourmet Guide to Lovemaking in the '90s. (Illus.). 256p. 1991. 32.00 (*0-517-58583-9*, Crown) Crown Pub Group.

— The New Joy of Sex - Compact Edition: A Gourmet Guide to Lovemaking in the Nineties. LC 94-9658. (Illus.). 224p. 1994. 12.00 (*0-517-59910-4*) Crown Pub Group.

— The New Joy of Sex - More Joy of Sex. 1994. pap. text 38.00 (*0-671-90619-4*) PB.

***Comfort, Alex.** Prepack 2 Joy of Sex Box Set 98: A Gourmet Guide to Lovemaking for the Nineties. 1998. per., boxed set 40.00 (*0-671-71782-0*) PB.

Comfort, Alex. Reality & Empathy: Physics, Mind, & Science in the 21st Century. LC 83-9318. 272p. (C). 1984. text 64.50 (*0-87395-762-8*); pap. text 21.95 (*0-87395-763-6*) State U NY Pr.

— Sexual Foreplay. LC 96-39786. 1997. 12.00 (*0-609-60032-X*) Random Hse Value.

— Sexual Positions. LC 96-48057. 1997. 12.00 (*0-609-60033-8*) Random Hse Value.

Comfort, Alex, tr. see Fowkes, Charles, ed.

Comfort, Barbara. The Cashmere Kid. (Tish McWhinny Mystery Ser.). 224p. 1994. pap. 6.95 (*0-88150-321-5*, Foul Play) Norton.

— Elusive Quarry. LC 94-47238. (Tish McWhinny Mystery Ser.). 224p. 1995. 19.00 (*0-88150-332-0*, Foul Play) Norton.

— Elusive Quarry. (Tish McWhinny Mystery Ser.). 224p. 1996. pap. 7.50 (*0-88150-370-3*, Foul Play) Norton.

— Grave Consequences. (Vermont Village Murders Ser.). 233p. (Orig.). 1989. pap. 5.95 (*0-9608726-4-7*) Norton.

— A Pair for the Queen. LC 97-34473. (Tish McWhinny Mystery Ser.: Vol. 5). 192p. 1998. 22.00 (*0-393-04627-3*) Norton.

— A Pair for the Queen. 1999. pap. 7.95 (*0-393-31913-X*) Norton.

***Comfort, Barbara.** A Pair for the Queen. large type ed. LC 99-50319. 335p. 1999. 26.95 (*0-7862-2297-2*) Thorndike Pr.

Comfort, Barbara. Phoebe's Knee. 220p. (Orig.). 1986. pap. 3.95 (*0-9608726-3-9*) Norton.

— Phoebe's Knee. LC 94-171443. (Tish McWhinny Mystery Ser.). 224p. (Orig.). 1994. pap. 7.95 (*0-88150-295-2*, Foul Play) Norton.

Comfort, Bonnie. Denial. 384p. 1996. mass mkt. 5.99 (*0-380-72716-1*, Avon Bks) Morrow Avon.

C

Comfort, Carol. Breaking Boundaries. LC 98-47828. 348p. 1999. pap. text 32.40 (*0-13-081350-8*) P-H.

Comfort, Carol, jt. ed. see Dunn, Carolyn.

Comfort, Claudette H. The Newbery & Caldecott Books in the Classroom. 160p. (J). (gr. 1-4). 1991. pap. text 12.95 (*0-86530-178-6*, IP 194-0) Incentive Pubns.

Comfort, David. The First Pet History of the World. LC 94-1219. 320p. 1994. pap. 10.95 (*0-671-89102-2*) S&S Trade.

— For Dogs Only. 1994. pap. write for info. (*0-9639602-0-2*) Freckles Fantasies.

Comfort, Iris T. Florida's Geological Treasures. LC 98-71261. (Illus.). 136p. 1998. pap. 11.95 (*0-935182-95-0*) Gem Guides Bk.

Comfort, J. M., et al. Business Reports in English. (Illus.). 96p. 1985. pap. text 15.95 (*0-521-27294-7*) Cambridge U Pr.

Comfort, Jeremy. Effective Meetings. (Illus.). 48p. 1996. pap. text, teacher ed. 7.50 (*0-19-457091-6*) OUP.

— Effective Meetings. (Illus.). 88p. 1996. pap. text, student ed. 13.95 (*0-19-457090-8*) OUP.

— Effective Telephoning. 56p. 1996. pap. text, teacher ed. 7.50 (*0-19-457094-0*) OUP.

— Effective Telephoning. (Illus.). 110p. 1996. pap. text, student ed. 13.95 (*0-19-457093-2*) OUP.

— Oxford Business English Skills: Effective Presentations. (Illus.). 48p. 1996. pap. text, teacher ed. 7.50 (*0-19-457089-4*) OUP.

Comfort, Jeremy & Utley, Derek. Effective Presentations. (Illus.). 80p. 1996. pap. text, student ed. 13.95 (*0-19-457065-7*) OUP.

— Effective Socializing. 48p. 1997. pap. text, teacher ed. 7.50 (*0-19-457097-5*) OUP.

— Effective Socializing. (Illus.). 88p. 1997. pap. text, student ed. 13.95 (*0-19-457096-7*) OUP.

Comfort, Jeremy, et al. Basic Technical English. (Illus.). 1983. pap. text, teacher ed. 9.75 (*0-19-457383-4*); pap. text, student ed. 10.75 (*0-19-457382-6*) OUP.

Comfort, Joseph R., et al, eds. Hadronic Probes & Nuclear Interactions, (Arizona State University, 1985) LC 85-72638. (AIP Conference Proceedings Ser.: No. 133). 432p. 1985. lib. bdg. 47.25 (*0-88318-332-3*) Am Inst Physics.

Comfort, Judith. Country Roads of the Maritimes. LC 93-44946. (Country Roads of... Ser.). (Illus.). 144p. (Orig.). 1994. pap. 9.95 (*1-56626-054-X*, 6054X, Cntry Rds Pr) NTC Contemp Pub Co.

Comfort, Judith. Writing Cookbooks. (Writing Ser.). 184p. (Orig.). 1997. pap. 15.95 (*1-55180-115-9*) Self-Counsel Pr.

***Comfort, Kenneth J.** The Ego & the Social Order. 360p. 1999. 29.95 (*0-9659144-1-0*) PAINYS.

Comfort, Kenneth J. Power, Politics & the Ego. LC 99-164645. v, 485p. 1997. 29.95 (*0-9659144-0-2*) PAINYS.

***Comfort, Louise K.** Shared Risk: Complex Systems in Seismic Response. LC 99-29391. 322p. 1999. 98.50 (*0-08-043211-5*, Pergamon Pr) Elsevier.

Comfort, Louise K., ed. Managing Disaster: Strategies & Policy Perspectives. LC 87-20049. (Illus.). xii, 420p. (C). 1988. text 69.95 (*0-8223-0800-2*) Duke.

— Managing Disaster: Strategies & Policy Perspectives. LC 87-20049. (Illus.). xii, 420p. (C). 1988. pap. text 29.95 (*0-8223-0816-9*) Duke.

Comfort, Mary, et al, eds. California Artichoke Cookbook: From the California Artichoke Advisory Board. LC 97-44106. 96p. 1998. pap. 4.95 (*0-89087-855-2*) Celestial Arts.

Comfort, Max, jt. auth. see Phillips, Maya.

Comfort, N. Lost City of Dunwich. 1994. 50.00 (*0-86138-086-X*, Pub. by T Dalton) St Mut.

Comfort, N. A. Mid-Suffolk Light Railway. 120p. (C). 1985. 60.00 (*0-85361-338-9*) St Mut.

Comfort, Phil. The One Year Book of Poetry. LC 99-38774. 1999. 19.99 (*0-8423-3712-1*) Tyndale Hse.

***Comfort, Phil.** The One Year Book of Poetry. LC 99-38774. 700p. 1999. pap. text 14.99 (*0-8423-3711-3*) Tyndale Hse.

Comfort, Phil. The Origin of the Bible. 320p. 1992. 15.99 (*0-8423-4735-6*) Tyndale Hse.

Comfort, Philip. Complete Guide to Bible Versions. LC 96-214248. 176p. 1996. mass mkt. 4.99 (*0-8423-1252-8*) Tyndale Hse.

***Comfort, Philip W.** The Essential Guide to Bible Versions. expanded ed. LC 00-37787. 2000. pap. 10.99 (*0-8423-3484-X*) Tyndale Hse.

Comfort, Philip W. & Barrett, David P. Quik Notes on the Books of the New Testament. LC 95-40490. 1999. pap. 6.99 (*0-8423-5984-2*) Tyndale Hse.

Comfort, Philip W., et al. Quik Notes on Christian Classics. LC 95-40488. 1999. pap. 6.99 (*0-8423-5986-9*) Tyndale Hse.

— Quik Notes on the Books of the Bible. LC 95-40489. 1999. pap. 6.99 (*0-8423-5985-0*) Tyndale Hse.

Comfort, Philip W., tr. see Douglas, J. D., ed.

***Comfort, Philip Wesley.** English Bible Versions. LC 99-51621. (Quiknotes Ser.). 2000. pap. 6.99 (*0-8423-3554-4*) Tyndale Hse.

— The Origin of the Bible. LC 99-51648. (Quiknotes Ser.). 2000. pap. 6.99 (*0-8423-3555-2*) Tyndale Hse.

Comfort, R. Lo Que el Diablo No Quiere Que Sepas.Tr. of Hell's Best Kept Secret. (SPA.). 224p. 1993. pap. 6.99 (*0-8297-0307-1*) Vida Pubs.

Comfort, Randall. History of Bronx Borough, City of New York. (Illus.). 422p. 1997. reprint ed. lib. bdg. 46.50 (*0-8328-7143-5*) Higginson Bk Co.

Comfort, Ray. Bride of Heaven, Pride of Hell. 1997. mass mkt. 6.99 (*0-88270-733-7*) Bridge-Logos.

— God Doesn't Believe in Atheists. LC 93-72222. 270p. 1993. mass mkt. 5.99 (*0-88270-677-2*) Bridge-Logos.

— God Doesn't Believe in Atheists: Proof the Atheist Doesn't Exist. 208p. (Orig.). (C). 1990. 6.00 (*1-878859-01-3*) Living Wat CA.

— Hell's Best Kept Secret. 191p. 1989. mass mkt. 5.99 (*0-88368-206-0*) Whitaker Hse.

***Comfort, Ray.** How to Win Souls & Influence People. LC 99-67198. 1999. pap. 10.99 (*0-88270-788-4*) Bridge-Logos.

Comfort, Ray. Key to Heaven. 190p. 1997. mass mkt. 5.99 (*0-88368-477-2*) Whitaker Hse.

— My Friends Are Dying! 224p. 1991. write for info. (*1-878859-32-3*) Living Wat CA.

— My Friends Are Dying! The Seductive Voice of Cocaine Whispers to the Simple, "Give Me Your Hand...& I Will Take Your Life!" 8th ed. Living Waters Pubns. Staff, ed. (Illus.). 210p. 1991. reprint ed. pap. write for info. (*1-878859-07-2*) Living Wat CA.

— 101 Things Children Can Do to Annoy Their Parents. LC 98-73143. (Illus.). 184p. 1998. pap. 7.99 (*0-88270-759-0*, Bridge) Bridge-Logos.

— 101 Things Husbands Do to Annoy Their Wives. (Illus.). 260p. 1998. pap. 5.00 (*1-878859-20-X*) Living Wat CA.

— The Secrets of Nostradamus Exposed: Undisclosed Secrets of the World's Greatest Prophet. (Illus.). 198p. (Orig.). 1996. pap. 5.95 (*1-878859-18-8*) Living Wat CA.

— You've Got to Be Choking & General Trivia. (Illus.). 80p. (Orig.). 1990. pap. write for info. (*1-878859-00-5*) Living Wat CA.

Comfort, W. W. & Negrepontis, S. Continuous Pseudometrics. (Lecture Notes in Pure & Applied Mathematics Ser.: Vol. 14). (Illus.). 136p. 1975. pap. text 110.00 (*0-8247-6294-0*) Dekker.

— The Theory of Ultra Filters. (Grundlehren der Mathematischen Wissenschaften Ser.: Vol. 211). 480p. 1974. 98.00 (*0-387-06604-7*) Spr-Verlag.

Comfort, Will L. Apache. 1976. reprint ed. lib. bdg. 23.95 (*0-89190-851-X*, Rivercity Pr) Amereon Ltd.

— Apache. LC 85-29021. 274p. 1986. reprint ed. pap. 11.95 (*0-8032-6319-8*, Bison Books) U of Nebr Pr.

— Routledge Rides Alone. 1976. reprint ed. lib. bdg. 24.95 (*0-89190-852-8*, Rivercity Pr) Amereon Ltd.

— Trooper Tales. LC 70-106271. (Short Story Index Reprint Ser.). 1977. 20.95 (*0-8369-3308-7*) Ayer.

— Trooper Tales. 1976. reprint ed. lib. bdg. 22.95 (*0-89190-853-6*, Rivercity Pr) Amereon Ltd.

Comfort, William W. William Penn & Our Liberties. (Illus.). 146p. (C). 1976. reprint ed. pap. 5.00 (*0-941308-02-2*) Phila Yrly Mtg RSOF.

Comforti, Pat & Carrie, Doreen. Health Beyond Belief: Breaking the Beliefs That Have Blocked Our Birthright for Radiant Health. LC 95-62012. 278p. (Orig.). 1997. pap. 14.95 (*0-9650464-0-0*) Life Zones.

Comhaire-Sylvain, Suzanne. Les Contes Haitiens, 2 vols. in 1. LC 78-67701. (Folktale Ser.). reprint ed. 33.50 (*0-404-16074-3*) AMS Pr.

***Comhlan Dannsa nan Eileanach.** Hebridgean Dances: Dannsa Nan Eileanach. 120p. 1999. pap. 52.00 (*0-86152-913-8*, Pub. by Acair Ltd) St Mut.

Comi, G., jt. auth. see International Congress of Electroencephalography & Clinical Neurophysiology Staff.

Comibam. Manual de Intercesion Misionera.Tr. of Manual for Missionary Intercession. (SPA.). 101p. 1986. pap. 3.99 (*1-56063-398-0*, 498548) Editorial Unilit.

Comic Staff. Archangels: The Saga, 10, No. 6. 1997. pap. 25.00 (*1-887814-08-6*) Eternal Stud.

Comics Buyers Guide Staff. Comics Buyer's Guide 1997 Annual. 6th ed. 104p. 1996. pap. 9.95 (*0-87341-473-X*) Krause Pubns.

Comics, D.C. Superman Action Comics: Archives, Vol. 1. (Illus.). 240p. 1998. 49.95 (*1-56389-335-5*, Pub. by DC Comics) Time Warner.

Comigan, ed. see Sewell.

Comin, F. A. & Northcote, T. G., eds. Saline Lakes. (Developments in Hydrobiology Ser.). (C). 1990. text 285.00 (*0-7923-0767-4*) Kluwer Academic.

Comin, Paula Ripple. Mixed Blessings. LC 98-37485. 160p. 1999. pap. 9.95 (*0-87793-666-8*) Ave Maria.

Comines, Philippe de. History of Comines, 2 vols. Danett, Thomas, tr. (Tudor Translations, First Ser.: Nos. 17-18). reprint ed. 115.00 (*0-404-51890-7*) AMS Pr.

Comings, David E. The Gene Bomb: Does Higher Education & Advanced Technology Accelerate the Selection of Genes for Learning Disorders, ADHD, Addictive & Disruptive Behaviors. LC 96-8110. 300p. 1996. 29.95 (*1-878267-38-8*); pap. 25.95 (*1-878267-39-6*) Hope Pr CA.

— Search for the Tourette Syndrome & Human Behavior Genes. 1996. 34.00 (*1-878267-36-1*); pap. 29.95 (*1-878267-41-8*) Hope Pr CA.

— Tourette Syndrome & Human Behavior. LC 89-83294. 828p. 1990. pap. 39.95 (*1-878267-28-0*) Hope Pr CA.

Comings, John. Participatory Communication in Nonformal Education. (Technical Notes Ser.: No. 17). 15p. (Orig.). 1981. pap. 2.00 (*0-932288-62-6*) Ctr Intl Ed U of MA.

Comings, John, jt. auth. see Cain, Bonnie.

Comini, Alessandra. Egon Schiele. LC 75-37328. 128p. 1976. pap. 19.95 (*0-8076-0820-3*, Pub. by Braziller) Norton.

— Egon Schiele's Portraits: With a New Preface. 463p. 1990. pap. 29.95 (*0-520-06869-6*, Pub. by U CA Pr) Cal Prin Full Svc.

— Nudes: Egon Schiele. LC 95-166232. (Illus.). 64p. 1995. 15.00 (*0-8478-1841-1*, Pub. by Rizzoli Intl) St Martin.

Comini, Alessandra, intro. National Museum of Women in the Arts. (Illus.). 256p. 1987. 39.95 (*0-685-43792-2*) Abrams.

Comini, Gianni & Nonino, Carlo. Finite Element Analysis in Heat Transfer: Basic Formulation & Linear Problems. LC 94-15973. (Computational & Physical Processes in Mechanics & Thermal Sciences Ser.). 1994. 85.00 (*1-56032-354-X*) Taylor & Francis.

***Comini, Gianni & Sunden, B., eds.** Computational Analysis of Convection Heat Transfer. (Developments in Heat Transfer Ser.). 350p. 2000. 180.00 (*1-85312-734-5*, 7345, Pub. by WIT Pr) Computational Mech MA.

Cominolli, Rita. Smokestacks Allegro: The Story of Solvay, a Remarkable Industrial - Immigrant Village (1880-1920) 250p. 1990. 19.50 (*0-934733-50-3*); pap. text 14.50 (*0-934733-51-1*) CMS.

***Comins, Neil F.** Lifeline to the Universe. 240p. 2000. text 22.00 (*0-7382-0127-8*, Pub. by Perseus Pubng) HarpC.

Cominsky, Karl J. Abortion & RU-486 - Mifepristone - Index of New Information & Research Bible. LC 95-17205. 1995. 47.50 (*0-7883-0684-7*); pap. 44.50 (*0-7883-0685-5*) ABBE Pubs Assn.

Cominsky, Ronald, et al. Level 1 Mix Design: Materials Selection, Compaction, & Conditioning. (SHRP Ser.: A-408). (Illus.). 121p. (C). 1994. pap. text 10.00 (*0-309-05824-4*, PA408) Natl Res Coun.

Cominsky, Ronald J. The Superpave Mix Design Manual for New Construction & Overlays. 172p. (C). 1994. pap. text 15.00 (*0-309-05804-X*, SHRP-A-407) SHRP.

Cominsky, Ronald J., et al. Quality Control & Acceptance of Superpave-Designed Hot Mix Asphalt. LC 98-60936. (NCHRP Report Ser.). 209p. 1998. 51.00 (*0-309-06269-1*, NR409) Natl Acad Pr.

Comish, Kathryn W., ed. see Williams, Jeannie S.

Comiskey, Andrew. Pursuing Sexual Wholeness. LC 89-80824. 1989. pap. 10.99 (*0-88419-259-8*) Creation House.

***Comiskey, Eugene E. & Mulford, Charles W.** Guide to Financial Reporting & Analysis. LC 99-87593. 622p. 2000. 75.00 (*0-471-35425-2*) Wiley.

Comiskey, Eugene E., jt. auth. see Mulford, Charles W.

Comiskey, J. A., jt. ed. see Dallmeier, F.

Comiskey, James A. El Ministerio de la Hospitalidad. Dees, Colette J., tr. (Ministry Ser.). (SPA.). 48p. 1994. pap. 1.95 (*0-8146-2070-1*) Liturgical Pr.

— The Ministry of Hospitality, 20 vols., Set. (Ministry Ser.). 48p. (C). 1989. pap. 1.95 (*0-8146-1812-X*) Liturgical Pr.

***Comiskey, James A.** This Is Our Church: A Guide for Children. (Illus.). 48p. 2000. pap. 4.95 (*0-8146-2597-5*) Liturgical Pr.

***Comiskey, Joel.** Groups of 12: A New Way to Mobilize Leades & Multiply Groups in Your Church. (Illus.). 1999. pap. 12.99 (*1-880828-15-4*) Touch Pubns.

— Home Cell Group Explosion: A Study Guide to Help You Grow & Multiply Your Small Group. 1999. pap. 5.99 (*1-880828-16-2*) Touch Pubns.

— Home Cell Group Explosion: How Your Small Group Can Grow & Multiply. (Illus.). 1999. pap. 12.97 (*1-880828-06-5*) Touch Pubns.

— Reap the Harvest: How a Small-Group System Can Grow Your Church. 236p. 1999. pap. 18.97 (*1-880828-13-8*) Touch Pubns.

Comiskey, Patrick. Bell & Us. 64p. (Orig.). 1988. pap. 7.00 (*0-945926-02-2*) Paradigm RI.

— Bell & Us. deluxe ed. 64p. (Orig.). 1988. pap. 12.00 (*0-945926-03-0*) Paradigm RI.

Comiskey, Stephen W. A Good Lawyer: Secrets Good Lawyers (& Their Best Clients) Already Know. LC 97-91879. xi, 172p. 1997. 25.00 (*0-9656804-0-1*) Chaos Limited.

Comiskey, Vickie M. The Foreign Syndication Handbook: A Guide to Selling Stock Photos All over the World. LC 86-81702. 220p. (Orig.). 1987. pap. 19.95 (*0-9617000-0-9*) Haberman Pr.

Comisky, Ian M. & Feld, Lawrence S. Tax Fraud & Evasion: Money Laundering, Asset Forfeiture, Sentencing Guidelines. 1056p. 1994. 150.00 (*0-7913-2033-2*) Warren Gorham & Lamont.

Comisky, Marvin, et al. Judiciary Law: Selection, Compensation, Ethics & Discipline. LC 86-619. 270p. 1987. 65.00 (*0-89930-168-1*, CJL/, Quorum Bks) Greenwood.

Comissiona, Robinne. A Practical Guide to Releasing Tension & Increasing Energy. LC 91-25701. (Illus.). 110p. 1992. pap. 10.95 (*0-944957-07-2*) Rivercross Pub.

Comissiong, Lynette. Ecoute-Moi Bien! (Mind Me Good Now!) (FRE., Illus.). 32p. (J). (ps-3). 1997. lib. bdg. 16.95 (*1-55037-415-X*, Pub. by Annick) Firefly Bks Ltd.

— Mind Me Good Now! A Caribbean Folktale. (Illus.). 32p. (J). (ps-4). 1997. pap. 6.95 (*1-55037-482-6*, Pub. by Annick) Firefly Bks Ltd.

— Mind Me Good Now! Caribbean Folktale. (Illus.). 32p. (J). (ps-4). 1997. 16.95 (*1-55037-483-4*, Pub. by Annick) Firefly Bks Ltd.

Comissiong, Wilesse. The Best Face of All. 1991. pap. 6.95 (*0-913543-19-5*) African Am Imag.

Comisso. Worker's Control under Plan & Market. 1979. 37.50 (*0-300-02334-0*) Yale U Pr.

Comisso, Ellen & Tyson, Laura D., eds. Power, Purpose & Collective Choice: Economic Strategy in Socialist States. LC 86-47639. (Cornell Studies in Political Economy). 424p. 1986. pap. text 21.95 (*0-8014-9435-4*) Cornell U Pr.

Comitas, Lambros, jt. auth. see Rubin, Vera.

Comite Arctique International Staff, et al. Proceedings of the Sixth Conference of the Comitbe Arctique International, 13-15 May 1985. LC 88-34085. vii, 637p. 1989. 243.00 (*90-04-08281-6*) Brill Academic Pubs.

Comite de Derechos Humanos de el Salvador Staff. Torture in El Salvador: September 1986. (Illus.). 150p. (Orig.). 1988. pap. text 25.00 (*0-929873-00-9*); 15.00 (*0-929873-01-7*) MITF Cent Am.

Comite de Terminologie de l'Audio-Video Staff. English - French Vocabulary of VCR's & Camcorders. (ENG & FRE.). 61p. 1991. pap. 29.95 (*0-8288-9397-7*) Fr & Eur.

Comite Del Sesquicentenario De Eugenio Maria de Ho. Imagenes De Hostos a Traves Del Tiempo. 78p. 1988. pap. 5.00 (*0-685-51574-5*) U of PR Pr.

Comite del Sesquicentenario de Eugenio Maria de Ho. Imagenes de Hostos a Traves del Tiempo. (SPA.). 78p. 1988. pap. 8.00 (*0-8477-4001-3*) U of PR Pr.

Comite Del Sesquicentenario Eugenio Maria de Hosto & Gonzalez, Jose E. Vivir a Hostos. 165p. 1989. pap. 10.00 (*0-685-51575-3*) U of PR Pr.

Comite des Sciences Sociales de la Republique Soci. Dictionnaire Francais-Vietnamien. (FRE & VIE.). 1988. write for info. (*0-7859-8712-6*, 9290280344) Fr & Eur.

Comite Euro-International du Beton. Coating Protection for Reinforcement: State of the Art Report. LC 95-220437. 51p. 1995. 5.00 (*0-7277-2021-X*) Am Soc Civil Eng.

Comite Euro-International du Beton (C. E. B.) Staf. Seismic Design of Concrete Structures: Part I--The CEB Model Code for the Seismic Design of Concrete Structures & Part II--Numerical Applications & Trial Calculations. 300p. 1987. text 99.95 (*0-291-39737-9*, Pub. by Gower) Ashgate Pub Co.

Comite Euro-International du Beton Staff. Fastenings to Concrete & Masonry Structures: State of the Art Report. LC 95-117847. 258p. 1994. 14.00 (*0-7277-1937-8*) Am Soc Civil Eng.

— RC Elements under Cyclic Loading: State of the Art Report. LC 96-187288. 224p. 1996. 115.00 (*0-7277-2086-4*) Am Soc Civil Eng.

— RC Frames under Earthquake Loading: State of the Art Report. LC 96-177539. 272p. 1996. 134.00 (*0-7277-2085-6*) Am Soc Civil Eng.

Comite Interentreprises de l'Industrie Petroliere. French - English Lexicon of Car Washing. (ENG & FRE.). 43p. 1984. pap. 14.95 (*0-8288-9385-3*) Fr & Eur.

Comite Interentreprises de l'Usinage et de la Mach. English - French Vocabulary of Metal Lathes & Metal Turning. (ENG & FRE.). 40p. 1991. pap. 19.95 (*0-8288-9394-2*) Fr & Eur.

Comite Interentreprises du Tabac Staff. English - French General Vocabulary of Tobacco. (ENG & FRE.). 83p. 1988. pap. 29.95 (*0-8288-9414-0*) Fr & Eur.

Comite International d'Histoire de l'Art, et al, eds. Glossarium Artis - Festungen-Forteresses-Fortifications, Vol. 7. 2nd ed. (Glossarium Artis - Worterbuch zur Kunst Dictionary of Art Terms Ser.). 407p. 1990. lib. bdg. 82.00 (*3-598-10806-0*) K G Saur Verlag.

Comite Para el Estudio de las Finanzas de Puerto R. Informe al Gobernador del Comite Para el Estudio de las Finanzas de Puerto Rico (Informe Tobin) Velilla, Robertin A., tr. from ENG. Orig. Title: Report to the Governor the Committee to Study P.R's Finances. (SPA., Illus.). 1976. pap. text 4.00 (*0-8477-2216-3*) U of PR Pr.

Comitini, Salvatore & Hardjolukito, Sutanto. Indonesian Marine Fisheries Development & Strategy under Extended Maritime Jurisdiction. LC 83-14208. (Research Reports: No. 13). (Illus.). vi, 69p. 1983. pap. text. write for info. (*0-86638-048-5*) EW Ctr HI.

Comito, Terry. In Defense of Winters: The Poetry & Prose of Yvor Winters. LC 85-40759. (Wisconsin Project on American Writers Ser.). 360p. 1986. reprint ed. pap. 111.60 (*0-608-01934-8*, 206258900003) Bks Demand.

Comito, Terry, ed. Touch of Evil: Orson Welles, Director. (Films in Print Ser.). (Illus.). 289p. (C). 1985. 35.00 (*0-8135-1096-1*); pap. 17.00 (*0-8135-1097-X*) Rutgers U Pr.

Comitz, Cindy, ed. see Barras, Jonetta R.

Comitz, Cindy, ed. see Becker, Anne.

Comitz, Cindy, ed. see Cavalieri, Grace.

Comitz, Cindy, ed. see James, Sonja.

Comitz, Cindy, ed. see Nordhaus, Jean, et al.

Comitz, Cynthia, ed. see Emerson, Jean.

Comitz, Cynthia, ed. see Tuthill, Stacy.

***Comizzoli, R. B., et al, eds.** Localized Corrosion & Reliability of Electronic Materials & Devices. 292p. 2000. 62.00 (*1-56677-252-4*, PV 99-29) Electrochem Soc.

Comizzoli, R. B. & Sinclair, J. D., eds. Proceedings of the International Symposium on Corrosion & Reliability of Electronic Materials & Devices, 2nd. LC 92-74540. (Proceedings Ser.: Vol. 93-1). 612p. 1993. 56.00 (*1-56677-051-3*) Electrochem Soc.

Comizzoli, R. B., et al. Corrosion Reliability of Electronic Materials & Devices: Third International Symposium. (Proceedings Ser.: Vol. 94-29). 428p. 1995. pap. 54.00 (*1-56677-088-2*) Electrochem Soc.

Comley. Fields of Reading. 5th ed. 1998. pap. text 23.00 (*0-312-17949-9*) St Martin.

— Fields of Reading. 5th ed. 2000. pap. text. write for info. (*0-312-17950-2*) St Martin.

— Fields of Writing. 5th ed. 832p. 1998. pap. 35.95 (*0-312-15314-7*) St Martin.

Comley, jt. auth. see Elia, Lewis M.

Comley, Nancy R. Hemingway's Genders: Rereading the Hemingway Text. 1996. pap. 12.00 (*0-300-06464-0*) Yale U Pr.

Comley, Nancy R., et al, eds. Fields of Writing: Readings Across the Disciplines. 3rd ed. LC 88-63057. (C). 1990. teacher ed. write for info. (*0-312-02098-8*); teacher ed. write for info. (*0-318-68121-8*) St Martin.

Comley, Nancy R. & Scholes, Robert. Hemingway's Genders: Rereading the Hemingway Text. LC 93-49752. 160p. 1994. 25.00 (*0-300-05967-1*) Yale U Pr.

Comline International Corporation Staff. Advanced Materials in Japan. 476p. 1992. 355.00 (*1-85617-158-2*, Pub. by Elsvr Adv Tech) Elsevier.

Comlit Inc. Staff. Stellar Twenty-Eight Constellation Game. (C). 1995. pap. text 25.95 (*0-8403-8189-1*) Kendall-Hunt.

Comm, Joel, jt. auth. see Bruno, Bonnie.

C

Comm, Walter E. The Desiring Self: Rooting Pastoral Counseling & Spiritual Direction in Self-Transcendence. LC 98-39635. 224p. 1998. pap. 19.95 (*0-8091-3831-X*) Paulist Pr.

Commachan, M., ed. The Flora of Jabalpur. 1994. pap. 100.00 (*0-7855-2849-0*, Pub. by Scientific Pubs) St Mut.

Commager, H. S. Theodore Parker: Yankee Crusader. 1990. 16.50 (*0-8446-1884-5*) Peter Smith.

***Commager, H. S., ed.** The Civil War Archive: The History of the Civil War in Documents. 800p. 2000. 29.98 (*1-57912-110-1*, 81110) Blck Dog & Leventhal.

Commager, Henry S. America in Perspective. 224p. Date not set. 21.95 (*0-8488-2566-7*) Amereon Ltd.

Commager, Henry S. The American Mind: An Interpretation of American Thought & Character Since the 1800s. (C). 1959. pap. 20.00 (*0-300-00046-4*, Y7) Yale U Pr.

— The Blue & the Gray Vol. I. 1995. pap. 14.95 (*0-452-01144-2*, Plume) Dutton Plume.

— Commager on Tocqueville. 144p. (C). 1993. pap. 14.95 (*0-8262-0941-6*) U of Mo Pr.

— Commager on Tocqueville. 144p. (C). 1993. text 24.95 (*0-8262-0897-5*) U of Mo Pr.

— The Defeat of the Confederacy. LC 78-25755. (Anvil Ser.). 189p. 1978. reprint ed. pap. 11.50 (*0-442-00071-5*) Krieger.

— The Era of Reform, 1830-1860. LC 82-15190. (Anvil Ser.). 192p. (Orig.). 1982. reprint ed. pap. 11.50 (*0-89874-498-9*) Krieger.

— Fifty Basic Civil War Documents. LC 82-15187. 192p. 1982. reprint ed. pap. 11.50 (*0-89874-497-0*) Krieger.

— St. Nicholas Anthology. Date not set. lib. bdg. 31.95 (*0-8488-1896-2*) Amereon Ltd.

— The Story of the Second World War. (World War II Commemorative & Association of the U. S. Army Book Ser.). 352p. 1991. 23.95 (*0-08-041066-9*, 4039M) Brasseys.

— The Story of the Second World War. (Association of the U. S. Army Book Ser.). 352p. 1998. pap. 23.95 (*1-57488-168-X*) Brasseys.

— Tocqueville: Centralization & Liberty. 16p. (Orig.). 1977. pap. text 11.00 (*0-8191-5828-3*) U Pr of Amer.

Commager, Henry S., ed. The Blue & the Grey: The Story of the Civil War As Told by Participants. LC 94-18223. 1994. pap. 14.95 (*0-452-01145-0*, Mer) NAL.

— Lester Ward & the Welfare State. LC 66-22579. 1967. 52.50 (*0-672-50998-9*) Irvington.

Commager, Henry S. & Morris, Richard B., eds. The Spirit of '76: The Story of the American Revolution As Told by Participants. (Illus.). 1436p. 1995. reprint ed. pap. 27.95 (*0-306-80620-7*) Da Capo.

Commager, Henry S., et al. Civil Liberties under Attack: Publications of the William J. Cooper Foundation, Swarthmore College. LC 68-14899. (Essay Index Reprint Ser.). 1977. 19.95 (*0-8369-0308-0*) Ayer.

Commager, Henry S., jt. auth. see Nevins, Allan.

Commager, Henry S., ed. see Hamilton, Alexander, et al.

Commager, Henry S., ed. see Jefferson, Thomas.

Commager, Henry S., ed. see Thomas, Emory M.

Commager, Steele. The Odes of Horace: A Critical Study. LC 94-39638. 384p. 1995. pap. 15.95 (*0-8061-2729-5*) U of Okla Pr.

Commager, Steele, ed. Needed Words. Incl. Arabic Words in English. Smith, Logan P., ed. 1979. B.B.L.'s Recommendations for Pronouncing Doubtful Words. Smith, Logan P., ed. 1979. Best English. Smith, Logan P., ed. 1979. Bull's Bellow. Smith, Logan P., ed. 1979. Colloquial Language in Literature. Smith, Logan P., ed. 1979. Index to Tracts XXI-XXIX. Smith, Logan P. 1979. lib. bdg. Oxford English. Smith, Logan P. 1979. lib. bdg. Possibility of a Universal Language. Smith, Logan P. 1979. lib. bdg. Robert Bridges Recollections. Smith, Logan P. 1979. lib. bdg. (Society for Pure English Ser.: Vol. 4). 1979. Set lib. bdg. 46.00 (*0-8240-3668-9*) Garland.

— Persian Words in English. Incl. American Variations. Daryusl, A. A., ed. 1979. Dutch Influence on English Vocabulary. Daryusl, A. A., ed. 1979. Fine Writing. Daryusl, A. A. 1979. lib. bdg. Formation & Use of Compound Epithets in English Poetry. Daryusl, A. A. 1979. lib. bdg. German Influence on the English Vocabulary. Daryusl, A. A. 1979. lib. bdg. H.W. Fowler. Daryusl, A. A. 1979. lib. bdg. Linguistic Self-Criticism. Daryusl, A. A. 1979. lib. bdg. Names, Designations, & Appelations. Daryusl, A. A. 1979. lib. bdg. Northern Words in Modern English. Daryusl, A. A. 1979. lib. bdg. (Society for Pure English Ser.: Vol. 5). 1979. Set lib. bdg. 46.00 (*0-8240-3669-7*) Garland.

Commager, Steele, ed. see Fowler, H. W., et al.

Commager, Steele, ed. see Lier, Bruno, et al.

Commance, Ashtar, ed. New World Order. (Illus.). 160p. (Orig.). 1990. 15.00 (*0-938294-11-3*) Inner Light.

***Command Magazine Editors.** Hitler's Army: The Evolution & Structure of German Forces, 1933-1945. 1999. pap. 21.95 (*1-58097-022-2*, 970222) Combined Pub.

Command of the Army Council Staff. Pistol: Browning, F. N. 9mm. No. 2, Mark 1. LC 83-6127. 1992. pap. text 5.00 (*0-86663-991-8*) Ide Hse.

***Commander, Bob.** Shiny Ice-Cream Truck. (Shiny Vehicles Ser.). (Illus.). 12p. (J). (ps-k). 2000. 3.99 (*0-8431-7591-5*, Price Stern) Peng Put Young Read.

Commander, Bob. Shiny Race Car: A Shiny Vehicles Book. (Shiny Vehicles Ser.). (Illus.). 12p. (J). (ps). 1998. pap. 3.99 (*0-8431-7846-9*) Putnam Pub Group.

***Commander, Bob.** Shiny Rocket Ship. (Shiny Vehicles Ser.). (Illus.). 12p. (J). (ps-k). 2000. 3.99 (*0-8431-7590-7*, Price Stern) Peng Put Young Read.

Commander, Bob. Shiny Fire Engine: A Shiny Vehicles Book. (Shiny Vehicles Ser.). 12p. (J). 1998. pap. 3.99 (*0-8431-7847-7*) Putnam Pub Group.

Commander, Lydia K. The American Idea. LC 77-169378. (Family in America Ser.). 352p. 1972. reprint ed. 20.95 (*0-405-03855-0*) Ayer.

Commander, Simon, ed. Enterprise Restructuring & Unemployment in Models of Transition. LC 97-46858. (EDI Development Studies). 240p. 1998. pap. 22.00 (*0-8213-4168-5*, 14168) World Bank.

— Structural Adjustment & Agriculture: Theory & Practice in Africa & Latin America. LC 89-1968. 250p. (C). 1989. pap. text 27.50 (*0-435-08037-7*, 08037) Heinemann.

Commander, Simon & Coricelli, Fabrizio, eds. Unemployment, Restructuring, & the Labor Market in Eastern Europe & Russia. LC 94-29583. (EDI Development Studies). 416p. 1995. pap. 25.00 (*0-8213-2988-X*, 12988) World Bank.

Commander, Simon, et al. Enterprise Restructuring & Economic Policy in Russia. LC 96-21160. (EDI Development). 308p. 1996. pap. 22.00 (*0-8213-3725-4*, 13725) World Bank.

Commander, William. Bustin' Miffs: An Expository Book of Poetry Dealing with the Urban Black Experience. (Illus.). 24p. 1997. pap. 8.00 (*0-9652316-3-1*) Griot Publns.

Commander X. The Commander X Files. 1997. 39.95 (*0-938294-32-6*) Inner Light.

— Incredible Technologies of the New World Order: UFOS-TESLA-Area 51. 1997. 14.95 (*0-938294-38-5*) Inner Light.

— Invisibility & Levitation: How-To Keys to Personal Performance. 1998. 14.95 (*0-938294-36-9*) Inner Light.

— Nikola Tesla: Free Energy & the White Dove. 148p. 1990. 15.00 (*0-938294-82-2*) Inner Light.

— Underground Alien Bases. 128p. 15.00 (*0-938294-92-X*) Inner Light.

Commander X, ed. The Controllers. 1997. 19.95 (*0-938294-42-3*) Inner Light.

— Cosmic Patriot Files, 2 vols., Set. 146p. 1993. 39.95 (*0-938294-06-7*) Inner Light.

— The Philadelphia Experiment Chronicles: Exploring the Strange Case of Alfred Bielek & Dr. M. K. Jessup. 15.00 (*0-938294-00-8*) Inner Light.

Commanille, Jacques & De Singly, Francois, eds. The European Family: The Family Question in the European Community. LC 97-35849. 256p. 1997. 113.50 (*0-7923-4757-9*) Kluwer Academic.

Commar, P. C., jt. ed. see Raha, Manis K.

Commarmond, Nicole, tr. see Calais-Germain, Blandine & Lamotte, Andree.

***Commemorative Association for the Japan World Exposition Staff, et al.** Extended Abstracts of 1998 6th International Workshop on Computational Electronics: Osaka University, Osaka, Japan, October 19-21, 1998. LC 97-80530. vii, 275 p. 1998. write for info. (*0-7803-4370-0*) IEEE Standards.

***Comment, Bernard.** The Painted Panorama. Glasheen, Anne-Marie, tr. LC 99-88310. (Illus.). 272p. 2000. 65.00 (*0-8109-4365-4*, Pub. by Abrams) Time Warner.

Comment, Jeffrey W. Mission in the Marketplace. Hughey, Jim & Stein, Shifra, eds. (Illus.). 200p. (Orig.). Date not set. pap. 11.95 (*0-9647405-0-8*) MITM.

Commentary Magazine Editors. The Condition of Jewish Belief. LC 88-33345. 292p. 1995. reprint ed. pap. text 30.00 (*1-56821-408-1*) Aronson.

Commerce Clearing House, Inc. Small Business Investment Companies. Bruchey, Stuart & Carosso, Vincent P., eds. LC 78-18958. (Small Business Enterprise in America Ser.). 1979. reprint ed. lib. bdg. 17.95 (*0-405-11462-1*) Ayer.

Commerce Department., Economics & Statistics Adm.., contrib. by. Foreign Direct Investment in the United States: Operations of United States Affiliates of Foreign Companies. 112p. 1996. pap. 8.50 (*0-16-053295-7*) USGPO.

— Foreign Direct Investment in the United States: Operations of United States Affiliates of Foreign Companies. rev. ed. 110p. 1996. pap. 8.50 (*0-16-053296-5*) USGPO.

— Foreign Direct Investment in the United States: Operations of United States Affiliates of Foreign Companies. rev. ed. 102p. 1997. per. 8.50 (*0-16-054659-1*) USGPO.

Commerce Department, Economics & Statistics Admini, contrib. by. Foreign Direct Investment in the United States: Establishment Data for 1992. 358p. 1997. per. 28.00 (*0-16-049068-5*) USGPO.

— Statistical Abstract of the United States, 1996: The National Data Book. 116th ed. (Illus.). 1036p. 1996. boxed set 47.00 (*0-16-048837-0*, 003-024-08810-0) USGPO.

— Statistical Abstract of the United States, 1997: The National Data Book. 117th ed. (Illus.). 1037p. 1997. boxed set 51.00 (*0-16-049281-5*) USGPO.

Commerce Dept., Census Bureau, Economics & Statist. Statistical Abstract of the United States, 1992: The National Data Book. 112th ed. (Illus.). 1992. pap., per. 38.00 (*0-16-038080-4*, 003-024-08159-8) USGPO.

Commerce Dept., Census Bureau, Economics & Statist, contrib. by. Congressional District Atlas: 103d Congress of the United States, Vol. 1-2. LC 72-600344. (Illus.). 1264p. 1993. per. 42.00 (*0-16-000489-6*, S/N003024086832) USGPO.

Commerce Dept., Economics & Statistics Administrat. Statistical Abstract of the United States, 1994. 114th ed. (Illus.). 1035p. 1994. 42.00 (*0-16-045174-4*, 003-024-08756-1); boxed set 49.00 (*0-16-045173-6*, 003-024-08757-0) USGPO.

— Statistical Abstract of the United States, 1995: The National Data Book. 115th ed. (Illus.). 1059p. 1995. 54.00 (*0-16-048288-7*, 003-024-08788-0); 48.00 (*0-16-048289-5*, 003-024-08787-1) USGPO.

— Statistical Abstract of the United States, 1996: The National Data Book. 116th ed. 1036p. 1996. 40.00 (*0-16-048836-2*, 003-024-08809-6) USGPO.

Commerce Dept., Economics & Statistics Administrat, contrib. by. Foreign Direct Investment in the United States: 1992 Benchmark Survey, Final Results. 279p. 1995. per. 20.00 (*0-16-026249-6*, S/N003010002590) USGPO.

Commerce Dept., Office of Federal Statistical Poli, contrib. by. Standard Occupational Classification Manual, 1980. rev. ed. 547p. 1980. boxed set 39.00 (*0-16-018462-2*, 041-001-00351-7) USGPO.

***Commerce Net Staff.** Online Auctions. LC 99-20605. 192p. 1999. pap. 14.95 (*0-07-134249-4*) McGraw.

Commerce Publishing Corporation Staff. Washington State Advanced Technology Directory. 15th ed. 1998. pap. text 34.00 (*0-9634596-5-1*) CCH INC.

CommerceNet PKI Task Force. Understanding Digital Signatures: Establishing Trust over the Internet & Other Networks. LC 97-39998. (Illus.). 304p. 1997. pap. 34.95 (*0-07-012554-6*) McGraw.

CommerceNet PKI Task Force Staff. Public Key Infrastructure. 1997. pap. 39.95 (*0-614-28496-1*) McGraw-Hill Prof.

CommerceNet Staff. Buying Travel Services on the Net. LC 99-16838. 179p. 1999. pap. 14.95 (*0-07-134871-9*) McGraw.

CommerceNet Staff & Little, Arthur D. The CommerceNet Guide to I-Commerce. (Illus.). 304p. 1997. pap. text 29.95 (*0-07-012373-X*) McGraw.

CommerceNet Staff, jt. auth. see Arthur D. Little Staff.

Commercial & Financial Trust Company Staff. British Virgin Islands Business Law. LC 82-176238. 259p. reprint ed. pap. 80.30 (*0-7837-2412-8*, 204009700006) Bks Demand.

Commercial Appeal Staff. All in a Day's Drive: A Guide to Memphis & the Mid-South. 2nd rev. ed. LC 95-79632. (Illus.). viii, 93p. 1997. pap. 8.95 (*1-891324-01-2*) Memphis Pub Co.

— I Am a Man: Photographs of the 1968 Memphis Sanitation Strike & Dr. Martin Luther King Jr. LC 92-63386. (Illus.). 142p. 1992. 21.60 (*1-891324-00-4*) Memphis Pub Co.

Commercial Appeal Staff, ed. Greatest Moments in Tennessee Vols Football History. 250p. 1998. 29.95 (*1-58261-019-3*) Sprts Pubng.

Commercial Law League of America Staff. Commercial Law & Practice Guide, 3 vols. 1991. ring bd. 370.00 (*0-8205-2048-9*) Bender.

Commercial Press, Beijing Staff, compiled by. Oxford Compact Chinese Dictionary. 2nd ed. 1176p. 1999. pap. 13.95 (*0-19-591151-2*) OUP.

Commercial Press Ltd. Staff. The Complete Collection of Treasures of the Palace Museum Jadeware. 1996. 580.00 (*962-07-5185-X*, Pub. by Commercial Pr) St Mut.

— The Complete Collection of Treasures of the Palace Museum Jadeware, Vol. 2. 1996. 580.00 (*962-07-5188-4*, Pub. by Commercial Pr) St Mut.

— The Complete Collection of Treasures of the Palace Museum Jadeware, Vol. 3. 1996. 580.00 (*962-07-5199-X*, Pub. by Commercial Pr) St Mut.

— The Complete Collection of Treasures of the Palace Museum Paintings by the Court Artists of the Qing Dynasty. 1996. 580.00 (*962-07-5206-6*, Pub. by Commercial Pr) St Mut.

— The Complete Collection of Treasures of the Palace Museum Paintings by Wang Shimin, Wang Tian, Wang Hui, Wang Yuangi, Wu Li & Yun Shouping. 1996. 580.00 (*962-07-5205-8*, Pub. by Commercial Pr) St Mut.

— The Complete Collection of Treasures of the Palace Museum Porcelain of the Jin & Tang Dynasties. 1996. 580.00 (*962-07-5204-X*, Pub. by Commercial Pr) St Mut.

— The Complete Collection of Treasures of the Palace Museum Porcelain of the Song Dynasty. 1996. 580.00 (*962-07-5215-5*, Pub. by Commercial Pr) St Mut.

— The Complete Collection of Treasures of the Palace Museum Porcelain of the Song Dynasty, Vol. 2. 1996. 580.00 (*962-07-5216-3*, Pub. by Commercial Pr) St Mut.

Commercial Press Staff. Chinese - English Medical Dictionary. (CHI & ENG.). 150.00 (*0-8288-2483-5*, F45700) Fr & Eur.

— Chinese-English Dictionary of Current Affairs. deluxe ed. (CHI & ENG.). 594p. 1977. 49.95 (*0-8288-5297-9*, M9247) Fr & Eur.

— Chinese-English Dictionary of Military Terms. (CHI & ENG.). 366p. 1977. 59.95 (*0-8288-5298-7*, M9275) Fr & Eur.

— Chinese-German Dictionary: Chinesie-Deutsch Worterbuch. deluxe ed. (CHI & GER.). 830p. 1980. 49.95 (*0-7859-0653-3*, M9272) Fr & Eur.

— A Concise English-Chinese Dictionary. (CHI & ENG.). 1211p. 1972. 19.95 (*0-8288-6803-4*, M-9563) Fr & Eur.

— Deutsch-Chinesisches Standard Handworterbuch: Standard German-Chinese Dictionary. (CHI & GER.). 1364p. 1979. 49.95 (*0-8288-4753-3*, M9265) Fr & Eur.

— Diccionario Abreviado Espanol-Chino: Spanish-Chinese Dictionary. deluxe ed. (CHI & SPA.). 1244p. 1979. 39.95 (*0-8288-4754-1*, S33189) Fr & Eur.

— Dictionary Arabic-Chinese. (ARA & CHI.). 1505p. 1978. 75.00 (*0-8288-5165-4*, M9288) Fr & Eur.

— Dictionary Industrial Chemistry: English-Chinese. (CHI & ENG.). 81p. 1977. pap. 19.95 (*0-8288-5373-8*, M9585) Fr & Eur.

— Dictionary Korean-Chinese. (CHI & KOR.). 1274p. 1978. 49.95 (*0-8288-5166-2*, M9289) Fr & Eur.

— Dictionary of Aerodynamics. (CHI & ENG.). 250p. 1974. pap. 49.95 (*0-8288-6001-7*, M9595) Fr & Eur.

— Dictionary of Astronomy. (CHI & ENG.). 103p. 1974. pap. 24.95 (*0-8288-6002-5*, M9574) Fr & Eur.

— Dictionary of Electronics Engineering. (CHI & ENG.). 785p. 1976. 49.95 (*0-8288-5632-X*, M956) Fr & Eur.

— Dictionary of Forestry - Chinese & English. (CHI & ENG.). 274p. 1977. pap. 19.95 (*0-8288-5375-4*, M9594) Fr & Eur.

— Dictionary of Measurement Technology for Computers. (CHI & ENG.). 161p. 1977. pap. 39.95 (*0-8288-5376-2*, M9565) Fr & Eur.

— Dictionary of Mechanical Engineering. (CHI & ENG.). 608p. 1974. pap. text 65.00 (*0-8288-6005-X*, M9586) Fr & Eur.

— Dictionary of Meteorology. (CHI & ENG.). 207p. 1974. pap. 39.95 (*0-8288-6007-6*, M9567) Fr & Eur.

— Dictionary of Physics. (CHI & ENG.). 1689p. 1978. 19.95 (*0-8288-5170-0*, M9287) Fr & Eur.

— Dictionary of Science & Technology: English & Chinese. (CHI & ENG.). 713p. 1979. pap. 25.00 (*0-8288-8431-5*, F45416) Fr & Eur.

— Dictionary of Spice Technology. (CHI & ENG.). 172p. 1978. pap. 19.95 (*0-8288-5171-9*, M9568) Fr & Eur.

— Dictionary of Telecommunications: English-Chinese. (CHI & ENG.). 721p. 1961. pap. 29.95 (*0-8288-6819-0*, M-9589) Fr & Eur.

— Dictionary of Zoology: English-Chinese. (CHI & ENG.). 52p. 1975. pap. 39.95 (*0-8288-5840-3*, M9571) Fr & Eur.

— Dictionnaire Chinois-Francais.Tr. of Chinese-French Dictionary. (CHI & FRE.). 673p. 1979. 39.95 (*0-8288-2283-2*, M9268) Fr & Eur.

— Dictionnaire de Poche Francais-Chinois. (CHI & FRE.). 558p. 1975. pap. 14.95 (*0-8288-5849-7*, M9579) Fr & Eur.

— Dictionnaire Francais-Chinois. (CHI & FRE.). 1498p. 1979. 24.95 (*0-8288-4797-5*) Fr & Eur.

— English-Chinese Architectural Engineering Dictionary. (CHI & ENG.). 441p. 1973. 29.95 (*0-8288-6289-3*, M-9254) Fr & Eur.

— An English-Chinese Dictionary of Abreviations & Acronyms. (CHI & ENG.). 1162p. 1979. lib. bdg. 49.95 (*0-8288-4747-9*, M9555) Fr & Eur.

— English-Chinese Dictionary of Aeronautical Engineering. (CHI & ENG.). 367p. 1975. 49.95 (*0-8288-5881-0*, M9257) Fr & Eur.

— English-Chinese Dictionary of Civil & Architectural Engineering Terms. (CHI & ENG.). 706p. 1981. 49.95 (*0-8288-0194-0*, M9271) Fr & Eur.

— English-Chinese Dictionary of Construction Engineering. (CHI & ENG.). 215p. 1980. 39.95 (*0-8288-0195-9*, M9279) Fr & Eur.

— An English-Chinese Dictionary of Engineering & Technology. (CHI & ENG.). 1036p. 1981. 95.00 (*0-8288-0609-8*, M9371) Fr & Eur.

— English-Chinese Dictionary of Mathematical Terms. (CHI & ENG.). 252p. 1980. 49.95 (*0-8288-1894-0*, M9293) Fr & Eur.

— English-Chinese Dictionary of Physical Geography. (CHI & ENG.). 279p. 1980. 59.95 (*0-8288-0955-0*, M9292) Fr & Eur.

— English-Chinese Dictionary of Railway Terms. (CHI & ENG.). 1025p. 1977. 39.95 (*0-8288-5427-0*, M9559) Fr & Eur.

***Commercial Press Staff.** English-chinese Dictionary of Science. 1999. 208.33 (*7-03-000434-5*) Freundlich.

Commercial Press Staff. English-Chinese Dictionary of Scientific & Technology Abreviations. (CHI & ENG.). 587p. 1979. pap. 29.95 (*0-8288-4748-7*, M9250) Fr & Eur.

— An English-Chinese Dictionary of Technology. (CHI & ENG.). 1098p. 1978. 49.95 (*0-8288-5236-7*, M9578) Fr & Eur.

— An English-Chinese Glossary of Social Sciences & Education. (CHI & ENG.). 238p. 1975. 39.95 (*0-8288-5882-9*, M9562) Fr & Eur.

— English-Chinese Maritime Dictionary. (CHI & ENG.). 678p. 1979. 39.95 (*0-8288-4749-5*, M9251) Fr & Eur.

— English-Chinese Medical Dictionary. (CHI & ENG.). 292p. 1977. pap. 39.95 (*0-8288-5428-9*, M9253) Fr & Eur.

— English-Chinese Medical Dictionary. 1665p. 1980. 150.00 (*0-8288-0558-X*, M9264) Fr & Eur.

— English-Chinese Microbiological Dictionary. (CHI & ENG.). 138p. 1979. pap. 29.95 (*0-8288-5453-X*, M9573) Fr & Eur.

— General Chinese-English Dictionary. (CHI & ENG.). 926p. 1979. 39.95 (*0-8288-4802-5*, M9583) Fr & Eur.

— German-Chinese Dictionary: Handwoerterbuch Deutsch-Chinesisch. (CHI & GER.). 1197p. 1980. 49.95 (*0-8288-1005-2*, M9270) Fr & Eur.

— Japanese-Chinese Dictionary. (CHI & JPN.). 569p. 1980. pap. 19.95 (*0-8288-4707-X*, M9252) Fr & Eur.

— Japanese-Chinese Dictionary. deluxe ed. (CHI & JPN.). 2587p. 1979. 95.00 (*0-8288-4814-9*, M9267) Fr & Eur.

— Japanese-Chinese Science & Technology Dictionary. (CHI & JPN.). 175p. 1976. 39.95 (*0-8288-5709-1*, M9260) Fr & Eur.

— Japanese-English-Chinese Radio Technology Dictionary. (CHI, ENG & JPN.). 1628p. 1974. 49.95 (*0-8288-6056-4*, M9590) Fr & Eur.

— A Junior English-Chinese Dictionary. (CHI & ENG.). 1023p. 1977. pap. 7.95 (*0-8288-5447-5*, M9557) Fr & Eur.

— Latin-English-Chinese Dictionary of Medical Terms. (CHI, ENG & LAT.). 761p. 1979. 95.00 (*0-8288-4815-7*, M9564) Fr & Eur.

— Model English-Chinese Dictionary with Illustrative Examples. (CHI & ENG., Illus.). 1674p. 1979. 24.95 (*0-8288-4821-1*, M9274) Fr & Eur.

— A New Chinese-English Dictionary. (CHI & ENG.). 718p. 1979. 49.95 (*0-8288-4826-2*, M9554) Fr & Eur.

C

— New Concise English-Japanese-English Computer Dictionary. 2nd ed. (ENG & JPN.). 254p. 1985. 95.00 (*0-8288-0251-3*, F16070) Fr & Eur.

— A New English-Chinese Dictionary. (CHI & ENG.). 1252p. 1979. 24.95 (*0-8288-4827-0*, M9290) Fr & Eur.

— A New English-Chinese Dictionary. deluxe ed. (CHI & ENG.). 1688p. 1975. 49.95 (*0-8288-5940-X*, M9556) Fr & Eur.

— New French-Chinese Dictionary: Nouveau Dictionnaire: Francais-Chinois. (CHI & FRE.). 1499p. 1981. 49.95 (*0-8288-4672-3*, M9372) Fr & Eur.

— Nouveau Dictionnaire: Francais-Chinois: French-Chinese. deluxe ed. (CHI & FRE.). 846p. 1980. 24.95 (*0-8288-4711-8*, M9278) Fr & Eur.

— Petit Dictionnaire de la Science et de la Technique Francais-Chinois. (CHI & FRE.). 407p. 1990. 10.95 (*0-7859-8574-3*, 7100008395) Fr & Eur.

— Un Petit Dictionnaire Francais-Chinois: A Small French-Chinese Dictionary. (CHI & FRE.). 177p. 1978. pap. 9.95 (*0-8288-5261-8*, M9280) Fr & Eur.

— A Pocket Concise Chinese-English Dictionary. (CHI & ENG.). 620p. 1978. pap. 14.95 (*0-8288-5262-6*, M9182) Fr & Eur.

— A Pocket English-Chinese Dictionary. (CHI & ENG.). 451p. 1980. 9.95 (*0-8288-1600-X*, M9580) Fr & Eur.

— A Practical English-Chinese Dictionary. (CHI & ENG.). 1674p. 1979. 29.95 (*0-8288-4831-9*, M9291) Fr & Eur.

— The Sino Chinese-English Dictionary. (CHI & ENG.). 564p. 1980. pap. 14.95 (*0-8288-1601-8*, M14526) Fr & Eur.

— Times Chinese-English Dictionary. (CHI & ENG.). 564p. 1980. pap. 14.95 (*0-8288-1602-6*, M9273) Fr & Eur.

***Commerse, Meta.** Landscapes of Abuse: Transforming Feminine Spirit from Powerlessness to Purpose. (Illus.). 128p. 1999. pap. 19.00 (*0-8059-4827-9*) Dorrance.

Comminel, George C. Rethinking the French Revolution: Marxism & the Revisionist Challenge. 240p. (C). 1991. pap. 19.00 (*0-86091-890-4*, A4979, Pub. by Verso) Norton.

***Commings, Karen.** Guide to Owning a Birman Cat. (Guide to Owning Ser.). (Illus.). 1999. pap. 7.95 (*0-7938-2163-0*) TFH Pubns.

— Guide to Owning an American Shorthair Cat. (Guide to Owning Ser.). (Illus.). 1999. pap. 6.95 (*0-7938-2189-4*) TFH Pubns.

— Guide to Owning an Exotic Shorthair Cat. (Guide to Owning Ser.). (Illus.). 1999. pap. 6.95 (*0-7938-2188-6*) TFH Pubns.

Commings, Karen. The Manx: Everything about Purchase, Care, Nutrition, Behavior & Training. LC 98-46012. 1999. 7.95 (*0-7641-0754-2*) Barron.

***Commings, Karen.** Manx Cats. (Complete Pet Owner's Manual Ser.). (Illus.). 104p. 1999. pap. 6.95 (*0-7641-0753-4*) Barron.

Commings, Karen. Shelter Cats. LC 97-51968. 192p. 1998. 12.95 (*0-87605-676-1*) Howell Bks.

— Shorthaired Cat: An Owner's Guide to a Happy Healthy Pet. LC 95-53973. 160p. 1996. 12.95 (*0-87605-475-0*) Howell Bks.

Commins, David. Historical Dictionary of Syria. LC 96-12372. (Asian Historical Dictionaries Ser.: No. 20). (Illus.). 336p. 1996. 49.50 (*0-8108-3176-7*) Scarecrow.

Commins, Dorothy. What Is an Editor? Saxe Commins at Work. LC 77-81716. 256p. 1981. pap. 5.95 (*0-226-11428-7*) U Ch Pr.

Commins, Dorothy, ed. see O'Neill, Eugene.

Commins, Elaine. The Big Book of Folder Games for the Primary Classroom. LC 88-9104. (Illus.). 256p. (Orig.). (J). (ps-3). 1989. lib. bdg. 27.95 (*0-89334-181-9*, 181-9) Humanics Ltd.

— Bloomin' Bulletin Boards. LC 83-81432. (Illus.). 160p. (Orig.). (J). (ps-7). 1984. lib. bdg. 25.95 (*0-89334-183-5*, 183-5) Humanics Ltd.

— Early Childhood Activities. LC 81-83051. (Illus.). 264p. (J). (ps-2). 1982. lib. bdg. 32.95 (*0-89334-169-X*, 169-X) Humanics Ltd.

— Folder Game Festival. LC 87-31203. 192p. (J). (ps-3). 1988. lib. bdg. 27.95 (*0-89334-224-6*) Humanics Ltd.

— Lessons from Mother Goose. LC 87-30130. (Illus.). 164p. (Orig.). 1989. lib. bdg. 28.95 (*0-89334-177-0*, 177-0) Humanics Ltd.

— Let's Learn About . . . Language Arts. LC 90-30477. (Illus.). 32p. (J). (gr. k-3). 1990. pap. 4.95 (*0-89334-147-9*) Humanics Ltd.

Commins, Gary. Spiritual People, Radical Lives: Spirituality & Justice in Four Twentieth Century American Lives. LC 93-47063. 1996. 69.95 (*1-883255-43-0*); pap. 49.95 (*1-883255-42-2*) Intl Scholars.

Commins, Lloyd T. Winning at Craps. 1965. pap. 10.00 (*0-87980-345-2*) Wilshire.

Commins, Patricia. Remembering Mother, Finding Myself: A Journey of Love & Self-Acceptance. LC 99-12511. 282p. (Orig.). 1999. pap. 11.95 (*1-55874-666-8*) Health Comm.

Commins, Patricia, jt. auth. see Borsellino, Lewis J.

Commins, Saxe, ed. see Stevenson, Robert Louis.

Commire, Anne. Historic World Leaders Vol. 1: Africa, Middle East, Australia, & Asia. 1993. 60.00 (*0-8103-8409-4*, 020651) Gale.

— Historic World Leaders Vols. 2 & 3, Pts. 1 & 2: Europe, 2 vols. 1993. 55.00 (*0-8103-8410-8*, 020652) Gale.

— Historic World Leaders Vols. 4 & 5, Pts. 1 & 2: North & South America, 2 vols. 1993. 55.00 (*0-8103-8412-4*, 020654) Gale.

— Historic World Leaders, Vol. 3: Asia - Pacific, Vol. 2. 2nd ed. 1993. 55.00 (*0-8103-8411-6*, 020653) Gale.

— Historic World Leaders, Vol. 5: North - South America, Vol. 5. 1993. 55.00 (*0-8103-8413-2*, 020655) Gale.

Commire, Anne. Something about the Author, Vol. 55. 275p. 1989. text 108.00 (*0-8103-2265-X*) Gale.

— Something about the Author, Vol. 56. 275p. 1989. text 108.00 (*0-8103-2266-8*) Gale.

— Something about the Author, Vol. 67. Olendorf, Donna, ed. 275p. 1992. text 108.00 (*0-8103-2277-3*) Gale.

— Something about the Author, Vol. 68. Olendorf, Donna, ed. 275p. 1992. text 108.00 (*0-8103-2278-1*) Gale.

— Something about the Author, Vol. 69. Olendorf, Donna, ed. 275p. 1992. text 108.00 (*0-8103-2279-X*) Gale.

— Something about the Author, Vol. 70. Oldendorf, Donna & Telgen, Diane, eds. 275p. 1992. text 108.00 (*0-8103-2280-3*) Gale.

Commire, Anne, ed. Historic World Leaders Vol. 1: Africa, Middle East, Australia & Asia, 5 Vols., Set. 1500p. 1993. 250.00 (*0-8103-8408-6*) Gale.

— Historic World Leaders, Europe, Vols. 2 & 3. (Historic World Leaders Ser.). 1602p. 1993. 110.00 (*0-8103-9777-3*) Gale.

Commire, Anne, ed. Something about the Author, Vol. 49. (Illus.). 315p. 1987. text 108.00 (*0-8103-2259-5*) Gale.

— Something about the Author, Vol. 50. (Illus.). 300p. 1987. text 108.00 (*0-8103-2260-9*) Gale.

— Something about the Author, Vol. 51. LC 72-27107. 300p. 1988. text 108.00 (*0-8103-2261-7*) Gale.

— Something about the Author, Vol. 52. 275p. 1988. text 108.00 (*0-8103-2262-5*) Gale.

— Something about the Author, Vol. 53. 275p. 1988. text 108.00 (*0-8103-2263-3*) Gale.

— Something about the Author, Vol. 54. 275p. 1988. text 108.00 (*0-8103-2264-1*) Gale.

— Something about the Author, Vol. 57. 275p. 1989. text 108.00 (*0-8103-2267-6*) Gale.

— Something about the Author, Vol. 58. 300p. 1989. text 108.00 (*0-8103-2268-4*) Gale.

— Something about the Author, Vol. 59. 300p. 1990. text 108.00 (*0-8103-2269-2*) Gale.

— Something about the Author: Facts & Pictures about Contemporary Authors & Illustrators of Books for Young People, Vol. 30. (Illus.). 304p. (YA). (gr. 9-12). 1983. text 108.00 (*0-8103-0055-9*) Gale.

— Something about the Author: Facts & Pictures about Contemporary Authors & Illustrators of Books for Young People, Vol. 34. (Illus.). 224p. (YA). (gr. 9-12). 1984. text 108.00 (*0-8103-0063-X*) Gale.

— Something about the Author: Facts & Pictures about Contemporary Authors & Illustrators of Books for Young People, Vol. 40. (Illus.). 321p. 1985. text 108.00 (*0-8103-2250-1*) Gale.

— Something about the Author: Facts & Pictures about Contemporary Authors & Illustrators of Books for Young People, Vol. 41. LC 72-27107. 348p. 1985. text 108.00 (*0-8103-2251-X*) Gale.

— Something about the Author: Facts & Pictures about Contemporary Authors & Illustrators of Books for Young People, Vol. 42. 299p. 1985. text 108.00 (*0-8103-2252-8*) Gale.

— Something about the Author: Facts & Pictures about Contemporary Authors & Illustrators of Books for Young People, Vol. 43. (Illus.). 300p. 1986. text 108.00 (*0-8103-2253-6*) Gale.

— Something about the Author: Facts & Pictures about Contemporary Authors & Illustrators of Books for Young People, Vol. 44. 300p. (J). (gr. 9-12). 1986. text 108.00 (*0-8103-2254-4*) Gale.

— Something about the Author: Facts & Pictures about Contemporary Authors & Illustrators of Books for Young People, Vol. 45. 304p. 1986. text 108.00 (*0-8103-2255-2*) Gale.

— Something about the Author: Facts & Pictures about Contemporary Authors & Illustrators of Books for Young People, Vol. 46. 313p. 1986. text 108.00 (*0-8103-2256-0*) Gale.

— Something about the Author: Facts & Pictures about Contemporary Authors & Illustrators of Books for Young People, Vol. 47. 315p. 1987. text 108.00 (*0-8103-2257-9*) Gale.

— Something about the Author: Facts & Pictures about Contemporary Authors & Illustrators of Books for Young People, Vol. 48. 323p. 1987. text 108.00 (*0-8103-2258-7*) Gale.

— Something about the Author Vol. 60: Facts & Pictures about Authors & Illustrators of Books for Young People, Vol. 60. LC 72-27107. (Illus.). 203p. 1990. text 108.00 (*0-8103-2270-6*, 001689) Gale.

— Something about the Author Vol. 61: Facts & Pictures about Authors & Illustrators of Books for Young People, Vol. 61. LC 72-27107. (Illus.). 275p. 1990. text 108.00 (*0-8103-2271-4*, 001690) Gale.

Commire, Anne, et al, eds. Authors & Artists for Young Adults, Vol. 1. (Illus.). 250p. 1988. text 82.00 (*0-8103-2763-5*) Gale.

— Authors & Artists for Young Adults, Vol. 2. 250p. 1989. text 82.00 (*0-8103-5051-3*) Gale.

***Commire, Anne & Klezmer, Deborah.** Women in World History: A Biographical Encyclopedia. LC 99-24692. 1999. write for info. (*0-7876-4063-8*) Gale.

Commire, Anne & Klezmer, Deborah, eds. Women in World History: A Biographical Encyclopedia, Vol. 1-3. LC 99-24692. 12500p. 1999. 995.00 (*0-7876-3736-X*, GML00299-113499, Gale Res Intl) Gale.

Commire, Anne, jt. ed. see Nagel, Rob.

Commisariat General de la Language Francaise Staff. Dictionnaire des Neologismes Officiels. (ENG & FRE.). 238p. 1988. pap. 49.95 (*0-8288-7664-9*) Fr & Eur.

Commision Nacional Defensa Idiama Comis Staff. Fundamental Dictionary of Mexican Spanish: Diccionario Fundamental del Espanol de Mexico. (SPA.). 1982. 29.95 (*0-8288-2035-X*, M3150) Fr & Eur.

Commissariat a l'Energie Atomique. Dictionnaire des Sciences et Techniques Nucleaires. 3rd ed. (FRE.). 492p. 1975. 125.00 (*0-7859-0650-9*, M6081) Fr & Eur.

Commissariat, M. S. Mandelso's Travels in Western India, AD 1638-1639. (C). 1995. reprint ed. 18.00 (*81-206-0714-7*, Pub. by Asian Educ Servs) S Asia.

Commission de Communautes Europeenne Staff. Glossary of Labor & the Trade Union Movement. (DAN, DUT, ENG, FRE & GER.). 216p. 1983. pap. 35.00 (*0-8288-1534-8*, M14218) Fr & Eur.

Commission des Avoyelles, jt. auth. see Eakin, Sue L.

***Commission for E U Economic.** Role of Foreign Direct Investment in the Gas Industry: Economies in Trasition & Southern Mediterranean Countries. 463p. 1998. 25.00 (*92-1-100768-2*) UN.

***Commission for EU Economic.** East-West Energy Efficiency Strandards & Labels. 14. 247p. 1998. 45.00 (*92-1-100772-0*) UN.

Commission for Labor Cooperation Staff. Fermetures d'Usines et Droits en Matiere de Travail.Tr. of Plant Closings & Labor Rights. (FRE.). 250p. 1997. pap. 27.50 (*0-89059-078-8*, BPF0788) Bernan Pr.

Commission for the Defence of Human Rights in Cent. This Is the Just Cause: Breaking the Silence: Testimony of the Panamanian People, Resulting from the U. S. A. Invasion. 2nd ed. (Illus.). 80p. (Orig.). 1991. pap. 9.95 (*0-945257-39-2*) Apex Pr.

Commission for the European Communities Staff. Multilingual Dictionary of Fishing Gear. 2nd ed. (Illus.). 360p. 1992. 85.00 (*0-85238-192-1*) Blackwell Sci.

— Multilingual Dictionary of Fishing Vessels & Safety on Board. 2nd ed. (Illus.). 1038p. 1992. 125.00 (*0-85238-191-3*) Blackwell Sci.

Commission for the Investigation of Health Hazards, ed. List of MAK & BAT Values 1995: Maximum Concentrations & Biological Tolerance Values at the Workplace, Report 31. (Reports: Vol. 31). (Illus.). 193p. 1995. pap. 59.95 (*3-527-27570-3*, Wiley-VCH) Wiley.

Commission for the Investigation of Health Hazards & Henschler, Dietrich, eds. Occupational Toxicants: Critical Data Evaluation for MAK Values & Classification of Carcinogens, Vol. 1. (Illus.). 398p. 1990. 165.00 (*3-527-27019-1*, Wiley-VCH) Wiley.

Commission for the Investigation of Health Hazards & Henschler, Dietrich, eds. Occupational Toxicants: Critical Data Evaluation for MAK Values & Classification of Carcinogens, Vol. 2. (Illus.). 349p. 1991. 165.00 (*3-527-27022-1*, Wiley-VCH) Wiley.

— Occupational Toxicants: Critical Data Evaluation for MAK Values & Classification of Carcinogens, Vol. 3. (Illus.). 380p. 1992. 165.00 (*3-527-27023-X*, Wiley-VCH) Wiley.

— Occupational Toxicants: Critical Data Evaluation for MAK Values & Classification of Carcinogens, Vol. 4. (Illus.). 385p. 1992. 165.00 (*3-527-27025-6*, Wiley-VCH) Wiley.

— Occupational Toxicants: Critical Data Evaluation for MAK Values & Classification of Carcinogens, Vol. 5. (Illus.). 390p. 1993. 165.00 (*3-527-27030-2*, Wiley-VCH) Wiley.

Commission for the Investigation of Health Hazards & Henschler, Dietrich, eds. Occupational Toxicants: Critical Data Evaluation for MAK Values & Classification of Carcinogens, Vol. 6. (Illus.). 368p. 1994. 165.00 (*3-527-27031-0*, Wiley-VCH) Wiley.

Commission for the Investigation of Health of Chemical Compunds in the Work Area Staff. List of MAK & BAT Values, 1998 No. 33: Maximum Concentrations & Biological Tolerance Values at the Workplace. (MAK & BAT Values Ser.). 220p. 1998. pap. 64.95 (*3-527-27585-1*) Wiley.

***Commission for the Investigation of Health of Chemical Compunds in the Work Area Staff, ed.** List of MAK & BAT Values 1999: Maximum Concentrations & Biological Tolerance Values at the Workplace, Report No. 35. 228p. 1999. 54.95 (*3-527-27590-8*) Wiley.

Commission Francaise du Guide des Sources de l'His, ed. Guide to the Sources for the History of the Nations: Sources de l'Histoire du Proche orient et de l'Afrique du Nord dans les Archives et Bibliotheque Francaise, Pt. 1: Archive, 2 vols., Vol. 5. 1200p. 1996. lib. bdg. 575.00 (*3-598-21478-2*) K G Saur Verlag.

Commission of Engineering & Technical Systems, Nat. The Economic Consequences of a Catastrophic Earthquake: Proceedings of a Forum, August 1-2, 1990. (Illus.). 196p. 1992. pap. text 21.00 (*0-309-04639-4*) Natl Acad Pr.

Commission of European Communities, ed. Plutonium Recycling Scenario in Light Water Reactors: Assessment of Environmental Impact in the European Community, Vol. 5. viii, 240p. 1982. text 156.00 (*3-7186-0118-4*) Gordon & Breach.

— Research & Development of Radioactive Waste Management & Storage, Vol. 3. 3rd ed. (Radioactive Waste Management Ser.: Vol. 12). iv, 402p. 1984. pap. text 225.00 (*3-7186-0191-5*) Gordon & Breach.

— Research & Development on Radioactive Waste Management & Storage: First Annual Progress Report of the European Community Programme 1980-84. (Radioactive Waste Management Ser.: Vol. 4). vi, 130p. 1982. text 90.00 (*3-7186-0115-X*) Gordon & Breach.

Commission of ICAO Staff, jt. auth. see Dangerous Goods Panel of Air Navigations Commissio.

Commission of International Trade & Investment Pol. United States International Economic Policy in an Interdependent World, 4 vols. (Final Reports & Compendium of Papers: Nos. 1 & 2). 1985. reprint ed. lib. bdg. 205.00 (*0-89941-420-6*, 201700) W S Hein.

***Commission of the European Communities.** Community Budget: The Facts in Figures Sec. (98) 1100-EN, 1998. (Illus.). 1998. pap. 35.00 (*92-828-3743-2*, Pub. by Comm Europ Commun) Bernan Associates.

— European Union Direct Investment: Analytical Aspects 1988-1998. 137p. 2000. pap. 38.00 (*92-828-8482-1*, Pub. by Comm Europ Commun) Balogh.

Commission of the European Communities. The Law & Practice Relating to Pollution Control in the Member States of the European Communities, 10 vols. 2nd ed. Environmental Resources, Ltd. Staff, ed. Incl. Vol. 1. 1986. 35.00 (*0-86010-040-5*); Vol. 2a. 1986. 35.00 (*0-86010-041-3*); Vol. 3. 1986. 35.00 (*0-86010-029-4*); Vol. 4. 1986. 35.00 (*0-86010-033-2*); Vol. 4a. 1986. 35.00 (*0-86010-035-9*); Vol. 5. 1986. 35.00 (*0-86010-032-4*); Vol. 5a. 1986. 35.00 (*0-86010-034-0*); Vol. 6. 1986. 35.00 (*0-86010-031-6*); Vol. 7. 1986. 35.00 (*0-86010-039-1*); Vol. 7a. 1986. 35.00 (*0-86010-042-1*); Vol. 8. 1986. 35.00 (*0-86010-030-8*); Vol. 9. 1986. 35.00 (*0-86010-037-5*); Vol. 11. 1986. 35.00 (*0-86010-038-3*); 1986. Set lib. bdg. 79.50 (*0-86010-806-6*) G & T Inc.

— New Technologies for Exploration & Exploitation for Oil & Gas Resources, 2 vols., Set. 338p. 1988. lib. bdg. 475.50 (*1-85333-226-7*) G & T Inc.

— Organophosphorus Pesticides Criteria (Dose-Effect Relationships) for Organophosphorus Compounds. Derache, R., ed. 1977. pap. 95.00 (*0-08-021993-4*, Pub. by Pergamon Repr) Franklin.

— Social Europe: Employee Representatives in Europe & Their Economic Prerogatives. 146p. 1996. pap., suppl. ed. 25.00 (*92-827-6312-9*, CENC-96-003-ENC, Pub. by Comm Europ Commun) Bernan Associates.

— Social Europe, National Seminars on Implementing the European Employment Strategy, 6/1996: Summary. LC 99-457847. 146p. 1997. pap. 25.00 (*92-827-9983-2*, CENC-96-006-ENC, Pub. by Comm Europ Commun) Bernan Associates.

— Social Europe, Work & Childcare, 5/1996: Implementing the Council Recommendation on Childcare. 146p. 1996. pap. 25.00 (*92-827-6318-8*, CENC-96-005-ENC, Pub. by Comm Europ Commun) Bernan Associates.

— Social Europe 7/1996 Outlook on Supplementary Pensions in the Context of Demographic Economic. LC 99-460423. 146p. 1997. pap. 25.00 (*92-828-0254-X*, CE-NC-96-007-EN, Pub. by Comm Europ Commun) Bernan Associates.

Commission of the European Communities, ed. Energy Research & Development Programme, Status Report, 1977. 1978. pap. text 71.50 (*90-247-2059-1*) Kluwer Academic.

— Medical Training in the European Community. viii, 87p. 1987. pap. 52.80 (*0-387-17761-2*) Spr-Verlag.

Commission of the European Communities, jt. auth. see Econstat Staff.

Commission of the European Communities, jt. auth. see Institut for Planungskybernetik Staff.

Commission of the European Communities, jt. auth. see Van Lierop, Ben.

Commission of the European Communities, Directorat. Energy Research & Development Programme, 2 vols. 1987. text 358.00 (*90-247-2220-9*) Kluwer Academic.

— Fusion Technology, 1918: Proceedings, 2 vols., Set. LC 79-40553. (Commission of the European Communities Ser.: EUR 6215). (Illus.). 1979. pap. 499.00 (*0-08-023439-9*, Pub. by Pergamon Repr) Franklin.

— Heating in Toroidal Plasmas: Proceedings, 2 vols. 1979. pap. 342.00 (*0-08-023400-3*, Pub. by Pergamon Repr) Franklin.

— Synopses of Results of the First Programme on Optimization of the Production & Utilisation of Hydrocarbons. 1000p. (C). 1993. lib. bdg. 396.50 (*1-85333-879-6*, Pub. by Graham & Trotman) Kluwer Academic.

Commission of the European Communities, Directorat, ed. Solar Energy for Development: Proceedings of the International Conference, Varese, Italy, March 26-29, 1979. 1979. pap. text 88.00 (*90-247-2239-X*) Kluwer Academic.

Commission of the European Communities, Luxembourg. Better Translation for Better Communication: A Survey of the Translation Market, Present & Future, Prepared for the Commission of the European Communities, Directorate-General Information Market & Innovation. (Commission of the European Communities Ser.). 200p. 1983. 96.00 (*0-08-030534-2*, Pub. by Pergamon Repr) Franklin.

— Fusion Technology: Proceedings of the 11th Symposium, Oxford, England, Sept. 15-19, 1980, 2 vols., Set. (Illus.). 1000p. 1979. pap. 576.00 (*0-08-025697-X*, Pub. by Pergamon Repr) Franklin.

Commission of the European Communities, Luxembourg, ed. Fusion Technology: Proceedings of the 12th Symposium (SOFT), Julich Laboratory, Federal Republic of Germany, 13-17 September 1982, 2 vols. (International School of Fusion Reactor Technology (CEC) Ser.). 1564p. 1983. pap. 753.00 (*0-08-029977-6*, Pub. by Pergamon Repr) Franklin.

Commission of the European Communities Staff. Decommissioning of Nuclear Power Plants. 462p. 1984. lib. bdg. 176.50 (*0-86010-558-X*) G & T Inc.

— European Community Oil & Gas Research & Development Projects. 222p. 1982. lib. bdg. 101.50 (*0-86010-393-5*) G & T Inc.

— Incineration of Radioactive Waste. 213p. 1985. lib. bdg. 112.00 (*0-86010-677-2*) G & T Inc.

— Law & Practice Concerning Occupational Health in the Member States of the European Community, 5 vols., 1. (Environmental Resources Limited Ser.). 1985. lib. bdg. 152.50 (*0-86010-626-8*) Kluwer Law Intl.

— Law & Practice Concerning Occupational Health in the Member States of the European Community, 5 vols., 2. (Environmental Resources Limited Ser.). 1985. lib. bdg. 152.50 (*0-86010-627-6*) Kluwer Law Intl.

— Law & Practice Concerning Occupational Health in the Member States of the European Community, 5 vols., 3. (Environmental Resources Limited Ser.). 1985. lib. bdg. 152.50 (*0-86010-628-4*) Kluwer Law Intl.

— Law & Practice Concerning Occupational Health in the

An Asterisk (*) at the beginning of an entry indicates that the title is appearing for the first time.

Member States of the European Community, 5 vols., 4. (Environmental Resources Limited Ser.). 1985. lib. bdg. 152.50 (*0-86010-794-9*) Kluwer Law Intl.

— Law & Practice Concerning Occupational Health in the Member States of the European Community, 5 vols., Set. (Environmental Resources Limited Ser.). 1987. lib. bdg. 33.00 (*0-86010-921-6*) G & T Inc.

— Multilingual Dictionary of Fishing Gear. 2nd ed. (DAN, DUT, ENG, FRE & GER.). 1360p. 1992. 150.00 (*0-7859-0549-9*, 0-852381921) Fr & Eur.

— Multilingual Dictionary of Fishing Vessels & Safety on Board. 2nd ed. (DAN, DUT, ENG, FRE & GER.). 1038p. 1992. 175.00 (*0-7859-0548-0*, 0-852381913) Fr & Eur.

— Roadway Drivage Techniques in the Coal Mines of the European Community. 392p. 1984. pap. text 108.00 (*0-86010-575-X*) G & T Inc.

— Safety & Health in the Oil & Gas Extractive Industries. 442p. 1983. pap. text 129.00 (*0-86010-452-4*) G & T Inc.

Commission of the European Communities Staff, ed. European Directory of Fisheries & Aquaculture Research. LC 92-20485. 1992. text 189.00 (*0-7923-1875-7*) Kluwer Academic.

— European Directory of Research Centers in the Fisheries Sector. 2nd ed. LC 93-47118. 624p. (C). 1994. text 255.50 (*0-7923-2691-1*) Kluwer Academic.

— Forward with Harmonized Conformance Testing Services. 177p. 1988. pap. 50.00 (*90-5199-001-4*, Pub. by IOS Pr) IOS Press.

— HERMES: Harmonised Econometric Research for Modelling Economic Systems. LC 92-41260. vi,720p. 1993. 130.00 (*0-444-89760-7*, North Holland) Elsevier.

— Scanning Microscopy: Symposium Proceedings, Wetzlar, October 1990. LC 92-24849. (ESPRIT Basic Research Ser.). 220p. 1992. 64.95 (*0-387-55696-6*) Spr-Verlag.

Commission of the European Communities Staff, et al, eds. Geographic Database Management Systems: Workshop Proceedings, Capri, Italy, May 1991. LC 92-24851. (ESPRIT Basic Research Ser.). vii, 317p. 1992. 69.00 (*0-387-55617-6*) Spr-Verlag.

Commission of the European Communities Staff & Directorate-General Telecommunications Staff, eds. Esprit '89: Proceedings of the 6th Annual Esprit Conference, Brussels, November 27 - December 1, 1989. (C). 1989. text 292.50 (*0-7923-0592-2*) Kluwer Academic.

Commission of the European Communities Staff, jt. auth. see P. A. Cambridge Economic Consultants Staff.

Commission of the European Community Staff, ed. see Banatre, J. P., et al.

Commission on Accreditation for Corrections Staff & Hutton, Scott D. Standards for Adult Local Detention Facilities. 3rd ed. American Correctional Association, ed. (Illus.). 156p. 1991. pap. 35.00 (*0-929310-47-0*, 316) Am Correctional.

Commission on Accreditation for Corrections Staff, jt. auth. see American Correctional Association.

Commission on Accreditation for Corrections Staff, jt. auth. see American Correctional Association Staff.

Commission on Accreditation Staff. Handbook of Accreditation Standards & Procedures. 1994. ring bd. 42.00 (*0-87293-043-2*) Coun Soc Wk Ed.

Commission on Behavioral & Social Sciences & Educa. Modeling Cost & Performance for Military Enlistment: Report of a Workshop. Green, Bert F. & Mavor, Anne S., eds. 172p. (Orig.). (C). 1994. pap. text 29.00 (*0-309-05041-3*) Natl Acad Pr.

Commission on Britain & Europe Staff. An Equal Partner: Britain's Role in a Changing Europe, Final Report of the Commission on Britain & Europe. Royal Institute Staff, ed. 100p. 1998. pap. 16.95 (*1-86203-066-9*, Pub. by Royal Inst Intl Affairs) Brookings.

Commission on Chronic Illness Staff. Commission on Chronic Illness, Vol. 2: Care of the Long-Term Patient, Vol. 2. (Illus.). 620p. 1956. 58.50 (*0-674-09650-9*) HUP.

— Commission on Chronic Illness, Vol. 3: Chronic Illness in a Rural Area: The Hunterdon Study, Vol. 3. 454p. 1956. 50.00 (*0-674-12901-6*) HUP.

— Commission on Chronic Illness, Vol. 4: Chronic Illness in a Large City: The Baltimore Study, Vol. 4. (Illus.). 642p. 1957. 56.00 (*0-674-12900-8*) HUP.

Commission on Country Life, Jr. Report of the Commission on Country Life. McCurry, Dan C. & Rubenstein, Richard E., eds. LC 74-30625. (American Farmers & the Rise of Agribusiness Ser.). 1975. reprint ed. 19.95 (*0-405-06787-9*) Ayer.

Commission on Dietetic Registration Staff. Study Guide for the Registration Examination for Dietitians. 5th ed. 50p. 1991. ring bd. 25.00 (*0-88091-086-0*, 0608) Am Dietetic Assn.

Commission on Engineering & Technical Systems Staf. Systems Panel Reports. (Star 21: Strategic Technologies for the Army in the Twenty-First Century Ser.: Vol. 3). 800p. 1992. pap. 66.00 (*0-309-04636-X*) World Scientific Pub.

— Technology Forecast Assessments. (Star 21: Strategic Technologies for the Army in the Twenty-First Century Ser.: Vol. 2). 600p. 1992. pap. 59.00 (*0-309-04637-8*) World Scientific Pub.

Commission on Engineering Staff, jt. auth. see National Research Council Staff.

Commission on Foundations & Private Philanthropy. Foundations: Private Giving & Public Policy. LC 78-139831. 1993. lib. bdg. 15.00 (*0-226-66286-1*) U Ch Pr.

Commission on Freedom of the Press, ed. see Leigh, Robert.

Commission on Geosciences, Environment, & Resource. Colorado River Ecology & Dam Management: Proceedings of a Symposium May 24-25, 1990, Santa Fe, New Mexico... 288p. 1991. pap. text 29.00 (*0-309-04535-5*) Natl Acad Pr.

Commission on Graduates of Foreign Nursing Schools. CGFNS Qualifying Exam: Practice English Test Audio Tape, No. 1. 20p. (C). 1992. write for info. incl. audio (*0-9630592-1-1*) Grads of For Nursing.

— CGFNS Qualifying Exam: Practice English Test Audio Tape, No. 2. 28p. (C). 1995. write for info. incl. audio (*0-9630592-3-8*) Grads of For Nursing.

— Official Study Guide for the CGFNS Qualifying Examination. 3rd ed. 200p. (C). 1995. write for info. (*0-9630592-2-X*) Grads of For Nursing.

Commission on Health Research for Development Staf. Health Research: Essential Link to Equity in Development. (Illus.). 160p. 1990. pap. text 17.95 (*0-19-520838-2*) OUP.

Commission on Jewish Education in North America St. A Time to Act: The Report of the Commission on Jewish Education in North America. 97p. (Orig.). (C). 1991. pap. text 16.00 (*0-8191-8104-8*); lib. bdg. 39.00 (*0-8191-8105-6*) U Pr of Amer.

Commission on Life Sciences, National Research Cou. The Scientific Bases for the Preservation of the Hawaiian Crow. 148p. (Orig.). (C). 1992. pap. text 21.00 (*0-309-04775-7*) Natl Acad Pr.

***Commission on Life Sciences, National Research Cou.** Strategies to Protect the Health Of: Assessing Health Risks to Deployed. 2000. pap. 75.50 (*0-309-06876-2*) Natl Acad Pr.

Commission on Medical Education, Sciences of Medic. Medical Education in Transition. Jones, Roseann M., ed. LC 92-64117. 146p. (Orig.). 1992. pap. write for info. (*0-942054-05-9*) R W Johnson Found.

Commission on National Parks & Protected Areas (CN, jt. auth. see International Union for Conservation of Nature & Natural Resources Staff.

Commission on Physical Science Staff, jt. auth. see National Research Council Staff.

Commission on Physical Sciences, Mathematics, & Ap & National Research Council Staff. National Collaboratories: Applying Information Technology for Scientific Research. 118p. (Orig.). (C). 1993. pap. text 29.00 (*0-309-04848-6*) Natl Acad Pr.

Commission on Precollege Guidance & Counseling. Keeping the Options Open: Recommendations. 44p. (Orig.). 1986. pap. 6.00 (*0-87447-282-2*) College Bd.

Commission on Preservation & Access Staff. The Commission on Preservation & Access Working Paper on the Future. 6p. 1994. pap. 5.00 (*1-887334-30-0*) Coun Lib & Info.

— The International Program & Its Global Mission. (Introduction to Report Ser.). 4p. 1995. pap. 10.00 (*1-887334-35-1*) Coun Lib & Info.

— Preserving the Illustrated Text: Report of the Joint Task Force on Text & Image. 31p. 1992. pap. 10.00 (*1-887334-15-7*) Coun Lib & Info.

— Preserving the Intellectual Heritage: A Report of the Bellagio Conference. 36p. 1993. pap. 10.00 (*1-887334-28-9*) Coun Lib & Info.

Commission on Professional & Hospital Activities S. Geriatric Length of Stay by Diagnosis & Operation, United States, 1987. LC 88-651323. 330p. reprint ed. pap. 102.30 (*0-8357-6834-1*, 203552100095) Bks Demand.

— Geriatric Length of Stay by Diagnosis & Operation, United States, 1988. LC 88-651323. 361p. reprint ed. pap. 112.00 (*0-7837-1814-4*, 204201400001) Bks Demand.

— Length of Stay by Diagnosis & Operation, North Central Region, 1986. LC 73-173193. 314p. pap. 97.40 (*0-8357-8610-2*, 203503500091) Bks Demand.

— Length of Stay by Diagnosis & Operation, North Central Region, 1987. LC 73-173193. 336p. reprint ed. pap. 104.20 (*0-8357-6831-7*, 203551800095) Bks Demand.

— Length of Stay by Diagnosis & Operation, North Central Region, 1988. LC 73-173193. 361p. reprint ed. pap. 112.00 (*0-7837-1811-X*, 204201100001) Bks Demand.

— Length of Stay by Diagnosis & Operation, Northeastern Region, 1986. LC 73-173193. 314p. reprint ed. pap. 97.40 (*0-8357-8609-9*, 203503400091) Bks Demand.

— Length of Stay by Diagnosis & Operation, Northeastern Region, 1987. LC 73-173193. 336p. reprint ed. pap. 104.20 (*0-8357-6832-5*, 203551900095) Bks Demand.

— Length of Stay by Diagnosis & Operation, Northeastern Region, 1988. LC 73-173193. 361p. reprint ed. pap. 112.00 (*0-7837-1812-8*, 204201200001) Bks Demand.

— Length of Stay by Diagnosis & Operation, Southern Region, 1986. LC 73-173193. 314p. reprint ed. pap. 97.40 (*0-8357-8611-0*, 203503600091) Bks Demand.

— Length of Stay by Diagnosis & Operation, Southern Region, 1987. LC 73-173193. 336p. reprint ed. pap. 104.20 (*0-8357-6830-9*, 203551700095) Bks Demand.

— Length of Stay by Diagnosis & Operation, Southern Region, 1988. LC 73-173193. 361p. reprint ed. pap. 112.00 (*0-7837-1810-1*, 204201000001) Bks Demand.

— Length of Stay by Diagnosis & Operation, United States, 1986. LC 73-173193. 314p. reprint ed. pap. 97.40 (*0-8357-8608-0*, 203503300091) Bks Demand.

— Length of Stay by Diagnosis & Operation, United States, 1987. LC 73-173193. 336p. reprint ed. pap. 104.20 (*0-8357-6299-8*, 203551500097) Bks Demand.

— Length of Stay by Diagnosis & Operation, United States, 1988. LC 73-173193. 361p. reprint ed. pap. 112.00 (*0-7837-1808-X*, 204200800001) Bks Demand.

— Length of Stay by Diagnosis & Operation, Western Region, 1986. LC 73-173193. 314p. reprint ed. pap. 97.40 (*0-8357-8612-9*, 203503700091) Bks Demand.

— Length of Stay by Diagnosis & Operation, Western Region, 1987. LC 73-173193. 336p. reprint ed. pap. 104.20 (*0-8357-6829-5*, 203551600095) Bks Demand.

— Length of Stay by Diagnosis & Operation, Western Region, 1988. LC 73-173193. 361p. reprint ed. pap. 112.00 (*0-7837-1809-8*, 204200900001) Bks Demand.

— Pediatric Length of Stay by Diagnosis & Operation, United States, 1986. LC 88-647491. 314p. reprint ed. pap. 97.40 (*0-8357-8614-5*, 203503900091) Bks Demand.

— Pediatric Length of Stay by Diagnosis & Operation, United States, 1987. LC 88-647491. 330p. reprint ed. pap. 102.30 (*0-8357-6833-3*, 203552000095) Bks Demand.

— Pediatric Length of Stay by Diagnosis & Operation, United States, 1988. LC 88-647491. 361p. reprint ed. pap. 112.00 (*0-7837-1813-6*, 204201300001) Bks Demand.

Commission on Reading Staff, jt. auth. see Anderson, Richard C.

Commission on Reform Jewish Outreach. The 1997 Idea Book. LC 98-142429. ix, 374p. 1997. write for info. (*0-8074-0644-9*) UAHC.

Commission on Roles & Missions of the Armed Forces. Directions for Defense: The Department of Defense Report. LC 97-209389. (Association of the U. S. Army Book Ser.). 148p. 1995. 39.95 (*1-57488-072-1*); pap. 21.95 (*1-57488-073-X*) Brasseys.

Commission on Standards for School Mathematics of. Curriculum & Evaluation Standards for School Mathematics. LC 89-9421. (Illus.). 258p. 1989. pap. 29.95 (*0-87353-273-2*) NCTM.

Commission on Synagogue Affiliation of Union of Am & Central Conference of American Rabbis Staff, eds. Engaging Generation Aleph: A Resource for Young Adults in the Synagogue. LC 98-102279. (Illus.). 158p. (YA). 1997. pap. text 12.00 (*0-8074-0641-4*, 280065) UAHC.

Commission on the Humanities. The Humanities in American Life: Report of the Commission on the Humanities. LC 80-14084. 1980. pap. 12.00 (*0-520-04208-5*, Pub. by U CA Pr) Cal Prin Full Svc.

Commission on the Relations Between Universities &. L' Universite, la Societe & le Gouvernment: Rapport de la Commission d'Etude sur les Relations Entre les Universites & les Gouvernements, Commissaires, Rene Hurtubise, Donald C. Rowat. LC 70-875960. (FRE.). 282p. 1970. reprint ed. pap. 87.50 (*0-608-02203-9*, 206287300004) Bks Demand.

Commission on United States-Latin American Relatio. The Americas in a Changing World. 1980. reprint ed. pap. 24.95 (*0-8129-0561-X*) Transaction Pubs.

Commission on Worship of the Lutheran Church, Miss, prod. Lutheran Worship Concordance. LC 94-41445. 1994. 19.95 (*0-570-01348-8*, 99-1527) Concordia.

Commission V, Testing, Measurement & Control of We, jt. auth. see International Institute of Welding Staff.

Committe for Public Art. Guide to Public Art in Downtown Cleveland. 1995. pap. text 5.95 (*0-9646067-0-4*) Comt Public Art.

Committe for Review of Oversight Mechanisms for Sp & National Research Council Staff. Assessment of Space Shuttle Flight Software Development Processes. 208p. (Orig.). (C). 1993. pap. text 35.00 (*0-309-04880-X*) Natl Acad Pr.

Committe of Maps Projections of the American Carto. Which Map Is Best? Projections for World Maps. 1986. 6.40 (*0-9613459-1-8*, C167) Am Congrs Survey.

Committee EuroInternational du Benton, contrib. by. Fastening for Seismic Retrofitting. LC 98-115154. 46p. 1996. 51.00 (*0-7277-2556-4*, Pub. by T Telford) RCH.

Committee for Economic Development. An Approach to Federal Urban Policy. LC 77-27893. 1977. pap. 2.50 (*0-87186-065-1*) Comm Econ Dev.

— Broadcasting & Cable Television: Policies for Diversity & Change. LC 75-6536. 120p. 1975. pap. 2.50 (*0-87186-058-9*) Comm Econ Dev.

— Budgeting for National Objectives. LC 66-17307. 72p. 1966. pap. 1.50 (*0-87186-021-X*); lib. bdg. 2.50 (*0-87186-721-4*) Comm Econ Dev.

— Congressional Decision Making for National Security. LC 74-12944. 1974. pap. 2.00 (*0-87186-055-4*) Comm Econ Dev.

— Economic Aspects of North Atlantic Security: A Statement on National Policy by the Research & Policy Committee of the Committee for Economic Development. LC 51-5321. 52p. reprint ed. pap. 30.00 (*0-608-30723-8*, 200700800060) Bks Demand.

— Employer Roles in Linking School & Work: Innovative Partnerships in Four Urban Districts. LC 98-24811. 1998. 18.00 (*0-87186-131-3*) Comm Econ Dev.

— The Employer's Role in Linking School & Work. LC 97-51686. 1998. 18.00 (*0-87186-128-3*); 18.00 (*0-87186-132-1*) Comm Econ Dev.

— Financing the Nation's Housing Needs. LC 73-77093. 69p. 1973. pap. 1.50 (*0-87186-050-3*) Comm Econ Dev.

— Helping Insure Our Energy Future: A Program for Developing Synthetic Fuel Plants Now. 1979. pap. 4.50 (*0-87186-069-4*); lib. bdg. 6.00 (*0-87186-769-9*) Comm Econ Dev.

— High Employment Without Inflation: A Positive Program for Economic Stabilization. LC 72-86317. 76p. 1972. pap. 1.50 (*0-87186-747-8*); lib. bdg. 2.50 (*0-87186-047-3*) Comm Econ Dev.

— Improving Federal Program Performance. LC 70-173676. 86p. 1971. pap. 1.50 (*0-87186-043-0*) Comm Econ Dev.

— Improving Productivity in State & Local Government. LC 76-2408. 92p. 1976. pap. 8.50 (*0-87186-060-0*) Comm Econ Dev.

— International Economic Consequences of High-Priced Energy. LC 75-22468. 116p. 1975. pap. 2.50 (*0-87186-059-7*) Comm Econ Dev.

— Military Manpower & National Security. LC 78-189538. 48p. 1972. pap. 1.00 (*0-87186-045-7*) Comm Econ Dev.

— Modernizing Local Government. LC 66-26939. 84p. 1966. pap. 1.50 (*0-87186-023-6*) Comm Econ Dev.

— Modernizing State Government. LC 67-27541. 85p. 1967. pap. 1.50 (*0-87186-028-7*); lib. bdg. 2.50 (*0-87186-728-1*) Comm Econ Dev.

— National Security & Our Individual Freedom: A Statement on National Policy by the Research & Policy Committee of the Committee for Economic Development. LC 50-2569. 50p. reprint ed. pap. 30.00 (*0-608-30726-2*, 200700100060) Bks Demand.

— A New U. S. Farm Policy for Changing World Food Needs. LC 74-84123. 1974. pap. 2.00 (*0-87186-056-2*) Comm Econ Dev.

— The Problem of National Security, Some Economic & Administrative Aspects: A Statement on National Policy by the Research & Policy Committee of the Committee for Economic Development. LC 58-13649. 86p. reprint ed. pap. 30.00 (*0-608-30720-3*, 200703300060) Bks Demand.

— Productivity Policy: Key to the Nation's Economic Future. (CED Statement on National Policy Ser.). 108p. (Orig.). 1983. 10.50 (*0-87186-776-1*); pap. 8.50 (*0-87186-076-7*) Comm Econ Dev.

***Committee for Economic Development.** Promoting Work Opportunities for Older Americans. LC 99-45902. 1999. write for info. (*0-87186-135-6*) Comm Econ Dev.

Committee for Economic Development. Reducing Crime & Assuring Justice. LC 72-81298. 86p. 1972. pap. 1.50 (*0-87186-046-5*); lib. bdg. 2.50 (*0-87186-746-X*) Comm Econ Dev.

— Toward a New International Economic System: A Joint Japanese-American View. LC 74-79477. 64p. 1974. pap. 2.00 (*0-87186-054-6*) Comm Econ Dev.

— Training & Jobs for the Urban Poor. LC 78-130757. 78p. 1970. pap. 1.50 (*0-87186-037-6*) Comm Econ Dev.

— U. S. Economic Policy Toward the Asia-Pacific Region: A Statement on National Policy. LC 97-22692. 1997. write for info. (*0-87186-126-7*) Comm Econ Dev.

***Committee for Economic Development.** Welfare Reform & Beyond: Making Work Work: A Statement on National Policy By the Research & Policy Committee of the Committee for Economic Development. LC 00-22963. 2000. write for info. (*0-87186-137-2*) Comm Econ Dev.

Committee for Economic Development & Conservation Foundation Staff. Energy Prices & Public Policy. LC 82-7428. (CED Statement on National Policy Ser.). 88p. 1982. pap. 7.50 (*0-87186-075-9*); lib. bdg. 9.50 (*0-87186-775-3*) Comm Econ Dev.

Committee for Economic Development & Keizai Doyuka. From Promise to Progress: Towards a New Stage in U. S.-Japan Economic Relations. LC 94-14782. 1994. 6.50 (*0-87186-099-6*) Comm Econ Dev.

Committee for Economic Development Staff. Connecting Inner-City Youth to the World of Work. LC 97-13964. 1997. 12.00 (*0-87186-125-9*) Comm Econ Dev.

***Committee for Economic Development Staff.** Improving Global Financial Stability: A Policy Statement. LC 00-31511. 2000. write for info. (*0-87186-138-0*) Comm Econ Dev.

Committee for Economic Development Staff. Modernizing Government Regulation: The Need for Action: A Statement. LC 97-51618. 1998. write for info. (*0-87186-127-5*) Comm Econ Dev.

— The New America: Prospects for Population & Policy in the 21st Century. 64p. 1989. pap. 7.50 (*0-87186-345-6*) Comm Econ Dev.

— Social Security: A Commitment Worth Keeping: Ensuring a Healthy Social Security System for America: A Statement on National Policy. LC 96-40029. 1997. write for info. (*0-87186-124-0*) Comm Econ Dev.

— Why Child Care Matters: Preparing Young Children for a More Productive America. Hamburg, Sandra K., ed. 144p. 1993. pap. 14.50 (*0-87186-096-1*) Comm Econ Dev.

Committee for Economic Development Staff, et al. America's Basic Research: Prosperity Through Discovery: A Policy Statement. LC 98-24814. 1998. 18.00 (*0-87186-130-5*) Comm Econ Dev.

Committee for Integrity in Science Education Staff. Teaching Science in a Climate of Controversy: A View from the American Scientific Affiliation. rev. ed. 48p. 1993. 7.00 (*1-881479-00-5*) Am Sci Affil.

Committee for National Security & Harriman, W. Averell, Institute for Advanced Study. A Guide to Films about the Soviet Union. 2nd ed. Lamberty, Kim & Halperin, Jonathan H., trs. 75p. 1987. pap. text 5.00 (*0-937115-06-1*) Comm Natl Security.

Committee for National Security Staff, ed. Citizen Attitudes on the Destruction & Disposal of Chemical Weapons Stockpiles: A Report from a Series of Community Dialogue Forums on Chemical Weapons Demilitarization. (Flowerree Series on Chemical Weapons Control). (Illus.). 56p. 1994. pap. text 10.00 (*1-884179-03-7*) Lawyers Alliance.

***Committee for Naval Hydromechanics Staff, et al.** An Assessment of Naval Hydromechanics Science & Technology. 74p. 2000. pap. 18.00 (*0-309-06927-0*) Natl Acad Pr.

***Committee for Oversight, et al.** Blast Mitigation for Structures: 1999 Status Report on the DTRA/TSWG Program. 86p. 2000. pap. 18.00 (*0-309-07048-1*) Natl Acad Pr.

Committee for Pro-Life Activities Staff & NCCB Staff. Nutrition & Hydration: Moral & Pastoral Reflections. 16p. 1992. pap. 1.95 (*1-55586-516-X*) US Catholic.

C

Committee for Study of Public Policy for Surface F. Paying Our Way: Estimating Marginal Social Costs of Feight Transportation Committee for Study of Public Policy for Surface Freight Transportation. LC 96-21831. (Special Reports: No. 246). 171p. 1996. 16.00 (*0-309-06217-9*) Transport Res Bd.

Committee for the Assessment of a National Hazardo. Hazardous Materials Shipment Information for Emergency Response. LC 93-15307. (Special Reports: No. 239). 1993. write for info. (*0-309-05421-4*) Transport Res Bd.

Committee for the Development of Subject Access to. A Cumulative Index to Selected Chicano Periodicals Published Between 1967 & 1978. 1981. 125.00 (*0-8161-0363-1*, G K Hall & Co) Mac Lib Ref.

Committee for the Protection of Human Participants. Ethical Principles in the Conduct of Research with Human Participants. 80p. 1982. pap. 12.95 (*0-912704-82-9*) Am Psychol.

Committee of Selected Works of Zhao Zhongyao Edito, ed. Selected Works of Zhao Zhongyao. 206p. 1996. 59.95 (*7-03-002958-5*, Pub. by Sci Pr) Lubrecht & Cramer.

Committee of the Association of Justices of the St. Bench Book for Trial Judges - New York. LC 89-63828. 1993. suppl. ed. 115.00 (*0-317-03808-7*) West Group.

Committee of the Grampian Club Staff, ed. Edgar: Genealogical Collections Concerning the Scottish House of Edgar, with a Memoir of James Edgar. (Illus.). 103p. 1997. reprint ed. pap. 17.00 (*0-8328-8444-8*); reprint ed. lib. bdg. 27.00 (*0-8328-8443-X*) Higginson Bk Co.

Committee of the Institute of Medicine Division of. Hip Fracture: Setting Priorities for Effectiveness Research. Heithoff, Kim & Lohr, Kathleen N., eds. 72p. 1990. pap. text 15.00 (*0-309-04299-2*) Natl Acad Pr.

Committee of the Town Staff. History of Washington, New Hampshire, from 1760 to 1886, with Genealogies. (Illus.). 696p. 1988. reprint ed. lib. bdg. 69.50 (*0-8328-0078-3*, NH0026) Higginson Bk Co.

Committee on Academic Careers for Experimental Com, jt. auth. see National Research Council Staff.

Committee on Adolescence Staff, jt. auth. see Group for the Advancement of Psychiatry Staff.

Committee on Alluvial Fan Flooding, National Resea. Alluvial Fan Flooding. 182p. (Orig.). 1996. pap. text 39.00 (*0-309-05542-3*) Natl Acad Pr.

Committee on Alternative Chemical Demilitarization, jt. auth. see National Research Council, Comm. on Engineering &.

Committee on Alternatives for Inspection of Outer. Alternatives for Inspecting Outer Continental Shelf Operations. 122p. 1990. pap. text 15.00 (*0-309-04227-5*) Natl Acad Pr.

Committee on American Legislatures, jt. auth. see American Political Science Association Staff.

Committee on an Aging Society Staff. Health in an Older Society. LC 85-15321. (America's Aging Ser.). (Illus.). 251p. reprint ed. pap. 77.90 (*0-8357-4269-5*, 203706500002) Bks Demand.

Committee on Applied & Theoretical Statistics, Nat. Modern Interdisciplinary University Statistics Education: Proceedings of a Symposium. 152p. (Orig.). (C). 1994. pap. text 29.00 (*0-309-05033-2*) Natl Acad Pr.

Committee on Assessing Alternative Birth Settings. Research Issues in the Assessment of Birth Settings: Report of a Study. LC 82-22481. 191p. 1983. reprint ed. pap. 59.30 (*0-608-02342-6*, 206298300004) Bks Demand.

Committee on Assessing Crop Yield, National Resear. Precision Agriculture in the 21st CEntury: Geospatial & Information Technologies in Crop Management. 260p. 1997. 39.95 (*0-309-05643-8*, Joseph Henry Pr) Natl Acad Pr.

Committee on Assessment of Technology & Opportunit. Marine Aquaculture: Opportunities for Growth. 304p. 1992. text 34.95 (*0-309-04675-0*) Natl Acad Pr.

Committee on Budget & Finance Staff. Diocesan Internal Controls: A Framework. LC 96-183153. 26p. (Orig.). 1995. pap. 3.95 (*1-57455-056-X*) US Catholic.

Committee on Care at the End of Life, Institute of. Approaching Death: Improving Care at the End of Life. Field, Marilyn J. & Cassel, Christine K., eds. LC 97-21175. 375p. 1997. 34.95 (*0-309-06372-8*) Natl Acad Pr.

Committee on CCCC Language Statement Staff, jt. auth. see Butler, Melvin A.

Committee on Clay Minerals Staff & Bradley, W. Clays & Clay Minerals: Proceedings of the 11th National Conference on Clays & Clay Minerals, Ottawa, August, 1962. (International Series of Monographs on Earth Sciences: Vol. 13). 168.00 (*0-08-009935-1*, Pub. by Pergamon Repr) Franklin.

Committee on Coastal Erosion Zone Management, Nati. Managing Coastal Erosion. 204p. 1990. text 24.50 (*0-309-04143-0*) Natl Acad Pr.

Committee on Coding. AAOS Guide to CPT Coding. 2nd ed. 65p. 1998. pap. 25.00 (*0-89203-210-3*) Amer Acad Ortho Surg.

Committee on College & University Archives. College & University Archives: Guidelines. 10p. (Orig.). 1979. pap. text 3.50 (*0-931828-32-5*) Soc Am Archivists.

Committee on Contraceptive Development, National R. Developing New Contraceptives: Obstacles & Opportunities. 212p. 1990. text 24.95 (*0-309-04147-3*) Natl Acad Pr.

Committee on Cultural Psychiatry & Group for the Advancement of Psychiatry Staff. Alcoholism in the United States: Racial & Ethnic Considerations. (Group for the Advancement of Psychiatry Ser.: No. 141). 142p. 1996. text 26.00 (*0-87318-209-X*, 7209) Am Psychiatric.

Committee on Developments in Business Financing, A. Term Loan Handbook. 282p. 1983. 55.00 (*0-13-903873-6*) Aspen Law.

Committee on DNA Technology in Forensic Science, N. DNA Technology in Forensic Science. (Illus.). 200p. (C). 1992. pap. text 29.95 (*0-309-04587-8*) Natl Acad Pr.

Committee on Doctrine Staff. The Teaching Ministry of the Diocesan Bishop: A Pastoral Reflection. 28p. (Orig.). (C). 1992. pap. 2.95 (*1-55586-484-8*) US Catholic.

***Committee on Earth Studies, et al.** The Role of Small Satellites in NASA & NOAA Earth Observation Programs. 104p. 2000. pap. 25.25 (*0-309-06982-3*) Natl Acad Pr.

Committee on Environmental Epidemiolgy, National R. Environmental Epidemiology Vol. 2: Use of the Gray Literature & Other Data in Environmental Epidemology. 200p. 1997. 39.95 (*0-309-05737-X*) Natl Acad Pr.

Committee on Financial Management, AHMA, ed. Hotel Internal Control Guide. (Illus.). 150p. 1997. pap. 40.95 (*0-86612-153-6*) Educ Inst Am Hotel.

Committee on Fire- & Smoke-Resistant Materials for, ed. see National Research Council Staff.

Committee on Fire & Smoke-Resistant Materials for. Fire & Smoke-Resistant Interior Materials for Commercial Transport Aircraft. LC 95-73091. 82p. 1996. pap. text 29.00 (*0-309-05389-7*) Natl Acad Pr.

Committee on Flood Control Alternatives in America, ed. see National Research Council Staff.

Committee on Food Chemicals Codex, Institute of Me, jt. auth. see Institute of Medicine (U. S.) Staff.

Committee on Foundations of Manufacturing, Nationa. Manufacturing Systems: Foundations of World-Class Practice. Compton, W. Dale & Heim, Joseph A., eds. 280p. 1991. 34.95 (*0-309-04588-6*) Natl Acad Pr.

— Manufacturing Systems: Foundations of World-Class Practice. Compton, W. Dale & Heim, Joseph A., eds. 288p. 1992. pap. 19.95 (*0-309-04678-5*) Natl Acad Pr.

Committee on Goals 2000 & the Inclusion of Student. Educating One & All: Students with Disabilities & Standards-Based Reform. McDonnell, Lorraine M. et al, eds. LC 97-4869. 304p. 1997. 42.95 (*0-309-05789-2*) Natl Acad Pr.

Committee on Government Policy, Group for the Adva. Forced into Treatment: The Role of Coercion in Clinical Practice. LC 93-26825. (Reports). 1993. 23.00 (*0-87318-205-7*) Grp Adv Psych.

Committee on High Speed Research, Aeronautics & Sp. U. S. Supersonic Commercial Aircraft: Assessing NASA's High Speed Research Program. LC 97-69127. 162p. 1997. pap. text 42.00 (*0-309-05878-3*) Natl Acad Pr.

Committee on Human Factors, ed. see National Research Council Staff.

Committee on Hydropower Intakes of the Energy Divi. Guidelines for Design of Intakes for Hydroelectric Plants. LC 95-1956. 476p. 1995. pap. 45.00 (*0-7844-0073-3*) Am Soc Civil Eng.

Committee on Insurance Coverage Litigation Task Fo, jt. auth. see Shugrue, John D.

Committee on International Banking. The International Monetary Fund & Private Markets. (Report Ser.). 32p. 1983. pap. 10.00 (*1-56708-060-X*) Grp of Thirty.

Committee on International Security & Arms Control. Management & Disposition of Excess Weapons Plutonium. 288p. (Orig.). (C). 1994. pap. text 39.00 (*0-309-05042-1*) Natl Acad Pr.

Committee on Issues in Transborder Flow of Scienti. Bits of Power: Issues in Global Access to Scientific Data. LC 97-4836. 210p. (C). 1997. 44.95 (*0-309-05635-7*, Joseph Henry Pr) Natl Acad Pr.

Committee on Juries of Six. Model Jury Instructions for Use in the District Court, 1997 Supplement: With Forms on Disk. LC 95-78127. 72p. 1997. ring bd., suppl. ed. 39.50 (*1-57589-047-X*, 97-06.16-SP) Mass CLE.

Committee on Juries of Six Staff. Model Jury Instructions for Use in the District Court. rev. ed. 1995. ring bd. 125.00 incl. disk (*0-944490-94-8*) Mass CLE.

***Committee on Labor & Public Welfare Staff.** Legislative History of the Employee Retirement Income Security Act of 1974, 3. 2000. reprint ed. 550.00 (*1-57588-623-5*, 324220) W S Hein.

Committee on Maintaining Privacy & Secruity in Hea. For the Record: Protecting Electronic Health Information. LC 97-65240. 288p. 1997. 29.95 (*0-309-05697-7*, Joseph Henry Pr) Natl Acad Pr.

Committee on Managing Global Genetic Resources, Ag. Forest Trees. (Managing Global Genetic Resources Ser.). 248p. 1991. text 24.95 (*0-309-04034-5*) Natl Acad Pr.

Committee on Medical Ethics. Wrestling with the Future: Our Genes & Our Choices. LC 98-27039. 144p. 1998. pap. 10.95 (*0-8192-1762-X*) Morehouse Pub.

Committee on Migration, U. S. Catholic Bishops Sta. Una Familia en Dios. Herrera, Marina, tr. (SPA.). 28p. (C). 1996. pap. text 1.95 (*1-57455-086-1*) US Catholic.

Committee on Native American Struggles. Rethinking Indian Law. 1983. 42.00 (*0-685-14957-9*) Natl Lawyers Guild.

Committee on Natural Disasters, National Research, ed. Hurricane Elena, Gulf Coast: August 29-September 2, 1985. (Natural Disaster Studies: Vol. 3). 138p. 1991. pap. text 19.00 (*0-309-04434-0*) Natl Acad Pr.

Committee on Natural Disasters Staff, National Res, ed. The Eruption of Nevado del Ruiz Volcano, Columbia, South America, November 13, 1985. (Natural Disaster Studies: Vol. 4). 128p. (C). 1991. pap. text 19.00 (*0-309-04477-4*) Natl Acad Pr.

Committee on Nutritional Status During Pregnancy &, ed. Nutrition During Pregnancy: Part I: Weight Gain, Part II: Nutrient Supplements, Pts. 1 & 2. 480p. 1990. 34.95 (*0-309-04138-4*) Natl Acad Pr.

Committee on Occupational Health Staff. A Physician's Primer on Workers' Compensation. 79p. 1992. pap. 25.00 (*0-89203-073-9*) Amer Acad Ortho Surg.

Committee on Opportunities in the Hydrologic Scien. Opportunities in the Hydrologic Sciences. 368p. 1990. text 29.95 (*0-309-04244-5*) Natl Acad Pr.

Committee on Opportunities to Improve Marine Obser, ed. Opportunities to Improve Marine Forecasting. 120p. 1989. pap. text 15.00 (*0-309-04090-6*) Natl Acad Pr.

Committee on Population, National Research Council. Changing Numbers, Changing Needs: American Indian Demography & Public Health. Sandfur, Gary D. et al, eds. LC 96-70052. 328p. (Orig.). (C). 1996. pap. text 49.00 (*0-309-05548-2*) Natl Acad Pr.

— From Death to Birth: Mortality Decline & Reproductive Change. Montgomery, Mark R. & Cohen, Barney, eds. LC 97-33802. 450p. 1997. pap. text 59.00 (*0-309-05896-1*) Natl Acad Pr.

***Committee on Population, National Research Council, et al.** The Consequences of Maternal Morbidity & Maternal: Report of a Workshop. 44p. 2000. pap. 12.00 (*0-309-06943-2*) Natl Acad Pr.

Committee on Price Determination. Cost Behavior & Price Policy. (Conference on Price Research Ser.: No. 4). 382p. 1943. reprint ed. 99.40 (*0-87014-190-2*) Natl Bur Econ Res.

Committee on Price Determination, jt. auth. see Conference on Price Research.

Committee on Production Technologies for Liquid Tr. Fuels to Drive Our Future. 244p. 1990. text 27.95 (*0-309-04142-2*) Natl Acad Pr.

Committee on Professional Liability, ed. Managing Orthopaedic Malpractice Risk. LC 97-102054. 80p. 1996. 25.00 (*0-89203-153-0*) Amer Acad Ortho Surg.

***Committee on Programmatic Review of the U. S. Department of Energy's Office of Power Technologies, et al.** Renewable Power Pathways: A Review of the U. S. Department of Energy's Renewable Energy Programs. 136p. 2000. pap. 30.75 (*0-309-06980-7*) Natl Acad Pr.

Committee on Psychopathology Staff. Beyond Symptom Suppression: Improving Long-Term Outcomes of Schizophrenia. Group for the Advancement of Psychiatry Staff, ed. LC 91-26231. (Group for the Advancement of Psychiatry Ser.). 125p. 1992. boxed set 27.50 (*0-87318-202-2*) Grp Adv Psych.

Committee on Recent Economic Changes of the Presid & National Bureau Special Staff. Recent Economic Changes in the United States, 2 vols., Vol. 1. (General Ser.: No. 13). 460p. 1929. reprint ed. 119.60 (*0-87014-012-4*) Natl Bur Econ Res.

Committee on Resource Sharing & Coordinated Acquis, ed. Resource Guide, 1987. 2nd ed. x, 56p. 1987. pap. 10.00 (*0-938435-01-9*) LI Lib Resources.

Committee on Reusable Launch Vehicle Technology &. Reusable Launch Vehicle: Technology Development & Test Program. LC 95-73106. 98p. 1996. pap. text 27.00 (*0-309-05437-0*) Natl Acad Pr.

Committee on Science, Engineering & Public Policy, et al. Research Briefings, 1986. 62p. 1986. pap. text 9.95 (*0-309-03689-5*) Natl Acad Pr.

Committee on Scientific Issues in the Endangered-A. Science & the Endangered Species Act. LC 95-33322. 1995. text 39.95 (*0-309-05291-2*) Natl Acad Pr.

Committee on Seismic Analysis of the Structural Di. Seismic Response of Buried Pipes & Structural Components. 58p. 1983. 13.00 (*0-87262-368-8*) Am Soc Civil Eng.

***Committee on Space Launch Staff, et al.** Streamlining Space Launch Range Safety. 70p. 2000. pap. 18.00 (*0-309-06931-9*) Natl Acad Pr.

Committee on Special Structures Staff, Structural, jt. auth. see International Association for Shell & Spatial Stru.

Committee on Technical Bases for Yucca Mountain St, ed. see National Research Council Staff.

Committee on the Assessment of Asthma & Indoor Air, et al. Clearing the Air: Asthma & Indoor Air Exposures. 456p. 2000. 57.95 (*0-309-06496-1*) Natl Acad Pr.

Committee on the Ethical & Legal Issues Relating t. Women & Health Research Vol. 2: Ethical & Legal Issues of Including Women in Clinical Studies: Workshop & Commissioned Papers. Mastroianni, Anna C. et al, eds. 264p. (Orig.). (C). 1994. pap. text 29.00 (*0-309-05040-5*) Natl Acad Pr.

Committee on the Future of Land Grant Colleges of. Colleges of Agriculture at the Land Grant Universities: A Profile. LC 95-31198. 1995. text 34.95 (*0-309-05295-5*) Natl Acad Pr.

Committee on the History of Law in California of t. California Legal History Manuscripts in the Huntington Library: A Guide. 247p. 1989. 35.00 (*0-87328-099-7*) Huntington Lib.

***Committee on the Impact Staff, et al.** The Impact of Selling the Federal Helium Reserve. 98p. 2000. 18.00 (*0-309-07038-4*) Natl Acad Pr.

Committee on the Liturgy, National Conference of C. Reflections on the Body, Cremation, & Catholic Funeral Rites. 16p. 1997. pap. text 1.50 (*1-57455-033-0*) US Catholic.

Committee on the Role of Alternative Farming Metho. Alternative Agriculture. 464p. 1989. pap. text 28.95 (*0-309-03985-1*) Natl Acad Pr.

Committee on the Status of Women in Librarianship. Women of Color in Librarianship: An Oral History. LC 92-42391. (Illus.). 1993. write for info. (*0-8389-7639-5*) ALA.

Committee on the Use of Volunteers in Schools, Nat. Volunteers in Public Schools. 160p. 1990. pap. text 14.95 (*0-309-04149-X*) Natl Acad Pr.

Committee on Therapeutic Care & Group for the Advancement of Psychiatry Staff. Mental Health in Remote Rural Developing Areas: Concepts & Cases. (GAP Report Ser.: No. 139). 230p. 1995. text 12.95 (*0-87318-207-3*, 7207) Am Psychiatric.

***Committee on Utilization of Technologies Developed at Russian Research & Educational Institutions Staff.** Technology Commercialization. LC 98-89705. viii, 138p. 1998. pap. 39.00 (*0-309-06194-6*) Natl Acad Pr.

Committee on Valuing Ground Water, National Resear. Valuing Ground Water: Economic Concepts & Approaches. LC 97-4837. 204p. (C). 1997. 37.95 (*0-309-05640-3*, Joseph Henry Pr) Natl Acad Pr.

Committee on Vision, National Research Council Sta. Reports on the Committee on Vision, 1947-1990. 124p. 1990. pap. text 15.00 (*0-309-04148-1*) Natl Acad Pr.

Committee on Xenograft Transplantation Institute o. Xenotransplantation: Science, Ethics, & Public Policy. LC 96-69850. 136p. (Orig.). (C). 1996. pap. text 29.00 (*0-309-05549-0*) Natl Acad Pr.

Committee Staff on Fuel Economy of Automobiles & L, ed. Automotive Fuel Economy: How Far Can We Go? 288p. 1992. pap. text 34.95 (*0-309-04530-4*) Natl Acad Pr.

Committee Staff on Restoration of Aquatic Ecosyte, ed. Restoration of Aquatic Ecosystems: Science, Technology, & Public Policy. 576p. 1992. text 39.95 (*0-309-04534-7*) Natl Acad Pr.

Committee to Evaluate Mass Balance Information for. Tracking Toxic Substances at Industrial Facilities: Engineering Mass Balance vs. Materials Accounting. 198p. 1990. pap. text 21.00 (*0-309-04086-8*) Natl Acad Pr.

Committee to Protect Journalist Staff & Article 19 (Organization) Staff. Journalism under Occupation: Israel's Regulation of the Palestinian Press. LC 98-104624. 224 p. 1988. write for info. (*0-938579-45-2*) Hum Rts Watch.

Committee to Study Foreign Investment in the Unite. A Guide to Foreign Investment under United States Law. 626p. 1979. 55.00 (*0-317-29404-0*, #H39808) Harcourt.

Committee to Study the Feasibility of, & Need for,, ed. see Institute of Medicine Staff.

Committee to Study the Use of Advisory Committees. Food & Drug Administration Advisory Committees, 1992. Rettig, Richard A. et al, eds. LC 92-62633. 238p. (Orig.). 1992. pap. text 33.00 (*0-309-04837-0*) Natl Acad Pr.

Committee 34, the Armored School Staff. The Armored Division As an Assault Landing Force. 3rd rev. ed. (World War II Monograph: Vol. 320). (Illus.). 60p. 1997. reprint ed. 15.95 (*1-57638-086-6*, M320H); reprint ed. pap. 5.95 (*1-57638-011-4*, M320S) Merriam Pr.

Commodore Business Machines, Inc. Staff. Amiga Rom Kernel Reference Manual: Exec. write for info. (*0-318-60215-6*) Addison-Wesley.

Commodore Business Machines Staff. Amiga Rom Kernel Reference Manual: Executive. 1986. pap. 24.95 (*0-201-11099-7*) Addison-Wesley.

Common, A. K., jt. ed. see Chisholm, J. S.

Common, Alfred F. How to Repair Violins. 1988. reprint ed. lib. bdg. 59.00 (*0-7812-0473-9*) Rprt Serv.

— How to Repair Violins. reprint ed. lib. bdg. 45.00 (*0-403-03871-5*) Scholarly.

Common Child Press Staff. Diana: Queen of Hearts. LC 97-76620. 1997. pap. 4.99 (*0-679-89214-1*) Random.

Common Council for American Unity. The Alien & the Immigration Law: A Study of 1446 Cases Arising under the Immigration & Naturalization Laws of the United States. LC 72-6923. 388p. reprint ed. lib. bdg. 22.50 (*0-8371-6503-2*, ALIL) Greenwood.

Common Desktop Environment Documentation Group Sta. Application Builder User's Guide. LC 95-11125. (Common Desktop Environment 1.0 Ser.). 176p. (C). 1995. pap. 29.95 (*0-201-48958-9*) Addison-Wesley.

— Programmer's Guide. LC 95-11123. (Common Desktop Environment 1.0 Ser.). 208p. (C). 1995. pap. 29.95 (*0-201-48954-6*) Addison-Wesley.

— Programmer's Overview. LC 95-11124. (Common Desktop Environment 1.0 Ser.). 112p. (C). 1995. pap. 27.95 (*0-201-48953-8*) Addison-Wesley.

— ToolTalk Messaging Overview. LC 95-11115. (Common Desktop Environment 1.0 Ser.). 176p. (C). 1995. pap. 29.95 (*0-201-48956-2*) Addison-Wesley.

— User's Guide. LC 95-11127. (Common Desktop Environment 1.0 Ser.). 368p. (C). 1995. pap. 29.95 (*0-201-48951-1*) Addison-Wesley.

Common Fund Staff. A Chartbook of Trends Affecting Higher Education Finance, 1960-1990, 3 vols., Set, Vol. 1. Wingerd, Dan, ed. 73p. 1992. pap. write for info. (*1-882778-03-0*) Common Fund.

— A Chartbook of Trends Affecting Higher Education Finance, 1960-1990, 3 vols., Vol. 1. Wingerd, Dan, ed. 73p. 1992. pap. write for info. (*1-882778-00-6*) Common Fund.

***Common Ground Staff.** The River's Voice: An Anthology of Poetry. King, Angela, ed. (Anthology of Poetry Ser.). 280p. 2000. 16.95 (*1-890132-69-1*) Chelsea Green Pub.

Common, Hubert, ed. see French Spring School of Theoretical Computer Scien.

Common, I. F. Moths of Australia. (Illus.). 535p. 1990. 236.00 (*90-04-09227-7*) Brill Academic Pubs.

— Oecophorine Genera of Australia Vol. II: The Chezala, Philobata, & Eulechria Groups (Lepidoptera: Oecophoridae) LC 97-175121. (Monographs on Australian Lepidoptera: No. 5). (Illus.). 404p. 1996. 130.00 (*0-643-05934-2*, Pub. by CSIRO) Accents Pubns.

— Oecophorine Genera of Australia I: The Wingia Group. (Monographs on Australian Lepidoptera: Vol. 3). 390p. 1994. 100.00 (*0-643-05524-X*, Pub. by CSIRO) Accents Pubns.

C

An Asterisk (*) at the beginning of an entry indicates that the title is appearing for the first time.

Common, I. F. & Waterhouse, D. F. Butterflies of Australia. expanded rev. ed. LC 95-225443. (Illus.). 682p. 1995. 69.95 (*0-643-05738-2*, Pub. by CSIRO) Accents Pubns.

Common, Ian. Moths of Australia. 544p. 1990. reprint ed. 150.00 (*0-522-84326-3*, Pub. by Melbourne Univ Pr) Paul & Co Pubs.

Common, Jack. Kiddar's Luck. LC 90-80811. 208p. 1990. pap. 15.95 (*1-85224-127-6*, Pub. by Bloodaxe Bks) Dufour.

Common, Michael. Sustainability & Policy: Limits to Economics. (Illus.). 360p. (C). 1995. pap. text 21.95 (*0-521-43605-2*) Cambridge U Pr.

Common, Michael S. Basic Econometrics. LC 76-7466. (Modern Economics Ser.). 527p. reprint ed. pap. 163.40 (*0-8357-5977-6*, 202524400043) Bks Demand.

— Environmental & Resource Economics: An Introduction. 2nd ed. LC 96-24368. 1995. pap. text. write for info. (*0-582-24632-6*) Longman.

Common, Richard, et al. Managing Public Services: Competition & Decentralization. 280p. 1993. pap. 47.95 (*0-7506-0977-X*) Buttrwrth-Heinemann.

Common Sense Press Staff. Great Editing Adventure Series, Vol. I. 61p. 1993. pap. 15.00 (*1-880892-75-8*) Com Sense FL.

Common, Thomas, tr. see Nietzsche, Friedrich Wilhelm.

Common Women Collective Staff. Women in U. S. History: An Annotated Bibliography. LC 77-350179. (Illus.). 2.60 (*0-9601122-1-9*) Common Women.

Commoner, Barry. Making Peace with the Planet. 304p. 1992. pap. 11.95 (*1-56584-012-7*, Pub. by New Press NY) Norton.

— Making Peace with the Planet. 1993. 24.00 (*0-8446-6701-3*) Peter Smith.

Commoner, Barry, jt. auth. see Cohen, Mark.

Commons, Harold & Amstutz, Harold E. Heritage & Harvest: The History of the Association of Baptist for World Evangelism, Inc., 2 vols., Set. (Illus.). (Orig.). 1992. pap. text 17.90 (*1-888796-02-2*) ABWE Pubng.

Commons, Harold T. Heritage & Harvest: The History of the Association of Baptist for World Evangelism, Inc., 2 vols., Set. (Illus.). 294p. (Orig.). 1981. pap. text 8.95 (*1-888796-08-1*) ABWE Pubng.

Commons, John R. Industrial Goodwill. LC 75-89726. (American Labor, from Conspiracy to Collective Bargaining Ser., No. 1). 213p. 1974. reprint ed. 18.95 (*0-405-02113-5*) Ayer.

— Institutional Economics: Its Place in Political Economy. 994p. (C). 1990. pap. 29.95 (*0-88738-797-7*) Transaction Pubs.

— Institutional Economics: Its Place in Political Economy, Vols. 1 & 2. 994p. (C). 1990. pap. 49.95 (*0-88738-832-9*) Transaction Pubs.

— Institutional Economics Vol. 2: It's Place in Political Economy. 994p. (C). 1990. pap. 29.95 (*0-88738-831-0*) Transaction Pubs.

— Labor & Administration. LC 64-17404. (Reprints of Economic Classics Ser.). ix, 431p. 1964. reprint ed. 49.50 (*0-678-00035-2*) Kelley.

— Legal Foundations of Capitalism. LC 75-184663. (Reprints of Economic Classics Ser.). x, 394p. 1974. reprint ed. lib. bdg. 49.50 (*0-678-00897-3*) Kelley.

— Legal Foundations of Capitalism. rev. ed. LC 94-12484. 438p. (C). 1994. pap. 29.95 (*1-56000-781-8*) Transaction Pubs.

— Myself: The Autobiography of John R. Commons. (Illus.). 222p. 1963. pap. 9.95 (*0-299-02924-7*) U of Wis Pr.

— Proportional Representation: With Chapters on the Initiative, the Referendum & Primary Elections. 2nd ed. LC 66-21662. xi, 369p. 1967. reprint ed. 45.00 (*0-678-00222-3*) Kelley.

— Races & Immigrants in America. 2nd ed. LC 67-27834. xxiv, 242p. 1967. reprint ed. 39.50 (*0-678-00321-1*) Kelley.

— Social Reform & the Church. LC 66-21663. (Illus.). x, 176p. 1967. reprint ed. 35.00 (*0-678-00286-X*) Kelley.

— A Sociological View of Sovereignty: A Series of Articles in the American Journal of Sociology, 1899-1900. LC 64-17405. (Reprints of Economic Classics Ser.). xiv, 107p. 1967. reprint ed. 29.50 (*0-678-00090-5*) Kelley.

Commons, John R., ed. Trade Unionism & Labor Problems. LC 66-21664. (Library of American Labor History). xiv, 628p. 1967. reprint ed. 65.00 (*0-678-00221-5*) Kelley.

— Trade Unionism & Labor Problems, Series 2. LC 66-21665. (Library of American Labor History). xiii, 838p. 1967. reprint ed. 75.00 (*0-678-00287-8*) Kelley.

Commons, John R. & Andrews, John B. Principles of Labor Legislation. 4th ed. LC 66-22620. (Reprints of Economic Classics Ser.). xviii, 606p. 1967. reprint ed. 57.50 (*0-678-00207-X*) Kelley.

Commons, John R., et al. A Documentary History of American Industrial Society, 10 vols., Set. Phillips, Ulrich B., ed. LC 88-47770. 1988. reprint ed. 920.00 (*0-404-20330-2*) AMS Pr.

— History of Labor in the United States, 4 vols., Set. LC 66-18557. (Reprints of Economic Classics Ser.). 1966. reprint ed. 250.00 (*0-678-00142-1*) Kelley.

— History of Labor in the United States (To 1896), Vol. 1. LC 66-18557. (Reprints of Economic Classics Ser.). xxv, 623p. 1966. reprint ed. 75.00 (*0-678-04036-2*) Kelley.

— History of Labor in the United States (To 1896), Vol. 2. LC 66-18557. (Reprints of Economic Classics Ser.). xx, 620p. 1966. reprint ed. 75.00 (*0-678-04037-0*) Kelley.

— History of Labor in the United States (1896-1932), Vol. 3. LC 66-18557. (Reprints of Economic Classics Ser.). xxx, 778p. 1966. reprint ed. 75.00 (*0-678-04038-9*) Kelley.

— Industrial Government. LC 79-89727. (American Labor, from Conspiracy to Collective Bargaining Ser., No. 1). 425p. 1974. reprint ed. 25.95 (*0-405-02114-3*) Ayer.

Commons, Michael L., et al, eds. Adult Development: Models & Methods in the Study of Adolescent & Adult Thought, Vol. 2. LC 88-27425. 304p. 1990. 65.00 (*0-275-92755-5*, C2755, Praeger Pubs) Greenwood.

Commons, Michael L., et al, eds. Beyond Formal Operations Vol. 2: Adolescent & Adult Development Models. LC 88-27425. 362p. 1989. 65.00 (*0-275-92748-2*, C2748, Praeger Pubs) Greenwood.

— Biological Determinants of Reinforcement: Quantitative Analyses of Behavior, Vol. 7. 312p. 1988. 69.95 (*0-89859-551-7*) L Erlbaum Assocs.

— The Effect of Delay of Intervening Events on Reinforcement Value: Quantitative Analyses of Behavior, Vol. 5. (Roitblat-Bever-Olton: Comparative Cognition & Neuroscience Ser.). 344p. 1986. text 69.95 (*0-89859-800-1*) L Erlbaum Assocs.

Commons, Michael L. & Nevin, J. A., eds. Discriminative Properties of Reinforcement Schedules: Quantitative Analyses of Behavior, Vol. 1. 480p. 1985. 99.95 (*0-89859-831-1*) L Erlbaum Assocs.

Commons, Michael L. & Shettleworth, A. Kacelnick, eds. Foraging: Qualitative Analysis of Behavior, Vol. 6. (Roitblat-Bever Olton: Comparative Cognition & Neuroscience Ser.). 312p. 1987. text 69.95 (*0-89859-550-9*) L Erlbaum Assocs.

Commons, Michael L., et al. Behavioral Approaches to Pattern Recognition & Concept Formation: Quantitative Analyses of Behavior, Vol. 8. 240p. 1990. 69.95 (*0-8058-0398-X*) L Erlbaum Assocs.

— Computational & Clinical Approaches to Pattern Recognition & Concept Formation: Quantitative Analyses of Behavior, Vol. 9. 176p. 1990. 59.95 (*0-8058-0399-8*) L Erlbaum Assocs.

— Qualitative Analysis of Behavior, Vol. 11: Neural Network Models of Conditioning & Action, Vol. 11. 376p. 1991. 79.95 (*0-8058-0842-6*); pap. 39.95 (*0-8058-0843-4*) L Erlbaum Assocs.

— Signal Detection: Mechanisms, Models, & Applications. 304p. (C). 1991. text 59.95 (*0-8058-0823-X*) L Erlbaum Assocs.

Commons, Michael L., jt. auth. see Stevens-Long, Judith.

Commons, Michael L., ed. see Chinen, Allan B., et al.

Commons, Michael L., ed. see Richards, Francis A. & Armon, Cheryl.

Commonwealth Expert Group Staff. Beyond Apartheid: Human Resources for a New South Africa. 133p. (C). 1991. pap. 17.50 (*0-435-08069-5*, 08069) Heinemann.

Commonwealth Fund Staff & Littlefield, John W. Variation, Senescence & Neoplasia in Cultured Somatic Cells. (Illus.). 147p. 1975. 23.95 (*0-674-93208-0*) HUP.

Commonwealth Institute Staff & Heathcote, David. The Arts of the Hausa. LC 77-4274. 72p. 1977. lib. bdg. 36.00 (*0-226-68899-2*) U Ch Pr.

Commonwealth of Pennsylvania Staff. Laws of Pennsylvania, 1987. Legislative Reference Bureau Staff, ed. 738p. 1988. text 8.70 (*0-8182-0102-9*) Commonweal PA.

— Oil & Gas Developments in Pennsylvania in 1986. Department of Environmental Resources Geological S, ed. (Progress Reports: No. 200). (Illus.). 93p. 1987. pap. text 3.05 (*0-8182-0098-7*) Commonweal PA.

Commonwealth Scientific & Industrial Research Orga. The Insects of Australia: A Textbook for Students & Research Workers. 2nd ed. LC 91-9407. (Comstock Ser.). (Illus.). 1500p. 1991. text 235.00 (*0-8014-2669-3*) Cornell U Pr.

— Scientific & Technical Research Centres in Australia. Crump, I., ed. 332p. 1975. 63.00 (*0-677-65210-0*) Gordon & Breach.

Commonwealth Secretariat Staff. Commonwealth National Bibliographies: An Annotated Directory. LC 77-377740. 97 p. 1977. 0.50 (*0-85092-125-2*) Comm Sec.

***Commonwealth Secretariat Staff.** Gender Mainstreaming in Education: A Reference Manual for Governments & Other Stakeholders. (Gender Management System Ser.). 2000. pap. 19.95 (*0-85092-598-3*, Pub. by Comm Sec) Stylus Pub VA.

Commonwealth Secretatiat Staff, jt. auth. see IFLA International Office for UBC Staff.

Communicating. Communicating, 6 vols. 6th ed. LC 94-76490. (C). 1994. pap. text 39.16 (*0-395-70865-6*) HM.

Communication Briefings Editors. The Best Ideas in Time Management. 44p. (Orig.). 1993. pap. 25.00 (*1-878604-10-4*) Briefings Pub Grp.

— 5 Minute Workshops for Effective Communication. 50p. 1996. pap. 25.00 (*1-878604-24-4*) Briefings Pub Grp.

***Communication Briefings Editors.** Glossary of (Even More) Misused Words & Phrases: Your Desktop Guide to Using the Right Terms in the Right Place at the Right Time. 50p. 1999. pap. 12.50 (*1-878604-34-1*) Briefings Pub Grp.

Communication Briefings Editors. How to Get Results with Business Writing. 48p. (Orig.). 1992. pap. 25.00 (*1-878604-07-4*) Briefings Pub Grp.

— How to Get Results with Publicity. 50p. (Orig.). 1992. pap. 25.00 (*1-878604-06-6*) Briefings Pub Grp.

***Communication Briefings Editors.** The 99 Most Common Grammar & Writing Errors . . . And How to Avoid Them. 48p. 1999. pap. 12.50 (*1-878604-33-3*) Briefings Pub Grp.

Communication Briefings Editors. 101 Ways to Influence People on the Job. 48p. 1998. pap. 25.00 (*1-878604-26-0*) Briefings Pub Grp.

— The Seventy-Six Most Common Grammar Errors. 48p. (Orig.). 1992. pap. 12.50 (*1-878604-08-2*) Briefings Pub Grp.

— 21 Workplace Personalities: How to Say the Right Things to the Right People. 46p. 1996. pap. 12.50 (*1-878604-23-6*) Briefings Pub Grp.

— Unlocking Your Leadership Potential. 48p. 1998. pap. 25.00 (*1-878604-27-9*) Briefings Pub Grp.

Communication Independence for the Neurologically. Communication & Swallowing Solutions for the ALS/MND Community: A CINI Manual. Kazandjian, Marta S., ed. LC 96-32631. (Illus.). 100p. (Orig.). 1996. pap. 39.95 (*1-56593-808-9*, 1580) Thomson Learn.

Communication Research Association Staff. Communicate: A Workbook for Interpersonal Communication. 5th ed. 416p. (C). 1996. pap. text, spiral bd. 27.95 (*0-8403-9541-8*) Kendall-Hunt.

Communication Skill Builders & VORT Corporation Editors, jt. auth. see Browne, Barbara C.

Communication Skill Builders Editorial & Consultan, compiled by. Clinician's Choice: Favorite Activities for Speech & Language. 66p. (Orig.). 1985. pap. text 25.00 (*0-7616-7011-4*) Commun Skill.

Communication Yearbook Staff. Communication Yearbook, Vol. 7, 1983. LC 76-45943. (Illus.). 927p. 1983. reprint ed. pap. 200.00 (*0-608-01107-X*, 205941600007) Bks Demand.

— Communication Yearbook, Vol. 8, 1984. LC 76-45943. (Illus.). 831p. 1984. reprint ed. pap. 200.00 (*0-608-01108-8*, 205941600008) Bks Demand.

— Communication Yearbook, Vol. 9, 1986. LC 76-45943. (Illus.). 853p. 1986. reprint ed. pap. 200.00 (*0-608-01109-6*, 205941600009) Bks Demand.

— Communication Yearbook, Vol. 10, 1987. LC 76-45943. (Illus.). 888p. 1987. reprint ed. pap. 200.00 (*0-608-01110-X*, 205941600010) Bks Demand.

— Communication Yearbook, Vol. 11, 1988. LC 76-45943. (Illus.). 640p. 1988. reprint ed. pap. 198.40 (*0-608-01111-8*, 205941600011) Bks Demand.

— Communication Yearbook, Vol. 12, 1989. LC 76-45943. (Illus.). 703p. reprint ed. pap. 200.00 (*0-608-01112-6*, 205941600012) Bks Demand.

Communications & Society Program (Aspen Institute) Staff, jt. auth. see Garmer, Amy K.

Communications Library Staff. Asi Es Nuestra Ley. 2nd ed. (SPA.). 70p. 1987. pap. text 25.00 (*0-934339-88-0*) Comm Lib.

— BCTV: Bibliography on Cable Television - 1987. LC 90-85810. 90p. (Orig.). 1987. pap. 40.00 (*0-934339-13-9*, 1987) Comm Lib.

— BCTV: Bibliography on Cable Television - 1988. LC 90-85810. 100p. (Orig.). 1988. pap. 40.00 (*0-934339-14-7*) Comm Lib.

— BCTV: Bibliography on Cable Television - 1990. Connelly, Theodore S., ed. LC 90-85810. 100p. (Orig.). 1990. pap. 40.00 (*0-934339-16-3*) Comm Lib.

— BCTV: Bibliography on Cable Television - 1991. Connelly, Theodore S., ed. LC 90-85810. 100p. (Orig.). 1991. pap. 40.00 (*0-934339-17-1*, 1991) Comm Lib.

— BCTV: Bibliography on Cable Television - 1992. Connelly, Theodore S., ed. LC 90-85810. 100p. (Orig.). 1992. pap. 40.00 (*0-934339-18-X*, 1992) Comm Lib.

— BCTV: Bibliography on Cable Television - 1994. Connelly, Theodore S., ed. LC 90-85810. 100p. (Orig.). 1994. pap. 40.00 (*0-934339-20-1*) Comm Lib.

— BCTV: Bibliography on Cable Television - 1996. Connelly, Theodore S., ed. LC 90-85810. 100p. (Orig.). 1996. pap. 40.00 (*0-934339-22-8*) Comm Lib.

— BCTV: Bibliography on Cable Television 1975. 52p. (C). 1975. pap. 40.00 (*0-934339-00-7*, 1975) Comm Lib.

— BCTV: Bibliography on Cable Television 1976. LC 90-85810. 35p. (Orig.). (C). 1976. pap. 40.00 (*0-934339-01-5*, 1976) Comm Lib.

— BCTV: Bibliography on Cable Television 1977. LC 90-85810. 31p. (Orig.). (C). 1977. pap. 40.00 (*0-934339-02-3*, 1977) Comm Lib.

— BCTV: Bibliography on Cable Television 1978. LC 90-85810. 29p. (Orig.). (C). 1978. pap. 40.00 (*0-934339-03-1*, 1978) Comm Lib.

— BCTV: Bibliography on Cable Television 1979. LC 90-85810. 29p. (Orig.). (C). 1979. pap. 40.00 (*0-934339-04-X*, 1979) Comm Lib.

— BCTV: Bibliography on Cable Television 1980. LC 90-85810. 35p. (Orig.). (C). 1980. pap. 40.00 (*0-934339-05-8*, 1980) Comm Lib.

— BCTV: Bibliography on Cable Television 1981. LC 90-85810. 41p. (Orig.). (C). 1981. pap. 40.00 (*0-934339-06-6*, 1981) Comm Lib.

— BCTV: Bibliography on Cable Television 1982. LC 90-85810. 59p. (Orig.). (C). 1982. pap. 40.00 (*0-934339-07-4*, 1982) Comm Lib.

— BCTV: Bibliography on Cable Television 1983. LC 90-85810. 60p. (Orig.). (C). 1983. pap. 40.00 (*0-934339-08-2*, 1983) Comm Lib.

— BCTV: Bibliography on Cable Television 1984. LC 90-85810. vi, 74p. (Orig.). (C). 1984. pap. 40.00 (*0-934339-09-0*, 1984) Comm Lib.

— BCTV: Bibliography on Cable Television 1985. LC 90-85810. vi, 80p. (Orig.). (C). 1985. pap. 40.00 (*0-934339-10-4*, 1985) Comm Lib.

— BCTV: Bibliography on Cable Television 1986. LC 90-85810. viii, 75p. (Orig.). (C). 1986. pap. 40.00 (*0-934339-12-0*, 1986) Comm Lib.

— BCTV: Bibliography on Cable Television 1989. LC 90-85810. 100p. (Orig.). 1989. pap. 40.00 (*0-934339-15-5*) Comm Lib.

— BCTV: Bibliography on Cable Television 1997. Connelly, Theodore S., ed. LC 90-85810. 100p. (Orig.). 1997. pap. 40.00 (*0-934339-23-6*) Comm Lib.

— This Is Your Law. 2nd ed. 70p. 1987. pap. text 25.00 (*0-934339-87-2*) Comm Lib.

Communications Research Council. Federal Government Frequency Assignments. 302p. 1995. pap. 24.95 (*0-917963-07-5*) Artsci Inc.

Communications Research Council Staff. Police & Fire Communications Handbook. 376p. 1995. pap. 19.95 (*0-917963-16-4*) Artsci Inc.

***Communications Theatre Staff.** Theatre Directory 1999-2000. 1999. pap. 9.95 (*1-55936-176-X*) Theatre Comm.

Communist Party Convention Staff. La Lucha de los Chicanos por la Liberacion: La Posicion del Portido Comunista, 20th National Convention.Tr. of Toward Chicano Liberation: the Communist Party Position. (SPA.). 24p. 1972. pap. 0.40 (*0-87898-092-X*) New Outlook.

— Our Nation's Crisis & How to Solve It: Main Political Resolution, Communist Party Twentieth National Convention. 96p. 1972. pap. 0.65 (*0-87898-087-3*) New Outlook.

Communist Party Convention Staff & Hall, Gus. For Peace, Jobs, Equality: Prevent "The Day after," Defeat Reaganism - Report to the 23rd Convention of the Communist Party, U. S. A., Cleveland, Ohio, November 10-13, 1983. LC 84-1976. 1983. 0.50 (*0-87898-156-X*) New Outlook.

Communist Party of China. Resolution on CPC History (1949-81) 126p. 1981. pap. 6.50 (*0-317-66867-6*, Pergamon Pr) Elsevier.

Communist Party Steel & Metal Workers Commission. Steel Mill or Treadmill? How to Stop the Big Steel Steal. 1971. pap. 0.15 (*0-87898-069-5*) New Outlook.

Communitarian Network Staff. Civic Repentance. Etzioni, Amitai, ed. LC 98-30411. (Rights & Responsibilities Ser.: Vol. 131). 240p. 1999. pap. 22.95 (*0-8476-9235-3*) Rowman.

Community Alliance Staff & Family Farmers Staff. National Organic Directory, 1999. 16th rev. ed. (Illus.). 396p. 1999. pap. 47.95 (*1-891894-03-X*) Commun Alliance.

Community Alliance with Family Farmers Staff, compiled by. Bios for Almonds: A Practical Guide to Biologically Integrated Orchard Systems Management. (Illus.). 104p. 1995. pap. 7.00 (*1-891894-02-1*) Commun Alliance.

— National Organic Directory, 1997. 14th rev. ed. (Illus.). xiii, 388p. 1997. pap. 24.95 (*1-891894-00-5*) Commun Alliance.

— National Organic Directory, 1998, Vol. 15. 15th rev. ed. (Illus.). 1998. pap. 44.95 (*1-891894-01-3*) Commun Alliance.

Community Arts Resources, Inc. Staff, jt. auth. see Fringe Festival-Los Angeles Staff.

Community Banker Staff. Community Banker: February Issue. 1995. per. write for info. (*0-7602-0040-8*, Irwn Prfssnl) McGraw-Hill Prof.

— Community Banker Q1. 96p. 1996. per. write for info. (*0-7602-0041-6*, Irwn Prfssnl) McGraw-Hill Prof.

— Community Banker Q3, 1996 Issue. 2nd ed. 1996. per. write for info. (*0-7863-0718-8*, Irwn Prfssnl) McGraw-Hill Prof.

Community College Roundtable Staff. Community Colleges: Core Indicators of Effectiveness. LC 94-185416. 32p. 1994. pap. 15.00 (*0-87117-272-0*, 1365) Comm Coll Pr Am Assn Comm Coll.

— Community Colleges: Core Indicators of Effectiveness: A Report of the Community College Roundtable. LC 94-185416. (AACC Special Reports: Vol. 4). (Illus.). 31p. pap. 30.00 (*0-608-20271-1*, 207153000012) Bks Demand.

Community Communications Staff, et al. Tuscaloosa: City Business Profiles. Turner, James E. & Hughes, Mary, eds. LC 94-30112. 165p. 1994. reprint ed. pap. 19.95 (*1-885352-05-0*) Community Comm.

Community Design Center of Pittsburgh, Inc. Staff. New Urban Housing: Fresh Thinking from the Pittsburgh Design Competition. (Illus.). 72p. 1994. pap. 21.95 (*0-9641302-0-3*) Comm Design.

Community Economics Corporation Staff & Cotter, Jim. Small & Micro Enterprise Credit: Recommendations & Case Studies Presented at the Best Practices Workshop. 138p. 1993. pap. text 25.00 (*0-9637044-2-7*) PACT Pubns.

Community Foundation of Greater Washington Staff. Directory of Foundations of the Greater Washington Area, 1984. 125p. 1984. 10.00 (*0-318-03830-7*) Comm Foun DC.

Community Garden Club of Johnson City Staff. Potluck on the Pedernales, Second Helping. 324p. 1993. 16.95 (*0-89015-909-2*) Sunbelt Media.

Community Garden Club of Johnson City, Texas Staff. Potluck on the Pedernales. 324p. 1991. 16.95 (*0-89015-829-0*) Sunbelt Media.

Community Home Health Section Staff. Guidelines for the Provision of Physical Therapy in the Home. 21p. 1996. pap. 15.00 (*1-887759-32-8*, P-131) Am Phys Therapy Assn.

Community Intervention, Inc. Staff. Athletes & Drugs: A No-Win Combination. 36p. (Orig.). 1986. pap. 3.95 (*0-9613416-2-9*) Comm Intervention.

— Participant Guidebook: My Life . . . Right Now. (Illus.). 52p. (YA). (gr. 7-12). 1988. student ed. 3.50 (*0-9613416-9-6*) Comm Intervention.

— Saying Yes, Saying No: You & Drugs--A Positive Approach to Staying Drug Free. 24p. (Orig.). (YA). (gr. 8-12). 1986. pap. 3.95 (*0-9613416-4-5*) Comm Intervention.

— Signs & Symptoms: Adolescent Drug & Alcohol Use: What to Look for, What to Do. 22p. (Orig.). 1986. pap. 3.95 (*0-9613416-3-7*) Comm Intervention.

Community Law Offices Staff, jt. ed. see Council of New York Law Associates Staff.

Community Maps Staff. Dane County Atlas. (Illus.). 72p. 1995. 11.95 (*0-9654175-1-4*) Community Maps.

Community of Jesus, Inc. Staff. The Starting Line. (Illus.). 118p. 1989. student ed. 19.95 (*0-685-29183-9*) Community Jesus.

C

Community Ownership Organizing Project Staff. The Cities' Wealth: Programs for Community Economic Control. 87p. 1976. pap. text 21.95 (*0-87855-665-6*) Transaction Pubs.
Community Resource Exchange Staff. From Vision to Reality: A Guide for Forming & Sustaining Community-Based Efforts. (Illus.). 240p. 1996. ring bd. 59.95 (*0-9655305-1-5*) Commun Res Exchange.
Community Resource Exchange Staff, ed. see Barrett, Fran, et al.
Community Scribes Staff, ed. see Carnegie Council on Adolescent Development Staff.
Community Service Editors. Bottom-up Democracy. 1954. pap. 1.50 (*0-910420-07-6*) Comm Serv OH.
— Community in Economic Pioneering. 1973. pap. 1.00 (*0-910420-21-1*) Comm Serv OH.
— Guidebook for Intentional Communities. Morgan, Griscom, ed. 1988. pap. 5.00 (*0-910420-01-7*) Comm Serv OH.
— Wholeness in Interaction. 1976. pap. 1.00 (*0-910420-10-6*) Comm Serv OH.
— World's Economic Plight & Community Responsibility. 1977. pap. 1.00 (*0-910420-24-6*) Comm Serv OH.
Community Service Society of New York Staff. Family in a Democratic Society. LC 77-167330. (Essay Index Reprint Ser.). 1977. reprint ed. 23.95 (*0-8369-2491-6*) Ayer.
Community Service Society Staff. Your Health Plan Handbook: How to Get the Health Care Your Family Needs from a Managed Care Plan. (SPA.). 36p. 1997. 5.00 (*0-88156-206-8*) Comm Serv Soc NY.
Community Service Staff. Intentional Community & the Folk Society. 1991. reprint ed. pap. 3.00 (*0-910420-11-4*) Comm Serv OH.
Community Workshop on Economic Development Staff. Economic Home Cookin' An Action Guide for Congregations on Community Economic Development. 90p. (C). 1989. pap. 20.00 (*0-945993-01-3*) Comm Wkshp Econ Dev.
Commynes, Phillippe De, see De Commynes, Phillippe.
Comnena, Anna. The Alexiad of Anna Comnena. Sewter, E. R., tr. (Classics Ser.). 560p. 1979. pap. 13.95 (*0-14-044215-4*, Penguin Classics) Viking Penguin.
— The Alexiad of the Princess Anna Comnena. Dawes, Elizabeth A., tr. LC 76-29821. reprint ed. 48.00 (*0-404-15414-X*) AMS Pr.
Comnes, Gregory. The Ethics of Indeterminacy in the Novels of William Gaddis. LC 93-30650. 200p. (C). 1994. 49.95 (*0-8130-1251-1*) U Press Fla.
Comnes, Leslie & Sly, Carolie. Toxics: Taking Charge. Bateson, John E., ed. LC 89-37364. (Illus.). 64p. (Orig.). 1989. write for info. (*0-88067-001-0*) Alameda Cnty Supr Schls.
Comnock, Robert M., compiled by. Comnock's School Speaker: Rhetorical Recitations for Boys & Girls. LC 73-2838. (Granger Index Reprint Ser.). 1977. reprint ed. 23.95 (*0-8369-6412-8*) Ayer.
Como, James. Branches to Heaven: The Geniuses of C. S. Lewis. LC 98-24612. 248p. 1998. 22.95 (*1-890626-01-5*) Spence Pub.
— Branches to Heaven: The Geniuses of C. S. Lewis. rev. ed. LC 98-24612. xiv, 226p. 2000. pap. 12.95 (*1-890626-15-5*) Spence Pub.
Como, James T. C. S. Lewis at the Breakfast Table. 372p. 1992. pap. 12.95 (*0-15-623207-3*, Harvest Bks) Harcourt.
Como, James T., ed. see Lewis, C. S.
Como, Mario & Grimaldi, Antonio. Theory of Stability of Continuous Elastic Structures. LC 94-37131. (CRC Press Library of Engineering Mathematics). 272p. 1995. boxed set 119.95 (*0-8493-8990-9*, 8990) CRC Pr.
***Comog, Evan.** The Birth of Empire. (Illus.). 256p. 2000. pap. 18.95 (*0-19-514051-6*) OUP.
Comoglio, P. M., ed. see Immunochemistry of the Cell Membrane, Ravello, 197.
Comola, Jacqueline, jt. auth. see Brown, J. H.
Comollo, Adriano, tr. see Allen, Diane & Frederick, Larry.
Comollo, Adriano, tr. see Colclazer, Susan.
Comollo, Adriano, tr. see Cook, Kayci.
Comollo, Adriano, tr. see Cox, W. Eugene.
Comollo, Adriano, tr. see Jackson, Victor L.
Comollo, Adriano, tr. see Rudd, Connie.
Comollo, Richard V. The Cellular Industry & Cellular Sales. (Illus.). 112p. 1995. pap. 49.95 (*0-9645905-0-6*) Pro Dig Mobile Comm.
Comolo, Jacqueline, jt. auth. see Brown, J. H.
Com.on Ground Water of Irrigation & Drainage Div. Operation & Maintenance of Ground Water Facilities. Fowler, Lloyd C., ed. (ASCE Manual of Professional Practice Ser.: Vol. 86). 192p. 1996. 48.00 (*0-7844-0139-X*) Am Soc Civil Eng.
Comon, Hubert, ed. Rewriting Techniques & Applications: Proceedings, 8th International Conference, RTA-97, Sitges, Spain, June 2-5, 1997, Vol. 123. LC 97-18882. (Lecture Notes in Computer Science Ser.: Vol. 1232). xi, 339p. 1997. pap. 55.00 (*3-540-62950-5*) Spr-Verlag.
Comon, Paul. Nikon Classic Cameras, Vol. 1. (Magic Lantern Guides). (Illus.). 176p. (Orig.). (C). 1998. pap. 19.95 (*1-883403-31-6*, H 191, Silver Pixel Pr) Saunders Photo.
— Nikon N6006-N8008s-N6000. LC 95-128074. (Magic Lantern Guides Ser.). (Illus.). 176p. (Orig.). (C). 1998. pap. 19.95 (*1-883403-11-1*, H 139, Silver Pixel Pr) Saunders Photo.
— Pentax Classic Cameras. LC 98-36473. (Magic Lantern Guides Ser.). 1999. pap. write for info. (*1-883403-53-7*, Silver Pixel Pr) Saunders Photo.
Comor, Edward A., ed. The Global Political Economy of Communication: Hegemony, Telecommunication & the Information Economy. LC 97-174643. (International Political Economy Ser.). 210p. 1996. pap. 21.95 (*0-312-16287-1*) St Martin.
Comora, jt. auth. see Chandra.
Comorovski, Ileana. Interrogative Phrases & the Syntax-Semantics Interface. (Studies in Linguistics & Philosophy: Vol. 59). 204p. (C). 1996. text 94.00 (*0-7923-3804-9*) Kluwer Academic.
Comotti, Giovanni. Music in Greek & Roman Culture. Munson, Rosaria V., tr. from ITA. LC 88-45413. (Ancient Society & History Ser.). 192p. 1991. reprint ed. pap. text 14.95 (*0-8018-4231-X*) Johns Hopkins.
Comp, T. Allan, jt. auth. see Pizor, Faith K.
Compa, Lance. Labor Rights in Haiti. 52p. 1989. pap. 5.00 (*1-880103-01-X*) Intl Labor Rghts.
Compa, Lance A. & Diamond, Stephen F., eds. Human Rights, Labor Rights, & International Trade. (Pennsylvania Studies in Human Rights). 320p. 1996. text 39.95 (*0-8122-3340-9*) U of Pa Pr.
Compact. Compact Bible. 1998. 27.99 (*0-529-11058-X*) World Publng.
Compact Classics Staff. Compact Classics, Vol. 3. 1994. pap. 19.95 (*1-880184-25-7*) Compact Classics.
— Compact Classics Leather, Vol. 1. 49.95 (*1-880184-15-X*) Compact Classics.
— Compact Classics Leather, Vol. 3. 1994. 39.95 (*1-880184-28-1*) Compact Classics.
— Compact Classics Planner Edition, Vol. 3. 1994. pap. 39.95 (*1-880184-27-3*) Compact Classics.
— Great Canadian Bathroom Book, Vol. 1. 1993. pap. 19.95 (*1-880184-06-0*) Compact Classics.
— Great Canadian Bathroom Book, Vol. 2. 1994. pap. 19.95 (*1-880184-13-3*) Compact Classics.
Compact Classics Staff & Anderson. Great American Bathroom, Vol. 3. 1994. pap. 19.95 (*1-880184-26-5*) Compact Classics.
Compact Reference Staff. New King James Version Compact Reference Snap Flap Bible Bonded Leather Blue, Supersaver ed. 1997. 19.97 (*0-7852-0209-9*) Nelson.
***Compact Slimline Staff.** Compact Slimline Bible. 2000. 24.99 (*0-8423-3908-6*); 24.99 (*0-8423-4092-0*); 35.99 (*0-8423-4093-9*); 35.99 (*0-8423-4094-7*) Tyndale Hse.
Compact Staff. Euro-Woerterbuch Computers, Information Science, EDV. (FRE, GER & SPA.). 448p. 1994. 29.95 (*0-7859-7535-7*, 3817472706) Fr & Eur.
— Euro-Woerterbuch Wirtschaft: German-English-French-Spanish-Italian. (FRE, GER & SPA.). 448p. 1991. 29.95 (*0-7859-7536-5*, 3817435568) Fr & Eur.
***Compact Youth Staff.** Extreme Faith Compact Youth Bible. (Illus.). (J). 2000. pap. 3.50 (*5-550-01011-9*) Nairi.
Compagni, Vittoria P., ed. see Agrippa, Henry Cornelius.
Compagno, Andrea. Intelligent Glass Facades: Material, Practice & Design. (Illus.). 128p. 1995. pap. 55.00 (*3-7643-5547-6*, Pub. by Birkhauser) Princeton Arch.
— Intelligent Glass Facades: Material, Practice, Design. 4th rev. ed. (Illus.). 160p. 1999. pap. 60.00 (*3-7643-5996-X*, Pub. by Birkhauser) Princeton Arch.
Compagno, G., et al. Atom-Field Interactions & Dressed Atoms. (Studies in Modern Optics: No. 17). (Illus.). 383p. (C). 1995. text 69.95 (*0-521-41948-4*) Cambridge U Pr.
Compagno, Leonard J. & Ebert, David. Field Guide to the Sharks & Rays of Southern Africa. (Illus.). 176p. (C). 1989. 100.00 (*0-7855-4045-8*) St Mut.
Compagno, Tony. A Slow Amassing Light. 67p. pap. write for info. (*0-9636625-0-3*) T Compagno.
Compagno, Tony, ed. see Diran, Edward.
Compagnon, Antoine. Five Paradoxes of Modernity. Philip, Franklin, tr. from FRE. LC 93-35830.Tr. of Cinq Paradoxes de la Modernite. 1994. 57.50 (*0-231-07576-6*) Col U Pr.
— Five Paradoxes of Modernity. Philip, Franklin, tr. from FRE. LC 93-35830.Tr. of Cinq Paradoxes de la Modernite. 1994. pap. 19.50 (*0-231-07577-4*) Col U Pr.
— Proust Between Two Centuries. Goodkin, Richard E., tr. from FRE. 320p. 1992. text 44.00 (*0-231-07264-3*) Col U Pr.
Compain. Business: An Introduction SIM. (C). 1984. wbk. ed. write for info. (*0-03-070282-8*) Harcourt Coll Pubs.
Compain, Rita. Giants: A Study Guide. Friedland, J. & Kessler, R., eds. (Novel-Ties Ser.). 1992. pap. text, student ed. 20.95 (*1-56982-038-4*) Lrn Links.
Compaine, Benjamin. Issues in New Information Technology. Dervin, Brenda, ed. LC 87-37443. (Communication & Information Science Ser.). 320p. 1988. pap. 39.50 (*0-89391-500-9*); text 73.25 (*0-89391-468-1*) Ablx Pub.
— Trans/acet Business: An Intro. (C). 1984. pap. text 772.50 (*0-03-063624-8*) Harcourt Coll Pubs.
***Compaine, Benjamin M. & Gomery, Douglas.** Who Owns the Media? Competition & Concentration in the Mass Media. 3rd ed. LC 99-89794. (Communication Ser.). 2000. pap. 49.95 (*0-8058-2936-9*) L Erlbaum Assocs.
Compaine, Benjamin M. & Read, William H., eds. The Information Resources Policy Handbook: Perspectives for the Information Age. LC 98-48229. (Illus.). 656p. 1999. 55.00 (*0-262-03264-3*) MIT Pr.
Compaine, Benjamin M., jt. ed. see Vogelsang, Ingo.
Compan, Charles. Dictionnaire de Danse. (FRE.). 420p. 1979. pap. 135.00 (*0-7859-8048-2*, 2826606778) Fr & Eur.
— Dictionnaire de Danse. fac. ed. (Monuments of Music & Music Literature in Facsimile Ser., Series II: Vol. 84). (FRE.). 1974. lib. bdg. 60.00 (*0-8450-2284-9*) Broude.
Companino. Palazzo Bricherasio. (Illus.). 48p. 1997. pap. 12.95 (*88-435-5484-0*, Pub. by Art Bks Intl) Partners Pubs Grp.
***Companjen, Johan.** Please Pray for Us: Praying for Persecuted Christians in 52 Nations. 192p. 2000. pap. 9.99 (*0-7642-2416-6*) Bethany Hse.
Compans, Richard W., jt. ed. see Mahy, Brian W.J.
Company, Merce. Don Gil y el Paraguas Magico: Sir Gil & the Magic Umbrella. Serra, Aurora M., tr. from GER. (Coleccion Barril Sin Fondo Ser.). (SPA., Illus.). 26p. (J). (gr. 1-4). 1990. 13.95 (*968-6465-03-0*) Hispanic Bk Dist.
Company of Mary Fathers, ed. see Saint Louis Grignon de Montfort.
Comparative Leukemia Research Symposium Staff. Comparative Leukemia Research, 1975: Proceedings of the Symposium, 7th International, Copenhagen, October 1975. Clemmesen, J. et al, eds. (Bibliotheca Haematologica Ser.: Vol. 43). (Illus.). 600p. 1976. 185.25 (*3-8055-2316-5*) S Karger.
Comparative Pathology of the Heart Symposium Staff. Comparative Pathology of the Heart: Proceedings of the Symposium, Boston, Sept. 1973. Homburger, F. & Lucas, I., eds. (Advances in Cardiology Ser.: Vol. 13). 250p. 1974. 226.25 (*3-8055-1697-5*) S Karger.
Comparative Study Staff. Comparative Study Bible. 3264p. 1999. 89.99 (*0-310-90336-X*); 49.99 (*0-310-90333-5*) Zondervan.
***Comparato, Doc.** La Guerra de las Imaginaciones. (SPA.). 1998. 26.95 (*84-08-02443-4*) Planeta Edit.
Comparato, Frank E. Books for the Millions: A History of the Men Whose Methods & Machines Packaged the Printed Word. LC 71-162441. (Illus.). 374p. 1971. 12.50 (*0-8117-0263-4*) Labyrinthos.
— Chronicles of Genius & Folly: R. Hoe & Company & the Printing Press As a Service to Democracy. LC 77-90647. (Illus.). 846p. 1979. 39.95 (*0-911437-00-2*); 24.95 (*0-911437-10-X*) Labyrinthos.
Comparato, Frank E., ed. see De Avendano y Loyola, Fray A.
Comparato, Frank E., ed. see De Leon Pinelo, Antonio.
Comparato, Frank E., ed. see Garcia De Palacios, Diego.
Comparato, Frank E., ed. see Seler, Eduard.
Comparato, Frank E., ed. see Villagutierre, Juan.
Comparette, T. Louis. Aes Signatum. (Illus.). 1978. 30.00 (*0-916710-39-4*) Obol Intl.
Comparetti, Domenico. Vergil in the Middle Ages. LC 96-3403. 392p. 1997. pap. text 19.95 (*0-691-02678-5*, Pub. by Princeton U Pr) Cal Prin Full Svc.
Compas. Introduction to Clinical Psychology. 2001. 69.95 (*0-07-012491-4*) McGraw.
Compas, Bruce E., jt. ed. see Bond, Lynne A.
COMPAS Staff, ed. With a Voice of Singing. (Illus.). 60p. (Orig.). 1992. pap. 5.00 (*0-927663-18-X*) COMPAS.
Compass America Staff. Coastal California. (Compass American Guides Ser.). 352p. 1998. pap. 19.95 (*0-679-03598-2*, Compass Amrcn) Fodors Travel.
— New Orleans. 3rd ed. LC 97-33361. (Compass American Guides Ser.). 320p. 1997. pap. 18.95 (*0-679-03597-4*, Compass Amrcn) Fodors Travel.
— Wine Country. 2nd ed. LC 97-52229. (Compass American Guides Ser.). 312p. 1998. pap. 19.95 (*0-679-00032-1*, Compass Amrcn) Fodors Travel.
— Wyoming. 3rd ed. LC 97-51360. (Compass American Guides Ser.). 392p. 1998. pap. 19.95 (*0-679-00034-8*, Compass Amrcn) Fodors Travel.
Compass America Staff, ed. Alaska. 2nd ed. LC 99-212981. (Compass American Guides Ser.). 1999. pap. 19.95 (*0-679-00230-8*) Fodors Travel.
— Chicago. 2nd ed. (Compass American Guides Ser.). 1999. pap. 0.19 (*0-679-00285-5*) Fodors Travel.
— Montana. 4th ed. LC 99-217843. (Compass American Guides Ser.). 320p. 1999. pap. 19.95 (*0-679-00281-2*) Fodors Travel.
— Santa Fe. 3rd ed. (Compass American Guides Ser.). 272p. 2000. pap. 19.95 (*0-679-00286-3*) Fodors Travel.
— Southern New England. (Compass American Guides Ser.). 1999. pap. 19.95 (*0-679-00184-0*) Fodors Travel.
— Vermont. (Compass American Guides Ser.). 1999. pap. 19.95 (*0-679-00183-2*) Fodors Travel.
Compass American Guides Staff. Georgia. (Compass American Guides Ser.). 320p. 1999. pap. 19.95 (*0-679-00245-6*) Fodors Travel.
Compass American Staff. Minnesota. LC 96-3086. (Compass American Guides Ser.). 348p. 1997. pap. 18.95 (*1-878867-48-2*, Compass Amrcn) Fodors Travel.
Compass Maps Staff. Highways & Streets of Shasta County. LC 93-676583. 42p. 1991. write for info. (*0-9615926-6-4*) Compass Maps.
Compass Productions Staff. Awesome Animal Actions. (Amazing Nature Pop-up Bks.). (Illus.). 10p. (J). (gr. k-4). 1992. 5.95 (*0-694-00409-X*, HarpFestival) HarpC Child Bks.
— Baffling Bird Behavior. (Amazing Nature Pop-up Bks.). (Illus.). 10p. (J). (gr. k-4). 1992. 5.95 (*0-694-00410-3*, HarpFestival) HarpC Child Bks.
— Dragons! The Giant Pop-Up Book of Fearsome Creatures. (Illus.). (J). 1994. write for info. (*0-316-15239-0*) Little.
— Freaky Fish Facts. (Amazing Nature Pop-up Bks.). (Illus.). 10p. (J). (gr. k-4). 1992. 5.95 (*0-694-00411-1*, HarpFestival) HarpC Child Bks.
— Grasslands & Deserts. (Vanishing Animal Pop-Up Ser.). (Illus.). 10p. (J). (gr. k-4). 1993. 5.95 (*0-694-00444-8*, HarpFestival) HarpC Child Bks.
— Incredible Insect Instincts. (Amazing Nature Pop-up Bks.). (Illus.). 10p. (J). (gr. k-4). 1992. 5.95 (*0-694-00412-X*, HarpFestival) HarpC Child Bks.
— Jungles & Islands. (Vanishing Animal Pop-Up Ser.). (Illus.). 10p. (J). (gr. k-4). 1993. 5.95 (*0-694-00443-X*) HarpC Child Bks.
— Oceans & Arctic. (Vanishing Animal Pop-Up Ser.). (Illus.). 10p. (J). (gr. k-4). 1993. 5.95 (*0-694-00441-3*) HarpC Child Bks.
Compassionate Friends Staff, jt. ed. see Mirren, Ena.
Compayre, Gabriel. Abelard & the Origin & Early History of the Universities. 1967. 10.00 (*0-403-00009-2*) Scholarly.
— Abelard & the Origin & Early History of the Universities. LC 75-90094. (BCL Ser.: II). 1969. reprint ed. 32.50 (*0-404-01639-1*) AMS Pr.
— History of Pedagogy. Payne, W. H., ed. LC 70-136417. (BCL Ser.: I). reprint ed. 45.00 (*0-404-01648-0*) AMS Pr.
— History of Pedagogy. 1988. reprint ed. lib. bdg. 69.00 (*0-7812-0392-9*) Rprt Serv.
Compbell, Paul. A Dose of My Own Medicine. (Illus.). 213p. (Orig.). 1992. pap. 6.95 (*0-9695852-0-9*) Grosvenor USA.
Compeau, Jane, tr. see Roels, Edwin D.
Comper, Frances M. The Life of Richard Rolle. 1988. reprint ed. lib. bdg. 59.00 (*0-7812-0348-1*) Rprt Serv.
Comper, Frances M. & Kastenbaum, Robert J., eds. The Book of the Craft of Dying & Other Early English Tracts Concerning Death. LC 76-19564. (Death & Dying Ser.). 1977. reprint ed. lib. bdg. 21.95 (*0-405-09560-0*) Ayer.
Comper, W. D., et al. Solar Energy Phase Transfer Catalysis Transport Processes. (Advances in Polymer Science Ser.: Vol. 55). (Illus.), 170p. 1984. 74.00 (*0-387-12592-2*) Spr-Verlag.
Comper, Wayne D. Extracellular Matrix, Vol. 1. 464p. 1996. text 57.00 (*3-7186-5842-9*, Harwood Acad Pubs); pap. text 28.00 (*3-7186-5915-8*, Harwood Acad Pubs) Gordon & Breach.
— Extracellular Matrix, Vol. 2. 384p. 1996. text 47.00 (*3-7186-5843-7*, Harwood Acad Pubs); text 96.00 (*3-7186-5844-5*, Harwood Acad Pubs); pap. text 23.00 (*3-7186-5916-6*, Harwood Acad Pubs); pap. text 47.00 (*3-7186-5917-4*, Harwood Acad Pubs) Gordon & Breach.
Compere, Edward L. Orthopaedic Surgery. LC 73-93801. (Handbook of Operative Surgery Ser.). 323p. reprint ed. pap. 100.20 (*0-608-15498-9*, 202973500064) Bks Demand.
Compere, Marie-Madeleine. L' Histoire de l'Education en Europe: Essai Comparatif sur la Facon Dont Elle S'Ecrit. (Exploration Ser.). (FRE.). 296p. 1995. 20.95 (*3-906754-28-6*, Pub. by P Lang) P Lang Pubng.
Compere, Newton. German Wirehaired Pointers. (Illus.). 192p. 1994. 9.95 (*0-86622-768-7*, KW187) TFH Pubns.
Compere, P. Flore Pratique des Algues d'eau Douce de Belgique, 4 vols. 1989. 60.00 (*1-878762-91-5*) Balogh.
***Compesi, Ronald J., ed.** Video Field Producting & Editing. 5th ed. LC 99-26738. 462p. 1999. 62.00 (*0-205-29556-8*) Allyn.
Compestine, Ying. Secrets of Fat-Free Chinese Cooking: Over 130 Fat-Free & Low-Fat Traditional Chinese Recipes - From Egg Rolls to Almond Cookies. LC 96-49697. (Illus.). 192p. 1996. pap. 14.95 (*0-89529-735-3*, Avery) Penguin Putnam.
***Compestine, Ying Chang.** Cooking with Green Tea: Delicious Recipes Enhanced by the Miraculous Healing Powers of Green Tea. 2000. pap. 14.95 (*1-58333-065-8*, Avery) Penguin Putnam.
— The Runaway Rice Cake. LC 99-462168. (Illus.). (J). 2000. write for info. (*0-689-82972-8*) S&S Childrens.
Competence Assurance Systems Staff. Advanced Arthritis Study Guide. 1986. pap. text 235.00 (*0-89147-068-9*) CAS.
— Advanced Dermatology Study Guide. 1980. pap. text 235.00 (*0-89147-062-X*) CAS.
— Advanced Obstetrics & Gynecology Study Guide. 1980. pap. text 235.00 (*0-89147-111-1*) CAS.
— Advanced Respiratory Education Course. (Illus.). 1985. pap. text 75.00 (*0-89147-106-5*) CAS.
— Arrhythmia Education Course. (Illus.). 1984. pap. text 40.00 (*0-89147-054-9*) CAS.
— Arthritis Education Course. (Illus.). 1984. pap. text 75.00 (*0-89147-067-0*) CAS.
— Cardiovascular Education Course. (Illus.). 1984. pap. text 60.00 (*0-89147-055-7*) CAS.
— Cardiovascular Education Course: Acute Care. (Illus.). 195p. pap. text 75.00 (*0-89147-112-X*) CAS.
— Cell Biology Course. (Illus.). 1978. pap. text 45.00 (*0-89147-057-3*) CAS.
— Circulatory System Course. (Illus.). 1981. pap. text 50.00 (*0-89147-053-0*) CAS.
— Clinical Pharmacology Course. (Illus.). 1985. pap. text 35.00 (*0-89147-071-9*) CAS.
— Dermatology Education Course. (Illus.). 1984. pap. text 75.00 (*0-89147-058-1*) CAS.
— Diabetes Education Course. (Illus.). 1986. pap. text 75.00 (*0-89147-064-6*) CAS.
— Endocrine System Course. (Illus.). 1981. pap. text 45.00 (*0-89147-063-8*) CAS.
— Estrogen Replacement Education Course. (Illus.). 1984. pap. text 65.00 (*0-89147-108-1*) CAS.
— Gastrointestinal System Course. (Illus.). 1981. pap. text 50.00 (*0-89147-065-4*) CAS.
— Hypertension Education Course. (Illus.). 1982. pap. text 80.00 (*0-89147-056-5*) CAS.
— I. V. Antibiotics Education Course. (Illus.). 1985. pap. text 85.00 (*0-89147-060-3*) CAS.
— Immunology Education Course. (Illus.). 1984. pap. text 80.00 (*0-89147-059-X*) CAS.
— Introduction to Anesthesiology. (Illus.). 1982. pap. text 45.00 (*0-89147-072-7*) CAS.
— Introduction to Hospital Selling. (Illus.). 1984. pap. text 50.00 (*0-89147-073-5*) CAS.
— Musculoskeletal System Course. (Illus.). 1981. pap. text 45.00 (*0-89147-066-2*) CAS.
— Nervous System Course. (Illus.). 1983. pap. text 60.00 (*0-89147-069-7*) CAS.
— Oral Antibiotics Education Course. (Illus.). 1984. pap. text 60.00 (*0-89147-061-1*) CAS.

C

An Asterisk (*) at the beginning of an entry indicates that the title is appearing for the first time.

— Oral Contraceptives Education Course. (Illus.). 1985. pap. text 85.00 (*0-89147-109-X*) CAS.
— Overview: Introduction to Ten Body Systems. (Illus.). 1985. pap. text 70.00 (*0-89147-070-0*) CAS.
— Renal System Course. (Illus.). 1981. pap. text 50.00 (*0-89147-074-3*) CAS.
— Reproductive System Course. (Illus.). 1984. pap. text 45.00 (*0-89147-107-3*) CAS.
— Respiratory System Course. (Illus.). 1981. pap. text 45.00 (*0-89147-105-7*) CAS.
— Vaginal Therapeutics Education Course. (Illus.). 1984. pap. text 55.00 (*0-89147-110-3*) CAS.
Compher, Catherine. Shoes on, Shoes Off. Gross, Karen, ed. (Illus.). 24p. (J). (ps). 1993. pap. text 3.99 (*1-56309-076-7*, N938101, New Hope) Womans Mission Union.
Compher, John V. Family Centered Practice: The Interactional Dance Beyond the Family System. 162p. 1989. 32.95 (*0-89885-422-9*, Kluwer Acad Hman Sci) Kluwer Academic.
***Compier, Don H.** What Is Rhetorical Theology? Textual Practice & Public Discourse. LC 99-33833. 112p. 1999. pap. 12.00 (*1-56338-290-3*) TPI PA.
Compilado. Llegando Al Hogar: Invitacion... (Serie Enfoque a la Familia - Focus on the Family Ser.).Tr. of Coming Home: Invitation.... (SPA.). 24p. 1991. 1.99 (*1-56063-052-3*, 497411) Editorial Unilit.
— La Predicacion Biblica - Biblical Preaching: Desarrollo de Mensajes Expositivos. pap. write for info. (*0-7899-0233-8*) Editorial Unilit.
— Viaje Maravilloso A los Tiempos Biblicos (Maes.) - Amazing Journey (Teacher) pap. write for info. (*1-56063-957-1*) Editorial Unilit.
Compiled by Poets & Writers, Inc. Literary Bookstores: A Cross-Country Guide. rev. ed. 1994. pap. 12.50 (*0-913734-27-6*) Norton.
Compiling Committee Staff, ed. China Machinery Industries Yearbook, 1987. 460p. 1988. 104.95 (*0-387-18725-1*) Spr-Verlag.
Compin, Isabelle, et al. Ecole Francaise, 3 vols., Set. (FRE., Illus.). 1072p. 1988. pap. 150.00 (*0-317-66904-4*) Abrams.
Compione, Mary, jt. auth. see McGilton, Henry.
Compleston, Frederick. A History of Philosophy: Hobbes to Hume. 1994. 75.00 (*0-85532-185-7*, Pub. by Srch Pr) St Mut.
Complete Hunter. Dressing & Cooking Wild Game. 160p. 1999. 19.95 (*0-86573-108-X*) Creat Pub Intl.
Complete Idiot Staff, ed. Complete Idiot's Guide to Dating. 352p. 1996. 16.95 (*0-02-861052-0*) Macmillan Gen Ref.
Complete Language Courses Staff & Mitchell, Carolyn B. Cassette German Course. (Cortina Ser.). (ENG & GER.). 1995. pap. 79.95 incl. audio (*0-8050-1887-5*) H Holt & Co.
Complete Language Courses Staff, et al. Cassette Italian Course. (Cortina Ser.). (ENG & ITA.). 1995. pap. 79.95 incl. audio (*0-8050-1888-3*) H Holt & Co.
— Cassette Spanish Course. (Cortina Ser.). (ENG & SPA.). 1995. pap. 79.95 incl. audio (*0-8050-1885-9*) H Holt & Co.
— Curso de Ingles en Cassette: For Spanish Speakers. (Cortina Ser.). (ENG & SPA.). 1995. pap. 89.95 incl. audio (*0-8050-1889-1*) H Holt & Co.
Complination. Crowned with Victory. 119p. (Orig.). 1998. pap. 9.99 (*1-84030-037-X*) Ambassador Prodns Ltd.
***Compo, Susan.** The Namedroppers. 200p. 2000. pap. 16.95 (*1-891241-12-5*) Verse Chorus Pr.
Composites Group of the Turner Moss Co. Staff. Composites, an Insider's Technical Guide to Corporate America's Activities: The Engineer's, the Marketer's & the Business Planner's Reference Book Containing Technical Profiles of over 400 Business Entities in the United States Currently Performing Significant Composites Work. (Orig.). 1989. pap. 127.00 (*0-9623228-4-9*, TM2284) Turner Moss Co.
Composites Institute of the Society of the Plastic, compiled by. The Composites Institute's FirstSource Directory. 248p. 1998. pap. 54.95 (*1-56676-658-3*) Technomic.
Composites Institute Staff. Introduction to Composites. 4th ed. (Illus.). 102p. 1998. pap. 50.00 (*1-56676-659-1*) Technomic.
***Compressed Gas Association, contrib. by.** Handbook of Compressed Gases. 4th ed. LC 98-36690. (Illus.). 1999. write for info. (*0-412-78230-8*) Kluwer Academic.
Comprone, Joseph J., jt. auth. see Greenberg, Ruth B.
COMPSEC International Staff. Proceedings of COMPSEC International 1996. LC 99-187067. vii, 624 p. 1996. write for info. (*1-85617-332-1*, Pub. by Elsvr Adv Tech) Elsevier.
Compsec Staff. COMPSEC 1995 - the Twelfth World Conference of Comp Security Audit. 1995. 200.50 (*1-85617-294-5*, Pub. by Elsvr Adv Tech) Elsevier.
Compston, Christine L., ed. see Holmes, Oliver W. & Frankfurter, Felix.
Compston, D. A., et al. McAlpine's Multiple Sclerosis. 3rd ed. (Illus.). 440p. 1998. text. write for info. (*0-443-05008-2*) Church.
Compston, Hugh. The New Politics of Unemployment: Radical Policy Initiatives in Western Europe. LC 96-26288. 240p. (C). 1996. 90.00 (*0-415-15054-X*); pap. 29.99 (*0-415-15055-8*) Routledge.
Compston, Juliet, jt. auth. see Agnusdei, Donato.
Compte, P., et al, eds. Computational Fluid Dynamics: Proceedings of the Les Houches Summer School. LC 95-50011. (Houches Summer School Proceedings Ser.: Vol. 59). 670p. 1996. 247.00 (*0-444-82292-5*) Elsevier.
Compte-Sponville, Andre. Small Treatise on Large Virtues. 1998. 27.50 (*0-8050-4555-4*) H Holt & Co.
— Small Treatise on Large Virtues. 1999. pap. write for info. (*0-8050-4556-2*) H Holt & Co.
CompTel Association Staff. Definitive Directory of Competitive Telecommunications Service Providers. (Illus.). 100p. 1999. 275.00 (*0-929870-49-2*) Advanstar Commns.
Comptex Associates Inc. Staff. Getting the Job You Want with the Audiovisual Portfolio: A Practical Guide for Job Hunters & Career Changers. 1981. 9.50 (*0-911849-00-9*) Comptex Assocs Inc.
Compton. Pathological Basis Disease. 5th ed. 1999. pap. text. write for info. (*0-7216-7857-2*, W B Saunders Co) Harcrt Hlth Sci Grp.
— Social Work Processes. 6th ed. LC 98-21140. (Social Work Ser.). 1998. pap. 75.95 (*0-534-35870-5*) Brooks-Cole.
— Social Work Processes. 7th ed. (Social Work Ser.). 2002. pap. 48.00 (*0-534-36559-0*) Brooks-Cole.
Compton & Ellis. Leisure & the American Dream. (Illus.). 425p. (C). (gr. 13). 2000. 22.95 (*0-8016-1028-1*, 01028) Mosby Inc.
Compton, A. J. Electromagnetismo Basico & sus Aplicaciones. (SPA.). 192p. (C). 1993. pap. text 12.33 (*0-201-60139-7*) Addison-Wesley.
Compton, Anita. Marriage Customs. LC 93-16317. (Comparing Religions Ser.). (Illus.). 32p. (J). (gr. 4-8). 1993. lib. bdg. 22.83 (*1-56847-033-9*) Raintree Steck-V.
Compton, Ann. Edward Halliday: Art for Life. LC 98-214532. (Illus.). 48p. 1998. pap. 12.95 (*0-85323-972-X*, Pub. by Liverpool Univ Pr) Intl Spec Bk.
***Compton, Ann, ed.** Edward Carter Preston, 1885-1965: Sculptor, Painter, Medalist. 72p. 1999. pap. 16.95 (*0-85323-792-1*, Pub. by Liverpool Univ Pr) Intl Spec Bk.
Compton, Ann & Ashton, Mary. Community Care for Health Professionals. (Illus.). 240p. 2000. pap. 45.00 (*0-7506-3290-9*) Buttrwrth-Heinemann.
Compton, Ann & Ashwin, Mary. Community Care for Health Professionals. 288p. 1992. pap. text 52.50 (*0-7506-0185-X*) Buttrwrth-Heinemann.
Compton, Anne. A. J. M. Smith: Canadian Metaphysical. (Illus.). 262p. 1994. pap. 25.00 (*1-55022-225-2*, Pub. by ECW) LPC InBook.
Compton, Arthur H. Man's Destiny in Eternity. LC 75-117821. (Essay Index Reprint Ser.). 1977. 21.95 (*0-8369-1762-6*) Ayer.
— Scientific Papers of Arthur Holly Compton. Shankland, Robert S., ed. 816p. 1974. lib. bdg. 60.00 (*0-226-11430-9*) U Ch Pr.
Compton, Beulah R. & Galaway, Burt. Social Work Processes. 3rd ed. 609p. (C). 1984. pap. 28.25 (*0-534-10509-2*) Brooks-Cole.
— Social Work Processes. 4th ed. 773p. (C). 1989. pap. 48.95 (*0-534-11096-7*) Brooks-Cole.
— Social Work Processes. 5th ed. LC 93-49529. 689p. 1994. pap. 49.50 (*0-534-17364-0*) Brooks-Cole.
Compton, Boyd, tr. see Tse-Tung, Mao.
Compton, Brian D., ed. see Smith, Harlan I.
Compton, Bridget R., jt. auth. see Albright, Ronald T.
Compton-Burnett, Ivy. Des Hommes et Des Femmes. (FRE.). 288p. 1984. pap. 11.95 (*0-7859-2004-8*, 2070376176) Fr & Eur.
Compton-Burnett, Ivy. First Omnibus. 768p. 1994. pap. 22.00 (*0-14-018662-X*, Pub. by Pnguin Bks Ltd) Trafalgar.
— A Heritage & Its History. LC 77-865602. 240 p. (J). 1969. write for info. (*0-575-00240-9*) V Gollancz.
Compton-Burnett, Juliet, tr. see Savitch, Marie.
Compton, C. & Jessop, J. Dictionary of Purchase & Supply Management. 150p. (C). 1989. 120.00 (*0-7855-5752-0*, Pub. by Inst Pur & Supply) St Mut.
Compton, Carl C. The Morning Cometh: Forty-Five Years with Anatolia College. Iatrides, John O. & Compton, William R., eds. xxii, 116p. 1986. lib. bdg. 25.00 (*0-89241-422-7*) Caratzas.
Compton, Carol & Hartmann, John, eds. Papers on Tai Languages, Linguistics, & Literatures (in Honor of Professor William J. Gedney) In Honor of Professor William J. Gedney on His 77th Birthday. (Occasional Papers: No. 16). 302p. 1992. pap. 26.95 (*1-877979-16-3*) SE Asia.
Compton, Carolyn C. Pathologic Basis of Disease: A Self-Assessment & Review. 4th ed. 250p. 1995. pap. text 23.00 (*0-7216-4041-9*, W B Saunders Co) Harcrt Hlth Sci Grp.
***Compton, Carrie.** Hammer Dulcimer Solos. 48p. 1998. pap. 17.95 (*0-7866-3452-9*, 94354BCD) Mel Bay.
Compton, Charles H. Who Reads What? LC 69-18923. (Essay Index Reprint Ser.). 1977. 17.95 (*0-8369-0012-X*) Ayer.
Compton, Cynthia L. Assistive Devices: Doorways to Independence. 67p. (YA). (gr. 7 up). 1991. pap. text 25.00 incl. VHS (*0-9638716-0-9*) SHHH Inc.
Compton, D. G. Farewell, Earth's Bliss. LC 79-12824. 188p. 1979. reprint ed. pap. 21.00 (*0-89370-235-8*) Millefleurs.
— Justice City. 256p. 1996. 27.00 (*0-575-05838-2*, Pub. by V Gollancz); pap. 10.95 (*0-575-05840-4*, Pub. by V Gollancz) Trafalgar.
— A Usual Lunacy. LC 78-14953. (Illus.). 191p. 1978. pap. 21.00 (*0-89370-225-0*) Millefleurs.
Compton, Dale W. Engineering Management: Creating & Managing World Class Operations. LC 96-43445. (Illus.). 350p. (C). 1997. text 82.00 (*0-02-324121-7*) Macmillan.
Compton, David. The Acolyte. LC 96-8933. 400p. 1996. 22.50 (*0-684-80430-1*) S&S Trade.
***Compton, David.** Impaired Judgment. LC 00-36079. 352p. 2000. 24.95 (*0-525-94457-5*) NAL.
Compton, David. Stammering: Its Nature, History, Causes & Cures. 152p. 1998. pap. 16.00 (*0-7881-5652-7*) DIANE Pub.
Compton, David M., ed. Issues in Therapeutic Recreation: Toward the New Millennium. 2nd ed. 400p. (C). 1997. text 42.95 (*1-57167-031-9*) Sagamore Pub.
***Compton, Dennis.** When in Doubt, Lead! The Leader's Guide to Enhanced Employee Relations in the Fire. Laughlin, Jerry, ed. LC 99-60152. 64p. 1999. pap. 12.50 (*0-87939-165-0*) Okla State U Fire Prot.
***Compton, Dennis, ed.** When in Doubt, Lead... Pt. 2: The Leaders Guide to Personal & Organizational Development. (Illus.). 64p. 2000. pap. 12.50 (*0-87939-179-0*) IFSTA.
Compton, Donna, ed. see Trumpeter Swan Society Staff.
Compton, Donna C. & Linck, Madeleine H., eds. Proceedings & Papers of the 15th Trumpeter Swan Society: A Vision for the 21st Century: Trumpeter Swans. (Illus.). 156p. (Orig.). 1996. pap. text 15.00 (*1-888377-00-3*) Trumpeter Swan Soc.
Compton, Donna C., ed. see Nelson, Harvey K.
Compton, Elizabeth L. The Saga of Saint Mary of the Mills. 70p. 1993. 15.00 (*0-9636115-2-6*) St Mary Mills.
***Compton, Ellen, et al, eds.** Pocket Change: The Towpath Anthology 2000. 48p. 2000. 5.00 (*1-893959-12-0*) Red Moon Pr.
Compton, Eric N. Principles of Banking. 4th rev. ed. Moss, Hunter V., ed. (Illus.). 400p. (C). 1991. text 45.00 (*0-89982-368-8*) Am Bankers.
Compton-Gooding, Ellen, jt. ed. see Schultz, Art.
Compton, H. K. Storehouse & Stockyard Management. 530p. (C). 1989. 180.00 (*0-7855-4646-4*, Pub. by Inst Pur & Supply) St Mut.
— Supplies & Materials Management. 518p. (C). 1985. 195.00 (*0-7855-5756-3*, Pub. by Inst Pur & Supply) St Mut.
— Supplies & Materials Management. 518p. (C). 1989. 175.00 (*0-7855-4615-4*, Pub. by Inst Pur & Supply) St Mut.
Compton, H. K. & Jessop, David A. Dictionary of Purchasing & Supply Management. 150p. (Orig.). (C). 1989. 115.00 (*0-7855-4609-X*, Pub. by Inst Pur & Supply) St Mut.
Compton-Hall, P. R. The Submariner's World. 144p. 1987. 49.00 (*0-85937-303-7*, Pub. by K Mason Pubns Ltd) St Mut.
Compton-Hall, Richard. Submarine Pioneers. 2000. 34.95 (*0-7509-2154-4*) Sutton Pub Ltd.
Compton, Henry. A Yogic Psalter. 64p. 1984. 60.00 (*0-7212-0679-4*, Pub. by Regency Pr GBR) St Mut.
***Compton-Hernandez, Maria.** Catholic Answers for Catholic Parents. (Illus.). 96p. 2000. pap. 7.95 (*1-891903-14-4*) St Andrew Prodns.
Compton-Hernandez, Maria. The Catholic Mother's Resource Guide: A Resource Listing of Hints & Ideas for Practicing & Teaching the Faith. LC 96-70666. 72p. (Orig.). 1996. pap. 3.50 (*1-877678-44-9*) Queenship Pub.
— Catholic Parents Internet Guide. (Illus.). 56p. 1998. pap. 3.00 (*1-891903-13-6*) St Andrew Prodns.
Compton, Ida L. Sinclair Lewis at Thorvale Farm: A Personal Memoir. LC 88-92777. (Illus.). 62p. (Orig.). 1988. pap. 5.00 (*0-915909-01-4*) Ruggles Pub.
Compton, Irene. Kritik des Kritikers: Bolls "Ansichten Eines Clowns" und Kleists "Marionettentheater" (Studies in Modern German Literature: Vol. 89). (GER.). 187p. (C). 1998. text 42.95 (*0-8204-3726-3*) P Lang Pubng.
Compton, J. A., jt. auth. see Coulter, J.
Compton, J. R., jt. auth. see Friendship, C. A.
Compton, James A. Military Chemical & Biological Agents: Chemical & Toxicological Properties. 440p. 1988. lib. bdg. 95.00 (*0-936923-11-3*) Telford Pr.
Compton, James V., compiled by. The New Deal. 39.00 (*1-56696-023-1*) Jackdaw.
Compton, Jeffery. The Las Vegas Advisor Guide to Slot Clubs. 2nd ed. (Illus.). 240p. 1999. pap. 12.95 (*0-929712-76-5*) Huntington Pr.
Compton, Jeffrey. The Las Vegas Advisor Guide to Slot Clubs. 118p. (Orig.). 1995. pap. 9.95 (*0-929712-75-7*) Huntington Pr.
Compton, Joan C. & Compton, Stephen B. Successful Business Forecasting. 204p. 1989. 21.95 (*0-8306-0207-0*) McGraw-Hill Prof.
Compton, Joanne, jt. auth. see Compton, Kenn.
Compton, K. C., ed. see Parker, Kathleene.
Compton, Katherine. Blue Moon Bayou. 352p. (Orig.). 1992. mass mkt. 4.50 (*0-380-76412-1*, Avon Bks) Morrow Avon.
— Eden's Angel. 384p. 1990. pap. 3.95 (*0-380-76121-1*, Avon Bks) Morrow Avon.
— The Lady & the Outlaw. 352p. (Orig.). 1994. mass mkt. 4.50 (*0-380-77454-2*, Avon Bks) Morrow Avon.
— Outlaw Bride. 400p. (Orig.). 1991. mass mkt. 4.50 (*0-380-76411-3*, Avon Bks) Morrow Avon.
— Whispers in the Wind. 368p. 1995. mass mkt. 4.99 (*0-380-77455-0*, Avon Bks) Morrow Avon.
Compton, Ken, jt. auth. see Reyes, Simone.
Compton, Kenn & Compton, Joanne. Granny Greenteeth & the Noise in the Night. LC 93-18232. (Illus.). 32p. (J). (gr. k-3). 1993. lib. bdg. 14.95 (*0-8234-1051-X*) Holiday.
Compton, LaNell. Happy Incidents along Life's Journey. LC 99-74072. 64p. 2000. 14.95 (*0-8158-0539-X*) Chris Mass.
— Looking Forward to a New Day. 1984. 7.95 (*0-8158-0418-0*) Chris Mass.
— Ozark Sketches: A Family Chronicle. LC 90-83321. 1991. 10.95 (*0-8158-0463-6*) Chris Mass.
Compton, Linda & Jester, Pamela J. California Elder Law - An Advocate's Guide, Set, Vols. 1 & 2. Sanders, Carol S., ed. LC 93-71394. 880p. 1993. 185.00 (*0-88124-633-6*, ES-32050) Cont Ed Bar-CA.
Compton, Linda & Peyrat, Paul I., eds. California Civil Procedure Before Trial, 3 vols., Set. 3rd rev. ed. LC 90-81348. 2553p. 1990. reprint ed. ring bd. 195.00 (*0-88124-271-3*, CP-31540) Cont Ed Bar-CA.
Compton, Linda, ed. see Christison, Randall B., et al.
Compton, Linda, ed. see Miles, Donald F. & Goff, Charles E.
Compton, Linda, ed. see Pitre, Frank M.
Compton, Linda, ed. see Raines, Richard C. & Marchiano, James J.
Compton, Linda A., ed. see Abbott, Mitchell E., et al.
Compton, Linda A., ed. see Chao, Cedric C.
Compton, Linda A., ed. see Flatt, Gail F.
Compton, Linda A., ed. see Flatt, Gail F., et al.
Compton, Linda A., ed. see McClain, Maureen E. & Polsky, Jeffrey D.
Compton, Linda A., ed. see Pitre, Frank M.
Compton, Linda A., ed. see Quackenbush, Willaim C. & Palefsky, Cliff.
Compton, Linda A., ed. see Robinson, William A.
Compton, Linda A., ed. see Wolf, Bernard N.
Compton, Linda A., ed. see Wright, Robert C.
Compton, M. R., Jr. Jason's Passage. 120p. (Orig.). 1993. pap. 7.95 (*1-886591-05-9*) Cabinet Crest Bks.
***Compton, Madonna S.** Herbal Gold: Healing Alternatives. LC 99-54457. 360p. 2000. pap. 12.95 (*1-56718-172-4*) Llewellyn Pubns.
Compton, Madonna S. Women at the Change: The Intelligent Woman's Guide to Menopause. LC 98-13884. 288p. 1999. pap. text 14.95 (*1-56718-171-6*) Llewellyn Pubns.
Compton, Mary F. & Hawn, Horace C. Exploration: The Total Curriculum. 180p. (C). 1993. pap. text 23.00 (*1-56090-067-9*) Natl Middle Schl.
Compton, Michael & Livingstone, Marco. Tilson. LC 93-61597. (Illus.). 184p. 1994. 45.00 (*0-500-97410-1*, Pub. by Thames Hudson) Norton.
Compton, Mike. Container Top Safety. 64p. (C). 1989. 350.00 (*1-85330-075-6*, Pub. by ICHCA) St Mut.
Compton, Nancy C. African American Children Who Have Experienced Homelessness: Risk, Vulnerability, & Resilience. rev. ed. LC 98-42315. (Children of Poverty Ser.). (Illus.). 180p. 1998. 49.00 (*0-8153-3232-7*) Garland.
Compton, Nancy L. Compton. Family & Direct Ancestors of Herman Everett Compton, 0006-1996. (Illus.). 504p. 1996. pap. 74.50 (*0-8328-5436-0*); lib. bdg. 84.50 (*0-8328-5435-2*) Higginson Bk Co.
Compton, Neil. The Battle for the Buffalo River: A Twentieth-Century Conservation Crisis in the Ozarks. LC 91-27540. (Illus.). 496p. 1992. pap. 34.00 (*1-55728-236-6*); text 58.00 (*1-55728-235-8*) U of Ark Pr.
***Compton, Neil.** The High Ozarks: A Vision of Eden. LC 82-60891. 105p. 1999. pap. 25.00 (*0-912456-22-1*) Ozark Soc Bks.
Compton, Neil, intro. Somewhere Apart: "My Favorite Place in Arkansas": Arkansas Residents Past & Present. LC 96-45409. 1997. pap. 16.00 (*1-55728-446-6*) U of Ark Pr.
Compton, P. & Pavey, N. L. Rules of Thumb - U. K.-France. 1995. pap. 100.00 (*0-86022-420-1*, Pub. by Build Servs Info Assn) St Mut.
Compton, P. A. & Pecsi, Marton. Environment Management: British & Hungarian Case Studies. (Studies in Geography in Hungary: No. 16). 263p. (C). 1984. 81.00 (*963-05-3696-X*, Pub. by Akade Kiado) St Mut.
— Theory & Practice in British & Hungarian Geography: Proceedings of the 4th British-Hungarian Geographical Seminar, Nyiregyhaza, August 18-19, 1987. No. 24. 351p. (C). 1989. 108.00 (*963-05-5589-1*, Pub. by Akade Kiado) St Mut.
Compton, P. A., tr. see Bernat, Tivadar.
Compton, Paul & Jansen, Bob, eds. The Knowledge Dictionary: Maintaining Knowledge Based Systems. (Knowledge Based Systems Ser.). (Illus.). 332p. 1998. text 59.95 (*0-12-380390-X*) Morgan Kaufmann.
Compton, Peter. Sailboat Diesel Maintenance. LC 97-10745. (International Marine Sailboat Library). (Illus.). 173p. 1997. 21.95 (*0-07-012354-3*) McGraw.
Compton, R. & Hancock, Gus. Research in Chemical Kinetics, Vol. IV. (Illus.). 256p. 1997. 195.00 (*0-86542-752-6*) Blackwell Sci.
Compton, R. G., ed. Comprehensive Chemical Kinetics Vol. 30: Electron Tunneling in Chemistry. 360p. 1989. 323.50 (*0-444-87364-3*) Elsevier.
— Electrode Kinetics: Reactions. (Comprehensive Chemical Kinetics Ser.: 27). xii,368p. 1988. 330.00 (*0-444-42879-8*) Elsevier.
— Reactions at the Liquid-Solid Interface. (Comprehensive Chemical Kinetics Ser.: 29). x,286p. 1989. 266.50 (*0-444-87363-5*) Elsevier.
Compton, R. G. & Hancock, G. Applications of Kinetic Modelling. LC 99-17977. (Comprehensive Chemical Kinetics Ser.). 736p. 1999. 421.50 (*0-444-50164-9*) Elsevier.
Compton, R. G. & Hancock, G., eds. Research in Chemical Kinetics, 1. LC 93-38643. 398p. 1993. 239.00 (*0-444-81751-4*) Elsevier.
— Research in Chemical Kinetics, 3. (Research in Chemical Kinetics Ser.: Vol. 3). (Illus.). 336p. 1995. 272.50 (*0-444-82036-1*) Elsevier.
— Research in Chemical Kinetics, Vol. 2. 378p. 1994. 253.50 (*0-444-82024-8*) Elsevier.
Compton, R. G., jt. auth. see Bamford, C. H.
Compton, Rae. Illustrated Dictionary of Knitting. (Illus.). 280p. 1989. pap. 18.95 (*0-934026-41-6*) Interweave.
Compton, Rae, jt. auth. see Harvey, Michael.
Compton, Ralph. Across the Rio Colorado. 1997. mass mkt. 5.99 (*0-312-96102-2*) St Martin.

C

— Autumn of the Gun. 1996. mass mkt. 5.99 (*0-451-19045-9*, Sig) NAL.
— The Bandera Trail. large type ed. (Niagara Large Print Ser.). 496p. 1996. 29.50 (*0-7089-5840-0*) Ulverscroft.
— Border Empire. 352p. 1997. mass mkt. 5.99 (*0-451-19209-5*, Sig) NAL.
— The California Trail. 1994. mass mkt. 5.99 (*0-312-95169-8*) St Martin.
— The California Trail. large type ed. (Niagara Large Print Ser.). 477p. 1996. 29.50 (*0-7089-5846-X*) Ulverscroft.
— The Chisholm Trail. large type ed. (Niagara Large Print Ser.). 466p. 1996. 29.50 (*0-7089-5829-X*) Ulverscroft.
***Compton, Ralph.** The Dakota Trail. 2000. mass mkt. write for info. (*0-312-97589-9*) St Martin.
Compton, Ralph. The Dawn of Fury. 352p. 1995. mass mkt. 5.99 (*0-451-18631-1*, Sig) NAL.
— The Deadwood Trail. 1999. mass mkt. 5.99 (*0-312-96816-7*) St Martin.
— Death Rides a Chestnut Mare. 320p. 1999. mass mkt. 5.99 (*0-451-19761-5*, Sig) NAL.
***Compton, Ralph.** Demon's Pass: A Ralph Compton Novel. 2000. mass mkt. 8.99 (*0-451-19763-1*, Pub. by Signet) Penguin Books.
Compton, Ralph. Devil's Canyon. 352p. 1998. mass mkt. 5.99 (*0-451-19519-1*, Sig) NAL.
***Compton, Ralph.** The Dodge City Trail. large type ed. 360p. 1999. 31.99 (*0-7089-9110-6*) Ulverscroft.
Compton, Ralph. Dodge City Trail, Vol. 1. 6th ed. 336p. 1995. mass mkt. 3.99 (*0-312-95380-1*) St Martin.
— The Goodnight Trail. large type ed. (Niagara Large Print Ser.). 507p. 1995. 29.50 (*0-7089-5812-5*) Ulverscroft.
— The Green River Trail. 304p. 1999. pap. 5.99 (*0-312-97092-7*, St Martins Paperbacks) St Martin.
— The Killing Season. 1996. mass mkt. 5.99 (*0-451-18787-3*, Sig) NAL.
— North to the Bitterroot. (Sundown Riders Ser.: No. 1). 1996. mass mkt. 5.99 (*0-312-95862-5*) St Martin.
— The Old Spanish Trail, Vol. 1. 1998. mass mkt. 5.99 (*0-312-96408-0*) St Martin.
***Compton, Ralph.** The Oregon Trail. large type ed. 360p. 2000. 31.99 (*0-7089-9135-1*) Ulverscroft.
Compton, Ralph. Oregon Trail: Trail Drive, No. 9. 1995. mass mkt. 5.99 (*0-312-95547-2*) St Martin.
— Santa Fe Trail. 1997. mass mkt. 5.99 (*0-312-96296-7*) St Martin.
***Compton, Ralph.** The Santa Fe Trail. 408p. 2000. 31.99 (*0-7089-9157-2*) Ulverscroft.
— The Shadow of a Noose. 311p. 2000. mass mkt. 5.99 (*0-451-19333-4*, Sig) NAL.
Compton, Ralph. The Shawnee Trail. 1994. mass mkt. 5.99 (*0-312-95241-4*) St Martin.
— The Shawnee Trail. large type ed. (Niagara Large Print Ser.). 438p. 1997. 29.50 (*0-7089-5861-3*, Charnwood) Ulverscroft.
— Six Guns & Double Eagles. 352p. 1998. mass mkt. 5.99 (*0-451-19331-8*, Sig) NAL.
***Compton, Ralph.** Skeleton Lodge, 3. 1999. mass mkt. 5.99 (*0-451-19762-3*, Sig) NAL.
Compton, Ralph. Sundown Riders Bk. 2: Whiskey River, 1 vol., Vol. 2. Vol. 2. 320p. 1999. mass mkt. 5.99 (*0-451-19332-6*) NAL.
— Train to Durango. (Border Empire Ser.: Bk. 3). 320p. 1998. mass mkt. 5.99 (*0-451-19237-0*, Sig) NAL.
— The Virginia City Trail. large type ed. (Niagara Large Print Ser.). 432p. 1997. 29.50 (*0-7089-5886-9*) Ulverscroft.
— Virginia City Trail, Vol. 1. 1994. mass mkt. 5.99 (*0-312-95306-2*) St Martin.
— The Western Trail. large type ed. (Niagara Large Print Ser.). 1996. 29.50 (*0-7089-5819-2*) Ulverscroft.
— The Winchester Run, Vol. 1. 1997. mass mkt. 5.99 (*0-312-96320-3*) St Martin.
Compton, Ralph H. Bandera Trail, Vol. 4. 1993. mass mkt. 3.99 (*0-312-95143-4*) St Martin.
— Chisholm Trail. 1993. mass mkt. 3.99 (*0-312-92953-6*) St Martin.
— The Goodnight Trail. 1992. mass mkt. 3.99 (*0-312-92815-7*) St Martin.
— The Western Trail. 1992. mass mkt. 3.99 (*0-312-92901-3*) St Martin.
Compton, Richard. Mountain Biking the Roaring Fork Valley: A Guidebook for Mountain Bikers Featuring Maps, Descriptions & Photographs for 65 Rides in the Mountains near Aspen, Colorado. Ohlrich, Warren H., ed. LC 96-60373. (Illus.). 128p. (Orig.). 1996. pap. 14.95 (*1-882426-04-5*) W H O Pr.
Compton, Richard G. & Sanders, Giles H. Electrode Potentials. (Oxford Chemistry Primers Ser.: No. 41). (Illus.). 96p. (C). 1996. pap. text 12.95 (*0-19-855684-5*) OUP.
Compton-Rickett, Arthur. Personal Forces in Modern Literature. LC 68-54367. (Essay Index Reprint Ser.). 1977. 19.95 (*0-8369-0824-4*) Ayer.
— Personal Forces in Modern Literature. LC 72-973. reprint ed. 34.50 (*0-404-01649-9*) AMS Pr.
Compton-Rickett, Arthur, jt. auth. see Short, Ernest H.
Compton, Robert R. Geology in the Field. LC 85-2325. (Illus.). 416p. 1985. text 73.95 (*0-471-82902-1*) Wiley.
***Compton, Robert W., Jr.** East Asian Democratization: Impact of Globalization, Culture & Economy. LC 00-22346. 224p. 2000. 55.00 (*0-275-96446-9*, C6446, Praeger Pubs) Greenwood.
***Compton, Ronald.** Stillpoint: Dance Photographs. 96p. 1999. 35.00 (*0-89381-873-9*) Aperture.
Compton, Sara. Daredevil Park. (Choose Your Own Adventure Ser.: No. 114). (J). (gr. 4-8). 1991. 8.60 (*0-606-04901-0*, Pub. by Turtleback) Demco.
Compton, Scott. SORD: The System of Role Development: Universal Rules for Roleplaying. Redick, Donald J. & Seymour, Kathleen D., eds. (Illus.). 96p. 1998. pap. 17.95 (*0-9655070-0-9*) Fractal Dimensions.

Compton, Stephen B., jt. auth. see Compton, Joan C.
Compton, Susan. Russian Avant-Garde Books, 1917-34. LC 92-22918. (Illus.). 175p. 1992. 32.00 (*0-262-03201-5*) MIT Pr.
***Compton, Susan, ed.** Chagall: Love & the Stage. (Illus.). 104p. 1998. 25.00 (*0-8276-0658-3*) JPS Phila.
Compton, Susan, et al, eds. British Art in the 20th Century: The Modern Movement. (Art in the Twentieth Century Ser.: Vol. 2). (Illus.). 457p. 1995. 80.00 (*3-7913-0798-3*, Pub. by Prestel) te Neues.
Compton, Susan, et al. Chagall: Love & the Stage. (Illus.). 104p. 1998. 29.95 (*1-85894-058-3*) U of Wash Pr.
— Marc Chagall: My Life - My Dream: Berlin & Paris, 1922-1940. (Illus.). 268p. 1990. 70.00 (*3-7913-1064-X*, Pub. by Prestel) te Neues.
Compton, Timothy G. Mexican Picaresque Narratives: Periquillo & Kin. LC 97-451. 152p. 1997. 32.50 (*0-8387-5348-5*) Bucknell U Pr.
Compton, Timothy G., tr. see Solares, Ignacio.
Compton, Todd. In Sacred Loneliness: The Plural Wives of Joseph Smith. LC 96-19033. (Illus.). 824p. 1997. 39.95 (*1-56085-085-X*) Signature Bks.
Compton, W., jt. auth. see Schulman, J.
Compton, W. Dale, ed. The Interaction of Science & Technology. LC 75-83548. 137p. 1969. text 19.95 (*0-252-00024-2*) U of Ill Pr.
Compton, W. Dale, ed. see Committee on Foundations of Manufacturing, Nationa.
Compton, W. H. Special Day Sermons. 1996. reprint ed. pap. 9.99 (*0-87148-753-5*) Pathway Pr.
Compton, William D. Where No Man Has Gone Before: A History of Apollo Lunar Exploration Missions. LC 88-600242. (NASA History Ser.: No. SP-2414). (Illus.). 429p. 1989. per. 25.00 (*0-16-004253-4*, S/N 033-000-01047-8) USGPO.
Compton, William D. Where No Man Has Gone Before: A History of Apollo Lunar Exploration Missions. (Illus.). 415p. 1996. reprint ed. pap. text 45.00 (*0-7881-3633-X*) DIANE Pub.
Compton, William R., ed. see Compton, Carl C.
CompuServe Staff, jt. auth. see Simkin, Mark G.
Computer & Automated Systems Association of SME st. Computer-Integrated Manufacturing. LC TJ0213.. 52p. 1986. reprint ed. pap. 30.00 (*0-7837-9730-3*, 206046000005) Bks Demand.
Computer & Communications Security Conference (198. Computer & Communications Security '86: Conference Proceeding, October 7-9, 1986. LC QA0076.9.A25. (Illus.). 334p. pap. 103.60 (*0-608-17395-9*, 203023500067) Bks Demand.
Computer & Engineering Services Staff, tr. see Wurth, Marilyn J. & Gannon, Maureen, eds.
Computer Conference (1969: Illinois Institute of Technology) Staff. Computational Approaches in Applied Mechanics: Presented at 1969 Computer Conference, Illinois Institute of Technology, Chicago, IL, June 19-20, 1969. Sevin, Eugene, ed. LC 75-105936. 293p. reprint ed. pap. 90.90 (*0-608-30358-5*, 201681200005) Bks Demand.
***Computer Confidence Inc. Staff.** Access 2000 Advanced. (Illus.). xxii, 132p. 1999. pap. 29.95 (*1-57533-099-7*); pap. 25.95 incl. disk (*1-57533-111-X*, 7948D) Comput Confidence.
— Access 2000 Intermediate. (Computer Confidence Ser.). (Illus.). xx, 132p. 1999. pap. 25.95 incl. disk (*1-57533-110-1*, 7947D) Comput Confidence.
— Access 2000 Introduction. (Computer Confidence Ser.). (Illus.). xx, 132p. 1999. pap. 25.95 incl. disk (*1-57533-109-8*, 7946D) Comput Confidence.
— Computer Hardware & Software Introduction. xiv, 108p. 1999. pap. 20.00 incl. disk (*1-57533-100-4*) Comput Confidence.
— Excel 2000 Advanced. (Computer Confidence Ser.). (Illus.). xxii, 142p. 1999. pap. 25.95 incl. disk (*1-57533-108-X*, 7208D) Comput Confidence.
— Excel 2000 Intermediate. (Illus.). xix, 130p. 1999. pap. 29.95 (*1-57533-095-4*); pap. 25.95 incl. disk (*1-57533-107-1*, 7207D) Comput Confidence.
— Excel 2000 Introduction. (Computer Confidence Ser.). (Illus.). xxii, 160p. 1999. pap. 25.95 incl. disk (*1-57533-106-3*, 7206D) Comput Confidence.
— PowerPoint 2000 Advanced. (Illus.). xx, 132p. 1999. pap. 29.95 (*1-57533-093-8*); pap. 25.95 incl. disk (*1-57533-105-5*, 7758D) Comput Confidence.
— PowerPoint 2000 Introduction. (Computer Confidence Ser.). (Illus.). xxii, 164p. 1999. pap. 25.95 (*1-57533-104-7*, 7756D) Comput Confidence.
— PowerPoint 2000 Introduction. (Illus.). xxii, 164p. 1999. spiral bd. 29.95 incl. disk (*1-57533-092-X*, 7756) Comput Confidence.
— Word 2000 Advanced. (Computer Confidence Ser.). (Illus.). xviii, 128p. 1999. pap. 25.95 (*1-57533-103-9*, 7918D); pap. 29.95 incl. disk (*1-57533-091-1*, 7918) Comput Confidence.
— Word 2000 Intermediate. deluxe ed. (Computer Confidence Ser.). (Illus.). xviii, 168p. 1999. pap. 25.95 (*1-57533-102-0*, 7917D) Comput Confidence.
— Word 2000 Introduction. (Computer Confidence Ser.). (Illus.). xvii, 146p. 1999. pap. 25.95 incl. disk (*1-57533-101-2*, 7916D); pap. 29.95 incl. disk (*1-57533-089-X*, 7916) Comput Confidence.
Computer Confidence Staff. Access 97 Advanced. (Illus.). xvi, 128p. 1998. spiral bd. 29.00 incl. disk (*1-57533-072-5*, 07973) Comput Confidence.
***Computer Confidence Staff.** Access 97 Advanced. deluxe ed. (Illus.). xvi, 128p. 1998. spiral bd. 25.95 incl. disk (*1-57533-122-5*, 7943D) Comput Confidence.
Computer Confidence Staff. Access 97 Intermediate. (Illus.). xviii, 134p. 1997. spiral bd. 29.00 incl. disk (*1-57533-062-8*, 07943) Comput Confidence.

Computer Confidence Staff. Access 97 Intermediate. deluxe ed. (Illus.). xviii, 134p. 1997. spiral bd. 25.95 incl. disk (*1-57533-121-7*, 7942D) Comput Confidence.
Computer Confidence Staff. Access 97 Introduction. (Illus.). xviii, 132p. 1997. spiral bd. 29.00 incl. disk (*1-57533-061-X*, 07941) Comput Confidence.
Computer Confidence Staff. Access 97 Introduction. deluxe ed. (Illus.). xviii, 132p. 1997. spiral bd. 25.95 incl. disk (*1-57533-120-9*, 7941D) Comput Confidence.
Computer Confidence Staff. Access 7.0 for Windows 95 Introduction. (Illus.). xvi, 124p. 1996. spiral bd. 29.00 incl. disk (*1-57533-080-6*, 07935) Comput Confidence.
***Computer Confidence Staff.** Access 2000 Intermediate. (Illus.). xx, 134p. 1999. pap. 29.95 incl. disk (*1-57533-098-9*) Comput Confidence.
Computer Confidence Staff. Access 2.0 Advanced. 100p. 1994. spiral bd. 29.95 incl. disk (*1-57533-031-8*) Comput Confidence.
— Access 2.0 Introduction. 150p. 1994. spiral bd. 29.95 incl. disk (*1-57533-030-X*) Comput Confidence.
— Enable 4.5 Introduction. (Illus.). 150p. 1993. spiral bd. 29.95 incl. disk (*1-57533-045-8*) Comput Confidence.
— Excel 97 Intermediate. (Illus.). xviii, 130p. 1998. spiral bd. 29.00 incl. disk (*1-57533-064-4*, 07202) Comput Confidence.
***Computer Confidence Staff.** Excel 97 Intermediate. deluxe ed. (Illus.). xviii, 130p. 1998. spiral bd. 25.95 incl. disk (*1-57533-118-7*, 7202D) Comput Confidence.
Computer Confidence Staff. Excel 97 Introduction. (Illus.). xviii, 164p. 1997. spiral bd. 29.00 incl. disk (*1-57533-063-6*, 07201) Comput Confidence.
Computer Confidence Staff. Excel 97 Introduction. deluxe ed. xviii, 164p. 1997. spiral bd. 25.95 incl. disk (*1-57533-117-9*, 7201D) Comput Confidence.
Computer Confidence Staff. Excel 7.0 for Windows 95 Introduction. (Illus.). xviii, 158p. 1996. spiral bd. 29.00 incl. disk (*1-57533-076-8*, 07198) Comput Confidence.
— Excel 5.0 Advanced. (Illus.). 150p. 1994. spiral bd. 29.95 incl. disk (*1-57533-011-3*) Comput Confidence.
— Excel 5.0 Introduction. (Illus.). 160p. 1994. spiral bd. 29.95 incl. disk (*1-57533-010-5*) Comput Confidence.
— Excel 97 Advanced. (Illus.). xviii, 118p. 1998. spiral bd. 29.00 incl. disk (*1-57533-073-3*, 07203) Comput Confidence.
***Computer Confidence Staff.** Excel 97 Advanced. deluxe ed. (Illus.). xviii, 118p. 1998. spiral bd. 25.95 incl. disk (*1-57533-119-5*, 7903D) Comput Confidence.
Computer Confidence Staff. FoxPro 2.5/2.6 Windows Advanced. (Illus.). 150p. 1993. spiral bd. 29.95 incl. disk (*1-57533-034-2*) Comput Confidence.
— FoxPro 2.5/2.6 Windows Intermediate. (Illus.). 150p. 1993. spiral bd. 29.95 incl. disk (*1-57533-033-4*) Comput Confidence.
— FoxPro 2.5/2.6 Windows Introduction. (Illus.). 150p. 1993. spiral bd. 29.95 incl. disk (*1-57533-032-6*) Comput Confidence.
— FoxPro 2.5 DOS Advanced. (Illus.). 150p. 1993. spiral bd. 29.95 incl. disk (*1-57533-037-7*) Comput Confidence.
— FoxPro 2.5 DOS Intermediate. (Illus.). 150p. 1993. spiral bd. 29.95 incl. disk (*1-57533-036-9*) Comput Confidence.
— FoxPro 2.5 DOS Introduction. (Illus.). 150p. 1993. spiral bd. 29.95 incl. disk (*1-57533-035-0*) Comput Confidence.
— Internet Introduction for Windows 95. (Illus.). xiv, 104p. 1996. spiral bd. 29.00 (*1-57533-087-3*, 09101) Comput Confidence.
— Internet Using MS Internet Explorer 3 Introduction. (Illus.). xvi, 126p. 1997. spiral bd. 29.00 incl. disk (*1-57533-065-2*, 09103) Comput Confidence.
— Introduction to Computers & DOS 6.2. (Illus.). 140p. 1994. spiral bd. 29.95 incl. disk (*1-57533-053-9*) Comput Confidence.
— Local Area Networks (LANs) Introduction. (Illus.). xiv, 114p. 1995. spiral bd. 29.00 (*1-57533-086-5*, 08030) Comput Confidence.
— Lotus 1-2-3 Version 5.0 Windows Introduction. (Illus.). 165p. 1994. spiral bd. 29.95 incl. disk (*1-57533-014-8*) Comput Confidence.
— Novell Groupwise 4.1 Introduction. (Illus.). xvi, 136p. 1996. spiral bd. 29.00 incl. disk (*1-57533-085-7*, 09601) Comput Confidence.
***Computer Confidence Staff.** Outlook 98 Introduction. (Illus.). xvii, 160p. 1998. spiral bd. 29.95 incl. disk (*1-57533-088-1*, 9811) Comput Confidence.
— Outlook 98 Introduction. deluxe ed. (Illus.). xviii, 160p. 1998. pap. 25.95 (*1-57533-126-8*) Comput Confidence.
Computer Confidence Staff. Outlook 97 Introduction. (Illus.). xviii, 140p. 1997. spiral bd. 29.00 incl. disk (*1-57533-066-0*, 07945) Comput Confidence.
— PageMaker 5.0 Windows Introduction. (Illus.). 160p. 1995. spiral bd. 29.95 incl. disk (*1-57533-003-2*) Comput Confidence.
— PowerPoint 97 Advanced. (Illus.). xviii, 126p. 1998. spiral bd. 29.00 incl. disk (*1-57533-069-5*, 07753) Comput Confidence.
***Computer Confidence Staff.** PowerPoint 97 Advanced. deluxe ed. (Illus.). xviii, 126p. 1998. spiral bd. 25.95 incl. disk (*1-57533-116-0*, 7753D) Comput Confidence.
Computer Confidence Staff. PowerPoint 97 Introduction. (Illus.). xviii, 164p. 1997. spiral bd. 29.00 incl. disk (*1-57533-068-7*, 07751) Comput Confidence.
Computer Confidence Staff. PowerPoint 97 Introduction. deluxe ed. (Illus.). xviii, 164p. 1997. spiral bd. 25.95 incl. disk (*1-57533-115-2*, 7951D) Comput Confidence.
Computer Confidence Staff. PowerPoint 7.0 for Windows 95 Introduction. (Illus.). xviii, 166p. 1996. spiral bd. 29.00 incl. disk (*1-57533-077-6*, 07747) Comput Confidence.

— PowerPoint 4.0 Windows Advanced. (Illus.). 160p. 1995. spiral bd. 29.95 incl. disk (*1-57533-021-0*) Comput Confidence.
— PowerPoint 4.0 Windows Introduction. (Illus.). 160p. 1994. spiral bd. 29.95 incl. disk (*1-57533-020-2*) Comput Confidence.
— Project 3.0 Advanced. (Illus.). 150p. 1993. spiral bd. 29.95 incl. disk (*1-57533-057-1*) Comput Confidence.
— Project 3.0 Windows Introduction. (Illus.). 150p. 1993. spiral bd. 29.95 incl. disk (*1-57533-056-3*) Comput Confidence.
— Project 4.0 Advanced. (Illus.). 160p. 1994. spiral bd. 29.95 incl. disk (*1-57533-055-5*) Comput Confidence.
— Project 4.0 Introduction. (Illus.). 160p. 1994. spiral bd. 29.95 incl. disk (*1-57533-054-7*) Comput Confidence.
— System 7.5 for Macintosh Introduction. (Illus.). 150p. 1995. spiral bd. 29.95 incl. disk (*1-57533-028-8*) Comput Confidence.
— Visual Basic 3.0 Windows Advanced. (Illus.). 160p. 1995. spiral bd. 29.95 incl. disk (*1-57533-051-2*) Comput Confidence.
— Visual Basic 3.0 Windows Introduction. (Illus.). 160p. 1995. spiral bd. 29.95 incl. disk (*1-57533-050-4*) Comput Confidence.
— Windows 98 Introduction. (Illus.). xviii, 148p. 1998. spiral bd. 29.95 incl. disk (*1-57533-067-9*, 09801) Comput Confidence.
***Computer Confidence Staff.** Windows 98 Introduction. deluxe ed. (Illus.). xviii, 148p. 1998. spiral bd. 25.95 incl. disk (*1-57533-124-1*, 9801D) Comput Confidence.
Computer Confidence Staff. Windows 95 Introduction. (Illus.). xvi, 122p. 1995. spiral bd. 29.00 incl. disk (*1-57533-075-X*, 09501) Comput Confidence.
Computer Confidence Staff. Windows NT 4.0 Workstation Introduction. deluxe ed. (Illus.). xx, 128p. 1997. spiral bd. 25.95 incl. disk (*1-57533-123-3*, 8203D) Comput Confidence.
Computer Confidence Staff. Windows NT v4.0 Workstation Introduction. (Illus.). xx, 128p. 1997. spiral bd. 29.00 incl. disk (*1-57533-081-4*, 08203) Comput Confidence.
— Windows NT v3.51 Introduction. (Illus.). xxvi, 170p. 1996. spiral bd. 29.00 incl. disk (*1-57533-084-9*, 08201) Comput Confidence.
— Windows 3.1. (Illus.). 160p. 1992. spiral bd. 29.95 incl. disk (*1-57533-052-0*) Comput Confidence.
— Word 97 Advanced. (Illus.). xviii, 124p. 1997. spiral bd. 29.00 incl. disk (*1-57533-074-1*, 07913) Comput Confidence.
Computer Confidence Staff. Word 97 Advanced. deluxe ed. (Illus.). xviii, 124p. 1997. spiral bd. 25.95 incl. disk (*1-57533-114-4*, 7913D) Comput Confidence.
Computer Confidence Staff. Word 97 Intermediate. (Illus.). xviii, 162p. 1997. spiral bd. 29.00 incl. disk (*1-57533-071-7*, 07912) Comput Confidence.
Computer Confidence Staff. Word 97 Intermediate. deluxe ed. (Illus.). xviii, 162p. 1997. spiral bd. 25.95 incl. disk (*1-57533-113-6*, 7912D) Comput Confidence.
Computer Confidence Staff. Word 97 Introduction. (Illus.). xviii, 158p. 1997. spiral bd. 29.00 incl. disk (*1-57533-070-9*, 07911) Comput Confidence.
Computer Confidence Staff. Word 97 Introduction. deluxe ed. (Illus.). xviii, 158p. 1997. spiral bd. 25.95 incl. disk (*1-57533-112-8*, 7911D) Comput Confidence.
Computer Confidence Staff. Word 7.0 for Windows 95 Introduction. (Illus.). xviii, 144p. 1996. spiral bd. 29.00 incl. disk (*1-57533-078-4*, 07857) Comput Confidence.
— Word 7.0 for Windows 95 Intermediate. (Illus.). xviii, 144p. 1997. spiral bd. 29.00 incl. disk (*1-57533-079-2*, 07858) Comput Confidence.
Computer Confidence Staff. Word 6.0 for Windows Introduction. deluxe ed. (Illus.). 160p. 1994. spiral bd. 25.95 incl. disk (*1-57533-125-X*, 7850D) Comput Confidence.
Computer Confidence Staff. Word 2000 Intermediate. (Illus.). xviii, 168p. 1999. pap. 29.95 incl. disk (*1-57533-090-3*, 7917) Comput Confidence.
— Word 5.1 for Macintosh Introduction. (Illus.). 150p. 1993. spiral bd. 29.95 incl. disk (*1-57533-026-1*) Comput Confidence.
— Word 6.0 Advanced. (Illus.). 160p. 1994. spiral bd. 29.95 incl. disk (*1-57533-001-6*) Comput Confidence.
— Word 6.0 for Macintosh Introduction. (Illus.). 160p. 1995. spiral bd. 29.95 incl. disk (*1-57533-025-3*) Comput Confidence.
— Word 6.0 Introduction. (Illus.). 160p. 1994. spiral bd. 29.95 incl. disk (*1-57533-000-8*) Comput Confidence.
— WordPerfect 6.1 for Windows Advanced. (Illus.). xviii, 138p. 1995. spiral bd. 29.00 incl. disk (*1-57533-083-0*, 07907) Comput Confidence.
— WordPerfect 6.1 for Windows Introduction. (Illus.). xvi, 158p. 1995. spiral bd. 29.00 incl. disk (*1-57533-082-2*, 07906) Comput Confidence.
Computer Consultants Ltd. Staff. European Computer Survey Nineteen Sixty-Eight to Nineteen Sixty-Nine, 2 vols. 5th ed. LC 68-21672. 1968. 197.00 (*0-08-013372-X*, Pub. by Pergamon Repr) Franklin.
— European Computer User's Handbook, 1969-70. 1969. write for info. (*0-318-55161-6*, Pub. by Pergamon Repr) Franklin.
Computer Graphics International 1998 Staff, et al. Proceedings: Computer Graphics International 1998 : Hannover, Germany, June 22-26, 1998. LC 98-84455. xxi, 800 p. 1998. write for info. (*0-8186-8447-X*) IEEE Comp Soc.
Computer Graphics 70 International Symposium Staff. Computer Graphics in Medical Research & Hospital Administration. Paslow, R. D. & Green, R. Elliot, eds. LC 75-137741. (Illus.). 99p. 1971. reprint ed. pap. 30.70 (*0-608-05485-2*, 206595400006) Bks Demand.
Computer Innovations Staff, jt. auth. see Pakin, Sandra.

Computer Institute Staff. IDEAS Operating & Reference Manual. (Illus.). 304p. 1983. pap. text 40.00 (*0-940090-03-1*) Haer Inst.
Computer Law Association Staff, ed. The 1995 Pacific Rim Computer Law Conference. 500p. 1995. 80.00 (*1-885169-01-9*) Computer Law.
Computer Law Institute Staff, et al. Fourth Annual Computer Law Institute. write for info. (*0-318-58020-9*) Harcourt.
Computer Law Reporter Editors. Computer Law Developments: 1984. 120.00 (*0-318-04463-3*) Comp Law Rep.
— The Semiconductor Chip Protection Act of 1984: Analysis, History & Practical Applications, 2 vols. 140.00 (*0-318-04464-1*) Comp Law Rep.
Computer Systems Research Group Staff. BSD 4.4, 5 vols., Vols. 1-5. (Orig.). 1994. pap. 120.00 (*1-56592-077-5*) Thomson Learn.
— BSD 4.4 Programmer's Reference Manual. 886p. (Orig.). 1994. pap. 30.00 (*1-56592-078-3*) Thomson Learn.
— BSD 4.4 Programmer's Supplementary Documents. 596p. (Orig.). 1994. pap. 30.00 (*1-56592-079-1*) Thomson Learn.
— BSD 4.4 System Manager's Manual. 804p. (Orig.). 1994. pap. 30.00 (*1-56592-080-5*) Thomson Learn.
— BSD 4.4 User's Reference Manual. 905p. (Orig.). 1994. pap. 30.00 (*1-56592-075-9*) Thomson Learn.
— BSD 4.4 User's Supplementary Documents. 712p. (Orig.). 1994. pap. 30.00 (*1-56592-076-7*) Thomson Learn.
Computer Technology Research Corp. Staff. The Complete Guide to High-Speed Networking & Communications. LC 95-47947. (Illus.). 266p. (Orig.). 1996. pap. 285.00 (*1-56607-963-2*) Comput Tech Res.
Computers in Aerodynamics Symposium Staff. Computers in Aerodynamics: Proceedings of the Symposium, Polytechnic Institute of New York, Aerodynamics Laboratories, 1979. Rubin, S. G. & Bloom, M. H., eds. 130p. 1980. pap. 46.00 (*0-08-025426-8*, Pergamon Pr) Elsevier.
Computing Environment Services Technical Committee. Computing Environment Services, Vol. 4. 160p. 1993. pap. text 100.00 (*1-882750-04-7*) CAD Framewk.
Computing Services Association Staff. Controlling Contractors' Services on a Prince Project. (Programme & Project Management Library). 98p. 1993. pap. 70.00 (*0-11-330588-5*, HM05885, Pub. by Statnry Office) Balogh.
Computing Smart Staff. PC Upgrading & Maintenance. 2nd ed. LC 98-83176. (No Experience Required Ser.). (Illus.). 704p. 1999. pap. 24.99 (*0-7821-2471-2*) Sybex.
Computype, Inc. Staff, ed. see Boland, Kevin.
Comrada, Norma, tr. see Capek, Karel.
Comras, Jay. Improving College Admission Test Scores: ACT English; Student Workbook. 136p. 1989. student ed. 5.50 (*0-88210-229-X*) Natl Assn Principals.
— Improving College Admission Test Scores: ACT English; Teacher Manual. 134p. 1989. teacher ed. 7.50 (*0-88210-227-3*) Natl Assn Principals.
— Improving College Admission Test Scores: ACT Reading. 88p. 1990. pap., teacher ed. 5.50 (*0-88210-233-8*); pap. text, student ed. 5.50 (*0-88210-232-X*) Natl Assn Principals.
— Improving College Admission Test Scores: ACT Science Reasoning. (Illus.). 88p. (Orig.). 1990. teacher ed. 5.50 (*0-88210-236-2*); pap. text, student ed. 5.50 (*0-88210-234-6*) Natl Assn Principals.
Comras, Jay & Zerowin, Jeffrey. Improving College Admission Test Scores: Math Workbook. Koerner, Thomas F. & Potter, Eugenia C., eds. (Orig.). (gr. 11-12). 1989. pap. text 5.50 (*0-88210-148-X*) Natl Assn Principals.
— Improving College Admission Test Scores: Math Workbook, Teachers Manual. Koerner, Thomas F. & Potter, Eugenia C., eds. (Orig.). (gr. 11-12). 1983. pap. text. write for info. (*0-88210-149-8*) Natl Assn Principals.
Comrey, Andrew. Handbook of Interpretations for the Comrey Personality Scales. LC 80-67424. 1980. pap. 23.75 (*0-912736-23-2*) EDITS Pubs.
Comrey, Andrew L. & Lee, Howard B. A First Course in Factor Analysis. 2nd ed. 448p. (C). 1992. text 55.00 (*0-8058-1062-5*) L Erlbaum Assocs.
Comrie, B. Aspect. (Cambridge Textbooks in Linguistics Ser.). 151p. 1976. pap. text 19.95 (*0-521-29045-7*) Cambridge U Pr.
Comrie, Bernard. Language Universals & Linguistic Typology. LC 81-52478. (Illus.). (C). 1981. pap. text 10.00 (*0-226-11436-8*); lib. bdg. 25.00 (*0-226-11434-1*) U Ch Pr.
— Language Universals & Linguistic Typology: Syntax & Morphology. 2nd ed. LC 89-40280. xii, 278p. 1989. pap. text 15.95 (*0-226-11433-3*) U Ch Pr.
— Tense. (Cambridge Textbooks in Linguistics Ser.). 149p. 1985. pap. text 17.95 (*0-521-28138-5*) Cambridge U Pr.
Comrie, Bernard, ed. The World's Major Languages. (Illus.). 1040p. 1990. reprint ed. pap. text 38.00 (*0-19-506511-5*) OUP.
Comrie, Bernard & Eid, Mushira, eds. Perspectives on Arabic Linguistics Vol. III: Papers from the 3rd Annual Symposium on Arabic Linguistics. Salt Lake City, Utah 1989. LC 91-7898. (Current Issues in Linguistic Theory Ser.: No. 80). xii, 274p. 1991. 71.00 (*1-55619-135-9*) J Benjamins Pubng Co.
Comrie, Bernard, et al. The Atlas of Languages: The Origins & Development of Languages Throughout the World. LC 95-15336. (Illus.). 244p. 1996. 35.00 (*0-8160-3388-9*) Facts on File.
— The Russian Language in the Twentieth Century. (Illus.). 396p. 1996. text 89.00 (*0-19-824066-X*) OUP.
Comrie, Bernard, jt. auth. see Vogel, Petra M.
Comrie, Bernard, jt. ed. see Nedjalkov, Vladimir P.
Comrie, R. G., jt. auth. see Gibson, J. T.
Comrie, Sandra M. & Crecelius, Allan M. Human Resources Policies & Procedures: Structuring Staff Guidelines for Your Credit Union. 285p. 1993. ring bd. 139.00 (*1-889394-06-8*) Credit Union Execs.
Comrie, Sandra M., jt. auth. see Crecelius, Allan M.
Comroe, J. H., Jr., et al, eds. Annual Review of Physiology, Vol. 34. LC 39-15404. (Illus.). 1972. text 42.00 (*0-8243-0334-2*) Annual Reviews.
— Annual Review of Physiology, Vol. 35. LC 39-15404. (Illus.). 1973. text 42.00 (*0-8243-0335-0*) Annual Reviews.
— Annual Review of Physiology, Vol. 36. LC 39-15404. (Illus.). 1974. text 42.00 (*0-8243-0336-9*) Annual Reviews.
— Annual Review of Physiology, Vol. 37. LC 39-15404. (Illus.). 1975. text 42.00 (*0-8243-0337-7*) Annual Reviews.
Comroe, Julius H., Jr. & Hall, Victor, eds. Annual Review of Physiology, Vol. 25. LC 39-15404. 1963. 42.00 (*0-8243-0325-3*) Annual Reviews.
Comsa, G., jt. auth. see Poelsema, B.
Comstantin, P., et al. Integral Manifolds & Inertial Manifolds for Dissipative Partial Differential Equations. (Applied Mathematical Sciences Ser.: Vol. 70). 165p. 1988. 65.95 (*0-387-96729-X*) Spr-Verlag.
Comstock. Public Communication & Behavior Series, Vol. 3. 1997. write for info. (*0-12-543203-8*) Acad Pr.
— Religious Autobiographies. 2nd ed. (Religion Ser.). 2000. pap. text 21.75 (*0-534-52641-1*) Thomson Learn.
— Television. LC 99-60584. 388p. (C). 1999. 54.95 (*0-12-183580-4*) Acad Pr.
Comstock, Anna B. Handbook of Nature Study. LC 85-29144. (Comstock Bk.). (Illus.). 912p. 1986. pap. text 24.95 (*0-8014-9384-6*) Cornell U Pr.
Comstock, Anthony. Frauds Exposed: or How People Are Deceived & Robbed, & Youth Corrupted. LC 69-16234. (Criminology, Law Enforcement, & Social Problems Ser.: No. 79). (Illus.). 1969. reprint ed. 30.00 (*0-87585-079-0*) Patterson Smith.
— Traps for the Young. Bremner, Robert H., ed. LC 67-17306. (John Harvard Library). (Illus.). 293p. 1967. 35.95 (*0-674-90555-5*) HUP.
Comstock, Ardis H., jt. auth. see Comstock, David A.
Comstock, Ariane, ed. see McLeod, Penn.
Comstock, Ariane C. The Young Person's Guide to the Opera. LC 96-78048. (Illus.). 288p. (YA). (gr. 5 up). 1997. lib. bdg. 29.95 (*1-889923-13-3*, Monarch Books) Monarch Westlake Village.
Comstock, Barbara. Anna's Adventure. 24p. (J). (gr. 3-6). 1997. pap. 7.00 (*0-8059-4212-2*) Dorrance.
Comstock, Christine M., jt. auth. see Bavolek, Stephen J.
Comstock, Craig, jt. auth. see Sanford, R. Nevitt.
Comstock, Cyrus. Comstock Diary. (Illus.). 408p. 1987. 37.50 (*0-89029-518-2*) Morningside Bkshop.
Comstock, Cyrus B. Comstock Genealogy: Descendants of William Comstock of New London, CT; Who Died after 1662, Ten Generations. (Illus.). 314p. 1994. reprint ed. lib. bdg. 57.50 (*0-8328-4309-1*); reprint ed. per. 47.50 (*0-8328-4310-5*) Higginson Bk Co.
Comstock, David A. Brides of the Gold Rush, 1851-1859. LC 86-73171. (Nevada County Chronicles Ser.: No. 2). (Illus.). xvi, 448p. 1987. 21.50 (*0-933994-05-2*) Comstock Bon.
***Comstock, David A.** Brides of the Gold Rush, 1851-1859. rev. ed. (The Nevada County Chronicles Ser.). (Illus.). 448p. 1999. 14.50 (*0-933994-26-5*) Comstock Bon.
Comstock, David A. Gold Diggers & Camp Followers, 1845-1851. LC 82-8176. (Nevada County Chronicles Ser.: No. 1). (Illus.). xvi, 413p. 1982. 35.00 (*0-933994-02-8*) Comstock Bon.
— Gold Diggers & Camp Followers, 1845-1851. LC 82-8176. (Nevada County Chronicles Ser.: No. 1). (Illus.). xvi, 413p. 1988. pap. 12.50 (*0-933994-08-7*) Comstock Bon.
— Greenbacks & Copperheads, 1859-1869. LC 95-38215. (Nevada County Chronicles Ser.: No. 3). (Illus.). xvi, 428p. 1995. 21.50 (*0-933994-12-5*) Comstock Bon.
— Greenbacks & Copperheads, 1859-1869. LC 95-38215. (Nevada County Chronicles Ser.: No. 3). (Illus.). xvi, 428p. 1996. pap. 12.50 (*0-933994-14-1*) Comstock Bon.
Comstock, David A. & Comstock, Ardis H. Nevada County, California, 1880 History Index. LC 79-115328. 84p. 1979. pap. 17.50 (*0-933994-00-1*) Comstock Bon.
— Nevada County Vital Statistics, 1850-1869: Births, Marriages, Separations, Divorces, Naturalizations & Deaths in Nevada County, California. (Nevada County Pioneers Ser.: No. 1). iv, 104p. (Orig.). 1996. pap. 17.50 (*0-933994-16-8*) Comstock Bon.
Comstock, E. B., jt. auth. see Wickersham, G. V.
Comstock, Ernest B. Harroun. History of the Harroun Family in America, Seven Generations: Descendants of Alexander Harroun of Colrain, Massachusetts, 1691-1784. (Illus.). 195p. 1997. reprint ed. pap. 29.00 (*0-8328-9008-1*); reprint ed. lib. bdg. 39.00 (*0-8328-9007-3*) Higginson Bk Co.
Comstock, Esther J. Feliciana's California Miracle. LC 85-9707. (Illus.). xiv, 178p. (J). (gr. 6). 1985. 10.00 (*0-933994-03-6*) Comstock Bon.
— Vallejo & the Four Flags: A True Story of Early California. LC 79-21636. (Illus.). xvi, 142p. (J). (gr. 4). 1988. pap. 10.00 (*0-933994-07-9*) Comstock Bon.
— Vallejo y las Cuatro Banderas: Una Historia Verdadera de la California de Antano. Pardo, Marcel & Velasco, Ana M., trs. LC 95-15440. Orig. Title: Vallejo & the Four Flags. (SPA., Illus.). xiv, 152p. (Orig.). (J). (gr. 4 up). 1996. pap. 12.50 (*0-933994-13-3*) Comstock Bon.
Comstock, Francis A. A Gothic Vision: F. L. Griggs & His Work. 1978. 65.00 (*0-89073-096-2*, 186) Boston Public Lib.
Comstock, Gary D. Gay Theology Without Apology. LC 92-42621. 192p. (Orig.). (C). 1993. pap. 15.95 (*0-8298-0944-9*) Pilgrim OH.
— Unrepentant, Self-Affirming, Practicing: Lesbian/Bisexual/Gay People Within Organized Religion. 336p. 1996. 29.95 (*0-8264-0881-8*) Continuum.
— Violence Against Lesbians & Gay Men. (Between Men - Between Women Ser.). 320p. (C). 1992. pap. 19.50 (*0-231-07331-3*) Col U Pr.
Comstock, Gary D. & Henking, Susan E., eds. Que(e)rying Religion: A Critical Anthology. LC 78-20932. 350p. 1996. pap. 29.95 (*0-8264-0924-5*) Continuum.
Comstock, Gary L. Religious Autobiographies. LC 94-20555. 375p. 1994. pap. 42.95 (*0-534-18780-3*) Wadsworth Pub.
Comstock, George. The Evolution of American Television. 2nd ed. 384p. (C). 1989. text 48.00 (*0-8039-3552-8*); pap. text 22.95 (*0-8039-3553-6*) Sage.
— Television in America. 2nd ed. (CommText Ser.: Vol. 1). 237p. (C). 1991. text 42.00 (*0-8039-3338-X*); pap. text 18.95 (*0-8039-3339-8*) Sage.
Comstock, George & Paik, Hae J. Television & the American Child. (Illus.). 386p. (C). 1991. text 45.00 (*0-12-183575-8*) Acad Pr.
Comstock, George A. The Evolution of American Television. LC 89-33253. 312p. 1989. reprint ed. pap. 96.80 (*0-608-01612-8*, 205959100003) Bks Demand.
— Television in America. LC 91-25358. (Sage Commtext Ser.: Vol. 1). 160p. 1991. reprint ed. pap. 49.60 (*0-608-03496-7*, 206421100008) Bks Demand.
Comstock, H. E. The Pottery of the Shenandoah Valley Region. LC 93-80689. (The Frank L. Horton Ser.). (Illus.). 538p. 1994. 125.00 (*0-945578-04-0*) Mus South Deco.
Comstock, Helen. American Furniture: Seventeenth, Eighteenth & Nineteenth Century Styles. LC 62-18074. (Illus.). 336p. 1980. reprint ed. 44.95 (*0-916838-28-5*) Schiffer.
Comstock, J. A. Comstock: A History & Genealogy of the Comstock Family in America. 715p. 1991. reprint ed. pap. 99.50 (*0-8328-2121-7*); reprint ed. lib. bdg. 109.50 (*0-8328-2120-9*) Higginson Bk Co.
***Comstock, Jim.** Poems of Love, Inspiration & Other Things. 120p. 2000. pap. write for info. (*0-7541-1035-4*, Pub. by Minerva Pr) Unity Dist.
Comstock, Joe. Erie in Photos. (Illus.). 112p. 1990. 9.95 (*0-910042-57-8*) Allegheny.
Comstock, John A. Butterflies of California. (Illus.). 334p. 1989. reprint ed. 32.50 (*0-945417-21-7*) Sci Pubs.
Comstock, John M. Chelsea: The Origin of Chelsea & a Record of Its Institutions & Individuals. (Illus.). 62p. 1996. reprint ed. pap. 12.00 (*0-8328-5126-4*); reprint ed. lib. bdg. 22.00 (*0-8328-5125-6*) Higginson Bk Co.
Comstock, John M., ed. List of the Principal Officers of Vermont, from 1777 to 1918. 411p. 1997. reprint ed. lib. bdg. 45.00 (*0-8328-6494-3*) Higginson Bk Co.
***Comstock, Kani & Thame, Marisa.** Journey into Love: Ten Steps to Wholeness. (Illus.). 2000. pap. 12.95 (*0-9679186-4-2*) Willow Pr OR.
***Comstock, Kathleen.** Orchid House. LC 99-75262. 272p. 2000. pap. 16.95 (*1-57197-201-3*, Pub. by Pentland Pr) Assoc Pubs Grp.
Comstock, Kathleen, jt. auth. see Hulit, Michael.
Comstock, Leila. Slektin - The Family. 132p. 1988. 14.95 (*0-87770-457-0*) Ye Galleon.
Comstock, Mary B., jt. auth. see Vermeule, Cornelius C., III.
Comstock, Mary C. Fortune's Mistress. 224p. 1996. mass mkt. 4.50 (*0-8217-5237-5*, Zebra Kensgtn) Kensgtn Pub Corp.
Comstock, R. Lawrence. Introduction to Magnetism & Magnetic Recording. LC 99-10811. 487p. (C). 1999. 95.00 (*0-471-31714-4*) Wiley.
Comstock, Ralph E. Quantitative Genetics with Special Reference to Plant & Animal Breeding. LC 94-48902. 436p. 1996. text 114.95 (*0-8138-2011-1*) Iowa St U Pr.
Comstock, Roger W., jt. ed. see Beard, Margaret L.
Comstock, Ruth B. Making Chair Seats from Cane, Rush & Other Natural Materials. rev. ed. (Illus.). 48p. 1988. reprint ed. pap. 3.95 (*0-486-25693-6*) Dover.
Comstock, Ruth B. & Garner, Clark E. Seats for Chairs: Cane, Hong Kong Grass, Rope, Twine, Rush & Splint. 3rd rev. ed. (Illus.). 62p. 1996. reprint ed. pap. 16.00 (*1-57753-087-X*, 327E) Corn Coop Ext.
Comstock, Sallyann. Belgians from Start to Finished. 2nd ed. Beyond Graphics Staff, ed. (Illus.). xii, 434p. 1998. 49.95 (*0-9670872-0-1*) Salcom Inc.
Comstock, Thomas W. Communicating in Business & Industry. 2nd ed. (C). 1990. teacher ed. 18.95 (*0-8273-3543-1*); text 41.95 (*0-8273-3542-3*) Delmar.
Comstock, Will. The Man from Wells Fargo. large type ed. LC 97-40849. 1998. 18.95 (*0-7862-0680-2*, G K Hall Lrg Type) Mac Lib Ref.
Comstock, Will A. Red Mountain. large type ed. (Linford Western Library). 320p. (Orig.). 1992. pap. 16.99 (*0-7089-7246-2*) Ulverscroft.
Comstock, William T. Country Homes & Seaside Cottages of the Victorian Era. (Illus.). 64p. 1999. pap. 6.95 (*0-486-25972-2*) Dover.
— Turn-of-the-Century House Designs: With Floor Plans, Elevations & Interior Details of 24 Residences. unabridged ed. LC 94-12113. Orig. Title: Suburban & Country Homes. (Illus.). 96p. 1994. reprint ed. pap. text 8.95 (*0-486-28186-8*) Dover.
— Victorian Domestic Architectural Plans & Details: Seven Hundred Thirty-Four Scale Drawings of Doorways, Windows, Staircases, Moldings, Cornices & Other Elements. (Illus.). 96p. 1987. reprint ed. pap. 8.95 (*0-486-25442-9*) Dover.
Comte. Dictionary of Mythology. (Reference Library). 256p. 1997. pap. 7.95 (*1-85326-337-0*, 3370WW, Pub. by Wrdsworth Edits) NTC Contemp Pub Co.
Comte, Auguste. Auguste Comte & Positivism: The Essential Writings. Lenzer, Gertrud, ed. LC 83-5122. ixiv, 506p. (C). 1984. pap. text 20.00 (*0-226-47217-5*) U Ch Pr.
— Comte: Early Political Writings. Jones, H. S., ed. LC 99-203405. (Cambridge Texts in the History of Political Thought Ser.). 290p. (C). 1998. text 54.95 (*0-521-46511-7*); pap. text 19.95 (*0-521-46923-6*) Cambridge U Pr.
— General View of Positivism. 1957. pap. 10.00 (*0-8315-0033-6*) Speller.
— General View of Positivism. (Reprint Series in Sociology). 1971. reprint ed. lib. bdg. 42.50 (*0-697-00214-4*) Irvington.
— Introduction to Positive Philosophy. Ferre, Frederick, ed. LC 73-84164. (Library of Liberal Arts). (Orig.). (C). 1970. pap. 3.05 (*0-672-60284-9*, LLA94, Bobbs) Macmillan.
— Introduction to Positive Philosophy. Ferre, Frederick, tr. from FRE. & intro. by. LC 87-34831. (HPC Classics Ser.). 86p. (Orig.). (C). 1988. reprint ed. pap. text 5.95 (*0-87220-050-7*); reprint ed. lib. bdg. 21.95 (*0-87220-051-5*) Hackett Pub.
— Passages from the Letters of Auguste Comte. 1972. 59.95 (*0-8490-0804-2*) Gordon Pr.
— Positive Philosophy. Martineau, Harriet, tr. LC 70-174979. reprint ed. 67.50 (*0-404-08209-2*) AMS Pr.
Comte, Auguste, jt. auth. see Mill, John Stuart.
Comte-Bellot, G. & Mathieu, J., eds. Advances in Turbulence: Proceedings of the First European Turbulence Conference, Lyon, France, 1-4, July 1986. (Illus.). 590p. 1987. 116.95 (*0-387-17586-5*) Spr-Verlag.
Comte, Edward Le, see Le Comte, Edward.
Comte, Edward S. Le, see Le Comte, Edward S.
Comte, G. & Marcelin, M., eds. Tridemensional Optical Spectroscopic Methods in Astrophysics. (ASP Conference Series Proceedings: Vol. 71). 398p. 1995. 34.00 (*0-937707-90-2*) Astron Soc Pacific.
Comte, Hubert. Tools: Making Things Around the World. Stevens, Molly & Marinelli, David, trs. from FRE. LC 98-22777. (Illus.). 363p. 1998. 75.00 (*0-8109-3899-5*, Pub. by Abrams) Time Warner.
***Comte, Michel.** Michel Comte: Aiko T. 2000. 195.00 (*3-88243-702-2*) Steidl.
— Michel Comte: People & Places Without Name. 400p. 2000. 65.00 (*3-88243-704-9*, Pub. by Steidl) Dist Art Pubs.
Comte, Michel, photos by. Stern Portfolio: Michel Comte - Contrasts. (Illus.). 112p. 1998. pap. 19.95 (*3-570-19165-6*) te Neues.
Comte, Michel, et al. Faces. (Illus.). 300p. 1999. 75.00 (*3-8238-0999-7*) te Neues.
Comte, Philippe. Klee. Marshall, Carol, tr. from FRE. (Illus.). 258p. 1991. 75.00 (*0-87951-438-8*, Pub. by Overlook Pr) Penguin Putnam.
Comte Pourtales, Guy De, see De Comte Pourtales, Guy.
Comte, R. & Pernin, A. Lexique des Industries Graphiques. (FRE.). 128p. 1975. pap. 39.95 (*0-8288-5930-2*, M6082) Fr & Eur.
Comte, Robert, jt. auth. see Lee, Leslie.
Comtesse de Segur. Malheurs de Sophie - Petites Filles Modeles. unabridged ed. (FRE.). pap. 7.95 (*2-87714-289-2*, Pub. by Bookking Intl) Distribks Inc.
***Comtesse De Segur, Sophie.** Les Petites Filles Modeles.Tr. of Perfect Little Girls. (FRE.). 1998. pap., boxed set 16.95 incl. audio compact disk (*2-921997-23-1*, Pub. by Coffragants) Penton Overseas.
Comtesse De Segur, Sophie. Les Petites Filles Modeles. (Coffragants Ser.).Tr. of Perfect Little Girls. (FRE., Illus.). 1998. boxed set 12.95 incl. audio (*2-921997-18-5*) Penton Overseas.
***Comtet, A., et al, eds.** Topological Aspects of Low Dimensional Systems. (Les Houches Summer School Ser.). xxxiii, 1030p. 2000. (*3-540-66909-4*) Spr-Verlag.
Comtet, L. Advanced Combinatorics: The Art of Finite & Infinite Expansions. enl. rev. ed. Nienhuys, J., tr. LC 73-86091. 1974. text 204.50 (*90-277-0380-9*) Kluwer Academic.
Comtois, M. F. & Miller, Lynn F. Contemporary American Theatre Critics: A Dictionary & Anthology of Their Works. LC 77-23063. 1977. 58.00 (*0-8108-1057-3*) Scarecrow.
Comton, R. G. & Hammett, A., eds. New Techniques for the Study of Electrodes & Their Reaction. (Comprehensive Chemical Kinetics Ser.: 29). xivi,504p. 1989. 411.50 (*0-444-42999-9*) Elsevier.
Comty, Christina M., jt. auth. see Bergerson, Betty.
Comunicadores, Kairos, ed. see Hernandez, Ruben.
Comus, Steve. The Gun Digest Book of 9mm Handguns. 2nd ed. LC 86-71043. (Illus.). 256p. 1993. pap. 18.95 (*0-87349-149-1*, 9MM2, DBI Bks) Krause Pubns.
Comuvir. Dictionary of Environment: French - English with English-French Index. (ENG & FRE.). 351p. 1992. 105.00 (*0-7859-7479-2*, 2853192431) Fr & Eur.
COMUVIR Staff. French-English Environmental Dictionary with English-French Glossary. 3rd ed. (ENG & FRE.). 351p. 1992. 110.00 (*2-85319-243-1*) IBD Ltd.
Comyn, G., et al, eds. Logic Programming in Action: Proceedings of Second International Logic Programming Summer School, Zurich, Switzerland, September 7-11, 1992. LC 92-28844. x, 324p. 1992. 52.00 (*0-387-55930-2*); pap. write for info. (*3-540-55930-2*) Spr-Verlag.
Comyn, J. Adhesion Science. (RSC Paperback Ser.). x, 150p. 1997. pap. 40.00 (*0-85404-543-0*) Am Chemical.
Comyn, J., jt. ed. see Brewis, D. M.

C

An Asterisk (*) at the beginning of an entry indicates that the title is appearing for the first time.

***Comyns.** Encyclopedic Dictionary of Named Processes. LC 98-41331. 320p. 1999. boxed set 99.95 (*0-8493-1205-1*) CRC Pr.

Comyns, Barbara. The House of Dolls. large type ed. 202p. 1991. reprint ed. lib. bdg. 18.95 (*1-56054-128-8*) Thorndike Pr.

Conable, Barbara. What Every Musician Needs to Know about the Body: The Practical Application of Body Mapping & the Alexander Technique to Making Music. (Illus.). 104p. 1998. pap. 21.50 (*0-9622595-5-1*) Andover Press OR.

***Conable, Barbara.** What Every Musician Needs to Know about the Body: The Practical Application of Body Mapping & the Alexander Technique to Making Music. (Illus.). 104p. 2000. pap. 21.50 (*0-9622595-6-X*) Andover Press OR.

Conable, Barbara & Conable, William. Aprendizaje de la Tecnica Alexander: Manual Del Alumno. Devoto, Alejandra, tr. (SPA., Illus.). 192p. (Orig.). 1995. pap. 21.50 (*0-9622595-3-5*) Andover Press OR.

— How to Learn the Alexander Technique: A Manual for Students. 3rd enl. rev. ed. (Illus.). 168p. (Orig.). 1995. pap. 21.50 (*0-9622595-4-3*) Andover Press OR.

Conable, Barber B., Jr. Congress & the Income Tax. LC 88-40542. (Julian J. Rothbaum Distinguished Lectures: Vol. 2). 160p. 1989. 24.95 (*0-8061-2195-5*) U of Okla Pr.

Conable, Charlotte W. Women at Cornell: The Myth of Equal Education. LC 77-3117. (Illus.). 176p. 1977. pap. text 14.95 (*0-8014-9167-3*) Cornell U Pr.

Conable, William, jt. auth. see Conable, Barbara.

Conaboy, Richard P. Cocaine & Federal Sentencing Policy. (Illus.). 242p. 1997. pap. text 45.00 (*0-7881-4674-2*) DIANE Pub.

Conaboy, Richard P., ed. Corporate Crime in America: Strengthening the "Good Citizen" Corporation - Proceedings. (Illus.). 473p. (C). 1998. pap. text 60.00 (*0-7881-7161-5*) DIANE Pub.

Conacher, A. J. & Sala, Maria. Land Degradation in Mediterranean Environments of the World: Nature & Extent, Causes & Solutions. LC 97-29313. 520p. 1998. 165.00 (*0-471-96317-8*) Wiley.

***Conacher, Arthur & Conacher, Jeanette.** Environmental Planning & Management in Australia. (Illus.). 352p. 2000. pap. text 60.00 (*0-19-553819-6*) OUP.

Conacher, Arthur & Conacher, Jeannettel, eds. Rural Land Degradation in Australia. LC 95-201864. (Meridian). (Illus.). 186p. (C). 1995. pap. text 26.95 (*0-19-553436-0*) OUP.

Conacher, D., ed. see Euripides.

Conacher, D. J. Aeschylus: The Earlier Plays & Related Studies. 208p. 1996. text 50.00 (*0-8020-0796-1*) U of Toronto Pr.

— Aeschylus: The Earlier Plays & Related Studies. 208p. 1996. pap. text 17.95 (*0-8020-7155-4*) U of Toronto Pr.

— Aeschylus' Oresteia: A Literary Commentary. 229p. 1987. pap. text 18.95 (*0-8020-6747-6*) U of Toronto Pr.

— Aeschylus' Oresteia: A Literary Commentary. LC 87-673186. 239p. reprint ed. pap. 74.10 (*0-8357-3776-4*, 203650600003) Bks Demand.

— Aeschylus' "Prometheus Bound" A Literary Commentary. 128p. 1980. text 30.00 (*0-8020-2391-6*); pap. text 12.95 (*0-8020-6416-7*) U of Toronto Pr.

Conacher, D. J., ed. & tr. see Euripides.

***Conacher, Duff.** More Canada Firsts: Another Collection of Canadian Firsts & Foremosts in the World. 224p. 2000. pap. 19.99 (*0-7710-2244-1*) McClelland & Stewart.

Conacher, Geoffrey N. Management of the Mentally Disordered Offender in Prisons. LC 97-156212. 144p. 1996. 49.95 (*0-7735-1419-8*, Pub. by McG-Queens Univ Pr) CUP Services.

Conacher, Gillian M., ed. see Maw, Geoffrey Waring.

Conacher, Gwen. Kitchen Sense for Disabled People. 192p. (Orig.). 1986. pap. 19.95 (*0-7099-4512-4*, Pub. by C Helm) Routldge.

Conacher, James B., ed. see Du Creux, Francois.

Conacher, Jeanette, jt. auth. see Conacher, Arthur.

Conacher, Jeannettel, jt. ed. see Conacher, Arthur.

Conaghan. Wrongs of Tort. (Law & Social Theory Ser.). (C). 83.95 (*0-7453-0526-1*, Pub. by Pluto GBR); pap. 28.95 (*0-7453-0527-X*, Pub. by Pluto GBR) Stylus Pub VA.

Conaghan, Catherine M. & Malloy, James M. Unsettling Statecraft: Democracy & Neoliberalism in the Central Andes. (Latin American Ser.). 320p. (Orig.). (C). 1994. pap. 22.95 (*0-8229-5532-6*); text 49.95 (*0-8229-3786-7*) U of Pittsburgh Pr.

***Conaghan, Joanne.** Wrongs of Tort. 2nd ed. LC 98-44294. 1999. write for info. (*0-7453-1298-5*) Pluto GBR.

Conaire, Brendan O., ed. see Hyde, Douglas.

***Conallen, Jim.** Building Web Applications with UML. LC 99-49970. (Object Technology Ser.). 352p. 2000. pap. 34.95 (*0-201-61577-0*) Addison-Wesley.

Conan, Allan. The Hemingway Sabbatical. LC 95-51005. 256p. 1996. 22.00 (*0-922811-24-5*) Mid-List.

— The PSI Delegation. 298p. 1989. 15.95 (*0-922811-04-0*) Mid-List.

Conan, Christa. All I Need. 1995. per. 3.75 (*0-373-07678-9*, 1-07678-5) Silhouette.

— One Night at a Time. (Intimate Moments Ser.: No. 839). 1998. per. 4.25 (*0-373-07839-0*, 1-07839-3) Silhouette.

Conan, Eric & Rousso, Henry. Vichy: An Ever-Present Past. Bracher, Nathan, tr. from FRE. LC 97-44597. (Contemporary French Culture & Society Ser.). 311p. 1998. 50.00 (*0-87451-795-8*) U Pr of New Eng.

Conan, Laure. Angeline de Montbrun. LC 73-82585. (Literature of Canada, Poetry & Prose in Reprint Ser.: No. 14). 202p. reprint ed. pap. 62.70 (*0-8357-5475-8*, 202360500033) Bks Demand.

Conan, Marcia & Heavers, Kathy. What You Need to Know about Developing Study Skills, Taking Notes & Tests, Using Dictionaries & Libraries. (NTC's Skill Builders Ser.). (Illus.). 96p. 1994. pap. 6.95 (*0-8442-5175-5*, Natl Textbk Co) NTC Contemp Pub Co.

***Conan, Michel.** Perspectives on Garden Histories. LC 98-30313. 1999. 35.00 (*0-88402-265-X*); pap. 20.00 (*0-88402-269-2*) Dumbarton Oaks.

Conan, Sally A. God Made Hugs. LC 94-72213. (Illus.). 32p. (J). (ps-3). 1994. pap. 5.99 (*0-8066-2725-5*, 9-2725, Augsburg) Augsburg Fortress.

— God's Best Gift. LC 97-7490. (Illus.). 32p. (J). (ps-2). 1998. pap. 7.95 (*0-8091-6644-5*, 6644-5) Paulist Pr.

— Little Blessings: A Child's First Book of Riddles. (Illus.). 32p. (J). (ps-1). 1996. pap. 6.95 (*0-8091-6632-1*, 6632-1) Paulist Pr.

— Look & See What God Gave Me. LC 97-7491. (Illus.). 32p. (J). (ps-2). 1998. pap. 7.95 (*0-8091-6645-3*, 6645-3) Paulist Pr.

— Thank You, God. LC 97-7497. (Illus.). 32p. (J). (ps-2). 1998. pap. 7.95 (*0-8091-6643-7*, 6643-7) Paulist Pr.

Conant, jt. auth. see Gloyd.

Conant, Arlene M. Never Trust a Skinny Cook. (Illus.). 316p. 1995. spiral bd. 24.95 (*0-9664418-0-X*) A M Conant.

Conant, Bessie, ed. see Conant, Edward.

Conant, Charles A. A History of Modern Banks of Issue. 6th ed. Nadler, Marcus, ed. LC 68-30519. (Library of Money & Banking History). xiii, 842p. 1969. reprint ed. 65.00 (*0-678-00505-2*) Kelley.

Conant, Charlotte H. A Girl of the Eighties at College & at Home. (American Biography Ser.). 261p. 1991. reprint ed. lib. bdg. 69.00 (*0-7812-8087-7*) Rprt Serv.

Conant, Craig, jt. auth. see Thomas, Carol G.

Conant, Edward. Memories of Gazos Creek & Pigeon Point, 1916-1918. Conant, Bessie, ed. LC 98-72358. (Illus.). 112p. 1998. 15.95 (*0-9637265-1-X*) Glenhaven Pr.

Conant, Ellen P. Nihonga: Transcending the Past: Japanese-Style Painting, 1868-1968. Rimer, J. Thomas & Owyoung, Stephen D., trs. (Illus.). 352p. 1996. 80.00 (*0-8348-0363-1*) Weatherhill.

Conant, Ellen P., et al. Nihonga, Transcending the Past: Japanese-Style Painting, 1868-1968. Tomii, Reiko & Steiner, Mary A., eds. (Illus.). 352p. 1995. pap. text 40.00 (*0-89178-044-0*) St Louis Art Mus.

Conant, F. O. A History & Genealogy of the Conant Family in England & America, Thirteen Generations, 1520-1887. (Illus.). 654p. 1989. reprint ed. pap. 98.00 (*0-8328-0417-7*); reprint ed. lib. bdg. 106.00 (*0-8328-0416-9*) Higginson Bk Co.

Conant, Francis, ed. Resource Inventory & Baseline Study Methods for Developing Countries. LC 83-15493. (AAAS Publication: No. 83-3). 565p. reprint ed. pap. 175.20 (*0-608-15670-1*, 203194800077) Bks Demand.

Conant, Helen S., tr. see Charnay, Desire.

Conant, James, ed. see Putnam, Hilary.

Conant, James B. Education in a Divided World: The Function of the Public Schools in Our Unique Society. LC 78-94580. 249p. 1970. reprint ed. lib. bdg. 35.00 (*0-8371-2548-0*, COEW, Greenwood Pr) Greenwood.

— Modern Science & Modern Man. LC 83-12753. 111p. 1983. reprint ed. lib. bdg. 49.75 (*0-313-24119-8*, CMOS, Greenwood Pr) Greenwood.

— My Several Lives: Memoirs of a Social Inventor. (American Biography Ser.). 701p. 1991. reprint ed. lib. bdg. 119.00 (*0-7812-8088-5*) Rprt Serv.

— The Overthrow of the Phlogiston Theory: The Chemical Revolution of 1775-1789. LC 50-8087. (Harvard Case Histories in Experimental Science Ser.: No. 2). 61p. reprint ed. pap. 30.00 (*0-608-10216-4*, 201768100007) Bks Demand.

Conant, James B., ed. Harvard Case Histories in Experimental Science, 2 vols., Vol. 1. LC 57-12843. 337p. reprint ed. pap. 104.50 (*0-7837-2239-7*, 205732900001) Bks Demand.

— Harvard Case Histories in Experimental Science, 2 vols., Vol. 2. LC 57-12843. 322p. reprint ed. pap. 99.90 (*0-7837-2240-0*, 205732900002) Bks Demand.

Conant, Janet L. Memory Change & Cognitive Function among the Elderly. (Studies on the Elderly in America). 250p. 1995. text 50.00 (*0-8153-1894-4*) Garland.

Conant, Jeff. Breathing Problems. 1991. pap. 4.00 (*0-938979-99-X*) EG Bksellers.

— On Becoming an Angel. (Illus.). 20p. 1993. pap. 125.00 (*0-945303-14-9*) Evanescent Pr.

Conant, Jonathan B. Cochran's German Review Grammar. 4th ed. 352p. (C). 1990. text 43.60 (*0-13-139965-9*) P-H.

Conant, Kenneth J. Carolingian & Romanesque Architecture: 800-1200. 4th ed. (Pelican History of Art Ser.). (Illus.). 522p. (C). 1959. reprint ed. 55.00 (*0-300-05297-9*); reprint ed. pap. 27.50 (*0-300-05298-7*) Yale U Pr.

Conant, Kim, jt. auth. see Conant, Phyllis.

Conant, Melvin. Heralds of Their Age. (Illus.). 24p. pap. 1.00 (*0-913344-04-4*) South St Sea Mus.

— The Long Polar Watch: Canada & the Defence of North America. LC 62-14889. 216p. reprint ed. pap. 67.00 (*0-608-30730-0*, 200215100012) Bks Demand.

Conant, Melvin A. Access to Energy: 2000 & After. LC 79-15015. (Illus.). 144p. (C). 1979. 20.00 (*0-8131-0401-7*) U Pr of Ky.

Conant, Michael. Antitrust in the Motion Picture Industry. Jowett, Garth S., ed. LC 77-11372. (Aspects of Film Ser.). (Illus.). 1978. reprint ed. lib. bdg. 21.95 (*0-405-11128-2*) Ayer.

***Conant, Michael.** Constitutional Structure & Purposes: Critical Commentary. 98. LC 00-33123. (Contributions in Legal Studies: No. 98). 224p. 2000. 64.00 (*0-313-31669-4*, GM1669, Greenwood Pr) Greenwood.

Conant, Michael. Railroad Mergers & Abandonments. LC 82-15834. (Publications of the Institute of Business & Economic Research, University of California). 212p. 1982. reprint ed. lib. bdg. 59.50 (*0-313-23694-1*, CORAM, Greenwood Pr) Greenwood.

Conant, Miriam B., ed. see Aron, Raymond.

Conant, Phyllis & Conant, Kim. I Am That I Am. LC 98-67421. 304p. 1999. pap. 23.95 (*1-57197-126-2*) Pentland Pr.

Conant, R. Luther. It's Getting Late - Early: A Primer for Those Who Have Procrastinated on Making Their Retirement Financial Plan. LC 92-18833. 9.95 (*0-9629159-3-9*) Pine Tree NY.

***Conant, Richard.** Natural Treatments for Varicose Veins. (Natural Pharmacist Ser.). 2000. pap. 9.99 (*0-7615-3012-6*) Prima Pub.

Conant, Roger. A Field Guide to the Life & Times of Roger Conant. (Illus.). 518p. 1997. 49.95 (*0-9657446-0-4*, Pub. by Cnyonlnds Pub TX) Bibliomania.

Conant, Roger. Introduction to PSpice with IBM. 1992. pap. text. write for info. (*0-318-68491-8*) HM.

— Mercer's Belles: The Journal of a Reporter. Deutsch, Lenna A., ed. LC 92-20225. (Washington State University Press Reprint Ser.). 168p. (Orig.). (C). 1992. reprint ed. 25.00 (*0-87422-089-0*) Wash St U Pr.

— Mercer's Belles: The Journal of a Reporter. 2nd ed. Deutsch, Lenna A., ed. LC 92-20225. (Washington State University Press Art Ser.). (Illus.). 168p. (Orig.). (C). 1992. reprint ed. pap. 16.95 (*0-87422-090-4*) Wash St U Pr.

— Peterson First Guide to Reptiles & Amphibians. (J). 1992. 10.05 (*0-606-05537-1*, Pub. by Turtleback) Demco.

***Conant, Roger, et al.** Reptiles & Amphibians. LC 91-33016. (Peterson First Guide Ser.). (Illus.). 128p. 1999. pap. 5.95 (*0-395-97195-0*) HM.

Conant, Roger, ed. see Ashby, W. Ross.

Conant, Susan. Animal Appetite: A Dog Lover's Mystery. 304p. 1998. reprint ed. mass mkt. 5.99 (*0-553-57186-9*, Crimeline) Bantam.

— The Barker Street Regulars: A Dog Lover's Mystery. 288p. 1999. mass mkt. 5.99 (*0-553-57655-0*) Bantam.

— The Barker Street Regulars: A Dog Lover's Mystery. large type ed. LC 98-22093. (Large Print Book Ser.). 1998. 22.95 (*1-56895-609-6*) Wheeler Pub.

— Bite of Death. 1994. mass mkt. 5.50 (*0-425-14542-5*) Berkley Pub.

— Black Ribbon: A Dog Lover's Mystery. large type ed. (Americana Series). 407p. 1995. 24.95 (*0-7862-0513-X*) Thorndike Pr.

— Black Ribbon: A Dog Lover's Mystery. 288p. 1995. reprint ed. pap. 5.99 (*0-553-29875-5*, Crimeline) Bantam.

— Bloodlines. 272p. 1993. mass mkt. 5.99 (*0-553-29886-0*) Bantam.

***Conant, Susan.** Creature Discomforts: A Dog Lover's Mystery. LC 99-36817. 256p. 2000. 22.95 (*0-385-49446-7*) Doubleday.

— Dead & Doggone. 1990. mass mkt. 5.50 (*0-425-14429-1*, Prime Crime) Berkley Pub.

— Evil Breeding. LC 98-11249. 256p. 1999. 21.95 (*0-385-48669-3*) Doubleday.

— Evil Breeding. LC 98-11249. (Dog Lover's Mystery Ser.). 224p. 2000. reprint ed. mass mkt. 5.99 (*0-553-58052-3*) Bantam.

— Financial Aspects of Annuities. LC 99-54029. 2000. pap. 54.95 (*1-57974-046-4*) Life Office.

Conant, Susan. Gone to the Dogs: A Dog Lover's Mystery. 272p. 1992. mass mkt. 5.99 (*0-553-29734-1*) Bantam.

— Living with Chronic Fatigue: New Strategies for Coping with & Conquering CFS. LC 89-77048. 148p. 1990. pap. 9.95 (*0-87833-709-1*) Taylor Pub.

— New Leash on Death. 1990. mass mkt. 5.99 (*0-425-14622-7*) Berkley Pub.

Conant, Susan. Paws Before Dying. 1991. mass mkt. 5.50 (*0-425-14430-5*) Berkley Pub.

Conant, Susan. Ruffly Speaking: A Dog Lover's Mystery. 304p. 1994. mass mkt. 5.99 (*0-553-29484-9*) Bantam.

— Ruffly Speaking: A Dog Lover's Mystery. large type ed. LC 94-28127. 410p. 1994. lib. bdg. 20.95 (*0-7862-0313-7*) Thorndike Pr.

— Stud Rites: A Dog Lover's Mystery. LC 95-44439. 272p. 1997. mass mkt. 5.99 (*0-553-57300-4*, Crimeline) Bantam.

— Test Preparation Guide for Regulatory Compliance: Companies, Producers, & Operations. LC 99-169919. (Associate, Insurance Regulatory Compliance Program Ser.). 101 p. 24.00 (*1-57974-013-8*, Pub. by Life Office) PBD Inc.

Conant, Susan, et al. Managing for Solvency & Profitability in Life & Health Insurance Companies. LC 96-76706. (FLMI Insurance Education Program Ser.). (Illus.). 732p. text 71.95 (*0-939921-80-4*, Pub. by Life Office) PBD Inc.

— Teaching Language-Disabled Children: A Communication Games Intervention. LC 83-27303. 188p. 1983. pap. 17.95 (*0-914797-38-7*) Brookline Bks.

Conant, Susan, ed. see Desouttes, Nicholas, et al.

Conant, Susan C. Came: Genealogy of the Came Family. (Illus.). 60p. 1997. reprint ed. pap. 12.00 (*0-8328-7823-5*); reprint ed. lib. bdg. 22.00 (*0-8328-7822-7*) Higginson Bk Co.

Conaola, Dara O. Night Ructions. Rosenstock, Gabriel, tr. from IRI. (Illus.). 58p. (Orig.). 1990. pap. 9.95 (*0-948259-93-0*, Pub. by Forest Bks) Dufour.

Conard, Alfred F. Corporations in Perspective. (University Textbook Ser.). 456p. 1991. reprint ed. text 29.00 (*0-88277-405-0*) Foundation Pr.

Conard, Alfred F., ed. Conference of Aims & Methods of Legal Research. (Michigan Legal Publications). x, 199p. 1986. reprint ed. lib. bdg. 37.50 (*0-89941-487-7*, 304140) W S Hein.

Conard, Alfred F. & Aaron, Richard I. Enterprise Organization: Adaptable to Courses Utilizing Materials by Conard. LC 87-114703. (Legalines Ser.). 314p. 11.95 (*0-685-18529-X*) Harcourt.

Conard, Alfred F., et al. Automobile Accident Costs & Payments: Studies in the Economics of Injury Reparation. LC 64-17437. (Michigan Legal Publications). xxviii, 506p. 1983. reprint ed. lib. bdg. 47.50 (*0-89941-315-3*, 303080) W S Hein.

Conard, Erik P., jt. ed. see Jones, Iris C.

Conard, Henry S. The Background of Plant Ecology: The Plant Life of the Danube Basin. Egerton, Frank N., 3rd, ed. LC 77-74234. (History of Ecology Ser.). 1978. reprint ed. lib. bdg. 21.95 (*0-405-10403-0*) Ayer.

— The Waterlilies - A Monograph of the Genus Nymphaea. fac. ed. (Illus.). 336p. 1991. 395.00 (*0-948697-17-2*, Pub. by Lark Pubns) St Mut.

Conard, Howard L., ed. History of Milwaukee: From Its First Settlement to the Year 1895, 2 vols. (Illus.). 1010p. 1997. reprint ed. lib. bdg. 105.00 (*0-8328-6973-2*) Higginson Bk Co.

Conard, J., jt. ed. see Tchoubar, D.

Conard, James. Internet & Internet Working Security. LC 97-109104. 1997. ring bd. write for info. (*0-7913-3022-2*) Warren Gorham & Lamont.

Conard, James, ed. Broadband Communications Systems. 1993. pap. 49.00 (*0-685-69688-X*, HCOX) Warren Gorham & Lamont.

— Handbook of Communications Systems Management. rev. ed. text 142.00 (*0-685-69686-3*) Warren Gorham & Lamont.

— Handbook of Communications Systems Management. 2nd ed. 1991. text 153.00 (*0-685-69685-5*, HCOM) Warren Gorham & Lamont.

Conard, James & Berk, Paul, eds. Data Communications Management. 1992. ring bd. 464.00 (*0-87769-264-5*) Warren Gorham & Lamont.

Conard, Joseph W. Behavior of Interest Rates: A Progress Report. (General Ser.: No. 81). 159p. 1966. 41.40 (*0-87014-081-7*) Natl Bur Econ Res.

— The Behavior of Interest Rates: A Progress Report. LC 66-22745. (National Bureau of Economic Research. General Ser.: No. 81). 159p. reprint ed. pap. 49.30 (*0-8357-3240-1*, 205713400011) Bks Demand.

Conard, Louisa S. Mosses & Liverworts. 2nd ed. (Pictured Key Nature Ser.). 316p. (C). 1979. text. write for info. (*0-697-04768-7*, WCB McGr Hill) McGrw-H Hghr Educ.

Conard, Rebecca. Places of Quiet Beauty: Parks, Preserves, & Environmentalism. LC 96-27207. (American Land & Life Ser.). (Illus.). 400p. (Orig.). 1997. pap. 15.95 (*0-87745-558-9*) U of Iowa Pr.

Conard, Richard T. What Should We Do about Mom? A New Look at Growing Old. (Illus.). 160p. 1992. pap. 8.95 (*0-8306-3957-8*, 4145, TAB-Human Servs Inst) TAB Bks.

Conard, Robert, ed. see Hesse, Hermann.

Conard, Robert C. Understanding Heinrich Boil. Hardin, James N., ed. LC 91-25072. (Understanding Modern European & Latin American Literature Ser.). 202p. 1992. text 29.95 (*0-87249-779-8*) U of SC Pr.

Conard, Ruth. Devotions for New Moms. 96p. 1996. pap. 6.99 (*0-87788-172-3*, H Shaw Pubs) Waterbrook Pr.

Conard, Sue S., jt. auth. see Chall, Jeanne S.

***Conari Press Editors.** Community of Kindness. LC 98-45502. 240p. 1999. pap. text 10.95 (*1-57324-148-2*) Conari Press.

Conari Press Editors. Kids' Random Acts of Kindness. (Practice of Kindness Ser.). (Illus.). 168p. (Orig.). (J). 1994. pap. 8.95 (*0-943233-62-3*) Conari Press.

— More Random Acts of Kindness. (Practice of Kindness Ser.). (Illus.). 180p. 1996. pap. 8.95 (*0-943233-82-8*) Conari Press.

— The Practice of Kindness: Meditations for Bringing More Peace, Love, & Compassion into Daily Life. 290p. (Orig.). 1996. pap. 9.95 (*1-57324-028-1*) Conari Press.

— Random Acts of Kindness. 176p. 1997. 6.98 (*1-56731-197-0*, MJF Bks) Fine Comms.

— Random Acts of Kindness. LC 92-38017. (Practice of Kindness Ser.). 150p. 1993. pap. 9.95 (*0-943233-43-7*) Conari Press.

***Conari Press Editors, ed.** More Random Acts of Kindness. 192p. 1998. 6.98 (*1-56731-277-2*, MJF Bks) Fine Comms.

***Conari Press Staff.** Random Acts of Kindness. Set. gif. ed. 160p. 1998. pap. 29.95 incl. audio (*1-57453-228-6*) Audio Lit.

Conarroe, Joel. Eight American Poets: An Anthology. 336p. 1997. pap. 14.00 (*0-679-77643-5*) Random.

Conason, Joe & Lyons, Gene. The Hunting of the President: The Ten Year Campaign to Destroy Bill & Hillary Clinton. (Illus.). 432p. 2000. text 25.95 (*0-312-24547-5*) St Martin.

Conaster. Spreadsheets for Small Business 2-3. 1991. pap. 24.95 (*0-13-785874-4*) P-H.

Conaster, Kelly. Excel 5.0 for the Mac Solutions. 471p. 1994. pap. 24.95 (*0-471-00952-0*) Wiley.

Conati, Marcello. Encounters with Verdi. Stokes, Richard, tr. from ITA. LC 83-73736. (Illus.). 472p. 1984. text 47.50 (*0-8014-1717-1*); pap. text 18.95 (*0-8014-9430-3*) Cornell U Pr.

Conati, Marcello & Medici, Mario, eds. The Verdi-Boito Correspondence. Weaver, William, tr. LC 93-22598. 386p. 1994. 29.95 (*0-226-85304-7*) U Ch Pr.

Conatser, Estee. Sterling Legend: Story of Lost Dutchman Mine. 2nd ed. (Illus.). 94p. 1987. pap. 7.95 (*0-935182-31-4*) Gem Guides Bk.

Conaty, Gerald T., jt. auth. see Boehme, Sarah E.

***Conaway, Charles F.** The Petroleum Industry: A Nontechnical Guide. LC 99-45825. 1999. write for info. (*0-87814-777-2*) PennWell Bks.

An Asterisk (*) at the beginning of an entry indicates that the title is appearing for the first time.

Conaway, Dale. Sex & the Bible. LC 96-166717. 222p. (Orig.). 1996. pap. 14.99 (*1-56043-256-X*, Treasure Hse) Destiny Image.

Conaway, Jack W., Jr. Bigger Than Life: A Place Where Hearts Run Free. LC 93-71259. (Illus.). 132p. (Orig.). 1993. pap. 6.95 (*0-9636627-0-8*) Crosspt Pub.

***Conaway, James.** America's Library: The Story of the Library of Congress, 1800-2000. LC 99-58751. (Illus.). 256p. 2000. 45.00 (*0-300-08308-4*) Yale U Pr.

Conaway, James. The Kingdom in the Country. 304p. 1993. reprint ed. pap. 11.00 (*0-380-71613-5*, Avon Bks) Morrow Avon.

— Memphis Afternoons. 224p. 1994. reprint ed. pap. 10.00 (*0-380-72298-4*, Avon Bks) Morrow Avon.

— Napa. 560p. 1992. pap. 15.00 (*0-380-71599-6*, Avon Bks) Morrow Avon.

— The Smithsonian: 150 Years of Adventure, Discovery, & Wonder. Date not set. write for info. (*0-614-13118-9*) Knopf.

— The Smithsonian: 150 Years of Adventure, Discovery, & Wonder. (Illus.). 432p. 1995. 60.00 (*0-679-44175-1*) Random.

Conaway, Joan W., jt. ed. see Conaway, Ronald C.

Conaway, John B. Call Out the Guard. (Illus.). 360p. 1998. 24.95 (*1-56311-372-4*) Turner Pub KY.

— Call Out the Guard! The Story of Lieutenant General John B. Conaway & the Modern Day National. LC 97-60384. 1997. 24.95 (*5-631-13724-0*, Pub. by AO) Turner Pub KY.

Conaway, Judith. Great Indoor Games from Trash & Other Things. (gr. k-4). 1977. 13.31 (*0-8172-0952-2*) Raintree Steck-V.

— Happy Haunting: Halloween Costumes You Can Make. LC 85-28840. (Illus.). 48p. (J). (gr. 1-5). 1986. lib. bdg. 16.65 (*0-8167-0666-2*) Troll Communs.

— Happy Haunting: Halloween Costumes You Can Make. LC 85-28840. (Illus.). 48p. (J). (gr. 1-5). 1997. pap. 3.95 (*0-8167-0667-0*) Troll Communs.

— Happy Thanksgiving: Things to Make & Do. LC 85-16463. (Illus.). 48p. (J). (gr. 1-5). 1986. lib. bdg. 16.65 (*0-8167-0668-9*) Troll Communs.

— Happy Thanksgiving: Things to Make & Do. LC 85-16463. (Illus.). 48p. (J). (gr. 4-7). 1996. pap. 3.95 (*0-8167-0669-7*) Troll Communs.

— Happy Thanksgiving! Things to Make & Do. (J). 1986. 9.15 (*0-606-02096-9*, Pub. by Turtleback) Demco.

— Match This, P. J. Funnybunny. 32p. (J). 1998. pap. 3.99 (*0-679-88165-4*, Pub. by Random Bks Yng Read) Random.

— Now Look at Numbers. (J). 1997. pap. 3.99 (*0-679-88167-0*) McKay.

— Put Me in the Alphabet. (J). 1997. pap., wbk. ed. 3.99 (*0-679-88164-6*) McKay.

Conaway, Judith. 20,000 Leagues under the Sea. (Bullseye Step into Classics Ser.). 1994. 9.09 (*0-606-08958-6*, Pub. by Turtleback) Demco.

Conaway, Judith. What's Next, PJ Funnybunny? 32p. (J). 1998. pap. 3.99 (*0-679-88166-2*) McKay.

Conaway, Judith, ed. see Doyle, Arthur Conan.

Conaway, Mary E. Circular Migration: A Summary & Bibliography. 1977. 1.50 (*0-686-19108-0*, 1250, Sage Prdcls Pr) Sage.

Conaway, Mary E., jt. ed. see Whitehead, Tony L.

Conaway, Roger N., jt. auth. see Schmidt, Wallace V.

Conaway, Ronald C. & Conaway, Joan W., eds. Transcription: Mechanisms & Regulation. LC 93-29738. (Series on Molecular & Cellular Biology: Vol. 3). 592p. 1994. text 141.00 (*0-7817-0126-0*) Lppncott W & W.

Conaway, Wayne A., jt. auth. see Morrison, Terri.

Conbhuidhe, Colmcille O. Cistercian Abbeys of Tipperary. Donovan, Finbarr, ed. LC 99-177238. 336p. 1999. pap. 29.95 (*1-85182-381-6*, Pub. by Four Cts Pr); boxed set 55.00 (*1-85182-380-8*, Pub. by Four Cts Pr) Intl Spec Bk.

Conboie, Joseph. Floating Air. 195p. 1996. reprint ed. spiral bd. 14.00 (*0-7873-1162-6*) Hlth Research.

Conboy, Fiona. Ghost Ship: 3-D Puzzle Storybook. (Illus.). 16p. (J). (ps-3). 1997. 5.95 (*0-590-36206-2*) Scholastic Inc.

— Haunted House: 3-D Puzzle Storybook. (Illus.). 16p. (J). (ps-3). 1997. 5.95 (*0-590-36205-4*) Scholastic Inc.

— Morty Mouse's Number Search. (Illus.). 5p. (J). 1997. pap. 9.99 (*1-58048-000-4*) Sandvik Pub.

— Mr. Mombo's Balloon Flight. (Illus.). (J). 1998. 15.99 (*1-884628-62-1*, Flyng Frog) Allied Pub MD.

— No, Monkey! No! LC 98-20026. (Illus.). 12p. (J). (ps-k). 1998. 8.95 (*0-7613-0390-1*, Copper Beech Bks) Millbrook Pr.

— Run, Mouse! Run! LC 98-20020. (Illus.). 12p. (J). (ps-k). 1998. 8.95 (*0-7613-0389-8*) Millbrook Pr.

— 10 Terrific Trains. 20p. (J). 1998. 8.99 (*0-525-45946-4*) NAL.

Conboy-Hill, Suzanne, ed. see Waitman, Alexis.

Conboy, James C., Jr. Law & Banking: Principles. 3rd ed. 423p. (C). 1990. text 57.00 (*0-89982-362-9*) Am Bankers.

— Law & Banking Principles. 2nd ed. 425p. (C). 1996. 60.00 (*0-89982-436-6*) Am Bankers.

Conboy, K. Elite Forces of India & Pakistan. (Elite Ser.: No. 41). (Illus.). 64p. pap. 12.95 (*1-85532-209-9*, 9456, Pub. by Ospry) Stackpole.

Conboy, K. & Bowra, K. The NVA & Viet Cong. (Elite Ser.: No. 38). (Illus.). 64p. pap. 12.95 (*1-85532-162-9*, 9453, Pub. by Ospry) Stackpole.

— The War in Cambodia, 1970-75. (Men-at-Arms Ser.: No. 209). (Illus.). 48p. pap. 11.95 (*0-85045-851-X*, 9142, Pub. by Ospry) Stackpole.

Conboy, Katie, et al. Writing on the Body: Female Embodiment & Feminist Theory. LC 96-48177. (Gender & Culture Reader Ser.). 1997. 52.00 (*0-231-10544-4*) Col U Pr.

— Writing on the Body: Female Embodiment & Feminist Theory. 7th ed. LC 96-48177. (Gender & Culture Reader Ser.). 1997. pap. 19.00 (*0-231-10545-2*) Col U Pr.

***Conboy, Kenneth.** Feet to the Fire: CIA Covert Operations in Indonesia, 1957-1958. LC 99-32286. 232p. 1999. 29.95 (*1-55750-193-9*) Naval Inst Pr.

Conboy, Kenneth. S. E. Asian Special Forces. (Elite Ser.: No. 33). (Illus.). 64p. pap. 12.95 (*1-85532-106-8*, 9433, Pub. by Ospry) Stackpole.

— Shadow War: The CIA's Secret War in Laos. (Illus.). 464p. 1995. text 49.95 (*0-87364-825-0*) Paladin Pr.

— The War in Laos, 1954-1975. LC 94-210137. (Vietnam Studies Group). (Illus.). 64p. 1994. pap. 10.95 (*0-89747-315-9*) Squad Sig Pubns.

— The War in Laos, 1960-1975. (Men-at-Arms Ser.: No. 217). (Illus.). 48p. pap. 11.95 (*0-85045-938-9*, 9150, Pub. by Ospry) Stackpole.

***Conboy, Kenneth J. & Andrade, Dale.** Spies & Commandos: How America Lost the Secret War in North Vietnam. LC 99-43457. (Modern War Studies). (Illus.). 360p. 2000. text 34.95 (*0-7006-1002-2*) U Pr of KS.

Conca, ed. Nili Ancyrani. (GRE.). 1983. 29.95 (*3-322-00150-4*, T1907, Pub. by B G Teubner) U of Mich Pr.

Conca, C. Numerical Methods in Mechanics. (Pitman Research Notes in Mathematics Ser.). 1997. pap. 47.95 (*0-582-31320-1*, Pub. by Addison-Wesley) Longman.

Conca, F., et al, eds. Lessico Dei Romanzieri Greci, Band 1. (GER.). 167p. 1983. 60.00 (*0-318-70474-9*) G Olms Pubs.

— Lessico Dei Romanzieri Greci, Band 3. (GER.). 250p. 55.00 (*3-487-09749-4*) G Olms Pubs.

— Lessico Dei Romanzieri Greci, Band 4. (Alpha-Omega, Reihe A Ser.: Bd. LXXVIII). (GER.). 250p. write for info. (*0-318-70477-3*) G Olms Pubs.

Conca, Fabricus, ed. Nicetas Eugenianus: De Drospillae et Chariclis Amoribus Libros IX. (London Studies in Classical Philology: Vol. 24). (GRE & LAT.). 295p. 1991. 94.00 (*90-70265-95-8*, Pub. by Gieben) J Benjamins Pubng Co.

Conca, Fabrizio, et al, eds. Lessico Dei Romanzieri Greci, 4 vols., Set. (Alpha-Omega, Reihe A Ser.: Bd. LXXVIII). (GER.). ii, 289p. 1989. 55.00 (*3-487-09080-5*) G Olms Pubs.

Conca, J. In Situ Remediation & Restoration Technology. 1992. text. write for info. (*0-442-01061-3*, VNR) Wiley.

Conca, Ken. Manufacturing Insecurity: The Rise & Fall of Brazil's Military-Industrial Complex. 290p. 1996. lib. bdg. 58.00 (*1-55587-695-1*, 876951) L Rienner.

Conca, Ken, jt. ed. see Lipschutz, Ronnie D.

***Conca, Kenneth & Dabelko, Geoffrey D., eds.** Green Planet Blues: Environmental Politics from Stockholm to Kyoto. 2nd ed. LC 98-19814. 400p. 1998. pap. text 32.00 (*0-8133-6882-0*, Pub. by Westview) HarpC.

Concannon, Dale. From Tee to Green: An Illustrated Anthology of Classic Golf Writing. (Illus.). 192p. 1997. 29.95 (*0-7472-1796-3*, Pub. by Headline Bk Pub) Trafalgar.

— Golfing Bygones, 233. (Shire Album Ser.). 1999. pap. text 4.75 (*0-7478-0035-9*) Severn Hse.

Concannon, G. J. George Orwell. 1976. lib. bdg. 250.00 (*0-87700-253-3*) Revisionist Pr.

Concannon, Matthew J., ed. Common Hand Problems in Primary Care. LC 98-37041. (Illus.). 350p. 1999. text 39.95 (*1-56053-209-2*) Hanley & Belfus.

Concannon, Tom. Using Media for Creative Teaching. 76p. 1979. pap. text 7.95 (*0-932720-85-4*) New Plays Inc.

***Concaro, Edoardo & Levi, Alberto, eds.** Sovereign Carpets: Unknown Masterpieces from European Collections. (Illus.). 240p. 2000. 50.00 (*88-8118-630-6*, Pub. by Skira IT) Abbeville Pr.

Concato, Cynthia. The Business Plan Workbook: A Workbook for the Entrepreneur to Plan the Start-Up of a Business Venture. (Illus.). xvii, 220p. spiral bd., wbk. ed. 99.95 (*0-9664029-4-4*); ring bd., wbk. ed. 99.95 (*0-9664029-3-6*) Bks & WorkBks.

— The Business Plan Workbook: A Workbook for the Entrepreneur to Plan the Start-Up of a Business Venture. 2nd ed. (Illus.). xvii, 220p. ring bd., wbk. ed. 29.95 (*0-9664029-2-8*) Bks & WorkBks.

Concato, Cynthia & Book & Workbooks, Corporation Staff. The Business Plan Workbook: A Workbook for the Entrepreneur to Plan the Start-Up of a Business Venture. (Illus.). xvii,220p. 1998. spiral bd., wbk. ed. 29.95 (*0-9664029-1-X*) Bks & WorkBks.

Conceicao, Maria Da, see Kitchen, K. A. & Da Conceicao, Maria.

Concepcion, Julio A. Carlitos y Pescaito. large type ed. LC 97-92296.Tr. of Carlitos & the Little Fish. (SPA., Illus.). 120p. 1998. pap. 10.00 (*0-9659592-1-X*) Nadir Pubn.

— Odyssey or Calvary? large type ed. LC 97-92297. (Illus.). 120p. 1998. pap. 12.95 (*0-9659592-0-1*) Nadir Pubn.

***Concepcion, Julio Antonio.** Dulce Miel: Regalo de Dios.Tr. of Sweet Honey: Gift of God. (SPA.). 53p. 1999. pap. 5.00 (*0-9659592-2-8*) Nadir Pubn.

Concepcion, Sara I., jt. auth. see Cordova, Gonzalo F.

Concepcion Valdes, Gabriel De La, see Manzano, Juan F. & De La Concepcion Valdes, Gabriel.

***Concept Publishing Staff.** Ayurveda Materia Medica. 1999. 39.95 (*81-7022-020-3*) Concept Pub.

Concepts & Standards for External Financial Report. Statement on Accounting Theory & Theory Acceptance. 61p. 1977. 12.00 (*0-86539-010-X*) Am Accounting.

***Concepts Coloring Staff.** The Marine Biology Coloring Book. 2nd ed. 272p. 2000. pap. 17.95 (*0-06-273718-X*) HarpC.

— The Physics Coloring Book. (Illus.). 128p. 2000. 17.95 (*0-06-273719-8*) HarpC.

Concepts, Triamond, ed. see Bissell, Ronald D.

Conceptual Frameworks Staff. Case Studies of the Third World. 1991. pap. text. write for info. (*0-05-004479-6*) Addison-Wesley.

Conces, Rory J. Blurred Visions: Philosophy, Science, & Ideology in a Troubled World. LC 94-36246. (San Francisco State University Series in Philosophy: Vol. 2). XXIV, 314p. (C). 1998. pap. text 34.95 (*0-8204-2468-4*) P Lang Pubng.

Concha, Victor Garcia De la, see Garcia de la Concha, Victor, ed.

Conchar, A. A. & Saff, Edward B., eds. Approximation Theory & Complex Analysis & Mathematical Physics. (Lecture Notes in Mathematics Ser.: Vol. 1550). iv, 222p. 1993. pap. write for info. (*3-540-56931-6*) Spr-Verlag.

Conchiero, Angel, jt. auth. see Martinez-Pacheco, Ramon.

Concho, Jaime, ed. see Blest Gana, Alberto.

Conchon, Georges. L' Amour en Face. (FRE.). 256p. 1987. pap. 11.95 (*0-7859-2077-3*, 2070378969) Fr & Eur.

— Colette Stern. (FRE.). 218p. 1989. pap. 10.95 (*0-7859-2125-7*, 2070381781) Fr & Eur.

Conciliis, Anthony J. De, see De Conciliis, Anthony J.

Concina, Ennio. A History of Venetian Architecture. LC 97-19201. (Illus.). 362p. (C). 1998. 80.00 (*0-521-57338-6*) Cambridge U Pr.

Conckle, Lenora. Hunting the Way It Was: An Alaskan Hunting Guides' Adventures on Pack Ice. LC 96-70834. (Illus.). 216p. 1997. 24.95 (*1-888125-08-X*) Publ Consult.

Concon. Food Toxicology, Contaminants & Additives, Pt. B. (Food Science & Technology Ser.: Vol. 26). (Illus.). 1830p. 1987. text 500.00 (*0-8247-7737-9*) Dekker.

Concon, Josw M. Food Toxicology, Principles & Concepts, Pt. A. (Food Science & Technology Ser.: Vol. 26). (Illus.). 696p. 1987. text 500.00 (*0-8247-7736-0*) Dekker.

Concone, G. Fifty Lessons Opus 9: High Voice. 92p. 1986. pap. 8.95 (*0-7935-5356-3*, 50259430) H Leonard.

— Fifty Lessons Opus 9: Low Vocal. 96p. 1986. per. 8.95 (*0-7935-4867-5*) H Leonard.

— Fifty Lessons Opus 9: Meduim Voice. 96p. 1986. pap. 8.95 (*0-7935-5344-X*) H Leonard.

— School of Sight Singing: Vocal Practical Method for Young Beginners. 64p. 1986. pap. 7.95 (*0-7935-5102-1*) H Leonard.

Conconi, Francesco, jt. auth. see Gregor, Robert J.

Conconi, Giorgio. When Jesus Smiled. Aumann, Jordan, tr. from ITA. LC 97-44733.Tr. of Quand Gesu Sorrise. 167p. (Orig.). 1998. mass mkt. 5.95 (*0-8189-0768-1*) Alba.

***Concord Reference Staff.** Concord Reference. 1999. 155.00 (*0-521-51297-2*) Cambridge U Pr.

Concord Reference Staff. Desk Encyclopedia 4 a New America. 1999. text. write for info. (*0-670-10010-2*) NAL.

— The New American Desk Encyclopedia. 1999. pap. write for info. (*0-451-17956-0*, Sig) NAL.

— The New American Desk Encyclopedia. 4th ed. 1424p. 1997. mass mkt. 9.99 (*0-451-19320-2*, Sig) NAL.

Concordance for Inner Peace Staff. Concordance. 1997. 29.95 (*0-614-20423-2*, Viking) Viking Penguin.

Concordia, Charles. Synchronous Machines Theory & Performance. LC TK2787.C65. (General Electric Ser.). (Illus.). 234p. reprint ed. pap. 72.60 (*0-608-10002-1*, 201186500079) Bks Demand.

Concordia Historical Institute Staff. Heritages of Cooking: A Collection of Recipes from East Perry County, Missouri. 5th rev. ed. Kramer, Gerhardt, ed. (Illus.). 226p. 1981. pap. 6.50 (*0-9659555-2-4*) Concordia Hist.

***Concordia House Publishing Staff.** Augsburg Confession & Its Apology, Leader's Guide. (Lutheran Confessions Bible Study Ser.). 1999. pap. 4.99 (*0-570-06840-1*) Concordia.

— Augsburg Confession & Its Apology, Study Guide. (Lutheran Confessions Bible Study Ser.). 1999. pap. 4.99 (*0-570-06839-8*) Concordia.

— Formula of Concord. (Lutheran Confessions Bible Study Ser.). 1999. pap., teacher ed. 4.99 (*0-570-07841-5*); pap., student ed. 4.99 (*0-570-07840-7*) Concordia.

Concordia House Staff. Advent, Christmas, Epiphany. 1995. pap. 5.50 (*0-570-09458-5*); pap. 7.75 (*0-570-09459-3*) Concordia.

— Lent Easter Ascension. 1995. pap. 5.50 (*0-570-09460-7*) Concordia.

Concordia Publishing. God Knows. (Illus.). 24p. (J). (ps). 1998. 3.00 (*0-570-05496-6*, 56-1959GJ) Concordia.

***Concordia Publishing Company Staff.** Bing! Bing! (Hear Me Read Ser.). (SPA., Illus.). 24p. (J). (ps-k). 2000. 2.95 (*0-570-09914-5*) Concordia.

— My Bible Story Coloring Book, 8. 1998. pap. 1.99 (*0-570-05085-5*) Concordia.

***Concordia Publishing Company Staff, contrib. by.** Membership Tools. 1998. cd-rom 129.95 (*0-570-09619-7*) Concordia.

Concordia Publishing House Staff. Born of Forgiveness. 1996. pap. 3.99 (*0-570-04927-X*) Concordia.

Concordia Publishing House staff. A Church Year. 1995. pap. text 5.50 (*0-570-09443-7*) Concordia.

Concordia Publishing House Staff. A Church Year. 1995. pap. 5.50 (*0-570-09444-5*); pap. text 5.50 (*0-570-09445-3*) Concordia.

— A Church Year. 1996. pap. 5.50 (*0-570-09446-1*) Concordia.

— A Church Year. 1996. pap. 5.50 (*0-570-09449-6*) Concordia.

— Communication with God & One Another, 3. 1997. pap., teacher ed. 5.75 (*0-570-09639-1*, 20-2805); pap., student ed. 4.75 (*0-570-09638-3*, 20-2804) Concordia.

***Concordia Publishing House Staff.** Date Prisa! (Hear Me Read Ser.). (SPA., Illus.). 32p. (J). (ps-3). 2000. 2.95 (*0-570-09911-0*) Concordia.

— Every Day Is Mother's Day. 1996. pap. 3.99 (*0-570-04930-X*) Concordia.

Concordia Publishing House Staff. Faith & Value Development, 2. 1996. pap. 4.75 (*0-570-09644-8*, 20-2810); pap., teacher ed. 5.75 (*0-570-09645-6*, 20-2811) Concordia.

Concordia Publishing House Staff. Father Who Is Following. 1996. pap. 3.99 (*0-570-04931-8*) Concordia.

— Juan, un Comentario Pastoral y Teologico. (SPA.). 640p. 2000. pap. 17.90 (*0-570-05125-8*) Concordia.

— Muy Alto Muy Bajito. (Hear Me Read Ser.). (SPA., Illus.). 24p. (J). (ps-k). 2000. 2.95 (*0-570-09917-X*) Concordia.

Concordia Publishing House Staff. One Hundred Bible Stories. (Illus.). 224p. (J). (gr. k-4). 1998. pap. 9.99 (*0-570-05465-6*, 56-1928) Concordia.

— One Hundred Bible Stories Activity Book. 1998. pap. text 5.50 (*0-570-00663-5*) Concordia.

***Concordia Publishing House Staff.** Plip, Plop. (Hear Me Read Ser.). (SPA., Illus.). 24p. (J). (ps-3). 2000. 2.95 (*0-570-09910-2*) Concordia.

— Que Sucedera Despues. (Hear Me Read Ser.). (SPA., Illus.). 24p. (J). (ps-3). 2000. 2.95 (*0-570-09909-9*) Concordia.

— Religious Myth New Age, Vol. 25. 1996. pap. text 3.99 (*0-570-04924-5*) Concordia.

— Remen la Barca. (Hear Me Read Ser.). (SPA., Illus.). 32p. (J). (ps-k). 2000. 2.95 (*0-570-09918-8*) Concordia.

Concordia Publishing House Staff. Romance & Sexuality: Leader's Guide, 2. 1996. pap. 5.75 (*0-570-09637-5*, 20-2803) Concordia.

— Romance & Sexuality: Study Guide, 2. 1996. pap. 4.75 (*0-570-09636-7*, 20-2802) Concordia.

***Concordia Publishing House Staff.** Ron, Ron. (Hear Me Read Ser.). (SPA., Illus.). 24p. (J). (ps-k). 2000. 2.95 (*0-570-09912-9*) Concordia.

— Sigue Esa Estrella. (Hear Me Read Ser.). (SPA., Illus.). 24p. (J). (ps-k). 2000. 2.95 (*0-570-09915-3*) Concordia.

— Tarara! Tarara! (Hear Me Read Ser.). (SPA., Illus.). 32p. (J). (ps-k). 2000. 2.95 (*0-570-09916-1*) Concordia.

— Way We Worship, Vol. 25. 1996. pap. text 3.99 (*0-570-04926-1*) Concordia.

— Whats Behind Lodge Door, 25. 1996. pap. text 3.99 (*0-570-04929-6*) Concordia.

Concordia Publishing House Staff, ed. God First: 52 Reproducible Single Session Stewardship Bible Studies. 1998. pap. 13.00 (*0-570-06849-5*) Concordia.

— One God, Many Gods: Bible Studies for Postmodern Times. 96p. (YA). 1998. pap. 16.00 (*0-570-06834-7*, 20-2427GJ) Concordia.

Concordia Publishing House Staff, ed. see Arch Books Staff.

***Concordia Publishing, PUBLISHING.** Bethlehem Inn. (J). (ps-3). 1999. 7.99 (*0-570-07046-5*) CPH Preserv Soc.

— Bethlehem Stable. 1999. 7.99 (*0-570-07047-3*) CPH Preserv Soc.

— Favorite Bible People, 1. 1999. pap. text 4.00 (*0-570-05598-9*) Concordia.

— Herod's Palace. 1999. 8.00 (*0-570-07051-1*) Concordia.

— Jesus & His Friends, 1. 1999. pap. text 4.00 (*0-570-05597-0*) Concordia.

— Mary's House. 1999. 8.00 (*0-570-07049-X*) Concordia.

— Noah's Ark Activity Set, 1. LC 99-21183. 1999. 12.99 (*0-570-05567-9*) Concordia.

— Shepherds' Fields. 1999. 8.00 (*0-570-07048-1*) Concordia.

— 2000 Years Since Then, 1. 1999. 6.99 (*0-570-05566-0*) Concordia.

— Where is Jesus?, 1. 1999. 7.00 (*0-570-05583-0*) Concordia.

— Where is Moses?, 1. 1999. 7.00 (*0-570-05584-9*) Concordia.

— Wise Men's Palace. 1999. 8.00 (*0-570-07050-3*) Concordia.

***Concordia Publishing Staff.** All about the Ark Giant Pop-Up Book. (Illus.). (J). 1999. 9.99 (*0-570-05588-1*) Concordia.

Concordia Publishing Staff. Called to Be: Devotions by Teens for Teens. 1998. pap. text 6.99 (*0-570-05063-4*) Concordia.

— Colossians Philemon. (God's Word for Today Ser.). 1994. pap. 5.50 (*0-570-09478-X*, 20-2649) Concordia.

— Colossians/Philemon: Take a New Look at Christ. 1994. pap. 5.50 (*0-570-09516-6*, 20-2648) Concordia.

***Concordia Publishing Staff.** Concordia Text Bible. 2000. 15.99 (*5-550-00881-5*) Nairi.

Concordia Publishing Staff. Coping with Stress. (Master's Touch Bible Study Ser.). 1996. pap. 4.50 (*0-570-09551-4*, 20-2592) Concordia.

— Cruisin' the River of Light: Devotions by Teens for Teens. LC 96-123295. (YA). 1995. 6.99 (*0-570-04828-1*, 12-3270) Concordia.

— The Day Jesus Died. (Arch Bks.). (Illus.). 16p. 1998. pap. text 1.99 (*0-570-07543-2*, 59-1516) Concordia.

— Deuteronomy. LC 96-181113. (People's Bible Commentary Ser.). 358p. 1996. pap. 12.99 (*0-570-04833-8*, 12-8043) Concordia.

— The Fishermen's Journey. (Illus.). 10p. (J). (ps-k). 1998. bds. 3.99 (*0-570-05467-2*, 56-1966GJ) Concordia.

— Forward in Faith Bk. 3. (Twenty-Something Ser.). 1997. pap. text 12.99 (*0-570-09899-8*, 20-3062) Concordia.

— Genesis. (God's Word for Today Ser.). 1994. pap. 5.50 (*0-570-09484-4*, 20-2642) Concordia.

— Jonah & the Very Big Fish. (Arch Bks.). 1998. pap. text 1.99 (*0-570-07541-6*, 59-1514) Concordia.

***Concordia Publishing Staff.** Just in Time Esther. (Arch Books Ser.). 1999. pap. 1.99 (*0-570-07558-0*) Concordia.

— Just Look in the Stable. (Arch Books Ser.). 1999. pap. 1.99 (*0-570-07559-9*) Concordia.

C

— Little Boy Jesus. LC 99-182962. (Small Big Bks.). (Illus.). 16p. (J). (ps-1). 1998. pap. 2.49 (*0-570-05544-X*, 54-0081GJ) Concordia.

Concordia Publishing Staff. Living with Change. (Master's Touch Bible Study Ser.). 1994. pap. 4.50 (*0-570-09439-9*, 20-2460) Concordia.

— Living with Chronic Pain. (Master's Touch Bible Study Ser.). 1994. pap. 4.50 (*0-570-09435-6*, 20-2456) Concordia.

— Living with Compulsive Behaviors. (Master's Touch Bible Study Ser.). 1994. pap. 4.50 (*0-570-09436-4*, 20-2457) Concordia.

— Living with Infertility. (Master's Touch Bible Study Ser.). 1994. pap. 4.50 (*0-570-09520-4*, 20-2461) Concordia.

— Living with Too Little Time. (Master's Touch Bible Study Ser.). 1996. pap. 4.50 (*0-570-09549-2*, 20-2590) Concordia.

— Love. (Connections Ser.). 1994. pap. 4.50 (*0-570-09369-4*, 20-2466) Concordia.

***Concordia Publishing Staff.** The Man Who Couldn't Speak. (Arch Books Ser.). (Illus.). 16p. (J). (gr. k-4). 1999. pap. 1.99 (*0-570-07560-2*) Concordia.

— Mary & Joseph's Journey to Bethlehem. (Folding Board Bks.). (Illus.). 10p. (J). (ps-k). 1998. bds. 3.99 (*0-570-05464-8*, 56-1964GJ) Concordia.

Concordia Publishing Staff. Matthew. (God's Word for Today Ser.). 1994. pap. 5.50 (*0-570-09486-0*, 20-2643) Concordia.

— My Bible Story Coloring Book No. 6. (Illus.). 32p. (ps-2). 1998. pap. 2.95 (*0-570-05073-1*) Concordia.

— Overcoming Depression. LC 96-173141. (Master's Touch Bible Study Ser.). 1996. pap. 4.50 (*0-570-09550-6*, 20-2591) Concordia.

— The Prodigal Son's Journey. (Illus.). 10p. (J). (ps-k). 1998. bds. 3.99 (*0-570-05466-4*, 56-1965GJ) Concordia.

— Psalms. (God's Word for Today Ser.). 1994. pap. 5.50 (*0-570-09476-3*, 20-2641) Concordia.

***Concordia Publishing Staff.** Quien Ayudara? (Hear Me Read Ser.). (SPA., Illus.). 24p. (J). (ps-k). 2000. 2.95 (*0-570-09913-7*) Concordia.

Concordia Publishing Staff. Revelation. (God's Word for Today Ser.). 1994. pap. 5.50 (*0-570-09470-4*, 20-2640) Concordia.

— Samuel. (People's Bible Commentary Ser.). 334p. 1996. pap. 12.99 (*0-570-04831-1*, 12-8041) Concordia.

***Concordia Publishing Staff.** Shepherd & the Lost Sheep. (Bible Soft Pockets Ser.). (Illus.). 10p. (J). (ps). 2000. 6.99 (*0-570-07065-1*) Concordia.

— The Story of Easter: Giant Flap Book. (Illus.). 10p. (J). (ps-k). 1999. 10.99 (*0-570-05551-2*, 56-1968GJ) Concordia.

Concordia Publishing Staff. Story of the Empty Tomb. LC 99-179137. 1998. pap. text 1.99 (*0-570-07544-0*) Concordia.

***Concordia Publishing Staff.** Ten Steps to Z-Z-Zing Development or Decline? 1999. pap. 11.94 (*0-570-07557-2*) Concordia U Pr.

— This Is the World That God Made. LC 99-182977. (Small Big Bks.). (Illus.). 16p. (J). (ps-1). 1998. pap. 2.49 (*0-570-05543-1*, 54-0080GJ) Concordia.

Concordia Publishing Staff. Time to Plant, a Time to Grow. (Rural & Small Town Issues Ser.). 1998. pap. text 12.99 (*0-570-09826-2*, 20-3015) Concordia.

— Twelve Who Followed Jesus. LC 98-189083. (Arch Bks.). 1998. pap. text 1.99 (*0-570-07542-4*, 59-1515) Concordia.

— Worry. (Connections Ser.). 1994. pap. 4.50 (*0-570-09373-2*, 20-2470) Concordia.

Concordia Publishing Staff, ed. Stories about Jesus for Little Ones. (Illus.). 35p. (J). (ps-1). 1998. 8.99 (*0-570-05476-1*) Concordia.

Concordia Staff. Adventures with Demetrius the Donkey. (J). 1994. pap. 8.25 (*0-570-04621-1*, 12-3202) Concordia.

— Jesus Returns to Heaven: Acts 1:3-12. (Arch Bks.). (Illus.). 24p. 1995. pap. 1.99 (*0-570-07503-3*, 59-1476) Concordia.

— My Confirmation Memories. 24p. 1994. 14.99 (*0-570-04693-9*, 12-3252) Concordia.

— The Night the Angels Sang: Luke 2: 8-20. 24p. (J). (ps-3). 1973. pap. 1.99 (*0-570-06095-8*, 59-1213) Concordia.

— Our Life in Christ. (Our Life in Christ Adult Bible Study Ser.). 1997. pap. 5.50 (*0-570-09729-0*, 20-3080) Concordia.

Concrete Construction, Concrete Producer and Concrete Repair Digest Editorial Staff. Concrete Problem Clinic. LC 99-200851. (Illus.). 249 p. 1999. pap. 20.00 (*0-924659-24-6*, 4061) Hanley.

Concrete Construction Magazine Editors. Concrete Repair, Vol. 3. (Illus.). 48p. 1988. pap. 11.95 (*0-924659-30-0*, 1320) Hanley.

Concrete Construction Magazine Editors, compiled by. Sawing, Drilling & Coring Concrete. rev. ed. 24p. 1997. pap. 11.95 (*0-924659-10-6*, 1230) Hanley.

Concrete Pole Task Committee of the Committee on E. Guide for the Design & Use of Concrete Poles. 60p. 1987. 13.00 (*0-87262-596-6*) Am Soc Civil Eng.

Concus, P. & Finn, R., eds. Variational Methods for Free Surface Interfaces. (Illus.). x, 204p. 1986. 72.95 (*0-387-96396-0*) Spr-Verlag.

Concus, P., ed. see Chern, Shiing-Shen.

Concus, Paul & Lancaster, Kirk, eds. Advances in Geometric Analysis & Continuum Mechanics. LC 95-79520. 1995. 42.00 (*1-57146-023-3*, INPR/18C) Intl Pr Boston.

Conda, Kandias & Ford, Karen. Get That Cutie in Commercials, Television, & Films: Breaking Your Talented Child into the Entertainment Industry: A Parents' Step-by-Step Beginners' Handbook & Guide to Show Business Success. LC 98-4557. 1998. 12.95 (*0-9655064-5-2*) Amber Books.

Condax, Kate D. One Hundred One Training Tips for Dogs. LC 94-6387. 256p. 1994. pap. 9.95 (*0-440-50568-2*) Dell.

Condax, Philip L. Selections from the Spira Collection: An Exhibition at George Eastman House Sept. 26, 1980 - Jan. 11, 1981. (Illus.). 24p. (Orig.). 1981. pap. 4.00 (*0-935398-04-X*) G Eastman Hse.

Condax, Philip L., pref. Evolution of the Japanese Camera. 100p. 1982. pap. 10.00 (*0-935398-11-2*) G Eastman Hse.

Conde. Caribbean Women Writers: Fiction in English. LC 98-28418. 248p. 1999. pap. 17.95 (*0-312-21863-X*) St Martin.

***Conde & Aguedas.** Spanish Proverbs, + Translations In E/f/g/i. (SPA & ENG.). 143p. 1999. pap. write for info. (*0-320-01759-1*) Fr & Eur.

Conde, A., et al. Trends in Non-Crystalline Solids: Proceedings of the 3rd International Workshop on Non-Crystalline Solids. 450p. 1992. text 124.00 (*981-02-1035-3*) World Scientific Pub.

Conde, Carmen. Woman Without Eden (Mujer Sin Eden) De Armas, Jose R. et al, trs. LC 85-80641. (Coleccion Alacran Azul).Tr. of Mujer Sin Eden. (SPA.). 175p. (Orig.). 1986. pap. 12.00 (*0-89729-375-4*) Ediciones.

Conde-Costas, Luis A. The Marxist Theory of Ideology: A Conceptual Analysis. (Studia Sociologica Upsaliensia: No. 33). 147p. (Orig.). 1991. pap. 35.00 (*91-554-2791-X*) Coronet Bks.

Conde-Guerri, Maria J., ed. see Jardiel, Poncela E.

Conde, H. Victor. A Handbook of International Human Rights Terminology. LC 98-37452. (Human Rights in International Perspective Ser.). 200p. 1999. text 35.00 (*0-8032-1501-0*) U of Nebr Pr.

***Conde, H. Victor & Cartwright, Rita Cantos.** Human Rights in the United States: A Sourcebook, 2 Vols. LC 00-22507. 750p. 2000. lib. bdg. 175.00 (*1-57607-109-X*) ABC-CLIO.

Conde, John A. Cars with Personalities. LC 82-73487. (Illus.). 256p. 1982. 24.95 (*0-9605048-1-8*) Arnold-Porter Pub.

Conde, Jose A. History of the Dominion of the Arabs in Spain, 3 vols. Foster, Jonathan, tr. reprint ed. 55.00 (*0-404-09270-5*) AMS Pr.

Conde, L. P. & Hart, S. M., eds. Feminist Readings on Spanish & Latin-American Literature. LC 91-40732. 216p. 1991. lib. bdg. 89.95 (*0-7734-9440-5*) E Mellen.

Conde, Lisa P. Stages of the Development of a Feminist Consciousness in Perez Galdos (1843-1920) A Biographical Sketch. LC 90-35014. (Hispanic Literature Ser.: Vol. 7). 392p. 1990. lib. bdg. 99.95 (*0-88946-375-1*) E Mellen.

— Women in the Theatre of Galdos: From Realidad (1892) to Voluntad (1895) LC 90-5916. 432p. 1990. lib. bdg. 109.95 (*0-88946-391-3*) E Mellen.

Conde, Lisa P., ed. see Galdos, Benito Perez.

Conde, Mabel. Memories Are Not Subject to Time. rev. unabridged ed. (Illus.). 70p. 1997. pap., per. 8.95 (*0-9658473-1-4*) M Conde.

— Religious Games to Sharpen Your Knowledge of the Roman Catholic Faith. unabridged ed. (Illus.). 20p. 1997. pap. write for info. (*0-9658473-0-6*) M Conde.

Conde, Maryse. The Children of Nya. LC 88-40486. 512p. 1989. 18.95 (*0-685-28276-7*) Viking Penguin.

— Crossing the Mangrove. Philcox, Richard, tr. from FRE. LC 94-35504.Tr. of Traversee de la Mangrove. 224p. 1995. pap. 11.95 (*0-385-47633-7*, Anchor NY) Doubleday.

***Conde, Maryse.** Desirada. 1998. pap. 11.95 (*2-266-08697-9*) Distribks Inc.

— Desirada. 256p. 2000. 24.00 (*1-56947-215-7*) Soho Press.

Conde, Maryse. I, Tituba, Black Witch of Salem. Philcox, Richard, tr. 256p. 1994. pap. 10.00 (*0-345-38420-2*) One Wrld.

— Land of Many Colors & Nanna-Ya: Pays Mele Suivi de Nanna-Ya. Ball, Nicole, tr. from FRE. LC 98-39182. 1999. pap. 12.00 (*0-8032-6395-3*) U of Nebr Pr.

— Land of Many Colors & Nanna-Ya (Pays Mele Suivi de Nanna-Ya) Pays Mele Suivi de Nanna-Ya. Ball, Nicole, tr. from FRE. LC 98-39182. 1999. text 30.00 (*0-8032-1488-X*) U of Nebr Pr.

— The Last of the African Kings. Philcox, Richard, tr. LC 97-7661. xiv, 216p. 1997. pap. 12.00 (*0-8032-6384-8*, Bison Books); text 40.00 (*0-8032-1489-8*) U of Nebr Pr.

— Moi, Tituba, Sorciere . . . (Folio Ser.: No. 1929). (FRE.). 277p. 1988. pap. 9.95 (*2-07-037929-9*) Schoenhof.

— Moi, Tituba Sorciere. (FRE.). 276p. 1988. pap. 11.95 (*0-7859-2087-0*, 2070379299) Fr & Eur.

— Season in Rihata. Philcox, Richard, tr. (Caribbean Writers Ser.). 192p. (Orig.). (C). 1988. pap. 9.95 (*0-435-98832-8*, 98832) Heinemann.

— Segou: Les Murailles de Terre, 2 vols., 1. 1987. pap. 12.95 (*0-7859-3125-2*) Fr & Eur.

— Segou: Les Murailles de Terre, 2 vols., 2. 1987. pap. 12.95 (*0-7859-3126-0*) Fr & Eur.

— Segou Vol. 3: La Terre en Mietes. (FRE.). 1987. pap. 16.95 (*0-7859-3137-6*) Fr & Eur.

— Segu. 512p. (C). 1998. pap. 14.95 (*0-14-025949-X*) Addson-Wesley Educ.

Conde, Maryse. Windward Heights. Philcox, Richard, tr. from FRE. LC 98-52071. 364p. 1999. 24.00 (*1-56947-161-4*) Soho Press.

***Conde, Maryse.** Windward Heights. 352p. 2000. pap. 12.00 (*1-56947-216-5*) Soho Press.

***Conde, Maryse & Philcox, Richard.** Heremakhonon. LC 99-34531. 168p. 1999. pap. 13.95 (*0-89410-886-7*, Three Contnts) L Rienner.

Conde, Nicholas. In the Deep Woods. large type ed. 576p. 1992. 27.99 (*0-7089-2568-5*) Ulverscroft.

Conde, Richard S. Shelburne, Vermont: A Novel. LC 98-29888. 1998. write for info. (*1-886166-06-4*) Pine Tree NY.

Conde, Rosina. Women on the Road. Segade, Gustavo et al, trs. from SPA. (Baja California Literature in Translation Ser.). 150p. (Orig.). 1994. pap. 12.50 (*1-879691-24-8*) SDSU Press.

***Conde, Yago.** Architecture of the Indeterminacy. (Illus.). 2000. pap. 25.00 (*84-89698-65-1*) Actar.

Conde, Yvonne. Operation Pedro Pan: The Untold Exodus of 14,000 Cuban Children. LC 99-17440. (Illus.). 256p. 1999. 27.50 (*0-415-92149-X*) Routledge.

***Conde, Yvonne M.** Operation Pedro Pan: The Untold Exodus of 14,000 Cuban Children. 2000. reprint ed. pap. 16.95 (*0-415-92823-0*) Routledge.

Condee, Nancy. Explosion in the Puzzle Factory: Poems. deluxe limited ed. (Poetry Ser.). 32p. 1983. pap. 15.00 (*0-930901-18-5*) Burning Deck.

Condee, Nancy, ed. Soviet Hieroglyphics: Visual Culture in Late Twentieth-Century Russia. LC 94-22839. (Illus.). 208p. 1995. 35.00 (*0-253-31402-X*); pap. 12.95 (*0-253-20945-5*) Ind U Pr.

Condee, William F. Theatrical Space: A Guide for Directors & Designers. LC 95-3311. (Illus.). 242p. 1995. 41.50 (*0-8108-3007-8*) Scarecrow.

Condell, Diana & Liddiard, Jean. Working for Victory? Images of Women in the First World War, 1914-18. (Illus.). 192p. 1987. 39.50 (*0-7102-0974-6*, A0747, Routledge Thoemms) Routledge.

Condelli, Pat. Royal Recipes from the Castle of the Cookie Queen. 280p. 1996. pap. 14.95 (*1-891231-00-6*) Word Assn.

Condeluci, Al. Beyond Difference. LC 94-73031. 302p. 1995. lib. bdg. 39.95 (*1-57444-022-5*) St Lucie Pr.

— Interdependence: The Route to Community. 2nd ed. LC 91-72030. 272p. 1995. per. 45.00 (*1-878205-11-0*) St Lucie Pr.

Conder, Claude R. The Latin Kingdom of Jerusalem. LC 78-180331. reprint ed. 72.50 (*0-404-56238-8*) AMS Pr.

— The Survey of Western Palestine, 3 vols., Set. Palmer, E. H. & Besant, Walter, eds. LC 78-63331. (Crusades & Military Orders Ser.: Second Series). (Illus.). reprint ed. 155.00 (*0-404-17010-2*) AMS Pr.

Conder, Claude R. & Kitchener, Horatio Herbert. Survey of Western Palestine, 1882-1888: 2nd Eastern. 1998. reprint ed. lib. bdg. 4995.00 (*1-85207-835-9*, Pub. by Archive Editions) N Ross.

Conder, Claude R., jt. auth. see Warren, Charles.

Conder, Forest E. You Are a Miracle: Why You Are Who You Are. (Illus.). 315p. (Orig.). 1989. pap. 7.95 (*0-685-25987-0*) F E Conder.

Conder, John. Formula of His Own: Henry Adam's Literary Experiment. LC 79-103427. 1970. lib. bdg. 8.50 (*0-226-11437-6*) U Ch Pr.

Conder, John J. Naturalism in American Fiction: The Classic Phase. LC 84-8661. 240p. 1984. pap. 16.00 (*0-8131-0169-7*) U Pr of Ky.

Conder, John R. & Young, C. L. Physicochemical Measurement by Gas Chromatography. LC 78-9899. (Illus.). 652p. reprint ed. pap. 200.00 (*0-8357-8984-5*, 203333200085) Bks Demand.

Conder, Joseph M. & Hopkins, Gilbert N. The Self-Insurance Decision. 119p. 1981. pap. 20.00 (*0-86641-002-3*, 81124) Inst Mgmt Account.

Conder, Josiah. Landscape Gardening in Japan. 1990. pap. 14.95 (*0-486-26559-5*) Dover.

Conder, Peter. RSPB Guide to Birdwatching. (Illus.). 1979. 12.50 (*0-600-31423-5*) Transatl Arts.

Conder, Russel. Handmade Houseboats: Independent Living Afloat. 240p. 1992. pap. 19.95 (*0-07-158022-0*) McGraw.

Conder, Russell. Handmade Houseboats: Independent Living Afloat. 240p. 1992. pap. 19.95 (*0-87742-307-5*, 60289) Intl Marine.

Conder, Susan. Dried Flowers: Drying & Arranging. LC 87-45830. (Illus.). 144p. 1988. 20.00 (*0-87923-719-8*) Godine.

Conder, Susan & Joyce, David. Variegated Leaves. (Illus.). 192p. 1994. text 25.00 (*0-02-273302-7*) Macmillan.

Condes, Santob De Carrion De Los, see De Carrion De Los Condes, Santob.

Condic, Dusko, tr. see Lasic, Vinko D.

Condie, A. Marshall Fowler Album. (Illus.). 104p. 1996. pap. 29.95 (*1-85638-005-X*, MBI 123494AE, Pub. by A T Condie Pubns) Motorbooks Intl.

Condie, Carol J. & Fowler, Catherine S., eds. The Anthropology of the Desert West: Essays in Honor of Jesse D. Jennings. LC 85-15810. (Anthropological Papers: No. 110). (Illus.). 336p. (C). 1993. reprint ed. pap. 27.50 (*0-87480-248-2*) U of Utah Pr.

Condie, Carol J. & Fowler, Don D., eds. Anthropology of the Desert West: Essays in Honor of Jesse D. Jennings. LC 85-15810. 339p. reprint ed. pap. 105.10 (*0-8357-5628-9*, 203191500077) Bks Demand.

Condie, David N. & Turner, M. S. An Atlas of Lower Limb Orthotic Practice. LC 96-84199. (Illus.). 104p. 1997. text 198.95 (*0-412-72770-6*, Pub. by E A) OUP.

Condie, K. C., ed. Proterozoic Crustal Evolution. LC 92-34776. (Developments in Precambrian Geology Ser.: No. 10). 538p. 1993. 192.50 (*0-444-88782-2*) Elsevier.

Condie, Kent & Sloan, Robert. The Origin & Evolution of Earth. LC 97-43759. 498p. 1998. 80.00 (*0-13-491820-7*) P-H.

Condie, Kent C. Plate Tectonics & Crustal Evolution. 4th ed. LC 97-4026. 288p. 1997. pap. text 49.95 (*0-7506-3386-7*) Buttrwrth-Heinemann.

Condie, Kent C., ed. Archean Crustal Evolution. LC 94-23508. (Developments in Precambrian Geology Ser.: Vol. 11). 542p. 1994. 184.00 (*0-444-81621-6*) Elsevier.

— Plate Tectonics & Crustal Evolution. (Illus.). 350p. 1982. pap. text 49.50 (*0-08-028075-7*) Elsevier.

— Plate Tectonics & Crustal Evolution. 2nd ed. (Illus.). 350p. 1982. text 110.00 (*0-08-028076-5*) Elsevier.

Condie, Spencer J. God of Comfort, God of Love. 1998. 16.95 (*1-57008-416-5*) Bookcraft Inc.

— Your Agency: Handle with Care. 1996. 13.95 (*1-57008-286-3*) Bookcraft Inc.

Condiff, John S., ed. Liquid Fuels & Industrial Products from Renewable Resources: Proceedings of the 3rd Liquid Fuel Conference. LC 96-86289. 375p. 1996. pap. 58.75 (*0-929355-79-2*, P0896) Am Soc Ag Eng.

Condillac. Condillac: Commerce & Government: Considered in Their Mutual Relationship. Eltis, Shelagh M. & Eltis, Walter, eds. & trs. by. LC 97-22294. 320p. 1998. 100.00 (*1-85898-171-9*) E Elgar.

Condillac, Etienne Bonnot de. Essay on the Origin of Human Knowledge. Nugent, Thomas, tr. LC 74-147960. reprint ed. 72.50 (*0-404-08210-6*) AMS Pr.

— Essay on the Origin of Human Knowledge. Nugent, Thomas, tr. from FRE. LC 76-161929. (History of Psychology Ser.). 424p. 1971. reprint ed. 60.00 (*0-8201-1090-6*) Schol Facsimiles.

Condillac, Etienne Bonnot De, see Bonnot de Condillac, Etienne.

Condini, Ned. Quartettsatz. LC 96-418808. (VIA Folios Ser.: Vol. 7). 51p. (C). 1996. pap. 7.00 (*1-884419-06-2*) Bordighera.

Condini, Ned. The Sky Below. 181p. mass mkt. 4.99 (*1-55197-369-3*) Picasso Publ.

Condino, Deanna, jt. auth. see Goldfarb, Marvin D.

Condit, Blackford. History of Early Terre Haute: From 1816 to 1840. (Illus.). 198p. 1997. reprint ed. lib. bdg. 27.50 (*0-8328-6666-0*) Higginson Bk Co.

Condit, Carl W. American Building: Materials & Techniques from the Beginning of the Colonial Settlements to the Present. (Illus.). xiv, 440p. (C). 1983. pap. text 18.95 (*0-226-11450-3*, CHAC25) U Ch Pr.

— American Building: Materials & Techniques from the First Colonial Settlements to the Present. 2nd ed. LC 82-13602. (Chicago History of American Civilization Ser.: No. 25). (Illus.). 431p. reprint ed. pap. 133.70 (*0-608-09288-6*, 205416200004) Bks Demand.

— Chicago. Incl. 1910-1929 - Building, Planning, & Urban Technology. 1976. pap. 5.45 1930-1970 - Building, Planning & Urban Technology. 1976. (Illus.). 1976. write for info. (*0-318-56022-4*) U Ch Pr.

— Chicago School of Architecture. LC 64-13287. (Illus.). 256p. 1973. pap. 28.50 (*0-226-11455-4*, P540) U Ch Pr.

— The Port of New York: A History of the Rail & Terminal System from the Grand Central Electrification to the Present, Vol. 2. LC 79-16850. 412p. 1981. 48.00 (*0-226-11461-9*) U Ch Pr.

Condit, Carl W., jt. auth. see Landau, Sarah B.

Condit, Celeste M. Decoding Abortion Rhetoric: The Communication of Social Change. LC 89-33469. (Illus.). 256p. 1990. text 24.95 (*0-252-01647-5*); pap. text 15.95 (*0-252-06403-8*) U of Ill Pr.

— The Meanings of the Gene: Public Debates about Human Heredity. LC 99-6274. (Rhetoric of the Human Sciences Ser.). 256p. 1999. pap. text 19.95 (*0-299-16364-4*) U of Wis Pr.

Condit, Celeste M. & Lucaites, John L. Crafting Equality: America's Anglo-African Word. LC 92-30215. (New Practices of Inquiry Ser.). (Illus.). 378p. (C). 1993. pap. text 18.95 (*0-226-11465-1*); lib. bdg. 56.00 (*0-226-11464-3*) U Ch Pr.

Condit, Celeste M., jt. ed. see Parrott, Roxanne L.

Condit, Celeste Michelle. The Meanings of the Gene: Determination, Discrimination & Perfectionism in U.S. Public Discourse. LC 99-6274. (Rhetoric of the Human Sciences Ser.). 256p. 1999. text 49.95 (*0-299-16360-1*) U of Wis Pr.

Condit, David L. The Hummingbird Brigade: A Novel of Healing. LC 89-85378. 165p. (Orig.). 1989. pap. 8.00 (*0-938513-05-2*) Amador Pubs.

Condit, E., jt. auth. see Condit, J. H.

Condit, Erin. Francois & Jean Claude Duvalier - Haitian Presidents. Schlesinger, Arthur Meier, Jr., ed. (World Leaders Past & Present Ser.). (Illus.). 128p. (YA). (gr. 5 up). 1989. 19.95 (*1-55546-832-2*) Chelsea Hse.

Condit, Ira M. The Chinaman As We See Him & Fifty Years of Work for Him. Daniels, Roger, ed. LC 78-54839. (Asian Experience in North America Ser.). (Illus.). 1979. reprint ed. lib. bdg. 23.95 (*0-405-11305-6*) Ayer.

Condit, J. H. & Condit, E. Genealogical Record of the Condit Family, Descendants of John Cunditt, a Native of Great Britan Who Settled in Newalk, N. J., 1678 to 1885. (Illus.). 470p. 1993. reprint ed. pap. 69.50 (*0-8328-3026-7*); reprint ed. lib. bdg. 79.50 (*0-8328-3025-9*) Higginson Bk Co.

Condit, Kenneth W. & Turnbladh, Edwin T. Hold High the Torch: A History of the 4th Marines. (Elite Unit Ser.: No. 18). (Illus.). 504p. 1989. reprint ed. 49.95 (*0-89839-130-X*) Battery Pr.

Condit, Kenneth W., et al. The History of the Joint Chiefs of Staff, Korean War Vol. 1: The Joint Chiefs of Staff & National Policy 1945-1947, 4 vols., Vol. 3, Pt. 2. Gough, Terrence J., ed. 555p. 1979. 60.00 (*0-89453-148-4*) Scholarly Res Inc.

— The History of the Joint Chiefs of Staff, Korean War Vol. 3, Pt. 1: The Joint Chiefs of Staff & National Policy. Gough, Terrence J., ed. 562p. 1979. 60.00 (*0-318-69511-1*) Scholarly Res Inc.

Condit, R. & Hubbell, S. P. Tropical Forest Census Plots: Methods & Results from Barro Colorado Island, Panama & a Comparison with Other Plots. (Environmental Intelligence Unit Ser.). 170p. 1998. 129.00 (*3-540-64144-0*) Spr-Verlag.

Condit, Richard. Field Guide for Tropical Forest Census Plots: Methods & Results from Barro Colorado Island, Panama & a Comparison with Other Plots. LC 96-52380. (Environmental Intelligence Unit Ser.). 1997. write for info. (*0-12-183940-0*) Acad Pr.

Condit, Tom. Ireland's Archaeology from the Air. LC 98-102683. (Illus.). 48p. 1997. pap. 8.95 (*0-946172-58-7*, Pub. by Town Hse) Roberts Rinehart.

An Asterisk (*) at the beginning of an entry indicates that the title is appearing for the first time.

Condit, William H. Transparent Watercolor: My Second Career. (Illus.). 128p. 1990. text 29.95 (*0-9624318-0-X*) Sand Dllr CO.

Condivi, Ascanio. Make a Splash: Swimming Holes & Waterfalls of the Green Mountains. LC 98-91299. (Travel Guide Ser.). 112 p. 1998. write for info. (*0-9663556-0-1*) Master Studios.

Condivi, Ascanio & Wohl, Hellmut. The Life of Michelangelo. 2nd ed. LC 98-37313. 442p. 1999. 19.00 (*0-271-01853-4*) Pa St U Pr.

Condliffe, John B. The Welfare State in New Zealand. LC 73-19123. (Illus.). 396p. 1975. reprint ed. lib. bdg. 38.50 (*0-8371-7298-5*, CONZ, Greenwood Pr) Greenwood.

***Condo, George.** Portraits Lost in Space. (Illus.). 96p. 1999. pap. write for info. (*1-878283-91-X*) PaceWildenstein.

Condominas, Georges. We Have Eaten the Forest: The Story of a Montagnard Village in the Central Highlands of Vietnam. Turner, Philip, ed. Foulke, Adrienne, tr. LC 94-25033. (Illus.). 464p. 1994. pap. 16.00 (*1-56836-023-1*) Kodansha.

Condon. Legal Terminology. (C). 1998. 28.95 (*1-56253-355-X*) Milady Pub.

— Manual of Surgery Asia, No. 7. 1988. 10.95 (*0-316-15260-9*, Little Brwn Med Div) Lppncott W & W.

— Manual of Surgery ISE, No. 7. 1988. 15.95 (*0-316-15259-5*, Little Brwn Med Div) Lppncott W & W.

Condon, Anne. Computational Models of Games. 150p. 1989. 25.00 (*0-262-03152-3*) MIT Pr.

Condon, Bill. Auntie Spells Trouble. 1998. pap. text 3.95 (*0-207-19086-0*) HarpC.

***Condon, Bill.** Gods & Monsters: The Shooting Script. (Shooting Script Ser.). (Illus.). 144p. 2000. pap. 16.95 (*1-55704-427-9*, Newmarket Shooting) Newmarket.

Condon, C. Japanese Guide to Fish Cooking. 1996. pap. 23.95 (*4-07-972619-8*) Shufu No.

Condon, C., jt. auth. see Condon, J.

Condon, Camy, jt. auth. see Nagasawa, Kimiko.

***Condon, Cynthia G., et al.** Freedman's Cemetery Site, Dallas Texas: Assessment of Sex, Age at Death, Stature & Date of Interment for Excavated Burials, 2 vols. (Archeology Studies Program: No. 9). (Illus.). 234p. 1998. 20.97 (*0-9660796-4-7*) TX Dept Transport.

Condon, Eddie & Gehman, Richard, eds. Treasury of Jazz. LC 75-2693. 488p. 1975. reprint ed. lib. bdg. 79.50 (*0-8371-8032-5*, COTJ, Greenwood Pr) Greenwood.

Condon, Eddie & Sugrue, Thomas. We Called It Music. (Roots of Jazz Ser.). (Illus.). 341p. 1987. reprint ed. lib. bdg. 35.00 (*0-306-76267-6*) Da Capo.

— We Called It Music: A Generation of Jazz. (Illus.). 375p. 1992. reprint ed. pap. 14.95 (*0-306-80466-2*) Da Capo.

Condon, Edward O. The Irish Race in America: Bicentennial Edition. LC 75-35480. 352p. reprint ed. pap. 4.95 (*0-916590-01-1*) Ogham Hse.

Condon, Edward U. & Sinanoglu, Oktay, eds. New Directions in Atomic Physics, 2 vols., Vol. 1: Theory. LC 78-140542. (Yale Series in the Sciences). 264p. 1972. reprint ed. pap. 81.90 (*0-608-08433-6*, 201680100001) Bks Demand.

— New Directions in Atomic Physics, 2 vols., Vol. 2: Experiments. LC 78-140542. (Yale Series in the Sciences). 179p. 1972. reprint ed. pap. 55.50 (*0-608-08434-4*, 201680100002) Bks Demand.

Condon, Edwyna, ed. see Schrier, Martha S.

Condon, Emmet, jt. auth. see Hansen, Gladys.

Condon, G. A., jt. auth. see Zoubek, Charles E.

Condon, George. The Man in the Arena: The Life & Times of A. C. Sutphin. unabridged ed. Leitch, Jeffrey, ed. (Illus.). 256p. 1996. 22.95 (*0-9649900-0-8*); pap. 18.50 (*0-9649900-1-6*) A C Sutphin.

Condon, Gerald M. & Condon, Jeffrey L. Beyond the Grave: The Right Way & the Wrong Way of Leaving Money to Your Children & Others. 384p. 1995. pap. 14.00 (*0-88730-797-3*, HarpBusn) HarpInfo.

Condon, Gregg. Condon Notetaking & Transcription Skills: Advanced Course. 256p. (C). 1991. teacher ed. 5.45 (*1-56118-043-2*); pap. text 18.95 (*1-56118-353-9*); student ed. 6.00 (*1-56118-356-3*); 12.00 (*1-56118-045-9*) Paradigm MN.

***Condon, Gregg.** Letters from the Attic. (Illus.). 248p. 1999. pap. 14.95 (*0-9637697-1-5*) Marsh Lake.

Condon, Gregg. Study Skills & Notetaking. 1990. 66.00 incl. audio (*1-56118-332-6*) Paradigm MN.

Condon, Gregg. Study Skills & Notetaking. 320p. (C). 1990. teacher ed. 8.00 (*1-56118-335-0*); pap. text 16.95 (*1-56118-334-2*); 8.80 (*1-56118-333-4*) Paradigm MN.

Condon, Gregg & Andera, Frank. Paradigm Guide to English Essentials. 60p. (C). 1991. teacher ed. 8.00 (*1-56118-037-8*); pap. text 10.95 (*1-56118-036-X*) Paradigm MN.

Condon, Gregg, et al. The Dinky: C&NW Narrow Gauge in Wisconsin. 64p. 1993. 17.95 (*0-9637697-0-7*) Marsh Lake.

Condon, Gregg, jt. auth. see Zoubek, Charles E.

Condon, J. What's Japanese about Japan? 1996. 23.95 (*4-07-972039-4*) Shufu No.

Condon, J. & Condon, C. Simple Pleasures of Japan. 1996. pap. 15.95 (*4-07-973843-9*) Shufu No.

Condon, Jackie, jt. auth. see Hofstede, David.

Condon, Jeffrey L., jt. auth. see Condon, Gerald M.

Condon, John C. Buenos Vecinos: Comunicadose con los Mexicanos. 2nd ed. Deneve, Carmen & Heusinkveld, Paula, trs. LC 98-7775. (SPA.). 124p. 1998. pap. text 14.95 (*1-877864-63-3*) Intercult Pr.

— Good Neighbors: Communicating with the Mexicans. 2nd ed. LC 97-19884. (Interact Ser.). 104p. 1997. pap. text 13.95 (*1-877864-53-6*) Intercult Pr.

— With Respect to the Japanese: A Guide for Americans. LC 81-85730. (InterAct Ser.). 110p. (Orig.). (C). 1984. pap. text 12.95 (*0-933662-49-1*) Intercult Pr.

Condon, John P. Corsairs & Flattops: Marine Carrier Air Warfare, 1944-1945. LC 97-31406. (Illus.). 160p. 1997. 27.95 (*1-55750-127-0*) Naval Inst Pr.

Condon, Judith. Chernobyl & Other Nuclear Accidents. LC 98-16931. (New Perspectives Ser.). 64 p. (J). 1999. 27.12 (*0-8172-5018-2*) Raintree Steck-V.

***Condon, Judith.** The Nineties. LC 99-37295. (Look at Life in Ser.). (Illus.). 48p. (J). (gr. 4-7). 2000. 25.69 (*0-7398-1342-0*) Raintree Steck-V.

Condon, Ken. Sky Scrape, City Scape: Poems of City Life. LC 92-61940. 32p. (J). (gr. 1-5). 1996. 15.95 (*1-56397-179-8*, Wordsong) Boyds Mills Pr.

Condon, Kent. Neighborhoods: A Guide to Communities along the Wasatch Front & Beyond. (Orig.). 1997. pap. 4.95 (*0-9656935-0-3*) Newspaper Agency.

Condon, Marie S., ed. see Deiler, J. Hanno.

Condon, Mark W., jt. auth. see Clyde, Jean A.

Condon, Mary G. Making Disclosure: Ideas & Interests in Ontario Securities Regulation. LC 99-188396. (Illus.). 384p. 1997. text 60.00 (*0-8020-2982-5*) U of Toronto Pr.

Condon, Matthew. Usher. (Orig.). 1993. pap. 14.95 (*0-7022-2421-9*, Pub. by Univ Queensland Pr) Intl Spec Bk.

Condon, Patrick M., ed. Sustainable Urban Landscapes: The Surrey Charette. (Illus.). 100p. 1996. pap. 19.95 (*0-88865-535-5*) UBC Pr.

Condon, Patrick M. & Neckar, Lance, eds. The Avant-Garde & the Landscape - Can They Be Reconciled? Proceedings of the Avant-Garde & the Landscape Conference, University of Minnesota, April 1989. (Illus.). 450p. (Orig.). 1990. pap. 42.95 (*0-9625360-0-8*) Landworks Pr.

***Condon, Pauline & Sangster, Jim.** The Complete Hitchcock. 1999. pap. 23.95 (*0-7535-0362-X*, Pub. by Virgin Bks) London Brdge.

Condon, Phil. River Street: A Novella & Stories. LC 94-10530. 240p. (Orig.). 1994. 22.50 (*0-87074-372-4*); pap. 10.95 (*0-87074-373-2*) SMU Press.

Condon, R. J. Our Pagan Christmas. 2nd ed. (Illus.). 20p. 1989. reprint ed. 3.00 (*0-910309-60-4*, 5064) Am Atheist.

Condon-Rall, Mary Ellen. Disaster on Green Ramp: The Army's Response. 161p. 1996. per. 8.50 (*0-16-048642-4*) USGPO.

***Condon-Rall, Mary Ellen & Cowdrey, Albert L.** Medical Department: Medical Service in the War Against Japan. (CMH Publication Ser.: Vol. 10-24). (Illus.). 505p. 1998. boxed set 37.00 (*0-16-049265-3*) USGPO.

Condon, Richard. The Manchurian Candidate. (Read-Along Ser.). (YA). pap., student ed. 34.95 incl. audio (*0-88432-966-6*, S23910) Audio-Forum.

— The Manchurian Candidate. 320p. 1988. mass mkt. 6.99 (*0-515-09441-2*, Jove) Berkley Pub.

— The Manchurian Candidate. 1993. pap. 5.25 (*0-8222-1339-7*) Dramatists Play.

— Prizzi's Money. 384p. 1995. mass mkt. 5.99 (*0-7860-0167-4*) Kensgtn Pub Corp.

— Prizzi's Money. large type ed. LC 94-4668. 401p. 1994. lib. bdg. 23.95 (*0-7862-0226-2*) Thorndike Pr.

— Winter Kills. large type ed. 419p. 1982. 27.99 (*0-7089-8030-9*) Ulverscroft.

Condon, Richard A. & Kurth, Burton O., eds. Writing from Experience. LC 72-8541. (Essay Index Reprint Ser.). 1977. reprint ed. 21.95 (*0-8369-7310-0*) Ayer.

Condon, Richard G. Inuit Youth: Growth & Change in the Canadian Arctic. (Adolescents in a Changing World Ser.). 275p. 1988. pap. text 20.00 (*0-8135-1364-2*) Rutgers U Pr.

— Inuit Youth: Growth & Change in the Canadian Arctic. LC 86-20257. (Adolescents in a Changing World Ser.). (Illus.). 275p. reprint ed. pap. 85.30 (*0-7837-5663-1*, 205908900005) Bks Demand.

Condon, Richard G., et al. The Northern Copper Inuit: A History. LC 95-39186. (Civilization of the American Indian Ser.: Vol. 220). (Illus.). 240p. (C). 1996. 29.95 (*0-8061-2811-9*, 2811) U of Okla Pr.

— The Northern Copper Inuit: A History. (Illus.). 240p. 1996. text 45.00 (*0-8020-0849-6*) U of Toronto Pr.

Condon, Robert E & DeCosse, Jerome, eds. Surgical Care, No. 2. LC 82-26127. 442p. reprint ed. pap. 137.10 (*0-7837-1483-1*, 205717800023) Bks Demand.

Condon, Robert E. & DeCosse, Jerome J., eds. Surgical Care: Physiologic Approach to Clinical Management. LC 79-21864. 487p. reprint ed. pap. 151.00 (*0-7837-1474-2*, 205716900022) Bks Demand.

Condon, Robert E. & Nyhus, Lloyd M. Manual of Surgical Therapeutics. 7th ed. 480p. 1988. 23.50 (*0-316-15261-7*, Little Brwn Med Div) Lppncott W & W.

— Manual of Surgical Therapeutics. 9th ed. LC 95-333. (Illus.). 439p. 1995. spiral bd. 34.95 (*0-316-15402-4*) Lppncott W & W.

Condon, Robert E. & Nyhus, Lloyd M., eds. Manual of Surgical Therapeutics. 9th ed. LC 95-333. 1996. 34.95 (*0-316-15396-6*, Little Brwn Med Div) Lppncott W & W.

Condon, Robert E., jt. auth. see Nyhus, Lloyd M.

Condon, Robert J. The Fifty Finest Athletes of the Twentieth Century: A Worldwide Reference. LC 89-43643. (Illus.). 160p. 1990. lib. bdg. 32.00 (*0-89950-374-8*) McFarland & Co.

— Great Women Athletes of the Twentieth Century. LC 91-52633. (Illus.). 190p. (YA). (gr. 9-12). 1991. lib. bdg. 32.50 (*0-89950-555-4*) McFarland & Co.

Condon, Sean. Lonely Planet Drive Thru America. (Illus.). 300p. (Orig.). 1998. pap. 12.95 (*0-86442-506-6*) Lonely Planet.

— Sean & David's Long Drive: Travel Literature. 304p. 1996. pap. 10.95 (*0-86442-371-3*) Lonely Planet.

Condon, Sue. Why I Left Boston Movement: (Diary 1984-1992) the Emperor's New Clothes. (Orig.). 1995. pap. 3.00 (*1-56794-103-6*, C-2403) Star Bible.

Condon, Thomas. Dynamic Enneagram: How to Work with Your Personality Style to Truly Grow & Change. 1997. pap. 16.00 (*0-06-251467-9*) Harper SF.

— The Enneagram Movie & Video Guide. (Everyday Enneagram Ser.). 232p. 1994. pap. 14.95 (*1-884305-85-7*) Changeworks.

— The Everyday Enneagram: Tools for Change. (Everyday Enneagram Ser.). 304p. 1995. 16.95 (*1-884305-86-5*) Changeworks.

***Condon, Thomas R.** The Dynamic Enneagram: How to Work with Your Personality Style to Truly Grow & Change. LC 00-40107. 2000. write for info. (*1-55552-101-0*) Metamorphous Pr.

Condon, William & Butler, Wayne. Writing the Information Superhighway. LC 96-43596. 318p. 1997. pap. text 40.00 (*0-205-19575-X*) Allyn.

Condon, William, jt. auth. see Hamp-Lyons, Liz.

Condor, Robert. Michael Jordan's 50 Greatest Games: From His NCAA Championship to Five NBA Titles. LC 98-30392. (Illus.). 224p. 1998. pap. 15.95 (*0-8065-2030-2*) Carol Pub Group.

Condoravdi, Cleo A. Descriptions in Context. Horn, Laurence, ed. LC 97-2202. (Outstanding Dissertations in Linguistics Ser.). 216p. 1997. text 55.00 (*0-8153-2871-0*) Garland.

Condorcet, Jean A. Esquisse d'Un Tableau Historique Des Progres De l'Esprit Humain. (FRE.). viii, 389p. 1981. reprint ed. 105.00 (*3-487-07041-3*) G Olms Pubs.

Condorcet, Marie J. Essai sur l'Application de l'Analyse aux Probabilites des Decisions Rendues a la Pluralite des Voix. LC 75-113124. (FRE.). 495p. 1973. reprint ed. 45.00 (*0-8284-0252-3*) Chelsea Pub.

Condordia Publishing House. Church Year-A Pentecost II Sg. 1996. pap. text 5.50 (*0-570-09448-8*) Concordia.

Condos, Theony. Star Myths of the Greeks & Romans: A Sourcebook. LC 97-29207. (Illus.). 300p. 1997. 35.00 (*1-890482-92-7*) Phanes Pr.

Condos, Theony, tr. Star Myths of the Greeks & Romans: A Sourcebook. LC 97-29207. (Illus.). 300p. 1997. pap. 18.95 (*1-890482-93-5*) Phanes Pr.

Condoyannis, George E. Scientific Russian. LC 77-16615. 238p. 1978. reprint ed. pap. 17.50 (*0-88275-643-5*) Krieger.

Condra, James J. & Slaton, Jeff. Pinpoint Guide to North & South Carolina Civil War Sites. (Pinpoint Guides to Civil War Sites Ser.). (Illus.). 1998. pap. 7.95 (*1-57587-085-1*) Crane Hill AL.

Condra, Anne. Life in the Mezzogiorno: Mongst Gazing Gargoyles. LC 97-92577. (Illus.). 247p. 1997. pap. 14.00 (*0-9660568-0-9*) Messapici Pub.

Condra, Estelle. See the Ocean. LC 94-4234. (Illus.). 32p. (J). (gr. k-3). 1994. 14.95 (*1-57102-005-5*, Ideals Child) Hambleton-Hill.

Condra, James J. & Slaton, Jeff. Pinpoint Guide to Alabama & Florida Civil War Sites. (Pinpoint Guides to Civil War Sites Ser.). (Illus.). 1998. pap. 7.95 (*1-57587-090-8*) Crane Hill AL.

— Pinpoint Guide to Atlanta: The March to the Sea. (Pinpoint Guides to Civil War Sites Ser.). (Illus.). 1998. pap. 7.95 (*1-57587-086-X*) Crane Hill AL.

— Pinpoint Guide to Mississippi Civil War Sites. (Pinpoint Guides to Civil War Sites Ser.). (Illus.). 1998. pap. 7.95 (*1-57587-089-4*) Crane Hill AL.

— Pinpoint Guide to the Atlanta Campaign. (Pinpoint Guides to Civil War Sites Ser.). (Illus.). 1998. pap. 7.95 (*1-57587-087-8*) Crane Hill AL.

— Pinpoint Guide to Virginia - From Richmond to Appomattox. (Pinpoint Guides to Civil War Sites Ser.). (Illus.). 1998. pap. 7.95 (*1-57587-088-6*) Crane Hill AL.

Condra, Lloyd N. Reliability Improvement with Design of Experiments. (Quality & Reliability Ser.: Vol. 41). (Illus.). 400p. 1993. text 75.00 (*0-8247-8888-5*) Dekker.

Condrau, G., ed. Phaenomenologie und Psychotheraprutische Praxis Vol. 12, Nos. 1-4, 1995: Journal: Daseinsanalyse. (Journal Ser.: Vol. 12, No. 1-4, 1995). (Illus.). 250p. 1995. pap. 73.25 (*3-8055-6230-6*) S Karger.

— Psychotherapie - Heilkunst Oder Heilslehre? Reprint from Journal: Daseinsanalyse, Vol. 9, No. 2-3, 1992. (Illus.). 212p. 1992. reprint ed. pap. 47.00 (*3-8055-5681-0*) S Karger.

Condray, Kathleen, jt. ed. see Lalande, John F., II.

Condray, Sydney. Assembled in Christ: Forty-Four Liturgies with Lay Presiders. LC 93-60025. 240p. (Orig.). 1993. pap. 29.95 (*0-89622-560-7*) Twenty-Third.

***Condre, R. Gates.** The Long Journey. unabridged ed. (Illus.). 190p. 2000. pap. 12.00 (*0-9679040-3-X*) Exlent Pubng.

Condrell, Kenneth N. How Not to Raise a Brat. 200p. 1985. reprint ed. pap. 12.95 (*0-933705-00-X*) Bonner Pr.

Condrell, Kenneth N. & Small, Linda L. Be a Great Divorced Dad. LC 97-35163. 160p. 1997. pap. 11.95 (*0-312-15549-2*) St Martin.

— Wimpy Parents: From Toddler to Teen - How Not to Raise a Brat. LC 97-39547. 208p. (Orig.). 1998. mass mkt. 13.99 (*0-446-67367-6*, Pub. by Warner Bks) Little.

Condren. Satire, Lies, & Politics. LC 97-7121. 256p. 1997. text 59.95 (*0-312-17515-9*) St Martin.

Condren, Conal. The Language of Political Theory in Seventeenth-Century England. LC 94-5979. 1994. text 65.00 (*0-312-12183-0*) St Martin.

— The Status & Appraisal of Classic Texts: An Essay on Political Theory, Its Inheritance, & the History of Ideas. LC 83-43065. 318p. 1985. reprint ed. pap. 98.60 (*0-608-03314-6*, 206402600008) Bks Demand.

Condren, Conal & Cousins, A. D. The Political Identity of Andrew Marvell. 256p. 1990. text 78.95 (*0-85967-818-0*, Pub. by Scolar Pr) Ashgate Pub Co.

Condren, Conal, ed. see Lawson, George.

Condren, Conel. Thomas Hobbes. LC 99-54906. 2000. 25.95 (*0-8057-1697-1*) S&S Trade.

Condren, Edward I. Chaucer & the Energy of Creation: The Design & the Organization of the Canterbury Tales. LC 99-18810. 1999. 49.95 (*0-8130-1679-7*) U Press Fla.

Condrescu, Andrei, et al. Walker Evans - Signs. LC 98-4270. (Illus.). 96p. 1998. 19.95 (*0-89236-376-2*, Pub. by J P Getty Trust) OUP.

Condrey, Jullianne. Faithful to the Cause. 78p. (J). 1999. pap. 9.99 (*0-88092-403-9*, 403-9) Royal Fireworks.

Condrey, Stephen B. Handbook of Human Resource Management in Government. LC 98-9093. 656p. 1998. 59.95 (*0-7879-4099-2*) Jossey-Bass.

***Condrill, Jo.** A Millennium Primer: Take Charge of Your Life. LC 99-91315. (Illus.). xv, 193p. 1999. 24.95 (*0-9661414-5-8*) GoalMinds.

Condrill, Jo & Bough, Bennie. 101 Ways to Improve Your Communication Skills Instantly. LC 97-97110. (Illus.). xii, 116p. 1998. pap. 14.95 (*0-9661414-7-4*) GoalMinds.

— 101 Ways to Improve Your Communication Skills Instantly. rev. ed. LC 99-90350. (Illus.). xii, 116p. 1999. reprint ed. pap. 14.95 (*0-9661414-9-0*) GoalMinds.

Condron, Barbara. The Dreamer's Dictionary. LC 95-230931. 308p. 1994. pap. 15.00 (*0-944386-16-4*) SOM Pub.

— First Opinion: Wholistic Health Care for the 21st Century. 320p. (Orig.). 1998. pap. 15.00 (*0-944386-18-0*) SOM Pub.

— Going in Circles: Search for a Satisfying Relationship. 138p. (C). 1987. reprint ed. pap. 5.95 (*0-944386-00-8*) SOM Pub.

— Kundalini Rising: Mastering Creative Energies. 224p. (Orig.). (C). 1992. pap. 13.00 (*0-944386-13-X*) SOM Pub.

— Spiritual Renaissance: Evaluating Your Consciousness for the Common Good. 1999. pap. 15.00 (*0-944386-22-9*) SOM Pub.

— What Will I Do Tomorrow? Probing Depression. 111p. (C). 1987. reprint ed. pap. 4.95 (*0-944386-02-4*) SOM Pub.

— Who Were Those Strangers in My Dream? 129p. (C). 1988. reprint ed. pap. 4.95 (*0-944386-08-3*) SOM Pub.

Condron, Barbara, ed. Uncommon Knowledge: An Introduction to Past Life & Health Readings. 208p. (Orig.). 1996. pap. 13.00 (*0-944386-19-9*) SOM Pub.

— The Work of the Soul: Past Life Recall & Spiritual Enlightenment. LC 97-104178. 208p. (Orig.). 1996. pap. 13.00 (*0-944386-17-2*) SOM Pub.

Condron, Bob. Easy Money. (Orig.). 1999. pap. text 10.95 (*0-352-33442-8*) London Brdge.

Condron, Daniel R. Dreams of the Soul: The Yogi Sutras of Patanjali. 208p. (C). 1991. pap. 9.95 (*0-944386-11-3*) SOM Pub.

— Permanent Healing. 224p. (Orig.). (C). 1992. pap. 13.00 (*0-944386-12-1*) SOM Pub.

— Superconscious Meditation: Kundalini & the Understanding of the Whole Mind. LC 99-175267. 1998. pap. text 13.00 (*0-944386-21-0*) SOM Pub.

— The Universal Language of Mind: The Book of Matthew Interpreted. 310p. 1994. pap. 13.00 (*0-944386-15-6*) SOM Pub.

Condry, John. The Psychology of Television. 336p. (C). 1989. pap. 39.95 (*0-8058-0621-0*) L Erlbaum Assocs.

Condry, Steve, ed. see Long, Harold & Wheeler, Allen.

Condry, William. Wales. (Illus.). 239p. (C). 1993. pap. 30.00 (*0-86383-781-6*, Pub. by Gomer Pr) St Mut.

— Wales, Vol. XII. 239p. 1993. pap. 29.95 (*0-8464-4649-9*) Beekman Pubs.

— A Welsh Country Diary. 176p. 1993. pap. 23.00 (*0-86383-872-3*, Pub. by Gomer Pr) St Mut.

— Welsh Country Essays. 136p. 1996. pap. 37.95 (*0-8464-4605-7*) Beekman Pubs.

— Wildlife: My Life. 216p. 1995. pap. 29.95 (*0-8464-4657-X*) Beekman Pubs.

Conduit, Andy, jt. auth. see Conduit, Anne.

Conduit, Anne & Conduit, Andy. Educating Andy: The Experiences of a Western Family in the Japanese Elementary School System. Sagar, Hilary, ed. (Illus.). 224p. 1996. pap. 12.00 (*4-7700-1921-1*) Kodansha.

Conduit, Brian. The Best Pathfinder Walks. (Ordnance Survey Pathfinder Guides Ser.). (Illus.). 120p. (Orig.). 1995. 24.95 (*0-7117-0813-4*, Pub. by JARR UK) Seven Hills Bk.

Conduit, Brian, compiled by. Chilterns & Thames Valley Walks. (Ordnance Survey Pathfinder Guides Ser.). (Illus.). 80p. (Orig.). 1994. pap. 14.95 (*0-7117-0674-3*) Seven Hills Bk.

Conduit, Brian, ed. Isle of Wight Walks. (Ordnance Survey Pathfinder Guides Ser.). (Illus.). 80p. (Orig.). 1994. pap. 14.95 (*0-7117-0672-7*) Seven Hills Bk.

Condy, Roy, jt. auth. see Sadu, Itah.

Cone & Hayes. Envir. Prob behav Solutions. 1980. pap. text 9.75 (*0-8185-0392-0*) Brooks-Cole.

Cone & Wilmore. By the Yard Fabric & Trim Source Book, 2 vols. 1995. 90.00 (*0-614-06058-3*) Bureau Style.

Cone, Arthur L. Fishing Basics: A Prize Catch for Fresh & Saltwater Fishermen (& Women) LC 98-11508. 256p. 1998. 19.98 (*1-57912-021-0*) Blck Dog & Leventhal.

Cone, Arthur L., Jr. Solid Gold Fund Raising Letters. LC 87-81191. (Illus.). 160p. 1987. 22.95 (*0-930807-04-9*, 600181) Fund Raising.

Cone, Billy. Sixty Days Under the Influence - A Photo Journal Through France. LC 97-65961. (Illus.). 135p. (Orig.). 1997. pap. 24.95 (*1-57197-064-9*) Pentland Pr.

Cone, Carl B. The University of Kentucky: A Pictorial History. LC 89-36823. 248p. 1989. text 35.00 (*0-8131-1696-1*) U Pr of Ky.

Cone, E. Christopher. Automotive Operation & Maintenance. rev. ed. 300p. 1991. 14.95 (*0-86619-310-3*) Vols Tech Asst.

Cone, Edward T. Music: A View from Delft: Selected Essays. Morgan, Robert P., ed. LC 88-20659. (Illus.). 352p. 1989. pap. text 22.00 (*0-226-11470-8*) U Ch Pr.

C

— Music: A View from Delft: Selected Essays. Morgan, Robert P., ed. LC 88-20659. (Illus.). 344p. 1998. lib. bdg. 78.00 (*0-226-11469-4*) U Ch Pr.

— Musical Form & Musical Performance. LC 68-11157. (Illus.). (C). 1968. pap. text 12.50 (*0-393-09767-6*) Norton.

Cone, Edward T., ed. see Berlioz, Hector.

Cone, Eric, et al. Planning for Windows 2000. LC 99-60311. (Illus.). 415p. 1999. pap. 29.99 (*0-7357-0048-6*) New Riders Pub.

Cone, Faye K. Making Sense of Menopause: Over One Hundred Fifty Women & Experts Share Their Wisdom, Experience & Common Sense Advice. LC 93-2526. 384p. 1993. per. 13.00 (*0-671-78638-5*, Fireside) S&S Trade Pap.

Cone, James & Bowler, Rosemarie, eds. Occupational Medicine Secrets. LC 99-19893. (Secrets Ser.). (Illus.). 400p. 1999. pap. text 39.00 (*1-56053-161-4*) Hanley & Belfus.

Cone, James H. Black Theology & Black Power. LC 97-220426. 200p. (Orig.). 1997. reprint ed. pap. 15.00 (*1-57075-157-9*) Orbis Bks.

— Black Theology of Liberation: Twentieth Anniversary with Critical Responses. LC 90-43041. 1990. pap. 15.00 (*0-88344-685-5*) Orbis Bks.

— For My People: Black Theology & the Black Church. LC 84-5195. (Bishop Henry McNeal Turner Studies in North American Black Religion: Vol. 1). 288p. (Orig.). 1984. pap. 17.00 (*0-88344-106-3*) Orbis Bks.

— God of the Oppressed. LC 97-30468. 280p. 1997. reprint ed. pap. 16.00 (*1-57075-158-7*) Orbis Bks.

— Martin & Malcolm & America: A Dream or a Nightmare. LC 90-14159. (Illus.). 358p. 1992. pap. 16.00 (*0-88344-824-6*) Orbis Bks.

— My Soul Looks Back. 144p. 1986. pap. 13.50 (*0-88344-355-4*) Orbis Bks.

***Cone, James H.** Risks of Faith: The Emergence of a Black Theology of Liberation, 1968-1998. 2000. pap. 15.00 (*0-8070-0951-2*) Beacon Pr.

— Risks of Faith: The Emergence of Black Theology of Liberation, 1968-1998. LC 99-28327. 240p. 1999. 25.00 (*0-8070-0950-4*) Beacon Pr.

Cone, James H. Speaking the Truth: Ecumenism, Liberation & Black Theology. LC 98-47100. 160p. 1999. pap. 15.00 (*1-57075-241-9*) Orbis Bks.

— The Spirituals & the Blues. 1984. 10.95 (*0-8164-2073-4*, SP74) Harper SF.

— The Spirituals & the Blues. 2nd ed. LC 91-19267. 152p. 1992. reprint ed. pap. 13.00 (*0-88344-843-2*) Orbis Bks.

Cone, James H. & Wilmore, Gayraud S. Black Theology, Set, Vol. 1: 1966-1979-Vol. 2: 1980-1992. 2nd ed. LC 92-44927. 1993. boxed set 42.00 (*0-88344-868-8*) Orbis Bks.

— Black Theology: A Documentary History, 1966-1979, Vol. 1. 2nd abr. rev. ed. LC 92-44927. 400p. 1993. pap. 23.00 (*0-88344-853-X*) Orbis Bks.

— Black Theology Vol. 2: A Documentary History, 1980-1992. LC 79-12747. 400p. (Orig.). 1993. pap. 23.00 (*0-88344-773-8*) Orbis Bks.

Cone, James H., jt. ed. see Wilmore, Gayraud S.

Cone, Jane H. Walter Darby Bannard. LC 73-87987. (Illus.). 1973. pap. 2.98 (*0-912298-34-0*) Baltimore Mus.

***Cone, John D.** Evaluating Outcomes: Empirical Tools for Effective Practice. LC 00-40608. 2000. write for info. (*1-55798-723-8*) Am Psychol.

Cone, John D. & Foster, Sharon L. Dissertations & Theses from Start to Finish: Psychology & Related Fields. LC 92-38195. 349p. (Orig.). 1993. pap. text 24.95 (*1-55798-194-9*) Am Psychol.

Cone, John F. Adelina Patti: Queen of Hearts. LC 92-39331. (Opera Biography Ser.: No. 3). (Illus.). 524p. 1993. 39.95 (*0-931340-60-8*, Amadeus Pr) Timber.

Cone, Joseph. A Common Fate: Endangered Salmon & the People of the Pacific Northwest. rev. ed. LC 96-26794. (Illus.). 352p. 1996. pap. 16.95 (*0-87071-391-4*) Oreg St U Pr.

Cone, Joseph & Ridlington, Sandy, eds. The Northwest Salmon Crisis: A Documentary History. (Illus.). 320p. (C). 1996. 29.95 (*0-87071-390-6*) Oreg St U Pr.

***Cone, Joseph & Ridlington, Sandy, eds.** The Northwest Salmon Crisis: A Documentary History. (Illus.). 384p. 2000. pap. 22.95 (*0-87071-472-4*) Oreg St U Pr.

Cone, Judson P. Heart: An Owner's Manual. 69p. (Orig.). 1974. pap. 1.95 (*0-685-52022-6*) Charing Cross.

— Tummy: An Owner's Manual. 63p. (Orig.). 1974. pap. 1.95 (*0-89074-008-9*) Charing Cross.

— Vagina: An Owner's Manual. 87p. (Orig.). 1974. pap. 1.95 (*0-89074-007-0*) Charing Cross.

Cone, Kate. What's Brewing in New England? LC 97-313. (Illus.). 160p. (Orig.). 1997. pap. 12.95 (*0-89272-387-4*) Down East.

Cone, Marcia, jt. auth. see Snyder, Thelma.

Cone, Margaret & Gombrich, Richard F., eds. The Perfect Generosity of Price Vessantara: A Buddhist Epic. (Illus.). 160p. 1977. text 48.00 (*0-19-826530-1*) OUP.

Cone, Michele. Artists under Vichy: A Case of Prejudice & Persecution. (Illus.). 300p. 1992. text 39.50 (*0-691-04088-5*, Pub. by Princeton U Pr) Cal Prin Full Svc.

Cone, Molly. About Belonging. (Hear, O Israel Ser.: Bk. 3). (Illus.). 64p. (J). (gr. k-3). 1972. pap. 6.00 (*0-8074-0234-6*, 101083) UAHC.

— About Learning. (Hear, O Israel Ser.: Bk. 2). (Illus.). (J). (gr. k-3). 1972. pap. 6.00 (*0-8074-0233-8*, 101082) UAHC.

— Come Back, Salmon: How a Group of Dedicated Kids Adopted Pigeon Creek & Brought It Back to Life. (Illus.). (J). (gr. 5). 1995. 9.32 (*0-395-73252-2*) HM.

— Come Back, Salmon: How a Group of Dedicated Kids Adopted Pigeon Creek & Brought It Back to Life. (Illus.). 48p. (J). (gr. k-3). 1992. 16.95 (*0-87156-572-2*, Pub. by Sierra Club Childrens) Little.

— Come Back, Salmon: How a Group of Dedicated Kids Adopted Pigeon Creek & Brought It Back to Life. LC 91-29023. (Illus.). 48p. (J). (gr. k-3). 1994. pap. 7.95 (*0-87156-489-0*, Pub. by Sierra Club Childrens) Little.

Cone, Molly. Come Back, Salmon: How a Group of Dedicated Kids Adopted Pigeon Creek & Brought It Back to Life. LC 91-29023. 1992. 13.15 (*0-606-06287-4*, Pub. by Turtleback) Demco.

Cone, Molly. Come Back, Salmon: How a Group of Dedicated Kids Adopted Pigeon Creek & Brought It Back to Life. large type ed. (Illus.). 70p. (J). (gr. 5). 17.50 (*0-614-20582-4*, L-38190-00 APHB) Am Printing Hse.

— First I Say the Shema. (Hear, O Israel Ser.: Bk. 1). (Illus.). (J). (gr. k-3). 1984. reprint ed. pap. text 6.00 (*0-8074-0232-X*, 101081) UAHC.

— Hello, Hello, Are You There, God? LC 98-54754. (Illus.). viii, 55p. (J). (gr. k-5). 1999. pap. 12.00 (*0-8074-0648-1*, 102553) UAHC.

***Cone, Molly.** Hello, Hello, Are You There God? (Illus.). (J). (ps-2). 1999. pap., teacher ed. 15.00 (*0-8074-0655-4*, 208048) UAHC.

Cone, Molly. Listen to the Trees: Jews & the Earth. (Illus.). (Orig.). (J). (gr. 4-6). 1995. pap. text 14.95 (*0-8074-0536-1*, 104064) UAHC.

— Mishmash, 001. 128p. (J). (gr. 4-7). 1962. 16.00 (*0-395-06711-1*) HM.

***Cone, Molly.** Mishmash. (Illus.). 128p. (J). 2000. pap. 4.95 (*0-618-05482-0*) HM.

Cone, Molly. Mishmash & the Sauerkraut Mystery. (Illus.). (J). (gr. 4-6). 1974. pap. 0.95 (*0-395-18556-4*) HM.

***Cone, Molly.** Mishmash & the Substitute Teacher. (Illus.). 96p. (J). 2000. pap. 4.95 (*0-618-05483-9*) HM.

Cone, Molly. Purim. LC 67-10071. (Harper Holiday Ser.). (Illus.). (J). (gr. k-3). 1967. lib. bdg. 10.89 (*0-690-65922-9*) HarpC Child Bks.

— The Story of Shabbat. LC 98-16626. (Illus.). 40p. (J). (gr. 2-5). 2000. 14.95 (*0-06-027944-3*); lib. bdg. 14.89 (*0-06-027945-1*) HarpC Child Bks.

— Who Knows Ten? Children's Tales of the Ten Commandments. rev. ed. LC 97-38462. (Illus.). 96p. (J). (gr. k-6). 1997. pap. 12.00 (*0-8074-0080-7*, 102551) UAHC.

Cone, Ollie, ed. see Papkoff, Lee.

Cone, Patrick. Grand Canyon. LC 93-31066. (Nature in Action Ser.). (Illus.). 48p. (J). (gr. 1-4). 1994. lib. bdg. 19.93 (*0-87614-820-8*, Carolrhoda) Lerner Pub.

— Grand Canyon. (Illus.). 48p. (J). (gr. 1-4). 1994. pap. 7.95 (*0-87614-628-0*, First Ave Edns) Lerner Pub.

— Wildfire. LC 95-40847. (Nature in Action Ser.). (J). 1996. 14.95 (*0-87614-936-0*, Carolrhoda) Lerner Pub.

— Wildfire. (Illus.). 48p. 1996. pap. text 7.95 (*1-57505-027-7*, Carolrhoda) Lerner Pub.

Cone, Paul R., et al. Strategic Resource Management: Allocation, Deployment, & Productive Use of Resources for Improved Performance Results. LC 85-73592. (Illus.). 420p. (C). 1986. text 32.99 (*0-943872-52-9*) Andrews Univ Pr.

Cone, Polly, ed. The Jack & Belle Linsky Collection in the Metropolitan Museum of Art. (Illus.). 364p. 1984. 19.95 (*0-87099-370-4*, 0-8109-6463-5) Metro Mus Art.

Cone, Richard A. & Dowling, John E., eds. Membrane Transduction Mechanisms. fac. ed. LC 78-65280. (Society of General Physiologists Ser.: No. 33). (Illus.). 248p. pap. 76.90 (*0-7837-7257-2*, 204704800005) Bks Demand.

Cone, Robert J. How the New Technology Works: A Guide to High-Tech Concepts. 2nd ed. LC 98-9169. (Illus.). 144p. 1998. pap. 32.50 (*1-57356-138-X*) Oryx Pr.

— Key to High-Tech. LC 87-81270. 153p. (Orig.). 1987. pap. 10.95 (*0-943075-17-3*) Galcon Pr.

Cone, Roger D. The Melanocortin Receptors. (Receptors Ser.). 568p. 2000. 145.00 (*0-89603-579-4*) Humana.

Cone, Stephen D. Biographical & Historical Sketches: Narrative of Hamilton & Its Residents, from 1792 to 1896. (Illus.). 468p. 1997. reprint ed. lib. bdg. 49.50 (*0-8328-6321-1*) Higginson Bk Co.

Cone, Sydney M. & ABA, Committee on Comparative Procedure & Practice. The Regulation of Foreign Lawyers. 3rd ed. LC 84-72263. 110p. 1984. pap. 15.00 (*0-89707-155-7*, 525-0035) Amer Bar Assn.

Cone, T., et al. Plays from Playwrights Horizons. 336p. (Orig.). 1987. pap. 14.95 (*0-88145-047-2*) Broadway Play.

Cone, Theresa P., et al. Interdisciplinary Teaching Through Physical Education. LC 98-7515. (Illus.). 280p. 1998. pap. text 27.00 (*0-88011-502-5*, BCON0502) Human Kinetics.

Cone, Thomas E., Jr. History of American Pediatrics. 1980. 27.00 (*0-316-15289-7*, Little Brwn Med Div) Lppncott W & W.

Cone, W. W. Cone: Some Account of the Cone Family in America, Principally the Descendants of Daniel Cone, Who Settled in Haddam, Conn., in 1662. (Illus.). 546p. 1992. reprint ed. pap. 83.00 (*0-8328-2312-0*); reprint ed. lib. bdg. 93.00 (*0-8328-2311-2*) Higginson Bk Co.

— Some Account of the Cone Family in America, Principally of the Descendants of Daniel Cone Who Settled in Haddam, Connecticut, in 1662. (Illus.). 547p. 1989. reprint ed. pap. 82.00 (*0-8328-0419-3*); reprint ed. lib. bdg. 90.00 (*0-8328-0418-5*) Higginson Bk Co.

Cone, W. W. & Root, G. A. Bishop: Records of the Descendants of John Bishop. (Illus.). 277p. 1991. reprint ed. pap. 42.50 (*0-8328-2098-9*); reprint ed. lib. bdg. 52.50 (*0-8328-2097-0*) Higginson Bk Co.

Cone, William. Stop Memory Loss: How to Fight Forgetfulness over Forty. LC 97-92937. 304p. (Orig.). 1997. pap. write for info. (*0-9655563-9-5*) Matteson Bks.

Cone, William P., jt. auth. see Randle, Kevin D.

Conefrey, Mick & Jordan, Tim. Icemen: A History of the Arctic & Its Explorers. (Illus.). 208p. 1999. 24.95 (*1-57500-038-5*, Pub. by TV Bks) HarpC.

Conejo, Carlos, jt. auth. see Whisler, Kirk.

Conejo Valley Genealogical Society, Inc. Staff. The Surname Register: Births, Marriages & Deaths of 15,000 Ancestors Researched by the Members of the Conejo Valley Genealogical Society. 2nd rev. ed. Marlatt, William P., ed. 1989. pap. text. write for info. (*0-9622138-0-2*) Conejo Val Geneal.

Conekin, Becky, et al, eds. Moments of Modernity? Reconstructing Britain, 1945-1964. (Illus.). 304p. 1998. text 50.00 (*1-85489-104-9*); pap. text 23.00 (*1-85489-105-7*) NYU Pr.

Coneley, Marshall S. I Did Try - Honestly I Did. 97p. (C). 1989. text 65.00 (*1-872795-94-3*, Pub. by Pentland Pr) St Mut.

Conely, James H. Organ Music for Celebration & Praise. LC 74-236614. 48p. reprint ed. pap. 30.00 (*0-7837-5882-0*, 204560200006) Bks Demand.

Conen, Judith L., jt. auth. see Ghez, Andrea.

Conen, W. & Neumann, G., eds. Coordination Technology for Collaborative Applications: Organizations, Processes, & Agents, Vol. 136. LC 98-10341. (Lecture Notes in Computer Science Ser.: Vol. 1364). viii, 282p. 1998. pap. 49.00 (*3-540-64170-X*) Spr-Verlag.

Coner-Edwards, Alice F. & Spurlock, Jeanne, eds. Black Families in Crisis: The Middle Class. LC 88-14642. 320p. 1988. text 35.95 (*0-87630-524-9*) Brunner-Mazel.

Coner, Kenyetta. The Mockingbirds. Richards, Lyn, ed. LC 98-93014. 250p. 1988. pap. 11.00 (*0-9665005-0-4*) Fifty-Two Wks.

Conerly, Donna. Forrest General Medical Center: Advanced Medical Terminology & Transcription Course. (Medical Assisting Ser.). 1986. 299.95 (*0-538-11316-2*) S-W Pub.

Conerly, Donna & Lott, Wanda. Forrest General Medical Center: Advanced Medical Terminology & Transcription Course. (C). 1986. pap. 32.95 (*0-538-11310-3*, K31) S-W Pub.

Conerly, Porter, et al, eds. Text & Concordances of Macer Herbolario Seville Colombina Manuscript 7-6-27. (Medieval Spanish Medical Texts Ser.: No. 7). 10p. 1986. 10.00 incl. fiche (*0-942260-78-3*) Hispanic Seminary.

Cones, Harold, jt. auth. see Bryant, John.

Cones, Harold N. & Bryant, John. Zenith Radio: The Early Years, 1919-1935. LC 97-24669. 223p. 1997. pap. 29.95 (*0-7643-0367-8*) Schiffer.

Cones, Harold N., jt. auth. see Bryant, John H.

Cones, James H., III, jt. auth. see White, Joseph L.

Cones, John W. The Feature Film Distribution Deal: A Critical Analysis of the Single Most Important Film Industry Agreement. LC 96-33733. (Illus.). 380p. (C). 1997. 49.95 (*0-8093-2081-9*); pap. 34.95 (*0-8093-2082-7*) S Ill U Pr.

— Film Finance & Distribution: A Dictionary of Terms. LC 92-23667. 638p. 1992. 24.95 (*1-879505-12-6*) Silman James Pr.

— Film Industry Contracts. (Hollywood Ser.). 640p. 1996. pap. 89.95 (*1-890341-00-2*) Rivas Canyon.

— 43 Ways to Finance Your Feature Film: A Comprehensive Analysis of Film Finance. rev. ed. LC 97-50007. 252p. 1998. pap. 16.95 (*0-8093-2202-1*) S Ill U Pr.

— Forty Three Ways to Finance Your Feature Film: A Comprehensive Analysis of Film Finance. LC 94-15308. 184p. (C). 1995. 24.95 (*0-8093-1968-3*) S Ill U Pr.

— Hollywood Corruption. (Hollywood Ser.). 205p. 1996. pap. 22.95 (*1-890341-08-8*) Rivas Canyon.

— How the Movie Wars Were Won. (Hollywood Ser.). 305p. 1996. pap. 27.95 (*1-890341-01-0*) Rivas Canyon.

— Legacy of the Hollywood Empire. (Hollywood Ser.). 335p. 1996. pap. 24.95 (*1-890341-07-X*) Rivas Canyon.

— Motion Picture Biographies: The Hollywood Spin on Historical Figures. (Hollywood Ser.). 283p. 1996. pap. 23.95 (*1-890341-04-5*) Rivas Canyon.

— Motion Picture Industry Reform. (Hollywood Ser.). 208p. 1996. pap. 22.50 (*1-890341-09-6*) Rivas Canyon.

— Patterns of Bias in Motion Picture Content. (Hollywood Ser.). (Illus.). 230p. 1996. pap. 24.95 (*1-890341-02-9*) Rivas Canyon.

— Politics, Movies & the Role of Government. (Hollywood Ser.). 298p. 1996. pap. 23.95 (*1-890341-05-3*) Rivas Canyon.

— A Study in Motion Picture Propaganda: Hollywood's Preferred Movie Messages. (Hollywood Ser.). 390p. 1996. pap. 28.95 (*1-890341-03-7*) Rivas Canyon.

— What's Really Going on in Hollywood. 318p. 1997. pap. 26.95 (*1-890341-10-X*) Rivas Canyon.

— Who Really Controls Hollywood? (Hollywood Ser.). 211p. 1996. pap. 21.95 (*1-890341-06-1*) Rivas Canyon.

Conesa, Eduardo R. The Argentine Economy: Policy Reform for Development. LC 89-8486. 144p. (Orig.). (C). 1989. pap. text 21.00 (*0-8191-7410-6*); lib. bdg. 42.00 (*0-8191-7409-2*) U Pr of Amer.

Conetta, Carl & Knight, Charles. After Desert Storm: Rethinking U. S. Defense Requirements. (Briefing Reports: No. 2). 26p. 1991. reprint ed. pap. 6.00 (*1-881677-00-1*) Commonwlth Inst.

— Defense Procurement Policy for the 1990s: Selected Army & Air Force Systems. (PDA Briefing Reports: No. 1). 43p. 1991. reprint ed. pap. 10.00 (*1-881677-03-6*) Commonwlth Inst.

— Defense Sufficiency & Cooperation: A U. S. Military Posture for the Post-Cold War Era. (Project on Defense Alternatives Briefing Report Ser.: Vol. 9). 1998. pap. 10.00 (*1-881677-07-9*) Commonwlth Inst.

— Reasonable Force Pt. 1: Adapting the U. S. Army & Marine Corps to the New Era, Threat Environment & Force Size Requirement. (Briefing Reports: No. 3). 82p. 1992. reprint ed. pap. 18.00 (*1-881677-01-X*) Commonwlth Inst.

— Vital Force: A Proposal for the Overhaul of the U. N. Peace Operating System & for the Creation of a U. N. Legion. 141p. 1995. pap. 22.00 (*1-881677-05-2*) Commonwlth Inst.

Conetta, Carl, et al. Toward Defensive Restructuring in the Middle East. (PDA Monograph: No. 1). 39p. 1991. reprint ed. pap. 8.00 (*1-881677-02-8*) Commonwlth Inst.

Coney, jt. auth. see Schultz.

Coney, Bettye S. My Soul Speaks Truth. (Illus.). 119p. (Orig.). 1996. pap. 14.95 (*0-9648337-0-0*) SteBreCo.

Coney, Judith. Sahaja Yoga. (Studies in New Religious Movements: Vol. 1). 288p. 1998. text 48.00 (*0-7007-1061-2*, Pub. by Curzon Pr Ltd) UH Pr.

Coney, M. & Holden, Paul. The Moon Looked Down & Laughed. pap. 9.95 (*1-56097-263-7*, Pub. by Fantagraph Bks) Seven Hills Bk.

Coney, Nancy S., jt. auth. see Mackey, Wade C.

Coney, Norma. The Complete Candlemaker: Techniques, Projects & Inspirations. LC 97-3615. (Illus.). 128p. 1997. 24.95 (*1-887374-42-6*, Pub. by Lark Books) Random.

— The Complete Candlemaker: Techniques, Projects & Inspirations. Morgenthal, Deborah, ed. LC 97-3615. (Illus.). 128p. 1997. pap. 16.95 (*1-887374-50-7*, Pub. by Lark Books) Random.

— Complete Candlemaker Book & Kit. LC 97-3615. 1997. 36.95 (*1-57990-006-2*) Lark Books.

— The Complete Soapmaker: Tips, Techniques & Recipes for Luxurious Handmade Soaps. (Illus.). 128p. 1997. pap. 14.95 (*0-8069-4869-8*) Sterling.

— Natural Decor: The Arranger's Garden & Project Book. LC 97-31825. (Illus.). 176p. 1998. 30.00 (*1-55821-664-2*); pap. 19.95 (*1-55821-541-7*) Lyons Pr.

Coney, Norma J. The Kitchen Garden: Fresh Ideas for Luscious Vegetables, Herbs, Flowers, & Fruit. LC 97-33083. 1998. write for info. (*1-56799-532-2*, Friedman-Fairfax) M Friedman Pub Grp Inc.

Coney, Sandra. The Menopause Industry: How the Medical Establishment Exploits Women. LC 94-11673. (Illus.). 384p. 1994. 24.95 (*0-89793-161-0*); pap. 14.95 (*0-89793-160-2*) Hunter Hse.

***Confair, Dana.** Learning to Love. LC 99-64078. 192p. 1999. pap. 12.95 (*1-56167-519-9*) Am Literary Pr.

Confalonieri, Pierluigi. The Clock of Vipassana Has Struck: A Tribute to the Saintly Life & Legacy of a Lay Master of Vipassana Meditation: Sayagyi U Ba Khin, 1899-1971. LC 99-67273. 256p. 1999. pap. 14.00 (*0-9649484-6-X*) Vipassana Res Pubns.

Confederate States of America - Constitutional Con. Constitution of the Confederate States of America with the Inaugural Address of President Jefferson Davis. Davis, Jefferson, ed. 1987. pap. 2.95 (*0-89979-005-4*) British Am Bks.

Confederate States of America, Congress Staff. Laws & Joint Resolutions of the Last Session of the Confederate Congress. reprint ed. 39.50 (*0-404-05222-3*) AMS Pr.

Confederated Salish & Kootenai Tribes of the Flathead Reservation Staff, jt. auth. see Kallowat, Howard.

Confederation of British Industry Staff. The Road to Recovery. LC 77-357052. 72p. 1976. write for info. (*0-85201-123-7*) Confed Brit Indus.

Confer, Chris. Geometry, Grades 1-2. (Math by All Means Ser.). (Illus.). 200p. 1994. pap. text 23.95 (*0-941355-08-X*) Math Solns Pubns.

Confer, Dennis W. Hunt Alaska Now: Self-Guiding for Trophy Moose & Caribou. rev. ed. LC 96-62088. (Illus.). 320p. 1999. 39.95 (*0-9656286-8-X*) Wily Ventures.

***Confer, Dennis W.** Hunt Alaska Now: Self-Guiding for Trophy Moose & Caribou. rev. ed. LC 96-62088. (Illus.). 320p. 1999. pap. 26.95 (*0-9656286-6-3*) Wily Ventures.

Confer, Grayce. Quilt of Many Colors: A Collage of Prose & Poetry. 116p. (Orig.). 1990. pap. 7.99 (*0-8341-1358-9*) Beacon Hill.

Confer, Grayce B. Alzheimer's ... Another Opportunity to Love. 64p. 1992. pap. 6.99 (*0-8341-1403-8*) Beacon Hill.

Confer, James A. Pele's Atlantis. (Illus.). v, 300p. 1998. pap. 14.95 (*0-9660391-0-6*) RTS Pub.

Confer, Robert G. Workplace Health Protection. 560p. 1994. lib. bdg. 104.95 (*0-87371-387-7*, L387) Lewis Pubs.

Confer, Robert G. & Confer, Thomas R. Occupational Health & Safety: Terms, Definitions, & Abbreviations. 2nd ed. LC 99-12086. 500p. 1999. 29.95 (*1-56670-361-1*) Lewis Pubs.

Confer, Robert G. & Confer, Thomas R., eds. Occupational Health & Safety Terms, Definitions, & Abbreviations. 224p. 1994. lib. bdg. 65.00 (*1-56670-077-9*, L1077) Lewis Pubs.

Confer, Thomas R., jt. auth. see Confer, Robert G.

Confer, Thomas R., jt. ed. see Confer, Robert G.

Confer, Vincent. France & Algeria: The Problem of Civil & Political Reform, 1870-1920. LC 66-24455. 1966. 29.95 (*0-8156-2099-3*) Syracuse U Pr.

Confer, William N. Intuitive Psychotherapy: The Role of Creative Therapeutic Intervention. LC 86-27506. 188p. 1987. 34.95 (*0-89885-337-0*, Kluwer Acad Hman Sci) Kluwer Academic.

Conference Board, jt. auth. see Garone, Stephen J.

Conference Board Antitrust Forum Staff, jt. auth. see Hall, Thomas.

Conference Board Staff, jt. auth. see Caropreso, Frank.

Conference Board Staff, jt. auth. see Csoka, Louis S.

Conference Board Staff, jt. auth. see Edelman, Karen A.

Conference Board Staff, jt. auth. see Garone, Stephen J.

Conference Board Staff, jt. auth. see Gates, Stephen M.

An Asterisk (*) at the beginning of an entry indicates that the title is appearing for the first time.

Conference Board Staff, jt. auth. see Hackett, Brian.

Conference Board Staff, jt. auth. see Logan, David.

Conference Board Staff, jt. auth. see Powell, Anna S.

Conference Board Staff, jt. auth. see Smith, Turner T.

Conference Board Staff, jt. auth. see Troy, Katherine.

Conference Board Staff, jt. auth. see Troy, Kathryn L.

Conference Board Staff, jt. auth. see Wheeler, Michael L.

***Conference for African-American Researchers in the Mathematical Sciences Staff.** African-Americans in Mathematics II: Fourth Conference for African-American Researchers in the Mathematical Sciences, June 16-19, 1998, Rice University, Houston, Texas. Dean, Nathaniel et al, eds. LC 99-53762. (Contemporary Mathematics Ser.: Vol. 252). 168p. 2000. 35.00 (*0-8218-1195-9*) Am Math.

Conference International High Temperature Electronics, et al. 1998 Fourth International High Temperature Electronics Conference: Hitec, Albuquerque, New Mexico, U.S.A, June 14-18, 1998. LC 98-84231. vii, 332 p. 1998. write for info. (*0-7803-4541-X*) IEEE Standards.

Conference, Oct. 18-21, 1970 & Gallardo, Jose M. Education of Puerto Rican Children on the Mainland: Proceedings. LC 74-14235. (Puerto Rican Experience Ser.). (Illus.). 200p. 1975. reprint ed. 16.95 (*0-405-06224-9*) Ayer.

Conference of Editors of Learned Journals Staff. Guidelines for Journal Editors & Contributors. fac. ed. LC 84-6684. 25p. 1984. reprint ed. pap. 30.00 (*0-7837-8027-3*, 204778300008) Bks Demand.

Conference of Research Library Directors & OCLC Staff. Tomorrow's Access, Today's Decisions: Ensuring Access to Today's Electronic Resources : Proceedings of the Fourteenth Annual Conference of Research Library Directors, March 11-12, 1996. LC 98-138951. v, 54 p. 1996. write for info. (*1-55653-219-9*) OCLC Online Comp.

Conference of State Bank Supervisors. A Profile of State-Chartered Banking. 11th rev. ed. 1995. ring bd. 60.00 (*0-916361-01-2*) Conf St Bank.

Conference of the Academy of Marketing Science. Developments in Marketing Science: Proceedings of the Annual Conference of the Academy of Marketing Science, 3rd, Miami, Florida, May 9-12, 1979, Vol. 8. Malhotra, Naresh K., ed. LC 78-106352. 523p. reprint ed. pap. 162.20 (*0-608-08169-8*, 202937900060) Bks Demand.

— Developments in Marketing Science: Proceedings of the Annual Conference of the Academy of Marketing Science, 3rd, Miami, Florida, May 9-12, 1979, Vol. 9. Malhotra, Naresh K., ed. LC 78-106352. 525p. 1986. reprint ed. pap. 162.80 (*0-608-08170-1*, 202938000060) Bks Demand.

— Developments in Marketing Science: Proceedings of the Seventh Annual Conference of the Academy of Marketing Science, 1983, Vol. 6. Rogers, John C., III, ed. LC HG5415.1.A53. 679p. 1983. reprint ed. pap. 200.00 (*0-608-08172-8*, 202398500006) Bks Demand.

— Developments in Marketing Science: Proceedings of the Sixth Annual Conference of the Academy of Marketing Science, 1982, Vol. 5. Kothari, Vinay N., ed. LC HG5415.1.A53. 641p. 1982. reprint ed. pap. 198.80 (*0-608-08171-X*, 202398400005) Bks Demand.

— Developments in Marketing Science Vol. 2: Proceedings of the Annual Conference of the Academy of Marketing Science, 3rd, Miami, Florida, May 9-12, 1979. Gitlow, Howard S. & Wheatley, Edward W., eds. LC 78-106352. 410p. 1979. reprint ed. pap. 127.10 (*0-608-08168-X*, 202937800060) Bks Demand.

Conference of the American Council of Learned Soci. Creating an Industrial Civilization: Proceedings. Stein, Leon & Staley, Eugene, eds. LC 77-70536. 1977. reprint ed. lib. bdg. 35.95 (*0-405-10204-6*) Ayer.

Conference of the Cryogenic Society of America, 5t. Application of Cryogenic Technology: Proceedings, Vol. 5. Carr, Robert H., ed. LC 68-57815. 352p. 1973. text 30.00 (*0-87936-001-1*) Scholium Intl.

— Applications of Cryogenic Technology: Proceedings, Vol. 6. Vance, Robert H. & Booth, Sterling H., eds. LC 68-57815. (Illus.). 290p. 1974. text 30.00 (*0-87936-003-8*) Scholium Intl.

Conference of the European Cooperation in Informat. Proceedings. Samelson, K. et al, eds. (Lecture Notes in Computer Science Ser.: Vol. 44). 1976. 21.95 (*0-387-07804-5*) Spr-Verlag.

Conference of the European Society for Microcircul. Recent Advances in Basic Microcirculatory Research: Proceedings, Pt. 1. Wolf-Heidegger, G. & Lewis, D. H., eds. (Bibliotheca Anatomica Ser.: No. 15). (Illus.). 1977. 172.25 (*3-8055-2757-8*) S Karger.

— Recent Advances in Basic Microcirculatory Research: Proceedings, Pt. 2. Wolf-Heidegger, G. & Lewis, D. H., eds. (Bibliotheca Anatomica Ser.: No. 16). (Illus.). 1977. 172.25 (*3-8055-2758-6*) S Karger.

Conference of the International Society for Psycho. Psychoneuroendocrinology: Proceedings. Hatotani, Noboru, ed. (Illus.). 450p. 1974. 116.75 (*3-8055-1711-4*) S Karger.

Conference of the Summer School, Banff Centre, Ban. Relativity, Astrophysics & Cosmology: Proceedings. Israel, Werner, ed. LC 72-97957. (Astrophysics & Space Science Library: Vol. 38). 340p. 1973. text 171.00 (*90-277-0369-8*) Kluwer Academic.

Conference of the Universities. Aspects of Labor Economics: Proceedings. LC 75-19698. (National Bureau of Economic Research Ser.). (Illus.). 1975. reprint ed. 30.95 (*0-405-07578-2*) Ayer.

— Business Concentration & Price Policy: Proceedings. LC 75-19699. (National Bureau of Economic Research Ser.). 1975. reprint ed. 42.95 (*0-405-07579-0*) Ayer.

— Capital Formation & Economic Growth: Proceedings. LC 75-19700. (National Bureau of Economic Research Ser.). (Illus.). 1975. reprint ed. 54.95 (*0-405-07580-4*) Ayer.

— Policies to Combat Depression: Proceedings. LC 75-19701. (National Bureau of Economic Research Ser.). (Illus.). 1975. reprint ed. 35.95 (*0-405-07581-2*) Ayer.

— The Rate & Direction of Inventive Activity: Economic & Social Factors: Proceedings. LC 75-19703. (National Bureau of Economic Research Ser.). (Illus.). 1975. reprint ed. 51.95 (*0-405-07583-9*) Ayer.

— The State of Monetary Economics: Proceedings. LC 75-19702. (National Bureau of Economic Research Ser.). (Illus.). 1975. reprint ed. 19.95 (*0-405-07582-0*) Ayer.

Conference of Western Attorneys General Staff. The American Indian Law Deskbook. 2nd ed. LC 98-10460. 502p. 1998. 85.00 (*0-87081-471-0*) Univ Pr Colo.

— American Indian Law Deskbook: 1994 Supplement. 32p. 1994. pap. 11.95 (*0-87081-339-0*) Univ Pr Colo.

— American Indian Law Deskbook: 1996 Supplement. 108p. 1996. pap. 16.95 (*0-87081-440-0*) Univ Pr Colo.

Conference on Advanced Composites Staff. Advanced Composites III: Expanding the Technology: Proceedings of the Third Annual Conference, 15-17 September 1987, Detroit, MI. LC 87-71917. (Illus.). 409p. 1987. reprint ed. pap. 126.80 (*0-608-02617-4*, 206327500004) Bks Demand.

— How to Apply Advanced Composites Technology: Proceedings of the Fourth Annual Conference on Advanced Composites, 13-15 September 1988, Dearborn, Michigan. LC 88-71675. (Illus.). 541p. 1988. reprint ed. pap. 167.80 (*0-608-03982-9*, 206471200010) Bks Demand.

Conference on Advanced Research in VLSI (1984: MIT. Conference on Advanced Research in VLSI: Proceedings - January, 23-25, 1984, Massachusetts Institute of Technology, Cambridge, MA. Penfield, Paul, Jr., ed. LC 83-73683. 235p. reprint ed. pap. 72.90 (*0-608-14986-1*, 202595800047) Bks Demand.

Conference on Ambulatory Monitoring, 3rd, 1977. The Scope of Ambulatory Monitoring in Ischemic Heart Disease: Proceedings. Jacobsen, Nancy K. et al, eds. 1978. 18.50 (*0-917054-15-6*) Med Communications.

Conference on Antenatal Diagnosis (1970: Universit. Antenatal Diagnosis. Dorfman, Albert, ed. LC 78-177973. 298p. reprint ed. pap. 92.40 (*0-8357-5623-8*, 202411200035) Bks Demand.

Conference on Application of X-Ray Analysis (10th,. Advances in X-Ray Analysis: Proceedings of the Tenth Annual Conference on Applications of X-Ray Analysis held August 7-9, 1961 - Sponsored by University of Denver, Denver Research Institute, Vol. 5. Mueller, William M., ed. LC 58-35928. 576p. reprint ed. pap. 178.60 (*0-8357-5195-3*, 202628000049) Bks Demand.

Conference on Applications of X-Ray Analysis. Advances in X-Ray Analysis: Proceedings of the Fourteenth Annual Conference of X-Ray Analysis held August 25-27, 1965 - Sponsored by University of Denver, Denver Research Institute, Vol. 9. Mallett, Gavin et al, eds. LC 58-35928. 554p. reprint ed. pap. 171.80 (*0-8357-5192-9*, 202628200009) Bks Demand.

— Advances in X-Ray Analysis: Proceedings of the Seventh Annual Conference on Applications of X-Ray Analysis held August 13-15, 1958 - Sponsored by University of Denver, Denver Research Institute, Vol. 2. Mueller, William M., ed. LC 58-35928. 359p. reprint ed. pap. 111.30 (*0-8357-5194-5*, 202627900002) Bks Demand.

— Advances in X-Ray Analysis: Proceedings of the Sixth Annual Conference on Applications of X-Ray Analysis held August 7-9, 1957 - Sponsored by University of Denver, Denver Research Institute, Vol. 1. Mueller, William M., ed. LC 58-35928. 504p. reprint ed. pap. 156.30 (*0-8357-5193-7*, 202627800001) Bks Demand.

— Advances in X-Ray Analysis: Proceedings of the Twelfth Annual Conference on Applications of X-Ray Analysis held August 7-9, 1963 - Sponsored by University of Denver, Denver Research Institute, Vol. 7. Mueller, William M. et al, eds. LC 58-35928. 672p. reprint ed. pap. 200.00 (*0-8357-5196-1*, 202628100007) Bks Demand.

— Advances in X-Ray Analysis, Vol. 3: Proceedings of the Eighth Annual Conference on Applications of X-Ray Analysis Held August 12-14, 1959. Mueller, William M., ed. LC 58-35928. (Illus.). 384p. reprint ed. pap. 119.10 (*0-8357-5197-X*, 201940700003) Bks Demand.

Conference on Bioavailability of Drugs, Washington. Bioavailability of Drugs: Proceedings. Brodie, B. B. & Heller, W. M., eds. (Pharmacology Journal: Vol. 8, Nos. 1-3). (Illus.). 1972. 56.75 (*3-8055-1456-5*) S Karger.

Conference on Biohazards in Cancer Research Staff, et al. Biohazards in Biological Research: Proceedings of a Conference Held at the Asilomer Conference Center, Pacific Grove, CA, January 22-24, 1973. Hellman, A., ed. LC 73-84153. 379p. reprint ed. pap. 117.50 (*0-7837-2083-1*, 204235700004) Bks Demand.

Conference on Blood Viscosity in Heart Disease, Th. Health Needs & Health Services in Rural Ghana. De Kadt, E. et al, eds. 140p. 1981. pap. 18.00 (*0-08-028136-2*, Pergamon Pr) Elsevier.

Conference on Book Publishing in Wisconsin, May 6,, et al. Book Publishing in Wisconsin: Proceedings. Clarke, Jack A. et al, eds. 101p. 1977. pap. 5.00 (*0-936442-06-9*) U Wis Sch Lib.

Conference on Canberra, 1973. The Myocardium: Proceedings. Reader, Ralph, ed. (Advances in Cardiology Ser.: Vol. 12). 300p. 1974. 117.50 (*3-8055-1690-8*) S Karger.

Conference on Cardiovascular Disease Staff. New Approaches in the Diagnosis & Management of Cardiovascular Disease: Proceedings of the Conference on Cardiovascular Disease, 9th, Snowmass-at-Aspen, Aspen, Colorado, January, 1978. Vogel, John H., ed. (Advances in Cardiology Ser.: Vol. 26). 1979. 71.50 (*3-8055-2914-7*) S Karger.

Conference on Cardiovascular Disease, 2nd, Snowmas. Long-Term Prognosis Following Valve Replacement: Proceedings. Vogel, J. H., ed. (Advances in Cardiology Ser.: Vol. 7). 1972. 86.25 (*3-8055-1299-6*) S Karger.

Conference on Category Theory Staff, et al. High Category Theory: Proceedings of a Conference on Category Theory, March 1997, Northwestern University, Evanston, Il. LC 98-32266. (Contemporary Mathematics Ser.). 134p. 1998. write for info. (*0-8218-1056-1*) Am Math.

Conference on Church and Media in Modern Ireland Staff & Conway, Eamonn. Twin Pulpits: Papers of the Conference on Church & Media in Modern Ireland, All Hallows College, July 1997. LC 98-119999. 216 p. 1997. write for info. (*1-85390-323-X*) Veritas Pubns.

Conference on Coastal Zone Staff. Coastal Zone, 1995: Extended Abstracts for the Ninth Conference: Sponsored by the U. S. Dept. of Agriculture, Natural Resources Conservation Service. Edge, Billy L., ed. LC 95-20791. (Proceedings). 616p. 1995. pap. 67.00 (*0-7844-0097-0*) Am Soc Civil Eng.

Conference on Coatings & Bimetallics for Energy Sy. Coatings & Bimetallics for Aggressive Environments: Conference Proceedings: Hilton Head, South Carolina, 12-14 November, 1984. LC 85-72288. (Illus.). 237p. reprint ed. pap. 73.50 (*0-8357-6060-X*, 203432500089) Bks Demand.

Conference on College Composition and Communication (U.S.), jt. ed. see Ede, Lisa S.

***Conference on Company Law & the Single Market Staff & European Commission.** Acts of the Conference on Company Law & the Single Market: 15 & 16 December, 1997, Albert Borschette Conference Centre, Brussels. LC 98-198063. 147p. 1998. write for info. (*92-828-3110-8*, Pub. by Comm Europ Commun) Bernan Associates.

Conference on Computation & Neural Systems Staff. The Neurobiology of Computation: Proceedings of the 3rd Annual Computation & Neural Systems Conference. Bower, James M., ed. LC 94-41228. 464p. (C). 1995. text 218.00 (*0-7923-9543-3*) Kluwer Academic.

Conference on Consumerism (1976: Baton Rouge, LA). Consumerism: New Challenges for Marketing. Kangun, Norman & Richardson, Lee, eds. LC 77-7370. (American Marketing Association, Proceedings Ser.). 220p. reprint ed. pap. 68.20 (*0-608-15106-8*, 202335900032) Bks Demand.

Conference on Contemporary Issues in Thematic Appe. Contemporary Issues in Thematic Apperceptive Methods. Kagan, Jerome & Lesser, Gerald S., eds. LC 76-7536. 328p. 1976. reprint ed. lib. bdg. 65.00 (*0-8371-8842-3*, KACI) Greenwood.

Conference on Control of Distributed Parameter & Stochastic Systems Staff & Choen, Shu-Poing. Control of Distributed Parameter & Stochastic Systems: Proceedings of the IFPIG 7.2 International Conference, June 19-22, 1999, Hangzhou, China. LC 99-18110. (International Federation for Information Processing Ser.). 1999. write for info. (*0-412-83790-0*) Kluwer Academic.

Conference on Creative Arts Therapies Staff. Conference on Creative Arts Therapies, June 28-30, 1979. LC RC0489.A72H8. 86p. pap. 30.00 (*0-8357-7798-7*, 203616200002) Bks Demand.

Conference on Critical Issues in the Development o. Critical Issues in the Development of High Temperature Structural Materials: Proceedings from the Conference on Critical Issues in the Development of High Temperature Structural Materials, Held in Kona, Hawaii, March 7-14, 1993. Stoloff, N. S. et al, eds. LC 93-86574. (Illus.). 505p. 1993. pap. 156.60 (*0-608-04888-7*, 206558000004) Bks Demand.

Conference on Cultural Preservation Staff. The Challenge to Our Cultural Heritage: Why Preserve the Past?: Proceedings of a Conference on Cultural Preservation, Washington, D. C., 8-10 April, 1984. Isar, Yudhishthir R., ed. LC 86-600111. (Illus.). 252p. reprint ed. pap. 78.20 (*0-7837-0546-8*, 204087400019) Bks Demand.

Conference on Culture & Mental Health Research in. Youth, Socialization & Mental Health. Lebra, William P., ed. LC 73-85581. (Mental Health Research in Asia & the Pacific Ser.: No. 3). 320p. reprint ed. pap. 99.20 (*0-7837-0995-1*, 204130100020) Bks Demand.

Conference on Database Theory Staff, et al. Database Theory - ICDT '99: 7th International Conference, Jerusalem, Israel, January 10-12, 1999: Proceedings. Beeri, C. Onal & Buneman, Peter, eds. LC 98-53821. xi, 489p. 1999. pap. 69.00 (*3-540-65452-6*) Spr-Verlag.

Conference on De Sitter & Conformal Groups & Their. De Sitter & Conformal Groups & Their Applications. Barut, Asim O. & Brittin, Wesley E., eds. LC 72-179661. (Lectures in Theoretical Physics: No. 13). (Illus.). 450p. reprint ed. pap. 139.50 (*0-8357-5510-X*, 203512500093) Bks Demand.

Conference on Depression in Childhood Staff. Depression in Childhood: Diagnosis, Treatment, & Conceptual Models. Schulterbrandt, Joy G. & Raskin, Allen, eds. LC 76-47122. 192p. 1977. reprint ed. pap. 59.60 (*0-608-00346-8*, 206106200007) Bks Demand.

Conference on Design Criteria & Equipment for Tran. Conference on Design Criteria & Equipment for Transmission at 400 KV & High Voltages: Contributions, Pt. 1. LC 66-1977. (Institution of Electrical Engineers Conference Report Ser.: No. 15). 234p. reprint ed. pap. 72.60 (*0-608-11056-6*, 200738900061) Bks Demand.

Conference on Development in the Non-Western World. Development in the Non-Western World: Proceedings of the Conference on Development in the Non-Western World, Held March 22-31, 1982, Tokyo, Japan. Nagai, Michio, ed. LC 84-225294. 261p. 1984. reprint ed. pap. 81.00 (*0-608-01251-3*, 206193900001) Bks Demand.

Conference on Differential Geometry Staff & Szenth, Jbanos. New Developments in Differential Geometry, Budapest 1996: Proceedings of the Conference on Differential Geometry, Budapest, Hungary, July 27-30, 1996. LC 98-31137. 1998. write for info. (*0-7923-5307-2*) Kluwer Academic.

Conference on Discontinuous Groups & Riemann Surfa. Discontinuous Groups & Riemann Surfaces: Proceedings of the 1973 Conference at the University of Maryland. Greenberg, Leon, ed. LC 73-16783. (Annals of Mathematics Studies: No. 79). (Illus.). 455p. 1974. reprint ed. pap. 141.10 (*0-608-06600-1*, 206679700009) Bks Demand.

Conference on Disposal of Solid Waste Materials (1. Geotechnical Practice for Disposal of Solid Waste Material: Proceedings of the Conference on June 13-15, 1977, University of Michigan, Ann Arbor, Michigan. LC 77-152066. (Illus.). 893p. reprint ed. pap. 200.00 (*0-608-11373-5*, 201954700013) Bks Demand.

Conference on Economic Development Staff & Nelson, Eastin. Economic Growth: Rationale, Problems, Cases. LC 70-157350. (Select Bibliographies Reprint Ser.). 1977. reprint ed. 23.95 (*0-8369-5811-X*) Ayer.

Conference on Economic Well-Being (1974: Universit. The Distribution of Economic Well-Being. Juster, E. Thomas, ed. LC 76-58909. (Studies in Income & Wealth: No. 41). 767p. reprint ed. pap. 200.00 (*0-608-15347-8*, 205636300061) Bks Demand.

Conference on Education & Income Staff. Education, Income & Human Capital. Hansen, W. Lee, ed. LC 75-106811. (Studies in Income & Wealth by the Conference on Research in Income & Wealth: No. 35). 332p. reprint ed. pap. 103.00 (*0-8357-3241-X*, 205713500011) Bks Demand.

Conference on Electronic Structures in Solids Staff. Electronic Structures in Solids. Haidemenakis, E. D., ed. LC 71-82759. 475p. reprint ed. pap. 147.30 (*0-608-30792-0*, 201939400011) Bks Demand.

Conference on Enzyme Economics Staff. Enzymes, the Interface Between Technology & Economics. Danehy, James P. & Wolnak, Bernard, eds. LC 80-10143. (Illus.). 216p. reprint ed. pap. 67.00 (*0-7837-0634-0*, 204097800019) Bks Demand.

C

Conference on Exchange Rate Flexibility & the Inte. Exchange Rate Flexibility. Dreyer, Jacob S., ed. LC 78-7379. (AEI Symposia Ser.: No. 78C). 306p. reprint ed. pap. 94.90 (*0-8357-4477-9*, 203732600008) Bks Demand.

Conference on Experimental Medicine & Surgery in P. Medical Primatology, 1970: Proceedings. Goldsmith, E. I. & Moor-Jankowski, J., eds. 1971. 243.50 (*3-8055-1227-9*) S Karger.

— Medical Primatology, 1972: Selected Papers, Proceedings, 3 pts. Set. Goldsmith, E. I. & Moor-Jankowski, J., eds. Incl. Pt. 1. General Primatology, Reproduction & Perinatal Studies, Genetics, Phylogenetics, & Evolution. 450p. 1973. 121.75 (*3-8055-1486-7*); Pt. 2. Surgery, Transplantation, Oral Medicine, Neurophysiology & Psychology. 350p. 1973. 104.50 (*3-8055-1487-5*); Pt. 3. Infectious Diseases, Oncology, Pharmacology & Toxicology, Cardiovascular Studies. 400p. 1973. 121.75 (*3-8055-1488-3*); 1972. 304.50 (*3-8055-1489-1*) S Karger.

Conference on Failure Modes in Composites Staff. Failure Modes in Composites Four: Proceedings of a Symposium Held at Fall Meeting Held in Chicago, Illinois, October 24-26, 1977. Cornie, James A. & Crossman, Frank W., eds. LC 79-89153. 471p. reprint ed. pap. 146.10 (*0-8357-2502-2*, 205238200013) Bks Demand.

Conference on Families & the Economy Staff. American Families & the Economy: The High Cost of Living. Nelson, Richard R. & Skidmore, Felicity, eds. LC 83-12134. 317p. reprint ed. pap. 98.30 (*0-8357-3449-8*, 203970900013) Bks Demand.

Conference on Fetal Homeostasis, 1964. Fetal Homeostasis: Proceedings, Vol. 2. Wynn, Ralph M., ed. LC RG0591.C6. 372p. reprint ed. pap. 115.40 (*0-608-12420-6*, 205570000002) Bks Demand.

Conference on Finite Elements Applied to Thin Shells & Curved Members (1974: Univ. College, Cardiff. Finite Elements for Thin Shells & Curved Members. Ashwell, D. G. & Gallagher, R. H., eds. LC 75-37654. (Illus.). 280p. reprint ed. pap. 86.80 (*0-608-30376-3*, 201644800004) Bks Demand.

Conference on Frequency Generation & Control for R. Conference on Frequency Generation & Control for Radio Systems. LC 67-112020. (Institution of Electrical Engineers Conference Report Ser.: No. 31). 199p. reprint ed. pap. 61.70 (*0-608-11024-8*, 200738300061) Bks Demand.

Conference on Function Spaces (2d: Edwardsville, I. Function Spaces, the Second Conference: Proceedings. Jarosz, Krzysztof, ed. LC 95-9482. (Lecture Notes in Pure & Applied Mathematics Ser.: Vol. 172). (Illus.). 408p. 1995. pap. text 175.00 (*0-8247-9665-9*) Dekker.

Conference on Function Spaces Staff & Jarosz, Krzysztof. Function Spaces: Proceedings of the Third Conference on Function Spaces, May 19-23, 1998, Southern Illinois University at Edwardsville. LC 99-13038. (Contemporary Mathematics Ser.). 20p. 1999. write for info. (*0-8218-0939-3*) Am Math.

Conference on Geochemical Transport & Kinetics (19. Geochemical Transport & Kinetics: Papers Presented at a Conference at Airlie House, Warrenton, Virginia, June 1973. Hofmann, A. W. et al, eds. LC 74-19286. (Carnegie Institution of Washington Publication Ser.: Vol. 634). (Illus.). 361p. reprint ed. pap. 112.00 (*0-608-06228-6*, 206655700008) Bks Demand.

An Asterisk (*) at the beginning of an entry indicates that the title is appearing for the first time.

Conference on Hokan Languages, San Diego, Californ. Hokan Studies: Proceedings. Langdon, Margaret & Silver, Shirley, eds. (Janua Linguarum, Series Practica: No. 181). 1976. pap. text 98.50 (*90-279-3124-0*) Mouton.

***Conference on Industrial Technologies Staff.** Proceedings of the Conference on Industrial Technologies, Toulouse 27-30 October, 1997. LC 98-231880. 253p. 1998. write for info. (*92-828-2974-X*, Pub. by Comm Europ Commun) Bernan Associates.

Conference on Intellectual Freedom, 1965, Washingt. Freedom of Inquiry: Supporting the Library Bill of Rights. LC 65-24954. 70p. 1965. reprint ed. pap. 30.00 (*0-608-08246-5*, 201551700094) Bks Demand.

Conference on Interference Problems Associated wit. Conference on Interference Problems Associated with the Operation of Microwave Communication Systems, 23rd-24th April, 1968. LC 71-586382. (Institution of Electrical Engineers Conference Report Ser.: No. 39). 208p. reprint ed. pap. 64.50 (*0-608-11047-7*, 200738800061) Bks Demand.

Conference on International Implications of Enviro. Environmental Problems & Their International Implications: Papers. Odabasi, Halis & Ulug, S. Erol, eds. LC 73-87538. (Illus.). 196p. reprint ed. pap. 60.80 (*0-8357-5592-4*, 203522900093) Bks Demand.

Conference on International Trade & Central Planni. International Trade & Central Planning: An Analysis of Economic Interactions. Brown, Alan A. & Neuberger, Egon, eds. LC 68-13821. 471p. reprint ed. pap. 146.10 (*0-608-15836-4*, 203142600074) Bks Demand.

Conference on Iranian Civilization & Culture Staff. Iranian Civilization & Culture: Essays in Honour of the 2500th Anniversary of the Founding of the Persian Empire. Adams, Charles J., ed. LC 75-302316. 171p. reprint ed. pap. 53.10 (*0-7837-1040-2*, 204135100020) Bks Demand.

Conference on Junior College Libraries (1967: Los. Junior College Libraries: Development, Needs, & Perspectives. LC 68-56370. (ACRL Monograph: No. 30). 116p. reprint ed. pap. 36.00 (*0-608-14069-4*, 202420600035) Bks Demand.

Conference on Large Body Impacts & Terrestrial Evo. Geological Implications of Impacts of Large Asteroids & Comets on the Earth. Silver, Leon T. et al, eds. LC 82-24164. (Geological Society of America, Special Paper: No. 190). (Illus.). 548p. reprint ed. pap. 169.90 (*0-8357-3148-0*, 203941100012) Bks Demand.

Conference on Lasers & Electro-Optics Staff, et al. Technical Digest: Summaries of Papers Presented at the Conference on Lasers & Electro-Optics, the Moscone Center, San Francisco, California, May 3-8, 1998. LC 98-84664. (1998 OSA Technical Digest Ser.). 559 p. 1998. write for info. (*1-55752-539-0*) Optical Soc.

Conference on Library Manpower (1967: Washington,. Library Manpower: Needs & Utilization. Asheim, Lester, ed. LC 72-3089. 39p. reprint ed. pap. 30.00 (*0-608-14077-5*, 202420900035) Bks Demand.

Conference on Local Governments' Decisions & the L. Local Governments' Decisions & the Local Tax Base: Proceedings of a Conference, February 9 & 10, 1979, U. S. C. Law Center, Los Angeles. Lefcoe, George, ed. LC HJ9204.C66. (Lincoln Institute Monograph: No. 79-8). 280p. reprint ed. pap. 86.80 (*0-7837-2169-2*, 204249100004) Bks Demand.

Conference on Magnetism & Magnetic Materials Staff. Magnetism & Magnetic Materials: Proceedings of the 7th Conference. Osborn, J. A., ed. LC 72-623469. 383p. reprint ed. pap. 118.80 (*0-608-30791-2*, 201938900011) Bks Demand.

Conference on Magnetism & Magnetic Materials 20th,. Magnetism & Magnetic Materials: Proceedings, 1974. Graham, C. D., Jr. et al, eds. LC 75-2647. (AIP Conference Proceedings Ser.: No. 24). 792p. 1975. 30.00 (*0-88318-123-1*) Am Inst Physics.

Conference on Manganese Containing Stainless Steel. High Manganese Austenitic Steels: Proceedings of a Conference on Manganese Containing Stainless Steels, Held in Conjunction with ASM's Materials Week '87, Cincinnati, OH, 10-15 October 1987. Lula, R. A., ed. LC 87-73382. (Illus.). 142p. reprint ed. pap. 44.10 (*0-8357-4088-9*, 203685400005) Bks Demand.

Conference on Marketing Management (6th: 1962: Uni. Changing Perspectives in Marketing Management: Sixth Annual Conference on Marketing Management, March 30, 1962. Warshaw, Martin R., ed. LC HF5415.13. (Michigan Business Studies: No. 37). 112p. reprint ed. pap. 34.80 (*0-608-13826-6*, 202208200024) Bks Demand.

Conference on Marmosets in Experimental Medicine,. Marmosets in Experimental Medicine: Proceedings. Moor-Jankowski, J. et al, eds. (Primates in Medicine Ser.: Vol. 10). (Illus.). 1978. 133.25 (*3-8055-2750-0*) S Karger.

Conference on Materials for Future Energy Systems. Materials for Future Energy Systems: Proceedings of a Conference. LC 85-73249. (Conference Proceedings Ser.). (Illus.). 488p. reprint ed. pap. 151.30 (*0-608-15995-6*, 203306700083) Bks Demand.

Conference on Microcirculation, 6th, Aalborg, 1970. European Conference on Microcirculation, 6th, Aalborg, 1970. Ditzel, J. & Lewis, D. H., eds. (Illus.). 1971. 204.50 (*3-8055-1234-1*) S Karger.

Conference on Microcirculation, 6th European, Aalb. Microcirculatory Approaches to Current Therapeutic Problems: Lung in Shock, Organ Transplantation, Diabetic Microangiopathy. Proceedings. Ditzel, J. & Lewis, D. H., eds. (Illus.). 1971. 45.25 (*3-8055-1186-8*) S Karger.

Conference on Modeling of Casting & Welding Proces. Modeling & Control of Casting & Welding Processes: Proceedings of the 3rd Conference on Modeling of Casting & Welding Processes. Sponsored by the Engineering Foundation & Held on January 12-17, 1986, in Santa Barbara, CA. Kou, Sindo & Mehrabian, Robert, eds. LC 86-16402. (Illus.). 636p. reprint ed. pap. 197.20 (*0-8357-8522-X*, 203481900091) Bks Demand.

Conference on Molecular Spectroscopy (6th: 1976: U. Molecular Spectroscopy: Proceedings of the 6th Conference on Molecular Spectroscopy, Organized by the Institute of Petroleum, Hydrocarbon Research Group, & Held at the University of Durham, 30 March-2 April, 1976. West, A. R., ed. LC 78-320788. 598p. reprint ed. pap. 185.40 (*0-608-14101-1*, 202401300035) Bks Demand.

Conference on Mononuclear Phagocytes, Third, Noorw. Functional Aspects of Mononuclear Phagocytes: Proceedings, 2 vols., Set. Van Furth, Ralph, ed. 1980. text 565.50 (*90-247-2211-X*) Kluwer Academic.

Conference on Montague Grammar, Philosophy, & Linguistics, 1977, State Univ. of NY at Albany, Staff. Linguistics, Philosophy, & Montague Grammar. Davis, Steven & Mithun, Marianne, eds. LC 79-13975. 352p. reprint ed. pap. 109.20 (*0-608-20101-4*, 207137300011) Bks Demand.

Conference on Natural Gas Research & Technology (2. Proceedings of the Second Conference on Natural Gas Research & Technology Sponsored by American Gas Association & Institute of Gas Technology, Atlanta, Georgia, June 5-7, 1972. White, Jack W. & Kragulski, Maryann, eds. LC TP0350.C65. 987p. reprint ed. pap. 200.00 (*0-608-12450-8*, 202423600036) Bks Demand.

Conference on Needs & Opportunities for the Study. Educating an Urban People: The New York City Experience. Ravitch, Diane & Goodenow, Ronald K., eds. LC 80-28478. (Illus.). 295p. reprint ed. pap. 91.50 (*0-8357-3032-8*, 203927900011) Bks Demand.

Conference on New Developments in Productivity Mea. New Developments in Productivity Measurement & Analysis. Kendrick, John W. & Vaccara, Beatrice N., eds. LC 79-20399. (Studies in Income & Wealth: No. 44). (Illus.). 726p. reprint ed. pap. 200.00 (*0-8357-8244-1*, 205679600087) Bks Demand.

Conference on Nineteenth Century Japanese Elites (. Modern Japanese Leadership: Transition & Change. Silberman, Bernard S. & Harootunian, H. D., eds. LC 66-18532. 445p. reprint ed. pap. 138.00 (*0-608-13996-3*, 205537200017) Bks Demand.

Conference on Nonlinear Dynamics in Particle Accel, et al. Nonlinear Dynamics in Particle Accelerators: Theory & Experiments: Proceedings. Chattopadhyay, Swapan et al, eds. LC 95-78135. (AIP Conference Proceedings Ser.: Vol. 344). (Illus.). 282p. 1995. 115.00 (*1-56396-446-5*) Am Inst Physics.

***Conference on Optical Fiber Communication Staff, et al.** OFC'98: Optical Fiber Communication Conference & Exhibit: Technical Digest: February 22-27, 1998, San Jose, California LC 97-81329. (Technical Digest Ser.). vii, 541p. 1998. write for info. (*1-55752-529-3*) Optical Soc.

Conference on Optimisation Techniques in Circuit &. Conference on Optimisation Techniques in Circuit & Control Applications, 29-30 June 1970. LC 71-595801. (Institution of Electrical Engineers Conference Report Ser.: No. 66). 82p. reprint ed. pap. 30.00 (*0-608-18594-9*, 205032900061) Bks Demand.

Conference on Ordered Groups (1978: Boise, ID) Sta. Ordered Groups: Proceedings of the Boise State Conference. Smith, Jo E. et al, eds. LC 80-24251. (Lecture Notes in Pure & Applied Mathematics Ser.: No. 62). (Illus.). 192p. 1980. reprint ed. pap. 59.60 (*0-608-05898-X*, 206623300007) Bks Demand.

Conference on Oriental Classics in General Educati. Approaches to the Oriental Classics: Asian Literature & Thought in General Education. De Bary, William T., ed. LC 59-9905. 275p. reprint ed. pap. 85.30 (*0-8357-5696-3*, 202374600033) Bks Demand.

Conference on Parallel Computing Technologies Staf. Parallel Computing Technologies: Proceedings, 4th International Conference, PaCT-97, Yaroslavl, Russia, September 8-12, 1997. Malyshkin, V. E., ed. LC 97-27823. (Lecture Notes in Computer Science Ser.: Vol. 1277). xiii, 455p. pap. 69.00 (*3-540-63371-5*) Spr-Verlag.

Conference on Periodical Publishing in Wisconsin,, et al. Periodical Publishing in Wisconsin: Proceedings. Arnold, Barbara J. et al, eds. 233p. 1980. pap. 7.00 (*0-936442-08-5*) U Wis Sch Lib.

Conference on Physics of the Magnetosphere, Boston. Physics of the Magnetosphere: Proceedings. Carovillano, R. L. et al, eds. (Astrophysics & Space Science Library: No.10). 686p. 1968. lib. bdg. 175.00 (*90-277-0111-3*) Kluwer Academic.

Conference on Planning & Short Term Macroeconomic. Short Term Macro-Economic Policy in Latin America. Behrman, Jere R. & Hanson, James A., eds. LC 78-24053. 392p. reprint ed. pap. 121.60 (*0-8357-3238-X*, 205713200011) Bks Demand.

Conference on Poverty in America. Poverty in America. Gordon, M. S., ed. (New Reprints in Essay & General Literature Index Ser.). 1977. reprint ed. 34.95 (*0-518-10197-5*, 10197) Ayer.

Conference on Power Applications of Controllable S. Conference on Power Applications of Controllable Semi-Conductor Devices: Contributions. LC 66-9749. (Institution of Electrical Engineers Conference Report Ser.: No. 17). 64p. reprint ed. pap. 30.00 (*0-608-11062-0*, 205032700061) Bks Demand.

Conference on Price Behavior (1974, Bethesda, Md). Analysis of Inflation, 1965-1974. LC 77-581. (Studies in Income & Wealth: No. 42). 519p. reprint ed. pap. 160.90 (*0-8357-5427-8*, 205636400061) Bks Demand.

Conference on Price Research & Committee on Price Determination. Cost Behavior & Price Policy. 1975. 26.95 (*0-405-19043-3*, 7) Ayer.

Conference on Process Control & Reliability Analys. Reliability & Process Control: Proceedings of a Conference on Process Control & Reliability Analysis Held in Conjunction with ASM's Materials Week '85, Toronto, Ontario, Canada, 14-17 October 1985. Ravindran, C. et al, eds. LC 86-70845. (Illus.). 279p. reprint ed. pap. 86.50 (*0-8357-4100-1*, 203686600005) Bks Demand.

Conference on Production Research & Technology. Computer-Based Factory Automation Conference Proceedings: May 21-23, 1984, Carnegie-Mellon University, Pittsburgh, Pennsylvania. LC 84-50766. 430p. reprint ed. pap. 133.30 (*0-608-14982-9*, 205609400048) Bks Demand.

Conference on Progress in Ion Exchange (1995: Wrex. Progress in Ion Exchange: Advances & Applications, Proceedings. Dyer, A. et al, eds. 498p. 1997. text 174.00 (*0-85404-791-3*, QD562) Am Chemical.

Conference on Propagation of Radio Waves at Freque. Conference on Propagation of Radio Waves at Frequencies above 10 GHz, 10-13 April, 1973. LC TK7876.C66. (Institution of Electrical Engineers Conference Report Ser.: N0. 98). 270p. reprint ed. pap. 83.70 (*0-608-10997-5*, 201213200080) Bks Demand.

Conference on Public Expenditure Decisions in the. Public Expenditure Decisions in the Urban Community: Papers Presented at a Conference, May 14-15, 1962, under the Sponsorship of the Committee on Urban Economics of Resources for the Future, Inc. Schaller, Howard G., ed. LC 63-22774. 208p. reprint ed. pap. 64.50 (*0-7837-3045-4*, 204287800006) Bks Demand.

Conference on Race Relations in World Perspective,. Race Relations in World Perspective: Papers. Lind, Andrew W., ed. LC 73-7074. 488p. 1973. reprint ed. lib. bdg. 69.50 (*0-8371-6907-0*, RRWP, Greenwood Pr) Greenwood.

Conference on Reading - University Of Chicago. Reading: 75 Years of Progress. Robinson, H. Alan, ed. LC 66-23696. 1967. lib. bdg. 7.50 (*0-226-72178-7*, SEM96) U Ch Pr.

Conference on Real Algebraic Geometry & Toplogy St. Real Algebraic Geometry & Topology: A Conference on Real Algebraic Geometry & Topology, December 17-21, 1993, Michigan State University. Akbulut, Selman, ed. LC 94-44468. (Contemporary Mathematics Ser.: Vol. 182). 158p. 1995. pap. 39.00 (*0-8218-0292-5*, CONM/182) Am Math.

Conference on Regional Accounts Staff. Design of Regional Accounts: Papers Presented at the Conference on Regional Accounts, 1960. Hochwald, Werner, ed. LC 61-17653. 301p. reprint ed. pap. 93.40 (*0-7837-3125-6*, 204286200006) Bks Demand.

— Elements of Regional Accounts: Papers Presented at the Conference on Regional Accounts, 1962. Hirsch, Werner Z., ed. LC 64-16309. 239p. reprint ed. pap. 74.10 (*0-7837-3128-0*, 202074000018) Bks Demand.

— Regional Accounts for Policy Decision: Papers Presented at the Conference on Regional Accounts, 1964. Hirsch, Werner Z., ed. LC 66-23000. 244p. reprint ed. pap. 75.70 (*0-7837-3127-2*, 204286000006) Bks Demand.

Conference on Reliability--Key to Industrial Succe & Kececioglu, Dimitri. Reliability, Key to Industrial Success: Proceedings of ASM's 1987 Conference on Reliability--Key to Industrial Success, Los Angeles, CA, 24-26 March 1987. Sundaresan, S., ed. LC 87-71238. (Illus.). 216p. reprint ed. pap. 67.00 (*0-8357-4093-5*, 203685900005) Bks Demand.

Conference on Religion & Peace 2nd Conference. World Religion - World Peace: Unabridges Proceedings. Homer, Jack A., ed. 200p. 1979. 3.95 (*0-317-61733-8*) World Confer Rel & Peace.

Conference on Remotely Manned Systems, 2nd, June 1. Robots & Manipulator Systems: Papers, 2 pts., Pt. 1. Heer, E., ed. LC 77-73105. 336p. 1977. pap. 35.00 (*0-08-021727-3*) Elsevier.

— Robots & Manipulator Systems: Papers, 2 pts., Pt. 2. Heer, E., ed. LC 77-73105. 336p. 1977. pap. 35.00 (*0-08-022681-7*, Pergamon Pr) Elsevier.

Conference on Research in Family Planning (1960: N. Research in Family Planning. Kiser, Clyde V., ed. LC 62-7409. 680p. reprint ed. pap. 200.00 (*0-608-14113-5*, 202429700036) Bks Demand.

Conference on Research in Income & Wealth. Input-Output Analysis: An Appraisal. LC 75-19705. (National Bureau of Economic Research Ser.). (Illus.). 1975. reprint ed. 31.95 (*0-405-07585-5*) Ayer.

— Measuring the Nation's Wealth: Proceedings. LC 75-19737. (National Bureau of Economic Research Ser.). (Illus.). 1975. reprint ed. 70.95 (*0-405-07614-2*) Ayer.

— Output, Input & Productivity Measurement. LC 60-12234. (National Bureau of Economic Research. Studies in International Economic Relations: Vol. 25). 516p. reprint ed. pap. 160.00 (*0-608-14417-7*, 205170200006) Bks Demand.

— Problems of Capital Formation: Concepts, Measurement, & Controlling Factors. LC 75-19707. (National Bureau of Economic Research Ser.). (Illus.). 1975. reprint ed. 50.95 (*0-405-07587-1*) Ayer.

— Trends in the American Economy in the Nineteenth Century. LC 75-19709. (National Bureau of Economic Research Ser.). (Illus.). 1975. reprint ed. 64.95 (*0-405-07588-X*) Ayer.

Conference on Research In Income And Wealth. Output, Input & Productivity Measurement. (Studies in Income & Wealth: No. 25). 516p. 1961. reprint ed. 129.00 (*0-87014-181-3*) Natl Bur Econ Res.

Conference on Research in National Income & Wealth. Studies in Income & Wealth. LC 75-19704. (National Bureau of Economic Research Ser.). (Illus.). 1975. reprint ed. 29.95 (*0-405-07589-8*) Ayer.

Conference on Research in Psychotherapy Staff. Research in Psychotherapy: Proceedings. Rubinstein, Eli A. & Parloff, Morris B., eds. LC 59-9192. 303p. reprint ed. pap. 94.00 (*0-7837-0493-3*, 204081700018) Bks Demand.

Conference on Research in Taxation & Boskin, Michael J. Research in Taxation: A Conference of the National Bureau of Economic Research. LC HJ2240.C6. (National Bureau of Economic Research, Conference Reports: No. 11). 160p. reprint ed. pap. 49.60 (*0-608-15348-6*, 205636500061) Bks Demand.

Conference on Residual Stress - in Design, Process. Residual Stress in Design, Process & Materials Selection: Proceedings of ASM's Conference on Residual Stress - in Design, Process, & Materials Selection: Cincinnati, Ohio, U. S. A., 27-29 April 1987. Young, William B., ed. LC 87-71686. (Illus.). 219p. pap. 67.90 (*0-7837-1871-3*, 204207200001) Bks Demand.

Conference on Resource Sharing in Libraries Staff. Library Resource Sharing: Proceedings of the 1976 Conference on Resource Sharing in Libraries, Pittsburgh, Pennsylvania. Kent, Allen & Galvin, Thomas J., eds. LC 77-5399. (Books in Library & Information Science: No. 21). (Illus.). 368p. reprint ed. pap. 114.10 (*0-7837-0832-7*, 204114600019) Bks Demand.

Conference on Riemann Surfaces & Related Topics (4. Riemann Surfaces & Related Topics: Proceedings of the 1978 Stony Brook Conference. Kra, Irwin & Maskit, Bernard, eds. LC 79-27823. (Annals of Mathematics Studies: No. 97). (Illus.). 528p. 1981. reprint ed. pap. 163.70 (*0-608-06499-8*, 206679600009) Bks Demand.

Conference on Robotics for Challenging Environment & American Society of Civil Engineers Staff. Robotics for Challenging Environments: Proceedings of the RCE II, the Second Conference, Albuquerque, New Mexico, June 1-6, 1996. Demsetz, Laura, ed. LC 96-8474. 336p. 1996. 40.00 (*0-7844-0178-0*) Am Soc Civil Eng.

Conference on Rock Engineering for Foundations & S. Rock Engineering for Foundations & Slopes: Proceedings of a Specialty Conference, University of Colorado, Boulder, Colorado, August 15-18, 1976, 2 vols., 1. LC 77-368041. 449p. reprint ed. pap. 139.20 (*0-608-11345-X*, 201955200001) Bks Demand.

— Rock Engineering for Foundations & Slopes: Proceedings of a Specialty Conference, University of Colorado, Boulder, Colorado, August 15-18, 1976, 2 vols., 2. LC 77-368041. 270p. reprint ed. pap. 83.70 (*0-608-11346-8*, 201955200002) Bks Demand.

Conference On Science - Philosophy And Religion -. Conflicts of Power in Modern Culture. Bryson, L. et al, eds. 703p. 1964. reprint ed. 75.50 (*0-8154-0037-3*) Cooper Sq.

Conference on Security & Cooperation in Europe (Or, jt. auth. see Bloed, Arie.

***Conference on Sensors & Their Applications Staff, et al.** Sensors & Their Applications: Proceedings of the 10th Conference on Sensors & Their Applications. LC 99-39941. (Sensors Ser.). 1999. 98.00 (*0-7503-0625-4*) IOP Pub.

Conference on Signal Processing, Communications, and Networking, et al. Signal Processing, Communications, & Networking: Proceedings of the Conference on Signal Processing, Communications, & Networking, Indian Institute of Science, Bangalore, July 16-19, 1997. LC 97-913725. (Illus.). 1997. write for info. (*0-07-463173-X*) McGrw-H Hghr Educ.

Conference on Software Engineering for Telecommuni. Conference on Software Engineering for Telecommunication Switching Systems. LC TK7868.S9C6. (Institution of Electrical Engineers Conference Report Ser.: No. 97). 346p. reprint ed. pap. 107.30 (*0-608-18591-4*, 201213100080) Bks Demand.

Conference on Software for Control Staff & Institution of Electrical Engineers Staff. Conference on Software for Control. LC 74-164766. (Ieee Conference Publication Ser.: Vol. 102). vi, 168p. 1973. write for info. (*0-85296-111-1*) INSPEC Inc.

Conference on Soviet Agricultural & Peasant Affair. Soviet Agricultural & Peasant Affairs, 1. LC 81-20287. (Slavic Studies: No. 1). 335p. 1982. reprint ed. lib. bdg. 65.00 (*0-313-23450-7*, COSO, Greenwood Pr) Greenwood.

Conference on Structural Integrity Technology, 197. Structural Integrity Technology. Gallagher, J. P. & Crooker, T. W., eds. LC 79-50210. (Illus.). 233p. reprint ed. pap. 72.30 (*0-8357-3553-2*, 205681600089) Bks Demand.

Conference on Structure & Function of Monoamine En. Structure & Function of Monoamine Enzymes: Proceedings of a Conference Held in Steamboat Springs, Colorado, March 10-13, 1977. Usdin, Earl et al, eds. LC 77-14089. (Modern Pharmacology-Toxicology Ser.: No. 10). 1025p. reprint ed. pap. 200.00 (*0-7837-0611-1*, 204095900019) Bks Demand.

***Conference on Summer Undergraduate Mathematics Research Programs Staff & Gallian, Joseph A.** Proceedings of the Conference on Summer Undergraduate Mathematics Research Programs. LC 00-29329. 2000. write for info. (*0-8218-2137-7*) Am Math.

Conference on Systems & Computer Science, 1965: Un. Systems & Computer Science. Hart, John F. & Takasu, Satoru, eds. LC 68-114245. 261p. reprint ed. pap. 81.00 (*0-608-11613-0*, 201424000090) Bks Demand.

Conference on Systems Simulation, Economic Analysi. Solar Engineering, 1981: Proceedings of the ASME Solar Energy Division Third Annual Conference on Systems Simulation, Economic Analysis - Solar Heating & Cooling Operational Results, Reno, Nevada, April 27-May 1, 1981. Reid, Robert L. et al, eds. LC 81-65532. (Illus.). 779p. reprint ed. pap. 200.00 (*0-8357-2890-0*, 203912600011) Bks Demand.

C

An Asterisk (*) at the beginning of an entry indicates that the title is appearing for the first time.

Conference on Telecommunication Transmission (1975. Conference on Telecommunication Transmission, September 9-11, 1975. LC 76-371266. (Institution of Electrical Engineers Conference Report Ser.: No. 131). 206p. reprint ed. pap. 63.90 (*0-608-11054-X*, 201212800080) Bks Demand.

Conference on the Application of Large Industrial. Conference on the Application of Large Industrial Drives. LC 67-2581. (Institution of Electrical Engineers Conference Report Ser.: No. 10). 275p. reprint ed. pap. 85.30 (*0-608-11717-X*, 205032600061); reprint ed. pap., suppl. ed. 30.00 (*0-608-11718-8*, 205032600062) Bks Demand.

Conference on the Beginnings of Modernization in t. Beginnings of Modernization in the Middle East: The Nineteenth Century. Polk, William R. & Chambers, Richard L., eds. LC 68-16712. (Publications of the Center for Middle Eastern Studies: No. 1). 437p. reprint ed. pap. 135.50 (*0-8357-8815-6*, 205675900085) Bks Demand.

Conference on the Concept of Academic Freedom Staf. The Concept of Academic Freedom: Papers. Pincoffs, Edmund L., ed. LC 74-20852. 296p. reprint ed. pap. 91.80 (*0-8357-7755-3*, 203611300002) Bks Demand.

Conference on the Electrical Transport & Optical P. Electrical Transport & Optical Properties of Inhomogeneous Media. Garland, J. C. & Tanner, D. B., eds. LC 78-54319. (AIP Conference Proceedings Ser.: No. 40). 1978. lib. bdg. 21.00 (*0-88318-139-8*) Am Inst Physics.

Conference on the Electrochemistry & Physics of Se. Semiconductor Liquid-Junction Solar Cells: Proceedings of a Conference on the Electrochemistry & Physics of Semiconductor Liquid Interfaces under Illumination Held at Airlie, VA, May 3-5, 1977. LC 77-79771. (Electrochemical Society Proceedings Ser.: Vol. 77-3). (Illus.). 339p. 1977. pap. 105.10 (*0-7837-8993-9*, 205925800002) Bks Demand.

Conference on the Federal Election Commission, jt. auth. see American Bar Association Staff.

Conference on the Foundations of Space-Time Theori. Foundations of Space-Time Theories. LC 77-83503. (Minnesota Studies in the Philosophy of Science: No. 8). (Illus.). 477p. reprint ed. pap. 147.90 (*0-8357-6535-0*, 203589700097) Bks Demand.

Conference on the History of Medicinal Drug Contro. Safeguarding the Public: Historical Aspects of Medicinal Drug Control. Blake, John B., ed. LC 76-84651. 213p. reprint ed. pap. 66.10 (*0-608-11892-3*, 202308400032) Bks Demand.

Conference on the Human Environment, Founex, Switz. Development & Environment: Proceedings. Strong, Maurice F., ed. LC 72-75446. (Illus.). 225p. (Orig.). 1973. pap. text 24.65 (*90-279-6990-6*) Mouton.

Conference on the Labour Market Staff, et al. The Economics of the Labour Market: Proceedings of a Conference on the Labour Market, Sponsored by Her Majesty's Treasury, the Department of Employment & the Manpower Services Commission, 10-12th September 1979 at Magdalen College, Oxford. Hornstein, Zmira, ed. LC 81-173192. 328 p. 1981. 8.95 (*0-11-630291-7*) Statnry Office.

Conference on the Measurement of Economic & Social. The Measurement of Economic & Social Performance. Moss, Milton, ed. LC 72-97766. (Studies in Income & Wealth: No. 38). (Illus.). 615p. reprint ed. pap. 190.70 (*0-8357-7669-7*, 205699700001) Bks Demand.

Conference on the Mechanical Properties of Materia. Mechanical Properties at High Rates of Strain, 1984: Proceedings of the Third Conference on the Mechanical Properties of Materials at High Rates of Strain Held in Oxford, 9-12 April 1984. Harding, J., ed. LC 86-102820. (Conference Ser.: No. 70). 568p. reprint ed. pap. 176.10 (*0-7837-3256-2*, 204327500007) Bks Demand.

Conference on the Nature of the Surface of the Moon Staff. The Nature of the Lunar Surface: Proceedings of the 1965 IAU-NASA Symposium, Greenbelt, MD. Hess, Wilmot N. et al, eds. LC 65-27671. (Illus.). 328p. reprint ed. pap. 101.70 (*0-608-30224-4*, 200384400037) Bks Demand.

Conference on the Neutron & Its Applications Staff. The Neutron & Its Applications, 1982: Plenary & Invited Papers from the Conference to Mark the 50th Anniversary of the Discovery of the Neutron Held at Cambridge, 13-17 September 1982. Schofield, P., ed. LC 82-40918. (Conference Ser.: No. 64). 536p. reprint ed. pap. 166.20 (*0-7837-3251-1*, 204327000007) Bks Demand.

Conference on the Optimal Preparation for the Stud. Preparation for the Study of Medicine: Proceedings. Page, Robert G. & Littlemeyer, Mary H., eds. LC 69-19280. 295p. reprint ed. pap. 91.50 (*0-608-12087-1*, 202412300035) Bks Demand.

Conference on the Philosophy of Mind & Psychology. Philosophical Aspects of the Mind-Body Problem: Proceedings. LC 75-17914. 232p. reprint ed. pap. 72.00 (*0-8357-6260-2*, 203463600090) Bks Demand.

Conference on the Present Status of Weak Interacti. Weak Interaction Physics: 1977 Proceedings. Lichtenberg, D. B., ed. LC 77-83344. (AIP Conference Proceedings Ser.: Vol. 37). (Illus.). 1977. lib. bdg. 13.00 (*0-88318-136-3*) Am Inst Physics.

Conference on the Princeton European Fertility Pro. The Decline of Fertility in Europe: The Revised Proceedings of a Conference on the Princeton European Fertility Project, 1979. Coale, Ansley J. & Watkins, Susan C., eds. LC 85-42682. 535p. reprint ed. pap. 165.90 (*0-7837-1408-4*, 204176200023) Bks Demand.

Conference on the Russian Revolution Staff, et al. Revolutionary Russian. Pipes, Richard, ed. LC 68-15641. (Russian Research Center Studies: No. 55). 379p. reprint ed. pap. 117.50 (*0-7837-3840-4*, 204366200010) Bks Demand.

Conference On the Scientific Spirit & Democratic F. Science for Democracy. LC 70-121459. (Essay Index Reprint Ser.). 1977. 20.95 (*0-8369-1793-6*) Ayer.

Conference on the Use of Computers in the Coal Ind. Proceedings of the Second Conference on the Use of Computers in the Coal Industry, April 15-17, the University of Alabama, Tuscaloosa, Alabama. fac. ed. Novak, Thomas et al, eds. LC 85-70438. (Illus.). 487p. 1985. reprint ed. pap. 151.00 (*0-7837-7840-6*, 204759900007) Bks Demand.

Conference on Tourism & the Environment Staff & British Tourist Authority Staff. Tourism & the Environment. LC 73-166949. 58 p. 1972. write for info. (*0-85630-018-7*) British Tour.

Conference on Trade Policies in the Americas Staff. Trade & Investment Policies in the Americas. Guisinger, Stephen E., ed. LC 73-84723. (Jno. E. Owens Memorial Foundation Publication Ser.). 113p. reprint ed. pap. 35.10 (*0-8357-7058-3*, 203343500086) Bks Demand.

Conference on Training Personnel for the Computing. Proceedings of the Conference on Training Personnel for the Computing Machine Field, 1st: Held at Wayne University, Detroit, Michigan, June 22 & 25, 1954. Jacobson, Arvid W., ed. LC 55-6746. 115p. reprint ed. pap. 35.70 (*0-7837-3805-6*, 204362500010) Bks Demand.

Conference on Training Psychologists for Work in A. Psychology & the Older Adult: Challenges for Training in the 1980s: Proceedings of the Conference on Training Psychologists for Work in Aging, Boulder, Colorado, June 14-18, 1981. Santos, John F. & VandenBos, Gary R., eds. LC 81-72065. 289p. reprint ed. pap. 89.60 (*0-7837-0490-9*, 204081400018) Bks Demand.

*__Conference on Transplantation & Clinical Immunology Staff, et al.__ Immunosuppression under Trial. LC 99-32565. (Transplantation & Clinical Immunology Ser.). 1999. write for info. (*0-7923-5804-X*) Kluwer Academic.

Conference on Trend in On-Line Computer Control Sy. Trend in On-Line Computer Control Systems, 21-24 April, 1975. LC 76-355944. (Institution of Electrical Engineers Conference Report Ser.: 127). (Illus.). 290p. reprint ed. pap. 89.90 (*0-608-11513-4*, 201212900080) Bks Demand.

Conference on Umbral Calculus & Hopf Algebras, 197. Umbral Calculus & Hopf Algebras. Morris, Robert, ed. LC 81-22756. (Contemporary Mathematics Ser.: No. 6). (Illus.). 92p. reprint ed. pap. 30.00 (*0-608-09192-8*, 205269600003) Bks Demand.

Conference on Understanding Profits (1964: Macales. Profits in the Modern Economy: Selected Papers. Stevenson, Harold W. & Nelson, J. Russell, eds. LC 67-13120. 214p. reprint ed. pap. 66.40 (*0-608-15957-3*, 203323800084) Bks Demand.

Conference on Vacuum Microbalance Techniques (9th:. Progress in Vacuum Microbalance Techniques: Proceedings of the Ninth Conference on Vacuum Microbalance Techniques, Technical University, Berlin, Germany, June, 1970, Vol. 1. Robens, Erich & Gast, T., eds. LC 72-82129. 419p. reprint ed. pap. 129.90 (*0-608-18636-8*, 202402200001) Bks Demand.

— Progress in Vacuum Microbalance Techniques: Proceedings of the 10th Conference on Vacuum Microbalance Techniques, Brunal University, Uxbridge, England, June 1972, Vol. 2. Bevan, Stanley C. & Gregg, S. J., eds. LC 72-82129. 266p. reprint ed. pap. 82.50 (*0-608-14057-0*, 202402300002) Bks Demand.

— Progress in Vacuum Microbalance Techniques: Proceedings of the 12th Conference on Vacuum Microbalance Techniques, Lyon University, Lyon, France, September 1974, Vol. 3. Eyraud, C. & Escoubes, M., eds. LC 72-82129. 481p. reprint ed. pap. 143.00 (*0-608-14058-9*, 202402400003) Bks Demand.

Conference on Very High Pressure. Progress in Very High Pressure Research: Proceedings of an International Conference. Bundy, F. P. et al, eds. LC 61-13156. 333p. reprint ed. pap. 103.30 (*0-608-16820-3*, 205617800054) Bks Demand.

Conference on Virginia Woolf Staff. Virginia Woolf & the Arts: Selected Papers from the Sixth Annual Conference on Virginia Woolf. Gillespie, Diane F. & Hankins, Leslie K., eds. LC 97-14185. 416p. (C). 1997. 67.00 (*0-944473-33-4*); pap. 39.50 (*0-944473-34-2*) Pace Univ Pr.

*__Conference on Virginia Woolf Staff, et al.__ Virginia Woolf: Turning the Centuries: Selected Papers from the 9th Annual Conference on Virginia Woolf: University of Delaware, June 10-13, 1999. LC 00-25621. 2000. pap. 30.00 (*0-944473-51-2*) Pace Univ Pr.

Conference on Weed Control in Rice Staff. Proceedings of the Conference on Weed Control in Rice: Jointly Sponsored by the International Rice Research Institute & the International Weed Science Society, Los Banos, Laguna, Philippines, 31 August-4 September 1981. LC SB0608.R5C66. (Illus.). 422p. 1983. reprint ed. pap. 130.90 (*0-608-07669-4*, 206704900010) Bks Demand.

Conference Proceedings Committee, jt. ed. see Biddle, Stanton F.

Conference Proceedings Staff. First International Conference on Induction Hardened Gears & Critical Components. (Orig.). 1995. pap. 150.00 (*0-9647898-0-9*) Gear Res Inst.

*__Conference Program Committee Staff, ed.__ Microorganisms in Activated Sludge & Biofilm Processes II. 630p. 1998. pap. 318.00 (*0-08-043382-0*, Excerpta Medica) Elsevier.

Conferencia General del Episcopado Latinoamericano Staff. Santo Domingo & Beyond: Documents & Commentaries from the 4th General Conference of Latin American Bishops, 1993. LC 93-36862. 256p. reprint ed. pap. 79.40 (*0-608-20261-4*, 207152000012) Bks Demand.

Conferenza GIFCO Staff, et al. Proceedings of the 8th GIFCO Conference, Cosmic Physics in the Year 2000: Scientific Perspectives & New Instrumentation: Como, 8-10 April 1997. LC 97-224591. (Conference Proceedings/Italian Physical Society Ser.). 326p. 1997. write for info. (*88-7794-097-2*) Compositori IT.

Confessore, Gary J. & Long, Huey B. Abstracts of Literature in Self-Directed Learning. 191p. (Orig.). 1992. pap. text 24.95 (*0-9622488-5-1*) U OK PMC.

Confessore, Gary J., jt. auth. see Long, Huey B.

Conffin, Peggy. Toby/Charlie's Game: A 2-in-1 Read & Color Book. (Illus.). 70p. (Orig.). (J). 1997. pap. write for info. (*1-57502-521-3*, P01547) Morris Pubng.

*__Confiant, Raphael.__ Mamzelle Dragonfly. Coverdale, Linda, tr. from FRE. LC 99-57740. 224p. 2000. 23.00 (*0-374-19932-9*) FS&G.

Confiant, R. Dictionary Titim et Sirandanes-Jeux de Mots Creoles. (CRP & FRE.). 1998. 79.95 (*0-320-00368-X*) Fr & Eur.

Confino, Alon. The Nation As a Local Metaphor: Wurttemberg, Imperial Germany & National Memory, 1871-1918. LC 96-52039. 296p. (C). (gr. 13). 1997. pap. text 19.95 (*0-8078-4665-1*); lib. bdg. 59.95 (*0-8078-2359-7*) U of NC Pr.

Confino, M. & Shamir, Shimon, eds. U. S. S. R. & the Middle East. 441p. 1973. 44.95 (*0-87855-160-3*) Transaction Pubs.

Confino, Vico. The Wrath of Condo. 171p. (Orig.). 1985. pap. 7.95 (*0-9615100-0-5*) Maxsell Corp.

Conford. Seven Days to a Brand New Life. (J). 1993. pap. 2.95 (*0-685-66035-4*) Scholastic Inc.

Conford, Ellen. The Alfred G. Graebner Memorial High School Handbook of Rules & Regulations. (J). (gr. 7-12). 1976. 14.95 (*0-316-15293-5*) Little.

— And This Is Laura. (Illus.). 192p. (J). (gr. 4-7). 1992. mass mkt. 4.95 (*0-316-15354-0*) Little.

— And This Is Laura. (J). (gr. 4-7). 1990. per. 2.95 (*0-671-72771-0*) PB.

— Annabel the Actress Starring in Gorilla My Dreams. LC 97-39449. (Illus.). 64p. (J). (gr. 2-5). 1999. lib. bdg. 14.00 (*0-689-81404-6*) S&S Childrens.

— Can Do, Jenny Archer. 58p. (J). (gr. k-3). 1993. pap. 4.50 (*0-316-15372-9*) Little.

— Can Do, Jenny Archer. (Springboard Bks.). (J). 1991. 9.70 (*0-606-05778-1*, Pub. by Turtleback) Demco.

— A Case for Jenny Archer. 61p. (J). (gr. k-3). 1990. pap. 4.50 (*0-316-15352-4*) Little.

— Case for Jenny Archer. (Springboard Bks.). (J). 1988. 9.70 (*0-606-04628-3*, Pub. by Turtleback) Demco.

— Crush: Stories by Ellen Conford. LC 97-34335. (Illus.). 144p. (J). (gr. 7-12). 1998. 14.95 (*0-06-025414-9*) HarpC.

— Crush: Stories by Ellen Conford. LC 97-34335. 144p. (YA). (gr. 5 up). 1999. pap. 4.95 (*0-06-440778-0*, HarpTrophy) HarpC Child Bks.

— Dear Lovey Hart: I Am Desperate. 224p. (J). (gr. 4-6). 1975. 14.95 (*0-316-15306-0*) Little.

— Diary of a Monster's Son. LC 98-24336. (Illus.). 80p. (J). (gr. 3-7). 1999. 14.95 (*0-316-15245-5*) Little.

— Felicia the Critic. large type ed. 1995. pap. 37.50 (*0-614-09579-4*, L-34848-00) Am Printing Hse.

— The Frog Princess of Pelham. LC 96-25046. 112p. (J). 1997. 15.95 (*0-316-15246-3*) Little.

*__Conford, Ellen.__ Get the Picture, Jenny Archer? 64p. (J). (gr. 3-7). 2000. pap. 4.95 (*0-316-15393-1*) Little.

Conford, Ellen. Hail, Hail Camp Timberwood. LC 78-18715. (Illus.). (J). (gr. 3-7). 1978. 14.95 (*0-316-15291-9*) Little.

— I Love You, I Hate You, Get Lost. (J). 1995. mass mkt. 3.50 (*0-590-45559-1*) Scholastic Inc.

— I Love You, I Hate You, Get Lost. 1995. 8.60 (*0-606-08552-1*, Pub. by Turtleback) Demco.

— Jenny Archer. 61p. (J). (gr. k-3). 1991. pap. 4.50 (*0-316-15353-2*) Little.

— Jenny Archer to the Rescue: What Happens When You Want to Be a Hero But Can't Find a Willing... 56p. (J). (gr. k-3). 1992. pap. 4.50 (*0-316-15369-9*) Little.

Conford, Ellen. Jenny Archer to the Rescue: What Happens When You Want to Be a Hero But Can't Find a Willing... (Springboard Bks.). (J). 1990. 9.70 (*0-606-02230-9*, Pub. by Turtleback) Demco.

Conford, Ellen. A Job for Jenny Archer. 76p. (J). (gr. k-3). 1990. pap. 4.50 (*0-316-15349-4*) Little.

Conford, Ellen. A Job for Jenny Archer. (Springboard Bks.). (J). 1988. 9.70 (*0-606-04452-3*, Pub. by Turtleback) Demco.

Conford, Ellen. My Sister the Witch. (Norman Newman Ser.). (Illus.). 96p. (J). (gr. 3-5). 1997. lib. bdg. 15.35 (*0-8167-3815-7*) Troll Communs.

— My Sister the Witch. (Norman Newman Ser.). (J). 1995. 7.60 (*0-606-07959-9*, Pub. by Turtleback) Demco.

— Nibble, Nibble, Jenny Archer. LC 92-34306. (Illus.). 61p. (J). (gr. k-3). 1993. 14.95 (*0-316-15371-0*) Little.

*__Conford, Ellen.__ Nibble, Nibble, Jerry Archer. 64p. (J). (gr. 3-7). 1999. pap. 4.50 (*0-316-15206-4*) Little.

Conford, Ellen. Norman Newman & the Werewolf of Walnut Street. LC 95-12758. (Illus.). 96p. (J). (gr. 2-5). 1995. lib. bdg. 15.35 (*0-8167-3849-1*, Little Rainbow) Troll Communs.

— Norman Newman & the Werewolf of Walnut Street. (Norman Newman Ser.). 1995. 8.15 (*0-606-07958-0*, Pub. by Turtleback) Demco.

— Seven Days to Brand New Me. 128p. (J). (gr. 7-9). 1990. pap. 3.50 (*0-590-43824-7*) Scholastic Inc.

— What's Cooking, Jenny Archer? 70p. (J). (gr. k-3). 1991. pap. 4.95 (*0-316-15357-5*) Little.

— What's Cooking, Jenny Archer? 1989. 9.15 (*0-606-00820-9*, Pub. by Turtleback) Demco.

— Why Me? 156p. (J). (gr. 5 up). 1985. 14.95 (*0-316-15326-5*) Little.

— You Never Can Tell. (Illus.). 156p. (J). (gr. 7 up). 1984. 14.95 (*0-316-15267-6*) Little.

Conford, Ellen, et al. A Night to Remember. 160p. (Orig.). (YA). (gr. 7 up). 1995. mass mkt. 3.99 (*0-380-78038-0*, Avon Bks) Morrow Avon.

Conford, Philip. Personal World: John MacMurray on Self & Society. 224p. 1997. pap. text 24.95 (*0-86315-236-8*, Pub. by Floris Bks) Anthroposophic.

Confort, Patricia, jt. auth. see Koelle, Ruth.

Conforth, Kellie. A Picture Book of Arctic Animals. LC 90-44896. (Picture Book of...Ser.). (Illus.). 24p. (J). (gr. 1-4). 1991. lib. bdg. 14.50 (*0-8167-2144-0*) Troll Communs.

— A Picture Book of Arctic Animals. LC 90-44896. (Picture Book of...Ser.). (Illus.). 24p. (J). (gr. 1-4). 1996. pap. 2.95 (*0-8167-2145-9*) Troll Communs.

— A Picture Book of Australian Animals. LC 91-18706. (Picture Book of...Ser.). (Illus.). 24p. (J). (gr. 1-4). 1992. pap. 2.95 (*0-8167-2471-7*); lib. bdg. 14.50 (*0-8167-2470-9*) Troll Communs.

Conforti & Francioni. Enforcing International Human Rights in Domestic Courts, Vol. ISHR 49. LC 97-10306. 1997. 179.00 (*90-411-0393-7*) Kluwer Law Intl.

Conforti, Benedetto. International Law & the Role of Domestic Legal Systems. Provost, Rene & Van Praagh, Shauna, trs. LC 93-13369. 1993. lib. bdg. 85.50 (*0-7923-2319-X*) Kluwer Academic.

— The Law & Practice of the United Nations. LC 96-14439. 310p. 1996. 97.00 (*90-411-0233-7*) Kluwer Law Intl.

*__Conforti, Benedetto.__ The Law & Practice of the United Nations. 2nd rev. ed. LC 00-42028. (Legal Aspects of International Organization Ser.). 2000. write for info. (*90-411-1414-9*) Kluwer Law Intl.

Conforti, Daniel A. Advanced Placement American Government: A Day to Day Approach. 62p. 1996. 29.95 (*1-930731-05-1*) DAC Ed Pubns.

— Advanced Placement American Government: A Practical Curriculum Guide for Teachers. 89p. 1989. teacher ed. write for info. (*1-930731-02-7*) DAC Ed Pubns.

Conforti, Daniel A. & Brown, Fredrick M. Advanced Placement Psychology: A Practical Guide for Teachers. 74p. 1991. teacher ed. 29.95 (*1-930731-12-4*) DAC Ed Pubns.

Conforti, Daniel A., jt. auth. see Brown, Fredrick M.

Conforti, Frank & Grabowski, Ralph. Micro Station for AUTOCAD Users. LC 98-8797. (CAD/CAM Ser.). 780p. 1998. text 55.95 (*0-7668-0656-1*) Delmar.

Conforti, Frank D. Food Selection & Preparation. LC 97-28050. 208p. 1997. pap., lab manual ed. 32.95 (*0-8138-2714-0*) Iowa St U Pr.

Conforti Guillermo, Guillermo y, et al. Euglenophyta Pigmentadas de la Argentina. (Bibliotheca Phycologica Ser.: Vol. 75). (SPA., Illus.). 301p. 1986. 71.00 (*3-443-60002-6*, Pub. by Gebruder Borntraeger) Balogh.

*__Conforti, John, ed.__ London After Midnight: Reconstruction of the Lost Classic Silent Film. 2nd rev. ed. (Lost Film Ser.: Vol. 1). (Illus.). 2000. pap. 24.95 (*1-882127-08-0*) Magicimage Filmbooks.

Conforti, John & Gorman, Christine. Confined Space Pocket Guide. (Illus.). 80p. (Orig.). 1993. pap. 41.80 (*0-931690-41-2*) Genium Pub.

Conforti, John, ed. see Mank, Gregory.

Conforti, John, ed. see Palumbo, Ron & Furmanek, Robert.

Conforti, John, ed. see Philip J., Riley.

Conforti, John, ed. see Seely, Lewis E. & Seely-Buell, Lorraine.

Conforti, John V. Lock Out - Tag Out Pocket Guide. Roy, Robert A., ed. (Illus.). 64p. (Orig.). 1993. pap. text 41.80 (*0-931690-59-5*) Genium Pub.

— Motor Vehicle Safety Pocket Guide. (Illus.). 63p. (Orig.). 1992. pap. 41.80 (*0-931690-48-X*) Genium Pub.

Conforti, Joseph A. Jonathan Edwards, Religious Tradition, & American Culture from the Second Great Awakening to the Twentieth Century. LC 94-49526. 1995. lib. bdg. 34.95 (*0-8078-2224-8*) U of NC Pr.

— Samuel Hopkins & the New Divinity Movement: Calvinism, the Congregational Ministry, & Reform in New England Between the Great Awakenings. LC 80-28268. 249p. reprint ed. pap. 77.20 (*0-608-30359-3*, 202084000019) Bks Demand.

Conforti, Jospeh A. Jonathan Edwards, Religious Tradition, & American Culture from the Second Great Awakening to the Twentieth Century. LC 94-49526. 1995. pap. text 15.95 (*0-8078-4535-3*) U of NC Pr.

Conforti, Michael. Art & Life on the Upper Mississippi, 1890-1915. (Illus.). 384p. 1994. 65.00 (*0-87413-560-5*) U Delaware Pr.

— Field, Form & Fate: Patterns in Mind, Psyche & Nature. LC 99-16065. 144p. 1999. pap. 19.00 (*0-88214-118-X*, Pub. by Spring Pubns) Continuum.

Conforti, Michael, et al. John Ringling, Dreamer - Builder - Collector: Legacy of the Circus King. Ormond, Mark et al, eds. LC 96-77907. (Illus.). 128p. (Orig.). 1996. pap., per. 29.95 (*0-916758-36-2*) Ringling Mus Art.

— Masterworks of European Sculpture. (Mead Art Museum Monographs: Vol. 4). (Illus.). 36p. 1983. pap. 3.00 (*0-914337-00-9*) Mead Art Mus.

Conforti, P., et al. Cerebral Revascularization by Microneurosurgical Bypass. 240p. 1984. text 64.00 (*1-57235-042-3*) Piccin Nuova.

Conforto, Giovanni. Breve e Facile Maniera. fac. ed. (Monuments of Music & Music Literature in Facsimile, I Ser.: Vol. 115). 1978. lib. bdg. 30.00 (*0-8450-2315-2*) Broude.

Conforto, Giovanni L. The Joy of Ornamentation: Being Conforto's "Treatise on Ornamentation" (Rome, 1593) 1989. pap. 8.95 (*0-912483-49-0*) Pro-Am Music.

Confreras, Moyra, tr. see Rodieck, Jorma.

Confrey, Jere, jt. ed. see Harel, Guershon.

Confucius. Analects. (Classics of World Literature Ser.). 1997. pap. 5.95 (*1-85326-462-8*, 4628WW, Pub. by Wrdsworth Edits) NTC Contemp Pub Co.
— The Analects. unabridged ed. Soothill, William E., tr. LC 94-24742. (Thrift Editions Ser.). (Illus.). 128p. 1995. pap. text 2.00 (*0-486-28484-0*) Dover.
— The Analects of Confucius. Lau, D. C., tr. 160p. 1998. pap. text 6.67 (*0-14-044348-7*) Addson-Wesley Educ.
— The Analects of Confucius. Hinton, David, tr. from CHI. 288p. 1999. pap. text 13.00 (*1-58243-038-1*, Pub. by Counterpt DC) HarpC.
— The Analects of Confucius. Leys, Simon, tr. & notes by. 258p. 1998. reprint ed. lib. bdg. 30.00 (*0-7351-0027-6*) Replica Bks.
— The Analects of Confucius. unabridged ed. Legge, James, tr. from CHI. LC 99-71178. 128p. 1999. pap. 14.95 (*0-87243-242-4*) Templegate.
— Confucian Analects, the Great Learning & the Doctrine of the Mean. Legge, James, ed. (CHI & ENG.). 503p. 1971. pap. 12.95 (*0-486-22746-4*) Dover.
— Confucius: The Analects (Lun Yu) 2nd ed. Lau, D. C., tr. from CHI. LC 98-129568. 288p. (C). 1997. 45.00 (*962-201-527-1*, Pub. by Chinese Univ) U of Mich Pr.
— The Wisdom of Confucius. LC 95-19792. 160p. 1995. pap. 6.95 (*0-8065-1702-6*, Citadel Pr) Carol Pub Group.
— Wisdom of Confucius. Yutang, Lin, ed. 290p. 1994. 15.95 (*0-679-60123-6*) Modern Lib NY.
***Confucius Staff.** Analects. (Oxford World Classics Ser.). 160p. 2000. pap. 9.95 (*0-19-283920-9*) OUP.
Cong, Dachang. When Heroes Pass Away: The Invention of a Chinese Communist Pantheon. LC 97-21811. 216p. (C). 1997. 47.00 (*0-7618-0809-4*); pap. 29.00 (*0-7618-0810-8*) U Pr of Amer.
Cong, Nguyen D. Topological Dynamics of Random Dynamical Systems. LC 97-19731. (Oxford Mathematical Monographs). 212p. 1997. text 89.00 (*0-19-850157-9*) OUP.
***Congalton, David.** Three Cats, Two Dogs: One Journey Through Multiple Pet Loss. LC 00-35123. (Illus.). 176p. 2000. pap. text 12.95 (*0-939165-37-6*) New Riders Pub.
Congalton, Russell G. Uncertainty Analysis in Environmental Science. ring bd. 64.95 (*1-56670-482-0*) Lewis Pubs.
Congalton, Russell G. & Green, Kass. Assessing the Accuracy of Remotely Sensed Data Principles & Practices. LC 98-29658. 160p. 1999. lib. bdg. 49.95 (*0-87371-986-7*, L986) Lewis Pubs.
Congar, Samuel H., ed. Records of the Town of Newark, New Jersey, from its Settlement in 1666 to its Incorporation as a City in 1836, Vol. 6. 308p. 1966. reprint ed. pap. 8.50 (*0-686-81799-0*) NJ Hist Soc.
Congar, Yves. Called to Life. (Orig.). (C). 1988. 55.00 (*0-85439-265-3*, Pub. by St Paul Pubns) St Mut.
— I Believe in the Holy Spirit. Smith, David, tr. LC 97-28324. 730p. 1997. pap. 29.95 (*0-8245-1696-6*) Crossroad NY.
— I Believe in the Holy Spirit, 3 Vols. Smith, David, tr. from FRE. Incl. Vol. I. Experience of the Spirit. 173p. 1984. 24.95 (*0-8164-0518-2*); Vol. 2. Lord & Giver of Life. 230p. 1984. 24.95 (*0-8164-0535-2*); Vol. 3. River of Life Flows in the East & in the West. 274p. 1984. 24.95 (*0-8164-0537-9*); 300p. 1984. 70.00 (*0-8164-0540-9*) Harper SF.
— Thomas d'Aquin: Sa Vision de Theologie et de l'Eglise. (Collected Studies: No. CS190). (ENG, FRE & LAT.). 334p. (C). 1984. reprint ed. text 124.95 (*0-86078-138-0*, Pub. by Variorum) Ashgate Pub Co.
Congar, Yves & Siegwalt, Gerard. Vocabulaire Oecumenique. 39.95 (*0-8288-7665-7*, M6083); pap. 39.95 (*0-686-56960-1*, M-6083) Fr & Eur.
Congar, Yves M. Tradition & Traditions. LC 98-135873. 536p. 1998. reprint ed. 15.80 (*0-536-00173-1*) Pearson Custom.
Congdom-Martin, Douglas, jt. auth. see Terranova, Jerry.
***Congdon.** Egg. Donovan, Jane, ed. (Essentials Ser.). 80p. 2000. 12.95 (*0-8092-2326-0*, 232600, Contemporary Bks) NTC Contemp Pub Co.
Congdon. Problems In Philosophy. 1996. pap. 16.00 (*0-07-217389-0*) McGraw.
— Tales of the Lost Formicans. 1990. pap. 6.95 (*0-88145-091-X*) Broadway Play.
Congdon, Charles T. Tribune Essays. LC 79-154147. (Select Bibliographies Reprint Ser.). 1977. reprint ed. 38.95 (*0-8369-5763-6*) Ayer.
Congdon, Clare, ed. Carmel vs. Flakey: A Comparison of Two Robots. (Technical Reports). (Illus.). 50p. 1994. spiral bd. 25.00 (*0-929280-61-X*) AAAI Pr.
Congdon, Constance. Tales of the Lost Formicans & Other Plays. LC 93-51495. 314p. 1994. pap. 14.95 (*1-55936-084-4*) Theatre Comm.
Congdon, Don. Combat WW II: Europe. 768p. 1996. 16.98 (*0-88365-945-X*) Galahad Bks.
— Combat WW II: Pacific. 768p. 1996. 16.98 (*0-88365-944-1*) Galahad Bks.
Congdon, Herbert W. Early American Homes for Today: A Treasury of Decorative Details & Restoration Procedures. (Illus.). xv, 236p. 1985. reprint ed. pap. 12.95 (*0-87233-065-6*) Bauhan.
Congdon, Kirby. Aipotu. 38p. 1998. pap. 7.95 (*1-892034-05-0*, Pub. by Missing Spoke) Partners Pubs Grp.
— Crank Letters. LC 85-61564. 84p. (Orig.). 1986. pap. 10.00 (*0-912292-79-2*) Smith.
Congdon, Kristin G., jt. ed. see Blandy, Doug E.
Congdon, Kristin G., jt. ed. see Blandy, Douglas E.
Congdon, Lee. Exile & Social Thought: Hungarian Intellectuals in Germany & Austria, 1919-1933. (Illus.). 392p. 1991. text 49.50 (*0-691-03159-2*, Pub. by Princeton U Pr) Cal Prin Full Svc.
— The Young Lukacs. LC 82-11162. xiii, 235p. (C). 1983. 39.95 (*0-8078-1538-1*) U of NC Pr.
Congdon-Martin, Douglas. America for Sale: Antique Advertising. LC 91-65650. (Illus.). 160p. 1991. pap. 29.95 (*0-88740-333-6*) Schiffer.
— Arts & Crafts: The California Home. LC 98-34697. 160p. 1998. 49.95 (*0-7643-0629-4*) Schiffer.
***Congdon-Martin, Douglas.** Arts & Crafts for the Home. (Illus.). 256p. 2000. 59.95 (*0-7643-1178-6*) Schiffer.
Congdon-Martin, Douglas. Basic Penknife Carving with Tom Wolfe. (Illus.). 48p. (Orig.). 1993. pap. 12.95 (*0-88740-499-5*) Schiffer.
— Camel Cigarette Collectibles: The Early Years, 1913-1963. LC 96-31484. (Illus.). 192p. (gr. 10). 1997. pap. 29.95 (*0-88740-948-2*) Schiffer.
— Camel Cigarette Collectibles: 1913-1963. LC 96-30074. (Illus.). 176p. 1997. pap. 29.95 (*0-7643-0196-9*) Schiffer.
— Drugstore & Soda Fountain Antiques. LC 91-65649. (Illus.). 160p. 1991. pap. 29.95 (*0-88740-334-4*) Schiffer.
— Figurative Cast Iron: A Collector's Guide. LC 94-65628. (Illus.). 176p. (Orig.). 1994. pap. 29.95 (*0-88740-622-X*) Schiffer.
— Hathaway Shirts: Their History, Design, & Advertising. LC 98-86372. (Illus.). 160p. 1998. pap. 29.95 (*0-7643-0628-6*) Schiffer.
— Images in Black: Three Hundred Years of Black Collectibles. LC 90-61509. (Illus.). 160p. (Orig.). 1990. pap. 24.95 (*0-88740-273-9*) Schiffer.
— Images in Black: 150 Years of Black Collectibles. 2nd rev. ed. LC 98-83289. (Illus.). 160p. (Orig.). 1999. pap. 24.95 (*0-7643-0806-8*) Schiffer.
— Masks of the World. LC 99-29934. (Illus.). 160p. 1999. 49.95 (*0-7643-0968-4*) Schiffer.
— The Navajo Art of Sandpainting. LC 90-61507. (Illus.). 64p. (Orig.). 1990. pap. 9.95 (*0-88740-271-2*) Schiffer.
— The Navajo Art of Sandpainting. 2nd rev. ed. LC 98-89784. (Illus.). 64p. (Orig.). 1999. pap. 9.95 (*0-7643-0810-6*) Schiffer.
— Out to the Ball Game with Tom Wolfe. LC 92-63110. (Illus.). 64p. (Orig.). 1993. pap. 12.95 (*0-88740-497-9*) Schiffer.
— Storytellers & Other Figurative Pottery. LC 90-61506. 144p. (Orig.). 1990. pap. 19.95 (*0-88740-270-4*) Schiffer.
— Storytellers & Other Figurative Pottery. 2nd rev. ed. LC 98-83093. (Illus.). 144p. (Orig.). 1999. pap. 19.95 (*0-7643-0805-X*) Schiffer.
— Tobacco Tins: A Collector's Guide. LC 92-60632. (Illus.). 160p. 1992. pap. 29.95 (*0-88740-429-4*) Schiffer.
— Traditional Windsor Chair Making with Jim Rendi. LC 93-83051. (Illus.). 128p. (Orig.). 1993. pap. 19.95 (*0-88740-503-7*) Schiffer.
Congdon-Martin, Douglas, ed. Country Store Antiques: From Cradles to Caskets. LC 91-65652. (Illus.). 160p. 1991. pap. 29.95 (*0-88740-331-X*) Schiffer.
***Congdon-Martin, Douglas, ed.** Monterey: Furnishings of California's Spanish Revival. LC 99-59827. (Illus.). 176p. 2000. 49.95 (*0-7643-1067-4*) Schiffer.
Congdon-Martin, Douglas, photos by. Carving a Kid's Size Rocking Horse. LC 95-30138. (Illus.). 64p. (Orig.). 1995. pap. 12.95 (*0-88740-852-4*) Schiffer.
— Carving Angels. LC 95-32236. (Illus.). 64p. (Orig.). 1995. pap. 12.95 (*0-88740-860-5*) Schiffer.
— Carving Caricature Heads & Faces: 33 Caricatures with Step-by-Step Carving Instructions. LC 95-15653. (Illus.). 64p. (Orig.). 1995. pap. 12.95 (*0-88740-784-6*) Schiffer.
— Georg Keilhofer's Traditional Carving: Basic Relief Carving. LC 95-24049. (Illus.). 64p. (Orig.). 1995. pap. 12.95 (*0-88740-785-4*) Schiffer.
— A Scroll-Saw Christmas with Frank Pozsgai: Step-by-Step to a 3-D Sleight & Reindeer, Plus 30 Tree Ornament Patterns. LC 95-19424. (Illus.). 64p. (Orig.). 1995. pap. 12.95 (*0-88740-786-2*) Schiffer.
— Tom Wolfe Carves . . . A Horse of a Different Color. LC 95-5962. (Illus.). 64p. (Orig.). 1995. pap. 12.95 (*0-88740-787-0*) Schiffer.
Congdon-Martin, Douglas & Biondi, Bob. Country Store Collectibles. LC 90-61510. (Illus.). 160p. (Orig.). 1990. pap. 24.95 (*0-88740-274-7*) Schiffer.
Congdon-Martin, Douglas & California Heritage Museum Staff. Aloha Spirit. LC 97-39000. 192p. 1998. 49.95 (*0-7643-0489-5*) Schiffer.
Congdon-Martin, Douglas & Kashmanian, John. Baseball Treasures: Memorabilia from the National Pastime. LC 92-83775. (Illus.). 256p. 1993. 59.95 (*0-88740-492-8*) Schiffer.
Congdon-Martin, Douglas, jt. auth. see Cooper, Mark.
Congdon-Martin, Douglas, jt. auth. see Gibson, Helen.
Congdon-Martin, Douglas, jt. auth. see Hawkins, Larry.
Congdon-Martin, Douglas, jt. auth. see Holland, William R.
Congdon-Martin, Douglas, jt. auth. see Kvetko, Edward C.
Congdon-Martin, Douglas, jt. auth. see Streams, Margaret.
Congdon-Martin, Douglas, jt. auth. see Terranova, Jerry.
Congdon-Martin, Douglas, jt. auth. see Toatley, Theodore.
Congdon-Martin, Douglas, jt. auth. see Veasey, Michael.
Congdon-Martin, Douglas, jt. auth. see Wolfe, Tom James.
Congdon-Martin, Douglas, ed. see Ditmer, Judith A.
Congdon-Martin, Douglas, ed. see Heller, Thomas & Clarkson, Ronald.
Congdon-Martin, Douglas, ed. see White, Paul.
Congdon, Peter. The Analysis of Small Area Social Change. (Progress in Planning Ser.: No. 34). (Illus.). 104p. 1991. pap. 44.50 (*0-08-040782-X*, Pergamon Pr) Elsevier.
Congdon, Peter & Batey, Peter. Advances in Regional Demography: Forecasts, Information, Models. 256p. 1989. 55.00 (*1-85293-046-2*) St Martin.
Congdon, Peter & Stillwell, John C. Migration Models. 308p. 1993. text 105.00 (*0-471-94804-7*, Pub. by P P Pubs) Wiley.
Congdon, Peter, jt. ed. see Shepherd, John.
Congdon, Tim & McWilliams, D. Economics Dictionary: Diccionario de Economia. 2nd ed. (SPA.). 232p. 1985. 29.95 (*0-7859-4918-6*) Fr & Eur.
Conge, Patrick. From Revolution to War: State Relations in a World of Change. (Illus.). 192p. Date not set. pap. text 21.95 (*0-472-08578-6*, 08578) U of Mich Pr.
Conge, Patrick J. From Revolution to War: State Relations in a World of Change. LC 96-10249. 192p. (C). 1996. text 39.50 (*0-472-10647-3*, 10647) U of Mich Pr.
Congebsi, James. Classroom Management Strategies. 4th ed. LC 99-22337. (C). 2000. pap. text. write for info. (*0-8013-3059-9*) Longman.
Congenital Heart Disease with Cyanosis Symposium S. Congenital Heart Disease with Cyanosis Symposium, Amsterdam 1968. Klinkhammer, A. C., ed. (Radiologia Clinica et Biologica Ser.: Vol. 39, No. 2). 1970. reprint ed. pap. 28.00 (*3-8055-0802-6*) S Karger.
Conger. Adolescence & Youth. 4th ed. (C). 1991. pap., student ed. 21.00 (*0-06-044579-3*) Addson-Wesley Educ.
Conger, Amy. Companeras de Mexico: Women Photograph Women. (ENG & SPA., Illus.). 80p. 1990. 18.95 (*0-932173-04-7*) Sweeney Art Gallery.
— Edward Weston: Photographs from the Collection of the Center for Creative Photography. (Illus.). 662p. 1992. 100.00 (*0-938262-21-1*) Ctr Creat Photog.
Conger, Amy & Poniatowska, Elena. Companeras de Mexico: Women Photograph Women. (Illus.). 80p. 1990. pap. 18.95 (*0-295-97051-0*) U of Wash Pr.
Conger, Arthur L. The Rise of U. S. Grant. LC 74-137371. (Select Bibliographies Reprint Ser.). (Illus.). 1977. 36.95 (*0-8369-5572-2*) Ayer.
— The Rise of U. S. Grant. (Illus.). 432p. 1996. reprint ed. pap. 15.95 (*0-306-80693-2*) Da Capo.
Conger, Arthur L., ed. see De Purucker, G.
Conger, B. V., ed. Cloning Agricultural Plants via In Vitro Techniques. 280p. 1981. 161.00 (*0-8493-5797-7*, SB123, CRC Reprint) Franklin.
Conger, Beach. Bag Balm & Duct Tape: Tales of a Vermont Doctor. 224p. 1988. 16.95 (*0-316-15258-7*, Little Brwn Med Div) Lppncott W & W.
— It's Not My Fault: Tales of a Vermont Doctor. 208p. 1995. 19.95 (*1-55591-223-0*) Fulcrum Pub.
Conger, Cathy. In the Wee Small Hours of the Morning. (Illus.). 49p. 1998. pap. 12.00 (*0-9671800-0-7*) Laura Alexandra.
Conger, David. C For Technology Students. 448p. (C). 2002. pap. 54.00 (*0-13-370172-7*, Macmillan Coll) P-H.
— C++ Software Development for Technology Students. LC 99-42696. (Illus.). 726p. (C). 1999. pap. text 85.00 (*0-13-370180-8*, Macmillan Coll) P-H.
— Fundamentals of Microcomputers for Technology Students. LC 98-14464. 452p. 1998. pap. text, student ed. 85.00 (*0-13-217019-1*) P-H.
Conger, Dorothy S., jt. auth. see Conger, Ivan A.
Conger, Dwight G., et al. Construction Accident Litigation. LC 90-62799. (Real Property-Zoning Ser.). 1990. 135.00 (*0-685-59797-0*) West Group.
Conger, Flora S. & Rose, Irene B. Child Care Aide Skills. (Careers in Home Economics Ser.). (Illus.). 1978. text 25.84 (*0-07-012420-5*) McGraw.
Conger, George P. Ideologies of Religion. LC 70-93329. (Essay Index Reprint Ser.). 1977. 21.95 (*0-8369-1283-7*) Ayer.
Conger, Ivan A. & Conger, Dorothy S. Timlick Family History: The Timlick, Timleck, Timlake, Timlock Family. deluxe ed. (Illus.). 544p. 1990. 40.00 (*0-9626440-0-5*) I A Conger.
Conger, James L. Windows API Bible: The Definitive Programmer's Reference. (Illus.). 1040p. (Orig.). 1992. pap. 39.95 (*1-878739-15-8*) Sams.
Conger, Jay A. The Charismatic Leader: Behind the Mystique of Exceptional Leadership. LC 89-45598. (Management Ser.). 236p. 1989. text 32.95 (*1-55542-171-7*) Jossey-Bass.
— Learning to Lead: The Art of Transforming Managers into Leaders. LC 92-16934. (Management Ser.). 254p. 1992. text 32.95 (*1-55542-474-0*) Jossey-Bass.
— Managing in the Age of Persuasion. LC 98-9632. 224p. 1998. 24.50 (*0-684-80772-6*) S&S Trade.
— Spirit at Work: Discovering the Spirituality in Leadership. (Business-Management Ser.). 264p. 1994. text 27.95 (*1-55542-639-5*) Jossey-Bass.
Conger, Jay A., et al, eds. The Leader's Change Handbook: An Essential Guide to Setting Direction & Taking Action. LC 98-40101. (Business & Management Ser.). 442p. 1998. 28.00 (*0-7879-4351-7*) Jossey-Bass.
Conger, Jay A. & Benjamin, Beth. Building Leaders: How Successful Companies Develop the Next Generation. LC 98-58113. 304p. 1999. 34.95 (*0-7879-4469-6*) Jossey-Bass.
Conger, Jay A. & Kanungo Rabindra Nath. Charismatic Leadership in Organizations. LC 98-9003. 280p. 1998. 40.00 (*0-7619-1633-4*); pap. 17.99 (*0-7619-1634-2*) Sage.
Conger, Jean. Velvet Paw. (Illus.). 1963. 14.95 (*0-8392-1125-2*) Astor-Honor.
Conger, John. The Body in Recovery: Somatic Psychotherapy & the Self. LC 93-37231. 277p. (Orig.). 1994. pap. 16.95 (*1-883319-06-4*) Frog Ltd CA.
Conger, John J. Adolescence & Youth: Psychological Development in a Changing World. 5th ed. (C). 1997. 24.00 (*0-673-97807-9*, GoodYrBooks) Addson-Wesley Educ.
— Adolescence & Youth: Psychological Development in a Changing World. 5th ed. (C). 1997. 24.00 (*0-673-55775-8*) S&S Trade.
Conger, John J. The Shape of the Tree: Selected Poems. 48p. (Orig.). 1993. pap. 6.95 (*0-9635839-0-5*) Equinox Mtn.
Conger, John J., ed. Adolescence & Youth. 5th ed. (C). 1997. pap. text, student ed. 26.00 (*0-673-99487-2*) Addison-Wesley.
Conger, John P. Jung & Reich: The Body As Shadow. 222p. (Orig.). 1988. 25.00 (*1-55643-038-8*); pap. 12.95 (*1-55643-037-X*) North Atlantic.
Conger, Margaret. Combined Chronology: For Use with the Mahatma & Blavatsky Letters. LC 73-92461. 61p. 1973. pap. 4.95 (*0-911500-17-0*) Theos U Pr.
Conger, Margaret M. Managed Care: Practice Strategies for Nursing. LC 98-40281. 290p. 1999. 55.00 (*0-7619-0964-8*) Sage.
Conger, Margaret M., jt. ed. see Artinian, Barbara M.
Conger, Marge. Managed Care: Practice Strategies for Nursing. LC 98-40281. 1999. 24.95 (*0-7619-0965-6*) Sage.
***Conger, Mary.** No Glamour Literature. 195p. (YA). (gr. 5-13). 1999. spiral bd. 41.95 (*0-7606-0301-4*) LinguiSystems.
Conger, Nancy. Sensuous Living: Expand Your Sensory Awareness. LC 95-12263. (Llewellyn's Whole Life Ser.). (Illus.). 216p. 1999. pap. 12.95 (*1-56718-160-0*) Llewellyn Pubns.
Conger, Rand D. & Elder, Glen H., Jr. Families in Troubled Times: Adapting to Change in Rural America. LC 93-38397. (Social Institutions & Social Change Ser.). 314p. 1994. pap. text 26.95 (*0-202-30488-4*); lib. bdg. 49.95 (*0-202-30487-6*) Aldine de Gruyter.
Conger, Rand D., jt. auth. see Elder, Glen H.
Conger, Roger. Pictorial History of Waco. (Illus.). 292p. 1969. 24.95 (*0-87244-026-5*) Texian.
Conger, Shelley, ed. see McDaniel, Nello.
Conger, Shelley, ed. see McDaniel, Nello & Thorn, George.
***Conger, Sue & Mason.** Planning & Designing Effective Web Sites. 10th ed. 160p. (C). 1998. pap. text, mass mkt. 32.95 incl. cd-rom (*0-7600-4988-2*) Course Tech.
Conger, Sue A. The New Software Engineering. 800p. 1994. pap. 55.95 (*0-534-17143-5*) Course Tech.
Conger, Sydny M., ed. see American Society for Eighteenth-Century Studies St.
Conger, Syndy, jt. ed. see Hay, Carla H.
Conger, Syndy M. Matthew G. Lewis, Charles Robert Maturin & the Germans: An Interpretative Study of the Influence of German Literature on Two Gothic Novels. Varma, Devendra P., ed. LC 79-8448. (Gothic Studies & Dissertations). 1980. reprint ed. lib. bdg. 35.95 (*0-405-12652-2*) Ayer.
Conger, Syndy M., et al, eds. Iconoclastic Departures: Mary Shelley after Frankenstein. LC 96-52067. (Illus.). 368p. 1997. 49.50 (*0-8386-3684-5*) Fairleigh Dickinson.
Conger, Syndy M. & Hayes, Julie C., eds. Studies in Eighteenth Century Culture, Vol. 25. (Illus.). 336p. 1997. text 40.00 (*0-8018-5462-8*) Johns Hopkins.
— Studies in Eighteenth Century Culture, Vol. 26. (Illus.). 352p. 1997. text 40.00 (*0-8018-5627-2*) Johns Hopkins.
Conger, Syndy M., jt. ed. see Hay, Carla H.
Conger, Syndy McMillen. Mary Wollstonecraft & the Language of Sensibility. LC 93-33718. 1994. 39.50 (*0-8386-3553-9*) Fairleigh Dickinson.
Conger, Yves M. After Nine Hundred Years: The Background of the Schism Between the Eastern & Western Churches. LC 78-6154. 150p. 1978. reprint ed. lib. bdg. 35.00 (*0-313-20493-4*, COAN, Greenwood Pr) Greenwood.
Conghail, Muiris Mac, see Mac Conghail, Muiris.
Congleton, Elizabeth, jt. auth. see Congleton, J. E.
Congleton, Henry B. On Financial Reform. 3rd ed. LC 68-56560. (Library of Money & Banking History). viii, 383p. 1968. reprint ed. 49.50 (*0-678-00452-8*) Kelley.
Congleton, J. E. Theories of Pastoral Poetry in England, 1684-1798. LC 68-29735. (Studies in Poetry: No. 38). 1969. reprint ed. lib. bdg. 75.00 (*0-8383-0329-3*) M S G Haskell Hse.
Congleton, J. E. & Congleton, Elizabeth. Johnson's Dictionary: A Bibliographical Survey, 1746-1984. LC 85-169578. 97p. 1985. 5.00 (*0-318-18658-6*); pap. 3.00 (*0-317-01174-X*) Dict Soc NA.
Congleton, Robert J., jt. auth. see Cassel, Jeris F.
Congleton, Roger D., ed. The Political Economy of Environmental Protection: Analysis & Evidence. LC 96-25. 304p. (C). 1996. text 57.50 (*0-472-10602-3*, 10602) U of Mich Pr.
Congleton, Roger D., jt. auth. see Buchanan, James M.
Congleton, Roger D., jt. ed. see Tollison, Robert D.
Congo, Jan, et al. The Woman Within: Daily Devotions for Women in Recovery. (Serenity Meditation Ser.). 372p. (Orig.). 1992. pap. 8.99 (*0-8407-3239-2*) Nelson.
Congregation Beth Israel Staff. Jewish Cooking from Here & Far: Traditions & Memories from Our Mothers Kitchens. (Illus.). 190p. 1994. 13.95 (*0-9642644-0-4*) Wimmer Bks.
***Congregation Bnai Jeshurun, New York, NY Staff.** My Prayer/Tefilati. 128p. 2000. pap. 15.00 (*0-87441-715-5*) Behrman.
Congregation for Catholic Education Staff. Directives Concerning the Preparation of Seminary Educators. 60p. pap. 1.75 (*0-8198-1871-2*) Pauline Bks.
— Educational Guidance in Human. 61p. pap. 1.25 (*0-8198-2322-8*) Pauline Bks.
Congregation for Divine Worship Staff. Christian Initiation of Adults. rev. ed. International Committee on English in the Liturgy., tr. from LAT. (Liturgy Documentary Ser.: No. 4). 138p. (Orig.). 1988. pap. 5.95 (*1-55586-895-9*) US Catholic.

C

An Asterisk (*) at the beginning of an entry indicates that the title is appearing for the first time.

Congregation for Institutes of Consecrated Life St & Societies of Apostolic Life Staff. Directives for Mutual Relations Between Bishops & Religious in the Church: Mutuae Relationes. 68p. pap. 0.50 (*0-8198-1860-7*) Pauline Bks.
— Directives on Formation in Religious Institutes. 95p. pap. 2.95 (*0-8198-1862-3*) Pauline Bks.
— Fraternal Life in Community: Congregavit Nos in Unum Christi Amor. 96p. pap. 1.95 (*0-8198-2658-8*) Pauline Bks.
— Letter to the Bishops of the United States & Essential Elements in the Church's Teaching on Religious Life As Applied to Works of the Apostolate. 55p. pap. 0.50 (*0-8198-2323-6*) Pauline Bks.
— Religious & Human Promotion & the Contemplative Dimension of Religious Life. 54p. pap. 0.50 (*0-8198-6432-3*) Pauline Bks.
Congregation for the Clergy Staff. Concluding Message to All Priests in the World: International Symposium Celebrating the 30th Anniversary of the Promulgation of the Conciliar Decree Presbyterorym Ordinis. 30p. (Orig.). 1996. pap. text 3.95 (*1-57455-088-8*) US Catholic.
— General Directory for Catechesis. United States Catholic Conference Staff, ed. 300p. 1998. pap. text 19.95 (*1-57455-225-2*) US Catholic.
Congregation for the Doctrine of the Faith. Instruction on Christian Freedom & Liberation. 72p. pap. 1.25 (*0-8198-3647-8*) Pauline Bks.
— Instruction on the Ecclesiastical Vocation of the Theologian. 32p. (Orig.). (C). 1990. pap. 1.75 (*1-55586-366-3*) US Catholic.
Congregation for the Doctrine of the Faith Staff. Instruction on Respect for Human Life in Its Origin & on the Dignity of Procreation: Replies to Certain Questions of the Day. 39p. 1987. pap. 4.95 (*1-55586-156-3*) US Catholic.
Congregation for the Doctrine of the Faith Staff, ed. From "Inter Insigniores" to "Ordinatio Sacerdotalis" Documents & Commentaries. 216p. (C). 1998. pap. 19.95 (*1-57455-163-9*) US Catholic.
Congregation for the Evangelization of Peoples. Guia para los Catequistas. Vatican, tr. (SPA.). 75p. (Orig.). 1995. pap. 5.95 (*1-55586-027-3*) US Catholic.
Congregation of Marians of the Immaculate Concepti, ed. see Kowalska, Faustina.
Congregation Shalar Zahav Staff. Out of Our Kitchen Closets: San Francisco Gay Jewish Cooking. LC 87-71707. (Illus.). 224p. (Orig.). 1987. pap. 12.95 (*0-9619242-0-9*) Cong Shaar Zahav.
Congres d'Ottawa sur Kant Dans les Traditions Angl. Actes du Congres d'Ottawa sur Kant dans les Traditions Anglo-Americaine & Continentale Tenu du 10-14 Octobre 1974: Proceedings of the Ottawa Congress on Kant in the Anglo-American & Continental Traditions, Held October 10-14, 1974. Laberge, Pierre et al, eds. LC 77-102. (Collection Philosophica: Vol. 5). (ENG & FRE.). 557p. 1976. reprint ed. pap. 172.70 (*0-608-02187-3*, 206285600003) Bks Demand.
Congres International de la Preparation des Minera, ed. Lexique Quadrilinque de la Preparation des Minerais. (ENG, FRE, GER & RUS.). 260p. 1963. pap. 25.00 (*0-686-56795-1*) Fr & Eur.
Congresional Quarterly Staff. Historic Documents of 1986. 1130p. 1987. 125.00 (*0-87187-399-0*) Congr Quarterly.
***Congreso Latinoamericano de Botanica, et al.** Proceedings of the VI Congreso Latinoamericano De Botanica, Mar Del Plata, Argentina, 2-8 October 1994. LC 99-191737. (Illus.). 1998. write for info. (*0-915279-58-4*) Miss Botan.
Congress, Elaine. Social Work Values & Ethics. LC 98-27940. 224p. (C). 1999. pap. text 33.95 (*0-8304-1492-4*) Thomson Learn.
Congress, Elaine P., ed. Multicultural Perspectives in Working with Families. LC 96-40363. (Social Work Ser.). (Illus.). 376p. 1997. 47.95 (*0-8261-9560-1*) Springer Pub.
Congress For Cultural Freedom-Berlin-1960. History & Hope. Jelenski, K. A., ed. LC 70-117773. (Essay Index Reprint Ser.). 1977. 20.95 (*0-8369-1794-4*) Ayer.
Congress for the New Urban Staff. Charter of New Urbanism. LC 99-51560. 160p. 1999. pap. 49.95 (*0-07-135553-7*) McGraw.
Congress, Joint Committee on Printing, contrib. by. Official Congressional Directory, 1997-1998. 1997. boxed set 43.00 (*0-16-055120-X*) USGPO.
Congress, Joint Committee on Printing Staff. Official Congressional Directory, 1997-1998. 1997. per. 30.00 (*0-16-055119-6*) USGPO.
Congress, Nita, ed. Sustainable America: A New Concensus for Prosperity, Opportunity, & a Healthy Environment for the Future. (Illus.). 186p. (Orig.). 1996. pap. text 35.00 (*0-7881-3351-9*) DIANE Pub.
Congress of Accountants, World Fair, St Louis, Sep. Official Record of the Congress of Accountants: Proceedings. Brief, Richard P., ed. LC 77-87266. (Development of Contemporary Accounting Thought Ser.). 1978. reprint ed. lib. bdg. 23.95 (*0-405-10895-8*) Ayer.
Congress of Colored Catholics of the United States. Three Catholic Afro-American Congresses. 1978. 21.95 (*0-405-10863-X*, 11829) Ayer.
Congress of Experimental Surgery Symposium Staff. Morphology in Lung Transplantation: Proceedings of the Congress of Experimental Surgery Symposium, 7th, Amsterdam, April 1972. Wildevuur, R. H., ed. (Illus.). 1973. 85.25 (*3-8055-1441-7*) S Karger.
Congress of International College of Psychosomatic. Mechanisms in Symptom Formation: Proceedings. Musaph, H., ed. (Psychotherapy & Psychosomatics Ser.: Vol. 23, No. 1-6). 300p. 1974. 83.50 (*3-8055-1689-4*) S Karger.
Congress of Neurological Surgeons Staff. Clinical Neurosurgery Vol. 42: Proceedings of the Congress of Neurological Surgeons, 42. (Illus.). 538p. 1996. write for info. (*0-683-02039-0*) Lppncott W & W.
Congress of Pediatric Dermatology, 2nd, Mexico Cit. Pediatric Dermatology & Internal Medicine: Internal Medicine & External Medicine, Proceedings. Ruiz-Maldonado, Ramon, ed. (Modern Problems in Pediatrics Ser.: Vol. 20). (Illus.). 1978. 85.25 (*3-8055-2703-9*) S Karger.
Congress of Psychosomatic Obstetrics & Gynecology. The Family: Proceedings. Hirsh, H. et al, eds. 600p. 1975. 153.25 (*3-8055-2206-1*) S Karger.
Congress of the European Society for Pediatric Neu. Pediatric Neurosurgery: Proceedings. Villani, R. & Giovanelli, M., eds. (Modern Problems in Pediatrics Ser.: Vol. 18). (Illus.). 1977. 121.75 (*3-8055-2668-7*) S Karger.
Congress of the International Association of Plant Tissue Culture & Biotechnology Staff, et al. Plant Biotechnolgy & in Vitro Biology in the 21st Century: Proceedings of the 21st International Congress of the International Association of Plant Tissue Culture & Biotechnology, Jerusalem, Israel, 14-19 June 1998. LC 99-33164. 1999. write for info. (*0-7923-5826-0*) Kluwer Academic.
Congress of the International Astronautical Federa. Astronautical Research 1971: Proceedings. Napolitano, Luigi G., ed. LC 72-92536. (Illus.). 586p. 1973. lib. bdg. 194.00 (*90-277-0306-X*) Kluwer Academic.
Congress of the United States, Office of Technolog. Groundwater from Contamination. 327p. (C). 1988. 100.00 (*0-7855-6708-9*, Pub. by Scientific) St Mut.
Congress of the United States Office of Technology. Mapping Our Genes: Genome Projects - How Big, How Fast? LC 88-45401. 224p. 1988. text 37.50 (*0-8018-3755-3*) Johns Hopkins.
— Protecting the Nation's Groundwater from Contamination. 1986. 90.00 (*81-85046-53-0*, Pub. by Scientific) St Mut.
Congress of the United States Office of Technology, ed. Protecting the Nation's Groundwater from Contamination, Vols. 1 & 2. (C). 1986. text 300.00 (*0-685-74016-1*) Scientific.
Congress of the United States Staff. Investigation of the Pearl Harbor Attack, with Added Index & Intelligence Memorandum: A Report Pursuant to S. Con. Res. 27, 79th Congress. 560p. 1946. pap. 38.80 (*0-89412-234-7*) Aegean Park Pr.
Congress On Africa. Africa & the American Negro. Bowen, J. W., ed. LC 74-79020. (Black Heritage Library Collection). 1977. 26.95 (*0-8369-8547-8*) Ayer.
Congress on Dynamical Systems Staff, et al. International Congress on Dynamical Systems. LC 96-45462. (Pitman Research Notes in Mathematics Ser.). 1997. pap. 59.95 (*0-582-30296-X*) Longman.
Congress on Electrocardiology, 1st, Wiesbaden, Oct. Congress on Electrocardiology, 1st, Wiesbaden, Oct. 1974. Abel, H., ed. (Advances in Cardiology Ser.: Vol. 16). 1976. 111.50 (*3-8055-2197-9*) S Karger.
Congress on Perinatal Medicine, 2nd European, Lond. Perinatal Medicine: Proceedings. Huntingford, P. J. et al, eds. 1971. 69.75 (*3-8055-1224-4*) S Karger.
Congress on Toxic Nephropathies, 6th, Parma, June. Toxic Nephropathies: Proceedings. Berlyne, Geoffrey M. et al, eds. (Contributions to Nephrology Ser.: Vol. 10). (Illus.). 1978. 29.75 (*3-8055-2832-9*) S Karger.
Congress, 75th, 1st Session, House Document No. 36. Technological Trends & National Policy, Including the Social Implications of New Inventions: National Resources Committee, Report of the Subcommittee on Technology. LC 72-5084. (Technology & Society Ser.). (Illus.). 398p. 1972. reprint ed. 33.95 (*0-405-04732-0*) Ayer.
Congressional Inforamtion Service, Inc. Staff, ed. CIS Index, 1979 Abstracts Volume. 1980. write for info. (*0-912380-75-6*) Cong Info.
— CIS Index, 1980 Index Volume. 1981. write for info. (*0-912380-81-0*) Cong Info.
Congressional Information Service. CIS Index to U.S. Executive Branch Documents, 1789-1909: Guide to Documents Listed in Checklist of U.S. Public Documents, 1789-1909, Not Printed in the U.S. Serial Set. LC 92-165613. 1997. write for info. (*0-88692-340-9*) Cong Info.
— CIS Index to U.S. Executive Branch Documents, 1910-1932: Guide to Documents Not Printed in the U.S. Serial Set. LC 97-151547. 1998. write for info. (*0-88692-377-8*) Cong Info.
Congressional Information Service, Inc., Staff. American Statistics Annual, 1994 Abstracts Volume. 2176p. 1995. write for info. (*0-88692-330-1*) Cong Info.
Congressional Information Service, Inc. Staff. CIS Index to Presidential Executive Orders & Proclamations Part II. LC 87-109975. 1986. write for info. (*0-88692-106-6*) Cong Info.
— CIS Index to Unpublished U. S. Senate Committee Hearings: 18th Congress-88th Congress, 1823-1964. LC 86-210230. 1986. 2085.00 (*0-88692-089-2*) Cong Info.
Congressional Information Service, Inc., Staff. CIS Index 1994 Annual, 3 vols. 1995. write for info. (*0-88692-309-3*) Cong Info.
— CIS Index, 1994 Annual: Abstracts Volume. 1995. write for info. (*0-88692-310-7*) Cong Info.
— CIS Index, 1994 Annual: Index Volume. 2092p. 1995. write for info. (*0-88692-311-5*) Cong Info.
Congressional Information Service, Inc., Staff, ed. American Foreign Policy Index, 1993, 2 vols. 1994. write for info. (*0-88692-280-1*) Cong Info.
— American Foreign Policy Index, 1993: Abstracts Volume. 1994. write for info. (*0-88692-281-X*) Cong Info.
— American Foreign Policy Index, 1993: Index Volume. 1994. write for info. (*0-88692-282-8*) Cong Info.
— American Foreign Policy Index, 1994, 2 vols. 1178p. 1995. write for info. (*0-88692-313-1*) Cong Info.
— American Foreign Policy Index, 1994: Abstracts Volume. 1995. write for info. (*0-88692-314-X*) Cong Info.
— American Foreign Policy Index, 1994: Index Volume. 1995. write for info. (*0-88692-315-8*) Cong Info.
Congressional Information Service, Inc. Staff, ed. American Statistics Annual, 1990: Abstracts Volume. 1991. write for info. (*0-88692-218-6*) Cong Info.
— American Statistics Annual, 1994, 2 vols. 2176p. 1995. write for info. (*0-88692-328-X*) Cong Info.
— American Statistics Annual, 1994: Index. 1995. write for info. (*0-88692-329-8*) Cong Info.
Congressional Information Service, Inc., Staff, ed. American Statistics Index Annual & Retrospective Edition, 3 vols. 1974. write for info. (*0-912380-16-0*) Cong Info.
— American Statistics Index Annual & Retrospective Edition Vol. 1. 1974. write for info. (*0-912380-18-7*) Cong Info.
— American Statistics Index Annual & Retrospective Edition, Abstract Volume 2. 1974. write for info. (*0-912380-19-5*) Cong Info.
— American Statistics Index Annual & Retrospective Edition, Index Volume. 1974. write for info. (*0-912380-17-9*) Cong Info.
— American Statistics Index, 1974, 2 vols. 1975. write for info. (*0-912380-23-3*) Cong Info.
— American Statistics Index, 1974: Abstracts Volume. 1975. write for info. (*0-912380-25-X*) Cong Info.
— American Statistics Index, 1974: Index Volume. 1975. write for info. (*0-912380-24-1*) Cong Info.
— American Statistics Index, 1974-1979: Cumulative Index, 4 vols. 1980. write for info. (*0-88692-189-9*) Cong Info.
— American Statistics Index, 1975, 2 vols. 1976. write for info. (*0-912380-35-7*) Cong Info.
— American Statistics Index 1975, Abstracts Volume. 1976. write for info. (*0-912380-37-3*) Cong Info.
— American Statistics Index, 1975: Index Volume. 1976. write for info. (*0-912380-36-5*) Cong Info.
— American Statistics Index, 1976, 2 vols. 1977. write for info. (*0-912380-44-6*) Cong Info.
— American Statistics Index, 1976: Abstracts Volume. 1977. write for info. (*0-912380-46-2*) Cong Info.
— American Statistics Index, 1976: Index Volume. 1977. write for info. (*0-912380-45-4*) Cong Info.
— American Statistics Index, 1977, 2 vols. 1978. write for info. (*0-912380-53-5*) Cong Info.
— American Statistics Index, 1977: Abstracts Volume. 1978. write for info. (*0-912380-55-1*) Cong Info.
— American Statistics Index, 1977: Index Volume. 1978. write for info. (*0-912380-54-3*) Cong Info.
— American Statistics Index, 1978, 2 vols. 1979. write for info. (*0-912380-64-0*) Cong Info.
— American Statistics Index 1978, Abstracts Volume. 1979. write for info. (*0-912380-66-7*) Cong Info.
Congressional Information Service, Inc. Staff, ed. American Statistics Index 1978, Index Volume. 1979. write for info. (*0-912380-65-9*) Cong Info.
Congressional Information Service, Inc., Staff, ed. American Statistics Index 1979, 2 vols. 1980. write for info. (*0-912380-76-4*) Cong Info.
— American Statistics Index 1979, Abstracts Volume. 1980. write for info. (*0-912380-78-0*) Cong Info.
— American Statistics Index 1979, Index Volume. 1980. write for info. (*0-912380-77-2*) Cong Info.
— American Statistics Index 1980, 2 vols. 1981. write for info. (*0-912380-83-7*) Cong Info.
— American Statistics Index 1980, Abstracts Volume. 1981. write for info. (*0-912380-85-3*) Cong Info.
— American Statistics Index 1980, Index Volume. 1981. write for info. (*0-912380-84-5*) Cong Info.
— American Statistics Index 1980-1984 Cumulative Index, 4 vols. 1985. write for info. (*0-88692-056-6*) Cong Info.
— American Statistics Index 1980-1984 Cumulative Index (A-E) 1985. write for info. (*0-88692-057-4*) Cong Info.
— American Statistics Index 1980-1984 Cumulative Index (F-M) write for info. (*0-88692-058-2*) Cong Info.
— American Statistics Index 1980-1984 Cumulative Index (N-Z) 1985. write for info. (*0-88692-059-0*) Cong Info.
— American Statistics Index 1980-1984 Cumulative Index (Supp) 1985. write for info. (*0-88692-060-4*) Cong Info.
— American Statistics Index 1981, 2 vols. 1982. write for info. (*0-912380-95-0*) Cong Info.
— American Statistics Index 1981, Abstracts Volume. 1982. write for info. (*0-912380-97-7*) Cong Info.
— American Statistics Index 1981, Index Volume. 1982. write for info. (*0-912380-96-9*) Cong Info.
— American Statistics Index 1982, 2 vols. 1983. write for info. (*0-88692-061-2*) Cong Info.
— American Statistics Index 1982, Abstracts Volume. 1983. write for info. (*0-88692-063-9*) Cong Info.
— American Statistics Index 1982, Index Volume. 1983. write for info. (*0-88692-062-0*) Cong Info.
— American Statistics Index 1983, 2 vols. 1984. write for info. (*0-88692-020-5*) Cong Info.
— American Statistics Index 1983, Abstracts Volume. 1984. write for info. (*0-88692-021-3*) Cong Info.
— American Statistics Index 1983, Index Volume. 1984. write for info. (*0-88692-022-1*) Cong Info.
— American Statistics Index 1984, 2 vols. 1985. write for info. (*0-88692-043-4*) Cong Info.
— American Statistics Index 1984, Abstracts Volume. 1985. write for info. (*0-88692-045-0*) Cong Info.
— American Statistics Index 1984, Index Volume. 1985. write for info. (*0-88692-044-2*) Cong Info.
— American Statistics Index 1985, 2 vols. 1986. write for info. (*0-88692-095-7*) Cong Info.
— American Statistics Index 1985, Abstracts Volume. 1986. write for info. (*0-88692-097-3*) Cong Info.
— American Statistics Index 1985, Index Volume. 1986. write for info. (*0-88692-096-5*) Cong Info.
— American Statistics Index 1985-1988 Cumulative Index, 4 vols. 1989. write for info. (*0-88692-178-3*) Cong Info.
— American Statistics Index 1986, 2 vols. 1987. write for info. (*0-88692-119-8*) Cong Info.
— American Statistics Index 1986, Abstracts Volume. 1987. write for info. (*0-88692-121-X*) Cong Info.
— American Statistics Index 1986, Index Volume. 1987. write for info. (*0-88692-120-1*) Cong Info.
— American Statistics Index 1987, 2 vols. 1988. write for info. (*0-88692-142-2*) Cong Info.
— American Statistics Index 1987, Abstracts Volume. 1988. write for info. (*0-88692-144-9*) Cong Info.
— American Statistics Index 1987, Index Volume. 1988. write for info. (*0-88692-143-0*) Cong Info.
— American Statistics Index 1988, 2 vols. 1989. write for info. (*0-88692-167-8*) Cong Info.
— American Statistics Index 1988, Abstracts Volume. 1989. write for info. (*0-88692-169-4*) Cong Info.
— American Statistics Index 1988, Index Volume. 1989. write for info. (*0-88692-168-6*) Cong Info.
— American Statistics Index 1988-1992 Cumulative Index, 4 vols. 1993. write for info. (*0-88692-279-8*) Cong Info.
— American Statistics Index 1989, 2 vols. 1990. write for info. (*0-88692-190-2*) Cong Info.
— American Statistics Index 1989, Abstracts Volume. 1990. write for info. (*0-88692-192-9*) Cong Info.
— American Statistics Index 1989, Index Volume. 1990. write for info. (*0-88692-191-0*) Cong Info.
— American Statistics Index 1990, 2 vols. 1991. write for info. (*0-88692-216-X*); write for info. (*0-88692-219-4*) Cong Info.
— American Statistics Index 1990, Index Volume. 1991. write for info. (*0-88692-217-8*) Cong Info.
— American Statistics Index 1991, 2 vols. 1992. write for info. (*0-88692-241-0*) Cong Info.
— American Statistics Index 1991, Abstracts Volume. 1992. write for info. (*0-88692-243-7*) Cong Info.
— American Statistics Index 1991, Index Volume. 1992. write for info. (*0-88692-242-9*) Cong Info.
— American Statistics Index 1992, 2 vols. 1993. write for info. (*0-88692-267-4*) Cong Info.
— American Statistics Index 1992, Abstracts Volume. 1993. write for info. (*0-88692-269-0*) Cong Info.
— American Statistics Index 1992, Index Volume. 1993. write for info. (*0-88692-268-2*) Cong Info.
— American Statistics Index 1993, 2 vols. 1994. write for info. (*0-88692-295-X*) Cong Info.
— American Statistics Index 1993, Abstracts Volume. 1994. write for info. (*0-88692-297-6*) Cong Info.
— American Statistics Index 1993, Index Volume. 1994. write for info. (*0-88692-296-8*) Cong Info.
— CIS Executive Branch Documents Pt. 1. LC 92-165613. 1990. write for info. (*0-88692-202-X*) Cong Info.
— CIS Executive Branch Documents Pt. 2. LC 92-165613. 1991. write for info. (*0-88692-225-9*) Cong Info.
— CIS Executive Branch Documents Pt. 3. LC 92-165613. 1992. write for info. (*0-88692-252-6*) Cong Info.
— CIS Executive Branch Documents Pt. 4. LC 92-165613. 1993. write for info. (*0-88692-274-7*) Cong Info.
— CIS Executive Branch Documents Pt. 5. 1994. write for info. (*0-88692-275-5*) Cong Info.
— CIS Federal Register Index: Jan-June, 1984. 1984. write for info. (*0-88692-074-4*) Cong Info.
— CIS Federal Register Index: Jan-June, 1985. 1985. write for info. (*0-88692-076-0*) Cong Info.
— CIS Federal Register Index: Jan-June, 1986. 1986. write for info. (*0-88692-100-7*) Cong Info.
— CIS Federal Register Index: Jan-June, 1987. 1987. write for info. (*0-88692-125-2*) Cong Info.
— CIS Federal Register Index: Jan-June, 1988. 1988. write for info. (*0-88692-149-X*) Cong Info.
— CIS Federal Register Index: Jan-June, 1989. 1989. write for info. (*0-88692-176-7*) Cong Info.
— CIS Federal Register Index: Jan-June, 1990. 1990. write for info. (*0-88692-198-8*) Cong Info.
— CIS Federal Register Index: Jan-June, 1991. 1991. write for info. (*0-88692-223-2*) Cong Info.
— CIS Federal Register Index: Jan-June, 1992. 1992. write for info. (*0-88692-250-X*) Cong Info.
— CIS Federal Register Index: Jan-June, 1993. 1993. write for info. (*0-88692-276-3*) Cong Info.
— CIS Federal Register Index: Jan-June, 1994. 1994. write for info. (*0-88692-304-2*) Cong Info.
— CIS Federal Register Index: July-Dec, 1984. 1985. write for info. (*0-88692-075-2*) Cong Info.
— CIS Federal Register Index: July-Dec, 1985. 1986. write for info. (*0-88692-081-7*) Cong Info.
— CIS Federal Register Index: July-Dec, 1986. 1987. write for info. (*0-88692-114-7*) Cong Info.
— CIS Federal Register Index: July-Dec, 1987. 1988. write for info. (*0-88692-131-7*) Cong Info.
— CIS Federal Register Index: July-Dec, 1988. 1989. write for info. (*0-88692-156-2*) Cong Info.
— CIS Federal Register Index: July-Dec, 1989. 1990. write for info. (*0-614-32345-2*) Cong Info.
— CIS Federal Register Index: July-Dec, 1990. 1991. write for info. (*0-88692-207-0*) Cong Info.
— CIS Federal Register Index: July-Dec, 1991. 1992. write for info. (*0-88692-229-1*) Cong Info.
— CIS Federal Register Index: July-Dec, 1992. 1993. write for info. (*0-88692-258-5*) Cong Info.
— CIS Federal Register Index: July-Dec, 1993. 1994. write for info. (*0-88692-293-3*) Cong Info.
— CIS Federal Register Index, July-December 1994. 810p. 1995. write for info. (*0-88692-324-7*) Cong Info.
— CIS Index Volume 1981, 2 vols. 1992. write for info. (*0-912380-92-6*) Cong Info.

C

An Asterisk (*) at the beginning of an entry indicates that the title is appearing for the first time.

Congressional Information Service, Inc. Staff, ed. CIS Index, 1970, 2 vols., Set. 1971. write for info. *(0-912380-00-4)* Cong Info.
— CIS Index, 1970: Index Volume. 1971. write for info. *(0-912380-01-2)* Cong Info.
Congressional Information Service, Inc., Staff, ed. CIS Index, 1970 Abstracts Volume. 1971. write for info. *(0-912380-02-0)* Cong Info.
— CIS Index, 1970-1974 Cumulative Index, 2 vols. 1975. write for info. *(0-912380-28-4)* Cong Info.
Congressional Information Service, Inc. Staff, ed. CIS Index, 1971, 2 vols., Set. 1972. write for info. *(0-912380-03-9)* Cong Info.
— CIS Index, 1971: Index Volume. 1972. write for info. *(0-912380-04-7)* Cong Info.
Congressional Information Service, Inc., Staff, ed. CIS Index, 1971 Abstracts Volume. 1972. write for info. *(0-912380-05-5)* Cong Info.
— CIS Index, 1972 Abstracts Volume. 1973. write for info. *(0-88692-073-6)* Cong Info.
Congressional Information Service, Inc. Staff, ed. CIS Index, 1973, 2 vols., Set. 1974. write for info. *(0-912380-12-8)* Cong Info.
— CIS Index, 1973: Index Volume. 1974. write for info. *(0-912380-13-6)* Cong Info.
Congressional Information Service, Inc., Staff, ed. CIS Index 1973, Abstracts Volume. 1979. write for info. *(0-912380-14-4)* Cong Info.
Congressional Information Service, Inc. Staff, ed. CIS Index, 1974, 2 vols., Set. 1975. write for info. *(0-912380-20-9)* Cong Info.
— CIS Index, 1974: Index Volume. 1975. write for info. *(0-912380-21-7)* Cong Info.
Congressional Information Service, Inc., Staff, ed. CIS Index, 1974 Abstracts Volume. 1975. write for info. *(0-912380-22-5)* Cong Info.
— CIS Index, 1975, 2 vols. 1976. write for info. *(0-912380-32-2)* Cong Info.
— CIS Index, 1975 Abstracts Volume. 1976. write for info. *(0-912380-34-9)* Cong Info.
— CIS Index, 1975 Index Volume. 1976. write for info. *(0-912380-33-0)* Cong Info.
— CIS Index, 1975-1978 Cumulative Index, 3 vols. 1979. write for info. *(0-912380-69-1)* Cong Info.
— CIS Index, 1975-1978 Cumulative Index (A-F) 1979. write for info. *(0-912380-70-5)* Cong Info.
— CIS Index, 1975-1978 Cumulative Index (G-Q) 1979. write for info. *(0-912380-71-3)* Cong Info.
— CIS Index, 1975-1978 Cumulative Index (R-Z) 1979. write for info. *(0-912380-72-1)* Cong Info.
— CIS Index, 1976, 2 vols. 1977. write for info. *(0-912380-41-1)* Cong Info.
— CIS Index, 1976 Abstracts Volume. 1977. write for info. *(0-912380-43-8)* Cong Info.
— CIS Index, 1976 Index Volume. 1977. write for info. *(0-912380-42-X)* Cong Info.
— CIS Index, 1977, 2 vols. 1978. write for info. *(0-912380-50-0)* Cong Info.
— CIS Index, 1977 Abstracts Volume. 1978. write for info. *(0-912380-52-7)* Cong Info.
— CIS Index, 1977 Index Volume. 1978. write for info. *(0-912380-51-9)* Cong Info.
— CIS Index, 1978, 2 vols. 1979. write for info. *(0-912380-60-8)* Cong Info.
— CIS Index, 1978 Abstracts Volume. 1979. write for info. *(0-912380-62-4)* Cong Info.
— CIS Index, 1978 Index Volume. 1979. write for info. *(0-912380-61-6)* Cong Info.
— CIS Index, 1979, 2 vols. 1980. write for info. *(0-912380-73-X)* Cong Info.
— CIS Index, 1979 Index Volume. 1980. write for info. *(0-912380-74-8)* Cong Info.
— CIS Index, 1979-1982 Cumulative Index, 3 vols. 1983. write for info. *(0-88692-000-0)* Cong Info.
— CIS Index, 1979-1982 Cumulative Index (A-F) 1983. write for info. *(0-88692-001-9)* Cong Info.
— CIS Index, 1979-1982 Cumulative Index (G-Q) 1983. write for info. *(0-88692-002-7)* Cong Info.
— CIS Index, 1979-1982 Cumulative Index (R-Z) 1983. write for info. *(0-88692-003-5)* Cong Info.
— CIS Index, 1980, 2 vols. 1981. write for info. *(0-912380-80-2)* Cong Info.
— CIS Index, 1980 Abstracts Volume. 1981. write for info. *(0-912380-82-9)* Cong Info.
— CIS Index, 1981 Abstracts Volume. 1982. write for info. *(0-912380-94-2)* Cong Info.
— CIS Index 1981, Index Volume. 1982. write for info. *(0-912380-93-4)* Cong Info.
— CIS Index, 1982, 2 vols. 1983. write for info. *(0-88692-064-7)* Cong Info.
— CIS Index, 1982 Abstracts Volume. 1983. write for info. *(0-88692-066-3)* Cong Info.
— CIS Index, 1982 Index Volume. 1983. write for info. *(0-88692-065-5)* Cong Info.
— CIS Index, 1983, 2 vols. 1984. write for info. *(0-88692-017-5)* Cong Info.
— CIS Index, 1983 Abstracts Volume. 1984. write for info. *(0-88692-019-1)* Cong Info.
— CIS Index, 1983 Index Volume. 1984. write for info. *(0-88692-018-3)* Cong Info.
— CIS Index, 1983-1986 Cumulative Index, 3 vols. 1987. write for info. *(0-88692-127-9)* Cong Info.
— CIS Index, 1984, 3 vols. 1985. write for info. *(0-88692-046-9)* Cong Info.
— CIS Index, 1984 Abstracts Volume. 1985. write for info. *(0-88692-048-5)* Cong Info.
— CIS Index, 1984 Index Volume. 1985. write for info. *(0-88692-047-7)* Cong Info.
— CIS Index, 1984 Legislative Histories Annual. 1985. write for info. *(0-88692-049-3)* Cong Info.
— CIS Index, 1985, 3 vols. 1986. write for info. *(0-88692-085-X)* Cong Info.
— CIS Index, 1985 Abstracts Volume. 1986. write for info. *(0-88692-087-6)* Cong Info.
— CIS Index, 1985 Index Volume. 1986. write for info. *(0-88692-086-8)* Cong Info.
— CIS Index, 1985 Legislative Histories Annual. 1986. write for info. *(0-88692-088-4)* Cong Info.
— CIS Index, 1986, 3 vols. 1987. write for info. *(0-88692-115-5)* Cong Info.
— CIS Index, 1986 Abstracts Volume. 1987. write for info. *(0-88692-117-1)* Cong Info.
— CIS Index, 1986 Index Volume. 1987. write for info. *(0-88692-116-3)* Cong Info.
— CIS Index, 1986 Legislative Histories Annual. 1987. write for info. *(0-88692-118-X)* Cong Info.
— CIS Index, 1987, 3 vols. 1988. write for info. *(0-88692-138-4)* Cong Info.
— CIS Index, 1987 Abstracts Volume. 1988. write for info. *(0-88692-140-6)* Cong Info.
— CIS Index, 1987 Index Volume. 1988. write for info. *(0-88692-139-2)* Cong Info.
— CIS Index, 1987 Legislative Histories Annual. 1988. write for info. *(0-88692-141-4)* Cong Info.
— CIS Index, 1987-1990 Cumulative Index, 3 vols. 1991. write for info. *(0-88692-226-7)* Cong Info.
— CIS Index, 1988, 3 vols. 1989. write for info. *(0-88692-163-5)* Cong Info.
— CIS Index, 1988 Abstracts Volume. 1989. write for info. *(0-88692-165-1)* Cong Info.
— CIS Index, 1988 Index Volume. 1989. write for info. *(0-88692-164-3)* Cong Info.
— CIS Index, 1988 Legislative Histories Annual. 1989. write for info. *(0-88692-166-X)* Cong Info.
— CIS Index, 1989, 3 vols. 1990. write for info. *(0-88692-185-6)* Cong Info.
— CIS Index, 1989 Abstracts Volume. 1990. write for info. *(0-88692-187-2)* Cong Info.
— CIS Index, 1989 Index Volume. 1990. write for info. *(0-88692-186-4)* Cong Info.
— CIS Index, 1989 Legislative Histories Annual. 1990. write for info. *(0-88692-188-0)* Cong Info.
— CIS Index, 1990, 3 vols. 1991. write for info. *(0-88692-212-7)* Cong Info.
— CIS Index, 1990 Abstracts Volume. 1991. write for info. *(0-88692-214-3)* Cong Info.
— CIS Index, 1990 Index Volume. 1991. write for info. *(0-88692-213-5)* Cong Info.
— CIS Index, 1990 Legislative Histories Annual. 1991. write for info. *(0-88692-215-1)* Cong Info.
— CIS Index, 1991, 3 vols. 1992. write for info. *(0-88692-236-4)* Cong Info.
— CIS Index 1991, Abstracts Volume. 1992. write for info. *(0-88692-238-0)* Cong Info.
— CIS Index, 1991 Index Volume. 1992. write for info. *(0-88692-237-2)* Cong Info.
— CIS Index, 1991 Legislative Histories Annual. 1992. write for info. *(0-88692-239-9)* Cong Info.
— CIS Index, 1992, 3 vols. 1993. write for info. *(0-88692-262-3)* Cong Info.
— CIS Index, 1992 Abstracts Volume. 1993. write for info. *(0-88692-264-X)* Cong Info.
— CIS Index, 1992 Index Volume. 1993. write for info. *(0-88692-263-1)* Cong Info.
— CIS Index, 1993, 3 vols. 1994. write for info. *(0-88692-283-6)* Cong Info.
— CIS Index 1993 Abstracts Volume. 1994. write for info. *(0-88692-285-2)* Cong Info.
— CIS Index, 1993 Index Volume. 1994. write for info. *(0-88692-284-4)* Cong Info.
Congressional Information Service, Inc. Staff, ed. CIS Index, 1994 Legislative Histories Annual. 1995. 265.00 *(0-88692-312-3)* Cong Info.
Congressional Information Service, Inc., Staff, ed. CIS Legislative Histories Annual. 1993. write for info. *(0-88692-265-8)* Cong Info.
— CIS Presidential Executive Orders & Proclamations: Part I 1789-1921. 1987. write for info. *(0-88692-123-6)* Cong Info.
— CIS Serial Set, Part I: 1789-1857. 1977. write for info. *(0-912380-47-0)* Cong Info.
— CIS Serial Set, Part II: 1857-1879. 1977. write for info. *(0-912380-48-9)* Cong Info.
— CIS Serial Set, Part III: 1879-1889. 1978. write for info. *(0-912380-56-X)* Cong Info.
— CIS Serial Set, Part IV: 1889-1897. 1978. write for info. *(0-912380-58-6)* Cong Info.
— CIS Serial Set, Part IX: 1925-1934. 1975. write for info. *(0-912380-27-6)* Cong Info.
— CIS Serial Set, Part V: 1897-1903. 1978. write for info. *(0-912380-59-4)* Cong Info.
— CIS Serial Set, Part VI: 1903-1909. 1979. write for info. *(0-912380-63-2)* Cong Info.
— CIS Serial Set, Part VII: 1909-1915. 1979. write for info. *(0-912380-68-3)* Cong Info.
— CIS Serial Set, Part VIII: 1915-1925. 1979. write for info. *(0-912380-67-5)* Cong Info.
— CIS Serial Set, Part X: 1935-1946. 1976. write for info. *(0-912380-31-4)* Cong Info.
— CIS Serial Set, Part XI: 1947-1958. 1976. write for info. *(0-912380-39-X)* Cong Info.
— CIS Serial Set, Part XII: 1959-1969. 1976. write for info. *(0-912380-40-3)* Cong Info.
— CIS Serial Set, Part XIII: Bill Numbers. 1994. write for info. *(0-88692-306-9)* Cong Info.
— CIS U. S. Congressional Committee Hearings, Part I: 1833-1917, 5 vols. 1985. write for info. *(0-88692-050-7)* Cong Info.
— CIS U. S. Congressional Committee Hearings, Part I: 1833-1917 (Names Index) 1985. write for info. *(0-88692-055-8)* Cong Info.
— CIS U. S. Congressional Committee Hearings, Part I: 1833-1917 (Ref. Bib. 1) 1985. write for info. *(0-88692-051-5)* Cong Info.
— CIS U. S. Congressional Committee Hearings, Part I: 1833-1917 (Ref. Bib. 2) 1985. write for info. *(0-88692-052-3)* Cong Info.
— CIS U. S. Congressional Committee Hearings, Part II: 1917-1925 (Ref. Bib. 1) 1984. write for info. *(0-88692-032-9)* Cong Info.
— CIS U. S. Congressional Committee Hearings, Part II: 1917-1925 (Ref. Bib. 2) 1984. write for info. *(0-88692-033-7)* Cong Info.
— CIS U. S. Congressional Committee Hearings, Part II: 1917-1925 (Subject Index 1) 1984. write for info. *(0-88692-034-5)* Cong Info.
— CIS U. S. Congressional Committee Hearings, Part II: 1917-1925 (Subject Index 2) 1984. write for info. *(0-88692-035-3)* Cong Info.
— CIS U. S. Congressional Committee Hearings, Part III: 1925-1934, 5 vols. 1984. write for info. *(0-88692-025-6)* Cong Info.
— CIS U. S. Congressional Committee Hearings, Part III: 1925-1934 (Ref. Bib. 1) 1984. write for info. *(0-88692-026-4)* Cong Info.
— CIS U. S. Congressional Committee Hearings, Part III: 1925-1934 (Ref. Bib. 2) 1984. write for info. *(0-88692-027-2)* Cong Info.
— CIS U. S. Congressional Committee Hearings, Part III: 1925-1934 (Subject Index 2) 1984. write for info. *(0-88692-029-9)* Cong Info.
— CIS U. S. Congressional Committee Hearings, Part IV: 1935-1944, 6 vols. 1983. write for info. *(0-88692-004-3)* Cong Info.
— CIS U. S. Congressional Committee Hearings, Part IV: 1935-1944 (Names Index 1) 1983. write for info. *(0-88692-009-4)* Cong Info.
— CIS U. S. Congressional Committee Hearings, Part IV: 1935-1944 (Names Index 2) 1983. write for info. *(0-88692-010-8)* Cong Info.
— CIS U. S. Congressional Committee Hearings, Part IV: 1935-1944 (Ref. Bib. 1) 1983. write for info. *(0-88692-005-1)* Cong Info.
— CIS U. S. Congressional Committee Hearings, Part IV: 1935-1944 (Ref. Bib. 2) 1983. write for info. *(0-88692-006-X)* Cong Info.
— CIS U. S. Congressional Committee Hearings, Part IV: 1935-1944 (Subject Index 1) 1983. write for info. *(0-88692-007-8)* Cong Info.
— CIS U. S. Congressional Committee Hearings, Part IV: 1935-1944 (Subject Index 2) 1983. write for info. *(0-88692-008-6)* Cong Info.
— CIS U. S. Congressional Committee Hearings, Part V: 1945-1952. 1983. write for info. *(0-88692-070-1)* Cong Info.
— CIS U. S. Congressional Committee Hearings, Part VI: 1953-1958. 1982. write for info. *(0-88692-069-8)* Cong Info.
— CIS U. S. Congressional Committee Hearings, Part VII: 1959-1964. 1982. write for info. *(0-88692-068-X)* Cong Info.
— CIS U. S. Congressional Committee Hearings, Part VIII: 1965-1969. 1981. write for info. *(0-88692-067-1)* Cong Info.
— CIS U. S. Congressional Committee Prints Index, 5 vols. 1980. write for info. *(0-912380-57-8)* Cong Info.
— CIS U. S. Congressional Committees Hearings, Part III: 1925-1934 (Subject Index 1) 1984. write for info. *(0-88692-028-0)* Cong Info.
— CIS U. S. Congrressional Committee Hearings, Part II: 1917-1925 (Names Index) 1984. write for info. *(0-88692-036-1)* Cong Info.
— CIS U. S. Senate Executive Documents & Reports, 2 vols. 1987. write for info. *(0-88692-130-9)* Cong Info.
— CIS U. S. Serial Set Index: Parts I-XII, 12 vols. 1979. write for info. *(0-912380-26-8)* Cong Info.
— CIS Unpublished U. S. House of Representatives Committee Hearings: 1833-1936. 1988. write for info. *(0-88692-152-X)* Cong Info.
— CIS Unpublished U. S. House of Representatives Committee Hearings: 1937-1946. 1990. write for info. *(0-88692-196-1)* Cong Info.
— CIS Unpublished U. S. House of Representatives Committee Hearings: 1947-1954. 1992. write for info. *(0-88692-253-4)* Cong Info.
— CIS Unpublished U. S. House of Representatives Committee Hearings: 1955-1958. LC 95-122402. 1994. write for info. *(0-88692-307-7)* Cong Info.
Congressional Information Service, Inc. Staff, ed. CIS Unpublished U. S. Senate Committee Hearings: 1823-1964 (Names) 1986. write for info. *(0-88692-094-9)* Cong Info.
Congressional Information Service, Inc., Staff, ed. CIS Unpublished U. S. Senate Committee Hearings: 1823-1964 (Ref. Bib. 1) 1986. write for info. *(0-88692-090-6)* Cong Info.
— CIS Unpublished U. S. Senate Committee Hearings: 1823-1964 (Ref. Bib. 2) 1986. write for info. *(0-88692-091-4)* Cong Info.
— CIS Unpublished U. S. Senate Committee Hearings: 1823-1964 (Subject Index 1) 1986. write for info. *(0-88692-092-2)* Cong Info.
— CIS Unpublished U. S. Senate Committee Hearings: 1823-1964 (Subject Index 2) 1986. write for info. *(0-88692-093-0)* Cong Info.
— CIS Unpublished U. S. Senate Committee Hearings: 1965-1968. 1989. write for info. *(0-88692-174-0)* Cong Info.
— CIS U.S. Congressional Committee Hearings, Part I: 1833-1917 (Subject Index 1) 1985. write for info. *(0-88692-053-1)* Cong Info.
— CIS U.S. Congressional Committee Hearings, Part I: 1833-1917 (Subject Index 2) 1985. write for info. *(0-88692-054-X)* Cong Info.
— CIS U.S. Congressional Committee Hearings, Part II: 1917-1925, 5 vols. 1984. write for info. *(0-88692-031-0)* Cong Info.
— Congressional Member Organizations & Caucuses, 1991. 1992. write for info. *(0-88692-248-8)* Cong Info.
— Congressional Member Organizations & Caucuses, 1992. 1993. write for info. *(0-88692-277-1)* Cong Info.
— Congressional Member Organizations & Caucuses, 1993. 1994. write for info. *(0-88692-308-5)* Cong Info.
— Environment Abstracts 1994, 3 vols. 3242p. 1995. write for info. *(0-88692-326-3)* Cong Info.
— Guide to 1980 U. S. Decennial Census Publications. 1986. write for info. *(0-88692-099-X)* Cong Info.
— Guide to 1990 U. S. Decennial Census Publications through March 1995. LC 95-233180. 246p. 1995. write for info. *(0-88692-335-2)* Cong Info.
— Index to Health Information 1988, 2 vols. 1989. write for info. *(0-88692-171-6)* Cong Info.
— Index to Health Information 1988: Abstracts Volume. 1989. write for info. *(0-88692-173-2)* Cong Info.
— Index to Health Information 1988: Index Volume. 1989. write for info. *(0-88692-172-4)* Cong Info.
— Index to Health Information 1989, 2 vols. 1990. write for info. *(0-88692-193-7)* Cong Info.
— Index to Health Information 1989: Abstracts Volume. 1990. write for info. *(0-88692-195-3)* Cong Info.
— Index to Health Information 1989: Index Volume. 1990. write for info. *(0-88692-194-5)* Cong Info.
— Index to Health Information 1990: Abstracts Volume. 1991. write for info. *(0-88692-221-6)* Cong Info.
— Index to Health Information 1990: Index Volume. 1991. write for info. *(0-88692-220-8)* Cong Info.
— Index to Health Information 1991, 2 vols. 1992. write for info. *(0-88692-244-5)* Cong Info.
— Index to Health Information 1991: Abstracts Volume. 1992. write for info. *(0-88692-246-1)* Cong Info.
— Index to Health Information 1991: Index Volume. 1992. write for info. *(0-88692-245-3)* Cong Info.
— Index to Health Information 1992, 2 vols. 1993. write for info. *(0-88692-271-2)* Cong Info.
— Index to Health Information 1992: Abstracts Volume. 1993. write for info. *(0-88692-273-9)* Cong Info.
— Index to Health Information 1992: Index Volume. 1993. write for info. *(0-88692-272-0)* Cong Info.
— Index to Health Information 1993, 2 vols. 1994. write for info. *(0-88692-300-X)* Cong Info.
— Index to Health Information 1993: Abstracts Volume. 1994. 875.00 *(0-88692-302-6)* Cong Info.
— Index to Health Information 1993: Index Volume. 1994. write for info. *(0-88692-301-8)* Cong Info.
— Index to Health Information 1994, 2 vols. 1112p. 1995. write for info. *(0-88692-332-8)* Cong Info.
— Index to Health Information 1994: Abstracts Volume. 1995. write for info. *(0-88692-334-4)* Cong Info.
— Index to Health Information 1994: Index Volume. 1995. write for info. *(0-88692-333-6)* Cong Info.
— Index to International Statistics 1983, 2 vols. 1984. write for info. *(0-88692-011-6)* Cong Info.
— Index to International Statistics 1983, Abstracts Volume. 1984. write for info. *(0-88692-012-4)* Cong Info.
— Index to International Statistics 1983, Index Volume. 1984. write for info. *(0-88692-013-2)* Cong Info.
— Index to International Statistics 1983-1987, Cumulative Index, 4 vols. 1988. write for info. *(0-88692-154-6)* Cong Info.
— Index to International Statistics 1984, 2 vols. 1985. write for info. *(0-88692-037-X)* Cong Info.
— Index to International Statistics 1984, Abstracts Volume. 1985. write for info. *(0-88692-038-8)* Cong Info.
— Index to International Statistics 1984, Index Volume. 1985. write for info. *(0-88692-039-6)* Cong Info.
— Index to International Statistics 1985, 2 vols. 1986. write for info. *(0-614-32342-8)* Cong Info.
— Index to International Statistics 1985, Abstracts Volume. 1986. write for info. *(0-614-32343-6)* Cong Info.
— Index to International Statistics 1985, Index Volume. 1986. write for info. *(0-614-32344-4)* Cong Info.
— Index to International Statistics 1986, 2 vols. 1987. write for info. *(0-88692-108-2)* Cong Info.
— Index to International Statistics 1986, Abstracts Volume. 1987. write for info. *(0-88692-109-0)* Cong Info.
— Index to International Statistics 1986, Index Volume. 1987. write for info. *(0-88692-110-4)* Cong Info.
— Index to International Statistics, 1987, 2 vols. 1988. write for info. *(0-88692-132-5)* Cong Info.
— Index to International Statistics 1987, Abstracts Volume. 1988. write for info. *(0-88692-133-3)* Cong Info.
— Index to International Statistics 1987, Index Volume. 1988. write for info. *(0-88692-134-1)* Cong Info.
— Index to International Statistics 1988, 2 vols. 1989. write for info. *(0-88692-157-0)* Cong Info.
Congressional Information Service, Inc. Staff, ed. Index to International Statistics, 1988: Abstracts Volume. 1989. write for info. *(0-88692-158-9)* Cong Info.
Congressional Information Service, Inc., Staff, ed. Index to International Statistics 1988, Index Volume. 1989. write for info. *(0-88692-159-7)* Cong Info.
— Index to International Statistics 1988-1991, Cumulative Index, 4 vols. 1992. write for info. *(0-88692-251-8)* Cong Info.
— Index to International Statistics 1989, 2 vols. 1990. write for info. *(0-88692-179-1)* Cong Info.
— Index to International Statistics 1989, Abstracts Volume. 1990. write for info. *(0-88692-180-5)* Cong Info.

— Index to International Statistics 1989, Index Volume. 1990. write for info. (*0-88692-181-3*) Cong Info.
— Index to International Statistics 1990, 2 vols. 1991. write for info. (*0-88692-204-6*) Cong Info.
— Index to International Statistics 1990, Abstracts Volume. 1991. write for info. (*0-88692-205-4*) Cong Info.
— Index to International Statistics 1990, Index Volume. 1991. write for info. (*0-88692-206-2*) Cong Info.
— Index to International Statistics 1991, 2 vols. 1992. write for info. (*0-88692-230-5*) Cong Info.
— Index to International Statistics 1991, Abstracts Volume. 1992. write for info. (*0-88692-231-3*) Cong Info.
— Index to International Statistics 1991, Index Volume. 1992. write for info. (*0-88692-232-1*) Cong Info.
— Index to International Statistics 1992, 2 vols. 1993. write for info. (*0-88692-255-0*) Cong Info.
— Index to International Statistics 1992, Abstracts Volume. 1993. write for info. (*0-88692-256-9*) Cong Info.
— Index to International Statistics 1992, Index Volume. 1993. write for info. (*0-88692-257-7*) Cong Info.
— Index to International Statistics 1993, 2 vols. 1994. write for info. (*0-88692-287-9*) Cong Info.
— Index to International Statistics 1993, Abstracts Volume. 1994. write for info. (*0-88692-288-7*) Cong Info.
— Index to International Statistics 1993, Index Volume. 1994. write for info. (*0-88692-289-5*) Cong Info.
— Index to International Statistics 1994 Annual, 2 vols. 1504p. 1995. write for info. (*0-88692-318-2*) Cong Info.
— Index to International Statistics 1994 Annual Abstracts Volume. 1995. write for info. (*0-88692-319-0*) Cong Info.
— Index to International Statistics 1994 Annual Index Volume. 1995. write for info. (*0-88692-320-4*) Cong Info.
— Index to the Code of Federal Regulations, 1981. 1982. write for info. (*0-88692-077-9*) Cong Info.
— Index to the Code of Federal Regulations, 1982. 1983. write for info. (*0-88692-078-7*) Cong Info.
— Index to the Code of Federal Regulations, 1983. 1984. write for info. (*0-88692-079-5*) Cong Info.
— Index to the Code of Federal Regulations, 1984. 1985. write for info. (*0-88692-080-9*) Cong Info.
— Index to the Code of Federal Regulations, 1985. 1986. write for info. (*0-614-32346-0*) Cong Info.
— Index to the Code of Federal Regulations, 1986. 1987. write for info. (*0-614-32347-9*) Cong Info.
— Index to the Code of Federal Regulations, 1987. 1988. write for info. (*0-614-32348-7*) Cong Info.
— Index to the Code of Federal Regulations, 1988. 1989. write for info. (*0-614-32349-5*) Cong Info.
— Index to the Code of Federal Regulations, 1989. 1990. write for info. (*0-614-32350-9*) Cong Info.
— Index to the Code of Federal Regulations, 1990. 1991. write for info. (*0-88692-211-9*) Cong Info.
— Index to the Code of Federal Regulations, 1991. 1992. write for info. (*0-614-32351-7*) Cong Info.
— Index to the Code of Federal Regulations, 1992. 1993. write for info. (*0-614-32352-5*) Cong Info.
— Index to the Code of Federal Regulations, 1993. 1994. write for info. (*0-88692-294-1*) Cong Info.
— Index to the Code of Federal Regulations, 1994, 4 vols. 3798p. 1995. write for info. (*0-88692-325-5*) Cong Info.
— Justice Current Documents, 1994. 116p. 1995. write for info. (*0-88692-331-X*) Cong Info.
— Records of the Judicial Conference, Common Rules of Practice & Procedures, 1989. 1992. write for info. (*0-88692-249-6*) Cong Info.
— Records of the U. S. Judicial Conference, Common Rules of Practice & Procedure: 1935-1988. 1991. write for info. (*0-88692-228-3*) Cong Info.
— Records of the U. S. Judicial Conference, Common Rules of Practice & Procedure, 1990. 176p. 1995. write for info. (*0-88692-316-6*) Cong Info.

Congressional Information Service, Inc. Staff, ed. Reports Required by Congress, 1994: CIS Guide to Executive Communications. 1995. 595.00 (*0-88692-337-9*) Cong Info.

Congressional Information Service, Inc., Staff, ed. Statistical Reference Index Annual, 1994, 2 vols. 1912p. 1995. write for info. (*0-88692-321-2*) Cong Info.
— Statistical Reference Index Annual, 1994 Abstracts Volume. 1995. write for info. (*0-88692-323-9*) Cong Info.
— Statistical Reference Index Annual, 1994, Index Volume. 1995. write for info. (*0-88692-322-0*) Cong Info.
— Statistical Reference Index, 1980-1985 Cumulative Index, 4 vols. 1986. write for info. (*0-88692-101-5*) Cong Info.
— Statistical Reference Index, 1980-1985 Cumulative Index (A-E) 1986. write for info. (*0-88692-102-3*) Cong Info.
— Statistical Reference Index, 1980-1985 Cumulative Index (F-N) 1986. write for info. (*0-88692-103-1*) Cong Info.
— Statistical Reference Index, 1980-1985 Cumulative Index (O-Z) 1986. write for info. (*0-88692-104-X*) Cong Info.
— Statistical Reference Index, 1980-1985 Cumulative Index (Supp.) 1986. write for info. (*0-88692-105-8*) Cong Info.
— Statistical Reference Index, 1986-1989, Cumulative Index, 4 vols. 1990. write for info. (*0-88692-201-1*) Cong Info.
— Statistical Reference Index, 1980, 2 vols. 1981. write for info. (*0-912380-86-1*) Cong Info.
— Statistical Reference Index, 1980, Index Volume. 1981. write for info. (*0-912380-87-X*) Cong Info.
— Statistical Reference Index, 1980, Abstracts Volume. 1981. write for info. (*0-912380-88-8*) Cong Info.
— Statistical Reference Index, 1981, 2 vols. 1982. write for info. (*0-912380-89-6*) Cong Info.
— Statistical Reference Index, 1981 Index Volume. 1982. write for info. (*0-912380-90-X*) Cong Info.
— Statistical Reference Index, 1981, Abstracts Volume. 1982. write for info. (*0-912380-91-8*) Cong Info.
— Statistical Reference Index, 1982, 2 vols. 1983. write for info. (*0-912380-06-3*) Cong Info.
— Statistical Reference Index, 1982, Index Volume. 1983. write for info. (*0-912380-07-1*) Cong Info.
— Statistical Reference Index, 1982, Abstracts Volume. 1983. write for info. (*0-912380-08-X*) Cong Info.
— Statistical Reference Index, 1983, 2 vols. 1984. write for info. (*0-88692-014-0*) Cong Info.
— Statistical Reference Index, 1983, Index Volume. 1984. write for info. (*0-88692-016-7*) Cong Info.
— Statistical Reference Index, 1983, Abstracts Volume. 1984. write for info. (*0-88692-015-9*) Cong Info.
— Statistical Reference Index, 1984, 2 vols. 1985. write for info. (*0-88692-040-X*) Cong Info.
— Statistical Reference Index, 1984, Index Volume. 1985. write for info. (*0-88692-042-6*) Cong Info.
— Statistical Reference Index, 1984, Abstracts Volume. 1985. write for info. (*0-88692-041-8*) Cong Info.
— Statistical Reference Index, 1985, 2 vols. 1986. write for info. (*0-88692-082-5*) Cong Info.
— Statistical Reference Index, 1985, Index Volume. 1986. write for info. (*0-88692-084-1*) Cong Info.
— Statistical Reference Index, 1985, Abstracts Volume. 1986. write for info. (*0-88692-083-3*) Cong Info.
— Statistical Reference Index, 1986, 2 vols. 1987. write for info. (*0-88692-111-2*) Cong Info.
— Statistical Reference Index, 1986, Index Volume. 1987. write for info. (*0-88692-113-9*) Cong Info.
— Statistical Reference Index, 1986, Abstracts Volume. 1987. write for info. (*0-88692-112-0*) Cong Info.
— Statistical Reference Index, 1987, 2 vols. 1988. write for info. (*0-88692-135-X*) Cong Info.
— Statistical Reference Index, 1987, Index Volume. 1988. write for info. (*0-88692-137-6*) Cong Info.
— Statistical Referene Index, 1987, Abstracts Volume. 1988. write for info. (*0-88692-136-8*) Cong Info.
— Statistical Reference Index, 1988, 2 vols. 1989. write for info. (*0-88692-160-0*) Cong Info.
— Statistical Reference Index, 1988, Index Volume. 1989. write for info. (*0-88692-161-9*) Cong Info.
— Statistical Reference Index, 1988, Abstracts Volume. 1989. write for info. (*0-88692-162-7*) Cong Info.
— Statistical Reference Index, 1989, 2 vols. 1990. write for info. (*0-88692-182-1*) Cong Info.
— Statistical Reference Index, 1989, Index Volume. 1990. write for info. (*0-88692-183-X*) Cong Info.
— Statistical Reference Index, 1989, Abstracts Volume. 1990. write for info. (*0-88692-184-8*) Cong Info.
— Statistical Reference Index, 1993, 2 vols. 1994. write for info. (*0-88692-290-9*) Cong Info.
— Statistical Reference Index, 1993, Index Volume. 1994. write for info. (*0-88692-291-7*) Cong Info.
— Statistical Reference Index, 1993, Abstracts Volume. 1994. write for info. (*0-88692-292-5*) Cong Info.
— Statistical Reference Index, 1990-1993, Cumulative Index, 4 vols. 1994. write for info. (*0-88692-305-0*) Cong Info.
— Statistical Reference Index, 1990, 2 vols. 1991. write for info. (*0-88692-208-9*) Cong Info.
— Statistical Reference Index, 1990, Index Volume. 1991. write for info. (*0-88692-209-7*) Cong Info.
— Statistical Reference Index, 1990, Abstracts Volume. 1991. write for info. (*0-88692-210-0*) Cong Info.
— Statistical Reference Index, 1991, 2 vols. 1992. write for info. (*0-88692-233-X*) Cong Info.
— Statistical Reference Index, 1991, Index Volume. 1992. write for info. (*0-88692-234-8*) Cong Info.
— Statistical Reference Index, 1991, Abstracts Volume. 1992. write for info. (*0-88692-235-6*) Cong Info.
— Statistical Reference Index, 1992, 2 vols. 1993. write for info. (*0-88692-259-3*) Cong Info.
— Statistical Reference Index, 1992, Index Volume. 1993. write for info. (*0-88692-260-7*) Cong Info.
— Statistical Reference Index, 1992, Abstracts Volume. 1993. write for info. (*0-88692-261-5*) Cong Info.
— U. S. Department of Justice Current Documents, 1988. 1989. write for info. (*0-88692-175-9*) Cong Info.
— U. S. Department of Justice Current Documents, 1989. 1990. write for info. (*0-88692-197-X*) Cong Info.
— U. S. Department of Justice Current Documents, 1990. 1991. write for info. (*0-88692-222-4*) Cong Info.
— U. S. Department of Justice Current Documents, 1991. 1992. write for info. (*0-88692-240-2*) Cong Info.
— U. S. Department of Justice Current Documents, 1992. 1993. write for info. (*0-88692-266-6*) Cong Info.
— U. S. Department of Justice Current Documents, 1993. 1994. write for info. (*0-88692-299-2*) Cong Info.

Congressional Information Service, Inc. Staff, ed. United States Government Periodicals Index, 1993. 1026p. 1995. write for info. (*0-88692-327-1*) Cong Info.

Congressional Information Service, Inc., Staff, ed. United States Government Periodicals Index, 1994, 2 vols. 1026p. 1995. write for info. (*0-88692-317-4*) Cong Info.

Congressional Information Service, Staff. CIS Index to U. S. Executive Branch Documents, 1910-1932: Guide to Documents Not Printed in the U. S. Serial Set. LC 97-151547. 1996. pap. text 17.50 (*0-88692-446-4*) Cong Info.

Congressional Information Service, Staff, ed. Index to Unpublished US Senate Committee Hearings: 93rd Congress-94th Congress, 1973-1976. LC 99-177560. 204 p. 1998. write for info. (*0-88692-445-6*) Cong Info.

***Congressional Quarterley Staff.** State Fact Finder 1999. 406p. 1999. pap. text 79.95 (*1-56802-453-3*) CQ Pr.

***Congressional Quarterly.** Congressional Staff Directory: Members, Committees, Staff Biographies, 1999 Summer Ed. 1300p. 1999. pap. 149.00 (*0-87289-157-7*) C Q Staff.

***Congressional Quarterly Book Staff.** CQ Almanac 1999. (Illus.). 2000. 370.00 (*1-56802-270-0*) Congr Quarterly.

Congressional Quarterly, Inc. Congressional Elections, 1946-1996. LC 97-35242. 375p. (C). 1997. text 37.95 (*1-56802-248-4*) Congr Quarterly.

Congressional Quarterly, Inc. Staff. America Votes, Vol. 11. 1975. 142.00 (*0-87187-125-4*) Congr Quarterly.
— America Votes, Vol. 14. LC 56-10132. 427p. 1981. 142.00 (*0-87187-218-8*) Congr Quarterly.
— America Votes, Vol. 15. LC 56-10132. 395p. 1983. 142.00 (*0-87187-265-X*) Congr Quarterly.
— American Leaders, 1789-1994: A Biographical Summary. rev. ed. LC 94-27169. 546p. 1994. 54.95 (*0-87187-841-0*) Congr Quarterly.
— Cabinets & Counselors: The President & the Executive Branch. 2nd ed. LC 97-1606. 205p. 1997. text 29.95 (*1-56802-309-X*) Congr Quarterly.
— Congress & the Great Issues 1945-1995. Elving, Ronald D., ed. LC 96-10595. 167p. (YA). (gr. 11). 1996. pap. text 14.97 (*1-56802-215-8*) Congr Quarterly.
— Congress & the Nation II, 1965-1968, Vol. 2. LC 65-22351. 1120p. 1969. 205.00 (*0-87187-004-5*) Congr Quarterly.
— Congress & the Nation III, 1969-1972, Vol. 3. LC 65-22351. 1178p. 1973. 205.00 (*0-87187-055-X*) Congr Quarterly.
— Congress & the Nation IV, 1973-1976. LC 65-22351. 1217p. 1977. 205.00 (*0-87187-112-2*) Congr Quarterly.

***Congressional Quarterly Inc. Staff.** Congress & the Nation IX, 1993-1997: A Review of Government & Politics, 9 vols. LC 65-22351. 1200p. (YA). (gr. 11). 1998. text 250.00 (*1-56802-240-9*) Congr Quarterly.

Congressional Quarterly, Inc. Staff. Congress & the Nation V, 1977-1980. 1240p. 1981. 209.00 (*0-87187-216-1*) Congr Quarterly.
— Congress & the Nation VI, 1981-1984. LC 65-22351. 1184p. 1985. 209.00 (*0-87187-334-6*) Congr Quarterly.
— Congress & the Nation VII, 1985-1988. 1194p. 1990. 209.00 (*0-87187-532-2*) Congr Quarterly.
— Congress & the Nation VIII, 1989-1992: A Review of Government & Politics. LC 65-22351. 1308p. 1993. 209.00 (*0-87187-789-9*) Congr Quarterly.
— Congressional Districts in the 1990's. LC 93-34324. 1016p. (YA). (gr. 11). 1994. text 123.00 (*0-87187-722-8*) Congr Quarterly.
— Congressional Roll Call, 1976. LC 72-77849. 1977. pap. text 33.95 (*0-87187-106-8*) Congr Quarterly.
— Congressional Roll Call, 1977. LC 72-77849. 1978. pap. text 33.95 (*0-87187-121-1*) Congr Quarterly.
— Congressional Roll Call, 1978. 1979. pap. text 33.95 (*0-87187-146-7*) Congr Quarterly.
— Congressional Roll Call, 1983. 296p. 1984. pap. 33.95 (*0-87187-313-3*) Congr Quarterly.
— Congressional Roll Call, 1984. 225p. 1985. pap. 33.95 (*0-87187-347-8*) Congr Quarterly.
— Congressional Roll Call, 1985. 260p. 1986. pap. 33.95 (*0-87187-386-9*) Congr Quarterly.
— Congressional Roll Call, 1986. 243p. 1987. pap. 33.95 (*0-87187-414-8*) Congr Quarterly.
— Congressional Roll Call, 1987. 306p. 1988. pap. 33.95 (*0-87187-460-1*) Congr Quarterly.
— Congressional Roll Call, 1994: A Chronology & Analysis of Votes in the House & Senate, 103rd Congress, 2nd Session. 219p. 1995. pap. 33.95 (*0-87187-854-2*) Congr Quarterly.
— CQ Almanac, 1984. (Almanac Ser.). 1000p. 1985. 330.00 (*0-87187-346-X*) Congr Quarterly.
— CQ Almanac, 1985. (Almanac Ser.). 1099p. 1986. 330.00 (*0-87187-388-5*) Congr Quarterly.
— CQ Almanac, 1986. (Almanac Ser.). 1200p. 1987. 330.00 (*0-87187-418-0*) Congr Quarterly.
— CQ Almanac, 1987. (Almanac Ser.). 1017p. 1988. 330.00 (*0-87187-463-6*) Congr Quarterly.
— CQ Almanac, 1988. (Almanac Ser.). 1000p. 1989. 330.00 (*0-87187-507-1*) Congr Quarterly.
— CQ Almanac, 1989. (Almanac Ser.). 1288p. 1990. 330.00 (*0-87187-549-7*) Congr Quarterly.
— CQ Almanac, 1990. (Almanac Ser.). 1200p. 1991. 330.00 (*0-87187-655-8*) Congr Quarterly.
— CQ Almanac 1991, Vol. 47. (Almanac Ser.). 1200p. 1992. 330.00 (*0-87187-743-0*) Congr Quarterly.
— CQ Almanac 1992, Vol. 48. (Almanac Ser.). 693p. 1993. 330.00 (*0-87187-931-X*) Congr Quarterly.
— The CQ Researcher 1994. 1151p. 1995. 147.00 (*1-56802-025-2*) Congr Quarterly.

Congressional Quarterly Inc. Staff. CQ's Federal PACs Directory 1998-1999. 700p. (C). 1998. pap. text 235.00 (*1-56802-425-8*) Congr Quarterly.

***Congressional Quarterly Inc. Staff.** Gubernatorial Elections, 1787-1997. LC 97-50560. 183p. (C). 1998. pap. text 24.95 (*1-56802-396-0*) Congr Quarterly.

Congressional Quarterly, Inc. Staff. Guide to Current American Government, Fall 1990. 160p. 1990. 17.95 (*0-87187-551-9*) Congr Quarterly.
— Guide to Current American Government, Fall 1991. 180p. 1991. 17.95 (*0-87187-524-1*) Congr Quarterly.
— Guide to Current American Government, Fall 1992. 180p. 1992. 17.95 (*0-87187-702-3*) Congr Quarterly.
— Guide to Current American Government, Fall 1993. 168p. 1993. pap. 17.95 (*0-87187-776-7*) Congr Quarterly.
— Guide to Current American Government, Fall 1994. 143p. 1994. pap. 17.95 (*0-87187-800-3*) Congr Quarterly.
— Guide to Current American Government, Fall 1996. LC 61-16893. 168p. 1996. pap. 17.95 (*0-87187-893-3*) Congr Quarterly.
— Guide to Current American Government, Spring 1990. 160p. 1989. 17.95 (*0-87187-523-3*) Congr Quarterly.
— Guide to Current American Government, Spring 1991. 1990. 17.95 (*0-87187-571-3*) Congr Quarterly.
— Guide to Current American Government, Spring, 1992. 180p. 1991. 17.95 (*0-87187-625-6*) Congr Quarterly.
— Guide to Current American Government, Spring 1993. 149p. 1992. pap. 17.95 (*0-87187-719-8*) Congr Quarterly.
— Guide to Current American Government, Spring 1994. 148p. 1993. 17.95 (*0-87187-790-2*) Congr Quarterly.
— Guide to Current American Government, Spring 1995. LC 61-16893. 160p. 1994. pap. 17.95 (*0-87187-812-7*) Congr Quarterly.
— Historic Documents of 1972-1976, Vol. 1. 987p. 1973. 125.00 (*0-87187-043-6*) Congr Quarterly.
— Historic Documents of 1972-1976, Vol. 2. 1020p. 1974. 125.00 (*0-87187-054-1*) Congr Quarterly.
— Historic Documents of 1972-1976, Vol. 3. 982p. 1975. 125.00 (*0-87187-069-X*) Congr Quarterly.
— Historic Documents of 1972-1976, Vol. 4. 982p. 1976. 125.00 (*0-87187-090-8*) Congr Quarterly.
— Historic Documents of 1972-1976, Vol. 5. 1003p. 1977. 125.00 (*0-87187-103-3*) Congr Quarterly.
— Historic Documents of 1972-1976, Vols. 1-5. 1977. write for info. (*0-318-56900-0*) Congr Quarterly.
— Historic Documents of 1982: 1982, Vol. XI. LC 72-97888. 1000p. 1983. 125.00 (*0-87187-257-9*) Congr Quarterly.
— Historic Documents of 1984. LC 85-6912. 1000p. 1985. 125.00 (*0-87187-324-9*) Congr Quarterly.
— Historic Documents of 1985. 856p. 1986. 125.00 (*0-87187-358-3*) Congr Quarterly.
— Historic Documents of 1987. LC 72-97888. 1100p. 1988. 125.00 (*0-87187-445-8*) Congr Quarterly.
— Historic Documents of 1994. LC 72-97888. 686p. 1995. 125.00 (*0-87187-803-8*) Congr Quarterly.

Congressional Quarterly Inc. Staff. Historic Documents of 1997. annuals LC 72-97888. 800p. (C). 1998. text 135.00 (*1-56802-385-5*) Congr Quarterly.

Congressional Quarterly, Inc. Staff. How Congress Works. 2nd ed. LC 91-11116. 157p. 1991. text 28.95 (*0-87187-598-5*) Congr Quarterly.
— National Party Conventions, 1831-1996. LC 97-20443. viii, 312p. (YA). 1997. 37.95 (*1-56802-280-8*) Congr Quarterly.
— Presidential Elections, 1789-1996. LC 97-19084. 280p. (YA). 1997. text 37.95 (*1-56802-065-1*) Congr Quarterly.
— Selecting the President: From 1789 to 1996. LC 97-6398. (Illus.). 240p. (C). (gr. 11). 1997. text 29.95 (*1-56802-312-X*) Congr Quarterly.

***Congressional Quarterly Inc. Staff.** 2000 Federal Staff Directory - Winter. 32nd ed. 1300p. 1999. pap. 234.75 (*0-87289-172-0*) C Q Staff.
— 2000 Judicial Staff Directory: Winter. 1300p. 2000. pap. text 211.25 (*0-87289-173-9*) C Q Staff.

Congressional Quarterly, Inc., Staff. Who's Who in Congress, 1999 Edition. 1998. pap. text 21.19 (*1-56802-088-0*) Congr Quarterly.

Congressional Quarterly, Inc. Staff. Who's Who in Washington Non-Profit Groups, 1995. 305p. (YA). (gr. 11). 1995. pap. text 16.95 (*1-56802-131-3*) Congr Quarterly.

Congressional Quarterly, Inc. Staff & Nelson, Michael. Congressional Quarterly's Guide to the Presidency. 2nd ed. LC 96-18543. 1996. write for info. (*1-56802-232-8*); write for info. (*1-56802-233-6*) Congr Quarterly.

Congressional Quarterly Inc. Staff, jt. auth. see Barnes, Patricia G.

Congressional Quarterly, Inc., Staff, jt. auth. see Lipset, Seymour M.

Congressional Quarterly, Inc. Staff, ed. see Mitchell, Ralph.

***Congressional Quarterly, QUARTERLY.** Federal Staff Directory 1999 Winter Ed. White House-departments-agencies-biographies, 1999 Winter Ed. 1999. pap. text 186.25 (*0-87289-150-X*) Congr Quarterly.

***Congressional Quarterly Staff.** American Political Leaders, 1789-2000. LC 00-25223. (Illus.). 600p. 2000. 49.95 (*1-56802-562-9*) CQ Pr.
— Concise Encyclopedia of Democracy. LC 99-54450. (Illus.). 400p. 2000. 95.00 (*1-56802-426-6*) CQ Pr.
— Congressional Quarterly Almanac 1998. 1999. 513.89 (*1-56802-269-7*) Congr Quarterly.
— Congressional Roll Call 1999: A Chronology & Analysis of Votes in the House & Senate. 300p. 2000. pap. 36.95 (*1-56802-502-5*) CQ Pr.

Congressional Quarterly Staff. Congressional Roll Call 1998: A Chronology & Analysis of Votes in the House & Senate 105th Congress, 2nd Session. LC 72-77849. 300p. 1999. pap. 35.95 (*1-56802-469-X*) CQ Pr.
— Congressional Roll Call 1997: A Chronology & Analysis of Votes in the House & Senate 105th Congress, First Session. annuals LC 72-77849. 300p. (C). 1998. pap. text 36.95 (*1-56802-409-6*) Congr Quarterly.

***Congressional Quarterly Staff.** Congressional Staff Directory 2000. 57th ed. 2000. 234.72 (*0-87289-175-5*) C Q Staff.
— CQ's State Fact Finder 2000. 2000. pap. 44.95 (*1-56802-547-5*) CQ Pr.
— Current American Government Fall 2000. 150p. 2000. 18.95 (*1-56802-559-9*) CQ Pr.

Congressional Quarterly Staff. Guide to Congress, 2 vols. , Set. 5th ed. 1200p. 1999. 39.95 (*1-56802-477-0*) CQ Pr.

***Congressional Quarterly Staff.** Historic Documents 1999. Vol. 28. 900p. 2000. 139.00 (*1-56802-489-4*) CQ Pr.

Congressional Quarterly Staff. How Congress Works. 3rd ed. LC 98-29616. 200p. (C). 1998. pap. text 29.95 (*1-56802-391-X*) Congr Quarterly.

***Congressional Quarterly Staff.** 1999 Congressional Staff Directory - Fall: Members Committees Staff Biographies. 56th ed. 1999. pap. 207.00 (*0-87289-160-7*) C Q Staff.
— 1999 Federal Staff Directory - Fall: White House Departments Agencies Biographies. 31st ed. 1999. pap. 207.00 (*0-87289-159-3*) C Q Staff.

— 1999 Judicial Staff Directory - Summer: Members Committees Staff Biographies. 14th ed. 1999. pap. 207.00 (*0-87289-167-4*) C Q Staff.

— State Information Directory 2000-2001. 500p. 2000. 79.95 (*1-56802-516-5*) CQ Pr.

— Washington Information Directory 2000-2001. 1100p. 2000. 119.00 (*1-56802-498-3*) CQ Pr.

Congressional Quarterly Staff. Watergate: Chronology of a Crisis. LC 75-660. 1039p. 1975. 349.00 (*0-87187-070-3*) Congr Quarterly.

***Congressional Quarterly Staff.** We the Students: Supreme Court Cases for & about Students. LC 00-29759. 250p. 2000. 34.95 (*1-56802-570-X*); pap. 19.95 (*1-56802-571-8*) CQ Pr.

Congressional Quarterly Staff. Who's Who in Congress: 105Th Congress, 2Nd Session, 1998 Edition. (Illus.). 344p. 1998. pap. text 17.95 (*1-56802-078-3*) Congr Quarterly.

***Congressional Quarterly Staff.** Who's Who in Congress 2000. 350p. 2000. pap. 17.95 (*1-56802-556-4*) CQ Pr.

***Congressional Quarterly Staff, ed.** Congressional Staff Directory 2000: Fall Edition. 59th ed. 2000. pap. 169.00 (*0-87289-183-6*) C Q Staff.

— Congressional Staff Directory 2000: Summer. 58th ed. 2000. pap. 169.00 (*0-87289-179-8*) C Q Staff.

Congressional Quarterly Staff, ed. Congressional Yearbook, 1996: 104th Congress, 2nd Session. 320p. 1997. pap. 23.95 (*1-56802-315-4*) Congr Quarterly.

— CQ Almanac, 1997. 1000p. 1998. 370.00 (*1-56802-268-9*) Congr Quarterly.

***Congressional Quarterly Staff, ed.** Federal Staff Directory 2000. 33rd ed. 2000. pap. 169.00 (*0-87289-177-1*) C Q Staff.

— Federal Staff Directory 2000: Fall Edition. 34th ed. 2000. pap. 169.00 (*0-87289-182-8*) C Q Staff.

— Judicial Staff Directory 2000: Summer Edition. 16th ed. 2000. pap. 169.00 (*0-87289-181-X*) C Q Staff.

Congressional Quarterly Staff & Cook, Rhodes. How Congress Gets Elected. LC 99-41561. 200p. 1999. pap. 29.95 (*1-56802-462-2*) Congr Quarterly.

***Congressional Quarterly Staff, et al.** CQ's State Fact Finder 2000. 406p. 2000. 89.95 (*1-56802-546-7*) CQ Pr.

Congressional Quarterly Staff, jt. auth. see Lipset, Seymour M.

Congressional Research Center Library of Congress, ed. Soviet Diplomacy & Negotiating Behavior, 4 vols., Set. LC 89-82366. 1604p. 1990. reprint ed. lib. bdg. 200.00 (*0-89941-732-9*, 201950) W S Hein.

Congressional Third World Debt Caucus Staff, jt. auth. see Washington Office on Latin America Staff.

***Congressionnal Quarterly Books Staff.** Judicial Staff Directory 1999. 1999. pap. 207.00 (*0-87289-151-8*) C Q Staff.

***Congreve, Bill.** Epiphanies of Blood: Tales of Desperation & Thirst. (Illus.). 182p. 1998. pap. 14.95 (*0-9586583-1-5*, Pub. by Mirrordanse Bks) Firebird Dist.

Congreve, Bill, ed. Intimate Armageddons. 144p. (Orig.). 1992. pap. 11.95 (*1-875604-03-0*, Pub. by Five Isl Pr) Firebird Dist.

Congreve, Bill & Hood, Robert, eds. Bonescribes: Year's Best Australian Horror: 1995. 148p. (Orig.). 1996. pap. 13.95 (*0-9586583-5-8*, Pub. by Mirrordanse Bks) Firebird Dist.

Congreve, William. Comedies. (BCL1-PR English Literature Ser.). 441p. 1992. reprint ed. lib. bdg. 99.00 (*0-7812-7334-X*) Rprt Serv.

— Complete Plays of William Congreve. Davis, Herbert, ed. LC 66-20598. 1967. lib. bdg. 35.00 (*0-226-11485-6*) U Ch Pr.

— The Complete Plays of William Congreve. Davis, Herbert, ed. LC 66-20598. (Curtain Playwrights Ser.). 511p. reprint ed. pap. 158.50 (*0-608-09289-4*, 205416300004) Bks Demand.

— Complete Works, 4 vols., Set. (BCL1-PR English Literature Ser.). 1992. reprint ed. lib. bdg. 300.00 (*0-7812-7333-1*) Rprt Serv.

— A Concordance to the Plays of William Congreve. Mann, David D., ed. LC 72-13384. (Cornell Concordances Ser.). 888p. 1973. text 105.00 (*0-8014-0767-2*) Cornell U Pr.

— Love for Love. Avery, Emmett L., ed. LC 66-20827. (Regents Restoration Drama Ser.). 165p. 1966. reprint ed. pap. 51.20 (*0-608-02042-7*, 206269500003) Bks Demand.

— The Mourning Bride, Poems, & Miscellanies. (BCL1-PR English Literature Ser.). 540p. 1992. reprint ed. lib. bdg. 99.00 (*0-7812-7335-8*) Rprt Serv.

— Rover. (New Mermaid Ser.). (C). 1996. pap. text 8.00 (*0-393-90076-2*, Norton Paperbks) Norton.

— The Way of the World. Perry, Henry T., ed. (Crofts Classics Ser.). 128p. 1951. pap. text 4.95 (*0-88295-024-X*) Harlan Davidson.

— The Way of the World. LC 59-1770. 128p. 1996. pap. 6.95 (*1-85459-198-3*, Pub. by N Hern Bks) Theatre Comm.

Congreve, William. The Way of the World. abr. ed. LC 73-751234. 1988. audio 30.00 (*0-694-50869-1*, SWC 339, Caedmon) HarperAudio.

Congreve, William. The Way of the World. 80p. 1993. reprint ed. pap. text 1.50 (*0-486-27787-9*) Dover.

— The Way of the World. Lynch, Kathleen M., ed. LC 65-10543. (Regents Restoration Drama Ser.). 136p. 1965. reprint ed. pap. 8.95 (*0-8032-5354-0*, Bison Books) U of Nebr Pr.

— The Way of the World. 2nd ed. Gibbons, Brian, ed. (New Mermaid Ser.). (C). 1995. pap. text 11.25 (*0-393-90074-6*) Norton.

Congreve, William, jt. auth. see Weldon, John.

Coni, Nicholas & Webster, Stephen. Lecture Notes on Geriatrics. 5th ed. LC 97-22533. (Lecture Notes Ser.). (Illus.). 1998. pap. 34.95 (*0-86542-750-X*) Blackwell Sci.

Coni, Nicholas, et al. Aging: The Facts. 2nd ed. (Facts Ser.). (Illus.). 214p. 1992. text 19.95 (*0-19-262150-5*) OUP.

Coniam, S. W. & Diamond, A. W. Practical Pain Management: A Guide for Practitioners. (Illus.). 116p. 1995. text 65.00 (*0-19-262405-9*); pap. text 29.95 (*0-19-262404-0*) OUP.

Coniam, Stephen, jt. auth. see Diamond, Andrew.

Coniaris, Anthony M. Achieving Your Potential in Christ: Plain Talks on Theosis. 1993. pap. 9.95 (*0-937032-93-X*) Light&Life Pub Co MN.

— Basic Orthodoxy: Key Words of the Faith. 1989. pap. 10.95 (*0-937032-63-8*) Light&Life Pub Co MN.

— Christ's Comfort for Those Who Sorrow: Orthodox Missionaries from the Early Church to the Twelfth Century. 1978. pap. 8.95 (*0-937032-00-X*) Light&Life Pub Co MN.

— Crown Them with Glory & Honor: Talks for Weddings. 1985. pap. 8.95 (*0-937032-40-9*) Light&Life Pub Co MN.

— Daily Vitamins for Spiritual Growth, Vol. 3. 377p. (Orig.). 1996. pap. 17.95 (*1-880971-15-1*) Light&Life Pub Co MN.

Coniaris, Anthony M. Daily Vitamins for Spiritual Growth Vol. 1: Day by Day with Jesus Through the Church Year. LC 93-81256. 377p. 1994. pap. 17.95 (*0-937032-97-2*) Light&Life Pub Co MN.

Coniaris, Anthony M. Daily Vitamins for Spiritual Growth Vol. 2: Day by Day with Jesus Though the Church Year. 377p. 1995. pap. 17.95 (*1-880971-03-8*) Light&Life Pub Co MN.

***Coniaris, Anthony M.** Daily Vitamins for Spiritual Growth Vol. 4: Daily Vitamins for Hurting Hearts. 298p. 1999. pap. 17.95 (*1-880971-50-X*) Light&Life Pub Co MN.

Coniaris, Anthony M. Discovering God Through the Daily Practice of His Presence: Claiming God's Presence. 1989. pap. 8.95 (*0-937032-68-9*) Light&Life Pub Co MN.

— Eastern Orthodoxy: A Way of Life. 1966. pap. 10.95 (*0-937032-14-X*) Light&Life Pub Co MN.

— Eighty Talks for Orthodox Young People. 1975. pap. 9.95 (*0-937032-16-6*) Light&Life Pub Co MN.

— Finding God in Time of Sorrow & Despair: Easy to Read Spiritual Gems Designed to Bring Strength to the Suffering. 240p. 1996. pap. 15.95 (*1-880971-21-6*) Light&Life Pub Co MN.

— Fitting Together the Pieces of Your Life. 1987. pap. 9.95 (*0-937032-48-4*) Light&Life Pub Co MN.

— Gems from the Sunday Gospel Lessons in the Orthodox Church, Vol. I. 1975. pap. 14.95 (*0-937032-12-3*) Light&Life Pub Co MN.

— Gems from the Sunday Gospel Lessons in the Orthodox Church, Vol. II. 1976. pap. 14.95 (*0-937032-13-1*) Light&Life Pub Co MN.

Coniaris, Anthony M. Getting Ready for Marriage in the Orthodox Church. 1972. pap. 3.95 (*0-937032-11-5*) Light&Life Pub Co MN.

Coniaris, Anthony M. God & You: Person to Person. LC 95-81050. 155p. (Orig.). 1995. pap. 9.95 (*1-880971-11-9*) Light&Life Pub Co MN.

— God Speaks from the Cross: Talks on the Last Seven Words of Jesus. 1984. pap. 9.95 (*0-937032-33-6*) Light&Life Pub Co MN.

***Coniaris, Anthony M.** God's Fullness for Our Emptiness. 140p. 1999. pap. 9.99 (*1-880971-44-5*) Light&Life Pub Co MN.

Coniaris, Anthony M. The Great I Came's of Jesus. 1980. pap. 12.95 (*0-686-27069-X*) Light&Life Pub Co MN.

— Homilies from an Orthodox Pulpit: Sermons. 1992. pap. 15.95 (*0-937032-88-3*) Light&Life Pub Co MN.

— Introducing the Orthodox Church. 1982. pap. 14.95 (*0-937032-25-5*) Light&Life Pub Co MN.

Coniaris, Anthony M. Let Us Commit Ourselves & One Another & Our Whole Life to Christ Our God. LC 97-73558. 75p. 1997. write for info. (*1-880971-30-5*) Light&Life Pub Co MN.

Coniaris, Anthony M. Let's Take a Walk Through Our Orthodox Church. LC 98-92087. (Illus.). 100p. (J). (gr. 3-6). 1998. pap. 16.95 (*1-880971-39-9*) Light&Life Pub Co MN.

***Coniaris, Anthony M.** Living a Balanced Life in an Unbalanced World. 105p. 2000. pap. 10.95 (*1-880971-62-3*) Light&Life Pub Co MN.

Coniaris, Anthony M. Living Responsibly in an Age of Excuses: Whatever Happened to Moral Responsibility? 105p. 1999. pap. 8.95 (*1-880971-43-7*) Light&Life Pub Co MN.

— Making God Real in the Orthodox Christian Home. 1977. pap. 11.95 (*0-937032-07-7*) Light&Life Pub Co MN.

— Meet Jesus in the Sunday Gospels: Sermons. 1986. pap. 15.95 (*0-937032-41-7*) Light&Life Pub Co MN.

— Meet Jesus in the Sunday Gospels: Sermons, Vol. 2. 1987. pap. 15.95 (*0-937032-45-X*) Light&Life Pub Co MN.

— The Message of the Sunday Gospel Readings, Vol. 1. 1982. pap. 15.95 (*0-937032-26-3*) Light&Life Pub Co MN.

— The Message of the Sunday Gospels, Vol. 2. 1983. pap. 15.95 (*0-937032-29-8*) Light&Life Pub Co MN.

— No Man Ever Spoke As This Man: The Great I Am's of Jesus. 1969. pap. 10.95 (*0-937032-18-2*) Light&Life Pub Co MN.

— Orthodoxy: A Creed for Today: Talks on the Nicene Creed. 1972. pap. 11.95 (*0-937032-19-0*) Light&Life Pub Co MN.

— Paradise on Your Doorstep: Brief Meditations on Revelation 3:20. LC 96-75549. 136p. 1996. pap. 10.95 (*1-880971-19-4*) Light&Life Pub Co MN.

— Perspectives on Living the Orthodox Faith. 1985. pap. 12.95 (*0-937032-36-0*) Light&Life Pub Co MN.

— Philokalia: The Bible of Orthodox Spirituality. LC 98-92036. 302 p. 1998. pap. 15.95 (*1-880971-38-0*) Light&Life Pub Co MN.

— Preaching the Word of God. LC 83-18416. 137p. 1983. pap. 6.95 (*0-916586-65-0*, Pub. by Holy Cross Orthodox) BookWorld.

— Reflections on the Priesthood: An Anthology on the Meaning of the Priesthood. 1993. pap. 11.95 (*0-937032-94-8*) Light&Life Pub Co MN.

Coniaris, Anthony M. Sacred Symbols That Speak: An Explanation of Symbols Used in the Eastern Orthodox Church. 1986. pap. 12.95 (*0-937032-39-5*) Light&Life Pub Co MN.

Coniaris, Anthony M. Sacred Symbols That Speak Vol. 2: An Explanation of the Meaning of Symbols Used in the Eastern Orthodox Church. 1987. pap. 12.95 (*0-937032-49-2*) Light&Life Pub Co MN.

— Sermons for the Church Year: Sermons. 1991. pap. 15.95 (*0-937032-76-X*) Light&Life Pub Co MN.

— Sermons on the Major Holy Days of the Orthodox Church. 1978. pap. 14.95 (*0-937032-03-4*) Light&Life Pub Co MN.

— Sixty-One Talks for Orthodox Funerals. 1969. pap. 10.95 (*0-937032-02-6*) Light&Life Pub Co MN.

— Surviving the Loss of a Loved One: Help for the Bereaved. 1992. pap. 11.95 (*0-937032-89-1*) Light&Life Pub Co MN.

— These Are the Sacraments. 1981. pap. 11.95 (*0-937032-22-0*) Light&Life Pub Co MN.

— This Is My Beloved Son - Listen to Him Vol. 1: Sermons. 1987. pap. 15.95 (*0-937032-55-7*) Light&Life Pub Co MN.

— This Is My Beloved Son - Listen to Him Vol. 2: Sermons. 1988. pap. 15.95 (*0-937032-50-6*) Light&Life Pub Co MN.

— Treasures from Paul's Letters, Vol. I. 1978. pap. 15.95 (*0-937032-05-0*) Light&Life Pub Co MN.

— Treasures from Paul's Letters, Vol. II. 1979. pap. 15.95 (*0-937032-06-9*) Light&Life Pub Co MN.

— Where Moth & Rust Do Not Consume. 1983. pap. 10.95 (*0-937032-30-1*) Light&Life Pub Co MN.

— Your Baby's Baptism in the Orthodox Church: A Pictorial Explanation. 1991. pap. 10.95 (*0-937032-83-2*) Light&Life Pub Co MN.

Coniaris, Anthony M., ed. Daily Readings from the Writings of St. John Chrysostom. 1988. pap. 10.95 (*0-937032-51-4*) Light&Life Pub Co MN.

Coniaris, Anthony M., jt. auth. see Harakas, Emily.

Conibear, Shirley. Medical Surveillance for Hazardous Waste. 1990. text. write for info. (*0-442-31901-0*, VNR) Wiley.

Conigliaro, Vincenzo. Dreams As a Tool in Psychodynamic Psychotherapy: Traveling the Royal Road to the Unconscious. LC 96-29393. 1997. 62.50 (*0-8236-1439-5*) Intl Univs Pr.

Coniglio, J. W. Economics of CNC Gashing vs. Large D. P. Hobbing. (Technical Papers: Vol. P129.26). (Illus.). 22p. 1982. pap. text 30.00 (*1-55589-542-5*) AGMA.

Coniglio, Jamie W. Introduction to Library Research. (C). 1996. text 22.50 (*0-86531-234-6*) Westview.

Conike, Jerome F., compiled by. Family Consecration Prayer Book. (Illus.). 224p. 1988. pap. text 3.95 (*0-932406-19-X*) AFC.

Coniker, Jerome F. Devotions & Prayers in Honor of St. Joseph. (Living Meditation & Prayerbook). (Illus.). 34p. (Orig.). 1978. pap. text 2.50 (*0-932406-04-1*) AFC.

— Peaceful Seed Living, Vols. 1 & 2. 2nd ed. LC 78-66369. (Living Meditation & Prayerbook Ser.). (Illus.). 156p. 1981. pap. text 3.00 (*0-932406-00-9*) AFC.

— Prayers & Recommended Practices. 2nd ed. LC 78-66374. (Living Meditation & Prayerbook Ser.). (Illus.). 91p. pap. text 3.00 (*0-932406-01-7*) AFC.

Coniker, Jerome F., ed. see Seeley, Burns K.

Conil, Christopher. New Vegetarian Tofu Recipes. 128p. 1995. pap. 5.95 (*0-572-01727-8*, Pub. by Foulsham UK) Assoc Pubs Grp.

Conil, Christopher & Conil, Jean, eds. All Colour Vegetarian Recipes. (Illus.). 64p. 1995. 9.95 (*0-572-01715-4*, Pub. by Foulsham UK) Assoc Pubs Grp.

Conil, Jean. Complete Book of Festive Vegetarian Recipes. 1994. pap. 11.95 (*0-572-01815-0*, Pub. by W Foulsham) Trans-Atl Phila.

— Complete Book of Vegetarian Recipes. 256p. 1996. pap. text 19.95 (*0-572-02120-8*, Pub. by W Foulsham) Trans-Atl Phila.

— Encyclopedia of Food. (Illus.). 346p. 1996. 9.99 (*1-57215-216-8*, JG1216) World Pubns.

— Let's Eat French at Home! (Let's Eat...at Home! Ser.). 160p. 1995. pap. 5.95 (*0-572-01834-7*, Pub. by Foulsham UK) Assoc Pubs Grp.

— The Master Chef. 256p. 1995. write for info. (*1-57215-136-6*) World Pubns.

— New Vegetarian Gourmet Recipes. 96p. (Orig.). 1995. pap. 6.95 (*0-572-01852-5*, Pub. by Foulsham UK) Assoc Pubs Grp.

Conil, Jean, jt. ed. see Conil, Christopher.

Coninck, J. De, see De Coninck, J., ed.

Coninck-Smith, Ning De, see De Coninck-Smith, Ning.

Conine, Jon. Fathers' Rights: The Sourcebook for Dealing with the Child Support System. 240p. 1989. 17.95 (*0-8027-1074-3*) Walker & Co.

Coning, Evelyn C. & Coning, William H. The Principle of Peace. Orig. Title: The Principle of Peace & Its Abuse. 128p. 1999. pap. 14.95 (*0-9670986-0-2*) Principle of Peace.

Coning, William H., jt. auth. see Coning, Evelyn C.

Conings, Clayne, et al. Miracle of Names: A 500 Word Description of Your Character. LC 94-67155. 220p. (Orig.). (YA). (gr. 10). 1996. pap. 13.95 (*1-887472-03-7*) Sunstar Pubng.

Conington, John, ed. see Virgil.

Coninx, Frans, jt. ed. see Elsendoorn, Ben A.

Conio, Gerard, jt. auth. see Forest, Philippe.

Conion, Tom & Cope, Peter. Computing in Scottish Education. 192p. 1990. 49.50 (*0-7486-0115-5*, Pub. by Edinburgh U Pr) Col U Pr.

Conisbee, Philip. Chardin. LC 84-23259. (Illus.). 240p. 1986. 75.00 (*0-8387-5091-5*) Bucknell U Pr.

— In the Light of Italy: Corot & Early Plein-Air Painting. LC 95-47753. 288p. 1996. 55.00 (*0-300-06794-1*) Yale U Pr.

Conisbee, Philip & Kloss, William. Discoveries! French Masterpieces from St. Etienne: Essays. LC 92-17435. 1992. write for info. (*0-89951-086-8*) Santa Barb Mus Art.

Conisbee, Philip, et al. The Ahmanson Gifts: European Masterpieces in the Collection of the Los Angeles County Museum of Art. LC 91-18247. (Illus.). 208p. 1991. pap. text 21.95 (*0-87587-160-7*) LA Co Art Mus.

— Monet to Matisse: French Art in Southern California Collections. (Illus.). 144p. (Orig.). 1991. pap. 29.95 (*0-87587-159-3*) LA Co Art Mus.

Conisbee, Philip, jt. auth. see Elsen, Albert E.

Conisbee, Philip, jt. ed. see Tinterow, Gary.

Conisbee, Philip. Georges de la Tour & His World. LC 96-49663. (Illus.). 356p. 1996. 60.00 (*0-300-06948-0*) Yale U Pr.

Conison, Jay. Employee Benefit Plans in a Nutshell. LC 93-19662. (Nutshell Ser.). 483p. (C). 1993. pap. 19.00 (*0-314-02253-8*) West Pub.

— Employee Benefit Plans in a Nutshell. 2nd ed. LC 98-173177. (Paralegal Ser.). (C). 1998. pap. 16.50 (*0-314-21165-9*) West Pub.

Conkel, Donald. Cichlids of North & Central America. (Illus.). 64p. 1997. 12.95 (*0-7938-0205-9*, WW-039) TFH Pubns.

***Conkelton, Sheryl.** Uta Barth: In Between Places. (Illus.). 178p. 2000. pap. 49.95 (*0-935558-37-3*) Henry Art.

Conkelton, Sheryl, ed. Frederick Sommer: Selected Texts & Bibliography. LC 94-45124. (World Photographers References Ser.: Vol. 7). 1995. 105.00 (*0-8161-0619-3*, G K Hall & Co) Mac Lib Ref.

***Conkelton, Sheryl, et al.** What It Meant to Be Modern: Seattle Art at Mid-Century. LC 00-26966. (Illus.). 80p. 2000. pap. 10.00 (*0-935558-38-1*) Henry Art.

Conkey, ed. see Swartwout, J. Baxter.

Conkey, Frances, ed. see Forrest, Elliott B.

Conkey, Kathleen. The Postal Precipice: Can the U. S. Postal Service Be Saved. 515p. 1983. pap. text 30.00 (*0-936758-09-0*) Ctr Responsive Law.

Conkey, Margaret W., et al, eds. Beyond Art: Pleistocene Image & Symbol. LC 97-68235. (Memoirs of the California Academy of Sciences Ser.: Vol. 23). (Illus.). 330p. (C). 1997. 48.00 (*0-940228-38-6*, Pub. by Calif Acad Sci); pap. 36.00 (*0-940228-37-8*, Pub. by Calif Acad Sci) U CA Pr.

Conkey, Margaret W., jt. ed. see Gero, Joan M.

Conkin & Stromberg. Heritage & Challenge: The History & Theory of History. 14.95 (*0-88295-286-2*) Forum Pr IL.

Conkin, Paul K. American Originals: Homemade Varieties of Christianity. LC 96-35270. 408p. (gr. 13). 1997. pap. 18.95 (*0-8078-4649-X*); lib. bdg. 59.95 (*0-8078-2342-2*) U of NC Pr.

— Big Daddy from the Pedernales: Lyndon B. Johnson. (Twayne's Twentieth Century American Biography Ser.: No. 1). 344p. (C). 1986. 26.95 (*0-8057-7762-8*, Twyne) Mac Lib Ref.

— Big Daddy from the Pedernales: Lyndon B. Johnson. (Twayne's Twentieth Century American Biography Ser.: No. 1). 344p. (C). 1987. pap. 20.00 (*0-8057-7772-5*, Twyne) Mac Lib Ref.

— Cane Ridge: America's Pentecost. LC 90-50081. (Curti Lectures). 198p. (C). 1991. text 34.95 (*0-299-12720-6*) U of Wis Pr.

— Cane Ridge, America's Pentecost. LC 90-50081. (Curti Lectures: No. 1989). (Illus.). 198p. reprint ed. pap. 61.40 (*0-608-09901-5*, 206923900003) Bks Demand.

— The Four Foundations of American Governments. 96p. (C). 1994. pap. text 11.95 (*0-88295-914-X*) Harlan Davidson.

— The New Deal. 3rd ed. Eisenstadt, A. S. & Franklin, John H., eds. (American History Ser.). (Illus.). 120p. 1992. pap. text 11.95 (*0-88295-889-5*) Harlan Davidson.

— Prophets of Prosperity: America's First Political Economists. LC 79-3251. 347p. reprint ed. pap. 107.60 (*0-608-18249-4*, 205669700081) Bks Demand.

— Puritans & Pragmatists: Eight Eminent American Thinkers. LC 75-34730. 505p. reprint ed. pap. 156.60 (*0-8357-6689-6*, 205686900094) Bks Demand.

***Conkin, Paul K.** A Requiem for the American Village. LC 99-40922. (American Intellectual Culture Ser.). 205p. 2000. text 30.00 (*0-8476-9736-3*) Rowman.

Conkin, Paul K. The Uneasy Center: Reformed Christianity in AnteBellum America. LC 94-12292. 352p. 1995. text 49.95 (*0-8078-2180-2*); pap. text 19.95 (*0-8078-4492-6*) U of NC Pr.

— When All the Gods Trembled: Darwinism, Scopes & American Intellectuals. LC 98-27694. (American Intellectual Culture Ser.). 192p. 1998. 22.95 (*0-8476-9063-6*, Pub. by Rowman) Natl Bk Netwk.

Conkin, Paul K. & Stromberg, Roland N. Heritage & Challenge: The History & Theory of History. 272p. (Orig.). (C). 1989. pap. text 14.95 (*0-88273-286-2*) Forum Pr IL.

Conkin, Paul K., jt. ed. see Hargrove, Erwin C.

Conkin, Paul K., ed. see Wingspread Conference on New Directions in America.

Conkle, Bud & Rearden, Jim. Trail of the Eagle: Hunting Alaska with Master Guide Bud Conkle. (Illus.). 252p. 1990. 29.50 (*0-937708-24-0*) Great Northwest.

Conkle, E. P. The Jewel in Papa's Crown: A Play in One Act for Women. 16p. 1990. pap. 3.25 (*0-88680-337-3*) I E Clark.

— No Time for Heaven: A Full-Length Play for the Whole Family. 76p. 1955. pap. 4.00 (*0-88680-140-0*) I E Clark.
— No Time for Heaven: Director's Script. 76p. 1955. pap. 15.00 (*0-88680-141-9*) I E Clark.
Conkle, Nancy. Renaissance Women. 48p. (YA). (gr. 7 up). 1996. pap. 4.95 (*0-88388-205-1*) Bellerophon Bks.
Conkle, Nancy E. Terrific Bee on Terrific Me. (Illus.). 32p. (Orig.). (J). (ps-1). 1993. pap. 9.50 (*0-9639061-0-0*) N Conkle.
Conklin, Alice L. A Mission to Civilize: The Republican Idea of Empire in France & West Africa, 1895-1930. LC 97-9868. 446p. 1997. 55.00 (*0-8047-2999-9*) Stanford U Pr.
***Conklin, Alice L.** Mission to Civilize: The Republican Idea of Empire in France & West Africa, 1895-1930. 2000. pap. text 24.95 (*0-8047-4012-7*) Stanford U Pr.
***Conklin, Alice L. & Fletcher, Ian Christopher, eds.** European Imperialism, 1830-1930: Climax & Contradiction. LC 98-72011. (Problems in European Civilization Ser.). 234p. 1999. pap. text 14.07 (*0-395-90385-8*) HM.
Conklin, Barbara. P. S. I Love You. (J). 1988. mass mkt. 3.95 (*0-553-19550-6*) BDD Bks Young Read.
***Conklin, Brian.** VX: It's Invisible, It's Odorless, It's Tasteless, It Has No Antidote, a Manman Threatens to Use It, & the World Has to Wait No Longer! LC 00-190400. 292p. 2000. 25.00 (*0-7388-1639-6*) Xlibris Corp.
— VX: It's Invisible, It's Odorless, It's Tasteless, It Has No Antidote, a Manman Threatens to Use It, & the World Has to Wait No Longer! LC 00-190400. 292p. 2000. pap. 18.00 (*0-7388-1640-X*) Xlibris Corp.
***Conklin, Caroline.** Meditations for Altar Guild Members. Webber, Christopher L., ed. 96p. 2000. pap. 6.95 (*0-8192-1845-6*, 6293) Morehouse Pub.
Conklin, Cheryl. Into the Fullness of Being: Tools for Spiritually Empowered Living. (Illus.). 111p. 1997. spiral bd. 29.75 (*1-890959-14-6*) Open Circle.
Conklin, David & Bergman, Paul, eds. Pay Equity in Ontario: A Manager's Guide. 115p. 1990. pap. text 23.95 (*0-88645-110-8*, Pub. by Inst Res Pub) Ashgate Pub Co.
Conklin, David & Lecraw, Dan. Foreign Ownership Restrictions & Liberalization Reforms. LC 97-71718. 150p. 1997. text 64.95 (*1-85972-620-8*, Pub. by Ashgate Pub) Ashgate Pub Co.
Conklin, David & St-Hilaire, France, eds. Provincial Tax Reforms: Options & Opportunities. 192p. 1990. pap. text 23.95 (*0-88645-111-6*, Pub. by Inst Res Pub) Ashgate Pub Co.
Conklin, David W. Comparative Economic Systems: Objectives, Decision Modes & the Process of Choice. (Illus.). 427p. (C). 1991. text 90.00 (*0-521-34439-5*); pap. text 33.95 (*0-521-34889-7*) Cambridge U Pr.
Conklin, David W. & St. Hilaire, Frances. Canadian High-Tech in a World Economy: A Case Study of Information Technology. 392p. 1988. 25.00 (*0-88645-054-3*, Pub. by Inst Res Pub) Ashgate Pub Co.
Conklin, Edmund S. Three Diagnostic Scorings for the Thurstone Personality Schedule. LC 37-28256. (Science Study Ser.: No. 6). 25p. reprint ed. pap. 30.00 (*0-608-30561-8*, 205522900011) Bks Demand.
Conklin, Edward. Getting Back into the Garden of Eden. LC 98-17222. (Illus.). 164p. 1998. 34.00 (*0-7618-1140-0*) U Pr of Amer.
Conklin, Eileen. Women at Gettysburg. (Illus.). 430p. 1998. pap. 22.95 (*1-57747-008-7*) Thomas Publications.
***Conklin, Eileen F.** Exile to Sweet Dixie: The Story of Euphemia Goldsborough. LC 98-86737. (Illus.). 208p. 2001. pap. 18.00 (*1-57747-044-3*) Thomas Publications.
Conklin, Eileen F. Women at Gettysburg, 1863. (Illus.). 430p. (C). 1993. text 29.95 (*0-939631-63-6*) Thomas Publications.
Conklin, Emma B., compiled by. A Brief History of Logan County, with Reminiscences by Pioneers. (Illus.). 354p. 1995. reprint ed. lib. bdg. 45.00 (*0-8328-4679-1*) Higginson Bk Co.
Conklin, George. Slithy Toves & Borogoves & Other Beasties. 1995. pap. 6.95 (*0-533-11381-4*) Vantage.
— The Story of Noah & His Ark. 1992. 10.00 (*0-533-10013-5*) Vantage.
Conklin, George W. Of Shoes & Ships & Sealing Wax, Cabbages & Kings, & Aspirin As Needed. 1997. 9.95 (*0-533-12263-5*) Vantage.
***Conklin, George W.** Under the Crescent & Star: The 134th New York Volunteer Infantry in the Civil War. LC 99-66056. (Illus.). xii, 370p. 2000. 29.95 (*0-9674985-0-3*) Axworthy.
Conklin-Halaj, Sara. Conklin's Guide, Maritime Auction Annual, July 4, 1988 - July 4, 1989. 460p. (Orig.). 1989. pap. 100.00 (*0-9623625-4-9*) Leeward Shore.
— Conklin's Guide, Maritime Auction Annual, July 4, 1989-May 12, 1990. 400p. 1990. 115.00 (*0-9623625-5-7*) Leeward Shore.
— Conklin's Guide Maritime Auction Annual, July 5, 1989 to May 12, 1990. 400p. (Orig.). 1990. pap. 110.00 (*0-685-45319-7*) Leeward Shore.
Conklin, Harold C. Ethnographic Atlas of Ifugao: A Study of Environment, Culture & Society in Northern Luzon. LC 79-689774. (Illus.). 122p. 1980. 295.00 (*0-300-02529-7*) Elliots Bks.
— Folk Classification: A Topically Arranged Bibliography of Contemporary & Background References Through 1971. rev. ed. LC 80-80582. 521p. 1980. reprint ed. pap. text 8.50 (*0-913516-02-3*) Yale U Anthro.
— Hanunoo Agriculture: A Report on an Integral System of Shifting Cultivation in the Phillipines FAO Forestry Development Paper No. 12. LC 75-28745. (Illus.). 209p. 1975. reprint ed. pap. text 29.50 (*0-911830-22-7*) Elliots Bks.
— Ifugao Bibliography. LC 68-29881. (Bibliography Ser.: No. 11). vi, 75p. 1968. 5.50 (*0-938692-18-6*) Yale U SE Asia.
Conklin, Henry. Through "Poverty's Vale" A Hardscrabble Boyhood in Upstate New York, 1832-1862. Tripp, Wendell, ed. LC 73-19980. (Illus.). 280p. 1974. 29.95 (*0-8156-0098-4*) Syracuse U Pr.
— Through "Poverty's Vale" A Hardscrabble Boyhood in Upstate New York, 1832-1862. Tripp, Wendell, ed. LC 73-19980. (Illus.). 280p. 1975. pap. 16.95 (*0-8156-0117-4*) Syracuse U Pr.
Conklin, J. C., jt. ed. see Ohadi, M. M.
***Conklin, Jean.** Music in the Midst of Chaos: One Family's Saga on the Human Rights Battlefield. LC 99-90747. (Illus.). 268p. 1999. pap. 16.95 (*0-9673440-0-X*, Pub. by Carico Pr) Good Shepherd Pubns.
Conklin, Jean, jt. auth. see Duff, Joey.
Conklin, Jeffrey S. Forging an East Asian Foreign Policy. 588p. (C). 1995. lib. bdg. 26.50 (*0-8191-9827-7*) U Pr of Amer.
Conklin, Jo-Ann & Messager, Annette, contrib. by. Annette Messager: Map of Temper, Map of Tenderness. (Illus.). 16p. 1998. pap. 7.50 (*0-933519-37-0*) D W Bell Gallery.
Conklin, Jo-Ann, ed. see Caneva, Caterina, et al.
Conklin, John E. Art Crime. LC 93-11869. 320p. 1994. 57.95 (*0-275-94771-8*, Praeger Pubs) Greenwood.
— Criminology. 6th ed. LC 97-1116. 626p. 1997. 70.00 (*0-205-26478-6*) P-H.
— Criminology: Instructor's Manual & Test Bank. 6th ed. (C). 1997. text, teacher ed. write for info. (*0-205-27122-7*, T7122-9) Allyn.
Conklin, John E. New Perspectives in Criminology: A Reader. LC 95-24524. 649p. 1995. pap. text 42.00 (*0-205-18388-3*) Allyn.
Conklin, Kathy, jt. auth. see Weiss, Kenneth.
Conklin, Les. Betting Horses to Win. LC 96-231954. 1980. pap. 10.00 (*0-87980-265-0*) Wilshire.
— Payday at the Races. 1982. pap. 7.00 (*0-87980-269-3*) Wilshire.
Conklin, Marie E. Genetic & Biochemical Aspects of the Development of Datura. Wolsky, A., ed. (Monographs in Developmental Biology: Vol. 12). (Illus.). 170p. 1976. 65.25 (*3-8055-2307-6*) S Karger.
Conklin, Nancy, jt. auth. see Lourie, Margaret.
Conklin, Nancy F., jt. auth. see Stiggins, Richard J.
Conklin, Paul. Tomorrow a New World. (FDR & the Era of the New Deal Ser.). 1976. reprint ed. lib. bdg. 39.50 (*0-306-70805-1*) Da Capo.
Conklin, Robert. Be Whole! LC 96-92796. ix, 229p. 1997. pap. 11.95 (*0-9654882-0-9*) CliffTop.
— Sell! Sell! Sell! 1995. pap. text 11.95 (*0-8087-7253-8*) Pearson Custom.
Conklin, Thomas. The Adventures of Hercules. (J). 1996. pap. 3.99 (*0-679-88263-4*, Pub. by Random Bks Yng Read) Random.
Conklin, Thomas. The Adventures of Hercules. (J). 1996. 9.09 (*0-606-11025-9*, Pub. by Turtleback) Demco.
Conklin, Thomas. Muhammad Ali: The Fight for Respect. (YA). 1992. pap. 5.70 (*0-395-63556-X*) HM.
— Muhammad Ali: The Fight for Respect. (New Directions Ser.). 1991. 11.15 (*0-606-07898-3*) Turtleback.
Conklin, Thomas. The Titanic Sinks. LC 97-4060. (J). 1997. pap. 3.99 (*0-679-88606-0*) Random.
— The Titanic Sinks. (J). 2000. lib. bdg. 11.99 (*0-679-98606-5*) Random.
***Conklin, Thomas.** The Titanic Sinks. 1999. pap. write for info. (*0-375-80920-1*, Pub. by Random Bks Yng Read) Random.
— The Titanic Sinks. 1997. 10.09 (*0-606-11992-2*, Pub. by Turtleback) Demco.
***Conklin, Tom.** Disasters! Background Information, Activities & Projects to Teach about Earthquakes, Hurricanes, Volcanoes & Other Forces. (Illus.). 80p. (J). (gr. 4-8). 2000. pap. 16.99 (*0-590-98823-9*) Scholastic Inc.
Conklin, Tom. Muhammad Ali: The Fight for Respect. LC 91-25950. (New Directions Ser.). (Illus.). 104p. (YA). (gr. 7 up). 1992. pap. 5.95 (*1-56294-832-6*); lib. bdg. 21.90 (*1-56294-112-7*) Millbrook Pr.
— Mystery Plays: 8 Plays for the Classroom Based on Stories by Famous Writers. 96p. (gr. 4-8). 1997. pap. 12.95 (*0-590-20939-6*) Scholastic Inc.
Conklin, W. E. In Defense of Fundamental Rights. 326p. 1979. lib. bdg. 131.50 (*90-286-0389-1*) Kluwer Academic.
Conklin, William. Finesse & Common Sense in School Administration. LC 97-28867. 217p. 1998. lib. bdg. 34.00 (*1-56072-463-3*) Nova Sci Pubs.
Conklin, William E. Images of a Constitution. 365p. 1989. text 47.50 (*0-8020-2669-9*) U of Toronto Pr.
— Images of a Constitution. 11th ed. 377p. 1993. pap. text 22.50 (*0-8020-6973-8*) U of Toronto Pr.
— The Phenomenology of Modern Legal Discourse: The Juridical Production & the Disclosure of Suffering. LC 97-40987. (Applied Legal Philosophy Ser.). 285p. 1998. 77.95 (*1-84014-071-2*, K213.C657, Pub. by Ashgate Pub) Ashgate Pub Co.
Conklin, William F. Nautical Rules of the Road Explained. 78p. 1997. pap. 9.95 (*0-9659647-0-1*) BBC Commun.
Conkling, Alfred. A Treatise on the Organization, Jurisdiction & Practice of the Courts of the United States. LC 85-80031. 538p. 1985. reprint ed. 110.00 (*0-912004-27-4*) Gaunt.
— A Treatise on the Organization, Jurisdiction & Practice of the Courts of the United States: With an Appendix of Practical Forms. 4th rev. ed. LC 86-83210. xii, 882p. 1987. reprint ed. 125.00 (*0-912004-61-4*) Gaunt.
Conkling, Alfred R. Appleton's Guide to Mexico. 1976. lib. bdg. 59.95 (*0-8490-1443-3*) Gordon Pr.
Conkling, Edgar C., jt. auth. see Berry, Brian J. L.
Conkling, Helen. Red Peony Night. LC 97-4919. (Pitt Poetry Ser.). 80p. 1997. pap. 12.95 (*0-8229-5647-0*); text 25.00 (*0-8229-4042-6*) U of Pittsburgh Pr.
Conkling, J. A. Chemistry of Pyrotechnics: Basic Principles & Theory. 2nd ed. Date not set. write for info. (*0-8247-9534-2*) Dekker.
Conkling, John A. Chemistry of Pyrotechnics & Explosives: Basic Principles & Theory. (Illus.). 216p. (C). 1985. text 79.75 (*0-8247-7443-4*) Dekker.
Conkling, Lori, jt. auth. see Gottlieb, Marvin R.
Conkling, Neil & Philip, Hilda. A Bird's Way of Singing. (J). Date not set. 12.95 (*0-8050-4795-6*) H Holt & Co.
Conkling, Philip. Islands in Time: A Natural & Cultural History of Islands in the Gulf of Maine. 2nd ed. LC 98-23981. (Illus.). 304p. 1998. pap. 19.95 (*0-89272-406-4*) Down East.
Conkling, Philip, jt. ed. see Bourgeault, Cynthia.
Conkling, Philip W., ed. From Cape Cod to the Bay of Fundy: An Environmental Atlas of the Gulf of Maine. (Illus.). 272p. 1995. 50.00 (*0-262-03227-9*); pap. text 29.95 (*0-262-53127-5*) MIT Pr.
Conkling, Philip W., et al, eds. Island Journal Vol. VI: An Annual Publication of the Island Institute. (Illus.). 88p. 1989. pap. 7.95 (*0-942719-07-7*) Island Inst.
— Island Journal Vol. VII: An Annual Publication of the Island Institute, Vol. VII. (Illus.). 88p. (C). 1990. pap. 7.95 (*0-942719-09-3*) Island Inst.
Conkling, Philip W. & Bourgeault, Cynthia, eds. Island Journal Vol. IX: An Annual Publication of the Island Institute. (Illus.). 92p. 1992. pap. 7.95 (*0-942719-11-5*) Island Inst.
Conkling, Philip W. & Platt, David D., eds. Island Journal Vol. XIII: An Annual Publication of the Island Institute. (Island Journals: No. 13). (Illus.). 96p. (Orig.). 1996. pap. 7.95 (*0-942719-15-8*) Island Inst.
Conkling, Philip W., jt. ed. see Bourgeault, Cynthia.
Conkling, Philip W., jt. ed. see Platt, David W.
Conkling, Philip W., jt. ed. see Putz, George.
***Conkling, Winifred.** The Carnitine Connection. 256p. 2000. pap. 5.99 (*0-312-97458-2*, St Martins Paperbacks) St Martin.
— The Expectant Mother's Checklist. 256p. 2000. mass mkt. 5.99 (*0-312-97304-7*) St Martin.
Conkling, Winifred. Getting Pregnant Naturally: Healthy Choices to Boost Your Chances of Conceiving Without Fertility Drugs. LC 98-45199. 224p. 1999. pap. 12.00 (*0-380-79633-3*, Avon Bks) Morrow Avon.
— Natural Healing for Children: An A-Z Guide to Easy Home Remedies. 1997. mass mkt. 6.99 (*0-312-96044-1*) St Martin.
— Natural Power Builders: A Pro & Con Look at Natural Steroids. 1999. mass mkt. 5.99 (*0-312-97103-6*) St Martin.
— Natural Power Builders Clip Strip. 1998. 71.88 (*0-312-97105-2*) St Martin.
— Secrets of Echinacea. 256p. 1999. mass mkt. 5.99 (*0-312-97086-2*, St Martins Paperbacks) St Martin.
— Secrets of 5HTP. LC 98-219509. 1998. mass mkt. 5.99 (*0-312-96859-0*) St Martin.
— Secrets of Ginseng. 256p. 1999. mass mkt. 5.99 (*0-312-97072-2*) St Martin.
— Securing Your Child's Future: A Financial & Legal Planner for Parents. 256p. (Orig.). 1995. pap. 12.95 (*0-449-90876-3*) Fawcett.
***Conkling, Winifred.** Smart Wiring Your Baby's Brain: What You Can Do to Stimulate Your Child During the Critical First Three Years. 160p. 2000. write for info. (*0-380-80251-1*, Quil) HarperTrade.
Conkling, Winifred, jt. auth. see Peterson, Esther.
Conklinn, JoAnn. Of Totems, Traps, Maps, & James Jesus Angleton: Richard Brothers, Yizhak Elyashiv, Harriet Pappas, Susannah Strong. 12p. 1997. pap. 5.00 (*0-933519-35-4*) D W Bell Gallery.
Conkright, Margarita E., et al. World Ocean Atlas, 1994 Vol. 1: Nutrients. (Illus.). 150p. (Orig.). 1996. pap. text 50.00 (*0-7881-3076-5*) DIANE Pub.
Conkwright, Nelson B. Introduction to Theory of Equations. LC 58-2094. 225p. reprint ed. pap. 69.80 (*0-608-30957-5*, 200050900028) Bks Demand.
Conlan, Craig. Fun Fur: Starring Hairy Mary. 1999. pap. text 9.95 (*1-899866-22-1*) Slab-O-Concrete Pubns.
***Conlan, Craig.** Inactivity Book. (Illus.). 2000. pap. 13.95 (*1-899866-42-6*) Slab-O-Concrete Pubns.
Conlan, James. Principles of Management in Export. Brooke, Michael Z., ed. LC 94-15839. (Principles of Export Guidebooks Ser.). 256p. (C). 1994. pap. text 43.95 (*0-631-19194-1*) Blackwell Pubs.
Conlan, Jim, jt. auth. see West, Bill.
Conlan, Jocko & Creamer, Robert W. Jocko. LC 96-51860. (Illus.). 246p. 1997. pap. 12.00 (*0-8032-6381-3*, Bison Books) U of Nebr Pr.
Conlan, Michael, jt. auth. see Kotas, Richard.
***Conlan, Roberta.** States of Mind: New Discoveries about How Our Brains Make Us Who We Are. LC 98-11719. 224p. 1999. 24.95 (*0-471-29963-4*) Wiley.
Conlan, Roberta, ed. Mind & Brain. LC 93-1152. (Journey Through the Mind & Body Ser.). (Illus.). 144p. 1993. lib. bdg. 17.99 (*0-7835-1001-2*) Time-Life.
Conlan, Roberta, ed. see Time-Life Books Editors.
Conlan, Terry. Lean Star Cuisine. Shirey, Trisha, ed. (Illus.). 304p. (C). 1993. reprint ed. text 19.95 (*0-9619476-1-6*) Lake Austin Resort.
Conlan, Timothy. New Federalism: Intergovernmental Reform from Nixon to Reagan. 274p. 1988. 36.95 (*0-8157-1540-4*); pap. 16.95 (*0-8157-1539-0*) Brookings.
Conlan, Timothy J. From New Federalism to Devolution: Twenty-Five Years of Intergovernmental Reform. LC 98-19780. 325p. 1998. 49.95 (*0-8157-1532-3*); pap. 19.95 (*0-8157-1531-5*) Brookings.
Conlan, Timothy J., et al. Taxing Choices. 275p. 1989. 21.95 (*0-87187-480-6*) Congr Quarterly.
Conlee, John, ed. Middle English Debate Poetry. 329p. 1991. 42.00 (*0-937191-18-3*) Mich St U Pr.
— Middle English Debate Poetry. 376p. 1997. pap. text 15.95 (*0-937191-23-X*) Mich St U Pr.
***Conlee, John, ed.** Prose Merlin. (Teams Middle English Text Ser.). 1998. pap. text 20.00 (*1-58044-015-0*) Medieval Inst.
Conlee, Ken, ed. & illus. see Houston, Jimmy.
Conlee, Ralph B. The Sun Will Shine - Again: An Orphan Boy's Journey Through the Great Depression & the "Big War" (Illus.). 328p. 1992. 22.00 (*0-9634046-0-1*) R B Conlee.
Conley. The Ion Channel FactsBook, 4 vols. 1997. write for info. (*0-12-184449-8*) Acad Pr.
Conley, jt. auth. see Clough.
Conley, jt. auth. see Schwartz, Stuart B.
Conley, Alston. Artists & Writers: Sculpture of Michael de Lisio. LC 98-66274. (Illus.). 16p. 1998. pap. 10.00 (*0-9640153-9-0*) McMullen Mus Art.
— Jack Tworkov, 1935-82: An Abstract Expressionist Inventing Form. 36p. 1993. pap. 15.00 (*0-9640153-0-7*) McMullen Mus Art.
Conley, Alston & Grinnell, Jennifer, eds. Redressing Cathleen: Contemporary Works from Irish Women Artists. LC 97-74589. (Illus.). 144p. 1997. pap. 29.95 (*0-9640153-8-2*) McMullen Mus Art.
Conley, Alston & Nahum, Katherine. Original Visions: Shifting the Paradigm, Women's Art, 1970-1996. (Illus.). 72p. (Orig.). (C). 1997. pap. text 12.95 (*0-9640153-6-6*) McMullen Mus Art.
Conley, Bayless. Cast Down but Not Destroyed. 31p. 1991. pap. text. write for info. (*0-9638534-0-6*) Cottonwood Chr.
— How to Make the Devil's Schemes Backfire. 47p. (Orig.). 1991. pap. text. write for info. (*0-9638534-2-2*) Cottonwood Chr.
— Nunca Se de Por Vencido (Cast down but Not Destroyed) Hernandez, Juan, tr. (SPA.). 32p. 1994. pap. text 2.95 (*1-57139-027-8*) Hernandez Translat.
— Ten Marks of a False Minister. 48p. 1991. pap. text. write for info. (*0-9638534-1-4*) Cottonwood Chr.
Conley, Billy D., ed. see Seifert, Janice A.
***Conley, Brian.** The Killer of Love. LC 98-74950. 207p. 1999. 21.00 (*0-9664329-0-8*, 010) Buckhead Pr.
Conley, Bruce H. Butterflies, Grandpa & Me. (Illus.). 25p. (J). (gr. 4 up). 1976. pap. 2.00 (*0-685-65885-6*) Conley Outreach.
Conley, C. Isolated Invariant Sets & the Morse Index. LC 78-1577. (CBMS Regional Conference Series in Mathematics: No. 38). 89p. 1978. reprint ed. pap. 23.00 (*0-8218-1688-8*, CBMS/38) Am Math.
Conley, Carla C., jt. auth. see De Sola Chervin, Ronda.
Conley, Carolyn. Melancholy Accidents: The Meaning of Violence in Post-Famine Ireland. LC 98-31624. 272p. 1999. 40.00 (*0-7391-0007-6*) Lxngtn Bks.
Conley, Carolyn A. The Unwritten Law: Criminal Justice in Victorian Kent. (Illus.). 256p. 1991. text 60.00 (*0-19-506338-4*) OUP.
***Conley, Chip & Branson, Richard.** The Rebel Rules: Daring to Be Yourself in Business. 2001. pap. 14.00 (*0-684-86516-5*, Fireside) S&S Trade Pap.
Conley, Cort. Idaho for the Curious: A Guide. (Illus.). 700p. (Orig.). 1982. pap. 19.95 (*0-9603566-3-0*) Backeddy Bks.
— Idaho Loners: Hermits, Solitaires & Individualists. 1994. pap. text 19.95 (*0-9603566-5-7*) Backeddy Bks.
Conley, Cort, selected by. Gathered Waters: An Anthology of River Poems. 1985. pap. 9.95 (*0-317-17262-X*) Backeddy Bks.
Conley, Cort & Carrey, John. The Middle Fork: A Guide. LC 80-17367. 1966. pap. 19.95 (*0-9603566-1-4*) Backeddy Bks.
— River of No Return. LC 78-52373. 1978. pap. 12.95 (*0-9603566-2-2*) Backeddy Bks.
— Snake River, of Hells Canyon. LC 79-55450. (Orig.). 1979. pap. 13.95 (*0-9603566-0-6*) Backeddy Bks.
Conley, Craig, jt. auth. see Schwartz, Stuart.
Conley, Craig, jt. auth. see Schwartz, Stuart B.
***Conley, Dalton.** Being Black, Living in the Red: Race, Wealth, & Social Policy in America. LC 98-49951. 208p. 1999. pap. 16.95 (*0-520-21673-3*, Pub. by U CA Pr) Cal Prin Full Svc.
— Being Black, Living in the Red: Race, Wealth, & Social Policy in America. LC 98-49951. (Illus.). 209p. 1999. 45.00 (*0-520-21672-5*, Pub. by U CA Pr) Cal Prin Full Svc.
— Honky. LC 00-23774. 242p. 2000. 22.50 (*0-520-21586-9*, Pub. by U CA Pr) Cal Prin Full Svc.
Conley, .Dan, et al. Ray of Hope: Story Teaching for Teachers, Parents & Children LC 93-87295. x, 184p. 1993. write for info. (*0-9639803-0-0*) Ray of Hope.
Conley, Darrell. The Gospel vs. Occultism. 77p. 1997. reprint ed. pap. 4.95 (*0-932859-30-5*) Apologetic Pr.
Conley, David T. Are You Ready to Restructure? A Guidebook for Educators, Parents, & Community Leaders. LC 95-40434. (Illus.). 184p. 1995. pap. 24.95 (*0-8039-6195-2*) Corwin Pr.
— Are You Ready to Restructure? A Guidebook for Educators, Parents, & Community Members. LC 95-40434. (Illus.). 184p. 1995. 55.95 (*0-8039-6194-4*) Corwin Pr.
— Roadmap to Restructuring: Charting the Course of Change in American Education. 2nd ed. LC 97-8610. xvi, 571p. 1997. 34.95 (*0-86552-136-0*); pap. 23.95 (*0-86552-137-9*) U of Oreg ERIC.
***Conley, Deane.** Angelino. Hunt, Christy, ed. (Butterfly Tree Ser.: Vol. 1). (Illus.). 32p. (J). (ps-3). 2000. 17.00 (*0-9664329-2-4*) Buckhead Pr.
— Butterflies. Hunt, Christy, ed. (Butterfly Tree Ser.: Vol. 2). (Illus.). 32p. (J). (ps-3). 2000. 17.00 (*0-9664329-4-0*) Buckhead Pr.
Conley, Edgar, jt. ed. see Robbillard, Jean.

C

An Asterisk (*) at the beginning of an entry indicates that the title is appearing for the first time.

Conley, Edward C., ed. The Ion Channel Factsbook. (Factsbooks Ser.: Vol. 2). (Illus.). 816p. 1996. pap. text 49.95 (*0-12-184451-X*) Acad Pr.
— The Ion Channel Factsbook. (Factsbooks Ser.: Vol. 3). (Illus.). 464p. 1999. pap. text 42.00 (*0-12-184452-8*) Morgan Kaufmann.
Conley, Edward C. & Brammar, William J. Ion Channel Factsbook Vol. IV: Volume-Gated Channels. LC 98-86472. (Illus.). 736p. 1998. pap. text 65.00 (*0-12-184453-6*) Acad Pr.
Conley, Edward C. & Brammer, William J., eds. The Ion Channel Factsbook Vol. 1: Extracellular Ligand-Gated Channels, Vol. 1. (Factsbooks Ser.). (Illus.). 416p. 1995. pap. text 42.00 (*0-12-184450-1*) Acad Pr.
Conley, Edward J. America Exhausted: Breakthrough Treatments of Fatigue & Fibromyalgia. 2nd rev. ed. LC 98-60288. 250p. 1998. 14.95 (*0-9652544-1-0*) Vitality Pr.
— America Exhausted Vol. 1: Breakthrough Treatments of Fatigue & Chronic Fatigue Syndrome. LC 96-60868. 256p. (Orig.). 1997. pap. 14.95 (*0-9652544-0-2*) Vitality Pr.
Conley, Frances K. Walking Out on the Boys. LC 97-46561. 240p. 1998. 24.00 (*0-374-28621-3*) FS&G.
***Conley, Frances K.** Walking Out on the Boys. 256p. 1999. pap. 13.00 (*0-374-52595-1*) FS&G.
Conley, Frank, ed. see Wallowa Resource Council Staff.
Conley, Gary. Tax Abatement. Sampson, Stephanie, ed. 12p. (Orig.). 1982. pap. 9.00 (*0-317-04833-3*) Natl Coun Econ Dev.
Conley, Jeff. Habits of the Heart: Simple Ideas for Taking Paths to Success Wide Enough for Family, Friends & Fun. LC 97-76830. 192p. 1998. pap. 14.95 (*1-885221-88-6*) BookPartners.
Conley, John. Teach Yourself Object-Oriented Programming with Visual Basic 5.1 21 Days. 1997. 39.99 (*0-672-31203-4*) Macmillan.
Conley, John & Dickinson, John T., eds. Plastic & Reconstructive Surgery of the Face & Neck, 2 vols. Incl. Vol. 1. Aesthetic Surgery. 264p. 1972. 58.25 (*0-8089-0750-6*, W B Saunders Co); (Illus.). 1972. write for info. (*0-318-52859-2*, Grune & Strat) Harcrt Hlth Sci Grp.
Conley, John A., ed. The President's Crime Commission Report, 1967: Its Impact 25 Years Later. LC 93-79360. (ACJS - Anderson Monographs). 160p. (C). 1993. pap. 19.95 (*0-87084-126-2*) Anderson Pub Co.
Conley, John D. Sams Teach Yourself OOP with Visual Basic in 21 Days. 1998. pap. 39.99 incl. audio compact disk (*0-672-31299-9*) Sams.
Conley, John J. Long Trail North. Grad, Doug, ed. 192p. (Orig.). 1993. mass mkt. 4.50 (*0-671-74930-7*) PB.
Conley, John J. & Koterski, Joseph W., eds. Prophecy & Diplomacy: The Moral Doctrine of John Paul II - A Jesuit Symposium. LC 99-41405. 306p. 1999. 35.00 (*0-8232-1975-5*, Pub. by Fordham) BookMasters.
***Conley, John J. & Koterski, Joseph W., eds.** Prophecy & Diplomacy: The Moral Doctrine of John Paul II - A Jesuit Symposium. LC 99-41405. 306p. 1999. pap. 17.50 (*0-8232-1976-3*, Pub. by Fordham) BookMasters.
Conley, John M. & O'Barr, William M. Rules vs. Relationships: The Ethnography of Legal Discourse. LC 89-20497. (Language & Legal Discourse Ser.). 236p. 1990. pap. text 17.95 (*0-226-11491-0*) U Ch Pr.
— Rules vs. Relationships: The Ethnography of Legal Discourse. LC 89-20497. (Language & Legal Discourse Ser.). 236p. 1999. lib. bdg. 41.00 (*0-226-11490-2*) U Ch Pr.
***Conley, John M., et al.** Just Words. LC 97-43227. (Illus.). 168p. 1998. pap. text 13.00 (*0-226-11487-2*); lib. bdg. 35.00 (*0-226-11486-4*) U Ch Pr.
Conley, John M., jt. auth. see Barnes, David W.
Conley, Joyce, jt. auth. see Clough, John.
Conley, Judy D. Shape-Up with Splash: Exercises to Be Done in the Water. (Illus.). 112p. 1988. 10.95 (*0-9619828-1-0*) Judys Splash Aerobics.
Conley, Julia V. The Conley Family in America. LC 90-63788. (Illus.). 242p. (Orig.). 1991. pap. 15.95 (*0-917012-95-X*) RI Pubns Soc.
Conley, Katharine. Automatic Woman: The Representation of Woman in Surrealism. LC 96-3379. (Illus.). xvi, 189p. 1996. text 45.00 (*0-8032-1474-X*) U of Nebr Pr.
Conley, Kevin. Benjamin Banneker: Scientist & Mathematician. Huggins, Nathan I., ed. (Black Americans of Achievement Ser.). (Illus.). 124p. (YA). (gr. 5 up). 1987. lib. bdg. 19.95 (*1-55546-573-0*) Chelsea Hse.
— Luftwaffe Field Divisions, 1941-45. (Men-at-Arms Ser.: No. 229). (Illus.). 48p. pap. 11.95 (*1-85532-100-9*, 9187, Pub. by Ospry) Stackpole.
***Conley, Lauren.** Meet Me Online: The #1 Practical Guide to Internet Dating. LC 99-67327. 130p. 1999. pap. 8.95 (*1-884778-78-X*, Pub. by Old Mountain) ACCESS Pubs Network.
Conley, Lucy. Gone to the Zoo. (Illus.). 208p. (J). (gr. 3-6). 1979. 8.30 (*0-7399-0086-2*, 2265) Rod & Staff.
— Little Jewel Bird. (Jewel Book Ser.: Set 1). (Illus.). 32p. (J). (ps-2). 1986. pap. 2.55 (*0-7399-0028-5*, 2311) Rod & Staff.
— The Lost Milk Jar. (Illus.). 24p. (J). (ps-2). 1986. pap. 2.55 (*0-7399-0029-3*, 2327) Rod & Staff.
— The Priceless Privilege. (Illus.). 242p. 1981. 9.25 (*0-7399-0146-X*, 2360) Rod & Staff.
— Tattletale Sparkie & Other Stories. (Illus.). 197p. (J). (gr. 3-6). 1983. 8.95 (*0-7399-0078-1*, 2427) Rod & Staff.
— Two Surprises. (Jewel Book Ser.: Set 1). (Illus.). 24p. (J). 1986. pap. 2.55 (*0-7399-0030-7*, 2453) Rod & Staff.
Conley, Mark W. Content Reading Instruction: A Communication Approach. 2nd ed. Date not set. pap. text, teacher ed. write for info. (*0-07-012497-3*) McGraw.
— Content Reading Instruction: A Communication Approach. 2nd ed. (C). 1995. 64.06 (*0-07-012496-5*) McGraw.
Conley, Marshall & Daborn, Graham, eds. Energy Options for Atlantic Canada, Vol. 1. 157p. 1983. pap. 9.95 (*0-88780-051-3*, Pub. by Formac Publ Co) Formac Dist Ltd.
Conley, Martha. Growing Light. 240p. 1995. mass mkt. 4.99 (*0-425-14792-4*) Berkley Pub.
Conley, Patrick. First in War, Last in Peace: Rhode Island & the Constitution, 1786-1790. (Illus.). 46p. (Orig.). 1987. pap. 5.95 (*0-917012-87-9*) RI Pubns Soc.
Conley, Patrick T. The Blackstone Valley: A Sketch of Its River, Its Canal & Its People. 19p. 1983. pap. 3.75 (*0-917012-41-0*) RI Pubns Soc.
— The Constitutional Significance of Trevett vs. Weeden (1786) (Illus.). 10p. 1976. pap. 2.50 (*0-917012-43-7*) RI Pubns Soc.
— Democracy in Decline: Rhode Island Constitutional Development, 1776-1841. LC 77-76314. (Illus.). 1977. 17.50 (*0-917012-09-7*) RI Pubns Soc.
— The Dorr Rebellion: Rhode Island's Crisis in Constitutional Government. 13p. 1976. pap. 3.75 (*0-917012-49-6*) RI Pubns Soc.
— The Irish in Rhode Island: A Historical Appreciation. (Rhode Island Ethnic Heritage Pamphlet Ser.). (Illus.). 46p. (Orig.). 1986. pap. 6.75 (*0-917012-83-6*) RI Pubns Soc.
— Liberty & Justice: Select Essays on Law & Lawyers in Rhode Island. LC 99-194540. (Illus.). 178p. 1998. 39.95 (*0-917012-99-2*) RI Pubns Soc.
***Conley, Patrick T.** Neither Separate Nor Equal: Legislature & Executive in Rhode Island Constitutional History. (Illus.). 218p. (C). 1999. 29.95 (*0-917012-06-2*) RI Pubns Soc.
Conley, Patrick T. North Kingstown: An Historical Sketch. (Illus.). 1976. pap. 3.95 (*0-917012-53-4*) RI Pubns Soc.
— Rhode Island Catholicism: A Historical Guide. 24p. (Orig.). 1984. pap. 2.95 (*0-917012-56-9*) RI Pubns Soc.
Conley, Patrick T. & Kaminski, John P., eds. The Bill of Rights & the States: The Colonial & Revolutionary Origins of American Liberties. (Illus.). 568p. 1992. text 39.95 (*0-945612-26-5*); pap. text 26.95 (*0-945612-29-X*) Madison Hse.
— The Constitution & the States: The Role of the Original Thirteen in the Framing & Adoption of the Federal Constitution. LC 88-9028. (Illus.). 352p. 1988. text 34.95 (*0-945612-02-8*); pap. text 18.95 (*0-945612-30-3*) Madison Hse.
Conley, Patrick T. & Klyberg, Albert T. Rhode Island's Road to Liberty. (Illus.). 24p. (Orig.). 1987. pap. 3.50 (*0-917012-85-2*) RI Pubns Soc.
Conley, Patrick T. & Smith, Matthew J. Catholicism in Rhode Island: The Formative Era. LC 76-62863. 1976. 17.50 (*0-917012-13-5*) RI Pubns Soc.
Conley, Patrick T., et al. The State Houses of Rhode Island. (Illus.). 79p. (Orig.). 1988. pap. 9.95 (*0-932840-04-3*) RI Hist Soc.
Conley, Patrick T., ed. see Cunha, M. Rachel, et al.
Conley, Patrick T., ed. see Foster, Geraldine S.
Conley, Patrick T., ed. see Sickinger, Raymond L. & Primeau, John K.
Conley, Pauline C. The Code Breaker. (J). (gr. 4 up). 1983. pap. 6.00 (*0-87602-241-7*) Anchorage.
Conley, Peter. Space Vehicle Mechanisms: Elements of Successful Design. LC 97-13993. 816p. 1998. 125.00 (*0-471-12141-X*) Wiley.
Conley, Phil, jt. auth. see Doherty, William T.
Conley, R. F. Practical Dispersion: A Guide to Understanding & Formulating Slurries. 464p. 1996. 165.00 (*0-471-18640-6*) Wiley.
***Conley, Robert.** Cherokee Dragon: A Novel of the Real People. LC 00-21276. 288p. 2000. text 23.95 (*0-312-20884-7*) St Martin.
Conley, Robert. War Woman: A Novel of the Real People. LC 97-18593. 1997. text 25.95 (*0-312-17058-0*) St Martin.
***Conley, Robert & Kelly, Deanna.** Pharmacologic Treatment of Schizophrenia. 200p. 2000. pap. text 19.95 (*1-884735-56-8*) Prof Comms.
Conley, Robert F. Practical Dispersion: A Guide to Understanding & Formulating Slurries. LC 95-38037. (Illus.). 500p. 1996. 135.00 (*1-56081-931-6*, Wiley-VCH) Wiley.
Conley, Robert J. The Actor. 192p. 1999. mass mkt. 3.99 (*0-8439-4498-6*) Dorchester Pub Co.
— Back to Malachi. 192p. 1997. reprint ed. mass mkt. 3.99 (*0-8439-4277-0*, Leisure Bks) Dorchester Pub Co.
***Conley, Robert J.** Barjack. 208p. 2000. mass mkt. 4.50 (*0-8439-4687-3*, Leisure Bks) Dorchester Pub Co.
Conley, Robert J. Border Line. Grad, Doug, ed. 192p. (Orig.). 1993. pap. 3.50 (*0-671-74931-5*) PB.
— Brass. 320p. 1999. mass mkt. 5.50 (*0-8439-4505-2*) Dorchester Pub Co.
***Conley, Robert J.** Broke Loose. 256p. 2000. pap. 4.50 (*0-8439-4756-X*, Leisure Bks) Dorchester Pub Co.
Conley, Robert J. Captain Dutch. 1995. mass mkt. 4.99 (*0-671-89868-X*) PB.
— Colfax. large type ed. LC 90-49541. 269p. 1990. reprint ed. lib. bdg. 15.95 (*1-56054-073-7*) Thorndike Pr.
— Crazy Snake. Grad, Doug, ed. 208p. (Orig.). 1994. mass mkt. 4.99 (*0-671-77902-8*) PB.
— Crazy Snake. large type ed. LC 95-38620. (Nightingale Ser.). 193p. (Orig.). 1996. pap. 17.95 (*0-7838-1539-5*, G K Hall Lrg Type) Mac Lib Ref.
***Conley, Robert J.** The Dark Island. LC 00-37396. Vol. 6. 192p. 2000. pap. 11.95 (*0-8061-3277-9*) U of Okla Pr.
— The Dark Way. LC 00-37400. Vol. 2. 192p. 2000. 11.95 (*0-8061-3273-6*) U of Okla Pr.
— Fugitive's Trial. 272p. 2000. mass mkt. 5.99 (*0-312-97508-2*, St Martins Paperbacks) St Martin.
Conley, Robert J. Geronimo. Miller, Tom, ed. LC 94-130863. 224p. (Orig.). 1994. mass mkt. 5.50 (*0-671-88982-6*) PB.
— Go-Ahead Rider. large type ed. LC 93-32281. (Evans Novel of the West Ser.). 1994. 16.95 (*0-8161-5853-3*, G K Hall Lrg Type) Mac Lib Ref.
— Go-Ahead Rider. Grad, Doug, ed. 192p. 1992. reprint ed. pap. 3.50 (*0-671-74365-1*) PB.
— Incident at Buffalo Crossing. 272p. 1998. mass mkt. 4.50 (*0-8439-4396-3*, Leisure Bks) Dorchester Pub Co.
— Killing Time. large type ed. 1990. pap. 16.99 (*0-7089-6862-7*) Ulverscroft.
— Killing Time. large type ed. LC 90-48257. 310p. 1991. reprint ed. lib. bdg. 15.95 (*1-56054-104-0*) Thorndike Pr.
***Conley, Robert J.** The Long Way Home. LC 00-37401. Vol. 5. 192p. 2000. pap. 11.95 (*0-8061-3276-0*) U of Okla Pr.
Conley, Robert J. The Meade Solution. LC 97-48703. 144p. 1998. 19.95 (*0-87081-479-6*) Univ Pr Colo.
— Mountain Windsong: A Novel of the Trail of Tears. LC 92-54150. 224p. 1995. pap. 11.95 (*0-8061-2746-5*) U of Okla Pr.
— Ned Christie's War. LC 91-10260. (Novel of the West Ser.). 180p. 1991. 16.95 (*0-87131-636-6*) M Evans.
— Ned Christie's War. Grad, Doug, ed. 208p. 1993. mass mkt. 3.99 (*0-671-75969-8*) PB.
— Outside the Law. (Illus.). (J). 1995. mass mkt. 4.99 (*0-671-89867-1*) PB.
— The Peace Chief: A Novel of the Real People. LC 98-21125. 336p. 1998. text 25.95 (*0-312-19314-9*) St Martin.
— Quitting Time. large type ed. LC 90-40666. 270p. 1990. reprint ed. lib. bdg. 15.95 (*1-56054-040-0*) Thorndike Pr.
— Quitting Time. Grad, Doug, ed. (Michigan Bks.). 192p. 1992. reprint ed. pap. 3.50 (*0-671-74364-3*) PB.
***Conley, Robert J.** The War Trail North. LC 00-37403. Vol. 7. 192p. 2000. pap. 11.95 (*0-8061-3278-7*) U of Okla Pr.
Conley, Robert J. War Woman: A Novel of the Real People. 368p. 1998. pap. 15.95 (*0-312-19361-0*) St Martin.
***Conley, Robert J.** The Way of the Priests. LC 00-37399. Vol. 1. 192p. 2000. 11.95 (*0-8061-3272-8*) U of Okla Pr.
— The Way South. LC 00-37398. Vol. 4. 192p. 2000. pap. 11.95 (*0-8061-3275-2*) U of Okla Pr.
Conley, Robert J. The Way South. large type ed. LC 94-16395. 254p. 1994. lib. bdg. 17.95 (*0-7862-0242-4*) Thorndike Pr.
***Conley, Robert J.** The White Path. LC 00-37402. Vol. 3. 192p. 2000. pap. 11.95 (*0-8061-3274-4*) U of Okla Pr.
Conley, Robert J. The Witch of Goingsnake & Other Stories. LC 88-4762. 182p. 1991. pap. 12.95 (*0-8061-2353-2*) U of Okla Pr.
— Zeke Proctor: Cherokee Outlaw. Grad, Doug, ed. 192p. (Orig.). 1994. mass mkt. 4.99 (*0-671-77901-X*) PB.
Conley, Robert T., ed. Thermal Stability of Polymers, Vol. 1. LC 74-107753. (Monographs in Macromolecular Chemistry). 656p. reprint ed. pap. 200.00 (*0-608-17089-5*, 202712500001) Bks Demand.
Conley, Ron. Drugs, Strangers & Other Dangers: Ron Conley's Complete Magical Say No Show. (Illus.). 98p. 1997. pap. 25.00 (*1-881099-17-2*) SPS Pubns.
Conley, Ronald W. The Economics of Mental Retardation. LC 72-12345. 400p. 1973. reprint ed. pap. 124.00 (*0-608-04069-X*, 206480100011) Bks Demand.
Conley, Rory T. Arthur Preuss: Journalist & Voice of German & Conservative Catholics in 1871-1934. Tolzmann, Don Heinrich, ed. (New German-American Studies: Vol. 16). (Illus.). XII, 361p. (C). 1998. text 58.95 (*0-8204-4002-7*) P Lang Pubng.
Conley, Sharon C., jt. auth. see Frase, Larry E.
Conley, Sunny. Cafe Hopping in the Southwest: 100 Great Places to Eat, Plus Tips for Tourists. 2nd ed. (Illus.). 136p. (Orig.). 1997. pap. 10.95 (*1-887045-02-3*) Arroyo Pr.
Conley, Susan C., ed. see Barnes, Jack.
Conley, Thomas M. Rhetoric in the European Tradition. 325p. (C). 1990. text 34.50 (*0-8013-0256-0*, 75909) Longman.
— Rhetoric in the European Tradition. LC 93-32600. 336p. 1993. pap. text 15.00 (*0-226-11489-9*) U Ch Pr.
Conley, Timothy G. Lafayette Square: An Urban Renaissance LC 74-21699. 116 p. 1974. write for info. (*0-9600796-1-0*) Lafayette Square Pr.
Conley, Tom. The Graphic Unconscious in Early Modern French Writing. (Cambridge Studies in French: No. 37). (Illus.). 238p. (C). 1992. text 69.95 (*0-521-41031-2*) Cambridge U Pr.
— The Self-Made Map: Cartographic Writing in Early Modern France. (Illus.). 448p. (C). 1996. 34.95 (*0-8166-2700-2*) U of Minn Pr.
Conley, Tom, jt. ed. see Ungar, Steven.
Conley, Tom, tr. see De Certeau, Michel.
Conley, Tom, tr. see De Certeau, Michel & Giard, Luce.
Conley, Tom, tr. see Schefer, Jean L.
Conley, Tom, tr. & afterword by see De Certeau, Michel.
Conley, Tom, tr. & frwd. see Deleuze, Gilles.
Conley, Valerie M. Characteristics & Attitudes of Instructional Faculty & Staff in the Humanities. LC 98-110465. 139p. 1997. pap. 13.00 (*0-16-049230-0*) USGPO.
Conley, Verena A. Ecopolitics: The Environment in Poststructuralist Thought. LC 96-17317. (Feminism for Today Ser.). 208p. (C). 1996. 75.00 (*0-415-10284-7*); pap. 21.99 (*0-415-10306-1*) Routledge.
— Helene Cixous. (Modern Cultural Theorists Ser.). 160p. 1992. text 45.00 (*0-8020-2879-9*); pap. text 16.95 (*0-8020-7387-5*) U of Toronto Pr.
— Helene Cixous: Writing the Feminine. LC 90-20323. xiv, 197p. 1991. pap. text 15.00 (*0-8032-6345-7*, Bison Books) U of Nebr Pr.
— Rethinking Technologies. LC 93-22415. 256p. 1993. pap. 17.95 (*0-8166-2215-9*) U of Minn Pr.
Conley, Verena A., et al, eds. Rethinking Technologies. LC 93-22415. 256p. 1993. text 47.95 (*0-8166-2214-0*) U of Minn Pr.
Conley, Verena A., tr. & intro. see Cixous, Helene.
***Conley-Weaver, Robyn.** What Really Matters to Me. (Guided Journals). 144p. 2000. 14.99 (*0-89879-994-5*, Walking Stick Pr) F & W Pubns Inc.
Conley, Will, ed. Advances in Resist Technology & Processing XV. (Proceedings of SPIE Ser.: Vol. 3333). 1500p. 1998. 166.00 (*0-8194-2778-0*) SPIE.
***Conley, Will E., ed.** Advances in Resist Technology & Processing XVI. 1438p. 1999. pap. text 171.00 (*0-8194-3152-4*) SPIE.
Conley, William. Optimization: A Simplified Approach. (Illus.). 272p. 1981. text 21.95 (*0-89433-121-3*) Petrocelli.
Conley, William C. BASIC II Advanced, Vol. II. 1983. pap. 12.95 (*0-685-07399-8*) Petrocelli.
Conley, William E. BASIC for Beginners. (Illus.). 144p. 1982. pap. text 12.95 (*0-89433-141-8*) Petrocelli.
Conlin. An American Harvest, Vol. 2. 2nd ed. (C). pap. text 19.50 (*0-15-501091-3*) Harcourt Coll Pubs.
— The American Past. 5th ed. (C). 1996. pap. text, student ed. 17.00 (*0-15-503140-6*, Pub. by Harcourt Coll Pubs); pap. text, student ed. 17.00 (*0-15-503143-0*, Pub. by Harcourt Coll Pubs) Harcourt.
— American Past. 5th ed. (C). 1997. pap. text, teacher ed. 28.00 (*0-15-505138-5*) Harcourt.
— American Past: Since 1865. 5th ed. (C). 1996. pap. text 26.95 (*0-15-503139-2*) Harcourt Coll Pubs.
— The American Past: Test Manual. 5th ed. (C). 1996. pap. text 33.50 (*0-15-503144-9*, Pub. by Harcourt Coll Pubs) Harcourt.
— Conlin the Working Reader. Date not set. pap. text 21.87 (*0-395-92920-2*) HM.
— Our Land - Our Time. 1991. text 67.25 (*0-03-030542-X*) Holt R&W.
— Patterns, 4 vols. (C). 1993. pap., teacher ed. 3.56 (*0-395-59344-1*) HM.
— Patterns. (C). 1993. pap., teacher ed. 60.76 (*0-395-68150-2*) HM.
— Patterns, 4 vols. 4th ed. LC 93-78632. (C). 1993. pap. text 30.36 (*0-395-59343-3*) HM.
— Patterns, 5 vols. 5th ed. (C). 1997. pap. text 30.36 (*0-395-86843-2*) HM.
— Patterns Plus. (C). Date not set. pap. text, teacher ed., suppl. ed. write for info. (*0-395-60774-4*) HM.
Conlin, C. Unternehmen Deutsch: Teacher's guide. text, teacher ed. 9.95 (*0-8219-1356-5*) EMC-Paradigm.
— Unternehmen Deutsch: Textbook. 22.95 (*0-8219-1354-9*) EMC-Paradigm.
— Unternehmen Deutsch: Workbook. 7.95 (*0-8219-1355-7*) EMC-Paradigm.
Conlin, Diane A. The Artists of the Ara Pacis & the Process of Hellenization in Roman Relief Sculpture. LC 96-41830. (Studies in the History of Greece & Rome). (Illus.). 360p. (C). (gr. 13). 1997. 69.95 (*0-8078-2343-0*) U of NC Pr.
Conlin, John. Buffalo City Hall: Americanesque Masterpiece. (Illus.). 40p. 1993. pap. 5.95 (*1-879201-14-3*) WNY Wares.
Conlin, Joseph R. An American Harvest, Vol. 1. 2nd ed. (C). pap. text 19.50 (*0-15-501090-5*) Harcourt Coll Pubs.
— The American Past. 6th ed. (C). 2000. pap. text 44.50 (*0-15-507536-5*) Harcourt Coll Pubs.
— The American Past: A Brief History. 672p. (C). 1991. pap. text 51.00 (*0-15-502382-9*, Pub. by Harcourt Coll Pubs) Harcourt.
— The American Past: A Survey of American History. 3rd ed. 964p. (C). 1990. student ed. write for info. (*0-318-67030-5*) Harcourt Coll Pubs.
— The American Past: A Survey of American History. 5th ed. LC 96-75916. 1028p. (C). 1996. text 39.95 (*0-15-503137-6*) Harcourt Coll Pubs.
— The American Past Pt. 1: A Survey of American History to 1877. 5th ed. 544p. (C). 1996. pap. text 26.95 (*0-15-503138-4*) Harcourt Coll Pubs.
— The American Past Pt. 2: A Survey of American History since 1865. 586p. (C). 1996. pap. text. write for info. (*0-614-19513-6*) Harcourt Coll Pubs.
— Big Bill Haywood & the Radical Union Movement. LC 79-80015. 264p. reprint ed. pap. 81.90 (*0-8357-3598-2*, 203011600067) Bks Demand.
— Bread & Roses Too, 1. LC 79-95505. (Contributions in American History Ser.: No. 1). 165p. 1970. 49.95 (*0-8371-2344-5*, COB/, Greenwood Pr) Greenwood.
Conlin, Joseph R., ed. At the Point of Production: The Local History of the I.W.W., 10. LC 80-1708. (Contributions in Labor History Ser.: No. 10). 329p. 1981. 55.00 (*0-313-22046-8*, CPP/, Greenwood Pr) Greenwood.
Conlin, Joseph R. & Peterson, C. H. An American Harvest: Readings in American History, 2 vols., Vol. 1. 208p. (C). 1986. pap. text 26.00 (*0-15-502304-7*, Pub. by Harcourt Coll Pubs) Harcourt.
— An American Harvest: Readings in American History, 2 vols., Vol. 2. 254p. (C). 1986. pap. text 26.00 (*0-15-502305-5*, Pub. by Harcourt Coll Pubs) Harcourt.
Conlin, Mary L. Patterns: A Short Prose Reader, 4 vols. 4th ed. (C). 1993. pap. text, teacher ed. 31.56 (*0-395-68425-0*) HM.
— Patterns Plus: A Short Prose Reader with Argumentation, 3 vols. 3rd ed. (C). 1989. pap. text 2.76 (*0-395-51690-0*) HM.
— Patterns Plus: A Short Prose Reader with Argumentation, 5 vols. 5th ed. (C). 1996. text, teacher ed. 11.96 (*0-395-71860-0*) HM.
— Simon Perkins of the Western Reserve. 215p. 1968. 15.95 (*0-911704-05-1*) Western Res.
Conlin, Mary Lou. Patterns Plus, 5 vols. 5th ed. LC 94-76496. (C). 1994. pap. text 27.56 (*0-395-69918-5*) HM.

An Asterisk (*) at the beginning of an entry indicates that the title is appearing for the first time.

— Patterns Plus: A Short Prose Reader with Argumentation 5th ed. LC 94-76496. xxix, 417p. 1995. write for info. (*0-395-71586-5*) HM.

— Patterns Plus: A Short Prose Reader with Argumentation. 6th ed. LC 98-72012. xxxii, 349p. 1999. pap. text 23.07 (*0-395-89959-1*) HM.

Conlin, Michael V. & Baum, Tom, eds. Island Tourism: Management Principles & Practice. LC 94-37087. 290p. 1995. 120.00 (*0-471-95556-6*) Wiley.

Conlin, P. Graham. Commercial Loan Review Procedures. 1978. 14.00 (*0-317-47027-2*) Robt Morris Assocs.

Conlin, Ross & Alvin, Pam. Pseudoscience in Biological Psychiatry: Blaming the Body. (Series in General & Clinical Psychology). 304p. 1994. 85.00 (*0-471-00776-5*) Wiley.

Conlin, Stephen. Rand McNally Fold-Out Skyscrapers. LC 94-24428. 16p. (J). 1995. 12.95 (*0-528-83724-9*) Rand McNally.

Conlin, Stephen, jt. auth. see Bardon, Jonathan.

Conlin, Susan & Friedman, Susan L. All My Feelings at Home: Ellie's Day. LC 89-60334. (Let's Talk about Feelings Ser.). (Illus.). 32p. (J). (ps-3). 1989. pap. 6.95 (*0-943990-44-0*); lib. bdg. 16.95 (*0-943990-45-9*) Parenting Pr.

— All My Feelings at Preschool: Nathan's Day. LC 90-62679. (Let's Talk about Feelings Ser.). (Illus.). 32p. (Orig.). (J). (ps-k). 1991. pap. 6.95 (*0-943990-60-2*); lib. bdg. 16.95 (*0-943990-61-0*) Parenting Pr.

Conlon. Colour Atlas & Text of Infectious Diseases. 1999. mass mkt. 42.95 (*0-7234-2434-9*) Wolfe Pubng AZ.

Conlon, Ann, ed. see Gayley, Rano.

Conlon, Denis J., ed. The Song of Dermot & Earl Richard Fitzgilbert: Le Chansun de Dermot e li Quens Ricard Fiz Gilbert. LC 92-37299. (Studien und Dokumente zur Geschichte der Romanischen Literaturen: Bd. 24). XVI, 254p. 1992. 51.00 (*3-631-45450-3*) P Lang Pubng.

Conlon, Dennis J., ed. see Chesterton, G. K.

Conlon, E. My Head Is Opening. (C). 1991. 34.95 (*0-946211-32-9*) St Mut.

Conlon, Evelyn. A Glassful of Letters. LC 98-145447. 208p. 1998. pap. 16.95 (*0-85640-618-X*, Pub. by Blackstaff Pr) Dufour.

— Taking Scarlet As a Real Colour. 176p. 1993. pap. 13.95 (*0-85640-501-9*, Pub. by Blackstaff Pr) Dufour.

Conlon, Faith, et al, eds. The Things That Divide Us: Stories by Women. LC 85-8290. 191p. (Orig.). 1985. pap. 10.95 (*0-931188-32-6*) Seal Pr WA.

Conlon, Frank S., ed. see Blee, Ben W.

Conlon, Ginger, ed. see Napolitano, Lisa & Pusateri, Mike.

Conlon, James. Earth Story, Sacred Story. LC 93-60951. 160p. (Orig.). 1994. pap. 12.95 (*0-89622-583-6*) Twenty-Third.

Conlon, James A. Lyrics for Re-Creation: Language for the Music of the Universe. 124p. 1996. pap. 14.95 (*0-8264-0921-0*) Continuum.

— Ponderings from the Precipice: Soulwork for the New Millennium. LC 98-6246. 143p. 1998. pap. 11.95 (*0-939516-40-3*) Forest Peace.

***Conlon, James A.** The Sacred Impulse: A Planetary Spirituality of Heart & Fire. 128p. 2000. pap. 14.95 (*0-8245-1865-9*, Pub. by Crossroad NY) Natl Bk Netwk.

Conlon, Jane. Fine Embellishment Techniques: Classic Details for Today's Clothing. LC 98-34694. (Illus.). 176p. 1999. 27.95 (*1-56158-231-X*, 070365) Taunton.

Conlon, John. Power of Two. LC 98-9057. 193p. 1998. 25.50 (*0-7879-0946-7*) Que.

Conlon, John J. Walter Pater & the French Tradition. LC 81-65458. 180p. 1982. 29.50 (*0-8387-5016-8*) Bucknell U Pr.

Conlon, John L. & Dombroff, Mark A. Trial Hearsay: Objections & Exceptions. 2nd ed. 304p. 1996. ring bd. 89.98 (*0-938065-97-1*) James Pub Santa Ana.

Conlon, Judith. Crossroads of the Heart. LC 96-20489. 224p. (Orig.). 1997. pap. 14.95 (*1-56474-194-X*) Fithian Pr.

***Conlon, Kathleen.** My Father's House. large type ed. 400p. 1999. 31.99 (*0-7089-4058-7*) Ulverscroft.

Conlon, Laura. Actors. LC 94-11603. (J). (gr. 4-7). 1994. lib. bdg. write for info. (*1-57103-063-8*) Rourke Pr.

— Dancers. LC 94-12387. (Performers Discovery Library). (J). 1994. lib. bdg. 14.60 (*1-57103-064-6*) Rourke Pr.

— Earthquakes. LC 92-43124. (Disasters Discovery Library). 24p. (J). (gr. k-4). 1993. lib. bdg. 10.95 (*0-86593-247-6*) Rourke Corp.

— Fire. LC 92-43123. (Disasters Discovery Library). 24p. (J). (gr. k-4). 1993. lib. bdg. 10.95 (*0-86593-246-8*) Rourke Corp.

— Floods. LC 92-43122. (Disasters Discovery Library). 24p. (J). (gr. k-4). 1993. lib. bdg. 10.95 (*0-86593-245-X*) Rourke Corp.

— Geografia de Mexico. Marcuse, Aida E., tr. LC 94-18332. (Al Sur de Nuestra Frontera Ser.).Tr. of Mexico: The Geography. (SPA.). 24p. (J). (gr. k-4). 1994. lib. bdg. 17.27 (*1-55916-077-2*) Rourke Bk Co.

— Maravillas de Mexico. (Al Sur de Nuestra Frontera Ser.).Tr. of Wonders of Mexico. 24p. (J). (gr. k-4). 1994. lib. bdg. 17.27 (*1-55916-075-6*) Rourke Bk Co.

— Mexico: The Geography. LC 94-15000. (South of the Border Discovery Library). 24p. (J). (gr. k-4). 1994. lib. bdg. 15.93 (*1-55916-056-X*) Rourke Bk Co.

— Musicians. LC 94-17029. (Performers Discovery Library). (J). 1994. 14.60 (*1-57103-062-X*) Rourke Pr.

— Painters. LC 94-11602. (Performers Discovery Library). (J). 1994. lib. bdg. 14.60 (*1-57103-065-4*) Rourke Pr.

— The People of Mexico. (South of the Border Discovery Library). 24p. (J). (gr. k-4). 1994. lib. bdg. 15.93 (*1-55916-052-7*) Rourke Bk Co.

— Productos de Mexico. (Al Sur de Nuestra Frontera Ser.).Tr. of Products of Mexico. 24p. (J). (gr. k-4). 1994. lib. bdg. 17.27 (*1-55916-074-8*) Rourke Bk Co.

— Products of Mexico. LC 94-15907. (South of the Border Discovry Library). 24p. (J). (gr. k-4). 1994. lib. bdg. 15.93 (*1-55916-053-5*) Rourke Bk Co.

— El Pueblo de Mexico. (Al Sur de Nuestra Frontera Ser.).Tr. of People of Mexico. 24p. (J). (gr. k-4). 1994. lib. bdg. 17.27 (*1-55916-073-X*) Rourke Bk Co.

— Una Visita a Mexico. Marcuse, Aida E., tr. LC 94-18335. (Al Sur de Nuestra Frontera Ser.).Tr. of Visiting Mexico. (SPA.). 24p. (J). (gr. k-4). 1994. lib. bdg. 17.27 (*1-55916-078-0*) Rourke Bk Co.

— Visiting Mexico. (South of the Border Discovery Library). 24p. (J). (gr. k-4). 1994. lib. bdg. 15.93 (*1-55916-057-8*) Rourke Bk Co.

— The Wonders of Mexico. (South of the Border Discovery Library). 24p. (J). (gr. k-4). 1994. lib. bdg. 15.93 (*1-55916-054-3*) Rourke Bk Co.

Conlon, Laurence. Differentiable Manifolds: A First Course. LC 92-31098. xiii, 395p. 1994. 54.50 (*0-8176-3626-9*) Birkhauser.

Conlon, Lawrence, jt. auth. see Candel, Alberto.

***Conlon, Lorraine.** Nursing & Mental Disorder: Clinical Practice. (Illus.). 256p. 2000. pap. text 45.00 (*0-7506-4309-9*) Buttrwrth-Heinemann.

Conlon-McKenna, Marita. The Blue Horse. 176p. 1997. pap. 6.95 (*0-86278-305-4*, Pub. by OBrien Pr) Irish Amer Bk.

Conlon-Mckenna, Marita. Fields of Home. LC 96-39132. (Illus.). 192p. (J). (gr. 4-6). 1997. pap. 15.95 (*0-8234-1295-4*) Holiday.

Conlon-McKenna, Marita. My First Holy Communion. 1989. pap. 22.00 (*1-85390-116-4*, Pub. by Veritas Pubns) St Mut.

— No Goodbye. 176p. 1997. pap. 6.95 (*0-86278-362-3*, Pub. by OBrien Pr) Irish Amer Bk.

— Safe Harbour: The Moving Story of Two Children Evacuated From The London Blitz. 176p. 1997. pap. 6.95 (*0-86278-422-0*, Pub. by OBrien Pr) Irish Amer Bk.

— Under the Hawthorn Tree. LC 90-55097. (Illus.). 160p. (J). (gr. 4-6). 1990. 13.95 (*0-8234-0838-8*) Holiday.

— Wildflower Girl. LC 92-52711. (Illus.). 176p. (J). (gr. 4-6). 1992. 14.95 (*0-8234-0988-0*) Holiday.

Conlon-Mckenna, Marita. Wildflower Girl. 1994. 10.09 (*0-606-06882-1*, Pub. by Turtleback) Demco.

Conlon, Patrick. Franciscan Ireland. 1996. pap. 16.95 (*0-946640-29-7*, Pub. by Lilliput Pr) Irish Bks Media.

Conlon, Patrick, jt. auth. see Manning, Michael.

***Conlon, Paul.** United Nations Sanctions Management: A Case Study of the Iraq Sanctions Committee, 1990-1994. (Procedural Aspects of International Law Monograph Ser.). 350p. 2000. 115.00 (*1-57105-059-0*) Transnatl Pubs.

***Conlon, Peter J., et al, eds.** Hemodialysis Vascular Access: Practice & Problems. LC 99-40691. (Oxford Clinical Nephrology Ser.). (Illus.). 304p. 2000. text 98.50 (*0-19-262942-5*) OUP.

***Conlon, Steven D. & Aquilino, Vincent M.** Principles of Financial Derivatives: U. S. & International Taxation. LC 99-62057. 1999. write for info. (*0-7913-3770-7*) Warren Gorham & Lamont.

— Tax-Exempt Derivatives: A Guide to Legal Considerations for Lawyers, Finance Professionals & Municipal Issuers. LC 93-73878. xviii, 377 p. 1994. write for info. (*0-89707-931-0*) Amer Bar Assn.

Conlon, Tom. Learning Micro-PROLOG: A Problem-Solving Approach. 39.95 (*0-685-43058-8*) Addison-Wesley.

— Programming in Parlog. (Illus.). (C). 1989. text 33.50 (*0-201-17450-2*) Addison-Wesley.

Conlon, Tom & Cope, Peter, eds. Computing in Scottish Education: The First Decade & Beyond. 200p. 1991. pap. text 25.00 (*0-7486-0150-3*, Pub. by Edinburgh U Pr) Col U Pr.

Conlon, Vincent, ed. see National Graves Association of Ireland Staff.

Conlow, Rick. Excellence in Management: Practical Applications for Success. Shotwell, Nancy, ed. LC 90-85864. (Illus.). 132p. (Orig.). 1991. pap. 15.95 (*1-56052-103-1*) Crisp Pubns.

Conly, Arlyn. Never Trust a White Man: I Am Makah, Son of Whaling Nation. LC 97-76424. (Illus.). 300p. 1998. pap. 16.95 (*1-880222-29-9*) Red Apple Pub.

Conly, Catherine H. Street Gangs: Current Knowledge & Strategies. 115p. (Orig.). (C). 1994. pap. text 25.00 (*0-7881-0880-8*) DIANE Pub.

Conly, Geoff & Conly, Maurice. New Zealand Pohutukawa. 88p. (C). 1988. 59.00 (*1-86934-016-7*, Pub. by Grantham Hse) St Mut.

Conly, Jane L. Crazy Lady! LC 92-18348. (Laura Geringer Bks.). 192p. (YA). (gr. 4-7). 1993. lib. bdg. 15.89 (*0-06-021360-4*) HarpC Child Bks.

— Crazy Lady! LC 92-18348. (Trophy Bk.). 192p. (YA). (gr. 4-7). 1995. pap. 5.95 (*0-06-440571-0*, HarpTrophy) HarpC Child Bks.

— Crazy Lady! (J). 1995. 9.60 (*0-606-07399-X*, Pub. by Turtleback) Demco.

— R-T, Margaret, & the Rats of NIMH. (Rats of NIMH Ser.). (J). (gr. 4-7). 1990. lib. bdg. 15.89 (*0-06-023647-7*) HarpC Child Bks.

— R-T, Margaret, & the Rats of NIMH. LC 89-19968. (Rats of NIMH Ser.). (Illus.). 288p. (J). (gr. 4-7). 1990. pap. 14.89 (*0-06-021364-7*) HarpC Child Bks.

— R-T, Margaret, & the Rats of NIMH. LC 89-19968. (Rats of NIMH Ser.). (Illus.). 272p. (J). (gr. 4-7). 1991. mass mkt. 4.95 (*0-06-440387-4*, HarpTrophy) HarpC Child Bks.

Conly, Jane L. R-T, Margaret, & the Rats of NIMH. (Rats of NIMH Ser.). (J). (gr. 4-7). 1991. 9.35 (*0-606-00844-6*, Pub. by Turtleback) Demco.

Conly, Jane L. Rasco & the Rats of NIMH. LC 85-42634. (Trophy Bk.). (Illus.). 288p. (J). (gr. 4-7). 1988. pap. 4.95 (*0-06-440245-2*, HarpTrophy) HarpC Child Bks.

— Rasco & the Rats of NIMH. LC 85-42634. (Rats of NIMH Ser.). (Illus.). 288p. (J). (gr. 4-7). 1986. 15.95 (*0-06-021361-2*); lib. bdg. 16.89 (*0-06-021362-0*) HarpC Child Bks.

— When No One Was Watching. LC 97-48718. 208p. (YA). (gr. 5 up). 1995. 16.95 (*0-8050-3934-1*) H Holt & Co.

Conly, Jane Leslie. Trout Summer. LC 95-16381. 208p. (J). (gr. 6-9). 1995. 15.95 (*0-8050-3933-3*) H Holt & Co.

— Trout Summer. (J). 1998. pap. text 4.50 (*0-590-93975-0*) Scholastic Inc.

— Trout Summer. (J). 1998. 9.60 (*0-606-13872-2*, Pub. by Turtleback) Demco.

— What Happened on Planet Kid. LC 99-16655. 160p. (gr. 5-9). 1999. 16.95 (*0-8050-6065-0*) H Holt & Co.

— While No One Was Watching. LC 99-30308. 240p. (J). (gr. 3-7). 2000. mass mkt. 4.95 (*0-06-440787-X*) HarpC Child Bks.

Conly, Maurice, jt. auth. see Conly, Geoff.

Conly, Maurice, jt. ed. see Bentley, Geoffrey.

Conly, Shanti R. Taking the Lead: The United Nations & Population Assistance. 68p. 1996. 8.00 (*1-889735-00-0*) Population Action.

Conly, Shanti R., ed. see Green, Cynthia P.

Conn. Museums & American Intellectual Life, 1876-1925. 1997. pap. text 13.95 (*0-226-11493-7*) U Ch Pr.

Conn, jt. auth. see Strumpf.

Conn, A. R., et al. Lancelot: A Fortran Package for Large-Scale Nonlinear Optimization (Release A) (Computational Mechanics Ser.: No. 17). 330p. 1992. 118.95 (*0-387-55470-X*) Spr-Verlag.

Conn, Aimee, ed. see Bryson, Breeze.

***Conn, Andrew R., et al.** Trust-Region Methods. (MPS SIAM Series on Optimization: No. 1). (Illus.). 951p. 2000. 119.00 (*0-89871-460-5*, MP0001) Soc Indus-Appl Math.

Conn, Barry, ed. Handbook of the Flora of Papua New Guinea, Vol. 3. (Illus.). 272p. 1996. 49.95 (*0-522-84582-7*, Pub. by Melbourne Univ Pr) Paul & Co Pubs.

Conn-Caffaro, Allison, jt. auth. see Caffaro, John V.

Conn, Carmelita J., ed. see Conn, Kenneth E.

Conn, Carmelita J., ed. see McGee, Therese.

***Conn, Charis.** Index Book, Vol. 3. 2000. pap. 14.95 (*1-879957-54-X*, Franklin Sq Pr) Harpers Mag Found.

Conn, Charles P. The Barbara Mandrell Story. 1989. 3.95 (*0-318-41967-X*) S&S Trade.

— The Dream That Will Not Die. (POL.). 198p. 1997. pap. 12.95 (*0-932877-45-1*); pap. 12.95 (*0-932877-46-X*); pap. 12.95 (*0-932877-49-4*); pap. 12.95 (*0-932877-48-6*); pap. 12.95 (*0-932877-47-8*) InterNET Serv.

— The Possible Dream. 1987. mass mkt. 4.99 (*0-425-10566-0*) Berkley Pub.

— Promises to Keep: The Amway Phenomenon & How it Works. 176p. 1986. mass mkt. 4.99 (*0-425-09856-7*) Berkley Pub.

— An Uncommon Freedom: The Amway Experience & Why It Grows. 208p. 1985. mass mkt. 5.99 (*0-425-08896-0*) Berkley Pub.

Conn, Charles P., jt. auth. see Devos, Richard M.

Conn, Charles P., jt. auth. see Eckerd, Jack.

Conn, Charles W. The Acts of the Apostles. 1996. reprint ed. pap. 8.99 (*0-87148-010-7*) Pathway Pr.

— Anatomy of Evil. 1996. reprint ed. pap. 9.99 (*0-87148-018-2*) Pathway Pr.

— A Balanced Church. 1996. reprint ed. pap. 9.99 (*0-87148-017-4*) Pathway Pr.

— Christ & the Gospels. 109p. 1981. reprint ed. pap. 4.95 (*0-87148-150-2*) Pathway Pr.

— A Guide to the Pentateuch. 109p. 1981. pap. 4.25 (*0-87148-005-0*) Pathway Pr.

— Like a Mighty Army: A History of the Church of God. 3rd ed. (Illus.). 615p. 1996. 26.99 (*0-87148-533-8*) Pathway Pr.

— When Your Upright World Turns Upside Down. LC 90-60594. 1990. pap. 9.99 (*0-87148-924-4*) Pathway Pr.

— Why Men Go Back. 1996. reprint ed. pap. 9.99 (*0-87148-917-1*) Pathway Pr.

Conn, Charles W., ed. Una Iglesia Blanceada. (SPA.). 165p. 1979. pap. 6.95 (*0-87148-882-5*) Pathway Pr.

Conn, D., et al, eds. Practical Psychiatry in the Nursing Home: A Handbook for Staff. (Illus.). 300p. 1992. text 34.50 (*0-88937-042-7*) Hogrefe & Huber Pubs.

***Conn, D., et al.** Practical Psychiatry in the Long Term Care Facility. 2nd rev. ed. 350p. 2000. 34.50 (*0-88937-222-5*) Hogrefe & Huber Pubs.

Conn, D. K., et al, eds. Psychiatric Consequences of Brain Disease in the Elderly: A Focus on Management. (Illus.). 224p. 1989. 65.00 (*0-306-43216-1*, Plenum Trade) Perseus Pubng.

Conn, David. The Football Business English Football in the 90's. (Illus.). 192p. 1997. 35.00 (*1-85158-916-3*, Pub. by Mainstream Pubng) Trafalgar.

Conn, David B. Atlas of Invertebrate Reproduction & Development. LC 90-19577. 272p. 1991. 195.00 (*0-471-56079-0*) Wiley.

— Atlas of Invertebrate Reproduction & Development. 2nd ed. LC 99-31030. 300p. 2000. 175.00 (*0-471-23796-5*) Wiley.

Conn, Didi. Frenchy's Grease Scrapbook: We'll Always Be Together. LC 97-36480. (Illus.). 182p. (J). 1998. pap. 15.95 (*0-7868-8345-6*, Pub. by Hyperion) Time Warner.

Conn, E. E., ed. Opportunities for Phytochemistry in Plant Biotechnology. (Recent Advances in Phytochemistry Ser.: Vol. 22). (Illus.). 190p. 1988. 65.00 (*0-306-42936-5*, Plenum Trade) Perseus Pubng.

Conn, E. E., jt. ed. see Stumpf, Paul K.

Conn, Eileen & Stewart, Jimmy, eds. Visions of Creation. 160p. 1998. pap. 19.95 (*1-897766-30-0*, Pub. by Jon Carpenter) Paul & Co Pubs.

Conn, Eric E., ed. The Shikimic Acid Pathway. LC 86-8885. (Recent Advances in Phytochemistry Ser.: Vol. 20). 356p. 1986. 75.00 (*0-306-42283-2*, Plenum Trade) Perseus Pubng.

Conn, Floyd & Conn, Sadie. They Followed the Rivers. (Illus.). 241p. 1981. 14.50 (*0-9607602-0-2*) Kiowa Pr.

Conn, George H. Horse Selection & Care for Beginners. 1978. pap. 10.00 (*0-87980-193-X*) Wilshire.

Conn, Hadley L. & Horwitz, Orville, eds. Cardiac & Vascular Diseases, 2 vols. LC 71-98493. 960p. reprint ed. pap. 200.00 (*0-608-18516-7*, 205599800001); reprint ed. pap. 200.00 (*0-608-18517-5*, 205599800002) Bks Demand.

***Conn, Harold O.** Spontaneous Bacterial Peritonitis: The Disease, Pathogenesis & Treatment. 311p. 2000. 165.00 (*0-8247-0355-3*) Dekker.

Conn, Harold O., et al, eds. Transjugular Intrahepatic Portal-Systemic Shunts. LC 95-48166. (Illus.). 400p. 1996. 108.00 (*0-89640-300-9*) Igaku-Shoin.

Conn, Harold O. & Bircher, Johannes, eds. Hepatic Encephalopathy: Syndromes & Therapies. LC 93-36530. 430p. 1994. text 63.95 (*0-936741-04-X*) Medi-Ed Pr.

Conn, Harold O., jt. auth. see Klatskin, Gerald.

Conn, Harvie. Evangelism: Doing Justice & Preaching Grace. 112p. (Orig.). (C). 1982. pap. 8.95 (*0-310-45311-9*, 11646P) Zondervan.

Conn, Harvie M. A Clarified Vision for Urban Mission. 1987. pap. 12.99 (*0-310-45441-7*) Zondervan.

— Eternal Word & Changing Worlds: Theology, Anthropology & Mission in Trialogue. 336p. 1984. pap. 19.95 (*0-310-45321-6*, 11647P) Zondervan.

— Eternal Word & Changing Worlds: Theology, Anthropology, & Mission in Trialogue. LC 92-16182. 1992. pap. 14.99 (*0-87552-204-1*) P & R Pubng.

— Evangelism: Doing Justice & Preaching Grace. 1992. pap. 8.99 (*0-87552-206-8*) P & R Pubng.

Conn, Harvie M., ed. Planting & Growing Urban Churches: From Dream to Reality. LC 97-3223. (Illus.). 272p. (Orig.). (gr. 12 up). 1997. pap. 19.99 (*0-8010-2109-X*) Baker Bks.

— Practical Theology & the Ministry of the Church, 1952-1984: Essays in Honor of Edmund P. Clowney. 328p. 1990. pap. 16.99 (*0-87552-207-6*) P & R Pubng.

Conn, Henry P., jt. auth. see Boyett, Joseph H.

Conn, Herb & Conn, Jan. The Jewel Cave Adventure. LC 76-41281. (Illus.). 240p. 1981. pap. 8.95 (*0-939748-01-0*) Cave Bks MO.

Conn, Jack F. Non-Abelian Minimal Closed Ideals of Transitive Lie Algebras. LC 79-24096. (Mathematical Notes Ser.: No. 25). 227p. 1981. reprint ed. pap. 70.40 (*0-608-06615-X*, 206681200009) Bks Demand.

Conn, Jan. What Dante Did with Loss. Harris, Michael, ed. LC 95-127982. (Signal Editions Ser.). 104p. (Orig.). 1994. pap. 9.95 (*1-55065-052-1*, Pub. by Vehicule Pr) Genl Dist Srvs.

Conn, Jan, jt. auth. see Conn, Herb.

Conn, Joann W. Spirituality & Maturity. 176p. 1994. reprint ed. pap. text 21.00 (*0-8191-9569-3*) U Pr of Amer.

— Women's Spirituality: Resources for Christian Development. 2nd ed. LC 96-17621. 352p. (Orig.). 1996. pap. 24.95 (*0-8091-3656-2*) Paulist Pr.

Conn, Joann W. & Conn, Walter E., eds. Horizons on Catholic Feminist Theology. LC 92-30435. 221p. reprint ed. pap. 68.60 (*0-608-07022-X*, 206722900009) Bks Demand.

Conn, Joey, compiled by. Robert Burton & the Anatomy of Melancholy: An Annotated Bibliography of Primary & Secondary Sources, 15. LC 88-24639. (Bibliographies & Indexes in World Literature Ser.: No. 15). 117p. 1988. lib. bdg. 55.00 (*0-313-26047-8*, CNB/) Greenwood.

Conn, Kenneth E. Settlement Conference: A Handbook for Judges & Lawyers. Conn, Carmelita J., ed. LC 88-2308. 96p. (Orig.). 1988. pap. 19.95 (*0-943663-01-6*) San Joaquin Eagle.

Conn, Marie A. Noble Daughters: Unheralded Women in Western Christianity, 13th To 18th Centuries, 60. LC 99-22142. 60. 144p. 2000. 49.95 (*0-313-30669-9*, Greenwood Pr) Greenwood.

Conn, Mary S. Have Family Will Travel: Mary Conn's Memories of a Girlhood Spent on the Move, from Wisconsin to Indian Country, Paleface Country & All Around the American West. abr. rev. ed. Warren, Bacil B., ed. Orig. Title: The Family. (Illus.). 64p. 1998. 10.50 (*1-887404-25-2*) A Griffin Pr.

Conn, Michael P., et al, eds. Methods in Enzymology Vol. 294, Pt. C: Ion Channels. (Illus.). 788p. (C). 1998. boxed set 115.00 (*0-12-182195-1*) Acad Pr.

Conn, Nicole. Angel Wings. LC 97-23523. 208p. 1997. 22.50 (*0-684-83205-4*) S&S Trade.

— Claire of the Moon. 172p. 1993. pap. 11.95 (*1-56280-038-8*) Naiad Pr.

— Passion's Shadow. 320p. 1995. 21.50 (*0-684-80326-7*, Fireside) S&S Trade Pap.

— Passion's Shadow. 336p. 1997. reprint ed. mass mkt. 5.99 (*0-425-15664-8*) Berkley Pub.

Conn, P. Jeffrey & Patel, Jitendra, eds. The Metabotropic Glutamate Receptors. LC 94-18190. (Receptors Ser.). (Illus.). 300p. 1994. text 120.00 (*0-89603-291-4*) Humana.

Conn, P. Michael. Neuroscience in Medicine. (Illus.). 752p. 1994. text 42.50 (*0-397-51279-1*) Lppncott W & W.

Conn, P. Michael, ed. Hormone Action Pt. H: Neuroendocrine Peptides. (Methods in Enzymology Ser.: Vol. 103). 1983. text 188.00 (*0-12-182003-3*) Acad Pr.

— Methods in Neurosciences, Vol. 12: Receptors: Molecular Biology, Receptor Subclasses, Localization, & Ligand Design. (Illus.). 419p. 1993. text 104.00 (*0-12-185273-3*) Acad Pr.

— Methods in Neurosciences, Vol. 2: Cell Culture. 424p. 1990. text 104.00 (*0-12-185253-9*) Acad Pr.

C

An Asterisk (*) at the beginning of an entry indicates that the title is appearing for the first time.

— Methods in Neurosciences, Vol. 3: Quantitative & Qualitative Microscopy. 494p. 1990. spiral bd. 52.00 (*0-12-185256-3*) Acad Pr.
— Methods in Neurosciences, Vol. 4: Electrophysiology & Microinjection. (Illus.). 504p. 1991. pap. 73.00 (*0-12-185258-X*) Acad Pr.
— Methods in Neurosciences, Vol. 7: Lesions & Transplantation. (Illus.). 496p. 1991. spiral bd. 48.00 (*0-12-185264-4*) Acad Pr.
— Methods in Neurosciences, Vol. 8: Neurotoxins. (Illus.). 423p. 1992. pap. 48.00 (*0-12-185266-0*) Acad Pr.
— Methods in Neurosciences, Vol. 9: Gene Expression in Neural Tissues. (Illus.). 492p. 1992. pap. 48.00 (*0-12-185268-7*) Acad Pr.
— Recent Progress in Hormone Research: Proceedings of the 1997 Conference, Vol. 53. (Illus.). 448p. (C). 1998. 115.00 (*1-879225-30-1*) Endocrine Soc.
— Recent Progress in Hormone Research Vol. 52: Proceedings of the 1996 Conference. (Illus.). 512p. (C). 1997. text 110.00 (*1-879225-26-3*) Endocrine Soc.
Conn, P. Michael, et al, eds. Methods in Neurosciences Vol. 24: Neuroimmunology. (Illus.). 434p. (C). 1995. text 59.95 (*0-12-185294-6*) Acad Pr.
Conn, P. Michael & Fain, John N., eds. Methods in Neurosciences Vol. 18: Lipid Metabolism in Signaling Systems. (Illus.). 357p. 1993. text 104.00 (*0-12-185285-7*) Acad Pr.
Conn, P. Michael & Freeman, Marc E., eds. Neuroendocrinology in Physiology & Medicine. LC 99-10139. 592p. 1999. 125.00 (*0-89603-725-8*) Humana.
Conn, P. Michael & Goodman, H. Maurice, eds. Endocrinology Section 7: Cellular Mechanisms, Vol. I. (Handbook of Physiology Ser.). (Illus.). 616p. 1998. text 165.00 (*0-19-510935-X*) OUP.
Conn, P. Michael & Maines, Mahin D., eds. Methods in Neurosciences Vol. 31: Nitric Oxide Synthase: Characterization & Functional Analysis. LC 96-200801. (Illus.). 354p. 1996. text 89.00 (*0-12-185301-2*) Acad Pr.
Conn, P. Michael & Means, Anthony R., eds. Cellular Regulators Pt. B: Calcium & Lipids. (Methods in Enzymology Ser.: Vol. 141). 469p. 1987. text 157.00 (*0-12-182041-6*) Acad Pr.
***Conn, P. Michael & Means, Anthony R., eds.** Principles of Molecular Regulation. 476p. 2000. 135.00 (*0-89603-630-8*) Humana.
Conn, P. Michael & Melmed, Shlomo, eds. Endocrinology: Basic & Clinical Principles. LC 96-43898. (Illus.). 460p. 1997. 125.00 (*0-89603-349-X*) Humana.
Conn, P. Michael & Perez-Polo, Jose R., eds. Methods in Neurosciences Vol. 30: Paradigms of Neural Injury. (Illus.). 335p. 1996. text 85.00 (*0-12-185300-4*) Acad Pr.
Conn, P. Michael & Sealfon, Stuart C., eds. Methods in Neurosciences Vol. 25: Receptor Molecular Biology. (Illus.). 519p. 1995. text 104.00 (*0-12-185295-4*) Acad Pr.
Conn, P. Michael, jt. auth. see Jennes, Lothar.
Conn, P. Michael, jt. auth. see Negro-Vilar, Andrea.
Conn, P. Michael, jt. ed. see Crowley, W. F., Jr.
Conn, P. Michael, jt. ed. see De Souza, Errol B.
Conn, P. Michael, jt. ed. see Levine, Jon E.
Conn, P. Michael, jt. ed. see Narahashi, Toshio.
Conn, P. Michael, jt. ed. see Negro-Vilar, Andrea.
Conn, P. Michael, jt. ed. see Sarkar, Gobinda.
Conn, P. Michael, jt. ed. see Smith, A. Ian.
Conn, Paul. Dad, Mom & the Church: Raising Children Together. LC 89-62865. 1989. 6.99 (*0-87148-267-3*); teacher ed. 3.50 (*0-87148-268-1*) Pathway Pr.
Conn, Peter. Pearl S. Buck: A Cultural Biography. (Illus.). 494p. (C). 1996. text 34.95 (*0-521-56080-2*) Cambridge U Pr.
— Pearl S. Buck: A Cultural Biography. (Illus.). 470p. (C). 1998. reprint ed. pap. 18.95 (*0-521-63989-1*) Cambridge U Pr.
Conn, Phoebe. Beloved Legacy. 416p. 1996. mass mkt. 5.50 (*0-8217-5371-1*, Zebra Kensgtn) Kensgtn Pub Corp.
— Captive Heart. 1985. mass mkt. 3.95 (*0-8217-1569-0*, Zebra Kensgtn) Kensgtn Pub Corp.
— Forbidden Legacy. 384p. 1998. pap. 5.99 (*0-8217-5985-X*, Zebra Kensgtn) Kensgtn Pub Corp.
— Hearts of Gold. 384p. (Orig.). 1988. mass mkt. 3.95 (*0-445-20812-0*, Pub. by Warner Bks) Little.
— Love's Elusive Flame. 1983. mass mkt. 3.75 (*0-8217-1267-5*, Zebra Kensgtn) Kensgtn Pub Corp.
— Loving Fury. 1986. mass mkt. 3.95 (*0-317-39260-3*, Zebra Kensgtn) Kensgtn Pub Corp.
— Paradise. 304p. 1995. mass mkt. 4.99 (*0-8217-5066-6*, Zebra Kensgtn) Kensgtn Pub Corp.
— Starfire. 448p. 1994. mass mkt. 5.99 (*0-7860-0033-3*, Pinncle Kensgtn) Kensgtn Pub Corp.
— Tender Savage. 480p. 1989. mass mkt. 3.95 (*0-8217-2572-6*, Zebra Kensgtn) Kensgtn Pub Corp.
— A Touch of Class. 416p. 1997. mass mkt. 5.50 (*0-8217-5662-1*, Zebra Kensgtn) Kensgtn Pub Corp.
— Wild Legacy. 400p. 1998. mass mkt. 5.99 (*0-8217-6097-1*) Kensgtn Pub Corp.
Conn, Rex B., et al. Current Diagnosis 9. 9th ed. Borer, William Z. & Kersey, Ray, eds. 1072p. 1996. text 120.00 (*0-7216-5843-1*, W B Saunders Co) Harcrt Hlth Sci Grp.
Conn, Richard. The ADA Software Repository & the DDN. 160p. (Orig.). 1986. pap. 16.95 (*0-918432-78-2*) Baseline Bks.
Conn, Robert & Clapp, Steve. Methods of Bible Study. (C-Four Youth Bible Materials Ser.). (Illus.). 91p. (Orig.). 1982. pap. 8.00 (*0-914527-14-2*) C-Four Res.
Conn, Robert H. Basic Bible Commentary Vol. 29: Revelation. Deming, Lynne M., ed. LC 94-10965. 160p. (Orig.). 1994. pap. 5.95 (*0-687-02649-0*) Abingdon.
— A Handbook for Higher Education & Campus Ministry in the Annual Conference. (Orig.). 1989. pap. text 3.50 (*0-938162-10-1*) United Meth Educ.
***Conn, Ronald J.** Rendezvous with Destiny: Discover the Ultimate Purpose of Your Life. (Illus.). 210p. 1999. pap. 14.95 (*0-9685132-0-4*) Str1ive Pub.
Conn, Sadie, jt. auth. see Conn, Floyd.
Conn, Stephen, tr. see Krumeich, Gerd.
Conn, Stetson. United States Army in World War 2, the Western Hemisphere, the Framework of the Hemisphere Defense. 494p. 1985. boxed set 16.00 (*0-16-061291-8*) USGPO.
***Conn, Steven.** Encounters with History. 2000. 29.00 (*0-226-11494-5*) U Ch Pr.
Conn, Steven. Museums & American Intellectual Life, 1876-1925. LC 98-16850. (Illus.). 301p. 1998. 32.50 (*0-226-11492-9*) U Ch Pr.
Conn, Steven R. Global Factor Pattern Interpretation of the 16PF Fifth Edition. (Illus.). 304p. (Orig.). 1997. pap. 195.00 (*0-918296-29-3*) Inst Personality & Ability.
Conn, Steven R. & Rieke, Mark L., eds. The Sixteen PF Fifth Edition: Technical Manual. 324p. (Orig.). (C). 1994. pap. 55.00 (*0-918296-22-6*) Inst Personality & Ability.
Conn, Stewart. In the Blood. 80p. 1996. pap. 16.95 (*1-85224-329-5*, Pub. by Bloodaxe Bks) Dufour.
— In the Kibble Palace: New & Selected Poems. LC 87-73048. 112p. (Orig.). 1988. pap. 14.95 (*1-85224-033-4*, Pub. by Bloodaxe Bks) Dufour.
— The Luncheon of the Boating Party. 64p. 1993. pap. 14.95 (*1-85224-142-X*, Pub. by Bloodaxe Bks) Dufour.
***Conn, Stewart.** Stolen Light: Selected Poems. 192p. 2000. pap. 23.95 (*1-85224-484-4*, Pub. by Bloodaxe Bks) Dufour.
Conn, Stewart, jt. ed. see McDonough, Ian.
Conn, Walter E., jt. ed. see Conn, Joann W.
Conn, Walter E., jt. ed. see Swidler, Arlene.
Connable & Newcomb. Genealogical Memoir of the Cunnabell, Conable or Connable Family, 1650-1886. (Illus.). 187p. 1993. reprint ed. pap. 34.50 (*0-8328-1387-7*); reprint ed. lib. bdg. 44.50 (*0-8328-1386-9*) Higginson Bk Co.
Connable, Ralph. Cunnabell: Pictorial Genealogy of the Cunnabell, Connable, Canable Family, 1886-1935, Vol. II. (Illus.). 190p. 1994. reprint ed. pap. 29.50 (*0-8328-4312-1*); reprint ed. lib. bdg. 39.50 (*0-8328-4311-3*) Higginson Bk Co.
Connah, Graham. African Civilizations: Precolonial Cities & States in Tropical Africa - An Archaeological Perspective. 2nd ed. (Illus.). 272p. 1987. pap. text 22.95 (*0-521-31992-7*) Cambridge U Pr.
— The Archaeology of Australia's History. (Illus.). 192p. (C). 1994. pap. text 29.95 (*0-521-45475-1*) Cambridge U Pr.
Connah, Graham, ed. Kibiro: The Salt of Bunyoro, Past & Present. (Memoir Ser.: Vol. 13). (Illus.). 256p. 1996. 65.00 (*1-872566-08-1*, Pub. by Brit Inst Estrn Africa) David Brown.
— Transformations in Africa: Essays on Africa's Later Past. LC 97-27703. 255p. 1998. 75.00 (*0-7185-0137-3*) Bks Intl VA.
Connah, Roger. Welcome to the Hotel Architecture. LC 97-47324. (Illus.). 160p. 1998. pap. text 17.50 (*0-262-53153-4*) MIT Pr.
Connaissance des Arts Editorial Staff. Connaissance des Arts Collection: Decoration, 2 vols., 1. 150.00 (*0-686-56194-5*) Fr & Eur.
— Connaissance des Arts Collection: Decoration, 2 vols., 2. 150.00 (*0-686-56195-3*) Fr & Eur.
— Connaissance des Arts Collection: French Cabinetmakers of the 18th Century. 150.00 (*0-8288-7388-7*) Fr & Eur.
— Connaissance des Arts Collection: Gardens & Flowers. 150.00 (*0-686-56197-X*) Fr & Eur.
— Les Ebenistes du Huitieme Siecle Francais.Tr. of French Cabinetmakers of the Eighteenth Century. (ENG & FRE., Illus.). 150.00 (*0-685-11206-3*) Fr & Eur.
— French Master Goldsmiths & Silversmiths from the Seventeenth to the Nineteenth Century. (Connaissance des Arts Collection). (FRE.). 280p. 1966. 150.00 (*0-685-57850-X*) Fr & Eur.
— Gardens & Flowers: Their Design & Arrangement. (Connaissance des Arts Collection). (Illus.). 280p. 1966. 150.00 (*0-8288-6723-2*) Fr & Eur.
— Les Oeuvres de Louis XIII a Charles X.Tr. of French Master Goldsmiths & Silversmiths from the Seventeenth to the Nineteenth Century. (Illus.). 150.00 (*0-685-11470-8*) Fr & Eur.
— Les Oeuvres de Louis XIII a Charles X.Tr. of French Master Goldsmiths & Silversmiths from the Seventeenth to the Nineteenth Century. (FRE.). 1966. 150.00 (*0-8288-7386-0*) Fr & Eur.
— Les Porcelainiers du Huitieme Siecle Francais. (FRE., Illus.). 150.00 (*0-685-11208-X*) Fr & Eur.
— Les Porcelainiers du Huitieme Siecle Francais: French Porcelain Makers of the 18th Century. 1966. write for info. (*0-8288-7387-9*) Fr & Eur.
Connaissance Staff. Dictionnaire Francais - Chinois en Automatique. (CHI & FRE.). 630p. 1990. 50.00 (*0-8288-9529-5*) Fr & Eur.
Connal, Mary E. & Johnson, Beverly A. Pediatric Emergencies: A Handbook for Nurses. 312p. 1990. 69.00 (*0-8342-0102-X*, 20102) Aspen Pub.
Connally, Eileen. Develop Your Psychic Powers. 235p. 1990. pap. 14.95 (*0-87877-151-4*) Newcastle Pub.
***Connally, Eric.** Functions Modeling Change. 554p. 1999. text 91.95 (*0-471-37918-2*) Wiley.
Connally, Eric. Functions Modeling Change: A Preparation for Calculus. 576p. 1999. pap. 80.95 (*0-471-17084-4*) Wiley.
***Connally, Eric.** Functions Modeling Change: A Preparation for Calculus: Preliminary Edition. 624p. 1998. text 80.95 (*0-471-31787-X*) Wiley.
Connally, Eric & Hughes-Hallett, Deborah. Functions Modeling Change: A Preparation for Calculus. 624p. 1997. pap. 65.95 (*0-471-17081-X*) Wiley.
***Connally, Eric, et al.** Functions Modeling Change: A Preparation for Calculus. 169p. 1999. pap., student ed. 31.95 (*0-471-29396-2*) Wiley.
Connally, Eugenia H., ed. National Parks in Crisis. 220p. 1982. 13.95 (*0-318-17829-X*) Natl Parks & Cons.
Connally, Eugenia H., pref. National Parks in Crisis. LC 82-81269. 220p. (C). 1982. 13.95 (*0-940091-11-9*) Natl Parks & Cons.
Connally, Eulalia H. Huffhines. John Huffhines Family History & Genealogy. (Illus.). 90p. 1997. reprint ed. pap. 18.00 (*0-8328-9243-2*); reprint ed. lib. bdg. 28.00 (*0-8328-9242-4*) Higginson Bk Co.
Connally, John & Herskowitz, Mickey. In History's Shadow: An American Odyssey. (Illus.). 400p. (J). 1994. pap. 12.45 (*0-7868-8068-6*, Pub. by Hyperion) Time Warner.
Connally, Runnoe, et al. Infoworld Windows 3.1 Connect Secrets. LC 93-81201. (WUGNET Windows Computing Secrets Ser.). (Illus.). 1000p. 1994. pap. 49.95 (*1-56884-030-6*) IDG Bks.
Connare, Carol, et al. Foghorn Outdoors: New England Camping: The Complete Guide to More Than 82,000 Campsites for Tenters, RVers, & Car Campers. 2nd ed. (Illus.). 540p. 1999. pap. 19.95 (*1-57354-058-7*, Foghorn Outdoors) Avalon Travel.
Connaroe, Joel, ed. Six American Poets: An Anthology. LC 92-50624. 320p. 1993. pap. 14.00 (*0-679-74525-4*) Vin Bks.
Connaughton, Dennis. Warren Cole, M. D., & the Ascent of Scientific Surgery. 272p. 1991. text 24.95 (*0-252-01884-2*) U of Ill Pr.
— Warren Cole, M. D., & the Ascent of Scientific Surgery. (Illus.). 272p. 1991. 24.95 (*0-9628799-0-8*) W & C Cole Found.
Connaughton, Janet, ed. see Stienstra, Tom.
Connaughton, Richard. Celebration of Victory: V-E Day 1945. (Illus.). 160p. 1995. 19.95 (*1-85753-181-7*, Pub. by Brasseys) Brasseys.
— Descent into Chaos: The Doomed Expedition to Low's Gully. (Illus.). 155p. 1996. 34.95 (*1-85753-147-7*, Pub. by Brasseys) Brasseys.
— The Nature of Future Conflict. 239p. 1995. 29.95 (*0-85052-460-1*, Pub. by Leo Cooper) Trans-Atl Phila.
— Shrouded Secrets: Japan's War on Mainland Australia 1942-1944. (Illus.). 150p. 1994. 30.00 (*1-85753-160-4*, Pub. by Brasseys) Brasseys.
Connaughton, Richard M. Military Intervention in the 1990s. LC 92-7938. (Operational Level of War Ser.). (Illus.). 208p. (C). 1993. pap. 27.99 (*0-415-07991-8*, A9791) Routledge.
— The War of the Rising Sun & Tumbling Bear: A Military History of the Russo-Japanese War (1904-1905) 320p. 1989. 49.95 (*0-415-00906-5*) Routledge.
Connaughton, Shane. A Border Station. 176p. 1991. reprint ed. mass mkt. 8.99 (*0-446-39302-9*, Pub. by Warner Bks) Little.
Connaway, John M. The Wilsford Site 22-Co-516, Coahoma County Mississippi. LC 84-620008. (Mississippi Department of Archives & History Archaeological Reports: No. 14). 222p. (Orig.). 1984. pap. 15.00 (*0-938896-40-7*) Mississippi Archives.
Connechen, James. Pharmacology for Nurses. 5th ed. 1983. text 17.00 (*0-7216-0803-5*, W B Saunders Co) Harcrt Hlth Sci Grp.
Connechen, James, et al. Pharmacology for Nurses. 5th ed. 384p. 1983. pap. text 17.95 (*0-7020-0868-0*) Bailliere Tindall.
Connecticut. Connecticut Related Laws to the Insurance Laws. LC 97-65524. 1997. write for info. (*0-89246-469-0*) NILS Pub.
Connecticut Division of the American Cancer Societ. Connecticut Cooks No. 2: Favorite Recipes. 318p. 1985. pap. 9.95 (*0-9608732-0-1*) Connecticut Bk.
Connecticut Division of the American Cancer Societ & Wimmer Brothers Books Staff. Connecticut Cooks No. 3: Favorite Recipes. LC 85-51321. (Illus.). 318p. (Orig.). (C). 1988. pap. 11.95 (*0-9608732-2-8*) ACS CT Div.
Connecticut Easter Seals Staff. Classic Connecticut Cuisine. 222p. 1994. 14.95 (*0-87197-406-1*) Connecticut Bk.
Connecticut General Assembly Staff. Minutes of the Testimony Taken Before John Q. Wilson, Joseph Eaton, & Morris Woodruff, Committee from the General Assembly, to Inquire into the Condition of the Connecticut State Prison. LC 74-3819. (Criminal Justice in America Ser.). 1974. reprint ed. 15.95 (*0-405-06140-4*) Ayer.
Connecticut Historical Society Staff. Catalogue of the Connecticut Historical Society Loan Collection. viii, 97p. 1987. pap. 7.00 (*0-940748-92-4*) Conn Hist Soc.
— Collections of the Connecticut Historical Society, 20 vols., Set. LC 74-19612. reprint ed. write for info. (*0-404-12383-X*) AMS Pr.
— Lists & Returns of Connecticut Men in the Revolution, 1775-1783. 489p. (Orig.). 1995. pap. 31.00 (*0-7884-0312-5*) Heritage Bk.
— Rolls & Lists of Connecticut Men in the Revolution, 1775-1783. 389p. 1993. reprint ed. pap. 26.00 (*0-7884-0300-1*) Heritage Bk.
Connecticut Historical Society Staff. Supplement to the Record of Connecticut Men... During the War of the Revolution: Vol. I: Rolls & Lists of Connecticut Men in the Revolution, 1775-1783; Vol. II: Lists & Returns of Connecticut Men in the Revolution, 1775-1783, 2 vols. 864p. 1997. reprint ed. pap. 65.00 (*0-8063-4752-X*) Clearfield Co.
Connecticut Historical Society Staff, jt. auth. see Avery, Amos G.
Connecticut Self-Help Network Staff. The Self-Help Directory: A Guide to Connecticut & National Groups 1996-1997. 8th rev. ed. 348p. 1996. pap. 22.00 (*0-9647301-1-1*) CT Self-Help Netwrk.
Connel, C. Mediterranean Maelstrom: The Story of HMS Jarvis. (C). 1986. text 130.00 (*0-7855-5304-5*, Pub. by Maritime Bks) St Mut.
Connell. Machiavel the Prince. 2000. pap. text. write for info. (*0-312-14978-6*) St Martin.
— Planning for Divorcing Couples. 95th ed. 1995. pap. text 35.00 (*0-15-601700-8*) Harcourt.
— Stations of the Cross for Sick. 32p. 1996. pap. 2.50 (*0-8198-6991-0*) Pauline Bks.
— Triumph of the Immaculate Heart. 1993. 29.95 (*1-882972-11-2*, 3121) Queenship Pub.
Connell, Bob. Process Instrumentation Applications Manual. LC 95-22624. 364p. 1995. 84.95 (*0-07-012353-5*) McGraw.
Connell, Brian, tr. see Von Papen, Franz.
Connell Brown, Susie & Connell Speck, Vicki. Going Hog Wild with Razorback Country Cooking. 192p. 1986. 10.95 (*0-9616573-0-8*) Connell & Connell.
Connell, Bruce & Arvaniti, Amalia, eds. Phonology & Phonetic Evidence: Papers in Laboratory Phonology IV. (Papers in Laboratory Phonology: Vol. IV). 417p. (C). 1995. text 74.95 (*0-521-48259-3*); pap. text 29.95 (*0-521-48388-3*) Cambridge U Pr.
***Connell, Bruce F. & Marten, Timothy J.** Atlas of Cervicofacial Rejuvenation. (Illus.). 500p. 2000. text 275.00 (*1-57626-123-9*) Quality Med Pub.
Connell, C. B. Gearmotors - Their Design & Application by AGMA Standards. (Technical Papers: Vol. P239). (Illus.). 25p. 1943. pap. text 30.00 (*1-55589-434-8*) AGMA.
— High Speed Industrial Gear Drives. (Technical Papers: Vol. P429.02). (Illus.). 28p. 1948. pap. text 30.00 (*1-55589-410-0*) AGMA.
— The Latest Developments in & Application of Industrial Gear Drives. (Technical Papers: Vol. P159.01). (Illus.). 30p. 1952. pap. text 30.00 (*1-55589-203-5*) AGMA.
— Relations Between Load Rating & Design Stresses of Gear Units. (Technical Papers: Vol. P141). (Illus.). 28p. 1936. pap. text 30.00 (*1-55589-242-6*) AGMA.
Connell, Charles W., jt. ed. see Berman, Constance H.
Connell, D. W. Basic Concepts of Environmental Chemistry. LC 97-7698. 528p. 1997. boxed set 64.95 (*0-87371-998-0*) CRC Pr.
— Introduction to Ecotoxicology. LC 98-53192. (Illus.). 1999. pap. 39.95 (*0-632-03852-7*) Blackwell Sci.
— Water Pollution: Causes & Effects in Australia & New Zealand. 3rd ed. 1993. pap. 29.95 (*0-7022-2337-9*, Pub. by Univ Queensland Pr) Intl Spec Bk.
Connell, D. W., jt. auth. see Vowles, P. D.
Connell, Dan. Against All Odds: A Chronicle of the Eritrean Revolution. LC 93-1010. (Illus.). 312p. 1993. 24.95 (*0-932415-89-X*) Red Sea Pr.
— Against All Odds: A Chronicle of the Eritrean Revolution with a New Afterword on the Postwar. LC 97-15552. 325p. 1997. pap. 14.95 (*1-56902-046-9*) Red Sea Pr.
Connell, Des W. Bioaccumulation of Xenobiotic Compounds. 240p. 1989. lib. bdg. 225.00 (*0-8493-4810-2*, QR4545) CRC Pr.
— Pollution in Tropical Aquatic Systems. 224p. 1991. lib. bdg. 149.00 (*0-8493-6581-3*, QH545) CRC Pr.
Connell, Des W. & Miller, Gregory. Chemistry & Exotoxicology of Pollution: Environmental Science & Technology. LC 83-16794. (Wiley-Interscience Series of Text & Monographs: No. 1121). 444p. 1984. 165.00 (*0-471-86249-5*) Wiley.
Connell, Desmond. Christ Our Life: Pastoral Letters. 1995. pap. 15.00 (*0-614-16416-8*, Pub. by Four Cts Pr) Intl Spec Bk.
— Essays in Metaphysics. 128p. 1996. pap. 14.95 (*1-85182-228-3*, Pub. by Four Cts Pr) Intl Spec Bk.
Connell, Donna. Writing Is Child's Play: A Guide for Teaching Young Children to Write. 2nd ed. (J). (ps-3). 1993. pap. 12.95 (*0-201-81884-1*) Addison-Wesley.
Connell, E. Jane. James Karsina: Transformations. (Illus.). 14p. (Orig.). 1996. pap. 9.95 (*0-942159-19-5*) Grnd Rpds Art Mus.
Connell, E. Jane, ed. see South, Will.
Connell, Ed. Reinsman of the West: Bridles & Bits. 1977. pap. 10.00 (*0-87980-333-9*) Wilshire.
Connell, Edgar N. Hackamore Reinsman. (Illus.). 93p. 1994. reprint ed. pap. 14.95 (*0-9648385-0-8*) Lennoche Pubs.
Connell, Evan S. Anatomy Lesson, & Other Stories. LC 79-38719. (Short Story Index Reprint Ser.). 1977. reprint ed. 18.95 (*0-8369-4132-2*) Ayer.
— Collected Stories of Evan S. Connell. 688p. 1997. pap. text 19.95 (*1-887178-39-2*, Pub. by Counterpt DC) HarpC.
***Connell, Evan S.** Deus Lo Volt! A Chronicle of the Crusades. LC 99-54831. 480p. 2000. 30.00 (*1-58243-065-9*, Pub. by Counterpt DC) HarpC.
Connell, Evan S. Mr. Bridge: A Novel. LC 81-81513. 367p. 1990. reprint ed. pap. 9.95 (*0-86547-054-5*) N Point Pr.
— Mrs. Bridge. LC 81-81514. 246p. 1990. reprint ed. pap. 9.95 (*0-86547-056-1*) N Point Pr.
— Mrs. Bridge: A Novel. large type ed. 1991. pap. 15.95 (*0-8161-5206-3*, G K Hall Lrg Type) Mac Lib Ref.
— Notes from a Bottle Found on the Beach at Carmel. LC 94-43666. 1995. pap. 13.00 (*0-88001-407-5*) HarpC.
— Son of the Morning Star: Custer & the Little Bighorn. 441p. (C). 1997. pap. text 8.93 (*0-06-502363-3*) Addison-Wesley.
— Son of the Morning Star: Custer & the Little Bighorn. LC 85-42560. 1991. pap. 10.95 (*0-06-097161-4*, Perennial) HarperTrade.
— Son of the Morning Star: Custer & the Little Bighorn. (Illus.). 448p. 1997. pap. text 15.00 (*0-86547-510-5*) N Point Pr.
Connell, Evan S. Son of the Morning Star: Custer & the Little Bighorn. 1993. 14.98 (*0-88394-088-4*) Promntory Pr.

C

An Asterisk (*) at the beginning of an entry indicates that the title is appearing for the first time.

***Connell, Gale O. & Connell, Kitty R.** Second Messenger. LC 00-190200. iv, 366p. 2000. pap. 13.95 (*0-9676852-0-6*) MythMaker Pr.

Connell, Gary, et al. Reshaping Family Relationships: The Symbolic Therapy of Carl Whitaker. LC 98-38283. 186p. 1998. 29.95 (*0-87630-878-7*) Brunner-Mazel.

Connell, George. To Be One Thing: Personal Unity in Kierkegaard's Thought. LC 85-4812. xx, 198p. 1985. 17.95 (*0-86554-156-6*, MUP/H146) Mercer Univ Pr.

Connell, Gerald F. The Chlorination - Chloramination Handbook. LC 96-37817. (Water Disinfection Ser.). (Illus.). 171p. 1997. 75.00 (*0-89867-886-2*) Am Water Wks Assn.

Connell, Helen Margaret. Essentials of Child Psychiatry. 2nd ed. (Illus.). 354p. (C). (gr. 13). 1985. 23.95 (*0-86793-144-2*, B-1017-6) Mosby Inc.

Connell, J. J. Control of Fish Quality. 1978. 65.00 (*0-7855-6913-8*) St Mut.

Connell, James E., Jr. Johnny Discovers Baseball & More. 118p. (J). (gr. 6-9). 1998. pap. 10.95 (*1-57532-198-X*) Press-Tige Pub.

***Connell, James G. & Valladares, Rene L.** Cultural Issues in Criminal Defense. LC 00-26404. 2000. write for info. (*1-57823-080-2*) Juris Pubng.

Connell, Jan. Queen of the Cosmos. LC 90-61665. (Illus.). 152p. 1990. pap. 9.95 (*1-55725-018-9*, 930-009, Pub. by Paraclete MA) BookWorld.

Connell, Jane, jt. auth. see Spence, Nancy.

Connell, Jane, ed. see Bulka, Michael, et al.

Connell, Janice T. Angel Power. 288p. (Orig.). 1995. pap. 12.00 (*0-345-39123-3*) Ballantine Pub Grp.

— Meetings with Mary: Visions of the Blessed Mother. 416p. 1996. pap. 10.00 (*0-345-39705-3*) Ballantine Pub Grp.

— Prayer Power. LC 98-19205. 1999. 13.00 (*0-06-061523-0*) HarpC.

— Prayer Power: Secrets of Healing & Protection. LC 98-19205. 320p. 1998. 18.00 (*0-06-061522-2*, Pub. by Harper SF) HarpC.

— Praying with Mary: A Treasury for All Occasions. 192p. 1999. pap. 12.00 (*0-06-061521-4*) HarpC.

— Praying with Mary: Sacred Prayers to the Blessed Mother for All Occasions. LC 97-41337. 192p. 1997. 18.00 (*0-06-061520-6*, Pub. by Harper SF) HarpC.

— Queen of Angels: Mary's Answers to Universal Questions. LC 99-34813. 224p. 1999. 19.95 (*0-87477-993-6*, Tarcher Putnam) Putnam Pub Group.

— Visions of Children Apparition. rev. ed. LC 98-105114. (Illus.). 320p. 1997. pap. 12.95 (*0-312-18204-X*) St Martin.

Connell, Janie B. & Ashley, William L. Helping the Dislocated Worker: Resources. 67p. 1984. 5.75 (*0-318-22113-6*, RD243C) Ctr Educ Trng Employ.

Connell, Jeanie. I Can Grow Up. (Illus.). 96p. (Orig.). 1995. pap. 10.00 (*1-885857-07-1*) Four Wnds Pubng.

***Connell, John.** Beginning Visual Basic 6 Coding Techniques. 700p. 2000. pap. 39.99 (*1-86100-279-3*) Wrox Pr Inc.

Connell, John. Beginning Visual Basic 6 Database Programming. LC 99-226260. 880p. 1998. pap. 39.99 (*1-86100-106-1*) Wrox Pr Inc.

— Homing Instinct: Using Your Lifestyle to Design & Build Your Home. rev. ed. (Illus.). 448p. 1999. pap. 34.95 (*0-07-012346-2*) McGraw.

— Papua New Guinea: Struggle for Development. LC 98-107783. (Routledge Studies in the Growth Economies of Asia Ser.). 368p. (C). 1997. 74.95 (*0-415-05401-X*) Routledge.

***Connell, John, ed.** Sydney: The Emergence of a World City. (Illus.). 256p. 2000. pap. 35.00 (*0-19-550748-7*) OUP.

Connell, John & Howitt, Richard, eds. Mining & Indigenous Peoples in Australasia. (Illus.). 216p. 1992. pap. text 28.00 (*0-424-00177-2*) OUP.

Connell, John & Lea, John P. Pacific 2010: Urbanisation in Polynesia LC 97-120511. (Pacific Policy Papers). viii, 161 p. 1995. write for info. (*0-7315-1954-X*) ANU Res Sch.

Connell, John, et al. Migration from Rural Areas: The Evidence from Village Studies. 1977. 7.50 (*0-19-560789-9*) OUP.

Connell, John, jt. auth. see Aldrich, Robert.

Connell, John, jt. auth. see King, Russell.

Connell, John, jt. ed. see Aldrich, Robert.

Connell, John L. & Shafer, Linda I. Object Oriented Rapid Prototyping. LC 94-5264. 224p. (C). 1994. 37.60 (*0-13-629643-2*, Yourdon) P-H.

Connell, John R., et al. Touche Ross Guide to Personal Financial Management. 2nd rev. ed. 336p. 1987. 39.95 (*0-13-925413-7*) P-H.

— The Touche Ross Personal Financial Planning & Investment Workbook. 3rd ed. 360p. 1989. 39.95 (*0-13-925844-2*) P-H.

Connell, Jonathan H., ed. Minimalist Mobile Robotics: A Colony-Style Architecture for an Artificial Intelligence. (Perspectives in Artificial Intelligence Ser.: Vol. 5). 192p. 1990. text 47.00 (*0-12-185230-X*) Acad Pr.

Connell, Jonathan H. & Mahadevan, Sridhar, eds. Robot Learning. LC 93-17570. (International Engineering & Computer Science Ser.: Vol. 233). 256p. (C). 1993. lib. bdg. 109.00 (*0-7923-9365-1*) Kluwer Academic.

Connell, K. H. Irish Peasant Society. 176p. 1996. 45.00 (*0-7165-2588-7*, Pub. by Irish Acad Pr); pap. 22.95 (*0-7165-2610-7*, Pub. by Irish Acad Pr) Intl Spec Bk.

Connell, Kate. Tales from the Underground Railroad. LC 92-14415. (Stories of America Ser.). (Illus.). 68p. (J). (gr. 2-5). 1992. lib. bdg. 24.26 (*0-8114-7223-X*) Raintree Steck-V.

— Tales from the Underground Railroad. LC 92-14415. (Stories of America Ser.). (Illus.). 68p. (J). (gr. 4-7). 1992. pap. 4.95 (*0-8114-8063-1*) Raintree Steck-V.

— These Lands Are Ours: Tecumseh's Fight for the Old Northwest. LC 92-14417. (Stories of America Ser.). (Illus.). 96p. (J). (gr. 2-5). 1992. pap. 4.95 (*0-8114-8067-4*); lib. bdg. 25.68 (*0-8114-7227-2*) Raintree Steck-V.

— They Shall Be Heard: The Story of Susan B. Anthony & Elizabeth Cady Stanton. Haley, Alex, ed. LC 92-18088. (Stories of America Ser.). (Illus.). 85p. (J). (gr. 2-5). 1993. lib. bdg. 25.68 (*0-8114-7228-0*) Raintree Steck-V.

— They Shall Be Heard: The Story of Susan B. Anthony & Elizabeth Cady Stanton. Haley, Alex, ed. LC 92-18088. (Stories of America Ser.). (Illus.). 85p. (J). (gr. 4-7). 1993. pap. write for info. (*0-8114-8068-2*) Raintree Steck-V.

Connell, Kenneth F. & Smith, Robert B. Analysis of Causes & Determination of Possible Means of Prevention of External Damage to Pipelines. 100p. 1968. 2.50 (*0-318-12584-6*, U78173) Am Gas Assn.

Connell, Kim, ed. from FRE. The Belgian School of the Bizarre: An Anthology of Short Stories. LC 97-38852. 224p. 1998. 38.50 (*0-8386-3717-5*) Fairleigh Dickinson.

Connell, Kim, tr. see Muno, Jean.

Connell, Kitty R., jt. auth. see Connell, Gale O.

Connell, Lee R. & Callahan, Michael T., Jr. Construction Defect Claims & Litigation, 1. LC 95-12833. (Construction Law Library). 544p. 1995. boxed set 150.00 (*0-471-11873-7*) Wiley.

***Connell, Martin.** Guide to the Revised Lectionary. LC 98-87345. (Basics of Ministry Ser.). 70p. 1998. 5.00 (*1-56854-256-9*) Liturgy Tr Pubns.

Connell, Martin. Introduction to the Church's Liturgical Year. 1998. pap. 3.15 (*0-8294-1024-4*) Loyola Pr.

Connell, Martin, ed. At Home with the Word, 1999. 1998. pap. 7.00 (*1-56854-223-2*) Liturgy Tr Pubns.

— The Catechetical Documents: A Parish Resource. 654p. (Orig.). 1996. pap. 22.00 (*1-56854-113-9*, CATDOC) Liturgy Tr Pubns.

— Eucharist: Toward the Third Millennium. LC 97-9976. 136p. 1997. pap. 9.00 (*1-56854-181-3*, V2EUCH) Liturgy Tr Pubns.

— The Renewal That Awaits Us. LC 97-73207. 184p. 1997. pap. 12.00 (*1-56854-087-6*, NDNEW) Liturgy Tr Pubns.

Connell, Martin, jt. ed. see Bernstein, Eleanor.

Connell, Martin, ed. see Philippart, David.

Connell, Mary U. Biological Investigations. 2nd rev. ed. (Illus.). 268p. 1999. pap. text 29.95 (*0-88725-240-0*) Hunter Textbks.

Connell, Michael. Technology & Math. (C). 1998. 25.00 (*0-205-18933-4*, Macmillan Coll) P-H.

***Connell, Nancy D. & Baker, Emanuel R.** Surfaces of Nanoparticles & Porous Materials. LC 98-49272. (Surfactant Science Ser.). (Illus.). 816p. 1999. text 235.00 (*0-8247-1933-6*) Dekker.

Connell, Nancy D., jt. auth. see Underwood Grant, Anne.

Connell, Paul. Parson, Priest & Master: National Education in Co. Meath, 1824-41. 64p. 1995. pap. 9.95 (*0-7165-2570-4*, Pub. by Irish Acad Pr) Intl Spec Bk.

Connell, R. W. Gender & Power: Society, the Person & Sexual Politics. LC 87-61426. xviii, 334p. 1987. 47.50 (*0-8047-1429-0*); pap. 17.95 (*0-8047-1430-4*) Stanford U Pr.

— Masculinities: Knowledge, Power & Social Change. LC 94-36172. 1995. pap. 18.95 (*0-520-08999-5*, Pub. by U CA Pr) Cal Prin Full Svc.

— Schools & Social Justice. LC 93-1616. 144p. (C). 1993. 44.95 (*1-56639-137-7*); pap. 19.95 (*1-56639-138-5*) Temple U Pr.

— Teacher's Work. 212p. (C). 1985. text 29.95 (*0-86861-752-0*, Pub. by Allen & Unwin Pty); pap. text 14.95 (*0-86861-760-1*, Pub. by Allen & Unwin Pty) Paul & Co Pubs.

— Which Way Is Up? 224p. 1984. pap. 12.95 (*0-86861-374-6*) Routledge.

Connell, R. W., et al, eds. Running Twice As Hard: The Disadvantage Schools Program in Australia. 299p. 1992. pap. 57.00 (*0-7300-1364-2*, ESA842, Pub. by Deakin Univ) St Mut.

Connell, R. W. & Dowsett, G. W., eds. Rethinking Sex: Social Theory & Sexuality Research. 182p. 1993. pap. 16.95 (*1-56639-073-7*) Temple U Pr.

Connell, R. W., et al. Making the Difference: Schools, Families & Social Division. 224p. 1982. pap. 14.95 (*0-86861-132-8*, Pub. by Allen & Unwin Pty) Paul & Co Pubs.

Connell, Richard E. Apes & Angels. LC 73-106272. (Short Story Index Reprint Ser.). 1977. 20.95 (*0-8369-3309-5*) Ayer.

— Sin of Monsieur Pettipon & Other Humorous Stories. LC 77-106273. (Short Story Index Reprint Ser.). 1977. 20.95 (*0-8369-3310-9*) Ayer.

Connell, Richard J. The Empirical Intelligence - The Human Empirical Mode: Philosophy as Originating in Experience. LC 88-11787. (Problems in Contemporary Philosophy Ser.: Vol. 10). 240p. 1988. lib. bdg. 89.95 (*0-88946-337-9*) E Mellen.

***Connell, Richard J.** From Observables to Unobservables in Science & Philosophy. 248p. 2000. 64.00 (*0-7618-1663-1*); pap. 37.50 (*0-7618-1664-X*) U Pr of Amer.

Connell, Richard J. Nature's Causes. LC 94-22404. (Revisioning Philosophy Ser.: Vol. 21). XX, 324p. (C). 1995. text 61.95 (*0-8204-2597-4*) P Lang Pubng.

— Substance & Modern Science. LC 87-73319. 280p. 1988. pap. 16.95 (*0-685-31940-7*) Ctr Thomistic.

— Substance & Modern Science. LC 87-73319. 1988. pap. text 19.50 (*0-268-01732-8*) U of Notre Dame Pr.

Connell, Robert Mac, see Naroola, Gurmeet & Mac Connell, Robert.

Connell, Roger. Measuring Customer & Service Profitability in the Finance Sector. (Illus.). 272p. 1996. mass mkt. 89.95 (*0-412-63180-6*) Chapman & Hall.

Connell, Royal W., jt. auth. see Mack, William P.

Connell Speck, Vicki, jt. auth. see Connell Brown, Susie.

Connell, Stan. How to Pronounce German Correctly: Beginning. (GER.). (C). 1991. 11.25 (*0-8442-2542-8*, X2542-8) NTC Contemp Pub Co.

Connell, Stanley. How to Pronounce Russian Correctly. (How to Pronounce...Ser.). (RUS.). 1995. pap. 21.95 incl. audio (*0-8442-4290-X*, 4290X, Passprt Bks) NTC Contemp Pub Co.

— How to Pronounce Spanish Correctly. (How to Pronounce...Ser.). (SPA.). 1995. pap. 19.95 incl. audio compact disk (*0-8442-7383-X*, 7383X, Passprt Bks) NTC Contemp Pub Co.

Connell, Stanley, et al. How to Pronounce German Correctly. (How to Pronounce...Ser.). (GER.). 1995. pap. 19.95 incl. audio compact disk (*0-8442-2507-X*, Natl Textbk Co) NTC Contemp Pub Co.

— How to Pronounce Japanese Correctly. (How to Pronounce...Ser.). (JPN.). 1995. pap. 19.95 incl. audio (*0-8442-8436-X*, Passprt Bks) NTC Contemp Pub Co.

Connell, Stanley W. How to Pronounce German Correctly. (How to Pronounce Ser.). (GER.). 64p. 1995. pap. 16.95 incl. audio (*0-8442-2541-X*, Passprt Bks) NTC Contemp Pub Co.

— How to Pronounce Italian Correctly. (How to Pronounce Ser.). (ITA.). (Orig.). 1995. pap. 16.95 incl. audio (*0-8442-8114-X*, 326409, Natl Textbk Co) NTC Contemp Pub Co.

Connell, Stanley W. & Poirell, Dominique. How to Pronounce French Correctly. (FRE.). 1989. pap. 16.95 incl. audio (*0-8442-1521-X*, Natl Textbk Co) NTC Contemp Pub Co.

Connell, Stanley W. & Poiriel, Doninique. How to Pronounce French Correctly. LC 98-13386. 1995. pap. 10.60 (*0-8442-1522-8*, Natl Textbk Co) NTC Contemp Pub Co.

Connell, Stanley W. & Rescigno, Federico. How to Pronounce Italian Correctly. 64p. (Orig.). 1994. pap. 10.60 (*0-8442-8112-3*, Natl Textbk Co) NTC Contemp Pub Co.

Connell, Stanley W., et al. How to Pronounce Spanish Correctly. (How to Pronounce...Ser.). (SPA.). 1995. pap. 16.95 incl. audio (*0-8442-7402-X*, 7402X, Passprt Bks) NTC Contemp Pub Co.

Connell, Stephen & Galbraith, Ian A. Electronic Mail: A Revolution in Business Communications. LC 82-44. (Professional Librarian Ser.). 141p. 1986. 35.00 (*0-86729-015-3*, Hall Reference); 25.00 (*0-86729-016-1*) Macmillan.

Connell, Susan. Exito en el Amor (Success at Love) (Deseo Ser.: No. 221). (SPA.). 1998. per. 3.50 (*0-373-35221-2*) Harlequin Bks.

— How to Succeed at Love. (Girls Most Likely To...Ser.). 1997. per. 3.50 (*0-373-76074-4*, 1-76074-3) Silhouette.

— Rebel's Spirit. 1996. per. 3.50 (*0-373-76044-2*, 1-76044-6) Silhouette.

— Reese: The Untamed. (Desire Ser.). 1996. per. 3.50 (*0-373-05981-7*, 1-05981-5) Silhouette.

— Tall, Dark & Temporary: The Girls Most Likely To . . . (Desire Ser.: No. 1120). 1998. per. 3.50 (*0-373-76120-1*, 1-76120-4) Silhouette.

Connell, Tim, jt. auth. see Kattan-Ibarra, Juan.

Connell, Tim, jt. auth. see Keble, Tony.

Connell, W. F. Reshaping Australian Education, 1960-1985. LC 99-458582. 1993. 175.00 (*0-86431-107-9*, Pub. by Aust Council Educ Res) St Mut.

***Connell, Will.** Prostate Cancer Treatment Options: A Guide to the Basics. LC 99-95100. (Illus.). xiv, 220p. 2000. pap. 19.95 (*0-9673892-1-6*) Edconco Pr.

***Connell, William & Zorzi, Andrea, eds.** Florentine Tuscany: Structures & Practices of Power. LC 99-33441. (Studies in Italian History & Culture). (Illus.). 404p. (C). 2000. 69.95 (*0-521-59111-2*) Cambridge U Pr.

Connell, William J., ed. Renaissance Essays II. (Library of the History of Ideas: Vol. 10). 383p. (C). 1993. 75.00 (*1-878822-23-3*, Pub. by Univ Rochester Pr); pap. 24.95 (*1-878822-28-4*, Pub. by Univ Rochester Pr) Boydell & Brewer.

***Connellan, Ian, et al.** Cycling Britain. (Cycling Guides Ser.). (Illus.). 352p. 2000. pap. 19.95 (*1-86450-037-9*) Lonely Planet.

Connellan, Leo. The Clear Blue Lobster-Water Country: A Trilogy. LC 84-12955. 160p. 1985. pap. 8.95 (*0-15-618054-5*, Harvest Bks) Harcourt.

— Crossing America. deluxe ed. (Illus.). 48p. 1976. 25.00 (*0-915778-11-4*) Penmaen Pr.

***Connellan, Leo.** Maine Poems. 132p. 1999. pap. 10.95 (*0-942396-83-9*) Blackberry ME.

Connellan, Leo. Massachusetts Poems. (Hollow Spring Poetry Ser.). 60p. (Orig.). 1981. pap. 6.95 (*0-685-02322-2*) Hollow Spring Pr.

— Provincetown & Other Poems. 77p. 1995. pap. 11.00 (*1-880684-29-2*) Curbstone.

— Shatterhouse. (Hollow Spring Poetry Ser.). (Illus.). 50p. (Orig.). 1983. pap. 6.95 (*0-936198-04-4*) Hollow Spring Pr.

— Short Poems, City Poems, 1944-1998. 64p. 1998. pap. text 10.00 (*1-887012-16-8*) Hanovr Pr.

Connellan, Thomas K. Getting Yours: Success Strategies for the 1980s. 244p. 1982. 12.95 (*0-8184-0330-6*) Carol Pub Group.

— How to Grow People into Self Starters. LC 80-65657. 238p. 1988. 34.95 (*0-936452-00-5*) Perf Pr MI.

Connellan, Thomas K. How to Improve Human Performance. (C). 1930. text. write for info. (*0-06-041349-2*) S&S Trade.

Connellan, Thomas K. Inside the Magic Kingdom: Seven Keys to Disney's Success. LC 97-780. 196p. 1997. 20.00 (*1-885167-23-7*) Bard Press.

Connellan, Thomas K., jt. auth. see Zemke, Ron.

Connellan, Tom, jt. auth. see Zemke, Ron.

Connelley, William E. The Founding of Harman's Station. (Illus.). iv, 177p. 1996. reprint ed. 22.50 (*0-7884-0522-5*, C565) Heritage Bk.

— John Brown. LC 71-164383. (Black Heritage Library Collection). 1977. reprint ed. 35.95 (*0-8369-8842-6*) Ayer.

— Quantrill & the Border Wars. (Illus.). 542p. (C). 1992. pap. 22.95 (*1-878882-04-X*) KS Heritage Pr.

Connelly. The French Revolution. 3rd ed. (C). Date not set. pap. 43.00 (*0-15-507866-6*, Pub. by Harcourt Coll Pubs) Harcourt.

— Management Skills for Clinical Supervisor. (Allied Health Ser.). 1998. pap. 31.50 (*0-8273-6154-8*) Delmar.

— Needs Assessmt & proj Plnn. 1999. pap. text 55.00 (*0-536-02353-0*) Pearson Custom.

— The Sundance Reader. (C). 1996. pap. text, teacher ed. write for info. (*0-15-503170-8*) Harcourt Coll Pubs.

— The Sundance Reader. 2nd ed. (C). 1999. pap. text 37.50 (*0-15-508052-0*, Pub. by Harcourt Coll Pubs) Harcourt.

— The Sundance Writer. (C). 1999. pap., teacher ed. 44.50 (*0-15-507343-5*) Harcourt.

— The Sundance Writer. (C). 1999. pap. text 46.00 (*0-15-507155-6*, Pub. by Harcourt Coll Pubs) Harcourt.

— Touch the Dragon: A Thai Journal. 205p. 1992. per. 10.95 (*0-88801-162-8*) LPC InBook.

Connelly, Bernardine. Follow the Drinking Gourd. LC 93-19247. (Illus.). (J). 1993. 14.95 (*0-88708-336-6*, Rabbit Ears); 19.95 incl. audio (*0-88708-335-8*, Rabbit Ears) Litle Simon.

— Follow the Drinking Gourd. LC 95-52467. (Rabbit Ears Ser.). (Illus.). 40p. (J). (gr. k-3). 1997. 22.00 incl. audio compact disk (*0-689-80242-0*) Macmillan.

Connelly, Berry. Annual Reports on the Progress of Chemistry Vol. 89: Inorganic. 1996. 72.00 (*0-85186-240-3*) CRC Pr.

Connelly, Bob, et al. Director Complete. 800p. 1997. 55.00 (*1-56830-348-3*) Hayden.

Connelly, Chris. Confessions of the Highest Bidder: Poems & Songwords, 1982-1996. LC 96-86156. 112p. 1999. 15.95 (*0-9664065-0-8*) K Blessing.

***Connelly, David, tr.** Carte Blanche: Selected Writings by Odysseus Elytis. (Greek Poetry Archives Ser.: Vol. 4). (Illus.). 96p. 1999. text 37.00 (*90-5755-100-4*, Harwood Acad Pubs) Gordon & Breach.

Connelly, David, tr. see Elytis, Odysseus.

Connelly, Dermot. A Book of Praises: A Workbook on the Psalms. 124p. (Orig.). 1987. pap. 7.95 (*0-86217-228-4*, Pub. by Veritas Pubns) St Mut.

Connelly, Diane M. All Sickness Is Homesickness. (Illus.). 167p. (Orig.). 1987. pap. 12.00 (*0-912379-02-2*) Ctr Traditional Acupuncture.

— All Sickness Is Homesickness. 2nd ed. (Illus.). (Orig.). 1993. reprint ed. pap. 16.00 (*0-912381-02-7*) Trad Acupuncture.

— Traditional Acupuncture: The Law of Five Elements. 3rd ed. (Illus.). 157p. pap. 12.00 (*0-912379-01-4*) Ctr Traditional Acupuncture.

Connelly, Dianne M. Traditional Acupuncture: The Law of Five Elements. 1994. pap. 16.00 (*0-912381-03-5*) Trad Acupuncture.

Connelly, Dixie, jt. auth. see Brown, Jacqueline M.

Connelly, Donald F. & Hamilton, William H. Small Business Planning & Management for the First-Time Entrepreneur. Stuts, Jacqueline A., ed. 160p. (Orig.). (C). 1996. pap. text, student ed., wbk. ed. 12.95 (*1-56502-012-X*, 8004W) Ohio Agri Educ.

Connelly, Donald F., jt. auth. see Hamilton, William H.

Connelly, Douglas. After Life: What the Bible Really Says. LC 95-22959. 180p. (Orig.). 1995. pap. 9.99 (*0-8308-1648-8*, 1648, Saltshaker Bk) InterVarsity.

— Angels. (LifeGuide Bible Studies). 64p. (Orig.). 1995. pap., wbk. ed. 4.99 (*0-8308-1074-9*, 1074) InterVarsity.

— Angels Around Us: What the Bible Really Says. LC 94-3574. 168p. (Orig.). 1994. pap. 9.99 (*0-8308-1695-X*, 1695) InterVarsity.

— Bible for Blockheads. LC 99-26110. 1999. pap. 17.99 (*0-310-22267-2*) Zondervan.

***Connelly, Douglas.** Daniel. (LifeGuide Bible Studies). 2000. pap. 4.99 (*0-8308-3031-6*) InterVarsity.

Connelly, Douglas. Daniel: Spiritual Living in a Secular World. (LifeGuide Bible Studies). 64p. (Orig.). 1986. pap., wbk. ed. 4.99 (*0-8308-1031-5*, 1031) InterVarsity.

***Connelly, Douglas.** Heaven: Finding Our True Home. (LifeGuide Bible Studies). 64p. 2000. pap. 4.99 (*0-8308-3051-0*) InterVarsity.

Connelly, Douglas. How Can I Pray When I'm Sick? 32p. 1999. pap. 0.99 (*0-87784-060-1*, 060) InterVarsity.

— John: The Way to True Life. (LifeGuide Bible Studies). 112p. (Orig.). 1990. pap., wbk. ed. 4.99 (*0-8308-1006-4*, 1006) InterVarsity.

— Mary: What the Bible Really Says. LC 97-49088. 132p. 1998. pap. 9.99 (*0-8308-1950-9*, 1950) InterVarsity.

— Meeting the Spirit. (LifeGuide Bible Studies). 64p. (Orig.). 1993. pap., wbk. ed. 4.99 (*0-8308-1068-4*, 1068) InterVarsity.

— Miracles: Signs of God's Glory. (Life Guide Bible Studies). 64p. 1999. pap. 4.99 (*0-8308-3087-1*, 3087) InterVarsity.

— Miracles: What the Bible Really Says. LC 96-43161. 168p. (Orig.). 1997. pap. 9.99 (*0-8308-1959-2*, 1959) InterVarsity.

***Connelly, Douglas.** Promise of Heaven: Discovering Our Eternal Home. 128p. 2000. 11.99 (*0-8308-2231-3*) InterVarsity.

Connelly, Douglas & Connelly, Karen. Mary: The Lord's Servant. (LifeGuide Bible Studies). 64p. 1996. pap., wbk. ed. 4.99 (*0-8308-1078-1*, 1078) InterVarsity.

Connelly, Elizabeth Russell. Conduct Unbecoming: Hyperactivity, Attention Deficit & Disruptive Behavior Disorders. Nadelson, Carol C., ed. LC 98-3756. (Encyclopedia of Psychological Disorders Ser.). 1998. 22.95 (*0-7910-4895-0*) Chelsea Hse.

*__Connelly, Elizabeth Russell.__ John Winthrop. (Colonial Leaders Ser.). 2000. 18.95 (*0-7910-5965-0*) Chelsea Hse.

— John Winthrop. (Colonial Leaders Ser.). (Illus.). 2000. pap. 8.95 (*0-7910-6122-1*) Chelsea Hse.

Connelly, Elizabeth Russell & Connolly, Beth. Through a Glass Darkly: The Psychological Effects of Marijuana & Hashish. Nadelson, Carol C., ed. LC 98-34150. (Encyclopedia of Psychological Disorders Ser.). 1998. 22.95 (*0-7910-4897-7*) Chelsea Hse.

— A World Upside down & Backwards. Nadelson, Carol C., ed. LC 98-42892. (Encyclopedia of Psychological Disorders Ser.). (Illus.). 144p. (J). 1998. 22.95 (*0-7910-4894-2*) Chelsea Hse.

Connelly, F. Michael & Clandinin, D. Jean, eds. Shaping A Professional Identity: Stories of Educational Practice. LC 98-56525. 192p. 1999. pap. 23.95 (*0-8077-3848-4*); text 50.00 (*0-8077-3849-2*) Tchrs Coll.

Connelly, F. Michael & Clandinin, Jean D. Teachers As Curriculum Planners: Narratives of Experience. 240p. (C). 1988. text 32.95 (*0-8077-2907-8*); pap. text 18.95 (*0-8077-2906-X*) Tchrs Coll.

Connelly, F. Michael, jt. auth. see Clandinin, Jean D.

Connelly, F. Michael, jt. ed. see Clandinin, Jean D.

Connelly, Frances S. The Sleep of Reason: Primitivism in Modern European Art & Aesthetics. 176p. 1995. 40.00 (*0-271-01305-2*) Pa St U Pr.

— The Sleep of Reason: Primitivism in Modern European Art & Aesthetics, 1725-1907. LC 93-27552. (Illus.). 154p. 1995. 35.00 (*0-271-01105-X*) Pa St U Pr.

— The Sleep of Reason: Primitivism in Modern European Art & Aesthetics, 1725-1907. (Illus.). 176p. 1999. pap. 22.50 (*0-271-01827-5*) Pa St U Pr.

Connelly, Gwen. El Alfabeto: A Child's Introduction to the Letters & Sounds of Spanish. (SPA.). 40p. (J). (gr. 1-6). 1990. 7.95 (*0-8442-7564-6*, 75646, Passprt Bks) NTC Contemp Pub Co.

Connelly, Gwen, jt. illus. see Ross, Kathy.

Connelly, J. A., jt. auth. see Motchenbacher, C. D.

Connelly, J. E., jt. ed. see White, K. L.

Connelly, J. J., jt. auth. see Weymer, H. J.

Connelly, James & Smith, Graham. Politics & the Environment. LC 98-28002. 1999. write for info. (*0-415-15067-1*); pap. 25.99 (*0-415-15068-X*) Routledge.

Connelly, James T., ed. see Sorin, Edward.

Connelly, Jerry H. The Hungry Person's Guide to Weight Control. LC 68-19964. 104p. 1997. pap. 10.00 (*0-8059-4281-5*) Dorrance.

Connelly, Joan Finn, see Braden-Whartenby, Geri & Finn Connelly, Joan.

*__Connelly, Joe.__ Bringing Out the Dead. 336p. 1999. pap. 12.00 (*0-676-58971-5*, Vin) Random.

Connelly, Joe. Bringing Out the Dead. 1999. pap. 12.00 (*0-375-70029-3*) Vin Bks.

Connelly, Joel, jt. auth. see Andrus, Cecil.

*__Connelly, John.__ Captive University: The Sovietization of East German, Czech, & Polish Higher Education, 1945-1956. 448p. 2000. pap. 24.95 (*0-8078-4865-4*); lib. bdg. 55.00 (*0-8078-2555-7*) U of NC Pr.

Connelly, John P. You're Too Sweet. (J). (gr. 4-9). 1968. 9.95 (*0-8392-1173-2*) Astor-Honor.

*__Connelly, Karen.__ The Border Surrounds Us. 96p. 2001. pap. 14.95 (*0-7710-2245-X*) McCland & Stewart.

— Disorder of Love. 112p. 1997. pap. text 12.95 (*1-896356-11-7*, Pub. by Gutter Pr) Dist Art Pubs.

— The Lizard Cage. 2001. write for info. (*0-679-31022-3*) Random.

Connelly, Karen. One Room in a Castle: Letters from Spain, France & Greece. LC 96-112670. 432p. 1995. 24.95 (*0-88801-194-6*, Pub. by Turnstone Pr) Genl Dist Srvs.

— This Brighter Prison: A Book of Journeys. 112p. 1993. pap. 11.95 (*0-919626-63-7*, Pub. by Brick Bks) Genl Dist Srvs.

Connelly, Karen, jt. auth. see Connelly, Douglas.

Connelly, Kathy & Whittlesey, Marrieta. Dressage Insights: Excerpts from Experts. LC 94-36096. (Illus.). 200p. 1994. 28.95 (*0-939481-38-3*) Half Halt Pr.

Connelly, Kevin. Gardener's Guide to California Wildflowers. (Illus.). 146p. (Orig.). 1991. pap. text 12.95 (*0-9627781-0-9*) T Payne FW&NP.

— Month by Month in a Waterwise Garden. (Illus.). 80p. (Orig.). 1991. pap. 5.00 (*0-914421-01-8*) Hist Soc So CA.

— Month by Month in a Waterwise Garden. LC 93-61036. (Illus.). 68p. (Orig.). 1993. pap. 12.95 (*0-914421-11-5*) Hist Soc So CA.

Connelly, Laurette. Hand Me My Pink Furry Slipper. (Illus.). 116p. 1998. pap. 10.95 (*1-883294-70-3*) Masthof Pr.

Connelly, Laurette M. Where Are You? . . . Where Are You Going? & How Are You Going to Get There? 120p. Date not set. pap. 9.95 (*1-880976-10-2*) Brookshire Pubns.

Connelly, Luella. Bears, Bears, Everywhere, Vol. 3646. (Emergent Reader Bks.). 16p. 1994. pap. 2.75 (*0-916119-60-2*) Creat Teach Pr.

— Bears, Bears, Everywhere, Vol. 3689. (Emergent Reader Big Bks.). (Illus.). 16p. (J). (gr. k-2). 1995. pap. 12.98 (*1-57471-072-9*) Creat Teach Pr.

— Dinosaurs Dancing, Vol. 4356. Graves, Kimberlee, ed. (Fun & Fantasy Ser.). (Illus.). 16p. (J). (ps-1). 1997. pap. 2.75 (*1-57471-253-5*, 4356) Creat Teach Pr.

— Let's Measure It!, Vol. 3735. (Emergent Reader Bks.). (Illus.). 16p. (J). (gr. k-2). 1995. pap. 2.75 (*1-57471-006-0*) Creat Teach Pr.

— Let's Measure It!, Vol. 3978. (Emergent Reader Big Bks.). (Illus.). 16p. (J). (gr. k-2). 1996. pap. 12.98 (*1-57471-116-4*) Creat Teach Pr.

— Mr. Noisy Builds a House, Vol. 3909. Williams, Rozanne L., ed. (Social Studies Learn to Read Ser.). (Illus.). 8p. (J). (ps-2). 1996. pap. 1.75 (*1-57471-128-8*, 3909) Creat Teach Pr.

— Mr. Noisy Builds a House, Vol. 3966. Williams, Rozanne L., ed. (Social Studies Big Bks.). (Illus.). 8p. (J). (ps-2). 1997. pap. 8.98 (*1-57471-174-1*, 3966) Creat Teach Pr.

— She'll Be Coming Around the Mountain, Vol. 4361. Graves, Kimberlee, ed. (Fun & Fantasy Ser.). (Illus.). 16p. (J). (ps-1). 1997. pap. 2.49 (*1-57471-258-6*, 4361) Creat Teach Pr.

Connelly, Marc. The Traveler: Manuscript Edition. 1939. pap. 13.00 (*0-8222-1418-0*) Dramatists Play.

Connelly, Margaret D., jt. auth. see Brown, Ruth A.

Connelly, Marie K. Martin Scorsese: An Analysis of His Feature Films, with a Filmography of His Entire Directorial Career. LC 92-56636. (Illus.). 192p. 1993. lib. bdg. 31.50 (*0-89950-845-6*) McFarland & Co.

*__Connelly, Mark.__ Christmas: A Social History. 1999. 39.50 (*1-86064-446-5*, Pub. by I B T) St Martin.

— Christmas at the Movies. 2000. text 29.95 (*1-86064-397-3*) I B T.

Connelly, Mark. The McGraw-Hill Workbook. 480p. (C). 1994. pap., wbk. ed. 18.13 (*0-07-012498-1*) McGraw.

— The McGraw-Hill Workbook. 1994. pap. text, teacher ed. write for info. (*0-07-012499-X*) McGraw.

— Orwell & Gissing. LC 97-8499. (American University Studies: Vol. 185, No. IV). 126p. (C). 1997. text 30.95 (*0-8204-3330-6*) P Lang Pubng.

Connelly, Mark, jt. auth. see Simons, Judith.

Connelly, Mark T. The Response to Prostitution in the Progressive Era. LC 79-24038. x, 261p. 1980. 45.00 (*0-8078-1424-5*) U of NC Pr.

Connelly, Mary J., et al. Critical Games: Four Games to Help Develop Critical Perspectives on Economic & Social Development. Cummings, James, ed. 46p. (Orig.). 1994. 8.00 (*0-932288-90-1*) Ctr Intl Ed U of MA.

Connelly, Maureen. Given in Love: For Mothers Releasing a Baby for Adoption. Johnson, Joy, ed. (Illus.). 24p. (Orig.). 1989. pap. 3.25 (*1-56123-010-3*, GILC) Centering Corp.

*__Connelly, Megan.__ Smart Approach to Kids' Rooms: Planning, Designing, Decorating. LC 00-101554. (Smart Approach To... Ser.). (Illus.). 176p. 2000. pap. text 19.95 (*1-58011-027-4*) Creative Homeowner.

Connelly, Michael. Angels Flight. (Harry Bosch Novel Ser.). 480p. 2000. mass mkt. 7.99 (*0-446-60727-4*, Pub. by Warner Bks) Little.

— Angels Flight: A Harry Bosch Novel. LC 98-28507. 400p. (gr. 8). 1999. 25.00 (*0-316-15219-6*) Little.

— Angels Flight: A Harry Bosch Novel. large type ed. LC 99-10431. (Paperback Bestsellers Ser.). 595p. 1950. pap. 27.95 (*0-7862-1865-7*) Thorndike Pr.

— Angels Flight: A Harry Bosch Novel. large type ed. LC 99-10431. 651p. 1999. pap. 30.00 (*0-7862-1864-9*) Thorndike Pr.

Connelly, Michael. The Black Echo. 10th ed. LC 91-10870. 432p. 1993. pap. 799.00 (*0-312-95048-9*) St Martin.

Connelly, Michael. The Black Ice. LC 92-33500. 384p. 1994. mass mkt. 7.50 (*0-312-95281-3*) St Martin.

— The Black Ice. large type ed. 1994. 90.95 (*0-7862-9985-1*, G K Hall Lrg Type) Mac Lib Ref.

— The Black Ice. large type ed. 561p. 1993. lib. bdg. 17.95 (*0-7862-0041-3*) Thorndike Pr.

— Blood Work. large type ed. LC 98-29230. (Large Print Book Ser.). 1998. 26.95 (*1-56895-622-3*) Wheeler Pub.

— Blood Work. 528p. 1998. reprint ed. mass mkt. 7.50 (*0-446-60262-0*, Pub. by Warner Bks) Little.

Connelly, Michael. The Concrete Blonde. LC 93-11802. 397p. 1995. mass mkt. 7.50 (*0-312-95500-6*) St Martin.

Connelly, Michael. The Concrete Blonde. large type ed. LC 94-31287. (Americana Series). 648p. 1995. 23.95 (*0-7862-0342-0*) Thorndike Pr.

*__Connelly, Michael.__ Darkness More Than Night. 2000. 25.95 (*0-316-15405-9*) Little.

— A Darkness More Than Night: A Novel. 400p. 2001. 25.95 (*0-316-15407-5*) Little.

Connelly, Michael. The Last Coyote. large type ed. (Large Print Bks.). 1995. pap. 23.95 (*1-56895-272-4*) Wheeler Pub.

— The Last Coyote, Vol. 1. 5th ed. LC 94-37437. Vol. 1. 416p. 1996. mass mkt. 7.99 (*0-312-95845-5*) St Martin.

— The Poet. 1996. 22.95 (*0-614-15483-9*) Little.

— The Poet. large type ed. LC 96-16366. 1996. 25.95 (*1-56895-330-5*, Compass) Wheeler Pub.

— The Poet. 512p. 1997. reprint ed. mass mkt. 7.99 (*0-446-60261-2*, Pub. by Warner Bks) Little.

— Trunk Music. 2002. 27.50 (*0-316-15391-5*) Little.

— Trunk Music. LC 96-18988. 438p. 1998. mass mkt. 6.99 (*0-312-96329-7*) St Martin.

— Trunk Music. large type ed. LC 97-2945. 1997. 26.95 (*1-56895-440-9*, Compass) Wheeler Pub.

— 26 Miles to Boston: The Boston Marathon Experience from Hopkins to Copley Square. LC 97-76269. (Illus.). 224p. 1998. 29.95 (*0-940160-78-1*) Parnassus Imprints.

Connelly, Michael. Void Moon. LC 99-37054. 400p. 1999. 24.95 (*0-316-15406-7*); pap. write for info. (*0-316-15232-3*) Little.

*__Connelly, Michael.__ Void Moon. LC 99-36462. 2000. 25.00 (*0-375-40862-2*) Random Hse Lrg Prnt.

— Void Moon. 480p. 2001. mass mkt. 7.99 (*0-446-60914-5*, Warner Vision) Warner Bks.

Connelly, Michael & Sims, Jean. Time & Space: A Basic Reader. 2nd ed. 224p. (C). 1990. pap. text 31.40 (*0-13-922014-3*) P-H.

Connelly, Naomi, ed. Stress at Work in the Social Services. 1995. pap. 40.00 (*1-899942-04-1*, Pub. by Natl Inst Soc Work) St Mut.

— Training Social Services Staff: Evidence from New Research. 1996. pap. 25.00 (*1-899942-12-2*) Natl Inst Soc Work.

Connelly, Naomi & Stubbs, Paul. Trends in Social Work & Social Work Educations Across Europe. 1996. pap. 23.00 (*1-899942-16-5*, Pub. by Natl Inst Soc Work) St Mut.

Connelly, Naomi, jt. ed. see Ballech, Susan.

Connelly, Neil Roy, jt. auth. see Silverman, David G.

Connelly, Owen. Blundering to Glory: Napoleon's Military Campaigns. rev. ed. 260p. 1999. 55.00 (*0-8420-2779-3*) Scholarly Res Inc.

— Blundering to Glory: Napoleon's Military Campaigns. rev. ed. LC 98-50626. 260p. 1999. pap. 18.95 (*0-8420-2780-7*) Scholarly Res Inc.

— The Epoch of Napoleon. LC 77-13473. 208p. 1977. reprint ed. pap. text 11.50 (*0-88275-622-2*) Krieger.

— The French Revolution & Napoleonic Era. 2nd ed. (Illus.). 416p. (C). 1991. pap. text 36.50 (*0-03-053329-5*, Pub. by Harcourt Coll Pubs) Harcourt.

— Napoleon's Satellite Kingdoms: Managing Conquered Peoples. 400p. (C). 1990. reprint ed. 21.50 (*0-89464-416-5*) Krieger.

Connelly, Owen, et al, eds. Historical Dictionary of Napoleonic France, 1799-1815. LC 83-22754. (Illus.). 586p. 1985. lib. bdg. 79.50 (*0-313-21321-6*, CNF/, Greenwood Pr) Greenwood.

Connelly, Owen & Hembree, Fred. The French Revolution. Eubank, Keith, ed. LC 92-30823. (European History Ser.). 176p. (C). 1993. pap. text 11.95 (*0-88295-898-4*) Harlan Davidson.

Connelly, Owen S., Jr. Leadership in War. 0.00 (*0-691-03186-X*) Princeton U Pr.

Connelly, Pat R., jt. auth. see Ladbury, John E.

Connelly, Pat R., jt. ed. see Ladbury, John E.

Connelly, Patrice, ed. see White, William.

Connelly, Paul. God's Dare. LC 94-166327. 80p. 1994. pap. 8.95 (*0-9639931-9-4*) Dawnstar Runelore.

— Practical Bakery. 342p. 1998. 44.95 (*0-470-25522-6*) Wiley.

Connelly, Richard D. & Grody, Mark S. Corporate Golf: How to Play the Game for Business Success. 192p. 1996. 19.95 (*0-9654995-2-9*) Mktg Golf Res.

Connelly, Rita, jt. auth. see Howell, Chris.

Connelly, Robert. Opportunities in Special Education Careers. LC 94-49079. (Opportunities In . . . Ser.). (Illus.). 160p. pap. 11.95 (*0-8442-4426-0*, 44260, VGM Career) NTC Contemp Pub Co.

— Opportunities in Special Education Careers. LC 94-49079. (Opportunities in...Ser.). (Illus.). 160p. 1995. 14.95 (*0-8442-4425-2*, 44252, VGM Career) NTC Contemp Pub Co.

— Opportunities in Technical Education Careers. LC 97-29001. (Opportunities in...Ser.). (Illus.). 160p. 1997. 14.95 (*0-8442-2310-7*, 23107, VGM Career) NTC Contemp Pub Co.

— Opportunities in Technical Education Careers. LC 97-29001. (Opportunities in... Ser.). 160p. 1998. pap. 11.95 (*0-8442-2311-5*, 23115) NTC Contemp Pub Co.

Connelly, Robert B. The Silents: Silent Feature Films, 1910-36. 2nd annot. rev. ed. LC 98-73041. Orig. Title: Motion Picture Guide, Vol. 10. 448p. 1998. pap. 49.50 (*0-913204-36-6*) December Pr.

Connelly, T. Garth. PT Boats in Action. LC 94-213847. (Warships in Action Ser.). (Illus.). 50p. 1994. pap. 9.95 (*0-89747-312-4*) Squad Sig Pubns.

*__Connelly, T. Garth.__ Vosper MTBs in Action. (Warships in Action Ser.: Vol. 13). (Illus.). 50p. 2000. pap. 9.95 (*0-89747-412-0*) Squad Sig Pubns.

Connelly, T. S. CINCOM-2000: Courses in Communications. LC 90-85811. 100p. 1999. spiral bd. 40.00 (*0-934339-77-5*, 2000) Comm Lib.

Connelly, Theodore S., ed. BCTV: Bibliography on Cable Television - 1993. LC 90-85810. 100p. (Orig.). 1993. pap. 40.00 (*0-934339-19-8*) Comm Lib.

— BCTV: Bibliography on Cable Television 1975-1992 - Eleven Thousand References. LC 90-85810. 1300p. (Orig.). 1993. pap. 600.00 (*0-934339-21-X*, 19751992) Comm Lib.

*__Connelly, Theodore S., ed.__ BCTV Bibliography on Cable Television - 1998. 23rd ed. LC 90-8510. 100p. 2000. 40.00 (*0-934339-24-4*) Comm Lib.

Connelly, Theodore S., ed. see Communications Library Staff.

Connelly, Thomas G., et al, eds. Morphogenesis & Pattern Formation. fac. ed. LC 80-5538. (Illus.). 312p. pap. 96.80 (*0-7837-7358-7*, 204716700005) Bks Demand.

Connelly, Thomas L. Army of the Heartland: The Army of Tennessee, 1861-1862. LC 67-21373. (Illus.). xvi, 306p. 1967. 29.95 (*0-8071-0404-3*) La State U Pr.

— Autumn of Glory: The Army of Tennessee, 1862-1865. LC 70-122353. (Illus.). x, 558p. 1971. 34.95 (*0-8071-0445-0*) La State U Pr.

— Civil War Tennessee: Battles & Leaders. LC 79-14885. (Tennessee Three Star Ser.). (Illus.). 114p. 1979. pap. 7.00 (*0-87049-261-6*) U of Tenn Pr.

— Marble Man: Robert E. Lee & His Image in American Society. LC 76-41778. 272p. 1978. pap. 14.95 (*0-8071-0474-4*) La State U Pr.

Connelly, Thomas L. & Bellows, Barbara L. God & General Longstreet: The Lost Cause & the Southern Mind. LC 82-33. 158p. 1995. pap. 12.95 (*0-8071-2014-6*) La State U Pr.

Connelly, Thomas L. & Jones, Archer. Politics of Command: Factions & Ideas in Confederate Strategy. LC 99-160634. (Illus.). 256p. 1998. pap. 14.95 (*0-8071-2349-8*) La State U Pr.

Connelly, Thomas L., et al. A Southern Renascence Man: Views of Robert Penn Warren. fac. ed. Edgar, Walter B., ed. LC 83-14922. (Southern Literary Studies). 132p. 1984. reprint ed. pap. 41.00 (*0-7837-7769-8*, 204752500007) Bks Demand.

Connelly, Thomas L., jt. auth. see McDonough, James L.

Connelly, Vincent, jt. auth. see Ricciotti, Hope.

Connelly, William E., jt. auth. see Root, Frank A.

Connelly, William F., Jr. & Pitney, John J., Jr. Congress' Permanent Minority? The Republicans in the U. S. House. 196p. (C). 1994. pap. text 16.95 (*0-8226-3032-X*); lib. bdg. 44.50 (*0-8476-7923-3*) Rowman.

*__Connely, Carrie.__ Like a Shoe That Pinches: How I Found Serenity Through the 12-Step Program of Emotions Anonymous. LC 99-63060. 70p. 1999. pap. 5.50 (*1-884778-66-6*) Old Mountain.

Connely, John. C Through Objects. 580p. (C). 1996. pap. text 50.54 (*1-881991-49-0*) Scott Jones Pubng.

Connely, Willard. Brawny Wycherley, First Master in English Modern Comedy. (BCL1-PR English Literature Ser.). 352p. 1992. reprint ed. lib. bdg. 89.00 (*0-7812-7419-2*) Rprt Serv.

Conner. Andre Gides Politics text 49.95 (*0-312-22708-6*) St Martin.

Conner & Huguley. The Auburn Experience. 3rd ed. 224p. (C). 1997. per. 22.95 (*0-7872-4205-5*) Kendall-Hunt.

— The Auburn Experience. 4th ed. 216p. (C). 1998. per. 27.95 (*0-7872-5149-6*, 41514901) Kendall-Hunt.

Conner, Alvin E. Sectarian Childrearing: The Dunkers, 1708-1900. (Illus.). 259p. 1987. 19.95 (*0-943429-00-5*) Brethren Heritage Pr.

*__Conner, Bobbi.__ The Book of Birthday Letters. LC 00-36261. (Illus.). 144p. 2000. pap. 10.95 (*0-7407-0994-1*) Andrews & McMeel.

— Everyday Opportunities for Extraordinary Parenting: Simple Ways to Make a Difference in Your Child's Life. LC 00-44042. 2000. write for info. (*1-57071-625-0*) Sourcebks.

*__Conner, Bobby.__ Shepherd's Rod 2000: A Prophetic Perspective as the Church Stands at the Gateway to the New Millenium. 72p. 1999. 9.99 (*1-929097-03-4*) Windmill Pubns.

Conner, Brook. Object Oriented Programming in Java. (C). 1998. pap. text. write for info. (*0-201-87013-4*) Addison-Wesley.

Conner, Bud. Great White Sturgeon Fishing. (Illus.). 72p. 1996. pap. 14.95 (*1-57188-067-4*) F Amato Pubns.

Conner, C. C., jt. auth. see Groover, David.

Conner, Catherine. From My Old Kentucky Home to the White House: The Political Journey of Catherine Conner. LC 98-49706. (Illus.). 192p. 1999. 24.00 (*0-8131-2102-7*) U Pr of Ky.

Conner, Claude C. Nothing Friendly in the Vicinity: My Patrols on the Submarine USS Guardfish in World War II. LC 99-63652. (Illus.). 240p. 1999. 24.95 (*1-882810-41-4*) Savas Pub.

Conner, Clifford D. Colonel Despard: The Life & Times of an Anglo-Irish Rebel. LC 99-58744. 1999. 29.95 (*1-58097-026-5*) Combined Pub.

— Jean Paul Marat: Scientist & Revolutionary LC 98-55993. 1999. 54.95 (*1-57392-607-8*, Humanity Bks) Prometheus Bks.

— Jean Paul Marat: Scientist & Revolutionary. LC 96-23026. (Revolutionary Studies). (Illus.). 268p. (C). 1997. text 55.00 (*0-391-03997-0*) Humanities.

Conner, Clint. Cures from the Counselor. 288p. 1995. mass mkt. 5.99 (*0-88368-349-0*) Whitaker Hse.

Conner, Cynthia, ed. see Aspen Health Law Center Staff.

*__Conner, Daniel & Miller, Lorraine.__ Master Mariner: Captain James Cook & the Peoples of the Pacific. 176p. 1999. pap. 18.95 (*1-55054-723-2*) DGL InfoWrite.

Conner, Darryl R., jt. auth. see Harrington, H. James.

Conner, Daryl, jt. ed. see Hughes, K. Scott.

Conner, Daryl R. Leading. LC 98-24357. 368p. 1998. 24.95 (*0-471-29557-4*) Wiley.

— Managing at the Speed of Change: Guidelines for Resilience in Turbulent Times. LC 92-20753. 1993. 24.95 (*0-679-40684-0*) Villard Books.

*__Conner, Deborah.__ The Auburn Experience. 5th ed. 210p. (C). 1999. per. 27.95 (*0-7872-6323-0*, 41632301) Kendall-Hunt.

Conner, Deborah & Huguley, Wendi. The Auburn Experience. 224p. (C). 1996. pap. text, per. 21.99 (*0-7872-2799-4*) Kendall-Hunt.

Conner, Dennis. Art of Winning, Vol. 1. 1990. mass mkt. 4.95 (*0-312-92098-9*) St Martin.

Conner, Dennis & Claflin, Edward. The Art of Winning. 212p. 1998. reprint ed. text 18.00 (*0-7881-5818-X*) DIANE Pub.

Conner, Dennis & Levitt, Michael. The America's Cup: The History of Sailing's Greatest Competition in the Twentieth Century. LC 98-12299. 320p. 1998. text 29.95 (*0-312-18567-7*) St Martin.

— Learn to Sail. 2nd ed. (Illus.). 256p. 1994. text 22.95 (*0-312-11020-0*) St Martin.

— Sail Like a Champion: Advanced Racing & Cruising Techniques. (Illus.). 416p. 1992. text 40.00 (*0-312-07078-0*) St Martin.

Conner, Dennis J. & Bueso, Alberto T. Managerial Finance: Theory & Techniques. (Illus.). 320p. 1981. text 54.70 (*0-13-550269-1*) P-H.

Conner, Diane, jt. auth. see Conner, Steve.

Conner, Donna B., ed. A Potpourri of Physics Teaching Ideas. (Illus.). 363p. (Orig.). 1987. spiral bd. 34.00 (*0-917853-27-X*, OP-57) Am Assn Physics.

Conner, Douglas, ed. see Sherman, Alana.

Conner, Douglas A., ed. see Saleh, Dennis.

Conner, Douglas L. & Marszalek, John F. A Black Physician's Story: Bringing Hope in Mississippi. LC 85-9106. (Illus.). 197p. reprint ed. pap. 61.10 (*0-8357-4339-X*, 203714100007) Bks Demand.

Conner, E., jt. auth. see Research & Education Association Staff.

Conner, Floyd. Fore! More Great Moments & Dubious Achievements in Golf History. 208p. 1996. pap. 6.95 (*0-8118-1138-7*) Chronicle Bks.

— Golf! Great Moments & Dubious Achievements in Golf History. 208p. (Orig.). 1992. pap. 6.95 (*0-8118-0128-4*) Chronicle Bks.

— Pretty Poison: The Tuesday Weld Story. LC 95-22145. 256p. 1995. 22.00 (*1-56980-015-4*) Barricade Bks.

Conner, Floyd & Snyder, John. The Cincinnati Reds. LC 85-90352. (Illus.). 1997. 32.00 (*0-88014-079-8*) Mosaic Pr OH.

Conner, Francis P. Letting Go: The Grief Experience. unabridged ed. 126p. 1996. pap. text 16.00 (*0-9656373-0-1*) AUM Prods.

Conner, Frank. AutoCAD Student Workbook & Instructor's Guide. 200p. 1992. 175.00 (*1-56205-024-9*) New Riders Pub.

Conner, Frederick. Cosmic Optimism: A Study of the Interpretation of Evolution. (BCL1-PS American Literature Ser.). 458p. 1993. reprint ed. lib. bdg. 99.00 (*0-7812-6584-3*) Rprt Serv.

Conner, Gary B. High-Involvement Training: How to Set up ISO-Complaint In-House Training Programs. Nickel, Amy J., ed. (Illus.). 131p. (C). 1994. pap. 44.00 (*1-881113-08-6*) Croydon Grp.

Conner, Gertrude V. Those Early Years. (Illus.). 48p. 1999. 24.95 (*1-885983-42-5*) Turtle Point Pr.

Conner, Harold W. Residential Concrete. 3rd ed. LC 98-43157. 1998. write for info. (*0-86718-450-7*) Home Builder.

Conner, Ivy. Is It a Sin to Be Rich? Is It a Sin to Be Poor? LC 89-64296. (Illus.). 80p. 1990. pap. text 9.95 (*1-878579-01-0*) SUN Pub Co.

— Revelation Revealed: Simple Studies in Revelation for Simple Students by a Simple Teacher. 96p. (Orig.). 1991. pap. text 7.95 (*1-878579-04-5*) SUN Pub Co.

— Revelation Revealed Workbook: Simple Studies in Revelation for Simple Students by a Simple Teacher. 24p. (Orig.). 1991. pap. text 4.95 (*1-878579-05-3*) SUN Pub Co.

— A Study of the Holy Spirit. 70p. 1998. pap. text 15.00 (*1-878579-12-6*) SUN Pub Co.

***Conner, Ivy.** Success Sparklers: A Treasury of Quips, Quotes & Sparkling Sayings for the Positive Person. 3rd rev. ed. 160p. 2000. pap. 10.95 (*1-878579-13-4*) SUN Pub Co.

Conner, Ivy, compiled by. Mighty Mini Success Sparklers: Education - Excellence - Einstein. 16p. (Orig.). 1997. pap. text 3.00 (*1-878579-11-8*) SUN Pub Co.

— Mighty Mini Success Sparklers: Goals - Success. 16p. (Orig.). 1997. pap. text 3.00 (*1-878579-10-X*) SUN Pub Co.

Conner, Ivy, ed. Book of Revelation Illustrations. (Illus.). 25p. (Orig.). 1997. pap. text 10.00 (*1-878579-09-6*) SUN Pub Co.

Conner, J. Married in Friendship. 1990. pap. 30.00 (*0-7220-5264-2*) St Mut.

Conner, J. Richard & Loehman, Edna, eds. Economics & Decision Making for Environmental Quality. LC 74-6056. (Illus.). 309p. reprint ed. pap. 95.80 (*0-7837-5097-8*, 204479600004) Bks Demand.

Conner, Jacob Elon. Christ Was Not a Jew: An Epistle to the Gentiles. 189p. 1997. pap. 5.00 (*0-944379-19-2*) CPA Bk Pub.

Conner, Jamie, jt. auth. see Kashiwagi, Dean T.

Conner, Janis C. A Dancer in Relief: Works by Malvina Hoffman. (Illus.). 40p. (Orig.). 1984. pap. 2.00 (*0-943651-15-8*) Hudson Riv.

Conner, Jeff. The Crow: The Movie. Amara, Philip & Eastman, Michael, eds. LC 96-130166. (Illus.). 112p. 1994. pap. 18.95 (*0-87816-285-2*) Kitchen Sink.

— The Crow - City of Angels: A Diary of the Film. Boyd, Robert, ed. LC 96-21434. (Illus.). 128p. (Orig.). 1996. pap. 15.95 (*0-87816-478-2*) Kitchen Sink.

Conner, Jesse R. Chemical Fixation & Solidification. 784p. (gr. 13). 1989. text 121.95 (*0-442-20511-2*) Chapman & Hall.

***Conner, Joan.** We Who Live Apart: Stories. 152p. 2000. pap. 17.95 (*0-8262-1293-X*) U of Mo Pr.

Conner, John & Folts, Cathy. Breaking the Spanish Barrier. (SPA.). 329p. 1997. pap. text 29.50 (*1-57790-401-X*) Book Tech.

— Breaking the Spanish Barrier. (SPA.). 374p. 1997. pap. text 29.50 (*1-57790-522-9*) Book Tech.

Conner, Jud. Alligators Don't Eat Yankees: And Other Fantasies for Yankees & Southerners Alike. (Illus.). 104p. (Orig.). 1996. pap. write for info. (*0-9643659-1-X*) Watermarks.

— Alligators Don't Eat Yankees: And Other Fantasies for Yankees & Southerners Alike. 2nd ed. (Orig.). 1997. reprint ed. pap. 9.95 (*0-9643659-3-6*) Watermarks.

***Conner, Jud.** Southern Yankees & the One-Eyed Alligator. (Illus.). 132p. 2000. pap. 9.95 (*0-941072-36-3*) Southern Herit.

Conner, Judson J. Vermont from A to Z. (Illus.). 48p. (Orig.). 1990. pap. 4.95 (*0-933050-79-8*) New Eng Pr VT.

Conner, Karen A. Aging America: Issues Facing An Aging Society. 240p. (C). 1991. pap. text 25.60 (*0-13-019621-5*) P-H.

***Conner, Karen Ann.** Continuing to Care: Older Americans & Their Families in the 21st Century LC 99-37922. (Garland Reference Library of Social Science). 1999. write for info. (*0-8153-2889-3*) Garland.

Conner, Ken & Heimerdinger, Debra. Horace Bristol: An American View. (Illus.). 144p. 1996. 60.00 (*0-8118-1262-6*) Chronicle Bks.

Conner, Kevin, jt. auth. see Malmin, Ken.

Conner, Kevin J. The Book of Acts. 2nd rev. ed. 176p. 1995. pap. 12.99 (*1-886849-02-1*) City Bible Pub.

— Church in the New Testament. 315p. 1982. pap. 21.99 (*1-886849-15-3*) City Bible Pub.

— The Epistle to the Romans: A Commentary. 409p. 1998. 27.95 (*1-886849-13-7*) City Bible Pub.

— The Epistle to the Romans: A Commentary. 409p. 1999. pap. 21.99 (*1-886849-65-X*) City Bible Pub.

— Feasts of Israel. (Illus.). 111p. (C). 1980. pap. 12.99 (*0-914936-42-5*) City Bible Pub.

— Foundations of Christian Doctrine. 309p. 1979. pap. 21.99 (*0-914936-38-7*) City Bible Pub.

— Interpreting the Book of Revelation. 203p. 1995. pap. 14.99 (*0-914936-10-7*) City Bible Pub.

— Interpreting the Symbols & Types. 2nd rev. ed. 200p. 1992. pap. 11.99 (*0-914936-51-4*) City Bible Pub.

— Mystery Parables of the Kingdom. 341p. 1998. pap. 24.99 (*0-949829-29-3*) City Bible Pub.

— Tabernacle of David. rev. ed. (Illus.). 270p. 1993. pap. 14.99 (*0-914936-94-8*) City Bible Pub.

— Tabernacle of Moses. (Illus.). 119p. 1988. pap. 12.99 (*0-914936-93-X*) City Bible Pub.

— The Temple of Solomon. (Illus.). 251p. 1988. pap. 14.99 (*0-914936-96-4*) City Bible Pub.

Conner, Kevin J. & Malmin, Ken. The Covenants. 120p. 1983. pap. 12.99 (*0-914936-77-8*) City Bible Pub.

Conner, Kevin J. & Malmin, Kenneth P. Interpreting the Scriptures. 165p. 1983. pap. 12.99 (*0-914936-20-4*) City Bible Pub.

Conner, Kiersten & Krol, Ed. The Whole Internet: The Next Generation. LC 99-45755. 480p. 1999. pap. 24.95 (*1-56592-428-2*) OReilly & Assocs.

Conner, Lester I. A Yeat's Dictionary: Persons & Places in the Poetry of William Butler Yeats. LC 97-34458. (Irish Studies). 1998. 39.95 (*0-8156-2769-6*) Syracuse U Pr.

Conner, Lester I., ed. A Yeat's Dictionary: Persons & Places in the Poetry of William Butler Yeats. 232p. 1999. pap. 19.95 (*0-8156-2770-X*) Syracuse U Pr.

Conner, Linda H., jt. ed. see Rubinstein, Raechelle.

Conner, Lynne. Spreading the Gospel of the Modern Dance: Newspaper Dance Criticism in the United States, 1850-1934. LC 96-45868. (Illus.). 177p. 1997. pap. 17.95 (*0-8229-5617-9*); text 35.00 (*0-8229-3963-0*) U of Pittsburgh Pr.

***Conner, Marc C., ed.** The Aesthetics of Toni Morrison: Speaking the Unspeakable. LC 00-21405. 192p. 2000. pap. 18.00 (*1-57806-285-3*); lib. bdg. 45.00 (*1-57806-284-5*) U Pr of Miss.

Conner, Maura, ed. see Kee, Joyce L. & Hayes, Evelyn R.

Conner, Maura, ed. see Nasrawi, Christina & Allender, Judith.

Conner, Michael. Archangel. 416p. 1996. mass mkt. 6.99 (*0-8125-4321-1*, Pub. by Tor Bks) St Martin.

Conner, Michael D. Cypress Land: A Late Archaic-Early Woodland Site in the Lower Illinois River Floodplain. LC 86-21567. (Kampsville Archeological Center Technical Reports: No. 2). (Illus.). 79p. (Orig.). 1986. pap. 5.95 (*0-942118-23-5*) Ctr Amer Arche.

Conner, Michael D., ed. The Hill Creek Homestead & the Late Mississippian Settlement in the Lower Illinois Valley. LC 85-2642. (Kampsville Archeological Center Research Ser.: No. 1). (Illus.). 239p. (Orig.). 1985. pap. 9.95 (*0-942118-18-9*) Ctr Amer Arche.

Conner, Michael D., jt. ed. see Atwell, Karen A.

***Conner, Michelle.** A Day in Morning. 1000. 66p. (YA). (gr. 9 up). 2000. pap. 9.95 (*0-9671603-0-8*) Amanda Lees Pubs.

Conner, Miguel. The Queen of Darkness. 288p. (Orig.). 1998. mass mkt. 5.99 (*0-446-60506-9*, Pub. by Warner Bks) Little.

Conner, Miguel O. Stargazer. (Orig.). 1997. pap. write for info. (*0-614-19754-6*, Aspect) Warner Bks.

Conner, Nancy, jt. auth. see Stevens, Barbara.

Conner, Nikki. Cardboard Boxes. LC 96-12639. (Use Your Junk Ser.). (Illus.). 24p. (J). (ps-2). 1996. lib. bdg. 19.90 (*0-7613-0538-6*, Copper Beech Bks) Millbrook Pr.

— Plastic Cups. LC 96-12632. (Use Your Junk Ser.). (Illus.). 24p. (J). (ps-2). 1996. lib. bdg. 19.90 (*0-7613-0539-4*, Copper Beech Bks) Millbrook Pr.

Conner, P. E. The Neumann's Problem for Differential Forms on Riemannian Manifolds. LC 52-42839. (Memoirs Ser.: No. 1/20). 58p. 1990. reprint ed. pap. 17.00 (*0-8218-1220-3*, MEMO/1/20) Am Math.

Conner, P. E. & Hurrelbrink, J. Class Number Parity. (Pure Mathematics Ser.: Vol. 8). 248p. 1988. text 48.00 (*9971-5-0669-6*) World Scientific Pub.

Conner, Patrick. George Chinnery, 1744-1852. (Illus.). 320p. 1993. 89.50 (*1-85149-160-0*) Antique Collect.

Conner, Patrick W. Anglo-Saxon Exeter: A Tenth-Century Cultural History. (Studies in Anglo-Saxon History: No. IV). (Illus.). 292p. (C). 1993. 90.00 (*0-85115-307-0*) Boydell & Brewer.

Conner, Patrick W., ed. The Anglo-Saxon Chronicle 10: The Abingdon Chronicle AD 956-1066 (MS C with Ref. 6BDE) (Illus.). 138p. (C). 1996. 75.00 (*0-85991-466-6*) Boydell & Brewer.

Conner, Paul M., jt. auth. see Cole, Basil.

Conner, Paul W. Poor Richard's Politicks: Benjamin Franklin & His New American Order. LC 80-21490. 285p. 1980. reprint ed. lib. bdg. 65.00 (*0-313-22695-4*, COPRP, Greenwood Pr) Greenwood.

Conner, Pierre E. The Neumann's Problem for Differential Forms on Riemannian Manifolds. LC 52-42839. (American Mathematical Society Ser.: Vol. 20). (Illus.). 62p. reprint ed. pap. 30.00 (*0-608-09601-6*, 205275900007) Bks Demand.

Conner, Pierre E. & Floyd, E. E. Torsion in SU-Bordism. LC 52-42839. (Memoirs Ser.: No. 1/60). 72p. 1969. reprint ed. pap. 17.00 (*0-8218-1260-2*, MEMO/1/60) Am Math.

Conner, Rachel. Jingle Bells Board Book. LC 95-133280. (Musical Board Bk.). 12p. (J). (ps up). 1994. 5.95 (*0-694-00656-4*, HarpFestival) HarpC Child Bks.

***Conner, Randall C., et al.** Pipeline Safety, Reliability & Rehabilitation: Proceedings of the Group of ASCE Technical Sessions at the 1999 American Public Works Association International Public Works Congress & Exposition, September 19-22. 1999, Denver, Colorado. LC 99-26671. 320p. 1999. pap. 40.00 (*0-7844-0452-6*) Am Soc Civil Eng.

Conner, Randy P., et al. Cassell's Encyclopedia of Queer Myth, Symbol, & Spirit: Gay, Lesbian, Bisexual, & Transgender Lore. LC 98-20180. 400p. 1998. pap. 15.95 (*0-304-70423-7*) Continuum.

Conner, Richard N., jt. ed. see Kulhavy, David L.

Conner, Rick. Harley-Davidson Data Book. LC 96-51113. (Data Bks.). (Illus.). 160p. 1996. pap. 15.95 (*0-7603-0226-X*) MBI Pubg.

Conner, Robert B. & Foster, Ruel. Buck: A Life Sketch of James H. Harless. (Illus.). 166p. 1992. 15.00 (*0-937058-30-0*) West Va U Pr.

Conner, Robert P., jt. auth. see Abedin, Zainul.

Conner, Roger & Burns, Patrick. The Winnable War: A Community Guide to Eradicating Street Drug Markets. (Illus.). 105p. (Orig.). 1991. pap. 12.50 (*0-9633620-0-3*) Am Alliance R & R.

Conner, Ross F. & Huff, C. Ronald. Attorneys As Activists: Evaluating the American Bar Association's BASICS Program. LC 79-19830. (Contemporary Evaluation Research Ser.: Vol. 1). 264p. reprint ed. pap. 81.90 (*0-8357-5869-9*, 202187800026) Bks Demand.

Conner, Steve & Conner, Diane. Programmer's Guide to the NCP (Netware Core Protocol) 650p. 1996. mass mkt. 49.95 (*0-929392-31-0*) Annabooks.

Conner, Susan & Uszler, Marienne, eds. The American Music Teacher. 84p. (Orig.). 1.50 (*0-318-17133-3*) Music Tchrs.

Conner, Susan L. & Freeman, Lloyd A. Drinking Water Quality: Taking Responsibility. LC 97-91387. (Illus.). 62p. 1998. pap. 16.95 (*0-9662520-9-8*) Waterwrks Pub.

***Conner, Susan L. & Freeman, Lloyd A.** Drinking Water Quality - Taking Responsibility Coloring Book. (Illus.). 36p. (J). (gr. k-12). 2000. pap. 4.95 (*0-9662520-2-0*) Waterwrks Pub.

Conner, T. Doctrina Cristiana. Robleto, Adolfo, tr.Tr. of Christian Doctrine. (SPA.). 408p. 1962. reprint ed. pap. 16.50 (*0-311-09012-5*) Casa Bautista.

Conner, Thomas, Jr. & Skinner, Robert E., eds. Above Ground: Stories about Life & Death by New Southern Writers. (Occasional Publications: No. 1). (Illus.). 200p. (Orig.). 1993. pap. 11.95 (*1-883275-00-8*) Xavier Rev.

Conner, Thomas L. & Fisek, M. Hamit. Expectation States Theory: A Theoretical Research Program. Berger, Joseph et al, eds. LC 81-40887. 256p. 1982. reprint ed. pap. text 24.50 (*0-8191-1999-7*) U Pr of Amer.

Conner, Tom. Chateaubriand's Memoires D'Outre-tombe: A Portrait of the Artist as Exile. LC 93-22139. (Age of Revolution & Romanticism Ser.: Vol. 7). XVIII, 180p. (C). 1995. text 55.95 (*0-8204-2232-0*) P Lang Pubng.

— Remember When, Pt. II. Nobels, Virginia, ed. (Illus.). 120p. (Orig.). 1993. pap. 9.95 (*1-882616-04-9*) Advertiser.

Conner, Valerie J. The National War Labor Board: Stability, Social Justice, & the Voluntary State in World War I. LC 82-13362. (Supplementary Volumes to the Papers of Woodrow Wilson). 247p. reprint ed. pap. 76.60 (*0-7837-2464-0*, 204261700005) Bks Demand.

Conner, W. T. The Teachings of "Pastor" Russell. 68p. 1988. reprint ed. pap. 2.95 (*1-883858-42-9*) Witness CA.

Conner, Walter T. Christian Doctrine. 1998. pap. text 24.99 (*0-8054-1859-8*) Broadman.

Conner, Wendy S. The "After 8" Elegant Beaded Jewelry Book: Techniques for Beadlovers. LC 97-93595. (Beading Books Ser.: Vol. 10). (Illus.). 52p. 1997. pap. 11.95 (*1-889599-01-8*) Interstell Pub.

Beads have been around since the beginning of time. Man's link with beads - prayer, spiritual & adornment - transcends culture & continent. This documentary explores this connection - showing history, contemporary aesthetics, how beads are made & the global impact beads have in our live. ***Publisher Paid Annotation.***

–The Cat Lover's Beaded Project Book: Techniques for Beadlovers. LC 97-93596. (Beading Books Ser.: Vol. 9). (Illus.). 52p. 1997. pap. 11.95 (*1-889599-00-X*) Interstell Pub.

Everyone loves cats, & cat jewelry is the hottest thing to come along in years! This fun book will keep you & your cat purring as you create a collection of necklaces, earrings, collars & more. You can make jewelry for yourself or your cat. Of course, it helps to have prehensile hands, but if your cat wants to try her paw at some of these projects, it's purrfectly okay! Be sure to look for the Beading Book Series: The Best Little Beading Book, The Beaded Lampshade Book, The Magical Beaded Medicine Bag Book, The "Knotty" Macrame & Beading Book, The Beaded Watchband Book, The Beaded Jewelry for a Wedding Book, The Children's Beading Book, The Chain & Crystal Book, The Cat Lover's Beaded Project Book, The Wirebending Book, The Beading on Fabric Book, and more soon to come! Many of these books are available in kit form, also. There is also a wonderful documentary which complements the series. The Bead Movement is a beautiful program which chronicles man's oldest artform, beads. It is available in 60 minutes, or a 30 min. director's cut. For information or ordering, contact The Intestellar Trading & Publishing Company, Post Office Box 2215, LaMesa, CA 91943; (858) 452-8181 or 292-8191, Order Dept. (800) 790-8730, Fax (858)452-0351 or 292-0373, email Interstlr@aol.com. Visit our website at www.interstellarpublishing.com. Available through Sunbelt Publications, Ingram Books, Baker & Taylor Books. ***Publisher Paid Annotation.***

Conner, Wendy Simpson. The Beaded Jewelry for a Wedding Book: Techniques for Beadlovers. LC 96-94611. (Beading Bks.). (Illus.). 52p. 1996. 11.95 (*0-9645957-5-3*) Interstell Pub.

Brides have a difficult time finding the perfect jewelry for their special day. This elegant book has many techniques on pearl knotting, basic stringing, working with chain, earrings, & more to ensure the perfect accessories for the bride & her wedding party. Included are special gifts to make for bridesmaids, & even a beautiful headpiece for the bride. This exciting book has so many ideas, that you'll want to make everything! Be sure to look for the other books in the series: The Best Little Beading Book, The Beaded Lampshade Book, The Magical Beaded Medicine Bag Book, The "Knotty" Macrame & Beading Book, The Beaded Watchband Book, The Beaded Jewelry for a Wedding Book, The Children's Beading Book, The Chain & Crystal Book, The Cat Lover's Beaded Project Book, The Wirebending Book, The Beading on Fabric Book, and more soon to come! Many of these books are available in kit form, also. There is also a wonderful documentary which complements the series. The Bead Movement is a beautiful program which chronicles man's oldest artform, beads. It is available in 60 minutes, or a 30 min. director's cut. For information or ordering, contact The Interstellar Trading & Publishing Company, Post Office Box 2215, La Mesa, CA 91943; (858) 452-8181 or 292-8191, Order Dept. (800) 790-8730, Fax (858) 452-0351 or 292-0373, email Interstlr@aol.com. Visit our website at www.interstellarpublishing.com. Available through Sunbelt Publications, Ingram Books, Baker & Taylor Books. ***Publisher Paid Annotation.***

–The Beaded Lampshade Book: Techniques for Beadlovers. LC 95-95201. (Beading Bks.). (Illus.). 52p. 1996. 11.95 (*0-9645957-1-0*) Interstell Pub.

Beadwork is one of the oldest & most global artforms. Considered one of the oldest styles of self-beautification, people have been adorning themselves with beads since prehistoric times. Today's beadwork is considered an exciting genre of art: many people are rediscovering the unlimited possibilities when it comes to beads. Beaded lampshades are very popular again. This beautiful book gives many different patterns & techniques for wonderful ways to dress up many styles of lamps. The easy-to-follow step-by-step diagrams & full-color photos make this a fun, exciting book! The author is a third-generation bead artist - her grandmother designed beaded gowns & jewelry for the Ziegfeld Follies. Wendy is the author of the immensely popular BEST LITTLE BEADING BOOK. Be sure to look for the other books in the series: THE MAGICAL BEADED MEDICINE BAG BOOK, THE "KNOTTY" MACRAME & BEADING BOOK, THE BEADED WATCHBAND BOOK, THE BEADED JEWELRY FOR A WEDDING BOOK, THE CHILDREN'S BEADING BOOK, THE CHAIN & CRYSTAL BOOK, THE CAT LOVER'S BEADING BOOK, THE WIREBENDING BOOK & more soon to come! Many of these books are available in kit form, also. For information or ordering, contact The Interstellar Trading & Publishing Company, Post Office Box 2215, La Mesa, CA 91943; (858) 452-8181 or 292-819, Order Dept. (800) 790-8730, Fax (858) 452-0351 or 292-0373, email: Interstlr@aol.com. Visit our website at www.interstellarpublishing.com. Available through: Sunbelt Publications, Ingram Books, Baker & Taylor Books. ***Publisher Paid Annotation.***

–The Beaded Watchband Book: Techniques for Beadlovers. LC 95-95204. (Beading Bks.). (Illus.). 52p. 1996. 11.95 (*0-9645957-3-7*) Interstell Pub.
A great member of the very popular Beading Books Series Tm, this how-to book on making your own beaded watchbands is as packed full of information as the other books in the series. This wonderful, informative book offers many patterns & a lot of inspiration for everyone. Beadlovers will delight in the variety of designs - there's a beaded watchband for everyone! The diagrams are very complete & easy to follow. This book is great for both beginners & pros...it makes you wish you owned more watches! The author is a third-generation bead artist, & knows her subject inside out. Be sure to look for the other books in the series: The Best Little Beading Book, The Beaded Lampshade Book, The Magical Beaded Medicine Bag Book, The "Knotty" Macrame & Beading Book, The Beaded Watchband Book, The Beaded Jewelry for a Wedding Book, The Children's Beading Book, The Chain & Crystal Book, The Cat Lover's Beaded Project Book, The Wirebending Book, The Beading on Fabric Book, and more soon to come! Many of these books are available in kit form, also. There is also a wonderful documentary which complements the series. The Bead Movement is a beautiful program which chronicles man's oldest artform, beads. It is available in 60 minutes, or a 30 min. director's cut. For information or ordering, contact The Interstellar Trading & Publishing Company, Post Office Box 2215, La Mesa, CA 91943; (858) 452-8181 or 292-8191, Order Dept. (800) 790-8730, Fax (858) 452-0351 or 292-0373, email Interstlr@aol.com. Visit our website at www.interstellarpublishing.com. Available through Sunbelt Publications, Ingram Books, Baker & Taylor Books. ***Publisher Paid Annotation.***

–The Best Little Beading Book: Techniques & More: A Practical Guide for Beadlovers. LC 95-94215. (Illus.). 280p. 1995. pap. 28.95 (*0-9645957-0-2*) Interstell Pub.
This complete how-to book is the "bible for beaders," considered the best on the market. Beadwork is one of the oldest artforms. Today's beadwork is considered an exciting genre of art: many are rediscovering the unlimited possibilities of beads. The author is a third-generation bead artist - her grandmother designed beaded gowns & jewelry for the Ziegfeld Follies. Many of these vintage techniques & designs are included. THE BEST LITTLE BEADING BOOK has thousands of illustrations, including step-by-step instructions for hundreds of projects, depicting beads, supplies & more. Chapters include: designing & creating jewelry; making beads with clay, glass, etc.; healing with gemstones; esoteric values & symbolism; starting a jewelry business; creating a portfolio; & lots more! The writing style & the diagrams are easy-to-understand. The photographs are beautiful, full-color celebrations of fabulous jewelry that the reader can very easily make. A must-have for beginners & pros. Look for the other books in the series: THE MAGICAL BEADED MEDICINE BAG BOOK, THE "KNOTTY" MACRAME & BEADING BOOK, THE BEADED WATCHBAND BOOK, THE BEADED JEWELRY FOR A WEDDING BOOK, THE CHILDREN'S BEADING BOOK, THE CHAIN & CRYSTAL BOOK, THE CAT LOVER'S BEADING BOOK & THE WIREBENDING BOOK. Many of these books are also in kits. For information or ordering, contact The Interstellar Trading & Publishing Company, P.O. Box 2215, La Mesa, CA 91943; (858) 452-818, Order Dept. (800) 790-8730, Fax (858) 452-0351 or 292-0373, email: Interstlr@aol.com. Visit our website at www.interstellarpublishing.com. Available through Sunbelt Publications, Ingram Books, Baker & Taylor Books. ***Publisher Paid Annotation.***

–The Chain & Crystal Book: Techniques for Beadlovers. (Beading Books Ser.: Vol. 6). (Illus.). 52p. 1997. pap. 11.95 (*0-9645957-7-X*) Interstell Pub.
Beadwork is one of the oldest & most global artforms. Considered one of the oldest styles of self-beautification, people have been adorning themselves with beads since prehistoric times. Today's beadwork is considered an exciting genre of art: many people are rediscovering the unlimited possibilities when it comes to beads. Chain & crystal jewelry is elegant & fun. Everyone loves the expensive look: here's a way to make the jewelry & not pay the retail prices! Easy step-by-step illustrations & full color photos make this a fun & fast project book! Includes the always popular "y" necklaces, & much, much more! The author is a third-generation bead artist - her grandmother designed beaded gowns & jewelry for the Ziegfeld Follies. Wendy is the author of the immensely popular Best Little Beading Book. Be sure to look for the other books in the series: The Best Little Beading Book, The Beaded Lampshade Book, The Magical Beaded Medicine Bag Book, The "Knotty" Macrame & Beading Book, The Beaded Watchband Book, The Beaded Jewelry for a Wedding Book, The Children's Beading Book, The Chain & Crystal Book, The Cat Lover's Beaded Project Book, The Wirebending Book, The Beading on Fabric Book, & more soon to come! Many of these books are available in kit form, also. There is also a wonderful documentary which complements the series. The Bead Movement is a beautiful program which chronicles man's oldest artform, beads. It is available in 60 minutes, or a 30 min. director's cut. For information or ordering, contact The Interstellar Trading & Publishing Company, Post Office Box 2215, La Mesa, CA 91943; (858) 452-8181 or 292-8191, Order Dept. (800) 790-8730, Fax (858) 452-0351 or 292-0373, e-mail Interstlr@aol.com. Visit our website at www.interstellarpublishing.com. Available through Sunbelt Publications, Ingram Books, Baker & Taylor Books. ***Publisher Paid Annotation.***

–The Children's Beading Book: Techniques for Little Beadlovers. LC 96-94612. (Beading Bks.). (Illus.). 52p. 1996. 11.95 (*0-9645957-6-1*) Interstell Pub.
A great new addition to the very popular Beading Book Series (TM), this new how-to bead book for children is a great way to introduce children to beads & their many facets! Beads are educational, ornamental, & beautiful to work with. This wonderful new book has many projects that children will love - from the simplest for young children to more advanced projects for older children & teens. Beautiful illustrations & bead-related stories & games make this a great rainy day book for hours of fun. There are many step-by-step illustrations, & full color photographs. The author writes in a way that children will understand & enjoy. A truly fun book for the entire family! The author is a third-generation bead artist, & knows her subject inside out. 52 pages. Be sure to look for the Beading Books Series: The Best Little Beading Book, The Beaded Lampshade Book, The Magical Beaded Medicine Bag Book, The "Knotty" Macrame & Beading Book, The Beaded Watchband Book, The Beaded Jewelry for a Wedding Book, The Children's Beading Book, The Chain & Crystal Book, The Cat Lover's Beaded Project Book, The Wirebending Book, The Beading on Fabric Book, & more soon to come! Many of these books are available in kit form, also. There is also a wonderful documentary which complements the series. The Bead Movement is a beautiful program which chronicles man's oldest art form, beads. It is available in 60 minutes, or a 30 min. director's cut. For information or ordering, contact The Interstellar Trading & Publishing Company, P.O. Box 2215, La Mesa, CA 91943; (858) 452-8181 or 292-8191, Order Dept. (800) 790-8730, Fax (858) 452-0351 or 292-0373, email Interstlr@aol.com. Visit our website at www.interstellarpublishing.com. Available through Sunbelt Publications, Ingram Books, Baker & Taylor Books. ***Publisher Paid Annotation.***

–The "Knotty" Macrame & Beading Book: Techniques for Beadlovers. LC 95-95203. (Beading Bks.). (Illus.). 52p. 1996. 11.95 (*0-9645957-4-5*) Interstell Pub.
A great new addition to the very popular BEADING BOOKS SERIES (TM), this new how-to book brings back a lot of popular techniques on macrame. Macrame jewelry is the latest thing, & this is the only book published recently which updates the 70s styles into a wonderful new look. Sixteen jewelry & other projects with step-by-step illustrations & full color photographs, & many diagrams of knots & other useful information. Many of these projects use hemp, jute, & other cordings, along with a variety of beads to achieve many different styles. 52 pages. The author is a third-generation bead artist, & knows her subject inside out. Be sure to look for the other books in the series: THE BEST LITTLE BEADING BOOK, THE BEADED LAMPSHADE BOOK, THE MAGICAL BEADED MEDICINE BAG BOOK, THE CHILDREN'S BEADING BOOK, THE BEADED WATCHBAND BOOK, THE BEADED JEWELRY FOR A WEDDING BOOK, THE CHAIN & CRYSTAL BOOK, THE CAT LOVER'S BEADING BOOK, THE WIREBENDING BOOK & more soon to come! Many of these books are available in kit form, also. For more information, or to order these books, please contact: The Interstellar Trading & Publishing Company, P.O. Box 2215, La Mesa, CA 91943. (619) 292-8191, Order Dept., (800) 790- 8730, FAX (619) 292-0373, email: Interstlr@aol.com. Available through Sunbelt Publications, Ingram Books, Baker & Taylor Books. ***Publisher Paid Annotation.***

–The Magical Beaded Medicine Bag Book: Techniques for Beadlovers. LC 95-95202. (Beading Bks.). (Illus.). 52p. 1996. 11.95 (*0-9645957-2-9*) Interstell Pub.
The concept of the "prayer pouch" (or medicine bag) is as old as time itself. There is a special magic in making one's own bag, & filling it with the amulets that symbolize the meaning of one's own life. This book has many styles of medicine bags to make - Chinese finger weaving, Peyote Stitch, beading on leather, plus much more; all shown with easy-to-follow step-by-step illustrations & beautiful full color photos. The projects help the reader to focus on positive energy, & taking control of one's life through the realization of one's own power. Make your own magic! The author is a third-generation bead artist - her grandmother designed beaded gowns & jewelry for the Ziegfeld Follies. Wendy is the author of the immensely popular Best Little Beading Book. ***Publisher Paid Annotation.***

–The Wirebending Book: Techniques for Beadlovers. LC 97-93597. (Beading Books Ser.: Vol. 11). (Illus.). 52p. 1997. pap. 11.95 (*0-9645957-9-6*) Interstell Pub.
Wire Bending in jewelry is the hot look that everyone wants. With simple wire & pliers, you can create elegant wearable art. This fabulous book has over 20 projects & techniques to give your jewelry a very special look. Techniques include wire wrapping, scrollwork, Peruvian style bead weaving, working with a jig, & much, much more. Be sure to look for the other books in the series: The Best Little Beading Book, The Beaded Lampshade Book, The Magical Beaded Medicine Bag Book, The "Knotty" Macrame & Beading Book, The Beaded Watchband Book, The Beaded Jewelry for a Wedding Book, The Children's Beading Book, The Chain & Crystal Book, The Cat Lover's Beaded Project Book, The Wirebending Book, The Beading on Fabric Book, & more soon to come! Many of these books are available in kit form, also. There is also a wonderful documentary which complements the series. The Bead Movement is a beautiful program which chronicles man's oldest artform, beads. It is available in 60 minutes, or a 30 min. director's cut. For information or ordering, contact The Interstellar Trading & Publishing Company, Post Office Box 2215, La Mesa, CA 91943; (858) 452-8181 or 292-8191, Order Dept. (800) 790-8730, Fax (858) 452-0351 or 292-0373, e-mail Interstlr@aol.com. Visit our website at www.interstellarpublishing.com. Available through Sunbelt Publications, Ingram Books, Baker & Taylor Books. ***Publisher Paid Annotation.***

Conner, William. Building a Successful Accounting Practice. 288p. (Orig.). 1995. pap. text 69.00 (*0-89447-312-3*) Cypress.

Conner, William B. Psycho-Mathematics: The Key to the Universe, Set. Incl. Vol. 1-Creativity through Calculator Harmonic Braiding. 140p. 1983. (*0-9603536-5-8*); Vol. 2-Creativity through Keyboard Harmonic Braiding. Orig. Title: Math's & Music's Metasonics. 213p. 1983. reprint ed. pap. 36.50 (*0-9603536-6-6*); Orig. Title: Math's & Music's Metasonics. (Orig.). 1983. Set pap. text 36.50 (*0-9603536-7-4*) Tesla Bk Co.

Conner, William F. Memory's Glass. LC 95-36729. (Appalachian Connection Ser.). (Illus.). 160p. 1995. pap. 12.95 (*0-936015-53-5*) Pocahontas Pr.

Conner, William H., jt. auth. see Messina, M. G.

Connerade, J. P., et al, eds. Giant Resonances in Atoms, Molecules & Solids. LC 87-7950. (NATO ASI Series B, Physical Sciences: Vol. 151). (Illus.). 582p. 1987. 125.00 (*0-306-42564-5*, Plenum Trade) Perseus Pubng.

Connerade, Jean P. Highly Excited Atoms. (Cambridge Monographs on Atomic, Molecular, & Chemical Physics Ser.: No. 9). (Illus.). 526p. (C). 1998. text 115.00 (*0-521-43232-4*) Cambridge U Pr.

Connerly, Ward. Creating Equal: My Fight Against Race Preferences. LC 99-88627. 248p. 2000. 24.95 (*1-893554-04-X*) Encounter Bks.

Conners. Dancehall. 1983. 14.95 (*0-02-527490-2*) Macmillan.

Conners, Aaron. The Pandora Directive: A Tex Murphy Novel. 336p. 1995. mass mkt. 5.99 (*0-7615-0068-5*) Prima Pub.

Conners, Aaron. Under a Killing Moon: A Tex Murphy Novel. 336p. 1996. mass mkt., per. 5.99 (*0-7615-0420-6*) Prima Pub.

Conners, C. K. Feeding the Brain: How Foods Affect Children. LC 89-16071. (Illus.). 288p. (C). 1989. 23.95 (*0-306-43306-0*, Plenum Trade) Perseus Pubng.

Conners, C. Keith. Food Additives & Hyperactive Children. LC 80-66. 182p. 1980. 35.00 (*0-306-40400-1*, Plenum Trade) Perseus Pubng.

Conners, C. Keith, et al, eds. Rating Scales & Assessment Instruments for Use in Pediatric Psychopharmacology Research. 415p. (Orig.). (C). 1995. pap. text 60.00 (*0-7881-2518-4*) DIANE Pub.

Conners, C. Keith & Jett, Juliet L. Attention Deficit Hyperactivity Disorder. LC 99-19853. (Condensed Reviews for Professionals Ser.). 116p. 1999. pap. 14.95 (*1-887537-11-2*) Compact Clinicals.

Conners, C. Keith & Wells, Karen C. Hyperkinetic Children. (Developmental Clinical Psychology & Psychiatry Ser.: Vol. 7). 160p. (C). 1986. text 42.00 (*0-8039-2278-7*); pap. text 18.95 (*0-8039-2279-5*) Sage.

— Hyperkinetic Children: A Neuropsychosocial Approach. LC 85-19626. (Developmental Clinical Psychology & Psychiatry Ser.: No. 7). (Illus.). 160p. 1986. reprint ed. pap. 49.60 (*0-7837-9899-7*, 206062500006) Bks Demand.

***Conners, Christine & Conners, Tim.** Lipsmackin' Backpackin' LC 99-54507. (Illus.). 256p. 2000. pap. 15.95 (*1-56044-881-4*) Falcon Pub Inc.

Conners, Erin, jt. auth. see Baumann, Kathy.

***Conners, Gail A.** Good News! How to Get the Best Possible Media Coverage for Your School. LC 99-50518. (One-Off Ser.). 128p. 2000. pap. 27.95 (*0-7619-7507-1*); lib. bdg. 61.95 (*0-7619-7506-3*) Corwin Pr.

Conners, Jo. Who's Who in Arizona, Vol. 1. (Illus.). 820p. 1998. reprint ed. lib. bdg. 85.00 (*0-8328-7010-2*) Higginson Bk Co.

Conners, John A. Shenandoah National Park: An Interpretive Guide. LC 88-23118. (Illus.). ix, 214p. (Orig.). 1988. pap. 15.95 (*0-939923-02-5*) M & W Pub Co.

Conners, John B., ed. Coastal Exposure & Community Protection: Hurricane Andrew's Legacy. (Illus.). 48p. (C). 1998. pap. text 25.00 (*0-7881-7178-X*) DIANE Pub.

Conners, John J., jt. auth. see Young, Woody.

Conners, John R. Advice to a Freshman. 104p. 1984. pap. text 12.25 (*0-89917-416-7*) Tichenor Pub.

Conners, Martin & Furtaw, Julia, eds. Videohound on CD IBM Single (VIP) 1993. 79.95 (*0-8103-4999-X*) Visible Ink Pr.

Conners, Ronald B., ed. Integrating the Practice of Medicine: A Decision Maker's Guide to Organizing & Managing Physician Services. LC 97-17762. 469p. 1997. 49.00 (*1-55648-206-X*) AHPI.

Conners, Ronald B. & Winters, Robert W., eds. Home Infusion Therapy Current Status & Future Trends. LC 95-36061. 276p. 1995. pap. 72.00 (*1-55648-146-2*, 079202) AHPI.

Conners, Russell B., Jr. & McCormick, Patrick T. Character, Choices & Community: The Three Faces of Christian Ethics. LC 98-89867. 288p. 1998. pap. 15.95 (*0-8091-3805-0*) Paulist Pr.

Conners, Terrance E. & Banerjee, Sujit, eds. Surface Analysis of Paper. 368p. 1995. boxed set 169.95 (*0-8493-8992-5*, 8992) CRC Pr.

Conners, Tim, jt. auth. see Conners, Christine.

***Conners, William W.** Aegis. (Alternity Ser.). (Illus.). 96p. 2000. pap. 18.95 (*0-7869-1620-6*) TSR Inc.

Conners, William W. Domains of Dread Rulebook. Horner, Miranda & Rice, Cindi, eds. 1997. 30.00 (*0-7869-0672-3*, Pub. by TSR Inc) Random.

Connerton & Reid. Linkages. (J). 1993. VHS 114.95 (*0-8384-5090-3*) Heinle & Heinle.

— Linkages. (J). 1993. mass mkt. 57.95 (*0-8384-4204-8*) Heinle & Heinle.

Connerton, Patrice & Reid. Linkages. (J). 1993. mass mkt., teacher ed. 9.95 (*0-8384-4205-6*) Heinle & Heinle.

Connerton, Patrice & Reid, Frances. Linkages. 280p. (J). 1993. mass mkt. 25.95 (*0-8384-3955-1*) Heinle & Heinle.

Connerton, Paul. How Societies Remember. (Themes in the Social Sciences Ser.). 128p. (C). 1989. pap. text 17.95 (*0-521-27093-6*) Cambridge U Pr.

Connery. Intro to Media Writing, Vol. 1. LC 98-84336. 1998. pap. text 31.95 (*0-312-15441-0*) St Martin.

Connery, Christopher L. The Empire of the Text: Writing & Authority in Early Imperial China. LC 98-22604. 246p. 1998. pap. 22.95 (0-8476-8739-2); text 65.00 (0-8476-8738-4) Rowman.

Connery, Clare. In an Irish Country Kitchen: A Cook's Celebration of Ireland. (Illus.). 160p. 1993. 32.00 (0-671-74945-5) S&S Trade.

— Quick & Easy Salads. (Illus.). 136p. (Orig.). 1993. pap. 9.95 (0-563-36253-7, BBC-Parkwest) Parkwest Pubns.

Connery, Donald S., ed. Convicting the Innocent: The Story of a Murder, a False Confession, & the Struggle to Free a "Wrong Man" LC 95-49419. 220p. 1995. pap. 16.95 (1-57129-021-4) Brookline Bks.

***Connery, Jan, ed.** Environmental Regulations & Technology: Control of Pathogens & Vector Attraction in Sewage Sludge. (Illus.). 152p. (C). 1999. reprint ed. pap. text 35.00 (0-7881-8234-X) DIANE Pub.

Connery, John R. Abortion: The Development of the Roman Catholic Perspective. LC 76-51217. 342p. reprint ed. pap. 106.10 (0-7837-5727-1, 204538700006) Bks Demand.

Connery, Liz N. Loving Letters. (Illus.). 60p. (Orig.). 1985. pap. text 7.00 (0-9614333-0-2) L Newkirk Connery.

Connery, Robert H. Governmental Problems in Wild Life Conservation. LC 68-58560. (Columbia University. Studies in the Social Sciences: No. 411). reprint ed. 32.50 (0-404-51411-1) AMS Pr.

Connery, Robert H. & Benjamin, Gerald. Rockefeller of New York: Executive Power in the Statehouse. LC 78-23947. (Illus.). 480p. reprint ed. pap. 148.80 (0-608-08085-3, 206904400002) Bks Demand.

Connery, Robert H. & Leach, Richard H. The Federal Government & Metropolitan Areas. LC 77-74936. (American Federalism-the Urban Dimension Ser.). 1978. reprint ed. lib. bdg. 26.95 (0-405-10483-9) Ayer.

Connery, Thomas B., ed. A Sourcebook of American Literary Journalism: Representative Writers in an Emerging Genre. LC 91-17127. 424p. 1992. lib. bdg. 79.50 (0-313-26594-1, CYJ, Greenwood Pr) Greenwood.

***Connery, Tom.** Honour Redeemed. (Markham of the Marines Ser.: Vol. 2). 328p. 2000. 21.95 (0-89526-255-X) Regnery Pub.

Connery, Tom. Shred of Honour: A Markham of the Marines Novel. LC 99-39754. 328p. 1999. 21.95 (0-89526-269-X) Regnery Pub.

Connes, Alain, ed. Noncommutative Geometry. LC 94-26550. (Illus.). 661p. 1994. text 70.00 (0-12-185860-X) Acad Pr.

Connes, Alain, et al. Operator Algebras, Unitary Representations, Enveloping Algebras & Invariant Theory. 1990. 109.00 (0-8176-3489-4) Birkhauser.

— Quantiques Symmetries/Symmetries Quantiques. LC 97-49073. (Les Houches Summer School Proceedings Ser.: 64). 1032p. 1998. 296.00 (0-444-82867-2) Elsevier.

Connes, G. Dictionary of the Characters & Scenes in the Novels, Romances & Short Stories of H. G. Wells. LC 73-174698. (Reference Ser.: No. 44). 1971. reprint ed. lib. bdg. 75.00 (0-8383-1353-1) M S G Haskell Hse.

Connes, Georges, jt. auth. see Merimee, Prosper.

Connes, Keith. The GPS, Loran & Navigation Communication Guide. 6th rev. ed. (Illus.). 192p. pap. 19.95 (0-932579-07-8) Butterfield Pr.

— Know Your Airplane! LC 85-19740. (Illus.). 210p. 1986. 16.95 (0-8138-1056-6) Iowa St U Pr.

Connett, Eugene V., III. My Friend the Trout. (Illus.). 176p. 1991. reprint ed. 50.00 (0-9620609-4-1) Meadow Run Pr.

***Connett, Eugene V., III, ed.** American Big Game Fishing. (Illus.). 251p. 1999. pap. 27.95 (1-56833-137-1, Pub. by Derrydale Pr) Natl Bk Netwk.

Connett, P. H. Inorganic Elements in Biochemistry. (Structure & Bonding Ser.: Vol. 54). (Illus.). 190p. 1983. 69.95 (0-387-12542-6) Spr-Verlag.

Connett, W. C. & Schwartz, Alan Lee. The Theory of Ultraspherical Multipliers. LC 76-58958. (Memoirs Ser.: No. 9/183). 92p. 1977. pap. 21.00 (0-8218-2183-0, MEMO/9/183) Am Math.

Connett, William C., et al, eds. Applications of Hypergroups & Related Algebras: A Joint Summer Research Conference, July 10-August 6, 1993, Seattle, WA. LC 94-42671. (Contemporary Mathematics Ser.: Vol. 183). 441p. 1995. pap. 69.00 (0-8218-0297-6, CONM/183) Am Math.

Connie, Pennedelton & Stunz Staff. This Was Virginia, 1900-1927: As Shown by the Glass Negatives of J. Harry Shannon, the Rambler. LC 98-46162. 1998. 34.95 (0-9653759-7-8) Hallmark Publng.

Conniff. Africans in Americas. 2nd ed. 2000. text. write for info. (0-312-15378-3) St Martin.

Conniff, Brian. The Lyric & Modern Poetry: Olson, Creeley, Bunting. (American University Studies: English Language & Literature: Ser. IV, Vol. 60). 218p. (C). 1988. text 39.90 (0-8204-0533-7) P Lang Pubng.

Conniff, James. The Useful Cobbler: Edmund Burke & the Politics of Progress. LC 93-16994. 363p. (C). 1994. text 59.50 (0-7914-1843-X); pap. text 19.95 (0-7914-1844-8) State U NY Pr.

Conniff, Michael L. Panama & the United States: The Forced Alliance. LC 91-7319. (United States & the Americas Ser.). 208p. 1992. 40.00 (0-8203-1359-9); pap. 20.00 (0-8203-1360-2) U of Ga Pr.

— Populism in Latin America. LC 98-40081. 272p. 1999. text 44.95 (0-8173-0959-4) U of Ala Pr.

— Populism in Latin America. LC 98-40081. 1999. pap. 22.50 (0-8173-0970-5) U of Ala Pr.

Conniff, Michael L., ed. Latin American Populism in Comparative Perspective. LC 80-54572. 271p. reprint ed. pap. 84.10 (0-8357-4641-0, 203757200008) Bks Demand.

Conniff, Michael L. & McCann, Frank D., eds. Modern Brazil: Elites & Masses in Historical Perspective. LC 88-19088. (Latin American Studies). xxviii, 306p. 1989. text 50.00 (0-8032-3131-8) U of Nebr Pr.

Conniff, Richard. Every Creeping Thing: True Tales of Faintly Repulsive Wildlife. LC 98-12700. (Illus.). 255p. 1998. 25.00 (0-8050-5697-1); pap. 13.50 (0-8050-5698-X, Owl) H Holt & Co.

***Conniff, Richard.** Ireland: Stone Walls & Fabled Landscapes. LC 99-176198. (Illus.). 144p. 2000. pap. 35.00 (0-7112-1372-0, Pub. by F Lincoln) Antique Collect.

Conniff, Richard. Spineless Wonders. 256p. 1997. pap. 12.95 (0-8050-5531-2) H Holt & Co.

— Spineless Wonders: Strange Tales from the Invertabrate World. LC 96-11748. (Illus.). 256p. 1995. 25.00 (0-8050-4218-0) H Holt & Co.

Connikie, Yvonne. Fashions of a Decade: The 1960s. Cumming, Valerie & Feldman, Elane, eds. (Illus.). 64p. (J). (gr. 4-9). 1990. 19.95 (0-8160-2469-3) Facts on File.

Connin, D. M., jt. auth. see Anderson.

Connin, Ray & Murphy, Betsy. The Story of Land Surveying. (Illus.). 24p. (Orig.). (J). (gr. 4-6). 1996. pap. 3.95 (0-932514-32-4) Red Rose Studio.

Conning. Twenty Years of Toxicology. (Food & Chemical Toxicology Ser.). 1982. pap. 48.00 (0-08-028856-1, Pergamon Pr) Elsevier.

Conning, D. M., jt. ed. see Anderson, Diana.

Conning, D. M., jt. ed. see Anderson, D.

Conning, D. M., jt. ed. see Goldberg, L.

Conningham, Jewell. Conflict & Triumph: Over Fifty Years with Missions. Biros, Florence K. & Libb, Melva, eds. (Illus.). 320p. (Orig.). 1988. pap. 6.95 (0-936369-12-4) Son-Rise Pubns.

Connington & Dupuis, Hector. Unit Based Quality Assurance: A Patient-Centered Approach. 180p. 1990. 79.00 (0-8342-0153-4, 20153) Aspen Pub.

Connirae, Andreas & Andreas, Tamara. Core Transformation: Reaching the Wellspring Within. LC 93-41068. 232p. 1997. reprint ed. pap. 13.50 (0-911226-33-8) Real People.

Connley, Mark & Dubois, Jennifer. Now Hiring! Destination Resort Jobs: The Insider's Guide to Seasonal & Year-Round Employment at America's Top Vacation Resorts. (Illus.). 274p. (Orig.). (C). 1994. pap. 17.95 (1-881199-56-8) Perpetual Pr.

Connnor, W. R., ed. see Taylor, Michael W.

Conno, F. De, see De Conno, F.

***Connock & Johns.** Ethical Leadership. 240p. 2000. pap. 59.95 (0-8464-5050-X) Beekman Pubs.

Connock, Stephen. HR Vision: Managing a Quality Workforce. 194p. (C). 1991. pap. 90.00 (0-85292-482-8, Pub. by IPM Hse) St Mut.

***Connolly.** Managing in the Public Sector. 2000. pap. write for info. (0-412-61380-8) Thomson Learn.

Connolly. Selected Writings. 1998. 40.00 (0-7453-1279-9, Pub. by Pluto GBR) Stylus Pub VA.

Connolly, et al. Instructor's Manual for Database Systems. Mosman, Karen & Harutunian, Katherine, eds. 1995. 15.94 (0-201-40343-9) Addison-Wesley.

Connolly, Ann M., jt. auth. see Munnell, Alicia H.

Connolly, Austin J. Keymath Attribute Blocks Manual. (Illus.). 58p. 1980. pap. text 19.95 (0-913476-93-5, 2701) Am Guidance.

— KeyMath Boards Manual. (Illus.). 110p. 1980. pap. text 29.95 (0-913476-96-X, 2757) Am Guidance.

— KeyMath Chips Manual. (Illus.). 71p. 1980. pap. text 24.95 (0-913476-98-6, 2837) Am Guidance.

— KeyMath Cubes Manual. (Illus.). 134p. 1980. pap. text 29.95 (0-913476-94-3, 2710) Am Guidance.

— KeyMath Teach & Practice. (J). (gr. k-6). 1985. 599.95 (0-88671-385-4, 6880) Am Guidance.

— KeyMath Tumblers Manual. (Illus.). 74p. 1980. pap. text 19.95 (0-913476-99-4, 2847) Am Guidance.

Connolly, Barbara, jt. ed. see Montgomery, Patricia C.

Connolly, Bernard. Rotten Heart of Europe: The Dirty War for Europe's Money. LC 97-180114. 432p. 1997. pap. 16.95 (0-571-17521-X) Faber & Faber.

Connolly, Beth, jt. auth. see Connelly, Elizabeth Russell.

Connolly, Billy. Billy Connolly's World Tour of Australia. (Illus.). 176p. 1997. 28.95 (0-563-38723-8, BBC-Parkwest) Parkwest Pubns.

Connolly, Bob, tr. see Romani, Cinzia.

Connolly, Brendan. Moving to Ireland: A Guide to Living & Investing. 1998. 24.95 (1-85915-150-7, Pub. by W & G) Motorbooks Intl.

Connolly, Carol. Payments Due: Onstage Offstage. rev. ed. LC 93-77632. (Illus.). 92p. 1995. pap. 12.00 (0-935697-06-3) Midwest Villages.

***Connolly, Castle.** America's Top Doctors. 960p. 2000. pap. 29.95 (1-883769-67-1, Pub. by Castle Connolly Med) IPG Chicago.

— How to Find the Best Doctors: Los Angeles Metropolitan Area/Orange County. 600p. 2000. pap. 24.95 (1-883769-15-9) Castle Connolly Med.

— How to Find the Best Doctors: San Francisco Bay Area. 600p. 2000. pap. 24.95 (1-883769-14-0) Castle Connolly Med.

Connolly, Christopher, jt. auth. see Syer, John.

Connolly, Claire & Copley, Stephen, eds. Wild Irish Girl by Lady Morgan. (Pickering Women's Classics Ser.). 400p. 1998. text 55.00 (1-85196-359-6, Pub. by Pickering & Chatto) Ashgate Pub Co.

Connolly, Claire, ed. see Edgeworth, Maria.

Connolly, Colleen, jt. auth. see Farrar, Eleanor.

Connolly, Colm. The Illustrated Life of Michael Collins. (Illus.). 96p. 1996. 24.95 (1-57098-112-4) Roberts Rinehart.

— Illustrated Life of Michael Collins. (Illus.). 96p. 1998. pap. text 17.95 (1-57098-215-5) Roberts Rinehart.

Connolly, Coyle & Bikowski, Joseph. Dermatological Atlas of Black Skin. (Illus.). 96p. 1998. 49.95 (1-873413-61-0, 8277) Merit Pub Intl.

***Connolly, Cresida.** Happiest Days: Short Stories. 192p. 2000. 21.00 (0-312-26171-3, Picador USA) St Martin.

Connolly, Cynthia, et al. Banned in D.C. Photos & Anecdotes from the D.C. Punk Underground (79-85) 5th ed. Ely, Lydia, ed. LC 88-92504. (Illus.). 176p. 1998. reprint ed. pap. 22.95 (0-9620944-0-4) Sun Dog Propaganda.

Connolly, Cyril. Enemies of Promise. 268p. (C). 1983. reprint ed. pap. 6.95 (0-89255-078-3) Persea Bks.

— The Rock Pool. LC 81-82928. 138p. 1996. reprint ed. pap. 9.95 (0-89255-059-7) Persea Bks.

— The Selected Essays of Cyril Connolly. Quennell, Peter, ed. 312p. (C). 1984. 17.95 (0-89255-072-4) Persea Bks.

— The Unquiet Grave. 156p. 1982. reprint ed. pap. 12.50 (0-89255-058-9) Persea Bks.

Connolly, Cyrill, tr. see Jarry, Alfred.

***Connolly, D. J.** The Temple of Karnak: How Rogue Judges Have Been Strangling Your Democracy. LC 99-95684. (Illus.). 256p. 2000. pap. 17.76 (0-9673798-0-6) Plum Crk Bk.

Connolly, David. In Search of Angels: A Celestial Sourcebook for Beginning Your Journey. LC 93-26752. (Illus.). 160p. (Orig.). 1994. pap. 8.95 (0-399-51851-7, Perigee Bks) Berkley Pub.

— Lost in America. (White Noise Poetry Ser.). 86p. (Orig.). (C). 1994. pap. 10.00 (0-9628524-9-X) Burning Cities Pr.

— Lost in America. (White Noise Poetry Ser.). 70p. (Orig.). 1994. pap. 12.00 (1-885215-00-2) Burning Cities Pr.

Connolly, David, tr. see Vatromanolakis, Voryis.

Connolly, David, tr. see Vrettakos, Nikiforos.

***Connolly, Dawn.** La Femme Peta: The Unauthorized Biography of Peta Wilson. (FRE., Illus.). 220p. 1999. pap. 16.95 (1-55022-385-2, ECWR & EC) Evangel Concern Wstrn.

Connolly, Dawn, jt. auth. see Adamson, Gil.

***Connolly, Deborah R.** Homeless Mothers: Face to Face with Women & Poverty. LC 99-50683. 2000. 24.95 (0-8166-3281-2); write for info. (0-8166-3282-0) U of Minn Pr.

Connolly, E. Sander, et al. Fundamentals of Operative Techniques in Neurosurgery. (Illus.). 800p. 2000. 59.00 (0-86577-836-1) Thieme Med Pubs.

Connolly, Edward & Harding, Christopher S. A Cop's Cop. 288p. 1987. pap. 3.95 (0-380-70169-3, Avon Bks) Morrow Avon.

Connolly, Eileen. Connolly Tarot. 1990. pap. 15.00 (0-88079-437-2, CN78) US Games Syst.

— Karma Without Stress. 1989. pap. 14.95 (0-87877-144-1) Newcastle Pub.

— Tarot: A New Handbook for the Apprentice. rev. ed. 254p. 1990. pap. 14.95 (0-87877-162-X) Newcastle Pub.

— Tarot: The First Handbook for the Master. Wisiroglo, Gina, ed. (Illus.). 320p. 1996. pap. 18.95 (0-87877-235-9) Newcastle Pub.

— Tarot Vol. 1: A New Handbook for the Apprentice (Classic Edition) LC 79-15303. (Illus.). 254p. 1979. pap. 14.95 (0-87877-045-3) Newcastle Pub.

— Tarot Vol. 2: The Handbook for the Journeyman. 288p. 1988. pap. 14.95 (0-87877-124-7) Newcastle Pub.

Connolly, Elaine & Self, Dian. Capitol Women: An Interpretive History of Women in Sacramento from 1850-1920. 185p. 1995. pap. text 12.95 (0-9645485-1-8) Capito Womens.

Connolly, Francis M. & Mullins, George J. Police Sergeant * Lieutenant * Captain. 336p. 1993. per. 19.95 (0-671-84686-8, Arc) IDG Bks.

Connolly, Francis X. St. Philip of the Joyous Heart. LC 92-74761. (Vision Bks.). (Illus.). 189p. (J). (gr. 4-9). 1993. pap. 9.95 (0-89870-431-6) Ignatius Pr.

Connolly, Frank B. Local Government in Connecticut. Pesci, David & Sembor, Edward C., eds. (Illus.). 76p. (Orig.). 1992. pap. text 10.00 (1-881866-00-9) U CT Inst Pub Serv.

Connolly, Geraldine. Food for the Winter. LC 89-70186. (Illus.). 64p. 1990. pap. 12.95 (1-55753-005-X) Purdue U Pr.

— Province of Fire. LC 98-88641. xi, 82 p. 1998. write for info. (0-916078-46-9) Iris Pr.

***Connolly, Graham & Jay, Christopher.** The Private World of Family Business, Vol. 1. 270p. (Orig.). 1999. pap. 29.95 (0-7299-0339-7) Pitman Pubng.

Connolly, Harold & Kelly, Madge. Iowa Pioneers. (History of Iowa Ser.). (Illus.). 51p. (Orig.). (YA). (gr. 5 up). 1988. pap. text 1.50 (0-924702-02-8) Grn Valley Area.

***Connolly, Harry, et al.** Fighting Chance: Journeys Through Childhood Cancer. LC 97-14834. (Illus.). 144p. 1998. 27.95 (0-9656342-5-6) Woodholme Hse.

Connolly, Holly & Connolly, Peter. Buddhism. Cole, W. Owen, ed. (World Religions Ser.). (Illus.). 140p. (Orig.). (YA). (gr. 9 up). 1992. pap. 21.00 (1-871402-07-7) Dufour.

Connolly, Hugh. The Irish Penitentials & the Sacrament of Penance Today. 240p. 1995. pap. 25.00 (1-85182-203-8, Pub. by Four Cts Pr) Intl Spec Bk.

— The Irish Penitentials & the Sacrament of Penance Today: And the Sacrament of Penance Today. 240p. 1995. 45.00 (1-85182-161-9, Pub. by Four Cts Pr) Intl Spec Bk.

Connolly, J. D. & Hill, R. A., eds. Dictionary of Terpenoids. 1800p. (C). (gr. 13). 1997. lib. bdg. 1995.00 (0-412-25770-X, A6858) Chapman & Hall.

Connolly, J. H., et al, eds. CSCW & Artificial Intelligence. (Computer Supported Cooperative Work Ser.). 216p. 1994. 54.95 (0-387-19816-4) Spr-Verlag.

Connolly, J. J., jt. auth. see Gilbert, D. G.

Connolly, J. L. John Gerson: Reformer & Mystic. (Medieval Studies). (Illus.). reprint ed. lib. bdg. 47.00 (0-697-00031-1) Irvington.

Connolly, James & Casthasaigh, Aindrias O. The Lost Writings. LC 97-28160. 256p. 1997. 59.95 (0-7453-1297-7, Pub. by Pluto GBR) Stylus Pub VA.

Connolly, James & Casthasaigh, Aindrias O. The Lost Writings. 256p. 1997. pap. 21.95 (0-7453-1296-9, Pub. by Pluto GBR) Stylus Pub VA.

Connolly, James A. Three Years in the Army of the Cumberland. Angle, Paul M, ed. 1996. pap. text 14.95 (0-253-21073-9) Ind U Pr.

Connolly, James B. Deep Sea's Toll. LC 78-37262. (Short Story Index Reprint Ser.). (Illus.). 1977. reprint ed. 23.95 (0-8369-4073-3) Ayer.

— Out of Gloucester. LC 70-94712. (Short Story Index Reprint Ser.). 1977. 20.95 (0-8369-3091-6) Ayer.

Connolly, James E., ed. Why the Possum's Tail Is Bare: And Other North American Indian Nature Tales. 4th ed. LC 84-26871. (Illus.). 64p. (J). (gr. 4-8). 1992. reprint ed. 15.95 (0-88045-069-X, Intl Design); reprint ed. pap. 7.95 (0-88045-107-6, Intl Design) Stemmer Hse.

Connolly, James J. The Triumph of Ethnic Progressivism: Urban Political Culture in Boston, 1900-1925. LC 97-38662. (Illus.). 304p. 1999. text 45.00 (0-674-90950-X) HUP.

Connolly, Jane E., et al, eds. Saints & Their Authors: Studies in Medieval Spanish Hagiography in Honor of John K. Walsh. (SPA.). xxviii, 216p. 1990. 30.00 (0-940639-61-0) Hispanic Seminary.

Connolly, Jane Ellen. Translation & Poetization in the Quaderna via. Study & Edition of the Libro de Miseria d'omme. (Spanish Ser.: No. 33). 260p. 1987. 20.00 (0-942260-81-3) Hispanic Seminary.

Connolly, Jay. Dancewater Blues. 1990. pap. text 11.95 (0-88982-099-6, Pub. by Oolichan Bks) Genl Dist Srvs.

Connolly, Joe, jt. auth. see Corcoran, Mary.

Connolly, Joe, jt. auth. see Doran, John.

Connolly, John. Every Dead Thing. LC 98-50085. 395p. 1999. 24.50 (0-684-85714-6) S&S Trade.

***Connolly, John.** Every Dead Thing. 480p. 2000. reprint ed. per. 6.99 (0-671-02731-X, Pocket Star Bks) PB.

Connolly, John A., jt. ed. see Kershner, Keith M.

Connolly, John F. Fractures & Dislocations - Closed Management. (Illus.). 1264p. 1995. text 150.00 (0-7216-2601-7, W B Saunders Co) Harcrt Hlth Sci Grp.

Connolly, John F., ed. Tibial Nonunion: Diagnosis & Treatment. LC 91-4558. 71p. 1991. pap. 35.00 (0-89203-048-8) Amer Acad Ortho Surg.

Connolly, John H., et al, eds. Discourse & Pragmatics in Functional Grammar. LC 96-43963. (Functional Grammar Ser.: Vol. 18). x, 235p. (C). 1997. lib. bdg. 105.75 (3-11-015153-7) Mouton.

Connolly, John H. & Pemberton, Lyn. Linguistic Concepts & Methods in CSCW. LC 96-24165. (Computer Supported Cooperative Work Ser.). (Illus.). 200p. 1996. pap. 59.95 (3-540-19984-5) Spr-Verlag.

Connolly, John J. The ABCs of HMOs: How to Get the Best from Managed Care. LC 95-70353. 228p. (Orig.). 1997. pap. 11.95 (1-883769-74-4) Castle Connolly Med.

— Buyer's Guide to the Best Health Care. Orig. Title: How to Find the Best Doctors, Hospitals & HMOs for You & Your Family - Pocket Guide. 464p. 1998. pap. 12.95 (1-883769-61-2) Castle Connolly Med.

— Castle Connelly Guide, How to Find the Best Doctors: Metropolitan Chicago, 1999. 600p. 1999. pap. 19.99 (1-883769-11-6) Castle Connolly Med.

— Castle Connolly Guide: How to Find the Best Doctors for You & Your Family in the New York Metro Area. Berkman, Sue & Beach, Sandra, eds. LC 93-72954. (Illus.). 608p. 1993. pap. 21.95 (1-883769-59-0) Castle Connolly Med.

— How to Find the Best Doctors: Florida Area. 500p. 1999. pap. 24.95 (1-883769-25-6) Castle Connolly Med.

— How to Find the Best Doctors: New York Metro Area. 3rd rev. ed. LC 98-92928. 1375p. 1998. pap. 19.95 (1-883769-07-8) Castle Connolly Med.

— How to Find the Best Doctors, Hospitals, & HMOs for You & Your Family: Castle Connolly Pocket Guide. Berkman, Sue, ed. LC 94-92449. 457p. (Orig.). 1994. pap. 9.95 (1-883769-70-1) Castle Connolly Med.

Connolly, John J., ed. How to Find the Best Doctors: New York Metro Area. 4th rev. ed. 1375p. 1999. pap. 24.95 (1-883769-66-3) Castle Connolly Med.

Connolly, John J., jt. auth. see Williams, Christine L.

Connolly, Joseph. Beside the Seaside. (Illus.). 1999. 29.95 (1-84000-164-X, Pub. by Mitchell Beazley) Trafalgar.

Connolly, Julian W. Invitation to a Beheading: A Critical Companion. LC 97-23097. (Northwestern - AATSEEL Critical Companions to Russian Literature Ser.). 1997. pap. 17.95 (0-8101-1271-X) Northwestern U Pr.

***Connolly, Julian W., ed.** Nabokov & His Fiction: New Perspectives. LC 98-47176. (Studies in Russian Literature). 256p. (C). 1999. write for info. (0-521-63283-8) Cambridge U Pr.

Connolly, Julian W. & Ketchian, Sonia I., eds. Studies in Russian Literature in Honor of Vsevolod Setchkarev. (Illus.). 288p. (Orig.). 1987. pap. 22.95 (0-89357-174-1) Slavica.

Connolly, Kathleen G. & Connolly, Paul M. Competing for Employees: Proven Marketing Strategies for Hiring & Keeping Exceptional People. 232p. 1999. reprint ed. text 25.00 (0-7881-6113-X) DIANE Pub.

Connolly, Ken. Biographical Sketch of C. H. Spurgeon. 1990. pap. 3.00 (1-56186-418-8) Pilgrim Pubns.

Connolly, Kevin, ed. The Psychobiology of the Hand. (Clinics in Developmental Medicine Ser.: No. 147). (Illus.). 250p. (C). 1999. text 69.95 (1-898683-14-X, Pub. by Mc Keith Pr) Cambridge U Pr.

Connolly, Kevin B. Buying & Selling Volatility with Disk. LC 96-46655. (Illus.). 230p. 1997. 84.95 (0-471-96884-6) Wiley.

— Pricing Convertible Bonds. LC 98-19146. 268p. 1998. 79.95 incl. disk (0-471-97872-8) Wiley.

C

An Asterisk (*) at the beginning of an entry indicates that the title is appearing for the first time.

Connolly, Kevin J. & Forssberg, Hans. Neurophysiology & Neuropsychology of Motor Development. LC 98-107760. (Illus.). 1997. write for info. (*0-521-01898-6*) Cambridge U Pr.

Connolly, Kevin J. & Forssberg, Hans, eds. The Neurophysiology & Neuropsychology of Motor Development. LC 98-107760. (Clinics in Developmental Medicine Ser.: No. 143). (Illus.). 350p. (C). 1997. 99.95 (*1-898683-10-7*, Pub. by Mc Keith Pr) Cambridge U Pr.

Connolly, Kieron, jt. auth. see Herrick, Clyde N.

Connolly-Lauder & Schwartz. Maternity Nursing. 3rd ed. 222p. (C). 1998. per. 44.95 (*0-7872-4568-2*, 41456801) Kendall-Hunt.

Connolly-Lauder, Barbara & Schwartz, Linda. Maternity Nursing: Student Workbook. 2nd ed. 208p. (C). 1996. pap. text, student ed., spiral bd. 20.95 (*0-8403-9496-9*) Kendall-Hunt.

Connolly, Leonard P. & Treves, S. T. Pediatric Skeletal Scintigraphy. LC 96-29796. 240p. 1997. text 135.00 (*0-387-94695-0*) Spr-Verlag.

Connolly, Liza. The Journey Back: The Emotional Process to Physical Healing. LC 97-91058. 1998. pap. 10.95 (*0-533-12553-7*) Vantage.

Connolly, M. J., ed. see Black, Henry C., et al.

Connolly, Margaret. John Shirley: Book Production in the Noble Household in Fifteenth-Century England. LC 98-23625. (Illus.). 247p. 1998. text 83.95 (*1-85928-462-0*, PR317.M34C66, Pub. by Scolar Pr) Ashgate Pub Co.

Connolly, Margaret, ed. Contemplations of the Dread & Love of God. (Early English Text Society-Original Ser.: Vol. 303).Tr. of Fervor Amoris. (Illus.). 176p. 1994. reprint ed. text 55.00 (*0-19-722305-2*) OUP.

Connolly, Marie & McKenzie, Margaret. Effective Participatory Practice: Empowering Families in Child Protection. LC 98-46483. (Modern Applications of Social Work Ser.). 156p. 1999. pap. text 19.95 (*0-202-36108-X*); lib. bdg. 42.95 (*0-202-36107-1*) Aldine de Gruyter.

Connolly, Maureen. Dragsters. (Cruisin' Ser.). (Illus.). 48p. (J). (gr. 3-6). 1992. 19.00 (*0-516-35074-9*) Childrens.

Connolly, Michael. Briefcase on Commercial Law. (Cavendish Briefcase Ser.). 226p. 1995. pap. 20.00 (*1-85941-241-6*, Pub. by Cavendish Pubng) Gaunt.

— Japan: From Shape to Mind. LC 98-89000. 337p. 1999. pap. 20.00 (*1-891218-05-0*) Watersign Pr.

— The Parish Cantor: Helping Catholics Pray in Song. 67p. 1991. pap. text 8.95 (*0-941050-24-6*, G-3626) GIA Pubns.

— The West That Nobody Knew. 94p. 1997. pap. 14.00 (*0-8059-4039-1*) Dorrance.

Connolly, Michael & De Melo, Jaime, eds. The Effects of Protectionism on a Small Country: The Case of Uruguay. (World Bank Ser.). 184p. 1996. 68.95 (*1-85972-231-8*, Pub. by Avebry) Ashgate Pub Co.

— The Effects of Protectionism on a Small Country: The Case of Uruguay. LC 94-7420. (Regional & Sectorial Studies). 184p. 1994. pap. 22.00 (*0-8213-2788-7*, 12788) World Bank.

Connolly, Michael B. International Trade & Lending. LC 84-26254. 144p. 1985. 49.95 (*0-275-90077-0*, I, Praeger Pubs) Greenwood.

Connolly, Michael B., et al, eds. The International Monetary System: Choices for the Future. LC 82-7483. 331p. 1982. 65.00 (*0-275-90774-0*, C0774, Praeger Pubs) Greenwood.

Connolly, Michael B. & Gonzalez-Vega, Claudio, eds. Economic Reform & Stabilization in Latin America. LC 86-9405. 374p. 1986. 69.50 (*0-275-92307-X*, C2307, Praeger Pubs) Greenwood.

Connolly, Michael B. & McDermott, John, eds. The Economics of the Caribbean Basin. LC 85-3419. 306p. 1985. 69.50 (*0-275-90076-2*, C0076, Praeger Pubs) Greenwood.

Connolly, Michael J., jt. auth. see Connolly, Walter B., Jr.

Connolly, Mike, jt. auth. see Weissman, Dick.

Connolly, Myles. Mr. Blue. LC 90-31948. 97p. 1990. 10.95 (*0-911519-20-3*) Richelieu Court.

***Connolly, Nancy Kennedy.** The Color of Dust. LC 99-67733. 90p. 1999. pap. 7.00 (*1-884778-79-8*) Old Mountain.

Connolly, Norma. Bilingual Dictionary of Domestic Relations & Juvenile Terms: English - Spanish. (ENG & SPA.). 185p. 1998. pap. 24.95 (*0-87526-540-5*) Gould.

— Bilingual Dictionary of Immigration Terms: English - Spanish. (ENG & SPA.). 120p. 1997. pap. 24.95 (*0-87526-541-3*) Gould.

Connolly, P. Research Racism in Education Set: Politics, Theory & Practice. LC 97-23199. 192p. 1997. 95.00 (*0-335-19663-2*); pap. 29.95 (*0-335-19662-4*) OpUniv Pr.

Connolly, Pamela. What Do You Say to a Naked Icebox? A Cookbook for College Students & Other Kitchen Virgins. (Illus.). 88p. 1997. pap. 10.00 (*0-8059-4178-9*) Dorrance.

***Connolly, Pat.** Candida Albicans Yeast-Free Cookbook: How Good Nutrition Can Help Fight the Epidemic of Yeast-Related Diseases. LC 99-86945. (Illus.). 256p. 2000. pap. 12.95 (*0-658-00292-9*, 002929, Keats Publng) NTC Contemp Pub Co.

Connolly, Pat. Coaching Evelyn: Fast, Faster, Fastest Woman in the World. LC 90-4835. (Illus.). 224p. (YA). (gr. 7 up). 1991. 15.95 (*0-06-021282-9*) HarpC Child Bks.

— Guide to Living Foods. rev. ed. LC 78-70856. (Illus.). 1978. 5.95 (*0-916764-05-2*) Price-Pottenger.

Connolly, Pat, jt. auth. see Associates of Price Pottinger Nutrition Foundation.

Connolly, Paul. Racism Gender Identities & Young Children: Social Relations in a Multi-Ethnic Inner City Primary School. LC 98-18322. 224p. (C). 1998. pap. 22.99 (*0-415-18319-7*) Routledge.

Connolly, Paul & Vilardi, Teresa, eds. New Methods in College Writing Programs: Theories in Practice. LC 86-16259. (Options for Teaching Ser.: No. 9). vii, 167p. 1987. pap. 19.75 (*0-87352-363-6*, J209C) Modern Lang.

— Writing to Learn Mathematics & Science. 336p. 1989. text 32.00 (*0-8077-2962-0*) Tchrs Coll.

Connolly, Paul H. Conflict & Decision Making: An Introduction to Political Science. LC 70-151333. xiv, 317p. 1971. write for info. (*0-06-041352-2*, HarpAudio) HarperTrade.

Connolly, Paul M. Entrepreneurs in Corporation. (Studies in Productivity: No. 47). 79p. 1986. pap. 55.00 (*0-08-029519-3*) Work in Amer.

— Promotional Practices & Policies. (Studies in Productivity: Highlights of the Literature Ser.: Vol. 41). 1985. 55.00 (*0-08-029515-0*) Work in Amer.

Connolly, Paul M., jt. auth. see Connolly, Kathleen G.

Connolly, Paula T. Winnie-the-Pooh & the House at Pooh Corner: Recovering Arcadia. LC 94-26329. (Twayne's Masterwork Studies). 160p. 1994. 29.00 (*0-8057-8810-7*, Twyne); per. write for info. (*0-8057-8811-5*, Twyne) Mac Lib Ref.

Connolly, Peter. Ancient Greece of Odysseus. rev. ed. (Illus.). 80p. 1999. pap. 12.95 (*0-19-910532-4*) OUP.

— The Cavalryman. 2nd ed. (The Roman World Ser.). (Illus.). 32p. (J). 1998. reprint ed. pap. 9.95 (*0-19-910424-7*) OUP.

— Greece & Rome at War. LC 97-40290. 1998. write for info. (*1-85367-303-X*, Pub. by Greenhill Bks) Stackpole.

— Holyland. LC 99-231799. (Illus.). 96p. 1999. pap. 12.95 (*0-19-910533-2*) OUP.

— The Legionary. 2nd ed. (The Roman World Ser.). (Illus.). 32p. (J). 1998. reprint ed. pap. 9.95 (*0-19-910425-5*) OUP.

— No Bland Facility: Selected Writings on Literature Religion & Censorship. 239p. 1991. 40.00 (*0-86140-315-0*, Pub. by Smyth) Dufour.

— Pompeii. (The Roman World Ser.). (Illus.). 78p. (J). (gr. 4-8). 1994. reprint ed. pap. 12.95 (*0-19-917158-0*) OUP.

— The Roman Fort. rev. ed. (The Roman World Ser.). (Illus.). 32p. (J). 1998. reprint ed. pap. 9.95 (*0-19-910426-3*) OUP.

— Vitalistic Thought in India: (A Study of the 'Prana' Concept in Vedic Literature & Its Development in the Vedanta, Samkhya & Pancaratra Traditions) (C). 1992. 19.00 (*81-7030-348-6*) S Asia.

Connolly, Peter, ed. Approaches to the Study of Religion. LC 97-180728. 224p. 1998. 69.95 (*0-304-33710-2*) Continuum.

— Literature & the Changing Ireland. (Irish Literary Studies: Vol. # 9). 230p. 1982. 35.00 (*0-86140-043-7*, Pub. by Smyth) Dufour.

Connolly, Peter & Dodge, Hazel. The Ancient City: Life in Classical Athens & Rome. LC 98-201131. (Illus.). 256p. (C). 1998. 35.00 (*0-19-917242-0*) OUP.

— The Ancient City: Life in Classical Athens & Rome. LC 98-201131. (Illus.). 256p. (gr. 5 up). 1998. lib. bdg. 37.50 (*0-19-521409-9*) OUP.

***Connolly, Peter & Dodge, Hazel.** The Ancient City: Life in Classical Athens & Rome. 256p. (YA). 2000. pap. 18.95 (*0-19-521582-6*) OUP.

Connolly, Peter, jt. auth. see Connolly, Holly.

***Connolly, Philomena & Martin, Geoffrey, eds.** The Dublin Guild Merchant Roll, c. 1190-1265. (Illus.). 186p. 1999. 37.50 (*0-946841-28-4*) Four Cts Pr.

Connolly, R. Chris. Millennium Superworld. 155p. 1997. reprint ed. pap. 8.95 (*0-9666506-0-3*) Megiddo Pr.

Connolly, Robert, tr. see Tafuri, Manfredo.

Connolly, Robert D. The New Collector's Directory. 56p. 1976. pap. 3.50 (*0-914598-36-8*) Intl Resources.

— The New Collector's Directory for the 1980's. 2nd rev. ed. (Illus.). 168p. 1980. pap. 5.95 (*0-914598-38-4*) Intl Resources.

Connolly, Robert E. Armalite & Ballot Box: An Irish-American Republican Primer. 130p. 1985. pap. 7.00 (*0-9614659-0-5*) Cuchullain Pubns.

— The Connolly Report: An Irish-American Republican Reader. 160p. 1988. 20.00 (*0-9614659-2-1*); pap. 7.50 (*0-9614659-1-3*) Cuchullain Pubns.

— A Time to Mend: An Irish-American Republican Solution. 145p. (Orig.). 1990. pap. 7.00 (*0-9614659-5-6*) Cuchullain Pubns.

Connolly, Robert E., ed. see Servatia, M.

Connolly, S. Modern Demonolatry. 98p. 1999. 40.00 (*0-9669788-0-3*) Darkerwd Pub Gp.

***Connolly, S. J.** Priests & People in Pre-Famine Ireland, 1780-1845. 2nd ed. 256p. 2000. pap. 29.95 (*1-85182-557-6*, Pub. by Four Cts Pr) Intl Spec Bk.

Connolly, S. J. Religion, Law, & Power: The Making of Protestant Ireland 1660-1760. (Illus.). 358p. 1995. pap. text 26.00 (*0-19-820587-2*) OUP.

Connolly, S. J., ed. Kingdoms United? LC 99-176026. 288p. 1999. pap. 24.95 (*1-85182-432-4*, Pub. by Four Cts Pr); boxed set 55.00 (*1-85182-401-4*, Pub. by Four Cts Pr) Intl Spec Bk.

— The Oxford Companion to Irish History. LC 98-150895. (Illus.). 636p. (YA). 1998. 49.95 (*0-19-211695-9*) OUP.

— The Oxford Companion to Irish History. (Illus.). 636p. 1999. pap. 19.95 (*0-19-866240-8*) OUP.

Connolly, Seamus G. Finding, Entering & Succeeding in a Foreign Market. 304p. 1987. text 39.95 (*0-13-316951-0*) P-H.

Connolly, Sean. AIDS Pastoral Care: An Introductory Guide. LC 94-70579. 96p. (Orig.). 1994. pap. 7.95 (*0-9636183-1-8*) Arc Res.

***Connolly, Sean.** Amelia Earhart. LC 99-89879. (Profiles Ser.). (Illus.). (J). 2000. lib. bdg. write for info. (*1-57572-223-2*) Heinemann Lib.

— Amphetamines. LC 00-26789. (Just the Facts Ser.). (Illus.). 2000. lib. bdg. write for info. (*1-57572-254-2*) Heinemann Lib.

Connolly, Sean. Bill Gates. LC 98-23409. (Heinemann Profiles Ser.). (J). 1998. (*1-57572-691-2*) Heinemann Lib.

***Connolly, Sean.** Claude Monet. LC 99-14546. (Life & Work of...Ser.). (Illus.). 32p. (J). (gr. k-3). 1999. lib. bdg. 13.95 (*1-57572-956-3*) Heinemann Lib.

— Cocaine. LC 00-26790. (Just the Facts Ser.). 2000. lib. bdg. write for info. (*1-57572-255-0*) Heinemann Lib.

Connolly, Sean. Drawing & Painting with Color. 160p. 1995. 15.98 (*0-7858-0240-1*) Bk Sales Inc.

***Connolly, Sean.** Ecstasy. LC 00-24347. (Just the Facts Ser.). 2000. lib. bdg. write for info. (*1-57572-256-9*) Heinemann Lib.

Connolly, Sean. Gardening for Containers & Window Boxes. 1995. 14.98 (*0-7858-0246-0*) Bk Sales Inc.

— A Great Place to Die. LC 96-47194. (Hardscrabble Bks.). 175p. 1997. 21.95 (*0-87451-811-3*) U Pr of New Eng.

***Connolly, Sean.** Henry Moore. LC 99-14558. (Life & Work of...Ser.). (Illus.). 32p. (J). (gr. k-3). 1999. lib. bdg. 13.95 (*1-57572-953-9*) Heinemann Lib.

— Heroin. LC 00-25652. (Just the Facts Ser.). (YA). 2000. lib. bdg. write for info. (*1-57572-257-7*) Heinemann Lib.

— Leonardo Da Vinci. LC 99-10151. (Life & Work of...Ser.). (Illus.). 32p. (J). (gr. k-3). 1999. lib. bdg. 13.95 (*1-57572-954-7*) Heinemann Lib.

— LSD. LC 00-25655. 2000. lib. bdg. write for info. (*1-57572-258-5*) Heinemann Lib.

— Margaret Thatcher. LC 99-89880. (Profiles Ser.). (Illus.). 2000. lib. bdg. write for info. (*1-57572-224-0*) Heinemann Lib.

Connolly, Sean. Neil Armstrong. LC 98-7465. (Profiles Ser.). (Illus.). (J). 1998. 23.95 (*1-57572-692-0*) Heinemann Lib.

***Connolly, Sean.** Nelson Mandela. LC 99-85742. (Profiles Ser.). (Illus.). 2000. lib. bdg. write for info. (*1-57572-225-9*) Heinemann Lib.

— Paul Cezanne. LC 99-14545. (Life & Work of...Ser.). (Illus.). 32p. (J). (gr. k-3). 1999. lib. bdg. 13.95 (*1-57572-957-1*) Heinemann Lib.

— Steroids. LC 00-25654. 2000. lib. bdg. write for info. (*1-57572-259-3*) Heinemann Lib.

Connolly, Sean. Steven Spielberg. LC 98-7466. (Profiles Ser.). (Illus.). 56p. (J). 1998. write for info. (*1-57572-694-7*) Heinemann Lib.

***Connolly, Sean.** Tobacco. LC 00-25653. (Just the Facts Ser.). (YA). 2000. lib. bdg. write for info. (*1-57572-260-7*) Heinemann Lib.

Connolly, Sean, tr. Bede: On the Temple. 142p. (Orig.). 1996. pap. text 17.95 (*0-85323-049-8*) U of Pa Pr.

Connolly, Sean, tr. Bede: On Tobit & the Canticle of Habakkuk. LC 98-103949. 144p. 1997. pap. 15.00 (*1-85182-284-4*, Pub. by Four Cts Pr); boxed set 50.00 (*1-85182-283-6*, Pub. by Four Cts Pr) Intl Spec Bk.

Connolly, Shane. Table Flowers. (Illus.). 128p. 1996. 24.95 (*1-57076-041-1*, Trafalgar Sq Pub) Trafalgar.

— Wedding Flowers. LC 97-61777. (Illus.). 144p. 1998. 29.95 (*1-57076-108-6*, Trafalgar Sq Pub) Trafalgar.

Connolly, Steven, jt. auth. see Gershon, David.

Connolly, Susan R. Triplet Mania. LC 95-90369. 86p. (Orig.). 1995. pap. 10.95 (*0-9647132-0-9*) Full Moon Pubng.

Connolly, Sylvia. Math Problem-Solving Brain Teasers. (Brain Teasers Ser.). (Illus.). 80p. (J). (gr. 5-8). 1998. pap. 9.95 (*1-57690-219-6*, TCM2219) Tchr Create Mat.

— Pre-Geometry Brain Teasers. (Brain Teasers Ser.). 80p. (J). (gr. 5-8). 1998. pap. 9.95 (*1-57690-218-8*) Tchr Create Mat.

Connolly, Terence L., ed. see Thompson, Francis.

***Connolly, Terry, et al, eds.** Judgment & Decision Making: An Interdisciplinary Reader. 2nd ed. LC 98-51484. (Cambridge Series on Judgment & Decision Making). (Illus.). 992p. (C). 2000. 80.00 (*0-521-62355-3*); pap. 34.95 (*0-521-62602-1*) Cambridge U Pr.

Connolly, Theresa, et al. The Well-Managed Classroom: Promoting Student Success Through Social Skill Instruction. 162p. 1995. pap. text 24.95 (*0-938510-61-4*, 48-005) Boys Town Pr.

***Connolly, Thomas.** Database Solutions: A Step-by-Step Guide to Building Databases. (Illus.). 256p. 1999. pap. text 44.95 (*0-201-67476-9*) Addison-Wesley.

— Database Systems: A Practical Approach to Design, Implementation & Management. 2nd ed. LC 98-25198. 848p. (C). 1998. pap. 69.00 (*0-201-34287-1*) Addison-Wesley.

Connolly, Thomas. Mourning into Joy: Music, Raphael, & Saint Cecilia. LC 94-5325. 1995. 40.00 (*0-300-05901-9*) Yale U Pr.

Connolly, Thomas E. A Coeur D'Alene Indian Story. 85p. (J). 1990. pap. 4.50 (*0-87770-483-X*) Ye Galleon.

— Essays on Fiction-Dickens, Melville, Hawthorne & Faulkner. LC 98-54721. (Studies in Comparative Literature Ser.: Vol. 25). 156p. 1999. text 69.95 (*0-7734-8143-5*) E Mellen.

— Faulkner's World: A Directory of His People & Synopses of Actions in His Published Works. LC 88-5439. 634p. (Orig.). (C). 1988. lib. bdg. 62.00 (*0-8191-5703-1*) U Pr of Amer.

— A Neo-Aristotelian & Joycean Theory of Poetic Forms. LC 95-7457. (Studies in Comparative Literature: Vol. 6). 1995. 69.95 (*0-7734-8886-3*) E Mellen.

— Swinburne's Theory of Poetry. LC 64-17576. 144p. (C). 1965. text 19.50 (*0-87395-013-5*) State U NY Pr.

Connolly, Thomas E., ed. Joyce's "Portrait" Criticisms & Critiques. LC 62-14861. (Goldentree Books in English Literature). (Orig.). 1962. pap. text 17.95 (*0-89197-253-6*) Irvington.

Connolly, Thomas E., et al. James Joyce's Books, Portraits, Manuscripts, Notebooks, Typescripts, Page Proofs: Together with Critical Essays about Some of His Works. LC 97-17838. (Illus.). 296p. 1997. text 89.95 (*0-7734-8645-3*) E Mellen.

Connolly, Thomas F. George Jean Nathan & the Making of Modern American Drama Criticism. LC 99-10529. (Illus.). 176p. 2000. 35.00 (*0-8386-3780-9*) Fairleigh Dickinson.

Connolly, Thomas J. Newberry Crater: A Ten-Thousand-Year Record of Human Occupation & Environmental Change. LC 99-27479. (Anthropological Papers: No. 121). (Illus.). 287p. 1999. pap. 34.50 (*0-87480-574-0*) U of Utah Pr.

Connolly, Tom, jt. auth. see Meyer, Brian.

Connolly, Walter B., Jr. & Connolly, Michael J. A Practical Guide to Equal Employment Opportunity, 2 vols. 1100p. 1979. 135.00 (*0-317-01348-3*) NY Law Pub.

Connolly, Walter B., Jr. & Crowell, Donald R. A Practical Guide to the Occupational Safety & Health Act. 650p. 1982. 90.00 (*0-317-03299-2*, 00578) NY Law Pub.

Connolly, Walter B., Jr. & Peterson, David W. Use of Statistics in Equal Employment Opportunity Litigation. 750p. 1980. ring bd. 90.00 (*0-318-20279-4*, 00553) NY Law Pub.

Connolly, William. Politics & Ambiguity. LC 86-15819. (Rhetoric of the Human Sciences Ser.). 256p. 1987. text 27.95 (*0-299-10990-9*) U of Wis Pr.

Connolly, William E. The Augustinian Imperative: A Reflection on the Politics. (Modernity & Political Thought Ser.: Vol. 1). 176p. (C). 1993. text 44.00 (*0-8039-3636-2*); pap. text 19.95 (*0-8039-3637-0*) Sage.

— The Ethos of Pluralization. (Borderlines Ser.: Vol. 1). 256p. 1995. pap. 19.95 (*0-8166-2669-3*) U of Minn Pr.

— Identity-Difference: Democratic Negotiations of Political Paradox. LC 90-45789. 264p. 1991. text 39.95 (*0-8014-2506-9*) Cornell U Pr.

— Identity-Difference: Democratic Negotiations of Political Paradox. LC 90-45789. 264p. 1992. pap. text 16.95 (*0-8014-9744-2*) Cornell U Pr.

— Why I Am Not a Secularist. LC 98-43815. 1999. 29.95 (*0-8166-3331-2*) U of Minn Pr.

***Connolly, William E.** Why I Am Not a Secularist. LC 98-43815. 1999. pap. write for info. (*0-8166-3332-0*) U of Minn Pr.

Connolly, William E., epil. Political Theory & Modernity. 2nd ed. LC 93-193. 240p. 1993. pap. text 16.95 (*0-8014-8108-2*) Cornell U Pr.

Connolly, William G., jt. auth. see Barry, William A.

Connolly, William G., jt. auth. see Siegal, Allan M.

Connolly, William J., jt. auth. see Birmingham, Madeline.

Connoly, Cyril. Cien Libros, Clave Del Movimiento Moderno. (SPA.). pap. 5.99 (*968-16-4111-6*, Pub. by Fondo) Continental Bk.

Connoly, Joseph. Summer Things. LC 99-202022. 336p. 1999. pap. 16.95 (*0-571-19076-6*) Faber & Faber.

Connoly, William M., jt. auth. see Walkowski, Paul J.

Connon, ed. see Saurin.

***Connon, Bryan.** Beverley Nichols: A Life. LC 99-46819. (Illus.). 344p. 2000. 29.95 (*0-88192-444-X*, Amadeus Pr) Timber.

Connon, Bryan. Somerset Maugham & the Maughan Dynasty. LC 97-154890. (Illus.). 396p. 1998. 40.00 (*1-85619-274-1*, Pub. by Sinclair-Stevenson) Trafalgar.

Connon, Derek, jt. ed. see Cardy, Michael.

Connon, Derek, ed. see De Musset, Alfred.

Connon, Heather & Roper, Paul. Great Glen Way. (Illus.). 240p. 1997. 22.95 (*1-85158-864-7*, Pub. by Mainstream Pubng) Trafalgar.

— The Highland High Way: A High-Level Walking Route from Loch Lomond to Fort William. (Illus.). 240p. 1996. pap. 22.95 (*1-85158-791-8*, Pub. by Mainstream Pubng) Trafalgar.

Connor. Pathology of Infectious Diseases, Vol. I. (C). 1997. 176.00 (*0-8385-7693-1*) Appleton & Lange.

— Pathology of Infectious Diseases, Vol. II. (C). 1997. 176.00 (*0-8385-7694-X*) Appleton & Lange.

Connor, jt. auth. see Yogev.

***Connor, Alexandra.** Midnight's Smiling. large type ed. 400p. 1999. 31.99 (*0-7089-4096-X*, Linford) Ulverscroft.

Connor, Ann, jt. auth. see Griffith, Marlene.

Connor, Anna T. & Zajdel, Laura C. 1794: Janie Miller's Whiskey Rebellion Saga. (Illus.). (Orig.). (YA). 1994. pap. 11.95 (*0-9640994-0-3*) L C Zajdel.

Connor, Anne & Black, Stewart, eds. Performance Review & Quality Assurance in Social Work. (Research Highlights in Social Work Ser.: No. 20). 200p. 1994. 34.95 (*1-85302-017-6*) Taylor & Francis.

Connor, Anne, jt. ed. see Ulas, Marion.

Connor, Anthony, jt. auth. see Neff, Robert.

Connor, Anthony C. & Batchelor, Margaret A. Using Excelerator for Windows. LC 94-23579. 141p. (C). 1995. text 23.95 (*0-256-18187-X*, Irwn McGrw-H) McGrw-H Hghr Educ.

Connor, Anthony J. Baseball for the Love of It. 1982. 16.95 (*0-02-527500-3*) Macmillan.

— Voices from Cooperstown: Baseball's Hall of Famers Tell It Like It Was. 1998. pap. text 9.99 (*1-57866-016-5*) Promntory Pr.

Connor, Bernadette Y. Damaged! LC 98-61432. 352p. 1998. 23.95 (*0-9650970-3-X*); pap. 14.95 (*0-9650970-2-1*) Waverly Hse.

Connor, Beverly. Dressed to Die. LC 98-34125. (Lindsay Chamberlain Mystery Ser.). 320p. 1998. 20.95 (*1-888952-89-X*) Cumberland Hse.

— Questionable Remains. LC 97-24565. 288p. 1997. 20.95 (*1-888952-53-9*) Cumberland Hse.

— A Rumor of Bones. LC 96-31985. Vol. 1. (Illus.). 254p. 1996. 20.95 (*1-888952-08-3*) Cumberland Hse.

***Connor, Beverly.** Skeleton Crew. LC 99-46311. (Lindsay Chamberlin Novel Ser.: Vol. 3). 352p. 1999. 20.95 (*1-58182-042-9*, Cumberland Hearthside) Cumberland Hse.

An Asterisk (*) at the beginning of an entry indicates that the title is appearing for the first time.

Connor, Billie M. & Machedlover, Helene. Ottemiller's Index to Plays in Collections: An Author & Title Index to Plays Appearing in Collections Published Between 1900 & 1985. 7th ed. LC 87-34160. 576p. 1988. 52.00 (*0-8108-2081-1*) Scarecrow.

Connor, Brooke, jt. auth. see Kittelson, Pat.

Connor, C. Assessment Testing in the Primary School. 1990. 79.95 (*1-85000-551-6*, Falmer Pr); pap. 37.95 (*1-85000-552-4*, Falmer Pr) Taylor & Francis.

***Connor, C. J.** Wolves. (Wild Stickers Ser.). (Illus.). 2000. pap. 2.50 (*0-941042-27-8*) Dog Eared Pubns.

Connor, Carolyn & Connor, Robert. The Life & Miracles of St. Luke. (Archbishop Iakovos Library of Ecclesiastical & Historical Sources: No. 18). 178p. 1994. pap. 14.95 (*0-917653-36-X*, Pub. by Hellenic Coll Pr) BookWorld.

Connor, Carolyn L. Art & Miracles in Medieval Byzantium: The Crypt as Hosios Loukas & Its Frescoes. (Illus.). 136p. 1991. text 75.00 (*0-691-04084-2*, Pub. by Princeton U Pr) Cal Prin Full Svc.

— The Color of Ivory: Polychromy on Byzantine Ivories. LC 97-23914. 164p. 1998. text 79.50 (*0-691-04818-5*, Pub. by Princeton U Pr) Cal Prin Full Svc.

Connor, Carolyn L. & Connor, W. Robert. The Life & Miracles of Saint Luke of Steiris. Vaporis, Nomikos M., ed. LC 89-11153. (Archbishop Iacovos Library of Ecclesiastical & Historical Sources: No. 18). 178p. (C). 1994. 14.95 (*0-917653-35-1*, Pub. by Hellenic Coll Pr) BookWorld.

Connor, Catherine. Alison Goes for the Gold. (Magic Attic Club Ser.). (Illus.). 72p. (J). (gr. 2-6). 1995. 12.95 (*1-57513-002-5*); pap. 5.95 (*1-57513-003-3*) Magic Attic.

— Alison Goes for the Gold. (Magic Attic Club Ser.). (J). (gr. 2-6). 1995. 11.15 (*0-606-08473-8*, Pub. by Turtleback) Demco.

— Alison on the Trail. (Magic Attic Club Ser.). (Illus.). 72p. (J). (gr. 2-6). 1995. 12.95 (*1-57513-010-6*); pap. 5.95 (*1-57513-011-4*) Magic Attic.

— Alison on the Trail. (Magic Attic Club Ser.). (J). (gr. 2-6). 1995. 11.15 (*0-606-08474-6*, Pub. by Turtleback) Demco.

— Alison Saves the Wedding. (Magic Attic Club Ser.). (Illus.). 80p. (J). (gr. 2-6). 1996. 12.95 (*1-57513-018-1*); pap. 5.95 (*1-57513-019-X*) Magic Attic.

Connor, Cathy & O'Haire, Daniel. Roadside Geology of Alaska. LC 88-1651. (Roadside Geology Ser.). (Illus.). 256p. 1988. pap. 16.00 (*0-87842-213-7*) Mountain Pr.

***Connor, Celeste.** Democratic Visions: Art & Theory of the Steiglitz Circle, 1924-1934. LC 99-87355. (Illus.). 256p. 2000. 45.00 (*0-520-21354-8*, Pub. by U CA Pr) Cal Prin Full Svc.

***Connor, Chris.** Miller's Collector's Guide: Postcards. (Illus.). 64p. 2000. pap. 9.95 (*1-84000-190-9*, Pub. by Millers Pubns) Antique Collect.

Connor, D. J., jt. auth. see Loomis, R. S.

Connor, D. Russell. Benny Goodman: Wrappin' It Up. LC 95-39267. (Studies in Jazz: No. 23). 180p. 1996. 39.50 (*0-8108-3102-3*) Scarecrow.

Connor, Daniel, et al. Diagnostic Pathology of Infectious Diseases, Vol. 1/2. LC 96-31452. 1707p. (C). 1999. 320.00 (*0-8385-1601-7*, A1601-2, Apple Lange Med) McGraw.

Connor, Danny & Chun, Yip. Wing Chun Martial Arts: Principles & Techniques. LC 93-9998. (Illus.). 128p. (Orig.). 1993. pap. 12.95 (*0-87728-796-1*) Weiser.

Connor, Danny & Tse, Michael. Qigong: Chinese Movement & Meditation for Health. LC 92-1762. (Illus.). 96p. 1992. pap. 12.95 (*0-87728-758-9*) Weiser.

Connor, Darlene, ed. see Graham, Cary D.

Connor, Dennis. Life's Winning Tips. (Illus.). 78p. (Orig.). 1993. pap. 7.95 (*1-56245-066-2*) Great Quotations.

Connor, Dick & Davidson, Jeff. Getting New Clients. 2nd ed. LC 92-20197. 304p. 1992. 37.95 (*0-471-55528-2*) Wiley.

Connor, Dick & Davidson, Jeffrey P. Marketing Your Consulting & Professional Services. 3rd ed. LC 97-22965. 288p. 1997. 34.95 (*0-471-13392-2*) Wiley.

Connor, Dixie. Shining Mountain Shadows. (Illus.). 1977. pap. 5.00 (*0-918292-02-6*) Griggs Print.

Connor, E. S., jt. ed. see Bruce, A. M.

Connor, Edward. Prophecy for Today. LC 83-70408. 135p. 1984. reprint ed. pap. 5.50 (*0-89555-212-4*) TAN Bks Pubs.

Connor, Elizabeth. Methodist Trail Blazer: Philip Gatch. rev. ed. LC 76-101704. (Illus.). 260p. reprint ed. pap. 12.00 (*0-914960-51-2*) Academy Bks.

Connor, Elizabeth & Kinzler, Mary. Libby Meets the Bully. (Illus.). 100p. (J). (gr. 2-7). 1997. 12.95 (*0-9658468-0-6*) Adbeth Pr.

***Connor, Elizabeth & Kinzler, Mary.** Libby Saves Beauty's Colt. limited large type ed. LC 98-93720. (Illus.). 106p. (J). (gr. 2-6). 1999. 12.95 (*0-9658468-1-4*) Adbeth Pr.

Connor, Elizabeth, tr. see Aelred of Rievaulx.

Connor, Ellwood. I Am Irish American. LC 96-53128. (Our American Family Ser.). (J). (gr. k-3). 1997. lib. bdg. 15.93 (*0-8239-5005-0*, PowerKids) Rosen Group.

***Connor, Floyd.** Football's Most Wanted: The Top Ten Book of the Great Game's Outrageous Characters, Fortunate Fumbles & Other Oddities. 2000. pap. 12.95 (*1-57488-309-7*) Brasseys.

— Out of the Park: The Top 10 Book of Screwball Players, Lucky Bounces & Other Baseball Oddities. LC 99-86476. 2000. pap. 12.95 (*1-57488-229-5*) Brasseys.

— Wrestling's Most Wanted: The Top 10 Book of Pro Wrestling's Outrageous Performers, Punishing Piledrivers & Other Oddities. 2000. pap. 12.95 (*1-57488-308-9*) Brasseys.

Connor, Frances P., et al. Program Guide for Infants & Toddlers with Neuromotor & Other Developmental Disabilities. LC 77-28188. 408p. 1978. pap. 21.95 (*0-8077-2546-3*) Tchrs Coll.

Connor, Gary B. & Woods, John A. Sales: Games & Activities for Trainers. LC 97-9590. 256p. 1997. pap. 24.95 (*0-07-071847-4*) McGraw.

Connor, Gregory. Vehicle Stops: Tactical Procedures & Safety Strategies. (Illus.). 159p. 1999. pap. text 17.80 (*0-87563-799-X*) Stipes.

Connor, Gregory J. & Summers, Matthew. Tactical Neutralization Techniques. (Illus.). 300p. 1988. spiral bd. 24.80 (*0-87563-326-9*) Stipes.

Connor, H., ed. see National Conference on the Diabetic Foot Staff.

Connor, H. E., jt. auth. see Edgar, E.

Connor, Helen, ed. see Serwitz, Marshall & Serwitz, Jewel.

Connor, Helen V., jt. auth. see Mathis, Carla M.

Connor, J. Alexandra. The Hour of the Angel. 430p. 1990. 22.95 (*0-434-14218-2*) Trafalgar.

Connor, J. J. & Brebbia, Carlos A., eds. Betech 86. (BETECH Ser.: Vol. 2). 828p. 1986. 130.00 (*0-931215-30-7*) Computational Mech MA.

Connor, J. J. & Klink, B. S. A. Introduction to Motion Based Design. LC 96-83301. 440p. (C). 1996. text 146.00 (*1-85312-454-0*, 4540, Pub. by WIT Pr) Computational Mech MA.

Connor, J. J., jt. ed. see Brebbia, Carlos A.

Connor, J. J., ed. see Power, H.

Connor, J. M., jt. ed. see Whittle, M. J.

Connor, J. Michael & Ferguson-Smith, M. A. Essential Medical Genetics. 5th ed. LC 96-45181. (Essentials Ser.). (Illus.). 288p. 1997. pap. text 44.95 (*0-86542-666-X*) Blackwell Sci.

Connor, Jack. The Complete Birder: A Guide to Better Birding. LC 87-27217. (Illus.). 288p. 1988. pap. 14.95 (*0-395-46807-8*) HM.

— Leahy's Lads: The Story of the Famous Notre Dame Football Teams of the 1940s. LC 94-20706. (Illus.). 318p. 1994. 24.95 (*0-912083-75-1*) Diamond Communications.

— Leahy's Lads: The Story of the Famous Notre Dame Football Teams of the 1940s. LC 97-30224. 1997. pap. 16.95 (*0-912083-90-5*) Diamond Communications.

— Season at the Point: A Birder's Journal of Cape May. LC 91-9048. 304p. 1992. pap. 12.50 (*0-87113-475-6*, Atlntc Mnthly) Grove-Atltic.

Connor, James R., ed. Metals & Oxidative Damage in Neurological Disorders. LC 97-30552. (Illus.). 396p. (C). 1997. text 114.00 (*0-306-45534-X*, Kluwer Plenum) Kluwer Academic.

Connor, Jane Gardner. Children's Library Services Handbook. LC 89-8568. (Illus.). 144p. 1990. pap. 29.95 (*0-89774-489-6*) Oryx Pr.

Connor, Jeannette M., ed. Colonial Records of Spanish Florida: Letters & Reports of Governors & Secular Persons, 2 vols., Set. LC 74-19720. reprint ed. 105.00 (*0-404-12475-5*) AMS Pr.

***Connor, Jennifer.** Guardians of Medical Knowledge: The Genesis of the Medical Library Association. LC 99-57038. 248p. 2000. 65.00 (*0-8108-3470-7*) Scarecrow.

Connor, Joan. Here on Old Route 7: Stories. LC 97-15900. 152p. 1997. pap. 17.95 (*0-8262-1129-1*) U of Mo Pr.

Connor, John. Doctrina Wesleyana Aclarada: Instruccion Programada con el Suplemento. Bardsley, Sharon S. et al, trs. (Wesleyan Doctrine Made Plain Ser.). (SPA., Illus.). 316p. 1989. pap. 12.95 (*0-89827-063-4*, BK076) Wesleyan Pub Hse.

— Wesleyan Doctrine Made Plain: Programmed Instruction Text Plus Supplement. (Illus.). 336p. (Orig.). 1987. pap. 12.95 (*0-89827-048-0*, BK077) Wesleyan Pub Hse.

***Connor, John & Connor, Margie, eds.** Portraits of Grace: Stories of Salvation from Wesleyan World Missions. 255p. 1999. pap. text 9.95 (*0-89827-201-7*) Wesleyan Pub Hse.

Connor, John A., et al. Tier 2 Guidance Manual for Risk-Based Corrective Action. (Illus.). (Orig.). 1996. pap. 75.00 (*1-882713-03-6*) Grndwater Srv.

Connor, John J. ABCs of Performance Improvement: A Desktop Reference Guide. LC 98-75070. 250p. 1999. pap. 24.95 (*0-945820-10-0*) Harris & Connor.

— One-on-One - Step-by-Step: A Supervisor's Guide to Training in the Workplace. LC 89-110011. 128p. (Orig.). 1988. pap. 19.95 (*0-945820-03-8*) Harris & Connor.

— Problem Solving - Decision Making: A Workbook for Managers & Supervisors. (Illus.). 100p. 1998. pap. text 19.95 (*0-945820-09-7*) Harris & Connor.

Connor, John M. & Schiek, William A. Food Processing: An Industrial Powerhouse in Transition. 2nd ed. LC 96-43765. 688p. 1997. 89.95 (*0-471-15515-2*) Wiley.

Connor, Joseph. Marine Fire Prevention, Firefighting & Fire Safety. (Illus.). 404p. 1979. pap. text 21.95 (*0-87618-994-X*) P-H.

Connor, Judith. Seashore Life on Rocky Coasts. LC 92-42249. (Natural History Ser.). (Illus.). 64p. 1993. pap. 9.95 (*1-878244-05-1*) Monterey Bay Aquarium.

Connor, Judith & Baxter, Charles. Kelp Forests. LC 89-14553. (Natural History Ser.). (Illus.). 64p. 1989. pap. 9.95 (*1-878244-01-9*) Monterey Bay Aquarium.

Connor, Julia. A Canto for the Birds. (Illus.). 38p. 1995. pap. write for info. (*0-914485-14-8*) Trill Pr.

— The Delta Poem. limited ed. (Illus.). 46p. 1987. pap. write for info. (*0-9618584-1-9*) Vernacular Edit.

Connor, K. J. & McLintock, I. S. Radiation Protection: Handbook for Laboratory Workers. 202p. 1997. pap. 150.00 (*0-948237-21-X*, Pub. by H&H Sci Cnslts) St Mut.

Connor, Kathryn M. Kava: Nature's Stress Relief. LC 99-190569. 224p. 1999. mass mkt. 5.99 (*0-380-80641-X*, Avon Bks) Morrow Avon.

Connor, Kathryn M., jt. auth. see Davidson, Jonathan R. T.

***Connor, Ken.** Ghost Force: The Secret History of the SAS. (Illus.). 375p. 1999. 24.95 (*1-57098-314-3*, Pub. by Roberts Rinehart) Publishers Group.

Connor, Kenneth A. Salon Electromagnetic. (C). 1996. text. write for info. (*0-201-52744-8*) Addison-Wesley.

Connor, Kimberly R. Conversions & Visions in the Writings of African-American Women. LC 93-14499. 328p. (C). 1995. pap. text 18.00 (*0-87049-908-4*) U of Tenn Pr.

***Connor, Kimberly R.** Imagining Grace: Liberating Theologies in the Slave Narrative Tradition. LC 99-6615. 2000. 32.95 (*0-252-02530-X*) U of Ill Pr.

Connor, Larence J., ed. see Berthold, Robert, Jr.

Connor, Lawerence J., jt. ed. see Hoopingarner, Roger.

Connor, Lawrence J., et al, eds. Asian Apiculture: Proceedings of the First International Conference on the Asian Honey Bees & Bee Mites. LC 93-29190. 1993. 79.95 (*1-878075-03-9*) Wicwas Pr.

Connor, Leonard P. & O'Brien, R.L. Welding Handbook, (WHB-2.8) Welding Processes. 8th enl. ed. (Illus.). 955p. 1991. 118.00 (*0-87171-354-3*) Am Welding.

Connor, Linda. Linda Conner: Lux Three. limited ed. LC 94-61918. (Lux Ser.: Vol. III). (Illus.). 52p. 1998. pap. 19.95 (*0-9630393-3-4*) Ctr for Photo.

— Luminance: Lux Three. 58p. 1994. pap. 19.95 (*0-9630393-2-6*) Ctr for Photo.

Connor, Linda, et al. Jero Tapakan: Balinese Healer. 2nd rev. ed. Seaman, Gary, ed. LC 95-83303. (Illus.). 280p. 1996. pap. 20.00 (*1-878986-07-4*) Ethnographics Pr.

***Connor, Linda H. & Samuel, Geoffrey, eds.** Healing Powers & Modernity: Traditional Medicine, Shamanism & Science in Asian Societies. LC 00-29256. 266p. 2000. 67.00 (*0-89789-715-3*, H715, Bergin & Garvey) Greenwood.

Connor, Margaret K., jt. compiled by see Kelsey, Mavis P.

Connor, Margie, jt. ed. see Connor, John.

Connor, Mark & Norman, Paul, eds. Predicting Health Behaviour: Research & Practice with Social Cognition Models. LC 95-14732. 240p. 1995. pap. 34.95 (*0-335-19320-X*) OpUniv Pr.

Connor, Mary. Training the Counsellor: An Integrative Model. LC 94-16169. 240p. (C). 1994. pap. 25.99 (*0-415-10219-7*, B4079) Routledge.

— Training the Counsellor: An Integrative Model. LC 94-16169. 240p. (C). (gr. 13). 1994. 80.00 (*0-415-10218-9*, B4075) Routledge.

Connor, Mary K. Dick Connor Remembered: Writing on Sports & Life. LC 94-37940. (Illus.). 288p. 1995. 22.95 (*1-55591-216-8*) Fulcrum Pub.

Connor, Maura, ed. see American Society of PeriAnesthesia Nurses Staff.

Connor, Maura, ed. see Chitty, Kay K.

Connor, Maura, ed. see Curry, Katharine & Jaffe, Amy.

Connor, Maura, ed. see Gutierrez, Kathleen.

Connor, Maura, ed. see Hodgson, Barbara B. & Kizior, Robert J.

Connor, Maura, ed. see Kee, Joyce L. & Hayes, Evelyn R.

Connor, Maura, ed. see Kenner, Carole A.

Connor, Maura, ed. see Kost, Michael.

Connor, Maura, ed. see Lehne, Richard A.

Connor, Maura, ed. see Matarese, Laura E. & Gottschlich, Michele M.

Connor, Maura, ed. see Matassarin-Jacobs, Esther.

Connor, Maura, ed. see Mitchell, Mary K.

Connor, Maura, ed. see Myers Gorrie, Trula, et al.

Connor, Maura, ed. see Nagelhout, John J. & Zaglaniczny, Karen L.

Connor, Maura, ed. see Papanier Wells, MaryAnn & Bradley, Mary.

Connor, Maura, ed. see Peckenpaugh, Nancy J. & Poleman, Charlotte.

Connor, Maura, ed. see Peckenpaugh, Nancy J. & Poleman, Charlotte M.

Connor, Maura, ed. see Phippen, Mark L. & Wells, Maryann P.

Connor, Maura, ed. see Phippen, Mark L., et al.

Connor, Maura, ed. see Saunders Publishing Staff.

Connor, Maura, ed. see Sieh, April & Brentin, Louise.

Connor, Maura, ed. see Silvestri, Linda Anne.

Connor, Maura, ed. see Thureen, Patricia J., et al.

Connor, Michael. Forgive? Forget It! Creative Revenge at Its Best. (Illus.). 210p. 1988. pap. 19.95 (*0-87364-452-2*) Paladin Pr.

— How to Create a New Identity. (Illus.). 120p. 1987. pap. 8.95 (*0-8065-1034-X*, Citadel Pr) Carol Pub Group.

— How to Hide Anything. (Illus.). 120p. 1984. pap. 14.00 (*0-87364-289-9*) Paladin Pr.

Connor, Nikki. Cardboard Tubes. LC 96-45582. (Creative Crafts from Ser.). (Illus.). 24p. (J). (ps-2). 1997. lib. bdg. 19.90 (*0-7613-0552-1*, Copper Beech Bks) Millbrook Pr.

— Plastic Bottles. LC 96-45580. (Creative Crafts from Ser.). (Illus.). 24p. (J). (ps-2). 1997. lib. bdg. 19.90 (*0-7613-0553-X*, Copper Beech Bks) Millbrook Pr.

Connor, Noel. Talitha Cumi. 48p. 1983. pap. 9.95 (*0-906427-53-3*, Pub. by Bloodaxe Bks) Dufour.

Connor, Noel. Confounded Language: Images by Noel Connor: New Poems by Irish Writers. 47p. 1991. pap. 12.95 (*1-85224-143-8*, Pub. by Bloodaxe Bks) Dufour.

Connor, Noel, jt. auth. see Paulin, Tom.

Connor, P. E. & Perlis, R. A Survey of Trace Forms of Algebraic Number Fields. (Series in Pure Mathematics: Vol. 2). 328p. 1984. text 55.00 (*9971-966-04-2*); pap. text 30.00 (*9971-966-05-0*) World Scientific Pub.

Connor, Pat, jt. auth. see Bracegirdle, Hilary.

Connor, Patrick E. & Lake, Linda K. Managing Organizational Change. 2nd ed. LC 94-16461. 248p. 1994. 75.00 (*0-275-94652-5*, Praeger Pubs); pap. 22.95 (*0-275-94653-3*, Praeger Pubs) Greenwood.

Connor, Peter. The Patterns of Life. LC 98-85203. 185p. 1999. pap. 14.95 (*1-56315-110-3*, Pub. by SterlingHse) Natl Bk Netwk.

Connor, Peter, tr. see Bataille, Georges.

***Connor, Peter T.** Georges Bataille & the Mysticism of Sin. LC 99-32724. 2000. 34.95 (*0-8018-6268-X*) Johns Hopkins.

Connor, Pierre E. & Floyd, E. E. Torsion in SU-Bordism. LC 52-42839. (American Mathematical Society Ser.: No. 60). 76p. 1969. reprint ed. pap. 30.00 (*0-608-04437-7*, 205257300012) Bks Demand.

Connor, R. D. Ante-Bellum Builders of North Carolina. LC 70-149342. 123p. 1971. reprint ed. 20.00 (*0-87152-064-8*) Reprint.

Connor, R. W., ed. see Isocrates.

Connor, Ralph. The Doctor: A Tale of the Rockies. 1976. lib. bdg. 17.25 (*0-89968-015-1*, Lghtyr Pr) Buccaneer Bks.

— Glengarry School Days. 216p. 1996. pap. text 6.95 (*0-7710-9889-8*) McCland & Stewart.

— Jim Craig's Battle for Black Rock. Phillips, Michael, ed. 1988. pap. 7.99 (*0-940652-06-4*) Inhtce Pubns.

— The Man from Glengarry. 1976. lib. bdg. 19.50 (*0-89968-017-8*, Lghtyr Pr) Buccaneer Bks.

— The Man from Glengarry. 392p. 1996. pap. 7.95 (*0-7710-9890-1*) McCland & Stewart.

— The Sky Pilot, a Tale of the Foothills. 1976. 15.95 (*0-8488-1271-9*) Amereon Ltd.

— The Sky Pilot, a Tale of the Foothills. 1976. lib. bdg. 14.25 (*0-89968-019-4*, Lghtyr Pr) Buccaneer Bks.

— The Sky Pilot in No Man's Land. 1976. 16.95 (*0-8488-1270-0*) Amereon Ltd.

— The Sky Pilot in No Man's Land. 1976. lib. bdg. 15.75 (*0-89968-018-6*, Lghtyr Pr) Buccaneer Bks.

— Thomas Skyler: Foothills Preacher. Phillips, Michael R., ed. LC 87-82629. (Stories of Yesteryear Ser.: Vol. 2). Orig. Title: The Sky Pilot. 169p. 1988. pap. 6.95 (*0-940652-07-2*) Inhtce Pubns.

Connor, Randy P. The Encyclopedia of Queer Myth, Smybol & Spirit. LC 97-185203. (Sexual Politics Ser.). 400p. 1997. 21.95 (*0-304-33760-9*) Continuum.

Connor, Reardon. Shake Hands with the Devil. 312p. reprint ed. lib. bdg. 24.95 (*0-89190-449-2*, Rivercity Pr) Amereon Ltd.

Connor, Richard, jt. ed. see Nettles, Scott.

Connor, Richard C. Lives of Whales & Dolphins: From the American Museum of Natural History. 1995. 25.00 (*0-8050-1950-2*) H Holt & Co.

Connor, Richard C. & Micklethwaite Peterson, Dawn. The Lives of Whales & Dolphins: From the American Museum of Natural History. (Illus.). 288p. 1995. pap. 15.95 (*0-8050-4565-1*, Owl) H Holt & Co.

Connor, Robert, jt. auth. see Connor, Carolyn.

Connor, Robert D. Cornelius Harnett: An Essay in North Carolina History. LC 76-148876. (Select Bibliographies Reprint Ser.). 1977. reprint ed. 20.95 (*0-8369-5647-8*) Ayer.

Connor, Robert E., Jr., jt. auth. see Sarkesian, Sam C.

Connor, Robert E., Jr., jt. ed. see Sarkesian, Sam C.

***Connor, Russell.** Essays in the Foundations of Mathematics. 2000. pap. 8.00 (*0-8059-5007-9*) Dorrance.

Connor, Russell. Masters in Pieces: The Art of Russell Connor. LC 96-28289. 1997. pap. 49.95 (*1-885203-28-4*) Jrny Editions.

Connor, Russell D. Benny Goodman: Listen to His Legacy. LC 87-32069. (Studies in Jazz: No. 6). (Illus.). 409p. 1988. 62.50 (*0-8108-2095-1*) Scarecrow.

Connor, Ruth. The Scholastic Behavior of a Selected Group of Undergraduate Home Economics Students. LC 70-176667. (Columbia University. Teachers College. Contributions to Education Ser.: No. 497). reprint ed. 37.50 (*0-404-55497-0*) AMS Pr.

Connor, S. S. & Fuenzalida-Puelma, H. L., eds. Bioethics: Issues & Perspectives. (PAHO Scientific Publications: No. 527). (ENG & SPA.). xii, 238p. 1990. pap. text. write for info. (*92-75-31527-2*, 1610527) World Health.

Connor, S. S., jt. ed. see Fuenzalida-Puelma, H. L.

Connor, Samuel R. The Handbook for Effective Job Development. 101p. 1981. pap. 14.95 (*0-89361-027-5*) Work in Amer.

Connor, Seymour V. Texas in 1776: A Historical Description. LC 75-37049. 112p. 1975. 20.00 (*0-8363-0136-6*, V24-10-7228) Jenkins.

Connor, Sheila. New England Natives: A Celebration of People & Trees. (Illus.). 312p. 1993. text 39.95 (*0-674-61350-3*) HUP.

— New England Natives: A Celebration of People & Trees. (Illus.). 312p. (C). 1995. pap. 24.95 (*0-674-61351-1*) HUP.

Connor, Sonja, jt. auth. see Connor, William.

Connor, Sonja L. & Connor, William E. The New American Diet. 416p. 1989. pap. 14.00 (*0-671-66375-5*, Fireside) S&S Trade Pap.

Connor, Stephen R. Hospice: Practice, Pitfalls, & Promise. LC 97-28959. 1997. write for info. (*1-56032-512-7*); pap. write for info. (*1-56032-513-5*) Hemisp Pub.

Connor, Steven. Charles Dickens. LC 96-1912. (Critical Readers Ser.). 248p. (C). 1996. text 51.95 (*0-582-21016-X*, Pub. by Addison-Wesley); pap. text 22.50 (*0-582-21015-1*, Pub. by Addison-Wesley) Longman.

***Connor, Steven.** A Cultural History of Ventriloquism. 448p. 2000. 35.00 (*0-19-818433-6*) OUP.

Connor, Steven. English Novel in History, 1950 to the Present. LC 95-4304. (Novel in History Ser.). 272p. (C). 1995. pap. 24.99 (*0-415-07231-X*) Routledge.

— James Joyce. LC 96-161402. (Writers & Their Works). 110p. (Orig.). 1996. pap. 22.50 (*0-7463-0753-5*, Pub. by Northcote House) Trans-Atl Phila.

— Postmodernist Culture: An Introduction to Theories of the Contemporary. 2nd ed. LC 96-16125. 304p. 1996. pap. 24.95 (*0-631-20052-5*) Blackwell Pubs.

An Asterisk (*) at the beginning of an entry indicates that the title is appearing for the first time.

Connor, Steven, intro. Oliver Twist. 432p. 1994. 3.95 (*0-460-87490-X*, Everyman's Classic Lib) Tuttle Pubng.
Connor, Steven, ed. see Dickens, Charles.
Connor, Susan F., et al. A Comprehensive Review Manual for the Adult Nurse Practitioner. 2nd ed. (Illus.). 569p. (C). 1989. spiral bd. 42.00 (*0-673-39860-9*) Lppncott W & W.
Connor, Thomas, jt. ed. see Fox, Frederick.
Connor, Tim. The Ancient Scrolls. LC 98-89277. 148p. 1998. pap. 12.95 (*0-937539-34-1*) Executive Bks.
— The Road to Happiness Is Full of Potholes. LC 98-84573. 174p. 1998. reprint ed. pap. 11.95 (*0-937539-28-7*) Executive Bks.
— Soft Sell: The New Art of Selling, Self-Empowerment & Persuasion. 3rd rev. ed. LC 98-7187. 256p. 1998. pap. 12.95 (*1-57071-393-6*) Sourcebks.
***Connor, Tim.** Soft Sell: The New Art of Selling, Self-Empowerment & Persuasion, Set. (Learn in Your Car - Discovery Ser.). 2000. pap. 15.95 incl. audio (*1-56015-212-5*) Penton Overseas.
Connor, Tim. The Voyage, a Journey of Self Discovery. Bolick, Jann, ed. 234p. (Orig.). 1994. pap. 15.00 (*0-9606296-4-5*) Connor Res.
— Walk Easy with Me Through Life. (Illus.). 175p. (Orig.). 1992. pap. 15.00 (*0-9606296-1-0*) Connor Res.
Connor, Tim & Downey, Jim. Re>Wired: A Parody. (Illus.). 64p. 1999. pap. 12.00 (*0-7881-6055-9*) DIANE Pub.
Connor, Timothy J. That Does Not Compute: A Handbook for the Baffled Computer Owner. (Illus.). 204p. (Orig.). 1992. pap. 19.95 (*0-9632910-1-7*) Disk Org Srvs.
Connor, Tom. Martha Stuart's Excruciatingly Perfect Weddings. LC 98-3808. 64p. 1998. pap. 10.00 (*0-06-095238-5*, Perennial) HarperTrade.
— Smyth & Hawk'em: Parody, A. LC 97-186334. 64p. 1997. pap. 10.00 (*0-06-095239-3*, Perennial) HarperTrade.
***Connor, Tom.** Suburban Renewal: Transforming Standard Capes, Ranches & Builders' Colonials into Classic Homes. (Illus.). 176p. 2000. 34.95 (*0-670-89217-3*, Viking) Viking Penguin.
Connor, Tom & Downey, Jim. The Handmade Cigar Collector's Guide & Journal. LC 97-1043. 128p. 1997. 25.00 (*0-00-649169-3*) Collins SF.
— Martha Stuart's Better Than You at Entertaining: A Parody. LC 96-155402. (Illus.). 64p. 1996. pap. 10.00 (*0-06-095171-0*, Perennial) HarperTrade.
— Smythe & Hawk 'Em. (Orig.). 1997. pap. 12.50 (*0-614-27410-9*, Perennial) HarperTrade.
— Zeguts. LC 97-170666. 96p. 1997. pap. 9.00 (*1-57566-152-7*, Knsington) Kensgtn Pub Corp.
Connor, Tom, ed. see Kramer, Russell.
Connor, Tony. Metamorphic Adventures. LC 96-143964. 118p. 1997. pap. 15.95 (*0-85646-261-6*, Pub. by Anvil Press) Dufour.
— New & Selected Poems. 138p. 1982. pap. 14.95 (*0-85646-069-9*, Pub. by Anvil Press) Dufour.
— Spirits of the Place. 88p. 1986. 21.95 (*0-85646-164-4*, Pub. by Anvil Press); pap. 14.95 (*0-85646-165-2*, Pub. by Anvil Press) Dufour.
Connor, Ulla. Contrastive Rhetoric: Cross-Cultural Aspects of Second Language Writing. (Cambridge Applied Linguistics Ser.). (Illus.). 217p. (C). 1996. text 54.95 (*0-521-44145-5*); pap. text 22.95 (*0-521-44688-0*) Cambridge U Pr.
Connor, Ulla & Johns, Ann M., eds. Coherence in Writing: Research & Pedagogical Perspectives. LC 88-50781. 263p. 1990. pap. 14.95 (*0-939791-34-X*) Tchrs Eng Spkrs.
Connor, Ursula. How to Select & Buy a Personal Computer: For Small Business, for Department Heads, for the Home, for Self-Employed Professionals. (Illus.). 177p. 1983. pap. 5.95 (*0-8159-5717-3*) Devin.
Connor, W. R., ed. The Acts of the Pagan Martyrs. LC 78-18588. (Greek Texts & Commentaries Ser.). 1979. reprint ed. lib. bdg. 38.87 (*0-405-11430-3*) Ayer.
— Ancient Religion & Mythology, 32 vols. (Illus.). 1976. 1039.00 (*0-405-07001-2*) Ayer.
— Chion of Heraclea. LC 78-18571. (Greek Texts & Commentaries Ser.). 1979. reprint ed. lib. bdg. 21.95 (*0-405-11415-X*) Ayer.
— Greek History, 27 bks., Set. 1973. 881.00 (*0-405-04775-4*) Ayer.
— Greek Texts & Commentaries Series, 40 bks., Set. (Illus.). 1979. lib. bdg. 1007.50 (*0-405-11412-5*) Ayer.
— Latin Texts & Commentaries Series, 30 bks., Set. (Illus.). 1979. lib. bdg. 940.00 (*0-405-11594-6*) Ayer.
— Roman Augury & Etruscan Divination. LC 75-10649. (Ancient Religion & Mythology Ser.). 1979. 18.95 (*0-405-07273-2*) Ayer.
Connor, W. R., et al, eds. Monographs in Classical Studies, 32 vols., Set. 1981. lib. bdg. 1055.00 (*0-405-14025-8*) Ayer.
Connor, W. R. & Dilke, O. A., eds. Statius Achilled. LC 78-67127. (Latin Texts & Commentaries Ser.). (ENG & LAT.). 1979. reprint ed. lib. bdg. 23.95 (*0-405-11598-9*) Ayer.
Connor, W. R. & Magnus, Hugo, eds. Metamorphoseon, Libri XV. LC 78-67140. (Latin Texts & Commentaries Ser.). (ENG & LAT.). 1979. reprint ed. lib. bdg. 61.95 (*0-405-11609-8*) Ayer.
Connor, W. R., ed. see Adler, Eve.
Connor, W. R., ed. see Aeschines.
Connor, W. R., ed. see Aeschylus.
Connor, W. R., ed. see Alcman.
Connor, W. R., ed. see Apollonius, Rhodius.
Connor, W. R., ed. see Aristophanes.
Connor, W. R., ed. see Arnould, Dominique.
Connor, W. R., ed. see Block, Elizabeth.
Connor, W. R., ed. see Bowie, Angus M.
Connor, W. R., ed. see Brooks, Robert A.
Connor, W. R., ed. see Brumfield, Allaire C.
Connor, W. R., ed. see Caesar, Julius.
Connor, W. R., ed. see Callimachus.
Connor, W. R., ed. see Carey, Christopher.
Connor, W. R., ed. see Cicero, Marcus Tullius.
Connor, W. R., ed. see David, Ephraim.
Connor, W. R., ed. see Davies, John K.
Connor, W. R., ed. see Demetrius, C.
Connor, W. R., ed. see Demosthenes.
Connor, W. R., ed. see Doenges, Norman A.
Connor, W. R., ed. see Euripides.
Connor, W. R., ed. see Furley, William D.
Connor, W. R., ed. see Geffcken, John.
Connor, W. R., ed. see Ginsberg, Judith.
Connor, W. R., ed. see Hall, Jennifer.
Connor, W. R., ed. see Hammond, Nicholas G.
Connor, W. R., ed. see Herodas.
Connor, W. R., ed. see Hesiod.
Connor, W. R., ed. see Hillyard, Brian P.
Connor, W. R., ed. see Hine, Harry M. & Seneca, Lucius Annaeus.
Connor, W. R., ed. see Hippocrates.
Connor, W. R., ed. see Homer.
Connor, W. R., ed. see Horace.
Connor, W. R., ed. see Horrocks, Geoffrey C.
Connor, W. R., ed. see Isaeus.
Connor, W. R., ed. see Isocrates.
Connor, W. R., ed. see Juvenal.
Connor, W. R., ed. see Lipovsky, James.
Connor, W. R., ed. see Longus.
Connor, W. R., ed. see Lucan, D.
Connor, W. R., ed. see Lycophron.
Connor, W. R., ed. see Lysias.
Connor, W. R., ed. see McCabe, Donald F.
Connor, W. R., ed. see Nicander.
Connor, W. R., ed. see Parry, Adam M.
Connor, W. R., ed. see Pernot, Laurent.
Connor, W. R., ed. see Persius.
Connor, W. R., ed. see Philippides, Dia M.
Connor, W. R., ed. see Philo.
Connor, W. R., ed. see Pindar, Peter.
Connor, W. R., ed. see Plautus.
Connor, W. R., ed. see Plautus, Titus Maccius.
Connor, W. R., ed. see Plutarch.
Connor, W. R., ed. see Propertius.
Connor, W. R., ed. see Rash, James N.
Connor, W. R., ed. see Robinson, Thomas M.
Connor, W. R., ed. see Skinner, Marilyn B.
Connor, W. R., ed. see Spofford, Edward W.
Connor, W. R., ed. see Stone, Laura M.
Connor, W. R., ed. see Suetonius.
Connor, W. R., ed. see Suetonius, T.
Connor, W. R., ed. see Szegedy-Maszak, Andrew.
Connor, W. R., ed. see Terence.
Connor, W. R., ed. see Theognis.
Connor, W. R., ed. see Theophrastus of Eresus.
Connor, W. R., ed. see Tibullus.
Connor, W. R., ed. see Varro, Marcus T.
Connor, W. R., ed. see Walker, B.
Connor, W. R., ed. see White, F. C.
Connor, W. R., ed. see Xenophon.
Connor, W. R., ed. see Zetzel, James E.
Connor, W. R., ed. see Ziolkowiski, John E.
Connor, W. Robert. The New Politicians of Fifth-Century Athens. LC 92-23958. 232p. (C). 1992. reprint ed. pap. text 14.95 (*0-87220-142-2*); reprint ed. lib. bdg. 34.95 (*0-87220-143-0*) Hackett Pub.
Connor, W. Robert, ed. History of the Peloponnesian War. 545p. 1993. pap. 7.95 (*0-460-87153-6*, Everyman's Classic Lib) Tuttle Pubng.
Connor, W. Robert, jt. auth. see Connor, Carolyn L.
Connor, Walker. Ethnonationalism: The Quest for Understanding. LC 93-17829. 264p. 1993. pap. text 17.95 (*0-691-02563-0*, Pub. by Princeton U Pr) Cal Prin Full Svc.
— The National Question in Marxist-Leninist Theory & Strategy. LC 83-43067. 633p. reprint ed. pap. 196.30 (*0-8357-3699-7*, 203642300003) Bks Demand.
Connor, Walter, et al, eds. The Polish Road from Socialism: The Economics, Sociology & Politics of Transition. LC 91-27626. 320p. (C). (gr. 13). 1992. text 87.95 (*0-87332-886-8*) M E Sharpe.
Connor, Walter D. The Accidental Proletariat: Workers, Politics, & Crisis in Gorbachev's Russia. (Illus.). 382p. 1991. text 55.00 (*0-691-07787-8*, Pub. by Princeton U Pr) Cal Prin Full Svc.
Connor, Walter D. Socialism's Dilemmas: State & Society in the Soviet Bloc. 320p. 1988. text 57.50 (*0-231-06606-6*) Col U Pr.
Connor, Walter R. Theopompus & Fifth-Century Athens. LC 68-14253. (Center for Hellenic Studies). 327p. reprint ed. 101.40 (*0-8357-9180-7*, 201654300004) Bks Demand.

Connor, Wendy Simpson. The Beading on Fabric Book. (Beading Books Ser.). 11.95 (*0-9645957-8-8*) Interstell Pub.
This informative how-to-book covers every facet of beading on fabric. From the Kuba-style beading in Africa, to elegant beaded dresses, to Victorian netted embellishments, to solid bead embroidery, & much, much more. A must-have for anyone who works with costumes or clothing. There's so many wonderful ideas & projects in this book, that you'll want to make it all. Be sure to look for the Beading Book Series: The Best Little Beading Book, The Beaded Lampshade Book, The Magical Beaded Medicine Bag Book, The "Knotty Macrame & Beading Book, The Beaded Watchband Book, The Beaded Jewelry for a Wedding Book, The Children's Beading Book, The Chain & Crystal Book, The Cat Lover's Beaded Project Book, The Wirebending Book, The Beading on Fabric Book, & more soon to come! Many of these books are available in kit form, also. There is also a wonderful documentary which complements the series. The Bead Movement is a beautiful program which chronicles man's oldest artform, beads. It is available in 60 minutes, or a 30 min. director's cut. For information or ordering, contact The Interstellar Trading & Publishing Company, P.O. Box 2215, LaMesa, CA 91943; (858) 452-8181 or 292-8191, Order Dept. (800) 790-8730, Fax (858) 452-0351 or 292-0373, e-mail Interstlr@aol.com. Visit our website at www.Interstellarpublishing.com. Available through Sunbelt Publications, Ingram Books, Baker & Taylor Books. *Publisher Paid Annotation.*

***Connor, William.** The Achievement of Gerald Warner Brace. LC 98-26874. (American University Studies XXIV: Vol. 71). 162p. (C). 1999. text 40.95 (*0-8204-4145-7*) P Lang Pubng.
Connor, William & Connor, Sonja. The New Century Cookbook. 1996. 24.00 (*0-614-19398-2*) S&S Trade.
Connor, William E., jt. auth. see Connor, Sonja L.
Connor, William S. D., jt. auth. see Hacinli, Cynthia.
***Connors.** Assessment, Diagnosis & Treatment of ADHD in Children, Adolescents & Adults. (LEA/DLN Mental Health Professionals Video Reference Library). 1999. VHS 169.95 (*0-8058-3301-3*) L Erlbaum Assocs.
— The Nonprofit Handbook: Management Supplement , 1998. (Nonprofit Law, Finance, & Management Ser.). 172p. 1998. pap. 57.00 (*0-471-19594-4*) Wiley.
Connors. Volunteer Management Handbook. 407p. 1999. pap. 34.95 (*0-471-37142-4*) Wiley.
Connors & Furtan. Videohound's Golden Movie Retriever, 1994. 3rd ed. 1500p. 1993. pap. 17.95 (*0-8103-9131-7*, 089402) Visible Ink Pr.
Connors & Hickman. The Oz Principle: What the Management Wizards Can't or Won't Tell You about Getting Results. (C). 1995. 12.95 (*0-13-254301-X*) P-H.
Connors, jt. auth. see Lunsford, Andrea.
Connors, Andree. Amateur People. LC 76-47836. 1977. 10.95 (*0-914590-30-8*); pap. 6.95 (*0-914590-31-6*) Fiction Coll.
***Connors, Andrew.** La Luz: Contemporary Latino Art in the United States. 2000. pap. 20.00 (*0-89013-375-1*) Museum NM Pr.
Connors, Betsy, jt. auth. see Friis-Hansen, Dana.
Connors, Catherine. Petronius the Poet: Verse & Literary Traditions in the Satyricon. LC 97-6743. 180p. (C). 1998. text 54.95 (*0-521-59231-3*) Cambridge U Pr.
Connors, Dean & Duppler, Dana. The 1834 Prairie Spring Hotel: Biography of a Building. Calvert, Stephen, ed. (Illus.). 80p. 1997. pap. 18.95 (*0-9622783-2-7*) Cottonwood Hill Pub.
Connors, Dean M. Going for the Iron. 80p. 1994. 40.00 (*0-938627-23-6*) New Past Pr.
***Connors, Dennis.** Greater Syracuse. (Images of America Ser.). 128p. 1999. pap. 18.99 (*0-7385-0194-8*) Arcadia Publng.
Connors, Dennis, ed. Onondaga: Portrait of a Native People. LC 85-27686. (Iroquois Bks.). (Illus.). 120p. (Orig.). 1986. pap. 19.95 (*0-8156-0198-0*) Syracuse U Pr.
Connors, Dorsey. Helpful Hints for Hurried Homemakers: Time & Money Saving Shortcuts. 176p. 1988. pap. 7.95 (*0-933893-53-1*) Bonus Books.
***Connors, Edward, et al.** Building Bulk. LC 98-43699. (Gold's Gym Essentials Ser.). 176p. 1999. pap. 16.95 (*0-8092-2789-4*, 278940, Contemporary Bks) NTC Contemp Pub Co.
Connors, Edward, et al. Convicted by Juries, Exonerated by Science: Case Studies in the Use of DNA Evidence to Establish Innocence after Trial. (Illus.). 85p. (Orig.). (C). 1997. pap. text 25.00 (*0-7881-3125-7*) DIANE Pub.
— The Gold's Gym Encyclopedia of Bodybuilding. LC 97-42287. (Illus.). 416p. 1997. pap. 18.95 (*0-8092-3006-2*, 300620, Contemporary Bks) NTC Contemp Pub Co.
— Total Torso Training. LC 99-21573. (Gold's Gym Essentials Ser.). 176p. 1999. pap. 16.95 (*0-8092-2788-6*, 278860, Contemporary Bks) NTC Contemp Pub Co.
— Urban Street Gang Enforcement. (Illus.). 126p. (C). 1998. pap. text 30.00 (*0-7881-7255-7*) DIANE Pub.
Connors, Eugene, jt. auth. see Valesky, Thomas C.
Connors, Florence M. Osteoporosis - Phases, Conditions & Therapy: Index of New Information with Authors, Subjects & References. 150p. 1994. 47.50 (*1-55914-724-5*); pap. 44.50 (*1-55914-725-3*) ABBE Pubs Assn.
Connors, Gerald J., intro. Innovations in Alcoholism Treatment: State of the Art Reviews & Their Implications for Clinical Practice. LC 93-49064. (Drugs & Society Ser.). Orig. Title: Drugs & Society. (Illus.). 134p. 1994. reprint ed. 39.95 (*1-56024-657-X*) Haworth Pr.
Connors, Gerilynn A. How to Assess for Rehabilitation of the Pulmonary Patient, Vol. 6 No. 1. (Master Module Ser.). 1987. 14.99 (*0-931263-35-2*) Educ Res Consortium.
***Connors, Ginny Lowe, ed.** Essential Love: Poems about Mothers & Fathers, Daughters & Sons. 341p. 2000. 21.95 (*0-9675554-1-8*); pap. 14.95 (*0-9675554-2-6*) Grayson Bks.
Connors, J. C. & Lawrence, Chris. RuneQuest: Slayers. Knight, Ben, ed. (Illus.). 240p. 1998. pap. text 24.95 (*1-56038-213-9*) Avalon Hill.
Connors, J. J. & Wojak, Joan C. Practice of Interventional Neuroradiology. LC 97-28810. (Illus.). xxiv, 795p. (C). 1999. text 190.00 (*0-7216-7147-0*, W B Saunders Co) Harcrt Hlth Sci Grp.
Connors, Jimmy & LaMarche, Robert J. Winning Tennis My Way. write for info. (*0-318-60257-1*) S&S Trade.
Connors, John. S. E. 5a in Action. (Aircraft in Action Ser.: Vol. 69). (Illus.). 50p. 2000. pap. 9.95 (*0-89747-191-1*, 1069) Squad Sig Pubns.
Connors, John M., jt. auth. see Perlin, Marc G.
Connors, Joseph, ed. Memoirs of the American Academy in Rome. 248p. (C). 1996. text 59.50 (*0-472-10720-8*, 10720) U of Mich Pr.
Connors, Joseph & Wright, Frank Lloyd. The Robie House of Frank Lloyd Wright. LC 83-4891. (Illus.). 1984. 30.00 (*0-226-11541-0*); pap. 18.00 (*0-226-11542-9*) U Ch Pr.
Connors, Judith. Beads in Tatting. (Illus.). 56p. 1997. pap. 15.00 (*0-916896-83-8*) Lacis Pubns.
***Connors, Judith.** Tatting: Adventures with Beads, Shuttle & Heedle. (Illus.). 80p. 2000. pap. 16.00 (*1-891656-22-8*, LE77) Lacis Pubns.
Connors, Kenneth A. Binding Constants: The Measurement of Molecular Complex Stability. 432p. 1987. 189.00 (*0-471-83083-6*) Wiley.
— Chemical Kinetics: The Study of Reaction Rates in Solution. 480p. 1990. 95.00 (*1-56081-006-8*, Wiley-VCH) Wiley.
Connors, Kenneth A. Chemical Kinetics: The Study of Reaction Rates in Solution. 1990. 169.00 (*0-471-72021-6*); pap. 69.95 (*0-471-72020-8*) Wiley.
Connors, Kenneth A. Chemical Kinetics: The Study of Reaction Rates in Solution. 480p. 1990. pap. 49.50 (*1-56081-053-X*, Wiley-VCH) Wiley.
— A Textbook of Pharmaceutical Analysis. 3rd ed. LC 81-19742. 680p. 1982. 149.00 (*0-471-09034-4*) Wiley.
Connors, Kenneth A., et al. Chemical Stability of Pharmaceutricals: A Handbook for Pharmacists. 2nd ed. LC 85-31455. 864p. 1986. 195.00 (*0-471-87955-X*) Wiley.
***Connors, Laurence A.** Connors on Advanced Trading Strategies. 268p. 1998. 150.00 (*0-9650461-5-X*) M Gordon Pubng.
Connors, Laurence A. The Will to Win. 156p. 1997. 14.95 (*0-9650461-4-1*) M Gordon Pubng.
Connors, Laurence A., ed. The Best of the Professional Traders Journal: Day Trading. (Illus.). 56p. 1999. pap. 39.95 (*1-893756-00-9*) M Gordon Pubng.
— The Best of the Professional Traders Journal Vol. II: Best Trading Patters. (Illus.). 70p. 1999. pap. 39.95 (*1-893756-01-7*) M Gordon Pubng.
— Best Trading Patterns Vol. I: Best Trading Patterns. (Best of the Professional Traders Journal Ser.). 70p. 1999. pap. 39.95 (*0-9650461-9-2*) M Gordon Pubng.
— Market Timing: Market Timing. (Best of the Professional Traders Journal Ser.). 56p. 1999. pap. 39.95 (*0-9650461-8-4*) M Gordon Pubng.
— Options Trading & Volatiligy Trading: Options Trading & Volatility Trading. (Best of the Professional Traders Journal Ser.). 64p. 1999. pap. 39.95 (*0-9650461-7-6*) M Gordon Pubng.
Connors, Laurence A. & Hayward, Blake E. Investment Secrets Hedge Fund Manager: Exploiting the Herd Mentality of the Financial Markets. 300p. 1995. 50.00 (*1-55738-900-4*, Irwn Prfssnl) McGraw-Hill Prof.
Connors, Laurence A. & Raschke, Linda B. Street Smarts: High Probability Short Term Trading Strategies. (Illus.). 240p. 1996. 175.00 (*0-9650461-0-9*) M Gordon Pubng.
Connors, Lesley. The Emperor's Adviser: Saionji Kinmochi & Prewar Japanese Politics. 1987. 65.00 (*0-7099-3449-1*, Pub. by C Helm) Routldge.
Connors, Libby, et al. Australia's Frontline: Remembering the 1939-45 War. (Orig.). 1992. pap. 16.95 (*0-7022-2446-4*, Pub. by Univ Queensland Pr) Intl Spec Bk.
Connors, Libby, jt. auth. see Hutton, Drew.
***Connors, Martin.** Videohound's Golden Movie Retriever 2000. 1800p. 1999. pap. text 21.95 (*1-57859-042-6*) Visible Ink Pr.
Connors, Martin & Craddock, Jim, eds. Golden Movie Retriever: The Complete Guide to Movies on Videocassette, Laserdisc, & DVD. 8th ed. (Videohound's Golden Movie Retriever Ser.). 1815p. 1998. pap. 21.95 (*1-57859-041-8*) Visible Ink Pr.
Connors, Martin, jt. ed. see Craddock, Jim.
Connors, Martin, ed. see Gottschalk, Jack A.
Connors, Mary. Lao Textiles & Traditions. (Images of Asia Ser.). (Illus.). 96p. (C). 1997. text 18.95 (*983-56-0001-5*) OUP.
Connors, Mary & Herweck, Dona. Native American Arts & Culture. (Illus.). 1994. 14.95 (*1-55734-619-4*) Tchr Create Mat.
Connors, Michael. How to Hide Anything. (Illus.). 120p. 1987. reprint ed. pap. 5.95 (*0-8065-1036-6*, Citadel Pr) Carol Pub Group.
Connors, Michael P., et al. Nonqualified Deferred Compensation Answer Book: Forms & Checklists. 2nd ed. 344p. pap. 96.00 (*1-56706-369-1*, 63691) Panel Pubs.
Connors, Neila. Homework: A New Direction. 92p. 1991. pap. text 15.00 (*1-56090-057-1*) Natl Middle Schl.
***Connors, Neila.** If You Don't Feed the Teachers They Eat the Students: Guide to Success for Administrators & Teachers. Streams, Jennifer J., ed. (Illus.). 144p. 2000. pap. 14.95 (*0-86530-457-2*) Incentive Pubns.
***Connors, Nellie Nally & Drury, Patricia M.** Recipes from Hammond Castle. (Illus.). 104p. 1999. pap. 9.95 (*1-878452-23-1*, Pub. by Quincannon) Hammond Castle.

An Asterisk (*) at the beginning of an entry indicates that the title is appearing for the first time.

Connors, Patricia & Perucci, Dorianne. Runaways: Coping at Home & on the Street. Rosen, Ruth C., ed. (Coping Ser.). (YA). (gr. 7-12). 1989. lib. bdg. 16.95 (*0-8239-1019-9*) Rosen Group.

Connors, Patrick, jt. auth. see Timms, Robert.

Connors, Rhea M., ed. Making a Difference: A Directory of Northwest Environmental Non-Profit Organizations. Date not set. pap. 7.00 (*0-9665952-1-1*) Sugar Mtn Press.

— 10,000 Free Recipes for Baking! 38p. 1998. pap. 5.00 (*0-9665952-0-3*) Sugar Mtn Press.

Connors, Richard J. & Dunham, William J. The Government of New Jersey: An Introduction. rev. ed. LC 92-40303. (Orig.). 1993. 57.50 (*0-8191-9022-5*); pap. 29.50 (*0-8191-9023-3*) U Pr of Amer.

Connors, Robert, jt. auth. see Lunsford, Andrea.

Connors, Robert J. Composition-Rhetoric: Backgrounds, Theory, & Pedagogy. LC 96-51259. (Composition, Literacy, & Culture Ser.). 320p. 1997. pap. 19.95 (*0-8229-5630-6*); text 45.00 (*0-8229-3979-7*) U of Pittsburgh Pr.

Connors, Robert J., et al, eds. Essays on Classical Rhetoric & Modern Discourse. LC 83-14718. 308p. 1984. pap. 19.95 (*0-8093-1134-8*) S Ill U Pr.

***Connors, Robert J. & Glenn, Cheryl.** The New St. Martin's Guide to Teaching Writing LC 98-86514. xi, 548p. 1999. pap. text 19.95 (*0-312-19762-4*) St Martin.

Connors, Robert J. & Glenn, Cheryl. The St. Martin's Guide to Teaching Writing. 2nd ed. 256p. (C). 1992. pap. text. write for info. (*0-318-68813-1*) St Martin.

Connors, Robert J., jt. auth. see Corbett, Edward P.

Connors, Robert J., jt. auth. see Lunsford, Andrea A.

Connors, Robert J., ed. see Corbett, Edward P. J.

Connors, Robin, jt. auth. see Trautmann, Kristy.

Connors, Roger & Smith, Tom. Journey to the Emerald City. 320p. 1999. 26.00 (*0-7352-0052-1*) PH Pr.

Connors, Roger, et al. The Oz Principle: Getting Results Through Individual & Organizational Accountability. 320p. 1998. pap. text 14.00 (*0-7352-0043-2*) PH Pr.

— The Oz Principle: What the Management Wizards Can't or Won't Tell You about Getting Results. 304p. (C). 1994. text 22.95 (*0-13-032129-X*) P-H.

Connors, Thomas E. Abstract Relations. LC 79-50423. (Illus.). 128p. 1980. pap. 15.00 (*0-913204-12-9*) December Pr.

Connors, Tom. Bud the Spud. LC 94-170424. (Illus.). 24p. (J). (ps up). 1994. pap. 5.95 (*0-921556-43-8*, Pub. by Gynergy-Ragweed) U of Toronto Pr.

— Hockey Night Tonight. (Illus.). 24p. (J). (ps up). 1995. pap. 5.95 (*0-921556-57-8*, Pub. by Gynergy-Ragweed) U of Toronto Pr.

Connors, Tracy D. The Nonprofit Management Handbook: Operating Policies & Procedures. LC 92-10811. 943p. 1996. pap. 59.95 (*0-471-15177-7*) Wiley.

Connors, Tracy D., ed. The Nonprofit Organization Handbook. 2nd ed. 784p. 1988. 89.50 (*0-07-012432-9*) McGraw.

Connors, Tracy D. & Callaghan, Christopher T., eds. Financial Management for Nonprofit Organizations. LC 81-69355. 346p. reprint ed. pap. 107.30 (*0-608-12699-3*, 202351700033) Bks Demand.

Connors, Tracy D. & Greenfield, James M., eds. The Nonprofit Handbook, 2 vols. 2nd ed. LC 96-54804. 576p. 1997. 240.00 (*0-471-15400-8*) Wiley.

— The Nonprofit Handbook: Management, Vol. 1. 2nd ed. LC 96-54804. 832p. 1997. 130.00 (*0-471-17967-1*) Wiley.

***Connors, Tracy D. & Greenfield, James M., eds.** The Nonprofit Management Handbook: 1999 Edition. 2nd ed. 256p. 1999. pap. 65.00 (*0-471-29907-3*) Wiley.

***Connors, Tracy Daniel, ed.** The Nonprofit Handbook, Fund Raising. 2nd ed. (Wiley Nonprofit Law, Finance, & Management Ser.). 112p. 2000. pap. 65.00 (*0-471-36133-X*) Wiley.

— The Nonprofit Handbook, Management: February 2000 Supplement. 2nd ed. 208p. 2000. pap. 65.00 (*0-471-36142-9*) Wiley.

***Connors, Tracy Daniel & Greenfield, James M., eds.** Fund Raising Handbook: 1999 Supplement. 2nd ed. 184p. 1999. pap. 65.00 (*0-471-29902-2*) Wiley.

Connors, W. Best Of The Barrelman. 96p. 1998. pap. 9.55 (*1-895387-99-X*) Creative Bk Pub.

Connors, W. & Smedman, Lisa. Requiem: Grim Harvest. 1996. 30.00 (*0-7869-0431-3*, Pub. by TSR Inc) Random.

Connors, W. & Weinlein, S. Last Tower: Legacy of Raistlin. 1997. 20.00 (*0-7869-0538-7*, Pub. by TSR Inc) Random.

Connors, William. The Street Cars of Old Saint John's: A Photo History. (Illus.). 100p. 1989. pap. 9.55 (*0-920021-65-4*) Creative Bk Pub.

— Winds of History: Notable Newfoundland Events. 160p. 1995. pap. 11.95 (*1-895387-53-1*) Creative Bk Pub.

Connors, William W. Children of the Night: Werebeasts. 1998. 16.95 (*0-7869-1202-2*, Pub. by TSR Inc) Random.

— Gothic Earth Gazetteer: Ravenloft Masque of the Red Death Accessory. 1995. 9.95 (*0-7869-0193-4*, Pub. by TSR Inc) Random.

— Night of the Walking Dead. (Advanced Dungeons & Dragons, Second Edition; Al-Qadim Ser.). 1992. 10.95 (*1-56076-351-5*) TSR Inc.

***Connors, William W., et al.** Alien Compendium II: The Exploration of 2503. (Alternity Ser.). (Illus.). 96p. 2000. pap. 19.95 (*0-7869-1617-6*) TSR Inc.

Connors, William W., et al. Masque of the Red Death & Other Tales. (Advanced Dungeons & Dragons, 2nd Edition: Ravenloft Campaign World Ser.). 1994. 25.00 (*1-56076-877-0*) TSR Inc.

Conny, Beth M. Mom, You're the Best! LC 97-220798. (Charming Petites Ser.). (Illus.). 80p. 1997. 4.95 (*0-88088-813-X*) Peter Pauper.

— Pearls of Wisdom. (Charming Petites Ser.). (Illus.). 80p. 1996. 4.95 (*0-88088-801-6*) Peter Pauper.

— Simple Gifts, Abundant Treasures: A Woman's Companion. LC 97-198546. (Gift Editions Ser.). (Illus.). 56p. 1997. 8.99 (*0-88088-499-1*) Peter Pauper.

— What Highly Effective Women Know. LC 99-162745. 1998. 4.95 (*0-88088-075-9*) Peter Pauper.

Conny, Beth M., compiled by. Gentle Thoughts. (Charming Petites Ser.). (Illus.). 80p. 1993. 4.95 (*0-88088-760-5*) Peter Pauper.

— Inspiration for Living. (Charming Petites Ser.). 80p. 1992. 4.95 (*0-88088-756-7*) Peter Pauper.

Conny, Beth M. Principals for Our Changing Schools: The Knowledge & Skill Base. 590p. (C). 1998. pap. text 39.95 (*1-56676-303-7*) Scarecrow.

***Conny, Beth Mende, ed.** Dare to Believe. (Charming Petites Ser.). (Illus.). 80p. 2000. 4.95 (*0-88088-328-6*) Peter Pauper.

Conny, Beth Mende & Bedford-Pierce, Sophie. Believe in Yourself: A Key to Life Guided Journal. (Guided Journals Ser.). 1998. 11.99 (*0-88088-203-4*) Peter Pauper.

***Conny, Beth Mende & Conny, Julia Mende.** Girls Rule! A Guided Journal with Silver Gel Pen. (Guided Journals). 128p. (YA). 2000. 14.99 (*0-88088-261-1*) Peter Pauper.

***Conny, Beth Mende & Conny, Julia Mende, eds.** Girls Rule! (Charming Petites Ser.). (Illus.). 80p. (YA). 2000. 4.95 (*0-88088-327-8*) Peter Pauper.

Conny, Julia Mende, jt. auth. see Conny, Beth Mende.

Conny, Julia Mende, jt. auth. see Conny, Beth Mende.

Conoley, Collie W., jt. auth. see Conoley, Jane Close.

Conoley, Gillian. Beckon. LC 95-67965. (Poetry Ser.). 80p. (C). 1996. 20.95 (*0-88748-218-X*); pap. 11.95 (*0-88748-219-8*) Carnegie-Mellon.

— Some Gangster Pain. LC 86-70209. (Poetry Ser.). 80p. (C). 1987. 20.95 (*0-88748-026-8*); pap. 11.95 (*0-88748-027-6*) Carnegie-Mellon.

— Tall Stranger. (Poetry Ser.). 64p. (Orig.). (C). 1991. pap. 11.95 (*0-88748-108-6*) Carnegie-Mellon.

— Woman Speaking Inside Film Noir. LC 84-14317. 26p. 1984. 4.50 (*0-89924-043-7*) Lynx Hse.

Conoley, Jane C., ed. The Eleventh Mental Measurements Yearbook. LC 39-3422. xvi, 1183p. 1992. 125.00 (*0-910674-33-7*) Buros Inst Mental.

— Home - School Collaboration: Enhancing Children's Academic & Social Competence. 531p. 1992. pap. text 49.00 (*0-932955-04-5*) Natl Assn Schl Psych.

Conoley, Jane C., et al, eds. The Supplement to the Ninth Mental Measurements Yearbook. (Mental Measurements Yearbook Ser.). xiii, 279p. (Orig.). 1988. pap. 55.00 (*0-910674-30-2*) Buros Inst Mental.

Conoley, Jane C. & Impara, James C., eds. Supplement to the Eleventh Mental Measurements Yearbook. LC 39-3422. (Mental Measurements Yearbook Ser.). 323p. 1994. pap. 55.00 (*0-910674-34-5*) Buros Inst Mental.

— 12th Mental Measurements Yearbook. (Mental Measurements Yearbook Ser.). 1200p. (C). 1995. text 150.00 (*0-910674-40-X*) Buros Inst Mental.

Conoley, Jane C. & Kramer, Jack J., eds. The Tenth Mental Measurements Yearbook. 1000p. 1989. 125.00 (*0-910674-31-0*) Buros Inst Mental.

Conoley, Jane C. & Werth, Elaine, eds. Family Assessment. (Buros-Nebraska Series on Measurement & Testing). 275p. (C). 1995. text 49.95 (*0-910674-38-8*) Buros Inst Mental.

Conoley, Jane C., jt. ed. see Goldstein, Arnold P.

Conoley, Jane C., jt. ed. see Kramer, Jack J.

Conoley, Jane Close & Conoley, Collie W. School Consultation. 2nd ed. 180p. (C). 1992. pap. text 41.00 (*0-205-14561-2*, H4561) Allyn.

Conoley, William N., Jr. Waterfowl Heritage: North Carolina Decoys & Gunning Lore. (Illus.). 336p. 1983. 39.95 (*0-9610358-1-1*) Webfoot Inc.

Conolly & Cox. World & People, Vol. 3. 1991. pap. text. write for info. (*0-582-87052-6*, Pub. by Addison-Wesley) Longman.

Conolly, Brian & Pierce, John G. Information Mechanics: Transformation of Information in Management, Command, Control & Communication. 160p. 1988. text 47.95 (*0-470-21136-9*) P-H.

Conolly, Brian & Vajda, Steven. A Mathematical Kaleidoscope: Applications in Industry, Business & Science. (Illus.). 256p. 1995. pap. 25.00 (*1-898563-21-7*) Paul & Co Pubs.

Conolly, Bruce W. Atlas of Hand Surgery. LC 97-36173. 1997. text 105.00 (*0-443-05077-5*) Church.

Conolly, John. Indications of Insanity. 1964. reprint ed. 44.95 (*0-8464-0507-5*) Beekman Pubs.

— A Study of Hamlet. LC 72-942. reprint ed. 32.50 (*0-404-01695-2*) AMS Pr.

— The Treatment of the Insane Without Mechanical Restraints. LC 73-2392. (Mental Illness & Social Policy; the American Experience Ser.). 1973. reprint ed. 28.95 (*0-405-05200-6*) Ayer.

Conolly, John, jt. ed. see Dik, Simon.

Conolly, John H. Constituent Order in Functional Grammar: Synchronic & Diachronic Perspectives. LC 91-30409. (Functional Grammar Ser.: No. 14). x, 206p. (C). 1991. lib. bdg. 75.40 (*3-11-013389-X*) Mouton.

Conolly, L. W., ed. Canadian Drama & the Critics. rev. ed. LC 96-108170. 383p. 1995. pap. 21.95 (*0-88922-359-9*) Genl Dist Srvs.

— Theatrical Touring & Founding in North America, 5. LC 81-23766. (Contributions in Drama & Theatre Studies: No. 5). (Illus.). 245p. 1982. 59.95 (*0-313-22595-8*, CTH/, Greenwood Pr) Greenwood.

Conolly, L. W., jt. ed. see Benson, Eugene.

Conolly, Leonard, jt. ed. see Benson, Eugene.

Conolly, Leonard W. The Censorship of English Drama, 1737-1824. LC 75-32840. (Illus.). 235p. 1976. reprint ed. pap. 72.90 (*0-608-03160-7*, 206361300007) Bks Demand.

Conolly, Peter, ed. Approaches to the Study of Religion. 256p. 1998. pap. 21.95 (*0-304-33709-9*) Continuum.

Conoly, David Z., ed. see State Bar of Texas Real Estate Forms Manual Committee.

Conomis, ed. Lycurgi. (GRE.). 1970. 27.50 (*3-322-00152-0*, T1520, Pub. by B G Teubner) U of Mich Pr.

Conomos, Dimitri. Byzantine Hymnography & Byzantine Chant. (Nicholas E. Kulukundis Lectures in Hellenism). 56p. (Orig.). 1984. pap. text 2.00 (*0-917653-04-1*, Pub. by Hellenic Coll Pr) BookWorld.

Conomos, Dimitri, ed. Studies in Eastern Chant, Vol. 5. 186p. (Orig.). 1991. pap. 15.95 (*0-913836-79-6*) St Vladimirs.

Conomos, Dimitri E. The Late Byzantine & Slavonic Communion Cycle: Liturgy & Music. LC 84-12176. (Dumbarton Oaks Studies: Vol. 21). (Illus.). 222p. 1985. 35.00 (*0-88402-134-3*) Dumbarton Oaks.

Conomy, John P., ed. see Brandt, T.

Conomy, John P., ed. see Hughes, R. A.

Cononelos, Louis J. In Search of Gold Paved Streets: Greek Immigrant Labor in the Far West, 1900-1920. LC 88-36493. (Immigrant Communities & Ethnic Minorities in the U. S. & Canada Ser.: No. 55). 1989. 54.00 (*0-404-19465-6*) AMS Pr.

Conor, Bernard E. Japan's New Colony - America: How We Americans Have Been Brainwashed & Compromised by Japan. 168p. 1991. 19.95 (*0-9631145-0-6*) Perkins Pr.

— Japan's New Colony - America: How We Americans Have Been Brainwashed & Compromised by Japan. 168p. 1992. reprint ed. pap. 9.95 (*0-9631145-1-4*) Perkins Pr.

***Conor, William.** Titan A. E. How to Draw. (Illus.). 48p. (YA). (gr. 4-7). 2000. pap. 6.99 (*0-8431-7586-9*, Price Stern) Peng Put Young Read.

Conord, Bruce & Conord, June. Cancun & Cozumel Alive. (Alive Guides Ser.). (Illus.). 350p. 1998. pap. 15.95 (*1-55650-830-1*) Hunter NJ.

***Conord, Bruce & Conord, June.** The Yucatan: Cancun & Cozumel. 2nd ed. (Adventure Guides Ser.). (Illus.). 400p. 2000. pap. 16.95 (*1-55650-908-1*) Hunter NJ.

Conord, Bruce W. Bill Cosby: Family Man. LC 91-31711. (Junior Black Americans of Achievement Ser.). (Illus.). 76p. (J). (gr. 4-7). 1993. lib. bdg. 15.95 (*0-7910-1761-3*) Chelsea Hse.

Conord, June, jt. auth. see Conord, Bruce.

Conot, Robert. Thomas A. Edison: A Streak of Luck. (Series in Science). (Illus.). 608p. 1986. pap. 15.95 (*0-306-80261-9*) Da Capo.

Conot, Robert E. Justice at Nuremberg. Date not set. lib. bdg. 34.95 (*0-8488-1898-9*) Amereon Ltd.

— Justice at Nuremberg. 594p. 1984. pap. 13.95 (*0-88184-032-7*) Carroll & Graf.

Conover & Wellens, Hein J. The ECG in Emergency Decision Making. 272p. 1991. pap. text 36.95 (*0-7216-3214-9*, W B Saunders Co) Harcrt Hlth Sci Grp.

Conover, Alexandra, jt. auth. see Conover, Garrett.

Conover, C. Todd. The Art of Astute Investing. LC 98-5918. 224p. 1998. 27.95 (*0-8144-0406-5*) AMACOM.

Conover, Charlotte. Dayton, Ohio: An Intimate History, with One Hundred Twenty-Six Illustrations. (Illus.). 311p. 1997. reprint ed. lib. bdg. 39.50 (*0-8328-7151-6*) Higginson Bk Co.

Conover, Charlotte R. Dayton, Ohio: An Intimate History, Vol. 1. LC 95-78178. (Becentennial Bookshelf Ser.: No. 1). (Illus.). 304p. 1971. reprint ed. 34.95 (*0-913428-00-0*) Landfall Pr.

— A History of the Beck Family. (Illus.). 259p. 1988. reprint ed. pap. 39.00 (*0-8328-0219-0*); reprint ed. lib. bdg. 47.00 (*0-8328-0218-2*) Higginson Bk Co.

Conover, Chris. The Adventures of Simple Simon. 32p. 1989. pap. 4.95 (*0-374-40096-2*) FS&G.

— Froggie Went A-Courting. 32p. (ps-3). 1988. pap. 4.95 (*0-374-42474-8*) FS&G.

***Conover, Chris.** The Lion's Share. (Illus.). 40p. (J). 2000. 16.00 (*0-374-39974-3*) FS&G.

***Conover, David & Conover, Patricia.** Humphrey the Hugganite. LC 00-190584. (Illus.). 32p. (J). (ps-3). 2000. pap. 7.99 (*0-9677987-0-1*) Hugganite Pubng.

Conover, Ernie. The Lathe Book. (Illus.). 208p. 1993. pap. 25.95 (*1-56158-057-0*, 70195) Taunton.

— Router Table Book. LC 94-24591. (Illus.). 128p. 1994. pap. 19.95 (*1-56158-084-8*) Taunton.

***Conover, Ernie.** Turn a Bowl with Ernie Conover: Getting Terrific Results the First Time Around. LC 99-47134. (Illus.). 160p. 2000. pap. 19.95 (*1-56158-293-X*) Taunton.

Conover, Ernie. Turning for Furniture - Creating Furniture Parts on Your Lathe. LC 96-22633. (Illus.). 144p. 1996. pap. 19.95 (*1-56158-117-8*, 070245) Taunton.

Conover, Garrett. Beyond the Paddle: The Canoeists Guide to Expedition Skills - Poling, Lining, Portaging & Maneuvering Through Ice. (Illus.). 112p. 1991. pap. 17.95 (*0-88448-066-6*) Tilbury Hse.

***Conover, Garrett.** Winter Wilderness Companion: Traditional & Native American Skills for the Undiscovered Season. rev. ed. (Illus.). 448p. 2000. pap. 19.95 (*0-07-136417-X*) McGraw.

Conover, Garrett & Conover, Alexandra. Snow Walker's Companion: Winter Trail Skills from the Far North. LC 94-3374. (Illus.). 272p. 1994. pap. 19.95 (*0-07-022892-2*, Ragged Mntain) McGraw-Hill Prof.

Conover, George S., ed. History of Ontario County, with Illustrations & Family Sketches of Some of the Prominent Men & Families. (Illus.). 915p. 1996. reprint ed. lib. bdg. 92.00 (*0-8328-5083-7*) Higginson Bk Co.

Conover, Grandin. Ten Years. LC 72-77578. 76p. 1972. 15.00 (*0-87023-116-2*); pap. 9.95 (*0-87023-117-0*) U of Mass Pr.

Conover, Helen F. A Guide to Bibliographic Tools for Research in Foreign Affairs, 2 vols. 1975. lib. bdg. 250.00 (*0-8490-1917-6*) Gordon Pr.

Conover, Helen F., jt. auth. see Mugridge, Donald H.

Conover, Hobart, et al. Business Dynamics. 481p. 1982. teacher ed. write for info. (*0-672-97978-0*); text. write for info. (*0-672-97973-X*); student ed. write for info. (*0-672-97977-2*) Macmillan.

Conover, Jim. Greenhorns & Killer Mountains. LC 99-90242. 450p. 1999. pap. 16.00 (*0-9669472-1-5*) Lynch Law.

Conover, Jim & Brecher, James. Lynch Law. (Illus.). vi, 297p. 1998. pap. 18.00 (*0-9669472-0-7*) Lynch Law.

Conover, John H. Blue Hill Meteorological Observatory: The First 100 Years, 1885-1985. (Illus.). 528p. 1990. 60.00 (*0-933876-89-0*) Am Meteorological.

Conover, John L., jt. auth. see Pachman, Stuart L.

Conover, Joseph A. How to Make Big Profits from Land in Transition. 1975. 59.50 (*0-13-418012-7*) Exec Reports.

Conover, K. Scott. Can I Play, Too? LC 98-67942. (Illus.). 70p. (J). (gr. 4-8). 1998. pap. 9.95 (*1-882792-69-6*) Proctor Pubns.

Conover, Kris & Gardner, Gayle M. Marriage Made Simple: 50 Hints on Building Long Lasting Love. LC 98-30257. 128p. 1999. pap. 10.95 (*0-452-28038-9*, Plume) Dutton Plume.

Conover, Marilyn. Hannah Jumper: A Legend of the New England Seacoast. (Illus.). 149p. (Orig.). (J). (gr. 4 up). 1994. pap. write for info. (*0-9639867-0-8*) Meristem Bks.

Conover, Mary B. Understanding Electrocardiography. 7th ed. (Illus.). 560p. (C). (gr. 13). 1995. pap. text 37.95 (*0-8151-1927-5*, 27202) Mosby Inc.

Conover, Mary B., jt. auth. see Marriott, Henry J. L.

Conover, Mary B., jt. auth. see Tilkian, Ara G.

Conover, Mary Boudreau. Pocket Guide to Electrocardiography. 4th ed. LC 97-39597. (Illus.). 288p. (C). (gr. 13). 1997. text 22.95 (*0-8151-3695-1*, 31037) Mosby Inc.

Conover, Milton. The Federal Power Commission: Its History, Activities & Organization. LC 72-3035. (Brookings Institution. Institute for Government Research. Service Monographs of the U. S. Government: No. 17). reprint ed. 24.00 (*0-404-57117-4*) AMS Pr.

— The General Land Office: Its History, Activities & Organization. LC 72-3026. (Brookings Institution. Institute for Government Research. Service Monographs of the U. S. Government: No. 13). reprint ed. 30.00 (*0-404-57113-1*) AMS Pr.

— The Office of Experiment Stations: Its History, Activities & Organization. LC 72-3047. (Brookings Institution. Institute for Government Research. Service Monographs of the U. S. Government: No. 32). reprint ed. 25.00 (*0-404-57132-8*) AMS Pr.

Conover, Pamela J. & Gray, Virginia. Feminism & the New Right: Conflict Over the American Family. LC 82-24643. 253p. 1983. 65.00 (*0-275-90960-3*, C0960, Praeger Pubs) Greenwood.

Conover, Patricia, jt. auth. see Conover, David.

***Conover, Sara.** Kindness: A Treasury of Buddhist Wisdom for Children & Parents. (Illus.). 120p. 2000. 39.95 (*0-910055-67-X*) East Wash Univ.

Conover, Steven G. Building an American Clock Movement. (Illus.). 88p. 1994. pap. 21.95 (*0-9624766-3-3*, 114) Clockmakers.

— Chime Clock Repair. 2nd rev. ed. (Illus.). 126p. 1997. pap. 28.50 (*0-9624766-6-8*, 100) Clockmakers.

— Clock Repair Basics. unabridged ed. (Illus.). 92p. 1996. 22.95 (*0-9624766-5-X*, 116) Clockmakers.

***Conover, Steven G.** How to Make a Foliot Clock. (Illus.). 88p. 2000. pap. 22.95 (*0-9624766-8-4*) Clockmakers.

Conover, Steven G. How to Repair Herschede Tubular Bell Clocks. LC 93-73238. (Illus.). 70p. 1993. reprint ed. pap. 12.95 (*0-9624766-2-5*, 110) Clockmakers.

***Conover, Steven G.** How to Repair Herschede Tubular Bell Clocks. 2nd rev. ed. (Illus.). 116p. 1999. 28.50 (*0-9624766-7-6*, 110) Clockmakers.

Conover, Steven G. Striking Clock Repair Guide. (Illus.). 90p. 1995. pap. 22.95 (*0-9624766-4-1*, 115) Clockmakers.

Conover, Ted. Alaskan Journey: In My Grandfather's Footsteps. (J). 1900. lib. bdg. 19.99 (*0-679-98588-3*, Pub. by Random Bks Yng Read) Random.

— Coyotes: A Journey Through the Secret World of America's Illegal Aliens. LC 87-40066. (Vintage Departures Ser.). 256p. 1987. pap. 13.00 (*0-394-75518-9*) Vin Bks.

— In My Grandfather's Footsteps. (YA). (gr. 6 up). 1999. 18.00 (*0-679-88588-9*, Pub. by Knopf Bks Yng Read) Random.

***Conover, Ted.** Newjack: Guarding Sing Sing. LC 99-87895. 352p. 2000. 24.95 (*0-375-50177-0*) Random.

Conover, Theodore E. Graphic Communications Today. 2nd ed. Perlee, Clyde, ed. 517p. (C). 1990. mass mkt. 46.50 (*0-314-66570-6*) West Pub.

— Graphic Communications Today. 3rd ed. LC 94-35459. 500p. (C). 1996. pap. 72.95 (*0-314-04424-8*) West Pub.

— Graphic Design in Action: A Workbook. Perlee, Clyde, ed. 500p. (C). 1992. pap. text 22.25 (*0-314-92850-2*) West Pub.

Conover, W. J. Practical Nonparametric Statistics. 3rd ed. LC 98-8521. 584p. 1998. text 100.95 (*0-471-16068-7*) Wiley.

Conow, B. Hoff. Baha'i Teachings: A Resurgent Model of the Universe. (Illus.). 184p. (Orig.). (C). 1990. pap. 13.95 (*0-85398-297-X*) G Ronald Pub.

Conoway, Douglas C., et al. Geriatrics. (National Medical Ser.). (Illus.). 112p. 1988. 37.00 (*0-683-06220-4*) Lppncott W & W.

Conoway, Judith, jt. auth. see Tilkin, Sheldon L.

Conquest. Ravaged Century. 2000. text 27.50 (*0-312-20338-1*) St Martin.

Conquest, Fay, jt. auth. see Katz, Nancy.

C

C

Conquest, John. Trouble Is Their Business: Private Eyes in Fiction, Film & Television, 1927-1988. LC 89-33039. 552p. 1989. text 35.00 (*0-8240-5947-6*, H1151) Garland.
Conquest, Ned. Achilles & Company. LC 88-192272. 185p. 1988. 22.50 (*0-9627485-0-1*) Apollonian Pr.
— Virginia, the Gray & the Green. LC 90-83455. 160p. 1990. 19.95 (*0-9627485-1-X*) Apollonian Pr.
— The Way of the Eagle. LC 94-72041. 319p. 1994. 19.95 (*0-9627485-2-8*) Apollonian Pr.
— The Widow's Might: Three Plays. LC 97-71095. 115p. (Orig.). 1997. pap. 9.95 (*0-9627485-3-6*) Apollonian Pr.
Conquest, Robert. The Great Terror: A Reassessment. 584p. 1991. reprint ed. pap. 19.95 (*0-19-507132-8*) OUP.
— The Harvest of Sorrow: Soviet Collectivization & the Terror-Famine. 430p. 1987. pap. 16.95 (*0-19-505180-7*) OUP.
— History, Humanity & Truth: Jefferson Lecture in Humanities. LC 93-30917. (Hoover Essays Ser.: No. 5). 17p. 1993. pap. 5.00 (*0-8179-3682-3*) Hoover Inst Pr.
Conquest, Robert. Reflections on a Ravaged Century. pap. 15.95 (*0-393-32086-3*) Norton.
Conquest, Robert. Stalin: Breaker of Nations. 368p. 1992. reprint ed. pap. 14.95 (*0-14-016953-9*, Penguin Bks) Viking Penguin.
Conquest, Robert, ed. The Last Empire: Nationality & the Soviet Future. (Publication Ser.: No. 325). 406p. 1986. lib. bdg. 27.95 (*0-8179-8251-5*) Hoover Inst Pr.
Conquest, Robert & Djordjevich, Dusan, eds. Political & Ideological Confrontations in 20th Century Europe: Essays in Honor of Milorad M. Drachkovitch. 300p. 1996. text 55.00 (*0-312-12373-6*) St Martin.
Conquest, Robert, et al. Reflections on a Ravaged Century. LC 99-31980. 336p. 1999. 27.95 (*0-393-04818-7*) Norton.
Conquest, Robert, jt. ed. see Amis, Kingsley.
Conrad. Be My Guest. 1983. mass mkt. 0.55 (*0-446-31254-1*, Pub. by Warner Bks) Little.
Conrad. The Coral Island. (Classics Library). pap. 3.95 (*1-85326-170-X*, 170XWW, Pub. by Wrdsworth Edits) NTC Contemp Pub Co.
Conrad. Differential Equations with Dynamic Systems & Boundary Value Problems. (Mathematics Ser.). 1998. text 65.95 (*0-534-95672-6*) PWS Pubs.
— How Meteorite Got to Museum, Vol. 1. (J). 1995. 14.95 (*0-8050-1977-4*) H Holt & Co.
— Kitchen Poem. 32p. (J). Date not set. 15.00 (*0-06-021512-7*) HarperTrade.
— Kitchen Poem. (Illus.). 32p. (J). Date not set. lib. bdg. 14.89 (*0-06-021513-5*) HarperTrade.
— Sea Stories. (Classics Library). 1998. pap. 3.95 (*1-85326-743-0*, 7430WW, Pub. by Wrdsworth Edits) NTC Contemp Pub Co.
— Strategic Organization Communication. 4th ed. LC 97-72835. 1997. text 48.50 (*0-15-503570-3*, Pub. by Harcourt Coll Pubs) Harcourt.
— Strategic Organizational. 3rd ed. (C). 1993. pap. text, teacher ed. 34.00 (*0-15-501595-8*) Harcourt Coll Pubs.
Conrad. The Tub People. 32p. (J). Date not set. 16.95 (*0-694-00604-1*, HarpFestival) HarpC Child Bks.
Conrad. Women in the West. 1996. 40.00 (*0-8161-1822-1*, G K Hall & Co) Mac Lib Ref.
Conrad & Lowenberg. Current Perspectives in Industrial Organization. LC 97-44531. 617p. 1997. 82.00 (*0-205-14252-4*) P-H.
Conrad, et al. 1987 Corporation & Partnership, Statutes, Rules, & Forms. 1987. pap. text 15.25 (*0-88277-597-9*) Foundation Pr.
Conrad, jt. auth. see Eckenrode, Hamilton J.
Conrad, Agnes C., ed. see Gast, Ross H.
Conrad, Alfred, et al. Agency & Partnership. 1987. text 31.95 (*0-88277-598-7*) Foundation Pr.
Conrad, Alfred F., et al. Enterprise Organization: Cases, Statutes & Analysis on Licensing, Employment, Agency, Partnerships, Associations & Corporations. 4th ed. (University Casebks.). 1197p. 1990. reprint ed. text 43.95 (*0-88277-562-6*) Foundation Pr.
Conrad, Allen. Double Crossfire. 256p. 1988. mass mkt. 2.95 (*0-8217-2363-4*, Zebra Kensgtn) Kensgtn Pub Corp.
Conrad, Andree & Clemens, John. Huckins the Living Legacy. unabridged ed. (Illus.). 216p. 1998. 49.95 (*0-9664092-0-5*) Huckins Yacht.
Conrad, Barnaby, III. Absinthe: History in a Bottle. LC 88-12669. (Illus.). 160p. 1988. 29.95 (*0-87701-566-X*) Chronicle Bks.
Conrad, Barnaby. Absinthe: History in a Bottle. 1997. pap. 19.95 (*0-8118-1650-8*) Chronicle Bks.
***Conrad, Barnaby.** The Blonde. LC 99-22312. 1999. write for info. (*0-8118-2262-1*) Chronicle Bks.
***Conrad, Barnaby, III.** The Blonde: A Celebration of the Golden Era from Harlowe to Monroe. LC 99-22312. (Illus.). 132p. 1999. 29.95 (*0-8118-2591-4*) Chronicle Bks.
Conrad, Barnaby, III. Les Chiens de Paris. LC 94-19721. (Illus.). 72p. 1995. 14.95 (*0-8118-0743-6*) Chronicle Bks.
— The Cigar: An Illustrated History of Fine Smoking. (Illus.). 132p. 1996. 29.95 (*0-8118-1449-1*) Chronicle Bks.
— John Register: Persistent Observer. Defendorf, Richard, ed. LC 98-61588. (Illus.). 180p. 1999. 45.00 (*0-942627-50-4*) Woodford Pubng.
Conrad, Barnaby. Learning to Write Fiction from the Masters. 1996. pap. 14.95 (*0-452-27657-8*, Plume) Dutton Plume.
Conrad, Barnaby, III. Martini: Shaken Not Stirred. LC 94-17325. (Illus.). 132p. 1995. 24.95 (*0-8118-0717-7*) Chronicle Bks.
Conrad, Barnaby. Monarch Notes on Conrad's Lord Jim & Other Works. (Orig.). (C). pap. 3.95 (*0-671-00605-3*, Arco) Macmillan Gen Ref.
— Name Dropping: Tales from My San Francisco Nightclub. LC 96-61771. (Illus.). 212p. 1997. pap. 14.95 (*0-9649701-4-7*) Wild Coconuts.
— Pan Am: An Aviation Legend. 200p. 1999. 39.95 (*0-942627-55-5*) Woodford Pubng.
— Time Is All We Have. 1992. 9.95 (*0-918684-37-4*) Cameron & Co.
Conrad, Barnaby, Sr. World of Herb Caen: San Francisco, 1938-1997. LC 97-26163. 144p. 1997. 35.00 (*0-8118-1859-4*) Chronicle Bks.
***Conrad, Barnaby.** World of Herb Caen: San Francisco, 1938-1997. 144p. 1999. pap. 18.95 (*0-8118-2575-2*) Chronicle Bks.
Conrad, Barnaby, III, ed. Les Chats de Paris. LC 95-23318. (Illus.). 72p. 1996. 14.95 (*0-8118-1186-7*) Chronicle Bks.
Conrad, Barnaby & Santa Barbara Writer's Conference Staff. The Complete Guide to Writing Fiction. (Illus.). 312p. 1990. 19.99 (*0-89879-395-5*, Wrtrs Digest Bks) F & W Pubns Inc.
Conrad, Bonnie H. When a Child Has Been Murdered: Ways You Can Help the Grieving Parents. LC 97-28443. (Death, Value & Meaning Ser.). 152p. 1997. text 32.95 (*0-89503-186-8*) Baywood Pub.
— When a Child Has Died: Ways You Can Help a Bereaved Parent. 56p. 1995. pap. 8.95 (*1-56474-141-9*) Fithian Pr.
— Who Will Sing to Me Now? LC 95-78166. 1995. pap. text 18.95 (*1-883612-04-7*) Bks Unltd.
Conrad, Bonnie H., jt. auth. see De Vries, Brian.
Conrad, Bryan, jt. auth. see Eckenrode, H. J.
Conrad, Bryce. Refiguring America: A Study of William Carlos Williams' In the American Grain. 192p. 1990. text 29.95 (*0-252-01704-8*) U of Ill Pr.
Conrad, C. A. Frank. 30p. 1993. pap. 5.00 (*1-882827-02-3*) Insight to Riot.
Conrad, C. Eugene & Newell, Leonard A., eds. Proceedings of the Session on Tropical Forestry for People of the Pacific. Seventeenth Pacific Science Congress. (Illus.). 88p. (Orig.). (C). 1994. pap. text 35.00 (*0-7881-0364-4*) DIANE Pub.
Conrad, C. Eugene, jt. ed. see Hamilton, Lawrence.
Conrad, Charles & Dervin, Brenda, eds. The Ethical Nexus: Communication, Values, & Organizational Decisions. (Communication & Information Science Ser.). 280p. (C). 1993. pap. 39.50 (*0-89391-844-X*); text 73.25 (*0-89391-795-8*) Ablx Pub.
Conrad, Charles F., jt. auth. see Urban, Matt.
Conrad, Chris. Hemp for Health: The Nutritional & Medicinal Uses of the World's Most Extraordinary Plant. LC 96-51628. (Illus.). 160p. 1997. pap. 14.95 (*0-89281-539-6*, Heal Arts VT) Inner Tradit.
— Hemp, Lifeline to the Future: The Unexpected Answer for Our Environmental & Economic Recovery. 2nd rev. ed. Richard, Roy, ed. (Illus.). 322p. (Orig.). 1994. pap. 13.00 (*0-9639754-1-2*) Creat Xpress.
Conrad, Chris, et al. Human Rights & the U. S. Drug War. LC 98-205091. (Illus.). x, 118 p. 1999. pap. 5.00 (*0-9639754-4-7*) Creat Express.
Conrad, Chris, ed. see Herer, Jack.
***Conrad, Christine.** A Woman's Guide to Natural Hormones. LC 99-88619. 2000. pap. 13.95 (*0-399-52581-5*, Perigee Bks) Berkley Pub.
***Conrad, Christine, ed.** Jerome Robbins: That Broadway Man, That Ballet Man. (Illus.). 304p. 2000. 49.95 (*1-86154-173-2*, Pub. by Booth-Clibborn) Dist Art Pubs.
Conrad, Christine, jt. auth. see Laux, Marcus.
Conrad, Clay S. Jury Nullification: The Evolution of a Doctrine. LC 98-87688. (Illus.). 336p. 1999. pap. 22.50 (*0-89089-702-6*) Carolina Acad Pr.
Conrad, Clifton. The Undergraduate Curriculum. 1979. 24.00 (*0-89158-196-0*) Westview.
Conrad, Clifton, ed. Curriculum in Transition: Perspectives on the Undergraduate Experience. 2nd ed. (C). 1990. pap. text 48.00 (*0-536-57792-7*) Pearson Custom.
Conrad, Clifton F., et al, eds. Qualitative Research in Higher Education: Experiencing Alternative Perspectives & Approaches. (ASHE Reader Ser.). 706p. (C). 1993. pap. text 54.00 (*0-536-58417-6*) Pearson Custom.
Conrad, Clifton F. & Wilson, Richard F. Academic Program Reviews: Institutional Approaches, Expectations, & Controversies. Fife, Jonathan D., ed. LC 85-73508. (ASHE-ERIC Higher Education Reports: No. 85-5). 96p. (Orig.). 1985. pap. 24.00 (*0-913317-24-1*) GWU Grad Schl E&HD.
Conrad, Clifton F., et al. A Silent Success: Master's Education in the United States. LC 92-1612. 384p. 1993. text 35.95 (*0-8018-4508-4*) Johns Hopkins.
Conrad, Clifton F., jt. auth. see Haworth, Jennifer G.
Conrad, Clifton F., jt. ed. see Haworth, Jennifer G.
Conrad, Daniel & Hedin, Diane, eds. Youth Participation & Experiential Education: Theory, Research, & Programs. LC 81-20114. (Child & Youth Services Ser.: Vol. 4, Nos. 3 & 4). 156p. 1982. text 49.95 (*0-917724-99-2*) Haworth Pr.
Conrad, David C. The Songhay Empire. LC 97-31288. (African Civilizations Ser.). (J). 1998. 22.00 (*0-531-20284-4*) Watts.
Conrad, David C., ed. A State of Intrigue: The Epic of Bamana Segu According to Tayiru Banbera. Diakite, Soumaila, tr. (Fontes Historiae Africanae, Series Varia: Vol. VI). (Illus.). 372p. 1990. pap. 85.00 (*0-19-726088-8*) OUP.
Conrad, David C. & Frank, Barbara E., eds. Status & Identity in West Africa: Nyamakalaw of Mande. LC 94-20215. (African Systems of Thought Ser.). 224p. 1995. 29.95 (*0-253-31409-7*); pap. 12.95 (*0-253-20929-3*) Ind U Pr.
Conrad, David E. The Forgotten Farmers: The Story of Sharecroppers in the New Deal. LC 82-955. 223p. 1982. reprint ed. lib. bdg. 35.00 (*0-313-23358-6*, COFF, Greenwood Pr) Greenwood.
Conrad, David R. Education for Transformation: Implications in Lewis Mumford's Ecohumanism. LC 75-25867. 1976. 23.95 (*0-88280-030-2*) ETC Pubns.
Conrad, Deborah K., et al. Telecommunications Making Sense Out of New Technology & New Legislation. Divilbiss, J. L., ed. 1985. text 10.00 (*0-87845-072-6*) U of Ill Grad Sch.
Conrad, Dennis M., ed. see Greene, Nathanael.
Conrad, Dennis M., jt. ed. see Showman, Richard K.
Conrad, Diane. Fables of Psyche. (Illus.). 70p. (Orig.). 1996. pap. 8.00 (*0-614-32385-1*) Phantsml Pr.
— Love's Lance. 46p. (Orig.). 1996. pap. 8.00 (*0-614-32387-8*) Phantsml Pr.
— MindShadows. (Illus.). 70p. (Orig.). 1996. pap. 8.00 (*0-614-32386-X*) Phantsml Pr.
— Ocean's Lure. (Illus.). vi, 52p. (Orig.). 1996. pap. 8.00 (*0-614-32388-6*) Phantsml Pr.
***Conrad, Donna.** See You Soon Moon! (J). 2001. mass mkt. 14.95 (*0-375-80656-3*, Pub. by Random Bks Yng Read) Random.
Conrad, Douglas. Integrated Delivery Systems: Creation, Management, & Governance. LC 97-27721. 1997. 45.00 (*1-56793-069-7*) Health Admin Pr.
Conrad, Douglas, et al. Managed Care Contracting: Concepts & Applications for the Health Care Executive. LC 96-3242. (Management Ser.). 146p. 1996. 20.00 (*1-56793-042-5*, 0979) Health Admin Pr.
Conrad, Douglas A. & Hoare, Geoffrey A., eds. Strategic Alignment: Managing Integrated Health Systems. LC 93-34353. 303p. (Orig.). (C). 1993. pap. text 20.00 (*1-56793-003-4*, 0937) Health Admin Pr.
Conrad, Earl. Gulf Stream North. LC 80-50244. 248p. 1980. reprint ed. 22.00 (*0-933256-13-2*); reprint ed. pap. 16.00 (*0-933256-17-5*) Second Chance.
— Harriet Tubman. (YA). 1990. 21.95 (*0-87498-036-4*); pap. 15.95 (*0-685-55179-2*) Assoc Pubs DC.
Conrad, Edgar W. Zechariah. (Readings Ser.). 219p. 1999. 57.50 (*1-85075-899-9*, Pub. by Sheffield Acad); pap. 23.75 (*1-85075-900-6*, Pub. by Sheffield Acad) CUP Services.
Conrad, Edgar W. & Newing, Edward G., eds. Perspectives on Language & Text: Essays & Poems in Honor of Francis I. Andersen's Sixtieth Birthday, July 28, 1985. LC 86-24349. xxviii, 443p. 1987. text 49.50 (*0-931464-26-9*) Eisenbrauns.
***Conrad, Eleanor & Hart, Michael.** Mastering the Uncommon Common Sense. 120p. 2000. pap. 9.95 (*0-615-11754-6*) Off Beat Tours.
Conrad, Elfi-Marein. Gedächtnis und Wissensrepräsentation. (Philosophische Texte und Studien: Vol. 37). (GER.). viii, 274p. 1993. write for info. (*3-487-09771-0*) G Olms Pubs.
Conrad, F., ed. Applied Control & Identification - ACI '83: Proceedings, IASTED Symposium, Copenhagen, Denmark, June 28-July 1, 1983, 2 vols., 1. 849p. 1983. write for info. (*0-88986-045-9*) Acta Pr.
— Applied Control & Identification - ACI '83: Proceedings, IASTED Symposium, Copenhagen, Denmark, June 28-July 1, 1983, 2 vols., Set. 849p. 1983. 120.00 (*0-318-22563-8*, 053) Acta Pr.
— Applied Control & Identification - ACI '83: Proceedings, IASTED Symposium, Copenhagen, Denmark, June 28-July 1, 1983, 2 vols., Vol. 2. 849p. 1983. write for info. (*0-88986-046-7*) Acta Pr.
Conrad, Frederick G., jt. ed. see Payne, David G.
Conrad, Geoffrey W. & Demarest, Arthur A. Religion & Empire: The Dynamics of Aztec & Inca Expansionism. LC 83-14414. (New Studies in Archaeology). 284p. 1984. pap. text 26.95 (*0-521-31896-3*) Cambridge U Pr.
Conrad, Geoffrey W., jt. auth. see Bawden, Garth.
Conrad, Geoffrey W., jt. ed. see Demarest, Arthur A.
Conrad, Glen R., jt. ed. see Becnel, Thomas A.
Conrad, Glenn. First Families of L. A., Vol. 2. 1970. 35.00 (*0-87511-355-9*, CFIRS2) Claitors.
— First Families of Louisiana, Vol. 1. 1970. 35.00 (*0-87511-020-7*, CFIRS1) Claitors.
Conrad, Glenn R. Land Records of the Attakapas Vol. 2, Pt. 1: Conveyance Records of Attakapas Country, 1804-1818. LC 90-81684. 430p. 1990. 24.95 (*0-940984-57-1*) Univ LA Lafayette.
Conrad, Glenn R., ed. The Cajuns: Essays on Their History & Culture. LC 83-70891. (U. S. L. History Ser.). 280p. (C). 1983. 20.00 (*0-940984-10-5*) Univ LA Lafayette.
— The Road to Louisiana: The Saint-Domingue Refugees, 1792-1809. Cheramie, David, tr. xviii, 306 p. 1992. 20.00 (*0-940984-76-8*) Univ LA Lafayette.
Conrad, Glenn R., ed. The French Experience in Louisiana, Vol. 1. LC 95-71051. (Louisiana Purchase Bicentennial Ser.). 674p. 1995. text 40.00 (*0-940984-97-0*) Univ LA Lafayette.
Conrad, Glenn R. & Brasseaux, Carl A. Crevasse! The 1927 Flood in Acadiana. (Illus.). 136p. 1994. 15.00 (*0-940984-88-1*) Univ LA Lafayette.
Conrad, Glenn R. & Lucas, Ray F. White Gold: A Brief History of the Louisiana Sugar Industry, 1795-1995. LC 94-74142. (Louisians Life Ser.: No. 8). (Illus.). 102p. (Orig.). 1995. pap. 5.00 (*0-940984-92-X*) Univ LA Lafayette.
Conrad, Glenn R., jt. auth. see Brasseaux, Carl A.
Conrad, Glenn R., jt. ed. see Baker, Vaughan Burdin.
Conrad, Glenn R., ed. see De la Harpe, Jean-Baptiste.
Conrad, Glenn R., jt. ed. see Din, Gilbert C.
Conrad, Glenn R., jt. ed. see Kurtz, Michael L.
Conrad, Glenn R., jt. ed. see Vincent, Charles.
Conrad, Glenn R., jt. ed. see Wade, Michael G.
Conrad, H., jt. ed. see Westbrook, J. H.
Conrad, H. C. Kunders: Some Scraps of History Regarding Thomas Kunders & His Children; Also, a List of the Descendants for Six Generations of His Youngest Son, Henry Cunreds of "Whitpain," 1683-1891. 128p. 1993. reprint ed. pap. 21.00 (*0-8328-2813-0*); reprint ed. lib. bdg. 31.00 (*0-8328-2812-2*) Higginson Bk Co.
Conrad, H. Edward. Heparin-Binding Proteins. LC 97-74397. (Illus.). 527p. 1997. text 89.95 (*0-12-186060-4*) Morgan Kaufmann.
Conrad, Helen. Jake's Promise. 1994. per. 3.50 (*0-373-70617-0*, 1-70617-5) Harlequin Bks.
— Joe's Miracle. (Superromance Ser.). 1993. per. 3.39 (*0-373-70544-1*, 1-70544-1) Harlequin Bks.
— The Reluctant Daddy. (Hometown Reunion Ser.). 1996. per. 4.50 (*0-373-82550-1*, 1-82550-4) Harlequin Bks.
— Those Baby Blues. (Hometown Reunion Ser.). 1997. per. 4.50 (*0-373-82553-6*, 1-82553-8) Silhouette.
Conrad, Henry C. Old Delaware Clockmakers. (Illus.). 34p. 1998. reprint ed. pap. 7.00 (*0-8328-9589-X*) Higginson Bk Co.
Conrad, Henry S., ed. & tr. see Braun-Blanquet, J.
Conrad, Herbert S., ed. Studies in Human Development: Selections from the Publications & Addresses of Harold Ellis Jones. (Century Psychology Ser.). (Illus.). 1966. 67.50 (*0-89197-581-0*) Irvington.
Conrad, Hy. Almost Perfect Crimes: Mini-Mysteries for You to Solve. LC 95-20065. (Illus.). 96p. 1995. pap. 5.95 (*0-8069-3807-2*) Sterling.
— Almost Perfect Murders: Mini-Mysteries for You to Solve. LC 96-50120. (Illus.). 96p. 1997. pap. 5.95 (*0-8069-9513-0*) Sterling.
— Whodunit - You Decide! Mini-Mysteries for You to Solve. LC 96-25416. (Illus.). 96p. 1996. pap. 5.95 (*0-8069-6150-3*) Sterling.
Conrad, Hy & LaFleur, Matt. Little Giant Book of Whodunits. LC 98-6165. (Illus.). 352p. (J). 1998. pap. 6.95 (*0-8069-0473-9*) Sterling.
Conrad, Hy & Peterson, Bob. Solve-It-Yourself Mysteries: Detective Club Puzzlers. LC 96-37010. (Illus.). 96p. (J). 1997. 14.95 (*0-8069-9400-2*) Sterling.
Conrad, J. Oeuvres, Vol. 3. (Pleiade Ser.). (FRE.). 1987. 135.00 (*0-8288-3467-9*, F41030) Fr & Eur.
Conrad, J. David. The Steam Locomotive Directory of North America, 2 vols., Set, Vols. 1&2. 1987. 47.00 (*0-933449-06-2*) Transport Trails.
Conrad, J. P., jt. auth. see Van den Haag, E.
***Conrad, Jake.** Yellowsnake: Son of Prophecy. 276p. 2000. 26.48 (*1-58721-553-5*) First Bks Lib.
Conrad, James. Making Love to the Minor Poets of Chicago. LC 99-55719. 496p. 2000. text 25.95 (*0-312-20472-8*) St Martin.
Conrad, James, jt. auth. see Singleton, Ralph S.
Conrad, James A. The Model-Actor's Dictionary. LC 88-60886. 160p. (Orig.). 1988. pap. 9.95 (*0-944957-00-5*) Rivercross Pub.
Conrad, James H., jt. auth. see Sitton, Thad.
Conrad, James L. The Young Lions: Confederate Cadets at War. LC 97-9907. (Illus.). 224p. 1997. 24.95 (*0-8117-1975-8*) Stackpole.
Conrad, James M. A Simple & Inexpensive Robot That You Can Build. LC 99-52734. 250p. 1999. 30.00 (*0-8186-7514-4*, BP07514) IEEE Comp Soc.
Conrad, James M. & Mills, Jonathan W. Stiquito: Advanced Experiments with a Simple & Inexpensive Robot. LC 96-29883. 250p. 1997. teacher ed. 35.00 (*0-8186-7408-3*) IEEE Comp Soc.
Conrad, James W. Environmental Science Deskbook. LC 97-52805. (Law Ser.). 1998. 140.00 (*0-8366-1220-5*) West Group.
— Handbook of Communications Systems Management 1999. 1998. 180.00 (*0-8493-9965-3*) CRC Pr.
Conrad, Jean. Applegate Landing, No. 22. (Serenade Saga Ser.). 1985. pap. 2.50 (*0-310-46832-9*, 15542P) Zondervan.
— Golden Gates. 224p. 1987. pap. 7.95 (*0-310-47811-1*, 15658P) Zondervan.
Conrad, Jessie. Joseph Conrad As I Knew Him. LC 76-128877. (Select Bibliographies Reprint Ser.). 1977. 18.95 (*0-8369-5497-1*) Ayer.
Conrad, Jillian, ed. Eco-Villages & Sustainable Communities: Models for 21st Century Living. 96p. (Orig.). 1996. pap. 11.95 (*1-899171-21-5*, Pub. by Findhorn Pr) Words Distrib.
Conrad, Jim. Discover Nature in the Garden: Things to Know & Things to Do. (Illus.). 224p. 1996. pap. 14.95 (*0-8117-2442-5*) Stackpole.
— Mexico: A Hiker's Guide to Mexico's Natural History. LC 94-45479. (Illus.). 224p. 1995. pap. 16.95 (*0-89886-424-0*) Mountaineers.
— On the Road to Tetlama: Mexican Adventures of a Wandering Naturalist. (Illus.). 196p. 1991. 21.95 (*0-8027-1152-9*) Walker & Co.
Conrad, Jobst. Environmental Management in European Countries: Success Stories & Evaluation. 370p. 1998. text 69.00 (*90-5699-085-3*) Gordon & Breach.
— Nitrate Pollution & Politics: Great Britain, the Federal Republic of Germany & the Netherlands. (Illus.). 88p. 1990. text 82.95 (*0-566-07147-9*, Pub. by Avebry) Ashgate Pub Co.
Conrad, John J., jt. auth. see Cox, Steven M.
Conrad, John P. The Future of Corrections. Sellin, Thorsten D., ed. LC 69-16927. (Annals Ser.: No. 381). 1969. pap. 18.00 (*0-87761-112-2*) Am Acad Pol Soc Sci.
Conrad, John P., jt. ed. see Flynn, Edith E.
Conrad, John W. Advanced Ceramic Manual, Technical Data for the Studio Potter. 278p. (Orig.). (C). 1988. pap. 34.05 (*0-935921-05-2*) Falcon Co.
— Ceramic Formulas: The Complete Compedium. 2nd ed. 112p. 1989. reprint ed. pap. text 23.75 (*0-935921-09-5*) Falcon Co.
— Ceramic Windchimes. (Illus.). 80p. (Orig.). 1985. pap. 10.70 (*0-935921-01-X*) Falcon Co.
— Cone Six Ceramics. (Illus.). 110p. (Orig.). 1998. pap. 25.00 (*0-935921-19-2*) Falcon Co.

An Asterisk (*) at the beginning of an entry indicates that the title is appearing for the first time.

— Studio Ceramic Dictionary. 90p. (Orig.). 1990. pap. 13.66 (*0-935921-12-5*) Falcon Co.

— Studio Potter's Ceramic Extruder. LC 97-61699. (Illus.). 110p. (Orig.). (C). 1998. pap. 30.00 (*0-935921-16-8*) Falcon Co.

Conrad, Jon M. Resource Economics. LC 98-49529. (Illus.). 232p. (C). 1999. 54.95 (*0-521-64012-1*) Cambridge U Pr.

— Resource Economics. LC 98-49529. (Illus.). 232p. (C). 1999. pap. 19.95 (*0-521-64974-9*) Cambridge U Pr.

Conrad, Jon M. & Clark, Colin W. Natural Resource Economics: Notes & Problems. (Illus.). 254p. 1987. text 85.00 (*0-521-33188-9*); pap. text 26.95 (*0-521-33769-0*) Cambridge U Pr.

***Conrad, Joseph.** Almayer. (Oxford World's Classics Ser.). (Illus.). 320p. 1999. pap. 8.95 (*0-19-283831-8*) OUP.

Conrad, Joseph. Almayer's Folly. 1976. 19.95 (*0-8488-0460-0*) Amereon Ltd.

— Almayer's Folly. 128p. 1991. pap. 9.95 (*0-14-018030-3*, Penguin Classics) Viking Penguin.

***Conrad, Joseph.** Almayer's Folly. (Classics Library). 1998. pap. 3.95 (*1-85326-297-8*, 2978WW, Pub. by Wrdsworth Edits) NTC Contemp Pub Co.

Conrad, Joseph. Almayer's Folly. LC 79-184735. 224p. 1971. reprint ed. lib. bdg. 20.00 (*0-8376-0408-7*) Bentley Pubs.

— Almayer's Folly. rev. ed. Knowles, Owen, ed. (Everyman Paperback Classics Ser.). 400p. (C). 1995. pap. 6.95 (*0-460-87634-1*, Everyman's Classic Lib) Tuttle Pubng.

— Almayer's Folly: A Story of an Eastern River. Higdon, David L. et al, eds. (Cambridge Edition of the Works of Joseph Conrad). (Illus.). 324p. (C). 1994. text 85.00 (*0-521-43205-7*) Cambridge U Pr.

***Conrad, Joseph.** The Arrow of Gold. 2000. pap. 7.95 (*0-460-87666-X*, Everyman's Classic Lib) Tuttle Pubng.

Conrad, Joseph. Chance. 400p. 1993. pap. 6.95 (*0-14-018654-9*, Penguin Classics) Viking Penguin.

***Conrad, Joseph.** Chance: A Tale in Two Parts. 512p. 2000. pap. 5.95 (*0-19-283637-4*) OUP.

Conrad, Joseph. The Collected Letters: 1903-1907, Vol. 3. Karl, Frederick R. & Davies, Laurence, eds. (Illus.). 576p. 1988. text 120.00 (*0-521-32387-8*) Cambridge U Pr.

— The Collected Letters: 1908-1911, Vol. 4. Karl, Frederick R. & Davies, Laurence, eds. (Illus.). 596p. (C). 1991. text 120.00 (*0-521-32388-6*) Cambridge U Pr.

— The Collected Letters of Joseph Conrad: 1861-1897, Vol. 1. Karl, Frederick R. & Davies, Laurence, eds. LC 82-14643. (Illus.). 512p. 1983. text 120.00 (*0-521-24216-9*) Cambridge U Pr.

— The Collected Letters of Joseph Conrad Vol. 5: 1912-1916. Karl, Frederick R. & Davies, Laurence, eds. (Cambridge Edition of the Works of Joseph Conrad Ser.). (Illus.). 781p. (C). 1996. text 125.00 (*0-521-32389-4*) Cambridge U Pr.

— Collected Stories Of Joseph Conrad. Hynes, Samuel, ed. (Companions Ser.). 630p. 1996. pap. 18.00 (*0-88001-464-4*) HarpC.

— Collected Tales. Hynes, Samuel, ed. 656p. 1995. pap. 18.00 (*0-88001-439-3*) HarpC.

— Complete Short Fiction, 2 vols. Date not set. lib. bdg. 46.95 (*0-8488-0968-8*) Amereon Ltd.

— Conrad's Prefaces to His Works. LC 70-163112. (English Literature Ser.: No. 33). 1971. lib. bdg. 75.00 (*0-8383-1304-3*) M S G Haskell Hse.

— Conrad's Prefaces to His Works. LC 72-160963. (Select Bibliographies Reprint Ser.). 1977. reprint ed. 18.95 (*0-8369-5831-4*) Ayer.

— Eastern Skies, Western Seas. 524p. 1990. pap. 12.95 (*0-88184-595-7*) Carroll & Graf.

— La Fleche d'Or. (FRE.). 404p. 1977. pap. 11.95 (*0-7859-1861-2*, 2070369781) Fr & Eur.

— La Folie-Almayer. (FRE.). 1975. pap. 10.95 (*0-7859-1806-X*, 2070366871) Fr & Eur.

— Fortune. (FRE.). 1989. pap. 13.95 (*0-7859-2105-2*, 2070380904) Fr & Eur.

— Le Frere-De-la-Cote. (FRE.). 1976. pap. 11.95 (*0-7859-1832-9*, 2070368319) Fr & Eur.

— Heart of Darkness. Goonetilleke, D. C. R. A., ed. 280p. 1995. pap. 7.95 (*1-55111-065-2*) Broadview Pr.

— Heart of Darkness. LC 90-3492. (Thrift Editions Ser.). 80p. 1990. pap. 1.00 (*0-486-26464-5*) Dover.

— Heart of Darkness. LC 93-1855. 1993. 15.00 (*0-679-42801-1*) Everymns Lib.

***Conrad, Joseph.** Heart of Darkness. (Cloth Bound Pocket Ser.). 1999. 7.95 (*3-8290-3003-7*) Konemann.

Conrad, Joseph. Heart of Darkness. LC 99-205953. (Penguin Great Books of the 20th Century Ser.). 146p. 1999. pap. 8.95 (*0-14-028163-0*) Viking Penguin.

— Heart of Darkness. (Classics Library). 316p. 1998. pap. 3.95 (*1-85326-240-4*, 2404WW, Pub. by Wrdsworth Edits) NTC Contemp Pub Co.

— Heart of Darkness. 1998. lib. bdg. 18.95 (*1-56723-033-4*) Yestermorrow.

— Heart of Darkness. large type ed. 1997. pap. 19.95 (*1-55701-210-5*) BNI Pubns.

— Heart of Darkness. large type ed. (Large Print Heritage Ser.). 156p. 1997. lib. bdg. 26.95 (*1-58118-004-7*, 21963) LRS.

— Heart of Darkness. LC 81-38511. 128p. 1982. reprint ed. 12.50 (*0-8376-0458-3*) Bentley Pubs.

— Heart of Darkness. 2nd ed. Murfin, Ross, ed. 315p. 1996. pap. text 11.95 (*0-312-11491-5*) St Martin.

***Conrad, Joseph.** Heart of Darkness, Vol. 58. 2000. pap. 10.95 (*1-892295-49-0*) Green Integer.

Conrad, Joseph. Heart of Darkness: An authoritative text, backgrounds & sources, criticism. 3rd ed. Kimbrough, Robert, ed. (Critical Editions Ser.). (Illus.). 320p. (C). 1987. pap. text 10.50 (*0-393-95552-4*) Norton.

— Heart of Darkness: And Other Tales. Watts, Cedric, ed. & intro. by. (Oxford World's Classics Ser.). 316p. 1998. pap. 6.95 (*0-19-283373-1*) OUP.

— Heart of Darkness: And, The Secret Sharer. 1983. 10.05 (*0-606-00787-3*, Pub. by Turtleback) Demco.

Conrad, Joseph. Heart of Darkness: Quayle,&Anthony, Set. abr. ed. 1991. audio 16.00 (*1-55994-390-4*, DCN 2043) HarperAudio.

Conrad, Joseph. Heart of Darkness: With the Congo Diary. (Penguin Great Books of the 20th Century Ser.). 166p. (Orig.). 1995. pap. 7.95 (*0-14-018652-2*, Penguin Classics) Viking Penguin.

— Heart of Darkness & Other Stories. large type ed. 433p. 1998. reprint ed. lib. bdg. 24.00 (*0-939495-68-6*) North Bks.

— Heart of Darkness & Secret Sharer. 1976. 18.95 (*0-8488-0461-9*) Amereon Ltd.

— Heart of Darkness & The Congo diary. LC 99-11703. 1999. pap. 7.95 (*0-375-75377-X*) Modern Lib NY.

— Heart of Darkness & the Secret Sharer. Walker, Franklin, ed. (Classics Ser.). 224p. 1982. mass mkt. 4.95 (*0-553-21214-1*, Bantam Classics) Bantam.

— Heart of Darkness & The Secret Sharer. (Signet Classics Ser.). 168p. (Orig.). 1997. mass mkt. 4.95 (*0-451-52657-0*, Sig Classics) NAL.

— Heart of Darkness & the Secret Sharer. 1978. reprint ed. lib. bdg. 17.95 (*0-89966-054-1*) Buccaneer Bks.

— Inquietude. (FRE.). 1984. pap. 11.95 (*0-7859-1983-X*, 2070375218) Fr & Eur.

— Joseph Conrad: Selected Literary Criticism & "The Shadow Line" Ingram, Allan, ed. 288p. (C). 1987. pap. 20.99 (*0-416-39350-0*, 1077) Routledge.

— Joseph Conrad on Fiction. Wright, Walter F., ed. LC 64-11355. (Regents Critic Ser.). 252p. 1964. reprint ed. pap. 78.20 (*0-608-02368-X*, 206301000004) Bks Demand.

— The Lagoon & Other Stories. Atkinson, William, ed. LC 97-9268. (The World's Classics Ser.). 322p. 1998. pap. 8.95 (*0-19-283222-0*) OUP.

***Conrad, Joseph.** The Lagoon & Other Stories. 328p. 2000. pap. 8.95 (*0-19-283619-6*) OUP.

Conrad, Joseph. Last Essays. LC 75-117777. (Essay Index Reprint Ser.). 1977. 19.95 (*0-8369-1795-2*) Ayer.

— Letters to William Blackwood & David S. Meldrum. LC 58-12588. 247p. reprint ed. pap. 76.60 (*0-608-15091-6*, 202619300048) Bks Demand.

— Lord Jim. (Classics Illustrated Notes Ser.). (Illus.). (J). 1997. pap. text 4.99 (*1-57840-066-X*, Pub. by Acclaim Bks) Penguin Putnam.

— Lord Jim. (J). Date not set. lib. bdg. 24.95 (*0-8488-1272-7*) Amereon Ltd.

— Lord Jim. 288p. (J). 1981. mass mkt. 4.95 (*0-553-21361-X*, Bantam Classics) Bantam.

— Lord Jim. (J). 1988. lib. bdg. 25.95 (*0-89966-057-6*) Buccaneer Bks.

— Lord Jim. LC 98-41019. (Dover Thrift Editions Ser.). 256p. (J). 1999. pap. text 2.00 (*0-486-40650-4*) Dover.

— Lord Jim. (FRE.). 512p. (J). 1982. pap. 13.95 (*0-7859-1962-7*, 2070374033) Fr & Eur.

Conrad, Joseph. Lord Jim. Zabel, Morton D., ed. LC 91-30904. (J). 1958. pap. 13.96 (*0-395-05121-5*, RivEd) HM.

Conrad, Joseph. Lord Jim. (J). 1992. 17.00 (*0-679-40544-5*) Knopf.

— Lord Jim. (Illus.). 1999. 7.95 (*3-8290-2842-3*) Konemann.

— Lord Jim. 320p. (J). 1961. mass mkt. 4.95 (*0-451-52234-6*, CJ1195, Sig Classics) NAL.

— Lord Jim. Batchelor, John, ed. & intro. by. (World's Classics Paperback Ser.). 448p. (J). 1983. pap. 4.95 (*0-19-281625-X*) OUP.

***Conrad, Joseph.** Lord Jim. (Oxford World's Classics Hardcovers Ser.). 368p. 2000. 15.00 (*0-19-210044-0*) OUP.

Conrad, Joseph. Lord Jim. (Now Age Illustrated V Ser.). (Illus.). 64p. (gr. 4-12). 1979. student ed. 1.25 (*0-88301-415-7*) Pendulum Pr.

— Lord Jim. (Now Age Illustrated V Ser.). (Illus.). 64p. (J). (gr. 4-12). 1979. pap. text 2.95 (*0-88301-391-6*) Pendulum Pr.

— Lord Jim. (J). 1998. pap. text 4.95 (*84-320-3974-8*) Planeta.

— Lord Jim. (Signet Classics). (J). 1961. 9.05 (*0-606-02758-0*, Pub. by Turtleback) Demco.

***Conrad, Joseph.** Lord Jim. 2000. pap. 7.95 (*0-460-87665-1*, Everyman's Classic Lib) Tuttle Pubng.

Conrad, Joseph. Lord Jim. (Classics Library). 272p. (J). 1998. pap. 3.95 (*1-85326-037-1*, 0371WW, Pub. by Wrdsworth Edits) NTC Contemp Pub Co.

— Lord Jim. large type ed. 493p. (J). 1981. 27.99 (*0-7089-8014-7*, Charnwood) Ulverscroft.

— Lord Jim. LC 75-184734. 320p. (J). 1971. reprint ed. lib. bdg. 14.00 (*0-8376-0409-5*) Bentley Pubs.

— Lord Jim. unabridged ed. (Wordsworth Classics). (J). (gr. 6-12). 1998. 5.27 (*0-89061-037-1*, R0371WW, Jamestwn Pub) NTC Contemp Pub Co.

— Lord Jim: A Tale. Batchelor, John, ed. (Oxford World's Classics Ser.). 352p. (J). 2000. pap. 4.95 (*0-19-283512-2*) OUP.

— Lord Jim: A Tale. Hampson, Robert, ed. 384p. 1989. pap. 5.95 (*0-14-018092-3*, Penguin Classics) Viking Penguin.

— Lord Jim: An Authoritative Text, Backgrounds, Essays in Criticism. 2nd ed. Moser, Thomas C. & Sherry, Norman, eds. LC 95-1667. (Critical Editions Ser.). (C). 1996. pap. text 14.75 (*0-393-96335-7*) Norton.

***Conrad, Joseph.** Lord Jim: 100th Anniversary. (Classics Ser.). 2000. mass mkt. 4.95 (*0-451-52767-4*, Sig) NAL.

Conrad, Joseph. Lord Jim & Nostromo. LC 99-39913. 800p. 1999. pap. 11.95 (*0-375-75489-X*) Modern Lib NY.

Conrad, Joseph. The Mirror of the Sea. Date not set. lib. bdg. 19.95 (*0-8488-1669-2*) Amereon Ltd.

Conrad, Joseph. The Mirror of the Sea. LC 87-62517. 196p. 1988. pap. 10.95 (*0-910395-34-9*) Marlboro Pr.

— The Mirror of the Sea & a Personal Record. (Oxford World's Classics Ser.). 216p. 2000. pap. 8.95 (*0-19-283748-6*) OUP.

— The Nigger of the Narcissus. LC 99-35223. (Thrift Editions Ser.). 128p. 1999. pap. text 1.50 (*0-486-40880-9*) Dover.

— The Nigger of the Narcissus. Kimbrough, Robert, ed. (Critical Editions Ser.). (Illus.). (C). 1979. pap. text 12.50 (*0-393-09019-1*) Norton.

— The Nigger of the Narcissus. Watts, Cedric P., ed. & intro. by. 208p. 1989. pap. 12.95 (*0-14-018094-X*, Penguin Classics) Viking Penguin.

— Nigger of the Narcissus. 1976. 22.95 (*0-8488-0969-6*) Amereon Ltd.

— Nigger of the Narcissus. 1991. lib. bdg. 21.95 (*0-89966-055-X*) Buccaneer Bks.

— The Nigger of the 'Narcissus' Simmons, Alan, ed. (Everyman Paperback Classics). 480p. 1997. pap. 4.95 (*0-460-87789-5*, Everyman's Classic Lib) Tuttle Pubng.

— The Nigger of the 'Narcissus' A Tale of the Sea. Berthoud, Jacques, ed. (World's Classics Ser.). 244p. 1985. pap. 6.95 (*0-19-281623-3*) OUP.

***Conrad, Joseph.** The Nigger of the 'Narcissus' A Tale of the Sea. (Oxford World Classics Ser.). 232p. 1999. pap. 7.95 (*0-19-283649-8*) OUP.

Conrad, Joseph. Nostromo. Nadelhaft, Ruth, ed. 440p. 1997. pap. 12.95 (*1-55111-074-1*) Broadview Pr.

— Nostromo. 1992. 20.00 (*0-679-41321-9*) Everymns Lib.

***Conrad, Joseph.** Nostromo. (Cloth Bound Pocket Ser.). 400p. 1998. 7.95 (*3-8290-0887-2*, 520659) Konemann.

— Nostromo. LC 99-43964. 600p. 1999. 34.95 (*1-56000-469-X*) Transaction Pubs.

Conrad, Joseph. Nostromo. 1990. pap. 12.95 (*0-14-118049-8*) Viking Penguin.

— Nostromo. 4p. 1999. audio 23.95 (*0-14-086453-9*) Viking Penguin.

— Nostromo. Smith, Martin S., ed. & intro. by. 480p. (C). 1999. pap. 8.95 (*0-14-018371-X*) Viking Penguin.

— Nostromo. (Classics Library). 1998. pap. 3.95 (*1-85326-174-2*, 170XWW, Pub. by Wrdsworth Edits) NTC Contemp Pub Co.

— Nostromo. 566p. 1983. reprint ed. lib. bdg. 37.95 (*0-89966-311-7*) Buccaneer Bks.

— Nostromo. rev. ed. Watts, Cedric, ed. (Everyman Paperback Classics Ser.). 416p. 1995. pap. 5.95 (*0-460-87191-9*, Everyman's Classic Lib) Tuttle Pubng.

— Nostromo: A Tale of the Seaboard. LC 91-53185. 1992. 20.00 (*0-679-40990-4*) Knopf.

— Nostromo: A Tale of the Seaboard. LC 96-6289. 1996. 18.50 (*0-679-60202-X*) Modern Lib NY.

***Conrad, Joseph.** Nostromo: A Tale of the Seaboard. Carabine, Keith, ed. (Oxford World Classics Ser.). 584p. 2000. pap. 7.95 (*0-19-283556-4*) OUP.

Conrad, Joseph. Notes on Life & Letters. LC 72-1327. (Essay Index Reprint Ser.). 1977. reprint ed. 18.95 (*0-8369-2842-3*) Ayer.

— Oeuvres, Vol. 1. (Pleiade Ser.). (FRE.). 1982. 110.00 (*0-8288-3465-2*, F60422) Fr & Eur.

— Oeuvres, Vol. 2. (Pleiade Ser.). (FRE.). 1985. 115.00 (*0-8288-3466-0*, F76970) Fr & Eur.

— Oeuvres, Vol. 4. (Pleiade Ser.). (FRE.). 1989. 135.00 (*0-8288-3468-7*, F41060) Fr & Eur.

— Oeuvres, Vol. 5. Monod, Maurice, ed. (FRE.). 1992. lib. bdg. 165.00 (*0-7859-3956-3*) Fr & Eur.

— An Outcast of the Islands. (Airmont Classics Ser.). (YA). (gr. 9 up). 1966. mass mkt. 1.50 (*0-8049-0113-9*, CL-113) Airmont.

— An Outcast of the Islands. 1976. 17.95 (*0-8488-1273-5*) Amereon Ltd.

***Conrad, Joseph.** An Outcast of the Islands. (Oxford World's Classics Ser.). (Illus.). 448p. 1999. pap. 7.95 (*0-19-283840-7*) OUP.

Conrad, Joseph. An Outcast of the Islands. 384p. 1996. pap. 7.95 (*0-460-87773-9*, Everyman's Classic Lib) Tuttle Pubng.

— An Outcast of the Islands. large type ed. LC 97-16032. 320p. 1997. text 24.95 (*1-56000-533-5*) Transaction Pubs.

— Un Paria des Iles. (FRE.). 1983. pap. 12.95 (*0-7859-2224-5*, 207037436X) Fr & Eur.

Conrad, Joseph. A Personal Record. Date not set. lib. bdg. 17.95 (*0-8488-1670-6*) Amereon Ltd.

Conrad, Joseph. A Personal Record. 2nd ed. LC 88-60728. 148p. 1988. reprint ed. pap. 8.95 (*0-910395-46-2*) Marlboro Pr.

— Personal Record & the Mirror of the Sea. LC 99-185223. 384p. 1998. pap. 13.99 (*0-14-018966-1*) Viking Penguin.

— Portable Conrad. rev. ed. Zabel, Morton D. & Karl, Frederick R., eds. (Portable Library: No. 33). 768p. 1976. pap. 15.95 (*0-14-015033-1*, P33, Penguin Bks) Viking Penguin.

— La Rescousse. (FRE.). 528p. 1985. pap. 13.95 (*0-7859-2015-3*, 2070376605) Fr & Eur.

— The Rescue. 384p. 1996. pap. 9.95 (*0-14-018034-6*) Penguin Putnam.

— The Rover. LC 99-14966. (Heart of Oak Sea Classics Ser.). 1999. write for info. (*0-8050-6262-9*) H Holt & Co.

***Conrad, Joseph.** The Rover. LC 99-14966. (Heart of Oak Sea Classics Ser.). 1999. pap. text 14.00 (*0-8050-6263-7*, Owl) H Holt & Co.

Conrad, Joseph. The Rover. Busza, Andrew & Stape, John H., eds. (Oxford World's Classics Ser.). (Illus.). 352p. 2001. pap. 8.95 (*0-19-282623-9*) OUP.

— The Secret Agent. 21.95 (*0-8488-0462-7*) Amereon Ltd.

— The Secret Agent. 1988. lib. bdg. 25.95 (*0-89966-058-4*) Buccaneer Bks.

— The Secret Agent. Harkness, Bruce & Reid, S. W., eds. (Cambridge Edition of the Works of Joseph Conrad). (Illus.). 469p. (C). 1990. text 95.00 (*0-521-34135-3*) Cambridge U Pr.

— The Secret Agent. LC 92-52924. 352p. 1992. 17.00 (*0-679-41723-0*) Everymns Lib.

— The Secret Agent. (Illus.). (J). (gr. k up). 1991. pap. 3.95 (*0-425-12524-6*) First Classics.

— The Secret Agent. LC 98-19549. (Modern Library Ser.). 1998. pap. 8.95 (*0-375-75252-8*) Modern Lib NY.

***Conrad, Joseph.** The Secret Agent. (Twelve-Point Ser.). 240p. 1999. lib. bdg. 24.00 (*1-58287-098-5*) North Bks.

Conrad, Joseph. The Secret Agent. Smith, Martin S., ed. & intro. by. 272p. 1990. pap. 9.95 (*0-14-018096-6*, Penguin Classics) Viking Penguin.

— The Secret Agent. (Classics Library). 1997. pap. 3.95 (*1-85326-065-7*, 0657WW, Pub. by Wrdsworth Edits) NTC Contemp Pub Co.

— The Secret Agent. unabridged ed. 1997. audio 69.95 (*0-7540-5301-6*, SAB 169) Chivers N Amer.

— The Secret Agent: A Simple Tale. Tennant, Roger, ed. & intro. by. LC 99-186624. (Oxford World's Classics Ser.). 356p. 1998. pap. 8.95 (*0-19-283477-0*) OUP.

— Secret Agent: Penguin Readers Level Three. 32p. 1998. pap. 7.00 (*0-14-081669-0*) Viking Penguin.

— The Secret Sharer. Schwarz, Daniel R., ed. LC 96-84946. 268p. 1997. pap. text 11.95 (*0-312-11224-6*) St Martin.

— The Secret Sharer. large type ed. (Large Print Heritage Ser.). 81p. 1997. lib. bdg. 19.95 (*1-58118-005-5*, 21487) LRS.

— The Secret Sharer. unabridged ed. 1986. pap. 7.95 incl. audio (*1-882071-09-3*, 011) B&B Audio.

— The Secret Sharer & Other Stories. LC 92-36764. (Thrift Editions Ser.). 128p. 1993. reprint ed. pap. 1.00 (*0-486-27546-9*) Dover.

— Selected Short Stories. (Classics Library). 1998. pap. 3.95 (*1-85326-190-4*, 1904WW, Pub. by Wrdsworth Edits) NTC Contemp Pub Co.

Conrad, Joseph. A Set of Six. 395p. 1983. lib. bdg. 18.95 (*0-89966-264-1*) Buccaneer Bks.

Conrad, Joseph. The Shadow-Line. 1976. 18.95 (*0-8488-0257-8*) Amereon Ltd.

— The Shadow-Line. Berthoud, Jacques, ed. & intro. by. 160p. 1993. pap. 10.95 (*0-14-018097-4*, Penguin Classics) Viking Penguin.

***Conrad, Joseph.** Shadow-Line: A Confession "Worthy of My Undying Regard" (Oxford World Classics Ser.). 176p. 1999. pap. text 9.95 (*0-19-283648-X*) OUP.

Conrad, Joseph. Shorter Tales. LC 71-128727. (Short Story Index Reprint Ser.). 1977. 24.95 (*0-8369-3618-3*) Ayer.

— A Sketch - With a Bibliography. 1976. 16.95 (*0-8488-0463-5*) Amereon Ltd.

— Tales of Unrest. 1973. 250.00 (*0-87968-086-5*) Gordon Pr.

Conrad, Joseph. Tales of Unrest. pap. 4.95 (*0-460-87656-2*, Everyman's Classic Lib) Tuttle Pubng.

Conrad, Joseph. Tales of Unrest. 202p. 1991. pap. 8.95 (*0-14-018036-2*, Penguin Classics) Viking Penguin.

— Three Great Tales. Incl. Heart of Darkness. 1958. pap. Nigger of the Narcissus. 1958. pap. Typhoon. 1958. pap. 1958. Set pap. 3.95 (*0-394-70155-0*, V-155) Vin Bks.

— Typhoon. LC 99-16769. 144p. 1999. pap. 16.95 (*0-312-87303-4*, Pub. by Forge NYC) St Martin.

Conrad, Joseph. Typhoon. (FRE.). 160p. 1973. pap. 10.95 (*0-7859-2203-2*, 207036416X) Fr & Eur.

Conrad, Joseph. Typhoon & Other Stories. Kirschner, Paul, ed. & intro. by. 320p. 1991. pap. 7.95 (*0-14-018257-8*, Penguin Classics) Viking Penguin.

— Typhoon & Other Tales. Watts, Cedric, ed. & intro. by. LC 99-186611. (Oxford World's Classics Ser.). 356p. 1998. pap. 7.95 (*0-19-283787-7*) OUP.

— Under Western Eyes. 1976. 17.95 (*0-8488-0749-9*) Amereon Ltd.

— Under Western Eyes. 512p. 1991. 20.00 (*0-679-40554-2*) Everymns Lib.

— Under Western Eyes. Hawthorn, Jeremy, ed. (World's Classics Ser.). 416p. (C). 1996. pap. 7.95 (*0-19-281619-5*) OUP.

***Conrad, Joseph.** Under Western Eyes. Hawthorn, Jeremy, ed. (Oxford World Classics Ser.). 424p. 2000. pap. 8.95 (*0-19-283933-0*) OUP.

Conrad, Joseph. Under Western Eyes. LC 97-129058. 352p. 1997. pap. 9.95 (*0-14-018849-5*) Viking Penguin.

— Victory. 426p. Date not set. 28.95 (*0-8488-2237-4*) Amereon Ltd.

— Victory. 464p. 1995. pap. 6.95 (*0-460-87478-0*, Everyman's Classic Lib) Tuttle Pubng.

— Victory. 192p. 1995. pap. 8.95 (*0-14-018978-5*, Viking) Viking Penguin.

— Victory. 1999. pap. 11.95 (*0-14-025519-2*, Viking) Viking Penguin.

***Conrad, Joseph.** Victory. (Classics Library). 1998. pap. 3.95 (*1-85326-256-0*, 2560WW, Pub. by Wrdsworth Edits) NTC Contemp Pub Co.

— Victory: An Island Tale. LC 98-27677. 1998. 20.00 (*0-375-40047-8*) Everymns Lib.

Conrad, Joseph. Victory: An Island Tale. LC 95-18067. 300p. (J). 1995. pap. 9.70 (*0-7868-8142-9*, Pub. by Hyperion) Little.

— Victory: An Island Tale. Batchelor, John, ed. (World's Classics Ser.). (Illus.). 464p. (C). 1996. pap. 5.95 (*0-19-281708-6*) OUP.

***Conrad, Joseph.** Victory: An Island Tale. (Oxford World Classics Ser.). (Illus.). 472p. 2000. pap. 7.95 (*0-19-283651-X*) OUP.

Conrad, Joseph. Wisdom & Beauty from Conrad. Capes, Harriett, ed. LC 76-51355. (Studies in Conrad: No. 8). 1977. lib. bdg. 75.00 (*0-8383-2125-9*) M S G Haskell Hse.

— The Works of Joseph Conrad, 22 vols., Set. 2nd ed. 8450p. (C). 1995. text, boxed set 2465.00 (*0-415-13485-4*) Routledge.

C

— Youth: A Narrative. 1976. 19.95 (*0-8488-0464-3*) Amereon Ltd.

— Youth-Heart of Darkness - The End of the Tether. Lyon, John, ed. & intro. by. 384p. 1995. pap. 7.95 (*0-14-018513-5*, Penguin Classics) Viking Penguin.

Conrad, Joseph & Ford, Ford Madox. The Inheritors. 228p. 1985. pap. 7.95 (*0-88184-136-6*) Carroll & Graf.

— Romance. 558p. 1985. pap. 8.95 (*0-88184-166-8*) Carroll & Graf.

***Conrad, Joseph & Goonetilleke, D. C. R. A.** Heart of Darkness. 2nd ed. (Literary Texts Ser.). 260p. 1999. pap. 7.95 (*1-55111-307-4*) Broadview Pr.

Conrad, Joseph & Snyder, John K., III. The Secret Agent. (Classics Illustrated Ser.). (Illus.). 52p. (YA). pap. 4.95 (*1-57209-017-0*) Classics Int Ent.

Conrad, Joseph, et al. Conrad under Familial Eyes. Zdzislaw, Najder, ed. Carroll-Najder, Halina, tr. LC 83-5187. 304p. 1984. text 80.00 (*0-521-25082-X*) Cambridge U Pr.

Conrad, Joseph, jt. auth. see Bartollas, Clemens.

Conrad, Joseph, jt. auth. see Center for Learning Network Staff.

Conrad, Joseph, jt. auth. see Defoe, Daniel.

Conrad, Joseph, ed. see Zielinski, Leszek.

Conrad, Joyner. The American Politician. LC 70-160811. 247p. reprint ed. pap. 76.60 (*0-8357-5391-3*, 202431800037) Bks Demand.

Conrad, Judy, ed. see Columbus-America Discovery Group, Inc. Staff.

Conrad, Kathryn K. Classical Tutu Construction. (Illus.). 42p. 1979. pap. text 20.00 (*0-9646987-0-6*) K K Angleman.

— Romantic Tutu Construction. (Illus.). 34p. 1979. pap. text 20.00 (*0-9646987-1-4*) K K Angleman.

Conrad, Kelley A., jt. ed. see Hansen, Curtiss P.

Conrad, Kendon J., ed. Critically Evaluating the Role of Experiments. LC 85-644749. (New Directions for Program Evaluation Ser.: No. PE 63). 111p. (Orig.). 1994. pap. 22.00 (*0-7879-9992-X*) Jossey-Bass.

***Conrad, Kendon J., et al, eds.** Homelessness Prevention in Treatment of Substance Abuse & Mental Illness: Logic Models & Implementation of Eight American Projects. LC 99-32742. 220p. 1999. 49.95 (*0-7890-0750-9*) Haworth Pr.

Conrad, Kendon J., et al, eds. Treatment of the Chemically Dependent Homeless: 14 American Projects. LC 95-4175. 1995. 19.95 (*1-56023-066-5*, Harrington Park) Haworth Pr.

Conrad, Kendon J. & Roberts-Gray, Cynthia, eds. Evaluating Program Environments. LC 85-644749. (New Directions for Evaluation Ser.: No. PE 40). 1988. 22.00 (*1-55542-895-9*) Jossey-Bass.

Conrad, Kevin, ed. see Morrison, Grant.

Conrad, L. J. Bibliography of Antarctic Exploration: Expedition Accounts from 1768-1960. xv, 424p. 1999. 99.95 (*0-9669627-0-2*) Parmer Bks.

Conrad, Lawrence, et al. The Western Medical Tradition: 800 B. C.-1800 A. D. (Illus.). 570p. (C). 1995. text 95.00 (*0-521-38135-5*); pap. text 38.95 (*0-521-47564-3*) Cambridge U Pr.

Conrad, Lawrence H. Temper. LC 74-22774. (Labor Movement in Fiction & Non-Fiction Ser.). 305p. 1976. reprint ed. 34.50 (*0-404-58414-4*) AMS Pr.

Conrad, Lawrence I. Muhammadanea Edessensis: The Rise of Islam in Eastern Christian Historiography under the Early 'Abbasids. (Studies in Late Antiquity & Early Islam: Vol. 12). 150p. 2000. text 24.95 (*0-87850-116-9*) Darwin Pr.

Conrad, Lawrence I., ed. History & Historiography in Early Islamic Times: Studies & Perspectives. (Studies in Late Antiquity & Early Islam: No. 9). 700p. 2000. text 49.95 (*0-87850-083-9*) Darwin Pr.

— Reflections on Islamic History & Civilization: The Complete Collected Essays of Sir Hamilton Gibb, 4 vols., Set. (Illus.). 2500p. 2001. 140.00 (*0-87850-054-5*) Darwin Pr.

— Reflections on Islamic History & Civilization: The Complete Collected Essays of Sir Hamilton Gibb, 4 vols., Vol. 1. (Illus.). 2001. 35.00 (*0-87850-055-3*) Darwin Pr.

— Reflections on Islamic History & Civilization: The Complete Collected Essays of Sir Hamilton Gibb, Vol. 2. (Illus.). 2001. 35.00 (*0-87850-057-X*) Darwin Pr.

— Reflections on Islamic History & Civilization: The Complete Collected Essays of Sir Hamilton Gibb, Vol. 3. (Illus.). 2001. 35.00 (*0-87850-058-8*) Darwin Pr.

— Reflections on Islamic History & Civilization: The Complete Collected Essays of Sir Hamilton Gibb, Vol. 4. (Illus.). 2001. 35.00 (*0-87850-059-6*) Darwin Pr.

Conrad, Lawrence I., jt. auth. see Noth, Albrecht.

Conrad, Lawrence I., ed. see Buheiry, Marwan R.

Conrad, Lawrence I., jt. ed. see Cameron, Averil.

Conrad, Lawrence I., ed. & tr. see Jabbur, Jibrail S.

Conrad, Lawrence I., tr. see Duri, A. A.

Conrad, Lawrence L., ed. The World of Ibn Tufayl: Interdisciplinary Studies on Hayy ibn Yaqzan. LC 95-6229. (Islamic Philosophy, Theology & Science, Studies & Texts Ser.: No. 24). 270p. 102.50 (*90-04-10135-7*) Brill Academic Pubs.

Conrad, Leo, jt. auth. see Zimmerman, Steven M.

Conrad, Les. Desperate Remedies: The Tragedy of Santa Maria, California. 5th ed. LC 97-13017. 328p. 1997. pap. 7.95 (*1-56474-235-0*) Fithian Pr.

Conrad, Lisa, jt. ed. see Grossinger, Richard.

***Conrad, Liz.** Bedtime Bear. 20p. (J). 1999. reprint ed. 16.95 (*1-892374-28-5*) Weldon Owen.

Conrad, Lynn. All Aboard Trucks. (All Aboard Bks.). (Illus.). 32p. (Orig.). (J). (ps-2). 1989. pap. 2.99 (*0-448-19094-X*, G & D) Peng Put Young Read.

Conrad, Lynne. Maternal-Neonatal Nursing. 3rd ed. LC 96-29145. (Springhouse Notes Ser.). (Illus.). 192p. (Orig.). 1996. 22.95 incl. disk (*0-87434-860-9*) Springhouse Corp.

Conrad, Lynne, et al. Essentials of Material Child Nursing. 3rd rev. ed. (Illus.). 246p. (Orig.). (C). 1998. pap. 39.95 (*1-57801-028-4*) Western Schls.

Conrad, Margaret. George Nowlan: Maritime Conservative in National Politics. 358p. 1986. text 37.50 (*0-8020-2600-1*) U of Toronto Pr.

— History of the Canadian Peoples: 1867-Present. (C). 1993. pap. text 38.50 (*0-7730-5189-9*) Addison-Wesley.

— The Joy of Ginger. (Illus.). 196p. 1998. 14.95 (*1-55109-198-4*) Nimbus Publ.

Conrad, Margaret, et al. No Place Like Home. (Illus.). 306p. 1995. pap. 19.95 (*0-88780-066-1*, Pub. by Formac Publ Co) Formac Dist Ltd.

***Conrad, Marjorie.** Five Senses, Vol. 2442. Blocher, Wendy, ed. (Illus.). 32p. 1999. pap. 6.98 (*1-57471-628-X*, 2442) Creat Teach Pr.

Conrad, Mark. Notes from Within: A Souls Awakening. 240p. 1998. 18.95 (*1-891569-22-8*, 00041198) Pura Vida.

Conrad, Mark & Varnum, Keith. Living the Dream: It's Time: A Chronicle of the Gathering of Equals. LC 97-75697. (Illus.). 256p. 1998. 22.95 (*1-891569-19-8*, 0001197) Pura Vida.

Conrad, Melinda, ed. see Nichols, Weta.

Conrad, Michael, ed. Adaptability: The Significance of Variability from Molecule to Ecosystem. LC 82-24558. (Illus.). 408p. (C). 1983. text 114.00 (*0-306-41223-3*, Kluwer Plenum) Kluwer Academic.

***Conrad, Michael, ed.** Real-Time Astrology: A Clear Case for Planetary Influence. 80p. 1998. pap. 17.00 (*0-9671981-0-0*) Cosmo Res Ctr.

***Conrad, Miriam B.** The Courage to Be Real: Becoming a Woman of Confidence & Integrity. LC 99-39991. (Women of Confidence Ser.). 180p. 1999. pap. 10.99 (*1-56955-102-2*, Vine Bks) Servant.

Conrad, Pam. Balancing Home & Career: A Fifty-Minute Program. 3rd ed. Crisp, Michael, ed. LC 95-68990. (Fifty-Minute Ser.). (Illus.). 88p. (Orig.). 1995. pap., wbk. ed. 10.95 (*1-56052-355-7*) Crisp Pubns.

— Blue Willow. LC 95-42867. (Illus.). 32p. (J). (gr. 2-5). 1999. 16.99 (*0-399-22904-3*) Peng Put Young Read.

— Call Me Ahnighito. LC 93-5080. (Laura Geringer Bks.). (Illus.). 32p. (J). (ps-3). 1995. 14.95 (*0-06-023322-2*) HarpC Child Bks.

— El Diario de Pedro.Tr. of Pedro's Journal. (SPA.). 96p. (J). (gr. 4-7). 1994. pap. 2.95 (*0-590-47402-2*) Scholastic Inc.

— Don't Go Near That Rabbit, Frank! LC 94-45773. (Laura Geringer Bks.). (Illus.). 48p. (J). (gr. 3-7). 1998. 14.95 (*0-06-021514-3*) HarpC Child Bks.

— Holding Me Here. LC 85-45254. 192p. (YA). (gr. 7 up). 1986. 11.95 (*0-06-021338-8*); lib. bdg. 12.89 (*0-06-021339-6*) HarpC Child Bks.

— Holding Me Here. LC 85-45254. 192p. (YA). (gr. 7 up). 1997. pap. 4.95 (*0-06-447166-7*, HarpTrophy) HarpC Child Bks.

— Holding Me Here. 1997. 9.60 (*0-606-11470-X*, Pub. by Turtleback) Demco.

***Conrad, Pam.** Is Anyone Here My Age? (J). 1999. 15.99 (*0-7868-0196-4*, Pub. by Hyperion) Little.

Conrad, Pam. Is Anyone Here My Age? (J). lib. bdg. 16.49 (*0-7868-2164-7*, Pub. by Hyprn Child) Little.

***Conrad, Pam.** The Lost Sailor. LC 91-39640. 32p. (J). (gr. k-4). 1999. pap. 4.95 (*0-06-443381-1*, HarpTrophy) HarpC Child Bks.

Conrad, Pam. My Daniel. LC 88-19850. 144p. (J). (gr. 4-7). 1989. lib. bdg. 15.89 (*0-06-021314-0*) HarpC Child Bks.

— My Daniel. LC 88-19850. 144p. (YA). (gr. 5 up). 1989. 13.95 (*0-06-021313-2*) HarpC Child Bks.

— My Daniel. LC 88-19850. (Trophy Bk.). 144p. (YA). (gr. 4-7). 1991. pap. 4.95 (*0-06-440309-2*, HarpTrophy) HarpC Child Bks.

— Old Man Hoover's Dead Rabbit. LC 94-45773. (Laura Geringer Bks.). (Illus.). 48p. (J). lib. bdg. 14.89 (*0-06-021515-1*) HarpC Child Bks.

— Our House: The Stories of Levittown. LC 94-42126. (Illus.). 80p. (J). (gr. 3-7). 1995. 14.95 (*0-590-46523-6*, Scholastic Hardcover) Scholastic Inc.

— Pedro's Journal. (Illus.). 96p. (J). (gr. 3-7). 1992. pap. 2.95 (*0-590-46206-7*, 058, Apple Paperbacks) Scholastic Inc.

— Pedro's Journal: A Voyage with Christopher Columbus, Aug. 3, 1492-Feb. 14, 1493. LC 90-85723. (Illus.). 96p. (J). (gr. 3-7). 1991. 15.95 (*1-878093-17-7*) Boyds Mills Pr.

— Pedro's Journal: A Voyage with Christopher Columbus, August 3, 1492-February 14, 1493. (J). 1991. 8.60 (*0-606-01924-3*, Pub. by Turtleback) Demco.

— Prairie Songs. 176p. (J). (gr. 7 up). 1985. lib. bdg. 15.89 (*0-06-021337-X*) HarpC.

— Prairie Songs. (Illus.). (J). (gr. 4-7). 1985. 14.00 (*0-06-021336-1*, 236070) HarpC.

— Prairie Songs. LC 85-42633. (Trophy Bk.). (Illus.). 176p. (J). (gr. 4-7). 1987. pap. 4.95 (*0-06-440206-1*, HarpTrophy) HarpC Child Bks.

— Prairie Songs. 1995. 19.25 (*0-8446-6812-5*) Peter Smith.

— Prairie Songs. LC 85-42633. (J). 1987. 9.60 (*0-606-03639-3*, Pub. by Turtleback) Demco.

— Prairie Visions: The Life & Times of Solomon Butcher. 1998. write for info. (*0-397-32482-0*); write for info. (*0-397-32483-9*) Lppncott W & W.

— The Rooster's Gift. LC 93-14490. (Illus.). 40p. (J). (ps-3). 1998. pap. text 6.95 (*0-06-443496-6*) HarpC Child Bks.

— The Rooster's Gift. 1998. 11.15 (*0-606-13750-5*, Pub. by Turtleback) Demco.

— Staying Nine. LC 87-45862. (Trophy Bk.). (Illus.). 80p. (J). (gr. 2-5). 1988. pap. 4.25 (*0-06-440377-7*, HarpTrophy) HarpC Child Bks.

— Staying Nine. 1988. 9.15 (*0-606-04809-X*, Pub. by Turtleback) Demco.

— Staying Nine. 1990. 9.05 (*0-606-13814-5*, Pub. by Turtleback) Demco.

— Stonewords: A Ghost Story. LC 89-36382. 144p. (J). (gr. 7 up). 1990. lib. bdg. 15.89 (*0-06-021316-7*) HarpC Child Bks.

— Stonewords: A Ghost Story. LC 89-36382. (Trophy Bk.). 144p. (YA). (gr. 5-9). 1991. pap. 4.95 (*0-06-440354-8*, HarpTrophy) HarpC Child Bks.

— Stonewords: A Ghost Story. 1991. 10.05 (*0-606-00845-4*, Pub. by Turtleback) Demco.

— This Mess. LC 97-28177. (Illus.). 32p. (J). (ps-2). 1998. 14.95 (*0-7868-0159-X*, Pub. by Hyprn Child); lib. bdg. 15.49 (*0-7868-2131-0*, Pub. by Hyprn Child) Little.

— The Tub Grandfather. LC 92-31770. (Laura Geringer Bks.). (Illus.). 32p. (J). (ps-3). 1993. 15.00 (*0-06-022895-4*); lib. bdg. 14.89 (*0-06-022896-2*) HarpC Child Bks.

— The Tub Grandfather. LC 92-31770. (Laura Geringer Bks.). (Illus.). 32p. (J). (gr. k-3). 1996. pap. 5.95 (*0-06-443469-9*, HarpTrophy) HarpC Child Bks.

— Tub Grandfather. (J). 1993. 11.15 (*0-606-09997-2*, Pub. by Turtleback) Demco.

— The Tub People. LC 88-32804. (Laura Geringer Bks.). (Illus.). 32p. (J). (ps-3). 1999. 15.95 (*0-06-021340-X*); pap. 6.95 (*0-06-443306-4*, HarpTrophy) HarpC Child Bks.

— The Tub People. (J). 1993. 10.15 (*0-606-08321-9*, Pub. by Turtleback) Demco.

— The Tub People. unabridged ed. (Illus.). 32p. (J). (ps-2). 1996. 7.95 incl. digital audio (*0-694-70058-4*) HarpC.

***Conrad, Pam.** The Tub People's Christmas. LC 98-53466. (Laura Geringer Ser.). (Illus.). 32p. (J). (ps-3). 1999. 15.95 (*0-06-026028-9*) HarpC.

— The Tub People's Christmas. LC 98-53466. (Illus.). 40p. (J). (ps-3). 1999. lib. bdg. 15.89 (*0-06-026029-7*, Pub. by Harper SF) HarpC.

Conrad, Pam. What I Did for Roman. LC 86-45497. 1996. 9.60 (*0-606-10044-X*, Pub. by Turtleback) Demco.

— Zoe Rising. LC 95-42663. (Illus.). 144p. (J). (gr. 4 up). 1996. lib. bdg. 14.89 (*0-06-027218-X*) HarpC Child Bks.

Conrad, Pam. Zoe Rising. 1997. 10.05 (*0-606-12137-4*, Pub. by Turtleback) Demco.

Conrad, Pam. Zoe Rising. LC 95-42663. (Trophy Bk.). (Illus.). 144p. (J). (gr. 4-7). 1997. reprint ed. pap. 4.95 (*0-06-440687-3*, HarpTrophy) HarpC Child Bks.

Conrad, Pamela J., jt. auth. see Maddox, Robert B.

Conrad, Paul. Conartist: Thirty Years with the Los Angeles Times. 208p. 1993. 35.00 (*0-9619095-5-2*) LA Times.

Conrad, Paul. Drawing the Line: The Collected Works of America's Premier Political Cartoonist. 208p. 1999. 24.95 (*1-883792-54-1*, Pub. by LA Times) Sunbelt Pubns.

Conrad, Peter. Modern Times, Modern Places. LC 98-15888. 1999. pap. 10.01 (*0-375-70105-2*) Knopf.

— Modern Times, Modern Places: A Monumental Study of the Transformation of Art & Life in the Twentieth Century. LC 98-15888. 752p. 1999. 40.00 (*0-375-40113-X*) Knopf.

— Romantic Opera & Literary Form. (Quantum Bks.: No. 9). (Illus.). 185p. 1977. pap. 15.95 (*0-520-04508-4*, Pub. by U CA Pr) Cal Prin Full Svc.

— The Sociology of Health & Illness: Critical Perspectives. 5th ed. LC 95-73192. 544p. 1996. pap. text 38.95 (*0-312-11229-7*) St Martin.

— A Song of Love & Death: The Meaning of Opera. LC 96-75707. (Graywolf Rediscovery Ser.). 384p. 1996. reprint ed. pap. 16.00 (*1-55597-241-1*) Graywolf.

— To Be Continued: Four Stories & Their Survival. 214p. 1995. text 26.00 (*0-19-818291-0*) OUP.

***Conrad, Peter & Gabe, Jonathan.** Sociological Perspectives on the New Genetics. (Sociology of Health & Illness Ser.). 1999. pap. text 32.95 (*0-631-21599-9*) Blackwell Pubs.

Conrad, Peter & Gallagher, Eugene B., eds. Health & Health Care in Developing Countries: Sociological Perspectives. LC 92-49629. 352p. (C). 1993. 59.95 (*1-56639-027-3*) Temple U Pr.

Conrad, Peter & Reinharz, Shulamit, eds. Computers & Qualitative Data: A Special Issue of Qualitative Sociology. 191p. (C). 1984. pap. 18.95 (*0-89885-218-8*, Kluwer Acad Hman Sci) Kluwer Academic.

Conrad, Peter & Schneider, Joseph W. Deviance & Medicalization: From Badness to Sickness. enl. ed. LC 92-13441. 352p. (C). 1992. reprint ed. pap. 24.95 (*0-87722-999-6*) Temple U Pr.

Conrad, Peter, jt. auth. see Schneider, Joseph W.

Conrad-Rice, Joy B. Dear Ming, Love, Mei-Ling. unabridged ed. 63p. (J). 1989. pap. 39.50 incl. audio (*0-88432-261-0*, SEN100) Audio-Forum.

***Conrad, Richard.** Safari Guide: A Guide to Planning Your Next Hunting Safari. (Illus.). 314p. 2001. 29.95 (*1-57157-208-2*) Safari Pr.

Conrad, Richard T. & Winkel, Steven R. Design Guide to the 1997 Uniform Building Code. 496p. 1998. 89.00 (*0-471-23641-1*) Wiley.

Conrad, Rob, ed. see Taylor, Steve.

Conrad, Robert E. Children of God's Fire: A Documentary History of Black Slavery in Brazil. LC 83-42553. (Illus.). 542p. reprint ed. pap. 168.10 (*0-8357-3687-3*, 203641100003) Bks Demand.

— The Destruction of Brazilian Slavery, 1850-1888. 2nd ed. LC 92-11285. 254p. (C). 1993. pap. 24.50 (*0-89464-750-4*) Krieger.

— World of Sorrow: The African Slave Trade to Brazil. fac. ed. LC 85-23160. 231p. 1986. reprint ed. pap. 71.70 (*0-7837-7727-2*, 204748300007) Bks Demand.

Conrad, Robert E., ed. Children of God's Fire: A Documentary History of Black Slavery in Brazil. 516p. (C). 1994. reprint ed. pap. text 22.50 (*0-271-01321-4*) Pa St U Pr.

Conrad, Robert E., jt. ed. see Ramirez, Sergio.

***Conrad, Robert Edgar.** In the Hands of Strangers: Readings on Foreign & Domestic Slave Trading & the Crisis of the Union. LC 00-32669. 2001. write for info. (*0-271-02090-3*) Pa St U Pr.

Conrad, Robert F. & Hool, R. Bryce. Taxation of Mineral Resources. LC 80-8392. 127p. reprint ed. pap. 39.40 (*0-7837-3261-9*, 204328000007) Bks Demand.

Conrad, Robert L. Confirmation: Engaging Lutheran Foundations & Practices. LC 99-19139. 1999. write for info. (*0-8006-3157-9*) Augsburg Fortress.

Conrad, Robert T., ed. General Scott & His Staff: Comprising Memoirs of General Scott, Twiggs, Smith, Quitman, Shields, Pillow, Lane, Cadwalader, Patterson, & Pierce, Colonels Childs, Riley, Harney, & Butler, & Other Distinguished Officers Attached to General Scott's Army. LC 77-109626. (Select Bibliographies Reprint Ser.). 1977. 29.95 (*0-8369-5235-9*) Ayer.

Conrad, Robert W. A Hunter's Guide to Mourning Doves. (Illus.). 28p. (Orig.). 1996. pap. 4.50 (*1-881399-08-7*) Beaver Pond P&P.

Conrad, Roger S., jt. auth. see Leeb, Stephen.

Conrad, Roseanne. An Owner's Guide to the Garden Pond. LC 97-45784. 128p. 1998. pap. 12.95 (*0-87605-447-5*) Howell Bks.

Conrad, Roxanne. Bridge of Shadows. 1998. mass mkt. 6.50 (*0-451-19166-8*, Onyx) NAL.

Conrad, Ruth, ed. The Art & Reflections of Rupert Conrad: The Naked Dawn. LC 89-24024. (Illus.). 216p. 1991. 40.00 (*0-8453-4824-8*, Cornwall Bks) Assoc Univ Prs.

Conrad, Scott W. Moving the Force: Desert Storm & Beyond. 88p. 1995. per. 3.50 (*0-16-061172-5*) USGPO.

Conrad, Scott W. Moving the Force: Desert Storm & Beyond. 81p. (C). 1996. reprint ed. pap. text 20.00 (*0-7881-3679-8*) DIANE Pub.

Conrad, Sheree D., jt. auth. see Milburn, Michael A.

Conrad, Stephen A. Citizenship & Common Sense: The Problem of Authority in the Social Background & Social Philosophy of the Wise Club of Aberdeen. (Modern European History Ser.). 504p. 1988. text 15.00 (*0-8240-7802-0*) Garland.

Conrad, Stephen A., et al, eds. Pulmonary Function Testing: Principles & Practice. (Illus.). 378p. 1984. pap. text 44.95 (*0-443-08182-4*) Church.

Conrad, Steven R. & Flegler, Daniel. Math Contests - Grades 4, 5, & 6 Vol. 3: School Years: 1991-92 Through 1995-96. (Math Contests Ser.). 154p. (Orig.). (J). (gr. 3-7). 1996. pap. 12.95 (*0-940805-09-X*) Math Leagues.

— Math Contests - Grades 7 & 8 Vol. 3: School Years: 1991-92 Through 1995-96. (Math Contests Ser.). 136p. (Orig.). (YA). (gr. 6-12). 1996. pap. 12.95 (*0-940805-10-3*) Math Leagues.

— Math Contests - Grades 4, 5, & 6 Vol. 1: School Years: 1979-80 Through 1985-86. rev. ed. 94p. 1992. pap. 12.95 (*0-940805-06-5*) Math Leagues.

— Math Contests - Grades 4, 5, & 6 Vol. 2: School Years: 1986-87 Through 1990-91. (Math Contests Ser.). 102p. (Orig.). (J). (gr. 3-8). 1991. pap. 12.95 (*0-940805-03-0*) Math Leagues.

— Math Contests - Grades 7 & 8: Surival, Vol. 1. rev. ed. 94p. 1992. pap. 12.95 (*0-940805-07-3*) Math Leagues.

— Math Contests - Grades 7 & 8 Vol. 2: School Years: 1982-83 Through 1990-91. (Math Contests Ser.). 166p. (Orig.). (J). (gr. 5-8). 1992. pap. 12.95 (*0-940805-05-7*) Math Leagues.

— Math Contests - High School Vol. 1: School Years: 1977-78 Through 1981-82. rev. ed. 70p. 1992. pap. 12.95 (*0-940805-08-1*) Math Leagues.

— Math Contests - High School Vol. 2: School Years: 1982-83 Through 1990-91. (Math Contests Ser.). 118p. (Orig.). (YA). (gr. 9-12). 1992. pap. 12.95 (*0-940805-04-9*) Math Leagues.

— Math Contests - High School Vol. 3: School Years: 1991-92 Through 1995-96. (Math Contests Ser.). 70p. (Orig.). (YA). (gr. 9-12). 1996. pap. 12.95 (*0-940805-11-1*) Math Leagues.

Conrad, Susan G., jt. auth. see Barro, Susan C.

Conrad, Tim. Almuric: An Adaptation of the Novel by Robert E. Howard. 72p. (Orig.). 1991. pap. 10.95 (*1-878574-18-3*) Dark Horse Comics.

Conrad, William. Disciples' Diary. LC 97-217533. 1997. pap. write for info. (*0-7880-0950-8*, Fairway Pr) CSS OH.

Conrad, William, ed. Boone County: Top of Kentucky. (Illus.). 64p. (Orig.). 1992. pap. 5.95 (*0-9624673-7-5*) Picture This Bks.

Conrad, William R., Jr. & Glenn, William E. The Effective Voluntary Board of Directors: What It Is & How It Works. rev. ed. LC 82-8240. (Illus.). 264p. 1983. pap. 14.95 (*0-8040-0836-1*) Swallow.

Conrad, Winston S. Fabled Isles of the South Seas: With Insights by Literary Greats. LC 96-61772. (Illus.). 168p. 1997. 49.95 (*0-9649701-1-2*) Wild Coconuts.

***Conrad, Winston S.** Hemingway's France. (Illus.). 2000. 39.95 (*0-942627-62-8*) Woodford Pubng.

Conrader, Constance, jt. auth. see Conrader, Jay.

Conrader, Jay & Conrader, Constance. The Northwoods Wildlife Region, Vol. 1. LC 83-6257. (Illus.). 192p. (C). 1983. pap. 8.95 (*0-87961-127-8*) Naturegraph.

Conradi, Katja. Malerei am Hofe der Este. (Studien Zur Kunstgeschichte: Bd. 110). (Illus.). 207p. 1997. 54.00 (*3-487-10246-3*) G Olms Pubs.

Conradi, Peter. Reuse of Electronic Design: From Information Modelling to Intellectual Properties. LC 98-47321. 314p. 1999. 115.00 (*0-471-98750-6*) Wiley.

An Asterisk (*) at the beginning of an entry indicates that the title is appearing for the first time.

Conradi, Peter J. Angus Wilson. Armstrong, Isobel & Loughrey, Bryan, eds. (Writers & Their Work Ser.). 1997. pap. 17.00 (0-7463-0803-5, Pub. by Northcote House) U Pr of Miss.
— John Fowles. (Contemporary Writers Ser.). 1982. pap. 7.95 (0-416-32250-6, NO. 3664) Routledge.
Conradi, Peter J., ed. see Murdoch, Iris.
Conradi, R., et al, eds. Advanced Programming Environments. (Lecture Notes in Computer Science Ser.: Vol. 244). vii, 603p. 1987. pap. 53.00 (0-387-17189-4) Spr-Verlag.
***Conradi, Reidar O., ed.** Software Process Technology: Proceedings, Seventh European Workshop, EWSPT 2000, Kaprun, Austria, February 21-25, 2000. LC 00-26539. (Lecture Notes in Computer Science Ser.: Vol. 1780). ix, 249p. 2000. pap. 52.00 (3-540-67140-4) Spr-Verlag.
Conradi, Reidar O., et al, eds. Software Configuration Management: ICSE'97 SCM-7 Workshop, Boston, MA, U. S. A., May 18-19, 1997, Proceedings. LC 97-14611. (Lecture Notes in Computer Science Ser.: No. 1235). viii, 234p. 1997. pap. 43.00 (3-540-63014-7) Spr-Verlag.
Conrads, David, ed. see Churchman, Michael & Erbes, Scott.
Conrads, David, ed. see Marquardt-Cherry, Janet.
Conrads, Margaret C. American Paintings & Sculpture at the Sterling & Francine Clark Art Institute. LC 90-80949. (Illus.). 224p. 1990. 50.00 (1-55595-050-7) Hudson Hills.
Conrads, Margaret C., jt. auth. see Baur, John I.
Conrads, T. J., ed. see Thomas, E. Donnall, Jr.
Conrads, Ulrich, ed. Programs & Manifestos on 20th-Century Architecture. 1975. pap. text 14.50 (0-262-53030-9) MIT Pr.
***Conradsen, David.** Useful Beauty: Early American Decorative Arts from St. Louis Collections. (Illus.). 100p. 1999. pap. 39.99 (0-89178-080-7) St Louis Art Mus.
Conradson, Diane, ed. see Muckle, James E.
Conradson, Diane R. Exploring Our Baylands. 3rd rev. ed. (Illus.). 72p. 1996. pap. 9.95 (0-9649328-0-6) SF Bay Wldlife.
Conradson, Shari. Just Junior High. rev. ed. 52p. (Orig.). (YA). (gr. 6-9). 1992. pap. 5.00 (0-9620445-1-2) KSJL Publishing.
Conradson, Shari, ed. see Muckle, James.
Conradson, Shari, ed. see Muckle, James E.
Conradson, Shari, ed. see Muckle, Jim.
Conradt, David, et al, eds. Germany's New Politics: Parties & Issues in the 1990s. LC 95-31588. (Modern German Studies: Vol. 1). (Illus.). 336p. 1995. 49.95 (1-57181-032-3); pap. 15.00 (1-57181-033-1) Berghahn Bks.
Conradt, David P. The German Polity. 5th rev. ed. LC 92-17069. 257p. (C). 1992. pap. text 26.95 (0-8013-0769-4, 78798) Longman.
— The German Polity. 7th ed. LC 00-20242. 352p. (C). 2000. pap. 47.00 (0-8013-1917-X) Addison-Wesley.
Conradt, David P., et al, eds. Power Shift in Germany: The 1998 Election & the End of the Kohl Era. LC 99-87840. (Modern German Studies: Vol. 5). 336p. 2000. pap. 19.95 (1-57181-200-8) Berghahn Bks.
— Power Shift in Germany: The 1998 Election & the End of the Kohl Era. LC 99-87840. (Modern German Studies: Vol. 5). 336p. 2000. 69.95 (1-57181-199-0) Berghahn Bks.
Conradt, Dirk-Michael. Porsche 356: Driving in Its Purest Form. (Illus.). 264p. (C). 1993. reprint ed. 64.95 (0-929758-09-9) Beeman Jorgensen.
Conradt, Mark & Dawson, Gregory. Great Scot! 1969. pap. 5.25 (0-8222-0483-5) Dramatists Play.
Conrady, A. E. Applied Optics & Optical Design, 2 vols., 1. (Illus.). 855p. 1992. reprint ed. pap. 14.95 (0-486-67007-4) Dover.
— Applied Optics & Optical Design, 2 vols., 2. (Illus.). 855p. 1992. reprint ed. pap. 14.95 (0-486-67008-2) Dover.
Conrah, T. & Pearson, D. The Essential Garden Book. LC 97-44390. 272p. 1998. pap. 40.00 (0-609-80022-1) Crown Pub Group.
Conran, Anthony. The Cost of Strangeness. 330p. 1998. 14.95 (0-8464-4751-7) Beekman Pubs.
— Frontiers in Anglo-Welsh Poetry. LC 97-216155. 284p. 1997. pap. 25.00 (0-7083-1395-7, Pub. by Univ Wales Pr) Paul & Co Pubs.
Conran, Anthony, ed. The Cost of Strangeness: Essays on the English Poets in Wales. 330p. (C). 1982. pap. text 20.00 (0-85088-865-4, Pub. by Gomer Pr) St Mut.
Conran, Elizabeth, et al. The Bowes Museum. (Illus.). 96p. 1997. 25.00 (1-870248-93-7) Scala Books.
***Conran, Sebastian & Bond, Mark.** Soma Basics--Lighting. LC 99-54702. (Soma Basics Ser.). (Illus.). 128p. 2000. pap. 16.95 (1-57959-063-2, SOMA) BB&T Inc.
***Conran, Sebastian, et al.** Soma Basics: Furniture. LC 99-54438. (Soma Basics Ser.). (Illus.). 128p. 2000. pap. 16.95 (1-57959-015-2, SOMA) BB&T Inc.
Conran, Shirley. Crimson. Rubenstein, Julie, ed. 576p. 1992. reprint ed. mass mkt. 5.99 (0-671-79161-3) PB.
— Lace. Rubenstein, Julie, ed. 608p. 1990. mass mkt. 5.99 (0-671-73745-7) PB.
— Lace. large type ed. LC 94-40739. 1994. pap. 22.95 (1-56895-085-3) Wheeler Pub.
— Lace II. Rubenstein, Julie, ed. 336p. (Orig.). 1988. mass mkt. 5.99 (0-671-66904-4) PB.
— Savages. Rubenstein, Julie, ed. 1990. mass mkt. 5.99 (0-671-72719-2) PB.
Conran, Sir T. Conran Design Gold Kitchen Utensils. 1990. pap. 7.98 (0-442-30294-0) Chapman & Hall.
— Conran Design Gold Lamps & Light. 1990. pap. 7.98 (0-442-30302-5) Chapman & Hall.
— Conran Design Gold Tableware. 1990. pap. 7.98 (0-442-30293-2) Chapman & Hall.
— Conran Design Guides: Home Office. 1990. pap. 7.98 (0-442-30292-4) Chapman & Hall.
***Conran, Terence.** The Chef's Garden. LC 99-39830. (Illus.). 144p. 2000. 25.00 (1-57959-050-0, SOMA) BB&T Inc.
Conran, Terence. The Essential House Book: Getting Back to Basics. LC 94-8955. (Illus.). 256p. 1994. pap. 39.95 (0-517-88231-0, Crown) Crown.
***Conran, Terence.** Garden Diary: Over 75 Projects & Design Ideas for Making the Most of Your Garden. (Illus.). 160p. 2000. pap. 19.95 (1-85029-723-1) Conran Octopus.
Conran, Terence. The New House Book. 1999. pap. text 24.95 (1-84091-112-3) Conran Octopus.
— Terence Conran on Design. LC 96-18134. 288p. 1996. 55.00 (0-87951-686-0, Pub. by Overlook Pr) Penguin Putnam.
***Conran, Terence.** Terence Conran on Restaurants. (Illus.). 2000. 45.00 (1-58567-045-6, Pub. by Overlook Pr) Penguin Putnam.
— Terence Conran's DIY by Design: Over 30 Projects to Make. (Illus.). 256p. 1999. pap. 24.95 (1-85029-460-7) Conran Octopus.
Conran, Terence. Terence Conran's Easy Living. LC 99-11594. (Illus.). 192p. 1999. 35.00 (1-57959-045-4, SOMA) BB&T Inc.
— Terence Conrans Home Furnishings. 1989. 29.95 (0-685-33239-X) Random Hse Value.
Conran, Terence, intro. The Cigar in Art. LC 96-36338. 176p. 1996. 35.00 (0-87951-693-3, Pub. by Overlook Pr) Penguin Putnam.
Conran, Terence, et al. Terence Conran's Kitchen Book. (Illus.). 224p. 1993. 45.00 (0-87951-513-9, Pub. by Overlook Pr) Penguin Putnam.
— Terence Conran's Kitchen Book. 224p. 1995. pap. 28.95 (0-87951-623-2, Pub. by Overlook Pr) Penguin Putnam.
Conran, Tony. All Hallows. 61p. 1998. pap. 13.95 (0-8464-4755-X) Beekman Pubs.
— Castles: Variations on an Original Theme. 90p. 1998. pap. 15.00 (0-8464-4754-1) Beekman Pubs.
***Conran, Tony.** Eros Proposes a Toast: Collected Public Poems & Gifts. 108p. 1999. pap. (1-85411-235-X, Pub. by Seren Bks) Dufour.
Conran, Tony. Life Fund. 120p. (C). 1979. pap. 30.00 (0-85088-651-1, Pub. by Gomer Pr) St Mut.
— Visions & Praying Mantids. 1997. pap. 23.95 (0-8464-4592-1) Beekman Pubs.
— Visions & Praying Mantids. 1997. pap. 30.00 (1-85902-477-7, Pub. by Gomer Pr) St Mut.
Conran, Tony, et al, eds. from WEL. Welsh Verse: Translations. 3rd rev. ed. 355p. 1993. pap. 17.95 (1-85411-081-0, Pub. by Seren Bks) Dufour.
Conran, Tony, jt. auth. see Williams, Waldo.
Conran, Tony, tr. see Williams, Waldo.
Conran, Una. New Life in Christ. (C). 1988. 60.00 (0-85439-131-2, Pub. by St Paul Pubns) St Mut.
Conrans, T. & Pearson, D. The Essential Garden Book. 272p. 1998. 55.00 (0-517-70810-8) Crown Pub Group.
Conrat, Maisie & Conrat, Richard. Executive Order 9066: The Internment of 110,000 Japanese Americans. (Illus.). 120p. 1992. 15.00 (0-934052-19-0) UCLA Asian Am Studies Ctr.
Conrat, Richard, jt. auth. see Conrat, Maisie.
Conrath & Pittman. Competition Law & Enforcement in Transition & Development. 71.95 (1-84014-756-3) Ashgate Pub Co.
***Conrath, Edward J. & Structural Engineering Institute Staff.** Structural Design for Physical Security. LC 99-46356. 250p. 1999. write for info. (0-7844-0457-7) Am Soc Civil Eng.
Conrath, Regina, et al. Provocative Thoughts & Pleasures in Poetry. (Illus.). 193p. 1992. per. 15.00 (0-614-24755-1) Tesseract SD.
Conrey, Kathleen & St. John, Leigh. Human Anatomy Lab Text. 256p. 1995. spiral bd. 80.95 (0-7872-1593-7, 41159301) Kendall-Hunt.
Conrick, Brian, ed. see Rajanayagam, M. J.
***Conron, John.** American Picturesque. LC 98-51056. (Illus.). 320p. 2000. 45.00 (0-271-01920-4) Pa St U Pr.
Conrotto, Eugene L. Lost Gold & Silver Mines of the Southwest. unabridged ed. LC 96-20462. (Illus.). 288p. 1996. reprint ed. pap. text 7.95 (0-486-29275-4) Dover.
***Conrow, E. H.** Effective Risk Management: Some Keys to Success. LC 00-26650. 2000. write for info. (1-56347-383-6) AIAA.
***Conroy.** Jean Jacques Rousseau. LC 98-23266. 171p. 1998. 32.00 (0-8057-1616-5) S&S Trade.
Conroy, Andy, jt. auth. see Wilby, Pete.
Conroy, Barbara J. Restaurant China Vol. I: Identification & Value Guide for Restaurant, Airline, Ship & Railroad. LC 98-198501. 1998. 24.95 (1-57432-059-9, 5056) Collector Bks.
— Restaurant China Vol. 2: Identification & Value Guide for Restaurant, Airline, Ship & Railroad Dinnerwa. LC 98-198501. 657p. 1999. 39.95 (1-57432-148-X) Collector Bks.
Conroy, Daniel F. Over Forty MPH. LC 90-32393. 1991. pap. 13.95 (0-87949-342-9) Ashley Bks.
Conroy, David L. Out of the Nightmare: Recovery from Depression & Suicidal Pain. LC 90-63398. 364p. (Orig.). 1991. reprint ed. pap. 12.95 (1-879204-00-2) New Liberty Pubns.
Conroy, David W. The Defense of Indian Land Rights: William Bollan & the Mohegan Case 1743. 20p. (Orig.). 1994. reprint ed. pap. 6.50 (0-944026-52-4) Am Antiquarian.
— In Public Houses: Drink & the Revolution of Authority in Colonial Massachusetts. LC 94-32658. (Institute of Early American History & Culture Ser.). (Illus.). 368p. 1995. text 49.95 (0-8078-2207-8); pap. text 18.95 (0-8078-4521-3) U of NC Pr.
Conroy, Dennis L. & Hess, Karen M. Officers at Risk: How to Identify & Cope with Stress. LC 91-73969. (Illus.). 271p. (C). 1991. pap. 19.95 (0-942728-48-3) Copperhouse.
Conroy, Don. The Bat Who Was All in A Flap. (Illus.). 78p. (J). (ps-3). 1997. pap. 6.95 (0-86278-416-6, Pub. by OBrien Pr) Irish Amer Bk.
— Cartoon Fun. (Illus.). 96p. 1997. pap. 7.95 (0-86278-358-5, Pub. by OBrien Pr) Irish Amer Bk.
— The Hedgehog's Prickly Problem. (Illus.). 80p. (J). 1997. pap. 6.95 (0-86278-415-8, Pub. by OBrien Pr) Irish Amer Bk.
— On Silent Wings. (Illus.). 240p. 1997. pap. 7.95 (0-86278-369-0, Pub. by OBrien Pr) Irish Amer Bk.
— Sky Wings. (Illus.). 208p. 1997. pap. 6.95 (0-86278-419-0, Pub. by OBrien Pr) Irish Amer Bk.
— Wild Wings. (Illus.). 160p. (J). (gr. 4-7). 1997. pap. 6.95 (0-86278-418-2, Pub. by OBrien Pr) Irish Amer Bk.
— Wildlife Fun. (Illus.). 96p. (YA). 1997. pap. 7.95 (0-86278-385-2, Pub. by OBrien Pr) Irish Amer Bk.
Conroy, Don, et al. The Owl Who Couldn't Give A Hoot. (Illus.). 80p. (J). (gr. 1-4). 1995. pap. 8.95 (0-86278-370-4) Dufour.
— The Tiger Who Was A Roaring Success. 80p. (J). (gr. 1-4). 1995. pap. 0.95 (0-86278-371-2) Dufour.
***Conroy, Donald B. & Peterson, Rodney L., eds.** Earth at Risk: Advancing the Environmental Dialogue Between Religion & Science. LC 99-57948. 350p. 2000. 59.95 (1-57392-817-8, Humanity Bks) Prometheus Bks.
Conroy, Ed. Report on Communion. 446p. 1990. mass mkt. 4.95 (0-380-70811-6, Avon Bks) Morrow Avon.
Conroy, Ellen. The Symbolism of Color. (Illus.). 80p. 1996. reprint ed. pap. 9.95 (0-87877-236-7) Newcastle Pub.
— The Symbolism of Color (1921) 66p. 1998. reprint ed. pap. 8.95 (0-7661-0241-6) Kessinger Pub.
Conroy, Ellen, tr. see Camus, Albert & Viallaneix, Paul.
Conroy, Ellen M. The Four Great Initiations. 143p. 1992. pap. 12.00 (0-89540-207-6, SB-207) Sun Pub.
Conroy, Frank. Body & Soul. 464p. 1998. pap. 11.95 (0-385-31986-X) Doubleday.
— Stop-Time. 288p. 1977. pap. 12.95 (0-14-004446-9, Penguin Bks) Viking Penguin.
***Conroy, Frank, ed.** The Eleventh Draft: Craft & the Writing Life from the Iowa Writers' Workshop. LC 99-28758. 256p. 1999. 23.00 (0-06-273639-6) HarpC.
Conroy, Frank, frwd. Autobiography of a Schizophrenic Girl: An Astonishing Memoir of Reality Lost & Regained. 192p. 1994. pap. 12.95 (0-452-01133-7, Mer) NAL.
Conroy, Frank, selected by. The Iowa Award: The Best Stories from Twenty Years. LC 90-5220. 342p. 1991. pap. 15.95 (0-87745-333-0); text 24.95 (0-87745-313-6) U of Iowa Pr.
Conroy, G. C. Primate Postcranial Remains from the Oligocene of Egypt. (Contributions to Primatology Ser.: Vol.8). 140p. 1976. 55.00 (3-8055-2333-5) S Karger.
Conroy, Glenn. Primate Evolution. (Illus.). 492p. (C). 1990. pap. text 55.75 (0-393-95649-0) Norton.
— Reconstructing Human Origins: A Modern Synthesis. LC 96-25161. (C). 1997. pap. text 58.50 (0-393-97042-6) Norton.
Conroy, Harry. Off the Record: A Life of Journalism. LC 96-212586. 239p. 1997. write for info. (1-874640-67-X) Argyll Pubng.
Conroy, Hilary. The Japanese Frontier in Hawaii, 1868-1898. Daniels, Roger, ed. LC 78-54840. (Asian Experience in North America Ser.). 1979. reprint ed. lib. bdg. 16.95 (0-405-11306-4) Ayer.
Conroy, Hilary, et al, eds. Japan in Transition: Thought & Action in the Meiji Era, 1868-1912. LC 83-48577. (Illus.). 320p. 1985. 44.50 (0-8386-3169-X) Fairleigh Dickinson.
Conroy, Hilary & Wray, Harry, eds. Pearl Harbor Reexamined: Prologue to the Pacific War. LC 89-37487. (Illus.). 224p. 1989. text 24.00 (0-8248-1235-2) UH Pr.
Conroy, Hilary, jt. ed. see Coox, Alvin D.
Conroy, Hilary, jt. ed. see Kim, Roy.
Conroy, Hilary, jt. ed. see Wray, Harry.
***Conroy, J. Patrick.** Intellectual Leadership in Education. LC 99-47096. 312p. 1999. 120.00 (0-7923-8658-2) Kluwer Academic.
Conroy, Jack. The Disinherited. LC 78-26296. 1979. reprint ed. lib. bdg. 18.00 (0-8376-0426-5) Bentley Pubs.
— The Disinherited: A Novel of the 1930s. 19th ed. 296p. (C). 1991. reprint ed. pap. 17.95 (0-8262-0770-7) U of Mo Pr.
***Conroy, Jack.** A World to Win. (Radical Novel Reconsidered Ser.). 392p. 2000. reprint ed. pap. 17.95 (0-252-06927-7) U of Ill Pr.
Conroy, Jack, jt. auth. see Bontemps, Arna.
Conroy, James. The Night Is Once Before. LC 97-14673. 48p. 1997. pap. 14.95 (0-7734-2830-5, Mellen Poetry Pr) E Mellen.
Conroy, Joanne M. & Dorman, B. Hugh, eds. Anesthesia for Orthopedic Surgery. 480p. 1994. text 147.00 (0-7817-0165-1) Lppncott W & W.
Conroy, John. Belfast Diary: War As a Way of Life. rev. ed. LC 94-41937. (Illus.). 240p. 1995. pap. 14.00 (0-8070-0217-8) Beacon Pr.
***Conroy, John.** Unspeakable Acts, Ordinary People: The Dynamics of Torture. LC 99-28509. 304p. 2000. 26.00 (0-679-41918-7) Knopf.
Conroy, Joseph. Basque-English, English-Basque Dictionary & Phrasebook. Aran, Aitor & Jansen, Wim, eds. (BAQ & ENG.). 240p. 1998. pap. 11.95 (0-7818-0622-4) Hippocrene Bks.
— Beginner's Esperanto. (Beginner's Language Ser.). (ENG & ESP.). 342p. (Orig.). 1994. pap. 14.95 (0-7818-0230-X) Hippocrene Bks.
— Breton-English - English-Breton Dictionary & Phrasebook. (Dictionary & Phrasebook Ser.). 131p. 1997. pap. 9.95 (0-7818-0540-6) Hippocrene Bks.
— Tajik-English, English-Tajik: Dictionary & Phrasebook. (TAJ.). 176p. 1998. pap. 11.95 (0-7818-0662-3) Hippocrene Bks.
Conroy, Joseph F. A l'Aventure sur Route Contreband: Reader 3. text 3.75 (0-88436-856-4) EMC-Paradigm.
Conroy, Joseph F. La Chanson de Roland: An Adaptation for Intermediate Students. (FRE & ENG.). 128p. 1994. pap. 12.65 (0-8442-1234-2) NTC Contemp Pub Co.
Conroy, Joseph F. Danger sur la Cote d Azur! Reader 4. 3.75 (0-88436-857-2) EMC-Paradigm.
Conroy, Joseph F. Esperanto-English/English-Esperanto Dictionary & Phrasebook. 1999. pap. text 13.95 (0-7818-0736-0) Hippocrene Bks.
Conroy, Joseph F. La Famille Marais un Sejour en France. text 4.95 (0-8219-1035-3) EMC-Paradigm.
— A l aventure! Aventure en Normandie, Reader 2. 3.75 (0-88436-855-6) EMC-Paradigm.
— A l aventure! Destination: France! Reader 1. 3.75 (0-88436-854-8) EMC-Paradigm.
Conroy, Kathleen. Valuing the Timeshare Property. 97p. 1981. 17.00 (0-911780-50-5) Appraisal Inst.
Conroy, Larry & O'Connell, Paul. The Consumer Cost Guide to Car Repair. (Illus.). 144p. 1983. pap. 11.00 (0-13-168864-2); pap. text 17.00 (0-13-168872-3) P-H.
Conroy, Lois. The Gardner Museum Cafe Cookbook. LC 85-16803. (Illus.). 160p. (Orig.). 1985. pap. 10.95 (0-916782-71-9) Harvard Common Pr.
Conroy, M. Catherine. Dementia Care: Keeping Intact & in Touch: A Search for Occupational Therapy Interventions. LC 96-85505. 252p. 1996. text 72.95 (1-85972-036-6, Pub. by Avebry) Ashgate Pub Co.
Conroy, Maggie. A World of Love. LC 96-79082. 256p. 1997. 23.00 (1-57566-159-4, Knsington) Kensgtn Pub Corp.
Conroy, Maggie F. International Adoption Sourcebook. 224p. 1998. 21.95 (1-55972-458-7, Birch Ln Pr) Carol Pub Group.
Conroy, Mark. Modernism & Authority: Strategies of Legitimation in Flaubert & Conrad. LC 84-21848. 204p. 1985. reprint ed. pap. 63.30 (0-608-03647-1, 206447300009) Bks Demand.
***Conroy, Mary Ann.** 101 Ways to Integrate Personal Development into Core Curriculum: Lessons in Character Education for Grades K-12. LC 99-462072. 320p. 1999. pap. 29.50 (0-7618-1642-9) U Pr of Amer.
Conroy, Mary S. In Health & in Sickness: Pharmacy, Pharmacists & the Pharmaceutical Industry in Late Imperial, Early Soviet Russia. LC 94-70069. viii, 702p. 1994. 62.00 (0-88033-283-2, 386, Pub. by East Eur Monographs) Col U Pr.
Conroy, Mary S., ed. Emerging Democracy in Late Imperial Russia: Case Studies on Local Self-Government (the Zemstvos), State Duma Elections, the Tsarist Government, & the State Council Before & During World War I. LC 97-48794. 352p. 1998. 39.95 (0-87081-470-2) Univ Pr Colo.
Conroy, Maureen. The Discerning Heart: Discovering a Personal God. LC 93-12508. 272p. (Orig.). (C). 1993. pap., per. 13.95 (0-8294-0752-9, TDH) Loyola Pr.
— Growing in Love & Freedom: Personal Experiences of Counseling & Spiritual Direction. 1985. pap. 9.95 (0-87193-263-6) Dimension Bks.
Conroy, Maureen A., jt. ed. see Brown, William H.
Conroy, Michael, jt. auth. see Walbek, Norman V.
Conroy, Michael E., et al. A Cautionary Tale: Failed U. S. Development Policy in Central America. LC 95-26189. 212p. 1996. lib. bdg. 46.50 (1-55587-630-7) L Rienner.
Conroy, Michael R. Don't Tell America! LC 92-72812. (Illus.). 500p. (Orig.). 1992. 29.95 (1-879027-06-2) Eagle Red Bluff.
Conroy, Pat. Beach Music. 1996. mass mkt. 7.99 (0-614-98034-8) Bantam.
— Beach Music. 640p. 1995. 27.50 (0-385-41304-1, N A Talese) Doubleday.
— Beach Music. 1996. 13.09 (0-606-11096-8, Pub. by Turtleback) Demco.
— Beach Music. 816p. 1996. reprint ed. mass mkt. 7.99 (0-553-57457-4) Bantam.
— Boo. 1976. 21.95 (0-8488-1274-3) Amereon Ltd.
— The Boo. (Orig.). 1983. reprint ed. 22.95 (0-937036-02-1) Old NY Bk Shop.
— Great Santini. 1976. 12.60 (0-606-03795-0, Pub. by Turtleback) Demco.
— The Great Santini. abr. ed. 1995. audio 16.99 (0-553-47387-5) BDD Aud Pub.
— The Great Santini. 440p. 1987. reprint ed. mass mkt. 7.99 (0-553-26892-9) Bantam.
— The Great Santini. 536p. 1989. reprint ed. 25.00 (0-937036-00-5) Old NY Bk Shop.
— The Lords of Discipline. 512p. 1982. mass mkt. 7.99 (0-553-27136-9) Bantam.
— The Lords of Discipline. 1980. 25.00 (0-937036-01-3) Old NY Bk Shop.
— Lords of Discipline. 1995. 13.50 (0-606-01637-6, Pub. by Turtleback) Demco.
— The Lords of Discipline, Set. abr. ed. 1988. audio 18.00 (0-553-45152-9) BDD Aud Pub.
— The Prince of Tides. 672p. 1987. mass mkt. 7.99 (0-553-26888-0) Bantam.
— The Prince of Tides, 001. 576p. 1986. 30.00 (0-395-35300-9) HM.
— Prince of Tides. LC 86-10689. 1991. 12.60 (0-606-03895-7, Pub. by Turtleback) Demco.
— The Prince of Tides, Set. abr. ed. 1987. audio 16.99 (0-553-45096-4, 391403) BDD Aud Pub.

C

Conroy, Pat. Water Is Wide. 1972. 11.60 (*0-606-03948-1*, Pub. by Turtleback) Demco.
— The Water Is Wide. 272p. 1987. reprint ed. mass mkt. 7.50 (*0-553-26893-7*) Bantam.
Conroy, Pat. The Water Is Wide. (Illus.). 288p. 1990. reprint ed. 25.00 (*0-937036-03-X*) Old NY Bk Shop.
Conroy, Pat, frwd. Gullah Images: The Art of Jonathan Green. LC 96-25200. (Illus.). 224p. 1996. 49.95 (*1-57003-145-2*) U of SC Pr.
Conroy, Pat, jt. auth. see Wolfe, Thomas.
Conroy, Peter V., Jr. Intimate, Intrusive, & Triumphant: Readers in the Liasons Dangereuses. LC 87-9185. (Purdue University Monographs in Romance Languages: No. 23). xi, 139p. (C). 1987. pap. 40.00 (*0-915027-72-0*) J Benjamins Pubng Co.
— Montesquieu Revisited. LC 92-18575. (Twayne's World Authors Ser.). 170p. 1992. 32.00 (*0-8057-8273-7*, Twayne) Mac Lib Ref.
Conroy, Richard T. Our Man in Belize: A Memoir. LC 97-14778. 352p. 1997. 27.50 (*0-312-16959-0*, Thomas Dunne) St Martin.
Conroy, Roisin. So You Want to Be Published? A Guide to Getting into Print. 1992. 65.00 (*1-85549-056-0*) St Mut.
Conroy, Sandra. Sarcoidosis Resource Guide & Directory. (Illus.). 304p. (Orig.). 1992. pap. 19.95 (*0-9631222-5-8*) PC Pubns.
— Sarcoidosis Resource Guide & Directory for Health Care Professionals. (Illus.). 250p. 1991. pap. write for info. (*0-9631222-6-6*) PC Pubns.
Conroy, Susan, tr. see De Meester, Conrad.
Conroy, Teddie B., et al. A Garland of Poems & Short Stories Vol. 1: Anthology. 4th ed. Moore, Michael, ed. 164p. 1997. pap. 12.95 (*0-9610702-7-7*) Mstrd Seed Pr.
Conroy-Teri, Jeannette. Rap-a-Matics: Math Rap Multiplication Through Song. (Illus.). 32p. (J). (gr. 2-4). 1993. wbk. ed. 11.95 (*0-933243-01-4*) Laurel Pubns New York.
Conroy, Thomas F., ed. Markets of the United States for Business Planners: Historical & Current Profiles of 183 U. S. Urban Economies by Major Section & Industry with Maps, Graphics & Commentary. 2nd ed. (Illus.). 1688p. 1995. lib. bdg. 240.00 (*0-7808-0019-2*) Omnigraphics Inc.
Conroy, Tim. How to Become a Star Athlete. (Illus.). 88p. (Orig.). (YA). write for info. (*0-9636706-7-0*) Coach Ent.
Conroy, Timothy, jt. ed. see Kegler, Richard.
***Conroy, Timothy Richard.** Our Man in Vienna. 2000. text 24.95 (*0-312-26493-3*) St Martin.
Conroy, W. J. Challenging the Boundaries of Reform: Socialism in Burlington. 288p. 1990. 49.95 (*0-87722-702-0*) Temple U Pr.
Conroy, William B. Map Skills for Texas History & Geography Students. 48p. 1995. pap. 8.95 (*0-937460-36-2*) Hendrick-Long.
Conru, Paula, et al. Speaking of Language: An International Guide to Language Service Organizations. (Language in Education Ser.). (Illus.). 191p. 1993. pap. text 16.50 (*0-937354-80-5*) Delta Systems.
Conry, Barbara, jt. ed. see Carpenter, Ted G.
Conry, Edward J. Ethics & Evidence: Developing Ethical Character in Professionals. abr. ed. 325p. (C). 1997. text. write for info. (*1-887959-04-1*) Sage CO.
— Moral Partners: Building Moral Character for Business. 750p. (C). 1995. text. write for info. (*1-887959-00-9*) Sage CO.
— Moral Partners: Building Moral Character for Business. abr. ed. 265p. (C). 1995. write for info. (*1-887959-01-7*) Sage CO.
Conry, Edward J., et al. The Legal Environment of Business. 2nd ed. 650p. 1989. text 54.00 (*0-205-12192-6*, H21926) Allyn.
— The Legal Environment of Business. 2nd ed. 650p. 1989. teacher ed. write for info. (*0-318-66388-0*, H21934); student ed. 19.00 (*0-685-29841-8*, H21942); write for info. (*0-318-66389-9*, H21959) P-H.
Conry-Murray, Andrew, ed. see Seabourne, Tom.
***Cons, Jean.** Pathways to Sexual Behavior. 2000. pap. text. write for info. (*0-7167-3749-3*) W H Freeman.
Cons, Louis L. Auteur de la Farce de Pathelin. (Elliott Monographs: Vol. 17). 1926. 25.00 (*0-527-02620-4*) Periodicals Srv.
***Consagra, Francesca, et al.** Landscapes of Retrospection: The Magoon Collection of British Prints & Drawings, 1739-1760. Schwartz, Sheila, ed. (Illus.). 150p. 1999. pap. text. write for info. (*0-9644263-3-1*) F L Loeb Art Ctr.
Consalvi, Peter, Sr. Collector Steiff Values: 1980-1990 Limited Editions & Replicas Including Disney. 2nd ed. LC 97-180059. (Illus.). 128p. 1996. 19.95 (*0-87588-447-4*) Hobby Hse.
Consalvo, Carmine M. Changing Pace: Outdoor Games for Experiential Learning. LC 96-212608. 1996. pap. text 34.95 (*0-87425-354-3*) HRD Press.
— Experiential Training Activities for Outside & In. 445p. 1994. ring bd. 139.95 (*0-87425-962-2*) HRD Press.
— Training with Outdoor Activities. 344p. 1993. ring bd. 239.95 (*1-85904-041-1*, Pub. by Gower) Ashgate Pub Co.
— WorkPlay: Playing to Learn & Learning to Play. 2nd ed. LC 91-67971. 132p. (Orig.). 1996. ring bd. 95.00 (*0-925652-12-1*) Orgn Design & Dev.
Consalvo, Domenick S. The Eagle That Did Not Fly: Memories of a Prisoner of War Survivor. (Illus.). 163p. (Orig.). 1989. pap. 8.50 (*0-9623989-0-X*) D S Consalvo.
Consbruch, ed. Hephaestionis. (GRE.). 1971. reprint ed. 53.50 (*3-519-01399-1*, T1399, Pub. by B G Teubner) U of Mich Pr.
Conscable, Todd A. Lift up Your Hearts: Musical Settings for Holy Communion. 39p. 1998. pap. 10.00 (*0-9664162-0-1*, PSC1015) Paradoxology.
Consei International de la Langue Francaise Staff. Dictionary of Spatiologie: Terms & Definitions. 3rd ed. (ENG, GER, RUS & SPA.). 352p. 1992. 150.00 (*0-7859-1010-7*, 2853192393) Fr & Eur.
Conseil de la Musique, Belgique Staff. Dictionnaire du Jazz a Bruxelles et en Wallonie. (FRE.). 327p. 1991. pap. 95.00 (*0-7859-8662-6*, 287009468x) Fr & Eur.
Conseil International de la Langue Francaise Sta. Diccionario de la Industrias: Industrial Dictionary. (SPA.). write for info. (*0-8288-7667-3*) Fr & Eur.
— Dictionnaire de la Presse et des Medias.Tr. of French-Arabic, Arabic-French Dictionary of the Press & Media. (ARA & FRE.). pap. write for info. (*0-8288-7675-4*) Fr & Eur.
— Dictionnaire des Noms d'Agents Pathogenes.Tr. of French & English Dictionary of Pathogenic Agents. (ENG & FRE.). write for info. (*0-8288-7671-1*) Fr & Eur.
— Dictionnaire Encyclopedique d'Agrometeorology: French, English & Spanish Dictionary of Agrometeorology. (ENG, FRE & SPA.). write for info. (*0-8288-7672-X*) Fr & Eur.
— Dictionnaire Francais-Arabe de la Presse et des Medias.Tr. of French & Arabic Dictionary of the Press & Media. (ARA & FRE.). write for info. (*0-8288-7673-8*) Fr & Eur.
— Dictionnaire Quadrilingue de la Presse et des Medias: French, Portuguese, Italian & Spanish Dictionary of the Press & Media. (FRE, ITA, POR & SPA.). write for info. (*0-8288-7674-6*) Fr & Eur.
— French & English Dictionary of the Environment. 3rd ed. (ENG & FRE.). 351p. 1992. 150.00 (*0-8288-7666-5*, 2853192431) Fr & Eur.
— French, German, Spanish & English Dictionary of Architectural Planning. (ENG, FRE, GER & SPA.). 704p. 1992. 295.00 (*0-8288-7668-1*, 2853192458) Fr & Eur.
Conseil International de la Langue Francaise Sta & Abouriche, Nouredine. Thesaurus de l'Education et de son Environment Socio-Economique: French-Arabic, Arabic-French. (ARA & FRE.). 105p. 1991. write for info. (*0-8288-7582-0*, 285319288) Fr & Eur.
Conseil International de la Langue Francaise Sta & Zezeze-Kalonji, M. T. Conseil International de la Langue Francaise, Dictionnaire Francophone des Organizations Panafricaines: French Speaker's Dictionary of Pan-African Organizations. 291p. 1992. write for info. (*0-8288-6167-6*, 2853192385) Fr & Eur.
Conseil International de la Langue Francaise Staff. Industrial Dictionary - English & Spanish. (FRE & POR.). 484p. 1992. pap. 395.00 (*0-8288-6160-9*, 2853192482) Fr & Eur.
Conseil International de la Langue Francaise Staff, ed. Vocabulaire de la Publicite. (FRE.). 1976. pap. 19.95 (*0-8288-5760-1*, M6559) Fr & Eur.
— Vocabulaire de L'Environnement. 3rd ed. (ENG & FRE.). 351p. 1992. 135.00 (*0-7859-4780-9*, M4648) Fr & Eur.
— Vocabulaire d'Ecologie: Ecological Vocabulary. (FRE.). 1974. pap. 39.95 (*0-8288-6218-4*, M-4641) Fr & Eur.
— Vocabulaire du Breton. (FRE.). 192p. 1976. pap. 45.00 (*0-8288-5761-X*, M6084) Fr & Eur.
Conseil International des Machines a Combustion St. Lexique: Machines a Combustion. (DUT, FRE, GER, ITA & SPA.). 96p. pap. 29.95 (*84-600-0836-3*, S-30858) Fr & Eur.
Conseil Quebecois de la Recherche Sociale, jt. auth. see Brown, Thomas G.
Conseiller, C., et al, eds. Curare & Curarisation. 368p. 1980. 97.50 (*90-219-0443-8*, Excerpta Medica) Elsevier.
Consentino, Phyllis. Teddy Bear Junction: Stop Here for Fine Collector Bears. (Illus.). 104p. (Orig.). (YA). 1985. pap. 10.95 (*0-935855-00-9*) T B J Pubns.
Conser, Anne, jt. auth. see Berger, Robert.
***Conser, James A. & Russell, Gregory D.** Law Enforcement in the United States. LC 99-45510. 2000. write for info. (*0-8342-1724-4*) Aspen Pub.
Conser, Walter H., Jr. Church & Confession: Conservative Theologians in Germany, England, & America, 1815-1866. LC 84-18990. viii, 360p. 1984. text 28.95 (*0-86554-119-1*, MUP/H109) Mercer Univ Pr.
— God & the Natural World: Religion & Science in Antebellum America. LC 93-1422. 201p. (C). 1993. text 39.95 (*0-87249-893-X*) U of SC Pr.
***Conser, Walter H., Jr.** Sacred Spaces: Architecture & Religion in Historic Wilmington. (Illus.). 64p. 1999. pap. 9.00 (*0-9673037-0-2*) Bellamy Mansion.
Conser, Walter H., Jr. & Twiss, Sumner B., eds. Religious Diversity & American Religious History: Studies in Traditions & Cultures. LC 97-26767. 312p. 1997. text 55.00 (*0-8203-1917-1*) U of Ga Pr.
— Religious Diversity & American Religious History: Studies in Traditions & Cultures. LC 97-26767. 312p. 1998. pap. text 25.00 (*0-8203-1918-X*) U of Ga Pr.
Conser, Walter H., Jr., jt. ed. see Twiss, Sumner B.
***Conservancy Garden Staff.** Garden Conservancy's Open Days Directory: The Guide to Visiting 100s of American's Best Private Gardens. (Illus.). 464p. 2000. pap. 14.95 (*0-8109-6694-8*, Pub. by Abrams) Time Warner.
Conservation Foundation Staff. Groundwater Protection. Groundwater, Saving the Unseen Resource: The Final Report of the National Groundwater Policy Forum. A Guide to Groundwater Pollution - Problems, Causes, & Government Responses. LC 86-24084. (Illus.). 256p. reprint ed. pap. 79.40 (*0-608-08877-3*, 206951400006) Bks Demand.
— Paying for Pollution: Water Quality & Effluent Charges. LC 78-52289. (Conservation Foundation: Issue Reports). 64p. reprint ed. pap. 30.00 (*0-608-11748-X*, 201578400097) Bks Demand.
— State of the Government: A View Toward the '90s. LC 87-15193. (Illus.). 664p. reprint ed. pap. 200.00 (*0-8357-2931-1*, 203917000011) Bks Demand.
Conservation Foundation Staff, et al. Resource Guide for Creating Successful Communities. LC 89-15473. (Illus.). 206p. 1989. text 45.00 (*1-55963-031-0*) Island Pr.
Conservation Foundation Staff, jt. auth. see Committee for Economic Development.
***Conservation Fund Staff.** The Civil War Battlefield Guide. 2nd ed. (Illus.). 1998. 40.00 (*0-395-74013-4*) HM.
Conservation of Human Resources Project Staff & Ginzberg, Eli, eds. From Health Dollars to Health Services: New York City, 1965-1985. (Conservation of Human Resources Ser.: No. 25). 176p. 1986. text 50.00 (*0-8476-7440-1*) Rowman.
Conservation Unit Staff & Museums & Galleries Commission Staff. The Science for Conservators Series: Adhesives & Coatings, Vol. 3. (Heritage: Care-Preservation-Management Program Ser.). (Illus.). 140p. (C). 1992. pap. 22.99 (*0-415-07163-1*, A9587) Routledge.
— The Science for Conservators Series: An Introduction to Materials, Vol. 1. (Heritage: Care-Preservation-Management Program Ser.). (Illus.). 116p. (C). 1992. pap. 22.99 (*0-415-07167-4*, A9604) Routledge.
— The Science for Conservators Series: Cleaning, Vol. 2. (Heritage: Care-Preservation-Management Program Ser.). (Illus.). 132p. (C). 1992. pap. 22.99 (*0-415-07165-8*, A7855) Routledge.
Consibee, Philip. Masterpiece in Focus: Soap Bubbles by Jean-Simeon Chardin. LC 91-107248. (Illus.). 28p. 1990. pap. text 8.95 (*0-87587-154-2*) LA Co Art Mus.
Considerant, Victor P. Au Texas: With the Great West & European Colonization in Texas. LC 74-32216. (American Utopian Adventure Ser.). (FRE.). 432p. 1975. reprint ed. lib. bdg. 57.50 (*0-87991-021-6*) Porcupine Pr.
***Considine.** Scientific Encyclopedia, 1. 9th ed. 2000. write for info. (*0-471-33197-X*) Wiley.
— Scientific Encyclopedia, 2. 9th ed. 2000. write for info. (*0-471-33196-1*) Wiley.
— Van Nostrand's Scientific Encyclopedia, 2. 8th ed. 1594p. 1994. 149.50 (*0-471-28638-9*) Wiley.
— Von Nostrand's Scientific Encyclopedia, Vol. 1. 8th ed. 1861p. 1994. 149.50 (*0-471-28636-2*) Wiley.
Considine, Bob, ed. see Stripling, Robert E.
Considine, David M. & Haley, Gail E. Visual Messages: Integrating Imagery into Instruction. 2nd ed. LC 98-52727. 10p. 1999. pap. 45.00 (*1-56308-575-5*) Libs Unl.
Considine, Douglas M. Desk Science. text. write for info. (*0-471-36331-6*) Wiley.
— Process-Industrial Instruments & Controls Handbook. 4th ed. (Illus.). 1008p. 1991. 99.50 (*0-07-012445-0*, 6394U) McGraw.
***Considine, Douglas M.** Scientific Encyclopedia. 8th ed. 4p. 1999. cd-rom 200.00 (*0-471-29323-7*) Wiley.
Considine, Douglas M. Van Nostrand's Scientific Dictionary, 2 vols. 7th ed. 1990. text. write for info. (*0-442-31816-2*, VNR) Wiley.
— Van Nostrand's Scientific Encyclopedia, 2 vols., Set. 8th ed. (Illus.). 3488p. 1995. text 269.95 (*0-442-01864-9*, VNR) Wiley.
— Van Nostrand's Scientific Encyclopedia, Vol. 1. 7th ed. (General Science & Technology Ser.). 1989. text. write for info. (*0-442-31814-6*, VNR) Wiley.
— Van Reinhold Encyclopedia of Chemistry. 5th ed. 1990. text 140.00 (*0-442-23978-5*, VNR) Wiley.
Considine, Douglas M. & Considine, Glenn D. Van Nostrand's Scientific Encyclopedia, 2 Vols. 8th ed. (General Science & Technology Ser.). 3455p. 1994. 200.00 (*0-471-28635-4*, VNR) Wiley.
Considine, Douglas M. & Considine, Glenn D., eds. Van Nostrand's Scientific Encyclopedia, 2 vols., Vol. 1. 8th ed. 3200p. 1995. text 199.95 (*0-442-01865-7*, VNR) Wiley.
— Van Nostrand's Scientific Encyclopedia, 2 vols., Vol. 2. 8th ed. 3200p. 1995. text 199.95 (*0-442-01868-1*, VNR) Wiley.
Considine, Douglas M. & Ross, S. D., eds. Handbook of Applied Instrumentation. LC 81-19336. 1180p. 1982. reprint ed. 86.50 (*0-89874-397-4*) Krieger.
***Considine, Dougles M.** Van Nostrand's Scientific Encyclopedia, 3 vols. 1999. 385.00 (*0-471-34770-1*) Wiley.
Considine, Glenn D., jt. auth. see Considine, Douglas M.
Considine, Glenn D., jt. ed. see Considine, Douglas M.
Considine, John J. Marketing Your Church: Concepts & Strategies. 136p. (Orig.). 1995. pap. 14.95 (*1-55612-800-2*) Sheed & Ward WI.
— New Horizons in Latin America. LC 74-93330. (Essay Index Reprint Ser.). 1977. 30.95 (*0-8369-1561-5*) Ayer.
Considine, June. When the Luvenders Came to Merrick Town. 240p. (Orig.). 1990. pap. 6.95 (*1-85371-055-5*) Dufour.
— When the Luvenders Came to Merrick Town. LC 89-82487. 240p. (Orig.). (YA). (gr. 8-12). 1990. pap. 6.95 (*0-685-46916-6*, Pub. by Poolbeg Pr) Dufour.
Considine, Mark. The Politics of Reform: Works Compensation from Woodhouse to Workcare, Vol. 1. 118p. 1991. pap. 52.50 (*0-7855-2673-0*, PTSSSO, Pub. by Deakin Univ) St Mut.
— The Politics of Reform No. 1: Workers Compensation from Woodhouse to Workcare. 118p. (C). 1991. 53.00 (*0-7300-1472-X*, Pub. by Deakin Univ) St Mut.
— Public Policy: A Critical Approach. 350p. 1995. 64.95 (*0-7329-1297-0*, Pub. by Macmill Educ); pap. 32.95 (*0-7329-1296-2*, Pub. by Macmill Educ) Paul & Co Pubs.
Considine, Mark & Painter, Martin. Managerialism: The Great Debate. 256p. 1998. pap. 24.95 (*0-522-84759-5*, Pub. by Melbourne Univ Pr) Paul & Co Pubs.
Considine, Mark, jt. auth. see Marginson, Simon.
Considine, Robert, ed. see Wainwright, Jonathan M.
Considine, Tim. An American Grand Prix History: A Century of Drivers & Cars. LC 97-27507. (Illus.). 196p. 1997. 39.95 (*0-7603-0210-3*) MBI Pubg.
Consigleri, Pederoso. Portuguese Folk-Tales. Montfiro, H., tr. 1974. reprint ed. pap. 25.00 (*0-8115-0503-0*) Periodicals Srv.
Consigliere-Pedroso, Z. Portuguese Folk Tales. LC 68-57186. 1972. reprint ed. 12.95 (*0-405-08375-0*, Pub. by Blom Pubns) Ayer.
Consiglio, William. Homosexual No More. (Personal Growth Bookshelf). 168p. 1991. pap. 10.99 (*0-89693-935-9*, 6-1935, Victor Bks) Chariot Victor.
Consiglio, William E. Spirit-Led Helping. Keith-Lucas, Alan, ed. (Practice Monograph Ser.: No. 3). 52p. 1987. 10.00 (*0-685-35658-2*) N American Assn.
Consigny, Elisabeth, et al, eds. Pocket Gastronomical Dictionary: France. 225p. 1999. pap. 12.95 (*0-9666899-1-7*, Pub. by Mariposa Pr NM) Consort Bk Sales.
Conso, P. Diccionario de la Gestion Financiera. (SPA.). 1991. write for info. (*0-7859-3705-6*, 8428318514) Fr & Eur.
— Robert Dictionnaire des Anglicismes. 7th ed. (FRE.). 352p. 1985. pap. 49.95 (*0-7859-4815-5*) Fr & Eur.
Conso, Pierre, et al. Dictionary of Financial Management: Dictionnaire de la Gestion Financiere. 3rd ed. (ENG & FRE.). 496p. 1984. 125.00 (*0-8288-0316-1*, M7776) Fr & Eur.
Consolazio, C. F. Nutrition & Performance, Vol 7/1-2. (Illus.). 200p. 1983. pap. 92.00 (*0-08-031013-3*, 38, Pergamon Pr) Elsevier.
Console, Rodolfo & Nikolaev, Alexei, eds. Earthquakes Induced by Underground Nuclear Explosions: Environmental & Ecological Problems, Vol. XI. LC 95-31117. (NATO ASI Ser.: Vol. 4). 452p. 1995. 262.95 (*3-540-60185-6*) Spr-Verlag.
Console, William A., et al. The First Encounter: The Beginnings in Psychotherapy. LC 76-25708. 384p. 1993. pap. 50.00 (*1-56821-141-4*) Aronson.
Consoli, Joseph P. & Wilhelm, James J., eds. The Novellino or One Hundred Ancient Tales: A Edition & Translation Based on the 1525 Gualteruzzi Editio Princeps. LC 96-41562. (Garland Library of Medieval Literature: Vol. 105A). 224p. 1997. text 50.00 (*0-8153-1080-3*) Garland.
Consolidated Capital Communications Group Editors. The Financial Deskbook: Taxation Investment & Financial Planning. 1985. 59.95 (*0-671-54797-6*) S&S Trade.
***Consolmagno, Guy.** Brother Astronomer: Adventures of a Vatican Scientist. LC 99-86237. 256p. 2000. 24.95 (*0-07-135428-X*) McGraw.
Consolmagno, Guy. Worlds Apart: A Textbook in Planetary Sciences. 496p. 1994. text 50.20 (*0-13-964131-9*) P-H.
Consolmagno, Guy J. Way to the Dwelling of Light. (From the Vatican Observatory Foundation Ser.). 180p. 1999. pap. text 15.00 (*0-268-01954-1*, Pub. by U of Notre Dame Pr) Chicago Distribution Ctr.
***Consolmagno, Guy J. & Davis, Dan M.** Turn Left at Orion: A Hundred Night Sky Objects to See in a Small Telescope--And How to Find Them. 3rd ed. LC 99-86087. (Illus.). 224p. 2000. 24.95 (*0-521-78190-6*) Cambridge U Pr.
Consolmagno, Guy J. & Davis, Daniel M. Turn Left at Orion: One Hundred Night Sky Objects to See in a Small Telescope & How to Find Them. 2nd rev. ed. (Illus.). 205p. (C). 1995. 24.95 (*0-521-48211-9*) Cambridge U Pr.
Consolo, Bonnie. Bonnie, Vol. 1. 2nd ed. (Illus.). 147p. (Orig.). 1990. reprint ed. pap. 12.50 (*0-9641198-0-3*) B Consolo.
***Consolo-Murphy, Sue & Murphy, Kerry.** WildLife @ Yellowstone: The Story Behind the Scenery. LC 99-60067. (Illus.). 64p. 1999. pap. 8.95 (*0-88714-149-8*) KC Pubns.
Consolo, Vincenzo. The Smile of the Unknown Mariner. Farrell, Joseph, tr. from ITA. 128p. 1995. 27.95 (*1-85754-051-4*, Pub. by Carcanet Pr) Paul & Co Pubs.
Consorte, Linda, et al. The InSights Manual: Vision Education for Older Adults. 1995. 9.95 (*1-888504-12-9*, P950) Lighthouse NYC.
Consortium CCE-CNMA Staff. MMS: The Communication Language of Manufacturing. (Research Reports ESPRIT, Project 7096, CCE-CNMA: Vol. 2). 185p. 1996. pap. 37.00 (*3-540-59061-7*) Spr-Verlag.
Consortium CCE/CNMA, ESPRIT Editors, ed. CCE an Integration Platform for Distributed Manufacturing Applications: A Survey for Advanced Computing Technologies. (Research Reports ESPRIT: Vol. 1). 207p. 1995. 43.00 (*3-540-59060-9*) Spr-Verlag.
Consortium for Longitudinal Studies Staff. As the Twig Is Bent: Lasting Effects of Preschool Programs. 512p. (C). 1983. text 89.95 (*0-89859-271-2*) L Erlbaum Assocs.
Consortium for Mathematics & Its Applications. For All Practical Purposes: Introduction to Contemporary Mathematics. 2nd ed. LC 87-21453. (Illus.). 550p. (C). 1990. student ed. 9.60 (*0-7167-2181-3*) W H Freeman.
— For All Practical Purposes: Introduction to Contemporary Mathematics. 2nd ed. LC 87-21453. (Illus.). 550p. (C). 1990. trans. 40.00 (*0-7167-2182-1*) W H Freeman.
— For All Practical Purposes: Introduction to Contemporary Mathematics. 5th ed. LC 99-32012. 1999. pap. text 77.95 (*0-7167-3514-8*) W H Freeman.
Consortium for Research on Black Adolescence Staff & Bell-Scott, Patricia. Black Adolescence: Current Issues & Annotated Bibliography. 168p. 1990. 40.00 (*0-8161-9080-1*, Hall Reference) Macmillan.
Consortium for Spinal Cord Medicine Staff. Acute Management of Autonomic Disreflexia: Adults with Spinal Cord Injury Presenting to Health-Care Facilities. (Clinical Practice Guidelines Ser.). 18p. 1997. pap. write for info. (*0-929819-07-1*) Paralyzed Vets.

An Asterisk (*) at the beginning of an entry indicates that the title is appearing for the first time.

— Prevention of Thromboembolism in Spinal Cord Injury. unabridged ed. (Clinical Practice Guidelines Ser.). 18p. (Orig.). 1997. pap. write for info. (*0-614-30208-0*) Paralyzed Vets.

***Consortium for the Foundation of Mathematics Staff.** Mathematics in Action: An Introduction to Algebraic, Graphical & Trigonometric Problem Solving. LC 00-25664. (Illus.). 2000. write for info. (*0-201-66043-1*) Addison-Wesley.

Consortium for the Teaching of the Middle Ages Sta, jt. auth. see DeWindt, Edwin B.

Consortium for the Teaching of the Middle Ages Sta, jt. auth. see Nicholas.

Consortium of National Arts Education Associations. Setting the Record Straight: Give & Take on the National Standards for Arts Education. 12p. 1994. pap. 1.50 (*1-56545-065-5*, 1608) MENC.

Consortium on Revolutionary Europe Staff. The Consortium on Revolutionary Europe, 1750-1850: 1972 Proceedings. Kennett, Lee B. & Sturgill, Claude C., eds. LC 73-15970. 137p. reprint ed. pap. 42.50 (*0-8357-6724-8*, 203536200095) Bks Demand.

— The Consortium on Revolutionary Europe, 1750-1850: 1973 Proceedings. Sturgill, Claude C., ed. LC D 0913.C6. 206p. reprint ed. pap. 63.90 (*0-8357-6725-6*, 203536300095) Bks Demand.

— The Consortium on Revolutionary Europe, 1750-1850: 1974 Proceedings. Horward, Donald D. & Sturgill, Claude C., eds. LC D 0913.C6. 202p. reprint ed. pap. 62.70 (*0-8357-6729-9*, 203537000095) Bks Demand.

Constabel, Fred, jt. ed. see Fowke, Larry C.

Constable, Archibald, tr. see Bernier, Francois.

Constable, David. Beginner's Guide to Candlemaking. 64p. 1997. pap. 15.95 (*0-85532-832-0*, 8320, Pub. by Srch Pr) A Schwartz & Co.

— Candlemaking. (Illus.). 80p. (Orig.). (J). 1993. pap. 16.95 (*0-85532-683-2*, 683-2, Pub. by Srch Pr) A Schwartz & Co.

Constable, David, et al. Beeswax Craft. (Illus.). 80p. (Orig.). 1996. pap. 18.95 (*0-85532-816-9*, 169, Pub. by Srch Pr) A Schwartz & Co.

Constable, E. C. Metals & Ligard Reactivity: An Introduction to the Organic Chemistry of Metal Complexes. 308p. 1996. 150.00 (*3-527-29278-0*); pap. 74.95 (*3-527-29277-2*) Wiley.

Constable, E. C., jt. auth. see Gerloch, M.

***Constable, Edwin C.** Coordination Chemistry of Macrocyclic Compounds. LC 98-50107. 72. (Illus.). 96p. 1999. pap. text 12.95 (*0-19-855692-6*) OUP.

Constable, Frank C. The Curse of the Intellect. LC 79-8297. reprint ed. 44.50 (*0-404-61835-9*) AMS Pr.

Constable, Freda. John Constable: A Biography, 1776-1837. 152p. (C). 1988. 30.00 (*0-900963-54-9*, Pub. by T Dalton) St Mut.

Constable, Freda, et al, texts. John Constable, R. A. Eugene Delacroix, Peter Paul Reubens. (Illus.). 1989. pap. 75.00 (*1-58821-009-X*) Salander OReilly.

Constable, George. The XI, XII & XIII Olympiads: Berlin, 1936; St., Moritz, 1948. LC 96-10657. (Olympic Century Ser.: No. 11). (Illus.). 184p. 1996. write for info. (*1-888383-11-9*, Wrld Spt) Wld Sport Resch.

Constable, George, ed. see Russell, Francis.

Constable, George W. Gospel Postscripts: Tales of Encounters with Christ. (Illus.). 102p. (Orig.). 1990. pap. 9.75 (*0-911726-52-7*, GPB) Alleluia Pr.

***Constable, Giles.** Cluny from the 10th to the 12th Centuries: Further Studies. LC 99-42063. (Variorum Collected Studies: Vol. CS671). 320p. 2000. text 97.95 (*0-86078-815-6*, Pub. by Ashgate Pub) Ashgate Pub Co.

Constable, Giles. Culture & Spirituality in Medieval Europe. (Collected Studies: No. CS541). 330p. 1996. 98.95 (*0-86078-609-9*, Pub. by Variorum) Ashgate Pub Co.

— Medieval Monasticism: A Select Bibliography. LC 75-42284. (Toronto Medieval Bibliographies Ser.: No. 6). 196p. reprint ed. pap. 60.80 (*0-8357-4019-6*, 203670900005) Bks Demand.

— Monks, Hermits & Crusaders in Medieval Europe. (Collected Studies: No. CS273). 346p. (C). 1988. reprint ed. lib. bdg. 108.95 (*0-86078-221-2*, Pub. by Variorum) Ashgate Pub Co.

— The Reformation of the Twelfth Century. (Illus.). 427p. (C). 1998. reprint ed. pap. text 24.95 (*0-521-63871-2*) Cambridge U Pr.

— Three Studies in Medieval Religious & Social Thought: The Interpretation of Mary & Martha, the Ideal of the Imitation of Christ, the Orders of Society. (Illus.). 443p. (C). 1995. text 69.95 (*0-521-30515-2*) Cambridge U Pr.

— Three Studies in Medieval Religious & Social Thought: The Interpretation of Mary & Martha, the Ideal of the Imitation of Christ, the Orders of Society. (Illus.). 443p. (C). 1998. reprint ed. pap. text 24.95 (*0-521-63874-7*) Cambridge U Pr.

Constable, Giles, jt. auth. see Kazhdan, Alexander P.

Constable, Giles, jt. ed. see Benson, Robert L.

Constable, Giles, jt. ed. see Evergates, Theodore.

Constable, Giles, ed. see Peter The Venerable.

Constable, Hilary, et al, eds. Change in Classroom Practice. LC 93-37807. 168p. 1994. 85.00 (*0-7507-0198-6*, Falmer Pr); pap. 29.95 (*0-7507-0199-4*, Falmer Pr) Taylor & Francis.

Constable, Ian, jt. auth. see Lim, Arthur S.

Constable, Ian J. & Lim, Arthur S. Laser: Its Clinical Uses in Eye Diseases. 2nd ed. (Illus.). 207p. 1990. text 149.00 (*0-443-04450-3*) Church.

***Constable, John.** I. A. Richards: Selected Works, 1919-1938. (Illus.). 2000. 865.00 (*0-415-21731-8*) Routledge.

Constable, John. Shamanic Plays. (Oberon Bks.). 288p. 1997. pap. 18.95 (*1-870259-90-4*) Theatre Comm.

***Constable, John.** Southwark Mysteries. (Oberon Bks.). 2000. pap. text 22.95 (*1-84002-099-7*) Theatre Comm.

Constable, John, ed. Critical Essays on William Empson. (Critical Thoughts Ser.: Vol. 3). 567p. 1993. 69.95 (*0-85967-884-9*, Pub. by Scolar Pr) Ashgate Pub Co.

Constable, John, ed. see Richards, I. A.

Constable, Kate. Carolyn Quartermaine Revealed. LC 97-66474. (Illus.). 160p. 1997. 55.00 (*0-8478-2033-5*, Pub. by Rizzoli Intl) St Martin.

Constable, Liz, ed. Perennial Decay: On the Aesthetics & Politics of Decadence. LC 98-34373. (New Cultural Studies). (Illus.). 320p. 1998. 45.00 (*0-8122-3470-7*); pap. 19.95 (*0-8122-1678-4*) U of Pa Pr.

Constable, Marianne. The Law of the Other: The Mixed Jury & Changing Conceptions of Citizenship, Law, & Knowledge. LC 93-28838. (New Practices of Inquiry Ser.). 208p. 1993. pap. text 15.95 (*0-226-11498-8*) U Ch Pr.

— The Law of the Other: The Mixed Jury & Changing Conceptions of Citizenship, Law, & Knowledge. LC 93-28838. (New Practices of Inquiry Ser.). 208p. 1994. lib. bdg. 38.00 (*0-226-11496-1*) U Ch Pr.

Constable, Marianne, ed. see Sarat, Austin.

Constable, N. Ancient Ireland. 144p. 1997. 14.98 (*0-7858-0689-X*) Bk Sales Inc.

***Constable, Nick.** The History of Archaeology. (Illus.). 192p. 2000. 35.00 (*1-58574-091-8*) Lyons Pr.

Constable, Nick. St. Patrick's Day: A Celebration. (Illus.). 144p. 1998. 14.99 (*0-7858-0950-3*) Bk Sales Inc.

Constable, Nick & Constantino, Maria. Worlds Biggest Buildings. LC 98-36376. (Illus.). 104p. 1998. 14.99 (*1-57145-164-1*, Thunder Bay) Advantage Pubs.

Constable, Nicole. Christian Souls & Chinese Spirits: A Hakka Community in Hong Kong. LC 93-24006. 274p. 1994. 48.00 (*0-520-08384-9*, Pub. by U CA Pr) Cal Prin Full Svc.

— Maid to Order in Hong Kong: Stories of Filipina Workers. LC 96-48241. (Illus.). 256p. 1996. text 39.95 (*0-8014-3331-2*); pap. text 16.95 (*0-8014-8382-4*) Cornell U Pr.

Constable, Nicole, ed. Guest People: Hakka Identity in China & Abroad. LC 95-17857. (Studies on Ethnic Groups in China). (Illus.). 280p. 1996. 35.00 (*0-295-97469-9*) U of Wash Pr.

Constable, Olivia R. Trade & Traders in Muslim Spain: The Commercial Realignment of the Iberian Peninsula, 900-1500. (Cambridge Studies in Medieval Life & Thought: No. 24). (Illus.). 348p. 1996. pap. text 22.95 (*0-521-56503-0*) Cambridge U Pr.

Constable, Olivia R., ed. Medieval Iberia: Readings from Christian, Muslim, & Jewish Sources. (Middle Ages Ser.). 448p. 1997. text 49.95 (*0-8122-3333-6*) U of Pa Pr.

— Medieval Iberia: Readings from Christian, Muslim, & Jewish Sources. LC 97-4097. (Middle Ages Ser.). 448p. 1997. pap. text 26.50 (*0-8122-1569-9*) U of Pa Pr.

Constable, Pamela & Valenzuela, Arturo. A Nation of Enemies: Chile under Pinochet. 368p. 1993. pap. 15.95 (*0-393-30985-1*) Norton.

Constable, Randi E. Novell's ManageWise Administrator's Handbook: Networks with Management. LC 96-80451. 300p. 1997. pap. 29.99 (*1-56884-817-X*) IDG Bks.

Constable, Robert. Prerogativa Regis: Tertia Lectura Roberti Constable De Lyncolnis Inne. Thorne, Samuel E., ed. 1949. 79.50 (*0-685-69876-9*) Elliots Bks.

Constable, Robert & Mehta, Vera, eds. Social Work Education in Eastern Europe: Changing Horizons. LC 93-43668. 136p. 1994. pap. text 30.00 (*0-925065-10-2*) Lyceum IL.

Constable, Robert L., et al. An Introduction to the Pl-CV2 Programming Logic. (Lecture Notes in Computer Science Ser.: Vol. 135). 292p. 1982. 30.00 (*0-387-11492-0*) Spr-Verlag.

Constable, Robert T., et al. School Social Work: Practice, Policy, & Research Perspectives. 4th ed. LC 98-26474. 1998. 46.95 (*0-925065-50-1*) Lyceum IL.

Constable, Robin, jt. auth. see Clapham, Adam.

Constable, Thomas. Archibald Constable & His Literary Correspondents, 3 vols., Set. LC 70-148766. reprint ed. 210.00 (*0-404-07640-8*) AMS Pr.

Constable, Trevor J. The Cosmic Pulse of Life: The Revolutionary Biological Power Behind UFOs. rev. ed. LC 90-60345. (Illus.). 504p. 1990. pap. 24.95 (*0-945685-07-6*) Borderland Sciences.

— Loom of the Future: Weather Engineering. 18.95 (*0-945685-19-X*) Borderland Sciences.

Constable, Trevor J., jt. auth. see Toliver, Raymond F.

Constable, W. G. The Painter's Workshop. (Illus.). 148p. 1979. reprint ed. pap. 6.95 (*0-486-23836-9*) Dover.

Constain. Amplificadores Realimentados. 672p. (C). 1994. text 38.33 (*0-201-62921-6*) Addison-Wesley.

Constales, D., jt. auth. see Brackx, F.

Constalie, Rand & Steen, Johan B. A Breed Apart. (Illus.). 216p. (Orig.). 1987. pap. 12.95 (*0-9618900-0-2*) Sira Pub.

Constance. Early History of Israel Study Guide, Bk. 1. 100p. 1988. pap., student ed. 12.99 (*1-889015-41-5*) Explrs Bible.

— Early History of Israel Study Guide, Bk. 2. 104p. 1988. pap., student ed. 12.99 (*1-889015-42-3*) Explrs Bible.

— Early History of Israel Study Guide, Bk. 3. 86p. 1988. pap., student ed. 12.99 (*1-889015-43-1*) Explrs Bible.

— Genesis Study Guide, Bk. 1. 82p. 1988. pap., student ed. 12.99 (*1-889015-38-5*) Explrs Bible.

— Genesis Study Guide, Bk. 2. 85p. 1988. pap., student ed. 12.99 (*1-889015-39-3*) Explrs Bible.

— Genesis Study Guide, Bk. 3. 80p. 1988. pap., student ed. 12.99 (*1-889015-40-7*) Explrs Bible.

— The Gospel of John Study Guide, Bk. 1. 83p. 1988. pap., student ed. 12.99 (*1-889015-53-9*) Explrs Bible.

— The Gospel of John Study Guide, Bk. 2. 100p. 1988. pap., student ed. 12.99 (*1-889015-54-7*) Explrs Bible.

— The Gospel of John Study Guide, Bk. 3. 88p. 1988. pap., student ed. 12.99 (*1-889015-55-5*) Explrs Bible.

— The Gospel of Matthew Study Guide, Bk. 1. 98p. 1997. pap., student ed. 12.99 (*1-889015-56-3*) Explrs Bible.

— The Gospel of Matthew Study Guide, Bk. 2. 91p. 1997. pap., student ed. 12.99 (*1-889015-57-1*) Explrs Bible.

— The Gospel of Matthew Study Guide, Bk. 3. 92p. 1997. pap., student ed. 12.99 (*1-889015-58-X*) Explrs Bible.

— Isaiah Study Guide, Bk. 1. 96p. 1988. pap., student ed. 12.99 (*1-889015-62-8*) Explrs Bible.

— Isaiah Study Guide, Bk. 2. 102p. 1988. pap., student ed. 12.99 (*1-889015-63-6*) Explrs Bible.

— Isaiah Study Guide, Bk. 3. 93p. 1988. pap., student ed. 12.99 (*1-889015-64-4*) Explrs Bible.

— Jeremiah Study Guide, Bk. 1. 102p. 1995. pap., student ed. 12.99 (*1-889015-59-8*) Explrs Bible.

— Jeremiah Study Guide, Bk. 2. 86p. 1995. pap., student ed. 12.99 (*1-889015-60-1*) Explrs Bible.

— Jeremiah Study Guide, Bk. 3. 78p. 1995. pap., student ed. 12.99 (*1-889015-61-X*) Explrs Bible.

— Job, Psalms & Proverbs Study Guide, Bk. 1. 120p. 1990. pap., student ed. 12.99 (*1-889015-65-2*) Explrs Bible.

— Job, Psalms & Proverbs Study Guide, Bk. 2. 116p. 1990. pap., student ed. 12.99 (*1-889015-66-0*) Explrs Bible.

— Job, Psalms & Proverbs Study Guide, Bk. 3. 124p. 1990. pap., student ed. 12.99 (*1-889015-67-9*) Explrs Bible.

— Later History of Israel Study Guide, Bk. 1. 102p. 1988. pap., student ed. 12.99 (*1-889015-44-X*) Explrs Bible.

— Later History of Israel Study Guide, Bk. 2. 108p. 1988. pap., student ed. 12.99 (*1-889015-45-8*) Explrs Bible.

— Later History of Israel Study Guide, Bk. 3. 108p. 1988. pap., student ed. 12.99 (*1-889015-46-6*) Explrs Bible.

— Luke & Acts Study Guide, Bk. 1. 97p. 1988. pap., student ed. 12.99 (*1-889015-47-4*) Explrs Bible.

— Luke & Acts Study Guide, Bk. 2. 89p. 1988. pap., student ed. 12.99 (*1-889015-48-2*) Explrs Bible.

— Luke & Acts Study Guide, Bk. 3. 92p. 1988. pap., student ed. 12.99 (*1-889015-49-0*) Explrs Bible.

— New Testament Epistles Study Guide, Bk. 1. 86p. 1988. pap., student ed. 12.99 (*1-889015-50-4*) Explrs Bible.

— New Testament Epistles Study Guide, Bk. 2. 95p. 1988. pap., student ed. 12.99 (*1-889015-51-2*) Explrs Bible.

— New Testament Epistles Study Guide, Bk. 3. 130p. 1988. pap., student ed. 12.99 (*1-889015-52-0*) Explrs Bible.

***Constance, A.** The Ride of Man: A Quest for Man's Beginning & His Ultimate Destinity. Brown, Fiona, ed. 300p. 1999. pap. 19.95 (*1-930024-07-X*, Pub. by Serpent Bks) Bookpeople.

Constance Anderson. Robin Hood: The Truth Behind the Green Tights: A Play. LC 85-143478. ii, 74 p. 1984. 0.00 (*0-573-11381-5*) S French Trade.

Constance Anderson, et al. Lifekeys Discovery Workbook. 32p. 1998. pap. 6.99 (*0-7642-2081-0*, 212081) Bethany Hse.

Constance, Anita. Advent Thirst...Christmas Hope: Prayer & Meditation for the Journey. LC 94-16328. 88p. 1994. pap. 4.95 (*0-8091-3511-6*) Paulist Pr.

Constance, Anita M. Night Vision: Praying Through Change. LC 98-5152. 96p. 1998. pap. 11.95 (*0-8091-3783-6*) Paulist Pr.

— A Time to Turn . . . The Paschal Experience. LC 95-35390. 96p. (Orig.). 1996. pap. 5.95 (*0-8091-3613-9*) Paulist Pr.

Constance, Anita M., ed. Living the Days of Lent 2000. 54p. 2000. pap. 3.95 (*0-8091-3917-0*) Paulist Pr.

Constance, Diana. Introduction to Drawing & Painting with Pastels. 1990. 12.98 (*1-55521-567-X*) Bk Sales Inc.

Constance, Douglas, jt. auth. see Bonanno, Alessandro.

Constance, Harry & Fuerst, Randall. Good to Go: The Life & Times of a Decorated Member of the U. S. Navy's Elite SEAL Team Two. LC 97-303. 388p. 1997. 24.00 (*0-688-15249-X*, Wm Morrow) Morrow Avon.

— Good to Go Vol. 2: The Life & Times of a Decorated Member of the U. S. Navy's Elite SEAL Team. 432p. 1998. mass mkt. 6.99 (*0-380-72966-0*, Avon Bks) Morrow Avon.

Constance, John. Controlling In-Plant Airborne Contaminants. (Mechanical Engineering Ser.: Vol. 21). (Illus.). 368p. 1983. text 145.00 (*0-8247-1900-X*) Dekker.

***Constance, John D.** Mechanical Engineering License Review: For the Professional P. E. Exam. 5th ed. (Illus.). 630p. 1999. pap. 59.50 (*1-57645-022-8*, 228) Engineering.

Constance, L., jt. auth. see Mathias, M. E.

Constance, Lincoln, jt. auth. see Mukherjee, P. K.

Constance, Nellie E., ed. see Constance, Tom M.

Constance, Nellie E., ed. see McKenzie, Marni S.

Constance, Nellie E., ed. see Russell, Patricia C.

Constance, Tom M. Bible Quest: Genesis. Eades, Lois B. & Constance, Nellie E., eds. 215p. (Orig.). (YA). (gr. 7-12). 1996. pap. 18.95 (*1-889015-06-7*) Explrs Bible.

Constance, Tom M., ed. see Bridges, Nancy S.

***Constanda, C.** Direct & Indirect Boundary Integral Equation Methods LC 99-41796. (Monographs & Surveys in Pure & Applied Mathematics). 216p. 1999. boxed set 69.95 (*0-8493-0639-6*, Chap & Hall CRC) CRC Pr.

Constanda, C. Integral Methods in Science & Engineering. 1994. pap. 64.95 (*0-582-23921-4*, Pub. by Addison-Wesley) Longman.

— Integral Methods in Science & Engineering. 1994. write for info. (*0-318-72599-1*) Longman.

Constanda, C., jt. auth. see Chudinovich, Igor.

Constanda, C., tr. see Shubin, M. A., ed.

Constandse, William. Dewi. 168p. 1983. pap. 6.95 (*0-317-01757-8*) Utama Pubns Inc.

— Inside Indonesia. 128p. (Orig.). 1983. pap. 6.95 (*0-911527-00-1*) Utama Pubns Inc.

— A Tribute to the Women of Santa Fe. 149p. (Orig.). 1983. pap. 6.95 (*0-911527-01-X*) Utama Pubns Inc.

— Why I Became a Buddhist. 130p. (Orig.). (C). 1985. pap. 6.95 (*0-911527-02-8*) Utama Pubns Inc.

Constanduros, Denis. My Grandfather. (Illus.). 136p. 1989. pap. 8.95 (*0-563-20864-3*, Pub. by BBC) Parkwest Pubns.

— My Grandfather. large type ed. (Illus.). 112p. 1991. 19.95 (*1-85089-471-X*, Pub. by ISIS Lrg Prnt) Transaction Pubs.

***Constans, Gabriel.** The Goddess of Cancer & Other Plays. 130p. 2000. pap. 12.95 (*1-883938-44-9*) Dry Bones Pr.

Constans, Gabriel. Great American Smoothies: The Ultimate Blending Guide for Shakes, Slushes, Desserts & Thirst Quenchers. LC 97-7712. 160p. 1997. pap. 9.95 (*0-89529-784-1*, Avery) Penguin Putnam.

— Just a Heartbeat Away: When a Mother Dies of AIDS. 1996. 5.95 (*1-56123-088-X*) Centering Corp.

Constant. Materials Processing: A Multimedia Approach. (General Engineering Ser.). (C). 1909. pap. 50.00 (*0-534-95111-2*) PWS Pubs.

Constant, A. Escape to Hong Kong. (J). (gr. 7). 4.99 (*1-85792-063-5*, Pub. by Christian Focus) Spring Arbor Dist.

***Constant, Alan.** Close-Up Photography. LC 99-30127. 152p. 2000. pap. text 32.95 (*0-240-80380-9*, Focal) Buttrwrth-Heinemann.

Constant, Alberta W. Does Anyone Care about Lou Emma Miller? LC 78-4774. 256p. (J). (gr. 5-8). 1979. 11.95 (*0-690-01335-3*) HarpC Child Bks.

Constant, Benjamin. Adolphe. (FRE.). 1973. pap. 10.95 (*0-685-73250-9*, F59309) Fr & Eur.

— Adolphe. (FRE.). 282p. 1988. pap. 11.95 (*0-7859-2190-7*, 2253045888) Fr & Eur.

— Adolphe. Tancock, Leonard W., tr. (Classics Ser.). 128p. 1980. pap. 11.95 (*0-14-044134-4*, Penguin Classics) Viking Penguin.

— Adolphe. unabridged ed. (FRE.). Date not set. reprint ed. pap. 6.95 (*2-87714-346-5*, Pub. by Bookking Intl) Distribks Inc.

— Adolphe & the Red Notebook. large type ed. LC 99-12183. 240p. 1999. 24.95 (*1-56000-491-6*) Transaction Pubs.

— Adolphe, Le Cahier Rouge, Cecile. (Folio Ser.: No. 514). (FRE.). pap. 9.95 (*2-07-036514-X*) Schoenhof.

— De l'Esprit de Conquete. (FRE.). 72p. 1980. pap. 16.95 (*0-7859-4585-7*) Fr & Eur.

— Political Writings. Fontana, Biancamaria, ed. (Cambridge Texts in the History of Political Thought Ser.). 368p. 1988. pap. text 19.95 (*0-521-31632-4*) Cambridge U Pr.

***Constant, Caroline.** Elleen Gray. (Illus.). 2000. 59.95 (*0-7148-3905-1*) Phaidon Pr.

Constant, Caroline. The Palladio Guide. 2nd rev. ed. LC 93-23987. (Illus.). 160p. 1998. pap. 19.95 (*1-878271-85-7*) Princeton Arch.

Constant, Christine & Ogden, Steve. The Potter's Palette: A Practical Guide to Creating over 700 Illustrated Glazes & Slip Covers. LC 96-142140. (Illus.). 80p. 1996. pap. 19.95 (*0-8019-8753-9*) Krause Pubns.

Constant de Rebecque, Henri B. Cours de Politique Constitutionnelle, 2 vols., Set. Mayer, J. P., ed. LC 78-67347. (European Political Thought Ser.). (FRE.). 1979. reprint ed. lib. bdg. 88.95 (*0-405-11686-1*) Ayer.

Constant, D'Estaurnelles De, see De Constant, D'Estaurnelles.

Constant, Edward W. The Origins of the Turbojet Revolution. fac. ed. LC 80-11802. (Johns Hopkins Studies in the History of Technology; New Ser.: No. 5). (Illus.). 327p. 1980. pap. 101.40 (*0-7837-7636-5*, 204738900007) Bks Demand.

Constant, F. Woodbridge. Theoretical Physics: Mechanics of Particles, Rigid & Elastic Bodies & Heat Flow. LC 78-14353. 296p. 1979. reprint ed. lib. bdg. 18.50 (*0-88275-738-5*) Krieger.

Constant, Gustave L. The Reformation in England. Scantlebury, R. E., tr. LC 83-45576. reprint ed. 85.00 (*0-404-19895-3*) AMS Pr.

Constant, Jacques G. Amsterdam: Portrait of an Exceptional City. 1998. pap. 15.00 (*1-873329-29-6*, Pub. by Sheldrake Pr) Interlink Pub.

Constant, James. Gravitational Action. 114p. (Orig.). 1978. 14.95 (*0-914330-16-0*) RCS Assocs.

— Uncertainty & Relativity of Knowledge & Survival. 300p. (Orig.). 1996. pap. 29.95 (*0-930293-01-0*) RCS Assocs.

Constant, James N. Fundamentals of Strategic Weapons. 940p. 1981. 140.00 (*90-286-0129-5*) Kluwer Academic.

— Fundamentals of Strategic Weapons, 2 Vols. 1981. lib. bdg. 481.00 (*90-247-2545-3*) Kluwer Academic.

— Uncertainty of Law & Constitutional Government. limited ed. 260p. (Orig.). 1993. pap. 29.95 (*0-930293-00-2*) RCS Assocs.

Constant, Jan. MacKenzie's Woman. large type ed. LC 93-14408. 269p. 1993. lib. bdg. 15.95 (*0-8161-5842-8*, G K Hall Lrg Type) Mac Lib Ref.

— Master of Craigraven. large type ed. LC 93-34649. 230p. 1994. lib. bdg. 16.95 (*0-8161-5844-4*, G K Hall Lrg Type) Mac Lib Ref.

Constant, Jules. Bedside Cardiology. 4th ed. LC 93-20239. 384p. 1993. text 65.00 (*0-316-15385-0*) Lppncott W & W.

— Essentials of Bedside Cardiology: For Students & House Staff. 304p. 1989. pap. text 20.00 (*0-316-15337-0*); pap. text 20.00 (*0-316-15338-9*) Lppncott W & W.

— Essentials of Bedside Cardiology for Students & House Staff. 304p. 1989. pap. text 44.95 (*0-316-15335-4*) Lppncott W & W.

— Essentials of Learning Electrocardiography: A Complete Course for the Non-Cardiologist. 4th ed. LC 97-5800. (Illus.). 232p. 1997. pap. 34.95 (*1-85070-921-1*) Prthnon Pub.

Constant, Jules, ed. Learning Echocardiography. 3rd ed. 648p. (C). text 45.00 (*0-317-53596-X*, Little Brwn Med Div) Lppncott W & W.

Constant, Mews & Flint, Valerie I. Authors of the Middle Ages Vol. II, Nos. 5-6: Historical & Religious Writers of the Latin West. Geary, Patrick J., ed. 192p. 1995. 63.95 (*0-86078-488-6*, Pub. by Variorum) Ashgate Pub Co.

Constant, Nancy, jt. auth. see Offenburger, Jeffrey.

Constant, Nicholas J. Improved Recovery. LC 83-62119. (Oil & Gas Production Ser.). (Illus.). 123p. (Orig.). 1983. pap. text 15.00 (*0-88698-044-5*, 3.30810) PETEX.

Constant, Paule. Balta. (FRE.). 292p. 1986. pap. 11.95 (*0-7859-2053-6*, 2070377830) Fr & Eur.

— The Governor's Daughter. Wing, Betsy, tr. from FRE. LC 97-18926. (European Women Writers Ser.).Tr. of La Fille du Gobernator. xv, 152p. 1998. pap. 15.00 (*0-8032-6385-6*) U of Nebr Pr.

— The Governor's Daughter (La Fille du Gobernator) Wing, Betsy, tr. from FRE. LC 97-18926. (European Women Writers Ser.).Tr. of La Fille du Gobernator. xv, 152p. 1998. text 40.00 (*0-8032-1478-2*) U of Nebr Pr.

— Ouregano. (FRE.). 256p. 1985. pap. 11.95 (*0-7859-2006-4*, 2070376230) Fr & Eur.

— Propriete Privee. (FRE.). 248p. 1989. pap. 11.95 (*0-7859-2130-3*, 2070382036) Fr & Eur.

Constant, Pierre. Galapagos: Darwin's Islands of Evolution. LC 94-80161. (Latin American Guides Ser.). (Illus.). 300p. 1995. pap. 19.95 (*0-8442-8951-5*, Passprt Bks) NTC Contemp Pub Co.

— The Galapagos Islands. 2nd ed. (Illus.). 300p. 1997. pap. 19.95 (*0-8442-4755-3*, Passprt Bks) NTC Contemp Pub Co.

Constant, Pierre. Galapagos Islands. 4th ed. pap. 23.95 (*962-217-653-4*) China Guides.

Constant, Pierre. Galapagos Islands: A Natural History Guide. 3rd ed. LC 98-52795. 1999. pap. 19.95 (*962-217-580-5*) Norton.

Constantaras, Kalliope. Stillness: Poems. (ENG & GRE.). 83p. (Orig.). 1995. pap. 8.00 (*0-9652259-0-9*) Kalliope Constantaras.

Constante, Lena. The Silent Escape: Three Thousand Days in Romanian Prisons. Philip, Franklin, tr. from FRE. LC 94-10627. (Society & Culture in East Central Europe Ser.: No. 9).Tr. of Evasion Silencieuse. 257p. 1995. 27.50 (*0-520-08209-5*, Pub. by U CA Pr) Cal Prin Full Svc.

Constantelos, Demetria J. Understanding the Greek Orthodox Church Its Faith, History & Life. 3rd ed. LC 97-45878. 291p. 1998. pap. 14.95 (*0-917653-50-5*, Pub. by Hellenic Coll Pr) BookWorld.

Constantelos, Demetrios J. Byzantine Philanthropy & Social Welfare, Vol. I. 2nd enl. rev. ed. (Studies in the Social & Religious History of the Mediaeval Greek World). (Illus.). xviii, 282p. (C). 1991. lib. bdg. 60.00 (*0-89241-402-2*) Caratzas.

— Christian Hellenism: Essays & Studies in Continuity & Change. (Hellenism Ser.: Vol. 13). xii, 302p. 1999. pap. 30.00 (*0-89241-588-6*) Caratzas.

— Christian Hellenism: Essays & Studies in Continuity & Change. LC 95-52590. (Hellenism Ser.: Vol. 13). xii, 302p. (C). 1999. 50.00 (*0-89241-523-1*) Caratzas.

— The Greeks: Their Heritage & Its Value Today. LC 96-21691. (Illus.). 65p. (Orig.). 1996. pap. 4.95 (*0-917653-47-5*, Pub. by Hellenic Coll Pr) BookWorld.

— Marriage, Sexuality & Celibacy: A Greek Orthodox Perspective. 1975. pap. 8.95 (*0-937032-15-8*) Light&Life Pub Co MN.

— Poverty, Society & Philanthropy in the Late Mediaeval Greek World. (Studies in the Social & Religious History of the Mediaeval Greek World: Vol. II). 190p. (C). 1992. lib. bdg. 60.00 (*0-89241-401-4*) Caratzas.

— Studies in the Social & Religious History of the Medieval Greek World, 3 vols., Set. Date not set. 165.00 (*0-89241-511-8*) Caratzas.

Constantelos, Demetrios J., ed. Issues & Dialogues: In the Orthodox Church since World War II. 90p. (Orig.). 1986. pap. 5.00 (*0-917651-27-8*, Pub. by Holy Cross Orthodox) BookWorld.

Constantelos, Demetrios J., intro. Orthodox Theology & Diakonia: Trends & Prospects. 398p. (C). 1981. 17.95 (*0-916586-79-0*, Pub. by Hellenic Coll Pr) BookWorld.

Constantelos, Demetrios J., jt. auth. see Iakovos.

Constanten, Tom. Between Rock & Hard Places: A Musical Autobiodyssey. 256p. (Orig.). 1992. pap. 17.00 (*0-938493-16-7*) Hulogosi Inc.

Constanti, Andrew, et al. Basic Endocrinology for Students of Pharmacy & Allied Health Sciences. 156p. 1998. text 49.00 (*90-5702-250-8*, Harwood Acad Pubs); pap. text 15.00 (*90-5702-251-6*, Harwood Acad Pubs) Gordon & Breach.

Constantian, Mark B., ed. Pressure Ulcers: Principles & Techniques of Management. 320p. 1980. text 50.00 (*0-316-15330-3*, Little Brwn Med Div) Lppncott W & W.

***Constantian, Mark B. & Hammersley, Richard.** The Original Homeowner's Remodeling Price Guide. 43p. 1998. pap. 15.00 (*0-9676899-0-2*) Beacon Data Serv.

Constantin, Gheorghe & Istratescu, Ioana. Elements of Probabilistic Analysis with Applications. (C). 1989. text 341.00 (*90-277-2838-0*) Kluwer Academic.

Constantin, James A. Understanding Resource Management: How to Deploy Your People, Products, & Processing. 264p. 1994. text 35.00 (*0-7863-0360-3*, Irwn Prfssnl) McGraw-Hill Prof.

Constantin, James A. & Lusch, Robert F. Understanding Resource Management: How to Deploy Your People, Products, & Processes for Maximum Productivity. 1994. write for info. (*0-318-72930-X*, Irwn Prfssnl) McGraw-Hill Prof.

Constantin, P. S., et al. Attractors Representing Turbulent Flows. LC 84-24623. (Memoirs of the AMS Ser. No. 314: No. 53/314). 67p. 1988. reprint ed. pap. 18.00 (*0-8218-2315-9*, MEMO/53/314) Am Math.

Constantin, Peter & Foias, Ciprian. Navier-Strokes Equations. (Chicago Lectures in Mathematics). 200p. 1988. pap. text 18.00 (*0-226-11549-6*) U Ch Pr.

— Navier-Strokes Equations. (Chicago Lectures in Mathematics). 200p. 1996. lib. bdg. 42.00 (*0-226-11548-8*) U Ch Pr.

***Constantine.** Kiquito & the Coati. 40p. (J). (gr. k-3). 2001. 15.95 (*0-06-028309-2*) HarpC Child Bks.

— Kiquoti & the Coati. 40p. (J). (gr. k-3). 2001. pap. 5.95 (*0-06-443552-0*) HarpC Child Bks.

***Constantine.** Kiquoti & the Coati. 40p. (J). (gr. k-3). 2001. lib. bdg. 15.89 (*0-06-028310-6*) HarpC Child Bks.

Constantine & Hobbs. Know Your Woods. 1975. text 23.92 (*0-02-664790-7*) Glencoe.

Constantine, Albert J., Jr. Know Your Woods: A Complete Guide to Trees, Woods, & Veneers. 2nd rev. ed. 360p. 1987. pap. 14.00 (*0-684-18778-7*, Scribners Ref) Mac Lib Ref.

***Constantine, Alex.** The Covert War Against Rock: What You Don't Know about the Deaths of Jim Morrison, Tupac Shakur, Michael Hutchence, Brian Jones, Jimi Hendrix, Phil Ochs, Bob Marley, Peter Tosh, John Lennon, the Notorious B. I. G. 260p. 2000. pap. 14.95 (*0-922915-61-X*, Pub. by Feral Hse) Publishers Group.

Constantine, Alex. Psychic Dictatorship in the U. S. A. 221p. 1995. pap. 12.95 (*0-922915-28-8*) Feral Hse.

— Virtual Government: CIA Mind Control Operations in America. LC 98-168791. (Illus.). 284p. 1997. pap. 14.95 (*0-922915-45-8*) Feral Hse.

Constantine, Archimandrite. Antichrist, Orthodoxy or Heterodoxy. 1980. pap. 0.25 (*0-89981-007-1*) Eastern Orthodox.

— Ecumenism, Communism & Apostasy: The Spiritual State of the Contemporary World. 19p. (Orig.). 1985. pap. 1.50 (*0-912927-15-1*, X015) St John Kronstadt.

— A Spiritual Portrait of St. John of Kronstadt. (Illus.). 94p. (Orig.). 1982. pap. 6.00 (*0-912927-02-X*, X002) St John Kronstadt.

Constantine, Brad. Fraud Prevention/Detection Kit (Manual), Vol. 1. (Illus.). 180p. (C). 1996. ring bd. 99.95 (*1-877858-82-X*, FPDK) Amer Focus Pub.

***Constantine, Brendan & Buck, Janet.** Maytag Heights. unabridged ed. Armstrong, R. D., ed. (Little Red Books Ser.). 56p. 1999. pap. 5.00 (*1-929878-15-X*) Lummox.

***Constantine, Crissa.** Banished from the Homeland. LC 99-65235. 192p. 2000. pap. 12.95 (*1-58501-019-7*, Pub. by CeShore Pubg) Natl Bk Netwk.

Constantine, David. Davies. 1985. 19.95 (*0-906427-91-6*, Pub. by Bloodaxe Bks) Dufour.

— Holderlin. (Illus.). 422p. 1988. text 95.00 (*0-19-815788-6*) OUP.

— Madder. LC 87-73052. 80p. (Orig.). 1988. pap. 11.95 (*1-85224-039-3*, Pub. by Bloodaxe Bks) Dufour.

— The Pelt of Wasps. 96p. 1998. pap. 15.95 (*1-85224-428-3*, Pub. by Bloodaxe Bks) Dufour.

— Selected Poems. 160p. (Orig.). 1992. pap. 18.95 (*1-85224-166-7*, Pub. by Bloodaxe Bks) Dufour.

Constantine, David, ed. German Short Stories 2. 288p. 1976. pap. 11.95 (*0-14-004119-2*, Penguin Bks) Viking Penguin.

Constantine, David, et al. Caspar Hauser: A Poem in Nine Cantos. 96p. 1995. pap. 14.95 (*1-85224-299-X*, Pub. by Bloodaxe Bks) Dufour.

Constantine, David, ed. see Von Kleist, Heinrich.

Constantine, David, tr. see Holderlin, Friedrich.

Constantine, David, tr. see Jaccottet, Philippe.

Constantine, David, tr. see Michaux, Henri.

Constantine, David, tr. & intro. see Goethe, Johann Wolfgang Von.

***Constantine, George H.** Tyler's Tips: The Shopper's Guide for Herbal Remedies. LC 00-39706. 132p. 2000. pap. 14.95 (*0-7890-0949-8*, Haworth Herbal Pr); lib. bdg. 39.95 (*0-7890-0948-X*, Haworth Herbal Pr) Haworth Pr.

Constantine, Helen. Plant Communities of the Mono Basin. (Mono Lake Committee Field Guide Ser.). (Illus.). 50p. 1993. pap. text 3.95 (*0-939716-04-6*) Mono Lake Comm.

Constantine, Helen, tr. see Michaux, Henri.

Constantine I. A Treatise of the Donation of Gyfts & Endowment of Possessyons Gyven & Graunted Unto Sylvester Pope of Rome by Constantyne Emperour of Rome. Marshall, William, tr. LC 79-84096. (English Experience Ser.: No. 916). 152p. 1979. reprint ed. lib. bdg. 35.00 (*90-221-0916-X*) Walter J Johnson.

Constantine, J. Robert, ed. Gentle Rebel: Letters of Eugene V. Debs. LC 93-48601. (Illus.). 360p. 1994. 15.95 (*0-252-06324-4*); text 34.95 (*0-252-02018-9*) U of Ill Pr.

Constantine, J. Robert, ed. see Debs, Eugene V.

Constantine, K. C. Always a Body to Trade: A Mario Balzic Mystery. 248p. 1993. reprint ed. pap. 5.95 (*0-87923-952-2*) Godine.

— Blood Mud. LC 98-34909. 375p. 1999. 23.00 (*0-89296-647-5*, Pub. by Mysterious Pr) Little.

— Blood Mud. LC 99-30875. 1999. 27.95 (*0-7862-2031-7*) Thorndike Pr.

***Constantine, K. C.** Blood Mud. 384p. 2000. mass mkt. 13.95 (*0-446-67640-3*, Mysterious Paperbk) Warner Bks.

Constantine, K. C. Bottom Liner Blues. 256p. 1993. 18.95 (*0-89296-289-5*) Mysterious Pr.

— Bottom Liner Blues. 272p. 1994. mass mkt. 5.99 (*0-446-40372-5*, Pub. by Warner Bks) Little.

— Brushback. LC 97-10130. 288p. 1998. 21.50 (*0-89296-646-7*, Pub. by Mysterious Pr) Little.

— Brushback. 1999. mass mkt. write for info. (*0-446-60675-8*) Warner Bks.

— Cranks & Shadows. 320p. 1995. 19.45 (*0-89296-543-6*, Pub. by Mysterious Pr) Little.

— Family Values. 1997. 22.00 (*0-614-27891-0*) Mysterious Pr.

— Family Values. 1998. mass mkt. write for info. (*0-446-40355-5*, Mysterious Paperbk) Warner Bks.

— Family Values. large type ed. 256p. 1998. mass mkt. 5.99 (*0-446-60594-8*, Pub. by Warner Bks) Little.

— Good Sons. 304p. 1997. mass mkt. 5.99 (*0-446-40354-7*, Pub. by Warner Bks) Little.

***Constantine, K. C.** Grievance. LC 99-41380. 279p. 2000. 23.95 (*0-89296-648-3*, Pub. by Mysterious Pr) Little.

Constantine, K. C. Joey's Case. 224p. 1989. mass mkt. 4.50 (*0-445-40786-7*, Pub. by Warner Bks) Little.

— Joey's Case: A Mario Balzic Novel. 1988. 15.45 (*0-89296-347-6*, Pub. by Mysterious Pr) Little.

Constantine, K. C. The Man Who Liked Slow Tomatoes. (Mario Balzic Detective Novel Ser.). 192p. 1993. pap. 5.95 (*0-87923-953-0*) Godine.

Constantine, Larry, jt. auth. see Swonger, Alvin K.

Constantine, Larry, jt. ed. see Ambler, Scott.

Constantine, Larry L. Constantine on Peopleware: Practical Insights into the Human Side of Software Development. 219p. (C). 1995. pap. text 19.95 (*0-13-331976-8*) P-H.

Constantine, Larry L. & Lockwood, Lucy A.D. Software Use: A Practical Guide to the Models & Methods of Usage-Centered Design. LC 98-46573. (ACM Press Ser.). 608p. (C). 1999. 44.95 (*0-201-92478-1*) Addison-Wesley.

Constantine, Larry L., jt. auth. see Yourdon, Edward.

Constantine, Mildred. Tina Modotti: A Fragile Life. LC 93-1154. (Illus.). 200p. 1993. pap. 18.95 (*0-8118-0502-6*) Chronicle Bks.

— Tina Modotti: Una Vida Fragil (A Fragile Life) (SPA., Illus.). 247p. 1996. pap. 46.99 (*968-16-4833-1*, Pub. by Fondo) Continental Bk.

— Whole Cloth. LC 97-28737. 1997. 60.00 (*1-885254-75-X*, Pub. by Monacelli Pr) Penguin Putnam.

Constantine, Mildred & Reuter, Laurel J. Frontiers in Fiber: The Americans. (Illus.). 106p. (Orig.). 1988. pap. 18.00 (*0-943107-01-6*) ND Mus Art.

Constantine, Mildred, jt. ed. see Selz, Peter H.

Constantine, Murray. The Devil, Poor Devil: A Novel. Reginald, R. & Melville, Douglas, eds. LC 77-84214. (Lost Race & Adult Fantasy Ser.). 1978. reprint ed. lib. bdg. 24.95 (*0-405-10969-5*) Ayer.

Constantine, Neil T. Retroviral Testing: Essentials of Quality Control & Lab Diagnosis. 256p. 1992. boxed set 115.95 (*0-8493-4429-8*, RC607) CRC Pr.

Constantine, Peter. Japanese Slang. 224p. 1995. pap. text 12.95 (*4-900737-03-8*, Pub. by Yen Bks) Tuttle Pubng.

— Japanese Street Slang. (JPN.). 216p. (Orig.). (C). 1992. pap. 9.95 (*0-8348-0250-3*, Tengu Bks) Weatherhill.

— Japan's Sex Trade. (Illus.). 208p. (Orig.). 1994. pap. 8.95 (*4-900737-00-3*) Tuttle Pubng.

— Making Out in Indonesian. (IND.). 228p. (Orig.). 1994. pap. 6.95 (*4-900737-02-X*) Tuttle Pubng.

— Making Out in Korean. (ENG & KOR., Illus.). 104p. (Orig.). 1995. pap. 6.95 (*4-900737-33-X*) Tuttle Pubng.

— Making Out in Vietnamese. 104p. 1998. pap. 6.95 (*4-900737-48-8*) Tuttle Pubng.

— What's Your Type? How Blood Types Are the Keys to Unlocking Your Personality. LC 97-587. 208p. 1997. pap. 10.95 (*0-452-27802-3*, Plume) Dutton Plume.

Constantine, Peter, jt. ed. see Morrow, Bradford.

Constantine, Peter, tr. see Chekhov, Anton.

Constantine, Peter, tr. see Deichmann, Hans.

Constantine, Peter, tr. see Kadare, Ismail.

Constantine, Peter, tr. see Kustenmacher, Werner.

Constantine, Peter, tr. see Mann, Thomas.

Constantine, Peter, tr. see Messner, Reinhold.

Constantine, R., ed. see DiNapoli, Carlo.

Constantine, R., ed. see Woe, Jonathan.

***Constantine-Simms, Delroy.** The Greatest Taboo: Homosexuality in Black Communities. 504p. 2001. pap. 16.95 (*1-55583-564-3*, Pub. by Alyson Pubns) Consort Bk Sales.

Constantine, Stephen. Making of British Colonial Development Policy, 1914-1940. (Illus.). 340p. 1984. text 47.50 (*0-7146-3204-X*, BHA-03204, Pub. by F Cass Pubs) Intl Spec Bk.

Constantine, Stephen, et al, eds. The First World War in British History. 256p. 1995. pap. text 19.95 (*0-340-57053-9*, B4150, Pub. by E A) Routldge.

Constantine, Stephen, jt. ed. see Cockshut, A. O. J.

Constantine, Storm. The Enchantments of Flesh & Spirit. (Wraeththu Ser.: No. 1). 1990. pap. 3.95 (*0-8125-0554-9*, Pub. by Tor Bks) St Martin.

— Fulfillments of Fate & Desire. 1991. mass mkt. 4.95 (*0-8125-0558-1*) Tor Bks.

— The Oracle Lips: A Collection. aut. limited num. ed. 398p. 1999. 45.00 (*0-9667848-0-4*, Pub. by Stark Hse Pr) Firebird Dist.

— Scenting Hollowed Blood. (Grigori Trilogy Ser.: No. 2). 488p. 1999. pap. 16.00 (*0-9658345-5-7*) Meisha Merlin.

***Constantine, Storm.** Sea Dragon Heir. 2001. pap. 14.95 (*0-312-87366-2*) St Martin.

— Sea Dragon Heir. LC 99-59314. 384p. 2000. 24.95 (*0-312-87306-9*, Pub. by Tor Bks) St Martin.

— Sea Dragon Heir. 2001. pap. write for info. (*0-312-87751-X*) Tor Bks.

Constantine, Storm. Stalking Tender Prey. (Grigori Trilogy Ser.: Vol. 1). 488p. 1998. pap. 16.00 (*0-9658345-4-9*) Meisha Merlin.

***Constantine, Storm.** Stealing Sacred Fire. (Grigori Trilogy Ser.: Vol. 3). 456p. 2000. pap. 16.00 (*0-9658345-6-5*) Meisha Merlin.

— The Thorn Boy. 1999. pap. 12.95 (*0-9586864-3-2*, Pub. by Eidolon Pubns) Firebird Dist.

Constantine, Storm. Three Heralds of the Storm. 332p. 1997. pap. 5.00 (*0-9658345-2-2*) Meisha Merlin.

— Wraeththu. 800p. 1993. pap. 18.95 (*0-312-89000-1*) Orb NYC.

Constantine, Susan. Student Computer Study Skills Notebook. large type ed. (Illus.). 98p. 1998. spiral bd. 15.00 (*1-893916-17-0*, 3002) Project Pr.

***Constantine, Susan.** Student Study Skills Notebook: A Guide to Better Study Habits. large type ed. (Illus.). 58p. 1998. pap. 7.95 (*1-893916-16-2*, 3001) Project Pr.

Constantinesco, Nicholas. Romania on the European Stage, 1875-1880. LC 98-71535. 200p. 1998. 28.00 (*0-88033-396-0*, 499, Pub. by East Eur Monographs) Col U Pr.

Constantinescu, C. & Cornea, A. Potential Theory on Harmonic Spaces. LC 72-86117. (Grundlehren der Mathematischen Wissenschaften Ser.: Vol. 158). 1973. 103.95 (*0-387-05916-4*) Spr-Verlag.

Constantinescu, Corneliu. Advanced Integration Theory. LC 98-34119. (Mathematics & Its Applications Ser.). 1998. write for info. (*0-7923-5234-3*) Kluwer Academic.

— Spaces of Measures. LC 84-5815. (Studies in Mathematics: Vol. 4). 444p. 1984. 99.95 (*3-11-008784-7*) De Gruyter.

Constantinescu, Corneliu, et al. Integration Theory Vol. 1: Measure & Integral. 534p. (C). 1985. reprint ed. text 63.95 (*0-471-04479-2*) Krieger.

Constantinescu, F. & Magyari, E. Problems in Quantum Mechanics. 1976. 185.00 (*0-08-006826-X*, Pub. by Pergamon Repr); pap. text 194.00 (*0-08-019008-1*, Pub. by Pergamon Repr) Franklin.

Constantinescu, I. English-Romanian Dictionary. (ENG & ROM.). 186p. (C). 1991. text 30.00 (*0-7855-0115-0*, Pub. by Collets) St Mut.

Constantinescu, Tiberiu. Schur Parameters, Factorization, & Dilation Problems. LC 96-15524. (Operator Theory, Advances & Application Ser.: Vol. 82). 264p. 1996. 122.50 (*3-7643-5285-X*) Birkhauser.

Constantinescu, V. N., et al. Sliding Bearings. xx, 543p. 1984. 80.00 (*0-89864-011-3*) Allerton Pr.

Constantinescu, Virgiliu N. Gas Lubrication. Wehe, Robert L., ed. Scripta Technica Staff, tr. LC 78-93540. 645p. reprint ed. pap. 200.00 (*0-608-12385-4*, 205212000035) Bks Demand.

Constantinescu, Virgilu N. Laminar Viscous Flow. LC 95-16333. (Mechanical Engineering Ser.). (Illus.). 480p. 1995. 69.95 (*0-387-94528-8*) Spr-Verlag.

Constantini, Naama W., jt. ed. see Warren, Michelle P.

***Constantinides.** Critical Pathways in Otolaryngology. (Illus.). 608p. 2000. pap. 89.00 (*0-86577-847-7*) Thieme Med Pubs.

Constantinides, A. Dictionary Savoyard. (FRE.). 514p. 1994. 95.00 (*0-320-03036-9*) Fr & Eur.

Constantinides, A. G., jt. ed. see Bogner, R. E.

Constantinides, Alkis. Applied Numerical Methods with Personal Computers. (C). 1987. text 80.00 incl. disk (*0-07-079690-4*) McGraw.

Constantinides, Damon. Bigelow's PC Upgrade Pocket Reference. 1999. pap. 19.95 (*0-07-012603-8*) McGraw.

Constantinides, E. The Priest's Service Book. (ENG & GRE.). 1997. 20.00 (*0-9623833-0-9*) E Constantinides.

Constantinides, Evagoras. Mikpon Exxonorion H Ariaematapion: The Priest's Service Book. (Illus.). 426p. (C). 1989. 20.00 (*0-685-28020-9*) E Constantinides.

Constantinides, George, jt. auth. see Bhattacharya, Sudipto.

Constantinides, George M., ed. see Bhattacharya, Sudipto.

Constantinides, George M., jt. ed. see Bhattacharya, Sudipto.

Constantinides, Paris. General Pathobiology. (Illus.). 307p. (C). 1994. pap. text 44.95 (*0-8385-3119-9*, A3119-3, Apple Lange Med) McGraw.

Constantinidis, George. A User's Manual for Living in the World: A Book about Personal Empowerment. 240p. (Orig.). 1998. pap. 22.95 (*0-9660470-3-6*) Crazy Horse Bks.

Constantinidis, Stratos E. Theatre under Deconstruction? A Question of Approach. LC 92-24320. (Studies in Modern Drama: Vol. 2). 360p. 1993. text 25.00 (*0-8153-0872-8*, H1605) Garland.

Constantinidis, Stratos E., ed. Greece in Modern Times: An Annotated Bibliography of Works Published in English in 22 Academic Disciplines During the Twentieth Century. LC 99-24674. 656p. 2000. 115.00 (*0-8108-3658-0*) Scarecrow.

Constantino, Anthony O. Windows of Perception. 64p. 1993. pap. 4.95 (*1-57087-177-9*) Prof Pr NC.

Constantino, Cathy A. & Merchant, Christina S. Designing Conflict Management Systems: A Guide to Creating Productive & Healthy Organizations. (Conflict Resolution Ser.). 272p. 1995. text 30.95 (*0-7879-0162-8*) Jossey-Bass.

Constantino, Ernesto. Ilokano Dictionary. (PALI Language Texts, Philippines Ser.). 510p. (Orig.). (C). 1971. pap. text 24.00 (*0-87022-152-3*) UH Pr.

Constantino, Maria, jt. auth. see Constable, Nick.

Constantino, Mario. Italian at a Glance. 2nd ed. Wald, Heywood, ed. LC 92-26541. (ITA & ENG., Illus.). 277p. 1992. pap. 6.95 (*0-8120-1396-4*) Barron.

***Constantino, Mario.** Italian at a Glance. 3rd ed. 2000. pap. text 6.95 (*0-7641-1256-2*) Barron.

Constantino, Mario, et al. Traveler's Dictionary. 1985. pap. 7.95 (*0-8120-3557-7*) Barron.

— Traveler's Phrasebook. 1985. pap. 9.95 (*0-8120-3558-5*) Barron.

Constantino, Rebecca. Literacy, Access & Libraries among the Language Minority Community. LC 97-24393. 264p. 1998. 36.00 (*0-8108-3418-9*) Scarecrow.

Constantinon, P. How to Say It in Modern Greek. (ENG & GRE.). 22.50 (*0-87559-171-X*) Shalom.

An Asterisk (*) at the beginning of an entry indicates that the title is appearing for the first time.

Constantinou, Chris. Protocol & Procedures for Quality Assurance of Linear Accelerators. (Illus.). (Orig.). (C). 1993. pap. write for info. (*0-9638266-0-3*); text. write for info. (*0-9638266-1-1*) CNC Med Physics.

Constantinou, Costas M. On the Way to Diplomacy. LC 96-6310. (Borderlines Ser.: Vol. 7). 208p. (C). 1996. pap. 19.95 (*0-8166-2685-5*); text 49.95 (*0-8166-2684-7*) U of Minn Pr.

Constantinou, Michael, et al. Passive Energy Dissipation Systems for Structural Design & Retrofit. (NCEER Monograph Ser.: Vol. 1). 300p. 1998. pap. write for info. (*0-9656682-1-5*, MN-0001) Multidisciplinary Ctr.

Constantopoulos, G. First Greek Reader. (ENG & GRE., Illus.). 96p. 4.70 (*0-686-79626-8*) Divry.

— Second Greek Reader. (GRE., Illus.). 96p. 4.70 (*0-686-79627-6*) Divry.

Constantopoulos, James. Earth Resources. 229p. (C). 1997. pap. text 32.00 (*0-13-531393-7*) P-H.

Constantz, Brent, jt. ed. see Brown, Paul W.

Constantz, George. Hollows, Peepers, & Highlanders: An Appalachian Mountain Ecology. Ort, Kathleen, ed. LC 94-2315. (Illus.). 288p. 1993. pap. 14.00 (*0-87842-263-3*) Mountain Pr.

Constanza, Malacheck. A Modern Day Recipe for Duck Soup: Sleuthing & Sightseeing with 100 Poetic Slopes. (Self Realization Bks.: Bk. XII). (Illus.). 100p. 1986. pap. 10.00 (*0-938582-06-2*) Sensitive Man.

— Taking the Sky Out of the Box. (Self Realization Bks.: Bk. X). 100p. 1986. pap. 10.00 (*0-938582-14-3*) Sensitive Man.

Constanzo. Programmable Logic Controllers. (Food Science & Technology Ser.). 1997. pap. text 23.95 (*0-340-69258-8*, VNR) Wiley.

Constanzo, Mariangela, jt. auth. see Sajeva, Maurizio.

Constas, Dimitri & Stavrou, Theofanis G., eds. Greece Prepares for the Twenty-First Century. 304p. 1995. text 55.00 (*0-943875-67-6*); pap. text 17.50 (*0-943875-68-4*) Johns Hopkins.

Constas, Michael & Harroch, Richard D. Private Real Estate Syndications. LC 83-9417. 600p. 1983. ring bd. 90.00 (*0-317-03225-9*, 00581) NY Law Pub.

Constas, Michael, jt. auth. see Shim, Jae.

Consterdine, Guy. Readership Research. 200p. 1987. text 76.95 (*0-566-05071-4*, Pub. by Gower) Ashgate Pub Co.

Consterdine, Peter. Fit to Fight: The Manual of Intense Training for Combat. 1998. pap. 25.95 (*1-873475-42-X*, Pub. by Summers) Howell Pr VA.

— Modern Bodyguard: The Manual of Close Protection Training. 1998. pap. 39.95 (*1-873475-09-8*, Pub. by Summers) Howell Pr VA.

— Streetwise: The Complete Manual of Personal Security & Self Defence. 1998. pap. text 44.95 (*1-873475-52-7*, Pub. by Summers) Howell Pr VA.

Constine, Louis S., jt. auth. see Halperin, Edward C.

Constitution Works Staff, jt. auth. see American History Workshop Staff.

Constitutional Convention of South Carolina Staff. Proceedings of the Constitutional Convention of South Carolina. LC 68-29018. (American Negro: His History & Literature. Series 1). 1968. reprint ed. 39.95 (*0-405-01837-1*) Ayer.

***Construction Audit Ltd. Staff.** Hapm Guide to Defect Avoidance. (Hapm Ser.). (Illus.). 128p. (Orig.). (C). 2000. pap. 49.99 (*0-419-24890-0*, E & FN Spon) Routledge.

***Construction Congress Staff & Walsh, Kenneth D.** Construction Congress VI: Building Together for a Better Tomorrow in an Increasingly Complex World, Proceedings of the Congress, Orlando, Florida, February 20-22, 2000. LC 99-88589. 2000. write for info. (*0-7844-0475-5*) Am Soc Civil Eng.

Construction Education Foundation Staff. Exploring Careers in Construction. 120p. 1995. pap. 11.95 (*1-886831-00-9*) Constrct Educ.

— Wheels of Learning - Core Curricula. (Wheels of Learning Ser.). 398p. (Orig.). (C). 1992. pap. 50.00 (*1-886831-01-7*) Constrct Educ.

Construction Industry Board Staff. Selecting Consultants for the Team: Balancing Quality & Price. 36p. 1996. 24.00 (*0-7277-2543-2*) Am Soc Civil Eng.

Construction Industry Research & Information Assoc. Water-Resisting Basements, Report 139. 189p. 1995. 14.00 (*0-7277-2042-2*) Am Soc Civil Eng.

Construction Industry Research Staff. Design & Construction of Joints in Concrete Structures. LC 96-136367. 80p. 1996. 96.00 (*0-7277-2092-9*) Am Soc Civil Eng.

— Formwork Striking Times: Criteria, Prediction & Methods of Assessment. LC 96-142384. 72p. 1996. 86.00 (*0-7277-2090-2*) Am Soc Civil Eng.

— Underground Service Reservoirs: Waterproofing & Repair Manual. 168p. 1996. 99.00 (*0-7277-2095-3*) Am Soc Civil Eng.

Consuegra, Diosdado. El Emperador Frente Al Espejo. LC 89-80697. (Coleccion Caniqui). (SPA.). 86p. (Orig.). 1990. pap. 9.95 (*0-89729-542-0*) Ediciones.

Consul. Generalized Poisson Distributions: Properties & Applications. (Statistics: Textbooks & Monographs: Vol. 99). (Illus.). 320p. 1988. text 155.00 (*0-8247-7863-4*) Dekker.

Consul, Wilma, tr. see Lucas, Alice, ed.

Consultant Dietitians in Health Care Facilities St. Nutrition Care of the Older Adult: A Handbook for Dietetics Professionals Working Throughout the Continuum of Care. LC 98-42196. 250p. 1998. 34.95 (*0-88091-167-0*) Am Dietetic Assn.

— Resource Guide for the Consultant Dietitian. 3rd rev. ed. 209p. 1993. ring bd. 49.95 (*1-884675-00-X*) Cnslt Dietitians.

Consultant Dietitians in Health Care Facilities St, jt. auth. see Gerwick, Clara L.

Consultants Bureau Staff. Contemporary Equipment for Work with Radioactive Isotopes: Collected Reports. LC 59-14767. (Soviet Journal of Atomic Energy: Supplement Ser.: No. 5, 1958). 72p. reprint ed. pap. 30.00 (*0-608-13321-3*, 205580000038) Bks Demand.

— The Geology of Uranium. LC 59-24987. (Soviet Journal of Atomic Energy: Supplement Ser.: 1957; No. 6). 134p. reprint ed. 41.60 (*0-608-12929-1*, 202470500038) Bks Demand.

— Physics & Heat Technology of Reactors. LC 59-958. (Soviet Journal of Atomic Energy: No. 1, 1958). 180p. reprint ed. pap. 55.80 (*0-608-30740-8*, 202065400018) Bks Demand.

— Primary Acts in Radiation Chemical Processes: A Portion of Proceedings of the 1st All-Union Conference on Radiation Chemistry, Moscow, 1957 in English Translation. LC QD601.. 34p. reprint ed. pap. 30.00 (*0-608-30046-2*, 202068800018) Bks Demand.

— Production of Isotopes: A Portion of the Proceedings of the All-Union Scientific & Technical Conference on Applications of Radioactive Isotopes. LC 59-14487. 139p. reprint ed. pap. 43.10 (*0-608-10233-4*, 202065500018) Bks Demand.

Consultation on Common Texts Association Staff. Christian Celebration of Marriage: An Ecumenical Liturgy. rev. ed. LC 95-20292. 1995. pap. 7.50 (*0-8066-2831-6*, 10-28316) Augsburg Fortress.

Consultative Council of the Lawyers Committee on A. Vietnam & International Law: An Analysis of International Law & the Use of Force, & the Precedent of Vietnam for Subsequent Interventions. 3rd ed. Fried, John H., ed. LC 90-36599. (Normative International Relations Ser.). 208p. 1990. reprint ed. pap. text 12.50 (*0-9623718-0-7*); reprint ed. lib. bdg. 27.50 (*0-9623718-3-1*) Aletheia Pr.

***Consultative Steering Group on the Scottish Parliament & Great Britain. Scottish Office.** Report of the Consultative Steering Group on the Scottish Parliament: Presented to the Secretary of State for Scotland. LC 99-180541. (Illus.). 1999. write for info. (*0-11-496125-5*) Statnry Office.

ConsultWare, Inc. Staff, jt. auth. see Goldman, Don.

***Consumer Guide Editors.** America's Best Hotels & Restaurants. 2000. 12.00 (*0-7853-4401-2*) Penguin Putnam.

Consumer Guide Editors. Auto Book, '97. 1996. mass mkt. 10.99 (*0-451-82334-6*) NAL.

— Automobile Book 1998. (Consumer Guide Ser.). 1998. mass mkt. 10.99 (*0-451-82341-9*) NAL.

***Consumer Guide Editors.** Automobile Book 2000. (Consumer Guide Automobile Bks.). (Illus.). 1999. pap. 10.99 (*0-7853-4036-X*) Pubns Intl Ltd.

Consumer Guide Editors. Automobiles of the '50s. (Illus.). 96p. 1993. 12.98 (*0-7853-0110-0*, 1013500) Pubns Intl Ltd.

— Automobiles of the '60s. (Illus.). 96p. 1993. 19.95 (*0-7853-0143-7*, 1002800) Pubns Intl Ltd.

— The Baseball Almanac: 1996 Edition. 608p. 1996. mass mkt. 6.99 (*0-451-18755-5*, Sig) NAL.

***Consumer Guide Editors.** Baseball Chronology, 1900-1999. (Illus.). 2000. pap. 6.99 (*0-7853-3960-4*) Pubns Intl Ltd.

Consumer Guide Editors. Basketball Almanac, 97-98. 1997. mass mkt. 6.99 (*0-451-19245-1*, Sig) NAL.

— Best Buy Book 1999. 192p. 1999. mass mkt. 9.99 (*0-451-19453-5*) NAL.

— Best of Baseball. 1997. mass mkt. 5.99 (*0-451-19072-6*, Sig) NAL.

— The Best of Hockey. 384p. 1998. mass mkt. 5.99 (*0-451-19431-4*, Sig) NAL.

— The Big Book of Questions & Answers. (Illus.). 192p. 14.98 (*1-56173-411-X*) Pubns Intl Ltd.

— Braids. 128p. (Orig.). 1994. mass mkt. 7.99 (*0-451-82271-4*, Sig) NAL.

***Consumer Guide Editors.** Cars, 1 vol. 1999th ed. (Consumer Guide Cars Ser.). (Illus.). 544p. 1999. mass mkt. 6.99 (*0-451-19917-0*, Sig) NAL.

— Cars 2000. (Illus.). 2000. mass mkt. 6.99 (*0-7853-4037-8*) Pubns Intl Ltd.

Consumer Guide Editors. Chevrolet, 1955-1957. (Illus.). 96p. 1991. 6.98 (*1-56173-311-3*) Pubns Intl Ltd.

***Consumer Guide Editors.** Children's Prescription Drugs: A Parent's Guide to the Most Commonly Recommended Drugs for Children. (Illus.). 2000. pap. 8.99 (*0-7853-3962-0*) Pubns Intl Ltd.

Consumer Guide Editors. Cholesterol. 1989. pap. 3.95 (*0-451-15932-2*, Sig) NAL.

— Cholesterol: Your Guide for a Healthy Heart. 256p. 1989. 7.98 (*0-88176-584-8*) Pubns Intl Ltd.

— Christmas Crafts Made Easy. 128p. (Orig.). 1994. mass mkt. 6.99 (*0-451-82287-0*, Sig) NAL.

— Collectible & Classic Trucks. (Illus.). 96p. 1993. 19.95 (*0-7853-0108-9*, 1013100) Pubns Intl Ltd.

— Complete Baby Name Book. (Illus.). 160p. 1993. spiral bd. 9.98 (*0-88176-814-6*, 4003001) Pubns Intl Ltd.

— The Complete Book of Collectible Cars. (Illus.). 320p. 1993. 29.95 (*0-88176-934-7*, 1010200) Pubns Intl Ltd.

— The Complete Book of Collectible Cars, 1930-1990. LC 97-120766. 804p. 1997. mass mkt. 8.99 (*0-451-19058-0*, Sig) NAL.

— The Complete Book of Vitamins & Minerals. 288p. (Orig.). 1989. 7.98 (*0-88176-497-3*) Pubns Intl Ltd.

— Complete Guide to Used Cars: The Complete Buying Guide to the Best Used Car & Truck Values. (Consumer Guide Ser.). 448p. 1998. mass mkt. 6.99 (*0-451-19445-4*, Sig) NAL.

***Consumer Guide Editors.** Complete Guide to Used Cars: The Complete Guide to the Best Used Car, Truck, SUV. 544p. 2000. mass mkt. 6.99 (*0-7853-4040-8*) Pubns Intl Ltd.

Consumer Guide Editors. Computer Buyer's Guide 98. 1997. mass mkt. 9.99 (*0-451-82342-7*) Viking Penguin.

***Consumer Guide Editors.** Computer Buying Guide. (Illus.). 1999. mass mkt. 9.99 (*0-7853-3930-2*) Pubns Intl Ltd.

— Computer Buying Guide: 2001 Edition. annuals 2000. pap. 9.99 (*0-7853-4042-4*) Pubns Intl Ltd.

— Consumer Buying Guide, 2000 Ed. 2000. mass mkt. 6.99 (*0-7853-3951-5*) Pubns Intl Ltd.

Consumer Guide Editors. The Consumer Guide - "Coin World" Guide to U. S. Coins, Prices & Value Trends, 1989. 1989. pap. 4.50 (*0-317-02796-4*) NAL.

***Consumer Guide Editors.** Consumer Guide Automobile Book: All New 1999 Edition. (Consumer Guide Ser.). 224p. 1998. pap. 10.99 (*0-451-19452-7*, Sig) NAL.

Consumer Guide Editors. Corvette. (Illus.). 96p. 1993. 12.95 (*1-56173-273-7*, 1011400) Pubns Intl Ltd.

— Deluxe Family Medical Library, 2 bks., Set. rev. ed. (Illus.). 1993. 29.95 (*1-56173-296-6*, 9006101) Pubns Intl Ltd.

— Elvis: A Tribute to His Life. (Illus.). 1989. 29.95 (*0-88176-665-8*) Pubns Intl Ltd.

— Elvis Album, 1 vol. 1999. pap. text 9.99 (*0-451-19923-5*) NAL.

— Emergency First Aid for Your Child. (Illus.). 128p. 1993. spiral bd. 9.98 (*0-88176-815-4*, 3203000) Pubns Intl Ltd.

— Encyclopedia of American Cars from 1930: Sixty Years of Automotive History. (Illus.). 816p. 1993. 29.95 (*0-7853-0175-5*) Pubns Intl Ltd.

— Family Medical & Health Guide. (Illus.). 384p. 1993. pap. 9.98 (*1-56173-451-9*, 4005500) Pubns Intl Ltd.

— Family Medical & Prescription Drug Guide. (Illus.). 864p. 1993. 39.95 (*0-7853-0084-8*, 3211400) Pubns Intl Ltd.

— Fat Reduction: Trim Fat from Your Life. (Illus.). 160p. 1993. spiral bd. 9.98 (*0-7853-0187-9*, 3211800) Pubns Intl Ltd.

— Fifty Years of American Automobiles, 1939-1989. (Illus.). 720p. 1989. 49.95 (*0-88176-592-9*) Pubns Intl Ltd.

— Folk Remedies: Healing Wisdom of Days Gone By. LC 99-208427. 1999. mass mkt. 7.99 (*0-451-19903-0*) NAL.

— Food Processor Cookbook. 1976. 13.95 (*0-671-22675-4*, Fireside) S&S Trade Pap.

***Consumer Guide Editors.** Foods that Make You Lose Weight: Fat-fighting Foods for a Healthier You, Vol. 1. 192p. 1999. mass mkt. 5.99 (*0-7853-3933-7*) Pub Intl.

Consumer Guide Editors. The Football Almanac. 1999. pap. 5.99 (*0-451-17788-6*, Sig) NAL.

— Football Greats: 100 Legendary Stars. 320p. 1998. mass mkt. 5.99 (*0-451-19429-2*, Sig) NAL.

— Ford: The Complete History. (Illus.). 512p. 1989. 39.95 (*0-88176-639-9*) Pubns Intl Ltd.

***Consumer Guide Editors.** 4x4s, Pickups & Vans: 2000 Buying Guide. 160p. 2000. pap. 8.99 (*0-7853-4039-4*) Pubns Intl Ltd.

Consumer Guide Editors. 4x4's, Pickups & Vans Buying Guide, 1999. 160p. 1999. mass mkt. 8.99 (*0-451-19914-6*, Sig) NAL.

— Frugal Almanac. LC 97-150449. 1997. mass mkt. 5.99 (*0-451-19071-8*, Sig) NAL.

***Consumer Guide Editors.** Healing Garden: Growing Your Own Natural Remedies Indoors or Outdoors. (Illus.). 2000. mass mkt. 6.99 (*0-7853-3934-5*) Pubns Intl Ltd.

— Healing Power of Touch: The Many Ways Physical Contact Can Cure, 1 vol. (Illus.). 256p. 1999. mass mkt. 5.99 (*0-451-19904-9*) NAL.

— Home Electronic Buying Guide. (Illus.). 1999. pap. 5.99 (*0-7853-3928-0*) Pubns Intl Ltd.

— Home Electronic Buying Guide. 1999. pap. text 5.99 (*0-451-19910-3*) Signet.

Consumer Guide Editors. Home Electronics Buying Guide. 192p. 1998. mass mkt. 5.99 (*0-451-19900-6*, Sig) NAL.

— The Home Remedies Handbook. (Illus.). 400p. 1993. 19.98 (*1-56173-747-X*, 3211000) Pubns Intl Ltd.

— How It Works & How to Fix It. 1985. pap. 4.50 (*0-451-13871-6*, Sig) NAL.

***Consumer Guide Editors.** How to Be a TV Quiz Show Millionaire. 2000. pap. 4.99 (*0-7853-4046-7*) Pubns Intl Ltd.

Consumer Guide Editors. How to Operate a VCR. 1999. 6.99 (*0-451-82302-8*) NAL.

— How to Win at Apple Computer Games. 64p. 1984. spiral bd. 8.95 (*0-671-49559-3*) S&S Trade.

— Jesus: His Life, Times & Teachings. 576p. 1999. pap. 7.99 (*0-7853-3929-9*) Pubns Intl Ltd.

— Lamborghini. (Illus.). 256p. 1993. 21.95 (*0-88176-931-2*, 1010400) Pubns Intl Ltd.

— The Low Fat Handbook. 1996. mass mkt. 7.99 (*0-451-82314-1*) NAL.

— Meet Charles Barkley. 1999. pap. 3.99 (*0-451-18228-6*, Sig) NAL.

— Meet Emmitt Smith. 1999. pap. 3.99 (*0-451-18350-9*, Sig) NAL.

— Miracle of Birth. (Illus.). 128p. 1993. 9.98 (*0-88176-560-0*, 3201900) Pubns Intl Ltd.

— Muscle Cars of the '50s. (Illus.). 96p. 1993. 12.98 (*1-56173-301-6*, 1011700) Pubns Intl Ltd.

— Muscle Cars of the '60s. (Illus.). 96p. 1993. 19.95 (*1-56173-308-3*, 1011800) Pubns Intl Ltd.

— Mustang. (Illus.). 96p. 1993. 12.98 (*1-56173-276-1*, 1011900) Pubns Intl Ltd.

— Nature's Miracle Medicines: Amazing Remedies from Mother Earth. 1999. mass mkt. 5.99 (*0-451-19925-1*) NAL.

— Nature's Miracle Medicines: Amazing Remedies from Mother Earth. LC 98-68003. 256p. 1999. mass mkt. 5.99 (*0-7853-3923-X*) Pubns Intl Ltd.

***Consumer Guide Editors.** Nature's Miracle Medicines: Amazing Remedies from Mother Earth. 2000. mass mkt. 5.99 (*0-7853-4048-3*) Pubns Intl Ltd.

Consumer Guide Editors. New Car Price Guide: Retail & Dealer Invoice Prices. (Consumer Guide Ser.). 1998. mass mkt. 5.99 (*0-451-19447-0*, Sig) NAL.

— New Car Price Guide: 1999 Edition, 1 vol. 1999. mass mkt. 5.99 (*0-451-19911-1*) NAL.

— The New Illustrated Family Medical & Health Guide. rev. ed. (Illus.). 448p. 1993. 14.98 (*1-56173-600-7*, 3210102) Pubns Intl Ltd.

— The New Prescription Drug Reference Guide. (Illus.). 448p. 1993. 14.98 (*1-56173-601-5*, 3210801) Pubns Intl Ltd.

— 1998 Used Cars Book. 160p. 1998. mass mkt. 9.99 (*0-451-19438-1*, Sig) NAL.

***Consumer Guide Editors.** 1999 Used Car Book. (Consumer Guide Used Car Book). 192p. 1999. mass mkt. 9.99 (*0-451-19916-2*) NAL.

Consumer Guide Editors. Nondescription Drug. 1997. mass mkt. 7.99 (*0-451-19063-7*, Sig) NAL.

***Consumer Guide Editors.** 101 Best Websites for Kids. 2000. mass mkt. 5.99 (*0-7853-4047-5*) Pubns Intl Ltd.

Consumer Guide Editors. Piano Playing Made Easy. (Illus.). 64p. 1993. spiral bd. 5.98 (*1-56173-737-2*, 3615000) Pubns Intl Ltd.

— The Players of Cooperstown: Baseball's Hall of Fame. LC 99-230474. 432p. 1998. mass mkt. 6.99 (*0-451-19525-6*, Sig) NAL.

***Consumer Guide Editors.** Pokemon Card Collector's Guide. (Illus.). 2000. pap. 7.99 (*0-7853-4045-9*) Pubns Intl Ltd.

Consumer Guide Editors. Practical Guide to Dog Care. 192p. 1995. mass mkt. 4.99 (*0-451-18575-7*, Sig) NAL.

— Practical Hints & Tips: Household. 256p. 1995. mass mkt. 4.99 (*0-451-18358-4*, Sig) NAL.

— Prescription Drugs. 1997. mass mkt. 7.99 (*0-451-19240-0*, Sig) NAL.

— Prescription Drugs. (Illus.). 384p. 1993. pap. 9.95 (*1-56173-452-7*, 4005200) Pubns Intl Ltd.

— Prescription Drugs. rev. ed. (Illus.). 1024p. 1995. mass mkt. 8.99 (*0-451-18364-9*, Sig) NAL.

— Prescription Drugs over 40. 1997. mass mkt. 6.99 (*0-451-19273-7*, Sig) NAL.

— Prevention. LC 96-208567. 1996. mass mkt. 5.99 (*0-451-18810-1*, Sig) NAL.

— Profiles of Great African-Americans. 1998. mass mkt. 6.99 (*0-451-19275-3*, Sig) NAL.

— Step into Shape. (Illus.). 64p. 1993. spiral bd. 5.98 (*1-56173-748-8*, 3210900) Pubns Intl Ltd.

— 365 Gardening Hints & Tips: Down to Earth. 384p. 1999. mass mkt. 6.99 (*0-451-19905-7*) NAL.

***Consumer Guide Editors.** Used Car & Truck Book 2000: 1990-1999 Cars, Trucks, Minivans, SUVs. (Illus.). 2000. pap. 9.99 (*0-7853-4038-6*) Pubns Intl Ltd.

Consumer Guide Editors. Viper: Pure Performance by Dodge. (Illus.). 80p. 1993. 12.98 (*0-7853-0109-7*, 1002900) Pubns Intl Ltd.

— The Vitamin Book. 1979. pap. 5.95 (*0-671-24819-7*, Fireside) S&S Trade Pap.

— Whole Car Catalog. (Illus.). 1978. pap. 7.95 (*0-671-23022-0*, Fireside) S&S Trade Pap.

— Wit & Wisdom for Fishing: Funny Lines & Fishy Advice. (Illus.). 192p. 1998. mass mkt. 4.99 (*0-451-19427-6*, Sig) NAL.

— Wit & Wisdom of Golf: Insightful Truths & Bad Lies. 192p. 1998. mass mkt. 4.99 (*0-451-19428-4*, Sig) NAL.

— Women's Book of Home Remedies. 576p. (Orig.). 1994. mass mkt. 6.99 (*0-451-18230-8*, Sig) NAL.

— Women's Home Remedy Health Guide. (Illus.). 400p. 1994. 19.98 (*0-7853-0185-2*, 3212100) Pubns Intl Ltd.

— You Can Draw Animals. (Illus.). 80p. 1989. 5.95 (*0-88176-601-1*) Pubns Intl Ltd.

— You Can Draw Cars, Planes, Boats & Other Vehicles. (Illus.). 80p. 1989. 5.95 (*0-88176-605-4*) Pubns Intl Ltd.

— You Can Draw Dinosaurs & Other Prehistoric Animals. (Illus.). 80p. 1989. 5.95 (*0-88176-604-6*) Pubns Intl Ltd.

— You Can Draw People. (Illus.). 80p. 1989. 5.95 (*0-88176-603-8*) Pubns Intl Ltd.

— Your VCR: Easy Step-by-Step Instructions to Operate, Maintain, & Repair. 96p. 1996. mass mkt. 7.99 (*0-451-82308-7*) NAL.

— Your VCR: How to Operate, Maintain, & Repair. (Illus.). 64p. 1993. spiral bd. 5.98 (*1-56173-739-9*, 3615200) Pubns Intl Ltd.

Consumer Guide Editors, contrib. by. Children's Prescription Drugs: A Parent's Guide to the Most Commonly Recommended Drugs for Children. LC 96-70997. (Illus.). 400p. 1997. write for info. (*0-7853-2163-2*) Pubns Intl Ltd.

— Corvette: The American Legend. LC 97-65094. (Illus.). 144p. 1997. write for info. (*0-7853-2402-X*) Pubns Intl Ltd.

Consumer Guide Editors, ed. The Complete Guide to Used Cars: 1996 Edition. 1996. mass mkt. 6.99 (*0-451-18782-2*, Sig) NAL.

***Consumer Guide Editors, ed.** Consumer Guide New Car Price Guide 2000. 2000. mass mkt. 5.99 (*0-7853-4041-6*) Pubns Intl Ltd.

Consumer Guide Editors, ed. 4X4s, Pickups & Vans 1998 Buying Guide. 160p. 1998. mass mkt. 8.99 (*0-451-19444-6*, Sig) NAL.

***Consumer Guide Editors, ed.** Golf Chronology. 2000. mass mkt. 6.99 (*0-7853-3961-2*) Pubns Intl Ltd.

— Hear Charmers. 96p. 1999. mass mkt. 5.95 (*0-451-19936-7*, Sig) NAL.

Consumer Guide Editors, ed. Irish Wit & Wisdom, 1 vol. 192p. 1999. mass mkt. 5.99 (*0-451-19906-5*) NAL.

— 1998 Cars. 448p. 1998. mass mkt. 6.99 (*0-451-19436-5*, Sig) NAL.

— Walk into Shape. 1997. mass mkt. 5.99 (*0-451-19068-8*, Sig) NAL.

— Wit & Wisdom of Baseball. 192p. 1998. mass mkt. 4.99 (*0-451-19426-8*, Sig) NAL.

Consumer Guide Editors & Berko, Robert L. Food Additives Explained: What Those Long Names on Food Labels Tell Us. LC 82-71122. 80p. 1983. 5.00 (*0-685-18143-X*) Consumer Ed Res.

Consumer Guide Editors & Chasnoff, Ira J. Your Child: A Medical Guide. (Illus.). 576p. 1993. 9.98 (*0-88176-391-8*, 3200700) Pubns Intl Ltd.

Consumer Guide Editors & Dugan, Ann. Fitness over Forty: For Men Only. (Illus.). 64p. 1993. spiral bd. 5.98 (*0-88176-219-9*, 3201400) Pubns Intl Ltd.

— Slimming Your Hips & Thighs. (Illus.). 64p. 1993. spiral bd. 5.98 (*0-88176-083-8*, 3200000) Pubns Intl Ltd.

Consumer Guide Editors & Flammang, James M. Camaro: Style, Speed, & Spirit. (Illus.). 128p. 1993. 12.98 (*1-56173-538-8*, 1012200) Pubns Intl Ltd.

— Corvette Chronicle. (Illus.). 192p. 1993. 19.98 (*0-7853-0068-6*, 1013800) Pubns Intl Ltd.

Consumer Guide Editors & Holmes, Randee. Additive Alert: What Have They Done to Our Food. 4th ed. 1994. pap. 14.99 (*0-7710-7139-6*) McCland & Stewart.

Consumer Guide Editors & Lansky, Vicki. Complete Pregnancy & Baby Book. (Illus.). 448p. 1993. 14.98 (*0-7853-0230-1*, 3211600) Pubns Intl Ltd.

Consumer Guide Editors & Lyons, Pete. Jaguar: Performance & Pride. (Illus.). 256p. 1993. 19.98 (*0-88176-983-5*, 1010300) Pubns Intl Ltd.

Consumer Guide Editors, et al. Chevrolet Chronicle - A Pictorial History from 1904. (Illus.). 320p. 1993. 29.98 (*1-56173-272-9*, 1010000) Pubns Intl Ltd.

— Family Medical Guide: The Illustrated Medical & Health Advisor. (Illus.). 576p. 1993. 9.98 (*0-7853-0184-4*, 3212000) Pubns Intl Ltd.

— Ford Chronicle. (Illus.). 320p. 1993. 29.98 (*1-56173-730-5*, 1012700) Pubns Intl Ltd.

— Great American Automobiles of the '50s. (Illus.). 320p. 1993. 29.95 (*0-88176-593-7*, 1001300) Pubns Intl Ltd.

— Great American Automobiles of the '60s. (Illus.). 320p. 1992. 29.95 (*1-56173-274-5*) Pubns Intl Ltd.

— Great Cars of the Twentieth Century. (Illus.). 420p. 1993. 49.98 (*1-56173-089-0*, 1010800) Pubns Intl Ltd.

Consumer Guide Editors, jt. auth. see Chasnoff, Ira J.

Consumer Guide Staff. Hockey Almanac 1996-1997. 1999. mass mkt. 5.99 (*0-451-19044-0*, Sig) NAL.

C

Consumer Information Experts Staff. New Cars: American & Imports. (Edmunds New Car Prices Ser.). 1998. pap. text 8.99 (*0-87759-629-8*) Edmund Pubns.

Consumer Information Express Staff. New Trucks: Vans, Pickups & Sport Utilities. (Edmunds New Trucks Ser.). 1998. pap. text 8.99 (*0-87759-630-1*) Edmund Pubns.

Consumer Information Services Incorporated Staff. National Foreclosure Catalog: Nationwide Access to Foreclosed Real Estate. 3rd ed. LC 99-175992. 128 p. 1996. write for info. (*0-9647365-1-9*) Public Infor Servs.

Consumer Law Foundation Staff. The Complete Small Business Loan Kit. (Consumer Law Foundation Ser.). 192p. 1989. pap. 12.95 (*1-55850-996-8*) Adams Media.

Consumer Protective Services, Inc. Staff. Fraud Prevention on Automobile & Small Truck Purchase & Repair. (Illus.). 1995. pap. 12.95 (*0-9642681-2-4*) Torocin Ent.

Consumer Protective Services, Inc. Staff. Fraud Prevention on Central Air-Conditioning & Heatpump Systems. LC 94-61171. (Illus.). 56p. (Orig.). 1994. pap. 12.95 (*0-9642681-0-8*) Torocin Ent.

Consumer Protective Services, Inc. Staff. Fraud Prevention on Siding, Soffit & Fascia, & Replacement Window Purchase & Installation. (Illus.). 1994. pap. 12.95 (*0-9642681-1-6*) Torocin Ent.

***Consumer Reports Books Editors.** Best Buys for Your Home: 2000 Edition. 1999. mass mkt. 9.99 (*0-89043-924-9*) Consumer Reports.

Consumer Reports Books Editors. Consumer Reports Buying Guide 1994. 1993. pap. 8.99 (*0-89043-709-2*) Consumers Union.

— Consumer Reports 1998. 1999. 29.95 (*0-89043-915-X*) St Martin.

***Consumer Reports Books Editors.** Consumer Reports, 1999. 2000. 29.95 (*0-89043-935-4*) Consumer Reports.

— Consumer Reports 1999 New Car Buying Guide. 1999. pap. text 9.99 (*0-89043-922-2*) Consumer Reports.

— Consumer Reports 2000 Buying Guide. 350p. 1999. pap. 9.99 (*0-89043-925-7*) Consumer Reports.

— Consumer Reports Used Car Buying Guide 2000. (Used Car Buying Guide Ser.). (Illus.). 252p. 2000. pap. 9.99 (*0-89043-930-3*) Consumer Reports.

Consumer Reports Books Editors. The Facts about Drug Use: Coping with Drugs & Alcohol in Your Family, at Work, in Your Community. Stimmel, Barry, ed. LC 92-40886. 1992. pap. 14.95 (*1-56024-401-1*) Haworth Pr.

***Consumer Reports Books Editors.** New Car Buying Guide 2000. (Consumer Reports New Car Buying Guide Ser.). (Illus.). 256p. 2000. pap. 9.99 (*0-89043-937-0*) Ed Devel Corp.

Consumer Reports Books Editors. 2000 Complete Drug Reference. 1999. 44.95 (*0-89043-928-1*) Consumer Reports.

Consumer Reports Books Editors & Kippell, Edward. How to Clean Practically Anything. 4th ed. LC 95-37498. 226p. 1996. 11.95 (*0-89043-843-9*) Consumer Reports.

Consumer Reports Books Editors, ed. see Bradley, Edward L., III.

Consumer Reports Editors, jt. auth. see Lieberman, Trudy.

Consumers' Checkbook Magazine Editors & Collins, Geneva. Guide to Washington Area Restaurants. rev. ed. LC 97-117767. 128p. 1995. pap. 7.95 (*0-9611432-8-2*) Ctr Study Serv.

Consumers' Checkbook Magazine Editors & Remick, Sue. Guide to Bay Area Restaurants. rev. ed. 128p. (Orig.). 1995. pap. 7.95 (*0-9611432-9-0*) Ctr Study Serv.

Consumers' Checkbook Magazine Editors, jt. auth. see Francis, Walter.

Consumers Power Company Staff. Fundamentals of Natural Gas. LC 74-100858. (Supervision Ser.). 1970. pap. 14.00 (*0-201-01180-8*) Addison-Wesley.

***Consurmer Guide Editors.** Consumer Buying Guide 2000. (Illus.). 2000. pap. 9.99 (*0-7853-3950-7*) Pubns Intl Ltd.

Conta, Lewis D. Energy Conservation in Space Conditioning. (Industrial Energy-Conservation Manuals Ser.: No. 7). (Illus.). 120p. 1982. 20.00 (*0-262-03084-5*) MIT Pr.

Contact, pseud. Cavalry of the Clouds. LC 76-169411. (Literature & History of Aviation Ser.). 1972. reprint ed. 24.95 (*0-405-03756-2*) Ayer.

Contadini, Anna. Fatimid Art at the Victoria & Albert Museum. (Illus.). 160p. 1998. 99.00 (*1-85177-178-6*, Pub. by V&A Ent) Antique Collect.

Contadini, Anna, jt. auth. see Bayani, Manijeh.

Contadino, Darlene, jt. auth. see Boyles, Nancy S.

Contag, Kimberly. Mockery in Spanish Golden Age Literature: Analysis of Burlesque Representation. LC 96-8239. 260p. 1996. pap. text 32.00 (*0-7618-0374-2*); lib. bdg. 52.00 (*0-7618-0373-4*) U Pr of Amer.

Contag, Victoria & Wang Chi-ch'ien. Seals of Chinese Painters & Collectors of the Ming & Ch'ing Periods. (Illus.). 794p. (C). 1982. pap. text 75.00 (*962-209-034-6*, Pub. by HK Univ Pr) Coronet Bks.

Contal, Marie-Helene. Christian Hauvette. (Current Architecture Catalogues Ser.). (Illus.). 96p. 1997. pap. 29.95 (*84-252-1657-5*) Watsn-Guptill.

Contamine, Philippe. War in the Middle Ages. Jones, Michael, tr. 420p. 1992. reprint ed. pap. 29.95 (*0-631-14469-2*) Blackwell Pubs.

***Contamine, Philippe, ed.** War & Competition Between States. (The Origins of the Modern State in Europe Ser.). (Illus.). 360p. 2001. text 74.00 (*0-19-820214-8*) OUP.

Contamine, Philippe, ed. see Corvisier, Andre.

Contant-Astrom, Birgitta. Aging & Spatial Memory: Assessment of Age-Related Alterations of Spatial Memory in Rats. (Illus.). 305p. (Orig.). 1994. pap. 64.50 (*91-7081-079-6*, Pub. by P Astroms) Coronet Bks.

Contant, Clement & De Filippi, Joseph. Parallele des Principaux Theatres Moderns de L'Europe, 2 vols., 1 bk. LC 68-21209. (Illus.). 1972. reprint ed. 64.95 (*0-405-08376-9*) Ayer.

Contant, George W. Each Bee Was a Bullet: Corporal Thomas Geer & Color Sergeant Judson Hicks, Co. A, 111th NY Vols., at the Battles of Harper's Ferry & Gettysburg. (Illus.). 70p. 1998. pap. 9.95 (*0-9659177-2-X*) G W Contant.

Contant, H. & Duthie, H. C. The Phytoplankton of Lac St-Jean, Quebec. (Bibliotheca Phycologica Ser.: No. 40). (Illus.). 1978. pap. text 40.00 (*3-7682-1198-3*) Lubrecht & Cramer.

***Contardi, Bruno.** Baroque in Italy: From Bernini to Guarini. Stierlin, Henri, ed. (World Architecture Ser.: Vol. 13). (Illus.). 240p. 2000. 29.99 (*3-8228-7648-8*) Taschen Amer.

Contardi, Bruno, jt. auth. see Amendola, Aurelio.

Contardi, Bruno, jt. auth. see Argan, Guilio C.

Contarella, Raffaele, jt. auth. see Garzya, Antonio.

Contasdim, Bruno. St. Peters. (GER., Illus.). 192p. 1999. 60.00 (*3-8238-0961-X*) te Neues.

Contat, Michel, et al, eds. Yale French Studies, 89. 1996. pap. 18.00 (*0-300-06708-9*) Yale U Pr.

Contat, Michel, jt. ed. see Rybalka, Michel.

Contat, Michel, ed. see Sartre, Jean-Paul.

Conte. Cognitive & Social Action. 192p. 1995. 54.95 (*1-85728-186-1*, Pub. by UCL Pr Ltd) Taylor & Francis.

***Conte.** Compiler Design. 2001. 54.39 (*0-07-239352-1*, McGraw-H College) McGrw-H Hghr Educ.

Conte. Earth Science: An Holistic Approach. 1994. 77.50 (*0-697-17428-X*, WCB McGr Hill) McGrw-H Hghr Educ.

— Elementary Numerical Analysis. 2002. 21.75 (*0-07-012466-3*) McGraw.

— Physical Geography. 1997. pap. text, student ed. 14.00 (*0-697-38532-9*) McGraw.

Conte, et al. Earth Science. 2nd ed. 1996. 60.00 (*0-697-26926-4*, WCB McGr Hill) McGrw-H Hghr Educ.

— Earth Science. 2nd ed. 1996. student ed. 52.25 (*0-697-27941-3*, WCB McGr Hill) McGrw-H Hghr Educ.

Conte, Alba. Attorney Fee Awards: 1996 Supplement. 2nd ed. Davis, Russ, ed. 470p. 1996. pap. text, suppl. ed. write for info. (*0-7620-0073-2*) West Group.

— Newberg on Class Actions: 1996 Supplement. 3rd ed. Davis, Russ, ed. 600p. 1996. pap. text. write for info. (*0-7620-0094-5*) West Group.

***Conte, Alba.** Sexual Harassment in the Workplace: Law & Practice, 2. 3rd ed. LC 99-53917. 2150p. 1999. boxed set 265.00 (*0-7355-1092-X*) Panel Pubs.

Conte, Alba. Sexual Orientation & Legal Rights, 2 vols., Vol. 2. LC 97-31198. (Civil Rights Library Ser.). 1500p. 1998. boxed set 265.00 (*0-471-16311-2*) Wiley.

Conte, Alba, et al. Computational Geometry: Proceedings of the Workshop. 264p. 1993. text 95.00 (*981-02-1229-1*) World Scientific Pub.

Conte, Anna Del, see Del Conte, Anna.

Conte, Anna Del, see Treuille, Eric & Del Conte, Anna.

Conte, Anna Del, see Del Conte, Anna.

Conte, Antonio T. The Anesthesiology Resident's Guide to Gaining Employment. (Illus.). 112p. 1996. pap. text 22.00 (*0-397-58762-7*) Lppncott W & W.

Conte, Christine. Maya Culture & Costume: A Catalogue of the Taylor Museum's E. B. Ricketson Collection of Guatemalan Textiles. LC 84-40115. (Illus.). 120p. (Orig.). 1984. pap. 15.00 (*0-916537-00-5*, Taylor Museum) CO Springs Fine Arts.

Conte, Cynthia M., jt. auth. see MacDonald, Paxson C.

Conte-Deboor. Elementary Numerical Analysis. 4th ed. 2002. 21.75 (*0-07-012465-5*) McGraw.

Conte, Donald J., et al. Earth Science: An Holistic Approach. 464p. (C). 1994. per. write for info. (*0-697-22762-6*, WCB McGr Hill) McGrw-H Hghr Educ.

— Earth Science: An Integrated Perspective. 2nd ed. 480p. (C). 1996. text. write for info. (*0-697-26922-1*, WCB McGr Hill) McGrw-H Hghr Educ.

— Earth Science: Solutions Manual. 2nd ed. 160p. (C). 1996. text, student ed. 20.62 (*0-697-26924-8*, WCB McGr Hill) McGrw-H Hghr Educ.

Conte, Ellen La, see La Conte, Ellen.

Conte, Frances. Christian Rakovski: A Political Biography. (East European Monographs: No. 256). 517p. 1989. text 101.50 (*0-88033-153-4*, Pub. by East Eur Monographs) Col U Pr.

Conte, Francis. The Slavs. 250p. 1995. 37.00 (*0-88033-310-3*, 413, Pub. by East Eur Monographs) Col U Pr.

Conte, Francis, ed. Great Dates in Russian & Soviet History. 368p. 1994. 29.95 (*0-8160-2687-4*) Facts on File.

Conte, Fred S., et al. Hatchery Manual for the White Sturgeon. LC 88-50176. (Illus.). 120p. 1988. pap. 15.00 (*0-931876-84-2*, 3322) ANR Pubns CA.

Conte, G. Woerterbuch Recht und Wirtschafts: English-German. 4th ed. (ENG & GER.). 416p. 1993. 150.00 (*0-7859-7537-3*, 3406377289) Fr & Eur.

Conte, G., et al. New Trends in Systems Theory. (Progress in Systems & Control Theory Ser.: Vol. 7). xvii, 722p. 1991. 181.00 (*0-8176-3548-3*) Birkhauser.

— Nonlinear Control Systems: An Algebraic Setting. LC 98-52362. (Lecture Notes in Control & Information Sciences). xvi, 166p. 1999. pap. 59.00 (*1-85233-151-8*) Spr-Verlag.

Conte, Gian B. The Hidden Author: An Interpretation of Petronius's Satyricon. LC 96-17101. (Sather Classical Lectures: Vol. 60). 224p. 1997. 38.00 (*0-520-20715-7*, Pub. by U CA Pr) Cal Prin Full Svc.

— Latin Literature: A History. Most, Glenn W., ed. Solodow, Joseph B., tr. LC 93-20985. (C). 1994. 65.00 (*0-8018-4638-2*) Johns Hopkins.

— The Rhetoric of Imitation: Genre & Poetic Memory in Virgil & Other Latin Poets. Segal, Charles, ed. (Studies in Classical Philology). 224p. 1996. pap. text 16.95 (*0-8014-8359-X*) Cornell U Pr.

Conte, Gian Biagio. Genres & Readers: Lucretius, Love Elegy, Pliny's Encyclopedia. Most, Glenn W., tr. LC 93-19631. 224p. (C). 1993. text 38.50 (*0-8018-4679-X*) Johns Hopkins.

— Latin Literature: A History. Solodow, Joseph B., tr. 864p. 1999. pap. 29.95 (*0-8018-6253-1*) Johns Hopkins.

Conte, Gianni & Del Corso, Dante, eds. Multi-Microprocessor Systems for Real-Time Applications. 1985. text 144.00 (*90-277-2054-1*) Kluwer Academic.

Conte, Giuseppe. The Ocean & the Boy. Stortoni, Laura, tr. from ITA. 208p. (Orig.). 1997. pap. 15.00 (*0-9641003-0-4*) Hesperia Pr.

Conte, Giuseppe & Hans, Boss. German & Italian Legal & Commercial Dictionary: Woerterbuch der Deutschen und Italienischen Wirtschafts und Rechtssprache, Vol. 1. 3rd ed. (GER & ITA.). 416p. 1983. 125.00 (*0-8288-0815-5*, M7028) Fr & Eur.

— German & Italian Legal & Economics Dictionary: Woerterbuch der Deutschen und Italeinischen Wirtschafts und Rechtssprache, Vol. 2. 3rd ed. (GER & ITA.). 500p. 1981. 150.00 (*0-8288-0816-3*, M7027) Fr & Eur.

Conte-Helm, Marie. Japan & the North East of England: From 1862 to the Present Day. 2nd ed. LC 88-36615. (Illus.). 240p. (C). 1989. text 45.00 (*0-485-11367-8*, Pub. by Athlone Pr) Humanities.

— The Japanese & Europe: Economic & Cultural Encounters. LC 95-23893. (Illus.). 200p. (C). 1996. text 60.00 (*0-485-11461-5*, Pub. by Athlone Pr) Humanities.

Conte, Hope R. & Plutchik, Robert, eds. Ego Defenses: Theory & Measurement. (Einstein Psychiatry Publication Ser.: No. 10). 340p. 1994. 75.00 (*0-471-05233-7*, Pub. by Interscience) Wiley.

Conte, Hope R., jt. ed. see Plutchik, Robert.

***Conte, Jeanne.** Advent Anticipations: Drawing Nearer to the Christ-Child. LC 99-51396. 1999. write for info. (*1-56072-741-1*, Nova Troitsa Bks) Nova Sci Pubs.

Conte, John E., Jr. Manual of Antibiotics & Infectious Diseases. 8th ed. LC 94-23078. (Illus.). 384p. 1995. pap. 32.00 (*0-683-02068-4*) Lppncott W & W.

Conte, John E., Jr. Manual of Antibiotics & Infectious Diseases. 9th ed. 512p. pap. text 39.95 (*0-7817-2316-7*) Lppncott W & W.

Conte, John E. Le, see Le Conte, John E.

Conte, Jon R. & Shore, David A., eds. Social Work & Child Sexual Abuse. LC 82-11952. (Journal of Social Work & Human Sexuality: Vol. 1, Nos. 1-2). 184p. 1982. text 39.95 (*0-917724-98-4*) Haworth Pr.

Conte, Joseph Le, see Le Conte, Joseph.

Conte, Joseph M. Unending Design: The Forms of Postmodern Poetry. LC 90-55732. (Illus.). 336p. 1991. pap. text 18.95 (*0-8014-9914-3*) Cornell U Pr.

Conte, Joseph M., ed. American Poets since World War II. (Dictionary of Literary Biography Ser.: Vol. 165). 400p. 1996. text 155.00 (*0-8103-9360-3*) Gale.

Conte, Marie, ed. see Borba, Michele.

Conte, Marie-Elisabeth, et al, eds. Text & Discourse Connectedness: Proceedings of the Conference on Connexity & Coherence, Urbino, July 16-21, 1984. LC 88-7543. (Studies in Language Companion Ser.: Vol. 16). xxiv, 584p. (C). 1989. 156.00 (*90-272-3017-X*) J Benjamins Pubng Co.

Conte, Mario, jt. auth. see MacKay, William M.

Conte, Michael, et al. Employee Ownership. LC 81-150054. (Institute for Social Research, Research Report). 71p. (Orig.). reprint ed. pap. 30.00 (*0-7837-5268-7*, 204500600005) Bks Demand.

Conte, Paul. Common-Sense C: Advice & Warnings for C & C ++ Programmers. LC 92-36412. 100p. 1993. pap. 24.95 (*1-882419-00-6*) News Four-Hund.

— Database Design & Programming for DB2/400. LC 96-35673. 772p. (C). 1996. pap. text 65.00 (*1-882419-06-5*) News Four-Hund.

***Conte, Paul, et al.** The Essential AS/400 Library, 4 vols. 850p. 1999. 224.00 (*1-58304-043-9*) News Four-Hund.

Conte, Paul, jt. auth. see Otey, Michael.

Conte, R., ed. The Painleve Property: One Century Later. LC 99-16039. (CRM Series in Mathematical Physics). (Illus.). 600p. 1999. 98.00 (*0-387-98888-2*) Spr-Verlag.

Conte, Robert & Boccara, Nino, eds. Partially Integrable Evolution Equations in Physics. (C). 1990. text 309.50 (*0-7923-0752-6*) Kluwer Academic.

***Conte, Robert V.** Black Sabbath: The Ozzy Years. 2000. pap. 12.95 (*1-890313-99-8*, Silver Skull) Studio Chikara.

Conte, Robert V., ed. see Barbi Twins.

Conte, Robert V., ed. see Criss, Lydia.

Conte, Robert V., ed. see Dayton, Chip R.

Conte, Robert V., ed. see Levine, Barry.

Conte, Robert V., ed. see Schwab, Steven D.

Conte, Rosaria, et al, eds. Simulating Social Phenomena. LC 97-29950. (Lecture Notes in Economics & Mathematical Systems Ser.: Vol. 456). viii, 536p. 1997. pap. 96.00 (*3-540-63329-4*) Spr-Verlag.

Conte, Rosaria, jt. ed. see Ahrweiler, Petra.

Conte, S. D. & De Boor, C. W. Elementary Numerical Analysis: An Algorithmic Approach. 3rd ed. 408p. (C). 1980. 87.19 (*0-07-012447-7*) McGraw.

Conte, Samuel D., et al. Software Engineering. 500p. (C). 1986. text 51.75 (*0-8053-2162-4*) Benjamin-Cummings.

Conte, Thomas M., ed. Fast Simulation of Computer Architectures. 256p. (C). 1995. text 118.50 (*0-7923-9593-X*) Kluwer Academic.

Conte, Yvonne F. Serious Laughter: A Guide Book to a Happier, Healthier, More Productive Life. rev. ed. (Illus.). 156p. (Orig.). 1998. pap. 16.95 (*0-9665336-0-7*) Amstrdm-Berwck.

Conteh-Morgan, Earl. American Foreign Aid & Global Power Projection. 246p. 1990. 61.95 (*1-85521-006-1*, Pub. by Dartmth Pub) Ashgate Pub Co.

— Democratization in Africa: The Theory & Dynamics of Political Transitions. LC 96-33193. 208p. 1997. 55.00 (*0-275-95780-2*, Praeger Pubs) Greenwood.

— Japan & the United States: Global Dimensions of Economic Power. LC 92-13191. (American University Studies: Political Science: Ser. X, Vol. 36). XII, 170p. (C). 1993. text 39.95 (*0-8204-1915-X*) P Lang Pubng.

***Conteh-Morgan, Earl & Dixon-Fyle, Mac.** Sierra Leone at the End of the Twentieth Century: History, Politics in Africa. LC 98-26873. (Society & Politics in Africa Ser.: Vol. 8). (Illus.). XVI, 175p. (C). 1999. pap. text 27.00 (*0-8204-4172-4*) P Lang Pubng.

Conteh-Morgan, Jane. Guess Who Love Me? (First Blessings Flap Bks.). (Illus.). 20p. (J). 1998. bds. 4.99 (*0-8054-1249-2*) Broadman.

***Conteh-Morgan, Jane.** I Love My Grandma! (First Blessings Flap Bks.). (Illus.). 20p. (J). 1998. bds. 4.99 (*0-8054-1264-6*) Broadman.

Conteh-Morgan, Jane. Colors. (So Tall Board Bks.). 18p. (J). (ps up). 1993. bds. 4.99 (*0-448-40522-9*, G & D) Peng Put Young Read.

— Eyes, Nose, Ears & Toes. (First Blessings Flap Bks.). 20p. (J). 1998. bds. 4.99 (*0-8054-1250-6*) Broadman.

— Night, Night, God Bless! (First Blessings Flap Bks.). 20p. (J). 1998. bds. 4.99 (*0-8054-1263-8*) Broadman.

— Noah's Ark. (Pudgy Pal Board Bks.). 18p. (J). (ps up). 1994. bds. 3.99 (*0-448-40185-1*, G & D) Peng Put Young Read.

Conteh-Morgan, John. Theatre & Drama in Francophone Africa: A Critical Introduction. 255p. (C). 1995. text 74.95 (*0-521-43453-X*) Cambridge U Pr.

Contemp Bks Staff. Basic Dictionary. 1996. 13.26 (*0-8092-0847-4*); pap. 7.93 (*0-8092-0848-2*) NTC Contemp Pub Co.

— Put English to Work. 100p. (J). (gr. 1). 1996. pap., teacher ed. 4.50 (*0-8092-3352-5*) NTC Contemp Pub Co.

— Put English to Work. 100p. (J). (gr. 2). 1996. pap., teacher ed. 4.50 (*0-8092-3279-0*) NTC Contemp Pub Co.

— Put English to Work. 100p. (J). (gr. 3). 1996. pap., teacher ed. 4.50 (*0-8092-3295-2*) NTC Contemp Pub Co.

— Put English to Work. 100p. (J). (gr. 4). 1996. pap., teacher ed. 4.50 (*0-8092-3296-0*) NTC Contemp Pub Co.

— Put English to Work. 100p. (J). (gr. 5). 1996. pap., teacher ed. 4.50 (*0-8092-3293-6*) NTC Contemp Pub Co.

— Put English to Work. 100p. (J). (gr. 6). 1996. pap., teacher ed. 4.50 (*0-8092-3294-4*) NTC Contemp Pub Co.

— Put English to Work, Bk. 3. 100p. 1996. pap. 11.93 (*0-8092-3357-6*) NTC Contemp Pub Co.

— Put English to Work, Vol. 1. 100p. 1996. pap. 11.93 (*0-8092-3359-2*) NTC Contemp Pub Co.

— Put English to Work, Vol. 2. 100p. 1996. pap. 11.93 (*0-8092-3358-4*) NTC Contemp Pub Co.

— Word Power A. 1997. pap. 10.60 (*0-8092-0835-0*) NTC Contemp Pub Co.

— Word Power B. 1997. pap. 10.60 (*0-8092-0836-9*) NTC Contemp Pub Co.

— Word Power C. 1997. pap. 10.60 (*0-8092-0837-7*) NTC Contemp Pub Co.

— Word Power D. 1997. pap. 10.60 (*0-8092-0838-5*) NTC Contemp Pub Co.

— Word Power E. 1997. pap. 10.60 (*0-8092-0839-3*) NTC Contemp Pub Co.

— Workplace English, Bk. 4. 100p. 1996. pap. 11.93 (*0-8092-3356-8*) NTC Contemp Pub Co.

— Workplace English, Bk. 6. 100p. 1996. pap. 11.93 (*0-8092-3353-3*) NTC Contemp Pub Co.

Contemporary Biography Editorial Staff. Contemporary Biography-Artists. (Contemporary Biography Ser.). (Illus.). 320p. 1987. lib. bdg. 60.00 (*0-317-59247-5*) Rprt Serv.

— Contemporary Biography-Athletes. (Contemporary Biography Ser.). (Illus.). 320p. 1987. lib. bdg. 60.00 (*0-317-59245-9*) Rprt Serv.

— Contemporary Biography-Blacks. (Contemporary Biography Ser.). (Illus.). 1987. lib. bdg. 60.00 (*0-317-59240-8*) Rprt Serv.

— Contemporary Biography-California. 180p. 1987. pap. 28.00 (*0-317-59238-6*); lib. bdg. 35.00 (*0-317-59237-8*) Rprt Serv.

— Contemporary Biography-Entertainers. (Contemporary Biography Ser.). (Illus.). 320p. 1987. lib. bdg. 60.00 (*0-317-59241-6*) Rprt Serv.

— Contemporary Biography-Religion. (Contemporary Biography Ser.). (Illus.). 320p. 1987. lib. bdg. 60.00 (*0-317-59249-1*) Rprt Serv.

— Contemporary Biography-Women. (Contemporary Biography Ser.). (Illus.). 320p. 1987. 60.00 (*0-317-59234-3*); lib. bdg. 60.00 (*0-317-59235-1*) Rprt Serv.

Contemporary Book Editors. Amazing Century. 96p. 1992. pap., teacher ed. 4.10 (*0-8092-3871-3*) NTC Contemp Pub Co.

— Building Punctuation Skills. 30p. 1993. pap. 2.50 (*0-8092-3742-3*) NTC Contemp Pub Co.

— Connections: Pre & Post Tests. 1992. pap. 3.00 (*0-8092-3869-1*) NTC Contemp Pub Co.

— Discoveries: Pre & Post Tests. 1992. pap. 3.00 (*0-8092-3868-3*) NTC Contemp Pub Co.

— Expressing Your Viewpoints, 2 vols. 1994. pap., teacher ed. 7.95 (*0-8092-3645-1*) NTC Contemp Pub Co.

— Expressions 2, Vol. 2. 1994. pap. 10.60 (*0-8092-3648-6*) NTC Contemp Pub Co.

— Improving Spelling & Capitalization. 30p. 1993. pap. 2.50 (*0-8092-3745-8*) NTC Contemp Pub Co.

— Improving Writing Styles & Paragraghs. 30p. 1993. pap. 2.50 (*0-8092-3740-7*) NTC Contemp Pub Co.

— Insights: Pre-Test & Post-Test. 1992. pap. 3.00 (*0-8092-3870-5*) NTC Contemp Pub Co.

— Look at U. S. Literacy Level. 1989. pap., teacher ed. 8.75 (*0-8092-4328-8*) NTC Contemp Pub Co.

— Mastering Parts of Speech. 30p. 1993. pap. 2.50 (*0-8092-3749-0*) NTC Contemp Pub Co.

— Pre-GED Literature & The Arts. 1995. pap. 11.93 (*0-8092-3491-2*) NTC Contemp Pub Co.

— Pre-GED Mathematics. 1995. pap. 11.93 (*0-8092-3490-4*) NTC Contemp Pub Co.

— Pre-GED Social Studies Skills. 1995. pap. 11.93 (*0-8092-3493-9*) NTC Contemp Pub Co.

— Pre-GED Writing Skills. 1995. pap. 11.93 (*0-8092-3494-7*) NTC Contemp Pub Co.

— Reader's Choice: Connections Pre & Post Tests. 1992. pap. 14.85 (*0-8092-3866-7*) NTC Contemp Pub Co.

— Reader's Choice: Discoveries Pre & Post Tests. 1992. pap. 14.85 (*0-8092-3865-9*) NTC Contemp Pub Co.

— Reader's Choice: Insights Pre & Post Tests. 1992. pap. 14.85 (*0-8092-3867-5*) NTC Contemp Pub Co.

— Using Correct Sentence Structure. 30p. 1993. pap. 2.50 (*0-8092-3747-4*) NTC Contemp Pub Co.

— Viewpoints, Vol. 2. LC 91-30924. 1994. pap. 10.60 (*0-8092-3647-8*) NTC Contemp Pub Co.

— Writing Program Viewer's Guide. 1986. pap. 9.50 (*0-8092-4933-2*) NTC Contemp Pub Co.

Contemporary Book Editors, ed. Look at U. S., 2 bks., Bks. 1 & 2. 1989. pap., teacher ed. 8.75 (*0-8092-4380-6*) NTC Contemp Pub Co.

— Managing Basic Skills Program. 1977. pap. 0.40 (*0-8092-7398-5*) NTC Contemp Pub Co.

Contemporary Books Editors. The Contemporary Reader, Bk. 2. LC 94-32588. 1994. pap. 5.95 (*0-8092-3462-9*) NTC Contemp Pub Co.

Contemporary Books, Inc., Staff. Pre-GED Science. LC 95-9123. 1995. pap. 11.93 (*0-8092-3492-0*) NTC Contemp Pub Co.

Contemporary Books Staff. Beginning Language Skills for the World of Work, Bk. 2. 150p. 1990. pap., teacher ed. 8.45 (*0-8092-4146-3*) NTC Contemp Pub Co.

— Catch of the Day: Swimmingly Sassy Seafood & Freshwater Fish Recipes. (Illus.). 128p. 2000. pap. 19.95 (*0-8092-9917-8*, 991780, Contemporary Bks) NTC Contemp Pub Co.

Contemporary Books Staff. Chase's Annual Events, 1995: Calendar of Events. (Illus.). 592p. 1994. pap. 47.95 (*0-8092-3634-6*) NTC Contemp Pub Co.

***Contemporary Books Staff.** Chase's Calendar of Events: The Day-By-Day Directory to Special Days, Weeks & Months 2001. (Chase's Calendar of Events Ser.). (Illus.). 2000. pap. 59.95 (*0-8092-2775-4*, Contemporary Bks); pap. 49.95 (*0-8092-9554-7*, Contemporary Bks) NTC Contemp Pub Co.

Contemporary Books Staff. Contemporary's Complete Pre-GED. LC 97-44080. 1024p. 1998. pap. 15.95 (*0-8092-2887-4*, 288740, Contemporary Bks) NTC Contemp Pub Co.

— London: A City Revealed. LC 98-39198. (Illus.). 176p. 1998. 60.00 (*0-8092-2802-5*, 280250, Contemporary Bks) NTC Contemp Pub Co.

— Monthly Interest Amortization Tables. 283p. 1994. pap. 6.95 (*0-8092-3564-1*) NTC Contemp Pub Co.

Contemporary Books Staff. A Picture-Based Approach for the World of Work, Bk. 1. 150p. 1991. pap., teacher ed. 8.45 (*0-8092-4167-6*) NTC Contemp Pub Co.

***Contemporary Club Staff.** Collierville, a Place Called Home. 96p. 1999. write for info. (*0-9674398-0-9*) Contemp Club.

Contemporary Editors, Staff. Skills: Pre-Tests Book. 1992. pap. 16.95 (*0-8092-3864-0*) NTC Contemp Pub Co.

— Skills: Progress. 1992. pap. 12.70 (*0-8092-3876-4*) NTC Contemp Pub Co.

— Skills: Progress Tests. 1992. pap., wbk. ed. 16.95 (*0-8092-3863-2*) NTC Contemp Pub Co.

— Skills: Scoring. 1992. pap. 6.35 (*0-8092-3874-8*) NTC Contemp Pub Co.

Contemporary Mathematics Staff, jt. auth. see Shapiro, Victor L.

Contemporary Museum Staff. Satoru Abe: A Retrospective, 1948-1998. LC 98-73422. (Illus.). 84p. 1998. 35.00 (*1-888254-02-5*) Contemp Museum.

***Contemporary Museum Staff & Lerner, Adam.** Making Sense: Ellen Gallagher, Christian Marclay & Liliana Porter, 4 vols. (Illus.). 2000. pap. 25.00 (*0-9700986-0-X*) Contemp Mus.

Contemporary Music Project for Creativity in Music. Comprehensive Musicianship: An Anthology of Evolving Thought: A Discussion of the First Ten Years (1959-1969) of the Contemporary Music Project. LC 76-157384. (Contemporary Music Project Ser.: No. 5). 129p. 1971. reprint ed. pap. 40.00 (*0-608-04217-X*, 206495800011) Bks Demand.

Contemporary Perspectives Staff. Mastering Reading, Commercial Truck Driving. (YA - Adult Education Ser.). 1991. pap. 12.95 (*0-538-70976-6*); pap. 12.95 (*0-538-70977-4*); pap. 12.95 (*0-538-70978-2*); pap. 12.95 (*0-538-70979-0*) S-W Pub.

Contemporary Reader Editors. The Contemporary Reader. 1994. pap. 46.33 (*0-8092-3461-0*); pap., teacher ed. 23.30 (*0-8092-3469-6*) NTC Contemp Pub Co.

— The Contemporary Reader, Tape 1. 1994. pap. 11.00 (*0-8092-3459-9*) NTC Contemp Pub Co.

— The Contemporary Reader, Tape 2. 1994. pap. 11.00 (*0-8092-3460-2*) NTC Contemp Pub Co.

— The Contemporary Reader, Vol. 3. 1994. pap. 5.95 (*0-8092-3464-5*) NTC Contemp Pub Co.

— The Contemporary Reader, Vol. 4. 1994. pap. 5.95 (*0-8092-3465-3*) NTC Contemp Pub Co.

— The Contemporary Reader, Vol. 5. 1994. pap. 5.95 (*0-8092-3466-1*) NTC Contemp Pub Co.

— The Contemporary Reader, Vol. 6. 1994. pap. 5.95 (*0-8092-3468-8*) NTC Contemp Pub Co.

Contemporary Reader Editors, ed. The Contemporary Reader, Vol. 2. 1994. pap. 5.95 (*0-8092-3463-7*) NTC Contemp Pub Co.

Contemporary Research, Inc. Staff. An Investigation of the Application of Programmed Inert Gas Multiple Electrode Arc Welding to the Fabrication of Automotive Heat Exchangers. 63p. 9.45 (*0-317-34534-6*, 134) Intl Copper.

Contemporary Staff. Contemporary's Amazing Century Bk. 1: 1900-1929, Bk. 1. 96p. 1992. pap. 9.86 (*0-8092-4020-3*) NTC Contemp Pub Co.

— Contemporary's Amazing Century Bk. 2: 1929 to 1945. 96p. 1992. pap. 9.86 (*0-8092-4018-1*) NTC Contemp Pub Co.

— Contemporary's Amazing Century Bk. 3: 1945 to 1960. 96p. 1992. pap. 9.86 (*0-8092-4017-3*) NTC Contemp Pub Co.

— Contemporary's Amazing Century Bk. 4: 1960 to 1975. 96p. 1992. pap. 9.86 (*0-8092-4016-5*) NTC Contemp Pub Co.

— Contemporary's Amazing Century Vol. 5: 1975 to 1992. 96p. 1992. pap. 9.86 (*0-8092-4015-7*) NTC Contemp Pub Co.

Contemporary, Staff. Post-Test: Scoring Set GED. 1987. pap. 16.20 (*0-8092-4567-1*) NTC Contemp Pub Co.

— Post-Test: Starter Set GED. 1998. pap. 33.95 (*0-8092-4566-3*) NTC Contemp Pub Co.

Contemporary Staff. Working in English Bk. 1: A Picture-Based Approach for the World of Work, Bk. 1. 150p. 11.26 (*0-8092-4170-6*) NTC Contemp Pub Co.

— You're Hired. 1991. pap., teacher ed. 7.40 (*0-8092-4029-7*) NTC Contemp Pub Co.

— You're Hired: Getting the Right Job, No. 2. 1991. pap. 9.86 (*0-8092-4030-0*) NTC Contemp Pub Co.

— You're Hired: Your Career Path, No. 1. 1991. pap. 9.86 (*0-8092-4031-9*) NTC Contemp Pub Co.

Contemporary Testimony Committee of the Christian. Our World Belongs to God: A Contemporary Testimony. rev. ed. 92p. 1987. pap. text, student ed. 3.75 (*0-930265-31-9*) CRC Pubns.

Contemporary Testimony Committee of the Christian. Our World Belongs to God: A Contemporary Testimony. rev. ed. 92p. 1988. pap. text 1.95 (*1-56212-672-5*) CRC Pubns.

***Contensou, Francois & Vranceanu, Radu.** Working Time: Theory & Policy Implications. LC 99-88518. 256p. 2000. 90.00 (*1-85898-996-5*) E Elgar.

Contensou, P., jt. auth. see Lunc, M.

Content, C. S. A Geologist's Sketch Book. 56p. 1977. pap. 3.00 (*0-87262-089-1*) Am Soc Civil Eng.

Content, D. J. & Stark, P., eds. Gold: Important Ancient & Ethnic Jewellery & Works of Art in Precious Metal. (Illus.). 240p. 1990. 45.00 (*0-685-60653-8*) D J Content.

Content, Derek J. Glyptic Arts, Ancient Jewelry: An Annotated Bibliography. 158p. (Orig.). 1985. pap. text. write for info. (*0-935681-00-0*) D J Content.

— Islamic Rings & Gems: The Zucker Collection. (Illus.). 552p. 1987. 115.00 (*0-85667-333-1*, Pub. by P Wilson) Hoovers TX.

***Content, Derek J., et al.** The Pearl & the Dragon: A Study of Vietnamese Pearls & a History of the Oriental Pearl Trade. 125p. 1999. write for info. (*0-935681-07-8*) D J Content.

Contento, William G. & Greenberg, Martin H. Index to Crime & Mystery Anthologies. 760p. 1990. 65.00 (*0-8161-8629-4*, Hall Reference) Macmillan.

Contento, William G., jt. auth. see Ashley, Michael.

Contento, William G., jt. auth. see Brown, Charles N.

Conterio, Karen. Bodily Harm: The Breakthrough Healing Program for Self-Injurers. LC 98-38171. 320p. (J). 1998. 24.95 (*0-7868-6464-8*, Pub. by Hyperion) Time Warner.

Conterio, Karen, et al. Bodily Harm: The Breakthrough Healing Program for Self-Injurers. 320p. 1999. reprint ed. pap. text 14.95 (*0-7868-8504-1*, Pub. by Hyperion) Time Warner.

***Contessa, Fabrizio.** Padre Pio. Lane, Edmund C., tr. from ITA. LC 99-35027. (Illus.). xii, 80p. 1999. pap. 6.95 (*0-8189-0826-2*) Alba.

Contestabile, E., ed. see Kosanke, Kenneth L. & Kosanke, Bonnie J.

Conteurs Francais du XVI Siecle Staff. Les Cent Nouvelles Nouvelles. 1520p. 89.95 (*0-7859-0699-1*, F27560) Fr & Eur.

Context Software Staff. Codelink - Plastic Surgery. 3rd ed. 850p. 1997. pap. text 79.95 (*1-57066-112-X*, 9755) Practice Mgmt Info.

— Context Color-Coded ICD-9-CM 1998, 2 vols. annuals rev. ed. 890p. 1997. pap. text 44.95 (*1-57066-118-9*, 9827) Practice Mgmt Info.

Context Software Staff, ed. Context Color-Coded ICD-9-CM, 1997. 5th ed. 650p. 1996. pap. text 44.95 (*1-57066-073-5*, 9727) Practice Mgmt Info.

Context Software Systems, Inc. Staff. HCPCS 1997: Medicare Level II National Codes. 1996. pap. 29.95 (*0-07-600824-X*) McGraw.

— ICD-9-CM, 1997: International Classification of Diseases, Vols. 1-3. 9th rev. ed. 1996. pap. 44.95 (*0-07-600826-6*) McGraw.

— ICD-9-CM, 1997: International Classification of Diseases, Vols. 1 & 2. 9th rev. ed. 1996. pap. 39.95 (*0-07-600825-8*) McGraw.

***Contexx, Inc. Staff.** Office 2000 QuickPro. (QuickPro Ser.: Vol. 2). (Illus.). 36p. (C). 1999. pap. 14.99 (*1-929445-01-6*) Contexx.

— QuickPro 97. (Illus.). 36p. 1999. pap. text, wbk. ed. 14.99 (*1-929445-00-8*) Contexx.

***Conti, Peter E. & Finkel, David M.** How to Create Multiple Streams of Income: Buying Homes in Nice Areas with Nothing Down! 2nd ed. 2000. 19.95 (*1-893384-15-2*) Mentor Financial.

Conti, A., jt. ed. see Maestroni, G. J. M.

Conti, C. Richard, ed. Coronary Artery Spasm: Pathophysiology, Diagnosis & Treatment. LC 86-4592. (Basic & Clinical Cardiology Ser.: No. 6). 363p. reprint ed. pap. 112.60 (*0-7837-3352-6*, 204331000008) Bks Demand.

Conti, Charles. Metaphysical Personalism: An Examination of Austin Farrer's Philosophical Theism. 326p. 1995. text 65.00 (*0-19-826338-4*) OUP.

Conti, Charles R. Introduction to Clinical Cardiology. LC 88-43396. (Illus.). 304p. 1991. reprint ed. pap. 94.30 (*0-608-05792-4*, 205975700007) Bks Demand.

Conti, Claudio J., et al, eds. Skin Tumors: Experimental & Clinical Aspects. LC 88-26435. (Carcinogenesis - A Comprehensive Survey Ser.: Vol. 11). 407p. 1989. reprint ed. pap. 126.20 (*0-608-03399-5*, 206409600008) Bks Demand.

***Conti-D'Antonio, Marcia, et al.** Self Efficacy: Raising the Bar for Students with Learning Needs. LC 99-55007. 200p. 2000. pap. text 29.95 (*1-883001-90-0*) Eye On Educ.

Conti-D'Antonio, Marcia, et al. Supporting Students with Learning Needs in the Block. LC 97-51879. (Teaching in the Block Ser.). 220p. 1998. pap. 29.95 (*1-883001-54-4*) Eye On Educ.

Conti, Delia B. Reconciling Free Trade, Fair Trade & Interdependence: The Rhetoric of Presidential Economic Leadership. LC 97-27925. (Praeger Series in Political Communication). 200p. 1998. 55.00 (*0-275-96109-5*, Praeger Pubs) Greenwood.

Conti, Edmund. The Ed C. Scrolls. 43p. 1995. pap. 3.00 (*1-57141-011-2*) Runaway Spoon.

— Eddies. (Illus.). 33p. (Orig.). 1994. pap. 3.00 (*1-57141-000-7*) Runaway Spoon.

Conti-Entin, Carol. Improvisation & Spiritual Disciples. LC 89-62589. (Orig.). 1989. pap. 4.00 (*0-87574-288-2*) Pendle Hill.

Conti-Fine, Bianca M., et al. Myasthenia Gravis: The Immunobiology of an Autoimmune Disease. LC 96-41316. (Neuroscience Intelligence Unit Ser.). 212p. 1996. 99.00 (*1-57059-406-6*) Landes Bioscience.

Conti, Fiorenzo & Hicks, T. Philip, eds. Excitatory Amino Acids & the Cerebral Cortex. LC 95-43192. (Illus.). 512p. (C). 1996. 85.00 (*0-262-03238-4*, Bradford Bks) MIT Pr.

Conti, Franco, ed. see North Atlantic Treaty Organization Staff, et al.

Conti, Gary J., jt. auth. see Feilenz, Robert A.

Conti, Gregory, tr. see Deaglio, Enrico.

Conti, Gregory, tr. see Loy, Rosetta.

Conti, Joseph G. & Stetson, Brad. Challenging the Civil Rights Establishment: Profiles of a New Black Vanguard. LC 92-31851. 264p. 1993. 22.95 (*0-275-94460-3*, C4460, Praeger Pubs) Greenwood.

Conti, Louis T. Florida Limited Liability Company Forms & Manual. LC 99-18185. 672p. 1999. ring bd. 219.90 (*1-57400-015-2*) Data Trace Pubng.

Conti, M., et al. Metropolitan Area Networks. 440p. 1997. 89.00 (*0-7803-3471-X*, PC5728-QOE) Inst Electrical.

Conti, Marco, et al. Metropolitan Area Networks. LC 96-46893. (Telecommunications Networks & Computer Systems Ser.). (Illus.). 440p. 1996. 89.95 (*3-540-19883-0*) Spr-Verlag.

Conti, Michael E. In the Line of Fire: A Working Cop's Guide to Pistolcraft. LC 97-226715. (Illus.). 184p. 1997. pap. 30.00 (*0-87364-930-3*) Paladin Pr.

Conti, P., jt. auth. see Pansini, A.

Conti, Paolo. Ducati Superbikes: 851, 888, 916. LC 96-134541. (Illus.). 94p. 1995. pap. 24.95 (*0-7603-0222-7*) MBI Pubg.

Conti, Peter S. & De Loore, Camiel W., eds. Mass Loss & Evolution of O-Type Stars. (International Astronomical Union Symposia Ser.: No. 83). 1979. pap. text 82.50 (*90-277-0989-0*); lib. bdg. 158.50 (*90-277-0988-2*) Kluwer Academic.

***Conti, Peter S. & Finkel, David.** How to Create Multiple Streams of Income: Buying Homes in Nice Areas with Nothing Down!, 1. (Illus.). 287p. 1999. pap. 19.95 (*1-893384-00-4*) Mentor Financial.

Conti, R., et al, eds. Optimization & Related Fields. (Lecture Notes in Mathematics Ser.: Vol. 1190). vii, 419p. 1986. 53.95 (*0-387-16476-6*) Spr-Verlag.

Conti, R., jt. auth. see Sansone, G.

Conti-Ramsden, Gina & Snow, Catherine E. Children's Language, Vol. 7. 352p. (C). 1990. text 89.95 (*0-8058-0523-0*) L Erlbaum Assocs.

Conti-Ramsden, Gina, jt. auth. see Beveridge, Michael.

Conti-Ramsden, Gina, jt. ed. see McTear, Michael F.

Conti, Sergio, et al, eds. The Industrial Enterprise & Its Environment Spatial Perspectives. LC 94-73479. 255p. (C). 1995. 72.95 (*1-85628-876-5*, Pub. by Avebury) Ashgate Pub Co.

Conti, Sergio & Taylor, Michael, eds. Interdependent & Uneven Development: Global-Local Perspectives. LC 97-72314. (Organization of Industrial Space Ser.). (Illus.). 328p. 1997. text 73.95 (*1-85972-445-0*, Pub. by Avebry) Ashgate Pub Co.

Conti, Vittorio & Hamaui, Rony, eds. Financial Markets Liberalisation & the Role of Banks. (Illus.). 398p. (C). 1993. text 64.95 (*0-521-41982-4*) Cambridge U Pr.

Contine, Tom. Blueprints for Successful Teaching, Pt. One: Setting the Stage for Instruction. 103p. 1994. teacher ed. 30.00 (*1-878276-47-6*) Educ Systs Assocs Inc.

— Blueprints for Successful Teaching, Pt. Two: Elements of Effective Instruction. 96p. 1994. teacher ed. 30.00 (*1-878276-48-4*) Educ Systs Assocs Inc.

— Current Brain Research: Classroom Applications: "Brain Friendly" Teaching. (Illus.). 113p. (C). 1995. 30.00 (*1-878276-51-4*) Educ Systs Assocs Inc.

— The Effective Teacher Series Pt. 1: Traits & Characteristics. 201p. (C). 1992. teacher ed. 50.00 (*1-878276-25-5*) Educ Systs Assocs Inc.

— The Effective Teacher Series Pt. II: Ingredients of Lesson Design. 163p. 1992. teacher ed. 35.00 (*1-878276-26-3*) Educ Systs Assocs Inc.

— A First Step in School Renewal Pt. 1: A School Climate Survey for Schools in Rural Settings. 45p. 1991. teacher ed. 40.00 (*1-878276-45-X*) Educ Systs Assocs Inc.

— A First Step in School Renewal Pt. 2: A School Climate Survey for Schools in Rural Settings: For Students Grades 2-12. 91p. 1992. teacher ed. 40.00 (*1-878276-29-8*) Educ Systs Assocs Inc.

— A First Step in School Renewal Pt. 3: A School Climate Survey for Schools in Rural Settings: For Parents, Support Staff, Community. 57p. 1992. teacher ed. 40.00 (*1-878276-30-1*) Educ Systs Assocs Inc.

— Outcomes Based Education: An Introduction for Teachers, Administrator, Parents & Patrons. 59p. 1993. teacher ed. 25.00 (*1-878276-33-6*) Educ Systs Assocs Inc.

— Questions: The Tool Most Used. 45p. (C). 1995. 10.00 (*1-878276-52-2*) Educ Systs Assocs Inc.

Contine, Tom, ed. A Book of Readings Selected to Nurture & Enrich Effective Teaching. (Effective Teacher Ser.: Vol. 1). 201p. (Orig.). (C). 1992. 30.00 (*1-878276-27-1*) Educ Systs Assocs Inc.

Contine, Tom & Christensen, Douglas D. Effective Schools & School Climate: A Synthesis of Research for Classroom Teachers & School Administrators. 102p. 1992. teacher ed. 25.00 (*1-878276-28-X*) Educ Systs Assocs Inc.

Continental Historical Society Staff. Queen Victoria's "Alice in Wonderland" 2nd ed. Orig. Title: Queen Victoria's Secret Diaries. (Illus.). 290p. 1984. pap. 9.95 (*0-9609900-1-1*) Cont Hist Soc.

— Queen Victoria's "Alice in Wonderland" 2nd ed. (Queen Victoria's Secret Diaries Ser.: Vol. 1). Orig. Title: Queen Victoria's Secret Diaries. (Illus.). 476p. (C). 1990. pap. text 16.95 (*0-9609900-3-8*) Cont Hist Soc.

— Queen Victoria's Through the Looking Glass. (Illus.). 319p. 1986. pap. 10.95 (*0-9609900-2-X*) Cont Hist Soc.

Continetti, R. E., jt. ed. see Suits, Arthur G.

***Contingency Planning & Recovery Consulting Group Staff.** E-Commerce & Internet Risk Management, Contingency Planning & Business Continuity: Best Practices for E-Commerce & ASP Risk Control. (Information Technologies Management, Security & Business Continuity Ser.). (Illus.). 145p. 2000. ring bd. 299.00 (*0-940706-48-2*, CP-10) Management Advisory Pubns.

Contingency Planning & Recovery Institute Staff. Standards for Establishing an Effective Contingency Planning & Disaster Recovery Function. Kuong, Javier F., ed. (Illus.). 100p. 1990. student ed., ring bd. 179.00 (*0-940706-25-3*) Management Advisory Pubns.

Contini, Lisa. Assert Yourself! Developing Power-Packed Communication Skills to Make Your Points Clearly, Confidently & Persuasively. Scanlon, Kelly & Guthrie, Jane D., eds. LC 95-7132. (Illus.). 101p. (Orig.). 1996. pap. 12.95 (*1-878542-84-2*, 12-0013) SkillPath Pubns.

Contini-Morava, Ellen & Goldberg, Barbara S., eds. Meaning As Explanation: Advances in Linguistic Sign Theory. (Trends in Linguistics, Studies & Monographs: No. 84). xii, 487p. (C). 1995. lib. bdg. 190.80 (*3-11-014122-1*) Mouton.

***Contini-Morava, Ellen & Tobin, Yishai, eds.** Between Grammar & Lexicon. LC 99-43482. (Current Issues in Linguistic Theory Ser.: 183). xxxii, 365p. 2000. 95.00 (*1-55619-960-0*) J Benjamins Pubng Co.

C

Contini, Paolo. Somali Republic: An Experiment in Legal Integration. 92p. 1969. 30.00 (*0-7146-2395-4*, Pub. by F Cass Pubs) Intl Spec Bk.
Contino, Richard. Complete Book of Equipment Leasing Agreements, Forms, Worksheets & Checklists. LC 96-52974. 640p. 1997. 125.00 (*0-8144-0338-7*) AMACOM.
Contino, Richard M. Decision Maker's Guide to Equipment Leasing. 320p. (Orig.). 1988. text 49.00 (*0-13-283268-2*, Busn) P-H.
— Handbook of Equipment Leasing: A Deal Maker's Guide. 2nd ed. Vlamis, Tony, ed. LC 96-15977. 400p. 1996. 65.00 (*0-8144-0317-4*) AMACOM.
— Negotiating Business Equipment Leases. rev. ed. 320p. 1998. 49.95 (*0-8144-0417-0*) AMACOM.
Continuing Education Center Staff. Microcomputer Literacy Program: All about Personal Computers. 89p. 1982. student ed. 99.99 (*0-07-010297-X*) McGraw.
Continuous Electron Beam Accelerator Facility Staff, jt. auth. see Goity, Jose L.
Continuum Staff. The Complete Book of Christian Prayer. LC 79-48080. (Illus.). 512p. (C). 1996. 29.95 (*0-8264-0872-9*) Continuum.
Contis, Ellene T., et al. Food Flavors: Formation, Analysis, & Packaging Influences: Proceedings of the 9th International Flavor Conference, the George Charalambous Memorial Symposium. LC 98-16165. (Developments in Food Science Ser.: 40). 812p. 1998. 342.00 (*0-444-82590-8*) Elsevier.
Contiti-Morava, Ellen. Discourse Pragmatics & Semantic Categorization: The Case of Negation & Tense-Aspect with Special Reference to Swahili. (Discourse Perspectives on Grammar Ser.: No. 1). xii, 205p. (C). 1989. lib. bdg. 79.25 (*0-89925-436-5*) Mouton.
***Conto, Richard A.** Measuring the Democratic Prospect of Mediating Structures. 27p. 1999. pap. 10.00 (*0-929556-16-X*) Ind Sector.
Contogenis, Constantine & Choe, Wolhee, trs. Songs of the Kisaeng. LC 96-80160. (New American Translations Ser.: Vol. 10). (Illus.). 70p. (Orig.). 1997. pap. 11.50 (*1-880238-53-5*) BOA Edns.
Contopoulos, G., ed. Reports on Astronomy, 3 pts., Pt. 1. (Transactions of the International Astronomical Union Ser.: Vol. XVIA). 1976. lib. bdg. 129.50 (*90-277-0739-1*) Kluwer Academic.
— Reports on Astronomy, 3 pts., Pt. 3. (Transactions of the International Astronomical Union Ser.: Vol. XVIA). 1976. lib. bdg. 129.50 (*90-277-0741-3*) Kluwer Academic.
Contopoulos, G. & Kotsakis, D. Cosmology. (Illus.). 250p. 1987. 49.95 (*0-387-16922-9*) Spr-Verlag.
Contopoulos, G., et al. Galactic Dynamics & N-Body Simulations: Lectures Held at the Astrophysics School VI, Organized by the European Astrophysics Doctoral Network (EADN) in Thessaloniki, Greece, 13-23 July 1993. Spyrou, N. & Vlahos, L., eds. LC 94-21973. 1994. 86.95 (*0-387-57983-4*) Spr-Verlag.
Contopoulos, G., ed. see International Astronomical Union Staff.
Contopoulos, G., ed. see International Astronomical Union Staff & Extraordinary General Assembly, Poland, 1973.
Contopoulos, George. Waves in Astrophysics. 345p. 1999. pap. text 22.50 (*0-8018-6303-1*) Johns Hopkins.
Contopoulos, Michael. The Greek Community of New York City: Early Years to 1910. (Hellenism: Ancient, Mediaeval, Modern Ser.: No. 11). xvi, 232p. 1992. lib. bdg. 40.00 (*0-89241-518-5*) Caratzas.
***Contorno, Joann.** Pathway to Passion: From the Pits to Passion. 2000. pap. 14.95 (*0-9678157-0-3*) J Contorno.
Contos, Leonidas, tr. see Kalokyris, Konstantin.
Contos, Leonidas C. The Psalms Translated from the Greek Septuagint. De Vinck, Jose M., tr. from GRE. LC 93-72528. 202p. 1993. 18.75 (*0-911726-60-8*, SPS) Alleluia Pr.
— Two Thousand & One the Church in Crisis. 60p. (C). 1981. pap. 2.95 (*0-916586-46-4*) Holy Cross Orthodox.
Contoski, Edmund. Maker & Takers: How Wealth & Progress Are Made - & How They Are Taken Away or Prevented. LC 96-78787. 480p. (Orig.). 1997. pap. 24.95 (*0-9655007-4-8*) Am Liberty Pubs.
— The Trojan Project. LC 96-78788. 256p. (Orig.). 1997. pap. 17.95 (*0-9655007-5-6*) Am Liberty Pubs.
***Contoski, Victor.** Homecoming: Poems. 120p. 2000. pap. 13.95 (*0-89823-210-4*, Pub. by New Rivers Pr) Consort Bk Sales.
Contoski, Victor, tr. see Rozewicz, Tadeusz.
***Contosta, David R.** Lancaster, Ohio, 1800-2000: Frontier Town to Edge City. Miller, Zane L., ed. & frwd. by. LC 99-21549. (Urban Life & Urban Landscape Ser.). (Illus.). 352p. 1999. text 37.50 (*0-8142-0825-8*) Ohio St U Pr.
— Lancaster, Ohio, 1800-2000: Frontier Town to Edge City. (Urban Life & Urban Landscape Ser.). (Illus.). 360p. 2000. pap. 19.95 (*0-8142-5027-0*) Ohio St U Pr.
Contosta, David R. A Philadelphia Family: The Houstons & Woodwards of Chestnut Hill. LC 88-21596. (Illus.). 226p. (C). 1988. 25.95 (*0-8122-8136-5*); pap. 15.95 (*0-8122-1406-4*) U of Pa Pr.
— Philadelphia's Progressive Orphanage: The Carson Valley School. LC 97-6406. 1997. 34.95 (*0-271-01714-7*) Pa St U Pr.
— The Private Life of James Bond. LC 93-15237. (Illus.). 130p. 1993. 16.95 (*0-915010-38-0*) Sutter House.
***Contosta, David R.** Saint Joseph's, Philadelphia's Jesuit University. LC 00-9878. 2000. write for info. (*0-916101-37-1*) St Joseph.
Contosta, David R. Suburb in the City: Chestnut Hill, Philadelphia, 1850-1990. LC 92-9820. (Illus.). 351p. 1992. reprint ed. pap. text 18.95 (*0-8142-0581-X*) Ohio St U Pr.
— Villanova University, 1842-1992: American-Catholic-Augustinian. LC 94-45427. (Illus.). 328p. 1995. 40.00 (*0-271-01459-8*) Pa St U Pr.
Contosta, David R. & Gallagher, Dennis J. Ever Ancient, Ever New: Villanova University 1842-1992. LC 92-24373. 1992. write for info. (*0-89865-847-0*) Donning Co.
Contosta, David R. & Muccigrosso, Robert, eds. Henry Adams & His World. LC 92-76199. (Transactions Ser.: Vol. 83, Pt. 4). 120p. (C). 1993. pap. 15.00 (*0-87169-834-X*, T834-COD) Am Philos.
Contractor, Farok. International Corporate Finance. 1997. pap. 24.95 (*0-415-10522-6*) Thomson Learn.
Contractor, Farok J. Licensing in International Strategy: A Guide for Planning & Negotiations. LC 84-22756. (Illus.). 254p. 1985. 69.50 (*0-89930-024-3*, CLI/, Quorum Bks) Greenwood.
***Contractor, Farok J., ed.** Valuation of Intangible Assets in Global Operations. 2001. write for info. (*1-56720-412-0*) Greenwood.
Contractor, Farok J. & International Trade & Finance Association Staff. Economic Transformation in Emerging Countries: The Role of Investment, Trade, & Finance. LC 98-11833. (International Business & Economics Ser.). 1998. 65.00 (*0-08-043429-0*, Pergamon Pr) Elsevier.
Contractor, M. H., jt. ed. see Kapadia, Harish.
Contractors' Service Center, Inc. Staff. Rules of the Road. 372p. 1990. 29.95 (*0-9627309-0-4*) Contractors Srvc Ctr.
Contractors' Service Center, Inc., Staff. Rules of the Road. rev. ed. 372p. 1991. 29.95 (*0-9627309-1-2*) Contractors Srvc Ctr.
Contrada, Richard J. & Ashmore, Richard D., eds. Self, Social Identity, & Physical Health: Interdisciplinary Explorations. LC 98-20149. (Rutgers Series on Self & Social Identity). (Illus.). 296p. 1999. text 60.00 (*0-19-512730-7*); pap. text 29.95 (*0-19-512731-5*) OUP.
Contratto, Susan & Gutfreund, M. Janice, eds. A Feminist Clinician's Guide to the Memory Debate. LC 96-38179. (Women & Therapy Ser.: Vol. 19, No. 1). 140p. (C). 1996. 29.95 (*1-56024-822-X*, Haworth Pastrl); pap. 14.95 (*1-56023-085-1*) Haworth Pr.
Contreni, John J. Carolingian Learning, Masters & Manuscripts. (Collected Studies: No. CS363). 1000p. 1992. text 115.95 (*0-86078-317-0*, Pub. by Variorum) Ashgate Pub Co.
Contreni, John J., jt. ed. see Noble, Thomas F.
Contreras, Alan. Northwest Birds in Winter. LC 97-26736. (Illus.). 288p. 1997. pap. 17.95 (*0-87071-425-2*) Oreg St U Pr.
— A Pocket Guide to Oregon Birds. 65p. 1996. 5.00 (*1-877693-23-5*) Oregon Field.
Contreras, Alan & Kindschy, Robert R. Birds of Malheur County, Oregon. (Illus.). 104p. (Orig.). 1996. pap. 12.00 (*1-877693-22-7*) Oregon Field.
Contreras, Alonso de. Discurso de Mi Vida. Ettinghausen, Henry, ed. (Nueva Austral Ser.: Vol. 66). (SPA.). 1991. pap. text 24.95 (*84-239-1866-1*) Elliots Bks.
***Contreras, Andrew.** Voice of the 7th Angel: The End Is Not Yet. LC 99-59029. 512p. 1999. pap. 14.95 (*0-86534-310-1*) Sunstone Pr.
Contreras, Arnoldo, jt. auth. see Gregersen, Hans M.
Contreras, Belisario R. Tradition & Innovation in New Deal Art. LC 81-65861. (Illus.). 256p. 1984. 45.00 (*0-8387-5032-X*) Bucknell U Pr.
Contreras, Carlos A., jt. ed. see Wilkie, James W.
Contreras, Don, photos by. We Dance Because We Can: People of the Powwow. LC 95-82240. (Illus.). 149p. 1996. 29.95 (*1-56352-287-X*) Longstreet.
Contreras, Francisco. Health in the 21st Century: Will Doctors Survive? Lowe, Pamela M., ed. Ruiz, Luisa, tr. from SPA.Tr. of Salud en el Siglo XXI, "Sobreviviran Los Medicos?. (Illus.). 392p. (Orig.). 1997. mass mkt. 19.95 (*1-57946-000-3*) Interpacific Pr.
***Contreras, Francisco.** Hope of Living Cancer Free: Breakthrough Strategies for Preventing & Reversing Cancer, Vol. 1. 1999. 17.99 (*0-88419-655-0*) Creation House.
— Hope of Living Long & Well. 224p. 2000. pap. 12.99 (*0-88419-695-X*) Creation House.
Contreras, Francisco. Saludo en el Siglo: Sobreviviran los Medicas? Lowe, Pamela M., ed. Ruiz, Luisa, tr.Tr. of Health in the 21st Century: Will Doctors Survive?. (SPA., Illus.). 456p. (Orig.). 1997. mass mkt. 19.95 (*1-57946-001-1*) Interpacific Pr.
— Todo Para la Mujer, el Papel de la Progesterona Natural en el Bienestar Femenino. Kennedy, Daniel, ed. Ruiz, Luisa, tr.Tr. of Everything for the Woman, the Role of Natural Progesterone in Feminine Well Being. (SPA.). 32p. 1998. pap. 3.95 (*1-57946-002-X*) Interpacific Pr.
Contreras, Gloria, ed. Latin American Culture Studies: Information & Materials for Teaching about Latin America. rev. ed. (Latin American Culture Studies Project). 310p. (J). (gr. k-12). 1987. pap. text 19.95 (*0-86728-020-4*) U TX Inst Lat Am Stud.
Contreras, Gonzalo. El Nadador (The Swimmer)Tr. of Swimmer. 240p. 1996. pap. 12.50 (*0-679-76549-2*) Random.
Contreras-Hermosilla, Arnoldo, jt. ed. see Shen, Susan.
Contreras, Josefina M., ed. see Kerns, Kathryn A.
Contreras, Josefina M., ed. see Neal-Barnett, Angela M.
Contreras, M., jt. ed. see Leikola, J.
Contreras, Marcela. ABC of Transfusion. 2nd ed. (Illus.). 76p. 1992. pap. text 28.00 (*0-7279-0754-9*, Pub. by BMJ Pub) Login Brothers Bk Co.
Contreras, Olga, tr. see Quinby, Marge M.
Contreras-Ramos, Atilano. Systematics of the Dobsonfly Genus Corydalus: (Megaloptera: Corydalidae) (Monographs, Thomas Say Publications in Entomology Ser.). (Illus.). 360p. 1998. pap. 35.00 (*0-938522-70-1*) Entomol Soc.
Control Zed Staff. The Revolutionary Guide to Bitmapped Graphics. 550p. 1994. pap. 44.95 incl. cd-rom (*1-874416-31-1*) Wrox Pr Inc.
Controvich, James T. The Central Pacific Campaign, 1943-1944: A Bibliography, Vol. 2. LC 90-5508. (Bibliographies of Battles & Leaders Ser.: No. 2). 160p. 1990. lib. bdg. 55.00 (*0-313-28074-6*, CCY, Greenwood Pr) Greenwood.
Controvich, James T., compiled by. United States Army Unit Histories: A Reference & Bibliography. 600p. 1983. pap. 82.00 (*0-89126-121-4*) MA-AH Pub.
— United States Army Unit Histories: A Reference & Bibliography, Suppl. C. LC 97-112310. 115p. 1996. pap. 29.95 (*0-89126-195-8*) MA-AH Pub.
— United States Army Unit Histories: A Reference & Bibliography, Suppl. A. 136p. 1987. pap. 32.00 (*0-89126-166-4*) MA-AH Pub.
— United States Army Unit Histories: A Reference & Bibliography, Suppl. B. 600p. 1992. pap. 32.00 (*0-89126-174-5*) MA-AH Pub.
Contrucci, Joyce, jt. auth. see Collard, Andree.
Contry, ed. see Dueck, Robert K.
Conture, Edward G. Stuttering. 2nd ed. 320p. (C). 1989. 81.00 (*0-13-853631-7*) P-H.
Conture, Edward G., jt. auth. see Guitar, Barry.
Conture, Edward G., jt. ed. see Fraser, Jane.
Conty, ed. see Assadipour, Hossein.
Conty, ed. see Flore, James M.
Conty, ed. see Gendell, Julien.
Conty, ed. see Granger, Frank.
Conty, ed. see Lamit, L. Gary.
Conty, ed. see Lamit, L. Gary & Kitto, Kathleen L.
Conty, ed. see Miller, Michael A.
Conty, ed. see Walls, Ron & Johnstone, Wesley.
Conuel, Thomas. Quabbin: The Accidental Wilderness. rev. ed. LC 90-11048. (Illus.). 120p. 1990. reprint ed. pap. 13.95 (*0-87023-730-6*) U of Mass Pr.
Conus, Leon & Conus, Olga. Fundamentals of Piano Technique, Bks. 1 & 2. rev. ed. McKeever, James M., ed. 60p. 1957. pap. text 9.95 (*0-87487-660-5*) Summy-Birchard.
Conus, Olga, jt. auth. see Conus, Leon.
Convention for the Protection of Human Rights & Fu, jt. auth. see Fawcett, J. E.
Convergence Multimedia Corporation Staff. Career Paths in Marketing. (Prentice Hall College Titles Ser.). (C). 1996. cd-rom 33.33 (*0-13-531344-9*, Macmillan Coll) P-H.
Convergence Multimedia Staff. Management Consulting Cd-Rom. 1996. 39.95 (*0-87584-752-8*) Harvard Busn.
Convers, Howard. The Promised Land. LC 96-225333. (Illus.). 185p. (Orig.). 1996. pap., per. 23.95 (*0-9653430-0-6*) H Convers.
Convers, Howard. That Convers Kid from Turlock. (Illus.). 232p. 1998. pap. 25.00 (*0-9653430-1-4*) H Convers.
Conversa-phone Institute Staff. Basic French. unabridged ed. (Round the World Basic Language Program Ser.). (ENG & FRE.). 1997. pap. 9.95 incl. audio (*1-56752-001-4*) Conversa-phone.
Converse, C. A. Some of the Ancestors & Descendants of Samuel Converse, Jr., Major James Convers, Hon. Heman Allen, Captain Jonathan Bixby, Sr., 2 vols. (Illus.). 989p. 1989. reprint ed. pap. 148.00 (*0-8328-0421-5*); reprint ed. lib. bdg. 156.00 (*0-8328-0420-7*) Higginson Bk Co.
Converse, Carolyn A. & Skinner, Roy, eds. Lipoprotein Analysis: A Practical Approach. (Practical Approach Ser.). (Illus.). 272p. 1992. pap. text 42.00 (*0-19-963231-6*) OUP.

Converse, Elliott V., et al. The Exclusion of Black Soldiers from the Medal of Honor in World War II: The Study Commissioned by the United States Army to Investigate Racial Bias in the Awarding of the Nation's Highest Military Decoration. LC 96-50355. 208p. 1997. lib. bdg. 29.95 (*0-7864-0277-6*) McFarland & Co.
Converse, Frank. Deluxe Concertina Book. 52p. 1981. pap. 8.95 (*0-87166-869-6*, 93758) Mel Bay.
Converse, Frank B. Frank B. Converse's Method for the Banjo: With Or Without a Master. LC 92-61251. (Illus.). 84p. (Orig.). (C). 1993. reprint ed. pap. 18.00 (*0-9633593-2-0*) Tuckahoe Music.
Converse, George, jt. auth. see Peddicord, Richard G.
Converse, Howard H. Handbook of Paleo-Preparation Techniques. 109p. 1989. pap. 13.00 (*1-883167-00-0*) FL Paleo Soc.
Converse, Jane. Accused Nurse. large type ed. 1990. 27.99 (*0-7089-2293-7*) Ulverscroft.
— Condemned Nurse. large type ed. (Linford Romance Library). 256p. 1996. pap. 16.99 (*0-7089-7828-2*, Linford) Ulverscroft.
— Hostage Nurse. large type ed. (Linford Romance Library). 224p. 1993. pap. 16.99 (*0-7089-7467-8*) Ulverscroft.
— Nurse Against the Town. large type ed. (Linford Romance Library). 208p. 1993. pap. 16.99 (*0-7089-7456-2*, Linford) Ulverscroft.
— Nurse in Panic. large type ed. LC 93-27183. 204p. 1994. lib. bdg. 14.95 (*0-7862-0046-4*) Thorndike Pr.
— Nurse in Rome. large type ed. (Linford Romance Library). 240p. 1994. pap. 16.99 (*0-7089-7523-2*, Linford) Ulverscroft.
— Paradise Postponed. large type ed. 1994. 27.99 (*0-7089-3183-9*) Ulverscroft.
— Penthouse Nurse. large type ed. (Linford Romance Library). 224p. 1993. pap. 16.99 (*0-7089-7411-2*, Linford) Ulverscroft.
***Converse, Jane.** Pleasure Cruise Nurse. LC 00-23528. 2000. write for info. (*0-7862-2508-4*) Five Star.
Converse, Jane. Psychiatric Nurse. large type ed. (Linford Romance Library). 256p. 1993. pap. 16.99 (*0-7089-7329-9*, Linford) Ulverscroft.
— Recruiting Nurse. large type ed. (Linford Romance Library). 256p. 1993. pap. 16.99 (*0-7089-7394-9*, Linford) Ulverscroft.
— Second-Chance Nurse. large type ed. 1991. 27.99 (*0-7089-2387-9*) Ulverscroft.
— Thrill Show Nurse. large type ed. (Linford Romance Library). 288p. 1994. pap. 16.99 (*0-7089-7505-4*, Linford) Ulverscroft.
Converse, Jane B. How to Sprinkler Installation Guide. (Illus.). 16p. 1989. pap. 5.00 (*0-685-29960-0*) L R Nelson.
***Converse, Jane Bodman, ed.** The Peoria Collection: A Book of Engravings from 1886. 58p. 1999. ring bd. 30.00 (*1-893525-01-5*) Converse Pubg.
Converse, Jean M. & Presser, Stanley. Survey Questions. (Quantitative Applications in the Social Sciences Ser.: Vol. 63). 96p. (Orig.). 1986. pap. text 10.95 (*0-8039-2743-6*) Sage.
Converse, John M., ed. Reconstructive Plastic Surgery: Principles & Procedures in Correction Reconstruction & Transplantation, 7 vols., 1. 2nd ed. LC 74-21010. (Illus.). 1977. text 140.00 (*0-7216-2680-7*, W B Saunders Co) Harcrt Hlth Sci Grp.
— Reconstructive Plastic Surgery: Principles & Procedures in Correction Reconstruction & Transplantation, 7 vols., 2. 2nd ed. LC 74-21010. (Illus.). 1977. text 140.00 (*0-7216-2681-5*, W B Saunders Co) Harcrt Hlth Sci Grp.
— Reconstructive Plastic Surgery: Principles & Procedures in Correction Reconstruction & Transplantation, 7 vols., 3. 2nd ed. LC 74-21010. (Illus.). 1977. text 140.00 (*0-7216-2682-3*, W B Saunders Co) Harcrt Hlth Sci Grp.
— Reconstructive Plastic Surgery: Principles & Procedures in Correction Reconstruction & Transplantation, 7 vols., 4. 2nd ed. LC 74-21010. (Illus.). 1977. text 140.00 (*0-7216-2683-1*, W B Saunders Co) Harcrt Hlth Sci Grp.
— Reconstructive Plastic Surgery: Principles & Procedures in Correction Reconstruction & Transplantation, 7 vols., 5. 2nd ed. LC 74-21010. (Illus.). 1977. text 140.00 (*0-7216-2684-X*, W B Saunders Co) Harcrt Hlth Sci Grp.
— Reconstructive Plastic Surgery: Principles & Procedures in Correction Reconstruction & Transplantation, 7 vols., 6. 2nd ed. LC 74-21010. (Illus.). 1977. text 140.00 (*0-7216-2685-8*, W B Saunders Co) Harcrt Hlth Sci Grp.
— Reconstructive Plastic Surgery: Principles & Procedures in Correction Reconstruction & Transplantation, 7 vols., 7. 2nd ed. LC 74-21010. (Illus.). 1977. text 140.00 (*0-7216-2686-6*, W B Saunders Co) Harcrt Hlth Sci Grp.
— Reconstructive Plastic Surgery: Principles & Procedures in Correction Reconstruction & Transplantation, 7 vols., Set. 2nd ed. LC 74-21010. (Illus.). 1977. text 900.00 (*0-7216-2691-2*, W B Saunders Co) Harcrt Hlth Sci Grp.
Converse, John M., jt. auth. see Ballantyne, D. L.
***Converse, Kimberley, tr.** God's Comfort Food for New Beginnings: Satisfying, Solid Words of Hope in Times of Change. LC 99-229877. (Illus.). 160p. 1999. pap. 7.95 (*1-893689-01-8*, 701) Elim.
Converse of International School of Languages Staf, tr. Panorama of Tapestry. LC 86-71250. (ENG., Illus.). 40p. (Orig.). 1986. pap. 9.95 (*0-945858-00-0*) Am Tapestry Alliance.
Converse, Parker L. Legends of Woburn, 1642-1892, Second Series. (Illus.). 252p. 1995. reprint ed. lib. bdg. 35.00 (*0-8328-4699-6*) Higginson Bk Co.

— Legends of Woburn, 1642-1892: Now First Written & Preserved in Collected Form...to Which Is Added a Chrono-Indexical History of Woburn. (Illus.). 174p. 1995. reprint ed. lib. bdg. 29.00 (*0-8328-4700-3*) Higginson Bk Co.

Converse, Paul D. The Beginning of Marketing Thought in the United States, 2 vols. Assael, Henry, ed. LC 78-282. (Century of Marketing Ser.). 1979. reprint ed. lib. bdg. 21.95 (*0-405-11161-4*) Ayer.

Converse, Paul D. symposium Staff. Proceedings: 13th Paul D. Converse Symposium, 1992, University of Illinois. Sudharsan, Devanathan, ed. LC 94-46837. (Proceedings Ser.). 1995. 35.00 (*0-87757-254-2*) Am Mktg.

Converse, Philip, et al. Canadian National Election Study, 1965. 1972. write for info. (*0-89138-058-2*) ICPSR.

Converse, Philip E. & Pierce, Roy. Political Representation in France. LC 85-15789. (Illus.). 1040p. 1986. 83.00 (*0-674-68660-8*) Belknap Pr.

Converse, Philip E., et al. American Social Attitudes Data Sourcebook: 1947-1978. (Illus.). 441p. 1980. 43.50 (*0-674-02880-5*) HUP.

Converse, Philip E., jt. ed. see Campbell, Angus.

Converse, Phillip E., jt. auth. see Campbell, Angus.

Converse Staff. Converse 3 All-Star Basketball: How to Play Like a Pro. LC 96-21551. (Illus.). 96p. (J). (gr. 3 up). 1996. pap. 12.95 (*0-471-15977-8*) Wiley.

— Converse 3 All-Star Football: How to Play Like a Pro. LC 96-20833. (Illus.). 96p. (J). (gr. 3 up). 1996. pap. 12.95 (*0-471-15978-6*) Wiley.

— Converse 3 All Star Soccer: How to Play Like a Pro. LC 96-39054. (Converse All Star Sports Ser.). 96p. 1997. pap. 12.95 (*0-471-15992-1*) Wiley.

Converse, Terry J. Directing for the Stage: A Workshop Guide for 42 Creative Training Exercises & Projects. Zapel, Theodore O., ed. LC 95-35414. (Illus.). 328p. (YA). (gr. 9 up). 1995. pap. 19.95 (*1-56608-014-2*, B169) Meriwether Pub.

— The Psychology of the Grotesque in August Strindberg's The Ghost Sonata. LC 98-50017. (Studies in Comparative Literature: Vol. 24). 268p. 1999. text 89.95 (*0-7734-8207-5*) E Mellen.

***Converse, Tim.** PHP 4 Bible. (Bible Ser.). (Illus.). 750p. 2000. pap. text 39.99 (*0-7645-4716-X*) IDG Bks.

***Converse, Tracey C.** Lonoke County, Arkansas, Will Books A & B, 1873-1913. 65p. 1999. pap. 15.00 (*1-56546-147-9*) Arkansas Res.

***Conversi, Daniele.** The Basques, the Catalans, & Spain: Alternative Routes to Ethnic Autonomy. LC 95-45484. (Ethnonationalism in Comparative Perspective Ser.). 338p. (C). 2000. pap. 21.95 (*0-87417-362-0*) U of Nev Pr.

Conversino da Ravenna, Giovanni Di, see Di Conversino da Ravenna, Giovanni.

Conversino, Mark J. Fighting with the Soviets: The Failure of Operation FRANTIC, 1944-1945. LC 96-32956. (Modern War Studies). (Illus.). 288p. 1996. 35.00 (*0-7006-0808-7*) U Pr of KS.

Convert-Chalmers, Claudine, jt. auth. see Rochester, Myrna B.

Convert, Pierre & Forsyth, J. Bruce, eds. Position-Sensitive Detection of Thermal Neutrons. 1984. text 123.00 (*0-12-186180-5*) Acad Pr.

Convery, Anne. Pupils' Perceptions of Europe. LC 97-179435. (Illus.). 1997. 89.50 (*0-304-33637-8*) Continuum.

Convery, Frank J. Applying Environmental Economics in Africa. LC 95-1897. (World Bank Technical Papers: No. 277). 176p. 1995. pap. 22.00 (*0-8213-3190-6*, 13190) World Bank.

Convery, Frank J., ed. A Guide to Policies for Energy Conservation: The European Experience. LC 98-6256. 192p. 1999. 80.00 (*1-85898-635-4*) E Elgar.

Convery, Frank J., et al, eds. Reorganization: Issues, Implications & Opportunities for U. S. Natural Resources Policy: Symposium Proceedings, April 19-20, 1979. LC HC0103.7.R39. 212p. reprint ed. pap. 65.80 (*0-7837-6036-1*, 204584900008) Bks Demand.

Convery, Frank J. & Davis, Jean E., eds. Centers of Influence & U. S. Forest Policy. LC SD0565.C40. 168p. reprint ed. pap. 52.10 (*0-7837-6041-8*, 20458540008) Bks Demand.

Convery, Frank J. & European Foundation for the Improvement of Living & Working Staff. Challenges for Urban Infrastructure in the European Union LC 99-169432. 6p. 1998. write for info. (*92-828-3673-8*) Intl Pubns Serv.

Convery, Frank J. & Ralston, Charles W., eds. Forestry & Long Range Planning. LC SD0561.F60. (Illus.). 243p. reprint ed. pap. 75.40 (*0-7837-6035-3*, 204584800008) Bks Demand.

Convery, Frank J. & Strain, Boyd R., eds. United States Dependency on Canadian Natural Resources: Extent & Significance: Seminar Proceedings, April 7, 1979. LC E 0183.8.C2U. 72p. reprint ed. pap. 30.00 (*0-7837-6047-7*, 204586000008) Bks Demand.

Convery, Frank J., jt. ed. see Royer, Jack P.

Convery, Fredric R. Behind the Lines: From North Africa to Germany During World War II. 225p. 1995. pap. 16.95 (*1-880222-21-3*) Red Apple Pub.

***Convery, William J.** Pride of the Rockies: The Life of Colorado's Premiere Irish Patron, John Kernan Mullen. (Illus.). 256p. 2000. 22.50 (*0-87081-591-1*) U of Okla Pr.

Convey, John. Online Information Retrieval: An Introductory Manual to Principles & Practice. 4th ed. LC 93-150072. (Illus.). 318p. 1992. reprint ed. pap. 98.60 (*0-608-07773-9*, 206786100010) Bks Demand.

Convey, John J. Catholic Schools Make a Difference: Twenty-Five Years of Research. (Illus.). 219p. 1992. pap. 10.00 (*1-55833-123-9*) Natl Cath Educ.

Convey, John J. & Ciriello, Maria J. Strategic Planning for Catholic Schools: A Diocesan Model of Consultation. 239p. (Orig.). (C). 1996. pap. 44.95 (*1-57455-055-1*) US Catholic.

Convey, John J. & Haney, Regina. Benchmarks of Excellence: Effective Boards of Catholic Education. LC 98-206980. 218p. 1997. pap. 36.00 (*1-55833-192-1*) Natl Cath Educ.

***Convey, John J. & Thompson, Andrew D.** Assessment of Catholic Religious Education: Weaving Christ's Seamless Garment. 127p. 1999. pap. 13.00 (*1-55833-228-3*) Natl Cath Educ.

Convey, John J., jt. auth. see Youniss, James.

Convey, Stephen R. & Pain, Andrew J. A Practical Guide to Effective Protection at the Land Registry. 232p. 1991. 75.00 (*1-85190-121-3*, Pub. by Tolley Pubng) St Mut.

Convicer, Richard G. & Schatz, Louis B. Connecticut Limited Liability Company Forms & Practice Manual, 2 vols. LC 95-12574. 674p. 1995. ring bd. 239.90 (*1-57400-001-2*) Data Trace Pubng.

Conville, Richard L. Relational Transitions: The Evolution of Personal Relationships. LC 91-4089. 208p. 1991. 55.00 (*0-275-93523-X*, C3523, Praeger Pubs) Greenwood.

Conville, Richard L., ed. Uses of "Structure" in Communication Studies. LC 93-19112. 240p. 1993. 62.95 (*0-275-94407-7*, C4407, Praeger Pubs) Greenwood.

Conville, Richard L. & Rogers, L. Edna, eds. The Meaning of 'Relationship' in Interpersonal Communication. LC 97-14472. 216p. 1998. 59.95 (*0-275-95211-8*, Praeger Pubs) Greenwood.

Convington, Robert N. & Decker, Kurt H. Individual Employee Rights in a Nutshell. (Nutshell Ser.). 386p. (C). 1995. pap. 21.00 (*0-314-04743-3*) West Pub.

Convis, Charles L. Dogs & Masters. (True Tales of the Old West Ser.: Vol. 10). (Illus.). ii, 62p. 1999. pap. 7.95 (*1-892156-00-8*, Pub. by Pioneer Pr NV) Sunbelt Pubns.

— Entertainers. (True Tales of the Old West Ser.: Vol. 9). (Illus.). ii, 62p. 1998. pap. 7.95 (*0-9651954-9-X*) Pioneer Pr NV.

— Frontiers Men. (True Tales of the Old West Ser.: Vol. 12). (Illus.). ii, 62p. 1999. pap. 7.95 (*1-892156-02-4*, Pub. by Pioneer Pr NV) Sunbelt Pubns.

***Convis, Charles L.** Gamblers. LC 96-68502. (True Tales of the Old West Ser.: Vol. 13). (Illus.). ii, 62p. 2000. pap. 7.95 (*1-892156-03-2*) Pioneer Pr NV.

Convis, Charles L. The Honor of Arms: A Biography of Myles W. Keogh. (Great West & Indian Ser.: Vol. 55). (Illus.). 1990. 26.95 (*0-87026-076-6*) Westernlore.

— Horses & Riders. (True Tales of the Old West Ser.: Vol. 7). (Illus.). ii, 62p. 1998. pap. 7.95 (*0-9651954-7-3*) Pioneer Pr NV.

***Convis, Charles L.** Lawmen. LC 96-68502. (True Tales of the Old West Ser.: Vol. 14). (Illus.). ii, 62p. 2000. pap. 7.95 (*1-892156-04-0*) Pioneer Pr NV.

Convis, Charles L. Miners. (True Tales of the Old West Ser.: Vol. 8). (Illus.). ii, 62p. 1998. pap. 7.95 (*0-9651954-8-1*) Pioneer Pr NV.

— Mountain Men. (True Tales of the Old West Ser.: Vol. 4). (Illus.). 62p. 1997. pap. 7.95 (*0-9651954-4-9*) Pioneer Pr NV.

— Native Women. (True Tales of the Old West Ser.: Vol. 3). (Illus.). ii, 62p. (Orig.). 1996. pap. 7.95 (*0-9651954-3-0*) Pioneer Pr NV.

— Outlaws. (True Tales of the Old West Ser.: Vol. 11). ii, 62p. 1999. pap. 7.95 (*1-892156-01-6*, Pub. by Pioneer Pr NV) Sunbelt Pubns.

— Pioneer Women. (True Tales of the Old West Ser.: Vol. 5). (Illus.). 62p. 1997. pap. 7.95 (*0-9651954-5-7*) Pioneer Pr NV.

— Ranchers & Cowboys. (True Tales of the Old West Ser.: Vol. 6). (Illus.). 62p. 1997. pap. 7.95 (*0-9651954-6-5*) Pioneer Pr NV.

***Convis, Charles L.** Scouts. LC 96-68502. (True Tales of the Old West Ser.: Vol. 15). (Illus.). ii, 62p. 2000. pap. 7.95 (*1-892156-05-9*) Pioneer Pr NV.

Convis, Charles L. Soldiers. (True Tales of the Old West Ser.: Vol. 2). (Illus.). ii, 62p. (Orig.). 1996. pap. 7.95 (*0-9651954-2-2*) Pioneer Pr NV.

— Warriors & Chiefs. (True Tales of the Old West Ser.: Vol. 1). (Illus.). ii, 62p. (Orig.). 1996. pap. 7.95 (*0-9651954-1-4*) Pioneer Pr NV.

Conviser. Gilbert Agency & Partnership. 4th ed. 1982. 16.95 (*0-15-900001-7*) Harcourt Legal.

— Gilbert Agency & Partnerships. 5th ed. 1998. pap. text 16.95 (*0-15-900327-X*) Harcourt Legal.

— Gilbert Multistate Bar Examination. 4th ed. 2000. pap. text 19.95 (*0-15-900246-X*) Harcourt.

Convissor, Kate. Young Widow: Learning to Live Again. 176p. 1992. pap. 8.99 (*0-310-54941-8*) Zondervan.

Conwat, Mary, ed. Crop Protection Reference, 1998. 14th ed. 1998. 165.00 (*1-57009-061-0*, 1108) Chem & Pharmac.

Conway. Domestic Violence. 1997. pap. 14.95 (*0-7459-3722-5*, Pub. by Lion Pubng) Trafalgar.

Conway. Information Disease. 352p. 1999. text 19.95 (*0-670-82223-X*) Viking Penguin.

— Nietzsche Critical Assessments, 4 vols. Conway, Daniel, ed. 1608p. (C). 1998. reprint ed. 660.00 (*0-415-13561-3*) Routledge.

***Conway.** Soul of All Things Cyber. 2000. pap. 30.00 (*0-7382-0368-8*, Pub. by Perseus Pubng) HarpC.

— Strategies for Mentoring. LC 98-24567. 208p. 1998. 67.50 (*0-471-98438-8*) Wiley.

Conway & Bourque. Politics of Women's Education. 272p. (C). 1995. pap. text 18.95 (*0-472-08328-7*, 08328) U of Mich Pr.

Conway & Conway, Malloy, eds. Hazardous Solid Waste Testing: First Conference - STP 760. 352p. 1983. 39.00 (*0-8031-0795-1*, STP760) ASTM.

Conway, jt. auth. see Munson.

Conway, jt. auth. see Valentine.

Conway, Agnes J., tr. see St. Leo the Great.

Conway, Ainslie. Enchanted Islands: American Autobiography. 287p. 1995. lib. bdg. 79.00 (*0-7812-8488-0*) Rprt Serv.

Conway, Alan. The Reconstruction of Georgia. LC 66-18867. 254p. reprint ed. pap. 78.80 (*0-608-16690-1*, 205619300055) Bks Demand.

Conway, Alan, jt. ed. see Baylen, Joseph O.

Conway, Alice. The Green Branch. 257p. pap. 9.95 (*0-89697-254-2*) Intl Univ Pr.

Conway, Amy. A Woman's Own Remedy Box: Natural Remedies for Self-Healing. (Illus.). 84p. 1996. boxed set 24.95 (*0-8048-3067-3*) Tuttle Pubng.

Conway, Amy J. The Remedy Box. LC 94-7706. 48p. 1994. boxed set 24.95 (*0-8048-3015-0*) Tuttle Pubng.

Conway, Amy J., jt. auth. see Sanderford, Laura.

***Conway, Andrew.** The Bullwhip Book. 140p. 2000. pap. 11.95 (*1-890159-18-2*) Greenery Pr.

Conway, Anne. Anne Conway: The Principles of the Most Ancient & Modern Philosophy. Coudert, Allison P. & Corse, Taylor, eds. (Cambridge Texts in the History of Philosophy Ser.). 112p. (C). 1996. text 54.95 (*0-521-47335-7*); pap. text 17.95 (*0-521-47904-5*) Cambridge U Pr.

— The Conway Letters: Being the Correspondence of Anne, Viscountess Conway, Henry More & Their Friends. Nicolson, Marjorie H., ed. 1930. 100.00 (*0-685-89745-1*) Elliots Bks.

— The Principles of the Most Ancient & Modern Philosophy. 256p. 1982. text 153.00 (*90-247-2671-9*, Pub. by M Nijhoff) Kluwer Academic.

Conway, Anne & Loptson, Peter. The Principles of the Most Ancient & Modern Philosophy. 2nd ed. LC 98-16731. (ENG & LAT.). 268p. 1998. 50.00 (*0-8201-1509-6*) Schol Facsimiles.

Conway, Anne, jt. auth. see Eggers, De A.

Conway, Anne S. Instant People Reading Through Handwriting. 224p. 1991. pap. 9.95 (*0-87877-161-1*) Newcastle Pub.

Conway, Arthur L. The Poetic Vibrations of a Matured Butterfly. 2nd rev. ed. LC 92-73855. (Illus.). 120p. (Orig.). 1992. pap. 10.95 (*0-9633352-1-9*) A L Conway.

— The Poetic Vibrations of a Matured Butterfly, Poems & Parables. LC 92-90290. (Illus.). 117p. (Orig.). 1992. pap. 10.95 (*0-9633352-0-0*) A L Conway.

***Conway, B. E.** Electrochemical Supercapacitors: Scientific Fundamentals & Technological Applications. LC 98-48209. 1999. write for info. (*0-306-45736-9*, Kluwer Plenum) Kluwer Academic.

Conway, B. E. & Jerkiewicz, G. Electrochemistry & Materials Science of Cathodic Hydrogen Absorption & Adsorption. (Proceedings Ser.: Vol. 94-21). 478p. 1995. 56.00 (*1-56677-078-5*) Electrochem Soc.

Conway, B. E. & Korzeniewski, C., eds. The Electrochemical Double-Layer: Commemorating 50 Years of D. C. Grahame's Ground-Breaking Paper. LC 98-110293. (Proceedings Ser.: Vol. 97-17). 458p. 1997. 85.00 (*1-56677-144-7*) Electrochem Soc.

Conway, B. E., et al. Modern Aspects of Electrochemistry, Vol. 23. (Illus.). 432p. (C). 1992. text 110.00 (*0-306-44164-0*, Kluwer Plenum) Kluwer Academic.

— Modern Aspects of Electrochemistry, Vol. 26. (Illus.). 356p. (C). 1994. text 110.00 (*0-306-44608-1*, Kluwer Plenum) Kluwer Academic.

— Modern Aspects of Electrochemistry, Vol. 28. (Illus.). 373p. (C). 1996. text 114.00 (*0-306-45146-8*, Kluwer Plenum) Kluwer Academic.

***Conway, B. E., et al.** Modern Aspects of Electrochemistry, Vol. 32. 420p. 1999. write for info. (*0-306-45964-7*, Kluwer Plenum) Kluwer Academic.

— Modern Aspects of Electrochemistry, Vol. 33. 555p. 1999. write for info. (*0-306-45968-X*, Kluwer Plenum) Kluwer Academic.

Conway, B. E., jt. ed. see Bockris, John O.

Conway, B. E., ed. see Gurevich, Iurii I., et al.

Conway, B. E., tr. see Pleskov, Yu V. & Filinovskii, V. Yu, eds.

Conway, Barbara. Maritime Fraud. 170p. 1990. 75.00 (*1-85044-257-6*) LLP.

***Conway, Bernita.** The Ascended Life. 1999. pap. 7.99 (*1-56043-337-X*, Treasure Hse) Destiny Image.

Conway, Bob & Kulik, Robert. Microsoft Frontpage Quickstart. LC 98-160271. 1996. 24.99 (*1-56276-465-9*, Ziff-Davis Pr) Que.

Conway, Brian E. Electrochemical Data. write for info. (*0-318-56697-4*) Elsevier.

— Electrochemical Data. LC 69-10078. (Illus.). 374p. 1971. reprint ed. lib. bdg. 69.50 (*0-8371-1630-9*, COED, Greenwood Pr) Greenwood.

Conway, Brian E., et al, eds. Modern Aspects of Electrochemistry, Vol. 16. LC 54-12732. 528p. 1985. 115.00 (*0-306-42024-4*, Plenum Trade) Perseus Pubng.

— Modern Aspects of Electrochemistry, Vol. 19. (Illus.). 414p. (C). 1989. text 132.00 (*0-306-42954-3*, Kluwer Plenum) Kluwer Academic.

Conway, Bruce A., jt. auth. see Prussing, John E.

Conway, Bryan. Christ's Commandment: "Love One Another"; an Examination of the Biblical Teaching on Unity. LC 92-22778. 60p. (Orig.). 1992. pap. text 3.50 (*1-880573-07-5*) Bible Search Pubns.

Conway, Bryant W. Successful Hints on Hunting White Tail Deer. 2nd ed. 1967. pap. 4.95 (*0-87511-589-6*) Claitors.

Conway, Byron. Expatriate Effectiveness: A Study of European Expatriates in South East Asia. 92p. 1998. pap. 126.95 (*0-471-96283-X*) Wiley.

Conway, Carle. The Joy of Soaring. rev. ed. 154p. 1993. text 18.00 (*1-883813-02-6*) Soaring Soc.

Conway, Carol & Nothdurft, William E. The International State: Crafting a Statewide Trade Development System. 160p. 1996. pap. 15.00 (*0-89843-186-7*) The Aspen Inst.

Conway, Cecelia. African Banjo Echoes in Appalachia: A Study of Folk Traditions. LC 95-4362. (Publications of the American Folklore Society). (Illus.). 424p. (C). 1995. pap. text 25.00 (*0-87049-893-2*) U of Tenn Pr.

Conway, Chad, jt. auth. see Vincent, Norah.

Conway, Christopher M., jt. auth. see Schwartz, Jane W.

***Conway, Colleen M.** Men & Women in the Fourth Gospel: Gender & Johannine Characterization. LC 99-45667. (Dissertation Studies). 224p. 1999. 35.00 (*0-88414-002-4*, 062167) Soc Biblical Lit.

***Conway, Cyril Francis.** While the Banshee Cried. unabridged ed. 518p. 1999. pap. 25.95 (*0-9674415-0-1*, 2502) Emerald Isle Pubs.

***Conway, D. J.** Advanced Celtic Shamanism. 2000. pap. 16.95 (*1-58091-073-4*) Crossing Pr.

Conway, D. J. Animal Magick: The Art of Recognizing & Working with Familiars. LC 95-10721. (Illus.). 288p. 1995. pap. 13.95 (*1-56718-168-6*) Llewellyn Pubns.

— By Oak, Ash & Thorn: Modern Celtic Shamanism. LC 94-40820. (Illus.). 320p. 1995. reprint ed. pap. 12.95 (*1-56718-166-X*) Llewellyn Pubns.

***Conway, D. J.** The Celtic Book of Names: Traditional Names from Ireland, Scotland & Wales. LC 99-22594. 2p. 1999. pap. 12.00 (*0-8065-2096-5*, Citadel Pr) Carol Pub Group.

Conway, D. J. Celtic Magic. LC 90-32139. (Llewellyn's New World Magic Ser.). (Illus.). 240p. (Orig.). 1990. mass mkt. 4.99 (*0-87542-136-9*) Llewellyn Pubns.

***Conway, D. J.** Crystal Enchantments: A Complete Guide to Stones & Their Magical Properties. LC 99-36233. 352p. 2000. pap. 16.95 (*1-58091-010-6*) Crossing Pr.

Conway, D. J. Dancing with Dragons: Invoke Their Ageless Wisdom & Power. LC 94-28370. (Illus.). 320p. 1999. pap. 14.95 (*1-56718-165-1*) Llewellyn Pubns.

— The Dream Warrior: Book One of the Dream Warrior Trilogy, Bk. 1. LC 95-47961. Vol. 1. 320p. 1996. pap. 14.95 (*1-56718-169-4*) Llewellyn Pubns.

— Falcon Feather & Valkyrie Sword: Feminine Shamanism, Witchcraft & Magick. LC 95-44526. (Llewellyn's Women's Spirituality Ser.). (Illus.). 352p. 1995. pap. 19.95 (*1-56718-163-5*) Llewellyn Pubns.

C

***Conway, D. J.** Feminine Shamanism, Witchcraft & Magick: Invoking Woman's Power. 2nd ed. LC 99-88566. 384p. 2000. pap. 19.95 (*1-56718-158-9*) Llewellyn Pubns.

Conway, D. J. Flying Without a Broom: Astral Projection & the Astral World. LC 95-16124. (Illus.). 224p. 1999. pap. 13.00 (*1-56718-164-3*) Llewellyn Pubns.

***Conway, D. J.** A Guide to the Celtic Dragon Tarot. LC 99-40420. 1999. write for info. (*1-56718-185-6*) Llewellyn Pubns.

— Laying on of Stones. LC 99-36232. (Illus.). 96p. 2000. pap. 10.95 (*1-58091-029-7*) Crossing Pr.

— A Little Book of Altar Magic. (Little Book Ser.). (Illus.). 2000. pap. 9.95 (*1-58091-052-1*) Crossing Pr.

— A Little Book of Candle Magic. (Little Book Ser.). 130p. 2000. pap. 9.95 (*1-58091-043-2*, Pub. by Crossing Pr) Publishers Group.

Conway, D. J. Lord of Light & Shadow: The Many Faces of God. LC 96-39222. (Illus.). 224p. 1999. pap. 14.95 (*1-56718-177-5*) Llewellyn Pubns.

— Magic of the Gods & Goddesses: How to Invoke Their Powers. LC 97-17438. (Illus.). 448p. 1999. pap. 17.95 (*1-56718-179-1*) Llewellyn Pubns.

— Magickal, Mythical, Mystical Beasts: How to Invite Them into Your Life. LC 96-9051. (Illus.). 272p. (Orig.). 1999. pap. 14.95 (*1-56718-176-7*) Llewellyn Pubns.

— Maiden, Mother, Crone: The Myth & Reality of the Triple Goddess. LC 94-6807. (Illus.). 240p. 1999. pap. 12.95 (*0-87542-171-7*) Llewellyn Pubns.

— Moon Magick: Myth & Magic, Crafts & Recipes, Rituals & Spells. LC 95-18474. (Illus.). 320p. 1995. pap. 16.95 (*1-56718-167-8*) Llewellyn Pubns.

***Conway, D. J.** The Mysterious, Magical Cat. LC 00-37143. (Illus.). 224p. (J). 2000. pap. 8.99 (*0-517-16301-2*) Bell T.

Conway, D. J. Norse Magic. LC 90-6204. (Llewellyn's New World Magic Ser.). (Illus.). 240p. (Orig.). 1990. mass mkt. 4.99 (*0-87542-137-7*) Llewellyn Pubns.

— Perfect Love: Find Intimacy on the Astral Plane. 2nd ed. LC 97-42432. (Illus.). 192p. 1999. pap. 12.95 (*1-56718-181-3*) Llewellyn Pubns.

— Soothslayer: A Magickal Fantasy. LC 97-3558. (Illus.). 400p. (Orig.). 1999. pap. 9.95 (*1-56718-162-7*) Llewellyn Pubns.

— Warrior of Shadows: The Final Battle. LC 98-5868. (Dream Warrior Ser.: vol. 3). 336p. 1999. pap. 9.95 (*1-56718-178-3*) Llewellyn Pubns.

***Conway, D. J. & Hunt, Lisa.** The Celtic Dragon Tarot. LC 99-40420. (Illus.). 216p. 1999. 29.95 (*1-56718-182-1*) Llewellyn Pubns.

Conway, D. J. & Knight, Sirona. Shapeshifter Tarot. LC 97-43797. 1998. write for info. (*1-56718-388-3*); pap. write for info. (*1-56718-389-1*) Llewellyn Pubns.

— Shapeshifter Tarot. LC 97-43797. (Illus.). 264p. 1999. 29.95 (*1-56718-384-0*) Llewellyn Pubns.

Conway, Damian. Object Oriented Perl. LC 99-27793. 490p. 1999. pap. 42.95 (*1-884777-79-1*, Pub. by Manning Pubns) IPG Chicago.

Conway, Daniel, ed. see Conway.

Conway, Daniel W. Nietzsche: Critical Assessments. LC 97-29031. 1998. write for info. (*0-415-13562-1*) Routledge.

— Nietzsche & the Political. LC 96-7867. (Thinking the Political Ser.). 176p. (C). 1997. 70.00 (*0-415-10068-2*); pap. 20.99 (*0-415-10069-0*) Routledge.

— Nietzsche's Dangerous Game: Philosophy in the Twilight

of the Idols. LC 96-46726. (Modern European Philosophy Ser.). 279p. 1997. text 57.95 (*0-521-57371-8*) Cambridge U Pr.

Conway, Daniel W. & Seery, John E., eds. The Politics of Irony: Essays in Self-Betrayal. LC 91-44679. 288p. 1992. text 39.95 (*0-312-04801-7*) St Martin.

Conway, David. The Complete Magic Primer: An Occult Primer. (Illus.). 304p. 1992. reprint ed. pap. 18.00 (*1-85538-174-5*, Pub. by Aqrn Pr) Harper SF.

— Help ??? Help !!! Solving Learning Problems (Even Dyslexia) LC 91-66597. (Illus.). 152p. (Orig.). 1992. pap. 12.95 (*0-9630681-6-4*) Gander Educ.

***Conway, David.** The Rediscovery of Wisdom: From Here to Antiquity in Quest of. 2000. text 69.95 (*0-312-23406-6*) St Martin.

Conway, David. Secret Widsom: The Occult Universe Explored. 1991. pap. 13.95 (*0-85030-590-X*, Pub. by Aqrn Pr) HarpC.

Conway, David, et al. Free-Market Feminism. (Choices in Welfare Ser.: No. 43). 104p. 1998. pap. 18.95 (*0-255-36435-0*, Pub. by Inst Economic Affairs) Coronet Bks.

Conway, David A. & Munson, Ronald. The Elements of Reasoning. 225p. 1989. mass mkt. 15.25 (*0-534-12162-4*) Wadsworth Pub.

— The Elements of Reasoning. 2nd ed. LC 96-22769. (Philosophy Ser.). 249p. (C). 1996. 22.95 (*0-534-51672-6*) Wadsworth Pub.

***Conway, Denise.** Nurse at Smokey River. large type ed. 272p. 1999. pap. 20.99 (*1-85389-967-4*, Dales) Ulverscroft.

Conway, Dennis. Demographic Issues & Policy Options to Ameliorate Caribbean Population-Development Conflicts. (Series on Environment & Development). 67p. (Orig.). 1991. pap. 2.00 (*1-881157-06-7*) In Ctr Global.

Conway, Dennis & Cuffel, Victoria, eds. Series on Environment & Development. 579p. 1992. pap. 25.00 (*1-881157-15-6*) In Ctr Global.

Conway, Dennis & White, James C., II, eds. Global Change: How Vulnerable Are North & South Communities? (Series on Environment & Development). 122p. (Orig.). 1995. pap. 6.00 (*1-881157-29-6*) In Ctr Global.

C

Conway, Dennis, jt. auth. see Boswell, Thomas D.

Conway, Dennis, jt. auth. see Shrestha, Nanda R.

Conway, Dennis, ed. see Baker, Randall.

Conway, Dennis, ed. see Catanese, Anthony V.

Conway, Dennis, ed. see Hopkins, Jack W.

Conway, Dennis, ed. see McElroy, Jerome L. & De Albuquerque, Klaus.

Conway, Dennis, ed. see Moran, Emilio F.

Conway, Dennis, jt. ed. see Potter, Robert B.

Conway, Dennis, ed. see Stolnitz, George J.

Conway, Diana C. Northern Lights: A Hanukkah Story. (Illus.). 32p. (J). (ps-3). 1994. pap. 6.95 (*0-929371-80-1*) Kar-Ben.

Conway, Diane. The Fairy Godmother's Guide to Dating & Mating. LC 95-79683. 100p. 1995. pap. 11.00 (*1-885221-26-6*) BookPartners.

Conway, D.J. The Mysterious, Magickal Cat. LC 98-2501. (Illus.). 256p. 1998. pap. 15.95 (*1-56718-180-5*) Llewellyn Pubns.

Conway, Donal P. & McKenzie, M. Elizabeth. Poultry Coccidiosis: Diagnostic & Testing Procedures. 2nd ed. (Illus.). 66p. (C). 1991. pap. text. write for info. (*0-9602652-2-8*) Pfizer Intl.

Conway, Donald, jt. auth. see Hydge, Debra M.

Conway, Douglas R. Human Experimentation: Index of Modern Authors & Subjects with Guide for Rapid Research. LC 90-56253. 200p. 1991. 47.50 (*1-55914-288-X*); pap. 44.50 (*1-55914-289-8*) ABBE Pubs Assn.

— Human Rights: Index of Modern Information with Bibliography. LC 89-18603. 150p. (Orig.). 1990. 47.50 (*1-55914-134-4*); pap. 44.50 (*1-55914-135-2*) ABBE Pubs Assn.

— Human Rights & Social Justice: Index of Modern Authors & Subjects. LC 92-37538. 1992. 47.50 (*1-55914-962-0*); pap. 44.50 (*1-55914-963-9*) ABBE Pubs Assn.

Conway, Eamonn. The Anonymous Christian - A Relativised Christianity? An Evaluation of Hans Urs von Balthasar's Criticism of Karl Rahner's Theory of the Anonymous Christian. (European University Studies: Series 23, Vol. 485). 189p. 1993. 36.95 (*3-631-46209-3*) P Lang Pubng.

Conway, Eamonn, jt. auth. see Conference on Church and Media in Modern Ireland Staff.

Conway, Edward S. Comprehending Comprehensives: The JFS Experience. (Illus.). 163p. 1983. text 27.50 (*0-7130-0172-0*, Pub. by Woburn Pr); pap. text 18.50 (*0-7130-4008-4*, Pub. by Woburn Pr) Intl Spec Bk.

Conway, Elliot. The Blue-Belly Sergeant. large type ed. (Linford Western Large Print Ser.). 240p. 1997. pap. 16.99 (*0-7089-5124-4*, Linford) Ulverscroft.

— The Last of the Old Guns. large type ed. (Dales Large Print Ser.). 1995. pap. 18.99 (*1-85389-545-8*, Dales) Ulverscroft.

— The Law-Bringers. large type ed. (Linford Western Large Print Ser.). 240p. 1998. pap. 17.99 (*0-7089-5274-7*, Linford) Ulverscroft.

— The Loner. large type ed. (Linford Western Library). 288p. 1992. pap. 16.99 (*0-7089-7253-5*, Linford) Ulverscroft.

— The Man from Clay County. large type ed. (Dales Large Print Ser.). 224p. 1998. pap. 19.99 (*1-85389-821-X*, Dales) Ulverscroft.

— The Maverick. large type ed. (Linford Western Library). 1991. pap. 16.99 (*0-7089-7038-9*) Ulverscroft.

— The Peace Officer. large type ed. (Linford Western Library). 272p. 1993. pap. 16.99 (*0-7089-7433-3*, Linford) Ulverscroft.

— The President's Man. large type ed. (Dales Large Print Ser.). 224p. 1996. pap. 18.99 (*1-85389-645-4*, Dales) Ulverscroft.

— The Return of the Gringo. large type ed. (Linford Western Library Ser.). 240p. 1997. pap. 16.99 (*0-7089-5149-X*) Ulverscroft.

Conway, Elliot. The San Pedro Ring. large type ed. 240p. pap. 18.99 (*0-7089-5424-3*) Ulverscroft.

Conway, Elliot. Trouble on the Lordsburg Trail. large type ed. (Dales Large Print Ser.). 200p. 1997. pap. 18.99 (*1-85389-710-8*) Ulverscroft.

***Conway, Elliot.** Tucumcari Shoot-out. 240p. 1999. 20.99 (*1-85389-972-0*) Ulverscroft.

Conway, Elliot. Woodrow's Last Heist. large type ed. (linford Western Library). 240p. 1997. pap. 16.99 (*0-7089-5136-8*) Ulverscroft.

Conway, Eric D. An Introduction to Satellite Image Interpretation. LC 96-53574. (Illus.). 256p. 1997. text 65.00 (*0-8018-5576-4*); pap. text 29.95 (*0-8018-5577-2*) Johns Hopkins.

Conway, Eugenia D., ed. & des. see Cyrs, Thomas E.

Conway, Flo & Siegelman, Jim. Holy Terror: The Far Right War on America's Freedoms in Religion, Politics & Our Private Lives. 2nd expanded rev. ed. 450p. Date not set. pap. 14.95 (*0-9647650-1-2*) Stillpt Pr NY.

— Snapping: America's Epidemic of Sudden Personality Change. 2nd expanded rev. ed. LC 95-69831. 400p. 1995. pap. 14.95 (*0-9647650-0-4*) Stillpt Pr NY.

Conway, George L. Garment & Textile Dictionary. abr. rev. ed. LC 96-13600. 256p. (C). 1996. pap. 37.95 (*0-8273-7986-2*) Delmar.

Conway, Gerry. Spider-Man: Death of Gwen Stacy. 112p. 1999. pap. text 14.95 (*0-7851-0716-9*) Marvel Entrprs.

— Spider-Man Clone Genesis. (Illus.). 192p. 1995. pap. 16.95 (*0-7851-0134-9*) Marvel Entrprs.

Conway, Gerry & Claremont, Chris. Marvel - DC Crossover Classics. (Illus.). 320p. 1991. pap. 24.95 (*0-87135-858-1*) Marvel Entrprs.

Conway, Gordon. Doubly Green Revolution: Food for All in the Twenty-First Century. LC 98-32350. 1999. pap. text 16.95 (*0-8014-8610-6*) Cornell U Pr.

Conway Greene Editorial Staff. Athletic Scholarships: A Complete Guide. 2nd ed. 1998. pap. 23.95 (*1-884669-17-4*) Conway Greene.

— Music, Dance & Theater Scholarships: A Guide to Undergraduate Awards. 1998. pap. 24.95 (*1-884669-18-2*) Conway Greene.

Conway Greene Publishing Co. Editorial Staff, et al. Sports, Everyone! Recreation & Sports for the Physically Challenged of All Ages. (Illus.). 272p. (Orig.). 1995. pap. 16.95 (*1-884669-10-7*) Conway Greene.

Conway, H. Bugatti Le Pur Sang. 5th ed. LC 96-75170. (Illus.). 416p. 1997. 75.00 (*0-85429-970-X*, Pub. by J H Haynes & Co) Motorbooks Intl.

Conway, H. McKinley. Disaster Survival: How to Choose Secure Sites & Make Practical Escape Plans. LC 80-68816. (Illus.). 297p. 1981. 14.95 (*0-910436-17-7*) Conway Data.

— A Glimpse of the Future: Technology Forecasts for Global Stratigists. (Illus.). 103p. 1992. 95.00 (*0-910436-31-2*) Conway Data.

— Pitfalls in Development. LC 78-62198. 350p. 1981. pap. 11.95 (*0-910436-06-1*) Conway Data.

— Site World. (Illus.). 608p. 1991. 95.00 (*0-910436-30-4*) Conway Data.

Conway, H. McKinley & Liston, Linda L. The Good Life Index: How to Compare Quality of Life Throughout the U. S. & Around the World. LC 81-68204. (Illus.). 422p. 1981. 13.95 (*0-910436-22-3*) Conway Data.

Conway, H. McKinley & Liston, Linda L., eds. Corporate Facility Planning. 450p. 1981. 14.95 (*0-910436-21-5*) Conway Data.

— Facility Planning Technology. (Illus.). 935p. 1987. 33.95 (*0-910436-26-6*) Conway Data.

— Industrial Park Growth. 554p. 1981. 11.95 (*0-910436-23-1*) Conway Data.

— The Weather Handbook. rev. ed. LC 90-82037. (Illus.). 548p. 1990. 39.95 (*0-910436-29-0*) Conway Data.

Conway, H. McKinley, et al. The SiteNet World Guide. (Illus.). 530p. 1989. 95.00 (*0-910436-28-2*) Conway Data.

Conway, Hazel. Ernest Race. 80p. 1987. 60.00 (*0-85072-128-8*) St Mut.

— Public Parks. (Garden History Ser.: No. 9). (Illus.). 96p. 1996. pap. 12.50 (*0-7478-0332-3*, Pub. by Shire Pubns) Parkwest Pubns.

Conway, Hazel, ed. Design History: A Student's Handbook. (Illus.). 224p. 1987. text 49.95 (*0-04-709019-7*); pap. text 16.95 (*0-04-709020-0*) Routledge.

Conway, Hazel & Roenisch, Rowan. Understanding Architecture: An Introduction to Architecture & Architectural History. LC 93-47002. (Illus.). 272p. (C). 1994. pap. 22.99 (*0-415-10466-1*, B4445) Routledge.

Conway, Helen. Sir John Pritchard: His Life in Music. (Illus.). 434p. 1994. 45.00 (*0-233-98845-9*, Pub. by Andre Deutsch) Trafalgar.

Conway, Helen L. Domestic Violence & the Church. viii, 198p. 1998. reprint ed. pap. 25.00 (*0-85364-817-4*, Pub. by Paternoster Pub) OM Literature.

Conway, J. The Theory of Subnormal Operators. LC 90-26659. (Mathematical Surveys & Monographs: Vol. 36). 436p. 1991. text 133.00 (*0-8218-1536-9*, SURV/36) Am Math.

Conway, J. A., et al, eds. A Study in the Determination of Quality - Value Relationships in Rice. 1992. pap. 25.00 (*0-85954-314-5*, Pub. by Nat Res Inst) St Mut.

Conway, J. A. & Tyler, P. S. Practical Implications of Grain Market Liberalization in Southern Africa. 194p. 1995. pap. 60.00 (*0-85954-398-6*, Pub. by Nat Res Inst) St Mut.

Conway, J. B. A Course in Functional Analysis. (Graduate Texts in Mathematics Ser.: Vol. 96). 350p. 1984. 46.00 (*0-387-96042-2*) Spr-Verlag.

— A Course in Functional Analysis. 2nd ed. Halmos, P. R. et al, eds. (Graduate Texts in Mathematics Ser.: Vol. 96). (Illus.). xvi, 402p. 1997. 49.50 (*0-387-97245-5*) Spr-Verlag.

— Functions of One Complex Variable. Halmos, P. R., ed. LC 72-96938. (Lecture Notes in Mathematics Ser.: Vol. 11). (Illus.). xiv, 314p. 1989. 19.95 (*0-387-07028-1*) Spr-Verlag.

— Functions of One Complex Variable. 2nd ed. (Graduate Texts in Mathematics Ser.: Vol. 11). (Illus.). xiii, 317 p. 1997. 48.95 (*0-387-90328-3*) Spr-Verlag.

Conway, J. B. & Olin, R. F. A Functional Calculus for Subnormal Operators II. LC 77-3937. (Memoirs Ser.: No. 10/184). 61p. 1977. pap. 19.00 (*0-8218-2184-9*, MEMO/10/184) Am Math.

Conway, J. H. & Sloane, N. J. Sphere Packings, Lattices & Groups. (Grundlehren der Mathematischen Wissenschaften Ser.: Vol. 290). (Illus.). 550p. 1987. 89.90 (*0-387-96617-X*) Spr-Verlag.

— Sphere Packings, Lattices & Groups. 2nd ed. Berger, M. et al, eds. (Grundlehren der Mathematischen Wissenschaften Ser.: Vol. 290). (Illus.). xliv, 679p. 1992. 99.95 (*0-387-97912-3*) Spr-Verlag.

— Sphere Packings, Lattices & Groups, Vol. 290. 3rd ed. LC 98-26950. (Grundlehren der Mathematischen Wissenschaften Ser.). (Illus.). 710p. 1998. 89.00 (*0-387-98585-9*) Spr-Verlag.

Conway, J. North. New England Visionaries: 12 Who Changed America. 192p. (Orig.). 1998. pap. 12.95 (*0-924771-93-3*, Covered Brdge Pr) Douglas Charles Ltd.

— New England Women: In Their Own Words. (New England Gift Bks.: Vol. 3). (Illus.). 64p. 2000. 4.95 (*1-58066-008-8*, Covered Brdge Pr) Douglas Charles Ltd.

— New England Women of Substance: 15 Who Made a Difference. 176p. (Orig.). 1996. pap. 12.95 (*0-924771-81-X*, Covered Brdge Pr) Douglas Charles Ltd.

— Shipwrecks of New England. (Illus.). 160p. 2000. pap. 12.95 (*1-58066-026-6*) Douglas Charles Ltd.

Conway, James A., jt. auth. see Shipengrover, Judith A.

Conway, James J., jt. auth. see Balsley, Howard L.

Conway, James V. Evidential Documents. fac. ed. (Illus.). 288p. 1978. 49.95 (*0-398-00342-4*) C C Thomas.

Conway, James V. P. Evidential Documents. (Illus.). 288p. 1978. pap. 35.95 (*0-398-06073-8*) C C Thomas.

Conway, Jill K. When Memory Speaks: Exploring the Art of Autobiography. LC 97-49452. 192p. 1998. 24.00 (*0-679-44593-5*) Knopf.

— When Memory Speaks: Exploring the Art of Autobiography. LC 97-49452. 224p. 1999. pap. 13.00 (*0-679-76645-6*) Random.

Conway, Jill Ker. In Her Own Words: Women's Memoirs from Australia, Vol. 3. LC 98-44745. 656p. 1999. pap. 18.00 (*0-679-78153-6*) Vin Bks.

— The Road from Coorain. LC 89-40547. 238p. 1990. pap. 11.00 (*0-679-72436-2*) Vin Bks.

— The Road from Coorain: An Autobiography. 1989. 26.50 (*0-394-57456-7*) Knopf.

— The Road from Coorain: Recollections of a Harsh & Beautiful Journey into Adulthood. large type ed. (General Ser.). 394p. 1991. lib. bdg. 21.95 (*0-8161-5204-7*, G K Hall Lrg Type) Mac Lib Ref.

— True North: A Memoir. 1995. pap. 13.00 (*0-679-74461-4*) Random.

— Written by Herself Vol. II: Women's Memoirs from Four Continents. 1996. pap. 16.00 (*0-679-75109-2*) Vin Bks.

Conway, Jill Ker, et al, eds. Earth, Air, Fire, Water: Humanistic Studies of the Environment. LC 99-16970. 368p. 2000. pap. 50.00 (*1-55849-220-8*) U of Mass Pr.

Conway, Jill Ker, intro. Written by Herself: Autobiographies of American Women: an Anthology. LC 92-50081. 656p. 1992. pap. 16.00 (*0-679-73633-6*) Vin Bks.

Conway, Jill Kerr. True North: A Memoir. large type ed. LC 96-2652. 296p. 1996. lib. bdg. 22.95 (*1-57490-060-9*, Beeler LP Bks) T T Beeler.

***Conway, JillKer, et al, eds.** Earth, Air, Fire, Water: Humanistic Studies of the Environment. LC 99-16970. 368p. 2000. pap. 17.95 (*1-55849-221-6*) U of Mass Pr.

Conway, Jim. Making Real Friends in a Phony World. Orig. Title: Friendship. 208p. 1991. pap. 8.95 (*0-310-54251-0*) Zondervan.

— Making Real Friends in a Phony World. Orig. Title: Friendship. 208p. 1991. reprint ed. pap. 8.99 (*0-310-54841-1*) Zondervan.

— Men in Mid-Life Crisis. LC 78-67098. 322p. 1976. pap. 9.99 (*0-89191-145-6*, LifeJourney) Chariot Victor.

— Men in Midlife Crisis. rev. ed. LC 97-29004. 336p. 1997. 11.99 (*1-56476-698-5*, Victor Bks) Chariot Victor.

— The Superific Science Series, 12 bks., Set. teacher ed. 106.99 (*1-56417-131-0*, GA1110) Good Apple.

Conway, Jim & Conway, Sally. Basta Ya de Acosamiento Sexual!Tr. of Sexual Harassment No More. (SPA.). 176p. 1996. pap. text 9.99 (*0-311-46144-1*, Edit Mundo) Casa Bautista.

Conway, Jim & Conway, Sally. Moving on after He Moves Out. LC 94-23856. 220p. (Orig.). 1995. pap. 10.99 (*0-8308-1643-7*, 1643) InterVarsity.

— La Mujer en su etapa de Media Vida: Women in Mid-Life Crisis. De Zorzoli, Alicia S., tr. from SPA. 352p. 1986. pap. 9.99 (*0-311-46105-0*) Casa Bautista.

— Traits of a Lasting Marriage. LC 91-21244. 200p. (Orig.). 1991. pap. 10.99 (*0-8308-1293-8*, 1293, Saltshaker Bk) InterVarsity.

— Women in Mid-Life Crisis. 1997. pap. 5.99 (*0-8423-8383-2*) Tyndale Hse.

Conway, Jim, jt. auth. see Conway, Sally.

Conway, John. Debts to Pay: A Fresh Approach to the Quebec Question. rev. ed. LC 97-185537. 291p. 1997. pap. 19.95 (*1-55028-544-0*, Pub. by J Lorimer); bds. 34.95 (*1-55028-545-9*, Pub. by J Lorimer) Formac Dist Ltd.

— Retrospect: An Anecdotal History of Sullivan County, New York. LC 96-14374. (Illus.). 148p. (Orig.). 1996. pap. 15.00 (*0-935796-72-X*) Purple Mnt Pr.

— Surfing. (Illus.). 128p. 1989. pap. 18.95 (*0-8117-2278-3*) Stackpole.

— The West: The History of a Region in Confederation. rev. ed. LC 94-211748. 372p. 29.95 (*1-55028-408-8*, Pub. by J Lorimer); pap. 19.95 (*1-55028-409-6*, Pub. by J Lorimer) Formac Dist Ltd.

Conway, John & Maguire, Jon A. American Flight Jackets, Airmen & Aircraft: A History of U. S. Flyers' Jackets from World War I to Desert Storm. LC 93-84498. (Illus.). 256p. 1994. 59.95 (*0-88740-511-8*) Schiffer.

***Conway, John B.** A Course in Operator Theory. LC 99-41229. (Graduate Studies in Mathematics: Vol. 21). 372p. 1999. 49.00 (*0-8218-2065-6*) Am Math.

Conway, John B. Functions of One Complex Variable II. LC 95-2331. (Graduate Texts in Mathematics Ser.: Vol. 158). 1995. 49.95 (*0-387-94460-5*) Spr-Verlag.

— On Being a Department Head, a Personal View. LC 96-22067. 107p. 1996. pap. 24.00 (*0-8218-0615-7*, AHEAD) Am Math.

Conway, John B. & Morrel, B. B., eds. Operator Theory: Proceedings of the 1988 GPOTS - Wabash Conference. LC 89-38852. (Pitman Research Notes in Mathematics Ser.: Vol. 225). 197p. 1990. reprint ed. pap. 61.10 (*0-608-03602-1*, 206442500009) Bks Demand.

Conway, John B., et al. Completing the Riesz-Dunford Functional Calculus. LC 89-17740. 104p. 1989. pap. 19.00 (*0-8218-2480-5*, MEMO/82/417) Am Math.

Conway, John F. The Canadian Family in Crisis. 3rd rev. ed. (Illus.). 248p. 1997. bds. 34.95 (*1-55028-563-7*, Pub. by J Lorimer) Formac Dist Ltd.

— Canadian Family In Crisis. 3rd rev. ed. LC 98-108175. (Illus.). 281p. 1997. pap. 19.95 (*1-55028-562-9*, Pub. by J Lorimer) Formac Dist Ltd.

Conway, John H. The Sensual (Quadratic) Form. LC 97-74335. (Carus Mathematical Monographs: No. 26). 228p. 1997. 35.95 (*0-88385-030-3*) Math Assn.

Conway, John H., et al, eds. Atlas of Finite Groups: Maximal Subgroups & Ordinary Characters for Simple Groups. LC 85-11559. (Illus.). 284p. (C). 1986. spiral bd. 65.00 (*0-19-853199-0*) OUP.

Conway, John H. & Guy, Richard K. The Book of Numbers. 1996. 29.00 (*0-614-97166-7*) Copernicus Systs.

— The Book of Numbers. LC 95-32588. 310p. 1996. 32.00 (*0-387-97993-X*) Spr-Verlag.

Conway, John P., jt. auth. see Maguire, Jon A.

Conway, John S. The Nazi Persecution of the Churches, 1933-1945. 474p. 1997. reprint ed. pap. 29.95 (*1-57383-080-1*) Regent College.

Conway, John T., jt. ed. see Grogan, John C.

Conway, Julie, jt. auth. see Conway, Thor.

Conway, Katherine, ed. see Marchok, Janice M.

Conway, Kathlyn. Ordinary Life: A Memoir of Illness. LC 96-273316. 250p. 1996. pap. text 22.95 (*0-7167-3036-7*) W H Freeman.

Conway, Kathryn M., jt. auth. see Leslie, Russell P.

Conway, Kathy, jt. auth. see Charney, Cy.

Conway, Katrina. To Dance a Tango. (Rainbow Romances Ser.). 160p. 1993. 14.95 (*0-7090-4912-9*) Parkwest Pubns.

Conway, Linda. A Teacher Is Better Than Two Books. 168p. (Orig.). 1992. pap. 5.95 (*1-56245-055-7*) Great Quotations.

Conway, Linda G., ed. Party Receipts: From the Charleston Junior League: Hors d'Oeuvres, Savories, Sweets. 224p. 1993. pap. 13.95 (*0-945575-84-X*) Algonquin Bks.

Conway, Lois, jt. auth. see Rehberg, Linda.

Conway, Lorie. Boston the Way It Was: Pictures & Memories from the Thirties & Forties. (Illus.). 132p. (Orig.). 1996. pap. 16.95 (*1-884738-89-3*) WGBH.

Conway, Lorraine. Ancient Egypt. (Gifted Learning Ser.). (Illus.). 64p. (J). (gr. 4-8). 1987. pap. 8.99 (*0-86653-399-0*, GA 1021) Good Apple.

— Animals. 64p. (J). (gr. 5 up). 1980. 8.99 (*0-916456-68-4*, GA 177) Good Apple.

— Body Systems. (Illus.). 64p. (J). (gr. 5 up). 1984. student ed. 7.99 (*0-86653-153-X*, GA 552) Good Apple.

— Chemistry Concepts. (Illus.). 64p. (J). (gr. 5 up). 1983. student ed. 8.99 (*0-86653-100-9*, GA 460) Good Apple.

— Earth Science: Tables & Tabulations. (Illus.). 64p. (J). (gr. 5 up). 1984. student ed. 8.99 (*0-86653-154-8*, GA 553) Good Apple.

— Energy. (Superific Science Ser.). (Illus.). 64p. (J). (gr. 5 up). 1985. student ed. 7.99 (*0-86653-267-6*, GA 639) Good Apple.

— Heredity & Embryology. (J). (gr. 5 up). 1980. 8.99 (*0-916456-90-0*, GA 179) Good Apple.

— The Human Body. 64p. (J). (gr. 5 up). 1980. 8.99 (*0-916456-67-6*, GA 178) Good Apple.

— Marine Biology. 64p. (J). (gr. 5 up). 1982. 7.99 (*0-86653-056-8*, GA 400) Good Apple.

— Oceanography. 64p. (J). (gr. 5 up). 1982. 7.99 (*0-86653-066-5*, GA401) Good Apple.

— Plants. 64p. (J). (gr. 5 up). 1980. 8.99 (*0-916456-69-2*, GA 176) Good Apple.

— Plants & Animals in Nature, Set. (Superific Science Ser.). (Illus.). 64p. (J). (gr. 5 up). 1986. student ed. 7.99 (*0-86653-356-7*, GA 797) Good Apple.

— Science Graphs & Word Games. (Superific Science Ser.: Bk. V). 48p. (J). (gr. 5 up). 1981. 8.99 (*0-86653-029-0*, GA 257) Good Apple.

***Conway, Lydia.** Evening Standard Childrens London 1999. 240p. 2000. per. 14.50 (*0-684-86841-5*) S&S Trade.

An Asterisk (*) at the beginning of an entry indicates that the title is appearing for the first time.

Conway, Lynda L., jt. auth. see Conway, William H.

Conway, M. E. Conway House. 240p. (Orig.). (C). 1995. pap. 9.95 (*0-9638758-7-6*) Brockton Pubng.

— The Horses of Mare Creek: The Story of Two Brothers Who Helped Make Texas a Nation. 240p. (Orig.). 1994. pap. 9.95 (*0-9638758-2-5*) Brockton Pubng.

Conway, M. Margaret. Political Participation in the United States. 2nd ed. LC 90-47357. 204p. 1990. text 24.95 (*0-87187-539-X*) Congr Quarterly.

***Conway, M. Margaret.** Political Participation in the United States. 3rd rev. ed. 200p. 2000. pap. text 24.95 (*0-87187-792-9*) Congr Quarterly.

Conway, M. Margaret, et al. Women & Public Policy: A Revolution in Progress. LC 95-30134. 213p. (YA). 1994. text 22.95 (*0-87187-923-9*) Congr Quarterly.

— Women & Public Policy: A Revolution in Progress. 2nd ed. LC 98-31147. 220p. 1998. pap. text 24.95 (*1-56802-406-1*) Congr Quarterly.

Conway, Malloy, jt. ed. see Conway.

Conway, Mandi D., jt. auth. see Kertes, Peter J.

Conway, Martin. Catholic Politics in Europe: 1918-1945. (Historical Connections Ser.). 128p. (C). 1997. pap. 16.99 (*0-415-06401-5*) Routledge.

— The Outer Banks: From a Flying Machine. LC 89-60752. (Illus.). 46p. 1989. pap. write for info. (*0-938634-09-7*) Carabelle.

Conway, Martin, jt. ed. see Buchanan, Tom.

Conway, Martin, jt. ed. see Campbell, Ruth.

Conway, Martin A. Theories of Memory II. 1998. 54.95 (*0-86377-805-4*, Pub. by Psychol Pr) Taylor & Francis.

Conway, Martin A., ed. Cognitive Models of Memory. LC 96-43748. (Studies in Cognition Ser.). (Illus.). 320p. 1997. 55.00 (*0-262-03245-7*) MIT Pr.

— Cognitive Models of Memory. LC 96-43748. (Studies in Cognition Ser.). (Illus.). 320p. 1997. pap. text 27.50 (*0-262-53148-8*) MIT Pr.

— Recovered Memories & False Memories. (Debates in Psychology Ser.). (Illus.). 312p. 1997. pap. text 29.95 (*0-19-852386-6*) OUP.

— Theoretical Perspectives on Autobiographical Memory: Proceedings of the NATO Advanced Research Workshop, Grange-over-Sands, U. K. 4-12 July, 1991. (NATO Advanced Science Institutes Series C: Mathematical & Physical Sciences). 516p. (C). 1992. lib. bdg. 251.00 (*0-7923-1646-0*) Kluwer Academic.

Conway, Martin A., jt. ed. see Gathercole, Susan E.

Conway, Martin E., jt. ed. see Morris, Peter E.

Conway, Martin R. Shepherdstown: An American Treasure. LC 90-83219. (Illus.). 72p. 1998. text 14.95 (*0-938634-10-0*) Carabelle.

Conway, Mary, ed. American Indian & Alaska Native Health: Bibliography: January 1990 Through September 1996. 123p. 1999. reprint ed. pap. text 40.00 (*0-7881-8058-4*) DIANE Pub.

— MSDS Reference for Crop Protection Products, 1998. 10th ed. 1998. pap. 170.00 (*1-57009-064-5*, 2108) Chem & Pharmac.

— Turf & Ornamental Reference for Plant Protection Products, 1998. 7th ed. 1998. pap. 128.00 incl. cd-rom (*1-57009-063-7*, 3108) Chem & Pharmac.

Conway, Mary E. Effective Medical Treatment of Heroin Addiction, January 1994 Through September 1997 Plus Selected Earlier Citations, CBM 97-7. 56p. 1997. pap. 7.50 (*0-16-061585-2*) USGPO.

Conway, McKinley. Airport Cities Twenty-One: The New Global Transport Centers of the Twenty-First Century. (Illus.). 113p. 1992. write for info. (*0-910436-32-0*) Conway Data.

— The Airport City: Development Concepts for the Twenty-First Century. rev. ed. LC 80-65254. (Illus.). 288p. 1980. 11.95 (*0-910436-14-2*) Conway Data.

— Development Highlights of the Twentieth Century: With Lessons for Century 21. (Illus.). 114p. 1997. pap. 24.00 (*0-910436-35-5*) Conway Data.

Conway, Michael. The Odyssey Singer. 88p. (Orig.). 1985. pap. 6.00 (*0-912449-17-9*) Floating Island.

Conway, Michael & Ricci, Mark. The Complete Films of Marilyn Monroe. (Illus.). 160p. 1986. reprint ed. pap. 15.95 (*0-8065-1016-1*, Citadel Pr) Carol Pub Group.

— Films of Marilyn Monroe. (Illus.). 1968. pap. 14.95 (*0-8065-0145-6*, C265, Citadel Pr) Carol Pub Group.

Conway, Michael, jt. ed. see Clark, Joseph F.

Conway, Moncure. Demonology & Devil Lore, Vol. II. Templar, Thorguard, ed. 435p. 1994. 45.00 (*1-57179-023-3*) Intern Guild ASRS.

Conway, Moncure D. Addresses & Reprints. (Works of Moncure Daniel Conway). 1990. reprint ed. lib. bdg. 90.00 (*0-7812-2347-4*) Rprt Serv.

— Autobiography: Memoirs, & Experiences of Moncure Daniel Conway, 2 vols. LC 76-87495. (American Public Figures Ser.). (Illus.). 1970. reprint ed. lib. bdg. 115.00 (*0-306-71402-7*) Da Capo.

— Autobiography Memories & Experiences. (Works of Moncure Daniel Conway). 1990. reprint ed. lib. bdg. 79.00 (*0-7812-2346-6*) Rprt Serv.

— Centenary History of South Place Chapel. (Works of Moncure Daniel Conway). 1990. reprint ed. lib. bdg. 90.00 (*0-7812-2344-X*) Rprt Serv.

— Demonology & Devil Lore, 2 vols., Set. (Works of Moncure Daniel Conway). 1990. reprint ed. lib. bdg. 150.00 (*0-7812-2333-4*) Rprt Serv.

— The Earthward Pilgrimage. (Works of Moncure Daniel Conway). 1990. reprint ed. lib. bdg. 90.00 (*0-7812-2330-X*) Rprt Serv.

— Emerson at Home & Abroad. LC 68-24934. (Studies in Emerson: No. 12). 1969. reprint ed. lib. bdg. 75.00 (*0-8383-0930-5*) M S G Haskell Hse.

— Emerson at Home & Abroad. (Works of Moncure Daniel Conway). 1990. reprint ed. lib. bdg. 90.00 (*0-7812-2337-7*) Rprt Serv.

— George Washington & Mt. Vernon. (Works of Moncure Daniel Conway). 1990. reprint ed. lib. bdg. 90.00 (*0-7812-2340-7*) Rprt Serv.

— The Golden Hour. (Works of Moncure Daniel Conway). 1990. reprint ed. lib. bdg. 90.00 (*0-7812-2328-8*) Rprt Serv.

— Idols & Ideals. (Works of Moncure Daniel Conway). 1990. reprint ed. lib. bdg. 90.00 (*0-7812-2332-6*) Rprt Serv.

— Life of Nathaniel Hawthorne. LC 68-24935. (Studies in Hawthorne: No. 15). 1969. reprint ed. lib. bdg. 75.00 (*0-8383-0931-3*) M S G Haskell Hse.

— Life of Nathaniel Hawthorne. (Works of Moncure Daniel Conway). 1990. reprint ed. lib. bdg. 79.00 (*0-7812-2341-5*) Rprt Serv.

— The Life of Thomas Paine. 1972. 30.95 (*0-405-09114-1*, 1707) Ayer.

— The Life of Thomas Paine. (Works of Moncure Daniel Conway). 1990. reprint ed. lib. bdg. 79.00 (*0-7812-2343-1*) Rprt Serv.

— A Necklace of Stories. (Works of Moncure Daniel Conway). 1990. reprint ed. lib. bdg. 79.00 (*0-7812-2334-2*) Rprt Serv.

— Omitted Chapters of History. (Works of Moncure Daniel Conway). 1990. reprint ed. lib. bdg. 79.00 (*0-7812-2339-3*) Rprt Serv.

— Pine & Palm. (Works of Moncure Daniel Conway). 1990. reprint ed. lib. bdg. 79.00 (*0-7812-2338-5*) Rprt Serv.

— Prisons of Air. (Works of Moncure Daniel Conway). 1990. reprint ed. lib. bdg. 79.00 (*0-7812-2342-3*) Rprt Serv.

— The Rejected Stone. (Works of Moncure Daniel Conway). 1990. reprint ed. lib. bdg. 79.00 (*0-685-44755-3*) Rprt Serv.

— Republican Superstitions. (Works of Moncure Daniel Conway). 1990. reprint ed. lib. bdg. 79.00 (*0-685-44752-9*) Rprt Serv.

— Solomon & Solomonic Literature. LC 72-2032. (Studies in Comparative Literature: No. 35). 1972. reprint ed. lib. bdg. 75.00 (*0-8383-1478-3*) M S G Haskell Hse.

— Solomonic Literature. (Works of Moncure Daniel Conway). 1990. reprint ed. lib. bdg. 79.00 (*0-7812-2345-8*) Rprt Serv.

— Testimonies Concerning Slavery. LC 77-82187. (Anti-Slavery Crusade in America Ser.). 1977. reprint ed. 20.95 (*0-405-00625-X*) Ayer.

— Thomas Carlyle. (Works of Moncure Daniel Conway). 1990. reprint ed. lib. bdg. 79.00 (*0-7812-2336-9*) Rprt Serv.

— Tracts for Today. (Works of Moncure Daniel Conway). 1990. reprint ed. lib. bdg. 79.00 (*0-7812-2327-X*) Rprt Serv.

— The Wandering Jew & the Pound of Flesh. (Works of Moncure Daniel Conway). 1990. reprint ed. lib. bdg. 79.00 (*0-7812-2335-0*) Rprt Serv.

— The Works of Moncure Daniel Conway. 1990. reprint ed. lib. bdg. 63.00 (*0-685-44757-X*) Rprt Serv.

Conway, Moncure D., ed. Dial: A Monthly Magazine for Literature, Philosophy & Religion, Vol. 1, Nos. 1-12. reprint ed. lib. bdg. 76.50 (*0-404-19515-6*) AMS Pr.

Conway, Moncure D., ed. see Paine, Thomas.

Conway, Moncure D., tr. see Phillips, John T., II.

Conway Morris, Simon. The Crucible of Creation: The Burgess Shale & the Rise of Animals. (Illus.). 276p. 2000. pap. 16.95 (*0-19-286202-2*) OUP.

Conway, Nancy. Speech Evaluation of the Patient with a Tracheostomy Tube. Drolet, Cindy, ed. (Illus.). 124p. 1997. 44.95 (*1-883315-23-9*, 7097) Imaginart Intl.

Conway, Nancy Jessop, see Roth-Nelson, Stephanie.

Conway, Nancy Jessop, see Roth-Nelson, Stephanie & Jessop Conway, Nancy.

Conway, Nancy Jessop, see Roth-Nelson, Stephanie.

Conway, Nancy Jessop, jt. auth. see Roth-Nelson, Stephanie.

Conway, Neal J. Tales from Old Bethesda. 208p. 1996. 23.95 (*0-9649472-1-8*) C M S MD.

Conway, Pat. Instant Guitar! (Illus.). 16p. (Orig.). 1995. pap. 12.95 incl. cd-rom (*0-8256-2266-2*, AM32517, Amsco Music) Music Sales.

— Learn Blues Harp Effects in 60 Minutes. 19p. 1998. pap. text 5.95 (*0-7119-5634-0*, AM 936122) Music Sales.

— Learn Blues Harp Note Bending in 60 Minutes. 19p. 1998. pap. text 5.95 (*0-7119-5631-6*, AM 936090) Music Sales.

— Learn Guitar Tunings in 60 Minutes. 19p. 1998. pap. text 5.95 (*0-7119-5633-2*, AM 936111) Music Sales.

— One Hundred Great Scottish Songs. 112p. 1986. pap. 17.95 (*0-7866-1590-7*, 95175WW) Mel Bay.

— Play Blues Harp in 60 Minutes. (Illus.). 19p. 1998. pap. text 5.95 (*0-7119-5640-5*, AM 936188) Music Sales.

— Play Essential Guitar Scales in 60 Minutes. 19p. 1998. pap. text 5.95 (*0-7119-5637-5*, AM 936155) Music Sales.

— Play Essential Rock Chords in 60 Minutes. 19p. 1998. pap. text 5.95 (*0-7119-5635-9*, AM 936133) Music Sales.

— Play Famous Blues Guitar Rhythms in 60 Minutes. (Illus.). 19p. 1998. pap. text 5.95 (*0-7119-5630-8*, AM 936089) Music Sales.

— Play Guitar in 60 Minutes. 19p. 1998. pap. text 5.95 (*0-7119-5632-4*, AM 936100) Music Sales.

— Play Jam Tracks for Guitar in 60 Minutes. 19p. 1998. pap. text 5.95 (*0-7119-5629-4*, AM 936078) Music Sales.

— Play Your First Blues Riffs in 60 Minutes. (Illus.). 19p. 1998. pap. text 5.95 (*0-7119-5639-1*, Am 936177) Music Sales.

— Play Your First Rock Riffs in 60 Minutes. (Illus.). 19p. 1998. pap. text 5.95 (*0-7119-5638-3*, AM 936166) Music Sales.

Conway, Pat, ed. Children's Songs for Harmonica. (Illus.). 48p. 1992. pap. 9.95 (*0-7119-2831-2*, AM87060) Music Sales.

— Irish Songs for Harmonica. (Illus.). 48p. 1992. pap. 7.95 (*0-7119-2790-1*, AM90151) Music Sales.

— Scottish Songs for Harmonica. (Illus.). 48p. 1992. pap. 9.95 (*0-7119-2791-X*, AM86520) Music Sales.

Conway, Patrick. Currency Proliferation: The Monetary Legacy of the Soviet Union. LC 95-18713. (Essays in International Finance: No. 197). 64p. 1995. pap. 10.00 (*0-88165-104-4*) Princeton U Int Finan Econ.

— Deluxe Tinwhistle Songbook. 1983. spiral bd. 6.95 (*0-87166-670-7*, 93819) Mel Bay.

— Guitar Chords Pocket Book. 32p. 1980. pap. 0.95 (*0-87166-544-1*, 93702) Mel Bay.

— Irish Tinwhistle Pocketbook. 32p. 1981. pap. 0.95 (*0-87166-547-6*, 93752) Mel Bay.

***Conway, Patrick J. & Conway, Patrick S.** The Awful Truth: For Those Who Dare to Know. (Illus.). 288p. 1999. pap. 19.95 (*1-880959-39-9*) Pragmatic Pr.

Conway, Patrick S., jt. auth. see Conway, Patrick J.

Conway, Paul & Weaver, Shari. The Setup Phase of Project Open Book. 24p. 1994. pap. 10.00 (*1-887334-34-3*) Coun Lib & Info.

Conway, Pierre. Aristotelian Formal & Material Logic. 330p. (Orig.). (C). 1995. pap. text 39.50 (*0-8191-9906-0*); lib. bdg. 59.00 (*0-8191-9905-2*) U Pr of Amer.

— Faith Views the Universe: A Thomistic Perspective. Spangler, Mary M., ed. LC 97-20070. 232p. 1997. 49.50 (*0-7618-0786-1*); pap. 29.50 (*0-7618-0787-X*) U Pr of Amer.

— Metaphysics of Aquinas: A Summary of Aquinas' Exposition of Aristotle's Metaphysics. Spangler, Mary M., ed. (C). 1996. pap. text 36.50 (*0-7618-0293-2*); lib. bdg. 54.00 (*0-7618-0292-4*) U Pr of Amer.

Conway Quality Inc. Staff. Waste Chasers: A Pocket Companion to Quality & Productivity. (Illus.). 105p. (Orig.). 1992. pap. write for info. (*0-9631464-1-6*) Conway Qual.

Conway, R. A., et al, eds. Hazardous & Industrial Solid Waste Minimization Practices. LC 89-33965. (Special Technical Publication Ser.: No. STP 1043). (Illus.). 225p. 1989. pap. text 39.00 (*0-8031-1269-6*, STP1043) ASTM.

Conway, R. A. & Gulledge, W. P., eds. Hazardous & Industrial Solid Waste Testing 2nd Symposium-STP 805. LC 84-70420. 332p. 1983. text 44.00 (*0-8031-0246-1*, STP805) ASTM.

Conway, R. S. The Making of Latin: An Introduction to Latin, Greek & English Etymology. 1983. 32.50 (*0-89241-335-2*) Caratzas.

— The Making of Latin: An Introduction to Latin, Greek & English Etymology. 1995. pap. 18.00 (*0-89241-341-7*) Caratzas.

Conway, R. S. & Walters, C. F., eds. Ab Ube Condita, Vol. II, Bks. VI-X. (Oxford Classical Text Ser.). 410p. 1920. text 42.00 (*0-19-814621-3*) OUP.

— Ab Ube Condita, Vol. III, Bks. XXI-XXV. (Oxford Classical Texts Ser.). 438p. 1929. text 42.00 (*0-19-814622-1*) OUP.

Conway, Richard A. Environmental Risk Analysis of Chemicals. LC 90-24622. 584p. 1993. reprint ed. 72.50 (*0-89464-566-8*) Krieger.

Conway, Rita S. NoteWriter. (Illus.). 328p. 1996. vinyl bd. 29.95 (*0-9655195-3-8*) Sandpiper Pubs Inc.

Conway, Robert & Izard, John. Student Behaviour Outcomes: Choosing Appropriate Paths. 1995. pap. 65.00 (*0-86431-200-8*, Pub. by Aust Council Educ Res) St Mut.

Conway, Robert, jt. auth. see Ashman, Adrian F.

Conway, Robert N., jt. auth. see Ashman, Adrian F.

Conway, Robert S. Ancient Italy & Modern Religion. LC 77-27141. (Hibbert Lectures: 1932). reprint ed. 32.50 (*0-404-60428-5*) AMS Pr.

— Harvard Lectures on the Vergilian Age. LC 67-13861. 1928. 32.00 (*0-8196-0182-9*) Biblo.

— Makers of Europe: Dickinson College, James Henry Morgan Lectures, 1930. LC 67-28748. (Essay Index Reprint Ser.). 1977. 16.95 (*0-8369-0330-7*) Ayer.

Conway, Robert S., et al. The Prae-Italic Dialects of Italy, 3 vols. (Illus.). xlvii, 1277p. 1967. reprint ed. 400.00 (*0-318-71103-6*) G Olms Pubs.

— The Prae-Italic Dialects of Italy, 3 vols., Set. (Illus.). 1967. reprint ed. 400.00 (*0-685-66454-6*, 05101889) G Olms Pubs.

Conway, Rosanne, jt. auth. see Scott, Kenneth.

Conway, Russ. Game Misconduct: Alan Eagleson & The Corruption Of Hockey. rev. ed. LC 96-125662. (Illus.). 304p. 1996. text 24.95 (*0-921912-78-1*) London Brdge.

— Game Misconduct: Alan Eagleson & The Corruption Of Hockey. rev. ed. LC 98-135078. (Illus.). 304p. 1997. pap. 15.95 (*1-55199-018-0*) MW&R.

***Conway, Ruth.** The Choices at the Heart of Technology: A Christian Perspective. LC 99-45070. (Christian Mission in Modern Culture Ser.). 144p. 1999. pap. 12.00 (*1-56338-287-3*) TPI PA.

Conway, Sally & Conway, Jim. When a Mate Wants Out: Secrets for Saving a Marriage. 224p. 1992. 15.99 (*0-310-57370-X*) Zondervan.

Conway, Sally, jt. auth. see Conway, Jim.

Conway, Sheelegh. The Faraway Hills Are Green: Voices of Irish Women in Canada. 338p. pap. 16.95 (*0-88961-176-9*, Pub. by Womens Pr) LPC InBook.

***Conway, Simon.** Damaged. 2000. pap. 15.00 (*0-86241-760-0*, Pub. by Canongate Books); pap. 15.00 (*0-86241-895-X*) Canongate Books.

***Conway, Stephen.** The British Isles & the War of American Independence. LC 99-45407. 424p. 2000. text 90.00 (*0-19-820659-3*) OUP.

— The War of American Independence, 1775-1783. (Modern Wars Ser.). 296p. 1995. pap. text 17.95 (*0-340-57626-X*, Pub. by E A) OUP.

— The War of American Independence, 1775-1783. 256p. 1995. text 49.95 (*0-340-62520-1*, Pub. by E A) St Martin.

Conway, Stephen, ed. The Correspondence of Jeremy Bentham: July 1820 to December 1821, Vol. 10. (Collected Works of Jeremy Bentham). 518p. 1995. text 95.00 (*0-19-822617-9*) OUP.

Conway, Stephen, ed. see Bentham, Jeremy.

Conway, Stephen, jt. ed. see Stokes, Melvyn.

Conway, Stephen, tr. see Theweleit, Klaus.

Conway, Steve J., jt. auth. see Fisher, Charles F.

Conway, Thomas, Jr. & Patterson, Ernest M. The Operations of the New Bank Act. Bruchey, Stuart, ed. LC 80-1141. (Rise of Commercial Banking Ser.). 1981. reprint ed. lib. bdg. 42.95 (*0-405-13643-9*) Ayer.

Conway, Thomas, jt. auth. see Doern, G. Bruce.

Conway, Thor. Painted Dreams: Native American Rock Art. LC 93-19666. (Illus.). 1996. 29.95 (*1-55971-213-9*, NorthWord Pr) Creat Pub Intl.

Conway, Thor & Conway, Julie. Spirits on Stone: The Agawa Pictographs. LC 90-82538. (Illus.). (Orig.). 1990. pap. 8.95 (*1-878094-00-9*) Heritage Discover.

Conway, Tim, Jr., photos by. Hearts of Gold: A Collection of Recipes from 'Doctors Who Cook' & Friends of the Medical College of Georgia Children's Health Program. (Illus.). 192p. 1998. 19.95 (*0-9659707-0-1*) Med Coll of GA.

Conway, Timothy. Women of Power & Grace: Nine Astonishing, Inspiring Luminaries of Our Time. (Illus.). 352p. 1995. 22.95 (*1-882978-26-9*) Wake Up Pr.

— Women of Power & Grace: Nine Astonishing, Inspiring Luminaries of Our Time. (Illus.). 352p. 1995. reprint ed. pap. 16.95 (*1-882978-27-7*) Wake Up Pr.

Conway, Timothy, jt. auth. see Pearson, Gayle.

Conway, Tom, jt. auth. see Doern, G. Bruce.

Conway-Turner, Kate, et al, eds. Women's Studies in Transition: The Pursuit of Interdisciplinarity. LC 97-47689. 344p. 1998. 52.50 (*0-87413-643-1*) U Delaware Pr.

Conway-Turner, Kate & Cherrin, Suzanne. Women, Families, & Feminist Politics: A Global Exploration. (Illus.). 260p. 1998. pap. 29.95 (*1-56023-935-2*, Harrington Park); lib. bdg. 49.95 (*0-7890-0482-8*, Harrington Park) Haworth Pr.

Conway, W. D. Countercurrent Chromatography: Apparatus, Theory & Applications. 475p. 1990. 125.00 (*0-471-18677-5*) Wiley.

Conway, W. Fred. Chemical Fire Engines. (Fire Service History Ser.). (Illus.). 127p. 1987. 24.95 (*0-925165-20-4*) Fire Buff Hse.

Conway, W. Fred, Sr. Corydon - The Forgotten Battle of the Civil War. (Illus.). 128p. (Orig.). 1991. pap. 9.95 (*0-925165-03-4*) Fire Buff Hse.

Conway, W. Fred. Firefighting Lore. (Illus.). 188p. (Orig.). 1992. pap. 9.95 (*0-925165-14-X*) Fire Buff Hse.

— The Incredible Adventures of Daniel Boone's Kid Brother - Squire. (Illus.). 112p. 1992. pap. 9.95 (*0-925165-08-5*) Fire Buff Hse.

— More Firefighting Lore: Forty More Strange but True Stories from Firefighting History. LC 98-220582. (Illus.). 176p. 1998. pap. 9.95 (*0-925165-23-9*) Fire Buff Hse.

— The Most Incredible Prison Escape of the Civil War. (True Adventure Stories from the Civil War Ser.). (Illus.). 120p. (Orig.). 1991. pap. 9.95 (*0-925165-04-2*) Fire Buff Hse.

— Those Magnificent Old Steam Fire Engines. LC 96-83534. (Illus.). 304p. 1996. 29.95 (*0-925165-19-0*) Fire Buff Hse.

Conway, W. Fred, Sr. What the Bible Says about Prehistoric Man. (Illus.). 96p. (Orig.). 1993. pap. 4.99 (*0-925165-13-1*) Fire Buff Hse.

Conway, W. Fred. Young Abe Lincoln - His Teenage Years in Indiana. (Illus.). 136p. (Orig.). 1992. pap. 9.95 (*0-925165-09-3*) Fire Buff Hse.

Conway, W. Fred, ed. Discovering America's Fire Museums. rev. ed. (Illus.). 200p. 1999. pap. 12.95 (*0-925165-24-7*) Fire Buff Hse.

Conway, Walter D. Countercurrent Chromatography: Apparatus, Theory & Applications. LC 89-14697. 475p. 1990. text 80.00 (*0-89573-331-5*, Wiley-VCH) Wiley.

Conway, Walter D. & Petroski, Richard J., eds. Modern Countercurrent Chromatography. LC 95-7048. (Symposium Ser.: No. 593). 238p. 1995. text 75.00 (*0-8412-3167-2*, Pub. by Am Chemical) OUP.

Conway, Walter D., jt. ed. see Ito, Yoichiro.

***Conway, Wilbur.** Manhood God's Style. 112p. 1999. pap. 8.99 (*1-56043-318-3*) Destiny Image.

Conway, William E. Winning the War on Waste: Changing the Way We Work. (Illus.). 239p. 1996. text 26.95 (*0-9631464-2-4*) Conway Qual.

— Winning the War on Waste: Changing the Way We Work. 2nd ed. 250p. 1996. 6.95 (*0-9631464-4-0*) Conway Qual.

Conway, William H. & Conway, Lynda L. Canonical Crime Scenes & Investigations, Vol. 1. 55p. 1995. pap. 14.95 (*1-888728-02-7*) Clssic Spclties.

— Canonical Crime Scenes & Investigations, Vol. 2. 53p. 1997. pap. 14.95 (*1-888728-04-3*) Clssic Spclties.

— Canonical Crime Scenes & Investigations, Vol. 3. 58p. 1998. pap. text 14.95 (*1-888728-08-6*) Clssic Spclties.

— Valley of Fear & the Molly Maguires. 77p. 1996. pap. 14.95 (*1-888728-06-X*) Clssic Spclties.

Conway, William M. The Van Eycks & Their Followers. LC 75-41065. (BCL Ser.: Ii). reprint ed. 47.50 (*0-404-14657-0*) AMS Pr.

Conwell, Charles A., et al. Rise 'n Shine: Catholic Education & the African-American Community. Chineworth, Mary A., ed. 90p. (Orig.). 1996. pap. 10.00 (*1-55833-177-8*) Natl Cath Educ.

Conwell, E. Proceedings of the Symposium on Photoinduced Charge Transfer. iv, 362p. 1991. pap. text 1300.00 (*2-88124-483-1*) Gordon & Breach.

Conwell, E. M., jt. auth. see Epstein, A. J.

***Conwell, Kent.** The Alamo Trail. LC 99-91314. 192p. 2000. 18.95 (*0-8034-9401-7*, Avalon Bks) Bouregy.

Conwell, Kent. Blood Brothers. LC 99-90152. 192p. 1997. lib. bdg. 18.95 (*0-8034-9361-4*, Avalon Bks) Bouregy.

— Bumpo, Bill, & the Girls. LC 96-97057. 192p. 1996. 18.95 (*0-8034-9186-7*, Avalon Bks) Bouregy.

— The Ghost of Blue Bone Mesa. LC 97-97221. 192p. 1998. lib. bdg. 18.95 (*0-8034-9291-X*, Avalon Bks) Bouregy.

— Glitter of Gold. LC 98-97007. 192p. 1999. lib. bdg. 18.95 (*0-8034-9350-9*, Avalon Bks) Bouregy.

***Conwell, Kent.** The Gold of Black Mountain. LC 99-90723. 192p. 1999. 18.95 (*0-8034-9380-0*, Avalon Bks) Bouregy.

Conwell, Kent. Painted Comanche Tree. LC 97-94023. 192p. 1997. 18.95 (*0-8034-9261-8*, Avalon Bks) Bouregy.

— Panhandle Gold. large type ed. 178p. 1992. reprint ed. lib. bdg. 14.95 (*1-56054-571-2*) Thorndike Pr.

— Texas Orphan Train. LC 98-96619. 192p. 1998. 18.95 (*0-8034-9330-4*, Avalon Bks) Bouregy.

— Valley of Gold. LC 97-93462. 192p. 1997. 18.95 (*0-8034-9240-5*, Avalon Bks) Bouregy.

Conwell, Marilyn & Juilland, Alphonse. Louisiana French Grammar, Vol. 1, Phonology, Morphology, & Syntax. (Janua Linguarum, Ser. Practica: No. 1). 1963. text 55.40 (*90-279-0621-1*) Mouton.

Conwell, R. Acres of Diamonds. 1987. 8.95 (*0-933062-23-0*) R H Sommer.

Conwell, Russell H. Acres of Diamonds. 1986. mass mkt. 4.50 (*0-515-09028-X*, Jove) Berkley Pub.

— Acres of Diamonds. 54p. pap. 4.50 (*0-87516-405-6*) DeVorss.

— Acres of Diamonds: All Good Things Are Possible, Set. deluxe ed. Leonardo, Bianca, ed. & intro. by. (Illus.). 160p. 1998. pap. 20.00 incl. audio (*0-930852-38-9*) Tree Life Pubns.

— Acres of Diamonds: All Good Things Are Possible, Right Where You Are, & Now! Leonardo, Bianca, ed. 160p. 1993. reprint ed. pap. text 10.95 (*0-930852-25-7*) Tree Life Pubns.

Conwell, Russell H., intro. 1000 Thoughts for Funeral Occasions. LC 99-28070. 1999. 48.00 (*0-7808-0303-5*) Omnigraphics Inc.

Conwell, Thomas, 3rd. Consumer's Guide to Credit Reporting: The Next Person to Read Your Credit Report...Should Be You. 55p. (Orig.). 1995. pap. 3.95 (*0-9643168-0-3*) T Patrick.

Conwell, Yeates, jt. ed. see Pearson, Jane L.

Cony, Frances, et al. Old MacDonald Had a Farm. LC 98-67008. (Illus.). 12p. (J). (ps-k). 1999. 9.95 (*0-531-30129-X*) Orchard Bks Watts.

***Conybeare, Catherine.** Paulinus Noster: Self & Symbols in the Letters of Paulinus of Nola. (Oxford Early Christian Studies). 300p. 2001. text 74.00 (*0-19-924072-8*) OUP.

Conybeare, Charles A. Place of Iceland in the History of European Institutions, Being the Lothian Prize Essay, 1877. reprint ed. 34.50 (*0-404-01696-0*) AMS Pr.

Conybeare, F. C. & Stock, George, eds. Selections from the Septuagint. (College Classical Ser.). vi, 313p. (C). 1981. reprint ed. pap. 17.00 (*0-89241-114-7*); reprint ed. lib. bdg. 32.50 (*0-89241-366-2*) Caratzas.

Conybeare, F. C. & Stock, S. George. Grammar of Septuagint Greek, with Selected Readings, Vocabularies, & Updated Indexes. 382p. 1995. 19.95 (*1-56563-150-1*) Hendrickson MA.

Conybeare, Fred C. Myth, Magic, & Morals. 184p. 1996. reprint ed. spiral bd. 32.00 (*0-7873-0196-5*) Hlth Research.

Conybeare, Frederick C. & Stock, G. A Grammar of Septuagint Greek. 80p. (C). 1980. pap. 7.95 (*0-310-43001-1*, 6652P) Zondervan.

Conybeare, John A. Trade Wars: The Theory & Practice of International Commercial Rivalry. (Political Economy of International Change Ser.). (Illus.). 352p. 1987. text 57.50 (*0-231-06234-6*) Col U Pr.

Conybeare, John J. Illustrations of Anglo-Saxon Poetry. LC 65-15875. (Studies in Poetry: No. 38). 1969. reprint ed. lib. bdg. 75.00 (*0-8383-0530-X*) M S G Haskell Hse.

Conybeare, W. D. & Phillips, William R. Outlines of the Geology of England & Wales: General Principles of That Science, & Comparative Views of the Structure of Foreign Countries. Albritton, Claude C., Jr., ed. LC 77-6516. (History of Geology Ser.). 1978. reprint ed. lib. bdg. 41.95 (*0-405-10438-3*) Ayer.

Conybeare, W. J. & Howson, J. S. The Life & Epistles of St. Paul. 1977. lib. bdg. 59.95 (*0-8490-2160-X*) Gordon Pr.

Conyers, A. J. A Basic Christian Theology. LC 94-25096. 272p. 1995. pap. 19.99 (*0-8054-1092-9*, 4210-92) Broadman.

— Eclipse of Heaven: The Loss of Transcendence & Its Effect on Modern Life. LC 99-19019. 202p. 1999. reprint ed. pap. 19.00 (*1-890318-21-3*) St Augustines Pr.

— The End: What the Gospels Really Say about the Last Things. LC 95-32672. 160p. (Orig.). 1995. pap. 9.99 (*0-8308-1617-8*, 1617) InterVarsity.

— God, Hope & History: Jurgen Moltman's & the Christian Concept of History. LC 88-4858. xiii, 227p. (C). 1988. text 39.95 (*0-86554-297-X*, H255) Mercer Univ Pr.

Conyers, D. Rural Regional Planning: Towards an Operational Theory. 66p. 1984. pap. 22.00 (*0-08-032351-0*, Pergamon Pr) Elsevier.

Conyers, Diana. An Introduction to Social Planning in the Third World. LC 81-14717. (Social Development in the Third World Ser.). (Illus.). 238p. reprint ed. pap. 67.90 (*0-8357-7527-5*, 2036033) Bks Demand.

Conyers, Diana, et al. The Role of Integrated Rural Development Projects in Developing Local Institutional Capacity. (Studies in Technology & Social Change: No. 2). 50p. (Orig.). (C). 1988. pap. 6.00 (*0-945271-02-6*) ISU-CIKARD.

Conyers, Diane. Guidelines on Social Analysis for Rural Area Development Planning. (Training Materials for Agricultural Planning Ser.: 34). 232p. 1994. pap. 27.00 (*92-5-103439-7*, F34397, Pub. by FAO) Bernan Associates.

Conyers, James E. & Wallace, Walter L. Black Elected Officials: A Study of Black Americans Holding Governmental Office. LC 74-30881. 208p. 1976. 30.00 (*0-87154-206-4*) Russell Sage.

Conyers, James L., Jr. Charles H. Wesley: The Intellectual Tradition of a Black Historian. rev. ed. LC 96-37837. (Studies in African American History & Culture). (Illus.). 336p. 1997. text 73.00 (*0-8153-2754-4*) Garland.

— The Evolution of African American Studies: A Descriptive & Evaluative Analysis of Selected African American Studies Departments & Programs. (Illus.). 254p. (Orig.). (C). 1994. pap. text 29.50 (*0-8191-9687-8*); lib. bdg. 57.50 (*0-8191-9686-X*) U Pr of Amer.

Conyers, James L., Jr., ed. African Studies: A Disciplinary Quest for Both Theory & Method. LC 96-36256. 247p. 1997. lib. bdg. 45.00 (*0-7864-0278-4*) McFarland & Co.

***Conyers, James L., Jr., ed.** Black American Intellectualism & Culture. LC 99-40707. (Comporary Studies in Sociology). 311p. 1999. 78.50 (*0-7623-0603-3*) Jai Pr.

Conyers, James L., Jr., ed. Black Lives: Essays in African American Biography. LC 98-5996. 240p. (C). (gr. 13). 1998. text 60.95 (*0-7656-0329-2*) M E Sharpe.

Conyers, James L., ed. Black Lives: Essays in African American Biography. LC 98-5996. 240p. 1998. pap. text 21.95 (*0-7656-0330-6*) M E Sharpe.

Conyers, James L., Jr. & Barnett, Alva. Africana History, Culture & Social Policy: A Collection of Critical Essays. LC 99-21698. 424p. 1999. 64.00 (*1-57309-211-8*, U Pr W Africa); pap. 44.50 (*1-57309-210-X*, U Pr W Africa) Intl Scholars.

Conyers, James L. & Barnett, Alva, eds. African American Sociology: A Social Study of the Pan-African Diaspora. LC 97-43072. (Illus.). 230p. (C). 1999. pap. text 38.95 (*0-8304-1525-4*) Thomson Learn.

Conyers, James L., jt. auth. see Woodson, Carter Godwin.

Conyers, Lawrence B. & Goodman, Dean. Ground-Penetrating Radar: An Introduction for Archaeologists. LC 97-4828. (Illus.). 232p. 1997. pap. 26.95 (*0-7619-8928-5*) AltaMira Pr.

— Ground-Penetrating Radar: An Introduction for Archaeologists. LC 97-4828. (Illus.). 232p. 1997. 69.00 (*0-7619-8927-7*) AltaMira Pr.

Conyers, Marcus A., jt. auth. see Berg, Howard S.

Conyers, Maria. Vision for the Future: Meeting the Challenge of Sight Loss. 1992. 34.00 (*1-85302-110-5*) Taylor & Francis.

Conyne, Robert, et al. Comprehensive Group Work: What It Means & How to Teach It. 306p. (Orig.). 1997. pap. text 33.95 (*1-55620-158-3*, 72629) Am Coun Assn.

Conyne, Robert K. Failures in Group Work: How We Can Learn from Our Mistakes LC 98-40210. 1999. write for info. (*0-7619-1290-8*) Sage.

***Conyne, Robert K.** Failures in Group Work: How We Can Learn from Our Mistakes LC 98-40210. 1999. 46.00 (*0-7619-1289-4*) Sage.

Conyne, Robert K. How Personal Growth & Task Groups Work. (Human Services Guides Ser.: Vol. 55). 160p. (C). 1989. pap. text 18.95 (*0-8039-3340-1*) Sage.

Conyne, Robert K. & Clack, R. James. Environmental Assessment & Design: A New Tool for the Applied Behavioral Scientist. LC 80-24816. 183p. 1981. 36.95 (*0-275-90598-5*, C0598, Praeger Pubs) Greenwood.

Conyne, Robert K. & O'Neil, James M., eds. Organizational Consultation: A Casebook. LC 92-20917. (Counseling Psychologist Casebook Ser.: Vol. 1). (Illus.). 232p. (C). 1992. 42.00 (*0-8039-4201-X*) Sage.

— Organizational Consultation: A Casebook. LC 92-20917. (Counseling Psychologist Casebook Ser.: Vol. 1). 220p. 1992. reprint ed. pap. 68.20 (*0-608-07684-8*, 206777400010) Bks Demand.

— Organizational Consultation: A Casebook, No. 1. LC 92-20917. (Counseling Psychologist Casebook Ser.: Vol. 1). (Illus.). 232p. (C). 1992. pap. 19.95 (*0-8039-4202-8*) Sage.

Conyngton, Mary. How to Help: A Manual of Practical Charity. LC 77-137160. (Poverty U. S. A. Historical Record Ser.). 1975. reprint ed. 24.95 (*0-405-03099-1*) Ayer.

Conyngton, Thomas. A Manual of Partnership Relations. LC 06-693. (Business Enterprises Reprint Ser.). 221p. 1982. reprint ed. lib. bdg. 40.00 (*0-89941-178-9*, 302130) W S Hein.

Conynham, David P. The Irish Brigade & Its Campaigns. 599p. 1989. reprint ed. 35.00 (*0-942211-39-1*) Olde Soldier Bks.

***Conza, Tony.** Success - It's a Beautiful Thing: Lessons on Life from the Founder of Blimpie International. 256p. 2000. 24.95 (*0-471-38147-0*) Wiley.

***Conze.** Buddhism: It's Essence & Development. 1999. reprint ed. pap. 18.50 (*81-215-0905-X*, Pub. by M Manoharial) S Asia.

Conze, Edward. Buddha's Law among the Birds. (Illus.). 65p. 1986. reprint ed. 10.00 (*81-208-0198-9*, Pub. by Motilal Bnarsidass) S Asia.

— Buddhist Meditation. (C). 1997. reprint ed. text 22.50 (*81-215-0781-2*, Pub. by M Manoharial) Coronet Bks.

— Buddhist Studies Nineteen Thirty-Four to Nineteen Seventy-Two. 512p. 1977. reprint ed. 20.00 (*0-686-48400-2*) Wheelwright Pr.

— Buddhist Texts Through the Ages. (C). 1992. 28.00 (*81-215-0574-7*, Pub. by M Manoharial) Coronet Bks.

— Buddhist Thought in India. 304p. 1967. pap. text 19.95 (*0-472-06129-1*, 06129, Ann Arbor Bks) U of Mich Pr.

— Buddhist Thought in India: Three Phases of Buddhist Philosophy. 1996. reprint ed. 29.50 (*81-215-0722-7*, Pub. by M Manoharial) Coronet Bks.

— A Short History of Buddhism. 160p. 1994. pap. 13.95 (*1-85168-066-7*, Pub. by Onewrld Pubns) Penguin Putnam.

***Conze, Edward.** Thirty Years of Buddhist Studies. 2nd ed. 2000. reprint ed. 27.50 (*81-215-0960-2*, Pub. by M Manoharial) S Asia.

Conze, Edward. Thirty Years of Buddhist Studies: Selected Essays. 274p. 1967. 69.50 (*0-614-01821-8*) Elliots Bks.

— The Way of Wisdom. 56p. 1993. 3.00 (*955-24-0110-0*, Pub. by Buddhist Pub Soc) Vipassana Res Pubns.

Conze, Edward, ed. The Large Sutra on Perfect Wisdom: With the Divisions of the Abhisamayalankara. LC 71-189224. (Center for South & Southeast Asia Studies, UC Berkeley: No. 18). 697p. 1974. pap. 24.95 (*0-520-05321-4*, Pub. by U CA Pr) Cal Prin Full Svc.

Conze, Edward, tr. Perfect Wisdom: The Short Prajnaparamita Texts. 224p. 1995. pap. 14.95 (*0-946672-28-8*, Pub. by Buddhist Pub) Assoc Pubs Grp.

— The Perfection of Wisdom in Eight Thousand Lines & Its Verse Summary. (C). 1994. text 28.50 (*81-7030-405-9*, Pub. by Sri Satguru Pubns) S Asia.

Conze, Edward, tr. from SAN. The Perfection of Wisdom in Eight Thousand Lines & Its Verse Summary. LC 72-76540. (Wheel Ser.: No. 1). 348p. 1973. pap. 17.95 (*0-87704-049-4*) Four Seasons Foun.

Conze, Edward, et al. Buddhist Texts Through the Ages. 323p. 1995. pap. 22.95 (*1-85168-107-8*, Pub. by Onewrld Pubns) Penguin Putnam.

Conze, Edward, jt. auth. see Wilkinson, Ellen C.

Conze, Edward, ed. & intro. see Wyatt, Thomas.

Conzelman, Hans. Gentiles-Jews-Christians: Polemics & Apologetics in the Graeco-Roman Era. Boring, M. Eugene, tr. from GER. LC 91-37936. 432p. 1991. 52.00 (*0-8006-2520-X*, 1-2520, Fortress Pr) Augsburg Fortress.

Conzelmann, H. & Lindemann, A. Interpreting the New Testament: An Introduction to the Principles & Methods of N. T. Exegesis. Schatzmann, Siegfried S., tr. from GER.Tr. of Arbeitsbuch zum Neuen Testament. 390p. Date not set. pap. 29.95 (*1-56563-140-4*) Hendrickson MA.

— Interpreting the New Testament: An Introduction to the Principles & Methods of N. T. Exegesis. Schatzmann, Siegfried S., tr. from GER.Tr. of Arbeitsbuch zum Neuen Testament. 390p. 1988. text 19.95 (*0-913573-80-9*) Hendrickson MA.

Conzelmann, Hans. Acts of the Apostles. LC 86-45203. (Hermeneia: A Critical & Historical Commentary on the Bible Ser.). 288p. 1987. 48.00 (*0-8006-6018-8*, 1-6018, Fortress Pr) Augsburg Fortress.

— I Corinthians. MacRae, George W., ed. Leitch, James W., tr. from GER. LC 73-88360. (Hermeneia: a Critical & Historical Commentary on the Bible Ser.). 328p. 1975. 48.00 (*0-8006-6005-6*, 1-6005, Fortress Pr) Augsburg Fortress.

Conzelmann, Hans, jt. auth. see Dibelius, Martin.

Conzemius, Anne & O'Neill, Jan. Creating Meaning Through Measurement: How Our School Got SMART about Accountability. Reynard, Susan, ed. 135p. 1998. 425.00 incl. VHS, cd-rom (*1-893542-00-9*) Quantum Learn.

Conzemius, Edward, ed. Ethnographical Survey of the Miskito & Suma Indians of Honduras & Nicaragua. (Bureau of American Ethnology Bulletins Ser.). 191p. 1995. lib. bdg. 79.00 (*0-7812-4106-5*) Rprt Serv.

Conzen, Kathleen N. Immigrant Milwaukee, 1836-1860: Accommodation & Community in a Frontier City. LC 75-37557. (Harvard Studies in Urban History). 315p. reprint ed. pap. 97.70 (*0-7837-2059-9*, 204233400004) Bks Demand.

Conzen-Meiars, Ina, et al, texts. Latham, John: Art after Physics. (Illus.). 128p. 1991. pap. 70.00 (*0-905836-75-8*, Pub. by Museum Modern Art) St Mut.

Conzen, Michael P., ed. Chicago Mapmakers: Essays on the Rise of the City's Map Trade. LC 84-5853. (Illus.). 76p. 1984. 12.00 (*0-916789-01-2*) Chicago Map.

— Focus on Ottawa: A Historical & Geographical Survey of Ottawa, Illinois, in the Twentieth Century. fac. ed. LC 87-11744. (Studies on the Illinois & Michigan Canal Corridor: No. 1). (Illus.). 242p. 1987. reprint ed. pap. 75.10 (*0-7837-7834-1*, 204759000007) Bks Demand.

— Making of the American Landscape. LC 89-20047. (Illus.). 449p. (C). 1990. pap. 36.99 (*0-415-91178-8*) Routledge.

— The Making of the American Landscape. 256p. 1990. pap. text 20.95 (*0-04-917010-4*) Routledge.

— Time & Place in Joliet: Essays on the Geographical Evolution of the City. fac. ed. LC 88-6108. (Studies on the Illinois & Michigan Canal Corridor: No. 2). (Illus.). 221p. 1988. reprint ed. pap. 68.60 (*0-7837-8041-9*, 204759100007) Bks Demand.

Conzen, Michael P., et al, eds. The Industrial Revolution in the Upper Illinois Valley. LC 94-1426. (Studies on the Illinois & Michigan Canal Corridor: Vol. 6). 1994. 15.00 (*0-89065-141-8*) U Chicago Comm Geo.

— A Scholar's Guide to Geographical Writing on the American & Canadian Past. (Geography Research Papers: No. 235). 760p. 1993. pap. text 33.00 (*0-226-11569-0*) U Ch Pr.

— Settling the Upper Illinois Valley: Patterns of Change in the I & M Canal Corridor, 1830-1900. LC 89-15702. (Studies on the Illinois & Michigan Canal Corridor: Vol. 3). 1989. pap. 15.00 (*0-89065-134-5*) U Ch Pr.

Conzen, Michael P. & Carr, Kay J., eds. The Illinois & Michigan Canal National Heritage Corridor: A Guide to Its History & Sources. (Illus.). 251p. 1988. 50.00 (*0-87580-128-5*) N Ill U Pr.

Conzen, Michael P. & Daniel, Adam R., eds. Lockport Legacy: Themes in the Historical Geography of an Illinois Canal Town. fac. ed. LC 90-1711. (Studies on the Illinois & Michigan Canal Corridor: No. 4). (Illus.). 174p. 1990. reprint ed. pap. 54.00 (*0-7837-7835-X*, 204759200007) Bks Demand.

Conzen, Michael P. & Mckay, Valerie M., eds. Canal Town & Country Seat: The Historical Geography of Morris. LC 94-3798. (Studies on the Illinois & Michigan Canal Corridor: Vol. 8). 1994. 15.00 (*0-89065-143-4*) U Chicago Comm Geo.

Conzen, Michael P. & Wenjun Liu, eds. Historical Geography & the Life of the Mind in the Upper Illinois Valley. LC 95-52329. (Studies on the Illinois & Michigan Canal Corridor: No. 9). 1995. write for info. (*0-89065-144-2*) U Chicago Comm Geo.

Conzen, Michale P., et al, eds. Looking for Lemont: Place & People in an Illinois Canal Town. LC 94-20130. (Studies on the Illinois & Michigan Canal Corridor: No. 7). 1994. 15.00 (*0-89065-142-6*) U Chicago Comm Geo.

Coo, jt. auth. see Jani.

Cooch, Francis A. Little Known History of Newark Delaware, & Its Environments. (Illus.). 297p. 1997. reprint ed. lib. bdg. 35.00 (*0-8328-7055-2*) Higginson Bk Co.

Cooch, Mary E. Allyn. Ancestry & Descendants of Nancy Allyn (Foote) Webb, Rev. Edward Webb & Joseph Wilkins Cooch. 157p. 1997. reprint ed. pap. 24.00 (*0-8328-7251-2*); reprint ed. lib. bdg. 34.00 (*0-8328-7250-4*) Higginson Bk Co.

Coode, Carole. Labrador Retrievers Today. (Illus.). 192p. 1993. 27.95 (*0-87605-207-3*) Howell Bks.

Coode, Thomas H. & Bauman, John F. People, Poverty, & Politics: Pennsylvanians During the Great Depression. LC 78-75198. (Illus.). 276p. 1981. 32.50 (*0-8387-2320-9*) Bucknell U Pr.

Coode, Thomas H., jt. auth. see Bauman, John F.

Coodley, Eugene L. Odyssey of a Physician: A Life of Adventure & Exploration. LC 93-40536. (Illus.). 128p. (Orig.). 1994. pap. 9.95 (*1-56474-092-7*) Fithian Pr.

Coodley, Eugene L., ed. Diagnostic Enzymology. LC 78-85839. 336p. reprint ed. pap. 104.20 (*0-608-30504-9*, 205541700022) Bks Demand.

Coody, Betty. Using Literature with Young Children. 5th ed. LC 95-81130. 320p. (C). 1996. text. write for info. (*0-697-24142-4*) Brown & Benchmark.

Coody, Marie, et al. Nehemiah: Man of Radical Obedience. LC 99-25025. (Wisdom of the Word Bible Study Ser.). 88p. 1999. pap. 12.99 (*0-8341-1820-3*) Beacon Hill.

Cooey, J. & Sebek, O. Developments in Industrial Microbiology Vol. 30: Symposium of the 45th General Meeting of the Society for Industrial Microbiology, Vol. 30. (Illus.). 270p. 1989. lib. bdg. 156.00 (*0-945345-25-9*) Lubrecht & Cramer.

Cooey, Paula, et al, eds. After Patriarchy: Feminist Transformations of the World Religions. LC 91-3287. (Faith Meets Faith Ser.). 175p. (Orig.). 1991. pap. 18.00 (*0-88344-748-7*) Orbis Bks.

Cooey, Paula M. Family, Freedom & Faith: Building Community Today. 160p. (Orig.). 1996. pap. 15.95 (*0-664-25663-5*) Westminster John Knox.

— Jonathan Edwards on Nature & Destiny: A Systematic Analysis. LC 85-21499. (Studies in American Religion: Vol. 16). 296p. 1985. lib. bdg. 89.95 (*0-88946-660-2*) E Mellen.

Coogan, Beatrice. The Big Wind: A Novel of Ireland. rev. ed. 684p. 1995. pap. 14.95 (*1-57098-031-4*) Roberts Rinehart.

Coogan, David. Electronic Writing Centers: Computing in the Field of Composition. LC 98-55723. (New Directions in Computers & Composition Studies). 1999. pap. 24.95 (*1-56750-429-9*) Ablx Pub.

***Coogan, David.** Electronic Writing Centers: Computing the Field of Composition. LC 98-55723. (New Directions in Computers & Composition Studies). 146p. 1999. 73.25 (*1-56750-428-0*) Ablx Pub.

Coogan, Gertrude. Lawful Money Explained. 1979. lib. bdg. 59.95 (*0-8490-2956-2*) Gordon Pr.

Coogan, Gertrude M. Money Creators. 1979. 250.00 (*0-87968-317-1*) Gordon Pr.

Coogan, Harold, jt. auth. see Cate, Michael.

Coogan, James C. Geologic Map of the Bear Lake South Quadrangle, Rich County, Utah. (Miscellaneous Publication of the Utah Geological Survey Ser.: Vol. 97-1). (Illus.). 16p. 1997. pap. 9.00 (*1-55791-383-8*, MP-97-1) Utah Geological Survey.

— Geologic Map of the Sheeppen Creek Quadrangle, Rich County, Utah. (Miscellaneous Publication of the Utah Geological Survey Ser.: Vol. 97-2). (Illus.). 17p. 1997. pap. 9.00 (*1-55791-381-1*, MP-97-2) Utah Geological Survey.

Coogan, Jim, jt. auth. see Sheedy, Jack.

Coogan, John W. A Workbook of Words. (J). 1987. pap. text 16.20 (*0-8013-0116-5*, 75780) Longman.

Coogan, Kevin. Dreamer of the Day: Francis Parker Yockey & the Postwar Fascist International. LC 98-18591. 644p. 1998. pap. 15.00 (*1-57027-039-2*, Pub. by Autonomedia) SPD-Small Pr Dist.

Coogan, Michael D. The Oxford History of the Biblical World. (Illus.). 672p. 1999. 49.95 (*0-19-508707-0*) OUP.

Coogan, Michael D., ed. The Illustrated Guide to World Religions. LC 98-6784. (Illus.). 288p. 1998. 39.95 (*0-19-521366-1*) OUP.

Coogan, Michael D., et al, eds. Scripture & Other Artifacts: Essays on Archaeology & the Bible in Honor of Philip J. King. LC 94-9998. 480p. 1994. 28.95 (*0-664-22036-3*) Westminster John Knox.

Coogan, Michael D., tr. Stories from Ancient Canaan. LC 77-20022. 120p. 1978. pap. 16.95 (*0-664-24184-0*) Westminster John Knox.

Coogan, Michael D., jt. ed. see Metzger, Bruce M.

Coogan, Michael David, jt. ed. see Metzger, Bruce M.

An Asterisk (*) at the beginning of an entry indicates that the title is appearing for the first time.

Coogan, Peter & Hogan, William E. Secured Transaction under the Uniform Commercial Code, 5 vols., Vol. 1, 1a, 1b, 1c & 1d. (Bender's Uniform Commercial Code Service Ser.). 1963. ring bd. 1080.00 (*0-8205-1615-5*) Bender.

Coogan, Tim P. The IRA: A History. LC 93-85475. (Illus.). 542p. 1994. pap. 18.95 (*1-879373-99-8*) Roberts Rinehart.

— Michael Collins: The Man Who Made Ireland. LC 95-72787. (Illus.). 480p. 1996. pap. text 16.95 (*1-57098-075-6*) Roberts Rinehart.

— On the Blanket: The Inside Story of the IRA Prisoners "Dirty" Protest. 264p. 1997. pap. 14.95 (*1-57098-133-7*) Roberts Rinehart.

— The Troubles: Ireland's Ordeal 1966-1995 & the Search for Peace. LC 96-67091. 488p. 1996. 29.95 (*1-57098-092-6*) Roberts Rinehart.

— The Troubles: Ireland's Ordeal 1966-1996 & the Search for Peace. (Illus.). 488p. 1997. pap. 18.95 (*1-57098-144-2*) Roberts Rinehart.

— The Troubles: Ireland's Ordeal, 1966-1999 & the Search for Peace. rev. ed. 520p. 1999. pap. 18.95 (*1-57098-286-4*) Roberts Rinehart.

Coogan, Tim Pat. Eamon de Valera: The Man Who Was Ireland. (Illus.). 772p. 1995. 30.00 (*0-614-32314-2*) HarpC.

— Irish: The Story of the Irish Diaspora. 1999. 35.00 (*1-57098-300-3*) Roberts Rinehart.

Coogan, Timothy P. Ireland since the Rising. LC 75-35333. (Illus.). 355p. 1976. reprint ed. lib. bdg. 35.00 (*0-8371-8560-2*, COIR, Greenwood Pr) Greenwood.

Coogle, Diana. Fire from the Dragon's Tongue: Essays about Living with Nature in the Siskiyou Mountains. LC 98-75670. 109p. 1999. pap. 14.00 (*0-9669364-0-X*) Laugh Dog.

Coogler, J. Gordon. Purely Original Verse. limited ed. (Illus.). 1974. reprint ed. 6.00 (*0-686-09908-7*) C H Neuffer.

***Coohill, Joe.** Ireland: A Short History. (Illus.). 2000. pap. 15.95 (*1-85168-238-4*, Pub. by Onewrld Pubns) Element MA.

Coohman, Tim. Test Process Improvement: Step-by-Step Guide to Structured Testing. 192p. 1999. text 34.95 (*0-201-59624-5*) Addison-Wesley.

***Cooijer, C., et al.** Shpol'skii Spectroscopy & Other Site Selection Methods: Applications in Environmental Analysis, Bioanalytical Chemistry & Chemical Physics. LC 99-55651. 584p. 2000. 125.00 (*0-471-24508-9*) Wiley.

Cook. Bankruptcy Litigation Manual: 1996-97 Edition. 1065p. 1996. 160.00 (*1-56706-334-9*) Panel Pubs.

— Biocomputers. (ITCP-UK Computer Science Ser.). (C). 1991. pap. 64.95 (*0-412-35770-4*) Thomson Learn.

Cook. Charts & Publications of Alexander Dalrymple. 85.95 (*0-85967-936-5*) Ashgate Pub Co.

Cook. Chinese Economy Under Transition. LC 99-33850. 1999. text 85.00 (*0-312-22621-7*) St Martin.

Cook. Computerized Study Guide for Introductory Psychology. 1994. student ed. 20.00 incl. cd-rom (*0-205-16003-4*) Allyn.

Cook. Dennis Potter: A Life on Screen. (Illus.). 350p. 1998. pap. 29.95 (*0-7190-5423-0*, Pub. by Manchester Univ Pr) St Martin.

— Dying & Grieving. 2nd ed. (C). 1997. text, teacher ed. 31.00 (*0-15-505450-3*) Harcourt Coll Pubs.

— Dying & Grieving: Lifespan & Family. 2nd ed. LC 97-77278. (C). 1998. text 74.00 (*0-15-501506-0*) Harcourt.

Cook. Enamines: Their Synthesis, Structure, Reactions. 2nd ed. (Illus.). 720p. 1987. text 295.00 (*0-8247-7764-6*) Dekker.

Cook. Good Night, Pillow Fight. (J). Date not set. 14.95 (*0-06-205189-X*); pap. 5.95 (*0-06-205932-7*); lib. bdg. 14.89 (*0-06-205190-3*) HarpC Child Bks.

— Governing with the News: The News Media as a Political Institution. LC 97-23716. 264p. 1999. lib. bdg. 48.00 (*0-226-11499-6*) U Ch Pr.

— History of the American Cinema, Vol. 8. 1998. 69.00 (*0-684-18416-8*) Mac Lib Ref.

— History of the American Cinema, Vol. 9. LC 99-21371. 500p. 1999. 85.00 (*0-684-80463-8*) S&S Trade.

— Introduction to Semiconductors. 1995. pap. text, lab manual ed. 38.20 (*0-13-250010-8*) P-H.

— Introductory DC-AC Circuits. 4th ed. LC 98-21136. 848p. (C). 1998. 100.00 (*0-13-896036-4*) P-H.

— Machine Designed Mathcad Solutions. 1998. pap. text 38.00 (*0-13-287434-2*) P-H.

— Management & Organizational Behavior. 2nd ed. 1996. 43.75 (*0-256-26372-8*, WCB McGr Hill) McGrw-H Hghr Educ.

— Manson's Tropical Disease. 20th ed. 1995. text 125.00 (*0-7020-1764-7*, W B Saunders Co) Harcrt Hlth Sci Grp.

Cook. Manual of Archival Description 2nd Edition. 1990. 78.95 (*0-566-03634-7*) Ashgate Pub Co.

— Milton Spenser & the Epic Tradition. 208p. 1999. pap. 19.95 (*0-7546-0048-3*) Ashgate Pub Co.

— More Structured Workshops for Customer Care. 264p. 1993. ring bd. 262.95 (*1-85904-005-5*) Ashgate Pub Co.

Cook. Practical Electricity. 1996. pap. text, lab manual ed. 38.20 (*0-13-268210-9*) P-H.

— Private Health Care. 1991. pap. text. write for info. (*0-582-06775-8*, Pub. by Addison-Wesley) Longman.

***Cook.** Qualitative Research in Occupational Therapy. 2001. pap. 35.25 (*0-7693-0079-0*) Thomson Learn.

Cook. Quasi-Experimentation, 2 vols. (C). Date not set. pap. write for info. (*0-395-61556-9*) HM.

***Cook.** Rhinoplasty. 452p. 2000. 185.00 (*0-86577-763-2*, C3687) Thieme Med Pubs.

Cook. St. Martin's Guide to Contemporary British History. 1994. text 75.00 (*0-312-12076-1*) St Martin.

— Supporting Sick Children. (C). 1999. pap. text 15.00 (*0-7020-2207-1*, Pub. by W B Saunders) Saunders.

— Wizard War. 1987. mass mkt. 3.95 (*0-445-20700-0*, Pub. by Warner Bks) Little.

Cook, ed. American History Through Documents, Vol. 1. (C). 1991. write for info. (*0-673-46134-3*) Addison-Wesley.

— American History Through Documents, Vol. 2. (C). 1991. write for info. (*0-673-46135-1*) Addison-Wesley.

— Book of 18th Century Verse. (Poetry Library). 1998. pap. 7.95 (*1-85326-450-4*, 4504WW, Pub. by Wrdsworth Edits) NTC Contemp Pub Co.

***Cook, ed.** Introductory Computer Mathematics. LC 99-28231. (Illus.). 373p. 1999. pap. text 57.00 (*0-13-013151-2*) P-H.

Cook, ed. Maleshop: Men, Consumerism & Shopping Culture. 1995. pap. 22.50 (*0-85315-805-3*, Pub. by Lawrence & Wishart) NYU Pr.

Cook & Fuller. Nutrition 1996/97. 8th annot. ed. 1996. teacher ed. (*0-697-31607-6*, WCB McGr Hill) McGrw-H Hghr Educ.

Cook & Marchant. Advanced Greek Unseens: From Cook & Marchant. Bowen, Anthony, ed. 92p. 1980. pap. 18.95 (*0-906515-47-5*, Pub. by Brist Class Pr) Focus Pub-R Pullins.

Cook & Weber. The Crisis: How the Hunger & Disaster Fund Is Helping. 1987. pap. 3.50 (*0-8341-1200-0*) Nazarene.

Cook & Yale. Tourism: The Business of Trave; 347p. (C). 1998. pap. text 62.00 (*0-13-271032-3*) P-H.

Cook, jt. auth. see Blance.

Cook, jt. auth. see Hinks.

Cook, jt. auth. see Rhodes.

Cook, jt. auth. see Sweney.

Cook, jt. auth. see Wigley, Richard.

Cook, ed. see Chenier.

Cook, ed. see Marion, Sheila.

Cook, A. Gilbert, ed. Enamines: Synthesis, Structure, & Reactions. LC 69-18431. 527p. reprint ed. pap. 163.40 (*0-8357-3824-8*, 203654600004) Bks Demand.

Cook, A. H. Gravity & the Earth. (Wykeham Science Ser.: No. 6). 108p. 1970. pap. 18.00 (*0-85109-070-2*) Taylor & Francis.

Cook, A. H. & Saunders, V. T. Gravity & the Earth. (Wykeham Science Ser.: No. 6). 108p. (C). 1969. 18.00 (*0-8448-1108-4*, Crane Russak) Taylor & Francis.

Cook, A. S., ed. The Dream of the Rood: An Old English Poem Attributed to Cynewulf. 1977. lib. bdg. 59.95 (*0-8490-1733-5*) Gordon Pr.

Cook, A. S., intro. Survey of the Shores & Islands of the Persian Gulf, 1820-1829, 5 vols. (Illus.). 378p. (C). 1989. reprint ed. lib. bdg. 995.00 (*1-85207-190-7*, Pub. by Archive Editions) N Ross.

Cook, Alan. Edmond Halley: Charting the Heavens & the Seas. LC 97-12596. (Illus.). 556p. (C). 1998. text 37.50 (*0-19-850031-9*) OUP.

— The Motion of the Moon. (Illus.). 236p. 1988. 137.00 (*0-85274-348-3*) IOP Pub.

— The Observational Foundations of Physics. LC 93-36901. (Illus.). 176p. (C). 1994. text 64.95 (*0-521-45450-6*); pap. text 22.95 (*0-521-45597-9*) Cambridge U Pr.

Cook, Alan & Chen, Y. T. Gravitational Experiments in the Laboratory. (Illus.). 282p. (C). 1993. text 80.00 (*0-521-39171-7*) Cambridge U Pr.

Cook, Alan, ed. see Good, Mary B.

Cook, Alan D., ed. Pruning Techniques. (Plants & Gardens Ser.). (Illus.). 1994. per. 7.95 (*0-945352-61-1*) Bklyn Botanic.

Cook, Alan H. The Astronomer As Natural Philosopher: An Inaugural Lecture. LC 73-89007. (Illus.). 39p. reprint ed. pap. 25.00 (*0-8357-5822-2*, 2051372) Bks Demand.

Cook, Alan R., ed. New Cancer Sourcebook. LC 95-33730. (Health Reference Ser.: Vol. 12). 1996. lib. bdg. 78.00 (*0-7808-0041-9*) Omnigraphics Inc.

Cook, Alan R., ed. see Dresser, Peter D.

Cook, Albert. Affibility Blues. LC 93-36166. 204p. 1994. pap. 24.95 (*0-7734-2799-6*, Mellen Poetry Pr) E Mellen.

— Canons & Wisdoms. LC 93-16781. 200p. (C). 1993. text 32.95 (*0-8122-3204-6*) U of Pa Pr.

— Concordance to Beowulf. LC 68-26349. (Beowulf & the Literature of the Anglo-Saxons Ser.: No. 2). 1969. reprint ed. lib. bdg. 75.00 (*0-8383-0273-4*) M S G Haskell Hse.

— Delayed Answers: Poems. LC 92-20422. 164p. 1992. pap. 24.95 (*0-7734-9566-5*) E Mellen.

— The Future Invests. LC 97-342. 140p. 1997. pap. 24.95 (*0-7734-2816-X*, Mellen Poetry Pr) E Mellen.

— Haiku. LC 97-32887. (Illus.). 88p. 1998. pap. 19.95 (*0-7734-2825-9*) E Mellen.

— Modulars: Poems. LC 92-20742. 112p. 1992. pap. 14.95 (*0-7734-9564-9*) E Mellen.

— The Reach of Poetry. LC 94-44602. 349p. 1995. 42.95 (*1-55753-068-8*); pap. 21.95 (*1-55753-069-6*) Purdue U Pr.

— Reasons for Waking. LC 95-43093. 184p. 1996. pap. 24.95 (*0-7734-2674-4*, Mellen Poetry Pr) E Mellen.

— The Something Master. LC 98-42602. 144p. 1998. pap. 24.95 (*0-7734-3092-X*) E Mellen.

— The Stance of Plato. 266p. 1996. 62.50 (*0-8226-3048-6*); pap. 24.95 (*0-8226-3049-4*) Littlefield.

Cook, Albert & Perkins, Pamela, trs. from RUS. The Burden of Sufferance: Women Poets in Russia. LC 92-10597. (Library of World Literature in Translation: Vol. 19). 218p. 1993. text 54.00 (*0-8240-3325-6*) Garland.

Cook, Albert, ed. & tr. see Homer.

Cook, Albert M. & Hussey, Susan M. Assistive Technologies: Principles & Practice. LC 94-30291. 736p. (C). (gr. 13). 1994. text 61.00 (*0-8016-1038-9*, 01038) Mosby Inc.

Cook, Albert M. & Webster, John G., eds. Therapeutic Medical Devices: Application & Design. (Illus.). 656p. 1982. text 72.00 (*0-13-914796-9*) P-H.

Cook, Albert S. Beowulfian & Odyssean Voyages. (Connecticut Academy of Arts & Sciences Ser., Trans.: Vol. 28). 1926. pap. 39.50 (*0-685-22813-4*) Elliots Bks.

— The Burden of Prophecy: Poetic Utterance in the Prophets of the Old Testament. LC 96-17804. 192p. (C). 1997. 29.95 (*0-8093-2083-5*) S Ill U Pr.

— Chaucerian Papers. (Connecticut Academy of Arts & Sciences Ser., Trans.: Vol. 23, No. 1). 1919. pap. 49.50 (*0-685-22836-3*) Elliots Bks.

— Chaucerian Papers. LC 72-1040. reprint ed. 29.50 (*0-404-01697-9*) AMS Pr.

— Christ of Cynewulf: A Poem in Three Parts; the Advent, the Ascension, & the Last Judgement. (Select Bibliographies Reprint Ser.). 1982. reprint ed. lib. bdg. 16.95 (*0-8290-0846-2*) Irvington.

— A Concordance to Beowulf. (BCL1-PR English Literature Ser.). 436p. 1992. reprint ed. lib. bdg. 99.00 (*0-7812-7161-4*) Rprt Serv.

— A Concordance to the English Poems of Thomas Gray. 1990. 18.50 (*0-8446-1124-7*) Peter Smith.

— A Concordance to the English Poems of Thomas Gray. (BCL1-PR English Literature Ser.). 160p. 1992. reprint ed. lib. bdg. 69.00 (*0-7812-7362-5*) Rprt Serv.

— Cynewulf's Part in Our Beowulf. (Connecticut Academy of Arts & Sciences Ser., Trans.: Vol. 27). 1925. pap. 39.50 (*0-685-22816-9*) Elliots Bks.

— Figural Choice in Poetry & Art. LC 84-40582. (Illus.). 268p. reprint ed. pap. 83.10 (*0-608-09075-1*, 206970900005) Bks Demand.

— A Glossary of the Old Northumbrian Gospels. 275p. 1969. reprint ed. lib. bdg. 55.00 (*0-685-13871-2*, 05102731) G Olms Pubs.

— The Historical Background of Chaucer's Knight. (Connecticut Academy of Arts & Sciences Ser., Trans.: Vol. 20). 1916. pap. 49.50 (*0-685-22845-2*) Elliots Bks.

— Historical Background of Chaucer's Knight. LC 68-1564. (Studies in Chaucer: No. 6). (C). 1969. reprint ed. lib. bdg. 75.00 (*0-8383-0531-8*) M S G Haskell Hse.

— The Last Months of Chaucer's Earliest Patron. (Connecticut Academy of Arts & Sciences Ser., Trans.: Vol. 21). 1916. pap. 75.00 (*0-685-22843-6*) Elliots Bks.

— The Last Months of Chaucer's Earliest Patron. LC 72-1000. reprint ed. 29.50 (*0-404-01698-7*) AMS Pr.

— The Meaning of Fiction. LC 60-9591. 330p. reprint ed. pap. 102.30 (*0-7837-3793-9*, 204361300010) Bks Demand.

— Modes. LC 93-6534. 108p. 1993. pap. 24.95 (*0-7734-2788-0*) E Mellen.

— The Old English Andreas & Bishop Acca of Hexham. (Connecticut Academy of Arts & Sciences Ser., Trans.: Vol. 26). 1924. pap. 49.50 (*0-685-22820-7*) Elliots Bks.

— The Possible Begetter of the Old English Beowulf & Widsith. (Connecticut Academy of Arts & Sciences Ser., Trans.: Vol. 25). 1922. pap. 20.00 (*0-685-22825-8*) Elliots Bks.

— The Possible Begetter of the Old English Beowulf & Widsith. (Beowulf & the Literature of the Anglo-Saxons Ser.: No. 2). (C). 1970. reprint ed. pap. 22.95 (*0-8383-0018-9*) M S G Haskell Hse.

— Progressions & Other Poems. LC 63-11976. 128p. reprint ed. pap. 39.70 (*0-608-13693-X*, 205534800017) Bks Demand.

— Select Translations from Old English Poetry. (BCL1-PR English Literature Ser.). 195p. 1992. reprint ed. lib. bdg. 69.00 (*0-7812-7157-6*) Rprt Serv.

— Select Translations from Old English Prose. (BCL1-PR English Literature Ser.). 296p. 1992. reprint ed. lib. bdg. 79.00 (*0-7812-7158-4*) Rprt Serv.

— Soundings: On Shakespeare, Modern Poetry, Plato & Other Subjects. LC 90-22103. 254p. reprint ed. pap. 78.80 (*0-608-10613-5*, 207123500009) Bks Demand.

— Sources of the Biography of Aldhelm. (Connecticut Academy of Arts & Sciences Ser., Trans.: Vol. 28). 1927. pap. 39.50 (*0-685-22809-6*) Elliots Bks.

— Temporalizing Space: The Triumphant Strategies of Piero della Francesca. LC 91-43126. (Literature & the Visual Arts Ser.: Vol. 8). (Illus.). XII, 207p. (C). 1992. text 47.95 (*0-8204-1865-X*) P Lang Pubng.

— Thresholds: Studies in the Romantic Experience. LC 85-40365. 320p. reprint ed. pap. 99.20 (*0-608-09163-4*, AU0050200005) Bks Demand.

Cook, Albert S., ed. Judith, an Old English Epic Fragment. LC 70-144441. (Belles Lettres Ser., Section I: No. 7). reprint ed. 27.50 (*0-404-53608-5*) AMS Pr.

Cook, Albert S. & Tinker, Chauncey B., eds. Select Translations from Old English Poetry. rev. ed. LC 68-59036. 195p. (C). 1968. reprint ed. 45.00 (*0-87752-024-0*) Gordian.

— Select Translations from Old English Prose. LC 68-57700. 304p. (C). 1968. reprint ed. 45.00 (*0-87752-025-9*) Gordian.

Cook, Albert S., ed. see Cynewulf.

Cook, Albert S., tr. see Sievers, Eduard.

Cook, Alexandra P. & Cook, Noble D. Good Faith & Truthful Ignorance: A Case of Transatlantic Bigamy. LC 90-36173. 224p. 1991. text 49.95 (*0-8223-1086-4*) Duke.

— Good Faith & Truthful Ignorance: A Case of Transatlantic Bigamy. LC 90-36173. 224p. 1992. pap. text 17.95 (*0-8223-1222-0*) Duke.

Cook, Alice H. Comparable Worth: A Case Book ... 1986 Supplement. (Occasional Publications: No. 155). 174p. 1986. 5.00 (*0-318-23506-4*) U Hawaii.

— Comparable Worth: A Case Book of Experiences in States & Localities. (Occasional Publications: No. 151). 264p. 1985. 20.00 (*0-318-19011-7*) U Hawaii.

— Comparable Worth: The Problem & States' Approaches to Wage Equity. (Occasional Publications: No. 145). 84p. 1983. 3.00 (*0-318-04752-7*) U Hawaii.

***Cook, Alice H.** Lifetime Labor. 354p. 2000. 15.95 (*1-55861-257-2*) Feminist Pr.

Cook, Alice H. A Lifetime of Labor: The Autobiography of Alice H. Cook. LC 98-18433. (Cross Cultural Memoir Ser.). (Illus.). 368p. 1999. 29.95 (*1-55861-189-4*) Feminist Pr.

— The Working Mother: A Survey of Problems & Programs in Nine Countries. 2nd rev. ed. LC 78-620004. 84p. 1978. pap. text 6.95 (*0-87546-067-4*, ILR Press) Cornell U Pr.

Cook, Alice H., et al. Public Employee Labor Relations in Japan: Three Aspects. LC 71-634401. (Comparative Studies in Public Employment Labor Relations Ser.). 1971. 10.00 (*0-87736-019-7*); pap. 5.00 (*0-87736-020-0*) U of Mich Inst Labor.

Cook, Alice R. Haywood County, North Carolina, Families. viii, 154p. (Orig.). 1993. pap. text 18.50 (*1-55613-808-3*) Heritage Bk.

— Haywood County North Carolina Families. rev. ed. 160p. 1998. pap. 14.50 (*0-7884-0877-1*, C554) Heritage Bk.

Cook, Alicia S. & Dworkin, Daniel S. Helping the Bereaved: Therapeutic Interventions for Children, Adolescents, & Adults. LC 91-57905. (Illus.). 193p. 1992. 34.00 (*0-465-02717-2*, Pub. by Basic) HarpC.

Cook, Alicia S. & Oltjenbruns, Kevin A. Dying & Grieving: Lifespan & Family Perspectives. (Illus.). 512p. (C). 1989. text 34.75 (*0-03-000512-4*) Harcourt Coll Pubs.

Cook, Alison H., jt. ed. see Dimitrious, Harry T.

Cook, Allan. Burns Sourcebook. LC 99-24510. (Health Reference Ser.). 595p. 1999. lib. bdg. 78.00 (*0-7808-0204-7*) Omnigraphics Inc.

— Ophthalmic Disorders Sourcebook. LC 96-3345. (Health Reference Ser.: Vol. 17). 1996. lib. bdg. 78.00 (*0-7808-0081-8*) Omnigraphics Inc.

Cook, Allan, ed. Allergies Sourcebook. LC 96-30992. (Health Reference Ser.: Vol. 19). 1997. lib. bdg. 78.00 (*0-7808-0036-2*) Omnigraphics Inc.

— Arthritis Sourcebook. (Health Reference Ser.). 650p. 1998. lib. bdg. 75.00 (*0-7808-0201-2*) Omnigraphics Inc.

— Immune System Disorders Sourcebook. LC 96-33469. (Health Reference Ser.: Vol. 18). 1997. lib. bdg. 78.00 (*0-7808-0209-8*) Omnigraphics Inc.

— Oral Health Sourcebook. LC 97-28301. (Health Reference Ser.: Vol. 30). 1997. lib. bdg. 78.00 (*0-7808-0082-6*) Omnigraphics Inc.

— Pain Sourcebook. LC 97-37833. (Health Reference Ser.: Vol. 32). 1997. lib. bdg. 78.00 (*0-7808-0213-6*) Omnigraphics Inc.

— Skin Diseases & Disorders Sourcebook. LC 97-6570. (Health Reference Ser.: Vol. 22). 1997. lib. bdg. 78.00 (*0-7808-0080-X*) Omnigraphics Inc.

Cook, Allan R., ed. Alternative Medicine Sourcebook. LC 99-37612. (Health Reference Ser.). 600p. 1999. 75.00 (*0-7808-0200-4*) Omnigraphics Inc.

— Environmentally Induced Disorders Sourcebook. LC 97-14614. (Health Reference Ser.: Vol. 28). (Illus.). 632p. 1997. 78.00 (*0-7808-0083-4*) Omnigraphics Inc.

— Men's Health Concerns Sourcebook. LC 98-33612. (Health Reference Ser.: Vol. 38). (Illus.). 600p. 1998. 78.00 (*0-7808-0212-8*) Omnigraphics Inc.

***Cook, Allan R., ed.** Osteoporosis Sourcebook. (Health Reference Ser.). (Illus.). 600p. 2000. lib. bdg. 78.00 (*0-7808-0239-X*) Omnigraphics Inc.

Cook, Allan R. & Dresser, Peter D., eds. Repiratory Diseases & Disorders Sourcebook. LC 95-19214. (Health Reference Ser.: Vol. 6). 771p. 1995. lib. bdg. 78.00 (*0-7808-0037-0*) Omnigraphics Inc.

Cook, Allison M. & Dacre, Maxwell W. Excavations at Portway, Andover 1973-1975. (Illus.). 192p. 1986. pap. 19.98 (*0-947816-04-6*, Pub. by Oxford Univ Comm Arch) David Brown.

Cook, Alton, ed. Type & Color: A Handbook of Creative Combinations. (Design Sourcebook Ser.). (Illus.). 160p. 1989. 39.99 (*0-935603-19-0*, 30166) Rockport Pubs.

***Cook, Andra.** What's Cooking America. (Illus.). 448p. 2000. pap. 22.95 (*1-56044-792-3*) Falcon Pub Inc.

Cook, Andra, jt. auth. see Stradley, Linda.

Cook, Andrew. Least of These: Religion, Race, & Law in America. LC 96-48799. 264p. (C). 1997. pap. 20.99 (*0-415-91647-X*) Routledge.

Cook, Angel G. Antologia de Tlaxcala. (SPA., Illus.). 280p. 1996. pap. 19.00 (*968-29-9050-5*, IN94, Pub. by Dir Gen Pubicaiones) UPLAAP.

Cook, Angel Garcia, see Garcia Cook, Angel, compiled by.

Cook, Angelique S. & Hawk, G. A. Shamanism & the Esoteric Tradition. LC 92-5607. (New Worlds Spirituality Ser.). (Illus.). 240p. 1992. pap. 12.95 (*0-87542-325-6*) Llewellyn Pubns.

Cook, Ann. American Accent Training. 1997. 12.95 (*0-8120-4602-1*) Barron.

***Cook, Ann.** American Accent Training. 2nd ed. 162p. 2000. pap. 39.95 incl. cd-rom (*0-7641-7369-3*) Barron.

— American Accent Training: A Guide to Speaking & Pronouncing Colloquial American English, 3 cassettes. 1991. 39.95 incl. audio (*0-8120-7763-6*) Barron.

Cook, Ann. How Well Does Your Child Do Math: A Step-by-Step Assessment of Your Child's Math Skills. LC 97-13344. (How Well Does Your Child Do in School Ser.). 160p. 1997. pap. 9.99 (*1-56414-302-3*) Career Pr Inc.

— How Well Does Your Child Read? A Step-by-Step Assessment of Your Child's Reading Skills. (Twenty Minute Ser.: Vol. 1). (Illus.). iv, 144p. 1996. pap., per. 9.95 (*1-889229-15-6*) Am Accent Trng.

— How Well Does Your Child Read: A Step-by-Step

C

Assessment of Your Child's Reading Skills. LC 97-13343. (How Well Does Your Child Do in School Ser.). 160p. 1997. pap. 9.99 (*1-56414-303-1*) Career Pr Inc.

***Cook, Ann.** How Well Does Your Child Read, Write & Do Math? 576p. 1999. 29.97 (*1-57866-074-2*) Galahad Bks.

Cook, Ann. How Well Does Your Child Write: A Step-by-Step Assessment of Your Child's Writing Skills. LC 97-25084. (How Well Does Your Child Do in School Ser.). 160p. 1997. pap. 9.99 (*1-56414-304-X*) Career Pr Inc.

Cook, Ann J. Making a Match: Courtship in Shakespeare & His Society. ix, 273p. 1991. text 47.50 (*0-691-06842-9*, Pub. by Princeton U Pr) Cal Prin Full Svc.

Cook, Ann Mariah. Running North: A Yukon Adventure. LC 98-25598. 324p. 1999. 21.95 (*1-56512-213-5*) Algonquin Bks.

— Running North: A Yukon Adventure. LC 99-10601. 1999. 25.95 (*1-56895-638-X*, Compass) Wheeler Pub.

***Cook, Ann Mariah.** Running North: A Yukon Adventure. 324p. 1999. reprint ed. pap. 12.95 (*1-56512-253-4*) Algonquin Bks.

Cook, Ann T., et al. A Collector's Guide to the Gerber Baby Vol. 1: Featuring Gerber Baby Dolls & Advertising Collectibles. LC 96-94986. (Illus.). 224p. 1996. 39.95 (*0-9654647-0-9*, H19 622 4411) G-B Pubns.

Cook, Anna. How Increased Competition from Generic Drugs Has Affected Prices & Returns in the Pharmaceutical Industry. (Illus.). 75p. (C). 1998. pap. text 20.00 (*0-7881-7351-0*) DIANE Pub.

Cook, Anna & Webre, Philip. How Health Care Reform Affects Pharmaceutical Research & Development. (Illus.). 65p. (Orig.). (C). 1994. pap. text 40.00 (*0-7881-1092-6*) DIANE Pub.

Cook, Anna L. Identification & Value Guide to Textile Bags: Feed, Flour, Sugar, Burlap, Clothing, Quilts & More. (Illus.). 216p. 1998. reprint ed. pap. text 13.00 (*0-7881-5219-X*) DIANE Pub.

Cook, Anna M. History of Baldwin County Georgia. (Illus.). 484p. 1997. reprint ed. lib. bdg. 52.50 (*0-8328-7062-5*) Higginson Bk Co.

Cook, Anthony. Least of These: Religion, Race, & Law in America. LC 96-48799. 264p. (C). 1997. 75.00 (*0-415-91646-1*) Routledge.

***Cook, Arnold L.** Historical Drift: Must My Church Die. 2000. pap. 14.99 (*0-87509-901-7*) Chr Pubns.

Cook, Arthur, jt. auth. see Hollingsworth, Brian.

Cook, Arthur N. British Enterprise in Nigeria. 330p. 1964. reprint ed. 47.50 (*0-7146-1644-3*, Pub. by F Cass Pubs) Intl Spec Bk.

Cook, B. F. The Elgin Marbles. (Illus.). 72p. 1984. pap. 11.95 (*0-674-24626-8*) HUP.

— Greek Inscriptions. (Reading the Past Ser.: Vol 5). (C). 1988. pap. 13.95 (*0-520-06113-6*, Pub. by U CA Pr) Cal Prin Full Svc.

Cook, B. M., et al, eds. Transputer Applications & Systems, '95. LC 95-7902. 614p. (YA). (gr. 12). 1995. 127.00 (*90-5199-235-1*, 235-1) IOS Press.

Cook, B. W. & Jones, K. A Programmed Introduction to Infrared Spectroscopy. LC 72-189960. (Illus.). 216p. reprint ed. pap. 67.00 (*0-8357-3052-2*, 203930800012) Bks Demand.

Cook, Barbara C., ed. see Pulci, Antonia.

Cook, Barbara W. & Cook, Grafton H., II. Pokagon Township Reflections. (Illus.). v, 252p. 1998. pap. 20.00 (*0-9601340-1-8*) The Cooks.

***Cook, Ben.** 52-Week Football Training. LC 99-27996. (Illus.). 200p. (YA). 1999. pap. 17.95 (*0-7360-0085-2*, PCOO0085) Human Kinetics.

Cook, Ben, ed. see Thames, Joseph B.

Cook, Benjamin L. Freemasonry Condemned from Its Own Sources: Freemasonry vs. Christianity & Phallic Worship of Freemasonry Unveiled. rev. ed. 90p. (C). reprint ed. pap. 6.95 (*0-88418-005-0*) Omni Hawthorne.

Cook, Bernadine. The Little Puppy That Lost Its Tail. LC 94-90799. (Illus.). 16p. (J). (ps-3). 1995. pap. 4.00 (*0-9604726-7-3*) Enterprise Pr.

— Looking for Susie. LC 90-41001. (Illus.). 32p. (J). (gr. 1-3). 1991. lib. bdg. 15.00 (*0-208-02241-4*, Linnet Bks) Shoe String.

Cook, Bernard A. German Americans. (American Voices Ser.). 112p. (J). 1991. lib. bdg. 18.95 (*0-86593-140-2*) Rourke Corp.

Cook, Bertha E. L' Enseignement du Francais au Moyen de l'Action. (FRE.). 1995. teacher ed. 19.99 (*0-938395-36-X*) B Segal.

— Teaching Russian Through Action. Galeev, Aidar, tr. (RUS.). (Orig.). 1994. pap., teacher ed. 19.99 (*0-938395-33-5*) B Segal.

Cook, Beryl. Happy Days. (Illus.). 64p. 1996. 29.95 (*0-575-06192-8*, Pub. by V Gollancz) Trafalgar.

Cook, Bev. In God's House: A Guidebook for Children on Using Good Manners at Church. (Illus.). iv, 32p. (J). (gr. k-5). 1998. pap. 5.95 (*0-9667718-0-X*) Bright Eyes Inc.

Cook, Beverly B., et al. Women in the Judicial Process. (Women & American Politics Ser.). 54p. (Orig.). (C). 1988. pap. text 3.90 (*0-915654-80-6*) Am Political.

Cook, Bill R., jt. auth. see Hennessee, Odus M.

Cook, Billie J. Black Gold. LC 98-90059. 1998. pap. 11.95 (*0-533-12695-9*) Vantage.

Cook, Blaise. Fuchsias: A Complete Guide to Cultivation & Care. 1998. pap. text 12.95 (*1-85967-667-7*, Lorenz Bks) Anness Pub.

Cook, Blanche Wiesen. Eleanor Roosevelt: 1884-1933, vol. 1. 608p. 1993. pap. 16.95 (*0-14-009460-1*, Penguin Bks) Viking Penguin.

Cook, Blanche Wiesen. Eleanor Roosevelt Vol. 2: 1933-1938. LC 87-40632. (Illus.). 748p. 1999. 34.95 (*0-670-84498-5*) Viking Penguin.

***Cook, Blanche Wiesen.** Eleanor Roosevelt Vol. 2: 1933-1938, Vol. 2. (Illus.). 704p. 2000. pap. 17.95 (*0-14-017894-5*, Penguin Bks) Viking Penguin.

Cook, Blanche Wiesen & Markowitz, Gerald. Main Problems in American History Vol. 7: The Fifties. abr. ed. (PaperBook Series in History). (Illus.). 128p. (C). 1996. pap. text 2.25 (*1-877891-38-X*) Paperbook Pr Inc.

Cook, Bob. Disorderly Elements. 1988. pap. 3.50 (*0-317-67527-3*) St Martin.

— Disorderly Elements. large type ed. 320p. 1989. 27.99 (*0-7089-1992-8*) Ulverscroft.

***Cook, Bob.** Paper Chase. large type ed. 320p. 2000. 20.99 (*1-84137-040-1*, Pub. by Mgna Lrg Print) Ulverscroft.

Cook, Bob. Questions of Identity. large type ed. 426p. 1989. 27.99 (*0-7089-1927-8*) Ulverscroft.

Cook, Bob, et al. The Baby Book for Grandparents. (Illus.). 40p. 1985. pap. 4.95 (*0-916043-02-9*) Light Hearted Pub Co.

***Cook, Bree, et al.** Victims' Need, Victims' Rights: Policies & Programs for Victims of Crime in Australia. (Research & Public Policy Series: Vol. 19). 160p. 1999. pap. text 75.00 (*0-642-24119-8*, Pub. by Aust Inst Criminology) St Mut.

Cook, Brian, ed. The Electronic Journal: The Future of Serials-Based Information. LC 93-19969. (Australian & New Zealand Journal of Serials Librarianship: Vol. 3, No. 2). (Illus.). 106p. 1993. lib. bdg. 39.95 (*1-56024-452-6*) Haworth Pr.

Cook, Brian B., jt. auth. see Stewart, Gordon W.

Cook, Brian J. Bureaucracy & Self-Government: Reconsidering the Role of Public Administration in American Politics. LC 96-20325. (Interpreting American Politics Ser.). 184p. 1996. text 45.00 (*0-8018-5409-1*); pap. text 14.95 (*0-8018-5410-5*) Johns Hopkins.

— Bureaucratic Politics & Regulatory Reform: The EPA & Emissions Trading, 196. LC 87-15032. (Contributions in Political Science Ser.: No. 196). 181p. 1988. 49.95 (*0-313-25493-1*, CBC/, Greenwood Pr) Greenwood.

Cook, Bridget M. Practical Skills in Bobbin Lace. (Illus.). 192p. 1987. pap. 16.95 (*0-486-25561-1*) Dover.

— The Torchon Lace Workbook. (Color Craft Workbooks Ser.). (Illus.). 96p. 1988. pap. 18.95 (*0-312-02119-4*) St Martin.

Cook, Bridget M., jt. auth. see Stott, Geraldine.

Cook, Bruce. Celebrity Homes Tour of Los Angeles. 1998. pap. 72.00 (*0-7871-1783-8*, Dove Audio) NewStar Media.

— Celebrity Homes Tour of Los Angeles. (Illus.). 208p. 1998. pap. 12.00 (*0-7871-1770-6*, Dove Audio) NewStar Media.

— Dalton Trumbo. LC 76-42141. 343 p. 1977. write for info. (*0-684-14750-5*) Free Pr.

— The Town That Country Built: Welcome to Branson, Missouri. 280p. (Orig.). 1993. mass mkt. 4.99 (*0-380-77095-4*, Avon Bks) Morrow Avon.

Cook, C., jt. auth. see Sked, A.

Cook, C. D. Aquatic & Wetland Plants of India. (Illus.). 392p. 1996. text 165.00 (*0-19-854821-4*) OUP.

— Water Plants of the World. (Illus.). 1974. 318.00 (*90-6193-024-3*, Pub. by Kluwer Academic) Kluwer Academic.

Cook, C Donald, ed. The Future of the Union Catalogue: Proceedings of the International Symposium on the Future of the Union Catalogue, University of Toronto. LC 82-6238. (Cataloging & Classification Quarterly Ser.: Vol. 2, Nos. 1-2). 130p. 1982. text 4.95 (*0-86656-175-7*) Haworth Pr.

Cook, C. Lee, Jr. Cordage: Industry & Trade Summary. (Illus.). 31p. (Orig.). (C). 1995. pap. text 25.00 (*0-7881-1565-0*) DIANE Pub.

Cook, C. W., jt. auth. see Hunsaker, Philip L.

Cook, Carl. PostScripts. LC 94-23596. 80p. 1994. 10.00 (*1-880729-09-1*) Vega Pr.

— The Tranquil Lake of Love: Love Letters. LC 92-85179. 80p. (Orig.). 1993. pap. 8.00 (*1-880729-04-0*) Vega Pr.

Cook, Carloyn. Gene. LC 99-200337. (Illus.). 128p. 1998. 24.95 (*0-87588-523-3*, 5502) Hobby Hse.

Cook, Carole. Math Learning Centers for the Primary Grades. 224p. 1991. pap. text 27.95 (*0-87628-574-4*) Ctr Appl Res.

Cook, Carole & Carlisle, Jody. Practical Activities for Practically Everything. 1990. 12.99 (*0-8224-5576-5*) Fearon Teacher Aids.

***Cook, Carolyn.** Gene. 2nd rev. ed. (Illus.). 152p. 1999. 24.95 (*0-87588-558-6*, H5701) Hobby Hse.

Cook, Carrie Ann, jt. see Gregath, Anna M.

***Cook, Catherine.** Managing PeopleSoft with Tivoli: Planning, Design, Management, & Optimization! 634p. 2000. pap. text 59.00 incl. cd-rom (*0-13-016889-0*) P-H.

Cook, Catherine Halloran & Pfiefer, Janet McGinney. Internet Adventures for Young Children: 101 Websites & Hands-On Activities. Janke, Jennifer E., ed. LC 99-71590. (Illus.). 125p. (J). (gr. k-2). 1999. pap. text 12.95 (*0-86530-435-1*) Incentive Pubns.

***Cook, Catherine Holloran & Pfeifer, Janet McGivney.** Internet Quest: 101 Adventures Around the World Wide Web. Reiner, Angela & Streams, Jennifer, eds. LC 99-75427. (Illus.). 144p. (J). (gr. 2-4). 2000. pap. text 14.95 (*0-86530-456-4*, IP 456-4) Incentive Pubns.

Cook, Cathy, jt. auth. see Simosko, Susan.

Cook, Cecil. Marquette: The Biography of an Iowa Railroad Town. LC 75-7184. (Illus.). 240p. 1975. 9.95 (*0-942240-03-0*) D Rehder.

Cook, Cecil M. God's World. 280p. 1971. reprint ed. spiral bd. 17.50 (*0-7873-0197-3*) Hlth Research.

Cook, Charles. The Battle of Cape Esperance: Encounter at Guadalcanal. LC 92-4658. (Illus.). 176p. 1992. reprint ed. 29.95 (*1-55750-126-2*) Naval Inst Pr.

— Essential Guide to Cross-Country Skiing & Snowshoeing in the United States. LC 97-19140. 256p. 1997. pap. 17.95 (*0-8050-4113-3*) St Martin.

— The Essential Guide to Hiking in the U. S. LC 92-34801. (Illus.). 228p. (Orig.). 1995. pap. 19.95 (*0-935576-41-X*) Kesend Pub Ltd.

— The Essential Guide to Nature Walking in the United States. LC 96-23411. 240p. (Orig.). 1995. pap. 19.95 (*0-8050-4111-7*, Owl) H Holt & Co.

— The Essential Guide to Wilderness Camping & Backpacking in the U. S. (Illus.). 324p. 1995. pap. 24.95 (*0-935576-46-0*) Kesend Pub Ltd.

— Millennium Mania. 150p. (Orig.). 1980. pap. 2.50 (*0-933672-68-3*, C-1914) Star Bible.

***Cook, Charles.** Trapping the Boundary Waters: A Tenderfoot's Year in the Border Country, 1919-1920. LC 99-40555. (Midwest Reflections Ser.). (Illus.). 194p. 2000. 29.95 (*0-87351-378-9*, 378-9, Borealis Book) Minn Hist.

Cook, Charles C. All about One Russell. 48p. 1988. reprint ed. pap. 2.95 (*1-883858-37-2*) Witness CA.

— More Data on "Pastor Russell" 30p. 1988. reprint ed. pap. 1.95 (*1-883858-38-0*) Witness CA.

***Cook, Charles Ira.** Trapping the Boundary Waters: A Tenderfoot's Year in the Border Country, 1919-1920. LC 99-40555. (Midwest Reflections Ser.). (Illus.). 194p. 2000. pap. 16.95 (*0-87351-379-7*, 379-7, Borealis Book) Minn Hist.

Cook, Charles M. The American Codification Movement: A Study of Antebellum Legal Reform, 14. LC 80-662. (Contributions in Legal Studies: No. 14). 234p. 1981. 62.95 (*0-313-21314-3*, CAC/, Greenwood Pr) Greenwood.

***Cook, Charles Orson, ed.** Horatio Alger: Gender & Success in the Gilded Age. 212p. (Orig.). (C). 2000. pap. text 16.50 (*1-881089-66-5*) Brandywine Press.

Cook, Charles T., ed. see Spurgeon, Charles H.

Cook, Chas, jt. auth. see Taulor, Joe.

Cook, Chas, jt. auth. see Taylor, Joe.

Cook, Chester L. Inventor's Guide in a Series of Four Parts: How to Protect, Search, Compile Facts & Sell Your Invention. rev. ed. (Illus.). 52p. 1981. reprint ed. 11.95 (*0-9604670-1-7*) C L Cook.

Cook, Chris. Dictionary of Historical Terms. lib. bdg. 24.95 (*0-8488-0794-4*) Amereon Ltd.

— Dictionary of Historical Terms. 1998. lib. bdg. 24.95 (*1-56723-034-2*) Yestermorrow.

— Dictionary of Historical Terms. 2nd ed. LC 89-14934. 352p. (C). 1990. 34.95 (*0-87226-331-2*, P Bedrick Books) NTC Contemp Pub Co.

— Dictionary of Historical Terms. 2nd ed. LC 97-30835. 352p. 1998. 7.99 (*0-517-18871-6*) Random Hse Value.

— The Facts on File World Political Almanac. LC 88-11208. 463p. reprint ed. pap. 143.60 (*0-7837-2671-6*, 204303900006) Bks Demand.

***Cook, Chris.** The Facts on File World Political Almanac: From 1945 to the Present. 4th rev. ed. (Illus.). 576p. 2001. pap. 21.95 (*0-8160-4296-9*) Facts on File.

— The Facts on File World Political Almanac: The Facts & Figures of Governments & Leaders, Political Parties & Constitutions, Wars & Treaties. 4th rev. ed. 576p. 2001. 60.00 (*0-8160-4295-0*) Facts on File.

Cook, Chris. From the Skies of Paradise Hawaii. (Illus.). 160p. 1991. 25.95 (*0-935180-61-3*) Mutual Pub HI.

***Cook, Chris.** A Kaua'i Reader. 396p. 1999. mass mkt. 6.95 (*1-56647-066-8*) Mutual Pub HI.

Cook, Chris. The Kauai Movie Book: Films Made on the Beautiful Garden Island. LC 96-77564. (Illus.). 128p. 1996. 27.95 (*1-56647-141-9*); pap. 22.95 (*1-56647-129-X*) Mutual Pub HI.

***Cook, Chris.** Kauai's Hollywood Moments. (Illus.). 112p. 1999. 17.95 (*1-56647-287-3*) Mutual Pub HI.

— The Longman Companion to Nineteenth Century Britain. LC 99-21551. (Companions to History Ser.). 368p. (C). 1999. 79.95 (*0-582-27991-7*) Longman.

— The Longman Companion to Nineteenth Century Britain. LC 99-21551. (Companions to History Ser.). 368p. (C). 1999. pap. text 25.95 (*0-582-27990-9*) Longman.

Cook, Chris. The Longman Handbook of Modern European History, 1763-1991: Longman Handbooks to History. (C). 1992. text 57.50 (*0-582-07291-3*) Addison-Wesley.

— The Making of Modern Africa: A Guide to Archives. 224p. 1995. 35.00 (*0-8160-2071-X*) Facts on File.

***Cook, Chris.** Pears Cyclopedia. 107th ed. 1056p. 1998. text 29.95 (*0-14-027737-4*, Pub. by Pnguin Bks Ltd) Trafalgar.

Cook, Chris. A Short History of the Liberal Party, 1900-1984. 2nd ed. write for info. (*0-318-59186-3*) Macmillan.

Cook, Chris, compiled by. The Facts on File Asian Political Almanac. LC 93-26319. (Political Almanacs Ser.). 272p. 1994. 35.00 (*0-8160-2585-1*) Facts on File.

Cook, Chris, ed. Dictionary of Historical Terms. 2nd ed. LC 89-14934. 352p. 1991. pap. 14.95 (*0-87226-241-3*, P Bedrick Books) NTC Contemp Pub Co.

— The Garden Island Guide to Kauai. (Illus.). 160p. 1998. pap. 6.95 (*0-9664754-0-2*) Kauai Pubg Co.

— Sources in European Political History Vol. 3: War & Resistance. 260p. 1992. lib. bdg. 40.00 (*0-8160-1757-3*) Facts on File.

Cook, Chris & Boynton, David. Kauai, the Garden Island: A Pictorial History of the Commerce & Work of the People LC 99-34463. 1999. write for info. (*1-57864-072-5*) Donning Co.

Cook, Chris & Paxton, John. European Political Facts, 1918-1990. 3rd ed. 1992. 40.00 (*0-8160-2766-8*) Facts on File.

Cook, Chris & Ramsden, John, eds. By-Elections in British Politics. LC 97-224395. 352p. 1997. 75.00 (*1-85728-534-4*, Pub. by UCL Pr Ltd); pap. 24.95 (*1-85728-535-2*, Pub. by UCL Pr Ltd) Taylor & Francis.

***Cook, Chris & Stevenson, John.** Britain Since 1945. 368p. 2000. pap. 25.95 (*0-582-35674-1*) Longman.

Cook, Chris & Stevenson, John. LONG HDBK MOD BRIT 1714. 3rd ed. LC 96-18356. (Longman Handbooks to History Ser.). 560p. (C). 1996. pap. text 26.25 (*0-582-29304-9*) Addison-Wesley.

***Cook, Chris & Stevenson, John.** Longman Handbook of the Modern World: International History & Politics since 1945. LC 98-19337. (C). 1998. 74.95 (*0-582-30412-1*) Longman.

Cook, Chris & Stevenson, John, eds. The Longman Companion to Britain since 1945. LC 94-49608. (Companions to History Ser.). 272p. (C). 1995. text 62.95 (*0-582-07030-9*, Pub. by Addison-Wesley) Longman.

— The Longman Companion to Britain since 1945. LC 94-49608. (Companions to History Ser.). 272p. (C). 1995. pap. text 30.94 (*0-582-07031-7*) Longman.

Cook, Chris & Waller, David. The Longman Handbook of Modern American History, 1763-1996. LC 97-14206. (Companions to History Ser.). (C). 1997. text 76.88 (*0-582-08489-X*) Longman.

Cook, Chris, jt. ed. see Martino, Wayne.

Cook, Chris, ed. see Renshaw, Patrick.

***Cook, Chris M.** Japan's System of Official Development Assistance. 160p. 1999. pap. 16.95 (*0-88936-883-X*, Pub. by IDRC Bks) Stylus Pub VA.

Cook, Chrisopher C. Tradition - Transition - New Vision: Exhibition of Phillips Academy Alumni. (Illus.). 88p. (Orig.). 1983. pap. 15.00 (*1-879886-24-3*) Addison Gallery.

Cook, Christine, jt. ed. see Borgman, Dean.

Cook, Christopher. Collectible American Yo-Yos: 1920s to 1970s Identification & Value Guide. LC 97-181931. (Illus.). 128p. (Orig.). 1997. pap. 16.95 (*0-89145-761-5*, 4849) Collector Bks.

***Cook, Christopher.** Robbers. 320p. 2000. 24.95 (*0-7867-0776-3*, Pub. by Carroll & Graf) Publishers Group.

Cook, Christopher, ed. see Powell, Dilys.

Cook, Christopher C. The Fishing Room. (Illus.). 20p. (Orig.). 1990. pap. 8.00 (*1-879886-29-4*) Addison Gallery.

— Possibles. 56p. (Orig.). 1970. pap. 10.00 (*1-879886-20-0*) Addison Gallery.

Cook, Christopher D. Aquatic Plant Book. 2nd rev. ed. (Illus.). 228p. 1996. 70.00 (*90-5103-132-7*, Pub. by SPB Acad Pub) Balogh.

Cook, Chuck. Chubby Engine. (Chubby Shape Bks.). (J). 1984. pap. 3.50 (*0-671-50951-9*) Litle Simon.

***Cook, Claire.** Ready to Fall: A Novel. LC 99-55389. 200p. 2000. 22.95 (*1-882593-32-4*, Pub. by Bridge Wrks) Natl Bk Netwk.

Cook, Claire K. Line by Line: How to Improve Your Own Writing. pap. 8.95 (*0-685-54946-1*, H-01031) HM.

— Line by Line: The MLA's Guide to Improving Your Writing, 001. Reference Division Staff, ed. LC 85-8346. 240p. 1986. pap. 10.00 (*0-395-39391-4*) HM.

Cook, Clarence. The House Beautiful: An Unabridged Reprint of the Classic Victorian Stylebook. LC 94-48289. (Illus.). 336p. 1995. pap. text 9.95 (*0-486-28586-3*) Dover.

Cook, Clarence C. A Description of the New York Central Park. LC 70-174831. (Illus.). 206p. 1972. reprint ed. 18.95 (*0-405-08377-7*, Pub. by Blom Pubns) Ayer.

Cook, Clarice D., jt. auth. see Cook, Lanny K.

Cook, Cliff E. Bank Secrecy. Smith, Mary L., ed. (Illus.). 292p. 1991. 46.00 (*0-89982-374-2*, 050350) Am Bankers.

***Cook Communication Ministry Staff.** Nuevo Testamento Ilustrado.Tr. of Illustrated New Testament. (SPA., Illus.). 256p. (J). 1999. pap. 8.99 (*0-311-38642-3*, Edit Mundo) Casa Bautista.

Cook Communications Ministries International Staff. Article Writing: How to Plan an Article, Learn from Models, & Polish Your Final Words. (Interlit Imprint Ser.: Unit 3). 40p. 1993. pap. text 6.00 (*1-884752-02-0*, 44636) Cook Min Intl.

— Book Selling: How to Know Your Target Audience, Plan Special Sales Strategies & Develop Flexible Marketing Methods. (Interlit Imprint Ser.: Unit 4). 40p. 1993. pap. text 6.00 (*1-884752-03-9*, 44628) Cook Min Intl.

— Books for Your Readers. (Illus.). 24p. 1997. pap. text 6.00 (*1-884752-55-1*) Cook Min Intl.

— Bookwriting: How to Decide if You Are Ready for a Book, Develop Working Strategies & Prepare for Publication. (Interlit Imprint Ser.: Vol. 19). 40p. 1996. pap. 6.00 (*1-884752-28-4*, 44347) Cook Min Intl.

— Business Planning for Publishing. (Illus.). 24p. 1997. pap. text 6.00 (*1-884752-52-7*) Cook Min Intl.

— Co-Editions That Work. (Illus.). 24p. 1997. pap. text 6.00 (*1-884752-54-3*) Cook Min Intl.

— Creative Writing: How to Draw Inspiration from Everyday Life & Channel It into Drama, Poetry & Short Fiction. (Interlit Imprint Ser.: Vol. 15). (Illus.). 40p. (Orig.). 1996. pap. 6.00 (*1-884752-24-1*, 44263) Cook Min Intl.

— Design: How to Create Eye-Catching Publications Through Creative Layout, Thoughtful Color, Strong Graphics & Readable Type. (Interlit Imprint Ser.: Unit 2). 44p. 1993. pap. text 6.00 (*1-884752-01-2*, 44644) Cook Min Intl.

— Desktop Publishing: How to Get Started, Build Skills & Plan for the Future. (Interlit Imprint Ser.: Unit 6). 40p. 1994. pap. text 6.00 (*1-884752-08-X*, 44529) Cook Min Intl.

— Editor-Writer Relationships: How to Use Editorial Principles & Working Tools to Build Better Relationships. (Interlit Imprint Ser.: Vol. 13). (Illus.). 40p. (Orig.). 1996. pap. 6.00 (*1-884752-22-5*, 44271) Cook Min Intl.

— Editorial Planning for Books: How to Define Your Organization's Mission, Make Sound Strategy Decisions

An Asterisk (*) at the beginning of an entry indicates that the title is appearing for the first time.

& Be Prepared for Each Step of the Publishing Process. (Interlit Imprint Ser.: Unit 5). 40p. 1994. pap. text 6.00 (*1-884752-07-1*, 44610) Cook Min Intl.

— Editorial Planning for Magazines: How to Define Purpose, Develop Strategy & Provide Creative Direction. (Interlit Imprint Ser.: Unit 9). 40p. (Orig.). 1995. pap. text 6.00 (*1-884752-16-0*, 44032) Cook Min Intl.

— Editorial Roles: How the Editor Relates to Readers, Writers, Staff, Management & the Product. (Interlit Imprint Ser.: Unit 1). 40p. 1993. pap. text 6.00 (*1-884752-00-4*, 44669) Cook Min Intl.

— Evaluate Your Publishing. (Illus.). 24p. 1997. pap. text 6.00 (*1-884752-53-5*) Cook Min Intl.

— Fiction: How to Write Fiction with Strong Plot, Believable Characters, Settings, Dialogue, Flashbacks & Endings. (Interlit Imprint Ser.: Unit 7). 40p. 1994. pap. text 6.00 (*1-884752-09-8*, 44511) Cook Min Intl.

— Leadership Development: How to Identify Qualities, Use Planning Tools & Choose Models for Good Leadership. (Interlit Imprint Ser.: Vol. 20). (Illus.). 40p. (Orig.). 1996. pap. 6.00 (*1-884752-29-2*, 44420) Cook Min Intl.

— Magazine Marketing: How to Use Traditional Methods & Explore Creative Models. (Interlit Imprint Ser.: Vol. 12). 40p. 1995. pap. text 6.00 (*1-884752-17-9*, 44156) Cook Min Intl.

— Mechanics of Editing: How to Keep a Manuscript Focused with Substantive Editing & Improve Details Through Copy Editing. (Interlit Imprint Ser.: Vol. 17). (Illus.). 40p. (Orig.). 1996. pap. 6.00 (*1-884752-26-8*, 44354) Cook Min Intl.

— Money Matters. (Interlit Imprint Ser.: Unit 8). 40p. 1994. pap. text 6.00 (*1-884752-10-1*, 44495) Cook Min Intl.

— Production: How to Organize Your Production Office, Increase Efficiency & Make Informed Production Decision. (Interlit Imprint Ser.: Unit 10). 40p. 1995. pap. text 6.00 (*1-884752-15-2*, 44099) Cook Min Intl.

— Research & Evaluation: How to Plan Research Instruments & Use the Results to Evaluate Your Effectiveness & Guide Decisions. (Interlit Imprint Ser.: Vol. 18). (Illus.). 40p. (Orig.). 1996. pap. 6.00 (*1-884752-27-6*, 44362) Cook Min Intl.

— Staff Development: How to Assess Staff Needs, Choose Training Models & Plan Development Cycles. (Interlit Imprint Ser.: Vol. 16). (Illus.). 40p. (Orig.). 1996. pap. 6.00 (*1-884752-25-X*, 44313) Cook Min Intl.

— Typesetting & Printing: How to Recognize Superior Typesetting, Choose the Right Paper & Avoid Printing Propblems. (Interlit Imprint Ser.: Vol. 14). (Illus.). 40p. (Orig.). 1996. pap. 6.00 (*1-884752-23-3*, 44297) Cook Min Intl.

— Vision for Self Sufficiency. (Illus.). 24p. 1997. pap. text 6.00 (*1-884752-51-9*) Cook Min Intl.

— Where There Are No Writers. (Illus.). 24p. 1997. pap. text 6.00 (*1-884752-56-X*) Cook Min Intl.

— Writing for Children: How to Apply Writing Basics, Target Children's Needs & Communicate in Fresh Formats. (Interlit Imprint Ser.: Unit 11). 40p. 1995. pap. text 6.00 (*1-884752-18-7*, 44131) Cook Min Intl.

Cook, Constance A., ed. see Blakeley, Barry B.

Cook, Constance E. Lobbying for Higher Education: How Colleges & Universities Influence Federal Policy. LC 98-8885. (Issues in Higher Education Ser.). (Illus.). 272p. (C). 1998. 45.00 (*0-8265-1316-6*); pap. 19.95 (*0-8265-1317-4*) Vanderbilt U Pr.

Cook, Corey. Campaign Finance Reform. 109p. 1994. pap. write for info. (*1-58703-030-6*) CA St Librry.

Cook, Corey. Campaign Finance Reform (in California) (Illus.). 109p. (Orig.). (C). 1994. pap. text 40.00 (*0-7881-1608-8*) DIANE Pub.

Cook, Corey. Preliminary Annotated Bibliography Related to State Government Reform. 16p. 1994. pap. write for info. (*1-58703-028-4*) CA St Librry.

Cook, Corey & Simmons, Charlene Wear. California Political Reform: Selected Research. 49p. 1994. pap. write for info. (*1-58703-019-5*, CRB-94-001) CA St Librry.

Cook, Corin B., see Phillips, Alan, pseud.

Cook, Cornelia. Joyce Cary: Liberal Principles. (Critical Studies). 242p. 1981. 44.00 (*0-389-20201-0*, N6975) B&N Imports.

***Cook, Curtis.** Aboriginal Rights & Self-Government: The Canadian & Mexican Experience in North American Perspective. 350p. 2000. text 49.95 (*0-7735-1884-3*) McG-Queens Univ Pr.

Cook, Curtis, ed. Constitutional Predicament: Canada after the Referendum of 1992. LC 94-231392. 304p. (C). 1994. 65.00 (*0-7735-1192-X*, Pub. by McG-Queens Univ Pr); pap. text 22.95 (*0-7735-1202-0*, Pub. by McG-Queens Univ Pr) CUP Services.

Cook, Curtis, et al. Management & Organizational Behavior. 2nd ed. LC 96-44030. 640p. (C). 1996. text 68.95 (*0-256-20807-7*, Irwn McGrw-H) McGraw-H Hghr Educ.

Cook, Curtis, jt. auth. see Coffey, Robert.

Cook, Cynthia C., ed. Involuntary Resettlement in Africa: Selected Papers from a Conference on Environment & Settlement Issues in Africa. LC 93-23727. (Technical Papers: No. 227). 246p. 1994. pap. 22.00 (*0-8213-2632-5*) World Bank.

Cook, D. The Ax Book: The Lore & Science of the Woodcutter. LC 99-52674. Orig. Title: Keeping Warm with an Ax. (Illus.). 144p. 1999. reprint ed. pap. 22.50 (*0-911469-16-8*) A C Hood.

Cook, D., et al, eds. Social Work Treatment of Alcohol Problems. LC 82-620033. (NIAAA-RUCAS Alcoholism Treatment Ser.: No. 5). 1983. pap. 15.00 (*0-911290-15-X*) Rutgers Ctr Alcohol.

Cook, D. B., ed. Schrodinger's Mechanics. (Lecture Notes in Physics Ser.: Vol. 28). 164p. (C). 1989. text 40.00 (*9971-5-0760-9*) World Scientific Pub.

Cook, D. J. Cellular Pathology. LC 98-28024. (Biomedical Sciences Explained Ser.). 368p. 1998. pap. text 37.50 (*0-7506-3111-2*) Buttrwrth-Heinemann.

— Cook & Deal: Great Recipes for Easy Entertaining Plus Challenging Bridge Hands. exp. rev. ed. (Illus.). 288p. 1993. 17.95 (*0-9621351-0-0*) D J Cook.

Cook, D. Ryan & Davis, Peter J., eds. Anesthetic Principles for Organ Transplantation. LC 94-9865. 400p. 1994. text 129.00 (*0-7817-0011-6*) Lppncott W & W.

Cook, D. Ryan & Marcy, Joseph H., eds. Neonatal Anesthesia. LC 87-27309. 300p. 1988. text 52.50 (*0-941022-10-2*) Davies Pubng.

Cook, Daisy L. Adam's Eden. LC 89-36802. 1993. pap. 14.95 (*0-87949-303-8*) Ashley Bks.

Cook, Daniel. Language in the Philosophy of Hegel. (Janua Linguarum, Ser. Minor: No. 135). 198p. (Orig.). 1973. pap. text 36.95 (*90-279-2402-3*) Mouton.

Cook, Daniel J., ed. see Leibniz, Gottfried Wilhelm.

Cook, Dave. Dwellers of Forbidden City. 1981. 5.50 (*0-394-51424-6*) Random.

Cook, David. Blizzard Pass M1. 1983. 8.00 (*0-394-53070-5*) Random.

Cook, David. Book of Artifacts. (AD&D Accessory Ser.). (Illus.). 1997. pap. 22.95 (*0-7869-1150-6*) TSR Inc.

— Coloured Pencils: Everything You Need to Know to Get Started. (Learn to Paint Ser.). (Illus.). 64p. 1999. pap. 15.95 (*0-00-413320-X*, Pub. by HarpC) Trafalgar.

Cook, David. Drug Free Challenge: Feeling Good about the Way You're Made. 1999. pap. 13.99 (*0-7814-5459-X*) Cook.

— Extreme Friendship: Feeling Good about the Way You're Made. 1999. pap. 13.99 (*0-7814-5460-3*) Cook.

— A History of Narrative Film. (C). 1996. pap. text. write for info. (*0-393-96939-8*) Norton.

— King Pinch. (Nobles Ser.). 320p. (Orig.). 1995. pap. 4.95 (*0-7869-0127-6*, Pub. by TSR Inc) Random.

— Launching a Business on the Web. 3rd ed. 1997. 39.99 (*0-7897-1277-6*) Macmillan.

***Cook, David.** Learn to Draw Buildings. (Learn to Draw Ser.). (Illus.) 64p. 1999. pap. 14.95 (*0-00-413353-6*, Pub. by HarpC) Trafalgar.

Cook, David. Lost Conquistador Mine. 1982. 5.50 (*0-394-52594-9*) Random.

— Master of Desert Nomads. 1983. 5.50 (*0-394-53161-2*) Random.

— Studies on Neotropical Water Mites. (Memoir Ser.: No. 31). (Illus.). 544p. 1980. 75.00 (*1-56665-029-1*) Assoc Pubs FL.

— Sunrising. 1990. pap. 9.95 (*0-87951-261-X*, Pub. by Overlook Pr) Penguin Putnam.

— The Temple of Death. 1983. 5.50 (*0-394-53166-3*) Random.

— Thinking about Faith: An Introductory Guide to Philosophy & Religion. 1986. pap. 9.45 (*0-310-44131-5*, 18401P) Zondervan.

— Tome of Magic. (Advanced Dungeons & Dragons Ser.). 1991. 20.00 (*1-56076-107-5*, Pub. by TSR Inc) Random.

— Walter. LC 84-5116. 206p. 1985. 15.95 (*0-87951-972-X*, Pub. by Overlook Pr) Penguin Putnam.

— Walter. 216p. 1988. pap. 8.95 (*0-87951-205-9*, Pub. by Overlook Pr) Penguin Putnam.

— Water Mite Genera & Subgenera. (Memoir Ser.: No. 21). (Illus.). 860p. 1974. 75.00 (*1-56665-019-4*) Assoc Pubs FL.

— Water Mites from Australia. (Memoir Ser.: No. 40). (Illus.). 568p. 1986. 55.00 (*1-56665-038-0*) Assoc Pubs FL.

— Water Mites from Chile. (Memoir Ser.: No. 42). (Illus.). 356p. 1988. 45.00 (*1-56665-040-2*) Assoc Pubs FL.

— Winter Doves: A Love Story. LC 84-22678. 225p. 1983. 15.95 (*0-87951-994-0*, Pub. by Overlook Pr) Penguin Putnam.

— Winter Doves: A Love Story. LC 84-22678. 225p. 1985. pap. 8.95 (*0-87951-225-3*, Pub. by Overlook Pr) Penguin Putnam.

Cook, David, ed. Maleshop: Men, Consumerism & Shopping Culture. 256p. (C). 1996. pap. 22.50 (*0-85315-821-5*, Pub. by Lawrence & Wishart) NYU Pr.

Cook, David, et al, eds. Psychosocial Issues in the Treatment of Alcoholism. LC 84-28966. (Alcoholism Treatment Quarterly Ser.: Vol. 2, No. 1). 134p. 1985. text 39.95 (*0-86656-363-6*) Haworth Pr.

— Psychosocial Issues in the Treatment of Alcoholism. LC 84-28966. (Alcoholism Treatment Quarterly Ser.: Vol. 2, No. 1). 134p 1985. pap. text 14.95 (*0-86656-401-2*) Haworth Pr.

Cook, David & Okenimkpe, Michael. Ngugi Wa Thiong'o: An Exploration of His Writings. LC 97-219198. 283p. 1997. pap. write for info. (*0-435-07430-X*) Heinemann.

Cook, David & Sellers, Deborah. Launching a Business on the Web. LC 95-69233. (Illus.). 550p. 1995. 39.99 (*0-7897-0188-X*) Que.

Cook, David, jt. auth. see Kroker, Arthur.

Cook, David, ed. see Null, Kathleen Christopher.

Cook, David, ed. see Oetken, Rachel C.

Cook, David A. A History of Narrative Film. 3rd ed. LC 95-31987. (Illus.). 950p. (C). 1996. pap. 57.75 (*0-393-96819-7*, Norton Paperbks) Norton.

Cook, David A., jt. ed. see McLean, Adrienne L.

Cook, David B. Handbook of Computational Quantum Chemistry. (Illus.). 768p. (C). 1998. text 140.00 (*0-19-850114-5*) OUP.

Cook, David C. My Primer Libro Devocional de la Biblia.Tr. of My First Book of Bible Devotions. (SPA.). 80p. (J). 1981. write for info. (*0-614-27082-0*) Editorial Unilit.

Cook, David J. Planescape Campaign Setting. (Advanced Dungeons & Dragons, 2nd Edition: Planescape Campaign World Ser.). 1994. 30.00 (*1-56076-834-7*, Pub. by TSR Inc) Random.

Cook, David L. When Your Child Struggles: The Myths of 20/20. 4th ed. (Illus.). 173p. (Orig.). 1991. reprint ed. pap. text 15.00 (*0-9632657-0-9*) Cook Vision.

Cook, David N. Build Your Dream House for a Song: And Own It Free & Clear in Five Years. LC 98-195016. (Illus.). 160p. (Orig.). 1998. pap. 24.95 (*1-890824-36-4*) Warbeck Pub.

Cook, David R. Water Mites from India. (Memoir Ser.: No. 9). (Illus.). 411p. 1967. 45.00 (*1-56665-007-0*) Assoc Pubs FL.

— The Water Mites of Liberia. (Memoir Ser.: No. 6). (Illus.). 418p. 1966. 45.00 (*1-56665-004-6*) Assoc Pubs FL.

Cook, David S. Indian Canoe Routes of Maine. (Illus.). 128p. 2000. pap. 12.95 (*1-58066-021-5*, Covered Brdge Pr) Douglas Charles Ltd.

Cook, David W., jt. ed. see Onsrud, Harlan J.

Cook, Dean. Information Engineering with the IEF. (DC - Introduction to Computing Ser.). 1996. pap. 49.95 (*0-7895-0555-X*) Course Tech.

***Cook, Deanna.** Family Fun Cookbook: Special Edition for Troll Associates. 1999. pap. 24.95 (*0-7868-8535-1*, Pub. by Hyperion) Time Warner.

— FamilyFun Tricks & Treats: 100 Creepy Costumes Crafts & Recipes. (Illus.). 96p. 2000. 14.95 (*0-7868-6610-1*, Pub. by Disney Pr) Time Warner.

Cook, Deanna. The Kids' Multicultural Cookbook: Food & Fun Around the World. LC 94-44231. (Kids Can! Ser.: No. 15). 160p. (J). (ps-5). 1995. pap. 12.95 (*0-913589-91-8*) Williamson Pub Co.

Cook, Deanna & FamilyFun Magazine Staff. Family Fun's Parties: 100 Party Plans for Birthdays, Holidays & Every Day. LC GV1205.C66 1999. (FamilyFun Ser.). (Illus.). 256p. 1998. pap. 24.95 (*0-7868-6454-0*, Pub. by Hyperion) Time Warner.

Cook, Deanna F. FamilyFuns Cookies for Christmas: 75 Recipes for You & Your Kids. LC 98-219957. (Illus.). 64p. (J). 1998. 9.70 (*0-7868-6469-9*, Pub. by Hyperion) Time Warner.

— Kids' Pumpkin Projects: Planting & Harvesting Fun. LC 97-48366. (Kids Can! Ser.: Vol. 20). (Illus.). 96p. (J). (gr. k-4). 1998. pap. 8.95 (*1-885593-21-X*) Williamson Pub Co.

Cook, Deanna F. & Family Fun Magazine Staff. Disney's FamilyFun Crafts: 500 Creative Activities for You & Your Kids. LC 97-40453. (Illus.). 256p. (J). 1997. 24.45 (*0-7868-6304-8*, Pub. by Hyperion) Time Warner.

Cook, Deanna F. & Family Fun Magazine Staff. Familyfun Cookbook: Irresistible Recipes for You & Your Kids. (Illus.). 256p. (J). 1996. 24.45 (*0-7868-6112-6*, Pub. by Hyperion) Time Warner.

Cook, Deborah. The Culture Industry Revisited: Adorno on Mass Culture. 206p. (C). 1996. pap. text 24.95 (*0-8476-8155-6*); lib. bdg. 60.50 (*0-8476-8154-8*) Rowman.

Cook, Deborah, jt. ed. see Mulrow, Cynthia D.

Cook, Deborah E. The Subject Finds a Voice: Foucalt's Turn Towards Subjectivity. LC 91-39555. (Revisioning Philosophy Ser.: Vol. 11). X, 152p. (C). 1993. text 39.95 (*0-8204-1821-8*) P Lang Pubng.

Cook, Dee. Rich Law, Poor Law: Different Response to Tax & Supplementary Benefit Fraud. 192p. 1989. 113.00 (*0-335-15878-1*); pap. 35.95 (*0-335-15877-3*) OpUniv Pr.

Cook, Dee & Hudson, Barbara A. Racism & Criminology. (C). 1994. text 59.95 (*0-8039-8762-5*); pap. text 19.95 (*0-8039-8763-3*) Sage.

Cook, Dee, jt. auth. see Carlen, Pat.

Cook-Deegan, Robert. The Gene Wars: Science, Politics & the Human Genome. LC 93-10762. 1994. 25.00 (*0-393-03572-7*) Norton.

— The Gene Wars: Science, Politics & the Human Genome. 416p. 1996. pap. 14.95 (*0-393-31399-9*, Norton Paperbks) Norton.

Cook, Deirdre & Finlayson, Helen. Interactive Children, Communicative Teaching: ICT & Classroom Teaching. LC 99-12583. (Enriching the Primary Curriculum - Child, Teacher, Context Ser.). 1999. 22.95 (*0-335-20020-6*) OpUniv Pr.

Cook, Dennis & Sheilds, Donald. Saga of Darkness: Vision of Light. Spears-Stewart, Reta, ed. 200p. 1998. pap. 12.95 (*1-892477-02-5*) Barnabs Pub.

Cook, Desmond L. Program Evaluation & Review Technique: Applications in Education. LC 78-57981. 1978. pap. text 16.00 (*0-8191-0657-7*) U Pr of Amer.

Cook, Diana. Wisconsin Capitol: Fascinating Facts. LC 91-7976. (Illus.). 120p. 1991. pap. 7.95 (*1-879483-02-5*) Prairie Oak Pr.

Cook, Diana, jt. auth. see Feldman, Michael.

Cook, Diana, jt. auth. see Hansen, John R.

Cook, Diane J., ed. Proceedings: Eleventh International Florida Artificial Intelligence Research Symposium Conference. LC 98-196524. (Illus.). 485p. 1998. pap. text 50.00 (*1-57735-051-0*) AAAI Pr.

Cook Doel Li Wang. Dislocating the Pacific-transpacific Linkages. 59.95 (*1-85972-197-4*) Ashgate Pub Co.

— Sustainable Development in Pacific Asia. 59.95 (*1-85972-195-8*) Ashgate Pub Co.

Cook, Don. The Long Fuse: How England Lost the American Colonies: 1760-1785. LC 94-43632. 432p. 1996. pap. 14.00 (*0-87113-661-9*, Atlntc Mnthly) Grove-Atltic.

Cook, Don L., ed. see Howells, William Dean.

Cook, Donald. Light Reflected: A Four Petal Trillium. (Illus.). 7p. 1999. ring bd. 54.90 (*0-9614887-4-3*) DRC Graphics Serv.

Cook, Donald, tr. see Standiford, Natalie.

Cook, Donald J., jt. auth. see Walsh, Daniel E.

Cook, Donald L., ed. see Tyler, Royall.

Cook, Donald R. The Light, the Tree & the Artist: Inspirational Images. 16p. (Orig.). 1994. pap. 28.95 (*0-9614887-2-7*) DRC Graphics Serv.

Cook, Donelda A., jt. auth. see Helms, Janet E.

Cook, Doris E. Sherlock Holmes & Much More. (Illus.). 112p. 1970. pap. 3.50 (*0-940748-42-8*) Conn Hist Soc.

Cook, Doris M. A Guide to Curriculum Planning in Reading. 186p. (C). 1986. pap. text 30.00 (*1-57337-014-2*) WI Dept Pub Instruct.

— Strategic Learning in the Content Areas. 203p. (C). 1989. pap. text 30.00 (*1-57337-015-0*) WI Dept Pub Instruct.

Cook, Dorothy E. & Monro, Isabel S., eds. Supplement, 1953. LC 75-649762. 1533p. 1953. 55.00 (*0-8242-0384-4*) Wilson.

Cook, Douglas. Cases & Materials on Nonprofit, Tax-Exempt Organizations, 1993. 440p. 1999. ring bd. 59.00 (*1-879581-68-X*) Lupus Pubns.

Cook, Douglas A. The Illustrated Guide to BTRIEVE. Brann, Jane T., ed. (Illus.). 300p. (Orig.). 1992. pap. 29.95 (*0-9623397-7-6*) Midi Amer.

Cook, Dutton. A Book of the Play: Studies & Illustrations of Histrionic Story, Life, & Character, 2 Vols. LC 72-13278. (Essay Index Reprint Ser.). 1977. reprint ed. 41.95 (*0-8369-8152-9*) Ayer.

Cook, E. A. Scottish Rite Masonry, 2 vols., Set. 32.00 (*0-685-22097-4*) Wehman.

Cook, E. A. & Van Lier, Hubert N. Landscape Planning & Ecological Networks. LC 95-117329. (Developments in Landscape Management & Urban Planning Ser.: Vol. 6F). 368p. 1994. 215.50 (*0-444-82084-1*) Elsevier.

Cook, E. H. Knight Templarism. pap. 15.00 (*0-911164-15-4*) Powner.

Cook, E. R. & Kairiukstis, L. A., eds. Methods of Dendrochronology: Applications in the Environmental Sciences. (C). 1990. text 186.00 (*0-7923-0586-8*) Kluwer Academic.

Cook, E. U. The First Mortgage. (Illus.). 254p. Date not set. reprint ed. 10.00 (*0-9628571-0-6*) B H Short.

Cook, Edward. The Deficient Cause of Moral Evil According to St. Thomas Aquinas. LC 94-40760. (Cultural Heritage & Contemporary Change Ser.: Vol. 14). 1997. pap. text 17.50 (*1-56518-070-4*) Coun Res Values.

Cook, Edward, et al. The Interrelationship Between Federal & State Wetlands & Riparian Protection Programs. 200p. 1991. spiral bd. 30.00 (*1-884320-02-3*) ASU Herberger Ctr.

— Verde River Reclamation Survey: Verde River Corridor Study, Tapco to Beasley Flat. 43p. 1991. spiral bd. 25.00 (*1-884320-07-4*) ASU Herberger Ctr.

— Verde River Visual Assessment: Verde River Corridor Study, Tapco to Beasley Flat. 100p. 1991. spiral bd. 45.00 (*1-884320-06-6*) ASU Herberger Ctr.

Cook, Edward, tr. see Myles, W. C.

Cook, Edward M. Love Made Manifest. LC 94-79089. 230p. 1994. 14.95 (*0-914927-21-3*) Higher Ed Pubns.

Cook, Edward M., ed. Sopher Mahir: Northwest Semitic Studies Presented to Stanislav Segert. LC 90-2924. 384p. 1990. text 37.50 (*0-931464-56-0*) Eisenbrauns.

Cook, Edward T. The Life of John Ruskin, 2 vols. LC 68-24903. (English Biography Ser.: No. 31). 1969. reprint ed. lib. bdg. 150.00 (*0-8383-0155-X*) M S G Haskell Hse.

— The Life of John Ruskin, 2 vols., Set. (BCL1-PR English Literature Ser.). 1992. reprint ed. lib. bdg. 150.00 (*0-7812-7638-1*) Rprt Serv.

— Literary Recreations. LC 68-54340. (Essay Index Reprint Ser.). 1977. 20.95 (*0-8369-0331-5*) Ayer.

— More Literary Recreations. LC 76-105005. (Essay Index Reprint Ser.). 1977. 29.95 (*0-8369-1457-0*) Ayer.

Cook, Edwin F., jt. auth. see Maschwitz, David E.

Cook, Eleanor. Against Coercion: Games Poets Play. LC 97-27591. 1998. write for info. (*0-8047-2937-9*) Stanford U Pr.

— Poetry, Word-Play, & Word-War in Wallace Stevens. LC 88-4817. 339p. 1988. reprint ed. pap. 105.10 (*0-608-04582-9*, 206535200003) Bks Demand.

Cook, Eleanor, et al, eds. Centre & Labyrinth: Essays in Honour of Northrop Frye. 360p. 1982. pap. 17.95 (*0-8020-6594-5*) U of Toronto Pr.

Cook, Elin K., jt. auth. see Teacher Created Materials Staff.

Cook, Elisabeth. Duet & Ensemble in the Early Opera-Comique. LC 95-14167. (Outstanding Dissertations in Music from British Universities Ser.). (Illus.). 344p. 1995. text 94.00 (*0-8153-1893-6*) Garland.

Cook, Elizabeth. Holy Places of the Buddha: Visual Aids for Teaching Buddhism. Tulku, Tarthang, ed. LC 94-2497. (Crystal Mirror Ser.: Vol. 9). (Illus.). 500p. (Orig.). (C). 1996. pap. 25.00 (*0-89800-244-3*) Dharma Pub.

— The Roaring Girl. 2nd ed. (New Mermaids Ser.). (C). 1998. pap. text. write for info. (*0-393-90085-1*) Norton.

— Seeing Through Words: The Scope of Late Renaissance Poetry. LC 85-29502. 192p. 1986. 25.00 (*0-300-03675-2*) Yale U Pr.

— Visual Play: A Green Dance in Three Acts. (Illus.). 30p. 1983. ring bd. 15.00 (*0-915066-53-X*) Assembling Pr.

Cook, Elizabeth, ed. Ozone Protection in the United States: Elements of Success. 130p. 1996. pap. 20.00 (*1-56973-088-1*) World Resources Inst.

Cook, Elizabeth & Yeshe De Project Staff. The Stupa: Sacred Symbol of Enlightenment. LC 97-12563. (Crystal Mirror Ser.: Vol. 12). 1997. 50.00 (*0-89800-288-5*); pap. 35.00 (*0-89800-284-2*) Dharma Pub.

Cook, Elizabeth, jt. ed. see Dow, Michael.

Cook, Elizabeth, ed. see Keats, John.

Cook, Elizabeth, jt. ed. see Wallace, Zara.

***Cook, Elizabeth Amy.** Backyard Living-Outdoor Style. 128p. 2000. pap. 16.95 (*0-7370-0623-4*) Time-Life Educ.

Cook, Elizabeth H. Epistolary Bodies: Gender & Genre in the Eighteenth-Century Republic of Letters. LC 95-32390. 220p. (C). 1996. 35.00 (*0-8047-2538-1*) Stanford U Pr.

Cook, Ellen P. Psychological Androgny. (C). 1985. 25.95 (*0-205-14432-2*, Macmillan Coll) P-H.

C

— Women, Relationships & Power: Implications for Counseling. 296p. (C). 1993. pap. text 35.95 (*1-55620-100-1*, 72515) Am Coun Assn.

Cook, Ellen Piel, see Piel Cook, Ellen.

Cook, Ellie. Watercolor Journey. (Illus.). 1997. pap. 10.50 (*1-56770-381-X*) S Scheewe Pubns.

Cook, Elspeth & Donald, Anna. Hard Time. 198p. 1998. pap. 12.95 (*1-86368-233-3*, Pub. by Fremantle Arts) Intl Spec Bk.

Cook, Emily W., ed. Research in Parapsychology, 1992: Abstracts & Papers from the 35th Annual Convention of the Parapsychological Association, 1992. LC 95-35064. 192p. 1996. 34.00 (*0-8108-3041-8*) Scarecrow.

Cook, Emily W. & Delanoy, Deborah L., eds. Research in Parapsychology, 1991: Abstracts & Papers from the 34th Annual Convention of the Parapsychological Association. LC 66-28580. (Illus.). 240p. 1994. 34.00 (*0-8108-2827-8*) Scarecrow.

Cook, Erwin F. The Odyssey in Athens: Myths of Cultural Origins. (Myth & Poetics Ser.). 232p. 1995. text 37.50 (*0-8014-3121-2*) Cornell U Pr.

Cook, Esky. Jewish Artwork by Esky: Children, Borders, Hebrew Alphabets. (Illus.). 128p. (Orig.). (J). (gr. 1-8). pap. 19.95 (*1-885143-02-8*) Preferred Ent.

— Jewish Artwork by Esky: Complete Set of Jewish Graphics. (Illus.). 384p. (Orig.). (J). (gr. 1-8). pap. 59.95 (*1-885143-00-1*) Preferred Ent.

— Jewish Artwork by Esky: Mitzvot, Animals, Food & Brachot. Whitman, Jonathan, ed. (Illus.). 128p. (Orig.). (J). (gr. 1-8). pap. 19.95 (*1-885143-03-6*) Preferred Ent.

Cook, Esme, tr. see Maurois, Andre.

Cook, Eung D. & Rice, Keren, eds. Athapaskan Linguistics: Current Perspectives on a Language Family. (Trends in Linguistics, State-of-the-Art Reports). viii, 645p. (C). 1989. lib. bdg. 176.95 (*0-89925-282-6*) Mouton.

Cook, Eung-Do & Gerdts, Donna B . Syntax & Semantics Vol. 16: The Syntax of Native American Languages. LC 83-17265. (Serial Publication Ser.). 1984. text 125.00 (*0-12-613516-9*) Acad Pr.

Cook, Evelyn, jt. auth. see Choy, Sam.

Cook, F. Seeing the Invisible. 1998. pap. text 10.99 (*0-85234-407-4*) P & R Pubng.

Cook, F., et al. Gregg Junior High Typing. 3rd ed. 1979. text 19.96 (*0-07-012477-9*) McGraw.

Cook, Faith. Grace in Winter: Rutherford in Verse. (Illus.). 96p. 1989. 13.99 (*0-85151-555-X*) Banner of Truth.

— Samuel Rutherford & His Friends. 157p. 1993. reprint ed. pap. 8.99 (*0-85151-635-1*) Banner of Truth.

— Singing in the Fire. 193p. (Orig.). 1995. pap. 9.99 (*0-85151-684-X*) Banner of Truth.

***Cook, Faith.** Sound of Trumpets. 176p. 2000. pap. 9.99 (*0-85151-778-1*) Banner of Truth.

— William Grimshaw of Haworth. 1997. 39.99 (*0-85151-732-3*) Banner of Truth.

Cook, Faith. William Grimshaw of Haworth. 342p. 1997. pap. 25.99 (*0-85151-734-X*) Banner of Truth.

Cook, Fay L. & Barrett, Edith J. Support for the American Welfare State: The View of Congress & the Public. (Illus.). 320p. 1992. text 64.00 (*0-231-07618-5*); pap. text 21.00 (*0-231-07619-3*) Col U Pr.

Cook, Ferris. Garden Dreams. (Illus.). 104p. 1995. bds. 6.75 (*1-55670-396-1*) Stewart Tabori & Chang.

— The Garden Trellis: Designs to Build & Vines to Cultivate. LC 95-21060. (Illus.). 96p. 1996. 15.95 (*1-885183-18-6*) Artisan.

— Invitation to the Garden: A Literary & Photographic Celebration. (Illus.). 240p. 1995. pap. 13.50 (*1-55670-397-X*) Stewart Tabori & Chang.

***Cook, Ferris, ed.** Gifts of Love: A Selection of Unusual Love Poetry. LC 99-46421. 80p. 2000. 12.95 (*1-55670-983-8*) Stewart Tabori & Chang.

***Cook, Ferris.** Bark: Selected Poems about Dogs. 72p. 2000. 18.95 (*0-8212-2664-9*) Bulfinch Pr.

Cook, Ferris, jt. auth. see Dickinson, Emily.

Cook, Frances E. Economic Botany Data Collection Standard. x, 146p. 1995. pap. 30.00 (*0-947643-71-0*, Pub. by Royal Botnic Grdns) Balogh.

Cook, Francis, tr. & intro. see Numata Center for Buddhist Translation & Research.

Cook, Francis D. How to Raise an Ox: Zen Practice As Taught in Zen Master Dogen's Shobogenzo (Including Ten Newly Translated Essays) 3rd ed. LC 78-12025. 230p. 1990. reprint ed. pap. 10.95 (*0-916820-07-6*) Center Pubns.

Cook, Francis H. The Record of Transmitting the Light: Zen Master Keizan's Denkoroku. 300p. 1991. text. write for info. (*0-916820-19-X*); pap. text. write for info. (*0-916820-20-3*) Center Pubns.

— Sounds of Valley Streams: Enlightenment in Dogen's Zen: Translation of Nine Essays from Shobogenzo. LC 88-12180. (SUNY Series in Buddhist Studies). 164p. (C). 1988. pap. text 19.95 (*0-88706-924-X*) State U NY Pr.

Cook, Frank X., jt. auth. see Maxim, L. Daniel.

Cook, Franklin R. Reza: His Life & Times. 1988. pap. 5.50 (*0-8341-1241-8*) Nazarene.

Cook, Fred, jt. auth. see Jaffery, Sheldon.

Cook, Fred B., Jr. Apostle Paul Pressing on to Greece. 111p. (Orig.). 1987. pap. 9.95 (*0-9614001-1-0*) Cook MO.

— Cyprus & Beyond. LC 84-90790. (Orig.). 1984. pap. write for info. (*0-9614001-0-2*, 24A) Cook MO.

Cook, Fred J. A Two-Dollar Bet Means Murder. LC 72-854. 248p. 1972. reprint ed. lib. bdg. 22.50 (*0-8371-5927-X*, COTD, Greenwood Pr) Greenwood.

Cook, Frederick, jt. auth. see Sullivan, John.

***Cook, Frederick A.** Through the First Antarctic Night. rev. ed. Gibbons, Russell W., ed. (Illus.). 520p. 1998. reprint ed. 49.95 (*0-9665613-0-9*); reprint ed. pap. 19.95 (*0-9665613-1-7*) Polar Publ.

Cook, Frederick A. Through the First Antarctic Night, 1898-1899: A Narrative of the Voyage of the Belgica among Newly Discovered Lands & over an Unknown Sea about the South Pole. LC 81-129738. 582p. reprint ed. pap. 180.50 (*0-7837-1043-7*, 204135400020) Bks Demand.

— To the Top of the Continent: The First Ascent of Mt. McKinley, 1903-1906. Gibbons, Russell W., ed. (Illus.). 368p. 1996. reprint ed. 49.95 (*0-9653995-0-8*); reprint ed. pap. 19.95 (*0-9653995-1-6*) F A Cook.

Cook, Fredrea Marlyn Hermann. The Crowder Family Collection. x, 135p. 1993. lib. bdg. 45.00 (*0-944619-04-5*) Gregath Pub Co.

Cook-Fuller. Nutrition 1999-2000 Edition. 11th ed. 1999. pap., student ed. 16.56 (*0-07-040354-6*) McGraw.

Cook-Fuller, Charlotte. Annual Editions: Nutrition, 95-96. annuals 7th rev. ed. Barrett, Stephen, ed. (Illus.). 256p. (C). 1995. text 12.95 (*1-56134-365-X*, Dshkn McG-Hill) McGrw-H Hghr Educ.

Cook-Fuller, Charlotte & Barrett, Stephen. Annual Editions: Nutrition, 97-98. 9th ed. 256p. (C). 1997. text 12.25 (*0-697-37331-2*) Brown & Benchmark.

— Nutrition, 1996-1997. annuals 8th ed. 256p. (C). 1996. text. write for info. (*0-697-31606-8*) Brown & Benchmark.

— Nutrition, 98-99. 10th ed. (Annual Ser.). (Illus.). 240p. 1998. pap. text 12.25 (*0-697-39176-0*, Dshkn McG-Hill) McGrw-H Hghr Educ.

Cook, G. C. From the Greenwich Hulks to Old St. Pancras: A History of Tropical Disease in London. LC 92-10542. 400p. (C). 1992. text 75.00 (*0-485-11411-9*, Pub. by Athlone Pr) Humanities.

Cook, G. C., ed. Gastroenterological Problems from the Tropics. 152p. (Orig.). (C). 1995. pap. text 12.00 (*0-7279-0902-9*, Pub. by BMJ Pub) Login Brothers Bk Co.

Cook, G. D., & Co. Staff. Illustrated Catalogue of Carriages & Special Business Advertiser. (Illus.). 226p. 1970. reprint ed. pap. 9.95 (*0-486-22364-7*) Dover.

Cook, G. K. & Hinks, A. J. Appraising Building Defects. (Illus.). 320p. (Orig.). 1992. text 72.50 (*0-582-05108-8*, Pub. by Addison-Wesley) Trans-Atl Phila.

Cook, G. Ramsay. The Dictionary of Canadian Biography, Vol. XIV. 1100p. 1998. text 100.00 (*0-8020-3476-4*) U of Toronto Pr.

— The Regenerators: Social Criticism in Late Victorian English Canada. 304p. 1984. pap. 19.95 (*0-8020-6609-7*) U of Toronto Pr.

— The Regenerators: Social Criticism in Late Victorian English Canada. LC 86-194918. (Illus.). 301p. reprint ed. pap. 93.40 (*0-8357-4136-2*, 203690800006) Bks Demand.

Cook, G. Ramsay, ed. Confederation. LC 23-16213. (Canadian Historical Readings Ser.: No. 3). 1967. pap. text 9.95 (*0-8020-1456-9*) U of Toronto Pr.

— Dictionary of Canadian Biography - Dictionnaire Biographique du Canada, Vol. XIII: 1901-1910. (ENG & FRE.). 1300p. 1994. text 85.00 (*0-8020-3998-7*) U of Toronto Pr.

Cook, G. Ramsay & Mitchinson, Wendy, eds. The Proper Sphere: Woman's Place in Canadian Society. 1976. pap. 8.95 (*0-19-540272-3*) OUP.

Cook, G. T., et al, eds. Liquid Scintillation Spectrometry, 1994. LC 96-45900. (Illus.). 396p. (C). 1997. text 20.00 (*0-9638314-3-7*) Radiocarbon.

Cook-Gait, Helen, jt. auth. see Valle, Ramon.

Cook, Gary. The Old Man. 1988. 17.50 (*0-913150-58-4*) Pioneer Pr.

***Cook, Gary, et al.** B-Movie Survival Guide. (Illus.). 72p. 1999. pap. 9.95 (*0-9669817-0-7*) Wild Things.

Cook, Gary, jt. auth. see Thompson, Jack.

Cook, Gary A. George Herbert Mead: The Making of a Social Pragmatist. LC 92-22923. 240p. (C). 1993. text 31.95 (*0-252-01969-5*) U of Ill Pr.

Cook, Gary D., ed. see Hardenbrook, Harry.

Cook, Gary W. Oakseeds: Stories from the Land. LC 92-43364. (Outdoor Tennessee Ser.). (Illus.). 208p. (C). 1993. pap. 17.95 (*0-87049-802-9*); text 30.00 (*0-87049-801-0*) U of Tenn Pr.

***Cook, Gay.** Mrs. Cook's Kitchen: Basics & Beyond. 256p. 2000. pap. 16.95 (*1-55285-014-5*) Carlton Bks Ltd.

Cook, Gene R. Living by the Power of Faith. 110p. 1991. reprint ed. pap. 8.95 (*0-87579-526-9*) Deseret Bk.

— Raising up a Family to the Lord. LC 93-8928. xxvii, 340p. 1993. 17.95 (*0-87579-713-X*) Deseret Bk.

— Raising up a Family to the Lord. 1999. pap. write for info. (*1-57345-514-8*) Deseret Bk.

— Receiving Answers to Our Prayers. LC 96-21309. 128p. 1996. 14.95 (*0-87579-803-9*) Deseret Bk.

— Searching the Scriptures: Bringing Power to Your Personal & Family Study. LC 97-13603. xii, 228p. 1997. 16.95 (*1-57345-247-5*) Deseret Bk.

Cook, Geoffrey. Azrael. 56p. (Orig.). 1992. pap. text 5.00 (*1-879594-17-X*) Androgyne Bks.

Cook, George. Poor Man's Cookbook: Old-Fashioned Country Cooking for Today's Budget. 144p. 1995. pap. 9.95 (*0-943231-95-7*) Howell Pr VA.

Cook, Gerald W. Howard: Descendants of Claiborne Howard, Soldier of the American Revolution, Including Barnard, Brindle, Campbell, Clemons, Cook, Denny, Etc. (Illus.). 186p. 1993. reprint ed. pap. 29.50 (*0-8328-2973-0*); reprint ed. lib. bdg. 39.50 (*0-8328-2972-2*) Higginson Bk Co.

Cook, Gillian P. Spatial Dynamics of Business Growth in the Witwatersrand. LC 73-92654. (University of Chicago, Department of Geography, Research Paper Ser.: No. 157). 156p. 1975. reprint ed. pap. 48.40 (*0-608-02253-5*, 206289400004) Bks Demand.

Cook, Glen. Black Company. (Chronicles of the Black Company Ser.: No. 1). 320p. 1992. mass mkt. 5.99 (*0-8125-2139-0*, Pub. by Tor Bks) St Martin.

— Bleak Seasons. (Glittering Stone: 1). 320p. 1996. 22.95 (*0-312-86105-2*) Tor Bks.

— Bleak Seasons. (Glittering Stone: 1). 1997. mass mkt. 5.99 (*0-8125-5532-5*, Pub. by Tor Bks) St Martin.

— Darkwar Trilogy No. 2: Warlock. 1985. mass mkt. 2.95 (*0-445-20049-9*, Pub. by Warner Bks) Little.

— Dreams of Steel: The Fifth Chronicle of the Black Company, Vol. 5. 320p. 1990. pap. 3.95 (*0-8125-0210-8*, Pub. by Tor Bks) St Martin.

— Faded Steel Heat. 1999. mass mkt. 6.99 (*0-451-45479-0*, ROC) NAL.

— An Ill Fate Marshalling. 320p. 1988. pap. 3.50 (*0-8125-5379-9*) Tor Bks.

— An Ill Fated Marshalling. 1999. mass mkt. 3.50 (*0-8125-3379-8*) Tor Bks.

— Shadow Games, Vol. 4. Vol. 4. 320p. 1989. pap. 3.95 (*0-8125-3382-8*, Pub. by Tor Bks) St Martin.

— Shadows Linger, Vol. 2. Vol. 2. 320p. (Orig.). 1990. pap. 3.95 (*0-8125-0842-4*, Pub. by Tor Bks) St Martin.

— She Is Darkness. 1998. mass mkt. 6.99 (*0-8125-5533-3*, Pub. by Tor Bks) St Martin.

— She Is the Darkness. LC 97-13701. (Glittering Stone: 2). 384p. 1997. text 23.95 (*0-312-85907-4*) St Martin.

***Cook, Glen.** Soldiers Live: A Novel. (Black Company Ser.: Vol. 4). 528p. 2000. 25.95 (*0-312-89057-5*, Pub. by Tor Bks) St Martin.

Cook, Glen. Swordbearer. 1992. mass mkt. 4.99 (*0-8125-3330-5*, Pub. by Tor Bks) St Martin.

— Tower of Fear. 1991. mass mkt. 4.99 (*0-8125-1933-7*, Pub. by Tor Bks) St Martin.

***Cook, Glen.** Water Sleeps. 480p. 2000. mass mkt. 6.99 (*0-8125-5534-1*, Pub. by Tor Bks) St Martin.

Cook, Glen. Water Sleeps, No. 3. LC 98-43786. (Glittering Stone: 3). 464p. 1999. 24.95 (*0-312-85909-0*, Pub. by Tor Bks) St Martin.

— The White Rose, Vol. 3. 320p. 1990. pap. 3.95 (*0-8125-0844-0*, Pub. by Tor Bks) St Martin.

Cook, Gloria. Pengarron Land. large type ed. 1995. 27.99 (*0-7505-0692-X*, Pub. by Mgna Lrg Print) Ulverscroft.

— Roscarrock. 384p. 1997. pap. 11.95 (*0-7472-5396-X*, Pub. by Headline Bk Pub) Trafalgar.

— Trevallion. 512p. 1995. pap. 10.95 (*0-7472-4708-0*, Pub. by Headline Bk Pub) Trafalgar.

Cook, Grace T. Ruth: A Story of God's Love. (Great Big Bks.). 16p. (J). (gr. k-1). 1997. pap. text 14.95 (*0-687-00007-6*) Abingdon.

Cook, Grafton H., II, jt. auth. see Cook, Barbara W.

***Cook, Greg D.** Catch As Catch Can. 1999. 9.95 (*0-9665363-6-3*) Highwater Bks.

Cook, Gregory A., jt. auth. see Falstrom, Pauline.

Cook, Gregory M. Ernest Buckler. LC 72-1350. (Critical Views on Canadian Writers Ser.). 145 p. 1972. write for info. (*0-07-092958-0*) McGraw.

Cook-Greuter, Susanne, jt. ed. see Miller, Melvin E.

Cook-Greuter, Susanne R., jt. auth. see Miller, Melvin E.

Cook, Guillermo, ed. Crosscurrents in Indigenous Spirituality: Interface of Maya, Catholic & Protestant Worldviews. LC 96-49379. (Studies in Christian Mission: Vol. 18). xviii, 331p. 1997. 109.00 (*90-04-10622-7*) Brill Academic Pubs.

— New Face of the Church in Latin America: Between Tradition & Change. LC 94-2812. (American Society of Missiology Ser.: No. 18). 250p. (Orig.). 1994. pap. 20.00 (*0-88344-937-4*) Orbis Bks.

Cook, Guillermo & Foulkes, Ricardo. Marcos. (Comentario Biblico Hispanoamericano Ser.). 372p. 1990. 19.99 (*0-89922-377-X*) Caribe Betania.

Cook, Guillermo, tr. see De Carvalho Azevedo, Marcello.

Cook-Gumperz, Jenny, et al, eds. Children's Worlds & Children's Language. (New Babylon Studies in the Social Sciences: No. 47). (Illus.). 487p. 1986. lib. bdg. 161.55 (*0-89925-089-0*) Mouton.

Cook, Guy. Discourse. Widdowson, H. G. & Candlin, C. N., eds. (Illus.). 176p. 1989. pap. text 14.95 (*0-19-437140-9*) OUP.

— Discourse & Literature: The Interplay of Form & Mind. (Illus.). 296p. 1995. pap. text 18.95 (*0-19-437185-9*) OUP.

— Discourse of Advertising. LC 92-2778. (Interface Ser.). (Illus.). 242p. (C). 1992. pap. 24.99 (*0-415-04171-6*, A7861) Routledge.

— Principle & Practice in Applied Linguistics: Studies in Honour of H. G. Widdowson. (Illus.). 442p. 1995. pap. text 23.95 (*0-19-442148-1*) OUP.

Cook, Hadrian. The Protection & Conservation of Water Resources: A U. K. Perspective. LC 97-41191. 354p. 1998. 165.00 (*0-471-97681-4*) Wiley.

Cook, Harold E. Shaker Music: A Manifestation of American Folk Culture. LC 71-161507. (Illus.). 312p. 1975. 39.50 (*0-8387-7953-0*) Bucknell U Pr.

Cook, Harold J. The Decline of the Old Medical Regime in Stuart London. LC 85-26932. (Illus.). 311p. reprint ed. pap. 96.50 (*0-608-08086-1*, 206904500002) Bks Demand.

— Tales of the 04 Ranch: Recollections of Harold J. Cook, 1887-1909. LC 68-25320. 251p. 1968. reprint ed. pap. 77.90 (*0-8357-2536-7*, 205715700015) Bks Demand.

— Trials of an Ordinary Doctor: Joannes Groenevelt in Seventeenth-Century London. LC 93-39733. (Illus.). 301p. 1994. 45.00 (*0-8018-4778-8*) Johns Hopkins.

Cook, Harriet N. The Bible Alphabet of Animals. (Illus.). 128p. (YA). (gr. 7-10). 1976. pap. 5.65 (*0-7399-0118-4*, 2130) Rod & Staff.

Cook, Harry. Samurai: The Story of a Warrior Tradition. (Illus.). 144p. 1998. 16.95 (*0-8069-0670-7*) Sterling.

Cook, Harry C., jt. auth. see Bancroft, John D.

Cook, Harry E. & Enos, Paul, eds. Deep-Water Carbonate Environments: Based on a Symposium Sponsored by the Society of Economic Paleontologists & Mineralogists. LC 79-109186. (Society of Economic Paleontologists & Mineralogists Ser.: No. 25). (Illus.). 342p. 1977. reprint ed. pap. 106.10 (*0-608-02971-8*, 206343900006) Bks Demand.

Cook, Harry E., et al. Platform Margin & Deep Water Carbonates No. 12: Lecture Notes for Short Course. LC QE0471.15.C3. (SEPM Short Course Ser.: No. 12). (Illus.). 581p. reprint ed. pap. 180.20 (*0-8357-6266-1*, 203417800089) Bks Demand.

Cook, Harry N., ed. Waterway User Taxes: The Public Value of Navigation Programs, the Rationale for Cost Recovery...Major Arguments, Pro & Con. 48p. (Orig.). 1994. pap. 7.50 (*0-934292-12-4*) Natl Waterways.

Cook, Harry N., ed. Implementing Public Law 99-662 (H.R. 6) The Water Resources Development Act of 1986 - Proceedings of a Seminar. 243p. 1987. pap. text 40.00 (*0-934292-06-X*) Natl Waterways.

Cook, Harry N., frwd. Personal Injury Liability under the Jones Act: Background Materials. 158p. (Orig.). (C). 1992. pap. text 25.00 (*0-934292-11-6*) Natl Waterways.

Cook, Harry T. Christianity Beyond Creeds. Chevalier, Susan M., ed. LC 97-77496. 93p. (Orig.). 1997. pap. 12.95 (*0-9660728-0-4*, 97-1) Ctr Ratnl Chrstnity.

— Sermons of a Devoted Heretic: A Priest Offers Messages of Hope to Faithful Doubters. Chevalier, Susan M., ed. 1999. pap. 12.95 (*0-9660728-1-2*, Pub. by Ctr Ratnl Chrstnty) Partners Pubs Grp.

Cook, Haruko M., et al, eds. New Trends & Issues in Teaching Japanese Language & Culture. (Technical Report Ser.: Vol. 15). 184p. 1998. pap. text 20.00 (*0-8248-2067-3*) Sec Lang Tching.

Cook, Haruko T. Japan at War: An Oral History. LC 92-53731. 1993. pap. 14.95 (*1-56584-039-9*, Pub. by New Press NY) Norton.

Cook, Haruko T. & Cook, Theodore F. Japan at War: An Oral History. LC 92-53731. 496p. 1992. 27.50 (*1-56584-014-3*, Pub. by New Press NY) Norton.

Cook, Harvey A. & Pederson, Duane E. Scientific Success. Nickell, Samila S. & Bushnell, Holly W., eds. (Scientific Selling Ser.). 179p. (Orig.). 1989. pap. write for info. (*0-9626547-0-1*) Sell Perfect.

Cook, Harvey T. Rambles in the Pee Dee Basin, South Carolina. (Illus.). 512p. 1991. reprint ed. 37.50 (*0-89308-447-6*, SC 90) Southern Hist Pr.

Cook, Herbert R. One Man's Walk with God: A Lifetime of Christian Witness. LC 94-44920. (Illus.). 304p. (Orig.). 1994. pap. 18.00 (*0-88196-006-3*) Oak Woods Media.

Cook, Howard, ed. Continua: With the Houston Problem Book. LC 95-4002. (Lecture Notes in Pure & Applied Mathematics Ser.: Vol. 170). (Illus.). 416p. 1995. pap. text 165.00 (*0-8247-9650-0*) Dekker.

Cook, Hugh. Cracked Wheat & Other Stories. LC 84-18878. 127p. (YA). (gr. 7 up). 1984. 12.95 (*0-931940-09-5*); pap. 6.95 (*0-931940-08-7*) Middleburg Pr.

— Cracked Wheat & Other Stories. 122p. 1994. pap. 9.95 (*0-88962-265-5*) Mosaic.

— The Homecoming Man. 324p. 1996. pap. 12.95 (*0-88962-428-3*) Mosaic.

— The Walrus & the Warwolf. 1992. 30.00 (*0-8023-1287-X*) Dufour.

— The Walrus & the Warwolf. LC 88-70886. (Chronicles of an Age of Darkness Ser.: No. 4). (Illus.). 486p. 1993. 30.00 (*0-86140-294-4*, Pub. by Smyth) Dufour.

— Wizard War Chronicles III: The Hero's Return. 208p. 1988. mass mkt. 3.95 (*0-445-20664-0*, Pub. by Warner Bks) Little.

— The Wizards & the Warriors. (Chronicles of an Age of Darkness Ser.). 352p. 1987. 30.00 (*0-86140-244-8*, Pub. by Smyth) Dufour.

— The Women & the Warlords. LC 87-73288. (Chronicles of an Age of Darkness Ser.: Vol. 3). 275p. 1988. 30.00 (*0-8023-1286-1*) Dufour.

Cook, Hulet H. Paul Hervieu & French Classicism. LC 45-37189. (Indiana University Humanities Ser.: No. 14). 56p. reprint ed. pap. 30.00 (*0-608-10180-X*, 205522300011) Bks Demand.

Cook, Hull. Fifty Years a Country Doctor. LC 97-50636. vii, 203p. 1998. pap. 12.00 (*0-8032-6389-9*) U of Nebr Pr.

***Cook, Ian.** Liberalism in Australia. 272p. 2000. pap. text 22.00 (*0-19-553702-5*) OUP.

Cook, Ian, et al, eds. Fragmented Asia: Regional Integration & National Disintegration in Pacific. LC 95-83728. (Pacific Rim Research Ser.). 256p. 1996. 72.95 (*1-85972-194-X*, Pub. by Avebry) Ashgate Pub Co.

Cook, Ian G., et al, eds. Dynamic Asia: Business, Trade & Economics Development in Pacific Asia. LC 97-77888. (Pacific Rim Research Ser.). (Illus.). 246p. 1998. text 67.95 (*1-85972-196-6*, Pub. by Ashgate Pub) Ashgate Pub Co.

Cook Inlet Historical Society Staff & Anchorage Museum of History & Art Staff. Enlightenment & Exploration in the North Pacific, 1741-1805. Haycox, Stephen W. et al, eds. LC 96-37993. (Illus.). 240p. 1997. pap. 19.95 (*0-295-97583-0*) U of Wash Pr.

***Cook, Isabelle.** In Times of War: Memoirs of a World War II Nurse. 384p. (C). 1999. 15.95 (*0-9670352-0-1*) Ivy Pub.

***Cook, J.** Categorizing & Transporting Low Specific Activity Materials & Surface Contaminated Objects. 57p. 1998. pap. 5.00 (*0-16-062753-2*) USGPO.

— How Things Are Made. (Illus.). 24p. (J). (gr. 2-4). 1989. pap. 4.95 (*0-7460-0276-9*, Usborne) EDC.

Cook, J. How to Draw Robots. (Young Artist Ser.). (Illus.). 32p. (J). (gr. 4-7). 1993. pap. 4.95 (*0-7460-0745-0*, Usborne) EDC.

— How to Draw Robots. (Young Artist Ser.). (Illus.). 32p. (J). (gr. 4 up). 1993. lib. bdg. 12.95 (*0-88110-538-4*, Usborne) EDC.

— Mountain Bikes. (Superskills Ser.). (Illus.). xp. (YA). (gr. 6-10). 1990. pap. 5.95 (*0-7460-0520-2*, Usborne) EDC.

An Asterisk (*) at the beginning of an entry indicates that the title is appearing for the first time.

— Mountain Bikes. (Superskills Ser.). (Illus.). 48p. (YA). (gr. 6-10). 1999. lib. bdg. 13.95 (*0-88110-426-4*, Usborne) EDC.

— Understanding Modern Art. (Understanding the Arts Ser.). (Illus.). 64p. (J). (gr. 6-12). 1992. pap. 9.95 (*0-7460-0475-3*, Usborne) EDC.

— Understanding Modern Art. (Understanding the Arts Ser.). (Illus.). 64p. (J). (gr. 6 up). 1999. lib. bdg. 17.95 (*0-88110-512-0*, Usborne) EDC.

***Cook, J.** United States-specific Schedules of Requirements for Transport of Specified Types of Radioactive Material Consignments. 113p. 1998. per. 9.50 (*0-16-062779-6*) USGPO.

— Where Food Comes From. (Explainers Ser.). (Illus.). 24p. (gr. 2-4). 1989. pap. 4.95 (*0-7460-0280-7*, Usborne) EDC.

Cook, J., et al, eds. General Surgery at the District Hospital. (ENG, FRE, RUS & SPA., Illus.). 230p. 1988. pap. text 27.00 (*92-4-154235-7*, 1150300) World Health.

— Surgery at the District Hospital: Obstetrics, Gynaecology, Orthopaedics, & Traumatology. (ENG, FRE, RUS & SPA.). 207p. 1991. pap. text 22.50 (*92-4-154413-9*, 1150351) World Health.

Cook, J., et al. A Guide to Commonwealth Government Information Sources. (Guides to Australian Information Sources Ser.). 120p. 1988. pap. text 13.00 (*0-08-034421-6*, Pergamon Pr) Elsevier.

Cook, J., jt. auth. see McComb, Gordon.

Cook, J. D. & Hughes, D. FumeCupboards Revisited. (Handbook Ser.: No. 2). (C). 1989. 105.00 (*0-948237-01-5*, Pub. by H&H Sci Cnslts) St Mut.

Cook, J. D., et al. Laboratory Design Issues: Technical Guide. (Technical Guide Ser.: No. 10). 123p. (C). 1994. pap. 150.00 (*0-948237-11-2*, Pub. by H&H Sci Cnslts) St Mut.

Cook, J. F., ed. NDE Engineering Codes & Standards & Materials Characterization. 95p. 1996. pap. text 70.00 (*0-7918-1769-5*, TS283) ASME Pr.

Cook, J. G. Handbook of Textile Fibres Vol. 1: Natural Fibres. 240p. 1984. pap. text 29.00 (*1-85573-484-2*, Pub. by Woodhead Pubng) Am Educ Systs.

Cook, J. G. Handbook of Textile Fibres Vol. 1: Natural Fibres. 5th ed. (Merrow Technical Library: Vol. 1). 1984. pap. 18.00 (*0-904095-39-8*, Pub. by Textile Inst) St Mut.

Cook, J. G. Handbook of Textile Fibres Vol. 2: Man-Made Fibres, 760p. 1984. pap. text 58.00 (*1-85573-485-0*, Pub. by Woodhead Pubng) Am Educ Systs.

Cook, J. G. Handbook of Textile Fibres Vol. 2: Man-Made Fibres. 5th ed. (Merrow Technical Library: Vol. 1). 1984. pap. 40.00 (*0-904095-40-1*, Pub. by Textile Inst) St Mut.

Cook, J. Lennox. 6 Great Travellers. (Illus.). 200p. (gr. 4-8). 1960. 7.00 (*0-8023-9031-5*) Dufour.

Cook, J. Sue & Fontaine, Karen L. Essentials of Mental Health Nursing. 2nd ed. McCormick, Mark, ed. (Illus.). 768p. (C). 1991. text 45.25 (*0-201-12597-8*) Addison-Wesley.

Cook, Jacquelyn. Image in the Looking Glass. 224p. 1986. pap. 5.95 (*0-310-47641-0*, 15616P) Zondervan.

— The River Between, No. 17. (Serenade Saga Ser.). 1985. pap. 1.49 (*0-310-46762-4*, 15535P) Zondervan.

— The Wind along the River. (Serenade Saga Ser.: No. 31). 1986. pap. 1.49 (*0-310-47072-2*, 15560P) Zondervan.

Cook, James. Arizona Landmarks. Holden, John W., ed. LC 84-73392. (Illus.). 160p. 1999. 35.00 (*0-916179-04-4*) Ariz Hwy.

— Bibliography of the Writings of Charles Dickens. 1972. 59.95 (*0-87968-744-4*) Gordon Pr.

— Explorations of Captain James Cook in the Pacific, as Told by Selections of His Own Journals, 1768-1779. Price, A. Grenfell, ed. (Illus.). 292p. 1971. pap. 9.95 (*0-486-22766-9*) Dover.

— Fellow Travelers. LC 98-34201. 248p. 1999. pap. 18.00 (*1-57962-052-3*) Permanent Pr.

***Cook, James.** Journals of Captain Cook. abr. ed. Edwards, Philip, ed. (Penguin Classics Ser.). 672p. 2000. pap. 9.95 (*0-14-043647-2*, Penguin Bks) Viking Penguin.

Cook, James. Remedies & Rackets: The Truth about Patent Medicines Today. LC 75-39284. (Getting & Spending: The Consumer's Dilemma Ser.). 1976. reprint ed. 23.95 (*0-405-08059-X*) Ayer.

— Voyages of Discovery. (Illus.). 555p. 1993. pap. 16.95 (*0-89733-316-0*) Academy Chi Pubs.

Cook, James D., ed. Iron. LC 80-22756. (Methods in Hematology Ser.: No. 1). 190p. reprint ed. pap. 58.90 (*0-7837-2576-0*, 204273500006) Bks Demand.

Cook, James D., ed. see Bothwell, Thomas H. & Carlton, Robert W.

Cook, James D., ed. see Bothwell, Thomas H. & Charlton, Robert W.

Cook, James E. The Arizona Trivia Book. Shepherd, Robin, ed. LC 91-70239. 200p. (Orig.). 1991. pap. 6.95 (*0-935182-51-9*) Gem Guides Bk.

— Arizona 101: An Irreverent Short Course for New Arrivals. 3rd rev. ed. LC 96-78396. (Illus.). 80p. (Orig.). 1997. pap. 7.95 (*0-935182-80-2*) Gem Guides Bk.

— Dry Humor: Tales of Arizona Weather. Shepherd, Robin, ed. LC 92-52500. (Illus.). 103p. (Orig.). 1992. pap. 6.95 (*0-935182-54-3*) Gem Guides Bk.

Cook, James E., ed. Charles Sanders Peirce: Contributions to the Nation, Pt. 2 : 1894-1900. (Graduate Studies: No. 16). 281p. 1978. 20.00 (*0-89672-065-9*); pap. 14.00 (*0-89672-064-0*) Tex Tech Univ Pr.

— Charles Sanders Peirce: Contributions to the Nation, Pt. 3 : 1901-1908. (Graduate Studies: No. 19). 306p. 1979. 22.00 (*0-89672-070-5*); pap. 16.00 (*0-89672-069-1*) Tex Tech Univ Pr.

***Cook, James E., et al.** Travel Arizona: The Back Roads. (Illus.). 1999. pap. 12.95 (*1-893860-09-4*) Ariz Hwy.

Cook, James F. Carl Sanders: Spokesman of the New South. LC 93-36314. (C). 1994. 24.99 (*0-86554-433-6*, MUP-H345) Mercer Univ Pr.

— The Governors of Georgia, 1754-1995. expanded rev. ed. LC 95-32393. (C). 1996. pap. 17.95 (*0-86554-537-5*, MUP-P152) Mercer Univ Pr.

Cook, James G. Thomas Edison Book of Easy & Incredible Experiments. LC 88-20669. (Science Editions Ser.). 160p. 1988. pap. 14.95 (*0-471-62090-4*) Wiley.

Cook, James H. Fifty Years on the Old Frontier. (American Biography Ser.). 253p. 1991. reprint ed. lib. bdg. 69.00 (*0-7812-8089-3*) Rprt Serv.

Cook, James I. Shared Pain & Sorrow: The Reflections of a Secondary Sufferer. (Looking up Ser.). 24p. (Orig.). 1991. pap. 1.95 (*0-8298-0903-1*) Pilgrim OH.

Cook, James I., ed. Saved by Hope: Essays in Honor of Richard C. Oudersluys. LC 78-5416. 198p. reprint ed. 61.40 (*0-8357-9132-7*, 201606000097) Bks Demand.

Cook, James L. Conversion Factors. (Illus.). 176p. 1991. text 35.00 (*0-19-856349-3*, 12269) OUP.

***Cook, James R.** Full Faith & Credit: A Novel about Financial Collapse. 304p. 2000. pap. 22.95 (*1-886768-49-8*) Blue Bk Pubns.

Cook, James W., tr. The Autobiography of Lorenzo de' Medici The Magnificent: A Commentary on My Sonnets. LC 94-11190. (Medieval & Renaissance Texts & Studies: Vol. 129). 304p. 1995. 28.00 (*0-86698-136-5*, MR129) MRTS.

— Petrarch's Songbook: Rerum Vulgarium Fragmenta. A Verse Translation. (Medieval & Renaissance Texts & Studies: Vol. 151). 464p. 1995. 30.00 (*0-86698-191-8*, MR151) MRTS.

— Petrarch's Songbook: Rerum Vulgarium Fragmenta. A Verse Translation, Bilingual edition. (Medieval & Renaissance Texts & Studies: Vol. 151). 464p. 1996. pap. 19.95 (*0-86698-192-6*, P32) Pegasus Pr.

Cook, James W., ed. see Pulci, Antonia.

Cook, James W., ed. & tr. see Pulci, Antonia.

Cook, Jamice A., et al. The Learning Organization in the Public Services. LC 96-52107. 264p. 1997. text 78.95 (*0-566-07773-6*, Pub. by Gower) Ashgate Pub Co.

Cook, Jane, ed. Innovations in Activities for the Elderly: Proceedings of the National Association of Activity Professionals Convention. LC 84-28996. (Activities, Adaptation & Aging Ser.: Vol. 6, Nos. 3 & 4). 120p. 1985. text 39.95 (*0-86656-389-X*) Haworth Pr.

***Cook, Jane L.** Coalescence of Styles: The Ethnic Heritage of St. John River Valley Regional Furniture, 1763-1851. (McGill-Queen's Studies in Ethnic History). (Illus.). 288p. 2000. 45.00 (*0-7735-2056-2*, Pub. by McG-Queens Univ Pr) CUP Services.

Cook, Janet & Kent, Jessica. Hotshots Bikes. (Hotshots Ser.). (Illus.). 32p. (J). (gr. 2 up). 1996. pap. 2.95 (*0-7460-2550-5*, Usborne) EDC.

Cook, Janet E. Radiologic Sciences Examination Review. (Illus.). 350p. 1999. pap. 31.95 (*0-07-012604-6*) McGraw-Hill HPD.

Cook, Janet P., intro. Berkshire Victuals. (Illus.). 202p. (Orig.). 1993. pap. 19.95 (*0-9639206-0-X*) Berkshire Cnty Hist.

Cook, Jean G. & Jimmie, Elsie. How the Crane Got Its Blue Eyes. (Illus.). (J). pap. 12.00 (*1-55036-505-3*) Todd Commns.

Cook, Jean G., jt. ed. see Tuttle, Marcia.

Cook, Jean T. Room for a Stepdaddy. LC 95-3128. (Albert Whitman Concept Bks.). (Illus.). 32p. (J). (ps-2). 1995. lib. bdg. 14.95 (*0-8075-7106-7*) A Whitman.

Cook, Jeannette. Beady Eyed Women's Guide to Exquisite Beadwork: A Sculptural Peyote Project Primer. (Illus.). 35p. 1996. spiral bd., wbk. ed. 14.95 (*1-889789-05-4*, 005) Beady Eyed Women.

***Cook, Jeannette & Star, Vicki.** Beading with Peyote Stitch: A Beadwork How-To Book. (Illus.). 2000. 21.95 (*1-883010-71-3*) Interweave.

Cook, Jeannette & Star, Vicki. Beady Eyed Women's Guide to Exquisite Beadwork: A Bead & Weave Primer. (Illus.). 17p. 1995. spiral bd., wbk. ed. 14.95 (*1-889789-03-8*, 003) Beady Eyed Women.

— Beady Eyed Women's Guide to Exquisite Beadwork: A Peyote Stitch Primer. (Illus.). 14p. (Orig.). 1994. spiral bd., wbk. ed. 14.95 (*1-889789-01-1*, 001) Beady Eyed Women.

— Beady Eyed Women's Guide to Exquisite Beadwork: An Off-Loom Bead Weaving Primer. (Illus.). 28p. 1996. spiral bd., wbk. ed. 14.95 (*1-889789-06-2*, 006) Beady Eyed Women.

Cook, Jeannie, et al. Buffalo Bill's Town in the Rockies: A Pictorial History of Cody, Wyoming. LC 96-747. 1996. write for info. (*0-89865-967-1*) Donning Co.

Cook, Jeff. A Collective Concern: Setting Policies & Procedures for Credit Union Collections. 80p. (Orig.). 1993. pap. 59.00 (*1-889394-12-2*) Credit Union Execs.

— Credit Union Mergers: A Professional Analysis & Real-Life Examples. 72p. (Orig.). 1994. pap. 79.00 (*1-889394-30-0*) Credit Union Execs.

Cook, Jeff S. Elements of Speechwriting & Public Speaking. 192p. 1996. 9.95 (*0-02-861452-6*) Macmillan Gen Ref.

***Cook, Jeffrey.** Passive Cooling. (Illus.). 593p. 2000. pap. 55.00 (*0-262-53171-2*) MIT Pr.

Cook, Jeffrey. Seeking Structure from Nature: The Organic Architecture of Hungary. (Illus.). 192p. 1996. 66.00 (*3-7643-5178-0*, Pub. by Birkhauser) Princeton Arch.

Cook, Jeffrey, text. Anasazi Places: The Photographic Vision of William Current. LC 91-35194. (Illus.). 152p. 1992. 45.00 (*0-292-76515-0*) U of Tex Pr.

Cook, Jeffrey S. The Elements of Speechwriting & Public Speaking: An Indispensable Guide for Anyone Who Speaks in Public. 192p. 1991. reprint ed. pap. 9.95 (*0-02-042782-4*) Macmillan Gen Ref.

***Cook, Jennifer.** Flight Across the Mekong. 181p. (YA). 1999. pap. 10.95 (*0-920661-79-3*, Pub. by TSAR Pubns) SPD-Small Pr Dist.

Cook, Jeremy. Hatfield Photographic Lunar Atlas, 1. LC 98-29308. (Illus.). vi, 122p. 1999. pap. text 44.95 (*1-85233-018-X*) Spr-Verlag.

Cook, Jerry O. Worship Resources for Youth. 132p. 1983. pap. 12.95 (*0-87178-948-5*) Brethren.

Cook, Jerry O., jt. auth. see Clapp, Steve.

Cook, Jerry O., ed. see Taylor, Blaine, et al.

Cook, Jerry Van, see VanCook, Jerry.

Cook, Jerry W. Once a Fighter Pilot. (Illus.). 223p. 1996. 22.95 (*0-07-012549-X*) McGraw.

Cook, Jim. Do You Know the Symbols. 1997. pap. 6.99 (*0-929987-26-8*) Culinary Collections.

— Into the Fire. (C). 1993. pap. text 25.00 (*1-881592-47-2*) Hayden-McNeil.

Cook, Jim, jt. auth. see Bratton, Jacky.

Cook, Jim, ed. see Lo Russo, Andrew P.

***Cook, Jo.** Internet Explorer Version 5.0: Session One. Dietz, Kevin C. et al, eds. (YA). 2000. pap. write for info. (*0-7423-0469-8*, MSIE5001ALG) ComputerPREP.

— Internet Explorer Version 5.0: Session Two. Dietz, Kevin C. et al, eds. (Illus.). (YA). 2000. pap. write for info. (*0-7423-0470-1*, MSIE5001BLG) ComputerPREP.

— Using Microsoft Internet Explorer 5.0. Dietz, Kevin C. & Tillman, Jamie, eds. (Illus.). 230p. (YA). 1999. pap. write for info. (*0-7423-0415-9*) ComputerPREP.

Cook, Joan E. Hannah's Desire, God's Design: Early Interpretations of the Story of Hannah. (JSOTS Ser.: Vol. 282). 136p. 1999. 46.50 (*1-85075-909-X*, Pub. by Sheffield Acad) CUP Services.

***Cook, JoAnne, et al.** Towards a Gendered Political Economy. LC 99-53563. 2000. text 69.95 (*0-312-23133-4*) St Martin.

***Cook, Joe & Cook, Monica.** River Songs: A Journey down the Chattahoochee & Apalachicola Rivers. (Illus.). 224p. 2000. 39.95 (*0-8173-1034-7*) U of Ala Pr.

Cook, Joel. Rat's Daughter: From an Old Tale. LC 92-71871. (Illus.). 32p. (J). (ps-3). 1993. 14.95 (*1-56397-140-2*) Boyds Mills Pr.

Cook, Joel. Favorite Fairy Tales Told in Poland. LC 94-1500. 96p. (J). (gr. 3-7). 1995. reprint ed. mass mkt. 4.95 (*0-688-12602-2*, Wm Morrow) Morrow Avon.

Cook, Johann. The Septuagint of Proverbs - Jewish &/or Hellenistic Proverbs? Concerning the Hellenistic Colouring of LXX Proverbs. LC 97-37344. (Vetus Testamentum Ser.: Suppl. 69). xxi, 391p. 1997. 134.00 (*90-04-10879-3*) Brill Academic Pubs.

***Cook, John.** Air Transport: The First Fifty Years. (Transport Ser.). 1999. pap. 18.99 (*0-7524-0790-2*) Arcadia Publng.

Cook, John. The Book of Positive Quotations. LC 98-45374. 1999. 10.99 (*0-517-20216-6*) Random Hse Value.

— The Book of Positive Quotations. LC 97-15078. Orig. Title: The Fairview Guide to Positive Quotations. 560p. 1997. reprint ed. pap. 15.95 (*1-57749-053-3*) Fairview Press.

— How to Help Someone Who Is Depressed, or Suicidal: Practical Suggestions from a Survivor. 157p. 12.95 (*0-9630359-5-9*) Rubicon Pr.

— How to Keep Going When Everything's Going Against You. 192p. 14.95 (*0-9630359-4-0*) Rubicon Pr.

— The Rubicon Dictionary of Positive, Motivational, Life-Affirming & Inspirational Quotations. 445p. 19.95 (*0-9630359-3-2*) Rubicon Pr.

— Wills & Estates. 80p. pap. 7.50 (*0-685-23171-2*, 41,575W) NCLS Inc.

Cook, John, compiled by. Faith & Belief. LC 97-31319. (Pocket Positives Ser.). 256p. 1997. pap. 8.95 (*1-57749-060-6*) Fairview Press.

— Hope. LC 97-31318. (Pocket Positives Ser.). 256p. 1997. pap. 8.95 (*1-57749-059-2*) Fairview Press.

— Living One Day at a Time. LC 97-31317. (Pocket Positives Ser.). 256p. 1997. pap. 8.95 (*1-57749-058-4*) Fairview Press.

— Overcoming Challenges. LC 97-31315. (Pocket Positives Ser.). 256p. 1997. pap. 8.95 (*1-57749-061-4*) Fairview Press.

— Peace of Mind. LC 97-31316. (Pocket Positives Ser.). 256p. 1997. pap. 8.95 (*1-57749-057-6*) Fairview Press.

— Success. LC 97-31299. (Pocket Positives Ser.). 256p. 1997. pap. 8.95 (*1-57749-062-2*) Fairview Press.

Cook, John, ed. School Librarianship. (Illus.). 272p. 1981. 34.00 (*0-08-024814-4*, Pergamon Pr); pap. 22.00 (*0-08-024813-6*, Pergamon Pr) Elsevier.

***Cook, John & Szwec, Jeanette.** Day Trade Part-Time. LC 00-36650. (Online Trading for a Living Ser.). (Illus.). 224p. 2000. 29.95 (*0-471-39310-X*) Wiley.

Cook, John, jt. auth. see McComb, Gordon.

Cook, John, ed. see Hazlitt, William.

Cook, John, ed. see Tolliver, Roland & Spyrison, Stephen.

Cook, John A. Neo-Classic Drama in Spain. LC 74-5771. 576p. 1974. reprint ed. lib. bdg. 85.00 (*0-8371-7518-6*, CONC, Greenwood Pr) Greenwood.

Cook, John A. & Strong, William F. Persuasion: Strategies for Public Influence. 3rd ed. 208p. 1996. per. 26.95 (*0-8403-8037-2*) Kendall-Hunt.

Cook, John E. Wearing of the Gray. 601p. 1987. reprint ed. 30.00 (*0-942211-69-3*) Olde Soldier Bks.

***Cook, John Granger.** The Interpretation of the New Testament in Greco-Roman Paganism. (Studies & Texts in Antiquity & Christianity). 400p. 1999. 112.50 (*3-16-147195-4*, Pub. by JCB Mohr) Coronet Bks.

Cook, John H. A Study of the Mill Schools of North Carolina. LC 73-176668. (Columbia University. Teachers College. Contributions to Education Ser.: No. 178). reprint ed. 37.50 (*0-404-55178-5*) AMS Pr.

Cook, John L. The Advisor: The Phoenix Program in Vietnam. LC 96-69811. (Illus.). 352p. 1997. 35.00 (*0-7643-0137-3*) Schiffer.

— The Illustrated History of the Vietnam War, Vol. 16. 1988. pap. 6.95 (*0-318-37493-5*) Bantam.

— Rescue under Fire: The Story of Dustoff in Vietnam. LC 97-80322. (Illus.). 208p. 1998. pap. 24.95 (*0-7643-0461-5*) Schiffer.

— A Visual Novel of the War of Tomorrow: Armor at Fulda Gap, Vol. 2. (Illus.). 224p. 1990. pap. 6.95 (*0-380-75843-1*, Avon Bks) Morrow Avon.

Cook, John Lee. Standard Operating Procedures & Guidelines. LC 98-43459. 318p. 1998. pap. 45.00 (*0-912212-69-1*) Fire Eng.

Cook, John M. Inside Four Ninety-Five. Haye, Caroline, ed. (Illus.). 128p. (YA). 1989. write for info. (*0-318-64984-5*) J M Cook Pub.

— The Sanctuary of Hemithea at Kastabos. Plommer, William H., ed. LC 66-10449. 222p. reprint ed. pap. 63.30 (*0-608-11799-4*, 2051471) Bks Demand.

Cook, John P. Composite Construction Methods. LC 84-5770. 346p. (C). 1985. reprint ed. lib. bdg. 47.95 (*0-89874-760-0*) Krieger.

Cook, John P., jt. auth. see Panek, Julian R.

Cook, John R. The Border & the Buffalo: An Untold Story of the Southwest Plains. LC 89-36507. (Illus.). 374p. 1989. reprint ed. 21.95 (*0-938349-39-2*); reprint ed. pap. 14.95 (*0-938349-40-6*) State House Pr.

— Dennis Potter: A Life on Screen. LC 95-2169. 1995. text 24.95 (*0-7190-4602-5*, Pub. by Manchester Univ Pr) St Martin.

Cook, John R. & Fulmer, Scott G., eds. The Archaeology of the McCain Valley Study Area in Eastern San Diego County, California. (Illus.). 275p. (C). 1981. reprint ed. pap. text 28.75 (*1-55567-402-X*) Coyote Press.

***Cook, John Raymond.** Asphalt Justice: A Critique of the Criminal Justice System in America. LC 00-22345. (Praeger Series in Criminology & Crime Control Policy). 244p. 2000. 64.00 (*0-275-96827-8*, C6827, Praeger Pubs) Greenwood.

Cook, John S., ed. Biogenesis & Turnover of Membrane Macromolecules. LC 75-25111. (Society of General Physiologists Ser.: No. 31). (Illus.). 304p. reprint ed. pap. 94.30 (*0-7837-7090-1*, 204691500004) Bks Demand.

***Cook, John W.** Morality & Cultural Differences. LC 98-27685. 224p. 1999. 29.95 (*0-19-512679-3*) OUP.

Cook, John W. Wittgenstein, Empiricism & Language. LC 99-10740. 240p. 1999. text 39.95 (*0-19-513298-X*) OUP.

— Wittgenstein's Metaphysics. 376p. (C). 1994. text 80.00 (*0-521-46019-0*) Cambridge U Pr.

— Wittgenstein's Metaphysics. LC 93-28603. (C). 1994. write for info. (*0-521-45536-7*) Cambridge U Pr.

Cook, Joie. Acts of Submission. 28p. (Orig.). 1990. pap. 4.00 (*0-916397-04-1*) Manic D Pr.

— My Body Is a War Toy. 24p. (Orig.). 1990. pap. 3.00 (*0-929730-26-7*) Zeitgeist Pr.

Cook, Joie & Redo. A Picture Is Worth 62 Words. 36p. 1998. pap. 4.95 (*1-893084-04-3*) Benway Inst.

Cook, Jon, et al. The Prelude. Wood, Nigel, ed. LC 92-32420. (Theory in Practice Ser.). 1993. pap. 25.00 (*0-335-09624-7*) OpUniv Pr.

***Cook, Jonathan.** DB2 Cluster Certification Guide. LC 98-30447. 544p. 1998. pap. text 54.99 (*0-13-081900-X*) P-H.

— DB2 Universal Database Version 6.1 Certification Guide. 3rd ed. 1014p. 1999. pap. text 59.99 (*0-13-086755-1*) P-H.

Cook, Jonathan. The Universal Guide to DB2 for Windows NT. LC 98-46933. 528p. 1998. pap. 54.99 incl. cd-rom (*0-13-099723-4*) P-H.

***Cook, Jonathan & Harbus, Robert.** DB2 Universal Replication Certification Guide. (IBM DB2 Certification Ser.). (Illus.). 432p. 1999. pap. text 54.99 (*0-13-082424-0*) P-H.

***Cook, Jonathan, et al.** Db2 Universal Database in Application Environments. 400p. 2000. pap. 54.99 (*0-13-086987-2*) P-H.

Cook, Jonathan A. Satirical Apocalypse: An Anatomy of Melville's the Confidence Man. 67. LC 95-40033. (Contributions to the Study of World Literature Ser.: Vol. 67). 296p. 1996. 65.00 (*0-313-29404-6*, Greenwood Pr) Greenwood.

Cook, Joseph G. & Marcus, Paul. Criminal Law. 2nd ed. 1988. teacher ed. write for info. (*0-8205-0067-4*) Bender.

***Cook, Joseph G. & Marcus, Paul.** Criminal Law. 4th ed. LC 99-201785. (Casebook Ser.). 1999. 57.00 (*0-8205-4056-0*) Bender.

— Criminal Procedure. 4th ed. LC 98-150175. 1997. text. write for info. (*0-8205-3072-7*) Bender.

Cook, Joseph G. & Sobieski, John L. Civil Rights Actions, 7 vols. 1983. ring bd. 980.00 (*0-8205-1199-4*) Bender.

Cook, Joseph R. Constitutional Rights of the Accused, 3 vols., Set. 2nd ed. LC 85-51443. 1985. 345.00 (*0-685-59838-1*) West Group.

Cook, Juanita V., jt. auth. see Filberth, Ernest W.

Cook, Judith. Apprentices of Freedom. 7.95 (*0-7043-3368-6*, Pub. by Quartet) Charles River Bks.

— Priestley LC 98-145693. 314p. 1997. write for info. (*0-7475-3036-X*, Pub. by Blmsbury Pub) AMACOM.

Cook, Judith A., jt. ed. see Fonow, Mary M.

Cook, Julian A., Jr., et al. Federal Civil Procedure Before Trial in the 6th Circuit: Federal Practice Guide. LC 96-75688. (American Inns of Court Ser.). 2500p. 1996. text. write for info. (*0-7620-0050-3*) West Group.

Cook, K. M., tr. see Anikin, Andrei V.

***Cook, Karen, ed.** Trust in Society. 464p. 2000. 45.00 (*0-87154-248-X*) Russell Sage.

Cook, Karen, et al, eds. Sociological Perspectives on Social Psychology. LC 94-1890. 816p. 1994. 85.00 (*0-205-13716-4*) Allyn.

Cook, Karen S., ed. Social Exchange Theory. LC 86-6613. 248p. reprint ed. pap. 76.90 (*0-7837-6589-4*, 204615400011) Bks Demand.

C

***Cook, Karen S. & Hagan, John, eds.** Annual Review of Sociology, Vol. 25. LC 75-648500. 744p. 1999. 120.00 (*0-8243-2225-8*) Annual Reviews.

Cook, Karen S. & Levi, Margaret, eds. The Limits of Rationality. 432p. 1993. lib. bdg. 49.95 (*0-226-74238-5*) U Ch Pr.

— The Limits of Rationality. 438p. 1998. pap. text 23.95 (*0-226-74239-3*) U Ch Pr.

Cook, Karen S., jt. ed. see Borgatta, Edgar F.

Cook, Karen S., jt. ed. see Messick, David M.

Cook, Karin. What Girls Learn. LC 96-30315. 1997. 23.00 (*0-679-44828-4*) Pantheon.

— What Girls Learn. 1998. pap. 13.00 (*0-679-76944-7*) Random.

Cook, Kate. Wildlife Law & the Environment. (Environmental Law Ser.). 220p. 1995. 125.00 (*1-874698-01-5*, Pub. by Cameron May) Gaunt.

Cook, Kate, tr. see Lobanova, Marina.

***Cook, Kathleen N.** Cape Cod on My Mind. (America on My Mind Ser.). (Illus.). 2000. 32.95 (*1-56044-787-7*) Falcon Pub Inc.

— Grand Canyon on My Mind. (America on My Mind Ser.). (Illus.). 2000. 32.95 (*1-56044-969-1*) Falcon Pub Inc.

— Yosemite on My Mind. (America on My Mind Ser.). (Illus.). 2000. 32.95 (*1-56044-970-5*) Falcon Pub Inc.

Cook, Kathleen Norris, photos by. Spirit of the San Juans. LC 98-60195. (Illus.). 160p. 1998. 49.95 (*1-890437-10-7*) Western Reflections.

Cook, Kayci. In Pictures Death Valley: The Continuing Story. LC 89-80843. (Illus.). 48p. (Orig.). 1989. pap. 7.95 (*0-88714-039-4*) KC Pubns.

— In Pictures Death Valley: The Continuing Story. (GER., Illus.). 48p. (Orig.). 1990. pap. 8.95 (*0-88714-708-9*) KC Pubns.

— In Pictures Death Valley: The Continuing Story. Le Bras, Yvon, tr. (FRE., Illus.). 48p. (Orig.). 1990. pap. 8.95 (*0-88714-709-7*) KC Pubns.

— In Pictures Death Valley: The Continuing Story. Petzinger, Saori, tr. (JPN., Illus.). 48p. (Orig.). 1991. pap. 8.95 (*0-88714-710-0*) KC Pubns.

— In Pictures Death Valley: The Continuing Story. Comollo, Adriano, tr. (ITA., Illus.). 48p. (Orig.). 1993. pap. 8.95 (*0-88714-711-9*) KC Pubns.

Cook, Kaye V. & Bray-Garretson, Helen. Chaotic Eating: A Guide to Recovery From... 128p. 1992. pap. 8.99 (*0-310-57401-3*) Zondervan.

***Cook, Keith.** Paradise on the Plains. LC 98-75677. 258p. (Orig.). 1999. pap. 14.95 (*1-890622-61-3*) Leathers Pub.

Cook, Kelly F. & Kitchel, Dwain L. The Other Capri. (Illus.). 201p. (Orig.). 1992. pap. 10.00 (*1-882194-00-4*) TN Valley Pub.

Cook, Ken, Company Staff. International Small Craft Owners Manual. LC 98-70705. (Illus.). 224p. 1998. pap. text 5.95 (*0-9652491-4-X*) Ken Cook.

Cook, Kenneth. Play Little Victims. LC 79-303356. 1978. 8.00 (*0-08-023123-3*, Pergamon Pr) Elsevier.

Cook, Kenneth J. AMA Complete Guide to Small Business Marketing. (AMA Complete Guide to...Ser.). (Illus.). 192p. 1994. pap. 17.95 (*0-8442-3596-2*, NTC Business Bks) NTC Contemp Pub Co.

— AMA Complete Guide to Strategic Planning for Small Business. LC 93-42166. (Illus.). 204p. 1995. 29.95 (*0-8442-3587-3*, NTC Business Bks) NTC Contemp Pub Co.

— AMA Complete Guide to Strategic Planning for Small Business. (Illus.). 204p. 1995. pap. 17.95 (*0-8442-3585-7*, NTC Business Bks) NTC Contemp Pub Co.

— AMA Guide to Small Business Marketing. LC 92-18353. (AMA Complete Guide to...Ser.). (Illus.). 192p. 1994. 29.95 (*0-8442-3590-3*, NTC Business Bks) NTC Contemp Pub Co.

Cook, Kevin, jt. auth. see Woodard, Lynette.

Cook, Kevin, tr. see Dembinski, Pawe.

Cook, Kevin L. Dubester's U. S. Census Bibliography with SuDocs Class Numbers & Indexes. LC 95-43247. 450p. 1996. lib. bdg. 85.00 (*1-56308-295-0*) Libs Unl.

Cook, Kim. Communicate: A Guide to Basic PR for Christians. (C). 1989. 25.00 (*0-9510086-7-6*, Pub. by Jay Bks) St Mut.

Cook, Kimberly J. Divided Passions: Public Opinions on Abortion & the Death Penalty. LC 97-20960. 320p. 1997. text 45.00 (*1-55553-330-2*) NE U Pr.

Cook, Kirtley R. Beast of Balibago. unabridged ed. 260p. 1998. pap. 15.95 (*1-892896-57-5*) Buy Books.

***Cook, Kirtley R.** Oldman's Ordeal. 159p. 1999. pap. 13.95 (*0-7414-0127-4*) Buy Books.

Cook, Kristi, jt. auth. see Lowder, Eleanor A.

***Cook, Kristin & Williams, Lisa.** Wit & Whimsy. (Illus.). 30p. 1999. write for info. (*1-58050-085-4*, 40-6214) Provo Craft.

Cook, L. B. Bull Shoals Memories. (Illus.). 80p. 1997. pap. 10.95 (*0-9638648-4-X*) Barnabs Pub.

Cook, L. M. & Callow, R. S. Genetic & Ecological Diversity: The Sport of Nature. 2nd ed. (Illus.). 256p. 1999. pap. 42.50 (*0-7487-4336-7*) Standard Pub.

Cook, L. P. Transonic Aerodynamics: Problems in Asymptotic Theory. LC 93-3092. (Frontiers in Applied Mathematics Ser.: No. 12). x, 90p. 1993. pap. 33.00 (*0-89871-310-2*) Soc Indus-Appl Math.

Cook, L. P. & McMurdie, Howard F., eds. Phase Diagrams for Ceramists Vol. VII: Salts. 592p. 1989. 150.00 (*0-944904-04-1*, PH07) Am Ceramic.

Cook, L. P., jt. auth. see Cole, J. D.

Cook, L. Pamela, et al, eds. Mathematics Is for Solving Problems: A Volume in Honor of Julian Cole on his 70th Birthday. (Proceedings in Applied Mathematics Ser.: No. 84). xxxiv, 249p. 1996. pap. 52.50 (*0-89871-371-4*, PR84) Soc Indus-Appl Math.

Cook, Lanny K. & Cook, Clarice D. Wings of the Dawn. 181p. 1997. pap. write for info. (*1-57502-657-0*, PO1863) Morris Pubng.

Cook, Laurel O., ed. see Swanson, John H.

Cook, Lee. The Skull & Cross Bones Squadron: VF-17 in World War II. LC 97-80198. (Illus.). 240p. 1998. 45.00 (*0-7643-0475-5*) Schiffer.

Cook, Lee, jt. auth. see Cook, Marvin.

Cook, Lenora L. & Lodge, Helen C., eds. Voices in English Classrooms Vol. 28: Honoring Diversity & Change Classroom Practices in Teaching English. 247p. 1995. 14.95 (*0-8141-1645-0*) NCTE.

Cook, Leonard R. Computer Fundamentals. LC 99-96666. 19.95 (*0-533-13322-X*) Vantage.

Cook, LeRoy. One Hundred & One Things to Do with Your Private License. (Illus.). 224p. (Orig.). 1985. pap. 13.95 (*0-8306-2359-0*, 2359) McGraw-Hill Prof.

— One Hundred One Things to Do with Your Private License. 2nd ed. 256p. 1990. pap. 24.95 (*0-07-155914-0*) McGraw.

Cook, Lesley, ed. see Johnson, Adrianne & Hirst, Rachel.

Cook, Lewis C., ed. see Pollard, Stewart M.

Cook, Linda. Night Fires. (Zebra Bks.). 352p. 1998. mass mkt. 4.99 (*0-8217-6043-2*, Zebra Kensgtn) Kensgtn Pub Corp.

Cook, Linda J. Labor & Liberalization: Trade Unions in the New Russia. LC 97-8847. 129p. (C). 1997. pap. 9.95 (*0-87078-377-7*) Century Foundation.

— The Soviet Social Contract & Why It Failed: Welfare Policy & Workers' Politics from Brezhnev to Yeltsin. LC 93-19068. (Russian Research Center Studies: No. 86). (Illus.). 272p. 1994. text 51.95 (*0-674-82800-3*) HUP.

***Cook, Liz & Rothwell, Brian.** The X & Y of Leadership: How Men & Women Make a Difference at Work. 224p. 2000. pap. 19.95 (*1-85835-895-7*, Indust Soc) Stylus Pub VA.

Cook, Lloyd A., ed. Toward Better Human Relations. LC 70-90626. (Essay Index Reprint Ser.). 1977. 19.95 (*0-8369-1284-5*) Ayer.

Cook, Lori A., ed. see Cook, Ralph T.

Cook, Lurana H., et al. Provincetown Massachusetts Cemetery Inscriptions. 255p. (Orig.). 1980. pap. 20.00 (*0-917890-18-3*) Heritage Bk.

Cook, Lyndon. David Whitmer Interviews. 277p. (C). 1994. 18.95 (*0-910523-38-X*) Grandin Bk Co.

— Nauvoo Deaths & Marriages. 145p. (C). 1994. 29.95 (*0-910523-08-8*) Grandin Bk Co.

— William Law: Nauvoo, Dissenter. 164p. (C). 1994. 16.95 (*0-910523-01-0*) Grandin Bk Co.

— Words of Joseph Smith: Nauvoo Contemporary Accounts. 468p. (C). 1993. 24.95 (*0-910523-39-8*) Grandin Bk Co.

Cook, Lyndon & Backman, Milton V., Jr. Kirtland Elders Quorum Record. 136p. (C). 1991. 9.95 (*0-910523-10-X*) Grandin Bk Co.

Cook, Lyndon W. Joseph Smith & the Law of Consecration. 100p. 1985. 8.95 (*0-910523-24-X*) Grandin Bk Co.

— Joseph Smith & the Law of Consecration. (Personal Enrichment Ser.). 99p. 1991. pap. write for info. (*0-929985-77-X*) Jackman Pubng.

Cook, Lynn. A Canadian ABC: An Alphabet Book for Kids. (Illus.). 60p. (J). 1990. pap. 8.95 (*0-921254-24-5*, Pub. by Penumbra Pr) U of Toronto Pr.

Cook, Lynn, jt. auth. see Choy, Sam.

***Cook-Lynn, Elizabeth.** Aurelia: A Crow Creek Trilogy. LC 99-44821. 416p. 1999. 27.50 (*0-87081-539-3*) Univ Pr Colo.

Cook-Lynn, Elizabeth. I Remember the Fallen Trees: New & Selected Poems. LC 98-39668. 1998. write for info. (*0-910055-46-7*); pap. 15.95 (*0-910055-45-9*) East Wash Univ.

— Why I Can't Read Wallace Stegner & Other Essays: A Tribal Voice. LC 96-18557. 172p. 1996. pap. 17.95 (*0-299-15144-1*) U of Wis Pr.

Cook-Lynn, Elizabeth, jt. auth. see Gonzalez, Mario.

Cook, M., ed. Beaumarchais: Le Barbier de Seville. (French Texts Ser.). (FRE.). 152p. 1994. pap. 18.95 (*1-85399-384-0*, Pub. by Brist Class Pr) Focus Pub-R Pullins.

Cook, M. & Vallese, R. Faction War. 128p. 1998. 19.95 (*0-7869-1203-0*, Pub. by TSR Inc) Random.

Cook, M. A., ed. Studies in the Economic History of the Middle East: From the Rise of Islam to the Present Day. 1970. 32.00 (*0-19-713561-7*) OUP.

Cook, M. C., ed. Dialogues Revolutionnaires EFT. (Exeter French Texts Ser.: No. 89). (FRE.). 90p. pap. text 19.95 (*0-85989-399-5*, Pub. by Univ Exeter Pr) Northwestern U Pr.

Cook, M. Garfield. Cornerstones of the Restoration. LC 98-73936. 144 p. 1998. write for info. (*1-56713-325-8*) APP.

Cook, M. J. Cook on Costs - A Guide to Legal Remuneration in Civil Contentious & Non-Contentious Business. 406p. 1991. pap. 63.00 (*0-406-00460-9*, UK, MICHIE) LEXIS Pub.

Cook, M. V. Flight Dynamics Principles. 379p. pap. text 54.95 (*0-340-63200-3*, Pub. by E A) OUP.

— Flight Dynamics Principles. LC 98-100252. 379p. 1997. pap. 75.00 (*0-470-23590-X*) Wiley.

Cook, M. V. & Rycroft, Michael J., eds. Aerospace Vehicle Dynamics & Control: Based on the Proceedings of a Conference Organized by the Institute of Mathematics & Its Applications on Aerospace Vehicle Dynamics & Control, Held at the Cranfield Institute of Technology, September 1992. LC 93-35620. (Institute of Mathematics & Its Applications Conference Series, New Ser.: Vol. 47). (Illus.). 448p. (C). 1994. text 145.00 (*0-19-853473-6*, Clarendon Pr) OUP.

Cook, Malcolm. Fictional France: Social Reality in the French Novel, 1775-1800. (French Studies). 160p. 1993. 37.50 (*0-85496-765-6*) Berg Pubs.

***Cook, Malcolm.** 101 Youth Soccer Drills. (Illus.). 128p. (J). (gr. 2-5). 1999. pap. 14.95 (*1-890946-22-2*) Reedswain.

— 101 Youth Soccer Drills. (Illus.). 128p. (YA). (gr. 7-11). 1999. pap. 14.95 (*1-890946-23-0*) Reedswain.

— Soccer Training Games: Drills & Fitness Practices. (Illus.). 126p. 1999. pap. 14.95 (*1-890946-19-2*) Reedswain.

Cook, Malcolm. Soccer Coaching & Team Management. 2nd ed. (Illus.). 128p. 1998. pap. 18.95 (*0-7136-4458-3*) A & C Blk.

***Cook, Malcolm, et al, eds.** Journalisme et Fiction au 18e Siecle. (French Studies of the Eighteenth & Nineteenth Centuries). 241p. 1999. 49.95 (*0-8204-4221-6*) P Lang Pubng.

***Cook, Malcolm & Davie, Grace, eds.** Modern France: Society in Transition. LC 98-21808. 279p. 1999. pap. 22.99 (*0-415-15432-4*) Routledge.

***Cook, Malcolm & Jourdan, Annie, eds.** Journalisme et Fiction au 18e Siecle. 241p. 1999. 49.95 (*3-906761-50-9*, Pub. by P Lang) P Lang Pubng.

Cook, Malcolm, jt. auth. see Whitehead, Nick.

Cook, Malcolm, ed. see Langford, Rachael.

Cook, Manuela. Portuguese: A Complete Course for Beginners. (POR., Illus.). 240p. 1995. pap. 12.95 (*0-8442-3819-8*, Teach Yrslf) NTC Contemp Pub Co.

— Teach Yourself Portuguese. (Teach Yourself Ser.). 1992. 14.95 (*0-8288-8379-3*) Fr & Eur.

— Teach Yourself Portuguese: Quick & Easy. (Teach Yourself Ser.). 1992. 12.95 (*0-8288-8382-3*); 29.95 incl. audio (*0-8288-8381-5*) Fr & Eur.

— Teach Yourself Portuguese Complete Course. (Teach Yourself Ser.). (POR.). 240p. 1995. pap. 21.95 incl. audio (*0-8442-3869-4*, Teach Yrslf) NTC Contemp Pub Co.

— Teach Yourself Portuguese Pack. (Teach Yourself Ser.). 1992. 37.95 (*0-8288-8380-7*) Fr & Eur.

Cook, Marc. Accessories for Harley-Davidson Motorcycles. LC 98-26271. (Illus.). 192p. 1998. 29.95 (*0-9649722-7-1*) D Bull.

Cook, Marcy. Daily Math Adventures. 1987. pap. 9.50 (*0-201-48001-8*) Addison-Wesley.

— Daily Math Adventures. (Illus.). 64p. (J). (gr. 3-8). 1987. pap. text 9.50 (*0-914040-51-0*) Cuisenaire.

— Numbers & Words: A Problem Per Day. (J). (gr. 4-7). 1995. pap. 9.50 (*0-201-48002-6*) Addison-Wesley.

— Numbers & Words: A Problem Per Day. (Illus.). 64p. 1987. pap. text 9.50 (*0-914040-52-9*) Cuisenaire.

***Cook, Margaret.** Slight & Delicate Creature. 1999. 45.00 (*0-297-84293-5*, Pub. by Weidenfeld & Nicolson) Trafalgar.

Cook, Margaret, tr. see Couliano, Ioan P.

Cook, Margaret, tr. see Detienne, Marcel.

Cook, Margaret G. The New Library Key. 3rd ed. LC 75-11754. (Illus.). 264p. (C). 1975. pap. 10.00 (*0-8242-0541-3*) Wilson.

Cook, Margarite, jt. auth. see Hawk, Diane.

Cook, Margie. Ways You Can Help. (Orig.). 1995. pap. write for info. (*0-446-60227-2*) Warner Bks.

— Ways You Can Help. (Orig.). 1995. pap. write for info. (*0-446-67149-5*) Warner Bks.

Cook, Maria L. Organizing Dissent: The Politics of Protest in the Mexican Teachers' Union. LC 95-26109. 1996. 60.00 (*0-271-01560-8*); pap. 19.95 (*0-271-01561-6*) Pa St U Pr.

Cook, Maria L. & Katz, Harry C., eds. Regional Integration & Industrial Relations in North America. LC 94-23338. 1994. pap. 29.95 (*0-87546-851-9*, ILR Press) Cornell U Pr.

***Cook, Mariana.** Couples: Speaking from the Heart. (Illus.). 2000. 40.00 (*0-8118-2873-5*) Chronicle Bks.

Cook, Mariana, photos by. Fathers & Daughters: In Their Own Words. LC 93-31739. (Illus.). 132p. 1994. 40.00 (*0-8118-0648-0*); pap. 22.95 (*0-8118-0619-7*) Chronicle Bks.

— Generations of Women: In Their Own Words. (Illus.). 108p. 1998. 27.50 (*0-8118-1907-8*) Chronicle Bks.

— Mothers & Sons: In Their Own Words. LC 95-30152. (Illus.). 132p. 1996. 40.00 (*0-8118-1194-8*); pap. 22.95 (*0-8118-1170-0*) Chronicle Bks.

***Cook, Mariana Ruth.** Couples: Speaking from the Heart. LC 00-31503. 2000. pap. write for info. (*0-8118-2874-3*) Chronicle Bks.

Cook, Mariss. Club Venus. Scherer, Judy, ed. LC 97-90130. 64p. (Orig.). 1997. pap. 6.95 (*0-9657569-0-4*) Edgewater Pub.

Cook, Mark. Levels of Personality. 2nd ed. LC 88-47779. 276p. 1993. 85.00 (*0-304-32425-6*); pap. 40.00 (*0-304-32438-8*) Weidner & Sons.

— Personnel Selection: Adding Value Through People. 3rd ed. LC 97-44532. 366p. 1998. pap. 37.00 (*0-471-98158-3*) Wiley.

Cook, Mark. Personnel Selection: Adding Value Through People. 3rd ed. LC 97-44532. 366p. 1998. 87.95 (*0-471-98156-7*) Wiley.

Cook, Mark, jt. auth. see Piggott, Judith.

Cook, Mark, jt. ed. see Piggott, Judith.

Cook, Marshall. Adams Streetwise Time Management. LC 98-50808. 1999. pap. 17.95 (*1-58062-131-7*) Adams Media.

— Hometown Series. 1994. pap. 11.95 (*1-886028-01-X*) Savage Pr.

— Hometown Wisconsin. (Hometown Ser.). 1994. pap. 11.95 (*1-886028-02-8*) Savage Pr.

Cook, Marshall, ed. Wisconsin Fiction: Wisconsin Sesquicentennial Issue. 144p. 1997. pap. 12.95 (*1-882280-01-6*) WI Acad Sci.

Cook, Marshall J. Adams Time Managment. LC 97-46962. 304p. 1998. pap. 9.95 (*1-55850-799-X*) Adams Media.

— Effective Coaching. LC 98-41551. (Briefcase Bks.). (Illus.). 186p. 1998. pap. 14.95 (*0-07-071864-4*) McGraw.

— Freeing Your Creativity: A Writer's Guide. 176p. 1995. pap. 14.99 (*0-89879-664-4*, Wrtrs Digest Bks) F & W Pubns Inc.

— How to Handle Worry: A Catholic Approach. LC 99-25895. 128p. 1999. pap. 5.95 (*0-8198-3379-7*) Pauline Bks.

— Leads & Conclusions. LC 94-23650. (Elements of Article Writing Ser.). 176p. 1995. 15.99 (*0-89879-661-X*, Wrtrs Digest Bks) F & W Pubns Inc.

— Ten Minute Guide to Motivating People. 144p. 1997. 10.95 (*0-02-861738-X*) Macmillan Gen Ref.

***Cook, Marshall J.** 10 Minute Guide to Motivating People. 2nd ed. 168p. 2000. pap. text 10.95 (*0-02-863612-0*) Macmillan.

Cook, Marshall J. Writing for the Joy of It. 134p. (Orig.). 1990. pap. 7.95 (*0-9625546-0-X*) Will Beymer Pr.

— The Year of the Buffalo: A Novel of Love & Minor League Baseball. (Illus.). 160p. (Orig.). 1997. pap. 13.95 (*1-886028-22-2*) Savage Pr.

Cook, Marshall J., jt. auth. see Camenson, Blythe.

Cook, Martha, ed. Colorado Court Rules: September 1998 Update. 150p. 1998. ring bd. write for info. (*0-327-05798-X*, 41039-33, MICHIE) LEXIS Pub.

Cook, Martin. The Birds of Moray & Nairn. 280p. 1989. pap. 60.00 (*1-873644-05-1*, Pub. by Mercat Pr Bks) St Mut.

***Cook, Martin.** Medieval Bridges. (Archaeology Ser.: Vol. 77). (Illus.). 1999. pap. text 10.50 (*0-7478-0384-6*, Pub. by Shire Pubns) Parkwest Pubns.

Cook, Martin, ed. French Culture Since 1945. LC 92-28669. 327p. (C). 1995. pap. 53.00 (*0-582-08806-2*, 79860) Addison-Wesley.

Cook, Martin L., jt. auth. see Gelber, Steven M.

Cook, Marvin & Cook, Lee. Blue Goose Passport. (Illus.). 256p. 1999. 5.95 (*0-9671292-0-6*) Wilderness Graph.

Cook, Mary. Consulting on the Side: How to Start a Part-Time Consulting Business While Still Working at Your Full-Time Job. LC 95-46269. 242p. 1996. pap. 19.95 (*0-471-12029-4*) Wiley.

— Consulting on the Side: How to Start a Part-Time Consulting Business While Still Working at Your Full-Time Job. LC 95-46269. 256p. 1996. 59.95 (*0-471-12028-6*) Wiley.

Cook, Mary A. Traditional Portuguese Recipes from Provincetown. 2nd rev. ed. Drake, Gillian, ed. LC 97-40526. (Illus.). 96p. 1997. 9.50 (*0-9609814-3-8*) Shank Painter Pub.

Cook, Mary F. Human Resource Director's Handbook. LC 83-17810. 320p. 1984. text 59.95 (*0-13-445859-1*, Busn) P-H.

— The Human Resource Manager's Daily Planner, 1988. 272p. 1988. text 32.50 (*0-13-445883-4*, Busn) P-H.

— Outsourcing Human Resources Functions: Strategies for Providing Enhanced HR Services at Lower Cost. LC 98-26302. 350p. 1998. 107.95 (*0-8144-0419-7*) AMACOM.

— Personnel Manager's Portfolio of Model Letters. LC 84-15065. 198p. 1984. 60.00 (*0-13-659251-1*, Busn) P-H.

Cook, Marylou. Now That You Are Grandparents. (Christian Living Ser.). 40p. 1988. pap. 3.50 (*0-8341-1242-6*) Beacon Hill.

Cook, Matthew & Duncan, Paul. The British Season. LC 96-137230. (Illus.). 128p. 1995. write for info. (*0-316-90986-6*) Little.

Cook, Meira. The Blood Girls. LC 99-10236. 215p. 1999. 22.95 (*0-87951-945-2*, Pub. by Overlook Pr) Penguin Putnam.

— A Fine Grammar of Bones. 1997. pap. 7.95 (*0-88801-171-7*, Pub. by Turnstone Pr) Genl Dist Srvs.

— Toward a Catalogue of Falling. 112p. 1996. pap. 12.95 (*0-919626-88-2*, Pub. by Brick Bks) Genl Dist Srvs.

Cook, Mel. Home Business, Big Business. rev. ed. LC 98-13889. 304p. 1998. 14.95 (*0-02-862252-9*) Macmillan.

Cook, Melissa. Building Enterprise Information Architectures. 1996. 25.95 (*0-614-14489-2*) P-H.

— Las Vegas Weddings: A Guide for Every Bride. (Illus.). 150p. 1999. pap. 12.95 (*0-929712-80-3*) Huntington Pr.

— Reengineering Information Systems. 224p. (C). 1996. pap. text 29.95 (*0-13-440256-1*) P-H.

Cook, Melvin A. The Science of High Explosives. LC 58-10260. (ACS Monograph Ser.: Vol. 139). (Illus.). 455p. reprint ed. pap. 141.10 (*0-608-06937-X*, 206714500009) Bks Demand.

Cook, Mercer. Five French Negro Authors. 1990. 15.00 (*0-87498-026-7*) Assoc Pubs DC.

Cook, Mercer, ed. & tr. see Diop, Cheikh Anta.

***Cook, Michael.** Commanding Right & Forbidding Wrong in Islamic Thought. LC 99-54807. 800p. 2000. write for info. (*0-521-66174-9*) Cambridge U Pr.

Cook, Michael. Empowering Women: Critical Views on the Beijing Conference. LC 95-217235. 167 p. 1995. write for info. (*1-86315-092-7*) Little Hills.

— Illustrated Jaguar Buyers Guide. (Illustrated Buyer's Guide Ser.). (Illus.). 160p. 1996. pap. 17.95 (*0-7603-0169-7*) MBI Pubg.

— Information Management & Archival Data. LC 93-159994. (Illus.). 224p. reprint ed. pap. 69.50 (*0-608-20967-8*, 207183900002) Bks Demand.

— Jacob's Wake. 144p. 1975. reprint ed. pap. 12.95 (*0-88922-097-2*, Pub. by Talonbks) Genl Dist Srvs.

***Cook, Michael.** The Koran: A Very Short Introduction. LC 99-57686. (Illus.). 144p. 2000. pap. 8.95 (*0-19-285344-9*) OUP.

Cook, Michael. The Management of Information from Archives. LC 98-32250. 1999. 96.95 (*0-566-07993-3*) Ashgate Pub Co.

— Maximum Distrust: Unusual Stories of Injustice,

C

An Asterisk (*) at the beginning of an entry indicates that the title is appearing for the first time.

Unbalanced Thinking & Mob Psychology in America. LC 96-25970. (Illus.). 181p. (Orig.). 1998. pap. 18.95 (*1-56072-341-6*, Nova Kroshka Bks) Nova Sci Pubs.
— Muhammad. (Past Masters Ser.). (Illus.). 96p. 1983. pap. text 9.95 (*0-19-287605-8*) OUP.
— Tiln & Other Plays. 1976p. 1976. pap. 11.95 (*0-88922-107-3*, Pub. by Talonbks) Genl Dist Srvs.
Cook, Michael, et al, eds. Butterworths Costs Service. ring bd. write for info. (*0-406-99644-X*, BCS1ASET, MICHIE) LEXIS Pub.
— Butterworths Costs Service, 2 vols. 1991. ring bd. 420.00 (*0-406-10749-1*, UK, MICHIE) LEXIS Pub.
Cook, Michael & Procter, Margaret. A Mad User Guide. 1989. text 19.95 (*0-566-03621-5*) Ashgate Pub Co.
Cook, Michael, jt. auth. see King, Lawrence.
Cook, Michael, jt. auth. see Procter, Margaret.
Cook, Michael B., contrib. by. A Plain English Guide to the EPA Part 503 Biosolids Rule. (Illus.). 176p. (C). 1998. reprint ed. pap. text 40.00 (*0-7881-4260-7*) DIANE Pub.
***Cook, Michael B., ed.** Combined Sewer Overflows: Guidance for Financial Capability Assessment & Schedule Development. 59p. (C). 1999. pap. text 20.00 (*0-7881-8545-4*) DIANE Pub.
Cook, Michael J. Cook on Costs: Guide to Legal Remuneration in Civil Contentious & Non-Contentious Business. 2nd ed. LC 95-171301. 1995. pap. write for info. (*0-406-04807-X*, CC2, MICHIE) LEXIS Pub.
Cook, Michael J., ed. Bankruptcy Litigation Manual, 1994-1995. LC 94-40149. 1994. ring bd. write for info. (*0-13-361908-7*) Aspen Law.
Cook, Michael L. Bankruptcy Litigation Manual: 1995-96 Edition. 1996. write for info. (*1-56706-290-3*) Panel Pubs.
— Christology As Narrative Quest. LC 96-51701. 256p. (Orig.). 1997. pap. 21.95 (*0-8146-5854-7*, M Glazier) Liturgical Pr.
— Dime Novel Roundup: Annotated Index 1931-1981. LC 82-73847. 1983. 13.95 (*0-87972-227-4*); pap. 7.95 (*0-87972-228-2*) Bowling Green Univ Popular Press.
— Mystery, Detective, & Espionage Magazines. LC 82-20977. (Historical Guides to the World's Periodicals & Newspapers Ser.). 793p. 1983. lib. bdg. 105.00 (*0-313-23310-1*, CMD/, Greenwood Pr) Greenwood.
— Mystery Fanfare: A Composite Annotated Index to Mystery & Related Fanzines 1963-1981. LC 82-73848. 1983. pap. 13.95 (*0-87972-230-4*) Bowling Green Univ Popular Press.
— Responses to One Hundred One Questions about Jesus. LC 93-25492. 144p. (Orig.). 1993. pap. 8.95 (*0-8091-3428-4*) Paulist Pr.
Cook, Michael L., ed. Bankruptcy Litigation Manual. 725p. 1988. write for info. (*0-318-65475-X*, P05654) P-H.
— Bankruptcy Litigation Manual. annuals 1065p. ring bd. 165.00 (*1-56706-733-6*, 63350) Panel Pubs.
— Monthly Murders: A Checklist & Chronological Listing of Fiction in the Digest-size Mystery Magazines in the United States & England. LC 81-6986. 1147p. 1982. lib. bdg. 69.50 (*0-313-23126-5*, CMM/, Greenwood Pr) Greenwood.
Cook, Michael L. & Ross, Wilbur L. Workouts & Bankruptcy Reorganization Workshop. 265p. write for info. (*0-318-61659-9*) Harcourt.
Cook, Michael L., jt. auth. see King, Lawrence P.
Cook, Michael L., jt. auth. see Miller, Harvey R.
Cook, Molly. Roach Motel. LC 98-10142. 13p. (J). (ps-3). 1996. pap. 1.95 (*1-56763-170-3*) Ozark Pub.
Cook, Monica, jt. auth. see Cook, Joe.
***Cook, Monica Hay.** Kickin' up Some Cowboy Fun: 130 Activities for Cowboys & Cowgirls. LC 99-91466. (Illus.). 144p. (J). (gr. k-7). 1999. pap. 14.95 (*0-9662738-1-8*) Monjeu Pr.
***Cook, Monte.** Dungeon Master's Guide. 224p. 2000. 19.95 (*0-7869-1551-X*) Wizards Coast.
Cook, Monte. Glass Prison. (Forgotten Realms Ser.). 1999. pap. 5.99 (*0-7869-1343-6*, Pub. by TSR Inc) Random.
— A Paladin in Hell. 1998. 0.13 (*0-7869-1210-3*, Pub. by TSR Inc) Random.
— The Planewalker's Handbook. 1996. 20.00 (*0-7869-0460-7*, Pub. by TSR Inc) Random.
— Vecna Reborn. 64p. 1998. 13.95 (*0-7869-1201-4*, Pub. by TSR Inc) Random.
Cook, Monte & McComb, Colin. The Great Modron March. (Planescape Game World Ser.). 1997. 24.95 (*0-7869-0648-0*, Pub. by TSR Inc) Random.
Cook, N. D. Stability & Flexibility: An Analysis of Natural Systems. (Systems Science & World Order Library). (Illus.). 246p. 1982. 32.00 (*0-317-66881-1*, Pub. by Pergamon Repr) Franklin.
Cook, Nancy. Classifying Fingerprints. Stenstedt, Katarina, ed. (Real-World Mathematics Through Science Ser.). 112p. (Orig.). (YA). (gr. 6-8). 1995. pap. 18.95 (*0-201-49310-1*) Supplementary Div.
— In the Pharmacy. Stenstedt, Katarina, ed. (Real-World Mathematics Through Science Ser.). 112p. (Orig.). (YA). (gr. 6-8). 1994. pap. 18.95 (*0-201-86123-2*) Supplementary Div.
— Measuring Earthquakes. Stenstedt, Katarina, ed. (Real-World Mathematics Through Science Ser.). 87p. (Orig.). (YA). (gr. 6-8). 1994. pap. 18.95 (*0-201-86122-4*) Supplementary Div.
— Secret Codes. Gideon, Joan, ed. (Real-World Mathematics Through Science Ser.). (Illus.). 136p. (Orig.). (J). (gr. 6-8). 1996. pap. text 18.95 (*0-201-49607-0*, 22733) Seymour Pubns.
Cook, Nancy & Hermann, Michele G. Criminal Defense Checklists LC 95-124652. xiv, 279 p. 1994. write for info. (*0-87632-204-6*) West Group.
Cook, Nancy & Johnson, Christine V. Measuring Dinosaurs. Anderson, Cathy & Stenstedt, Katarina, eds. (Real-World Mathematics Through Science Ser.). 127p. (Orig.). (J). (gr. 6-8). 1995. pap. 24.95 (*0-201-49312-8*) Addison-Wesley.
Cook, Nicholas. Analysing Musical Multimedia. LC 97-2414. (Illus.). 292p. 1998. text 65.00 (*0-19-816589-7*) OUP.
***Cook, Nicholas.** Analysing Musical Multimedia. (Illus.). 296p. 2000. pap. 19.95 (*0-19-816737-7*) OUP.
Cook, Nicholas. Analysis Through Composition: Principles of the Classical Style. LC 94-44695. (Illus.). 258p. 1997. spiral bd. 38.00 (*0-19-879013-9*) OUP.
— Beethoven "Symphony No. 9" LC 92-20451. (Cambridge Music Handbooks Ser.). 143p. (C). 1993. pap. text 12.95 (*0-521-39924-6*) Cambridge U Pr.
— Guide to Music Analysis. (C). 1992. pap. text 16.00 (*0-393-96255-5*, Norton Paperbks) Norton.
— Music: A Very Short Introduction. LC 98-12197. (Very Short Introductions Ser.). (Illus.). 156p. 1998. pap. 8.95 (*0-19-285340-6*) OUP.
— Music, Imagination & Culture. (Illus.). 272p. 1992. pap. text 21.00 (*0-19-816303-7*) OUP.
Cook, Nicholas & Everist, Mark, eds. Rethinking Music. (Illus.). 592p. 1999. pap. text 29.95 (*0-19-879004-X*) OUP.
— Rethinking Music. (Illus.). 592p. 1999. text 110.00 (*0-19-879003-1*) OUP.
***Cook, Nicholas, et al.** Theory into Practice: Composition, Performance & the Listening Experience: Collected Writings of the Orpheus Institute. (Illus.). 120p. 1999. pap. 35.00 (*90-6186-994-3*, Pub. by Leuven Univ) Coronet Bks.
Cook, Nick. Aggressor. 1993. 239.40 (*0-312-07925-7*) St Martin.
***Cook, Nick.** Downhill In-Line Skating. LC 99-53303. (Extreme Sports Ser.). (Illus.). 50p. (YA). (gr. 5 up). 2000. lib. bdg. 21.26 (*0-7368-0482-X*, Capstone Bks) Capstone Pr.
Cook, Nick. Roller Coasters: or I Had So Much Fun, I Almost Puked. LC 97-14394. (J). 1997. 22.60 (*1-57505-071-4*, Carolrhoda) Lerner Pub.
***Cook, Nick.** The World's Fastest Boats. LC 00-22397. (Built for Speed Ser.). (Illus.). 48p. (YA). (gr. 5 up). 2000. lib. bdg. 21.26 (*0-7368-0569-9*, Capstone Bks) Capstone Pr.
— The World's Fastest Cars. (Built for Speed Ser.). 48p. (YA). (gr. 5 up). 2000. lib. bdg. 21.26 (*0-7368-0570-2*, Capstone Bks) Capstone Pr.
Cook, Nigel P. Electronics. 1996. pap. text, lab manual ed. 35.00 (*0-13-268228-1*) P-H.
— A First Course in Digital Electronics. LC 98-19390. 814p. (C). 1998. 90.00 (*0-13-779836-9*) P-H.
— Introductory DC-AC Electronics. 4th ed. LC 98-14637. 1080p. (C). 1998. 99.00 (*0-13-896044-5*) P-H.
— Introductory Digital Electronics. LC 97-10713. (Illus.). 719p. (C). 1997. 99.00 (*0-675-21334-7*, Merrill Coll) P-H.
— Introductory Mathematics. 2nd ed. LC 97-1557. 257p. 1997. pap. 35.40 (*0-13-270018-2*) P-H.
***Cook, Nigel P.** Introductory Mathematics. 3rd ed. LC 99-58689. 320p. 2000. 34.67 incl. cd-rom (*0-13-016132-2*) P-H.
— Introductory Semiconductor Electronics. LC 95-14481. 1168p. 1995. 105.00 (*0-13-249855-3*) P-H.
Cook, Nigel P. Practical Electricity. 464p. (C). 1996. 63.00 (*0-13-243296-X*) P-H.
— Practical Electronics. 447p. (C). 1996. 63.00 (*0-13-243304-4*) P-H.
Cook, Nigel S. Potassium Channels: Structure, Classification, Function & Therapeutic Potential. 1990. text 123.00 (*0-470-21605-0*) P-H.
Cook, Noble D. Born to Die: Disease & New World Conquest (1492-1650) LC 97-25064. (New Approaches to the Americas Ser.). (Illus.). 272p. (C). 1998. text 54.95 (*0-521-62208-5*); pap. text 15.95 (*0-521-62730-3*) Cambridge U Pr.
— Demographic Collapse: Indian Peru, 1520-1620. LC 81-9950. (Cambridge Latin American Studies: No. 41). (Illus.). 320p. 1982. text 85.00 (*0-521-23995-8*) Cambridge U Pr.
Cook, Noble D. & Lovell, W. George, eds. Secret Judgments of God: Old World Disease in Colonial Spanish America. LC 91-50301. (Civilization of the American Indian Ser.: Vol. 205). (Illus.). 256p. 1992. 29.95 (*0-8061-2372-9*) U of Okla Pr.
Cook, Noble D., jt. auth. see Cook, Alexandra P.
Cook, Norma B., jt. auth. see Fisher, Fran.
Cook, Norman D. The Brain Code Mechanisms of Information Transfer & the Role of the Corpus Callosum. 300p. 1986. 42.50 (*0-416-40840-0*, 9834) Routledge.
Cook, Olive. English Cathedrals. (Illus.). 285p. 1990. 40.00 (*0-906969-62-X*, NAB) I R Dee.
Cook, Olive & Hutton, Graham. English Parish Churches. LC 78-55192. (World of Art Ser.). (Illus.). 252p. 1989. reprint ed. pap. 14.95 (*0-500-20139-0*, Pub. by Thames Hudson) Norton.
Cook, Olive R. Trails to Poosey. LC 86-8602. (Illus.). 200p. (Orig.). (J). (gr. 3-6). 1986. pap. 5.95 (*0-930079-01-9*) Misty Hill Pr.
Cook, P., et al. Archigram. (Illus.). 144p. 1991. pap. 44.00 (*0-8176-2447-3*, Pub. by Birkhauser) Princeton Arch.
Cook, P. A. Nonlinear Dynamical Systems. 2nd ed. LC 93-42976. (Series in Systems & Control Engineering). (C). 1994. pap. text 50.00 (*0-13-625161-7*) P-H Intl.
Cook, P. Dan, jt. ed. see Sanghvi, Yogesh S.
Cook, Paddy. Drugs & Pregnancy: It's Not Worth the Risk. rev. ed. LC 86-70944. 36p. 1991. pap. 3.00 (*0-942348-17-6*) Am Council Drug Ed.
Cook, Paddy S., et al. Alcohol, Tobacco & Other Drugs May Harm the Unborn. Haase, Tineke B., ed. 80p. (Orig.). (C). 1993. pap. text 20.00 (*1-56806-548-5*) DIANE Pub.
Cook, Pam. Fashioning the Nation: Costume & Identity in British Cinema. (Distributed for the British Film Institute Ser.). (Illus.). 152p. 1996. 49.95 (*0-85170-469-7*, Pub. by British Film Inst); pap. 19.95 (*0-85170-574-X*, Pub. by British Film Inst) Ind U Pr.
Cook, Pam, ed. The Cinema Book. (Illus.). 384p. 1992. pap. 35.00 (*0-85170-144-2*, Pub. by British Film Inst) Ind U Pr.
***Cook, Pam & Bernink, Mieke, eds.** The Cinema Book. 2nd expanded rev. ed. (British Film Institute Ser.). 1999. 75.00 (*0-85170-729-7*); pap. 35.00 (*0-85170-726-2*) Ind U Pr.
Cook, Pam & Dodd, Philip, eds. Women & Film: A Sight & Sound Reader. LC 93-31694. (Culture & the Moving Image Ser.). 320p. 1993. pap. 22.95 (*1-56639-143-1*) Temple U Pr.
— Women & Film: A Sight & Sound Reader. LC 93-31694. (Culture & the Moving Image Ser.). 320p. 1994. text 69.95 (*1-56639-142-3*) Temple U Pr.
Cook, Pamela J., ed. see Cook, Stephen P.
Cook, Pat. Baker's Dozen. 31p. 1989. pap. 3.50 (*0-87129-696-9*, B62) Dramatic Pub.
— Boo! Thirteen Scenes from Halloween. 1994. 5.50 (*0-87129-436-2*, B77) Dramatic Pub.
— The Christmas Express. 1995. 5.50 (*0-87129-562-8*, C45) Dramatic Pub.
— Clockwork. 67p. 1990. pap. 5.50 (*0-87129-007-3*, C76) Dramatic Pub.
— Dad's Christmas Miracle. 1993. pap. 5.50 (*0-87129-212-2*, D55) Dramatic Pub.
— Death & Taxes. 1994. 5.50 (*0-87129-409-5*, D60) Dramatic Pub.
— Every Little Crook & Nanny. 1995. pap. 8.99 (*0-8341-9436-8*, MP-775) Lillenas.
— The Great Pandemonium. 28p. 1996. pap. 3.50 (*0-87129-746-9*, G61) Dramatic Pub.
— Honeymoon at Graveside Manor. 1993. pap. 5.50 (*0-87129-236-X*, H64) Dramatic Pub.
— If It's Monday, This Must Be Murder! 1994. 5.50 (*0-87129-448-6*, I52) Dramatic Pub.
— If the Good Lord's Willing & the Creek Don't Rise: A Comedy in Two-Acts. 1995. pap. 8.99 (*0-8341-9289-6*, MP-764) Lillenas.
— In Praise of Miss Brown. 1997. 8.99 (*0-8341-9651-4*, MP-807) Lillenas.
— It's Murder in the Wings. 80p. 1991. pap. 5.50 (*0-87129-119-3*, I46) Dramatic Pub.
— Just a Stage He's Going Through. 28p. 1996. pap. 3.50 (*0-87129-648-9*, J25) Dramatic Pub.
— The Long Red Herring. LC 94-226409. 1994. 5.50 (*0-87129-336-6*, L78) Dramatic Pub.
— The Middleton Zephyr. 1995. 5.50 (*0-87129-501-6*, M89) Dramatic Pub.
— Much Ado about Murder: Audience Plays Detective. (Illus.). 64p. 1988. pap. 4.50 (*0-88680-282-2*) I E Clark.
— Murder's Bad But Monday Can Kill You! 79p. (YA). (gr. 10 up). 1998. pap. 5.60 (*0-87129-866-X*, MA8) Dramatic Pub.
— Old Faith, Hope & Charityy: A Two-Act Comedy with Lots of Heart. 1998. pap. 8.99 (*0-8341-9087-7*) Lillenas.
— Pandora's Revenge. 27p. (J). 1998. pap. 3.50 (*0-87129-859-7*, P64) Dramatic Pub.
— Rest in Peace. 34p. 1976. pap. 3.50 (*0-87129-672-1*, R14) Dramatic Pub.
— Those Crazy Ladies in the House on the Corner. 1993. pap. 5.50 (*0-87129-301-3*, T94) Dramatic Pub.
— Three Murders & It's Only Monday. 71p. 1990. pap. 5.50 (*0-87129-068-5*, T82) Dramatic Pub.
— You Can't Get There from Here. 1993. pap. 5.50 (*0-87129-213-0*, Y19) Dramatic Pub.
***Cook, Pat.** You Have the Right to Remain Dead. 78p. 2000. pap. 5.60 (*0-87129-808-2*, Y23) Dramatic Pub.
Cook, Patricia, ed. Philosophical Imagination & Cultural Memory: Appropriating Historical Traditions. LC 92-34703. (Illus.). 257p. 1993. text 49.95 (*0-8223-1307-3*); pap. text 18.95 (*0-8223-1322-7*) Duke.
Cook, Patricia A., jt. auth. see O'Dell, Nancy E.
Cook, Patrick J. Milton, Spenser & the Epic Tradition. 208p. 1996. 65.95 (*1-85928-271-7*, Pub. by Scolar Pr) Ashgate Pub Co.
Cook, Paul. Engines of Dawn. 1999. mass mkt. 5.99 (*0-451-45736-6*, ROC) NAL.
Cook, Paul, et al, eds. Privatization, Enterprise Development & Economic Reform: Experiences of Developing & Transitional Economies. LC 97-52045. 320p. 1998. 95.00 (*1-85898-376-2*) E Elgar.
***Cook, Paul & Kirkpatrick, C. H.** Privatisation in Developing Countries. LC 00-34797. (International Library of Critical Writings in Economics). 2000. write for info. (*1-85898-358-4*) E Elgar.
Cook, Paul, jt. ed. see Nixson, Frederick I.
Cook, Paul H. Enzyme Mechanism from Isotope Effects. 1991. lib. bdg. 259.00 (*0-8493-5312-2*, QP601) CRC Pr.
Cook, Paul J. Business Management for Contractors: How to Make Profits in Today's Market. Orig. Title: Business Management for the General Contractor. (Illus.). 229p. 1991. pap. 35.95 (*0-87629-269-4*, 67250) R S Means.
— Estimating for Contractors: How to Make Estimates That Win Jobs. Orig. Title: Estimating for the General Contractor. 225p. 1991. pap. 35.95 (*0-87629-271-6*, 67160) R S Means.
— Quantity Takeoff for Contractors: How to Get Accurate Material Counts. Orig. Title: Quantity Takeoff for the General Contractor. (Illus.). 250p. 1991. pap. 35.95 (*0-87629-268-6*, 67262) R S Means.
— Superintending for Contractors: How to Bring Jobs in on Time, on Budget. Orig. Title: Superintending for the General Contractor: Field Project Management. 220p. 1991. pap. 35.95 (*0-87629-272-4*, 67233) R S Means.
Cook, Penny A., jt. auth. see Wheater, C. Philip.
***Cook, Perrin H.** Bible Facts: Concealed in the Old Darkness, Revealed in the New Light. 174p. 1999. pap. write for info. (*0-7392-0401-7*, PO3632) Morris Pubng.
Cook, Perry R., ed. Music, Cognition & Computerized Sound: An Introduction to Psychoacoustics. LC 98-16783. (Illus.). 734p. 1999. 60.00 (*0-262-03256-2*) MIT Pr.
Cook, Peter. Best Practice Creativity. LC 97-6783. 150p. 1998. 78.95 (*0-566-08027-3*, Pub. by Gower) Ashgate Pub Co.
— Dominique Perrault. 2nd ed. (Illus.). 120p. 1994. pap. 45.00 (*3-7643-5543-3*, Pub. by Birkhauser) Princeton Arch.
— The Industrial Craftsman: Skill, Managerial Strategies & Workplace Relationships. (Employment & Work Relations in Context Ser.). 352p. 1996. 100.00 (*0-7201-2264-3*) Continuum.
— Morphosis. 1995. boxed set. write for info. (*0-8478-1948-5*) Rizzoli Intl.
— Power of Contemporary Architecture. 128p. 1999. pap. 45.00 (*0-471-98419-1*) Wiley.
Cook, Peter. Primer. LC 98-116516. 1p. 1995. pap. 30.00 (*1-85490-388-8*, Pub. by Wiley) Wiley.
***Cook, Peter, ed.** Archigram. LC 99-39255. (Illus.). 152p. 1999. pap. 29.95 (*1-56898-194-5*) Princeton Arch.
Cook, Peter, ed. Morphosis: Buildings & Projects. LC 88-43453. (Illus.). 240p. 1990. 60.00 (*0-8478-1030-5*, Pub. by Rizzoli Intl); pap. 40.00 (*0-8478-1031-3*, Pub. by Rizzoli Intl) St Martin.
Cook, Peter & Hawley, Christine. Zero Point 4: Light Registers London. (Illus.). 96p. (Orig.). 1997. pap. write for info. (*1-889629-03-0*) Form Zero.
Cook, Peter & Manning, Scott. Why Doesn't My Floppy Disk Flop: And Other Kids Computer Question Answered by the CompuDudes. LC 98-42151. 90p. (J). (gr. 3). 1999. pap. text 12.95 (*0-471-18429-2*) Wiley.
Cook, Peter A., jt. auth. see Fisher, Joseph C.
Cook, Peter G. John Folinsbee. LC 92-80512. (Illus.). 148p. (C). 1994. 40.00 (*0-9639104-0-X*) Kubaba Bks.
— John Folinsbee, an Artist's Life, 1892-1972. LC 93-80512. (Illus.). 1993. 40.00 (*0-87233-104-0*) Bauhan.
***Cook, Peter G. & Herczeg, Andrew Leslie.** Environmental Tracers in Subsurface Hydrology. LC 99-48102. 1999. write for info. (*0-7923-7707-9*) Kluwer Academic.
Cook, Peter S. Red Barrister: A Biography of Ted Laurie. LC 94-236090. 1995. pap. 29.95 (*1-86324-414-X*, Pub. by LaTrobe Univ) Intl Spec Bk.
Cook, Petronelle. Queen Consorts of England: The Power Behind the Throne. LC 93-16463. (Illus.). 320p. 1993. 35.00 (*0-8160-2900-8*) Facts on File.
Cook, Petronelle, see Arnold, Margot, pseud.
Cook, Phil F., jt. auth. see Hollis, Margaret.
Cook, Philip, jt. ed. see Coward, Harold.
Cook, Philip J. & Lambert, Richard D., eds. Gun Control. (Annals of the American Academy of Political & Social Science Ser.: No. 455). 250p. (C). 1981. pap. 18.00 (*0-87761-263-3*) Am Acad Pol Soc Sci.
***Cook, Philip J. & Ludwig, Jens.** Gun Violence: The Real Cost. (Studies in Crime & Public Policy). (Illus.). 256p. 2000. 25.00 (*0-19-513793-0*) OUP.
Cook, Philip J. & Ludwig, Jens. Guns in America: Results of a Comprehensive National Survey on Firearms Ownership & Use. LC 97-66573. (Illus.). 100p. (Orig.). 1997. pap. write for info. (*1-884614-14-0*) Police Found.
Cook, Philip J., jt. auth. see Clotfelter, Charles T.
Cook, Philip J., jt. auth. see Frank, Robert H.
Cook, Philip L. Zion City, Illinois: Twentieth-Century Utopia. LC 95-33571. (Utopianism & Communitarianism Ser.). (Illus.). (C). 1996. pap. 19.95 (*0-8156-0349-5*, COZCP) Syracuse U Pr.
— Zion City, Illinois: Twentieth-Century Utopia. LC 95-33571. (Utopianism & Communitarianism Ser.). (Illus.). 260p. (C). 1996. text 39.95 (*0-8156-2621-5*, COZC) Syracuse U Pr.
Cook, Philip S., ed. Liberty of Expression. 130p. (C). 1990. lib. bdg. 25.25 (*0-943875-14-5*) W Wilson Ctr Pr.
Cook, Philip S., et al, eds. American Media: The Wilson Quarterly Reader. 296p. (Orig.). (C). 1989. pap. text 12.95 (*0-943875-09-9*); lib. bdg. 32.00 (*0-943875-10-2*) W Wilson Ctr Pr.
— The Future of News: Television, Newspapers, Wires, Newsmagazines. 288p. 1992. pap. text 13.95 (*0-943875-34-X*) Johns Hopkins.
Cook, Philip W. Abused Men: The Hidden Side of Domestic Violence. LC 97-5581. 216p. 1997. 26.95 (*0-275-95862-0*, Praeger Pubs) Greenwood.
Cook, Preston. The Railroad Night Scene. (Illus.). 128p. 1991. 44.00 (*1-879314-06-1*) Old Line Graph.
Cook Publishers Incorporated Staff, jt. auth. see Boynton.
Cook, R. Southampton. (Best of Britain in Old Photographs Ser.). (Illus.). 128p. 1998. pap. 15.95 (*0-7509-1315-0*, Pub. by Sutton Pub Ltd) Intl Pubs Mktg.
Cook, R. & Dickens, B. Abortion Laws in Commonwealth Countries. (International Digest of Health Legislation Offprints: Vol. 30, No. 3). 108p. 1979. 14.00 (*92-4-169303-7*) World Health.
Cook, R. Dennis. Regression Graphics: Ideas for Studying Regressions Through Graphics. LC 98-3628. (Probability & Statistics Ser.). 349p. 1998. 84.95 (*0-471-19365-8*) Wiley.
Cook, R. Dennis & Weisberg, Sanford. Applied Regression Including Computing & Graphic. LC 99-17200. (Series in Probability & Statistics Texts & References Section). 600p. 1999. 89.95 (*0-471-31711-X*) Wiley.
— An Introduction to Regression Graphics. (Probability & Mathematical Statistics Ser.). 280p. 1994. 79.95 incl. disk (*0-471-00839-7*) Wiley.

C

Cook, R. Franklin & Weber, Steve. The Greening: The Story of Nazarene Compassionate Ministries. 104p. (Orig.). 1986. pap. 5.99 (*0-8341-1130-6*) Beacon Hill.
Cook, R. J. Women's Health & Human Rights: The Promotion & Protection of Women's Health Through International Human Rights Law. LC 94-234143. (ENG, FRE & SPA.). vii, 62p. 1994. pap. text 14.00 (*92-4-156166-1*, 1150412) World Health.
Cook, R. J., et al, eds. Annual Review of Phytopathology, Vol. 24. LC 63-8847. (Illus.). 1986. text 42.00 (*0-8243-1324-0*) Annual Reviews.
— Annual Review of Phytopathology, Vol. 25. LC 63-8847. (Illus.). 1987. text 42.00 (*0-8243-1325-9*) Annual Reviews.
— Annual Review of Phytopathology, Vol. 26. LC 63-8847. (Illus.). 1988. text 42.00 (*0-8243-1326-7*) Annual Reviews.
— Annual Review of Phytopathology, Vol. 27. LC 63-8847. 1989. text 42.00 (*0-8243-1327-5*) Annual Reviews.
— Annual Review of Phytopathology, Vol. 28. LC 63-8847. 1990. text 42.00 (*0-8243-1328-3*) Annual Reviews.
— Annual Review of Phytopathology, Vol. 29. LC 63-8847. 1991. text 42.00 (*0-8243-1329-1*) Annual Reviews.
Cook, R. James, et al, eds. Annual Review of Phytopathology, Vol. 23. LC 63-8847. (Illus.). (C). 1985. 42.00 (*0-8243-1323-2*) Annual Reviews.
— Annual Review of Phytopathology, Vol. 30. LC 63-8847. 1992. text 46.00 (*0-8243-1330-5*) Annual Reviews.
— Annual Review of Phytopathology, Vol. 31. (Illus.). 1993. text 46.00 (*0-8243-1331-3*) Annual Reviews.
— Annual Review of Phytopathology, Vol. 32. LC 63-8847. (Illus.). 1994. text 49.00 (*0-8243-1332-1*) Annual Reviews.
Cook, R. James & Baker, Kenneth F. Nature & Practice of Biological Control of Plant Pathogens. LC 83-71224. 539p. 1983. text 58.00 (*0-89054-053-5*) Am Phytopathol Soc.
Cook, R. James & Veseth, Roger J. Wheat Health Management. LC 90-85253. (Plant Health Management Ser.). (Illus.). 168p. 1991. pap. 55.00 (*0-89054-111-6*) Am Phytopathol Soc.
Cook, R. James, jt. auth. see Baker, Kenneth F.
Cook, R. M. Greek Painted Pottery. 2nd ed. (Illus.). 400p. 1972. 125.00 (*0-416-76170-4*, NO. 2153) Routledge.
Cook, R. M. & Nicholls, R. V. Old Smyrna Excavations: The Temples of Athena. (BSA Supplementary Volumes Ser.: Vol. 30). (Illus.). 246p. 1999. lib. bdg. 90.00 (*0-904887-28-6*, Pub. by Brit Sch Athens) David Brown.
Cook, R. Michael, jt. ed. see Gifford, Eli.
Cook, Rae G., et al. The International Dimensions of Technical Communication. 135p. (Orig.). 1996. pap. 30.00 (*0-914548-91-3*, 167-96) Soc Tech Comm.
Cook, Ralph T. City Lights Books: A Descriptive Bibliography. Cook, Lori A., ed. (Illus.). 361p. 1992. 45.00 (*0-8108-2621-6*) Scarecrow.
— The City Lights Pocket Poets Series: A Descriptive Bibliography. 104p. 1982. pap. 12.50 (*0-910938-89-X*); lib. bdg. 22.50 (*0-910938-90-3*) McGilvery.
Cook, Ramsey. The Voyages of Jacques Cartier. LC 92-95268. 177p. 1993. pap. text 16.95 (*0-8020-6000-5*) U of Toronto Pr.
Cook, Ray. Art & Science of Putting. 1997. pap. text 9.95 (*1-888170-03-4*) Advent Quest.
— The Dance Director. 2nd rev. ed. (Illus.). 178p. (Orig.). (C). 1981. pap. text 15.00 (*0-9602002-1-5*) Ray Cook.
— Labanotation Quiz Book. (Illus.). 72p. (Orig.). 1976. pap. text 10.00 (*0-932582-57-5*, Pub. by Dance Notation) Princeton Bk Co.
— One Hundred & Sixteen Modern Classroom Combinations. (Illus.). 40p. (Orig.). (C). 1979. pap. text 7.00 (*0-9602002-2-3*) Ray Cook.
— Theme & Variation. 59p. (Orig.). (C). 1981. pap. text 15.00 (*0-9602002-3-1*) Ray Cook.
Cook, Ray, jt. auth. see Brainard, Ingrid.
Cook, Ray, ed. see Becker, Svea & Winn, Laurie.
Cook, Ray G. The Three Ivans Choreography Nijinska. (Illus.). 30p. (Orig.). (C). 1988. ring bd. 20.00 (*0-9602002-8-2*) Ray Cook.
Cook, Ray G., ed. The Wombat Duet. (Illus.). 22p. (C). 1984. pap. 10.00 (*0-9602002-6-6*) Ray Cook.
Cook, Ray L. & Ellis, Boyd G. Soil Management: A World View of Conservation & Production. LC 91-38873. 428p. (C). 1992. reprint ed. 63.50 (*0-89464-682-6*) Krieger.
Cook, Raymond A. Mountain Singer: The Life & the Legacy of Byron Herbert Reece. LC 80-8067. (Illus.). 368p. 1980. pap. 14.95 (*0-87797-246-X*) Cherokee.
Cook, Rebecca J., ed. Human Rights of Women: National & International Perspectives. LC 94-20682. (Pennsylvania Studies in Human Rights). (Illus.). 634p. (Orig.). (C). 1994. pap. text 22.95 (*0-8122-1538-9*) U of Pa Pr.
Cook, Rhodes. America Votes 23: A Handbook of Contemporary Election Statistics. Vol. 23. 500p. 1999. 155.00 (*1-56802-456-8*) CQ Pr.
— America Votes 22: A Handbook of Contemporary Election Statistics. 542p. (C). 1998. text 147.00 (*0-87187-918-2*) Congr Quarterly.
***Cook, Rhodes.** Race for the Presidency: Winning the Year 2000 Nomination. 200p. 1999. pap. 29.95 (*1-56802-475-4*) CQ Pr.
Cook, Rhodes & McGillivray, Alice V. U. S. Primary Elections, 1995-1996. LC 97-27322. 409p. (YA). 1997. text 189.00 (*0-87187-900-X*) Congr Quarterly.
— U.S. Primary Elections: President, Congress, Governors: 1997-1998. 400p. 1999. 189.00 (*1-56802-455-X*) CQ Pr.
Cook, Rhodes, jt. auth. see Congressional Quarterly Staff.
Cook, Richard, Sr. New York Central's Mercury. 60p. 1996. pap. 14.95 (*0-9622003-4-4*) TLC VA.
— The Twentieth Century Limited, 1938-1967. (Illus.). 154p. 1996. pap. 19.95 (*1-883089-26-3*) TLC VA.
***Cook, Richard & Lange, Deborah.** Glen Echo Park: A Story of Survival. (Illus.). 128p. 2000. pap. 29.95 (*0-615-11340-0*) Bethesda Comm Grp.
Cook, Richard, ed. see Alden, Chevy.
Cook, Richard, jt. ed. see Smith, Harry.
Cook, Richard J. The Beauty of Railroad Bridges. 4th ed. LC 87-11998. (Illus.). 208p. 1987. reprint ed. 44.95 (*0-87095-097-5*) Gldn West Bks.
— The Twentieth-Century Limited, 1938-1967. LC 93-60647. 154p. 1993. 25.95 (*0-685-70804-7*) TLC VA.
Cook, Richard J., et al. How to Design & Build Thermosiphoning Air Panels. iv, 36p. (Orig.). 1982. pap. 2.00 (*0-939294-13-3*, TH-7413-C66) Beech Leaf.
Cook, Rick. Mall Purchase Night. 352p. 1993. per. 4.99 (*0-671-72198-4*) Baen Bks.
— Wiz Biz. 624p. 1997. per. 6.99 (*0-671-87846-8*) Baen Bks.
— The Wizardry Compiled. 320p. 1991. mass mkt. 4.95 (*0-671-72078-3*) Baen Bks.
— The Wizardry Consulted. 1995. mass mkt. 5.99 (*0-671-87700-3*) Baen Bks.
— Wizardry Cursed. 1991. mass mkt. 4.95 (*0-671-72049-X*) Baen Bks.
— The Wizardry Quested. 288p. 1996. mass mkt. 5.99 (*0-671-87708-9*) Baen Bks.
Cook, Rob. The Complete History of the Leedy Drum Company. (Illus.). 178p. (C). 1993. pap. 29.95 (*0-931759-74-9*) Centerstream Pub.
— The Rogers Book. (Illus.). 250p. 1998. pap. 35.00 (*1-888408-04-9*) Rebeats Pubns.
— The Slingerland Book. (Illus.). vi, 292p. (Orig.). 1996. pap. 34.95 (*1-888408-00-6*) Rebeats Pubns.
Cook, Rob & Aldridge, John. Leedy Drum Topics: Complete from 1923 to 1941. (Illus.). 300p. 1997. pap. 29.95 (*0-931759-78-1*) Centerstream Pub.
Cook, Robert. Ahora que Creo. Orig. Title: Now That I Believe. (SPA.). 128p. 1981. mass mkt. 4.99 (*0-8254-1137-8*, Edit Portavoz) Kregel.
— Baptism of Fire: The Republican Party in Iowa, 1838-1878. LC 93-31825. (Illus.). 324p. 1993. text 46.95 (*0-8138-1938-5*) Iowa St U Pr.
— Finite Element Modeling for Stress Analysis. LC 94-34421. 336p. 1994. text 89.95 (*0-471-10774-3*) Wiley.
— Sweet Land Liberty. LC 97-8579. (Studies in Modern History). 336p. (C). 1998. 66.00 (*0-582-21531-5*) Longman.
— Sweet Land of Liberty. LC 97-8579. (Studies in Modern History). 336p. (C). 1997. pap. 24.60 (*0-582-21532-3*) Longman.
Cook, Robert & Roberts. Mother Jones & Her Sisters. 290p. (C). 1999. per. 33.95 (*0-7872-5809-1*, 41580902) Kendall-Hunt.
Cook, Robert, jt. auth. see Herbert, Lynden.
Cook, Robert A. Now That I Believe. mass mkt. 4.99 (*0-8024-5983-8*, 233) Moody.
Cook, Robert C. Human Fertility: The Modern Dilemma. LC 72-156185. 380p. 1971. reprint ed. lib. bdg. 69.50 (*0-8371-6128-2*, COHU, Greenwood Pr) Greenwood.
Cook, Robert D. & Young, Warren C. Advanced Mechanics of Materials. 2nd ed. LC 98-24374. 496p. 1998. 105.00 (*0-13-396961-4*) P-H.
Cook, Robert D., et al. Concepts & Applications of Finited Element Analysis. 3rd ed. LC 88-27929. 656p. 1989. text 102.95 (*0-471-84788-7*) Wiley.
Cook, Robert E., ed. see Jackson, Jeremy B.
Cook, Robert F. The Sense of the Song of Roland. LC 87-5407. 296p. (C). 1987. text 47.50 (*0-8014-1930-1*) Cornell U Pr.
Cook, Robert F., ed. Worker Dislocation: Case Studies of Causes & Cures. LC 87-31717. 219p. 1987. text 23.00 (*0-88099-053-8*); pap. text 13.00 (*0-88099-052-X*) W E Upjohn.
Cook, Robert F., et al. Public Service Employment: The Experience of a Decade. LC 85-22495. 131p. 1985. text 22.00 (*0-88099-030-9*); pap. text 12.00 (*0-88099-031-7*) W E Upjohn.
Cook, Robert F., tr. see Murat, Ines.
Cook, Robert Francis. Chanson d'Antioche, Chanson de Geste: Le Cycle de la Croisade Est-Il Epique? (Purdue University Monographs in Romance Languages: No. 2). vi, 107p. 1980. 29.00 (*90-272-1712-2*) J Benjamins Pubng Co.
Cook, Robert J. Leasing Office Space You Can Afford: Everything Companies Need to Know - from Finding Great Space & Negotiating the Lease to Moving In. 350p. 1992. per. 29.95 (*1-55738-457-6*, 457, Irwn Prfssnl) McGraw-Hill Prof.
Cook, Robert M. Greek Painted Pottery. 3rd ed. LC 96-18748. (Illus.). 416p. (C). 1997. 125.00 (*0-415-13859-0*); pap. 32.99 (*0-415-13860-4*) Routledge.
Cook, Robert M. & Dupont, Pierre. East Greek Pottery. LC 97-7494. (Illus.). 256p. (C). 1998. 85.00 (*0-415-16601-2*) Routledge.
Cook, Robert S., ed. Ecological Issues on Reintroducing Wolves into Yellowstone National Park. (Illus.). 328p. (C). 1997. reprint ed. pap. text 40.00 (*0-7881-3890-1*) DIANE Pub.
Cook, Robin. Acceptable Risk. 400p. 1996. mass mkt. 7.50 (*0-425-15186-7*) Berkley Pub.
— Acceptable Risk. large type ed. LC 95-3699. 1995. 26.95 (*1-56895-173-6*) Wheeler Pub.
— Blindsight. 352p. 1993. mass mkt. 7.50 (*0-425-13619-1*) Berkley Pub.
— Brain. 4.95 (*0-685-47356-2*) NAL.
— Brain. 320p. 1982. mass mkt. 7.99 (*0-451-15797-4*, Sig) NAL.
— Chromosome 6. 512p. 1998. mass mkt. 7.50 (*0-425-16124-2*) Berkley Pub.
— Chromosome 6. LC 96-53133. 400p. 1997. 24.95 (*0-399-14207-X*, G P Putnam) Peng Put Young Read.
— Chromosome 6. large type ed. LC 97-10885. 1999. pap. 26.95 (*0-7862-1099-0*) Thorndike Pr.
— Coma. 320p. 1977. mass mkt. 7.99 (*0-451-15953-5*, Sig) NAL.
— Coma. 1994. reprint ed. lib. bdg. 29.95 (*1-56849-266-9*) Buccaneer Bks.
— Coma: A Novel. (Signet Bks.). 1977. 11.60 (*0-606-01135-8*, Pub. by Turtleback) Demco.
— Contagion. 384p. 1996. 24.95 (*0-399-14106-5*, G P Putnam) Peng Put Young Read.
— Contagion. large type ed. 1997. pap. 24.95 (*0-7862-0650-0*) Thorndike Pr.
— Contagion. 496p. 1999. reprint ed. mass mkt. 6.99 (*0-425-15594-3*) Berkley Pub.
— Il Est Mort les Yeux Ouverts (On Ne Meurt Que Deux Fois) (FRE.). 246p. 1989. pap. 10.95 (*0-7859-2123-0*, 2070381668) Fr & Eur.
— Fatal Cure. 464p. 1995. pap. text 7.50 (*0-425-14563-8*) Berkley Pub.
***Cook, Robin.** Fever. 2000. mass mkt. 7.99 (*0-425-17420-4*) Berkley Pub.
Cook, Robin. Fever. 1983. 11.09 (*0-606-07509-7*, Pub. by Turtleback) Demco.
***Cook, Robin.** Godplayer. 2000. mass mkt. 7.99 (*0-425-17638-X*) Berkley Pub.
Cook, Robin. Godplayer. 320p. 1984. mass mkt. 7.99 (*0-451-15728-1*, Sig) NAL.
— Harmful Intent. 1991. mass mkt. 7.50 (*0-425-12546-7*) Berkley Pub.
***Cook, Robin.** Harmful Intent. LC 00-25973. 2000. write for info. (*0-7862-2504-1*) Thorndike Pr.
— Harmful Intent. 1991. 12.09 (*0-606-00927-2*, Pub. by Turtleback) Demco.
Cook, Robin. Invasion. 352p. 1997. mass mkt. 7.50 (*0-425-15540-4*) Berkley Pub.
***Cook, Robin.** Invasion. large type ed. LC 00-23519. (Famous Authors Ser.). 2000. 28.95 (*0-7862-2505-X*, MML06400-171917) Thorndike Pr.
Cook, Robin. Mindbend. LC 85-5804. 352p. 1986. mass mkt. 7.99 (*0-451-14108-3*, Sig) NAL.
— Mortal Fear. 1989. mass mkt. 7.99 (*0-425-11388-4*) Berkley Pub.
— Mortal Fear. 1989. 12.60 (*0-606-00930-2*, Pub. by Turtleback) Demco.
— Mutation. 1990. mass mkt. 7.50 (*0-425-11965-3*) Berkley Pub.
— Mutation. 1990. 12.09 (*0-606-00933-7*, Pub. by Turtleback) Demco.
— Outbreak. 400p. 1988. mass mkt. 6.99 (*0-425-10687-X*) Berkley Pub.
— Outbreak. 1988. 12.09 (*0-606-00934-5*, Pub. by Turtleback) Demco.
— Robin Cook - Three Complete Novels: Acceptable Risk-Fatal Cure-Terminal. LC 97-6480. 832p. 1997. 12.98 (*0-399-14319-X*, G P Putnam) Peng Put Young Read.
— Robin Cook - Three Complete Novels: Harmful Intent; Vital Signs; Blindsight. unabridged ed. LC 94-5134. 800p. 1994. 11.98 (*0-399-13964-8*, G P Putnam) Peng Put Young Read.
— Robin Cook - Three Complete Novels: Outbreak; Mortal Fear; Mutation. LC 93-3230. 720p. 1993. 11.98 (*0-399-13876-5*, G P Putnam) Peng Put Young Read.
***Cook, Robin.** Shock. 368p. 2000. 24.95 (*0-399-14600-8*) Putnam Pub Group.
Cook, Robin. Sphinx. 1994. lib. bdg. 21.95 (*1-56849-490-4*) Buccaneer Bks.
— Sphinx. 320p. 1983. mass mkt. 7.99 (*0-451-15949-7*, Sig) NAL.
— Terminal. 1996. mass mkt. 6.99 (*0-425-15506-4*) Berkley Pub.
— Terminal. 1994. 12.09 (*0-606-06051-0*, Pub. by Turtleback) Demco.
— Terminal. large type ed. LC 93-18332. 604p. 1993. 23.95 (*1-56054-689-1*) Thorndike Pr.
— Terminal. large type ed. LC 93-18332. 604p. 1994. pap. 15.95 (*1-56054-880-0*) Thorndike Pr.
— Three Complete Novels: Contagion, Invasion, Chromosome 6. LC 99-24694. 752p. 1999. 12.98 (*0-399-14538-9*, G P Putnam) Peng Put Young Read.
— Toxin. large type ed. LC 98-5792. 504p. 1998. 29.95 (*0-7838-0130-0*, G K Hall & Co) Mac Lib Ref.
— Toxin. large type ed. LC 98-5792. 1999. pap. 20.00 (*0-7838-0131-9*, G K Hall Lrg Type) Mac Lib Ref.
***Cook, Robin.** Toxin. 1999. reprint ed. pap. 7.99 (*0-425-16661-9*) Berkley Pub.
Cook, Robin. Toxin Display. 1999. mass mkt. 255.68 (*0-425-16647-3*) Berkley Pub.
— Vector. LC 98-49058. 416p. 1999. 24.95 (*0-399-14471-4*) Putnam Pub Group.
— Vector. large type ed. LC 99-18829. 589p. 1950. pap. 27.95 (*0-7838-8599-7*, G K Hall Lrg Type) Mac Lib Ref.
***Cook, Robin.** Vector. large type ed. LC 99-18829. 589p. 1999. 29.95 (*0-7838-8598-9*, G K Hall & Co) Mac Lib Ref.
— Vector. 2000. reprint ed. mass mkt. 7.99 (*0-425-17299-6*) Berkley Pub.
Cook, Robin. Vital Signs. 1992. mass mkt. 7.50 (*0-425-13176-9*) Berkley Pub.
— Vital Signs. 1992. 12.09 (*0-606-00935-3*, Pub. by Turtleback) Demco.
— Vital Signs. large type ed. 560p. 1991. pap. 16.95 (*0-8161-5304-3*, G K Hall Lrg Type) Mac Lib Ref.
— Vital Signs. 1994. reprint ed. lib. bdg. 32.95 (*1-56849-267-7*) Buccaneer Bks.
— The Year of the Intern. 224p. 1973. mass mkt. 7.50 (*0-451-16555-1*, Sig) NAL.
— The Year of the Intern. LC 72-75414. 220p. 1995. reprint ed. lib. bdg. 29.95 (*0-89968-317-7*, Lghtyr Pr) Buccaneer Bks.
***Cook, Rod.** Rod Cook's How to Start Your Network Marketing or Internet Multi-Affiliate Company. 8th rev. ed. (Illus.). 1999. pap. 149.00 (*0-9672915-1-8*) Americas M L M.
Cook, Roger & Zimmermann, Karl. The Western Maryland Railway: Fireballs & Black Diamonds. LC 92-25390. xii, 332p. 1992. 50.00 (*0-9620844-4-1*) Garrigues Hse.
Cook, Roger, jt. auth. see Rohler, Lloyd E.
Cook, Roger, jt. auth. see Zimmermann, Karl.
Cook, Roger, ed. see Brown, Sally.
Cook, Roger, ed. see Jacobs, Andy.
Cook, Roger, jt. ed. see Rohler, Lloyd.
Cook, Roger F. By the Rivers of Babylon: Heinrich Heine's Late Songs & Reflections. LC 98-10790. 1998. 39.95 (*0-8143-2760-5*) Wayne St U Pr.
— The Demise of the Author: Autonomy & the German Writer, 1770-1848. LC 92-30153. (Studies in Modern German Literature: Vol. 52). (Illus.). 229p. (C). 1993. text 46.95 (*0-8204-2012-3*) P Lang Pubng.
Cook, Roger F. & Gemunden, Gerd, eds. The Cinema of Wim Wenders: Image, Narrative, & the Postmodern Condition. (Contemporary Film & Television Ser.). (Illus.). 288p. (Orig.). 1997. pap. 19.95 (*0-8143-2578-5*) Wayne St U Pr.
Cook, Ron. Ground Zero: Getting in Touch with God a 28-Day Journey to Intimacy with Your Creator, 1. LC 99-21289. 1999. pap. 12.99 (*0-8499-3724-8*) Word Pub.
Cook, Ronald, Sr. Personal Convictions Philosopoetry. 1998. pap. write for info. (*1-57553-859-8*) Watermrk Pr.
Cook, Ronald A. & Soltani, Mehrdad, eds. Hurricanes of Nineteen Ninety Two: Lessons Learned & Implications for the Future: Proceedings of a Symposium Organized by the American Society of Civil Engineers, December 1-3, 1993. LC 94-24896. 820p. 1994. 67.00 (*0-7844-0046-6*, ASCE Press) Am Soc Civil Eng.
Cook, Rosemarie S. Counseling the Families of Children with Disabilities. (Resources for Christian Counseling Ser.: Vol. 25). 208p. 18.99 (*0-8499-0738-1*) Word Pub.
***Cook, Roy A., et al.** Tourism: The Business of Travel. LC 98-8160. (Illus.). 1999. write for info. (*0-01-327103-2*) P-H.
Cook, Roy B. The Annals of Fort Lee. (Illus.). 132p. 1998. pap. 15.00 (*0-7884-0956-5*, C553) Heritage Bk.
Cook, Roy J. One Hundred & One Famous Poems. 202p. Date not set. 20.95 (*0-8488-2238-2*) Amereon Ltd.
— 101 Famous Poems. 186p. 1985. 12.95 (*0-8092-5096-9*, 509690, Contemporary Bks) NTC Contemp Pub Co.
Cook, Roy J., compiled by. One Hundred One Famous Poems. 186p. 1919. reprint ed. 14.95 (*0-8092-8833-8*, 883380); reprint ed. pap. 11.00 (*0-8092-8834-6*, 883460) NTC Contemp Pub Co.
— One Hundred One Famous Poems. LC 97-514. 186p. 1984. reprint ed. 12.95 (*0-8092-8831-1*, 883110) NTC Contemp Pub Co.
Cook, Roy J., ed. One Hundred & One Famous Poems. (Illus.). 186p. (YA). (gr. 9-12). 1990. reprint ed. lib. bdg. 21.95 (*0-89966-667-1*) Buccaneer Bks.
***Cook, Rupert.** Leveraging Competitive Advantage from the Euro. (Management Briefings Ser.). (Illus.). 1999. pap. 127.50 (*0-273-64324-X*, Pub. by F T P-H) Trans-Atl Phila.
Cook, Ruth B. North Across the River: A Civil War Trail of Tears. LC 97-49449. 224p. 1999. 24.95 (*1-57587-070-3*) Crane Hill AL.
***Cook, Ruth Beaumont.** North Across the River: A Civil War Trail of Tears. (Illus.). 224p. 2000. pap. 14.95 (*1-57587-166-1*, Pub. by Crane Hill AL) Blair.
***Cook, Ruth E., et al.** Adapting Early Childhood Curricula for Children in Inclusive Settings. 5th ed. LC 99-15564. (Illus.). 477p. 1999. pap. text 43.00 (*0-13-083201-4*, Merrill Coll) P-H.
Cook, S. A. The Religion of Ancient Palestine in the Light of Archaeology. (British Academy, London, Schweich Lectures on Biblical Archaeology Series, 1930). 1974. reprint ed. pap. 30.00 (*0-8115-1267-3*) Periodicals Srv.
Cook, S. B. Imperial Affinities: Nineteenth Century Analogies & Exchanges Between India & Ireland. LC 93-19206. (Illus.). 162p. (C). 1993. 39.95 (*0-8039-9121-5*) Sage.
Cook, S. Chrystal, jt. auth. see Travis, Curtis C.
Cook, S. F. The Aboriginal Population of Alameda & Contra Costa Counties, California. fac. ed. Rowe, J. H. et al, eds. (University of California Publications: No. 16:4). 79p. (C). 1957. reprint ed. pap. 9.06 (*1-55567-145-4*) Coyote Press.
— The Aboriginal Population of the North Coast of California. fac. ed. Olson, Ronald L. et al, eds. (University of California Publications: No. 16:3). 54p. (C). 1956. reprint ed. pap. 6.56 (*1-55567-144-6*) Coyote Press.
— The Aboriginal Population of the San Joaquin Valley, California. fac. ed. Olson, Ronald L. et al, eds. (University of California Publications: No. 16:2). 54p. (C). 1955. reprint ed. pap. 6.56 (*1-55567-143-8*) Coyote Press.
— Colonial Expeditions of the Interior of California: Central Valley, 1800-1820. fac. ed. Rowe, J. H. et al, eds. (University of California Publications: No. 16:6). 57p. (C). 1960. reprint ed. pap. 6.88 (*1-55567-147-0*) Coyote Press.
— The Epidemic of 1830-1833 in California & Oregon. fac. ed. Gifford et al, eds. (University of California Publications in American Archaeology & Ethnology: No. 43:3). 27p. (C). 1955. reprint ed. pap. 3.13 (*1-55567-320-1*) Coyote Press.
— Erosion Morphology & Occupation History in Western

C

An Asterisk (*) at the beginning of an entry indicates that the title is appearing for the first time.

Mexico. fac. ed. Rowe, J. H. et al, eds. (University of California Publications: No. 17:3). (Illus.). 57p. (C). 1963. reprint ed. pap. 6.88 (*1-55567-153-5*) Coyote Press.

— Expeditions to the Interior of California, Central Valley, 1820-1840. fac. ed. Rowe, J. H. et al, eds. (University of California Publications: No. 20:5). 64p. (C). 1962. reprint ed. pap. 7.50 (*1-55567-156-X*) Coyote Press.

— The Fossilization of Human Bone: Calcium, Phosphate & Carbonate. fac. ed. Gifford et al, eds. (University of California Publications in American Archaeology & Ethnology: No. 40:6). 27p. (C). 1951. reprint ed. pap. 3.13 (*1-55567-316-3*) Coyote Press.

Cook, S. F. The Mechanism & Extent of Dietary Adaptation among Certain Groups of California & Nevada Indians. fac. ed. (Ibero-Americana Ser.: Vol. 18). 68p. (C). 1941. reprint ed. pap. text 8.13 (*1-55567-805-X*) Coyote Press.

Cook, S. F. & Heiger, R. F. The Quantitative Approach to the Relation Between Population & Settlement Size, No. 64. (University of California Archaeological Research Facility Ser.). 105p. 1965. pap. text 11.56 (*1-55567-815-7*) Coyote Press.

Cook, S. F. & Heizer, R. F. The Fossilization of Bone: Organic Components & Water. fac. ed. (Reports of the University of California Archaeological Survey: No. 17). (Illus.). 28p. 1952. reprint ed. pap. 3.13 (*1-55567-338-4*) Coyote Press.

— Studies on the Chemical Analysis of Archaeological Sites. (University of California Publications in American Archaeology & Ethnology: Vol. 2). (Illus.). 107p. 1964. reprint ed. pap. text 11.88 (*1-55567-479-8*) Coyote Press.

Cook, S. F. & Treganza, Adam E. The Quantative Investigation of Indian Mounds: With Special Reference to the Relation of the Physical Components to the Probable Material Culture. fac. ed. Gifford, Edward W. et al, eds. (University of California Publications in American Archaeology & Ethnology: No. 40:5). 43p. (C). 1950. reprint ed. pap. 4.69 (*1-55567-315-5*) Coyote Press.

Cook, S. F., et al. Chemical Analysis of the Hotchkiss Site (CCO-138) - The Rustler Rockshelter Site (SBr-288), a Culturally Stratified Site in the Mohave Desert, CA, Set, Pts. I & II. fac. ed. (Reports of the University of California Archaeological Survey: No. 57). (Illus.). 71p. 1962. reprint ed. pap. 8.44 (*1-55567-372-4*) Coyote Press.

Cook, S. F., jt. auth. see Heizer, R. F.

Cook, S. J., jt. auth. see Enz, Billie.

Cook, Sadie, ed. Ella Fitzgerald/Essential: 20 Ella Fitzgerald Classics Arranged for Piano, Vocal & Chords. 88p. (Orig.). 1996. pap. 19.95 (*0-7692-0131-8*, 4977A) Wrner Bros.

Cook, Sally. Inherit Your Love. (Presents Ser.: No. 440). 1992. pap. 2.89 (*0-373-11440-0*, 1-11440-4) Harlequin Bks.

Cook, Sally, jt. auth. see Stallings, Gene.

Cook, Sam. CampSights. LC 91-62787. (Illus.). 192p. 1991. 16.95 (*0-938586-49-1*) Pfeifer-Hamilton.

— Friendship Fires. LC 98-86234. (Illus.). 192p. 1998. 19.95 (*1-57025-170-3*) Pfeifer-Hamilton.

— If This Is Mid-Life, Where's the Crisis? (Illus.). 192p. (Orig.). 1993. pap. 12.95 (*0-938586-90-4*) Pfeifer-Hamilton.

— Quiet Magic. LC 88-62599. (Illus.). 192p. 1989. 16.95 (*0-938586-17-3*) Pfeifer-Hamilton.

— Up North. LC 86-62906. (Illus.). 192p. 1987. 18.95 (*0-938586-09-2*) Pfeifer-Hamilton.

***Cook, Samantha.** Best Little Knitter in the West: The Bin Saad, Sermsah. (Illus.). 32p. (J). 2000. pap. 12.95 (*1-875641-52-1*, Pub. by Magabala Bks) Intl Spec Bk.

Cook, Samantha. Estados Unidos en Vivo. (SPA.). 995p. 1993. pap. 49.95 (*0-7859-7563-2*, 8420749109) Fr & Eur.

— The Mini Rough Guide to New Orleans. (Illus.). 288p. 1999. 9.95 (*1-85828-440-6*, Pub. by Rough Guides) Penguin Putnam.

Cook, Samantha, et al. The Rough Guide to the U. S. A. 1996. pap. 19.95 (*0-614-97945-5*, Penguin Bks) Viking Penguin.

Cook, Samantha, jt. ed. see Thomas, Nicholas.

***Cook, Samuel D., ed.** Black - Jewish Relationships: Dillard University National Conference Papers, 1989-1997. LC 99-61482. 1999. pap. 22.95 (*1-57736-082-6*) Providence Hse.

***Cook, Samuel R.** Monacans & Miners: Native American & Coal Mining Communities in Appalachia. LC 00-36502. (Illus.). 368p. 2000. text 65.00 (*0-8032-1505-3*); pap. text 29.95 (*0-8032-6412-7*, Bison Books) U of Nebr Pr.

***Cook, Sandy.** Nicholas Claus Hollyberry: A Christmas Story. large type ed. (Illus.). 59p. 1999. pap. 24.99 (*0-9674142-0-2*, 001) Roseheart Pubng.

Cook, Sandy & Bessant, Judith. Women's Encounters with Violence: Australian Experiences. LC 97-4601. (Sage Series on Violence Against Women). 268p. 1997. 49.00 (*0-7619-0431-X*); pap. 22.95 (*0-7619-0432-8*) Sage.

***Cook, Sandy & Davies, Susanne, eds.** Harsh Punishment: International Experiences of Women's Imprisonment. LC 99-31173. (Northeastern Series on Gender, Crime, & Law). 352p. 1999. 50.00 (*1-55553-412-0*) NE U Pr.

Cook, Sandy & Davies, Susanne, eds. Harsh Punishment: International Experiences of Women's Imprisonment. LC 99-31173. 326p. 2000. pap. text 22.50 (*1-55553-411-2*) NE U Pr.

Cook, Sarah. Compendium of Questionnaires & Inventories. LC 99-234025. 200p. 1999. ring bd. 166.95 (*0-566-08088-5*) Ashgate Pub Co.

— Process Improvement: A Handbook for Managers. 176p. 1996. 61.95 (*0-566-07633-0*, Pub. by Gower) Ashgate Pub Co.

— Training for Empowerment. 484p. 1994. 306.95 (*0-566-07514-8*, Pub. by Gower) Ashgate Pub Co.

— Twenty Training Workshops for Customer Service, Vol. 2. 1993. ring bd. 139.95 (*0-87425-226-1*) HRD Press.

Cook, Sarah & Maurer-Fazio, Margaret, eds. The Workers State Meets the Market: Labour in China's Transition. LC 99-12625. 160p. 1999. 45.00 (*0-7146-4942-2*, Pub. by F Cass Pubs); pap. 24.50 (*0-7146-8001-X*, Pub. by F Cass Pubs) Intl Spec Bk.

Cook, Sarah S., et al. Children & Dying: An Exploration & Selective Bibliographies. LC 73-383. 106p. 1977. pap. 5.95 (*0-930194-87-X*) Ctr Thanatology.

Cook, Scott. Gingerbread Boy. (Illus.). 1996. pap. 5.99 (*0-679-88089-5*) Random.

— Gingerbread Boy. 1996. 11.19 (*0-606-10819-X*, Pub. by Turtleback) Demco.

— Mexican Brick Culture in the Building of Texas, 1800s-1980s. (Illus.). 400p. 1998. 44.95 (*0-89096-792-X*) Tex A&M Univ Pr.

— Zapotec Stoneworkers: The Dynamics of Rural Simple Commodity Production in Modern Mexican Capitalism. LC 81-40584. (Illus.). 454p. (Orig.). 1982. pap. text 32.00 (*0-8191-2420-6*); lib. bdg. 67.00 (*0-8191-2419-2*) U Pr of Amer.

Cook, Scott & Binford, Leigh. Obliging Need: Rural Petty Industry in Mexican Capitalism. (Illus.). 336p. 1990. text 37.50 (*0-292-76032-9*) U of Tex Pr.

Cook, Scott S. Colonial Encounters in the Age of High Imperialism: Harpercollins World History Series. LC 95-20933. (World History Ser.). 128p. (C). 1997. pap. 23.33 (*0-673-99229-2*) Addson-Wesley Educ.

***Cook, Sharon.** All Things Bright & Beautiful. (Illus.). 52p. 2000. write for info. (*1-58050-091-9*, 40-6218) Provo Craft.

Cook, Sharon. The Great Stake Out. 36p. 1998. 9.99 (*1-58050-023-4*, 40-6152) Provo Craft.

Cook, Sharon & Rusting, Jean. Jouanah: A Hmong Cinderella. 1996. teacher ed., ring bd. 9.95 (*1-885008-04-X*) Shens Bks.

Cook, Sharon Anne. Through Sunshine & Shadow: The Woman's Christian Temperance Union, Evangelicalism & Reform in Ontario, 1874-1930. (Illus.). 304p. 1995. 49.95 (*0-7735-1305-1*, Pub. by McG-Queens Univ Pr) CUP Services.

Cook, Sharon C. & Gale, Elizabeth. A Personal Wedding Planner. (Illus.). 192p. 1992. 20.00 (*1-55850-048-0*) Adams Media.

Cook, Sharon L. & Sholander, Graciela B. Return to the Child of Light. (Illus.). 150p. 1996. pap. 14.95 (*0-9652299-0-4*) Triangle Publng.

Cook, Sharon T. Creating Web Pages for Business Communication: Macintosh Edition. Young, Natalie, ed. (Illus.). 72p. 1997. pap. 225.00 (*1-56562-099-2*) OneOnOne Comp Trng.

— How to Use the Internet As a Research Tool. Young, Natalie B., ed. 86p. 1996. pap. text 225.00 incl. audio (*1-56562-082-8*) OneOnOne Comp Trng.

— How to Use the Internet As a Research Tool - CD: Netscape Edition. Aquino, James, ed. (Illus.). 75p. 1998. pap. 225.00 incl. cd-rom (*1-56562-102-6*) OneOnOne Comp Trng.

Cook, Sharon Touhy. How to Use the Internet As a Research Tool: Microsoft Internet Explorer Edition. Aquino, James, ed. 97p. 1997. pap. 225.00 incl. cd-rom (*1-56562-152-2*) OneOnOne Comp Trng.

Cook, Sharon Touhy, jt. auth. see Rinehart, Janice S.

Cook, Shelby, ed. see Perry, Bryon A.

Cook, Sherburne F. The Conflict Between the California Indian & White Civilization, 4 vols. in 1. LC 76-43678. (Ibero-Americana Ser.: No. 21-24). reprint ed. 27.50 (*0-404-15512-X*) AMS Pr.

Cook, Sherburne F. & Borah, Woodrow. Essays in Population History, 3 vols. Incl. Vol. 3. Essays in Population History. 333p. 1979. 65.00 (*0-520-03560-7*, Pub. by U CA Pr); write for info. (*0-318-56008-9*) U CA Pr.

Cook, Sherburne F. & Simpson, Lesley B. The Population of Central Mexico in the Sixteenth Century. LC 76-29408. (Ibero-Americana Ser.: No. 31). reprint ed. 37.50 (*0-404-15333-X*) AMS Pr.

Cook, Sherburne F., et al. Papers on California Archaeology, Nos. 1-5. fac. ed. (Reports of the University of California Archaeological Survey: No. 7). 25p. 1950. reprint ed. pap. 2.81 (*1-55567-333-3*) Coyote Press.

Cook, Sherry. Winning the War: How to Pray Prayers That God Answers. 250p. (Orig.). 1996. pap. 8.00 (*1-57502-246-X*, P0923) Morris Pubng.

Cook, Sherwin L. Torchlight Parade. LC 70-128227. (Essay Index Reprint Ser.). 1977. 23.95 (*0-8369-1911-4*) Ayer.

Cook, Sheryl & Moore, Farrar. Help! Am I the Parent Now? A Practical Resource Kit for Caregivers of Aging Parents or Relatives. 106p. 1998. ring bd. 39.95 (*0-9666356-0-4*) Instrctional Tech.

— Help! Where Are All My Papers? A Practical Guide for Caregivers & Seniors to Identify & Organize "Must-Know" Information. Orig. Title: Help! Am I the Parent Now?. 106p. 1998. ring bd. 39.95 (*0-9666356-1-2*) Instrctional Tech.

Cook, Shirley. Endangered Species: Linking Environmental Studies with Everyday Life. Britt, Leslie, ed. (Illus.). 64p. (Orig.). (J). (gr. 2-6). 1993. pap. text, teacher ed. 8.95 (*0-86530-272-3*, 269-5) Incentive Pubns.

— Environmental Impact: Linking Environmental Studies with Everyday Life. Britt, Leslie, ed. (Illus.). 64p. (Orig.). (J). (gr. 2-6). 1993. pap. text, teacher ed. 8.95 (*0-86530-273-1*, 269-6) Incentive Pubns.

— Learning Through Research. Aldy, Catherine & Keeling, Jan, eds. (Illus.). 128p. (Orig.). (J). (gr. 1-6). 1995. pap. text 12.95 (*0-86530-334-7*, IP 334-7) Incentive Pubns.

— Linking Literature & Comprehension. Keeling, Jan, ed. (Integrating Literature into Basic Skills Programs Ser.). (Illus.). 240p. (Orig.). (J). (gr. k-4). 1992. pap. text 16.95 (*0-86530-205-7*, IP193-3) Incentive Pubns.

— Linking Literature with Self-Esteem. Keeling, Jan, ed. (Integrating Literature into Basic Skills Programs Ser.). (Illus.). 160p. (Orig.). (J). (gr. k-4). 1992. pap. text 14.95 (*0-86530-196-4*, IP194-6) Incentive Pubns.

— The Marriage Puzzle. 128p. (Orig.). 1985. pap. 4.70 (*0-310-33611-2*, 11718P) Zondervan.

— Math in the Real World of Architecture: Dimensions, Quantities, Shapes, & Patterns. Aldy, Catherine, ed. (Illus.). 96p. (Orig.). (J). (gr. 5-8). 1996. pap. text 10.95 (*0-86530-342-8*, IP 343-5) Incentive Pubns.

— Math in the Real World of Business & Living: Probability, Graphing, & Statistics. Quinn, Anna, ed. (Illus.). 96p. (Orig.). (J). (gr. 5-8). 1996. pap. text 10.95 (*0-86530-343-6*, IP 343-6) Incentive Pubns.

— Math in the Real World of Design & Art: Geometry, Measurements, & Projections. Quinn, Anna, ed. (Illus.). 96p. (Orig.). (J). (gr. 5-8). 1996. pap. text 10.95 (*0-86530-344-4*, IP 344-4) Incentive Pubns.

— On the Loose with Dr. Seuss: Using the Works of Theodor Geisel to Develop Reading, Writing, & Thinking Skills. Britt, Leslie, ed. (Illus.). 96p. (J). (gr. k-6). 1994. pap. text 10.95 (*0-86530-233-2*) Incentive Pubns.

— 180 Days Around the World: Learning about Countries & Cultures Through Research & Thinking-Skills Activities. Keeling, Jan, ed. (Illus.). 240p. (J). (gr. 4-8). 1993. pap. text 16.95 (*0-86530-253-7*, 253-7) Incentive Pubns.

— Rain Forest: Linking Environmental Studies with Everyday Life. Britt, Leslie, ed. (Illus.). 64p. (Orig.). (J). (gr. 2-6). 1993. pap. text, teacher ed. 8.95 (*0-86530-275-8*, 269-7) Incentive Pubns.

— Through the Valley of Love. 224p. 1987. pap. 5.95 (*0-310-47381-0*, 15584P) Zondervan.

— 20th-Century American Heroes: A Thematic Approach to Cultural Awareness. Keeling, Jan, ed. (Illus.). 80p. (J). (gr. 3-6). 1993. pap. text 9.95 (*0-86530-259-6*, 259-6) Incentive Pubns.

Cook, Shirley & Carl, Kathy. Linking Literature & Writing. (Illus.). 240p. (J). (gr. 1-4). 1989. pap. text 16.95 (*0-86530-064-X*, IP 166-5) Incentive Pubns.

Cook, Shirley, jt. auth. see Forte, Imogene.

Cook, Stanley A. A Glossary of the Aramaic Inscriptions. viii, 127p. 1974. reprint ed. 45.00 (*3-487-05314-4*) G Olms Pubs.

Cook, Stanley A., ed. see Smith, William Robertson.

Cook, Stanley J. & Suter, Richard W. The Scope of Grammar: A Study of Modern English. Talkington, William A., ed. (Illus.). 321p. (C). 1980. 60.00 (*0-07-012460-4*) McGraw.

Cook, Stephen. Coming of Age in the Global Village: The Science & Technology, Politics, Economics, Environment & Ethics Literacy Book. LC 90-62089. (Illus.). 400p. (Orig.). 1990. pap. 14.95 (*0-9627349-0-X*) Parthenon Bks.

— Laundromat. unabridged ed. Landes, William-Alan, ed. LC 98-15586. (Illus.). 55p. 1998. pap. 15.00 (*0-88734-205-1*) Players Pr.

Cook, Stephen, ed. ECOOP, 1989: Proceedings of the European Conference on Object-Oriented Programming, 1989. (British Computer Society Workshop Ser.). 400p. (C). 1990. text 115.00 (*0-521-38232-7*) Cambridge U Pr.

***Cook, Stephen & Russell, Stuart.** Heinrich Himmler's Camelot: Pictorial Documentary: The Wewelsburg, Ideological Center of the SS 1934-1945. LC 99-71545. (Illus.). vii, 258p. 2000. 65.00 (*0-9670443-0-8*) Kress Backm.

Cook, Stephen L. Prophecy & Apocalypticism: The Postexilic Social Setting. LC 95-23148. 240p. 1995. pap. 23.00 (*0-8006-2839-X*, 1-2839) Augsburg Fortress.

Cook, Stephen L., ed. see Landes, George M.

Cook, Stephen P. Physical Science in the Laboratory: An STS Approach. 3rd ed. (Illus.). 128p. (C). 1993. pap. 7.50 (*0-9627349-2-6*) Parthenon Bks.

— Physical Science in the Laboratory: An STS Approach. 4th rev. ed. Cook, Pamela J., ed. (Illus.). 144p. (C). 1995. pap. 9.25 (*0-9627349-3-4*) Parthenon Bks.

Cook, Sterling, et al. Annette Covington: Paintings & Drawings. LC 82-82113. (Illus.). 50p. (Orig.). 1982. pap. 5.00 (*0-940784-02-5*) Miami Univ Art.

***Cook, Steve.** Utah Fishing Guide, 2000 ed. 1999. pap. text 24.95 (*0-9671738-1-7*) Utah Outdoors.

Cook, Steve & Daniels, John D. Designing Object Systems: Object-Oriented Modelling with Syntropy. 317p. 1994. 62.00 (*0-13-203860-9*) P-H.

Cook, Steve, ed. see Heim, Judy & Hansen, Gloria.

Cook, Steve H., ed. The Correspondence Between Hart Crane & Waldo Frank. LC 96-61967. xxii, 212p. 1998. 39.00 (*0-87875-493-8*) Whitston Pub.

Cook, Stuart D. Handbook of Multiple Sclerosis. 2nd ed. LC 96-24682. (Neurological Disease & Therapy Ser.: Vol. 43). (Illus.). 640p. 1996. text 190.00 (*0-8247-9726-4*) Dekker.

— Universe Lost: Reclaiming a World View. 192p. (Orig.). (C). 1992. pap. 8.99 (*0-89900-404-0*) College Pr Pub.

***Cook, Sue.** Art Nouveau in Cross Stitch. (Cross Stitch Ser.). (Illus.). 40p. 1999. pap. 6.95 (*1-85391-764-8*) Merehurst Ltd.

— Cross Stitch Inspirations: 27 Design Form Psalm & Verses. 128p. 1999. 24.95 (*0-7153-0798-3*) Strlng Pub CA.

Cook, Sue C. The Numbers Book: Student Syllabus, 2 vols. (J). (gr. k-2). 1974. audio 19.95 (*0-89420-208-1*, 193000) Natl Book.

— The Numbers Book: Student Syllabus, 2 vols., 1. (J). (gr. k-2). 1974. pap. text 19.95 (*0-89420-081-X*, 193050) Natl Book.

— The Numbers Book: Student Syllabus, 2 vols., 2. (J). (gr. k-2). 1974. pap. text 19.95 (*0-89420-082-8*, 193051) Natl Book.

Cook, Susan, jt. auth. see Dow, Roger.

Cook, Susan C. & Tsou, Judy S., eds. Cecilia Reclaimed: Feminist Perspectives on Gender & Music. LC 93-18463. (Illus.). 296p. 1994. text 34.95 (*0-252-02036-7*); pap. text 15.95 (*0-252-06341-4*) U of Ill Pr.

Cook, Susan J., jt. auth. see Lamb, Norman.

Cook, Susan P., jt. auth. see Dow, Roger J.

Cook, Suzan D. Too Blessed to Be Stressed: Words of Wisdom for Women on the Move. LC 97-45839. 192p. 1998. pap. 12.99 (*0-7852-7070-1*) Nelson.

Cook, Suzan D., ed. Sister to Sister: Devotion for & from African American Women. 256p. 1995. pap. 11.00 (*0-8170-1221-4*) Judson.

Cook, Suzan D., jt. auth. see Watley, William D.

Cook, Suzan J., compiled by. SisterStrength: A Collection of Devotions for & from African-American Women. LC 98-8561. 256p. 1998. pap. 10.99 (*0-7852-7072-8*) Nelson.

Cook, Sybilla. Library Flipper: A Dewey Decimal System Guide. 49p. (YA). (gr. 5 up). 1988. 6.95 (*1-878383-08-6*) C Lee Pubns.

— Reference Flipper: A Guide to Reference Material. 49p. (YA). (gr. 5 up). 1988. reprint ed. 6.95 (*1-878383-09-4*) C Lee Pubns.

Cook, Sybilla A. Walking Portland. LC 98-26162. (Illus.). 281p. 1998. pap. 12.95 (*1-56044-604-8*) Falcon Pub Inc.

Cook, Sybilla A. & Page, Cheryl A. Books, Battles & Bees: Questions on Intermediate Level Children's Books. LC 93-29756. 180p. 1993. pap. 22.00 (*0-8389-0626-5*) ALA.

Cook, Sylvia J. Erskine Caldwell & the Fiction of Poverty: The Flesh & the Spirit. LC 90-28655. (Southern Literary Studies). 336p. 1991. pap. text 19.95 (*0-8071-1693-9*) La State U Pr.

— From Tobacco Road to Route 66: The Southern Poor White in Fiction. LC 75-35822. 222p. reprint ed. pap. 68.90 (*0-8357-3879-5*, 203661100004) Bks Demand.

Cook, T. A. The Story of Rouen. (Mediaeval Towns Ser.: Vol. 24). 1974. reprint ed. pap. 58.00 (*0-8115-0866-8*) Periodicals Srv.

Cook, T. D., ed. Underground Waste Management & Environmental Implications: Proceedings. LC 72-96385. (American Association of Petroleum Geologists. Memoir Ser.: No. 18). 420p. 1972. pap. 130.20 (*0-608-05610-3*, 206606800006) Bks Demand.

Cook, T. G., ed. History of Education in Europe. 99p. (C). 1974. 15.00 (*0-8464-1163-6*) Beekman Pubs.

Cook, Terence E. The Great Alternatives of Social Thought: Aristocrat, Saint, Capitalist, Socialist. 320p. (C). 1991. text 57.50 (*0-8476-7683-8*); pap. text 24.95 (*0-8476-7684-6*) Rowman.

Cook, Terrence E. Criteria of Social Scientific Knowledge: Interpretation, Prediction, Praxes. 208p. (C). 1994. pap. text 66.00 (*0-8476-7883-0*); lib. bdg. 25.95 (*0-8476-7884-9*) Rowman.

Cook, Terry. The Mark of the New World Order. 280p. 1995. pap. 29.95 (*0-9647860-0-1*) Virtue Intl Pubng.

— The Mark of the New World Order. LC 97-108. 385p. 1996. pap. 12.99 (*0-88368-466-7*) Whitaker Hse.

***Cook, Terry L.** Big Brother Nsa & It's Little Brother: National Security Agencys Gobal Survellance Network. 1999. pap. text 14.95 (*1-57558-036-5*) Hearthstone OK.

Cook, Theodore A. The Curves of Life. (Illus.). 512p. 1979. pap. 11.95 (*0-486-23701-X*) Dover.

***Cook, Theodore Andrea.** Old Provence. (Illus.). 2000. pap. 16.00 (*1-56656-372-0*) Interlink Pub.

Cook, Theodore F., jt. auth. see Cook, Haruko T.

Cook, Thomas. China. 2nd ed. (Illustrated Travel Guides from Thomas Cook Ser.). 1994. pap. 16.95 (*0-8442-9958-8*, Passprt Bks) NTC Contemp Pub Co.

— Iran: Historic & Cultural Persia. (Illustrated Travel Guides from Thomas Cook Ser.). (Illus.). 288p. 1994. pap. 17.95 (*0-8442-9457-8*, Passprt Bks) NTC Contemp Pub Co.

***Cook, Thomas.** Ireland. 2nd ed. (Passport's Illustrated Travel Guides Ser.). (Illus.). 192p. 1999. pap. 14.95 (*0-8442-4845-2*, 48452, Passprt Bks) NTC Contemp Pub Co.

Cook, Thomas. London. (Passport's Illustrated Travel Guides from Thomas Cook Ser.). (Illus.). 192p. 1994. pap. 12.95 (*0-8442-9040-8*, Passprt Bks) NTC Contemp Pub Co.

— London. 3rd ed. (Passport's Illustrated Travel Guides Ser.). (Illus.). 192p. 1998. pap. 14.95 (*0-8442-4823-1*, 48231, Passprt Bks) NTC Contemp Pub Co.

— Mortal Memory. 320p. 1994. mass mkt. 5.99 (*0-553-56532-X*) Bantam.

— New York. 2nd ed. (Passport's Illustrated Travel Guides Ser.). (Illus.). 192p. 1998. pap. 14.95 (*0-8442-4846-0*, 48460, Passprt Bks) NTC Contemp Pub Co.

— On the Rails Around Europe. 416p. 1995. pap. 14.95 (*0-8442-9037-8*, Passprt Bks) NTC Contemp Pub Co.

— Paris: Passport's Illustrated Travel Guides. 3rd ed. LC 96-70699. (Illus.). 192p. 1996. pap. text 14.95 (*0-8442-4840-1*) NTC Contemp Pub Co.

— Passport's Illustrated Guide to Caribbean Cruising. 2nd ed. (Passport's Illustrated Ser.). (Illus.). 192p. 2000. pap. 14.95 (*0-8442-1176-1*, 11761, Passprt Bks) NTC Contemp Pub Co.

— Passport's Illustrated Guide to Mexico. 2nd ed. (Passport's Illustrated Ser.). (Illus.). 192p. 2000. pap. 14.95 (*0-8442-1154-0*, 11540, Passprt Bks) NTC Contemp Pub Co.

— Passport's Illustrated Paris. (Passport's Illustrated Travel Guides from Thomas Cook Ser.). (Illus.). 192p. 1994. pap. 12.95 (*0-8442-9041-6*, Passprt Bks) NTC Contemp Pub Co.

— Prague. 2nd ed. LC 96-70698. (Passport's Illustrated Travel Guides Ser.). (Illus.). 192p. 1998. pap. 14.95 (*0-8442-4842-8*, 48428, Passprt Bks) NTC Contemp Pub Co.

C

— Rome. 2nd ed. (Passport's Illustrated Travel Guides Ser.). (Illus.). 192p. 1998. pap. 14.95 (*0-8442-4821-5*, 48215, Passprt Bks) NTC Contemp Pub Co.
— Soul-Saving Preaching. 1993. reprint ed. pap. 5.99 (*0-88019-304-2*) Schmul Pub Co.
— Sydney & New South Wales. 2nd ed. (Passport's Illustrated Travel Guides Ser.). (Illus.). 192p. 1998. pap. 14.95 (*0-8442-4820-7*, 48207, Passprt Bks) NTC Contemp Pub Co.
— Thomas Cook European Airport's Directory. 208p. 1994. pap. 15.95 (*0-8442-9039-4*, Passprt Bks) NTC Contemp Pub Co.
— Thomas Cook International Air Travel Handbook: A Guide to the World's Major Airports, Their Facilities & Transport Connections. LC 96-72070. (Illus.). 208p. 1997. pap. 24.95 (*0-8442-9188-9*) NTC Contemp Pub Co.
— Turkey. (Essential Guides Ser.). 1994. 7.95 (*0-8442-8939-6*, Passprt Bks) NTC Contemp Pub Co.
— Yunnan. 2nd ed. (Illustrated Travel Guides from Thomas Cook Ser.). (Illus.). 204p. 1995. pap. 19.95 (*0-8442-9664-3*, 96643, Passprt Bks) NTC Contemp Pub Co.

Cook, Thomas & Scioli, Frank P., eds. The Methodology of Policy Studies. (C). 1973. pap. 15.00 (*0-918592-05-4*) Pol Studies.
Cook, Thomas, et al. Meta-Analysis for Explanation: A Casebook. LC 91-17999. 1992. 45.00 (*0-87154-220-X*) Russell Sage.
— Meta-Analysis for Explanation: A Casebook. (Illus.). 392p. 1994. reprint ed. pap. 19.95 (*0-87154-228-5*) Russell Sage.
Cook, Thomas D. Qualitative & Quantitative Methods in Evaluation Research. Reichardt, Charles S., ed. LC 79-20962. (Sage Research Progress Series in Evaluation: Vol. 1). 160p. 1979. reprint ed. pap. 49.60 (*0-608-03379-0*, 205964300008) Bks Demand.
Cook, Thomas D., et al. Sesame Street Revisited. LC 74-25853. 420p. 1975. 39.95 (*0-87154-207-2*) Russell Sage.
Cook, Thomas G. Koster: An Artifact Analysis. LC 82-101459. (Prehistoric Records Ser.: No. 1). (Illus.). 218p. 1976. 9.00 (*0-942118-04-9*); pap. 6.00 (*0-942118-05-7*) Ctr Amer Arche.
***Cook, Thomas H.** Blood Innocents. LC 98-56127. 1999. 20.95 (*0-7862-1813-4*) Thorndike Pr.
Cook, Thomas H. Breakheart Hill. 320p. 1996. mass mkt. 5.99 (*0-553-57192-3*) Bantam.
— Breakheart Hill. large type ed. (Large Print Bks.). 1995. pap. 22.95 (*1-56895-251-1*) Wheeler Pub.
— The Chatham School Affair. LC 96-4021. 336p. 1997. mass mkt. 5.99 (*0-553-57193-1*) Bantam.
— Evidence of Blood. large type ed. LC 91-38371. 589p. 1992. reprint ed. lib. bdg. 21.95 (*1-56054-328-0*) Thorndike Pr.
— Evidence of Blood. 400p. 1998. reprint ed. mass mkt. 5.99 (*0-553-57836-7*) Bantam.
— Instruments of Night. 336p. 1999. mass mkt. 5.99 (*0-553-57820-0*) Bantam.
— Instruments of Night. large type ed. 1999. 28.95 (*0-7862-1825-8*) Mac Lib Ref.
— Mortal Memory. large type ed. LC 93-1388. (Cloak & Dagger Ser.). 431p. 1993. lib. bdg. 22.95 (*1-56054-707-3*) Thorndike Pr.
— Night Secrets. 1991. mass mkt. 5.99 (*0-446-36177-1*, Pub. by Warner Bks) Little.
***Cook, Thomas H.** Places in the Dark. LC 99-89644. 256p. 2000. 23.95 (*0-553-10563-9*, Spectra) Bantam.
Cook, Thomas H. Streets of Fire. 1991. mass mkt. 4.95 (*0-446-35972-6*, Pub. by Warner Bks) Little.
Cook, Thomas H. & Campbell, Donald T. Quasi-Experimentation, 001. (C). 1979. pap. 58.76 (*0-395-30790-2*) HM.
Cook, Thomas J., ed. Performance Measurement in Public Agencies. 196p. (Orig.). 1986. pap. 15.00 (*0-918592-87-9*) Pol Studies.
Cook, Thomas J., jt. auth. see Scioli, Frank P., Jr.
Cook, Thomas J., jt. ed. see Scioli, Frank P., Jr.
Cook, Thomas R., ed. Essays in Modern Thought. LC 68-16922. (Essay Index Reprint Ser.). 1977. 18.95 (*0-8369-0332-3*) Ayer.
Cook, Thomas W. Ants of California. (Illus.). xvi, 462p. 1953. 29.95 (*0-87015-036-7*) Pacific Bks.
***Cook, Tim.** No Place to Run: The Canadian Corps & Gas Warfare in the First World War. (Illus.). 352p. 1999. text 85.00 (*0-7748-0739-3*) UBC Pr.
— No Place to Run: The Canadian Corps & Gas Warfare in the First World War. (Illus.). 352p. 2000. pap. 24.95 (*0-7748-0740-7*, Pub. by UBC Pr) U of Wash Pr.
Cook, Tim, jt. auth. see Brooks, Benjamin.
Cook, Timothy. Making Laws & Making News: Media Strategies in the U. S. House of Representatives. 240p. 1989. 34.95 (*0-8157-1558-7*); pap. 14.95 (*0-8157-1557-9*) Brookings.
Cook, Timothy E. Governing with the News: The News Media as a Political Institution. LC 97-23716. 1997. pap. text 18.00 (*0-226-11500-3*) U Ch Pr.
Cook, Tom, ed. see Ferber, Kae.
***Cook, Tony & Prater, Robin.** Abc's of Architectural & Interior Design Drafting. 528p. 2000. pap. 46.67 (*0-13-086637-7*, Prentice Hall) P-H.
Cook, Trevor. Beginners Introduction to Homeopathy: Good Health Guide. 31p. 1987. pap. 3.95 (*0-87983-394-7*, 33947K, Keats Publng) NTC Contemp Pub Co.
Cook, Veronica L. Collection of Short Stories: Love, Romance & Desire. 200p. (Orig.). 1989. pap. 10.00 (*0-685-29995-3*) Ronnie Two Pub.
— Editorials of My Mind: Inpirational Messages. 100p. (Orig.). (YA). (gr. 9-12). 1989. pap. 7.00 (*0-685-29992-9*) Ronnie Two Pub.
— The Hardest Decision - Abortion: An Inside Story. 50p. (Orig.). 1989. pap. 7.00 (*0-685-29994-5*) Ronnie Two Pub.
— Mike the Copycat: Adventures & Stories of Cat Tails. (Illus.). 50p. (Orig.). (J). (ps up). 1989. pap. text. write for info. (*0-318-66532-8*) Ronnie Two Pub.
— My Collection of Poems: Expressions. 70p. (Orig.). 1989. pap. text 10.00 (*0-685-29993-7*) Ronnie Two Pub.
Cook, Victor J. & Larreche, Jean-Claude. Readings in Marketing Strategy. 2nd ed. 320p. (C). 1990. mass mkt. 31.75 (*0-89426-139-8*) Course Tech.
Cook, Vivian. Inside Language. LC 96-35490. 304p. 1997. text 70.00 (*0-340-69270-7*, Pub. by E A) OUP.
— Inside Language. LC 96-35490. (Illus.). 304p. 1997. pap. text 24.95 (*0-340-60761-0*) OUP.
— Second Language Learning & Language Teaching. 176p. 1995. pap. text 16.95 (*0-340-52626-2*, A5878, Pub. by E A) St Martin.
— Second Language Learning & Language Teaching. 2nd ed. LC 95-36369. 240p. 1996. pap. text 18.95 (*0-340-65202-0*, Pub. by E A) OUP.
***Cook, Vivian E.** Alaska Adventure. LC 99-96919. (Adventures of Spencer, Private Eye & His Psychic Sister, Tiffany Ser.: No. 6). (Illus.). 66p. (J). (gr. 3-5). 1999. pap. 8.95 (*1-928659-05-5*) Two Sisters Pubg.
— Danger under the Big Top. LC 99-93904. (Adventures of Spencer, Private Eye & His Psychic Sister, Tiffany Ser.: No. 4). (Illus.). 66p. (J). (gr. 3-5). 1999. pap. 8.95 (*1-928659-03-9*) Two Sisters Pubg.
Cook, Vivian E. The Journey Home. LC 99-93584. (Adventures of Spencer, Private Eye & His Psychic Sister, Tiffany Ser.: No. 2). (Illus.). 50p. (J). (gr. 3-5). 1999. pap. 7.95 (*1-928659-01-2*) Two Sisters Pubg.
— Rescue from Rapid Gully. LC 99-93777. (Adventures of Spencer, Private Eye & His Psychic Sister, Tiffany Ser.: No. 3). (Illus.). 56p. (J). (gr. 3-5). 1999. pap. 7.95 (*1-928659-02-0*) Two Sisters Pubg.
— The Search for Charming Carletta. LC 99-93583. (Adventures of Spencer, Private Eye & His Psychic Sister, Tiffany Ser.: No. 1). (Illus.). 43p. (J). (gr. 3-5). 1999. pap. 7.95 (*1-928659-00-4*) Two Sisters Pubg.
***Cook, Vivian E.** Trapped in Haunted Castle. LC 99-95082. (Adventures of Spencer, Private Eye & His Psychic Sister, Tiffany Ser.: No. 5). (Illus.). 58p. (J). (gr. 3-5). 1999. pap. 8.95 (*1-928659-04-7*) Two Sisters Pubg.
Cook, Vivian J. & Newson, Mark. Chomsky's Universal Grammar: An Introduction. 2nd ed. LC 95-30630. 336p. (C). 1996. 69.95 (*0-631-19796-6*); pap. 29.95 (*0-631-19556-4*) Blackwell Pubs.
Cook, W. & Seymour, P., eds. Polyhedral Combinatorics: Proceedings of the DIMACS Workshop. LC 90-49139. (DIMACS Series in Discrete Mathematics & Theoretical Computer Science: Vol. 1). 288p. 1991. text 57.00 (*0-8218-6591-9*, DIMACS/1) Am Math.
Cook, W. George, jt. auth. see McCoy, Dell A.
Cook, W. Robert. Specifications for Speed in the Racehorse: The Airflow Factors. (Illus.). 253p. (Orig.). (C). 1989. pap. 25.00 (*0-929346-05-X*) R Meerdink Co Ltd.
Cook, Wade. Cook's Book on Creative Real Estate. 2nd ed. LC 98-28111. 1998. 14.95 (*0-910019-37-1*) Lighthouse Pubns.
— 101 Ways to Buy Real Estate Without Cash. 2nd ed. LC 98-37362. 320p. 1996. pap. 16.95 (*0-910019-74-6*) Lghthse Pub Gp.
— Real Estate for Real People. rev. ed. 288p. 1998. boxed set 24.95 (*0-910019-93-2*) Lghthse Pub Gp.
— Real Wealth. 1986. mass mkt. 9.95 (*0-446-37037-1*, Pub. by Warner Bks) Little.
— Stock Market Miracles. 1996. 24.95 (*0-910019-71-1*) Lghthse Pub Gp.
— Wealth 101. 2nd ed. LC 97-37898. 312p. 1999. 24.95 (*0-910019-83-5*) Lighthouse Pubns.
Cook, Wade B. A+ LC 97-46964. 124p. 1998. 21.95 (*0-910019-39-8*) Lghthse Pub Gp.
— Bear Market Baloney. 1997. boxed set 22.95 (*0-910019-77-0*) Lghthse Pub Gp.
— Brilliant Deductions. LC 97-31549. 1997. boxed set 26.95 (*0-910019-89-4*) Lghthse Pub Gp.
***Cook, Wade B.** Bulls & Bears. (Wall Street Money Machine Ser.: No. 3). Orig. Title: Bear Market Baloney. 2000. 22.95 (*1-892008-65-3*, Pub. by Lghthse Pub Gp) Origin Bk Sales.
Cook, Wade B. Business Buy the Bible. LC 97-19664. 192p. 1997. text 16.95 (*0-910019-68-1*, Pub. by Lghthse Pub Gp) Origin Bk Sales.
— Don't Set Goals: The Old Way. LC 97-4402. 120p. (Orig.). 1997. pap. 14.95 (*0-910019-50-9*) Lghthse Pub Gp.
— How to Pick up Foreclosures. 2nd ed. 130p. (Orig.). 1996. pap. text 16.95 (*0-910019-66-5*) Lghthse Pub Gp.
— The Incorporation Handbook. 1997. reprint ed. 49.95 (*0-910019-20-7*) Lghthse Pub Gp.
— Owner Financing. 1997. reprint ed. pap. 5.95 (*0-910019-05-3*) Lghthse Pub Gp.
— Real Estate Money Machine. 4th rev. ed. (Illus.). 210p. 1996. reprint ed. text 24.95 (*0-910019-43-6*) Lghthse Pub Gp.
***Cook, Wade B.** Safety 1st Investing. LC 99-20560. 368p. 1999. boxed set 22.00 (*1-892008-59-9*, Pub. by Lghthse Pub Gp) Origin Bk Sales.
— Safety 1st Investing. (Wall Street Money Machine Ser.: No. 4). 2000. 26.95 (*1-892008-66-1*, Pub. by Lghthse Pub Gp) Origin Bk Sales.
Cook, Wade B. Wade Cook's Power Quotes: To Whom Are You Listening. 1998. 9.95 (*0-910019-78-9*) Lghthse Pub.
— Wall Street Money Machine: New & Incredible Strategies for Cash Flow & Wealth. rev. ed. LC 99-17010. 304p. 1999. boxed set 24.95 (*1-892008-60-2*, Pub. by Lghthse Pub Gp) Origin Bk Sales.
***Cook, Wade B.** Wall Street Money Machine: Stock Market Miracles, 9, Vol. 2. 2000. 24.95 (*1-892008-64-5*, Pub. by Lghthse Pub Gp) Origin Bk Sales.
Cook, Wade B. Wall Street Money Machine/Dynamic Dollars. 1997. 24.95 incl. audio (*0-910019-73-8*) Lghthse Pub Gp.
— Y2K Gold Rush. LC 98-31994. 152p. 1998. pap. 16.95 (*1-882723-36-8*, Pub. by Gold Leaf Pr) Origin Bk Sales.
Cook, Wade B., compiled by. Wade Cook's Power Quotes. LC 98-28818. 440p. 1998. boxed set 29.95 (*0-910019-90-8*) Lghthse Pub Gp.
***Cook, Wade B., et al.** Success: American Style. 168p. 2000. pap. 16.95 (*1-892008-63-7*) Lghthse Pub Gp.
***Cook Waldron, Kathleen.** Loon Lake Fishing Derby. LC 98-89929. (Illus.). 32p. (J). (gr. k-3). 1999. 14.95 (*1-55143-142-4*) Orca Bk Pubs.
Cook Waldron, Kathleen & Turney Zagwyn, Deborah. A Winter's Yarn. (Illus.). 40p. (J). (ps-3). 1989. pap. 6.95 (*0-88995-048-2*, Pub. by Red Deer) Genl Dist Srvs.
Cook, Walter A. Case Grammar Applied. LC 97-62075. (Publications in Linguistics: Vol. 127). 291p. 1998. pap. 29.00 (*1-55671-046-1*) S I L Intl.
— Case Grammar Theory. LC 88-33553. 234p. (Orig.). 1989. reprint ed. pap. 72.60 (*0-7837-9389-8*, 206013400005) Bks Demand.
— Introduction to Tagmemic Analysis. fac. ed. LC 78-1268. 220p. 1978. reprint ed. pap. 68.20 (*0-7837-7802-3*, 204755800007) Bks Demand.
Cook, Walter W. The Logical & Legal Bases of the Conflict of Laws. LC 43-268. (Harvard Studies in the Conflict of Laws: Vol. 5). xx, 473p. 1978. reprint ed. lib. bdg. 50.00 (*0-89941-130-4*, 300170) W S Hein.
Cook, Wanda D., jt. auth. see Edwards, Ronald R.
Cook, Warren L. Epigraphic Society Occasional Publications: A Guide to Volumes 1-17. Smith, Roberta C., ed. 106p. 1991. lib. bdg. 15.00 (*1-880820-00-5*) ISAC Pr.
Cook, Wayne, ed. see Towns, Elmer L.
Cook, Wendy, et al, eds. The Big Green Book: Northwest Music Industry Directory & Guide, 1992. 3rd ed. 208p. 1992. pap. 19.95 (*0-9632474-3-3*) NW Intl Enter.
Cook, Wendy, jt. ed. see Ormsby, Gregory.
***Cook, Will.** Apache Ambush. 2000. 19.00 (*0-7540-8076-5*, Gunsmoke) Chivers N Amer.
Cook, Will. Apache Ambush. large type ed. (Sagebrush Large Print Westerns Ser.). 282p. 1995. lib. bdg. 17.95 (*1-57490-001-3*) T T Beeler.
— Elizabeth, by Name. 320p. 1995. pap. text, mass mkt. 4.99 (*0-8439-3868-4*) Dorchester Pub Co.
— Fury at Painted Rock. large type ed. (Western Ser.). 384p. 1994. pap. 16.99 (*0-7089-7584-4*) Ulverscroft.
— The Last Scout. large type ed. LC 97-17585. 1997. lib. bdg. 17.95 (*1-57490-055-2*, Sagebrush LP West) T T Beeler.
— The Rain Tree. large type ed. LC 97-24019. 1997. 20.95 (*0-7838-1676-6*, G K Hall Lrg Type) Mac Lib Ref.
— The Rain Tree: A Western Story. LC 96-5872. 1996. 16.95 (*0-7862-0665-9*) Five Star.
***Cook, Will.** A Saga of Texas: Until Shadows Fall. LC 99-55127. 2000. 30.00 (*0-7862-1847-9*) Mac Lib Ref.
Cook, Will. A Saga of Texas: Until Shadows Fall. large type ed. 2001. pap. 30.00 (*0-7862-1852-5*) Thorndike Pr.
***Cook, Will.** The Texas Pistol. 2000. 20.95 (*1-57490-269-5*, Sagebrush LP West) T T Beeler.
Cook, Will. Texas Yankee - Bullets for the Doctor. LC 98-50923. 1999. write for info. (*1-57490-183-4*) T T Beeler.
— Until Day Breaks. LC 98-52077. 1999. 19.95 (*0-7862-1794-4*) Thorndike Pr.
***Cook, Will.** Until Day Breaks Book 1: A Saga of Texas. large type ed. Macmillan Library Reference Staff, ed. LC 99-58958. (Thorndike Western Ser.). 2000. 21.95 (*0-7862-1795-2*) Thorndike Pr.
Cook, Will. The Wind River Kid. large type ed. (Linford Western Library). 368p. 1995. pap. 16.99 (*0-7089-7696-4*, Linford) Ulverscroft.
— The Wranglers. LC 98-33783. 241 p. 1999. write for info. (*0-7540-3540-9*) Chivers N Amer.
— The Wranglers. large type ed. LC 98-33783. 1999. 30.00 (*0-7838-0356-7*, G K Hall Lrg Type) Mac Lib Ref.
Cook, Will M., et al. The Music & Scripts of "In Dahomey" Riis, Thomas L., ed. (Music of the United States of America Ser.: Vol. MUSA5). (Illus.). lxxii, 245p. 1996. pap. 130.00 (*0-89579-342-3*) A-R Eds.
***Cook, William, ed.** Ha Bloody Ha: Comedians Talking. 2000. pap. 19.95 (*1-85702-180-0*, Pub. by Fourth Estate) Trafalgar.
Cook, William, et al, eds. Combinatorial Optimization: Papers from the DIMACS Special Year. LC 95-1957. (DIMACS Series in Discrete Mathematics & Theoretical Computer Science: Vol. 20). 441p. 1995. text 98.00 (*0-8218-0239-9*, DIMACS/20) Am Math.
Cook, William, jt. auth. see Ostrom, John.
***Cook, William A.** A Time to Know. LC 00-100846. 192p. 2000. pap. 13.95 (*1-58244-066-2*) Rutledge Bks.
Cook, William B., Jr., compiled by. Catalogue of the Egyptological Library of the Late Charles Edwin Wilbour. 802p. 1996. reprint ed. 80.00 (*1-888262-30-3*) Martino Pubng.
Cook, William E. Avian Desert Predators. Cloudsley-Thompson, J. L., ed. LC 97-12159. (Adaptations of Desert Organisms Ser.). (Illus.). 125p. 1997. 64.95 (*3-540-59262-8*) Spr-Verlag.
Cook, William H. Road to the 707: The Inside Story of Designing the 707. 288p. 1991. pap. 18.00 (*0-9629605-0-0*) TYC Pub.
Cook, William H. Success, Motivation & the Scriptures. LC 74-82582. 224p. 1974. 9.99 (*0-8054-5226-5*, 4252-26) Broadman.
***Cook, William J., Jr.** The Evolving Corporation: A Humanist Interpretation. LC 99-462242. 300p. 2000. 67.00 (*1-56720-279-9*, Q279, Quorum Bks) Greenwood.
Cook, William J., Jr. Masks, Modes, & Morals: The Art of Evelyn Waugh. LC 73-118125. 352p. 1975. 39.50 (*0-8386-7707-X*) Fairleigh Dickinson.
— Strategic Planning for America's Schools. 2nd ed. 131p. 1995. 23.95 (*0-87652-132-4*, 021-0295) Am Assn Sch Admin.
***Cook, William J.** Strategics: The Art & Science of Creating Holistic Strategy. LC 99-33205. 320p. 2000. 69.50 (*1-56720-278-0*) Greenwood.
Cook, William J., Jr. The Urgency of Change. Hirsch, Stephanie, ed. 73p. (Orig.). 1988. pap. 6.95 (*0-317-91172-4*) Underdog Pr.
— The Urgency of Change: America's Schools in Transition. Hirsch, Stephanie, ed. LC 88-50676. 80p. 1988. pap. 4.95 (*0-929570-00-6*) Underdog Pr.
Cook, William J., et al. Combinatorial Optimization. LC 97-35774. (Series in Discrete Mathematics). 368p. 1997. 64.95 (*0-471-55894-X*, Wiley-Interscience) Wiley.
Cook, William R. Francis in America: A Catalog of Early Paintings of St. Francis of Assisi in the United States & Canada. LC 98-16416. 1998. 39.95 (*0-8199-0984-X*) Franciscan Pr.
— Manual of Tumescent Liposculpture & Laser Cosmetic Surgery: Including the Weekend Alternative to the Facelift. LC 98-50220. 217p. 1999. write for info. (*0-7817-1987-9*) Lppncott W & W.
— Specifications for Speed in the Racehorse: The Airflow Factors. 1993. pap. text 25.00 (*0-929346-21-1*) R Meerdink Co Ltd.
Cook, William R. & Herzman, Ronald B. The Medieval World View: An Introduction. (Illus.). 394p. 1983. pap. text 23.95 (*0-19-503090-7*) OUP.
Cook, William W. Adrift in the Unknown: Queer Adventures in a Queer Realm. LC 74-15957. (Science Fiction Ser.). 305p. 1975. reprint ed. 25.95 (*0-405-06283-4*) Ayer.
— Cast Away at the Pole. Reginald, R. & Melville, Douglas, eds. LC 77-84215. (Lost Race & Adult Fantasy Ser.). 1978. reprint ed. lib. bdg. 29.95 (*0-405-10970-9*) Ayer.
— Hudson Hornet. 42p. (Orig.). 1989. pap. 3.95 (*0-918408-27-X*) Ishmael Reed.
***Cook, William W.** Spiritual. 56p. 1999. pap. 10.95 (*0-918408-33-4*) Ishmael Reed.
Cook, Zeb. The Dungeon Master's Guide. 2nd rev. ed. (Advanced Dungeons & Dragons, 2nd Edition Ser.). (Illus.). 1995. 24.95 (*0-7869-0328-7*, Pub. by TSR Inc) Random.
— The New Player's Handbook. 2nd rev. ed. (Advanced Dungeons & Dragons, 2nd Edition Ser.). (Illus.). 1995. 29.95 (*0-7869-0329-5*, Pub. by TSR Inc) Random.
Cookbook Committee, National Park Service, Western. What's Cooking in Our National Parks? LC 89-8541. (Illus.). 254p. 1989. reprint ed. pap. 9.95 (*0-89646-081-9*) Vistabooks.
Cookbook Committee of Holy Trinity Episcopal Churc, ed. Not by Bread Alone. (Illus.). 304p. 1985. pap. 11.95 (*0-9615284-0-0*) Holy Episcopal.
Cookbook Committee Staff. Diamonds in the Desert. LC 87-90525. (Illus.). 350p. 1989. reprint ed. 13.95 (*0-9618029-0-1*) Ozona Womans.
— Jubilee Cookbook: The Jubilee of Our Many Blessings. (Illus.). 254p. 1994. text 14.95 (*0-9641283-0-6*) Dallas Bethlehem.
Cookbook Committee Staff, ed. Heavenly Hosts. (Illus.). 350p. 1991. write for info. (*0-9629583-0-1*) Bryn Mawr Pres.
Cookbook Committee Staff & Cape Cod Academy Staff, eds. Scoops from the Bay. (Illus.). 376p. 1989. 15.95 (*0-9623316-1-9*) Cape Cod Acad.
Cookbook Committee Staff, jt. ed. see Stonewall Jackson House Staff.
Cookbook Committee, 1979, ed. Indianapolis Collects & Cooks. (Illus.). 208p. 1980. pap. text 6.00 (*0-936260-00-9*) Ind Mus Art.
Cookbook Consortium. Fruits, Nuts, Etc: Snack Mix Ingredient Substitution Recipe Book. 1984. ring bd. 19.95 (*0-318-04312-2*) Prosperity & Profits.
— Honey Basic Information Rhyme. 1984. pap. text 4.00 (*0-318-01298-7*) Prosperity & Profits.
Cookbook Consortium Educational Division Staff. Recipe Research Correspondence Course. 1984. ring bd. 25.95 (*0-318-04319-X*) Prosperity & Profits.
— Recipe Research Correspondence Course for Pastries & Desserts. 1984. ring bd. 21.95 (*0-318-04320-3*) Prosperity & Profits.
— Regional Cookbook, Recipe & Cookbook Research Correspondence Course. 1985. ring bd. 26.95 (*0-318-04321-1*) Prosperity & Profits.
Cookbook Consortium Information Division Staff, ed. Baby Food Cookbooks & Recipe References: A How to Find or Locate Workbook. 60p. 1993. ring bd. 21.95 (*0-318-00119-5*) Prosperity & Profits.
— Singles Cookbooks: How to Find or Locate Cookbooks for Singles Cooking. 70p. 1992. ring bd. 24.95 (*0-318-00120-9*) Prosperity & Profits.
Cookbook Consortium Staff. Coffee Substitutes with Medicinal Additives: A Recipe Book. 1993. pap. text 19.95 (*0-318-04305-X*) Prosperity & Profits.
— Dump Cake, Twenty-Five & More Ways to Make a Dump Cake. 1984. ring bd. 21.95 (*0-318-04310-6*) Prosperity & Profits.
— Family Meals Recipe & Cookbook Research Correspondence Course. 1993. ring bd. 26.95 (*0-318-04311-4*) Prosperity & Profits.
— Food Variations Suggestion Rhymes, Bk. 1. 1993. pap. text 4.50 (*0-318-01300-2*) Prosperity & Profits.
— Mock Champagne Ingredient Substitution Recipe Book. 1984. ring bd. 19.95 (*0-318-04313-0*) Prosperity & Profits.

C

An Asterisk (*) at the beginning of an entry indicates that the title is appearing for the first time.

An Asterisk (*) at the beginning of an entry indicates that the title is appearing for the first time.

— Minesta's Vision: A Centenary Collection of Grace Cooke's Writing. (Illus.). 60p. (Orig.). 1992. pap. (*0-85487-089-X*) White Eagle.

— The New Mediumship. 88p. 1965. pap. 8.95 (*0-85487-068-7*) White Eagle.

— Sun Men of the Americas. 120p. 1975. pap. (*0-85487-057-1*) White Eagle.

Cooke, Grace & Cooke, Ivan. The Light in Britain. (Illus.). 128p. 1971. pap. (*0-85487-056-3*) White Eagle.

Cooke, Grace M. The Grapple. LC 74-22775. (Labor Movement in Fiction & Non-Fiction Ser.). reprint ed. 42.50 (*0-404-58415-2*) AMS Pr.

***Cooke, Graham.** Desarrolle Sus Dones Profeticus. (SPA.). 2000. mass mkt. 11.99 (*0-7899-0586-8*) Editorial Unilit.

— A Divine Confrontation. 1999. pap. 14.99 (*0-7684-2039-3*) Destiny Image.

Cooke, Grant & Cox, Maureen, eds. Teaching Young Children to Draw: Imaginative Approaches to Representational Drawing. LC 98-104125. 160p. 1997. pap. 22.95 (*0-7507-0653-8*, Falmer Pr) Taylor & Francis.

Cooke, Gwen C. Toward Excellence in Secondary Vocational Education: Improving Teaching. 43p. 1985. 4.75 (*0-318-22219-1*, IN293) Ctr Educ Trng Employ.

Cooke, H. B., jt. ed. see Maglio, Vincent J.

Cooke, H. P. Osiris. 180p. 1979. reprint ed. pap. 15.00 (*0-89005-287-5*) Ares.

Cooke, H. R. Driver Family: A Genealogical Memoir of the Descendants of Robert & Phebe Driver of Lynn, Mass. with Appendix Containing 83 Allied Families. 556p. 1989. reprint ed. pap. 85.00 (*0-8328-0497-5*); reprint ed. lib. bdg. 95.00 (*0-8328-0496-7*) Higginson Bk Co.

***Cooke, Hannah.** When Someone Dies: A Practical Guide to Holistic Care for the Terminally Ill. LC 99-58768. 192p. 2000. pap. 35.00 (*0-7506-4094-4*) Buttrwrth-Heinemann.

Cooke, Hannah, jt. auth. see Williams, Anne.

Cooke, Henry, ed. Iron & Manganese Ore Databook. 1992. pap. text. write for info. (*0-947671-62-5*) Metal Bulletin.

Cooke, Henry M., IV. Beneath the Elms: A Pictorial History of Randolph, Massachusetts. LC 93-26531. 1993. write for info. (*0-89865-865-9*) Donning Co.

Cooke, Hope. Seeing New York: History Walks for Armchair & Footloose Travelers. (Critical Perspectives on the Past Ser.). (Illus.). 416p. (Orig.). (C). 1995. pap. 18.95 (*1-56639-289-6*); lib. bdg. 69.95 (*1-56639-288-8*) Temple U Pr.

Cooke, I. D., jt. ed. see Barratt, Christopher L.

Cooke, Ian. Plantfinder's Guide to Tender Perennials. LC 98-22940. (Illus.). 192p. 1998. 34.95 (*0-88192-450-4*) Timber.

Cooke, Ian & Mayes, Paul. Introduction to Innovation & Technology Transfer. LC 95-48910. 365p. 1995. 65.00 (*0-89006-832-1*) Artech Hse.

Cooke, Ian, jt. ed. see Barratt, Christopher L.

Cooke, Ivan. Arthur Conan Doyle's Book of the Beyond. rev. ed. (Illus.). 256p. (Orig.). 1994. pap. (*0-85487-093-8*) White Eagle.

— Bright New Year: A Centenary Collection of Ivan Cooke's Writing. 64p. (Orig.). 1989. pap. (*0-85487-079-2*) White Eagle.

— Healing by the Spirit. 208p. 1955. pap. 11.95 (*0-85487-069-5*) White Eagle.

Cooke, Ivan, jt. auth. see Cooke, Grace.

Cooke, J., et al. Voyage Charters. 930p. 1993. 260.00 (*1-85044-263-0*) LLP.

Cooke, J. C. & Elevatorski, E. A. Latin American Gold. LC 98-92274. 336p. 1999. 435.00 (*0-942218-35-3*) Minobras.

Cooke, J. F. Music Masters Old & New. 1972. 59.95 (*0-8490-0682-1*) Gordon Pr.

Cooke, J. R. Architects, Engineers & the Law: Commentary & Materials. xxxiv, 314p. 1989. pap. 45.50 (*0-455-20946-4*, Pub. by LawBk Co) Gaunt.

Cooke, J. W. The American Tradition of Liberty, 1800-1860: From Jefferson to Lincoln. LC 86-18081. (Studies in Social & Political Theory: Vol. 1). 236p. 1986. lib. bdg. 89.95 (*0-88946-101-5*) E Mellen.

Cooke, Jacob E. Pennsylvania & the American Constitution. (Illus.). 14p. (Orig.). 1989. pap. 3.00 (*1-877701-00-9*) NCH&GS.

— Tench Coxe & the Early Republic. LC 77-28832. (Institute of Early American History & Culture Ser.). (Illus.). xiv, 573p. 1978. 59.95 (*0-8078-1308-7*) U of NC Pr.

Cooke, Jacob E., ed. The Federalist. LC 82-2815. 702p. 1982. pap. 25.00 (*0-8195-6077-4*, Wesleyan Univ Pr) U Pr of New Eng.

Cooke, James F. Great Pianists on Piano Playing. LC 74-27332. reprint ed. 43.50 (*0-404-12885-8*) AMS Pr.

— Great Singers on the Art of Singing. LC 74-27333. (Orig.). reprint ed. 45.00 (*0-404-12886-6*) AMS Pr.

Cooke, James F., jt. auth. see Brower, Harriette M.

Cooke, James Francis. Great Pianist on Piano Playing: Godowsky, Hofmann, Lhevinne, Paderewski & 24 Other Legendary Pianists. LC 99-38221. 418p. 1999. pap. text 12.95 (*0-486-40845-0*) Dover.

Cooke, James J. The All-Americans at War. LC 98-21782. 168p. 1999. 55.00 (*0-275-95740-3*, Praeger Pubs) Greenwood.

— Back Roads: Twenty Back Road Tours for the Whole Family. 1999. pap. 12.95 (*0-916179-54-0*) Ariz Hwy.

— One Hundred Miles from Bagdad: With the French in Desert Storm. LC 92-39282. 256p. 1993. 47.95 (*0-275-94528-6*, C4528, Praeger Pubs) Greenwood.

— Pershing & His Generals: Command & Staff in the AEF. LC 97-12319. 192p. 1997. 59.95 (*0-275-95363-7*, Praeger Pubs) Greenwood.

— The Rainbow Division in the Great War, 1917-1919. LC 93-37024. 304p. 1994. 65.00 (*0-275-94768-8*, Praeger Pubs) Greenwood.

— The U. S. Air Service in the Great War: An International Exploration. LC 95-34093. 272p. 1996. 65.00 (*0-275-94862-5*, Praeger Pubs) Greenwood.

Cooke, James J., ed. see French Colonial Historical Society Staff.

Cooke, Jane K. & Haipt, Mildred. Thinking with the Whole Brain: An Integrative Teaching & Learning Model (K-8) 56p. 1986. pap. 6.95 (*0-8106-0687-9*); pap. 6.95 (*0-8106-1831-1*) NEA.

Cooke, Janette & Finneran, Kathleen. A Clearing in the Crowd: Innovations in Emergency Services. LC 94-2739. (Papers). 48p. 1994. 10.00 (*1-881277-11-9*) United Hosp Fund.

***Cooke, Janice.** Peckham Cry. 290p. 1999. pap. 8.95 (*1-901442-05-5*) Seven Hills Bk.

***Cooke, Jim.** Charles Dickens' Ireland: An Anthology. 200p. 1999. pap. 24.95 (*0-9528453-8-5*, Pub. by Woodfield Pr) Irish Bks Media.

Cooke, Jo. Greene's Tu Quoque. LC 72-133649. (Tudor Facsimile Texts. Old English Plays Ser.: No. 131). reprint ed. 59.50 (*0-404-53431-7*) AMS Pr.

***Cooke, Jocelyne.** Secrets of the Body: Your Character & Future Revealed. (Illus.). 128p. 2000. pap. 6.95 (*965-494-101-5*) Astrolog Pub.

— Secrets of the Face: Your Character & Future Revealed. 128p. 2000. pap. 6.95 (*965-494-106-6*) Astrolog Pub.

Cooke, John. Building & the Law. (Illus.). 210p. 24.95 (*0-86840-244-3*, Pub. by New South Wales Univ Pr) Intl Spec Bk.

— Constructing Correct Software: The Basics. Schuman, S. A., ed. LC 97-26050. (Formal Approaches to Computing & Information Technology Ser.). 410p. 1998. pap. 54.95 (*3-540-76156-X*) Spr-Verlag.

— The Influence of Painting on Five Canadian Writers: Alice Munro, Hugh Hood, Timothy Findley, Margaret Atwood, & Michael Ondaatje. LC 95-34705. (Canadian Studies: Vol. 10). 264p. 1996. text 89.95 (*0-7745-8838-1*) E Mellen.

— The Influence of Painting on Five Canadian Writers: Alice Munro, Hugh Hood, Timothy Findley, Margaret Atwood, & Michael Ondaatje, Vol. 10. LC 95-34705. (Canadian Studies). 1996. write for info. (*0-7734-8838-3*) E Mellen.

— Janis Joplin: A Performance Diary, 1966-1970. (Illus.). 160p. 1997. 24.95 (*1-888358-11-4*) Acid Test Prodns.

Cooke, John B. The Snowblind Moon. 864p. 1993. mass mkt. 5.99 (*0-8125-2461-6*, Pub. by Tor Bks) St Martin.

Cooke, John E. The Life of Stonewall Jackson: From Official Papers, Contemporary Narratives, & Personal Acquaintance. LC 76-179511. (Select Bibliographies Reprint Ser.). 1977. reprint ed. 25.95 (*0-8369-6640-6*) Ayer.

— Mohun. LC 68-20008. (Americans in Fiction Ser.). (Illus.). reprint ed. pap. text 6.95 (*0-89197-856-9*); reprint ed. lib. bdg. 22.00 (*0-8398-0271-4*) Irvington.

— My Lady Pocahontas. LC 68-20009. (Americans in Fiction Ser.). reprint ed. pap. text 5.95 (*0-89197-862-3*) Irvington.

— My Lady Pokahontas. LC 68-20009. (Americans in Fiction Ser.). reprint ed. lib. bdg. 22.00 (*0-8398-0272-2*) Irvington.

— Pretty Mrs. Gaston & Other Stories. LC 74-94713. (Short Story Index Reprint Ser.). 1977. 20.95 (*0-8369-3092-4*) Ayer.

— Surry of Eagle's Nest: Or, the Memoirs of a Staff Officer Serving in Virginia. LC 68-23718. (Americans in Fiction Ser.). 484p. reprint ed. lib. bdg. 37.00 (*0-8398-0273-0*) Irvington.

— Surry of Eagle's Nest: Or, the Memoirs of a Staff Officer Serving in Virginia. (Americans in Fiction Ser.). 484p. (C). 1986. reprint ed. pap. text 8.95 (*0-8290-2037-3*) Irvington.

— Virginia: A History of the People. LC 72-3765. (American Commonwealths Ser.: No. 1). reprint ed. 49.50 (*0-404-57201-4*) AMS Pr.

— The Virginia Comedians: Or, Old Days in the Old Dominion, 2 vols. in 1. LC 68-23717. (Americans in Fiction Ser.). 625p. reprint ed. lib. bdg. 50.00 (*0-8398-0274-9*) Irvington.

— The Virginia Comedians: Or, Old Days in the Old Dominion, 2 vol. in 1. 625p. (C). 1986. reprint ed. pap. text 9.95 (*0-8290-2048-9*) Irvington.

— The Virginia Comedians: or Old Days in the Old Dominion. (BCL1-PS American Literature Ser.). 1992. reprint ed. lib. bdg. 99.00 (*0-7812-6691-2*) Rprt Serv.

— Wearing of the Gray: Being Personal Portraits, Scenes & Adventures of the War. LC 97-30013. (Illus.). 624p. 1997. pap. 24.95 (*0-8071-2216-5*) La State U Pr.

Cooke, John E., ed. The Dublin Book of Irish Verse, Seventeen Twenty-Eight - Nineteen Hundred Nine. LC 70-152148. (Granger Index Reprint Ser.). 1977. reprint ed. 42.95 (*0-8369-6251-6*) Ayer.

***Cooke, John Esten.** Hilt to Hilt. 252p. 2000. pap. 9.95 (*0-594-02831-0*) Eightn Hundrd.

— A Life of General Robert E. Lee. 252p. 2000. pap. 9.95 (*0-594-00576-0*) Eightn Hundrd.

— My Lady Pocahontas. 252p. 2000. pap. 9.95 (*0-594-00027-0*) Eightn Hundrd.

— Surry of Eagle's Nest. 252p. 2000. pap. 9.95 (*0-594-00129-3*) Eightn Hundrd.

— The Virginia Comedians. 252p. 2000. pap. 9.95 (*0-594-03640-2*) Eightn Hundrd.

Cooke, John Peyton. The Chimney Sweeper. 288p. 1996. mass mkt. 5.99 (*0-446-40388-1*, Pub. by Warner Bks) Little.

— Haven: A Novel of Anxiety. 1998. mass mkt. write for info. (*0-446-40465-9*, Mysterious Paperbk) Warner Bks.

— The Lake. 224p. 1989. pap. 3.95 (*0-380-75768-0*, Avon Bks) Morrow Avon.

— Out for Blood. 320p. 1991. pap. 3.95 (*0-380-75927-6*, Avon Bks) Morrow Avon.

Cooke, John R. Architects, Engineers & the Law. 2nd ed. 320p. 1997. pap. 54.00 (*1-86287-229-5*, Pub. by Federation Pr) Gaunt.

Cooke, John S. The Word of One: Tarot Wisdom of the Ages. rev. ed. (Illus.). 70p. 34.95 (*0-9634800-2-2*) Catalyst Ent.

Cooke, Joseph R. Celebration of Grace: Living in Freedom. 176p. 1991. pap. 8.99 (*0-310-52961-1*) Zondervan.

— Enconters with Truth: Bible Characters Tell Their Own Story. 1998. pap. 12.00 (*1-885193-05-X*) Good Samaritan.

Cooke, K., jt. auth. see Castillo-Chavez, C.

Cooke, Kaz. Great Hysterical Figures California 9. 1997. pap. 9.95 (*0-393-31665-3*) Norton.

Cooke, Kaz. Real Gorgeous: The Truth about Body & Beauty. 288p. (Orig.). 1996. pap. 13.00 (*0-393-31355-7*, Norton Paperbks) Norton.

Cooke, Kelly, jt. auth. see Andres, Dayna.

Cooke, Kenneth, jt. auth. see Busenberg, Stavros N.

Cooke, Kenneth L., jt. auth. see Bellman, Richard.

Cooke, Kenneth L., jt. auth. see Bellman, Richard Ernest.

Cooke, LeRoy & Rimmer, Steve W. Canned Code for DOS & Windows. LC 93-34624. 1994. 39.95 incl. disk (*0-8306-4511-X*, Windcrest) TAB Bks.

Cooke, LeRoy, jt. auth. see Dashefsky, H. Steven.

Cooke, Leslie N. Polytetrafluoroethylene (Teflon, Gore-Tex, Polytef, PTFE) Index of New Information with Authors, Subjects & References. 150p. 1996. 47.50 (*0-7883-1254-5*); pap. 44.50 (*0-7883-1255-3*) ABBE Pubs Assn.

Cooke, Lucy R. Crossing the Plains in 1852. 148p. 1987. 19.95 (*0-87770-430-9*) Ye Galleon.

Cooke, Lynn & van Gelder, Kees, texts. Marijke Van Warmerdam: Single, Double, Crosswise. LC 99-213630. (Illus.). 96p. 1999. 44.00 (*90-70149-70-2*, 915028, Pub. by S V Abbemuseum) Dist Art Pubs.

Cooke, Lynne. Juan Munoz. 1999. 28.00 (*0-944521-39-8*) Dia Ctr Arts.

***Cooke, Lynne.** Roni Horn. (Contemporary Artists Ser.). 2000. pap. 29.95 (*0-7148-3865-9*) Phaidon Pr.

Cooke, Lynne & Wollen, Peter, eds. Visual Display: Culture Beyond Appearances. (Discussions in Contemporary Culture Ser.: Vol. 10). (Illus.). 240p. 1998. pap. 16.95 (*1-56584-495-5*, Pub. by New Press NY) Norton.

Cooke, Lynne, et al. Ann Hamilton: Tropos. LC 93-73429. (Illus.). 152p. (C). 1995. 40.00 (*0-944521-27-4*) Dia Ctr Arts.

— Doubletake: Collective Memory & Current Art. 1992. pap. 39.95 (*3-907509-18-8*, Pub. by Parkett Verlag AG) Dist Art Pubs.

— Julian Opie. LC 93-61543. (Illus.). 128p. (Orig.). 1994. pap. 29.95 (*0-500-27766-4*, Pub. by Thames Hudson) Norton.

— Katharina Fritsch: Rattenkonig (Rat-King) Niesluchowski, Warren, tr. LC 93-71631. (Illus.). 34p. (Orig.). 1993. pap. 15.00 (*0-944521-26-6*) Dia Ctr Arts.

— Richard Serra: Torqued Elipses. LC 97-76918. (Illus.). 80p. 1998. pap. 27.50 (*0-944521-35-5*) Dia Ctr Arts.

— Tracey Moffatt: Free-Falling. Kelly, Karen, ed. LC 98-84518. (Illus.). 60p. 1998. pap. text 25.00 (*0-944521-36-3*, 810523) Dia Ctr Arts.

— Worlds Envisioned: Alighiero e Boetti & Frederic Bruly Bouabre. LC 94-62122. (Illus.). 102p. 1995. 40.00 (*0-944521-32-0*) Dia Ctr Arts.

Cooke, Lynne, ed. see Amelio, Lucio, et al.

Cooke, Lynne, ed. see Colomina, Beatriz, et al.

Cooke, Lynne, ed. see Kort, Pamela, et al.

Cooke, Lynne, ed. see Temkin, Ann, et al.

Cooke, M. Brazil on the March. 1976. lib. bdg. 59.95 (*0-8490-1546-4*) Gordon Pr.

Cooke, M., et al, eds. Polynuclear Aromatic Hydrocarbons: Measurements, Means, & Metabolism: Proceedings of the 11th PAH International Symposium. LC 90-39041. 1220p. 1990. text 82.50 (*0-935470-58-1*) Battelle.

Cooke, M. & Beet, S. W. Visual Representations of Speech Signals. LC 92-40219. 396p. 1993. 175.00 (*0-471-93537-9*) Wiley.

Cooke, M. & Dennis, A. J. Polynuclear Aromatic Hydrocarbons: Chemistry, Characterization & Carcinogenesis. LC 86-18430. (Ninth International Symposium on Polynuclear Aromatic Hydrocarbons Ser.). 987p. 1986. 75.00 (*0-935470-25-5*) Battelle.

Cooke, Maeve. Language & Reason: A Study of Habermas's Pragmatics. (Studies in Contemporary German Social Thought). (Illus.). 232p. 1997. reprint ed. pap. text 15.00 (*0-262-53145-3*) MIT Pr.

Cooke, Marcus, et al, eds. Polynuclear Aromatic Hydrocarbons: Physical & Biological Chemistry. LC 82-16439. (Sixth International Symposium on Polynuclear Aromatic Hydrocarbons Ser.). 947p. 1982. 65.00 (*0-935470-13-1*) Battelle.

Cooke, Marcus & Dennis, Anthony J. Polynuclear Aromatic Hydrocarbons: Formation, Metabolism & Measurement. LC 83-12734. (Seventh International Polynuclear Aromatic Symposium on Hydrocarbons Ser.). 1301p. 1983. 65.00 (*0-935470-16-6*) Battelle.

— Polynuclear Aromatic Hydrocarbons: Mechanisms, Methods & Metabolism. LC 84-24254. (Eighth International Symposium on Polynuclear Aromatic Hydrocarbons Ser.). 1464p. 1984. 75.00 (*0-935470-22-0*) Battelle.

Cooke, Marcus & Dennis, Anthony J., eds. Polynuclear Aromatic Hydrocarbons: A Decade of Progress. LC 79-642622. (Proceedings of the Tenth Polynuclear Aromatic Hydrocarbons International Symposiums Ser.). 960p. 1987. text 75.00 (*0-935470-34-4*) Battelle.

— Polynuclear Aromatic Hydrocarbons: Chemical Analysis & Biological Fate. LC 81-3669. (Fifth International Symposium on Polynuclear Aromatic Hydrocarbons Ser.). 770p. 1981. 65.00 (*0-935470-09-3*) Battelle.

Cooke, Marjorie B. Dramatic Episodes. LC 79-50023. (One-Act Plays in Reprint Ser.). 1980. reprint ed. 25.00 (*0-8486-2047-X*) Roth Pub Inc.

Cooke, Martin. Modelling Auditory Processing & Organisation. (Distinguished Dissertations in Computer Science Ser.: No. 7). (Illus.). 134p. (C). 1993. text 44.95 (*0-521-45094-2*) Cambridge U Pr.

Cooke, Matthew, et al. Minor Injuries Unit Handbook: A Guide for A&E Senior House Officers Emergency Nurse Practitioners & General Practitioners. LC 98-26929. 194p. 1998. pap. text 28.00 (*0-7506-3451-0*) Buttrwrth-Heinemann.

Cooke, Mervyn. Britten: War Requiem. (Cambridge Music Handbooks Ser.). (Illus.). 124p. (C). 1996. text 39.95 (*0-521-44089-0*); pap. text 13.95 (*0-521-44633-3*) Cambridge U Pr.

— Britten & the Far East: Asian Influences in the Music of Benjamin Britten. LC 97-32608. (Aldeburgh Studies in Music). (Illus.). 304p. 1998. 90.00 (*0-85115-579-0*, Boydell Pr) Boydell & Brewer.

— The Chronicle of Jazz. (Illus.). 256p. 1998. 45.00 (*0-7892-0399-5*) Abbeville Pr.

— Jazz. LC 98-60193. (World of Art Ser.). (Illus.). 200p. 1999. pap. 14.95 (*0-500-20318-0*, Pub. by Thames Hudson) Norton.

Cooke, Mervyn, ed. The Cambridge Companion to Benjamin Britten. LC 98-30683. (Cambridge Companions to Music Ser.). (Illus.). 350p. (C). 1999. pap. 22.95 (*0-521-57476-5*); text 64.95 (*0-521-57384-X*) Cambridge U Pr.

Cooke, Mervyn & Reed, Philip, eds. Benjamin Britten: "Billy Budd" LC 92-25834. (Cambridge Opera Handbooks Ser.). (Illus.). 192p. (C). 1993. text 49.95 (*0-521-38328-5*); pap. text 18.95 (*0-521-38750-7*) Cambridge U Pr.

Cooke, Michael. Acts of Inclusion: Studies Bearing on an Elementary Theory of Romanticism. LC 78-21909. (Illus.). 1979. 42.50 (*0-300-02303-0*) Yale U Pr.

— The Ancient Curse of the Baskervilles. LC 82-83499. 63p. Date not set. 11.95 (*0-934468-14-1*) Gaslight.

— Tasmania. 1998. pap. text 14.95 (*1-86315-086-2*) Little Hills.

***Cooke, Michael.** Tasmania. 3rd ed. (Shorter Stay Guides Ser.). (Illus.). 2000. pap. 14.95 (*1-86315-141-9*) Little Hills.

Cooke, Michael G. Afro-American Literature in the Twentieth Century: The Achievement of Intimacy. LC 84-5066. 256p. 1986. pap. 18.00 (*0-300-03624-8*, Y-561) Yale U Pr.

***Cooke, Miriam.** Hayati, My Life: A Novel. 160p. 2000. 22.95 (*0-8156-0671-0*) Syracuse U Pr.

Cooke, Miriam. War's Other Voices: Women Writers in the Lebanese Civil War. (Cambridge Middle East Library: No. 14). 218p. 1988. text 59.95 (*0-521-34192-2*) Cambridge U Pr.

— War's Other Voices: Women Writers on the Lebanese Civil War. 228p. (C). 1996. pap. 17.95 (*0-8156-0377-0*, COWOP) Syracuse U Pr.

— Women & the War Story. LC 96-11601. (Illus.). 340p. 1997. 55.00 (*0-520-20612-6*, Pub. by U CA Pr); pap. 19.95 (*0-520-20613-4*, Pub. by U CA Pr) Cal Prin Full Svc.

***Cooke, Miriam.** Women Claim Islam: Creating Islamic Feminism Through Literature. 2000. 80.00 (*0-415-92553-3*); pap. text 20.99 (*0-415-92554-1*) Routledge.

Cooke, Miriam & Woollacott, Angela, eds. Gendering War Talk. LC 92-27190. 360p. (C). 1993. text 55.00 (*0-691-06980-8*, Pub. by Princeton U Pr); pap. text 17.95 (*0-691-01542-2*) Princeton U Pr.

Cooke, Miriam, jt. ed. see Badran, Margot.

Cooke, Miriam, tr. see Haqqi, Yahya.

Cooke, Mordecai. The Seven Sisters of Sleep: The Celebrated Drug Classic. LC 97-22404. 304p. 1997. pap. 16.95 (*0-89281-748-8*) Inner Tradit.

Cooke, Mordicai C. The Seven Sisters of Sleep. LC 89-90881. 407p. 1991. 45.00 (*0-88000-146-1*) Quarterman.

Cooke, Morris L. & Murray, Philip. Organized Labor & Production: Next Steps in Industrial Democracy. LC 73-156409. (American Labor Ser., No. 2). 1971. reprint ed. 23.95 (*0-405-02918-7*) Ayer.

Cooke, Nathalie. Margaret Atwood: A Biography. LC 98-225308. (Illus.). 336p. 1998. text 24.95 (*1-55022-308-9*, Pub. by ECW) Genl Dist Srvs.

Cooke, Ned & Dunnigan, John. Furniture Studio: The Heart of the Functional Arts. Kelsey, John & Mastelli, Rick, eds. LC 99-29702. (Furniture Studio Ser.). (Illus.). 144p. 1999. pap. 30.00 (*0-9671004-0-2*, Pub. by Furniture Socy) Lyons Pr.

Cooke, Nelson M., et al. Basic Mathematics for Electronics. 6th ed. 736p. 1986. text 87.32 (*0-07-012521-X*) McGraw.

— Basic Mathematics for Electronics. 7th ed. 736p. 1992. text 55.48 (*0-02-800853-7*) Glencoe.

— Basic Mathematics for Electronics with Calculus. 816p. (C). 1989. text 93.68 (*0-07-012523-6*) McGraw.

Cooke, Nicholas F. Satan in Society. LC 73-20617. (Sex, Marriage & Society Ser.). 412p. 1974. reprint ed. 34.95 (*0-405-05796-2*) Ayer.

Cooke, Nym, ed. see Swan, Timothy.

Cooke, Olga M., ed. After Plattling. (Illus.). 69p. (Orig.). 1996. pap. 8.00 (*1-57201-021-5*) Berkeley Slavic.

Cooke, P. Region, Class & Gender: A European Comparison. (Illus.). 62p. 1984. pap. 22.00 (*0-08-032303-0*, Pergamon Pr) Elsevier.

Cooke, P., jt. auth. see Loveday, Peter.

Cooke, Patty G. B. Louisa & Louisa County, Virginia. (Images of America Ser.). (Illus.). 128p. 1996. pap. 16.99 (*0-7524-0560-8*) Arcadia Publng.

An Asterisk (*) at the beginning of an entry indicates that the title is appearing for the first time.

Cooke, Paul & Cooke, Sunita. Natural Wonders of Texas. LC 94-32680. (Natural Wonders of... Ser.). (Illus.). 180p. (Orig.). 1995. pap. 9.95 (*1-56626-109-0*, 61090, Cntry Rds Pr) NTC Contemp Pub Co.

Cooke, Paul D. Hobbes & Christianity: Reassessing the Bible in "Leviathan" 304p. (C). 1996. lib. bdg. 66.00 (*0-8476-8196-3*) Rowman.

— Hobbes & Christianity: Reassessing the Bible in Leviathan. 304p. (C). 1996. pap. text 25.95 (*0-8476-8197-1*) Rowman.

Cooke, Phil, ed. Localities: The Changing Face of Urban Britain. 320p. 1989. text 60.00 (*0-04-445502-X*) Routledge.

Cooke, Philip, ed. Localities: Changing Face of Urban Britain. LC 88-26991. 334p. (C). 1989. pap. 27.99 (*0-04-445300-0*) Routledge.

— The Rise of the Rustbelt. (Illus.). x, 262p. 1995. text 65.00 (*0-312-12943-2*) St Martin.

Cooke, Philip, et al, eds. Regional Innovation Systems: The Role of Governances in a Globalized World. 272p. 1996. 75.00 (*1-85728-689-8*, Pub. by UCL Pr Ltd); pap. 26.95 (*1-85728-690-1*, Pub. by UCL Pr Ltd) Taylor & Francis.

Cooke, Philip & Fox, Jonathan, eds. Effective Tax Strategies for Corporate Acquisitions. 184p. 23.00 (*90-6544-255-3*) Kluwer Academic.

Cooke, Philip & Morgan, Kevin. The Associational Economy: Firms, Regions, & Innovation. (Illus.). 256p. (C). 1998. text 65.00 (*0-19-829018-7*) OUP.

— The Associational Economy: Firms, Regions & Innovation. (Illus.). 264p. 2000. pap. text 24.95 (*0-19-829659-2*) OUP.

Cooke, Philip, et al. The Governance of Innovation in Europe: Regional Perspectives on Global Competitiveness. LC 99-17501. (Science, Technology & the International Political Economy Ser.). 1999. 26.95 (*1-85567-628-1*) P P Pubs.

— Towards Global Localization: The Computing & Communication Industries in Britain & France. 240p. 1992. 55.00 (*1-85728-000-8*, Pub. by UCL Pr Ltd) Taylor & Francis.

***Cooke, Philip E.** Fenoglio's Binoculars, Johnny's Eyes: History, Language & Narrative Technique in Fenoglio's "Il Partigiano Johnny" LC 99-43012. (Studies in Italian Culture: Vol. 30). 176p. (C). 2000. 44.95 (*0-8204-4878-8*) P Lang Pubng.

Cooke, Philip P. Froissart Ballads, & Other Poems. LC 72-4959. (Romantic Tradition in American Literature Ser.). 220p. 1972. reprint ed. 23.95 (*0-405-04631-6*) Ayer.

Cooke, Philip S. The Conquest of New Mexico & California: An Historical & Personal Narrative. 1977. reprint ed. lib. bdg. 59.00 (*0-403-07682-X*) Scholarly.

Cooke, Philip St George. The Conquest of New Mexico & California: An Historical & Personal Narrative. Cortes, Carlos E., ed. LC 76-1244. (Chicano Heritage Ser.). 1977. reprint ed. 26.95 (*0-405-09497-3*) Ayer.

Cooke, R. The Mathematics of Sonya Kovalevskaya. (Illus.). 275p. 1984. 87.95 (*0-387-96030-9*) Spr-Verlag.

Cooke, R., tr. see Arnol'd, V. I.

Cooke, R., tr. see Egorov, Yu V., et al, eds.

Cooke, R., tr. see Havin, V. P. & Nikol'skij, N. K., eds.

Cooke, R. C. & Whipps, J. M. Eco-Physiology of Fungi. LC 92-31283. 337p. 1993. 99.95 (*0-632-02168-3*) Blackwell Sci.

Cooke, R. H., ed. see Weeks, H. M.

Cooke, R. J., jt. auth. see Trevena, D. H.

Cooke, R. U. Geomorphological Hazards in Los Angeles: A Study of Slope & Sediment Problems in a Metropolitan County. LC 84-9234. (London Research Series in Geography: No. 7). (Illus.). 192p. (C). 1984. text 60.00 (*0-04-551090-3*) Routledge.

Cooke, Raymond. Velimir Khlebnikov: A Critical Study. (Cambridge Studies in Russian Literature). 256p. 1987. text 74.95 (*0-521-32670-2*) Cambridge U Pr.

Cooke, Rhonda. HR Digest: Updated Articles by Rhonda Cooke. 128p. (Orig.). 1995. pap. 79.00 (*1-889394-18-1*) Credit Union Execs.

— Succession Planning: An Ongoing Approach. (CUES HR Development Ser.). 48p. 1995. pap. 99.00 (*1-889394-21-1*) Credit Union Execs.

Cooke, Richard A., III. Molokai, an Island in Time. 196p. 1987. 75.00 (*0-941831-13-2*) Beyond Words Pub.

— Molokai, an Island in Time. 1987. 95.00 (*0-941831-06-X*) Beyond Words Pub.

— Molokai, an Island in Time. deluxe ed. 196p. 1987. 2250.00 (*0-941831-07-8*) Beyond Words Pub.

***Cooke, Robert.** Healer: Dr. Judah Folkman's War on Cancer. 312p. 2000. 25.95 (*0-375-50244-0*) Random.

Cooke, Robert. Personal Finance for Busy People. LC 98-65407. 272p. 1998. pap. 16.95 (*0-07-012556-2*) McGraw.

— Taxes for Busy People, 1998. LC 97-75820. 224p. 1997. pap. 14.95 (*0-07-012557-0*) McGraw.

— Tools for Individual & Group Learning: Constructive Negotiations Challenge. (The Challenge Ser.). 56p. 1998. spiral bd. 49.95 (*0-8144-1214-9*) AMACOM.

— Tools for Individual & Group Learning: Critical Thinking Challenge. (The Challenge Ser.). 56p. 1998. spiral bd. 49.95 (*0-8144-1210-6*) AMACOM.

— Tools for Individual & Group Learning: Ethical Decision Challenge. (The Challenge Ser.). 56p. 1998. spiral bd. 49.95 (*0-8144-1206-8*) AMACOM.

— Tools for Individual & Group Learning: Performance Appraisal Challenge. (The Challenge Ser.). 56p. 1998. spiral bd. 49.95 (*0-8144-1202-5*) AMACOM.

Cooke, Robert A. Doing Business Tax-Free: Perfectly Legal Techniques to Reduce or Eliminate Your Federal Business Taxes. 256p. 1995. pap. 19.95 (*0-471-03416-9*) Wiley.

— How to Start Your Own (Subchapter) S Corporation. LC 94-40401. 256p. 1995. pap. 19.95 (*0-471-11022-1*) Wiley.

— McGraw-Hill Thirty-Six Hour Course in Finance for Non-Financial Managers. 266p. 1993. pap. 19.95 (*0-07-012538-4*) McGraw.

Cooke, Robert A., jt. auth. see Cooke, Robert E.

Cooke, Robert A., jt. auth. see Georgopoulos, Basil S.

***Cooke, Robert E. & Cooke, Robert A.** Small Business Formation Handbook. LC 98-48157. (Illus.). 245p. 1999. pap. 22.95 (*0-471-31475-7*) Wiley.

Cooke, Robert E., jt. ed. see Osler, Sonia F.

Cooke, Robin, ed. The Laws of New Zealand, 20 vols., Set. 1992. ring bd. 2120.00 (*0-318-72509-6*, MICHIE) LEXIS Pub.

Cooke, Robin A. & Stewart, Brian. Colour Atlas of Anatomical Pathology. 2nd ed. LC 95-7285. 1995. pap. text 55.00 (*0-443-05062-7*) Church.

Cooke, Roderic C. The Biology of Symbiotic Fungi. LC 76-56175. (Illus.). 294p. reprint ed. pap. 91.20 (*0-8357-7244-6*, 203049600069) Bks Demand.

— Fungi, Man & His Environment. LC 79-37316. (Illus.). 158p. reprint ed. pap. 49.00 (*0-8357-6125-8*, 203450800090) Bks Demand.

Cooke, Roger. The History of Mathematics: A Brief Course. LC 97-6046. 552p. 1997. 84.95 (*0-471-18082-3*) Wiley.

Cooke, Roger & Costantini, Domenico, eds. Statistics in Science: The Foundations of Statistical Methods in Biology, Physics & Economics. 200p. (C). 1990. lib. bdg. 139.00 (*0-7923-0797-6*, Pub. by Kluwer Academic) Kluwer Academic.

Cooke, Roger, ed. see Mendel, Max, et al.

Cooke, Roger, tr. see Kolmogorov, A. N. & Ushkevich, A. P.

Cooke, Roger, tr. see Kolmogorov, A. N. & Yushkevich, A. P., eds.

Cooke, Roger, tr. see Monastyrskii, Mikhailiich.

Cooke, Roger, tr. see Monastyrsky, Michael.

Cooke, Roger, tr. see Yushkevich, A. P. & Kolmogorov, Andrei N., eds.

Cooke, Roger M. Experts in Uncertainty: Opinion & Subjective Probability in Science. (Environmental Ethics & Science Policy Ser.). (Illus.). 336p. 1991. text 85.00 (*0-19-506465-8*, 11551) OUP.

Cooke, Ronald U. & Doornkamp, John C. Geomorphology in Environmental Management: A New Introduction. 2nd ed. (Illus.). 434p. (C). 1990. 82.95 (*0-19-874150-2*); pap. text 46.95 (*0-19-874151-0*) OUP.

— Geomorphology in Environmental Management: An Introduction. (Illus.). (C). 1974. pap. text 15.95 (*0-19-874021-2*) OUP.

Cooke, Ronald U., et al. Urban Geomorphology in Drylands. 1983. 35.00 (*0-19-823239-X*) OUP.

— Urban Geomorphology in Drylands. 1985. pap. 15.95 (*0-19-823258-6*) OUP.

Cooke, Rose. Huckleberries Gathered from New England Hills. 1972. reprint ed. 29.50 (*0-8422-8029-4*) Irvington.

— Root-Bound & Other Sketches. LC 68-23719. (Americans in Fiction Ser.). (Illus.). 264p. reprint ed. pap. text 6.95 (*0-89197-924-7*); reprint ed. lib. bdg. 24.00 (*0-8398-0275-7*) Irvington.

— Somebody's Neighbors. 1972. reprint ed. lib. bdg. 46.00 (*0-8422-8028-6*) Irvington.

Cooke, Rose T. How Celia Changed Her Mind & Selected Stories. Ammons, Elizabeth, ed. (American Women Writers Ser.). 400p. (C). 1986. text 40.00 (*0-8135-1165-8*); pap. text 16.00 (*0-8135-1166-6*) Rutgers U Pr.

Cooke, Sarah A. Wayside Sketches. pap. 7.99 (*0-88019-196-1*) Schmul Pub Co.

Cooke, Sarah E. & Ramadhyani, Rachel, compiled by. Indians & a Changing Frontier: The Art of George Winter. LC 92-43041. (Illus.). xiv, 270p. 1993. 24.95 (*0-87195-097-9*) Ind Hist Soc.

Cooke, Sarah S., ed. A Field Guide to the Common Wetland Plants of Western Washington & Northwestern Oregon. (Trailside Ser.). (Illus.). 403p. (Orig.). 1997. pap. 24.95 (*0-914516-11-6*) Seattle Audubon Soc.

Cooke, Stanley G., ed. It Wasn't All Work: An Autobiography. 230p. (C). 1983. 45.00 (*0-7212-0686-7*, Pub. by Regency Pr GBR) St Mut.

Cooke, Steve & Slack, Nigel. Making Management Decisions. 2nd ed. LC 90-20450. 1992. write for info. (*0-13-543406-8*) P-H.

Cooke, Stewart J., jt. auth. see Burney, Fanny.

Cooke, Sunita, jt. auth. see Cooke, Paul.

Cooke, Susan M. Law of Hazardous Waste: Management, Cleanup, Liability & Litigation, 4 vols. 1987. ring bd. 760.00 (*0-8205-1307-5*) Bender.

Cooke, Susette T., tr. see Bei Dao.

Cooke, T. E. An Empirical Study of Financial Disclosures by Swedish Companies. (Accounting History & Thought Ser.). 400p. 1990. reprint ed. text 15.00 (*0-8240-3315-9*) Garland.

Cooke, T. H. Concrete Pumping & Spraying. 1990. text 57.95 (*0-442-30352-1*) Chapman & Hall.

Cooke, Terence. Prayers for Today. 190p. 1991. pap. 6.95 (*0-8189-0628-6*) Alba.

Cooke, Terence C. Meditations on Mary: Conferences. LC 93-26373. 152p. (Orig.). 1993. pap. 7.95 (*0-8189-0683-9*) Alba.

Cooke, Terence Cardinal. His Words Shall Guide Us. McBride, M. Aloysius, ed. & compiled by by. (Illus.). 48p. 1995. pap. 2.95 (*0-8189-0757-6*) Alba.

Cooke, Terence E. & Parker, Robert H. Financial Reporting in the West Pacific Rim. LC 93-13081. 450p. (C). (gr. 13). 1994. pap. 92.95 (*0-415-10223-5*) Thomson Learn.

Cooke, Thomas, tr. see Hesiod.

***Cooke, Timothy.** History of the Modern World, 10 vols. LC 99-14780. (Illus.). 144p. 1999. 657.07 (*0-7614-7147-2*, Benchmark NY) Marshall Cavendish.

Cooke, Tom. Sesame Street Cookie Monster's Little Kitchen: A Chunky Book. LC 94-66510. (Illus.). (J). 1995. 3.99 (*0-679-85456-8*) Random.

Cooke, Tom. Bert's Little Garden: A Sesame Street Book. LC 90-61311. (Chunky Shape Bks.). 22p. (J). (ps). 1991. 3.25 (*0-679-81061-7*, Pub. by Random Bks Yng Read) Random.

— Grover's Adventure under the Sea. LC 88-61629. (Peek-a-Boo Board Bks.). 14p. (J). (ps). 1989. 3.99 (*0-394-81951-9*, Pub. by Random Bks Yng Read) Random.

— Hide-&-Seek with Big Bird: A Sesame Street Book. LC 89-64284. (Peek-a-Boo Board Bks.). 14p. (J). (ps). 1991. 4.99 (*0-679-80785-3*, Pub. by Random Bks Yng Read) Random.

— Open Sesame Picture Dictionary. (Open Sesame Ser.). (ENG & JPN.). (J). 1987. pap. text 8.50 (*0-19-434170-4*) OUP.

Cooke, Tom & Tk. I Want a Hat Like That. 24p. 2000. pap. 3.25 (*0-375-80438-2*) Random.

Cooke, Tricia, jt. auth. see Robertson, William P.

***Cooke, Trish.** The Grandad Tree. LC 99-28783. (Illus.). 32p. (J). 2000. 15.99 (*0-7636-0815-7*) Candlewick Pr.

Cooke, Trish. Mr. Pam Pam & the Hullabazoo. LC 93-32382. (Illus.). 32p. (J). (ps up). 1994. 14.95 (*1-56402-411-3*) Candlewick Pr.

— So Much. LC 94-13435. (Illus.). 32p. (J). (ps up). 1994. 16.99 (*1-56402-344-3*) Candlewick Pr.

— So Much. LC 94-13435. (Illus.). 48p. (J). (ps-1). 1997. reprint ed. pap. 6.99 (*0-7636-0296-5*) Candlewick Pr.

— When I Grow Bigger. LC 93-42601. (Illus.). 32p. (J). (ps up). 1994. 13.95 (*1-56402-430-X*) Candlewick Pr.

Cooke, Virginia, et al, eds. File on Shaffer. (Methuen Writer-Files Ser.). 88p. (Orig.). (C). 1988. pap. 9.95 (*0-413-42000-0*, A0101, Methuen Drama) Methn.

Cooke, W. Alfred. Caledonia: From Antebellum Plantation, 1713-1892 to State Prison & Farm, 1892-1988. (Illus.). 325p. 1989. vinyl bd. write for info. (*0-318-64671-4*) W A Cooke.

Cooke, Warren F. Tomorrow's Banks: Developments Shaping the 1990's. 1989. pap. 59.95 (*1-55840-279-9*) Exec Ent Pubns.

Cooke, William. The Elements of Dramatic Criticism. (Anglistica & Americana Ser.: No. 133). (Illus.). vii, 216p. 1976. reprint ed. 80.00 (*3-487-04277-0*) G Olms Pubs.

— Memoirs of Charles Macklin. LC 72-82822. 444p. 1972. 30.95 (*0-405-08378-5*, Pub. by Blom Pubns) Ayer.

Cooke, William, ed. Edward Thomas. (Everyman's Poetry Ser.). 128p. 1997. pap. 3.50 (*0-460-87877-8*, Everyman's Classic Lib) Tuttle Pubng.

Cooke, William A. Caledonia: From Antebellum Plantation, 1713-1892 To State Prison & Farm, 1892-1988. LC 88-63379. (Illus.). 329p. (Orig.). 1988. pap. 20.00 (*0-9622121-0-5*) W A Cooke.

Cooke, William B. The Fungi of Our Mouldy Earth: A Compilation. (Nova Hedwigia, Beihefte/Supplementary Issues Ser.: Beih 85). (Illus.). vi, 467p. 1986. pap. 95.00 (*3-443-51006-X*, Pub. by Gebruder Borntraeger) Balogh.

Cooke, William N. Labor-Management Cooperation: New Partnerships or Going in Circles? LC 90-46159. 192p. 1990. text 35.00 (*0-88099-099-6*); pap. text 17.00 (*0-88099-100-3*) W E Upjohn.

— Union Organizing & Public Policy: Failure to Secure First Contracts. LC 85-3239. 159p. (C). 1985. text 22.00 (*0-88099-026-0*); pap. text 12.00 (*0-88099-027-9*) W E Upjohn.

***Cooke-Yarborough, Ann.** Paris Hotels. 3rd ed. (Alastair Sawday's Special Places to Stay Ser.). (Illus.). 2001. pap. 14.95 (*0-7627-0773-9*) Globe Pequot.

Cooke-Yarborough, Ann, ed. see Alastair Sawday Staff.

Cooke-Yarborough, Anne, ed. see Alastair Sawday Staff.

Cooke-Zimmerman, Ruth. Abyssinians. (KW Ser.). (Illus.). 96p. 1992. 9.95 (*0-86622-197-2*, KW-223) TFH Pubns.

Cookenboo, Leslie, Jr. Crude Oil Pipe Lines & Competition in the Oil Industry & Costs of Operating Crude Oil Pipe Lines. Bruchey, Stuart, ed. LC 78-22669. (Rice Institute Pamphlet: Energy in the American Economy Ser.: Vol. 41, No. 1). (Illus.). 1979. reprint ed. lib. bdg. 28.95 (*0-405-11973-9*) Ayer.

Cookerly, J. Richard. Recovering Love: Codependency to CoRecovery. 192p. 1992. pap. write for info. (*0-8306-3837-7*, 4121) McGraw-Hill Prof.

— Recovering Love: Codependency to Corecovery. 1993. 17.95 (*0-07-012700-X*) McGraw.

Cookerly, J. Richard, jt. auth. see Martin, Daniel R.

Cookey, S. J. S. King Jaja of the Niger Delta: His Life & Times, 1821-1891. LC 73-88683. 192p. 1974. text 18.95 (*0-88357-026-2*) NOK Pubs.

Cookfair, Arthur S., jt. auth. see Gordon, Thomas T.

Cooking Light Magazine Staff. Cooking Light Annual Recipes, 1997. LC 96-71335. 352p. 1996. 29.95 (*0-8487-1528-4*) Oxmoor Hse.

— Cooking Light Desserts. 1991. mass mkt. 5.95 (*0-446-39180-8*, Pub. by Warner Bks) Little.

— Cooking Light Fish & Shellfish. 1991. mass mkt. 5.95 (*0-446-39184-0*, Pub. by Warner Bks) Little.

— Cooking Light Microwave. 1991. mass mkt. 5.95 (*0-446-39181-6*, Pub. by Warner Bks) Little.

— Cooking Light Poultry. 1991. mass mkt. 5.95 (*0-446-39183-2*, Pub. by Warner Bks) Little.

— Cooking Light Tex-Mex. LC 91-35920. (Illus.). (Orig.). 1992. mass mkt. 5.99 (*0-446-39404-1*, Pub. by Warner Bks) Little.

***Cooking Light Magazine Staff, ed.** Christmas Gifts of Good Taste Vol. 6: Festive Bags & Baskets for Yummy Treats. (Illus.). 128p. 2000. 19.95 (*1-57486-177-8*) Leisure AR.

Cookinham, Henry J. History of Oneida County, from 1700 to the Present Time, 2 vols. (Illus.). 1267p. 1997. reprint ed. lib. bdg. 128.00 (*0-8328-6187-1*) Higginson Bk Co.

Cooklin, Gerry. Fusing Technology. 92p. (C). 1990. 110.00 (*1-870812-20-4*, Pub. by Textile Inst); pap. text 75.00 (*1-870812-22-0*, Pub. by Textile Inst) St Mut.

— Garment Technology for Fashion Designers. LC 97-34199. 1997. pap. 32.95 (*0-632-04775-5*) Blackwell Sci.

— Introduction to Clothing Manufacture. (Illus.). 190p. 1991. pap. 32.95 (*0-632-02661-8*) Blackwell Sci.

— Master Patterns & Grading for Women's Outsizes: Pattern Sizing Technology. 228p. 1995. pap. 34.95 (*0-632-03915-9*) Blackwell Sci.

— Pattern Cutting for Women's Outerwear. LC 94-16577. (Illus.). 192p. 1994. 36.95 (*0-632-03797-0*, Pub. by Blckwll Scitfc UK) Blackwell Sci.

— Pattern Grading for Men's Clothes: The Technology of Sizing. (Illus.). 304p. 1992. pap. 39.95 (*0-632-03305-3*) Blackwell Sci.

Cookman, Lesley. Writing a Pantomime: How to Write & Deliver a Successful Traditional Script. 112p. 1998. pap. 19.95 (*1-85703-249-7*, Pub. by How To Bks) Trans-Atl Phila.

***Cookman, Scott.** Ice Blink: The Tragic Fate of Sir John Franklin's Last Polar Expedition. LC 99-47620. (Illus.). 246p. 2000. text 24.95 (*0-471-37790-2*) Wiley.

Cook's Choice Staff. The Cook's Choice Southern Gourmet Newsletter Collection, Vol. 1. (Illus.). 107p. 1988. ring bd. 16.95 (*0-945686-00-5*) Cooks Choice.

***Cook's Illustrated Editors.** The Complete Book of Pasta & Noodles. LC 99-40076. (Illus.). 496p. 2000. 32.50 (*0-609-60064-8*) C Potter.

Cook's Illustrated Editors. Cook's Illustrated Recipe Index, 1993-1998. 96p. 1998. pap. 12.95 (*0-936184-36-1*) Boston Common Pr.

— How to Barbecue & Roast on the Grill: An Illustrated Step-by-Step Guide to Preparing Ribs, Brisket. (How to Cook Master Ser.). (Illus.). 96p. 1999. 14.95 (*0-936184-31-0*) Boston Common Pr.

— How to Cook Holiday Roasts & Birds: An Illustrated Step-by-Step Guide to Roast Turkey, Goose, Cornish Hen. (How to Cook Master Ser.). (Illus.). 96p. 1998. 14.95 (*0-936184-28-0*) Boston Common Pr.

— How to Cook Shrimp & Other Shellfish: An Illustrated Step-by-Step Guide to Preparing Shrimp, Scallops. (How to Cook Master Ser.). (Illus.). 96p. 1999. 14.95 (*0-936184-30-2*) Boston Common Pr.

— How to Make a Pie: An Illustrated Step-by-Step Guide to Perfect Pie Crusts... (How to Cook Master Ser.). (Illus.). 96p. 1996. 14.95 (*0-936184-16-7*) Boston Common Pr.

— How to Make an American Layer Cake: An Illustrated Step-by-Step Guide to Perfect Cakes & Frosting. (How to Cook Master Ser.). (Illus.). 96p. 1997. 14.95 (*0-936184-17-5*) Boston Common Pr.

— How to Make Cookie Jar Favorites: An Illustrated Step-by-Step Guide to the Simplest & Best. (How to Cook Master Ser.). (Illus.). 96p. 1998. 14.95 (*0-936184-27-2*) Boston Common Pr.

— How to Make Ice Cream: An Illustrated Step-by-Step Guide to Perfect Ice Cream... (How to Cook Master Ser.). (Illus.). 96p. 1997. 14.95 (*0-936184-19-1*) Boston Common Pr.

— How to Make Pizza: An Illustrated Step-by-Step Guide to Thin-Crust & Deep-Dish Pizza. (Illus.). 96p. 1997. 14.95 (*0-936184-20-5*) Boston Common Pr.

— How to Make Simple Fruit Desserts: An Illustrated Step-by-Step Guide to Crisps, Cobblers, Shortcakes. (How to Cook Master Ser.). (Illus.). 96p. 1998. 14.95 (*0-936184-26-4*) Boston Common Pr.

— How to Make Stew: An Illustrated Step-by-Step Guide to Beef, Lamb, Pork, Chicken. (How to Cook Master Ser.). (Illus.). 96p. 1999. 14.95 (*0-936184-29-9*) Boston Common Pr.

Cook's Illustrated Editors, ed. Cook's Illustrated, 1998. (Illus.). 216p. 1998. 24.95 (*0-936184-32-9*) Boston Common Pr.

— Cook's Illustrated, 1997. (Illus.). 216p. 1997. 24.95 (*0-9640179-7-0*) Boston Common Pr.

— Cook's Illustrated, 1996. (Illus.). 216p. 1996. 24.95 (*0-9640179-5-4*) Boston Common Pr.

— How to Grill: An Illustrated Step-by-Step Guide to Cooking Steaks, Chops... (How to Cook Master Ser.). (Illus.). 96p. 1998. 14.95 (*0-936184-25-6*) Boston Common Pr.

— How to Make Holiday Desserts: An Illustrated Step-by-Step Guide to Plum Pudding... (How to Cook Master Ser.). (Illus.). 96p. 1997. 14.95 (*0-936184-21-3*) Boston Common Pr.

— How to Make Pasta Sauces: An Illustrated Step-by-Step Guide to Perfect Sauces with Tomatoes. (How to Cook Master Ser.). (Illus.). 96p. 1998. 14.95 (*0-936184-23-X*) Boston Common Pr.

— How to Make Salad: An Illustrated Step-by-Step Guide to Perfect Salads & Dressings. (How to Cook Master Ser.). (Illus.). 96p. 1998. 14.95 (*0-936184-24-8*) Boston Common Pr.

— How to Stir-Fry: An Illustrated Step-by-Step Guide to Adapting a Chinese Technique. (How to Cook Master Ser.). (Illus.). 96p. 1997. 14.95 (*0-936184-18-3*) Boston Common Pr.

Cook's Illustrated Staff. The Cook's Illustrated Complete Book of Poultry. LC 98-43305. 469p. 1999. 32.50 (*0-609-60063-X*) C Potter.

***Cook's Illustrated Staff, ed.** The Best Recipe: Would You Make 38 Versions of Creme Carmel to Find the Absolute. (Illus.). 560p. 1999. 29.95 (*0-936184-38-8*) Boston Common Pr.

***Cooksey.** Molecular Approaches to the Study of the Ocean. LC 97-75088. 568p. 1998. write for info. (*0-412-72960-1*) Kluwer Academic.

C

An Asterisk (*) at the beginning of an entry indicates that the title is appearing for the first time.

Cooksey, Cynthia. Shelby. 48p. 1995. 4.50 (*1-887945-01-6*) CTTC.

Cooksey, John. France: Calais. (Battleground Europe Ser.). 1999. pap. text 16.95 (*1-58097-011-7*) Combined Pub.

Cooksey, Karen, jt. auth. see Gitnick, Gary L.

Cooksey, Ray W., ed. Judgment Analysis: Theory, Methods, & Applications. (Illus.). 407p. 1996. text 59.95 (*0-12-187575-X*) Acad Pr.

Cooksey, Robert & Bramwell, Paul. The Art of the Cabinet Maker. (Illus.). 160p. 1996. 35.00 (*1-85223-982-4*, Pub. by Cro1wood) Trafalgar.

Cookshaw, Marlene. The Whole Elephant. 80p. 1989. pap. 9.95 (*0-919626-44-0*, Pub. by Brick Bks) Genl Dist Srvs.

Cooksley, Peter. BE2 in Action. (Aircraft in Action Ser.). (Illus.). 50p. 1992. pap. 9.95 (*0-89747-275-6*, 1123) Squad Sig Pubns.

— Bristol Fighter in Action. (Aircraft in Action Ser.). (Illus.). 50p. 1993. pap. 9.95 (*0-89747-301-9*) Squad Sig Pubns.

— Croydon Airport Flypast: Historic Aircraft Profiles in Colour. 44p. (C). 1985. 60.00 (*0-907335-10-1*, Pub. by Sutton Libs & Arts) St Mut.

— DeHavilland DH-9 in Action. (Aircraft in Action Ser.: No. 164). (Illus.). 50p. 1996. pap. 9.95 (*0-89747-365-5*, 1164) Squad Sig Pubns.

*__Cooksley, Peter.__ DeHavilland DH.2 in Action. (Aircraft in Action Ser.: Vol. 171). (Illus.). 50p. 1999. pap. 9.95 (*0-89747-408-2*) Squad Sig Pubns.

Cooksley, Peter. Encyclopedia of 20th Century Conflict: Air Wars. LC 98-115327. (Illus.). 320p. 1998. 34.95 (*1-85409-223-5*, Pub. by Arms & Armour) Sterling.

*__Cooksley, Peter.__ German Bombers of WWI. (Aircraft in Action Ser.: Vol. 173). (Illus.). 50p. 2000. pap. 9.95 (*0-89747-416-3*, 1173) Squad Sig Pubns.

Cooksley, Peter J. The Air VCs. (VCs of the First World War Ser.). (Illus.). 240p. 1997. 33.95 (*0-7509-1212-X*, Pub. by Sutton Pub Ltd) Intl Pubs Mktg.

Cooksley, Valerie. Aromatherapy: A Lifetime Guide to Healing with Essential Oils. 220p. 1996. pap. 13.95 (*0-13-349432-2*) P-H.

— Comforting Scents. LC 97-32868. 192p. 1998. pap. 15.95 (*0-7352-0002-5*) PH Pr.

Cooksley, Valerie G. Comforting Scents: Your Personal Aromatherapy Journal. 192p. (C). 1998. mass mkt. 15.95 (*0-13-793456-4*) P-H.

Cooksley, Valerie Gennari. Aromatherapy: A Lifetime Guide to Healing with Essential Oils. 400p. (C). 1996. text 27.95 (*0-13-349424-1*) P-H.

C

*__Cookson.__ Bill Bailey Omnibus. 2000. pap. 12.95 (*0-552-14624-2*, Pub. by Transworld Publishers Ltd) Trafalgar.

— Charter Schools. 2000. 25.00 (*0-8133-6631-3*, Pub. by Westview) HarpC.

— Fenwick Houses. 2000. pap. 8.95 (*0-552-14069-4*, Pub. by Transworld Publishers Ltd) Trafalgar.

— Gambling Man. 2000. pap. 8.95 (*0-552-14341-3*, Pub. by Transworld Publishers Ltd) Trafalgar.

— Hamilton Trilogy. 2000. pap. 12.95 (*0-552-14703-6*, Pub. by Transworld Publishers Ltd) Trafalgar.

— House of Men. 2000. pap. 10.95 (*0-552-14088-0*, Pub. by Transworld Publishers Ltd) Trafalgar.

— The Invisible Cord. 2000. pap. 10.95 (*0-552-10267-9*, Pub. by Transworld Publishers Ltd) Trafalgar.

— Iron Facade & House Men Omnib. 2000. pap. 10.95 (*0-552-14700-1*, Pub. by Transworld Publishers Ltd) Trafalgar.

— Joe & the Gladiator. 2000. 16.95 (*0-385-40178-7*, Pub. by Transworld Publishers Ltd) Trafalgar.

— Matty Doolin. 2000. 17.95 (*0-385-40138-8*, Pub. by Transworld Publishers Ltd) Trafalgar.

— Mrs. Flanagan's Trumpet. 2000. 17.95 (*0-385-40134-5*, Pub. by Transworld Publishers Ltd) Trafalgar.

Cookson, ed. Measure for Measure. 1991. pap. text. write for info. (*0-582-07576-9*, Pub. by Addison-Wesley) Longman.

— Midsummer Night Dream. 1991. pap. text. write for info. (*0-582-07580-7*, Pub. by Addison-Wesley) Longman.

Cookson, jt. ed. see Loughrey.

*__Cookson, Catherine.__ Bill & The Mary Ann Shaughne-p(f. 2000. pap. 5.95 (*0-552-52725-4*, Pub. by Transworld Publishers Ltd) Trafalgar.

Cookson, Catherine. Bill Bailey's Daughter, Vol. 3. large type ed. (General Ser.). 321p. 1990. lib. bdg. 20.95 (*0-8161-4768-X*, G K Hall Lrg Type) Mac Lib Ref.

— The Black Candle. 608p. 1990. mass mkt. 8.99 (*0-552-13576-3*) Bantam.

— The Black Candle. large type ed. 1991. 24.95 (*0-7089-8571-8*) Ulverscroft.

— The Black Velvet Gown. 480p. 1985. mass mkt. 6.99 (*0-552-12473-7*) Bantam.

— The Blind Miller. 288p. 1988. mass mkt. 4.50 (*0-552-08700-9*) Bantam.

— The Blind Miller. 289p. 1996. mass mkt. 7.99 (*0-552-14064-3*) Bantam.

*__Cookson, Catherine.__ Bondage of Love. 2000. mass mkt. 10.95 (*0-552-14533-5*, Pub. by Transworld Publishers Ltd) Trafalgar.

— The Bondage of Love. LC 97-187848. 2000. 29.95 (*0-593-04125-9*, Pub. by Transworld Publishers Ltd) Trafalgar.

Cookson, Catherine. The Bonny Dawn. LC 97-154922. 192p. 1996. 19.95 (*0-593-04092-9*) Bantam.

— The Bonny Dawn. 1997. mass mkt. 7.99 (*0-552-14531-9*) Bantam.

— The Branded Man. 1997. 32.95 (*0-593-03880-0*) Bantam.

*__Cookson, Catherine.__ The Branded Man. 2000. pap. 10.95 (*0-552-14348-0*, Pub. by Transworld Publishers Ltd) Trafalgar.

Cookson, Catherine. The Cinder Path. 256p. 1983. mass mkt. 7.99 (*0-552-14260-3*) Bantam.

— Colour Blind. 1987. pap. 3.95 (*0-552-13164-4*) Bantam.

*__Cookson, Catherine.__ Colour Blind. 2000. pap. 10.95 (*0-552-14633-1*, Pub. by Transworld Publishers Ltd) Trafalgar.

Cookson, Catherine. Colour Blind. large type ed. 1990. 27.99 (*0-7089-8545-9*) Ulverscroft.

*__Cookson, Catherine.__ Cultured Handmaiden. (J). 2000. mass mkt. 10.95 (*0-552-12476-1*, Pub. by Transworld Publishers Ltd) Trafalgar.

Cookson, Catherine. The Desert Crop. 2000. per. 5.99 (*1-55166-583-2*) Harlequin Bks.

— The Desert Crop. LC 98-40561. 319p. 1999. 23.00 (*0-684-85683-2*) Scribner.

— The Desert Crop. LC 98-55244. 1999. 28.95 (*0-7862-1830-4*) Thorndike Pr.

*__Cookson, Catherine.__ The Desert Crop. (Illus.). 512p. 1998. mass mkt. 10.95 (*0-552-14156-9*, Pub. by Transworld Publishers Ltd) Trafalgar.

— The Desert Crop. 320p. 2000. 29.95 (*0-593-03476-7*, Pub. by Transworld Publishers Ltd) Trafalgar.

Cookson, Catherine. The Devil & Mary Ann. large type ed. 1976. 15.95 (*0-85456-419-5*) Ulverscroft.

— A Dinner of Herbs. 736p. 1986. pap. 8.99 (*0-552-12551-2*) Bantam.

— The Dwelling Place. 416p. 1994. mass mkt. 7.99 (*0-552-14066-X*) Bantam.

— Fanny McBride. 384p. 1996. mass mkt. 7.99 (*0-552-14067-8*) Bantam.

— The Fifteen Streets. 336p. 1994. mass mkt. 7.99 (*0-552-14070-8*) Bantam.

*__Cookson, Catherine.__ The Gambling Man. 2000. mass mkt. 8.95 (*0-552-10450-7*, Pub. by Transworld Publishers Ltd) Trafalgar.

Cookson, Catherine. The Garment. 1976. 22.95 (*0-8488-0970-X*) Amereon Ltd.

*__Cookson, Catherine.__ The Garment. 288p. 2000. pap. 10.95 (*0-552-13716-2*, Pub. by Transworld Publishers Ltd); pap. 10.95 (*0-552-14705-2*, Pub. by Transworld Publishers Ltd) Trafalgar.

Cookson, Catherine. The Girl. 384p. 1998. mass mkt. 16.95 (*0-552-14468-1*) Bantam.

— The Glass Virgin. 352p. 1989. pap. 6.99 (*0-552-08849-8*) Bantam.

— The Glass Virgin. 1998. mass mkt. 16.95 (*0-552-14328-6*) Bantam.

— The Glass Virgin. LC 70-81283. 1969. write for info. (*0-672-50685-8*, 9675) Macmillan.

— The Glass Virgin. 1986. pap. 6.95 (*0-02-527810-X*) Macmillan.

— The Golden Straw. 416p. 1995. mass mkt. 8.99 (*0-552-13685-9*) Bantam.

— The Golden Straw. large type ed. 795p. 1996. 25.95 (*0-7862-0588-1*) Thorndike Pr.

— The Golden Straw: A Novel. 496p. 1995. 23.00 (*0-684-81177-4*) Simon & Schuster.

— The Gullyvors. 240p. 1991. mass mkt. 7.99 (*0-552-13621-2*) Bantam.

Cookson, Catherine. Hannah Massey. (J). pap. 10.95 (*0-552-13715-4*, Pub. by Transworld Publishers Ltd) Trafalgar.

— Hannah Massey. (J). 2000. pap. 10.95 (*0-552-14704-4*, Pub. by Transworld Publishers Ltd) Trafalgar.

— Harold. (J). mass mkt. 8.95 (*0-552-12789-2*, Pub. by Transworld Publishers Ltd) Trafalgar.

Cookson, Catherine. The Harrogate Secret. 464p. 1991. mass mkt. 7.99 (*0-552-13300-0*) Bantam.

— Heritage of Folly. LC 95-133497. 288p. 1995. mass mkt. 7.99 (*0-552-14087-2*) Bantam.

*__Cookson, Catherine.__ Heritage of Folly/The Fen Tiger. 2000. pap. 10.95 (*0-552-14701-X*, Pub. by Transworld Publishers Ltd) Trafalgar.

— A House Divided: A Novel. LC 99-54730. 368p. 2000. 23.50 (*0-684-87121-1*) S&S Trade.

Cookson, Catherine. House of Women. 384p. 1993. mass mkt. 6.99 (*0-552-13303-5*) Bantam.

— The Invitation. 384p. 1996. mass mkt. 7.99 (*0-552-14090-2*) Bantam.

— The Iron Facade. 224p. 1991. mass mkt. 7.99 (*0-552-10780-8*) Bantam.

*__Cookson, Catherine.__ The Iron Facade. large type ed. LC 00-31475. 260p. 2000. lib. bdg. 28.95 (*1-58547-046-5*) Ctr Point Pubg.

— Joe & the Gladiator. (Orig.). 2000. pap. 5.95 (*0-552-52617-7*, Pub. by Transworld Publishers Ltd) Trafalgar.

Cookson, Catherine. Justice Is a Woman. 384p. 1995. mass mkt. 7.99 (*0-552-13622-0*) Bantam.

*__Cookson, Catherine.__ Kate Hannigan. 224p. 2000. pap. 10.95 (*0-552-14091-0*, Pub. by Transworld Publishers Ltd) Trafalgar.

— Kate Hannigan: Long Corridor. (J). 2000. pap. 10.95 (*0-552-14702-8*) Transworld Publishers Ltd.

Cookson, Catherine. Katie Mullholland. 528p. 1994. mass mkt. 8.99 (*0-552-14092-9*) Bantam.

*__Cookson, Catherine.__ Lady on My Left. 2000. mass mkt. 17.95 (*0-552-14569-6*, Pub. by Transworld Publishers Ltd) Trafalgar.

— Let Me Make Myself Plain. pap. 10.95 (*0-552-13407-4*, Pub. by Transworld Publishers Ltd) Trafalgar.

— The Long Corridor. 2000. pap. 8.95 (*0-552-14078-3*, Pub. by Transworld Publishers Ltd) Trafalgar.

Cookson, Catherine. Love & Mary Ann. large type ed. 1970. 15.95 (*0-85456-657-0*) Ulverscroft.

— The Love Child. large type ed. 512p. 1992. lib. bdg. 14.95 (*1-56054-935-1*) Thorndike Pr.

— Maggie Rowan. 384p. (Orig.). 1995. mass mkt. 7.99 (*0-552-14081-3*) Bantam.

— The Mallen Girl. 288p. 1988. mass mkt. 6.99 (*0-552-09896-5*) Bantam.

— The Mallen Girl. large type ed. LC 99-38129. (Thorndike Romance Ser.). 411p. 2000. 28.95 (*0-7862-2140-2*) Thorndike Pr.

— The Mallen Litter. 320p. 1988. mass mkt. 6.99 (*0-552-10151-6*) Bantam.

— The Mallen Litter. LC 99-38128. 2000. pap. 30.00 (*0-7862-2139-9*) Mac Lib Ref.

— The Mallen Streak. 256p. 1984. mass mkt. 6.99 (*0-552-09720-9*) Bantam.

*__Cookson, Catherine.__ The Mallen Streak. (J). 2000. pap. 12.95 (*0-552-14699-4*) Transworld Publishers Ltd.

Cookson, Catherine. The Mallen Streak. large type ed. LC 99-16641. (Thorndike Romance Ser.). 1999. 27.95 (*0-7862-2141-0*) Thorndike Pr.

— The Maltese Angel: A Novel. 528p. 1994. mass mkt. 6.99 (*0-552-13684-0*) Bantam.

— The Maltese Angel: A Novel. large type ed. LC 94-42977. 739p. 1995. 24.95 (*0-7862-0386-2*) Thorndike Pr.

Cookson, Catherine. The Man Who Cried. mass mkt. 6.95 (*0-552-11350-6*, Pub. by Transworld Publishers Ltd) Trafalgar.

Cookson, Catherine. Mary Ann & Bill. large type ed. 1983. 15.95 (*0-7089-0984-1*) Ulverscroft.

— The Menagerie. Date not set. lib. bdg. 21.95 (*0-8488-2140-8*) Amereon Ltd.

— The Menagerie. 1987. pap. 3.95 (*0-552-13163-6*) Bantam.

— The Menagerie. 224p. 1987. mass mkt. 4.50 (*0-552-08653-3*) Bantam.

— The Moth. 432p. 1987. mass mkt. 7.99 (*0-552-12524-5*) Bantam.

*__Cookson, Catherine.__ The Moth. 2000. pap. 10.95 (*0-552-14545-9*) Transworld Publishers Ltd.

Cookson, Catherine. The Moth. large type ed. 480p. 1987. 18.95 (*0-7089-8386-3*, Charnwood) Ulverscroft.

— My Beloved Son. 432p. 1992. mass mkt. 6.99 (*0-552-13302-7*) Bantam.

— My Beloved Son. large type ed. 524p. 1993. reprint ed. lib. bdg. 22.95 (*1-56054-694-8*) Thorndike Pr.

— My Beloved Son: A Novel. LC 92-10143. 1993. 22.00 (*0-671-75865-9*) S&S Trade.

*__Cookson, Catherine.__ Nice Bloke. 2000. pap. 10.95 (*0-552-14086-4*, Pub. by Transworld Publishers Ltd) Trafalgar.

Cookson, Catherine. La Obsesion. 1999. pap. text 9.95 (*84-08-02526-0*) Planeta Edit.

— The Obsession. 529p. 1996. 29.95 (*0-593-03479-1*) Bantam.

— The Obsession. 1996. mass mkt. 7.99 (*0-552-14157-7*) Bantam.

— The Obsession. (Mira Bks.). 1998. mass mkt. 5.99 (*1-55166-454-2*, 1-66454-9, Mira Bks) Harlequin Bks.

— The Obsession. LC 97-18868. 320p. 1997. 22.50 (*0-684-84241-6*) S&S Trade.

— Our John Willie. LC 73-22687. 224p. 1974. 6.95 (*0-672-51897-X*) Macmillan.

*__Cookson, Catherine.__ Our John Willie. 2000. 17.95 (*0-385-40132-9*, Pub. by Transworld Publishers Ltd) Trafalgar.

Cookson, Catherine. Our Kate. LC 74-161241. 1971. 5.95 (*0-672-51618-7*, Bobbs) Macmillan.

*__Cookson, Catherine.__ Our Kate. (J). 2000. pap. 10.95 (*0-552-14093-7*, Pub. by Transworld Publishers Ltd) Trafalgar.

Cookson, Catherine. The Parson's Daughter. 464p. 1988. mass mkt. 7.99 (*0-552-13088-5*) Bantam.

*__Cookson, Catherine.__ Plainer Still. 2000. mass mkt. 10.95 (*0-552-14384-7*, Pub. by Transworld Publishers Ltd) Trafalgar.

Cookson, Catherine. Pure As the Lily. 320p. 1988. mass mkt. 4.50 (*0-552-09596-6*) Bantam.

— Pure As the Lily. 1998. mass mkt. 7.99 (*0-552-14073-2*) Bantam.

— The Rag Nymph. 432p. 1992. mass mkt. 7.99 (*0-552-13683-2*) Bantam.

*__Cookson, Catherine.__ The Rag Nymph: A Novel. 2000. pap. 10.95 (*0-552-14546-7*, Pub. by Transworld Publishers Ltd) Trafalgar.

Cookson, Catherine. The Rag Nymph: A Novel. large type ed. 507p. 1994. lib. bdg. 24.95 (*0-7862-0167-3*) Thorndike Pr.

*__Cookson, Catherine.__ Rooney. 2000. pap. 10.95 (*0-552-14074-0*, Pub. by Transworld Publishers Ltd); pap. 10.95 (*0-552-14706-0*) Transworld Publishers Ltd.

Cookson, Catherine. The Round Tower. 1986. mass mkt. 4.95 (*0-552-13009-5*) Bantam.

— The Round Tower. 336p. 1994. mass mkt. 7.99 (*0-552-14075-9*) Bantam.

*__Cookson, Catherine.__ The Round Tower. 2000. pap. 10.95 (*0-552-14620-X*, Pub. by Transworld Publishers Ltd) Trafalgar.

— A Ruthless Need. 2000. pap. 10.95 (*0-552-14039-2*, Pub. by Transworld Publishers Ltd) Trafalgar.

— Slinky Jane. 288p. (J). 2000. pap. 10.95 (*0-552-13714-6*, Pub. by Transworld Publishers Ltd) Trafalgar.

— Solace of Sin. 2000. pap. 10.95 (*0-552-14583-1*, Pub. by Transworld Publishers Ltd) Trafalgar.

Cookson, Catherine. The Tide of Life. 512p. 1993. mass mkt. 7.99 (*0-552-10630-5*) Bantam.

— The Tide of Life. 1997. mass mkt. 8.99 (*0-552-14446-0*) Bantam.

— Tilly Trotter. 1997. mass mkt. 7.99 (*0-552-11737-4*) Bantam.

*__Cookson, Catherine.__ Tilly Trotter. 2000. pap. 12.95 (*0-552-14683-8*) Transworld Publishers Ltd.

Cookson, Catherine. Tilly Trotter Wed. 352p. 1989. mass mkt. 7.99 (*0-552-11960-1*) Bantam.

— Tilly Trotter Widowed. 1997. mass mkt. 7.99 (*0-552-12200-9*) Bantam.

— The Tinker's Girl. 384p. 1996. mass mkt. 7.99 (*0-552-14038-4*) Bantam.

— The Unbaited Trap. rev. ed. 336p. 1995. mass mkt. 7.99 (*0-552-14076-7*) Bantam.

— The Upstart. LC 96-197122. 1997. 29.95 (*0-593-02848-1*) Bantam.

— The Upstart. 1997. mass mkt. 8.99 (*0-552-14037-6*) Bantam.

*__Cookson, Catherine.__ The Upstart. 1999. per. 5.99 (*1-55166-527-1*, Mira Bks) Harlequin Bks.

Cookson, Catherine. The Upstart. LC 97-28621. 352p. 1998. 22.50 (*0-684-84315-3*) S&S Trade.

— The Upstart. large type ed. LC 98-9955. (Basic Ser.). 1998. 27.95 (*0-7862-1401-5*) Thorndike Pr.

*__Cookson, Catherine.__ The Whip. 2000. mass mkt. 10.95 (*0-552-12368-4*, Pub. by Transworld Publishers Ltd) Trafalgar.

Cookson, Catherine. The Wingless Bird. 512p. 1998. mass mkt. 7.99 (*0-552-14515-7*) Bantam.

— The Wingless Bird. large type ed. LC 91-18382. 601p. 1991. reprint ed. lib. bdg. 21.95 (*1-56054-211-X*) Thorndike Pr.

— The Year of the Virgins. 352p. 1994. mass mkt. 6.99 (*0-552-13247-0*) Bantam.

— The Year of the Virgins. large type ed. LC 95-34857. 1995. 24.95 (*1-56895-247-3*, Compass) Wheeler Pub.

Cookson, Christopher. The Stranger. LC 97-75383. 80p. 1999. 14.95 (*1-56167-373-0*) Am Literary Pr.

Cookson, David. Robbie. (C). 1989. text 40.00 (*0-948929-18-9*) St Mut.

*__Cookson, Dawn.__ Painting with Annigoni: Florence, 1958-68. (Illus.). 128p. 2000. pap. 35.00 (*0-906290-37-6*, Pub. by Unicorn Pr Lon) Boydell & Brewer.

Cookson, Gillian, jt. auth. see Hempstead, Colin.

Cookson, J. E. The British Armed Nation, 1793-1815. LC 96-44824. (Illus.). 296p. (C). 1997. text 95.00 (*0-19-820658-5*) OUP.

Cookson, J. E. The Friends of Peace: Anti-War Liberalism in England, 1793-1815. LC 81-3909. 336p. reprint ed. pap. 95.80 (*0-608-17012-7*, 2027273) Bks Demand.

— Lord Liverpool's Administration: The Crucial Years, 1815-1822. xiii, 422p. 1975. 89.50 (*0-208-01495-0*) Elliots Bks.

Cookson, James, tr. see Gendron, Francois.

*__Cookson, Janet.__ Masquerade. large type ed. 200p. 1999. pap. 18.99 (*0-7089-5612-2*, Linford) Ulverscroft.

— Quest of the Heart. large type ed. 208p. 1999. pap. 18.99 (*0-7089-5526-6*, Linford) Ulverscroft.

— Sweet Surrender. LC 99-90979. 192p. 1999. 18.95 (*0-8034-9384-3*, Avalon Bks) Bouregy.

Cookson, John & Nottingham, Judith. A Survey of Chemical & Biological Warfare. LC 79-128595. 428p. reprint ed. pap. 132.70 (*0-8357-3560-5*, 203433800089) Bks Demand.

Cookson, John & Richmond, Iain. Programming in BASIC. LC 85-621. 128p. reprint ed. pap. 39.70 (*0-8357-2770-X*, 203989500014) Bks Demand.

Cookson, John T., Jr. Bioremediation Engineering: Design & Applications. 524p. 1994. 94.95 (*0-07-012614-3*) McGraw.

Cookson, L., jt. auth. see Ogden, P. H.

Cookson, Linda. Brian Patten. (Writers & Their Work Ser.). 112p. (Orig.). 1996. pap. 17.00 (*0-7463-0809-4*, Pub. by Northcote House) U Pr of Miss.

Cookson, Linda, ed. see Shakespeare, William.

*__Cookson, Lorraine Marie.__ A Caution of a Boy. 2000. pap. 5.95 (*0-533-13164-2*) Vantage.

*__Cookson, Paul.__ Father's Hands. viii, 56p. 1998. reprint ed. pap. 11.99 (*1-900507-75-7*, Pub. by Solway) OM Literature.

Cookson, Peter, ed. see Epstein, Jon.

Cookson, Peter J., Jr., et al, eds. A New Understanding of Parent Involvement: Family - Work - School, Conference Proceedings. 91p. (Orig.). (C). 1997. pap. text 30.00 (*0-7881-4569-X*) DIANE Pub.

Cookson, Peter S., ed. Program Planning for the Training & Continuing Education of Adults: North American Perspectives. LC 97-35031. (Illus.). 528p. (C). 1998. 63.50 (*0-89464-767-9*) Krieger.

Cookson, Peter S., jt. auth. see Rothwell, William J.

*__Cookson, Peter W.__ Parent's Guide to 1st Grade: What Your Kids Are Being Taught-And How You Can Help Them Learn. (Illus.). 2000. pap. text 14.95 (*1-57685-310-1*) LrningExprss.

— Parent's Guide to 2nd Grade: What Your Kids Are Being Taught-And How You Can Help Them Learn. (Illus.). 2000. pap. text 14.95 (*1-57685-311-X*) LrningExprss.

Cookson, Peter W., Jr. School Choice: The Struggle for the Soul of American Education. LC 93-35450. 184p. 1994. 27.50 (*0-300-05791-1*) Yale U Pr.

Cookson, Peter W. School Choice: The Struggle for the Soul of American Education. 1995. pap. 10.00 (*0-300-06499-3*) Yale U Pr.

Cookson, Peter W., Jr., ed. The Choice Controversy. LC 92-17348. 234p. 1992. pap. 72.60 (*0-608-05607-3*, 206606500006) Bks Demand.

Cookson, Peter W., Jr., et al, eds. International Handbook of Educational Reform. LC 91-30586. 640p. 1992. lib. bdg. 105.00 (*0-313-27277-8*, CER/, Greenwood Pr) Greenwood.

Cookson, Peter W., Jr. & Persell, Caroline H. Preparing for Power: America's Elite Boarding Schools. LC 85-47559. 272p. 1987. pap. 17.50 (*0-465-06269-5*, Pub. by Basic) HarpC.

Cookson, Peter W., Jr. & Schneider, Barbara, eds. Transforming Schools. LC 94-36371. (Reference Library of Social Science: Vol. 888). 632p. 1995. text 109.00 (*0-8153-1257-1*, SS888) Garland.

— Transforming Schools. LC 94-36371. (Reference Library of Social Science: Vol. 888). 632p. 1995. pap. text 24.95 (*0-8153-1533-3*, SS888) Garland.

Cookson, Peter W., Jr., jt. auth. see Hanus, Jerome J.

Cookson, Peter W., jt. auth. see Shapira, Rina.
Cookson, William. Agenda: An Anthology. 320p. (Orig.). 1997. pap. 24.95 (*1-85754-302-5*, Pub. by Carcanet Pr) Paul & Co Pubs.
— Ford Madox Ford. Saunders, Max, ed. 1988. pap. 20.00 (*0-933806-51-5*) Black Swan.
— A Guide to the Cantos of Ezra Pound. (Lamplighter Ser.). 224p. 1985. 24.95 (*0-89255-081-3*); pap. 14.95 (*0-89255-082-1*) Persea Bks.
***Cookson, William.** A Guide to the Cantos of Ezra Pound. rev. ed. 256p. 2000. pap. 17.95 (*0-89255-246-8*, Pub. by Persea Bks) Norton.
Cookson, William, ed. Agenda: An Anthology, the First Four Decades 1959-1993. LC 94-210398. 1994. 35.00 (*1-85754-069-7*, Pub. by Carcanet Pr) Paul & Co Pubs.
Cookson, William, ed. see Pound, Ezra.
***Cool Breeze Systems Staff.** Digital Audio Dictionary. LC 99-66347. 228p. 1999. 29.95 (*0-7906-1201-1*) Prompt Publns.
Cool J, LL. I Make My Own Rules. 1998. mass mkt. 5.99 (*0-312-96786-1*) St Martin.
Cool, Jesse. The Vegetarian Slow Cooker Cook Book. 1924. write for info. (*0-688-16275-4*, Hearst) Hearst Commns.
Cool, Jesse Z. Breakfast in Bed: 90 Recipes for Creative Indulgences. LC 97-1052. (Illus.). 128p. 1997. 19.95 (*0-00-225098-5*) Collins SF.
***Cool, Jesse Ziff.** Your Organic Kitchen: Essential Guide to Selecting & Cooking Organic Foods. 304p. 2000. 30.00 (*1-57954-166-6*) Rodale Pr Inc.
Cool, John C., jt. ed. see Hemmi, Kenzo.
Cool, Joyce. The Kidnapping of Courtney Van Allen & What's-Her-Name. 176p. (YA). 1988. pap. 2.75 (*0-553-15597-0*, Starfire BDD) BDD Bks Young Read.
Cool, Lisa C. How to Write Irresistible Query Letters. 136p. 1990. pap. 12.99 (*0-89879-391-2*, Wrtrs Digest Bks) F & W Pubns Inc.
Cool Root, Margaret, jt. auth. see Garrison, Mark B.
***Cool Springs Press Publications Staff.** My Florida Garden: A Gardener's Journal. 2000. 19.95 (*1-888608-84-6*) Cool Springs Pr.
— My Georgia Garden: A Gardener's Journal. 2000. 19.95 (*1-888608-82-X*) Cool Springs Pr.
— My Illinois Garden: A Gardener's Journal. 2000. 19.95 (*1-888608-88-9*) Cool Springs Pr.
— My Kentucky Garden: A Gardener's Journal. 2000. 19.95 (*1-888608-93-5*) Cool Springs Pr.
— My Missouri Garden: A Gardener's Journal. 2000. 19.95 (*1-888608-90-0*) Cool Springs Pr.
— My New York Garden: A Gardener's Journal. 2000. 19.95 (*1-888608-94-3*) Cool Springs Pr.
— My North Carolina Garden: A Gardener's Journal. 2000. 19.95 (*1-888608-85-4*) Cool Springs Pr.
— My Ohio Garden: A Gardener's Journal. 2000. 19.95 (*1-888608-81-1*) Cool Springs Pr.
— My Pennsylvania Garden: A Gardener's Journal. 2000. 19.95 (*1-888608-89-7*) Cool Springs Pr.
— My Texas Garden: A Gardener's Journal. 2000. 19.95 (*1-888608-83-8*) Cool Springs Pr.
— My Wisconsin Garden: A Gardener's Journal. 2000. 19.95 (*1-888608-86-2*) Cool Springs Pr.
Cool, Tom. Infectress. 352p. 1997. per. 5.99 (*0-671-87763-1*) Baen Bks.
— Secret Realms. LC 98-11422. 304p. 1998. text 22.95 (*0-312-86417-5*) St Martin.
— Secret Realms. 1999. mass mkt. 6.99 (*0-8125-4526-5*, Pub. by Tor Bks) St Martin.
Cool, Tom, jt. auth. see De Lancie, John.
Cool, Wouter. With the Dutch in the East: An Outline of the Military Operations in Lombock, 1894. Taylor, E. J., tr. from DUT. LC 77-86968. (Illus.). reprint ed. 47.50 (*0-404-16702-0*) AMS Pr.
***Coolbaugh, James.** DDS Keyword Reference. LC 99-6158. (Illus.). 212p. 1999. pap. 59.95 (*1-58304-042-0*) News Four-Hund.
Coolbaugh, James. DDS Programming for Display & Printer Files. 2nd ed. LC 98-58130. 429p. 1999. pap. 89.00 (*1-58304-037-4*) News Four-Hund.
— SQL/400 by Example. rev. ed. LC 98-58126. 204p. 1999. pap. 59.95 (*1-58304-030-7*) News Four-Hund.
Coolbrith, Ina, ed. see Stoddard, Charles W.
Coole, Arthur B. A Trouble Shooter for God in China. (Illus.). 1976. 20.00 (*0-912706-05-8*) M Akers.
***Coole, Diana.** Negativity & Politics: Dionysus & Dialectics from Kant to Poststructuralism. 240p. 2000. 85.00 (*0-415-03176-1*) Routledge.
***Coole, Diana H.** Negativity & Politics: Dionysus & Dialectics from Kant to Poststructuralism. LC 99-52690. 240p. 2000. pap. 25.99 (*0-415-03177-X*) Routledge.
Coole, Diana H. Women in Political Theory: From Misogyny to Contemporary Feminism. 2nd ed. LC 93-11082. 312p. (C). 1993. pap. text 22.00 (*1-55587-457-6*) L Rienner.
Coole, Walter A. A Mentor's Soiree. 1988. pap. text 7.00 (*0-926725-06-8*) Scaramouche.
Coole, Walter A., et al. Teach Me Tomorrow. 39p. (Orig.). 1986. pap. text 4.00 (*0-926725-04-1*) Scaramouche.
Cooledge, Harold. Supporting Roles. LC 98-89004. 325p. 1998. 25.00 (*0-7388-0193-3*); pap. 15.00 (*0-7388-0194-1*) Xlibris Corp.
Cooledge, Harold N. Samuel Sloan, Architect of Philadelphia, 1815-1884. LC 85-22496. 274p. 1986. reprint ed. pap. 85.00 (*0-608-03636-6*, 206446200009) Bks Demand.
Coolen, Edward. Nicholl's Concise Guide to the Navigation Examinations, Vol. 2. 12th ed. (Illus.). 492p. 1995. 125.00 (*0-85174-635-7*) Sheridan.
Coolen, E. J., rev. Nicholls's Concise Guide to the Navigation Examinations, Vol. 1. 10th rev. ed. (Illus.). 1012p. 1987. reprint ed. text 155.00 (*0-85174-539-3*, Pub. by Brown Son & Ferguson) Sheridan.
Coolen, John & Roddy, Dennis J. Electronic Communications. 4th ed. LC 94-14041. 820p. (C). 1995. 87.00 (*0-13-312083-X*) P-H.
Cooler, Richard & Zehner, Edwin, eds. The Journal of Burma Studies, Vol. 1. 124p. 1997. pap. 16.00 (*1-877979-35-X*) SE Asia.
— The Journal of Burma Studies Vol. 3: General Issue. 91p. 1999. pap. 16.00 (*1-877979-37-6*) SE Asia.
Cooler, Richard M. The Karen Bronze Drums of Burma: Types, Iconography, Manufacture & Use. LC 94-23144. (Studies in Asian Art & Archaeology: Vol. 16). xx, 235p. 1994. 182.50 (*90-04-09933-6*) Brill Academic Pubs.
Cooley. Basic Econometrics. (HQ - Econometrics Ser.). Date not set. pap. 62.95 (*0-538-86248-3*) S-W Pub.
— Life Choices. LC 96-76884. (C). 1996. pap. text 28.76 (*0-395-73865-2*) HM.
— Life Choices. (C). 1997. pap., teacher ed. 11.96 (*0-395-73866-0*) HM.
— Norton's Guide to Writing Short Stories with MAC. (C). 1992. pap. text 37.50 (*0-393-96269-5*) Norton.
— On Self & Social Organization. LC 98-13172. 259p. 1998. pap. text 19.00 (*0-226-11509-7*) U Ch Pr.
— On Self & Social Organization. LC 98-13172. 1998. lib. bdg. 48.00 (*0-226-11508-9*) U Ch Pr.
— Surgery of the Heart & Aorta. pap. text. write for info. (*0-7216-4371-X*, W B Saunders Co) Harcrt Hlth Sci Grp.
Cooley, ed. The Norton Sampler: Short Essays for Composition. 5th ed. LC 96-24245. 1997. pap. write for info. (*0-393-97090-6*) Norton.
Cooley, ed. see Moore, Schuyler M.
Cooley, Le Roy C. Elements of Natural Philosophy (1873) 192p. 1999. reprint ed. pap. 14.95 (*0-7661-0778-7*) Kessinger Pub.
Cooley, A. S. Cooley: The Descendants of Dr. Asahel & Sally Wilbur Cooley. Cooley, L. A., ed. (Illus.). 153p. 1991. reprint ed. pap. 23.00 (*0-8328-2124-1*) Higginson Bk Co.
Cooley, Arnold J. Brewing Science: The Early Days. Thompson, Jack C., ed. & frwd. by. LC 95-71507. iv, 50p. (C). 1995. reprint ed. pap. 8.95 (*1-887719-03-2*) Caber Pr.
Cooley, Barbara. Macintosh Online Handbook. pap. 13.50 (*0-393-96279-2*) Norton.
Cooley, Brandon & Torrence, Elizabeth. Can Rice Grow in Oklahoma? (The/Sunflower Ser.). 132p. (Orig.). (J). (gr. 5-8). 1995. pap., per. 9.95 (*0-943487-48-X*) Sevgo Pr.
***Cooley, Brian & Wilson, Mary Ann.** Make-a-Saurus: My Life with Raptors & Other Dinosaurs. (Illus.). 64p. (J). (gr. 3-6). 2000. lib. bdg. 24.95 (*1-55037-645-4*, Pub. by Annick Pr); per. 14.95 (*1-55037-644-6*, Pub. by Annick Pr) Firefly Bks Ltd.
Cooley, Carletta, ed. see Davis, Alvis O.
Cooley, Charles H. Human Nature & the Social Order. LC 82-11002. (Social Science Classics Ser.). (Illus.). 482p. 1991. reprint ed. pap. 24.95 (*0-87855-918-3*) Transaction Pubs.
— The Roots of Social Knowledge. (Reprint Series in Social Sciences). (C). 1993. reprint ed. pap. text 1.90 (*0-8290-2690-8*, S-50) Irvington.
— Social Organization: A Study of the Larger Mind. LC 80-15746. (Social Science Classics Ser.). 457p. (C). 1983. pap. 29.95 (*0-87855-824-1*) Transaction Pubs.
***Cooley, Chris.** Passions. Boodry, Sharon, ed. 100p. 1999. pap. 11.95 (*0-9677802-0-9*) Coolio.
***Cooley, Clare.** The Book of Cranes. (Illus.). 30p. 2000. reprint ed. boxed set 17.00 (*0-7881-9323-6*) DIANE Pub.
Cooley, Dennis. Eli Mandel & His Works. (Canadian Author Studies). 89p. (C). 1992. pap. 9.95 (*1-55022-071-3*, Pub. by ECW) Genl Dist Srvs.
— Sunfall: New & Selected Poems. LC 97-113086. 160p. (Orig.). 1996. pap. 13.95 (*0-88784-580-0*, Pub. by Hse of Anansi Pr) Genl Dist Srvs.
— This Only Home. 1997. pap. 9.95 (*0-88801-164-4*, Pub. by Turnstone Pr) Genl Dist Srvs.
Cooley, Dennis, ed. Inscriptions: A Prairie Poetry Anthology. 1997. pap. 15.95 (*0-88801-168-7*, Pub. by Turnstone Pr) Genl Dist Srvs.
— Replacing. 323p. (C). 1980. pap. text 3.75 (*0-920802-34-6*, Pub. by ECW) Genl Dist Srvs.
Cooley, Donald G. Science Book of Wonder Drugs. LC 72-99627. (Essay Index Reprint Ser.). (Illus.). 1977. 23.95 (*0-8369-1562-3*) Ayer.
Cooley, Doris H., ed. Ritual of Music. 1968. pap. text 1.00 (*0-88053-318-8*, S-79) Macoy Pub.
Cooley, Grace J. Lost in Silence & Forgot. 208p. 1992. 17.50 (*0-87244-083-4*) Texian.
Cooley, Gregory M., jt. auth. see Van Wynsberghe, Donna M.
Cooley, Henry B. Chartering & Charter Parties. LC 47-27566. 166p. reprint ed. pap. 51.50 (*0-608-16174-8*, 202255200028) Bks Demand.
Cooley, Henry S. A Study of Slavery in New Jersey. LC 78-63853. (Johns Hopkins University. Studies in the Social Sciences. Thirtieth Ser. 1912: 9-10). reprint ed. 32.50 (*0-404-61109-5*) AMS Pr.
Cooley, J. H., ed. see Havlin, D L.
Cooley, John. Callaghan's Appellate Advocacy Manual (Lawyer's Edition), 2 vols., Set. 1989. 160.00 (*0-318-41453-8*) West Group.
— Savages & Naturals: Black Portraits by White Writers in Modern American Literature. 208p. 1982. 32.50 (*0-87413-167-7*) U Delaware Pr.
Cooley, John, ed. Earthly Words: Essays on Contemporary American Nature & Environmental Writers. 300p. 1994. pap. 19.95 (*0-472-06537-8*, 06537); text 42.50 (*0-472-09537-4*, 09537) U of Mich Pr.
Cooley, John K. Payback: America's Long War in the Middle East. 257p. 1997. reprint ed. text 20.00 (*0-7881-5137-1*) DIANE Pub.
— Unholy Wars: The CIA in Afghanistan, the Taliban & International Terrorism. LC 98-50370. 256p. 1999. 29.95 (*0-7453-1328-0*) Pluto GBR.
***Cooley, John W.** The Arbitrator's Handbook. LC 99-189419. 447 p. 1998. 49.95 (*1-55681-616-2*) Natl Inst Trial Ad.
— Mediation Advocacy. 320p. 1996. 37.95 (*1-55681-503-4*) Natl Inst Trial Ad.
Cooley, John W. Queen of Battle. LC 98-89880. 365p. 1999. 25.00 (*0-7388-0313-8*); pap. 15.00 (*0-7388-0314-6*) Xlibris Corp.
— Retirement Decisions Made Easier: For Federal Employees under the Civil Service Retirement System. 4th ed. 200p. 1995. reprint ed. student ed., ring bd. 29.95 (*1-883336-00-7*) CCL.
Cooley, John W. & Lubet, Steven. Arbitration Advocacy. 372p. 1996. 37.95 (*1-55681-527-1*) Natl Inst Trial Ad.
***Cooley, John W. & National Institute for Trial Advocacy Staff.** The Mediator's Handbook: Advanced Practice Guide for Civil Litigation. LC 99-88515. 2000. pap. write for info. (*1-55681-681-2*) Natl Inst Trial Ad.
Cooley, Julia, jt. auth. see Altrocchi, Julia.
Cooley, L. A., ed. see Cooley, A. S.
Cooley, Laura, jt. ed. see Elder, John.
Cooley, Lindell. A Touch of Glory. LC 97-215143. 182p. 1997. pap. 10.99 (*1-56043-689-1*, Revival Pr) Destiny Image.
Cooley, M. E. Cooley Genealogy: Descendants of Ensign Benjamin Cooley. 1199p. 1991. reprint ed. pap. 149.00 (*0-8328-2123-3*); reprint ed. lib. bdg. 159.00 (*0-8328-2122-5*) Higginson Bk Co.
Cooley, Martha. The Archivist: A Novel. LC 97-38385. 336p. (gr. 8). 1998. 22.95 (*0-316-15872-0*) Little.
***Cooley, Martha.** The Archivist: A Novel. 336p. 1999. pap. 13.00 (*0-316-15846-1*, Back Bay) Little.
Cooley, Mason. The Comic Art of Barbara Pym. LC 87-45807. (Studies in Modern Literature: No. 18). 1988. 42.50 (*0-404-61588-0*) AMS Pr.
Cooley, Maurice E., jt. auth. see Eddy, Frank W.
Cooley, Mel. The Bride Wore Combat Boots. 144p. 1989. pap. 5.95 (*0-88144-146-5*) Christian Pub.
Cooley, Michael E. The Inventive Writer: Using Critical Thinking to Persuade. 464p. (C). 1993. pap. text 32.76 (*0-669-24492-9*) HM Trade Div.
Cooley, Mike. Architect or Bee? The Human-Technology Relationship. 134p. 1982. reprint ed. pap. 7.00 (*0-89608-131-1*) South End Pr.
Cooley, Mortimer E. Scientific Blacksmith. LC 72-5041. (Technology & Society Ser.). (Illus.). 290p. 1972. reprint ed. 20.95 (*0-405-04693-6*) Ayer.
Cooley, Nicole. Judy Garland & Ginger Love. 2000. pap. 13.00 (*0-06-098744-8*) HarpC.
— Resurrection. LC 96-2242. 96p. (C). 1996. pap. 10.95 (*0-8071-2059-6*) La State U Pr.
Cooley, Peter. The Astonished Hours. LC 91-72055. (Poetry Ser.). 70p. (Orig.). 1992. pap. 11.95 (*0-88748-131-0*) Carnegie-Mellon.
— The Company of Strangers. 1991. 10.00 (*0-941038-07-6*) Coyne & Chenoweth.
— Nightseasons. LC 82-74302. 1983. 20.95 (*0-915604-82-5*); pap. 11.95 (*0-915604-83-3*) Carnegie-Mellon.
— The Room Where Summer Ends. LC 79-51605. (Poetry Ser.). 1979. 16.95 (*0-915604-27-2*); pap. 11.95 (*0-915604-28-0*) Carnegie-Mellon.
— Sacred Conversations. LC 97-65563. (Poetry Ser.). 104p. 1998. 24.95 (*0-88748-255-4*); pap. 11.95 (*0-88748-256-2*) Carnegie-Mellon.
Cooley, Philip L. Advances in Business Financial Management. 2nd ed. LC 95-69072. 669p. (C). 1995. pap. text 62.00 (*0-03-015717-X*) Dryden Pr.
Cooley, Philip L., et al. Business Financial Management. 4th ed. (Illus.). 530p. (C). 1997. pap. text 39.95 (*0-9659459-0-1*) JLH Enter.
— Study Guide for Business Financial Management. 4th ed. 288p. 1997. pap. text 12.00 (*0-9659459-1-X*) JLH Enter.
Cooley, Regina F. The Magic Christmas Pony. LC 91-76342. (Illus.). 36p. (J). (gr. 1-5). 1991. 19.95 (*1-880450-04-6*) Capstone Pub.
Cooley, Richard K. & Vanderwolf, C. H. The Sheep Brain: A Basic Guide. 1979. pap. 10.95 (*0-920700-01-2*) A J Kirby.
Cooley, Richard K. & Vanderwolf, C.H. Stereotaxic Surgery in the Rat: A Photographic Series. 2nd ed. 1990. pap. 29.95 (*0-920700-00-4*) A J Kirby.
Cooley, Richard K., jt. auth. see Vanderwolf, C. H.
Cooley, Rossa B. School Acres: An Adventure in Rural Education. LC 71-106853. (Illus.). 166p. 1970. reprint ed. lib. bdg. 49.50 (*0-8371-3475-7*, CSC&, Greenwood Pr) Greenwood.
Cooley, Shannon, ed. Eye Wuz Here: Women Writers under 30. 288p. (Orig.). 1997. pap. 16.95 (*1-55054-524-8*, Pub. by DGL) Orca Bk Pubs.
Cooley, Sheila. Why the Hymen? 144p. 1997. pap. 10.00 (*1-57502-595-7*, P01707) Morris Pubng.
Cooley, Sheryl L., jt. ed. see Hart, Roger D.
Cooley, Sue, ed. see Wilson, Ann.
Cooley, T. M., et al. Constitutional History of the United States As Seen in the Development of American Law: A Course of Lectures Before the Political Science Association of the University of Michigan. 296p. 1993. reprint ed. 42.50 (*0-8377-2022-2*, Rothman) W S Hein.
Cooley, Talmage & Spade, Andy. Public Love. LC 98-42891. (Illus.). 96p. 1999. 14.95 (*0-8118-2153-6*) Chronicle Bks.
***Cooley, Thomas.** The Ivory Leg in the Ebony Cabinet: Madness, Race, & Gender in Victorian America. 2001. 34.95 (*1-55849-284-4*) U of Mass Pr.
Cooley, Thomas. The Norton Guide to Writing. (Illus.). 650p. (C). 1992. text 34.50 (*0-393-96232-6*); pap. text 45.25 (*0-393-95320-3*) Norton.
— The Norton Guide to Writing. (Illus.). 650p. (C). 1992. pap. text. write for info. (*0-393-95324-6*) Norton.
— The Norton Guide to Writing with the Mac. (C). 1992. pap. text 39.50 (*0-393-96266-0*) Norton.
Cooley, Thomas, ed. Huckleberry Finn: An Authoritative Text, Contexts & Sources, Criticism. 3rd ed. LC 98-6901. (Critical Editions Ser.). (Illus.). 402p. (C). 1998. pap. text 11.25 (*0-393-96640-2*, Norton Paperbks) Norton.
Cooley, Thomas, ed. The Norton Sampler: Short Essays for Composition. 4th ed. LC 92-26173. 427p. (C). 1993. pap. text 22.25 (*0-393-95739-X*) Norton.
Cooley, Thomas F., ed. Frontiers of Business Cycle Research. LC 94-22131. 464p. 1995. text 55.00 (*0-691-04323-X*, Pub. by Princeton U Pr) Cal Prin Full Svc.
Cooley, Thomas M. Elements of Torts. lxxv, 335p. 1995. reprint ed. 52.50 (*0-8377-2056-7*, Rothman) W S Hein.
— Michigan, a History of Governments. rev. ed. LC 72-3764. (American Commonwealths Ser.: No. 5). reprint ed. 42.50 (*0-404-57205-7*) AMS Pr.
— A Treatise on the Constitutional Limitations Which Rest Upon the Legislative Power of the States of the American Union, 1868. LC 99-20589. 1999. 95.00 (*1-886363-92-7*) Lawbk Exchange.
— Treatise on the Law of Torts: or The Wrongs Which Arise Independent of Contract. ci, 755p. 1993. reprint ed. 85.00 (*0-8377-2049-4*, Rothman) W S Hein.
Cooley, Timothy J., jt. ed. see Barz, Gregory F.
Cooley, W. Carl, jt. auth. see Wilson, Golder N.
Cooley, W. D. Negroland of the Arabs. rev. ed. 143p. 1966. 35.00 (*0-7146-1799-7*, Pub. by F Cass Pubs) Intl Spec Bk.
Cooley, William & Bickel, William. Decision-Oriented Educational Research. 1985. lib. bdg. 84.50 (*0-89838-201-7*) Kluwer Academic.
Cooley, William W. & Lohnes, Paul R. Evaluation Research in Education: Theory, Principles & Practice. 368p. (C). 1976. text 22.95 (*0-8290-0410-6*) Irvington.
Coolican. Introduction to Research Methods & Statistics in Psychology. 1996. text 19.95 (*0-340-67937-9*) St Martin.
Coolican, Hugh. Research Methods & Statistics in Psychology. 320p. 1993. pap. 16.95 (*0-340-52404-9*, B0100, Pub. by E A) Routledge.
— Research Methods & Statistics in Psychology. 2nd ed. 512p. 1995. text 16.95 (*0-340-60082-9*, Pub. by E A) St Martin.
Coolidge. General Psychology: Paradigmatic Approach. 336p. 1997. pap. text 49.00 (*0-536-00326-2*) Pearson Custom.
Coolidge, Archibald C., Jr. English Laws & American Problems. LC 95-12246. 96p. 1995. pap. 9.95 (*0-944266-24-X*) Maecenas Pr.
***Coolidge, Archibald C., Jr.** Political Metaphors. 80p. (C). 1999. pap. 7.95 (*0-944266-26-6*) Maecenas Pr.
Coolidge, Archibald C., Jr. A Theory of Story. LC 89-90740. 112p. (Orig.). 1989. pap. 9.95 (*0-944266-02-9*) Maecenas Pr.
— The U. S. As a World Power. 1988. reprint ed. lib. bdg. 59.00 (*0-7812-0460-7*) Rprt Serv.
— The U. S. As a World Power. 1981. reprint ed. lib. bdg. 69.00 (*0-403-00907-3*) Scholarly.
Coolidge, Archibald C. United States As a World Power. (History - United States Ser.). 385p. 1992. reprint ed. lib. bdg. 89.00 (*0-7812-6211-9*) Rprt Serv.
Coolidge, Archibald C., jt. auth. see Channing, Edward.
Coolidge, Archibald C., ed. see Harris, Joel Chandler.
Coolidge, Calvin. The Autobiography of Calvin Coolidge. LC 84-72055. (Illus.). 246p. (Orig.). (C). 1989. reprint ed. pap. 14.95 (*0-944951-03-1*) C Coolidge Memorial.
— The Autobiography of Calvin Coolidge. (History - United States Ser.). 246p. (Orig.). 1992. reprint ed. lib. bdg. 79.00 (*0-7812-6229-1*) Rprt Serv.
— Foundations of the Republic. LC 68-8450. (Essay Index Reprint Ser.). 1977. 23.95 (*0-8369-0333-1*) Ayer.
Coolidge, Charles H. Accident Investigation Board Report: U. S. Air Force CT-43A, 73-1149, 3 April 1996, Dubrovnik, Croatia - Executive Summary. (Illus.). 94p. (Orig.). (C). 1996. pap. text 30.00 (*0-7881-3375-6*) DIANE Pub.
***Coolidge, Clark.** Alien Tatters. unabridged ed. 208p. 2000. pap. 12.95 (*1-891190-08-3*, Pub. by Atelos) SPD-Small Pr Dist.
Coolidge, Clark. American Ones. 48p. (Orig.). 1981. pap. 5.00 (*0-939180-17-0*) Tombouctou.
— At Egypt. 1988. per. 10.00 (*0-935724-35-4*) Figures.
***Coolidge, Clark.** Bomb. (Illus.). 48p. 2000. pap. 12.00 (*1-887123-32-6*, Pub. by Granary Bks) DAP Assocs.
Coolidge, Clark. The Book of During. 1991. per. 15.00 (*0-935724-43-5*) Figures.
— The Book of During. deluxe ed. 1991. per. 25.00 (*0-935724-49-4*) Figures.
— The Crystal Text. (Sun & Moon Classics Ser.: No. 99). 168p. 1995. pap. 11.95 (*1-55713-230-5*) Sun & Moon CA.
***Coolidge, Clark.** A Geology. 28p. (Orig.). 1999. pap. 8.00 (*1-893541-19-3*, Pub. by Potes Poets) SPD-Small Pr Dist.
Coolidge, Clark. Keys to the Caverns. 1995. pap. 8.00 (*84-87467-23-7*, Pub. by Zasterle Pr) SPD-Small Pr Dist.
— Mesh. 48p. 1988. pap. 4.95 (*0-932597-05-X*) In Camera.
***Coolidge, Clark.** Now It's Jazz: Writings on Kerouac & the Sounds. 136p. 1999. 14.00 (*0-945953-09-7*, Pub. by Living Batch Bks) SPD-Small Pr Dist.
Coolidge, Clark. Odes of Roba. 1991. 12.00 (*0-935724-46-X*) Figures.
— Odes of Roba. deluxe limited ed. 1991. 25.00 (*0-935724-47-8*) Figures.

C

*__Coolidge, Clark.__ On the Nameways. 128p. 2000. pap. 13.95 (*1-930589-02-6*, Pub. by Figures) SPD-Small Pr Dist.

__Coolidge, Clark.__ On the Slates. limited ed. 62p. 1992. 65.00 (*1-880392-05-4*) Flockophobic Pr.

— Registers. 88p. (Orig.). (C). 1994. pap. 9.95 (*0-939691-10-8*) Avenue B.

— The Rova Improvisations. LC 94-209422. (Sun & Moon Classics Ser.: No. 34). 170p. (Orig.). 1993. pap. 11.95 (*1-55713-149-X*) Sun & Moon CA.

— Smithsonian Depositions & Subject to a Film. 84p. 1980. 6.00 (*0-931428-30-0*) Vehicle Edns.

— Solution Passage: Poems 1978-1981. deluxe limited ed. 390p. 1986. 30.00 (*0-940650-59-2*) Sun & Moon CA.

__Coolidge, Clark & Guston, Philip.__ Baffling Means: Writings-Drawings. (Orig.). 1991. 80.00 (*1-879645-00-9*); pap. 19.95 (*1-879645-01-7*) o-blek editions.

__Coolidge, Clark, et al.__ Joglars, 1964-1966. 1974. 20.00 (*0-685-43164-9*, 14183) Ayer.

__Coolidge, Clark, jt. auth. see Padgett, Ron.__

__Coolidge, Clark, ed. see Brodey, Jim.__

__Coolidge, Dane.__ Death Valley Prospectors. LC 85-62283. (Illus.). 128p. (Orig.). 1985. reprint ed. 20.00 (*0-930704-18-5*) Sagebrush Pr.

— The Desert Trail. 1975. lib. bdg. 13.85 (*0-89966-059-2*) Buccaneer Bks.

— Fighting Men of the West. LC 68-24846. (Essay Index Reprint Ser.). (Illus.). 1977. reprint ed. 22.95 (*0-8369-0334-X*) Ayer.

*__Coolidge, Dane.__ Gun-Smoke. 2000. 19.00 (*0-7540-8077-3*, Gunsmoke) Chivers N Amer.

__Coolidge, Dane.__ Hidden Water. 1975. lib. bdg. 20.10 (*0-89966-062-2*) Buccaneer Bks.

— Rawhide Johnny. large type ed. LC 98-48134. 1999. 18.95 (*1-57490-170-2*, Sagebrush LP West) T T Beeler.

— The Texican. 1975. lib. bdg. 16.30 (*0-89966-065-7*) Buccaneer Bks.

— Under the Sun. large type ed. LC 94-33480. (Nightingale Ser.). 312p. 1995. pap. 16.95 (*0-7838-1147-0*, G K Hall Lrg Type) Mac Lib Ref.

— Wally Laughs-Easy. large type ed. LC 93-44661. 270p. 1994. lib. bdg. 15.95 (*0-7862-0160-6*) Thorndike Pr.

__Coolidge, Dane & Coolidge, Mary R.__ Last of the Seris: The Aboriginal Indians of Kino Bay, Sonora, Mexico. LC 71-153199. (Beautiful Rio Grande Classics Ser.). (Illus.). 340p. 1973. reprint ed. lib. bdg. 17.50 (*0-87380-078-8*) Popular E Commerce.

— The Navajo Indians. LC 76-43679. reprint ed. 52.50 (*0-404-15513-8*) AMS Pr.

__Coolidge, Daniel S.__ Survival Guide for Road Warriors: Essentials for the Mobile Lawyer. LC 96-83727. (Illus.). 176p. 1996. pap. text 29.95 (*1-57073-298-1*) Amer Bar Assn.

__Coolidge, G. B.__ SAT, TOEFL Vocabulary: English Vocabulary - The Effective Learning. LC 98-71328. 315p. 1998. pap. text 19.50 (*0-9664017-0-0*) GMAI Pubng.

__Coolidge, Guy O.__ The French Occupation of the Champlain Valley from 1609 to 1759. 3rd ed. LC 99-18316. 218p. 1999. reprint ed. pap. 18.00 (*0-916346-68-4*) Purple Mnt Pr.

__Coolidge, Gypsy A.__ Celestial Gems Books, 2. LC 73-88209. (Illus.). 48p. 1972. 10.00 (*0-914154-01-X*) Celestial Gems.

— Celestial Gems Books, Set, Vols. 5-6. LC 73-88209. (Illus.). 150p. 1975. 10.00 (*0-914154-05-2*) Celestial Gems.

— Celestial Gems Books, Vol. 1. rev. ed. LC 73-88209. 150p. 1971. 10.00 (*0-914154-00-1*) Celestial Gems.

— Celestial Gems Books, Vol. 4. LC 73-88209. 65p. 1974. spiral bd. 10.00 (*0-914154-03-6*) Celestial Gems.

— Cosmic Folly. 1990. write for info. (*0-318-66955-2*) Celestial Gems.

— Feet of Clay. 1990. write for info. (*0-318-66954-4*) Celestial Gems.

— A Gypsy Lover's Kiss. 1990. write for info. (*0-318-66957-9*) Celestial Gems.

— Gypsy Passion. 1990. write for info. (*0-318-66953-6*) Celestial Gems.

— Moonlight Stars Candles Wine Roses Romance. 1990. write for info. (*0-318-66958-7*) Celestial Gems.

— The Only Right Solution to Control Sex Offenders & Drug Addicts. 1990. write for info. (*0-318-66956-0*) Celestial Gems.

__Coolidge, Harold J. & Lord, Robert H.__ Archibald Cary Coolidge: Life & Letters. LC 70-179512. (Select Bibliographies Reprint Ser.). 1977. reprint ed. 26.95 (*0-8369-6641-4*) Ayer.

__Coolidge, Jane T.__ Growing up with Chapel Hill. unabridged ed. (Illus.). 112p. 1988. reprint ed. pap. 5.95 (*0-940715-01-5*) Chapel Hill Hist.

__Coolidge, Joe, tr. see McDiarmid, Jim.__

__Coolidge, John.__ Gustave Dore's London: A Study of the City in the Age of Confidence, 1848-1873. LC 93-28385. (Illus.). 1994. 10.95 (*0-87233-107-5*) Bauhan.

— Mill & Mansion: A Study of Architecture & Society in Lowell, Massachusetts, 1820-1865. 2nd ed. LC 92-14978. (Illus.). 336p. 1993. reprint ed. pap. 18.95 (*0-87023-819-1*) U of Mass Pr.

__Coolidge, Julian L.__ The Mathematics of Great Amateurs. 2nd ed. (Illus.). 236p. 1990. pap. text 45.00 (*0-19-853939-8*) OUP.

— Treatise on the Circle & the Sphere. LC 78-128872. 1971. text 45.00 (*0-8284-0236-1*) Chelsea Pub.

__Coolidge, Katherine, ed. see Gallo, Jon J., et al.__

__Coolidge, Lillie P.__ History of Prescott, Mass., One of the Four Townships in the Swift River Valley Which Was "Born, Lived & Died" to Make Way for Metro. Water Basin (Quabbin Reservoir). With Genealogies & Biographies. (Illus.). 288p. 1995. reprint ed. lib. bdg. 39.50 (*0-8328-4468-3*) Higginson Bk Co.

__Coolidge, Louis A.__ Ulysses S. Grant. Morse, John T., Jr., ed. LC 75-128953. (American Statesmen Ser.: No. 32). xix, 596 p. 1972. reprint ed. 49.50 (*0-404-50894-4*) AMS Pr.

__Coolidge, Mary E.__ The Rain-Makers: Indians of Arizona & New Mexico. LC 76-43681. (Illus.). 376p. reprint ed. 49.50 (*0-404-15514-6*) AMS Pr.

__Coolidge, Mary R.__ Chinese Immigration. LC 69-18768. (American Immigration Collection. Series 1). (Illus.). 1978. reprint ed. 26.95 (*0-405-00516-4*) Ayer.

— Chinese Immigration. 1992. reprint ed. lib. bdg. 75.00 (*0-7812-5017-X*) Rprt Serv.

— Why Women Are So. LC 72-2595. (American Women Ser.: Images & Realities). 376p. 1974. reprint ed. 25.95 (*0-405-04452-6*) Ayer.

__Coolidge, Mary R., jt. auth. see Coolidge, Dane.__

__Coolidge, Matthew.__ Commonwealth of Technology: Extrapolations on the Contemporary Landscape of Massachusetts. Simons, Sarah, ed. (Illus.). 72p. 1999. pap. 10.00 (*0-9650962-1-1*) Ctr Land Use Interpret.

*__Coolidge, Nancy & Spencer, R.__ Killingly. (Images of America Ser.). 128p. 1999. pap. 18.99 (*0-7385-0211-1*) Arcadia Publng.

__Coolidge, Nellie & Manutoli, Sophie.__ Ellaliuryaraq.Tr. of Weather. (ESK., Illus.). 28p. (J). (gr. k-3). 1998. pap. text 8.00 (*1-58084-048-5*) Lower Kuskokwim.

__Coolidge, Olivia.__ Caesar's Gallic War. LC 91-33962. (Illus.). x, 246p. (YA). (gr. 8-12). 1991. reprint ed. lib. bdg. 23.50 (*0-208-02334-8*, Linnet Bks) Shoe String.

— Lives of Famous Romans. LC 91-40360. (Illus.). 248p. (YA). (gr. 8-12). 1992. reprint ed. lib. bdg. 25.00 (*0-208-02333-X*, Linnet Bks) Shoe String.

__Coolidge, Olivia E.__ The Apprenticeship of Abraham Lincoln LC 74-11713. viii, 242 p. 1974. 6.95 (*0-684-14003-9*) Scribner.

— Colonial Entrepreneur: Silvester Gardiner & the Settlement of the Kennebec River Valley. LC 98-32359. (Illus.). 304p. 1999. 20.00 (*0-88448-205-7*) Tilbury Hse.

__Coolidge, Olivia E.__ Greek Myths, 001. (Illus.). 256p. (J). (gr. 7 up). 1949. 16.00 (*0-395-06721-9*) HM.

— Trojan War. 256p. (YA). 1990. pap. 7.95 (*0-395-56151-5*) HM.

__Coolidge, Orville W.__ Twentieth Century History of Berrien County. (Illus.). 1007p. 1997. reprint ed. lib. bdg. 99.50 (*0-8328-6749-7*) Higginson Bk Co.

__Coolidge, Susan.__ What Katy Did. (Andre Deutsch Classics). 175p. (J). (gr. 5-8). 1996. 9.95 (*0-233-99036-4*, Pub. by Andre Deutsch) Trafalgar.

— What Katy Did. 160p. 1999. 24.95 (*1-85149-705-6*) Antique Collect.

— What Katy Did. LC 98-41709. (Chapter Book Charmers Ser.). 80p. (J). (gr. 2-5). 1999. 2.99 (*0-694-01283-1*, HarpFestival) HarpC Child Bks.

— What Katy Did. (Illus.). (YA). (gr. 5 up). 1997. pap. 4.99 (*0-14-036697-0*) Viking Penguin.

— What Katy Did. 190p. (J). 1988. reprint ed. lib. bdg. 19.95 (*0-89966-585-3*) Buccaneer Bks.

— What Katy Did Next. 1999. lib. bdg. 21.95 (*1-56723-169-1*) Yestermorrow.

__Coolik, Eugene.__ Simply Shooters: A. K. A. Coast to Coast Shooter Collection - The Professional Bartender's Directory. 2nd rev. ed. 144p. 1998. pap. 12.95 (*0-944057-02-0*) Just Bev Pubns.

__Cooling.__ Modula-2 for Microcomputer Systems. (C). 1988. mass mkt. 39.95 (*0-412-43730-9*) Chapman & Hall.

— Software Design Realtime Systems. (C). 1990. mass mkt. 98.50 (*0-412-34180-8*) Chapman & Hall.

__Cooling, jt. auth. see Lundy.__

__Cooling, B. F., jt. auth. see Millett, Allan R.__

__Cooling, B. Franklin.__ Monocacy: The Battle That Saved Washington. LC 97-6135. (Illus.). 333p. 1997. 34.95 (*1-57249-032-2*) White Mane Pub.

*__Cooling, B. Franklin.__ Monocacy: The Battle That Saved Washington. (Illus.). 335p. 2000. pap. 19.95 (*1-57249-229-5*) White Mane Pub.

— U. S. S. Olympia: Herald of Empire. LC 00-42391. 2000. write for info. (*1-55750-148-3*) Naval Inst Pr.

__Cooling, B. Franklin, 3rd, ed.__ New American State Papers, 1789 to 1860: Military Affairs, 19 vols., Set. LC 79-110. 1979. lib. bdg. 1200.00 (*0-8420-2137-X*) Scholarly Res Inc.

__Cooling, Benjamin F.__ Fort Donelson's Legacy: War & Society in Kentucky & Tennessee, 1862-1863. LC 96-10012. (Illus.). 423p. 1997. 38.00 (*0-87049-949-1*) U of Tenn Pr.

— Forts Henry & Donelson: The Key to the Confederate Heartland. LC 87-5910. (Illus.). 368p. 1988. 32.00 (*0-87049-538-0*) U of Tenn Pr.

__Cooling, Benjamin F., III.__ Jubal Early's Raid on Washington, 1864. LC 89-60483. (Illus.). 320p. 1989. 28.95 (*0-933852-86-X*) Nautical & Aviation.

__Cooling, Benjamin F., ed.__ Case Studies in the Development of Close Air Support. (Illus.). 616p. 1990. 39.00 (*0-912799-65-X*) AFH & MP.

__Cooling, J. E.__ Software Design for Real-Time Systems. (Illus.). 528p. (C). 1991. mass mkt. 39.95 (*1-85032-279-1*) ITCP.

__Cooling, Jeffrey, jt. auth. see Drakeford, Brian.__

__Cooling, Jim.__ Software Engineering for Real-Time Systems. (C). 2000. pap. text. write for info. (*0-201-59620-2*) Addison-Wesley.

__Cooling, W. Colebrook.__ Low-Cost Maintenance Control. LC 73-75670. (Illus.). 71p. reprint ed. pap. 30.00 (*0-608-11638-6*, 205152900085) Bks Demand.

__Cooling, Wendy.__ Book of Stories for Five Year Olds. pap. 8.95 (*0-14-037458-2*, Pub. by Pnguin Bks Ltd) Trafalgar.

— Book of Stories for Six Year Olds. pap. 7.95 (*0-14-037459-0*, Pub. by Pnguin Bks Ltd) Trafalgar.

__Cooling, Wendy.__ Farmyard Tales from Far & Wide. (Illus.). 48p. (J). (ps-2). 1998. 15.95 (*1-901223-38-8*) Barefoot Bks NY.

__Cooling, Wendy.__ Puffin Book of Stories for Eight Year Olds. (Illus.). 128p. (J). (gr. 3). pap. 8.95 (*0-14-038052-3*, Pub. by Pnguin Bks Ltd) Trafalgar.

— Puffin Book of Stories for Seven Year Olds. (Illus.). 176p. (J). 1996. pap. 8.95 (*0-14-037460-4*, Pub. by Pnguin Bks Ltd) Trafalgar.

__Cooling, Wilmer.__ Simplified Low-Cost Maintenance Control. LC 82-18380. 122p. reprint ed. pap. 37.90 (*0-608-11964-4*, 202350100033) Bks Demand.

__Coolman, Anne, ed. see Snow, Diane.__

__Cools, A. R., jt. ed. see Ellenbroek, B. A.__

__Coolsaet, B., ed. see Annual Meeting of the International Continence Soc.__

__Coolwell, Wayne.__ My Kind of People: Achievement, Identity & Aboriginality. 1993. pap. 14.95 (*0-7022-2543-6*, Pub. by Univ Queensland Pr) Intl Spec Bk.

*__Coomans, Fons, et al.__ Human Rights from Exclusion to Inclusion. 520p. 2000. 182.00 (*90-411-1377-0*) Kluwer Law Intl.

__Coomans, H. E., ed. see Rombouts, A.__

__Coomara, Swamy M., intro.__ Sutta Nipata: Or Dialogues & Discourses of Gotama Buddha. LC 78-70125. 1980. reprint ed. 34.00 (*0-404-17384-5*) AMS Pr.

__Coomaraswami, Ananda K.__ The Dance of Siva: Essays on Indian Art & Culture. (Fine Art Ser.). 192p. 1985. reprint ed. pap. 7.95 (*0-486-24817-8*) Dover.

__Coomaraswamy, A. K.__ The Arts & Crafts of India & Ceylon. (Illus.). xxiv, 265p. 1987. reprint ed. 19.00 (*0-88065-044-3*) Scholarly Pubns.

__Coomaraswamy, Amanda K.__ The Door in the Sky: Coomaraswamy on Myth & Meaning, Vol. 89. Coomaraswamy, R. P., ed. LC 98-156083. (Mythos Ser.). 256p. 1997. pap. text 15.95 (*0-691-01747-6*, Pub. by Princeton U Pr) Cal Prin Full Svc.

— Essays in Early Indian Architecture. Meister, Michael W., ed. (Illus.). 180p. 1994. text 29.95 (*0-19-563094-7*) OUP.

__Coomaraswamy, Anand K.__ Jaina Art. LC 94-905051. (Illus.). 120p. 1994. 33.50 (*81-215-0539-9*, Pub. by M Manoharial) Coronet Bks.

__Coomaraswamy, Ananda.__ Early Indian Architecture: Cities & City Gates. (C). 1991. 14.00 (*0-685-54513-X*, Pub. by M Manoharial) S Asia.

__Coomaraswamy, Ananda & Duggirala, Gopala K.__ Mirror of Gesture. (C). 1997. 14.00 (*81-215-0021-4*, Pub. by M Manoharial) Coronet Bks.

*__Coomaraswamy, Ananda & Horner, I. B.__ The Living Thoughts of Gotama the Buddha. 2000. pap. 8.95 (*0-486-41439-6*) Dover.

__Coomaraswamy, Ananda K.__ Am I My Brother's Keeper? LC 67-23196. (Essay Index Reprint Ser.). 1977. 15.95 (*0-8369-0335-8*) Ayer.

— Art & Swadeshi. (C). 1994. text 22.00 (*81-215-0638-7*, Pub. by M Manoharial) Coronet Bks.

— Buddha & the Gospel of Buddhism. 1988. pap. 12.95 (*0-8065-1101-X*, Citadel Pr) Carol Pub Group.

— The Bugbear of Literacy. rev. ed. 150p. 1979. pap. 17.95 (*0-900588-19-5*) S Perennis.

— Christian & Oriental Philosophy of Art. 146p. 1956. pap. 6.95 (*0-486-20378-6*) Dover.

— Christian & Oriental Philosophy of Art. 1974. reprint ed. 12.75 (*0-8364-2574-X*, Pub. by M Manoharial) S Asia.

— Coomaraswamy Vol. 1: Selected Papers - Traditional Art & Symbolism. Lipsey, Roger, ed. LC 86-206309. (Bollingen Ser.: Vol. 89). (Illus.). 619p. reprint ed. pap. 191.90 (*0-608-07797-6*, 205986400001) Bks Demand.

— Coomaraswamy Vol. 2: Selected Papers, Metaphysics. LC 76-41158. (Bollingen Ser.: Vol. 89). 497p. 1977. reprint ed. pap. 154.10 (*0-608-02949-1*, 206401500002) Bks Demand.

— Coomaraswamy Vol. 3: His Life & Work. Lipsey, Roger, ed. LC 76-41158. (Bollingen Ser.: No. 89). 331p. reprint ed. pap. 102.70 (*0-7837-0234-5*, 204054200003) Bks Demand.

— Elements of Buddhist Iconography. (Illus.). 1979. text 28.50 (*0-685-13842-9*) Coronet Bks.

— Essays in Architectural Theory. Meister, Michael W., ed. LC 96-219814. (Illus.). 146p. 1996. text 39.95 (*0-19-563805-0*) OUP.

— Figures of Speech or Figures of Thought. (C). 1981. reprint ed. 14.00 (*0-8364-2421-2*, Pub. by M Manoharial) S Asia.

— Hinduism & Buddhism. (C). 1986. 20.00 (*81-215-0037-0*, Pub. by M Manoharial) Coronet Bks.

— History of Indian & Indonesian Art. (Illus.). 304p. 1985. reprint ed. pap. 11.95 (*0-486-25005-9*) Dover.

— The Indian Craftsman. (C). 1989. 15.00 (*0-685-30854-5*, Pub. by M Manoharial) S Asia.

*__Coomaraswamy, Ananda K.__ Introduction to Indian Art. (Illus.). 250p. 1999. 27.50 (*81-215-0389-2*, Pub. by Munshiram) Coronet Bks.

__Coomaraswamy, Ananda K.__ New Approach to the Vedas: An Essay in Translation & Exegesis. 126p. (C). 1994. reprint ed. 22.00 (*81-215-0630-1*, Pub. by M Manoharial) Coronet Bks.

— Rajput Painting, 2 vols. in 1. LC 72-87768. 1975. reprint ed. lib. bdg. 85.00 (*0-87817-118-5*) Hacker.

— Selected Examples of Indian Art. vii, 20p. 1971. 25.00 (*0-88065-045-1*, Pub. by Today Tomorrow) Scholarly Pubns.

— Selected Letters of Ananda K. Coomaraswamy. Coomaraswamy, Rama P. & Moore, Alvin, Jr., eds. (Illus.). 512p. 1989. text 39.95 (*0-19-562306-1*) OUP.

— Time & Eternity. 1993. reprint ed. 20.00 (*81-215-0059-1*, Pub. by M Manoharial) Coronet Bks.

— Time & Eternity. 2nd ed. (C). 1990. 14.00 (*0-685-59777-6*, Pub. by Usha) S Asia.

— Time & Eternity. 2nd rev. ed. (C). 1989. 18.50 (*0-8364-2488-3*) S Asia.

— Transformation of Nature in Art. (C). 1994. text 20.00 (*81-215-0325-6*, Pub. by M Manoharial) Coronet Bks.

— What Is Civilization? Keeble, Brian, ed. 194p. (Orig.). 1989. pap. 14.50 (*0-940262-06-1*, Lindisfarne) Anthroposophic.

__Coomaraswamy, Ananda K. & Horner, I. B.__ The Living Thoughts of Gotama, the Buddha. LC 78-72397. reprint ed. 34.50 (*0-404-17256-3*) AMS Pr.

__Coomaraswamy, Ananda K. & Nivedita, Sr.__ Myths of the Hindus & Buddhists. (Illus.). 400p. (J). (gr. 4-8). 1967. pap. 10.95 (*0-486-21759-0*) Dover.

*__Coomaraswamy, Ananda K., et al.__ Hinduism & Buddhism. enl. ed. LC 99-933384. xxi, 87 p. 1999. write for info. (*81-7304-227-6*, Pub. by Manohar) S Asia.

__Coomaraswamy, R. P., ed. see Coomaraswamy, Amanda K.__

*__Coomaraswamy, Rama P.__ Invocation of the Name of Jesus: As Practiced in the Western Church. 2000. pap. 19.95 (*1-887752-26-9*) Fons Vitae.

— The Invocation of the Name of Jesus As Practiced in the Western Church. LC 99-68060. 256p. 2000. pap. 19.95 (*1-887752-25-0*, Pub. by Fons Vitae) Words Distrib.

__Coomaraswamy, Rama P.__ The Problems with the New Mass: A Brief Overview of the Major Theological Difficulties Inherent in the Novus Ordo Missae. rev. ed. LC 90-71558. Orig. Title: The Problems of the New Mass. 86p. 1993. reprint ed. pap. 7.00 (*0-89555-412-7*) TAN Bks Pubs.

*__Coomaraswamy, Rama P.__ The Problems with the New Sacraments. LC 98-61408. 224p. 1999. pap. 12.00 (*0-89555-637-5*, 1585) TAN Bks Pubs.

__Coomaraswamy, Rama P., ed. see Coomaraswamy, Ananda K.__

__Coomarawaswamy, A.__ Dance of Siva. 1974. 300.00 (*0-87968-245-0*) Gordon Pr.

*__Coombe, Jack.__ Gunfire Around the Gulf. 256p. 2000. pap. 13.95 (*0-553-38106-7*) Bantam.

__Coombe, Jack D.__ Derailing the Tokyo Express: The Naval Battles for the Solomon Islands That Sealed Japan's Fate. LC 91-7799. (Illus.). 192p. 1991. pap. 14.95 (*0-8117-3030-1*) Stackpole.

*__Coombe, Jack D.__ Gunfire Around the Gulf: The Last Major Naval Campaigns of the Civil War. LC 98-55774. (Illus.). 256p. 1999. 23.95 (*0-553-10731-3*) Bantam.

__Coombe, Jack D.__ Thunder along the Mississippi: The River Battles That Split the Confederacy. LC 96-18422. (Illus.). 304p. 1996. 24.95 (*1-885119-25-9*) Sarpedon.

__Coombe, Jack D.__ Thunder along the Mississippi: The River Battles That Split the Confederacy. 304p. 1997. 80.00 (*1-873376-69-3*, Pub. by Spellmnt Pubs) St Mut.

__Coombe, Jack D.__ Thunder Along the Mississippi: The River Battles That Split the Confederacy. 288p. 1998. reprint ed. pap. 12.95 (*0-553-37967-4*) Bantam.

__Coombe, Kate.__ Folk Art & Tole Painting: New Designs for Decorative Paintwork. (Illus.). 84p. 1992. pap. 12.95 (*1-86351-057-5*, Pub. by Sally Milner) Sterling.

*__Coombe, Kate.__ Painted Garden: Designs for Folk Art & Tole Painting. (Milner Craft Ser.). (Illus.). 2000. pap. 16.95 (*1-86351-236-5*) Sally Milner.

__Coombe, Marten, jt. auth. see Gunson, Jonathan.__

__Coombe, Rosemary J.__ The Cultural Life of Intellectual Properties: Authorship, Appropriation & the Law. LC 97-32525. (Post-Contemporary Interventions Ser.). 462p. 1998. 59.95 (*0-8223-2103-3*) Duke.

— The Cultural Life of Intellectual Properties: Authorship, Appropriation & the Law. LC 97-32525. (Post-Contemporary Interventions Ser.). 462p. 1998. pap. 19.95 (*0-8223-2119-X*) Duke.

__Coombe, Tucker.__ The Shoresaver's Handbook: A Citizen's Guide. 128p. (Orig.). 1996. pap. 12.95 (*1-55821-401-1*, 14011) Lyons Pr.

__Coomber, I. M.__ Haynes Datsun 310 Owners Workshop Manual, No. 679: 1978-1982. 16.95 (*0-85696-977-X*) Haynes Manuals.

— Haynes Toyota Celica Owners Workshop Manual, No. 935: 1982 thru 1985. (Illus.). 388p. (Orig.). 1986. pap. 16.95 (*0-85696-935-4*) Haynes Manuals.

— Haynes Toyota Corolla Owners Workshop Manual, No. 961: '80-'87. LC 90-81412. 336p. 1920. 17.95 (*1-85010-632-0*) Haynes Manuals.

— Haynes Triumph GT6 Vitesse Owners' Workshop Manual, No. 112: 1962-1974. 1983. 16.95 (*0-85696-612-6*) Haynes Manuals.

__Coomber, I. M., jt. auth. see Haynes, J. H.__

__Coomber, James.__ Magnificent Churches on the Prairie: A Story of Immigrant Priests, Builders & Homesteaders. LC 97-76915. (Illus.). 102p. 1996. pap. 29.95 (*0-911042-45-8*) NDSU Inst Reg.

*__Coomber, Richard.__ Birds of the World. 1999. 24.99 (*0-86283-806-1*) Quadrillion Pubng.

__Coomber, Ross, ed.__ The Control of Drugs & Drug Users: Reason or Reaction? 252p. 1997. text 35.00 (*90-5702-187-0*, Harwood Acad Pubs); pap. text 14.00 (*90-5702-188-9*, Harwood Acad Pubs) Gordon & Breach.

— Drugs & Drug Use in Society: A Critical Reader. 426p. (C). 1996. pap. 35.00 (*1-874529-30-2*, Pub. by Greenwich Univ Pr) NYU Pr.

__Coombes, A. R., ed.__ Conveyancing. 240p. (C). 1991. 100.00 (*1-85352-905-2*, Pub. by HLT Pubns); 80.00 (*1-85352-394-1*, Pub. by HLT Pubns) St Mut.

__Coombes, Allen J.__ Dictionary of Plant Names. 207p. 1985. lib. bdg. 10.95 (*0-600-35770-8*) Lubrecht & Cramer.

— Dictionary of Plant Names: Botanical Names & Their Common Name Equivalents. rev. ed. 207p. 1994. 12.95 (*0-88192-294-3*) Timber.

— Trees. LC 92-52782. (Eyewitness Handbooks Ser.). (Illus.). 320p. 1992. 29.95 (*1-56458-075-X*); pap. 18.95 (*1-56458-072-5*) DK Pub Inc.

Coombes, Annie E. Reinventing Africa: Museums, Material Culture, & Popular Imagination in Late Victorian & Edwardian England. (Illus.). 288p. 1997. pap. 27.00 (*0-300-06890-5*) Yale U Pr.

— Reinventing Africa: Museums, Material Culture & Popular Imagination in Late Victorian & Edwardian England. (Illus.). 256p. 1994. 57.00 (*0-300-05972-8*) Yale U Pr.

Coombes, Annie E., jt. auth. see Brah, A.

Coombes, Archie J. Some Australian Poets. LC 76-107688. (Essay Index Reprint Ser.). 1977. 15.95 (*0-8369-1492-9*) Ayer.

Coombes, C. G., ed. Printed Circuits Handbook. 2nd ed. 536p. 1979. 63.00 (*0-318-12558-7*) Am Electro Surface.

Coombes, David. Representative Government & Economic Power. (Policy Studies Institute). vi, 208p. 1982. text 72.95 (*0-435-83180-1*, Pub. by Dartmth Pub) Ashgate Pub Co.

Coombes, David, jt. ed. see Verheijen, Tony.

Coombes, K., ed. Proceedings of the Ergonomics Society's Conference, 1983. 214p. 1983. pap. 36.00 (*0-85066-252-4*) Taylor & Francis.

— Proceedings of the Ergonomics Society's Conference, 1983. 214p. 1983. pap. 36.00 (*0-8002-3087-6*) Taylor & Francis.

Coombes, Kevin R., et al. Differential Equations with MapleTM, 2E. 2nd ed. LC 97-130653. 248p. 1997. pap. 37.95 (*0-471-17645-1*) Wiley.

Coombes, Kevin R., et al. Differential Equations with Mathematica. 2nd ed. 240p. 1997. pap. 34.95 (*0-471-17696-6*) Wiley.

— Differential Equations with Matlabtm. 256p. 1999. pap. 34.95 (*0-471-32227-X*) Wiley.

Coombes, Kevin R., et al. The Mathematica Primer. LC 97-51989. (Illus.). 256p. (C). 1998. text 64.95 (*0-521-63130-0*); pap. text 24.95 (*0-521-63715-5*) Cambridge U Pr.

— Multivariable Calculus & Mathematica(r) With Applications to Geometry & Physics. LC 97-44764. (Illus.). 272p. 1998. pap. text 34.95 incl. disk (*0-387-98360-0*) Spr-Verlag.

Coombes, R. A. America, the Babylon: America's Destiny Foretold in Biblical Prophecy. 250p. 1998. pap. 19.95 (*1-890622-33-8*) Leathers Pub.

***Coombes, R. A.** America the Babylon: America's Destiny, Foretold in Biblical Prophecy. 250p. 1998. pap. 20.00 (*1-58538-001-6*) Prophecy Club.

Coombes, Yolande, jt. ed. see Thorogood, Margaret.

Coombs. Pitman 2000 Phrasebuilder. 1992. pap. text. write for info. (*0-273-03822-2*) Addison-Wesley.

Coombs & Alston. The Biotechnology Directory, 1998. 600p. 1998. pap. 295.00 (*1-56159-221-8*) Groves Dictionaries.

Coombs & Jenkins. Public Sector Financial Management. 2nd ed. (ITBP Textbooks Ser.). 1994. pap. 34.95 (*1-86152-206-1*) Thomson Learn.

Coombs, Bryan. Pitman Two Thousand Shorthand: Rapid Review & Speed Development. 96p. 1991. pap. 26.00 (*0-582-29170-4*, Pub. by Addison-Wesley) Trans-Atl Phila.

Coombs, Candace R., jt. ed. see Hixon, Jonathan D.

Coombs, Charles. All-Terrain Bicycling. LC 86-14980. (Illus.). 144p. (J). (gr. 5-9). 1995. 14.95 (*0-8050-0204-9*) H Holt & Co.

Coombs, Charles A. The Arena of International Finance. LC 76-19093. (Illus.). 263p. reprint ed. pap. 81.60 (*0-8357-5728-5*, 201646300004) Bks Demand.

Coombs, Charles A., jt. auth. see Guindey, Guillaume.

Coombs, Clyde F. Communications Network Test & Measurement Handbook. LC 97-13329. (Illus.). 813p. 1996. 89.50 (*0-07-012617-8*) McGraw.

***Coombs, Clyde F., Jr.** Electronic Instrument Handbook. 3rd ed. LC 99-35923. (Engineering Handbks.). (Illus.). 1264p. 1999. 125.00 (*0-07-012618-6*) McGraw.

***Coombs, Clyde F.** Electronic Instrument Handbook 3rd ed. LC 99-35923. 1999. write for info. (*0-07-135016-0*) McGrw-H Intl.

Coombs, Clyde F., Jr. Printed Circuit Handbook. 4th ed. LC 95-25131. (Illus.). 1088p. 1995. 99.00 (*0-07-012754-9*) McGraw.

Coombs, Clyde F. Printed Circuits Vol. 1: Engineering & Fundamentals. 1990. pap. text 26.95 (*0-07-012739-5*) McGraw.

Coombs, Clyde F., Jr., ed. Electronic Instrument Handbook. 2nd ed. (Illus.). 944p. 1992. 89.50 (*0-07-012616-X*) McGraw.

Coombs, Clyde H. & Avrunin, George S. The Structure of Conflict. 264p. 1988. text 55.00 (*0-8058-0011-5*) L Erlbaum Assocs.

Coombs, Colby. Denali's West Buttress: A Climber's Guide to Mt. McKinley's Classic Route. LC 97-30735. (Illus.). 144p. 1997. pap. 16.95 (*0-89886-516-6*) Mountaineers.

***Coombs, Corinne.** My Brother Sam Is Dead: Literature Unit. (Illus.). 48p. 1999. pap., teacher ed. 7.95 (*1-57690-507-1*, TCM2507) Tchr Create Mat.

Coombs, Dennis W., jt. ed. see Rawal, Narinder.

Coombs, Elizabeth, et al. Pasteprints: A Technical & Art Historical Investigation. (Illus.). 46p. 1986. pap. 12.00 (*0-916724-62-X*, 362X) Harvard Art Mus.

Coombs, Ernie & Tanaka, Shelley. Mr. Dress-Up's Fifty More Things to Make & Do. (Illus.). 62p. 1991. pap. 9.95 (*0-7737-5460-1*) Genl Dist Srvs.

Coombs, Fliss. The Making of Rhodes. (Illus.). 128p. 1997. pap. 17.95 (*0-563-38785-8*, BBC-Parkwest) Parkwest Pubns.

Coombs, Fred, jt. auth. see Branson, Margaret.

Coombs, Gary B. The Archeology of the Northeast Mojave Desert. (Illus.). 156p. (C). 1979. reprint ed. pap. text 16.88 (*1-55567-392-9*) Coyote Press.

— The Archeology of the Western Mojave. (Illus.). 122p. (C). 1979. reprint ed. pap. text 13.75 (*1-55567-395-3*) Coyote Press.

— Goleta Depot: The History of a Rural Railroad Station. LC 82-83472. (Illus.). 96p. 1982. pap. 5.00 (*0-911773-01-0*) Inst Am Res.

Coombs, Gary B. & Olsen, Phyllis J. In the Grand Manor: The Story of Devereux Hall. 40p. 1987. pap. 3.00 (*0-911773-05-3*) Inst Am Res.

— Sentinel at Ellwood: The Barnsdall-Rio Grande Gasoline Station. (Illus.). 24p. 1985. pap. 2.50 (*0-911773-06-1*) Inst Am Res.

Coombs, Gary B. & Sullivan, Steve. Golden Deeds Remembered. 1988. pap. 2.00 (*0-911773-10-X*) Inst Am Res.

Coombs, Gary B., et al. Those Were the Days: Landmarks of Old Goleta. LC 86-81698. (Illus.). 1986. 15.00 (*0-911773-08-8*); pap. 8.50 (*0-911773-09-6*) Inst Am Res.

Coombs, Gary B., jt. auth. see Everett, William B.

Coombs, Gilbert G. The Young Man & the Sea. LC 91-71742. 224p. 1993. pap. 14.95 (*0-942963-17-2*) Distinctive Pub.

Coombs, Graham H., ed. Biochemical Protozoology As a Basis for Drug Design. 500p. 1991. 180.00 (*0-7484-0000-1*, Pub. by Tay Francis Ltd); pap. 69.00 (*0-7484-0001-X*, Pub. by Tay Francis Ltd) Taylor & Francis.

Coombs, Graham H., et al, eds. Evolutionary Relationships Among Protozoa. 486p. 1998. text. write for info. (*0-412-79800-X*) Kluwer Academic.

Coombs, H. & Jenkins, E. Public Sector Financial Management. (Series in Accounting & Finance). 288p. (C). 1991. mass mkt. 52.95 (*0-412-38550-3*, A5664) Chapman & Hall.

Coombs, H. C. The Return of Scarcity: Strategies for an Economic Future. 181p. (C). 1990. text 59.95 (*0-521-36373-X*); pap. text 19.95 (*0-521-36896-0*) Cambridge U Pr.

Coombs, H. C., et al. Land of Promises: Aborigines & Development in the East Kimberley. LC 89-203658. 165 p. 1989. write for info. (*0-85575-200-9*) AIB & TSIS.

Coombs, H. M. Public Sector Financial Management. 2nd ed. 1994. pap. 31.95 (*0-412-56560-9*) Chapman & Hall.

— Public Sector Financial Management: Teachers' Manual. 2nd ed. 88p. (Orig.). 1994. pap. text 52.00 (*0-412-57130-7*, Chap & Hall NY) Chapman & Hall.

Coombs, H. Samm. Teenage Survival Manual: A Safe Landing Place for Kamikaze Kids. 5th rev. ed. LC 97-21273. (Illus.). 288p. (Orig.). (YA). (gr. 9-12). 1998. pap. 14.95 (*1-879904-18-7*) Halo Bks.

— Time Happens: You Could Not Have Picked a Better Time to Be Fiftysomething. LC 94-34061. 248p. (Orig.). 1995. pap. 13.95 (*1-879904-13-6*) Halo Bks.

Coombs, H. Samm, ed. see Veltri, Raylene.

Coombs, Hugh, et al, eds. Double Entry Bookkeeping in British Central Government, 1822-1856. LC 97-30590. (New Works in Accounting History). 366p. 1997. text 98.00 (*0-8153-3036-7*) Garland.

Coombs, Hugh J. & Edwards, John. Local Authority Accounting Methods: The Early Debate, 1884-1908. LC 90-25398. (New Works in Accounting History). 336p. 1991. text 10.00 (*0-8153-0003-4*) Garland.

Coombs, Hugh M. & Edwards, John R. Accounting Innovation: Municipal Corporations, 1835-1935. LC 95-33793. (New Works in Accounting History). 224p. 1996. text 66.00 (*0-8153-2244-5*) Garland.

Coombs, Isabel & Crompton, David W. A Guide to Human Helminths. 203p. 1991. 55.00 (*0-85066-807-7*, Pub. by Tay Francis Ltd) Taylor & Francis.

Coombs, J. Solar Energy in Agriculture: A European Perspective. (C). 1983. 100.00 (*0-7855-4194-2*, Pub. by Interntl Solar Energy Soc) St Mut.

— Solar Energy in Agriculture: A European Perspective (C33) 89p. (C). 1983. 125.00 (*0-7855-3797-X*, Pub. by Interntl Solar Energy Soc) St Mut.

Coombs, J. & Alston, Y. R., eds. The Biotechnology Directory, 1998. 782p. 1998. 295.00 (*1-56159-232-3*) Groves Dictionaries.

***Coombs, J. & Hall, K.** Dictionary of Biological Control & Integrated Pest Management. 3rd ed. 248p. 2000. write for info. (*1-872691-17-X*, CPL Pr) CPL Sci Pub.

***Coombs, J. & Hall, K., eds.** AIR Programme Final Project Results: Disseminated under FAIR-CT96-1904; NF-2000 Non-Food Agro-Industrial Research Information. 312p. 2000. 65.00 (*1-872691-22-6*, CPL Pr) CPL Sci Pub.

— Dictionary of Biological Control & Integrated Pest Management. 2nd ed. LC 99-492148. 206p. 1998. 72.00 (*1-872691-76-5*, CPL Pr) CPL Sci Pub.

Coombs, J., et al, eds. Plants As Solar Collectors: Optimizing Productivity for Energy. 1983. text 106.00 (*90-277-1625-0*) Kluwer Academic.

Coombs, James. Setting up an Internet Site for Dummies. 384p. 1996. pap. 19.99 (*1-56884-335-6*) IDG Bks.

Coombs, James & Coombs, Ted. Database 5 for Windows Programming for Dummies. LC 94-72738. (For Dummies Ser.). 416p. 1994. pap. 19.99 (*1-56884-215-5*) IDG Bks.

Coombs, James & Coombs, Ted. PowerBuilder 4 Program for Dummies. 384p. 1995. pap. 19.99 (*1-56884-325-9*) IDG Bks.

Coombs, James H., et al, eds. A Pre-Raphaelite Friendship: The Correspondence of William Holman Hunt & John Lucas Tupper. LC 86-1486. (Nineteenth-Century Studies). 357p. reprint ed. 110.70 (*0-8357-1745-3*, 207047200095) Bks Demand.

***Coombs, Jason, et al.** Bioinformatics: An Introduction to Computational Biology, Medicine & the Internet. 300p. 1999. 79.95 (*0-8493-1188-8*) CRC Pr.

Coombs, Jason, et al. Inside Windows Sockets. 400p. 1996. pap. text 34.95 incl. cd-rom (*1-57231-346-3*) Microsoft.

— Setting up an Internet Site for Dummies. 3rd ed. LC 98-84490. (For Dummies Ser.). 408p. 1998. pap. 29.99 incl. cd-rom (*0-7645-0358-8*) IDG Bks.

Coombs, Jason, jt. auth. see Coombs, Ted.

***Coombs, Joseph E.** International Strategy & Market Performance in New Biotechnology Firms LC 99-32275. (Transnational Business & Corporate Culture Ser.). 1999. write for info. (*0-8153-3501-6*) Garland.

Coombs, Karen. Flush! Treating Wastewater. LC 94-37676. (Photo Bks.). (Illus.). 56p. (J). (gr. 3-6). 1995. lib. bdg. 22.60 (*0-87614-879-8*, Carolrhoda) Lerner Pub.

Coombs, Karen M. Jackie Robinson: Baseball's Civil Rights Legend. LC 96-20584. (African-American Biographies Ser.). (Illus.). 128p. (YA). (gr. 6 up). 1997. lib. bdg. 20.95 (*0-89490-690-9*) Enslow Pubs.

— Samantha Gill, Belly Dancer. 128p. (J). 1989. pap. 2.75 (*0-380-75737-0*, Avon Bks) Morrow Avon.

— Sarah on Her Own. (American Dreams Ser.). 1996. 9.09 (*0-606-09818-6*, Pub. by Turtleback) Demco.

— Saving Casey. 192p. (Orig.). (J). 1992. pap. 3.50 (*0-380-76634-5*, Avon Bks) Morrow Avon.

***Coombs, Karen Mueller.** Children of the Dust Days. LC 98-49041. (Picture the American Past Ser.). (Illus.). 48p. (J). (gr. 3-6). 2000. 22.60 (*1-57505-360-8*, Carolrhoda) Lerner Pub.

Coombs, Karen Mueller. Sarah on Her Own. (American Dreams Ser.). 240p. (YA). (gr. 7 up). 1996. mass mkt. 3.99 (*0-380-78275-8*, Avon Bks) Morrow Avon.

Coombs, Katherine. Portrait Miniature in England. LC 99-215417. 1998. 50.00 (*1-85177-206-5*, Pub. by V&A Ent) Antique Collect.

Coombs, L. F. E. Fighting Cockpits 1914-2000: Design & Development of Military Aircraft Cockpits. LC 99-14623. (Illus.). 192p. 1999. 39.95 (*0-7603-0742-3*, Pub. by MBI Pubg) Motorbooks Intl.

— The Lion Has Wings: The Race to Prepare the RAF for World War II, 1935-1940. LC 98-108337. x, 176 p. 1997. write for info. (*1-85310-805-7*) Airlife Publishing.

Coombs, Leslie. Aircraft Cockpit: From Stick & String to Fly-by-Wire. (Illus.). 240p. 1990. 34.95 (*1-85260-281-3*) Thorsons PA.

***Coombs, LuAnn.** Critters in the Corn Patch. (Illus.). 32p. 1999. 8.99 (*1-58050-058-7*, 40-6187) Provo Craft.

Coombs, M. J. & Alty, Jim L. Computing Skills & the User Interface. LC 80-2768. (Computers & People Ser.). 1981. text 107.00 (*0-12-186520-7*) Acad Pr.

Coombs, M. J., jt. ed. see Bolc, Leonard.

Coombs, Malcolm & Edwards, J. R., eds. Accountability of Local Authorities in England & Wales, 1831-1935, 2 vols. LC 89-71467. (Accounting History & Thought Ser.). 742p. 1990. reprint ed. text 20.00 (*0-8240-3316-7*) Garland.

Coombs, Margaret. Regards to the Czar. LC 87-23177. 186p. (Orig.). 1989. pap. 15.95 (*0-7022-2108-2*, Pub. by Univ Queensland Pr) Intl Spec Bk.

Coombs, Marie T. & Nemeck, Francis K. Called by God: A Theology of Vocation & Lifelong Commitment. 160p. (Orig.). 1992. pap. text 11.95 (*0-8146-5909-8*, M Glazier) Liturgical Pr.

Coombs, Marie T., jt. auth. see Nemeck, Francis K.

***Coombs, Mark & Coombs, Matthew.** Honda CBR600 F2 & F3. LC 98-72826. 1998. write for info. (*1-85960-538-9*) Haynes Manuals.

Coombs, Mark, jt. auth. see Churchill, Jeremy.

Coombs, Mark, jt. auth. see Rendle, Steve.

Coombs, Martha, jt. auth. see Karr, Paul.

Coombs, Matthew. Hyns Suzuki GSF600 & GSF1200 Bandit 600 & 1200cc, 1996-1997. LC 97-72742. (Motorcycle Repair Manual Ser.). (Illus.). 256p. 1998. pap. 23.95 (*1-85960-367-X*, Pub. by J H Haynes & Co) Motorbooks Intl.

Coombs, Matthew, jt. auth. see Coombs, Mark.

Coombs, Matthew, jt. auth. see Cox, Penny.

Coombs, Nina. Man's Best Friend. 368p. (Orig.). 1997. mass mkt. 5.50 (*0-505-52205-5*, Love Spell) Dorchester Pub Co.

Coombs, Norman, jt. auth. see Cunningham, Carmela.

Coombs, Patricia. Dorrie & the Haunted Schoolhouse. (Illus.). 32p. (J). (ps-3). 1992. 13.95 (*0-395-60116-9*, Clarion Bks) HM.

***Coombs, Peter.** Painting With Pastels. 2000. pap. text 10.95 (*0-85532-899-1*) Srch Pr.

Coombs, Philip H. Attacking Rural Poverty: How Nonformal Education Can Help. Israel, Barbara B., ed. LC 73-19350. 308p. reprint ed. pap. 95.50 (*0-7837-4256-8*, 204394600012) Bks Demand.

— New Strategies for Improving Rural Family Life. 72p. 1981. 3.00 (*0-318-16926-6*) ICED Pubns.

Coombs, Richard & Robinson, Dennis. Nanotechnology in Medicine & the Biosciences. (Developments in Nanotechnology Ser.). 320p. 1996. text 54.00 (*2-88449-080-9*) Gordon & Breach.

Coombs, Rob, et al, eds. Technological Collaboration: The Dynamics of Cooperation in Industrial Innovation. LC 95-18024. 256p. 1996. 100.00 (*1-85898-235-9*) E Elgar.

***Coombs, Robert.** Mystical Themes in Le Corbuster's architecture in the Chapel Notre Dame Du Hout at Ronchamp: The Ronchamp Riddle. LC 00-23741. (Mellen Studies in Architecture: 2). 232p. 2000. 89.95 (*0-7734-7746-2*) E Mellen.

Coombs, Robert, et al, eds. Socialization in Drug Abuse. LC 75-37067. 496p. 1976. pap. text 24.95 (*0-87073-489-X*) Transaction Pubs.

Coombs, Robert H. Drug-Impaired Professionals. 384p. 1997. 41.50 (*0-674-21673-3*) HUP.

***Coombs, Robert H.** Drug-Impaired Professionals. 2000. pap. text 19.95 (*0-674-00174-5*) HUP.

Coombs, Robert H. Surviving Medical School. LC 97-33951. 197p. 1998. 51.00 (*0-7619-0528-6*); pap. 23.50 (*0-7619-0529-4*) Sage.

Coombs, Robert H., ed. The Family Context of Adolescent Drug Use. LC 88-10965. (Journal of Chemical Dependency Treatment: Vol. 1, No. 2). (Illus.). 273p. (Orig.). 1988. pap. text 24.95 (*0-86656-828-X*) Haworth Pr.

— The Family Context of Adolescent Drug Use. LC 88-10965. (Journal of Chemical Dependency Treatment: Vol. 1, No. 2). (Illus.). 273p. (Orig.). 1989. text 49.95 (*0-86656-799-2*) Haworth Pr.

Coombs, Robert H., et al, eds. Inside Doctoring: Stages & Outcomes in the Professional Development of Physicians. LC 86-15083. 315p. 1986. pap. 22.95 (*0-275-92173-5*, B2173, Praeger Pubs) Greenwood.

— Inside Doctoring: Stages & Outcomes in the Professional Development of Physicians. LC 86-15683. 315p. 1986. 65.00 (*0-275-92172-7*, C2172, Praeger Pubs) Greenwood.

Coombs, Robert H. & West, Louis J., eds. Drug Testing: Issues & Options. 272p. 1991. text 47.95 (*0-19-505414-8*) OUP.

Coombs, Robert H. & Ziedonis, Douglas, eds. Handbook on Drug Abuse Prevention: A Comprehensive Strategy to Prevent the Abuse of Alcohol & Other Drugs. LC 94-45871. 608p. 1995. 64.00 (*0-13-377557-7*) Allyn.

Coombs, Robert S. Enlightening Object Lessons for Children. (Object Lessons Ser.). 114p. (Orig.). (gr. 10). 1992. pap. 7.99 (*0-8010-2567-2*) Baker Bks.

Coombs, Rod, et al, eds. Technological Change & Company Strategies. (Economic & Social Analysis of Technology Ser.). (Illus.). 255p. 1992. pap. text 55.00 (*0-12-187582-2*) Acad Pr.

***Coombs, Rod, et al, eds.** Technological Change & Organization. LC 97-35416. 272p. 1998. 90.00 (*1-85898-589-7*) E Elgar.

Coombs, Rod, et al. Economics & Technological Change. 256p. (C). 1987. 61.50 (*0-8476-7545-9*); pap. 27.95 (*0-8476-7546-7*) Rowman.

Coombs, S., et al, eds. The Mechanosensory Lateral Line. (Illus.). 655p. 1989. 262.00 (*0-387-96837-7*) Spr-Verlag.

Coombs, Samm, ed. see Spalding, Albert G.

Coombs, Steven L., jt. auth. see MacKuen, Michael B.

Coombs, Ted. Internet Programming with Visual Basic 5.0 & Active X. 400p. 1997. pap. text 29.95 (*0-471-17822-5*) Wiley.

Coombs, Ted & Coombs, Jason. Java: Secrets of the Java Masters: Java Developer's Journal. (Java Training Ser.). (Illus.). 480p. (Orig.). 1996. pap. 38.95 (*1-886141-06-1*) SYS-Con Pubns.

***Coombs, Ted & DeLeon, Roderico.** Conquering E-Commerce: The Complete Guide to Setting up Shop on the Web. 368p. 2000. pap. 34.95 (*1-929685-07-6*) Muska Lipman.

— ICQ FYI. 2000. pap. 14.95 (*1-929685-04-1*) Muska Lipman.

***Coombs, Ted & Pickslay, Pat.** Home Recording Power! Set up Your Own Recording Studio for Personal & Professional Use. (Illus.). 352p. 2000. pap. 29.95 (*1-929685-08-4*, Pub. by Muska Lipman) IPG Chicago.

Coombs, Ted, et al. ActiveX Sourcebook: Build an ActiveX-Based Web Site. LC 96-27530. 392p. 1996. pap. 24.95 (*0-471-16714-2*) Wiley.

Coombs, Ted, jt. auth. see Coombs, James.

Coombs, Urban R. Magical Tales about Willie the Wizard. (Illus.). 216p. (YA). 1994. pap. 12.95 (*1-57087-081-0*) Prof Pr NC.

Coombs, W. C. The Story of Anthony Coombs & His Descendants. (Illus.). 226p. 1993. reprint ed. pap. 38.00 (*0-8328-3028-3*); reprint ed. lib. bdg. 48.00 (*0-8328-3027-5*) Higginson Bk Co.

Coombs, Whitney. Wages of Unskilled Labor in Manufacturing Industries in the United States, 1890-1924. LC 76-76686. (Columbia University. Studies in the Social Sciences: No. 283). reprint ed. 32.50 (*0-404-51283-6*) AMS Pr.

Coomer, Captain James. Life on the Ohio. LC 97-14526. (Ohio River Valley Ser.). (Illus.). 200p. 1997. 24.95 (*0-8131-2000-4*) U Pr of Ky.

***Coomer, David.** UFO Investigator's Guide. 192p. 1999. pap. text 14.95 (*0-7137-2782-9*) Strlng Pub CA.

Coomer, Donna. Barney's Animal Homes. LC 97-74900. (Barney Ser.). 18p. (J). (ps-k). 1998. 5.95 (*1-57064-258-3*) Lyrick Pub.

Coomer, Gerald. The Coasts of Southern Indiana: Twelve Reflections. LC 98-72875. 144p. 1998. pap. 12.95 (*0-9666024-0-4*) Hue Pr.

Coomer, Joe. Apologizing to Dogs. LC 99-26937. 288p. 1999. 22.00 (*0-684-85946-7*) Scribner.

***Coomer, Joe.** Apologizing to Dogs. LC 99-55065. 2000. 26.95 (*0-7862-2367-7*) Thorndike Pr.

Coomer, Joe. Beachcombing for a Shipwrecked God. 304p. 1995. 22.95 (*1-55597-228-4*) Graywolf.

— Beachcombing for a Shipwrecked God. LC 96-38328. 1997. per. 11.00 (*0-684-82440-X*) S&S Trade Pap.

— The Loop. 216p. 1999. pap. 11.00 (*0-684-85904-1*) S&S Trade Pap.

— Sailing in a Spoonful of Water. LC 96-53645. 256p. 1997. text 22.00 (*0-312-15646-4*) St Martin.

— Sailing in a Spoonful of Water. 256p. 1998. pap. 13.00 (*0-312-18697-5*) St Martin.

***Coomer, Martin.** Art in Focus: London. 1999. pap. 12.95 (*1-899858-75-X*, Pub. by Ellipsis) Norton.

Coomer, Silas E. Poems: About People & Rivers of Appalachia. (Illus.). 46p. 1993. pap. text 8.95 (*1-883045-00-2*) Trning Materials.

***Coomes, A. Francis.** Mothers' Manual. (Illus.). 2000. pap. 3.95 (*1-929198-18-3*) W J Hirten.

C

Coomes, Michael D. & Gehring, Donald D., eds. Student Services in a Changing Federal Climate. LC 85-644751. (New Directions for Student Services Ser.: No. SS 68). 110p. (Orig.). 1995. pap. 22.00 (0-7879-9997-0) Jossey-Bass.

Coomes, Oliver T., jt. auth. see Barham, Bradford L.

Coomler, David. The Icon Handbook. LC 95-60055. (Illus.). 320p. 1995. pap. 23.95 (0-87243-210-6) Templegate.

Coon. Essential Psychology. 6th ed. Date not set. pap. text, teacher ed. write for info. (0-314-03331-9) West Pub.

— Essentials of Psychology. 5th ed. Date not set. pap. text, student ed. 15.75 (0-314-83332-3) West Pub.

— Essentials of Psychology. 5th ed. (Psychology Ser.). (C). 1991. mass mkt. write for info. (0-314-89884-0) West Pub.

— Essentials of Psychology. 6th ed. Date not set. pap. text, student ed. 17.25 (0-314-03686-5) West Pub.

— Essentials of Psychology. 7th ed. (Psychology Ser.). 1997. student ed. 15.75 (0-314-20944-1) Brooks-Cole.

— Essentials of Psychology. 7th ed. 1996. pap. 30.00 (0-314-20630-2) Wadsworth Pub.

— Essentials of Psychology. 8th ed. (Psychology). 1999. 33.75 (0-534-26426-3); text 72.95 (0-534-26425-5) Thomson Learn.

— Essentials of Psychology: Testbank. 6th ed. Date not set. pap. text, suppl. ed. write for info. (0-314-03332-7) West Pub.

— Essentials of Psychology (Case) with InfoTrac. 7th ed. (Psychology Ser.). 1998. pap. 46.50 (0-534-36331-8) Brooks-Cole.

— Essentials of Psychology Exploration & Application. 6th ed. (Psychology Ser.). 1994. 33.75 (0-314-04189-3) Brooks-Cole.

— Essentials of Psychology with InfoTrac. 7th ed. (Psychology Ser.). 1998. pap. 31.00 (0-534-36332-6); pap. 42.00 incl. cd-rom (0-534-36333-4) Brooks-Cole.

— Intro to Psychology. 8th ed. 1997. mass mkt., student ed. 15.75 (0-534-35402-5) Brooks-Cole.

— Intro to Psychology: Exploration & Applications. 7th ed. 1995. mass mkt. 19.50 (0-314-06211-4) Wadsworth Pub.

— Intro to Psychology: Exploration & Applications. 8th ed. LC 97-34738. (Psychology). 733p. (C). 1997. pap. 73.95 (0-534-34966-8) Brooks-Cole.

— Intro to Psychology. 7th ed. (Psychology). 1995. pap. 2.50 (0-314-07582-8) Wadsworth Pub.

— Introduction to Psychology. 6th ed. (Psychology Ser.). Date not set. 6.75 (0-314-11142-5) Brooks-Cole.

— Introduction to Psychology. 7th ed. Date not set. pap. text, teacher ed. write for info. (0-314-06206-8) West Pub.

— Introduction to Psychology. 7th ed. 1995. mass mkt., student ed. 15.75 (0-314-05969-5) West Pub.

***Coon.** Introduction to Psychology. 9th ed. 2000. 15.50 (0-534-57674-5) Wadsworth Pub.

— Introduction to Psychology. 9th ed. (Psychology Ser.). (C). 2000. text 21.00 (0-534-57676-1) Wadsworth Pub.

Coon. Introduction to Psychology: ESL Developmental Readers Guide. 8th ed. (Psychology Ser.). 1998. pap. 7.25 (0-534-35403-5) Brooks-Cole.

— Introduction to Psychology: E.S.L. Reader Guide. 7th ed. (Psychology Ser.). 1995. pap. 7.25 (0-314-05891-5) Brooks-Cole.

***Coon.** Introduction to Psychology Exploration & Application. 9th ed. (Psychology). 2000. pap. text 57.25 (0-534-57672-9) Wadsworth Pub.

Coon. Introduction to Psychology Exploration & Application with InfoTrac. 8th ed. (Psychology Ser.). 1998. pap. 52.00 incl. cd-rom (0-534-36334-2) Brooks-Cole.

***Coon.** Language Development Guide: An Introduction to Psychology. 9th ed. (Psychology Ser.). 2000. 8.00 (0-534-57675-3) Wadsworth Pub.

Coon. Psychological Organizations in Community & Culture. Date not set. pap. text. write for info. (0-314-81022-6) West Pub.

— Psychology. Date not set. pap. text. write for info. (0-314-77166-2) West Pub.

— Psychology. 6th ed. Date not set. pap. text, teacher ed. write for info. (0-314-01114-5); pap. text, student ed. 17.75 (0-314-00693-1); pap. text, wbk. ed. write for info. (0-314-00691-5) West Pub.

— Psychology. 6th ed. 1992. pap. text, teacher ed. write for info. (0-314-00689-3) West Pub.

— Psychology. 7th ed. Date not set. pap. text, teacher ed. write for info. (0-314-06859-7) West Pub.

— Psychology: Reader's Guide. 6th ed. Date not set. pap. 8.25 (0-314-00692-3) West Pub.

— Psychology Mastery. 6th ed. 1993. pap. text, student ed. 20.50 (0-314-00738-5) West Pub.

Coon, Alma S. Amy, Ben, & Catalpa the Cat: A Fanciful Story of This & That. (Illus.). 40p. (J). (ps-2). 1990. 8.95 (0-87935-079-2) Colonial Williamsburg.

— The Mouse & the Mill & the Bottle Babies. (Illus.). 44p. (J). (ps-1). 1982. 6.95 (0-87935-061-X) Colonial Williamsburg.

Coon, Anne C. Hear Me Patiently: The Reform Speeches of Amelia Jenks Bloomer. 138. LC 93-31611. (Contributions in Women's Studies: No. 138). 224p. 1994. 62.95 (0-313-29086-5, Greenwood Pr) Greenwood.

Coon, Anthony. Town Planning under Military Occupation: An Explanation of the Law & Practice of Town Planning. 180p. 1992. 68.95 (1-85521-287-0, Pub. by Dartmth Pub) Ashgate Pub Co.

Coon, Arthur M. The Nature of the Soul. 40p. 1996. reprint ed. pap. 9.00 (0-7873-1232-0) Hlth Research.

Coon, Betty. Seaward. 36p. (Orig.). 1978. pap. 9.95 (0-917658-08-6) BPW & P.

Coon, Carl. Creatures of the Earth & the Mind. LC 98-74392. 60p. 1998. pap. 6.00 (1-892379-08-2) Five & Ten.

***Coon, Carl.** Culture Wars & the Global Village: A Diplomat's Perspective. LC 99-45207. 245p. 2000. 26.95 (1-57392-801-1) Prometheus Bks.

— Sic Transit. LC 99-97010. 68p. 1999. pap. 6.00 (1-892379-11-2) Five & Ten.

Coon, Carleton S. The Hunting Peoples. (Illus.). 384p. 1987. pap. 15.95 (0-941130-27-4) Lyons Pr.

— Mountains of Giants: A Racial & Cultural Study of the North Albanian Mountain Ghegs. (HU PMP Ser.: Vol. 23, No. 3). 1974. reprint ed. 25.00 (0-527-01258-0) Periodicals Srv.

— The Races of Europe. LC 76-184840. (Illus.). 739p. 1972. reprint ed. lib. bdg. 69.50 (0-8371-6328-5, CORE, Greenwood Pr) Greenwood.

Coon, Carleton S., Jr., ed. Daniel Bliss & the Founding of the American University in Beirut. LC 89-28561. 96p. 1989. 12.00 (0-916808-35-1) Mid East Inst.

Coon, Carleton S., et al. Races: A Study of the Problems of Race Formation in Man, Publication Number 77. LC 80-24479. (American Lecture Ser.: No. 77). (Illus.). 153p. 1981. reprint ed. lib. bdg. 55.00 (0-313-22878-7, CORA, Greenwood Pr) Greenwood.

— Yengema Cave Report. (University Museum Monographs: No. 31). (Illus.). 77p. 1968. pap. 15.00 (0-934718-23-7) U Museum Pubns.

Coon, Carlton. Daily Things of Christian Living. (Orig.). 1994. pap. 8.00 (0-9642348-0-7) Truth Pubns.

Coon, Crawford D. Christian Development Course: A Reason of the Hope, 3 vols., Set, Vol. I. LC 87-71134. 313p. (C). 1987. ring bd. write for info. (0-9618853-3-5) Christian Development.

— Christian Development Course: A Reason of the Hope, Vol. I. LC 87-71134. 313p. (C). 1987. 19.95 (0-9618853-0-0) Christian Development.

Coon, David L. The Development of Market Agriculture in South Carolina, 1670-1785. (Outstanding Studies in Early American History). 394p. 1989. reprint ed. 25.00 (0-8240-6176-4) Garland.

Coon, Dennis. Dimensions of Psychology. (Psychology). 550p. (C). 2001. 30.00 (0-314-07157-1) West Pub.

— Essentials of Psychology. 7th ed. LC 96-35206. 1996. pap. 44.50 (0-314-20479-2) West Pub.

***Coon, Dennis.** Essentials of Psychology. 8th ed. (Psychology Ser.). 1999. 16.75 (0-534-36967-7) Brooks-Cole.

Coon, Dennis. Essentials of Psychology: Exploration & Application. 6th ed. Perlee, Clyde, ed. LC 93-32251. 600p. (C). 1993. mass mkt. 39.25 (0-314-02768-8) West Pub.

— Essentials of Psychology: Exploration & Application. 7th ed. LC 96-35206. 682p. 1996. pap. 45.50 (0-314-20629-9) West Pub.

— Essentials of Psychology: Exploration & Applications. 8th ed. LC 99-24490. (Psychology Ser.). 665p. 1999. mass mkt. 50.95 (0-534-36291-5) Brooks-Cole.

***Coon, Dennis.** Introduction to Psychology. 8th ed. 1998. pap. 21.00 (0-534-35401-7) Thomson Learn.

Coon, Dennis. Introduction to Psychology: Exploration & Application. 6th ed. Perlee, Clyde, ed. 726p. (C). 1992. text 57.50 (0-314-92211-3) West Pub.

— Introduction to Psychology: Exploration & Application. 7th ed. LC 94-46124. 844p. (C). 1995. mass mkt. 50.75 (0-314-04450-7) West Pub.

Coon, Elizabeth, ed. see Johnson, E. M.

Coon, F. N., ed. Proceedings of the 1993 Industrial Power Conference. LC 89-46157. (PWR Ser.: Vol. 20). 120p. 1993. pap. 40.00 (0-7918-0679-0, I00342) ASME.

Coon, Glenn A. Path to the Heart: Informal Talks on Personal Soul Winning. LC BV3790.C66. 191p. reprint ed. pap. 59.30 (0-7837-6434-0, 204643200012) Bks Demand.

Coon, Horace. American Tel & Tel: The Story of a Great Monopoly. 1977. 24.95 (0-8369-5691-5) Ayer.

— Money to Burn: Great American Foundations & Their Money. 393p. (C). 1990. 49.95 (0-88738-334-3) Transaction Pubs.

— Money to Burn: What the Great American Philanthropic Foundations Do with Money. 352p. 1977. 21.95 (0-8369-2843-1) Ayer.

Coon, James A., jt. auth. see Damsky, Sheldon W.

Coon, Jeannette Saxon. Trilogy: A Family's Voyage of Faith. (Illus.). ix, 451p. 1998. 29.95 (0-9614443-8-X) Jungle Pr.

***Coon, Jon.** Blackwolf. LC 98-31483. 440p. 1999. pap. 11.95 (1-881652-15-7) Aqua Quest.

Coon, Jon. Thief of the Deep. LC 93-16853. 400p. (Orig.). 1993. pap. 11.95 (0-9623389-9-0) Aqua Quest.

Coon, Juanita, et al, compiled by. Excelsior Township Cemetery, Kalkaska County, Michigan. (Illus.). 74p. 1990. pap. 8.00 (0-940133-25-3) Kinseeker Pubns.

Coon, Lynda L. Sacred Fictions: Holy Women & Hagiography in Late Antiquity. LC 97-3136. (Middle Ages Ser.). (Illus.). 232p. 1997. text 39.95 (0-8122-3371-9) U of Pa Pr.

***Coon, Norma Jean.** It All Started Here: The Breen Family. LC 99-67286. (Illus.). 75p. 1999. lib. bdg. 175.00 (1-890698-05-9) N Coon.

Coon, Norma Jean. It All Started Here: The Burris Family. LC 97-67263. (Illus.). 675p. 1998. 225.00 (1-890698-02-4) N Coon.

— It All Started Here: The Family: The Strachan Family, 10 vols. LC 99-72532. (Illus.). 200p. 1999. lib. bdg. 175.00 (1-890698-08-3) N Coon.

***Coon, Norma Jean.** It All Started Here: The Ferguson Family. LC 97-67287. (Illus.). 200p. 1999. lib. bdg. 175.00 (1-890698-06-7) N Coon.

Coon, Norma Jean. It All Started Here: The Guenther Family, the Gunther Family, the Ginther Family. LC 97-67264. (Illus.). 200p. 1997. write for info. (1-890698-01-6) N Coon.

— It All Started Here: The Rempe Family, the Lampe Family. LC 97-67263. (Illus.). 200p. 1997. write for info. (1-890698-00-8) N Coon.

Coon, Norma Jean, contrib. by. It All Started Here: The Mahurin Family, 10 vols. LC 99-72533. (Illus.). 250p. 1999. write for info. (1-890698-09-1) N Coon.

Coon, Reva P. & Harris, Grace M., eds. Dunsmuir Centennial Book. LC 85-50084. (Illus.). (Orig.). 1985. 39.95 (0-9614838-0-6) Dunsmuir Centennial.

Coonan, Delia & Holt, Richard. Law of International Trade in Practice. 259p. 1998. pap. 48.00 (1-85431-721-0, Pub. by Blackstone Pr) Gaunt.

***Coonan, Delia & Holt, Richard.** Law of International Trade in Practice. 3rd ed. (Inns of Court School of Law Ser.). 237p. 2000. pap. 46.00 (1-84174-008-X, Pub. by Blackstone Pr) Gaunt.

Coonan, Thomas, tr. see Praskiewicz, Szczepan T.

***Coone, Mira K.** Mira's Food Planner/Journal. 68p. 1999. 4.95 (1-928824-00-5) JMC Pubg.

Cooner, Donna. Barney & Baby Bop Go to the Grocery Store. LC 96-86246. (Barney's Go to Ser.). (Illus.). 20p. (J). (ps-3). 1997. pap. 3.25 (1-57064-117-X, Barney Publ) Lyrick Pub.

Cooner, Donna. Barney & BJ's Treehouse. Larsen, Margie, ed. LC 95-83154. (Barney Ser.). (Illus.). 22p. (J). (ps-k). 1996. bds. 5.95 (1-57064-080-7) Lyrick Pub.

***Cooner, Donna.** Barney Makes Music. Davis, Guy, ed. (Barney Ser.). (Illus.). 22p. (J). (ps-k). 1999. 4.95 (1-57064-461-6, Barney Publ) Lyrick Pub.

Cooner, Donna. Bedtime for Baby Bop. Larsen, Margie, ed. LC 95-83153. (Barney Ser.). (Illus.). 20p. (J). (ps-k). 1996. bds. 4.95 (1-57064-078-5, Barney Publ) Lyrick Pub.

***Cooner, Donna.** Here Is Christmas. 32p. (J). (ps-2). 2000. 14.95 (1-57856-298-8) Waterbrook Pr.

Cooner, Donna. I Know an Old Texan Who Swallowed a Fly. LC 96-24769. (Illus.). 32p. (Orig.). (J). (ps-2). 1996. pap. 9.95 (1-885777-14-0) Hendrick-Long.

Cooner, Donna D. Baby Bop's Purse. LC 97-75560. (Barney Ser.). (Illus.). 14p. (J). (ps-k). 1998. bds. 5.95 (1-57064-245-1, Barney Publ) Lyrick Pub.

— Barney's Toolbox. LC 97-75561. (Barney Ser.). (Illus.), 14p. (J). (ps-k). 1998. bds. 5.95 (1-57064-244-3) Lyrick Pub.

***Cooner, Donna D.** Bible 1, 2, 3. (Illus.). 20p. 1998. pap. 4.99 (0-8054-1280-8) Broadman.

Cooner, Donna D. Count Your Blessings. LC 94-45281. (Illus.). 28p. (J). (ps-2). 1995. 12.99 (0-8499-1199-0) Tommy Nelson.

— Twelve Days in Texas. (Illus.). 32p. (J). (ps up). 1994. pap. 7.95 (0-937460-85-0) Hendrick-Long.

— The World God Made. LC 94-3333. (Illus.). 28p. (J). (ps-2). 1994. 12.99 (0-8499-1162-1) Tommy Nelson.

Cooney. Developing a Topic Across the Curriculum: Functions, 6 vols., Vol. 2. 1996. pap. text 20.00 (0-435-07108-4) Heinemann.

— Mathematics, Pedagogy & Secondary Teacher Education. 1998. pap. text 23.00 (0-325-00115-4) Heinemann.

— The Place of Mind. LC 99-12987. (Philosophy Ser.). 1999. mass mkt. 52.95 (0-534-52825-2) Wadsworth Pub.

— Thinking about Being a Mathematics Teacher, 6 vols., Vol. 1. 1996. pap. text 15.00 (0-435-07107-6) Heinemann.

Cooney & Wittman. Mathematics, Pedagogy & Secondary Teacher Education: An Introduction. 1996. text. write for info. (0-435-07113-0) Heinemann.

Cooney, Craig & Lawren, Bill. Methyl Magic: Maximum Health Through Methylation. LC 98-45810. 1999. 19.95 (0-8362-3585-1) Andrews & McMeel.

***Cooney, Anthony.** C. H. Douglas. 16p. (C). 2000. pap. 6.00 (0-9679707-4-1) Third Way.

— Distributism. 42p. (C). 2000. pap. 6.50 (0-9679707-5-X) Third Way.

— G. K. Chesterton - One Sword at Least. (C). 2000. 6.50 (0-9679707-1-7) Third Way.

— Hilaire Belloc, 1870-1953. 25p. (C). 2000. pap. 6.50 (0-9679707-2-5) Third Way.

— Social Credit Asterisks. 43p. (C). 2000. pap. 7.00 (0-9679707-3-3) Third Way.

Cooney, Barbara. Eleanor. (Illus.). (J). (gr. k up). 1999. pap. 5.99 (0-14-055583-8, PuffinBks) Peng Put Young Read.

— Eleanor. (Illus.). 40p. (J). (ps up). 1996. 15.99 (0-670-86159-6) Viking Penguin.

— Hattie & the Wild Waves. LC 90-32577. (Illus.). (J). (ps-3). 1990. 15.99 (0-670-83056-9, Viking Child) Peng Put Young Read.

— Hattie & the Wild Waves: A Story from Brooklyn. LC 92-40723. (Illus.). 40p. (J). (ps-3). 1993. pap. 5.99 (0-14-054193-4, PuffinBks) Peng Put Young Read.

— Hattie & the Wild Waves: A Story from Brooklyn. (Picture Puffin Ser.). (Illus.). (J). 1993. 11.19 (0-606-05343-3, Pub. by Turtleback) Demco.

— Island Boy. LC 88-175. (Illus.). (J). (ps-3). 1988. 16.99 (0-670-81749-X, Viking Child) Peng Put Young Read.

— Island Boy. LC 88-175. (Illus.). 40p. (J). (ps-3). 1991. pap. 5.99 (0-14-050756-6, PuffinBks) Peng Put Young Read.

Cooney, Barbara. Island Boy. (Picture Puffin Ser.). 1991. 10.19 (0-606-04946-0, Pub. by Turtleback) Demco.

Cooney, Barbara. Miss Rumphius. LC 82-2837. (Illus.). 32p. (J). (gr. k-3). 1982. 15.99 (0-670-47958-6, Viking Child) Peng Put Young Read.

— Miss Rumphius. (Illus.). (J). (ps-3). 1994. pap. 9.99 incl. audio (0-14-095026-5, PuffinBks) Peng Put Young Read.

— Miss Rumphius. (Picture Puffin Ser.). (J). 1985. 10.19 (0-606-00345-2, Pub. by Turtleback) Demco.

— La Senorita Rumfio. (SPA., Illus.). 32p. (ps-3). 1997. pap. 4.99 (0-14-056231-1) Penguin Putnam.

— La Senorita Runfio. (Picture Puffin Ser.). 1997. 10.19 (0-606-11544-7, Pub. by Turtleback) Demco.

— The Story of Christmas. LC 94-18687. (Illus.). 32p. (J). (gr. 2-5). 1998. pap. 5.95 (0-06-443512-1) HarpC.

— The Story of Christmas. rev. ed. LC 94-18687. (Illus.). 32p. (J). (gr. 2-5). 1995. 14.95 (0-06-023433-4) HarpC Child Bks.

Cooney, Barbara, tr. see Becker, John.

Cooney, Barbara, tr. see Hall, Donald.

Cooney, Brian. A Hylomorphic Theory of Mind. LC 90-24986. (New Perspectives in Philosophical Scholarship Series: Texts & Issues: Vol. 2). 226p. (C). 1992. text 44.95 (0-8204-1545-6) P Lang Pubng.

Cooney, Caroline. Driver's Ed. (J). 1995. mass mkt. 5.99 (0-440-91078-1) BDD Bks Young Read.

— Driver's Ed. 208p. (YA). (gr. 7 up). 1996. mass mkt. 5.50 (0-440-21981-7) Dell.

— Driver's Ed. (J). 1995. 20.95 (0-385-30974-0) Doubleday.

— Night School. LC 95-235817. 176p. (YA). (gr. 7-9). 1995. pap. 3.50 (0-590-47878-8) Scholastic Inc.

— A Prisoner of Time. 208p. (YA). 1999. mass mkt. 4.99 (0-440-22019-X) BDD Bks Young Read.

— 20 Pagents. 192p. (YA). 1994. mass mkt. 4.80 (0-440-21962-0) Dell.

Cooney, Caroline B. Among Friends. 176p. (YA). 1988. mass mkt. 4.50 (0-440-22692-9) BDD Bks Young Read.

Cooney, Caroline B. Among Friends. (J). 1987. 9.09 (0-606-04044-7, Pub. by Turtleback) Demco.

Cooney, Caroline B. Both Sides of Time. 224p. (YA). 1997. mass mkt. 4.99 (0-440-21932-9, LLL BDD) BDD Bks Young Read.

— Both Sides of Time. LC 94-32538. 1997. 9.60 (0-606-11158-1, Pub. by Turtleback) Demco.

***Cooney, Caroline B.** Burning Up. (YA). 2001. mass mkt. 5.50 (0-440-22687-2) Bantam Dell.

Cooney, Caroline B. Burning Up: A Novel. LC 98-19343. 240p. (YA). (gr. 6 up). 1999. 15.95 (0-385-32318-2) BDD Bks Young Read.

— Cheerleader. 192p. (YA). (gr. 7-9). 1991. pap. 3.25 (0-590-44316-X, Point) Scholastic Inc.

— Driver's Ed. LC 94-445. 192p. (YA). (gr. 6 up). 1994. 16.95 (0-385-32087-6) Delacorte.

— Driver's Ed. (J). 1996. 10.09 (0-606-08731-1, Pub. by Turtleback) Demco.

— Emergency Room. 176p. (YA). (gr. 7-12). 1994. pap. 3.25 (0-590-45740-3) Scholastic Inc.

Cooney, Caroline B. Emergency Room. (Point Ser.). 1994. 9.60 (0-606-06361-7, Pub. by Turtleback) Demco.

Cooney, Caroline B. The Face on the Milk Carton. (J). 1994. mass mkt. 4.99 (0-440-91009-X, LLL BDD) BDD Bks Young Read.

— The Face on the Milk Carton. 192p. (YA). (gr. 7 up). 1996. 15.95 (0-385-32328-X, Delacorte Pr Bks) BDD Bks Young Read.

— The Face on the Milk Carton. 208p. (YA). (gr. 7 up). 1991. mass mkt. 5.50 (0-440-22065-3) Dell.

Cooney, Caroline B. The Face on the Milk Carton. (J). 1991. 10.09 (0-606-04871-5, Pub. by Turtleback) Demco.

Cooney, Caroline B. The Fire. (YA). (gr. 7 up). 1990. pap. 3.25 (0-590-41641-3) Scholastic Inc.

— Fire. (J). 1990. 8.60 (0-606-03284-3, Pub. by Turtleback) Demco.

— Flash Fire. LC 94-43805. 176p. (YA). (gr. 7 up). 1995. 14.95 (0-590-25253-4, Scholastic Hardcover) Scholastic Inc.

— Flash Fire. LC 94-43805. (YA). (gr. 7 up). 1996. mass mkt. 4.50 (0-590-48496-6) Scholastic Inc.

— Flash Fire. LC 94-43805. 1995. 9.60 (0-606-09284-6, Pub. by Turtleback) Demco.

— Flight Number 116 Is Down. 208p. (J). (gr. 7-9). 1992. 14.95 (0-590-44465-4, Scholastic Hardcover) Scholastic Inc.

Cooney, Caroline B. Flight Number 116 Is Down. LC 91-9796. (Point Ser.). 201p. (YA). (gr. 7-12). 1993. mass mkt. 4.50 (0-590-44479-4) Scholastic Inc.

Cooney, Caroline B. Flight Number 116 Is Down. (Point Ser.). (J). 1992. 9.60 (0-606-02642-8, Pub. by Turtleback) Demco.

— Hush Little Baby. 258p. (YA). (gr. 6-10). 1999. pap. 4.99 (0-590-81974-7) Scholastic Inc.

***Cooney, Caroline B.** Mummy. (Illus.). 176p. (J). (gr. 7-12). 2000. mass mkt. 4.50 (0-590-67450-1) Scholastic Inc.

Cooney, Caroline B. Night School. 1995. 8.60 (0-606-07950-5, Pub. by Turtleback) Demco.

— Operation - Homefront. 1996. 9.09 (0-606-00717-2, Pub. by Turtleback) Demco.

— Out of Time. 1996. pap. 10.95 (0-385-21933-4) Delacorte.

— Out of Time. LC 95-22186. (Romantic Time Travel Ser.: No. 2). 224p. (YA). (gr. 7-12). 1997. mass mkt. 4.99 (0-440-21933-7) Dell.

Cooney, Caroline B. Out of Time. LC 95-22186. 1997. 9.60 (0-606-11716-4, Pub. by Turtleback) Demco.

Cooney, Caroline B. The Party's Over. (J). 1991. 8.35 (0-606-01919-7, Pub. by Turtleback) Demco.

— The Party's Over. 192p. (YA). (gr. 7-9). 1992. reprint ed. pap. 3.25 (0-590-42553-6, Point) Scholastic Inc.

— The Perfume. 176p. (YA). (gr. 7-9). 1992. pap. 3.50 (0-590-45402-1, Point) Scholastic Inc.

— Prisoner of Time. LC 97-24073. 208p. (YA). 1998. 15.95 (0-385-32244-5) Delacorte.

***Cooney, Caroline B.** The Ransom of Mercy Carter. (YA). 2001. mass mkt. 15.95 (0-385-32615-7, Pub. by Random Bks Yng Read) Random.

Cooney, Caroline B. Saturday Night. (Point Romance Ser.). 240p. (J). (gr. 7-9). 1992. pap. 3.25 (0-590-45784-5, Point) Scholastic Inc.

— Stranger. 176p. (YA). (gr. 7 up). 1993. pap. 3.50 (0-590-45680-6) Scholastic Inc.

— Summer Nights. (Point Romance Ser.). 176p. (J). (gr. 7-9). 1992. pap. 3.25 (0-590-45786-1, Point) Scholastic Inc.

An Asterisk (*) at the beginning of an entry indicates that the title is appearing for the first time.

***Cooney, Caroline B.** The Terrorist. 198p. (YA). (gr. 7-12). 1999. reprint ed. mass mkt. 4.50 (*0-590-22854-4*) Scholastic.

Cooney, Caroline B. Tune in Anytime. LC 99-20025. 192p. (J). 1999. 8.95 (*0-385-32649-1*, Delacorte Pr Bks) BDD Bks Young Read.

— Twenty Pageants Later. (Bantam Starfire Bks.). (J). 1993. 9.09 (*0-606-02953-2*, Pub. by Turtleback) Demco.

— Twins. 176p. (YA). (gr. 7-12). 1994. pap. 3.50 (*0-590-47478-2*) Scholastic Inc.

Cooney, Caroline B. Twins. 1994. 9.60 (*0-606-06832-5*, Pub. by Turtleback) Demco.

Cooney, Caroline B. Unforgettable. 272p. (J). (gr. 7-9). 1994. pap. 3.95 (*0-590-47877-X*) Scholastic Inc.

— Vampires Promise. 176p. (J). (gr. 7-9). 1993. pap. 3.50 (*0-590-45682-2*) Scholastic Inc.

— The Voice on the Radio. 192p. (YA). (gr. 7 up). 1998. mass mkt. 5.50 (*0-440-21977-9*) BDD Bks Young Read.

— The Voice on the Radio. (Illus.). 183p. (YA). (gr. 7-12). 1996. 15.95 (*0-385-32213-5*) Delacorte.

— The Voice on the Radio. (J). 1998. 10.09 (*0-606-13886-2*, Pub. by Turtleback) Demco.

— Wanted! LC 49-255390. 230p. (YA). (gr. 6-12). 1997. mass mkt. 4.50 (*0-590-98849-2*) Scholastic Inc.

Cooney, Caroline B. Wanted! 1997. 10.34 (*0-606-12048-3*) Turtleback.

Cooney, Caroline B. What Child Is This? 160p. (YA). 1999. mass mkt. 5.50 (*0-440-22684-8*) Bantam.

— What Child Is This? A Christmas Story. LC 96-54891. 160p. (YA). (gr. 7). 1997. 14.95 (*0-385-32317-4*) Delacorte.

— What Ever Happened to Janie? LC 92-32334. 208p. (YA). (gr. 7 up). 1993. 15.95 (*0-385-31035-8*) Delacorte.

— What Ever Happened to Janie? LC 92-32334. 224p. (YA). (gr. 5-9). 1994. mass mkt. 5.50 (*0-440-21924-8*, Dell Trade Pbks) Dell.

— What Ever Happened to Janie? (J). 1994. 10.09 (*0-606-07136-9*, Pub. by Turtleback) Demco.

***Cooney, Caroline B.** What Janie Found. LC 99-37409. 192p. (YA). (gr. 7 up). 2000. 15.95 (*0-385-32611-4*) Delacorte.

Cooney, Cedric X., jt. auth. see Jacobs, Steven E.

Cooney, David, ed. Biomedical Engineering Principles: An Introduction to Fluid, Heat & Mass Transport Processes. (Biomedical Engineering & Instrumentation Ser.: Vol. 2). (Illus.). 464p. 1976. text 125.00 (*0-8247-6347-5*) Dekker.

Cooney, David O. Activated Charcoal: Antidotal & Other Medical Uses. LC 79-26211. (Drugs & the Pharmaceutical Sciences Ser.: Vol. 9). (Illus.). 172p. reprint ed. pap. 53.40 (*0-608-08925-7*, 206956000005) Bks Demand.

— Activated Charcoal: Antidote, Remedy & Health Aid. LC 95-61283. 80p. 1995. per. 7.95 (*1-57258-047-X*) Teach Servs.

— Activated Charcoal in Medical Applications. 2nd ed. LC 94-40860. (Illus.). 584p. 1995. text 210.00 (*0-8247-9300-5*) Dekker.

— Adsorption Design for Wastewater Treatment. LC 98-5694. 176p. 1998. lib. bdg. 44.95 (*1-56670-333-6*) Lewis Pubs.

***Cooney, David O.** Purification of Wilderness Waters: A Practical Guide. LC 99-75562. (Illus.). 80p. 1999. pap. 12.95 (*0-9675854-1-4*) Balsam Bks.

Cooney, David O., ed. Advances in Biomedical Engineering, 2 pts., Pt. 1. LC 80-10862. (Biomedical Engineering & Instrumentation Ser.: No. 6). (Illus.). 358p. reprint ed. pap. 111.00 (*0-7837-0844-0*, 204115700001) Bks Demand.

— Advances in Biomedical Engineering, 2 pts., Pt. 2. LC 80-10862. (Biomedical Engineering & Instrumentation Ser.: No. 6). (Illus.). 366p. reprint ed. pap. 113.50 (*0-7837-0845-9*, 204115700002) Bks Demand.

Cooney, Denise. A Plea from the Angels: Messages from Michael the Archangel. 2nd ed. (Orig.). 1996. pap. 12.95 (*0-944256-74-0*) ACCESS Pubs Network.

Cooney, Denise R. Beyond a Master. 1987. pap. 9.95 (*0-9673784-1-9*, Pub. by Angel Work Pr) ACCESS Pubs Network.

— A Plea from the Angels: Messages from Michael, the Archangel. 2nd ed. 160p. 1996. pap. 12.95 (*0-9673784-0-0*, Pub. by Angel Work Pr) ACCESS Pubs Network.

Cooney, Eleanor & Altieri, Daniel. Court of the Lion. 1024p. 1990. mass mkt. 6.50 (*0-380-70985-6*, Avon Bks) Morrow Avon.

— Deception. 640p. 1994. reprint ed. mass mkt. 5.99 (*0-380-70872-8*, Avon Bks) Morrow Avon.

Cooney, Ellen. For the City Is Father. 100p. pap. write for info. (*0-9602912-9-6*) Duir Press.

— Horns: Hunting & Drinking Poems. LC 97-94759. 1999. pap. 12.00 (*0-9602912-5-3*) Duir Press.

— House Holding. LC 83-72996. (Illus.). 120p. (Orig.). 1984. pap. 7.95 (*0-9602912-6-1*) Duir Press.

— The Old Ballerina. LC 99-35462. 208p. 1999. 23.95 (*1-56689-086-1*, Pub. by Coffee Hse) Consort Bk Sales.

— The Quest for the Holy Grail. LC 80-67333. 104p. (Orig.). 1981. pap. 5.95 (*0-9602912-3-7*) Duir Press.

— The Silver Rose. LC 79-52862. 104p. (Orig.). 1979. pap. 5.95 (*0-9602912-8-8*) Duir Press.

— Within the Labyrinth All. LC 91-72921. 104p. (Orig.). 1992. pap. 10.00 (*0-9602912-7-X*) Duir Press.

***Cooney, Gabriel.** Landscapes of Neolithic Ireland. LC 99-23710. 272p. (C). 1999. text 85.00 (*0-415-16976-3*) Routledge.

***Cooney, Gabriel A.** Landscapes of Neolithic Ireland. LC 99-23710. 272p. 1999. pap. 27.99 (*0-415-16977-1*) Routledge.

Cooney, Helen. Underwater Animals. LC 96-16966. (Nature Company Young Discoveries Ser.). (Illus.). 32p. (J). (ps-2). 1999. 10.00 (*0-7835-4841-9*) Time-Life.

Cooney, James, ed. see Krampf, Thomas.

Cooney, James P., jt. auth. see Strasburg, William E.

Cooney, Jerry W., jt. auth. see Whigham, Thomas.

Cooney, Joe, jt. auth. see Ward, Charlie.

Cooney, Joe, jt. auth. see Williams, Terrie.

Cooney, John. Acts of Contrition. 1994. mass mkt. 5.99 (*0-671-78316-5*) PB.

***Cooney, John.** John Charles McQuaid: Ruler of Catholic Ireland. LC 99-87755. 560p. 2000. 34.95 (*0-8156-0642-7*) Syracuse U Pr.

Cooney, John D. Late Egyptian & Coptic Art: An Introduction to the Collections in the Brooklyn Museum. (Illus.). 1974. reprint ed. 15.00 (*0-913696-23-4*) Bklyn Mus.

***Cooney, Judd.** Advance Scouting for Whitetails. (Whitetail Secrets Ser.). 2000. pap. 10.95 (*1-58667-026-3*) Derrydale Pr.

— Advanced Scouting for Whitetails. (Illus.). 171p. 2000. 19.95 (*1-56416-162-5*) Derrydale Pr.

Cooney, Judith. Coping with Sexual Abuse. 1987. 17.95 (*0-8239-0684-1*) Rosen Group.

— Coping with Sexual Abuse. rev. ed. Rosen, Roger, ed. (Coping Ser.). 118p. (YA). (gr. 7-12). 1991. lib. bdg. 17.95 (*0-8239-1336-8*) Rosen Group.

Cooney-Lazaneo, Mary B., jt. auth. see Lyons, Kathleen.

Cooney, Linda A. Samantha Crane on Her Own. 272p. (Orig.). (J). 1996. mass mkt. 4.50 (*0-06-106412-2*, Harp PBks) HarpC.

Cooney, Mark. Warriors & Peacemakers: How Third Parties Shape Violence. 216p. 1998. text 50.00 (*0-8147-1514-1*); pap. text 19.00 (*0-8147-1567-2*) NYU Pr.

Cooney, Miriam P., ed. Celebrating Women in Mathematics & Science. LC 96-14119. (Illus.). 225p. (J). 1996. pap. 25.95 (*0-87353-425-5*) NCTM.

Cooney, Nancy Evans. The Umbrella Day. LC 87-16730. (J). 1997. 11.15 (*0-606-12023-8*, Pub. by Turtleback) Demco.

Cooney, Nancy H., jt. auth. see Cannon, Nancy A.

Cooney, Nicky. Decorating Ceramics: Over 300 Easy-to-Paint Patterns. LC 98-48690. 1999. 24.95 (*0-8069-6325-5*) Sterling.

Cooney, Patrick. Discovering the Mid-Atlantic: Historical Tours. LC 90-23764. (Illus.). 350p. (C). 1991. pap. 15.00 (*0-8135-1704-4*); text 45.00 (*0-8135-1703-6*) Rutgers U Pr.

Cooney, Ray & Chapman, John. Not Now, Darling. 1971. pap. 5.25 (*0-8222-0832-6*) Dramatists Play.

Cooney, Seamus, jt. auth. see Morrow, Bradford.

Cooney, Seamus, ed. see Bukowski, Charles.

Cooney, Seamus, ed. see Lewis, Wyndham.

Cooney, Seamus, ed. see Reznikoff, Charles.

Cooney, Seamus, ed. & intro. see Fante, John.

Cooney, Terry A. Balancing Acts: American Thought & Culture in the 1930s. (Twayne's American Thought & Culture Ser.). (Illus.). 288p. 1995. 33.00 (*0-8057-9060-8*, Twayne) Mac Lib Ref.

— Balancing Acts: American Thought & Culture in the 1930s. (Twayne's American Thought & Culture Ser.). (Illus.). 288p. 1995. pap. 20.00 (*0-8057-9069-1*, Twayne) Mac Lib Ref.

— The Rise of the New York Intellectuals: Partisan Review & Its Circle. LC 86-40049. (History of American Thought & Culture Ser.). 352p. 1986. 25.00 (*0-299-10710-8*) U of Wis Pr.

Cooney, Thomas J., ed. Teaching & Learning Mathematics in the 1990s: 1990 Yearbook. LC 89-14410. (Illus.). 248p. 1990. 22.50 (*0-87353-285-6*) NCTM.

Cooney, Thomas J. & Brown. Mathematics, Pedagogy & Secondary Teacher Education: Reweaving the Frayed Braid. 2nd ed. LC 96-19145. 1997. text, teacher ed. 100.00 (*0-435-07101-7*) Heinemann.

Cooney, Tim & Preddy, Beth. Connections & Disconnections: Between Linguistics, Morality, Religion & Democracy. LC 98-73465. 225p. 1999. 28.95 (*0-940121-50-6*, H318) Cross Cultural Pubns. A lively dialogue, this analysis leads to many fresh insights into the cause of anger within families & between nations. It is dedicated to bringing about rights & democracy in all the neighborhoods of our world village, without bloodshed. *Publisher Paid Annotation.*

Cooney, Timothy, ed. see Brooks, John R. & Wiant, Harry V., Jr.

Cooney, Timothy J. The Difference Between Truth & Opinion: How the Misuse of Language Can Lead to Disaster. LC 90-23842. 127p. (C). 1991. 25.95 (*0-87975-668-3*) Prometheus Bks.

— Telling Right from Wrong: What Is Moral, What Is Immoral & What Is Neither One Nor the Other. LC 85-61123. 160p. 1985. 29.95 (*0-87975-297-1*) Prometheus Bks.

Cooney, Timothy M., ed. Forestry in a Brave New World. 30p. (Orig.). 1984. pap. text 7.50 (*0-9615391-1-9*) Forest Res Syst.

Cooney, Timothy M., jt. auth. see Hartel, Dudley R.

Cooney, Tom & Faulkner, Crystal. 96 Ways You Can Save Taxes in '96: Cincinnati, OH Edition. 128p. (Orig.). Date not set. pap. 9.95 (*1-888303-05-0*) Loopholes Pr.

***Cooney, William.** The Quest for Meaning: A Journey Through Philosophy, the Arts, & Creative Genius. LC 99-48692. 288p. 1999. pap. 32.50 (*0-7618-1526-0*) U Pr of Amer.

Cooney, William, et al. From Plato to Piaget: The Greatest Educational Theorists from Across the Centuries & Around the World. LC 92-41787. 1993. 47.50 (*0-8191-9009-8*); pap. 19.50 (*0-8191-9010-1*) U Pr of Amer.

Cooney, William P., III, jt. ed. see Saffar, Philippe.

Cooney, William Patrick, ed. see Linscheid, R. L., et al.

Coonfield, Ed. Enduro Secrets Revealed. LC 84-62945. (Illus.). 176p. (Orig.). 1985. pap. 11.95 (*0-932479-24-3*) Hourglass Pub.

Coonfield-Ward, Martha. A World Full of Women. 2nd ed. LC 98-6779. 322p. 1998. pap. 37.00 (*0-205-28135-4*) Allyn.

Coonradt, Charles. Managing the Obvious. 215p. 1993. 22.00 (*1-883004-01-2*, Pub. by Game of Work) Origin Bk Sales.

Coonradt, Charles, jt. auth. see Harris, Blaine.

Coonradt, Charles A. Managing the Obvious: How to Get What You Want Using What You Know. 2nd rev. ed. LC 93-80954. 215p. 1997. reprint ed. pap. 14.95 (*1-883004-04-7*) Game of Work.

Coonradt, Charles A. & Benson, Lee. Scorekeeping for Success. (Illus.). 187p. 1998. 19.95 (*1-883004-05-5*, Pub. by Game of Work) Origin Bk Sales.

Coonradt, Charles A. & Nelson, Lee. The Game of Work: How to Enjoy Work As Much As Play. 3rd rev. ed. LC 85-14241. 148p. 1997. reprint ed. 19.95 (*1-883004-00-4*, Pub. by Game of Work) Origin Bk Sales.

Coonradt, Charles A. & Nelson, Lee. The Game of Work: How to Enjoy Work As Much As Play. 3rd rev. ed. LC 85-14241. 146p. 1997. reprint ed. pap. 14.95 (*1-883004-03-9*) Game of Work.

Coonrod, Janice A., jt. auth. see Pimentel, George C.

Coons. Tourist Third Cabin. 1999. text. write for info. (*0-312-21429-4*) St Martin.

Coons, Dale E. Country Boy. 37p. (J). (gr. 2-8). 1993. pap. text 8.95 (*1-882241-75-4*) Alleycat.

Coons, Dorothy H., ed. Specialized Dementia Care Units. LC 90-4743. (Series in Contemporary Medicine & Public Health). (Illus.). 288p. 1990. text 50.00 (*0-8018-4076-7*) Johns Hopkins.

Coons, Dorothy H., et al. Quality of Life in Long-Term Care. LC 96-356. (Illus.). 160p. 1996. lib. bdg. 39.95 (*0-7890-6039-6*) Haworth Pr.

Coons, E. N. How to Stop Crime in America in Ninety Days. (Illus.). 82p. 1998. pap. 7.50 (*0-9624037-1-7*) E N Coons.

Coons, Elizabeth, ed. see Johnson, E. M.

Coons, John E. By Nature Equal. LC 98-41031. 7p. 1999. 35.00 (*0-691-05922-5*, Pub. by Princeton U Pr) Cal Prin Full Svc.

Coons, John E. & Monahan, Frank J. Political Action, Public Policy & Catholic Schools. (National Congress Catholic Schools for the 21st Century Ser.). 37p. 1991. pap. 2.00 (*1-55833-070-4*) Natl Cath Educ.

Coons, John E. & Sugarman, Stephen D. Education by Choice: The Case for Family Control. LC 99-10059. 274p. 1999. pap. 30.95 (*1-891928-02-3*) Educ Intl Pr.

Coons, John E., et al. Private Wealth & Public Education. LC 73-102667. (Illus.). 548p. reprint ed. pap. 169.90 (*0-7837-4101-4*, 205792400011) Bks Demand.

***Coons, Linda.** The Artist's Soul: Daily Nourishment to Support Creative Growth. LC 99-37588. 512p. 2000. pap. 14.95 (*1-58542-016-6*, Tarcher Putnam) Putnam Pub Group.

Coons, Linda. Daily Nourishment for the Artist's Soul: Ideas, Prayers, & Meditations to Support Creative Growth. 200p. (Orig.). 1996. pap. 15.00 (*1-57502-287-7*, PO994) Morris Pubng.

Coons, Mary H. The Teacher's Classroom Companion: A Handbook for Primary Teachers. LC 92-85215. (Illus.). 320p. (Orig.). (J). (ps). 1993. per. 24.95 (*0-9634938-0-9*) Teachers Handbk.

Coons, Patricia Courtright. Event Planner. 1998. pap. 12.95 (*0-8038-9427-9*) Publishers Group.

***Coons, Patty.** Gala! The Fund-Raisers Event Planner for Professionals & Volunteers. LC 99-38962. 1999. pap. 12.95 (*1-892123-13-4*) Capital VA.

Coons, Richard R. Robert Clunie: Plein-Air Painter of the Sierra. LC 98-93128. (Illus.). v, 289p. 1998. 85.00 (*0-9665414-0-5*) Coons Gal.

Coons, Robert D., jt. auth. see Martin, Dennis G.

Coons, Robert O. Geriatric Assessments in Health & Disease Including Life-Styles & Happiness Quality. 150p. 1996. 47.50 (*0-7883-1284-7*); pap. 44.50 (*0-7883-1285-5*) ABBE Pubs Assn.

— Geriatric Assessments in Health & Disease Including Life-Styles & Happiness Quality: Index of New Information. rev. ed. 129p. 1997. 47.50 (*0-7883-1848-9*); pap. 44.50 (*0-7883-1849-7*) ABBE Pubs Assn.

Coons, Ronald E., ed. see Ritter Von Hohnel, Ludwig.

Coons, Stephen J., jt. ed. see Arndt, Jack R.

Coons, Stephen J., jt. ed. see Smith, Harry A.

Coons, W. S. Coon: The Koon-Coons Families of Eastern N.Y. (Illus.). 502p. 1991. reprint ed. pap. 78.50 (*0-8328-6554-0*); reprint ed. lib. bdg. 88.50 (*0-8328-2126-8*) Higginson Bk Co.

Coonse, Marian. Onions, Leeks & Garlic: A Handbook for Gardeners. LC 95-16659. (W. L. Moody, Jr. Natural History Ser.: No. 19). (Illus.). 156p. (C). 1995. 29.95 (*0-89096-675-3*); pap. 16.95 (*0-89096-676-1*) Tex A&M Univ Pr.

***Coonse, Marian.** Onions, Leeks & Garlic: A Handbook for Gardeners. (Illus.). 136p. 2000. reprint ed. text 20.00 (*0-7881-6963-7*) DIANE Pub.

Coonts, Stephen. The Cannibal Queen. McCarthy, Paul, ed. 392p. 1993. mass mkt. 6.50 (*0-671-74885-8*) PB.

***Coonts, Stephen.** Cannibal Queen: A Flight into the Heart of America. 1999. per. 14.95 (*0-671-03849-4*) PB.

— Cuba. LC 99-22070. 461p. 2000. mass mkt. 7.99 (*0-312-97139-7*) St Martin.

Coonts, Stephen. Cuba. 2nd ed. LC 99-22070. 384p. 1999. text 24.95 (*0-312-20521-X*) St Martin.

— Final Flight. 400p. 1989. mass mkt. 6.99 (*0-440-20447-X*) Dell.

— Flight of the Intruder. LC 86-16440. 329p. 1986. 21.95 (*0-87021-200-1*) Naval Inst Pr.

— Flight of the Intruder. McCarthy, Paul, ed. 448p. 1990. per. 6.99 (*0-671-70960-7*) PB.

— Fortunes of War. LC 97-52793. 368p. 1998. text 24.95 (*0-312-18583-9*) St Martin.

— Fortunes of War. 1999. mass mkt. 7.99 (*0-312-96941-4*) St Martin.

***Coonts, Stephen.** Fortunes of War. large type ed. LC 98-6491. 1998. 27.95 (*0-7862-1463-5*) Thorndike Pr.

— Hong Kong. 384p. 2000. 25.95 (*0-312-25339-7*) St Martin.

Coonts, Stephen. The Intruders. (Illus.). 1995. per. 6.99 (*0-671-87061-0*) PB.

— The Intruders. large type ed. LC 94-40976. 25.95 (*1-56895-164-7*) Wheeler Pub.

— The Intruders (Export) McCarthy, Paul, ed. (Orig.). 1995. mass mkt. 6.50 (*0-671-51953-0*) PB.

— The Minotaur. 448p. 1990. mass mkt. 6.99 (*0-440-20742-8*) Dell.

— The Minotaur. large type ed. LC 90-10806. 719p. 1990. 13.95 (*0-89621-982-8*) Thorndike Pr.

— The Minotaur. large type ed. LC 90-10806. 719p. 1990. reprint ed. 21.95 (*1-56054-020-6*) Thorndike Pr.

— The Red Horseman. 1993. pap. 6.50 (*0-671-88413-1*) PB.

— The Red Horseman. McCarthy, Paul, ed. 416p. 1994. reprint ed. mass mkt. 6.99 (*0-671-74888-2*) PB.

***Coonts, Stephen.** Technothriller Anthology. 2000. text 24.95 (*0-312-87190-2*) St Martin.

Coonts, Stephen. Under Siege. McCarthy, Paul, ed. 1991. per. 6.99 (*0-671-74294-9*) PB.

— Under Siege. large type ed. LC 90-28432. 847p. 1991. pap. 16.95 (*1-56054-991-2*) Thorndike Pr.

— War in the Air: True Accounts of the 20th Century's Most Dramamtic Air Battles by the Men Who Fought Them. 1997. per. 14.00 (*0-671-88191-4*) PB.

— War in the Air: True Accounts of the 20th Century's Most Dramatic Air Battles - By The Men Who Fought Them. large type ed. LC 96-49227. 578p. 1997. 26.95 (*0-7862-0973-9*) Thorndike Pr.

***Coontz.** Technoanthology. 1999. mass mkt. write for info. (*0-8125-7615-2*) Tor Bks.

— Technoanthology. 2nd ed. 1999. mass mkt. write for info. (*0-8125-7616-0*) Tor Bks.

— Technoanthology. 3rd ed. 1999. mass mkt. write for info. (*0-8125-7617-9*) Tor Bks.

Coontz, Stephanie. American Families: A Multicultural Reader. LC 98-6092. 480p. (C). (gr. 13). 1998. pap. 27.99 (*0-415-91574-0*) Routledge.

— American Families: A Multicultural Reader. LC 98-6092. 544p. (C). 1999. 80.00 (*0-415-91573-2*) Routledge.

Coontz, Stephanie. The Way We Never Were: American Families & the Nostalgia Trap. LC 91-59009. 400p. 1993. reprint ed. pap. 16.00 (*0-465-09097-4*, Pub. by Basic) HarpC.

Coontz, Stephanie. The Way We Really Are: Coming to Terms with America's Changing Families. 256p. 1998. pap. 15.00 (*0-465-09092-3*, Pub. by Basic) HarpC.

Coontz, Sydney H. Productive Labour & Effective Demand, Including a Critique of Keynesian Economics. LC 66-15567. (Illus.). ix, 174p. 1966. 35.00 (*0-678-06511-X*) Kelley.

Coop, jt. auth. see Rotella, Robert J.

Coop, D. W. & Gonzalez, M. R. Read the New Testament in Spanish. (IQ Bks.). (SPA., Illus.). 256p. (YA). (gr. 9-12). 1996. wbk. ed. 14.95 (*1-883316-52-9*) K K & G.

Coop, Dwight W. Camelot General Chemistry Primer. (IQ Bks.). (Illus.). 416p. (YA). (gr. 12). 1994. wbk. ed. 15.95 (*1-883316-19-7*) K K & G.

— Camelot General Chemistry Teaching Guide & Assessment Battery. (IQ Bks.). (Illus.). 96p. 1995. teacher ed. 12.95 (*1-883316-77-4*) K K & G.

Coop, Mahlon, ed. see Bales, Eugene H.

Coop, Mahlon, ed. see Cokinos, Christopher.

Coop, Richard. Mind over Golf: How to Use Your Head to Lower Your Score. 194p. 1997. 12.95 (*0-02-861683-9*) Macmillan.

Coop, Richard & Fields, Bill. Mind over Golf: How to Use Your Head to Lower Your Score. Wolff, Rick, ed. 256p. 1993. 20.00 (*0-02-527830-4*) Macmillan.

Coop, Richard, jt. auth. see Wiren, Gary.

Coop, William L., ed. Pacific People Sing Out Strong. LC 81-22211. (Illus.). 99p. 1982. reprint ed. pap. 30.70 (*0-608-01656-X*, 206230800002) Bks Demand.

Coope, A. E. Malay-English - English-Malay Standard Dictionary. 631p. (Orig.). 1993. pap. 16.95 (*0-7818-0103-6*) Hippocrene Bks.

Coope, Geoffrey G., jt. ed. see Beckwith, John A.

Coope, Jean, jt. auth. see Hunter, Myra.

Coope, Jessica A. The Martyrs of Cordoba: Community & Family Conflict in an Age of Mass Conversion. LC 94-30425. xvii, 115p. 1995. text 35.00 (*0-8032-1471-5*) U of Nebr Pr.

Coope, Marian G. Reality & Time in the Oleza Novels of Gabriel Miro. (Monografias A Ser.: Vol. CII). (Illus.). 235p. (C). 1984. 69.00 (*0-7293-0182-6*, Pub. by Tamesis Bks Ltd) Boydell & Brewer.

Coope, Peter M., jt. auth. see Peterson, William N.

Cooper. Act of Exposure. mass mkt. 6.95 (*0-7472-5400-1*, Pub. by Headline Bk Pub) Trafalgar.

Cooper. Agricultural Mechanics. 3rd ed. (Agriculture Ser.). 40p. 1996. text, teacher ed., lab manual ed. 12.75 (*0-8273-6929-8*) Delmar.

— Agricultural Mechanics. 3rd ed. (Agriculture Ser.). 336p. 1996. text, lab manual ed. 17.00 (*0-8273-6928-X*) Delmar.

— Agricultural Mechanics. 3rd ed. (Agriculture Ser.). 448p. 1996. teacher ed., ring bd. 96.95 (0-8273-6895-X) Delmar.
— Agricultural Mechanics: Fundamentals/Applications. 3rd ed. (Agriculture Ser.). 88p. 1996. text, teacher ed. 13.95 (0-8273-6855-0) Delmar.
— Agriscience. (Agriculture Ser.). 1993. pap., teacher ed. 12.00 (0-8273-5585-8) Delmar.
— Agriscience: Fundamentals & Application. 2nd ed. (Agriculture Ser.). 96p. 1996. teacher ed. 12.75 (0-8273-6280-3) Delmar.
— Agriscience: Fundamentals & Applications. (Agriculture Ser.). 1990. 12.00 (0-8273-3395-1) Delmar.
— Agriscience: Fundamentals & Applications Training. 2nd ed. (Agriculture Ser.). 432p. 1996. 89.95 (0-8273-6957-3) Delmar.
— Agriscience: Fundamentals/Applications. 2nd ed. (Agriculture Ser.). 40p. 1996. teacher ed., lab manual ed. 12.75 (0-8273-6942-5) Delmar.
— Agriscience: Fundamentals/Applications. 2nd ed. (Agriculture Ser.). 192p. 1996. lab manual ed. 17.00 (0-8273-6941-7) Delmar.
— Agriscience CTB. 2nd ed. (Agriculture Ser.). 1997. text 100.00 (0-8273-7487-9) Delmar.
— Business Research Methods. 7th ed. 2001. 66.00 (0-07-231451-6) McGraw.
— Cardiac Pacing. 188p. (gr. 13). 1988. text 26.95 (0-944132-17-0) Mosby Inc.
— Change Your Voice, Change Your Life. 1984. 13.95 (0-02-528040-6) Macmillan.
— Chemistry 1998. pap., lab manual ed. 6.25 (0-07-230407-3) McGraw.
— Creeping Ivy. LC 99-15493. 1999. text 23.95 (0-312-20520-1) St Martin.
— Criminology. 2000. pap. text 11.97 (0-395-97313-9) HM.
— Le Dernier des Mohicans. (FRE.). 1996. pap. 7.95 (2-87714-323-6, Pub. by Bookking Intl) Distribks Inc.
— Engaging Questions. 736p. 2000. pap. text 35.95 (0-312-11159-2) St Martin.
*Cooper. Guess Again: Short Stories. 208p. 2000. 20.50 (0-684-86586-6) S&S Trade.
Cooper. The Hong Kong Connection. 1992. pap. text. write for info. (0-582-02524-9, Pub. by Addison-Wesley) Longman.
— International Review of Industrial & Organizational Psychology, 1987, Vol. 87. LC 86-643874. 378p. 1987. 300.00 (0-471-91352-9) Wiley.
— Islam & Modernity. 1998. text 55.00 (1-86064-175-X) I B T.
— Langston Hughes. 1997. 24.95 (0-8057-4022-8) Macmillan.
— The Leatherstocking, 5 vols., Set. 1993. pap. 21.00 (0-19-521063-8) OUP.
— Literacy, 2 vols. 2nd ed. (C). 1992. pap. text 41.56 (0-395-64782-7) HM.
— Management of Facial, Head, & Neck Pain. 352p. 1989. text 115.00 (0-7216-2841-9, W B Saunders Co) Harcrt Hlth Sci Grp.
— Managerial Accounting for Managers. (SWC-Accounting). 2002. pap. 62.00 (0-324-02809-1) Thomson Learn.
— Occupational Therapy in Oncology & Palliative Care. 1997. pap. 36.00 (1-86156-015-X) Thomson Learn.
— Principles of Cell Growth & Division. 384p. 1999. 69.95 (0-12-188010-9) Acad Pr.
— Principles of Marketing. 4th ed. (C). 1995. pap. text, student ed. 22.95 (0-673-46556-X) Addson-Wesley Educ.
— Public Administration & Government. LC 97-72037. (C). 1997. text 53.00 (0-15-500481-6, Pub. by Harcourt Coll Pubs) Harcourt.
— Russia & World. LC 98-21077. 26p. 1999. text 65.00 (0-312-21569-X) St Martin.
— Science, Level 1. 1985. 26.50 (0-15-365491-0) Harcourt Schl Pubs.
— Science, Level 2. 1985. 29.50 (0-15-365492-9) Harcourt Schl Pubs.
— Science, Level 3. 1985. 29.95 (0-15-365493-7) Harcourt Schl Pubs.
— Science, Level 5. 1985. 34.50 (0-15-365494-5) Harcourt Schl Pubs.
— Science, Level R. enl. ed. 1985. 323.25 (0-15-365488-0) Harcourt Schl Pubs.
— Science, 1985, Level 1. 1985. 69.00 (0-15-365502-X) Harcourt Schl Pubs.
— Science, 1985, Level 5. 1985. teacher ed. 96.75 (0-15-365506-2) Harcourt Schl Pubs.
— Science, 1985, Level 6. 1985. student ed. 35.00 (0-15-365495-3) Harcourt Schl Pubs.
— Science, 1985, Level R. 1985. teacher ed. 57.00 (0-15-365501-1) Harcourt Schl Pubs.
— Science, 1989, Nova Level 6. 1989. 35.25 (0-15-364326-9) Harcourt Schl Pubs.
— Science, 1989, Nova Level R. 1989. teacher ed. 57.00 (0-15-364327-7) Harcourt Schl Pubs.
— The Science of Agriculture: Biological Applications. (Agriculture Ser.). 1996. 100.00 (0-8273-7490-9) Delmar.
— Science 1985. 1985. pap., teacher ed., wbk. ed. 12.75 (0-15-365527-5); pap., teacher ed., wbk. ed. 12.75 (0-15-365528-3); pap., teacher ed., wbk. ed. 13.25 (0-15-365529-1); pap., teacher ed., wbk. ed. 13.25 (0-15-365530-5); pap., teacher ed., wbk. ed. 13.50 (0-15-365531-3); pap., teacher ed., wbk. ed. 13.50 (0-15-365532-1); pap., wbk. ed. 9.00 (0-15-365523-2) Harcourt Schl Pubs.
— Science 1985. 1985. pap. 12.25 (0-15-365489-9) Harcourt Schl Pubs.
— Science 1985: Tests. 1985. pap. 5.75 (0-15-365538-0); pap. 5.75 (0-15-365539-9); pap. 5.75 (0-15-365540-2); pap. 5.75 (0-15-365541-0) Harcourt Schl Pubs.
— Software Quality Management. 1979. text 25.95 (0-89433-093-4) Petrocelli.
— Teachers' Stress. (C). 1996. text 65.00 (0-415-09483-6) Routledge.
— Tourism Principles & Practice. 1995. pap. 37.92 (0-582-28694-8, Pub. by Addison-Wesley) Longman.
*Cooper. Trends in Organizational Behaviour, Vol. 5. 182p. 1999. pap. 54.95 (0-471-98405-1) Wiley.
Cooper. Viruses & the Environment. 2nd ed. 58.50 (0-412-45120-4) Kluwer Academic.
— When Lean Enterprises Collide. 1995. 35.00 (0-07-103632-6) McGraw.
Cooper, ed. The Basic Writing Process. (C). 1993. text. write for info. (0-321-01560-6) Addson-Wesley Educ.
— Professional Selling in the 21st Century. (C). 1999. text. write for info. (0-321-01410-3) Addson-Wesley Educ.
Cooper & Gibson. An Introduction to Paralegal Studies. 2nd ed. LC 97-26789. 496p. (C). 1998. mass mkt. 63.95 (0-8273-8339-8) Delmar.
Cooper & Melanie, M. Cooperative Chemistry. 208p. (C). 1996. spiral bd., lab manual ed. 28.13 (0-07-012771-9) McGraw.
*Cooper & Palmer. Conquer Your Stress. 96p. 2000. pap. 17.95 (0-8464-5162-X) Beekman Pubs.
Cooper & Simic. Readings in Cultural Anthropology. 2nd ed. 264p. 1997. per. 45.95 (0-7872-4533-X) Kendall-Hunt.
Cooper, et al. English Water Gardens. (Illus.). 160p. 1993. pap. 17.95 (0-297-83150-X, Pub. by Weidenfeld & Nicolson) Trafalgar.
Cooper, et al. Human Anatomy & Physiology: Laboratory Manual for Zoology. 136p. (C). 1998. text 22.95 (0-7872-5417-7) Kendall-Hunt.
— Keys to Excellence. 4th ed. 328p. (C). 1997. per. 35.95 (0-7872-4302-7, 41430201) Kendall-Hunt.
Cooper, et al. Modernising Social Welfare. 74.95 (1-84014-387-8) Ashgate Pub Co.
Cooper, et al. New Financial Instruments. 1987. 120.00 (0-85297-190-7, Pub. by Chartered Bank) St Mut.
— When Teachers Lead. Clark, David L., ed. 84p. (Orig.). (C). 1993. pap. text 7.00 (1-55996-157-0) Univ Council Educ Admin.
— Workbook for the Medical Assistant. 6th ed. 320p. 1993. pap. text 19.95 (0-8016-1011-7) Mosby Inc.
Cooper, jt. auth. see Adrian.
Cooper, jt. auth. see Axelrod.
Cooper, jt. auth. see Blakstad.
Cooper, jt. auth. see Cartwright.
Cooper, jt. auth. see Drew.
Cooper, jt. auth. see Earnshaw.
Cooper, jt. auth. see Novak, M.
Cooper, jt. auth. see Patton.
Cooper, jt. auth. see Robertson, Jr.
Cooper, jt. auth. see Slauson, David O.
Cooper, jt. intro. see Grahame, Kenneth.
*Cooper & Lee. Warm Air Heating for Climate Control. 4th ed. LC 98-53501. 542p. 1999. text 80.00 (0-13-095964-2) S&S Trade.
Cooper, A., et al, eds. The Enzyme Catalysis Process: Energetics, Mechanism & Dynamics. (NATO ASI Series A, Life Sciences: Vol. 178). (Illus.). 504p. 1989. 135.00 (0-306-43331-1, Plenum Trade) Perseus Pubng.
Cooper, A., jt. auth. see Whitehead, M. I.
Cooper, A., jt. ed. see Parker, P.
Cooper, A. Edward. The Triumph of the Third Reich. LC 99-60980. 302p. 1999. pap. 11.95 (1-888106-99-9) Agreka Bks.
Cooper, A. H., ed. see HMSO Staff.
*Cooper, Adaline. Drawing from God's Strength. 31p. 1999. pap. 12.95 (0-9679109-2-7) Straght From The Heart.
Cooper, Adam. Eddie Irvine. (Illus.). 176p. 1996. pap. 19.95 (1-85260-560-X, Pub. by J H Haynes & Co) Motorbooks Intl.
Cooper, Adrian. Sacred Mountains: Ancient Wisdom & Modern Meanings. 1998. 49.95 (0-86315-235-X, Pub. by Floris Bks) Gryphon Hse.
*Cooper, Adrian. Sacred Nature: Ancient Wisdom & Modern Meanings. (Illus.). 1998. pap. 29.95 (1-86163-038-7, Pub. by Capall Bann Pubng) Holmes Pub.
Cooper, Afua. Memories Have Tongue: Poetry. 128p. 1993. per. write for info. (0-920813-50-X) Sister Vis Pr.
— The Red Caterpillar on College Street. (Illus.). 32p. (J). (ps-3). Date not set. pap. write for info. (0-920813-87-9) Sister Vis Pr.
Cooper, Al. World of Logotypes, Vol. 1. LC 75-29774. 1976. pap. 25.95 (0-910158-20-7) Art Dir.
— World of Logotypes, Vol. 2. LC 75-29774. (Illus.). 1978. 32.50 (0-910158-34-7) Art Dir.
— World of Logotypes, Vol. 3. LC 75-29774. (Illus.). 356p. 1982. 32.50 (0-910158-82-7) Art Dir.
Cooper, Alan. About Face: The Essentials of User Interface Design. 600p. 1995. pap. 29.99 (1-56884-322-4) IDG Bks.
— The Inmates are Running the Asylum: Why High Tech Products Drive Us Crazy & How to Restore the Sanity. 20p. 1999. 25.00 (0-672-31649-8) Sams.
— Logo. (C). 1989. 35.00 (0-7223-2348-4, Pub. by A H S Ltd) St Mut.
— Philip Roth & the Jews. LC 95-19591. (SUNY Series in Modern Jewish Literature & Culture). 319p. (C). 1996. pap. text 19.95 (0-7914-2910-5) State U NY Pr.
Cooper, Alan, ed. How to Plan Advertising. LC 98-118533. (Illus.). 160p. 1997. pap. 28.95 (0-304-70143-2) Continuum.
Cooper, Alan & Walker, Norman. Getting the Measure of the Stars. (Illus.). 308p. 1987. 49.00 (0-85274-830-2) IOP Pub.
Cooper, Alan K., et al, eds. Geology & Seismic Stratigraphy of the Antarctic Margin. LC 95-43568. (Antarctic Research Ser.: Vol. 68). 1995. 65.00 (0-87590-884-5) Am Geophysical.
Cooper, Alan K. & Davey, Frederick, eds. The Antarctic Continental Margin: Geology & Geophysics of the Western Ross Sea. (Earth Science Ser.: Vol. 5B). (Illus.). 253p. 1987. pap. 10.00 (0-933687-05-2, 831-28) Circum-Pacific.
Cooper-Alarcon, Daniel. The Aztec Palimpsest: Mexico in the Modern Imagination. LC 96-45805. 224p. 1997. 45.00 (0-8165-1655-3) U of Ariz Pr.
— The Aztec Palimpsest: Mexico in the Modern Imagination. LC 96-45805. 224p. 1997. pap. 19.95 (0-8165-1656-1) U of Ariz Pr.
Cooper, Aldwyn, jt. auth. see Blakstad, Michael.
Cooper, Alice H. Paradoxes of Peace: German Peace Movements since 1945. LC 94-48681. (Social History, Popular Culture, & Politics in Germany Ser.). 344p. (C). 1996. text 57.50 (0-472-10624-4, 10624) U of Mich Pr.
Cooper, Alice P. Authors & Others. LC 70-107689. (Essay Index Reprint Ser.). 1977. 21.95 (0-8369-1493-7) Ayer.
Cooper, Alison. International Business in South Africa, 1993: A Directory of Non-U. S. Corporations with Business Links to South Africa. 7th ed. 288p. 1993. pap. 50.00 (1-879775-14-X) IRRC Inc DC.
— International Business in South Africa, 1995. LC 99-186632. 241p. (Orig.). 1995. pap. 50.00 (1-879775-23-9) IRRC Inc DC.
— Media Power? LC 96-53429. (Viewpoints Ser.). (Illus.). 32p. (J). 1997. 20.00 (0-531-14452-6) Watts.
— A Punishment to Fit the Crime? LC 96-2138. (Viewpoints Ser.). (J). 1997. lib. bdg. 22.00 (0-531-14411-9) Watts.
— U. S. Business in South Africa, 1993. 9th ed. 237p. (Orig.). 1993. pap. text 50.00 (1-879775-05-0) IRRC Inc DC.
Cooper, Allan. The Deer is Thirsty for the Mountain Stream. 9.75 (0-920635-07-5) Genl Dist Srvs.
— Heaven of Small Moments. LC 98-232086. 80p. 1998. pap. 9.75 (0-921411-79-0) Genl Dist Srvs.
— The Pearl Inside the Body: Poems Selected & New. (Poetry Ser.). 1991. pap. 11.25 (0-920187-04-8) Genl Dist Srvs.
Cooper, Allan D. The Occupation of Namibia: Afrikanerdom's Attack on the British Empire. 226p. (Orig.). (C). 1990. pap. text 26.50 (0-8191-7955-8) U Pr of Amer.
Cooper, Allen D., et al. Cecil Review of General Internal Medicine. 6th ed. Kersey, Ray, ed. 288p. 1996. pap. text 39.95 (0-7216-6264-1, W B Saunders Co) Harcrt Hlth Sci Grp.
Cooper, Allene. Thinking & Writing by Design: A Cross-Disciplinary Rhetoric & Reader. (C). 1996. pap., teacher ed. write for info. (0-02-324703-7, U1534-9) Allyn.
— Thinking & Writing by Design: A Cross-Disciplinary Rhetoric & Reader. LC 95-36508. 700p. 1995. pap. text 38.00 (0-02-324702-9, Macmillan Coll) P-H.
Cooper, Amy, tr. see Cardinal, Marie.
Cooper, Amy J. Dream Quest: Stories from Spirit Bay. (Illus.). 128p. (J). (gr. 3-7). 1996. 7.95 (0-920303-86-2, Pub. by Annick); pap. 4.95 (0-920303-84-6, Pub. by Annick) Firefly Bks Ltd.
*Cooper, Andre R., Sr. Air CFRS Made Easy. LC 99-51395. 339p. 1999. pap. 89.00 (0-86587-630-4) Gov Insts.
Cooper, Andre R., Sr. Cooper's Comprehensive Environmental Desk Reference: With Supplemental Spell Check Disk. LC 95-38571. (Industrial Health & Safety Ser.). 1040p. 1997. text 104.95 (0-442-02159-3, VNR) Wiley.
— Cooper's Pocket Environmental Compliance Dictionary. LC 94-24689. 352p. (Orig.). 1994. pap. 36.95 (0-442-02017-1, VNR) Wiley.
Cooper, Andre R. Cooper's Pocket Environmental Compliance Dictionary. (Industrial Health & Safety Ser.). 340p. 1994. pap. 49.95 (0-471-28691-5, VNR) Wiley.
Cooper, Andre R., Sr. Cooper's Toxic Exposures Desk Reference. LC 96-35221. 2016p. 1996. pap. 199.00 (1-56670-220-8) Lewis Pubs.
Cooper, Andre R., Sr. Environmental Compliance Made Easy: A Checklist Approach to Industry. LC 98-13131. 300p. 1998. pap. text 69.00 (0-86587-599-5, 599) Gov Insts.
— ESAs Made Easy: A Checklist Approach to Phase I Environmental Site Assessments. LC 96-182382. 206p. 1996. pap. text 59.00 (0-86587-536-7) Gov Insts.
— Properties of Hazardous Industrial Materials. 1998. 250.00 (1-56670-236-4, L1236) CRC Pr.
*Cooper, Andre R., Sr. Water CFRs Made Easy. 350p. 2000. pap. text 89.00 (0-86587-631-2, 631) Gov Insts.
Cooper, Andre R., ed. Cooper's Comprehensive Environmental Desk Reference. (Industrial Health & Safety Ser.). 1039p. 1996. 140.00 (0-471-28735-0, VNR) Wiley.
Cooper, Andrew. Playing in the Zone. LC 98-5799. 1998. pap. 13.00 (1-57062-151-9, Pub. by Shambhala Pubns) Random.
— Secret Nature of the Channel Shore. (Illus.). 224p. (Orig.). 1994. pap. 17.95 (0-563-36906-X, BBC-Parkwest) Parkwest Pubns.
Cooper, Andrew, ed. Active Welfare, Issue 8. 128p. 1998. pap. 19.50 (0-85315-869-X, Pub. by Lawrence & Wishart) NYU Pr.
Cooper, Andrew F. Canadian Culture: International Dimensions. LC 86-105590. (Contemporary Affairs Ser.: No. 50). 168p. 1985. reprint ed. pap. 52.10 (0-608-04225-0, 206496900012) Bks Demand.
— In Between Countries: Australia, Canada & the Search for Order in Agricultural Trade. 288p. 1997. text 55.00 (0-7735-1667-0, Pub. by McG-Queens Univ Pr) CUP Services.
Cooper, Andrew M. Doubt & Identity in Romantic Poetry. LC 87-10651. 244p. (C). 1988. 40.00 (0-300-04004-0) Yale U Pr.
*Cooper, Ann. Bitter Harvest: A Chef's Perspective on Hidden Dangers in Foods We Eat & What You Can Do About It. LC 99-56123. 272p. 2000. 29.95 (0-415-92227-5) Routledge.
Cooper, Ann. Eagles: Hunters of the Sky. (Wonder Ser.). (Illus.). 64p. (Orig.). (J). (gr. 4-6). 1992. pap. 7.95 (1-879373-11-4) Roberts Rinehart.
— In the Desert. (Wild Wonder Ser.). (Illus.). 48p. (Orig.). (J). (gr. k-3). 1997. pap. 9.95 (1-57098-174-4) Roberts Rinehart.
— On the Wing: Jessie Woods & the Flying Aces Air Circus. (Illus.). 159p. 1993. 23.95 (1-879630-17-6) Black Hawk Pub.
— Owls: On Silent Wings. LC 94-65092. (Wonder Ser.). (Illus.). 64p. (Orig.). (J). 1994. pap. 7.95 (1-879373-78-5) Roberts Rinehart.
Cooper, Ann. A Woman's Place Is in the Kitchen: The Evolution of Women Chefs. 336p. 1997. pap. 29.95 (0-471-29208-7, VNR) Wiley.
Cooper, Ann. A Woman's Place Is in the Kitchen: The Evolution of Women Professional Chefs. LC 97-17963. (Culinary Arts Ser.). (Illus.). 300p. 1997. pap. 29.95 (0-442-02370-7, VNR) Wiley.
Cooper, Ann, jt. auth. see Cooper, Charlie.
Cooper, Ann C. Above the Treeline. LC 95-72983. (Wild Wonders Ser.). (Illus.). 48p. (Orig.). (J). (gr. k-3). 1996. pap. 7.95 (0-916278-70-0) Denver Mus.
— Along the Seashore. (Wild Wonder Ser.). (Illus.). 48p. (Orig.). (J). (gr. k-3). 1997. pap. 9.95 (1-57098-121-3) Roberts Rinehart.
— Around the Pond: The Wild Wonders Series. LC 98-25065. (Wild Wonder Ser.). (Illus.). 48p. (J). (gr. k-4). 1998. pap. 9.95 (1-57098-223-6) Roberts Rinehart.
— Bats: Swift Shadows in the Twilight. (Wonder Ser.). (Illus.). 64p. (J). (gr. 3-6). 1993. pap. text 7.95 (1-879373-52-1) Roberts Rinehart.
*Cooper, Ann C. In the City. LC 99-31231. (Illus.). 48p. (J). (ps-3). 1999. pap. 9.95 (1-57098-298-8, Pub. by Roberts Rinehart) Publishers Group.
Cooper, Ann C. In the Forest. LC 95-72984. (Wild Wonders Ser.). (Illus.). 48p. (Orig.). (J). (gr. k-3). 1996. pap. 7.95 (0-916278-71-9) Denver Mus.
*Cooper, Ann Goode. Zebordee's Miracle. 32p. 1999. 9.95 (1-57072-099-1) Overmountain Pr.
Cooper, Ann K. Essays of Ann Klein Cooper. 64p. (C). 1993. pap. text. write for info. (1-883331-00-5) Anderie Poetry.
— Gallery of Pioneers. 68p. (YA). (gr. 9-12). 1986. pap. text. write for info. (0-910463-05-0) Edit Heliodor.
— How Ya Doin Funny Face. 110p. (Orig.). 1989. pap. text. write for info. (0-910463-08-5) Edit Heliodor.
— The Psychiatrist's Daughter. 108p. (Orig.). 1987. pap. text. write for info. (0-910463-06-9) Edit Heliodor.
— Reflections of an Enlightened Blond. 120p. (Orig.). 1988. pap. text. write for info. (0-910463-07-7) Edit Heliodor.
Cooper, Ann L., jt. auth. see Wagstaff, Patty.
Cooper, Ann R. The Trendy Traveler. (Illus.). 140p. (Orig.). 1989. pap. text. write for info. (0-910463-10-7) Edit Heliodor.
Cooper, Anna J. Slavery & the French Revolutionists, 1788-1805. Keller, Frances R., ed. & tr. by. from FRE. LC 87-24704. (French Civilization Ser.: Vol. 1). (Illus.). 220p. 1988. lib. bdg. 89.95 (0-88946-637-8) E Mellen.
— A Voice from the South. LC 77-78762. 304p. 1969. reprint ed. lib. bdg. 65.00 (0-8371-1384-9, COV&, Greenwood Pr) Greenwood.
— A Voice from the South. (Schomburg Library of Nineteenth-Century Black Women Writers). 368p. 1988. reprint ed. text 35.00 (0-19-505246-3) OUP.
— A Voice from the South. (Schomburg Library of Nineteenth-Century Black Women Writers). 368p. 1990. reprint ed. pap. text 13.95 (0-19-506323-6) OUP.
Cooper, Anne. Ishmael My Brother. rev. ed. 1998. 14.99 (1-85424-233-4) O M Lit.
Cooper, Annie. Ruby's Miracle. 384p. 2000. mass mkt. 5.99 (0-06-101375-7) HarpC.
Cooper, Anthony A. Characteristics of Men, Manners, Opinions, Times, Vol. 1. Ayres, Philip, ed. (Illus.). 368p. 1999. text 115.00 (0-19-812376-0) OUP.
— Characteristics of Men, Manners, Opinions, Times, Vol. II. Ayres, Philip, ed. (Illus.). 404p. 1999. text 115.00 (0-19-812377-9) OUP.
— An Inquiry Concerning Virtue. LC 91-14925. 258p. 1991. reprint ed. 50.00 (0-8201-1455-3) Schol Facsimiles.
Cooper, Anthony J., ed. The Black Experience, 1865-1978: A Documentary Reader. 444p. (C). 1996. pap. 29.00 (1-874529-51-5, Pub. by Greenwich Univ Pr) NYU Pr.
Cooper, Anthony R., ed. Determination of Molecular Weight. LC 88-25881. (Chemical Analysis). 526p. 1989. 275.00 (0-471-05893-9) Wiley.
Cooper, Antonya & Harpin, Valerie. This Is Our Child: How Parents Experience the Medical World. 160p. 1991. pap. 14.95 (0-19-261899-7, 12169) OUP.
Cooper, Arlene, jt. auth. see School, Beverly.
Cooper, Arnold. Psychoanalysis: Toward the Second Century. 248p. (C). 1990. 40.00 (0-300-04558-1) Yale U Pr.
Cooper, Arnold C. Challenges in Predicting New Firm Performance. 25p. (Orig.). (C). 1993. pap. text 30.00 (1-56806-662-7) DIANE Pub.
— Entrepreneurship: Starting a New Business. 19p. reprint ed. pap. 1.00 (0-940791-01-3) NFIB Found.
*Cooper, Artemis. Writing at the Kitchen Table: The Authorized Biography of Elizabeth David. LC 00-37603. 384p. 2000. 27.50 (0-06-019828-1, Ecco Press) HarperTrade.
Cooper, Arthur, tr. & intro. see Li Po, et al.

An Asterisk (*) at the beginning of an entry indicates that the title is appearing for the first time.

Cooper, Ashley, jt. auth. see Shaftesbury, Anthony Ashley Cooper.

Cooper, Astrid. Crystal Dreams. pap. 6.99 (*0-9586998-3-6*) Life on Paper.

— Shadows Embrace. 1998. mass mkt. 6.99 (*0-9586998-4-4*) Life on Paper.

Cooper, Austin. The Cloud: On the Cloud of Unknowing. 184p. 1990. pap. 8.95 (*0-8189-0573-5*) Alba.

— The Cloud of Unknowing: Reflections on Selected Texts. 184p. 1994. pap. 21.00 (*0-86012-188-7*, Pub. by Srch Pr) St Mut.

— Julian of Norwich: Reflections on Selected Texts. 144p. (Orig.). 1994. pap. 40.00 (*0-86012-159-3*, Pub. by Srch Pr) St Mut.

Cooper, B. Marriage in Maradi: Gender & Culture in a Hausa Society in Niger, 1900-1989. LC 97-1610. (Social History of Africa Ser.). 1997. pap. 23.95 (*0-435-07413-X*, 07413) Heinemann.

— Marriage in Maradi: Gender & Culture in a Hausa Society in Niger, 1900-1989. LC 97-1610. (Social History of Africa Ser.). 1997. 60.00 (*0-435-07414-8*, 07414) Heinemann.

Cooper, B. & Lane, D. R., eds. Veterinary Nursing, 2 vols. 2nd ed. 1994. pap. text. write for info. (*0-08-042289-6*, Pergamon Pr) Elsevier.

Cooper, B., jt. auth. see Lane, D. R.

Cooper, B., jt. ed. see Lane, D. R.

Cooper, B. A. & Whitehead, V. Michael, eds. Chemistry & Biology of Pteridines, 1986 - Pteridines & Folic Acid Derivatives: Proceedings of the 8th International Symposium. xxviii, 1048p. (C). 1986. lib. bdg. 292.35 (*3-11-010771-6*) De Gruyter.

Cooper, B. A. & Zittoun, J., eds. Folates & Cobalamines. (Illus.). 305p. 1989. 126.00 (*0-387-50653-5*) Spr-Verlag.

Cooper, B. Lee. Images of American Society in Popular Music: A Guide to Reflective Teaching. LC 81-18790. 1982. text 33.95 (*0-88229-514-4*) Burnham Inc.

— Popular Music Perspectives: Ideas, Themes, & Patterns in Contemporary Lyrics. LC 90-83700. 216p. (C). 1991. 39.95 (*0-87972-505-2*); pap. 19.95 (*0-87972-506-0*) Bowling Green Univ Popular Press.

— A Resource Guide to Themes in Contemporary American Song Lyrics, 1950-1985. LC 85-21933. (Illus.). 481p. 1986. lib. bdg. 85.00 (*0-313-24516-9*, CPI/, Greenwood Pr) Greenwood.

Cooper, B. Lee & Haney, Wayne S. Response Recordings: An Answer Song Discography, 1950-1990. LC 90-8728. 296p. 1990. 36.00 (*0-8108-2342-X*) Scarecrow.

Cooper, B. Lee & Haney, Wayne S. Rock Music in American Popular Culture: Rock & Roll Resources. LC 93-15554. (Illus.). 320p. 1995. pap. 29.95 (*1-56023-853-4*, Harrington Park) Haworth Pr.

Cooper, B. Lee & Haney, Wayne S. Rock Music in American Popular Culture: Rock & Roll Resources. LC 93-15554. (Illus.). 386p. 1995. lib. bdg. 49.95 (*1-56024-861-0*) Haworth Pr.

— Rock Music in American Popular Culture No. II: More Rock 'N' Roll Resources. LC 96-7919. (Illus.). 404p. (C). 1997. 39.95 (*1-56023-877-1*, Harrington Park) Haworth Pr.

— Rock Music in American Popular Culture No. II: More Rock 'n Roll Resources. 1996. 39.95 (*0-614-20831-9*) Haworth Pr.

— Rock Music in American Popular Culture No. III: More Rock 'n' Roll Resources. LC 99-10097. 358p. 1999. pap. 29.95 (*0-7890-0490-9*) Haworth Pr.

— Rock Music in American Popular Culture No. III: More Rock n' Roll Resources. LC 99-10097. 358p. 1999. lib. bdg. 59.95 (*0-7890-0489-5*) Haworth Pr.

— Rockabilly: A Bibliographic Resource Guide. LC 90-49760. 372p. 1990. 45.00 (*0-8108-2386-1*) Scarecrow.

Cooper, B. Lee, jt. auth. see Hoffmann, Frank.

Cooper, B. Lee, jt. auth. see Walker, Donald E.

Cooper, B. R. & Petrakis, L., eds. Chemistry & Physics of Coal Utilization - 1980 (APS, Morgantown) LC 81-65106. (AIP Conference Proceedings Ser.: No. 70). 472p. 1981. lib. bdg. 34.50 (*0-88318-169-X*) Am Inst Physics.

Cooper, B. Z. The Idea of God: A Whiteheadian Critique of St. Thomas Aquinas' Concept of God. 136p. 1974. pap. text 50.50 (*90-247-1591-1*, Pub. by M Nijhoff) Kluwer Academic.

Cooper Back, Mary W., jt. auth. see Lamb, Ruth M.

***Cooper, Barbara.** The Choosing. large type ed. LC 99-41389. 219p. 1999. 30.00 (*0-7862-2177-1*) Thorndike Pr.

Cooper, Barbara. Fortune's Kiss. large type ed. 432p. 1997. 27.99 (*0-7089-3806-X*) Ulverscroft.

— Multiple Choice Questions in Veterinary Nursing, Vol. 1. LC 97-185352. 132p. 1997. pap. text 25.00 (*0-7506-3611-4*) Buttrwrth-Heinemann.

— Multiple Choice Questions in Veterinary Nursing, Vol. 2. LC 97-185352. 132p. 1997. pap. text 25.00 (*0-7506-3612-2*) Buttrwrth-Heinemann.

***Cooper, Barbara.** The Penny Road. 392p. 2000. 31.99 (*0-7089-4214-8*) Ulverscroft.

Cooper, Barbara A. Winds of Passion. 1981. mass mkt. 2.75 (*0-89083-778-3*, Zebra Kensgtn) Kensgtn Pub Corp.

Cooper, Barbara E., jt. auth. see Somer, John.

Cooper, Barbara M. Marriage in Maradi: Gender & Culture in a Hausa Society in Niger, 1900-1989. LC 97-1610. l, 228 p. 1997. pap. write for info. (*0-85255-627-6*) Heinemann.

Cooper, Barbara T. & Donaldson-Evans, Mary, eds. Modernity & Revolution in Late Nineteenth-Century France. LC 91-50645. (Illus.). 176p. 1992. 35.00 (*0-87413-447-1*) U Delaware Pr.

***Cooper, Barry.** Beethoven. (Master Musicians Ser.). (Illus.). 400p. 2000. 35.00 (*0-19-816598-6*) OUP.

Cooper, Barry. Beethoven & the Creative Process. (Illus.). 336p. 1993. reprint ed. pap. text 28.00 (*0-19-816353-3*) OUP.

— Beethoven's Folksong Settings: Chronology, Sources, Style. (Illus.). 282p. 1994. text 55.00 (*0-19-816283-9*) OUP.

— Dictionnaire Beethoven. (FRE.). 600p. 1991. 195.00 (*0-8288-9447-7*) Fr & Eur.

***Cooper, Barry.** Eric Voegelin & the Foundations of Modern Political Science. LC 99-24837. 488p. 1999. 44.95 (*0-8262-1229-8*) U of Mo Pr.

Cooper, Barry. Merleau-Ponty & Marxism: From Terror to Reform. LC 78-16829. 239p. reprint ed. pap. 74.10 (*0-8357-3635-0*, 203636300003) Bks Demand.

— Michel Foucault: An Introductory Study of His Thought. LC 82-8260. (Studies in Religion & Society: Vol. 2). 170p. (C). 1982. lib. bdg. 79.95 (*0-88946-867-2*) E Mellen.

— The Political Theory of Eric Voegelin. LC 86-23517. (Toronto Studies in Theology: Vol. 27). 256p. 1986. lib. bdg. 89.95 (*0-88946-771-4*) E Mellen.

— The Restoration of Political Science & the Crisis of Modernity. LC 89-12335. (Studies in Social & Political Theory: Vol. 6). 320p. 1990. lib. bdg. 99.95 (*0-88946-106-6*) E Mellen.

— Sins of Omission: Critical Studies of CBC Television News. 224p. (C). 1994. text 29.95 (*0-8020-0597-7*) U of Toronto Pr.

Cooper, Barry, et al, eds. The Resurgence of Conservatism in Anglo-American Democracies. LC 87-22270. vii, 468p. (C). 1987. text 59.95 (*0-8223-0709-X*); pap. text 22.95 (*0-8223-0793-6*) Duke.

Cooper, Barry & Mairead, Dunne. Assessing Children's Mathematical Knowledge: Social Class, Sex & Problem-Solving. LC 99-21687. 1999. 28.95 (*0-335-20316-7*) OpUniv Pr.

Cooper, Barry, jt. ed. see Emberley, Peter.

Cooper, Barry, ed. see Schlosser, Johann A.

Cooper, Barry, ed. & intro. see Voegelin, Eric.

Cooper, Basil. No Letters from the Grave. large type ed. (Linford Mystery Library). 240p. 1998. pap. 17.99 (*0-7089-5223-2*, Linford) Ulverscroft.

Cooper, Belinda, ed. War Crimes: The Legacy of Nuremberg. (Illus.). 352p. 1998. 29.95 (*1-57500-009-1*, Pub. by TV Bks) HarpC.

Cooper, Belinda, tr. see Aly, Gotz, et al.

Cooper, Belinda, tr. see Pross, Christian.

***Cooper, Belton Y.** Death Traps: The Survival of an American Armor Division in World War II. 352p. 2000. pap. 19.95 (*0-89141-722-2*) Presidio Pr.

Cooper, Belton Y. Death Traps: The Survival of an American Armored Division in World War II. LC 98-16672. 352p. 1998. 28.95 (*0-89141-670-6*, Pub. by Presidio Pr) Natl Bk Netwk.

Cooper, Ben. Blind Luck. LC 98-92759. 355p. 1998. 24.00 (*0-9663548-7-7*) Heritage Prod.

Cooper, Bernard. Maps to Anywhere. LC 89-11864. 160p. 1997. pap. 12.95 (*0-8203-1946-5*) U of Ga Pr.

— Truth Serum: Memoirs. 224p. 1997. pap. 11.00 (*0-395-85994-8*, Mariner Bks) HM.

Cooper, Bernard R., ed. Scientific Problems of Coal Utilization: Proceedings. LC 78-9553. (DOE Symposium Ser.). 409p. 1978. pap. 18.50 (*0-87079-400-0*, CONF-770509); fiche 9.00 (*0-87079-378-0*, CONF-770509) DOE.

Cooper, Bernard R. & Ellingson, William A., eds. The Science & Technology of Coal & Coal Utilization. 682p. 1984. 135.00 (*0-306-41436-8*, Plenum Trade) Perseus Pubng.

Cooper, Bill. Imitators of God: A Study of Seventeen Qualities of Spiritual Growth. 258p. (Orig.). 1996. pap. text 12.00 (*1-57502-316-4*) Morris Pubng.

***Cooper, Bill.** Outdoor Celebrities Cookbook. (Illus.). 270p. 1999. 21.95 (*0-9672035-0-3*) Dry Creek Pr.

Cooper, Bill. The Rider's Guidebook. 2nd ed. (Illus.). 32p. 1994. pap. 4.95 (*1-884313-00-0*) Whitehorse NH.

Cooper, Bill & Cooper, Laurel. Back Door to Byzantium: To the Black Sea by the Great Rivers of Europe. LC 97-28393. (Illus.). 224p. 1997. pap. 17.95 (*1-57409-043-7*) Sheridan.

— Sail into the Sunset. (Illus.). 160p. 1994. pap. 27.50 (*0-7136-3951-2*) Sheridan.

— Sell up & Sail: Taking the Ulysses Option. 2nd ed. 1996. pap. text 29.95 (*0-07-021529-4*) McGraw.

— Sell up & Sail: Taking the Ulysses Option. 3rd ed. LC 97-37677. (Illus.). 336p. 1998. pap. 29.95 (*1-57409-046-1*) Sheridan.

— Watersteps Round Europe: From Greece to England by Barge. LC 96-8267. (Illus.). 176p. 1996. pap. 17.95 (*1-57409-016-X*) Sheridan.

— Watersteps Through France: To the Camargue by Canal. (Illus.). 192p. 1996. pap. 17.95 (*1-57409-017-8*) Sheridan.

Cooper, Bo & Cooper, Lacey. Epictetus: The Discourses: A Classical Guide to Freedom & Happiness. LC 91-158556. 339p. (Orig.). 1990. pap. 19.90 (*0-9628187-5-5*) B&L Cooper.

Cooper, Bob. San Francisco Running Guide. LC 97-47673. (City Running Guide Ser.). (Illus.). 160p. 1998. pap. 16.95 (*0-88011-703-6*, PCOO0703) Human Kinetics.

— Saxophone Method. 136p. 1984. pap. 10.95 (*0-7866-0530-8*, 93472) Mel Bay.

Cooper, Bob, jt. auth. see McCormack, Bill.

Cooper, Brenda. Magical Realism in West African Fiction: Seeing with a Third Eye. LC 97-35008. (Routledge Research in Postcolonial Studies). 264p. (C). 1998. 75.00 (*0-415-18239-5*) Routledge.

Cooper, Brenda & Steyn, Andrew, eds. Transgressing Boundaries: New Directions in the Study of Culture in Africa. 240p. 1997. pap. text 27.95 (*0-8214-1183-7*) Ohio U Pr.

***Cooper, Brian.** Searching the Internet. 72p. 2000. pap. 6.95 (*0-7894-6370-9*) DK Pub Inc.

Cooper, Brian, ed. Assessing the Handicaps & Needs of Mentally Retarded Children. LC 81-66374. 1981. text 104.00 (*0-12-188020-6*) Acad Pr.

— The Epidemiology of Psychiatric Disorders. LC 86-21372. 421p. 1987. reprint ed. pap. 130.60 (*0-608-05936-6*, 206627300008) Bks Demand.

Cooper, Brian & Eastwood, Robin. Primary Health Care & Psychiatric Epidemiology. 320p. (C). 1992. text 110.00 (*0-415-07073-2*, A6619) Routledge.

Cooper, Brian G. Meeting Famous Christians. (Illus.). 111p. 1977. pap. 6.50 (*0-85597-205-X*) Attic Pr.

Cooper, Bruce, jt. auth. see Vitullo-Martin, Thomas.

Cooper, Bruce C. & Hart, Gene. The Hockey Trivia Book. LC 84-757. (Illus.). 144p. (Orig.). reprint ed. pap. 44.70 (*0-608-20822-1*, 207192100003) Bks Demand.

Cooper, Bruce E. & Cumming, Jeffrey M. Diptera Types in the National Collection of Insects Pt. 2: Brachycera. 112p. (Orig.). 1993. pap. 32.45 (*0-660-57979-0*, Pub. by Canadian Govt Pub) Accents Pubns.

Cooper, Bruce S., ed. Labor Relations in Education: An International Perspective, 54. LC 91-37121. (Contributions to the Study of Education Ser.: No. 54). 384p. 1992. 65.00 (*0-313-26707-3*, CIH/, Greenwood Pr) Greenwood.

Cooper, Bruce S. & Randall, E. Vance. Accuracy of Advocacy: The Politics of Research in Education. (Yearbook of the Politics of Education Association Ser.). (Illus.). 232p. 1999. 55.95 (*0-8039-6777-2*); pap. 24.95 (*0-8039-6778-0*) Corwin Pr.

Cooper, Bruce S., jt. auth. see Doyle, Denis P.

Cooper, Bryan. The Tenth Irish Division in Gallipoli. 172p. 1993. pap. 22.95 (*0-7165-2517-8*, Pub. by Irish Acad Pr) Intl Spec Bk.

Cooper, Burton Z. Why God? LC 87-21499. 132p. 1988. pap. 17.95 (*0-8042-0731-3*) Westminster John Knox.

Cooper, C. Change Partners. mass mkt. 6.95 (*0-7472-5401-X*, Pub. by Headline Bk Pub) Trafalgar.

— Green Silk. mass mkt. 6.95 (*0-7472-5289-0*, Pub. by Headline Bk Pub) Trafalgar.

— Liaison Intoxication. 1998. mass mkt. 6.95 (*0-7472-5820-1*, Pub. by Headline Bk Pub) Trafalgar.

— Liaison Seduction. 1997. mass mkt. 6.95 (*0-7472-5627-6*, Pub. by Headline Bk Pub) Trafalgar.

— Liaison Temptation. 1997. mass mkt. 6.95 (*0-7472-5628-4*, Pub. by Headline Bk Pub) Trafalgar.

Cooper, C. David & Alley, F. C. Air Pollution Control: A Design Approach. 2nd rev. ed. (Illus.). 694p. (C). 1994. text 63.95 (*0-88133-758-7*) Waveland Pr.

Cooper, C. David, et al. Foundations of Environmental Engineering. 369p. 1999. 54.95 (*1-57766-048-X*) Waveland Pr.

Cooper, C. David, ed. see Wanielista, Martin P., et al.

Cooper, C. E., jt. ed. see Brown, G. C.

Cooper, C. Everett. Up Your Asteroid! A Science Fiction Farce. LC 77-866. 47p. 1977. pap. 13.00 (*0-89370-206-4*) Millefleurs.

Cooper, C. L. Psychosocial Factors at Work & Their Relation to Health. Kalimo, R. et al, eds. 254p. 1987. pap. text 39.00 (*92-4-156102-5*, 1150264) World Health.

Cooper, C. L., ed. Group Training for Individual & Organizational Development. (Interpersonal Development Ser.: Vol. 3, Nos. 1-4). (Illus.). 1973. 52.25 (*3-8055-1481-6*) S Karger.

Cooper, C. L. & Robertson, Ivan T., eds. International Review of Industrial & Organizational Psychology, 1991, Vol. 6. LC 86-643874. 412p. 1991. 300.00 (*0-471-92819-4*) Wiley.

Cooper, C. L., jt. auth. see Sloan, S. J.

Cooper, C. P. Progress in Tourism, Recreation & Hospitality Management, Vol. 4. Lockwood, A., ed. (Progress in Tourism, Recreation & Management Ser.: Vol. 4). 224p. 1993. 195.00 (*0-471-94512-9*) Wiley.

Cooper, C. P., ed. Progress in Tourism, Recreation & Hospitality Management, Vol. 1. (Progress in Tourism, Recreation & Management Ser.: Vol. 1). 224p. 1993. 185.00 (*0-471-94509-9*) Wiley.

Cooper, C. P. & Lockwood, A, eds. Progress in Tourism, Recreation & Hospitality Management, Vol. 5. (Progress in Tourism, Recreation & Management Ser.: Vol. 5). 327p. 1994. 185.00 (*0-471-94433-5*) Wiley.

Cooper, C. P. & Lockwood, A., eds. Progress in Tourism, Recreation & Hospitality Management, Vol. 6. (Progress in Tourism, Recreation & Management Ser.: Vol. 6). 314p. 1995. 185.00 (*0-471-94859-4*) Wiley.

Cooper, C. S. & Grover, P. L., eds. Chemical Carcinogenesis & Mutagenesis I. (Handbook of Experimental Pharmacology Ser.: Vol. 94-I). (Illus.). 656p. 1989. 421.95 (*0-387-51182-2*, 3138) Spr-Verlag.

— Chemical Carcinogenesis & Mutagenesis II. (Handbook of Experimental Pharmacology Ser.: Vol. 94, Pt. 2). (Illus.). 510p. 1990. 348.95 (*0-387-51183-0*, 3316) Spr-Verlag.

Cooper, Camille. Liquorlicious: Alcohol Beverage Cookbook. Wittig, Robert, ed. (Illus.). (Orig.). 1994. pap. 19.95 (*0-9640349-3-X*) Unorthodox Pr.

Cooper, Carey L., ed. Psychosocial Stress & Cancer. LC 84-5264. 280p. 1985. 340.00 (*0-471-90477-5*) Wiley.

Cooper, Carl, jt. auth. see Humble, Lance.

Cooper, Carl R., jt. auth. see Grieco, Peter L., Jr.

***Cooper, Carol.** Baby & Child Question & Answer Book. LC 99-59614. (Illus.). 240p. 2000. pap. text 19.95 (*0-7894-5155-7*, D K Ink) DK Pub Inc.

Cooper, Carol, et al. Keys to Excellence. 3rd ed. 336p. (C). 1996. pap. text, per. 28.29 (*0-7872-1352-7*) Kendall-Hunt.

Cooper, Carole L., jt. auth. see Stanley, David T.

Cooper, Caroline, et al. Differentiated Case Management: Implementation Manual. (Illus.). 137p. (Orig.). (C). 1994. pap. text 40.00 (*0-7881-1302-X*) DIANE Pub.

***Cooper, Carolyn.** The Art of Nursing: A Practical Introduction. LC 00-33000. (Illus.). 2001. write for info. (*0-7216-8216-2*) Saunders.

Cooper, Carolyn. Noises in the Blood: Orality, Gender, & the "Vulgar" Body of Jamaican Popular Culture. LC 94-37826. 240p. 1995. text 49.95 (*0-8223-1580-7*); pap. text 17.95 (*0-8223-1595-5*) Duke.

Cooper, Carolyn, ed. see Hodge, Jeffrey.

Cooper, Carolyn, ed. see Watkins, Dawn L.

Cooper, Cary. Essence of Stress Management. 208p. (C). 1999. pap. 19.95 (*0-13-312042-2*) P-H.

Cooper, Cary & Lewis, Suzan. How to Manage Your Career & Family: Getting the Balance Right. (Daily Telegraph Lifeplanner Ser.). 160p. 1998. pap. 19.95 (*0-7494-2528-8*) Kogan Page Ltd.

Cooper, Cary & Travers, Cheryl. Teachers under Pressure: Stress in the Teaching Profession. LC 95-9587. 248p. (C). 1995. pap. 25.99 (*0-415-09484-4*) Routledge.

Cooper, Cary, jt. auth. see Earnshaw, Jill.

***Cooper, Cary L.** Industrial/Organizational Psychology. 440p. 1999. 212.50 (*0-471-98666-6*) Wiley.

Cooper, Cary L. Learning from Others in Groups: Experimental Learning Approaches. LC 78-26987. (Illus.). 304p. 1979. 55.00 (*0-313-20922-7*, COL/, Greenwood Pr) Greenwood.

***Cooper, Cary L.** Organizational Psychology. (Manchester Business & Management Series). 432p. 2000. pap. 54.95 (*0-631-20992-1*) Blackwell Pubs.

— Theories of Organizational Stress. LC 99-88862. 296p. 2000. pap. 29.95 (*0-19-829705-X*) OUP.

— Who's Who in the Management Sciences. LC 00-34799. 2000. write for info. incl. cd-rom (*1-84064-488-5*) E Elgar.

***Cooper, Cary L., ed.** Classics in Management Thought, 2 vols. LC 00-25514. (Mini Ser.). 1440p. 2000. 495.00 (*1-85898-911-6*) E Elgar.

Cooper, Cary L., ed. Handbook of Stress, Medicine, & Health. LC 95-7307. 400p. 1995. boxed set 139.95 (*0-8493-2908-6*, 2908C2W) CRC Pr.

— Industrial & Organizational Psychology, 2 vols., Set. (International Library of Critical Writings in Business History). 1280p. (C). 1992. lib. bdg. 325.00 (*0-8147-1457-9*) NYU Pr.

— Industrial Organ Psychology, Vol. I. (C). 1992. lib. bdg. 175.00 (*0-8147-1455-2*) NYU Pr.

— Industrial Organ Psychology, Vol. 2. (C). 1992. lib. bdg. 175.00 (*0-8147-1456-0*) NYU Pr.

— Organizational Development in the U. K., U. S. A. A Joint Evaluation. LC 77-15084. 1978. text 12.00 (*0-89433-069-1*) Petrocelli.

— Stress & Breast Cancer. LC 87-19000. (Wiley Medical Publication Ser.). (Illus.). 229p. reprint ed. pap. 71.00 (*0-608-07299-0*, 206752700009) Bks Demand.

— Stress Research: Issues for the Eighties. LC 82-11049. (Illus.). 159p. reprint ed. pap. 49.30 (*0-8357-3105-7*, 203936100012) Bks Demand.

— Theories of Group Processes. LC 74-28089. 289p. reprint ed. pap. 89.60 (*0-608-30161-2*, 205185500011) Bks Demand.

— Theories of Organizational Stress. LC 98-35996. (Illus.). 294p. 1999. text 65.00 (*0-19-852279-7*) OUP.

***Cooper, Cary L., ed.** Who's Who in the Management Sciences. LC 00-20570. 512p. 2000. write for info. (*1-84064-237-8*) E Elgar.

Cooper, Cary L. & Alderfer, Clayton P., eds. Advances in Experiential Social Processes. LC 77-22060. 235p. reprint ed. pap. 72.90 (*0-8357-5162-7*, 203037300001) Bks Demand.

Cooper, Cary L. & Argyris, Chris, eds. The Blackwell Encyclopedia of Management, 12 vols. (C). 1997. 1200.00 (*1-57718-035-6*) Blackwell Pubs.

— The Concise Blackwell Encyclopedia of Management. LC 98-9489. 880p. 1998. 100.00 (*0-631-20885-2*); pap. 39.95 (*0-631-20911-5*) Blackwell Pubs.

***Cooper, Cary L. & Burke, Ronald J., eds.** Organizational Psychology. (Manchester Business & Management Series). 432p. 2000. 74.95 (*0-631-20991-3*) Blackwell Pubs.

Cooper, Cary L. & Cartwright, Susan. Managing Workplace Stress. LC 96-25274. 185p. 1996. 34.00 (*0-7619-0192-2*); pap. 15.95 (*0-7619-0193-0*) Sage.

Cooper, Cary L. & Jackson, Susan E. Creating Tomorrow's Organizations: A Handbook for Future Research in Organizational Behavior. LC 96-53015. 536p. 1997. 165.50 (*0-471-97239-8*) Wiley.

Cooper, Cary L. & Kompier, Michiel. Preventing Stress, Improving Productivity: European Case Studies in the Workplace. LC 98-35612. 10p. 1999. write for info. (*0-415-16556-3*); pap. write for info. (*0-415-16557-1*) Routledge.

Cooper, Cary L. & Marshall, Judi. Understanding Executive Stress. LC 77-16077. 1978. text 17.50 (*0-89433-059-4*) Petrocelli.

Cooper, Cary L. & Marshall, Judi, eds. White Collar & Professional Stress. LC 79-41779. (Wiley Series on Studies in Occupational Stress). 271p. reprint ed. pap. 84.10 (*0-608-18143-9*, 203283000081) Bks Demand.

Cooper, Cary L. & Mumford, Enid, eds. The Quality of Working Life in Western & Eastern Europe, 25. LC 78-27692. (Contributions in Economics & Economic History Ser.: No. 25). 348p. 1979. 75.00 (*0-313-20957-X*, CWL/, Greenwood Pr) Greenwood.

Cooper, Cary L. & Payne, Roy, eds. Stress at Work. LC 77-9626. (Wiley Series on Studies in Occupational Stress). (Illus.). 305p. reprint ed. pap. 94.60 (*0-608-18142-0*, 203282900081) Bks Demand.

Cooper, Cary L. & Pervin, Lawrence A. Personality: Critical Concepts, 4 vols. LC 97-32757. 1664p. (C). 1998. reprint ed. 700.00 (*0-415-13504-4*) Routledge.

Cooper, Cary L. & Robertson, Ivan T., eds. International Review of Industrial & Organizational Psychology, Vol. 95. 384p. 1995. 250.00 (*0-471-95241-9*) Wiley.

***Cooper, Cary L. & Robertson, Ivan T., eds.** International Review of Industrial & Organizational Psychology Vol. 15: 2000, Vol. 15, 2000. 456p. 2000. 195.00 (0-471-85855-2) Wiley.

Cooper, Cary L. & Robertson, Ivan T., eds. International Review of Industrial & Organizational Psychology, 1986. LC 86-643874. 352p. pap. 109.20 (0-7837-0112-8, 2040389000016) Bks Demand.

— International Review of Industrial & Organizational Psychology, 1996, Vol. 96. 332p. 1997. 250.00 (0-471-96111-6) Wiley.

— International Review of Industrial & Organizational Psychology, 1997, Vol. 199. 422p. 1997. 250.00 (0-471-97004-2) Wiley.

— Key Reviews in Managerial Psychology: Concepts & Research for Practice. LC 93-47088. 368p. 1994. pap. 89.95 (0-471-95010-6) Wiley.

Cooper, Cary L. & Smith, Michael J., eds. Job Stress & Blue Collar Work. LC 85-12022. (Wiley Series on Studies in Occupational Stress). (Illus.). 253p. 1985. reprint ed. pap. 78.50 (0-608-00193-7, 206097600006) Bks Demand.

Cooper, Cary L. & Sutherland, Valerie. Understanding Stress: A Psychological Perspective for Health Professionals. 250p. 1990. 19.95 (0-412-33930-7, A4406) Chapman & Hall.

Cooper, Cary L. & Torrington, Derek P., eds. After Forty: The Time for Achievement? LC 82-105750. (Illus.). 219p. reprint ed. pap. 67.90 (0-8357-4911-8, 203784100009) Bks Demand.

Cooper, Cary L. & Williams, Steve, eds. Creating Healthy Organizations. LC 92-2441. (Work, Well-Being & Stress Ser.). 266p. 1994. 109.95 (0-471-94345-2) Wiley.

Cooper, Cary L., jt. auth. see Davidson, Marilyn J.

Cooper, Cary L., jt. auth. see Hingley, Peter.

Cooper, Cary L., jt. auth. see Jones, Andrew N.

Cooper, Cary L., jt. auth. see Kahn, Howard.

Cooper, Cary L., jt. auth. see Marshall, Judi.

Cooper, Cary L., jt. auth. see Murphy, Lawrence R.

Cooper, Cary L., jt. auth. see Roney, Alex.

Cooper, Cary L., jt. auth. see Wills, Geoff.

Cooper, Cary L., jt. ed. see Alderfer, Clayton P.

Cooper, Cary L., jt. ed. see Davidson, Marilyn J.

Cooper, Cary L., jt. ed. see Markides, Kyriakos S.

Cooper, Cary L., jt. ed. see Marshall, Judi.

Cooper, Cary L., jt. ed. see Payne, Roy.

C

***Cooper, Catherine, et al, eds.** Amino Acid Analysis Protocols. LC 00-23798. (Methods in Molecular Biology Ser.: Vol. 159). 254p. 2000. 84.50 (0-89603-656-1) Humana.

Cooper, Cathie. The Storyteller's Cornucopia. 2nd ed. LC 98-39884. 1998. pap. 19.95 (1-57950-025-0, Alleyside) Highsmith Pr.

Cooper, Cathie H. ABC Books & Activities: From Preschool to High School. LC 95-9728. (School Library Media Ser.: No. 5). 164p. 1996. pap. 27.50 (0-8108-3013-2) Scarecrow.

— Counting Your Way Through 1-2-3: Books & Activities. LC 95-50639. (School Library Media Ser.: No. 8). 224p. 1997. pap. 33.50 (0-8108-3125-2) Scarecrow.

Cooper, Cathryn. Obsession. mass mkt. 6.95 (0-7472-5288-2, Pub. by Headline Bk Pub) Trafalgar.

***Cooper, Cecilia Romero.** Pearl/La Perla. 1999. mass mkt. 5.99 (0-7860-1036-3) Kensgtn Pub Corp.

Cooper, Charles. Researching Response to Literature & the Teaching of Literature: Points of Departure. LC 83-11826. 352p. 1985. pap. 39.50 (0-89391-323-5); text 73.25 (0-89391-184-4) Ablx Pub.

Cooper, Charles, ed. Science, Technology & Development: Political Economy of Technical Advance in Underdeveloped Countries. 204p. 1973. 45.00 (0-7146-2999-5, Pub. by F Cass Pubs) Intl Spec Bk.

— Technology & Innovation in the International Economy. 256p. 1994. 90.00 (1-85898-027-5) E Elgar.

Cooper, Charles & Kaplinsky, Raphael, eds. Technology & Development in the Third Industrial Revolution. 113p. 1990. text 35.00 (0-7146-3389-5, Pub. by F Cass Pubs) Intl Spec Bk.

Cooper, Charles & Odell, Lee. Evaluating Writing: The Role of Teacher's Knowledge about Text Learning, & Culture. LC 98-37174. 422p. (C). 1998. 29.95 (0-8141-1625-6) NCTE.

Cooper, Charles, jt. ed. see Anderson, Sara L.

Cooper, Charles L. & Fitzgerald, Eur, eds. Development Studies Revisited: Twenty-Five Years of the Journal of Development Studies. 548p. 1989. text 65.00 (0-7146-3376-3, Pub. by F Cass Pubs) Intl Spec Bk.

Cooper, Charles R. & Greenbaum, Sidney, eds. Studying Writing: Linguistic Approaches. LC 87-33673. (Written Communication Annual Ser.: No. 1). 272p. 1986. reprint ed. pap. 84.40 (0-608-01485-0, 205952900001) Bks Demand.

Cooper, Charles R., jt. auth. see Axelrod, Rise B.

Cooper, Charles W., jt. auth. see Zingaro, Ralph.

Cooper, Charlie & Cooper, Ann. Tuskegee's Heroes: As Depicted in the Aviation Art of Roy E. La Grone. LC 96-2735. (Illus.). 156p. 1996. 29.95 (0-7603-0254-5) MBI Pubg.

Cooper, Charlie, jt. ed. see Hawtin, Murray.

Cooper, Charlotte. Fat & Proud. pap. 15.95 (0-7043-4473-4, Pub. by Womens Press) Trafalgar.

Cooper, Charlotte. 50 Object Stories for Children. (Object Lesson Ser.). 126p. 1987. pap. 7.99 (0-8010-2523-0) Baker Bks.

Cooper-Chen, Anne. Games in the Global Village. pap. 15.95 (0-87972-599-0) Bowling Green Univ Popular Press.

Cooper-Chen, Anne. Games in the Global Village: A 50-Nation Study of Entertainment Television. LC 93-73820. (Illus.). 319p. 1994. 36.95 (0-87972-598-2) Bowling Green Univ Popular Press.

Cooper-Chen, Anne & Kodama, Miiko. Mass Communication in Japan. LC 97-9167. (Illus.). 1997. 39.95 (0-8138-2710-8) Iowa St U Pr.

Cooper, Chester L., ed. Growth in America, 21. LC 75-35359. (Contributions in American Studies: No. 21). (Illus.). 262p. 1976. 59.95 (0-8371-8596-3, CGA/, Greenwood Pr) Greenwood.

Cooper, Chip, photos by. Silent in the Land. (Illus.). 192p. 1993. 45.00 (0-9636713-0-8) CKM Pr.

***Cooper, Chris.** Devil's Advocate: The Art of COOP. (Illus.). 2000. pap. 25.00 (0-9670566-6-7) Westhampton Hse.

Cooper, Chris. Matter. LC 92-6928. (Eyewitness Books). (Illus.). 64p. (J). (gr. 4-7). 1992. 15.95 (1-879431-88-2) DK Pub Inc.

Cooper, Chris, jt. auth. see Boniface, Brian G.

Cooper, Chris P., jt. auth. see Boniface, Brian G.

Cooper, Christine, jt. auth. see Schaffer, Matt.

***Cooper, Christopher.** Mediation & Arbitration by Patrol Police Officers. LC 99-18895. 88p. 1999. pap. 14.50 (0-7618-1368-3) U Pr of Amer.

— The Solar System. LC 99-44322. (Science Fact Files Ser.). 2001. 27.12 (0-7398-1006-5) Raintree Steck-V.

***Cooper, Christopher B. & Storer, Thomas W.** Exercise Testing & Interpretation: A Practical Guide. (Illus.). 250p. (C). 2000. pap. write for info. (0-521-64842-4) Cambridge U Pr.

Cooper, Christopher P., et al. Educating the Educators in Tourism: A Manual of Tourism & Hospitality Education. LC 97-108124. (Tourism Education & Training Ser.). xxi, 221p. 1996. pap. 30.00 (92-844-0151-8, Pub. by Wrld Tourism Org) Bernan Associates.

Cooper, Clancy B. Condensed Pascal with Oh Lightspeed. (C). 1989. pap. text 55.00 (0-393-96021-8) Norton.

Cooper, Clancy J. B. Using Quickmod. pap. 96.00 (0-393-99531-3) Norton.

Cooper, Clare. Ashar of Qarius. LC 89-24522. 163p. (J). (gr. 3-7). 1990. 14.95 (0-15-200409-2, Gulliver Bks) Harcourt.

— The Black Horn. (Simon Jones & the Wizard Trilogy Ser.: Vol. I). 145p. (J). (gr. 4). 1994. pap. 11.95 (0-8464-4834-3) Beekman Pubs.

— Cat of Morfa. 128p. (J). (gr. 4-12). 1998. pap. 14.95 (0-8464-4907-2) Beekman Pubs.

— The Kings of the Mountain. (Simon Jones & the Wizard Trilogy Ser.: Vol. III). 124p. (J). (gr. 4). 1994. pap. 10.95 (0-8464-4809-2) Beekman Pubs.

— Marya's Emmets. 151p. (J). (gr. 4-8). 1996. pap. 14.95 (0-8464-4632-4) Beekman Pubs.

— Marya's Emmets LC 97-202606. 152p. (YA). (gr. 5-8). 1996. write for info. (1-85902-289-8) Gomer Pr.

— Miracles & Rubies. 69p. (J). (gr. 4). 1992. pap. 7.95 (0-8464-4847-5) Beekman Pubs.

— Time Loft. 2nd ed. 127p. (J). (gr. 4). 1997. reprint ed. pap. 12.95 (0-8464-4810-6) Beekman Pubs.

— A Wizard Called Jones. (Simon Jones & the Wizard Trilogy Ser.: Vol. II). 124p. (J). (gr. 4). 1994. pap. 10.95 (0-8464-4808-4) Beekman Pubs.

Cooper, Clarence, Jr. Black. LC 96-30313. 320p. 1997. pap. 12.00 (0-393-31541-X) Norton.

— The Farm. LC 95-42494. 236p. 1998. pap. 13.00 (0-393-31785-4) Norton.

— The Farm. 240p. 1996. reprint ed. pap. 12.95 (0-86241-600-0, Pub. by Payback Pr) AK Pr Dist.

Cooper, Clarence L., Jr. The Scene. LC 96-8036. (Old School Bks.). 1996. pap. 11.00 (0-393-31463-4, Norton Paperbks) Norton.

Cooper, Clifford D. The Runt Pig Principle: A Fundamental Approach to Solving Problems & Creating Value. LC 92-81924. 184p. (Orig.). 1992. pap. 12.95 (0-9633046-0-7) Alliance Prog.

Cooper Clinic, Nutrition Department Staff. What's Cooking at the Cooper Clinic. 1992. pap. 14.95 (0-9633862-0-4) Its Cooking.

***Cooper, Colin.** Individual Difference Reader. 448p. 2000. 55.00 (1-85343-447-7, Pub. by Free Assoc Bks); pap. 25.00 (1-85343-453-1, Pub. by Free Assoc Bks) Intl Spec Bk.

Cooper, Colin. Individual Differences. LC 97-12827. 368p. 1997. pap. text 19.95 (0-340-66274-3, Pub. by E A) OUP.

— Individual Differences. LC 97-12827. (Illus.). 368p. 1997. text 60.00 (0-340-66273-5) OUP.

— Intelligence & Abilities. LC 98-42127. (Psychology Focus Ser.). 1999. 50.00 (0-415-18868-7); pap. 16.99 (0-415-18869-5) Routledge.

Cooper, Colin & Varma, Ved P. Processes in Individual Differences. LC 96-52970. (Illus.). 192p. (C). 1997. 75.00 (0-415-14119-2) Routledge.

***Cooper, Colin S. & Fletcher, Jonathan A.** Translocations in Solid Tumors. (Medical Intelligence Unit Ser.). 262p. 2000. 99.00 (1-58706-033-7, Pub. by Eurekah) Landes Bioscience.

Cooper, Constance J. Curtis Paper Company: From Thomas Meeteer to the James River Corporation, Vol. 1. (Illus.). 64p. 1991. 23.95 (0-9657328-2-7, 50415) Cedar Tree Bks.

— To Market, To Market, in Wilmington Vol. 1: King Street & Beyond. (Illus.). xi, 54p. 1993. 23.95 (0-9657328-3-5, 103) Cedar Tree Bks.

***Cooper, Corinne.** The New Article 9. LC 99-35859. 1999. write for info. (1-57073-699-5) Amer Bar Assn.

— The New Article 9. 2nd ed. LC 00-33219. 2000. pap. write for info. (1-57073-831-9) Amer Bar Assn.

Cooper, Craig. Ohio. (Color My State Ser.). (J). 1994. pap. 6.95 (0-89133-249-9) Wiley.

Cooper, Cynthia. Magnificent Entertainments: Fancy Dress Balls of Canada's Governors General, 1876-1898. LC 98-151437. (Illus.). 185p. 1997. 36.95 (0-86492-187-X, Pub. by Goose Ln Edits) Genl Dist Srvs.

Cooper, Cynthia. She Got Game: My Personal Odyssey. LC 99-18907. (Illus.). 256p. 1999. 20.00 (0-446-52566-9, Pub. by Warner Bks) Little.

***Cooper, Cynthia.** She Got Game: My Personal Odyssey. (Illus.). 304p. 2000. mass mkt. 6.99 (0-446-60839-4) Warner Bks.

Cooper, Cynthia A. Violence on Television: Congressional Inquiry, Public Criticism & Industry Response: A Policy Analysis. LC 96-32884. 214p. 1996. pap. text 24.50 (0-7618-0477-3); lib. bdg. 44.50 (0-7618-0476-5) U Pr of Amer.

Cooper, Cynthia L. Insider's Guide to the Top Fifteen Law Schools. 416p. 1990. pap. 12.95 (0-385-24932-2) Doubleday.

— A Mockery of Justice: The True Story of the Sheppard Murder Case. LC 97-201401. 1997. mass mkt. 7.99 (0-451-40763-6, Onyx) NAL.

Cooper, Cynthia L. & Sheppard, Sam R. A Mockery of Justice: The True Story of the Sheppard Murder Case. LC 95-15809. 1995. 30.00 (1-55553-241-1) NE U Pr.

Cooper, D. & Kemp, E., eds. Xenotransplantation: The Transplantation of Organs & Tissues Between Species. 2nd ed. LC 96-39074. (Illus.). 850p. 1997. 355.00 (3-540-61777-9) Spr-Verlag.

Cooper, D. Jason. Esoteric Rune Magic: The Elder Futhark in Magic, Astral Projection, & Spiritual Development. LC 94-10749. (World Magic Ser.). (Illus.). 240p. 1994. pap. 12.00 (1-56718-174-0) Llewellyn Pubns.

— Mithras: Mysteries & Initiations Rediscovered. LC 96-10326. (Illus.). 192p. 1996. pap. 12.95 (0-87728-865-8) Weiser.

— The Power of Dreaming: Messages from Your Inner Self. LC 95-31175. (Llewellyn's Strategies for Success Ser.). 224p. 1999. pap. 12.00 (1-56718-175-9) Llewellyn Pubns.

***Cooper, D. Jason.** Power of Dreaming: Messages from Your Inner Self. 2000. 7.99 (0-7858-1195-8) Bk Sales Inc.

Cooper, D. K., et al, eds. The Transplantation & Replacement of Thoracic Organs: The Present Status of Biological & Mechanical Replacement of the Heart & Lungs. 2nd ed. LC 97-136519. 830p. 1997. text 350.00 (0-7923-8898-4) Kluwer Academic.

Cooper, D. K. & Lanza, R. P., eds. Heart Transplantation. 1984. text 193.50 (0-85200-862-7) Kluwer Academic.

Cooper, D. Mark & Dean, Rose B. Get a Life: A Second Chance after 50. LC 96-77885. 300p. (Orig.). 1997. pap. 15.95 (1-882480-23-6) Info Intl.

Cooper, D. N. & Krawczak, M. Human Gene Mutation. (Human Molecular Genetics Ser.). (Illus.). 416p. 1993. 142.50 (1-872748-41-4, Pub. by Bios Sci) Coronet Bks.

Cooper, D. N. & Krawczak, M., eds. Venous Thrombosis: From Genes to Clinical Medicine. (Human Molecular Genetics Ser.). (Illus.). 352p. 1997. 150.00 (1-872748-94-5, Pub. by Bios Sci) Bks Intl VA.

Cooper, D. N., jt. auth. see Farzaneh, F.

Cooper, D. N., jt. auth. see Lemoine, N.

Cooper, Dale. Ephesians: Uniting Against Evil. LC 96-46428. (Revelation Ser.). 64p. (Orig.). 1996. pap., student ed. 4.95 (1-56212-223-1, 1310-0400) CRC Pubns.

— First & Second Thessalonians: Longing for the Lord: Study Guide. LC 93-14319. (Revelation Series for Adults). 1995. pap., student ed. 4.95 (1-56212-045-X) CRC Pubns.

— Psalms: Speaking Honestly with God (Study) 2nd ed. LC 97-45091. (Revelation Series for Adults). 64p. 1998. pap. text, student ed. 4.95 (1-56212-333-5, 1312-8800) CRC Pubns.

Cooper, Dan. Enrico Fermi: And the Revolutions of Modern Physics. Gingerich, Owen, ed. LC 98-34471. (Oxford Portraits in Science Ser.). (Illus.). 120p. (YA). (gr. 7 up). 1999. 22.00 (0-19-511762-X) OUP.

Cooper, Dana, ed. see Dean, James & Hait, Pam.

Cooper, Darien. Hinds Feet on High Places: Devotional. 1999. pap. text 13.99 (0-7684-2035-0) Destiny Image.

Cooper, Darien, ed. The Beauty of Beholding God. 196p. 1992. pap. 10.99 (0-914903-83-7) Destiny Image.

Cooper, Darien B. The Christian Woman's Planner. 160p. (Orig.). 1986. spiral bd. 9.95 (0-310-44621-X, 11742P) Zondervan.

— You Can Be the Wife of a Happy Husband. 156p. 1996. pap. text 9.99 (1-56476-711-6) Chariot Victor.

***Cooper, Darius.** The Cinema of Satyajit Ray: Between Tradition & Modernity. (Cambridge Studies in Film). (Illus.). 288p. 2000. 59.95 (0-521-62026-0) Cambridge U Pr.

— The Cinema of Satyajit Ray: Between Tradition & Modernity. LC 99-24768. (Cambridge Studies in Film). (Illus.). 288p. 2000. pap. 22.95 (0-521-62980-2) Cambridge U Pr.

Cooper, Darlen. You Can Be the Happy Mom of an Empty Nest. 1999. pap. 11.99 (1-56043-333-7, Treasure Hse) Destiny Image.

***Cooper, Dave.** Crumple. 2000. pap. 14.95 (1-56097-321-8) Fantagraph Bks.

Cooper, Dave. Suckle: The Status of Basil. 136p. 1996. pap. 14.95 (1-56097-301-3) Fantagraph Bks.

Cooper, David. Bartok: Concerto for Orchestra. (Cambridge Music Handbks.). 111p. (C). 1996. text 39.95 (0-521-48004-3); pap. text 13.95 (0-521-48505-3) Cambridge U Pr.

— A Companion to Aesthetics. 466p. 1995. pap. 31.95 (0-631-19659-5) Blackwell Pubs.

— Jazz Trumpet Solos. 48p. 1997. pap. 9.95 (0-7935-7011-5) H Leonard.

Cooper, David, et al, eds. Growing Diversity: Genetic Resources & Local Food Security. 166p. 1992. pap. 21.00 (1-85339-119-0, Pub. by Intermed Tech); text 47.50 (1-85339-123-9, Pub. by Intermed Tech) Stylus Pub VA.

Cooper, David & French, Peter, eds. The Manson Murders: A Philosophical Inquiry. LC 73-78119. 141p. 1974. pap. text 15.95 (0-87073-533-0) Schenkman Bks Inc.

Cooper, David, et al. Cultivando Diversidad. 208p. 1994. pap. 27.00 (1-85339-168-9, Pub. by Intermed Tech) Stylus Pub VA.

Cooper, David, et al. Z in Practice. 408p. 1995. pap. 48.00 (0-13-124934-7) P-H.

Cooper, David A. God Is a Verb: Kabbalah & the Practice of Mystical Judaism. 333p. 1998. pap. 14.00 (1-57322-694-7, Riverhd Trade) Berkley Pub.

***Cooper, David A.** The Handbook of Jewish Meditation Practices: A Guide for Enriching the Sabbath & Other Days of Your Life. 2000. pap. 16.95 (1-58023-102-0) Jewish Lights.

— A Heart of Stillness: A Complete Guide to Learning the Art of Meditation. LC 99-13433. 272p. 1999. pap. 16.95 (1-893361-03-9) SkyLight Paths.

Cooper, David A. Renewing Your Soul: A Guided Retreat for the Sabbath & Other Days of Rest. LC 95-7183. (Illus.). 160p. 1995. pap. 12.00 (0-06-061471-4, Pub. by Harper SF) HarpC.

— Silence, Simplicity & Solitude: A Complete Guide to Spiritual Retreat at Home. LC 99-17384. 336p. 1999. pap. 16.95 (1-893361-04-7) SkyLight Paths.

***Cooper, David A.** Three Gates to Meditation Practice: A Personal Journey into Sufism, Buddhism & Judaism. 2000. pap. 16.95 (1-893361-22-5) SkyLight Paths.

***Cooper, David B.** Human Gene Evolution. 500p. 2000. 115.00 (0-12-187870-8) Acad Pr.

***Cooper, David C.** Apocalypse! A New Look at the Book of Revelation. 2000. pap. 10.99 (0-87148-043-3) Pathway Pr.

Cooper, David D., ed. Thomas Merton & James Laughlin: Selected Letters. LC 96-39819. 320p. (C). 1997. 35.00 (0-393-04069-0) Norton.

Cooper, David E. Authenticity & Learning: Nietzhe's Educational Philosophy. (Modern Revivals in Philosophy Ser.). 161p. 1992. 51.95 (0-7512-0012-3, Pub. by Gregg Revivals) Ashgate Pub Co.

— Existentialism: A Reconstruction. LC 98-52529. (Introducing Philosophy Ser.). 245p. 1999. 59.95 (0-631-21322-8); pap. 26.95 (0-631-21323-6) Blackwell Pubs.

— Heidegger. LC 96-207904. 99p. pap. 14.95 (1-870626-12-5, Pub. by Claridge Pr) Paul & Co Pubs.

— Philosophy & the Nature of Language, 14. LC 86-29423. (Longman Linguistics Library). 233p. 1987. reprint ed. lib. bdg. 59.50 (0-313-25641-1, COPN, Greenwood Pr) Greenwood.

— Presupposition. (Janua Linguarum, Ser. Minor: No. 203). 130p. 1974. pap. text 33.85 (90-279-3152-6) Mouton.

— World Philosophies: An Historical Introduction. LC 95-5864. 400p. (C). 1995. pap. 29.95 (0-631-18867-3) Blackwell Pubs.

Cooper, David E., ed. Aesthetics: Classic Readings. LC 96-40885. (Classic Readings in Philosophy Ser.). 288p. 1997. 57.95 (0-631-19568-8) Blackwell Pubs.

— Aesthetics: The Classic Readings. LC 96-40885. (Philosophy Ser.). 288p. (C). 1997. pap. text 24.95 (0-631-19569-6) Blackwell Pubs.

— A Companion to Aesthetics. LC 92-38691. (Companions to Philosophy Ser.). 480p. 1993. 99.95 (0-631-17801-5) Blackwell Pubs.

— Education, Values, & Mind Essays for R. S. Peter. (International Library of the Philosophy of Education). 218p. (C). 1986. 37.50 (0-7100-9905-3, Routledge Thoemms) Routledge.

— Epistemology: The Classic Readings. LC 98-28675. (Philosophy Ser.). 368p. 1999. 59.95 (0-631-21087-3); pap. 24.95 (0-631-21088-1) Blackwell Pubs.

— Ethics: The Classic Readings. LC 97-8622. (Philosophy Ser.). 224p. 1997. text 57.95 (0-631-20632-9); pap. text 24.95 (0-631-20633-7) Blackwell Pubs.

***Cooper, David E., ed.** Metaphysics. LC 99-16130. (Philosophy Ser.: Vol. 4). 304p. 2000. text 59.95 (0-631-21324-4); pap. text 24.95 (0-631-21325-2) Blackwell Pubs.

Cooper, David E. & Palmer, Joy. Spirit of the Environment: Religion, Value & Environmental Concern. LC 97-22308. (Illus.). 224p. (C). 1998. 75.00 (0-415-14201-6); pap. 20.99 (0-415-14202-4) Routledge.

Cooper, David E. & Palmer, Joy A., eds. The Environment in Question: Ethics & Global Issues. (Illus.). 272p. (C). 1992. pap. 22.99 (0-415-04968-7, A6474) Routledge.

Cooper, David E., jt. auth. see Palmer, Joy A.

Cooper, David G. Finding & Signing Profitable Contracts: A Guide for Architects, Engineers, & Contractors. 328p. 1993. 80.00 (0-471-55841-9) Wiley.

Cooper, David G. & Gibson, Michael J. An Introduction to Paralegal Studies. 362p. 1994. teacher ed. write for info. (0-538-70731-3) S-W Pub.

Cooper, David K. & Novitzky, Dimitry, eds. The Transplantation & Replacement of Thoracic Organs: The Present Status of Biological & Mechanical Replacement. (C). 1990. text 398.00 (0-7923-8909-3) Kluwer Academic.

***Cooper, David K. C. & Lanza, Robert P.** Xeno: The Promise of Transplanting Animal Organs into Humans. LC 99-14437. (Illus.). 304p. 2000. 30.00 (0-19-512833-8) OUP.

***Cooper, David L.** Linguistic Attractors: The Cognitive Dynamics of Language Aquisition & Change. LC 99-10761. (Human Cognitive Processing Ser.: Vol. 2). xv, 375p. 1999. 90.00 (1-55619-202-9) J Benjamins Pubng Co.

Cooper, David M. Child Abuse Revisited: Children, Society, & Social Work. LC 92-19315. 1993. pap. 34.95 (0-335-15726-2) OpUniv Pr.

— The Race. LC 87-50096. 100p. (Orig.). 1987. pap. 6.95 (0-933571-02-X) Ure Pr.

An Asterisk (*) at the beginning of an entry indicates that the title is appearing for the first time.

*Cooper, David N. Human Gene Mutation. (Illus.). 412p. 1999. 105.00 (0-12-220439-5) Acad Pr.

— Venous Thrombosis: From Genes to Clinical Medicine. (Human Molecular Genetics Ser.). 352p. 1999. 120.00 (0-12-220446-8) Acad Pr.

Cooper, David N., jt. auth. see Tuddenham, Edward G.

Cooper, David Y. & Ledger, Marshall A. Innovation & Tradition at the University of Pennsylvania School of Medicine: An Anecdotal Journey. LC 90-12050. (Illus.). 360p. (C). 1990. text 34.95 (0-8122-8242-6) U of Pa Pr.

Cooper, Davina. Governing Out of Order: Space, Law & the Politics of Belonging. 256p. 1998. text 50.00 (1-85489-102-2); pap. text 19.50 (1-85489-103-0) NYU Pr.

— Power in Struggle: Feminism, Sexuality & the State. LC 96-34339. 192p. (C). 1995. text 50.00 (0-8147-1526-5); pap. text 19.00 (0-8147-1527-3) NYU Pr.

— Power in Struggle: Feminism, Sexuality & the State. LC 94-49576. 192p. 1995. pap. 22.95 (0-335-19211-4); text 88.00 (0-335-19212-2) OpUniv Pr.

Cooper, Deborah. Understanding Your Lover: Avoiding Rejection. 21p. 1989. pap., spiral bd. 9.95 (0-9636566-0-0) Schaefer Pubns.

Cooper, Deborah L. Developing Utilities in Assembly Language. LC 94-12424. (Popular Applications Ser.). 160p. 1994. pap. 15.95 incl. disk (1-55622-429-X) Wordware Pub.

— Developing Utilities in Visual Basic 4.0. (Popular Applications Ser.). 192p. 1995. pap. 15.95 incl. disk (1-55622-467-2) Wordware Pub.

Cooper, Denis R. Coins & Minting. (Album Ser.: No. 106). (Illus.). 32p. 1989. pap. 4.75 (0-7478-0069-3, Pub. by Shire Pubns) Parkwest Pubns.

Cooper, Denise. Wrong: Stories. LC 91-29524. 176p. 1993. pap. 11.00 (0-8021-3367-3, Grove) Grove-Atltic.

Cooper, Dennis. All Ears. 176p. 1999. pap. 13.25 (1-887128-33-6, Pub. by Soft Skull Pr) SPD-Small Pr Dist.

— Closer. LC 82-27396. 144p. 1990. pap. 11.00 (0-8021-3212-X, Grove) Grove-Atltic.

— The Dream Police. 144p. 1996. reprint ed. pap. 11.00 (0-8021-3457-2, Grove) Grove-Atltic.

— Frisk: A Novel. LC 91-6699. 144p. 1992. pap. 11.00 (0-8021-3289-8, Grove) Grove-Atltic.

— Guide. 192p. 1998. reprint ed. pap. 12.00 (0-8021-3580-3, Grove) Grove-Atltic.

— He Cried: Poems & Stories. 32p. 1984. pap. 5.00 (0-9607630-1-5) Black Star.

— Horror Hospital: Unplugged. (Illus.). 256p. 1996. pap. 24.95 (0-9651042-1-4) Juno Bks.

— Jerk. (Illus.). 64p. 1992. 15.00 (0-9631095-1-0) Artspace Bks.

***Cooper, Dennis.** Period. LC 99-42765. 128p. 2000. 21.00 (0-8021-1656-6, Pub. by Grove-Atltic) Publishers Group.

Cooper, Dennis. Try. LC 93-31364. 208p. 1995. pap. 11.00 (0-8021-3338-X, Grove) Grove-Atltic.

Cooper, Dennis, jt. auth. see Barnes, Lucinda.

Cooper, Dennis, jt. auth. see Reust, Hans R.

Cooper, Derek. Little Book of Scotch Whiskies. (Illus.). 60p. 1992. 7.95 (0-8118-0253-1) Chronicle Bks.

— Skye. (Traditional Scotland Ser.). (Illus.). 324p. pap. 16.95 (1-874744-37-8, Pub. by Birlinn Ltd) Dufour.

Cooper, Dermont M. F., ed. Now Distributing the Following Volumes in the Serial: Adenylyl Cyclases. Vol. 32. 240p. 99.95 (0-12-036132-9) Acad Pr.

Cooper, Dermot M., ed. Adenylyl Cyclases. (Advances in Second Messenger & Phosphoprotein Research Ser.). 400p. 1997. text 115.00 (0-397-51850-1) Lppncott W & W.

Cooper, Dermot M. & Seamon, Kenneth B., eds. Advances in Cyclic Nucleotide & Protein Phosphorylation Research Vol. 19: 1985. LC 84-649078. (Illus.). 352p. 1985. reprint ed. pap. 109.20 (0-7837-9246-8, 204714800019) Bks Demand.

Cooper, Diana. Autobiography: The Rainbow Comes & Goes, the Lights of Common Day, Trumpets from the Steep. (Illus.). 752p. 1985. pap. 13.95 (0-88184-131-5) Carroll & Graf.

— Contemporary Japanese Painting. (Illus.). 40p. 1991. 10.00 (0-942746-17-1) SUNYP R Gibson.

— Golden Footsteps. 132p. 1997. pap. 17.95 (1-899171-71-1, Pub. by Findhorn Pr) Words Distrib.

— Light up Your Life: Discover Your True Purpose & Potential. LC 97-108279. 186p. 1996. pap. text 12.95 (0-7499-1557-9, Pub. by Piatkus Bks) London Brdge.

***Cooper, Diana.** Light up Your Life: Discover Your True Purpose & Potential. 192p. 2000. pap. 9.95 (0-7499-1986-8, Pub. by Piatkus Bks) London Brdge.

Cooper, Diana. A Little Light on Angels. (Illus.). 128p. (Orig.). 1996. pap. 10.95 (1-899171-51-7, Pub. by Findhorn Pr) Words Distrib.

— A Little Light on Ascension. (A Little Light On...Ser.). (Orig.). 1997. pap. 10.95 (1-899171-81-9, Pub. by Findhorn Pr) Words Distrib.

— The Power of Inner Peace. 234p. 1995. pap. 12.95 (0-7499-1435-1, Pub. by Piatkus Bks) London Brdge.

— A Time for Transformation: How to Awaken to Your Soul's Purpose & Claim Your Power. 170p. (Orig.). 1996. pap. 12.95 (0-7499-1556-0, Pub. by Piatkus Bks) London Brdge.

***Cooper, Diana.** Time for Transformation: How to Awaken to Your Soul's Purpose & Claim Your Power. 176p. 2000. 9.95 (0-7499-1943-4, Pub. by Piatkus Bks) London Brdge.

Cooper, Diana. Transform Your Life: A Step-by-Step Programme for Change. 176p. (Orig.). 1995. pap. text 14.95 (0-7499-1310-X, Pub. by Piatkus Bks) London Brdge.

***Cooper, Diana.** Transform Your Life: A Step-by-Step Programme for Change. 176p. (Orig.). 2000. pap. 11.95 (0-7499-1944-2, Pub. by Piatkus Bks) London Brdge.

Cooper, Diana S. Night after Night. LC 93-44947. (Illus.). 1994. 20.00 (1-55963-306-9) Island Pr.

Cooper, Dolores O., jt. auth. see Knott, Thomas A.

Cooper, Dominic. Improving Safety Culture: A Practical Guide. LC 97-25693. 318p. 1997. pap. 96.95 (0-471-95821-2) Wiley.

Cooper, Dominic, jt. auth. see Robertson, Ivan T.

Cooper, Dominic, ed. see Cooper, Martin.

Cooper, Don. Atoms in the Field. (Illus.). 218p. (C). 1989. text 29.95 (1-55059-000-6) Temeron Bks.

Cooper, Don, et al. Search & Rescue Fundamentals. (Illus.). 396p. 1996. per. 30.00 (0-913724-37-8) Emerg Response Inst.

Cooper, Dona. American Film Institute's Guide to Writing Great Screenplays for Film & TV, 2 vols. 2nd ed. (Illus.). 208p. 1997. pap. 14.95 (0-02-861555-7, Arc) IDG Bks.

Cooper, Donald. Theatre World, 1983. (Illus.). 132p. 1988. pap. write for info. (0-413-75783-8, A0291, Methuen Drama) Methn.

Cooper, Donald & Schindler, Pamela S. Business Research Methods: Casebook. 6th ed. 60p. (C). 1997. pap. 7.81 (0-07-290610-3) McGrw-H Hghr Educ.

Cooper, Donald C. Fundamentals of Mantracking. (Illus.). 134p. 1992. per. 15.00 (0-685-50889-7) Emerg Response Inst.

Cooper, Donald H. & Mohn, Paul O. The Greenbelt Cooperative: Success & Decline. (Illus.). 258p. (Orig.). (C). 1992. pap. 13.00 (1-885641-01-X, B2) U CA Ctr Cooperatives.

Cooper, Donald R. & Emory, C. William. Business Research Methods. 5th ed. LC 95-5000. (Statistics Ser.). 681p. (C). 1994. text 69.25 (0-256-13777-3, Irwn Prfssnl) McGraw-Hill Prof.

Cooper, Donald R. & Schindler, Pamela S. Business Research Methods. 6th ed. LC 97-30873. 1997. write for info. (0-256-23952-5, Irwn Prfssnl) McGraw-Hill Prof.

Cooper, Donna. Tudors & Stuarts: A Fact Finder Book. (J). 1994. pap. 8.95 (0-563-35376-7, BBC-Parkwest) Parkwest Pubns.

Cooper, Doug. Condensed Pascal. rev. ed. 550p. (C). 1987. pap. text 61.25 (0-393-95540-0) Norton.

Cooper, Doug. Oh My! Modula-2! (C). 1990. pap. 65.50 (0-393-96009-9) Norton.

Cooper, Doug. Oh My! Modula-2! (Illus.). (C). 1991. pap. 73.75 incl. disk (0-393-96115-X) Norton.

— Oh My! Modula-2! Stony Brook's QuickMod Complier for DOS. (Illus.). (C). 1991. write for info. (0-393-96090-0) Norton.

Cooper, Doug. Oh My! Modula-2! With Macintosh Data Disk. (Illus.). (C). 1991. 65.50 incl. mac hd (0-393-96107-9) Norton.

Cooper, Doug. Oh My! Modula-2! 5.25 Disks & Reference Manual. (Illus.). (C). 1991. write for info. incl. disk (0-393-96091-9) Norton.

— Oh! Pascal! LC 92-31207. (C). 1993. pap. text. write for info. (0-393-96400-0) Norton.

— Oh! Pascal! 3rd ed. LC 92-31207. (C). 1993. write for info. (0-393-96397-7) Norton.

— Oh! Pascal! With DOS Program Disk. 3rd ed. LC 92-31207. (C). 1993. pap. text 62.50 incl. 3.5 hd (0-393-96398-5) Norton.

— Oh! Pascal! With Macintosh Program Disk. 3rd ed. LC 92-31207. (C). 1993. pap. text 62.50 incl. mac hd (0-393-96399-3) Norton.

— Oh! Pascal! (Turbo Pascal 6.0) With IBM 5.25 Program Disk. 3rd ed. 735p. (C). 1992. 61.25 incl. 5.25 hd (0-393-96249-0) Norton.

Cooper, Doug. Oh! Pascal! (Turbo Pascal 6.0) 3rd ed. 735p. (C). 1992. pap. 61.25 (0-393-96077-3) Norton.

— Standard Pascal User Reference Manual. 1983. pap. 15.95 (0-393-30121-4) Norton.

Cooper, Douglas. Amnesia. LC 93-27929. 240p. 1994. 19.45 (1-56282-748-0, Pub. by Hyperion) Time Warner.

Cooper, Douglas. The Cubist Epoch. rev. ed. (Illus.). 320p. (C). 1995. reprint ed. pap. 22.95 (0-7148-3242-1, Pub. by Phaidon Press) Phaidon Pr.

— Delirium. LC 97-28778. 256p. (J). 1998. 21.45 (0-7868-6341-2, Pub. by Hyperion) Time Warner.

Cooper, Douglas. Drawing & Perceiving. 2nd ed. 224p. 1992. pap. 44.95 (0-471-28466-1, VNR) Wiley.

Cooper, Douglas. Drawing & Perceiving. 2nd ed. (Illus.). 224p. 1992. pap. 36.95 (0-442-00994-1, VNR) Wiley.

***Cooper, Douglas.** Drawing & Perceiving: Life Drawing for Students of Architecture & Design. 3rd ed. LC 99-89639. 240p. 2000. pap. 44.95 (0-471-35714-6) Wiley.

— Living God's Love: Being a Source of Refreshment in a Dry World. 158p. 1995. pap. 5.97 (0-8163-1260-5) Pacific Pr Pub Assn.

— Steel Shadows: Murals & Drawings of Pittsburgh. 144p. 2000. 35.00 (0-8229-4144-9); pap. 17.50 (0-8229-5748-5) U of Pittsburgh Pr.

Cooper, Douglas. Toulouse-Lautrec. (Masters of Art Ser.). (Illus.). 128p. 1983. 24.95 (0-8109-1678-9, Pub. by Abrams) Time Warner.

Cooper, Duff. Sergeant Shakespeare. LC 76-30696. (Studies in Shakespeare: No. 24). 1977. lib. bdg. 75.00 (0-8383-2152-6) M S G Haskell Hse.

Cooper, Duff, tr. see De Vilmorin, Louise.

Cooper, E., ed. see Martin, Lance & Dicke, Robert, Jr.

Cooper, E. Crawley. Laboratory Design Handbook. 256p. 1994. boxed set 99.95 (0-8493-8996-8, 8996) CRC Pr.

Cooper, E. I., ed. Invertebrate Immune Responses. (Advances in Comparative & Environmental Physiology: Vol. 24). (Illus.). 210p. 1996. 190.00 (3-540-59468-X) Spr-Verlag.

Cooper, E. L. General Immunology. LC 80-42218. (Illus.). 300p. 1982. 161.00 (0-08-026368-2, Pub. by Pergamon Repr) Franklin.

Cooper, E. L., ed. Carp in North America. LC 87-71550. 84p. 1987. pap. 22.00 (0-913235-44-X, 550.12P) Am Fisheries Soc.

— Invertebrate Immune Responses: Cells & Molecular Products. (Advances in Comparative & Environmental Physiology Ser.: Vol. 23). (Illus.). 216p. 1996. 159.00 (3-540-59154-0) Spr-Verlag.

Cooper, Edith, ed. see Miller, Michael D.

Cooper-Edwards, Ellen. God Will Rebuke the Devourer for You. (Illus.). 81p. 1997. pap. 10.00 (0-9660639-0-2) Straight & Narrow.

Cooper, Edwin L. Fishes of Pennsylvania & the Northeastern United States. LC 82-18052. (Illus.). 256p. 1983. 40.00 (0-271-00337-5) Pa St U Pr.

Cooper, Edwin L. Stress, Immunity & Aging. (Immunology Ser.: Vol. 24). (Illus.). 336p. 1984. text 155.00 (0-8247-7114-1) Dekker.

Cooper, Edwin L. & Nisbet-Brown, Eric. Developmental Immunology. (Illus.). 496p. 1993. text 98.00 (0-19-504353-7) OUP.

***Cooper, Eleanor & Liu, William.** Grace in China: An American Woman Beyond the Great 1934-1974. 350p. 1999. 28.95 (1-57966-024-X, Black Belt) Black Belt Communs.

Cooper, Elisha. Ballpark. LC 97-18756. (Illus.). 40p. (J). (gr. k-3). 1998. 15.00 (0-688-15755-6, Grenwillow Bks) HarpC Child Bks.

— Building. LC 98-18902. (Illus.). 40p. (J). (ps-3). 1999. 16.00 (0-688-16494-3, Grenwillow Bks) HarpC Child Bks.

***Cooper, Elisha.** California: A Sketchbook. LC 99-41297. 144p. 2000. 17.95 (0-8118-2697-X) Chronicle Bks.

Cooper, Elisha. Country Fair. LC 96-52583. (Illus.). 40p. (J). (ps-3). 1997. 15.00 (0-688-15531-6, Grenwillow Bks) HarpC Child Bks.

— Henry. LC 98-52341. (Illus.). 96p. 1999. 14.95 (0-8118-2402-0) Chronicle Bks.

— A Year in New York. 96p. 1995. 20.00 (1-885492-24-3) City & Co.

Cooper, Elizabeth. A Primer of Cooking & Housekeeping. (Illus.). 192p. 1979. 10.95 (0-89496-023-7); pap. 9.95 (0-89496-015-6) Ross Bks.

Cooper, Elmer. Agriscience: Fundamentals & Applications. 1992. teacher ed., lab manual ed. 12.00 (0-8273-5321-9) Delmar.

Cooper, Elmer L. Agricultural Mechanics: Fundamentals & Applications. 3rd rev. ed. LC 95-15152. 672p. 1995. mass mkt. 70.95 (0-8273-6854-2) Delmar.

Cooper, Elmer L. Agriscience: Fundamentals & Applications. 2nd ed. LC 95-15156. 784p. (J). 1995. pap. 74.95 (0-8273-6278-1) Delmar.

Cooper, Elmer L. & Hamilton, William. Agricultural Mechanics: Fundamentals & Applications. 2nd ed. LC 85-20568. 532p. 1991. pap., teacher ed. 12.00 (0-8273-3470-2) Delmar.

— Agricultural Mechanics: Fundamentals & Applications. 2nd ed. LC 85-20568. 532p. 1991. text 43.45 (0-8273-3469-9) Delmar.

— Agricultural Mechanics: Fundamentals & Applications. 2nd ed. LC 85-20568. 532p. 1991. student ed. 16.50 (0-8273-3471-0) Delmar.

Cooper, Elner L. Agriscience: Fundamentals & Applications. (Agriculture Ser.). 1990. pap. 41.95 (0-8273-3394-3) Delmar.

Cooper, Emanuel & Royle, Derek. Glazes for the Potter. (Encore Edition Ser.). (Illus.). 1979. 3.95 (0-684-17714-5, Scribners Ref) Mac Lib Ref.

Cooper, Emerson A. To the Unknown God: The God of Science & the Bible. LC 97-90079. 252p. (Orig.). 1998. pap. 12.95 (0-533-12278-3) Vantage.

Cooper, Emmanuel. Fully Exposed: The Male Nude in Photography. 2nd ed. LC 95-20088. (Illus.). 304p. (gr. 13). 1995. pap. 27.99 (0-415-03280-6) Routledge.

— The Life & Work of Henry Scott Tuke 1858-1929. 1995. 35.00 (0-85449-069-8, Pub. by Gay Mens Pr) LPC InBook.

— The Life & Work of Henry Scott Tuke, 1858-1929. (Illus.). 72p. 1997. 30.00 (0-85449-068-X, Pub. by Gay Mens Pr) LPC InBook.

— The Sexual Perspective: Homosexuality & Art in the Last 100 Years in the West. 2nd ed. LC 93-41921. (Illus.). 388p. (gr. 13). 1994. pap. 25.99 (0-415-11101-3, B4374) Routledge.

— The Sexual Perspective: Homosexuality & Art in the Last 100 Years in the West. 2nd ed. LC 93-41921. (Illus.). 388p. (C). (gr. 13). 1994. 80.00 (0-415-11100-5, B4370) Routledge.

Cooper, Emmeline, jt. auth. see Cooper, Polly.

Cooper, Emmett & Wamberg, Steve. Making God's Word Stick. 168p. 1996. pap. 9.99 (0-7852-7506-1) Nelson.

***Cooper, Eugene.** Adventures in Chinese Bureaucracy: A Meta-Anthropological Saga. 257p. 2000. lib. bdg. 34.00 (1-56072-776-4) Nova Sci Pubs.

Cooper, Eugene & Jiang, Yinhuo. The Artisans & Entrepreneurs of Dongyang County: Economic Reform & Flexible Production in China. LC 98-11092. (Studies on Contemporary China). (Illus.). 296p. (C). (gr. 13). 1998. text 68.95 (0-7656-0321-7, East Gate Bk) M E Sharpe.

— The Artisans & Entrepreneurs of Dongyang County: Economic Reform & Flexible Production In China. LC 98-11092. (Studies on Contemporary China). (Illus.). 296p. 1999. pap. text 24.95 (0-7656-0322-5, East Gate Bk) M E Sharpe.

Cooper, Eugene & Simic, Andrei. Readings in Anthropology. 240p. (C). 1994. pap. text, per. 45.95 (0-8403-9193-5) Kendall-Hunt.

Cooper, F., et al, eds. The State of Physics at the End of the 20th Century: In Honor of Peter Carruthers' 61st Birthday Santa Fe, New Mexico, U. S. A. 26-29 October, 1996. 300p. 1998. 68.00 (981-02-3251-9) World Scientific Pub.

Cooper, F., et al. Intermittency in High Energy Collisions: Santa Fe Workshop. 488p. 1990. text 118.00 (981-02-0404-3) World Scientific Pub.

***Cooper, F. D.** Stones Unturned: The Soul Poetic. Martin, Regina, ed. LC 99-91588. 96p. 2000. pap. 12.99 (1-930269-00-5) Alimayu.

Cooper, F. T. Some American Story Tellers. 1977. lib. bdg. 59.95 (0-8490-2623-7) Gordon Pr.

Cooper, F. T., tr. see Donauer, Friedrich.

Cooper, Fiona. Blossom at the Mention of Your Name. 272p. 1996. pap. 13.99 (1-85242-399-4) Serpents Tail.

— I Believe in Angels. 154p. 1994. pap. 12.99 (1-85242-284-X) Serpents Tail.

— Jay Loves Lucy. 160p. (Orig.). 1992. pap. 14.99 (1-85242-218-1) Serpents Tail.

— Rotary Spokes. 256p. 1996. pap. 13.99 (1-85242-507-5) Serpents Tail.

— Skyhook in the Midnight Sun. (Masks Ser.). 432p. (Orig.). 1995. pap. 14.99 (1-85242-357-9) Serpents Tail.

Cooper, Floyd. Coming Home: From the Life of Langston Hughes. LC 93-36332. (Illus.). 32p. (J). (ps-5). 1994. 15.95 (0-399-22682-6, Philomel) Peng Put Young Read.

— Coming Home: From the Life of Langston Hughes. (Illus.). 32p. (J). (gr. k-3). 1998. pap. 6.99 (0-698-11612-7, PapStar) Peng Put Young Read.

***Cooper, Floyd.** Coming Home: From the Life of Langston Hughes. 1998. 11.19 (0-606-12908-1, Pub. by Turtleback) Demco.

Cooper, Floyd. Cumbayah. LC 96-44323. (Illus.). 32p. (J). 1998. 16.00 (0-688-13543-9, Wm Morrow) Morrow Avon.

***Cooper, Floyd.** Cumbayah. LC 96-44323. (Illus.). 32p. (J). 1998. lab manual ed. 16.89 (0-688-13544-7, Wm Morrow) Morrow Avon.

Cooper, Floyd. Mandela: From the Life of the South African Statesman. LC 95-19639. (Illus.). 40p. (J). (gr. 1-5). 1996. 15.95 (0-399-22942-6, Philomel) Peng Put Young Read.

***Cooper, Floyd.** Mandela: From the Life of the South African Statesman. LC 95-19639. (Illus.). 40p. (J). (gr. k-5). 1999. pap. 6.99 (0-698-11816-2) Putnam Pub Group.

Cooper, Floyd. How Sweet the Sound: African-American Songs for Children. LC 95-2406. 48p. (J). (ps-3). 1995. 15.95 (0-590-48030-8, Scholastic Hardcover) Scholastic Inc.

— Pass It On: African-American Poetry for Children. LC 92-16034. 32p. (J). (gr. k-4). 1993. 15.95 (0-590-45770-5) Scholastic Inc.

Cooper, Floyd, jt. auth. see Littlesugar, Amy.

Cooper, Forrest L. In Hometown Mississippi: An Address & Date Book. LC 92-25011. (Illus.). 142p. 1992. pap. 7.50 (0-87805-608-4) U Pr of Miss.

Cooper, Frank. Astronomy Physics 113/317. (C). 1995. pap. text 22.61 (1-56870-217-5) RonJon Pub.

Cooper, Frank & Knight, Jesse F. The Romantic Revival - Setting the Record Straight. Villegas, Roberto, ed. LC 79-50797. (YA). (gr. 7 up). 1980. pap. 2.95 (0-930962-02-8) Villegas Pub.

Cooper, Frank M. Oriental Carpets in Miniature: Charted Designs for Needlepoint, Cross-Stitch, or What You Will. Ligon, Linda C., ed. (Illus.). 120p. 1994. pap. 16.95 (0-934026-98-X) Interweave.

Cooper, Fred. Ballads of American History. (Illus.). 160p. (Orig.). (J). (gr. 4-7). 1997. pap. 24.95 (1-56857-033-3, 1775) Noble Pub Assocs.

— Cooper's Corner: Revisited. 253p. (Orig.). 1995. pap. text 11.95 (0-9644767-0-3) S & F Pub.

Cooper, Frederic T. Some American Story Tellers. LC 68-8451. (Essay Index Reprint Ser.). 1977. reprint ed. 23.95 (0-8369-0336-6) Ayer.

— Some English Story Tellers. LC 68-54341. (Essay Index Reprint Ser.). 1977. 23.95 (0-8369-0337-4) Ayer.

— Some English Story Tellers: A Book of the Younger Novelists. 1977. lib. bdg. 59.95 (0-8490-2627-X) Gordon Pr.

— Word Formation in the Roman Sermo Plebeius: An Historical Study of the Development of Vocabulary in Vulgar & Later Latin, with Special Reference to the Romance Languages. xlvii, 330p. 1975. reprint ed. 80.00 (3-487-05917-7) G Olms Pubs.

***Cooper, Frederick.** Beyond Slavery: Explorations of Race, Labor & Citizenship in Post-Emancipation Societies. LC 99-53083. (Illus.). 224p. 2000. lib. bdg. 34.95 (0-8078-2541-7) U of NC Pr.

Cooper, Frederick. Decolonization & African Society: The Labor Question in French & British Africa. (African Studies: No. 89). 694p. (C). 1996. text 69.95 (0-521-56251-1); pap. text 28.95 (0-521-56600-2) Cambridge U Pr.

— From Slaves to Squatters: Plantation Labor & Agriculture in Zanbiar & Costal Kenya, 1890. LC 97-9727. 1997. pap. 27.50 (0-435-07420-2) Heinemann.

— From Slaves to Squatters: Plantation Labor & Agriculture in Zanibar & Coastal Kenya, 1890-1925. LC 80-5391. 352p. 1981. 52.00 (0-300-02454-1) Yale U Pr.

— Plantation Slavery on the East Coast of Africa. LC 97-5082. 314p. 1997. pap. 27.50 (0-435-07419-9) Heinemann.

Cooper, Frederick, ed. Struggle for the City: Migrant Labor, Capital, & the State in Urban Africa. LC 83-11196. (Sage Series on African Modernization & Development: No. 8). (Illus.). 319p. reprint ed. pap. 98.90 (0-8357-4778-6, 203771500009) Bks Demand.

C

Cooper, Frederick & Packard, Randall M. International Development & the Social Sciences: Essays on the History & Politics of Knowledge. LC 97-26697. 344p. 1997. 50.00 (*0-520-20956-7*, Pub. by U CA Pr); pap. 20.00 (*0-520-20957-5*, Pub. by U CA Pr) Cal Prin Full Svc.

Cooper, Frederick & Stoler, Ann L., eds. Tensions of Empire: Colonial Cultures in a Bourgeois World. LC 96-32968. (Illus.). 463p. 1997. 58.00 (*0-520-20540-5*, Pub. by U CA Pr); pap. 22.50 (*0-520-20605-3*, Pub. by U CA Pr) Cal Prin Full Svc.

***Cooper, Frederick, et al.** Beyond Slavery: Explorations of Race, Labor & Citizenship in Post-Emancipation Societies. LC 99-53083. (Illus.). 224p. 2000. pap. 15.95 (*0-8078-4854-9*) U of NC Pr.

Cooper, Frederick, et al. Confronting Historical Paradigms: Peasants, Labor, & the Capitalist World System in Africa & Latin America. LC 92-39242. 416p. (Orig.). (C). 1993. lib. bdg. 60.00 (*0-299-13680-9*) U of Wis Pr.

— Confronting Historical Paradigms: Peasants, Labor & the Capitalist World System in Africa & Latin America. LC 92-39242. 416p. (C). 1993. pap. 19.95 (*0-299-13684-1*) U of Wis Pr.

Cooper, Frederick A. The Temple of Apollo Bassitas Vol. 3: Photographs for Vol. 1: Notebook of Baron Haller Von Hallerstein; & Inventory of Blocks. (Illus.). 480p. 1996. 90.00 (*0-87661-948-0*) Am Sch Athens.

— The Temple of Apollo Bassitas Vol. 4: Maps, Plans & Other Drawings. LC 92-23979. (Illus.). 68p. 1992. 80.00 (*0-87661-949-9*) Am Sch Athens.

Cooper, Frederick A. & Kelly, Nancy J. The Temple of Apollo Bassitas Vol. 1: The Architecture. (Illus.). 430p. 1996. 110.00 (*0-87661-946-4*) Am Sch Athens.

Cooper, G., et al. Income Taxation: Commentary & Materials. 2nd ed. 1300p. 1993. 115.00 (*0-455-21164-7*, Pub. by LawBk Co); pap. 89.50 (*0-455-21165-5*, Pub. by LawBk Co) Gaunt.

Cooper, G. A. & Dutro, J. T., Jr. Bulletins of American Paleontology Vols. 82 & 83: Devonian Brachiopods of New Mexico, Vol. 315. 215p. 1982. 50.00 (*0-87710-390-9*) Paleo Res.

Cooper, G. Burns. Mysterious Music: Rhythm & Free Verse. LC 97-49161. 262p. 1998. 49.50 (*0-8047-2938-7*) Stanford U Pr.

Cooper, G. David, jt. auth. see York, Michael W.

Cooper, G. R. & McGillem, C. D. Modern Communications & Spread Spectrum. 544p. (C). 1985. text 83.00 (*0-07-012951-7*) McGraw.

Cooper, G. S. & Inglis, M. W. Australian Capital Gains Tax. 2nd ed. 1992. pap. 66.00 (*0-409-30492-1*, AT, MICHIE) LEXIS Pub.

Cooper, Gabriele V. Natzmer. Kafka & Language: In the Stream of Thoughts & Life. LC 91-2360. (Studies in Austrian Literature, Culture, & Thought). 208p. 1992. 29.00 (*0-929497-38-4*) Ariadne CA.

Cooper, Gail. Air-Conditioning America: Engineers & the Controlled Environment, 1900-1960. LC 97-37148. (Johns Hopkins Studies in the History of Technology). (Illus.). 248p. 1998. text 35.00 (*0-8018-5716-3*) Johns Hopkins.

— Don't Get Caught in the Web: An Internet Guide for Real Estate Professionals. 2nd ed. LC 96-35893. 221p. 1997. spiral bd. 31.00 (*0-922154-33-3*) Appraisal Inst.

— Don't Get Caught in the Web: An Internet Guide for Real Estate Professionals. 2nd ed. LC 97-50091. xiv, 221 p. 1997. 31.00 (*0-922154-45-7*) Appraisal Inst.

Cooper, Gail & Cooper, Garry. Virtual Field Trips. LC 97-26028. 168p. 1997. 24.00 (*1-56308-557-7*) Libs Unl.

Cooper, Gail B., jt. auth. see Davis, Dee.

Cooper, Gale & Schiller, Alan L. Anatomy of the Guinea Pig. LC 74-81866. (Commonwealth Fund Publications). (Illus.). 392p. 1975. 67.50 (*0-674-03159-8*) HUP.

***Cooper, Garry.** Introduction to Planning. 60p. (C). 2000. spiral bd. 25.95 (*0-7872-7202-7*) Kendall-Hunt.

Cooper, Garry, jt. auth. see Cooper, Gail.

Cooper, Garry, jt. auth. see Cooper Markunas, Gail.

Cooper, Gary J. Take a Chance. (J). (gr. 2-8). 1993. 18.95 (*0-937857-46-7*, 1544) Speech Bin.

Cooper, Geoffrey. Elements of Human Cancer. 2nd ed. (Life Science Ser.). 1999. 47.50 (*0-7637-0619-1*) Jones & Bartlett.

Cooper, Geoffrey & Wortham, Christopher, eds. Everyman. 64p. 1988. pap. 12.95 (*0-85564-167-3*, Pub. by Univ of West Aust Pr) Intl Spec Bk.

Cooper, Geoffrey M. The Cancer Book: A Guide to Understanding the Causes, Prevention, & Treatment of Cancer. LC 93-16282. 248p. 1993. pap. text 18.75 (*0-86720-770-1*) Jones & Bartlett.

— The Cell: A Molecular Approach. (Illus.). 636p. (C). 1996. text 72.95 incl. cd-rom (*0-87893-119-8*) Sinauer Assocs.

— Elements of Human Cancer. (Biology Ser.). 1992. 46.25 (*0-86720-191-6*) Jones & Bartlett.

— Oncogenes. 2nd ed. LC 94-42582. (Biology Ser.). (Illus.). 400p. 1995. 58.75 (*0-86720-937-2*) Jones & Bartlett.

Cooper, Geoffrey M., et al. The DNA Provirus: Howard Temin's Scientific Legacy. LC 95-12355. 1995. 75.00 (*1-55581-098-5*) ASM Pr.

Cooper, George. Poison Widow: A True Story of Witchcraft, Arsenic, & Murder. LC 98-43796. 288p. 1999. text 24.95 (*0-312-19947-3*) St Martin.

— A Voluntary Tax? New Perspectives on Sophisticated Estate Tax Avoidance. LC 78-20853. (Studies of Government Finance). 115p. 1979. pap. 8.95 (*0-8157-1551-X*) Brookings.

Cooper, George & Daws, Gavan. Land & Power in Hawaii: The Democratic Years. 528p. 1990. reprint ed. pap. 18.95 (*0-8248-1303-0*) UH Pr.

Cooper, George R. & McGillem, Clare D. Continuous & Discrete Signal & System Analysis. 3rd ed. (The/Oxford Series in Electrical & Computer Engineering). (Illus.). 512p. 1995. text 84.00 (*0-19-510750-0*) OUP.

— Probabilistic Methods of Signal & System Analysis. 2nd ed. 408p. (C). 1986. student ed. write for info. (*0-03-070616-5*) SCP.

— Probabilistic Methods of Signal & System Analysis. 3rd ed. (The Oxford Series in Electrical & Computer Engineering). (Illus.). 496p. 1998. text 84.00 (*0-19-512354-9*) OUP.

Cooper, George R., jt. auth. see McGillem, Clare D.

Cooper, Gib, ed. see Lewis, Daphne B.

Cooper, Gil, jt. auth. see Drew, Shirley.

Cooper, Giles & Albee, Edward. Everything in the Garden. adapted ed. 1968. pap. 5.25 (*0-8222-0371-5*) Dramatists Play.

Cooper, Gladys E. Eulogy to Happiness. 64p. 1993. pap. 6.99 (*1-881379-06-X*) Samaritan Pr.

Cooper, Glenn. The Two-Day Diet. 1990. mass mkt. 5.99 (*0-449-21848-1*) Fawcett.

Cooper-Goldenberg, Julianna. A Spirituality for Late Life. (Older Adult Issues Ser.). 50p. 1999. pap. 4.50 (*0-664-50084-6*) Geneva Press.

Cooper, Gordon. Festivals of Europe. (Illus.). 172p. 1994. reprint ed. lib. bdg. 44.00 (*0-7808-0005-2*) Omnigraphics Inc.

— Leap of Faith: An Astronaut's Journey into the Unknown. LC 99-86433. 288p. 2000. 25.00 (*0-06-019416-2*, HarpCollins) HarperTrade.

Cooper, Graham, et al. Scientific Foundations of Trauma. LC 97-199803. (Illus.). 848p. 1997. text 310.00 (*0-7506-1585-0*) Buttrwrth-Heinemann.

Cooper, Gregory. Collectible Compact Disc Price Guide. (Illus.). 600p. 1993. pap. 24.95 (*1-883907-10-1*) Special Collectibles.

— Collectible Compact Disc Price Guide: Including Rare & Valuable, Vol. 2. 2nd rev. ed. (Illus.). 560p. 1998. pap. 17.95 (*0-89145-764-X*, 4852) Collector Bks.

Cooper, Gregory F., jt. ed. see Glymour, Clark.

Cooper, Grosvenor. Learning to Listen: A Handbook for Music. LC 57-8579. 176p. 1962. pap. text 15.00 (*0-226-11519-4*, P79) U Ch Pr.

Cooper, Grosvenor & Meyer, Leonard B. Rhythmic Structure of Music. LC 60-14068. 221p. 1963. pap. text 15.00 (*0-226-11522-4*, P118) U Ch Pr.

Cooper, Gustav A. Jurassic Brachiopods of Saudi Arabia. LC 88-600170. (Smithsonian Contributions to Paleobiology Ser.: No. 65). (Illus.). 217p. reprint ed. pap. 67.30 (*0-8357-5553-3*, 203518300093) Bks Demand.

***Cooper, Guy & Taylor, Gordon.** Gardens of the Future: Gestures Against the Wild. LC 99-53855. (Illus.). 224p. 2000. 50.00 (*1-58093-063-8*, Pub. by Monacelli Pr) Penguin Putnam.

— Mirrors of Paradise: The Gardens of Fernando Caruncho. (Illus.). 224p. 2000. 65.00 (*1-58093-071-9*, Pub. by Monacelli Pr) Penguin Putnam.

Cooper, Guy & Taylor, Gordon. Paradise Transformed: The Private Garden for the Twenty-First Century. LC 96-24485. (Illus.). 224p. 1996. 50.00 (*1-885254-35-0*, Pub. by Monacelli Pr) Penguin Putnam.

Cooper, Guy, et al. English Herb Gardens. (Illus.). 160p. 1996. pap. 19.95 (*0-297-79131-1*, Pub. by Weidenfeld & Nicolson) Trafalgar.

Cooper, H. H. Business Intelligence: A Primer. 175p. (Orig.). 1996. pap. 22.00 (*0-9628411-2-9*) Exec Protect Inst.

Cooper, H. H., jt. auth. see Kobetz, Richard W.

Cooper, H. R. Practical Dredging. (C). 1987. 90.00 (*0-85174-079-0*) St Mut.

Cooper, Hannah. Time Will Not Wait. large type ed. (Linford Romance Library). 304p. 1993. pap. 16.99 (*0-7089-7395-7*, Linford) Ulverscroft.

Cooper, Harold. Heaven All Around Us. 142p. (Orig.). 1992. pap., teacher ed. 9.95 (*0-89114-186-3*) Baptist Pub Hse.

Cooper, Harris. The Battle over Homework: An Administrator's Guide to Setting Sound & Effective Policies. LC 94-17155. (Road Maps to Success Ser.). 72p. 1994. pap. 14.95 (*0-8039-6163-4*) Corwin Pr.

— Homework. (Research on Teaching Monograph). 218p. (C). 1989. pap. text 19.16 (*0-8013-0207-2*, 75866) Longman.

***Cooper, Harris.** Making the Most of Summer School: A Meta-Analytic & Narrative Review. (Monographs of the Society for Research in Children Development). 120p. 2000. pap. 32.95 (*0-631-22152-2*) Blackwell Pubs.

Cooper, Harris & Hedges, Larry V., eds. The Handbook of Research Synthesis. (Illus.). 576p. 1993. 49.95 (*0-87154-226-9*) Russell Sage.

Cooper, Harris M. Synthesizing Research: A Guide for Literature Reviews. 3rd ed. LC 97-33792. (Applied Social Research Methods Ser.). 1998. write for info. (*0-7619-1347-5*); pap. write for info. (*0-7619-1348-3*) Sage.

Cooper, Harry, jt. auth. see Kelly, Ellsworth.

Cooper, Helen. The Baby Who Wouldn't Go to Bed. LC 98-143578. (Illus.). 32p. 1997. 18.95 (*0-385-40793-9*) Doubleday.

— The Basic Guide to How to Read Music. (Illus.). 80p. (Orig.). 1985. pap. 8.95 (*0-399-51122-9*, Perigee Bks) Berkley Pub.

— The Basic Guide to How to Read Music. (Orig.). 1996. 19.95 incl. audio compact disk (*0-8256-1658-1*, OP 47450) Music Sales.

— The Basic Guide to How to Read Music. (Illus.). 80p. (Orig.). pap. 9.95 (*0-8256-2309-X*, AM 34893) Omnibus NY.

***Cooper, Helen.** The Boy Who Wouldn't Go to Bed: Pictures & Story. (Illus.). 32p. (J). (ps-2). 2000. pap. 5.99 (*0-14-056771-2*, PuffinBks) Peng Put Young Read.

— Ella & the Rabbit. 32p. (J). 1999. 6.99 (*0-7112-0635-X*) F Lincoln.

Cooper, Helen. Ella & the Rabbit. LC 90-34499. (Illus.). 32p. (J). (ps-3). 1990. 12.95 (*0-940793-62-8*, Crocodile Bks) Interlink Pub.

— Little Monster Did. 32p. (J). 1996. pap. 17.95 (*0-385-40620-7*) Doubleday.

— Little Monster Did It! (J). 1999. pap. 5.99 (*0-14-055883-7*, PuffinBks) Peng Put Young Read.

— Oxford Guides to Chaucer: The Canterbury Tales. 2nd ed. (Oxford Guides to Chaucer Ser.). 452p. (C). 1996. pap. text 26.00 (*0-19-871155-7*) OUP.

— Pumpkin Soup. LC 98-18677. 32p. (J). (ps-3). 1999. 15.00 (*0-374-36164-9*) FS&G.

— Sopa de Calabaza. Reyes, Christiane, tr.Tr. of Pumpkin Story. (Illus.). 30p. (gr. k-3). 1998. 17.50 (*84-261-3095-X*) Juventud Edit.

— The Tale of Bear. LC 94-21054. (Illus.). 24p. (J). (ps up). 1995. pap. 6.95 (*0-688-13990-6*) Lothrop.

***Cooper, Helen.** Toy Tales. LC 99-56713. (Illus.). (J). 2000. pap. 7.95 (*0-374-47944-5*) FS&G.

Cooper, Helen & Mapstone, Sally, eds. The Long Fifteenth Century: Essays for Douglas Gray. (Illus.). 374p. 1997. text 85.00 (*0-19-818365-8*) OUP.

Cooper, Helen, et al. Thomas Eakins: The Rowing Pictures. Schwartz, Shelia, ed. LC 96-15716. (Illus.). 139p. (C). 1996. pap. 20.95 (*0-89467-076-X*) Yale Art Gallery.

Cooper, Helen, ed. see Burnham, Patricia M., et al.

Cooper, Helen, ed. see Harrison, Keith.

Cooper, Helen, ed. & intro. see Malory, Thomas.

Cooper, Helen A. Thomas Eakins: The Rowing Pictures. LC 96-15716. (Illus.). 144p. 1998. 40.00 (*0-300-06939-1*); pap. 20.00 (*0-300-07785-8*) Yale U Pr.

— Winslow Homer Watercolors. (Illus.). 260p. 1987. reprint ed. pap. 30.00 (*0-300-03997-2*, Y-687) Yale U Pr.

Cooper, Helen M. Elizabeth Barrett Browning, Woman & Artist. LC 87-40538. xiii, 219p. (C). 1988. pap. 15.95 (*0-8078-4217-6*) U of NC Pr.

Cooper, Helen M., et al. Arms & the Woman: War, Gender, & Literary Representation. LC 89-5246. xxii, 348p. (C). 1989. pap. 18.95 (*0-8078-4256-7*) U of NC Pr.

Cooper, Henry R., Jr., tr. from CRO. Judith: The Book of Marko Marulic of Split. 1991. text 43.50 (*0-88033-199-2*, Pub. by East Eur Monographs) Col U Pr.

Cooper, Henry R., Jr., jt. ed. see Lencek, Rado L.

Cooper, Henry S., Jr. Before Lift-Off: The Making of a Space Shuttle Crew. LC 87-2761. (New Series in NASA History). (Illus.). 288p. 1987. 34.95 (*0-8018-3524-0*) Johns Hopkins.

— The Evening Star: Venus Observed. LC 92-36347. 1993. text 22.00 (*0-374-15000-1*) FS&G.

— Thirteen: The Apollo Flight That Failed. LC 94-39726. 208p. 1995. pap. 14.95 (*0-8018-5097-5*) Johns Hopkins.

Cooper, Herbert, jt. auth. see Mullish, Henry.

Cooper-Hewitt Museum., jt. auth. see Rohrer, Judith C.

Cooper-Hewitt Museum Staff & Yelavich, Susan. Design for Life: Our Daily Lives, the Spaces We Shape & the Ways We Communicate, as Seen through the Collections of the Cooper Hewitt National Design Museum. LC 96-53981. 1997. write for info. (*0-910503-63-X*); pap. write for info. (*0-910503-64-8*) Cooper-Hewitt Museum.

Cooper, Hilary. The Teaching of History: Implementing the National Curriculum. (Studies in Primary Education Ser.). 160p. 1992. pap. 29.95 (*1-85346-186-5*, Pub. by David Fulton) Taylor & Francis.

— The Teaching of History in Primary Schools: Implementing the Revised National Curriculum. 2nd ed. 208p. 1995. pap. 25.95 (*1-85346-403-1*, Pub. by David Fulton) Taylor & Francis.

Cooper, Hilary, et al. Display in the Classroom: Principles, Practice, & Learning Theory. LC 96-217274. 160p. 1996. pap. text 24.95 (*1-85346-404-X*, Pub. by David Fulton) Taylor & Francis.

Cooper-Hilbert, Beth. Infertility & Involuntary Childlessness: Helping Couples Cope. LC 98-24233. 256p. 1998. 30.00 (*0-393-70262-6*) Norton.

Cooper, Howard, jt. auth. see Diamant, Anita.

Cooper-Hunt, C. L. Radiesthetic Analysis. 40p. 1996. reprint ed. spiral bd. 9.00 (*0-7873-0199-X*) Hlth Research.

Cooper, Huw, ed. Cochlear Implants: A Practical Guide. (Illus.). 400p. (Orig.). (C). 1991. pap. text 75.00 (*1-879105-32-2*, 0014) Thomson Learn.

Cooper, I. J. Life & Public Services of James Logan. 1993. reprint ed. lib. bdg. 89.00 (*0-7812-5443-4*) Rprt Serv.

Cooper, I. S., jt. ed. see Collins, M. F.

Cooper, Ilay. The Painted Towns of Shekhawati: A Mapin Guide to India. LC 96-146445. (Illus.). 230p. 1994. pap. 17.50 (*81-85822-17-4*, Pub. by Mapin Pubng) Antique Collect.

— Traditional Buildings of India. LC 97-61642. (Illus.). 192p. 1998. 50.00 (*0-500-34161-3*, Pub. by Thames Hudson) Norton.

Cooper, Ilay & Gillow, John. Arts & Crafts of India. LC 95-61618. (Illus.). 160p. (Orig.). 1996. pap. 24.95 (*0-500-27863-6*, Pub. by Thames Hudson) Norton.

***Cooper, Ilene.** Absolutely Lucy. LC 99-36118. (Road to Reading Ser.). 80p. 2000. 10.99 (*0-307-46502-0*) Gldn Bks Pub Co.

— Absolutely Lucy. LC 99-36118. (Road to Reading Ser.). (Illus.). 80p. (J). 2000. pap. 3.99 (*0-307-26502-1*, Golden Books) Gldn Bks Pub Co.

Cooper, Ilene. Buddy Love - Now on Video. LC 95-1767. 192p. (J). (gr. 5 up). 1995. lib. bdg. 13.89 (*0-06-024664-2*) HarpC Child Bks.

— Buddy Love--Now on Video. LC 95-1767. 192p. (YA). (gr. 5-9). 1998. pap. 4.95 (*0-06-440724-1*) HarpC.

— Choosing Sides. LC 89-13669. 224p. (J). (gr. 4-7). 1990. 15.00 (*0-688-07934-2*, Wm Morrow) Morrow Avon.

— The Dead Sea Scrolls. LC 96-21983. (Illus.). 64p. (J). 1997. 15.00 (*0-688-14300-8*, Wm Morrow) Morrow Avon.

— I'll See You in My Dreams. LC 96-54049. 128p. (gr. 5 up). 1997. 15.99 (*0-670-86322-X*) Viking Penguin.

***Cooper, Ilene.** Lucy on the Loose. LC 00-21432. (Road to Reading Ser.). (Illus.). (J). 2000. pap. 3.99 (*0-307-26508-0*, Goldn Books) Gldn Bks Pub Co.

— Lucy on the Loose. (Road to Reading Mile 5 Ser.). (Illus.). (J). 2000. 10.99 (*0-307-46508-X*) Gldn Bks Pub Co.

Cooper, Ilene. No Thanks Thanksgiving. 1999. pap. 3.99 (*0-14-037087-0*) Viking Penguin.

— Star Spangled Summer. 144p. 1999. pap. 3.99 (*0-14-037086-2*) Penguin Putnam.

— Trick or Trouble. (J). (gr. 4 up). 1994. write for info. (*0-318-72462-6*) Viking Penguin.

Cooper, Ilene, jt. ed. see Wilms, Denise.

Cooper, Inez S. Sojourn in Israel. LC 89-50414. (Illus.). 77p. (Orig.). 1989. pap. 6.95 (*0-935615-06-7*) S Utah U Pr.

Cooper, Inglath. The Last Good Man. (Superromance Ser.). 1997. per. 3.99 (*0-373-70728-2*, 1-70728-0) Harlequin Bks.

Cooper, Irving S. Cerebellar Stimulation in Man. fac. ed. LC 77-76925. (Illus.). 232p. pap. 72.00 (*0-7837-7536-9*, 204696800005) Bks Demand.

— Methods of Psychic Development. 113p. 1996. reprint ed. spiral bd. 12.50 (*0-7873-0198-1*) Hlth Research.

— Methods of Psychic Development (1919) 116p. 1996. reprint ed. pap. 11.00 (*1-56459-868-3*) Kessinger Pub.

— Theosophy Simplified. rev. ed. 107p. (C). 1989. pap. 6.95 (*0-8356-0651-1*, Quest) Theos Pub Hse.

Cooper, Irving S. & Bekken, Dean. Ceremonies of the Liberal Catholic Rite. 3rd ed. (Illus.). 275p. 1997. ring bd. 20.00 (*0-935461-54-X*) St Alban Pr CA.

Cooper, Irving S., et al. Ceremonies of the Liberal Catholic Rite. 3rd rev. ed. 200p. 1996. 25.00 (*0-935461-50-7*) St Alban Pr CA.

Cooper, Isabella M. Bibliography on Educational Broadcasting. LC 76-161184. (History of Broadcasting: Radio to Television Ser.). 1977. reprint ed. 51.95 (*0-405-03587-X*) Ayer.

Cooper, Iver P. Biotechnology & the Law, 2 vols. LC 82-12957. (IP Ser.). 1982. ring bd. 260.00 (*0-87632-311-5*) West Group.

Cooper, J. Crisis Admission Units & Emergency Psychiatric Services. (Public Health in Europe Ser.: No. 11). 118p. 1979. 11.00 (*92-9020-130-4*, 1320011) World Health.

— Microprocessor Background for Management Personnel. 208p. 1981. 32.00 (*0-13-580829-4*) P-H.

— Plastic Containers for Pharmaceuticals: Testing & Control. (Offset Publications: No. 4). 1974. pap. text 28.80 (*92-4-170004-1*, 1120004) World Health.

Cooper, J., ed. Logistics & Distribution Planning: Strategies for Management. (C). 1990. 305.00 (*0-7855-5726-1*, Pub. by Inst Pur & Supply) St Mut.

***Cooper, J., et al, eds.** Assessment in Psychotherapy. 176p. 1998. pap. 29.00 (*1-85575-158-5*, Pub. by H Karnac Bks Ltd) Other Pr LLC.

Cooper, J. & Dobson, H. Aerial Spraying for Tsetse Fly Control: A Handbook of Aerial Spray Calibration & Monitoring for the Sequential Aerosol Technique. 1993. pap. 25.00 (*0-85954-348-X*, Pub. by Nat Res Inst) St Mut.

Cooper, J., et al. Mackintosh Architecture. 1984. 35.00 (*0-312-50244-3*) St Martin.

Cooper, J., tr. see Langensiepen, Bernd & Guleryuz, Ahmet.

Cooper, J. Allen D. & Pappas, Peter G. Cecil Review of General Internal Medicine. 7th ed. (Illus.). 255p. pap. text. write for info. (*0-7216-7789-4*, W B Saunders Co) Harcrt Hlth Sci Grp.

Cooper, J. C. Dictionary of Symbolic & Mythological Animals. (Illus.). 272p. 1995. pap. 14.00 (*0-7225-3238-5*) Harper SF.

— An Illustrated Encyclopaedia of Traditional Symbols. LC 78-55429. (Illus.). 208p. 1987. pap. 16.95 (*0-500-27125-9*, Pub. by Thames Hudson) Norton.

— Taoism: The Way of the Mystic. pap. write for info. (*0-85030-096-7*, Pub. by Aqrn Pr) HarpC.

— Taoism: The Way of the Mystic. 1990. pap. 10.00 (*1-85274-071-X*, Pub. by Crucible Pr) Cavendish Bks.

Cooper, J. California. Family. 240p. 1990. 21.00 (*0-385-41171-5*) Doubleday.

— Family. 240p. 1991. pap. 11.95 (*0-385-41172-3*, Anchor NY) Doubleday.

***Cooper, J. California.** The Future Has a Past: Stories. 288p. 2000. 23.95 (*0-385-49680-X*) Doubleday.

Cooper, J. California. Homemade Love. 192p. 1998. pap. 10.95 (*0-312-19465-X*) St Martin.

— In Search of Satisfaction. 368p. 1995. reprint ed. pap. 11.95 (*0-385-46786-9*, Anchor NY) Doubleday.

— The Matter Is Life. LC 92-15970. 240p. 1992. pap. 12.00 (*0-385-41174-X*, Anchor NY) Doubleday.

— A Piece of Mine. 144p. 1991. reprint ed. pap. 9.95 (*0-385-42087-0*, Anchor NY) Doubleday.

— Some Love, Some Pain, Some Time. large type ed. 1996. lib. bdg. 24.95 (*0-7862-0639-X*) Thorndike Pr.

— Some Love, Some Pain, Some Time: Stories. 288p. 1996. pap. 11.95 (*0-385-46788-5*, Anchor NY) Doubleday.

— Some Soul to Keep. 1998. pap. 10.95 (*0-312-19337-8*) St Martin.

— Wake of the Wind. 384p. 1999. pap. 12.95 (*0-385-48705-3*) Doubleday.

Cooper, J. D., ed. Ordovician of the Great Basin: Fieldtrip Guidebook & Volume for the 7th International Symposium on the Ordovician System, Las Vegas, Nevada. 151p. 1995. 12.00 (*1-878861-71-9*) Pac Section SEPM.

Cooper, J. D., et al, eds. Ordovician Odyssey: Short Papers for the 7th International Symposium on the Ordovician System, Las Vegas, Nevada. 498p. 1995. 30.00 (*1-878861-70-0*) Pac Section SEPM.

Cooper, J. David. Literacy: Helping Children Construct Meaning, 3 vols. (C). 1997. text, teacher ed. 11.96 (*0-395-79003-4*) HM.

An Asterisk (*) at the beginning of an entry indicates that the title is appearing for the first time.

— Literacy: Helping Children Construct Meaning, 3 vols. 3rd ed. 608p. (C). 1996. pap. text 41.56 (*0-395-79002-6*) HM.

Cooper, J. David, et al. Celebrate. (J). (gr. 3). 1995. text 35.00 (*0-395-71955-0*) HM.

— Celebrate, 2 vols. large type ed. 380p. (J). (gr. 3). 92.00 (*0-614-20581-6*, L-38223-00 APHB) Am Printing Hse.

— Celebrate: Literacy Activity Book. (J). (gr. 3). 1995. student ed. 5.84 (*0-395-74367-2*) HM.

— Celebrate: Literacy Activity Book. large type ed. 190p. (J). (gr. 3). 47.50 (*0-614-20580-8*, L-38228-00 APHB) Am Printing Hse.

— Enjoy. (J). (gr. 3). 1995. text 35.00 (*0-395-71954-2*) HM.

— Enjoy. large type ed. 319p. (J). (gr. 3). 79.75 (*0-614-20586-7*, L-38224-00 APHB) Am Printing Hse.

— Enjoy: Literacy Activity Book. (YA). 1995. student ed. 5.84 (*0-395-72484-8*) HM.

— Enjoy: Literacy Activity Book. large type ed. 174p. (J). (gr. 3). 43.50 (*0-614-20585-9*, L-38229-00 APHB) Am Printing Hse.

— Explore. (J). (gr. 5). 1995. text 50.64 (*0-395-71957-7*) HM.

— Explore. large type ed. 756p. (J). (gr. 5). 181.00 (*0-614-20590-5*, L-38226-00 APHB) Am Printing Hse.

— Explore: Literacy Activity Book. (J). (gr. 5). 1995. student ed. 8.64 (*0-395-72486-4*) HM.

— Explore: Literacy Activity Book. large type ed. 330p. (J). (gr. 5). 82.50 (*0-614-20589-1*, L-38231-00 APHB) Am Printing Hse.

— Imagine. (J). (gr. 5). 1996. write for info. (*0-395-71956-9*) HM.

— Imagine, 3 vols. large type ed. 720p. (J). (gr. 5). 172.50 (*0-614-20596-4*, L-38225-00 APHB) Am Printing Hse.

— Imagine: Literacy Activity Book. (J). (gr. 5). 1995. student ed. 8.64 (*0-395-72485-6*) HM.

— Imagine: Literacy Activity Book. large type ed. 330p. (J). (gr. 4). 82.50 (*0-614-20597-2*, L-38230-00 APHB) Am Printing Hse.

— Quest. (J). (gr. 6). 1995. text 51.96 (*0-395-71958-5*) HM.

— Quest, 3 vols. large type ed. 752p. 188.00 (*0-614-20613-8*, L-38227-00 APHB) Am Printing Hse.

— Quest: Literacy Activity Book. (J). (gr. 6). 1995. student ed. 8.64 (*0-395-72487-2*) HM.

— Quest: Literacy Activity Book, 2 vols. large type ed. 368p. (J). (gr. 6). 92.00 (*0-614-20612-X*, L-38232-00 APHB) Am Printing Hse.

Cooper, J. E. Disease & Threatened Birds. 216p. 1989. pap. 34.95 (*1-56098-434-1*) Smithsonian.

— SAPT in Veterinary Medicine: Exotics. (C). (gr. 13). 1994. text 32.95 (*0-8151-1861-9*, 22825) Mosby Inc.

Cooper, J. E., compiled by. Who Pocket Guide to Classification of Mental & Behavioural Disorders: With Glossary & Diagnostic Criteria for Research. LC 94-26148. 422p. 1994. pap. text 27.95 (*0-88048-983-9*, 8983) Am Psychiatric.

Cooper, J. E., ed. see World Health Organization Staff.

Cooper, J. G., jt. auth. see Prout, Brian J.

Cooper, J. M. & Benedetto, J. J., eds. Introduction to Partial Differential Equations with MATLAB. LC 97-32251. (Applied & Numerical Harmonic Analysis Ser.). 380p. 1997. 59.95 (*0-8176-3967-5*) Birkhauser.

Cooper, J. P. Land, Men & Beliefs: Studies in Early-Modern History. 300p. (C). 1983. 55.00 (*0-907628-26-5*) Hambledon Press.

— Wentworth Papers, 1597-1628. (Camden Fourth Ser.: No. 12). 347p. 27.00 (*0-901050-20-2*) David Brown.

Cooper, J. R., jt. ed. see Bulman, R. S.

Cooper, J. S. Reconstructing History from Ancient Inscriptions: The Lagash-Umma Border Conflict. (Sources from the Ancient Near East Ser.: Vol. 2-1). (Illus.). 61p. (C). 1983. pap. text 11.00 (*0-89003-059-6*) Undena Pubns.

Cooper, J. W. Game Fowls: Their Origin & History - How to Breed. 125p. 1911. pap. 25.00 (*0-87556-809-2*) Saifer.

Cooper, Jack, ed. see Boyd, Robert G.

Cooper, Jack, ed. see Boyd, Robert G. & Adams, Vivian.

Cooper, Jack R., et al. The Biochemical Basis of Neuropharmacology. 7th ed. (Illus.). 528p. (C). 1996. text 57.50 (*0-19-510398-X*); pap. text 32.50 (*0-19-510399-8*) OUP.

Cooper, Jackie, et al. Mackintosh Architecture. (Illus.). 128p. 1984. pap. 25.00 (*0-312-50243-5*) St Martin.

Cooper, Jackie, jt. auth. see Beck, Haig.

Cooper, Jackie, jt. auth. see Emery Vincent Design Staff.

***Cooper, Jackie K.** Journey of a Gentle Southern Man: Reflections from the Road. LC 99-65742. 176p. 1999. 22.00 (*1-892298-15-5*) Abique.

Cooper, James. Logistics & Distribution Planning: Strategies for Management. (C). 1988. 145.00 (*0-7855-3770-8*, Pub. by Inst Pur & Supply) St Mut.

— Welding the Tracks of Time: The Progress of Humanity. 240p. 1999. 24.95 (*0-947993-72-X*, Pub. by Mlvrn Pubg Co) Brit Bk Co Inc.

Cooper, James, et al. European Logistics: Markets, Management & Strategy. 2nd ed. 344p. 1994. pap. 43.95 (*0-631-19226-3*) Blackwell Pubs.

Cooper, James, jt. ed. see Chisholm, Marie A.

Cooper, James A. & Weaver, David K., eds. A Trumpeter Swan Bibliography. 55p. (Orig.). 1986. pap. text 10.00 (*0-9619936-3-4*); disk 25.00 (*0-9619936-5-0*) Trumpeter Swan Soc.

Cooper, James D., ed. Lifeline Earthquake Engineering: Performance, Design & Construction: Proceedings of a Symposium Sponsored by the Technical Council on Lifeline Earthquake Engineering. 260p. 1984. 30.00 (*0-87262-414-5*) Am Soc Civil Eng.

Cooper, James D., jt. ed. see Cassaro, Michael A.

Cooper, James F. The Spy. large type ed. (G. K. Hall Perennial Bestsellers Ser.). 2000. 26.95 (*0-7838-8490-7*, G K Hall Lrg Type) Mac Lib Ref.

Cooper, James F., Jr. Tenacious of Their Liberties: The Congregationalists in Colonial Massachusetts. LC 97-42441. (Religion in America Ser.). 304p. 1999. text 55.00 (*0-19-511360-8*) OUP.

Cooper, James Fenimore. Afloat & Ashore. (Works of James Fenimore Cooper). 1990. reprint ed. lib. bdg. 79.00 (*0-7812-2392-X*) Rprt Serv.

— Afloat & Ashore: A Sea Tale. 549p. 1980. reprint ed. lib. bdg. 18.25 (*0-89968-212-X*, Lghtyr Pr) Buccaneer Bks.

— The American Democrat. LC 80-83794. 280p. 1981. reprint ed. 14.00 (*0-913966-91-6*); reprint ed. pap. 6.00 (*0-913966-92-4*) Liberty Fund.

***Cooper, James Fenimore.** The American Democrat & Other Essays. 2000. 35.00 (*0-89526-242-8*) Regnery Pub.

Cooper, James Fenimore. The Bravo. Ringe, Donald A., ed. (Masterworks of Literature Ser.). 1963. 21.95 (*0-8084-0065-7*); pap. 16.95 (*0-8084-0066-5*) NCUP.

— The Bravo. (Works of James Fenimore Cooper). 1990. reprint ed. lib. bdg. 79.00 (*0-7812-2380-6*) Rprt Serv.

— The Chainbearer. (Works of James Fenimore Cooper). 1990. reprint ed. lib. bdg. 79.00 (*0-7812-2394-6*) Rprt Serv.

— Chainbearer: Or, the Littlepage Manuscripts, 2 vols. in 1. LC 70-37651. reprint ed. 39.50 (*0-404-01704-5*) AMS Pr.

— Chainbearer or the Littlepage Manuscripts, 2 vols. in 1. LC 06-32149. 1981. reprint ed. 19.00 (*0-403-00135-8*) Scholarly.

— Correspondence of James Fenimore Cooper, 2 vols, Set. LC 70-164597. (Select Bibliographies Reprint Ser.). 1977. reprint ed. 58.95 (*0-8369-5881-0*) Ayer.

— Correspondence of James Fenimore Cooper, 2 Vols, Set. LC 71-160159. (American Biography Ser.: No. 32). 1971. reprint ed. lib. bdg. 150.00 (*0-8383-1295-0*) M S G Haskell Hse.

— Correspondence of James Fenimore Cooper, 2 vols., Set. (American Biography Ser.). 1991. reprint ed. lib. bdg. 148.00 (*0-7812-8090-7*) Rprt Serv.

— The Crater. (Works of James Fenimore Cooper). 1990. reprint ed. lib. bdg. 79.00 (*0-7812-2396-2*) Rprt Serv.

— The Crater: Or, Vulcan's Peak; a Tale of the Pacific. LC 76-42723. reprint ed. 47.50 (*0-404-60058-1*) AMS Pr.

— The Deerslayer. 528p. (YA). (gr. 9-12). 1991. mass mkt. 5.95 (*0-553-21085-8*, Bantam Classics) Bantam.

— The Deerslayer. 1976. lib. bdg. 27.95 (*0-89968-162-X*, Lghtyr Pr) Buccaneer Bks.

— The Deerslayer. 544p. (J). (gr. 7). 1963. mass mkt. 5.95 (*0-451-52484-5*, CE1645, Sig Classics) NAL.

— The Deerslayer, 4 vols. 40.00 (*0-614-30524-1*) NAVH.

***Cooper, James Fenimore.** The Deerslayer. Peck, Daniel H., ed. (Oxford World's Classics Ser.). (Illus.). 592p. 2000. pap. 9.95 (*0-19-283725-7*) OUP.

Cooper, James Fenimore. The Deerslayer. 560p. 1993. pap. 6.95 (*0-460-87186-2*, Everyman's Classic Lib) Tuttle Pubng.

— The Deerslayer. Pease, Donald, ed. & intro. by. 384p. 1996. pap. 10.95 (*0-14-039061-8*, Penguin Classics) Viking Penguin.

— The Deerslayer. (Classics Library). 1998. pap. 3.95 (*1-85326-552-7*, 5527WW, Pub. by Wrdsworth Edits) NTC Contemp Pub Co.

Cooper, James Fenimore. Deerslayer. 410p. Date not set. 27.95 (*0-8488-2517-9*) Amereon Ltd.

Cooper, James Fenimore. The Deerslayer. (Works of James Fenimore Cooper). 1990. reprint ed. lib. bdg. 79.00 (*0-7812-2387-3*) Rprt Serv.

— The Deerslayer: or the First Warpath. Schachterle, Lance, ed. & intro. by. LC 87-9928. (Writings of James Fenimore Cooper). 682p. (C). 1987. text 59.50 (*0-87395-361-4*) State U NY Pr.

— The Deerslayer: or the First Warpath. Schachterle, Lance, ed. & intro. by. LC 87-9928. (Writings of James Fenimore Cooper). 682p. (C). 1987. pap. text 19.95 (*0-87395-790-3*) State U NY Pr.

— The Deerslayer: or the First Warpath. 1987. 11.05 (*0-606-00553-6*, Pub. by Turtleback) Demco.

— Early Critical Essays, Eighteen Twenty to Eighteen Twenty-Two. LC 55-11038. 160p. 1977. reprint ed. 50.00 (*0-8201-1228-3*) Schol Facsimiles.

— Gleanings in Europe: England. LC 80-16993. (Writings of James Fenimore Cooper). 375p. (C). 1981. text 59.50 (*0-87395-367-3*) State U NY Pr.

— Gleanings in Europe: England. LC 80-16993. (Writings of James Fenimore Cooper). 375p. (C). 1983. pap. text 24.95 (*0-87395-459-9*) State U NY Pr.

— Gleanings in Europe: France. LC 82-669. (Writings of James Fenimore Cooper). 348p. (C). 1983. text 59.50 (*0-87395-368-1*); pap. text 24.95 (*0-87395-596-X*) State U NY Pr.

— Gleanings in Europe: Italy. LC 79-15177. (Writings of James Fenimore Cooper). 377p. 1981. text 59.50 (*0-87395-365-7*) State U NY Pr.

— Gleanings in Europe: Italy. LC 79-15177. (Writings of James Fenimore Cooper). 377p. 1983. pap. text 24.95 (*0-87395-460-2*) State U NY Pr.

— Gleanings in Europe: Switzerland. LC 79-13133. (Writings of James Fenimore Cooper). 361p. (C). 1983. pap. text 24.95 (*0-87395-422-X*) State U NY Pr.

— Gleanings in Europe: The Rhine. LC 86-14402. (Writings of James Fenimore Cooper). 326p. (C). 1983. pap. text 24.95 (*0-87395-928-0*) State U NY Pr.

— Gleanings in Europe: The Rhine. LC 86-14402. (Writings of James Fenimore Cooper). 326p. (C). 1986. text 59.50 (*0-87395-366-5*) State U NY Pr.

***Cooper, James Fenimore.** The Headman. (Notable American Authors Ser.: Pt. I). 444p. 2000. reprint ed. lib. bdg. 79.00 (*0-7812-2402-0*) Rprt Serv.

— The Heidenmauer. (Notable American Authors Ser.: Pt. I). 399p. 2000. reprint ed. lib. bdg. 79.00 (*0-7812-2400-4*) Rprt Serv.

Cooper, James Fenimore. The History of the Navy of the United States of America. LC 87-33697. 560p. 1988. 75.00 (*0-8201-1430-8*) Schol Facsimiles.

— The History of the Navy of the United States of America. (Works of James Fenimore Cooper). 1990. reprint ed. lib. bdg. 79.00 (*0-7812-2385-7*) Rprt Serv.

— Home As Found. (Works of James Fenimore Cooper). 1990. reprint ed. lib. bdg. 79.00 (*0-7812-2384-9*) Rprt Serv.

— Homeward Bound. LC 88-26464. 471p. 1988. reprint ed. 28.00 (*0-933249-11-X*) Mid-Peninsula Lib.

— Homeward Bound. (Works of James Fenimore Cooper). 1990. reprint ed. lib. bdg. 79.00 (*0-7812-2383-0*) Rprt Serv.

— Last of Mohicans. 1991. mass mkt. 3.95 (*0-425-12674-9*) Berkley Pub.

— Last of the Mohicans. 432p. (J). (gr. 7). 1962. mass mkt. 4.95 (*0-451-52503-5*, Sig Classics) NAL.

***Cooper, James Fenimore.** Last of the Mohicans. (Signet Classics Ser.). (Illus.). 416p. 2000. mass mkt. 4.95 (*0-451-52765-8*, Sig Classics) NAL.

Cooper, James Fenimore. Last of the Mohicans. 1980. 10.05 (*0-606-02760-2*, Pub. by Turtleback) Demco.

— Last of the Mohicans. (Step-Up Classics). (J). 1993. 9.09 (*0-606-02705-X*, Pub. by Turtleback) Demco.

— The Last of the Mohicans. (Classics Illustrated Study Guides Ser.). (Illus.). 1997. mass mkt. 4.99 (*1-57840-053-8*, Pub. by Acclaim Bks) Penguin Putnam.

— The Last of the Mohicans. (Illustrated Classics Collection 3). 64p. 1994. pap. 4.95 (*0-7854-0699-9*, 40459) Am Guidance.

— The Last of the Mohicans. 27.95 (*0-89190-895-1*) Amereon Ltd.

— The Last of the Mohicans. (Bantam Classics Ser.). (Illus.). 377p. 1982. mass mkt. 4.95 (*0-553-21329-6*, Bantam Classics) Bantam.

— The Last of the Mohicans. (J). 1989. 26.95 (*0-89968-254-5*) Buccaneer Bks.

— The Last of the Mohicans, 3 vols. 30.00 (*0-614-30530-6*) NAVH.

— The Last of the Mohicans. McWilliams, John, ed. & intro. by. (Oxford World's Classics Ser.). (Illus.). 458p. 1998. pap. 8.95 (*0-19-283505-X*) OUP.

— The Last of the Mohicans. Peters, Sally, ed. 432p. 1992. mass mkt. 5.99 (*0-671-75931-0*) PB.

— The Last of the Mohicans. Vogel, Malvina, ed. (Great Illustrated Classics Ser.: Vol. 24). (Illus.). 240p. (J). (gr. 3-6). 1992. 9.95 (*0-86611-975-2*) Playmore Inc.

— The Last of the Mohicans. LC 92-35775. (Step into Classics Ser.). (Illus.). 96p. (J). (gr. 4-7). 1993. pap. 3.99 (*0-679-84706-5*, Pub. by Random Bks Yng Read) Random.

— The Last of the Mohicans. LC 86-17694. (Illus.). 376p. (J). 1986. 28.00 (*0-684-18711-6*) Scribner.

— The Last of the Mohicans. Beard, James F., ed. & intro. by. LC 82-21890. (Writings of James Fenimore Cooper). 418p. 1983. text 19.50 (*0-87395-362-2*) State U NY Pr.

— The Last of the Mohicans. Beard, James F., ed. & intro. by. LC 82-21890. (Writings of James Fenimore Cooper). 418p. (C). 1983. pap. text 19.95 (*0-87395-470-X*) State U NY Pr.

— The Last of the Mohicans. 480p. 1992. mass mkt. 3.99 (*0-8125-2297-4*, Pub. by Tor Bks) St Martin.

— The Last of the Mohicans. Slotkin, Richard, ed. & intro. by. LC 86-2570. (Classics Ser.). (Illus.). 688p. 1986. pap. 13.99 (*0-14-039024-3*, Penguin Classics) Viking Penguin.

— The Last of the Mohicans. (Classics Library). 432p. 1997. pap. 3.95 (*1-85326-049-5*, 0495WW, Pub. by Wrdsworth Edits) NTC Contemp Pub Co.

— The Last of the Mohicans. abr. ed. Farr, Naunerle C., ed. (Now Age Illustrated III Ser.). (Illus.). (J). (gr. 4-12). 1977. pap. text 2.95 (*0-88301-267-7*) Pendulum Pr.

— The Last of the Mohicans. adapted ed. (Living Classics Ser.). (Illus.). 32p. (J). (gr. 3-7). 1997. 14.95 (*0-7641-7048-1*) Barron.

— The Last of the Mohicans. (Works of James Fenimore Cooper). 1990. reprint ed. lib. bdg. 79.00 (*0-7812-2374-1*) Rprt Serv.

— The Last of the Mohicans. rev. ed. 432p. 1994. pap. 5.95 (*0-460-87545-0*, Everyman's Classic Lib) Tuttle Pubng.

— The Last of the Mohicans. 2nd ed. (Illustrated Classic Book Ser.). (Illus.). 61p. (J). (gr. 3 up). 1998. reprint ed. pap. text 4.95 (*1-56767-249-3*) Educ Insights.

— The Last of the Mohicans Read-Along. (Illustrated Classics Collections 3). 64p. 1994. pap. 14.95 incl. audio (*0-7854-0740-5*, 40461) Am Guidance.

— The Leatherstocking Saga. (J). (gr. 5-6). 44.95 (*0-8488-0059-1*) Amereon Ltd.

— The Leatherstocking Tales: The Pathfinder; The Deerslayer. Navius, Blake, ed. LC 84-25060. (Library of America Ser.: Vol. 2). 1051p. 1985. 35.00 (*0-940450-21-6*, C12048, Pub. by Library of America) Penguin Putnam.

— The Leatherstocking Tales Vol. 1: The Pioneers; The Last of the Mohicans; The Prairie. Nevius, Blake, ed. LC 84-25060. (Library of America Ser.). 1347p. 1985. 40.00 (*0-940450-20-8*, C10461, Pub. by Library of America) Penguin Putnam.

— A Letter to His Countryman. (Works of James Fenimore Cooper). 1990. reprint ed. lib. bdg. 79.00 (*0-7812-2381-4*) Rprt Serv.

— Letters & Journals, Vol. 2. Beard, James F., ed. LC 60-5388. (Illus.). 442p. 1960. reprint ed. pap. 137.10 (*0-7837-3082-9*, 205746500002) Bks Demand.

— Letters & Journals, Vol.1. Beard, James F., ed. LC 60-5388. (Illus.). 500p. 1994. reprint ed. pap. 155.00 (*0-7837-3081-0*, 205746500001) Bks Demand.

— Letters & Journals of James Fenimore Cooper, 6 vols. Beard, James F., ed. Incl. Set. JF Cooper's Letters, 8 Journals. 895p. 1968. 80.00 (*0-674-52552-3*); Set. 992p. 1964. 79.95 (*0-674-52551-5*); (Illus.). write for info. (*0-318-53093-7*) Belknap Pr.

— Lionel Lincoln. (Works of James Fenimore Cooper). 1990. reprint ed. lib. bdg. 79.00 (*0-7812-2373-3*) Rprt Serv.

— Lionel Lincoln: or The Leaguer of Boston. LC 84-8675. (Writings of James Fenimore Cooper). 437p. (C). 1985. text 59.50 (*0-87395-416-5*); pap. text 24.95 (*0-87395-671-0*) State U NY Pr.

***Cooper, James Fenimore.** Miles Wallingford. (Notable American Authors Ser.: Pt. I). 454p. 2000. reprint ed. lib. bdg. 79.00 (*0-7812-2399-7*) Rprt Serv.

Cooper, James Fenimore. The Monikins. Hedger, James S., ed. (Masterworks of Literature Ser.). pap. 15.95 (*0-8084-0421-0*) NCUP.

— The Monikins. (Works of James Fenimore Cooper). 1990. reprint ed. lib. bdg. 79.00 (*0-685-44762-6*) Rprt Serv.

— Ned Myers. (Works of James Fenimore Cooper). 1990. reprint ed. lib. bdg. 79.00 (*0-7812-2391-1*) Rprt Serv.

— Ned Myers: A Life Before the Mast. Sweetman, Jack, ed. LC 89-30546. (Classics of Naval Literature Ser.). 320p. 1989. reprint ed. 32.95 (*0-87021-417-9*) Naval Inst Pr.

— Notions of the Americans: Picked up by a Travelling Bachelor. Williams, Gary, ed. LC 89-4493. (Writings of James Fenimore Cooper). 807p. (C). 1991. pap. text 24.95 (*0-7914-0214-2*) State U NY Pr.

— Notions of the Americans: Picked up by a Travelling Bachelor. Williams, Gary, ed. LC 89-4493. (Writings of James Fenimore Cooper). 807p. (C). 1991. text 59.50 (*0-7914-0213-4*) State U NY Pr.

— Notions of the Americans: Picked up by a Travelling Bachelor. (Works of James Fenimore Cooper). 1990. reprint ed. lib. bdg. 79.00 (*0-7812-2377-6*) Rprt Serv.

— The Oak Openings. 520p. 1984. reprint ed. 40.00 (*0-938190-33-4*) North Atlantic.

— The Pathfinder. (Airmont Classics Ser.). (YA). (gr. 6 up). 1964. mass mkt. 2.95 (*0-8049-0035-3*, CL-35) Airmont.

— The Pathfinder. 1976. lib. bdg. 26.95 (*0-89968-159-X*, Lghtyr Pr) Buccaneer Bks.

— The Pathfinder. (Illus.). 488p. (J). (gr. k-10). 1961. mass mkt. 5.95 (*0-451-52257-5*, Sig Classics) NAL.

— The Pathfinder. House, Kay S., ed. & intro. by. LC 88-32956. 496p. 1989. pap. 9.95 (*0-14-039071-5*, Penguin Classics) Viking Penguin.

— Pathfinder. 1961. 11.05 (*0-606-02759-9*, Pub. by Turtleback) Demco.

— The Pathfinder. (Works of James Fenimore Cooper). 1990. reprint ed. lib. bdg. 79.00 (*0-7812-2386-5*) Rprt Serv.

***Cooper, James Fenimore.** The Pathfinder: Or the Inland Sea. Kelly, William P., ed. (Oxford World's Classics Ser.). 528p. 2000. pap. 8.95 (*0-19-283989-6*) OUP.

— The Pathfinder: or the Inland Sea. 351p. Date not set. 25.95 (*0-8488-2541-1*) Amereon Ltd.

Cooper, James Fenimore. The Pathfinder: or the Inland Sea. LC 79-15598. (Writings of James Fenimore Cooper). 569p. (C). 1980. pap. text 19.95 (*0-87395-477-7*) State U NY Pr.

— The Pilot. Seymour-House, Kay, ed. LC 84-8765. (Writings of James Fenimore Cooper). 479p. (C). 1986. pap. text 19.95 (*0-87395-791-1*) State U NY Pr.

— The Pilot. 1990. reprint ed. lib. bdg. 27.95 (*0-89966-704-X*) Buccaneer Bks.

— The Pilot. (Works of James Fenimore Cooper). 1990. reprint ed. lib. bdg. 79.00 (*0-7812-2372-5*) Rprt Serv.

— The Pilot. (BCL1-PS American Literature Ser.). 339p. 1993. reprint ed. lib. bdg. 89.00 (*0-7812-6953-9*) Rprt Serv.

— The Pilot: A Tale of the Sea. Seymour House, Kay, ed. LC 84-8765. (Writings of James Fenimore Cooper). 479p. (C). 1986. text 59.50 (*0-87395-415-7*) State U NY Pr.

— Pioneers. 346p. Date not set. 25.95 (*0-8488-2544-6*) Amereon Ltd.

— Pioneers. 448p. (YA). 1964. mass mkt. 5.95 (*0-451-52521-3*, Sig Classics) NAL.

— The Pioneers. 1976. lib. bdg. 26.95 (*0-89968-157-3*, Lghtyr Pr) Buccaneer Bks.

— The Pioneers. Wallace, James D., ed. & intro. by. (Oxford World's Classics Ser.). (Illus.). 496p. 2000. pap. 8.95 (*0-19-283667-6*) OUP.

— The Pioneers. Beard, James F., ed. LC 77-21795. (Writings of James Fenimore Cooper). 460p. (C). 1980. pap. text 18.95 (*0-87395-423-8*) State U NY Pr.

— The Pioneers. Clark, Robert, ed. (Illus.). 444p. 1993. pap. 6.95 (*0-460-87187-0*, Everyman's Classic Lib) Tuttle Pubng.

— The Pioneers. Ringe, Donald A., ed. & intro. by. LC 87-31694. 448p. 1988. pap. 9.95 (*0-14-039007-3*, Penguin Classics) Viking Penguin.

— The Pioneers. (Works of James Fenimore Cooper). 1990. reprint ed. lib. bdg. 79.00 (*0-7812-2371-7*) Rprt Serv.

— Places in the Sun. Place, Lew, ed. (Illus.). 1989. 19.95 (*0-87026-070-7*) Westernlore.

— Prairie. 411p. Date not set. 27.95 (*0-8488-2546-2*) Amereon Ltd.

— The Prairie. 1976. lib. bdg. 28.95 (*0-89968-160-3*, Lghtyr Pr) Buccaneer Bks.

***Cooper, James Fenimore.** The Prairie. Ringe, Donald A., ed. (Oxford World's Classics Ser.). 432p. 2000. pap. 10.95 (*0-19-283766-4*) OUP.

Cooper, James Fenimore. The Prairie. Elliott, James P., ed. LC 84-24096. 566p. (C). 1985. pap. text 19.95 (*0-87395-672-9*) State U NY Pr.

— The Prairie. Elliott, James P., ed. & intro. by. LC 84-24096. 566p. (C). 1985. text 59.50 (*0-87395-363-0*) State U NY Pr.

— The Prairie. Nevius, Blake, ed. & intro. by. 384p. 1987. pap. 11.95 (*0-14-039026-X*, Penguin Classics) Viking Penguin.

— The Prairie. (Works of James Fenimore Cooper). 1990. reprint ed. lib. bdg. 79.00 (*0-7812-2375-X*) Rprt Serv.

C

An Asterisk (*) at the beginning of an entry indicates that the title is appearing for the first time.

— Precaution. (Works of James Fenimore Cooper). 1990. reprint ed. lib. bdg. 79.00 (0-7812-2369-5) Rprt Serv.

— Precaution. LC 06-29686. reprint ed. 11.00 (0-403-00101-3) Scholarly.

— Precaution, 2 vols., Set. LC 73-1898. (BCL Ser.: No. I). reprint ed. 47.50 (0-404-01707-X) AMS Pr.

— The Red Rover. Date not set. lib. bdg. 28.95 (0-8488-1966-7) Amereon Ltd.

— The Red Rover. 1976. 30.95 (0-8488-1407-X) Amereon Ltd.

— The Red Rover. 1976. lib. bdg. 29.95 (0-89968-158-1, Lghtyr Pr) Buccaneer Bks.

— The Red Rover. (Works of James Fenimore Cooper). 1990. reprint ed. lib. bdg. 79.00 (0-7812-2376-8) Rprt Serv.

— The Red Rover: A Tale. Philbrick, Thomas & Philbrick, Marianne, eds. LC 89-31289. 676p. 1991. text 59.50 (0-7914-0188-X) State U NY Pr.

— The Red Rover: A Tale. Philbrick, Thomas & Philbrick, Marianne, eds. LC 89-31289. 676p. (C). 1991. pap. text 19.95 (0-7914-0189-8) State U NY Pr.

— The Redskins. (Works of James Fenimore Cooper). 1990. reprint ed. lib. bdg. 79.00 (0-7812-2395-4) Rprt Serv.

— Representative Selections. (BCL1-PS American Literature Ser.). 350p. 1993. reprint ed. lib. bdg. 89.00 (0-7812-6952-0) Rprt Serv.

— Representative Selections, with Introduction, Bibliography & Notes. Spiller, Robert E., ed. & intro. by. LC 76-48040. (Illus.). 350p. 1977. reprint ed. lib. bdg. 35.00 (0-8371-9317-6, CORES, Greenwood Pr) Greenwood.

— Satanstoe. LC 62-9515. (Bison Bk.: BB138). 442p. reprint ed. pap. 137.10 (0-608-14266-2, 202220500025) Bks Demand.

— Satanstoe. (Works of James Fenimore Cooper). 1990. reprint ed. lib. bdg. 79.00 (0-7812-2393-8) Rprt Serv.

— Satanstoe, or the Littlepage Manuscripts: A Tale of the Colony. LC 88-12196. (Writings of James Fenimore Cooper). 500p. 1990. pap. text 24.95 (0-88706-904-5) State U NY Pr.

— Satanstoe, or the Littlepage Manuscripts: A Tale of the Colony. LC 88-12196. (Writings of James Fenimore Cooper). 500p. 1990. text 59.50 (0-88706-903-7) State U NY Pr.

— Sea Lions. Walker, Warren S., ed. LC 65-18416. (Illus.). 533p. reprint ed. 165.30 (0-8357-9714-7, 201602700097) Bks Demand.

***Cooper, James Fenimore.** The Sea Lions. (Notable American Authors Ser.: Pt. I). 457p. 2000. reprint ed. lib. bdg. 79.00 (0-7812-2401-2) Rprt Serv.

Cooper, James Fenimore. Sea Tales: The Pilot; The Red Rover. House, Kay S. & Philbrick, Thomas L., eds. 902p. 1991. 35.00 (0-940450-70-4, Pub. by Library of America) Penguin Putnam.

— The Spy. 1976. lib. bdg. 28.95 (0-89968-161-1, Lghtyr Pr) Buccaneer Bks.

— The Spy. Pickering, James H., ed. (Masterworks of Literature Ser.). 1971. pap. 17.95 (0-8084-0027-4) NCUP.

— Spy. 348p. Date not set. 25.95 (0-8488-2552-7) Amereon Ltd.

— The Spy. (Works of James Fenimore Cooper). 1990. reprint ed. lib. bdg. 79.00 (0-7812-2370-9) Rprt Serv.

***Cooper, James Fenimore.** The Spy: A Tale of the Neutral Ground. LC 99-88709. (Writings of James Fenimore Cooper Ser.). 2000. write for info. (0-404-64454-6) AMS Pr.

Cooper, James Fenimore. The Spy: A Tale of the Neutral Ground. LC 97-12074. 412p. 1997. pap. 12.95 (0-14-043628-6) Viking Penguin.

— Tales for Fifteen. LC 59-6525. 240p. 1977. reprint ed. 50.00 (0-8201-1247-X) Schol Facsimiles.

— The Two Admirals. LC 88-12190. 511p. (gr. 9-12). 1990. text 59.50 (0-88706-905-3); pap. text 19.95 (0-88706-907-X) State U NY Pr.

— The Two Admirals. (Works of James Fenimore Cooper). 1990. reprint ed. lib. bdg. 79.00 (0-7812-2388-1) Rprt Serv.

— Water-Witch. (BCL Ser.). reprint ed. 37.50 (0-404-00629-9) AMS Pr.

— The Water Witch. (Works of James Fenimore Cooper). 1990. reprint ed. lib. bdg. 79.00 (0-7812-2379-2) Rprt Serv.

— Water-Witch: or The Skimmer of the Seas. LC 04-15437. 1997. 13.00 (0-403-00244-3) Scholarly.

— The Ways of the Hour. LC 98-119082. (Pocket Classics Ser.). 336p. 1996. pap. 10.95 (0-7509-1158-1, Pub. by Sutton Pub Ltd) Intl Pubs Mktg.

— The Ways of the Hour. (Works of James Fenimore Cooper). 1990. reprint ed. lib. bdg. 79.00 (0-7812-2397-0) Rprt Serv.

— The Wept of Wish-Ton-Wish, 2 vols. in 1. (BCL Ser. I). reprint ed. 42.50 (0-404-01715-0) AMS Pr.

— The Wept of Wish-Ton-Wish. (Works of James Fenimore Cooper). 1990. reprint ed. lib. bdg. 79.00 (0-7812-2378-4) Rprt Serv.

— The Wept of Wish-Ton-Wish, 2 vols. in 1. LC 74-107169. 1971. reprint ed. 39.00 (0-403-00432-2) Scholarly.

— The Wing & Wing. (Works of James Fenimore Cooper). 1990. reprint ed. lib. bdg. 79.00 (0-7812-2389-X) Rprt Serv.

— The Wing-&-Wing, No. 4. LC 98-6699. 412p. 1998. pap. 15.00 (0-8050-5567-3, Owl) H Holt & Co.

— The Wing-&-Wing, No. 5. LC 98-14088. 470p. 1998. pap. 15.00 (0-8050-5568-1, Owl) H Holt & Co.

— The Wing-& Wing: or Le Feu-Follet: A Tale. LC 98-14088. (Heart of Oak Sea Classics Ser.). 448p. 1998. 30.00 (0-8050-5987-3) H Holt & Co.

— The Works of James Fenimore Cooper. 1990. reprint ed. lib. bdg. 63.00 (0-685-27629-5) Rprt Serv.

— Wyandotte, or the Hutted Knoll: A Tale. Philbrick, Thomas & Philbrick, Marianne, eds. LC 81-1132. 434p. (C). 1981. text 59.50 (0-87395-414-9); pap. text 19.95 (0-87395-469-6) State U NY Pr.

— Wyandotte, or the Hutted Knoll: A Tale. (Works of James Fenimore Cooper). 1990. reprint ed. lib. bdg. 79.00 (0-7812-2390-3) Rprt Serv.

Cooper, James Fenimore & Turner, Frederick. Knights of the Brush: The Hudson River School & the Moral Landscape. LC 99-16549. (Illus.). 109p. 1999. 35.00 (1-55595-180-5, Pub. by Hudson Hills) Natl Bk Netwk.

Cooper, James Fenimore, jt. auth. see Steele, Alexander.

***Cooper, James Ford.** On the Finland Watch: An American Diplomat in Finland During the Cold War. rev. ed. LC 99-51717. Orig. Title: Asemamaana Suomi. (Illus.). 416p. 1999. 39.50 (0-941690-94-6) Regina Bks.

— On the Finland Watch: An American Diplomat in Finland During the Cold War. rev. ed. LC 99-51717. Orig. Title: Asemamaana Suomi. (Illus.). 416p. 1999. pap. 19.50 (0-941690-95-4) Regina Bks.

Cooper, James H. & Cooper, Vera D., eds. Shepard's Contemporary Health Care Issues. LC 94-19056. 1994. write for info. (0-07-172577-6) Shepards.

Cooper, James L. Artistry & Ingenuity in Artificial Stone: Indiana's Concrete Bridges, 1900-1942. (Illus.). 280p. 1997. pap. 19.95 (0-936631-13-9) DePauw Univ.

***Cooper, James L. & Hamre, R. H., eds.** Warmwater Fisheries: Symposium I (1991) (Illus.). 407p. (C). 1999. reprint ed. pap. text 45.00 (0-7881-8244-7) DIANE Pub.

Cooper, James M., ed. Classroom Teaching Skills. 5th ed. (C). 1994. text, teacher ed. 2.66 (0-669-34964-X); pap. text 52.36 (0-669-34963-1) HM Trade Div.

— Teachers' Problem Solving: A Casebook of Award-Winning Teaching Cases. LC 94-12554. 128p. 1995. pap. 26.00 (0-205-15203-1) Allyn.

Cooper, James M. & Cognition & Technology Group at Vandenberg University Staff. Classroom Teaching Skills. 6th ed. LC 98-72013. xviii, 381p. 1999. pap. text 41.07 (0-395-90413-7) HM.

Cooper, James M. & DeVault, M. Vere. Competency Based Teacher Education. LC 72-83478. 123p. 1973. 32.00 (0-8211-0010-6) McCutchan.

Cooper, James R. The Sermon Notebook of Samuel Parris, 1689-1694. Minkema, Kenneth P., ed. (Publication: Vol. 66). (Illus.). 322p. (C). 1993. text 50.00 (0-9620737-1-7) Colonial MA.

— Twilight's Last Gleaming: The Price of Happiness in America. LC 92-16854. 372p. (C). 1992. 32.95 (0-87975-719-1) Prometheus Bks.

***Cooper, James Thomas.** The First Christmas Teddy Bear. (Illus.). 32p. 1999. pap. 6.95 (0-9675037-0-1) Cooper Pubg Co.

Cooper, James W., Jr. Community & Nursing Home Practice Drug Therapy OBRA Monitoring & Patient Education Guidelines, 1993. LC 93-70156. 350p. (C). 1993. pap. text 42.50 (0-9635702-4-2) J W Cooper Cnslt.

Cooper, James W. Drug-Related Problems in Geriatric Nursing Home Patients. (Pharmaceutical Sciences Ser.). 101p. 1991. text 39.95 (1-56024-085-7); pap. text 19.95 (1-56024-086-5) Haworth Pr.

— Microsoft QuickBASIC for Scientists: Guide to Writing Better Programs. LC 88-10140. 281p. 1988. pap. 68.50 (0-471-61301-0) Wiley.

— Visual Basic for DOS: Building Scientific & Technical Applications. LC 93-16839. 424p. (Orig.). 1993. pap. 37.95 (0-471-59772-4) Wiley.

***Cooper, James W.** The Visual Basic Programmer's Guide to Java: Your Professional Toolkit for Object-Oriented Programming. LC 99-61416. (Illus.). 564p. 1999. pap. write for info. (5-8348-2172-3) iUniversecom.

Cooper, James W. Writing Scientific Programs under the OS-2 Presentation Manager. 403p. 1990. pap. 115.00 (0-471-51928-6) Wiley.

Cooper, James W., ed. Antiinfectives in the Elderly. LC 95-39976. (Journal of Geriatric Drug Therapy: Vol. 10, No. 1). 78p. 1996. 39.95 (1-56024-793-2, Pharmctl Prods) Haworth Pr.

— Antivirals in the Elderly. LC 96-3445. (Journal of Geriatric Drug Therapy: Vol. 10, No. 2). 79p. (C). 1996. 39.95 (1-56024-820-3, Pharmctl Prods) Haworth Pr.

— Antivirals in the Elderly. LC 96-3445. (Journal of Geriatric Drug Therapy: Vol. 10, No. 2). 79p. (C). 1997. pap. 14.95 (0-7890-0219-1, Pharmctl Prods) Haworth Pr.

— Diabetes Mellitus in the Elderly. LC 99-12436. 84p. 1999. 39.95 (0-7890-0682-0, Pharmctl Prods) Haworth Pr.

— Geriatric Drug Therapy Interventions. LC 97-46982. 90p. 1998. 29.95 (0-7890-0394-5) Haworth Pr.

***Cooper, James W., ed.** Geriatric Drug Therapy Interventions. 73p. 2000. pap. 19.95 Haworth Pr.

Cooper, James W., ed. Urinary Incontinence in the Elderly: Pharmacotherapy Treatment. LC 97-16252. (Journal of Geriatric Drug Therapy Ser.). 72p. 1997. 24.95 (0-7890-0327-9) Haworth Pr.

Cooper, James W. & Lam, Richard B. A Jump Start Course in C Plus Plus Programming. 296p. 1994. pap. 29.95 (0-471-03171-2) Wiley.

Cooper, James W. & Wade, William E., eds. Gastrointestinal Drug Therapy in the Elderly. LC 97-42595. (Journal of Geriatric Drug Therapy Ser.). 144p. 1998. 29.95 (0-7890-0395-3, Pharmctl Prods) Haworth Pr.

Cooper, James W. & Wilent, Steve. Object-Oriented Programming in Visual BASIC. LC 96-27179. (Special Reports). 1996. write for info. (1-880935-49-X) Pinnacle WA.

Cooper, James W., jt. ed. see Chisolm, Marie A.

Cooper, Jamie. Midwest Voter Registration Laws: A Comparative Overview. 60p. 1990. 12.00 (0-685-56592-0) CPA Washington.

Cooper, Jamie & Smith, Burek, eds. Agenda, 1993: Progressive Policies That Work. (C). 1992. pap. write for info. (0-89788-115-X) CPA Washington.

Cooper, Jamie, et al. Voter Registration & the States: Effective Policy Approaches to Increase Registration. 100p. 1991. 15.00 (0-685-56593-9) CPA Washington.

Cooper, Jan. Argument with An Angel. 128p. (Orig.). 1996. pap. 11.95 (0-944031-63-3) Aslan Pub.

— Argument with An Angel. 80p. (Orig.). 1993. pap. 15.95 (1-880365-65-0) Prof Pr NC.

Cooper, Jan, ed. see Laden, Elizabeth.

Cooper, Jan, ed. & illus. see Stephenson, E. L.

Cooper, Jane. Flashboat. pap. 13.00 (0-393-32087-1) Norton.

Cooper, Jane. Flashboat: Poems Collected & Reclaimed. LC 99-31822. 256p. 1999. text 23.95 (0-393-04777-6) Norton.

— Woodstove Cookery: At Home on the Range. LC 77-10640. (Illus.). 208p. 1983. pap. 12.95 (0-88266-108-6, Garden Way Pub) Storey Bks.

Cooper, Jane R., ed. Reading Adrienne Rich: Reviews & Re-Visions, 1951-81. LC 83-23377. (Under Discussion Ser.). 384p. 1984. pap. text 21.95 (0-472-06350-2, 06350) U of Mich Pr.

Cooper, Janet, ed. The Battle of Maldon: Fiction & Fact. LC 93-38742. 1993. 55.00 (1-85285-065-5) Hambledon Press.

— A History of the County Essex Vol. 9: The Borough of Colchester. (Victoria History of the Counties of England Ser.). (Illus.). 484p. 1994. 195.00 (0-19-722784-8) OUP.

Cooper, Janet E. Three Proud Princesses. LC 93-36897. (Illus.). 64p. (J). 2000. 19.95 (0-913720-86-0) Beil.

Cooper, Jason. Airports. LC 92-8677. (Great Places to Visit Ser.). 24p. (J). (gr. k-4). 1992. lib. bdg. 10.95 (0-86593-208-5) Rourke Corp.

— The Alaska Brown Bear. LC 96-52097. (Giants Among Us Discovery Library). 24p. (J). (gr. k-4). 1997. lib. bdg. 15.93 (1-55916-183-3) Rourke Bk Co.

— Apples. LC 97-13037. (Farm to Market Discovery Library). 24p. (J). (gr. k-4). 1997. lib. bdg. 14.60 (0-86625-622-9) Rourke Pubns.

— Arboles (Trees) (Spanish Language Books, Set 3: Los Jardines de la Tierra (The Earth's Garden)). (J). 1991. 14.60 (0-86592-498-8) Rourke Enter.

— Automoviles. (Maquinas de Viaje Ser.).Tr. of Automobiles. 24p. (J). (gr. k-4). 1991. lib. bdg. 14.60 (0-86592-510-0) Rourke Enter.

— Aviones. (Maquinas de Viaje Ser.).Tr. of Airplanes. 24p. (J). (gr. k-4). 1991. lib. bdg. 14.60 (0-86592-507-0) Rourke Enter.

— Baleen Whales. LC 96-19191. (Read All About Whales Ser.). 24p. (J). (gr. 1-4). 1996. lib. bdg. 12.95 (0-86593-450-9) Rourke Corp.

— Beef. LC 97-13038. (Farm to Market Discovery Library). 24p. (J). (gr. k-4). 1997. lib. bdg. 15.93 (0-86625-617-2) Rourke Pubns.

— Botes y Barcos. (Maquinas de Viaje Ser.).Tr. of Boats & Ships. 24p. (J). (gr. k-4). 1991. lib. bdg. 14.60 (0-86592-474-0) Rourke Enter.

— Bridges. (Man-Made Wonders Ser.). 24p. (J). (gr. k-4). 1991. lib. bdg. 14.60 (0-86592-628-X) Rourke Enter.

— Cactos (Cactus) (Spanish Language Books, Set 3: Los Jardines de la Tierra (The Earth's Garden)). (J). 1991. write for info. (0-86592-546-1) Rourke Enter.

— Camiones. (Maquinas de Viaje Ser.).Tr. of Trucks. 24p. (J). (gr. k-4). 1991. lib. bdg. 14.60 (0-86592-509-7) Rourke Enter.

— Canales. (Maravillas de la Humanidad Ser.: Set VI).Tr. of Canals. (SPA.). 24p. (J). (gr. k-4). 1991. lib. bdg. 14.60 (0-86592-923-8) Rourke Enter.

— Canals. (Man-Made Wonders Ser.). 24p. (J). (gr. k-4). 1991. lib. bdg. 14.60 (0-86592-638-7) Rourke Enter.

***Cooper, Jason.** Canoes & Kayaks. LC 99-15110. (Boats Ser.). 24p. 1999. lib. bdg. write for info. (0-86593-560-2) Rourke Corp.

— Cargo Ships. LC 99-15112. (Boats Ser.). 24p. 1999. lib. bdg. write for info. (0-86593-561-0) Rourke Corp.

Cooper, Jason. Castillos. (Maravillas de la Humanidad Ser.: Set VI).Tr. of Castles. (SPA.). 24p. (J). (gr. k-4). 1991. lib. bdg. 14.60 (0-86592-937-8) Rourke Enter.

— Centipedes. (Animals Without Bones Discovery Library). 24p. (J). (gr. k-4). Date not set. lib. bdg. 14.60 (1-57103-574-5) Rourke Pr.

— Centipedes. LC 95-46037. (Animals Without Bones Ser.). (J). 1996. write for info. (0-86625-574-5) Rourke Pubns.

— Coral Reef. LC 92-16077. (Sea Discovery Library). 24p. (J). (gr. k-4). 1992. lib. bdg. 10.95 (0-86593-229-8) Rourke Corp.

— Corn. LC 97-13056. (Farm to Market Discovery Library). (Illus.). 24p. (J). (gr. k-4). 1998. lib. bdg. 14.60 (0-86625-620-2) Rourke Pubns.

— Crabs. LC 95-26008. (Animals Without Bones Discovery Library). (Illus.). 24p. (J). (gr. k-4). 1996. lib. bdg. 14.60 (0-86625-571-0) Rourke Pubns.

***Cooper, Jason.** Cruise Ships. LC 99-15111. (Boats Ser.). 24p. 1999. lib. bdg. write for info. (0-86593-563-7) Rourke Corp.

Cooper, Jason. Dairy Products. LC 97-13231. (Farm to Market Discovery Library). 24p. (J). (gr. k-4). 1998. lib. bdg. 14.60 (0-86625-619-9) Rourke Pubns.

— Dams. (Man-Made Wonders Ser.). 24p. (J). (gr. k-4). 1991. lib. bdg. 14.60 (0-86592-627-1) Rourke Enter.

— Death Valley. LC 95-12306. (Natural Wonders Ser.). (J). (gr. 2-6). 1995. lib. bdg. 14.60 (1-57103-015-8) Rourke Pr.

— Death Valley. (Natural Wonders Discovery Library). 24p. (J). (gr. k-4). Date not set. lib. bdg. 10.95 (0-86625-015-8) Rourke Pubns.

— The Earth's Garden Series, 6 bks., Set. (J). 1991. 83.70 (0-86592-619-0) Rourke Enter.

— Electricdad. (Secretos de la Ciencia Ser.).Tr. of Electricity. 24p. (J). (gr. k-4). Date not set. lib. bdg. 10.95 (0-86593-327-8) Rourke Corp.

— Electricity. (Science Secrets Discovery Library). 24p. (J). (gr. k-4). 1992. lib. bdg. 10.95 (0-86593-169-0) Rourke Corp.

— Estaciones de Policia. (Lugares Divertidos Para Visitar Ser.).Tr. of Police Stations. 24p. (J). (gr. k-4). 1994. lib. bdg. 10.95 (0-86593-240-9) Rourke Corp.

— The Everglades. LC 95-12303. (Natural Wonders Ser.). (J). (gr. 2-6). 1995. lib. bdg. 14.60 (1-57103-017-4) Rourke Pr.

— Farm Cats. LC 94-39535. (Barnyard Friends Discovery Library). 24p. (J). (gr. k-4). 1995. lib. bdg. 15.93 (1-55916-094-2) Rourke Bk Co.

— Farm Dogs. LC 94-39534. (Barnyard Friends Discovery Library). 24p. (J). (gr. k-4). 1995. lib. bdg. 15.93 (1-55916-091-8) Rourke Bk Co.

— Farms. LC 92-10078. (Great Places to Visit Ser.). 24p. (J). (gr. k-4). 1992. lib. bdg. 10.95 (0-86593-211-5) Rourke Corp.

— Faros. (Maravillas de la Humanidad Ser.: Set VI).Tr. of Lighthouses. (SPA.). 24p. (J). (gr. k-4). 1991. lib. bdg. 14.60 (0-86592-936-X) Rourke Enter.

— Fire Stations. LC 92-8676. (Great Places to Visit Ser.). 24p. (J). (gr. k-4). 1992. lib. bdg. 10.95 (0-86593-210-7) Rourke Corp.

***Cooper, Jason.** Fishing Boats. LC 99-15115. (Boats Ser.). 24p. 1999. lib. bdg. write for info. (0-86593-562-9) Rourke Corp.

Cooper, Jason. Flowers. (Earth's Garden Discovery Library). 24p. (J). (gr. k-4). 1991. lib. bdg. 14.60 (0-86592-620-4) Rourke Enter.

— Geese. LC 94-38413. (Barnyard Friends Discovery Library). 24p. (J). (gr. k-4). 1995. lib. bdg. 15.93 (1-55916-089-6) Rourke Bk Co.

***Cooper, Jason.** Gettysburg. LC 99-27476. (American Landmarks Ser.). 1999. write for info. (0-86593-545-9) Rourke Corp.

Cooper, Jason. Goats. LC 94-39536. (Barnyard Friends Discovery Library). 24p. (J). (gr. k-4). 1995. lib. bdg. 15.93 (1-55916-093-4) Rourke Bk Co.

— Granjas. (Lugares Divertidos Para Visitar Ser.).Tr. of Farms. 24p. (J). (gr. k-4). 1994. lib. bdg. 10.95 (0-86593-237-9) Rourke Corp.

— Great Smoky Mountains. LC 95-12304. (Natural Wonders Ser.). (J). (gr. 2-6). 1995. lib. bdg. 14.60 (1-57103-014-X) Rourke Pr.

— The Great White Shark. LC 96-52098. (Giants Among Us Discovery Library). 24p. (J). (gr. k-4). 1997. lib. bdg. 15.93 (1-55916-185-X) Rourke Bk Co.

— Historic Boston. LC 99-27477. (American Landmarks Ser.). (Illus.). 24p. (J). (gr. 3-5). 1999. lib. bdg. 13.45 (0-86593-546-7) Rourke Corp.

***Cooper, Jason.** Historic Philadelphia. LC 00-38729. (Historic Landmarks Ser.). (J). 2000. write for info. (1-55916-326-7) Rourke Bk Co.

— Historic St. Augustine. LC 00-38728. (Historic Landmarks Ser.). 2000. write for info. (1-55916-328-3) Rourke Bk Co.

Cooper, Jason. Imanes. (Secretos de la Ciencia Ser.).Tr. of Magnets. 24p. (J). (gr. k-4). Date not set. lib. bdg. 10.95 (0-86593-325-1) Rourke Corp.

— Insect-Eating Plants. (Earth's Garden Discovery Library). 24p. (J). (gr. k-4). 1991. lib. bdg. 14.60 (0-86592-624-7) Rourke Enter.

— Large Sea Creatures. LC 92-16072. (Discovery Library of the Sea). (J). 1992. 9.50 (0-685-59714-8) Rourke Corp.

— Large Sea Creatures. LC 92-16072. (Sea Discovery Library). 24p. (J). (gr. k-4). 1992. lib. bdg. 10.95 (0-86593-231-X) Rourke Corp.

— Light. LC 92-8808. (Science Secrets Ser.). (J). 1992. 9.50 (0-685-59295-2) Rourke Corp.

— Light. LC 92-8808. (Science Secrets Discovery Library). 24p. (J). (gr. k-4). 1992. lib. bdg. 10.95 (0-86593-166-6) Rourke Corp.

— Lighthouses. (Man-Made Wonders Ser.). 24p. (J). (gr. k-4). 1991. lib. bdg. 14.60 (0-86592-630-1) Rourke Enter.

***Cooper, Jason.** Little Bighorn Battlefield. LC 00-38727. (Historic Landmarks Ser.). (Illus.). (J). 2000. write for info. (1-55916-325-9) Rourke Bk Co.

Cooper, Jason. Lobsters. LC 95-26010. (Animals Without Bones Discovery Library). (Illus.). 24p. (J). (gr. k-4). 1996. lib. bdg. 15.93 (0-86625-572-9) Rourke Pubns.

— Luz. (Secretos de la Ciencia Ser.).Tr. of Light. 24p. (J). (gr. k-4). Date not set. lib. bdg. 10.95 (0-86593-326-X) Rourke Corp.

— Magnetism. LC 92-8807. (Science Secrets Ser.). (J). 1992. 8.95 (0-685-59294-4) Rourke Corp.

— Magnets. LC 92-8807. (Science Secrets Discovery Library). 24p. (J). (gr. k-4). 1992. lib. bdg. 10.95 (0-86593-165-8) Rourke Corp.

— Man-Made Wonders Series, 6 bks., Set. (J). 1991. lib. bdg. 87.60 (0-86592-626-3) Rourke Enter.

— Maravillas de la Humanidad (Man-Made Wonders) Series, 6 bks., Set VI. (SPA.). (J). 1991. 87.60 (0-86592-899-1) Rourke Enter.

— The Mississippi Delta. LC 95-12305. (Natural Wonders Ser.). (J). (gr. 2-6). 1995. lib. bdg. 14.60 (1-57103-016-6) Rourke Pr.

— Moose. LC 96-52094. (Giants Among Us Discovery Library). 24p. (J). (gr. k-4). 1997. lib. bdg. 15.93 (1-55916-184-1) Rourke Bk Co.

— Motocicletas. (Maquinas de Viaje Ser.).Tr. of Motorcycles. 24p. (J). (gr. k-4). 1991. lib. bdg. 14.60 (0-86592-508-9) Rourke Enter.

— Mount Vernon. LC 99-27475. (American Landmarks Ser.). (Illus.). 24p. 1999. lib. bdg. write for info. (0-86593-548-3) Rourke Corp.

— Museos. (Lugares Divertidos Para Visitar Ser.).Tr. of Museums. 24p. (J). (gr. k-4). 1994. lib. bdg. 10.95 (0-86593-239-5) Rourke Corp.

— Museums. LC 92-12556. (J). 1992. 9.50 (*0-685-59389-4*) Rourke Corp.

— Museums. LC 92-12556. (Great Places to Visit Ser.). 24p. (J). (gr. k-4). 1992. lib. bdg. 10.95 (*0-86593-209-3*) Rourke Corp.

— Mushrooms. (Earth's Garden Discovery Library). 24p. (J). (gr. k-4). 1991. lib. bdg. 14.60 (*0-86592-623-9*) Rourke Enter.

— Oranges. LC 97-13232. (Farm to Market Discovery Library). 24p. (J). (gr. k-4). 1997. lib. bdg. 15.93 (*0-86625-621-0*) Rourke Pubns.

— Police Stations. LC 92-12575. (J). 1992. 9.50 (*0-685-59406-8*) Rourke Corp.

— Police Stations. LC 92-12575. (Great Places to Visit Ser.). 24p. (J). (gr. k-4). 1992. lib. bdg. 10.95 (*0-86593-213-1*) Rourke Corp.

— Poultry. LC 97-13233. (Farm to Market Discovery Library). 24p. (J). (gr. k-4). 1997. lib. bdg. 15.93 (*0-86625-618-0*) Rourke Pubns.

***Cooper, Jason.** Power Boats. LC 99-15114. (Boats Ser.). 24p. 1999. lib. bdg. write for info. (*0-86593-564-5*) Rourke Corp.

Cooper, Jason. Puentes. (Maravillas de la Humanidad Ser.: Set VI).Tr. of Bridges. (SPA.). 24p. (J). (gr. k-4). 1991. lib. bdg. 14.60 (*0-86592-934-3*) Rourke Enter.

— Rabbits. LC 94-39533. (Barnyard Friends Discovery Library). 24p. (J). (gr. k-4). 1995. lib. bdg. 15.93 (*1-55916-090-X*) Rourke Bk Co.

— Rascacielos. (Maravillas de la Humanidad Ser.: Set VI).Tr. of Skyscrapers. (SPA.). 24p. (J). (gr. k-4). 1991. lib. bdg. 14.60 (*0-86592-935-1*) Rourke Enter.

— The Redwood Coast. LC 95-12307. (Natural Wonders Ser.). (J). (gr. 2-6). 1995. lib. bdg. 14.60 (*1-57103-018-2*) Rourke Pr.

— Represas. (Maravillas de la Humanidad Ser.: Set VI).Tr. of Dams. (SPA.). 24p. (J). (gr. k-4). 1991. lib. bdg. 14.60 (*0-86592-924-6*) Rourke Enter.

***Cooper, Jason.** Sail Boats. LC 99-15113. (Boats Ser.). 24p. 1999. lib. bdg. write for info. (*0-86593-559-9*) Rourke Corp.

Cooper, Jason. Scorpions. LC 95-46038. (Animals Without Bones Discovery Library). 24p. (J). (gr. k-4). 1996. lib. bdg. 15.93 (*0-86625-573-7*) Rourke Pubns.

— Sea Plants. LC 92-16076. (Sea Discovery Library). 24p. (J). (gr. k-4). 1992. lib. bdg. 10.95 (*0-86593-232-8*) Rourke Corp.

— Sea Shells. LC 92-16075. (Sea Discovery Library). 24p. (J). (gr. k-4). 1992. lib. bdg. 10.95 (*0-86593-233-6*) Rourke Corp.

— Sea Stars. LC 95-26011. (Animals Without Bones Discovery Library). (Illus.). 24p. (J). (gr. k-4). 1996. lib. bdg. 15.93 (*0-86625-569-9*) Rourke Pubns.

— Sea Urchins. LC 95-26009. (Animals Without Bones Discovery Library). (Illus.). 24p. (J). (gr. k-4). 1996. lib. bdg. 15.93 (*0-86625-570-2*) Rourke Pubns.

— The Siberian Tiger. LC 96-52095. (Giants Among Us Discovery Library). 24p. (J). (gr. k-4). 1997. lib. bdg. 15.93 (*1-55916-186-8*) Rourke Bk Co.

— Skyscrapers. (Man-Made Wonders Ser.). 24p. (J). (gr. k-4). 1991. lib. bdg. 14.60 (*0-86592-637-9*) Rourke Enter.

— Small Sea Creatures. LC 92-16073. (Sea Discovery Library). (J). 1992. 9.50 (*0-685-59715-6*) Rourke Corp.

— Small Sea Creatures. LC 92-16073. (Sea Discovery Library). 24p. (J). (gr. k-4). 1992. lib. bdg. 10.95 (*0-86593-230-1*) Rourke Corp.

— Sound. LC 92-8809. (Science Secrets Ser.). (J). 1992. 9.50 (*0-685-59296-0*) Rourke Corp.

— Sound. LC 92-8809. (Science Secrets Discovery Library). 24p. (J). (gr. k-4). 1992. lib. bdg. 10.95 (*0-86593-167-4*) Rourke Corp.

— The Southern Elephant Seal. LC 96-52193. (Giants Among Us Discovery Library). 24p. (J). (gr. k-4). 1997. lib. bdg. 15.93 (*1-55916-188-4*) Rourke Bk Co.

— Spanish Language Books Set 5: Maquinas de Viaje (Traveling Machines), 6 bks. (J). 1991. 87.60 (*0-86592-473-2*) Rourke Enter.

— Strange Plants. (Earth's Garden Discovery Library). 24p. (J). (gr. k-4). 1991. lib. bdg. 14.60 (*0-86592-625-5*) Rourke Enter.

— Tide Pools. LC 92-16074. (Sea Discovery Library). 24p. (J). (gr. k-4). 1992. lib. bdg. 10.95 (*0-86593-234-4*) Rourke Corp.

— Toothed Whales. LC 96-19190. (Read All About Whales Ser.). 24p. (J). (gr. 1-4). 1996. lib. bdg. 12.95 (*0-86593-448-7*) Rourke Corp.

— Traveling Machines Series, 6 bks. (J). 1991. 87.60 (*0-86592-489-9*) Rourke Enter.

— Trees. (Earth's Garden Discovery Library). 24p. (J). (gr. k-4). 1991. lib. bdg. 14.60 (*0-86592-621-2*) Rourke Enter.

— Trees. LC 97-16927. (Guide to State Symbols Ser.). 48p. (J). 1998. lib. bdg. 22.60 (*1-57103-195-2*) Rourke Pr.

— Trees, 6 bks., Set II. (The Rourke Guide to State Symbols Ser.). (Illus.). 48p. (J). (gr. 3-8). 1991. lib. bdg. 16.95 (*0-86625-195-2*) Rourke Pubns.

— Trenes. (Maquinas de Viaje Ser.).Tr. of Trains. 24p. (J). (gr. k-4). 1991. lib. bdg. 14.60 (*0-86592-515-1*) Rourke Enter.

— The Trumpeter Swan. LC 96-52096. (Giants Among Us Discovery Library). 24p. (J). (gr. k-4). 1997. lib. bdg. 15.93 (*1-55916-187-6*) Rourke Bk Co.

— Turkeys. LC 94-39537. (Barnyard Friends Discovery Library). 24p. (J). (gr. k-4). 1995. lib. bdg. 15.93 (*1-55916-092-6*) Rourke Bk Co.

***Cooper, Jason.** U. S. Holocaust Memorial Museum. LC 00-30377. (Historic Landmarks Ser.). (Illus.). (J). 2000. write for info. (*1-55916-330-5*) Rourke Bk Co.

— The U. S. S. Constitution. LC 00-30589. (Historic Landmarks Ser.). (Illus.). (J). 2000. write for info. (*1-55916-329-1*) Rourke Pr.

Cooper, Jason. U. S. Treasury. LC 99-15316. (American Landmarks Ser.). 1999. write for info. (*0-86593-550-5*) Rourke Corp.

— Valley Forge. LC 99-27474. (American Landmarks Ser.). (Illus.). 24p. (J). (gr. 3-5). 1999. lib. bdg. 13.45 (*0-86593-547-5*) Rourke Corp.

***Cooper, Jason.** Vietnam Veterans Memorial. LC 99-29411. (American Landmarks Ser.). 1999. write for info. (*0-86593-549-1*) Rourke Corp.

Cooper, Jason. Watching Whales. LC 96-19192. (Read All About Whales Ser.). 24p. (J). (gr. 1-4). 1996. lib. bdg. 12.95 (*0-86593-451-7*) Rourke Corp.

— Water. (Science Secrets Discovery Library). 24p. (J). (gr. k-4). 1992. lib. bdg. 15.93 (*0-86593-168-2*) Rourke Corp.

— Whales & People. LC 96-19194. (Read All About Whales Ser.). 24p. (J). (gr. 1-4). 1996. lib. bdg. 12.95 (*0-86593-452-5*) Rourke Corp.

— Whales of the Seas. LC 96-19193. (Read All About Whales Ser.). 24p. (J). (gr. 1-4). 1996. lib. bdg. 12.95 (*0-86593-453-3*) Rourke Corp.

— Whales' World. LC 96-19189. (Read All About Whales Ser.). 24p. (J). (gr. 1-4). 1996. lib. bdg. 12.95 (*0-86593-449-5*) Rourke Corp.

— Wind. LC 92-8811. (Science Secrets Ser.). (J). 1992. 9.50 (*0-685-59297-9*) Rourke Corp.

— Wind. LC 92-8811. (Science Secrets Discovery Library). 24p. (J). (gr. k-4). 1992. lib. bdg. 10.95 (*0-86593-171-2*) Rourke Corp.

— Yellowstone. LC 95-13262. (Natural Wonders Ser.). (Illus.). (J). (gr. 2-6). 1995. lib. bdg. 14.60 (*1-57103-013-1*) Rourke Pr.

— Zoos. LC 92-12555. (J). 1992. 9.50 (*0-685-59388-6*) Rourke Corp.

— Zoos. LC 92-12555. (Great Places to Visit Ser.). 24p. (J). (gr. k-4). 1992. lib. bdg. 10.95 (*0-86593-212-3*) Rourke Corp.

Cooper, Jason D. Numerology: The Power to Know. 1988. 5.95 (*0-85030-472-5*, Pub. by Aqrn Pr) Harper SF.

— Using the Runes: A Comprehensive Introduction to the Art of Runecraft. 191p. 1989. pap. 7.95 (*0-85030-568-3*, Pub. by Aqrn Pr) HarpC.

Cooper, Jay & Lance, Kathryn. The Body Code: A Personalized Wellness & Weight Loss Plan Developed at the World Famous Green Valley Spa. LC 99-18027. 320p. 2001. 13.95 (*0-671-02619-4*, PB Hardcover) PB.

Cooper, Jay L., jt. compiled by see Spiegel, Irwin O.

Cooper, Jay S. & Pizzarello, Donald J. Concepts in Cancer Care: A Practical Explanation of Radiotherapy & Chemotherapy for Primary Care Physicians. LC 80-10334. (Illus.). 285p. reprint ed. pap. 88.40 (*0-8357-7642-5*, 205696700096) Bks Demand.

Cooper, J.C., ed. Dictionary of Christianity. 304p. 1996. lib. bdg. 45.00 (*1-884964-49-4*) Fitzroy Dearborn.

Cooper, Jean. Aquarian Dictionary of Festivals. 1990. pap. 14.95 (*0-85030-848-8*, Pub. by Aqrn Pr) Harper SF.

— The Stain & Spot Remover Handbook. LC 95-12056. 160p. 1995. pap. 12.95 (*0-88266-811-0*, Garden Way Pub) Storey Bks.

Cooper, Jean C. Cassell Dictionary of Christianity. LC 96-147561. 320p. 1998. 33.95 (*0-304-34286-6*) Continuum.

Cooper, Jeannie. Amex: Boston. (Illus.). 304p. 1996. 13.95 (*0-02-860901-8*) Macmillan.

Cooper, Jeff. The Art of the Rifle. LC 97-225316. (Illus.). 104p. 1997. text 29.95 (*0-87364-931-1*) Paladin Pr.

— Building a Recording Studio: The Complete Guide to Studio Design & Construction. rev. ed. LC 84-90061. (Illus.). 209p. 1984. spiral bd. 30.00 (*0-916899-00-4*) Synergy Group.

— Firearms: A Gunsite Anthology. (Illus.). 192p. 1998. pap. 25.00 (*0-87364-996-6*) Paladin Pr.

— The 5 Day Momentum Method. 61p. 1997. ring bd. 50.00 (*0-9650461-3-3*) M Gordon Pubng.

— The 5 Day Momentum Method. 2nd ed. (Illus.). 64p. 1999. pap. 50.00 (*1-893756-03-3*) M Gordon Pubng.

***Cooper, Jeff.** Hit & Run Lessons: Mastering the Trading Strategies. (Illus.). 156p. 1999. pap. 75.00 (*1-893756-05-X*) M Gordon Pubng.

Cooper, Jeff. Hit & Run Trading: The Short-Term Stock Traders Bible. LC 97-126097. 152p. 1996. 100.00 (*0-9650461-2-5*) M Gordon Pubng.

— Hit & Run Trading Vol. II: Capturing Explosive Short-Term Moves in Stocks. 212p. 1998. 100.00 (*0-9650461-6-8*) M Gordon Pubng.

— Principles of Personal Defense. rev. ed. 56p. 1988. pap. 14.00 (*0-87364-497-2*) Paladin Pr.

— To Ride, Shoot Straight & Speak the Truth. LC 88-82323. (Illus.). 400p. 1988. 26.00 (*0-9621342-0-1*) Gunsite Trng Ctr.

Cooper, Jeff & Lagerstrom, James. The Effective Public Speaker: A Guide to Researching, Composing, & Delivering Public Speeches. 2nd ed. 192p. 1994. per. 19.16 (*0-8403-9792-5*) Kendall-Hunt.

Cooper, Jeff, jt. auth. see Suarez, Gabriel.

Cooper, Jeffery. Introduction to Partial Differential Equations with MATLAB. LC 97-32251. (Applied & Numerical Harmonic Analysis Ser.). 1997. write for info. (*3-7643-3967-5*) Birkhauser.

Cooper, Jeffrey. The Rise of Instrumental Music & Concert Series in Paris, 1828-1871. LC 83-1062. (Studies in Musicology: No. 65). (Illus.). 401p. reprint ed. pap. 124.40 (*0-8357-1403-9*, 207047900096) Bks Demand.

Cooper, Jeffrey, jt. auth. see Cooper, Rhonda.

Cooper, Jeremy. Disability & the Law. 300p. 1996. pap. 39.95 (*1-85302-318-3*, Pub. by Jessica Kingsley) Taylor & Francis.

— Keyguide to Information Sources in Public Interest Law. 220p. 1991. text 120.00 (*0-7201-2084-5*) Continuum.

— The Legal Rights Manual: A Guide for Social Workers & Advice Centres. 2nd ed. 448p. 1994. pap. 36.95 (*1-85742-136-1*, Pub. by Arena) Ashgate Pub Co.

Cooper, Jeremy. No Fun Without U. 50.00 (*1-899858-50-6*, Pub. by Ellipsis) Norton.

Cooper, Jeremy. Victorian & Edwardian Decor: From the Gothic Revival to Art Nouveau. (Illus.). 256p. 1988. pap. 39.95 (*0-7892-0446-0*) Abbeville Pr.

Cooper, Jeremy & Trubek, Louise G. Educating for Justice: Social Values & Legal Education. LC 97-18968. 220p. 1997. text 82.95 (*1-85521-967-0*, Pub. by Dartmth Pub) Ashgate Pub Co.

Cooper, Jeremy, jt. ed. see Trubek, Louise G.

Cooper, Jerrold S. & Schwartz, Glenn, eds. The Study of the Ancient Near East in the Twenty-First Century: The William Foxwell Albright Centennial Conference. 432p. 1996. text 42.50 (*0-931464-96-X*) Eisenbrauns.

Cooper, Jerry. Alley Oops. 24p. (Orig.). 1996. pap. 3.95 (*1-889419-17-6*) J Cooper.

— Bagels: The Hole Story. 24p. (Orig.). 1996. pap. 3.95 (*1-889419-08-7*) J Cooper.

— Computer Illiteracy Made Easy. 24p. (Orig.). 1996. pap. 3.95 (*1-889419-11-7*) J Cooper.

— Eekology. 24p. (Orig.). 1996. pap. 3.95 (*1-889419-02-8*) J Cooper.

— Everybody's Doin' "It" 24p. (Orig.). 1996. pap. 3.95 (*1-889419-03-6*) J Cooper.

— The Fab Fun Diet. 24p. (Orig.). 1996. pap. 3.95 (*1-889419-01-X*) J Cooper.

— Fore Play. 24p. 1996. pap. 3.95 (*1-889419-15-X*) J Cooper.

— Funny 4s. 24p. (Orig.). 1996. pap. 3.95 (*1-889419-20-6*) J Cooper.

— Funny 8s. 24p. (Orig.). 1996. pap. 3.95 (*1-889419-21-4*) J Cooper.

— Holy Moses. 24p. (Orig.). 1996. pap. 3.95 (*1-889419-24-9*) J Cooper.

— Messed up Pieces. 24p. (Orig.). 1996. pap. 3.95 (*1-889419-19-2*) J Cooper.

— Old Is . . . 24p. (Orig.). 1996. pap. 3.95 (*1-889419-05-2*) J Cooper.

— Oy. 24p. (Orig.). 1996. pap. 3.95 (*1-889419-16-8*) J Cooper.

— Reel Ism. 24p. (Orig.). 1996. pap. 3.95 (*1-889419-23-0*) J Cooper.

— The Rise of the National Guard: The Evolution of the American Militia, 1865-1920. LC 97-7630. (Studies in War, Society, & the Military). xviii, 246p. 1997. text 50.00 (*0-8032-1486-3*) U of Nebr Pr.

— The S-E-X Word. 24p. (Orig.). 1996. pap. 3.95 (*1-889419-22-2*) J Cooper.

— Seniors' Tennis Quiz. 24p. (Orig.). 1996. pap. 3.95 (*1-889419-04-4*) J Cooper.

— Sexism: Going, Going, Gone but Not Forgotten. 24p. (Orig.). 1996. pap. 3.95 (*1-889419-18-4*) J Cooper.

— Silly Signs & Stuff. 24p. (Orig.). 1996. pap. 3.95 (*1-889419-14-1*) J Cooper.

— So You Think You're Macho. 24p. (Orig.). 1996. pap. 3.95 (*1-889419-10-9*) J Cooper.

— 10-S NE-1? 24p. 1996. pap. 3.95 (*1-889419-12-5*) J Cooper.

— 2-Bits Worth of Tennis Tips: For Just a Few Bucks. 24p. (Orig.). 1996. pap. 3.95 (*1-889419-06-0*) J Cooper.

— What's It Like Being Jewish? Besides Having Heartburn? 24p. (Orig.). 1996. pap. 3.95 (*1-889419-13-3*) J Cooper.

— You're a Dirty Old Man. 24p. (Orig.). 1996. pap. 3.95 (*1-889419-09-5*) J Cooper.

— Zoo: Ology. 24p. (Orig.). 1996. pap. 3.95 (*1-889419-07-9*) J Cooper.

Cooper, Jerry A. Birdfinder: A Birder's Guide to Planning North American Trips. Baicich, Paul J., ed. LC 95-75100. (ABA Birdfinding Guides Ser.). (Illus.). 384p. (Orig.). 1996. pap. 21.95 (*1-878788-10-8*, 233) Amer Birding Assn.

Cooper, Jerry C. & Dethloff, Henry C. Footsteps: A Guided Tour of the Texas A&M University Campus. LC 90-40744. (Centennial Series of the Association of Former Students: No. 38). (Illus.). 200p. 1991. 13.95 (*0-89096-459-9*); pap. 7.95 (*0-89096-462-9*) Tex A&M Univ Pr.

Cooper, Jerry M. The Army & Civil Disorder: Federal Military Intervention in Labor Disputes, 1877-1900, 19. LC 79-7064. (Contributions in Military History Ser.: No. 19). 284p. 1980. 55.00 (*0-313-20958-8*, CAD/, Greenwood Pr) Greenwood.

— The Militia & the National Guard in America since Colonial Times: A Research Guide, 7. LC 93-14047. (Research Guides in Military Studies: No. 7). 200p. 1993. lib. bdg. 65.00 (*0-313-27721-4*, CMN/, Greenwood Pr) Greenwood.

Cooper, Jill. Occupational Therapy in Oncology & Palliative Care. (Illus.). 200p. 1997. pap. 45.00 (*1-56593-884-4*, 1732) Singular Publishing.

Cooper, Jill, jt. ed. see Aspray, William.

Cooper, Jilly. Appasionata. 1997. mass mkt. 9.99 (*0-552-14323-5*) Bantam.

— Appassionata. 416p. 1996. 32.95 (*0-593-03861-4*) Bantam.

— Araminta's Wedding or a Fortune Secured - A Country House Extravaganza. (Illus.). 65p. 1996. pap. 14.99 (*0-7493-2420-1*) Buttrwrth-Heinemann.

***Cooper, Jilly.** The Complete Illustrated Works of Oscar Wilde. (Illus.). 864p. 2000. 12.95 (*1-85152-102-X*) Cha2ncellor.

— Lisa & Co. 2000. pap. 8.95 (*0-552-12041-3*, Pub. by Transworld Publishers Ltd) Trafalgar.

Cooper, Jilly. The Man Who Made Husbands Jealous. 736p. 1994. mass mkt. 7.99 (*0-552-13895-9*) Bantam.

***Cooper, Jilly.** Octavia. 2000. pap. 8.95 (*0-552-10717-4*, Pub. by Transworld Publishers Ltd) Trafalgar.

Cooper, Jilly. Polo. LC 91-58983. 608p. 1992. 20.00 (*0-345-37557-2*) Ballantine Pub Grp.

— Polo. 768p. 1992. pap. 8.99 (*0-552-13552-6*) Bantam.

— Riders. 928p. 1986. mass mkt. 9.99 (*0-552-12486-9*) Bantam.

Cooper, Jilly. Rivals. 720p. 1989. mass mkt. 8.99 (*0-552-13264-0*) Bantam.

***Cooper, Jilly.** Rivals. 2000. 29.95 (*0-593-01368-9*, Pub. by Transworld Publishers Ltd) Trafalgar.

***Cooper, Jim.** Log Homes Made Easy. 2nd ed. LC 00-39492. (Illus.). 2000. write for info. (*0-8117-2847-1*) Stackpole.

Cooper, Jim. Log Homes Made Easy: Contracting & Building Your Own Log Home. LC 92-32751. (Illus.). 256p. (Orig.). 1993. pap. 14.95 (*0-8117-2422-0*) Stackpole.

— SNA Server 4. (MCSE Ser.). 1998. student ed. 49.99 (*0-7821-2347-3*) Sybex.

***Cooper, Jim.** Using MS-DOS 6.22. 2nd ed. (Special Edition Using... Que Ser.). 1200p. 1999. pap. text 34.99 (*0-7897-2040-X*) Que.

Cooper, Jo. Pioneer Pilot: Early Aviation, 1911-1931. 176p. 1993. pap. 19.95 (*0-9638147-0-2*) Converse Pubng.

Cooper, JoAnn. Boys & Girls Study Skills Bingo: A Program to Help Students in Grades Kindergarten Through Third Grade to Learn, Understand, & Apply Good Study Skills. LC 94-77207. 16p. (J). (gr. k-3). 1991. 13.95 (*1-884063-28-4*) Mar Co Prods.

— Stepfamilies , 2 vol. LC 93-79230. (Changing Family Ser.). 1993. write for info. (*1-884063-13-6*) Mar Co Prods.

Cooper, JoAnn & Martenz, Arden. Classroom Guidance: Intermediate Level for Grades 4-8. 84p. 1993. 14.95 (*1-884063-84-5*) Mar Co Prods.

— Classroom Guidance: Primary Level for Grades K-3. 92p. 1993. 14.95 (*1-884063-83-7*) Mar Co Prods.

— Creative Bulletin Boards: Twenty Bulletin Boards Designed for Classroom or Small-Group Counseling Use. (Illus.). 59p. 1990. 1.00 (*1-884063-57-8*) Mar Co Prods.

— Divorce I: Small-Group Counseling Programs for Students in Grades Two Through Four. LC 93-79231. (Changing Family Ser.). 36p. 1993. 5.95 (*1-884063-11-X*) Mar Co Prods.

— Divorce II: Small-Group Counseling for Students in Grades Five Through Eight. LC 93-79231. (Changing Family Ser.). 36p. 1993. 5.95 (*1-884063-12-8*) Mar Co Prods.

— Rap, Rock, & Role into Conflict Resolution: Conflict Resolution Presented Through Lessons & Music for Middle, Junior High, & High School Students. LC 93-79190. 32p. 1993. 14.95 (*1-884063-05-5*) Mar Co Prods.

— Stepfamilies I: Small Group Counseling Programs for Students in Grades Two Through Four. LC 93-79230. (Changing Family Ser.). 36p. 1993. 5.95 (*1-884063-09-8*) Mar Co Prods.

— Stepfamilies II: Small Group Counseling Program for Students in Grades Five. LC 93-79230. (Changing Family Ser.). 36p. 1993. 5.95 (*1-884063-10-1*) Mar Co Prods.

Cooper, JoAnne. Handling Anger: A Program for 2-4 Grades. LC 94-77657. (Illus.). 76p. (Orig.). (J). (gr. 2-5). 1994. pap. 13.95 (*1-884063-37-3*) Mar Co Prods.

Cooper, Joanne E., jt. auth. see Nee-Benham, Maenette K.

Cooper, Joel, jt. auth. see Worchel, Stephen.

Cooper, Joel, jt. ed. see Darley, John M.

Cooper, Joel D., jt. auth. see Urschel, Harold C., Jr.

Cooper, John. The Child in Jewish History. LC 96-9603. 448p. 1996. 50.00 (*1-56821-956-3*) Aronson.

— Eat & Be Satisfied: A Social History of Jewish Food. LC 92-45772. 280p. 1993. pap. 30.00 (*0-87668-316-2*) Aronson.

— The Fugitive: A Complete Episode Guide, 1963-1967. Schultheiss, Thomas, ed. (Illus.). 288p. 1994. lib. bdg. 40.00 (*1-56075-038-3*) Popular Culture.

— Historical & Statistical Sketch of Croyden, from Its Incorporation to the Year 1852, Containing Much Local Information Which Must Be Highly Interesting to Every Inhabitant of the Town. (Illus.). 52p. 1997. reprint ed. pap. 11.00 (*0-8328-5985-0*) Higginson Bk Co.

***Cooper, John.** Islam & Modernity. 2000. pap. 24.50 (*1-86064-531-3*, Pub. by I B T) St Martin.

Cooper, John & Cooper, Jonathan. Children's Fiction, 1900-1950: A Pictorial Survey of 1st Editions. LC 97-19547. (Illus.). 350p. 1998. text 78.95 (*1-85928-289-X*) Ashgate Pub Co.

Cooper, John & Pike, B. A. Artists in Crime: An Illustrated Survey of Crime Fiction Dust Wrappers, 1920-1970. (Illus.). 217p. 1995. 86.95 (*1-85928-188-5*, Pub. by Scolar Pr) Ashgate Pub Co.

Cooper, John & Pike, Barry A. Detective Fiction: The Collector's Guide. 2nd ed. (Illus.). 352p. 1994. 69.95 (*0-85967-991-8*, Pub. by Scolar Pr) Ashgate Pub Co.

Cooper, John C. The Gesture. LC 87-62810. 253p. 1988. 22.00 (*0-933256-69-8*) Second Chance.

— The Roots of the Radical Theology. 174p. (C). 1988. reprint ed. pap. text 22.50 (*0-8191-7115-8*) U Pr of Amer.

Cooper, John C. The Spiritual Presence in the Theology of Paul Tillich: Tillich's Use of Paul. LC 97-30334. (C). 1997. text 35.00 (*0-86554-535-9*, MUP/H440) Mercer Univ Pr.

Cooper, John C., jt. auth. see McManus, Una.

Cooper, John D., ed. Cavalcade of Carbonates. (Illus.). 144p. (Orig.). 1989. pap. 11.00 (*1-878861-08-5*) Pac Section SEPM.

Cooper, John D. & Stevens, Calvin H., eds. Paleozoic Paleogeography of the Western United States - II, 2 vols., 1. (Illus.). 872p. (Orig.). 1991. pap. write for info. (*1-878861-01-8*) Pac Section SEPM.

C

— Paleozoic Paleogeography of the Western United States - II, 2 vols., 2 (Illus.). 872p. (Orig.). 1991. pap. write for info. (*1-878861-02-6*) Pac Section SEPM.

— Paleozoic Paleogeography of the Western United States - II, 2 vols., Set. (Illus.). 872p. (Orig.). 1991. pap. 55.00 (*1-878861-03-4*) Pac Section SEPM.

Cooper, John E., jt. ed. see Beynon, Peter H.

***Cooper, John F.** Historical Dictionary of Taiwan (Republic of China) 2nd ed. Woronoff, Jon, ed. LC 99-27946. (Asian Historical Dictionaries Ser.: No. 34). (Illus.). 368p. 1999. 49.50 (*0-8108-3665-3*) Scarecrow.

Cooper, John F. A Primer of Brief Psychotherapy. 160p. (C). 1995. 23.00 (*0-393-70189-1*) Norton.

— Taiwan's 1991 & 1992 Non-Supplemental Elections: Reaching a Higher State of Democracy. LC 94-6040. 180p. 1994. pap. text 21.50 (*0-8191-9480-8*); lib. bdg. 46.50 (*0-8191-9479-4*) U Pr of Amer.

Cooper, John F. & Lee, Ta-ling. One Step Forward, One Step Back, Human Rights in the People's Republic of China in 1987-88, No. 3. 140p. 1989. 6.00 (*0-925153-02-8*, 92) Occasional Papers.

Cooper, John F. & Marks, Thomas C., Jr. Florida Constitutional Law: Cases & Materials. 2nd ed. LC 96-85851. 764p. 1996. boxed set 70.00 (*0-89089-755-7*) Carolina Acad Pr.

Cooper, John F., jt. auth. see Marks, Thomas C., Jr.

Cooper, John F., jt. auth. see Ta-Ling Lee.

Cooper, John G., jt. auth. see Prout, Brian J.

Cooper, John J., Jr. Pivotal Decades: The United States, 1990-1920. 432p. 1990. pap. 16.95 (*0-393-95655-5*) Norton.

***Cooper, John K., ed.** T.S. Eliot's Orchestra: Critical Essays on Poetry & Music. (Border Crossings Ser.: 7). 440p. 2000. 75.00 (*0-8153-2577-0*) Garland.

Cooper, John M. East Suffolk Railway. 56p. (C). 1985. 45.00 (*0-7855-3515-2*, Pub. by Oakwood) St Mut.

— The Northern Algonquian Supreme Being. LC 76-43682. (Catholic University of America Anthropological Ser.: No. 2). reprint ed. 34.50 (*0-404-15515-4*) AMS Pr.

— Reason & Emotion: Essays on Ancient Moral Psychology & Ethical Theory. LC 98-11851. 1999. 75.00 (*0-691-05874-1*, Pub. by Princeton U Pr); 26.95 (*0-691-05875-X*, Pub. by Princeton U Pr) Cal Prin Full Svc.

— Reason & Human Good in Aristotle. LC 74-30852. 206p. reprint ed. pap. 63.90 (*0-7837-3852-8*, 204367400010) Bks Demand.

— Reason & Human Good in Aristotle. LC 86-19468. 216p. (C). 1986. reprint ed. pap. text 12.95 (*0-87220-022-1*); reprint ed. lib. bdg. 34.95 (*0-87220-115-5*) Hackett Pub.

— Snares, Deadfalls & Other Traps of the Northern Algonquians & Northern Athapaskans. LC 76-43683. (Catholic University of America Anthropological Ser.: No. 5). reprint ed. 37.50 (*0-404-15516-2*) AMS Pr.

Cooper, John M., Jr. The Vanity of Power: American Isolationism & the First World War, 3. LC 70-95508. (Contributions in American History Ser.: No. 3). 271p. 1970. 59.95 (*0-8371-2342-9*, COP/, Greenwood Pr) Greenwood.

— Walter Hines Page: The Southerner As American, 1855-1918. LC 77-4390. (Illus.). 490p. reprint ed. pap. 151.90 (*0-8357-3884-1*, 203661600004) Bks Demand.

— The Warrior & the Priest: Woodrow Wilson & Theodore Roosevelt. (Illus.). 456p. 1985. pap. text 18.00 (*0-674-94751-7*) Belknap Pr.

Cooper, John M., ed. Analytical & Critical Bibliography of the Tribes of Tierra Del Fuego & Adjacent Territory. (Bureau of American Ethnology Bulletins Ser.). 233p. 1995. lib. bdg. 89.00 (*0-7812-4063-8*) Rprt Serv.

Cooper, John M., Jr. & Neu, Charles E., eds. The Wilson Era: Essays in Honor of Arthur S. Link. 380p. (C). 1991. text 26.95 (*0-88295-877-1*); pap. text 18.95 (*0-88295-872-0*) Harlan Davidson.

Cooper, John M. & Siedentop, Daryl. The Theory & Science of Basketball. 2nd ed. LC 74-4376. (Health Education, Physical Education, & Recreation Ser.). (Illus.). 275p. reprint ed. pap. 85.30 (*0-608-17895-0*, 205668000080) Bks Demand.

Cooper, John M., jt. auth. see Adrian.

Cooper, John M., jt. auth. see Adrian, Marlene J.

Cooper, John M., ed. see Plato.

Cooper, John M., ed. see Seneca, Lucius Annaeus.

Cooper, John O., et al. Applied Behavior Analysis. 672p. (C). 1987. suppl. ed. write for info. (*0-318-61564-9*, Merrill Pub Co) Macmillan.

Cooper, John O., et al. Applied Behavior Analysis. 672p. (C). 1990. 120.00 (*0-675-20223-X*, Merrill Coll) P-H.

Cooper, John S. Rough Notes of Seven Campaigns in Portugal, Spain, France & America During the Years 1809-1815. 1996. 29.95 (*1-885119-35-6*) Sarpedon.

— Rough Notes on Seven Campaigns in Portugal, Spain, France & America During the Years 1809-1815. 150p. 1997. 80.00 (*1-873376-65-0*, Pub. by Spellmnt Pubs) St Mut.

Cooper, John W. Body, Soul & Life Everlasting: Biblical Anthropology & the Monism-Dualism Debate. 262p. (C). 1995. reprint ed. pap. 25.95 (*1-57383-048-8*) Regent College.

— Our Father in Heaven: Christian Faith & Inclusive Language for God. LC 98-40633. 304p. (C). (gr. 13). 1999. pap. 19.99 (*0-8010-2188-X*) Baker Bks.

— The Theology of Freedom: The Legacy of Jacque Maritain & Reinhold Niebuhr. LC 85-13852. ix, 186p. 1985. text 19.95 (*0-86554-172-8*, MUP-H162) Mercer Univ Pr.

Cooper, John X. T. S. Eliot & the Ideology of Four Quartets. 249p. (C). 1996. text 59.95 (*0-521-49629-2*) Cambridge U Pr.

— T. S. Eliot & the Politics of Voice: The Argument of the Waste Land. LC 87-10896. (Studies in Modern Literature: No. 79). 133p. reprint ed. pap. 41.30 (*0-8357-1824-7*, 207064000012) Bks Demand.

Cooper, Jonathan, jt. auth. see Cooper, John.

Cooper, Jonni. ICU Pocket Professor. (C). (gr. 13). 1991. text 16.95 (*0-944132-45-6*) Mosby Inc.

Cooper, Joseph. Lost Continent: or Slavery & the Slave Trade in Africa. 130p. 1968. reprint ed. 49.50 (*0-7146-1890-X*, BHA-01890, Pub. by F Cass Pubs) Intl Spec Bk.

***Cooper, Joseph, ed.** Why Can't the Government Do What's Right? Congress & the Decline of Public Trust. LC 99-21970. (Transforming American Politics Ser.). 256p. 1999. 64.00 (*0-8133-6837-5*, Pub. by Westview); pap. 25.00 (*0-8133-6838-3*, Pub. by Westview) HarpC.

Cooper, Joseph & MacKenzie, G. Calvin, eds. The House at Work. LC 81-2987. (Dan Danciger Publications). 276p. reprint ed. pap. 85.60 (*0-608-15861-5*, 203073200070) Bks Demand.

Cooper, Joseph & Maisel, Louis S., eds. The Impact of the Electoral Process. LC 76-47088. (Sage Electoral Studies Yearbook: Vol. 3). (Illus.). 304p. reprint ed. pap. 94.30 (*0-608-10076-5*, 202192600026) Bks Demand.

Cooper, Joseph, jt. auth. see Meisel, Louis.

Cooper, Joseph B. Comparative Psychology. LC 70-190204. (Illus.). 472p. reprint ed. pap. 146.40 (*0-608-11264-X*, 201247700081) Bks Demand.

Cooper, Josephine, ed. see Sullivan-Sorrento Historical Society Staff.

Cooper, Judith. Ubu Roi: An Analytical Study, Vol. 6. 120p. 1974. pap. 7.00 (*0-912788-05-4*) Tulane Romance Lang.

Cooper, Judy. Speak of Me As I Am: The Life & Work of Masud Khan. 176p. 1993. pap. 26.00 (*1-85575-044-9*, Pub. by H Karnac Bks Ltd) Other Pr LLC.

Cooper, Judy & Maxwell, Nilda. Narcissistic Wounds: Clinical Perspectives. LC 95-35828. 280p. 1995. pap. 25.00 (*1-56821-747-1*) Aronson.

Cooper, Julian, jt. ed. see Amann, Ronald.

Cooper, Julie Anne. 301 Ways to Stay Young at Heart. 1999. pap. text 5.95 (*1-56245-355-6*) Great Quotations.

Cooper, K., et al, eds. Homeostasis & Thermal Stress: International Symposium on Pharmacology of Thermoregulation, 6th, Jasper, Alta, August 1985. (Illus.). xiv, 210p. 1986. 101.00 (*3-8055-4228-3*) S Karger.

Cooper, K. E., ed. see Pharmacology of Thermoregulation Symposium Staff, et al.

Cooper, K. E., ed. see Symposium, Calgary, Alberta Staff.

Cooper, Karen. Tribal Museum Directory. 48p. 1998. pap. 15.00 (*0-9667033-0-8*) Smithson Inst Ctr Museum Studs.

Cooper, Karol. Love Is Forever. 1999. pap. text 6.95 (*1-58334-000-9*) Walnut Gr Pr.

Cooper, Kate. Virgin & the Bride: Idealized Womanhood in Late Antiquity. LC 96-2256. 256p. 1996. 39.00 (*0-674-93949-2*) HUP.

— Virgin & the Bride: Idealized Womanhood in Late Antiquity. 1999. pap. text 16.95 (*0-674-93950-6*) HUP.

Cooper, Kate, ed. see St. John, Bill.

Cooper, Kate M., tr. see Leupin, Alexandre.

Cooper, Kathie, jt. auth. see Funnell, Warwick.

Cooper, Kathy. Painting Floor Cloths: 20 Canvas Rugs to Stamp, Stencil, Sponge & Spatter in a Weekend. Morgenthal, Deborah, ed. LC 99-25458. (Illus.). 80p. 1999. pap. 14.95 (*1-57990-134-4*) Lark Books.

Cooper, Kathy & Hersey, Jan. The Complete Book of Floorcloths: Designs & Techniques for Painting Great-Looking Canvas Rugs. Dierks, Leslie, ed. LC 96-41383. (Illus.). 144p. 1997. 24.95 (*1-887374-19-1*, Pub. by Lark Books) Random.

***Cooper, Katy.** Prince of Hearts. (Historical Ser.). 2000. mass mkt. 4.99 (*0-373-29125-6*, 1-29125-1) Harlequin Bks.

Cooper, Kay. Discover It Yourself: Where Did You Get Those Eyes? 80p. (J). 1993. pap. 3.50 (*0-380-71304-7*, Avon Bks) Morrow Avon.

— Discover It Yourself: Where in the World Are You? (Illus.). 96p. (J). 1993. reprint ed. pap. 3.50 (*0-380-71299-7*, Avon Bks) Morrow Avon.

— Discover It Yourself: Who Put the Canon in the Courthouse Square? 96p. (J). 1993. pap. 3.50 (*0-380-71298-9*, Avon Bks) Morrow Avon.

— Neal-Schuman Index to Fingerplays. Roginski, Jim, ed. LC 93-40099. 320p. 1993. 32.95 (*1-55570-149-3*) Neal-Schuman.

— Where Did You Get Those Eyes: A Guide to Discovering Your Family History. (American History Series for Young People). (Illus.). (J). (gr. 5 up). 1988. 13.95 (*0-8027-6802-4*); lib. bdg. 14.85 (*0-8027-6803-2*) Walker & Co.

— Where in the World Are You? (Illus.). 80p. (J). (gr. 3-7). 1990. 13.95 (*0-8027-6912-8*); lib. bdg. 14.85 (*0-8027-6913-6*) Walker & Co.

— Who Put the Cannon in the Courthouse Square? A Guide to Uncovering the Past. LC 84-17251. (Illus.). (J). (gr. 4 up). 1984. lib. bdg. 12.85 (*0-8027-6561-0*) Walker & Co.

— Why Do You Speak As You Do? A Guide to Learning about Language - A Discovery Book. 66p. 1992. 13.95 (*0-8027-8164-0*); lib. bdg. 14.85 (*0-8027-8165-9*) Walker & Co.

Cooper, Keith E. Fever & Antipyresis: The Role of the Nervous System. (Illus.). 198p. (C). 1995. text 59.95 (*0-521-41924-7*) Cambridge U Pr.

Cooper, Ken, jt. ed. see Christensen, Burke A.

Cooper, Kenneth. Advanced Nutritional Therapies: Evaluates Hundreds of Foods, Supplements, & Nutrients, & Shows How to Use Them to Achieve Maximal Health & Long Life. 368p. 1998. pap. 12.99 (*0-7852-7073-6*) Nelson.

Cooper, Kenneth, ed. American Classical Music. (Three Centuries of Music in Score Ser.: vol.13). 264p. 1988. text 25.00 (*0-8240-0940-1*) Garland.

— Baroque Vocal Music II: Italian & Spanish Sacred & Secular Music. (Three Centuries of Music in Score Ser.: Vol. 12). 232p. 1988. text 25.00 (*0-8240-0939-8*) Garland.

— Concerto I Vol. II: Italy: Three Ground-Breaking Italian Concerto Styles. (Three Centuries of Music in Score Ser.). 216p. 1988. text 25.00 (*0-8240-0929-0*) Garland.

***Cooper, Kenneth Carlton.** Effective Competency Modeling & Reporting: A Step-by-Step Guide for Improving Individual & Organizational Performance. LC 00-27350. 368p. 2000. 95.00 incl. audio compact disk (*0-8144-0548-7*) AMACOM.

Cooper, Kenneth H. Aerobics Program. 320p. 1985. pap. 17.95 (*0-553-34677-6*) Bantam.

— Can Stress Heal? Converting a Major Health Hazard into a Surprising Health Benefit. LC 97-33082. 288p. 1998. 19.99 (*0-7852-8315-3*) Nelson.

— Controlling Cholesterol: Preventive Medicine Program. 416p. 1989. mass mkt. 6.99 (*0-553-27775-8*) Bantam.

— Dr. Kenneth H. Cooper's Antioxidant Revolution. 256p. 1997. pap. 14.99 (*0-7852-7525-8*) Nelson.

— Dr. Kenneth H. Cooper's Preventive Medicine Program: Preventing Osteoporosis. 1989. 18.95 (*0-685-24550-0*) Bantam.

— Faith-Based Fitness. LC 97-19280. Orig. Title: It's Better to Believe. (Illus.). 256p. 1997. pap. 12.99 (*0-7852-7137-6*, J Thoma Bks) Nelson.

— It's Better to Believe. LC 95-14457. (Illus.). 256p. 1995. 22.99 (*0-7852-8314-5*) Nelson.

***Cooper, Kenneth H.** Kid Fitness. rev. ed. LC 99-32126. (Illus.). 384p. 1999. pap. 14.99 (*0-8054-1878-4*) Broadman.

Cooper, Kenneth H. Overcoming Hypertension. 464p. 1991. mass mkt. 6.99 (*0-553-28937-3*) Bantam.

— Regaining the Power of Youth at Any Age. LC 98-45029. 288p. 1999. 19.99 (*0-7852-7142-2*) Nelson.

***Cooper, Kenneth H. & Proctor.** Controlling Cholesterol the Natural Way: Eat Your Way to Better Health with New Breakthrough Food Discoveries. 272p. 1999. mass mkt. 6.99 (*0-553-58210-0*) Bantam.

Cooper, Kerry. The Financial Marketplace. 5th ed. 1996. text. write for info. (*0-201-54287-0*) Addison-Wesley.

Cooper, Kerry & Fraser, Donald. Banking Deregulation & the New Competition in Financial Services: Student Edition. LC 85-29655. 344p. 1986. pap. text 16.95 (*0-88730-090-1*, HarpBusn) HarpInfo.

Cooper, Khershed P., et al, eds. Liquid Metal Atomization: Fundamentals & Practice. (Illus.). 250p. 62.00 (*0-87339-465-8*) Minerals Metals.

***Cooper, Kim, et al.** Human Anatomy & PhysiologyL: Laboratory Manual for Biology 201 & 202. 132p. (C). 1999. spiral bd. 27.95 (*0-7872-6237-4*) Kendall-Hunt.

Cooper, L. Horse Show Organization. (Illus.). 25.00 (*0-87556-587-5*) Saifer.

Cooper, L. & Cooper, Mary W. Introduction to Dynamic Programming. LC 79-42640. (International Series in Modern Applied Mathematics & Computer Science: Vol. 1). (Illus.). 256p. 1981. 129.00 (*0-08-025065-3*, Pub. by Pergamon Repr) Franklin.

Cooper, L. C. Horse Show Organisation. 120p. (C). 1990. 21.00 (*0-85131-310-8*, Pub. by J A Allen) St Mut.

Cooper, L. E. Eck: The Zacharias Eck Family Record. 126p. 1991. reprint ed. pap. 19.50 (*0-8328-1812-7*); reprint ed. lib. bdg. 29.50 (*0-8328-1811-9*) Higginson Bk Co.

Cooper, Lacey, jt. auth. see Cooper, Bo.

Cooper, Lamar E., Sr. Ezekiel. LC 93-49996. (New American Commentary Ser.: Vol. 17). 432p. 1994. 27.99 (*0-8054-0117-2*, 4201-17) Broadman.

Cooper, Lane. A Concordance of the Latin, Greek, & Italian Poems of John Milton. (BCL1-PR English Literature Ser.). 212p. 1992. reprint ed. lib. bdg. 79.00 (*0-7812-7381-1*) Rprt Serv.

— A Concordance to the Poems of William Wordsworth. (BCL1-PR English Literature Ser.). 1136p. 1992. reprint ed. lib. bdg. 248.00 (*0-7812-7654-3*) Rprt Serv.

— Evolution & Repentance: Mixed Essays & Addresses. LC 78-152166. (Essay Index Reprint Ser.). 1977. reprint ed. 20.95 (*0-8369-2222-0*) Ayer.

Cooper, Lane, ed. Art of the Writer: Essays, Excerpts, & Translations. enl. rev. ed. LC 73-37837. (Essay Index Reprint Ser.). 1977. reprint ed. 25.95 (*0-8369-2586-6*) Ayer.

Cooper, Lane, tr. The Rhetoric of Aristotle. (Orig.). (C). 1960. pap. text 19.20 (*0-13-780692-2*) P-H.

Cooper, Larry & Harrison, Yvonne. Program Administration, Vol. 1. (Restorative Nursing for Long Term Care Ser.). 544p. 1994. ring bd. 60.00 (*1-885506-02-3*) Cooper & Harrison.

— Therapy for the Humerus: A Collection of Jokes Told by Nursing Home Residents to Their Therapists. 4th ed. 217p. 1992. pap., spiral bd. 10.00 (*1-885506-00-7*) Cooper & Harrison.

***Cooper, Laura.** Insurance Protection Planning: A Guide for People with Chronic Illness or Disability. 176p. 2000. pap. 24.95 (*1-888799-44-7*, Pub. by Demos Medical) SCB Distributors.

Cooper, Laura J. & Nolan, Dennis R. Labor Arbitration: A Coursebook. (American Casebook Ser.). 557p. (C). 1994. 47.50 (*0-314-04023-4*) West Pub.

Cooper, Laurel, jt. auth. see Cooper, Bill.

Cooper, Lauremce D. Rousseau, Nature & the Problem of the Good Life. LC 98-50149. 358p. 2000. 18.95 (*0-271-01923-9*) Pa St U Pr.

Cooper, Laurie. Ethiopia: Technical Assistance Project, September 1994-July 1995. ii, 212p. 1995. pap. text 23.00 (*1-879720-14-0*) Intl Fndt Elect.

— Malawi: Strengthening Democratic Institutions, Final Activity Report, May 31, 1995. ii, 144p. 1996. pap. text 16.00 (*1-879720-01-9*) Intl Fndt Elect.

— Nyali Means Change: The June 14, 1993 Referendum in Malawi: IFES Monitoring, Voter Education & Pollworker Training Projects. vi, 100p. 1993. pap. text 12.00 (*1-879720-23-X*) Intl Fndt Elect.

Cooper, Laurie & Henderson, Jerry. Uganda: A Pre-Election Assessment Report, January, 1996. LC 96-16751. viii, 56p. 1996. pap. text 8.00 (*1-879720-10-8*) Intl Fndt Elect.

Cooper, Laurie, ed. see Butler, Vic, et al.

Cooper, Lee. Chinese Language for Beginners. LC 70-151121. 1971. pap. 6.95 (*0-8048-0918-6*) Tuttle Pubng.

— Fun with German. (Illus.). (J). (gr. 3 up). 1972. lib. bdg. 15.95 (*0-316-15588-8*) Little.

Cooper, Lela N. Nelsons in the Revolutionary War. LC 94-195484. (Orig.). 1994. pap. text 23.50 (*1-55613-970-5*) Heritage Bk.

Cooper, Leland R. & Cooper, Mary L., eds. The Pond Mountain Chronicle: Self-Portrait of a Southern Appalachian Community. LC 97-38306. 252p. 1997. pap. 25.00 (*0-7864-0391-8*) McFarland & Co.

Cooper, Leo. Seneca Indian Stories. 1995. pap. 9.95 (*0-912678-89-5*) Greenfld Rev Lit.

Cooper, Leon N. How We Learn, How We Remember - Toward an Understanding of the Brain & Neural Systems: Selected Papers. 400p. 1995. text 99.00 (*981-02-1814-1*); pap. text 53.00 (*981-02-1815-X*) World Scientific Pub.

***Cooper, Lesley, ed.** Fieldwork in the Human Services: Theory & Practice for Field Educators, Practice Teachers & Supervisors. 288p. 2000. pap. 39.95 (*1-86448-830-1*, Pub. by Allen & Unwin Pty) Paul & Co Pubs.

Cooper, Leslie L. The Low-Fat Living Cookbook: 250 Easy, Great-Tasting Recipes. LC 97-41540. 400p. 1998. 27.95 (*0-87596-435-4*) Rodale Pr Inc.

***Cooper, Leslie L.** The Low-Fat Living Cookbook: 250 Easy, Great-Tasting Recipes. LC 97-41540. (Illus.). 448p. 2000. pap. 17.95 (*0-87596-436-2*) Rodale Pr Inc.

Cooper, Leslie L., jt. auth. see Cooper, Robert K.

Cooper, Lettice. Unusual Behavior. large type ed. 248p. 1990. 20.95 (*0-7451-1140-8*, G K Hall Lrg Type) Mac Lib Ref.

***Cooper-Lewter, Nicholas C.** Black Grief & Soul Therapy LC 99-71529. 149 p. 1999. write for info. (*1-893562-00-X*) Harriet Tubman Pr.

Cooper, Linn, et al. Training the Time Sense - Hypnosis & Conditioning: The Millenial Edition. Morgan, Robert F., ed. 239p. 1999. pap. 85.00 (*1-885679-10-6*) Morgan Fnd Pubs.

Cooper, Linn F. & Erickson, Milton H. Time Distortion in Hypnosis: An Experimental & Clinical Investigation. 2nd ed. LC 82-663. (Illus.). 206p. 1982. reprint ed. text 29.50 (*0-8290-0702-4*) Irvington.

Cooper, Lisa. The Ballad in Memory. deluxe limited ed. 1991. pap. 75.00 (*0-925904-15-5*) Chax Pr.

— Calling It Home. LC 98-22725. 96p. (Orig.). 1997. pap. 12.95 (*0-925904-17-1*) Chax Pr.

Cooper, Lisa H., ed. see Kline, Thomas L.

Cooper, Lloyd G. & Maltby, Gregory P., eds. New Directions for Education. 249p. 1975. pap. text 12.75 (*0-8422-0504-7*) Irvington.

Cooper, Louis & Waltman, Franklin M., eds. La Gran Conquista de Ultramar, Biblioteca Nacional MS 1187. (Spanish Ser.: No. 41). xxxii, 278p. 1989. text 25.00 (*0-942260-85-6*) Hispanic Seminary.

Cooper, Louise. Aisling. (Indigo Ser.: Vol. 7). 384p. (Orig.). 1994. mass mkt. 4.99 (*0-8125-0808-4*) Tor Bks.

— Avatar. 1992. mass mkt. 4.99 (*0-8125-0802-5*) Tor Bks.

***Cooper, Louise.** Creatures: Once I Caught a Fish Alive. 1999. 16.95 (*0-7540-6076-4*) Chivers N Amer.

— Heart of Fire. (Illus.). 160p. (J). pap. 7.95 (*0-14-038771-4*, Pub. by Pnguin Bks Ltd) Trafalgar.

Cooper, Louise. Inferno. (Indigo Ser.: No. 2). 1989. pap. 3.95 (*0-8125-0246-9*, Pub. by Tor Bks) St Martin.

— The Initiate. 288p. (Orig.). 1985. pap. 2.95 (*0-8125-3392-5*, Pub. by Tor Bks) St Martin.

— Nemesis. (Indigo Ser.: No. 1). 1989. pap. write for info. (*0-8125-3401-8*, Pub. by Tor Bks) St Martin.

— Nocturne. (Indigo Ser.: No. 4). 1990. mass mkt. 4.95 (*0-8125-0798-3*, Pub. by Tor Bks) St Martin.

— Outcast No. 2: Time Master. 1992. mass mkt. 4.99 (*0-8125-1973-6*, Pub. by Tor Bks) St Martin.

— The Revenant. 320p. (Orig.). 1993. mass mkt. 4.99 (*0-8125-0807-6*) Tor Bks.

— Star Ascendant, Vol. 1. 1996. mass mkt. 5.99 (*0-8125-5175-3*, Pub. by Tor Bks) St Martin.

***Cooper, Louise.** The Summer Witch. 2000. pap. 11.00 (*0-7472-5950-X*, Pub. by Headline Bk Pub) Trafalgar.

Cooper, Louise. Troika. (Indigo Ser.: No. 5). 1991. mass mkt. 4.50 (*0-8125-0799-1*) Tor Bks.

Cooper, Lowell B. The Fresno & San Francisco Bicycle Mail of 1894. Hartmann, Leonard H., ed. LC 82-84657. (Illus.). 152p. 1983. 50.00 (*0-917528-05-0*) L H Hartmann.

Cooper, Lucy. Southern Entertaining Cookbook with a New Twist. 1988. pap. 16.95 (*0-942084-90-X*) SeaSide Pub.

Cooper, Lucy & Hosmon, Bob. The Miami Herald Dining Guide. (Illus.). 144p. (Orig.). 1984. pap. text 3.95 (*0-685-09725-0*) S&S Trade.

Cooper, Lucy, ed. see Costa Cruises, Inc. Staff.

Cooper, Lynda S. Bouquet of Unguarded Hearts. 1999. mass mkt. 3.99 (*0-8217-6374-1*, Zebra Kensgtn) Kensgtn Pub Corp.

— True Blue: An Insider's Guide to Street Cops for Writers. Clough, Judy, ed. 240p. 1999. 21.95 (*0-9654371-3-2*) Gryphon Bks Writers.

Cooper, Lynn A., jt. ed. see Nadel, Lynn.

Cooper, Lynn B., jt. ed. see Van Den Bergh, Nan.

Cooper, Lynna. Forgotten Love. (Orig.). 1979. mass mkt. 1.75 (*0-451-08569-8*, E8569, Sig) NAL.

— Forgotten Love. (Orig.). 1982. mass mkt. 2.75 (*0-451-11361-6*, AE1361, Sig) NAL.

C

— The Hired Wife. 1981. mass mkt. 2.75 (*0-451-11089-7*, AE1089, Sig) NAL.

Cooper, M. Health & Safety Training. 1996. pap. 129.00 (*1-85953-005-2*, Pub. by Tech Comm) St Mut.

Cooper, M. & Hammer, G. L., eds. Plant Adaptation & Crop Improvement. LC 97-142325. (CAB International Publication). (Illus.). 656p. 1997. text 130.00 (*0-85199-108-4*) OUP.

Cooper, M. & Wallace, E. King Kong. 1982. reprint ed. lib. bdg. 17.95 (*0-89966-440-7*) Buccaneer Bks.

Cooper, M., et al. Community Social Work: A Paradigm for Change. (C). 1988. 50.00 (*0-7855-0092-8*, Pub. by Natl Inst Soc Work) St Mut.

— Community Social Work: A Paradigm for Change. Wardle, M. & Crosbie, D., eds. (C). 1988. 39.00 (*0-7855-5894-2*, Pub. by Natl Inst Soc Work) St Mut.

Cooper, M. A. Control Surveys in Civil Engineering. 396p. 1987. 26.00 (*0-614-16825-2*, BSP833) Am Soc Civil Eng.

Cooper, M. A. & Williams, G. D., eds. Inversion Tectonics. (Geological Society Special Publication Classic Ser.: No. 44). (Illus.). viii, 375p. 1993. pap. 34.00 (*0-903317-97-4*, 292, Pub. by Geol Soc Pub Hse) AAPG.

Cooper, M. E. Blood & Pity: A True Story of Deceit & Murder. LC 94-70390. (Illus.). 216p. (Orig.). 1994. pap. 11.95 (*0-918751-37-3*, 24) Delta Pr.

Cooper, M. Frances. A Checklist of American Imprints, 1820 - 1829. (Checklist of American Imprints Ser.). 562p. 1972. 58.00 (*0-8108-0513-8*) Scarecrow.

Cooper, M. J., jt. auth. see Campbell, Bruce.

Cooper, M. J., jt. auth. see Williamson, R. C.

Cooper, M. McG. & Thomas, R. J. Profitable Sheep Farming. 5th ed. (Illus.). 192p. 1982. 32.95 (*0-85236-117-3*, Pub. by Farming Pr) Diamond Farm Bk.

Cooper, M. S. & Wanerman, Leon R. Children in Treatment: A Primer for Beginning Therapists. LC 77-7637. 191p. 1988. pap. text 19.95 (*0-87630-333-5*) Brunner-Mazel.

Cooper, M. Truman. Substantial Holdings. 20p. 1987. pap. 7.95 (*0-944754-12-0*) Pudding Hse Pubns.

Cooper, M. Wayne. Cardiology Handbook for Health Professionals. (Illus.). 186p. 1988. pap. 22.50 (*0-87527-366-1*) Green.

Cooper Madlener, Judith. The Sea Vegetable Gelatin Cookbook. LC 80-29228. (Illus.). 154p. (Orig.). 1981. pap. 7.95 (*0-912800-76-3*) Woodbridge Pr.

Cooper, Majorie. Test Yourself Principles of Marketing. (Test Yourself Ser.). (Illus.). 176p. (Orig.). 1996. pap. 11.95 (*0-8442-2373-5*, NTC Learningworks) NTC Contemp Pub Co.

Cooper, Malcolm. The Birth of Independent Air Power: British Air Policy in the First World War. (Illus.). 224p. (C). 1986. text 55.00 (*0-04-942204-9*) Routledge.

Cooper, Manda, ed. see Repp, Gloria.

***Cooper, Marc.** Pinochet & Me: A Chilean Anti-Memoir. 144p. 2000. 22.00 (*1-85984-785-4*, Pub. by Verso) Norton.

Cooper, Marc, et al. Zapatistas: Spreading Hope for Grassroots Change Starting from Chiapas. Ruggiero, Greg & Sahulka, Stuart, eds. (Open Magazine Pamphlet Ser.). 24p. (Orig.). 1994. 4.00 (*1-884519-06-7*) Open Media.

Cooper, Marc C. Blues Jam Along. 1996. pap., pap. text 12.95 incl. audio compact disk (*0-8256-1497-X*, AM931348) Music Sales.

— Hard Rock Jam Along. 1996. pap., pap. text 12.95 incl. audio compact disk (*0-8256-1498-8*, AM931359) Music Sales.

Cooper, Marcia M. Evaluation of the Mother's Advisory Service. (SRCD M Ser.: Vol. 12, No. 1). 1947. pap. 25.00 (*0-527-01540-7*) Periodicals Srv.

Cooper Marcus, Clare & Sarkissian, Wendy. Housing As If People Mattered: Site Design Guidelines for the Planning of Medium-Density Family Housing. (California Studies in Urban Development: Vol. 4). (Illus.). 280p. 1986. pap. 24.95 (*0-520-06330-9*, Pub. by U CA Pr) Cal Prin Full Svc.

Cooper, Margaret. Exploring the Ice Age. LC 99-44202. (J). 2000. 19.00 (*0-689-82556-0*) Atheneum Yung Read.

Cooper, Margaret E. An Introduction to Animal Law. 110p. 1988. 69.00 (*0-12-188030-3*) Acad Pr.

Cooper, Marian, ed. The World's Top Retirement Havens. 3rd ed. 480p. 1991. 15.95 (*0-945332-25-4*) Agora Inc MD.

Cooper, Marian G., et al. The Medical Assistant. 6th ed. LC 92-48690. 1992. text 36.95 (*0-8016-1012-5*) Mosby Inc.

Cooper, Marian G., et al. The Medical Assistant. 6th ed. 1993. teacher ed. write for info. (*0-8151-2663-8*) Mosby Inc.

Cooper, Marian G., et al. The Medical Assistant. 6th ed. (Illus.). 624p. (C). (gr. 13). 1993. text 43.00 (*0-8016-7445-X*, 01012) Mosby Inc.

Cooper, Marian R. & Johnson, Anthony W. Poisonous Plants & Fungi: An Illustrated Guide. (Illus.). 134p. 1998. pap. 115.00 (*0-11-242981-5*, Pub. by Statnry Office) Bernan Associates.

Cooper, Marian V., ed. Undiscovered Europe. 610p. 1988. 14.95 (*0-945332-07-6*) Agora Inc MD.

— The World Catalogue. 256p. 1990. 16.95 (*0-945332-20-3*) Agora Inc MD.

— The World's Best. 3rd ed. 600p. 1988. 19.95 (*0-945332-08-4*) Agora Inc MD.

Cooper, Marilyn M. & Holzman, Michael. Writing As Social Action. LC 88-31483. 243p. (Orig.). (C). 1989. pap. text 24.00 (*0-86709-244-0*, 0244, Pub. by Boynton Cook Pubs) Heinemann.

Cooper, Mario. Flower Painting in Watercolor. rev. ed. LC 72-186773. 143p. reprint ed. pap. 44.40 (*0-608-18583-3*, 20058090054) Bks Demand.

Cooper, Marion D. Dean. Descendants of John Dean, 1650-1727, of Dedham, Massachusetts. 217p. 1997. reprint ed. pap. 30.00 (*0-8328-8244-5*); reprint ed. lib. bdg. 40.00 (*0-8328-8243-7*) Higginson Bk Co.

Cooper, Marion R. & Johnson, Anthony R. Poisonous Plants & Fungi: An Illustrated Guide. 4th ed. (Illus.). 134p. 1996. pap. 21.95 (*0-11-242718-9*, Pub. by Statnry Office) Bernan Associates.

Cooper, Mark. Roll over, Che Guevara: Travels of a Radical Reporter. (Haymarket Ser.). 320p. 1996. pap. 19.00 (*1-85984-065-5*, Pub. by Verso) Norton.

Cooper, Mark & Congdon-Martin, Douglas. The Baseball Games: Home Versions of the National Pastime, 1860's-1960's. LC 95-1297. (Illus.). 160p. 1995. 39.95 (*0-88740-767-6*) Schiffer.

Cooper, Mark A., ed. Dear Father...Letters to Frederick Douglass from his Children. write for info. (*0-318-68429-2*) Fulmore Pr.

Cooper, Mark B., jt. auth. see Lewis, Morris.

Cooper, Mark N. The Transformation of Egypt. LC 82-15317. 282p. 1982. reprint ed. pap. 87.50 (*0-608-03648-X*, 206447400009) Bks Demand.

Cooper Markunas, Gail & Cooper, Garry. More Virtual Field Trips. 2nd ed. LC 99-19355. 200p. 1999. pap. 25.50 (*1-56308-770-7*) Libs Unl.

Cooper, Marshall, ed. see Norris, Michael K. & Goodhead, Giles.

Cooper, Martha. Analyzing Public Discourse. (Illus.). 231p. (C). 1989. pap. text 14.95 (*0-88133-407-3*) Waveland Pr.

— R. I. P. Memorial Wall Art. 89p. 1995. pap. write for info. (*0-8050-3316-5*) H Holt & Co.

Cooper, Martha & Chalfant, Henry. Subway Art. LC 84-620. (Illus.). 104p. 1995. pap. 17.95 (*0-8050-0678-8*, Owl) H Holt & Co.

Cooper, Martha D. & Nothstine, William L. Power Persuasion: Moving an Ancient Art into the Media Age. 2nd rev. ed. 357p. (Orig.). 1997. pap. text 20.95 (*0-9616489-8-8*) Alistair Pr IN.

Cooper, Martha R., jt. auth. see Levitan, Sar A.

Cooper, Martin. Georges Bizet. LC 71-138216. (Illus.). 136p. 1971. reprint ed. lib. bdg. 49.50 (*0-8371-5571-1*, COGB, Greenwood Pr) Greenwood.

— Georges Bizet. (Music Book Index Ser.). 136p. 1992. reprint ed. lib. bdg. 69.00 (*0-7812-9490-8*) Rprt Serv.

— Gluck. 1988. reprint ed. lib. bdg. 59.00 (*0-7812-0124-1*) Rprt Serv.

— Gluck. LC 74-181129. 293p. 1935. reprint ed. 55.00 (*0-403-01526-X*) Scholarly.

— Judgements of Value: Selected Writings on Music by Martin Cooper. Cooper, Dominic, ed. (Illus.). 360p. 1989. 70.00 (*0-19-311929-3*) OUP.

— Opera Comique. 1988. reprint ed. lib. bdg. 75.00 (*0-7812-0105-5*) Rprt Serv.

— Opera Comique. LC 70-181128. 1949. reprint ed. 45.00 (*0-403-01527-8*) Scholarly.

— Russian Opera. 1988. reprint ed. lib. bdg. 49.00 (*0-7812-0142-X*) Rprt Serv.

— Russian Opera. LC 77-181127. 65p. 1951. reprint ed. 59.00 (*0-403-01528-6*) Scholarly.

— Stop Committing Voice Suicide. 172p. 1996. pap. text 10.00 (*0-87980-437-8*) Wilshire.

Cooper, Martin & Larson, John. Lasers in Conservation: An Introduction. LC 98-156459. (Illus.). 112p. 1998. 79.95 (*0-7506-3117-1*, Butterwrth Archit) Buttrwrth-Heinemann.

Cooper, Martin, jt. auth. see Campbell, Bruce.

Cooper, Martin, tr. see Boucourechliev, Andre.

Cooper, Martin, tr. see Boulez, Pierre.

Cooper, Marva. So Beautiful De Swatches. 48p. (Orig.). 1991. pap. 6.95 (*1-56411-011-7*) Untd Bros & Sis.

Cooper, Mary L. A Rebel Made a Child. unabridged ed. (Children's Heritage Ser.). (Illus.). 76p. (J). (gr. 4-6). 1996. pap. 5.00 (*1-58339-130-4*, D30) Triangle Press.

Cooper, Mary L. & Slayman, Toby. School-to-Work in the West: A Survey of the States. (Illus.). 93p. 1998. pap. text 25.00 (*0-7881-4039-6*) DIANE Pub.

Cooper, Mary L., jt. ed. see Cooper, Leland R.

Cooper, Mary W., jt. auth. see Cooper, L.

***Cooper, Mason Y.** Norfolk & Western Electrics. (Illus.). (C). 2000. write for info. (*0-9633254-9-3*) Norfolk & Wstrn HS.

Cooper, Mason Y. Norfolk & Western's Shenandoah Valley Line. LC 97-76580. (Illus.). 260p. 1998. 49.95 (*0-9633254-7-7*) Norfolk & Wstrn HS.

Cooper, Matthew. The German Army, 1933-1945. 640p. 1990. pap. 17.95 (*0-8128-8519-8*, Scrbrough Hse) Madison Bks UPA.

Cooper, Matthew & Rodman, Margaret C. New Neighbours: A Case Study of Cooperative Housing in Toronto. 368p. (Orig.). 1992. text 50.00 (*0-8020-5992-9*); pap. text 19.95 (*0-8020-6925-8*) U of Toronto Pr.

Cooper, Matthew, jt. ed. see Rodman, Margaret.

Cooper, Max D. & Dayton, Delbert H., eds. Development of Host Defenses. fac. ed. LC 76-51866. (Illus.). 320p. pap. 99.20 (*0-7837-7519-9*, 204698600005) Bks Demand.

Cooper, Melrose. Gettin' Through Thursday. LC 98-13083. (Illus.). 32p. (J). (gr. 1-3). 1998. 15.95 (*1-880000-67-9*) Lee & Low Bks.

***Cooper, Melrose.** Gettin' Through Thursday. 2000. pap. 6.95 (*1-58430-014-0*) Lee & Low Bks.

Cooper, Melrose. I Got a Family. LC 92-1689. (Illus.). 88p. (J). (ps-2). 1995. 14.95 (*0-8050-1965-0*, Bks Young Read) H Holt & Co.

— I Got a Family. 1997. 11.15 (*0-606-13503-0*, Pub. by Turtleback) Demco.

— I Got a Family. (Illus.). 32p. (J). (ps-2). 1997. reprint ed. pap. text 5.95 (*0-8050-5542-8*) H Holt & Co.

— I Got Community. (J). 1995. 14.95 (*0-8050-3179-0*) H Holt & Co.

***Cooper, Melrose.** Kwanzaa. LC 99-72743. (Illus.). 24p. (J). (gr. 2-6). 1999. pap. text 9.95 (*1-58521-002-1*) Bks Black Chldn.

Cooper, Melrose. Life Magic. 128p. (J). (gr. 4-7). 1995. 14.95 (*0-8050-4114-1*, B Martin BYR) H Holt & Co.

— Life Riddles. 88p. (J). (gr. 5-7). 1995. 14.95 (*0-8050-2613-4*, Bks Young Read) H Holt & Co.

— "Pets!" LC 97-16173. (Illus.). 32p. (J). (ps-2). 1998. text 15.95 (*0-8050-3893-0*) St Martin.

Cooper, Michael. Exploring Kamakura: A Guide for the Curious Traveler. LC 79-11997. (Exploring Japan Ser.). (Illus.). 160p. 1979. pap. 11.95 (*0-8348-0144-2*) Weatherhill.

— Klondike Fever: The Famous Gold Rush of 1898. (Illus.). (J). (gr. 4-7). 1990. pap. 6.95 (*0-395-54784-9*, Clarion Bks) HM.

— Klondike Fever: The Famous Gold Rush of 1898. (J). 1989. 12.15 (*0-606-04724-7*, Pub. by Turtleback) Demco.

— 1998 Michael Cooper's Buyer's Guide to New Zealand Wines. LC 98-202319. 314p. 1997. write for info. (*1-86958-570-4*) Moa Beckett.

— Rodriques the Interpreter: An Early Jesuit in Japan & China. (Illus.). 416p. (Orig.). 1994. pap. 17.95 (*0-8348-0319-4*) Weatherhill.

— The Wines of New Zealand. (Mitchell Beazley Pocket Guides Ser.). 1998. 14.95 (*1-84000-020-1*, Pub. by Mitchell Beazley) Antique Collect.

Cooper, Michael, ed. They Came to Japan: An Anthology of European Reports on Japan, 1543-1640. LC 95-41563. (Michigan Classics in Japanese Studies: No. 15) xviii, 439p. 1995. reprint ed. pap. 18.95 (*0-939512-73-4*) U MI Japan.

Cooper, Michael D. Design of Library Automation Systems: File Structures, Data Structures, & Tools. LC 95-45827. 638p. 1996. 69.99 (*0-471-13884-3*) Wiley.

Cooper, Michael H. Dues: A Novel of War & After. LC 94-26056. 248p. (Orig.). 1994. pap. 11.95 (*1-880684-19-5*) Curbstone.

Cooper, Michael L. Bound for Promise. 1999. pap. write for info. (*0-14-038226-7*) Viking Penguin.

***Cooper, Michael L.** Fighting for Honor: Japanese Americans & World War II. LC 00-26855. (Illus.). 128p. (gr. 4-7). 2000. 16.00 (*0-395-91375-6*, Clarion Bks) HM.

— Indian School: Teaching the White Man's Way. LC 98-43640. (Illus.). 103p. (YA). (gr. 4-7). 1999. 15.00 (*0-395-92084-1*, Clarion Bks) HM.

Cooper, Michael R., ed. see Bath, Markus.

Cooper, Mike, jt. ed. see Pickell, David.

Cooper, Mimi & Mathews, Arlene. Color Smart: How to Use Color to Enhance Your Business & Personal Life. (Illus.). 184p. 2000. per. 12.95 (*0-671-03459-6*, PB Trade Paper) PB.

Cooper, Molly. Classic Mysteries: A Collection of Mind-Bending Masterpieces. LC 96-140. 1996. 11.05 (*0-606-09151-3*, Pub. by Turtleback) Demco.

Cooper, Morley. The Cruising Yacht: What to Buy, How to Equip It & How to Handle It on Long & Short Cruises. 1977. lib. bdg. 69.95 (*0-8490-1688-6*) Gordon Pr.

***Cooper, Morton.** Change Your Voice, Change Your Life. 1999. 9.95 (*1-55927-042-X*) Audio Renaissance.

Cooper, Morton. Change Your Voice, Change Your Life. 180p. 1996. pap. 10.00 (*0-87980-441-6*) Wilshire.

— Winning with Your Voice. 1996. pap. 10.00 (*0-87980-442-4*) Wilshire.

Cooper, Ms Carol D. Cooper Communications & Its Skills for Nursing & Health Care. (C). 2000. pap. text. write for info. (*0-201-36059-4*) Addison-Wesley.

Cooper-Mullin, Alison & Coye, Jennifer Marmaduke. Once upon a Heroine. LC 97-32121. 320p. 1998. pap. 16.95 (*0-8092-3020-8*, 302080, Contemporary Bks) NTC Contemp Pub Co.

***Cooper, Muriel.** The Music of Memory. 64p. 2000. pap. 7.50 (*0-920635-13-X*) Genl Dist Srvs.

Cooper, Murphy R. Cooper Family History & Genealogy, 1681-1931. (Illus.). 116p. 1997. reprint ed. pap. 18.50 (*0-8328-8038-8*); reprint ed. lib. bdg. 28.50 (*0-8328-8037-X*) Higginson Bk Co.

***Cooper, Myra.** Bulimia Nervosa: A Cognitive Manual. 2000. pap. 24.95 (*1-85302-717-0*) Jessica Kingsley.

Cooper, Myrtle E. From Tent Town to City: A Chronological History of Billings, Montana 1882-1935. Von Vogt, Janice, ed. (Illus.). 79p. (Orig.). (J). (gr. 6-8). 1982. pap. 5.95 (*0-9613224-0-3*) Parmly Lib.

Cooper, N. R., ed. Thirteenth International Complement Workshop, San Diego, Calif., September 1989 Abstracts. (Journal: Complement & Inflammation: Vol. 6, No. 5). 128p. 1990. pap. 36.75 (*3-8055-5089-8*) S Karger.

Cooper, N. V. The Fighting General. (Heritage Library Ser.). (Illus.). 362p. 1987. 14.95 (*0-940328-08-9*, Marine Corps.

Cooper, Nancy. The Convenience Foods Cookbook: Over 200 Quick & Healthy Recipes Based on Brand-Name Foods. LC 98-12638. 256p. 12.95 (*1-885115-46-6*) IDC Pub.

Cooper, Nancy, jt. auth. see Monk, Arlene.

Cooper, Nancy K. The Development of Roof Revetment in the Peloponnese. (Studies in Mediterranean Archaeology & Literature: Pocket-Book 88). (Illus.). 192p. (Orig.). 1989. pap. 42.50 (*91-85058-44-0*, Pub. by P Astroms) Coronet Bks.

Cooper, Nanthapa, jt. ed. see Cooper, Robert.

Cooper, Natasha. Bitter Herbs. large type ed. 1995. 25.99 (*0-7089-3291-6*) Ulverscroft.

— Bloody Roses. large type ed. LC 93-22677 467p. 1993. lib. bdg. 17.95 (*1-56054-901-7*) Thorndike Pr.

— A Common Death. large type ed. Orig. Title: Festering Lillies. 1991. 25.99 (*0-7089-2458-1*) Ulverscroft.

***Cooper, Natasha.** Creeping Ivy. large type ed. 376p. 1999. 31.99 (*0-7089-4144-3*) Ulverscroft.

Cooper, Natasha. The Drowning Pool. (WWL Mystery Ser.). 1998. per. 4.99 (*0-373-26271-X*, 1-26271-6, Wrldwide Lib) Harlequin Bks.

***Cooper, Natasha.** Fault Lines. LC 99-462108. 352p. 2000. 23.95 (*0-312-25316-8*, Minotaur) St Martin.

Cooper, Natasha. Poison Flowers. large type ed. (Mystery Ser.). 544p. 1992. 25.99 (*0-7089-2726-2*) Ulverscroft.

***Cooper, Natasha.** Prey to All. 2000. 23.95 (*0-312-26636-7*) St Martin.

Cooper, Natasha. Rotten Apples. (Worldwide Library Mysteries: No. 244). 1997. per. 4.99 (*0-373-26244-2*, 1-26244-3, Wrldwide Lib) Harlequin Bks.

— Sour Grapes. Vol. 319. 1999. pap. 4.99 (*0-373-26319-8*, Wrldwide Lib) Harlequin Bks.

— Sour Grapes. LC 98-3716. 304p. 1998. text 22.95 (*0-312-18666-5*) St Martin.

***Cooper, Natasha.** The Telephone in Business & Daily Life. (Learn Telephone English Ser.). 120p. 2000. pap. 19.00 (*0-9677755-0-7*) Cooper Learn Syst.

***Cooper, Nathaniel.** Scribble - Letters from the Heart. 1999. pap. write for info. (*1-58235-191-0*) Watermrk Pr.

Cooper, Necia, ed. The Human Genome Project. rev. ed. LC 93-85290. (Illus.). 327p. (C). 1994. text 48.50 (*0-935702-29-6*) Univ Sci Bks.

Cooper, Neil. The Business of Death: Britain's Arms Trade at Home & Abroad. LC 95-62308. 256p. 1997. text 59.50 (*1-85043-953-2*, Pub. by I B T) St Martin.

Cooper, Neil. The Diversity of Moral Thinking. (CLLP Ser.). (Illus.). 314p. (C). 1981. text 75.00 (*0-19-824423-1*) OUP.

Cooper, Neil, et al, eds. Integrating Perspectives on Health. LC 95-47214. 192p. (C). 1996. 98.95 (*0-335-19357-9*); pap. 28.95 (*0-335-19356-0*) OpUniv Pr.

Cooper, Neil H. & Jarvis, Rebecca E. Recognition & Enforcement of Cross-Border Insolvency: A Guide to International Practice. LC 96-22533. (Wiley Series in Commercial Law). 1996. text 121.00 (*0-471-96310-0*) Wiley.

***Cooper, Nic & McCoy, Rick.** How to Keep Being a Parent When Your Child Stops Being a Child: A Practical Guide for Parents of Adolescents. LC 99-68057. (Illus.). xx, 185p. 1999. pap. 12.95 (*0-9675426-0-X*) Willow Creek MI.

***Cooper, Nicholas.** Houses of the Gentry,1480-1680. LC 99-14919. 344p. 1999. 75.00 (*0-300-07390-9*) Yale U Pr.

Cooper, Nicholas & Majerus, Marianne. English Manor Houses. (Country Ser.). (Illus.). 160p. 1996. pap. 17.95 (*0-297-83106-2*, Pub. by Weidenfeld & Nicolson) Trafalgar.

***Cooper, Nicola J.** France in Indochina: Colonial Encounters. 224p. 2001. 65.00 (*1-85973-476-6*, Pub. by Berg Pubs); pap. 19.50 (*1-85973-481-2*, Pub. by Berg Pubs) NYU Pr.

C

Cooper, Norman P. Collaborative Ministry: Communion, Contention, Commitment. LC 92-38074. 192p. 1993. pap. 14.95 (*0-8091-3376-8*) Paulist Pr.

Cooper, Norman W. Finding Your Self. 96p. 1974. pap. 6.50 (*0-87516-183-9*) DeVorss.

— Love That Heals. 1977. pap. 7.00 (*0-87516-228-2*) DeVorss.

Cooper, O. William. Discovering the Message of Scripture: A Step by Step Guide to How to Do Inductive Bible Study. 260p. (Orig.). 1996. pap. write for info. (*1-57502-168-4*, PO777) Morris Pubng.

— Partakers of the Divine Nature: A Study of 13 Qualities of Spiritual Growth. LC 98-93153. 214p. 1998. pap. write for info. (*1-57502-860-3*, PO2349) Morris Pubng.

Cooper-Oakley, Isabal. Masonry & Medieval Mysticism: Traces of a Hidden Tradition. 192p. 1996. reprint ed. pap. 16.95 (*1-56459-643-5*) Kessinger Pub.

Cooper-Oakley, Isabel. The Count of Saint-Germain. LC 70-137422. 260p. 1988. pap. 12.95 (*0-89345-239-4*, Steinerbks) Garber Comm.

— The Count of Saint-Germain. 254p. 1997. reprint ed. pap. 19.95 (*0-7661-0101-0*) Kessinger Pub.

— Mystical Traditions (1909) 305p. 1998. reprint ed. pap. 24.95 (*0-7661-0346-3*) Kessinger Pub.

***Cooper, P.** That's Disgusting! LC 99-27896. 208p. 1999. pap. 8.95 (*1-58008-094-4*) Ten Speed Pr.

Cooper, P., ed. Colour in Dyehouse Effluent. 1995. pap. 79.00 (*0-901956-69-4*, Pub. by Textile Inst) St Mut.

— Pumping Machinery, 1993. LC 89-84349. (FED Ser.: Vol. 154). 395p. 1993. pap. 60.00 (*0-7918-0962-5*, H00794) ASME.

Cooper, P., jt. auth. see Garbage, Greta.

Cooper, P. F. & Atkinson, Bernard, eds. Biological Fluidised Bed Treatment of Water & Wastewater. LC 80-41740. 411p. 1981. text 131.00 (*0-470-27112-4*) P-H.

Cooper, P. J., jt. ed. see Rothe, J. Peter.

Cooper, P. W. Explosives Engineering. 480p. 1997. 94.50 (*0-471-18636-8*) Wiley.

Cooper, P. W. & Kurowski, S. R. Introduction to the Technology of Explosives. LC 95-52613. 224p. 1997. 64.95 (*0-471-18635-X*) Wiley.

Cooper, Pamela. The American Marathon. LC 97-45156. (Sports & Entertainment Ser.). 226p. 1998. 34.95 (*0-8156-0520-X*) Syracuse U Pr.

— The American Marthon. 240p. 1999. pap. 17.95 (*0-8156-0573-0*) Syracuse U Pr.

Cooper, Pamela & Galvin, Kathleen M., eds. The Future of Speech Communication Education: Proceedings of the 1988 Speech Communication Association Flagstaff Conference. LC 89-62176. 96p. (C). 1989. pap. text 13.00 (*0-944811-02-7*) Natl Comm Assn.

Cooper, Pamela, jt. auth. see Stewart, Lea P.

Cooper, Pamela, jt. ed. see Galvin, Kathleen.

Cooper, Pamela J. & Simonds, Cheri. Communication for the Classroom Teacher. 6th ed. LC 98-7273. 333p. 1998. pap. text 51.00 (*0-205-28805-7*) Allyn.

Cooper, Pamela J., jt. auth. see Collins, Rives.

Cooper, Pamela J., jt. auth. see Galvin, Kathleen M.

Cooper, Parley. Conspiracy. 384p. (Orig.). 1988. spiral bd. 3.95 (*0-373-97088-9*) Harlequin Bks.

Cooper, Pat & Dancyger, Ken. Writing the Short Film. 224p. 1994. pap. 26.95 (*0-240-80165-2*, Focal) Buttrwrth-Heinemann.

— Writing the Short Film. 2nd ed. LC 99-27623. 256p. 1999. pap. 22.95 (*0-240-80369-8*, Focal) Buttrwrth-Heinemann.

Cooper, Patricia A. Once a Cigar Maker: Men, Women, & Work Culture in American Cigar Factories, 1900-1919. LC 86-11207. (Working Class in American History Ser.). (Illus.). 376p. 1987. text 23.95 (*0-252-01333-6*) U of Ill Pr.

— Understanding Genital Warts: A Guide for Women. (Women's Health Care Ser.). (Illus.). 103p. (Orig.). 1997. pap. 6.95 (*1-880906-29-5*) IDI Pub.

Cooper, Patricia J. & Allen, Norma B. The Quilters: Women & Domestic Art.: An Oral History. LC 98-41324. 1999. 17.95 (*0-89672-410-7*) Tex Tech Univ Pr.

Cooper, Patrick. Never Trust a Squirrel. LC 98-23251. (Illus.). (J). (ps-2). 1999. 15.99 (*0-525-46009-8*, Dutton Child) Peng Put Young Read.

Cooper, Patsy. When Stories Come to School: Telling, Writing, & Performing Stories in the Early Childhood Classroom. (Illus.). 144p. (Orig.). 1993. pap. 13.95 (*0-915924-77-3*) Tchrs & Writers Coll.

***Cooper, Patty & Zillner, Dian.** Toy Buildings, 1880-1980. LC 99-40538. 222p. 1999. 49.95 (*0-7643-1011-9*) Schiffer.

Cooper, Patty, jt. auth. see Zillner, Dian.

Cooper, Paul. Effective Schools for Disaffected Students: Integration & Segregation. LC 92-15266. 288p. 1993. pap. write for info. (*0-415-06484-8*) Routledge.

***Cooper, Paul.** Helping Children with Attention Deficit/Hyperactivity Disorder. (Illus.). 1998. pap. 29.95 (*1-86156-074-5*) Whurr Pub.

— Positive Alternatives to Exclusion. LC 00-28197. 2000. pap. write for info. (*0-415-19758-9*) Routledge.

Cooper, Paul. Pupils with Attention Deficit. 1999. pap. text 29.95 (*1-86156-108-3*) Whurr Pub.

— Understanding & Supporting Children with Emotional & Behavioral Difficulties. 1998. 75.00 (*1-85302-665-4*); pap. 26.95 (*1-85302-666-2*) Taylor & Francis.

Cooper, Paul & Ideus, Katherine. Attention Deficit/Hyperactivity Disorder: A Practical Guide for Teachers. LC 96-224076. 128p. 1996. pap. 24.95 (*1-85346-431-7*, Pub. by David Fulton) Taylor & Francis.

Cooper, Paul & McIntyre, Donald. Effective Teaching & Learning: Teachers' & Pupils' Perspectives. LC 95-19491. 192p. 1995. 113.95 (*0-335-19380-3*); pap. 29.95 (*0-335-19379-X*) OpUniv Pr.

Cooper, Paul, et al. Emotional & Behavioural Difficulties: Theory to Practice. LC 93-25943. 176p. (C). 1994. text 59.95 (*0-415-07198-4*) Routledge.

Cooper, Paul, jt. auth. see Olsen, Jerry.

Cooper, Paul, jt. auth. see Sammarco, G. James.

Cooper, Paul, jt. auth. see Siggins, Paul.

Cooper, Paul L. Archaeological Investigations in the Heart Butte Reservoir Area, North Dakota, Paper No. 9. fac. ed. (Smithsonian Institution, Bureau of American Ethnology Ser.: Bulletin 169). (Illus.). 58p. (C). 1958. reprint ed. pap. text 7.20 (*1-55567-692-8*) Coyote Press.

— Weekend Warriors. (Illus.). 250p. 1996. pap. 23.95 (*0-89745-202-X*) Sunflower U Pr.

Cooper, Paul R. Head Injury. 3rd ed. LC 92-16760. (Illus.). 544p. 1992. 135.00 (*0-683-02108-7*) Lppncott W & W.

Cooper, Paul R., ed. Degenerative Disease of the Cervical Spine. (Neurosurgical Topics Ser.: Bk. 12). (Illus.). 175p. 1994. 95.00 (*1-879284-04-9*) Am Assn Neuro.

Cooper, Paul R. & Golfinos, John. Head Injury. 4th ed. (Illus.). 564p. (C). 2000. pap. 140.00 (*0-8385-3687-5*) McGraw.

Cooper, Paul W. Explosives Engineering. (Illus.). 320p. 1996. 79.95 (*1-56081-927-8*, Wiley-VCH) Wiley.

Cooper, Paul W. & Kurowski, Stanley R. Introduction to the Technology of Explosives. LC 95-52613. (Illus.). 350p. 1996. 49.95 (*1-56081-926-X*, Wiley-VCH) Wiley.

Cooper, Paulette. 277 Secrets Your Cat Wants You to Know. 208p. (Orig.). 1997. pap. 8.95 (*0-89815-952-0*) Ten Speed Pr.

— 277 Secrets Your Dog Wants You to Know. rev. ed. (Illus.). 208p. 1998. pap. 8.95 (*1-58008-014-6*) Ten Speed Pr.

— 277 Secrets Your Snake & Lizard Want You to Know: Unusual & Useful Information for Snake Owners & Snake Lovers. LC 99-20517. 208p. 1999. pap. 8.95 (*1-58008-035-9*) Ten Speed Pr.

Cooper, Paulette & Noble, Paul. The 100 Top Psychics in America: Their Stories, Specialties & How to Contact Them. 186p. 1996. mass mkt. 6.99 (*0-671-53401-7*) PB.

Cooper, Paulette, tr. see Kagan, Spencer.

***Cooper, Peter.** Children of the Amulet. 2000. pap. 18.00 (*0-7388-2124-1*) Xlibris Corp.

Cooper, Peter. Complete Irish Fiddle Player. (Complete Bks.). 160p. 1995. pap. 17.95 (*0-7866-0329-1*, MB95406) Mel Bay.

Cooper, Peter. Complete Irish Fiddle Player. 160p. 1995. pap. 38.95 incl. audio compact disk (*0-7866-1319-X*, 95406CDP) Mel Bay.

Cooper, Peter. Hub City Music Makers: One Southern Town's Popular Music Legacy. (Illus.). 288p. (Orig.). 1997. pap. 19.95 (*0-9638731-9-9*) Hub City Writers.

***Cooper, Peter.** Valley of My Eastern Heart. 300p. 2000. pap. 16.00 (*1-58776-032-0*) Vivisphere.

— The Valley of My Western Heart. LC 00-101734. 376p. 2000. pap. 20.00 (*1-58776-033-9*, Straw Hse Pr) Vivisphere.

Cooper, Peter, et al. Agroecological Constraints to Crop Production in West Asia & North Africa, & Their Impact on Fertilizer Use. Roth, E. N., ed. LC 89-15447. (Papers: No. P-9). (Illus.). 30p. (Orig.). 1989. pap. text 4.00 (*0-88090-074-1*) Intl Fertilizer.

Cooper, Peter, jt. auth. see Buchanan, Neil.

Cooper, Peter J. Bulimia Nervosa & Binge-Eating: A Guide to Recovery. (Illus.). 160p. (C). 1995. pap. 13.95 (*0-8147-1523-0*) NYU Pr.

— Bulimia Nervosa & Binge-Eating: A Guide to Recovery. LC 95-8359. (Illus.). 160p. (C). 1995. text 35.00 (*0-8147-1522-2*) NYU Pr.

— Feeding Problems & Eating Disorders in Children & Adolescents, Vol. 5. (Monographs in Clinical Pediatrics). xiii, 205p. 1992. text 132.00 (*3-7186-5158-0*, Harwood Acad Pubs); pap. text 48.00 (*3-7186-5166-1*, Harwood Acad Pubs) Gordon & Breach.

— Forever Farnborough: Flying the Limits, 1904-1996. Ketley, Barry, ed. (Illus.). 174p. 1999. pap. 39.95 (*0-9519899-3-6*, Pub. by Hikoki Pubns) Howell Pr VA.

Cooper, Peter J., jt. auth. see Miller, Edgar.

Cooper, Peter J., jt. auth. see Rothe, J. Peter.

Cooper, Peter J., jt. ed. see Murray, Lynne.

Cooper, Philip. Cubism. (Color Library). (Illus.). 128p. (C). 1995. pap. 14.95 (*0-7148-3250-2*, Pub. by Phaidon Press) Phaidon Pr.

Cooper, Philip D., ed. Health Care Marketing: A Foundation for Managed Quality. 3rd ed. 544p. 1994. 51.00 (*0-8342-0527-0*) Aspen Pub.

Cooper, Philip D., et al, eds. Marketing & Preventive Health Care: Interdisciplinary & Interorganizational Perspectives. LC 77-25849. (American Marketing Association, Proceedings Ser.). 142p. reprint ed. pap. 44.10 (*0-608-13822-3*, 201777900008) Bks Demand.

Cooper, Philip D. & Robinson, Larry M. Health Care Marketing Management: A Case Approach. LC 82-3904. 368p. (C). 1981. 79.00 (*0-89443-394-6*) Aspen Pub.

Cooper, Phillip. Basic Magick: A Practical Guide. 224p. (Orig.). 1996. pap. 12.95 (*0-87728-832-1*) Weiser.

***Cooper, Phillip.** Candle Magic: A Coveted Collection of Spells, Rituals & Magical Paradigms. LC 99-59296. (Illus.). 176p. 2000. pap. 12.95 (*1-57863-121-1*) Weiser.

Cooper, Phillip. The Magickian: A Study in Effective Magick. LC 93-18793. (Illus.). 240p. (Orig.). 1993. pap. 12.95 (*0-87728-777-5*) Weiser.

— Secrets of Creative Visualization. LC 98-51029. (Illus.). 224p. 1999. pap. 14.95 (*1-57863-102-5*) Weiser.

Cooper, Phillip J. Battles on the Bench: Conflict Inside the Supreme Court. LC 95-31618. 240p. 1999. pap. 16.95 (*0-7006-0966-0*) U Pr of KS.

— Battles on the Bench: Conflict Inside the Supreme Court. LC 95-31618. 240p. (C). 1999. 35.00 (*0-7006-0737-4*) U Pr of KS.

— Handbook of Public Law & Public Administration. LC 97-28390. 1997. 59.95 (*0-7879-0930-0*) Jossey-Bass.

— Hard Judicial Choices: Federal Court Orders & State & Local Officials. LC 87-7901. (Illus.). 384p. 1988. pap. text 27.95 (*0-19-504192-5*) OUP.

Cooper, Phyllis. Euthenics: A Stress Reduction Worktext. 208p. (C). 1996. pap. text, spiral bd. 31.95 (*0-7872-2753-6*) Kendall-Hunt.

Cooper, Phyllis S. & Trnka, Milan. Teaching Basic Gymnastics: A Coeducational Approach. 3rd ed. LC 93-7874. 307p. (C). 1993. pap. text 59.00 (*0-02-324701-0*, Macmillan Coll) P-H.

Cooper, Polly. Como Guiar a los Adultos. Martinez, Carol, tr. from ENG. Orig. Title: How to Guide Adults. (SPA.). 160p. 1990. pap. 6.99 (*0-311-11823-2*) Casa Bautista.

Cooper, Polly & Cooper, Emmeline. Savannah Safari: A Self-Guided Walking Adventure in Search of Architectural Animals. 16p. 1995. pap. text 5.00 (*0-9647471-0-3*) Perry St Bks.

Cooper, Polly, jt. ed. see Dolling, Yolanda.

***Cooper, Polly Wylly & Lawton, Laura Connerat.** Savannah Movie Memories. 50p. 2000. pap. 7.50 (*0-9647471-2-X*) Perry St Bks.

Cooper, Pressley. Bone Appetite. (Illus.). 64p. (Orig.). 1997. pap. 8.95 (*1-56550-055-5*) Vis Bks Intl.

Cooper Publishing Group Staff. Ice Hockey: A Guide for Parents & Coaches. (USOC Sports Education Ser.). (Illus.). 128p. 1999. pap. 18.00 (*1-884125-56-5*) Cooper Pubng.

— Soccer: A Guide for Parents & Coaches. LC 96-96088. (U. S. O. C. Sports Education Ser.). (Illus.). 138p. (Orig.). 1996. pap. 18.00 (*1-884125-54-9*) Cooper Pubng.

— Weightlifting: A Guide for Parents & Coaches. (USOC Sports Education Ser.). (Illus.). 128p. 1999. pap. 18.00 (*1-884125-59-X*) Cooper Pubng.

— Wrestling: A Guide for Parents & Coaches. (USOC Sports Education Ser.). (Illus.). 128p. 1999. pap. 18.00 (*1-884125-58-1*) Cooper Pubng.

***Cooper, R.** Practical Guide to Alterations & Improvements. 170p. (C). (gr. 13). 1998. pap. text 29.99 (*1-85032-006-3*) ITCP.

Cooper, R., jt. ed. see Wagman, G. H.

Cooper, R. A. & Weekes, A. J. Data, Models & Statistical Analysis. LC 82-25110. (Illus.). 416p. 1983. pap. text 30.00 (*0-389-20383-1*, N7256) B&N Imports.

Cooper, R. A. & Weeks, A. J. Data, Models & Statistical Analysis. LC 82-25110. (Illus.). 416p. 1983. 57.00 (*0-389-20382-3*, N7255) B&N Imports.

Cooper, R. C. & Cambie, R. C. New Zealand's Economic Native Plants. (Illus.). 248p. 1992. text 55.00 (*0-19-558229-2*) OUP.

Cooper, R. C., jt. auth. see Vivienne, Cassie.

Cooper, R. John & Sanford, Bruce W. First Amendment & Libel: The Experts Look at Print, Broadcast & Cable. Law & Business Inc. Staff, ed. write for info. (*0-318-58019-5*) Harcourt.

Cooper, R. K. & Pellegrini, C. Modern Analytic Mechanics. LC 99-37364. (Illus.). 290p. (C). 1998. text. write for info. (*0-306-45958-2*, Kluwer Plenum) Kluwer Academic.

Cooper, R. Scott. Ready, Willing & Enabled: Easy Guidelines for Living Your Dreams. LC 96-94692. (Illus.). 235p. (Orig.). 1997. pap. 14.95 (*0-9654444-0-6*) Life Guides.

Cooper, Rachel & Press, Mike. The Design Agenda: A Guide to Successful Design Management. LC 94-13491. 304p. 1995. 99.95 (*0-471-94106-9*) Wiley.

Cooper, Rachel, jt. auth. see Bruce, Margaret.

Cooper, Ralph L., et al, eds. Aging & Environmental Toxicology: Biological & Behavioral Perspectives. LC 90-5134. (Johns Hopkins Series in Environmental Toxicology). (Illus.). 312p. reprint ed. pap. 96.80 (*0-608-05986-2*, 206627200007) Bks Demand.

Cooper, Ralph L., jt. ed. see Walker, Richard F.

Cooper, Rand R. The Last to Go. 320p. 1990. pap. 7.95 (*0-380-70862-0*, Avon Bks) Morrow Avon.

— The Last to Go: A Family Chronicle. 304p. 1988. 16.95 (*0-15-148430-9*) Harcourt.

Cooper, Raymond D., ed. see AEC Technical Information Center Staff.

Cooper, Rebecca. The Logical Influence of Hegel on Marx. 1974. lib. bdg. 250.00 (*0-8490-0550-7*) Gordon Pr.

Cooper, Redmond. Butterworths Construction Law Manual. 300p. 1993. 96.00 (*0-406-00635-0*, UK, MICHIE) LEXIS Pub.

Cooper, Remi. Amino Acids. 1999. pap. 3.95 (*1-885670-55-9*) Woodland UT.

— Antioxidants. (The Woodland Health Ser.). 1997. pap. text 3.95 (*1-885670-52-4*) Woodland UT.

— Dha: The Essential Omega-3 Fatty Acid. (Woodland Health Ser.). 1998. pap. 3.95 (*1-58054-021-X*) Woodland UT.

— Pyruvate. 1999. pap. 3.95 (*1-885670-80-X*) Woodland UT.

— Thermogenics. 1999. pap. 3.95 (*1-885670-85-0*) Woodland UT.

***Cooper, Rhonda & Cooper, Jeffrey.** Masterpiece of Chinese Art. 128p. 1998. 16.98 (*1-57717-060-1*) Todtri Prods.

Cooper, Richard. Video. (Illus.). 120p. 1991. pap. text 13.95 (*0-19-437102-6*) OUP.

Cooper, Richard, ed. Maurice Sceve, the Entry of Henri II into Lyon, September 1548. (Medieval & Renaissance Texts & Studies: Vol. 160). (Illus.). 328p. 1997. 36.00 (*0-86698-200-0*, MR160) MRTS.

Cooper, Richard L., ed. Interfaces to Database Systems: Proceedings of the 1st International Workshop on Interfaces to Database Systems, Glasgow, 1-3 July 1992. (Workshops in Computing Ser.). (Illus.). 480p. 1993. pap. write for info. (*3-540-19802-4*) Spr-Verlag.

— Interfaces to Database Systems - IDS 92: Proceedings of the 1st International Workshop on Interfaces to Database Systems, Glasgow, 1-3 July 1992. LC 93-7749. (Workshops in Computing Ser.). 1993. 79.95 (*0-387-19802-4*) Spr-Verlag.

Cooper, Richard N. Economic Stabilization & Debt in Developing Countries. (Ohlin Ser.). (Illus.). 216p. 1992. 27.50 (*0-262-03187-6*) MIT Pr.

— Economic Stabilization in Developing Countries. 102p. 1991. pap. 9.95 (*1-55815-148-6*) ICS Pr.

— The Economics of Interdependence. (Council on Foreign Relations Ser.). 316p. 1980. reprint ed. pap. text 25.50 (*0-231-05071-2*) Col U Pr.

— The Economics of Interdependence: Economic Policy in the Atlantic Community. LC 80-398. (Illus.). 311p. reprint ed. pap. 96.50 (*0-8357-6869-4*, 203556700095) Bks Demand.

— Environment & Resource Policies for the World Economy. (Integrating National Economies Ser.). 94p. (C). 1995. 34.95 (*0-8157-1546-3*); pap. 14.95 (*0-8157-1545-5*) Brookings.

***Cooper, Richard N.** Prospects for the World Economy. (New Ser.: Vol. 26). 26p. 2000. pap. 15.00 (*0-86682-112-0*) Ctr Intl Relations.

Cooper, Richard N. & Gacs, Janos, eds. Trade Growth in Transition Economies: Export Impediments for Central & Eastern Europe. 384p. 1997. 95.00 (*1-85898-608-7*) E Elgar.

Cooper, Richard N., et al. Lower Oil Prices: Mapping the Impact. LC 87-83646. (International Energy Studies: No. 4). x, 109p. (Orig.). 1988. pap. 21.50 (*0-942781-03-1*) Harvard EEPC.

Cooper, Robb, jt. auth. see Florestal, Ketleen.

***Cooper, Robert.** Around the World with Mark Twain. 2000. 26.95 (*1-55970-522-1*, Pub. by Arcade Pub Inc) Time Warner.

— Bahrain. (Cultures of the World Ser.). (Illus.). (J). 2000. 35.64 (*0-7614-1161-5*, Benchmark NY) Marshall Cavendish.

— Bhutan. (Cultures of the World Ser.). (Illus.). (J). 2001. 35.64 (*0-7614-1191-7*, Benchmark NY) Marshall Cavendish.

— Croatia. (Cultures of the World Ser.). (Illus.). (J). 2000. 35.64 (*0-7614-1156-9*, Benchmark NY) Marshall Cavendish.

Cooper, Robert. In the Realm of Organization. 224p. 1996. pap. 19.95 (*0-415-12757-2*) Routledge.

— In the Realm of Organization. LC 98-28454. 224p. (C). 1998. 85.00 (*0-415-12756-4*) Routledge.

— Portfolio Management for New Products. LC 97-49937. 1998. 38.00 (*0-201-32814-3*) Addison-Wesley.

— Winning at New Products. 1986. 21.95 (*0-201-13665-1*) Addison-Wesley.

— Winning big with New Products. 1998. 1.00 (*0-201-33979-X*) Addison-Wesley.

Cooper, Robert & Cooper, Nanthapa, eds. Culture Shock! Thailand. LC 90-85620. (Illus.). 256p. 1991. pap. 12.95 (*1-55868-058-6*) Gr Arts Ctr Pub.

Cooper, Robert & Sawaf, Ayman. Executive E. Q. Emotional Intelligence in Leadership & Organizations. LC 96-54909. 256p. 1997. 24.95 (*0-399-14294-0*, Grosset-Putnam) Putnam Pub Group.

Cooper, Robert, jt. auth. see Sroufe, Alan.

Cooper, Robert, ed. see Fidler, Brian.

Cooper, Robert B. Introduction to Queueing Theory. 2nd ed. LC 80-16481. 365p. 1981. reprint ed. pap. 113.20 (*0-608-07976-6*, AU0049800012) Bks Demand.

— Solutions Manual for Robert B. Cooper's Introduction to Queueing Theory - by Borge Tilt. 2nd ed. LC T 0057.C66. 188p. 1981. reprint ed. pap. 58.30 (*0-608-07975-8*, AU0049700012) Bks Demand.

Cooper, Robert B., Jr., jt. auth. see Harrington, Thomas P.

Cooper, Robert B., jt. ed. see Lai, Wai S.

Cooper, Robert F. Serenade to the Blue Lady: The Story of Bert Stiles. LC 92-82993. (Illus.). 256p. (Orig.). 1993. pap. 12.95 (*1-879384-21-3*) Cypress Hse.

***Cooper, Robert G.** Product Leadership: Creating & Launching Superior New Products. 336p. 1999. pap. text 20.00 (*0-7382-0156-1*, Pub. by Perseus Pubng) HarpC.

Cooper, Robert G. Winning at New Products: Strategy & Process. 2nd ed. 1993. pap. 20.00 (*0-201-56381-9*) Addison-Wesley.

Cooper, Robert G. & Kleinschmidt, Elko J. New Products: The Key Factors in Success. LC 90-49464. 52p. 1990. pap. text 20.00 (*0-87757-213-5*) Am Mktg.

Cooper, Robert G., jt. auth. see Edgett, Scott J.

Cooper, Robert K. Executive EQ: Emotional Intelligence in Leadership & Organizations. 368p. 1998. pap. 14.95 (*0-399-52404-5*, Perigee Bks) Berkley Pub.

— Health & Fitness Excellence: The Scientific Action Plan. 544p. 1990. pap. 16.00 (*0-395-54453-X*) HM.

***Cooper, Robert K.** High Energy Living: Activate Your Energy Igniters Feel 100Alive. (Illus.). 448p. 2000. 29.95 (*1-57954-126-7*) Rodale Pr Inc.

— Vivir Bien (Low Fat Living) (SPA.). 528p. 2000. pap. 17.95 (*1-57954-300-6*) Rodale Pr Inc.

Cooper, Robert K. & Cooper, Leslie L. Low-Fat Living: Turn off the Fat Makers, Turn on the Fat Burners for Longevity, Energy, Weight Loss, Freedom from Disease. (Illus.). 496p. 1996. text 27.95 (*0-87596-295-5*) Rodale Pr Inc.

— Low-Fat Living: Turn off the Fat-Makers; Turn on the Fat-Burners for Longevity, Energy, Weight Loss, Freedom from Disease. (Illus.). 478p. 1998. pap. 14.95 (*1-57954-021-X*) Rodale Pr Inc.

Cooper, Robert K., jt. auth. see Bloomfield, Harold H.

Cooper, Robert L. Language Planning & Social Change. (Illus.). 224p. (C). 1990. text 59.95 (*0-521-33359-8*) Cambridge U Pr.

— Language Spread: Studies in Diffusion & Social Change. LC 81-47567. 368p. 1982. reprint ed. pap. 114.10 (*0-7837-6098-1*, 205914400008) Bks Demand.

Cooper, Robert L. & Spolsky, Bernard J., eds. The Influence of Language on Culture & Thought: Essays in Honor of Joshua A. Fishman's 65th Birthday. vi, 290p. 1991. lib. bdg. 121.55 (*3-11-012806-3*) Mouton.

Cooper, Robert L., jt. auth. see Spolsky, Bernard J.

Cooper, Robert M. The Literary Guide & Companion to Middle England. LC 92-13580. (Illus.). 398p. (C). 1992. text 34.95 (*0-8214-1032-6*) Ohio U Pr.

— The Literary Guide & Companion to Middle England. LC 92-13580. (Illus.). 398p. (C). 1993. reprint ed. pap. 16.95 (*0-8214-1033-4*) Ohio U Pr.

— The Literary Guide & Companion to Northern England. (Illus.). 398p. 1994. text 34.95 (*0-8214-1095-4*) Ohio U Pr.

— The Literary Guide & Companion to Northern England. LC 94-21981. (Illus.). 398p. 1995. pap. 16.95 (*0-8214-1096-2*) Ohio U Pr.

— The Literary Guide & Companion to Southern England. LC 97-49201. xxi, 389p. 1998. pap. 19.95 (*0-8214-1226-4*) Ohio U Pr.

— The Literary Guide & Companion to Southern England. rev. ed. LC 97-49201. 350p. 1998. reprint ed. text 39.95 (*0-8214-1225-6*) Ohio U Pr.

Cooper, Robert M., compiled by. A Concordance to the English Poetry of Richard Crashaw. LC 80-51219. lx, 477p. 1980. 54.00 (*0-87875-188-2*) Whitston Pub.

Cooper, Robert W. An Historical Analysis of the Tontine Principle. LC 72-92061. (S. S. Huebner Foundation Monographs: No. 1). 69p. (C). 1972. pap. 12.00 (*0-918930-01-4*) Huebner Foun Insur.

Cooper, Roberta K. The American Shakespeare Theatre: Stratford, 1955-1985. LC 85-45578. (Illus.). 352p. 1987. 48.50 (*0-918016-88-6*) Folger Bks.

Cooper, Robin. Design of Cost Management Systems. 2nd ed. LC 98-37654. 536p. 1998. 100.00 (*0-13-570417-0*) P-H.

— The Evolving Mind: Buddhism, Biology, & Consciousness. (Illus.). 288p. (Orig.). 1996. pap. 21.95 (*0-904766-74-8*) Windhorse Pubns.

— Implementing Activity-Based Cost Management: Moving from Analysis to Action. 1993. pap. 40.00 (*0-86641-206-9*) Inst Mgmt Account.

— When Lean Enterprises Collide: Competing Through Confrontation. 400p. 1995. 35.00 (*0-87584-540-1*) Harvard Busn.

Cooper, Robin, et al, eds. Situation Theory & Its Applications, Vol. 1. LC 90-82189. (CSLI Lecture Notes Ser.: No. 22). 515p. 1991. 64.95 (*0-937073-55-5*); pap. 24.95 (*0-937073-54-7*) CSLI.

Cooper, Robin & Slagmulder, Regine. Supply Chain Development for the Lean Enterprise: Interorganizational Cost Management. LC 99-19428. (Strategies in Confrontational Cost Management Systems Ser.: Vol. 2). 512p. 1999. 50.00 (*1-56327-218-0*) Productivity Inc.

An Asterisk (*) at the beginning of an entry indicates that the title is appearing for the first time.

— Target Costing & Value Engineering. LC 97-15146. (Strategies in Confrontational Cost Management Ser.: Vol. I). (Illus.). 379p. 1997. pap. 50.00 (*1-56327-172-9*, 97319) Productivity Inc.

Cooper, Robin & Vitale, Michael. CABIS: Computer-Aided Bookkeeping Instruction System. LC 86-32148. 80p. (C). 1987. 25.00 (*0-201-11306-6*); text, teacher ed. 30.00 (*0-317-60800-2*) Addison-Wesley.

Cooper, Robin, jt. auth. see Kaplan, Robert S.

Cooper, Robin S., et al. Triathlon. Crane, Carla J., ed. (Next Level Preteen Electives Ser.). (Illus.). 128p. 1996. teacher ed. 14.99 (*0-7847-0502-X*, 42102) Standard Pub.

Cooper, Rod. Journey Through Australia. LC 91-46173. (Illus.). 32p. (J). (gr. 3-5). 1997. lib. bdg. 18.60 (*0-8167-2757-0*) Troll Communs.

Cooper, Rod N. Abbeys & Priories of Wales. (Illus.). 100p. (C). 1992. 70.00 (*0-7154-0712-0*, Pub. by C Davies Pubs) St Mut.

Cooper, Rodney H., et al. Augustinus - Concordantia in Libros XIII Confessionum S. Aurelii Augustini, 2 vols., Set. (Alpha-Omega, Reihe A Ser.: Bd. CXXIV). (GER.). xx, 1191p. 1991. 320.00 (*3-487-09489-4*) G Olms Pubs.

***Cooper, Rodney L.** Mark. (Holman New Testament Commentary Ser.: Vol. 2). 2000. 16.99 (*0-8054-0202-0*) Broadman.

Cooper, Roger, ed. see Christie, Agatha.

Cooper, Ron L. Heidegger & Whitehead: A Phenomenological Examination into the Intelligibility of Experience. LC 93-21562. (Series in Continental Thought : Vol. 19). 160p. (C). 1993. text 34.95 (*0-8214-1060-1*) Ohio U Pr.

Cooper, Ronald S. & Pols, Cynthia M. Flsa: The Public Employer's Guide. 542p. 1993. 65.00 (*0-87326-089-9*) Intl City-Cnty Mgt.

Cooper, Rory A. Rehabilitation Engineering Applied to Mobility & Manipulation. LC 95-38066. (Medical Science Ser.). (Illus.). 516p. 1995. 200.00 (*0-7503-0343-3*, RM950) IOP Pub.

— Wheelchair Selection & Configuration. LC 98-22858. (Illus.). 424p. 1998. 34.95 (*1-888799-18-8*) Demos Medical.

Cooper, Rosalind. The Wine Almanac. (Illus.). 184p. 1998. pap. text 25.00 (*0-7881-5371-4*) DIANE Pub.

Cooper, Roscoe. The Great Pyramid. LC 98-140556. (Illus.). 10p. (J). 1998. 18.95 (*0-8167-4390-8*) BrdgeWater.

Cooper, Roy. Calf Roping. Witte, Randy, ed. (Illus.). 144p. (Orig.). 1984. pap. 12.95 (*0-911647-04-X*) Western Horseman.

Cooper, Ruskin. Ludwig Schuncke (1810-1834) & His Piano Music: Robert Schumann's Closest "Jugendfreund" Draheim, Joachim & Schuncke, Michael, eds. (GER., Illus.). 278p. 1997. write for info. (*3-926435-16-X*, Pub. by Fischer & Partner) Lichtental Pubns.

Cooper, Russell M. & Fisher, Margaret B. The Vision of a Contemporary University: A Case Study of Expansion & Development in American Higher Education, 1950-75. LC 80-29022. 332p. reprint ed. pap. 103.00 (*0-7837-5088-9*, 204478600004) Bks Demand.

Cooper, Russell W. Coordination Games: Complementarities & Macroeconomics. LC 98-20151. (Illus.). 184p. (C). 1999. text 54.95 (*0-521-57017-4*); pap. text 17.95 (*0-521-57896-5*) Cambridge U Pr.

— Wage & Employment Patterns in Labor Contracts: Micro-Foundations & Macroeconomics Implications. (Fundamentals of Pure & Applied Economics Ser.: Vol. 19). viii, 80p. 1987. pap. text 36.00 (*3-7186-0378-0*) Gordon & Breach.

Cooper, S., ed. Blackstone's Guide to the Road Traffic Act, 1991. vii, 190p. (C). 1991. pap. 33.00 (*1-85431-120-4*, Pub. by Blackstone Pr) Gaunt.

Cooper, S. B., et al, eds. Computability, Enumerability, Unsolvability: Directions in Recursion Theory. (London Mathematical Society Lecture Note Ser.: No. 224). 355p. (C). 1996. pap. text 47.95 (*0-521-55736-4*) Cambridge U Pr.

Cooper, S. Barry & Truss, John K., eds. Models & Computability. LC 99-19677. (London Mathematical Society Lecture Note Ser.: No. 259). 300p. (C). 1999. pap. text 44.95 (*0-521-63550-0*) Cambridge U Pr.

— Sets & Proofs. LC 99-19676. (London Mathematical Society Lecture Note Ser.: No. 258). 300p. (C). 1999. pap. text 44.95 (*0-521-63549-7*) Cambridge U Pr.

Cooper, S. Clement & Thron, W. J., eds. Continued Fractions & Orthogonal Functions: Theory & Applications. LC 93-33234. (Lecture Notes in Pure & Applied Mathematics Ser.: Vol. 154). (Illus.). 400p. 1993. pap. text 185.00 (*0-8247-9071-5*) Dekker.

Cooper, S. J. & Hendrie, C. A., eds. Ethology & Psychopharmacology. LC 94-15718. 370p. 1995. 294.95 (*0-471-95213-3*) Wiley.

Cooper, S. J., jt. auth. see Levens, A. S.

Cooper, S. Kerry & Fraser, Donald R. The Financial Marketplace. 1982. 30.25 (*0-201-00196-9*) Addison-Wesley.

— The Financial Marketplace. 2nd ed. LC 84-28327. 720p. (C). 1989. text. write for info. (*0-201-10548-9*) Addison-Wesley.

Cooper, S. Kerry, et al. Money: The Financial System & Economic Policy. (Finance Ser.). 576p. 1983. text. write for info. (*0-201-03994-X*) Addison-Wesley.

Cooper, S. L., et al, eds. Polymer Biomaterials in Solution, As Interfaces & As Solids. 1100p. 1995. 260.00 (*90-6764-180-4*, Pub. by VSP) Coronet Bks.

Cooper, S. R., ed. Crown Compounds: Toward Future Applications. 325p. 1992. 175.00 (*0-471-18783-6*) Wiley.

Cooper, Sally. New Strategies for Free Children: A Leader's Manual of the Child Assault Prevention Projects. Britton, Jan, ed. LC 91-62365. (Illus.). 220p. 1991. 21.25 (*1-880326-49-3*) Natl Assault.

Cooper, Samuel W. Think & Thank: A Tale. LC 74-27975. (Modern Jewish Experience Ser.). 1975. reprint ed. 17.95 (*0-405-06704-6*) Ayer.

Cooper, Sandi E. Patriotic Pacifism: Waging War on War in Europe, 1815-1914. 352p. 1991. text 60.00 (*0-19-505715-5*, 8865) OUP.

Cooper, Sarah. Girls! Girls! Girls! Essays on Women & Music. (Illus.). 180p. (C). 1996. text 45.00 (*0-8147-1540-0*); pap. text 18.50 (*0-8147-1541-9*) NYU Pr.

***Cooper, Sarah.** Relating to Queer Theory: Re-Reading Sexual Self Definition with Irigaray, Kristeva, Wittig & Cixous, 3. Collier, Peter, ed. LC 99-87570. 231p. 2000. 38.95 (*3-906764-46-X*, Pub. by P Lang) P Lang Pubng.

— Relating to Queer Theory: Rereading Sexual Self-Definition with Irigaray, Kristeva, Wittig & Cixous. LC 99-87570. (Modern French Identities Ser.: Vol. 3). 231p. 2000. pap. 38.95 (*0-8204-4636-X*) P Lang Pubng.

Cooper, Saul & Hodges, William F., eds. The Mental Health Consultation Field. (Community Psychology Ser.: Vol. XI). 247p. (C). 1983. 34.95 (*0-89885-130-0*, Kluwer Acad Hman Sci); pap. 24.95 (*0-89885-286-2*, Kluwer Acad Hman Sci) Kluwer Academic.

Cooper, Saul & Lentner, Timothy H., eds. Innovations in Community Mental Health. LC 92-5819. 256p. 1992. pap. 28.95 (*0-943158-76-1*, ICMBP, Prof Resc Pr) Pro Resource.

***Cooper, Scott.** Sticks & Stones: 7 Ways Your Child Can Deal with Teasing, Conflict, & Other Hard Times. LC 99-54856. 160p. 2000. pap. 13.00 (*0-8129-3240-4*, Times Bks) Crown Pub Group.

Cooper, Scott W., jt. auth. see Hiebing, Roman.

Cooper, Scott W., jt. auth. see Hiebing, Roman G.

Cooper, Scott W., jt. auth. see Hiebing, Roman G., Jr.

Cooper, Shawn. The Clinical Use & Interpretation of the Wechsler Intelligence Scale for Children. 3rd rev. ed. LC 95-14202. (Illus.). 466p. (C). 1995. text 78.95 (*0-398-06523-3*); pap. text 56.95 (*0-398-06524-1*) C C Thomas.

***Cooper, Sheila & Patton, Rosemary.** Writing Logically, Thinking Critically. 3rd ed. LC 00-30458. 2000. write for info. (*0-321-07237-5*) Addison-Wesley Educ.

Cooper, Shelley. Cross-Border Savings Flows & Capital Mobility in the G7 Economies. LC HG0136.D57. (Bank of England, Discussion Papers: Vol. 54). 39p. 1991. reprint ed. pap. 30.00 (*0-608-00498-7*, 206131700007) Bks Demand.

***Cooper, Shelley.** Dad in Blue. (Intimate Moments Ser.: Bk. 1044). 2000. mass mkt. 4.50 (*0-373-27114-X*, 1-27114-7) Silhouette.

Cooper, Shelley. Guardian Groom. (Intimate Moments Ser.: Bk. 942). 1999. per. 4.25 (*0-373-07942-7*, 1-07942-5) Silhouette.

— Major Dad. (Intimate Moments Ser.). 1998. per. 4.25 (*0-373-07876-5*, 1-07876-5) Silhouette.

Cooper, Sherod. Liberty Ship: The Voyages of the "John W. Brown," 1942-1946. LC 97-1519. (Illus.). 264p. 1997. 34.95 (*1-55750-135-1*) Naval Inst Pr.

Cooper, Shirley & Wanerman, Leon R. A Casebook of Child Psychotherapy: Strategies & Techniques. LC 93-31139. 272p. 1993. pap. 40.00 (*1-56821-116-3*) Aronson.

Cooper, Simon. Welcome to the Mardi Gras Experience. 1999. 26.00 (*1-85782-351-6*, Pub. by Blake Publng) Seven Hills Bk.

Cooper, Simon, ed. Evidence & Criminal Procedure. (C). 1991. text 22.00 (*1-85431-132-8*, Pub. by Blackstone Pr) Gaunt.

Cooper, Simon & Mackey, Sally. Theatre Studies: An Approach for Advanced Level. (Illus.). 329p. 1995. pap. 47.50 (*0-7487-2121-5*, Pub. by S Thornes Pubs) Trans-Atl Phila.

Cooper, Simon, et al. Cases & Materials on Evidence. 3rd ed. 614p. 1994. pap. 50.00 (*1-85431-279-0*, Pub. by Blackstone Pr) Gaunt.

— Cases & Materials on Evidence. 4th ed. 572p. 1997. pap. 52.00 (*1-85431-638-9*, Pub. by Blackstone Pr) Gaunt.

Cooper, Simon, jt. auth. see Johnson, Nick.

Cooper, Simon, jt. auth. see Mackey, Sally.

***Cooper-Sinykin, Sheri.** Heather's Fashion World. (Magic Attic Club Ser.). (Illus.). 80p. (J). (gr. 2-6). 1999. 12.95 (*1-57513-171-4*, Pub. by Magic Attic); pap. 5.95 (*1-57513-170-6*, Pub. by Magic Attic) Millbrook Pr.

Cooper, Sonja Flating, see Flating Cooper, Sonja.

Cooper, Sonni. Black Fire. 1986. per. 3.50 (*0-671-62747-3*) PB.

Cooper, Stephanie, et al. The Children's Year: Crafts & Clothes for Children & Parents to Make. (Lifeways Ser.). (Illus.). 220p. 1990. pap. 18.95 (*1-869890-00-0*, 1187, Pub. by Hawthorn Press) Anthroposophic.

Cooper, Stephen. Bacterial Growth & Division: Biochemistry & Regulation of Prokaryotic & Eukaryotic Division Cycles. (Illus.). 501p. (C). 1991. text 77.00 (*0-12-187905-4*) Acad Pr.

***Cooper, Stephen.** Full of Life: A Biography of John Fante. LC 99-56197. (Illus.). 496p. 2000. 30.00 (*0-86547-554-7*) N Point Pr.

Cooper, Stephen. A House Divided. (C). 1989. 65.00 (*0-947934-12-X*, Pub. by Bridge Pubns) St Mut.

— Perspectives on John Huston. LC 93-46640. (Perspectives on Film Ser.). (Illus.). 224p. 1994. 55.00 (*0-8161-1985-6*, G K Hall & Co) Mac Lib Ref.

— The Politics of Ernest Hemingway. LC 87-5872. (Studies in Modern Literature: No. 71). 174p. reprint ed. pap. 54.00 (*0-8357-1799-2*, 207064400012) Bks Demand.

Cooper, Stephen, et al, eds. Financial Aid for Study Abroad: A Manual for Advisers & Administrators. 105p. (Orig.). 1989. pap. text 12.00 (*0-912207-55-8*) NAFSA Washington.

Cooper, Stephen & Fine, David M., eds. John Fante: A Critical Gathering. LC 99-20894. 160p. 1999. 33.50 (*0-8386-3778-7*) Fairleigh Dickinson.

Cooper, Stephen, ed. see Fante, John.

Cooper, Stephen A. Metaphysics & Moral in Marius Victorinus' Commentary on the Letter to the Ephesians Vol. 155: A Contribution to the History of Neoplatonism & Christianity. LC 94-16095. (American University Studies: Series V). XIII, 248p. (C). 1996. text 44.95 (*0-8204-2330-0*) P Lang Pubng.

Cooper, Stephen R., ed. Crown Compounds: Toward Future Applications. LC 92-26923. 1992. 125.00 (*1-56081-024-6*, Wiley-VCH) Wiley.

Cooper, Stephen V., et al. Forest Habitat Types of Northern Idaho: A Second Approximation. (Illus.). 152p. 1997. reprint ed. 23.00 (*0-89904-634-7*, Bear Meadows Resrch Grp); reprint ed. pap. 18.00 (*0-89904-635-5*, Bear Meadows Resrch Grp) Crumb Elbow Pub.

***Cooper, Steven.** Objects of Hope: Exploring Possibility & Limit in Psychoanalysis. LC 00-26949. Vol. 18. 244p. 2000. 49.95 (*0-88163-271-6*) Analytic Pr.

Cooper, Steven J. & Clifton, Peter G., eds. Drug Receptor Subtypes & Ingestive Behavior. (Illus.). 416p. 1996. text 95.00 (*0-12-187620-9*) Acad Pr.

Cooper, Steven J. & Dourish, Colin T., eds. Neurobiology of Stereotyped Behavior. (Illus.). 320p. 1990. 75.00 (*0-19-852160-X*) OUP.

Cooper, Steven J., jt. auth. see Liebman, Jeffrey M.

Cooper, Stewart, jt. auth. see Archer, James, Jr.

Cooper, Stuart L. Polyurethanes in Biomedical Devices. LC 97-41911. 1997. boxed set 139.95 (*0-8493-4517-0*) CRC Pr.

Cooper, Stuart L. & Estes, Gerald M., eds. Multiphase Polymers. LC 79-10972. (Advances in Chemistry Ser.: No. 176). 1979. 71.95 (*0-8412-0457-8*) Am Chemical.

— Multiphase Polymers. LC 79-10972. (Advances in Chemistry Ser.: Vol. 176). 656p. 1979. reprint ed. pap. 200.00 (*0-608-03869-5*, 206431600008) Bks Demand.

Cooper, Stuart L. & Peppas, Nicholas A., eds. Biomaterials: Interfacial Phenomena & Applications. LC 82-6763. (ACS Advances in Chemistry Ser.: No. 199). 539p. 1982. lib. bdg. 76.95 (*0-8412-0631-7*) Am Chemical.

— Biomaterials, Interfacial Phenomena & Applications. LC 82-6763. (Advances in Chemistry Ser.: Vol. 199). 554p. 1982. reprint ed. pap. 171.80 (*0-608-03503-3*, 206422200008) Bks Demand.

Cooper, Stuart L., jt. auth. see Lelah, Michael D.

Cooper, Susan. The Boggart. LC 92-15527. 196p. (J). (gr. 3-7). 1995. pap. 3.95 (*0-689-80173-4*) Aladdin.

Cooper, Susan. The Boggart. 196p. (YA). (gr. 5 up). pap. 3.95 (*0-8072-1465-5*) Listening Lib.

Cooper, Susan. The Boggart. LC 92-15527. 208p. (J). (gr. 3-7). 1993. text 15.00 (*0-689-50576-0*) McElderry Bks.

— The Boggart. (J). 1995. 9.05 (*0-606-07305-1*, Pub. by Turtleback) Demco.

***Cooper, Susan.** Boggart. (2000 Kids Picks Ser.). (J). (gr. 4-7). 2000. mass mkt. 2.99 (*0-689-83864-6*) Aladdin.

Cooper, Susan. The Boggart & the Monster. LC 96-42389. (Illus.). 192p. (J). (gr. 3-7). 1998. per. 4.50 (*0-689-82286-3*) Aladdin.

Cooper, Susan. The Boggart & the Monster. 185p. (J). (gr. 4-6). pap. 3.95 (*0-8072-1531-7*) Listening Lib.

Cooper, Susan. The Boggart & the Monster. LC 96-42389. 192p. (J). (gr. 3-7). 1997. per. 16.00 (*0-689-81330-9*) McElderry Bks.

— Danny & the Kings. LC 92-22744. (Illus.). 32p. (J). (ps-3). 1993. 14.95 (*0-689-50577-9*) McElderry Bks.

— The Dark Is Rising. (Dark Is Rising Sequence Ser.). 1999. pap. 2.99 (*0-689-82989-2*) Aladdin.

— The Dark Is Rising. LC 86-3647. (Illus.). 232p. (J). (gr. 5-9). 1999. per. 4.99 (*0-689-82983-3*) Aladdin.

Cooper, Susan. The Dark Is Rising. 244p. (YA). (gr. 5 up). pap. 4.99 (*0-8072-1533-3*) Listening Lib.

Cooper, Susan. The Dark Is Rising. LC 72-85916. (Dark Is Rising Sequence Ser.). (Illus.). 232p. (YA). (gr. 5 up). 1973. 17.00 (*0-689-30317-3*) McElderry Bks.

— The Dark Is Rising. (Dark Is Rising Sequence Ser.). (J). 1986. 9.05 (*0-606-00687-7*, Pub. by Turtleback) Demco.

— The Dark Is Rising. LC 86-3647. (Dark Is Rising Sequence Ser.). 256p. (YA). (gr. 7 up). 1999. reprint ed. mass mkt. 3.95 (*0-689-71087-9*) Aladdin.

— The Dark Is Rising Sequence Box, 5 bks. (YA). (gr. 7 up). 1993. reprint ed. pap., boxed set 19.75 (*0-02-042565-1*, Pub. by Macmillan) S&S Trade.

— Dawn of Fear. (J). 1970. 9.60 (*0-606-04195-8*, Pub. by Turtleback) Demco.

— Dawn of Fear. LC 89-6820. (Illus.). 224p. (J). (gr. 3-7). 1989. reprint ed. mass mkt. 4.50 (*0-689-71327-4*) Aladdin.

Cooper, Susan. Dreams & Wishes: Essays on Writing for Children. LC 95-31077. 208p. (YA). (gr. 8-12). 1996. pap. 18.00 (*0-689-80736-8*) McElderry Bks.

Cooper, Susan. Greenwitch. LC 73-85319. (Dark Is Rising Sequence Ser.). (Illus.). 148p. (J). (gr. 4-7). 1985. 17.00 (*0-689-30426-9*) McElderry Bks.

— Greenwitch. (Dark Is Rising Sequence Ser.). 1974. 9.05 (*0-606-00700-8*, Pub. by Turtleback) Demco.

— Greenwitch. LC 86-3324. (Dark Is Rising Sequence Ser.). 148p. (J). (gr. 4-7). 1986. reprint ed. mass mkt. 3.95 (*0-689-71088-7*, Collier Bks Young) S&S Childrens.

***Cooper, Susan.** The Grey King. LC 86-3613. (Illus.). 224p. (J). (gr. 5-9). 1999. per. 4.99 (*0-689-82984-1*) Aladdin.

Cooper, Susan. The Grey King. LC 75-8526. (Dark Is Rising Sequence Ser.). (Illus.). 224p. (J). (gr. 4-8). 1975. 17.00 (*0-689-50029-7*) McElderry Bks.

— The Grey King. (Dark Is Rising Sequence Ser.). (J). 1986. 9.05 (*0-606-01150-1*, Pub. by Turtleback) Demco.

— The Grey King. LC 86-3613. (Dark Is Rising Sequence Ser.). 224p. (YA). (gr. 6 up). 1986. reprint ed. mass mkt. 3.95 (*0-689-71089-5*, Collier Bks Young) S&S Childrens.

— The Grey King, Vol. 1. (Dark Is Rising Sequence Ser.). 1999. pap. 2.99 (*0-689-82988-4*) Aladdin.

— Matthew's Dragon. LC 90-31532. (Illus.). 32p. (J). (ps-3). 1991. 14.95 (*0-689-50512-4*) McElderry Bks.

— Matthew's Dragon. (J). 1994. 11.19 (*0-606-05921-0*, Pub. by Turtleback) Demco.

— Matthew's Dragon. LC 93-26574. (Illus.). 32p. (J). (gr. k-3). 1994. reprint ed. mass mkt. 5.99 (*0-689-71794-6*) Aladdin.

— Over Sea, under Stone. LC 66-11199. (Dark is Rising Sequence Ser.). (Illus.). 252p. (YA). (gr. 5 up). 1966. 17.00 (*0-15-259034-X*, Harcourt Child Bks) Harcourt.

Cooper, Susan. Over Sea, under Stone. (Dark Is Rising Sequence Ser.). (J). 1989. 9.05 (*0-606-04293-8*, Pub. by Turtleback) Demco.

— Over Sea, under Stone. LC 88-37690. (Dark is Rising Sequence Ser.). 243p. (J). (gr. 4-7). 1989. reprint ed. pap. 3.95 (*0-02-042785-9*) Harcourt.

Cooper, Susan. Seaward. LC 83-7055. 180p. (YA). (gr. 5 up). 1983. lib. bdg. 16.00 (*0-689-50275-3*) McElderry Bks.

— Seaward. 1987. 9.05 (*0-606-03459-5*, Pub. by Turtleback) Demco.

— Seaward. LC 86-23234. 180p. (YA). (gr. 5 up). 1987. reprint ed. mass mkt. 3.95 (*0-02-042190-7*) Macmillan.

Cooper, Susan. The Silver Cow: A Welsh Tale. 1991. 11.44 (*0-606-12516-7*) Turtleback.

Cooper, Susan. The Silver Cow: A Welsh Tale. LC 91-234. (Illus.). 32p. (J). (gr. k-4). 1991. reprint ed. mass mkt. 5.99 (*0-689-71512-9*) Aladdin.

— Silver on the Tree. LC 77-5361. (Dark Is Rising Sequence Ser.). 256p. (J). (gr. 4-8). 1977. 17.00 (*0-689-50088-2*) McElderry Bks.

Cooper, Susan. Silver on the Tree. (Dark Is Rising Sequence Ser.). (J). 1986. 9.05 (*0-606-02257-0*, Pub. by Turtleback) Demco.

Cooper, Susan. Silver on the Tree. LC 86-3341. (Dark Is Rising Sequence Ser.). 288p. (YA). (gr. 6 up). 1987. reprint ed. mass mkt. 3.95 (*0-689-71152-2*, Collier Bks Young) S&S Childrens.

***Cooper, Susan.** Staging Dance. LC 97-35293. (Theatre Arts Ser.). (Illus.). 1998. pap. 21.99 (*0-87830-081-3*) Routledge.

***Cooper, Susan & Clapp, John.** King of Shadows. LC 98-51127. 186p. (YA). (gr. 5-9). 1999. per. 16.00 (*0-689-82817-9*) McElderry Bks.

***Cooper, Susan & Glazer, Ellen S.** Choosing Assisted Reproduction: Social, Emotional & Ethical Considerations. LC 97-36563. 1999. pap. text 15.00 (*0-944934-22-6*) Perspect Indiana.

Cooper, Susan & Houghton Mifflin Company Staff. The Dark Is Rising. (Literature Experience 1993 Ser.). (J). (gr. 8). 1992. pap., student ed. 11.04 (*0-395-61880-0*) HM.

Cooper, Susan, jt. auth. see Listening Library Staff.

Cooper, Susan B. & Dunn, Pete J. Magnificent Rocks: The Story of Mining, Men, & Minerals at Franklin & Sterling Hill, N. J. 2nd rev. ed. 74p. (J). (gr. 4-8). 1997. pap. text 15.00 (*0-9662132-0-3*) S Cooper.

Cooper, Susan F. Rural Hours. 380p. 1995. pap. 16.95 (*0-8156-0317-7*) Syracuse U Pr.

— Rural Hours. unabridged ed. Johnson, Rochelle & Patterson, Daniel, eds. LC 98-2689. 376p. 1998. reprint ed. pap. 16.95 (*0-8203-2000-5*); reprint ed. text 50.00 (*0-8203-1974-0*) U of Ga Pr.

Cooper, Susan L. Dawn of Fear. LC 71-115755. (Illus.). 157p. (YA). (gr. 5 up). 1988. 14.95 (*0-15-266201-4*, Harcourt Child Bks) Harcourt.

Cooper, Susan L. & Glazer, Ellen S. Beyond Infertility: The New Paths to Parenthood. 376p. 1994. 19.95 (*0-02-911813-1*) Jossey-Bass.

— Choosing Assisted Reproduction: Social, Emotional & Ethical Considerations. LC 97-36563. 400p. 1998. 24.95 (*0-944934-19-6*) Perspect Indiana.

Cooper, Susan L., jt. auth. see Glazer, Ellen S.

Cooper, Susan M., jt. auth. see Farris, Pamela J.

Cooper, Susan R. Chasing Away the Devil. (Mystery Ser.). 1993. per. 3.99 (*0-373-26129-2*, 1-26129-6) Harlequin Bks.

— A Crooked Little House. (E. J. Pugh Mystery Ser.: No. 6). 352p. 1999. mass mkt. 5.99 (*0-380-79469-1*, Avon Bks) Morrow Avon.

— Hickory Dickory Stalk. LC 96-96173. 224p. (Orig.). 1996. mass mkt. 5.50 (*0-380-78155-7*, Avon Bks) Morrow Avon.

— Home Again, Home Again. (E. J. Pugh Mystery Ser.). 256p. 1997. mass mkt. 5.99 (*0-380-78156-5*, Avon Bks) Morrow Avon.

— Houston in the Rearview Mirror. (Worldwide Library Mysteries: No. 95). 1992. per. 3.99 (*0-373-26095-4*, 1-26095-9) Harlequin Bks.

— The Man in the Green Chevy. 1991. reprint ed. per. 3.50 (*0-373-26071-7*) Harlequin Bks.

— One, Two What Did Daddy. 1996. mass mkt. 5.50 (*0-380-78417-3*, Avon Bks) Morrow Avon.

— Other People's Houses. 1993. per. 3.99 (*0-373-26112-8*, 1-26112-2) Harlequin Bks.

— Other People's Houses. pap. 3.99 (*0-373-05139-5*) St Martin.

— There Was a Little Girl. 224p. 1998. mass mkt. 5.50 (*0-380-79468-3*, Avon Bks) Morrow Avon.

***Cooper, Susan Rogers.** Don't Drink the Water. (E. J. Pugh Mysteries Ser.). 192p. 2000. mass mkt. 5.99 (*0-380-80533-2*) Morrow Avon.

— Not in My Backyard. (E. J. Pugh Mystery Ser.). 256p. 1999. mass mkt. 5.99 (*0-380-80532-4*, Avon Bks) Morrow Avon.

Cooper, Suzanne, jt. auth. see Schulze, Donna.

Cooper, Ted & Glennon, Amy. Side by Side. 24p. 1994. pap. text 4.95 (*0-913277-32-0*) Summy-Birchard.

— Side by Side, Pt. A. 32p. 1997. pap. text 5.95 (*0-913277-33-9*) Summy-Birchard.

C

Cooper, Terrance C. The Tools of Biochemistry. 448p. 1977. 110.00 (0-471-17116-6) Wiley.

Cooper, Terry D. Accepting the Troll Underneath the Bridge: Overcoming Our Self-Doubts. 96p. (Orig.). 1996. pap. 6.95 (0-8091-3670-8) Paulist Pr.

— I'm Judgmental, You're Judgmental: Healing Our Condeming Attitudes. LC 99-14353. (Illus.). 80p. 1999. pap. 5.95 (0-8091-3870-0) Paulist Pr.

Cooper, Terry L. Handbook of Administrative Ethics. (Public Administration & Public Policy Ser.: Vol. 52). (Illus.). 608p. 1993. text 195.00 (0-8247-9095-2) Dekker.

— The Responsible Administrator: An Approach to Ethics for the Administrative Role. 4th ed. LC 98-28113. (Nonprofit & Public Administration Ser.). 240p. 1998. 27.95 (0-7879-4133-6) Jossey-Bass.

Cooper, Terry L. & Wright, N. Dale, eds. Exemplary Public Administrators: Character & Leadership in Government. LC 91-34296. (Public Administration Ser.). 380p. 1992. 29.95 (1-55542-428-7) Jossey-Bass.

Cooper, Thomas. Bankrupt Law of America Compared with the Bankrupt Law of England: Compared with the Bankrupt Law of England. xx, 399p. 1991. reprint ed. 75.00 (0-8377-2019-2, Rothman) W S Hein.

— Introductory Lecture & Discourse on the Connexion Between Chemistry & Medicine, 2 vols. Cohen, I. Bernard, ed. LC 79-7956. (Three Centuries of Science in America Ser.). 1980. reprint ed. lib. bdg. 25.95 (0-405-12537-2) Ayer.

— Lectures on the Elements of Political Economy. 2nd ed. LC 66-21666. (Reprints of Economic Classics Ser.). 360p. 1971. reprint ed. lib. bdg. 49.50 (0-678-00776-4) Kelley.

— A Small Garden. 1996. 35.00 (0-8050-4916-9) H Holt & Co.

— Some Information Respecting America. LC 67-29498. (Illus.). iv, 240p. 1969. reprint ed. 39.50 (0-678-00570-2) Kelley.

— Television & Ethics: A Bibliography. 300p. 1988. 55.00 (0-8161-8966-8, Hall Reference) Macmillan.

— Thesaurus Linguae Romanae et Britannicae. (Anglistica & Americana Ser.: No. 111). 1808p. 1975. reprint ed. 480.00 (3-487-05439-6) G Olms Pubs.

— Treatise on the Law of Libel & the Liberty of the Press, Showing the Origin, Use & Abuse of the Law of Libel. LC 78-125688. (American Journalists Ser.). 1977. reprint ed. 23.95 (0-405-01665-4) Ayer.

— Two Essays: On the Foundation of Civil Government & On the Constitution of the United States. LC 72-99477. (American Constitutional & Legal History Ser.). 1970. reprint ed. lib. bdg. 19.50 (0-306-71852-9) Da Capo.

Cooper, Thomas, ed. Cooper's Journal: Or Unfettered Thinker & Plain Speaker for Truth, Freedom & Progress, Vol. 1, Nos. 1-30. LC 78-119473. 476p. 1970. reprint ed. 57.50 (0-678-00671-7) Kelley.

Cooper, Thomas & Wogrin, Nancy. Rule-Based Programming with OPS5. 349p. (C). 1988. text 54.95 (0-934613-51-6) Morgan Kaufmann.

Cooper, Thomas, jt. auth. see Fischer, Joseph.

Cooper, Thomas, jt. auth. see Hill, Paul.

Cooper, Thomas, jt. auth. see Navone, John.

Cooper, Thomas J. Guidebook to Biblical Truth. Cooper, Willia S., ed. (Make the Path Clear Ser.: Vol. 1). 99p. (Orig.). 1984. pap. 4.95 (0-685-09739-0) Cooper & Cooper Pub.

— Guidebook to Biblical Truth. Cooper, Willia S., ed. (Master of Light & Darkness Ser.: Vol. 5). 70p. (Orig.). 1985. pap. 4.75 (0-931429-05-6) Cooper & Cooper Pub.

— Guidebook to Biblical Truth. Cooper, Willia S., ed. (Ministry of Women in God's Plan Ser.: Vol. 6). 50p. (Orig.). 1985. pap. 4.00 (0-931429-06-4) Cooper & Cooper Pub.

— Handful of Stones. 1997. 24.95 (0-906630-06-1, Pub. by Coracle Pr) Dist Art Pubs.

— Investigate the Demons (Did Jesus Have a Christology?) Cooper, Willia S., ed. (Guidebook to Biblical Truth Ser.: Vol. 2). 45p. (Orig.). 1984. pap. 3.75 (0-931429-02-1, TXU 104-636) Cooper & Cooper Pub.

Cooper, Thomas J. & Cooper, Willia S. Christian Message for Today. (Guidebook to Biblical Truth Ser.: Vol. 3). 60p. (Orig.). 1984. pap. 4.50 (0-931429-03-X, TXU 109-949) Cooper & Cooper Pub.

— Guidebook to Biblical Truth, 4. (Stewardship Ser.: Vol. 4). 60p. (Orig.). 1985. pap. 4.50 (0-931429-04-8) Cooper & Cooper Pub.

— Guidebook to Biblical Truth, Set. (Stewardship Ser.: Vol. 4). 60p. (Orig.). 1985. write for info. (0-931429-00-5) Cooper & Cooper Pub.

Cooper, Thomas M. & Clayton, Richard R. The Cooper-Clayton Method to Stop Smoking: New Hope for Heavy Smokers. 160p. (Orig.). 1988. pap. 10.00 (0-9621398-0-7) SBC SBC.

— How Heavy Smokers Can Become Nonsmokers Using a Comprehensive Behavioral Smoking-Cessation Program with Nicoderm. (Illus.). 160p. (Orig.). 1992. pap. text 12.00 (0-9621398-1-5) SBC SBC.

— You Can Become a Nonsmoker: Here's How! rev. ed. 156p. (Orig.). 1998. 12.00 (0-9621398-2-3) SBC SBC.

Cooper, Thomas W. The Records of the Court of Sessions of Suffolk County in the Province of New York, 1670-1688. xix, 331p. (Orig.). 1993. pap. 26.50 (1-55613-799-0) Heritage Bk.

— A Time Before Deception: Truth in Communication, Culture & Ethics. LC 94-43547. (Illus.). 256p. (C). 1997. 24.95 (0-940666-59-6) Clear Light.

— A Time Before Deception: Truth in Communication Culture & Ethics. LC 94-43547. (Illus.). 256p. (C). 1997. pap. text 14.95 (0-940666-89-8) Clear Light.

Cooper, Thomas W., jt. ed. see Christians, Clifford G.

***Cooper, Tim.** The Last Generation of English Catholic Clergy: Parish Priests in the Diocese of Coventry & Lichfield in the Early Sixteenth Century. LC 99-32793. (Studies in the History of Medieval Religion). 224p. 1999. 81.00 (0-85115-752-1, Suffolk Records Soc) Boydell & Brewer.

Cooper, Tim, jt. auth. see Chen, John.

Cooper, Timothy. Sonia. LC 91-73764. 304p. (J). 1991. 19.95 (0-9619914-1-0) Americus Pr.

— World One. LC 87-73424. 1990. 19.95 (0-9619914-0-2) Americus Pr.

Cooper, Tom. Triad of Knives. 384p. 1986. mass mkt. 3.50 (0-373-97020-X) Harlequin Bks.

— War Moon. 384p. 1987. per. 3.50 (0-373-97031-5) Harlequin Bks.

Cooper, Ursula. Mini Walks on the Mesa: A Story for Children. LC 89-4448. (Illus.). 32p. (Orig.). (J). (gr. 3-6). 1989. pap. 6.95 (0-86534-133-8) Sunstone Pr.

Cooper, V. Students Manual of Auditing. 3rd ed. 1985. mass mkt. 41.75 (0-85258-237-4) Chapman & Hall.

Cooper, Val. 1000 Plus Stationery Designs: Dynamic Matching Business Cards, Letterheads & Envelopes. (Illus.). 200p. (Orig.). 1995. pap. 19.95 (0-9646108-3-3) Point Pac Pr.

Cooper, Vera D., jt. ed. see Cooper, James H.

Cooper, Victor. A Dangerous Woman: New York's First Lady Liberty; The Life & Times of Lady Deborah Moody (1586-1659?) (Illus.). 187p. (Orig.). 1995. pap. 18.50 (0-7884-0303-6) Heritage Bk.

Cooper, Victoria. Dilemma. 120p. 1997. pap. write for info. (1-57502-572-8, PO1652) Morris Pubng.

Cooper, Violet M. How to Find Those Hidden Jobs. LC 94-40677. 220p. (Orig.). 1995. pap. 13.95 (0-931625-25-4) DIMI Pr.

***Cooper, Virgil R.** A New Threat: Honest Rustlers. 218p. 2000. 4.99 (0-9668804-2-0) A-bar-V.

Cooper, W. C. & Dreisinger, D. B. The Principles & Practice of Leadhing: 25th Annual Hydrometallurgy Meeting. (Illus.). 398p. 1995. 226.50 (0-444-82255-0) Elsevier.

Cooper, W. E. Delictual Liability in Motor Law Vol. 2: Principles of Liability. rev. ed. 519p. 1996. 107.50 (0-7021-3647-6, Pub. by Juta & Co) Gaunt.

— Landlord & Tenant. 2nd ed. LC 94-197944. 439p. 1994. pap. 47.50 (0-7021-3079-6, Pub. by Juta & Co) Gaunt.

— Motor Law, Vol. 1. 740p. 1982. 50.00 (0-7021-1253-4, Pub. by Juta & Co) Gaunt.

— Motor Law, Vol. 2. 507p. 1987. 68.00 (0-7021-1906-7, Pub. by Juta & Co) Gaunt.

— Road Traffic Legislation: Padverkeerwetgewing. 1990. ring bd. 84.00 (0-7021-2430-3, Pub. by Juta & Co) Gaunt.

— Road Transport. 400p. 1985. ring bd. 55.50 (0-7021-1652-1, Pub. by Juta & Co) Gaunt.

— The South African Law of Landlord & Tenant. 570p. 1973. write for info. (0-7021-0407-8, Pub. by Juta & Co) Gaunt.

Cooper, W. Fordham. Electrical Safety Engineering. 3rd ed. LC 93-4310. (Illus.). 544p. 1994. 105.00 (0-7506-1645-8) Buttrwrth-Heinemann.

— Electrical Safety Engineering. 3rd ed. LC 98-147899. (Illus.). 544p. 1998. pap. text 69.95 (0-7506-3965-2, Newnes) Buttrwrth-Heinemann.

Cooper, W. Norman. Dance with God. LC 81-69932. 128p. (Orig.). 1982. 9.50 (0-87516-491-9); pap. 6.50 (0-87516-468-4) DeVorss.

— The Flower & the Honeybee. 310p. pap. 8.50 (0-87516-596-6) DeVorss.

— The Non-Thinking Self. 112p. 1980. 9.50 (0-87516-414-5); pap. 6.50 (0-87516-403-X) DeVorss.

— The Ultimate Destination. 95p. 1980. 9.50 (0-87516-413-7) DeVorss.

Cooper, W. Norman. The Ultimate Destination. 95p. 1980. pap. 6.50 (0-87516-381-5) DeVorss.

Cooper, W. W., et al, eds. Impact: How IC2 Institute Research Affects Public Policy & Business Practices, 6. LC 95-50748. (IC2 Management & Management Science Ser.: Vol. 6). 352p. 1997. 65.00 (1-56720-030-3, Quorum Bks) Greenwood.

Cooper, W. W., et al. Kohler's Dictionary for Accountants. 6th ed. 593p. 1983. 95.00 (0-8288-4417-8, M7773) Fr & Eur.

Cooper, W. W., jt. auth. see Charnes, Abraham.

***Cooper, Walter.** Briefs: A Virile Display of Verse Witty & Gay. (Illus.). 80p. 2000. text 19.95 (0-7893-0406-6) Universe.

— A Most Desperate Situation 1854-1864: Frontier Adventures of a Young Scout. 328p. 2000. 29.95 (1-56044-891-1, Falcon) Falcon Pub Inc.

Cooper, Walter G. Official History of Fulton County. LC 78-12918. 1978. reprint ed. 35.00 (0-87152-280-2) Reprint.

Cooper, Wayne F. Claude McKay, Rebel Sojourner in the Harlem Renaissance: A Biography. LC 86-18505. (Illus.). 456p. (C). 1996. reprint ed. pap. 16.95 (0-8071-2074-X) La State U Pr.

Cooper, Weldon & Morris, Thomas R., eds. Virginia Government & Politics: Readings & Comments. LC 75-44333. 454p. reprint ed. pap. 140.80 (0-8357-2707-6, 203982000013) Bks Demand.

Cooper, Wendy A. Classical Taste in America, 1800-1840. (Illus.). 256p. 1993. 85.00 (1-55859-385-3) Abbeville Pr.

Cooper-White, Pamela. The Cry of Tamar: Violence Against Women & the Church's Response. LC 94-23086. 320p. 1995. pap. 24.00 (0-8006-2730-X, 1-2730, Fortress Pr) Augsburg Fortress.

Cooper-Wiele, Jonathan K. The Totalizing Act: Key to Husserl's Early Philosophy. 160p. (C). 1989. lib. bdg. 111.00 (0-7923-0077-7, Pub. by Kluwer Academic) Kluwer Academic.

Cooper, Willa, jt. auth. see Schultheis, Nancy.

Cooper, Willia S., jt. auth. see Cooper, Thomas J.

Cooper, Willia S., ed. see Cooper, Thomas J.

Cooper, William. Behold a Pale Horse. 499p. (Orig.). 1991. pap. 25.00 (0-929385-22-5) Light Tech Pubng.

Cooper, William. From Early Life: Childhood in Crewe. large type ed. (Reminiscence Ser.). 22.95 (1-85695-117-0, Pub. by ISIS Lrg Prnt) Transaction Pubs.

— Guide in the Wilderness. LC 79-140352. (Select Bibliographies Reprint Ser.). 1977. 15.95 (0-8369-5595-1) Ayer.

— A Guide to the Wilderness. 41p. 1993. reprint ed. lib. bdg. 69.00 (0-7812-5211-3) Rprt Serv.

— Liberty & Slavery: Southern Politics to 1860. LC 83-4311. 320p. (C). 1983. pap. 27.81 (0-07-553588-2) McGraw.

Cooper, William, ed. see Oana, Katherine.

Cooper, William, ed. see Philatethes, Eirenaeus.

Cooper, William A., tr. see Bielschowsky, Albert.

Cooper, William B. Commercial, Industrial, & Institutional Refrigeration: Design, Installation & Troubleshooting. (Illus.). 576p. (C). 1986. text 63.80 (0-13-152018-0) P-H.

— Tales of a Warrior. unabridged ed. Baty, Wayne, ed. (Illus.). 533p. 1998. pap. 19.95 (0-9665591-0-X) W B Cooper.

Cooper, William B. & Quinlan, Raymond A. Warm Air Heating for Climate Control: Lincoln Technical Institute Edition. 3rd ed. LC 92-41644. 576p. 1993. text 84.00 (0-13-102369-1, Pub. by P-H) S&S Trade.

Cooper, William D., ed. Lists of Foreign Protestants & Aliens Resident in England, 1618-1688. LC 17-1252. (Camden Society, London. Publications, First Ser.: No. 82). reprint ed. 35.00 (0-404-50182-6) AMS Pr.

Cooper, William E. Speech Perception & Production: Studies in Selective Adaptation. LC 79-17281. (Language & Being Ser.). 208p. 1979. text 73.25 (0-89391-027-9) Ablx Pub.

Cooper, William E., ed. Cognitive Aspects of Skilled Typewriting. (Illus.). 417p. 1983. 118.00 (0-387-90774-2) Spr-Verlag.

Cooper, William E. & Paccia-Cooper, Jeanne. Syntax & Speech. LC 80-16614. (Cognitive Science Ser.: No. 3). 284p. 1980. 42.00 (0-674-86075-6) HUP.

Cooper, William H., II. God's Last Day Armour Bearers. 94p. Date not set. pap. 9.99 (1-892352-13-3, Blooming Hse Pubs) Blooming Bks.

Cooper, William H., ed. see Butrick, Lyn M.

Cooper, William H., ed. see McCarthy, Donald W.

Cooper, William H., ed. see Oana, Katherine.

Cooper, William H., ed. see Shuster, Albert H. & Miller, Russell R.

Cooper, William H., ed. see Shuster, Albert H., et al.

Cooper, William J., Jr. The Conservative Regime: South Carolina, 1877-1890. LC 91-17958. 239p. 1991. pap. text 14.95 (0-8071-1718-8) La State U Pr.

Cooper, William J. The Conservative Regime: South Carolina, 1877-1890. LC 67-26859. (Johns Hopkins University Studies in Historical & Political Science). (Illus.). 239p. reprint ed. pap. 74.10 (0-608-15145-9, 202581000046) Bks Demand.

***Cooper, William J., Jr.** Jefferson Davis, American: A Biography. (Illus.). 784p. 2000. 35.00 (0-394-56916-4) Knopf.

Cooper, William J., Jr. South & the Politics of Slavery, 1828-1856. LC 78-751. 456p. 1978. pap. text 19.95 (0-8071-0775-1) La State U Pr.

Cooper, William J., et al, eds. Environmental Applications of Ionizing Radiation. LC 98-10932. 752p. 1998. 98.50 (0-471-17086-0, Wiley-Interscience) Wiley.

Cooper, William J., Jr. & Terrill, Thomas E. The American South: A History. 1990. 50.00 (0-394-58948-3) Knopf.

— The American South: A History. 2nd ed. LC 95-41856. 834p. (C). 1995. 46.98 (0-07-064440-3) McGraw.

Cooper, William J. & Terrill, Thomas E. The American South: A History, Vol. 1. 2nd ed. 400p. (C). 1995. pap. 33.75 (0-07-064438-1) McGraw.

— The American South: A History, Vol. 2. 2nd ed. 416p. (C). 1995. pap. 33.75 (0-07-064439-X) McGraw.

Cooper, William J., Jr., ed. see Cowdrey, Albert E.

Cooper, William J., Jr., ed. see Hundley, Daniel R.

Cooper, William J., Jr., jt. ed. see McPherson, James M.

Cooper, William J., Jr., ed. see Peter, Frances D.

Cooper, William J., jt. ed. see Saltzman, Eric S.

Cooper, William J., jt. ed. see Zika, Rod G.

***Cooper, William M.** Unraveling the Rapture: The Book. 3rd ed. 237p. (C). 1999. pap. 18.00 (1-929416-17-2) Magner Pubg.

***Cooper, William P.** Terminus & the House of Beth-El. LC 00-131336. 208p. 2000. pap. 14.95 (1-57197-198-X, Pub. by Pentland Pr) Assoc Pubs Grp.

Cooper, William R., ed. see Butrick, Lyn M.

Cooper, William S. Coastal Dunes of California. LC 67-29290. (Geological Society of America, Memoir Ser.: No. 104). 189p. reprint ed. pap. 58.60 (0-608-15641-8, 203180600077) Bks Demand.

— Foundations of Logico-Linguistics. (Synthese Language Library: No. 2). 264p. 1978. lib. bdg. 93.00 (90-277-0864-9, D Reidel) Kluwer Academic.

— Foundations of Logico-Linguistics. (Synthese Language Library: No. 2). 264p. 1978. pap. text 51.50 (90-277-0876-2, D Reidel) Kluwer Academic.

— Set Theory & Syntactic Description. (Janua Linguarum, Ser. Minor: No. 34). 52p. 1974. pap. text 53.85 (90-279-2704-9) Mouton.

Cooper, William W., et al, eds. Eric Louis Kohler: A Collection of His Writings (1919-1975) (Monograph Series of the Academy of Accounting Historians: Monograph 3). 573p. 1980. 15.00 (1-879750-01-5); pap. 10.00 (1-879750-05-8) Acad Acct Hist.

Cooper, William W. & Whinston, Andrew B., eds. New Directions in Computational Economics. LC 93-23548. (Advances in Computational Economics Ser.: Vol. 4). 1994. lib. bdg. 153.00 (0-7923-2539-7) Kluwer Academic.

Cooper, William W., jt. ed. see Charnes, Abraham.

Cooper, Wilmer. A Living Faith: An Historical Study of Quaker Beliefs. LC 89-28708. 217p. 1990. pap. 14.00 (0-944350-12-7) Friends United.

— The Quaker Testimony of Integrity. LC 91-60175. 32p. (Orig.). 1991. pap. 4.00 (0-87574-296-3) Pendle Hill.

***Cooper, Wilmer A.** Growing up Plain: The Journey of a Public Friend. LC 99-15856. (Illus.). 200p. 1999. 16.50 (0-944350-44-5) Friends United.

***Cooper, Wolfgang.** Snapper. LC 00-190846. 115p. 2000. 25.00 (0-7388-2021-0); pap. 18.00 (0-7388-2022-9) Xlibris Corp.

— Trials in Youngstown, Ohio. LC 00-190408. 123p. 2000. 25.00 (0-7388-1649-3); pap. 18.00 (0-7388-1650-7) Xlibris Corp.

— Wehrmacht Diary: The Story of Siegfried Knappe (1936-1999) LC 00-190389. 234p. 2000. 25.00 (0-7388-1623-X); pap. 18.00 (0-7388-1624-8) Xlibris Corp.

Cooper, Wyn. The Country of Here Below. 2nd ed. Boyer, Dale K., ed. LC 87-71263. (Ahsahta Press Modern & Contemporary Poets of the West Ser.). 70p. (Orig.). 1987. pap. 6.95 (0-916272-34-6) Ahsahta Pr.

***Cooper, Wyn.** The Way Back. 2000. pap. 14.00 (1-893996-03-4) White Pine.

Cooper, Zachary. Black Settlers in Rural Wisconsin. 2nd ed. (Ethnic Ser.). (Illus.). 32p. 1994. pap. 3.95 (0-87020-170-0, BLWI) State Hist Soc Wis.

Cooper, Zoe. Brides: Sherri's Perfect Day. 128p. (YA). (gr. 7 up). 1997. mass mkt. 3.99 (0-380-78699-0, Avon Bks) Morrow Avon.

— Corinne's Family Affair, Vol. 2. (Brides Ser.). (J). (gr. 7). 1997. mass mkt. 3.99 (0-380-78700-8, Avon Bks) Morrow Avon.

— Heather's Change of Heart. (Brides Ser.: No. 3). 128p. (YA). (gr. 5 up). 1997. mass mkt. 3.99 (0-380-78701-6, Avon Bks) Morrow Avon.

Cooperative Central Exchange Staff. The Cooperative Pyramid Builder: Published in the Interest of the Consumer's Cooperative Movement, 3 vols., Set. McCurry, Dan C. & Rubenstein, Richard E., eds. LC 74-30626. (American Farmers & the Rise of Agribusiness Ser.). (Illus.). 1975. reprint ed. 125.95 (0-405-06824-7) Ayer.

— The Cooperative Pyramid Builder: Published in the Interest of the Consumer's Cooperative Movement, 3 vols., Vol. 1. McCurry, Dan C. & Rubenstein, Richard E., eds. LC 74-30626. (American Farmers & the Rise of Agribusiness Ser.). (Illus.). 1975. reprint ed. 41.95 (0-405-06825-5) Ayer.

— The Cooperative Pyramid Builder: Published in the Interest of the Consumer's Cooperative Movement, 3 vols., Vol. 2. McCurry, Dan C. & Rubenstein, Richard E., eds. LC 74-30626. (American Farmers & the Rise of Agribusiness Ser.). (Illus.). 1975. reprint ed. 53.95 (0-405-06826-3) Ayer.

— The Cooperative Pyramid Builder: Published in the Interest of the Consumer's Cooperative Movement, 3 Vols., Vol. 3. McCurry, Dan C. & Rubenstein, Richard E., eds. LC 74-30626. (American Farmers & the Rise of Agribusiness Ser.). (Illus.). 1975. reprint ed. 27.50 (0-686-67166-X) Ayer.

Cooperative Children's Book Center Staff. The Multicolored Mirror: Cultural Substance in Literature for Children & Young Adults. Lindgren, Merri V. & Kruse, Ginny M., eds. LC 91-76433. (Illus.). 195p. 1991. pap. 19.00 (0-917846-05-2, 95506) Highsmith Pr.

Cooperative Whole Grain Education Association Staf, ed. Uprisings: The Whole Grain Bakers Book. LC 90-1030. (Illus.). 288p. (Orig.). 1990. pap. 14.95 (0-913990-70-1) Book Pub Co.

Cooperberg, Peter L., jt. ed. see Winsberg, Fred.

Cooperman. Advanced Laparoscopic Surgery. (C). 2000. text. write for info. (0-7216-5611-0) Harcrt Hlth Sci Grp.

— Professional Office Procedures. 2nd ed. LC 98-30199. 270p. 1998. pap. text 48.00 (0-13-979576-6) P-H.

Cooperman, Avram M. Laparoscopic Cholecystectomy: Difficult Cases & Creative Solutions. (Illus.). 192p. 1992. 100.00 (0-942219-28-7) Quality Med Pub.

Cooperman, Bernard D., ed. In Iberia & Beyond: Hispanic Jews Between Cultures. LC 97-19839. (Illus.). 408p. 1998. 47.50 (0-87413-601-6) U Delaware Pr.

— Jewish Thought in the Sixteenth Century. (Judaic Texts & Studies). 500p. 1983. 30.00 (0-674-47461-9) HUP.

— Jewish Thought in the Sixteenth Century. (Judaic Texts & Studies). 500p. 1984. pap. 14.95 (0-674-47462-7) HUP.

Cooperman, Bernard D., jt. auth. see Katz, Jacob.

Cooperman, Bernard D., jt. ed. see Berlin, Adele.

Cooperman, Bernard D., tr. & afterword by see Katz, Jacob.

Cooperman, Bob. Gold Camp in the Colorado Gold Fever Mountains. LC 99-60187. (Illus.). 212p. 1999. pap. 16.95 (1-890437-32-8) Western Reflections.

Cooperman, Carolyn & Rhoades, Chuck. New Methods for Puberty Education. (Illus.). 176p. 1992. pap. 25.00 (0-9609366-0-2) Plan Parenthood.

Cooperman, Curtis L., ed. see Martin, Riley L. & Wann, O-Qua T.

***Cooperman, G., et al, eds.** Workshop on Wide Area Networks & High Performance Computing. LC 99-42438. (Lecture Notes in Control & Information Sciences Ser.: Vol. 249). (Illus.). viii, 344p. 1999. pap. 89.80 (1-85233-642-0, Pub. by Spr-Verlag) Spr-Verlag.

An Asterisk (*) at the beginning of an entry indicates that the title is appearing for the first time.

Cooperman, G., IGH Performanomputing & Gigabit, et al. Workshop on High Perfince Computing & Gigabit Local Area Networks. 226. LC 97-19340. (Lecture Notes in Control & mation Sciences). viii, 237p. 1997. pap. text. write ffo. (*3-540-76169-1*) Spr-Verlag.

Cooperman, Matthew. Surge. LC55674. (Wick Poetry Chapbook Ser.). 1999. write nfo. (*0-87338-642-6*) Kent St U Pr.

Cooperman, Robert. Caseworkers, 1968-1970, No. 82. 40p. (Orig.). 1997. pap. 7.95(44754-08-2) Pudding Hse Pubns.

— Clifford Odets: An Annotated iography of Criticism, 1935-1989. 168p. 1990. lib. 55.00 (*0-313-27669-2*) Greenwood.

— In the Household of Percy By Shelley. LC 92-27087. (University of Central Floriontemporary Poetry Ser.). 120p. 1993. 19.95 (*0-8130-1180-9*); pap. 10.95 (*0-8130-1181-7*) U Press Fla

Cooperman, Saul. How Schoolsally Work: Practical Advice for Parents from an der. 178p. (Orig.). 1996. pap. 18.95 (*0-8126-9335-3*)n Court.

Cooperman, Stanley. Monarch es on Hemingway's Major Novels. (Orig.). (C). 5 (*0-671-00621-5*, Arco) Macmillan Gen Ref.

— Old Man & the Sea. (C). 3.9-671-00673-8, Arco) Macmillan Gen Ref.

— World War I & the Americanvel. LC 66-28506. 285p. 1967. reprint ed. pap. 88.4(608-07547-7, 200384600037) Bks Dema

Cooperrider, Allen & Nosee, H F. Saving Nature's Legacy: Protecting & Restg Biodiversity. 1994. text 55.00 (*1-55963-247-X*) IslPr.

Cooperrider, Allen & Noss, R F. Saving Nature's Legacy: Protecting & Resng Biodiversity. 1994. pap. text 29.95 (*1-55963-248-8*land Pr.

Cooperrider, Craig C., jt. autee Lawson, Gary W.

Cooperrider, David, jt. auth. Srivastva, Suresh.

***Cooperrider, David L., et als.** Appreciative Inquiry: Rethinking Human Organion Toward a Positive Theory of Change. 287p. . 1999. pap. text 19.80 (*0-87563-931-3*) Stipes.

Cooperrider, David L. & Dun, Jane E. Organizational Dimensions of Global Che: No Limits to Cooperation. LC 98-4006(Human Dimensions of Global Change Ser.). 4321999. 65.00 (*0-7619-1528-1*); pap. 34 (*0-7619-1529-X*) Sage.

Cooperrider, Tom S. The Dioledoneae of Ohio Pt. 2: Linaceae Through Campilaceae. LC 87-31257. (Vascular Flora of Ohio : Vol. II). (Illus.). 656p. 1995. text 80.00 (*0-814228-X*) Ohio St U Pr.

Cooperrider, Tom S., ed. Engered & Threatened Plants of Ohio. LC 81-82268. (ological Notes Ser.: No. 16). 1982. pap. text 10.00 (*0-727-091-8*) Ohio Bio Survey.

Coopers & Lybrand. Emploient Law in Europe: A Country by Country Gui for Employers. 2nd ed. 512p. 1995. 113.95 (*0-566-076-6*, Pub. by Gower) Ashgate Pub Co.

— Fit to Design? (C). 1988. t 120.00 (*0-85072-219-5*) St Mut.

— Understanding Options: Wkbook 1, Bk. 1. (Self-Study Swaps Ser.). 1997. wbkd. 122.00 (*1-873446-13-6*, Pub. by IFR Pub) Am Ec Systs.

Coopers & Lybrand & Instite for Internal Auditors. Research Foundation. AP R/3: Its Use, Control, & Audit. LC 98-122912. (us.). 1997. write for info. (*0-89413-385-3*) Inst Inr Aud.

Coopers & Lybrand, jt. au. see Donaghy, Peter.

Coopers & Lybrand Deloit Staff, compiled by. Coopers & Lybrand Deloitte: Maging Company Growth. 1990. pap. 70.00 (*0-406-67829*, UK, MICHIE) LEXIS Pub.

Coopers & Lybrand Forei Exchange Tax Team Staff. Tolley's Taxation of Foign Exchange Gains & Losses. 432p. (C). 1995. 195.0(*0-85459-851-0*, Pub. by Tolley Pubng) St Mut.

— Tolley's Taxation of Foren Exchange Gains & Losses Fourth Edition. 4th ed.998. pap. 275.00 (*1-86012-833-5*) TolleyPubng.

Coopers & Lybrand Institte of Petroleum Accountin. Coopers & Lybrand Svey of Accounting Practices in the Oil & Gas Industry1994. 218p. 1994. pap. 100.00 (*0-926969-02-1*) UNT?A.

Coopers & Lybrand, L. LP. Staff, jt. auth. see American Psychological Association Practice Direct.

Coopers & Lybrand L. LP. Staff, jt. auth. see Culpepper & Associates Inc. Staff.

Coopers & Lybrand LLPStaff. UNIX: Its Use, Control & Audit. Campbell, Lee A., ed. 136p. 1995. pap. 65.00 (*0-89413-344-6*, A899 Inst Inter Aud.

Coopers & Lybrand LLPStaff, et al. Reinventing the University: Managing& Financing Institutions of Higher Education. Johson, Sandra L. & Rush, Sean C., eds. LC 94-45421. (Nnprofit Law, Finance, & Management Ser.). 432p. 1995. 160.00 (*0-471-10452-3*) Wiley.

Coopers & Lybrand Staf. Closing Plants: Planning & Implementing Strategies. LC 86-80051. 103p. 1986. 20.00 (*0-910586-57-8*) Finan Exec.

— Equity Swaps: A Self-Study Guide to Mastering & Applying Equity Swaps. 1994. per. 55.00 (*1-55738-591-2*, Irwn Prfssnl) McGraw-Hill Prof.

— The Financial Jungle: A Guide to Financial Instruments. 2nd ed. (Illus.). 684p. 1991. 153.00 (*1-873446-85-3*, Pub. by IFR Pub) Am Educ Systs.

— A Guide to VAT in the EU, 1996-1997 Update. 368p. 1997. 100.00 (*90-411-0658-8*) Kluwer Law Intl.

— Interest Rate Swaps: A Self-Study Guide to Mastering & Applying Interest Rate Swaps. 1994. per. 55.00 (*1-55738-589-0*, Irwn Prfssnl) McGraw-Hill Prof.

***Coopers & Lybrand Staff.** 1998 Global Telecoms Tax Profiles: A Resource for Business, Tax, & Market Strategies. 446p. 1998. pap. 175.00 (*0-471-31841-8*) Wiley.

Coopers & Lybrand Staff. The Software Directory for Retailers. 5th ed. LC 96-203373. 733p. 1995. pap. 125.00 (*0-471-13531-3*) Wiley.

— The Swap Mechanism: Using Swaps, Trading Swaps, Valuing Swaps, Swap Risk & Regulation. (Self-Study Swaps Ser.). 1997. 285.00 (*1-873446-11-X*, Pub. by IFR Pub) Am Educ Systs.

— Swaps & Financial Engineering: A Self-Study Guide to Mastering & Applying Swaps & Financial Engineering. 1994. per. 55.00 (*1-55738-592-0*, Irwn Prfssnl) McGraw-Hill Prof.

— Tolley's Manual of Accounting Vol. I: Primarily Individual Companies. 1160p. 1990. 110.00 (*0-85459-473-6*, Pub. by Tolley Pubng) St Mut.

— Tolley's Manual of Accounting Vol. II: Groups of Companies. 576p. 1990. 60.00 (*0-85459-467-1*, Pub. by Tolley Pubng) St Mut.

— Tolley's Manual of Accounting Vol. III: Specialised Businesses. 1180p. 1991. 90.00 (*0-85459-474-4*, Pub. by Tolley Pubng) St Mut.

— Using Options: Workbook 2. (Self-Study Options Ser.). 1997. wbk. ed. 122.00 (*1-873446-18-7*, Pub. by IFR Pub) Am Educ Systs.

Coopers & Lybrand Staff, jt. auth. see American Psychological Association Practice Direct.

Coopers & Lybrand, Trust Department Staff. Trust Practice Manual. 2nd ed. 250p. 1992. pap. text 78.00 (*0-406-50361-3*, UK, MICHIE) LEXIS Pub.

Coopers, C. & Lyrand, L. International Insurance Industry Guide. 4th ed. (C). 1988. 250.00 (*0-7855-4121-7*, Pub. by Witherby & Co) St Mut.

Coopers, Lybrand, et al. Auditing E4 Sm. 4th ed. (ITBP Textbooks). 900p. 1999. pap. 42.95 (*0-412-36490-5*) Chapman & Hall.

***Coopers, P. W.** Corporate Taxes 1999: Worldwide Summaries. 864p. 1999. pap. 95.00 (*0-471-35557-7*) Wiley.

— Individual Taxes 1999: Worldwide Summaries, 2. 608p. 1999. pap. 95.00 (*0-471-35554-2*) Wiley.

Coopers, P. W. 1999-2000 Global Telecommunications. 2nd ed. (C). 2000. pap. text 150.00 (*0-471-32854-5*) Wiley.

— Tax Summaries 99. 1344p. 1999. text 160.00 incl. cd-rom (*0-471-32858-8*) Wiley.

Coopersmith, Georgia. Directions in Metal: Work Produced at the Johnson Atelier Technical Institute of Sculpture. (Illus.). 24p. (Orig.). 1982. pap. 8.00 (*0-942746-02-3*) SUNYP R Gibson.

— Robert Plumb. 1985. pap. text 5.00 (*0-942746-09-0*) SUNYP R Gibson.

— Twentieth Anniversary Exhibition of the Vogel Collection. (Illus.). 94p. 1982. pap. 12.50 (*0-942746-03-1*) SUNYP R Gibson.

— Twenty Years: Harriet FeBland. (Illus.). 17p. 1986. pap. 0.75 (*0-942746-12-0*) SUNYP R Gibson.

— Variations on a Theme: Figurative Painting. (Illus.). 32p. 1985. pap. 8.00 (*0-942746-08-2*) SUNYP R Gibson.

Coopersmith, Georgia, ed. Contemporary Fiber Arts: From the Mid-Atlantic Region. (Illus.). 17p. 1997. pap. 2.00 (*1-890327-02-6*) Longwood Ctr.

Coopersmith, Georgia & Ellis, Sharon. An Uncommon Subject: Drawings & Prints by Sharon Ellis. 1986. pap. 0.75 (*0-942746-11-2*) SUNYP R Gibson.

Coopersmith, Georgia, jt. ed. see Hildreth, Joseph.

Coopersmith, Harry. Companion Volume to the Songs We Sing. 1950. 3.50 (*0-8381-0210-7*) USCJE.

— Songs We Sing. (Illus.). 1950. 22.50 (*0-8381-0723-0*) USCJE.

Coopersmith, Harry, compiled by. New Jewish Songbook. LC 65-14593. (Illus.). pap. 16.95 (*0-87441-060-6*) Behrman.

Coopersmith, Harry, ed. More of the Songs We Sing. (ENG & HEB., Illus.). 288p. (J). (gr. 4-10). 1970. 9.50 (*0-8381-0217-4*) USCJE.

Coopersmith, Jonathan. The Electrification of Russia, 1880-1926. LC 92-5735. (Illus.). 288p. 1992. text 47.50 (*0-8014-2723-1*) Cornell U Pr.

Coopersmith, Penina. Toronto, 1999-2000. 2nd ed. 240p. 1999. pap. 16.95 (*0-88780-472-1*, Pub. by Formac Publ Co) Seven Hills Bk.

Coopersmith, Yitzchak. Eye of the Needle. 1993. 16.95 (*0-87306-640-5*); pap. 13.95 (*0-87306-641-3*) Feldheim.

***Cooperson, Michael.** Classical Arabic Biography: The Heirs of the Prophets. 256p. 2000. 59.95 (*0-521-66199-4*) Cambridge U Pr.

Cooperstein, Bruce & Mason, Geoffrey, eds. Proceedings, Santa Cruz Conference on Finite Groups, Vol. 37. LC 80-26879. (Proceedings of Symposia in Pure Mathematics Ser.). 634p. 1981. text 62.00 (*0-8218-1440-0*, PSPUM/37) Am Math.

Cooperstein, Claire. Johanna: A Novel of Johanna van Gogh-Bonger. LC 94-35517. 1995. 22.00 (*0-684-80234-1*) S&S Trade.

Coopey, R., et al, eds. The Wilson Governments, 1964-1970. LC 92-42167. 288p. 1993. text 59.00 (*0-86187-188-X*) St Martin.

Coopey, Richard, et al, eds. Defence Science & Technology: Adjusting to Change. LC 93-1362. (Studies in Defence Economics: Vol. 3). 242p. 1993. text 48.00 (*3-7186-5400-8*) Gordon & Breach.

— The Wilson Governments, 1964-1970. 226p. 1995. pap. 29.95 (*1-85567-343-6*) Bks Intl VA.

Coopey, Richard & Clarke, Donald. 3i: Fifty Years of Investing in Industry. (Illus.). 488p. 1995. 39.95 (*0-19-828944-8*) OUP.

***Coopmans, Peter, et al, eds.** Lexical Specification & Insertion. LC 99-58274. (Current Issues in Linguistic Theory Ser.: Vol. 197). 458p. 2000. 85.00 (*1-55619-975-9*) J Benjamins Pubng Co.

Coopmans, Peter, jt. auth. see Bok-Bennema, Reineke.

Cooprider, Dan H., et al, eds. Certification Study Guide. (Illus.). 320p. 1996. pap. text, student ed. 49.50 (*1-885517-05-X*) AACE Intl.

Cooray, L. J. Conventions, the Australian Constitution & the Future. xix, 235p. 1979. reprint ed. 30.00 (*0-9596568-1-2*) W S Hein.

Coords, Arthur E. The Space Apple Story: The Children's Tribute to the Seven Challenger Astronauts. (Illus.). 32p. (J). (gr. 2-6). 1992. lib. bdg. 7.70 (*0-9631106-0-8*) A E Coords.

Cooreman, Ann M. Transitivity & Discourse Continuity in Chamorro Narratives. (Empirical Approaches to Language Typology Ser.: No. 4). 246p. 1987. lib. bdg. 81.50 (*3-11-011307-4*) Mouton.

***Cooren, Francois.** The Organizing Property of Communication. LC 99-52671. (Pragmatic & Beyond New Ser.: Vol. 65). xvi, 255p. 2000. 50.00 (*1-55619-943-0*) J Benjamins Pubng Co.

Coorey, Sunil F. Principles of Administrative Law in Sri Lanka. LC 99-933001. lxvi, 750p. 1998. pap. 125.00 (*955-96262-0-5*, Pub. by Simmonds & Hill Pubng) Gaunt.

Coormaraswamy, A. K. Early Indian Architecture: Palaces. (Illus.). 1975. text 22.00 (*0-685-13844-5*) Coronet Bks.

Coornaert, Michel & Papadopoulos, Athanase. Symbolic Dynamics & Hyperbolic Groups. LC 93-9394. (Lecture Notes in Mathematics Ser.: Vol. 1539). 1993. 30.95 (*0-387-56499-3*) Spr-Verlag.

Coornaert, Michel, et al. Geometrie et Theorie des Groupes: Les Groupes Hyperboliques de Gromov. Dold, A. et al, eds. (Lecture Notes in Mathematics Ser.: Vol. 1441). x, 165p. 1990. 34.95 (*0-387-52977-2*) Spr-Verlag.

Coorough, Calleen. Getting Started with Multimedia. LC 98-70996. 336p. (C). 1998. pap. text. write for info. (*0-03-023671-1*) Harcourt Coll Pubs.

— Getting Started with Multimedia. 1998. pap. text 68.50 (*0-03-023681-9*, Pub. by Harcourt Coll Pubs) Harcourt.

Coorpender, Bruce. Peace Officer's Pocket Guide to the Criminal Code of Oregon: Edition 2000. 160p. 2000. per. 4.95 (*1-884493-28-9*) Pocket Pr.

— Peace Officer's Pocket Guide to the Oregon Vehicle Code: Edition 2000. 160p. 2000. per. 4.95 (*1-884493-29-7*) Pocket Pr.

***Coorpender, Bruce, ed.** Peace Officer's Pocket Guide to the Criminal Code of Alabama: Edition 2000. 128p. 1999. pap. 4.95 (*1-884493-47-5*) Pocket Pr.

— Peace Officer's Pocket Guide to the Criminal Code of Alaska: Edition 2000. 144p. 2000. pap. 4.95 (*1-884493-49-1*) Pocket Pr.

— Peace Officer's Pocket Guide to the Criminal Code of Florida: Edition 2000. 192p. 1999. pap. 4.95 (*1-884493-46-7*) Pocket Pr.

— Peace Officer's Pocket Guide to the Criminal Code of Indiana: Edition 2000. 128p. 1999. pap. 4.95 (*1-884493-44-0*) Pocket Pr.

— Peace Officer's Pocket Guide to the Criminal Code of Missouri: Edition 2000. 144p. 2000. pap. 4.95 (*1-884493-53-X*) Pocket Pr.

— Peace Officer's Pocket Guide to the Criminal Code of New Jersey: Edition 2000. 160p. 1999. pap. 4.95 (*1-884493-45-9*) Pocket Pr.

— Peace Officer's Pocket Guide to the Criminal Code of New York: Edition 2000. 160p. 2000. pap. 4.95 (*1-884493-57-2*) Pocket Pr.

— Peace Officer's Pocket Guide to the Criminal Code of Ohio: Edition 2000. 160p. 1999. pap. 4.95 (*1-884493-48-3*) Pocket Pr.

— Peace Officer's Pocket Guide to the Criminal Code of Pennsylvania: Edition 2000. 128p. 2000. pap. 4.95 (*1-884493-56-4*) Pocket Pr.

— Peace Officer's Pocket Guide to the Criminal Code of Tennessee: Edition 2000. 144p. 1999. pap. 4.99 (*1-884493-50-5*) Pocket Pr.

Coorpender, Bruce, ed. Peace Officer's Pocket Guide to the Criminal Code of Texas: Edition 2000. 176p. 1998. per. 4.95 (*1-884493-32-7*) Pocket Pr.

***Coorpender, Bruce, ed.** Peace Officer's Pocket Guide to the Criminal Code of the United States: Edition 2000. 192p. 2000. pap. 4.95 (*1-884493-58-0*) Pocket Pr.

— Peace Officer's Pocket Guide to the Criminal Code of Washington: Edition 2000. 160p. 1999. pap. 4.95 (*1-884493-42-4*) Pocket Pr.

— Peace Officer's Pocket Guide to the Criminal Code of Wisconsin: Edition 1999. 160p. 1999. pap. 4.95 (*1-884493-54-8*) Pocket Pr.

— Peace Officer's Pocket Guide to the Criminal Code of Wyoming: Edition 2000. 92p. 1999. pap. 4.95 (*1-884493-41-6*) Pocket Pr.

— Peace Officer's Pocket Guide to the Vehicle Code of Alabama: Edition 2000. 128p. 1999. pap. 4.95 (*1-884493-52-1*) Pocket Pr.

— Peace Officer's Pocket Guide to the Vehicle Code of New Jersey: Edition 2000. 160p. 1999. pap. 4.95 (*1-884493-55-6*) Pocket Pr.

— Peace Officer's Pocket Guide to the Vehicle Code of Tennessee: Edition 2000. 144p. 1999. pap. 4.95 (*1-884493-51-3*) Pocket Pr.

— Peace Officer's Pocket Guide to the Vehicle Code of Washington: Edition 2000. 92p. 1999. pap. 4.95 (*1-884493-43-2*) Pocket Pr.

Coosey, Marshall R. & Magill, Robert E., eds. A Dictionary of Mosses. (C). 1988. 60.00 (*0-7855-3338-9*, Pub. by Scientific) St Mut.

Coote, Belinda & LeQuesne, Caroline. The Trade Trap. 256p. (C). 1996. pap. 17.50 (*0-85598-351-5*, Pub. by Oxfam Pub) Stylus Pub VA.

Coote, Jack, ed. Total Loss. (Illus.). 322p. 1992. pap. 19.95 (*0-924486-33-3*) Sheridan.

Coote, Jeremy & Shelton, Anthony, eds. Anthropology, Art, & Aesthetics. (Oxford Studies in the Anthropology of Cultural Forms). (Illus.). 294p. 1994. reprint ed. pap. text 22.00 (*0-19-827945-0*) OUP.

Coote, John. Altering Course: A Submariner in Fleet Street. (Illus.). 156p. 1992. 49.50 (*0-85052-348-6*, Pub. by Leo Cooper) Trans-Atl Phila.

Coote, John O. The Norton Book of the Sea. 1989. 22.50 (*0-393-02778-3*) Norton.

Coote, Mary P., jt. auth. see Coote, Robert B.

Coote, Robert B. & Coote, Mary P. Power, Politics, & the Making of the Bible: An Introduction. LC 89-29954. 208p. (Orig.). 1990. pap. 18.00 (*0-8006-2441-6*, 1-2441) Augsburg Fortress.

Coote, Robert B. & Whitelam, Keith. The Emergence of Early Israel in Historical Perspective. (Social World of Biblical Antiquity Ser.: Vol. 5). 212p. 1987. 49.00 (*1-85075-073-4*, Pub. by Sheffield Acad) CUP Services.

Coote, Robert B., jt. auth. see Ord, David R.

Coote, Robert T., jt. ed. see Phillips, James M.

Coote, Roger. The Anglo-Saxons. LC 93-34486. (Look into the Past Ser.). (Illus.). 32p. (J). (gr. 4-6). 1994. lib. bdg. 22.83 (*1-56847-062-2*) Raintree Steck-V.

— The Egyptians. LC 93-8466. (Look into the Past Ser.). (Illus.). 32p. (J). (gr. 4-6). 1993. lib. bdg. 22.83 (*1-56847-061-4*) Raintree Steck-V.

— The Sailor Through History. LC 92-43640. (Journey Through History Ser.). (Illus.). 48p. (J). (gr. 5-8). 1993. lib. bdg. 22.83 (*1-56847-012-6*) Raintree Steck-V.

Coote, S. H., ed. see Shakespeare, William.

Coote, Stephen. The Penguin Short History of English Literature. 784p. 1994. pap. 16.95 (*0-14-012531-0*, Penguin Bks) Viking Penguin.

***Coote, Stephen.** Royal Survivor: The Life of Charles II. LC 99-38614. 396p. 2000. text 27.95 (*0-312-22687-X*) St Martin.

Coote, Stephen, ed. & intro. see Goldsmith, Oliver.

***Cooter, Robert.** Law & Economics. 3rd ed. LC 99-26824. 545p. (C). 1999. 90.00 (*0-321-06482-8*) Addison-Wesley.

Cooter, Robert & Ulen, Thomas. Law Economics. 2nd ed. (Illus.). 481p. (C). 1997. text 84.00 (*0-673-46332-X*) Addson-Wesley Educ.

Cooter, Robert, jt. auth. see Reutzel.

Cooter, Robert, jt. auth. see Rubin, Edward L.

Cooter, Robert, jt. ed. see Schmidtchen, Dieter.

Cooter, Robert B. Botany: An Introductory Survey of the Plant Kingdom. (Illus.). 384p. 1996. 68.95 (*0-471-36551-3*) Wiley.

Cooter, Robert B., Jr. & Flynt, E. Sutton. Teaching Reading in the Content Areas: Developing Content Literacy for All Students. 448p. (C). 1996. pap. text 63.00 (*0-02-324711-8*, Macmillan Coll) P-H.

Cooter, Robert B. & Reutzel, D. Ray. Balanced Reading Strategies & Practices: Assessing & Assisting Readers with Special Needs. LC 98-8778. 320p. 1998. text 42.00 (*0-02-324715-0*, Pub. by Macmillan) S&S Trade.

Cooter, Robert B., jt. auth. see Flynt, E. Sutton.

***Cooter, Robert D.** Strategic Constitution. LC 99-58556. 2000. 45.00 (*0-691-05864-4*, Pub. by Princeton U Pr) Cal Prin Full Svc.

Cooter, Roger. Phrenology in the British Isles: An Annotated, Historical Biobibliography & Index. LC 88-31828. 449p. 1989. 52.00 (*0-8108-2165-6*) Scarecrow.

— War, Medicine & Modernity. 256p. 2000. 81.00 (*0-7509-1801-2*) Sutton Publng.

Cootes, R. J. Middle Ages. 2nd ed. (Longman Secondary Histories Ser.). 208p. (YA). (gr. 6-12). 1989. pap. text 21.52 (*0-582-31783-5*, 78446) Longman.

Cootes, R. J. & Snellgrove, L. E. Ancient World. 2nd ed. (Longman Secondary Histories Ser.). (Illus.). 208p. (YA). (gr. 6-12). 1991. student ed. 11.72 (*0-582-36690-9*, 72482); pap. text 23.00 (*0-582-31785-1*, 79165) Longman.

Cootner, Cathryn. Tent & Town: Rugs & Embroideries from Central Asia. LC 82-49068. (H. McCoy Jones Collection). (Illus.). 16p. 1982. pap. 2.95 (*0-88401-043-0*) Fine Arts Mus.

Cootner, Cathryn M. Anatolian Kilims: The Caroline & H. McCoy Jones Collection. LC 90-39305. (Illus.). 276p. (Orig.). (C). 1990. pap. 39.95 (*0-88401-068-6*) Fine Arts Mus.

Cootner, Cathryn M., et al. Flat-Woven Textiles: The Arthur D. Jenkins Collection. LC 81-84336. (Illus.). 224p. 1981. 110.00 (*0-87405-018-9*) Textile Mus.

Cootner, Cathyrn M. Anatolian Kilims. (Illus.). 276p. 1990. 80.00 (*0-85667-390-0*, Pub. by P Wilson) Hoovers TX.

Cootner, Paul H. & Lof, George O. Water Demand for Steam Electric Generation: An Economic Projection Model. LC 65-27669. 156p. reprint ed. pap. 48.40 (*0-7837-3137-X*, 202095900020) Bks Demand.

Coots, Max. Seasons of the Self. 1994. pap. 7.00 (*1-55896-285-9*, Skinner Hse Bks) Unitarian Univ.

Coursen, Valerie. Stars Notes. (Notes Ser.). (Illus.). 80p. 1996. pap. text 4.95 (*1-56138-758-4*) Running Pr.

Covelis, Mark. Gloria. 256p. 1995. pap. 10.00 (*0-671-73925-5*, WSP) PB.

Coover. Adventures of Lucky Pierre. Date not set. 23.00 (*0-8050-5886-9*) H Holt & Co.

— Child Again. 1999. 23.00 (*0-8050-5885-0*) H Holt & Co.

Coover, Edwin R. ATM Switches. LC 97-12575. (Communications Engineering Ser.). 272p. 1997. 87.00 (*0-89006-783-X*) Artech Hse.

Coover, J. Music Publishing, Copyright & Piracy in Victorian England, 1881-1906: A Twenty-Five Year Chronicle from the Pages of the Musical Times & Other English Music Journals of the Period. 184p. 1985. text 120.00 (*0-7201-1749-6*) Continuum.

C

Coover, James B., ed. Richard S. Hill: Tributes from Friends. LC 87-23292. (Detroit Studies in Music Bibliography: No. 58). xv, 397p. 1987. 45.00 (*0-89990-035-6*) Harmonie Park Pr.

Coover, John E. Experiments in Psychical Research at Leland Stanford Junior University. LC 75-7372. (Perspectives in Psychical Research Ser.). (Illus.). 1975. reprint ed. 54.95 (*0-405-07023-3*) Ayer.

Coover, Robert. After Lazarus: A Filmscript. limited ed. 1980. 50.00 (*0-89723-020-5*) Bruccoli.

— Briar Rose. 96p. 1998. reprint ed. pap. 11.00 (*0-8021-3541-2*, Grove) Grove-Atltic.

— Gerald's Party. LC 97-30905. 320p. 1997. pap. 12.00 (*0-8021-3528-5*, Grove) Grove-Atltic.

***Coover, Robert.** Ghost Town: A Novel. 160p. 2000. pap. 12.00 (*0-8021-3666-4*, Grove) Grove-Atltic.

— Ghost Town: A Novel. LC 98-5713. 160p. 1998. 25.00 (*0-8050-5884-2*) H Holt & Co.

Coover, Robert. Hair O'The Chine. limited ed. 1979. 55.00 (*0-89723-019-1*) Bruccoli.

— John's Wife. 1997. per. 13.00 (*0-684-83043-4*, Scribner Pap Fic) S&S Trade Pap.

— A Night at the Movies: or You Must Remember This. 2nd ed. LC 92-14178. 197p. 1997. reprint ed. pap. 11.95 (*1-56478-160-7*) Dalkey Arch.

***Coover, Robert.** Origin of the Brunists. 2000. pap. 12.00 (*0-8021-3743-1*, Grove) Grove-Atltic.

Coover, Robert. Pinocchio in Venice. LC 96-19879. 336p. 1997. reprint ed. pap. 12.00 (*0-8021-3485-8*, Grove) Grove-Atltic.

***Coover, Robert.** Pricksongs & Descants. 1999. pap. 12.95 (*0-8050-6169-X*) St Martin.

— Pricksongs & Descants: Fictions. LC 99-51707. 256p. 2000. reprint ed. pap. 12.00 (*0-8021-3667-2*, Grove) Grove-Atltic.

Coover, Robert. The Public Burning. LC 97-28954. 560p. 1998. pap. 14.00 (*0-8021-3527-7*, Grove) Grove-Atltic.

— Spanking the Maid. 112p. 1998. pap. text 11.00 (*0-8021-3540-4*, Grove) Grove-Atltic.

— Spanking the Maid. deluxe limited ed. 1981. 125.00 (*0-89723-024-8*) Bruccoli.

— Spanking the Maid. limited ed. 1981. 75.00 (*0-89723-023-X*) Bruccoli.

— The Universal Baseball Association Inc., J. Henry Waugh, Prop. 1971. pap. 12.95 (*0-452-26030-2*, Plume) Dutton Plume.

Coover, Robert & Kinsella, W. P. Baseball & the Game of Life: Stories for the Thinking Fan. deluxe limited ed. Bjarkman, Peter C., ed. 232p. 1990. 30.00 (*0-913559-15-6*) Birch Brook Pr.

Coover, Shriver L. Programmed Blueprint Reading. 3rd ed. 1975. text 22.92 (*0-07-013063-9*) McGraw.

Coovert, Gary A. A Revision of the Genus Pipiza Fallen (Diptera: Syrphidae) of America North of Mexico: With Notes on the Placement of the Tribe Pipizini. LC 95-73108. (Bulletin Ser.: Vol. 11, No. 3). (Illus.). (C). 1996. pap. text 15.00 (*0-86727-120-5*) Ohio Bio Survey.

Coox, Alvin D. The Anatomy of a Small War: The Soviet-Japanese Struggle for Changkufeng-Khasan, 1938. 13. LC 76-51924. (Contributions in Military History Ser.: No. 13). 409p. 1977. 79.50 (*0-8371-9479-2*, CSJ/, Greenwood Pr) Greenwood.

— Nomonhan: Japan Against Russia, 1939, 2 vols. LC 81-85447. (Illus.). 1296p. 1985. pap. 4.95 (*0-8047-1835-0*) Stanford U Pr.

— Nomonhan: Japan Against Russia, 1939, 2 vols., Set. LC 81-85447. (Illus.). 1296p. 1985. 135.00 (*0-8047-1160-7*) Stanford U Pr.

— The Unfought War: Japan 1941-1942. 65p. 1992. 27.50 (*1-879691-06-X*) SDSU Press.

Coox, Alvin D. & Conroy, Hilary, eds. China & Japan: A Search for Balance since World War I. LC 77-10006. (Topics in Diplomatic History Ser.). 468p. 1978. 12.50 (*0-87436-275-X*) Regina Bks.

Cooze, Sandra. Roses in December: A Treasury of Children's Verse. (Illus.). 72p. (J). (gr. k-2). 1996. pap. 9.95 (*1-895387-69-8*) Creative Bk Pub.

Copa, George H. Vocational Education & Youth Employment. 73p. 1984. 7.25 (*0-318-22236-1*, IN274) Ctr Educ Trng Employ.

Copacino, William C. Supply Chain Management. LC 97-152801. 224p. 1997. boxed set 54.95 (*1-57444-074-8*) St Lucie Pr.

Copacino, William C. & Robeson, James F., eds. The Logistics Handbook. 1000p. 1994. 100.00 (*0-02-926595-9*) Free Pr.

Copage, Eric V. Black Pearls: Daily Meditations, Affirmations, & Inspirations for African Americans. LC 92-33186. 1993. pap. 10.00 (*0-688-12291-4*, Quil) HarperTrade.

Copage, Eric V. Black Pearls: Meditations, Affirmations & Inspirations for African-Americans. abr. ed. 1994. audio 11.00 (*1-55994-859-0*, CPN 1996) HarperAudio.

Copage, Eric V. Black Pearls Book of Love: Romantic Meditations & Inspirations for African Americans. LC 95-46094. 1996. pap. 10.00 (*0-688-13970-1*, Quil) HarperTrade.

— Black Pearls Journal: Quotes from the National Bestseller Black Pearls with Space to Record Your Own Daily Meditations, Reflections, Aspirations, & Plans: Inspired by the Timeless Wisdom of People of African Decent. LC 94-3417. (Illus.). 388p. 1995. pap. 12.95 (*0-688-13967-1*, Wm Morrow) Morrow Avon.

— Kwanzaa: An African-American Celebration of Culture & Cooking. 1993. pap. 15.00 (*0-688-12835-1*, Quil) HarperTrade.

— Parents-Black Pearls. LC 94-33073. (Illus.). 388p. 1995. pap. 10.00 (*0-688-13098-4*, Quil) HarperTrade.

— Soul Food: Inspirational Stories for African-Americans. LC 00-27226. 224p. 2000. pap. 11.95 (*0-7868-8499-1*, Pub. by Hyperion) Time Warner.

Copaken, Nina, tr. see Soffer, Arnon.

***Copan, Lil.** Arms of Love: Mothers & Daughters. LC 99-50225. 2000. write for info. (*0-87788-401-3*, H Shaw Pubs) Waterbrook Pr.

Copan, Lil. Finding God Between a Rock & a Hard Place: Stories of Gratitude & Grace. LC 99-23194. 160p. 1999. pap. 10.99 (*0-87788-329-7*, H Shaw Pubs) Waterbrook Pr.

— Little Book of Love Letters. (Shaw Greetings Ser.). 80p. 1998. pap. text 5.99 (*0-87788-471-4*, H Shaw Pubs) Waterbrook Pr.

— Promises of Heaven. (Pocket Pac Ser.). 1997. pap. text 2.99 (*0-87788-618-0*, H Shaw Pubs) Waterbrook Pr.

— Sisters: A Shared Childhood, a Shared Friendship. LC 97-15008. 1997. pap. text 5.99 (*0-87788-744-6*, H Shaw Pubs) Waterbrook Pr.

Copan, Lil, compiled by. The Fabric of Friendship. LC 96-34949. 96p. (Orig.). 1996. pap. 5.99 (*0-87788-242-8*, H Shaw Pubs) Waterbrook Pr.

***Copan, Lil & Neubacher, Helen Copan, compiled by.** Mothers & Daughters Together. LC 98-33140. (Shaw Greetings Ser.). 96p. 1999. pap. 5.99 (*0-87788-186-3*, H Shaw Pubs) Waterbrook Pr.

Copan, Paul. True for You, but Not for Me: Answering the Comebacks That Leave You Speechless. LC 97-45477. 192p. 1998. pap. 9.99 (*0-7642-2091-8*) Bethany Hse.

***Copan, Paul & Tacelli, Ronald, eds.** Jesus' Resurrection: Fact or Figment?: A Debate Between William Lane Craig & Gerd Ludemann. 200p. 2000. pap. 12.99 (*0-8308-1569-4*) InterVarsity.

Copan, Paul, ed. see Crossan, John Dominic & Craig, William L.

Copani, Peter. Peter Copani's Handbook for People in Search of Love, Money, Power, Happiness, Inspiration, Sound Health, &-or Peace of Mind. LC 92-45724. 164p. (Orig.). 1993. pap. 14.95 (*1-56825-001-0*) Rainbow Bks.

Copans, Stuart, et al. Smart Moves: Your Guide Through the Emotional Maze of Relocation. LC 96-24012. 224p. (Orig.). 1996. pap. 16.95 (*1-57525-079-9*) Smith & Kraus.

Copans, Stuart, jt. auth. see Rich, Phil.

Copans, Stuart, jt. auth. see Singer, Thomas.

Copans, Stuart A., jt. auth. see Rich, Phil.

***Copas, Cheryl A., et al, eds.** From the Mouth of the Shenandoah: The William Copas Family of Tennessee & Kentucky. unabridged ed. LC 98-74404. (Illus.). viii, 1094p. 1998. ring bd. 70.00 (*0-9668028-0-2*) C A Copas.

Copass, Jake. I'll Be Satisfied. (Illus.). 136p. 1998. 25.00 (*0-933380-13-5*) Olive Pr Pubns.

— It Don't Hurt to Laugh: Cowboy Poetry. LC 92-28168. (Illus.). 96p. (Orig.). 1993. pap. 10.00 (*0-933380-12-7*) Olive Pr Pubns.

Copass, Michael K., et al. EMT Manual. 3rd ed. LC 97-47600. (Illus.). 432p. (C). 1998. pap. text 29.00 (*0-7216-6965-4*, W B Saunders Co) Harcrt Hlth Sci Grp.

Copcutt, L., jt. ed. see Clark, J. E.

Cope. Current Techniques in Interventional Radiology. 2nd ed. 200p. (C). 1996. pap. 125.00 (*0-8385-1503-7*, Apple Lange Med) McGraw.

— Higher Classification of Frogs. 1979. write for info. (*0-916984-08-7*) SSAR.

Cope, A. C. Organic Reactions, Vol. 14. (Organic Reactions Ser.). 512p. 1965. 99.95 (*0-471-17166-2*) Wiley.

— Organic Reactions, Vol. 15. (Organic Reactions Ser.). 592p. 1967. 99.95 (*0-471-17168-9*) Wiley.

— Organic Reactions, Vol. 16. (Organic Reactions Ser.). 444p. 1968. 99.95 (*0-471-17169-7*) Wiley.

Cope, A. C. Organic Reactions, Vol. 11. (Organic Reactions Ser.). 501p. 1960. 99.95 (*0-471-17127-1*) Wiley.

— Organic Reactions, Vol. 12. (Organic Reactions Ser.). 538p. 1962. 99.95 (*0-471-17160-3*) Wiley.

— Organic Reactions, Vol. 13. (Organic Reactions Ser.). 382p. 1963. 99.95 (*0-471-17163-8*) Wiley.

Cope, A. T., tr. see Wessels, Allison & Champion, George.

Cope, Alexis. The Fifteenth Ohio Volunteers & Its Campaigns: War of 1861-5. (Illus.). 872p. 1993. reprint ed. 45.00 (*0-9626034-2-2*) Generals Bks.

Cope, Becky, jt. ed. see Cope, Jerry.

Cope, Bill & Kalantzis, Mary. Multiliteracies: Literacy Learning & the Design of Social Futures. LC 99-32355. (Literacies Ser.). 288p. 1999. pap. 29.99 (*0-415-21421-1*) Routledge.

***Cope, Bill & Kalantzis, Mary, eds.** Multiliteracies: Literacy Learning & Design of Social Futures. LC 99-32355. 368p. (C). 1999. text. write for info. (*0-415-21420-3*) Routledge.

Cope, Bill & Kalantzis, Mary, eds. The Powers of Literacy: A Genre Approach to Teaching Writing. (Series in Composition, Literacy, & Culture). 296p. (C). 1993. pap. 19.95 (*0-8229-6104-0*); text 49.95 (*0-8229-1179-5*) U of Pittsburgh Pr.

Cope, Brian, jt. ed. see Kinnamon, Michael.

Cope, C. & Thomas, P. A. Dane & Thomas Vol. 1: How to Use a Law Library: An Introduction to Research Skills. 3rd ed. LC 95-171305. 1994. pap. text 28.00 (*0-421-46090-3*, Pub. by Sweet & Maxwll) Gaunt.

Cope, Constantin. Current Techniques in Interventional Radiology. (Illus.). 216p. 1993. text 99.95 (*1-878132-02-4*) Current Med.

— Current Techniques in Interventional Radiology. 3rd ed. (Illus.). 208p. 1994. text 109.95 (*1-878132-59-8*) Current Med.

***Cope, David.** The Algorithmic Composer. LC 99-59109. 2000. write for info. (*0-89579-454-3*) A-R Eds.

Cope, David. Coming Home. LC 93-21783. (Vox Humana Ser.). 119p. 1993. 18.95 (*0-89603-262-0*); pap. 9.95 (*0-89603-263-9*) Humana.

— Computers & Musical Style. LC 91-11494. (Computer Music & Digital Audio Ser.: Vol. 6). (Illus.). 246p. (C). 1991. 45.95 (*0-89579-256-7*) A-R Eds.

— Experiments in Musical Intelligence. LC 95-6042. (Computer Music & Digital Audio Ser.: No. 12). 263p. 1996. pap. 49.95 incl. cd-rom (*0-89579-314-8*) A-R Eds.

— Fragments from the Stars. LC 89-20027. (Vox Humana Ser.). 128p. 1990. 21.95 (*0-89603-172-1*); pap. 12.95 (*0-89603-174-8*) Humana.

— New Directions in Music. 6th ed. (Illus.). 399p. (C). 1998. reprint ed. pap. text 38.95 (*0-88133-992-X*) Waveland Pr.

— On the Bridge. LC 86-21074. (Vox Humana Ser.). 90p. 1986. 14.95 (*0-89603-113-6*); pap. 12.95 (*0-89603-114-4*) Humana.

— Quiet Lives. LC 83-172. (Vox Humana Ser.). 92p. 1983. 14.95 (*0-89603-048-2*); pap. 11.95 (*0-89603-049-0*) Humana.

— Silences for Love. LC 97-49975. (Vox Humana Ser.). 128p. 1998. pap. 9.95 (*0-89603-631-6*) Humana.

— Silences for Love. LC 97-49975. (Vox Humana Ser.). (Illus.). 128p. 1998. 19.50 (*0-89603-508-5*) Humana.

— Techniques of the Contemporary Composer. LC 97-5415. 1997. 32.00 (*0-02-864737-8*) Mac Lib Ref.

***Cope, David.** Virtual Music: Computer Synthesis of Musical Style. (Illus.). 292p. (C). 2000. 39.95 (*0-262-03283-X*) MIT Pr.

Cope de Wyatt, Joyce. Soy Mujer, Soy Especial: I'm a Woman I'm Special. (SPA.). 112p. (Orig.). 1988. pap. 7.99 (*0-311-12100-4*) Casa Bautista.

Cope, Doric K., et al, eds. Anesthesia History Association Newsletters: 1982-1995. (Illus.). 664p. 1996. lib. bdg. write for info. (*0-88135-172-5*) Watson Pub Intl.

Cope, E. A. Pinophyta (Gymnospers) of New York State. (New York State Museum Bulletin Ser.: No. 483). (Illus.). 80p. (Orig.). 1992. pap. 8.50 (*1-55557-198-0*) NYS Museum.

Cope, E. M. Introduction to Aristotle's Rhetoric with Analysis, Notes, & Appendices. (Classical Studies). reprint ed. lib. bdg. 47.00 (*0-697-00032-X*) Irvington.

— The Rhetoric of Aristotle with a Commentary, 3 vols., 1. Sandys, John E., ed. (Classical Studies). (ENG & GRE.). reprint ed. lib. bdg. 62.00 (*0-697-00033-8*) Irvington.

— The Rhetoric of Aristotle with a Commentary, 3 vols., 2. Sandys, John W., ed. (Classical Studies). (ENG & GRE.). reprint ed. lib. bdg. 62.00 (*0-697-00034-6*) Irvington.

— The Rhetoric of Aristotle with a Commentary, 3 vols., 3. Sandys, John E., ed. (Classical Studies). (ENG & GRE.). reprint ed. lib. bdg. 62.00 (*0-697-00035-4*) Irvington.

— The Rhetoric of Aristotle with a Commentary, 3 vols., Set. Sandys, John E., ed. (Classical Studies). (ENG & GRE.). reprint ed. lib. bdg. 177.00 (*0-89197-922-0*) Irvington.

Cope, E. S. Proceedings of the Short Parliament, 1640. (Camden Fourth Ser.: Vol. 19). 343p. 27.00 (*0-901050-37-7*) David Brown.

Cope, Eddie. Agatha Christie Made Me Do It: A Mystery Comdy in 3 Acts. (Illus.). 62p. 1975. pap. 4.50 (*0-88680-001-3*) I E Clark.

— Don't Print That! A Three-Act Melodrama. (Illus.). 40p. 1983. pap. 3.50 (*0-88680-042-0*) I E Clark.

— Don't Touch My Tutu: 2-Act Comedy. (Illus.). 40p. (J). (gr. 4 up). 1985. pap. 4.00 (*0-88680-242-3*) I E Clark.

— Frankenstein's Centerfold: 2-Act Comedy. 40p. 1984. pap. 4.00 (*0-88680-222-9*) I E Clark.

— The Invisible Man: Comedy Thriller in 3-Acts. (Illus.). 48p. 1980. pap. 4.00 (*0-88680-094-3*) I E Clark.

Cope, Eddie & Cearley, Buster. Airport Nineteen Hundred Four: A 2-Act Musical. (Illus.). 40p. 1981. pap. 4.50 (*0-88680-002-1*) I E Clark.

— Last Tango in Pango Pango. (Illus.). 36p. (Orig.). 1988. pap. 4.00 (*0-88680-293-8*) I E Clark.

***Cope, Edward A.** Muenscher's Keys to Woody Plants: An Expanded Guide to Native & Cultivated Species. rev. ed. (Illus.). 2001. 50.00 (*0-8014-3852-7*, Comstock Pub); pap. 22.95 (*0-8014-8702-1*, Comstock Pub) Cornell U Pr.

Cope, Edward A. Native & Cultivated Conifers of Northeastern North America: A Guide. LC 85-24338. (Illus.). 224p. 1986. text 47.50 (*0-8014-1721-X*); pap. text 18.95 (*0-8014-9360-9*) Cornell U Pr.

Cope, Edward D. The Origin of the Fittest: Essays on Evolution & the Primary Factors of Organic Evolution, 2 vols. LC 73-17813. (Natural Sciences in America Ser.). 1066p. 1974. reprint ed. 76.95 (*0-405-05729-6*) Ayer.

— The Vertebrata of the Tertiary Formations of the West, 1vol., 2 bks. Sterling, Keir B., ed. LC 77-81093. (Biologists & Their World Ser.). (Illus.). 1978. reprint ed. lib. bdg. 95.95 (*0-405-10672-6*) Ayer.

— The Vertebrata of the Tertiary Formations of the West, 1 vol., 2 bks., 1. Sterling, Keir B., ed. LC 77-81093. (Biologists & Their World Ser.). (Illus.). 1978. reprint ed. lib. bdg. 45.95 (*0-405-10673-4*) Ayer.

— The Vertebrata of the Tertiary Formations of the West, 1 vol., 2 bks., Vol. 2. Sterling, Keir B., ed. LC 77-81093. (Biologists & Their World Ser.). (Illus.). 1978. reprint ed. 50.95 (*0-405-10674-2*) Ayer.

Cope, Edward M. An Introduction to Aristotle's Rhetoric: With Analysis, Notes & Appendices. xvi, 464p. 1970. reprint ed. 105.00 (*0-685-66429-5*, 05103086) G Olms Pubs.

Cope, Emma E. Cope. Records of the Family of Cope. 31p. 1997. reprint ed. pap. 6.00 (*0-8328-8042-6*); reprint ed. lib. bdg. 16.00 (*0-8328-8041-8*) Higginson Bk Co.

Cope, Esther S. Handmaid of the Holy Spirit: Dame Eleanor Davies, Never Soe Mad a Ladie. (Illus.). 272p. (C). 1993. text 47.50 (*0-472-10303-2*, 10303) U of Mich Pr.

— Politics Without Parliaments, 1629-1640. 256p. (C). 1987. text 55.00 (*0-04-941020-2*) Routledge.

Cope, Esther S., ed. see Davies, Eleanor.

Cope, Fred O., jt. ed. see Tomei, L. David.

Cope, Frederick O., jt. ed. see Tomei, L. David.

Cope, G. Genealogy of tharpless Family, Descendants from John & Jane Sess, Settlers near Chester, Pennsylvania, 1682.s.). 1349p. 1989. reprint ed. pap. 198.00 (*0-83283-0*); reprint ed. lib. bdg. 206.00 (*0-8328-1062-2*) Higon Bk Co.

— Genealogy of the Sme Family Descended from George & Sarah Sm, Settlers in Chester County, Pennsylvania with BNotices of Other Families. (Illus.). 1011p. 1989:int ed. pap. 144.00 (*0-8328-1085-1*); reped. lib. bdg. 152.00 (*0-8328-1084-3*) Higgn Bk Co.

Cope, G., jt. auth. see Fu, J. S.

Cope, G., ed. see Robert, S.

Cope, Gilbert. Baily. Gengy of the Baily Family of Bromham, Wiltshire, land, & More Particulary of the Descendants of Jcaily, Who Came from Bromham about 1682ettled in Chester County, Pa. (Illus.). 672p. 1997. rat ed. pap. 95.00 (*0-8328-7333-0*); reprd. lib. bdg. 105.00 (*0-8328-7332-2*) Higgn Bk Co.

— Cope. Record of the Colamily, As Established in America by Oliver CoWho Came from England to Pennsylvania about 16(Illus.). 251p. 1997. reprint ed. pap. 38.00 (*0-83284-2*); reprint ed. lib. bdg. 48.00 (*0-8328-8043-4*)gginson Bk Co.

Cope, Gilbert & Ashmeadenry G. Historic Homes & Institutions & Genealol & Personal Memoirs of Chester & Delaware Cies, Pennsylvania, 2 vols. (Illus.). 1198p. 1994. rat ed. lib. bdg. 115.00 (*0-8328-3920-5*) Higgi Bk Co.

Cope, Gilbert, jt. auth. seethey, J. Smith.

Cope, Glen C. & Keel, Ths. Budget Imbalance & the External Influences: A Sy of the Legislative Budget Board of Texas. (Policysearch Project Report: No. 99). 46p. 1992. pap. 8.5*0-89940-707-2*) LBJ Sch Pub Aff.

Cope, Glen H., ed. Diffusior Innovations in the Public Sector: Proceedings of anference. (Institute & Seminar Proceedings Se145p. 1992. pap. 8.50 (*0-89940-101-5*) LBJ Scub Aff.

Cope, Glen H. & Keel, Thos M. Constitutional Authority for & Limitations on TeState Govt Finance, Appropriations & Spendi (Working Paper Ser.: Vol. 73). 170p. 1993. pap. 6.5*0-89940-563-0*) LBJ Sch Pub Aff.

Cope, Glen H. & Wilson, Rert. The Effects of State Government on Economievelopment in Texas Cities. LC 84-81929. (Policy Rerch Project Report: No. 63). 248p. 1985. pap. 9.00 (*0-940-665-3*) LBJ Sch Pub Aff.

Cope, J. A. & Winch, F. E. Kw Your Trees. 6th ed. (4-H Ser.). (Illus.). 72p. (Orig.)996. reprint ed. pap. 3.95 (*1-57753-033-0*, 147185) rn Coop Ext.

Cope, J. C., et al, eds. Atlas oalaeogeography & Lithofacies. Ingham, J. K. Rawson, P. F., trs. (Geological Society Meme Ser.: No. 13). (Illus.). 176p. 1992. 493.00 (*0-9037-65-6*, 264, Pub. by Geol Soc Pub Hse) AAPG.

***Cope, J. C., et al, eds.** Atlas Palaeogeography & Lithofacies. 2nd ed. (Geolcal Society Memoir Ser.: No. 13). 154p. 1999. 115.0*1-86239-055-X*, Pub. by Geol Soc Pub Hse) AAPG.

Cope, Jackson I. Dramaturgy che Daemonic: Studies in Anti-Generic Theater fromuzante to Grimaldi. LC 83-23886. 183p. 1984. repnt ed. pap. 56.80 (*0-608-05937-4*, 2066274008) Bks Demand.

— Joyce's Cities: Archaeologiesf the Soul. LC 80-8056. 176p. (C). 1981. text 30.00-*8018-2543-1*) Johns Hopkins.

— Robert Coover's Fictions. LC6-45445. 168p. 1986. reprint ed. pap. 52.10 (*0-6005938-2*, 206627500008) Bks Demand.

— Secret Sharers in Italian Comly: From Machiavelli to Goldoni. LC 95-49319. 232 1996. text 39.95 (*0-8223-1760-5*) Duke.

Cope, Jackson I. & Green, Georey, eds. Novel vs. Fiction. 166p. 1981. 8.50 (*0-9376646-1*) Pilgrim Bks OK.

Cope, James B., jt. auth. see Hmphrey, Stephen R.

Cope, Jane. A Treasury of JewisStories. LC 96-363. 160p. (J). (gr. k-4). 1996. pap. 5.950-*7534-5028-3*, Kingfisher) LKC.

Cope, Janet, jt. auth. see Harpe Shannon.

Cope, Jeffrey T., jt. auth. see Trble, Curtis G.

Cope, Jerry & Cope, Becky, eds Potlucks & Petticoats. 1986. 11.95 (*0-9617157-0-7*) opside Pubs.

***Cope, John.** A Warrior's Way: Inights for Cancer Patients, cancer Survivors & Those Wb Love Them. 112p. 2000. pap. 12.95 (*0-9678284-2-2*) Harts Care.

Cope, John A. International Militry Education & Training: An Assessment. 72p. 1996. rarint ed. pap. text 30.00 (*0-7881-3040-4*) DIANE Pub.

Cope, Judith, ed. see Parker, Nacy.

***Cope, Julian.** Head on & Reposesed. 2000. pap. 18.95 (*0-7225-3882-0*) Thorsons PA

— The Modern Antiquarian: A PreMillennial Odyssey Through Megalithic Britain. 412p. 1999. pap. text 45.00 (*0-7225-3599-6*) Thorsons PA.

Cope, June. A Matter of Choice: Aortion Law Reform in Apartheid South Africa. 190p. 1994. pap. 40.00 (*0-86980-887-7*, Pub. by Univ Natal Pr) Intl Spec Bk.

Cope, Kathy. Malnutrition in the Elderly: A National Crisis: A Focus on the Problems, Causes, Consequences, & Solutions. (Illus.). 77p. 1998. pap. text 20.00 (*0-7881-4814-1*) DIANE Pub.

Cope, Kathy. Malnutrition in the Elderly, a National Crisis. 95p. 1996. pap. 9.00 (*0-16-061595-X*) USGPO.

***Cope, Kenneth A.** Alaskan Deep Sea Fish Tales: A Selected Group of Short Stories about Guided Charter Boat Operations in Alaska. LC 99-94691. 113 p. (J). 1999. write for info. (*0-9670108-0-2*) Fantasy N.

C

An Asterisk (*) at the beginning of an entry indicates that the title is appearing for the first time.

Cope, Kenneth L. American Machinist's Tools: An Illustrated Directory of Patents. (Illus.). 424p. (Orig.). 1993. pap. 29.95 (*1-879335-40-9*) Astragal Pr.

— American Wrench Makers, 1830-1915. LC 98-74739. 284p. 1999. pap. 24.95 (*1-879335-87-5*) Astragal Pr.

***Cope, Kenneth L.** Collectable Tools: Tool Ads, 1841-1920. (Illus.). 117p. 1999. pap. 16.95 (*0-9653719-9-9*) Osage Pr IL.

— Kitchen Collectibles: An Identification Guide. (Illus.). 320p. 2000. pap. 29.95 (*1-879335-93-X*) Astragal Pr.

Cope, Kenneth L. Makers of American Machinist Tools. (Illus.). 320p. (Orig.). 1994. pap. 27.50 (*1-879335-55-7*) Astragal Pr.

— More Makers of American Machinist Tools. unabridged ed. (Illus.). 165p. 1998. pap. 19.95 (*1-879335-83-2*) Astragal Pr.

Cope, Kenneth L., intro. A Brown & Sharpe Catalog Collection, 1868 to 1899. LC 97-70456. (Illus.). 291p. 1997. pap. 19.95 (*1-879335-76-X*) Astragal Pr.

Cope, Kevin, ed. see Panagopoulos, Nic.

Cope, Kevin L. Criteria of Certainty: Truth & Judgment in the English Enlightenment. LC 90-12264. 232p. 1990. text 29.95 (*0-8131-1750-X*) U Pr of Ky.

***Cope, Kevin L.** John Locke Revisited. LC 99-11815. (English Authors Ser.: Vol. 554). xi, 147 p. 1999. 32.00 (*0-8057-1657-2*, Twayne) Mac Lib Ref.

Cope, Kevin L., ed. Compendious Conversations: The Method of Dialogue in the Early Enlightenment. LC 92-16289. 424p. 1992. 79.00 (*3-631-43714-5*) P Lang Pubng.

— Enlightening Allegory: Theory, Practice & Contexts of Allegory in the Late Seventeenth & Eighteenth Centuries. LC 91-75412. (Studies in the Eighteenth Century: No. 18). (Illus.). 405p. 1993. 45.00 (*0-404-63518-0*) AMS Pr.

— Ideas, Aesthetics & Inquiries in the Early Modern Era, 1650-1850, Vol. 2. 366p. 1993. 62.50 (*0-404-64400-7*) AMS Pr.

— 1650-1850 Vol. 3: Ideas, Aesthetics, & Inquiries in the Early Modern Era. 445p. 1997. 74.50 (*0-404-64403-1*) AMS Pr.

***Cope, Kevin Lee & Ahrens, Rhudiger.** Talking Forward, Talking Back: Critical Dialogues with the Enlightenment. LC 99-59955. (Studies in the Eighteenth Century). 2000. write for info. (*0-404-63535-0*) AMS Pr.

Cope, L. & Rice, L., eds. Practical Placer Mining. LC 91-66951. (Illus.). 112p. (Orig.). 1992. pap. 47.00 (*0-87335-105-3*, 105-3) SMM&E Inc.

Cope, Landa. Clearly Communicating Christ: Breaking Down Barriers to Effective Communication. 178p. (Orig.). 1996. pap. 8.99 (*0-927545-47-0*) YWAM Pub.

Cope, Lloyd. Astrologer's Forecasting Workbook. LC 82-73127. 182p. 1995. 29.95 (*0-86690-041-1*, C2642-014) Am Fed Astrologers.

— Your Stars Are Numbered: Your Birthdate Secrets Revealed Through Astronumerology. LC 99-36833. 368p. 1999. pap. 16.95 (*1-86204-363-9*, Pub. by Element MA) Penguin Putnam.

Cope, Malcolm. Constructive Trusts. 1011p. 1992. 205.00 (*0-455-21071-3*, Pub. by LawBk Co) Gaunt.

— Proprietary Claims & Remedies. 218p. 1997. 64.00 (*1-86287-253-8*, Pub. by Federation Pr) Gaunt.

Cope, Malcolm, ed. Equity: Issues & Trends. 272p. 1995. 64.00 (*1-86287-159-0*, Pub. by Federation Pr) Gaunt.

Cope, Mick. Leading the Organisation to Learn: The 10 Levers for Putting Knowledge & Learning to Work. (Illus.). 301p. 1998. pap. 45.00 (*0-273-63524-7*, Pub. by F T P-H) Trans-Atl Phila.

***Cope, Mick.** The Seven C's of Consulting. 240p. 2000. pap. 29.00 (*0-273-64511-0*) F T P-H.

***Cope, Mike.** One Holy Hunger: When God Is All You Want. 200p. 2000. pap. 11.95 (*0-89112-443-8*, Hill Crest Pubg) Abilene Christ U.

Cope, Mike, jt. auth. see Shelly, Rubel.

Cope, Nicholas. To Bind the Nation: Solomon kaDinuzulu & Zulu Nationalism, 1913-1933. (Illus.). 328p. 1993. pap. 31.95 (*0-86980-888-5*, Pub. by Univ Natal Pr) Intl Spec Bk.

Cope, Nigel. Retail in the Digital Age. 1997. pap. text 19.95 (*0-906097-59-2*, Pub. by Bowerdean Pub) Capital VA.

Cope, O. Lamar. Matthew: A Scribe Trained for the Kingdom of Heaven. LC 75-36778. (Catholic Biblical Quarterly Monographs: No. 5). 142p. 1976. pap. 4.50 (*0-915170-04-3*) Catholic Bibl Assn.

Cope, Pamela. Introductory Grammar: A Stratificational Approach. LC 94-66237. 110p. (Orig.). 1994. pap. text 12.00 (*1-55671-001-1*) S I L Intl.

Cope, Peter, jt. auth. see Conion, Tom.

Cope, Peter, jt. ed. see Conlon, Tom.

Cope, R. Douglas. The Limits of Racial Domination: Plebeian Society in Colonial Mexico City, 1660-1720. LC 93-23344. 1994. 50.00 (*0-299-14040-7*); pap. 19.95 (*0-299-14044-X*) U of Wis Pr.

Cope, R. J. & Clark, L. A., eds. Concrete Slabs: Analysis & Design. (Illus.). 512p. 1984. mass mkt. 157.50 (*0-85334-254-7*, I-216-84) Elsevier.

***Cope, Ray.** From Mersey to Missouri: A Doctor's Reflections on Life in the U. K. & U. S. A. (Illus.). 382p. 2000. 32.50 (*1-85776-441-2*, Pub. by Book Guild Ltd) Trans-Atl Phila.

***Cope, Richard.** The Ploughshare of War: The Origins of the Anglo-Zulu War of 1879. LC 99-456901. (Illus.). 282p. 1999. pap. 12.75 (*0-86980-944-X*, Pub. by Univ Natal Pr) Intl Spec Bk.

Cope, Robert. High Involvement Strategic Planning: When People & Their Ideas Really Matter. 128p. 1989. pap. 19.95 (*0-912841-30-3*) Planning Forum.

Cope-Robinson, Lyn. Beginning Scottish Country Dance: A Dancer's Manual (with Glossary) Milton, June, ed. (Illus.). 115p. (Orig.). 1995. pap. 13.00 (*1-887774-00-9*) Canmore Pr.

— The Little Quaker Sociology Book with Glossary. (Illus.). 165p. (Orig.). (C). 1995. pap. 14.99 (*1-887774-01-7*) Canmore Pr.

Cope, Sandy & Dillbeck, Sandy. Instant Christmas Pageant: The Fumbly Bumbly Angels. Brolsma, Jody, ed. LC 96-51868. 48p. (Orig.). (J). 1997. pap. 24.99 (*1-55945-498-9*) Group Pub.

***Cope, Stephen.** Yoga & the Quest for the True Self. LC 99-33236. 384p. 1999. 24.95 (*0-553-10313-X*) Bantam.

— Yoga & the Quest for the True Self. 384p. 2000. pap. 14.95 (*0-553-37835-X*) Bantam.

Cope, T. A. & Hosni, H. A. A Key to Egyptian Grasses. (Illus.). vi, 75p. 1991. pap. 20.00 (*0-947643-35-4*, Pub. by Royal Botnic Grdns) Balogh.

Cope, T. A., jt. ed. see Miller, A. G.

Cope, Thom. Executive Guide to Employment Practices. 2nd ed. 200p. (Orig.). 1990. pap. 14.95 (*0-939644-78-9*) Media Pub.

Cope, Thom K. Executive Guide to Employment Practices. 3rd rev. ed. Dageforde, Linda J., ed. LC 98-37429. 224p. (Orig.). 1998. pap. 15.95 (*1-886225-22-2*, 2000) Dageforde Pub.

Cope, Todd F. The Shift. vi, 74p. 1998. pap. 5.95 (*0-9663413-0-9*) T F Cope.

Cope, Vern. The Oregon Earthquake Handbook: An Easy-to-Understand Information & Survival Guide. LC 92-97560. (Illus.). 152p. (Orig.). 1993. pap. text 11.95 (*0-9635564-3-6*) V Cope.

— The Washington Earthquake Handbook: An Easy-to-Understand Information & Survival Guide. LC 93-91101. (Illus.). 152p. (Orig.). 1994. pap. 11.95 (*0-9635564-4-4*) V Cope.

Cope, William, ed. A Glossary of Hampshire Words & Phrases. (English Dialect Society Publications: No. 40). 1969. reprint ed. pap. 25.00 (*0-8115-0465-4*) Periodicals Srv.

Copel, Joshua A. & Reed, Kathryn L., eds. Doppler Ultrasound in Obstetrics & Gynecology. LC 93-48969. 368p. 1994. text 142.00 (*0-7817-0206-2*) Lppncott W & W.

***Copel, Linda.** Nurse's Clinical Guide to Psychiatric & Mental Health Care. 2nd ed. LC 99-35195. 1999. write for info. (*0-87434-986-9*) Springhouse Corp.

Copel, Linda. Psychiatric Nursing. Ballard, Karen A. et al, eds. LC 98-49716. (Nursing Core Ser.). (Illus.). 504p. 1999. pap. text 37.00 (*0-07-105479-0*) McGraw-Hill HPD.

Copel, Linda C. Nurse's Clinical Guide to Psychiatric & Mental Health Care. LC 95-32425. (Illus.). 384p. 1995. pap. 27.95 (*0-87434-720-3*) Springhouse Corp.

Copelan. Our Covenant with God. 1988. pap. 2.95 (*0-938458-02-7*) K Copeland Pubns.

— Proverbs. 1997. 14.99 (*0-89274-951-2*) Harrison Hse.

***Copelan, Rachel.** Fell's Official Know-It-All Guide to Hypnotism. 224p. 2000. pap. 16.95 (*0-88391-015-2*) F Fell Pubs Inc.

Copeland. Antique Airplanes Coloring Book. (Illus.). (J). 1975. pap. 2.95 (*0-486-21524-5*) Dover.

— Arnold Adoff. 1998. 22.95 (*0-8057-4599-8*, Twyne) Mac Lib Ref.

— Civil War Uniforms. 1980. pap. text 2.95 (*0-486-23535-1*) Dover.

— Computer Aided Legal Research. (Paralegal Ser.). (C). 2001. pap. 29.75 (*0-7668-1780-6*) Delmar.

— Conversacion y Repaso. 6th ed. (SPA.). (C). 1997. pap. text 50.00 (*0-03-017517-8*) Harcourt.

— Conversacion y Repaso. 6th ed. (C). 1997. wbk. ed. 32.50 (*0-03-017522-4*, Pub. by Harcourt Coll Pubs) Harcourt.

— Conversacion Y Repaso. 6th ed. 1997. pap. text, teacher ed. 35.00 (*0-03-017519-4*) Harcourt Coll Pubs.

— Great Native Americans. 1998. pap. 2.95 (*0-486-29607-5*) Dover.

— KITCONVERSACIONY REPASO6E+LI 6th ed. (SPA.). 1997. 52.50 (*0-03-023881-1*) Harcourt Coll Pubs.

— Measuring & Managing the Value of Companies: Teacher's Manual to Valuation. 2nd ed. 232p. 1996. pap. write for info. (*0-471-13989-0*) Wiley.

— Mythical Beasts Stained Glass Coloring Book. (Illus.). pap. 3.95 (*0-486-28899-4*) Dover.

— North American Indian Dances & Rituals. 1998. pap. 2.95 (*0-486-29913-9*) Dover.

— Prayers That Avail Much: WWJD. 101p. 1994. pap. 6.99 (*1-57794-119-5*) Harrison Hse.

— Prayers That Avail Much for Women. 19.99 (*1-57794-124-1*) Harrison Hse.

— Princess Sister. 2000. text 24.95 (*0-312-19948-1*) St Martin.

— Shoulder Surgery. 1996. text 102.00 (*0-7020-2063-X*, W B Saunders Co) Harcrt Hlth Sci Grp.

— The Titanic Coloring Book. (Illus.). pap. 2.50 (*0-486-29756-X*) Dover.

Copeland, et al. Managerial Accounting. 8th ed. LC 98-70890. 1998. 63.95 (*0-87393-764-3*) Dame Pubns.

— Managerial Accounting: Student Solutions Manual. 8th ed. LC 98-70890. 1998. pap., student ed. 24.95 (*0-87393-767-8*) Dame Pubns.

— Managerial Accounting: Study Guide. 8th ed. LC 98-70890. 1998. pap., student ed. 21.95 (*0-87393-765-1*) Dame Pubns.

— Managerial Accounting: Working Papers. 8th ed. LC 98-70890. 1998. pap. 20.95 (*0-87393-766-X*) Dame Pubns.

Copeland, Alexandra. An Artist's Travel Guide to the Ceramics Museums of Europe. (Illus.). 192p. 1999. pap. 13.95 (*0-9586098-0-2*) Seven Hills Bk.

***Copeland, Bill.** Absolutely Complete Retail Loss Prevention Guide, 4 vols. 1478p. 2000. 160.00 (*1-893763-51-X*) Absolutely Zero.

— BBC Academy of Private Investigation & Loss Prevention Vol. I: Professional Text Set. 1650p. 2000. 200.00 (*1-893763-76-5*) Absolutely Zero.

Copeland, Bill. Investigations in Retail. 444p. 1999. 40.00 (*1-893763-99-4*) Absolutely Zero.

— Loss Prevention Professional. 404p. 1999. 40.00 (*0-9657659-5-4*) Absolutely Zero.

***Copeland, Bill.** Loss Prevention Trilogy How to Achieve Success!, 3 vols. 1212p. 1999. 120.00 (*1-893763-46-3*) Absolutely Zero.

— LP for HR: The Loss Prevention Guide for Human Resources Professionals. xii, 182p. 2000. 40.00 (*1-893763-00-5*) Absolutely Zero.

— Private Investigaiton Trilogy: The Retail Community Connection!, 3 vols. 1106p. 1999. 120.00 (*1-893763-36-6*) Absolutely Zero.

Copeland, P. T. I Liked You at Ten... I'll Like You Again: Reflections of Mommy Years. (Illus.). 56p. 1998. 14.95 (*1-890753-02-5*) Ganas Co.

Copeland, A. Copeland Financial Theory Plus Student Solutions Manual. 1998. write for info. (*0-201-36269-4*) Addison-Wesley.

Copeland, Aaron. What to Listen for in Music. rev. ed. LC 98-53893. 288p. 1999. mass mkt. 6.99 (*0-451-62880-2*, Sig) NAL.

Copeland, Alfred M. A History of Hampden County, Massachusetts, Set, Vols. I-III. (Illus.). 1993. reprint ed. lib. bdg. 145.00 (*0-8328-3205-7*) Higginson Bk Co.

— History of the Town of Murrayfield, Mass. Earlier Known as Township No. 9 & Comprising the Present Towns of Chester & Huntington, the Northern Part of Montgomery, & the Southeast Corner of Middlefield, 1760-1783. (Illus.). 175p. 1997. reprint ed. pap. 22.50 (*0-8328-5547-2*); reprint ed. lib. bdg. 32.50 (*0-8328-5546-4*) Higginson Bk Co.

Copeland, Amelia. Snatch. 1. 1999. mass mkt. 7.95 (*1-58419-010-8*) Masq Bks.

Copeland, Andy, jt. auth. see Copeland, Liza.

Copeland, Ann. The ABCs of Writing Fiction. 256p. 1996. 18.99 (*1-884910-12-2*, Story Press) F & W Pubns Inc.

— The Golden Thread. 274p. 1995. reprint ed. pap. 12.95 (*0-86492-159-4*, Pub. by Goose Ln Edits) Genl Dist Srvs.

— Season of Apples. 216p. 1996. pap. 13.95 (*0-86492-210-8*, Pub. by Goose Ln Edits) Genl Dist Srvs.

Copeland, Anne P. & White, Kathleen M. Studying Families. (Applied Social Research Methods Ser.: Vol. 27). (Illus.). 160p. 1991. text 42.00 (*0-8039-3247-2*); pap. text 18.95 (*0-8039-3248-0*) Sage.

Copeland, Barry. Funding Sources in Physical Education, Exercise & Sport Science. 125p. (C). 1995. pap. text 19.00 (*0-9627926-7-5*) Fit Info Tech.

Copeland, Bobby. B-Western Boot Hill: A Final Tribute to the Cowboys & Cowgirls Who Rode the Saturday Matinee Movie Range. 200p. 1999. pap. 15.00 (*0-944019-28-5*) Empire NC.

Copeland-Brooks, Candice, jt. auth. see Tirabassi, Becky.

Copeland, C. T., ed. see Carlyle, Thomas.

Copeland, C. W. & Fisher, Robert L. Know Credit . . . No Problem! 2nd rev. ed. (Illus.). 80p. (Orig.). 1995. pap. 14.95 (*0-9652131-0-2*) Mddle Passage.

Copeland, Carole, ed. see De Lafayette, J. Maximillien.

Copeland, Carole, ed. see De LaFayette, Jean M.

Copeland, Carolyn. Tankas from the Koelz Collection: Museum of Anthropology, University of Michigan. rev. ed. (Michigan Papers on South & Southeast Asia: No. 18). (Illus.). 100p. (Orig.). (C). 1986. pap. 17.95 (*0-89148-018-8*) Ctr S&SE Asian.

Copeland, Carolyn F. Language & Time & Gertrude Stein. LC 75-16491. 191p. reprint ed. pap. 59.30 (*0-8357-8902-0*, 202593900047) Bks Demand.

Copeland, Charles. Video Codecs by Example: The Cross-Platform Digital Video Cookbook. (C). 1997. pap. text. write for info. (*0-201-63491-0*) Addison-Wesley.

Copeland, Charlie, Jr., jt. auth. see German, John L.

Copeland, Cody C. & Bacon, Jonathan P. Understanding & Using MS DOS - PC DOS: A Complete Guide. (Microcomputing Ser.). 262p. (C). 1987. pap. text 28.75 (*0-314-34747-X*) West Pub.

Copeland, Cody T. & Bacon, Jonathan P. Understanding & Using WordPerfect Release 5.1. Leyh, ed. 435p. (C). 1991. mass mkt. 28.25 (*0-314-81983-5*) West Pub.

***Copeland, Colene.** Evan's Well. (Illus.). 181p. (J). (gr. 2-6). 1999. 4.95 (*0-939810-23-9*) Jordan Valley.

Copeland, Colene. Little Prissy & T. C. LC 88-81916. (Priscilla Ser.: No. 2). (Illus.). 114p. (Orig.). (J). (gr. 2 up). 1988. 8.95 (*0-939810-07-7*); pap. 3.95 (*0-939810-08-5*) Jordan Valley.

— Magic Cellar. (Illus.). 94p. (J). (gr. 1-7). 1995. 8.95 (*0-938810-17-0*) Jordan Valley.

— Mystery in the Farrowing Barn. LC 91-62326. (Priscilla Ser.: No. 4). (Illus.). 150p. (Orig.). (J). (gr. 3-7). 1991. 9.95 (*0-939810-13-1*); pap. 3.95 (*0-939810-14-X*) Jordan Valley.

— Piston & the Porkers. LC 89-84652. (Illus.). 127p. (Orig.). 1989. 8.95 (*0-939810-09-3*); pap. 3.95 (*0-939810-10-7*) Jordan Valley.

Copeland, Colene. Potsy. (Priscilla Pig Ser.: Vol. 6). 103p. (J). (gr. 1-6). 1997. pap. 4.95 (*0-939810-20-4*) Jordan Valley.

Copeland, Colene. Priscilla. LC 81-80663. (Illus.). 212p. (Orig.). (J). (gr. 3 up). 1981. 8.95 (*0-939810-01-8*); pap. 3.95 (*0-939810-02-6*) Jordan Valley.

— Wanted: Pot Bellied Pigs. LC 93-78897. (Illus.). 158p. (J). (gr. 1-7). 1993. 9.95 (*0-939810-15-8*); pap. 4.95 (*0-939810-16-6*) Jordan Valley.

Copeland, Colene M. Family Trees & Pedigrees. LC 84-81951. (Illus.). 104p. 1984. pap. 5.95 (*0-939810-03-4*) Jordan Valley.

Copeland, Craig, jt. auth. see Copeland, Kathy.

Copeland, Curtis. Regulatory Burden: Some Agencies' Claims Regarding Lack of Rule Making Discretion Have Merit. 92p. (C). 1999. pap. text 25.00 (*0-7881-8137-8*) DIANE Pub.

***Copeland, Curtis W.** Regulatory Accounting: Analysis of OMB's Reports on the Costs & Benefits of Federal Regulation. 76p. 1999. pap. text 20.00 (*0-7881-8619-1*) DIANE Pub.

Copeland, Curtis W. Regulatory Reform: Implementation of the Small Business Advocacy Review Panel Requirements. 49p. 1999. pap. text 20.00 (*0-7881-7972-1*) DIANE Pub.

Copeland, Curtis W., et al, eds. Regulatory Burden: Measurement Challenges & Concerns Raised by Selected Companies. (Illus.). 128p. (Orig.). (C). 1997. pap. text 40.00 (*0-7881-4056-6*) DIANE Pub.

Copeland, D. R., jt. auth. see Van Eys, J.

***Copeland, Dale C.** The Origins of Major War: Hegemonic Rivalry & the Fear of Decline. LC 00-24040. (Studies in Security Affairs). 2000. write for info. (*0-8014-3750-4*) Cornell U Pr.

Copeland, David, jt. auth. see Louis, Ron.

Copeland, David A. Colonial American Newspapers: Character & Content. LC 96-17172. 392p. 1996. 49.50 (*0-87413-591-5*) U Delaware Pr.

***Copeland, David A.** Debating the Issues in Colonial Newspapers: Primary Documents on Events of the Period. LC 99-89070. 2000. write for info. (*0-313-30982-5*, Greenwood Pr) Greenwood.

Copeland, David S. History of Clarendon, New York. 382p. 1993. reprint ed. lib. bdg. 41.00 (*0-8328-2911-0*) Higginson Bk Co.

Copeland, Douglas & Colander, David. Economics. 2nd ed. 552p. (C). 1995. text, student ed. 20.00 (*0-256-16812-1*, Irwn McGrw-H) McGrw-H Hghr Educ.

Copeland, Douglas, jt. auth. see Colander, David.

Copeland, E. B. Ferns of Fiji. (BMB Ser.: No. 59). 1972. reprint ed. 25.00 (*0-527-02165-2*) Periodicals Srv.

— Genera Filicum: The Genera of Ferns. (Illus.). 247p. 1984. reprint ed. text 35.00 (*0-945345-64-X*, Pub. by Mahendra Pal Singh) Lubrecht & Cramer.

— Hymenophyllum: Trichomanes - Manila, 1933, Genera Hymenophyllacearum - Manila, 1938, 3 vols. in 1. (Phil. Journal of Science Ser.: Vols. 51, 64, 67). (Illus.). 460p. 1975. reprint ed. 149.60 (*3-87429-079-4*, 003327, Pub. by Koeltz Sci Bks) Lubrecht & Cramer.

— Pteridophytes of the Society Islands. (BMB Ser.). 1974. reprint ed. 25.00 (*0-527-02199-7*) Periodicals Srv.

Copeland, E. Luther. A New Meeting of the Religions: Interreligious Relationships & Theological Questioning. LC 99-12735. 195p. 1999. 26.95 (*0-918954-71-1*) Baylor Univ Pr.

— The Southern Baptist Convention & the Judgement of History: The Taint of an Original Sin. LC 95-12894. 198p. (Orig.). 1995. lib. bdg. 47.50 (*0-8191-9934-6*) U Pr of Amer.

— The Southern Baptist Convention & the Judgement of History: The Taint of an Original Sin. 198p. (Orig.). (C). 1995. pap. text 28.00 (*0-8191-9935-4*) U Pr of Amer.

Copeland, Edna D. & Copps, Stephen C. Medications for Attention Disorders & Related Medical Problems. 2nd rev. ed. (Illus.). 406p. 1995. 37.00 (*1-886941-00-9*) Spec Pr FL.

Copeland, Edna D. & Love, Valerie L. Attention, Please! A Comprehensive Guide for Successfully Parenting Children with Attention Disorders & Hyperactivity. 2nd rev. ed. (Illus.). 352p. 1995. 25.00 (*1-886941-02-5*) Spec Pr FL.

— Attention Without Tension: A Teacher's Handbook on Attention Deficit Disorders. 2nd rev. ed. (Illus.). 178p. 1995. pap. 28.00 (*1-886941-01-7*) Spec Pr FL.

Copeland, Edward. 1996 Resident Year Book of Surgery. 5th ed. LC 98-4103. (Illus.). 528p. (C). (gr. 13). 1998. text 67.00 (*0-8151-2952-1*, 31833) Mosby Inc.

— Surgery Two Thousand. (Illus.). 624p. 2000. text 74.00 (*0-8151-1502-4*, 29695) Mosby Inc.

— Women Writing about Money: Women's Fiction in England, 1790-1820. (Studies in Romanticism: No. 9). (Illus.). 309p. (C). 1995. text 64.95 (*0-521-45461-1*) Cambridge U Pr.

Copeland, Edward & McMaster, Juliet, eds. The Cambridge Companion to Jane Austen. (Cambridge Companions to Literature Ser.). 267p. (C). 1997. text 54.95 (*0-521-49517-2*); pap. text 17.95 (*0-521-49867-8*) Cambridge U Pr.

Copeland, Edward M. 1998 Year Book of Surgery. 2nd ed. (Illus.). 576p. (C). (gr. 13). 1998. text 74.00 (*0-8151-9743-8*, 25030) Mosby Inc.

— 1997 Year Book of Surgery. (Illus.). 672p. (C). (gr. 13). 1997. text 74.00 (*0-8151-9742-X*, 25029) Mosby Inc.

Copeland, Edward M., III, jt. auth. see Bland, Kirby I.

Copeland, Elsa, tr. see Hyvrard, Jeanne.

Copeland, Eric. Milton, My Father's Dog. LC 93-61795. (Illus.). 24p. (J). (gr. 1-5). 1994. 13.95 (*0-88776-339-1*) Tundra Bks.

Copeland, Evelyn. But a Brown Bird Sang. 1993. 16.95 (*0-533-10562-5*) Vantage.

Copeland, Evelyn, tr. see Verne, Jules.

Copeland, Fayette. Kendall of the Picayune. LC 96-33330. 384p. 1997. pap. 16.95 (*0-8061-2924-7*) U of Okla Pr.

***Copeland, G. A.** Oraciones con Poder, Vol. 1.Tr. of Prayers That Avail Much. (SPA.). 2000. 8.99 (*0-7899-0539-6*, 550104) Editorial Unilit.

Copeland, G. A., jt. ed. see Johnson-Cartee, K. S.

Copeland, G. E. Prayers That Avail - Fathers Gift. mass mkt. 19.99 (*0-89274-965-2*) Harrison Hse.

— Prayers That Avail - Mothers Gift. mass mkt. 17.99 (*0-89274-840-0*) Harrison Hse.

Copeland, Gail. Spring Winds of Beijing. LC 92-73014. (Illus.). 330p. 1993. 21.95 (*0-944435-20-3*) Glenbridge Pub.

Copeland, Gary A., jt. auth. see Johnson-Cartee, Karen S.

Copeland, Gary W., et al, eds. The Almanac of Oklahoma Politics, 1998. (Illus.). 1997. pap. 17.50 (*0-9662388-0-X*) OK Poli Sci.

C

An Asterisk (*) at the beginning of an entry indicates that the title is appearing for the first time.

Copeland, Gary W. & Patterson, Samuel C., eds. Parliaments in the Modern World: Changing Institutions. LC 94-1743. 192p. (C). 1994. pap. text 20.95 (*0-472-08255-8*, 08255) U of Mich Pr.

Copeland, Germaine. Mastering the Art of Intercessory Prayer. 144p. (Orig.). 1997. pap. 6.99 (*0-89274-988-1*, HH-988) Harrison Hse.

***Copeland, Germaine.** Oraciones Con Ponder. Vol. 2. (SPA.). 2000. pap. 8.99 (*0-7899-0691-0*) Spanish Hse Distributors.

— Prayers That Avail Much. 576p. 1999. 24.99 (*1-57794-263-9*) Harrison Hse.

Copeland, Germaine. Prayers That Avail Much, Vol. 1. 1999. pap. 9.99 (*1-57794-064-4*) Dake Pub.

***Copeland, Germaine.** Prayers That Avail Much, Vol. 1. 2000. pap. 7.99 (*1-57794-282-5*) Harrison Hse.

Copeland, Germaine. Prayers That Avail Much, Vol. 2. 1999. pap. 9.99 (*1-57794-062-8*) Dake Pub.

***Copeland, Germaine.** Prayers That Avail Much, Vol. 2. 2000. pap. 7.99 (*1-57794-283-3*) Harrison Hse.

Copeland, Germaine. Prayers That Avail Much, Vol. 3. 1999. pap. 9.99 (*1-57794-063-6*) Dake Pub.

***Copeland, Germaine.** Prayers That Avail Much, Vol. 3. 2000. pap. 7.99 (*1-57794-284-1*) Harrison Hse.

Copeland, Germaine. Prayers That Avail Much for Men. gif. ed. 1999. 14.99 (*1-57794-182-9*) Harrison Hse.

— Prayers That Avail Much for Mothers. 1998. mass mkt. 10.99 (*1-57794-120-9*) Harrison Hse.

***Copeland, Germaine.** Ptam Comm. 1999. 24.99 (*1-57794-121-7*) Harrison Hse.

Copeland, Germaine, jt. auth. see Word Ministries Staff.

Copeland, Glenn. The Foot Book: Relief for Overused, Abused & Ailing Feet. LC 91-43125. 208p. 1992. pap. 14.95 (*0-471-55840-0*) Wiley.

Copeland, Glenn & Solomon, Stan. The Foot Book: A Complete Guide for Men & Women. 208p. 1997. pap. 5.99 (*0-471-19917-6*) Wiley.

***Copeland, Glenn & Solomon, Stan.** The Foot Doctor: Lifetime Relief for Your Aching Feet. rev. ed. (Illus.). 282p. 2000. pap. 20.00 (*0-7881-9315-5*) DIANE Pub.

Copeland, Gloria. El Amor el Secreto de Su Exito (Love the Secret to Your Success) (SPA.). 24p. 1997. 1.00 (*1-57562-015-4*, 30-0523S) K Copeland Pubns.

— And Jesus Healed Them All. 1997. pap. 3.95 (*1-57562-204-1*) K Copeland Pubns.

— Andar en el Espiritu. Copeland, Kenneth, Publications Staff, tr. (SPA.). 83p. (Orig.). 1986. pap. 5.95 (*0-88114-712-5*) K Copeland Pubns.

***Copeland, Gloria.** Are You Listening? Hearing His Word & Doing His Will. 2000. 19.99 (*1-57794-195-0*) Harrison Hse.

Copeland, Gloria. Are You Ready? 14p. 1995. pap. 1.00 (*0-88114-983-7*) K Copeland Pubns.

— Build Your Financial Foundation. (Orig.). 1997. pap. 1.00 (*1-57562-147-9*, 30-0544) K Copeland Pubns.

— Build Yourself an Ark: A Blueprint for Deliverance from Danger. 60p. 1992. mass mkt. 2.95 (*0-88114-839-3*) K Copeland Pubns.

— Cosecha de Salud - Harvest of Health. (SPA.). 32p. (Orig.). 1996. pap. 1.00 (*1-57562-105-3*, S30-0527) K Copeland Pubns.

— Fight On! 22p. 1996. pap. 1.00 (*1-57562-054-5*) K Copeland Pubns.

— God's Prescription for Divine Health. 79p. (Orig.). 1996. reprint ed. pap. 2.25 (*0-88114-986-1*) K Copeland Pubns.

— God's Success Formula. 14p. 1994. pap. 1.00 (*0-88114-957-8*) K Copeland Pubns.

— God's Will for You. 163p. 1972. pap. 6.95 (*0-938458-10-8*) K Copeland Pubns.

— God's Will for Your Healing. 39p. 1972. pap. 3.95 (*0-938458-09-4*) K Copeland Pubns.

— God's Will Is Prosperity. 109p. 1978. pap. 6.95 (*0-938458-08-6*) K Copeland Pubns.

— God's Will Is the Holy Spirit. 28p. 1990. pap. 1.00 (*0-88114-826-1*) K Copeland Pubns.

— Harvest of Health. 12p. 1992. pap. 1.00 (*0-88114-841-5*) K Copeland Pubns.

— Hidden Treasures: Abundant Life in the Riches of Proverbs. 1998. 14.99 (*1-57794-129-2*) Harrison Hse.

— A Journey of Faith: The First 30 Years. LC 98-102701. 1997. 24.95 (*1-57562-189-4*) K Copeland Pubns.

— Living Contact. LC 97-170884. 131p. (Orig.). 1997. pap. 8.95 (*1-57562-149-5*, 30-0533) K Copeland Pubns.

— Living in Heaven's Blessings Now, 10. 48p. 1999. pap. text 15.00 (*1-57794-161-6*) Harrison Hse.

— Love: The Secret to Your Success. 13p. 1992. pap. 1.00 (*0-88114-798-2*) K Copeland Pubns.

— No Deposit No Return. 15p. 1994. pap. 1.00 (*0-88114-969-1*) K Copeland Pubns.

— Pleasing the Father: Minibook. (Illus.). 25p. (Orig.). 1996. pap. 1.00 (*1-57562-121-5*, 30-0543) K Copeland Pubns.

— The Power to Live a New Life. 15p. 1986. pap. 1.00 (*1-57562-056-1*) K Copeland Pubns.

— Pressing In: It's Worth It All. 29p. 1992. pap. 1.00 (*0-88114-842-3*) K Copeland Pubns.

— This Same Jesus. 32p. 1998. pap. 1.00 (*1-57562-243-2*, 30-0547) K Copeland Pubns.

— The Unbeatable Spirit of Faith. 20p. 1995. pap. 1.00 (*1-57562-014-6*) K Copeland Pubns.

— La Voluntad de Dios Es el Espiritu Santo (God's Will Is the Holy Spirit) (SPA.). 48p. 1997. 1.00 (*1-57562-129-0*, 30-0524S) K Copeland Pubns.

— La Voluntad de Dios es Prosperidad. Copeland, Kenneth, Publications Staff, tr. (SPA.). 123p. (Orig.). 1984. pap. 5.95 (*0-88114-314-6*) K Copeland Pubns.

— La Voluntad de Dios para Usted. Copeland, Kenneth, Publications Staff, tr. (SPA.). 170p. (Orig.). 1985. pap. 5.95 (*0-88114-312-X*) K Copeland Pubns.

— Walk in the Spirit. 90p. 1986. pap. 5.95 (*0-88114-280-8*) K Copeland Pubns.

— Walk with God. 116p. 1995. pap. 6.95 (*0-88114-985-3*) K Copeland Pubns.

— Walk with God & Obedience, 6 tapes, Set. 30p. 1984. 30.00 incl. audio (*0-88114-705-2*, 03-1100) K Copeland Pubns.

— Well Worth the Wait. 15p. 1996. pap. 1.00 (*0-88114-980-2*) K Copeland Pubns.

— Y Jesus Sanaba a Todos. Copeland, Kenneth, Publications Staff, tr. (SPA.). 43p. (Orig.). 1985. pap. 3.95 (*0-88114-315-4*) K Copeland Pubns.

Copeland, Gloria, jt. auth. see Copeland, Kenneth.

***Copeland, Grant.** Acts of Balance: Profits, People & Place. 176p. 2000. pap. 14.95 (*0-86571-410-X*, Pub. by New Soc Pubs) Consort Bk Sales.

Copeland, Helen M. Endangered Speciman & Other Poems from a Lay Naturalist. (Illus.). 60p. (Orig.). 1988. pap. 10.00 (*0-932662-78-1*) St Andrews NC.

Copeland, Herbert F. Classification of Lower Organisms. LC 56-7944. (Illus.). x, 302p. 1956. 27.95 (*0-87015-059-6*) Pacific Bks.

Copeland, Ian C. The Making of the Backward Pupil in Education in England, 1870-1914. Gordon, Peter, ed. LC 98-30483. (Education Ser.). 256p. 1999. 57.50 (*0-7130-0216-6*, Pub. by Woburn Pr); pap. 27.50 (*0-7130-4037-8*, Pub. by Woburn Pr) Intl Spec Bk.

Copeland, Jack. Artificial Intelligence: A Philosophical Introduction. LC 92-44278. 288p. 1993. pap. 25.95 (*0-631-18385-X*) Blackwell Pubs.

Copeland, Jack, ed. Logic & Reality: Essays on the Legacy of Arthur Prior. LC 97-164768. (Illus.). 556p. 1997. text 112.00 (*0-19-824060-0*) OUP.

Copeland, James, jt. auth. see Osborn, Marvin S.

Copeland, Janet H., jt. ed. see Copeland, Peter A.

Copeland, Janet H., ed. see Marek, Don.

Copeland, Janice. Handbook for Health Records in LTC. 259p. (C). 1986. 52.00 (*0-929442-00-8*, 2205pp) Prof Prnting & Pub.

Copeland, Jeffrey S. Speaking of Poets: Interviews with Poets Who Write for Children & Young Adults. 128p. 1993. pap. 12.95 (*0-8141-4622-8*) NCTE.

Copeland, Jeffrey S., et al. Speaking of Poets 2: More Interviews with Poets Who Write for Children & Young Adults. LC 94-47005. 204p. 1995. pap. 15.95 (*0-8141-4620-1*) NCTE.

***Copeland, John.** Retribution. 320p. 2000. 24.95 (*1-929175-10-8*, Corinthian Bks); pap. 19.95 (*1-929175-21-3*, Corinthian Bks) Cote Lit Grp.

Copeland, John, tr. see Montemayor, Carlos.

Copeland, John A. A Study of Daniel. 1973. pap. 6.15 (*0-89137-703-4*) Quality Pubns.

— A Study of the Revelation. unabridged ed. 1971. pap. 4.50 (*0-89137-702-6*, 77026) Quality Pubns.

Copeland, John D. Understanding the Farmers Comprehensive Personal Liability Policy: A Guide for Farmers, Attorneys & Insurance Agents. 150p. 1992. pap. 25.00 (*1-882461-00-2*) Natl Ctr Agricult LR&I.

Copeland, John G., et al. Civilzacion Y Cultura. 6th ed. (SPA.). 288p. (C). 1997. pap. text 35.50 (*0-03-017514-3*) Holt R&W.

— Literature y Arte: Intermediate Spanish. 6th ed. (SPA.). 304p. (C). 1996. pap. text 34.00 (*0-03-017513-5*) Holt R&W.

— Puertas a la Comunicacion: An Activities Manual. 3rd ed. (C). 1990. pap. text 32.25 (*0-07-540846-5*) McGraw.

— Puertas a la Lengua Espanola: An Introductory Course. 1990. teacher ed., student ed. write for info. incl. audio (*0-318-67200-6*) McGraw.

— Puertas a la Lengua Espanola: An Introductory Course. 3rd ed. 1988. pap. text. write for info. (*0-07-540855-4*) McGraw.

— Puertas a la Lengua Espanola: An Introductory Course. 3rd ed. 479p. (C). 1990. pap. 65.63 (*0-07-540845-7*) McGraw.

— Puertas a la Lengua Espanola: An Introductory Course. 3rd ed. (C). 1990. teacher ed. 22.18 (*0-07-540851-1*); pap. text 20.62 (*0-07-540852-X*) McGraw.

— Puertas a la Lengua Espanola: An Introductory Course. 3rd ed. 1990. write for info. (*0-07-909484-8*) McGraw.

— Puertas a la Lengua Espanola: An Introductory Course. 3rd ed. (C). 1990. pap., wbk. ed. 27.50 (*0-07-540848-1*); pap., lab manual ed. 28.13 (*0-07-540849-X*) McGraw.

— Puertas a la Lengua Espanola: An Introductory Course. 3rd ed. (C). 1990. audio 52.19 (*0-07-540850-3*) McGraw.

— Puertas al Mundo Hispanico: A Cultural Reader. 3rd ed. (C). 1990. pap. text 27.25 (*0-07-540847-3*) McGraw.

Copeland, John R., et al. Principles & Practice of Geriatric Psychiatry. LC 92-48920. 1084p. 1994. 575.00 (*0-471-92654-X*, Wiley-Interscience) Wiley.

Copeland, Judith. Modular Crochet: A Revolutionary New Method of Creating Custom-Design Pullovers. LC 78-3704. (Illus.). 192p. 1978. 17.50 (*0-87131-256-5*) M Evans.

Copeland, K. The Laws of Prosperity. 1975. pap. 5.95 (*0-8007-0725-7*) K Copeland Pubns.

— The Miraculous Realm of God's Love. 1987. pap. 5.95 (*0-938458-11-6*) K Copeland Pubns.

***Copeland, Kathy.** Don't Waste Your Time in the Canadian Rockies. 376p. 1998. pap. 16.95 (*0-9698016-4-5*) VWPI.

***Copeland, Kathy & Copeland, Craig.** Don't Waste Your Time in the B. C. Coast Mountains: An Opinionated Hiking Guide to Help You Get the Most from This Magnificent Wilderness. 1999. pap. text 14.95 (*0-9698016-3-7*) VWPI.

Copeland, Kathy & Copeland, Craig. Don't Waste Your Time in the North Cascades: An Opinionated Hiking Guide to Help You Get the Most from This Magnificent Wilderness. LC 96-13488. (Illus.). 256p. (Orig.). 1996. pap. 14.95 (*0-89997-182-2*) Wilderness Pr.

Copeland, Kenneth. La Actitud Triunfadora. Orig. Title: The Winning Attitude. (SPA.). 28p. (Orig.). 1996. pap. 1.00 (*0-88114-996-9*, 30-0031S) K Copeland Pubns.

— Actualmente Estamos en Christo Jesus. Copeland, Kenneth, Publications Staff, tr. (SPA.). 26p. (Orig.). 1985. pap. 1.00 (*0-88114-308-1*) K Copeland Pubns.

— Bienvenido a la Familia. Copeland, Kenneth, Publications Staff, tr. (SPA.). 29p. (Orig.). 1984. pap. 1.00 (*0-88114-304-9*) K Copeland Pubns.

— Una Ceremonia de Matrimonio. Gonzales, Luis, tr. (ENG & SPA.). 13p. 1984. pap. 2.50 (*0-88114-305-7*) K Copeland Pubns.

— A Ceremony of Marriage. 20p. 1978. pap. 2.50 (*0-938458-15-9*) K Copeland Pubns.

— La Decision es Suya. Copeland, Kenneth, Publications Staff, tr. (SPA.). 28p. (Orig.). 1985. pap. 1.00 (*0-88114-303-0*) K Copeland Pubns.

— The Decision Is Yours. 25p. 1981. pap. 1.00 (*0-938458-01-9*) K Copeland Pubns.

***Copeland, Kenneth.** Decision Is Yours, 10 vols. 2000. pap. text 15.00 (*1-57562-127-4*) K Copeland Pubns.

Copeland, Kenneth. Die Entscheidung Liegt Bei Dir. (GER.). 29p. 1981. pap. 0.75 (*0-88114-814-8*) K Copeland Pubns.

— Faith & Patience: The Power Twins. 14p. 1992. pap. 1.00 (*0-88114-835-0*) K Copeland Pubns.

— Family Promises. LC 97-172110. 1997. pap. 6.95 (*1-57562-118-5*) K Copeland Pubns.

— Fasting & Prayer. 22p. 1982. 20.00 incl. audio (*0-938458-18-3*, 01-1000) K Copeland Pubns.

— The Force of Faith. 29p. 1983. pap. 3.95 (*0-938458-14-0*) K Copeland Pubns.

— The Force of Righteousness. 24p. 1984. pap. 3.95 (*0-938458-12-4*) K Copeland Pubns.

— Freedom from Fear. 31p. 1980. pap. 1.00 (*0-938458-05-1*) K Copeland Pubns.

— Frei von Angst. Des Glaubens, Wort, tr. (ENG & GER.). 31p. 1980. pap. 0.75 (*0-88114-811-3*) K Copeland Pubns.

— From Faith to Faith: A Daily Guide to Victory. 384p. 1991. pap. 8.95 (*0-88114-843-1*) K Copeland Pubns.

— La Fuerza de la Fe. Copeland, Kenneth, Publications Staff, tr. (SPA.). 24p. (Orig.). 1984. pap. 3.95 (*0-88114-298-0*) K Copeland Pubns.

— La Fuerza de la Justicia. Copeland, Kenneth, Publications Staff, tr. (SPA.). 24p. (Orig.). 1984. pap. 3.95 (*0-88114-299-9*) K Copeland Pubns.

— Giving & Receiving. 16p. 1986. pap. 1.00 (*0-88114-744-3*) K Copeland Pubns.

— Honor. 144p. 1995. pap. 7.99 (*0-89274-923-7*, HH-923) Harrison Hse.

— How to Build Your Firm Foundation. 19p. 1982. 20.00 incl. audio (*0-938458-17-5*, 020100) K Copeland Pubns.

— How to Conquer Strife. rev. ed. 14p. 1987. pap. 1.00 (*1-57562-103-7*) K Copeland Pubns.

Copeland, Kenneth. How to Discipline Your Flesh. 28p. 1991. pap. 2.95 (*0-88114-830-X*) K Copeland Pubns.

Copeland, Kenneth. How to Receive Communion. 11p. 1987. pap. 1.00 (*0-88114-796-6*) K Copeland Pubns.

— The Image of God in You. 11p. 1989. pap. 1.00 (*0-88114-789-3*) K Copeland Pubns.

— Kenneth Copeland Collection: Songbook. 98p. 1992. pap. 8.98 (*0-88114-954-3*) K Copeland Pubns.

— The Laws of Prosperity. 28p. 1974. pap. 5.95 (*0-88114-952-7*) K Copeland Pubns.

— Libertad del Temor. Copeland, Kenneth, Publications Staff, tr. (SPA.). 30p. (Orig.). 1985. pap. 1.00 (*0-88114-309-X*) K Copeland Pubns.

— Love Never Fails. 24p. 1987. pap. 0.75 (*1-57562-094-4*) K Copeland Pubns.

— Love Never Fails. 12p. 1987. pap. 1.00 (*0-88114-792-3*) K Copeland Pubns.

— Managing God's Mutual Funds: Yours & His - Understanding True Prosperity. LC 97-148010. 192p. 1997. 14.95 (*0-88114-970-5*) K Copeland Pubns.

— A Matter of Choice. 19p. 1994. pap. 1.00 (*0-88114-971-3*) K Copeland Pubns.

— The Mercy of God. 47p. 1986. pap. 3.95 (*0-88114-725-7*) K Copeland Pubns.

— The Miraculous Realm of God's Love. 71p. 1987. pap. 5.95 (*0-88114-784-2*) K Copeland Pubns.

— La Misericordia De Dios. Copeland, Kenneth, Publications Staff, tr. (SPA.). 47p. (Orig.). 1986. pap. 3.95 (*0-88114-726-5*) K Copeland Pubns.

***Copeland, Kenneth.** No Os Entristezcais. (SPA.). 32p. 1999. pap. write for info. (*1-58633-008-X*) Libros Intern.

Copeland, Kenneth. Now Are We in Christ Jesus. 26p. 1980. pap. 1.00 (*0-938458-03-5*) K Copeland Pubns.

— Nuestro Pacto Con Dios. Gonzales, Luis, tr. (ENG & SPA.). 39p. 1984. pap. 2.95 (*0-88114-302-2*) K Copeland Pubns.

— One Nation under God. 1996. 17.95 incl. VHS (*1-57562-128-2*) K Copeland Pubns.

***Copeland, Kenneth.** One Word From God Can Change Your Destiny. (One Word From God Ser.). 1999. pap. 6.99 (*1-57794-147-0*) Harrison Hse.

— One Word From God Can Change Your Family. (One Word From God Ser.). 1999. pap. 6.99 (*1-57794-148-9*) Harrison Hse.

— One Word From God Can Change Your Finances. (One Word From God Ser.). 1999. pap. 6.99 (*1-57794-146-2*) Harrison Hse.

— One Word from God Can Change Your Formula for Success. 144p. 1999. pap. text 6.99 (*1-57794-197-7*) Harrison Hse.

— One Word From God Can Change Your Health. (One Word From God Ser.). 1999. pap. 6.99 (*1-57794-145-4*) Harrison Hse.

— One Word from God Will Change Your Nation. 144p. 1999. pap. text 6.99 (*1-57794-200-0*) Harrison Hse.

— One Word from God Will Change Your Prayer Life. 144p. 1999. pap. text 6.99 (*1-57794-198-5*) Harrison Hse.

— One Word from God Will Change Your Relationships. 144p. 1999. pap. text 6.99 (*1-57794-199-3*) Harrison Hse.

Copeland, Kenneth. Oracion: Su Fundamento Para el Exito. Copeland, Kenneth, Publications Staff, ed. (SPA.). 106p. (Orig.). 1984. pap. 5.95 (*0-88114-311-1*) K Copeland Pubns.

Copeland, Kenneth. Oracion Intercesora, Set. Kenneth Copeland Publications Staff, tr. from ENG. (SPA.). 1984. pap., student ed. 20.00 incl. audio (*0-88114-318-9*) K Copeland Pubns.

Copeland, Kenneth. Our Covenant with God. 32p. 1976. mass mkt. 2.95 (*0-88114-742-7*) K Copeland Pubns.

***Copeland, Kenneth.** Our Covenant with God. 66p. 1999. pap. 4.99 (*1-57562-242-4*) K Copeland Pubns.

Copeland, Kenneth. The Outpouring of the Spirit. 1993. mass mkt. 30.00 incl. audio (*0-88114-288-3*) K Copeland Pubns.

— The Outpouring of the Spirit: The Result of Prayer. 20p. 1983. mass mkt. 3.95 (*0-88114-297-2*) K Copeland Pubns.

***Copeland, Kenneth.** Over the Edge Xtreme Planner for Students. 2000. pap. 9.99 (*1-57794-290-6*) Harrison Hse.

Copeland, Kenneth. El Poder de la Lengua. Copeland, Kenneth, Publications Staff, tr. (SPA.). 32p. (Orig.). 1985. pap. 0.75 (*0-88114-307-3*) K Copeland Pubns.

— El Poder de la Lengua (The Power of the Tongue) (SPA.). 62p. 1996. 1.00 (*0-88114-997-7*, S30-0014) K Copeland Pubns.

— The Power of the Tongue. 1996. pap. text 1.00 (*1-57562-113-4*) K Copeland Pubns.

— The Power to Be Forever Free. 11p. 1987. pap. 1.00 (*1-57562-058-8*) K Copeland Pubns.

— The Power to Be Forever Free. 1996. pap. text 1.00 (*0-88114-787-7*) K Copeland Pubns.

***Copeland, Kenneth.** Prayer: Your Foundation for Success. 1999. pap. 8.99 (*1-57794-155-1*) Harrison Hse.

Copeland, Kenneth. Prayer, Your Foundation for Success. 112p. 1983. pap. 5.95 (*0-88114-704-4*) K Copeland Pubns.

— Prosperity: The Choice Is Yours. 35p. 1985. pap. 3.95 (*0-88114-728-1*) K Copeland Pubns.

— Prosperity Promises. 48p. 1985. pap. 2.50 (*0-88114-731-1*) K Copeland Pubns.

***Copeland, Kenneth.** Protection Promises. 2000. pap. 9.99 (*1-57794-201-9*) Harrison Hse.

Copeland, Kenneth. Pursuit of His Presence. 1998. 19.99 (*1-57794-137-3*) Harrison Hse.

— Pursuit of His Presence Daily Devotional. 1998. 12.99 (*1-57794-139-X*) Harrison Hse.

— Quest for the Second Half. 1999. pap. text 7.99 (*1-57794-150-0*) Harrison Hse.

— Real People. Real Needs. Real Victories. 230p. 1997. pap. 8.95 (*1-57562-112-6*) K Copeland Pubns.

— Rumors of War. 13p. 1991. pap. 1.00 (*0-88114-832-6*) K Copeland Pubns.

— Sensitividad de Corazon. Copeland, Kenneth, Publications Staff, tr. (SPA.). 27p. (Orig.). 1984. pap. 2.50 (*0-88114-722-2*) K Copeland Pubns.

— Sensitivity of Heart. 28p. 1983. pap. 2.50 (*0-88114-711-7*) K Copeland Pubns.

— Six Steps to Excellence in Ministry. 64p. 1987. pap. 4.95 (*1-57562-104-5*) K Copeland Pubns.

— Sorrow Not! Winning over Grief & Sorrow. 18p. 1992. pap. 1.00 (*0-88114-813-X*) K Copeland Pubns.

— The Troublemaker. 33p. 1978. pap. 2.95 (*0-938458-13-2*) K Copeland Pubns.

— Turn Your Hurts into Harvests. 40p. 1998. pap. 15.00 (*1-57562-236-X*, 30-0058) K Copeland Pubns.

— Usted Es Sanado. Copeland, Kenneth, Publications Staff, tr. (SPA.). 18p. (Orig.). 1985. pap. 1.00 (*0-88114-306-5*) K Copeland Pubns.

— Welcome to the Family. 26p. 1979. pap. 1.00 (*0-938458-06-X*) K Copeland Pubns.

— Willkommenin der Familie Gottes. (GER.). 30p. 1970. pap. 0.75 (*0-88114-801-6*) K Copeland Pubns.

— The Winning Attitude. 18p. 1987. pap. 1.00 (*0-88114-791-5*) K Copeland Pubns.

— You Are Healed. 23p. 1979. pap. 1.00 (*0-88114-733-8*) K Copeland Pubns.

— Your Right-Standing with God. 16p. 1983. pap. 1.00 (*0-88114-795-8*) K Copeland Pubns.

***Copeland, Kenneth & Copeland, Gloria.** Crezcamos De Fe En Fe: Una Guia Diaria para la Victoria. (SPA., Illus.). 384p. 1999. 12.99 (*1-58633-000-4*) Libros Intern.

Copeland, Kenneth & Copeland, Gloria. From Faith to Faith: A Daily Guide to Victory/Female. 384p. 1992. 16.95 (*0-88114-833-4*) K Copeland Pubns.

— From Faith to Faith: A Daily Guide to Victory/Male. 384p. 1992. 16.95 (*0-88114-829-6*) K Copeland Pubns.

— Healing Promises. 190p. 1994. pap. 6.95 (*0-88114-949-7*) K Copeland Pubns.

— Over the Edge: Youth Devotional. 1998. pap. 14.99 (*1-57794-138-1*) Harrison Hse.

— Prosperity Promises. expanded ed. 288p. 1997. pap. 6.95 (*1-57562-036-7*) K Copeland Pubns.

Copeland, Kenneth, Editors. How to Discipline Your Flesh. mass mkt. 2.95 (*1-57562-116-9*) K Copeland Pubns.

Copeland, Kenneth Ministries Staff. Baby Praise. LC 97-221538. (Illus.). (J). 1997. 4.95 (*1-57562-192-4*, 30-1202) K Copeland Pubns.

Copeland, Kenneth, Ministries Staff. John G. Lake: His Life, His Sermons, His Boldness of Faith. LC 94-72505. (Illus.). 547p. 1994. pap. 17.95 (*0-88114-962-4*) K Copeland Pubns.

Copeland, Kenneth Ministries Staff. Pursuit of the Enemy. (Superkids Novels Ser.). 1999. pap. text 6.99 (*1-57794-152-7*) Harrison Hse.

An Asterisk (*) at the beginning of an entry indicates that the title is appearing for the first time.

Copeland, Kenneth, Publications Staff. Real People, Real Needs, Real Victories. LC 97-110155. (Illus.). 225p. 1996. pap. write for info. (*1-57562-095-2*) K Copeland Pubns.

Copeland, Kenneth, Publications Staff, ed. see Copeland, Kenneth.

Copeland, Kenneth, Publications Staff, tr. see Copeland, Gloria.

Copeland, Kenneth, Publications Staff, tr. see Copeland, Kenneth.

Copeland, Kim, jt. auth. see Tucker, Susan.

Copeland, L. Exchange Rules & International Finance. (C). 2000. pap. text. write for info. (*0-201-39850-8*) Addison-Wesley.

Copeland, L. O., jt. auth. see McDonald, M. B.

Copeland, Larry D. Textbook of Gynecology. 2nd ed. 1999. text. write for info. (*0-7216-5526-2*, W B Saunders Co) Harcrt Hlth Sci Grp.

Copeland, Larry J. Study Guide for the Textbook of Gynecology. 304p. 1993. pap. text, student ed. 39.95 (*0-7216-3383-8*, W B Saunders Co) Harcrt Hlth Sci Grp.

Copeland, Larry J., ed. Textbook of Gynecology. (Illus.). 1216p. 1993. text 120.00 (*0-7216-3401-X*, W B Saunders Co) Harcrt Hlth Sci Grp.

— Textbook of Gynecology: Incls. Study Guide. (Illus.). 1276p. 1993. text, student ed. write for info. (*0-7216-5581-5*, W B Saunders Co) Harcrt Hlth Sci Grp.

Copeland, Lennie. Happy Hands: A Book-N-Glove Experience. (Illus.). 32p. (J). (gr. k). 1997. pap. text 11.95 (*0-8362-2718-2*) Andrews & McMeel.

— The Lice-Buster Book: What to Do When Your Child Comes Home with Head Lice. (Illus.). 128p. (Orig.). 1996. mass mkt. 8.99 (*0-446-67249-1*, Pub. by Warner Bks) Little.

Copeland, Lennie & Griggs, Lewis. Going International. 304p. 1986. pap. 14.95 (*0-452-25864-2*, Plume) Dutton Plume.

Copeland, Lewis. Popular Quotations for All Uses. 36.95 (*0-89190-474-3*) Amereon Ltd.

— World's Great Speeches. 4th enl. ed. LC 99-32880. 2000. pap. text 15.95 (*0-486-40903-1*) Dover.

Copeland, Lewis, ed. Ten Thousand Jokes, Toasts & Stories. LC 66-737. 1040p. 1965. 24.95 (*0-385-00163-0*) Doubleday.

Copeland, Lewis & Lamm, Lawrence, eds. World's Great Speeches. 3rd rev. ed. 842p. 1972. pap. 14.95 (*0-486-20468-5*) Dover.

Copeland-Lewis, Cynthia. Dilly's Big Sister Diary. LC 97-47431. (Illus.). (J). (gr. 2-4). 1998. lib. bdg. 19.90 (*0-7613-0414-2*) Millbrook Pr.

Copeland, Liza. Just Cruising: Europe to Australia. (Family Travels the World Ser.). (Illus.). 336p. 1993. pap. 16.95 (*0-9697690-0-8*, Pub. by Romany Ent) R Hale & Co.

— Still Cruising: Australia to Asia, Africa & America. (Family Travels the World Ser.). (Illus.). 336p. 1995. pap. 16.95 (*0-9697690-1-6*) R Hale & Co.

Copeland, Liza & Copeland, Andy. Cruising for Cowards: Strategies, Boats & Equipment Preferred by Experienced Cruisers. LC 96-910601. (Illus.). 288p. 1997. pap. 24.95 (*0-9697690-3-2*, Pub. by Romany Ent) R Hale & Co.

Copeland, Lois & Wolfe, Leslie R. Violence Against Women As Bias Motivated Hate Crime: Defining the Issues. (Violence Against Women Ser.). 50p. (Orig.). (C). 1991. pap. 15.00 (*1-877966-05-3*) Ctr Women Policy.

Copeland, Lori. Angelface & Amazing Grace. 1997. mass mkt. 5.99 (*0-449-14886-6*, GM) Fawcett.

— AngelFace & Amazing Grace. 1997. mass mkt. write for info. (*0-614-20503-4*, GM) Fawcett.

— Courtship of Cade Kolby. 1997. mass mkt. 5.99 (*0-380-79156-0*, Avon Bks) Morrow Avon.

***Copeland, Lori.** Courtship of Cade Kolby. LC 98-46991. 1999. 22.95 (*1-56895-627-4*) Wheeler Pub.

Copeland, Lori. Dates & Other Nuts. (Love & Laughter Ser.). 1996. per. 3.50 (*0-373-44002-2*, 1-44002-3) Silhouette.

— Faith. LC 98-23844. (Brides of the West Ser.: No. 1). 350p. 1998. pap. 9.99 (*0-8423-0267-0*) Tyndale Hse.

— Fudgeballs & Other Sweets. (Love & Laughter Ser.). 1998. per. 3.50 (*0-373-44041-3*, 1-44041-1) Harlequin Bks.

***Copeland, Lori.** Glory No. 4: Brides of the West. 2000. pap. 9.99 (*0-8423-3749-0*) Tyndale Hse.

— Hope, Vol. 3. LC 99-34162. (Brides of the West Ser.). 1999. pap. 9.99 (*0-8423-0269-7*) Tyndale Hse.

Copeland, Lori. June. LC 98-46117. (Brides of the West Ser.: Bk. 2). 259p. 1999. pap. 9.99 (*0-8423-0268-9*) Tyndale Hse.

***Copeland, Lori.** Marrying Walker McKay. 384p. 2000. mass mkt. 5.99 (*0-380-80249-X*, Avon Bks) Morrow Avon.

Copeland, Lori. Out of Control - A Winning Combination, 2 bks. in 1. 368p. 1994. mass mkt. 4.99 (*0-505-51951-8*, Love Spell) Dorchester Pub Co.

— Promise Me Today. large type ed. LC 93-17004. 401p. 1993. lib. bdg. 17.95 (*1-56054-735-9*) Thorndike Pr.

— Promise Me Tomorrow. large type ed. LC 94-599. (Orig.). 1994. pap. text 22.95 (*1-56895-064-0*) Wheeler Pub.

— With This Ring. LC 97-49337. 1998. 9.99 (*0-8423-7822-7*) Tyndale Hse.

***Copeland, Lori.** With This Ring: A Quartet of Charming Stories about Four Very Special Weddings. LC 98-14362. 1999. 26.95 (*0-7862-1921-1*) Thorndike Pr.

***Copeland, Lori & Raye, Kimberly.** Fruitcakes & Other Leftovers/Christmas, Texas Style, No. 15. (Duets 2-in-1 Ser.). 1999. mass mkt. 5.99 (*0-373-44081-2*) Harlequin Bks.

Copeland, Lori, et al. Avon Books Presents: Timeless Love. 384p. (Orig.). 1993. mass mkt. 4.99 (*0-380-76853-4*, Avon Bks) Morrow Avon.

Copeland, Lorraine. Deeds of Darkness. LC 98-90299. 1998. pap. 12.95 (*0-533-12760-2*) Vantage.

Copeland, M. J. Early Silurian Ostracodes from Southeastern Quebec & Northern New Brunswick. (Geological Survey of Canada Bulletin Ser.). (Illus.). 75p. (Orig.). 1993. pap. 11.05 (*0-660-15127-8*, Pub. by Canadian Govt Pub) Accents Pubns.

Copeland, M. J. & Bolton, Thomas E. Fossils of Ontario Pt. 3: The Eurypterids & Phyllocarids. (Illus.). 48p. pap. 16.00 (*0-88854-314-X*) Brill Academic Pubs.

Copeland, M. Shawn & Fiorenza, Elisabeth S., eds. Violence Against Women - Concilium. LC 94-213252. 1994. pap. 15.00 (*0-88344-876-9*) Orbis Bks.

Copeland, M. Shawn, jt. ed. see Fiorenza, Elisabeth S.

Copeland, Marion W. Charles Alexander Eastman (Ohiyesa) LC 78-52562. (Western Writers Ser.: No. 33). 43p. 1978. pap. 4.95 (*0-88430-057-9*) Boise St U W Writ Ser.

Copeland, Mark. After This Manner Pray. LC 92-70135. 227p. (Orig.). 1992. pap. 7.99 (*0-88270-653-5*) Bridge-Logos.

Copeland, Mary E. The Depression Workbook: A Guide for Living with Depression & Manic Depression. LC 92-81725. (Illus.). 320p. 1992. pap. 18.95 (*1-879237-32-6*) New Harbinger.

— Living Without Depression & Manic Depression: A Workbook for Maintaining Mood Stability. LC 94-67047. 288p. (Orig.). 1994. pap. 18.95 (*1-879237-74-1*) New Harbinger.

— Winning Against Relapse: A Workbook of Action Plans for Recurring Health & Emotional Problems. LC 98-68745. 176p. 1999. pap. 14.95 (*1-57224-130-6*) New Harbinger.

— The Worry Control Workbook. 208p. 1998. pap. 15.95 (*1-57224-120-9*) New Harbinger.

Copeland, Mary E., jt. auth. see Starlanyl, Devin J.

***Copeland, Mary Ellen.** The Loneliness Workbook: A Guide to Developing & Maintaining Lasting Connections. (Illus.). 170p. 2000. pap. 14.95 (*1-57224-203-5*) New Harbinger.

***Copeland, Mary Ellen & Harris, Maxine.** Healing the Trauma of Abuse: A Woman's Workbook. 390p. 2000. pap. 19.95 (*1-57224-199-3*) New Harbinger.

Copeland, Melvin T. The Cotton Manufacturing Industry of the United States. LC 66-23981. (Library of Early American Business & Industry: Vol. XVII). xii, 415p. 1966. reprint ed. lib. bdg. 49.50 (*0-678-00196-0*) Kelley.

— Principles of Merchandising. Assael, Henry, ed. LC 78-277. (Century of Marketing Ser.). 1979. reprint ed. lib. bdg. 33.95 (*0-405-11182-7*) Ayer.

Copeland, Michael, jt. auth. see Schuster, Camille.

Copeland, Morris A. Concerning a New Federal Financial Statement. (Technical Papers: No. 5). 71p. 1947. reprint ed. 20.00 (*0-87014-450-2*) Natl Bur Econ Res.

— Fact & Theory in Economics. Morse, Chandler, ed. LC 73-8564. 347p. 1973. reprint ed. lib. bdg. 89.50 (*0-8371-6965-8*, COFA, Greenwood Pr) Greenwood.

— A Study of Moneyflows in the United States. 1976. 33.95 (*0-405-07586-3*, 16432) Ayer.

— A Study of Moneyflows in the United States. (General Ser.: No. 54). 620p. 1952. reprint ed. 160.00 (*0-87014-053-1*) Natl Bur Econ Res.

— Toward Full Employment in Our Free Enterprise Economy. LC 66-16972. (Moorhouse I.X. Millar Lecture Ser.: No. 7). 96p. reprint ed. pap. 30.00 (*0-7837-0441-0*, 204076400018) Bks Demand.

— Trends in Government Financing. LC 75-19710. (National Bureau of Economic Research Ser.). (Illus.). 1975. reprint ed. 20.95 (*0-405-07590-1*) Ayer.

— Trends in Government Financing. (Studies in Capital Formation & Financing: No. 7). 236p. 1961. reprint ed. 61.40 (*0-87014-105-8*) Natl Bur Econ Res.

Copeland, Nancy, ed. see Centlivre, Susanna.

Copeland, Nichlaus, ed. see Swift, Duncan.

Copeland, Nicklaus, ed. see Swift, Duncan.

Copeland, Ola, ed. Black Families in Cherokee County South Carolina, As Taken from 1910-1920 Federal Census. rev. ed. LC 92-47427. 1993. pap. 25.00 (*0-87152-465-1*) Reprint.

***Copeland, P.** Historic North American Forts. 2000. pap. 2.95 (*0-486-41036-6*) Dover.

Copeland, P. Mammals, 10 bks., Set. (Smithsonian Coloring Bks.). (Illus.). 32p. (J). (ps-8). 1984. pap. 29.50 (*0-87474-335-4*) Smithsonian.

— Story of the American Revolution. 1988. text 2.95 (*0-486-25648-0*) Dover.

***Copeland, P.** Story of the Underground Railroad. 2000. pap. 2.95 (*0-486-41158-3*) Dover.

Copeland, P. A. Pacific Electric in Color, Vol. 1. LC 97-73625. (Illus.). 128p. 1997. 49.95 (*1-878887-88-2*) Morning NJ.

***Copeland, P. A.** Pacific Electric in Color, Vol. 2. (Illus.). 128p. 1999. 54.95 (*1-58248-024-9*) Morning NJ.

Copeland, Pamela C. & MacMaster, Richard K. The Five George Masons: Patriots & Planters of Virginia & Maryland. LC 75-8565. 358p. reprint ed. pap. 111.00 (*0-608-16961-7*, 202772700056) Bks Demand.

Copeland, Pamela C. & Macmaster, Richard K. The Five George Masons: Patriots & Planters of Virginia & Maryland. viii, 341p. 1989. reprint ed. 22.95 (*1-884085-03-2*) Bd Regents.

Copeland, Paul, et al. DeBriefing the Rose. rev. ed. 112p. 1976. pap. 2.95 (*0-88784-611-4*) Genl Dist Srvs.

Copeland, Paul W. The Land & People of Jordan. rev. ed. LC 72-5362. (Portraits of the Nations Ser.). (Illus.). (J). (gr. 6 up). 1972. 11.74 (*0-397-31403-5*) HarpC Child Bks.

— The Land & People of Syria. rev. ed. LC 77-37732. (Portraits of the Nations Ser.). (Illus.). (J). (gr. 5-9). 1972. lib. bdg. 11.89 (*0-397-31537-6*) HarpC Child Bks.

Copeland, Peter A. & Copeland, Janet H., eds. The Indian Splint Manufacturing Company 1909 & 1910-11 Catalogs. (Illus.). 88p. 1994. pap. 19.95 (*0-9638771-1-9*) Parchment NJ.

— 1912 Quaint Furniture Catalog. (Illus.). 96p. (Orig.). 1993. pap. 23.50 (*0-9638771-0-0*) Parchment NJ.

Copeland, Peter A., ed. see Marek, Don.

Copeland, Peter F. Civil War Coloring Book. (Illus.). (YA). (gr. 7-10). 1991. pap. 2.95 (*0-486-26532-3*) Dover.

— Everyday Dress of the American Colonial Period Coloring Book. (Illus.). (J). (gr. k-3). 1975. pap. 2.95 (*0-486-23109-7*) Dover.

— Exploration of North America Coloring Book. 1992. text 2.95 (*0-486-27123-4*) Dover.

— From Antietam to Gettysburg Book. 1983. pap. 2.95 (*0-486-24476-8*) Dover.

— Indian Tribes of North America Coloring Book. (Illus.). (J). (gr. 4-7). 1990. pap. 2.95 (*0-486-26303-7*) Dover.

— North American Indian Crafts. (J). (gr. 1-5). 1996. pap. 2.95 (*0-486-29283-5*) Dover.

— Pirates & Buccaneers Coloring Book. (Illus.). (J). (gr. k-3). 1977. pap. 2.95 (*0-486-23393-6*) Dover.

— Sea Monsters Coloring Book. 1999. pap. text 2.95 (*0-486-40562-1*) Dover.

— Shipwrecks & Sunken Treasures Coloring Book. (Illus.). (J). (gr. k-3). 1992. pap. 2.95 (*0-486-27286-9*) Dover.

— Southeast Indians Coloring Book. (Illus.). 44p. (J). 1996. pap. 2.95 (*0-486-29164-2*) Dover.

— Story of the California Gold Rush Coloring Book, Vol. 181. (Illus.). (J). (gr. k-3). 1988. pap. 2.95 (*0-486-25814-9*) Dover.

— Working Dress in Colonial & Revolutionary America. 58. LC 76-15309. (Contributions in American History Ser.: No. 58). (Illus.). 224p. 1977. 55.00 (*0-8371-9033-9*, COD/, Greenwood Pr) Greenwood.

Copeland, Peter F., jt. auth. see Hamer, Dean.

Copeland, R. Rhetoric, Hermeneutics & Translation in the Middle Ages: Academic Traditions & Vernacular Texts. 309p. 1995. pap. text 24.95 (*0-521-48365-4*) Cambridge U Pr.

Copeland, Rachel. Sexually Fulfilled Man. 1983. pap. 5.00 (*0-87980-403-3*) Wilshire.

— Sexually Fulfilled Woman. 1983. pap. 5.00 (*0-87980-402-5*) Wilshire.

Copeland, Rebecca, tr. & intro. see Chiyo, Uno.

***Copeland, Rebecca L.** Lost Leaves: Women Writers of Meiji Japan. LC 99-58864. (Illus.). 320p. 2000. text 49.00 (*0-8248-2229-3*); pap. text 24.95 (*0-8248-2291-9*) UH Pr.

Copeland, Rebecca L. The Sound of the Wind: The Life & Works of Uno Chiyo. LC 91-48130. (Illus.). 256p. 1992. text 23.00 (*0-8248-1409-6*) UH Pr.

Copeland, Reid. Building Service Management Program Vol. 3: Motivation & Training. vii, 163p. 1995. pap. 50.00 (*1-892725-20-7*, CBSMP3) Building Serv.

Copeland, Reid, ed. Building Service Management Program Vol. 1: Accident Management - Trainer's Manual. i, 44p. 1995. 20.00 (*1-892725-17-7*, BSMP1T) Building Serv.

— Building Service Management Program Vol. 1: Account Management. vii, 193p. 1995. pap. 50.00 (*1-892725-16-9*, CBSMP1) Building Serv.

— Building Service Management Program Vol. 2: Hiring & Firing. vii, 172p. 1995. pap. 50.00 (*1-892725-18-5*, CBSMP2) Building Serv.

— Building Service Management Program Vol. 2: Hiring & Firing - Trainer's Manual. i, 47p. 1996. 20.00 (*1-892725-19-3*, RSMP2T) Building Serv.

— Building Service Management Program Vol. 3: Motivation & Training - Trainer's Manual. i, 35p. 1995. 20.00 (*1-892725-21-5*, BSMP3T) Building Serv.

— Building Service Management Program Vol. 3: Personnel Policies - Trainer's Manual. i, 28p. 1995. 20.00 (*1-892725-23-1*, BSMP4T) Building Serv.

— Building Service Management Program Vol. 4: Personnel Policies. vii, 156p. 1995. pap. 50.00 (*1-892725-22-3*, CBSMP4) Building Serv.

— Building Service Management Program Vol. 5: Safety & Security. vii, 156p. 1995. pap. 50.00 (*1-892725-24-X*, CMSMP5) Building Serv.

— Building Service Management Program Vol. 5: Safety & Security - Trainer's Manual. i, 31p. 1995. pap. 20.00 (*1-892725-25-8*, BSMP5T) Building Serv.

Copeland, Richard. Piagetian Activities: A Diagnostic & Developmental Approach. 225p. 1988. spiral bd. 35.00 (*0-930599-17-9*) Thinking Pubns.

Copeland, Rita, ed. Criticism & Dissent in the Middle Ages. (Illus.). 343p. (C). 1996. text 64.95 (*0-521-45315-1*) Cambridge U Pr.

Copeland, Rita, et al, eds. New Medieval Literatures, Vol. II. (Illus.). 290p. 1998. text 82.00 (*0-19-818476-X*) OUP.

Copeland, Robert. Blue & White Transfer-Printed Pottery. (C). 1989. pap. 6.25 (*0-85263-620-2*, Pub. by Shire Pubns) St Mut.

— Spode. LC 98-184216. (Illus.). 40p. 1998. pap. 25.00 (*0-7478-0364-1*, Pub. by Shire Pubns) Parkwest Pubns.

***Copeland, Robert.** Spode's Willow Pattern: And Other Designs after the Chinese. 3rd ed. (Illus.). 2000. 60.00 (*0-289-80177-X*) SVista Bks.

Copeland, Robert. Wedgwood Ware. (Illus.). 32p. 1995. pap. 25.00 (*0-7478-0296-3*, Pub. by Shire Pubns) Parkwest Pubns.

Copeland, Robert A. Enzymes: A Practical Introduction to Structure, Mechanism, & Data Analysis. (Illus.). xv, 306p. 1996. 59.95 (*1-56081-903-0*, Wiley-VCH) Wiley.

***Copeland, Robert A.** Enzymes: A Practical Introduction to Structure, Mechanism & Data Analysis. 2nd ed. LC 99-50087. 400p. 2000. text 99.95 (*0-471-35929-7*, Wiley-VCH) Wiley.

Copeland, Robert M. Isaac Baker Woodbury: The Life & Works of an American Musical Populist. LC 95-24543. (Composers of North America Ser.). 298p. 1995. 41.50 (*0-8108-3060-4*) Scarecrow.

— Spare No Exertions: One Hundred Seventy-Five Years of the Reformed Presbyterian Theological Seminary. LC 86-60501. (Illus.). 144p. 1986. 5.00 (*0-9616417-0-3*) Ref Presby Theo.

Copeland, Roger & Cohen, Marshall. What Is Dance? Readings in Theory & Criticism. (Illus.). 600p. 1983. pap. text 18.95 (*0-19-503197-0*) OUP.

Copeland, Roger & Cohen, Marshall, eds. What Is Dance? Readings in Theory & Criticism. (Illus.). 582p. 1998. reprint ed. pap. text 18.00 (*0-7881-5612-8*) DIANE Pub.

Copeland, Ronald M. & Ingram, Robert W. Municipal Financial Reporting & Disclosure Quality. LC 82-11580. (Illus.). 156p. 1983. pap. text. write for info. (*0-201-10197-1*) Addison-Wesley.

Copeland, Ronald M., jt. auth. see Ingram, Robert W.

Copeland, Sarah. Dreamers in Time. (Black Lace Ser.). 288p. (Orig.). 1996. mass mkt. 5.95 (*0-352-33064-3*, Pub. by Virgin Bks) London Brdge.

Copeland, Sheila. Chocolate Star. LC 97-1158. 1997. text 23.95 (*0-312-15493-3*) St Martin.

Copeland, Stephen. Operative Shoulder Surgery. (Illus.). 1995. text 150.00 (*0-443-04640-9*) Church.

***Copeland, Sue M. & Hamilton, John A.** Hands-on Dog Care: The Complete Book of Canine First Aid. (Illus.). 400p. 2000. pap. 34.95 (*0-944875-68-8*, Pub. by Doral Pub) Natl Bk Netwk.

Copeland, Sue M., ed. see Hayes, Karen E.

Copeland, Thomas. Financial Theory & Corporate Policy. 3rd ed. 240p. (C). 1988. pap. text, student ed. 30.00 (*0-201-10649-3*) Addison-Wesley.

Copeland, Thomas, ed. Women in History, Literature & the Arts: A Festschrift for Hilegard Schnuttgen in Honor of Her Thirty Years of Outstanding Service at Youngstown State University. 420p. (Orig.). (C). 1989. pap. 19.95 (*0-9623146-1-7*) Youngstown State Univ.

Copeland, Thomas E. Financial Theory. 4th ed. (C). 2000. text. write for info. (*0-201-53892-X*) Addison-Wesley.

— Financial Theory & Corporate Policy: Student Solutions Manual. 4th ed. (C). 2000. pap. text. write for info. (*0-201-58658-4*) Addison-Wesley.

Copeland, Thomas E. & Weston, J. Fred. Financial Theory & Corporate Policy. 2nd ed. LC 82-11662. (Illus.). 704p. 1983. student ed. write for info. (*0-201-10292-7*); text 43.25 (*0-201-10291-9*) Addison-Wesley.

— Financial Theory & Corporate Policy. 3rd ed. LC 87-12595. (Illus.). 946p. (C). 1988. 95.00 (*0-201-10648-5*) Addison-Wesley.

Copeland, Thomas W. Our Eminent Friend Edmund Burke, Six Essays. LC 76-104217. 251p. 1970. reprint ed. lib. bdg. 49.50 (*0-8371-3334-3*, COEB, Greenwood Pr) Greenwood.

Copeland, Tim. Ancient Greece. LC 98-142989. (Primary History Ser.). (Illus.). 49p. (C). 1997. pap. 9.95 (*0-521-55808-5*) Cambridge U Pr.

Copeland, Tom. The Basic Guide to Family Child Care Record Keeping. 5th ed. LC 95-24577. 1995. pap. 9.95 (*1-884834-06-X*, 1005) Redleaf Pr.

— Centralia Tragedy, 1919: Elmer Smith & the Wobblies. LC 93-13453. (Illus.). 256p. (C). 1993. pap. 17.50 (*0-295-97274-2*) U of Wash Pr.

— Family Child Care Contracts & Policies: How to Be Businesslike in a Caring Profession. LC 91-33658. (Illus.). (Orig.). 1991. pap. 9.95 (*0-934140-70-7*, 1076) Redleaf Pr.

***Copeland, Tom.** Family Child Care Inventory-Keeper: The Complete Log for Depreciating & Insuring Your Property. 1999. pap. 7.95 (*1-884834-76-0*) Redleaf Pr.

— Family Child Care Marketing Guide: How to Build Enrollment & Promote Your Business as a Child Care Professional. (Illus.). 120p. 1999. pap. 12.95 (*1-884834-75-2*, 107201, Pub. by Redleaf Pr) Gryphon Hse.

Copeland, Tom. Teaching Family Child Care Record Keeping & Tax Preparation: A Curriculum for Trainers. 1997. pap. text 25.95 (*0-934140-91-X*) Redleaf Pr.

***Copeland, Tom.** Teaching Family Child Care Record Keeping & Tax Preparation: A Curriculum for Trainers. 2nd ed. 1999. pap. text 25.95 (*1-884834-63-9*) Redleaf Pr.

Copeland, Tom. Valuation: Measuring & Managing the Value of Companies. 2nd ed. 1994. 99.95 (*0-471-01313-7*) Wiley.

Copeland, Tom, et al. Valuation: Measuring & Managing the Value of Companies. 2nd ed. (Professional Banking & Finance Ser.). 576p. 1994. 69.95 (*0-471-00993-8*); text 169.95 incl. disk (*0-471-00994-6*) Wiley.

— Valuation: Measuring & Managing the Value of Companies. 2nd rev. ed. LC 94-8304. 576p. 1995. pap. 69.95 (*0-471-08627-4*) Wiley.

***Copeland, Valire Carr, et al, compiled by.** Approaches to Teaching Health Care in Social Work: A Compendium of Model Syllabi. (Teaching Social Work Ser.). 149p. 1999. pap. text 14.00 (*0-87293-068-8*) Coun Soc Wk Ed.

Copeland, Vince. The Built-in U. S. War Drive. 106p. 1980. 4.00 (*0-89567-038-0*) World View Forum.

— Expanding Empire. 68p. 1972. pap. 3.00 (*0-89567-001-1*) World View Forum.

— Lenin: Thinker, Fighter. 26p. 1989. pap. 0.50 (*0-89567-095-X*) World View Forum.

***Copeland, Vincent.** Market Elections: How Democracy Serves the Rich. LC 99-53590. 2000. write for info. (*0-89567-134-4*) World View Forum.

Copeland, W. J., et al, eds. Library of Anglo-Catholic Theology, 18 titles in 81 vols., Set. reprint ed. write for info. (*0-404-52010-3*) AMS Pr.

C

An Asterisk (*) at the beginning of an entry indicates that the title is appearing for the first time.

Copeland, Warren R. And the Poor Get Welfare: The Ethics of Poverty in the U. S. Matthews, Rex, ed. LC 94-9873. (Churches Center for Theology & Public Policy Ser.). 224p. (Orig.). 1994. pap. 14.95 (*0-687-01386-0*) Abingdon.

Copeland, William D. Absolutely Zero Loss. v, 324p. 1997. 40.00 (*0-9657659-4-6*) Absolutely Zero.

— Private Investigator: How to Be Successful. v, 220p. 1997. 40.00 (*0-9657659-9-7*) Absolutely Zero.

Copeley, William. New Hampshire Family Records. 834p. (Orig.). 1995. pap. text 50.00 (*0-7884-0068-1*) Heritage Bk.

Copelin, David. Practical Playwriting. LC 98-36275. 204p. 1998. pap. 12.95 (*0-87116-185-0*) Writer.

***Copella, Sue.** State & County Detailed Population Estimates: Pennsylvania 1998. Sweigart, Wendy, ed. (Illus.). 102p. 2000. pap. 30.00 (*1-58036-140-4*) Penn State Data Ctr.

Copella, Sue, jt. auth. see Lichter, Don.

Copella, Susan. Detailed County Population Projections: Pennsylvania, 1990-2020. Shoop, Diane, ed. (Illus.). 282p. 1998. pap. 35.00 (*1-58036-061-0*) Penn State Data Ctr.

***Copello, Richard J.** American Car Haulers. LC 99-54249. (Crestline Ser.). (Illus.). 224p. 2000. pap. 24.95 (*0-7603-0694-X*, 129827AP, Pub. by MBI Pubg) Motorbooks Intl.

Copelman, Dina. London's Women Teachers: Gender, Class & Feminism 1870-1930. LC 95-32403. 312p. (C). 1996. 75.00 (*0-415-01312-7*) Routledge.

Copelon, Dianne, ed. see Glueck, Grace, et al.

Copely, Ursula E., ed. Directory of Homosexual Organizations & Publications: 1985-1986. 7th ed. 100p. (Orig.). pap. 6.00 (*0-686-26160-7*) Homosexual Info.

Copeman, Geoff D. Bomber Squadrons at War: Nos. 57 & 630 Squadrons. LC 98-175325. (Illus.). 160p. 1998. 34.95 (*0-7509-1710-5*, Pub. by Sutton Pub Ltd) Intl Pubs Mktg.

Copeman, Gwendolyn. The Girls In Greece. unabridged ed. 125p. 1998. pap. 11.95 (*1-892896-30-3*) Buy Books.

Copeman, Harold. The Pocket Singing in Latin. (C). 1988. spiral bd. 30.00 (*0-9515798-1-9*, Pub. by H Copeman) St Mut.

— Singing in Latin. (C). 1988. 65.00 (*0-9515798-2-7*, Pub. by H Copeman) St Mut.

— Singing the Meaning. 200p. 1996. pap. 39.95 (*0-9515798-6-X*, Pub. by H Copeman) St Mut.

Copeman, June. Nutritional Care for Older People: A Handbook. 160p. pap. 45.00 (*0-86242-284-1*, Pub. by Age Concern Eng) St Mut.

Copeman, June, jt. auth. see Webb, Geoffrey P.

***Copen, Lynn M.** Preparing Children for Court: A Practitioner's Guide. LC 00-8184. (Interpersonal Violence Ser.). 2000. pap. write for info. (*0-7619-2182-6*) Sage.

Copen, Lynn M. & Pucci, Linda. Getting Ready for Court: A Book for Children. (Criminal Court Edition Ser.). (Illus.). 22p. (Orig.). (J). (ps-6). 1991. reprint ed. pap., student ed. 3.50 (*0-9647796-0-9*) Kids Kourt Pubns.

Copen, Lynn M. & Pucci, Linda M. Getting Ready for Court, a Book for Children: Criminal Court & Civil Court Editions, 2 vols., Set. (Illus.). (J). (gr. k-6). 1995. pap., wbk. ed. 7.00 (*0-9647796-2-5*) Kids Kourt Pubns.

Copen, Lynn M., et al. Getting Ready for Court: A Book for Children. large type ed. (Civil Court Edition Ser.). (Illus.). 21p. (Orig.). (J). (ps-6). 1995. pap., student ed. 3.50 (*0-9647796-1-7*) Kids Kourt Pubns.

Copen, Lynn M., jt. auth. see Pucci, Linda M.

Copenhagen University, Center for Research in the. Literacy & Society. Schousboe, Karen & Larsen, M. T., eds. 248p. (Orig.). 1989. pap. 87.50 (*87-500-2784-0*) Coronet Bks.

Copenhaver, Brian. Symphorien Champier & the Reception of the Occultist Tradition in Renaissance France. 1978. text 102.35 (*90-279-7647-3*) Mouton.

Copenhaver, Brian P. Renaissance Philosophy. (History of Western Philosophy Ser.: No. 3). (Illus.). 464p. 1992. pap. 21.00 (*0-19-289184-7*) OUP.

Copenhaver, Brian P., ed. Hermetica: The Greek Corpus Hermeticum & the Latin Asclepius in a New English Translation with Notes & Introduction. 404p. (C). 1995. pap. 19.95 (*0-521-42543-3*) Cambridge U Pr.

Copenhaver, Carl. Intelligent Choices in Mutual Funds: Risk & Reward, 1. 1996. 24.95 (*0-9654547-8-9*) P & C Pubs.

Copenhaver, Howard. Copenhaver Country. (Montana Legacy Ser.: No. 1). (Illus.). 160p. 1996. 17.95 (*0-912299-65-7*); pap. 12.95 (*0-912299-66-5*) Stoneydale Pr Pub.

— More Tracks: 78 Years of Mountains, People & Happiness. (Illus.). 1991. pap. 13.95 (*0-912299-50-9*) Stoneydale Pr Pub.

— More Tracks: 78 Years of Mountains, People & Happiness. (Illus.). 1992. 18.95 (*0-912299-49-5*) Stoneydale Pr Pub.

— They Left Their Tracks. (Illus.). 190p. 1990. pap. text 13.95 (*0-912299-46-0*) Stoneydale Pr Pub.

— They Left Their Tracks: Recollections of 60 Years As a Bob Marshall Wilderness Outfitter. (Illus.). 190p. 1990. 18.95 (*0-912299-45-2*) Stoneydale Pr Pub.

Copenhaver, John D. Prayerful Responsibility: Prayer & Social Responsibility in the Religious Thought of Douglas Steere. 216p. (Orig.). (C). 1992. lib. bdg. 44.00 (*0-8191-8530-2*) U Pr of Amer.

Copenhaver, Martin B. To Begin at the Beginning: An Introduction to the Christian Faith. LC 94-3891. 312p. (Orig.). 1994. pap. 12.95 (*0-8298-0992-9*) Pilgrim OH.

Copenhaver, Martin B., et al. Good News in Exile. LC 98-49967. 128p. 1999. pap. 12.00 (*0-8028-4604-1*) Eerdmans.

***Coper, Jennifer I., et al.** Reengineering Verbal Orders: New Team-Based Strategies. (Illus.). 96p. 1999. pap. text 87.00 (*1-57839-074-5*) Opus Communs.

Coper, M. The Franklin Dam Case. 260p. 1983. pap. 29.00 (*0-409-49431-3*, AT, MICHIE) LEXIS Pub.

— Freedom of Interstate Trade. 1983. 76.00 (*0-409-49180-2*, AT, MICHIE) LEXIS Pub.

Coper, Michael & Williams, George. Power, Parliament & the People. 223p. 1997. pap. 29.00 (*1-86287-247-3*, Pub. by Federation Pr) Gaunt.

Coper, Michael & Williams, George, eds. How Many Cheers for Engineers. LC 97-179784. 159p. 1997. pap. 44.00 (*1-86287-228-7*, Pub. by Federation Pr) Gaunt.

— Justice Lionel Murphy: Influential or Merely Prescient? 293p. 1997. 64.00 (*1-86287-262-7*, Pub. by Federation Pr) Gaunt.

Copernicus, Nicolaus. On the Revolutions. LC 92-16304. (Foundations of Natural History Ser.). (Illus.). 475p. reprint ed. pap. 147.30 (*0-608-06276-6*, 206660500008) Bks Demand.

— On the Revolutions of Heavenly Spheres. Wallis, Charles G., tr. LC 95-35654. (Great Minds Ser.). 444p. 1995. pap. 8.95 (*1-57392-035-5*) Prometheus Bks.

Copertino, John. New York Canudo on Criminal Law. annuals 1000p. ring bd. 44.95 (*0-87526-201-5*) Gould.

Copes, Lawrence E. Investigating Algebra: A Novel Approach to Abstract Algebra, Preliminary Edition. 748p. (C). 1998. pap. text 55.00 (*0-201-32584-5*) Addison-Wesley.

Copes, Wayne, et al. Graph Theory: Euler's Rich Legacy. (Contemporary Applied Mathematics Ser.). (Illus.). 78p. (Orig.). (YA). (gr. 7 up). 1987. pap. text 11.95 (*0-939765-09-8*, G106) Janson Pubns.

***Copestake, Ann.** Implementing Typed Feature Structure Grammars. (Lecture Notes Ser.: Vol. 110). 200p. (C). 2000. 59.95 (*1-57586-261-1*); pap. 22.95 (*1-57586-260-3*) CSLI.

Copestake, James, jt. auth. see Moris, Jon.

Copestake, James G., jt. ed. see Wellard, Kate.

Copestick, Joanna. The Family Home: Relaxed, Informal Living for All Ages. LC 98-7288. 256p. 1998. 40.00 (*1-55670-851-3*) Stewart Tabori & Chang.

Copestick, Joanna, jt. auth. see Wilhide, Elizabeth.

Copet-Rougier, E., jt. auth. see Heritier-Auge, F.

Copet-Rougier, Elisabeth, jt. auth. see Hiritier-Augi, Frangoise.

Copher, Charles B. Black Biblical Studies: An Anthology of Charles B. Copher. LC 92-43566. (Biblical & Theological Issues on the Black Presence in the Bible Ser.). (Illus.). 150p. (Orig.). 1993. pap. 14.95 (*0-933176-38-4*) Black Light Fellow.

Copi. Et Moi, Pourquoi J'ai Pas une Banane. (FRE.). 1978. pap. 10.95 (*0-7859-1868-X*, 2070370089) Fr & Eur.

— Introduction to Logic. 10th ed. 264p. (C). 1997. pap. text, student ed. 19.60 (*0-13-887720-3*) P-H.

Copi, Irving & Burgess-Jackson, Keith. Informal Logic. 3rd ed. (C). 1996. pap. text 35.00 (*0-02-325061-5*, Macmillan Coll) P-H.

Copi, Irving M. An Introduction to Logic. 10th ed. 1998. text 51.33 (*0-13-010202-4*) P-H.

— Symbolic Logic. 5th ed. 411p. (C). 1979. 73.00 (*0-02-324980-3*, Macmillan Coll) P-H.

Copi, Irving M. & Burgess-Jackson, Keith. Informal Logic. 3rd ed. LC 95-33207. 314p. 1995. pap. text 57.00 (*0-13-229048-0*) P-H.

Copi, Irving M. & Cohen, Carl. An Introduction to Logic. 10th ed. LC 96-52297. 714p. 1997. 51.33 (*0-13-242587-4*) P-H.

Copic, Spelca, et al. Outdoor Sculpture in Ljubljana. Fras, Gerda, tr. LC 95-123496. 186 p. 1991. write for info. (*86-341-0672-1*) Drazvna Zaloba.

Copiffet, Philippe, jt. auth. see Burdea, Grigore C.

Copinger, H. B., ed. see Merryweather, F. Somner.

Copinschi, G. & Jaquet, P., eds. Lipo-Corticotropic Hormones & Cushing's Disease. (Journal: Hormone Research Ser.: Vol. 13, No. 4-5). (Illus.). 152p. 1981. pap. 57.50 (*3-8055-3410-8*) S Karger.

Copinschi, G., jt. ed. see Van Cauter, E.

Copinschi, Georges & Van Cauter, Eve, eds. Endocrine Rhythms: Roles of the Sleep-Wake Cycle, the Circadian Clock & the Environment: Diagnostic & Therapeutic Implications 40th International Henri-Pierre Klotz Symposium on Clinical Endocrinology, Paris, May 1997. (Hormone Research Ser.: Vol. 49, Nos. 3-4). (Illus.). 98p. 1998. pap. 85.25 (*3-8055-6666-2*) S Karger.

Copioli, Rosita. The Blazing Lights of the Sun. Treitel, Renata, tr. from ITA. LC 96-24334. (Sun & Moon Classics Ser.: No. 84). 116p. 1995. pap. 11.95 (*1-55713-195-3*) Sun & Moon CA.

Copjec, Joan. Radical Evil. 288p. (C). 1996. pap. 20.00 (*1-85984-006-X*, Pub. by Verso) Norton.

— Read My Desire: Lacan Against the Historicists. LC 94-383. (October Bk.). (Illus.). 288p. 1994. 35.00 (*0-262-03219-8*) MIT Pr.

— Read My Desire: Lacan Against the Historicists. (Illus.). 288p. 2000. reprint ed. pap. 32.00 (*0-262-53140-2*) MIT Pr.

Copjec, Joan, ed. Radical Evil. 288p. (C). (gr. 13 up). 1996. 60.00 (*1-85984-911-3*, Pub. by Verso) Norton.

— Shades of Noir. 320p. (C). (gr. 13). 1993. pap. 22.00 (*0-86091-625-1*, B0531, Pub. by Verso) Norton.

— Shades of Noir. 320p. (C). (gr. 13). 1993. 60.00 (*0-86091-460-7*, B0527, Pub. by Verso) Norton.

— Supposing the Subject. 288p. (C). (gr. 13). 1994. 60.00 (*1-85984-980-6*, B4678, Pub. by Verso); pap. 20.00 (*1-85984-075-2*, B4682, Pub. by Verso) Norton.

Copjec, Joan & Sorkin, Michael, eds. Giving Ground: The Politics of Propinquity. LC 99-17417. 312p. 1999. 60.00 (*1-85984-892-3*, Pub. by Verso); pap. 20.00 (*1-85984-134-1*, Pub. by Verso) Norton.

Coplakova, Eva & Hart, Klaas Pieter, eds. Papers on General Topology & Applications: Tenth Summer Conference at Amsterdam. LC 96-15559. (Annals of the New York Academy of Sciences Ser.). 1996. pap. 110.00 (*0-89766-964-9*) NY Acad Sci.

Coplan, David B. In the Time of Cannibals: The Word Music of South Africa's Basotho Migrants. LC 94-9093. (Chicago Studies in Ethnomusicology). 336p. 1994. pap. text 18.95 (*0-226-11574-7*); lib. bdg. 55.00 (*0-226-11573-9*) U Ch Pr.

Coplan, David B., ed. Lyrics of Basotho Migrants. Santho, Seakhi, tr. 1995. write for info. (*0-942615-27-1*) U Wis African Stud.

Coplan, Jeff, jt. auth. see Ferguson, Sarah.

Copland, Aaron. Como Escuchar la Musica. (Breviarios Ser.). (SPA.). 282p. 1999. pap. 5.99 (*968-16-4151-5*) Fondo CA.

— Music & Imagination. LC 52-9385. (Charles Eliot Norton Lectures: 1951-1952). 116p. 1952. pap. text 10.95 (*0-674-58915-7*) HUP.

— The New Music, 1900-1960. 194p. reprint ed. lib. bdg. 39.00 (*0-685-14848-3*) Rprt Serv.

Copland, Aaron & Perlis, Vivian. Copland: Since 1943. (Illus.). 480p. 1990. pap. 17.95 (*0-312-05066-6*) St Martin.

— Copland: 1900 Through 1942. (Illus.). 402p. 1999. pap. 19.95 (*0-312-01149-0*) St Martin.

Copland, Douglas B. Australia in the World Crisis, 1929-1933. LC 74-111474. (BCL Ser. I). reprint ed. 40.00 (*0-404-01718-5*) AMS Pr.

— The Changing Structure of the Western Economy. LC 65-9230. (Beatty Memorial Lectures). 96p. reprint ed. pap. 30.00 (*0-608-12127-4*, 202382700034) Bks Demand.

Copland, Ian. The Burden of Empire: Perspectives on Imperialism & Colonialism. (Illus.). 224p. 1991. pap. 26.00 (*0-19-553208-2*) OUP.

— The Princes of India in the Endgame of Empire, 1917-1947. (Cambridge Studies in Indian History & Society: No. 2). 316p. 1997. text 59.95 (*0-521-57179-0*) Cambridge U Pr.

Copland, Ian, et al. Federalism: Comparative Perspectives from India & Australia. LC 99-932412. 299p. 1999. 32.00 (*81-7304-239-X*, Pub. by Manohar) S Asia.

Copland, J. Draught Animal Power. 170p. (C). 1985. text 120.00 (*0-7855-6907-3*, Pub. by ACIAR) St Mut.

Copland, J. W. Draught Animal Power. 170p. (Orig.). 1985. pap. 81.00 (*0-949511-17-X*) St Mut.

Copland, J. W. & Lucas, J. S. Giant Clams in Asia & the Pacific. 274p. 1988. pap. 162.00 (*0-949511-70-6*, Pub. by ACIAR) St Mut.

Copland, J. W., et al. Agroforestry & Animal Production for Human Welfare. 125p. 1994. pap. 75.00 (*1-86320-133-5*, Pub. by ACIAR) St Mut.

— Diagnosis & Epidemiology of Foot & Mouth Disease in Southeast Asia. 209p. 1994. pap. 114.00 (*1-86320-123-8*, Pub. by ACIAR) St Mut.

Copland, J. W., jt. auth. see Blaber, S. J.

Copland, Jean B. Grandma's Legacy & Other Poems. Knight, Jane D., ed. (Illus.). 112p. (Orig.). 1992. pap. 9.95 (*0-9632498-0-0*) Legacy Columbus.

Copland, Robert, tr. see Aristotle.

Coplans, John. James Turrell: Occluded Front. LC 85-81089. (Illus.). 158p. 1985. pap. 20.00 (*0-932499-11-2*, Pub. by Fellows Cont Art) RAM Publications.

Coplans, John, ed. Weegee: Naked New York. (Illus.). 80p. Date not set. 19.95 (*3-8238-2122-9*) te Neues.

***Coplans, P.** Frightened Fred. (Illus.). 32p. 1999. pap. text 8.95 (*0-86264-821-1*, Pub. by Andersen Pr) Trafalgar.

— Hippos River Cafe. (J). 1999. 19.95 (*0-86264-804-1*, Pub. by Andersen Pr) Trafalgar.

Coplen, Dotty T. Parenting a Path Through Childhood. 1988. pap. 8.50 (*0-903540-61-4*, 20239, Pub. by Floris Bks) Gryphon Hse.

— Parenting for a Healthy Future. 126p. 1995. 14.95 (*1-869890-53-1*, Pub. by Hawthorn Press) Anthroposophic.

Coplen, Jim. The Wild Bird's Song. LC 98-96689. (Illus.). 183p. 1998. pap. 14.95 (*0-9667137-0-2*) Amer Bison Pubg.

Coplen, Tyler B., jt. auth. see Davis, George H.

Copleston, Frederick C. Aquinas. 1956. pap. 12.95 (*0-14-013674-6*, Viking) Viking Penguin.

— A History of Medieval Philosophy. LC 89-40756. 399p. (C). 1990. reprint ed. pap. text 16.50 (*0-268-01091-9*) U of Notre Dame Pr.

— A History of Philosophy, 9 vols., Set. 1994. 495.00 (*0-85532-438-4*, Pub. by Srch Pr) St Mut.

— A History of Philosophy Vol. 1: Greece & Rome. 1994. 80.00 (*0-85532-181-4*, Pub. by Srch Pr) St Mut.

— History of Philosophy Vol. 1: Greece & Rome. 35.00 (*0-8091-0065-7*) Paulist Pr.

— A History of Philosophy Vol. 2: Augustine to Scotus. 1994. 60.00 (*0-85532-182-2*, Pub. by Srch Pr) St Mut.

— History of Philosophy Vol. 2: Medieval Philosophy - Augustine to Scotus. 35.00 (*0-8091-0066-5*) Paulist Pr.

— A History of Philosophy Vol. 3: Ockham to Suarez. 1994. 60.00 (*0-85532-183-0*, Pub. by Srch Pr) St Mut.

— History of Philosophy Vol. 3: Ockham to Suarez. 29.00 (*0-8091-0067-3*) Paulist Pr.

— A History of Philosophy Vol. 4: Descartes to Leibniz. 1994. 60.00 (*0-85532-184-9*, Pub. by Srch Pr) St Mut.

— History of Philosophy Vol. 4: Descartes to Leibniz. 35.00 (*0-8091-0068-1*) Paulist Pr.

— History of Philosophy Vol. 5: Hobbes to Hume. 35.00 (*0-8091-0069-X*) Paulist Pr.

— A History of Philosophy Vol. 6: Wolff to Kant. 1994. 75.00 (*0-85532-186-5*, Pub. by Srch Pr) St Mut.

— History of Philosophy Vol. 6: Wolff to Kant. 29.00 (*0-8091-0070-3*) Paulist Pr.

— A History of Philosophy Vol. 7: Fichte to Nietzsche. 1994. 75.00 (*0-85532-187-3*, Pub. by Srch Pr) St Mut.

— History of Philosophy Vol. 7: Fichte to Nietzsche. 29.00 (*0-8091-0071-1*) Paulist Pr.

— A History of Philosophy Vol. 8: Bentham to Russell. 1994. 75.00 (*0-85532-188-1*, Pub. by Srch Pr) St Mut.

— History of Philosophy Vol. 8: Bentham to Russell. 35.00 (*0-8091-0072-X*) Paulist Pr.

— History of Philosophy Vol. 9: Maine de Bira to Sartre. 1976. 35.00 (*0-8091-0196-3*) Paulist Pr.

— A History of Philosophy Vol. 9: Maine de Biran to Sartre. 1994. 75.00 (*0-85532-341-8*, Pub. by Srch Pr) St Mut.

Copleston, Frederick C. Medieval Philosophy. LC 53-2190. (Methuen's Home Study Bks.). 200p. reprint ed. pap. 62.00 (*0-608-30089-6*, 201315300086) Bks Demand.

Copleston, Frederick C. Memoirs of a Philosopher. LC 93-7810. 240p. (Orig.). 1993. 19.95 (*1-55612-570-4*); pap. 14.95 (*1-55612-621-2*) Sheed & Ward WI.

— Modern Philosophy: Empiricism, Idealism & Pragmatism in Britain & America, Vol. 8. 592p. 1994. pap. 17.95 (*0-385-47045-2*) Doubleday.

— Modern Philosophy: From the French Revolution to Sartre, Camus & Levi-Strauss, Vol. 9. LC 92-34997. Vol. 9. 496p. 1994. pap. 17.95 (*0-385-47046-0*) Doubleday.

— Modern Philosophy: From the Post-Kantian Idealists to Marx, Kierkegaard & Nietzsche, Vol. 7. 512p. 1994. pap. 17.95 (*0-385-47044-4*) Doubleday.

— The Philosophical Assessment of Theology: Essays in Honour of Frederick C. Copleston. fac. ed. Hughes, Gerard J., ed. LC 87-94. 227p. pap. 70.40 (*0-7837-7394-3*, 204689600006) Bks Demand.

— Philosophy in Russia: From Herzen to Lenin to Berdyaev. 480p. 1994. 75.00 (*0-85532-577-1*, Pub. by Srch Pr) St Mut.

— Religion & the One: Philosophies East & West. 288p. 1994. 45.00 (*0-85532-514-3*, Pub. by Srch Pr) St Mut.

— Russian Religious Philosophy. 192p. 1994. 45.00 (*0-85532-630-1*, Pub. by Srch Pr) St Mut.

— Russian Religious Philosophy: Selected Aspects. (C). 1988. text 29.00 (*0-268-01635-6*) U of Notre Dame Pr.

Copleston, Frederick J. History of Philosophy: Greece & Rome, Vol. 1. 544p. 1993. pap. 17.95 (*0-385-46843-1*) Doubleday.

— Late Medieval & Renaissance Philosophy Vol. 3: Ockham, Francis Bacon & the Beginning of the Modern World. LC 92-34997. 496p. 1993. pap. 16.95 (*0-385-46845-8*, Image Bks) Doubleday.

— Medieval Philosophy Vol. 2: From Augustine to Duns Scotus. LC 92-34997. 624p. 1993. pap. 17.95 (*0-385-46844-X*, Image Bks) Doubleday.

— Modern Philosophy: From Descartes to Leibniz, No. 4. 384p. 1993. pap. 17.95 (*0-385-47041-X*) Doubleday.

— Modern Philosophy Vol. 5: The British Philosophers from Hobbes to Hume. 448p. 1993. pap. 16.95 (*0-385-47042-8*) Doubleday.

— Modern Philosophy Vol. 6: From the French Enlightenment to Kant. 528p. 1993. pap. 16.95 (*0-385-47043-6*) Doubleday.

— Philosophies & Cultures. 1980. 26.00 (*0-19-213960-6*) OUP.

Copleston, Reginald S. Buddhism: Primitive & Present in Magadha & in Ceylon. 2nd ed. (C). 1984. reprint ed. 18.00 (*0-8364-2412-3*, Pub. by Asian Educ Servs) S Asia.

— Buddhism, Primitive & Present in Magdha & in Ceylon. 2nd ed. LC 78-72398. reprint ed. 42.50 (*0-404-17257-1*) AMS Pr.

— Theravada Buddhism. Sobti, Harcharan S., ed. xxv, 206p. (C). 1993. reprint ed. 20.00 (*81-85133-80-8*, Pub. by Eastern Bk Linkers) Nataraj Bks.

Copley, A., ed. Biorheology: Abstracts of the Second International Congress, No. 2. 1975. pap. 29.00 (*0-08-019962-3*, Pergamon Pr) Elsevier.

— Biorheology: Proceedings of the Second International Congress. 1975. pap. 47.00 (*0-08-019963-1*, Pergamon Pr) Elsevier.

Copley, Antony. Gandhi: Against the Tide. 124p. 1996. pap. 10.95 (*0-19-563190-0*) OUP.

— Religions in Conflict: Ideology, Cultural Contact & Conversion in Late-Colonial India. (Oxford India Paperbacks). (Illus.). 308p. 2000. pap. text 11.95 (*0-19-564910-9*) OUP.

— Religions in Conflict: Ideology, Cultural Contact & Conversions in Late-Colonial India. LC 97-914024. (Illus.). 296p. (C). 1998. text 32.00 (*0-19-563676-7*) OUP.

— Sexual Moralities in Modern France, 1780-1980: New Ideas on the Family, Divorce & Homosexuality. 288p. 1989. 49.95 (*0-415-00360-1*) Routledge.

Copley, Antony, ed. Gurus & Their Followers: New Religious Reform Movements in Colonial India. 352p. 2000. text 29.95 (*0-19-564958-3*) OUP.

Copley-Braves, Lynn, compiled by. Great-Grandmother's Recipes: Cookies, Candies, & Nut Confections. (Great-Grandmother's Recipes Ser.). 58p. 1992. pap. 12.95 (*0-9631758-4-X*) Platoro Pr.

Copley, Eleanor. The User Friendly Cookbook: Easy to Use Recipes for Busy People. 200p. 1985. 14.95 (*0-943066-05-0*) CareerTrack Pubns.

Copley, F. O. Set of Alphabets of Various Hands. (Illus.). 40p. 25.00 (*0-87556-588-3*) Saifer.

Copley, Frank B. Frederick W. Taylor, Father of Scientific Management, 2 Vols, Set. LC 68-55515. (Library of Early American Business & Industry: No. 36). (Illus.). 1969. reprint ed. 95.00 (*0-678-00461-7*) Kelley.

Copley, Frank O., tr. The Nature of Things. (C). 1977. pap. text 14.00 (*0-393-09094-9*) Norton.

Copley, Frank O., tr. see Terence.

Copley, Frank S. A Set of Alphabets in Modern Use with Examples of Each Style: Letters, Cyphers, Figures, Monograms, Borders, Compasses & Flourishes. 200p. 1989. pap. 15.00 (*0-87556-490-9*) Saifer.

Copley-Graves, L., ed. see Moskuina, Tamara.

Copley-Graves, Lynn. Figure Skating History: The Evolution of Dance on Ice. (Figure Skating History Ser.). (Illus.). 415p. (Orig.). 1992. pap. 38.00 (*0-9631758-1-5*) Platoro Pr.

Copley-Graves, Lynn, compiled by. Great-Grandmother's Recipes: Vegetables. (Great-Grandmother's Recipes Ser.). 58p. 1994. pap. 12.95 (*0-9631758-8-2*) Platoro Pr.

Copley-Graves, Lynn, ed. see Tchaikovskaya, Yelena.

Copley, Gregory R., ed. Defense & Foreign Affairs Handbook, 1988-89. (Illus.). 1400p. 1988. 197.00 (*0-9605932-6-8*) Intl Strtgc Stds Assn.

***Copley, Helen F.** The Christy Quest. LC 99-34825. (Illus.). 196p. 1999. pap. 12.95 (*1-880397-30-7*) Patrice Pr.

***Copley, Jodie & Kuipers, Kathy.** Management of Upper Limb Hypertonicity. LC 98-54875. 308p. 1999. 45.00 (*0-7616-1529-6*) Commun Skill.

Copley, John S. Letters & Papers of John Singleton Copley & Henry Pelham, 1739-1776. LC 78-100615. (Library of American Art). (Illus.). 1970. reprint ed. lib. bdg. 49.00 (*0-306-71406-X*) Da Capo.

— Letters & Papers of John Singleton Copley & Henry Pelham, 1739-1776. (American Biography Ser.). 253p. 1991. reprint ed. lib. bdg. 69.00 (*0-7812-8091-5*) Rprt Serv.

Copley, John S. & Pelham, Henry. Letters & Papers of John Singleton Copley & Henry Pelham, 1739-1776. LC 72-456. reprint ed. 54.00 (*0-404-01719-3*) AMS Pr.

Copley, Juanita V., ed. Mathematics in the Early Years. LC 99-34458. (Illus.). 226p. 1999. pap. 30.95 (*0-87353-469-7*) NCTM.

Copley, Lynn. Platoro Area Wildflowers: Food, Medicinal, & Craft Uses of 125 Montane, Subalpine, & Alpine Wildflowers of Southeastern Colorado. (Illus.). 112p. 1998. pap. 15.95 (*1-882849-06-X*) Platoro Pr.

***Copley, Paul.** Routledge Critical Dictionary of Semiotics & Linguistics. 416p. 2000. pap. 22.95 (*0-415-92520-7*) Routledge.

***Copley, Paul A., ed.** Research in Governmental & Nonprofit Accounting, Vol. 5. 1999. 78.50 (*0-7623-0521-5*) Jai Pr.

Copley, R. Evan. Harmony Pt. 1: Baroque to Contemporary. 198p. 1991. pap. 21.80 (*0-87563-373-0*) Stipes.

— Harmony Pt. 2: Baroque to Contemporary. 198p. 1991. pap. 24.80 (*0-87563-377-3*) Stipes.

Copley, Stephen, ed. Joseph Andrews: Henry Fielding. (Routledge English Texts Ser.). 416p. (C). (gr. 13). 1987. pap. 20.99 (*0-416-41240-8*) Routledge.

Copley, Stephen & Sutherland, Kathryn, eds. Adam Smith The Wealth of Nations: New Interdisciplinary Essays. LC 94-16671. (Texts in Culture Ser.). 205p. 1995. text 24.95 (*0-7190-3943-6*, Pub. by Manchester Univ Pr) St Martin.

Copley, Stephen, jt. ed. see Connolly, Claire.

Copley, Stephen, ed. see Hume, David.

Copley, Steve M., jt. ed. see Singh, Jogender.

***Copley, Terence.** Spiritual Development in the State School: A Perspective on Worship & Spirituality in the Education System of England & Wales. 176p. 1999. 80.00 (*0-85989-600-5*, Pub. by Univ Exeter Pr); pap. 28.95 (*0-85989-601-3*, Pub. by Univ Exeter Pr) Northwestern U Pr.

Copley, Terence. Teaching Religion: Fifty Years of Religious Education in England & Wales. (Illus.). 256p. 1998. 60.00 (*0-85989-489-4*, Pub. by Univ Exeter Pr); pap. 26.95 (*0-85989-510-6*, Pub. by Univ Exeter Pr) Northwestern U Pr.

Coplien, James O. Advanced C Plus Plus Programming Styles & Idioms. (Illus.). 544p. (C). 1991. pap. 49.95 (*0-201-54855-0*) Addison-Wesley.

— Multiparadigm Design for C++ LC 98-36336. 304p. (C). 1998. pap. text 34.95 (*0-201-82467-1*) Addison-Wesley.

— Software Patterns: Management Briefings. 61p. 1996. pap. 85.00 (*1-884842-50-X*) SIGS Bks & Multimedia.

Coplien, James O. & Schmidt, Douglas C. Pattern Languages of Program Design, Vol. 1. 576p. (C). 1995. pap. text 41.95 (*0-201-60734-4*) Addison-Wesley.

Coplin, Maxine. A National Guide to Guest Homes. (Illus.). (Orig.). 1981. pap. 4.95 (*0-686-29699-0*, 0-96057804) Home on Arrange.

Coplin, William. Teaching Policy Studies. (C). 1978. pap. 15.00 (*0-918592-26-7*) Pol Studies.

Coplin, William, et al, eds. A Teacher's Guide to Students Shopping for a Better World. (Illus.). 84p. (Orig.). 1993. pap. text 25.00 (*0-936826-40-1*) PS Assocs Croton.

Coplin, William D. How You Can Help: Easy Guide to Doing Good Deeds in Your Everyday Life. LC 99-20659. 444p. 2000. pap. 14.95 (*0-415-92297-6*) Routledge.

Coplin, William D. & O'Leary, Michael K. Effective Participation in Government: A Problem-Solving Manual. (Illus.). 66p. (Orig.). 1988. pap. text 12.50 (*0-936826-32-0*) PS Assocs Croton.

— Introduction to Political Risk Analysis. (Learning Packages in the Policy Sciences Ser.: No. 24). (Illus.). 104p. (Orig.). 1983. pap. text 10.75 (*0-936826-19-3*) PS Assocs Croton.

— Political Analysis Through the Prince System. (Learning Packages in the Policy Sciences Ser.: No. 23). (Illus.). 100p. (Orig.). 1983. pap. text 10.75 (*0-936826-18-5*) PS Assocs Croton.

— Public Policy Skills. 3rd rev. ed. (Illus.). 206p. 1998. text 38.00 (*0-936826-42-8*) PS Assocs Croton.

Coplin, William D. & O'Leary, Michael K., eds. The Handbook of Country & Political Risk Analysis. 370p. Date not set. 89.00 (*1-85271-383-6*) PRS Grp.

Coplin, William D. & Rochester, J. Martin. Dyadic Disputes, 1920-1968. 2nd ed. 1976. write for info. (*0-89138-021-3*) ICPSR.

Coplin, William D., et al. Effective Participation in Government: A Guide to Policy Skills. rev. ed. (Illus.). 170p. 1987. reprint ed. text 22.50 (*0-936826-27-4*) PS Assocs Croton.

— Effective Participation in Government Workbook. (Illus.). 117p. (Orig.). 1987. pap. 8.75 (*0-936826-28-2*) PS Assocs Croton.

Coplon, Jeff. Gold Buckle: The Grand Obsession of Rodeo Bull Riders. 1999. pap. 10.00 (*0-06-258608-4*) HarpC.

— Gold Buckle: The Grand Obsession of Rodeo Bull Riders. LC 95-12563. (Illus.). 304p. 1995. 23.00 (*0-06-258545-2*, Pub. by Harper SF) HarpC.

Coplon, Jeff & Cher. The First Time. 272p. 1999. per. 14.00 (*0-671-03488-X*, PB Trade Paper) PB.

Coplon, Jeff, jt. auth. see Cher.

Coplon, Jeff, jt. auth. see O'Grady, Scott.

Coplon, Jeff, jt. auth. see Parcells, Bill.

Coplon, Jeff, jt. auth. see Sinatra, Tina.

Coplon, Jeff, jt. auth. see York, Sarah M.

Coplon, Jennifer K. Single Older Women in the Workforce: By Necessity, or Choice? rev. ed. LC 97-9289. (Studies in the History of American Labor). (Illus.). 192p. 1997. text 55.00 (*0-8153-2837-0*) Garland.

Coply, Jodie & Kuipers, Kathy. Management of Upper Limb Hypertonicity. (Illus.). 308p. 1999. pap. 45.00 (*0-12-784596-8*) Acad Pr.

Copney, Claudette. Jamaican Culture & International Folklore, Superstitions, Beliefs, Dreams, Proverbs & Remedies. LC 98-65638. 95 p. 1998. pap. 14.95 (*1-57197-117-3*) Pentland Pr.

Copney, Claudette V. The Little Handbook of Office Humors. (Illus.). 48p. 1998. pap. 8.95 (*1-56167-453-2*) Am Literary Pr.

Copney, Nancy Jane. African-American Life in Preston County. (Images of America Ser.). (Illus.). 128p. 1999. pap. 18.99 (*0-7385-0133-6*) Arcadia Publng.

Copoloff-Mechanic, Susan. Pilgrim's Progress: A Study of the Short Stories of Hugh Hood. 161p. (C). 1988. text 25.00 (*1-55022-001-2*, Pub. by ECW); pap. text 15.00 (*1-55022-000-4*, Pub. by ECW) Genl Dist Srvs.

***Coposu, Corneliu.** Corneliu Coposu. LC 98-72876. 224p. 1998. text 31.50 (*0-88033-405-3*, 507, Pub. by East Eur Monographs) Col U Pr.

Copp. Effective Health Management Guides. pap. text. write for info. (*0-7730-5180-5*) Addison-Wes.

Copp. Introduction to Business. 1993. pap. text. write for info. (*0-7730-5337-9*) Addison-Wesley.

Copp, Dan. Dragons Live Forever. (Mac & Mel Ser.: Vol. 1). 115p. 1997. pap. write for info. (*0-9660217-0-3*, Bellyache Bks) Topa Pub.

Copp, David. Morality, Normativity & Society. 280p. 1995. text 49.95 (*0-19-507879-9*) OUP.

Copp, David, et al, eds. The Idea of Democracy. 461p. 1995. pap. text 22.95 (*0-521-48326-3*) Cambridge U Pr.

Copp, David & Wendell, Susan, eds. Pornography & Censorship. LC 83-61031. 414p. 1983. pap. 24.95 (*0-87975-182-7*) Prometheus Bks.

Copp, DeWitt S. A Few Great Captains: The Men & Events That Shaped the Development of U. S. Air Power. (Illus.). 535p. 1989. pap. 19.95 (*0-939009-29-3*) EPM Pubns.

Copp, Dewitt S. A Matter of Concealment. 384p. 1991. mass mkt. 4.50 (*0-8217-3269-2*, Zebra Kensgtn) Kensgtn Pub Corp.

Copp, Gerry. Great Paper Mache: Furniture, Masks, Animals, Hats. 64p. (Orig.). 1997. pap. 15.95 (*0-85532-815-0*, 8150, Pub. by Srch Pr) A Schwartz & Co.

— Paper into Pots: And Other Fun Objects Using Hand-Made Recycled Paper & Papier-Mache Techniques. (Illus.). 48p. 1995. pap. 11.95 (*0-85532-772-3*, 772-3, Pub. by Srch Pr) A Schwartz & Co.

Copp, Henry N. American Mining Code: Embracing the United States, State, & Territorial Mining Laws. 160p. 1994. reprint ed. 35.00 (*0-8377-2052-4*, Rothman) W S Hein.

— Manual for the Use of Prospectors on the Mineral Lands of the U. S. 5th ed. Bruchey, Stuart, ed. LC 78-53538. (Development of Public Land Law in the U. S. Ser.). 1979. reprint ed. lib. bdg. 16.95 (*0-405-11371-4*) Ayer.

— Public Land Laws. Bruchey, Stuart, ed. LC 78-53559. (Development of Public Land Law in the U. S. Ser.). 1979. reprint ed. lib. bdg. 69.95 (*0-405-11372-2*) Ayer.

— United States Mineral Lands. Bruchey, Stuart, ed. LC 78-53539. (Development of Public Land Law in the U. S. Ser.). 1979. reprint ed. lib. bdg. 49.95 (*0-405-11373-0*) Ayer.

Copp, James H., jt. ed. see Wardwell, John M.

Copp, Jay. The Liguori Guide to Catholic U. S. A. A Treasury of Churches, Schools, Monuments, Shrines, & Monasteries. LC 98-43555. 336p. 1999. pap. 15.95 (*0-7648-0371-9*) Liguori Pubns.

Copp, John D. & Pula, Faafouina I. The Samoan Dance of Life: An Anthropological Narrative. LC 83-26370. 176p. 1984. reprint ed. lib. bdg. 55.00 (*0-313-24244-5*, COSD, Greenwood Pr) Greenwood.

Copp, Martha A., jt. auth. see Kleinman, Sherryl.

Copp, Michael, ed. From Emmanuel to the Somme: The War Writings of A. E. Tomlinson. LC 98-127433. 190p. 1998. 47.95 (*0-7188-2963-8*, Lutterworth-Parkwest) Parkwest Pubns.

Copp, Nelson, jt. auth. see Schad, Jerry.

Copp, Newton H. & Zanella, Andrew W. Discovery, Innovation, & Risk: Case Studies in Science & Technology. (Illus.). 400p. 1992. pap. text 29.50 (*0-262-53111-9*) MIT Pr.

Copp, Richard P., jt. auth. see Bajaria, Hans J.

Copp, Tara, jt. auth. see Rogers, Robert L.

Copp, Terry & McAndrew, Bill. Battle Exhaustion: Soldiers & Psychiatrists in the Canadian Army, 1939-1945. 280p. (C). 1990. 49.95 (*0-7735-0774-4*, Pub. by McG-Queens Univ Pr) CUP Services.

Coppa, Frank J. Cardinal Giacomo Antonelli & Papal Politics in European Affairs. LC 89-4357. 299p. (C). 1990. pap. text 24.95 (*0-7914-0185-5*) State U NY Pr.

***Coppa, Frank J.** County Government: A Guide to Efficient & Accountable Government. LC 99-45988. 216p. 2000. write for info. (*0-275-96829-4*) Greenwood.

— MODERN PAPACY 1789 1995. LC 98-18988. (History of the Papacy Ser.). (C). 1998. 87.00 (*0-582-09629-4*) Longman.

Coppa, Frank J. The Modern Papacy, 1798-1995. LC 98-18988. (History of the Papacy Ser.). 296p. (C). 1998. pap. 33.53 (*0-582-09630-8*) Addison-Wesley.

— The Papacy Confronts the Modern World. Date not set. pap. write for info. (*1-57524-101-3*) Krieger.

— Planning, Protectionism, & Politics in Liberal Italy: Economics & Politics in the Giolittian Age. LC 73-148346. 292p. reprint ed. pap. 90.60 (*0-608-17278-2*, 202952300061) Bks Demand.

Coppa, Frank J., ed. Controversial Concordats: The Vatican's Relations with Napoleon, Mussolini, & Hitler. LC 98-23276. 245p. (C). 1999. text 44.95 (*0-8132-0908-0*); pap. text 24.95 (*0-8132-0920-X*) Cath U Pr.

— Dictionary of Modern Italian History. LC 84-6704. 496p. 1985. lib. bdg. 115.00 (*0-313-22983-X*, CMI/, Greenwood Pr) Greenwood.

— Encyclopedia of the Vatican & Papacy. LC 98-15328. 496p. 1999. lib. bdg. 99.50 (*0-313-28917-4*) Greenwood.

— Screen & Society: The Impact of Television upon Aspects of Contemporary Civilization. LC 79-13500. 248p. 1980. text 36.95 (*0-88229-413-X*) Burnham Inc.

Coppa, Frank J. & Repetto-Alaia, Margherita, eds. The Formation of the Italian Republic: Proceedings of the International Symposium on Postwar Italy. LC 92-26677. (Studies in Modern European History: Vol. 5). VIII, 354p. 1993. 42.95 (*0-8204-1530-8*) P Lang Pubng.

Coppa, Frank J. & Roberts, William C., compiled by. Modern Italian History: An Annotated Bibliography, 18. LC 89-78122. (Bibliographies & Indexes in World History Ser.: No. 18). 236p. 1990. lib. bdg. 65.00 (*0-313-24812-5*, CPM/, Praeger Pubs) Greenwood.

Coppa, Frank J., ed. see Wolff, Richard J.

***Coppack, Glyn.** White Monks. (Illus.). 176p. 1998. 29.99 (*0-7524-1413-5*, Pub. by Tempus Pubng) Arcadia Publng.

— The White Monks: The Cistercians in Britain 1128-1540. (Illus.). 176p. 2000. pap. 24.99 (*0-7524-1493-3*, Pub. by Tempus Pubng) Arcadia Publng.

Coppage, jt. auth. see Maxim, A.

Coppage, A. Maxim. Searching for Scottish Ancestors. 1983. 28.35 (*0-318-03039-X*); pap. 28.25 (*0-318-03040-3*) A M Coppage.

— Virginia Settlers, Vol. II. 1988. 30.00 (*0-318-32890-9*); pap. 25.00 (*0-318-32891-7*) A M Coppage.

***Coppage, Keith.** Roller Derby to Rollerjam: The Authorized Story of an Unathorized Sport. (Illus.). 148p. 1999. pap. 19.95 (*0-916290-80-8*, Pub. by Squarebooks) Publishers Group.

Coppage, Nora. An Ormsbee Odyssey. 350p. 1990. 38.00 (*0-317-02848-0*); 32.50 (*0-317-02849-9*) A M Coppage.

Coppage, William E. Elementary Algebra: Guide for Students in Mastery-Learning Classes. 3rd ed. 224p. (C). 1994. spiral bd. 13.95 (*0-8403-8905-1*) Kendall-Hunt.

Coppard. Splinting. 2nd ed. 2000. spiral bd. 33.00 (*0-323-00934-4*) Mosby Inc.

Coppard, A. E. Adam & Eve & Pinch Me: Tales. 1976. 23.95 (*0-8488-0971-8*) Amereon Ltd.

— The Higgler & Other Stories. large type ed. 227p. 1991. 22.95 (*1-85290-014-8*, Pub. by ISIS Lrg Prnt) Transaction Pubs.

Coppard, Alfred E. Adam & Eve & Pinch Me: Tales. LC 70-106274. (Short Story Index Reprint Ser.). 1977. 21.95 (*0-8369-3451-2*) Ayer.

— Black Dog & Other Stories. LC 74-106275. (Short Story Index Reprint Ser.). 1977. 20.95 (*0-8369-3312-5*) Ayer.

— The Collected Tales of A. E. Coppard. Reginald, R. & Menville, Douglas A., eds. LC 75-26260. (Supernatural & Occult Fiction Ser.). 1976. reprint ed. lib. bdg. 44.95 (*0-405-08119-7*) Ayer.

— Fishmonger's Fiddle. LC 78-106276. (Short Story Index Reprint Ser.). 1977. 20.95 (*0-8369-3313-3*) Ayer.

— Ninepenny Flute: Twenty-One Tales. LC 71-106277. (Short Story Index Reprint Ser.). 1977. 20.95 (*0-8369-3314-1*) Ayer.

— Polly Oliver. LC 70-132114. (Short Story Index Reprint Ser.). 1977. 17.95 (*0-8369-3671-X*) Ayer.

Coppard, Brenda M. & Lohman, Helene. Introduction to Splinting: A Critical Thinking & Problem-Solving Approach. Colditz, Judy C., ed. LC 95-42842. (Illus.). 352p. (C). (gr. 13). 1996. spiral bd. 39.95 (*0-8151-7126-9*, 26607) Mosby Inc.

Coppe, Bernard. French Cuisine under Pressure: Two Hundred One Easy Family Recipes for Pressure Cookers. (FRE., Illus.). 184p. (Orig.). 1993. pap. text 16.95 (*0-9634974-3-X*) Club Paris.

— French Cuisine under Pressure: Two Hundred One Easy Family Recipes for Pressure Cookers. (SPA., Illus.). 184p. (Orig.). 1993. pap. text 16.95 (*0-685-64834-6*) Club Paris.

— French Cuisine under Pressure: Two-Hundred One Easy Family Recipes for Pressure Cookers. 2nd rev. ed. (Illus.). 184p. 1993. pap. text 16.95 (*0-9634974-1-3*) Club Paris.

Coppedge, Allan. The Biblical Principles of Discipleship. 176p. 1989. 16.99 (*0-310-75350-3*) Zondervan.

— John Wesley in Theological Debate. 289p. 1987. text 17.95 (*0-915143-03-8*) F A Society.

Coppedge, Michael. Strong Parties & Lame Ducks: Presidential & Factionalism in Venezuela. 258p. 1997. pap. text 16.95 (*0-8047-2961-1*) Stanford U Pr.

— Strong Parties & Lame Ducks: Presidential Patriarchy & Factionalism in Venezuela. LC 93-36656. 264p. 1994. 45.00 (*0-8047-2278-1*) Stanford U Pr.

Coppedge, Robert O. & Davis, Carlton G., eds. Rural Poverty & the Policy Crisis. LC 76-53751. (Illus.). 232p. 1977. reprint ed. pap. 72.00 (*0-608-00060-4*, 206082600006) Bks Demand.

Coppedge, Walter. Henry King's America. LC 86-22066. (Filmmakers Ser.: No. 15). (Illus.). 182p. 1987. 23.50 (*0-8108-1957-0*) Scarecrow.

Coppee, Francois. Ten Tales. Learned, Walter, ed. LC 76-86140. (Short Story Index Reprint Ser.). (Illus.). 1977. 19.95 (*0-8369-3044-4*) Ayer.

Coppee, G. H., jt. auth. see Forssman, S.

Coppee, H. History of the Conquest of Spain by the Moors, 2 vols. 1976. lib. bdg. 250.00 (*0-8490-1992-3*) Gordon Pr.

Coppejans, E. Iconographie d'Algues Mediterraneennes: (Chlorophyta, Phaeophyta, Rhodophyta) (Bibliotheca Phycologica Ser.: No. 63). (Illus.). 1983. text 175.00 (*3-7682-1357-9*) Lubrecht & Cramer.

— Scripta Botanica Belgica Vol. 17: Flora Can de Noord-Franse en Belgische Zeewieren. (DUT., Illus.). 462p. 1998. pap. 52.40 (*90-72619-41-2*, Pub. by Natl Botanic Grdn Belgium) Balogh.

Coppejans, E. & Kling, R. Flore Algologique des Cotes du Nord de la France et de la Belgique. (Scripta Botanica Belgica Ser.: Vol. 9). (Illus.). 454p. 1995. 54.00 (*90-72619-16-1*, Pub. by Natl Botanic Grdn Belgium) Balogh.

Coppel. Linocuts of the Machine Age: Claude Flig. limited ed. 205p. 1995. 795.00 (*1-85928-179-6*) Ashgate Pub Co.

Coppel, Aldred. Glory's People. 1997. mass mkt. 5.99 (*0-8125-2395-4*, Pub. by Tor Bks) St Martin.

Coppel, Alec & Coppel, Myra. The Gazebo. 1959. pap. 5.25 (*0-8222-0434-7*) Dramatists Play.

Coppel, Alfred. Glory. 384p. 1994. mass mkt. 5.99 (*0-8125-2393-8*, Pub. by Tor Bks) St Martin.

— Glory's War. 288p. 1996. pap. write for info. (*0-614-05534-2*); mass mkt. 5.99 (*0-8125-2394-6*, Pub. by Tor Bks) St Martin.

— A Land of Mirrors. 320p. 1988. 18.95 (*0-15-147682-9*) Harcourt.

— Show Me a Hero. LC 86-26961. 320p. 1987. 16.95 (*0-15-182080-5*) Harcourt.

Coppel, Alfred, ed. see Knox, Donald.

Coppel, H. C. & Mertins, J. W. Biological Insect Press Suppression. LC 76-42188. (Advanced Series in Agricultural Sciences: Vol. 4). (Illus.). 1977. 47.00 (*3-540-07931-9*) Spr-Verlag.

Coppel, Jonathan & De Serres, Alain. EMU: Facts, Challenges & Policies. LC 99-221597. 220p. (Orig.). 1999. pap. 36.00 (*92-64-17027-8*, 11 1999 01 1 P, Pub. by Org for Econ) OECD.

Coppel, Myra, jt. auth. see Coppel, Alec.

Coppel, R. & Nossal, G. J. Reshaping Life: Key Issues in Genetic Engineering. 2nd ed. (Illus.). 191p. (C). 1990. pap. text 17.95 (*0-521-38969-0*) Cambridge U Pr.

Coppel, Stephan. Linocuts of the Machine Age A Catalogue Raisonne: Claude Flight & His Followers. 205p. 1995. 139.95 (*0-85967-945-4*, Pub. by Scolar Pr) Ashgate Pub Co.

Coppel, Stephen. Picasso & Printmaking in Paris. (Illus.). 128p. 1999. pap. 29.95 (*1-85332-180-X*, Pub. by U CA Pr) Cal Prin Full Svc.

Coppel, W. A. Foundations of Convex Geometry. (Australian Mathematical Society Lecture Ser.: No. 12). (Illus.). 236p. (C). 1998. pap. text 39.95 (*0-521-63970-0*) Cambridge U Pr.

Coppel, William A., jt. auth. see Block, Louis S.

Coppell & Stratigos, Susan. Pacific Island Theses & Dissertations: A Bibliography. (Australian National University Press Ser.). 1996. pap. write for info. (*0-08-032989-6*, Pergamon Pr) Elsevier.

Coppell, W. G. & Stratigos, Susan. A Bibliography of Pacific Island Theses & Dissertations. 528p. (C). 1984. pap. text 22.95 (*0-939154-33-1*) Inst Polynesian.

Coppen-Gardner, Sylvia. A Background for Glass Collectors. (Illus.). 172p. 1976. 14.95 (*0-7207-0624-6*) Transatl Arts.

Coppen, J. J. & Dyer, L. R. Eucalyptus & Its Leaf Oils: An Indexed Bibliography. 205p. 1993. pap. 30.00 (*0-85954-347-1*, Pub. by Nat Res Inst) St Mut.

Coppen, J. J. & Hone, G. A. Eucalyptus Oils: A Review of Production & Markets. 1992. pap. 35.00 (*0-85954-308-0*, Pub. by Nat Res Inst) St Mut.

— Gum Naval Stores: Turpentine & Rosin from Pine Resin. LC 96-125264. (Non-Wood Forest Products: Vol. 2). 72p. 1995. pap. 12.00 (*92-5-103684-5*) Food & Agri Org UN.

***Coppen, Peter-Arno, ed.** Computational Linguistics in the Netherlands, 1997: Proceedings: CLIN Meeting (8th: 1997: Nijmegen, Netherlands) (Language & Computers: No. 25). 239p. 1998. pap. 22.00 (*90-420-0494-0*) Editions Rodopi.

Coppenrath, Robert A. The Leadership Legacy. 376p. Date not set. text 24.95 (*1-889534-30-7*) Jay St Pubs.

***Coppens, Christian, ed.** Leuven in Books - Books in Leuven: The Oldest University of the Low Countries & Its Library. Dreisbach, Ardis, tr. (Illus.). 323p. 1999. pap. 77.50 (*90-6186-951-X*, Pub. by Leuven Univ) Coronet Bks.

C

Coppens, Christian, ed. Reading in Exile: The Libraries of John Ramridge, Thomas Harding & Henry Joliffe, Recusants in Louvain. (Title Libri Pertinentes Ser.: Vol. 2). 250p. 1993. pap. text 26.00 (*0-9518811-1-6*, MRLP2, Pub. by Libri Pertinentes) MRTS.

Coppens, Francoise, jt. auth. see Mari, Jean-Luc.

Coppens, Patrick, et al, eds. Aphasia in Atypical Populations. LC 97-41461. 300p. 1997. write for info. (*0-8058-1738-7*) L Erlbaum Assocs.

Coppens, Philip. X-Ray Charge Densities & Chemical Bonding. LC 96-48736. (International Union of Crystallography Texts on Crystallography: No. 4). (Illus.). 368p. (C). 1997. text 95.00 (*0-19-509823-4*) OUP.

Coppens, Philip, ed. Experimental & Theoretical Studies of Electron Densities. (Transactions of the American Crystallographic Association Ser.: Vol. 8). 155p. 1972. pap. 25.00 (*0-686-60379-6*) Polycrystal Bk Serv.

Coppens, Yves, et al, eds. Earliest Man & Environments in the Lake Rudolf Basin: Stratigraphy, Paleoecology, & Evolution. LC 75-5075. (Prehistoric Archeology & Ecology Ser.). (Illus.). 656p. 1976. pap. text 18.00 (*0-226-11579-8*) U Ch Pr.

Copper. Automotive Scopes & Scanners. (Automotive Technology Ser.). 1998. teacher ed. 14.00 (*0-8273-7353-8*); pap. 30.95 (*0-8273-7352-X*) Delmar.

***Copper, Basil.** Bad Scene. large type ed. LC 00-21438. 238p. 2000. 20.95 (*0-7838-8997-6*, G K Hall & Co) Mac Lib Ref.

Copper, Basil. Bad Scene. large type ed. 1991. pap. 16.99 (*0-7089-7021-4*) Ulverscroft.

— The Black Death. (Illus.). 380p. (C). 1991. 32.00 (*1-878252-04-6*) Fedogan & Bremer.

— The Black Death. limited ed. (Illus.). 380p. (C). 1991. 60.00 (*1-878252-05-4*) Fedogan & Bremer.

— The Breaking Point. large type ed. (Linford Mystery Large Print Ser.). 1995. pap. 16.99 (*0-7089-7805-3*, Linford) Ulverscroft.

***Copper, Basil.** The Caligari Complex. large type ed. 304p. 1999. pap. 18.99 (*0-7089-5504-5*, Linford) Ulverscroft.

Copper, Basil. Crack in the Sidewalk. large type ed. (Linford Mystery Library). 320p. 1997. pap. 16.99 (*0-7089-5065-5*, Linford) Ulverscroft.

— The Dark Mirror. large type ed. (Linford Mystery Library). 416p. 1997. pap. 16.99 (*0-7089-5101-5*, Linford) Ulverscroft.

— Dead File. large type ed. 1991. pap. 16.99 (*0-7089-7001-X*) Ulverscroft.

***Copper, Basil.** Death Squad. large type ed. 304p. 1999. pap. 18.99 (*0-7089-5460-X*, Linford) Ulverscroft.

Copper, Basil. Die Now, Live Later. large type ed. (Linford Mystery Library). 336p. 1993. pap. 16.99 (*0-7089-7341-8*) Ulverscroft.

— Don't Bleed on Me. large type ed. (Linford Mystery Library). 1991. pap. 16.99 (*0-7089-7081-8*) Ulverscroft.

— The Dossier of Solar Pons. (Solar Pons Ser.). 278p. 1987. pap. 7.95 (*0-89733-252-0*) Academy Chi Pubs.

— The Empty Silence. large type ed. 320p. 1994. pap. 16.99 (*0-7089-7569-0*) Ulverscroft.

— Exploits of Solar Pons. (Illus.). 256p. (C). 1993. 25.00 (*1-878252-11-9*) Fedogan & Bremer.

— Exploits of Solar Pons. limited ed. (Illus.). 256p. (C). 1993. 45.00 (*1-878252-14-3*) Fedogan & Bremer.

— The Far Horizon. large type ed. (Linford Mystery Library). 336p. 1993. pap. 16.99 (*0-7089-7378-7*) Ulverscroft.

— Feedback. large type ed. (Linford Mystery Library). 1991. pap. 16.99 (*0-7089-7129-6*) Ulverscroft.

— The Further Adventures of Solar Pons. (Solar Pons Ser.). 256p. (Orig.). 1987. pap. 7.95 (*0-89733-273-3*) Academy Chi Pubs.

— A Good Place to Die. large type ed. (Linford Mystery Library). 1989. pap. 16.99 (*0-7089-6742-6*) Ulverscroft.

— A Great Year for Dying. large type ed. (Linford Mystery Library). 352p. 1993. pap. 16.99 (*0-7089-7349-3*) Ulverscroft.

— Hard Contract. large type ed. (Linford Mystery Library). 272p. 1988. pap. 16.99 (*0-7089-6504-0*) Ulverscroft.

Copper, Basil. Heavy Iron. large type ed. 272p. pap. 18.99 (*0-7089-5457-X*) Ulverscroft.

Copper, Basil. The High Wall. large type ed. (Linford Mystery Library). 304p. 1987. pap. 16.99 (*0-7089-6455-9*, Linford) Ulverscroft.

— The Hook. large type ed. (Linford Mystery Large Print Ser.). 1995. pap. 16.99 (*0-7089-7810-X*, Linford) Ulverscroft.

***Copper, Basil.** House-Dick. 288p. 2000. 18.99 (*0-7089-5719-6*) Ulverscroft.

Copper, Basil. Impact. large type ed. (Linford Mystery Library). 320p. 1997. pap. 16.99 (*0-7089-5070-1*, Linford) Ulverscroft.

— Jet-Lag. large type ed. (Linford Mystery Library). 1990. pap. 16.99 (*0-7089-6837-6*) Ulverscroft.

— The Lonely Place. large type ed. (Linford Mystery Library). 304p. 1997. pap. 16.99 (*0-7089-5060-4*) Ulverscroft.

— The Long Rest. large type ed. LC 94-12705. 221p. 1994. lib. bdg. 16.95 (*0-8161-7421-0*, G K Hall Lrg Type) Mac Lib Ref.

— The Marble Orchard. large type ed. (Linford Mystery Large Print Ser.). 256p. 1998. pap. 17.99 (*0-7089-5265-8*, Linford) Ulverscroft.

— Night Frost. large type ed. (Linford Mystery Library). 368p. 1996. pap. 16.99 (*0-7089-7868-1*, Linford) Ulverscroft.

— Pressure Point. large type ed. (Linford Mystery Library). 1991. pap. 16.99 (*0-7089-7085-0*) Ulverscroft.

— Print-Out. large type ed. (Dales Mystery Ser.). 246p. 1993. pap. 18.99 (*1-85389-380-3*, Dales) Ulverscroft.

— Print-Out. large type ed. (Linford Mystery Library). 304p. 1996. pap. 16.99 (*0-7089-7861-4*, Linford) Ulverscroft.

— A Quiet Room in Hell. large type ed. (Linford Mystery Large Print Ser.). 288p. 1998. pap. 17.99 (*0-7089-5294-1*, Linford) Ulverscroft.

— The Recollections of Solar Pons. 1995. 25.00 (*1-878252-20-8*) Fedogan & Bremer.

— The Recollections of Solar Pons. limited ed. 1995. 75.00 (*1-878252-21-6*) Fedogan & Bremer.

— Ricochet. large type ed. (Linford Mystery Library). 304p. 1993. pap. 16.99 (*0-7089-7382-5*, Linford) Ulverscroft.

***Copper, Basil.** Scratch on the Dark. 264p. 2000. 18.99 (*0-7089-5767-6*) Ulverscroft.

Copper, Basil. Shock-Wave. large type ed. (Linford Mystery Library). 1994. pap. 16.99 (*0-7089-7629-8*, Linford) Ulverscroft.

— Snow-Job. large type ed. (Linford Mystery Library). 260p. 1989. pap. 16.99 (*0-7089-6636-5*, Linford) Ulverscroft.

— Strong-Arm. large type ed. (Linford Mystery Library). 319p. 1989. pap. 16.99 (*0-7089-6629-2*, Linford) Ulverscroft.

— Tight Corner. large type ed. (Linford Mystery Library). 304p. 1994. pap. 16.99 (*0-7089-7564-X*, Linford) Ulverscroft.

— Trigger-Man. large type ed. (Linford Mystery Library). 320p. 1994. pap. 16.99 (*0-7089-7561-5*, Linford) Ulverscroft.

— Tuxedo Park. large type ed. (Linford Mystery Library). 1990. pap. 16.99 (*0-7089-6845-7*) Ulverscroft.

— A Voice from the Dead. large type ed. (Linford Mystery Large Print Ser.). 304p. 1998. pap. 17.99 (*0-7089-5287-9*, Linford) Ulverscroft.

***Copper, Basil.** Whispers in the Night. 274p. 1999. 27.00 (*1-878252-40-2*) Fedogan & Bremer.

Copper, Basil. The Year of the Dragon. large type ed. (Linford Mystery Library). 1991. pap. 16.99 (*0-7089-7077-X*) Ulverscroft.

***Copper, Basil.** You Only Die Once. large type ed. 296p. 2000. pap. 18.99 (*0-7089-5678-5*, Linford) Ulverscroft.

Copper, Basil & Maugham, W. Somerset. The Narrow Corner. large type ed. (Linford Mystery Library). 1989. pap. 16.99 (*0-7089-6749-3*, Linford) Ulverscroft.

Copper Beech Books Staff, ed. Knowledge Network. LC 98-28529. 352p. (YA). (gr. 5 up). 1998. 24.95 (*0-7613-0779-6*, Copper Beech Bks) Millbrook Pr.

Copper, Carolyn M., et al. Defense Industry: Trends in DOD Spending, Industrial Productivity, & Competition. (Illus.). 70p. (C). 1999. reprint ed. pap. text 20.00 (*0-7881-4362-X*) DIANE Pub.

Copper, Cary, jt. auth. see McGoldrick, Ann.

***Copper in Drinking Water Committee, et al.** Copper in Drinking Water. 162p. 2000. pap. 35.00 (*0-309-06939-4*) Natl Acad Pr.

Copper, James G. Ornithology: Land Birds. Baird, Spencer F. & Whitney, J. D., eds. LC 73-17812. (Natural Sciencs in America Ser.). (Illus.). 608p. 1974. reprint ed. 51.95 (*0-405-05728-8*) Ayer.

***Copper, John.** Taiwan Approaches the New Millennium: Essays on Politics & Foreign Affairs. LC 99-30463. 200p. 1999. pap. 26.50 (*0-7618-1432-9*) U Pr of Amer.

Copper, John F. Taiwan: Nation-State or Province? 3rd ed. LC 99-26974. 272p. 1999. pap. 24.00 (*0-8133-3388-1*, Pub. by Westview) HarpC.

Copper, John Franklin. China's Global Role: An Analysis of Peking's National Power Capabilities in the Context of an Evolving International System. (Publication Ser.: No. 226). 181p. 1980. pap. 3.58 (*0-8179-7262-5*) Hoover Inst Pr.

— Historical Dictionary of Taiwan. LC 92-32868. (Asian Historical Dictionaries Ser.: No. 12). (Illus.). 336p. 1993. 29.00 (*0-8108-2608-9*) Scarecrow.

— A Quiet Revolution: Political Development in the Republic of China. LC 87-32930. 76p. (Orig.). (C). 1988. pap. text 12.75 (*0-89633-128-8*) Ethics & Public Policy.

— Taiwan: Nation-State or Province? 2nd ed. (Nations of the Modern World: Asia Ser.). 250p. (C). 1996. pap. 26.00 (*0-8133-2091-7*, Pub. by Westview) HarpC.

— The Taiwan Political Miracle: Essays on Political Development, Elections & Foreign Relations. 1995. pap. text. write for info. (*0-7618-0113-8*) U Pr of Amer.

— The Taiwan Political Miracle: Essays on Political Development, Elections & Foreign Relations. LC 95-25161. 612p. 1997. lib. bdg. 72.50 (*0-7618-0112-X*) U Pr of Amer.

***Copper, John Franklin.** Taiwan's Mid-1990's Elections: Taking the Final Step to Democracy. LC 98-4949. 256p. 1998. 59.95 (*0-275-96207-5*, Praeger Pubs) Greenwood.

Copper, John Franklin. Taiwan's Recent Elections: Fulfilling the Democratic Process. No. 6. 174p. 1990. 8.00 (*0-925153-12-5*, 101) Occasional Papers.

— Words Across the Strait: A Critique of Beijing's "White Paper" on China's Reunification. 138p. (Orig.). (C). 1995. pap. text 17.50 (*0-8191-9909-5*); lib. bdg. 39.00 (*0-8191-9908-7*) U Pr of Amer.

Copper, John Franklin & Chen, George P. Taiwan's Elections: Political Development & Democratization in the Republic of China. LC 84-62053. (Reprints Series in Contemporary Asian Studies). iv, 180p. 1984. write for info. (*0-942182-65-0*) Occasional Papers.

Copper, John Franklin & Lee, Ta-ling. Coping with a Bad Global Image: Human Rights in the People's Republic of China, 1993-1994. LC 97-18988. 328p. 1997. 64.00 (*0-7618-0788-8*); pap. 29.50 (*0-7618-0789-6*) U Pr of Amer.

Copper, John Franklin, jt. auth. see Kintner, William R.

Copper, John Franklin, jt. auth. see Lee, Ta-Ling.

Copper, Paul. Brachiopods: Proceedings of the Third International Brachiopod Congress, Sudbury, Ontario, Canada, 2-5 September 1995. Jin, Jisuo, ed. (Illus.). 380p. (C). 1996. text 110.00 (*90-5410-816-9*, Pub. by A A Balkema) Ashgate Pub Co.

***Copperman, Cara.** After School Activities. (60 Super Simple Ser.). (Illus.). 80p. (J). (gr. 2-6). 2000. pap. 6.95 (*0-7373-0485-5*, 04855W, Pub. by Lowell Hse Juvenile) NTC Contemp Pub Co.

Copperman, Cara. Dragon School. 1997. per. 3.50 (*0-671-01180-4*) PB.

Copperman, Rena, ed. see Chandler, Arline.

Copperman, William H. A Guide to the Contractual Aspects of Value Engineering. (Illus.). 115p. (Orig.). (C). 1986. pap. text 25.00 (*1-56049-011-X*) NCSU CE IES.

Coppernoll. Soul 2 Soul. LC 98-24506. 1998. pap. 12.99 (*0-8499-4029-X*) Word Pub.

Coppernoll, Marilyn. Miami County, Indiana: A Pictorial History. LC 95-33444. (Illus.). 1995. write for info. (*0-89865-951-5*) Donning Co.

Coppersmith, D., et al, eds. Advances in Cryptology - CRYPTO '95: 15th Annual International Cryptology Conference, Santa Barbara, CA, August 27-31, 1995, Proceedings, Vol. XII. (Lecture Notes in Computer Science Ser.: Vol. 963). 467p. 1995. pap. 75.00 (*3-540-60221-6*) Spr-Verlag.

Copperud, Roy H. & Nelson, Roy P. Editing the News. 304p. (C). 1983. text. write for info. (*0-697-04353-3*) Brown & Benchmark.

Coppes, Charles H. Millennium Time Bomb: How to Prepare & Survive the Coming Technological Disaster. LC 98-75121. 25690-075121p. 1998. pap. 12.99 (*1-56384-158-4*) Huntington Hse.

Coppes, Leonard J. Daddy, May I Take Communion? Paedocommunion vs The Bible. 288p. (Orig.). 1988. pap. 14.95 (*0-9612862-4-5*) R E F Typesetting Pub.

Copess, Marcia, jt. auth. see Gage, Diane.

Coppett, John I. & Staples, William A. Professional Selling: A Relationship Management Process. 512p. (C). 1990. text. write for info. (*0-538-80367-3*, SD60AA) S-W Pub.

Coppi, B., ed. Theory of Magnetically Confined Plasmas: Proceedings. (Commission of the European Communities Ser.: EUR 5737). (Illus.). 1979. pap. 236.00 (*0-08-023434-8*, Pub. by Pergamon Repr) Franklin.

***Coppi, B., et al, eds.** Plasma Astrophysics. (International School of Physics Enrico Fermi Ser.: Vol. 142). 500p. 2000. 126.00 (*1-58603-073-6*) IOS Press.

Coppieters, Bruno, ed. Contested Borders in the Caucasus. 200p. 1996. pap. 25.00 (*90-5487-117-2*, Pub. by VUB Univ Pr) Paul & Co Pubs.

— The World of the Enlightenment: Die Welt der Aufklarung. 128p. 1994. pap. 19.95 (*90-5487-039-7*) Paul & Co Pubs.

Coppieters, Bruno, et al, eds. Commonwealth & Independence in Post-Soviet Eurasia. LC 97-49408. 216p. 1998. 52.50 (*0-7146-4881-7*, Pub. by F Cass Pubs); pap. 24.50 (*0-7146-4480-3*, Pub. by F Cass Pubs) Intl Spec Bk.

***Coppin, Brigitte.** The Compass: Steering Towards the New World. (Illus.). 47p. (YA). (gr. 6-8). 2000. pap. text 10.00 (*0-7881-6878-9*) DIANE Pub.

Coppin, Brigitte. Inventing Our World. Gibson, Sarah et al, trs. LC 97-27525. (Discoveries Ser.). Orig. Title: The Great Inventions. (Illus.). 80p. (J). (gr. 2-9). 1998. lib. bdg. 23.95 (*0-88682-948-8*, Creat Educ) Creative Co.

Coppin, Clayton & High, Jack. The Politics of Purity: Harvey Washington Wiley & the Origins of Federal Food Regulation. LC 99-13530. 232p. 1999. text 49.50 (*0-472-10984-7*, 10984) U of Mich Pr.

Coppin, Ezra. Murder on the Mountain. LC 88-61490. 148p. 1988. pap. 6.95 (*0-89221-158-X*) New Leaf.

Coppin, Fanny J. Reminiscences of School Life & Hints on Teaching. Vol. 8. LC 94-19855. (African American Women Writers, 1910-1940 Ser.). 1995. 25.00 (*0-8161-1633-4*, G K Hall & Co) Mac Lib Ref.

— Reminiscences to School Life Hints Teaching. Gates, Henry Louis, Jr., ed. (African American Women Writers 1910-1940 Ser.). 1995. 15.95 (*0-7838-1396-1*, Hall Reference) Macmillan.

Copping, A. E. Gotty & the Guv'nor. 231p. 1990. 24.00 (*0-904623-98-X*, Pub. by T Dalton) St Mut.

Copping, L. G. & Hewitt, H. G. Chemistry & Mode of Action of Crop Protection Agents. 160p. 1998. pap. 39.95 (*0-85404-559-7*) Spr-Verlag.

Copping, Lois, jt. ed. see Copping, Wilf.

Copping, Wilf & Copping, Lois, eds. The Country Innkeepers' Cookbook. LC 92-74911. (Illus.). 224p. 1992. pap. 12.95 (*1-56626-015-9*, Cntry Rds Pr) NTC Contemp Pub Co.

Coppinger. IRS Service Center. LC 95-77099. 1995. 125.00 (*0-316-15633-7*) Little.

Coppini, Pompeo. From Dawn to Sunset: American Autobiography. 404p. 1995. lib. bdg. 99.00 (*0-7812-8489-9*) Rprt Serv.

Coppins, Richard, jt. auth. see Wu, Nesa.

Coppins, Richard J. & Umberger, Paul M. Applied Finite Mathematics. LC 85-1228. (C). 1986. text. write for info. (*0-201-10312-5*); student ed. write for info. (*0-201-10215-3*) Addison-Wesley.

— College Mathematics. LC 85-26884. (C). 1986. student ed. write for info. (*0-201-10319-2*); text. write for info. (*0-201-10311-7*) Addison-Wesley.

***Copple, Barbara.** How are We Doing? A Guide to Local Program Evaluation. Kirby, Judy, ed. 86p. (Orig.). 1998. pap. 18.95 (*0-934513-73-2*) Natl Crime DC.

Copple, Carol, et al. Educating the Young Thinker: Classroom Strategies for Cognitive Growth. LC 79-89436. 266p. (Orig.). 1984. pap. 32.50 (*0-89859-523-1*) L Erlbaum Assocs.

— Educating the Young Thinker: Classroom Strategies for Cognitive Growth. LC 79-89436. 286p. (Orig.). 1979. reprint ed. pap. 16.50 (*0-442-27924-8*) Krieger.

Copple, Carol, jt. ed. see Bredekamp, Sue.

Copple, Currey, ed. The Magic of the Medals. 160p. (Orig.). 1996. pap. 12.95 (*0-9650432-0-7*) KatMar.

Copple, Currey, ed. see Holt, Reba W.

Copple, Curry, ed. see Maughon, Robert M.

Copple, David. Heaps. 112p. 1987. pap. text 5.25 (*0-88144-086-8*) Christian Pub.

***Copple, Jim.** Safer Schools. Kirby, Judy, ed. 12p. (Orig.). 1998. pap. Price not set. (*0-934513-85-6*) Natl Crime DC.

Copple, Rudolf, tr. see Mitchell, David, ed.

Copple, Rudolf, tr. see Uehli, Ernst.

Coppleson, M., jt. ed. see Stegner, H. E.

Coppleson, Malcolm, et al, eds. Gynecologic Oncology. 2nd ed. (Illus.). 1052p. 1991. text 360.00 (*0-443-04114-8*) Church.

Coppleson, Malcolm, et al. Colposcopy: A Scientific & Practical Approach to the Cervix, Vagina & Vulva in Health & Disease. 3rd ed. (Illus.). 624p. (C). 1986. 102.95 (*0-398-05153-4*) C C Thomas.

Copplestone, Irewin. Behind Facades: A Dramatic Cutaway Look into Five of the World's Architectural Treasures. (Illus.). 79p. 1998. text 25.00 (*0-7881-5441-9*) DIANE Pub.

Copplestone, Trewin. Frank Lloyd Wright: A Retrospective View. 1999. 14.99 (*0-7628-2431-X*) Alva Pr.

— History & Techniques of the Masters: Monet. 1997. 8.98 (*0-7858-0794-2*) Bk Sales Inc.

Coppo, Giovanni Di, see Di Coppo, Giovanni.

Coppo, Mario, jt. auth. see Berardi, Stefano.

***Coppo, R. & Peruzzi, L., eds.** Moderately Proteinuric IgA Nephropathy in the Young. (Biomedical & Health Research Ser.: Vol. 44). 100p. 2000. 74.00 (*1-58603-059-0*) IOS Press.

Coppo, Timothy. Reproductive Technology: A Research Guide to the Legal Status of the Frozen Human Embryo. LC 95-33288. (Legal Research Guides Ser.: Vol. 25). (9) 40 (12)p. 1996. 42.00 (*0-89941-982-8*, 308900) W S Hein.

***Coppoc, Loran E.** The Rebirth of America: "People Power" & the Constitution. 380p. 2000. pap. text 40.00 (*1-55605-299-5*) Wyndham Hall.

Coppock, Bertram A., jt. auth. see Warfield-Coppock, Nsenga.

Coppock, D. J., jt. auth. see Prest, A. R.

Coppock, D. J., jt. ed. see Prest, A. R.

Coppock, Dawn. Coppock on Tennessee Adoption Law. 2nd ed. LC 99-169687. 541p. 1998. 95.00 (*0-327-06648-2*, 332511) LEXIS Pub.

Coppock, J. T., ed. Second Homes: Curse or Blessing. 1977. 105.00 (*0-08-021371-5*, Pub. by Pergamon Repr) Franklin.

Coppock, J. T., ed. see Royal Scottish Geographical Society Staff.

Coppock, J. T., jt. ed. see Sewell, W. Derrick.

Coppock, James A. The Strategic Management Handbook: Managing Growth with High Performance. LC 98-9234. (Illus.). 200p. 1998. pap. 29.95 (*1-883999-08-1*) Pressmark Intl.

Coppock, Joseph. Foreign Trade of the Middle East: Instability & Growth, 1946-1962. 1966. pap. 11.95 (*0-8156-6022-7*, Pub. by Am U Beirut) Syracuse U Pr.

Coppock, Joseph D. Government Agencies of Consumer Instalment Credit. (Financial Research Program II: Studies in Consumer Installment Financing: No. 5). 240p. 1940. reprint ed. 62.40 (*0-87014-464-2*) Natl Bur Econ Res.

***Coppock, Lillian.** Outstanding Art. (Illus.). 2000. pap. 15.95 (*0-947882-30-8*) Belair Pubns Ltd.

Coppock, Ray & Kreith, Marcia, eds. Farmers & Neighbors: Land Use, Pesticides & Other Issues. 78p. (Orig.). 1996. pap. text 13.00 (*1-885976-03-8*) U CA Agricult Issues.

Coppock, Ray & Smith, Stephanie W., eds. Shaping Agriculture in the 21st Century. 130p. (Orig.). 1995. pap. text 15.00 (*1-885976-02-X*) U CA Agricult Issues.

Coppock, Ray & Weber, Stephanie, eds. Animal Agriculture Impacts on Water Quality in California. 87p. (Orig.). 1995. pap. text 15.00 (*1-885976-00-3*, AA-1) U CA Agricult Issues.

Coppock, Ray, ed. see Butler, L. J. & Ekboir, Javier.

Coppock, Rob, jt. ed. see Hammond, P. Brett.

Coppock, S. Dawn. Tennessee Adoption Law with Forms & Statutes: 1996-1997 Edition. 466p. 1997. pap. text 90.00 (*1-55834-488-8*, 33235-10, MICHIE) LEXIS Pub.

Coppock, Terry, ed. Information Technology & Scholarship: Applications in the Humanities & Social Sciences. (Illus.). 300p. 2000. pap. text 45.00 (*0-19-726205-8*) OUP.

***Coppock, Terry, ed.** Making Information Available in Digital Format: Perspectives from Practitioners. (Illus.). vii, 168p. 1999. 30.00 (*0-11-497276-1*, Pub. by Statnry Office) Balogh.

***Coppock, Vicki & Hopton, John.** Critical Perspectives on Mental Health. LC 99-46626. 2000. pap. write for info. (*1-85728-880-7*) Routledge.

Coppock, Vicki, et al. The Illusion of Post-Feminism: New Women, Old Myths. (Gender & Society Ser.). 224p. 1995. 85.00 (*0-7484-0237-3*); pap. 29.95 (*0-7484-0238-1*) Taylor & Francis.

Coppola, Alan C. Fit & Trim: A How-to-Guide for Diet & Fitness. Wnorowski, Thomas, ed. LC 86-82815. 78p. (Orig.). 1986. pap. 7.95 (*0-931543-03-7*) IM-Pr.

Coppola, Andrew J. Law of Business Contracts. (Quality Paperback Ser.: No. 230). 190p. (Orig.). 1981. reprint ed. pap. 9.95 (*0-8226-0230-X*) Littlefield.

— The Law of Commercial Paper. rev. ed. LC 69-14862. (Quality Paperback Ser.: No. 232). (C). 1977. reprint ed. pap. 9.95 (*0-8226-0232-6*) Littlefield.

Coppola, Anthony H. They Raced Horses on Main Street: Recollection of an Era. limited ed. Coppola, Peter A., ed. LC 90-93489. (Illus.). 200p. (Orig.). 1990. pap. 32.00 (*0-9627978-0-4*) C E Coppola.

Coppola, Brian P., jt. auth. see Krajcik, Joseph.

C

An Asterisk (*) at the beginning of an entry indicates that the title is appearing for the first time.

Coppola, Carlo, ed. Marxist Influences & South Asian Literature. (C). 1988. 38.50 (*81-7001-011-X*, Pub. by Chanakya) S Asia.

Coppola, Eleanor. Notes: On the Making of Apocalypse Now. LC 91-24001. (Illus.). 292p. 1991. reprint ed. pap. 17.95 (*0-87910-150-4*) Limelight Edns.

Coppola, Eli. As Luck Would Have It. (Orig.). 1993. pap. 3.00 (*0-929730-43-7*) Zeitgeist Pr.

Coppola, Francis F. & Hart, James. Bram Stoker's Dracula: The Film & the Legend. LC 92-28191. (Illus.). 176p. 1992. 29.95 (*1-55704-140-7*, Pub. by Newmarket) Norton.

Coppola, Francis F. & Hart, James V. Bram Stoker's Dracula: The Film & the Legend. LC 92-28191. (Illus.). 176p. 1992. pap. 14.95 (*1-55704-139-3*, Pub. by Newmarket) Norton.

***Coppola, Francis Ford.** Francis Ford Coppola's Zoetrope: All Story. Brodeur, Adrienne & Schnee, Samantha, eds. LC 99-57273. (Harvest Original Ser.). 320p. 2000. pap. 14.00 (*0-15-601110-7*, Harvest Bks) Harcourt.

Coppola, G. M. & Schuster, H. F. Chiral A-Hydroxy Acids in Enantioselective Synthesis. LC 97-172561. 524p. 1997. 260.00 (*3-527-29093-1*, Wiley-VCH) Wiley.

Coppola, Gary M. & Schuster, Herbert F. Asymmetric Synthesis: Construction of Chiral Molecules Using Amino Acids. LC 86-22472. 416p. 1987. 159.00 (*0-471-82874-2*) Wiley.

Coppola, Gary M. & Schuster, Herbert F., eds. Isoquinolines, Pt. 3, The Chemistry of Heterocyclic Compounds, Vol. 38, Pt. 3, The Chemistry of Heterocyclic Comp. 2nd ed. LC 80-11510. (Chemistry of Heterocyclic Compounds, a Series of Monographs: Vol. 38, Pt. 3). 568p. 1995. 325.00 (*0-471-62855-7*) Wiley.

Coppola, Joann M. & Frechette, Michael. Study Guide - Self Test for Physiological Chemistry I. 112p. 1995. spiral bd. 15.95 (*0-8403-8942-6*) Kendall-Hunt.

***Coppola, Nancy & Karis, Bill.** Technical Communication, Deliberative Rhetoric & Environmental Discourse: Connections & Directions. LC 99-38153. (ATTW Contemporary Studies in Technical Communications). 2000. pap. write for info. (*1-56750-481-7*) Ablx Pub.

Coppola, Peter A., ed. see Coppola, Anthony H.

Coppola, Pietro Antonio. La Pazza Per Amor & Exerpts from il Postilglione Di Longjumeaux. (Italian Opera II Ser.: Vol. 5). 288p. 1986. text 30.00 (*0-8240-6554-9*) Garland.

Coppola, Ralph. Planetary Emergencies: The Collision of an Asteroid or Comet with the Earth. LC 96-11736. 1996. write for info. (*0-387-94669-1*) Spr-Verlag.

Coppola, Regina. Jin Soo Kim: From Tacit Transit. LC 93-61862. (Illus.). 44p. 1994. pap. 10.00 (*0-929597-04-4*) UMass Univ Gallery.

Coppola, Vincent. Dragons of God: A Journey Through Far-Right America. LC 96-76508. (Illus.). 216p. 1997. 20.00 (*1-56352-327-2*) Longstreet.

— Uneasy Warriors: Coming Back Home: The Perilous Journey of the Green Berets. LC 94-74244. 185p. 1995. 19.95 (*1-56352-197-0*) Longstreet.

Coppolillo, Henry P. Psychodynamic Psychotherapy of Children. 1987. 60.00 (*0-8236-4455-3*, BN#04455) Intl Univs Pr.

Coppolino, Joseph, compiled by. A Book of Devotions. 68p. (Orig.). 1986. pap. 1.75 (*0-8189-0502-6*) Alba.

Coppolino, Robert, jt. auth. see Stroud, Richard C.

Copps, David H. Views from the Road: A Community Guide for Assessing Rural Historic Landscapes. (Orig.). 1995. pap. text 27.50 (*1-55963-412-X*) Island Pr.

Copps, Stephen C., jt. auth. see Copeland, Edna D.

Coppula, Susan. Winterbourne. 1998. pap. 5.99 (*0-449-45876-8*); mass mkt. 5.99 (*0-449-00456-2*, GM) Fawcett.

Coprario, John. John Coprario: Twelve Fantasias for Two Bass Viols & Organ & Eleven Pieces for Three Lyra Viols. Charteris, Richard, ed. (Recent Researches in Music of the Baroque Era Ser.: Vol. RRB41). (Illus.). xxi, 110p. 1982. pap. 45.00 (*0-89579-180-3*) A-R Eds.

Copray, Frans J., jt. ed. see Van Geijn, Herman P.

COPS Subcommittee Staff, jt. auth. see Association's Municipal Credit Research Committee.

Copsey, Ian. Integrated Technical Analysis. LC 99-19108. (Trading Advantage Ser.). 314p. 1999. 59.95 (*0-471-82539-5*) Wiley.

***Copsey, Nigel.** Anti-Fascism in Britain. LC 99-33827. 2000. text 65.00 (*0-312-22765-5*) St Martin.

Copson, E. T., jt. auth. see Baker, Bevan B.

Copson, Edward T. Partial Differential Equations. LC 74-12965. 288p. reprint ed. pap. 82.10 (*0-608-15708-2*, 2031635) Bks Demand.

Copson, Raymond W. Africa's Wars & Prospects for Peace. LC 93-28928. 232p. (C). (gr. 13). 1994. text 75.95 (*1-56324-300-8*); pap. text 34.95 (*1-56324-301-6*) M E Sharpe.

Copstead, Lee-Ellen C. Perspectives on Pathophysiology. LC 94-21277. (Illus.). 1258p. 1995. text 65.00 (*0-7216-3846-5*, W B Saunders Co) Harcrt Hlth Sci Grp.

Copstead, Lee-Ellen C. & Banasik, Jacquelyn L. Pathophys Biological/Behaviora. 2nd ed. Carter, Robin, ed. LC 98-53145. (Illus.). 1230p. 1999. text 66.00 (*0-7216-7178-0*, W B Saunders Co) Harcrt Hlth Sci Grp.

— Pathophysiology: Biological & Behavioral: Study Guide for Copstead/Banasik. 2nd ed. (Illus.). 350p. 1999. text, student ed. write for info. (*0-7216-7183-7*, W B Saunders Co) Harcrt Hlth Sci Grp.

Coptcoat, M. J. & Joyce, M. R. Laparoscopy in Urology, Pt. 1. LC 93-11903. (Illus.). 192p. 1994. 99.95 (*0-632-03664-8*) Blackwell Sci.

Coptcoat, M. J., jt. ed. see Oliver, R. T.

Coptcoat, Malcolm J. The Management of Advanced Prostate Cancer. 64p. 1996. pap. 54.95 (*0-86542-929-4*) Blackwell Sci.

Coptic Church Staff. Coptic Morning Service for the Lord's Day. Crichton-Stuart, John P., tr. LC 72-39871. reprint ed. 47.50 (*0-404-01247-7*) AMS Pr.

Copulsky, Jonathan & Wertheimer, David. Comparative Religion. 1979. 8.00 (*1-881678-23-7*) CSEE.

Copur, Halil. Local Organization Dimensions of Rural Development in Turkey: Socio-Economic Stratification Orientations toward Participation, & Attitudinal Modernity. (Special Series on Rural Local Organization: No. 5). 77p. 1980. pap. 7.50 (*0-86731-032-4*) Cornell CIS RDC.

Copus, David A. Employment Law 101 Deskbook: The Essential Foundation in the Law for Business Executives, HR Professionals & Employment Counsel. 246p. (Orig.). 1996. pap. text 100.00 (*1-890487-01-5*) Ntl Employ Law.

Copus, Julia. The Shuttered Eye. 64p. 1996. pap. 16.95 (*1-85224-338-4*, Pub. by Bloodaxe Bks) Dufour.

Copway, George. Indian Life & Indian History. LC 76-43684. reprint ed. 49.50 (*0-404-15517-0*) AMS Pr.

— Life, Letters & Speeches. Ruoff, A. LaVonne & Smith, Donald B., eds. LC 96-35888. (American Indian Lives Ser.). x, 255p. (C). 1997. text 45.00 (*0-8032-1470-7*) U of Nebr Pr.

Coquereaux, R. & Jadczyk, A. Riemannian Geometry, Fibre Bundles, Kaluza-Klein Theories & All That. 360p. (C). 1988. text 85.00 (*9971-5-0426-X*); pap. text 49.00 (*9971-5-0427-8*) World Scientific Pub.

Coquereaux, R., et al. Infinite Dimensional Geometry, Noncommutative Geometry, Operator Algebra & Fundamental Interactions. 370p. 1995. text 101.00 (*981-02-2244-0*) World Scientific Pub.

Coquery-Vidrovitch, Catherine. Africa: Endurance & Change South of the Sahara. Maisel, David, tr. (Illus.). 448p. 1988. 60.00 (*0-520-05679-5*, Pub. by U CA Pr); pap. 19.95 (*0-520-07881-0*, Pub. by U CA Pr) Cal Prin Full Svc.

— African Women: A Modern History. Raps, Beth G., tr. LC 96-47847. 336p. (C). 1997. pap. 30.00 (*0-8133-2361-4*, Pub. by Westview) HarpC.

Coquery-Vidrovitch, Catherine & Lovejoy, Paul E., eds. The Workers of African Trade. LC 85-2259. (Sage Series on African Modernization & Development: No. 11). (Illus.). 304p. reprint ed. pap. 94.30 (*0-8357-8449-5*, 203471300091) Bks Demand.

Coquet, Michele. African Royal Court Art. Todd, Jane M., tr. LC 98-5071. (Illus.). 179p. 1998. 55.00 (*0-226-11575-5*) U Ch Pr.

Coquillette, Daniel R. The Anglo-American Legal Heritage: Introductory Materials. LC 99-60392. 664p. 1998. boxed set 70.00 (*0-89089-725-5*) Carolina Acad Pr.

— Francis Bacon. LC 92-80405. (Jurists: Profiles in Legal Theory Ser.). 320p. (C). 1992. 45.00 (*0-8047-2089-4*) Stanford U Pr.

— Lawyers & Fundamental Moral Responsibility. LC 94-45186. 344p. (C). 1995. 48.95 (*0-87084-401-6*) Anderson Pub Co.

Coquillette, Daniel R., ed. Law in Colonial Massachusetts, 1630 to 1800. (Illus.). 608p. 1984. text 40.00 (*0-8139-1052-8*) U Pr of Va.

Cora. Cora's Country Cookbook. 1985. 11.95 (*0-02-528150-X*) Macmillan.

Cora, Bruno. Castellani. 1997. pap. 35.00 (*88-8158-071-3*, Pub. by Charta) Dist Art Pubs.

Cora, Helena S. Shaker Sisters Drawings. LC 96-40516. 1997. 24.95 (*1-885254-52-0*, Pub. by Monacelli Pr) Penguin Putnam.

Corada, Monica, jt. auth. see Dejana, Elisabetta.

Coradini, A. & Fulchignoni, M., eds. The Comparative Study of the Planets. 1982. text 199.50 (*90-277-1406-1*) Kluwer Academic.

Corado, Cristina, et al. Foreign Direct Investment, East & West: The Experiences of the Czech Republic, Hungary, Poland, Spain & Portugal. LC 97-194362. 186p. 1996. write for info. (*83-7016-945-7*) Lodzki Univ Pr.

Coradry, Mary U. Maryland's Eastern Shore: A Guide for Wanderers. 224p. (Orig.). 1997. pap. 14.95 (*0-937692-14-X*) Literary Hse Pr.

Coraggio, Jose L. Nicaragua: Revolution & Democracy. 160p. (C). 1986. pap. text 13.95 (*0-04-497019-6*) Routledge.

***Coram, Alex Talbot.** State, Anarchy & Collective Decisions. LC 00-33299. 2000. write for info. (*0-312-23783-9*) St Martin.

Coram, Christopher. A Call to Danger. large type ed. (Linford Mystery Library). 304p. 1988. pap. 16.99 (*0-7089-6621-7*, Linford) Ulverscroft.

— A Call to Die. large type ed. (Linford Mystery Library). 1990. pap. 16.99 (*0-7089-6842-2*, Linford) Ulverscroft.

— Death in Ptarmigan Forest. large type ed. (Linford Mystery Library). 1990. pap. 16.99 (*0-7089-6850-3*) Ulverscroft.

— Death on the Motorway. large type ed. (Linford Mystery Library). 1991. pap. 16.99 (*0-7089-7065-6*) Ulverscroft.

— Prisoner on the Dam. large type ed. (Dales Large Print Ser.). 256p. 1996. pap. 18.99 (*1-85389-623-3*, Dales) Ulverscroft.

— Prisoner on the Run. large type ed. (Dales Large Print Ser.). 265p. 1997. pap. 18.99 (*1-85389-627-6*) Ulverscroft.

Coram, Robert. Dead South. 336p. 1999. mass mkt. 5.99 (*0-451-19688-0*, Sig) NAL.

— Drug Warriors. 1989. pap. 4.50 (*0-318-42580-7*, Sig) NAL.

Coran & Spitz, Lewis. Pediatric Surgery. 5th ed. (Operative Surgery Ser.). Date not set. write for info. (*0-7506-1704-7*) Chapman & Hall.

Coran, Arnold G., jt. auth. see Spitz, Lewis.

Coran, Dan & Schmidt, Julie, eds. The Annual Review of Communications, 1998, Vol. 51. Orig. Title Telecommunication & Information Industry: Proceedings of the National Communications Forum. (Illus.). 1300p. 1998. 295.00 (*0-933217-48-X*) Prof Educ Intl.

Coran, Pierre. The Crying Cat. (Child's World Library). (Illus.). 32p. (J). (gr. k-5). 1992. lib. bdg. 18.50 (*0-89565-745-7*) Childs World.

— Family Tree. LC 97-33062. (Illus.). 32p. (J). 1999. 15.95 (*1-57505-219-9*, Carolrhoda) Lerner Pub.

— The Lazy Beaver. (Child's World Library). (Illus.). 32p. (J). (gr. k-5). 1992. lib. bdg. 18.50 (*0-89565-743-0*) Childs World.

— Old Mr. Bennet's Carrots. (Child's World Library). (Illus.). 32p. (J). (gr. k-5). 1992. lib. bdg. 18.50 (*0-89565-749-X*) Childs World.

— The Ranger Smokes Too Much. (Child's World Library). (Illus.). 32p. (J). (gr. k-5). 1992. lib. bdg. 18.50 (*0-89565-748-1*) Childs World.

— River at Risk. (Child's World Library). (Illus.). 32p. (J). (gr. k-5). 1992. lib. bdg. 18.50 (*0-89565-747-3*) Childs World.

— The Tree Poachers. (Child's World Library). (Illus.). 32p. (J). (gr. k-5). 1992. lib. bdg. 18.50 (*0-89565-746-5*) Childs World.

Coran, Stanley. Why We Love the Dogs We Do: How to Find the Dog That Matches Your Personality. LC 97-50333. 320p. 1998. 24.00 (*0-684-83901-5*) Free Pr.

Coran, Terence. Enciclopedia de la Decoracion. 3rd ed. (SPA.). 343p. 1978. 75.00 (*0-8288-5213-8*, S50463) Fr & Eur.

Corapcioglu, M. Y. Advances in Porous Media, Vol. 1. xiv,310p. 1992. 168.00 (*0-444-88909-4*) Elsevier.

Corapcioglu, M. Y., ed. Advances in Porous Media, Vol. 2. 468p. 1994. text 226.50 (*0-444-81723-9*) Elsevier.

— Advances in Porous Media, Vol. 3. 454p. 1996. text 204.00 (*0-444-82500-2*) Elsevier.

Corapcioglu, M. Yavuz, jt. ed. see Bear, Jacob.

Coraro, Paulo D. Hyperfunctions on Hypo-Analytic Manifolds. LC 94-29391. (Annals of Mathematics Studies). 378p. 1995. pap. text 35.00 (*0-691-02992-X*, Pub. by Princeton U Pr) Cal Prin Full Svc.

Coraro, Paulo D. & Treves, Francois. Hyperfunctions on Hypo-Analytic Manifolds. LC 94-29391. (Annals of Mathematics Studies: 136). 378p. 1995. text 79.50 (*0-691-02993-8*, Pub. by Princeton U Pr) Cal Prin Full Svc.

Corasco, Francesco, ed. see Matulich, Loretta K.

Corathiel, Elizabethe, tr. see Feret, H. M.

Coray, G., jt. ed. see Vanoirbeek, C.

Coray, Henry. Son of Tears. LC 99-18263. 350p. 1999. reprint ed. pap. 9.95 (*1-889542-07-5*) Augustinian Pr.

Coray, Henry W. Against the World: The Odyssey of Athanasius. LC 92-36828. 111p. (Orig.). 1992. pap. 7.90 (*0-921100-35-3*) Inhtce Pubns.

Corazziari, Enrico, ed. Neurogastroenterology. (Illus.). xix, 410p. (Orig.). (C). 1996. pap. text 91.45 (*3-11-015343-2*) De Gruyter.

Corbalan, R., jt. ed. see Vilaseca, R.

Corbalis, Judy. The Cuckoo Bird. LC 90-22576. (Illus.). 32p. (J). (gr. 1-4). 1991. 14.95 (*0-06-021697-2*) HarpC Child Bks.

Corballis, Michael C. Descent of Mind: Psychological Perspectives on Hominid Evolution. LC 98-45132. (Illus.). 376p. 1999. text 65.00 (*0-19-852415-6*) OUP.

***Corballis, Michael C.** Twin Lateralisation: Biology & Psychology. 1999. pap. text 34.95 (*0-86377-543-4*) L Erlbaum Assocs.

Corballis, Michael C. & Beale, Ivan L. The Psychology of Left & Right. 240p. 1976. text 49.95 (*0-89859-114-7*) L Erlbaum Assocs.

— The Psychology of Left & Right. LC 76-13233. (Illus.). 239p. 1976. reprint ed. pap. 74.10 (*0-608-07972-3*, 206794400012) Bks Demand.

Corbally, C. J., et al, eds. The MK Process at 50 Years No. 60: A Powerful Tool for Astrophysical Insight. 440p. 1994. 34.00 (*0-937707-79-1*) Astron Soc Pacific.

Corbally, John E., jt. ed. see Sergiovanni, Thomas J.

Corban, Jay. "I'm Not Dreaming If It's Not about You!" 1998. pap. 15.95 (*1-892896-60-5*) Buy Books.

Corban, Herbert C. Classical & Quantum Theories of Spinning Particles. LC 68-5706. 293p. reprint ed. pap. 90.90 (*0-608-30731-9*, 201628800005) Bks Demand.

Corban, Michele, et al, contrib. by. Philadelphia Creative Directory. 334p. 1998. write for info. (*1-885512-04-X*) Phila Creat.

Corbascio, Aldo N., jt. auth. see Smith, Norman T.

Corbeil & Archambault. Dictionnaire des Termes de la Cuisine. (FRE.). 1998. 49.95 (*0-320-00384-1*) Fr & Eur.

Corbeil, Carole. In the Wings: A Novel. LC 98-108328. 272p. 1999. pap. text 15.95 (*0-7737-5997-2*, Pub. by Stoddart Publ) Genl Dist Srvs.

Corbeil, J. C. Pons Pictorial Dictionary: German-English-French-Spanish. (ENG, FRE, GER & SPA., Illus.). 959p. 1992. 117.00 (*0-7859-8917-X*) Fr & Eur.

— Visual Dictionary Italian-English - English-Italian. (ENG & ITA., Illus.). 896p. 1992. 99.00 (*88-08-14032-6*, Pub. by Zanichelli) IBD Ltd.

***Corbeil, Jean C. & Archambault, Ariane.** Scholastic Visual Dictionary. LC 99-14870. (Illus.). 224p. (ps-3). 2000. 20.01 (*0-439-05940-2*) Scholastic Inc.

Corbeil, Jean-Claude. The Facts on File Visual Dictionary of English. 800p. 1986. 49.95 (*0-8288-1926-2*, M2242) Fr & Eur.

— Visual Dictionary, English-Hebrew/Hebrew-English. (ENG & HEB.). 748p. 1992. 125.00 (*0-7859-9637-0*) Fr & Eur.

— Visual Dictionary in English & Danish. (DAN & ENG.). 1993. 150.00 (*0-7859-9373-8*) Fr & Eur.

— Visual Dictionary in English & German. (ENG & GER.). 1993. 150.00 (*0-7859-9378-9*) Fr & Eur.

— Visual Dictionary in English & Italian. (ENG & ITA.). 896p. 1993. 150.00 (*0-7859-9371-1*) Fr & Eur.

— Visual Dictionary in English & Korean. (ENG & KOR.). 1993. 150.00 (*0-7859-9380-0*) Fr & Eur.

— Visual Dictionary in English & Norwegian. (ENG & NOR.). 1993. 150.00 (*0-7859-9376-2*) Fr & Eur.

— Visual Dictionary in English & Polish. (ENG & POL.). 1993. 150.00 (*0-7859-9379-7*) Fr & Eur.

— Visual Dictionary in English & Portuguese. (ENG & POR.). 1993. 150.00 (*0-7859-9374-6*) Fr & Eur.

— Visual Dictionary in English & Slovenian. (ENG & SLO.). 1993. 150.00 (*0-7859-9377-0*) Fr & Eur.

— Visual Dictionary in English, French, German & Spanish. (ENG, FRE, GER & SPA.). 964p. 1992. 150.00 (*0-7859-9370-3*) Fr & Eur.

— Visual Junior Dictionary in English & French. (ENG & FRE.). 232p. 1993. 39.95 (*0-7859-9375-4*) Fr & Eur.

— Le Visuel: Dictionnaire Thematique: French & English. (ENG & FRE.). 928p. 1992. 115.00 (*0-7859-8025-3*, 2761910834) Fr & Eur.

Corbeil, Jean-Claude & Archambault, Ariane. The MacMillan Visual Dictionary: Spanish/English. 896p. 1997. 39.95 (*0-02-861434-8*) Macmillan.

Corbeil, Jean-Claude & Archambault, Ariane, compiled by. The Macmillan Visual Dictionary. LC 95-20838. (Illus.). 864p. 1996. 65.00 (*0-02-860814-3*) Macmillan.

— The Macmillan Visual Dictionary. abr. ed. LC 95-20838. (Illus.). 864p. 1995. 24.95 (*0-02-860810-0*) Macmillan.

Corbeil, Jean-Claude, ed. see Viller, M. & Drollet, A.

Corbeil, Pierre, jt. auth. see Ritz, Stacy.

Corbeill, Anthony. Controlling Laughter: Political Humor in the Late Roman Republic. 280p. 1996. text 35.00 (*0-691-02739-0*, Pub. by Princeton U Pr) Cal Prin Full Svc.

Corbeiller, Clare Le, see Le Corbeiller, Clare.

Corbel. Little Greenish-Brown Book of Slugs. 96p. 1993. per. 4.95 (*0-88978-267-9*, Pub. by Arsenal Pulp) LPC InBook.

Corbel, Christopher. Options in Teaching English to Adult Speakers of Other Languages: (A Collection of Essays) 131p. (C). 1989. 80.00 (*0-7300-0697-2*, Pub. by Deakin Univ) St Mut.

Corbel, Michael J., jt. ed. see Young, Edward J.

Corbell, Jean-Claude. Visual Dictionary in English & Japanese. (ENG & JPN.). 1993. 195.00 (*0-7859-9372-X*) Fr & Eur.

Corbell, Tony, ed. see Brooks Institute Staff.

Corben, H. C. & Stehle, Philip. Classical Mechanics. 2nd ed. (Illus.). 416p. 1994. reprint ed. pap. 10.95 (*0-486-68063-0*) Dover.

Corben, Herbert C. The Struggle to Understand: A History of Human Wonder & Discovery. LC 91-26727. 398p. 1991. 34.95 (*0-87975-683-7*) Prometheus Bks.

Corben, Richard. Richard Corben's Art Book. (Illus.). 64p. (Orig.). 1990. pap. 14.95 (*0-9623841-2-7*) Fantagor Pr.

— Richard Corben's Art Book, Vol. 2. (Illus.). 64p. (Orig.). 1994. pap. write for info. (*1-884924-00-X*) Fantagor Pr.

Corben, Richard & Strnad, Jan. Jeremy Brood. (Illus.). 64p. (Orig.). 1989. pap. 11.95 (*0-9623841-0-0*) Fantagor Pr.

Corben, Richard, jt. auth. see Jones, Bruce.

Corben, Richard, jt. auth. see Revelstroke, Simon.

Corber, Robert J. Homosexuality in Cold War America: Resistance & the Crisis of Masculinity. LC 96-53408. (New Americanists Ser.). x, 240p. 1997. pap. text 16.95 (*0-8223-1964-0*); lib. bdg. 49.95 (*0-8223-1956-X*) Duke.

— In the Name of National Security: Hitchcock, Homophobia, & the Political Construction of Gender in Postwar America. LC 93-19816. (New Americanists Ser.). (Illus.). 272p. 1993. text 49.95 (*0-8223-1380-4*); pap. text 17.95 (*0-8223-1386-3*) Duke.

Corberan, V. Cortes & Bellon, S. Vic, eds. New Developments in Selective Oxidation II: Proceedings of the 2nd World Congress & Fourth European Workshop Meeting, Benalmadena, Spain, September 20-24, 1993. LC 94-10954. (Studies in Surface Science & Catalysis: Vol. 82). 900p. 1994. 316.50 (*0-444-81552-X*) Elsevier.

Corbet, Colleen. Captivated. 384p. (Orig.). 1996. mass mkt. 5.50 (*0-380-78027-5*, Avon Bks) Morrow Avon.

— Dark Eyes. 384p. (Orig.). 1995. mass mkt. 4.99 (*0-380-78026-7*, Avon Bks) Morrow Avon.

Corbet, Edward P J. The Writing Teacher's Sourcebook. 4th ed. LC 98-45377. 391p. 1999. pap. 29.95 (*0-19-512377-8*) OUP.

Corbet, G. B. & Hill, J. E. Mammals of the Indo-Malayan Region: A Systematic Review. (Illus.). 496p. 1992. text 125.00 (*0-19-854693-9*) OUP.

Corbet, Hugh, jt. ed. see Streeten, Paul.

Corbet, John. Physical Geography Manual. 4th ed. 425p. 1998. 36.95 (*0-7872-4908-4*, 41490801) Kendall-Hunt.

Corbet, John & Walter, Tom. Abridged Version of Physical Geography Manual. abr. ed. 174p. (C). 1996. spiral bd. 19.95 (*0-7872-2925-3*, 41292501) Kendall-Hunt.

***Corbet, Philip S.** Dragonflies: Behavior & Ecology of Odonata. LC 98-45290. 1999. 95.00 (*0-8014-2592-1*) Cornell U Pr.

Corbet, Stephen & King, John, III, eds. Geotextiles in Filtration & Drainage: Proceedings of the Conference Geofad '92: Geotextiles in Filtration & Drainage Organized by the U. K. Chapter of the International Geotextile Society, Held at Churchill College, Cambridge, U. K. September 23, 1992. 142p. 1993. 67.00 (*0-7277-1924-6*) Am Soc Civil Eng.

Corbett. Business & Computer Careers. Date not set. pap. text, teacher ed. 21.95 (*0-314-90183-3*) West Pub.

Corbett. Drake & the Tudor Navy. 1988. 91.95 (*0-566-05616-X*) Ashgate Pub Co.

— Echo. (Illus.). (C). pap. text. write for info. (*0-472-06657-9*) U of Mich Pr.

C

Corbett. Lab Tests & Diagnose Procedure. 5th ed. LC 99-52568. 80p. 1999. pap. 34.96 (0-8385-5588-8, Medical Exam) Appleton & Lange.

***Corbett.** Little English Handbook. 8th ed. 273p. 1998. pap. text 23.53 (0-321-04965-9) Addison-Wesley.

Corbett. Modernity English Art, 1914-30. (Illus.). 250p. 1997. pap. 29.95 (0-7190-3733-6, Pub. by Manchester Univ Pr) St Martin.

Corbett, ed. Politics & Religion in the U. S. (C). 1998. text. write for info. (0-321-01151-1) Addson-Wesley Educ.

Corbett & Young, eds. That Various Field for James Schuyler. (Illus.). 56p. 1991. pap. 7.50 (0-935724-51-6) Figures.

Corbett, jt. auth. see Bell.

Corbett, jt. auth. see Digre.

Corbett, Alan, et al. Witnessing, Nurturing, Protecting: Therapeutic Responses to Sexual Abuse. LC 96-219391. 160p. 1996. pap. 24.95 (1-85346-338-8, Pub. by David Fulton) Taylor & Francis.

Corbett, Barbara. The Day Before Yesterday. LC 95-112180. 1995. pap. 9.95 (0-7022-2537-1, Pub. by Univ Queensland Pr) Intl Spec Bk.

— No Ordinary Childhood. LC 94-152972. 169p. 1994. pap. 16.95 (0-7022-2592-4, Pub. by Univ Queensland Pr) Intl Spec Bk.

***Corbett, Bill.** The Big Slam. LC 99-224321. 1999. pap. 5.95 (0-8222-1692-2) Dramatists Play.

Corbett, Bob. The Cheater's Handbook: The Naughty Student's Guide. LC 99-222926. (Illus.). 160p. 1999. pap. 12.00 (0-06-098812-6) HarpC.

Corbett, Brenda. More Than a Game: A New Focus on Senior Activity Services. LC 97-80848. (Illus.). 210p. 1998. 25.95 (0-910251-94-0, MTG99) Venture Pub PA.

Corbett, Charles R. Lowndes County, Georgia, Probate Records: Recorded July Term 1847-January Term 1852. (Illus.). xxvi, 259p. 1998. 35.00 (0-9661041-0-2) C R Corbett.

Corbett Curtis, C. S. Brave Winds: Native American Experiences. (Petites Major Ser.). 134p. 1996. pap. 9.95 (1-884754-17-1) Potpourri Pubns.

Corbett, D. A. The Regimental Badges of New Zealand. (Illus.). 320p. (C). 1987. 140.00 (0-7855-2170-4, Pub. by Picton) St Mut.

— The Regimental Badges of New Zealand. 320p. (C). 1990. 90.00 (0-908596-05-7, Pub. by Picton) St Mut.

Corbett, David. Australian Public Sector Management. 2nd ed. 304p. 1997. pap. 32.95 (1-86448-160-9, Pub. by Allen & Unwin Pty) Paul & Co Pubs.

Corbett, David P. The Modernity of English Art, 1914-1930. (Illus.). 250p. 1997. 74.95 (0-7190-3732-8, Pub. by Manchester Univ Pr) St Martin.

Corbett, Dick, jt. auth. see Wilson, Bruce L.

Corbett, Don C. Mary Fielding Smith: Daughter of Britain. LC 66-29293. 310p. 1995. 17.95 (0-87579-990-6) Deseret Bk.

Corbett, Donald L., et al, eds. Teaching Stringed Instruments: A Course of Study. (Illus.). 32p. 1991. teacher ed. 16.00 (0-940796-99-6, 1604) MENC.

— Teaching Wind & Percussion Instruments: A Course of Study. 72p. (C). 1991. teacher ed. 20.00 (1-56545-004-3, 1603) MENC.

Corbett, Doris Crowley, ed. see Sullivan, Eileen.

Corbett, Doris R. Outstanding Athletes of Congress. (Outstanding Members of Congress Ser.). (Illus.). 80p. (Orig.). (YA). (gr. 7-12). 1997. pap. 4.95 (0-916200-21-3) US Capitol Hist.

Corbett, Doris S., jt. auth. see Wright, J. E.

Corbett, Edward. The Elements of Reasoning. 90p. (C). 1991. pap. text 14.00 (0-02-325071-2, Macmillan Coll) P-H.

Corbett, Edward P. The Little Rhetoric & Handbook. 2nd ed. LC 81-43604. 637p. 1982. reprint ed. pap. 197.50 (0-7837-8337-X, 204912400010) Bks Demand.

Corbett, Edward P. & Burke, Virginia M., eds. The New Century Composition-Rhetoric. LC 73-150594. (C). 1971. 37.50 (0-8290-2384-4) Irvington.

Corbett, Edward P. & Connors, Robert J. Classical Rhetoric for the Modern Student. 4th ed. LC 97-26686. (Illus.). 578p. 1998. text 39.95 (0-19-511542-2) OUP.

— Style & Statement. LC 97-26751. 160p. 1998. pap. text 16.95 (0-19-511543-0) OUP.

Corbett, Edward P. & Finkle, Sheryl L. The Essay: Old & New. 2nd ed. LC 92-34201. 464p. (C). 1993. pap. text 19.80 (0-13-284621-7) P-H.

— The Little English Handbook: Choices & Conventions. LC 97-9865. 1997. write for info. (0-673-98048-0) Addison-Wesley.

Corbett, Edward P., jt. auth. see Golden, James L.

Corbett, Edward P. J. Essays on the Rhetoric of the Western World. 400p. 1990. pap. text 40.95 (0-8403-5660-9) Kendall-Hunt.

— Selected Essays of Edward P. J. Corbett. Connors, Robert J., ed. LC 87-42940. (SMU Studies in Composition & Rhetoric). 384p. 1989. 26.95 (0-87074-264-7); pap. 14.95 (0-87074-271-X) SMU Press.

Corbett, Edward P. J. & Finkle, Sheryl L. The Little English Handbook: Choices & Conventions. LC 94-18590. (C). 1995. pap. 10.50 (0-673-99323-X) HarpC.

Corbett, Edward P.J. & Finkle, Sheryl L. The Little English Handbook: Choices & Conventions. 7th ed. 288p. 1995. pap. 14.95 (0-8230-5002-5) Watsn-Guptill.

Corbett, Gary M. Didja' Ever Make Butter? And Other Hilarious Childhood Survival Tales. 217p. 19.95 (1-886882-00-2) Polo Springs.

Corbett, Gordon, jt. auth. see Burgess, David R.

Corbett, Grahame. Fantastic Animals. 1998. pap. 4.95 (0-7894-3889-5) DK Pub Inc.

***Corbett, Grahame.** Jonah & the Big Fish. (Bible Sticker Activity Bks.). 2000. pap. 5.95 (0-7894-5329-0) DK Pub Inc.

Corbett, Greville. Hierarchies, Targets & Controllers: Agreement Patterns in Slavic. LC 83-61325. 272p. (C). 1983. text 30.00 (0-271-00354-5) Pa St U Pr.

Corbett, Greville G. Gender. (Cambridge Textbooks in Linguistics Ser.). (Illus.). 383p. (C). 1991. text 74.95 (0-521-32939-6); pap. text 25.95 (0-521-33845-X) Cambridge U Pr.

Corbett, H. Dickson. On the Meaning of Restructuring. 15p. 1990. pap. 5.95 (1-56602-035-2) Research Better.

Corbett, H. Dickson & D'Amico, Joseph J. Training for School Improvement: Understanding Context & Change. 205p. 1985. pap. 24.95 (1-56602-010-7) Research Better.

Corbett, H. Dickson & Wilson, Bruce L. Testing, Reform & Rebellion. Nobilt, George & Pink, William, eds. (Interpretive Perspectives on Education & Policy Ser.). 192p. 1991. pap. 39.50 (1-56750-083-8); text 73.25 (0-89391-719-2) Ablx Pub.

Corbett, H. Dickson, jt. auth. see D'Amico, Joseph J.

Corbett, H. Roger, Jr. Virginia White Water. 1988. pap. text 12.50 (0-686-22838-3) Seneca Pr Rockville.

Corbett, J., ed. see Musalem, M. & Vazquez, O. Riosz.

Corbett, J., jt. ed. see Williams, Aubrey.

Corbett, J. Martin, jt. auth. see Scarbrough, Harry.

Corbett, J. W., et al, eds. Oxygen, Carbon, Hydrogen, & Nitrogen in Crystalline Silicon, Vol. 59. (Materials Research Society Symposium Proceedings Ser.). 1986. text 17.50 (0-931837-24-3) Materials Res.

Corbett, Jack. Death on the Wild Side. 465p. (Orig.). 1995. pap. 19.95 (0-9647143-0-2) Nirvana Pubng.

Corbett, James. Through French Windows: An Introduction to France in the Nineties. LC 93-41808. (Illus.). 320p. (C). 1994. pap. 22.95 (0-472-06469-X, 06469) U of Mich Pr.

Corbett, James A., tr. see Simon, Yves R.

Corbett, James J. The Roar of the Crowd. LC 76-6330. (Irish Americans Ser.). 1976. reprint ed. 29.95 (0-405-09326-8) Ayer.

Corbett, James J., jt. auth. see Martin, Timothy J.

Corbett, James M., jt. auth. see Bentley, William K.

Corbett, James W. & Ianniello, Louis C., eds. Radiation-Induced Voids in Metals: Proceedings. LC 72-600048. (AEC Symposium Ser.). 878p. 1972. pap. 30.00 (0-87079-320-9, CONF-710601); fiche 9.00 (0-87079-321-7, CONF-710601) DOE.

Corbett, Jane. Laboratory & Diagnostic Procedures with Nursing Diagnoses. 4th ed. LC 95-36448. (C). 1995. pap. text 34.95 (0-8385-5595-0, A5595-2) Appleton & Lange.

Corbett, Jenny. Bad-Mouthing: The Language of Special Needs. 114p. 1995. 69.95 (0-7507-0501-9, Falmer Pr); pap. 27.95 (0-7507-0502-7, Falmer Pr) Taylor & Francis.

— Special Education Needs in the 20th Century: A Cultural Analysis. LC 98-190457. (Institute of Education Ser.). 1998. pap. 24.95 (0-304-70081-9) Continuum.

— Special Education Needs in the 20th Century: A Cultural Analysis. LC 98-190457. (Institute Of Education). 1998. 75.00 (0-304-70080-0) Continuum.

— Uneasy Transitions: Disaffection in Post-Compulsory Education & Training. (Education & Alienation Ser.). 208p. 1990. 69.95 (1-85000-795-0, Falmer Pr); pap. 32.95 (1-85000-796-9, Falmer Pr) Taylor & Francis.

***Corbett, Jenny & Clough, Peter.** Theories of Inclusive Education: A Student's Guide. 256p. 2000. pap. 25.95 (0-7619-6941-1, Pub. by P Chapman); lib. bdg. 74.00 (0-7619-6940-3, Pub. by P Chapman) Sage.

Corbett, Jenny, jt. ed. see Wolfendale, Sheila.

Corbett, Jim, jt. auth. see Elford, Ricardo.

Corbett, Jim, pseud. English for International Banking & Finance. 122p. (C). 1991. pap. text 16.95 (0-521-31999-4) Cambridge U Pr.

— English for International Banking & Finance: Guide for Teachers. 87p. (C). 1991. pap. text 17.95 (0-521-32000-3) Cambridge U Pr.

— Jungle Lore. 2nd ed. (Illus.). 110p. 1990. text 15.95 (0-19-562487-4) OUP.

***Corbett, Jim, pseud.** Jungle Lore. 2nd ed. 184p. 2000. pap. 12.95 (0-19-565185-5) OUP.

Corbett, Jim, pseud. Man-Eaters. (Adventure Library: Vol. 11). (Illus.). 288p. 1997. lib. bdg. 35.00 (1-885283-11-3) Advent Library.

— Man-Eaters of Kumaon. Date not set. lib. bdg. 21.95 (0-8488-1967-5) Amereon Ltd.

— Man-Eaters of Kumaon. (Oxford India Paperbacks Ser.). (Illus.). 228p. (C). 1993. pap. 8.95 (0-19-562255-3) OUP.

— Man-Eaters of Kumaon. 238p. 1985. reprint ed. lib. bdg. 31.95 (0-89966-574-8) Buccaneer Bks.

— The Man-Eating Leopard of Rudraprayag. (Illus.). 198p. 1989. pap. 9.95 (0-19-562256-1) OUP.

— The Man-Eating Leopard of Rudraprayag. 200p. 1991. reprint ed. lib. bdg. 19.95 (0-89966-798-8) Buccaneer Bks.

— More Man-Eaters of Kumaon. 210p. 1991. lib. bdg. 23.95 (0-89966-797-X) Buccaneer Bks.

— The Sanctuary Church. LC 86-63044. (Orig.). 1986. pap. 4.00 (0-87574-270-X) Pendle Hill.

— The Temple Tiger. 210p. 1991. reprint ed. lib. bdg. 19.95 (0-89966-799-6) Buccaneer Bks.

— The Temple Tiger & More Man Eaters of Kumaon. (Illus.). 190p. 1989. pap. 8.95 (0-19-562257-X) OUP.

— A White Stone. LC 98-112934. 1997. pap. 12.00 (0-9657268-0-0); pap., wbk. ed. 12.00 (0-9657268-1-9) J Corbett.

Corbett, Jim, pseud & Corbett, Merry. From Our Father's Heart to You. 1998. pap. 12.00 (0-9657268-2-7) J Corbett.

Corbett, John. Extended Play: Sounding off from John Cage to Dr. Funkenstein. LC 93-43239. (Illus.). 408p. 1994. pap. 17.95 (0-8223-1473-8); text 49.95 (0-8223-1456-8) Duke.

Corbett, John. Language & Scottish Literature: Teaching Scottish Language & Literature. 288p. 1997. pap. 25.00 (0-7486-0826-5, Pub. by Edinburgh U Pr) Col U Pr.

Corbett, John. Written in the Language of the Scottish Nation: A History of Literary Translation into Scots. LC 98-37721. (Topics in Translation Ser.). 210p. 1999. 59.00 (1-85359-431-8) Multilingual Matters.

Corbett, Julia. Sea Life at the Ocean's Edge. Moore, Shirley T. & Warren, Hank, eds. (Illus.). 24p. (J). (gr. 4-6). 1984. pap. text 2.95 (0-914019-04-X) NW Interpretive.

Corbett, Julia M., jt. auth. see Corbett, Michael.

Corbett, Julian. Monk. LC 72-154148. (Select Bibliographies Reprint Ser.). 1977. reprint ed. 20.95 (0-8369-5764-4) Ayer.

— Naval Operations, Vol. III. 2nd ed. (Great War Ser.: No. 41). (Illus.). 486p. 1995. reprint ed. 49.95 (0-89839-231-4) Battery Pr.

Corbett, Julian S. The Campaign of Trafalgar, 2 vols. in 1. LC 70-154131. (Illus.). reprint ed. 67.50 (0-404-09234-9) AMS Pr.

— England in the Mediterranean: A Study of the Rise & Influence of British Power Within the Straits 1603-1713. LC 86-25733. (Illus.). 639p. 1987. reprint ed. lib. bdg. 125.00 (0-313-25417-6, CENM, Greenwood Pr) Greenwood.

— England in the Seven Years War, 2 vols. 2nd ed. LC 76-154130. reprint ed. 125.00 (0-404-09224-1) AMS Pr.

— England in the Seven Years' War, 2 vols., Vol. 1. LC 92-26684. 448p. 1992. reprint ed. 50.00 (1-85367-133-9) Stackpole.

— England in the Seven Years' War, 2 vols., Vol. 2. LC 92-26684. 416p. 1992. reprint ed. 50.00 (1-85367-134-7) Stackpole.

— Maritime Operations in the Russo-Japanese War, 1904-1905, 2 vols., Set. LC 94-34316. 1072p. 1994. 79.95 (1-55750-129-7) Naval Inst Pr.

— Naval Operations, Vol. I. (Great War Ser.: Vol. 55). (Illus.). 528p. 1997. reprint ed. 49.95 (0-89839-256-X) Battery Pr.

— Naval Operations, Vol. II. (Great War Ser.: Vol. 56). (Illus.). 460p. 1997. reprint ed. 54.95 (0-89839-257-8) Battery Pr.

— Naval Operations, 1914-1918, 5 vols. Incl. Vol. 1, Pt. 1. (0-404-09281-0); Vol. 1, Pt. 2. (0-404-09282-9); Vol. 2. (0-404-09283-7); Vol. 3, Pt. 1. (0-404-09284-5); Vol. 3, Pt. 2. (0-404-09285-3); Vol. 4, Pt. 1. (0-404-09286-1); Vol. 4, Pt. 2. (0-404-09287-X); Vol. 5, Pt. 1. (0-404-09288-8); Vol. 5, Pt. 2. (0-404-09289-6); (Illus.). reprint ed. write for info. (0-404-09280-2) AMS Pr.

— Signals & Instructions, 1776-1794. (C). 1987. 115.00 (0-7855-6042-4) St Mut.

— Sir Francis Drake. LC 77-105513. (BCL Ser. II). reprint ed. 29.50 (0-404-01725-8) AMS Pr.

— Sir Francis Drake. LC 68-25228. (English Biography Ser.: No. 31). 1969. reprint ed. lib. bdg. 75.00 (0-8383-0932-1) M S G Haskell Hse.

— Some Principles of Maritime Strategy. LC 76-154122. (BCL Ser. II). reprint ed. 32.50 (0-404-09227-6) AMS Pr.

Corbett, Julian S., ed. Papers Relating to the Spanish War, 1585-1587. 420p. 1987. text 86.95 (0-566-05565-1, Pub. by Scolar Pr) Ashgate Pub Co.

Corbett, Katharine I. In Her Place: A Guide to St. Louis Women's History. LC 99-43356. (Illus.). 320p. 1999. 39.95 (1-883982-30-8); pap. 22.50 (1-883982-26-X) MO Hist Soc.

Corbett, Katharine T. & Miller, Howard S. St. Louis in the Gilded Age. LC 93-79982. (Illus.). 102p. 1993. pap. 12.95 (1-883982-01-4) MO Hist Soc.

Corbett, Kathryn, tr. see Doumerc, Beatriz & Alcantara, Ricardo.

Corbett, Kathryn, tr. see Rondon, Javier.

Corbett, Kathryn L. & Preston, Kathleen. From the Catbird Seat: A History of Women's Studies at Humboldt State University, 1971-1996. (Illus.). 216p. 1998. pap. 11.95 (0-9663867-0-1) C & P Publ.

Corbett, Laurie. The Dingo: In Australia & Asia. (Comstock Bk.). (Illus.). 216p. 1995. pap. text 27.50 (0-8014-8264-X) Cornell U Pr.

— The Dingo in Australia & Asia. LC 97-117568. (Illus.). 200p. 1994. pap. 27.95 (0-86840-230-3, Pub. by New South Wales Univ Pr) Intl Spec Bk.

Corbett, Lionel. The Religious Function of the Psyche. LC 95-25778. 272p. (C). 1996. 85.00 (0-415-14400-0); pap. 25.99 (0-415-14401-9) Routledge.

Corbett, Lionel, jt. ed. see Stein, Murray.

Corbett, Lynn & Leone, Bill. Sextrology. 2000. 37.50 (0-688-16757-8, Wm Morrow) Morrow Avon.

Corbett, M. J., et al. Crossing the Border: The Social & Engineering Design in Computer Integrated Manufacturing Systems. Gill, Karamjit S., ed. (Artificial Intelligence & Society Ser.). (Illus.). 136p. 1991. pap. 44.00 (0-387-19613-7) Spr-Verlag.

Corbett, M. M., et al. Law of Succession in South Africa: Includes the 1994 Supplement. lvi, 739p. 1980. pap., suppl. ed. 58.50 (0-7021-1096-5, 15598, Pub. by Juta & Co) Gaunt.

Corbett, Margaret D. Help Yourself to Better Sight. 1980. pap. 10.00 (0-87980-048-8) Wilshire.

Corbett, Margery & Norton, Michael. Engraving in England in the Reign of Charles I: A Catalogue Raisonne. (Illus.). 630p. 1999. reprint ed. 160.00 (1-55660-182-4) A Wofsy Fine Arts.

Corbett, Marjorie, ed. see Lienesch, William C.

Corbett, Marjorie R., pref. Greenline Parks: Land Conservation Trends for the Eighties & Beyond. (Illus.). 142p. (Orig.). 1984. pap. 9.95 (0-940091-12-7) Natl Parks & Cons.

***Corbett, Mary Jean.** Allegories of Union in Irish & English Writing, 1790-1870: Politics, History & the Family from Edgeworth to Arnold. LC 99-86658. 260p. 2000. Price not set. (0-521-66132-3) Cambridge U Pr.

Corbett, MaryAnn, ed. Directory of Indexing & Abstracting Courses & Seminars. LC 98-21546. 40p. 1998. pap. 18.00 (1-57387-056-0) Info Today Inc.

Corbett, Maurice N. Harp of Ethiopia. LC 74-152918. (Black Heritage Library Collection). 1977. 26.95 (0-8369-8762-4) Ayer.

Corbett, Merry, jt. auth. see Corbett, Jim, pseud.

Corbett, Michael. American Public Opinion. 381p. (Orig.). (C). 1991. pap. text 34.95 (0-8013-0323-0, 78091) Longman.

— Research Methods in Political Science: An Introduction Using MicroCase. 3rd ed. (C). 1999. pap. text 26.00 (0-922914-30-3) Thomson Learn.

— 33 Ruthless Rules of Local Advertising. 1999. pap. text 14.95 (0-9667383-9-X) Pinnacle Books.

Corbett, Michael & Corbett, Julia M. Politics & Religion in the United States. LC 98-19364. (Garland Reference Library of Social Science). 488p. 1998. 60.00 (0-8153-3141-X); pap. 24.95 (0-8153-3143-6) Garland.

Corbett, Mike, jt. auth. see Boga, Steven.

Corbett, Nancy. Inner Cleansing. 163p. (Orig.). 1993. pap. 15.95 (1-85327-083-0, Pub. by Prism Pr) Assoc Pubs Grp.

Corbett, Nancy A. & Beveridge, Phyllis. Computer Simulations for Clinical Nursing, Vol. 2. 1986. 783.00 (0-7216-1368-3, W B Saunders Co); text 783.00 (0-7216-1343-8, W B Saunders Co) Harcrt Hlth Sci Grp.

— Computer Simulations in Clinical Nursing, Vol. 1. 1983. 665.00 (0-7216-1023-4, W B Saunders Co); pap. text, student ed. 16.00 (0-7216-1154-0, W B Saunders Co) Harcrt Hlth Sci Grp.

Corbett, Nancy A., jt. auth. see Hole, John W., Jr.

Corbett, Nancy A. S., jt. auth. see Hole, John W., Jr.

Corbett, Noel, tr. see Margolis, Maxine L. & Murphy, Martin F., eds.

Corbett, P. Scott. Quiet Passages: The Exchange of Civilians Between the United States & Japan During the Second World War. LC 87-2069. 235p. 1987. reprint ed. pap. 72.90 (0-608-07556-6, 205265600009) Bks Demand.

Corbett, Patricia. The Prayer Book of Michelino Da Besozzo. (Illus.). 1995. 45.00 (0-8076-1389-4) Braziller.

— The Prayer Book of Michelino Da Besozzo. LC 81-68186. (Illus.). 1981. boxed set 65.00 (0-8076-1016-X) Braziller.

Corbett, Paula & Huntsman, Leslee. Quick Change Displays. (Teacher Aid Ser.). 43p. 1985. 6.95 (0-513-01772-0) Denison.

Corbett, Pearson H. Hyrum Smith: Patriarch. (Classics in Mormon Literature Ser.). xxii, 472p. 1995. 17.95 (0-87579-950-7) Deseret Bk.

Corbett, Percy E. The Growth of World Law. LC 70-132236. 228p. 1971. reprint ed. pap. 70.70 (0-7837-9325-1, 206006500004) Bks Demand.

Corbett, Robert B., ed. Rolls for the Metalworking Industries. LC 89-82593. 357p. 1990. reprint ed. pap. 110.70 (0-608-00481-2, 206130000007) Bks Demand.

Corbett, Roger & Matacia, Louis J. An Illustrated Guide to Ten Beginner & Intermediate Canoe Trips. 4th rev. ed. (Blue Ridge Voyages Ser.: Vol. 1). (Illus.). (Orig.). 1973. pap. 3.50 (0-686-08918-9) Matacia.

Corbett, Roger, jt. auth. see Matacia, Louis J.

Corbett, Ron, jt. auth. see Karsh, Malak.

Corbett, Ruth, ed. How to Be a Professional Line Artist. LC 87-72469. 126p. 1988. pap. 9.50 (0-88108-046-2); text 12.50 (0-88108-045-4) Art Dir.

Corbett, S. E. The Diver's Reference Dictionary. 1986. text 22.50 (0-941332-03-9, D053) Best Pub Co.

Corbett, Sandra. Educating Students with Traumatic Brain Injuries, a Resource & Planning Guide. LC 96-622120. 184p. 1996. pap. text, teacher ed. 27.00 (1-57337-031-2) WI Dept Pub Instruct.

Corbett, Sandra L., jt. auth. see Bober, Patricia A.

Corbett, Sara. Animals & Us. LC 95-7024. (World of Difference Ser.). (Illus.). 32p. (J). (gr. 3-7). 1995. lib. bdg. 21.00 (0-516-08177-2) Childrens.

— Animals & Us. (World of Difference Ser.). (Illus.). 32p. (J). (gr. 3-7). 1996. pap. 6.95 (0-516-48177-0) Childrens.

— Hats off to Hats! LC 95-2394. (World of Difference Ser.). (Illus.). 32p. (J). (gr. 4-6). 1995. lib. bdg. 21.00 (0-516-08176-4) Childrens.

— Hats off to Hats. (World of Difference Ser.). (Illus.). 32p. (J). (gr. 4-6). 1996. reprint ed. pap. 6.95 (0-516-48176-2) Childrens.

— Hold Everything! LC 95-39665. (World of Difference Ser.). (Illus.). 32p. (J). (gr. 4-6). 1996. lib. bdg. 21.00 (0-516-08212-4) Childrens.

— Hold Everything! (World of Difference Ser.). (Illus.). 32p. (J). (gr. 4-6). 1996. pap. 6.95 (0-516-20221-9) Childrens.

— Shake, Rattle, & Strum. LC 94-36343. (World of Difference Ser.). (Illus.). 32p. (J). (gr. 4-6). 1995. lib. bdg. 21.00 (0-516-08194-2) Childrens.

— Shake, Rattle & Strum. (World of Difference Ser.). (Illus.). 32p. (J). 1995. pap. 6.95 (0-516-48194-0) Childrens.

— Venus to the Hoop: A Gold Medal Year in Women's Basketball. LC 97-184758. 342p. 1997. 23.95 (0-385-48682-0) Doubleday.

— Venus to the Hoop: A Gold Medal Year in Women's Basketball. (Illus.). 352p. 1998. pap. 12.95 (0-385-49352-5) Doubleday.

— What a Doll! LC 95-39664. (World of Difference Ser.). (Illus.). 32p. (J). (gr. 4-6). 1996. lib. bdg. 21.00 (0-516-08211-6) Childrens.

— What a Doll! LC 95-39664. (World of Difference Ser.). (Illus.). 32p. (J). (gr. 4-6). 1996. pap. 6.95 (*0-516-20080-1*) Childrens.

Corbett, Sara & Flanagan, Alice K. Masks! LC 95-39672. (World of Difference Ser.). (Illus.). 32p. (J). (gr. 3-7). 1996. lib. bdg. 21.00 (*0-516-08213-2*) Childrens.

Corbett, Sarah. The Red Wardrobe. LC 99-164603. 64p. 1998. pap. 17.95 (*1-85411-216-3*, Pub. by Seren Bks) Dufour.

Corbett, Scott. Lemonade Trick. (J). 1960. 9.09 (*0-606-03600-8*, Pub. by Turtleback) Demco.

Corbett, Scott. The Lemonade Trick. LC 59-7361. (Illus.). 112p. (J). (gr. 4-7). 1988. reprint ed. pap. 2.99 (*0-590-32197-8*, Apple Paperbacks) Scholastic Inc.

— We Chose Cape Cod. LC 52-13127. 1970. reprint ed. pap. 9.95 (*0-85699-007-8*) Chatham Pr.

— We Chose Cape Cod. 320p. 1984. reprint ed. pap. 8.95 (*0-940160-27-7*) Parnassus Imprints.

Corbett, Scott & Vasiliu, Mircea. Ever Ride a Dinosaur? LC 69-11174. 113p. (J). 1969. write for info. (*0-03-074605-1*) Holt R&W.

***Corbett, Suzanne.** Pushcarts & Stalls: The Soulard Market History Cookbook. (Illus.). 235p. 1999. pap. 16.95 (*0-911921-38-9*, 1-300-04) Palmerston & Reed.

***Corbett, Terry.** Nicholas & the Elves. (Illus.). 20p. (Orig.). (J). 1999. pap. 5.99 (*1-929731-03-5*) Rowfant.

***Corbett, Theodore.** The Making of American Resorts: Saratoga Springs, Ballston Spa & Lake George. LC 00-28074. (Illus.). 288p. (C). 2001. text 59.00 (*0-8135-2841-0*); pap. text 28.00 (*0-8135-2842-9*) Rutgers U Pr.

Corbett, Thomas. Throughput Accounting. 160p. 1998. pap. 25.00 (*0-88427-158-7*) North River.

Corbett, Tiffany K., ed. see Summit Junior Fortnightly Club Staff.

Corbett, Tom, jt. auth. see Robinson, Lady S.

Corbett, W. Ark of the People. mass mkt. 8.95 (*0-340-69965-5*, Pub. by Hodder & Stought Ltd) Trafalgar.

— Battle of Chinnbrook Wood. mass mkt. 8.95 (*0-340-69964-7*, Pub. by Hodder & Stought Ltd) Trafalgar.

— Dragon's Egg & Other Stories. (Illus.). (J). mass mkt. 8.95 (*0-340-65576-3*, Pub. by Hodder & Stought Ltd) Trafalgar.

Corbett, William. Boston Vermont. LC 99-34172. 96p. 1999. pap. 14.00 (*1-58195-011-X*, Pub. by Zoland Bks) SPD-Small Pr Dist.

— The Collected Poems of William Corbett. LC 84-71923. (Poets Ser.). 153p. (Orig.). 1984. 25.00 (*0-915032-45-7*); pap. 12.95 (*0-915032-46-5*) Natl Poet Foun.

— Don't Think: Look. LC 91-65385. 128p. (Orig.). 1991. pap. 9.95 (*0-944072-17-8*) Zoland Bks.

— Furthering My Education. LC 96-37563. 208p. 1997. 21.95 (*0-944072-74-7*) Zoland Bks.

— New & Selected Poems. LC 94-23652. 288p. 1995. pap. 18.75 (*0-944072-54-2*) Zoland Bks.

— New York Literary Lights: William Corbett. LC 97-80077. 338p. 1998. pap. 16.95 (*1-55597-272-1*) Graywolf.

— Philip Guston's Late Work: A Memoir. LC 94-14571. (Illus.). 128p. 1994. 17.50 (*0-944072-43-7*) Zoland Bks.

— Remembrances. 1987. pap. 5.00 (*0-935724-29-X*) Figures.

— Surplus Population. abr. rev. ed. 48p. 1994. pap. 5.95 (*0-948688-07-6*, Pub. by Pelagian Pr) AK Pr Dist.

***Corbett, William, et al, eds.** The Blind See Only This World: Poems for John Wieners. 104p. 2000. pap. write for info. (*1-887123-34-2*, Pub. by Granary Bks) DAP Assocs.

Corbett, William & Hunter, Sam. John Raimondi: Sculptor. LC 99-16550. (Illus.). 128p. 1999. 45.00 (*1-55595-179-1*) Hudson Hills.

Corbett, William R. Adventures at Mitchell Lake: Retreating & Recharging in Canada's Wilderness, Vol. 1. LC 95-198114. (Illus.). 102p. (Orig.). 1997. pap. 11.95 (*0-919574-92-0*) Gordon Soules Bk.

Corbett-Winder, Kate. The Barn Book: Creative Conversions for Country Living. (Illus.). 128p. 1996. 29.95 (*0-09-180928-2*, Pub. by Ebury Pr) Trafalgar.

Corbetta, Piergiorgio, jt. ed. see Leonardi, Robert.

Corbi, Angel L. Leukocyte Integrins: Structure, Expression & Function. LC 96-22039. (Molecular Biology Intelligence Unit Ser.). 200p. 1996. 99.00 (*1-57059-358-2*) Landes Bioscience.

Corbi, Josep E. & Prades, Josep L. Minds, Causes & Mechanisms: A Case Against Physicalism. LC 99-16131. (Aristotelian Society Monographs: Vol. 17). 288p. 1999. text 64.95 (*0-631-21801-7*) Blackwell Pubs.

***Corbi, Josep E. & Prades, Josep L.** Minds, Causes & Mechanisms: A Case Against Physicalism. LC 99-16131. (Aristotelian Society Monographs: Vol. 17). 288p. 1999. pap. text 29.95 (*0-631-21802-5*) Blackwell Pubs.

Corbian, Francisco L. Diccionario de Immunologia. (SPA.). 256p. 1991. pap. 25.95 (*0-7859-6502-5*) Fr & Eur.

Corbiere. The Centenary Corbiere. Warner, Val, tr. from FRE. LC 74-18607. 171p. 1975. 21.00 (*0-8023-1256-X*) Dufour.

Corbiere-Cros, Tristan. Oeuvres Completes. Forestier, Michel, ed. (FRE.). 1970. lib. bdg. 105.00 (*0-7859-3919-9*) Fr & Eur.

Corbiere, Tristan. Poems. McElroy, Walter, tr. from FRE. LC 77-10257. 80p. reprint ed. 27.50 (*0-404-16312-2*) AMS Pr.

Corbiere, Tristan, jt. auth. see Cros, Charles.

***Corbijn, Anton.** Anton Corbijn: 33 Still Lives. 2000. 55.00 (*3-8238-5448-8*) te Neues.

Corbijn, Anton. Star Trak. 144p. 1996. 55.00 (*3-88814-857-X*) Stewart Tabori & Chang.

Corbijn, Anton, photos by. Famouz Photographs 1976-88. (Illus.). 105p. 1997. 80.00 (*1-55670-598-0*) Stewart Tabori & Chang.

Corbijn, Anton, photos by. Star Trak. (Illus.). 144p. 1996. 55.00 (*1-55670-519-0*) Stewart Tabori & Chang.

Corbin. Concepts Physical Fitness Test. 8th ed. 1993. 23.69 (*0-697-23346-4*) McGraw.

— Fitness & Wellness Concept. 2nd ed. 1998. 21.50 (*0-07-229608-9*) McGraw.

— Fitness Wellness , 1. 1999. pap. 7.00 (*0-07-235783-5*) McGraw.

— Stress Management. 2000. pap. text 11.97 (*0-395-97328-7*) HM.

Corbin & Lindsay. Concepts of Fitness & Wellness. 3rd ed. LC 99-14990. 1999. pap. text 25.00 (*0-697-29566-4*) McGraw.

Corbin & Lindsey. Con. Course Org. Concepts of Physical Fitness. 9th ed. 1996. 30.00 (*0-697-25891-2*, WCB McGr Hill) McGrw-H Hghr Educ.

— Concepts Physical Fitness. 10th ed. LC 99-14989. 1999. pap. text 20.50 (*0-697-29567-2*) McGraw.

— Fitness & Wellness Concepts. 2nd ed. 1997. text 18.00 (*0-697-29574-5*) McGraw.

— Menu Guide: Physical Fitness. 1995. 11.25 (*0-697-31440-5*, WCB McGr Hill) McGrw-H Hghr Educ.

— Physical Fitness: Test Item File. 1996. teacher ed. 21.87 (*0-697-31432-4*, WCB McGr Hill) McGrw-H Hghr Educ.

Corbin & Perillo. Corbin on Contracts, 13 vols. LC 93-60572. 1998. text 728.00 (*0-314-09259-5*, 63310, MICHIE) LEXIS Pub.

Corbin, Alain. The Foul & the Fragrant. LC 86-7684. 384p. 1986. 37.50 (*0-674-31175-2*) HUP.

— The Foul & the Fragrant: Odor & the French Social Imagination. Kochan, Miriam L., tr. LC 86-7684. 384p. 1988. pap. text 17.50 (*0-674-31176-0*) HUP.

— The Lure of the Sea: The Discovery of the Seaside in the Western World. Phelps, Jocelyn, tr. from FRE. (Illus.). 380p. (C). 1994. 45.00 (*0-520-06638-3*, Pub. by U CA Pr) Cal Prin Full Svc.

— Time, Desire, & Horror: Towards a History of the Senses. Birrell, Jean, tr. from FRE. 224p. 1996. 53.95 (*0-7456-1131-1*, Pub. by Polity Pr) Blackwell Pubs.

— Village Bells: The Culture of the Senses in the Nineteenth-Century French Countryside. Thom, Martin, tr. from FRE. LC 98-13799. 416p. 1998. 35.00 (*0-231-10450-2*) Col U Pr.

— The Village of Cannibals: Rage & Murder in France, 1870. Goldhammer, Arthur, tr. from FRE. (Illus.). 176p. 1992. text 22.95 (*0-674-93900-X*) HUP.

— The Village of Cannibals: Rage & Murder in France, 1870. 176p. 1993. pap. text 13.50 (*0-674-93901-8*) HUP.

— Women for Hire: Prostitution & Sexuality in France after 1850. Sheridan, Alan, tr. from FRE. (Illus.). 512p. 1990. 46.00 (*0-674-95543-9*) HUP.

— Women for Hire: Prostitution & Sexuality in France after 1850. Sheridan, Alan, tr. (Illus.). 496p. 1996. pap. 18.00 (*0-674-95544-7*) HUP.

***Corbin, Annalies.** The Material Culture of Steamboat Passengers: Archaeological Evidence from the Missouri River. LC 99-48649. (Series in Underwater Archaeology). 237p. 1999. write for info. (*0-306-46168-4*) Kluwer Academic.

Corbin, Arthur L. Contracts. 2nd ed. (Text Ser.). 1224p. (C). 1952. reprint ed. student ed. 38.00 (*0-314-28433-8*) West Pub.

Corbin, Arthur L. & Perillo, Joseph M. Corbin on Contracts. LC 93-60572. 1993. write for info. (*0-314-22815-2*) West Pub.

Corbin, B. J., et al. The Explorers of Ararat: And the Search for Noah's Ark. 2nd ed. Wakefield, Tad & Craig, Brian, eds. (Illus.). 450p. 1999. pap. 24.95 (*0-9653469-8-6*) GCI Books.

Corbin, Barry. Throckmorton, TX 76083. 1984. pap. 5.25 (*0-8222-1145-9*) Dramatists Play.

Corbin, Bill. Your Second Mattress Will Last Forever: And Other Guarantees of Marriage & Parenting. (Illus.). 144p. (Orig.). 1996. pap. 10.95 (*0-9634373-9-9*) Beckett-Highland.

Corbin, Bill & Wright, Shelbi. The Edge Resume & Job Search Strategy: A New Approach to the Reality of the 90's Job Market. 2nd ed. LC 92-62613. (Illus.). 168p. 1997. pap. 23.95 (*0-9634373-8-0*) Beckett-Highland.

Corbin, Carol, ed. Rhetoric in Postmodern America: Conversations with Michael Calvin McGee. (Revisioning Rhetoric Ser.). 198p. 1997. pap. text 22.00 (*1-57230-327-1*, C0327); lib. bdg. 45.00 (*1-57230-278-X*, C0278) Guilford Pubns.

Corbin, Carol & Candow, James E., eds. How Deep is the Ocean? Historical Essays on Canada's East Coast Fishery. (Illus.). 300p. 1997. pap. 20.95 (*0-920336-86-8*, Pub. by U Coll Cape Breton) Genl Dist Srvs.

***Corbin, Carolyn.** Great Leaders See the Future First. LC 00-22732. (Illus.). 227p. 2000. 25.00 (*0-7931-3685-7*) Dearborn.

Corbin, Charles B. & Corbin, David E. Homemade Play Equipment. 2nd ed. (Illus.). 135p. 1991. pap. text 12.95 (*0-89641-221-0*) American Pr.

Corbin, Charles B. & Laurie, David R. Teaching Lifetime Fitness, 5 vols., 1. LC 81-81868. (Advanced Ser.). (C). 1981. write for info. (*0-914607-08-1*) Master Tchr.

— Teaching Lifetime Fitness, 5 vols., 2. LC 81-81868. (Advanced Ser.). (C). 1981. write for info. (*0-914607-09-X*) Master Tchr.

— Teaching Lifetime Fitness, 5 vols., 3. LC 81-81868. (Advanced Ser.). (C). 1981. write for info. (*0-914607-10-3*) Master Tchr.

— Teaching Lifetime Fitness, 5 vols., 4. LC 81-81868. (Advanced Ser.). (C). 1981. write for info. (*0-914607-11-1*) Master Tchr.

— Teaching Lifetime Fitness, 5 vols., 5. LC 81-81868. (Advanced Ser.). (C). 1981. write for info. (*0-914607-12-X*) Master Tchr.

— Teaching Lifetime Fitness, 5 vols., Set. LC 81-81868. (Advanced Ser.). (C). 1981. ring bd. 695.00 incl. audio, sl. (*0-914607-07-3*) Master Tchr.

Corbin, Charles B. & Lindsey, Ruth. Concepts of Fitness & Wellness with Laboratories. 2nd ed. LC 95-83958. 464p. (C). 1996. text. write for info. (*0-697-25877-7*) Brown & Benchmark.

— Concepts of Physical Fitness. 7th ed. 384p. (C). 1992. write for info. (*0-697-20503-7*) Brown & Benchmark.

— Concepts of Physical Fitness. 9th ed. LC 95-83959. 408p. (C). 1996. text. write for info. (*0-697-25890-4*, WCB McGr Hill) McGrw-H Hghr Educ.

— Concepts of Physical Fitness with Laboratories. 8th ed. 408p. (C). 1993. text 23.49 (*0-697-12611-0*) Brown & Benchmark.

— Concepts of Physical Fitness with Laboratories. 9th ed. 392p. (C). 1997. per. write for info. (*0-07-114293-2*) McGraw.

— Core Physical Fitness Concepts: Toward Active Lifestyles. LC 95-78143. 192p. (C). 1995. text. write for info. (*0-697-31789-7*) Brown & Benchmark.

— Physical Fitness Concepts: Toward Active Lifestyles. 600p. (C). 1995. text. write for info. (*0-697-27842-5*) Brown & Benchmark.

— The Ultimate Fitness Book: Physical Fitness Forever. LC 84-47519. (Illus.). 272p. 1984. reprint ed. pap. 84.40 (*0-608-04285-4*, 206506400012) Bks Demand.

Corbin, Charles B. & Pangrazi, Robert B. Toward a Better Understanding of Physical Fitness & Activity: Selected Topics. LC 98-38693. 1999. 32.95 (*1-890871-08-7*) Holcomb Hath.

Corbin, David & Metal-Corbin, Josie. Reach for It: A Handbook of Health, Exercise & Dance Activities for Older Adults. 3rd ed. 324p. 1997. pap. 34.95 (*0-945483-76-7*) E Bowers Pub.

Corbin, David A. Life, Work & Rebellion in the Coal Fields: Southern West Virginia Miners, 1880-1922. LC 80-25493. (Working Class in American History Ser.). (Illus.). 328p. 1990. pap. text 15.95 (*0-252-00895-2*) U of Ill Pr.

Corbin, David A., ed. The West Virginia Mine Wars: An Anthology. LC 90-64144. 165p. (Orig.). 1997. reprint ed. pap. 9.95 (*0-9627486-0-9*) Applchin Eds

Corbin, David E., jt. auth. see Corbin, Charles B.

Corbin, David R. Solving Your Year 2000 Problem. LC 99-162271. vi, 66 p. 1998. pap. 12.50 (*1-891935-00-3*, Y2K) Corbin OR.

Corbin, David R., jt. ed. see Herron, Norman.

Corbin, Don & Williams, Ellen. Recreation. 5th ed. (C). 1996. text 61.33 (*0-205-18125-2*) Allyn.

Corbin, Ernest, ed. see Corbin, Joyce.

Corbin, Frederick T., ed. World Soybean Research Conference II: Proceedings. 1980. text 59.00 (*0-89158-678-4*) Westview.

Corbin, George A. Native Arts of North America. LC 87-45606. (Illus.). 352p. 1988. pap. 38.00 (*0-06-430174-5*, IN-174, Icon Edns) HarpC.

Corbin, Henri. Man of Light in Iranian Sufism. 174p. 1996. pap. 14.00 (*0-614-21308-8*, 1428) Kazi Pubns.

Corbin, Henry. Alone with the Alone: Creative Imagination in the Sufism of Ibn 'Arabi. Manheim, R., tr. from FRE. LC 99-177431. (Mythos Ser.). 454p. 1998. pap. text 19.95 (*0-691-05834-2*, Pub. by Princeton U Pr) Cal Prin Full Svc.

— Avicenna & the Visionary Recital. Trask, Willard R., tr. from FRE. LC 90-41820. (Bollingen Ser.: No. 66). 439p. 1988. reprint ed. pap. 136.10 (*0-7837-8582-8*, 204939700011) Bks Demand.

— Creative Imagination in the Sufism of Ibn Arabi. Manheim, Ralph, tr. 405p. 1996. pap. 19.95 (*0-614-21261-8*, 178) Kazi Pubns.

— Creative Imagination in the Sufism of Ibn Arabi. Manheim, R., tr. (Bollingen Ser.: Vol. 91). 423p. 1969. pap. 19.95 (*0-691-01828-6*, Pub. by Princeton U Pr) Cal Prin Full Svc.

— Cyclical Time & Ismaili Gnosis. (Islamic Texts & Contexts Ser.). 193p. 1983. 47.50 (*0-7103-0047-6*); pap. 19.95 (*0-7103-0048-4*) Routledge.

— History of Islamic Philosophy. Sherrard, Liadain & Sherrard, Philip, trs. 450p. 1993. 65.00 (*0-7103-0416-1*, A5643) Routledge.

— The Man of Light in Irenian Sufism. 2nd ed. Pearson, Nancy, tr. from FRE. 174p. 1999. reprint ed. pap. 14.00 (*0-930872-48-7*) Omega Pubns NY.

— Swedenborg & Esoteric Islam. 150p. 1996. pap. 11.00 (*0-614-21242-1*, 1424); pap. 11.00 (*0-614-21585-0*, 1424) Kazi Pubns.

— Swedenborg & Esoteric Islam: Two Studies. Fox, Leonard, tr. from FRE. LC 94-30687. (Swedenborg Studies: No. 4). 168p. 1995. pap. text 14.95 (*0-87785-183-2*) Swedenborg.

— Temple & Contemplation. Sherrard, Philip & Sherrard, Liadain, trs. (Illus.). 390p. (C). 1986. text 65.00 (*0-7103-0129-4*); pap. text 17.95 (*0-7103-0130-8*) Routledge.

— The Voyage & the Messenger: Iran & Philosophy. Rowe, Joseph H., tr. from FRE. LC 97-49580. 250p. 1998. pap. 14.95 (*1-55643-269-0*) North Atlantic.

Corbin, Jackie D. & Francis, Sharron H., eds. Signal Transduction in Health & Disease. Vol. 31. 336p. 99.95 (*0-12-036131-0*) Acad Pr.

— Signal Transduction in Health & Disease. (Advances in Second Messenger & Phosphoprotein Research Ser.: Ser. 31). 500p. 1997. text 131.00 (*0-397-51685-1*) Lppncott W & W.

Corbin, Jackie D. & Hardman, Joel D., eds. Hormone Action Pt. F: Protein Kinases. (Methods in Enzymology Ser.: Vol. 99). 1983. text 188.00 (*0-12-181999-X*) Acad Pr.

Corbin, Jackie D. & Johnson, Roger A., eds. Initiation & Termination of Cyclic Nucleotide Action. (Methods in Enzymology Ser.). 850p. 1988. text 139.00 (*0-12-182060-2*) Acad Pr.

Corbin, James. The Anarchist Passion: Class Conflict in Southern Spain 1810-1965. (Studies in Spanish Anthropology). 224p. 1993. 68.95 (*1-85628-431-X*, Pub. by Avebry) Ashgate Pub Co.

Corbin, Jay S., et al. Centennial Souvenir History of Gouverneur with Personal Sketches. (Illus.). 384p. 1997. reprint ed. lib. bdg. 45.00 (*0-8328-6150-2*) Higginson Bk Co.

Corbin, John. Directory of Automated Library Systems. 2nd ed. 315p. 1989. pap. text 60.00 (*1-55570-050-0*) Neal-Schuman.

— Elizabethan Hamlet. LC 70-134608. reprint ed. 29.50 (*0-404-01726-6*) AMS Pr.

— Find the Law in the Library: A Guide to Legal Research. 1989. text 35.00 (*0-8389-0502-1*) ALA.

— Snakes & Lizards: Their Care & Breeding in Captivity. (Illus.). 208p. 21.95 (*3-89356-036-X*, 16047) Tetra Pr.

Corbin, John R. The Art of Distributed Applications: Programming Techniques for Remote Procedure Calls. (Sun Technical Reference Library). ix, 321p. 1990. 39.95 (*0-685-48006-2*) Spr-Verlag.

— Remote Procedure Call Programming: Writing Networked Applications. 321p. 1990. 59.95 (*0-387-97247-1*) Spr-Verlag.

— Unknown Washington. LC 72-1273. (Select Bibliographies Reprint Ser.). 1977. reprint ed. 23.95 (*0-8369-6823-9*) Ayer.

Corbin, John R. & Corbin, Marie P. Compromising Relations: Kith, Kin & Class in Southern Spain. LC 83-20729. (Studies in Spanish Anthropology, 1). 153p. 1984. text 72.95 (*0-566-00669-3*) Ashgate Pub Co.

Corbin, Jonathan, jt. auth. see Corbin, Richard.

Corbin, Joyce. Reading Success for Children: What Every Parent Should Know. Corbin, Ernest, ed. LC 91-75990. 96p. (Orig.). 1999. reprint ed. pap. 8.95 (*0-9630773-0-9*) Learn Strat.

Corbin, Juliet, jt. auth. see Strauss, Anselm.

Corbin, Juliet M., jt. auth. see Hyman, Ruth Bernstein.

Corbin, Juliet M., jt. auth. see Strauss, Anselm L.

Corbin, Juliet M., jt. ed. see Strauss, Anselm L.

Corbin, Katharine, ed. see Knight, E. Leslie & Reaume, Chuck.

Corbin, Kim, jt. auth. see Corbin, William G.

Corbin, L. W. Feedback Loop Analysis: A Systemic Approach to Process Improvement. 128p. 1994. pap. text 19.95 (*0-9640199-0-6*) Syst Sci Inst.

Corbin, Linda. Seven Ways to Pray for Spiritual Leaders. (Christian Living Ser.). 1996. pap. 1.99 (*0-87509-608-5*) Chr Pubns.

Corbin-Lindsey. Interactive Personal Trainer. 9th ed. 1997. 11.25 (*0-697-38468-3*, WCB McGr Hill) McGrw-H Hghr Educ.

Corbin, Marie P., jt. auth. see Corbin, John R.

Corbin, Michael D., ed. see Lapidus, Mikhail K. & Van De Waal-Palms, Pyotr J.

Corbin, Mike. Family Trees: The Peach Culture of the Piedmont. (Illus.). 136p. 1998. 100.00 (*1-891885-08-1*); pap. 23.00 (*1-891885-02-2*) Hub City Writers.

***Corbin, Peter.** Witch of Edmonton: By William Rowly Thom Dekker & John Ford. 1999. pap. 9.95 (*0-7190-5247-5*, Pub. by Manchester Univ Pr) St Martin.

Corbin, Peter & Sedge, Douglas, eds. Three Jacobean Witchcraft Plays: Sophonisba, The Witch, & The Witch of Edmonton. (Revels Plays Companion Library). (Illus.). 272p. 1989. reprint ed. text 19.95 (*0-7190-1953-2*, Pub. by Manchester Univ Pr) St Martin.

Corbin, Raymond M. Nineteen Hundred Ninety-Nine Facts about Blacks. 1995. pap. 14.95 (*0-931761-53-0*) Beckham Pubns.

— 1999 Facts about Blacks: A Sourcebook of African-American Accomplishment. rev. ed. 263p. 1995. pap. 10.95 (*0-931761-06-9*) Beckham Pubns.

— 1,999 Facts about Blacks. 2nd rev. ed. 228p. 1996. pap. 16.95 (*1-56833-081-2*) Madison Bks UPA.

Corbin, Richard & Corbin, Jonathan. Research Papers: A Guided Writing Experience for Senior High Students. 2nd rev. ed. 1978. pap. text 2.00 (*0-930348-00-1*) NY St Eng Coun.

Corbin, Richard W. Letters of a Confederate Officer to His Family in Europe During the Last Year of the War of Secession. 99p. (C). 1993. text 22.50 (*0-935523-34-0*) Butternut & Blue.

Corbin-Schuffels, Anne-Marie. Manes Sperber: Un Combat Contre la Tyrannie (1934-1960) (Contacts Ser.: Series III, Vol. 34). (FRE.). 568p. 1996. 63.95 (*3-906754-39-1*, Pub. by P Lang) P Lang Pubng.

Corbin, Steven. Fragments That Remain. 318p. 1995. pap. 9.95 (*1-55583-274-1*) Alyson Pubns.

Corbin, Verda S., jt. auth. see Hutchinson, Shane.

Corbin, William. Me & the End of the World. LC 90-2355. 256p. (YA). (gr. 5-9). 1991. pap. 15.00 (*0-671-74223-X*) S&S Bks Yung.

Corbin, William G. & Corbin, Kim. Getting, Keeping & Growing in Your Job: A Practical Guide to Success in the 90s Workplace. LC 93-61745. (Illus.). 128p. (Orig.). (YA). 1994. pap. 9.95 (*0-9634373-1-3*) Beckett-Highland.

Corbineau-Hoffmann, Angelika. Paradoxie der Fiktionen: Literarische Venedig-Bilder, 1797-1984. (Komparatistische Studien: No. 17). (GER.). x, 638p. (C). 1993. lib. bdg. 296.95 (*3-11-012937-X*) De Gruyter.

Corbishley, Anne M., jt. auth. see Yost, Elizabeth B.

Corbishley, M. Anne, jt. auth. see Yost, Elizabeth B.

Corbishley, Mike. Ancient Rome. (Cultural Atlas for Young People Ser.). (Illus.). 96p. (YA). 1989. 19.95 (*0-8160-1970-3*) Facts on File.

— Growing up in Ancient Rome. LC 91-14851. (Growing up in Ser.). (Illus.). 32p. (J). (gr. 3-5). 1997. pap. 4.95 (*0-8167-2722-8*) Troll Communs.

— How Do We Know Where People Came From? LC 94-16651. (How Do We Know? Ser.). (Illus.). 48p. (J). (gr. 4-8). 1995. lib. bdg. 24.26 (*0-8114-3880-5*) Raintree Steck-V.

— The Medieval World. LC 92-31445. (Timelink Ser.). (Illus.). 60p. (YA). (gr. 5 up). 1993. lib. bdg. 18.95 (*0-87226-362-2*, P Bedrick Books) NTC Contemp Pub Co.

— The Middle Ages. (Cultural Atlas for Young People Ser.). (Illus.). 96p. (J). (gr. 4-9). 1990. 17.95 (*0-8160-1973-8*) Facts on File.

— Rome & the Ancient World. (Illustrated History of the World Ser.). (Illus.). 80p. (J). (gr. 4-9). 1993. 19.95 (*0-8160-2786-2*) Facts on File.

— Vikings at a Glance. LC 98-12939. (At a Glance Ser.). (Illus.). 32p. (YA). (gr. 3 up). 1998. 14.95 (*0-87226-558-7*, 65578B, P Bedrick Books) NTC Contemp Pub Co.

— What Do We Know About Prehistoric People? LC 95-11224. (What Do We Know about...? Ser.). (Illus.). 44p. (J). (gr. 3 up). 1995. lib. bdg. 18.95 (*0-87226-383-5*) NTC Contemp Pub Co.

— What Do We Know about the Romans? LC 91-28763. (What Do We Know about...? Ser.). (Illus.). 40p. (YA). (gr. 2 up). 1992. lib. bdg. 18.95 (*0-87226-352-5*, 63525B, P Bedrick Books) NTC Contemp Pub Co.

— The World of Architectural Wonders. LC 96-47596. (World of...Ser.). (Illus.). 64p. (YA). (gr. 5 up). 1997. lib. bdg. 19.95 (*0-87226-279-0*, P Bedrick Books) NTC Contemp Pub Co.

Corbishley, Mike, et al. The Young Oxford History of Britain & Ireland No. 9. Morgan, Kenneth O., ed. LC 97-19451. (Illus.). 416p. (YA). (gr. 7 up). 1997. 45.00 (*0-19-910035-7*) OUP.

C

Corbit, Irene E., jt. auth. see Fryrear, Jerry L.

Corbit, R. M. History of Jones County: Past & Present, 2 vols. (Illus.). 1997. reprint ed. lib. bdg. 135.00 (*0-8328-6685-7*) Higginson Bk Co.

— History of Jones County, Iowa Past & Present, Vol. 1. (Illus.). 742p. 1994. reprint ed. lib. bdg. 74.50 (*0-8328-3820-9*) Higginson Bk Co.

— History of Jones County, Iowa Past & Present, Vol. 2. (Illus.). 662p. 1994. reprint ed. lib. bdg. 66.50 (*0-8328-3819-5*) Higginson Bk Co.

Corbitt. Information Technology & Its Application. 2nd ed. 1994. pap. text. write for info. (*0-582-23309-7*, Pub. by Addison-Wesley) Longman.

Corbitt, D. L. & Wilborn, Elizabeth W. Civil War Pictures. (Illus.). xiii, 55p. 1991. pap. 5.00 (*0-86526-074-5*) NC Archives.

Corbitt, David L. Formation of the North Carolina Counties, 1663-1943. xxix, 323p. 1996. pap. 15.00 (*0-86526-032-X*) NC Archives.

Corbitt, Gretchen. Journey Back to God. 72p. 1997. pap. 8.00 (*0-8059-4189-4*) Dorrance.

***Corbitt, Helen.** The Best from Helen Corbitt's Kitchens. MacDonald, Patty Vineyard, ed. LC 99-53514. (Evelyn Oppenheimer Ser.: Vol. 1). (Illus.). 353p. 2000. 29.95 (*1-57441-076-8*, Pub. by UNTX Pr) Tex A&M Univ Pr.

Corbitt, J. Nathan. GAPtest: Global Awareness Profile, Facilitator's Manual. LC 98-10757. 68p. 1998. ring bd. 35.00 (*1-877864-55-2*) Intercult Pr.

— The Sound of the Harvest: Music's Mission in Church & Culture. LC 98-28640. (Illus.). 352p. 1998. pap. 18.99 (*0-8010-5829-5*, Bridgept Bks) Baker Bks.

Corbitt, John H. Black Churches Reaching College Students. LC 95-3511. 1995. write for info. (*0-910683-30-1*) Townsnd-Pr.

Corbitt, Norma. Inorganic Membranes: Markets, Technologies, Players. LC 98-100573. 239p. 1997. 2950.00 (*1-56965-457-3*, GB-112N) BCC.

Corbitt, R. A. Standard Handbook of Environmental Engineering. (Illus.). 1152p. 1990. 110.00 (*0-07-013158-9*) McGraw.

Corbitt, Robert A. Standard Handbook of Environmental Engineering. 2nd ed. LC 98-31045. (Illus.). 1532p. 1998. 179.95 (*0-07-013160-0*) McGraw-Hill Prof.

Corblin, Francis, et al, eds. Empirical Issues in Formal Syntax & Semantics: Selected Papers from the Colloque de Syntaxe et de Semantique de Paris (CSSP 1995) LC 97-37981. 355p. (C). 1997. pap. text 52.95 (*0-8204-3419-1*) P Lang Pubng.

Corbman, B. P. Textiles: Fiber to Fabric. 6th ed. 1983. pap. 35.00 (*0-07-066236-3*) McGraw.

Corbo, V. & De Melo, Jaime. Liberalization with Stabilization in the Southern Cone of Latin America. 1985. pap. 26.00 (*0-08-033412-1*, Pub. by PPL) Elsevier.

Corbo, Vittorio. Development Strategies & Policies in Latin America: A Historical Perspective. 30p. 1992. pap. 9.95 (*1-55815-181-8*) ICS Pr.

Corbo, Vittorio, et al, eds. Growth-Oriented Adjustment Programs: Proceedings of an IMF-World Bank Seminar. xiii, 533p. 1987. pap. 25.00 (*0-939934-92-2*) Intl Monetary.

Corbo, Vittorio & Sang-Mok Suh. Structural Adjustment in a Newly Industrialized Country: The Korean Experience. 376p. 1992. text 39.95 (*0-8018-4328-6*, 44328) Johns Hopkins.

Corbon, Jean. The Wellspring of Worship. 208p. 1988. pap. 14.95 (*0-8091-2968-X*) Paulist Pr.

Corbonars, Robert S., jt. ed. see Lee, Peter W.

Corboy, John M. The Retinoscopy Book: An Introductory Manual for Eye Care Professionals. 4th ed. LC 79-65451. (Illus.). 160p. 1995. pap. 40.00 (*1-55642-271-7*, 62717) SLACK Inc.

Corboy, Philip H. Components of a Trial: Final Arguments. 126p. 1989. 32.00 (*0-941916-54-5*) West Group.

Corboy, W. G., Jr., ed. Yankee Dryer & Drying: A TAPPI Press Anthology of Published Papers. 275p. (Orig.). 1993. pap. 103.00 (*0-89852-310-9*, 0101R217) TAPPI.

Corboy, W. G., ed. see Allevato, Claudio & Williams, David.

Corboy, William G., Jr. Guidelines for the Safe Operation of Yankee Dryers. 2nd rev. ed. (Illus.). 38p. 1995. pap. 29.00 (*0-89852-289-7*, 0101R244) TAPPI.

Corboy, William G., Jr., ed. see Technical Association of the Pulp & Paper Industry.

Corboz, Andre. Looking for a City in America: Down These Mean Streets a Man Must Go . . . LC 91-14796. (Illus.). 96p. 1992. pap. 10.95 (*0-89236-211-1*, Getty Res Inst) J P Getty Trust.

— Looking for a City in America: Down These Mean Streets a Man Must Go. (Illus.). 128p. 1992. pap. 17.95 (*0-87923-935-2*) Godine.

Corbridge & Patkaniowska, M. Teach Yourself Polish. (Teach Yourself Ser.). 1992. 15.95 (*0-8288-8378-5*) Fr & Eur.

Corbridge, D. E. Phosphorus: An Outline of Its Chemistry, Biochemistry & Technology. 5th ed. LC 94-48222. (Inorganic Chemistry Ser.: Vol. 20). 1220p. 1995. 560.00 (*0-444-89307-5*) Elsevier.

***Corbridge, D. E. C.** Phosphorus 2000: Chemistry, Biochemistry & Technology. LC 00-28838. 2000. write for info. (*0-444-82550-9*) Elsevier.

***Corbridge, James N., Jr.** Vranesh's Colorado Water Law. rev. ed. 536p. 2000. 75.00 (*0-87081-543-1*) Univ Pr Colo.

Corbridge, James N., Jr. & Weber, William A. A Rocky Mountain Lichen Primer. LC 97-48870. (Illus.). 56p. 1998. pap. 19.95 (*0-87081-490-7*) Univ Pr Colo.

Corbridge, Marjorie, et al. Employment Resourcing. 320p. 1998. pap. 52.50 (*0-273-62527-6*, Pub. by Pitman Pub) Trans-Atl Phila.

Corbridge-Patkaniowska, M. Teach Yourself Polish: A Complete Course for Beginners. (ENG & POL.). 300p. 1995. pap. 12.95 (*0-8442-3816-3*, Teach Yrslf) NTC Contemp Pub Co.

Corbridge, Rogan. Essential ENT Practice: A Clinical Text. LC 98-3603. (Illus.). 192p. 1998. pap. text 32.50 (*0-340-67704-X*, Pub. by E A) OUP.

Corbridge, Stuart. Capitalist World Development: A Critique of Radical Development. 304p. (C). 1986. 66.50 (*0-8476-7509-2*, R7509); pap. 26.50 (*0-8476-7510-6*, R7510) Rowman.

***Corbridge, Stuart.** Development: Critical Concepts. LC 98-46663. 1999. write for info. (*0-415-20541-7*) Routledge.

— International Debt, 4 vols. 1998. 625.00 (*1-86064-274-8*, Pub. by I B T) St Martin.

Corbridge, Stuart, ed. Development Studies: A Reader. (Arnold Publications). (Illus.). 496p. 1995. pap. text 35.00 (*0-340-61452-8*) OUP.

Corbridge, Stuart, et al, eds. Money, Power & Space. (Illus.). 288p. (C). 1994. 65.95 (*0-631-18199-7*); pap. 29.95 (*0-631-19201-8*) Blackwell Pubs.

Corbridge, Stuart, jt. auth. see Agnew, John.

Corbusier, Harold Dunbar. A Boy at Fort Mackinac: The Diary of Harold Dunbar Corbusier 1883-1884, 1892. Porter, Phil, ed. (Illus.). vi, 97p. 1994. pap. text 7.00 (*0-911872-62-0*) Mackinac St Hist Pks.

***Corby, Brian.** Child Abuse. 2nd ed. LC 00-37507. 2000. pap. write for info. (*0-335-20567-4*) Taylor & Francis.

Corby, Brian. Child Abuse: Towards a Knowledge Base. LC 92-34683. 192p. 1993. 110.00 (*0-335-15747-5*); pap. 34.95 (*0-335-15746-7*) OpUniv Pr.

— Working with Child Abuse: Social Work Practice & the Child Abuse System. 192p. 1987. 123.00 (*0-335-15396-8*); pap. 34.95 (*0-335-15395-X*) OpUniv Pr.

Corby, Jane. Focus on Love. large type ed. (Linford Romance Library). 336p. 1989. pap. 16.99 (*0-7089-6685-3*, Linford) Ulverscroft.

— Nurse Liza Hale. large type ed. 1991. pap. 16.99 (*0-7089-6972-0*) Ulverscroft.

— Nurse of Green. large type ed. (Linford Romance Library). 272p. 1994. pap. 16.99 (*0-7089-7519-4*, Linford) Ulverscroft.

— Nurse with the Red-Gold Hair. large type ed. (Linford Romance Library). 256p. 1993. pap. 16.99 (*0-7089-7457-0*, Linford) Ulverscroft.

— Peril at Stone Hall. large type ed. (Linford Mystery Library). 272p. 1993. pap. 16.99 (*0-7089-7427-9*, Linford) Ulverscroft.

Corby, Jill, jt. auth. see Dwyer, Derek.

Corby, Richard, et al. Life in Sierra Leone, West Africa. (J). (gr. 6-9). 1991. pap., teacher ed. 21.95 (*0-943804-83-3*) U of Denver Teach.

Corby, Susan & White, Geoff. Employee Relations in the Public Services: Themes & Issues. LC 98-36487. 1999. 90.00 (*0-415-17444-9*); pap. 32.99 (*0-415-17445-7*) Routledge.

Corcao, Gustavo. Who If I Cry Out. Wilson, Clotilde, tr. LC 67-64317. (Texas Pan-American Ser.). 229p. reprint ed. pap. 71.00 (*0-8357-7733-2*, 203609000002) Bks Demand.

Corcelle, Guy, jt. auth. see Johnson, Stanley P.

Corchon. Theory of Implementation of Society. LC 96-7685. 192p. 1996. text 69.95 (*0-312-15953-6*) St Martin.

Corchon, Justo. Dictionary of Geography & Language: Diccionario de Geografia y Lenguaje. (ENG & SPA.). 230p. 1983. pap. 33.95 (*0-7859-4932-1*) Fr & Eur.

Corchon, Luis C. Theories of Imperfectly Competitive Markets. LC 96-27345. (Lecture Notes in Economics & Mathematical Systems Ser.: Vol. 442). 163p. 1996. 52.00 (*3-540-61553-9*) Spr-Verlag.

Corcineq, Phyllis P., ed. Space. 1992. 4.95 (*1-55708-342-8*, R746) McDonald Pub Co.

Corcker, Joanne, ed. see Allen, Margaret.

Corcodilos, Nick A. Ask the Headhunter: Reinventing the Interview to Win the Job. (Orig.). 1997. pap. 16.95 (*0-614-28123-7*, Plume) Dutton Plume.

Corcoran. Awaiting Apocalypse. LC 99-39492. 2000. text 59.95 (*0-312-22425-7*) St Martin.

— Maneuvering the Maze of Managed Care: A Survival Guide for Clinicians in Public & Private Settings. 1995. 18.00 (*0-02-874062-9*) Free Pr.

***Corcoran.** Measures For Clinical Practice A Sourcebook: Volume 2 Adults Third Edition. 3rd ed. LC 00-37132. Vol. 2. 960p. 2000. 54.95 (*0-684-84831-7*) S&S Trade.

— Pga Tour Ultimate Book of Golf. 1999. pap. 25.00 (*0-8050-5769-2*) St Martin.

***Corcoran, et al.** Pak: Critical Thinking Through Debate. 368p. (C). 1999. pap. text 52.95 (*0-7872-5569-6*, 41556902) Kendall-Hunt.

Corcoran, Adele. Miniature Quilts. Date not set. write for info. (*1-897954-55-7*) Sterling.

Corcoran, Adele & Wilkinson, Caroline. Mini Quilts from Traditional Designs. LC 95-24068. (Illus.). 128p. 1995. 27.95 (*0-8069-1322-3*) Sterling.

— Mini Quilts from Traditional Designs. (Illus.). 128p. 1997. pap. 16.95 (*0-8069-1323-1*) Sterling.

Corcoran, Adele, jt. auth. see Hart, Carol.

Corcoran, Alan, jt. auth. see Green, Joey.

Corcoran, Barbara. Family Secrets. LC 91-13104. 176p. (J). (gr. 3-7). 1992. lib. bdg. 13.95 (*0-689-31744-1*) Atheneum Yung Read.

— The Hideaway. 128p. (J). 1989. pap. 2.75 (*0-380-70635-0*, Avon Bks) Morrow Avon.

— The Potato Kid. 176p. (J). 1993. pap. 3.50 (*0-380-71213-X*, Avon Bks) Morrow Avon.

— The Sky Is Falling. 192p. (J). 1990. pap. 2.95 (*0-380-70837-X*, Avon Bks) Morrow Avon.

— Wolf At The Door. LC 92-45108. 192p. (J). (gr. 3-7). 1993. 16.00 (*0-689-31870-7*) Atheneum Yung Read.

— You Put up with Me, I'll Put up with You. 176p. (J). (gr. 3-7). 1989. pap. 2.50 (*0-380-70558-3*, Avon Bks) Morrow Avon.

Corcoran, Bill. Preparing the Initiation Rites with Adults & Children of Catechetical Age. (Preparing for Liturgy Ser.). 48p. (Orig.). 1997. pap. 3.95 (*0-8146-2498-7*) Liturgical Pr.

Corcoran, Bill & Evans, Emrys, eds. Readers, Texts, Teachers. LC 86-17556. 264p. (Orig.). (C). 1987. pap. text 23.50 (*0-86709-187-8*, 0187, Pub. by Boynton Cook Pubs) Heinemann.

Corcoran, Bill, et al. Knowledge in the Making: Challenging the Text in the Classroom. LC 94-16776. 326p. 1994. text 33.00 (*0-86709-326-9*, 0326, Pub. by Boynton Cook Pubs) Heinemann.

Corcoran, Brendan, jt. auth. see Martin, Mike.

Corcoran, Brent. Park City Underfoot: Self-Guided Tours of Historic Neighborhoods. LC 94-36029. (Illus.). 180p. (Orig.). 1995. pap. 10.95 (*1-56085-065-5*) Signature Bks.

Corcoran, Clodagh. Baker's Dozen: An Anthology of New Fiction for Young People. 272p. (J). 1990. pap. 7.95 (*1-85371-050-4*, Pub. by Poolbeg Pr) Dufour.

— Pornography: The New Terrorism. (C). 1989. 29.00 (*0-946211-84-1*) St Mut.

— Take Care! Preventing Child Sexual Abuse. 132p. 1987. pap. 7.95 (*1-85371-000-8*, Pub. by Poolbeg Pr) Dufour.

Corcoran, Desmond P. The Mayor & His Council. 168p. 1998. 24.95 (*0-944551-32-7*) Sundance Pr TX.

Corcoran, Eileen L. Meeting Basic Competencies in Communications. 68p. 1979. teacher ed. 0.50 (*0-88323-156-5*, 246); pap. 2.50 (*0-88323-152-2*, 242) Pendergrass Pub.

— Meeting Basic Competencies in Math. 72p. 1984. teacher ed. 0.50 (*0-88323-141-7*, 230); pap. text 2.50 (*0-88323-203-0*, 227) Pendergrass Pub.

— Meeting Basic Competencies in Practical Science & Health: A Workstudy Book to Improve Daily Living Skills. (Illus.). 72p. 1985. 2.50 (*0-88323-210-3*, 237); teacher ed. 0.50 (*0-88323-154-9*, 245) Pendergrass Pub.

Corcoran, Eileen L. & Pavka, John. What Is Electricity? (Science Ser.). 32p. 1966. pap. 1.00 (*0-88323-080-1*, 177) Pendergrass Pub.

Corcoran, Eileen L., jt. auth. see Kranich, Roger E.

Corcoran, Farrel & Preston, Paschal, eds. Democracy & Communication in the New Europe: Change & Continuity in East & West. LC 94-45447. (IAMCR Bks.). 320p. 1995. text 67.50 (*1-881303-88-8*); pap. text 24.95 (*1-881303-89-6*) Hampton Pr NJ.

Corcoran, Frances, jt. auth. see Karp, Rashelle.

Corcoran Gallery of Art Staff & Hartwell, Dare M. The Salon. LC 98-4628. 1998. pap. write for info. (*0-88675-055-5*) Corcoran.

***Corcoran Gallery of Art Staff, et al.** American Treasures of the Corcoran Gallery of Art. LC 99-46577. (Tiny Folios Ser.). (Illus.). 288p. (J). 2000. 11.95 (*0-7892-0625-0*, Abbeville Kids) Abbeville Pr.

Corcoran, Irma. Thomas Holme, 1624-1695: Surveyor General of Pennsylvania. LC 91-76987. (Memoirs Ser.: Vol. 200). (Illus.). 414p. (C). 1992. 10.00 (*0-87169-200-7*, M200-COI) Am Philos.

Corcoran, J., ed. see Buffalo Symposium on Modernist Interpretation of A.

Corcoran, J. E. The Target Rifle in Australia. (Illus.). 223p. 1995. 40.00 (*1-884849-17-2*) R&R Bks.

***Corcoran, Jacqueline.** Evidence-Based Social Work Practice with Families: A Lifespan Approach. LC 99-51496. (Series on Social Work). (Illus.). 424p. 2000. text 44.95 (*0-8261-1303-6*) Springer Pub.

Corcoran, James, jt. auth. see Dees, Morris.

Corcoran, John. The American Council on Martial Arts Instructor Certification Manual LC 99-165176. 261p. 1998. write for info. (*0-9655539-3-0*) Graden Media Grp.

Corcoran, John & Carlson, Carole C. The Teacher Who Couldn't Read. LC 94-9250. 1994. 15.99 (*1-56179-249-7*) Focus Family.

Corcoran, John & Farkas, Emil. The Original Martial Arts Encyclopedia: Tradition - History - Pioneers. rev. ed. Sobel, Stuart, ed. LC 92-81677. (Illus.). 450p. 1993. reprint ed. 29.95 (*0-9615126-3-6*) Pro Action Pub.

Corcoran, John & Hackler, Lewis R. Let's Name It: Ten Thousand Boat Names, an Ingenious Reference Source for Beginners & "Old Salts" Alike. LC 87-90745. (Illus.). 144p. 1987. 9.95 (*0-931595-02-9*) Seascape Enters.

— Let's Name It: Ten Thousand Boat Names for All Types of Watercraft. 1987. pap. text 9.95 (*0-07-155340-1*) Intl Marine.

Corcoran, John, jt. auth. see Farkas, Emil.

Corcoran, John, ed. see Colasanti, Robert.

Corcoran, John, ed. see Graden, John.

Corcoran, John, ed. see Soo, Kim Pyung.

Corcoran, John, ed. see Tarski, Alfred.

Corcoran, John, ed. see Tulleners, Tonny.

Corcoran, Julie A., ed. see Stranges, Frank E.

Corcoran, Kathleen M. Look, Ma, No Meat! 786 Hearty Vegetarian Main Dishes, No Meat, No Fish, No Eggs. LC 88-70769. 550p. (Orig.). 1988. pap. 25.95 (*1-882055-01-2*) Butternut MN.

Corcoran, Kelvin. Lyric Lyric. 1993. pap. 9.00 (*1-874400-00-8*, Pub. by Reality St Edits) SPD-Small Pr Dist.

Corcoran, Kevin. Kerry Walks. (Illus.). 176p. 1997. pap. 10.95 (*0-86278-293-7*, Pub. by OBrien Pr) Irish Amer Bk.

— Maneuvering the Maze of Managed Care: A Survival Guide for Clinicians in Public & Private Settings. 1996. 35.00 (*0-684-82310-1*) Free Pr.

***Corcoran, Kevin.** Measures for Clinical Practice: A Sourcebook: Couples, Families & Children, Vol. 1. 3rd ed. LC 00-37132. Vol. 1. 704p. 2000. 44.95 (*0-684-84830-9*) S&S Trade.

Corcoran, Kevin. West Cork Walks. (Illus.). 112p. 1997. pap. 10.95 (*0-86278-254-6*, Pub. by OBrien Pr) Irish Amer Bk.

— West of Ireland Walks. (Illus.). 156p. 1997. pap. 10.95 (*0-86278-345-3*, Pub. by OBrien Pr) Irish Amer Bk.

Corcoran, Kevin & Fischer, Joel. Measures for Clinical Practice: A Sourcebook. 576p. 1987. 45.00 (*0-02-906681-6*) Free Pr.

Corcoran, Kevin & Vandiver, Vicki. Maneuvering the Maze of Managed Care: A Survival Guide for Clinicians in Public & Private Settings. 224p. 1996. 20.00 (*0-684-82309-8*) Free Pr.

Corcoran, Kevin, jt. auth. see Fischer, Joel.

Corcoran, Kevin J., ed. Structuring Change: Effective Practice for Common Client Problems. LC 91-43836. 340p. (C). 1992. pap. text 39.95 (*0-925065-14-5*) Lyceum IL.

Corcoran, Kevin J., et al. High Performance Sales Organization: Creating Competitive Advantage in the Global Marketplace. 192p. 1995. text 27.50 (*0-7863-0352-2*, Irwn Prfssnl) McGraw-Hill Prof.

Corcoran, L. H. Portrait Mummies from Roman Egypt (I-IV Centuries A. D.) with a Catalog of Portrait Mummies in Egyptian Museums. LC 94-69121. (Studies in Ancient Oriental Civilization: No. 56). (Illus.). xxx, 250p. 1995. pap. text 55.00 (*0-918986-99-0*) Orient Inst.

Corcoran, Lawrence. Outboard Service Guide. Corcoran, Lynn, ed. 1977. pap. text 3.25 (*0-686-24789-2*) L Corcoran.

Corcoran, Lois. He Leadeth Me: Autobiography of a Missionary to Pakistan. LC 91-9910. (Illus.). 272p. (Orig.). 1991. pap. 4.99 (*0-932581-86-2*) Word Aflame.

Corcoran, Lynn, ed. see Corcoran, Lawrence.

Corcoran, M. E. & Moshe, S. L. Kindling 5: Proceedings of the Fifth International Conference Held in Victoria, Canada, June 27-30, 1996. LC 98-134876. (Advances in Behavioral Biology Ser.: Vol. 48). (Illus.). 510p. 1998. 135.00 (*0-306-45805-5*, Kluwer Plenum) Kluwer Academic.

***Corcoran, Malcolm.** Waxing for Skiers. LC 99-33962.Tr. of Fartage de Ski de Fond. 1999. pap. text 12.95 (*0-8117-3126-X*) Stackpole.

Corcoran, Marlena G., jt. ed. see Wawrzycka, Jolanta W.

***Corcoran, Mary & Connolly, Joe.** Gaining Market Intelligence Using the World Wide Web. McKenna, Jill, ed. (Illus.). 1999. pap. write for info. (*1-58143-007-8*, PSG1GMI) Prosoft I-net.

Corcoran, Mary B., tr. see Thalmann, Marianne.

***Corcoran, Mary E.** Time Management for People with No Time. 237p. 1999. pap. 14.95 (*1-893544-18-4*, 1-82346, Pub. by W Waldron Pubs) Quality Bks IL.

Corcoran, Mary H., ed. see De Hojeda, Diego.

Corcoran, Mary I. Milton's Paradise with Reference to the Hexameral Background. LC 45-3381. 159p. reprint ed. pap. 49.30 (*0-608-18735-6*, 202951800061) Bks Demand.

Corcoran, Mary P. Irish Illegals: Transients Between Two Societies. 32. LC 92-42671. (Contributions in Ethnic Studies: No. 32). 224p. 1993. 57.95 (*0-313-28624-8*, CIO, Greenwood Pr) Greenwood.

Corcoran, Maura. Vrndavana in Vaisnava Literature: History - Mythology - Symbolism. (Illus.). xi, 178p. 1995. 24.00 (*81-246-0024-4*, Pub. by D K Printwrld) Nataraj Bks.

Corcoran, Maureen E. Managed Care Contracting: Advising the Managed Care Organization. (BNA's Health Law & Business Ser.: No. 1700). 1996. 125.00 (*1-55871-332-8*) BNA.

Corcoran, Maureen E., jt. auth. see Wolff, Ernst A.

Corcoran, Michael. The Golf Dictionary. LC 96-54061. (Illus.). 320p. 1997. 29.95 (*0-87833-951-5*) Taylor Pub.

An Asterisk (*) at the beginning of an entry indicates that the title is appearing for the first time.

— The PGA Tour Complete Book of Golf: Wisdom & Advice from The Best Players in The Game. LC 99-10390. (Illus.). 416p. 1999. 45.00 (*0-8050-5768-4*) H Holt & Co.

Corcoran, N., tr. see Manenc, J.

Corcoran, N., tr. see Tremillon, B.

Corcoran, Neil. After Yeats & Joyce: Reading Modern Irish Literature. LC 97-2971. 206p. (Orig.). 1997. pap. 15.95 (*0-19-289231-2*) OUP.

— ENGLSH POETRY SINCE 1940. LC 92-28298. (Literature in English Ser.). (C). 1993. text 72.95 (*0-582-00323-7*, 79777) Longman.

Corcoran, Neil, ed. Chosen Ground: Essays on the Contemporary Poetry of N. Ireland. LC 90-24815. 288p. 1992. 35.00 (*0-8023-1291-8*) Dufour.

Corcoran, Neil, ed. Poets of Modern Ireland: Text, Context, Intertext. LC 99-30718. 200p. 1988. pap. 21.95 (*0-8093-2290-0*) S Ill U Pr.

Corcoran, P. B., jt. auth. see Kormondy, E.

Corcoran, Patrick, tr. see Martin, Xavier D.

***Corcoran, Paul.** Four Knights in Knaresborough. (Nick Hern Books, Drama Classics). 104p. 2000. pap. 16.95 (*1-85459-481-8*) Theatre Comm.

***Corcoran, Paul & Spencer, Vicki, eds.** Disclosures. LC 99-75549. 206p. 2000. text 69.95 (*1-84014-796-2*, Pub. by Ashgate Pub) Ashgate Pub Co.

Corcoran, Peter B. & Pennock, Margaret T. Living Voices: Proceedings of Common Ground: A Conference on Progressive Education. (Illus.). 212p. (Orig.). 1993. pap. 7.50 (*0-9635242-0-8*) Schl Rose Valley.

Corcoran, Ross. Joint Custody with a Jerk. 4th ed. 304p. 1996. pap. 14.95 (*0-312-14113-0*) St Martin.

Corcoran, S. G., et al, eds. Electrochemical Synthesis & Modification of Materials. LC 97-23814. (Materials Research Society Symposium Proceedings Ser.: No. 451). 592p. 1997. text 66.00 (*1-55899-355-X*) Materials Res.

Corcoran, Sandy. She Who Walks the Sunrise, Vol. 1. LC 95-623. (Illus.). 32p. (J). 1996. 16.95 (*0-9629978-4-6*) Sights Prods.

Corcoran, Simon. The Empire of the Tetrarchs: Imperial Pronouncements & Government, AD 284-324. LC 95-40305. (Oxford Classical Monographs). (Illus.). 420p. (C). 1996. text 85.00 (*0-19-814984-0*, Clarendon Pr) OUP.

***Corcoran, Simon.** The Empire of the Tetrarchs: Imperial Pronouncements & Government A.D. 284-324. (Illus.). 424p. 2000. pap. 29.95 (*0-19-815304-X*) OUP.

***Corcoran, Theresa.** Mount Saint Vincent University: A Vision Unfolding, 1873-1988. LC 99-36526. (Illus.). 384p. 1999. 57.00 (*0-7618-1473-6*) U Pr of Amer.

Corcoran, Thom. Mount St. Helens: The Story Behind the Scenery. LC 85-50108. (Illus.). 48p. (Orig.). 1985. pap. 7.95 (*0-88714-000-9*) KC Pubns.

Corcoran, Thomas B. Competency Testing & At-Risk Youth. 20p. 1985. pap. 5.95 (*1-56602-008-5*) Research Better.

— Curriculum Reform & At-Risk Youth. 17p. 1985. pap. 5.95 (*1-56602-007-7*) Research Better.

Corcoran, Thomas B. & Wilson, Bruce L. The Search for Successful Secondary Schools: The First Three Years of the Secondary School Recognition Program. 106p. 1986. pap. 21.95 (*1-56602-012-3*) Research Better.

Corcoran, Thomas B., et al. Working in Urban Schools. 160p. 1988. 12.00 (*0-937846-74-0*) Inst Educ Lead.

Corcoran, Thomas B., jt. auth. see Wilson, Bruce L.

Corcoran, Thomas H., tr. see Seneca, Lucius Annaeus.

Corcoran, Thomas J. Outline of Classical Origins: Rome. (Illus.). 77p. 5.75 (*0-939507-10-2*, B305) Amer Classical.

***Corcoran, Tom.** Gumbo Limbo. LC 99-23848. 304p. 1999. text 23.95 (*0-312-24194-1*, Thomas Dunne) St Martin.

— Gumbo Limbo. 2000. mass mkt. 5.99 (*0-312-97570-8*) St Martin.

Corcoran, Tom. Hoofbeats: The Pulse of the Mustang World. LC 94-94494. 135p. 1994. pap. 11.95 (*0-9641735-0-6*) Ketch & Yawl.

***Corcoran, Tom.** The Mango Opera. 1999. mass mkt. 5.99 (*0-312-96988-0*, Minotaur) St Martin.

Corcoran, Tom. The Mango Opera, Vol. 1. LC 98-4804. 304p. 1998. text 22.95 (*0-312-18628-2*) St Martin.

— Mustang 1964 1/2-73 Restoration Guide. 2nd ed. LC 98-19123. (Illus.). 448p. 1998. pap. 29.95 (*0-7603-0552-8*) MBI Pubg.

— Mustang Sixty-Four & One Half - Sixty-Eight. (Muscle Car Color History Ser.). (Illus.). 128p. 1993. pap. 21.95 (*0-87938-630-4*) MBI Pubg.

— Shelby Mustang. (Muscle Car Color History Ser.). (Illus.). 128p. 1992. pap. 21.95 (*0-87938-620-7*) MBI Pubg.

Corcoran, W. J. Economic Impact of Eppley & Millard Airfields on the Omaha Metropolitan Statistical Area. 13p. (Orig.). 1986. pap. 2.00 (*1-55719-164-6*) U NE CPAR.

Corcoran, William J. Omaha Metropolitan Statistical Area Input-Output Tables & Multipliers: A User's Manual: A Guide for Identifying & Assessing the Effects of Business Changes on the Omaha Economy. (Illus.). 63p. (C). 1988. ring bd. 29.95 (*1-55719-179-4*) U NE CPAR.

Corcordia. Family Life Issues-Growing As a Christian Father. 1994. pap. 4.50 (*0-570-09494-1*, 20-2706) Concordia.

Corcorin, James, ed. see Francis, Sam.

Corcos, Alain F. The Myth of Human Races. LC 97-17769. 1997. pap. 17.95 (*0-87013-439-6*) Mich St U Pr.

Corcos, Alain F. & Monaghan, Floyd V. Gregor Mendel's Experiments on Plant Hybrids: A Guided Study. LC 92-30887. (Masterworks of Discovery: Guided Studies of Great Texts in Science Ser.). (Illus.). 200p. (C). 1993. pap. 17.00 (*0-8135-1921-7*); text 34.00 (*0-8135-1920-9*) Rutgers U Pr.

Corcos, Christine. Bibliography of Law & Literature. LC 96-25036. Date not set. write for info. (*1-57588-116-0*, 30812) W S Hein.

Corcos, Daniel M., jt. auth. see Christina, Robert W.

Corcos, Daniel M., jt. ed. see Newell, Karl M.

Corcos, Gilles. Air in Water Pipes: A Manual for Designers of Spring-Supplied, Gravity-Driven Drinking Water Rural Delivery Systems. (Illus.). 71p. (Orig.). 1992. pap. write for info. (*0-9634980-0-2*) Agua Para La Vida.

Corcostegui, Lisa, tr. see Aulestia, Gorka.

Cord. A-cord Algebra. 1997. pap. 24.75 (*0-538-67465-2*) Thomson Learn.

— Air & Other Gases: Applications in Biology & Chemistry. 2nd ed. 1998. pap. 7.25 (*1-57837-087-6*) Thomson Learn.

— Animal Life Processes. 2nd ed. 1998. pap. 7.25 (*1-57837-073-6*) Thomson Learn.

— Applications in Biology & Chemistry. 2nd ed. 1998. pap. 7.25 (*1-55502-837-3*) Thomson Learn.

— Applications in Biology & Chemistry: Disease & Wellness. 2nd ed. 1998. pap. 7.25 (*1-57837-071-X*) Thomson Learn.

— Applications in Biology & Chemistry: Plant Growth & Reproduction. 2nd ed. 1998. pap. 6.75 (*1-57837-075-2*) Thomson Learn.

— Applications in Biology & Chemistry: Waste & Waste Management. 2nd ed. 1998. pap. 7.25 (*1-57837-089-2*) Thomson Learn.

— B-cord Algebra. 1997. pap. 24.75 (*0-538-67466-0*) Thomson Learn.

Cord. Committee Adoption Kit. (Ma - Academic Math Ser.). (C). 1998. pap. 181.95 (*0-538-68187-X*) S-W Pub.

***Cord.** Community of Life: Applications in Biology & Chemistry. 2nd ed. 1998. pap. 7.25 (*1-57837-079-5*) Thomson Learn.

— Continuity of Life. 2nd ed. 1998. pap. 7.25 (*1-55502-839-X*) Thomson Learn.

Cord. Cord Algebra. (MA - Academic Math Ser.). 1997. mass mkt., student ed. 56.95 (*0-538-67121-1*) S-W Pub.

— Cord Geometry. (MA - Academic Math Ser.). (C). 1998. mass mkt. 56.95 (*0-538-68127-6*) S-W Pub.

***Cord.** Microorganisms: Applications in Biology & Chemistry. 2nd ed. 1998. pap. 7.25 (*1-57837-081-7*) Thomson Learn.

— Natrual Resources: Applications in Biology & Chemistry. 2nd ed. 1998. pap. 7.25 (*1-57837-085-X*) Thomson Learn.

— Nutrition: Applications in Biology & Chemistry. 2nd ed. 1998. pap. 7.25 (*1-57837-077-9*) Thomson Learn.

— Principles of Technology: Unit 10 Energy Converters. 2nd ed. 1996. pap. 4.75 (*1-55502-381-9*) Thomson Learn.

— Principles of Technology: Unit 11 Transducers. 2nd ed. 1996. pap. 4.75 (*1-55502-382-7*) Thomson Learn.

— Principles of Technology: Unit 12 Radiation. 2nd ed. 1996. pap. 4.75 (*1-55502-383-5*) Thomson Learn.

— Principles of Technology: Unit 13 Optical Systems. 2nd ed. 1996. pap. 4.75 (*1-55502-384-3*) Thomson Learn.

— Principles of Technology: Unit 14 Time Constants. 2nd ed. 1996. pap. 4.75 (*1-55502-385-1*) Thomson Learn.

— Principles Of Technology: Unit 8 Momentum. 2nd ed. 1996. pap. 4.75 (*1-55502-379-7*) Thomson Learn.

— Principles of Technology: Unit 9 Wave & Vibrations. 2nd ed. 1996. pap. 4.75 (*1-55502-380-0*) Thomson Learn.

— Principles of Technology: Year 1. 2nd ed. 1996. pap. 33.75 (*1-55502-913-2*) Thomson Learn.

— Supplementary Wrksht Part B,Cord Algebra, Complete. 1998. pap. 39.75 (*0-538-68386-4*) Thomson Learn.

— Synthetic Materials: Applications in Biology & Chemistry. 2nd ed. 1998. pap. 7.25 (*1-57837-083-3*) Thomson Learn.

***Cord, Barry.** Gallows Ghost. large type ed. LC 00-39595. 2000. write for info. (*0-7838-9097-4*, G K Hall & Co) Mac Lib Ref.

Cord, Barry. The Guns of Hammer. LC 99-19637. 1999. 19.95 (*0-7838-8580-6*, G K Hall & Co) Mac Lib Ref.

***Cord, Barry.** Hell in Paradise Valley, 1. large type ed. LC 99-36807. 1999. pap. text 21.95 (*0-7838-8739-6*) Macmillan Gen Ref.

Cord, Barry. Last Chance at Devil's Canyon. large type ed. LC 98-37552. 1999. 30.00 (*0-7838-0413-X*, G K Hall Lrg Type) Mac Lib Ref.

— Last Stage to Gomorrah. large type ed. (Linford Western Library). 240p. 1985. pap. 16.99 (*0-7089-6075-8*) Ulverscroft.

— Slade large type ed. LC 99-13802. 188p. 1999. 21.95 (*0-7838-8568-7*, G K Hall & Co) Mac Lib Ref.

— The Third Rider. large type ed. (Linford Western Library). 240p. 1988. pap. 16.99 (*0-7089-6521-0*, Linford) Ulverscroft.

— Trail Boss from Texas. large type ed. (Linford Western Library). 288p. 1989. pap. 16.99 (*0-7089-6708-6*, Linford) Ulverscroft.

Cord Communications Corporation Staff. ABC Mini Modules & Minilabs. 1996. pap. 20.75 (*1-55502-773-3*) CORD Commns.

— Applied Mathematics. 1996. pap. 84.75 (*1-55502-854-3*) CORD Commns.

— Skills & Drills, Practice Problem Units 16-33. 1996. pap. 32.75 (*1-55502-732-6*) CORD Commns.

— Skills & Drills, Practice Problems Units A-15. 1996. pap. 32.75 (*1-55502-731-8*) CORD Commns.

Cord, John. Revelation Earth: The Book of Revelation Based upon Edgar Cayce's Prophecies. 336p. pap. 24.95 (*0-9666116-0-8*) EternaLight.

Cord, Robert L. Separation of Church & State: Historical Fact & Current Fiction. LC 94-20242. 307p. 1995. 19.95 (*0-931186-03-X*) Lambeth Pr.

Cord, Steven B. Henry George: Dreamer or Realist? LC 84-40169. 272p. 1984. reprint ed. pap. 7.00 (*0-911312-26-9*) Schalkenbach.

Cord, William O. In Introduction to Richard Wagner's Der Ring Des Nibelungen: A Handbook. 2nd rev. ed. (Illus.). 232p. 1995. pap. text 19.95 (*0-8214-1112-8*) Ohio U Pr.

— The Teutonic Mythology of Richard Wagner's "The Ring of the Nibelung" Nine Properties. LC 89-12612. (Studies in the History & Interpretation of Music: Vol. 16). 160p. 1989. 69.95 (*0-88946-441-3*) E Mellen.

— The Teutonic Mythology of Richard Wagner's "The Ring of the Nibelung", Vol. 2: The Family of Gods. LC 89-12612. (Studies in the History & Interpretation of Music: Vol. 17). 1990. 89.95 (*0-88946-442-1*) E Mellen.

— The Teutonic Mythology of Richard Wagner's "The Ring of the Nibelung", Vol. 3: The Natural & Supernatural Worlds, 2 pts. LC 89-12612. (Studies in the History & Interpretation of Music: Vol. 18). 604p. 1990. 129.95 (*0-88946-443-X*) E Mellen.

Cordaire, Christina. Beloved Stranger. 192p. (Orig.). 1995. mass mkt. 4.50 (*0-515-11550-9*, Jove) Berkley Pub.

— Loving a Lowly Stranger. large type ed. LC 97-51959. (Romance Ser.). 1998. 24.95 (*0-7862-1372-8*) Thorndike Pr.

— Spring Enchantment. 1996. mass mkt. 5.99 (*0-515-11876-1*, Jove) Berkley Pub.

— Winter Longing. 288p. (Orig.). 1996. mass mkt. 5.50 (*0-515-11811-7*, Jove) Berkley Pub.

Cordano, Vira. Levi Scott: Oregon Trailblazer. LC 81-70857. (Illus.). 1982. pap. 7.50 (*0-8323-0400-X*) Binford Mort.

***Cordara, Giulio Cesare.** On the Suppression of the Society of Jesus: A Contemporary Account (1704-1785) Murphy, John P., tr. from LAT. LC 99-24712. (Illus.). 200p. 1999. pap. 21.95 (*0-8294-1295-6*, Jesuit Way) Loyola Pr.

Cordaro, Connie. Be Your Own Business: The Definitive Guide to Entrepreneurial Success. Fox, Marcia R., ed. LC 97-42956. (Illus.). 304p. 1997. pap. 16.95 (*1-57112-082-3*, PO823) Park Ave.

Cordaro, Philip, ed. L' Attualita di Pirandello: Atti Del Simposio Diretto Da Philip Cordaro. LC 91-38800. (ITA.). 88p. 1991. lib. bdg. 49.95 (*0-7734-9709-9*) E Mellen.

Cordaro, Philip, ed. see Dante Alighieri.

Cordasco, Edward M., et al, eds. Environmental Respiratory Diseases. (Industrial Health & Safety Ser.). 619p. 1994. 195.00 (*0-471-29072-6*, VNR) Wiley.

Cordasco, Francesco. American Medical Imprints, 1820-1910: A Checklist of Publications Illustrating the History & Progress of Medical Science, Medical Education, & the Healing Arts in the United States: A Preliminary Contribution, 2 vols. 1654p. 1985. 275.00 (*0-940198-01-0*) St Aedans Pr & Bk.

— A Brief History of Education. 2nd rev. ed. (Quality Paperback Ser.: No. 67). 192p. 1976. pap. 8.95 (*0-8226-0067-6*) Littlefield.

— Equality of Educational Opportunity: A Bibliography of Selected References. 139p. 1973. pap. 13.50 (*0-87471-202-5*) St Aedans Pr & Bk.

— Homoeopathy in the United States: A Bibliography of Homoeopathic Medical Imprints, 1825-1925. (Illus.). 230p. 1991. 54.00 (*0-940198-07-X*) St Aedans Pr & Bk.

— Immigrant Children in American Schools: A Classified & Annotated Bibliography with Selected Source Documents. LC 76-45096. 1976. lib. bdg. 57.50 (*0-678-00743-8*) Kelley.

— The Immigrant Woman in North America: An Annotated Bibliography of Selected References. LC 85-11746. 245p. (C). 1985. 29.00 (*0-8108-1824-8*) Scarecrow.

— The Italian Community & Its Language in the United States: The Annual Reports of the Italian Teachers Association. 464p. 1975. 32.00 (*0-87471-585-7*) St Aedans Pr & Bk.

— Italian Mass Emigration: The Exodus of a Latin People: A Bibliographical Guide to the Bollettino dell'Emigrazione, 1902-1927. 307p. 1980. 37.00 (*0-8476-6283-7*) St Aedans Pr & Bk.

— The Italians: Social Backgrounds of an American Group. 598p. 1974. 29.50 (*0-678-01366-7*) St Aedans Pr & Bk.

— Italians in the United States: A Bibliography of Reports, Texts, Critical Studies & Related Materials. LC 78-180898. 137p. 1972. 25.00 (*0-685-45321-9*) St Aedans Pr & Bk.

— Junius: A Bibliography of the Letters of Junius with a Checklist of Junian Scholarship & Related Studies. 253p. 1986. 45.00 (*0-940198-04-5*) St Aedans Pr & Bk.

— Junius & His Works: A History of the Letters of Junius & the Authorship Controversy. 450p. 1986. 52.00 (*0-940198-03-7*) St Aedans Pr & Bk.

— Medical Publishing in Nineteenth Century America: Lea of Philadelphia, William Wood & Company of New York City & F. E. Boericke of Philadelphia with a Checklist of Wood's Library of Standard Medical Authors & Specimen Catalogues. (Illus.). 225p. 1990. 47.50 (*0-940198-06-1*) St Aedans Pr & Bk.

— The Puerto Ricans: Migration & General Bibliography. LC 74-14245. (Puerto Rican Experience Ser.). (Illus.). 1979. reprint ed. 39.95 (*0-405-06232-X*) Ayer.

— Puerto Ricans & Educational Opportunity: An Orginal Anthology. LC 74-14246. (Puerto Rican Experience Ser.). (Illus.). 1979. reprint ed. 23.95 (*0-405-06231-1*) Ayer.

— The Role of the Immigrant Woman in the U. S. Labor Force, 1890-1910. Dickinson, Joan Y., ed. LC 80-852. (American Ethnic Groups Ser.). 1981. lib. bdg. 26.95 (*0-405-13415-0*) Ayer.

— Tobias George Smollett: A Bibliographical Guide. LC 77-83136. (Studies in the Eighteenth Century: No. 2). lib. bdg. 32.50 (*0-404-16018-2*) AMS Pr.

— The United States Senate Report on Equal Educational Opportunity: A Neglected Plan for Education Reform. 35p. (C). 1998. pap. text 7.50 (*0-9660056-1-9*) E Vaughn Pub.

— Useful Spanish for Medical & Hospital Personnel. 146p. 1977. pap. 14.95 (*1-879170-62-0*) St Aedans Pr & Bk.

Cordasco, Francesco, ed. American Ethnic Groups, 47 bks., Set. (European Heritage Ser.). 1981. lib. bdg. 1580.00 (*0-405-13400-2*) Ayer.

— A Bibliography of Vocational Education: An Annotated Guide. LC 76-5961. (Studies in Education: No. 4). 47.50 (*0-404-10125-9*) AMS Pr.

— The Bilingual-Bicultural Child & the Question of Intelligence: An Original Anthology. LC 77-90568. (Bilingual-Bicultural Education in the U. S. Ser.). 1978. lib. bdg. 47.95 (*0-405-11107-X*) Ayer.

— Bilingual-Bicultural Education in the U. S. Series, 37 bks., Set. (Illus.). 1978. lib. bdg. 1090.00 (*0-405-11071-5*) Ayer.

— Bilingual Education in New York City. LC 77-92284. (Bilingual-Bicultural Education in the U. S. Ser.). 1978. lib. bdg. 36.95 (*0-405-11081-2*) Ayer.

— Bilingualism & the Bilingual Child: Challenges & Problems (an Original Anthology) LC 77-90569. (Bilingual-Bicultural Education in the U. S. Ser.). 1978. lib. bdg. 51.95 (*0-405-11108-8*) Ayer.

— Dictionary of American Immigration History. LC 89-37041. 810p. 1990. 102.50 (*0-8108-2241-5*) Scarecrow.

— The Italian American Experience, 39 vols., Set. (Illus.). 1975. 867.00 (*0-405-06390-3*, 457) Ayer.

— Italians in the City: An Original Anthology. LC 74-17933. (Italian American Experience Ser.). (Illus.). 1975. reprint ed. 16.95 (*0-405-06405-5*) Ayer.

— Italians in the United States: An Original Anthology. LC 74-17934. (Italian American Experience Ser.). (Illus.). 1975. reprint ed. 47.95 (*0-405-06406-3*) Ayer.

— Materials & Human Resources for Teaching Ethnic Studies. LC 77-17706. (Bilingual-Bicultural Education in the U. S. Ser.). 1978. reprint ed. lib. bdg. 29.95 (*0-405-11088-X*) Ayer.

— Protestant Evangelism among Italians in America. LC 74-17943. (Italian American Experience Ser.). (Illus.). 276p. 1975. reprint ed. 23.95 (*0-405-06414-4*) Ayer.

— The Puerto Rican Experience. (Illus.). 10610p. 1975. 827.50 (*0-405-06210-9*) Ayer.

— La Societa Italiana Di Fronte Alle Prime Migrazioni Di Massa: Italian Society at the Beginnings of the Mass Migrations. LC 74-17954. (Italian American Experience Ser.). (Illus.). 524p. 1975. reprint ed. 35.95 (*0-405-06423-3*) Ayer.

— Studies in Italian American Social History: Essays in Honor of Leonard Covello. 264p. 1975. 32.50 (*0-87471-705-1*) St Aedans Pr & Bk.

— Theodore Besterman, Bibliographer & Editor: A Selection of Representative Texts. LC 91-45136. (Great Bibliographers Ser.: No. 9). 497p. 1992. 71.00 (*0-8108-2497-3*) Scarecrow.

Cordasco, Francesco, et al, eds. History of American Education: A Guide to Information Sources. LC 79-23010. (Education Information Guide Ser.: Vol. 7). 328p. 1979. 68.00 (*0-8103-1382-0*) Gale.

Cordasco, Francesco & Alloway, David N. American Ethnic Groups: The European Heritage. LC 80-28775. 376p. 1981. 29.00 (*0-8108-1405-6*) Scarecrow.

Cordasco, Francesco & Brickman, William W., eds. A Bibliography of American Educational History: An Annotated & Classified Guide. LC 74-29140. (Studies in Education: No. 3). 47.50 (*0-404-12661-8*) AMS Pr.

Cordasco, Francesco & Bucchioni, Eugene. The Puerto Rican Community & Its Children on the Mainland: A Source Book for Teachers, Social Workers & Other Professionals. 3rd rev. ed. LC 81-21250. 469p. 1982. 34.50 (*0-8108-1506-0*) Scarecrow.

Cordasco, Francesco & Cordasco, Michael V. The Italian Emigration to the United States, 1880-1930: A Bibliographical Register of Italian Views Including Selected Numbers of the Italian Commissariat of Emigration, Bollettino Del'Emigrazione. (Illus.). 210p. 1990. 47.50 (*0-940198-05-3*) St Aedans Pr & Bk.

— Italians in the United States: An Annotated Bibliography of Doctoral Dissertations Completed at American Universities. 229p. 1981. 37.00 (*0-940198-00-2*) St Aedans Pr & Bk.

Cordasco, Francesco, ed. see Allen, Harold B.

Cordasco, Francesco, ed. see Allen, Virginia F. & Forman, Sidney.

Cordasco, Francesco, ed. see Appel, John J.

Cordasco, Francesco, ed. see Aucamp, A. J.

Cordasco, Francesco, ed. see Axelrod, Herman C.

Cordasco, Francesco, ed. see Bayer, Alan E.

Cordasco, Francesco, ed. see Bengelsdorf, Winnie.

Cordasco, Francesco, ed. see Berger, Morris I.

Cordasco, Francesco, ed. see Berman, Myron.

Cordasco, Francesco, ed. see Berrol, Selma C.

Cordasco, Francesco, ed. see Buxbaum, Edwin C.

Cordasco, Francesco, ed. see Castelli, Joseph R.

Cordasco, Francesco, ed. see Costantakos, Chrysie M.

Cordasco, Francesco, ed. see Dissemination Center for Bilingual-Bicultural Educ.

Cordasco, Francesco, ed. see Dobbert, Guido A.

Cordasco, Francesco, ed. see Farrell, John J.

Cordasco, Francesco, ed. see Ferroni, Charles D.

Cordasco, Francesco, ed. see Fishman, Joshua A., et al.

Cordasco, Francesco, ed. see Flores, Solomon H.

Cordasco, Francesco, ed. see Gabriel, Richard A.

Cordasco, Francesco, ed. see Galvan, Robert R.

Cordasco, Francesco, ed. see Glasco, Laurence A.

Cordasco, Francesco, ed. see Gobetz, Giles E.

Cordasco, Francesco, ed. see Hansen, Judith E.

Cordasco, Francesco, ed. see Harper, Richard C.

Cordasco, Francesco, ed. see Hill, Robert F.

Cordasco, Francesco, ed. see Hosay, Philip M.

Cordasco, Francesco, ed. see Illinois State Advisory Committee, the United Stat.

Cordasco, Francesco, ed. see Iorizzo, John L.

C

Cordasco, Francesco, ed. see Juliani, Richard N.
Cordasco, Francesco, ed. see Knoche, Carl H.
Cordasco, Francesco, ed. see Kolm, Richard.
Cordasco, Francesco, ed. see Kraus, Harry P.
Cordasco, Francesco, ed. see Leder, Hans H.
Cordasco, Francesco, ed. see Leonard, Henry B.
Cordasco, Francesco, ed. see Levy-Salomone, Rosemary.
Cordasco, Francesco, ed. see Lindberg, Duane R.
Cordasco, Francesco, ed. see Malherbe, Ernest G.
Cordasco, Francesco, ed. see Mandera, Franklin R.
Cordasco, Francesco, ed. see Medina, Amelia C.
Cordasco, Francesco, ed. see Mondello, Salvatore A.
Cordasco, Francesco, ed. see Mostwin, Danuta.
Cordasco, Francesco, ed. see Munguia, Juan C.
Cordasco, Francesco, ed. see Nam, Charles B.
Cordasco, Francesco, ed. see National Advisory Council on Bilingual Education.
Cordasco, Francesco, ed. see Neuringer, Sheldon M.
Cordasco, Francesco, ed. see Newton, Lewis W.
Cordasco, Francesco, ed. see Obidinski, Eugene E.
Cordasco, Francesco, ed. see Olson, Audrey L.
Cordasco, Francesco, ed. see Peebles, Robert W.
Cordasco, Francesco, ed. see Reyes, Vinicio H.
Cordasco, Francesco, ed. see Romano, Louis A.
Cordasco, Francesco, ed. see Royal Commission on Bilingualism & Biculturalism.
Cordasco, Francesco, ed. see Scarpaci, Jean A.
Cordasco, Francesco, ed. see Schelbert, Leo.
Cordasco, Francesco, ed. see Scherini, Rose D.
Cordasco, Francesco, ed. see Scourby, Alice.
Cordasco, Francesco, ed. see Spengler, Paul A.
Cordasco, Francesco, ed. see Stein, Howard F.
Cordasco, Francesco, ed. see Streiff, Virginia.
Cordasco, Francesco, ed. see Streiff, Paul R.
Cordasco, Francesco, ed. see Theriault, George F.
Cordasco, Francesco, ed. see Thompson, Bryan.
Cordasco, Francesco, ed. see U. S. Bureau of Indian Affairs Staff.
Cordasco, Francesco, ed. see U. S. Commission on Civil Rights Staff.
Cordasco, Francesco, ed. see U. S. House of Representative Committee on Educati.
Cordasco, Francesco, ed. see U. S. House of Representatives General Subcommitte.
Cordasco, Francesco, ed. see U. S. Office of Education, Bureau of Research Staf.
Cordasco, Francesco, ed. see U. S. Senate Committee on Labor & Public Welfare.
Cordasco, Francesco, ed. see Ulrich, Robert J.
Cordasco, Francesco, ed. see United Kingdom Department of Education & Science N.
Cordasco, Francesco, ed. see United Nations Educational, Scientific & Cultural Staff.
Cordasco, Francesco, ed. see Viereck, Louis.
Cordasco, Francesco, ed. see Wilhelm, Hubert G.
Cordasco, Michael V., jt. auth. see Cordasco, Francesco.
Cordato, A. J. Australian Travel & Tourism Law. 2nd ed. xii, 315 p. 1993. pap. 39.00 (*0-409-49082-2*, Austral, MICHIE) LEXIS Pub.
Cordato, Caridad. Now & Always/Para Siempre. (Encanto Ser.). (SPA & ENG.). 1999. mass mkt. 5.99 (*0-7860-0666-8*) Kensgtn Pub Corp.
Cordato, Roy E. Social Costs, Public Policy, & Freedom of Choice. 32p. 1992. pap. 4.95 (*0-614-04373-5*) IRET.
— Welfare Economics & Externalities in an Open-Ended Universe: A Modern Austrian Perspective. LC 92-19778. 160p. 1992. lib. bdg. 94.00 (*0-7923-9246-9*, Pub. by Kluwer Academic) Kluwer Academic.
Cordavero, Moses. Or Nerev: Hebrew Text. 100p. 1980. 10.00 (*0-943688-17-5*) Res Ctr Kabbalah.
Corddry, Mary. City on the Sand: Ocean City, Maryland, & the People Who Built It. LC 91-50178. (Illus.). 208p. 1991. 19.95 (*0-87033-420-4*, Tidewtr Pubs) Cornell Maritime.
Corddry, Thomas. Kibby & the Red Elephant. LC 72-13771. (Illus.). (J). (gr. 3-6). 1973. 6.95 (*0-87955-106-2*) O'Hara.
Corde, Betty, ed. see Wiebe, Arthur J. & Wilson, Jim.
Cordeiro, Aquiles, jt. auth. see Jackins, Harvey.
Cordeiro, Daniel R., ed. A Bibliography of Latin American Bibliographies: Social Sciences & Humanities, Supplement No. 2 to Arthur E. Gropp's A Bibliography of Latin American Bibliographies, Vol. 1. LC 78-11935. 1979. lib. bdg. 31.00 (*0-8108-1170-7*) Scarecrow.
Cordeiro, Pat. Whole Learning: Whole Language & Content in the Upper Elementary Grades. LC 91-39407. 288p. (C). 1992. pap. text 19.95 (*1-878450-15-8*, 502) R Owen Pubs.
Cordeiro, Pat, ed. Endless Possibilities: Generating Curriculum in Social Studies & Literacy. LC 94-48367. 138p. 1995. pap. text 20.00 (*0-435-08903-X*, 08903) Heinemann.
Cordeiro, Paula A., et al. Multiculturalism & TQE: Addressing Cultural Diversity in Schools. LC 93-42325. (Total Quality Education for the World's Best Schools Ser.: Vol. 7). 128p. 1994. pap. 19.95 (*0-8039-6107-3*) Corwin Pr.
***Cordeiro, Wayne.** Developing an Attitude That Attracts Success. O'Brien, Dawn, ed. 1999. pap. write for info. (*0-9654251-8-5*) New Hope HI.
Cordeiro, Wayne. Doing Church As a Team. LC 98-233950. 196p. 1998. pap. 15.00 (*0-9654251-1-8*) New Hope HI.
— Gems along the Way. 144p. 1997. pap. 9.95 (*0-9654251-0-X*) New Hope HI.
***Cordeiro, Wayne.** How's Your Love Life? O'Brien, Dawn, ed. 1999. pap. write for info. (*1-929351-00-3*) New Hope HI.
Cordel, Betty, et al. Floaters & Sinkers: Mass, Volume, & Density. rev. ed. (J). (gr. 5-9). 1995. 16.95 (*1-881431-58-4*, 1306) AIMS Educ Fnd.
Cordel, Betty, ed. see Erickson, Sheldon.
Cordel, Betty, ed. see Erickson, Sheldon, et al.
Cordel, Betty, ed. see Gazlay, Suzy.
Cordel, Betty, ed. see Gossett, Carol.
Cordel, Betty, ed. see Gossett, Carol S.
Cordel, Betty, ed. see Hoover, Evalyn & Mercier, Sheryl.
Cordel, Betty, ed. see Novelli, Barbara A., et al.
Cordel, Betty, ed. see Wiebe, Ann.
Cordel, Betty, ed. see Wiebe, Arthur J.
Cordel, Betty, ed. see Wilson, Jim.
Cordel, Betty, ed. see Youngs, Dave & Youngs, Michelle.
Cordeli, Cleo. The Captive Flesh. (Black Lace Ser.). 1995. mass mkt. 5.95 (*0-352-32872-X*, Pub. by Virgin Bks) London Brdge.
— Path of the Tiger. (Black Lace Ser.). 1995. mass mkt. 5.95 (*0-352-32959-9*, Pub. by Virgin Bks) London Brdge.
Cordelier, M., jt. auth. see Harrison, P. W.
Cordell. The Alkaloids, Vol. 29. 1986. 167.00 (*0-12-469529-9*) Acad Pr.
Cordell, Alexander. Beloved Exile. large type ed. 608p. 1995. 27.99 (*0-7089-3200-2*) Ulverscroft.
— The Bright Cantonese. large type ed. 342p. 1977. 27.99 (*0-7089-0058-5*) Ulverscroft.
— The Dreams of Fair Women. large type ed. 624p. 1995. 27.99 (*0-7089-3255-X*) Ulverscroft.
— Land of Heart's Desire. 1994. lib. bdg. 20.00 (*0-7278-4715-5*) Severn Hse.
— Land of Heart's Desire. large type ed. 512p. 1996. 27.99 (*0-7089-3610-5*) Ulverscroft.
— The Love That God Forgot. large type ed. (Ulverscroft Large Print Ser.). 496p. 1997. 27.99 (*0-7089-3770-5*) Ulverscroft.
— Send Her Victorious. 224p. 25.00 (*0-7278-5205-1*) Severn Hse.
— Send Her Victorious. large type ed. (Ulverscroft Large Print Ser.). 336p. 1998. 29.99 (*0-7089-3936-8*) Ulverscroft.
— This Sweet & Bitter Earth. 1996. 24.00 (*0-7278-4950-6*) Severn Hse.
— To Slay the Dreamer. large type ed. 511p. 1982. 27.99 (*0-7089-0766-0*) Ulverscroft.
— Tunnel Tigers. large type ed. 480p. 1988. 27.99 (*0-7089-1818-2*) Ulverscroft.
Cordell, Barbara, et al, eds. Understanding the Legislative & Regulatory Process. unabridged ed. (Regional Conference Ser.). Date not set. ring bd. 475.00 (*0-935890-29-7*) Emerg Nurses IL.
Cordell, Bruce. A Darkness Gathering. 1998. 9.95 (*0-7869-1208-1*, Pub. by TSR Inc) Random.
***Cordell, Bruce.** Diablo II: The Monastery of the Sightless Eye. (AD & D Odyssey Adventure Ser.). (Illus.). 128p. 2000. pap. 22.95 (*0-7869-1612-5*) TSR Inc.
Cordell, Bruce. Gates of Firestorm Peak. 1996. 20.00 (*0-7869-0435-6*, Pub. by TSR Inc) Random.
— A Guide to the Ethereal Plane. 1998. 16.95 (*0-7869-1205-7*, Pub. by TSR Inc) Random.
***Cordell, Bruce.** Killing Jar. (Alternity Ser.). (Illus.). 64p. 2000. pap. 13.95 (*0-7869-1615-X*) TSR Inc.
Cordell, Bruce. Night of the Shark. Rateliff, John, ed. 1997. 9.95 (*0-7869-0718-5*, Pub. by TSR Inc) Random.
Cordell, Bruce, jt. auth. see Miller, Steve.
Cordell, Bruce R. Dawn of the Overmind. 64p. 1998. 13.95 (*0-7869-1211-1*, Pub. by TSR Inc) Random.
— Dungeon Builder's Guidebook. 1998. 14.95 (*0-7869-1207-3*, Pub. by TSR Inc) Random.
— Evil Tide. (Monstrous Arcana Adventure Ser.). 1997. 9.95 (*0-7869-0678-2*, Pub. by TSR Inc) Random.
— The Illithiad. 1998. 19.95 (*0-7869-1206-5*, Pub. by TSR Inc) Random.
— Masters of Eternal Night. 1998. pap. 9.95 (*0-7869-1253-7*, Pub. by TSR Inc) Random.
— Priest's Temple. 1999. 18.95 (*0-7869-1442-4*) TSR Inc.
— Return to White Plume Mountain. 1999. 12.95 (*0-7869-1434-3*) TSR Inc.
***Cordell, Bruce R.** The Sunless Citadel. 32p. 2000. pap. 9.95 (*0-7869-1640-0*) Wizards Coast.
Cordell, Bruce R. Tangents. (Alternity Ser.). 1999. 18.95 (*0-7869-1352-5*, Pub. by TSR Inc) Random.
Cordell, Charles E. Green Five. Smith, Frank K., ed. (Illus.). 214p. (Orig.). 1989. pap. 9.95 (*0-9619184-1-1*) E P Lay Assocs.
Cordell, Cleo. The Flesh Constrained. 320p. 1998. mass mkt. 6.95 (*0-7867-0602-3*) Carroll & Graf.
— Opal Darkness. (Black Lace Ser.). 1995. mass mkt. 5.95 (*0-352-33033-3*, Pub. by Virgin Bks) London Brdge.
— Temptation & Torment. 320p. 1998. mass mkt. 5.95 (*0-7867-0551-5*) Carroll & Graf.
Cordell, Crystal, jt. auth. see Cordell, Joan.
Cordell, David M., ed. Fundamentals of Financial Planning. 4th ed. LC 98-74662. 525p. (C). 1999. text 65.00 (*1-57996-013-8*) Amer College.
***Cordell, David M., ed.** Readings in Financial Planning. 4th ed. LC 99-75333. 475p. 1999. pap. text 34.00 (*1-57996-019-7*) Amer College.
Cordell, Dennis & Gregory, Joel. Hoe & Wage: A Social History of a Circular Migration System in West Africa. (African Modernization & Development Ser.). 384p. 2000. pap. text 28.00 (*0-8133-3608-2*, Pub. by Westview) HarpC.
Cordell, Dennis D. Dar Al-Kuti & the Last Years of the Trans-Saharan Slave Trade. LC 84-40147. (Illus.). 352p. 1985. 40.00 (*0-299-09520-7*) U of Wis Pr.
Cordell, Dennis D. & Gregory, Joel W., eds. African Population & Capitalism: Historical Perspectives. LC 93-39164. 1994. 40.00 (*0-299-14270-1*); pap. 19.95 (*0-299-14274-4*) U of Wis Pr.
Cordell, Geoffrey A. The Alkaloids Vol. 52: Chemistry & Biology. (Illus.). 391p. (C). 1998. boxed set. write for info. (*0-12-469552-3*) Acad Pr.
Cordell, Geoffrey A., ed. The Alkaloids, Vol. 42. (Illus.). 314p. 1992. text 129.00 (*0-12-469542-6*) Acad Pr.
— The Alkaloids: Chemistry & Biology. (Illus.). 439p. 1998. boxed set 135.00 (*0-12-469551-5*) Acad Pr.
— The Alkaloids Vol. 45: Chemistry & Pharmacology. (Illus.). 280p. 1994. text 133.00 (*0-12-469545-0*) Acad Pr.
— The Alkaloids Vol. 46: Chemistry & Pharmacology, Vol. 46. (Illus.). 364p. 1995. text 116.00 (*0-12-469546-9*) Acad Pr.
Cordell, Geoffrey A., ed. The Alkaloids Vol. 47: Chemistry & Pharmacology, Vol. 47. (Illus.). 381p. 1995. text 116.00 (*0-12-469547-7*) Acad Pr.
Cordell, Geoffrey A., ed. The Alkaloids Vol. 48: Chemistry & Pharmacology. (Illus.). 374p. 1996. text 99.95 (*0-12-469548-5*) Acad Pr.
— The Alkaloids Vol. 49: Chemistry & Pharmacology, Vol. 49. (Illus.). 405p. 1997. text 120.00 (*0-12-469549-3*) Morgan Kaufmann.
— The Alkaloids Vol. 50: Chemistry & Pharmacology, Vol. 50. (Illus.). 590p. 1997. text 125.00 (*0-12-469550-7*) Morgan Kaufmann.
Cordell, Helen. Laos. LC 92-146773. (World Bibliographical Ser.). 254p. 1992. lib. bdg. 82.00 (*1-85109-075-4*) ABC-CLIO.
Cordell, J. Business Within Europe for GNVQ Advanced Business. 200p. 1995. pap. 59.95 (*1-85805-084-7*, Pub. by DP Publns) St Mut.
Cordell, Joan. Desperate Images. LC 97-93448. 72p. (Orig.). 1997. pap. 12.95 (*1-890713-01-5*) Banquet Bks.
Cordell, Joan & Cordell, Crystal. The Adventurous Tales of the Allspot Family. LC 97-93447. (Illus.). 100p. (J). (gr. 3-6). 1997. 16.95 (*1-890713-00-7*) Banquet Bks.
Cordell, John, ed. A Sea of Small Boats. (Cultural Survival Reports: No. 26). 300p. 1988. 34.95 (*0-939521-37-7*); pap. 15.00 (*0-939521-31-8*) Cultural Survival.
Cordell, Karl. Ethnicity & Democratisation in the New Europe. LC 98-27618. 1999. 85.00 (*0-415-17311-6*) Routledge.
***Cordell, Karl.** Ethnicity & Democratisation in the New Europe. LC 98-27618. 1999. pap. 27.99 (*0-415-17312-4*) Routledge.
— The Politics of Ethnicity in Central Europe. LC 99-39505. 2000. text 65.00 (*0-312-22790-6*) St Martin.
***Cordell, Karl & Antoszewski, Andrzej.** Poland & the European Union. LC 00-20055. (Studies of Societies in Transition). 2000. write for info. (*0-415-23885-4*) Routledge.
Cordell, Ken. Integrating Social Sciences with Ecosystem Management. (Illus.). 400p. 1999. pap. 44.95 (*1-57167-247-8*) Sagamore Pub.
— Outdoor Recreation in American Life. LC 98-83130. (Illus.). 400p. 1999. pap. 49.95 (*1-57167-246-X*) Sagamore Pub.
Cordell, Ken & Stanley-Saunders, Barbara. The Private Sector Role in Rural Outdoor Recreation in the United States: An Annotated Bibliography. (CPL Bibliographies Ser.: No. 106). 118p. 1983. 10.00 (*0-86602-106-X*, Sage Prdcls Pr) Sage.
Cordell, Linda. Archaeology of the Southwest. 2nd ed. LC 97-80320. (Illus.). 522p. 1997. text 85.00 (*0-12-188225-X*); pap. text 39.95 (*0-12-188226-8*) Morgan Kaufmann.
***Cordell, Linda, ed.** The Alkaloids Vol. 53: Chemistry & Biology. 475p. 1999. text 140.00 (*0-12-469553-1*) Acad Pr.
— The Alkaloids Vol. 54. 384p. 2000. 140.00 (*0-12-469554-X*) Acad Pr.
Cordell, Linda S. Ancient Pueblo Peoples. LC 94-2308. (Exploring the Ancient World Ser.). (Illus.). 176p. 1995. text 24.95 (*0-89599-038-5*) Smithsonian.
— Before Pecos: Settlement Aggregation at Rowe, New Mexico. 1999. pap. text 28.00 (*0-912535-12-1*) Max Mus.
Cordell, Linda S. & Gumerman, George J., eds. Dynamics of Southwest Prehistory. LC 89-5954. (Series in Archaeological Inquiry). (Illus.). 389p. (C). 1993. reprint ed. pap. text 24.95 (*1-56098-307-8*) Smithsonian.
Cordell, Linda S., jt. ed. see Foster, Nelson.
Cordell, Robert J., jt. ed. see Roberts, W. H., III.
Cordell, Rose. Forget the ABC's until after Your Child Has Learned to Read. (Children's Alphabet Reading Ser.). (Illus.). 211p. (Orig.). 1983. 17.95 (*0-940047-00-4*); teacher ed. 31.95 (*0-940047-04-7*); teacher ed. write for info. (*0-940047-06-3*); student ed. 7.00 (*0-940047-05-5*); pap. 14.95 (*0-940047-03-9*); text 17.95 (*0-940047-02-0*); lib. bdg. 25.95 (*0-940047-01-2*) Child Alphabet.
Cordell, Victor V., et al, eds. Globalization & Regionalization: Strategies, Policies, & Their Economic Environment. LC 98-16143. 350p. 1998. 79.95 (*0-7890-0513-1*, Intl Busn Pr) Haworth Pr.
Cordella, Peter, jt. ed. see Siegel, Larry J.
Cordellos, Harry C. Breaking Through. LC 78-23270. (Illus.). 240p. (Orig.). 1981. pap. 7.95 (*0-89037-168-7*) Anderson World.
Cordemoy, Geraud De. A Philosophical Discourse Concerning Speech. LC 78-147961. reprint ed. 15.00 (*0-404-08211-4*) AMS Pr.
Cordemoy, Geraud de. Philosophical Discourse Concerning Speech (1668) & a Discourse Written to a Learned Frier (1670) LC 72-6400. (History of Psychology Ser.). 232p. 1972. reprint ed. 50.00 (*0-8201-1106-6*) Schol Facsimiles.
Corden, A., jt. auth. see Boden, R.
Corden, Anne, jt. auth. see Eardley, Tony.
Corden, John & Preston-Shoot, Michael. Contracts in Social Work. (Community Care Practice Handbook Ser.). 100p. 1987. text 16.95 (*0-566-05130-3*, Pub. by Gower) Ashgate Pub Co.
***Corden, Roy.** Literacy & Learning Through Talk: Strategies for the Primary Classroom LC 99-44708. 2000. pap. write for info. (*0-335-20451-1*) OpUniv Pr.
Corden, W. M. Inflation, Exchange Rates, & the World Economy: Lectures on International Monetary Economics. 3rd ed. LC 76-5833. (Studies in Business & Society). viii, 208p. 1986. pap. text 12.95 (*0-226-11582-8*); lib. bdg. 22.50 (*0-226-11580-1*) U Ch Pr.
— The Revival of Protectionism. (Occasional Paper Ser.: No. 14). 28p. 1984. pap. 7.00 (*1-56708-013-8*) Grp of Thirty.
Corden, W. Max. Economic Policy, Exchange Rates, & the International System. 336p. 1994. pap. text 22.00 (*0-226-11591-7*) U Ch Pr.
— Economic Policy, Exchange Rates, & the International System. 336p. 1997. lib. bdg. 60.00 (*0-226-11590-9*) U Ch Pr.
— International Trade Theory & Policy: Selected Essays of W. Max Corden. (Economists of the Twentieth Century Ser.). 592p. 1992. 110.00 (*1-85278-732-5*) E Elgar.
— Protection & Liberalization: A Review of Analytical Issues. (Occasional Papers: No. 54). 28p. 1987. pap. 7.50 (*0-939934-94-9*) Intl Monetary.
— Trade Policy & Economic Welfare. 2nd ed. (Illus.). 318p. 1997. text 85.00 (*0-19-829223-6*) OUP.
— Trade Policy & Economic Welfare. 2nd ed. (Illus.). 318p. 1997. pap. text 19.95 (*0-19-877534-2*) OUP.
Cordenoy, E. Jacob De. Flore de l'Ile de la Reunion (Mascarene Islands) 1972. reprint ed. 120.00 (*3-7682-0758-7*) Lubrecht & Cramer.
Corder, Billie F. Structured Adolescent Psychotherapy Groups. LC 93-44822. 164p. (Orig.). 1994. pap. 23.95 (*0-943158-74-5*, SAPGBP, Prof Resc Pr) Pro Resource.
***Corder, Billie Farmer.** Structured Psychotherapy Groups for Sexually Abused Children & Adolescents. LC 00-27227. 272p. 2000. pap. 34.95 (*1-56887-058-2*, SCABP, Prof Resc Pr) Pro Resource.
Corder, Brice W., ed. Medical Professions Admission Guide: Strategy for Success. 3rd ed. 142p. (C). 1994. pap. 15.95 (*0-911899-11-1*) NAAHP Inc.
***Corder, Cathy, ed.** It Couldn't Happen Here: Recognizing & Helping Desperate Kids. 1999. pap. 12.95 (*0-87868-774-2*, CWLA Pr) Child Welfare.
Corder, Cliff. HTML: A Textbook Guide: An Introduction to Programming for the World Wide Web. (Illus.). 170p. 1998. spiral bd. 30.00 (*0-9663151-0-3*) GINS.
Corder, Colin. Teaching Hard, Teaching Soft. 200p. 1990. text 74.95 (*0-566-02865-4*, Pub. by Gower) Ashgate Pub Co.
Corder, Frederick. Ferencz (Francois) Liszt. LC 74-24062. reprint ed. 34.50 (*0-404-12888-2*) AMS Pr.
Corder, H. Judges at Work: The Role & Attitudes of the South African Appellate Judiciary, 1910-1950. 280p. 1984. 22.00 (*0-7021-1435-9*, 15605, Pub. by Juta & Co) Gaunt.
Corder, H., ed. Essays on Law & Social Practice in South Africa. 368p. 1988. pap. 15.00 (*0-7021-2005-7*, 15599, Pub. by Juta & Co) Gaunt.
Corder, Henry, ed. New Voices from West Africa. 1979. 11.00 (*0-686-33149-4*) Arden Assocs.
Corder, Hugh, jt. auth. see Du Plessis, Lourens.
Corder, Jim W. Chronicle of a Small Town. LC 89-4464. (Wardlaw Book Ser.). (Illus.). 192p. 1989. 15.95 (*0-89096-414-9*) Tex A&M Univ Pr.
Corder, Jim W. & Ruszkiewicz, John J. Handbook of Current English. 7th ed. (C). 1989. 31.60 (*0-673-15968-X*, Scott Frsmn) Addson-Wesley Educ.
Corder, Jim W., et al. Handbook Current English. 8th ed. (C). 1989. text 41.25 (*0-673-18971-6*) Addson-Wesley Educ.
Corder, Joan. A Dictionary of Suffolk Crests Vol. 40: Heraldic Crests of Suffolk Families. (Suffolk Records Society Ser.). (Illus.). 272p. 1998. 55.00 (*0-85115-554-5*, Boydell Pr) Boydell & Brewer.
Corder, John A., jt. auth. see McCall, Gene H.
Corder, Kevin. Central Bank Autonomy: The Federal Reserve System in American Politics. rev. ed. LC 98-25627. (Financial Sector of the American Economy Ser.). 200p. 1998. 53.00 (*0-8153-3197-5*) Garland.
Corder, Matthew, jt. auth. see Brooker, Richard.
Corder, S. Pit. Introducing Applied Linguistics. 1994. pap. 22.95 (*0-14-013208-2*, Pub. by Pnguin Bks Ltd) Trafalgar.

Corderman, Esther B. Out of the Night. 340p. 1994. pap. 12.95 (*0-87012-519-2*) McClain.
Set in the Appalachian mountains in the early 1900s, OUT OF THE NIGHT is a vivid portrayal of the many facets of passion exploding within one high-spirited young woman & the people who make up her world. It is not only the story of the woman's turmoil; it touches upon the growing pains of a nation in crisis. The author has skillfully recaptured some revealing realities of a bygone era. *Publisher Paid Annotation.*

Corderman, John P. & Knapel, Carole. Court Security & the Transportation of Prisoners: A National Study. 55p. (C). 1998. pap. text 20.00 (*0-7881-7385-5*) DIANE Pub.
Cordero. Game. 2nd ed. 1998. pap. text 24.00 incl. disk (*0-471-32596-1*) Wiley.
Cordero, Adelle M., ed. see Kendrick, Teresa A.
Cordero, Alberto, jt. ed. see Agazzi, E.
Cordero, Kristina, tr. see Frei, Irene G.
Cordero, Kristina, tr. see Loriga, Ray.

Cordero, Kristina, tr. see Prado, Benjamin.
Cordero, L. Luis, et al. Differential Geometry of Frame Bundles. (C). 1988. text 153.00 (*0-7923-0012-2*) Kluwer Academic.
Cordero, Marco, jt. auth. see Nasr, Isam.
Cordero, P., et al, eds. Nonlinear Phenomena in Fluids, Solids & Other Complex Systems: Proceedings of the 2nd Latin American Workshop on Nonlinear Phenomena, Santiago, Chile, 6-14 September, 1990. (North-Holland Delta Ser.: Vol. 9). xii, 482p. 1991. 165.00 (*0-444-88791-1*, NHD 9, North Holland) Elsevier.
Cordero, Richard. The Creation of a European Banking System: A Study of Its Legal & Technical Aspects. LC 89-13890. (American University Studies: Political Science: Ser. X, Vol. 27). XXXVI, 390p. (C). 1990. text 67.50 (*0-8204-1315-1*) P Lang Pubng.
Cordero, Wilma, jt. auth. see Kintisch, Shelly.
Cordes, jt. auth. see Ibrahim.
Cordes, Anne K. & Ingham, Roger J. Treatment Efficacy for Stuttering: A Search for Empirical Bases. LC 98-5956. 1998. write for info. (*1-56543-904-X*) Mt SA Coll Philos.
— Treatment Efficacy for Stuttering: A Search for Empirical Buses. (Illus.). 304p. 1998. pap. 65.00 (*1-56593-904-2*, 1790) Thomson Learn.
Cordes, Betty, et al. Pocket Guide to Emergency First Aid. (Illus.). 28p. 1993. spiral bd. 12.95 (*0-9633024-2-6*) Greycliff Pub.
— Pocket Guide to Safe Babysitting. (Illus.). 28p. 1995. spiral bd. 12.95 (*1-886127-09-3*) Greycliff Pub.
Cordes, Christopher, ed. Bruce Nauman Prints 1970-89. (Illus.). 236p. 1989. text 75.00 (*0-9625240-0-X*); pap. text 40.00 (*0-685-40656-3*) Castelli Graphics.
Cordes, Christopher & Yau, John. Bruce Nauman: Prints 1970-1989. Taylor, Debbie, ed. (Illus.). 128p. 1989. write for info. (*0-318-66699-5*) Castelli Graphics.
Cordes, Claire C. Ranch Trails & Short Tales. Wilson, Bruce M. et al, eds. LC 91-71942. (Illus.). 112p. 1991. pap. 10.95 (*0-9627573-1-4*) Crown King Pr.
Cordes, H. O. The Technique of Pseudodifferential Operators. (London Mathematical Society Lecture Note Ser.: No. 202). 394p. (C). 1995. pap. text 44.95 (*0-521-37864-8*) Cambridge U Pr.
Cordes, H. O., et al, eds. Pseudo-Differential Operators. (Lecture Notes in Mathematics Ser.: Vol. 1256). x, 479p. 1987. 62.95 (*0-387-17856-2*) Spr-Verlag.
Cordes, Helen. Girl Power in the Mirror: Your Body, Your Self. LC 97-1085. 64p. (YA). (gr. 6-9). 1999. lib. bdg. 25.26 (*0-8225-2691-3*, Lerner Publctns) Lerner Pub.
— In the Classroom. LC 99-28298. (Girl Power Ser.). 96p. (J). (gr. 6-9). 1999. 25.26 (*0-8225-2693-X*, Lerner Publctns) Lerner Pub.
Cordes, J. Chalom Des, see Chalom Des Cordes, V. & Chalom Des Cordes, J.
Cordes, J. M., et al, eds. Radio Wave Scattering in the Interstellar Medium. LC 88-72092. (AIP Conference Proceedings Ser.: No. 174). 245p. 1988. lib. bdg. 60.00 (*0-88318-374-9*) Am Inst Physics.
Cordes, Jayne A. The Hope Star. 1999. 16.95 (*0-9662670-0-1*) J Kid Prodns.
***Cordes, Jayne A.** The Hope Star. Hudson, Loretta, ed. LC 97-95119. (Illus.). 32p. (YA). (ps up). 1999. 16.95 (*0-9662670-1-X*) J Kid Prodns.
Cordes, Joseph, et al. Human Service Delivery in a Changing Funding Environment: Washington Area Nonprofits in an Era of Donor Choice. 1997. pap. 6.00 (*1-888028-30-0*) GWU Ctr WAS.
Cordes, Joseph J. Democracy, Social Values & Public Policy. Carrow, Milton M. & Churchill, Robert P., eds. LC 97-34748. 224p. 1998. 55.00 (*0-275-95985-6*, Praeger Pubs) Greenwood.
Cordes, Joseph J., et al, eds. The Encyclopedia of Taxation & Tax Policy. LC 98-40996. 462p. 1999. lib. bdg. 75.00 (*0-87766-682-2*) Urban Inst.
***Cordes, Kathleen A.** America's National Historic Trails. LC 98-45075. 1999. pap. text 19.95 (*0-8061-3103-9*) U of Okla Pr.
Cordes, Kathleen A. & Ibrahim, Hilmi. Applications in Recreation & Leisure: For Today & the Future. 2nd ed. LC 98-23795. 368p. 1998. 54.69 (*0-07-092132-6*) McGraw.
Cordes, Kathleen A., jt. auth. see Ibrahim, Hilmi.
Cordes, Lester, II, et al. Pocket Guide to Walleye Fishing in Lakes. (Illus.). 28p. 1995. spiral bd. 12.95 (*1-886127-08-5*) Greycliff Pub.
Cordes, Liane. Reflecting Pond. (Illus.). 140p. 1985. pap. 9.00 (*0-89486-121-2*, 1068A) Hazelden.
Cordes, Paul J. Born of the Spirit: Renewal Movements in the Life of the Church. 2nd ed. 138p. 1995. 11.95 (*0-937779-30-X*) Greenlawn Pr.
— Charisms & New Evangelization. 171p. (C). 1996. pap. 39.95 (*0-85439-403-6*, Pub. by St Paul Pubns) St Mut.
Cordes, Paul J. & Cantalamessa, Raniero. Call to Holiness: Reflections on the Catholic Charismatic Renewal. LC 97-37799. 72p. (Orig.). 1997. pap. 4.95 (*0-8146-5887-3*) Liturgical Pr.
Cordes, R. A. Backpacker's Guide to Fly Fishing. 96p. 1992. pap. text 8.95 (*0-9633024-0-X*) Troutbeck Pub.
Cordes, Ron & LaFontaine, Gary. Pocket Guide to Basic Fly Tying Techniques. (Illus.). 28p. 1995. spiral bd. 12.95 (*1-886127-11-5*) Greycliff Pub.
— Pocket Guide to Dry Fly Fishing. (Illus.). 28p. 1994. spiral bd. 12.95 (*0-9633024-3-4*) Greycliff Pub.
— Pocket Guide to Fly Fishing. (Illus.). 26p. 1992. spiral bd. 12.95 (*1-886127-16-6*) Greycliff Pub.
— Pocket Guide to Fly Fishing for Largemouth Bass. (Illus.). 28p. 1999. spiral bd. 12.95 (*1-886127-12-3*) Greycliff Pub.
— Pocket Guide to Fly Fishing the Lakes. (Illus.). 28p. 1993. spiral bd. 12.95 (*0-9633024-4-2*) Greycliff Pub.
— Pocket Guide to Hiking - Backpacking. (Illus.). 28p. 1993. spiral bd. 12.95 (*0-9633024-7-7*) Greycliff Pub.
— Pocket Guide to Nymph Fishing. (Illus.). 28p. 1994. spiral bd. 12.95 (*0-9633024-6-9*) Greycliff Pub.
— Pocket Guide to Saltwater Fly Fishing. (Illus.). 28p. 1994. spiral bd. 12.95 (*0-9633024-8-5*) Greycliff Pub.
Cordes, Ron, et al. Pocket Guide to Animal Tracks. (Illus.). 28p. 1995. spiral bd. 12.95 (*1-886127-03-4*) Greycliff Pub.
Cordes, Ron, ed. see Kaufmann, Randall.
Cordes, V. Chalom Des, see Chalom Des Cordes, V.
Cordesman, Anthony H. Bahrain, Oman, Qatar & the UAE: Challenges of Security. LC 96-46288. (CSIS Middle East Dynamic Net Assessment Ser.). 448p. (C). 1997. pap. text 35.00 (*0-8133-3240-0*, Pub. by Westview) HarpC.
— Iran's Military Forces in Transition. LC 98-41448. 448p. 1999. 69.50 (*0-275-96529-5*, Praeger Pubs) Greenwood.
— Iraq & the War of Sanctions. LC 98-41447. 712p. 1999. 75.00 (*0-275-96528-7*, Praeger Pubs) Greenwood.
— Jordanian Arms & the Middle East Balance: Update. LC 85-221948. 25p. (Orig.). 1985. pap. 5.00 (*0-916808-30-0*) Mid East Inst.
— Kuwait: Recovery & Security after the Gulf War. LC 96-44401. (CSIS Middle East Dynamic Net Assessment Ser.). 176p. (C). 1997. pap. text 25.00 (*0-8133-3244-3*, Pub. by Westview) HarpC.
— The Lessons of Modern War: The Gulf War, Vol. 4. (C). 1998. pap. 40.00 (*0-8133-8602-0*, Pub. by Westview) HarpC.
— Saudi Arabia: Guarding the Desert Kingdom. LC 96-46048. (CSIS Middle East Dynamic Net Assessment Ser.). 240p. (C). 1997. pap. text 27.00 (*0-8133-3242-7*, Pub. by Westview) HarpC.
***Cordesman, Anthony H.** Transnational Threats from the Middle East: Crying Wolf or Crying Havoc? LC 99-460641. 236p. 1999. pap. write for info. (*1-58487-001-X*) SSI US Army.
Cordesman, Anthony H. U. S. - Arab Relations: The Iran-Iraq War & U. S.-Iraq Relations: An Iraqi Perspective, No. 11. 40p. (Orig.). pap. 4.00 (*0-685-10615-2*) Natl Coun Arab.
— U. S. Forces in the Middle East: Resources & Capabilities. LC 96-46615. (CSIS Middle East Dynamic Net Assessment Ser.). 160p. (C). 1997. pap. text 26.00 (*0-8133-3246-X*, Pub. by Westview) HarpC.
— U. S. Strategic Interests & the India Pakistan Military Balance. (C). 1988. pap. 45.00 (*81-7002-035-2*, Pub. by Himalayan Bks) St Mut.
Cordesman, Anthony H. & Hashim, Ahmed S. Iraq: Sanctions & Beyond. LC 96-46046. 416p. 1997. text 85.00 (*0-8133-3235-4*, Pub. by Westview) HarpC.
— Iraq: Sanctions & Beyond. LC 96-46046. (CSIS Middle East Dynamic Net Assessment Ser.). 416p. (C). 1997. pap. text 35.00 (*0-8133-3236-2*, Pub. by Westview) HarpC.
Cordesman, Anthony H. & Parker, Richard. Jordanian Arms & the Middle East Balance. (Illus.). 186p. (Orig.). 1983. pap. 5.00 (*0-916808-20-3*) Mid East Inst.
Cordess, Christopher. Forensic Psychotherapy: Crime, Psychodynamics & the Offender Patient. 1100p. 1995. 299.00 (*1-85302-240-3*) Taylor & Francis.
— Forensic Psychotherapy: Crime, Psychodynamics & the Offender Patient, 1, 1. LC 98-184738. (Forensic Focus Ser.). 1998. 75.00 (*1-85302-634-4*) Taylor & Francis.
***Cordess, Christopher.** Violence, Victims & Crime: Readings in Forensic Psychotherapy. 2000. pap. 32.95 (*1-85302-729-4*) Jessica Kingsley.
Cordevero, Moshe. Tomer Devorah. Miller, Moshe, tr. (ENG & HEB.). 1994. 16.95 (*1-56871-027-5*) Feldheim.
Cordiano, C. Color Atlas of Gastrointestinal Surgery, 2 vols. (Illus.). 896p. 1989. text 528.00 (*88-299-0238-1*, Pub. by Piccin Nuova) Gordon & Breach.
— Staging & Treatment of Gastric Cancer. (Illus.). 330p. 1991. write for info. (*88-299-0976-9*, Pub. by Piccin Nuova) Gordon & Breach.
Cordiano, C. & De Manzoni, D. Staging & Treatment of Gastric Cancer. 330p. 1991. text 60.00 (*1-57235-016-4*) Piccin Nuova.
Cordiano, C. & Nardi, G. L. Color Atlas of Gastrointestinal Surgery, 2 vols., Set. 896p. 1989. text 480.00 (*1-57235-039-3*) Piccin Nuova.
Cordier, Andrew W. & Foote, Wilder, eds. Public Papers of the Secretaries-General of the United Nations Vol. 1: Trygve Lie, 1946-1953. LC 68-8873. 535p. 1978. text 81.00 (*0-231-03137-8*) Col U Pr.
— Public Papers of the Secretaries-General of the United Nations Vol. 4: Dag Hammarskjold, 1958-1960, Vol. 4. LC 68-8873. 659p. 1978. text 81.00 (*0-231-03810-0*) Col U Pr.
— Public Papers of the Secretaries-General of the United Nations, Vol. 2: Dag Hammarskjold, 1953-1956. LC 68-8873. 115p. 1978. text 81.00 (*0-231-03633-7*) Col U Pr.
— Public Papers of the Secretaries-General of the United Nations, Vol. 3: Dag Hammarskjold, 1956-1957. LC 68-88873. 729p. 1978. text 81.00 (*0-231-03735-X*) Col U Pr.
— Public Papers of the Secretaries-General of the United Nations, Vol. 5: Dag Hammarskjold, 1960-1961. LC 68-8873. 592p. 1978. text 81.00 (*0-231-03897-6*) Col U Pr.
Cordier, Andrew W. & Harrelson, Max, eds. Public Papers of the Secretaries-General of the United Nations, Vol. 6: U Thant, 1961-1964. LC 68-8873. 708p. 1978. text 81.00 (*0-231-03966-2*) Col U Pr.
— Public Papers of the Secretaries-General of the United Nations, Vol. 7: U Thant, 1965-1967. LC 68-8873. 633p. 1978. text 81.00 (*0-231-04098-9*) Col U Pr.
Cordier, Henri. Bibliotheca Indosinica, 5 pts. in 2, Set. vii, 3030p. 1972. reprint ed. 640.00 (*3-487-04196-0*) G Olms Pubs.
— Bibliotheca Indosinica: Dictionnaire Bibliographique, 5 vols. (FRE.). 3719p. 1998. reprint ed. 175.00 (*1-57898-075-5*) Martino Pubng.
— Bibliotheca Japonica. xii, 762p. 1992. reprint ed. 150.00 (*3-487-02193-5*) G Olms Pubs.
— Bibliotheca Japonica: Dictionnaire Bibliographique des Ouvrages Relatifs a l'Empire Japonais. (FRE.). 774p. 1997. reprint ed. 60.00 (*1-57898-036-4*) Martino Pubng.
— Bibliotheca Sinica, 5 vols. in 3. 1971. reprint ed. 785.00 (*0-318-71760-3*) G Olms Pubs.
— Bibliotheca Sinica: Dictionnaire Bibliographique, 3 vols. 2993p. 1997. reprint ed. 225.00 (*1-57898-038-0*) Martino Pubng.
— L' Expedition de Chine de 1857-1858: Histoire diplomatique. LC 72-38062. (China Classic & Contemporary Works in Reprint Ser.). reprint ed. 72.50 (*0-404-56922-6*) AMS Pr.
— L' Expedition de Chine de 1860: Histoire diplomatique. LC 76-38063. (China Classic & Contemporary Works in Reprint Ser.). reprint ed. 72.50 (*0-404-56923-4*) AMS Pr.
Cordier, Henri, jt. auth. see Yule, Henry.
Cordier, J., jt. auth. see Boutillier, Michel.
Cordier, J. M. & Porter, T. Shape Theory: Categorical Methods of Approximation. 1989. text 59.95 (*0-470-21345-0*) P-H.
Cordier, Jean, jt. ed. see Boutillier, Michel.
Cordier, Jean-Pierre. Velocities in Reflection Seismology. 1985. text 145.50 (*90-277-2024-X*) Kluwer Academic.
Cordier, Mary H. School Women of the Prairies & Plains: Personal Narratives from Iowa, Kansas, & Nebraska, 1860-1920s. 365p. 1997. pap. 17.95 (*0-8263-1774-X*) U of NM Pr.
Cordier, Mary H. & Perez-Stable, Maria A. Peoples of the American West: Historical Perspectives Through Children's Literature. LC 89-10284. 244p. 1989. 29.00 (*0-8108-2240-7*) Scarecrow.
— Understanding American History Through Children's Literature: Instructional Units, & Activities for Grades K-8. LC 94-2636. 328p. 1994. pap. 27.50 (*0-89774-795-X*) Oryx Pr.
Cordier, Sherwood S. The Defense of NATO's Northern Front & U. S. Military Policy. LC 88-33696. 90p. (Orig.). (C). 1989. pap. text 15.00 (*0-8191-7341-X*); lib. bdg. 31.00 (*0-8191-7340-1*) U Pr of Amer.
***Cordiero, Wayne.** Doing Church as a Team. 2000. 17.99 (*0-8307-2666-7*, Regal Bks) Gospel Lght.
Cordilia, Ann. The Making of an Inmate. 133p. 1983. 22.95 (*0-87073-722-8*); pap. 13.95 (*0-87073-723-6*) Schenkman Bks Inc.
Cordilos, Nicholas. Ask the Headhunter: Reinventing the Interview to Win the Job. LC 97-22987. 166p. 1997. pap. 14.95 (*0-452-27801-5*, Plume) Dutton Plume.
Cording, Edward J., ed. see Rock Mechanics Symposium Staff.
Cording, Robert. Heavy Grace. (Orig.). 1996. pap. 9.95 (*1-882295-09-9*) Alice James Bks.
— What Binds Us to This World. LC 91-4688. 71p. (Orig.). 1991. pap. 9.95 (*0-914278-57-6*) Copper Beech.
Cording, Robert, et al, eds. In My Life: Encounters with the Beatles. LC 98-17672. (Illus.). 352p. 1998. 25.00 (*0-88064-192-4*) Fromm Intl Pub.
***Cording, Robert, et al.** In My Life: Encounters with the Beatles. (Illus.). 304p. 2000. pap. 16.00 (*0-88064-248-3*) Fromm Intl Pub.
***Cording, Ruth James.** C. S. Lewis: A Celebration of His Early Life. LC 99-89615. (Illus.). 144p. 2000. pap. 14.99 (*0-8054-2200-5*) Broadman.
***Cordingley, Bill.** In Your Face: What Facial Features Reveal about the People You Know & Love. LC 00-132566. 160p. 2001. pap. 13.95 (*0-88282-201-2*, Pub. by New Horizon NJ) Natl Bk Netwk.
Cordingley, Ernest W. Principles & Practice of Naturopathy. 25p. 1996. reprint ed. spiral bd. 8.50 (*0-7873-0200-7*) Hlth Research.
Cordingley, Pat & Limb, Sue. Captain Oates Soldier & Explorer. large type ed. (Ulverscroft Large Print Ser.). (Illus.). 528p. 1997. 27.99 (*0-7089-3758-6*) Ulverscroft.
Cordingly, David. The Complete Book of Maritime Design: A Compendium of Naval Art & Painting. LC 98-2753. 192p. 1998. 19.99 (*0-517-16072-2*) Gramercy Bks.
— Painters of the Sea. (Illus.). 1980. pap. 20.00 (*0-85331-425-X*) Eastview.
— Ships & Seascapes: An Introduction to Maritime Prints, Drawings & Watercolours. (Illus.). 160p. 1997. 65.00 (*0-85667-484-2*, Pub. by P Wilson) Antique Collect.
— Under the Black Flag: The Romance & Reality of Life Among the Pirates. LC 97-15048. (Illus.). 320p. 1997. pap. 13.00 (*0-15-600549-2*) Harcourt.
***Cordingly, David.** Worldwide Illustrated History of Pirates. 256p. 1998. write for info. (*1-57215-264-8*) World Pubns.
Cordingly, David & Falconer, John. Pirates: Fact & Fiction. (Illus.). 128p. 1993. 15.98 (*0-89660-034-3*, Artabras) Abbeville Pr.
Cordingly, Norman. From a Cat's Whisker Beginning. (C). 1989. 39.00 (*0-86303-431-4*) St Mut.
Cordingly, Phillippa & Kogan, Maurice. In Support of Education: Governing the Reformed System. 120p. 1993. pap. 24.95 (*1-85302-536-4*) Taylor & Francis.
Cordish, Allan. Delta Zee Minimum Entropy Theory. rev. ed. (Illus.). ix, 122p. 1998. pap. 19.95 (*0-9661315-0-9*) FreeStar Pr.
***Cordish, Allan M.** Riemann's Hypothesis Defines the Natural Numbers As Solution & Other Papers. (Illus.). ii, 50p. 1999. pap. 12.00 (*0-9661315-2-5*) FreeStar Pr.
— The Strange Beauty of the Natural Numbers. (Illus.). 56p. (C). 2000. pap. 12.00 (*0-9661315-3-3*) FreeStar Pr.
Cordish, Janet L. Blessed Are They. large type ed. LC 97-90963. (Illus.). 320p. 1998. 22.95 (*0-9661315-1-7*) FreeStar Pr.
***Cordle, Daniel.** Postmodern Postures: Literature, Science & the Two Cultures Debate. LC 99-52631. 202p. 2000. 78.95 (*0-7546-0095-5*, Pub. by Ashgate Pub) Ashgate Pub Co.
Cordle, Thomas. Andre Gide Revisited. (Twayne's World Authors Ser.). 160p. 1992. 32.00 (*0-8057-8283-4*, Twyne) Mac Lib Ref.
Cordner, Gary W. & Hale, Donna C. What Works in Policing? Operations & Administration Examined. LC 91-70612. (ACJS - Anderson Monographs). 198p. (C). 1991. pap. 19.95 (*0-87084-015-0*) Anderson Pub Co.
Cordner, Gary W. & Kenney, Dennis J. Managing Police Organizations. LC 95-75512. 188p. (C). 1995. pap. 19.95 (*0-87084-142-4*) Anderson Pub Co.
Cordner, Gary W. & Sheehan, Robert. Police Administration. 4th ed. LC 98-51021. 1998. pap. 45.95 (*0-87084-794-5*) Anderson Pub Co.
Cordner, Gary W., et al. Police Operations: Analysis & Evaluation. LC 96-84653. 538p. (C). 1996. pap. 36.95 (*0-87084-118-1*) Anderson Pub Co.
Cordner, Gary W., jt. auth. see Hudzik, John.
Cordner, Gary W., jt. auth. see Sheehan, Robert.
Cordner, Gary W., jt. ed. see Gaines, Larry K.
Cordner, Gary W., jt. ed. see Kenny, Dennis J.
Cordner, John. "But Try the Spirits Whether They Be of God . . ." 39p. 1996. pap. 3.00 (*0-9617224-1-X*) Popham Pr.
— Dear Laddie. 306p. (Orig.). 1986. pap. 8.00 (*0-9617224-0-1*) Popham Pr.
Cordner, Michael, et al, eds. English Comedy. (Illus.). 337p. (C). 1994. text 74.95 (*0-521-41917-4*) Cambridge U Pr.
Cordner, Michael, ed. see Farquhar, George.
Cordner, Michael, ed. see Otway, Thomas, et al.
Cordner, Michael, ed. see Sheridan, Richard Brinsley.
Cordner, R., jt. auth. see Sheehan, Robert.
Cordner, Stephen M., jt. auth. see Plueckhahn, Vernon D.
Cordo, Paul & Harnad, Stevan R., eds. Movement Control. (Illus.). 288p. (C). 1994. pap. text 32.95 (*0-521-45607-X*) Cambridge U Pr.
— Movement Control. (Illus.). 288p. (C). 1994. text 85.00 (*0-521-45241-4*) Cambridge U Pr.
Cordo, Paul J., et al, eds. Motor Learning & Synaptic Plasticity in the Cerebellum. LC 97-1229. (Illus.). 206p. (C). 1997. text 80.00 (*0-521-59286-0*); pap. text 34.95 (*0-521-59705-6*) Cambridge U Pr.
Cordoba, D. A., et al, eds. The Border Region: Chihuahua, Mexico & the United States. (Guidebook Ser.: No. 20). (Illus.). 228p. 1969. 20.00 (*1-58546-050-8*) NMex Geol Soc.
Cordoba, Federico C. Diccionario Espanol-Arabe. 2nd ed.Tr. of Spanish-Arabic Dictionary. (ARA & SPA.). 862p. 1986. pap. 36.95 (*0-7859-5118-0*) Fr & Eur.
Cordoba, Federico Carlos Corriente, see De Robles, Sainz & Corriente Cordoba, Federico Carlos.
Cordoba, Guadalupe. La Morenita: The Story of Lupe Cordoba. 104p. 1998. pap. 10.00 (*0-8059-4452-4*) Dorrance.
Cordoba, Maria, tr. see Cole, Joanna.
Cordoba, Mariano. A Folksinger's Guide to Flamenco Guitar. (Illus.). 160p. 1971. pap. 19.95 (*0-8256-0064-2*, AM64014) Music Sales.
— Traditional Flamenco Guitar, Vol. 1. (ENG & SPA., Illus.). 219p. 1982. pap. text 30.00 (*0-9664134-0-7*) M Cordoba.
— Traditional Flamenco Guitar, Vol. 2. (ENG & SPA., Illus.). 143p. 1986. pap. text 30.00 (*0-9664134-1-5*) M Cordoba.
— Traditional Flamenco Guitar, Vol. 3. (ENG & SPA., Illus.). 149p. 1986. pap. text 30.00 (*0-9664134-2-3*) M Cordoba.
***Cordoba, Yasmine A.** Igloo. LC 00-38721. (Native American Homes Ser.). (Illus.). 2000. write for info. (*1-55916-277-5*) Rourke Bk Co.
Cordon Bleu Chefs Staff, jt. auth. see Wright, Jeni.
Cordon Bleu Cooking School Staff, Carole, ed. Le Cordon Bleu Home Collection Vol. 11: Italian. LC 98-85714. 64 p. 1999. 12.00 (*962-593-441-3*) Periplus.
— Le Cordon Bleu Home Collection Vol. 12: Cakes. LC 98-85715. 64 p. 1999. 12.00 (*962-593-442-1*) Periplus.
— Le Cordon Bleu Home Collection Vol. 13: Cookies. LC 98-85716. (Illus.). 64 p. 1999. 12.00 (*962-593-443-X*) Periplus.
— Le Cordon Bleu Home Collection Vol. 14: Finger Food. LC 98-85717. (Illus.). 64 p. 1999. 12.00 (*962-593-444-8*) Periplus.
— Le Cordon Bleu Home Collection Vol. 15: Muffins. LC 98-85718. (Illus.). 64 p. 1999. 12.00 (*962-593-445-6*) Periplus.
— Le Cordon Bleu Home Collection Vol. 16: Pasta. LC 98-85719. (Illus.). 64p. 1999. pap. 12.00 (*962-593-446-4*) Tuttle Pubng.
— Le Cordon Bleu Home Collection Vol. 17: Casseroles. LC 98-85722. (Illus.). 64 p. 1999. 12.00 (*962-593-447-2*) Periplus.
— Le Cordon Bleu Home Collection Vol. 19: Brunch. (Illus.). 1999. 12.00 (*962-593-449-9*) Tuttle Pubng.
— Le Cordon Bleu Home Collection Vol. 20: Summer. LC 98-85726. (Illus.). 64 p. 1999. 12.00 (*962-593-450-2*) Periplus.
Cordon, Faustino. Dictionary of Biology: Diccionario de Biologia. (ENG & SPA.). 389p. 1985. 49.95 (*0-8288-0784-1*, S16351) Fr & Eur.
— An Introduction to the Biological Basis of Feeding: Essential Biological Ideas Necessary to a Study of Living Beings from the Evolutionary Standpoint. LC 79-40933. (Illus.). 250p. 1980. pap. 41.00 (*0-08-025484-5*, Pergamon Pr) Elsevier.

C

Cordon, Mary J. Clinical Calculations for Nurses. 3rd ed. (Illus.). 285p. 1994. teacher ed. write for info. (*0-8385-1371-9*, A1371-2) Appleton & Lange.
— Clinical Calculations for Nurses with Basic Mathematics Review. 3rd ed. LC 93-23473. (Illus.). 300p. (C). 1994. pap. text 29.95 (*0-8385-1367-0*, A1367-0) Appleton & Lange.
Cordon, Mary J., jt. auth. see Yamato, Yoshiko.
***Cordon, O Herrera F.** Genetic Fuzzy Systems: Evolutionary Tuning & Learning of Fuzzy Knowledge Bases. 2000. pap. text 41.00 (*981-02-4017-1*) WSC Inst MA Studies.
Cordon, Patrick J., jt. auth. see Torok, Robert M.
Cordon, William A. Freezing & Thawing of Concrete: Mechanisms & Control. LC 66-14390. (American Concrete Institute Monographs: No. 3). 111p. reprint ed. pap. 34.50 (*0-608-30869-2*, 201229900082) Bks Demand.
— Properties, Evaluation & Control of Engineering Materials. 550p. (C). 1979. 108.44 (*0-07-013123-6*) McGraw.
Cordone, Richard P., jt. auth. see Johnson, Elvin R.
Cordones-Cook, Junamaria. Poetica de Transgresion en la Novelistica de Luisa Valenuela. LC 91-27570. (American University Studies: Romance Languages & Literature: Ser. II, Vol. 173). (SPA.). 118p. (C). 1992. text 35.95 (*0-8204-1584-7*) P Lang Pubng.
Cordoni, Barbara. Living with a Learning Disability. rev. ed. 1991. pap. 17.95 (*0-8093-1668-4*) S Ill U Pr.
Cordoni, Tatiana I., ed. see Baillie, Virginia & Trygstad, Louise.
Cordonnier, J., jt. auth. see Berne, Francois.
Cordonnier, Jean, jt. auth. see Berne, Francois.
Cordor, Henry & Brown, Robert T. Facing the Realities of the Liberian Nation. 1980. 12.00 (*0-686-34401-4*) Arden Assocs.
Cordor, S. Henry. Africa, from People to People: Six Short Stories from Contemporary Africa. 71p. 1979. 8.50 (*0-686-33168-0*) Arden Assocs.
Cordova, Amy. Abuelita's Heart. LC 96-12082. (ENG & SPA., Illus.). 32p. (J). (ps-3). 1997. per. 16.00 (*0-689-80181-5*) S&S Bks Yung.
Cordova, Chris De, see De Cordova, Chris.
Cordova, Dodie. Forms for Easy Home Management: Ready-Made Forms, Charts & Checklists...Complete with Easy Instructions & Suggestions. 80p. 1988. ring bd. 19.95 (*0-929550-05-6*) Swanova Pubns.
Cordova, Dorothy C. L., ed. see Fugita, Stephen.
Cordova, Efren. Clase Trabajadora y Movimiento Sindical en Cuba Vol. 2: 1959-1996. LC 94-61930. (Coleccion Cuba y sus Jueces). (SPA.). 462p. (Orig.). 1996. pap. 29.95 (*0-89729-766-0*) Ediciones.
— Clase Trabajadora y Movimiento Sindical en Cuba I, 1819-1959. (SPA.). 1995. pap. 29.95 (*0-89729-765-2*) Ediciones.
— El Trabajador Cubano en el Estado de Obreros y Campesinos. LC 89-81223. (Coleccion Cuba y sus Jueces). (SPA.). 219p. (Orig.). 1990. pap. 16.00 (*0-89729-553-6*) Ediciones.
Cordova Frunz, Jose L. La Quimica y la Cocina. (Ciencia para Todos Ser.). (SPA.). pap. 6.99 (*968-16-3568-X*, Pub. by Fondo) Continental Bk.
Cordova, Gonzalo F. Resident Commisioner Santiago Iglesias & His Times. 1993. 28.50 (*0-8477-0899-3*) U of PR Pr.
Cordova, Gonzalo F. & Concepcion, Sara I. Santiago Iglesias: Creador del Movimiento Obrero de Puerto Rico. LC 78-14404. (SPA., Illus.). 231p. 1980. pap. 6.00 (*0-8477-0857-8*) U of PR Pr.
Cordova-Iturregui, Felix. Militancia Contra la Soledad. LC 87-83311. (Flor del Agua Ser.). (SPA.). 77p. 1987. 8.50 (*0-940238-95-0*) Ediciones Huracan.
— Para Llenar de Dias el Dia. LC 85-80201. (Flor del Agua Ser.). (SPA.). 56p. 1985. pap. 6.95 (*0-940238-80-2*) Ediciones Huracan.
— El Rabo de Lagartija de Aquel Famoso Senor Rector & Otros Cuentos de Orilla. LC 85-72325. (SPA.). 109p. 1986. pap. 6.95 (*0-940238-84-5*) Ediciones Huracan.
Cordova, Jacqueline, jt. auth. see Velez Roman, Lydia.
Cordova, Jeanne, et al. Kicking the Habit: A Lesbian Nun Story. 264p. (Orig.). 1990. pap. 9.95 (*0-9625080-0-4*) Multiple Dimensions.
Cordova, Jorge C. La Familia y el Nuevo Milenio.Tr. of Family & the New Millennium. (SPA.). 224p. 1994. 9.99 (*0-88113-276-4*, B090-2764) Caribe Betania.
Cordova, Lieban. Luis Munoz Marin y Sus Campanas Politicas: Memorias de Su Secretario-Taquigrafo Personal. LC 83-26083. (SPA., Illus.). 175p. (Orig.). 1985. pap. 7.00 (*0-8477-2472-7*) U of PR Pr.
Cordova, Loretta Phelps De, see Phelps De Cordova, Loretta.
***Cordova, Maria.** The Witness to the Coming of Jesus Christ. Lacy, Sarah C., ed. (Illus.). 170p. 1999. 19.95 (*0-9676763-0-4*) Fathers House Pubng.
***Cordova, Regina & Carrasco, Emma.** Celebracion: Recipes & Traditions Celebrating Latino Family Life. 214p. 1999. reprint ed. pap. text 19.00 (*0-7881-6707-3*) DIANE Pub.
Cordova-Rios, Manuel, jt. auth. see Lamb, F. Bruce.
Cordova, Ruben C., jt. auth. see Bassham, Ben.
Cordova, Sarah D. Paris Dances: Textual Choreographies in the Nineteenth Century French Novel. (Illus.). 341p. 1998. 74.95 (*1-57309-335-1*) Intl Scholars.
Cordova, Senor. A Man's Guide to Mexico & Central America, 1996-97. annuals Torres, Joe, 3rd, ed. LC 95-70191. (Illus.). 204p. (Orig.). 1996. pap. 18.95 (*0-9639054-2-2*) Centurion CA.
— A Man's Guide to Mexico & Central America, 1998-99. (Illus.). 225p. (Orig.). 1997. pap. text 18.95 (*0-9639054-3-0*) Centurion CA.
— A Man's Guide to Mexico, 1995-96. Torres, Joe, 3rd, ed. (Illus.). 192p. 1995. pap. 16.95 (*0-9639054-1-4*) Centurion CA.
— A Man's Guide to the Caribbean, 1998-99. (Illus.). 225p. (Orig.). 1997. pap. text 18.95 (*0-9639054-4-9*) Centurion CA.
Cordova, Teresa, et al, eds. Chicana Voices: Intersections of Class, Race, & Gender. LC 86-70088. 236p. 1993. reprint ed. pap. 15.95 (*0-8263-1404-X*) U of NM Pr.
Cordovero, R. Moshe. Shiur Koma. (HEB.). 1983. 10.00 (*0-943688-38-8*) Res Ctr Kabbalah.
Cordoves, Barbara, pseud & Cordoves, Gladys M. The Legend of Zias. (Zias' Adventures Ser.). (Illus.). 44p. (J). (gr. k). pap. 7.99 (*0-9637252-0-3*) B & G Cordoves.
Cordoves, Gladys M., jt. auth. see Cordoves, Barbara, pseud.
Cordovez, Carlos, jt. ed. see Biebesheimer, Christina.
Cordovez, Diego & Harrison, Selig S. Out of Afghanistan: The Inside Story of the Soviet Withdrawal. (Illus.). 450p. Date not set. 35.00 (*0-614-19494-6*) OUP.
Cordoza, J. Poland Spring to Summer. (Images of America Ser.). Date not set. pap. 16.99 (*0-7524-0442-3*) Arcadia Publng.
Cordrey, Cindy. Hidden Treasures: Music & Memory Activities for People with Alzheimer's. 99p. (Orig.). 1994. pap. text 16.95 (*1-879633-18-3*) Eldersong.
Cordry, Donald B. Mexican Indian Costumes. LC 68-20363. (Texas Pan American Ser.). (Illus.). 425p. reprint ed. pap. 131.80 (*0-7837-0092-X*, 204036700016) Bks Demand.
Cordry, Donald B. & Cordry, Dorothy M. Costumes & Textiles of the Aztec Indians of the Cuetzalan Region, Puebla, Mexico. LC 40-11239. 60p. 1964. reprint ed. pap. 5.00 (*0-916561-15-1*) Southwest Mus.
— Costumes & Weaving of the Zoque Indians of Chiapas, Mexico. LC 42-6243. 130p. 1941. pap. 5.00 (*0-916561-17-8*) Southwest Mus.
Cordry, Dorothy M., jt. auth. see Cordry, Donald B.
Cordry, Harold V. Dictionary of American-English Pronunciation. LC 96-31976. 324p. 1997. pap. 24.95 (*1-57292-054-8*) Austin & Winfield.
— A Dictionary of American-English Pronunciation. LC 96-31976. 288p. 1997. 50.00 (*1-57292-055-6*) Austin & Winfield.
— Everything Crossword & Puzzle Book. (Everything Ser.). (Illus.). 352p. 1998. pap. text 12.95 (*1-55850-764-7*) Adams Media.
— The Multicultural Dictionary of Proverbs: Over 20,000 Adages from More Than 120 Languages, Nationalities & Ethnic Groups. LC 96-33264. 416p. 1997. lib. bdg. 47.50 (*0-7864-0251-2*) McFarland & Co.
***Cordry, Harold V.** Tobacco: A Reference Handbook. 2000. lib. bdg. 45.00 (*0-87436-967-3*) ABC-CLIO.
Cords, Marina. Mixed-Species Association of Cercopithecus Monkeys in the Kakamega Forest, Kenya. LC 86-30822. (University of California Publications in Zoology: Vol. 117). 123p. 1987. reprint ed. pap. 38.20 (*0-608-00714-5*, 206148800009) Bks Demand.
Cords, Nicholas, jt. ed. see Gerster, Patrick.
***Cordsen, Andreas, et al.** Planning Land 3-D Seismic Surveys. LC 00-26159. (Geophysical Developments Ser.). 2000. write for info. (*1-56080-089-5*) Soc Expl Geophys.
Cordua, Carla & Torretti, Roberto. Variedad en la Razon. 248p. 1992. 18.00 (*0-8477-2835-8*) U of PR Pr.
Corduan, Winfred. Mysticism: An Evangelical Option? 160p. 1991. pap. 10.99 (*0-310-52901-8*) Zondervan.
Corduan, Winfried. I & II Chronicles. LC 97-51488. (Shepherd's Notes Ser.). 1998. pap. 5.95 (*0-8054-9064-7*) Broadman.
— Neighboring Faiths: A Christian Introduction to World Religions. LC 97-36552. (Illus.). 320p. 1998. 24.99 (*0-8308-1524-4*, 1524) InterVarsity.
Corduan, Winfried. No Doubt about It: The Case for Christianity. LC 97-8569. 1997. 19.99 (*0-8054-1647-1*) Broadman.
Corduneanu, C. Qualitative Problems for Differential Equations & Control Theory. 320p. 1995. text 85.00 (*981-02-2257-2*) World Scientific Pub.
***Corduneanu, C. & Sandberg, I., eds.** Volterra Equations & Applications. (Illus.). 512p. 1999. text 120.00 (*90-5699-171-X*) Gordon & Breach.
Corduneanu, Constantin. Principles of Differential & Integral Equations. 2nd ed. LC 77-2962. 1977. text 19.95 (*0-8284-0295-7*) Chelsea Pub.
Corduneau, Constantin. Almost Periodic Functions. 2nd rev. ed. Tomer, Eugene, tr. LC 87-72946. (Illus.). 261p. (C). 1988. 19.95 (*0-8284-0331-7*, 331) Chelsea Pub.
Cordwell, Justine, ed. The Visual Arts: Plastic & Graphic. (World Anthropology Ser.). (Illus.). xii, 818p. 1979. text 107.70 (*90-279-7820-4*) Mouton.
Cordy-Collins, Alana, jt. ed. see Moseley, Michael E.
Cordy, J. T., ed. see Vacuum Metallurgy Conference on the Melting & Proc.
Cordy, Meta. Not for Johnny Only: Recollections for My American Son. LC 97-6886. Orig. Title: Nich Nur Fur Johnny. 272p. (Orig.). 1997. pap. 12.95 (*1-56474-223-7*) Fithian Pr.
Cordy, Michael. Crime Zero: A Novel. LC 98-56284. 432p. 1999. 25.00 (*0-688-15509-X*, Wm Morrow) Morrow Avon.
— Miracle Strain. 400p. 1998. mass mkt. 6.99 (*0-380-73042-1*, Avon Bks) Morrow Avon.
Cordy, Michael. The Miracle Strain: Larson,&Darrell, Set. abr. ed. 1997. audio. write for info. (*0-694-51859-X*, 395357, Pub. by HarperAudio) Lndmrk Audiobks.
Cordy, Ross. The Lelu Stone Ruins (Kosrae, Micronesia), 1978-81: Historical & Archaeological Research. (Asian & Pacific Archaeology Ser.: No. 10). 472p. (C). 1993. pap. text 36.00 (*0-8248-1134-8*) U HI SSRI.
***Core, Deborah.** Seminary Student Writes. 2000. pap. 15.99 (*0-8272-3447-3*) Chalice Pr.
***Core, Don.** Senior Moments: Growing Old Is Not for Sissies. LC 99-90399. (Illus.). 128p. 2000. pap. 10.95 (*1-879752-03-4*) SOFITS.

Core, Earl L. Chronicles of Core. 3rd ed. (Illus.). 320p. 1975. 10.00 (*0-87012-227-4*) McClain.
The third edition of a book published by mimeograph in 1937 & in 1960. This volume of 310 pages provides a detailed history of the community of Core, in Monongalia County, West Virginia, with genealogical records of many of its pioneer families. *Publisher Paid Annotation.*

–The Monongalia Story: Prelude, Vol. 1. 484p. 1974. 35.00 (*0-87012-169-3*) McClain.
Probably the most voluminous of all the West Virginia county histories is THE MONONGALIA STORY. The first volume (subtitled Prelude) contains a general description of the county, including its geology, flora, fauna, & an account of the aborigines, followed by a record of more than 1,000 early settlers. Volume II (The Pioneers) presents the history from the establishment of the county, in 1776, up to 1826.
Probably the most voluminous of all the West Virginia country histories is THE MONONGALIA STORY. The first volume (subtitled Prelude) contains a general description of the county, including its geology, flora, fauna & an account of the aborigines, followed by a record of more than 1,000 early settlers. Volume II (The Pioneers) presents the history from the establishment of the county in 1776, up to 1826. VOLUMES III, IV & V are currently out-of-print. Will be available in 2001. *Publisher Paid Annotation.*

— The Monongalia Story Vol. II: The Pioneers. 595p. 1977. 35.00 (*0-87012-245-2*) McClain.
— Spring Wild Flowers of West Virginia. LC 81-50933. 104p. 1981. pap. 5.00 (*0-937058-02-5*) West Va U Pr.
Core, Earl L. & Ammons, Nelle P. Woody Plants in Winter. (Illus.). (Orig.). (YA). (gr. 9 up). 1958. pap. text 12.50 (*0-910286-02-7*) Boxwood.
Core, Earl L., jt. auth. see Strausbaugh, P. D.
Core, Francoise, ed. The Future of Female-Dominated Occupations. LC 99-204590. 248p. 1998. pap. 38.00 (*92-64-16149-X*, 8198101P) OECD.
Core, George, ed. The Critics Who Made Us: Essays from Sewanee Review. LC 93-4857. 328p. 1993. text 39.95 (*0-8262-0916-5*) U of Mo Pr.
— Revelation & Other Fiction from the Sewane Review: A Centennial Anthology. LC 92-81354. 304p. 1992. 23.95 (*1-56469-012-1*) Harmony Hse Pub.
— Revelations & Other Fiction from the Sewanee Review: A Centennial Anthology. 304p. 1992. 24.95 (*1-56469-020-2*) Harmony Hse Pub.
Core, George & Sullivan, Walter. Writing from the Inside. (C). 1983. pap. text, teacher ed. write for info. (*0-393-95337-8*) Norton.
Core, George, ed. see Ransom, John Crowe.
Core, Graham, ed. see Lease, John R.
Core Knowledge Foundation Staff & Holdren, John. Books to Build On: A Grade-by-Grade Resource Guide for Parents & Teachers. LC 96-17200. 384p. 1996. pap. 12.95 (*0-385-31640-2*, Delta Trade) Dell.
Core, Lucy & Lyman, Clara, eds. Cathedral Cooking School Cookbook. LC 75-312985. (Illus.). 208p. (Orig.). 1974. spiral bd. 12.95 (*0-88289-033-6*) Pelican.
Core, Philip. Camp: The Lie that Tells the Truth. 256p. 1994. per. 14.95 (*0-85965-044-8*, Pub. by Plexus) Publishers Group.
Core-Plus Mathematics Project Staff, jt. auth. see Coxford, Arthur F.
Corea, Gamani. Need for Change: Towards the New International Economic Order. LC 80-40800. 350p. 1981. pap. 6.00 (*0-08-028120-6*, Pub. by Pergamon Repr) Franklin.
***Coreil, Jeannine, et al.** Social & Behavioral Foundations of Public Health. LC 00-9519. 2000. write for info. (*0-7619-1744-6*) Sage Pub.
Corel Corporation Staff. CorelDRAW Art & Artistry. 1998. pap. text 49.99 incl. cd-rom (*0-07-211879-2*) Osborne-McGraw.
Corelis, Jon, tr. Roman Erotic Elegy: Selections from Tibullus, Propertius, Ovid & Sulpicia. 166p. pap. write for info. (*3-7052-0424-6*, Pub. by Poetry Salzburg) Intl Spec Bk.
Corell, Cynthia, ed. see Feygin, Bella.
Corell, Cynthia, ed. see Tuzhilin, Avgustin.
Corell, R. W. & Anderson, P. A., eds. Global Environmental Change. (NATO ASI Series I: Global Environmental Change: Vol. 1). (Illus.). 264p. 1991. 119.00 (*0-387-53128-9*) Spr-Verlag.
Corelli, Arcangelo. Badinerie. 1971. 2.00 (*0-685-51176-6*, CM1010) Consort Music.
— Complete Concerti Grossi in Full Score. 240p. 1988. pap. 12.95 (*0-486-25606-5*) Dover.
— Complete Violin Sonatas & Trio Sonatas. Joachim, Joseph & Chrysander, Friedrich, eds. 352p. 1992. 16.95 (*0-486-27241-9*) Dover.
Corelli, Marie. Angel's Wickedness, a True Story. 54p. 1978. spiral bd. 9.00 (*0-7873-0203-1*) Hlth Research.
— Ardath: The Story of a Dead Self (1925) 610p. 1996. reprint ed. pap. 29.95 (*1-56459-782-2*) Kessinger Pub.
— Ardath, the Story of a Dead Self. 602p. 1993. pap. 30.00 (*0-7873-0208-2*) Hlth Research.
— Barabbas: A Dream of the World's Tragedy (1907) 300p. 1998. reprint ed. pap. 19.00 (*0-7661-0142-8*) Kessinger Pub.
— Boy: A Sketch (1900) 350p. 1999. reprint ed. pap. 24.95 (*0-7661-0733-7*) Kessinger Pub.
— Cameos. LC 75-106278. (Short Story Index Reprint Ser.). 1977. 20.95 (*0-8369-3316-8*) Ayer.
— Cameos. 291p. 1971. reprint ed. spiral bd. 17.50 (*0-7873-0216-3*) Hlth Research.
— Cameos (1896) 291p. 1996. reprint ed. pap. 17.00 (*1-56459-759-8*) Kessinger Pub.
— A Christmas Greeting (1902) 340p. 1998. reprint ed. pap. 24.95 (*0-7661-0254-8*) Kessinger Pub.
— The Devil's Motor. 40p. 1996. spiral bd. 10.00 (*0-7873-0221-X*) Hlth Research.
— The Devil's Motor: A Fantasy. 50p. 1996. reprint ed. pap. 9.95 (*1-56459-969-8*) Kessinger Pub.
— Free Opinions Freely Expressed on Certain Phases of Modern Social Life & Conduct. LC 76-37685. reprint ed. 37.50 (*0-404-56739-8*) AMS Pr.
— Free Opinions, Freely Expressed on Certain Phases of Modern Social Life & Conduct. 353p. 1972. reprint ed. spiral bd. 18.00 (*0-7873-0201-5*) Hlth Research.
— Free Opinions Freely Expressed on Certain Phases of Modern Social Life & Conduct (1905) 360p. 1996. reprint ed. pap. 17.95 (*1-56459-740-7*) Kessinger Pub.
— God's Good Man. 524p. 1998. reprint ed. pap. 36.00 (*0-7661-0170-3*) Kessinger Pub.
— Holy Orders: The Tragedy of a Quiet Life. 494p. 1998. reprint ed. pap. 33.00 (*0-7661-0433-8*) Kessinger Pub.
— Jane: A Social Incident. (Illus.). 148p. 1996. reprint ed. pap. 9.95 (*1-56459-945-0*) Kessinger Pub.
— Jane, a Social Incident. 148p. 1969. reprint ed. spiral bd. 10.00 (*0-7873-0213-9*) Hlth Research.
— Life Everlasting. 1966. pap. 13.00 (*0-87505-092-1*) Borden.
— The Life Everlasting: A Novel of the Eternal Life & How to Attain It, a Love Story. (Longevity Ser.). 1991. lib. bdg. 75.00 (*0-8490-4135-X*) Gordon Pr.
— The Life Everlasting: A Reality of Romance (1911) 439p. 1996. reprint ed. pap. 29.95 (*1-56459-728-8*) Kessinger Pub.
— The Life Everlasting, a Reality of Romance. 439p. 1973. reprint ed. spiral bd. 17.50 (*0-7873-0205-8*) Hlth Research.
— Love, - & the Philosopher: A Study in Sentiment (1923) 287p. 1996. reprint ed. pap. 17.95 (*1-56459-727-X*) Kessinger Pub.
— Love & the Philosopher, a Study in Sentiment. 287p. 1972. reprint ed. spiral bd. 18.50 (*0-7873-0204-X*) Hlth Research.
— The Love of Long Age & Other Stories. 271p. 1978. reprint ed. 17.50 (*0-7873-0222-8*) Hlth Research.
— The Master Christian (1900) 600p. 1998. reprint ed. pap. 36.00 (*0-7661-0161-4*) Kessinger Pub.
— The Mighty Atom. 310p. 1972. reprint ed. spiral bd. 19.00 (*0-7873-0212-0*) Hlth Research.
— The Mighty Atom, 1906. 310p. 1996. reprint ed. pap. 17.95 (*1-56459-755-5*) Kessinger Pub.
— The Murder of Delicia. 274p. 1971. reprint ed. spiral bd. 16.50 (*0-7873-0217-1*) Hlth Research.
— The Murder of Delicia, 1896. 274p. 1996. reprint ed. pap. 15.95 (*1-56459-949-3*) Kessinger Pub.
— Open Confession to a Man from a Woman. 190p. 1971. reprint ed. spiral bd. 14.00 (*0-7873-0202-3*) Hlth Research.
— Open Confession to a Man from a Woman. 190p. 1996. reprint ed. pap. 12.95 (*1-56459-737-7*) Kessinger Pub.
— A Romance of Two Worlds. 1986. 15.95 (*0-87505-333-5*) Borden.
— A Romance of Two Worlds. 370p. 1971. reprint ed. pap. 21.50 (*0-7873-0207-4*) Hlth Research.
— A Romance of Two Worlds. 366p. 1996. reprint ed. pap. 19.95 (*1-56459-763-6*) Kessinger Pub.
— A Romance of Two Worlds. 3rd ed. LC 85-81601. 320p. 1986. reprint ed. pap. 12.95 (*0-8334-0018-5*, Spir Lit Lib) Garber Comm.
— The Secret Power. 342p. 1971. reprint ed. spiral bd. 15.50 (*0-7873-0218-X*) Hlth Research.
— The Secret Power (1921) 342p. 1996. reprint ed. pap. 15.00 (*1-56459-739-3*) Kessinger Pub.
— The Silence of the Maharajah. 74p. 1972. reprint ed. spiral bd. 8.00 (*0-7873-0206-6*) Hlth Research.
— The Silence of the Maharajah (1895) 74p. 1996. reprint ed. pap. 7.95 (*1-56459-916-7*) Kessinger Pub.
— The Song of Miriam & Other Stories. 234p. 1971. reprint ed. spiral bd. 16.50 (*0-7873-0215-5*) Hlth Research.
— The Song of Miriam & Other Stories. 234p. 1996. reprint ed. pap. 16.00 (*1-56459-760-1*) Kessinger Pub.
— The Song of Miriam & Other Stories, Vol. 1. LC 71-37263. (Short Story Index Reprint Ser.). 1977. reprint ed. 18.95 (*0-8369-4074-1*) Ayer.
— The Sorrows of Satan. (Oxford Popular Fiction Ser.). 412p. 1996. pap. 10.95 (*0-19-283220-4*) OUP.
— The Sorrows of Satan. Keating, Peter, ed. (Oxford World's Classics Ser.). 426p. 1999. pap. 10.95 (*0-19-283324-3*) OUP.
— The Sorrows of Satan (1896) 450p. 1998. reprint ed. pap. 27.00 (*0-7661-0146-0*) Kessinger Pub.
— The Soul of Lilith. 431p. 1972. reprint ed. pap. 24.00 (*0-7873-0211-2*) Hlth Research.
— The Soul of Lilith. 446p. 1996. reprint ed. pap. 23.50 (*1-56459-681-8*) Kessinger Pub.
— The Strange Visitation. 188p. 1970. reprint ed. spiral bd. 16.50 (*0-7873-0214-7*) Hlth Research.

— The Strange Visitation. 190p. 1996. reprint ed. pap. 15.95 (*1-56459-783-0*) Kessinger Pub.
— Swagger Religionists: The Great Unrest. 10p. 1996. reprint ed. spiral bd. 8.00 (*0-7873-0220-1*) Hlth Research.
— Temporal Power: A Study in Supremacy (1902) 560p. 1998. reprint ed. pap. 36.00 (*0-7661-0193-2*) Kessinger Pub.
— Vendetta! The Story of One Forgotten. 405p. 1972. reprint ed. pap. 21.50 (*0-7873-0209-0*) Hlth Research.
— Vendetta: or The Story of One Forgotten (1896) 410p. 1996. reprint ed. pap. 19.95 (*1-56459-938-8*) Kessinger Pub.
— The Young Diana: An Experiment of the Future (1918) 381p. 1996. reprint ed. pap. 19.95 (*1-56459-917-5*) Kessinger Pub.
— The Young Diana, an Experiment of the Future: An Experiment of the Future. 381p. 1972. reprint ed. spiral bd. 22.00 (*0-7873-0210-4*) Hlth Research.
— Ziska. 88p. 1985. reprint ed. spiral bd. 16.50 (*0-7873-0219-8*) Hlth Research.
— Ziska. 316p. 1998. reprint ed. pap. 15.95 (*0-7661-0212-2*) Kessinger Pub.
Corelli, Toni & Chandik, Zoe. The Rare & Endangered Plants of San Mateo & Santa Clara County. (Illus.). 150p. 1996. pap. 25.00 (*0-9646994-0-0*) T Corelli.
Coremans, G. Deep Inelastic Scattering & QCD. 1998. 130.00 (*981-02-3557-7*) World Scientific Pub.
Coren. Sensation & Perception. 4th ed. (C). 1994. text, teacher ed. 35.00 (*0-15-500773-4*) Harcourt Coll Pubs.
— Sensation & Perceptions. 2nd ed. LC 98-72167. (C). 1998. text 82.50 (*0-15-508050-4*, Pub. by Harcourt Coll Pubs) Harcourt.
— Understanding Sensation & Perception. (C). 1996. write for info. (*0-15-501643-1*) Harcourt Coll Pubs.
***Coren, A.** Cricklewood Dome. 168p. 1999. text 25.95 (*1-86105-223-5*) Robson.
Coren, Alan. Animal Passions: Featuring the Finer Feelings of the Famous for Their Furred, Finned & Feathered Friends. LC 98-148827. (Illus.). 186p. 1997. pap. 11.95 (*0-86051-984-8*, Robson-Parkwest) Parkwest Pubns.
— A Bit on the Side. 158p. 1996. 21.95 (*0-86051-990-2*, Robson-Parkwest) Parkwest Pubns.
— A Bit on the Side. LC 96-71893. 158p. 1999. pap. 10.95 (*1-86105-127-1*, Pub. by Robson Bks) Parkwest Pubns.
— Toujours Cricklewood? (Illus.). 1995. pap. 10.95 (*0-86051-941-4*, Robson-Parkwest) Parkwest Pubns.
Coren, Alan, ed. Animal Passions: Featuring the Finer Feeling of the Famous for Their Furred, Finned & Feathered Friends. large type ed. 240p. 1997. 24.95 (*1-85695-094-8*, Pub. by ISIS Lrg Prnt) Transaction Pubs.
— Animal Passions: Featuring the Finer Feelings of the Famous for Their Furred, Finned, & Feathered Friends. LC 95-73118. (Illus.). 186p. 1996. 21.95 (*0-86051-918-X*, Robson-Parkwest) Parkwest Pubns.
Coren, Michael. Gilbert: The Man Who Was G.K. Chesterton. LC 89-149919. 270p. 1989. write for info. (*0-224-02507-4*) Jonathan Cape.
Coren, Richard L. The Evolutionary Trajectory: The Growth of Information in the History & Future of Earth. (World Futures General Evolution Studies). 224p. 1998. text 36.00 (*90-5699-601-0*) Gordon & Breach.
Coren, S., jt. auth. see Porac, C.
***Coren, Stanley.** How to Speak Dog: Mastering the Art of Dog-Human Communication. LC 00-23768. (Illus.). 272p. 2000. 23.50 (*0-684-86534-3*) Free Pr.
Coren, Stanley. The Intelligence of Dogs: Canine Consciousness & Capabilities. LC 94-22159. 288p. 1995. pap. 14.95 (*0-553-37452-4*) Bantam.
— The Intelligence of Dogs: Canine Consciousness & Capabilities. 292p. 1994. 22.95 (*0-02-906683-2*) Free Pr.
— The Left-Hander Syndrome: The Causes & Consequences of Left-Handedness. (Illus.). 375p. 1991. 27.95 (*0-02-906682-4*) Free Pr.
— The Left-Hander Syndrome: The Causes & Consequences of Left-Handedness. LC 92-50646. 1993. pap. 14.00 (*0-679-74468-1*) Vin Bks.
— Sleep Thieves. 1997. pap. 12.00 (*0-684-83184-8*) Free Pr.
***Coren, Stanley.** Sleep Thieves: An Eye-Opening Exploration into the Science & Mysteries of Sleep. 304p. 1999. reprint ed. text 24.00 (*0-7881-6475-9*) DIANE Pub.
Coren, Stanley. What Do Dogs Know? LC 97-31661. 160p. 1997. 14.95 (*0-684-84860-0*) Free Pr.
— What Do Dogs Know? 160p. 1997. 14.95 (*0-87605-613-3*) Howell Bks.
— Why We Love the Dogs We Do. large type ed. LC 98-26519. 1998. 26.95 (*0-7862-1551-8*) Thorndike Pr.
Coren, Stanley, ed. Left-Handedness: Behavioral Implications & Anomalies. (Advances in Psychology Ser.: No. 67). xviii,574p. 1990. 201.50 (*0-444-88438-6*, North Holland) Elsevier.
Coren, Stanley, et al. Sensation & Perception. 4th ed. (Illus.). (C). 1994. text 82.50 (*0-15-500103-5*) Harcourt Coll Pubs.
Corenthal, Michael G. Baseball on Record: A Recorded History of Americas National Pasttime from the Cylinder to the Compact Disc. (Illus.). 226p. 1998. pap. 20.00 (*0-9617673-6-7*, 5000) Yester Memories.
— Cohen on the Telephone: A History of Jewish Recorded Music, 1892-1942. (Illus.). 120p. 1984. 12.00 (*0-9617673-0-8*) Yester Memories.
— The Czarnina Kid & Other Weird Tales: A Collection of Short Stories to Please, Tease & Appease. (Illus.). 120p. 1996. 12.50 (*0-9617673-5-9*) Yester Memories.
— The Iconography of Recorded Sound: 100 Years of Commercial Entertainment & Collecting Opportunity. (Illus.). 250p. 1986. 20.00 (*0-9617673-1-6*) Yester Memories.
— The Iconography of Recorded Sound 1886-1986: One Hundred Years of Commercial Entertainment & Collecting Opportunity. 252p. (Orig.). 1986. pap. 20.00 (*0-318-21565-9*) Yester Memories.
— Owed to Milwaukee: Mr. Mike's Personal Poems for the Masses, the Misses & the Mouses. (Illus.). 56p. 1992. 20.00 (*0-9617673-4-0*) Yester Memories.
Corenthal, Michael G., ed. The Illustrated History of Wisconsin Music, 1840-1990: 150 Years of Melodies & Memories. (Illus.). 460p. 1990. 25.00 (*0-9617673-2-2*) Yester Memories.
Corenthal, Michael G., ed. see Epley, Anna P.
Corentin, Philipe. Papa! LC 96-27138. (Illus.). 32p. (J). (ps-1). 1997. 13.95 (*0-8118-1640-0*) Chronicle Bks.
Cores, Lucy. Fatal Passion. 212p. 1989. 18.95 (*0-8027-1084-0*) Walker & Co.
Coresti, Gerald R. SuccessMaster Real Estate Math Tutorial Software. 1996. pap. 42.95 incl. disk (*0-7931-1523-X*) Dearborn.
Coret, Andre. L' A-Prehension du Reel -- La Physique en Questions. 284p. 1997. pap. text 37.00 (*90-5709-004-X*, Harwood Acad Pubs) Gordon & Breach.
Coret, Harriette. In & Out the Windows: Reading Level 3. (Sundown Fiction Collection). 64p. 1993. 3.95 (*0-88336-201-5*); audio 17.95 (*0-88336-251-1*) New Readers.
Corey. Becoming a Helper. 4th ed. (Counseling Ser.). 2002. pap. text 30.25 (*0-534-35614-1*) Brooks-Cole.
— Becoming a Helper, Umissouri-Columbia. (Adaptable Courseware Ser.). 1997. 23.50 (*0-534-49927-9*) Brooks-Cole.
— Case Approach to Counseling & Psychotherapy. (Counseling Ser.). 1982. pap. 13.25 (*0-8185-0464-1*) Brooks-Cole.
— Going to Market. 394p. 1989. 39.95 (*0-07-103225-8*) McGraw.
— Groups-Process & Practice. (Counseling Ser.). 1977. pap. 12.75 (*0-8185-0235-5*) Brooks-Cole.
— Groups Process & Practice. 6th ed. (Counseling Ser.). 2001. mass mkt. 40.95 (*0-534-34789-4*) Brooks-Cole.
— I Never Knew I Had a Choice. (Counseling Ser.). Date not set. pap., teacher ed. write for info. (*0-534-02088-7*) Brooks-Cole.
— I Never Knew I Had a Choice. (Counseling Ser.). 1978. pap. 13.50 (*0-8185-0263-0*) Brooks-Cole.
— I Never Knew I Had a Choice. 4th ed. (Counseling Ser.). 1989. pap. write for info. (*0-534-11587-X*) Brooks-Cole.
— Politics in America. 2nd ed. 240p. 1997. pap. text, student ed. 20.80 (*0-13-258369-0*) P-H.
— Theory & Practice of Counseling & Psychology. (Counseling Ser.). 1977. pap. 17.75 (*0-8185-0191-X*) Brooks-Cole.
— Theory & Practice of Counseling & Psychotherapy. 5th ed. 1995. teacher ed. write for info. (*0-534-33858-5*) Thomson Learn.
— Theory & Practice of Counselng & Psychotherapy. 6th ed. (Counseling Ser.). 2000. pap. text, student ed. 19.50 (*0-534-34824-6*) Brooks-Cole.
— Theory & Practice of Group Counseling. (Counseling Ser.). 1981. pap. 25.50 (*0-8185-0400-5*) Brooks-Cole.
— Theory & Practice of Group Counseling. 3rd ed. 1985. pap. 12.75 (*0-534-05077-8*) Brooks-Cole.
— Theory & Practice of Group Counseling. 5th ed. LC 99-25736. (Counseling Ser.). 1999. mass mkt. 14.95 (*0-534-34822-X*) Brooks-Cole.
— Theory of Practicing Counseling & Psychology. (Counseling Ser.). 1977. pap., student ed. 8.00 (*0-8185-0208-8*) Brooks-Cole.
— Theory of Practicing Group Counseling. (Counseling Ser.). 1981. pap., student ed. 9.50 (*0-8185-0432-3*) Brooks-Cole.
Corey & Callahan. Issues & Ethics in the Help Profession. 6th ed. (Counseling Ser.). 2002. pap. text 36.50 (*0-534-35615-X*) Brooks-Cole.
Corey & University St Thomas. Christian Theologcal Trade. 435p. 1996. pap. 36.40 (*0-536-59579-8*) Pearson Custom.
Corey, jt. auth. see Gardner.
Corey, jt. auth. see Taliaferro.
Corey, A. Raymond. The Development of Markets for New Materials: A Study of Building New End-Product Markets for Aluminum, Fibrous Glass, & the Plastics. LC 56-9764. 279p. reprint ed. pap. 86.50 (*0-608-14432-0*, 205184000009) Bks Demand.
Corey, Arthur. Behind the Scenes with the Metaphysicians. 1968. pap. 14.95 (*0-87516-014-X*) DeVorss.
— More Class Notes. 1962. pap. 4.00 (*0-87516-016-6*) DeVorss.
Corey, Arthur, jt. auth. see Merritt, Robert E.
Corey, Arthur T. Mechanics of Immersible Fluids in Porous Media. LC 86-50589. 1994. 38.00 (*0-918334-83-7*) WRP.
Corey, Barry. About Divorce & Dissolution: 83 Questions & Answers. rev. ed. 32p. 1984. pap. 1.80 (*0-88450-052-7*, 6110-N) Lawyers & Judges.
Corey, Barry, jt. auth. see Abele, Jon R.
Corey, Beverly, ed. see Economopoulos, Karen, et al.
Corey-Bloom, Jody. Adult Neurology. 4th ed. LC 97-27321. (Neurology Psychiatry Access Ser.). (Illus.). 456p. (C). (gr. 13). 1997. text 64.95 (*0-8151-1854-6*, 28571) Mosby Inc.
Corey, Carolyn, jt. auth. see Miller, Preston.
Corey, Carolyn, jt. auth. see Miller, Preston E.
Corey, Christopher R., jt. auth. see Freeman, Howard E.
Corey, Cindy. Exploring the Lighthouses of North Carolina. rev. ed. (Illus.). 1982. pap. 11.95 (*0-936179-03-1*) Provincial NC.
Corey, Clark L. A Guide for Exuberant Living. LC 94-93978. (Illus.). 379p. 1995. 24.98 (*0-9644698-0-4*); pap. 14.98 (*0-9644698-1-2*) C L Corey.
Corey, D. P. Waite Family of Malden, Massachusetts. (Illus.). 129p. 1993. reprint ed. pap. 19.50 (*0-8328-3427-0*); reprint ed. lib. bdg. 29.50 (*0-8328-3426-2*) Higginson Bk Co.
Corey, D. Steven & MacKenzie, Julia. Eric Gill: A Bibliography. (Illus.). 383p. 1991. 60.00 (*0-906795-53-2*) Oak Knoll.
Corey, Dale. Inventing English: Imaginative Origins of Everyday Expression. 416p. 1997. mass mkt. 6.99 (*0-425-15228-6*) Berkley Pub.
***Corey, David.** Pain: Learning to Live Without It. (Illus.). 211p. 1999. reprint ed. pap. text 14.00 (*0-7881-6796-0*) DIANE Pub.
Corey, Deborah J. Losing Eddie: A Novel. LC 00-9. (Front Porch PB Ser.). (Illus.). 238p. 1994. pap. 8.95 (*1-56512-091-4*) Algonquin Bks.
Corey, Deirdre. Remember Me When This You See. (Friends 4-Ever Ser.: No. 4). 144p. (J). (gr. 4-7). 1990. pap. 2.75 (*0-590-42624-9*) Scholastic Inc.
Corey, Del. Bloodline Poems. (Illus.). 56p. (Orig.). 1994. pap. 5.00 (*1-56439-043-8*) Ridgeway.
— Pardon My Allusion. (Illus.). 64p. (Orig.). 1997. pap. 10.00 (*1-56439-064-0*) Ridgeway.
Corey, Deloraine P. History of Malden, Massachusetts, 1633-1785. (Illus.). 870p. 1989. reprint ed. lib. bdg. 87.00 (*0-8328-0841-5*, MA0199) Higginson Bk Co.
— The History of Malden, Massachusetts, 1633-1785, Pt. 1 & 2. (Illus.). xvii, 870p. 1898. reprint ed. pap. 50.00 (*1-55613-562-9*) Heritage Bk.
Corey, Donna. Manatee: A First BIG Book. large type ed. (Illus.). 32p. (Orig.). (J). 1997. pap. 7.00 (*1-879488-07-8*) Sundiver.
— Manatee: A First Book. 3rd rev. ed. LC 96-70668. (Illus.). 48p. (J). 1997. 7.00 (*1-879488-08-6*) Sundiver.
— Manatee Mania! A Teaching Guide. (Illus.). 48p. 1997. pap., teacher ed. 12.00 (*1-879488-12-4*) Sundiver.
— Manati: Un Libro Inicial. LC 92-64397. (Illus.). 48p. (J). (ps-6). 1992. pap. 5.00 (*1-879488-01-9*) Sundiver.
Corey, Donna S. Manatee Book & Toy. 1997. 12.00 (*1-879488-16-7*) Sundiver.
Corey, Dorothy. Will It Ever Be My Birthday? LC 86-1565. (Illus.). 32p. (J). (ps-3). 1986. lib. bdg. 14.95 (*0-8075-9106-8*) A Whitman.
— Will There Be a Lap for Me? Levine, Abby, ed. LC 91-20324. (Illus.). 24p. (J). (ps-1). 1992. pap. 5.95 (*0-8075-9110-6*); lib. bdg. 13.95 (*0-8075-9109-2*) A Whitman.
— You Go Away. LC 75-33015. (Self Starter Bks.). (Illus.). 32p. (J). (ps-k). 1976. lib. bdg. 11.95 (*0-8075-9441-5*) A Whitman.
— You Go Away. 2nd rev. ed. LC 98-54656. (Illus.). 32p. (J). (ps-k). 1999. lib. bdg. 14.95 (*0-8075-9442-3*) A Whitman.
Corey, E. R., et al, eds. Silicon Chemistry. 570p. 1988. text 105.00 (*0-470-21081-8*) P-H.
Corey, E. Raymond. Technology Fountainheads: The Management Challenge of R&D Consortia. 192p. 1996. 29.95 (*0-87584-723-4*) Harvard Busn.
Corey, E. Raymond, ed. MBA Field Studies: A Guide for Students & Faculty. 80p. 1990. pap. 5.95 (*0-87584-251-8*) Harvard Busn.
Corey, E. Raymond & Star, Steven H. Organization Strategy: A Marketing Approach. LC 79-132151. (Illus.). 447p. reprint ed. pap. 138.60 (*0-8357-6307-2*, 203558000096) Bks Demand.
Corey, Elias James & Cheng, Xue-Min. The Logic of Chemical Synthesis. LC 89-5335. 464p. 1995. pap. 32.95 (*0-471-11594-0*) Wiley.
— The Logic of Chemistry Synthesis. LC 89-5335. 436p. 1989. 59.95 (*0-471-50979-5*) Wiley.
Corey, Faris J. Exploring the Country Inns of North Carolina. rev. ed. (Illus.). 1987. pap. 8.95 (*0-936179-08-2*) Provincial NC.
Corey, Frank. Americans & Their Homes First: A Mandate for a National Real Estate Act. LC 96-96461. 130p. 1996. 25.00 (*0-9652911-0-3*) F Corey.
Corey, George S., et al, eds. The First One Hundred Years: A Centennial Anthology Celebrating Antiochian Orthodoxy in North America. LC 95-14094. 1995. write for info. (*0-9624190-2-8*) Antakya Pr.
***Corey, Gerald.** The Art of Integrative Counseling. LC 00-22465. 147p. 2000. pap. 17.95 (*0-534-57636-2*) Thomson Learn.
Corey, Gerald. The Art of Integrative Counseling & Psychotherapy. 1995. mass mkt., teacher ed. write for info. (*0-534-34100-4*) Brooks-Cole.
— A Case Approach to Counseling & Psychotherapy. 2nd ed. LC 85-9683. (Psychology-Counseling Ser.). 320p. (C). 1985. pap. 19.50 (*0-534-05262-2*) Brooks-Cole.
— A Case Approach to Counseling & Psychotherapy. 4th ed. LC 95-15146. 364p. 1995. pap. 41.95 (*0-534-26580-4*) Brooks-Cole.
— I Never Knew I Had a Choice. 3rd ed. LC 85-11306. (Psychology-Counseling Ser.). 520p. (C). 1985. pap. 30.50 (*0-534-05418-8*) Brooks-Cole.
Corey, Gerald. I Never Knew I Had a Choice. 6th ed. LC 96-5075. (Counseling Ser.). 464p. (C). 1996. pap. 61.95 (*0-534-34339-2*) Brooks-Cole.
Corey, Gerald. I Never Knew I Had a Choice. 7th ed. (Counseling Ser.). 2001. mass mkt. 49.95 (*0-534-34790-8*) Brooks-Cole.
Corey, Gerald. Manual for Theory & Practice of Counseling & Psychotherapy. 5th ed. LC 95-15144. 230p. 1995. pap., student ed. 16.50 (*0-534-33857-7*) Brooks-Cole.
Corey, Gerald. Manual for Theory & Practice of Group Counseling. 2nd ed. (Psychology-Counseling Ser.). 160p. (C). 1984. pap. 12.00 (*0-534-03428-4*) Brooks-Cole.
— Student Manual for Theory & Practice of Counseling & Psychotherapy. LC 84-5026. (Psychology-Counseling Ser.). 192p. 1984. pap. 8.50 Brooks-Cole.
— Theory & Practice of Counseling & Psychology. 6th ed. LC 99-52087. (Counseling). 556p. 2000. mass mkt. 68.95 (*0-534-34823-8*) Brooks-Cole.
— Theory & Practice of Counseling & Psychotherapy. 5th ed. LC 95-15145. (Psychology-Counseling Ser.). 526p. 1995. pap. 71.95 (*0-534-33856-9*) Brooks-Cole.
— Theory & Practice of Group Counseling. 2nd ed. LC 84-5026. (Psychology-Counseling Ser.). 600p. (C). 1984. pap. 32.75 (*0-534-03223-0*) Brooks-Cole.
— Theory & Practice of Group Counseling. 4th ed. 1994. pap., teacher ed. write for info. (*0-534-24068-2*) Brooks-Cole.
Corey, Gerald. Theory & Practice of Group Counseling. 4th ed. LC 94-1915. 506p. 1994. 43.00 (*0-534-24066-6*) Brooks-Cole.
Corey, Gerald. Theory & Practice Of Group Counseling. 5th ed. LC 98-52471. (Counseling). 530p. 1999. pap. 64.95 (*0-534-34821-1*) Wadsworth Pub.
Corey, Gerald, ed. Theory & Practice of Counseling & Psychotherapy. 4th ed. LC 90-33124. (Counseling Ser.). 512p. (C). 1991. pap., student ed. 13.50 (*0-534-13316-9*); text 43.25 (*0-534-13314-2*) Brooks-Cole.
Corey, Gerald & Corey, Marianne. Becoming a Helper. 2nd ed. 376p. (Orig.). (C). 1993. pap. 33.95 (*0-534-19440-0*) Brooks-Cole.
— Issues in Ethics in the Helping Profession. 5th ed. LC 97-9363. (Counseling Ser.). 520p. 1997. 50.95 (*0-534-34689-8*) Brooks-Cole.
Corey, Gerald & Corey, Marianne S. Groups: Process & Practice. 2nd ed. LC 82-4117. (Psychology Ser.). 352p. (C). 1982. pap. 19.50 (*0-534-01174-8*) Brooks-Cole.
— I Never Knew I Had a Choice. 4th ed. LC 89-32330. (Psychology-Counseling Ser.). 464p. (C). 1989. pap. 38.50 (*0-534-11586-1*) Brooks-Cole.
— I Never Knew I Had a Choice. 5th ed. LC 92-35589. 402p. 1993. pap. 33.75 (*0-534-20166-0*) Brooks-Cole.
— I Never Knew I Had a Choice. 5th ed. 1996. teacher ed. write for info. (*0-534-20167-9*) Brooks-Cole.
— I Never Knew I Had a Choice. 6th ed. (C). 1996. pap., teacher ed. write for info. (*0-534-34340-6*) Brooks-Cole.
Corey, Gerald, et al. Group Techniques. rev. ed. LC 87-15129. 181p. (C). 1987. pap. 18.50 (*0-534-08586-5*) Brooks-Cole.
— Issues & Ethics in the Helping Professions. 2nd ed. LC 83-10119. (Psychology-Counseling Ser.). 480p. (C). 1984. pap. 19.75 (*0-534-02819-5*) Brooks-Cole.
— Issues & Ethics in the Helping Professions. 3rd ed. LC 87-13194. 441p. (C). 1987. mass mkt. 28.00 (*0-534-08082-0*) Brooks-Cole.
— Issues & Ethics in the Helping Professions. 4th ed. LC 91-37997. 438p. (C). 1993. pap. 36.95 (*0-534-18762-5*) Brooks-Cole.
— Living & Learning. LC 96-21357. (Freshman Orientation Ser.). 384p. (C). 1996. 37.95 (*0-534-50500-7*) Wadsworth Pub.
Corey, Gerald, jt. auth. see Corey, Marianne.
Corey, Gerald, jt. auth. see Corey, Marianne S.
Corey, Gerald, jt. auth. see Corey, Richard.
Corey, Gerald, jt. auth. see Herlihy, Barbara.
Corey, Gerald, jt. ed. see Herlihy, Barbara.
Corey, Helen E. The Art of Syrian Cookery. 190p. 1996. pap. 12.95 (*0-9626376-2-9*) CharLyn Pub Hse.

C

PREVENT FAILURE. BOOK INCLUDES DISHES THAT FIT IN WITH TODAY'S SEARCH FOR HEALTHFUL LOW-FAT, HIGH FIBER PROTEIN DISHES. The chapter on "Fascinating to watch an expert work with filo dough." ON BOOK & LECTURE TOUR. DISTRIBUTORS; BAKER & TAYLOR, THE DISTRIBUTORS, PARTNERS BOOK DIST. CO., QUALITY BOOKS DIST. AMAZON.COM-CHARLYN PUBLISHING HSE., 146 S. 23RD ST., TERRE HAUTE, IN. 47803. FAX; 812-232-7743 BOOK & VIDEO; WEB SITE; Http://members.aol.com/hcoreyfood/ *Publisher Paid Annotation.*

Corey, Irene. The Face Is a Canvas: A Complete Guide to Theatrical Make-Up. LC 86-12246. 1987. 19.95 (*0-13-298589-6*) P-H.

— The Face Is a Canvas: The Design & Technique of Theatrical Make-up. (Illus.). 275p. (C). 1991. 60.00 (*0-87602-031-7*) Anchorage.

— The Magic Garden. (J). (gr. k-3). 2000. pap. 7.00 (*0-87602-376-6*) Anchorage.

— The Mask of Reality: An Approach to Design for Theatre. (Illus.). 1968. 37.50 (*0-87602-007-4*) Anchorage.

Corey, Jack & Abramoff, Larry. Tatnuck Bookseller's Totally Irreverent Cookbook. 128p. 2000. pap. 6.99 (*1-886284-07-5*, Tatnuck) Chandler Hse.

Corey, Jacquelynne. AAOA Homestudy Course in Otolaryngic Allergy. 2nd ed. 416p. 1995. pap. text, student ed. 135.00 (*1-887064-01-X*) J M Ryan.

Corey, Jacquelynne P., ed. see Emanuel, Ivor A.

Corey, Jacquelynne P., ed. see Trevino, Richard J.

Corey, Jane. Exploring the Seacoast of North Carolina. (Illus.). 1984. pap. 9.95 (*0-936179-02-3*) Provincial NC.

— Exploring the Waterfalls of North Carolina. (Exploring North Carolina Ser.). (Illus.). 54p. (Orig.). 1992. pap. 9.95 (*0-936179-10-4*) Provincial NC.

Corey, Jane, ed. North Carolina: A Camera Profile. (Illus.). 1978. pap. 8.95 (*0-936179-06-6*) Provincial NC.

Corey, Jasper W. Soul Its Organ & Development (1913) 148p. 1998. reprint ed. pap. 17.95 (*0-7661-0599-7*) Kessinger Pub.

Corey, Jim, jt. auth. see Chew, Joe.

Corey, Judy. Storysharing: A Bridge Between Generations. 43p. 1998. pap. 7.95 (*0-9666031-0-9*) North Ctry Pr.

Corey, Lawrence, ed. see Stern, Jerry O., et al.

Corey, Lewis. Crisis of the Middle Class. 1994. pap. 22.50 (*0-231-09977-0*) Col U Pr.

— The Decline of American Capitalism. LC 70-38265. (Evolution of Capitalism Ser.). 628p. 1972. reprint ed. 38.95 (*0-405-04116-0*) Ayer.

— House of Morgan. LC 78-94469. reprint ed. 72.50 (*0-404-01728-2*) AMS Pr.

Corey, Lillian, ed. see Letson, Tom.

Corey, M. A. Back to Darwin: The Scientific Case for Deistic Evolution. 448p. (Orig.). (C). 1994. pap. text 37.00 (*0-8191-9307-0*); lib. bdg. 67.50 (*0-8191-9306-2*) U Pr of Amer.

— Job, Jonah, & the Unconscious: A Psychological Interpretation of Evil & Spiritual Growth in the Old Testament. 160p. (Orig.). (C). 1994. pap. text 22.50 (*0-8191-9685-1*); lib. bdg. 47.50 (*0-8191-9684-3*) U Pr of Amer.

— The Natural History of Creation: Biblical Evolutionism & the Return of Natural Theology. 460p. (Orig.). (C). 1995. pap. text 42.00 (*0-8191-9923-0*); lib. bdg. 67.50 (*0-8191-9922-2*) U Pr of Amer.

Corey, Marianne & Corey, Gerald. Becoming a Helper. 3rd ed. LC 96-41520. (Counseling Ser.). 400p. 1997. mass mkt. 42.95 (*0-534-34794-0*) Brooks-Cole.

Corey, Marianne, jt. auth. see Corey, Gerald.

Corey, Marianne S. Groups: Process & Practice. 5th ed. (Counseling Ser.). 450p. (C). 1996. pap. 55.95 (*0-534-34224-8*) Brooks-Cole.

Corey, Marianne S. & Corey, Gerald. Becoming a Helper. LC 88-10897. 247p. (Orig.). (C). 1988. pap. 20.75 (*0-534-09282-9*) Brooks-Cole.

— Groups: Process & Practice. 3rd ed. LC 86-2595. (Counseling Ser.). 381p. (C). 1986. pap. 26.75 (*0-534-06540-6*) Brooks-Cole.

— Groups: Process & Practice. 4th ed. LC 90-26069. 464p. (C). 1992. pap. 29.50 (*0-534-16122-7*) Brooks-Cole.

— Groups: Process & Practice. 5th ed. (C). 1997. pap. text, teacher ed. write for info. (*0-534-34225-6*) Brooks-Cole.

Corey, Marianne S., et al. Group Techniques. 2nd ed. LC 91-10852. 198p. (C). 1991. mass mkt. 30.95 (*0-534-16248-7*) Brooks-Cole.

Corey, Marianne S., jt. auth. see Corey, Gerald.

Corey, Mary F. The World Through a Monocle: The New Yorker at Midcentury. LC 98-41167. 212p. 1999. 25.95 (*0-674-96193-5*) HUP.

***Corey, Mary F.** The World Through a Monocle: The New Yorker at Midcentury. 2000. pap. text 14.95 (*0-674-00208-3*) HUP.

Corey, Melinda. Let's Visit a Spaghetti Factory. LC 89-5110. (Let's Visit Ser.). (Illus.). 32p. (J). (gr. 2-4). 1990. lib. bdg. 15.35 (*0-8167-1741-9*) Troll Communs.

— Model Railroader's Catalogue. 265p. 1991. per. 19.95 (*0-671-70949-6*, Fireside) S&S Trade Pap.

Corey, Melinda & Ochoa, George. The Dictionary of Film Quotations. LC 94-44227. 1995. pap. 24.00 (*0-517-88067-9*) Random.

— The Encyclopedia of the Victorian World: A Reader's Companion to the People, Places, Events & Everyday Life of the Victorian Era. LC 95-21077. (Illus.). 672p. (YA). (gr. 9 up). 1995. 50.00 (*0-8050-2622-3*) H Holt & Co.

— Literature: The New York Public Library Book of Answers. 256p. (Orig.). 1993. pap. 11.00 (*0-671-78164-2*, Fireside) S&S Trade Pap.

— The New York Public Library Book of Answers: Movies & TV. 256p. (Orig.). (J). (gr. 5-9). 1992. pap. 10.00 (*0-671-77538-3*, Fireside) S&S Trade Pap.

— The NYPL Book of American History. 240p. 1993. pap. 11.00 (*0-671-79634-8*, Fireside) S&S Trade Pap.

Corey, Melinda, jt. auth. see Berliner, Barbara.

Corey, Melinda, jt. auth. see Ochoa, George.

Corey, Melinda, ed. see Fulghum, Robert.

Corey, Melinda, ed. see Tan, Amy.

Corey, Michael, et al. Oracle8 Data Warehousing. LC 98-161689. 686p. 1998. pap. text 44.99 (*0-07-882511-3*) Osborne-McGraw.

— SQL Server 7 Data Warehousing. 478p. 1999. pap. 49.99 incl. cd-rom (*0-07-211921-7*) McGraw.

Corey, Michael J. & Abbey, Michael. Oracle Data Warehousing: The Practical Guide to Building a Data Warehouse. LC 97-107179. 560p. 1996. pap. text 34.95 (*0-07-882242-4*) Osborne-McGraw.

Corey, Michael J., et al. Oracle 8 Tuning. LC 98-113989. (Illus.). 293p. (Orig.). 1997. pap. text 44.99 (*0-07-882390-0*, Oracle Press) Osborne-McGraw.

— Tuning Oracle. (Oracle Press Ser.). 544p. 1994. pap. text 29.95 (*0-07-881181-3*) Osborne-McGraw.

Corey, Michael J., jt. auth. see Abbey, Michael.

Corey, Orlin. The Book of Job. 1961. 10.00 (*0-87602-000-7*) Anchorage.

— An Odyssey of Masquers: The Everyman Players. (Illus.). 296p. 1990. text 50.00 (*1-878281-09-7*) Rivendell Hse Ltd.

— The Towers of the Brazos. 80p. (Orig.). 1987. pap. text 5.00 (*0-685-28900-1*) Rivendell Hse Ltd.

Corey, Orlin, ed. Aurand Harris Remembered. 130p. 1999. pap. 12.50 (*0-87602-036-8*) Anchorage.

Corey, Paul. Do Cats Think? 1990. pap. 4.98 (*0-89009-616-3*) Bk Sales Inc.

Corey, Peter, ed. see Black, Lydia T., et al.

Corey, Richard & Corey, Gerald. A Case Approach to Counseling & Psychotherapy. 5th ed. LC 99-52781. (Counseling). 309p. 2000. pap. 39.95 (*0-534-34820-3*) Brooks-Cole.

Corey, Ron, ed. see Letson, Tom.

***Corey, Ryanne.** Lady with a Past. (Desire Ser.: Vol. 1319). 2000. mass mkt. 3.99 (*0-373-76319-0*, 1-76319-2) Harlequin Bks.

Corey, Ryanne. When She Was Bad. 1995. per. 3.25 (*0-373-05950-7*) Harlequin Bks.

Corey, Shana. Babe. (Early Step into Reading Ser.). (J). 1998. 9.19 (*0-606-13967-2*, Pub. by Turtleback) Demco.

— Babe: Oops, Pig. LC 97-40800. (Early Step into Reading Ser.). (Illus.). (J). (ps-3). 1998. pap. 3.99 (*0-679-88967-1*) Random.

— Babe: The Funniest Pig in the World. LC 97-40851. 24p. 1998. pap. 3.25 (*0-679-88965-5*) Random.

— Babe: The Mudhole Trick. LC 97-40801. 24p. 1998. pap. 3.25 (*0-679-88966-3*) Random.

— Babe Magic Bath Book. 10p. (J). 1998. 4.99 (*0-679-89416-0*, Pub. by Random Bks Yng Read) Random.

— Babe the Brave. LC 98-53768. (Step into Reading Ser.: A Step 1 Book). (J). (gr. k-3). 1999. lib. bdg. 11.99 (*0-375-90204-X*) Random.

— Babe the Brave. LC 98-53768. (Step into Reading Ser.: A Step 1 Book). (Illus.). 32p. (J). (ps-1). 1999. pap. 3.99 (*0-375-80204-5*) Random.

— Babe's La-la-Bye. (Jellybean Bks.). (Illus.). 24p. (J). (ps-k). 1999. 1.99 (*0-375-80144-8*, Pub. by Random Bks Yng Read); lib. bdg. 7.99 (*0-375-90144-2*, Pub. by Random Bks Yng Read) Random.

***Corey, Shana.** Ballerina Bear. (Jellybean Bks.). (Illus.). 24p. (J). (ps-k). 1999. lib. bdg. 7.99 (*0-375-90098-5*, Pub. by Random Bks Yng Read) Random.

— Ballerina Bear. (Jellybean Bks.). (Illus.). 24p. (J). (ps-k). 2000. 2.99 (*0-375-80098-0*, Pub. by Random Bks Yng Read) Random.

— Boats. (J). 2001. pap. 3.99 (*0-375-80221-5*) Random.

— Boats. (J). 2001. mass mkt. 11.99 (*0-375-90221-X*, Pub. by Random Bks Yng Read) Random.

Corey, Shana. I Spy Blue, Lizzy Lou. LC 99-219523. (J). 1998. 3.99 (*0-679-89180-3*, Pub. by Random Bks Yng Read) Random.

— Little Airplane Book. (J). 2000. 4.99 (*0-679-89480-2*) Random.

— 101 Grouchland Surprises. 1999. 5.99 (*0-375-80137-5*, Pub. by Random Bks Yng Read) Random.

***Corey, Shana.** Sesame Street: Let's Go to the Fun Park. (Let's Go Lift & Peek Bks.). (Illus.). 7p. (J). (ps). 1999. 4.99 (*0-679-89483-7*, Pub. by Random Bks Yng Read) Random.

Corey, Shana. Where Is Elmo's Blanket. (Nifty Lift-&-Look Book Ser.). 6p. (J). 1999. 5.99 (*0-375-80138-3*) Random Hse Chldrns.

***Corey, Shana.** You Forgot Your Skirt, Amelia Bloomer! LC 99-27181. (Illus.). 40p. (J). (gr. k-3). 2000. 16.95 (*0-439-07819-9*, Scholastic Ref) Scholastic Inc.

Corey, Sheila. Rock the House: A Creative Study of the Book of Ezra. LC 97-49915. (Empowered Youth Products Ser.). (Illus.). 48p. 1998. pap. text 8.99 (*0-7847-0770-7*, 23310) Standard Pub.

— X-Treme Altitude - Equipping Yourself to Scale Life's Challenges: A Creative Study of the Book of Nehemiah. Reeves, Dale, ed. (Empowered Youth Products Ser.). (Illus.). 64p. 1998. pap. 8.99 (*0-7847-0761-8*, 26-23311) Standard Pub.

Corey, Stephen. All These Lands You Call One Country: Poems. 64p. (C). 1992. pap. 10.95 (*0-8262-0838-X*); text 18.95 (*0-8262-0837-1*) U of Mo Pr.

— Gentle Iron Lace. 28p. 1984. pap. 12.50 (*0-912960-16-7*) Nightowl.

— The Last Magician. LC 87-60412. 61p. (Orig.). 1987. pap. 7.95 (*0-930501-16-0*) Swallows Tale Pr.

— The Last Magician. 2nd rev. ed. LC 97-60412. (Illus.). 61p. (Orig.). 1987. pap. 7.95 (*0-930501-17-9*) Swallows Tale Pr.

— Synchronized Swimming. 66p. (Orig.). 1984. pap. 9.95 (*0-942979-14-1*) Livingston U Pr.

— Synchronized Swimming. LC 85-50561. 88p. (Orig.). 1985. pap. 9.95 (*0-930501-01-2*) Swallows Tale Pr.

Corey, Stephen, et al. Award Highlights. (Illus.). (Orig.). 1983. 60.00 (*0-931956-07-2*); pap. 15.00 (*0-931956-08-0*) Water Mark.

Corfield, Anthony P., ed. Glycoprotein Methods & Protocols: The Mucins. LC 99-25785. (Methods in Molecular Biology Ser.: Vol. 125). (Illus.). 506p. 2000. 119.50 (*0-89603-720-7*) Humana.

Corfield, David. Mathematics for Beginners, 1. LC 98-75004. 176p. 1999. pap. 10.95 (*1-84046-011-3*) Icon Bks.

***Corfield, P. J.** Power & the Professions in Britain, 1700-1850. LC 99-33041. 280p. 1999. pap. 29.99 (*0-415-22265-6*) Routledge.

Corfield, Penelope & Evans, Chris. Youth & Revolution in the 1790s: Letters of William Pattisson, Thomas Amyot & Henry Crabb Robinson. LC 96-218626. (Illus.). 192p. 1996. 35.95 (*0-7509-1163-8*, Pub. by Sutton Pub Ltd) Intl Pubs Mktg.

Corfield, Penelope J. & Keene, Derek J. Work in Towns. 250p. 1990. 45.00 (*0-7185-1313-4*) St Martin.

Corfis, Ivy, ed. Historia Delos Nobles Caballeros Oliueros de Castilla y Artus D'Algarve. 279p. 1997. 40.00 (*1-56954-072-1*) Hispanic Seminary.

Corfis, Ivy A. Diego de San Pedro's Carcel de Amor: A Critical Edition. (ENG & SPA.). 1987. pap. 51.00 (*0-7293-0206-7*, Pub. by Tamesis Bks Ltd) Boydell & Brewer.

Corfis, Ivy A., ed. Text & Concordance of the Vatican Manuscript 6428 Cuento de Tristan de Leonis. (Spanish Ser.: No. 26). 8p. 1985. 10.00 incl. fiche (*0-942260-68-6*) Hispanic Seminary.

Corfis, Ivy A. & Petit, Carlos, eds. Text & Concordance of the Ordenanzas Reales, I-1338: Biblioteca Nacional, Madrid. (Spanish Legal Texts Ser.: No. 7). (SPA.). 24p. 1990. 10.00 incl. fiche (*0-940639-42-4*) Hispanic Seminary.

Corfis, Ivy A. & Wolfe, Michael, eds. The Medieval City under Siege. (Medieval Archaeology Ser.). (Illus.). 302p. 1999. pap. 35.00 (*0-85115-756-4*, Suffolk Records Soc) Boydell & Brewer.

Corfis, Ivy A., ed. see D'Arras, Jean.

Corfis, Ivy A., ed. see De San Pedro, Diego.

Corfis, Ivy A., ed. see Solalinde, Antonio G.

Corfman, Ann, ed. see Parks, Nancy.

Corfman, J. Numbers & Shapes Revisited: More Problems for Young Mathematicians. (Illus.). 320p. 1995. pap. text 29.95 (*0-19-853460-4*) OUP.

Corfman, Kim & Lynch, John, eds. Advances in Consumer Research: Proceedings of the 1995 Conference, Vol. 23. 1996. 59.00 (*0-915552-36-1*) Assn Consumer Res.

Corfman, R. S., ed. see DeCherney, Alan H., et al.

Corfman, Randle S., et al. Complications of Laparoscopy & Hysteroscopy. 2nd ed. LC 97-15481. (Illus.). 304p. 1997. 105.00 (*0-86542-507-8*) Blackwell Sci.

Corgan, James X. The Geological Sciences in the Antebellum South. LC 81-2993. (Illus.). 203p. 1982. pap. 63.00 (*0-7837-8367-1*, 205917700009) Bks Demand.

Corgan, Verna C. Controversy, Courts, & Community: The Rhetoric of Judge Miles Welton Lord. 79. LC 94-39472. (Contributions in Legal Studies: Vol. 79). 216p. 1995. 62.95 (*0-313-29247-7*, Greenwood Pr) Greenwood.

***Corganati, Martina, ed.** Absolut Mail Art. 85p. 1998. 31.95 (*88-435-6265-7*, Pub. by Electa) Gingko Press.

Corgel. Real Estate Perspective Ready Note. 3rd ed. 1997. pap. 13.75 (*0-256-26335-3*) McGraw.

— Real Estate Perspectives. 4th ed. 2000. student ed. 15.74 (*0-07-231824-4*) McGraw.

— Real Estate Perspectives. 4th ed. 2001. 64.74 (*0-07-231822-8*) McGraw.

Corgel, John, et al. Real Estate Perspectives: An Introduction to Real Estate. 3rd ed. LC 97-25721. 768p. (C). 1997. per. 73.13 (*0-256-15245-4*, Irwn McGrw-H) McGrw-H Hghr Educ.

Corgel, John B. & Smith, Halbert C. Real Estate Perspectives: An Introduction to Real Estate. 2nd ed. 747p. (C). 1991. text 69.25 (*0-256-07914-5*, Irwn McGrw-H) McGrw-H Hghr Educ.

Cori, Jasmin L. Freefall to the Beloved: Mystical Poetry for God's Lovers. 113p. (Orig.). 1996. pap. 10.95 (*1-889245-00-3*) Glden Reed.

***Cori, Jasmin Lee.** The Tao of Contemplation: Re-Sourcing the Inner Life. LC 99-58156. 160p. 2000. pap. 12.95 (*1-57863-131-9*) Weiser.

Cori, R. & Wirsing, M., eds. STACS, '88. (Lecture Notes in Computer Science Ser.: Vol. 294). ix, 404p. 1988. 46.00 (*0-387-18834-7*) Spr-Verlag.

Cori, R., jt. ed. see Monien, B.

***Cori, Rene & Lascar, Daniel.** Mathematical Logic : A Course with Exercises Part 1: Propositional Calculus. Pelletier, Donald H., tr. 352p. 2000. pap. text 39.95 (*0-19-850048-3*) OUP.

— Mathematical Logic : A Course with Exercises Part 1: Propositional Calculus. Pelletier, Donald H., tr. 352p. 2000. text 70.00 (*0-19-850049-1*) OUP.

Coriat, Isador H. The Meaning of Dreams. 194p. 1996. pap. 17.00 (*0-89540-313-7*, SB-313) Sun Pub.

— What Is Psychoanalysis? LC 73-2393. (Mental Illness & Social Policy; the American Experience Ser.). 1973. reprint ed. 14.95 (*0-405-05201-4*) Ayer.

Coriat, Lbeon & Gus. What's Wrong with Me: A Guide to Common Symptoms. LC 77-500389. 160 p. 1970. write for info. (*0-207-95394-5*) Angus & Roberts.

Coriat, Pierre, et al, eds. Clinical Cardiovascular Medicine in Anaesthesia. 300p. 1997. pap. text 59.00 (*0-7279-1127-9*, Pub. by BMJ Pub) Login Brothers Bk Co.

Coric, Simun S. Listen, Iris! Letters from Croatia 199. Ziral Staff & Lasic, Vinko D., eds. Crnkovic, Z. & Tinskamper, B., trs. from GER. (Ziral Bks.: No. 69). (Illus.). 88p. 1995. pap. 16.00 (*1-880829-05-3*) Z I R A L.

Coricelli. Growth & Development: Theories, Empirical Evidence & Policy Issues. LC 97-8583. 336p. 1998. text 69.95 (*0-312-17621-X*) St Martin.

Coricelli, Fabrizio. Macroeconomic Policies & the Development of Markets in Transition Economies. 176p. (C). 1998. pap. text 16.95 (*963-9116-08-4*) Ctrl Europ Univ.

— Macroeconomic Policies & the Development of Markets in Transition Economies. (Illus.). 176p. (C). 1998. 39.95 (*963-9116-05-X*) Ctrl Europ Univ.

Coricelli, Fabrizio & Revenga, Ana, eds. Wage Policy During the Transition to a Market Economy: Poland, 1990-91. LC 92-12835. (Discussion Paper Ser.: Vol. 158). 132p. 1992. pap. 22.00 (*0-8213-2114-5*, 12114) World Bank.

Coricelli, Fabrizio, et al. Fiscal Policy in Central & Eastern Europe No. 3: Forum Report of the Economic Policy Initiative. 96p. 1997. pap. 14.95 (*1-898128-30-8*, Pub. by Ctr Econ Policy Res) Brookings.

Coricelli, Fabrizio, jt. ed. see Blejer, Mario I.

Coricelli, Fabrizio, jt. ed. see Commander, Simon.

***Coriden, James A.** Canon Law as Ministry: Freedom & Good Order for the Church. 256p. 2000. pap. 14.95 (*0-8091-3978-2*) Paulist Pr.

Coriden, James A. An Introduction to Canon Law. 1991. pap. 16.95 (*0-8091-3231-1*) Paulist Pr.

— The Parish in the Catholic Tradition: History, Theology & Canon Law. LC 96-33120. 192p. 1996. pap. 12.95 (*0-8091-3685-6*) Paulist Pr.

Coriden, James A., et al, eds. The Code of Canon Law: A Text & Commentary, Study Edition. 1184p. 1986. pap. text 44.95 (*0-8091-2837-3*) Paulist Pr.

Coriell, Jack, et al, eds. Appalachian Trail Guide to North Carolina - Georgia. 11th ed. (Illus.). 208p. 1998. pap. 24.95 (*1-889386-06-5*) Appalachian Trail.

Coriell, Rebekah, jt. auth. see Coriell, Ron.

Coriell, Ron & Coriell, Rebekah. A Child's Book of Character Building Bk. 1: Growing up in God's World - at Home, at School, at Play. (Illus.). 128p. (Orig.). (J). (ps-2). 1995. pap. 14.99 (*0-8007-5494-8*) Revell.

— A Child's Book of Character Building Bk. 2: Growing up in God's World - at Home, at School, at Play. (Illus.). 128p. (J). (ps-2). 1995. pap. 14.99 (*0-8007-5495-6*) Revell.

Corijn, Eric, ed. Leisure in Europe. 200p. 1994. pap. 29.50 (*90-5487-073-7*, Pub. by VUB Univ Pr) Paul & Co Pubs.

Corillion, Robert. Les Charophycees de France et d'Europe Occidentale. (FRE., Illus.). 499p. 1972. reprint ed. 160.00 (*3-87429-014-X*, 003344, Pub. by Koeltz Sci Bks) Lubrecht & Cramer.

Corin, Andrew R. The New York Missal: A Paleographic & Phonetic Analysis. (UCLA Slavic Studies: Vol. 21). 272p. 1991. 29.95 (*0-89357-224-1*) Slavica.

Corin, Ellen, jt. ed. see Bibeau, Gilles.

Corin, James. Mating, Marriage & the Status of Women. LC 72-9633. reprint ed. 39.50 (*0-404-57432-7*) AMS Pr.

***Corinaldesi, Ernesto.** Classical Mechanics for Physics Graduate Students. LC 98-48670. (Theoretical Physics Ser.). 300p. 1999. 38.00 (*981-02-3625-5*) World Scientific Pub.

Corinaldi, Michael. Jewish Identity: The Case of Ethiopian Jewry. LC 98-210084. 255p. 1998. write for info. (*965-223-993-3*) Magnes Pr.

Corinchock, Drew & Russell, James. Quick Guide: Gazebos. Schiff, David, ed. LC 95-70916. (Quick Guide Ser.). (Illus.). 80p. (Orig.). 1995. pap. 7.95 (*1-880029-52-9*) Creative Homeowner.

Corinchock, John A. Technician's Guide to Refrigeration Systems. LC 96-42366. 477p. 1996. 59.95 (*0-07-013159-7*) McGraw.

Coringold, Sally M., ed. see Skeffington, A. M.

Corinna, Joyce, jt. auth. see Petschulat, Neub.

Corinne, Dee. Cunt Coloring Book. 48p. 1989. 7.95 (*0-86719-371-9*) Last Gasp.

Corinne, Tee A. Dreams of the Woman Who Loved Sex. LC 98-51150. (Illus.). (Orig.). 1999. pap. 13.95 (*1-892281-01-5*) New Victoria Pubs.

— Women Who Loved Women: An Illustrated Bibliography. (Illus.). 112p. (Orig.). 1984. pap. write for info. (*0-930143-00-0*) Pearlchild.

Corinne, Tee A., ed. Riding Desire. LC 91-3657. 160p. (Orig.). 1991. pap. 8.95 (*0-934411-44-1*, Banned Bks) Edward-William Austin.

Corinth, Kay. Fashion Showmanship: Everything You Need to Know to Give a Fashion Show. LC 83-19446. 288p. 1984. reprint ed. 32.50 (*0-89874-697-3*) Krieger.

Corinthius, Gregorius. Gregorii Corinthii Et Aliorum Grammaticorum Libri de Dialectis Linguae Graecae. liv, 1072p. 1970. reprint ed. 240.00 (*0-318-70929-5*) G Olms Pubs.

Corio, David & Goldman, Vivien. Visions of the Groove: Connections Between Afrobeats, Rhythm & Blues, Hip Hop & More. LC 99-31952. (Illus.). 176p. 1999. 45.00 (*0-7893-0337-X*, Pub. by Universe); pap. 29.95 (*0-7893-0375-2*, Pub. by Universe) St Martin.

***Corio, Laura E. & Kahn, Linda G.** The Change Before the Change: Everything You Need to Know to Stay Healthy in the Decade Before Menopause. LC 00-31205. 2000. 24.95 (*0-553-10876-X*) Bantam.

An Asterisk (*) at the beginning of an entry indicates that the title is appearing for the first time.

C

Coriolan, John. Christy Dancing. rev. ed. LC 83-22665. 224p. 1984. pap. 7.95 (*0-912516-87-9*) Grey Fox.
— A Sand Fortress: A Novel. rev. ed. 224p. 1984. reprint ed. pap. 8.95 (*0-917342-46-1*) Gay Sunshine.
— The Smile of Eros: A Novel. 192p. (Orig.). 1984. pap. 7.95 (*0-917342-39-9*) Gay Sunshine.
***Coriolis Group Staff.** CCNA Routing & Switching Exam Cram. 2000. pap. text 129.99 (*1-57610-630-6*) Coriolis Grp.
— CCNA Routing & Switching Exam Cram Audio Review. 2000. audio 39.99 (*1-57610-629-2*) Coriolis Grp.
— Linux Internet Server: Visual Black Book. LC 00-22693. (Illus.). 250p. 1999. pap. write for info. (*1-57610-569-5*) Coriolis Grp.
— Setting Up a Linux Server: Visual Black Book. LC 99-45421. (Illus.). 247p. 1999. pap. 24.99 (*1-57610-568-7*) Coriolis Grp.
— Windows 2000 Active Directory & LDAP Little Black Book. (Little Black Book Ser.). 400p. 1999. pap. 49.99 (*1-57610-256-4*) Coriolis Grp.
***Coriolis Group Staff, ed.** MCSE Networking Essentials Exam Cram Personal Trainer. 3rd ed. (Illus.). 2000. pap. 69.99 incl. cd-rom (*1-57610-644-6*) Coriolis Grp.
— MCSE NT Server 4 Exam Cram Personal Trainer. 3rd ed. (Illus.). 2000. pap. text 69.99 incl. cd-rom (*1-57610-645-4*) Coriolis Grp.
— MCSE NT Server 4 in the Enterprise Exam Cram Personal Trainer. 3rd ed. (Illus.). 2000. pap. text 69.99 incl. cd-rom (*1-57610-646-2*) Coriolis Grp.
— MCSE Workstation 4 Exam Cram Personal Trainer. 3rd ed. (Illus.). 2000. pap. text 69.99 incl. cd-rom (*1-57610-647-0*) Coriolis Grp.
Coriolis Group Staff, ed. Windows 98 Professional Productivity Kit. 1998. pap. 79.99 (*1-57610-321-8*) Coriolis Grp.
Coriolis Publishing Staff. Kickass Visual J++ Programming. 1997. pap. text 49.99 (*1-57610-093-6*) Coriolis Grp.
Coriolis Technology Press Staff. Visual C++ 98 Black Book. 1200p. 1998. 49.99 incl. cd-rom (*1-57610-323-4*) Coriolis Grp.
— Visual C++ 6.0 Programming Explorer. LC 98-29350. 653p. 1998. 49.99 incl. cd-rom (*1-57610-324-2*) Coriolis Grp.
Coripio Perez, Fernando. Diccionario Etimologico Abreviado. 2nd ed. (SPA.). 320p. 1976. pap. 9.95 (*0-8288-5608-7*, S50161) Fr & Eur.
Corippus. Concordantia in Flavii Corippi Ioannida. Andres, Jean U., ed. (Alpha-Omega, Reihe A Ser.: Vol. 134). (GER.). 614p. 1993. write for info. incl. 3.5 hd (*3-487-09714-1*) G Olms Pubs.
Corish, Patrick. The Irish Martyrs. 1989. pap. 15.00 (*1-85390-066-4*, Pub. by Veritas Pubns) St Mut.
Corish, Patrick J., ed. Concise Encyclopedia of Polymer Processing & Applications. (Advances in Materials Science & Engineering Ser.: No. 10). (Illus.). 792p. 1991. 263.75 (*0-08-037064-0*, Pergamon Pr) Elsevier.
***Corish, Patrick J. & Sheehy, David.** Records of the Catholic Church in Ireland. (Maynooth Guides for Local History Research Ser.). (Illus.). 52p. 2000. pap. 14.50 (*0-7165-2698-0*, Pub. by Irish Acad Pr) Intl Spec Bk.
***Coristine, Philip.** Serena & the Wild Doll. (Illus.). 32p. (J). (ps-2). 2000. lib. bdg. 19.95 (*1-55037-649-7*, Pub. by Annick Pr); per. 6.95 (*1-55037-648-9*, Pub. by Annick Pr) Firefly Bks Ltd.
Cork, jt. auth. see Cox, Mike.
Cork, jt. auth. see Cox, Rosamund.
Cork, B. & Bramwell, M. Rocks & Fossils. (Hobby Guides Ser.). (Illus.). 32p. (J). (gr. 5-9). 1983. pap. text 6.95 (*0-7460-1975-0*) EDC.
— Rocks & Fossils. (Hobby Guides Ser.). (Illus.). 32p. (J). (gr. 5 up). 1999. lib. bdg. 14.95 (*0-88110-159-1*) EDC.
Cork, Barbara. Archaeology. (Young Scientist Ser.). (Illus.). 32p. (J). (gr. 4-8). 1985. pap. 6.95 (*0-86020-865-6*, Usborne) EDC.
— Archaeology. (Young Scientist Ser.). (Illus.). 32p. (J). (gr. 5-8). 1985. lib. bdg. 14.95 (*0-88110-220-2*, Usborne) EDC.
— Plant Life. (Mysteries & Marvels Ser.). (Illus.). 32p. (YA). (gr. 3-7). 1984. pap. 5.95 (*0-86020-755-2*); lib. bdg. 14.95 (*0-88110-169-9*) EDC.
— Wild Animals. (First Nature Bks.). (J). (gr. k up). 1982. lib. bdg. 12.95 (*0-88110-077-3*, Usborne) EDC.
— Wild Animals. (First Nature Bks.). (Illus.). 24p. (J). (gr. k-3). 1982. pap. 4.50 (*0-86020-628-9*, Usborne) EDC.
Cork, Barbara & Morris, R. Mysteries & Marvels of Nature. (Mysteries & Marvels Ser.). (Illus.). 192p. (J). (gr. 3-7). 1983. 24.95 (*0-7460-0421-4*) EDC.
Cork, Barry. Endangered Species. large type ed. 1995. 27.99 (*0-7089-3019-0*) Ulverscroft.
Cork, David & Lightstone, Susan. The Pig & the Python. LC 97-37319. 256p. 1997. per. 14.00 (*0-7615-1275-6*) Prima Pub.
Cork, Dorothy. Butterfly Montane. large type ed. 1990. 27.99 (*0-7089-2294-5*) Ulverscroft.
— Outback Runaway. large type ed. (Linford Romance Library). 327p. 1984. pap. 16.99 (*0-7089-6045-6*, Linford) Ulverscroft.
***Cork, Judson & Cork, Marilyn, eds.** The Heritage of Greene County, Alabama. (Heritage of Alabama Ser.: Vol. 32). 300p. 2001. 59.95 (*1-891647-50-4*) Herit Pub Consult.
Cork, Marilyn, ed. Bonner, ID. (Illus.). 1991. text 75.00 (*0-88107-189-7*) Curtis Media.
Cork, Marilyn, jt. ed. see Cork, Judson.
Cork, Patrick, jt. auth. see Cox, Rosamund K.
Cork, Richard. Art Beyond the Gallery in Early Twentieth Century England. LC 84-52240. (Illus.). 352p. 1985. 80.00 (*0-300-03236-6*) Yale U Pr.
— A Bitter Truth: The Avant-Garde Art & the Great War. LC 93-42951. (Illus.). 256p. 1994. 65.00 (*0-300-05704-0*) Yale U Pr.
— Bottle of Notes: Claes Oldenburg & Coosje Van Bruggen. (Illus.). 72p. 1997. pap. 25.95 (*0-85331-708-9*, Pub. by Lund Humphries) Antique Collect.
— British Sculpture of the 1980s & 1990s: From the Weltkunst Foundation. (Illus.). 120p. 1997. 59.95 (*0-85331-744-5*, Pub. by Lund Humphries) Antique Collect.
Cork, Richard. David Bomberg. LC 86-23402. 352p. 1987. 115.00 (*0-300-03827-5*) Yale U Pr.
Cork, Richard. David Bomberg. LC 86-23402. 352p. 1988. pap. 45.00 (*0-300-04194-2*) Yale U Pr.
— Jacob Epstein. (British Artists Ser.). (Illus.). 1999. pap. 13.95 (*0-691-02945-8*, Pub. by Princeton U Pr) Cal Prin Full Svc.
Cork, Richard, jt. auth. see Burdett, Richard.
Cork, Sarah G. The Bottlestopper's Christmas Tree Farm. (Illus.). 50p. (J). (gr. k-3). 1991. pap. 4.95 (*0-943487-35-8*) Sevgo Pr.
Cork, Seamus. Irish Erotic Art. 96p. 1981. text 7.95 (*0-312-43601-7*) St Martin.
Corke, Bettina, ed. Who's Who in Latin America: Government, Politics, Banking & Industry, 2 vols., Set. 4th rev. ed. 531p. 1997. lib. bdg. 149.00 (*0-88354-225-0*) N Ross.
— Who's Who in Latin America Vol. 1: South America, 2 vols., Set. 4th rev. ed. 1997. lib. bdg. 99.00 (*0-88354-226-9*) N Ross.
— Who's Who in Latin America Vol. 2: Central America & the Caribbean, 2 vols., Set. 4th rev. ed. 1997. lib. bdg. 99.00 (*0-88354-227-7*) N Ross.
Corke, C. F. Self Assessment for MRCP, Pt. I. 4th ed. LC 95-32582. 1995. pap. 29.95 (*0-86542-937-5*) Blackwell Sci.
Corke, C. F. & Jackson, I. J. Companion to Clinical Anaesthesia Exams. LC 94-1429. 1994. text 28.95 (*0-443-04962-9*) Church.
***Corke, Charlie.** Practical Intensive Care Medicine: Problem Solving in the ICU. (Illus.). 160p. 2000. pap. text 32.50 (*0-7506-4752-3*) Buttrwrth-Heinemann.
Corke, Harold & Lin, Rufa, eds. Asian Food Product Development - Focus on Specialty Grains & Grain Products: Proceedings of the 1st International Conference. 443p. 1998. pap. 50.00 (*1-880132-35-4*) Sci Pr NY.
Corke, Helen. Lawrence & Apocalypse. 130p. (C). 1966. lib. bdg. 75.00 (*0-8383-0655-1*) M S G Haskell Hse.
Corke, J. Tourism Law. (C). 1989. 90.00 (*0-946139-96-2*, Pub. by Elm Pubns) St Mut.
Corke, Philip. Handicrafts of the Arab World. (J). (gr. 2-9). 1988. 9.95 (*0-86685-496-7*) Intl Bk Ctr.
Corke, Philip. Rivers. (Butterfly Bks.). 32p. (J). (gr. 3-5). 1985. 9.95 (*0-86685-452-5*) Intl Bk Ctr.
Corker, I. R. Nevis: Resource Assessment & Zoning Plan. 65p. 1990. pap. 30.00 (*0-85954-271-8*, Pub. by Nat Res Inst) St Mut.
Corker, Jeanne, ed. see Benton, Linda, et al.
Corker, Joanne, ed. see Allen, Margaret.
Corker, Joanne, ed. see Burdick, Kathy, et al.
Corker, Joanne, ed. see Hildrum, Kristin K.
Corker, M. Deaf & Disabled, or Deafness Disabled? Towards a Human Rights Perspective. LC 97-20448. (Disability, Human Rights, & Society Ser.). 166p. 1997. 85.00 (*0-335-19700-0*) OpUniv Pr.
Corker, Mairian. Counselling: The Deaf Challenge. LC 94-209514. 272p. 1994. write for info. (*1-85302-223-3*, Pub. by Jessica Kingsley) Taylor & Francis.
— Counselling - The Deaf Challenge. LC 94-209514. 262p. 1995. pap. 24.95 (*1-85302-321-3*) Taylor & Francis.
— Deaf & Disabled, or Deafness Disabled? Towards a Human Rights Perspective. LC 97-20448. (Disability, Human Rights, & Society Ser.). 176p. 1997. pap. 25.95 (*0-335-19699-3*) OpUniv Pr.
— Deaf Transitions: Images & Origins of Deaf Families, Deaf Communities & Deaf Identities. 250p. 1996. pap. text 26.95 (*1-85302-326-4*, Pub. by Jessica Kingsley) Taylor & Francis.
Corker, Mairian & French, Sally. Disability Discourse. LC 98-20844. (Disability, Human Rights, & Society Ser.). 1998. 85.00 (*0-335-20223-3*) OpUniv Pr.
Corker, Mairian & French, Sally, eds. Disability Discourse. LC 98-20844. (Disability, Human Rights, & Society Ser.). 192p. 1998. pap. 29.95 (*0-335-20222-5*) OpUniv Pr.
Corker, Robert, et al. United Germany the First Five Years: Performance & Policy Issues. LC 95-18140. (Occasional Papers: No. 125). 1995. 15.00 (*1-55775-472-1*) Intl Monetary.
Corker, Robert, jt. auth. see Tseng, Wanda.
Corkery, Daniel. Fohnam the Sculptor. (Lost Play Ser.). 1973. pap. 1.25 (*0-912262-32-X*) Proscenium.
— The Hidden Ireland. (C). 1983. pap. 17.95 (*0-7171-0079-0*, Pub. by Gill & MacMill) Irish Bks Media.
— Hounds of Banba. LC 75-128728. (Short Story Index Reprint Ser.). 1977. 17.95 (*0-8369-3619-1*) Ayer.
— Nightfall & Other Stories. 204p. 1988. pap. 12.95 (*0-85640-414-4*, Pub. by Blackstaff Pr) Dufour.
— The Wager & Other Stories. (Illus.). (J). 1950. 8.50 (*0-8159-7200-8*) Devin.
***Corkery, James F.** Starting Law. 1999. pap. 22.95 (*0-9586727-4-1*) Gaunt.
Corkery, Jim. A Career in Law. 270p. 1989. pap. 25.00 (*1-86287-017-9*, Pub. by Federation Pr) Gaunt.
Corkery, Jim, jt. ed. see Lessing, John.
Corkery, Simon. The Golden Years of an Irish Emigrant: Step by Step. (C). 1990. text 40.00 (*0-7223-2532-0*, Pub. by A H S Ltd) St Mut.
Corkery, Tom. Tom Corkery's Dublin. (Illus.). 128p. 1989. reprint ed. pap. 15.95 (*0-900068-75-2*, Pub. by Anvil Books Ltd) Irish Bks Media.
Corkett, Ann, tr. see Jenkins, Dafydd.
Corkhill, Alan. Antipodean Encounters: Australia & the German Literary Imagination, 1754-1918. Jurgensen, Manfred, ed. (German-Australian Studies - Deutsch-Australische Studien: Vol. 2). (Illus.). XIX, 277p. 1990. pap. 48.00 (*3-261-04248-6*) P Lang Pubng.
Corkhill, J. W., jt. auth. see Park, W. W.
***Corkill, David.** Development of Portuguese Economy: Case of Europeanization. LC 98-47959. (Contemporary Economic History of Europe Ser.). 1999. text. write for info. (*0-415-14574-0*) Routledge.
Corkill, P. A., et al. Structure & Architectural Design. 4th rev. ed. (Illus.). 224p. (C). Date not set. reprint ed. pap. write for info. (*0-9674690-0-7*) Market Pubg.
Corkin, B., jt. auth. see Averill, M.
Corkin, Bud & Averill, Mary. Network Marketing: The Business of the 90's. Reider, Andrea, ed. LC 93-73201. (Fifty-Minute Ser.). (Illus.). 78p. (Orig.). 1994. pap. 10.95 (*1-56052-244-5*) Crisp Pubns.
Corkin, Jane, ed. Andre Kertesz: A Lifetime of Perception. 162p. 1993. write for info. (*0-9637867-0-9*) Andalusian.
Corkin, S., et al. Handbook of Neuropsychology, Vol. 5. 396p. 1991. 116.50 (*0-444-81233-4*) Elsevier.
— Handbook of Neuropsychology, Vol. 5. 396p. 1993. pap. 119.25 (*0-444-81501-5*) Elsevier.
Corkin, S., jt. ed. see Nebes, R. D.
Corkin, Stanley. Realism & the Birth of the Modern United States: Literature, Cinema, & Culture. LC 94-23968. 1996. 40.00 (*0-8203-1730-6*) U of Ga Pr.
Corkindale, J., jt. ed. see Willis, K. G.
Corkindale, John, ed. Reforming Land-Use Planning: Property Rights Approaches. (IEA Studies on the Environment: No. 12). 88p. 1998. pap. 19.95 (*0-255-36446-6*, Pub. by Inst Economic Affairs) Coronet Bks.
Corkish, Jo & Miles, David. Inflation, Inflation Risks & Asset Returns. LC HG0229.. (Bank of England, Economics Division. Working Paper Ser.: No. 27). (Illus.). 41p. reprint ed. pap. 30.00 (*0-608-20165-0*, 207142900011) Bks Demand.
Corkran, Charlotte & Thoms, Chris. Amphibians of Washington, Oregon & British Columbia. (Illus.). 176p. 1996. pap. 16.95 (*1-55105-073-0*, 1-55105) Lone Pine.
Corkrean, Mary, jt. auth. see Joiner, Carl.
Corkum, Paul B., jt. ed. see Perry, Michael D.
Corl, Kathryn A., et al. Sprechen wir Deutsch! 2nd ed. LC 88-19105. (GER., Illus.). 528p. (C). 1989. teacher ed. write for info. (*0-03-014102-8*); audio. write for info. (*0-318-64064-3*) Harcourt Coll Pubs.
Corl, Kathy & Jurasek. I.m. Ubergange: Texte Erfassen (reader) (Collge German). (GER.). (C). 1994. text, teacher ed. 13.95 (*0-8384-5372-4*) Heinle & Heinle.
— Ubergange. (College German Ser.). (GER.). (C). 1994. text, teacher ed. 13.95 (*0-8384-4640-X*) Heinle & Heinle.
Corl, Kathy, et al. Ubergange: Texte Erfassen. (Bridging the Gap Ser.). (GER.). (C). 1994. mass mkt. 36.95 (*0-8384-5370-8*) Heinle & Heinle.
— Ubergange: Texte Verfassen. (Bridging the Gap Ser.). (GER.). (C). 1994. mass mkt. 36.95 (*0-8384-4638-8*) Heinle & Heinle.
Corlac. In Search of Orlovsky: A Video Mystery & Resource Manual. 1997. 79.95 (*0-7872-3942-9*) Kendall-Hunt.
— Mir Russkikh: The World of the Russians Exercise Book. 192p. 1997. per. 29.95 (*0-7872-2733-1*, 41273301) Kendall-Hunt.
Corlac, jt. auth. see ACTR Staff.
Corle, Clyde G. Teaching Mathematics in the Elementary School. LC 64-13943. 395p. reprint ed. pap. 122.50 (*0-608-30961-3*, 201247900081) Bks Demand.
Corle, Clyde G., jt. auth. see Bouwsma, Ward D.
Corle, Edwin. Fig Tree John. 1971. reprint ed. 7.95 (*0-87140-518-0*, Pub. by Liveright) Norton.
— Fig Tree John. 1971. reprint ed. pap. 2.95 (*0-87140-242-4*, Pub. by Liveright) Norton.
— The Man in the Dog Suit. adapted ed. Wright, William H., ed. 1959. pap. 5.25 (*0-8222-0723-0*) Dramatists Play.
Corle, Edwin, ed. see Armitage, Merle.
Corle, Timothy R. & Kino, Gordon S. Confocal Scanning Optical Microscopy & Related Imaging Systems. (Illus.). 335p. 1996. text 79.95 (*0-12-408750-7*) Acad Pr.
Corless, Barrie, et al. Rugby Training. LC 96-144523. (Illus.). 128p. 1996. pap. 19.95 (*1-85223-897-6*, Pub. by Cro1wood) Trafalgar.
Corless, Colm. Birthway: Poems. pap. 8.95 (*1-874700-04-4*, Pub. by Clo Iar-Chonnachta) Dufour.
Corless, Hank. The Weiser Indians: Shoshoni Peacemakers. (Illus.). 170p. (Orig.). 1996. reprint ed. pap. 14.95 (*0-87004-376-5*, 037650) Caxton.
Corless, Inge. A Challenge for Living: Dying Death Bereavement. (Death & Dying Ser.). 428p. 1995. 40.00 (*0-86720-817-1*) Jones & Bartlett.
***Corless, Inge B. & Foster, Zelda, eds.** The Hospice Heritage: Celebrating Our Future. LC R726.8.H67125 1999. (Hospice Journal Monograph Ser.: Vol. 14, No. 3/4). 279p. (C). 1999. pap. text 29.95 (*0-7890-0847-5*, Hawrth Medical) Haworth Pr.
— The Hospice Heritage: Celebrating Our Future. LC R726.8.H67125 1999. (Hospice Journal Monograph Ser.: Vol. 14, No. 3/4). 279p. (C). 1999. 59.95 (*0-7890-0837-8*, Hawrth Medical) Haworth Pr.
Corless, Inge B. & Pittman-Lindeman, Mary, eds. AIDS: Principles, Practices & Politics. (Death Education, Aging & Health Care Ser.). 780p. 1989. 89.95 (*0-89116-716-1*, 66-56086) Hemisp Pub.
— AIDS: Principles, Practices & Politics. abr. ed. (Death Education, Aging & Health Care Ser.). 400p. 1987. 63.95 (*0-89116-795-1*, 66-57001); pap. 29.95 (*0-89116-772-2*, 66-56813) Hemisp Pub.
Corless, Inge B., et al. Dying, Death & Bereavement: Theoretical Perspectives & Other Ways of Knowing. (Illus.). 412p. (C). 1999. reprint ed. pap. text 30.00 (*0-7881-6349-3*) DIANE Pub.
Corless, R. M. Essential Maple: A Guide for Scientific Programmers. (Illus.). 218p. 1994. 34.95 (*0-387-94209-2*) Spr-Verlag.
— Symbolic Recipes: Scientific Computing with Maple. (Illus.). 300p. 1997. 39.00 (*0-387-94210-6*) Spr-Verlag.
Corless, Roger J. The Vision of Buddhism: The Space under the Tree. 362p. 1992. pap. 16.95 (*1-55778-200-8*) Paragon Hse.
Corless-Smith, Martin. The Garden: A Theophany or Eccohome: A Dialectical Lyric. deluxe ed. 36p. 1999. pap. 10.00 (*0-9666303-2-7*) A A Arts.
— Of Piscator: Poems by Martin Corless-Smith. LC 97-18690. (Contemporary Poetry Ser.). 1998. pap. 15.95 (*0-8203-1947-3*) U of Ga Pr.
Corless,R.N., Inge B., et al. Dying, Death & Bereavement. (Nursing-Health Science Ser.). 432p. (C). 1994. pap. text 41.25 (*0-86720-631-4*) Jones & Bartlett.
Corlett, Donald A. HACCP User's Manual. LC 97-46781. 512p. 1998. 79.00 (*0-8342-1200-5*) Aspen Pub.
Corlett, Donald A., Jr., jt. ed. see Pierson, Merle D.
Corlett, E. N., et al, eds. The Ergonomics of Working Postures: The First International Symposium on Occupational Ergonomics Zadar, Yugoslavia April 1985. LC 86-14459. 300p. 1986. 138.00 (*0-85066-338-5*) Taylor & Francis.
Corlett, E. N. & Clark, T. S. The Ergonomics of Workspaces & Machines: A Design Manual. 2nd ed. 100p. 1995. pap. 19.95 (*0-7484-0320-5*, Pub. by Tay Francis Ltd) Taylor & Francis.
Corlett, E. N. & Richardson, J., eds. Stress, Work Design & Productivity. LC 81-13075. (Wiley Series on Studies in Occupational Stress). (Illus.). 287p. reprint ed. pap. 89.00 (*0-8357-3049-2*, 203930500012) Bks Demand.
Corlett, E. N., et al. The Guide to the Handling of Patients. 4th ed. (Illus.). 134p. (C). 1994. reprint ed. pap. text 27.95 (*1-879864-01-0*) IMPACC USA.
Corlett, E. N., jt. auth. see Clark, T. S.
Corlett, Eleanor & Millner, Nancy. Navigating Midlife: Using Typology As a Guide. LC 93-4374. 272p. 1993. pap. 17.95 (*0-89106-061-8*, 7394, Davies-Black Pub) Consulting Psychol.
Corlett, J. Angelo. Analyzing Social Knowledge. 174p. 1996. pap. text 23.95 (*0-8476-8294-3*); lib. bdg. 55.50 (*0-8476-8293-5*) Rowman.
Corlett, J. Angelo, ed. Equality & Liberty: Analyzing Rawls & Nozick. 368p. 1991. text 45.00 (*0-312-06018-1*) St Martin.
Corlett, Jim. Super Natural Cookery: Recipes for Vegetarian Gourmets LC 75-318705. 96p. 1974. write for info. (*0-7153-6737-4*) D & C Pub.
Corlett, M. & McGregor, R. M. An Annotated List of the Published Names in Mycosphaerella & Sphaerella. (Mycologia Memoirs Ser.: No. 18). 250p. 1991. text 91.00 (*0-945345-35-6*, Pub. by Gebruder Borntraeger) Balogh.
***Corlett, Mary Lee & Fine, Ruth E.** The Prints of Roy Lichtenstein: A Catalogue Raisonne 1948-1997. (Illus.). 376p. 2000. 125.00 (*1-55595-196-1*, Pub. by Hudson Hills) Natl Bk Netwk.
Corlett, Michael. An Annotated List of the Published Names in Mycosphaerella & Sphaerella. (Mycologia Memoir Ser.: No. 18). (Illus.). 328p. 1991. 76.00 (*3-443-76008-2*, Pub. by Gebruder Borntraeger) Balogh.
Corlett, N., jt. ed. see Di Martino, V.
Corlett, Nigel, jt. ed. see Wilson, John R.
Corlett, Richard, jt. auth. see Chin, Wee Y.
Corlett, Richard, jt. auth. see Dudgeon, David.
Corlett, William. The Bloxworth Blue. LC 85-42916. 192p. (YA). (gr. 7 up). 1985. 12.95 (*0-06-021343-4*) HarpC Child Bks.
— Class Action: Reading Labor, Theory & Value. LC 98-8357. (Contestations Ser.). (Illus.). 256p. 1998. pap. 18.95 (*0-8014-8355-7*); text 45.00 (*0-8014-3278-2*) Cornell U Pr.
— Community Without Unity: A Politics of Derridean Extravagance. LC 89-1120. (Post-Contemporary Interventions Ser.). 280p. 1993. pap. text 17.95 (*0-8223-1335-9*) Duke.
— Community Without Unity: A Politics of Derridian Extravagance. LC 89-1120. 277p. 1993. text 49.95 (*0-8223-0732-4*) Duke.
***Corlett, William.** The Door in the Tree. (Maghousquar Ser.: Vol. 2). 2000. 4.99 (*0-7434-1002-5*, Archway) PB.
Corlett, William. Now & Then. 2nd ed. LC 98-148577. 300p. 1998. reprint ed. pap. 11.95 (*1-55583-424-8*) Alyson Pubns.
***Corlett, William.** The Steps up the Chimney. (Maghousquar Ser.). (J). 2000. per. 4.99 (*0-7434-1001-7*, Archway) PB.
— Two Gentlemen Sharing. LC 99-39914. 392p. 1999. pap. 12.95 (*1-55583-527-9*, Pub. by Alyson Pubns) Consort Bk Sales.
Corlett, William & Moore, John. The Buddha Way: An Inner Quest. 156p. (Orig.). 1997. pap. 10.95 (*1-85398-033-1*, Pub. by Ashgrove Pr) Words Distrib.
Corlett, William T. The Medicine-Man of the American Indian & His Cultural Background. LC 75-23699. reprint ed. 47.50 (*0-404-13249-9*) AMS Pr.
Corlew, Robert E. Tennessee: A Short History. LC 80-13553. (Illus.). 652p. 1990. pap. text 18.95 (*0-87049-647-6*) U of Tenn Pr.
Corlew, Robert W. A History of Dickson County, Tennessee. (Illus.). 243p. 1994. reprint ed. lib. bdg. 29.50 (*0-8328-4153-6*) Higginson Bk Co.
Corley-Anderson, Catherine. Jackie Kennedy Onassis: Woman of Courage. (Illus.). 72p. (J). (gr. 4 up). 1996. pap. text 6.95 (*0-8225-9714-4*) Lerner Pub.

C

Corley, Brigitte. Conrad Von Soest: Painter among Merchant Princes. (Illus.). 312p. 1997. text 98.00 (*1-872501-58-3*, Pub. by Harvey Miller) Gordon & Breach.

***Corley, Brigitte.** Painting & Patronage in Cologne 1300-1500. (Illus.). 300p. 1999. text 98.00 (*1-872501-51-6*, Pub. by Harvey Miller) Gordon & Breach.

Corley, Bruce, et al. Second Corinthians: A Bible Study Commentary. 192p. 1989. pap. 6.99 (*0-310-36101-X*, 11023P) Zondervan.

Corley, Corin. Lancelot of the Lake. (World's Classics Ser.). 470p. 1989. pap. 12.95 (*0-19-281756-6*) OUP.

***Corley, Corin.** Lancelot of the Lake. (Oxford World's Classics Ser.). 472p. 1999. pap. 12.95 (*0-19-283793-1*) OUP.

Corley, De Witt C. Corley. Genealogy of Corleys Beginning with Caniel Corley of Bedford County, Virginia, Tracing All Lineal Descendants of His Son Jonathan Cheathem Corley. (Illus.). 222p. 1997. reprint ed. pap. 34.00 (*0-8328-8054-X*); reprint ed. lib. bdg. 44.00 (*0-8328-8053-1*) Higginson Bk Co.

Corley, Donald. Haunted Jester. LC 79-106279. (Short Story Index Reprint Ser.). 1977. 20.95 (*0-8369-3317-6*) Ayer.

— House of Lost Identity: Tales & Drawings. LC 73-106280. (Short Story Index Reprint Ser.). 1977. reprint ed. 23.95 (*0-8369-4007-5*) Ayer.

Corley, Felix, ed. Religion in the Soviet Union: An Archival Reader. (Illus.). 352p. (C). 1996. text 55.00 (*0-8147-1539-7*) NYU Pr.

Corley, Florence F. Confederate City, Augusta, Georgia 1860-1865. LC 95-25410. (Illus.). 130p. 1995. reprint ed. 35.00 (*0-87152-494-5*) Richmond Cty Hist Soc.

***Corley, Gianetta.** Older People & Their Needs, 1. 1999. pap. text 39.95 (*1-86156-083-4*) Whurr Pub.

Corley, Hugh. Organic Small Farming. Bargyla & Rateaver, Gylver, eds. LC 74-33122. (Conservation Gardening & Farming Ser.: Ser. C). (C). 1975. reprint ed. pap. 35.00 (*0-9600698-4-4*) Rateavers.

Corley, Jane. Texas Judge Reviews. 532p. 1997. pap. 99.00 (*1-58012-014-8*) James Pub Santa Ana.

Corley, Kathleen. Private Women, Public Meals: Social Conflict in the Synoptic Tradition. LC 93-5702. 240p. 1993. 19.95 (*1-56563-003-3*) Hendrickson MA.

Corley, Maria. Choices. 224p. 1996. pap. 4.99 (*0-7860-0245-X*, Pinncle Kensgtn) Kensgtn Pub Corp.

Corley, Mary A., jt. auth. see Coyle, Joseph M.

Corley, Mary Ann & Hancock, Charles. Speak English!, Text 3. (Illus.). 96p. (Orig.). 1992. pap. text 7.95 (*0-8325-0510-2*, Natl Textbk Co) NTC Contemp Pub Co.

Corley, Mary Ann & Smallwood, Betty. Speak English!, Text 2. (Illus.). 96p. (Orig.). 1992. pap. 7.95 (*0-8325-0506-4*, Natl Textbk Co) NTC Contemp Pub Co.

— Speak English!, Wkbk. 2. (Illus.). 72p. (Orig.). 1994. pap. 7.95 (*0-8325-0507-2*, Natl Textbk Co) NTC Contemp Pub Co.

Corley, Mary Ann & Steurer, Stephen. Basic Beginner Book. (Speak English Ser.). (Illus.). 80p. (Orig.). 1993. pap. text 7.95 (*0-8325-0500-5*, Natl Textbk Co) NTC Contemp Pub Co.

Corley, Paula, ed. see Khoury, Robin.

Corley, Robert N. The Legal & Regulatory Environment of Business. 11th ed. LC 98-20992. 572p. 1998. 86.25 (*0-07-365429-9*) McGraw.

Corley, Robert N. & Reed, Lee O. The Legal & Regulatory Environment of Business. 10th ed. (C). 1995. pap., student ed. 27.50 (*0-07-013390-5*) McGraw.

— The Legal & Regulatory Environment of Business: Case Brief. 10th ed. 1995. pap. text. write for info. (*0-07-013340-9*) McGraw.

Corley, Robert N., et al. The Legal & Regulatory Environment of Business. 10th rev. ed. LC 95-11279. 752p. (C). 1995. 84.37 (*0-07-013337-9*) McGraw.

Corley Roberts, Ida M. Rising above It All: A Tribute to the Rowan Slaves of Federal Hill. Strode, William, ed. (Illus.). 184p. 1994. 14.95 (*1-56469-022-9*) Harmony Hse Pub.

Corley, Thomas A. Democratic Despot: A Life a Napoleon III. LC 74-8651. (Illus.). 402p. 1974. reprint ed. lib. bdg. 35.00 (*0-8371-7587-9*, CODC, Greenwood Pr) Greenwood.

Corley, W. A. Paradise Is Full of Bugs. LC 97-5007. (Illus.). 173p. (Orig.). Date not set. 11.95 (*0-9656099-0-1*) Blue Heron Books.

Corley, Winnie. Echoes from the Hills. (C). 1981. lib. bdg. 14.95 (*0-934188-06-8*) Evans Pubns.

— The Tie That Binds. LC 83-61020. (Illus.). 155p. 1983. 14.95 (*0-9611478-0-6*) Evans Pubns.

Corliss. Pascal. Date not set. pap. text, teacher ed. write for info. (*0-314-65445-3*) West Pub.

Corliss, A. W., et al. A Genealogical Record of the Corliss Family of America. (Illus.). 343p. 1993. reprint ed. pap. 54.00 (*0-8328-1379-6*); reprint ed. lib. bdg. 64.00 (*0-8328-1378-8*) Higginson Bk Co.

Corliss, Dennis & Seagraves-Higdon, Kathy. Pascal: Exploring Problem Solving & Program Design. 564p. (C). 1988. mass mkt. 43.75 (*0-314-59360-8*) West Pub.

— Pascal: Exploring Problem Solving & Program Design (HC) 564p. (C). 1988. mass mkt. 45.50 (*0-314-59361-6*) West Pub.

Corliss, G. F., tr. see Klatte, R., et al.

Corliss, J. O. & Patterson, D. J. Progress in Protistology, Vol. 1. (Illus.). 419p. 1986. lib. bdg. 70.00 (*0-948737-01-8*, Pub. by Biopress) Balogh.

— Progress in Protistology, Vol. 2. (Illus.). 390p. 1987. lib. bdg. 70.00 (*0-948737-04-2*, Pub. by Biopress) Balogh.

Corliss, John O. The Ciliated Protozoa: Characterization, Classification & Guide to the Literature. 2nd ed. LC 78-41075. (Illus.). 1979. 203.00 (*0-08-018752-8*, Pub. by Pergamon Repr) Franklin.

Corliss, John O., jt. ed. see Patterson, David J.

Corliss, Julia C. Crossing Borders with Literature of Diversity. 96p. 1999. pap. text 12.95 (*0-926842-81-1*, 3003) CG Pubs Inc.

Corliss, Ralph & Chase, Richard. Backpaddlers Guide to the North Umpqua River, 3 bks., Bk. 1: Soda Springs Dam to Gravel Bin. (Illus.). 50p. (Orig.). 1990. pap., spiral bd. 6.95 (*1-878947-01-X*) Walk Water.

— Backpaddlers Guide to the North Umpqua River, 3 bks., Bk. 2: Gravel Bin to Cable Crossing. (Illus.). (Orig.). 1990. pap., spiral bd. 6.95 (*1-878947-02-8*) Walk Water.

— Backpaddlers Guide to the North Umpqua River, 3 bks., Bk. 3: Cable Crossing to Winchester Dam. (Illus.). (Orig.). Date not set. pap., spiral bd. write for info. (*1-878947-03-6*) Walk Water.

Corliss, Richard. Lolita. (BFI Film Classics Ser.). (Illus.). 72p. 1995. pap. 10.95 (*0-85170-368-2*) Ind U Pr.

***Corliss, Richard.** Talking Pictures. 2000. pap. write for info. (*0-375-75532-2*) Modern Lib NY.

Corliss, Richard. Talking Pictures: Screenwriters in the American Cinema. LC 72-94413. 1985. reprint ed. pap. 13.95 (*0-87951-159-1*, Pub. by Overlook Pr) Penguin Putnam.

Corliss, William R. Anomalies in Geology: Physical, Chemical, Biological. LC 89-90680. (Catalog of Geological Anomalies Ser.). (Illus.). 335p. 1989. 18.95 (*0-915554-23-2*) Sourcebook.

— Biological Anomalies No. I: Humans I. LC 91-68541. (Catalog of Biological Anomalies Ser.). (Illus.). 304p. 1992. 19.95 (*0-915554-26-7*) Sourcebook.

— Biological Anomalies No. II: Humans II. LC 91-68541. (Catalog of Biological Anomalies Ser.). (Illus.). 297p. (C). 1993. 19.95 (*0-915554-27-5*) Sourcebook.

— Carolina Bays, Mima Mounds, Submarine Canyons & Other Topographical Phenomena. LC 87-63408. (Catalog of Geological Anomalies Ser.). (Illus.). 245p. 1988. 17.95 (*0-915554-22-4*) Sourcebook.

— Earthquakes, Tides, Unidentified Sounds & Related Phenomena. LC 83-50781. (Catalog of Geophysical Anomalies Ser.). (Illus.). 214p. 1983. pap. text 16.95 (*0-915554-11-9*) Sourcebook.

— Inner Earth: A Search for Anomalies. LC 90-92347. (Catalog of Geological Anomalies Ser.). (Illus.). 230p. (C). 1991. 18.95 (*0-915554-25-9*) Sourcebook.

— Lightning, Auroras, Nocturnal Lights & Related Luminous Phenomena. LC 82-99902. (Catalog of Geophysical Anomalies Ser.). (Illus.). 248p. 1982. pap. 16.95 (*0-915554-09-7*) Sourcebook.

— Mysterious Universe: A Handbook of Astronomical Anomalies. LC 78-65616. (Illus.). 1979. 19.95 (*0-915554-05-4*) Sourcebook.

— Neglected Geological Anomalies: A Catalog of Geological Anomalies. LC 90-60568. (Illus.). 333p. (C). 1990. 18.95 (*0-915554-24-0*) Sourcebook.

— Rare Halos, Mirages, Anomalous Rainbows & Related Electromagnetic Phenomena. (Catalog of Geophysical Anomalies Ser.). (Illus.). 244p. 1984. 16.95 (*0-915554-12-7*) Sourcebook.

— Science Frontiers: Some Anomalies & Curiosities of Nature. LC 93-92800. 356p. (Orig.). (C). 1994. pap. text 18.95 (*0-915554-28-3*) Sourcebook.

— Stars, Galaxies, Cosmos. LC 87-60007. (Catalog of Astronomical Anomalies Ser.). (Illus.). 246p. 1987. 17.95 (*0-915554-21-6*) Sourcebook.

— Strange Artifacts: A Sourcebook on Ancient Man, Vol. M1. LC 74-75256. (Illus.). 268p. 1974. 16.95 (*0-9600712-2-9*) Sourcebook.

— Strange Artifacts: A Sourcebook on Ancient Man, Vol. M2. LC 74-75256. (Illus.). 275p. 1976. 16.95 (*0-9600712-6-1*) Sourcebook.

— Strange Phenomena: A Sourcebook of Unusual Natural Phenomena, Vol. G2. LC 73-9148. 1974. 16.95 (*0-9600712-5-3*) Sourcebook.

— Strange Planet: A Sourcebook of Unusual Geological Facts, Vol. E1. LC 74-26226. (Illus.). 283p. 1975. ring bd. 9.95 (*0-9600712-3-7*) Sourcebook.

— The Sun & Solar System Debris. LC 86-60231. (Catalog of Astronomical Anomalies Ser.). (Illus.). 300p. 1986. 17.95 (*0-915554-20-8*) Sourcebook.

— Tornadoes, Dark Days, Anomalous Precipitation & Related Weather Phenomena. LC 82-63156. (Catalog of Geophysical Anomalies Ser.). (Illus.). 196p. 1983. 16.95 (*0-915554-10-0*) Sourcebook.

Corliss, William R., compiled by. Biological Anomalies: Mammals II. LC 91-68541. (Catalogue of Anomalies Ser.: Vol. 16). (Illus.). 320p. 1996. 21.95 (*0-915554-31-3*) Sourcebook.

— Biological Anomalies Mammals I: A Catalog of Biological Anomalies. LC 91-68541. (Catalog of Anomalies Ser.: Vol. 15). (Illus.). 292p. (C). 1995. 21.95 (*0-915554-30-5*) Sourcebook.

— Biological Anomalies No. III: Humans III. LC 91-68541. (Catalog of Biological Anomalies Ser.). (Illus.). 206p. 1984. 19.95 (*0-915554-29-1*) Sourcebook.

— Birds: Biological Anomalies. LC 91-68541. (Catalog of Anomalies Ser.: No. 17). (Illus.). 486p. 1998. 27.50 (*0-915554-32-1*) Sourcebook.

Corliss, William R., ed. The Moon & the Planets. LC 85-61380. (Catalog of Astronomical Anomalies Ser.). (Illus.). 380p. 1985. 18.95 (*0-915554-19-4*) Sourcebook.

Corliss, William R. & Holden, John C. Ancient Man: A Handbook of Puzzling Artifacts. LC 77-99243. (Illus.). 1978. 23.95 (*0-915554-03-8*) Sourcebook.

Corlyn, Judith. Young Parents in Public Care: Pregnancy & Parenthood among Young People Looked after by Local Authorities. 200p. 1998. pap. 30.00 (*1-900990-19-9*, Pub. by Natl Childrens Bur) Paul & Co Pubs.

Corm, Georges. Le Proche-Orient Eclate. (FRE.). 559p. 1991. pap. 18.95 (*0-7859-1675-X*, 2070326144) Fr & Eur.

Corma, Arelino, jt. auth. see Wojciechowski, Bohdan W.

Corma, Avelino, jt. auth. see International Congress on Catalysis staff.

Cormac, Grada. Black '47 & Beyond: The Great Irish Famine in History, Economy, & Memory. LC 98-27291. (Princeton Economic History of the Western World Ser.). 272p. 1998. 21.50 (*0-691-01550-3*, Pub. by Princeton U Pr) Cal Prin Full Svc.

Cormaci, April, jt. auth. see Durand, Ian.

Cormack. Charting an Empire. LC 97-14831. 344p. 1997. lib. bdg. 68.00 (*0-226-11606-9*) U Ch Pr.

***Cormack.** Through The Looking Glass: Byzantium Through Britian. (Illus.). 280p. 2000. 79.95 (*0-86078-667-6*) Ashgate Pub Co.

Cormack, jt. auth. see New.

Cormack, Andrew. The Royal Air Force 1935-45. (Men-at-Arms Ser.: No. 225). (Illus.). 48p. pap. 11.95 (*0-85045-966-4*, 9183, Pub. by Ospry) Stackpole.

Cormack, Annabel. Definitions: Implications for Syntax, Semantics, & the Language of Thought. LC 98-28259. (Outstanding Dissertations in Linguistics Ser.). 362p. 1998. 83.00 (*0-8153-3131-2*) Garland.

Cormack, David. Team Spirit: A Management Handbook. 240p. 1989. pap. 9.99 (*0-310-52831-3*) Zondervan.

Cormack, David H. Clinically Integrated Histology. LC 97-26178. 352p. 1997. pap. text 42.95 (*0-7817-1211-4*) Lppncott W & W.

— Essential Histology. LC 92-13416. 448p. 1993. spiral bd. 39.95 (*0-397-51062-4*) Lppncott W & W.

***Cormack, Desmond.** The Research Process in Nursing 4th ed. LC 99-33656. 2000. write for info. (*0-632-05158-2*) Blackwell Sci.

Cormack, Desmond, ed. Developing Your Career in Nursing. 250p. 1990. pap. 34.95 (*0-412-32130-0*, A4882) Chapman & Hall.

Cormack, Desmond F. The Research Process in Nursing. 3rd ed. 432p. 1996. pap. 34.95 (*0-632-04019-X*) Blackwell Sci.

***Cormack, Douglas.** Response to Marine Oil Pollution: Review & Assessment LC 99-21368. (Environmental Pollution Ser.). 1999. write for info. (*0-7923-5674-8*) Kluwer Academic.

Cormack, Eivor, tr. see Edstrom, Vivi.

Cormack, George C. & Lamberty, B. George. The Arterial Anatomy of Skin Flaps. (Illus.). 484p. 1987. text 249.95 (*0-443-03214-9*) Church.

— The Arterial Anatomy of Skin Flaps. 2nd ed. LC 94-5558. (Illus.). 538p. 1994. text 249.00 (*0-443-04567-4*) Church.

Cormack, Ian. He Kupu Arotake: A List of Terms for Education Evaluators: Meaori-English, English-Meaori. LC 96-114809. 111p. 1995. spiral bd. write for info. (*0-478-04914-5*) Manaaki Whenua.

Cormack, Karen Mac, see Mac Cormack, Karen.

Cormack, Lesley B. Charting an Empire. LC 97-14831. 344p. 1997. pap. text 23.95 (*0-226-11607-7*) U Ch Pr.

Cormack, M. A., et al. Reducing Benzodiazepine Consumption. (Recent Research in Psychology Ser.). x, 96p. 1989. 59.95 (*0-387-97035-5*) Spr-Verlag.

Cormack, Malcolm. Champion Animals: Sculptures by Herbert Haseltine. LC 95-52719. (Illus.). 94p. (Orig.). 1997. pap. 14.95 (*0-917046-43-9*) Va Mus Arts.

— A Concise Catalogue of Paintings in the Yale Center for British Art. LC 85-51355. (Illus.). 271p. (Orig.). 1985. 47.50 (*0-930606-48-5*); pap. 22.00 (*0-685-38944-8*) Yale Ctr Brit Art.

— J. M. W. Turner: A Selection of Paintings & Watercolors in the Yale Center for British Art. (Illus.). 17p. (Orig.). 1977. pap. 5.00 (*0-685-59702-4*) Yale Ctr Brit Art.

— Oil on Water: Oil Sketches by British Watercolorists. LC 86-50385. (Illus.). 64p. (Orig.). 1986. pap. 8.00 (*0-930606-52-3*) Yale Ctr Brit Art.

— The Paintings of Thomas Gainsborough. (Illus.). 198p. (C). 1993. pap. text 24.95 (*0-521-38887-2*) Cambridge U Pr.

— Selection II: British Watercolors & Drawings from the Museum's Collection. LC 72-78344. 188p. 1972. pap. 6.50 (*0-685-65902-X*) Mus of Art RI.

— William Blake: Illustrations of the Book of Job. LC 97-29064. (Illus.). 88p. 1997. pap. 21.95 (*0-917046-49-8*) Va Mus Arts.

Cormack, Margaret L. The Hindu Woman. LC 74-6750. 207p. 1974. reprint ed. lib. bdg. 72.50 (*0-8371-7557-7*, COHW, Greenwood Pr) Greenwood.

Cormack, Michael J. Ideology. LC 91-42297. 112p. (C). 1992. pap. text 15.95 (*0-472-06491-6*, 06491) U of Mich Pr.

Cormack, Mike. Ideology & Cinematography in Hollywood, 1930-39. LC 93-17636. (Illus.). 170p. 1993. text 49.95 (*0-312-10085-X*) St Martin.

Cormack, R. M., et al, eds. Sampling Biological Populations. (Statistical Ecology Ser.: Vol. 5). 1979. 45.00 (*0-89974-002-2*) Intl Co-Op.

Cormack, R. M. & Ord, J. Keith, eds. Spatial & Temporal Analysis in Ecology. (Statistical Ecology Ser.: Vol. 8). 1979. 45.00 (*0-89974-005-7*) Intl Co-Op.

Cormack, Robert J. & Osborne, Robert D., eds. Discrimination & Public Policy in Northern Ireland. (Illus.). 304p. 1991. 69.00 (*0-19-827519-6*) OUP.

***Cormack, Robin.** Byzantine Art. (Oxford History of Art Ser.). (Illus.). 256p. 2000. pap. 17.95 (*0-19-284211-0*) OUP.

Cormack, Robin. The Byzantine Eye: Studies in Art & Patronage. (Collected Studies: No. CS296). (Illus.). 350p. (C). 1989. lib. bdg. 122.95 (*0-86078-244-1*, Pub. by Variorum) Ashgate Pub Co.

— Painting the Soul: Icons, Death Masks & Shrouds. (Essays in Art & Culture Ser.). (Illus.). 248p. 1997. pap. 24.95 (*1-86189-001-X*, Pub. by Reaktion Bks) Consort Bk Sales.

Cormack, Syd & Orwin, Joanna. Four Generations of Maoridom: The Memoirs of a South Island Kaumatua. 176p. 1997. 29.95 (*1-877133-34-5*, Pub. by Univ Otago Pr) Intl Spec Bk.

Cormack, William S. Revolution & Political Conflict in the French Navy, 1789-1794. LC 95-25116. (Illus.). 357p. (C). 1995. text 64.95 (*0-521-47209-1*) Cambridge U Pr.

Corman. Limitation of Actions, 2 vols., 1. 1991. 165.00 (*0-316-15757-0*) Little.

— Limitation of Actions, 2 vols., 2. 1991. 165.00 (*0-316-15759-7*, Aspen Law & Bus) Aspen Pub.

— Limitation of Actions, 2 vols., Set. 1208p. 1991. 295.00 (*0-316-15761-9*, Aspen Law & Bus) Aspen Pub.

Corman, Avery. Selected from Kramer vs. Kramer. abr. ed. (Writers' Voices Ser.). (Illus.). 64p. 1989. pap. text 3.95 (*0-929631-01-3*, Signal Hill) New Readers.

Corman, Brian. Genre & Generic Change in English Comedy, 1660-1710. 168p. 1993. text 60.00 (*0-8020-2885-3*) U of Toronto Pr.

Corman, Calvin W. Commercial Law: Cases & Materials. 2nd ed. 856p. 1983. 50.00 (*0-316-15746-5*) Little.

Corman, Cid. Aegis: Selected Poems, 1970-1980. LC 82-16923. 112p. 1983. 14.95 (*0-930794-57-5*); pap. write for info. (*0-930794-58-3*) Station Hill Pr.

— And the Word. LC 87-18182. 144p. (Orig.). 1987. pap. 8.95 (*0-918273-34-X*) Coffee Hse.

— At Least. 5.00 (*0-318-11910-2*) Great Raven Pr.

— At Their Word: Essays on the Arts of Language, Vol. 2. LC 76-48282. 220p. 1978. 14.00 (*0-87685-308-4*) Black Sparrow.

— At Their Word: Essays on the Arts of Language, Vol. 2. LC 76-48282. Vol. 2. 220p. 1978. pap. 10.00 (*0-87685-307-6*) Black Sparrow.

— At Their Word: Essays on the Arts of Language, Vol. 2, signed ed. deluxe ed. LC 76-48282. 220p. 1978. 17.50 (*0-87685-309-2*) Black Sparrow.

— How - Now. Daniel, Darrin, ed. (Spike Ser.: No. 6). (Illus.). 108p. (Orig.). 1995. pap. 10.00 (*1-885089-03-1*) Cityful Pr.

— Livingdying. LC 77-103369. 1970. 5.00 (*0-8112-0261-5*, Pub. by New Directions) Norton.

— Livingdying. aut. deluxe limited ed. LC 77-103369. 1970. 25.00 (*0-8112-0508-8*, Pub. by New Directions) Norton.

— Nothing at All. (Poetry New York Pamphlet Ser.: Vol. 11). 16p. 1999. pap. 5.00 (*0-923389-23-7*) Meet Eyes Bind.

— Nothing/Doing. LC 99-31894. 160p. 1999. pap. 13.95 (*0-8112-1425-7*, Pub. by New Directions) Norton.

— The Practice of Poetry: Reconsiderations of Louis Zukofsky's a Test of Poetry. 52p. 1998. pap. 10.00 (*0-9620575-4-1*) Origin Pr.

— Root Song. 96p. (Orig.). 1986. pap. 7.50 (*0-937013-15-3*) Potes Poets.

— Sun Rock Man. LC 73-140033. (Orig.). 1970. pap. 1.75 (*0-8112-0024-8*, NDP318, Pub. by New Directions) Norton.

— Together. 28p. 1999. pap. 10.00 (*1-929048-00-9*) Longhouse Pubs.

— Tributary. Briet, Philippe, ed. LC 96-86334. (Illus.). 64p. (Orig.). (C). 1997. pap. text 10.00 (*0-9646466-2-5*) Edgewise Pr.

— Word for Word: Essays on the Arts of Language, Vol.I, Vol. I. LC 76-48282. 169p. 1977. pap. 10.00 (*0-87685-275-4*) Black Sparrow.

Corman, Cid & Santoka. Walking into the Wind: Poems by Santoka - Versions of Cid Corman. LC 87-71413. (Illus.). 142p. pap. 15.00 (*0-932274-41-2*) Cadmus Eds.

Corman, Cid, ed. see Arnold, Bob.

Corman, Cid, ed. see Niedecker, Lorine.

Corman, Cid, tr. see Basho, Matsu.

Corman, Cid, tr. see Basho, Matsu, et al.

Corman, Cid, tr. see Cohen, Marcel.

Corman, Cid, tr. see Kusano, Shimpei.

Corman, Cid, tr. & intro. see Buson, et al.

Corman, Cid, tr. & pref. see Basho, Matsu, et al.

Corman, Clifford L. & Trevino, Esther. Eukee the Jumpy Jumpy Elephant. LC 95-8308. (Illus.). 22p. (J). (ps-3). 1995. 15.00 (*0-9621629-8-1*) Spec Pr FL.

Corman, Dick. Apple & Eve. LC 96-71659. 270p. (Orig.). 1996. mass mkt. 9.95 (*0-9655749-1-1*) Dume Pub.

— Zoo Savers. LC 96-71658. 248p. (Orig.). 1996. mass mkt. 9.95 (*0-9655749-0-3*) Dume Pub.

Corman, James W. Materialism & Sensations. LC 75-151570. 366p. reprint ed. pap. 113.50 (*0-608-30606-1*, 202199000024) Bks Demand.

Corman, Joel & Lussier, Robert N. Small Business Management: A Planning Approach. LC 95-21713. 464p. (C). 1995. text 64.95 (*0-256-14517-2*, Irwn Prfssnl) McGraw-Hill Prof.

Corman, Marvin. Colon & Rectal Surgery. 3rd ed. (Illus.). 1100p. 1993. text 195.00 (*0-397-51178-7*) Lppncott W & W.

Corman, Marvin L. Colon & Rectal Surgery. 4th ed. LC 98-3238. 1300p. 1998. text 225.00 (*0-7817-1013-8*) Lppncott W & W.

Corman, Nicole S., tr. see Ingold, Gerard.

Corman, Richard. Glory: Photographs of Athletes. LC 98-54381. (Illus.). 160p. 1999. 45.00 (*0-688-15898-6*, Wm Morrow) Morrow Avon.

Corman, Roger. How I Made a Hundred Movies in Hollywood & Never Lost a Dime. LC 98-4130. (Illus.). 256p. 1998. reprint ed. pap. 14.95 (*0-306-80874-9*) Da Capo.

***Corman, Roger.** How I Made a Hundred Movies in Hollywood & Never Lost a Dime. (Illus.). 320p. 2000. reprint ed. pap. 20.00 (*1-887664-40-8*, Pub. by Midnght Marquee Pr) Koen Bk Distributors.

Cormann, Enzo. Cabale. Schein, Gideon Y., tr. from FRE. 136p. (Orig.). 1985. pap. text 8.95 (*0-913745-09-X*) Ubu Repertory.

Cormany, Christine. Whippets. (Illus.). 160p. 1989. lib. bdg. 11.95 (*0-86622-686-9*, KW179) TFH Pubns.

An Asterisk (*) at the beginning of an entry indicates that the title is appearing for the first time.

— Whippets. (Illus.). 192p. 1994. 9.95 (*0-7938-0182-6*, KW179) TFH Pubns.

Cormany, Michael. Polaroid Man. 1991. 15.95 (*1-55972-069-7*, Birch Ln Pr) Carol Pub Group.

— Polaroid Man. 240p. 1993. reprint ed. mass mkt. 3.99 (*0-8439-3542-1*) Dorchester Pub Co.

— Red Winter. (Orig.). 1989. 14.95 (*0-8184-0497-3*) Carol Pub Group.

— Skin Deep Is Fatal: A New Dan Kruger Detective Novel. 224p. 1992. 15.95 (*1-55972-110-3*, Birch Ln Pr) Carol Pub Group.

Cormary, H., et al. Diccionarios del Saber Moderno: La Pedagogia: Dictionaries of Modern Knowledge; Pedagogy. 2nd ed. (SPA.). 580p. 1980. 59.95 (*0-8288-1398-1*, S35605) Fr & Eur.

Cormeau, Christoph, ed. see Von der Vogelweide, Walther.

Cormen. Introduction to Algorithms. 2nd ed. 2001. 60.00 (*0-07-013151-1*) McGraw.

Cormen, Thomas H., et al. Introduction to Algorithms. (Electrical Engineering & Computer Science Ser.). 500p. 1990. 65.00 (*0-262-03141-8*) MIT Pr.

— Introduction to Algorithms. 768p. (C). 1990. 69.06 (*0-07-013143-0*) McGraw.

— Introduction to Algorithms. 448p. (C). 1991. pap. text 36.25 (*0-07-013144-9*) McGraw.

Cormen, Thomas H., jt. auth. see Leiserson, Charles E.

Cormfeld, Dave L. & Brody, Lawrence. Missouri Estate Planning, Will Drafting & Estate Administration Forms. 1994. suppl. ed. 89.00 (*0-685-74625-9*, MICHIE) LEXIS Pub.

Cormick, G. W., jt. ed. see Chalmers, W. Ellison.

Cormick, Mary P., jt. auth. see Barrett, M. Edgar.

Cormier, jt. auth. see Hackney.

Cormier-Boudreau, Marielle & Gallant, Melvin. A Taste of Acadie. Bauer, Ernest, tr. (Illus.). 186p. 1991. pap. 14.95 (*0-86492-109-8*, Pub. by Goose Ln Edits) Genl Dist Srvs.

Cormier, Christine. Amor, Amor. 128p. 1998. pap. 12.00 (*2-89135-040-5*) Guernica Editions.

Cormier, Doran. Women's Naturopathic Medicine. 1999. pap. text 32.95 (*1-55082-231-4*) Rockport Pubs.

Cormier, Edmond P. The More . . . The Merrier: A Collection of 54 Original Old-Timey Style Fiddle Tunes. LC 98-96742. (Illus.). 84p. 1998. pap. 12.00 (*0-9668020-0-4*) Abundance Ltd.

Cormier, F. P., et al. Vocabulary of Radio & Television: Vocabulaire de la Radio et de la Television. (ENG & FRE.). 31p. 1983. 14.95 (*0-8288-1315-9*, F134401) Fr & Eur.

Cormier, Flora, tr. see Breau-Major, Germaine.

Cormier, Garth. Puddlestamp Records Acoustic Venue Directory, Vol. 1. 418p. 1997. pap. 39.95 (*0-9661375-0-7*); lib. bdg. 69.95 (*0-9661375-1-5*) Puddlestomp.

***Cormier, Harvey.** The Truth Is What Works: William James, Pragmatism & the Seed of Death. LC 99-59829. 176p. 2000. 63.00 (*0-8476-9272-8*); pap. 19.95 (*0-8476-9273-6*) Rowman.

Cormier, Henri. The Humor of Jesus. Heiman, David, tr. from FRE. LC 77-9887. Orig. Title: L Humour De Jesus. 1977. pap. 5.95 (*0-8189-0356-2*) Alba.

***Cormier, Jay.** Heaven Is Like... A Gospel Model for Writing, Preparing & Delivering the... LC 99-56813. 160p. 2000. pap. 12.95 (*1-58051-072-8*) Sheed & Ward WI.

Cormier, Jay. Lord, Hear Our Prayer: Prayer of the Faithful for Sundays, Holy Days, & Ritual Masses. 382p. 1995. text 49.95 (*0-8146-2166-X*) Liturgical Pr.

— New Bells for New Steeples: Communications Strategies. LC 90-62651. 160p. (Orig.). (C). 1990. pap. 9.95 (*1-55612-369-8*) Sheed & Ward WI.

— The Season of Light: Daily Prayer for the Lighting of the Advent Wreath. LC 97-13969. 96p. (Orig.). 1997. pap. 4.95 (*0-8146-2468-5*) Liturgical Pr.

— Seed Sown: Themes & Reflections on the Sunday Readings. 280p. (Orig.). 1996. pap. 29.95 (*1-55612-801-0*) Sheed & Ward WI.

— The Sower's Book: A Workbook & Planning Guide for Homilists & Preachers, Cycle A. 260p. (Orig.). (C). 1989. pap. 19.95 (*1-55612-254-3*) Sheed & Ward WI.

Cormier, Joan, et al. Advanced Digital Logic Concepts. (Illus.). 136p. (Orig.). 1983. pap. text 10.00 (*0-86657-002-0*) Lab-Volt.

Cormier, L. Sherilyn. Couseling Strategies & Interventions. 5th ed. LC 98-29304. 204p. 1998. pap. text 48.00 (*0-205-29347-6*) P-H.

Cormier, L. Sherilyn, et al. Interviewing & Helping Skills for Health Professionals. LC 83-14596. 352p. (C). 1984. pap. text 37.50 (*0-86720-363-3*) Jones & Bartlett.

Cormier, L. Sherilyn, jt. auth. see Hackney, Harold L.

Cormier, Larry. The Captain, the Gypsy & the Giant Bird. Bruni, Mary-Ann S., ed. (Texas Ser.: Vol. 3). (Illus.). 48p. (J). (gr. k-8). 1986. 12.95 (*0-935857-07-9*); pap. write for info. (*0-935857-08-7*) Texart.

Cormier, Louis-Philippe, jt. auth. see Margry, Pierre.

Cormier, Louise S. & Cormier, William H. Interviewing Strategies for Helpers: Fundamental Skills & Cognitive Behavioral Interventions. 4th ed. LC 97-17465. (Counseling Ser.). 681p. 1997. mass mkt. 81.95 (*0-534-34916-1*) Wadsworth Pub.

Cormier, M. J., ed. see International Conference on Chemiluminescence Staf.

Cormier, Michael J. A Second Thought. LC 91-41619. (Publish-a-Book Contest Ser.). (Illus.). 32p. (J). (gr. 1-6). 1992. lib. bdg. 22.83 (*0-8114-3578-4*) Raintree Steck-V.

Cormier, Michel & Michaud, Achille. Richard Hatfield. Ponder, Daphne, tr. 253p. 1992. pap. 16.95 (*0-86492-117-9*, Pub. by Goose Ln Edits) Genl Dist Srvs.

Cormier, Ramona, ed. International Directory of Philosophy & Philosophers, 1999-2000. 11th ed. 580p. (C). 1999. 110.00 (*1-889680-03-6*) Philos Document.

Cormier, Raymond J. One Heart, One Mind: The Rebirth of Virgil's Hero in Medieval French Romance. LC 73-81571. (Romance Monographs: No. 3). 1973. pap. 28.00 (*84-399-1292-7*) Romance.

Cormier, Robert. After the First Death. 240p. (YA). 1991. mass mkt. 5.50 (*0-440-20835-1*, LLL BDD) BDD Bks Young Read.

Cormier, Robert. After the First Death. 1991. 10.09 (*0-606-04855-3*, Pub. by Turtleback) Demco.

Cormier, Robert. Beyond the Chocolate. (J). 1996. mass mkt. 6.99 (*0-440-91278-4*) BDD Bks Young Read.

— Beyond the Chocolate War. 288p. (YA). (gr. 6 up). 1986. mass mkt. 4.99 (*0-440-90580-X*, LLL BDD) BDD Bks Young Read.

***Cormier, Robert.** Beyond the Chocolate War. (YA). 2000. 19.50 (*0-8446-7140-1*) Peter Smith.

Cormier, Robert. Beyond the Chocolate War: A Novel. 1985. 10.09 (*0-606-02521-9*, Pub. by Turtleback) Demco.

— The Bumblebee Flies Anyway. 256p. (YA). (gr. 5 up). 1991. mass mkt. 4.99 (*0-440-90871-X*, LLL BDD) BDD Bks Young Read.

— The Bumblebee Flies Anyway. (J). 1983. 10.09 (*0-606-03350-5*, Pub. by Turtleback) Demco.

— The Chocolate War. 192p. (YA). (gr. 6 up). 1986. mass mkt. 5.50 (*0-440-94459-7*, LLL BDD) BDD Bks Young Read.

— The Chocolate War. (YA). 1993. mass mkt. 3.99 (*0-440-90032-8*) Dell.

Cormier, Robert. The Chocolate War. 191p. (YA). (gr. 7 up). pap. 4.99 (*0-8072-1428-0*) Listening Lib.

Cormier, Robert. The Chocolate War. (Assessment Packs Ser.). 15p. 1998. pap. text 15.95 (*1-58303-041-7*) Pthways Pubng.

— The Chocolate War. 1974. 10.09 (*0-606-00169-7*, Pub. by Turtleback) Demco.

— The Chocolate War. 1993. reprint ed. lib. bdg. 18.95 (*1-56849-170-0*) Buccaneer Bks.

— Eight Plus One. 208p. (YA). 1991. mass mkt. 4.99 (*0-440-20838-6*, LLL BDD) BDD Bks Young Read.

— Fade. 304p. (YA). 1991. mass mkt. 4.99 (*0-440-21091-7*, YB BDD) BDD Bks Young Read.

— Frenchtown Summer. LC 99-12244. 112p. (J). (gr. 7-12). 1999. 16.95 (*0-385-32704-8*) Dela Pr.

— La Guerra Del Chocolate.Tr. of Chocalate War. (SPA.). (J). 1996. pap. text 12.95 (*1-56014-666-4*) Santillana.

— La Guerra del Chocolate. 1997. 18.05 (*0-606-10437-2*, Pub. by Turtleback) Demco.

***Cormier, Robert.** Heroes. 144p. (J). 2000. mass mkt. 5.50 (*0-440-22769-0*) Dell.

Cormier, Robert. Heroes: A Novel. LC 97-40326. 192p. (YA). (gr. 9). 1998. 15.95 (*0-385-32590-8*) Delacorte.

— I Am the Cheese. (Laurel-Leaf Library Ser.). 224p. (YA). (gr. 7-12). 1991. mass mkt. 4.99 (*0-440-94060-5*, LLL BDD) BDD Bks Young Read.

Cormier, Robert. I Am the Cheese. (Laurel-Leaf Library). (J). 1978. 10.09 (*0-606-01161-7*, Pub. by Turtleback) Demco.

Cormier, Robert. I Have Words to Spend: Reflections of a Small-Town Editor. 224p. (J). (gr. 7 up). 1994. 9.95 (*0-385-31204-0*) Delacorte.

— In the Middle of the Night. 192p. (YA). (gr. 7). 1997. mass mkt. 4.99 (*0-440-22686-4*) Dell.

— In the Middle of the Night. (J). 1997. 10.09 (*0-606-10998-6*, Pub. by Turtleback) Demco.

Cormier, Robert. Middle of the Night. (J). 1995. 19.95 (*0-385-44629-2*) BDD Bks Young Read.

— Other Bells for Us to Ring. 2000. mass mkt. 4.99 (*0-440-22862-X*, LE) Dell.

— Other Bells for Us to Ring. 1990. 9.09 (*0-606-02821-8*, Pub. by Turtleback) Demco.

Cormier, Robert. Robert Cormier. 1982. 17.28 (*0-676-30289-0*) Random.

— Tenderness. 240p. (YA). 1998. mass mkt. 5.50 (*0-440-22034-3*) BDD Bks Young Read.

— Tenderness: A Novel. LC 96-3110. 240p. (YA). 1997. 16.95 (*0-385-32286-0*, Delacorte Pr Bks) BDD Bks Young Read.

— Tunes for Bears. (YA). 1994. mass mkt. 3.99 (*0-440-90103-0*) Dell.

— Tunes for Bears to Dance To. 112p. (YA). 1994. mass mkt. 4.99 (*0-440-21903-5*) Dell.

— Tunes for Bears to Dance To. 1992. 9.09 (*0-606-06831-7*, Pub. by Turtleback) Demco.

Cormier, Robert. We All Fall Down. 208p. (YA). 1993. mass mkt. 5.50 (*0-440-21556-0*) Dell.

Cormier, Robert. We All Fall Down. (J). 1991. 10.09 (*0-606-05687-4*, Pub. by Turtleback) Demco.

— We All Fall Down. large type ed. LC 93-13717. (J). 1993. 16.95 (*1-56054-774-X*) Thorndike Pr.

Cormier, Robert, jt. auth. see Knopp, Malcolm.

Cormier, Robert J. A Faith That Makes Sense: Reflections for Peace, Purpose, & Joy. LC 99-33228. 1999. pap. 17.95 (*0-8245-1817-9*) Crossroad NY.

***Cormier, Robert J.** A Faith That Makes Sense: Reflections for Peace, Purpose & Joy. 240p. 2000. pap. 10.95 (*0-8245-1875-6*, Pub. by Crossroad NY) Natl Bk Netwk.

Cormier, Robin A. Error-Free Writing: A Lifetime Guide to Flawless Business Writing. LC 94-47978. 368p. (C). 1995. pap. text 16.95 (*0-13-303595-6*) P-H.

Cormier, Ruby. Get a Reality Check. 204p. 1997. pap. 13.95 (*1-885877-01-3*) R Cormier.

Cormier, Sherilyn, jt. auth. see Cormier, William H.

Cormier, Sherilyn N. & Hackney, Harold L. The Professional Counselor: A Process Guide to Helping. (Illus.). 352p. (C). 1987. text 27.95 (*0-13-725508-X*) P-H.

Cormier, Sherilyn N., jt. auth. see Cormier, William H.

Cormier, Stephen M. Basic Processes of Learning, Cognition & Motivation. 472p. (C). 1986. text 89.95 (*0-89859-689-0*) L Erlbaum Assocs.

Cormier, Stephen M. & Hagman, Joseph D., eds. Transfer of Learning: Contemporary Research & Applications. (Educational Technology Ser.). 281p. 1987. text 79.95 (*0-12-188950-5*) Acad Pr.

Cormier, Steve, jt. auth. see Collins, Dennis.

Cormier, Steven A. The Siege of Suffolk: The Forgotten Campaign April 11-May 4, 1863. (Virginia Civil War Battles & Leaders Ser.). (Illus.). 445p. 1989. 19.95 (*0-930919-82-3*) H E Howard.

Cormier, Susan M., jt. auth. see Horton, Wesley W.

Cormier, William A. Next Year in Salem: A Chronicle of the Home Front During W. W. II 1940-1945. LC 96-92726. (Illus.). xii, 206p. 1996. 28.50 (*0-9655477-0-1*) New Perth.

Cormier, William H. & Cormier, Sherilyn. Interviewing Strategies for Helpers. 2nd ed. LC 84-19837. (Family Studies). 640p. (C). 1985. pap. 40.00 (*0-534-04416-6*) Brooks-Cole.

Cormier, William H. & Cormier, Sherilyn N. Interviewing Strategies for Helpers - Fundamental Skills & Cognitive Behavioral Interventions. 3rd ed. (Counseling Ser.). 670p. (C). 1990. mass mkt. 52.25 (*0-534-13824-1*) Brooks-Cole.

Cormier, William H., jt. auth. see Cormier, Louise S.

Corn, Alfred Dewitt. Part of His Story. LC 96-50021. 264p. 1997. 24.00 (*0-922811-29-6*) Mid-List.

— The Poem's Heartbeat: A Manual of Prosody. LC 97-5766. (Story Line Writers Guide Ser.). 224p. (Orig.). 1997. pap. 12.00 (*1-885266-40-5*) Story Line.

— Present. LC 96-51671. 112p. 1997. 22.00 (*1-887178-31-7*, Pub. by Counterpt DC) HarpC.

— Present. 112p. 1998. pap. 13.50 (*1-887178-69-4*, Pub. by Counterpt DC) HarpC.

— Stake: Poems (1972-1992) LC 99-16302. 256p. 1999. text 26.00 (*1-58243-024-1*, Pub. by Counterpt DC) HarpC.

Corn, Anne L. & Henderson, Lynnette M., eds. Charting a New Course in Gifted Education Pt. II: Educational Responses to Giftedness, a Special Issue in the "Peabody Journal of Education" 128p. 1998. pap. 20.00 (*0-8058-9846-8*) L Erlbaum Assocs.

— Charting a New Course in Gifted Education Pts. I & II: A Special Issue of the Peabody Journal of Education. 264p. 1997. pap. 40.00 (*0-8058-9971-5*) L Erlbaum Assocs.

Corn, Anne L. & Huebner, Kathleen M. A Report to the Nation: The National Agenda for the Education of Children & Youth with Visual Impairments, Including Those with Multiple Disabilities. LC 98-13630. 1998. pap. 9.95 (*0-89128-319-6*) Am Foun Blind.

Corn, Anne L. & Koenig, Alan J., eds. Foundations of Low Vision: Clinical & Functional Perspectives. 496p. (C). 1996. text 59.95 (*0-89128-941-0*) Am Foun Blind.

***Corn, Anne L. & Rosenblum, L. Penny.** Finding Wheels: A Curriculum for Nondrivers with Visual Impairments for Gaining Control of Transportation Needs. LC 99-39483. (Illus.). 2000. pap. write for info. (*0-89079-827-3*) PRO-ED.

Corn, Charles. The Scents of Eden: A Narrative of the Spice Trade. LC 97-36839. 352p. 1998. 25.00 (*1-56836-202-1*) Kodansha.

— The Scents of Eden: A Narrative of the Spice Trade. 1999. pap. 16.00 (*1-56836-249-8*) Kodansha.

Corn, David. Blond Ghost. (Illus.). 512p. 1994. 27.50 (*0-671-69525-8*) S&S Trade.

— Deep Background. 2nd ed. LC 99-35864. 370p. 1999. text 25.95 (*0-312-20900-2*) St Martin.

Corn, Elaine. Chicken: 150 Great Recipes for All Seasons. LC 98-31672. (Illus.). 280p. 1999. pap. 17.95 (*0-8118-1772-5*) Chronicle Bks.

— Now You're Cooking: Everything a Beginner Needs to Know to Start Cooking Today. LC 94-19208. (Illus.). 320p. 1994. 24.95 (*1-883791-00-6*, Astolat Bks) Harlow & Ratner.

— Now You're Cooking: Everything a Beginner Needs to Know to Start Cooking Today. LC 94-19208. (Illus.). 320p. 1997. reprint ed. pap. 16.95 (*1-883791-05-7*, Astolat Bks) Harlow & Ratner.

***Corn, Elaine.** Now You're Cooking for Company: Everything a Beginner Needs to Know to Have People Over. 318p. 2000. text 25.00 (*0-7881-9090-3*) DIANE Pub.

Corn, Elaine. Now You're Cooking for Company: Everything a Beginner Needs to Know to Have People Over. LC 96-18683. (Illus.). 320p. 1996. 24.95 (*1-883791-03-0*, Astolat Bks) Harlow & Ratner.

Corn, Fred, jt. auth. see Chang, David W.

Corn, Herman, jt. ed. see Marks, Manuel H.

Corn, Ira, Jr. Scalpel. 1984. mass mkt. 3.50 (*0-8217-1371-X*, Zebra Kensgtn) Kensgtn Pub Corp.

— Scalpel. 1985. pap. 3.50 (*0-8217-1682-4*) NAL.

Corn, Jacqueline K. Environment & Health in Nineteenth Century America: Two Case Studies. (American University Studies: History: Ser. IX, Vol. 53). XXI, 308p. 1989. text 50.50 (*0-8204-1009-8*) P Lang Pubng.

***Corn, Jacqueline K.** Environmental Public Health Policy for Asbestos on Schools: Unintended Consequences. LC 99-32020. 141p. 1999. 49.95 (*1-56670-488-X*) Lewis Pubs.

Corn, Jacqueline K. Response to Occupational Health Hazards. 198p. 1992. text 48.95 (*0-442-00488-5*, VNR) Wiley.

Corn, Jacqueline K. Response to Occupational Health Hazards: A Historical Perspective. (Industrial Health & Safety Ser.). 200p. 1992. 65.95 (*0-471-28407-6*, VNR) Wiley.

Corn, John. Factfinders: Village, Town, City. (Fact Finders Ser.). (J). pap. 8.95 (*0-563-37506-X*, BBC-Parkwest) Parkwest Pubns.

Corn, Joseph J. & Horrigan, Brian. Yesterday's Tomorrows: Past Visions of the American Future. (Illus.). 176p. (Orig.). (C). 1996. reprint ed. pap. 24.95 (*0-8018-5399-0*) Johns Hopkins.

Corn, Laura. 52 Invitations to Great Sex: Opening the Mail Will Never Be the Same. 67p. 1998. pap. 29.95 (*0-9629628-9-9*) Park Ave Pubs.

— 52 Invitations to Great Sex: Opening the Mail Will Never Be the Same. deluxe ed. 1999. pap. text 34.95 (*0-9629628-6-4*) Park Ave Pubs.

— 101 Grrreat Quickies. 1997. pap. text 25.95 (*0-9629628-5-6*) Park Ave Pubs.

— 101 Nights of Grrreat Sex: Secret Sealed Seductions for Fun Loving Couples. (Illus.). 210p. 1995. pap. 29.95 (*0-9629628-1-3*) Park Ave Pubs.

— 101 Nights of Grrreat Romance: How to Make Love with Your Clothes On. (Illus.). 420p. 1996. pap. 29.95 (*0-9629628-2-1*) Park Ave Pubs.

— Two Hundred Thirty-Seven Intimate Questions Every Woman Should Ask a Man. 256p. (Orig.). 1991. pap. 9.95 (*0-9629628-0-5*) Park Ave Pubs.

***Corn, Laura.** 237 Intimate Questions Every Woman Should Ask a Man. 2000. pap. 19.95 (*0-9629628-8-0*) Park Ave Pubs.

Corn, M. & Roath, Stuart, eds. Adult T-Cell Leukemia in Japan. (Hematology Reviews & Communications Ser.: Vol. 3, No. 4). 102p. 1990. pap. text 225.00 (*3-7186-4933-0*) Gordon & Breach.

— Current Approaches to Bone Marrow Histopathology. (Hematology Reviews & Communications Ser.: Vol. 3, Nos. 2-3). 114p. 1989. pap. text 255.00 (*3-7186-4974-8*) Gordon & Breach.

— Hematology Reviews & Communications, Vol. 3, No. 1. 88p. 1989. pap. text 182.00 (*3-7186-4935-7*) Gordon & Breach.

Corn, M., ed. see Mauri, C.

Corn, Morton, ed. Handbook of Hazardous Materials. (Illus.). 772p. 1993. text 167.00 (*0-12-189410-X*) Acad Pr.

Corn, Paul E. Our Roots of Faith, Vol. 1. LC 99-94768. xiv, 255p. 1999. pap. 14.00 (*0-9672208-0-7*, 47671) Key Projects.

Corn-Revere, Robert. Unreasonable Access: Another Turn of the Regulatory Spin Cycle. 40p. 1998. pap. 9.95 (*0-937790-59-1*, 4540) Media Institute.

Corn-Revere, Robert, et al. Rationales & Rationalizations: Regulating the Electronic Media. LC 97-70475. 226p. 1997. pap. 15.95 (*0-937790-54-0*, 4480) Media Institute.

Corn, Shirley, jt. auth. see Corn, Si.

Corn, Si & Corn, Shirley. Corn. Our Family Tree Corn Family with Related Families of Barker, Perry, Leonard, Cole, Taylor, Glenn & Lewallen. 449p. 1997. reprint ed. pap. 67.00 (*0-8328-8056-6*); reprint ed. lib. bdg. 77.00 (*0-8328-8055-8*) Higginson Bk Co.

Corn, Tim H., jt. ed. see Montgomery, Stuart A.

Corn, Wanda M. Grant Wood: The Regionalist Vision. LC 83-3514. 184p. reprint ed. pap. 57.10 (*0-7837-3291-0*, 205769300006) Bks Demand.

— The Great American Thing: Modern Art & National Identity, 1915-1935. LC 99-24604. (Illus.). 425p. 1999. 50.00 (*0-520-21049-2*, Pub. by U CA Pr) Cal Prin Full Svc.

***Corn, Wanda M., ed.** Cultural Leadership in America: Art Matronage & Patronage. (Fenway Court Ser.: Vol. 27). (Illus.). 125p. 1998. pap. 24.95 (*0-9648475-5-8*, Pub. by I S Gardner Mus) U Pr of New Eng.

Cornacchia, Lorenzo J., jt. auth. see Bompa, Tudor O.

Cornacchione, Marco. Indian Creek Climbs. (Illus.). 60p. 1998. pap. 9.95 (*0-9657079-4-6*) Sharp End.

Cornago, Johannes. Johannes Cornago: Complete Works. Gerber, Rebecca L., ed. (Recent Researches in Music of the Middle Ages & Early Renaissance Ser.: Vol. RRM15). (Illus.). xxx, 73p. 1984. pap. 35.00 (*0-89579-193-5*) A-R Eds.

Cornall, James. Halifax: South End. LC 98-88254. (Images of America Ser.). 1998. write for info. (*0-7524-1350-3*) Arcadia Publng.

Cornare, Oreste De, see De Cornare, Oreste.

Cornaro, L. Discourses on the Sober Life: How to Live One Hundred Years. (Longevity Ser.). 1991. lib. bdg. 79.95 (*0-8490-4189-9*) Gordon Pr.

Cornaro, Louis. Discourses on the Sober Life: How to Live 100 Years. 72p. 1996. reprint ed. pap. 9.95 (*1-56459-655-9*) Kessinger Pub.

Cornaro, Luigi. Art of Living. 214p. 1998. reprint ed. pap. 19.95 (*0-7661-0208-4*) Kessinger Pub.

— The Art of Living Long. Kastenbaum, Robert J., ed. LC 78-22195. (Aging & Old Age Ser.). (Illus.). 1979. reprint ed. lib. bdg. 18.95 (*0-405-11812-0*) Ayer.

— Discourses on the Sober Life: How to Live 100 Years. 72p. 1996, spiral bd. 10.00 (*0-7873-0223-6*) Hlth Research.

Cornaro, Luigi, jt. auth. see Lessius, Leonard.

Cornatzer, W. E., jt. ed. see Mertz, Walter.

Cornbelth, Katherine & Waugh, Dexter. The Great Speckled Bird: Multicultural Politics & Education Policymaking. 256p. 1995. pap. text 13.00 (*0-312-10824-9*) St Martin.

Cornberg, David. Liquid Mirrors. (ENG.). 68p. 1986. pap. text 8.00 (*1-57833-022-X*) Todd Commns.

— Movable Roots. (ENG.). 80p. 1988. pap. text 8.00 (*1-57833-021-1*) Todd Commns.

Cornblath, Joan. Beyond the Tower: London for Return Travellers. 192p. (Orig.). 1996. pap. 11.95 (*0-89733-432-9*) Academy Chi Pubs.

— Beyond the Tower: London for Return Travellers. LC 93-81356. (Illus.). 210p. (Orig.). 1994. pap. 10.95 (*0-9640203-0-0*) J Cornblath.

Cornbleet, S. Microwave & Geometric Optics. (Techniques of Physics Ser.). (Illus.). 640p. 1994. text 143.00 (*0-12-189651-X*) Acad Pr.

C

— Microwave & Optical Ray Geometry. LC 83-16737. (Illus.). 162p. reprint ed. pap. 50.30 (*0-8357-4314-4*, 2037113000007) Bks Demand.

Cornbleth, Catherine. Curriculum in Context. 225p. 1990. 65.00 (*1-85000-452-8*, Falmer Pr); pap. 26.00 (*1-85000-453-6*, Falmer Pr) Taylor & Francis.

***Cornbleth, Catherine, ed.** Curriculum Politics, Policy, Practice: Cases in Comparative Context. LC 99-43440. (C). 2000. text 54.50 (*0-7914-4567-4*); pap. text 17.95 (*0-7914-4568-2*) State U NY Pr.

Cornbleth, Catherine, ed. An Invitation to Research in Social Education. LC 86-70312. (Bulletin Ser.: No. 77). 138p. (Orig.). 1986. pap. 7.95 (*0-87986-051-0*) Nat Coun Soc Studies.

Cornbleth, Catherine & Waugh, Dexter. The Great Speckled Bird: Multicultural Politics & Education Policymaking. 224p. 1995. pap. 19.50 (*0-8058-8012-7*) L Erlbaum Assocs.

Cornbleth, Catherine, et al. Understanding Teacher Knowledge - In-Use. (Special Studies in Teaching & Teacher Education: No. 6). 63p. (Orig.). (C). 1991. pap. text 10.00 (*0-937033-24-3*) Grad Schl of Educ.

Cornblit, Oscar. Power & Violence in a Colonial City: Oruro from the Mining Renaissance to the Rebellion of Tupac Amaru (1740-1782) (Cambridge Latin American Studies: No. 76). (Illus.). 244p. (C). 1995. text 74.95 (*0-521-44148-X*) Cambridge U Pr.

Corne, Alexander. Future Classics. 1991. 9.98 (*1-55521-725-7*) Bk Sales Inc.

Corne, David. Applied Evolutionary Computation: Solving Industrial & Scientific Optimisation Problems. LC 98-37197. 1999. pap. 64.95 (*3-540-76235-3*) Spr-Verlag.

***Corne, David.** Telecommunications Optimization: Heuristic & Adaptive Computation Techniques. (Illus.). 256p. 2000. text 149.95 (*0-471-98855-3*) Wiley.

Corne, David, ed. see Society for the Study of Artificial Intelligence &.

Corne, Jonathan. Chest X-Ray Made Easy. LC 96-24944. 1997. pap. text 16.95 (*0-443-05194-1*) Church.

Corne, Michele F. American Neptune Pictorial Supplements, Vol. 14. 1992. pap. 3.95 (*0-87577-101-7*, PEMP228, Peabody Museum) Peabody Essex Mus.

Corne, Peter H. Foreign Investment in China: The Administrative Legal System. LC 98-129177. 256p. 1997. pap. 43.50 (*962-209-394-9*, Pub. by HK Univ Pr) Coronet Bks.

— Foreign Investment in China: The Administrative Legal System. LC 96-52231. 1997. 95.00 (*1-57105-049-3*) Transnatl Pubs.

Corne, Shawn, ed. see Martin-Baro, Ignacio.

Cornea, A., jt. auth. see Constantinescu, C.

Corneal, Sherry, jt. auth. see Vondracek, Fred W.

Corneau, Guy. Absent Fathers, Lost Sons: The Search for Masculine Identity. Shouldice, Larry, tr. from FRE. LC 90-53373. (C. G. Jung Foundation Bks.). 208p. (Orig.). 1991. pap. 15.00 (*0-87773-603-0*, Pub. by Shambhala Pubns) Random.

— Lessons in Love: The Transformation of Spirit Through Intimacy. LC 98-20668. 224p. 1999. 22.50 (*0-8050-6024-3*) H Holt & Co.

— Lessons in Love: The Transformation of Spirit Through Intimacy. 320p. 2000. pap. 14.00 (*0-8050-6397-8*, Owl) H Holt & Co.

Cornebise, Alfred E. Art from the Trenches: America's Uniformed Artists in World War I. LC 90-23921. (Military History Ser.: No. 20). (Illus.). 176p. 1991. 50.00 (*0-89096-349-5*) Tex A&M Univ Pr.

— Ranks & Columns: Armed Forces Newspapers in American Wars, 38. LC 92-36605. (Contributions to the Study of Mass Media & Communications Ser.: No. 38). 232p. 1993. 57.95 (*0-313-26628-X*, CFO, Greenwood Pr) Greenwood.

— Soldier-Scholars: Higher Education in the American Expeditionary Forces, 1917-1919. LC 96-84045. (Memoirs Ser.: Vol. 221). (Illus.). 246p. 1977. 25.00 (*0-87169-221-X*, M221-coa) Am Philos.

— The Stars & Stripes: Doughboy Journalism in World War I, 37. LC 83-12863. (Contributions in Military History Ser.: No. 37). (Illus.). 221p. 1984. 55.00 (*0-313-24230-5*, COS/, Greenwood Pr) Greenwood.

— Typhus & Doughboys: The American Polish Typhus Relief Expedition, Nineteen Nineteen to Nineteen Twenty-One. LC 81-70530. (Illus.). 240p. 1983. 29.50 (*0-87413-216-9*) U Delaware Pr.

Corneil, Wayne, jt. ed. see McClellan, Keith.

Corneille. Le Cid. (FRE.). (C). 1984. pap. 7.95 (*0-8442-1984-3*, VF1984-3) NTC Contemp Pub Co.

— Le Cid, Horace, Polyeucte. unabridged ed. (FRE.). pap. 6.95 (*2-87714-152-7*, Pub. by Bookking Intl) Distribks Inc.

— Circe. Clarke, ed. (Exeter French Texts Ser.: No. 71). (FRE.). 254p. Date not set. pap. text 19.95 (*0-85989-301-4*, Pub. by Univ Exeter Pr) Northwestern U Pr.

— Polyeucte. (FRE.). (C). pap. 7.95 (*0-8442-1985-1*, VF1985-1) NTC Contemp Pub Co.

Corneille, et al. Landmarks of French Classical Drama. Bryer, David et al, trs. from FRE. 393p. (Orig.). (C). 1991. pap. write for info. (*0-413-63100-1*, A0542, Methuen Drama) Methn.

Corneille, Birgitta. Guide to Using Math. (Illus.). (J). 1996. pap. 12.95 (*0-590-27050-8*) NAL.

Corneille, Pierre. Attila. 1965. pap. 5.95 (*0-7859-0590-1*, F36030) Fr & Eur.

— Le Cid. 1965. pap. 5.95 (*0-7859-0591-X*, FC1219) Fr & Eur.

— Le Cid. Lapp, John C., ed. & tr. by. (Crofts Classics Ser.). 96p. 1955. pap. text 4.95 (*0-88295-026-6*) Harlan Davidson.

— Le Cid: A Translation in Rhymed Couplets. Cheng, Vincent J., tr. from FRE. LC 85-40877. 208p. 1987. 36.50 (*0-87413-294-0*) U Delaware Pr.

— Le Cid: The Text of the Original Edition, 1637. fac. ed. Nurse, Peter H., ed. LC 79-100489. (Illus.). 183p. 1978. reprint ed. pap. 56.80 (*0-7837-7939-9*, 204769500008) Bks Demand.

— Le Cid: Tragi-Comedie. Margitic, Milorad R., ed. LC 89-6655. (Purdue University Monographs in Romance Languages: Vol. 28). (FRE.). lxxxviii, 302p. 1989. pap. 27.95 (*1-55619-068-9*) J Benjamins Pubng Co.

— Le Cid, Cinna, Polyeuct. 224p. 1996. pap. 15.95 (*0-948230-57-6*, Pub. by Absolute Classics) Theatre Comm.

— The Cid, Cinna, the Theatrical Illusion. Cairncross, John, tr. from FRE. & intro. by. (Classics Ser.). 288p. 1976. pap. 11.95 (*0-14-044312-6*, Penguin Classics) Viking Penguin.

— Cinna. 1965. pap. 3.95 (*0-7859-0592-8*, F35880) Fr & Eur.

— Clitandre ou l'Innocence Delivree. (FRE.). 151p. 1949. pap. 24.95 (*0-7859-5372-8*) Fr & Eur.

— Corneille: Polyeucte. Sayce, R. A., ed. (Bristol French Texts Ser.). (FRE.). 112p. 1949. reprint ed. 16.95 (*0-631-00480-7*) Blackwell Pubs.

***Corneille, Pierre.** Corneille: Three Masterpieces. (Absolute Classics Ser.). 200p. 2000. pap. 20.95 (*1-84002-124-1*) Theatre Comm.

Corneille, Pierre. Epitres. (FRE.). 104p. 1990. 19.95 (*0-7859-1216-9*, 290672422X) Fr & Eur.

— Horace. 1966. pap. 5.95 (*0-7859-0599-5*, FC1213) Fr & Eur.

— The Illusion. Kushner, Tony, tr. from FRE. & adapted by by. LC 94-29131. (TCG Translations Ser.: Vol. 6). 96p. 1994. 22.50 (*1-55936-089-5*); pap. 8.95 (*1-55936-090-9*) Theatre Comm.

— L' Illusion Comique. (Univers des Lettres Bordas Ser.). pap. 5.95 (*0-685-34208-5*, F35900) Fr & Eur.

— L' Illusion Comique. (FRE.). 1987. pap. 10.95 (*0-7859-3135-X*, 2253041572) Fr & Eur.

— L' Imitation de Jesus-Christ. (FRE.). 562p. 1941. pap. 29.95 (*0-7859-5373-6*) Fr & Eur.

— Melite Ou les Fausses Lettres. 147p. 1950. 5.95 (*0-686-54619-9*) Fr & Eur.

— La Mort de Solon: Piece Attribuee a Corneille Par Elisabeth M. Fraser. (FRE.). 136p. 1949. 10.95 (*0-7859-5375-2*) Fr & Eur.

— Nicomede. (FRE.). 202p. 1977. pap. 8.95 (*0-7859-0924-9*, F36134) Fr & Eur.

Corneille, Pierre. Oeuvres Completes. (FRE.). 1970. 59.95 (*0-8288-9169-9*, F35830) Fr & Eur.

— Oeuvres Completes, Tome 1. deluxe ed. (Pleiade Ser.). (FRE.). 1769p. 1980. 76.95 (*2-07-010946-1*) Schoenhof.

— Oeuvres Completes, Tome 2. deluxe ed. (Pleiade Ser.). (FRE.). 82.95 (*2-07-011083-4*) Schoenhof.

— Oeuvres Completes, Tome 3. deluxe ed. (Pleiade Ser.). (FRE.). 1749p. 1987. 88.95 (*2-07-011121-0*) Schoenhof.

— Oeuvres Completes, Vol. 1. deluxe ed. Couton, Georges, ed. (FRE.). 1872p. 1980. 115.00 (*0-7859-3846-X*, 2070109461) Fr & Eur.

— Oeuvres Completes, Vol. 3. Couton, Georges, ed. (FRE.). 1987. lib. bdg. 135.00 (*0-7859-3878-8*) Fr & Eur.

Corneille, Pierre. Polyeucte. 1965. pap. 5.95 (*0-7859-0608-8*, FC1728) Fr & Eur.

— Rodogune. (FRE.). 128p. 1985. pap. 8.95 (*0-7859-4644-6*) Fr & Eur.

— Rodogune: The French Text with a Facing English Translation. Clubb, William G., ed. & tr. by. LC 73-86397. (Regents Continental Drama Ser.). 169p. reprint ed. pap. 52.40 (*0-7837-4657-1*, 204438100002) Bks Demand.

— Sertorius. (FRE.). 160p. 1959. pap. 14.95 (*0-7859-0692-4*, F35960) Fr & Eur.

— Surena, General des Parthes. 248p. 1970. 12.95 (*0-7859-0693-2*, F35970) Fr & Eur.

— Theatre Vol. 1: Melite; La Galerie du Palais. (FRE.). 1968. pap. 19.95 (*0-7859-2963-0*) Fr & Eur.

— Theatre Vol. 2: Clitandre; Medee; Le Cid. (FRE.). 1980. pap. 17.95 (*0-7859-2964-9*) Fr & Eur.

Corneille, Pierre & Brownjohn, Alan. Horace. LC 97-180734. 92p. 1997. pap. 13.95 (*0-946162-57-3*, Pub. by Angel Bks) Dufour.

Corneille, Pierre & Couton, Georges. Oeuvres Completes, Vol. 2. (FRE.). 1984. lib. bdg. 125.00 (*0-7859-3868-0*) Fr & Eur.

Corneille, Pierre, jt. ed. see Margitic, Milorad R.

Corneille, Thomas. Ariadne: A Tragedy in Five Acts. Mandel, Oscar, tr. LC 80-24597. (Illus.). 95p. reprint ed. pap. 27.10 (*0-7837-4948-1*, 2044614) Bks Demand.

Corneilson, Paul, ed. see De Majo, Gian F.

Corneilson, Paul E., jt. auth. see Haar, James.

Cornejo, Miguel Angel. Infinitud Humana; La Grandeza De Los Valores. 1997. pap. text 19.98 (*970-05-0866-8*) Grijalbo Edit.

— Una Metafora Mas (Rustica) 1997. pap. text 14.98 (*968-6210-08-3*) Edit Diana.

— Metaforas y Pergaminos de la Excelencia. (SPA.). 1997. pap. 14.98 (*968-6210-04-0*) Grijalbo Edit.

— Ser Excelente. 1997. pap. text 14.98 (*970-05-0657-6*) Grijalbo Edit.

Cornel-Avendano, Beverly, jt. auth. see Reteguiz, Jo-Ann.

***Cornel West Staff.** Cornel West Reader. 2000. pap. 18.00 (*0-465-09110-5*) Basic.

Cornelia, Mary P. & Tarr, G. Alan, eds. State Supreme Courts: Policymakers in the Federal System, 24. LC 81-13431. (Contributions in Legal Studies: No. 24). (Illus.). 221p. 1982. 62.95 (*0-313-22942-2*, PSC/, Greenwood Pr) Greenwood.

Cornelia, William, jt. auth. see Creer, Margaret.

Cornelio, Fernando. Neuromuscular Diseases During Development. 168p. 68.00 (*0-86196-541-8*, Pub. by J Libbey Med) Bks Intl VA.

***Cornelis, Gustaaf C., et al.** Metadebates on Science: The Blue Book of 'Einsteen Meets Magritte' LC 99-27062. (Einstein Meets Magritte Ser.). 328p. 1999. 156.00 (*0-7923-5762-0*) Kluwer Academic.

Cornelis, Jakob, tr. see Schottelndreier, Jerry.

Cornelis, Jakob, tr. see Stibbe, Max.

Cornelis, Jakob M., tr. see Soesman, Albert.

***Cornelison, Gayle.** The Cay. 43p. 1999. pap. 5.60 (*0-87129-956-9*, C90) Dramatic Pub.

Cornelison, Isaac J. The Relation of Religion to Civil Government in the United States. LC 75-107409. (Civil Liberties in American History Ser.). 1970. reprint ed. lib. bdg. 45.00 (*0-306-71890-1*) Da Capo.

Cornelison, Pam, jt. auth. see Yanak, Ted.

Cornelison, Robert T. The Christian Realism of Reinhold Niebuhr & the Political Theology of Jurgen Moltmann in Dialogue: The Realism of Hope. LC 92-35175. 240p. 1993. text 89.95 (*0-7734-9805-2*) E Mellen.

Cornelisse, Diana G. Remarkable Journey: The Wright Field Heritage in Photographs. 253p. 1991. per. 26.00 (*0-16-033672-4*) USGPO.

— Remarkable Journey: The Wright Field Heritage in Photographs. (Illus.). 215p. 1997. reprint ed. pap. text 40.00 (*0-7881-4721-8*) DIANE Pub.

Cornelissen, Cornelia. Soft Rain: A Story of the Cherokee Trail of Tears. LC 98-10250. 128p. (J). (gr. 3-5). 1998. 14.95 (*0-385-32253-4*) BDD Bks Young Read.

***Cornelissen, Cornelia.** Soft Rain: A Story of the Cherokee Trail of Tears. 128p. 1999. pap. 4.50 (*0-440-41242-0*) Bantam.

Cornelissen, Maarten, et al. PDM Selection Guide: From Needs to Selection; a Business Solution - Guide for the Selection of Product Data Management Systems. 204p. (Orig.). 1995. pap. 115.00 (*90-407-1142-9*, Pub. by Delft U Pr) Coronet Bks.

Cornelius. English-gurkhali Dictionary. (NEP & ENG.). 157p. 59.95 (*0-320-03413-5*) Fr & Eur.

Cornelius. Food Service Careers. 1979. teacher ed. 2.00 (*0-02-664020-1*) Glencoe.

— Food Service Careers. 2nd ed. 1976. student ed. 11.12 (*0-02-663990-4*) Glencoe.

Cornelius, jt. auth. see Luca.

Cornelius, Betty & Silver, Edith. Topics in Math. 1988. spiral bd. 53.00 (*0-88252-156-X*) Paladin Hse.

Cornelius, Betty, jt. auth. see Silver, Edith.

Cornelius, C. S. & Cornelius, S. F. Cornelius: History of the Cornelius Family in America: Historical, Genealogical & Biographical. (Illus.). 292p. 1991. reprint ed. 56.00 (*0-8328-1855-0*); reprint ed. pap. 46.00 (*0-8328-1856-9*) Higginson Bk Co.

Cornelius, Carol. Iroquois Corn in a Culture-Based Curriculum: A Framework for Respectfully Teaching about Cultures. LC 98-14900. (SUNY Series, Social Context of Education & SUNY Series, Teacher Empowerment & School Reform). (Illus.). 288p. (C). 1998. text 65.50 (*0-7914-4027-3*); pap. text 21.95 (*0-7914-4028-1*) State U NY Pr.

Cornelius, Charles E., et al, eds. Advances in Veterinary Science & Comparative Medicine, Vol. 37: Animal Models in Liver Research. (Illus.). 512p. (C). 1993. text 104.00 (*0-12-039237-2*) Acad Pr.

Cornelius, Charles E., jt. ed. see Brandly, C. A.

Cornelius, Chas. S. Cornelius Vol. 2: Containing Supplemental Information & Additions & Corrections to 1929, with Historical & Biographical Sketches. (Illus.). 116p. 1998. reprint ed. pap. 19.00 (*0-8328-8058-2*); reprint ed. lib. bdg. 29.00 (*0-8328-8057-4*) Higginson Bk Co.

Cornelius, Chuck. A Runner's Heart. (Illus.). 138p. (Orig.). 1996. pap. 12.00 (*0-9651241-1-8*) C E Cornelius.

***Cornelius, Deborah.** In Search of the Nation: The New Generation of Youth in Czechoslovakia, 1925-1934. LC 98-74099. 300p. 1998. 42.00 (*0-88033-409-6*, 511, Pub. by East Eur Monographs) Col U Pr.

Cornelius, Diana. A L. I. F. E. Blueprint: Spirituality Designed for the Non-Religious. Date not set. write for info. (*0-9702124-0-2*) One Mind.

Cornelius, Edwin T., Jr. ACT: Accomplishing Advanced Communicative Tasks: Perfecting Communicative Abilities. (New Technology English Ser.: Vol. 11). (Illus.). 247p. 1984. text 8.95 (*0-89209-117-7*); pap. text 6.95 (*0-89209-410-9*) Pace Grp Intl.

— ACT: Accomplishing Advanced Communicative Tasks: Perfecting Communicative Abilities, 12 vols., Set. (New Technology English Ser.: Vol. 11). (Illus.). 247p. 1984. audio 50.00 (*0-89209-118-5*) Pace Grp Intl.

— ACT Interaction. (New Technology English Ser.: Vol. 12). (Illus.). 173p. 1984. text 8.95 (*0-89209-169-X*); pap. text 6.25 (*0-89209-411-7*) Pace Grp Intl.

— ACT Interaction, 8 vols., Set. (New Technology English Ser.: Vol. 12). (Illus.). 173p. 1984. audio 36.00 (*0-89209-162-2*) Pace Grp Intl.

— American Business English, No. 1A. (American Business English (A.B.E.) Satellite Television Program Ser.). (Illus.). 110p. 1987. VHS 60.00 (*0-89209-775-2*) Pace Grp Intl.

— American Business English, No. 1B. (American Business English (A.B.E.) Satellite Television Program Ser.). (Illus.). 110p. 1987. VHS 60.00 (*0-89209-776-0*) Pace Grp Intl.

— American Business English, No. 2A. (American Business English (A.B.E.) Satellite Television Program Ser.). (Illus.). 133p. 1987. VHS 60.00 (*0-89209-777-9*) Pace Grp Intl.

— American Business English, No. 2B. (American Business English (A.B.E.) Satellite Television Program Ser.). (Illus.). 133p. 1987. VHS 60.00 (*0-89209-778-7*) Pace Grp Intl.

— American Business English, No. 3A. (American Business English (A.B.E.) Satellite Television Program Ser.). (Illus.). 161p. 1987. VHS 60.00 (*0-89209-779-5*) Pace Grp Intl.

— American Business English, No. 3B. (American Business English (A.B.E.) Satellite Television Program Ser.). (Illus.). 161p. 1987. VHS 60.00 (*0-89209-780-9*) Pace Grp Intl.

— American Business English, No. 4A. (American Business English (A.B.E.) Satellite Television Program Ser.). (Illus.). 181p. 1987. VHS 60.00 (*0-89209-781-7*) Pace Grp Intl.

— American Business English, No. 4B. (American Business English (A.B.E.) Satellite Television Program Ser.). (Illus.). 181p. 1987. VHS 60.00 (*0-89209-782-5*) Pace Grp Intl.

— American Business English, No. IA. (American Business English (A.B.E.) Satellite Television Program Ser.). (Illus.). 110p. 1987. audio 12.00 (*0-89209-785-X*) Pace Grp Intl.

— American Business English, No. IB. (American Business English (A.B.E.) Satellite Television Program Ser.). (Illus.). 110p. 1987. audio 12.00 (*0-89209-786-8*) Pace Grp Intl.

— American Business English, No. IIA. (American Business English (A.B.E.) Satellite Television Program Ser.). (Illus.). 133p. 1987. audio 12.00 (*0-89209-787-6*) Pace Grp Intl.

— American Business English, No. IIB. (American Business English (A.B.E.) Satellite Television Program Ser.). (Illus.). 133p. 1987. audio 12.00 (*0-89209-788-4*) Pace Grp Intl.

— American Business English, No. IIIA. (American Business English (A.B.E.) Satellite Television Program Ser.). (Illus.). 161p. 1987. audio 12.00 (*0-89209-789-2*) Pace Grp Intl.

— American Business English, No. IIIB. (American Business English (A.B.E.) Satellite Television Program Ser.). (Illus.). 161p. 1987. audio 12.00 (*0-89209-790-6*) Pace Grp Intl.

— American Business English, No. IVA. (American Business English (A.B.E.) Satellite Television Program Ser.). (Illus.). 181p. 1987. audio 12.00 (*0-89209-791-4*) Pace Grp Intl.

— American Business English, No. IVB. (American Business English (A.B.E.) Satellite Television Program Ser.). (Illus.). 181p. 1987. audio 12.00 (*0-89209-792-2*) Pace Grp Intl.

— American Business English, Vol. I. (American Business English (A.B.E.) Satellite Television Program Ser.). (Illus.). 110p. 1987. pap. text 8.00 (*0-89209-750-7*) Pace Grp Intl.

— American Business English, Vol. II. (American Business English (A.B.E.) Satellite Television Program Ser.). (Illus.). 133p. 1987. pap. text 8.00 (*0-89209-751-5*) Pace Grp Intl.

— American Business English, Vol. III. (American Business English (A.B.E.) Satellite Television Program Ser.). (Illus.). 161p. 1987. pap. text 8.00 (*0-89209-752-3*) Pace Grp Intl.

— American Business English, Vol. IV. (American Business English (A.B.E.) Satellite Television Program Ser.). (Illus.). 181p. 1987. pap. text 8.00 (*0-89209-753-1*) Pace Grp Intl.

— American English One, Bk. 1. (American English One Video Ser.). (Illus.). 150p. 1987. pap. text 8.00 (*0-89209-700-0*) Pace Grp Intl.

— American English One, Bk. 2. (American English One Video Ser.). (Illus.). 169p. 1987. pap. text 8.00 (*0-89209-701-9*) Pace Grp Intl.

— American English One, Bk. 3. (American English One Video Ser.). (Illus.). 171p. 1987. pap. text 8.00 (*0-89209-702-7*) Pace Grp Intl.

— American English One, Bk. 4. (American English One Video Ser.). (Illus.). 185p. 1987. pap. text 8.00 (*0-89209-703-5*) Pace Grp Intl.

— American English One, No. 1. (American English One Video Ser.). (Illus.). 150p. 1987. audio 12.00 (*0-89209-709-4*) Pace Grp Intl.

— American English One, No. 1A. (American English One Video Ser.). (Illus.). 150p. 1987. VHS 60.00 (*0-89209-725-6*) Pace Grp Intl.

— American English One, No. 2. (American English One Video Ser.). (Illus.). 150p. 1987. audio 12.00 (*0-89209-710-8*) Pace Grp Intl.

— American English One, No. 2A. (American English One Video Ser.). (Illus.). 169p. 1987. VHS 60.00 (*0-89209-727-2*) Pace Grp Intl.

— American English One, No. 2B. (American English One Video Ser.). (Illus.). 150p. 1987. VHS 60.00 (*0-89209-726-4*); VHS 60.00 (*0-89209-728-0*) Pace Grp Intl.

— American English One, No. 3. (American English One Video Ser.). (Illus.). 150p. 1987. audio 12.00 (*0-89209-711-6*) Pace Grp Intl.

— American English One, No. 3A. (American English One Video Ser.). (Illus.). 171p. 1987. VHS 60.00 (*0-89209-729-9*) Pace Grp Intl.

— American English One, No. 3B. (American English One Video Ser.). (Illus.). 171p. 1987. VHS 60.00 (*0-89209-730-2*) Pace Grp Intl.

— American English One, No. 4. (American English One Video Ser.). (Illus.). 150p. 1987. audio 12.00 (*0-89209-712-4*) Pace Grp Intl.

— American English One, No. 4A. (American English One Video Ser.). (Illus.). 185p. 1987. VHS 60.00 (*0-89209-731-0*) Pace Grp Intl.

— American English One, No. 4B. (American English One Video Ser.). (Illus.). 185p. 1987. VHS 60.00 (*0-89209-732-9*) Pace Grp Intl.

 An Asterisk (*) at the beginning of an entry indicates that the title is appearing for the first time.

— American English One, No. 5. (American English One Video Ser.). (Illus.). 169p. 1987. audio 12.00 (*0-89209-713-2*) Pace Grp Intl.

— American English One, No. 6. (American English One Video Ser.). (Illus.). 169p. 1987. audio 12.00 (*0-89209-714-0*) Pace Grp Intl.

— American English One, No. 7. (American English One Video Ser.). (Illus.). 169p. 1987. audio 12.00 (*0-89209-715-9*) Pace Grp Intl.

— American English One, No. 8. (American English One Video Ser.). (Illus.). 169p. 1987. audio 12.00 (*0-89209-716-7*) Pace Grp Intl.

— American English One, No. 9. (American English One Video Ser.). (Illus.). 171p. 1987. audio 12.00 (*0-89209-717-5*) Pace Grp Intl.

— American English One, No. 10. (American English One Video Ser.). (Illus.). 171p. 1987. audio 12.00 (*0-89209-718-3*) Pace Grp Intl.

— American English One, No. 11. (American English One Video Ser.). (Illus.). 171p. 1987. audio 12.00 (*0-89209-719-1*) Pace Grp Intl.

— American English One, No. 12. (American English One Video Ser.). (Illus.). 171p. 1987. audio 12.00 (*0-89209-720-5*) Pace Grp Intl.

— American English One, No. 13. (American English One Video Ser.). (Illus.). 185p. 1987. audio 12.00 (*0-89209-721-3*) Pace Grp Intl.

— American English One, No. 14. (American English One Video Ser.). (Illus.). 185p. 1987. audio 12.00 (*0-89209-722-1*) Pace Grp Intl.

— American English One, No. 15. (American English One Video Ser.). (Illus.). 185p. 1987. audio 12.00 (*0-89209-723-X*) Pace Grp Intl.

— American English One, No. 16. (American English One Video Ser.). (Illus.). 185p. 1987. audio 12.00 (*0-89209-724-8*) Pace Grp Intl.

— Comprehension. (New Technology English Ser.: Vol. 9). (Illus.). 155p. 1984. text 8.95 (*0-89209-157-6*); pap. text 6.25 (*0-89209-408-7*) Pace Grp Intl.

— Comprehension, Set. (New Technology English Ser.: Vol. 9). (Illus.). 155p. 1984. audio 36.00 (*0-685-09171-6*) Pace Grp Intl.

Cornelius, Edwin T. English 300, Bk. 1, Programs 1-8. large type ed. Ersan, Claire & Bentley, Carlota, eds. (Illus.). 162p. (J). (gr. k-5). 1997. pap. text, student ed. 15.00 (*0-89209-482-6*) Pace Grp Intl.

— English 300, Bk. 2, Programs 9-16. large type ed. Ersan, Claire & Bentley, Carlota, eds. (Illus.). 147p. (J). (gr. k-5). 1997. pap. text, student ed. 15.00 (*0-89209-483-4*) Pace Grp Intl.

— English 300, Bk. 3, Programs 17-24. large type ed. Ersan, Claire & Bentley, Carlota, eds. (Illus.). 139p. (J). (gr. k-5). 1997. pap. text, student ed. 15.00 (*0-89209-484-2*) Pace Grp Intl.

— English 300, Bk. 4, Programs 25-32. large type ed. Ersan, Claire & Bentley, Carlota, eds. (Illus.). 136p. (J). (gr. k-5). 1997. pap. text, student ed. 15.00 (*0-89209-485-0*) Pace Grp Intl.

— English 300, Bk. 5, Programs 33-38. large type ed. Ersan, Claire & Bentley, Carlota, eds. (Illus.). 101p. (J). (gr. k-5). 1997. pap. text, student ed. 15.00 (*0-89209-486-9*) Pace Grp Intl.

Cornelius, Edwin T. E2 Genius, Bk. 1, Lessons 1-10. large type ed. 117p. (YA). 1997. pap. text, student ed. 15.00 (*0-89209-530-X*) Pace Grp Intl.

— E2 Genius, Bk. 2, Lessons 11-20. large type ed. 121p. (YA). 1997. pap. text, student ed. write for info. (*0-89209-531-8*) Pace Grp Intl.

— E2 Genius, Bk. 3, Lessons 21-30. large type ed. 123p. (YA). 1997. pap. text, student ed. 15.00 (*0-89209-532-6*) Pace Grp Intl.

Cornelius, Edwin T., Jr. Interaction. (New Technology English Ser.: Vol. 8). (Illus.). 153p. 1984. text 8.95 (*0-89209-159-2*); pap. text 6.25 (*0-89209-407-9*) Pace Grp Intl.

— Interaction, Set. (New Technology English Ser.: Vol. 8). (Illus.). 153p. 1984. audio 17.00 (*0-89209-160-6*) Pace Grp Intl.

— Interview: Listening Comprehension for the High Intermediate & Advanced Students/Book & Cassette. (English As a Second Language Bk.). (Illus.). 128p. 1981. audio 37.99 (*0-582-79782-9*, 75036) Longman.

— New English Course, 6 bks. Incl. Book 1. Nicholason, Karl. 1979. 4.75 (*0-89285-125-2*); Book 1. Nicholason, Karl. 1979. 6.95 (*0-89285-137-6*); Book 1. Nicholason, Karl. 1979. 2.00 (*0-89285-131-7*); Book 1. Nicholason, Karl. 1979. teacher ed., student ed. 120.00 incl. VHS (*0-89285-119-8*); Book 1. Nicholason, Karl. 1979. audio 18.00 (*0-89285-113-9*); Book 2. Nicholason, Karl. 1979. 4.75 (*0-89285-126-0*); Book 2. Nicholason, Karl. 1979. 6.95 (*0-89285-138-4*); Book 2. Nicholason, Karl. 1979. 2.00 (*0-89285-132-5*); Book 2. Nicholason, Karl. 1979. audio 120.00 (*0-89285-120-1*); Eternal We. Nicholason, Karl. (Orig.). 1979. 4.75 (*0-89285-130-9*); Eternal We. Nicholason, Karl. (Orig.). 1979. 6.95 (*0-89285-142-2*); Eternal We. Nicholason, Karl. (Orig.). 1979. 2.00 (*0-89285-136-8*); Eternal We. Nicholason, Karl. (Orig.). 1979. audio 120.00 (*0-89285-124-4*); Eternal We. Nicholason, Karl. (Orig.). 1979. audio 18.00 (*0-89285-118-X*); Eternal We. Nicholason, Karl. (Orig.). 1979. Book 3. Nicholason, Karl. 1979. 4.75 (*0-89285-127-9*); Book 3. Nicholason, Karl. 1979. 6.95 (*0-89285-139-2*); Book 3. Nicholason, Karl. 1979. 2.00 (*0-89285-133-3*); Book 3. Nicholason, Karl. 1979. audio 120.00 (*0-89285-121-X*); Book 3. Nicholason, Karl. 1979. audio 18.00 (*0-89285-115-5*); Book 4. Nicholason, Karl. 1979. 4.75 (*0-89285-128-7*); Book 4. Nicholason, Karl. 1979. 6.95 (*0-89285-140-6*); Book 4. Nicholason, Karl. 1979. 2.00 (*0-89285-134-1*); Book 4. Nicholason, Karl. 1979. audio 120.00 (*0-89285-122-8*); Book 4. Nicholason, Karl. 1979. audio 18.00 (*0-89285-116-3*); Book 5. Nicholason, Karl. 1979. 4.75 (*0-89285-129-5*); Book 5. Nicholason, Karl. 1979. 6.95 (*0-89285-141-4*); Book 5. Nicholason, Karl. 1979. 2.00 (*0-89285-135-X*); Book 5. Nicholason, Karl. 1979. audio 120.00 (*0-89285-123-6*); Book 5. Nicholason, Karl. 1979. audio 18.00 (*0-89285-117-1*); 1979. pap. text. write for info. (*0-318-51856-2*) ELS Educ Servs.

— NTE (New Technology English) Bk. 1: Handling Social Conventions. (New Technology English Ser.: Vol. 4). (Illus.). 147p. 1984. text 8.95 (*0-89209-109-6*); pap. text 6.25 (*0-89209-403-6*) Pace Grp Intl.

— NTE (New Technology English) Bk. 1: Handling Social Conventions, Set of 6. (New Technology English Ser.: Vol. 4). (Illus.). 147p. 1984. audio 25.00 (*0-89209-113-4*) Pace Grp Intl.

— NTE (New Technology English) Bk. 2: Interacting in Social & Business Settings. (New Technology English Ser.: Vol. 5). (Illus.). 150p. 1984. text 8.95 (*0-89209-110-X*); pap. text 6.25 (*0-89209-404-4*) Pace Grp Intl.

— NTE (New Technology English) Bk. 2: Interacting in Social & Business Settings, 6 cass., Set. (New Technology English Ser.: Vol. 5). (Illus.). 150p. 1984. audio 25.00 (*0-89209-114-2*) Pace Grp Intl.

— NTE (New Technology English) Bk. 3: Expressing & Finding Out Attitudes. (New Technology English Ser.: Vol. 6). (Illus.). 151p. 1984. text 8.95 (*0-89209-111-8*); pap. text 6.25 (*0-89209-405-2*) Pace Grp Intl.

— NTE (New Technology English) Bk. 3: Expressing & Finding Out Attitudes, 6 cass., Set. (New Technology English Ser.: Vol. 6). (Illus.). 151p. 1984. audio 25.00 (*0-89209-115-0*) Pace Grp Intl.

— NTE (New Technology English) Bk. 4: Extending Personal Abilities. (New Technology English Ser.: Vol. 7). (Illus.). 152p. 1984. text 8.95 (*0-89209-112-6*); pap. text 6.25 (*0-89209-406-0*) Pace Grp Intl.

— NTE (New Technology English) Bk. 4: Extending Personal Abilities, 6 cass., Set. (New Technology English Ser.: Vol. 7). (Illus.). 152p. 1984. audio 25.00 (*0-89209-116-9*) Pace Grp Intl.

— NTE Progress & Performance. (New Technology English Ser.: Vol. 10). (Illus.). 249p. 1984. text 8.95 (*0-685-09168-6*); pap. text 6.95 (*0-89209-409-5*) Pace Grp Intl.

— NTE Progress & Performance, 8 cass., Set. (New Technology English Ser.: Vol. 10). (Illus.). 249p. 1984. audio 36.00 (*0-89209-158-4*) Pace Grp Intl.

— PAL (Preliminary Achievement Level) Book 1: Giving Information & Socializing. (New Technology English Ser.: Vol. 1). (Illus.). 148p. 1984. text 8.95 (*0-89209-105-3*); pap. text 6.25 (*0-89209-400-1*) Pace Grp Intl.

— PAL (Preliminary Achievement Level) Book 1: Giving Information & Socializing, 6 cass., Set. (New Technology English Ser.: Vol. 1). (Illus.). 148p. 1984. audio 25.00 (*0-89209-107-X*) Pace Grp Intl.

— PAL (Preliminary Achievement Level) Book 2: Taking an Active Role in Conversations. (New Technology English Ser.: Vol. 2). (Illus.). 151p. 1984. text 8.95 (*0-89209-106-1*); pap. text 6.25 (*0-89209-401-X*) Pace Grp Intl.

— PAL (Preliminary Achievement Level) Book 2: Taking an Active Role in Conversations, 6 cass., Set. (New Technology English Ser.: Vol. 2). (Illus.). 151p. 1984. audio 25.00 (*0-89209-108-8*) Pace Grp Intl.

— PowerTalk, Bk. 1. (PowerTalk Video Ser.). (Illus.). 150p. 1988. pap. text 9.95 (*0-89209-970-4*); audio 12.00 (*0-89209-947-X*); audio 12.00 (*0-89209-948-8*); digital audio 12.00 (*0-89209-946-1*); VHS 59.95 (*0-89209-916-X*); VHS 59.95 (*0-89209-917-8*); VHS 59.95 (*0-89209-918-6*) Pace Grp Intl.

Cornelius, Edwin T. PowerTalk, Bk. 2. (PowerTalk Video Ser.). (Illus.). 133p. 1988. pap. text 9.95 (*0-89209-971-2*); audio 12.00 (*0-89209-950-X*); audio 12.00 (*0-89209-951-8*); digital audio 12.00 (*0-89209-949-6*); VHS 59.95 (*0-89209-919-4*); VHS 59.95 (*0-89209-920-8*); VHS 59.95 (*0-89209-921-6*) Pace Grp Intl.

Cornelius, Edwin T., Jr. PowerTalk, Bk. 3. (PowerTalk Video Ser.). (Illus.). 133p. 1988. pap. text 9.95 (*0-89209-972-0*); audio 12.00 (*0-89209-952-6*); audio 12.00 (*0-89209-953-4*); audio 12.00 (*0-89209-954-2*); VHS 59.95 (*0-89209-922-4*); VHS 59.95 (*0-89209-923-2*); VHS 59.95 (*0-89209-924-0*) Pace Grp Intl.

— PowerTalk, Bk. 4. (PowerTalk Video Ser.). (Illus.). 197p. 1988. pap. 9.95 (*0-89209-973-9*); audio 12.00 (*0-89209-955-0*); audio 12.00 (*0-89209-956-9*); audio 12.00 (*0-89209-957-7*); audio 12.00 (*0-89209-958-5*); VHS 59.95 (*0-89209-925-9*); VHS 59.95 (*0-89209-926-7*); VHS 59.95 (*0-89209-927-5*) Pace Grp Intl.

— Progress & Performance. (New Technology English Ser.: Vol. 3). (Illus.). 125p. 1984. text 8.95 (*0-89209-164-9*); pap. text 6.25 (*0-89209-402-8*); audio 17.00 (*0-89209-165-7*) Pace Grp Intl.

Cornelius, Edwin T., Jr., et al. Magazine U. S. A. (Illus.). 160p. 1984. pap. text 6.95 (*0-89209-269-6*); audio 75.00 (*0-89209-270-X*) Pace Grp Intl.

Cornelius, Edwin T., Jr., jt. auth. see Pace International Research, Inc. Staff.

Cornelius, Ethelwyn G. Food Service Careers. 2nd ed. 1979. text 42.84 (*0-02-664010-4*) Glencoe.

***Cornelius, Gary F.** Corrections Officer Training Manual. LC 99-68952. 280p. 2000. pap. write for info. (*0-89089-700-X*) Carolina Acad Pr.

Cornelius, Gary F. Jails in America: An Overview of Issues. 2nd ed. LC 96-25771. (Illus.). 84p. 1996. pap. 15.95 (*1-56991-053-7*) Am Correctional.

— Stressed Out! Strategies for Working with Stress in Corrections. LC 95-126336. (Illus.). 138p. 1994. pap. 21.95 (*1-56991-010-3*, 257) Am Correctional.

Cornelius, Geoffrey. The Star Lore Handbook: An Essential Guide to the Night Sky. LC 96-28301. 1997. pap. 14.95 (*0-8118-1604-4*) Chronicle Bks.

Cornelius, Geoffrey, jt. auth. see Devereux, Paul.

Cornelius, Georgianna M., jt. auth. see Yawkey, Thomas D.

Cornelius, Helana & Faire, Shoshana. Everyone Can Win. 192p. 1999. per. 12.00 (*0-684-86851-2*) S&S Trade.

Cornelius, Helena. Everyone Can Win: How to Resolve Conflict. 1998. pap. write for info. (*0-7318-0111-3*) Simon & Schuster.

Cornelius, Ian V. Meaning & Method in Information Studies. LC 96-17290. (Information Management & Policy Ser.). 300p. 1996. pap. 39.50 (*1-56750-228-8*) Ablx Pub.

— Meaning & Method in Information Studies. LC 96-17290. (Information Management & Policy Ser.). 300p. 1996. text 73.25 (*1-56750-227-X*) Ablx Pub.

Cornelius, Izak. The Iconography of the Canaanite Gods Reshef & Baal: Late Bronze & Iron Age I Periods (c1500 - 1000BCE) LC 95-110413. (Orbis Biblicus et Orientalis Ser.: Vol. 140). 298p. 1994. text 84.00 (*3-7278-0983-3*, Pub. by Presses Univ Fribourg) Eisenbrauns.

Cornelius, Janet. Constitution Making in Illinois, 1818-1970. rev. ed. LC 72-76864. (Studies in Illinois Constitution Making). 191p. reprint ed. pap. 59.30 (*0-8357-3291-6*, 203951400013) Bks Demand.

Cornelius, Janet D. Slave Missions & the Black Church in the Antebellum South. LC 97-45291. (Illus.). 256p. 1999. text 34.95 (*1-57003-247-5*) U of SC Pr.

— When I Can Read My Title Clear: Literacy, Slavery & Religion in the Antebellum South. LC 90-28086. (Illus.). 228p. (C). 1992. pap. text 16.95 (*0-87249-871-9*) U of SC Pr.

Cornelius, Jeff. Duluth Tour Book: An Illustrated Guide to Historic & Fun Places. (Illus.). 24p. (Orig.). 1997. pap. 6.95 (*1-886028-29-X*) Savage Pr.

— The North Shore Tourbook: An Illustrated Guide. (Illus.). 32p. 1998. pap. 7.95 (*1-886028-31-1*) Savage Pr.

Cornelius, Judy & Eadington, William, eds. Indian Gaming & the Law. 2nd ed. 298p. 1998. reprint ed. pap. 14.95 (*0-942828-42-9*) U of Nev Bur Busn.

— They're Off! Quantitative Studies of Betting on Racing, Lottery, & Sport. 400p. 1998. 39.95 (*0-942828-41-0*) U of Nev Bur Busn.

Cornelius, Judy & Eadington, William R., eds. Finding the Edge: Mathematical & Quantitative Analysis of Gambling. 400p. 1998. 39.95 (*0-942828-40-2*) U of Nev Bur Busn.

Cornelius, Judy, jt. ed. see Eadington, William R.

Cornelius, Judy, jt. ed. see Eadington, William.

Cornelius, Judy A., jt. auth. see Eadington, William R.

Cornelius, Judy A., jt. ed. see Eadington, William R.

Cornelius, Kay. After the Whirlwind. Date not set. pap. write for info. (*0-345-40359-2*, Ballantine) Ballantine Pub Grp.

— Blood on the Land. Date not set. pap. write for info. (*0-345-40358-4*, Ballantine) Ballantine Pub Grp.

***Cornelius, Kay.** Chamique Holdsclaw. (Women Who Win Ser.). (Illus.). 2000. pap. 7.95 (*0-7910-6153-1*) Chelsea Hse.

— Chamique Holdsclaw. LC 00-22720. 2001. 17.95 (*0-7910-5793-3*) Chelsea Hse.

— Frances Marion. (Revolutionary War Leaders Ser.). 2000. 18.95 (*0-7910-5976-6*) Chelsea Hse.

Cornelius, Kay. Love's Gentle Journey, No. 21. (Serenade Saga Ser.). 1985. pap. 2.50 (*0-310-47002-1*, 15555P) Zondervan.

— Twin Willows. 1996. pap. 7.99 (*0-345-40356-8*, Ballantine) Ballantine Pub Grp.

— Twin Willows. 384p. 1999. mass mkt. 5.99 (*0-06-101376-5*, Harp PBks) HarpC.

— The Uncertain Earth. Date not set. pap. write for info. (*0-345-40357-6*, Ballantine) Ballantine Pub Grp.

Cornelius, Larry M., jt. ed. see Lorenz, Michael D.

Cornelius, M., jt. auth. see Melliss, C. L.

Cornelius, Madelaine. Katahdin with Love: An Inspirational Journey along the Appalachian Trail. (Illus.). 172p. 1991. 17.95 (*0-924234-25-3*) Milton Pub.

Cornelius, Martin P., III. Til Death Do Us Part: A Basic Education in Total Health: How to Keep Body & Soul Happily Together. 256p. (Orig.). (C). 1981. pap. 15.00 (*0-9607142-0-0*) Health Ed & Life Exp Res.

Cornelius, Michael, jt. auth. see Bell, Robbie.

Cornelius, Nathalie G. A Semiotic Analysis of Guillaume Apollinaire's Mythology in Alcools, Vol. 17. (Berkeley Insights in Linguistics & Semiotics Ser.). 190p. (C). 1995. text 45.95 (*0-8204-2834-5*) P Lang Pubng.

***Cornelius, Nelarine.** Managing Diversity & Multicultural Workforces E1. 2001. pap. write for info. (*1-86152-585-0*) Thomson Learn.

Cornelius, Nelarine & Maxwell-Plath, Susan. Human Resource Management: A Management Perspective. LC 99-171816. 192p. 1998. pap. 22.99 (*1-86152-150-2*) Thomson Learn.

Cornelius Nepos. Cornelius Nepos. Rolfe, J. C., tr. from LAT. (Loeb Classical Library: No. 467). 366p. 1929. text 18.95 (*0-674-99514-7*) HUP.

Cornelius, Paul F., jt. auth. see Groner, Julius.

Cornelius, Peter K. & Lenain, Patrick, eds. Ukraine Seminar Proceedings. LC 97-775. 1997. write for info. (*1-55775-619-8*) Intl Monetary.

Cornelius, R. M. & Morris, John. Scopes: Creation on Trial. LC 99-70691. 48p. 1999. pap. 3.99 (*0-89051-257-4*) Master Bks.

Cornelius, Randolph R. The Science of Emotion: Research & Tradition in the Psychology of Emotions. LC 95-37946. 260p. (C). 1995. pap. text 34.60 (*0-13-300153-9*) P-H.

Cornelius, Ruth. All Together: A Manual of Cooperative Games. 1950. 3.00 (*0-933061-00-5*) Lentz Peace Res.

Cornelius, S. F., jt. auth. see Cornelius, C. S.

Cornelius, Sarah, jt. auth. see Heywood, Ian.

Cornelius, Stephen. Contribution to the Life History of Black Drum & Analysis of the Commercial Fishery in Baffin Bay, Vol. 11. LC 83-71622. 75p. 1984. pap. 5.00 (*0-912229-07-1*) CK Wildlife Res.

— An Ecological Survey of Alazan Bay, Texas, Vol. 1. LC 83-71623. 160p. 1984. pap. 5.50 (*0-912229-06-3*) CK Wildlife Res.

Cornelius, Steven, jt. auth. see Amira, John.

Cornelius, Steven L. Leaving the Military & Landing on Your Feet. LC 93-28085. (Illus.). 144p. 1993. pap. 14.95 (*0-942963-38-5*) Distinctive Pub.

Cornelius, Temple H. & Marshall, John B. Golden Treasures of the San Juan. LC 61-9435. 235p. 1961. pap. 11.95 (*0-8040-0636-9*) Swallow.

Cornelius, V'ann, jt. auth. see Temko, Florence.

Cornelius, Wayne, et al, eds. Transforming State-Society Relations in Mexico: The National Solidarity Strategy. (Contemporary Perspectives Ser.: No. 6). 364p. (C). 1994. pap. 21.95 (*1-878367-14-5*) UCSD Ctr US-Mex.

Cornelius, Wayne A. America in the Era of Limits: Nativist Reaction to the "New" Immigration. fac. ed. (Research Reports: No. 3). 31p. (Orig.). (C). 1982. pap. 5.00 (*0-935391-02-9*, RR-03) UCSD Ctr US-Mex.

— The Future of Mexican Immigrants in California: A New Perspective for Public Policy. (Research Reports: No. 6). 73p. (Orig.). (C). 1981. ring bd. 5.00 (*0-935391-05-3*, RR-06) UCSD Ctr US-Mex.

— Immigration, Mexican Development Policy & the Future of U. S. - Mexican Relations. (Research Reports: No. 8). 39p. (Orig.). (C). 1981. ring bd. 5.00 (*0-935391-07-X*, RR-08) UCSD Ctr US-Mex.

— Interviewing Undocumented Immigrants: Methodological Reflections Based on Fieldwork in Mexico & the United States. (Research Reports: No. 2). 42p. (Orig.). (C). 1981. ring bd. 5.00 (*0-935391-01-0*, RR-02) UCSD Ctr US-Mex.

— Legalizing the Flow of Temporary Migrant Workers from Mexico: A Policy Proposal. (Research Reports: No. 7). 17p. (Orig.). (C). 1981. ring bd. 5.00 (*0-935391-06-1*, RR-07) UCSD Ctr US-Mex.

— Mexican Migration to the United States: The Limits of Government Intervention. (Research Reports: No. 5). 11p. (Orig.). (C). 1981. pap. 5.00 (*0-935391-04-5*, RR-05) UCSD Ctr US-Mex.

— Mexican Politics in Transition: The Breakdown of a One-Party-Dominant Regime. (Monographs: No. 41). 119p. 1996. pap. 11.95 (*1-878367-29-3*) UCSD Ctr US-Mex.

— The Political Economy of Mexico under de la Madrid: The Crisis Deepens, 1985-1986. (Research Reports: No. 43). 50p. (Orig.). (C). 1986. pap. 5.00 (*0-935391-65-7*, RR-43) UCSD Ctr US-Mex.

— Subnational Politics & Democratization in Mexico. LC 98-54805. (U. S. - Mexico Contemporary Perspectives Ser.). 1999. pap. write for info. (*1-878367-39-0*) UCSD Ctr US-Mex.

Cornelius, Wayne A., ed. Immigration & U. S. - Mexican Relations. (Research Reports: No. 1). 92p. (Orig.). (C). 1979. ring bd. 5.00 (*0-935391-00-2*, RR-01) UCSD Ctr US-Mex.

Cornelius, Wayne A., et al, eds. California's Immigrant Children: Theory, Research, & Implications for Educational Policy. (Contemporary Perspectives Ser.: No. 8). 1995. pap. 21.95 (*1-878367-17-X*, CP-08) UCSD Ctr US-Mex.

— Controlling Immigration: A Global Perspective. xiv , 442p. 1995. 49.50 (*0-8047-2497-0*); pap. 18.95 (*0-8047-2498-9*) Stanford U Pr.

— Mexico's Alternative Political Futures. 468p. 1989. 19.95 (*0-935391-84-3*, MN30C); pap. 11.95 (*0-935391-83-5*, MN-30) UCSD Ctr US-Mex.

Cornelius, Wayne A., et al, intros. Mexican Immigrants & Southern California: A Summary of Current Knowledge. (Research Reports: No. 36). 99p. (Orig.). (C). 1982. ring bd. 5.00 (*0-935391-35-5*, RR-36) UCSD Ctr US-Mex.

— Mexican Immigrants in the San Francisco Bay Area: A Summary of Current Knowledge. (Research Reports: No. 40). 86p. (Orig.). (C). 1982. ring bd. 5.00 (*0-935391-39-8*, RR-40) UCSD Ctr US-Mex.

Cornelius, Wayne A. & Anzaldua, Ricardo, eds. The Report of U. S. Select Commission on Immigration & Refugee Policy: A Critical Analysis. (Research Reports: No. 32). 34p. (Orig.). (C). 1983. pap. 5.00 (*0-935391-31-2*, RR-32) UCSD Ctr US-Mex.

Cornelius, Wayne A. & Bustamante, Jorge A., eds. Mexican Migration to the United States: Origins, Consequences, & Policy Options. (Dimensions of U. S.-Mexican Relations Ser.: Vol. 3). 177p. 1989. pap. 12.50 (*0-935391-92-4*, BC-03) UCSD Ctr US-Mex.

Cornelius, Wayne A. & Kemper, Robert V., eds. Metropolitan Latin America: The Challenge & the Response. LC 77-79867. (Latin American Urban Research Ser.: Vol. 6). 346p. reprint ed. pap. 107.30 (*0-608-14197-6*, 202188100026) Bks Demand.

Cornelius, Wayne A. & Myhre, David, eds. The Transformation of Rural Mexico: Reforming the Ejido Sector. LC 97-42490. 1997. pap. write for info. (*1-878367-31-5*) UCSD Ctr US-Mex.

Cornelius, Wayne A. & Trueblood, Felicity M., eds. Anthropological Perspectives on Latin American Urbanization. LC 73-86706. (Latin American Urban Research Ser.: Vol. 4). (Illus.). 296p. reprint ed. pap. 91.80 (*0-8357-5626-2*, 202188000026) Bks Demand.

— Urbanization & Inequality: The Political Economy of Urban & Rural Development in Latin America. LC 74-83000. (Latin American Urban Research Ser.: Vol. 5). (Illus.). 318p. reprint ed. pap. 98.60 (*0-608-10129-X*, 202187900026) Bks Demand.

C

Cornelius, William J. Swift & Sure: Bringing Certainty & Finality to Criminal Punishment. LC 96-34997. 1997. 22.95 (*1-57105-037-X*) Transnatl Pubs.

Corneliussen, Roger D., jt. auth. see Brostow, Witold.

***Cornell.** Visual Basic. (C). 1998. pap. text 145.00 (*0-13-011935-0*) P-H.

— Whose Right to Bear Arms? 2000. pap. text 11.95 (*0-312-24060-0*) St Martin.

Cornell & Silverman, J., eds. Arithmetic Geometry. LC 98-164766. 370p. 1986. 54.95 (*0-387-96311-1*) Spr-Verlag.

***Cornell, et al.** Avenger's Dossier. 1998. mass mkt. 10.99 (*0-86369-754-2*) Virgin Bks.

Cornell, jt. auth. see Horstmann, Cay S.

Cornell, Al. The Foreshadowed Cross. 96p. 1997. pap. 4.95 (*1-56794-138-9*, C2478) Star Bible.

Cornell, Alan, jt. ed. see Parkes, Geoffrey.

Cornell, Alexander H. International Collaboration in Weapons & Equipment Development & Production by the NATO Allies. (Atlantic Ser.: No. 2). 248p. 1981. lib. bdg. 125.50 (*90-247-2564-X*) Kluwer Academic.

***Cornell, Alice M., ed.** Art as Image: Prints & Promotion in Cincinnati. (Illus.). 296p. 2000. text 49.95 (*0-8214-1335-X*, Ohio U Ctr Intl) Ohio U Pr.

***Cornell, Ann W.** The Power of Focusing. 128p. 1999. 5.98 (*1-56731-297-7*, MJF Bks) Fine Comms.

Cornell, Ann W. Power of Focusing: A Practical Guide to Emotional Self-Healing. LC 95-72225. 120p. 1996. pap. text 12.95 (*1-57224-044-X*) New Harbinger.

Cornell, Brad. Best Texas Icehouses. (Illus.). 228p. 1998. pap. 4.95 (*0-88415-135-2*, 5135) Gulf Pub.

Cornell, Brad & Galles, Julie. The Flow of Matter & Energy Through Systems: A General Science Curriculum. (Illus.). 300p. 1996. ring bd. 35.00 (*0-9653906-0-8*) Harvard-Westlake.

Cornell, Bradford. Corporate Valuation: Tools for Effective Appraisal & Decision Making. LC 92-42519. 350p. 1993. text 65.00 (*1-55623-730-8*, Irwn Prfssnl) McGraw-Hill Prof.

— The Equity Risk Premium: The Long Run Future of the Stock Market. LC 98-51035. (Frontiers in Finance Ser.). 227p. 1999. 59.95 (*0-471-32735-2*) Wiley.

Cornell, Brenda, jt. auth. see Newbold, Bruce.

Cornell, C. A., jt. auth. see Benjamin, Jack.

Cornell, Christine. The Dogon of West Africa, 6 vols., Set. LC 96-18272. (Celebrating the Peoples & Civilizations of Africa Ser.). (Illus.). 24p. (J). (gr. k-4). 1996. lib. bdg. 15.93 (*0-8239-2331-2*, PowerKids) Rosen Group.

— The Zulu of Southern Africa. LC 96-18271. (Celebrating the Peoples & Civilizations of Africa Ser.). (Illus.). 24p. (J). (gr. k-4). 1996. lib. bdg. 15.93 (*0-8239-2333-9*, PowerKids) Rosen Group.

Cornell, Claire P., jt. auth. see Gelles, Richard J.

Cornell Club of Central New York Staff. Cornell Cooks: Recipes & Rememberances of Cornell University. (Illus.). 1995. 14.95 (*0-9644413-0-6*) Cornell Alum Assoc.

Cornell, Dale D. & Erickson, Frances G. Marriage: The Phoenix Contract. 175p. 1990. pap. 22.50 (*0-87527-264-9*) Green.

Cornell Department of Architecture Staff. The Cornell Journal of Architecture Vol. 5: Media of Representation. Goro, Stephanie A. et al, eds. LC 82-641225. (Illus.). 160p. (Orig.). 1996. pap. 30.00 (*0-9652795-0-2*) Cornell Jrnl.

Cornell, Dewey G. Families of Gifted Children. LC 84-3578. (Research in Clinical Psychology Ser.: No. 11). 140p. 1984. reprint ed. pap. 43.40 (*0-8357-1550-7*, 207037300088) Bks Demand.

Cornell, Dewey G., jt. ed. see Benedek, Elissa P.

Cornell, Donald. Ice Told Tales. Rosoff, Barbara, tr. (ENG & FRE., Illus.). 58p. (Orig.). (J). (ps-2). 1991. pap. 4.00 (*0-9620738-1-4*) D Cornell.

Cornell, Drucilla. At the Heart of Freedom: Feminism, Sex, & Equality. LC 98-3548. 240p. 1998. text 42.50 (*0-691-02897-4*, Pub. by Princeton U Pr); pap. text 14.95 (*0-691-02896-6*, Pub. by Princeton U Pr) Cal Prin Full Svc.

***Cornell, Drucilla.** Beyond Accommodation: Ethical Feminism, Deconstruction & the Law. LC 99-37738. 288p. 1999. pap. 19.95 (*0-8476-9269-8*); text 65.00 (*0-8476-9268-X*) Rowman.

— Freedom, Identity & Rights: Selected Essays. 192p. 2000. pap. 18.95 (*0-8476-9791-6*); text 65.00 (*0-8476-9790-8*) Rowman.

Cornell, Drucilla. Hegel & Legal Theory. 336p. (C). 1991. pap. 21.99 (*0-415-90163-4*) Routledge.

— The Imaginary Domain: Abortion, Pornography & Sexual Harrassment. 304p. (C). (gr. 13). 1995. pap. 19.99 (*0-415-91160-5*, B4920) Routledge.

— Transformations: Recollective Imagination & Sexual Difference. 264p. (C). 1993. pap. 19.99 (*0-415-90747-0*, B0259) Routledge.

***Cornell, Drucilla, ed.** Feminism & Pornography. LC 99-57755. (Oxford Readings in Feminism). (Illus.). 600p. 2000. pap. 24.95 (*0-19-878250-0*) OUP.

Cornell, Drucilla, ed. The Philosophy of the Limit. 260p. (Orig.). (C). 1992. pap. 21.99 (*0-415-90239-8*, A4267) Routledge.

Cornell, Drucilla, et al, eds. Deconstruction & the Possibility of Justice. 432p. (C). 1992. pap. 24.99 (*0-415-90304-1*, A4801) Routledge.

Cornell, Drucilla, jt. ed. see Benhabib, Seyla.

Cornell, Edward. Ferguson: Susanna Cornell Ferguson & Her Descendants. (Illus.). 78p. 1995. reprint ed. pap. 16.00 (*0-8328-4780-1*); reprint ed. lib. bdg. 26.00 (*0-8328-4779-8*) Higginson Bk Co.

***Cornell, Erik.** Turkey on the Threshold of the 21st Century: Opportunities, Challenges, Threats. 288p. 1999. 72.00 (*0-7007-1171-6*, Pub. by Curzon Pr Ltd) Paul & Co Pubs.

Cornell, Felix M. & Hoffman, Allan C. American Merchant Seaman's Manual. 6th ed. Hayler, William B., ed. LC 80-25488. (Illus.). 633p. 1981. text 50.00 (*0-87033-267-8*) Cornell Maritime.

Cornell, Francis G. A Measure of Tax Paying Ability of Local School Administrative Units. LC 71-176670. (Columbia University. Teachers College. Contributions to Education Ser.: No. 698). reprint ed. 37.50 (*0-404-55698-1*) AMS Pr.

***Cornell, G. & Jezak, D.** Visual Basic Add-Ins & Wizards: Increasing Software Productivity. 300p. 2000. pap. 39.95 incl. cd-rom (*1-893115-14-3*, Pub. by APress L P) Spr-Verlag.

***Cornell, G., et al.** Modular Forms & Fermat's Last Theorem. 587p. 2000. pap. 39.95 (*0-387-98998-6*) Spr-Verlag.

Cornell, G., tr. see Scharlau, Winfried & Opolka, H.

Cornell, Gary. CGI Programming with Java. 400p. (C). 2002. pap. text 44.95 incl. cd-rom (*0-13-287079-7*) P-H.

— QuickBASIC 4.5. 1991. 24.95 incl. disk (*0-8306-2576-3*); 24.95 incl. disk (*0-8306-2577-1*) McGraw-Hill Prof.

— Teach Yourself Word for Windows Version 6. 1994. pap. 24.95 (*0-07-882010-3*) Osborne-McGraw.

— Visual Basic 5 from the Ground Up. LC 97-156019. 778p. 1997. pap. text 34.99 (*0-07-882349-8*) Osborne-McGraw.

— Visual Basic 6 from the Ground Up. LC 98-228333. 932p. 1998. pap. 34.99 (*0-07-882508-3*) McGraw.

— Visual Basic 3 for Windows Handbook. 736p. 1993. pap. 29.95 (*0-07-881986-5*) McGraw.

Cornell, Gary & Cuthbertson, Joanne. The Visual Basic 4 for Windows 95 Handbook. 4th ed. LC 96-124186. 982p. 1995. pap. text 34.95 (*0-07-882091-X*) Osborne-McGraw.

Cornell, Gary & Hall, Marty. Core Web Programming. 1997. pap. 49.95 incl. cd-rom (*0-614-28519-4*) P-H.

— Core Web Programming with CD-ROM. LC 97-45522. 1328p. (C). 1997. pap. text 49.95 (*0-13-625666-X*) P-H.

Cornell, Gary & Horstmann, Cay S. Core Java 1.1 Vol. 2: Advanced Features. 3rd ed. (Sunsoft Press Java Ser.). 704p. (C). 1997. pap. text 39.95 (*0-13-766965-8*) P-H.

Cornell, Gary & Strain, Troy. Delphi Nuts & Bolts: For Experienced Programmers. Brown, Cindy, ed. 336p. 1995. pap. text 24.95 (*0-07-882136-3*) Osborne-McGraw.

— Visual Basic 4 Nuts & Bolts: For Experienced Programmers. 256p. 1995. pap. text 24.95 (*0-07-882141-X*) McGraw.

Cornell, Gary, et al. Modular Forms & Fermat's Last Theorem. LC 97-10930. 587p. 1997. 49.95 (*0-387-94609-8*) Spr-Verlag.

Cornell, Gary, jt. auth. see Horstmann, Cay S.

Cornell, Gwenda. Azores Cruising Guide. (Illus.). 1993. pap. 26.95 (*0-9517486-2-9*, Pub. by World Cruising) Bluewater Bks.

— Canary Islands Cruising Guide. (Illus.). 1995. pap. 26.95 (*0-9517486-1-0*, Pub. by World Cruising) Bluewater Bks.

— Cruising with Children. abr. ed. (Illus.). 112p. 1992. pap. 16.50 (*0-924486-27-9*) Sheridan.

Cornell, Howard V., jt. ed. see Hawkins, Bradford A.

Cornell, Hugh & Hoveling, Albert. Wheat: Chemistry & Utilization. LC 97-61636. 414p. 1997. text 104.95 (*1-56676-348-7*) Technomic.

Cornell, J. Genealogy of the Cornell Family, Being an Account of the Descendants of Thomas Cornell of Portsmouth, R. I. (Illus.). 468p. 1989. reprint ed. pap. 70.25 (*0-8328-0425-8*); reprint ed. lib. bdg. 78.25 (*0-8328-0424-X*) Higginson Bk Co.

Cornell, J., jt. auth. see Duyckinck, W. C.

Cornell, James, ed. Bubbles, Voids & Bumps in Time: The New Cosmology. (Illus.). 204p. (C). 1992. pap. 18.95 (*0-521-42673-1*) Cambridge U Pr.

Cornell, James & Abney, Russell. Texas Insurance Law Digest. 2nd ed. 1998. pap. write for info. (*1-58012-031-8*) James Pub Santa Ana.

Cornell, James & Gorenstein, Paul, eds. Astronomy from Space: Sputnik to Space Telescope. 264p. 1983. reprint ed. 30.00 (*0-262-03097-7*) MIT Pr.

— Astronomy from Space: Sputnik to Space Telescope. 264p. 1985. reprint ed. pap. text 10.95 (*0-262-53061-9*) MIT Pr.

Cornell, James L. & Abney, Russell T. Cornell's Texas Insurance Law Digest. 1997. pap. 89.98 (*1-58012-015-6*) James Pub Santa Ana.

Cornell, Jane. Lighting Your Home Inside & Out: Design, Select, Install. Gallos, Margaret, ed. LC 95-70917. (Illus.). 176p. 1996. pap. 14.95 (*1-880029-67-7*) Creative Homeowner.

Cornell, Jennifer C. Departures. (Drue Heinz Literature Prize Ser.). 176p. (C). 1995. text 22.50 (*0-8229-3855-3*) U of Pittsburgh Pr.

— Departures. 176p. (C). 1996. pap. 14.95 (*0-8229-5604-7*) U of Pittsburgh Pr.

Cornell, Jim & Matthews, John R. Atlas of the Roman World. (Cultural Atlas Ser.). (Illus.). 240p. 1982. 45.00 (*0-87196-652-2*) Facts on File.

Cornell, Jimmy. Around the World Rally: Thirty-Six World Cruising Skippers Interviewed in the Most Comprehensive Equipment Survey Ever Undertaken. (Illus.). 208p. (Orig.). 1993. pap. 16.50 (*0-924486-47-3*) Sheridan.

— World Cruising Guide: Port Facilities Around the World. (Illus.). 202p. (C). 1995. pap. 39.95 (*0-9517486-5-3*, Pub. by World Cruising) Bluewater Bks.

— World Cruising Handbook. 2nd ed. LC 97-133674. (Illus.). 560p. 1996. 69.95 (*0-07-013396-4*) McGrw-H Intl.

— World Cruising Routes. 4th ed. (Illus.). 512p. 1998. 49.95 (*0-07-013406-5*) Intl Marine.

Cornell, John A. Experiments with Mixtures. 2nd ed. 656p. 1990. 149.95 (*0-471-52221-X*) Wiley.

— How to Apply Response Surface Methodology. rev. ed. (Basic "How to" Ser.: Vol. 8). (Illus.). 82p. 1990. pap. 25.00 (*0-87389-066-3*, T3508) ASQ Qual Pr.

— How to Run Mixture Experiments for Product Quality. rev. ed. (Basic "How to" Ser.: Vol. 5). (Illus.). 96p. 1990. pap. 22.00 (*0-87389-021-3*, T3505) ASQ Qual Pr.

Cornell, John A., jt. auth. see Khuri, Andre I.

Cornell, John C. Cyclotrons & Their Applications: Proceedings of the 14Th International Conference, Cape Town, South Africa, 8-13 October 1995. LC 96-2854. 892p. 1996. write for info. (*981-02-2625-X*) World Scientific Pub.

Cornell, Joseph. Listening to Nature. (Illus.). 96p. 1987. pap. 13.95 (*0-916124-35-5*, ES3) Dawn CA.

— Ocean Animal Clue Game: Six Playful Nature Card Games about Animals & Their Lives. (Illus.). 60p. (YA). (gr. 2 up). 1995. boxed set 11.95 (*1-883220-27-0*) Dawn CA.

— Rainforest Animals Clue Game: Playful Nature Card Games about Animals & Their Lives. (Illus.). 72p. (YA). (gr. 2 up). 1996. boxed set 11.95 (*1-883220-44-0*) Dawn CA.

— Sharing Nature with Children: 20th Anniversary Edition. (Illus.). 176p. 1998. pap. 9.95 (*1-883220-73-4*) Dawn CA.

***Cornell, Joseph.** Sharing Nature with Children II. Orig. Title: Sharing the Joy of Nature. (Illus.). 168p. 1998. pap. 9.95 (*1-883220-87-4*) Dawn CA.

Cornell, Joseph. Sharing the Joy of Nature: Nature Activities for All Ages. (Illus.). 176p. 1989. pap. 9.95 (*0-916124-52-5*, ES4) Dawn CA.

Cornell, Joseph & Deranja, Michael. Journey to the Heart of Nature: A Guided Exploration. (Illus.). 128p. (YA). (gr. 5 up). 1994. pap., student ed. 9.95 (*1-883220-06-8*) Dawn CA.

Cornell, Joseph, jt. auth. see Hauptman, Jodi.

***Cornell, Joseph Barat.** With Beauty Before Me: An Inspirational Guide for Nature Walks. LC 00-9589. (Sharing Nature Pocket Guide Ser.). 2000. write for info. (*1-58469-012-7*) Dawn CA.

Cornell, Joseph Bharat, jt. auth. see Muir, John.

Cornell, Joseph W. Spinoff to Payoff: An Analysis Guide to Investing in Corporate Divestitures. LC 97-13945. 220p. 1997. 50.00 (*0-7863-1204-1*, Irwn Prfssnl) McGraw-Hill Prof.

Cornell, Judith. Drawing the Light from Within: Keys to Awaken Your Creative Power. LC 96-40111. (Illus.). 212p. 1997. pap. 22.95 (*0-8356-0756-9*, Quest) Theos Pub Hse.

— Mandala: Luminous Symbols for Healing. (Illus.). 154p. 1994. pap. 25.95 (*0-8356-0710-0*, Quest) Theos Pub Hse.

***Cornell, Judith.** Travelling the Miracle Highway. 2001. write for info. (*0-688-17079-X*) Morrow Avon.

Cornell, Julien. Conscience & the State. LC 70-147636. (Library of War & Peace; Conscrip. & Cons. Object.). 1973. lib. bdg. 46.00 (*0-8240-0412-4*) Garland.

Cornell, Julien D. The Conscientious Objector & the Law, Conscience & the State: Legal & Administrateive Problems of Conscientious Objectors 1943-1944, 2 vols. (Peace Movement in America Ser.). 264p. 1972. lib. bdg. 31.95 (*0-89198-060-1*) Ozer.

Cornell, Kari A., jt. auth. see Nelson, Libby.

Cornell Laboratory of Ornithology & Interactive Audio Staff. Peterson Field Guide to Western Bird Songs, Vol. 2. (Peterson Field Guide Ser.). 32p. 1992. pap. 35.00 incl. audio (*0-395-51746-X*, 684732) HM.

Cornell Laboratory of Ornithology Staff. Birder's Life List & Diary. Sibley, Steven C., ed. 214p. (Orig.). 1986. spiral bd. 8.25 (*0-938027-00-X*) Crows Nest Bird.

— Birding in the Cayuga Lake Basin. Comar, Mildred C. et al, eds. (Illus.). 108p. (Orig.). 1974. pap. 8.25 (*0-938027-04-2*) Crows Nest Bird.

Cornell, Laura. Here's How. 1996. 11.15 (*0-606-10842-4*, Pub. by Turtleback) Demco.

Cornell, Laura, jt. auth. see Curtis, Jamie Lee.

Cornell, Laura, jt. illus. see Whitney, Brooks.

Cornell, Leelia. Poetry of Life. 1998. pap. 10.49 (*0-9648730-9-5*) Shoe Hse.

Cornell, Margaret, jt. auth. see Belgrave, Robert.

***Cornell, Martyn.** Beer Memorabilia, Vol. 1. 1999. 14.99 (*0-7858-0940-6*) Bk Sales Inc.

Cornell, Mary D., ed. see Hayes, Mary B.

***Cornell, Nancy J.** 1864 Census for Re-Organizing the Georgia Militia. 840p. 2000. 65.00 (*0-8063-1627-6*) Genealog Pub.

Cornell, Pat. Search n Shade. Jacobs, Alan, ed. (Illus.). (J). (gr. 4-9). 1979. pap. text 8.95 (*0-918272-07-6*, 120) Jacobs.

Cornell, Paul. Oh No It Isn't. (New Adventures Ser.). 256p. (Orig.). 1997. mass mkt. 5.95 (*0-426-20507-3*, Pub. by Virgin Bks) London Brdge.

***Cornell, Paul.** Storming of Avalon. (Doctor Who Ser.). 288p. 2000. mass mkt. 6.95 (*0-563-55588-2*, Pub. by BBC Bks) Genl Dist Srvs.

Cornell, Paul, ed. Licence Denied. (Virgin Ser.). (Orig.). 1997. pap. text 7.95 (*0-7535-0104-X*, Pub. by Virgin Bks) London Brdge.

Cornell, Paul, et al. Discontinuity Guide. (Dr. Who Missing Adventures Ser.). 1995. mass mkt. 5.95 (*0-426-20442-5*, Pub. by Virgin Bks) London Brdge.

— New Trek Programme Guide. 1995. mass mkt. 5.95 (*0-86369-922-7*, Pub. by Virgin Bks) London Brdge.

— X-Treme Possibilities. 256p. (Orig.). 1997. mass mkt. 5.95 (*0-7535-0019-1*, Pub. by Virgin Bks) London Brdge.

— X-Treme Possibilities: A Comprehensively Expanded Rummage Through the X-Files. rev. ed. 474p. 1998. mass mkt. 7.95 (*0-7535-0228-3*, Pub. by Virgin Bks) London Brdge.

Cornell, Penny. The Liberated Canvas: A Creative Approach to Canvas Embroidery. 2nd ed. (Illus.). 64p. 1995. reprint ed. pap. 19.95 (*0-9583873-5-4*, Pub. by Triple T Pubng) Quilters Res.

Cornell, R. M. & Schwertmann, U. The Iron Oxides: A Comprehensive Account of a Rapidly Expanding Field. (Illus.). 604p. 1997. 360.00 (*3-527-28576-8*, Wiley-VCH) Wiley.

Cornell, R. Reynolds. Witnessing an Era: Georgette de Montenay & the Emblemes ou Devises Chrestiennes. LC 87-61487. (Illus.). 137p. 1987. lib. bdg. 19.95 (*0-917786-53-X*) Summa Pubns.

Cornell, Regine R., ed. International Colloquium Celebrating the 500th Anniversary of the Birth of Marguerite de Navarre: April 13 & 14, Agnes Scott College. LC 94-74075. (Illus.). 133p. 1995. lib. bdg. 34.95 (*1-883479-05-3*) Summa Pubns.

Cornell, Richard A. Technology in Instruction: Standards for College & University Learning Resources Programs. 2nd ed. 112p. 1988. pap. 13.95 (*0-89240-045-5*) Assn Ed Comm Tech.

Cornell, Richard G. Statistical Methods for Cancer Studies. (Statistics: Textbooks & Monographs: Vol. 51). (Illus.). 496p. 1984. text 165.00 (*0-8247-7169-9*) Dekker.

***Cornell-Richter, Peter.** Georgia O'Keefe & Alfred Stieglitz. 2000. 25.00 (*3-7913-2312-1*, Pub. by Prestel) te Neues.

Cornell, Rkia, tr. see as-Sulami.

Cornell, Robert H., jt. ed. see Cole, Donald B.

Cornell, Ross, jt. auth. see Dudick, Thomas S.

Cornell, Sarah, tr. see Cixous, Helene.

Cornell, Saul. The Other Founders: Anti-Federalism & the Dissenting Tradition in America, 1788-1828. LC 99-13685. 352p. 1999. 55.00 (*0-8078-2503-4*); pap. 19.95 (*0-8078-4786-0*) U of NC Pr.

***Cornell, Saul.** Whose Right to Bear Arms Did the Second Amendment Protect? LC 99-63833. (Illus.). 188p. 2000. text 35.00 (*0-312-22818-X*) St Martin.

Cornell, Stephen. The Return of the Native: American Indian Political Resurgence. 288p. 1990. pap. text 19.95 (*0-19-506575-1*) OUP.

Cornell, Stephen & Kalt, Joseph P., eds. What Can Tribes Do? Strategies & Institutions in American Indian Economic Development. LC 92-54417. (American Indian Hanbook & Manual Ser.: No. 4). 336p. 1992. pap. 15.00 (*0-935626-37-9*) U Cal AISC.

Cornell, Stephen E. Ethnicity & Race: Making Identities in a Changing World. LC 97-4892. (Sociology for a New Century Ser.). 304p. (Orig.). (C). 1997. pap. text 18.95 (*0-7619-8501-8*) Pine Forge.

***Cornell, Svante E.** Small Nations & Great Powers: A Study of Ethnopolitical Conflict in the Caucasus. 288p. 1999. (*0-7007-1162-7*, Pub. by Curzon Pr Ltd) Paul & Co Pubs.

Cornell, T. H., ed. see Jones, Cy K.

Cornell, T. H., ed. see King, Sheila.

Cornell, T. J., jt. auth. see Bowerstock, G. W.

Cornell, T. J., ed. see Momigliano, Arnaldo D.

Cornell, Thomas. Thomas Cornell Paintings: The Birth of Nature. LC 89-64317. 32p. (Orig.). 1990. pap. 15.00 (*0-916606-20-1*) Bowdoin Coll.

Cornell, Tim. Beginnings of Rome: Italy from the Bronze Age to the Punic Wars (circa 1000 to 264 Bc) LC 94-43757. (Routledge History of the Ancient World Ser.). (Illus.). 528p. (C). 1995. pap. 29.99 (*0-415-01596-0*) Routledge.

Cornell, Tim, ed. see University College, London Staff.

Cornell University Libraries Staff. Southeast Asia Catalog. 1981. 780.00 (*0-8161-1329-7*, G K Hall & Co) Mac Lib Ref.

Cornell University, Martin P. Catherwood Library S. Cumulation of the Library Catalog Supplements of the New York State School of Industrial & Labor Relations, First Supplement. 1977. 165.00 (*0-8161-0055-1*, G K Hall & Co) Mac Lib Ref.

Cornell University Medical College Staff. Manual of Rheumatology & Outpatient Orthopedic Disorders: Diagnosis & Therapy. 3rd ed. Pellicci, Paul M. et al, eds. LC 92-49265. (Illus.). 400p. 1993. spiral bd. 35.95 (*0-316-68846-0*) Lppncott W & W.

Cornell University, New York State School of Indus. Library Catalog of the Martin P. Catherwood Library of the New York State School of Industrial & Labor Relations, 12 vols., Set. 1970. 1365.00 (*0-8161-0757-2*, G K Hall & Co) Mac Lib Ref.

— Martin P. Catherwood Library of the New York State School of Industrial & Labor Relations: Cumulation of the Library Catalog Supplements, 9 vols., Set. 1977. suppl. ed. 1625.00 (*0-8161-0022-5*, G K Hall & Co) Mac Lib Ref.

— Third Supplement to the Cumulation of the Library Catalog Supplements of the New York State School of Industrial & Labor Relations, 2 vols. 1979. 240.00 (*0-8161-0260-0*, G K Hall & Co) Mac Lib Ref.

Cornell University, Programs for Employment & Work. A Fighting Chance: New Strategies to Save Jobs & Reduce Costs. Klingel, Sally & Martin, Ann, eds. 146p. 1988. pap. 10.95 (*0-87546-145-X*, ILR Press) Cornell U Pr.

Cornell University, Southeast Asia Program. Directory of the Cornell Southeast Asia Program, 1951-1976. LC 76-379099. (Cornell University, Southeast Asia Program, Data Paper Ser.: No. 103). 88p. reprint ed. pap. 30.00 (*0-608-15443-1*, 202929000059) Bks Demand.

Cornell University Staff. National Labor Relations Board. Nasrallah, Wahib, ed. (Research & Information Guides in Business, Industry, & Economic Institutions Ser.). 300p. Date not set. text 40.00 (*0-8153-0382-3*) Garland.

Cornell University, Summer Seminar Staff. Relativity Theory & Astrophysics: Galactic Structure, (Proceedings of the Cornell University, Summer Seminar, 1965), Vol.

C

An Asterisk (*) at the beginning of an entry indicates that the title is appearing for the first time.

Cornford, Francis M. Before & after Socrates. 144p. (C). 1932. pap. text 16.95 (*0-521-09113-6*) Cambridge U Pr.
— The Origin of Attic Comedy. LC 92-38813. (Ann Arbor Paperbacks Ser.). 344p. 1993. pap. text 16.95 (*0-472-08195-0*, 08195) U of Mich Pr.
— Plato's Cosmology. LC 97-74231. 390p. (C). 1997. reprint ed. lib. bdg. 39.95 (*0-87220-387-5*) Hackett Pub.
— Plato's Cosmology. 2nd ed. LC 97-74231. 390p. (C). 1997. reprint ed. pap. 16.95 (*0-87220-386-7*) Hackett Pub.
— Plato's Timaeus. Piest, Oskar, ed. 144p. (C). 1959. pap. text 6.00 (*0-02-325190-5*, Macmillan Coll) P-H.
— Unwritten Philosophy & Other Essays. LC 68-78120. 159p. reprint ed. pap. 45.40 (*0-608-16439-9*, 2026337) Bks Demand.
Cornford, Francis M., ed. Greek Religious Thought from Homer to the Age of Alexander. LC 79-98637. (Library of Greek Thought: No. 2). reprint ed. 42.50 (*0-404-01734-7*) AMS Pr.
Cornford, Francis M., ed. see Plato.
Cornford, James, jt. ed. see Stubbs, William.
Cornford, L. C. William Ernest Henley. 1972. 59.95 (*0-8490-1302-X*) Gordon Pr.
— William Ernest Henley. LC 72-3679. (English Biography Ser.: No. 31). 1972. reprint ed. lib. bdg. 55.00 (*0-8383-1580-1*) M S G Haskell Hse.
Cornford, Tony, jt. auth. see Avgerou, Chrisanthi.
Cornforth, Chris, et al. Developing Successful Worker Co-Operatives. 256p. (C). 1988. text 48.00 (*0-8039-8076-0*); pap. text 17.95 (*0-8039-8077-9*) Sage.
Cornforth, Fred & Lale, Tim. Ten Who Left: People Who Left the Church & Why. LC 95-36786. 1995. pap. 8.99 (*0-8163-1298-2*) Pacific Pr Pub Assn.
***Cornforth, J.** Country Houses of Britain. 1998. text 50.00 (*0-09-479150-3*, Pub. by Constable & Co) Trafalgar.
***Cornforth, John, ed.** London Interiors: From the Archives of Country Life. (Illus.). 192p. 2000. 60.00 (*1-85410-668-6*, Pub. by Aurum Pr) London Brdge.
Corngold, Sally M., ed. The Full Scope of Retinoscopy. rev. ed. (Introduction to Behavioral Optometry Ser.). 64p. reprint ed. pap. text 18.00 (*0-943599-07-5*) OEPF.
Corngold, Sally M., jt. auth. see Kahn, Howard D.
Corngold, Sally M., ed. see Edelman, Ellis S., et al.
Corngold, Sally M., ed. see Emery, Leonard C.
Corngold, Sally M., ed. see Forrest, Elliott B.
Corngold, Sally M., ed. see Getman, G. N.
Corngold, Sally M., ed. see Groffman, Sidney & Solan, Harold A.
Corngold, Sally M., ed. see Hatfield, Coleman.
Corngold, Sally M., ed. see Hendrickson, Homer H.
Corngold, Sally M., ed. see Lane, Kenneth A.
Corngold, Sally M., ed. see McGraw, Lora G.
Corngold, Sally M., ed. see Miller, Pamela.
Corngold, Sally M., ed. see Miller, Pamela J.
Corngold, Sally M., ed. see Padula, William V.
Corngold, Sally M., ed. see Press, Leonard J., et al.
Corngold, Sally M., ed. see Shankman, Albert L.
Corngold, Sally M., ed. see Skeffington, A. M.
Corngold, Sally M., ed. see Solan, Harold A. & Suchoff, Irwin B.
Corngold, Sally M., ed. see Spache, G. B., et al.
Corngold, Sally M., ed. see Swartwout, J. Baxter.
Corngold, Sally M., ed. see Trachtman, Joseph N.
Corngold, Sally M., ed. see Wunderlich, Ray C.
Corngold, Stanley. Complex Pleasure: Forms of Feeling in German Literature. LC 97-27866. 330p. 1997. 49.50 (*0-8047-2939-5*); pap. 18.95 (*0-8047-2940-9*) Stanford U Pr.
— The Fate of the Self: German Writers & French Theory. LC 85-11292. 279p. 1986. text 57.50 (*0-231-06174-9*) Col U Pr.
— The Fate of the Self: German Writers & French Theory. LC 94-25933. 312p. 1994. pap. text 18.95 (*0-8223-1523-8*) Duke.
Corngold, Stanley & Giersing, Irene. Borrowed Lives. LC 90-44138. (SUNY Series, the Margins of Literature). 196p. (C). 1991. pap. text 18.95 (*0-7914-0672-5*) State U NY Pr.
Corngold, Stanley, ed. & tr. see Kafka, Franz.
Corngold, Stanley, tr. & intro. see Kafka, Franz.
Cornhusker Press Staff, ed. see Mignery, Herb.
Cornhuskers Press Staff, ed. see Mignery, Herb.
Cornia, Giovanni A., et al, eds. Adjustment with a Human Face: Protecting the Vulnerable & Promoting Growth, Vol. I. (Illus.). 344p. 1987. 69.00 (*0-19-828610-4*); pap. text 19.95 (*0-19-828609-0*) OUP.
— Adjustment with a Human Face: Ten Country Case Studies, Vol. 2. (Illus.). 320p. 1988. text 62.00 (*0-19-828611-2*) OUP.
Cornia, Giovanni A. & Danziger, Sheldon, eds. Child Poverty & Deprivation in Industrialized Countries, 1945-1995. LC 96-36784. (Illus.). 444p. 1997. text 89.00 (*0-19-829075-6*) OUP.
Cornia, Giovanni A. & Sipos, Sandor. Children & the Transition to the Market Economy: Safety Nets & Social Policies in Central & Eastern Europe. 279p. 1991. 72.95 (*1-85628-241-4*, Pub. by Avebry) Ashgate Pub Co.
***Cornia, Giovanni Andrea & Paniccia, Renato, eds.** The Mortality Crisis in Transitional Economies. (Wider Studies in Development Economics). (Illus.). 528p. 2000. text 99.00 (*0-19-829741-6*) OUP.
Cornic. Computer Integrated Building Design. (Illus.). 216p. (C). 1995. pap. 49.99 (*0-419-19590-4*, E & FN Spon) Routledge.
Cornick, Delroy L. Auditing in the Electronic Environment: Theory, Practice & Literature. LC 80-81813. 316p. 1981. 29.75 (*0-912338-23-7*); fiche 14.75 (*0-912338-24-5*) Lomond.
***Cornick, Martyn & Crossley, Ceri.** Problems in French History. LC 00-40485. 2000. write for info. (*0-312-23780-4*) St Martin.
Cornick, Martyn & Morris, Peter. The French Secret Services: A Selected Bibliography. LC 93-12239. (International Organizations Ser.: Vol. 6). 160p. (C). 1993. text 54.95 (*1-56000-111-9*) Transaction Pubs.
***Cornick, Matthew S.** Practical Guide to Bankruptcy Law. (Paralegal Ser.). (C). 2000. pap. 32.00 (*0-7668-0437-2*) Delmar.
Cornick, Matthew S. Practical Guide To Family Law. LC 94-46248. (Paralegal). 422p. (C). 1995. mass mkt. 63.95 (*0-314-04451-5*) West Pub.
***Cornick, Nicola.** Lady Polly. large type ed. 320p. 2000. 25.99 (*0-263-16325-3*, Pub. by Mills & Boon) Ulverscroft.
— The Larkswood Legacy. large type ed. 320p. 1999. 25.99 (*0-263-16117-X*, Pub. by Mills & Boon) Ulverscroft.
***Cornick-Seahorn, Janyce.** Veterinary Anesthesia: The Practical Veterinarian. (Illus.). 250p. 2000. pap. 25.00 (*0-7506-7227-7*) Buttrwrth-Heinemann.
Cornick, Tim. Quality Management for Building Design. 200p. 1991. text 61.95 (*0-7506-1225-8*) Buttrwrth-Heinemann.
— Quality Management for Building Design. LC 90-47836. (Butterworth Architecture Management Guides Ser.). (Illus.). 234p. 1990. reprint ed. pap. 72.60 (*0-608-04417-2*, 206519800001) Bks Demand.
Cornie, James A., ed. see Conference on Failure Modes in Composites Staff.
***Cornil, J. M. & Testud, P.** An Introduction to Maple V. Effelterre, T. V., tr. from FRE. (Illus.). 470p. 2000. pap. 36.00 (*3-540-66442-4*) Spr-Verlag.
Cornille, Catherine. The Guru in Indian Catholicism: Ambiguity of Opportunity of Inculturation? (Louvain Theological & Pastoral Mongraphs). 214p. (Orig.). 1992. pap. 25.00 (*0-8028-0566-3*) Eerdmans.
Cornille, Catherine & Neckebrouck, Valeer, eds. A Universal Faith? Peoples, Cultures, Religions, & the Christ. (Louvain Theological & Pastoral Monographs). 198p. (Orig.). 1993. pap. 25.00 (*0-8028-0569-8*) Eerdmans.
Cornilliat, Francois, et al, eds. What Is Literature? France, 1100-1600. LC 91-73983. (Edward C. Armstrong Monographs on Medieval Literature: No. 7). 231p. (Orig.). 1993. pap. 17.95 (*0-917058-84-4*) French Forum.
Cornillier, Pierre. The Survival of the Soul & Its Evolution after Death. 1972. lib. bdg. 250.00 (*0-87968-498-4*) Krishna Pr.
Cornils, B. & Herrmann, W. A., eds. Applied Homogeneous Catalysis with Organometallic Compounds: A Comprehensive Handbook, 2 vols. (Illus.). 1286p. 1996. 695.00 (*3-527-29286-1*, Wiley-VCH) Wiley.
Cornils, Boy & Herrmann, Wolfgang, eds. Aqueous Phase Organometallic Catalysis: Concepts & Application. (Illus.). 632p. 1998. 385.00 (*3-527-29478-3*) Wiley.
***Cornils, Boy, et al.** Catalysis from A to Z: A Concise Encyclopedia. 658p. 2000. 345.00 (*3-527-29855-X*) Wiley.
Corning Museum of Glass Staff. History & Art of Glass Index of Periodical Literature 1956 to 1979. 1982. 150.00 (*0-8161-1409-9*) Mac Lib Ref.
— New Glass Review, Vol. 18. (Illus.). 72p. (Orig.). 1997. pap. 8.50 (*0-87290-140-8*) Corning.
— New Glass Review, Vol. 19. (Illus.). 72p. (Orig.). 1998. pap. 8.50 (*0-87290-141-6*) Corning.
— New Glass Review, Vol. 20. (Illus.). 72p. (Orig.). 1999. pap. 8.50 (*0-87290-145-9*) Corning.
— New Glass Review, Vol. 21. LC 81-641214. (Annual Compendium of Contemporary Glass Made in Previous Calendar Year Ser.). (Illus.). 104p. (Orig.). 2000. pap. 8.50 (*0-87290-147-5*) Corning.
— New Glass Review: Annual Compendium of Contemporary Glass Made in Previous Calendar Year, No. 13. LC 81-641214. (Illus.). 56p. 1992. pap. 2.50 (*0-87290-128-9*) Corning.
— New Glass Review: Annual Compendium of Contemporary Glass Made in Previous Calendar Year, No. 17. LC 81-641214. 72p. 1996. pap. 8.50 (*0-87290-137-8*) Corning.
Corning Staff. History & Art of Glass Index of Periodical Literature, 1980 to 1982. 1984. 175.00 (*0-8161-1482-X*, G K Hall & Co) Mac Lib Ref.
Cornini, Guido. Raphael - The Apartments of Pope Julius II & Pope Leo X. (Illus.). 351p. 1993. 250.00 (*0-00-507512-2*) Treasures Inc.
Cornis-Pope, Marcel, jt. ed. see Bogue, Ronald.
***Cornish, Alison.** Reading Dante's Stars LC 99-39103. (Illus.). 256p. 2000. 25.00 (*0-300-07679-7*) Yale U Pr.
Cornish-Bowden, A. Fundamentals of Enzyme Kinetics. 2nd rev. ed. 350p. (Orig.). (C). 1995. pap. text 30.60 (*1-85578-072-0*, Pub. by Portland Pr Ltd) Ashgate Pub Co.
Cornish-Bowden, A. & Cardenas, M. L. Control of Metabolic Processes. LC 90-7160. (NATO ASI Series A, Life Sciences: Vol. 190). (Illus.). 470p. (C). 1990. text 149.50 (*0-306-43582-9*) Plenum.
Cornish-Bowden, Athel. Analysis of Enzyme Kinetic Data. (Illus.). 210p. 1995. text 115.00 (*0-19-854878-8*); pap. text 55.00 (*0-19-854877-X*) OUP.
***Cornish-Bowden, Athel.** Basic Mathematics for Biochemists. 2nd ed. (Illus.). 240p. 2000. pap. text 24.95 (*0-19-850216-8*) OUP.
— Basic Mathematics for Biochemists. 2nd ed. (Illus.). 240p. 2000. text 60.00 (*0-19-850217-6*) OUP.
***Cornish-Bowden, Athel & Cbardenas, Marbia Luz.** Technological & Medical Implications of Metabolic Control Analysis. LC 00-21828. (NATO ASI Ser.). 2000. write for info. (*0-7923-6188-1*) Kluwer Academic.
***Cornish-Bowden, Athel J.** Technological & Medical Implications of Metabolic Control. 388p. 2000. pap. 64.00 (*0-7923-6189-X*) Kluwer Academic.
Cornish, Carol, jt. ed. see Fitzpatrick, Elyse.
Cornish, Clive G. Basic Accounting for the Small Business: Simple, Foolproof Techniques for Keeping Your Books Straight & Staying Out of Trouble. 9th rev. ed. (Business Ser.). 224p. (C). 1993. pap. 8.95 (*0-88908-998-1*) Self-Counsel Pr.
Cornish, D. B. & Clarke, R. V. The Reasoning Criminal: Rational Choice Perspectives on Offending. LC 86-1275. (Research in Criminology Ser.). 1986. 105.00 (*0-387-96272-7*) Spr-Verlag.
***Cornish, Dave.** How to Run a Quiz. (Illus.). 192p. 2001. pap. 8.95 (*0-7160-2004-1*, Pub. by Elliot RW Bks) Midpt Trade.
— How to Win Quizzes. (Illus.). 192p. 2001. pap. 8.95 (*0-7160-2111-0*, Pub. by Elliot RW Bks) Midpt Trade.
Cornish, Dudley T. The Sable Arm: Black Troops in the Union Army, 1861-1865. LC 87-50106. (Modern War Studies). (Illus.). xviii, 342p. 1987. reprint ed. pap. 14.95 (*0-7006-0328-X*) U Pr of KS.
Cornish, Edward. Habitats Tomorrow: Homes & Communities in an Exciting New Era. LC 84-50376. 160p. 1984. pap. 6.95 (*0-930242-24-6*) World Future.
— Study of the Future. 310p. 1977. pap. 15.95 (*0-930242-03-3*) Transaction Pubs.
Cornish, Edward, ed. Careers Tomorrow: The Outlook for Work in a Changing World. 160p. 1983. pap. 16.95 (*0-930242-19-X*) Transaction Pubs.
— Careers Tomorrow: The Outlook for Work in a Changing World. 1988. pap. 7.95 (*0-930242-33-5*) World Future.
— The Computerized Society: Living & Working in an Electronic Age. 160p. 1985. pap. 6.95 (*0-930242-27-0*) World Future.
— Exploring Your Future: Living, Learning & Working in the Information Age. LC 96-225073. 160p. (Orig.). 1996. pap. 12.95 (*0-930242-52-1*) World Future.
— Global Solutions: Innovative Approaches to World Problems. LC 84-50375. 160p. 1984. pap. 6.95 (*0-930242-22-X*) World Future.
— The Great Transformation. 1983. pap. 6.95 (*0-930242-20-3*) World Future.
— 1999: The World of Tomorrow. 160p. 1978. pap. 15.95 (*0-930242-04-1*) Transaction Pubs.
Cornish, Elizabeth. Natural Cooking. 128p. 1995. write for info. (*1-57215-058-0*) World Pubns.
Cornish, Francis. Anaphora, Discourse & Understanding: Evidence from English & French. LC 98-37676. (Illus.). 284p. 1999. text 98.00 (*0-19-823648-4*); pap. text 35.00 (*0-19-870028-8*) OUP.
Cornish, Francis W. Jane Austen. LC 78-37333. (Select Bibliographies Reprint Ser.). 1977. reprint ed. 18.95 (*0-8369-6680-5*) Ayer.
Cornish, Francis W., tr. see Catullus, Gaius Valerius.
Cornish, G. St. Paul from the Trenches. 1994. 10.95 (*0-933062-31-1*) R H Sommer.
Cornish, Geoffrey S., jt. auth. see Graves, Robert M.
***Cornish, Grace.** 10 Bad Choices That Ruin Black Women's Lives. 240p. 1999. pap. 12.00 (*0-609-80133-3*) Three Rivers Pr.
***Cornish, Gracie.** 10 Good Choices That Empower Black Women's Lives. 192p. 2000. 21.00 (*0-609-60506-2*) Crown Pub Group.
***Cornish, Graham P.** Copyright: Interpreting the Law for Libraries, Archives & Information Services. 3rd ed. 188p. 1999. 45.00 (*1-85604-344-4*, Pub. by Library Association) Bernan Associates.
Cornish, Graham P. Religious Periodicals Directory. (Clio Periodicals Directories Ser.). 330p. 1986. lib. bdg. 99.50 (*0-87436-365-9*) ABC-CLIO.
Cornish, J., jt. ed. see Arensman, Robert M.
Cornish, J. E. The History & Genealogy of the Cornish Family in America. (Illus.). 353p. 1989. reprint ed. pap. 51.50 (*0-8328-0427-4*); reprint ed. lib. bdg. 59.50 (*0-8328-0426-6*) Higginson Bk Co.
Cornish, Joe. Coast of England, Wales & Northern Ireland. LC 98-154873. (Illus.). 144p. 1998. 24.95 (*0-8109-6360-4*, Pub. by Abrams) Time Warner.
— Countryside: Of England, Wales & Northern Ireland. LC 98-154862. (Illus.). 144p. 1998. 24.95 (*0-8109-6361-2*, Pub. by Abrams) Time Warner.
Cornish, John. The Raising of Lazarus. 1979. pap. 3.50 (*0-916786-36-6*, Saint George Pubns) R Steiner Col.
***Cornish, Kimberley.** The Jew of Linz. 1999. pap. 15.95 (*0-09-926995-3*, Pub. by Arrow Bks) Trafalgar.
— The Jew of Linz. LC 99-210678. 298p. 29.95 (*0-7126-7935-9*, Pub. by Random) Trafalgar.
Cornish, Mary & Spink, Lynn. Organizing Unions. (Illus.). 350p. 1994. pap. 19.95 (*0-929005-55-4*, Pub. by Sec Story Pr) LPC InBook.
***Cornish, Patrick.** Western Australia in the 20th Century. (Illus.). 280p. 1999. pap. 19.95 (*1-86368-274-0*, Pub. by Fremantle Arts) Intl Spec Bk.
Cornish, Patty Jo. An Outrageous Idea: Natural Prayer: A Powerful Answer to America's Prayer Dilemma. (Illus.). 108p. 14.95 (*0-9613717-1-4*) Hilltop Hse.
Cornish, Patty Jo. The Prayer Primer: A Philosophy Book. Quintero, Roberto, ed. LC 84-81741. 68p. (Orig.). pap. 5.95 (*0-9613717-0-6*) Hilltop Hse.
Cornish, Paul. Arms Trade. 144p. 1996. pap. text 14.95 (*0-906097-44-4*, Pub. by Bowerdean Pub) Capital VA.
— The Arms Trade & Europe. (Chatham House Papers). 128p. 1995. 44.95 (*1-85567-284-7*); pap. 15.95 (*1-85567-285-5*) Bks Intl VA.
— British Military Planning for the Defence of Germany, 1945-50. LC 95-37739. (Studies in Military & Strategic History Ser.). 256p. 1996. text 65.00 (*0-312-12960-2*) St Martin.
— British Military Planning for the Defence of Germany, 1945-50 LC 95-37739. (Studies in Military & Strategic History). xi, 211 p. 1996. write for info. (*0-333-63995-2*) Macmillan Pr.
— Henry the Eighth's Army. (Men-at-Arms Ser.: No. 191). (Illus.). 48p. pap. 12.95 (*0-85045-798-X*, 9124, Pub. by Osprey) Stackpole.
— Partnership in Crisis? The United States, Europe & the Fall & Rise of NATO. LC 98-130156. (Chatham House Papers). 256p. 44.95 (*1-85567-466-1*) Continuum.
— Partnership in Crisis? The United States, Europe & the Fall & Rise of NATO. LC 98-130156. (Chatham House Papers). 256p. 1997. pap. 15.95 (*1-85567-467-X*) Continuum.
Cornish, Robert E. Vitamin & Mineral Deficiencies. 150p. 1996. reprint ed. spiral bd. 16.00 (*0-7873-0224-4*) Hlth Research.
Cornish, Roger & Ketels, Violet, eds. Landmarks of Modern British Drama, 2 vols., Vol. 2. 624p. (C). 1988. 29.95 (*0-413-59090-9*, A0144); pap. 12.95 (*0-413-57270-6*, A0145) Heinemann.
Cornish, Roger & Ketels, Violet, frwds. Landmarks of Modern British Drama: The Plays of the Sixties, Vol. 1. 732p. (Orig.). (C). 1988. pap. 12.95 (*0-413-57260-9*, A0143, Methuen Drama) Methn.
Cornish, Rory T. George Grenville, 1712-1770: A Bibliography, Vol. 3. LC 91-35219. (Bibliographies of British Statesmen Ser.: No. 3). 256p. 1992. lib. bdg. 79.50 (*0-313-28281-1*, CGD/, Greenwood Pr) Greenwood.
Cornish, Sam. Cross a Parted Sea. LC 96-16397. 128p. (Orig.). 1996. pap. 11.95 (*0-944072-71-2*) Zoland Bks.
— Folks Like Me. LC 92-43940. 128p. 1993. 12.95 (*0-944072-30-5*) Zoland Bks.
— Grandmother's Pictures. (Illus.). 1974. pap. 10.00 (*0-912846-04-6*) Bookstore Pr.
— 1935: A Memoir. 181p. (C). 1990. 19.95 (*0-933277-03-2*); pap. 9.95 (*0-933277-04-0*) Ploughshares.
— Songs of Jubilee: New & Selected Poems. 150p. (Orig.). 1986. 20.00 (*0-87775-195-1*); pap. 10.95 (*0-87775-196-X*) Unicorn Pr.
Cornish, Tim, ed. see Saunders, T. C.
Cornish, Tony & Bureau of National Affairs Communications Staff. Zero Tolerance: An Employer's Guide to Preventing Sexual Harassment & Healing the Workplace. LC 97-11665. 1997. 29.00 (*1-55871-354-9*) BNAC.
Cornish, Tony, ed. see D. C. Bureau of National Affairs Washington Staff.
Cornish, Vaughan. Great Capitals. LC 70-114503. (Illus.). 296p. 1971. reprint ed. lib. bdg. 65.00 (*0-8371-4782-4*, COGC, Greenwood Pr) Greenwood.
Cornish, W. R., ed. Piracy & Counterfeiting of Industrial Property & Copyright. 143p. 1983. pap. 26.00 (*0-903067-27-7*, Pub. by Brit Inst ICL) St Mut.
Cornish, W. R., et al, eds. Restitution - Past, Present & Future: Essays in Honour of Gareth Jones. LC 98-198229. 256p. 1998. 60.00 (*1-901362-42-6*, Pub. by Hart Pub) Northwestern U Pr.
Cornish, W. R., jt. auth. see Chisum, D. S.
Cornman, Chas. A. Cornman-Corman-Korman. Genealogical Record of Descendants of Ludwig Kornman, Sr., in America. 168p. 1997. reprint ed. pap. 26.00 (*0-8328-8062-0*); reprint ed. lib. bdg. 36.00 (*0-8328-8061-2*) Higginson Bk Co.
Cornman, James W. Metaphysics, Reference, & Language. LC 66-21512. 310p. reprint ed. pap. 96.10 (*0-8357-8739-7*, 203369700087) Bks Demand.
— Skepticism, Justification, & Explanation. (Philosophical Studies in Philosophy: No. 18). 362p. 1980. text 135.00 (*90-277-1041-4*, D Reidel) Kluwer Academic.
Cornman, James W., et al. Philosophical Problems & Arguments: An Introduction. rev. ed. 384p. (C). 1992. pap. text 18.95 (*0-87220-124-4*) Hackett Pub.
— Philosophical Problems & Arguments: An Introduction. 4th rev. ed. 384p. (C). 1992. lib. bdg. 37.95 (*0-87220-125-2*) Hackett Pub.
Cornman, John M. & Kincaid, Barbara. Lessons from Rural America: A Case History. LC 84-14107. 160p. 1984. 13.95 (*0-932020-24-0*) Seven Locks Pr.
Cornman, Robert, tr. see Modrzejewski, Joseph M.
Corner, Haydn. Dreams: A New Guide to the Secrets of the Mind, with Dream Cards & Book of Dream Symbols. 128p. 1998. 15.95 (*0-7624-0330-6*) Running Pr.
Cornog, Evan. The Birth of Empire: DeWitt Clinton & the American Experience, 1769-1828. LC 97-53112. (Illus.). 234p. 1998. 29.95 (*0-19-511949-5*) OUP.
Cornog, Evan, contrib. by. Come All You Gallant Heroes: The World of the Revolutionary Soldier. (Illus.). 72p. (Orig.). 1991. pap. 10.00 (*0-9616415-9-2*) Fraunces Tavern.
Cornog, Martha & Perper, Timothy. For Sex Education, See Librarian: A Guide to Issues & Resources. LC 95-42445. 432p. 1996. 45.00 (*0-313-29022-9*, Greenwood Pr) Greenwood.
Cornog, Mary W. Merriam Webster's Vocabulary Builder. 576p. 1994. mass mkt. 5.99 (*0-87779-910-5*) Merriam-Webster Inc.
Cornoldi, C. & McDaniel, M. A., eds. Imagery & Cognition. (Illus.). 320p. 1990. 71.95 (*0-387-97410-5*) Spr-Verlag.
Cornoldi, Cesare & Logie, Robert, eds. Stretching the Imagination: Representation & Transformation in Mental Imagery. (Counterpoints Ser.). (Illus.). 208p. (C). 1996. text 50.00 (*0-19-509947-8*); pap. text 24.95 (*0-19-509948-6*) OUP.
Cornoldi, Cesare & Oakhill, Jane, eds. Reading Comprehension Difficulties: Processes & Intervention. 350p. 1996. text 74.95 (*0-8058-1845-6*) L Erlbaum Assocs.

Cornoni-Huntley, Joan, et al. Health Status & Well-Being of the Elderly: National Health & Nutrition Examination, No. I: Epidemiologic Follow-up Survey. LC 89-9212. (Illus.). 320p. 1990. text 55.00 (*0-19-504962-4*) OUP.

Corns. Milton's Prose. LC 97-36419. 1998. 32.00 (*0-8057-4530-0*, Twyne) Mac Lib Ref.

Corns, David, jt. auth. see Boucher, Eric.

Corns, John B. Nickel Plate Road Publicity Photos, 1943-1952, Vol. 2. (Illus.). 126p. 1998. 25.95 (*1-883089-22-0*) TLC VA.

Corns, Marshall C. The Practical Operations & Management of a Bank. 2nd ed. LC 68-17247. (Illus.). 979p. reprint ed. pap. 200.00 (*0-608-18753-4*, 205222700065) Bks Demand.

Corns, T. N., jt. auth. see Rudall, B. H.

Corns, Thomas N. The Development of Milton's Prose Style. (Oxford English Monographs). (Illus.). 134p. (C). 1982. text 45.00 (*0-19-811717-5*) OUP.

— Regaining Paradise Lost. LC 94-2146. (Medieval & Renaissance Library). 168p. (C). 1994. text 61.25 (*0-582-06621-2*, 76863, Pub. by Addison-Wesley); pap. text 20.25 (*0-582-06620-4*, 76862, Pub. by Addison-Wesley) Longman.

— Uncloistered Virtue: English Political Literature, 1640-1660. 352p. 1992. 85.00 (*0-19-812883-5*) OUP.

Corns, Thomas N., ed. The Cambridge Companion to English Poetry, Donne to Marvell. LC 92-44508. (Cambridge Companions to Literature Ser.). 326p. (C). 1993. pap. text 19.95 (*0-521-42309-0*) Cambridge U Pr.

— Literature of Controversy: Polemical Strategy from Milton to Junius. 1987. 29.50 (*0-7146-3292-9*, Pub. by F Cass Pubs) Intl Spec Bk.

— The Royal Image: Representations of Charles I. LC 98-38093. (Illus.). 320p. (C). 1999. text 59.95 (*0-521-59047-7*) Cambridge U Pr.

Corns, Thomas N. & Loewenstein, David, eds. The Emergence of Quaker Writing: Dissenting Literature in Seventeenth-Century England. LC 95-21771. 160p. 1995. pap. 22.50 (*0-7146-4246-0*, Pub. by F Cass Pubs) Intl Spec Bk.

Corns, Thomas N., jt. ed. see Downie, J. A.

Corns, Thomas N., jt. ed. see Kitson, Peter J.

Cornthwaite, Robert, tr. see Balzac, Honore de.

Cornthwaite, Robert, tr. see Goldoni, Carlo.

Cornthwaite, Robert, tr. see Scribe, Eugene.

Cornu, A., jt. auth. see Leclerc, J. C.

Cornu, Aymbe & Massot, R. List of Conversion Factors for Atomic Impurities to PPM by Weight. LC 68-20754. 148p. reprint ed. pap. 45.90 (*0-608-14065-1*, 202400300035) Bks Demand.

Cornu, Gerard. Vocabulaire Juridique. 2nd ed. (FRE.). 880p. 1990. 295.00 (*0-7859-4658-6*) Fr & Eur.

Cornu, J. Consumable Electrode Processes in Welding Automation. (Advanced Welding Systems Ser.: Vol. 2). (Illus.). 300p. 1989. 118.95 (*0-387-50482-6*) Spr-Verlag.

— TIG & Related Processes in Welding Automation. (Advanced Welding Systems Ser.: Vol. 3). (Illus.). 350p. 1989. 111.95 (*0-387-50484-2*) Spr-Verlag.

Cornu, Philippe. Tibetan Astrology. Gregor, Hamish, tr. from FRE. LC 96-39527. 368p. 1997. 35.00 (*1-57062-217-5*, Pub. by Shambhala Pubns) Random.

Cornubert, Raymond. Dictionary of Chemistry English - French. (ENG & FRE.). 1977. 85.00 (*0-8288-9465-5*) Fr & Eur.

— Dictionnaire de Chimie Allemand-Francais. 3rd ed.Tr. of German-French Chemistry Dictionary. (FRE & GER.). 240p. 1977. pap. 65.00 (*0-8288-5381-9*, M6088) Fr & Eur.

Cornuejols, Antoine, ed. Training Issues in Incremental Learning: Papers from the 1993 Spring Symposium. (Technical Reports). (Illus.). 156p. 1993. spiral bd. 25.00 (*0-929280-44-X*) AAAI Pr.

Cornuejols, G., et al, eds. Integer Programming & Combinatorial Optimization: 7th International IPCO Conference, Graz, Austria, June 9-11, 1999, Proceedings. LC 99-32451. (Lecture Notes in Computer Science Ser.: Vol. 1610). ix, 453p. 1999. pap. 73.00 (*3-540-66019-4*) Spr-Verlag.

Cornuelle. Competency Manual: Radiographic Anatomy & Positioning. 200p. (C). 1997. pap. text 29.95 (*0-8385-8239-7*, A-8239-4, Apple Lange Med) McGraw.

Cornuelle, Andrea G. & Gronefeld, Dinae H. Radiographic Anatomy & Positioning: An Integrated Approach. LC 96-46591. 640p. (C). 1997. pap. text 98.00 (*0-8385-8238-9*, A8238-6, Apple Lange Med) McGraw.

Cornuelle, Richard C. Reclaiming the American Dream: The Role of Private Individuals & Voluntary Associations. rev. ed. LC 92-32936. (Philanthropy & Society Ser.). 258p. (C). 1993. pap. text 24.95 (*1-56000-655-2*) Transaction Pubs.

***Cornuke, Bob & Halbrook, David.** In Search of the Mountain of God: The Discovery of the Real Mt. Sinai. (Illus.). 240p. 2000. 21.99 (*0-8054-2052-5*) Broadman.

Cornulier, Benoit De, see De Cornulier, Benoit.

Cornum, Rhonda. She Went to War. large type ed. LC 98-51854. (American History Ser.). 1999. 26.95 (*0-7838-8516-4*, G K Hall Lrg Type) Mac Lib Ref.

Cornutus. Artis Rhetoricae Epitome. Graeven, Johannes, ed. 55p. 1973. 30.00 (*3-296-12010-6*) G Olms Pubs.

Cornwall, Andrea & Lindisfarne, Nancy, eds. Dislocating Masculinity: Comparative Ethnographies. LC 93-13078. (Male Orders Ser.). 256p. (C). 1994. pap. 24.99 (*0-415-07942-X*) Routledge.

Cornwall, E. William Cornwall & His Descendants; a Genealogical History of the Family of William Cornwall, Who Came to America in 1633 & Died in Middleton, Connecticut in 1678. 185p. 1993. reprint ed. pap. 28.00 (*0-8328-1381-8*); reprint ed. lib. bdg. 38.00 (*0-8328-1380-X*) Higginson Bk Co.

Cornwall, Jim. The Pearlmaker. 168p. (Orig.). 1997. pap. 7.99 (*0-88270-734-5*, Logos NJ) Bridge-Logos.

Cornwall, John. Access to Learning for Pupils with Disabilities. LC 97-196876. 112p. 1997. pap. 22.95 (*1-85346-496-1*, Pub. by David Fulton) Taylor & Francis.

— Economic Breakdown & Recovery: Theory & Policy. rev. ed. LC 93-22648. 320p. (gr. 13). 1994. text 81.95 (*1-56324-304-0*); pap. text 36.95 (*1-56324-305-9*) M E Sharpe.

— Growth Employment & Inflation: Essays in Honour of John Cornwall. Setterfield, Mark, ed. & intro. by. LC 98-43273. (Illus.). 278p. 1999. 79.95 (*0-312-22013-8*) St Martin.

— Individual Education Plans (IEPs) Emotional & Behavioural Difficulties. LC 98-203740. 102p. 1998. pap. 34.95 (*1-85346-521-6*, Pub. by David Fulton) Taylor & Francis.

— Modern Capitalism: Its Growth & Transformation. LC 82-5490. 240p. reprint ed. pap. 74.40 (*0-608-18123-4*, 203277600081) Bks Demand.

Cornwall, John, ed. After Stagflation: Alternatives to Economic Decline. LC 83-27140. 192p. 1984. reprint ed. pap. 59.60 (*0-7837-9993-4*, 206072000006) Bks Demand.

— The Capitalist Economies: Prospects for the 1990's. 224p. 1991. text 80.00 (*1-85278-378-8*) E Elgar.

***Cornwall, Judson.** Ascending to Glory: The Secret of Personal Prayer. 159p. 1999. pap. 9.97 (*1-883906-32-6*) Kingdom Prods.

Cornwall, Judson. The Best of Judson Cornwall: Anthology of Judson's Writings for the Last Twenty-Five Years. 180p. 1992. pap. 7.99 (*0-88270-655-1*) Bridge-Logos.

— David Worshiped a Living God. 182p. (Orig.). 1989. pap. 10.99 (*0-938612-38-7*) Destiny Image.

— David Worshipped with a Fervent Faith. LC 92-74509. 210p. 1993. pap. 10.99 (*1-56043-089-3*) Destiny Image.

— Elements of Worship. LC 85-61459. 200p. 1985. pap. 9.99 (*0-88270-594-6*) Bridge-Logos.

— En Sintonia con Dios.Tr. of Secret of Personal Prayer. (SPA.). 144p. (Orig.). 1992. pap. 7.99 (*0-88113-268-3*) Caribe Betania.

— Heaven. 139p. 1993. pap. 7.99 (*0-88270-659-4*) Bridge-Logos.

— Incense & Insurrection. 75p. (Orig.). 1986. pap. 4.95 (*0-917595-12-2*) Kingdom Pubns.

— It's God's War: A Biblical View of Spiritual Warfare. 1998. pap. text 9.99 (*1-884369-86-3*) McDougal Pubng.

— Jesus, a Living Example of Worship. LC 97-73690. 158p. 1997. pap. 9.99 (*0-88270-742-6*, Logos NJ) Bridge-Logos.

— Let Us Abide: How to Adjust Your Will & Stay in God's Presence. 155p. 1977. pap. 7.99 (*0-88270-626-8*) Bridge-Logos.

— Let Us Be Holy. LC 87-70993. 1978. pap. 7.99 (*0-88270-278-5*) Bridge-Logos.

— Let Us Draw Near: Spiritual Symbolism of the Old Testament Tabernacle. LC 77-24832. 168p. 1977. pap. 8.99 (*0-88270-226-2*) Bridge-Logos.

— Let Us Enjoy Forgiveness. 159p. 1992. reprint ed. pap. 8.99 (*0-88270-708-6*) Bridge-Logos.

— Let Us Praise: Principles & Practices of Scriptural Praise. LC 73-75957. 159p. 1973. pap. 9.99 (*0-88270-039-1*) Bridge-Logos.

— Let Us See Jesus. LC 80-20645. 160p. 1981. pap. 7.99 (*0-88270-628-4*) Bridge-Logos.

— Let Us Worship. LC 82-75089. 177p. 1983. pap. 9.99 (*0-88270-542-3*) Bridge-Logos.

— Lord, It's Me Again. 179p. (Orig.). 1994. pap. 7.99 (*0-88270-666-7*) Bridge-Logos.

— My Father & I: How the Bible Teaches Fatherhood. 1998. pap. 10.99 (*1-884369-78-2*) McDougal Pubng.

— Praying the Scriptures: Communicating with God in His Own Words. LC 89-82724. 223p. (C). 1998. pap. 11.99 (*0-88419-266-0*) Creation House.

— Profiles of a Leader: The Characteristics of Spiritual Leadership. LC 80-85161. 227p. (Orig.). 1980. pap. 8.99 (*0-88270-503-2*) Bridge-Logos.

***Cornwall, Judson.** Releasing the Glory: The Secret of Joy. 2000. 19.97 (*1-883906-42-3*); pap. 9.97 (*1-883906-38-5*) Kingdom Prods.

Cornwall, Judson. Worship As David Lived It. 196p. 1990. pap. 10.99 (*1-56043-700-6*) Destiny Image.

Cornwall, Judson & Sasser, Sam. The Priesthood of the Believer: Christ Calls Believers to be Worshipping Priests unto God. LC 98-74675. 194p. 1998. pap. 9.99 (*0-88270-765-5*, Bridge) Bridge-Logos.

Cornwall, Judson, jt. auth. see Cornwall, Robert.

Cornwall, Judson, jt. auth. see Foster, Glenn.

Cornwall, Judson, jt. auth. see Smith, Stelman.

Cornwall, Judson, jt. auth. see Tompkins, Iverna.

Cornwall, L. Peter & Smith, Carol A. Names First - Rails Later: New England's 700-Plus Railroads & What Happened to Them. (Illus.). 124p. (C). 1988. text. write for info. (*0-9621689-0-4*) Arden Valley.

Cornwall-Madsen, Carol, jt. ed. see Stovall, Mary E.

Cornwall, Marie, et al, eds. Contemporary Mormonism: Social Science Perspectives. LC 93-6438. (Illus.). 376p. 1994. text 32.50 (*0-252-02076-6*) U of Ill Pr.

Cornwall, Marie, jt. ed. see Anderson, Dawn H.

***Cornwall, Mark.** The Undermining of Austria-Hungary: The Battle for Hearts & Minds. LC 99-59429. 2000. 69.95 (*0-312-23151-2*) St Martin.

Cornwall, Mark, ed. The Last Years of Austria - Hungary. 192p. 1998. pap. text 23.95 (*0-85989-563-7*) Univ Exeter Pr.

— The Last Years of Austria-Hungary: Essays in Political & Military History, 1908-1918. (Illus.). 168p. 1990. pap. text 17.50 (*0-85989-306-5*, Pub. by Univ Exeter Pr) Northwestern U Pr.

Cornwall, Richard R. & Wunnava, Phanindra V., eds. New Approaches to Economic & Social Analyses of Discrimination. LC 91-15504. 432p. 1991. 65.00 (*0-275-93581-7*, C3581, Praeger Pubs) Greenwood.

Cornwall, Richard R., jt. auth. see Claudon, Michael P.

Cornwall, Robert & Cornwall, Judson. Five Foundations for Marriage. 147p. (Orig.). 1997. pap. 7.99 (*0-88270-737-X*) Bridge-Logos.

Cornwall, Robert D. Visible & Apostolic: The Constitution of the Church in High Church Anglican & Non-Juror Thought. LC 92-56626. (C). 1993. 36.50 (*0-87413-466-8*) U Delaware Pr.

Cornwall, Robert D., ed. see Burnet, Gilbert.

Cornwall, Susan, ed. see American Institute of Certified Public Accountants.

Cornwall, Susan, ed. see American Institute of Certified Public Accountants, et al.

Cornwallis, Graeme. Great Hikes & Treks in Norway. 1998. pap. 17.95 (*0-9520900-7-4*, Pub. by Compass Star) Seven Hills Bk.

***Cornwallis, Graeme.** Lonely Planet Sweden. (Travel Guides Ser.). (Illus.). 380p. 2000. pap. 17.95 (*0-86442-721-2*) Lonely Planet.

Cornwallis, Graeme, jt. auth. see Smallman, Tom.

Cornwallis, Kinahan. The New El Dorado: or British Columbia. LC 72-9437. (Far Western Frontier Ser.). (Illus.). 442p. 1973. reprint ed. 29.95 (*0-405-04967-6*) Ayer.

Cornwallis, William. Discourses upon Seneca the Tragedian. LC 52-10576. 144p. 1978. reprint ed. 50.00 (*0-8201-1220-8*) Schol Facsimiles.

Cornwell, Antonia & Creedy, John. Environmental Taxes & Economic Welfare: Reducing Carbon Dioxide Emissions. LC 97-7576. (New Horizons in Environmental Economics Ser.). 168p. 1997. 70.00 (*1-85898-622-2*) E Elgar.

Cornwell, Bernard. Battle Flag. (Starbuck Chronicles Ser.: Vol. 3). 448p. 1996. mass mkt. 6.99 (*0-06-109197-9*) HarpC.

— The Bloody Ground. Vol. 4. 400p. 1997. mass mkt. 6.50 (*0-06-109198-7*) HarpC.

— The Bloody Ground. large type ed. LC 96-34277. 1996. 24.95 (*1-56895-371-2*, Compass) Wheeler Pub.

— Copperhead. LC 94-749. 448p. 1995. mass mkt. 6.99 (*0-06-109196-0*, Harp PBks) HarpC.

— Copperhead. large type ed. LC 94-749. (Starbuck Chronicles Ser.: Vol. 2). 716p. 1994. lib. bdg. 23.95 (*0-7862-0186-X*) Thorndike Pr.

— Enemy of God: A Novel of Arthur. LC 96-51740. Vol. 2. 416p. 1997. text 24.95 (*0-312-15523-9*) St Martin.

— Enemy of God: A Novel of Arthur. 416p. 1998. pap. 14.95 (*0-312-18714-9*) St Martin.

— Excalibur: A Novel of Arthur. LC 98-10247. 448p. 1998. text 24.95 (*0-312-18575-8*) St Martin.

— Excalibur: A Novel of Arthur. 448p. 1999. pap. 14.95 (*0-312-20648-8*) St Martin.

— Excalibur: A Novel of Arthur. large type ed. LC 98-3721. 685p. 1998. 27.95 (*0-7862-1476-7*) Thorndike Pr.

— Excalibur, Enemy of God, The Winter King: Novels of Arthur. 1999. pap. write for info. (*0-312-19070-0*) St Martin.

— Rebel. LC 92-53344. Vol. 1. 512p. 1994. mass mkt. 6.99 (*0-06-109187-1*, Harp PBks) HarpC.

— Rebel. large type ed. LC 93-16473. (Starbuck Chronicles Ser.: Vol. 1). 673p. 1993. lib. bdg. 22.95 (*1-56054-693-X*) Thorndike Pr.

— Rebel. large type ed. LC 93-16473. (Starbuck Chronicles Ser.: Vol. 1). 673p. 1994. lib. bdg. 14.95 (*1-56054-879-7*) Thorndike Pr.

— Redcoat. (Illus.). 496p. 1998. reprint ed. mass mkt. 6.99 (*0-06-101264-5*, Harp PBks) HarpC.

— Sharpe's Battle. LC 99-29510. 368p. 1999. pap. 12.00 (*0-06-093228-7*) HarpC.

— Sharpe's Battle: Richard Sharpe & the Battle of Fuentes de Onoro, May 1811. large type ed. 534p. 1996. 23.95 (*0-7862-0572-5*) Thorndike Pr.

— Sharpe's Company: The Siege of Badajoz. 288p. 1984. pap. 11.95 (*0-14-007023-0*, Penguin Bks) Viking Penguin.

— Sharpe's Devil. 368p. 1993. mass mkt. 6.50 (*0-06-109028-X*, Harp PBks) HarpC.

— Sharpe's Devil: Richard Sharpe & the Emperor, 1820-1921. LC 99-30290. (Sharpe's Adventures Ser.). 336p. 1999. pap. 12.00 (*0-06-093229-5*) HarpC.

— Sharpe's Eagle. large type ed. 480p. 1983. 27.99 (*0-7089-0945-0*) Ulverscroft.

— Sharpe's Eagle. 1991. reprint ed. lib. bdg. 29.95 (*1-56849-076-3*) Buccaneer Bks.

— Sharpe's Eagle, No. 2. 270p. 1987. pap. 10.95 (*0-14-009921-2*, Penguin Bks) Viking Penguin.

— Sharpe's Enemy, No. 6. 368p. 1987. pap. 11.95 (*0-14-010430-5*, Penguin Bks) Viking Penguin.

***Cornwell, Bernard.** Sharpe's Fortress. 320p. 2000. 25.00 (*0-06-019424-3*) HarpC.

Cornwell, Bernard. Sharpe's Gold. 1987. pap. 11.95 (*0-14-024305-4*, Penguin Bks) Viking Penguin.

— Sharpe's Honor. 1990. pap. 10.95 (*0-14-014597-4*, Penguin Bks) Viking Penguin.

— Sharpe's Regiment. 1987. pap. 10.95 (*0-14-024306-2*, Penguin Bks) Viking Penguin.

— Sharpe's Revenge: Richard Sharpe & the Peace of 1814, No. 10. 320p. 1990. pap. 11.95 (*0-14-008472-X*, Penguin Bks) Viking Penguin.

— Sharpe's Rifles: Richard Sharpe & the French Invasion of Galicia, January 1809, No. 1. 304p. 1989. pap. 11.95 (*0-14-011014-3*, Penguin Bks) Viking Penguin.

— Sharpe's Siege, No. 9. 320p. 1990. pap. 11.95 (*0-14-014442-0*, Penguin Bks) Viking Penguin.

— Sharpe's Sword. 1987. pap. 10.95 (*0-14-024304-6*, Penguin Bks) Viking Penguin.

— Sharpe's Tiger. 496p. 1997. mass mkt. 6.50 (*0-06-101269-6*, Harp PBks) HarpC.

— Sharpe's Tiger. LC 99-30288. (Sharpe's Adventures Ser.). 400p. 1999. pap. 12.00 (*0-06-093230-9*) HarpC.

— Sharpe's Trafalgar. Date not set. 24.00 (*0-06-019425-1*); mass mkt. 6.99 (*0-06-109862-0*) HarpC.

— Sharpe's Triumph: Richard Sharpe & the Battle of Assaye, September 1803. LC 00-503081. (Sharpe's Adventures Ser.). 291p. 1999. 24.00 (*0-06-101270-X*) HarpC.

***Cornwell, Bernard.** Sharpe's Triumph: Richard Sharpe & the Battle of Assaye, September 1803. 304p. 2000. pap. 13.00 (*0-06-095197-4*, Perennial) HarperTrade.

— Stonehenge. large type ed. (Core Ser.). 646p. 2000. 28.95 (*0-7838-9038-9*, G K Hall Lrg Type) Mac Lib Ref.

— Stonehenge: 2000 B. C. 432p. 2000. 26.00 (*0-06-019700-5*) HarpC.

Cornwell, Bernard. Waterloo No. 11: Sharpe's Final Adventure. 384p. 1991. pap. 11.95 (*0-14-008473-8*, Penguin Bks) Viking Penguin.

— Wildtrack. large type ed. 460p. 1989. lib. bdg. 19.95 (*0-8161-4716-7*, G K Hall Lrg Type) Mac Lib Ref.

— The Winter King: A Novel of Arthur. large type ed. 664p. 1996. 26.95 (*0-7862-0729-9*) Thorndike Pr.

— The Winter King: A Novel of Arthur. 3rd ed. LC 96-1421. 448p. 1997. pap. 14.95 (*0-312-15696-0*) St Martin.

Cornwell, Betty. Moment Out of Time. (Illus.). 82p. (Orig.). 1984. pap. 7.50 (*0-918957-00-1*) Pika Oregon.

Cornwell, Bruce, jt. auth. see Turner, Geoff.

Cornwell, Charles, ed. see Sanders, Zoe.

Cornwell, Cynthia A. Beside the Waters of the Buffalo: A History of Milligan College to 1941. LC 88-63934. (Illus.). 225p. 1989. 20.00 (*0-9621740-0-9*) Milligan Coll Hist Proj.

Cornwell, David A., et al. Assessment of Gac Adsorption for Radon Removal. LC 98-38697. 1998. write for info. (*0-89867-976-1*) Am Water Wks Assn.

***Cornwell, David A., et al.** Commercial Application & Marketing of Water Plant Residuals. LC 00-44144. 2000. write for info. (*1-58321-030-X*) Am Water Wks Assn.

Cornwell, David A., jt. auth. see Vandermeyden, Carel.

Cornwell, Debbie & Cornwell, Stephen. Cooking in the Nude: For Golf Lovers. (Illus.). 96p. 1998. pap. 9.95 (*1-57427-083-4*) Howell Pr VA.

— Cooking in the Nude: For Wine Lovers. (Illus.). 96p. 1998. pap. 9.95 (*1-57427-082-6*) Howell Pr VA.

— Cooking in the Nude: Just Married. (Cooking in the Nude Ser.). (Illus.). 96p. 1997. pap. 9.95 (*0-943231-99-X*) Howell Pr VA.

— Cooking in the Nude: Playful Gourmets. (Cooking in the Nude Ser.). (Illus.). 96p. 1996. pap. 9.95 (*0-943231-97-3*) Howell Pr VA.

— Cooking in the Nude: Quickies. LC 95-80600. (Illus.). 96p. (Orig.). 1995. pap. 9.95 (*0-943231-96-5*) Howell Pr VA.

— Cooking in the Nude: Red Hot Lovers. LC 95-81868. (Cooking in the Nude Ser.). (Illus.). 96p. 1996. pap. 9.95 (*0-943231-98-1*) Howell Pr VA.

***Cornwell, Diane.** Arthur Andersen Guide to Navigating Intermediate Sanctions. LC 99-6705. 250p. 1999. 159.95 (*0-7879-5038-6*) Jossey-Bass.

Cornwell, Don M. Horace the Pony & You. (Illus.). (Orig.). (J). (ps-4). 1996. pap. 4.95 (*0-9646734-1-X*) D M Cornwell.

— Sense & Nonsense. Holiday, Glenna & Roby, Tom, eds. (Orig.). 1995. pap. 10.00 (*0-9646734-0-1*) D M Cornwell.

Cornwell, Elmer, jt. auth. see Moakley, Maureen.

Cornwell, Elmer E., Jr. Presidential Leadership of Public Opinion. LC 78-11946. (Illus.). 370p. 1979. reprint ed. lib. bdg. 38.50 (*0-313-21076-4*, COPL, Greenwood Pr) Greenwood.

Cornwell, Gary. Real Answers: The True Story Told by Gary Cornwell, Deputy Chief Counsel, in Charge of the John F. Kennedy Assassination Investigation. LC 98-92011. 228p. 1998. 24.95 (*0-9666541-0-2*) Paleface Press.

***Cornwell, Grant H. & Stoddard, Eve W.** Global Multiculturalism: Comparative Perspectives on Ethnicity, Race & Nation. LC 00-40304. 2000. pap. write for info. (*0-7425-0883-8*) Rowman.

Cornwell, Grant H., jt. auth. see Guarasci, Richard.

Cornwell, Gretchen, et al. The State of the Commonwealth, 1998. (Illus.). 36p. 1998. pap. 20.00 (*1-58036-062-9*) Penn State Data Ctr.

Cornwell, Ilene, ed. see Berryhill, Judy.

Cornwell, Ilene J. Travel Guide to the Natchez Trace Parkway Between Natchez, MS, & Nashville, TN. LC 83-51206. (Illus.). 104p. (Orig.). 1984. pap. 7.95 (*0-915575-00-0*) Southern Resources.

Cornwell, J. F., ed. Group Theory in Physics: An Introduction. (Illus.). 326p. 1997. pap. text 59.95 (*0-12-189800-8*) Morgan Kaufmann.

Cornwell, JoAnne. That Hair Thing: And the Sisterlocks Approach. LC 97-91747. (Illus.). 192p. (Orig.). 1997. pap. 19.95 (*0-9657426-5-2*) Sisterlocks.

Cornwell, Jocelyn. Hard Earned Lives: Accounts of Health & Illness from East London. 250p. (Orig.). 1984. pap. 13.95 (*0-422-78580-6*, 9246, Pub. by Tavistock) Routldge.

Cornwell, John. Earth to Earth. large type ed. (Illus.). 288p. 1987. 27.99 (*0-7089-1609-0*) Ulverscroft.

Cornwell, John. Hiding Places of God: A Personal Journey into the World of Religious Visions, Holy Objects, & Miracles. 302p. 1991. 19.95 (*0-446-51468-3*, Pub. by Warner Bks) Little.

***Cornwell, John.** Hitler's Pope: The Secret History of Pius XII. 2000. pap. 15.00 (*0-14-029627-1*) Penguin Putnam.

Cornwell, John. Hitler's Pope: The Secret History of Pius XII. LC 99-28311. (Illus.). 512p. 1999. 29.95 (*0-670-88693-9*, Viking) Viking Penguin.

C

***Cornwell, John.** Intro to the Agricultural Institute. 100p. (C). 2000. ring bd. 24.95 (*0-7872-7315-5*) Kendall-Hunt.

Cornwell, John. Nature's Imagination: The Frontiers of Scientific Vision. (Illus.). 224p. 1995. 25.00 (*0-19-851775-0*) OUP.

— The Power to Harm. 336p. 1998. pap. 14.95 (*0-14-025471-4*) Viking Penguin.

— Power to Harm: Mind, Medicine, & Murder on Trial. LC 96-6722. xii, 321p. 1998. pap. 14.95 (*0-14-026996-7*) Viking Penguin.

***Cornwell, John, ed.** Big Canyon Country Guide to Kayaking in WV. deluxe ed. (Illus.). 2001. pap. 16.95 (*0-9700165-6-5*) Twin Rivers NC.

Cornwell, John, ed. Consciousness & Human Identity. LC 98-18360. (Illus.). 248p. 1998. 24.95 (*0-19-850323-7*) OUP.

Cornwell, John F. Group Theory in Physics, Vol. 2. (Techniques in Physics Ser.). 1984. text 89.95 (*0-12-189802-4*) Acad Pr.

— Group Theory in Physics, Vol. 2. (Techniques of Physics Ser.). 608p. 1986. pap. text 59.95 (*0-12-189804-0*) Acad Pr.

Cornwell, John F., ed. Group Theory in Physics: Supersymmetries & Infinite - Dimensional Algebras, Vol. 3. (Techniques of Physics Ser.). 628p. 1989. text 89.95 (*0-12-189805-9*) Acad Pr.

— Group Theory in Physics: Supersymmetries & Infinite - Dimensional Algebras, Vol. 3. (Techniques of Physics Ser.). 628p. 1992. text 59.95 (*0-12-189806-7*) Acad Pr.

Cornwell, Judy. The Seventh Sunrise. large type ed. (Large Print Ser.). 560p. 1996. 27.99 (*0-7089-3586-9*) Ulverscroft.

Cornwell-Kelly, M. P., jt. auth. see Rawlinson, W.

Cornwell-Kelly, M. P., jt. auth. see Rawlinson, William.

Cornwell-Kelly, Malachy P., jt. auth. see Rawlinson, William.

Cornwell, Linda, jt. auth. see Flanagan, Alice.

Cornwell, Linda, jt. auth. see Marx, David F.

Cornwell, N. Pushkin's the Queen of Spades: Critical Study. (Critical Studies in Russian Literature Ser.). 100p. 1993. pap. 14.95 (*1-85399-342-5*, Pub. by Brist Class Pr) Focus Pub-R Pullins.

Cornwell, N., tr. Odoevsky: The Salamander & Other Gothic Tales. (ENG & RUS.). 221p. 1992. pap. 22.95 (*1-85399-227-5*, Pub. by Brist Class Pr) Focus Pub-R Pullins.

Cornwell, Nancy. Adventures with Polar Fleece: A Sewing Expedition. LC 97-74596. (Illus.). 160p. 1997. pap. 19.95 (*0-87341-555-8*, AWPF) Krause Pubns.

— More Polarfleece Adventures: Exciting New Fleece Techniques from the Best-Selling Author of Adventures. LC 99-61442. 160p. 1999. pap. 19.95 (*0-87341-791-7*) Krause Pubns.

Cornwell, Neil. Essays on Vladimir Odoevsky. LC 97-28797. 174p. 1998. 39.95 (*1-57181-907-X*) Berghahn Bks.

Cornwell, Neil. The Life, Times & Milieu of V. F. Odoyevsky, 1804-1869. LC 88-174597. xiv, 417p. 1986. write for info. (*0-485-11279-5*, Pub. by Athlone Pr) Transaction Pubs.

— Vladimir Nabokov. (Writers & Their Works Ser.). 160p. 1999. pap. text 21.00 (*0-7463-0868-X*, Pub. by Northcote House) U Pr of Miss.

Cornwell, Neil, ed. Reference Guide to Russian Literature. LC 97-169924. 972p. 1998. lib. bdg. 140.00 (*1-884964-10-9*) Fitzroy Dearborn.

Cornwell, Neil & Malone, Maggie. The Turn of the Screw & What Maisie Knew: Henry James. LC 98-11472. (New Casebooks Ser.). 1998. text 45.00 (*0-312-21466-9*) St Martin.

Cornwell, Neil, ed. see Lermontov, Mikhail.

Cornwell, Neil, ed. & tr. see Odoevsky, Vladimir F.

Cornwell, Patricia. All That Remains. 416p. 1992. 20.00 (*0-684-19395-7*, Scribners Ref) Mac Lib Ref.

— All That Remains. LC 91-32457. (Kay Scarpetta Mystery Ser.). 416p. 1993. mass mkt. 7.99 (*0-380-71833-2*, Avon Bks) Morrow Avon.

Cornwell, Patricia. All That Remains. abr. ed. 1992. audio 17.00 (*1-55994-526-5*) HarperAudio.

Cornwell, Patricia. All That Remains. large type ed. 416p. 1992. 21.95 (*0-684-19515-1*); 23.95 (*0-8161-5526-7*, G K Hall Lrg Type) Mac Lib Ref.

Cornwell, Patricia. All That Remains: Burton,&Kate, Set. abr. ed. (Kay Scarpetta Mystery Ser.). 1994. audio 18.00 (*0-694-51471-3*, 390332, Pub. by HarperAudio) Lndmrk Audiobks.

— Black Notice. 464p. 2000. mass mkt. 7.99 (*0-425-17540-5*) Berkley Pub.

Cornwell, Patricia. Black Notice. LC 99-28776. 415p. 1999. 25.95 (*0-399-14508-7*, G P Putnam) Peng Put Young Read.

***Cornwell, Patricia.** Black Notice. large type ed. 2000. pap. 13.95 (*0-375-70771-9*) Random.

— Black Notice. large type ed. LC 99-34287. 576p. 1999. 25.95 (*0-375-40845-2*) Random Hse Lrg Prnt.

Cornwell, Patricia. Black Notice. limited ed. LC 99-28776. 368p. 1999. 150.00 (*0-399-14522-2*, G P Putnam) Peng Put Young Read.

— The Body Farm. LC 00-3342. 352p. 1995. mass mkt. 6.99 (*0-425-14863-7*, Prime Crime) Berkley Pub.

— The Body Farm. 400p. 1994. 23.00 (*0-684-19597-6*, Scribners Ref) Mac Lib Ref.

***Cornwell, Patricia.** The Body Farm. 1999. pap. text 9.98 (*0-671-04687-X*) S&S Trade.

Cornwell, Patricia. The Body Farm. large type ed. LC 94-34500. 1996. 18.95 (*0-7838-1123-3*, G K Hall Lrg Type) Mac Lib Ref.

— Body of Evidence. 400p. 1991. 18.95 (*0-684-19240-3*, Scribners Ref) Mac Lib Ref.

— Body of Evidence. (Kay Scarpetta Mystery Ser.). 416p. 1992. mass mkt. 6.99 (*0-380-71701-8*, Avon Bks) Morrow Avon.

— Body of Evidence. Pocket Books Staff, ed. 1999. per. 6.99 (*0-671-03856-7*) PB.

— Body of Evidence. large type ed. LC 93-27186. 1994. lib. bdg. 24.95 (*0-8161-5866-5*, G K Hall Lrg Type) Mac Lib Ref.

Cornwell, Patricia. Body of Evidence: Crouse,&Lindsay. abr. ed. 1995. audio 18.00 (*0-694-51592-2*, CPN 2267) HarperAudio.

Cornwell, Patricia. Cause of Death. 368p. 1997. mass mkt. 7.50 (*0-425-15861-6*) Berkley Pub.

— Cause of Death. LC 96-12114. 352p. 1996. 25.95 (*0-399-14146-4*, G P Putnam) Peng Put Young Read.

— Cause of Death, 4 vols., abr. ed. 1996. 23.50 incl. audio (*0-679-44508-0*) Discovery.

— Cause of Death. large type ed. LC 96-12114. 1996. lib. bdg. 27.95 (*0-7838-1792-4*, G K Hall Lrg Type) Mac Lib Ref.

— Cruel & Unusual. 1993. 21.00 (*0-684-19599-2*, Scribners Ref) Mac Lib Ref.

— Cruel & Unusual. 384p. 1993. 21.00 (*0-684-19530-5*, Scribners Ref) Mac Lib Ref.

— Cruel & Unusual. 416p. 1994. mass mkt. 7.99 (*0-380-71834-0*, Avon Bks) Morrow Avon.

— Cruel & Unusual. large type ed. LC 92-38203. (General Ser.). 1993. 25.00 (*0-8161-5727-8*, G K Hall Lrg Type) Mac Lib Ref.

— Cruel & Unusual. large type ed. 448p. 1993. 23.00 (*0-684-19612-3*) Mac Lib Ref.

Cornwell, Patricia. Cruel & Unusual: Burton,&Kate, Set. abr. ed. (Kate Scarpetta Mystery Ser.). 3p. 1993. audio 18.00 (*1-55994-712-8*, 390583, Pub. by HarperAudio) Lndmrk Audiobks.

Cornwell, Patricia. From Potter's Field. 352p. 1996. mass mkt. 7.99 (*0-425-15409-2*) Berkley Pub.

— From Potter's Field. 1995. 29.50 (*0-684-81318-1*) S&S Trade.

— From Potter's Field. large type ed. LC 95-30611. 456p. 1995. 25.95 (*0-7838-1291-4*, G K Hall Lrg Type) Mac Lib Ref.

Cornwell, Patricia. From Potter's Field. large type ed. LC 95-30611. (Core Collection). 434p. 1997. 23.95 (*0-7838-1292-2*, G K Hall Lrg Type) Mac Lib Ref.

Cornwell, Patricia. From Potter's Field. large type ed. LC 95-30611. 416p. 1995. 23.50 (*0-684-19598-4*) S&S Trade.

— Hornet's Nest. 369p. 1998. mass mkt. 7.50 (*0-425-16098-X*) Berkley Pub.

— Hornet's Nest. LC 96-3208. 384p. 1997. 25.95 (*0-399-14228-2*, G P Putnam) Peng Put Young Read.

— Hornet's Nest. large type ed. LC 96-53887. 490p. 1998. pap. 25.95 (*0-7838-8086-3*, G K Hall Lrg Type) Mac Lib Ref.

***Cornwell, Patricia.** The Last Precinct. 432p. 2000. 26.95 (*0-399-14625-3*) Putnam Pub Group.

— The Last Precinct. large type ed. LC 00-21645. 688p. 2000. 26.95 (*0-375-43068-7*) Random Hse Lrg Prnt.

— The Last Precinct. limited ed. 432p. 2000. 150.00 (*0-399-14639-3*) Putnam Pub Group.

Cornwell, Patricia. Life's Little Fable. LC 98-3669. (Illus.). 40p. (J). 1999. 16.99 (*0-399-23316-4*) Putnam Pub Group.

Cornwell, Patricia. Patricia Cornwell: 3 Complete Novels: Postmortem; Body of Evidence; All That Remains. 832p. 1997. 14.98 (*0-7651-9112-1*) Smithmark.

— Point of Origin. LC 98-10479. 368p. 1999. 25.95 (*0-399-14394-7*, G P Putnam) Peng Put Young Read.

Cornwell, Patricia. Point of Origin. large type ed. LC 98-23618. 542p. 1998. write for info. (*0-7540-2149-1*) Chivers N Amer.

— Point of Origin. large type ed. LC 98-23618. 543p. 1998. pap. 20.00 (*0-7862-1478-3*) Thorndike Pr.

— Point of Origin. large type ed. LC 98-23618. 582p. 1998. 20.00 (*0-7862-1477-5*) Thorndike Pr.

***Cornwell, Patricia.** Point of Origin. limited ed. 350p. 1998. 150.00 (*0-399-14412-9*, G P Putnam) Peng Put Young Read.

Cornwell, Patricia. Point of Origin. 397p. 1999. reprint ed. mass mkt. 7.99 (*0-425-16986-3*) Berkley Pub.

***Cornwell, Patricia.** Postmortem. (SPA.). 1999. pap. 14.95 (*970-05-0943-5*) Distribks Inc.

Cornwell, Patricia. Postmortem. 352p. 1991. mass mkt. 6.49 (*0-380-71021-8*, Avon Bks) Morrow Avon.

— Postmortem. (Kay Scarpetta Mystery Ser.). 352p. 2000. mass mkt. 7.99 (*0-671-02361-6*, Pocket Books) PB.

— Ruth, a Portrait: The Story of Ruth Bell Graham. (Illus.). 304p. 1998. pap. 10.95 (*0-385-48900-5*) Bantam.

— Ruth, a Portrait: The Story of Ruth Bell Graham. LC 96-41961. (Illus.). 304p. 1997. 21.95 (*0-385-48879-3*) Doubleday.

— Ruth, a Portrait: The Story of Ruth Bell Graham. large type ed. LC 97-41242. 571p. 1997. 26.95 (*0-7838-8331-5*, G K Hall Lrg Type) Mac Lib Ref.

— Scarpetta's Winter Table. LC 98-35159. (Illus.). 96p. 1998. 19.95 (*0-941711-42-0*, Pub. by Wyrick & Co) Putnam Pub Group.

***Cornwell, Patricia.** Southern Cross. 1999. mass mkt. 7.99 (*0-425-17254-6*) Berkley Pub.

Cornwell, Patricia. Southern Cross. LC 98-39751. 368p. 1999. 25.95 (*0-399-14465-X*) Putnam Pub Group.

— Southern Cross. large type ed. LC 99-18706. 1999. pap. 28.95 (*1-56895-709-2*) Wheeler Pub.

***Cornwell, Patricia.** Southern Cross. large type ed. 2000. pap. 11.95 (*1-56895-973-7*) Wheeler Pub.

Cornwell, Patricia. Unnatural Exposure. 367p. 1998. mass mkt. 7.99 (*0-425-16340-7*) Berkley Pub.

— Unnatural Exposure. LC 96-38460. 352p. 1997. 25.95 (*0-399-14285-1*, G P Putnam) Peng Put Young Read.

— Unnatural Exposure. large type ed. LC 96-54064. (Core Ser.). 415p. 1997. lib. bdg. 28.95 (*0-7838-8087-1*, G K Hall Lrg Type) Mac Lib Ref.

— Unnatural Exposure. large type ed. LC 96-54064. 415p. 1999. pap. 26.95 (*0-7838-8088-X*, G K Hall Lrg Type) Mac Lib Ref.

— Unnatural Exposure. limited ed. 352p. 1997. 150.00 (*0-399-14295-9*, G P Putnam) Peng Put Young Read.

Cornwell, R. D. World History in the Twentieth Century. 2nd ed. (Illus.). 1981. text 24.80 (*0-582-33074-2*, 72032) Longman.

Cornwell, Roger & Staunton, Marie. Data Protection: Putting the Record Straight. (C). 1988. 30.00 (*0-946088-16-0*, Pub. by NCCL) St Mut.

Cornwell, S. & Kott, Mike. House of Collectibles Price Guide to Star Wars Collectibles. 4th ed. 288p. 1998. pap. 19.95 (*0-87637-995-1*) Hse Collectbls.

Cornwell, S. V. Curtis Jenkins Cornwell & Company: A Study in Professional Origins, 1816-1966. LC 90-14043. (New Works in Accounting History). 200p. 1991. text 15.00 (*0-8153-0004-2*) Garland.

Cornwell, Sherry. The Labyrinth Called Planet Earth. 120p. 1994. pap. 10.95 (*0-9644429-0-6*) Natarr Pr.

Cornwell, Stephen, jt. auth. see Cornwell, Debbie.

Cornwell, Steve, jt. ed. see Freeman, Donald.

***Cornwell, Steven, ed.** Ripe: New Design in Australia. (Illus.). 252p. 1999. text 55.00 (*90-5703-422-0*, Pub. by Craftsman House) Gordon & Breach.

Cornwell, T. & Perley, R., eds. Radio Interferometry: Theory, Techniques & Observations. (ASP Conference Series Proceedings: Vol. 19). 463p. 1991. 34.00 (*0-937707-38-4*) Astron Soc Pacific.

Cornwell, Terri L. Democracy & the Arts: The Role of Participation. LC 90-30004. 232p. 1990. 59.95 (*0-275-93070-X*, C3070, Praeger Pubs) Greenwood.

Cornyetz, Nina. Dangerous Women, Deadly Words: Phallic Fantasy & Modernity in Izumi Kyoka, Enchi Fumiko, & Nakagami Kenji. LC 98-30575. 336p. 1999. 45.00 (*0-8047-3212-4*) Stanford U Pr.

Cornyn, Anthony G. & Mays, Elizabeth, eds. Interest Rate Risk Models: Theory & Practice. 450p. 1997. 65.00 (*1-888998-04-0*) Glenlake Pub.

Cornyn, Anthony J., et al, eds. Controlling & Managing Interest-Rate Risk. LC 97-11437. 512p. (C). 1997. text 75.00 (*0-13-570466-9*) P-H.

Cornyn, Anthony J. & Mays, Elizabeth. Interest-Rate Models: Theory & Practice. (Glenlake Business Monographs). 450p. 1998. 65.00 (*1-884964-72-9*) Fitzroy Dearborn.

Cornyn, J. H. Mexican Fairy Tales. 1972. 59.95 (*0-8490-0614-7*) Gordon Pr.

Cornyn, John, et al. Noncommercial Foodservice Management: An Administrator's Handbook. LC 94-17566. 305p. 1994. 64.95 incl. disk (*0-471-00880-X*) Wiley.

Cornyn-Selby, Alyce P. Alyce's Fat Chance: How to Take off 100 Pounds & Keep It Off! 72p. (Orig.). 1989. pap. text 8.95 (*0-941383-13-X*) Beynch Pr.

— Coming Apart at the Seems. 166p. 1991. pap. 11.00 (*0-941383-16-4*) Beynch Pr.

— Did She Leave Me Any Money? 198p. 1991. pap. text 11.95 (*0-941383-11-3*) Beynch Pr.

— I Don't Have to & You Can't Make Me: What You Can Accomplish with Anger. (Illus.). 48p. (Orig.). 1988. pap. 8.95 (*0-941383-04-0*) Beynch Pr.

— I'm Going to Change My Name & Move Away! Ultimate Change Method for Behavior. 72p. (Orig.). 1988. pap. 8.95 (*0-941383-06-7*) Beynch Pr.

— Making Your Mark: That's Marketing (8 Step Checklist for Marketing Right) (Illus.). 74p. (Orig.). 1988. pap. 8.95 (*0-941383-05-9*) Beynch Pr.

— One Thing Worse Than Being Alone - Wishing You Were! Craving Solitude & Getting It. 78p. (Orig.). 1989. pap. 8.95 (*0-941383-07-5*) Beynch Pr.

— Procrastinator's Success Kit. 172p. 1987. pap. 12.95 (*0-941383-01-6*) Beynch Pr.

— Procrastinator's Success Kit: How to Get What You Really Want from Yourself. rev. ed. LC 86-33444. (Illus.). 196p. 1987. reprint ed. pap. 12.95 (*0-941383-03-2*) Beynch Pr.

— Self-Sabotage: Solve It! 80p. 1989. pap. 8.95 (*0-941383-09-1*) Beynch Pr.

— Take Your Hands off My Attitude: Your Right to a Bad Attitude. 48p. (Orig.). 1987. pap. 8.95 (*0-941383-02-4*) Beynch Pr.

— Teamwork & Team Sabotage: New Look at the Team Concept. Orig. Title: Whatever Happened to Teamwork?. 84p. 1994. pap. text 8.95 (*0-941383-22-9*) Beynch Pr.

***Cornyn-Selby, Alyce P.** What's Your Sabotage? The Last Word in Overcoming Self-Sabotage. (Illus.). 210p. 2000. boxed set 15.95 (*0-941383-28-8*, Pub. by Beynch Pr) Metamorphous Pr.

Cornyn-Selby, Alyce P. Why Do Winners Win? Can Anyone Be a Winner? 64p. (Orig.). (C). 1990. pap. 8.95 (*0-941383-12-1*) Beynch Pr.

— Why Winners Win: Winning: Can Anyone Be a Winner? rev. ed. Orig. Title: Why Do Winners Win?. (Illus.). 64p. 1996. pap. 8.95 (*0-941383-23-7*) Beynch Pr.

Cornyn, William S. Spoken Burmese, Bk. I. (Spoken Language Ser.). 165p. 1979. audio 75.00 (*0-87950-025-5*) Spoken Lang Serv.

Cornyn, William S. Spoken Burmese, Bk. 1. (Spoken Language Ser.). 165p. 1979. pap. 90.00 incl. audio (*0-87950-026-3*) Spoken Lang Serv.

— Spoken Burmese, Bk. 1, Units 1-12. (Spoken Language Ser.). 165p. 1979. pap. 15.00 (*0-87950-020-4*) Spoken Lang Serv.

Cornyn, William S. & Roop, D. Haigh. Beginning Burmese. LC 66-21513. (Yale Linguistic Ser.). 525p. reprint ed. pap. 162.80 (*0-8357-7100-8*, 201109100074) Bks Demand.

Corob, Alison. Working with Depressed Women. 1987. 39.95 (*0-566-05424-8*) Ashgate Pub Co.

Corob, Alison. Working with Depressed Women: A Feminist Approach. (Community Care Practice Handbook Ser.). Orig. Title: Social Work with Depressed Women. 200p. 1987. pap. 18.95 (*0-566-05100-1*) Ashgate Pub Co.

Corominas i Vigneaux, Joan. Diccionari Etimologic i Complementari de la Llengua Catalana, Vol. 1. 6th ed. (CAT.). 900p. 1991. 150.00 (*0-7859-6201-8*, 8472561747) Fr & Eur.

— Diccionari Etimologic i Complementari de la Llengua Catalana, Vol. 2. 5th ed. (CAT.). 1120p. 1990. 150.00 (*0-7859-6202-6*, 8472561917) Fr & Eur.

— Diccionari Etimologic i Complementari de la Llengua Catalana, Vol. 3. 3rd ed. (CAT.). 1054p. 1985. 150.00 (*0-7859-6203-4*, 8472562042) Fr & Eur.

— Diccionari Etimologic i Complementari de la Llengua Catalana, Vol. 4. 4th ed. (CAT.). 964p. 1991. 150.00 (*0-7859-6204-2*, 8472562190) Fr & Eur.

— Diccionari Etimologic i Complementari de la Llengua Catalana, Vol. 5. 3rd ed. (CAT.). 996p. 1990. 150.00 (*0-7859-6205-0*, 8472562484) Fr & Eur.

— Diccionari Etimologic i Complementari de la Llengua Catalana, Vol. 7. 3rd ed. (CAT.). 1007p. 1991. 150.00 (*0-7859-6206-9*, 8472562972) Fr & Eur.

— Diccionari Etimologic i Complementari de la Llengua Catalana, Vol. 8. 2nd ed. (CAT.). 1000p. 1988. 150.00 (*0-7859-6207-7*, 8472563154) Fr & Eur.

Corominas i Vigneaux, Joan & Pascual, J. A. Shorter Etymological Dictionary of the Spanish Language: Breve Diccionario Etimologico de la Lengua Espanola. 3rd ed. (SPA.). 628p. 1990. write for info. (*0-7859-4949-6*) Fr & Eur.

Corominas, J. Breve Diccionario Etimologico de la Lengua Castellana. (SPA.). 628p. 1993. 125.00 (*84-249-1332-9*) Elliots Bks.

— Diccionario Critico Etimologico Castellano E Hispanico, 6 vols., Set. (SPA.). 5710p. 1993. 1000.00 (*0-614-00134-X*) Elliots Bks.

— Diccionario Critico Etimologico Castellano e Hispanico, 6 vols., Set. (SPA.). 5710p. 1993. 1000.00 (*0-614-00239-7*) Elliots Bks.

— Diccionario Critico Etimologico Castellano e Hispanico, Vol. 1. (SPA.). 1993. write for info. (*84-249-1361-2*) Elliots Bks.

— Diccionario Critico Etimologico Castellano E Hispanico, Vol. 2. (SPA.). 1993. write for info. (*84-249-1363-9*) Elliots Bks.

— Diccionario Critico Etimologico Castellano e Hispanico, Vol. 3. (SPA.). 1993. write for info. (*84-249-1365-5*) Elliots Bks.

— Diccionario Critico Etimologico Castellano E Hispanico, Vol. 5. (SPA.). 1993. write for info. (*84-249-0879-1*) Elliots Bks.

— Diccionario Critico Etimologico Castellano e Hispanico, Vol. 6. (SPA.). 1993. write for info. (*84-249-1456-2*) Elliots Bks.

Corominas, J. & Pascual, J. A. Critical Etymological Dictionary of the Spanish Language (Diccionario Critico Etimologico de la Lengua Espanola), 6 vols. 2nd ed. (SPA.). 6000p. 1991. 695.00 (*0-7859-3343-3*, S11937) Fr & Eur.

— Diccionario Critico Etimologico Castellano E Hispanico, Vol. 4. (SPA.). 1993. write for info. (*84-249-0066-9*) Elliots Bks.

Corominas, Pedro. Obra Completa en Castellano. (SPA.). 640p. 1993. 100.00 (*84-249-3319-2*) Elliots Bks.

Coromines i Vigneaux, Joan. Diccionario Critico Etimologico Casteliano e Hispanico, 1. 2nd ed. (SPA.). write for info. (*0-7859-5793-6*) Fr & Eur.

— Diccionario Critico Etimologico Casteliano e Hispanico, 2. 2nd ed. (SPA.). write for info. (*0-7859-5794-4*) Fr & Eur.

— Diccionario Critico Etimologico Casteliano e Hispanico, 3. 2nd ed. (SPA.). write for info. (*0-7859-5795-2*) Fr & Eur.

— Diccionario Critico Etimologico Casteliano e Hispanico, 4. 2nd ed. (SPA.). write for info. (*0-7859-5785-5*) Fr & Eur.

— Diccionario Critico Etimologico Casteliano e Hispanico, 5. 2nd ed. (SPA.). write for info. (*0-7859-5786-3*) Fr & Eur.

— Diccionario Critico Etimologico Casteliano e Hispanico, 6. 2nd ed. (SPA.). write for info. (*0-7859-5796-0*) Fr & Eur.

Coron, Jean-Michel, et al, eds. Nematics: Mathematical & Physical Aspects. (C). 1991. text 208.50 (*0-7923-1113-2*) Kluwer Academic.

Corona, Angel. The Adventuresome Angels: A Story of Who We Are & Why We Are Here. (Illus.). 45p. (Orig.). 1987. pap. 5.10 (*0-685-29955-4*) Heaven On Earth.

Corona, Belva. Heaven, Home & Fireside: A Collection of Poetry. Wright, Regina M. & Tomerlin, Gayle, eds. 82p. 1986. pap. 6.95 (*0-9616840-0-3*) B Corona.

Corona, Deanna. GED Interpreting Literature & the Arts. 1989. pap. text, student ed. 14.95 (*1-56030-006-X*) Comex Systs.

Corona, Gyl. Basic Cardiac Anatomy: A Self-Learning Module. Clutter, Pat, ed. LC 97-62500. (Illus.). 128p. 1998. pap. 19.95 (*1-880254-50-6*) Vista.

***Corona, Laura E.** Aprendiendo a Vivir: No Importa Que Problemas Tengas, Puedes Apiendera Vivir Tranquilamante. 2nd ed. (SPA.). 128p. 1999. pap. 15.95 (*970-92299-0-7*) Corona.

***Corona, Laurel.** Brazil. LC 99-23478. (Overview Ser.). (Illus.). 144p. (YA). (gr. 6-9). 2000. lib. bdg. 23.70 (*1-56006-621-0*) Lucent Bks.

Corona, Laurel. Kenya. LC 99-25321. (Overview Ser.). (Illus.). 144p. (YA). (gr. 6-9). 2000. lib. bdg. 23.70 (*1-56006-590-7*) Lucent Bks.

***Corona, Laurel.** Life in Moscow, Russia. LC 00-9164. (Way People Live Ser.). (Illus.). (YA). 2000. write for info. (*1-56006-795-0*) Lucent Bks.

— Poland. LC 99-50797. (Modern Nations of the World Ser.). (Illus.). 144p. (YA). (gr. 4-12). 2000. 18.96 (*1-56006-600-8*) Lucent Bks.

— South Africa. LC 99-38763. (Overview Ser.). (Illus.). 144p. (YA). (gr. 6-9). 2000. lib. bdg. 23.70 (*1-56006-601-6*) Lucent Bks.

***Corona, Piermaria & Zeide, Boris, eds.** Contested Issues of Ecosystem Management. LC 99-51660. (Journal of Sustainable Forestry Ser.: Vol. 9, Nos. 1/2). 183p. 1999. 49.95 (*1-56022-065-1*); pap. text 24.95 (*1-56022-067-8*) Haworth Pr.

Corona, Rossana, jt. ed. see Glade, William P.

Corona, Rossana, jt. ed. see Sanchez, Manuel.

Corona, Simon, tr. see Yates, K. M.

Corona, Vicki. Advanced Belly Dancing, Vol. I, Bk. 12. (Celebrate the Cultures Ser.). (Illus.). 28p. 1989. pap. 14.95 (*1-58513-025-7*) Dance Fantasy.

— Advanced Hawaiian Dancing, Vol. II, Bk. 20. (Celebrate the Cultures Ser.). (Illus.). 32p. 1989. pap. 14.95 (*1-58513-010-9*) Dance Fantasy.

— Advanced Middle Eastern Choreographies, Vol. I, Bk. 13. (Celebrate the Cultures Ser.). (Illus.). 20p. 1989. pap. 14.95 (*1-58513-026-5*) Dance Fantasy.

— All about Middle Eastern Floor Dancing, Vol. I, Bk. 18. (Celebrate the Cultures Ser.). (Illus.). 28p. 1989. pap. 14.95 (*1-58513-031-1*) Dance Fantasy.

— Art of Samoan Dance, Vol. II, Bk. 23. (Celebrate the Cultures Ser.). (Illus.). 32p. 1989. pap. 14.95 (*1-58513-013-3*) Dance Fantasy.

— Ballet Folklorico, Vol. III, Bk. 12. (Celebrate the Cultures Ser.). (Illus.). 26p. 1989. pap. 14.95 (*1-58513-041-9*) Dance Fantasy.

— Belly Dance Costume Making, Vol. I, Bk. 21. (Celebrate the Cultures Ser.). (Illus.). 34p. 1989. pap. 15.95 (*1-58513-034-6*) Dance Fantasy.

— "Bertha Belly" Pincushion & Ragdoll Pattern, Vol. I, Bk. 25. (Celebrate the Cultures Ser.). (Illus.). 22p. 1990. pap. 6.95 (*1-58513-038-9*) Dance Fantasy.

Corona, Vicki. Braids, Buns, Bows & Fun. large type rev. ed. (Celebrate the Cultures Ser.: Vol. 3, Bk. 15). (Illus.). 1989. pap. 14.95 (*1-58513-077-X*) Dance Fantasy.

Corona, Vicki. Caribbean Fantasies, Vol. III, Bk. 13. (Celebrate the Cultures Ser.). (Illus.). 30p. 1989. pap. 14.95 (*1-58513-042-7*) Dance Fantasy.

— Children's Ethnic Crafts, Vol. IV, Bk. 17. (Celebrate the Cultures Ser.). (Illus.). 58p. 1989. pap. 19.95 (*1-58513-050-8*) Dance Fantasy.

— Children's Luau Event, 2 bks., Vol. II, Bk. 31. (Celebrate the Cultures Ser.). (Illus.). 34p. 1989. pap. 19.95 incl. audio (*1-58513-021-4*) Dance Fantasy.

— China Folk Dance, Vol. VI, Bk. 11. (Celebrate the Cultures Ser.). (Illus.). 32p. 1989. pap., wbk. ed. 14.95 (*1-58513-064-8*) Dance Fantasy.

— Ciao! Italian Dance, Vol. VIII, Bk. 12. (Celebrate the Cultures Ser.). (Illus.). 34p. 1989. pap. 14.95 (*1-58513-061-3*) Dance Fantasy.

— Costume Jewelry Making, Vol. IV, Bk. 11. (Celebrate the Cultures Ser.). (Illus.). 34p. 1989. pap. 14.95 (*1-58513-044-3*) Dance Fantasy.

— Dancers! How to Promote Yourself, Vol. V, Bk. 10. (Celebrate the Cultures Ser.). (Illus.). 42p. 1989. pap. 14.95 (*1-58513-052-4*) Dance Fantasy.

— Dances of Indonesia, Vol. VI, Bk. 12. (Celebrate the Cultures Ser.). (Illus.). 30p. 1989. pap. 14.95 (*1-58513-066-4*) Dance Fantasy.

— Dances of Kuwait, Vol. I, Bk. 15. (Celebrate the Cultures Ser.). (Illus.). 24p. 1989. pap. 14.95 (*1-58513-028-1*) Dance Fantasy.

— Dances of Switzerland, Vol. VIII, Bk. 12. (Celebrate the Cultures Ser.). (Illus.). 26p. 1990. pap. 14.95 (*1-58513-062-1*) Dance Fantasy.

— Ethnic Dancer's International Cookbook: Mid-East/Africa/India, Vol. VII, Bk. 10. (Celebrate the Cultures Ser.). (Illus.). 38p. 1989. pap. 16.95 (*1-58513-056-7*) Dance Fantasy.

— Even More International Recipes: Americas/Caribbean, Vol. VII, Bk. 12. (Celebrate the Cultures Ser.). (Illus.). 50p. 1990. pap. 16.95 (*1-58513-058-3*) Dance Fantasy.

— Exotic Dances of Tonga, Vol. II, Bk. 24. (Celebrate the Cultures Ser.). (Illus.). 24p. 1989. pap. 14.95 (*1-58513-014-1*) Dance Fantasy.

— Fitness Guide for Dancers, Vol. IV, Bk. 15. (Celebrate the Cultures Ser.). (Illus.). 42p. 1989. pap. 14.95 (*1-58513-048-6*) Dance Fantasy.

— Flamenco Basics, Vol. III, Bk. 10. (Celebrate the Cultures Ser.). (Illus.). 34p. 1989. pap. 14.95 (*1-58513-039-7*) Dance Fantasy.

— Flower Power, Vol. IV, Bk. 12. (Celebrate the Cultures Ser.). (Illus.). 42p. 1989. pap. 14.95 (*1-58513-045-1*) Dance Fantasy.

— Folk Dances of the Philippines, Vol. VI, Bk. 10. (Celebrate the Cultures Ser.). (Illus.). 30p. 1989. pap. 14.95 (*1-58513-063-X*) Dance Fantasy.

Corona, Vicki. French Cancan Costumes, Vol. VIII, Bk. 13. (Illus.). 34p. 1989. pap. 14.95 (*1-58513-074-5*) Dance Fantasy.

Corona, Vicki. Fun! Ethnic Dance Instruction, Vol. V, Bk. 11. (Celebrate the Cultures Ser.). (Illus.). 36p. 1989. pap. 14.95 (*1-58513-053-2*) Dance Fantasy.

— German Oom-Pah-Pah, Vol. VIII, Bk. 10. (Celebrate the Cultures Ser.). (Illus.). 30p. 1990. pap. 14.95 (*1-58513-060-5*) Dance Fantasy.

— Gourd Mania, Vol. IV, Bk. 18. (Celebrate the Cultures Ser.). (Illus.). 34p. 1989. pap. 14.95 (*1-58513-051-6*) Dance Fantasy.

— Greek Folk Dancing, Vol. 1, Bk. 23. (Celebrate the Cultures Ser.). (Illus.). 26p. 1989. pap. 14.95 (*1-58513-036-2*, 58513) Dance Fantasy.

— Hawaiian Choreographies, Vol. II, Bk. 25. (Celebrate the Cultures Ser.). (Illus.). 34p. 1989. pap. 14.95 (*1-58513-015-X*) Dance Fantasy.

— Hawaiian Costume Making, Vol. II, Bk. 15. (Celebrate the Cultures Ser.). (Illus.). 34p. 1989. pap. 15.95 (*1-58513-005-2*) Dance Fantasy.

— Hawaiian Implements (Ipus & Pu'ilis), Vol. II, Bk. 13. (Celebrate the Cultures Ser.). (Illus.). 28p. 1989. pap. 14.95 (*1-58513-003-6*) Dance Fantasy.

— Hawaiian Implements "2" Uli'Ulis & Ili'Ilis, Vol. II, Bk. 14. (Celebrate the Cultures Ser.). (Illus.). 28p. 1989. pap. 14.95 (*1-58513-004-4*) Dance Fantasy.

— Hawaiian Weddings, Vol. II, Bk. 29. (Celebrate the Cultures Ser.). (Illus.). 30p. 1989. pap. 14.95 (*1-58513-019-2*) Dance Fantasy.

— How to Create a World Dance Company, Vol. V, Bk. 13. (Celebrate the Cultures Ser.). (Illus.). 42p. 1990. pap. 14.95 (*1-58513-055-9*) Dance Fantasy.

— How to Perform for Children, Vol. IV, Bk. 14. (Celebrate the Cultures Ser.). (Illus.). 34p. 1989. pap. 14.95 (*1-58513-047-8*) Dance Fantasy.

— Hula Kahiko, Vol. II, Bk. 27. (Celebrate the Cultures Ser.). (Illus.). 34p. 1989. pap. 14.95 (*1-58513-017-6*) Dance Fantasy.

— Hula Kahiko Choreographies, Vol. II, Bk. 28. (Celebrate the Cultures Ser.). (Illus.). 30p. 1989. pap. 14.95 (*1-58513-018-4*) Dance Fantasy.

— "Hula Lula" & "Tahiti Sweetie" Pincushion Patterns, Vol. II, Bk. 30. (Celebrate the Cultures Ser.). (Illus.). 22p. 1989. pap. 6.95 (*1-58513-020-6*) Dance Fantasy.

— Intermediate Belly Dancing, Vol. I, Bk. 11. (Celebrate the Cultures Ser.). (Illus.). 28p. 1989. pap. 14.95 (*1-58513-024-9*) Dance Fantasy.

— Intermediate Hawaiian Dancing, Vol. II, Bk. 16. (Celebrate the Cultures Ser.). (Illus.). 32p. 1989. pap. 14.95 (*1-58513-006-0*) Dance Fantasy.

— International Birthdays, Etc., Vol. IV, Bk. 13. (Celebrate the Cultures Ser.). (Illus.). 40p. 1990. pap. 14.95 (*1-58513-046-X*) Dance Fantasy.

— Israeli Folk Dancing, Vol. I, Bk. 24. (Celebrate the Cultures Ser.). (Illus.). 30p. 1990. pap. 14.95 (*1-58513-037-0*) Dance Fantasy.

— Just One More International Cookbook: Asia/Polynesia, Vol. VII, Bk. 13. (Celebrate the Cultures Ser.). (Illus.). 38p. 1990. pap. 16.95 (*1-58513-059-1*) Dance Fantasy.

— Learn Hawaiian Dancing, Vol. II, Bk. 10. (Celebrate the Cultures Ser.). (Illus.). 28p. 1989. pap., student ed. 14.95 (*1-58513-000-1*) Dance Fantasy.

— Learn Maori Tribe of New Zealand Dance, Vol. II, Bk. 12. (Celebrate the Cultures Ser.). (Illus.). 28p. 1989. pap. 14.95 (*1-58513-002-8*) Dance Fantasy.

— Learn Tahitian Dancing, Vol. II, Bk. 11. (Celebrate the Cultures Ser.). (Illus.). 24p. 1989. pap. 14.95 (*1-58513-001-X*) Dance Fantasy.

— Learn to Belly Dance, Vol. I, Bk. 10. (Celebrate the Cultures Ser.). (Illus.). 34p. 1989. pap. 14.95 (*1-58513-023-0*) Dance Fantasy.

— Legend of the Jesus Candy. (Celebrate the Cultures Ser.: Vol. X, Bk. 10). (Illus.). 26p. (J). (ps-7). 1990. pap. 14.95 (*1-58513-999-8*) Dance Fantasy.

— Maori Tribe Choreographies, Vol. II, Bk. 21. (Celebrate the Cultures Ser.). (Illus.). 28p. 1989. pap. 14.95 (*1-58513-011-7*) Dance Fantasy.

— Maori Tribe of New Zealand Costume-Making, Vol. II, Bk. 22. (Celebrate the Cultures Ser.). (Illus.). 28p. 1989. pap. 15.95 (*1-58513-012-5*) Dance Fantasy.

— Mexican Folk Dance, Vol. III, Bk. 11. (Celebrate the Cultures Ser.). (Illus.). 22p. 1989. pap. 14.95 (*1-58513-040-0*) Dance Fantasy.

— Middle Eastern Candle Dancing, Vol. I, Bk. 22. (Celebrate the Cultures Ser.). (Illus.). 24p. 1989. pap. 14.95 (*1-58513-035-4*) Dance Fantasy.

— Middle Eastern Cane Dancing, Vol. I, Bk. 17. (Celebrate the Cultures Ser.). (Illus.). 24p. 1989. pap. 14.95 (*1-58513-030-3*) Dance Fantasy.

— Middle Eastern Folk Dance Costumes, Vol. I, Bk. 20. (Celebrate the Cultures Ser.). (Illus.). 44p. 1990. pap. 15.95 (*1-58513-033-8*) Dance Fantasy.

— More International Recipes: Europe, Vol. VII, Bk. 11. (Celebrate the Cultures Ser.). (Illus.). 50p. 1989. pap. 16.95 (*1-58513-057-5*) Dance Fantasy.

— No Sew Ethnic Wraps, Vol. IV, Bk. 16. (Celebrate the Cultures Ser.). (Illus.). 34p. 1989. pap. 14.95 (*1-58513-049-4*) Dance Fantasy.

— Ori Tahiti, Vol. II, Bk. 17. (Celebrate the Cultures Ser.). (Illus.). 32p. 1989. pap. 14.95 (*1-58513-007-9*) Dance Fantasy.

— Polynesian Dancing for Men, Vol. II, Bk. 26. (Celebrate the Cultures Ser.). (Illus.). 34p. 1989. pap. 14.95 (*1-58513-016-8*) Dance Fantasy.

— A Rhapsody in Veils, Vol. I, Bk. 19. (Celebrate the Cultures Ser.). (Illus.). 28p. 1989. pap. 14.95 (*1-58513-032-X*) Dance Fantasy.

— Stage Make-Up, Vol. IV, Bk. 10. (Celebrate the Cultures Ser.). (Illus.). 42p. 1989. pap. 14.95 (*1-58513-043-5*) Dance Fantasy.

— Tahitian Choreographies, Vol. II, Bk. 18. (Celebrate the Cultures Ser.). (Illus.). 32p. 1989. pap. 14.95 (*1-58513-008-7*) Dance Fantasy.

— Tahitian Costume-Making, Vol. II, Bk. 19. (Celebrate the Cultures Ser.). (Illus.). 38p. 1989. pap. 15.95 (*1-58513-009-5*) Dance Fantasy.

— Tunisian Jug Dancing, Vol. I, Bk. 14. (Celebrate the Cultures Ser.). (Illus.). 28p. 1989. pap. 14.95 (*1-58513-027-3*) Dance Fantasy.

— Turkish Scimitar Dancing, Vol. I, Bk. 16. (Celebrate the Cultures Ser.). (Illus.). 24p. 1989. pap. 14.95 (*1-58513-029-X*) Dance Fantasy.

— Wedding Promotions, Vol. V, Bk. 12. (Celebrate the Cultures Ser.). (Illus.). 32p. 1990. pap. 14.95 (*1-58513-054-0*) Dance Fantasy.

Coronado. Enrichment Program for Art in Action Grade 1. 1987. pap., teacher ed. 12.00 (*0-15-770058-5*) Harcourt Schl Pubs.

Coronado, Eugenio, ed. Molecular Magnetism - From Molecular Assemblies to the Devices: Proceedings of the NATO Advanced Study Institute on 'Localized & Itinerany Molecular Magnetism: From Molecular Assemblies to the Devices', Puerto de la Cruz, Tenerife, Spain, April 23-May 3, 1995. LC 96-26728. (NATO Advance Science Institutes Series E). 604p. (C). 1996. text 306.00 (*0-7923-4130-9*) Kluwer Academic.

Coronado, Karen & Mathis, Richard. Woolgathered & Fitified: A Native American People's Struggle for Identity. LC 92-50435. 280p. (Orig.). 1994. pap. 12.95 (*1-879360-23-3*) Noble Pr.

Coronado, Rosa. Cooking the Mexican Way. LC 82-254. (Easy Menu Ethnic Cookbooks Ser.). (Illus.). 48p. (J). (gr. 5 up). 1982. lib. bdg. 19.93 (*0-8225-0907-5*, Lerner Publctns) Lerner Pub.

— Cooking the Mexican Way. (Illus.). 48p. (YA). (gr. 5 up). 1992. pap. 5.95 (*0-8225-9614-8*, Lerner Publctns) Lerner Pub.

Coronado, Shirleigh, jt. compiled by see North State Cooperative Library System Staff.

Coronado, Veronica C. & Kirk, Patty. More of What's Cooking. 214p. (Orig.). 1995. 14.95 (*0-9649658-0-1*) Its Cooking.

Coronel, Carlos, jt. auth. see Rob, Peter.

***Coronel-Ferrer, Miriam, ed.** Peace Matters: A Philippine Peace Compendium. LC 97-946611. (Illus.). 308p. 1999. pap. text 30.00 (*971-8797-95-5*, Pub. by U of Philippines Pr) UH Pr.

Coronel, R. E., jt. ed. see Verheij, E. W.

Coronel, Shelia S., et al. Pork & Other Perks: Corruption & Governance in the Philippines. LC 98-947502. 293 p. 1998. write for info. (*971-8686-18-5*) PCFIJ.

Corones, Anthony, jt. auth. see Freeland, Guy.

Corones, James P., et al, eds. Invariant Imbedding & Inverse Problems. LC 92-2908. (Proceedings in Applied Mathematics Ser.: No. 63). xiii, 257p. 1992. pap. 43.00 (*0-89871-305-6*) Soc Indus-Appl Math.

Corones, Stephen. Competition Law & Policy: The Aviation & Telecommunications Industries. 248p. 1992. 83.00 (*1-86287-086-1*, Pub. by Federation Pr) Gaunt.

— Restrictive Trade Practices Law. 400p. 1994. 82.00 (*0-455-21271-6*, Pub. by LawBk Co); pap. 62.00 (*0-455-21270-8*, Pub. by LawBk Co) Gaunt.

Corones, Stephen & Clarke, Philip. Consumer Protection & Product Liability Law: Commentary & Materials. 544p. 1997. pap. 76.00 (*0-455-21442-5*, Pub. by LawBk Co) Gaunt.

Corones, Steven G. Competition Law & Policy in Australia. xix, 324p. 1990. 75.00 (*0-455-20990-1*, Pub. by LawBk Co); pap. 55.00 (*0-455-20991-X*, Pub. by LawBk Co) Gaunt.

Coronet Staff. CAS Is King a Killer OR. 1976. 16.66 (*0-676-40903-2*) Ballantine Pub Grp.

Coronetz, Melanie. Schipperkes. LC 98-10544. (Barron's Complete Pet Owner's Manuals). (Illus.). 1998. pap. 6.95 (*0-7641-0337-7*) Barron.

Coronil, Fernando. Magical State: Nature, Money & Modernity in Venezuela. LC 97-8000. 1997. pap. text 20.00 (*0-226-11602-6*); lib. bdg. 50.00 (*0-226-11601-8*) U Ch Pr.

Coroniti, Joseph. Poetry As Text in Twentieth Century Vocal Music: From Stravinsky to Reich. LC 91-43310. (Studies in the History & Interpretation of Music: Vol. 35). 112p. 1992. lib. bdg. 59.95 (*0-7734-9774-9*) E Mellen.

Coroniti, Samuel C. & Hughes, J., eds. Planetary Electrodynamics, 2 vols. (Illus.). xL, 1092p. (C). 1969. text 835.00 (*0-677-13600-5*) Gordon & Breach.

Corooran. Maneuvering the Maze of Managed Care. 1996. 28.00 (*0-02-874126-9*) Free Pr.

Corosso, Vincent, jt. auth. see Kane, Thomas P.

Corotto, Loren V. The Psychological Basis Underlying Common Stock Movements. LC 87-51166. 1987. pap. 14.95 (*0-941099-00-8*); lib. bdg. 17.95 (*0-941099-01-6*) Tourmaline Pub.

Corp, Edward. Lord Burlington - The Man & His Politics. LC 98-25036. (Studies in British History: Vol. 48). (Illus.). 252p. 1998. text 89.95 (*0-7734-8367-5*) E Mellen.

Corp, Edward T. Lord Burlington: The Man & His Politics : Questions of Loyalty. LC 98-25036. (Studies in British History Ser.). xi, 212p. 1998. write for info. (*0-88946-450-2*) E Mellen.

Corp, Rand, et al. Improving Team Performance: Proceedings of the Rand Team Performance Workshop, November 1979. LC 80-23733. x, 192 p. 1980. 15.00 (*0-8330-0249-X*) Rand Corp.

Corpany, Susan Law. Unfinished Business. 280p. Date not set. mass mkt. 4.99 (*1-55197-212-3*) Picasso Publ.

Corpening, Gene. Best Humor of the White Trash: The You-Know Book) LC 96-83959. 96p. (Orig.). 1996. pap. 9.95 (*1-887108-80-7*, 1887108) Alice Pub.

— Harlequin Hitler. LC 94-72502. 304p. 1994. 21.00 (*0-9636775-6-X*) Alice Pub.

— What the Self-Publishing Manuals Don't Tell You & You Didn't Know to Ask. LC 95-94210. 94p. (Orig.). 1995. pap. 19.95 (*1-887108-95-5*) Alice Pub.

— Whistle-Blower: How to Blow the IRS Out of the Water. LC 98-93200. 135p. 1998. pap. 14.95 (*1-887108-98-X*) Alice Pub.

Corpening, Gene S. I Love to Hear the Cold Wind Howl: (When I'm All Tucked in at Night) (Illus.). 40p. (Orig.). (J). 1993. pap. 7.95 (*0-9636775-9-4*) Alice Pub.

— I Love to Hear the Cold Wind Howl: (When I'm All Tucked in at Night) 2nd ed. LC 94-78674. (Illus.). 40p. (Orig.). (J). 1994. reprint ed. 13.95 (*0-9636775-3-6*) Alice Pub.

Corpening, Mary & Corpening, Sara. Simplify Entertaining: Less-Stress Solutions for Party Giving. LC 98-9189. (Simple Life Bks.). (Illus.). 144p. 1998. 17.95 (*0-7621-0064-8*, Pub. by RD Assn) Penguin Putnam.

Corpening, Sara, jt. auth. see Corpening, Mary.

Corpi, Lucha. Eulogy for a Brown Angel: A Mystery Novel. 200p. 1992. 9.00 (*1-55885-050-3*) Arte Publico.

— Where Fireflies Dance (Ahi, Donde Bailan las Luciernagas) (ENG & SPA., Illus.). (J). (gr. 2-4). 1997. 21.27 (*0-516-20547-1*) Childrens.

— Where Fireflies Dance (Ahi, Donde Bailan las Luciernagas) LC 96-29355. (SPA & ENG., Illus.). 32p. (J). (gr. 1 up). 1997. 15.95 (*0-89239-145-6*) Childrens Book Pr.

Corpini, Joe D., jt. auth. see Cangelosi, Don.

Corporaal, Henk. Microprocessor Architectures: From VLIW to TTA. LC 97-15958. 428p. 1997. 140.00 (*0-471-97157-X*) Wiley.

Corporate & International Perspectives Staff. The Culture Factor. 94p. (C). 1994. pap. 120.00 (*0-85292-564-6*, Pub. by IPM Hse) St Mut.

Corporate Agents, Inc. Staff. The Essential Limited Liability Company Handbook: The Newest Alternative in Business. Doyle, Kathleen, ed. (Successful Business Library). (Illus.). 276p. (Orig.). 1995. pap. 21.95 (*1-55571-361-0*, Oasis Pr) PSI Resch.

Corporate Aviation Safety Seminar Staff. Advancing Safety Through Effective Communication (Proceedings) of the 29th Annual Meeting April 1-3, 1984, Le Bonaventure Westin Hotel, Montreal, Canada. LC TL0553.5. 224p. reprint ed. pap. 69.50 (*0-8357-5198-8*, 202349200033) Bks Demand.

— Aviation Safety in the Nineties: Proceedings of the 36th Corporate Aviation Safety Seminar, April 17-19, 1991, White Plains, NY. LC 83-645693. 228p. reprint ed. pap. 70.70 (*0-7837-3161-2*, 204282000006) Bks Demand.

— Challenges & Choices in Corporate Aviation Safety: 35th Annual Corporate Aviation Safety Seminar: Proceedings, April 18-20, 1990, Four Seasons Hotel, Montreal, Quebec, Canada. LC TL0722.C6. 178p. reprint ed. pap. 55.20 (*0-8357-2647-9*, 204013500015) Bks Demand.

— Growing a Safety Culture: Proceedings of the 38th Annual Corporate Aviation Safety Seminar CASS; April 14-16, 1993, Irving, Texas. fac. ed. LC TL0722.C6. (Illus.). 122p. 1994. pap. 37.90 (*0-7837-7680-2*, 204743300007) Bks Demand.

— Identifying the Hazards: Thirty-Third Annual Corporate Aviation Safety Seminar: Proceedings, April 20-22, 1988, Williamsburg Hilton & National Conference Center, Williamsburg, Virginia, U. S. LC TL0722.C6. 128p. reprint ed. pap. 39.70 (*0-8357-2645-2*, 204013300015) Bks Demand.

— Managing Corporate Aviation Safety: Proceedings, 27th Annual Meeting, April 4-6, 1982, Houston Texas. LC TL0541.6.C68. 164p. reprint ed. pap. 50.90 (*0-608-13922-X*, 201782800010) Bks Demand.

— New Technologies & Corporation Aviation: 25th Annual Meeting of Corporate Aviation Safety Seminar, March 23-25, 1980 St. Louis, Missouri. LC TL0545.F55. 174p. reprint ed. pap. 54.00 (*0-608-13064-8*, 201463500096) Bks Demand.

— Safety in Our Environment: Proceedings of the 31st Annual Meeting, Corporate Aviation Safety Seminar, April 14-16, 1986, Cincinnati, OH. LC TL0545.F55. 212p. pap. 65.80 (*0-608-15344-3*, 205221400061) Bks Demand.

— Safety in the Terminal Environment: Proceedings, 23rd Annual Meeting, April 9-12, 1978, Arlington Va. LC TL0553.5C6. 134p. reprint ed. pap. 41.60 (*0-608-11044-2*, 201033900068) Bks Demand.

— Thirty Years & Still Training for Safety: Proceedings of the 30th Annual Meeting Corporate Aviation Safety Seminar, April 14-16 ,1985, AMFAC Hotel & Resort, Dallas - Fort Worth International Airport. LC TL0553.5. 224p. reprint ed. pap. 69.50 (*0-608-15119-X*, 202579700046) Bks Demand.

Corporate Aviation Safety Seminar, 34th, 1989, Dea. New Approaches & Answers to Aviation Safety: 34th Corporate Safety Seminar: Proceedings, April 19-21, 1989, Hyatt Regency Hotel, Dearborn, Michigan, U. S. LC TL0722.C6. 177p. reprint ed. pap. 54.90 (*0-8357-2646-0*, 204013400015) Bks Demand.

***Corporate Classrooms Firm Staff.** Get a Grip on Supervisory Skills. LC 00-37308. 2000. write for info. (*0-13-021238-5*) P-H.

Corporate Classrooms Staff. Prentice Hall's Get a Grip on Finance & Accounting. LC 98-12786. 192p. (C). 1998. pap. text 69.95 (*0-13-616483-8*) P-H.

— Prentice Hall's Get a Grip on Grammar. 160p. (C). 1992. ring bd. 69.95 (*0-13-012428-1*, Pub. by P-H) S&S Trade.

— Prentice Hall's Get a Grip on Grammar: Language Skills for Today's Business World. LC 92-22769. 1992. 99.95 (*0-685-60782-8*) P-H.

— Prentice Hall's Get a Grip on Writing: Critical Skills for Success in Today's Business World. 192p. (C). 1996. text 69.95 (*0-13-232414-8*) P-H.

Corporate Compliance Resource Center Staff, ed. Compliance Across the Continuum: A Comprehensive Look at Healthcare Corporate Compliance. LC 98-214672. 200p. 1998. pap. text 89.00 (*1-57839-024-9*) Opus Communs.

Corporate Publication Staff. Native American Colleges: Progress & Prospects. LC 97-13002. 100p. (Orig.). 1997. pap. 10.00 (*0-931050-63-4*) Carnegie Fnd Advan Teach.

Corporation for Com. Col. TV Staff. Contemporary Health Issues. 3rd ed. (C). 1984. pap. text, student ed. 17.50 (*0-07-554753-8*) McGraw.

Corporation for Enterprise Development Staff. The Development Report Card for the States, 1993: Economic Benchmarks for State & Corporate Decision-Makers. 7th rev. ed. LC 93-70699. 215p. 1993. pap. 45.00 incl. audio (*1-883187-00-1*) Corp Ent Dev.

C

***Corporation for Enterprise Development Staff.** The 1998 Development Report Card for the States: Economic Benchmarks for State & Corporate Decision-Makers. 111p. 1998. pap. 75.00 (*1-883187-20-6*) Corp Ent Dev.

Corporation for Enterprise Development Staff. The 1996 Development Report Card for the States: Economic Benchmarks for State & Corporate Decision-Makers. 10th ed. 202p. (C). 1996. ring bd. 45.00 (*1-883187-09-5*) Corp Ent Dev.

— Rethinking Rural Development. 43p. 1993. pap. 17.50 (*1-883187-02-8*) Corp Ent Dev.

— The Rural Performance Benchmarks System: Policymaker's Guide & User's Manual. 124p. 1993. spiral bd. 35.00 (*1-883187-03-6*) Corp Ent Dev.

Corporation Microsoft. Microsoft Jet Database Engine Programmer's Guide. 3rd ed. 1999. pap. text 49.99 (*0-7356-0585-8*) Microsoft.

***Corporation Microsoft.** Microsoft Windows NT 5 BETA Training Kit. LC 99-17058. (Illus.). 800p. 1999. pap. 79.99 (*0-7356-0644-7*) Microsoft.

Corporation Microsoft. Technical Reference, Microsoft Windows NT Terminal Server Edition. LC 99-33267. 500p. 1999. pap. 49.99 (*0-7356-0645-5*) Microsoft.

Corpus Christi College (University of Cambridge) S & Budny, Mildred. Insular, Anglo-Saxon, & Early Anglo-Norman Manuscript Art at Corpus Christi College, Cambridge: An Illustrated Catalogue, 2 vols. LC 97-33996. 1998. 300.00 (*1-879288-87-7*) Medieval Inst.

Corpus Juris Civilis Staff. The Institutes of Justinian. Sandars, Thomas C., tr. LC 71-98749. 608p. 1970. reprint ed. lib. bdg. 89.50 (*0-8371-2920-6*, INOJ, Greenwood Pr) Greenwood.

Corpuz, O. D. An Economic History of the Philippines. LC 97-946685. 324p. (C). 1999. pap. text 35.00 (*971-542-094-X*) UH Pr.

Corr. King: The Bullitts of Seattle & Their Communications Empire. LC 96-16521. (Illus.). 352p. 1996. pap. 14.95 (*0-295-97584-9*) U of Wash Pr.

Corr, Anders. No Trespassing! Squatting, Rent Strikes & Land Struggles Worldwide. LC 98-56182. 256p. 1999. 40.00 (*0-89608-596-1*, Pub. by South End Pr); pap. 17.00 (*0-89608-595-3*, Pub. by South End Pr) Consort Bk Sales.

Corr, Arthur V. The Capital Expenditure Decision. 107p. 1983. pap. 20.00 (*0-86641-091-0*, 83142) Inst Mgmt Account.

Corr, B. Essential Elements of Business Information Systems. 120p. 1995. pap. 59.95 (*0-7855-2772-9*, Pub. by DP Publns) St Mut.

Corr, Charles, et al, eds. Sudden Infant Death Syndrome: Who Can Help & How. 272p. 1991. 36.95 (*0-8261-6720-9*) Springer Pub.

***Corr, Charles, et al.** Living with Grief: Children, Adolescents & Loss. Doka, Kenneth A., ed. 288p. (Orig.). 2000. pap. 16.95 (*1-893349-01-2*, Pub. by Hospice Fndt Amer) Brunner-Mazel.

Corr, Charles A. & Balk, David E., eds. Handbook of Adolescent Death & Bereavement. (Illus.). 438p. 1996. 52.95 (*0-8261-9240-8*) Springer Pub.

Corr, Charles A. & Corr, Donna M. Handbook of Childhood Death & Bereavement. LC 96-5016. (Illus.). 352p. 1996. 48.95 (*0-8261-9320-X*) Springer Pub.

Corr, Charles A. & Corr, Donna M., eds. Hospice Care: Principles & Practice. (Death & Suicide Ser.: Vol. 5). 384p. (C). 1983. 34.95 (*0-8261-3540-4*) Springer Pub.

Corr, Charles A. & Nabe. Death & Dying: Life & Living. 3rd ed. LC 99-30555. (Psychology Ser.). 661p. 1999. 60.95 (*0-534-36538-8*) Brooks-Cole.

Corr, Charles A., et al. Death & Dying, Life & Living. LC 93-3208. 1994. pap. 33.75 (*0-534-21138-0*) Brooks-Cole.

— Death & Dying, Life & Living. 2nd ed. 1996. mass mkt., teacher ed. write for info. (*0-534-34421-6*) Brooks-Cole.

— Death & Dying, Life & Living: Life & Living. 2nd ed. LC 96-23673. (Psychology Ser.). 750p. (C). 1996. 39.25 (*0-534-34420-8*) Brooks-Cole.

Corr, Charles A., jt. ed. see Corr, Domma.

Corr, Charles A., jt. ed. see Wass, Hannelore.

Corr, Domma & Corr, Charles A., eds. Nursing Care in an Aging Society. LC 90-9601. 368p. 1990. 38.95 (*0-8261-6630-X*) Springer Pub.

Corr, Donna M., jt. auth. see Corr, Charles A.

Corr, Donna M., jt. ed. see Corr, Charles A.

Corr, Gerard H. The War of the Springing Tigers. 200p. 1979. 12.95 (*0-318-36623-1*) Asia Bk Corp.

Corr, Helen. Teachers & the Politics of Gender 1850-1914: A Study of Scottish & English Education. 1995. text 29.50 (*0-7130-0173-9*, Pub. by Woburn Pr); text. write for info. (*0-7130-4013-0*, Pub. by Woburn Pr) Intl Spec Bk.

Corr, John, jt. auth. see Mitchell, Mary.

Corr, John B. Bankruptcy Code Manual LC 98-151278. (West's Bankruptcy Ser.). 1378 p. 1998. 0.00 (*0-314-23009-2*) West Pub.

Corr, Michael, ed. Power Consumption & Human Welfare. 1975. write for info. (*0-318-57474-8*) Macmillan Info.

Corr, O. Casey. Money from Thin Air: The Story of Craig McCaw, the Billionaire Who Invented the Cell Phone Industry & His Next Billion Dollar Idea. LC 99-89068. (Illus.). 320p. 2000. 25.00 (*0-8129-2697-8*, Times Bks) Crown Pub Group.

Corr, Vincent P. Earth. 1998. pap. write for info. (*1-57553-691-9*) Watermrk Pr.

Corr, William. Adams the Pilot: The Life & Times of Captain William Adams, 1564-1620. (Japan Library). 256p. (C). 1996. text 45.00 (*1-873410-44-1*, Pub. by Curzon Pr Ltd) UH Pr.

— Twenty-Two Europeans in Japan & Much More. 208p. 1991. pap. 9.50 (*0-933704-90-9*) Dawn Pr.

— Twenty-Two Europeans in Japan & Much More. 2nd ed. 208p. 1992. pap. 9.50 (*0-933704-96-8*) Dawn Pr.

Corradi, Juan E., et al, eds. Fear at the Edge: State Terror & Resistance in Latin America. (C). 1992. 55.00 (*0-520-07704-0*, Pub. by U CA Pr); pap. 17.95 (*0-520-07705-9*, Pub. by U CA Pr) Cal Prin Full Svc.

Corradini, Enrico. Discorsi Politici, 1902-1923. LC 76-180395. (ITA.). reprint ed. 55.00 (*0-404-56116-0*) AMS Pr.

Corradini, M. L., ed. see American Society of Mechanical Engineers Staff.

Corrado. Cps Chs 1-3 from Investments. 1999. pap. text 6.50 (*0-07-236007-0*) McGraw.

— The Wall Street Journal Fundamentals of Investment. 1999. 79.50 (*0-07-232584-4*) McGraw.

***Corrado.** WSJ Fundamentals of Investment. 1999. 84.00 (*0-07-232615-8*) McGraw.

Corrado & Jordan. Investments. LC 99-27709. 1999. 66.25 (*0-256-15423-6*) McGraw.

Corrado, Anthony. Paying for Presidents: Public Financing in National Elections. LC 93-38548. (Orig.). 1993. pap. 9.95 (*0-87078-185-5*) Century Foundation.

Corrado, Anthony & Firestone, Charles M., eds. Elections in Cyberspace: Toward a New Era in American Politics. 104p. 1997. pap. 10.00 (*0-89843-202-2*) The Aspen Inst.

Corrado, Anthony, et al. Campaign Finance Reform: A Sourcebook. Sorauf, Frank, ed. LC 97-33765. 402p. (Orig.). 1997. pap. 24.95 (*0-8157-1581-1*) Brookings.

Corrado, Anthony, jt. auth. see Alexander, Herbert E.

***Corrado, Charles J.** Fundamentals of Investments: Valuation & Management. 1999. pap., student ed. 84.69 (*0-07-231941-0*) McGraw.

Corrado, Frank. Communicating with Employees: Improving Organizational Communication. Reider, Andrea, ed. LC 93-73208. (Fifty-Minute Ser.). (Illus.). 90p. 1994. pap. 10.95 (*1-56052-255-0*) Crisp Pubns.

Corrado, Frank M. Media for Managers. (Illus.). 224p. (C). 1984. pap. text 23.00 (*0-13-572446-5*) P-H.

Corrado, Joseph. The Perfect Crime: The Annihilation of My Family. LC 98-92396. 1088p. 1998. 27.00 (*0-9662873-0-4*) Joe Corrado.

Corrado, Michael. The Analytic Tradition in Philosophy: Background & Issues. LC 75-9801. 165p. reprint ed. pap. 51.20 (*0-8357-5448-0*, 202425000035) Bks Demand.

Corrado, Michael L., ed. Justification & Excuse in the Criminal Law: A Collection of Essays. LC 93-15044. (Studies in Applied Ethics: Vol. 1). (Illus.). 672p. 1994. text 15.00 (*0-8153-0825-6*, SS831) Garland.

Corrain, Aibhe O., jt. auth. see Mac Mathuna, Seamus.

Corrain, Ailbhe, jt. ed. see Bramsback, Birgit.

Corrain, Ailbhe O. & Rekdal, Jan E., eds. Proceedings of the Third Symposium of Societas Celtologica Nordica, Nov. 1991. LC 95-109124. (Studia Celtica Upsaliensia: No. 1). 149p. (Orig.). 1994. pap. 40.00 (*91-554-3325-1*) Coronet Bks.

Corrain, Ailbhe O., jt. ed. see Mathuna, Seamus M.

Corrain, Donnchadh. Irish Antiquity. LC 95-120265. 378p. 1994. 45.00 (*1-85182-145-7*, Pub. by Four Cts Pr); pap. 30.00 (*1-85182-174-0*, Pub. by Four Cts Pr) Intl Spec Bk.

Corrain, Donnchadh O. & Maguire, Fidelma. Irish Names. 188p. 1990. reprint ed. pap. 11.95 (*0-946640-66-1*, Pub. by Lilliput Pr) Irish Bks Media.

Corrain, Lucia. The Art of the Renaissance. LC 97-19338. (Masters of Art Ser.). (Illus.). 64p. (J). (gr. 4-7). 1997. lib. bdg. 22.50 (*0-87226-526-9*, 65269B, P Bedrick Books) NTC Contemp Pub Co.

— Giotto & Medieval Painting. LC 95-10518. (Masters of Art Ser.). (Illus.). 64p. (J). (gr. 4-7). 1995. lib. bdg. 22.50 (*0-87226-315-0*, 63150B, P Bedrick Books) NTC Contemp Pub Co.

Corral, C. Corral. El Razonamiento Medico. (SPA.). 204p. 1994. pap. 23.50 (*84-7978-125-4*, Pub. by Ediciones Diaz) IBD Ltd.

Corral, G. Herrera & Aquino, Modesto S., eds. Instrumentation in Elementary Particle Physics: The VII ICFA School. LC 98-72211. (AIP Conference Proceedings Ser.: Vol. 422). (Illus.). xiii, 428p. 1998. 120.00 (*1-56396-763-4*) Am Inst Physics.

Corral, Hannah, jt. auth. see Corral, Kimberly.

Corral, Kimberly. A Child's Glacier Bay. LC 97-44666. (Illus.). 32p. (J). (gr. 4-7). 1998. 15.95 (*0-88240-503-9*, Alaska NW Bks) Gr Arts Ctr Pub.

Corral, Kimberly & Corral, Hannah. My Denali: Exploring Alaska's Favorite National Park with Hannah Corral. LC 95-21169. (Illus.). 32p. (YA). (gr. 5 up). 1995. 15.95 (*0-88240-467-9*, Alaska NW Bks) Gr Arts Ctr Pub.

Corral, Pablo, jt. ed. see Langston, Loup.

Corral, Roy, jt. auth. see Brown, Tricia.

Corral Salvador, Carlos. Diccionario de Derecho Canonico. (SPA.). 696p. 1989. 125.00 (*0-7859-3354-9*, 8430916784) Fr & Eur.

Corrales, Jeanne Frankel De, see Frankel de Corrales, Jeanne.

Corrales, Jose. Las Hambres Terrestres. (SPA.). 76p. (Orig.). 1995. pap. 4.95 (*1-885901-90-9*) Presbyters Peartree.

— Nocturno de Canas Bravas. (SPA.). 49p. 1994. pap. text 3.95 (*1-885901-15-1*) Presbyters Peartree.

— El Palacio de los Gritos. (SPA.). 34p. 1993. pap. text 2.95 (*1-885901-00-3*) Presbyters Peartree.

— Teatro Y Poesia Vol. 1: UNO: Cuestion De Santidad. (SPA.). 78p. 1998. 4.50 (*1-885901-31-3*, Liberts) Presbyters Peartree.

— Teatro Y Poesia Vol. 2: DOS: Dos/Two Plays/Obras: El Vestido Rojo; A Chopin Waltz. Pereiras, Manuel, tr. from SPA. 76p. 1998. 4.50 (*1-885901-32-1*, Liberts) Presbyters Peartree.

— Teatro Y Poesia Vol. 3: TRES: Orlando. (SPA.). 76p. 1998. 4.50 (*1-885901-33-X*, Liberts) Presbyters Peartree.

— Teatro Y Poesia Vol. 4: CUATRO: Las Sabanas. (SPA.). 44p. 1998. 4.50 (*1-885901-34-8*, Liberts) Presbyters Peartree.

— Teatro Y Poesia Vol. 5: CINCO: Spics, Gringos, & Gracejo. (SPA.). 58p. 1998. 4.50 (*1-885901-35-6*, Liberts) Presbyters Peartree.

— Teatro Y Poesia Vol. 6: SEIS: Walter a Primera Vista. (SPA.). 80p. 1998. 4.50 (*1-885901-36-4*, Liberts) Presbyters Peartree.

— Teatro Y Poesia Vol. 7: SIETE: When the Mailman Comes. Pereiras, Manuel, tr. from SPA. 88p. 1998. 4.50 (*1-885901-37-2*, Liberts) Presbyters Peartree.

— Teatro Y Poesia Vol. 8: OCHO: Dos Poemarios: . . .Donde Estoy?; Muecas Y Palabrerias. (SPA.). 62p. 1998. 4.50 (*1-885901-38-0*, Liberts) Presbyters Peartree.

— Teatro Y Poesia Vol. 9. Pereiras, Manuel, tr. from SPA. 618p. 1998. 35.00 (*1-885901-30-5*, Liberts) Presbyters Peartree.

— Teatro Y Poesia Vol. 9: NUEVE: El Libro De Mario D Y Otras Ausencias. (SPA.). 56p. 1998. 4.50 (*1-885901-39-9*, Liberts) Presbyters Peartree.

— Temporal. (SPA.). 50p. 1993. pap. text 3.95 (*1-885901-09-7*) Presbyters Peartree.

— The Three Marios, 2 vols., Set. Presbyter's Peartree Staff, tr. from SPA. 103p. 1993. pap. text 7.90 (*1-885901-06-2*) Presbyters Peartree.

— The Three Marios Vol. I: Circus Maximus, Corpus Delicti. Presbyter's Peartree Staff, tr. from SPA. 60p. 1993. pap. text 3.95 (*1-885901-07-0*) Presbyters Peartree.

— The Three Marios Vol. II: In Absentia. Presbyter's Peartree Staff, tr. from SPA. 43p. 1993. pap. text 3.95 (*1-885901-08-9*) Presbyters Peartree.

Corrales, Jose, tr. see Garcia, Manuel P.

Corrales, Ramon G., jt. auth. see Barnard, Charles P.

Corrales, Scott. Chupacabras! And Other Mysteries. LC 97-68468. Orig. Title: The Chupacabras Diaries. (Illus.). 257p. 1997. pap. 19.95 (*1-883729-06-8*) Greenleaf Tenn.

Corrallo, Sal. National Assessment of College Student Learning: An Inventory f State-Level Assessment Activities, a Report of the Proceedings of the Third Study Design Workshop. 158p. 1996. per. 13.00 (*0-16-048923-7*) USGPO.

Corras, James, et al. Improving College Admission Test Scores: Verbal Workbook. 184p. (Orig.). (gr. 11-12). 1989. pap. write for info. (*0-88210-135-8*) Natl Assn Principals.

***Corre & Rees.** Agent Provocateur: A Celebration of Femininity. (Illus.). 192p. 2000. 39.95 (*1-85868-758-6*) Carlton Bks Ltd.

Corre, Alan D., ed. Quest for Social Justice II: The Morris Fromkin Memorial Lectures, 1981-1990. LC 92-81949. (Illus.). 217p. (C). 1992. 22.95 (*1-879281-05-8*) G Meir Lib.

Corre, Neil. Ball in Criminal Proceedings. 214p. 1990. 60.00 (*1-85190-113-2*, Pub. by Tolley Pubng) St Mut.

Corre, Neil & Wolchover, David. Bail in Criminal Proceedings. 345p. 1999. pap. 64.00 (*1-85431-921-3*, Pub. by Blackstone Pr) Gaunt.

***Correa, Carlos M.** Trips: Trade-Related Intellectual Property Rights. 1999. text 49.95 (*1-85649-736-4*); text 17.50 (*1-85649-737-2*) Zed Books.

***Correa, Charles.** Housing & Urbanization: Building Solutions for People & Cities. LC 99-68178. (Illus.). 144p. 2000. pap. 18.95 (*0-500-28210-2*, Pub. by Thames Hudson) Norton.

Correa, Charles, jt. auth. see Frampton, Kenneth.

Correa, Clara S., jt. auth. see Levine, Sarah.

Correa de Oliveira, Plinio. Nobility & Analogous Traditional Elites in the Allocutions of Pius XII: A Theme Illuminating American Social History. LC 93-60895. (Illus.). 592p. 1993. 29.95 (*0-8191-9310-0*) U Pr of Amer.

Correa-Diaz, Luis. Lengua Muerta: Poesia, Post Litertura & Erotismo en Enrique Linn. (SPA.). 120p. (Orig.). 1996. pap. 15.00 (*1-888135-00-X*) Ediciones Inti.

Correa Do Lago, Luiz, jt. ed. see Coffey, Peter.

Correa, Federico C. De Robles, see De Robles Correa, Federico C.

Correa, Francois, ed. La Selva Humanizada: Ecologia Alternativa en el Tropico Humedo Colombiano. (SPA.). 232p. 1989. pap. 12.00 (*958-612-024-4*, IC001) UPLAAP.

Correa, Hector. The Economics of Human Resources, XXXIV. LC 82-6260. (Contributions to Economic Analysis Ser.). 262p. 1982. reprint ed. lib. bdg. 65.00 (*0-313-23438-8*, COEH, Greenwood Pr) Greenwood.

Correa, Hector, ed. Abortion Policy, Vol. 13:1/2. 162p. 1994. pap. 15.00 (*0-944285-41-4*) Pol Studies.

— Unwanted Pregnancies & Public Policy: An International Perspective. 222p. 1994. lib. bdg. 115.00 (*1-56072-136-7*) Nova Sci Pubs.

***Correa, Hector, et al.** Population, Health & Nutrition: Selected Papers of Hector Correa. LC 00-28407. 2000. write for info. (*1-56072-785-3*) Nova Sci Pubs.

Correa, Henrique L. Linking Flexibility, Uncertainty & Variability in Manufacturing Systems: Managing Un-Planned Change in the Automotive Industry. 208p. 1994. 66.95 (*1-85628-620-7*, Pub. by Avebry) Ashgate Pub Co.

Correa, Lourdes. Solucionario Del Libro "Elementos de Matematica Comercial" de Ruperto. 251p. 1969. pap. 2.50 (*0-8477-2604-5*) U of PR Pr.

Correa, P. & Haenszel, W. Epidemiology of Cancer of the Digestive Tract. 1982. text 171.00 (*90-247-2601-8*) Kluwer Academic.

Correa, Rafael E., tr. see Berdan, Frances F. & Barber, Russell J.

Correa, Sonia & Reichmann, Rebecca L. Population & Reproductive Rights: Feminist Perspectives from the South. LC 94-32596. 136p. (C). 1994. text 19.95 (*1-85649-284-2*, Pub. by Zed Books) St Martin.

Correa, Vivian, jt. auth. see Thomas, Carol C.

Correal, Gonzalo. Aguazuque: Evidencias de Cazadores, Recolectores y Plantadores en la Altiplanicie de la Cordillera Oriental. (SPA., Illus.). 307p. 1990. pap. 8.50 (*1-877812-11-0*, BR001) UPLAAP.

Correard, Alexander, jt. auth. see Savigny, J. B.

Correard, M-H. & Grundy, Valerie. The Oxford-Hachette Dictionary French-English--English-French. (ENG & FRE.). 1943p. 1994. pap. 95.00 (*0-7859-8896-3*) Fr & Eur.

Correard, Marie H. & O'Neill, Mary, eds. The Oxford Starter French Dictionary. LC 97-24384. 416p. 1997. pap. 8.95 (*0-19-864527-9*) OUP.

***Correard, Marie-Helene.** Oxford French Cartoon-Strip Vocabulary Builder. (ENG & FRE., Illus.). 80p. 2000. pap. 11.95 (*0-19-860267-7*) OUP.

Correard, Marie-Helene. The Oxford-Hachette French Dictionary. 2nd ed. LC 98-104077. (FRE.). 2,008p. 1997. 45.00 (*0-19-860068-2*) OUP.

***Correard, Marie-Helene, ed.** The Oxford-Hachette College French Dictionary. 2nd ed. LC 98-49988. 800p. 2000. pap. 11.95 (*0-19-860279-0*) OUP.

Correard, Marie-Helene, ed. The Oxford-Hachette French Desk Dictionary. LC 98-118884. (FRE.). 800p. 1997. 16.95 (*0-19-860149-2*) OUP.

— The Pocket Oxford-Hachette French Dictionary. 800p. 1997. pap. 11.95 (*0-19-864534-1*) OUP.

***Correard, Marie-Helene & Grundy, Valerie, eds.** The Concise Oxford-Hachette French Dictionary: French-English, English French. rev. ed. 1447p. 2000. 27.95 (*0-19-860242-1*) OUP.

Correard, Marie-Helene & O'Neill, Mary, eds. The Compact Oxford French Dictionary. 1,024p. 1995. pap. 13.95 (*0-19-864535-X*) OUP.

Correard, Marie-Helene, jt. ed. see Grundy, Valerie.

Corredor, Eva L. Lukacs after Communism: Interviews with Contemporary Intellectuals. LC 96-34207. (Post-Contemporary Interventions Ser.). 248p. 1997. pap. text 15.95 (*0-8223-1763-X*); lib. bdg. 49.95 (*0-8223-1754-0*) Duke.

Corredor-Matheos, Jose. Antoni Tapies: Materia, Signo, Espiritu. (Grandes Monografias). (SPA., Illus.). 128p. 1993. 100.00 (*84-343-0681-6*) Elliots Bks.

— Metaporfosis. deluxe limited ed. (Ediciones Especiales y de Bibliofilo Ser.). (SPA., Illus.). 120p. 1993. 7500.00 (*84-343-0271-3*) Elliots Bks.

— Montserrat Gudiol: Reality & Symbol. (Great Monographs). (Illus.). 332p. 1993. 250.00 (*84-343-0637-9*) Elliots Bks.

Correge, Joy, et al, eds. The Future of Labor Arbitration in America. LC 76-18440. 320p. 1976. pap. 5.00 (*0-943001-15-3*) Am Arbitration.

***Correia.** Filling the Gap: Critical Readings of Criminal Justice. 412p. (C). 1998. pap. text 28.00 (*0-536-01613-5*) S&S Trade.

***Correia, A. Gomes, ed.** Unbound Granular Materials - Modelling, Laboratory & In-Situ Testing: Proceedings of an International Workshop, Lisbon, 21-22 January 1999. (Illus.). 231p. 1999. 75.00 (*90-5410-491-0*, Pub. by A A Balkema) Ashgate Pub Co.

Correia, A. Gomes & Balkema, A. A., eds. Flexible Pavements: Proceedings of the European Symposium on Flexible Pavements, Lisbon, September 1993. (Illus.). 369p. (C). 1996. text 149.00 (*90-5410-523-2*, Pub. by A A Balkema) Ashgate Pub Co.

Correia-Afonso, John, ed. Letters from the Mughal Court: The First Jesuit Mission to Akbar (1580-1583) LC 81-81766. (Jesuit Primary Sources in English Translation Series I: No. 4). (Illus.). xvi, 136p. 1981. 4.50 (*0-912422-57-2*) Inst Jesuit.

Correia-Afonso, John, ed. see Godinho, Manuel.

Correia, Edmund, Jr., jt. auth. see Selfridge-Field, Eleanor.

Correia, Francisco Nunes, see Nunes Correia, Francisco, ed.

Correia, Joanne, ed. see Fisher, Connie C.

Correia, Joanne, ed. see Fisher, Connie Correia.

***Correia, Jose Higino G.** Optical Microsystems in Silicon Based on a Fabry-Perot Resonance Cavity: Application for Spectral Analysis of Visible Light. (Illus.). 196p. 1999. pap. 46.50 (*90-407-1870-9*, Pub. by Delft U Pr) Coronet Bks.

Correia, Kristin. Communications Studies Workbook. 100p. (C). 1998. pap. text, wbk. ed. 11.95 (*0-7872-5099-6*, 41509901) Kendall-Hunt.

***Correia, N., et al, eds.** Multimedia '99: Proceedings of the Eurographics Workshop in Milan, Italy, September 7-8, 1999. (Eurographics Ser.). ix, 222p. 2000. pap. (*3-211-83437-0*) Spr-Verlag.

Correl, Donovan S., jt. auth. see Ames, Oakes.

Correlius, Carol. The Six Nations Series. (Illus.). 40p. (Orig.). Date not set. pap., teacher ed. 15.00 (*0-614-29684-6*); pap., student ed. 4.00 (*0-614-29685-4*) Akwe Kon Pr.

Correll, Barbara A. The End of Conduct: "Grobianus" & the Renaissance Text of the Subject. LC 96-13885. (Illus.). 248p. 1996. 39.95 (*0-8014-3101-8*) Cornell U Pr.

***Correll, Bob.** Creating Your First Web Site with Microsoft FrontPage 2000. (Illus.). 128p. 2000. pap. 8.99 (*0-7645-8622-X*, CPG Pr) IDG Bks.

Correll, D. S. & Correll, H. B. Flora of the Bahama Archipelago. 1692p. 1996. reprint ed. 275.00 (*3-904144-02-2*) Gantner Verlag.

Correll, Donovan S. Native Orchids of North America North of Mexico. LC 78-62270. (Illus.). xvi, 400p. 1950. 55.00 (*0-8047-0999-8*) Stanford U Pr.

— The Potato & Its Wild Relatives: Section Tuberarium of the Genus Solanum. (Illus.). 606p. 1962. lib. bdg. 50.00 (*0-934454-93-0*) Lubrecht & Cramer.

Correll, H. B., jt. auth. see Correll, D. S.

An Asterisk (*) at the beginning of an entry indicates that the title is appearing for the first time.

Correll, Helen. Lady Preacher: Can a Submissive Wife & Mother Be an Ordained Minister. (Illus.). 328p. (Orig.). 1995. pap. 12.95 (*0-9636177-8-8*) Rhymeo Ink.

Correll, James G. & Edson, Norris W. Gaining Control: Capacity Management & Scheduling. LC 90-70730. 208p. 1990. 107.00 (*0-939246-18-X*) Wiley.

— Gaining Control: Capacity Mangement & Scheduling. 2nd ed. LC 98-28269. 270p. 1998. 58.95 (*0-471-29167-6*) Wiley.

Correll, James H., II. The Evaluation, Vol. 1. viii, 192p. 1997. pap. 9.95 (*0-9660647-0-4*) J H Correll.

— The Illumination, Vol. 3. LC 98-126768. vi, 138p. 1997. pap. 9.95 (*0-9660647-2-0*) J H Correll.

— The Refiner's Fire. xii, 209p. 1993. pap. 7.95 (*1-56043-538-0*) J H Correll.

— The Tribulation, Vol. 2. viii, 152p. 1997. pap. 9.95 (*0-9660647-1-2*) J H Correll.

Correll, Robert C. Our Changing Planet: The Fiscal Year 1996 U. S. Global Change Research Program. (Illus.). 152p. (C). 1998. pap. text 35.00 (*0-7881-7540-8*) DIANE Pub.

Correll, Robert W. & Harris, Robert C. Our Changing Planet: The Fiscal Year 1997 U. S. Global Change Research Program. (Illus.). 162p. (C). 1998. pap. text 35.00 (*0-7881-7538-6*) DIANE Pub.

Correll, Timothy C. & Polk, Patrick A. The Cast-Off Recast: Recycling & the Creative Transformation of Mass-Produced Objects. LC 99-27652. (Illus.). 148p. 1999. pap. 29.00 (*0-930741-75-7*) UCLA Fowler Mus.

***Correll, Timothy Corrigan & Polk, Patrick Arthur.** Muffler Men. LC 00-27338. (Folk Art & Artists Ser.). (Illus.). 128p. 2000. pap. 18.00 (*1-57806-299-3*); lib. bdg. 38.00 (*1-57806-298-5*) U Pr of Miss.

***Correll, Timothy Corrigan, et al.** The Cast-Off Recast: Recycling & the Creative Transformation of Mass-Produced Objects. LC 99-27652. (Illus.). 148p. 1999. 50.00 (*0-930741-74-9*) UCLA Fowler Mus.

Corrente, Linda. Nathaniel Hawthorne's The House of the Seven Gables. (Barron's Book Notes Ser.). (C). 1985. pap. 2.50 (*0-8120-3519-4*) Barron.

Corrente, Linda, jt. auth. see Krailing, Tessa.

Correnty, Paul. The Art of Cidermaking. (Illus.). 86p. 1995. pap. 9.95 (*0-937381-42-X*) Brewers Pubns.

Corretjer, Juan A. Albizu Campos & the Ponce Massacre. 26p. 1993. pap. 2.50 (*0-89567-115-8*) World View Forum.

— Los Dias Contados. (SPA., Illus.). 51p. 1985. pap. 3.50 (*0-685-24435-0*) Editorial El Coqui.

Corrette, Michel. Le Maitre de Clavecin. fac. ed. (Monuments of Music & Music Literature in Facsimile Ser., Series II: Vol. 13). 1976. lib. bdg. 45.00 (*0-8450-2213-X*) Broude.

— Le Maitre de Clavecin pour l'Accompagnement, Methode Theoretique et Pratique. vi, 90p. 1974. reprint ed. 52.00 (*3-487-05431-0*) G Olms Pubs.

— Methode pour Apprendre Aisement a Jouer de la Flute Traversiere. 50p. 1975. reprint ed. 30.00 (*3-487-05714-X*) G Olms Pubs.

— Michel Corrette: Premier Livre D'Orgue & Nouveau Livre de Noels. Beechey, Gwilym, ed. (Recent Researches in Music of the Baroque Era Ser.: Vol. RRB18). (Illus.). x, 118p. 1974. pap. 45.00 (*0-89579-055-6*, RRB18) A-R Eds.

Corrick, James A. The Battle of Gettysburg: Battles of the Civil War. LC 95-31681. (Battle Ser.). (Illus.). 112p. (J). (gr. 5-12). 1996. lib. bdg. 26.20 (*1-56006-451-X*) Lucent Bks.

— The Byzantine Empire. LC 96-34600. (World History Ser.). (Illus.). (J). (gr. 4-12). 1996. lib. bdg. 22.45 (*1-56006-307-6*) Lucent Bks.

— The Early Middle Ages. LC 94-8778. (World History Ser.). (Illus.). 128p. (J). (gr. 6-9). 1995. lib. bdg. 22.45 (*1-56006-246-0*) Lucent Bks.

***Corrick, James A.** Encyclopedia of Scientific Expeditions. 288p. 2001. text 59.95 (*1-57356-240-8*) Oryx Pr.

— The Industrial Revolution. LC 98-6922. (World History Ser.). (Illus.). (YA). (gr. 4-12). 1998. lib. bdg. 22.45 (*1-56006-318-1*) Lucent Bks.

Corrick, James A. The Late Middle Ages. (World History Ser.). (Illus.). 128p. (J). (gr. 5-9). 1995. lib. bdg. 22.45 (*1-56006-279-7*, 2797) Lucent Bks.

***Corrick, James A.** Life among the Soldiers & Cavalry (Civil War) LC 99-28237. (American War Library). (Illus.). 144p. (YA). (gr. 6-9). 2000. lib. bdg. 23.70 (*1-56006-491-9*) Lucent Bks.

— The Louisiana Purchase. LC 00-9156. (World History Ser.). 2000. write for info. (*1-56006-637-7*) Lucent Bks.

Corrick, James A. The Renaissance. LC 97-27261. (World History Ser.). (Illus.). (YA). (gr. 5 up). 1997. lib. bdg. 22.45 (*1-56006-311-4*) Lucent Bks.

— The Scientific Revolution: A World History Companion. (ABC-CLIO World Companions Ser.). (Illus.). 256p. 2001. lib. bdg. 65.00 (*0-87436-875-8*) ABC-CLIO.

Corrick, James A., jt. auth. see Lovisi, Gary.

***Corrie, Chad.** The Restoration Trilogy. LC 00-190193. 2000. pap. 18.00 (*0-7388-1588-8*) Xlibris Corp.

— The Restoration Trilogy: The Vision Made Flesh. LC 00-190193. 2000. 25.00 (*0-7388-1587-X*) Xlibris Corp.

Corrie, Jane. Island Fiesta. large type ed. (Linford Romance Library). 327p. 1984. pap. 16.99 (*0-7089-6030-8*) Ulverscroft.

Corrie, Joe. Billy Shaw. LC 96-22159. 55p. (Orig.). 1996. pap. 5.00 (*0-88734-389-9*) Players Pr.

— A Bride for Heatherhill. 32p. (Orig.). 1996. pap. 5.00 (*0-88734-354-6*) Players Pr.

— The Bridge. unabridged ed. Lnades, William-Alan, ed. LC 98-36755. 20p. 1998. pap. 5.00 (*0-88734-819-X*) Players Pr.

— A Plumber & a Man. LC 96-8659. 55p. (Orig.). 1996. pap. 6.00 (*0-88734-380-5*) Players Pr.

***Corrie Ten Boom Library Staff.** In My Father's House. LC BR1725.T35A34 2000. (Corrie Ten Boom Library). 272p. 2000. 14.99 (*0-8007-1771-6*) Chosen Bks.

Corriente Cordoba, Federico Carlos, jt. auth. see De Robles, Sainz.

Corriente, F. A Dictionary of Andalusi Arabic. (Handbuch der Orientalistik Ser.: No. 1). (ARA & ENG.). 648p. 1997. 227.50 (*90-04-09846-1*, NLG 360) Brill Academic Pubs.

Corriente, Federico. Diccionario Arabe-Espanol. (ARA & SPA.). 880p. 1991. 125.00 (*0-7859-5828-2*, 8425417635) Fr & Eur.

Corriere, Charles A. & Ham, O. A. How to Romance Your Wife: And Recapture the Passion You Once Enjoyed! LC 92-90453. (Illus.). 100p. (Orig.). 1992. pap. 8.95 (*1-881976-00-9*) Bridge Pub CO.

Corriere, Charles A., ed. see Vollmer, Donald E.

Corriere, Joseph N., Jr., ed. Essentials of Urology. LC 85-19039. 365p. (Orig.). reprint ed. pap. 113.20 (*0-7837-1370-3*, 204151900021) Bks Demand.

Corrieri, Michael E., Jr. The Complete Guide to Buying an Older Existing Home - Buyer Beware - "If Homes Could Only Talk" Complete Exterior & Interior Home Inspection - Well Informed Consumer Most Likely to Buy Wisely. (Illus.). 106p. (Orig.). 1985. pap. 4.95 (*0-9615686-1-5*) M Corrieri.

Corriez, Paul, jt. auth. see Lanjalley, Paul.

Corrigan. Bio-Art: Human Biology. (C). 1999. pap. text 31.00 (*0-03-005802-3*) Harcourt Coll Pubs.

***Corrigan.** Film Experience. 2002. pap. text. write for info. (*0-312-25566-7*) St Martin.

Corrigan. Human Biology. (C). Date not set. 3.5 hd 209.50 (*0-03-005803-1*); mac hd 209.50 (*0-03-005807-4*) Harcourt Coll Pubs.

— Human Biology. (C). 1996. 5.25 hd 21.00 (*0-03-005804-X*) Harcourt Coll Pubs.

— Human Biology. (C). 1999. text 58.50 (*0-03-097883-1*); pap. text, student ed. 33.00 (*0-03-005797-3*); pap. text, lab manual ed. 23.00 (*0-03-005798-1*) Harcourt Coll Pubs.

***Corrigan.** Typical Girls: New Stories by Smart Women. LC 99-12777. 208p. 1999. pap. 11.95 (*0-312-20679-8*) St Martin.

Corrigan & Maitland. Vertebral Musculoskeletal Disorders. LC 98-20593. 288p. 1998. pap. text 95.00 (*0-7506-2965-7*) Buttrwrth-Heinemann.

***Corrigan, Ann M., et al.** Core Curriculum or Intravenous Nursing. 2nd ed. LC 99-21557. 352p. 1999. text. write for info. (*0-7817-2116-4*) Lppncott W & W.

Corrigan, Beatrice. Curious Annals: New Documents Relating to Browning's Roman Murder Story. LC 56-3780. (Scholarly Reprint Ser.). 202p. reprint ed. pap. 62.70 (*0-608-16271-X*, 202651800050) Bks Demand.

Corrigan, Beatrice, ed. Italian Poets & English Critics, 1755-1859: A Collection of Critical Essays. LC 68-54483. (Patterns of Literary Criticism Ser.). 1969. pap. text 5.00 (*0-226-11588-7*, PLC7) U Ch Pr.

Corrigan, Beatrice, ed. see Erasmus, Desiderius.

Corrigan, Beatrice, ed. & intro. see Ariosto, Ludovico & Trissino, Giovanni Giorgio.

Corrigan, Beatrice, tr. see Alfieri, Vittorio.

Corrigan, Brian & Maitland, G. D. Practical Orthopedic Medicine. 432p. 1985. pap. text 70.00 (*0-7506-0494-8*) Buttrwrth-Heinemann.

Corrigan, Brian J., ed. The Misfortunes of Arthur: A Critical, Old-Spelling Edition. rev. ed. LC 92-31784. (Renaissance Imagination Ser.). 256p. 1992. text 35.00 (*0-8153-1088-9*) Garland.

Corrigan, D. A. & Srinivasan, S., eds. Hydrogen Storage Materials, Batteries & Electrochemistry. LC 92-70850. (Proceedings Ser.: Vol. 92-5). 460p. 1992. 43.00 (*1-56677-006-8*) Electrochem Soc.

Corrigan, D. Felicitas, tr. see Augustine, Saint.

Corrigan, Dan. The Internet University: College Courses by Computer. (Illus.). 500p. (Orig.). 1998. pap. 26.95 (*0-9648112-0-0*) Cape Soft Pr.

Corrigan, Daniel, et al. Natwest Markets Handbook of International REPO. 195p. 1995. 100.00 (*1-873440-42-1*, Pub. by IFR Pub) Am Educ Systs.

Corrigan, Daniel, jt. auth. see Rollins, Leighton.

Corrigan, Dennis A., ed. see Symposium on Nickel Hydroxide Electrodes (1989: Ho.

Corrigan, Don H. The Public Journalism Movement in America: Evangelists in the Newsroom. LC 98-50240. 256p. 1999. 59.95 (*0-275-95781-0*, Praeger Pubs) Greenwood.

Corrigan, E. & Hollowood, T. J., eds. Affine Toda Field Theory. 650p. 1998. 108.00 (*981-02-3289-6*) World Scientific Pub.

Corrigan, E. Gerald. William Taylor Memorial Lecture No. I: The Financial Disruptions of the 1980's: A Central Banker Looks Back. 20p. 1993. pap. 6.00 (*1-56708-039-1*) Grp of Thirty.

Corrigan, Edward G. & Gordon, Pearl-Ellen, eds. The Mind Object: Precocity & Pathology of Self Sufficiency. LC 95-9997. 1995. 50.00 (*1-56821-480-4*) Aronson.

Corrigan, Eileen, tr. see Gruzinski, Serge.

Corrigan, Eileen M. Problem Drinkers Seeking Treatment. LC 73-620006. (Monographs: No. 8). 1974. 5.00 (*0-911290-39-7*) Rutgers Ctr Alcohol.

Corrigan, Erin, ed. see Mullen, Laura.

Corrigan, Esther. Whisperings of Life: Book of Poetry. 98p. 1993. pap. 9.95 (*0-9638825-0-3*) SUESTA.

Corrigan, Felicitas. The Nun, the Infidel, & the Superman: The Remarkable Friendships of Dame Laurentia McLachlan with Sydney Cockerell, Bernard Shaw & Others. LC 84-52822. (Illus.). viii, 152p. 1985. 21.00 (*0-226-11589-5*) U Ch Pr.

***Corrigan, Felicitas, ed.** The Saints Humanly Speaking. LC 99-86136. 300p. 2000. pap. 10.99 (*1-56955-205-3*, Charis) Servant.

Corrigan, Felicitas, tr. see Augustine, Saint.

***Corrigan, Gerald E.** Solutions to the International Financial Crisis. (New Ser.: Vol. 22). 19p. 1999. pap. 15.00 (*0-86682-108-2*) Ctr Intl Relations.

***Corrigan, Gordon.** Sepoys in the Trenches: The Indian Corps on the Western Front, 1914-1918. 328p. 1999. write for info. (*1-86227-054-6*, Pub. by Spellmnt Pubs) St Mut.

Corrigan, Grace G. A Journal for Christa: Christa McAuliffe, Teacher in Space. LC 93-437. (Illus.). xiv, 215p. 1993. text 27.50 (*0-8032-1459-6*) U of Nebr Pr.

***Corrigan, Grace G.** A Journal for Christa: Christa McAuliffe, Teacher in Space. (Illus.). 215p. 2000. pap. 14.95 (*0-8032-6411-9*) U of Nebr Pr.

Corrigan, Janet, ed. Quality First: Better Health Care for All Americans: Final Report to the President of the United States. 315p. (C). 1999. pap. text 35.00 (*0-7881-7796-6*) DIANE Pub.

Corrigan, Jeff, tr. see Segal-Cook, Bertha E.

Corrigan, John. Business Services. (C). 1996. pap. text. write for info. (*0-201-40355-2*) Addison-Wesley.

***Corrigan, John.** Gwen: A Novel. LC 99-97580. 2000. pap. 14.95 (*0-533-13436-6*) Vantage.

Corrigan, John. The Hidden Balance: Religion & the Social Theories of Charles Chauncy & Jonathan Mayhew. 178p. 1987. text 57.95 (*0-521-32777-6*) Cambridge U Pr.

***Corrigan, John, et al.** Emotion & Religion: A Critical Assessment & Annotated Bibliography. LC 00-35372. 224p. 2000. lib. bdg. 75.00 (*0-313-30600-1*) Greenwood.

Corrigan, John, et al. Jews, Christians, Muslims: A Comparative Introduction to Monotheistic Religion. LC 96-51045. 528p. (C). 1997. pap. text 38.00 (*0-02-325092-5*) Macmillan.

***Corrigan, John, et al.** Readings in Judaism, Christianity & Islam. LC 97-29976. 376p. (C). 1998. pap. text 37.00 (*0-02-325098-4*) P-H.

Corrigan, John, jt. auth. see Hudson, Winthrop S.

Corrigan, John D., jt. auth. see Bennett, Millard.

***Corrigan, Joseph M.** The Patriot's Way: Everything You Need to Know about the POW/MIA Issue! LC 00-190649. 284p. 2000. 25.00 (*0-7388-1902-6*); pap. 18.00 (*0-7388-1903-4*) Xlibris Corp.

***Corrigan, Julia, ed.** Get Out! You're Not College Material: Have You Allowed the Educational System to Strip You of Your Self-Esteem. 195p. 2000. reprint ed. pap. 15.95 (*0-9639996-3-X*) ImageMaker.

Corrigan, Kevin, tr. see Gregory of Nyssa.

Corrigan, Lesa C. Poems of Pure Imagination: Robert Penn Warren & the Romantic Tradition. LC 99-32057. (Southern Literary Studies). 160p. 1999. text 35.00 (*0-8071-2408-7*); pap. text 19.95 (*0-8071-2506-7*) La State U Pr.

Corrigan, Maureen, jt. ed. see Winks, Robin W.

***Corrigan, Michael.** Substance Abuse & the Shadow. 2000. pap. write for info. (*1-929342-11-X*) Olde Ridge Bk.

Corrigan, Mike. Frank Blunt's Display. 1999. pap. text 77.70 (*0-9643986-2-1*) Andrews & McMeel.

***Corrigan, Mike & An, Margaret.** Frank Blunt's Driving Book. (Illus.). 96p. 2000. pap. 12.95 (*1-889647-54-3*) Boston Am.

Corrigan, Mike & Au, Margaret. Frank Blunt's Driving Bits. 1995. spiral bd. 12.95 (*0-9643986-0-5*) Leapin Lizard.

Corrigan, Patricia. Beavers for Kids. LC 96-11586. (Wildlife for Kids Ser.). (Illus.). 48p. (Orig.). (J). (gr. 3-7). 1996. pap. 6.95 (*1-55971-576-6*, NorthWord Pr) Creat Pub Intl.

— Dolphins for Kids. (Wildlife for Kids Ser.). (Illus.). 48p. (Orig.). (J). (gr. 3-7). 1995. pap. 6.95 (*1-55971-460-3*, NorthWord Pr) Creat Pub Intl.

— Manatees for Kids. LC 95-32806. (Wildlife for Kids Ser.). (Illus.). 48p. (Orig.). (J). (gr. 3-7). 1996. pap. 6.95 (*1-55971-539-1*, NorthWord Pr) Creat Pub Intl.

— Sharks for Kids. LC 95-6206. (Wildlife for Kids Ser.). (Illus.). 48p. (Orig.). (J). (gr. 3-7). 1995. pap. 6.95 (*1-55971-476-X*, NorthWord Pr) Creat Pub Intl.

— The Whale Watchers Guide: Whale Watching Trips in North America. 2nd rev. ed. LC 98-44878. 1999. pap. text 12.95 (*1-55971-683-5*, NorthWord Pr) Creat Pub Intl.

Corrigan, Patrick H. Building Local Area Networks with Novell's NetWare, Versions 2.2 to 3.12. 3rd ed. (Illus.). 655p. 1999. reprint ed. pap. 30.00 incl. disk (*0-7881-6515-1*) DIANE Pub.

Corrigan, Patrick H. & Guy, Aisling. Building Local Area Networks with Novell's NetWare 3.12. 3rd ed. 89p. (Orig.). 1994. pap. 39.95 incl. disk (*1-55851-292-4*) IDG Bks.

Corrigan, Patrick W. & McCracken, Stanley G. Interactive Staff Training: Rehabilitation Teams That Work. LC 97-13636. (Series in Rehabilitation & Health). (Illus.). 292p. (C). 1997. 47.50 (*0-306-45523-4*, Plenum Trade) Perseus Pubng.

Corrigan, Patrick W. & Yudofsky, Stuart C., eds. Cognitive Rehabilitation for Neuropsychiatric Disorders. LC 96-13648. 477p. 1996. text 72.95 (*0-88048-551-5*, 8551) Am Psychiatric.

Corrigan, Patrick W., et al. Practice Guidelines for Extended Psychiatric Residential Care: From Chaos to Collaboration. (Illus.). 176p. 1995. 47.95 (*0-398-06535-7*) C C Thomas.

— Practice Guidelines for Extended Psychiatric Residential Care: From Chaos to Collaboration. (Illus.). 176p. (C). 1995. pap. text 31.95 (*0-398-06536-5*) C C Thomas.

Corrigan, Paul. At the Grave of the Unknown Riverdriver: Poems of the Upcountry. LC 92-3866. 78p. 1992. pap. 10.95 (*0-945980-35-3*) Nrth Country Pr.

***Corrigan, Paul.** Shakespeare on Management: Leadership Lessons for Managers. 244p. 1999. 22.95 (*0-7494-2845-7*) Kogan Page Ltd.

Corrigan, Paul. Waiting for the Spring Freshet. 1984. pap. 3.00 (*0-942396-33-2*) Blackberry ME.

Corrigan, Peter. The Sociology of Consumption: An Introduction. LC 97-69178. 224p. 1997. 69.95 (*0-7619-5010-9*); pap. 23.95 (*0-7619-5011-7*) Sage.

Corrigan, Peter, jt. auth. see Gurry, Mark.

Corrigan, Phillip, ed. Capitalism, State Formation & Marxist Theory. 9.95 (*0-7043-3311-2*, Pub. by Quartet) Charles River Bks.

Corrigan, Philomena, jt. auth. see Parsley, Karen.

Corrigan, Ralph. Karate Made Easy. LC 95-21954. (Illus.). 96p. (Orig.). 1995. 14.95 (*0-8069-1370-3*) Sterling.

— Karate Made Easy. (Illus.). 96p. (Orig.). 1996. pap. 6.95 (*0-8069-1371-1*) Sterling.

Corrigan, Robert W. The Making of Theatre: From Drama to Performance. LC 80-19046. 352p. reprint ed. pap. 109.20 (*0-7837-3952-4*, 204378100011) Bks Demand.

— The World of the Theatre. 2nd ed. 408p. (C). 1992. write for info. (*0-697-16926-X*) Brown & Benchmark.

Corrigan, Robert W., ed. Classical Comedy Greek & Roman: Six Plays. 488p. 1987. pap. 10.95 (*0-936839-85-6*) Applause Theatre Bk Pubs.

— Classical Tragedy Greek & Roman: Eight Plays with Critical Essays. 640p. 1990. pap. 12.95 (*1-55783-046-0*) Applause Theatre Bk Pubs.

Corrigan, Robert W., ed. see Tulane Drama Review Staff.

Corrigan, Roberta L., et al, eds. Linguistic Categorization: Proceedings of an International Symposium in Milwaukee, Wisconsin, April 10-11, 1987. LC 89-15193. (Current Issues in Linguistic Theory Ser.: No. 61). viii, 348p. 1989. 89.00 (*90-272-3558-9*) J Benjamins Pubng Co.

Corrigan, Sara A. Seasons of Seasonings: An Urban Herb Gardener Cooks. large type ed. 164p. 1999. ring bd. 12.00 (*0-9671483-0-8*) S A Corrigan.

Corrigan, Thom. Experiencing Community. 79p. 1997. pap. 6.00 (*0-89109-938-7*) NavPress.

— 101 Great Ideas to Create a Caring Group. LC 98-126700. (Pilgrimage Ser.). 84p. 1997. pap. 8.00 (*1-57683-072-1*) NavPress.

— The Small Group Fitness Kit. 1996. pap. 7.00 (*0-89109-939-5*) NavPress.

Corrigan, Timothy. A Cinema Without Walls: Movies & Culture after Vietnam. LC 90-48792. (Illus.). 250p. (C). 1991. pap. 14.95 (*0-8135-1668-4*); text 40.00 (*0-8135-1667-6*) Rutgers U Pr.

— Film & Literature: An Introduction & Reader. LC 98-31413. 374p. 1998. pap. text 38.60 (*0-13-526542-8*) P-H.

— The Films of Werner Herzog. 232p. 1986. pap. 14.95 (*0-416-41070-7*) Routledge.

— New German Film: The Displaced Image. rev. ed. LC 93-4971. 1994. pap. 14.95 (*0-253-20841-6*) Ind U Pr.

— New German Film: The Displaced Image. rev. ed. LC 93-4971. (Illus.). 248p. 1994. 35.00 (*0-253-31439-9*) Ind U Pr.

Corrigan, Timothy, ed. A Short Guide to Writing about Film. 3rd ed. LC 97-13118. 208p. (C). 1997. pap. 24.20 (*0-321-01110-4*) Addson-Wesley Educ.

Corriher, Shirley O. Cookwise: The Secrets of Cooking Revealed. LC 97-20209. (Illus.). 476p. 1997. 28.50 (*0-688-10229-8*, Wm Morrow) Morrow Avon.

***Corrin, B.** Pathology of the Lungs. (Illus.). 704p. 1999. text. write for info. (*0-443-05713-3*, W B Saunders Co) Harcrt Hlth Sci Grp.

Corrin, B. Tumors of the Lung: Contemporary Issues. LC 97-7855. 1997. text 105.00 (*0-443-05367-7*) Church.

Corrin, B., ed. The Lungs. 3rd ed. (Systemic Pathology Ser.: Vol. 5). (Illus.). 467p. 1990. text 185.00 (*0-443-03094-4*) Church.

***Corrin, Chris.** Feminist Perspectives on Politics. (Feminist Perspectives Ser.). 284p. (C). 1999. pap. text 24.95 (*0-582-35638-5*) Longman.

***Corrin, Chris, ed.** Gender & Identity in Central & Eastern Europe. LC 99-17015. 152p. 1999. 54.50 (*0-7146-5033-1*, Pub. by F Cass Pubs); pap. 24.50 (*0-7146-8087-7*, Pub. by F Cass Pubs) Intl Spec Bk.

Corrin, Chris, ed. Superwomen & the Double Burden: Women's Experience of Change in the Former Soviet Union, Central & Eastern Europe. (Illus.). 256p. (Orig.). 1992. pap. 16.95 (*0-929005-34-1*, Pub. by Sec Story Pr) LPC InBook.

— Women in a Violent World: Feminist Analyses & Resistance Across Europe. LC 97-165767. 260p. 1996. pap. 25.00 (*0-7486-0804-4*, 103215, Pub. by Edinburgh U Pr) Col U Pr.

Corrin, Chris, et al, eds. Desperately Seeking Sisterhood: Still Challenging & Building. LC 96-18072. 222p. 1996. 79.95 (*0-7484-0409-0*); pap. 24.95 (*0-7484-0410-4*) Taylor & Francis.

Corrin, Lisa G. Mark Dion. (Illus.). 160p. 1997. pap. 29.95 (*0-7148-3659-1*, Pub. by Phaidon Press) Phaidon Pr.

Corrin, Ruth. Charlie Best. LC 93-9229. (Illus.). (J). 1994. write for info. (*0-383-03681-X*) SRA McGraw.

— It Always Rains for Jackie. (Illus.). 32p. (J). (ps-2). 1990. bds. 8.95 (*0-19-558205-5*) OUP.

— Mr. Cat. LC 91-20236. (Illus.). 32p. (J). (ps-3). 1991. 13.95 (*0-940793-89-X*, Crocodile Bks) Interlink Pub.

Corrin, Sara. Stories for Five-Year-Olds. (J). (ps-3). 1989. pap. 11.95 (*0-571-12998-6*) Faber & Faber.

Corrin, Sara, ed. The Pied Piper of Hamelin. (Illus.). 32p. (J). (ps-5). 1989. 14.95 (*0-15-261596-2*, Harcourt Child Bks) Harcourt.

Corrin, Sara, et al, eds. Stories for Under-Fives. (Illus.). 158p. (J). (ps-5). 1989. pap. 11.95 (*0-571-12920-X*) Faber & Faber.

Corrin, Sara & Corrin, Stephen, eds. Stories for Eight-Year-Olds. (Illus.). 192p. (J). (gr. 2-4). 1989. pap. 11.95 (*0-571-12969-2*) Faber & Faber.

C

— Stories for Nine-Year-Olds. unabridged ed. LC 79-670371. (Illus.). 160p. (J). (gr. 4-5). 1990. reprint ed. pap. 11.95 (*0-571-12931-5*) Faber & Faber.

— Stories for Seven-Year-Olds. (Illus.). 188p. (J). (gr. 1-3). 1989. pap. 11.95 (*0-571-12910-2*) Faber & Faber.

— Stories for Six-Year-Olds. (Illus.). 198p. (J). (gr. k-2). 1989. pap. 11.95 (*0-571-12959-5*) Faber & Faber.

Corrin, Sarah & Corrin, Stephen, eds. Round the Christmas Tree. (J). (gr. 3-7). reprint ed. pap. 3.95 (*0-317-62263-3*, PuffinBks) Peng Put Young Read.

Corrin, Stephen, jt. ed. see Corrin, Sarah.

Corrin, Stephen, jt. ed. see Corrin, Sara.

Corrin, Stephen, tr. see Eliade, Mircea.

Corrington, John W. The Actes & Monuments: Stories. fac. ed. LC 78-15325. (Illinois Short Fiction Ser.). 153p. 1978. pap. 47.50 (*0-7837-7616-0*, 204736800007) Bks Demand.

— The Actes & Monuments. Stories. LC 78-15325. (Illinois Short Fiction Ser.). 146p. 1978. 9.95 (*0-252-00715-8*) U of Ill Pr.

— Bombardier. 1970. 25.00 (*0-399-10096-2*) Ultramarine Pub.

— The Southern Reporter, Stories. fac. ed. LC 80-26204. 200p. 1981. reprint ed. pap. 62.00 (*0-7837-7728-0*, 204748400007) Bks Demand.

Corrington, John W., ed. The Collected Stories of John William Corrington. 528p. 1990. 29.95 (*0-8262-0753-7*) U of Mo Pr.

Corrington, Leafy J., jt. auth. see Fink, Bruce.

Corrington, Pat R. Alive Again...Again...& Again: 43 Actual Past-Life Regressions & How They Can Help You. LC 95-78460. 272p. (Orig.). 1995. pap. 12.95 (*0-9647606-8-1*) Awakening CA.

Corrington, Robert S. The Community of Interpreters: On the Hermeneutics of Nature & the Bible in the American Philosophical Tradition. LC 87-24807. (Studies in American Biblical Hermeneutics: No. 3). 136p. (C). 1996. reprint ed. pap. text 16.95 (*0-86554-502-2*, MUP/P132) Mercer Univ Pr.

— An Introduction to the Thought of C. S. Peirce: Philosopher, Semiotician, & Ecstatic Naturalist. 240p. (Orig.). (C). 1993. pap. text 25.95 (*0-8476-7814-8*); lib. bdg. 66.00 (*0-8476-7813-X*) Rowman.

— Nature & Spirit: An Essay in Ecstatic Naturalism. LC 92-361. xiii, 207p. 1992. 30.00 (*0-8232-1362-5*); pap. 19.95 (*0-8232-1363-3*) Fordham.

— Nature's Religion. LC 97-17894. 212p. 1997. 61.00 (*0-8476-8699-X*); pap. 24.95 (*0-8476-8750-3*) Rowman.

— Nature's Self: Our Journey from Origin to Spirit. LC 95-38603. 192p. (C). 1996. pap. text 24.95 (*0-8476-8134-3*); lib. bdg. 58.50 (*0-8476-8133-5*) Rowman.

C

***Corrington, Robert S.** A Semiotic Theory of Theology & Philosophy. 313p. 2000. write for info. (*0-521-78271-6*) Cambridge U Pr.

Corrington, Robert S., et al, eds. Pragmatism Considers Phenomenology. LC 87-22995. (Current Continental Research Ser.). 256p. 1987. 52.50 (*0-8191-6581-6*); pap. 26.00 (*0-8191-6582-4*) U Pr of Amer.

Corripio, A. B. Tuning of Industrial Control Systems. 225p. 1990. 76.00 (*1-55617-253-2*, A253-2) ISA.

***Corripio, A. B.** Tuning of Industrial Control Systems. 2nd rev. ed. 225p. 2000. text 76.00 (*1-55617-718-6*) ISA.

Corripio, Armando B. Design & Application of Process Control Systems. LC 97-29091. 1997. 76.00 (*1-55617-639-2*) ISA.

Corripio, Armando B., jt. auth. see Smith, Carlos A.

Corripio, Fernando. Abbreviated Dictionary of Synonyms: Diccionario Abreviado de Sinonimos. 478p. 1980. pap. 17.95 (*0-8288-2038-4*, S50157) Fr & Eur.

— Etymological Dictionary of the Castilian Language (Spanish) Diccionario Etimologico de la Lengua Castellana. 3rd ed. (SPA.). 511p. 1984. 39.95 (*0-8288-2040-6*, S50158) Fr & Eur.

Corris, Peter. The Greenwich Apartments. LC 89-114925. 173p. 1986. pap. write for info. (*0-04-820030-1*, Pub. by Allen & Unwin Pty) Paul & Co Pubs.

Corriveau, Jean. A Step-by-Step Guide to C Programming. LC 97-36756. 825p. (C). 1997. pap. 58.60 (*0-13-339946-X*) P-H.

Corriveau, Jean-Pierre. Time-Constrained Memory: A Reader-Based Approach to Text Comprehension. 424p. 1995. pap. 39.95 (*0-8058-1712-3*); text 79.95 (*0-8058-1711-5*) L Erlbaum Assocs.

Corriveau, Linda, text. Pure Gesture: Macrodimensional Glimpses of Other Realities--Art of E. J. Gold. LC 89-23642. 128p. 1990. 35.00 (*0-89556-062-3*) Gateways Bks & Tapes.

Corriveau, Linda, ed. see Gold, E. J. & Lourie, Iven.

Corriveau, Robert J., et al, eds. Opto-Contact Vol. 3414: Workshop on Technology Transfers, Start-Up Opportunities & Strategic Alliances. LC 99-170367. 1998. 89.00 (*0-8194-2868-X*) SPIE.

Corriveau, Verna, ed. see Sanborn, Jeannie & Harlin, David.

Corroon, Willis. The Application of Quality to Risk Management Practices. 1994. pap. 40.00 (*0-88711-272-2*) Am Trucking Assns.

Corrothers, James D. In Spite of the Handicap. LC 75-170694. (Black Heritage Library Collection). 1977. reprint ed. 25.95 (*0-8369-8884-1*) Ayer.

— In Spite of the Handicap: An Autobiography. (American Biography Ser.). 238p. 1991. reprint ed. lib. bdg. 69.00 (*0-7812-8092-3*) Rprt Serv.

— Negro Humor & Folk-Lore. LC 72-1047. (Black Cat Club Ser.). (Illus.). reprint ed. 39.00 (*0-404-00023-1*) AMS Pr.

Corrsin, Stephen D. Sword Dancing: A History. LC 96-196483. (Illus.). 256p. 1996. 45.00 (*1-874312-25-7*, Pub. by Hisarlik Pr) Intl Spec Bk.

— Warsaw Before the First World War: Poles, & Jews in the Third City of the Russian Empire. 183p. 1989. text 55.50 (*0-88033-171-2*, Pub. by East Eur Monographs) Col U Pr.

Corruccini, Robert S. How Anthropology Informs the Orthodontic Diagnosis of Malocclusion's Causes. LC 99-24675. (Studies in Anthropology: Vol. 1). 216p. 1999. text 89.95 (*0-7734-7980-5*) E Mellen.

Corruccini, Robert S. & Ciochon, Russell L. Integrative Paths to the Past: Paleoanthropological Advances in Honor of F. Clark Howell. LC 93-36013. 736p. 1994. pap. text 88.00 (*0-13-706773-9*) P-H.

Corruccini, Robert S. & Kaul, Samvit S. Halla: Demographic Consequences of the Partition of the Punjab, 1947. 124p. (Orig.). (C). 1990. pap. text 19.50 (*0-8191-7850-0*); lib. bdg. 38.50 (*0-8191-7849-7*) U Pr of Amer.

Corruccini, Robert S., jt. ed. see Ciochon, Russell L.

Corrugated Containers Division, TAPPI, Engineering, compiled by. Rotary Diecutting: Dimensional Accuracy Control. LC 92-14356. 1992. 27.00 (*0-89852-274-9*, 0101R205) TAPPI.

Corruscini, Robert S., et al, eds. Anthropological Studies Related to Health Problems of North American Indians. LC 74-5180. (American Indian Health Ser.: Vol. 4). 148p. 1974. text 19.00 (*0-8422-7157-0*) Irvington.

Corry. Public Expenditure. 1998. pap. 19.99 (*1-86152-428-5*) Thomson Learn.

Corry, Bernard & Peston, Maurice H. The History & Practice of Economics: Essays in Honour of Bernard Corry & Maurice Peston, Vol. 2. Daniel, Sami et al, eds. LC 98-12475. (Essays in honour of Bernard Corry & Maurice Peston Ser.). 256p. (C). 1999. 95.00 (*1-85898-579-X*) E Elgar.

***Corry, Bernard & Peston, Maurice H.** Regulation Strategies & Economic Policies Vol. III: Essays in Honour of Bernard Corry & Maurice Peston, Vol. 3. Daniel, Sami et al, eds. LC 98-53419. 256p. (C). 1999. 95.00 (*1-85898-580-3*) E Elgar.

Corry, C. E., ed. see Herrin, H., et al.

Corry, Charles E. Laccoliths: Mechanics of Emplacement & Growth. LC 88-10166. (Geological Society of America Ser.: Vol. 220). (Illus.). 188p. 1988. reprint ed. pap. 58.30 (*0-608-07746-1*, 206783400010) Bks Demand.

Corry, Chris. Teach Yourself COM/DCOM in 14 Days. (Teach Yourself Ser.). 500p. 1999. pap. text 35.00 (*0-672-31279-4*) Sams.

Corry, J. E., et al, eds. Culture Media for Food Microbiology. 472p. 1996. 218.75 (*0-614-16306-4*) Elsevier.

Corry, James A. & Hodgetts, J. E. Democratic Government & Politics. 3rd rev. ed. LC JF0051.C64. (Canadian Government Ser.: No. 1). 699p. reprint ed. pap. 200.00 (*0-8357-3763-2*, 203649000003) Bks Demand.

Corry, John. Global Warming & the Media. LC 98-114880. 54p. 1997. pap. 12.95 (*0-937790-57-5*, 4520) Media Institute.

Corry, John, et al. Speaking Freely Vol. 1: The Public Interest in Unfettered Speech. LC 95-79861. 135p. (Orig.). (C). 1995. pap. 14.95 (*0-937790-51-6*, 4460) Media Institute.

Corry, John A. 1898: Prelude to a Century. LC 98-138149. (Illus.). 355p. 1998. 24.95 (*0-9661570-0-1*) J A Corry.

***Corry, John A. A Rough Ride to Albany: Teddy Runs for Governor. (Illus.). 320p. 2000. 24.95 (*0-9661570-1-X*) J A Corry.**

Just as essential to Theodore Roosevelt's accession to the Presidency as his charge up San Juan Hill was his election as Governor of New York four months later. A defeat would have seriously set back & perhaps even destroyed his chances to gain the White House. Yet, until a Rough Ridge To Albany, no book has devoted itself primarily to that hard fought uphill campaign, which he barely won only after a series of energetic "whistle stop" tours in which he displayed for the first time a unique power to stir audiences that has rarely been seen in American politics. The book also describes how Roosevelt had to balance his commitment to reform with the positions of New York's Republican leadership, which did not share many of his priorities. It thus provides lessons that are just as relevant today as they were more than one hundred years ago. A ROUGH RIDE TO ALBANY is "must" reading for anyone who is fascinated by the career of Theodore Roosevelt or by the details of a dramatic political campaign that helped set the course of Twentieth Century American history. To order: Fordham University Press: 800-247-6553. *Publisher Paid Annotation.*

Corry, John P. Indian Affairs in Georgia, 1732-1756. LC 76-43685. reprint ed. 39.50 (*0-404-15518-9*) AMS Pr.

Corry, Joseph. Observations upon the Windward Coast of Africa: Religion, Character, Customs, Etc., of the Natives. (Illus.). 163p. 1968. reprint ed. 45.00 (*0-7146-1800-4*, Pub. by F Cass Pubs) Intl Spec Bk.

Corry, Leo. Modern Algebra & the Rise of Mathematical Structures. LC 96-3974. (Science Networks, Historical Studies: Vol. 17). 460p. 1996. 139.00 (*0-8176-5311-2*) Birkhauser.

Corry, Steven D., ed. see Corry, Thomas M.

Corry, Thomas M. I Begin to See . . . Corry, Steven D. & Corry, Vincent D., eds. LC 90-91867. 132p. (Orig.). 1990. pap. 7.95 (*1-878089-03-X*) Long Run Prodns.

Corry, Tracy, jt. auth. see Puryear, Kay.

Corry, Vincent D., ed. see Corry, Thomas M.

Corsa, Helen S., ed. see Chaucer, Geoffrey.

***Corsan, John & Mackay, Mac.** Veterinary Receptionist: A Professional Handbook. (Illus.). 192p. 2000. pap. 42.50 (*0-7506-4225-4*) Buttrwrth-Heinemann.

Corsan, W. C. Two Months in the Confederate States: An Englishman's Travels Through the South. LC 96-20861. (Illus.). 216p. (C). 1996. 26.95 (*0-8071-2037-5*) La State U Pr.

— Two Months in the Confederate States: An Englishman's Travels Through the South. Trask, Benjamin H., ed. LC 96-20861. (Illus.). 184p. 1998. pap. 12.95 (*0-8071-2335-8*) La State U Pr.

Corsaro, Robert D., jt. ed. see Sperling, Leslie H.

Corsaro, William. Friendship & Peer Culture in the Early Years. Wallat, Cynthia & Green, Judith, eds. LC 84-28221. (Language & Learning for Human Service Professions Ser.: Vol. 5). 336p. 1985. pap. 39.50 (*0-89391-256-5*); text 73.25 (*0-89391-174-7*) Ablx Pub.

Corsaro, William A. & Miller, Peggy J., eds. Interpretive Approaches to Children's Socialization. LC 85-644581. (New Directions for Child Development Ser.: No. CD 58). 100p. 1992. pap. 25.00 (*1-55542-733-2*) Jossey-Bass.

Corse, Sandra. Opera & the Uses of Language: Mozart, Verdi, & Britten. LC 86-45865. (Illus.). 168p. 1987. 32.50 (*0-8386-3300-5*) Fairleigh Dickinson.

— Wagner & the New Consciousness: Language & Love in the Ring. LC 88-46186. (Illus.). 216p. 1990. 36.50 (*0-8386-3378-1*) Fairleigh Dickinson.

Corse, Sarah M. Nationalism & Literature: The Politics of Culture in Canada & the United States. LC 96-14151. (Cambridge Cultural Social Studies). 225p. (C). 1996. text 59.95 (*0-521-57002-6*) Cambridge U Pr.

— Nationalism & Literature: The Politics of Culture in Canada & the United States. LC 96-14151. (Cultural Social Studies). 224p. (C). 1997. pap. text 19.95 (*0-521-57912-0*) Cambridge U Pr.

Corse, Taylor. Dryden's Aeneid: The English Virgil. LC 89-40594. 151 p. 1991. 32.50 (*0-87413-385-8*) U Delaware Pr.

Corse, Taylor, ed. see Conway, Anne.

Corsel, Ralph. The Con Man. 1993. 19.95 (*0-9638205-0-8*) Bandam Pr.

Corsello, Serafina. The Ageless Woman. (Illus.). 300p. 1999. pap. 19.95 (*0-9672219-0-0*) Corsello Commns.

Corsello, Serafina & Gallup, James. Bacillus Latero Sporus Bod: The Revolutionary New Natural Approach to Control Candida & Yeast Infections. 16p. 1996. pap. 2.95 (*0-9647080-7-8*) Healing Wisdom.

Corser, Elwood S., jt. auth. see Corser, Samuel B.

Corser, Kira & Adler, Frances P. When the Bough Breaks: Pregnancy & the Legacy of Addiction. 112p. 1993. 39.95 (*0-939165-20-1*); pap. 22.95 (*0-939165-19-8*) NewSage Press.

Corser, Samuel B. & Corser, Elwood S. Corser. Genealogy of the Corser Family in America, Embracing Many of the Descendants of the Early Settlers of the Name in Massachusetts & New Hampshire, with Some Reminiscences of Their Trans-Atlantic Cousins. (Illus.). 336p. 1997. reprint ed. pap. 52.00 (*0-8328-8064-7*); reprint ed. lib. bdg. 62.00 (*0-8328-8063-9*) Higginson Bk Co.

***Corset, Caroline M.** Three Cheers for the Good Years: You're Not an Antique, but the Rocking Chair Is. 96p. 2000. pap. 19.95 (*0-9647732-1-X*) C W Prodns.

Corset, J. & Turrell, George, eds. Raman Microscopy: Developments & Applications. (Illus.). 528p. 1996. text 99.95 (*0-12-189690-0*) Acad Pr.

***Corsetty, Kathy & Pearson, Judith E.** Healthy Habits: Total Conditioning for a Healthy Body & Mind. LC 00-31641. 2000. write for info. (*1-886225-47-8*) Dageforde Pub.

Corsi, Carlo, ed. Science & Innovation As Strategic Tools for Industrial & Economic Growth: Proceedings of the NATO Advanced Research Workshop, Moscow, Russia, October 24-26, 1994. LC 95-26544. (NATO ASI: Partnership Sub-Series 4: Science & Technology Policy: Vol. 4). 192p. (C). 1996. lib. bdg. 107.00 (*0-7923-3903-7*) Kluwer Academic.

Corsi, Carlos & Kudrya, S. Globalization of Science & Technology: A Way for CIS Counties to New Markets: Proceedings of Research Workshop on Globalization of Science & Technology. LC 98-28191. (NATO ASI Ser.). 1998. 80.00 (*0-7923-5195-9*) Kluwer Academic.

Corsi, Edward. In the Shadow of Liberty: The Chronicle of Ellis Island. LC 69-18769. (American Immigration Collection. Series 1). (Illus.). 1969. reprint ed. 18.95 (*0-405-00517-2*) Ayer.

Corsi, Giovanna, et al, eds. Bridging the Gap: Lectures on the Foundations of Science. LC 92-12617. (Boston Studies in the Philosophy of Science: Vol. 140). 336p. 1992. lib. bdg. 166.50 (*0-7923-1761-0*, Pub. by Kluwer Academic) Kluwer Academic.

Corsi, Jerome R. New Banking. 1996. text 50.00 (*0-8133-0370-2*) Westview.

Corsi, Jerome R., ed. Marketing Life Insurance in a Bank or Thrift. (Professional Handbooks on the New Banking Ser.). 233p. 1986. pap. text 51.50 (*0-8133-7205-4*) Westview.

Corsi, Jerome R. & Hills, William F. Debugging Assembly Language on the IBM PC. 1986. pap. 21.95 (*0-89303-627-7*) P-H.

Corsi, Jone Gaillard, see Gaillard Corsi, Jone.

Corsi, Jorge, tr. see Sonkin, Daniel J. & Durphy, Michael.

Corsi, Marcella. Division of Labour, Technical Change & Economic Growth. 175p. 1991. 75.95 (*1-85628-231-7*, Pub. by Avebry) Ashgate Pub Co.

Corsi, Mario. Tamagno, Il Piu Grande Fenomeno Canoro Dell'novocento: Tamagno, the Greatest Singing Phenomenon of the Nineteenth Century. Farkas, Andrew, ed. LC 76-29931. (Opera Biographies Ser.). (ITA., Illus.). 1977. reprint ed. lib. bdg. 26.95 (*0-405-09673-9*) Ayer.

Corsi, Paolo, jt. ed. see Chow, Gregory C.

***Corsi, Pietro.** Winter in Montreal: A Novel. Di Giacomantonio, Antonio, tr. (Picas Ser.: No. 11). 155p. 2000. pap. 10.00 (*1-55071-117-2*, Pub. by Guernica Editions) Paul & Co Pubs.

Corsi, Sergio. Il Modus Digressivus Nella "Divina Commedia" 201p. 1990. 28.75 (*0-916379-46-9*) Scripta.

Corsi-Staub, Wendy. Possession. 1996. mass mkt. 3.99 (*0-8217-5153-0*) NAL.

Corsi, Thomas, jt. auth. see Winston, Clifford M.

Corsini, Anna R. & Segoloni, Maria P., eds. Medicina Plinii - Concordantiae in Medicinam Plinii. (Alpha-Omega, Reihe A Ser.: Bd. CI). vi, 351p. 1989. 160.00 (*3-487-09182-8*) G Olms Pubs.

Corsini, Carlo A. & Viazzo, Pier P., eds. The Decline of Infant & Child Mortality: The European Experience: 1750-1990. LC 97-23862. 292p. 1997. 84.00 (*90-411-0466-6*) Kluwer Academic.

***Corsini, Raymond J.** Dictionary of Psychology. LC 99-30502. 1999. pap. text 124.95 (*1-58391-028-X*) Brunner-Mazel.

— Handbook of Innovative Therapy. 2nd ed. 800p. 2001. 75.00 (*0-471-34819-8*) Wiley.

Corsini, Raymond J., ed. The Encyclopedia of Criminology, 4 vols. 1995. text 85.00 (*0-02-884002-X*) Macmillan.

— The Encyclopedia of Criminology, 4 vols., 1. 1995. 85.00 (*0-02-884001-1*) Macmillan.

— The Encyclopedia of Criminology, 4 vols., 3. 1995. text 85.00 (*0-02-884003-8*) Macmillan.

— The Encyclopedia of Criminology, 4 vols., 4. 1995. text 85.00 (*0-02-884004-6*) Macmillan.

— The Encyclopedia of Criminology, 4 vols., Set. 1995. text 310.00 (*0-02-884000-3*) Macmillan.

— Encyclopedia of Psychology, 4 vols. 2nd ed. 2408p. 1994. 900.00 (*0-471-55819-2*) Wiley.

— Encyclopedia of Psychology, 4 vols., Vol. 1. 2nd ed. 576p. (C). 1994. text 225.00 (*0-471-55823-0*) Wiley.

— Encyclopedia of Psychology, 4 vols., Vol. 2. 2nd ed. 544p. (C). 1994. text 225.00 (*0-471-55822-2*) Wiley.

— Encyclopedia of Psychology, 4 vols., Vol. 3. 2nd ed. 608p. (C). 1994. text 225.00 (*0-471-55824-9*) Wiley.

— Encyclopedia of Psychology, 4 vols., Vol. 4. 2nd ed. 680p. (C). 1994. text 225.00 (*0-471-55821-4*) Wiley.

Corsini, Raymond J. & Auerbach, Alan, eds. Concise Encyclopedia of Psychology. LC 95-26497. 1035p. 1996. 235.00 (*0-471-13159-8*) Wiley.

Corsini, Raymond J. & Auerbach, Alan J. Concise Encyclopedia of Psychology. 2nd abr. ed. LC 98-14293. 952p. 1998. pap. 65.00 (*0-471-19282-1*) Wiley.

Corsini, Raymond J. & Wedding, Danny. Case Studies in Psychotherapy. 2nd ed. LC 94-74614. 207p. (C). 1995. pap. text 27.50 (*0-87581-393-3*, CSP2) F E Peacock Pubs.

— Current Psychotherapies. 5th ed. 462p. (C). 1995. pap. text 52.50 (*0-87581-392-5*, CP5) F E Peacock Pubs.

Corsini, Raymond J., jt. auth. see Manaster, Guy J.

Corso, Dante Del, see Conte, Gianni & Del Corso, Dante, eds.

Corso, Gregory. Earth Egg. (Illus.). 1974. pap. 35.00 (*0-934450-01-3*) Unmuzzled Ox.

— Earth Egg. deluxe ed. (Illus.). 1974. pap. 20.00 (*0-934450-00-5*) Unmuzzled Ox.

— Elegiac Feelings American. LC 71-122104. (Illus.). (Orig.). 1970. pap. 8.95 (*0-8112-0026-4*, NDP299, Pub. by New Directions) Norton.

— Gasoline, the Vestal Lady on Brattle. LC 76-10440. (Pocket Poets Ser., No. 8). (Orig.). 1982. pap. 7.95 (*0-87286-088-4*) City Lights.

— The Happy Birthday of Death. LC 59-15018. (Orig.). 1960. pap. 9.95 (*0-8112-0027-2*, NDP86, Pub. by New Directions) Norton.

— Herald of the Autochthonic Spirit. LC 81-9486. 64p. 1981. pap. 5.95 (*0-8112-0808-7*, NDP522, Pub. by New Directions) Norton.

— Herald of the Autochthonic Spirit. LC 81-9486. 64p. 1981. 12.95 (*0-8112-0819-2*, Pub. by New Directions) Norton.

— The Japanese Notebook Ox. 1974. pap. 19.95 (*0-934450-05-6*) Unmuzzled Ox.

— Long Live Man. LC 62-16927. (Orig.). 1962. pap. 8.95 (*0-8112-0025-6*, NDP127, Pub. by New Directions) Norton.

— Mind Field. 56p. (Orig.). 1989. pap. 5.95 (*0-937815-26-8*) Hanuman Bks.

— Mindfield: New & Selected Poems. LC 99-178252. (Illus.). 288p. 1998. pap. 13.95 (*1-56025-201-4*, Thunders Mouth) Avalon NY.

— Mindfield: New & Selected Poems. aut. limited ed. (Illus.). 288p. Date not set. pap. 300.00 (*0-938410-90-3*, Thunders Mouth) Avalon NY.

— Mindfield: New & Selected Poems. limited ed. 288p. 1997. 50.00 (*0-938410-96-2*, Thunders Mouth) Avalon NY.

— Writings from Ox. Andre, Michael, ed. (Illus.). 160p. 1981. pap. 9.95 (*0-934450-10-2*) Unmuzzled Ox.

Corso, Gregory, et al. Beat Voices: An Anthology of Beat Poetry. Kherdian, David, ed. LC 96-1490. 176p. 1996. pap. 4.95 (*0-688-14916-2*, Wm Morrow) Morrow Avon.

Corso, John F. Aging Sensory Systems & Perception. LC 80-39579. 302p. 1981. 65.00 (*0-275-90599-3*, C0599, Praeger Pubs) Greenwood.

Corso, Michael J., jt. ed. see Groome, Thomas H.

Corso, P. J., jt. ed. see France, Anna K.

Corso, Pete, Jr. Getting Control of Your Weight & Your Life. Seavey, Donna, ed. (Illus.). 66p. (Orig.). 1989. pap. write for info. (*0-9623085-0-1*) P C Corso.

An Asterisk (*) at the beginning of an entry indicates that the title is appearing for the first time.

Corso, Philip J. & Birnes, William J. The Day after Roswell. (Illus.). 341p. 1999. text 24.00 (*0-7881-6044-3*) DIANE Pub.
— The Day after Roswell. LC 97-208349. 341p. 1997. 24.00 (*0-671-00461-1*, Pocket Books) PB.
***Corso, Philip J. & Birnes, William J.** The Day after Roswell. ed. 1998. per. 24.00 (*0-671-03695-5*, Pocket Books) PB.
Corso, Philip J., et al. The Day after Roswell. (Illus.). 371p. 1998. per. 6.99 (*0-671-01756-X*, Pocket Books) PB.
Corso, S. M. De, see Clark, J. S. & De Corso, S. M., eds.
Corso, Susan. The Peace Diet: The 44 Day Feast for Personal Peace. (Illus.). 64p. (Orig.). 1996. pap. 12.95 (*0-9651541-4-9*) Dona Nobis Pacem.
Corso, William & Joyce, Paul S. Oceanography. (Applied Science Review Ser.). (Illus.). 192p. 1994. pap. 12.95 (*0-87434-608-8*) Springhouse Corp.
Corson, Carol. Schoenhut Dolls: A Collector's Encyclopedia. 272p. 1993. 39.95 (*0-87588-400-8*) Hobby Hse.
Corson, D., ed. see Peierls, Rudolf E., et al.
Corson, Dan W., jt. auth. see Noel, Thomas J.
Corson, David. Changing Education for Diversity. LC 97-34976. (Changing Education Ser.). 256p. 1998. pap. 28.95 (*0-335-19587-3*) OpUniv Pr.
— Changing Education for Diversity. LC 97-34976. (Changing Education Ser.). 268p. 1998. 89.00 (*0-335-19588-1*) Taylor & Francis.
— Discourse & Power in Educational Institutions. Noblit, George W. & Pink, William T., eds. (Understanding Education & Policy Ser.). 368p. (C). 1995. text 69.50 (*1-881303-96-9*); pap. text 28.50 (*1-881303-97-7*) Hampton Pr NJ.
***Corson, David.** Language Diversity & Education. LC 00-20306. 256p. 2000. write for info. (*0-8058-3448-6*); pap. write for info. (*0-8058-3449-4*) L Erlbaum Assocs.
Corson, David. Language, Minority Education, & Gender: Linking Social Justice & Power. LC 93-8605. (Language & Education Library: Vol. 6). 1993. 74.95 (*1-85359-210-2*, Pub. by Multilingual Matters); pap. 29.95 (*1-85359-209-9*, Pub. by Multilingual Matters) Taylor & Francis.
— Language Policy Across the Curriculum. (Language & Education Library: No. 1). 328p. 1990. 79.00 (*1-85359-069-X*, Pub. by Multilingual Matters); pap. 24.95 (*1-85359-068-1*, Pub. by Multilingual Matters) Taylor & Francis.
— Language Policy in Schools: A Resource for Teachers & Administrators. LC 98-28702. 264p. 1998. 59.95 (*0-8058-3005-7*) L Erlbaum Assocs.
— Language Policy in Schools: A Resource for Teachers & Administrators. LC 98-28702. 264p. 1999. pap. 27.50 (*0-8058-3296-3*) L Erlbaum Assocs.
— Oral Language Across the Curriculum. 1988. 54.00 (*0-905028-97-X*, Pub. by Multilingual Matters); pap. 24.95 (*0-905028-96-1*, Pub. by Multilingual Matters) Taylor & Francis.
— Using English Words. LC 95-36587. (Illus.). 236p. (C). 1995. lib. bdg. 120.00 (*0-7923-3710-7*) Kluwer Academic.
— Using English Words. 1996. pap. text 49.95 (*0-7923-3711-5*) Kluwer Academic.
Corson, David, ed. Education for Work: Background to Policy & Curriculum. 256p. 1990. 24.95 (*1-85359-124-6*, Pub. by Multilingual Matters) Taylor & Francis.
Corson, David, jt. auth. see Clapham, Caroline.
Corson, David, jt. auth. see Cummins, Jim.
Corson, David, jt. auth. see Davies, Bronwyn.
Corson, David, jt. auth. see Edwards, Viv.
Corson, David, jt. auth. see Hornberger, Nancy H.
Corson, David, jt. auth. see Tucker, G. Richard.
Corson, David, jt. auth. see Van Lier, Leo.
Corson, David, jt. auth. see Wodak, Ruth.
Corson, David, jt. ed. see Wodak, Ruth.
Corson, Edward M. Introduction to Tensors, Spinors & Relativistic Wave Equations. 2nd ed. LC 80-85523. 222p. (C). 1988. lib. bdg. 22.00 (*0-8284-0315-5*, 315) Chelsea Pub.
Corson, Elizabeth O., ed. see Klimenko, Viktor M. & Shkhinek, Elenor K.
Corson, Elizabeth O., ed. & tr. see Korneva, Elena A., et al.
Corson-Finnerty, Adam D. & Blanchard, Laura. Fundraising & Friend-Raising on the Web. LC 97-51833. 122p. 1998. 50.00 (*0-8389-0727-X*) ALA.
Corson, Hiram. Introduction to the Study of Robert Browning's Poetry. LC 74-119929. (Select Bibliographies Reprint Ser.). 1977. 23.95 (*0-8369-5372-X*) Ayer.
Corson, J. M., et al. Infinite Groups & Group Ring. (Series in Automation). 150p. 1993. text 67.00 (*981-02-1379-4*) World Scientific Pub.
Corson, James C., ed. Notes & Index to Sir Herbert Grierson's Edition of the Letters of Sir Walter Scott. 716p. 1979. text 135.00 (*0-19-812718-9*) OUP.
***Corson, Jennifer.** The Resourceful Renovator: A Gallery of Ideas for Re-Using Building Materials. (Illus.). 250p. 2000. pap. 24.95 (*1-890132-51-9*) Chelsea Green Pub.
Corson, John A. Stress, Self-Concept, & Violence. Humphrey, James H., ed. LC 86-82026. (Stress in Modern Society Ser.: No. 11). 1989. 32.50 (*0-404-63271-8*); pap. 14.95 (*0-404-63263-7*) AMS Pr.
Corson, John J. & Paul, R. S. Men near the Top: Filling Key Posts in the Federal Service. LC 66-17010. (Committee for Economic Development, CED Supplementary Papers: No. 20). 208p. reprint ed. pap. 64.50 (*0-608-30045-4*, 202051000018) Bks Demand.
Corson, John J. & Steiner, George A. Measuring Business's Social Performance: Corporate Social Audit. LC 74-19382. 1975. pap. 4.00 (*0-87186-239-5*) Comm Econ Dev.
Corson, Judith A. All That Zucchini. 1998. 10.95 (*0-9664503-0-2*) Creative Cooking.
Corson, Lynea. Secrets of Superselling: How to Program Your Subconscious for Success. 1991. pap. 13.00 (*0-425-12661-7*) Berkley Pub.
Corson, Martha. Love Feud. 1983. pap. 1.95 (*0-373-46067-8*) Harlequin Bks.
Corson, Norman E., jt. auth. see Deneen, Lawrence J.
Corson, Richard. Fashions in Eyeglasses. (Illus.). 1980. reprint ed. 99.95 (*0-7206-3282-X*, Pub. by P Owen Ltd) Dufour.
— Fashions in Hair: The First Five Thousand Years. (Illus.). 720p. 1980. 120.00 (*0-7206-3283-8*, Pub. by P Owen Ltd) Dufour.
— Fashions in Makeup: From Ancient to Modern Times. (Illus.). 614p. 1972. 120.00 (*0-7206-0431-1*, Pub. by P Owen Ltd) Dufour.
— Stage Make-Up. 9th ed. (C). 2000. write for info. (*0-13-606153-2*, Macmillan Coll) P-H.
— Stage Makeup. 8th ed. 400p. 1990. 90.00 (*0-13-840539-5*) P-H.
— Stage Makeup: Special Edition. 8th ed. 416p. (C). 1992. 34.00 (*0-13-840174-8*, Macmillan Coll) P-H.
Corson, S. L. & Derman, R. J., eds. Fertility Control. 2nd ed. (Illus.). 526p. 1995. pap. 24.95 (*0-9697978-0-X*) Prthnon Pub.
Corson, Samuel A., ed. see Klimenko, Viktor M. & Shkhinek, Elenor K.
Corson, Samuel A., ed. & tr. see Korneva, Elena A., et al.
Corson, Stephen. Endometriosis: The Enigmatic Disease. 257p. 1992. pap. 12.95 (*0-929240-42-1*) EMIS.
Corson, Stephen L., et al. Fertility Control. 400p. 1984. 49.95 (*0-316-15748-1*, Little Brwn Med Div) Lppncott W & W.
Corson, Walter, et al. Nonmonetary Eligibility in State Unemployment Insurance Programs: Law & Practice. LC 86-10985. 138p. (C). 1986. 20.00 (*0-88099-039-2*); pap. text 10.00 (*0-88099-038-4*) W E Upjohn.
Corson, William R. The Consequences of Failure. 1974. 7.95 (*0-393-05492-6*) Norton.
Corsortini, Anna, ed. Trends in Optics: Research, Developments & Applications. (Lasers & Optical Engineering Ser.). (Illus.). 608p. 1996. text 89.95 (*0-12-186030-2*) Acad Pr.
Corss. Ancient Irish Tales. 1995. 12.50 (*0-8050-4408-6*) H Holt & Co.
Corssar, Constance. French Verbs & Vocabulary Bingo Games. 1995. pap. text 23.95 (*0-8442-1307-1*) NTC Contemp Pub Co.
Corstanje, Auspicius Van, see Van Corstanje, Auspicius.
Corstein, Severin, ed. see Feldmann, Reinhard & Seipt, Birgit.
Corsten, Severin, ed. see Feldmann, Reinhard & Seipt, Birgit.
***Corsten, Volker.** Von Hei & Betaen Tranen und Gro & Beta;en Gefuhlen: Funktionen des Melodramas im Gereinigten Theater Des 18, Jahrhunderts. (Europaische Hochschulschriften: Reihe 1, Deutsche Sprache und Literatur Ser.). (Illus.). x, 184p. 1999. 35.95 (*3-631-34974-2*) P Lang Pubng.
Corstius, H. Brandt, see Brandt Corstius, H., ed.
Corstjens. Store Wars. 314p. (C). 1999. pap. 38.50 (*0-471-98765-4*) Wiley.
***Corston, Rod.** Crash Course in SPSS for Windows. (Illus.). 208p. 2000. 59.95 (*0-631-21770-3*); pap. text 22.95 (*0-631-21771-1*) Blackwell Pubs.
Cort, J. H., ed. see Natriuretic Hormone Symposium Staff.
Cort, John C. Christian Socialism: An Informal History. LC 87-14046. 416p. (Orig.). 1988. pap. 22.00 (*0-88344-600-6*) Orbis Bks.
— Christian Socialism: An Informal History. LC 87-14046. 416p. (Orig.). reprint ed. pap. 129.00 (*0-608-20269-X*, 207152800012) Bks Demand.
***Cort, John E.** Jains in the World: Religious Values & Ideology in India. LC 99-28440. 288p. 2000. write for info. (*0-19-513234-3*) OUP.
Cort, John E., ed. Open Boundaries: Jain Communities & Cultures in Indian History. LC 97-46027. (SUNY Series, Hindu Studies). (Illus.). 278p. (C). 1998. text 73.50 (*0-7914-3785-X*); pap. text 24.95 (*0-7914-3786-8*) State U NY Pr.
Cort, John E. & Folkert, Kendall W., eds. Scripture & Community: Collected Essays on the Jains. (Studies in World Religions). 450p. (C). 1993. pap. 89.95 (*1-55540-858-3*, 030006) Harvard U Wrld Relig.
Cort, Louise A. Seto & Mino Ceramics. (Japanese Collections in the Freer Gallery of Art). (Illus.). 256p. 1992. text 45.00 (*0-8248-1437-1*) Freer.
— Seto & Mino Ceramics. (Japanese Collections in the Freer Gallery of Art). (Illus.). 240p. 1992. pap. text 25.00 (*0-8248-1436-3*) Freer.
Cort, Louise A. & Kenji, Nakamura. A Basketmaker in Rural Japan. LC 94-33582. (Illus.). 160p. 1995. pap. 34.95 (*0-8348-0336-4*) Weatherhill.
***Cort, Louise Allison.** Shigaraki: Potters' Valley. (Illus.). 2000. 80.00 (*0-8348-0431-X*) Weatherhill.
Cortada. Publishing Intellectual Capital: Getting Your Business into Print. LC 98-51906. 228p. 1999. 41.00 (*0-13-021438-8*, Pub. by P-H) S&S Trade.
Cortada, James. Rise of the Knowledge Worker. LC 98-14157. 264p. 1998. pap. text 19.95 (*0-7506-7058-4*) Buttrwrth-Heinemann.
Cortada, James & Woods, John. McGraw-Hill Encyclopedia of Quality Terms & Concepts. 392p. 1995. 34.95 (*0-07-024099-X*) McGraw.
— The 1998 ASTD Training & Performance Yearbook. 544p. 1997. 79.95 (*0-07-071855-5*) McGraw.
***Cortada, James & Woods, John A.** The Knowledge Management Yearbook, 2000-2001. 576p. 2000. text 89.95 (*0-7506-7258-7*) Buttrwrth-Heinemann.
Cortada, James N. & Cortada, James W. Can Democracy Survive in Western Europe? LC 96-2803. 192p. 1996. 59.95 (*0-275-95680-6*, Praeger Pubs) Greenwood.
— United States Foreign Policy in the Caribbean, Cuba, & Central America. LC 84-26629. 251p. 1985. 59.95 (*0-275-90078-9*, C0078, Praeger Pubs) Greenwood.
Cortada, James W. Archives of Data Processing History: A Guide to Major U. S. Collections. LC 89-17244. 195p. 1990. lib. bdg. 59.95 (*0-313-25923-2*, CVA/, Greenwood Pr) Greenwood.
***Cortada, James W.** Before the Computer: IBM, NCR, Burroughs & Remington Rand & the Industry They Created, 1865. 2000. pap. text 22.95 (*0-691-05045-7*, Pub. by Princeton U Pr) Cal Prin Full Svc.
Cortada, James W. Before the Computer: IBM, NCR, Burroughs, & Remington Rand & the Industry They Created, 1865-1956. LC 92-25399. (Studies in Business & Technology). (Illus.). 392p. 1992. text 69.50 (*0-691-04807-X*, Pub. by Princeton U Pr) Cal Prin Full Svc.
— Best Practices in Information Technology: How Corporations Get the Most Value from Exploiting Their Digital I. LC 97-26392. 304p. (C). 1997. 41.00 (*0-13-756446-5*) P-H.
— The Computer in the United States: From Laboratory to Market, 1930 to 1960. LC 93-4184. (Illus.). 208p. (gr. 13). 1993. 70.95 (*1-56324-234-6*); pap. 35.95 (*1-56324-235-4*) M E Sharpe.
— Historical Dictionary of Data Processing: Biographies. LC 86-31805. 334p. 1987. lib. bdg. 95.00 (*0-313-25651-9*, CBS/, Greenwood Pr) Greenwood.
— Historical Dictionary of Data Processing: Organizations. LC 86-19394. 320p. 1987. lib. bdg. 95.00 (*0-313-23303-9*, CDC, Greenwood Pr) Greenwood.
— Historical Dictionary of Data Processing: Technology. LC 86-22751. 428p. 1987. lib. bdg. 105.00 (*0-313-25652-7*, CTY/, Greenwood Pr) Greenwood.
— Information Technology As Business History: Issues in the History & Management of Computers, 177. LC 96-3644. (Contributions in Economics & Economic History Ser.: No. 177). 280p. 1996. 75.00 (*0-313-29950-1*, Greenwood Pr) Greenwood.
***Cortada, James W.** New Order of Business: Managing & Working in the Information Age. 350p. 2000. pap. 24.00 (*0-13-030569-3*) P-H.
— Quality Yearbook 2001. 2001. 89.95 (*0-07-135506-0*) McGraw.
— The Quality Yearbook 2000. 2nd ed. 784p. 1999. 89.95 (*0-07-135247-3*) Datapro Res.
Cortada, James W. Two Nations over Time: Spain & the United States, 1776-1977, 74. LC 77-94752 (Contributions in American History Ser.: No. 74). 305p. 1978. 59.95 (*0-313-20319-9*, CTN/, Greenwood Pr) Greenwood.
Cortada, James W., compiled by. An Annotated Bibliography on the History of Data Processing. LC 83-8539. 215p. 1983. lib. bdg. 69.50 (*0-313-24001-9*, CDP, Greenwood Pr) Greenwood.
— Bibliographic Guide to Spanish Diplomatic History: Fourteen Sixty to Nineteen Seventy-Seven. LC 77-4565. 390p. 1977. lib. bdg. 59.95 (*0-8371-9685-X*, CBG/, Greenwood Pr) Greenwood.
— A Bibliographic Guide to the History of Computer Applications, 1950-1990, 10. LC 95-37997. (Bibliographies & Indexes in Science & Technology Ser.: No. 10). 304p. 1996. lib. bdg. 89.50 (*0-313-29876-9*, Greenwood Pr) Greenwood.
— A Bibliographic Guide to the History of Computing, Computers & the Information Processing Industry, 6. LC 90-3093. (Bibliographies & Indexes in Science & Technology Ser.: No. 6). 656p. 1990. lib. bdg. 105.00 (*0-313-26810-X*, CBF, Greenwood Pr) Greenwood.
— Second Bibliographic Guide to the History of Computing, Computers, & the Information Processing Industry, 9. LC 95-20889. (Bibliographies & Indexes in Science & Technology Ser.: Vol. 9). 432p. 1996. lib. bdg. 95.00 (*0-313-29542-5*) Greenwood.
Cortada, James W., ed. A City in War: American Views on Barcelona & the Spanish Civil War, 1936-39. LC 84-20302. (Illus.). 224p. 1985. 45.00 (*0-8420-2229-5*) Scholarly Res Inc.
— Historical Dictionary of the Spanish Civil War, 1936-1939. LC 81-13424. (Illus.). 571p. 1982. lib. bdg. 85.00 (*0-313-22054-9*, CSP/, Greenwood Pr) Greenwood.
— Spain in the Nineteenth-Century World: Essays on Spanish Diplomacy, 1789-1898, 41. LC 93-2232. (Contributions to the Study of World History Ser.: No. 41). 192p. 1994. 55.00 (*0-313-27655-2*, CSW/, Greenwood Pr) Greenwood.
— Spain in the Twentieth-Century World: Essays on Spanish Diplomacy, 1898-1978, 30. LC 78-75257. (Contributions in Political Science Ser.: No. 30). 294p. 1980. 65.00 (*0-313-21326-7*, CST/, Greenwood Pr) Greenwood.
***Cortada, James W., ed.** Knowledge Management Yearbook, 1999-2000. (Knowledge Reader Ser.). (Illus.). 536p. 1999. 75.00 (*0-7506-7122-X*) Buttrwrth-Heinemann.
Cortada, James W. & Hargraves, Thomas S. Into the Networked Age: How IBM & Other Firms Are Getting There Now. LC 99-34841. (Illus.). 256p. 1999. 27.50 (*0-19-512449-9*) OUP.
Cortada, James W. & Woods, John A. The 1999 ASTD Training & Performance Yearbook. (ASQ Ser.). (Illus.). 528p. 1999. 128.95 (*0-07-024818-4*) McGraw-Hill Prof.
— The Quality Yearbook, 1998. 800p. 1997. 89.95 (*0-07-071853-9*) McGraw.
— The Quality Yearbook, 1999. (ASQ Ser.). (Illus.). 800p. 1999. 128.95 (*0-07-071874-1*) McGraw-Hill Prof.
— The Quality Yearbook, 1997. 787p. 1996. 89.95 (*0-07-913281-2*) McGraw.
Cortada, James W., jt. auth. see Cortada, James N.
Cortada, James W., jt. auth. see Woods, John A.
Cortada, James W., jt. ed. see Woods, John A.
Cortal, Jordi B. Diccionari Terminologic de l'Administracio Municipal. (CAT.). 100p. 1980. pap. 6.95 (*0-7859-6043-0*, 8450036704) Fr & Eur.
Cortassa, Sonia, jt. auth. see Aon, Miguel Antonio.
Cortazar, Julio. Las Armas Secretas (The Secret Weapon) (SPA.). 180p. 1995. pap. 12.50 (*0-679-76099-7*) Random Hse Value.
— Les Armes Sevretes. (FRE.). 1973. pap. 11.95 (*0-7859-1756-X*, 2070364488) Fr & Eur.
— La Autopista del Sur y Otros Cuentos: The Highway of the South & Other Stories. Bernardez, Aurora, ed. 400p. 1996. pap. 14.95 (*0-14-025580-X*, Penguin Bks) Viking Penguin.
— Blow up & Other Stories. Blackburn, Paul, tr. from SPA. LC 84-22792. 1985. pap. 13.00 (*0-394-72881-5*) Pantheon.
— Cronopios & Famas. Blackburn, Paul, tr. from SPA. LC 98-54270. (New Directions Classics Ser.). 161p. 1999. reprint ed. pap. 12.95 (*0-8112-1402-8*, NDP873, Pub. by New Directions) Norton.
***Cortazar, Julio.** Cuentos Completos. LC 96-103501. (SPA.). 1998. pap. 21.95 (*84-204-8139-4*) Santillana.
Cortazar, Julio. Final Del Juego. (SPA.). 224p. 1987. pap. 10.95 (*0-7859-5008-7*) Fr & Eur.
— Final Exam. MacAdam, Alfred, tr. from SPA. & intro. by. LC 99-33385. 256p. 1999. 24.95 (*0-8112-1417-6*, Pub. by New Directions) Norton.
— Les Gagnants. (FRE.). 1982. pap. 12.95 (*0-7859-1952-X*, 2070373541) Fr & Eur.
— Hopscotch. Rabassa, Gregory, tr. from SPA. LC 66-10409. 576p. 1987. pap. 16.00 (*0-394-75284-8*) Pantheon.
— Le Livre de Manuel. (FRE.). 416p. 1987. pap. 13.95 (*0-7859-2059-5*, 2070378128) Fr & Eur.
— Rayuela. (SPA.). 14.95 (*0-8288-3904-2*, S1108) Fr & Eur.
— Save Twilight: Selected Poems. Kessler, Stephen, tr. from SPA. LC 97-27592.Tr. of Salvo el Crepusculo. 160p. 1997. pap. 12.95 (*0-87286-333-6*) City Lights.
— Siete Cuentos. Beardsell, Peter, ed. & intro. by. 1994. text 19.95 (*0-7190-3923-1*) St Martin.
***Cortazar, Julio.** 62: A Model Kit. Rabassa, Gregory, tr. from SPA. LC 99-58526. 288p. 2000. pap. 14.00 (*0-8112-1437-0*, Pub. by New Directions) Norton.
Cortazar, Julio. The Winners. Kerrigan, Elaine, tr. from SPA. LC 99-15874. 310p. 1999. reprint ed. 12.95 (*0-940322-31-5*, Pub. by NY Rev Bks) Midpt Trade.
Cortazar, Julio, et al. Voicing. Wellman, Don, ed. Franzen, Cola et al, trs. 184p. (Orig.). 1989. pap. 8.00 (*0-942030-08-7*) O ARS.
***Cortazzi, Hugh.** Collected Writings of Sir Hugh Cortazzi. (Collected Writings of Modern Western Scholars on Japan: Vol. 2). 496p. 2000. text 140.00 (*1-873410-93-X*, Pub. by Japan Library) UH Pr.
Cortazzi, Hugh. Dr. Willis in Japan, 1862-1877: A British Medical Pioneer. LC 85-1334. (Illus.). 273p. (C). 1985. text 29.50 (*0-485-11264-7*, Pub. by Athlone Pr) Humanities.
— Isles of Gold: Antique Maps of Japan. (Illus.). 196p. 1983. 85.00 (*0-8348-0184-1*) Weatherhill.
***Cortazzi, Hugh.** Japan & Back & Places Elsewhere: A Memoir. 2000. 29.95 (*1-901903-20-6*) Global Oriental.
Cortazzi, Hugh. Modern Japan: A Concise Survey. LC 93-27056. 1993. text 45.00 (*0-312-10630-0*) St Martin.
***Cortazzi, Hugh.** Modern Japan: A Concise Survey. 1999. pap. 22.95 (*0-333-54340-8*) St Martin.
Cortazzi, Hugh. Victorians in Japan: In & Around the Treaty Ports. LC 87-1029. 280p. (C). 1987. text 49.95 (*0-485-11312-0*, Pub. by Athlone Pr) Humanities.
Cortazzi, Hugh, ed. Mitford's Japan: The Memoirs & Recollections, 1866-1906, of Algernon Bertram Mitford, the First Lord Redesdale. LC 85-15805. 270p. (C). 1985. text 36.50 (*0-485-11275-2*, Pub. by Athlone Pr) Humanities.
Cortazzi, Hugh & Bennett, Terry, intros. Japan: Caught in Time. (Illus.). 160p. 1995. 34.95 (*0-8348-0343-7*) Weatherhill.
Cortazzi, Hugh, ed. see Kipling, Rudyard.
Cortazzi, Martin. Narrative Analysis. (Social Research & Educational Studies: Vol. 12). 224p. 1993. pap. 29.95 (*1-85000-963-5*, Falmer Pr) Taylor & Francis.
***Cortbes, Vicente.** A New Construction of Homogeneous Quaternionic Manifolds & Related Geometric Structures. LC 00-34993. (Memoirs Ser.). 2000. write for info. (*0-8218-2111-3*) Am Math.
Corte, Andrea D., ed. Canto E Bel Canto P.F. Tosi: Opinioni De Cantori Antichi E Moderni 1723. LC 80-2268. reprint ed. 31.50 (*0-404-18823-0*) AMS Pr.
Corte, Andrea Della. L' Opera Comica Italiana nel Settecento, Studi ed Appunti, 2 vols., Set. LC 80-2269. reprint ed. 62.50 (*0-404-18830-3*) AMS Pr.
Corte, Erik De, see De Corte, Erik.
Corte, Erik De, see Kayser, Daniel & Vosniadou, Stella.
Corte, Erik De, see De Corte, Erik.
Corte, Erik De, see Vosniadou, Stella.
Corte, Erik De, see Vosniadou, Stella & De Corte, Erik, eds.
Corte, Frans De, see Haute, Peter & De Corte, Frans.
Corte, Jean-Francois, ed. Centrifuge Eighty-Eight - Centrifugeuse 88: Proceedings of the International Conference on Geotech-nical Centrifuge Modelling, Paris, 25-27 April 1988 - Comptes-rendus du Congres International sur la Modelisation Geotechnique en Centrifugeuse, Paris, 25-27 April 1988. 632p. (C). 1988. 207.00 (*90-6191-813-8*, Pub. by A A Balkema) Ashgate Pub Co.

C

An Asterisk (*) at the beginning of an entry indicates that the title is appearing for the first time.

Corte, Jolio. El Cor'an. LC 92-82545. (SPA.). 784p. 1997. pap. 12.00 (*1-879402-15-7*) Tahrike Tarsile Quran.

Corteccia, Francesco. Francesco Corteccia: Eleven Works to Latin Texts. McKinley, Ann, ed. (Recent Researches in Music of the Renaissance Ser.: Vol. RRR6). (Illus.). xii, 101p. 1969. pap. 40.00 (*0-89579-015-7*) A-R Eds.

Cortelazzo, Manlio & Zolli, Paolo. Etymological Dictionary of the Italian Language: Dizionario Etimilogico della Lingua Italiana, 5 vols., Set. (ITA.). 1988. lib. bdg. 395.00 (*0-8288-3360-5*) Fr & Eur.

Corten. Pentecostalism in Brazil. LC 99-21770. 1999. text 59.95 (*0-312-22506-7*) St Martin.

***Corten, Andre & Marshall-Fratani, Ruth.** Between Babel & Pentecost: Transnational Pentecostalism in Africa & Latin America. LC 99-58781. 2000. pap. 22.95 (*0-253-21378-9*); lib. bdg. 49.95 (*0-253-33730-5*) Ind U Pr.

Corten, Irina H. Vocabulary of Soviet Society & Culture: A Selected Guide to Russian Words, Idioms, & Expressions of the Post-Stalin Era, 1953-1991. LC 91-31876. 197p. 1992. text 32.95 (*0-8223-1213-1*) Duke.

***Cortenraad, Wouter H.** The Corporate Paradox: Economic Realities of the Corporate Form of Organization. LC 99-51942. 1999. write for info. (*0-7923-8695-7*) Kluwer Academic.

***Cortens, Andrew J.** Global Anti-Realism. 184p. 1999. pap. 59.00 (*0-8133-9130-X*) Westview.

Corter, James E. Tree Models of Similarity & Association. LC 95-50165. (Quantitative Applications in the Social Science Ser.: Vol. 112). 96p. (C). 1996. pap. 10.95 (*0-8039-5707-6*) Sage.

Cortes-Caben, David. Al Final de las Palabras. SLUSA Staff, ed. (SPA.). 110p. (Orig.). 1984. pap. 4.50 (*0-9606758-9-2*) SLUSA.

Cortes, Carlos. Longitude: A Novel LC 98-947580. xxiii, 410 p. 1998. write for info. (*971-542-154-7*) U of Philippines Pr.

***Cortes, Carlos E.** The Children Are Watching: How the Media Teach about Diversity. LC 99-57987. (Multicultural Education Ser.). 224p. 2000. write for info. (*0-8077-3938-3*); pap. 22.95 (*0-8077-3937-5*) Tchrs Coll.

Cortes, Carlos E. Cuban Minority in the U. S., Vol. 2. (Hispanics in the United States Ser.: Vol. 2). 1981. 41.95 (*0-405-13189-5*) Ayer.

Cortes, Carlos E., ed. Church Views of the Mexican American. LC 73-14198. (Mexican American Ser.). (Illus.). 58p. 1975. reprint ed. 49.95 (*0-405-05672-9*) Ayer.

— Cuban Exiles in the United States: An Original Anthology. LC 79-6236. (Hispanics in the United States Ser.). (Illus.). 1981. lib. bdg. 19.95 (*0-405-13183-6*) Ayer.

— The Cuban Experience in the United States: An Original Anthology. LC 79-6230. (Hispanics in the United States Ser.). 1981. lib. bdg. 56.95 (*0-405-13177-1*) Ayer.

— Cuban Refugee Programs: An Original Anthology. LC 79-6237. (Hispanics in the United States Ser.). (Orig.). 1981. lib. bdg. 91.95 (*0-405-13184-4*) Ayer.

— Education & the Mexican American. LC 73-14201. (Mexican American Ser.). 1975. reprint ed. 39.95 (*0-405-05675-3*) Ayer.

— Hispanics in the United States Series, 30 bks., Set. 1981. lib. bdg. 1080.00 (*0-405-13150-X*) Ayer.

— Hispanos & American Politics: A Sociological Analysis & Description of the Political Role, Status, & Voting Behavior of Americans with Spanish Names. LC 76-1613. (Chicano Heritage Ser.). 1977. 18.95 (*0-405-09531-7*) Ayer.

— Juan N. Cortina: Two Interpretations. LC 73-14204. (Mexican American Ser.). (Illus.). 1975. reprint ed. 18.95 (*0-405-05678-8*) Ayer.

— The Latin American Brain Drain to the United States: An Original Anthology. LC 79-6229. (Hispanics in the United States Ser.). (Illus.). 1981. lib. bdg. 19.95 (*0-405-13176-3*) Ayer.

— Latinos in the United States: An Original Anthology. LC 79-6232. (Hispanics in the United States Ser.). (Illus.). 1981. lib. bdg. 73.95 (*0-405-13179-8*) Ayer.

— The Mexican American, 21 vols., Set. 1974. 623.00 (*0-405-05670-2*) Ayer.

— The Mexican American & the Law. LC 73-14207. 1977. reprint ed. 26.95 (*0-405-05681-8*) Ayer.

— Mexican American Bibliographies. LC 73-14421. (Mexican American Ser.). 1975. reprint ed. 29.95 (*0-405-05682-6*) Ayer.

— Mexican Labor in the United States. LC 73-14208. (Mexican American Ser.). (Illus.). 480p. 1976. reprint ed. 35.95 (*0-405-05683-4*) Ayer.

— The Mexican Side of the Texan Revolution, 1836: By the Chief Mexican Participants. Castenada, Carlos E., tr. LC 76-1215. (Chicano Heritage Ser.). 1980. reprint ed. 33.95 (*0-405-09487-6*) Ayer.

— The New Mexican Hispano. LC 73-14210. (Mexican American Ser.). (Illus.). 510p. 1975. reprint ed. 39.95 (*0-405-05684-2*) Ayer.

— Nineteenth Century Latin Americans in the United States: An Original Anthology. LC 79-6234. (Hispanics in the United States Ser.). 1981. lib. bdg. 31.95 (*0-405-13182-8*) Ayer.

— The Penitentes of New Mexico. LC 73-14212. (Mexican American Ser.). (Illus.). 1976. reprint ed. 39.95 (*0-405-05686-9*) Ayer.

— Portuguese Americans & Spanish Americans: An Original Anthology. LC 79-6233. (Hispanics in the United States Ser.). 1981. lib. bdg. 31.95 (*0-405-13180-1*) Ayer.

— Protestantism & Latinos in the United States: An Original Anthology. LC 79-6266. (Hispanics in the United States Ser.). (Illus.). 1981. lib. bdg. 56.95 (*0-405-13173-9*) Ayer.

— Regional Perspectives on the Puerto Rican Experience. LC 79-6231. (Hispanics in the United States Ser.). 1981. lib. bdg. 81.95 (*0-405-13178-X*) Ayer.

— Report of the Select Commission on Western Hemisphere Immigration. LC 80-7574. (Hispanics in the United States Ser.). (Illus.). 1981. reprint ed. lib. bdg. 23.95 (*0-405-13185-2*) Ayer.

— Spanish & Mexican Land Grants. LC 73-14216. (Mexican American Ser.). (Illus.). 1975. reprint ed. 33.95 (*0-405-05690-7*) Ayer.

— Spanish & Portugese Languages in the United States: An Original Anthology. LC 79-6234. (Hispanics in the United States Ser.). 1981. lib. bdg. 36.95 (*0-405-13181-X*) Ayer.

Cortes, Carlos E., et al, eds. The Chicano Heritage, 55 vols. 1976. 1746.00 (*0-405-09480-9*) Ayer.

Cortes, Carlos E., ed. see Adams, Emma H.

Cortes, Carlos E., ed. see Anderson, Henry P.

Cortes, Carlos E., ed. see Avina, Rose H.

Cortes, Carlos E., ed. see Barker, Ruth L.

Cortes, Carlos E., ed. see Biberman, Herbert.

Cortes, Carlos E., ed. see Colton, Walter.

Cortes, Carlos E., ed. see Cooke, Philip St George.

Cortes, Carlos E., ed. see Cue Canovas, Agustin.

Cortes, Carlos E., ed. see Digges, Jeremiah.

Cortes, Carlos E., ed. see Duran, Daniel F.

Cortes, Carlos E., ed. see Fergusson, Harvey.

Cortes, Carlos E., ed. see Fernandez-Florez, Dario.

Cortes, Carlos E., ed. see Fernandez, Jose.

Cortes, Carlos E., ed. see Francis, Jessie D.

Cortes, Carlos E., ed. see Gallagher, Patrick L.

Cortes, Carlos E., ed. see Getty, Harry T.

Cortes, Carlos E., ed. see Guzman, Ralph C.

Cortes, Carlos E., ed. see Harding, George L.

Cortes, Carlos E., ed. see Hayes, Benjamin.

Cortes, Carlos E., ed. see Herrick, Robert.

Cortes, Carlos E., ed. see Jamieson, Stuart.

Cortes, Carlos E., ed. see Kernstock, Elwyn N.

Cortes, Carlos E., ed. see Landolt, Robert G.

Cortes, Carlos E., ed. see Lane, John H., Jr.

Cortes, Carlos E., ed. see Lewin, Ellen.

Cortes, Carlos E., ed. see Lewis & Emory.

Cortes, Carlos E., ed. see Livermore, Abiel A.

Cortes, Carlos E., ed. see Loyola, Mary.

Cortes, Carlos E., ed. see Macklin, Barbara J.

Cortes, Carlos E., ed. see McWilliams, Carey.

Cortes, Carlos E., ed. see Miyares, Marcelino.

Cortes, Carlos E., ed. see Morrison, J. Cayce.

Cortes, Carlos E., ed. see Murray, Winifred.

Cortes, Carlos E., ed. see Parigi, Sam F.

Cortes, Carlos E., ed. see Poldervaart, Arie W.

Cortes, Carlos E., ed. see Read, Benjamin M.

Cortes, Carlos E., ed. see Redden, Charlotte A.

Cortes, Carlos E., ed. see Richmond, Marie L.

Cortes, Carlos E., ed. see Rodriguez, Eugene, Jr.

Cortes, Carlos E., ed. see Ropka, Gerald W.

Cortes, Carlos E., ed. see Ross, Elmer L.

Cortes, Carlos E., ed. see Sanchez, Nellie V.

Cortes, Carlos E., ed. see Shulman, Irving.

Cortes, Carlos E., ed. see Tireman, Loyd S.

Cortes, Carlos E., ed. see Tovar, Federico R.

Cortes, Carlos E., ed. see Twitchell, Ralph E.

Cortes, Carlos E., ed. see U. S. House of Representatives Staff.

Cortes, Carlos E., ed. see West, Stanley A.

Cortes, Carlos E., ed. see Woods, Frances J.

Cortes, Carlos E., ed. & intro. see Campa, Arthur.

Cortes, Carlos E., ed. & intro. see Griffin & Foster.

Cortes, Carlos E., ed. & intro. see Griggs, George, et al.

Cortes, Carlos E., ed. & intro. see Hill, et al.

Cortes, Carlos E., ed. & intro. see Jarratt, Claudia J., et al.

Cortes, Carlos E., ed. & intro. see Lucero-White, et al.

Cortes, Carlos E., ed. & intro. see Smith, et al.

Cortes, Carlos E., ed. & intro. see Taylor, Paul S., et al.

Cortes, Carols E., ed. see Tireman, Loyd S. & Watson, Mary.

Cortes, Claudia J. & Enezcortes, Jim. GATT, WTO & the Regulation of International Trade in Textiles. Tulloch, Christopher D., tr. from ENG. LC 97-6071. 320p. 1997. text 82.95 (*1-85521-938-7*, Pub. by Ashgate Pub) Ashgate Pub Co.

Cortes, Eladio, ed. Dictionary of Mexican Literature. LC 91-10529. 816p. 1992. lib. bdg. 105.00 (*0-313-26271-3*, CMX/, Greenwood Pr) Greenwood.

Cortes, Eladio & Barrea-Marlys, Mirta, eds. Dictionary of Latin American Theater. LC 99-32529. 2000. lib. bdg. write for info. (*0-313-29041-5*) Greenwood.

Cortes, Ernesto, Jr. A Community of Stories. (Involving Citizens in Education Reform Partners in Learning Ser.). 1996. pap. 8.00 (*0-89333-147-3*) AACTE.

Cortes, F., et al. Systems Analysis for Social Scientists. LC 73-23061. 352p. reprint ed. pap. 109.20 (*0-8357-9990-5*, 201646400002) Bks Demand.

Cortes, Felix, tr. see Jacobs, Joseph, et al.

Cortes, Fernando M. La Medicina Cientifica en el Siglo XIX Mexico. (Ciencia para Todos Ser.). (SPA.). pap. 6.99 (*968-16-2709-1*, Pub. by Fondo) Continental Bk.

Cortes, Georges D. El Mundo de los Microbios. (Ciencia para Todos Ser.). (SPA.). pap. 6.99 (*968-16-2703-2*, Pub. by Fondo) Continental Bk.

Cortes, Hernan. Five Letters. Morris, J. Bayard, tr. 1977. lib. bdg. 59.95 (*0-8490-1841-2*) Gordon Pr.

— Five Letters from Mexico. (The Great Commanders Ser.). 388p. 1998. reprint ed. 30.00 (*1-56515-014-7*) Collect Reprints.

— Letters from Mexico. Pagden, Anthony, ed. & tr. by. LC 86-50363. 640p. 1986. 65.00 (*0-300-03724-4*) Yale U Pr.

— Letters from Mexico. Pagden, Anthony, ed. & tr. by. LC 86-50363. 640p. 1986. pap. 25.00 (*0-300-03799-6*) Yale U Pr.

Cortes, Hernan J., ed. Multidimensional Chromatography: Techniques & Applications. (Chromatographic Science Ser.: Vol. 50). (Illus.). 424p. 1989. text 170.00 (*0-8247-8136-8*) Dekker.

Cortes, J. E., et al, eds. The Birds of Gibraltar. (C). 1988. pap. text 50.00 (*0-948466-00-6*, Pub. by Gibraltar Bks) St Mut.

Cortes, Jose L., tr. see Cole, Joanna.

Cortes, Juan D. On Order: Two Addresses Newly Translated into English. Draghici, S., ed. & tr. by. from SPA. LC 89-3711. 90p. (C). 1989. pap. text 3.95 (*0-943045-03-7*) Plutarch Pr OR.

Cortes, Juan D. & Schramm, Edmund. Ensayo Sobre el Catolicismo, el Liberalismo y el Socialismo & Donoso Cortes, 2 vols. Mayer, J. P., ed. LC 78-67342. (European Political Thought Ser.). (SPA.). 1980. reprint ed. lib. bdg. 42.95 (*0-405-11687-X*) Ayer.

***Cortes, Julio.** El Coran. (SPA.). 1998. pap. 12.95 (*0-8245-2151-X*) Crossroad NY.

Cortes, Julio, tr. from ARA. El Coran. LC 85-52262. (SPA.). 672p. 1986. 24.00 (*0-940368-71-4*, 127); pap. 16.00 (*0-940368-70-6*, 127A) Tahrike Tarsile Quran.

Cortes, Leticia. Survey of the Environmental Knowledge, Comprehension, of the Secondary Level Students & Teachers in the Philippines. (Environment Problems & Solutions Ser.). 191p. 1991. text 20.00 (*0-8240-9298-8*) Garland.

Cortes, Mariluz & Bocock, Peter. North-South Technology Transfer: A Case Study of Petrochemicals in Latin America. LC 83-49365. 184p. reprint ed. pap. 57.10 (*0-7837-4250-9*, 204394000012) Bks Demand.

Cortes, Martin. The Arte of Navigation. LC 92-16475. (Scholars' Facsimiles & Reprints Ser.: Vol. 471). 216p. 1992. reprint ed. 75.00 (*0-8201-1471-5*) Schol Facsimiles.

Cortes, Rosario M. Pangasinan, 1801-1900: The Beginnings of Modernization. (Illus.). 191p. (Orig.). (C). 1991. pap. 17.50 (*971-10-0426-7*, Pub. by New Day Pub) Cellar.

— Pangasinan, 1572-1800, Vol. I. (Illus.). 189p. 1991. reprint ed. pap. 18.75 (*971-10-0458-5*, Pub. by New Day Pub) Cellar.

— Pangasinan, 1901-1986: A Political, Socioeconomic & Cultural History. (Illus.). 328p. (C). 1991. pap. 25.00 (*971-10-0425-9*, Pub. by New Day Pub) Cellar.

Cortes, T. Roca & Sanchez, F., eds. The Structure of the Sun. (Illus.). 417p. (C). 1996. text 80.00 (*0-521-56307-0*) Cambridge U Pr.

***Cortes, Ulises & Sanchez-Marre, Miquel, eds.** Environmental Decision Support Systems & Artificial Intelligence: Papers from the AAAI Workshop. (Technical Reports: Vol. WS-99-07). (Illus.). 100p. 1999. spiral bd. 25.00 (*1-57735-091-X*) AAAI Pr.

Cortesao, Armando, ed. The Suma Oriental of Tome Pires & the Book of Francisco Rodrigues. 1990. reprint ed. 64.00 (*81-206-0535-7*, Pub. by Asian Educ Servs) S Asia.

Cortese, Alfred W. "Sentence First, Verdict Afterwards" The Crisis of Mass Torts. LC 99-165589. 38p. 1997. pap. write for info. (*0-937299-53-7*) Natl Legal Ctr Pub Interest.

Cortese, Anthony J. Ethnic Ethics: The Restructuring of Moral Theory. LC 89-39656. 197p. (C). 1990. text 64.50 (*0-7914-0279-7*); pap. text 21.95 (*0-7914-0280-0*) State U NY Pr.

***Cortese, Anthony J.** Provocateur: Images of Women & Minorities in Advertising. LC 99-14501. 192p. 1999. 65.00 (*0-8476-9174-8*) Rowman.

Cortese, Anthony J. Provocateur: Images of Women & Minorities in Advertising. LC 99-14501. (Postmodern Social Futures Ser.). (Illus.). 192p. 1999. pap. 24.95 (*0-8476-9175-6*) Rowman.

Cortese, Bernard J. Perimenopause. LC 98-26905. (Vital Information Ser.). 112p. 1998. pap. 11.95 (*0-89594-914-8*) Crossing Pr.

Cortese, Charles F., ed. The Social Impact of Energy Development in the West. text. write for info. (*0-8290-0235-9*); pap. text. write for info. (*0-8290-1083-1*) Irvington.

***Cortese, Delia.** Arabic Ismaili Manuscripts. 1999. text 59.50 (*1-86064-433-3*, Pub. by I B T) St Martin.

Cortese, Delia. Mauritania. LC 93-189401. (World Bibliographical Ser.). 184p. 1992. lib. bdg. 71.50 (*1-85109-152-1*) ABC-CLIO.

Cortese, Enzo. Josua 13-21: Ein Priesterschriftlicher Abschnitt in Deuteronomistischen Geschichtswerk. (Orbis Biblicus et Orientalis Ser.: Vol. 94). (GER.). 122p. 1990. text 26.00 (*3-7278-0661-3*, Pub. by Presses Univ Fribourg) Eisenbrauns.

Cortese, Peter & Middleton, Kathleen, eds. The Comprehensive School Health Challenge: Promoting Health Through Education. LC 93-24711. 1993. 62.95 (*1-56071-344-5*) ETR Assocs.

Cortese, Riccardo, ed. Combinatorial Libraries: Synthesis, Screening, & Application Potential. LC 95-39772. xiv, 230p. (C). 1995. lib. bdg. 106.15 (*3-11-014395-X*) De Gruyter.

***Cortesi, Agostino & Filbe, Gilbertino, eds.** Static Analysis: 6th International Symposium, SAS'99, Venice, Italy, September 22-24, 1999, Proceedings. LC 99-44587. (Lecture Notes in Computer Science Ser.: Vol. 1694). viii, 356p. 1999. pap. 62.00 (*3-540-66459-9*) Spr-Verlag.

Cortesi, Carla. My Book of Prayers. 48p. (Orig.). (J). (gr. 1-4). pap. 3.50 (*0-8198-4776-3*) Pauline Bks.

— My First Missal. 56p. (J). (gr. 1-4). pap. 3.50 (*0-8198-4775-5*) Pauline Bks.

Cortesi, David. Dr. Dobb's Toolbook for Z-80. 250p. 1995. pap. 35.75 (*0-934375-07-0*, M&T Bks) IDG Bks.

Cortesi, Gerald R. Mastering Real Estate Principles. 2nd ed. LC 98-39821. 552p. 1999. pap. 43.95 (*0-7931-2990-7*, 15108002, G&C Learning) Dearborn.

Cortesi, Henry B., ed. Unilateral Application of Antitrust & Trade Laws: Toward a New Economic Relationship Between the United States & Japan. LC 93-47931. 1994. 95.00 (*1-883223-04-0*) Pacific NY.

Cortesi, Laurence. Target: Tokyo. 1983. mass mkt. 3.25 (*0-685-07872-8*, Zebra Kensgtn) Kensgtn Pub Corp.

Cortesi, Lawrence. D-Day Minus One. 1984. mass mkt. 3.25 (*0-8217-1318-3*, Zebra Kensgtn) Kensgtn Pub Corp.

— Last Bridge to Victory. 320p. 1984. mass mkt. 2.50 (*0-685-08594-5*, Zebra Kensgtn) Kensgtn Pub Corp.

— Pacific Strike. (World at War Ser.). (Orig.). 1982. mass mkt. 2.95 (*0-8217-1041-9*, Zebra Kensgtn) Kensgtn Pub Corp.

Cortez, Carlos. Crystal Gazing in the Amber Fluid & Other Wobbly Poems. 64p. (Orig.). 1992. pap. 7.00 (*0-88286-206-5*) C H Kerr.

— De Kansas a Califas & Back to Chicago: Poems & Art. LC 92-60876. (Illus.). 51p. (Orig.). 1992. pap. 6.50 (*1-877636-09-6*) March Abrazo.

— Where Are the Voices? And Other Wobbly Poems. (Illus.). 64p. (Orig.). 1997. pap. 10.00 (*0-88286-238-3*) C H Kerr.

Cortez, Carlos E., ed. United States Congress, Immigration Hearings. LC 80-7793. (Hispanics in the United States Ser.). 1981. reprint ed. lib. bdg. 25.95 (*0-405-13186-0*) Ayer.

— United States Congress, Immigration 1976. LC 80-7794. (Hispanics in the United States Ser.). 1981. lib. bdg. 28.95 (*0-405-13187-9*) Ayer.

— Unites States Congress, Western Hemisphere Immigration. LC 80-7795. (Hispanics in the United States Ser.). 1981. reprint ed. lib. bdg. 40.95 (*0-405-13188-7*) Ayer.

Cortez, Clifton J., Jr. & Long, Joel M., eds. Directory of Legal Resources for People with AIDS & HIV. LC 97-147134. 385p. 1997. pap. 20.00 (*1-57073-389-9*, 517-7000, ABA Indiv Rts) Amer Bar Assn.

***Cortez, Duanne Fry.** Hot Jams & Cold Showers: Scenes from the Kerrville Folk Festival. LC 00-190666. (Illus.). 312p. 2000. pap. 24.95 (*0-9700189-0-8*) Dos Puertas.

Cortez, Edwin & Smorch, Tom. Second Generation Automated Library Systems. LC 92-30039. (Library Management Collection). 248p. 1993. lib. bdg. 59.95 (*0-313-28361-3*, CSZ/, Greenwood Pr) Greenwood.

Cortez, Edwin M. & Kazlauskas, Edward J. Managing Information Systems & Technologies: A Basic Guide for Design, Selection, Evaluation & Use. LC 85-32013. 179p. 1986. pap. text 45.00 (*0-918212-92-8*) Neal-Schuman.

***Cortez, Jaime.** Que Alegria/I Rejoiced. 136p. 1998. pap. 8.95 (*0-915531-97-6*) OR Catholic.

***Cortez, Jaime, ed.** Virgins, Guerillas & Locas: Gay Latinos Writing about Love. LC 99-43946. 200p. (Orig.). 1999. pap. 14.95 (*1-57344-087-6*, Pub. by Cleis Pr) Publishers Group.

Cortez, Jayne. Somewhere in Advance of Nowhere. (High Risk Bks.). 124p. (Orig.). 1996. pap. 12.99 (*1-85242-422-2*) Serpents Tail.

***Cortez, Julio Garcia.** The OSHA: Secrets of the Yoruba Lucumi Santeria Religion in the United States & the Americas. Francis, Roger, ed. LC 00-132518. (Illus.). 473p. (C). 2000. pap. 34.95 (*1-890157-22-8*) Athelia-Henrietta.

Cortez, Kevin. Annihilating the Spirit of Compromise. 192p. 1999. pap. 8.99 (*1-889116-17-3*) Penbrooke Pub.

***Cortez, Martin Diaz.** Corel DRAW 9 Graphic Suite Manual de Uso en Espanol: Corel DRAW 9 Graphics Suite Users Manual in Spanish. deluxe ed. (Manuales PC Users Ser.). (SPA., Illus.). 297p. 2000. pap. 19.90 incl. cd-rom (*987-526-030-4*, Pub. by MP Ediciones) Downtown Bk.

***Cortez, Sarah.** How to Undress a Cop. 96p. 2000. pap. 9.95 (*1-55885-301-4*) Arte Publico.

Corthell, Ronald. Ideology & Desire in Renaissance Poetry: The Subject of Donne. LC 97-14777. 304p. (C). 1997. text 39.95 (*0-8143-2676-5*) Wayne St U Pr.

Corthron, Kia. Come down Burning. 1995. pap. 5.25 (*0-8222-1392-3*) Dramatists Play.

***Corti, A., ed.** Low-Calorie Sweeteners: Present & Future: ISA-IUFoST World Conference on Low-Calorie Sweeteners, Barcelona, April 1999. LC 99-48944. (World Review of Nutrition & Dietetics Ser.: Vol. 85). (Illus.). xiv, 244p. 1999. 198.25 (*3-8055-6938-6*) S Karger.

Corti, Doris. Successful Grand-Parenting: How to Manage Family Relationships & Practical Issues. (Family Reference Ser.). 112p. 1997. pap. 19.95 (*1-85703-307-8*, Pub. by How To Bks) Trans-Atl Phila.

Corti, E. Reign of the House of Rothschild. 1973. 300.00 (*0-87968-171-3*) Gordon Pr.

— Rise of the House of Rothschild. 1973. 300.00 (*0-87968-170-5*) Gordon Pr.

Corti, Egon. Downfall of Three Dynasties. LC 79-124230. (Select Bibliographies Reprint Ser.). (Illus.). 1977. 23.95 (*0-8369-5419-X*) Ayer.

Corti, Eugenio. Few Returned: Twenty-Eight Days on the Russian Front, Winter 1942-1943. Levy, Peter E., tr. LC 97-6121. 272p. 1997. pap. 19.95 (*0-8262-1115-1*) U of Mo Pr.

***Corti, Eugenio.** The Red Horse: A Novel. 1000p. 2000. 29.95 (*0-89870-747-1*, Pub. by Ignatius Pr) Midpt Trade.

Corti, G. & Frazer, F. The Nations Oil: A Story of Control. 237p. 1983. lib. bdg. 64.50 (*0-86010-437-0*) G & T Inc.

Corti, Lillian. The Myth of Medea & the Murder of Children. 89. LC 97-26892. (Contributions to the Study of World Literature Ser.: Vol. 89). 264p. 1998. 59.95 (*0-313-30536-6*, Greenwood Pr) Greenwood.

An Asterisk (*) at the beginning of an entry indicates that the title is appearing for the first time.

Corti, M. & Mallamace, F., eds. Trends in Colloid & Interface Science V. (Progress in Colloid & Polymer Science Ser.: Vol. 84). 250p. 1991. 169.00 (*0-387-91399-8*) Spr-Verlag.

Corti, Maria. Otranto. Bright, Jessie, tr. from ITA. LC 93-32681. 288p. (Orig.). 1993. pap. 12.50 (*0-934977-29-1*) Italica Pr.

Corti, Victor, tr. see Artaud, Antonin.

Corti, W., ed. The Philosophy of William James. 1977. pap. 45.95 (*3-7873-0352-9*) Adlers Foreign Bks.

Corti, Walter R., ed. The Philosophy of George Herbert Mead. 1977. pap. 37.95 (*3-7873-0353-7*) Adlers Foreign Bks.

***Cortiel, Jeanne.** Demand My Writing: Joanna Russ, Feminism, Science Fiction. (Science Fiction Texts & Studies: Vol. 18). 272p. 1999. pap. 24.95 (*0-85323-624-0*, Pub. by Liverpool Univ Pr) Intl Spec Bk.

— Demand My Writing: Joanna Russ, Feminism, Science Fiction. (Science Fiction Texts & Studies: Vol. 18). 254p. 1999. 47.95 (*0-85323-614-3*, Pub. by Liverpool Univ Pr) Intl Spec Bk.

Cortils, Eduardo. Poetics - Poetica. (Artists' Books Ser.). (Illus.). 96p. 1995. 20.00 (*0-89822-115-3*) Visual Studies.

Cortina. Opening Doors. 3rd ed. 2000. 26.25 (*0-07-231496-6*) McGraw.

— Traveler's French Course, Vol. 1. 1991. 14.95 incl. cd-rom (*0-8050-1519-1*) H Holt & Co.

— Vest Pocket Vietnamese. 1995. pap. 5.95 (*0-8050-3375-0*) H Holt & Co.

***Cortina, Lou.** Goal: The History of the Baltimore Blast Indoor Soccer Team. (Illus.). 128p. (Orig.). 2000. pap. 16.95 (*1-893116-12-3*) Baltimore Sun.

Cortina Famous Schools Staff. How to Draw & Paint Landscapes. (Illus.). 98p. 1995. pap. 7.95 (*0-8050-1529-9*) H Holt & Co.

— How to Draw & Paint Portraits. (Illus.). 98p. 1995. pap. 7.95 (*0-8050-1530-2*) H Holt & Co.

— How to Draw Animals. (Illus.). 114p. 1995. pap. 7.95 (*0-8050-1527-2*) H Holt & Co.

— How to Draw the Human Figure. (Illus.). 98p. 1995. pap. 7.95 (*0-8050-1528-0*) H Holt & Co.

***Cortina, Guadalupe.** Invenciones Multitudinarias: Escritoras Judfomexicanas Contemporaneas. (Estudios de Literatura Latinoamericana Ser.: Vol. 4). (SPA.). 160p. 2000. pap. 16.00 (*0-936388-90-0*) Juan de la Cuesta.

Cortina Institute of Languages Staff. Conversational Russian in Twenty Lessons. (Cortina Language Ser.). 488p. 1995. pap. 6.95 (*0-8050-1501-9*) H Holt & Co.

— Cortina Handy Spanish-English - English-Spanish Dictionary. (Cortina Language Ser.). (ENG & SPA.). 574p. 1995. pap. 7.95 (*0-8050-1505-1*, Owl) H Holt & Co.

— Vest Pocket English Language Phrasebook Dictionary. 188p. 1995. pap. 4.95 (*0-8050-1513-2*) H Holt & Co.

— Vest Pocket Japanese. 188p. 1995. pap. 4.95 (*0-8050-1512-4*) H Holt & Co.

— Vest Pocket Russian Language Phrasebook Dictionary. 132p. 1995. pap. 4.95 (*0-8050-1511-6*) H Holt & Co.

***Cortina, Joe & Elder, Janet.** New Worlds: An Introduction to College Reading. LC 99-43522. 2000. write for info. (*0-07-366029-9*) McGrw-H Hghr Educ.

Cortina, Joe & Elder, Janet. Opening Doors: Understanding College Reading. LC 94-37873. 1995. pap. text 26.25 (*0-07-024004-3*) McGraw.

— Opening Doors: Understanding College Reading. 2nd ed. LC 97-16752. 24p. 1997. pap. 34.00 (*0-07-024470-7*) McGraw.

Cortina, Joe, et al. Comprehending College Textbooks: Steps to Understanding & Remembering What You Read. 3rd ed. LC 95-9661. 544p. (C). 1995. pap. 35.00 (*0-07-024058-2*) McGraw.

Cortina Language Institute Staff. Cassette French Course. (Cortina Ser.). (ENG & FRE.). 1995. pap. 79.95 incl. audio (*0-8050-1886-7*) H Holt & Co.

Cortina Language Institute Staff. Passport French. (Passport Language Ser.). (ENG & FRE.). 1995. pap. 12.95 incl. audio (*0-8050-2129-9*) H Holt & Co.

— Passport German. (Passport Language Ser.). (ENG & GER.). 1995. pap. 12.95 incl. audio (*0-8050-2130-2*) H Holt & Co.

— Passport Italian. (Passport Language Ser.). (ENG & ITA.). 1995. pap. 12.95 incl. audio (*0-8050-2131-0*) H Holt & Co.

— Passport Spanish. (Passport Language Ser.). (ENG & SPA.). 1995. pap. 12.95 incl. audio (*0-8050-2128-0*) H Holt & Co.

— Traveler's French. (Traveler's Language Courses Ser.). (ENG & FRE.). 1995. pap. 19.95 incl. audio (*0-8050-3469-2*) H Holt & Co.

— Traveler's German. (Traveler's Language Courses Ser.). (ENG & GER.). 1995. pap. 19.95 incl. audio (*0-8050-3470-6*) H Holt & Co.

— Traveler's Italian. (Traveler's Language Courses Ser.). (ENG & ITA.). 1995. pap. 19.95 incl. audio (*0-8050-3471-4*) H Holt & Co.

— Traveler's Spanish. (Traveler's Language Courses Ser.). (ENG & SPA.). 1995. pap. 19.95 incl. audio (*0-8050-3468-4*) H Holt & Co.

Cortina, Maruicio & Maccoby, Michael, eds. A Prophetic Analyst: Erich Fromm's Contributions to Psychoanalysis. 480p. 1996. 50.00 (*1-56821-621-1*) Aronson.

Cortina, Nestor C. Por la Libertad de Cuba: Una Historia Inconclusa. LC 95-83996. (Coleccion Cuba y sus Jueces). (SPA., Illus.). 513p. (Orig.). 1996. pap. 29.95 (*0-89729-786-5*) Ediciones.

Cortina, Rodolfo. Hispanic American Literature: An Anthology. LC 97-15505. 448p. 1997. pap. 32.50 (*0-8442-5730-3*, 57303, Natl Textbk Co) NTC Contemp Pub Co.

— Hispanic American Literature: An Anthology. LC 97-15505. (ENG & SPA.). 1998. pap., teacher ed. 32.66 (*0-8442-5731-1*) NTC Contemp Pub Co.

Cortina Schools Staff. Conversational French in Twenty Lessons. 1990. pap. 7.95 (*0-8327-0011-8*) Cortina.

— Conversational German in Twenty Lessons. 1990. pap. 7.95 (*0-8327-0012-6*) Cortina.

— Conversational Russian in Twenty Lessons. 1990. pap. 7.95 (*0-8327-0015-0*) Cortina.

— Ingles en Veinte Lecciones.Tr. of English for Spanish Speakers. 1990. pap. 7.95 (*0-8327-0101-7*) Cortina.

Cortina Staff. Conversational Brazilian-Portuguese. (Cortina Language Ser.). 192p. 1995. pap. 7.95 (*0-8050-1503-5*) H Holt & Co.

— Conversational English. (Cortina Language Ser.). 192p. 1995. pap. 7.95 (*0-8050-1504-3*) H Holt & Co.

— Conversational French. (Cortina Language Ser.). 384p. 1995. pap. 7.95 (*0-8050-1497-7*) H Holt & Co.

— Conversational German. (Cortina Language Ser.). 384p. 1995. pap. 7.95 (*0-8050-1498-5*) H Holt & Co.

— Conversational Italian. (Cortina Language Ser.). 352p. 1995. pap. 7.95 (*0-8050-1499-3*) H Holt & Co.

— Conversational Japanese. (Cortina Language Ser.). 256p. 1995. pap. 7.95 (*0-8050-1502-7*) H Holt & Co.

— Conversational Modern Greek. (Cortina Language Ser.). 288p. 1995. pap. 7.95 (*0-8050-1500-0*) H Holt & Co.

— Conversational Spanish. (Cortina Language Ser.). 384p. 1995. pap. 7.95 (*0-8050-1496-9*) H Holt & Co.

— Two Thousand Five Hundred Palabras Mas Usadas en Ingles: Cortina Method: 2500 Most Common English Words. (Cortina Language Ser.). (SPA.). 145p. 1995. pap. 4.95 (*0-8050-1890-5*) H Holt & Co.

— Vest Pocket Arabic. (Cortina Language Ser.). 260p. 1995. pap. 5.95 (*0-8050-1514-0*) H Holt & Co.

— Vest Pocket French. (Cortina Language Ser.). (FRE.). 132p. 1995. pap. 3.95 (*0-8050-1507-8*) H Holt & Co.

— Vest Pocket German. (Cortina Language Ser.). (GER.). 132p. 1995. pap. 3.95 (*0-8050-1508-6*) H Holt & Co.

— Vest Pocket Italian. (Cortina Language Ser.). (ITA.). 132p. 1995. pap. 3.95 (*0-8050-1509-4*) H Holt & Co.

— Vest Pocket Modern Greek. (Cortina Language Ser.). 188p. 1995. pap. 4.95 (*0-8050-1510-8*) H Holt & Co.

— Vest Pocket Spanish. (Cortina Language Ser.). (SPA.). 132p. 1995. pap. 3.95 (*0-8050-1506-X*) H Holt & Co.

Cortinas, Cristina. Cancer: Herencia y Ambiente. (Ciencia Para Todos Ser.). (SPA.). pap. 6.99 (*968-16-3572-8*, Pub. by Fondo) Continental Bk.

Cortinez, Carlos, ed. Simply a Man of Letters: Panel Discussions & Papers from the Proceedings of a Symposium on Jorge Luis Borges Held at the University of Maine at Orono. 353p. 1982. 27.50 (*0-89101-052-1*); pap. 13.95 (*0-89101-051-3*) U Maine Pr.

Cortipassi, Dennis A. Never Give Up. LC 90-85169. 1992. 6.95 (*0-8158-0467-9*) Chris Mass.

Cortis, Bruno. Heart & Soul: A Psychological & Spiritual Guide to Preventing & Healing Heart Disease. LC 96-38556. 240p. 1997. per. 12.00 (*0-671-55140-X*) PB.

Cortissoz, Ellen M., jt. auth. see Stedman, Edmund C.

Cortissoz, Royal. American Artists. LC 74-128228. (Essay Index Reprint Ser.). 1977. 25.95 (*0-8369-1825-8*) Ayer.

— American Artists. LC 70-121282. (BCL Ser. I). reprint ed. 29.50 (*0-404-01736-3*) AMS Pr.

— Personalities in Art. LC 68-55844. (Essay Index Reprint Ser.). 1977. 31.95 (*0-8369-0339-0*) Ayer.

Cortit, L. Iglesias, ed. see Creatsas, G. & European Society of Contraception Staff.

Cortler, Hugh, ed. Shame & the Corporation. 200p. 1986. 65.00 (*0-930586-31-X*) Haven Pubns.

Cortner, David, jt. auth. see Hendrickson, Nancy L.

Cortner, Hanna J. & Moote, Margaret A. Politics of Ecosystem Management. LC 98-34883. (Illus.). 224p. 1998. pap. text 25.00 (*1-55963-672-6*, Shearwater Bks) Island Pr.

***Cortner, Hanna J. & Moote, Margaret A.** Politics of Ecosystem Management. LC 98-34883. (Illus.). 224p. 1998. text 50.00 (*1-55963-671-8*, Shearwater Bks) Island Pr.

Cortner, Hanna J., et al. Institutional Barriers & Incentives for Ecosystem Management: A Problem Analysis. (Illus.). 44p. 1997. reprint ed. pap. 5.40 (*0-89904-660-6*, Bear Meadows Resrch Grp) Crumb Elbow Pub.

Cortner, Max J. Digital Test Engineering. LC 87-8319. 337p. 1987. 165.00 (*0-471-85135-3*) Wiley.

Cortner, Richard C. Apportionment Cases. 283p. (C). 1972. reprint ed. pap. 4.25 (*0-393-00637-9*) Norton.

— The Apportionment Cases. LC 75-100408. 296p. reprint ed. pap. 91.80 (*0-8357-5692-0*, 202316800032) Bks Demand.

— The Iron Horse & the Constitution: The Railroads & the Transformation of the Fourteenth Amendment, 68. LC 92-25805. (Contributions in Legal Studies: No. 68). 248p. 1993. 65.00 (*0-313-28578-0*, CIN, Greenwood Pr) Greenwood.

— The Kingfish & the Constitution: Huey Long, the First Amendment & the Emergence of Modern Press Freedom in America, 365. LC 95-31340. (Contributions in Political Science Ser.: Vol. 365). 216p. 1996. 57.95 (*0-313-29842-4*, Greenwood Pr) Greenwood.

— A Mob Intent on Death: The NAACP & the Arkansas Riot Cases. LC 85-29511. 280p. 1988. reprint ed. pap. 86.80 (*0-608-02309-4*, 206295000004) Bks Demand.

— A Scottsboro Case in Mississippi: The Supreme Court & Brown vs. Mississippi. LC 85-20174. 188p. reprint ed. pap. 58.30 (*0-7837-1073-9*, 204159700021) Bks Demand.

— The Supreme Court & the Second Bill of Rights: The Fourteenth Amendment & the Nationalization of Civil Liberties. 374p. 1981. 40.00 (*0-299-08390-X*) U of Wis Pr.

Cortner, Richard C. The Supreme Court & the Second Bill of Rights: The Fourteenth Amendment & the Nationalization of Civil Liberties. LC 80-5112. 373p. reprint ed. pap. 115.70 (*0-608-20418-8*, 207167100002) Bks Demand.

Cortona, Pietro Da, see Da Cortona, Pietro.

Cortona, Pietro Grilli Di, see Grilli Di Cortona, Pietro.

Cortopassi, Joan & Cain, Annette. Fat Chance: Your Best Chance for Permanent Weight Loss. Ingram, Colin, ed. LC 95-48221. (Illus.). 384p. 1996. 24.95 (*0-9649496-0-1*) Cook & the Trainer.

Cortot, Alfred. In Search of Chopin. Clarke, Cyril & Clarke, Rena, trs. from FRE. LC 74-33504. (Illus.). 268p. 1975. reprint ed. lib. bdg. 38.50 (*0-8371-7971-8*, COSCH, Greenwood Pr) Greenwood.

— Rational Principles of Pianoforte Technique. 102p. 1990. reprint ed. lib. bdg. 59.00 (*0-7812-9174-7*) Rprt Serv.

— Studies in Musical Interpretation. (Music Reprint Ser.). 1989. 37.50 (*0-306-79715-1*) Da Capo.

Cortrada, John W. United States-Spanish Relations: Wolfram & World War II. 134p. 1971. 10.00 (*0-939738-11-2*) Zubal Inc.

Cortright, jt. auth. see Glenetske.

Cortright, Brant. Psychotherapy & Spirit: Theory & Practice in Transpersonal Psychotherapy. LC 96-46518. (SUNY Series in the Philosophy of Psychology). (Illus.). 257p. (C). 1997. text 54.50 (*0-7914-3465-6*); pap. text 19.95 (*0-7914-3466-4*) State U NY Pr.

Cortright, David. International Soldiers' Movement. 23p. 1975. pap. 2.00 (*0-916894-05-3*) Recon Pubns.

Cortright, David, ed. The Price of Peace: Incentives & International Conflict Prevention. LC 97-22989. (Carnegie Commission on Preventing Deadly Conflict Ser.). (Illus.). 320p. 1997. 68.50 (*0-8476-8556-X*); pap. 26.95 (*0-8476-8557-8*) Rowman.

Cortright, David & Ahmed, Samina, eds. Pakistan & the Bomb: Public Opinion & Nuclear Options. LC 97-3802. (Studies on International Peace). 1998. pap. 20.00 (*0-268-03818-X*) U of Notre Dame Pr.

***Cortright, David & Lopez, George A.** The Sanctions Decade: Assessing U. N. Strategies in the 1990s. LC 99-89665. 274p. 2000. pap. 17.95 (*1-55587-867-9*) L Rienner.

— The Sanctions Decade: Assessing UN Strategies in the 1990s. LC 99-89665. 274p. 2000. lib. bdg. 45.00 (*1-55587-891-1*) L Rienner.

Cortright, David & Mattoo, Amitabh, eds. India & the Bomb: Public Opinion & Nuclear Options. LC 95-50914. (From the Joan B. Kroc Institute for International Peace Studies). 180p. (C). 1996. text 29.95 (*0-268-01175-3*); pap. text 18.95 (*0-268-01176-1*) U of Notre Dame Pr.

Cortright, David & Watts, Max. Left Face: Soldier Unions & Resistance Movements in Modern Armies, 107. LC 90-46702. (Contributions in Military Studies Ser.: No. 107). 296p. 1991. 65.00 (*0-313-27626-9*, CLT/, Greenwood Pr) Greenwood.

Cortright, Robert S. Bridging. LC 94-94550. (Illus.). 116p. (Orig.). 1994. pap. 24.95 (*0-9641963-0-1*) Bridge Ink.

— Bridging: Discovering the Beauty of Bridges. LC 98-92665. (Illus.). 176p. 1998. 29.95 (*0-9641963-2-8*) Bridge Ink.

***Cortright, S. A.** Labor, Solidarity & the Common Good. LC 00-36106. 2000. write for info. (*0-89089-722-0*) Carolina Acad Pr.

***Cortright, S. A., ed.** Labor, Solidarity & the Common Good: Essays on the Ethical Foundations of Management. 168p. 2000. write for info. (*0-89089-718-2*) Carolina Acad Pr.

Cortright, Sandy & Pokriots, Will. Making Backyard Birdhouses: Attracting, Feeding & Housing Your Favorite Birds. (Illus.). 128p. 1997. pap. 14.95 (*0-8069-0893-9*) Sterling.

Cortright, Steven, jt. auth. see Plous, Phyllis.

Corts, C. Mark. ShareLife: A Conversational Plan for Sharing the New Testament Gospel. 2nd ed. Oviatt, Denise K., ed. 357p. 1998. pap. 10.00 (*0-9656209-1-3*) ShareLife.

Corts, Thomas E. Henry Drummond. 176p. 37.95 (*0-567-08667-4*) T&T Clark Pubs.

Cortsen, Susan. Reflections of a Poet's Eye. 1998. pap. write for info. (*1-58235-010-8*) Watermrk Pr.

Coruh, jt. auth. see Costain.

Coruh, Cahit, jt. auth. see Robinson, Edwin S.

Corum, ed. see Nostredame.

Corum, Ann K. Aunty Pua's Dilemma. LC 95-120612. 32p. 1994. 7.95 (*1-56647-086-2*) Mutual Pub HI.

— Aunty Pua's Keiki Cookbook. LC 91-70849. (Illus.). 80p. 1991. pap. 4.95 (*0-935848-88-6*) Bess Pr.

***Corum, Ann K.** Ethnic Foods of Hawaii. rev. ed. (Illus.). 240p. 2000. pap. 11.95 (*1-57306-117-4*) Bess Pr.

Corum, Ann K. Folk Wisdom from Hawaii: Or Don't Take Bananas on a Boat. (Illus.). 120p. 1985. pap. 8.95 (*0-935848-32-0*) Bess Pr.

— Hawaii's Spam Cookbook. LC 87-70924. (Illus.). 160p. (Orig.). 1987. pap. 9.95 (*0-935848-49-5*) Bess Pr.

Corum, Delbert, et al. Tale of Two Bridges & the Battle for the Skies over North Vietnam. (USAF Southeast Asia Monograph Ser.: Monographs 1 & 2). (Illus.). 193p. 1986. reprint ed. pap. write for info. (*0-912799-26-9*) AFH & MP.

Corum, J. M., ed. see National Congress on Pressure Vessels & Piping Staff.

Corum, James S. The Luftwaffe: Creating the Operational Air War, 1918-1940. LC 97-6943. (Modern War Studies). (Illus.). 378p. 1999. 39.95 (*0-7006-0836-2*); pap. 19.95 (*0-7006-0962-8*) U Pr of KS.

— The Roots of Blitzkrieg: Hans von Seeckt & German Military Reform. LC 92-5178. (Modern War Studies). (Illus.). xviii, 276p. 1992. 29.95 (*0-7006-0541-X*); pap. 16.95 (*0-7006-0628-9*) U Pr of KS.

Corum, James S., jt. tr. see Muller, Richard.

Corum, Michael. Adverse Actions: A Guide for Federal Managers & Personnel Specialists. 123p. 1996. pap. 25.00 (*1-878810-34-0*) Dewey Pubns.

— Combatting Sexual Harassment: Disciplining the Sexual Harasser. 66p. 1993. pap. 25.00 (*1-878810-17-0*) Dewey Pubns.

— EEO Settlements: Through Interest-Based Resolutions. (Illus.). 83p. 1996. pap. text 14.95 (*0-936295-68-6*) FPMI Comns.

— A Federal EEO Counselor's Manual. 110p. 1993. pap. 25.00 (*1-878810-16-2*) Dewey Pubns.

— Handling Performance Problems: A Federal Supervisor's Guide to Dealing with Poor Performers. 2nd ed. 116p. 1998. pap. 25.00 (*1-878810-42-1*) Dewey Pubns.

***Corum, Michael.** Managing Employees' Time: A Federal Supervisor's Guide to Work Schedules, Leave, Attendance & Overtime Administration. 2nd rev. ed. 106p. 1999. pap. 25.00 (*1-878810-54-5*) Dewey Pubns.

— Taking Disciplinary Action: A Federal Supervisor's Guide to Corrective Discipline. 2nd ed. 162p. 1999. pap. 25.00 (*1-878810-55-3*) Dewey Pubns.

Corum, Michael, jt. auth. see Uffindell, Andrew.

Corum, Richard. Understanding Hamlet: A Student Casebook to Issues, Sources & Historical Documents. LC 98-12147. (Greenwood Press Literature in Context Ser.). 296p. 1998. 39.95 (*0-313-29877-7*, Greenwood Pr) Greenwood.

Corum, Robert T., Jr. Other Worlds & Other Seas: Art & Vision in Saint-Amant's Nature Poetry. LC 78-73094. (French Forum Monographs: No. 13). (Illus.). 174p. (Orig.). 1979. pap. 10.95 (*0-917058-12-7*) French Forum.

— Reading Boileau: An Integrative Study of the Early "Satires" LC 97-16246. (Studies in Romance Literatures: Vol. 15). 170p. 1997. 36.95 (*1-55753-110-2*) Purdue U Pr.

Coruzzi, Gloria & Puigdomenech, Pedro, eds. Plant Molecular Biology: Molecular Genetic Analysis of Plant Development & Metabolism. LC 94-9638. (NATO ASI Ser.: Vol. 81). 1994. write for info. (*3-540-57733-5*) Spr-Verlag.

— Plant Molecular Biology: Molecular Genetic Analysis of Plant Development & Metabolism. LC 94-9638. (NATO ASI Ser.: Vol. 81). 1994. write for info. (*0-387-57733-5*) Spr-Verlag.

Corvalan-Vasquez, Oscar. Youth Employment & Training in Developing Countries: An Annotated Bibliography. vii, 172p. (Orig.). 1984. pap. 15.75 (*92-2-103420-8*) Intl Labour Office.

***Corvalban, C., et al.** Decision-Making in Environmental Health: From Evidence to Action. LC 00-21614. 2000. pap. 49.99 (*0-419-25950-3*, E & FN Spon) Routledge.

Corvasce, Mauro & Paglino, Joseph. Murder One: A Writer's Guide to Homicide. LC 97-26703. (Howdunit Ser.). (Illus.). 216p. 1997. pap. 16.99 (*0-89879-773-X*, Wrtrs Digest Bks) F & W Pubns Inc.

Corvasce, Mauro V. & Paglino, Joseph R. Modus Operandi: A Writer's Guide to How Criminals Work. LC 94-49705. (Howdunit Ser.). 224p. (Orig.). 1995. pap. 16.99 (*0-89879-649-0*, Wrtrs Digest Bks) F & W Pubns Inc.

Corvasse, Frances. Satire & Irony: A Jr. High-Intermediate Language Arts Unit. 1984. pap. 4.00 (*0-89824-103-0*); pap., teacher ed. 5.00 (*0-89824-102-2*) Trillium Pr.

Corvellec, Herve. Stories of Achievements: Narrative Features of Organizational Performance. LC 96-49383. 154p. 1996. text 29.95 (*1-56000-282-4*) Transaction Pubs.

Corver, Norbert & Van Riemsdijk, Henk, eds. Studies on Scrambling: Movement & Non-Movement Approaches to Free Word-Order Phenomena. LC 94-14409. (Studies in Generative Grammar: No. 41). vi, 531p. (C). 1994. lib. bdg. 152.35 (*3-11-013572-8*) Mouton.

Corvette, Nikki. Rock 'n Roll Heaven: The Death & Lives of Musical Legends from the Big Bopper to Kurt Cobain. LC 97-165685. 192p. 1997. pap. 13.00 (*1-57297-167-3*) Blvd Books.

Corvi, Roberta. Introduction to the Thought of Karl Popper. Camiller, Patrick, tr. LC 96-7922. 224p. (C). 1996. 70.00 (*0-415-12956-7*); pap. 24.99 (*0-415-12957-5*) Routledge.

Corvilain, H. & Fuss, M., eds. Hormones & Calcium Metabolism. (Journal: Hormone Research Ser.: Vol. 20, No. 1). 92p. 1984. pap. 34.00 (*3-8055-3888-X*) S Karger.

Corvin-Blackburn, Judith. Journey to Wholeness: A Guide to Inner Healing. 2nd rev. ed. 248p. (Orig.). 1996. pap. 14.95 (*0-9651519-0-5*) Healing Concepts.

Corvin, Michel. Dictionnaire Encyclopedique du Theatre. (FRE.). 940p. 1991. 195.00 (*0-8288-9496-5*) Fr & Eur.

— Dictionnaire Encyclopedique du Theatre, 2. (FRE.). 1024p. 1995. 225.00 (*0-7859-9931-0*) Fr & Eur.

— Dictionnaire Encyclopedique du Theatre. (FRE.). 1998. 69.95 (*0-320-00200-4*) Fr & Eur.

Corvin, R. O. David & His Mighty Men. LC 74-136646. (Biography Index Reprint Ser.). 1977. 19.95 (*0-8369-8041-7*) Ayer.

***Corvina Books Staff.** The History of Hungarian Art in the Twentieth Century. (Illus.). 288p. 1999. pap. 80.00 (*963-13-4809-1*, Pub. by Corvina Bks) St Mut.

— A Hungarian Quartet: Four Contemporary Short Novels. 176p. 1999. pap. 40.00 (*963-13-4357-X*, Pub. by Corvina Bks) St Mut.

— The Lost Rider: A Bilingual Anthology - The Corvina Book of Hungarian Verse. 432p. 1999. pap. 30.00 (*963-13-4784-2*, Pub. by Corvina Bks) St Mut.

Corvina Staff. ARSHungarica. 192p. 1989. 150.00 (*963-13-3845-2*, Pub. by Corvina Bks) St Mut.

C

An Asterisk (*) at the beginning of an entry indicates that the title is appearing for the first time.

Corvino, John, ed. Same Sex: Debating the Ethics, Science, & Culture of Homosexuality. LC 97-22315. (Studies in Social, Political, & Legal Philosophy: Vol. 70). 432p. 1997. 27.95 (*0-8476-8482-2*, Pub. by Rowman) Natl Bk Netwk.

— Same Sex: Debating the Ethics, Science, & Culture of Homosexuality. (Studies in Social, Political, & Legal Philosophy: Vol. 70). 432p. 1999. pap. 17.95 (*0-8476-8483-0*, Pub. by Rowman) Natl Bk Netwk.

Corvisier, André. Art Dictionary of Military History: Dictionnaire d'Art et d'Histoire Militaires. (FRE.). 896p. 1988. 195.00 (*0-8288-1905-X*, F33200) Fr & Eur.

— Histoire Militaire de la France, Vol. 1: Des Origines a 1715. Contamine, Philippe, ed. (FRE.). 648p. 1993. 195.00 (*0-7859-0473-5*, 2130438725) Fr & Eur.

— Histoire Militaire de la France, Vol. 2: De 1715 a 1871. Delmas, Jean, ed. (FRE.). 640p. 1993. 195.00 (*0-7859-0474-3*, 2130444156) Fr & Eur.

— Histoire Militaire de la France, Vol. 3: De 1871 a 1940. Pedroncini, Guy, ed. (FRE.). 528p. 1993. 195.00 (*0-7859-0475-1*, 2130448984) Fr & Eur.

Corvisier, Andre, ed. A Dictionary of Military History. rev. ed. Turner, Chris, tr. from FRE. LC 92-46136. (Illus.). 944p. 1994. 62.95 (*0-631-16848-6*) Blackwell Pubs.

Corvo, Joseph & Verner-Bonds, Lilian. Healing with Color Zone Therapy. rev. ed. LC 98-12119. (Healing Ser.). (Illus.). 176p. 1998. pap. 14.95 (*0-89594-925-3*) Crossing Pr.

Corvo, Max. The O. S. S. in Italy, 1942-1945: A Personal Memoir. LC 89-3801. 334p. 1989. 39.95 (*0-275-93333-4*, C3333, Praeger Pubs) Greenwood.

Corwen. Careers Without College. 1995. pap. 12.95 (*0-671-51730-9*) S&S Trade.

Corwen, Leonard. Your Resume: Key to a Better Job. 6th ed. 192p. 1995. 10.95 (*0-02-860343-5*, Arc) IDG Bks.

— Your Resume: Key to a Better Job. 6th ed. 200p. 1996. pap. 24.95 incl. 3.5 ld (*0-02-861315-5*, Arc) IDG Bks.

Corwin. Basic Chemistry. 7th ed. 1995. pap. text, teacher ed., lab manual ed. write for info. (*0-13-378498-3*) Allyn.

Corwin. Basic Chemistry Lab Manual. 7th ed. 1995. pap. text, lab manual ed. 45.00 (*0-13-378506-8*) P-H.

— Introductory Chemistry. 2nd ed. 1997. pap. text, student ed. 31.67 (*0-13-908914-4*) P-H.

Corwin, et al. Used Numbers - Measuring: From Paces to Feet. 100p. 1990. 12.95 (*0-86651-503-8*, DS01025) Seymour Pubns.

Corwin, jt. auth. see Reynolds.

Corwin, Arthur F., ed. Immigrants & Immigrants: Perspectives on Mexican Labor Migration to the United States, 17. LC 77-84756. (Contributions in Economics & Economic History Ser.: No. 17). (Illus.). 378p. 1978. 59.95 (*0-8371-9848-8*, CII/) Greenwood.

Corwin, B. R. A Trip to the Rockies. LC 78-39693. (Select Bibliographies Reprint Ser.). 1977. reprint ed. 11.95 (*0-8369-9934-7*) Ayer.

Corwin, Charles & Corwin, Elizabeth J. A Dictionary of Japanese & English Idiomatic Equivalents. Takenaka, Jiro et al, eds. (ENG & JPN.). 336p. 1994. pap. 19.00 (*4-7700-1843-6*) Kodansha.

Corwin, Charles H. Chemistry: Concepts & Connections. 768p. (C). 1993. text 76.00 (*0-13-481946-2*) P-H.

— Introductory Chemistry. 2nd ed. (Prentice Hall Series in Decision Science). 323p. 1998. pap. text, lab manual ed. 49.00 (*0-13-908922-5*) P-H.

— Introductory Chemistry: Concepts & Connections. 2nd ed. LC 97-16869. 773p. (C). 1997. 82.00 (*0-13-267766-0*) P-H.

Corwin, Consuelo, tr. see Fuentes, Norberto.

Corwin, D. L. & Loague, K. Applications of GIS to the Modeling of Non-Point Source Pollutants in the Vadose Zone. (SSSA Special Publications: No. 48). 319p. 1996. 47.00 (*0-89118-824-X*) Soil Sci Soc Am.

Corwin, Dennis L. Deterministic Modeling: CONTAM Transport Thru Vadose Zone. Date not set. 59.95 (*0-87371-833-X*, L833) Lewis Pubs.

***Corwin, Dennis L., et al, eds.** Assessment of Non-point Source Polution in the Vadose Zone. LC 99-13743. (Geophysical Monograph Ser.: Vol. 108). 16p. 1999. 62.00 (*0-87590-091-7*) Am Geophysical.

Corwin, Donna G. Parent Traps: Understanding & Overcoming the Pitfalls That All Parents Face. LC 97-11912. 208p. 1997. pap. 11.95 (*0-312-16961-2*) St Martin.

— Parent Traps: Understanding & Overcoming the Pitfalls That All Parents Face, Vol. 1. 1997. mass mkt. write for info. (*0-312-96166-9*) St Martin.

— The Tween Years. LC 98-6778. 176p. 1998. pap. 14.95 (*0-8092-2995-1*, 299510, Contemporary Bks) NTC Contemp Pub Co.

Corwin, Donna G., jt. auth. see Golant, Mitch.

Corwin, Donna G., jt. auth. see Varni, James W.

***Corwin, Doug, et al.** LOL Humorous Adventures from Cyberspace. (Illus.). 228p. 1999. pap. 14.95 (*0-9676980-0-6*) Ross Pubns CA.

Corwin, E. S. French Policy & the American Alliance of, 1778. 1990. 16.50 (*0-8446-0559-X*) Peter Smith.

***Corwin, E. T.** The Corwin Genealogy (Curwin, Curwen, Corwine) in the United States. xxxiv, 284p. 2000. reprint ed. pap. 31.50 (*0-8063-4976-X*, Pub. by Clearfield Co) ACCESS Pubns Network.

Corwin, E. T. The Corwin Genealogy (Curwin, Curwen, Corwine) in the United States. (Illus.). 318p. 1989. reprint ed. pap. 47.50 (*0-8328-0429-0*); reprint ed. lib. bdg. 57.50 (*0-8328-0428-2*) Higginson Bk Co.

Corwin, E. T., ed. Ecclesiastical Records of the State of New York, 7 vols. LC 74-19602. reprint ed. 440.00 (*0-404-12305-8*) AMS Pr.

Corwin, Edward S. American Constitutional History: Essays. Mason, Babbie & Garvey, eds. 1990. 16.50 (*0-8446-0558-1*) Peter Smith.

— Commerce Power Versus States Rights. 1959. 16.50 (*0-8446-1130-1*) Peter Smith.

— Constitution & World Organization. LC 73-117869. (Select Bibliographies Reprint Ser.). 1977. 16.95 (*0-8369-5322-3*) Ayer.

— Constitutional Revolution, Ltd. LC 77-805. ix, 121p. 1977. reprint ed. lib. bdg. 22.50 (*0-8371-9498-9*, Greenwood Pr) Greenwood.

— Corwin on the Constitution Vol. One: The Foundations of American Constitution & Political Thought, the Powers of Congress, & the President's Power of Removal. Loss, Richard, ed. 392p. 1981. text 52.50 (*0-8014-1381-8*) Cornell U Pr.

— Corwin on the Constitution Vol. Three: On Liberty against Government. Loss, Richard, ed. LC 80-69823. 272p. 1988. text 52.50 (*0-8014-2176-4*) Cornell U Pr.

— Court over Constitution. LC 94-76046. xi, 273p. 1994. reprint ed. 40.00 (*0-89941-876-7*, 308240) W S Hein.

— Court Over Constitution: A Study of Judicial As an Instrument of Popular Government. 1990. 16.50 (*0-8446-1129-8*) Peter Smith.

— Doctrine of Judicial Review. 1990. 16.50 (*0-8446-1128-X*) Peter Smith.

— The Doctrine of Judicial Review: Its Legal & Historical Basis & Other Essays, 1914. LC 99-32362. 1999. reprint ed. 60.00 (*1-58477-011-2*) Lawbk Exchange.

— Edward S. Corwin's, Constitution & What It Means Today. rev. ed. Chase, Harold W. & Ducat, Craig R., eds. LC 78-53809. 374p. 1978. pap. text 22.95 (*0-691-02758-7*, Pub. by Princeton U Pr) Cal Prin Full Svc.

— The "Higher Law" Background of American Constitutional Law. 101p. 1955. pap. text 14.95 (*0-8014-9012-X*) Cornell U Pr.

— Liberty Against Government: The Rise, Flowering, & Decline of a Famous Judicial Concept. LC 77-4090. 210p. 1979. reprint ed. lib. bdg. 59.50 (*0-8371-9589-6*, COLAG, Greenwood Pr) Greenwood.

— National Supremacy: Treaty Power vs. State Power. 1965. 16.50 (*0-8446-1127-1*) Peter Smith.

— The President: Office & Powers. rev. ed. Bland, Randall W. et al, eds. 600p. (C). 1984. pap. text 35.00 (*0-8147-1391-2*) NYU Pr.

— Presidential Power & the Constitution: Essays. Loss, Richard, ed. LC 75-38000. 185p. 1976. text 52.50 (*0-8014-0982-9*) Cornell U Pr.

— Total War & the Constitution. LC 70-127590. (Essay Index Reprint Ser.). 1977. 20.95 (*0-8369-1796-0*) Ayer.

Corwin, Edward S. & Crews, Kenneth D. Corwin's Constitution: Essays & Insights of Edward S. Corwin, 34. LC 86-7590. (Contributions in Legal Studies: No. 34). 285p. 1986. 55.00 (*0-313-24903-2*, CCU, Greenwood Pr) Greenwood.

***Corwin, Elizabeth J.** Handbook of Pathophysiology. 2nd ed. LC 99-37060. 688p. 1999. spiral bd. write for info. (*0-7817-1938-0*) Lppncott W & W.

Corwin, Elizabeth J., jt. auth. see Corwin, Charles.

Corwin, Gary, jt. ed. see Rommen, Edward.

Corwin, Gene, jt. auth. see Lewis, Adele B.

Corwin, H., Jr., jt. ed. see Capaccioli, Massimo.

Corwin, H. G. & Bottinelli, L., eds. The World of Galaxies. (Illus.). 592p. 1989. 79.00 (*0-387-97083-5*) Spr-Verlag.

Corwin, Harold E., ed. see Horacek, Robert G.

Corwin, Harold E., ed. see Ortner, Herbert E.

Corwin, Harold G., et al. Southern Galaxy Catalogue: A Catalogue of 5481 Galaxies South of Declination-17 Degress Found on 1.2m U. K. Schmidt IIIa-J Plates. LC 85-50556. (Monographs in Astromony: No. 4). 342p. (Orig.). 1985. pap. write for info. (*0-9603796-3-0*) U of Tex Dept Astron.

Corwin, Howard. Surgical Critical Care. Date not set. write for info. (*0-393-71031-9*) Norton.

Corwin, Jay. La Transposicion de Fuentes Indigenas en Cien Anos de Soledad. LC 97-75592. (Monographs: No. 52). 108p. 1997. 20.00 (*1-889441-02-3*) Romance.

Corwin, Jeff. Jeff Corwin's My Story of the Rainforest Chocolate Tree. LC 99-30039. 32p. (J). 2001. 12.99 (*0-7868-0455-6*, Pub. by Disney Pr) Time Warner.

***Corwin, Jeff.** Jeff Corwin's Mystery of the Rainforest Chocolate Tree. (Illus.). 32p. (J). 2001. bds. 12.99 (*0-7868-3270-3*, Pub. by Disney Pr) Time Warner.

Corwin, Jeff. Jeff Corwin's Mystery of the Rainforest Chocolate Tree. LC 99-30039. 32p. (J). 2001. lib. bdg. 14.49 (*0-7868-2397-6*, Pub. by Hyprn Child) Little.

Corwin, Judith. Easy-to-Make Applique Quilts for Children: Instructions & Full-Size Templates. (Illus.). 48p. 1982. pap. 3.95 (*0-486-24293-5*) Dover.

Corwin, Judith H. Christmas Crafts. LC 93-6366. (Holiday Craft Bks.). (Illus.). 48p. (J). (gr. 3-5). 1996. lib. bdg. 21.00 (*0-531-11149-0*) Watts.

— Christmas Crafts. LC 93-6366. (Holiday Craft Bks.). (Illus.). 48p. (J). (gr. 3-6). 1996. pap. 5.95 (*0-531-15756-3*) Watts.

— Christmas Fun. (Holiday Fun Ser.). (Illus.). 64p. (J). (gr. 3 up). 1982. pap. 5.95 (*0-671-49583-6*, Julian Messner) Silver Burdett Pr.

— Colonial American Crafts: The Home. LC 89-8958. (Illus.). 48p. (J). (gr. 3-5). 1989. lib. bdg. 22.00 (*0-531-10713-2*) Watts.

— Colonial American Crafts: The School. LC 89-32542. (Illus.). 48p. (J). (gr. 3-5). 1989. lib. bdg. 22.00 (*0-531-10714-0*) Watts.

— Cookie Fun. (Holiday Fun Ser.). (Illus.). 64p. (J). (gr. 3 up). 1985. pap. 5.95 (*0-671-55019-5*, Julian Messner) Silver Burdett Pr.

— Easter Crafts. LC 93-21258. 48p. (J). 1994. lib. bdg. 21.00 (*0-531-11145-8*) Watts.

— Easter Crafts. (Holiday Craft Bks.). (Illus.). 48p. (J). (gr. 3-5). 1994. pap. 5.95 (*0-531-15726-1*) Watts.

— Easter Fun. (Holiday Library). (Illus.). 64p. (J). (gr. 3 up). 1984. pap. 5.95 (*0-671-53108-5*, Julian Messner) Silver Burdett Pr.

— Halloween Crafts. (Holiday Craft Bks.). (Illus.). 48p. (J). (gr. 3-5). 1995. lib. bdg. 21.00 (*0-531-11148-2*) Watts.

— Halloween Crafts. LC 93-6367. (Holiday Craft Bks.). (Illus.). 48p. (J). (gr. 3-5). 1996. pap. 5.95 (*0-531-15734-2*) Watts.

— Halloween Fun. LC 83-8289. (Holiday Library). (Illus.). 64p. (J). (gr. 3 up). 1983. pap. 5.95 (*0-671-49756-1*, Julian Messner) Silver Burdett Pr.

— Hanukkah Crafts. LC 95-38077. (Holiday Craft Bk.). (Illus.). (J). (gr. 3-5). 1996. pap. 5.95 (*0-531-15757-1*) Watts.

— Harvest Festivals Around the World. LC 93-6567. (Messner Multicultural Library). (Illus.). 48p. (J). (gr. 2-5). 1995. pap. 7.95 (*0-614-25431-0*, Julian Messner); lib. bdg. 6.95 (*0-671-87240-0*, Julian Messner) Silver Burdett Pr.

— Jewish Holiday Fun. LC 86-16201. (Holiday Fun Ser.). (Illus.). 64p. (J). (gr. 3 up). 1987. pap. 5.95 (*0-671-60127-X*, Julian Messner) Silver Burdett Pr.

— My First Book of Embroidery: With 44 Iron-on Transfer Patterns. (Illus.). 80p. (Orig.). 1992. pap. 4.95 (*0-486-27100-5*) Dover.

— My First Riddles. LC 97-73144. (Illus.). 24p. (J). (ps up). 1998. 9.95 (*0-694-01109-6*) HarpC Child Bks.

— Thanksgiving Crafts. LC 93-6369. (Holiday Craft Bks.). (Illus.). 48p. (J). (gr. 3-5). 1996. pap. 5.95 (*0-531-15736-9*) Watts.

— Thanksgiving Fun. (Holiday Fun Ser.). (Illus.). 64p. (J). (gr. 3 up). 1984. pap. 5.95 (*0-671-50849-0*, Julian Messner) Silver Burdett Pr.

— Valentine Crafts. LC 93-11970. (Holiday Craft Bks.). 48p. (J). 1994. lib. bdg. 21.00 (*0-531-11146-6*) Watts.

— Valentine Crafts. (Holiday Craft Bks.). (Illus.). 48p. (J). (gr. 3-5). 1994. pap. 5.95 (*0-531-15727-X*) Watts.

— Valentine Fun. LC 82-6047. (Holiday Fun Ser.). (Illus.). 64p. (J). (gr. 3 up). 1983. pap. 5.95 (*0-671-49755-3*, Julian Messner) Silver Burdett Pr.

Corwin, Judith Hoffman. Kwanzaa Crafts. (Holiday Craft Bks.). (Illus.). 48p. (J). (gr. 3-5). 1996. pap. 5.95 (*0-531-15735-0*) Watts.

Corwin, L., et al, eds. The Gel'Fand Mathematical Seminars, 1990-1992. xxi, 235p. 1993. 69.00 (*0-8176-3689-7*) Birkhauser.

Corwin, Lawrence J. & Szczarba. Multivariable Calculus. (Pure & Applied Mathematics Ser.: Vol. 64). (Illus.). 544p. 1982. text 165.00 (*0-8247-6962-7*) Dekker.

Corwin, Lawrence J. & Szczarba, Robert H. Calculus in Vector Spaces. 2nd ed. (Monographs & Textbooks in Pure & Applied Mathematics: Vol. 189). (Illus.). 600p. 1994. text 179.50 (*0-8247-9279-3*) Dekker.

Corwin, Marshall, jt. auth. see Nutkins, Terry.

***Corwin, Miles.** And Still We Rise: The Trials & Triumphs of Twelve Gifted Inner-City High School Students. LC 99-46775. 432p. 2000. 25.00 (*0-380-97650-1*, Wm Morrow) Morrow Avon.

Corwin, Miles. The Killing Season. 1998. mass mkt. 6.99 (*0-449-00291-8*, Crest) Fawcett.

— The Killing Season: A Summer Inside an LAPD Homicide Division. LC 96-47429. (Illus.). 336p. 1997. 22.50 (*0-684-80235-X*) S&S Trade.

Corwin, Nancy A. Cynthia Schira: New Work. (Illus.). 16p. (Orig.). 1987. pap. 5.00 (*0-913689-14-9*) Spencer Muse Art.

***Corwin, Nina.** Conversations with Friendly Demons & Tainted Saints. 57p. 1999. pap. 10.00 (*0-9615879-6-2*) Puddinhead Pr.

Corwin, Norman. Greater Than the Bomb. (Santa Susana Press Ser.). 1981. 38.00 (*0-937048-31-3*) Santa Susana.

— Holes in a Stained Glass Window. 1978. 10.00 (*0-8184-0255-5*) Carol Pub Group.

— Norman Corwin's Letters. Langguth, A. J., ed. LC 93-15898. 480p. 1993. 29.95 (*0-9623032-5-9*) Barricade Bks.

— Our Lady of the Freedoms. abr. ed. 1998. pap. 12.00 incl. audio (*0-671-58218-6*, 892889) S&S Audio.

— Trivializing America. 256p. 1983. 14.95 (*0-8184-0341-1*) Carol Pub Group.

Corwin, Norman, as told by. Years of the Electric Ear. LC 94-5101. 1994. 47.50 (*0-8108-2885-5*) Scarecrow.

Corwin, Patty & O'Callahan, Cheryl. Problem Solving Strategies: Grades 6-8. Muffoletto, Mary L., ed. (Illus.). 64p. 1996. pap., teacher ed. 6.95 (*1-889369-04-7*, TI0007) Teaching Ink.

Corwin, Phillip. Binoculars: New & Selected Poems. 1997. 10.00 (*0-9615475-1-0*) Catnip Pr.

— Dubious Mandate: A Memoir of the U. N. in Bosnia, Summer 1995. LC 98-39289. 312p. 1999. 27.95 (*0-8223-2126-2*) Duke.

— Poems to Keep. 42p. 1985. 4.95 (*0-9615475-0-2*) Catnip Pr.

Corwin, R. D. Racial Minorities in Banking: New Workers in the Banking Industry. 1971. pap. 16.95 (*0-8084-0042-8*) NCUP.

Corwin, Rebecca, et al. Talking Mathematics: Resource Package. 1996. pap. text 450.00 (*0-435-08398-8*, 08398) Heinemann.

Corwin, Rebecca B., et al. Talking Mathematics: Supporting Children's Voices. LC 95-34652. 160p. 1995. pap. text 17.50 (*0-435-08377-5*, 08377) Heinemann.

Corwin, Ronald G. Education in Crisis: A Sociological Analysis of Schools & Universities in Transition. LC 73-12844. 396p. reprint ed. pap. 122.80 (*0-608-10779-4*, 205511100008) Bks Demand.

— The Entrepreneurial Bureaucracy Vol. 1: Bibliographies of Two Federal Programs in Education. LC 82-81210. (Contemporary Studies in Sociology: Vol. 1). 267p. 1983. 78.50 (*0-89232-314-0*) Jai Pr.

— The Organization-Society Nexus: A Critical Review of Models & Metaphors, 67. LC 87-7552. (Contributions in Sociology Ser.: No. 67). 358p. 1987. 55.00 (*0-313-25582-2*, CLU/, Greenwood Pr) Greenwood.

Corwin, Ronald G., jt. auth. see Namboodiri, Krishnan.

Corwin, Sheila. Marriage & the Family & Child-Rearing Practices. Zak, Therese A., ed. (Lifeworks Ser.). (Illus.). 160p. 1981. text 13.96 (*0-07-013198-8*) McGraw.

***Corwin, Stanley J.** Fell's Guide to Writing Bestsellers: Your Absolute, Quintessential, Everything You Wanted to Know, Complete Guide. (Official Know-It-All Guides Ser.). (Illus.). 224p. 2000. pap. 16.95 (*0-88391-011-X*) F Fell Pubs Inc.

Corwin, Stanley J. How to Be a Best-Selling Author: Turn Your Small Ideas into Blockbuster Hits. 1999. pap. text 14.95 (*0-8119-0917-4*) Lifetime Bks.

Corwin, Thomas M. & Wachowiak, Dale G. The Universe: From Chaos to Consciousness. 421p. (C). 1989. pap. text 64.00 (*0-15-592942-9*, Pub. by SCP) Harcourt.

Corwin, W. R. Heavy-Section Steel Irradiation Program: Progress Report for April-September 1996. 79p. 1997. pap. 7.50 (*0-16-054738-5*) USGPO.

— Heavy Section Steel Irradiation Program: Semiannual Progress Report For October 1995-March 1996. 71p. 1997. pap. 7.00 (*0-16-062833-4*) USGPO.

Corwin, W. R. & Lucas, G. E., eds. The Use of Small-Scale Specimens for Testing Irradiated Material- STP 888. LC 85-27487. (Illus.). 375p. 1986. text 52.00 (*0-8031-0440-5*, STP888) ASTM.

Corwin, W. R., et al. Small Specimen Test Techniques, Vol. 132. LC 98-25686. (Special Technical Publication Ser.). (Illus.). 630p. 1998. 147.00 (*0-8031-2476-7*, STP1329) ASTM.

Corwin, William R., et al, eds. Small Specimen Test Techniques Applied to Nuclear Reactor Vessel Thermal Annealing & Plant Life Extension, STP 1204. LC 93-20768. (Special Technical Publication Ser.). (Illus.). 470p. 1993. text 125.00 (*0-8031-1869-4*, STP1204) ASTM.

Corwin, William R., jt. ed. see Chona, Ravinder.

Corwing. Time-Limited Social Work Practice. (Social Work Ser.). 2001. pap. 32.00 (*0-534-36768-2*) Brooks-Cole.

***Cory, Alex & Hejinian, Lyn.** Shark. Shaw, Lytle & Clark, Emilie, eds. 119p. 1998. pap. 8.00 (*0-9664871-0-9*) Shark.

Cory, Angelica J. Reflections of the Heart: Harmonics from the Angelic Spheres. (Illus.). ii, 42p. 1998. reprint ed. pap. 11.00 (*0-9669074-9-3*) A Cory.

— Thoughts to Ponder: A Treasure Chest of Golden Rays of Light. (Illus.). 50p. 1998. pap. 15.00 (*0-9669074-8-5*) A Cory.

Cory, B., jt. auth. see Weedy, B. M.

Cory, Beverly, ed. see Battista, Michael T. & Berle-Carman, Mary.

Cory, Beverly, ed. see Battista, Michael T. & Clements, Douglas H.

Cory, Beverly, ed. see Berle-Carman, Mary, et al.

Cory, Beverly, ed. see Clements, Douglas H., et al.

Cory, Beverly, ed. see Economopoulos, Karen & Murray, Megan.

Cory, Beverly, ed. see Economopoulos, Karen, et al.

Cory, Beverly, ed. see Eston, Rebeka & Economopoulos, Karen.

Cory, Beverly, ed. see Kliman, Marlene & Russell, Susan J.

Cory, Beverly, ed. see Kliman, Marlene, et al.

Cory, Beverly, ed. see Mokros, Jan, et al.

Cory, Beverly, ed. see Prien, Margaret S.

Cory, Beverly, ed. see Rubin, Andee & Mokros, Jan.

Cory, Beverly, ed. see Russell, Susan J. & Mokros, Jan.

Cory, Beverly, ed. see Russell, Susan J. & Rubin, Andee.

Cory, Beverly, ed. see Russell, Susan J., et al.

Cory, Beverly, ed. see Tierney, Cornelia.

Cory, Beverly, ed. see Tierney, Cornelia, et al.

Cory, Beverly, ed. see Wright, Tracey & Makros, Jan.

Cory, Beverly, ed. see Wright, Tracey, et al.

Cory, C. H., Jr. Cory Pts. 1 & 2: Lineal Ancestors of Susan Mulford Cory. 437p. 1991. reprint ed. pap. 64.00 (*0-8328-2131-4*); reprint ed. lib. bdg. 74.00 (*0-8328-2130-6*) Higginson Bk Co.

— Cory Pts. 1 & 2: Lineal Ancestors of Rhoda Axtell Cory. (Illus.). 300p. 1991. reprint ed. pap. 44.00 (*0-8328-2133-0*); reprint ed. lib. bdg. 54.00 (*0-8328-2132-2*) Higginson Bk Co.

— Cory Pts. 1 & 2: Lineal Ancestors of Susan Kitchell Mulford. 295p. 1991. reprint ed. pap. 43.50 (*0-8328-2129-2*); reprint ed. lib. bdg. 53.50 (*0-8328-2128-4*) Higginson Bk Co.

Cory, Catherine A., et al, eds. Christian Theological Traditions. (C). 1998. pap. 35.50 (*0-536-01820-0*) Pearson Custom.

Cory, Charles B. Hunting & Fishing in Florida, Including a Key to the Water Birds. LC 75-125734. (American Environmental Studies). 1974. reprint ed. 57.95 (*0-405-02657-9*) Ayer.

Cory, Charles B., jt. auth. see Field Museum of Natural History Staff.

Cory, Charles E. Place Names of Bourbon County, Kansas. 2nd ed. (Illus.). 96p. 1994. reprint ed. pap. 6.95 (*1-882355-03-2*) Mostly Bks Pub.

Cory, Chris. The Rain Forest: Student Book. Curry, Don, ed. (Early Science Ser.). 16p. (Orig.). (J). (ps-2). 1998. pap. text, student ed. 3.33 (*1-56784-380-8*) Newbridge Educ.

Cory, Christopher. The Rain Forest. Curry, Don, ed. (Early Science Big Bks.). (Illus.). 16p. (J). (ps-2). 1998. pap. 16.95 (*1-56784-379-4*) Newbridge Educ.

Cory, Daniel, ed. see Santayana, George.

Cory, David M. Faustus Socinus. LC 83-45606. reprint ed. 28.50 (*0-404-19874-0*) AMS Pr.

Cory, Desmond. The Circe Complex LC 75-323905. 288 p. (J). 1975. 2.75 (*0-333-17889-0*) Macmillan.

C

An Asterisk (*) at the beginning of an entry indicates that the title is appearing for the first time.

Cory, Donald W. The Homosexual in America: A Subjective Approach. LC 75-12310. (Homosexuality Ser.). 1975. reprint ed. 23.95 (0-405-07365-8) Ayer.

Cory, Gerald A., Jr. Algorithms, Illusions, & Reality: The Algorithmic Basis of Human Thought, Behavior, & Social Life. (Illus.). 450p. (Orig.). 1996. pap. 19.95 (0-9631280-4-3) Ctr Behav Ecol.

— The Reciprocal Modular Brain in Economics & Politics: Shaping the Rational & Moral Basis of Organization, Exchange & Choice. LC 99-33092. (C). 1999. text. write for info. (0-306-46183-8, Kluwer Plenum) Kluwer Academic.

— Rescuing Capitalist Free Enterprise for the 21st Century. LC 91-77266. (Illus.). 160p. (Orig.). 1992. pap. 10.95 (0-9631280-1-9) Ctr Behav Ecol.

***Cory, Gerald A., Jr.** Toward Consilience: The Bioneurological Basis of Behavior, Thoughts, Experience & Language. LC 00-42337. 2000. write for info. (0-306-46436-5) Plenum.

Cory, H. T. Cory. Ancestral Lines of Thomas Judd Cory, Clarence Richard Cory & John Harry Cory, Also Ancestral Lines of Alice E. A. Cory & Roy L. Adams, Jr. (Illus.). 270p. 1997. reprint ed. pap. 42.00 (0-8328-8074-4); reprint ed. lib. bdg. 52.00 (0-8328-8073-6) Higginson Bk Co.

Cory, Hans. Sukuma Law. 1970. reprint ed. lib. bdg. 49.50 (0-8371-3453-6) Greenwood.

Cory, Hans & Hartnoll, M. M. Customary Law of the Hava Tribe, Tanganyika Territory. 362p. 1971. reprint ed. 47.50 (0-7146-2476-4, Pub. by F Cass Pubs) Intl Spec Bk.

— Customary Law of the Haya Tribe, Tanganyika Territory. LC 46-427. 399p. 1945. reprint ed. pap. 123.70 (0-8357-3215-0, 205708600010) Bks Demand.

Cory, Harry H. Cory Family Genealogy, with Brief Records of Many Branches of the Cory Family in America. 117p. 1997. reprint ed. pap. 19.00 (0-8328-8068-X); reprint ed. lib. bdg. 29.00 (0-8328-8067-1) Higginson Bk Co.

Cory, Herbert E. Critics of Edmund Spenser. LC 65-15901. (Studies in Spenser: No. 26). 1969. reprint ed. lib. bdg. 75.00 (0-8383-0532-6) M S G Haskell Hse.

Cory, J. F., Jr., ed. Finite Element Applications Non-linear, Optimization & Fatique & Fracture: Proceedings, ASME/JSME Joint Pressure Vessels & Piping Conference (1998, San Diego, CA) LC 98-73177. 370. 201p. 1998. pap. 96.00 (0-7918-1866-7) ASME.

Cory, J. F., Jr., et al, eds. Current Topics in Computational Mechanics. (Proceedings of the 1995 ASME/JSME Pressure Vessels & Piping Conference Ser.: PVP-Vol. 305). 456p. 1995. 140.00 (0-7918-1336-3, H00968) ASME.

Cory, Jean-Jacques. Exhaustive Combinations, No. 2. 26p. (Orig.). 1996. pap. 5.00 (1-57141-022-8) Runaway Spoon.

— Lists. deluxe ed. 64p. (Orig.). 1974. pap. 10.00 (0-915066-06-8) Assembling Pr.

***Cory, Jill & McAndless-Davis, Karen.** When Love Hurts: A Woman's Guide to Understanding Abuse in Relationships. (Illus.). 120p. (Orig.). 2000. pap. 13.95 (0-9686016-0-X) WomanKind.

Cory, Jim. Wife. 29p. 1993. pap. 6.00 (1-882827-01-5) Insight to Riot.

Cory, Jim, ed. see Broughton, James.

Cory, Josie, jt. auth. see Cory, Troy.

Cory, Kathleen B. Tracing Your Scottish Ancestry. 2nd ed. 1996. pap. 16.00 (0-7486-6215-4, Pub. by Polygon) Subterranean Co.

***Cory, Kathleen B.** Tracing Your Scottish Ancestry. 2nd ed. 228p. 1999. reprint ed. pap. 16.95 (0-8063-1534-2) Genealog Pub.

Cory, Kim D. Lilly's Way. Austin, Jane, ed. 187p. (J). (gr. 4 up). 1998. pap. 9.99 (0-88092-363-6, 3636) Royal Fireworks.

***Cory, Kim Delmar.** Charlie Boy. (Illus.). (J). (gr. 4-6). 1999. pap. 9.99 (0-88092-496-9, 4969) Royal Fireworks.

Cory, Mark, jt. ed. see Bjorklund, Beth.

Cory, Michael R., jt. auth. see Cory, Vernon.

Cory, Pepper. Mastering Quilt Marking: Marking Tools & Techniques - Choosing Stencils - Matching Borders & Corners. Rymer, Cyndy & Aune, Carolyn, eds. LC 99-6016. (Illus.). 80p. 1999. pap. text 19.95 (1-57120-077-0, 10197) C & T Pub.

— Multiblock Quilt Designs. LC 97-50338. 1998. pap. 8.95 (0-486-40047-6) Dover.

— 65 Drunkard's Path Quilt Designs. LC 97-50339. 64p. 1998. pap. 8.95 (0-486-40046-8) Dover.

Cory, Pepper & McKelvey, Susan. The Signature Quilt: Traditions, Techniques & Signature Block Collection. Penders, Mary, ed. (Illus.). 144p. 1995. pap. 29.95 (1-881588-14-9, 882670200) EZ Quilting.

Cory, Steve. Daily Life in Ancient & Modern Mexico City. LC 98-18312. (Cities Through Time Ser.). (Illus.). 64p. (J). (gr. 4-7). 1999. lib. bdg. 23.93 (0-8225-3212-3, Runestone Pr) Lerner Pub.

***Cory, Steve.** Deck Designs: Plus Planters, Railings, Benches. Bakke, Timothy O., ed. LC 99-62083. (Illus.). 192p. 1999. pap. 16.95 (1-58011-070-3) Creative Homeowner.

Cory, Steve. Decks: Plan, Design & Build. Schiff, David, ed. LC 96-72417. (Illus.). 176p. 1997. pap. 14.95 (1-880029-93-6) Creative Homeowner.

***Cory, Steve.** Decks: Planning, Designing, Building. (Illus.). 192p. 2001. pap. 16.95 (1-58011-045-2) Creative Homeowner.

Cory, Steve. Quick Guide: Decks. Day, Jeff et al, eds. LC 97-75261. (Quick Guide Ser.). (Illus.). 80p. 1998. pap. 7.95 (1-58011-000-2) Creative Homeowner.

***Cory, Steve & Slavik, Diane.** Daily Life in Ancient & Modern Jerusalem. LC 99-42574. (Cities Through Time Ser.). (Illus.). 64p. (J). (gr. 4-10). 2000. lib. bdg. 25.26 (0-8225-3218-2, Runestone Pr) Lerner Pub.

Cory, Steven. Easy Step Patios. Toht, David W., ed. (Illus.). 64p. 1996. pap. 6.95 (0-89721-297-5, Ortho Bks) Meredith Bks.

Cory, Steven. Pueblo Indian. LC 95-3739. (American Pastfinder Ser.). (Illus.). 48p. (J). (gr. 4-7). 1996. lib. bdg. 21.27 (0-8225-2976-9, Lerner Publctns) Lerner Pub.

Cory, Steven. Wallpapering. Toht, David W., ed. (Easy-Step Ser.). (Illus.). 64p. (Orig.). 1997. pap. 6.95 (0-89721-345-9, 05985, Ortho Bks) Meredith Bks.

— Wallpapering: How to Cover Walls, Archways, Stairs & Ceilings in Paper & Fabric. (Easy-Step Ser.). (Illus.). 64p. 1998. pap. 4.95 (0-8069-7061-8) Sterling.

Cory, Troy. Bank of America, the Tortfeasor. 288p. 1994. pap. 29.95 (1-883644-85-2) TV Int Pubs.

Cory, Troy & Cory, Josie. Bank of America, the Tortfeasor. 1993. 80.00 (1-883644-94-1) TV Int Pubs.

Cory, Troy, et al. Smart-Daaf Boys Vol. I: The Inventors of Radio & Television & Nathan B. Stubblefield, 4 vols. (Illus.). 500p. 1994. 250.00 (1-883644-00-3) TV Int Pubs.

— Smart DAAF Boys Vol. II: The Inventors of Radio & Television & Nathan B. Stubblefield, 4 vols. (Illus.). 500p. 1994. 49.00 (1-883644-02-X) TV Int Pubs.

— Smart DAAF Boys Vol. III: The Inventors of Radio & Television & Nathan B. Stubblefield, 4 vols. (Illus.). 500p. 1994. 49.00 (1-883644-03-8) TV Int Pubs.

— Smart DAAF Boys Vol. IV: The Inventors of Radio & Television & Nathan B. Stubblefield, 4 vols. (Illus.). 500p. 1994. 49.00 (1-883644-04-6) TV Int Pubs.

Cory, Vernon & Cory, Michael R. The American Corys: Their Settlement & Dispersion in the United States & Canada. (Illus.). 98p. (Orig.). 1991. pap. 17.00 (1-55613-464-9) Heritage Bk.

Coryat, Karl, ed. The Bass Player Book: Equipment, Technique, Styles, & Artists. LC 99-22675. (Illus.). 224p. 1999. pap. 22.95 (0-87930-573-8, Pub. by Miller Freeman) Publishers Group.

Corydon, Bent. L. Ron Hubbard: Messiah or Madman? LC 91-39368. 480p. 1992. pap. 12.95 (0-942637-57-7) Barricade Bks.

— L. Ron Hubbard: Messiah or Madman? LC 96-208515. 1994. 24.95 (1-56980-009-X) Barricade Bks.

Corydon, Bent & Hubbard, L. Ron. L. Ron Hubbard: Messiah or Madman? (Illus.). 288p. 1987. 20.00 (0-8184-0444-2) Carol Pub Group.

Corydon, Hammond. Integrative Hypnotherapy. Date not set. write for info. (0-393-70137-9) Norton.

Corydon, Jeff, III, ed. see Thomas, Cora H.

Coryell, Deborah Morris. Good Grief: Healing Through the Shadow of Loss. unabridged ed. Centofante, Jane, ed. 137p. (C). 1997. pap. 15.00 (0-9660697-8-1) Shiva Fnd.

***Coryell, Janet.** Adeline & Julia. Myers, Robert, ed. (Illus.). 265p. 2000. pap. 24.95 (0-87013-513-9) Mich St U Pr.

Coryell, Janet L. Neither Heroine nor Fool: Anna Ella Carroll of Maryland. LC 89-24403. (Illus.). 195p. 1990. reprint ed. pap. 60.50 (0-608-07348-2, 206757600009) Bks Demand.

Coryell, Janet L., et al, eds. Beyond Image & Convention: Explorations in Southern Women's History. LC 98-6206. (Southern Women Ser.). 240p. 1998. 37.50 (0-8262-1172-0); pap. 16.95 (0-8262-1173-9) U of Mo Pr.

***Coryell, Janet L., et al, eds.** Negotiating Boundaries of Southern Womanhood: Dealing with the Powers That Be. 256p. 2000. 34.95 (0-8262-1295-6) U of Mo Pr.

Coryell, John W. & Cearley, Jack E. PCB Compliance Guide for Electrical Equipment. LC 92-657320. 234p. reprint ed. pap. 72.60 (0-7837-6796-X, 204662800003) Bks Demand.

***Coryell, Julie.** Jazz-Rock Fusion: The People, the Music. (Illus.). 2000. pap. 19.95 (0-7935-9941-5) H Leonard.

Coryell, Keith R. Entertaining Aurora. LC 93-73466. (Illus.). 164p. 1994. pap. 19.95 (0-916445-39-9) Crossroads Comm.

Coryell, Larry. Jazz Guitar: Creative Comping, Soloing, & Improv. LC 98-41679. (Illus.). 96p. 1998. pap. 19.95 incl. audio compact disk (0-87930-550-9) Miller Freeman.

Coryell, Murali. Stand Alone Rhythm & Blues. (Alfred's Handy Guide Ser.). 1996. pap. 12.95 incl. audio compact disk (0-88284-726-0) Alfred Pub.

Coryell, Nancy G. An Evaluation of Extensive & Intensive Teaching of Literature. LC 75-176671. (Columbia University. Teachers College. Contributions to Education Ser.: No. 275). reprint ed. 37.50 (0-404-55275-7) AMS Pr.

Coryell, Susan. Eaglebait. 187p. (YA). (gr. 7 up). 1989. 14.95 (0-15-200442-4, Gulliver Bks) Harcourt.

Coryell, William & Winokur, George, eds. The Clinical Management of Anxiety Disorders. (Illus.). 176p. 1991. text 32.50 (0-19-505953-0) OUP.

***Corzine, Chaz.** Letters to Baby: A Keepsake of Blessings & Wisdom for New Babies. 137p. 2000. reprint ed. 17.00 (0-7881-9244-2) DIANE Pub.

***Corzine, Don.** Decoration or Dishonor? 212p. 2000. pap. 14.95 (0-7414-0363-3) Buy Books.

***Corzine, Linda & Pirozzolo, Dick.** Timberframe Interiors. LC 00-26043. (Illus.). 192p. 2000. 39.95 (0-87905-970-2) Gibbs Smith Pub.

Corzine, Phyllis. The Black Death. LC 96-19441. (World History Ser.). (Illus.). (J). (gr. 4-12). 1996. lib. bdg. 22.45 (1-56006-299-1) Lucent Bks.

— The French Revolution. (World History Ser.). (Illus.). 112p. (J). (gr. 5-9). 1995. lib. bdg. 22.45 (1-56006-248-7, 2487) Lucent Bks.

***Corzine, Phyllis.** The King James Bible: Christianity's Definitive Text. LC 99-44140. (Words That Changed History Ser.). (Illus.). 144p. (YA). (gr. 6-9). 2000. lib. bdg. 23.70 (1-56006-673-3) Lucent Bks.

Corzine, Phyllis. The Palestinian-Israeli Accord. LC 96-34886. (Overview Ser.). (Illus.). (YA). (gr. 4-12). 1996. lib. bdg. 22.45 (1-56006-181-2) Lucent Bks.

Corzine, S. W., jt. auth. see Coldren, Larry A.

Corzo, Miguel A., ed. Mortality Immortality? The Legacy of 20th-Century Art. LC 98-38695. (Illus.). 212p. 1999. pap. 39.95 (0-89236-528-5, Pub. by J P Getty Trust) OUP.

Corzo, Miguel A. & Valentin, Nieves, eds. Conservacion de Vidrieras Historicas: Analisis y Diagnostico de su Deterioro. (Illus.). 232p. 1998. pap. 50.00 (0-89236-492-0, Pub. by J P Getty Trust) OUP.

Cos, Patricia L. de, see de Cos, Patricia L.

Cosa Member Attorneys Staff, jt. auth. see Office of General Counsel Staff.

COSASYL COBOL Committee. CODASYL COBOL Committee Journal of Development, 1988. rev. ed. Nelson, Donald F., ed. (Illus.). 1200p. 1988. pap. 40.00 (0-9621665-0-2) D Nelson.

Cosbriffe-Meyers, Christene, ed. Ventriloquist in the Rain: A Collection of Poems by Bruce Meyers. LC 92-72999. (Illus.). 100p. 1992. 14.95 (0-9623036-3-1) ConAmore Pub.

Cosby, Bill. The Best Way to Play. LC 96-32792. (Little Bill Books for Beginning Readers Ser.). (Illus.). 40p. (J). (gr. 1-5). 1997. 13.95 (0-590-13756-5); pap. 3.99 (0-590-95617-5, Cartwheel) Scholastic Inc.

— The Best Way to Play. (Little Bill Books for Beginning Readers Ser.). (J). (gr. k-3). 1997. 9.19 (0-606-11116-6, Pub. by Turtleback) Demco.

— Childhood. large type ed. 197p. 1992. lib. bdg. 19.95 (1-56054-371-X) Thorndike Pr.

— Childhood. large type ed. 197p. 1993. pap. 12.95 (1-56054-934-3) Thorndike Pr.

***Cosby, Bill.** Congratulations! Now What? A Book for Graduates. 2001. mass mkt. write for info. (0-7868-8964-0, Pub. by Disney Pr) Little.

— Congratulations! Now What? A Book for Graduates. LC 99-24172. 144p. 1999. 15.95 (0-7868-6572-5, Pub. by Hyperion) Time Warner.

— Congratulations! Now What? A Book for Graduates. 208p. 2000. pap. write for info. (0-7868-8486-X, Pub. by Hyperion) Little.

— The Day I Saw My Father Cry. LC 99-25076. (Little Bill Books for Beginning Readers Ser.). (Illus.). 40p. (J). (gr. 1-4). 2000. 15.95 (0-590-52197-7, Cartwheel) Scholastic.

Cosby, Bill. The Day I Was Rich. LC 98-53062. (Little Bill Books for Beginning Readers Ser.). (Illus.). 40p. (J). (gr. k-3). 1999. 15.95 (0-590-52172-1, Pub. by Scholastic Inc); pap. 3.99 (0-590-52173-X, Pub. by Scholastic Inc) Penguin Putnam.

— Fatherhood. 178p. 1991. pap. 11.95 (0-425-09772-2) Berkley Pub.

— Fatherhood. large type ed. LC 87-23628. (General Ser.). 175p. 1987. 16.95 (0-8161-4450-8, G K Hall Lrg Type) Mac Lib Ref.

— Hooray for the Dandelion Warriors! (Little Bill Books for Beginning Readers Ser.). (J). (gr. 1-3). 1999. pap. text 47.88 (0-439-13496-X) Scholastic Inc.

***Cosby, Bill.** Hooray for the Dandelion Warriors! LC 99-19026. (Little Bill Books for Beginning Readers Ser.). (Illus.). 40p. (J). (gr. k-3). 1999. 15.95 (0-590-52191-8, Pub. by Scholastic Inc) Penguin Putnam.

— Hooray for the Dandelion Warriors! (Illus.). (J). 1999. 9.44 (0-606-18561-5) Turtleback.

— It's All Relative: A Field Guide to the Modern Family. 144p. 2000. 16.95 (0-7868-6655-1, Pub. by Hyperion) Little.

Cosby, Bill. Kids Say the Darndest Things. 176p. 1999. mass mkt. 6.50 (0-553-58126-0) Bantam.

***Cosby, Bill.** Little Bill's Punch-Out Valentines. (Illus.). 16p. (ps-3). 1999. pap. text 2.99 (0-439-05204-1) Scholastic Inc.

Cosby, Bill. Love & Marriage. 304p. 1990. mass mkt. 6.50 (0-553-28467-3) Bantam.

— The Meanest Thing to Say. LC 96-32791. (Little Bill Books for Beginning Readers Ser.). (Illus.). 40p. (J). (gr. 1-5). 1997. 13.95 (0-590-13754-9); pap. 3.99 (0-590-95616-7) Scholastic Inc.

Cosby, Bill. The Meanest Thing to Say. (Little Bill Books for Beginning Readers Ser.). (J). (gr. k-3). 1997. 9.19 (0-606-11610-9, Pub. by Turtleback) Demco.

Cosby, Bill. Money Troubles. LC 97-34106. (Little Bill Books for Beginning Readers Ser.). (Illus.). 40p. (J). (gr. k-3). 1998. 13.95 (0-590-16402-3); pap. 3.99 (0-590-95623-X) Scholastic Inc.

***Cosby, Bill.** Money Troubles. (Little Bill Books for Beginning Readers Ser.). (J). (gr. k-3). 1998. 9.19 (0-606-13615-0, Pub. by Turtleback) Demco.

Cosby, Bill. My Big Lie. LC 98-42049. (Little Bill Books for Beginning Readers Ser.). (Illus.). 40p. (J). (gr. k-3). 1999. 15.95 (0-590-52160-8) Scholastic Inc.

***Cosby, Bill.** My Big Lie. LC 98-42049. (Little Bill Books for Beginning Readers Ser.). (Illus.). 40p. (J). (gr. 1-5). 1999. pap. 3.99 (0-590-52161-6) Scholastic Inc.

Cosby, Bill. One Dark & Scary Night. LC 98-8813. (Little Bill Books for Beginning Readers Ser.). (Illus.). (J). (gr. k-3). 1999. 15.95 (0-590-51475-X); pap. 3.99 (0-590-51476-8) Scholastic Inc.

***Cosby, Bill.** One Dark & Scary Night. (Little Bill Books for Beginning Readers Ser.). (J). (gr. k-3). 1999. pap. text 47.88 (0-439-04655-6, Cartwheel) Scholastic Inc.

Cosby, Bill. Selected from Fatherhood & Time Flies. abr. ed. (Writers' Voices Ser.). (Illus.). 64p. (Orig.). 1989. pap. text 3.95 (0-929631-00-5, Signal Hill) New Readers.

— Shipwreck Saturday. LC 97-16833. (Little Bill Books for Beginning Readers Ser.). 40p. (J). (gr. k-3). 1998. 13.95 (0-590-16400-7); pap. 3.99 (0-590-95620-5) Scholastic Inc.

— Shipwreck Saturday. (Little Bill Books for Beginning Readers Ser.). (J). (gr. k-3). 1998. 9.19 (0-606-13773-4, Pub. by Turtleback) Demco.

— Super-Fine Valentine. LC 97-16563. (Little Bill Books for Beginning Readers Ser.). (Illus.). 40p. (J). (gr. k-3). 1997. 13.95 (0-590-16401-5); pap. 3.99 (0-590-95622-1) Scholastic Inc.

— Super-Fine Valentine. (Little Bill Books for Beginning Readers Ser.). (J). (gr. k-3). 1998. 9.19 (0-606-13046-2, Pub. by Turtleback) Demco.

— Time Flies. 192p. 1988. mass mkt. 6.50 (0-553-27724-3) Bantam.

— The Treasure Hunt. LC 96-52072. (Little Bill Books for Beginning Readers Ser.). (Illus.). 40p. (J). (gr. 1-5). 1997. 13.95 (0-590-16399-X); pap. 3.99 (0-590-95618-3) Scholastic Inc.

— The Treasure Hunt. (Little Bill Books for Beginning Readers Ser.). (J). (gr. k-3). 1997. 9.19 (0-606-12002-5, Pub. by Turtleback) Demco.

— The Worst Day of My Life. LC 98-54266. (Little Bill Books for Beginning Readers Ser.). (Illus.). 40p. (J). (gr. k-3). 1999. 15.95 (0-590-52175-6, Pub. by Scholastic Inc) Penguin Putnam.

— The Worst Day of My Life. LC 98-54266. (Little Bill Books for Beginning Readers Ser.). (Illus.). 40p. (J). (gr. 1-5). 1999. pap. 3.99 (0-590-52190-X, Pub. by Scholastic Inc) Penguin Putnam.

Cosby, Bill & Honeywood, Varnette P. Hooray for the Dandelion Warriors! LC 99-19026. (Little Bill Books for Beginning Readers Ser.). (Illus.). 40p. (J). (gr. k-3). 1999. mass mkt. 3.99 (0-590-52194-2, Pub. by Scholastic Inc) Penguin Putnam.

Cosby, Bill & Honeywood, Varnette P. The Day I Saw My Father Cry. LC 99-25076. (Little Bill Books for Beginning Readers Ser.). (J). (gr. k-3). 2000. 3.99 (0-590-52199-3) Scholastic Inc.

Cosby, Bill, et al. Universal Spanish - Cambios: Descubriendo lo Mejor Que Hay en Ti. Callejas, Juan et al, eds. Trevant, Pierre, tr. from ENG. (Destrezas para la Adolescencia Ser.). (SPA., Illus.). 181p. (Orig.). (YA). (gr. 6-8). 1988. pap. text 6.85 (0-933419-44-9) Quest Intl.

Cosby, Camille O. Television's Imageable Influences: The Self-Perceptions of Young African Americans. LC 94-9258. (Illus.). 192p. 1994. reprint ed. 27.95 (0-8191-9521-9) U Pr of Amer.

***Cosby, Eileen Tucker.** A Is for Adopted. (Illus.). 56p. (J). (ps-5). 2000. 14.95 (0-9676385-0-X, 1001) SWAK Pak.

Cosby, Eschol. Branded for Christ. (Illus.). 128p. 1998. pap. 7.95 (0-939497-47-6) Promise Pub.

Cosby, Jane & Cosby, Randy. Fun with the Family in Missouri: Hundreds of Ideas for Day Trips with the Kids. 2nd ed. LC 99-29535. (Fun with the Family Ser.). (Illus.). 208p. 1999. pap. text 12.95 (0-7627-0466-7) Globe Pequot.

Cosby, John, tr. see Coss, Richard.

Cosby, John, tr. see Roels, Edwin D.

Cosby, Michael R. Portraits of Jesus: An Inductive Approach to the Gospels. LC 99-32672. 224p. 1999. pap. 22.95 (0-664-25827-1) Westminster John Knox.

— The Rhetorical Composition & Function of Hebrews 11: In Light of Example Lists in Antiquity. LC 88-27570. 132p. (C). 1989. 25.00 (0-86554-320-8, MUP/H273) Mercer Univ Pr.

Cosby, N. Gordon. By Grace Transformed: Christianity for a New Millennium. LC 98-6084. 192p. 1999. pap. 15.95 (0-8245-1754-7, Crsrd) Crossroad NY.

Cosby, Randy, jt. auth. see Cosby, Jane.

Cosby, Richard C. The Organization & Administration of Smaller College Athletics: A Handbook for Athletic Directors & Administrators. LC 89-82049. 1990. pap. 14.95 (0-938991-50-7) Colonial Pr AL.

Cosby-Thurman, Allison, tr. see Johnson, Veronda R.

Cosca, Theresa. High Earning Workers Who Don't Have a Bachelor's Degree. 8p. 1995. pap. 1.25 (0-16-061760-X) USGPO.

Coscarelli, Diego, ed. Barron's Regents Exams & Answers: Italian. rev. ed. LC 75-39381. (ITA.). 250p. (gr. 10-12). 1996. pap. text 5.95 (0-8120-3149-0) Barron.

***Coscarelli, Jane Tenorio.** The Pinata Quilt. Coscarelli, Nicole, tr. LC 99-64894. (ENG & SPA.). 48p. (J). (gr. k-6). 1999. 13.95 (0-9653422-5-5, Pub. by Quarter-Inch); pap. 9.95 (0-9653422-6-3, Pub. by Quarter-Inch) Sunbelt Pubns.

Coscarelli, Kate. Heir Apparent. large type ed. LC 93-38924. 1994. lib. bdg. 23.95 (0-7862-0128-2) Thorndike Pr.

Coscarelli, Nichole, tr. see Tenorio-Coscarelli, Jane.

Coscarelli, Nicole, jt. auth. see Tenorio-Coscarelli, Jane.

Coscarelli, Nicole, tr. see Coscarelli, Jane Tenorio.

Coscarelli, Nicole, tr. see Tenorio-Coscarelli, Jane.

Coscarelli, William C., jt. auth. see Shrock, Sharon.

Coscas, Gabriel, et al. Retinal Pigment Epithelium & Macular Diseases. LC 98-22538. (Documenta Ophthalmologica Proceedings Ser.). 457p. 1998. write for info. (0-7923-5144-4) Kluwer Academic.

Coscas, Gabriel, jt. auth. see Singerman, Lawrence.

Coscas, Gabriel J., jt. ed. see Regenbogen, Lucian S.

Cosci, Stefania. Credit Rationing & Asymmetric Information. (Luiss Ser.). 133p. 1993. 67.95 (1-85521-095-9, Pub. by Dartmth Pub) Ashgate Pub Co.

Coscia, Donald R. Computer Applications for Finite Mathematics & Calculus. (C). 1986. pap. text 1.66 (0-673-18154-5, Scott Frsmn) Addson-Wesley Educ.

Coscia, Eileen C. Reflections. (Orig.). 1997. pap. write for info. (1-57553-359-6) Watermrk Pr.

Coscia, Stephen. Customer Service over the Phone. 3rd ed. 1995. 12.95 (0-936648-68-6) Telecom Bks.

***Coscia, Stephen.** Customer Service over the Phone: Techniques &Technology for Handling Customers over the Phone. 5th ed. 144p. 1999. pap. 15.95 (1-57820-046-6, Pub. by Telecom Bks) Publishers Group.

Coscia, Stephen. Customer Service over the Phone: Techniques for Handling Customers over the Phone. 4th rev. ed. 96p. 1997. per. 14.95 (1-57820-020-2) Telecom Bks.

***Coscia, Stephen.** Tele-Stress: Relief for Call Center Stress. 2nd ed. (Illus.). 128p. 1999. pap. text 14.95 (1-57820-029-6) Telecom Bks.

Coscica, Carmine J. Handbook of Chromatography: Terpenoids. LC 83-14333. (Series in Chromatography). 200p. 1984. 113.00 (0-8493-3004-1, QD416, CRC Reprint) Franklin.

Cosculluela, Victor. The Ethics of Suicide. LC 94-45150. (Garland Studies in Applied Ethics; Garland Reference Library of Social Science: Vol. 4; Vol. 1033). 184p. 1995. text 39.00 (0-8153-2031-0) Garland.

Cose, Ellis. The Best Defense. LC 98-16838. 272p. 1998. 24.00 (0-06-017496-X) HarpC.

— The Best Defense. 432p. 1999. mass mkt. 6.99 (0-06-093087-X) HarpC.

— Color-Blind: Seeing Beyond Race in a Race-Obsessed World. 288p. 1998. pap. 13.00 (0-06-092887-5, Perennial) HarperTrade.

— The Rage of a Privileged Class. 208p. 1995. pap. 13.00 (0-06-092594-9) HarperTrade.

Cose, Elsa T. Introduction to Silk & Metal Thread Embroidery. rev. ed. (Illus.). 40p. 1984. pap. 9.95 (0-9614004-0-4) E T Cose.

Cose, Peter. Deathly Waters & Hungry Mountains: Agrarian Ritual & Class Formation in an Andean Town. LC 95-168320. (Anthropological Horizons Ser.: No. 4). (Illus.). 376p. (C). 1994. text 60.00 (0-8020-0606-X); pap. text 22.95 (0-8020-7210-0) U of Toronto Pr.

Cosechi, Paolo, jt. auth. see Sneddon, Peta.

Cosell, H. Like It Is. Date not set. 2.99 (0-87223-414-2) Playboy Ent.

***Cosell, Howard & Bonventre, Peter.** I Never Played the Game. large type ed. LC 99-87213. 590p. 2000. 34.95 (1-56000-460-6) Transaction Pubs.

Cosell, Howard & Bonvenure, Peter. I Never Played the Game. 384p. 1986. mass mkt. 5.99 (0-380-70159-6, Avon Bks) Morrow Avon.

Coselli, Joseph S., et al, eds. The History of Surgery in Houston: Fifty Year Anniversary of the Hauston Surgical Society. LC 98-28964. 424p. 1998. 39.95 (1-57168-254-6, Eakin Pr) Sunbelt Media.

Cosentino, jt. auth. see Plumer, Ada L.

Cosentino, Alfred S. Abarth King of Small Cars. (Illus.). 344p. 1986. 46.95 (0-929991-11-7) A S Cosentino Bks.

— Abarth Owners International, No. 001-88. 108p. 1988. 12.95 (0-929991-12-5) A S Cosentino Bks.

— Abarth Owners International, No. 002-88. 110p. 1988. 12.95 (0-929991-13-3) A S Cosentino Bks.

— Abarth Owners International, No. 003-89. 110p. 1989. 12.95 (0-929991-14-1) A S Cosentino Bks.

— Abarth Owners International, No. 004-89. 112p. 1989. 12.95 (0-929991-15-X) A S Cosentino Bks.

— California Ferraris. 5th ed. 200p. 1976. 6.00 (0-929991-06-0) A S Cosentino Bks.

— Carlo Abarth Foto Storia. 384p. 1989. 49.00 (0-929991-16-8) A S Cosentino Bks.

— Faza-Car Graphic Abarth Guide. (Illus.). 432p. 1984. 125.00 (0-929991-10-9) A S Cosentino Bks.

— Shut up & Paint. 1989. write for info. (0-929991-17-6) A S Cosentino Bks.

— X1-9 Strada 128 Race World. 308p. 1992. 15.95 (0-929991-07-9) A S Cosentino Bks.

— X1-9 Strada 128 Race World & Repair Manual. 572p. 1983. 27.95 (0-929991-08-7) A S Cosentino Bks.

— X1-9 Strada 128 Race World & Repair Manual. 6th ed. 160p. 1984. 6.00 (0-929991-09-5) A S Cosentino Bks.

Cosentino, Andrew J. A Passion for Liberty: Alexis de Tocqueville on Democracy & Revolution. LC 89-13051. 61p. 1989. 4.95 (0-8444-0651-1) Lib Congress.

Cosentino, Anthony M. & Martin, Richard J., eds. Cardiothoracic Interrelationships in Clinical Practice. LC 96-38646. (Illus.). 232p. 1997. 47.00 (0-87993-655-X) Futura Pub.

Cosentino, Christine & Muller, Wolfgang, eds. Im Widerstand/in MoBverstand? Zur Literatur und Kunst des Prenzlauer Bergs. (DDR Studien - East German Studies: Vol. 8). (GER.). 216p. (C). 1995. text 49.95 (0-8204-2321-1) P Lang Pubng.

Cosentino, Donald J. Vodou Things: The Art of Pierrot Barra & Marie Cassaise. LC 97-17175. (Folk Art & Artists Ser.). (Illus.). 72p. 1998. 22.50 (1-57806-014-1) U Pr of Miss.

Cosentino, Donald J., ed. Sacred Arts of Haitian Vodou. (Illus.). 446p. 1995. 99.00 (0-930741-46-3); pap. 59.00 (0-930741-47-1) UCLA Fowler Mus.

Cosentino, Edmund, jt. auth. see Punancy, Karlene.

Cosentino, Frank. A Passing Game: A History of the CFL. 400p. 1995. 21.95 (0-921368-54-2, Pub. by Bain & Cox) Genl Dist Srvs.

Cosentino, Joe & Mondzak, Susan. Columbus! A Musical. 40p. (Orig.). (J). (gr. 2-8). 1996. pap. 4.00 (1-57514-174-4, 0092) Encore Perform Pub.

Cosentino, Lydia. A Woman Speaks: Monologues for Actresses from Women Famous, Infamous, & Unknown. LC 94-49323. 1995. pap. 12.95 (0-940669-30-7, D-36) Dramaline Pubns.

Cosentino, Lydia, ed. Classic Mouth: Monologues for Boys & Girls from Classic Literature. LC 96-36422. 96p. (J). (gr. 1-9). 1996. pap. 8.95 (0-940669-35-8, D-41) Dramaline Pubns.

Cosentino, Lydia, ed. Voices. LC 95-45223. 96p. (Orig.). 1995. pap. 9.95 (0-940669-32-3, D-38) Dramaline Pubns.

Cosentino, Marc. The Harvard College Guide to Investment Banking. 69p. (Orig.). 1990. pap. 9.00 (0-943747-04-X) Harvard OCS.

Cosentino, Marc, ed. The Harvard College Guide to Consulting. 2nd ed. 172p. 1993. pap. 13.00 (0-943747-05-8) Harvard OCS.

Cosentino, Marc P. The Harvard College Guide to Consulting Case Questions. 60p. (Orig.). 1996. pap. 9.00 (0-943747-17-1) Harvard OCS.

Cosentino, Peter. The Encyclopedia of Pottery Techniques. (Illus.). 192p. 1990. 24.95 (0-89471-892-4) Running Pr.

***Cosentino, Ralph, ed.** Colors: Preschool Activity Book. (Illus.). 32p. (J). (ps-k). 1999. pap., student ed. 2.95 (1-58610-002-5) Learn Horizon.

— Lowercase Abcs: Preschool Activity Book. (Illus.). 32p. (J). (ps-k). 1999. pap., student ed. 2.95 (1-58610-000-9) Learn Horizon.

— Shapes: Preschool Activity Book. (Illus.). 32p. (J). (ps-k). 1999. pap., student ed. 2.95 (1-58610-003-3) Learn Horizon.

— Uppercase ABCs: Preschool Activity Book. (Illus.). 32p. (J). (ps-k). 1999. pap., student ed. 2.95 (1-58610-001-7) Learn Horizon.

Cosenza. Biographic & Bibliographic Dictionary of Italian Humanists & the World of Classical Scholarship in Italy, Supplement 1. 1970. suppl. ed. 160.00 (0-8161-1490-0, G K Hall & Co) Mac Lib Ref.

Cosenza, Edoardo & Zandonini, Riccardo. Analysis & Design of Steel Concrete Composite Structures. (New Directions in Civil Engineering Ser.). 1999. 89.95 (0-8493-9124-5) CRC Pr.

Cosenza, Mario E., compiled by. Checklist of the Non-Italian Humanists, 1300-1800. 1970. 160.00 (0-8161-0839-0, G K Hall & Co) Mac Lib Ref.

Cosenza, Mario E., tr. see Pais, Ettore.

Cosenza, Robert, jt. auth. see Davis, Duane.

Cosenza, Robert M., jt. auth. see Davis, Duane.

Coseo, Marc. The Acupressure Warmup: A System of Athletic Preparation & Injury Prevention. Felt, Robert L., ed. (Illus.). 144p. (Orig.). 1993. pap. text 18.00 (0-912111-34-8) Paradigm Publns.

Coser, Lewis A. European Sociology: Historically Significant Works, 54 vols., Set. (Illus.). 1975. 1739.00 (0-405-06493-4) Ayer.

— Functions of Social Conflict. LC 56-6874. 1964. pap. 14.95 (0-02-906810-X) Free Pr.

— A Handful of Thistles: Collected Papers in Moral Conviction. 320p. 1988. 39.95 (0-88738-208-8) Transaction Pubs.

— Masters of Sociological Thought: Ideas in Historical & Social Context. 2nd ed. (Illus.). 611p. (C). 1977. text 72.00 (0-15-555130-2, Pub. by Harcourt Coll Pubs); write for info. (0-318-52970-X) Harcourt Coll Pubs.

— Men of Ideas. LC 97-19975. 1997. per. 14.00 (0-684-83328-X) S&S Trade.

— Refugee Scholars in America: Their Impact & Their Experiences. LC 84-40193. 369p. reprint ed. pap. 114.40 (0-7837-7139-8, 208029600004) Bks Demand.

— Social Conflict & the Theory of Social Change. (Reprint Series in Social Sciences). (C). 1993. reprint ed. pap. text 1.00 (0-8290-3839-6, S-51) Irvington.

Coser, Lewis A. & Powell, Walter W., eds. Perennial Works in Sociology, 34 bks., Set. (Illus.). 1979. lib. bdg. 1064.00 (0-405-12081-8) Ayer.

Coser, Lewis A. & Rosenberg, Bernard, eds. Sociological Theory: A Book of Readings. 5th ed. 603p. (C). 1989. reprint ed. pap. text 27.95 (0-88133-457-X) Waveland Pr.

Coser, Lewis A., et al. Books: The Culture & Commerce of Publishing. LC 84-28044. xiv, 412p. 1985. pap. text 16.95 (0-226-11593-3) U Ch Pr.

— Introduction to Sociology. 3rd ed. 700p. (C). 1990. text 57.50 (0-15-545919-8, Pub. by Harcourt Coll Pubs) Harcourt.

Coser, Lewis A., ed. see Abegglen, James C.

Coser, Lewis A., ed. see Aron, Raymond.

Coser, Lewis A., ed. see Bernard, Luther L.

Coser, Lewis A., ed. see Chapin, Francis S.

Coser, Lewis A., ed. see DeGre, Gerard.

Coser, Lewis A., ed. see Granick, David.

Coser, Lewis A., ed. see Hughes, Everett C.

Coser, Lewis A., ed. see Keller, Suzanne I.

Coser, Lewis A., ed. see Lazarsfeld, Paul F. & Kendall, Patricia L.

Coser, Lewis A., ed. see Levy-Bruhl, Lucien.

Coser, Lewis A., ed. see Pareto, Vilfredo.

Coser, Lewis A., ed. see Powdermaker, Hortense.

Coser, Lewis A., ed. see President's Research Committee on Social Trends.

Coser, Lewis A., ed. see Rainwater, Lee, et al.

Coser, Lewis A., ed. see Riesman, David & Glazer, Nathan.

Coser, Lewis A., ed. see Rogoff, Natalie.

Coser, Lewis A., ed. see Rosenberg, Bernard & Fliegel, Norris.

Coser, Lewis A., ed. see Roth, Guenther.

Coser, Lewis A., ed. see Selznick, Philip.

Coser, Lewis A., ed. see Simmel, Georg.

Coser, Lewis A., ed. see Sorokin, Pitirim A.

Coser, Lewis A., ed. see Sumner, William G.

Coser, Lewis A., ed. see Svalastoga, Kaare.

Coser, Lewis A., ed. see Tiryakian, Edward A.

Coser, Lewis A., ed. see United States Office of Education Staff, et al.

Coser, Lewis A., ed. see Walker, Charles R. & Guest, Robert H.

Coser, Lewis A., ed. see Warner, W. Lloyd & Abegglen, James C.

Coser, Lewis A., ed. see Wood, Robert C.

***Coser, Margaret, ed.** I Love You. 384p. 1999. 40.00 (0-85305-365-0, Pub. by Arthur James) St Mut.

Coser, Rose L. In Defense of Modernity: Role Complexity & Individual Autonomy. 216p. 1991. 35.00 (0-8047-1871-7) Stanford U Pr.

— Laughter Among Colleagues: A Study of the Social Functions of Humor Among the Staff of a Men. (Reprint Series in Social Sciences). (C). 1993. reprint ed. pap. text 5.00 (0-8290-3093-X, S-362) Irvington.

Coser, Rose Laub, et al. Women of Courage: Jewish & Italian Immigrant Women in New York, 173. LC 98-47755. (Contributions in Women's Studies: Vol. 173). 176p. 1999. 49.95 (0-313-30820-9) Greenwood.

Coser, Stelamaris. Bridging the Americas: The Literature of Paule Marshall, Toni Morrison, & Gayl Jones. LC 94-30421. 240p. (C). 1994. text 69.95 (1-56639-266-7); pap. text 22.95 (1-56639-267-5) Temple U Pr.

***Cosey, Alfred Bonito.** American & English Law on Title of Record: Practice & Procedure. 415p. 1999. reprint ed. 125.00 (1-56169-551-3, 18153) Gaunt.

Cosey, R. In Search of Shirley, Vol. 1. Koch, Michael, tr. from FRE. 1992. pap. 9.95 (1-56163-066-7, Comics Lit) NBM.

— In Search of Shirley, Vol. 2. Koch, Michael, tr. from FRE. 1993. pap. 9.95 (1-56163-068-3, Comics Lit) NBM.

— Lost in the Alps. (Illus.). 120p. 1996. pap. 13.95 (1-56163-160-4, Comics Lit) NBM.

Cosgrave, Patrick & Richey, George. NATO's Strategy: A Case of Outdated Priorities? (C). 1990. 45.00 (0-907967-40-X, Pub. by Inst Euro Def & Strat) St Mut.

Cosgriff, Gabrielle, et al. Chicks on Film: Video Picks for Women & Other Intelligent Forms of Life. LC 98-10435. 272p. 1998. pap. 12.00 (0-380-79365-2, Avon Bks) Morrow Avon.

Cosgriff, James H., Jr. & Anderson, Diann L. The Practice of Emergency Care. 2nd ed. (Illus.). 652p. 1984. text 39.75 (0-397-54357-3, 64-02994, Lippnctt) Lppncott W & W.

Cosgriff, John. Lower Triassic Temnospondyli of Tasmania. LC 73-87235. (Geological Society of America, Special Paper: No. 149). (Illus.). 140p. reprint ed. pap. 43.40 (0-608-15186-6, 202737300055) Bks Demand.

Cosgrove. Air Base Design & Performence. (C). 1992. text. write for info. (0-673-46791-0) Addison-Wesley.

Cosgrove, Art, ed. A New History of Ireland Vol. II: Medieval Ireland, 1169-1534. 2nd rev. ed. (New History of Ireland Ser.: No. 2). (Illus.). 1,064p. 1993. text 165.00 (0-19-821755-2) OUP.

Cosgrove, Benedict. Covering the Bases: The Most Unforgettable Moments in Baseball in the Words of the Writers & Broadcasters Who Were There. LC 96-14861. (Illus.). 208p. 1997. pap. 14.95 (0-8118-1150-6) Chronicle Bks.

Cosgrove, Betty. Shoalwater Bay: On the Tracks of the Early Explorers. LC 97-199087. (Illus.). 108p. 1996. pap. 19.95 (1-875998-16-0, Pub. by Central Queensland) Accents Pubns.

***Cosgrove, Bill.** The Noble Breed. LC 99-65960. 304p. 1999. 19.95 (1-58244-063-8) Rutledge Bks.

Cosgrove, Bill. Robert DeNiro & the Fireman. 80p. 1997. 13.95 (1-887750-63-0) Rutledge Bks.

Cosgrove, Brian. Pilot's Weather: A Commonsense Approach to Metereology. (Illus.). 192p. 1999. 34.95 (1-882663-41-1) Plymouth VT.

***Cosgrove, Brian.** Weather. (Eyewitness Books). (Illus.). (J). (gr. 4-7). 2000. 19.99 (0-7894-6577-9) DK Pub Inc.

— Weather. (Eyewitness Books). (J). (gr. 4-7). 2000. 15.95 (0-7894-5782-2) DK Pub Inc.

Cosgrove, Brian. The World of Weather. (Illus.). 160p. 1997. 29.95 (1-85310-765-4, Pub. by Swan Hill Pr) Voyageur Pr.

Cosgrove, Brian, ed. Literature & the Supernatural: Essays for the Maynooth Bicentenary. LC 95-225665. 175p. 1995. pap. 49.95 (1-85607-143-X, Pub. by Columba Press) Intl Scholars.

— Literature & the Supernatural: Essays for the Maynooth Bicentenary. 175p. 1995. 64.95 (1-85607-215-0) Intl Scholars.

Cosgrove, Charles & Hatfield, Dennis. Church Conflict: The Hidden Systems Behind the Fights. LC 93-33081. 160p. (Orig.). 1994. pap. 13.95 (0-687-08152-1) Abingdon.

Cosgrove, Charles H. Elusive Israel: The Puzzle of Election in Romans. LC 97-2542. 1997. pap. 17.95 (0-664-25696-1) Westminster John Knox.

— A History of the One Hundred & Thirty-Fourth New York Volunteer Infantry Regiment in the American Civil War. LC 97-36256. (Studies in American History: Vol. 16). 512p. 1997. text 119.95 (0-7734-8551-1) E Mellen.

Cosgrove, Cornelius B. Caves of the Upper Gila & Hueco Areas in New Mexico & Texas. (HU PMP Ser.: Vol. 24, No. 1). 1947. 45.00 (0-527-01261-0) Periodicals Srv.

Cosgrove, D. & Petts, G., eds. Water Engineering & Landscape: Water Control & Landscape Transformation in the Modern Period. (Illus.). 192p. 1992. 51.95 (1-85293-069-1, Pub. by P P Pubs) CRC Pr.

Cosgrove, Daniel J. & Knievel, Daniel P., eds. Physiology of Cell Expansion During Plant Growth: Proceedings of the Second Annual Penn State Symposium in Plant Physiology. LC 87-72933. (Illus.). 329p. (C). 1987. pap. 20.00 (0-943088-11-9) Am Soc of Plan.

Cosgrove, David O., jt. auth. see Fukuda, Morimichi.

Cosgrove, Denis. The Palladian Landscape: Geographical Change & Its Cultural Representations in Sixteenth-Century Italy. LC 92-33774. (Illus.). 352p. (C). 1993. 65.00 (0-271-00942-X) Pa St U Pr.

Cosgrove, Denis, ed. Mappings. (Critical Views Ser.). (Illus.). 320p. 1999. pap. 27.00 (1-86189-021-4, Pub. by Reaktion Bks) Consort Bk Sales.

Cosgrove, Denis & Daniels, Stephen, eds. The Iconography of Landscapes: Essays on the Symbolic Representation, Design & Use of Past Environments. (Cambridge Studies in Historical Geography: No. 9). (Illus.). 328p. (C). 1989. pap. text 22.95 (0-521-38915-1) Cambridge U Pr.

***Cosgrove, Denis E.** Apollo's Eye: A Cartographic Genealogy of the Earth in the Western Imagination. LC 00-9623. 2001. write for info. (0-8018-6491-7) Johns Hopkins.

Cosgrove, Denis E. Social Formation & Symbolic Landscape. LC 97-48823. (Illus.). xxxvii, 293p. 1998. pap. 19.95 (0-299-15514-5) U of Wis Pr.

Cosgrove, Frances. Scenes for Student Actors, 6 Vols, 1. 5.00 (0-573-69025-1) French.

— Scenes for Student Actors, 6 Vols, 2. 5.00 (0-573-69026-X) French.

— Scenes for Student Actors, 6 Vols, 3. 5.00 (0-573-69027-8) French.

— Scenes for Student Actors, 6 Vols, 4. 5.00 (0-573-69028-6) French.

— Scenes for Student Actors, 6 Vols, 5. 5.00 (0-573-69029-4) French.

— Scenes for Student Actors, 6 Vols, 6. 5.00 (0-573-69030-8) French.

Cosgrove, Francis A., jt. ed. see Hoerner, Earl F.

Cosgrove, Francis M., Jr. Essentials of Discipleship. LC 88-61796. 192p. 1988. reprint ed. pap. 6.95 (0-86606-259-9, 833) Treasure Pub.

— Essentials of New Life. LC 88-61795. 180p. (Orig.). 1988. reprint ed. pap. 6.95 (0-86606-258-0, 832) Treasure Pub.

Cosgrove, Hannelore & Cosgrove, William C. Graded German Reader: Erste Stufe. 3rd ed. (ENG & GER.). 218p. (C). 1992. pap. text 29.16 (0-669-20159-6) HM Trade Div.

***Cosgrove, Holli.** Encyclopedia of Careers & Vocational Guidance, 4 vols. 11th ed. LC 99-16438. 262p. 1999. 159.95 (0-89434-274-6) Ferguson.

Cosgrove, Holli, ed. Career Discovery Encyclopedia: 1997 Edition, 6 vols. 3rd ed. LC 96-52611. (Illus.). 1100p. (J). (gr. 4 up). 1997. lib. bdg. 129.95 (0-89434-184-7, 694) Ferguson.

Cosgrove, Hollie, ed. Funk & Wagnalls New International Dictionary of the English Language, 2 vol. LC 99-178254. 1930p. 2000. 149.50 (0-89434-157-X) Ferguson.

Cosgrove, Irene. My Recipes Are for the Birds: Finch Fries, Dove Delights, Robin Russe, Wren Rolls, & More! LC 99-24942. (Illus.). 96p. 1999. pap. 7.95 (0-385-49547-1, Main St Bks) Doubleday.

Cosgrove, J. J. History of Sanitation. 1977. lib. bdg. 59.95 (0-8490-1985-0) Gordon Pr.

***Cosgrove, J. W. & Ameen, M. S., eds.** Forced Folds & Fractures. (Special Publication Ser.: No. 169). 260p. 2000. 108.00 (1-86239-060-6, Pub. by Geol Soc Pub Hse) AAPG.

Cosgrove, James C., ed. Medicare HMOs: Potential Effects of a Limited Enrollment Period Policy. (Illus.). 48p. (C). 1999. pap. text 20.00 (0-7881-7645-5) DIANE Pub.

Cosgrove, John & Jones, Mervyn, eds. Neotonics & Resources. LC 91-14592. 320p. 1994. text 115.00 (0-471-94513-7) Wiley.

Cosgrove, John, jt. auth. see Vinson, Ronald W.

Cosgrove, John, jt. ed. see Jones, Mervyn.

Cosgrove, Laurie, et al, eds. Restoring the Land: Environmental Values, Knowledge & Action. 288p. 1994. pap. 29.95 (0-522-84546-0, Pub. by Melbourne Univ Pr) Paul & Co Pubs.

Cosgrove, Mark. Counseling & Anger. (Resources for Christian Counseling Ser.: Vol. 16). 198p. 18.99 (0-8499-0598-2) Word Pub.

Cosgrove, Mark. Good Medicine. 88p. 1997. pap. 17.95 incl. audio compact disk (0-7866-3188-0, 96782BCD) Mel Bay.

Cosgrove, Mark P. The Essence of Human Nature. (Christian Free University Curriculum Ser.). 77p. (Orig.). (C). 1977. pap. 2.95 (0-310-35711-X) Probe Bks.

Cosgrove, Maryellen S. Distance Education & Teacher Education at Armstrong Atlantic State University. (Fastback Ser.: No. 440). 40p. 1998. pap. 3.00 (0-87367-640-8, FB440) Phi Delta Kappa.

Cosgrove, Michael H. The Cost of Winning: Global Development Policies & Broken Social Contracts. 317p. (C). 1996. text 39.95 (1-56000-229-8) Transaction Pubs.

Cosgrove, Owen. Morris: The Life & Works of Don H. Morris. (Illus.). 155p. (Orig.). 1993. pap. 11.95 (0-940999-89-7, C2247) Star Bible.

***Cosgrove, Patrick.** Sacramento. (City Smart Ser.). 240p. 2000. pap. 14.95 (1-56261-533-5, Pub. by Avalon Travel) Publishers Group.

Cosgrove, Peter. Impartial Stranger: History & Intertextuality in Gibbon's Decline & Fall of the Roman Empire. LC 98-43955. 288p. 1999. 43.50 (0-87413-658-X) U Delaware Pr.

Cosgrove, Richard A. Scholars of the Law: English Jurisprudence from Blackstone to Hart. LC 95-41782. 296p. (C). 1996. text 47.50 (0-8147-1533-8) NYU Pr.

Cosgrove, Richard A., jt. auth. see Dicey, Albert V.

Cosgrove, Richard A., jt. ed. see Shinn, Ridgway F., Jr.

Cosgrove-Sacks, Carol & Scappucci, Gioia. The European Union & Developing Countries: The Challenges of Globalization. LC 97-40582. 388p. 1999. text 79.95 (0-312-21189-9) St Martin.

Cosgrove, Stephen. Ark Angels. (Illus.). 32p. (J). 14.69 (1-56239-997-7) ABDO Pub Co.

Cosgrove, Stephen. Balderdash. (Dreammaker Ser.). (Illus.). 32p. (J). (gr. 3-6). 1991. 14.95 (1-55868-045-4) Gr Arts Ctr Pub.

An Asterisk (*) at the beginning of an entry indicates that the title is appearing for the first time.

— Bangalee. (Serendipity Bks.). (Illus.). 32p. (J). (gr. k-4). 1978. pap. 4.99 (*0-8431-0550-X*, Price Stern) Peng Put Young Read.
— Buttermilk Bear. LC 89-832099. (Serendipity Bks.). (Illus.). 32p. (J). (gr. k-4). 1995. pap. 3.95 (*0-8431-3828-9*, Price Stern) Peng Put Young Read.
Cosgrove, Stephen. Butterwings. (Serendipity Bks.). (Illus.). 32p. (J). (ps-3). 1996. pap. 4.99 (*0-8431-3920-X*, Price Stern) Peng Put Young Read.
Cosgrove, Stephen. Catundra. (Serendipity Bks.). (Illus.). 32p. (J). (gr. k-4). 1978. pap. 4.99 (*0-8431-0571-2*, Price Stern) Peng Put Young Read.
— Crabby Gabby. LC 85-14351. (Serendipity Bks.). (Illus.). 32p. (J). (gr. k-4). 1985. pap. 4.99 (*0-8431-1441-X*, Price Stern) Peng Put Young Read.
— Crabby Gabby. 1985. 9.15 (*0-606-02377-1*, Pub. by Turtleback) Demco.
***Cosgrove, Stephen.** Creole. (Illus.). 32p. (ps-3). 2000. pap. 4.99 (*0-8431-7631-8*, Price Stern) Peng Put Young Read.
Cosgrove, Stephen. Crickle-Crack. (Serendipity Bks.). (Illus.). 32p. (J). (gr. 1-4). 1987. pap. 4.99 (*0-8431-1909-8*, Price Stern) Peng Put Young Read.
— Dragolin. LC 94-25729. (Serendipity Bks.). (Illus.). 32p. (J). (gr. 1-4). 1995. pap. 4.99 (*0-8431-3825-4*, Price Stern) Peng Put Young Read.
Cosgrove, Stephen. Dragolin. (Serendipity Ser.). (J). 1995. 9.15 (*0-606-02380-1*, Pub. by Turtleback) Demco.
Cosgrove, Stephen. The Dream Stealer. LC 89-83843. (Dreammaker Ser.). (Illus.). 32p. (J). (gr. 1-4). 1990. 16.95 (*1-55868-009-8*) Gr Arts Ctr Pub.
— The Dream Tree. (Serendipity Bks.). (Illus.). 32p. (J). (gr. 1-4). 1978. pap. 4.99 (*0-8431-0553-4*, Price Stern) Peng Put Young Read.
— The Dream Tree. 1974. 9.15 (*0-606-02381-X*, Pub. by Turtleback) Demco.
— Earth Angels: Birthday. (Illus.). 12p. (J). (ps up). 1994. 2.95 (*1-56288-481-6*) Checkerboard.
— Earth Angels: Finnigan Firewing. (Illus.). 32p. (J). (ps-2). 1994. pap. 2.95 (*1-56288-476-X*) Checkerboard.
— Earth Angels: Flutter Fly. (Illus.). 12p. (J). (ps up). 1994. 2.95 (*1-56288-480-8*) Checkerboard.
— Earth Angels: Hannah Go Brightly. (Illus.). 32p. (J). (ps-2). 1994. pap. 2.95 (*1-56288-477-8*) Checkerboard.
— Earth Angels: Jacob Jinglehinder. (Illus.). 32p. (J). (ps-2). 1994. pap. 2.95 (*1-56288-478-6*) Checkerboard.
— Earth Angels: One-Two-Three. (Illus.). 12p. (J). (ps up). 1994. 2.95 (*1-56288-483-2*) Checkerboard.
— Earth Angels: Rainbow. (Illus.). 12p. (J). (ps up). 1994. 2.95 (*1-56288-482-4*) Checkerboard.
— Earth Angels: The Ark Angels. (Illus.). 32p. (J). (ps-2). 1994. pap. 2.95 (*1-56288-475-1*) Checkerboard.
— Earth Angels Handbook. (Illus.). 64p. (J). (ps up). 1994. 2.95 (*1-56288-485-9*) Checkerboard.
— Easter Bunnies. (Illus.). 32p. (J). (gr. k-5). 1992. pap. 4.95 (*0-8249-8538-9*, Ideals Child) Hambleton-Hill.
— Fanny. (Serendipity Bks.). (Illus.). 32p. (Orig.). (J). (gr. 1-4). 1986. pap. 4.99 (*0-8431-1460-6*, Price Stern) Peng Put Young Read.
— Feather Fin. LC 84-15057. (Serendipity Bks.). (Illus.). 32p. (J). (gr. 2 up). 1983. pap. 4.99 (*0-8431-0593-3*, Price Stern) Peng Put Young Read.
— Feather Fin. (Serendipity Ser.). (J). 1985. 9.15 (*0-606-02382-8*, Pub. by Turtleback) Demco.
Cosgrove, Stephen. Finnigan FireWing. (Illus.). 32p. (J). (gr. k-4). 11.95 (*1-56239-996-9*) ABDO Pub Co.
Cosgrove, Stephen. Flutterby. LC 94-28341. (Serendipity Bks.). (Illus.). 32p. (J). (gr. 1-4). 1995. pap. 4.99 (*0-8431-3821-1*, Price Stern) Peng Put Young Read.
— Flutterby. (Serendipity Ser.). 1995. 9.15 (*0-606-02383-6*, Pub. by Turtleback) Demco.
— Frazzle. LC 90-60297. (Serendipity Bks.). (Illus.). 32p. (Orig.). (J). (gr. 1-4). 1990. pap. 4.99 (*0-8431-2838-0*, Price Stern) Peng Put Young Read.
— Gabby. (Serendipity Bks.). (Illus.). 32p. (J). (gr. 1-4). 1983. pap. 4.99 (*0-8431-1401-0*, Price Stern) Peng Put Young Read.
Cosgrove, Stephen. Gabby. (Serendipity Ser.). (J). 1985. 9.15 (*0-606-02386-0*, Pub. by Turtleback) Demco.
Cosgrove, Stephen. Gnome from Nome. (Serendipity Bks.). (Illus.). 32p. (J). (gr. 1-4). 1978. pap. 4.99 (*0-8431-0555-0*, Price Stern) Peng Put Young Read.
Cosgrove, Stephen. Gnome from Nome. (Serendipity Ser.). (J). 1986. 9.15 (*0-606-02388-7*, Pub. by Turtleback) Demco.
Cosgrove, Stephen. Grampa-Lop. LC 84-15078. (Serendipity Bks.). (Illus.). 32p. (J). (ps-3). 1981. pap. 4.99 (*0-8431-0586-0*, Price Stern) Peng Put Young Read.
Cosgrove, Stephen. Grampa-Lop. (Serendipity Ser.). (J). 1985. 9.15 (*0-606-02389-5*, Pub. by Turtleback) Demco.
Cosgrove, Stephen. The Grumpling. LC 89-60559. (Serendipity Bks.). (Illus.). 32p. (Orig.). (J). (ps-3). 1989. pap. 4.99 (*0-8431-2739-2*, Price Stern) Peng Put Young Read.
Cosgrove, Stephen. Hannah GoBrightly. (Illus.). 32p. (J). (gr. k-4). 11.95 (*1-56239-998-5*) ABDO Pub Co.
Cosgrove, Stephen. Harmony. LC 89-83842. (Song of the Sea Ser.). (Illus.). 72p. (J). (gr. 7 up). 1991. text 24.95 (*1-55868-008-X*) Gr Arts Ctr Pub.
— Heidi's Rose. LC 90-71079. (Illus.). 32p. (J). (gr. 3-6). 1991. 14.95 (*1-55868-033-0*) Gr Arts Ctr Pub.
— Hucklebug. (Serendipity Bks.). (Illus.). 32p. (J). (gr. 1-4). 1978. pap. 4.99 (*0-8431-0556-9*, Price Stern) Peng Put Young Read.
Cosgrove, Stephen. Hucklebug. (Serendipity Ser.). (J). 1986. 9.15 (*0-606-02393-3*, Pub. by Turtleback) Demco.
— Jacob Jinglehinder. (Illus.). 32p. 11.95 (*1-56239-995-0*) ABDO Pub Co.
Cosgrove, Stephen. Jingle Bear. (Serendipity Bks.). (Illus.). 32p. (J). (gr. 1-4). 1985. pap. 3.95 (*0-8431-1440-1*, Price Stern) Peng Put Young Read.
— Jingle Bear. (Serendipity Ser.). (J). 1986. 9.15 (*0-606-02395-X*, Pub. by Turtleback) Demco.
— Lady Rose. (Serendipity Bks.). (Illus.). 32p. (Orig.). (J). (ps-3). 1996. pap. 4.99 (*0-8431-3921-8*, Price Stern) Peng Put Young Read.
— Leo the Lop. LC 94-21448. (Serendipity Bks.). (Illus.). 32p. (J). (gr. 1-4). 1995. pap. 4.99 (*0-8431-3820-3*, Price Stern) Peng Put Young Read.
Cosgrove, Stephen. Leo the Lop. (Serendipity Bks.). 1978. 9.15 (*0-606-06122-3*, Pub. by Turtleback) Demco.
— Leo the Lop. (J). 1995. 9.15 (*0-606-02402-6*, Pub. by Turtleback) Demco.
Cosgrove, Stephen. Leo the Lop: Tail Three. (Serendipity Bks.). (Illus.). 32p. (J). (ps-3). 1980. pap. 4.99 (*0-8431-0577-1*, Price Stern) Peng Put Young Read.
Cosgrove, Stephen. Leo the Lop: Tail Two. (Serendipity Bks.). (J). 1978. 9.15 (*0-606-02403-4*, Pub. by Turtleback) Demco.
— Little Mouse on the Prairie. (Serendipity Bks.). (Illus.). 32p. (J). (ps-3). 2000. pap. 4.99 (*0-8431-7632-6*, Price Stern) Peng Put Young Read.
Cosgrove, Stephen. Little Mouse on the Prairie. (Serendipity Bks.). (J). 1978. 9.15 (*0-606-02404-2*, Pub. by Turtleback) Demco.
— Maui-Maui. LC 94-21449. (Serendipity Bks.). (Illus.). 32p. (J). (gr. k-4). 1995. pap. 4.99 (*0-8431-3829-7*, Price Stern) Peng Put Young Read.
— Memily. LC 99-158475. (Illus.). 1994. write for info. (*0-8431-3792-4*) Price Stern.
— Memily. rev. ed. LC 94-25728. (Serendipity Bks.). (Illus.). 32p. (J). (ps-3). 1995. pap. 4.99 (*0-8431-3822-X*, Price Stern) Peng Put Young Read.
— Ming Ling. (Serendipity Ser.). 1986. 9.15 (*0-606-02415-8*, Pub. by Turtleback) Demco.
***Cosgrove, Stephen.** Minikin. (Illus.). 32p. (Orig.). (ps-3). 2000. pap. 4.99 (*0-8431-7629-6*, Price Stern) Peng Put Young Read.
Cosgrove, Stephen. Morgan & Me. LC 78-101413. (Serendipity Bks.). (Illus.). 32p. (J). (ps-3). 1978. pap. 4.99 (*0-8431-0560-7*, Price Stern) Peng Put Young Read.
— Morgan & Me. (Serendipity Ser.). 1985. 9.15 (*0-606-02418-2*, Pub. by Turtleback) Demco.
— Morgan & Yew. (Serendipity Bks.). (Illus.). 32p. (Orig.). (J). (gr. 1-4). 1982. pap. 4.99 (*0-8431-0589-5*, Price Stern) Peng Put Young Read.
— Morgan Morning. (Serendipity Bks.). (Illus.). 32p. (Orig.). (J). (ps-3). 1996. pap. 3.95 (*0-8431-3923-4*, Price Stern) Peng Put Young Read.
— Muffin Muncher. (Serendipity Ser.). 1986. 9.15 (*0-606-02419-0*, Pub. by Turtleback) Demco.
— Nitter Pitter. (Serendipity Bks.). (Illus.). 32p. (J). (gr. 1-4). 1978. pap. 4.99 (*0-8431-0570-4*, Price Stern) Peng Put Young Read.
Cosgrove, Stephen. Persnickity. (Serendipity Bks.). (Illus.). 32p. (J). (gr. 1-4). 1988. pap. 4.99 (*0-8431-2303-6*, Price Stern) Peng Put Young Read.
Cosgrove, Stephen. Persnickity. (Serendipity Ser.). (J). 1988. lib. bdg. 18.60 (*0-86592-782-0*) Rourke Enter.
— Poppyseed. (Serendipity Bks.). (Illus.). 32p. (Orig.). (J). (ps-3). 1996. pap. 4.99 (*0-8431-3924-2*, Price Stern) Peng Put Young Read.
— Prancer. LC 89-83843. (Illus.). 32p. (J). (gr. k-7). 1990. 14.95 (*1-55868-019-5*); pap. 12.95 incl. audio (*1-55868-041-1*) Gr Arts Ctr Pub.
— Raz-Ma-Taz. (Serendipity Bks.). (Illus.). 32p. (J). (ps-3). 1982. pap. 4.99 (*0-8431-0588-7*, Price Stern) Peng Put Young Read.
Cosgrove, Stephen. Raz-Ma-Taz. (Serendipity Bks.). (J). 1984. 9.15 (*0-606-02425-5*, Pub. by Turtleback) Demco.
Cosgrove, Stephen. Read on Rita. (Stephen Cosgrove Storybook Readers Ser.). (Illus.). 32p. (J). (ps up). 1993. lib. bdg. 13.95 (*1-56674-042-8*, HTS Bks) Forest Hse.
— Rhubarb. (Serendipity Ser.). (J). 1989. lib. bdg. 18.60 (*0-86592-783-9*) Rourke Enter.
— Rhubarb. rev. ed. LC 95-163711. (Serendipity Bks.). (Illus.). 32p. (J). (ps-3). 1995. pap. 4.99 (*0-8431-3824-6*, Price Stern) Peng Put Young Read.
— Sassafras. (Serendipity Ser.). (J). lib. bdg. 18.60 (*0-86592-784-7*) Rourke Enter.
— Sassafras. rev. ed. LC 95-163717. (Serendipity Bks.). (Illus.). 32p. (J). (ps-3). 1995. pap. 3.95 (*0-8431-3830-0*, Price Stern) Peng Put Young Read.
— Serendipity. 1995. 9.15 (*0-606-02428-X*, Pub. by Turtleback) Demco.
— Serendipity. rev. ed. LC 94-25575. (Serendipity Bks.). (Illus.). 32p. (J). (ps-3). 1995. pap. 4.99 (*0-8431-3819-X*, Price Stern) Peng Put Young Read.
— Sharing. LC 91-71221. (Song of the Sea Triology Ser.: Bk. 3). (Illus.). 72p. 1991. 24.95 (*1-55868-066-7*) Gr Arts Ctr Pub.
— Sniffles. (Serendipity Ser.). (J). 1988. lib. bdg. 18.60 (*0-86592-785-5*) Rourke Enter.
— Sniffles (Relaunch) (Illus.). 32p. (J). (ps-3). 1995. pap. 4.99 (*0-8431-3827-0*, Price Stern) Peng Put Young Read.
— Squeakers. (Serendipity Bks.). (Illus.). 32p. (J). (ps-3). 1996. pap. 4.99 (*0-8431-3925-0*, Price Stern) Peng Put Young Read.
— Squeakers. (Serendipity Ser.). 1985. 9.15 (*0-606-02429-8*, Pub. by Turtleback) Demco.
— Stephen Cosgrove's Storybook Readers, 5, Set. (Illus.). 128p. Date not set. lib. bdg. 73.75 (*1-56674-921-2*) Forest Hse.
— Trapper. LC 84-15058. (Serendipity Bks.). (Illus.). 32p. (J). (ps-3). 1981. pap. 4.99 (*0-8431-0587-9*, Price Stern) Peng Put Young Read.
— Trapper. (Serendipity Ser.). 1986. 9.15 (*0-606-02439-5*, Pub. by Turtleback) Demco.
***Cosgrove, Stephen.** Zippity Zoom. (Illus.). 32p. (Orig.). (ps-3). 2000. pap. 4.99 (*0-8431-7630-X*, Price Stern) Peng Put Young Read.
Cosgrove, Stephen E. Gigglesnitcher. (Illus.). 32p. (J). (gr. k-9). 1991. 12.95 (*1-55868-034-9*) Gr Arts Ctr Pub.
— Laughter Ring. (Song of the Sea Trilogy Ser.: Bk. 2). (Illus.). 72p. 1990. 24.95 (*1-55868-032-2*) Gr Arts Ctr Pub.
— T. J. Flopp. LC 89-9329. (Stephen Cosgrove's Value Tales Ser.). (Illus.). 32p. (J). (gr. k-4). 1989. lib. bdg. 21.36 (*0-89565-660-4*) Childs World.
Cosgrove, Thomas H. Last Climb: A Novel of Suspense. LC 98-53467. 320p. 1999. 23.00 (*0-684-83414-6*) S&S Trade.
Cosgrove, Vincent, jt. auth. see Manca, John.
Cosgrove, William C., jt. auth. see Cosgrove, Hannelore.
Cosgrove, William M., III. Time on Target: The 945th Field Artillery Battalion in World War II. (Illus.). 225p. 1997. 35.00 (*0-9656892-0-4*) W Cosgrove.
***Cosgrove, William M., et al, eds.** RCRA Waste Management: Planning, Implementation & Assessment of Sampling Activities. LC 00-28895. (MNL, Manual Ser.: Vol. 42). (Illus.). 80p. 2000. pap. text 45.00 (*0-8031-2085-0*, MNL42) ASTM.
Cosh, Andy & Hughes, Alan. Takeovers, Vols. I-III. LC 98-3786. (International Library of Management). (Illus.). 1687p. 1998. text 538.95 (*1-85521-556-X*, Pub. by Dartmth Pub) Ashgate Pub Co.
Cosh, J. A. & Lever, J. L. Rheumatic Diseases & the Heart. (Illus.). 225p. 1989. 121.00 (*0-387-19524-6*) Spr-Verlag.
Cosh, Mary, jt. auth. see Lindsay, Ian G.
Cosh, O. Glenn. Cycling in the Slow Lane. 112p. 1993. pap. 6.95 (*0-9638094-0-7*) G M C Cycling.
Cosh, Sylvia. Crochet Workbook. 3rd ed. 1990. pap. 17.95 (*0-312-04032-6*) St Martin.
Cosi, V., et al, eds. Amyotrophic Lateral Sclerosis: Therapeutic, Psychological & Research Aspects. LC 87-1748. (Advances in Experimental Medicine & Biology Ser.: Vol. 209). 372p. 1987. 89.50 (*0-306-42546-7*, Plenum Trade) Perseus Pubng.
Cosialls. Admisiones Hospitalarias. (C). 1995. text 25.50 (*84-8174-080-2*) Mosby Inc.
Cosic, Bora. My Family's Role in the World Revolution & Other Prose. Bigelow, Ann C., tr. LC 97-15118. 1997. pap. text 16.95 (*0-8101-1368-6*) Northwestern U Pr.
— My Family's Role in the World Revolution & Other Prose. Bigelow, Ann C., tr. LC 97-15118. (Writings from an Unbound Europe Ser.). 1997. 49.95 (*0-8101-1367-8*) Northwestern U Pr.
Cosic, Dobrica. Reach to Eternity. Heppell, Muriel, tr. LC 79-2234. 480p. 1980. 14.95 (*0-15-175961-8*) Harcourt.
— South to Destiny. LC 80-8764. 480p. 1982. 19.95 (*0-15-184486-0*) Harcourt.
— This Land, This Time, 4 vols., Set. Heppell, Muriel, tr. Incl. Reach to Eternity. 1983. pap. 7.95 (*0-15-676012-6*, Harvest Bks); South to Destiny. 1983. pap. 7.95 (*0-15-683913-X*, Harvest Bks); Time of Death. 1983. pap. 7.95 (*0-15-690445-4*, Harvest Bks); 1983. reprint ed. Set pap. 29.95 (*0-15-690026-2*, Harvest Bks) Harcourt.
Cosic, I. The Resonant Recognition Model of Macromolecular Bioactivity: Theory & Applications. LC 96-43992. (Biomethods Ser.). 1996. write for info. (*0-8176-5487-9*) Birkhauser.
— The Resonant Recognition Model of Macromolecular Bioactivity: Theory & Applications. LC 96-43992. (BioMethods Ser.: Vol. 8). (Illus.). 160p. 1997. 79.50 (*3-7643-5487-9*) Birkhauser.
Cosimano, Charles. PSI Magick Course. Templar, Thorguard, ed. 240p. 1993. 120.00 (*1-883147-94-8*) Intern Guild ASRS.
— PSI Magick Course, 8 lessons, Set. Templar, Thorguard, ed. 240p. 1993. 120.00 (*1-883147-93-X*) Intern Guild ASRS.
— Psionic Combat. Templar, Thorguard, ed. (Illus.). 112p. 1993. 65.00 (*1-883147-59-X*); 65.00 (*1-883147-60-3*) Intern Guild ASRS.
— Psionic Gadget Book. Templar, Thorguard, ed. (Illus.). 110p. (Orig.). 1993. spiral bd. 29.95 (*1-883147-61-1*); spiral bd. 29.95 (*1-883147-62-X*) Intern Guild ASRS.
— Psionic Path: Psychotronic Path. (Illus.). 115p. 1997. 35.00 (*1-57179-058-6*) Intern Guild ASRS.
Cosimano, T. F., et al. The Changing Distribution of Income in an Open U.S. Economy. Bergstrand, Jeffrey H., ed. LC 94-3996. (Contributions to Economic Analysis Ser.: Vol. 223). 412p. 1994. 117.00 (*0-444-81559-7*, North Holland) Elsevier.
Cosimo, Mariano. Mariano Cosimo Italian-Latin Dictionary. (ITA & LAT.). 1644p. 1988. 95.00 (*0-8288-7341-0*) Fr & Eur.
Cosin, Elizabeth. Zen & the Art of Murder. LC 98-19402. (Zen Moses Ser.). 288p. 1998. text 22.95 (*0-312-19376-9*) St Martin.
— Zen & the Art of Murder. 304p. 1999. pap. 5.99 (*0-312-96948-1*, Minotaur) St Martin.
— Zen & the City of Angels. LC 99-15940. 288p. 1999. text 23.95 (*0-312-20611-9*) St Martin.
***Cosin, Elizabeth M.** Zen & the City of Angels. 304p. 2000. mass mkt. 5.99 (*0-312-97446-9*) St Martin.
Cosin, John. Complete Works of John Cosin, 5 vols. LC 72-1028. (Library of Anglo-Catholic Theology: No. 5). reprint ed. write for info. (*0-404-52080-4*) AMS Pr.
***Cosio, Robyn.** The Eyebrow. (Illus.). 208p. 2000. pap. 30.00 (*0-06-039326-2*, ReganBks) HarperTrade.
Cosker, Joanne, jt. ed. see Waigand, Ann H.
***Coski, John.** Capital Navy: The Men, Ships & Operations of the James River Squadron. 2000. pap. 18.95 (*1-882810-85-6*) Savas Pub.
Coski, John. Capital Navy: The Men, Ships & Operations of the James River Squadron. LC 97-121409. (Illus.). 343p. 1997. reprint ed. 29.95 (*1-882810-03-1*, 03-1) Savas Pub.
Coski, John, ed. The Museum of the Confederacy: Treasures from the Archives. (Civil War Regiments Ser.: Vol. 5). (Illus.). 190p. 1996. pap. 12.00 (*1-882810-51-1*) Savas Pub.
Coski, John, ed. see Fullerton, Christopher D.
Cosko, Lizette, ed. see Cosko, Tatjana.
Cosko, Tatjana. Scrumptious Swedish Recipes. Cosko, Lizette, ed. 104p. 1996. pap., spiral bd. 8.95 (*1-889028-00-2*, 1001) TALI Bks.
Coskran, Kathleen. The High Price of Everything. (Minnesota Voices Project Ser.: Vol. 33). 133p. 1988. pap. 7.95 (*0-89823-102-7*) New Rivers Pr.
Coskran, Kathleen & Truesdale, C. W., eds. An Inn near Kyoto: Writing by American Women Abroad. LC 97-68817. (New Rivers Abroad Ser.). 480p. 1998. pap. 21.95 (*0-89823-181-7*) New Rivers Pr.
— Tanzania on Tuesday: Writing by American Women Abroad. LC 96-72513. 436p. 1997. pap. 19.95 (*0-89823-179-5*) New Rivers Pr.
Coslet, Dorothy. Madame Jeanne Guyon: Child of Another World. 219p. 1992. pap. 6.99 (*0-87508-144-4*) Chr Lit.
Cosley, Betty. The Story of Tiny McShane. large type ed. LC 98-96207. (Illus.). viii, 24p. (J). (ps-3). 1998. 14.95 (*0-9664588-0-X*) Cosley Prod.
Coslick, Merlin B. Billing Center Directory of Forms & Marketing Materials. (Illus.). 135p. 1998. pap. 29.95 (*1-893978-01-X*) Electron Med Bill.
— How to Buy New Jersey Tax Liens That Earn 18 Percent. (Illus.). 139p. 1993. pap. 19.95 (*1-893978-00-1*) Electron Med Bill.
— Medical Billing Home-Based Business: Success in Marketing & Consulting, Vol. II. 64p. 1998. pap. 4.95 (*1-893978-03-6*) Electron Med Bill.
— Medical Billing Home-Based Business Vol. I: Success in Management & Business Strategies. 66p. 1998. pap. 4.95 (*1-893978-02-8*) Electron Med Bill.
— Medical Billing Home-Based Business Vol. III: More Success in Marketing & Consulting. 85p. 1999. pap. 7.95 (*1-893978-04-4*) Electron Med Bill.
— Setting up Your Medical Billing Business: Step by Step Procedures for Beginning a Computer-Based Home Business. (Illus.). 122p. 1999. pap. 49.95 (*1-893978-05-2*) Electron Med Bill.
Coslick, Ronald T., jt. auth. see Baroody, Arthur J.
Cosloy, Sharon, jt. auth. see Steinberg, Mark L.
Cosloy, Sharon D., jt. auth. see Steinberg, Mark L.
Cosma, Flavia. The Fire That Burns Us. Wilson, Don D., tr. from RUM. 120p. 1996. pap. 11.00 (*1-880286-34-3*) Singular Speech Pr.
— Forty-Seven Poems. Wilson, Don D., tr. from RUM. vii, 99p. 1992. 24.95 (*0-89672-304-6*) Tex Tech Univ Pr.
Cosman, Carol. Penguin Book of Women Poets. 1978. 19.05 (*0-606-02186-8*, Pub. by Turtleback) Demco.
Cosman, Carol, et al, eds. The Penguin Book of Women Poets. (Poetry Ser.). 400p. 1986. pap. 13.95 (*0-14-058533-8*, Penguin Bks) Viking Penguin.
Cosman, Carol, jt. auth. see Alter, Robert.
Cosman, Carol, tr. see Balzac, Honore de.
Cosman, Carol, tr. see Baudelaire, Charles.
Cosman, Carol, tr. see Bayard, Pierre.
Cosman, Carol, tr. see Bouveresse, Jacques.
Cosman, Carol, tr. see Delbo, Charlotte.
Cosman, Carol, tr. see Goldberg, Sylvie-Anne.
Cosman, Carol, tr. see LaPierre, Alexandra.
Cosman, Carol, tr. see Reza, Yasmina.
Cosman, Carol, tr. see Sartre, Jean-Paul.
Cosman, Madeleine P. Fabulous Feasts: Medieval Cookery & Ceremony. LC 76-15909. (Illus.). 1976. pap. 24.95 (*0-8076-0898-X*) Braziller.
— Kissing the Dragon: The Intelligent Work-Hunter's Companion. LC 84-71095. (Illus.). 128p. 1984. pap. 9.99 (*0-916491-07-2*) Bard Hall Pr.
— The Medieval Baker's Daughter: A Bilingual Adventure in Medieval Life with Costumes, Banners, Music, Food, & a Mystery Play. LC 84-71590.Tr. of La/Hija de la Panadera Medieval. (ENG & SPA., Illus.). 112p. (J). (gr. 3-12). 1984. pap. 7.95 (*0-916491-18-8*) Bard Hall Pr.
— Medieval Wordbook. LC 95-15335. 304p. 1996. 35.00 (*0-8160-3021-9*) Facts on File.
Cosman, Madeleine P., ed. see De Pizan, Christine.
***Cosman, Madeline Pelner.** Women at Work in Medieval Europe. LC 99-47886. (Illus.). 176p. 2000. 29.95 (*0-8160-3125-8*) Facts on File.
Cosman, Milein, jt. auth. see Keller, Hans.
Cosmann, Richard. Sacrifice & Other Stories. 72p. (Orig.). 1998. pap. write for info. (*0-9667236-5-1*) Azrael Pr.
Cosmao, Vincent. Changing the World: An Agenda for the Churches. LC 84-5153.Tr. of Changer le monde-une tache pour l'eglise. 127p. (Orig.). reprint ed. pap. 39.40 (*0-8357-8548-3*, 203486200091) Bks Demand.
Cosmatom Staff. Big Bang Theory - or Rotating Universe? (C). 1992. pap. 35.00 (*1-874686-06-8*, Pub. by Cosmatom) St Mut.
— The Genetic Code of the Oscillating 5D Atom: Space & Time - The Birth of Existence. (C). 1992. pap. 25.00 (*1-874686-04-1*, Pub. by Cosmatom) St Mut.
— Letter to a Non-Believer. (C). 1992. pap. 25.00 (*1-874686-05-X*, Pub. by Cosmatom) St Mut.
— Rotation of Spheres (TCP) in Five Dimensions: A Sphere or Charge (4D) Moves in a Cylinder of (4D) Time. (C). 1992. pap. text 25.00 (*1-874686-07-6*, Pub. by Cosmatom) St Mut.
Cosme, Felix. Junior Handling. (Illus.). 160p. 1993. 14.95 (*0-948955-51-1*, Pub. by Ringpr Bks) Seven Hills Bk.
Cosme, Flavia. Fata Morgana. Barkan, Stanley H., ed. Wilson, Donald, tr. (Review Chapbook Ser.: No. 25: Romanian Poetry 2).Tr. of Romanian & Eng. 48p. 1992. 15.00 (*0-89304-958-1*); pap. 5.00 (*0-89304-959-X*) Cross-Cultrl NY.
— Fata Morgana: Mini Book. Barkan, Stanley H., ed.

C

Wilson, Donald, tr. (Review Chapbook Ser.: No. 25: Romanian Poetry 2).Tr. of Romanian & Eng.. 48p. 1992. 15.00 (*0-89304-960-3*); pap. 5.00 (*0-89304-961-1*) Cross-Cultrl NY.

Cosmelli, C. & Diambrini-Palazzi, G. Phenomenology of Unification from Present to Future. 508p. 1995. text 106.00 (*981-02-2106-1*) World Scientific Pub.

Cosmi, E V. Recent Advances in Perinatal Medicine. (Science & Culture Series--Medicine Ser.). 170p. 1999. 49.00 (*981-02-3933-5*) World Scientific Pub.

Cosmi, E. V. & Di Renzo, G. C., eds. Current Progress in Perinatal Medicine: Proceedings of the World Congress of Perinatal Medicine, 1993, Rome & Florence, Italy. 2nd ed. (Illus.). 902p. (C). 1994. text 95.00 (*1-85070-560-7*) Prthnon Pub.

— Proceedings of XI European Congress of Perinatal Medicine. xvi, 874p. 1989. pap. text 249.00 (*3-7186-4919-5*) Gordon & Breach.

Cosmi, Ermelando V. New Technologies in Reproductive Medicine, Neonatology & Gynecology: The Proceedings of the 1st International Symposium, Folgaria, Italy. LC 99-21828. (Illus.). 368p. 1999. 88.00 (*1-85070-065-6*) Prthnon Pub.

Cosmi, Ermelando V., ed. Labor & Delivery: The Proceedings of the 2nd World Congress on Labor & Delivery, May 1997, Rome Italy. (Illus.). 586p. 1998. 80.00 (*1-85070-973-4*) Prthnon Pub.

Cosmi, Ermelando V., et al. Advances in Perinantal Medicine, Vol. 1. x, 314p. 1988. text 129.00 (*3-7186-0463-9*) Gordon & Breach.

Cosmi, Ermelando V., ed. see Scarpelli, Emile M.

Cosmi, Ermelando V., jt. ed. see Scarpelli, Emile M.

***Cosmides, Leda & Tooby, John.** What Is Evolutionary Psychology? Explaining the New Science of the Mind. 64p. 2000. 9.95 (*0-300-08309-2*) Yale U Pr.

Cosmochemistry Symposium Staff. Cosmochemistry: Proceedings of the Symposium, Cambridge, MA, Aug. 1972. Cameron, A. G., ed. LC 73-88588. (Astrophysics & Space Science Library: No. 40). 180p. 1973. lib. bdg. 78.00 (*90-277-0394-9*) Kluwer Academic.

Cosmopolitan Editors, ed. The Cosmopolitan Beauty Book. 1924. write for info. (*0-688-16596-6*, Hearst) Hearst Commns.

Cosmopolitan Editors, ed. Cosmo's Bedside Quiz Book. LC 98-49659. 1999. pap. 10.00 (*0-688-16623-7*, Hearst) Hearst Commns.

Cosmopoulos, Michael B. The Early Bronze Age 2 in the Aegean. (Studies in Mediterranean Archaeology: Vol. XCVIII). (Illus.). 341p. (Orig.). 1991. pap. 86.50 (*91-7081-019-2*, Pub. by P Astroms) Coronet Bks.

Cosmovici, ed. see International Conference on Supernovae Staff.

Cosnard, M. Parallel Algorithms & Architectures. LC 95-228378. 1995. pap. 49.95 (*1-85032-125-6*) Thomson Learn.

Cosnard, Michael, et al, eds. Parallel & Distributed Computing: Theory & Practice; First Canada-France Conference, Montreal, Canada, May 19-21, 1994, Proceedings. LC 94-15892. (Lecture Notes in Computer Science Ser.: Vol. 805). 1994. write for info. (*0-387-58078-6*) Spr-Verlag.

Cosnard, Michel, ed. see Working Conference on Parallel Architectures & Com & Silberman, Gabriel M.

Cosner, Shaaron. The Light Bulb: Inventions That Changed Our Lives. LC 83-40398. 64p. (J). (gr. 5 up). 1984. lib. bdg. 10.85 (*0-8027-6527-0*) Walker & Co.

Cosner, Shaaron. Rubber. 1987. 10.85 (*0-8027-6654-4*) Walker & Co.

Cosner, Shaaron. War Nurses. (American History Series for Young People). (YA). (gr. 7 up). 1988. 16.95 (*0-8027-6826-1*); 17.85 (*0-8027-6828-8*) Walker & Co.

Cosner, Shaaron & Cosner, Victoria. Women under the Third Reich: A Biographical Dictionary. LC 97-45641. 224p. 1998. 55.00 (*0-313-30315-0*, Greenwood Pr) Greenwood.

Cosner, Shaaron, jt. auth. see Scanlon, Jennifer.

Cosner, Victoria, jt. auth. see Cosner, Shaaron.

Cosnett, Jay. PageMaker 5.0 for the Macintosh: Techniques & Applications. 1995. pap. 29.95 incl. disk (*1-55828-286-6*, MIS Pr) IDG Bks.

Cosola, Mary. Independent Working Musician: A Complete Guide to Do-It-Yourself Success in the Music Industry. LC 98-67690. 1998. pap. 24.95 (*0-87288-687-5*) Intertec Pub.

Cosolo, Nicci. The Competency Primer. 133p. 1995. spiral bd. 130.00 (*1-879575-55-8*) Acad Med Sys.

C.O.S.P.A.R International Space Science Symposium - London - Jul 26-27 1967, et al. Cloning Vectors, a Laboratory Manual, Vol. 2. Dollfus, A., ed. 1968. 14.25 (*0-7204-0129-1*) Elsevier.

COSPAR Staff & Hsiao, Fei-Bin. Microsatellites as Research Tools: Proceedings of Cospar Colloquium on Microsatellites As Research Tools Held in Tainan, Taiwan, 14-17 December 1997. LC 98-54989. (COSPAR Colloquia Ser.). 398p. 1999. 215.50 (*0-444-50196-7*) Elsevier.

COSPAR, Twenty-Second Plenary Meeting Staff. Low Latitude Aeronomical Processes: Proceedings of the COSPAR 22nd Plenary Meeting, Bangalore, India, 1979. Mitra, A. P., ed. LC 79-41341. 1980. 84.00 (*0-08-024439-4*, Pergamon Pr) Elsevier.

— Non - Solar Gamma Rays: Proceedings of the COSPAR 22nd Plenary Meeting, Bangalore, India, 1979. Cowsik, R. & Wills, R. D., eds. 254p. 1980. 61.00 (*0-08-024440-8*, Pergamon Pr) Elsevier.

Cosper, E. M., et al, eds. Novel Phytoplankton Blooms. (Coastal & Estuarine Studies: Vol. 35). (Illus.). xi, 799p. 1990. 132.00 (*0-387-51961-0*) Spr-Verlag.

***Cosper, John, Jr.** Righteous Acts: Contemporary Drama Sketches for Youth Ministry. Reeves, Dale & Caldwell, Lise, eds. LC 99-23940. (Empowered Youth Products Ser.). 80p. 1999. pap. text 10.99 (*0-7847-1079-1*) Standard Pub.

Coss. Knitting with Cotton. 1999. text. write for info. (*0-312-02028-7*) St Martin.

Coss, Bill, jt. auth. see Coss, John P.

Coss, Clare, ed. Lillian D. Wald: Progressive Activist. LC 89-32110. 120p. (Orig.). 1989. pap. 7.95 (*1-55861-000-6*) Feminist Pr.

Coss, John P. & Coss, Bill. Tales from Mischief Mountain. 68p. 1996. pap. 10.00 (*0-87012-558-3*) McClain. This delightful book is about humorous tales & pranks that occurred on Mischief Mountain somewhere in West Virginia. The book sets the time in the late 1800s, in the early days of the railroad. Each character is fictitious but you might find the tales similar to incidents that have happened in your life or an old tale that has been handed down through your family. ***Publisher Paid Annotation.***

***Coss, Melinda.** Complete Book of Embroidery: Includes Crewelwork, Goldwork, Ribbon Embroidery & Embellishment. 1999. pap. text 18.95 (*0-7621-0273-X*, Pub. by RD Assn) Penguin Putnam.

Coss, Melinda. Country Woolwork. LC 96-62081. (Illus.). 128p. 1997. 24.95 (*1-57076-087-X*, Trafalgar Sq Pub) Trafalgar.

— Floral Needlepoint. LC 92-17550. (Illus.). 112p. 1992. pap. 14.95 (*0-8069-8792-8*) Sterling.

— Folk Knits: Traditional Patterns from Around the World. (Illus.). 112p. 1991. 24.95 (*0-943955-43-2*, Trafalgar Sq Pub) Trafalgar.

— The Handmade Soap Book. LC 98-4609. (Illus.). 80p. 1998. 22.95 (*1-58017-084-6*) Storey Bks.

— 101 Crafty Cats (& How to Make Them) (Illus.). 96p. (Orig.). 1995. 14.95 (*1-85410-340-7*, Pub. by Aurum Pr) London Brdge.

Coss, P. R. The Early Records of Medieval Coventry. (Records of Social & Economic History Ser.: Vol. XI). 560p. 1987. 140.00 (*0-19-726038-1*) OUP.

Coss, P. R. & Lloyd, S. D., eds. Thirteenth Century England IV: Proceedings of the Newcastle upon Tyne Conference 1991, 230p. (C). 1992. 75.00 (*0-85115-325-9*) Boydell & Brewer.

— Thirteenth-Century England II: Proceedings of the Newcastle upon Tyne Conference 1987. (Illus.). 190p. 1988. 75.00 (*0-85115-513-8*) Boydell & Brewer.

— Thirteenth Century England V: Proceedings of the Newcastle upon Tyne Conference 1993. (Illus.). 240p. (C). 1995. 75.00 (*0-85115-565-0*) Boydell & Brewer.

***Coss, Peter.** The Knight in Medieval England, 1000-1400. (Illus.). 191p. 2000. reprint ed. pap. text 20.00 (*0-7881-9170-5*) DIANE Pub.

Coss, Peter. Lady in Medieval England 1000-1500. LC 98-206650. (Illus.). 208p. 1998. 29.95 (*0-8117-0985-X*) Kitch Keepsakes.

***Coss, Peter, ed.** The Moral World of the Law. (Past & Present Publications). (Illus.). 270p. (C). 2000. 59.95 (*0-521-64059-8*) Cambridge U Pr.

Coss, Peter, ed. Thomas Wright's Political Songs of England: From the Reign of John to That of Edward II. (Camden Classic Reprints Ser.: No. 2). 487p. (C). 1996. text 69.95 (*0-521-55466-7*); pap. text 24.95 (*0-521-55587-6*) Cambridge U Pr.

Coss, Richard. Full Pardon: A Message of Hope for Those in Prison. (Friendship Ser.). (Illus.). 48p. (Orig.). 1993. reprint ed. pap. 0.70 (*1-882536-07-X*, A100-0021) Bible League.

— Pleno Perdon. Cosby, John, tr. from ENG. (Friendship Ser.). (SPA., Illus.). 48p. 1992. pap. 0.70 (*1-882536-29-0*, A110-0014) Bible League.

Coss, Richard David. Wanted. 2nd ed. LC 99-17429. (Illus.). 136p. 1999. pap. 6.95 (*1-56554-688-1*) Pelican.

Cossa, Ralph A. The Major Powers in Northeast Asian Security. (Illus.). 75p. (Orig.). (C). 1997. pap. text 25.00 (*0-7881-3647-X*) DIANE Pub.

Cossa, Ralph A. Major Powers in Northeast Asian Security. 77p. 1996. per. 4.50 (*0-16-061188-1*) USGPO.

— U. S.-Korea-Japan Relations: Building Toward a "Virtual Alliance" LC 99-47166. (Significant Issues Ser.). 240p. 1999. pap. text 21.95 (*0-89206-358-0*) CSIS.

Cossa, Ralph A., ed. Asia Pacific Confidence & Security Building Measures. LC 95-12882. (Significant Issues Ser.: Vol. 17, No. 3). 172p. (C). 1995. pap. 14.95 (*0-89206-307-6*) CSIS.

Cossa, Ralph A. & Douglas, Richard, eds. Restructuring the U. S. - Japan Alliance: Toward a More Equal Partnership. LC 97-37213. (Significant Issues Ser.: Vol. 19, No. 5). 153p. (C). 1997. pap. text 18.95 (*0-89206-294-0*) CSIS.

Cossa, Roberto M. Neustro Fin de Semana. Yates, Donald A., ed. (SPA.). (Orig.). 1966. pap. text. write for info. (*0-685-15661-3*) Macmillan.

Cossaboom, Robert T. Joint Contact Team Program: Contacts with Former Soviet Republics & Warsaw Pact Nations, 1992- 1994. LC 97-2425. 113p. 1998. per. 16.00 (*0-16-049110-X*) USGPO.

***Cossaboom, Robert T.** The Joint Contact Team Program: Contacts with Former Soviet Republics & Warsaw Pact Nations 1992-1994. (Illus.). 107p. (C). 1999. reprint ed. pap. text 25.00 (*0-7881-8282-X*) DIANE Pub.

Cossali, Paul & Robson, Clive. Stateless in Gaza. (Illus.). 172p. (C). 1986. pap. 9.95 (*0-86232-509-9*, Pub. by Zed Books); text 29.95 (*0-86232-508-0*, Pub. by Zed Books) St Martin.

Cossard & Salazar. Mastering French. (Foreign Service Institute Language Ser.). (FRE & ENG.). 1985. pap. 16.95 (*0-8120-2204-1*) Barron.

— Mastering French, 13 CDs. (Mastering Ser.). (ENG & FRE.). 1992. pap. 110.00 incl. audio compact disk (*0-8120-7874-8*) Barron.

***Cossard, Monique.** French Basic Course Level One with 15 Cassettes. (Multilingual Books Intensive Cassette Foreign Language Ser.). 173p. 1999. pap. text 180.00 (*1-58214-018-9*) Mltilingl Bks.

— French Basic Course Level Three with 29 Cassettes. (Multilingual Books Intensive Cassette Foreign Language Ser.). 307p. 1999. pap. text 240.00 (*1-58214-020-0*) Mltilingl Bks.

— French Basic Course Level Two with 29 Cassettes. (Multilingual Books Intensive Cassette Foreign Language Ser.). 320p. 1999. pap. text 210.00 (*1-58214-019-7*) Mltilingl Bks.

— French Complete Basic Course with 87 Cassettes: Foreign Service French Level 1 Through 4. (Multilingual Books Intensive Cassette Foreign Language Ser.). 1999. pap. text 750.00 (*1-58214-063-4*) Mltilingl Bks.

Cossard, Monique & Salazar. Mastering French. (Foreign Service Institute Language Ser.). (FRE & ENG.). 1985. 79.95 incl. audio (*0-8120-7321-5*) Barron.

Cossart, Pascale F., et al, eds. Cellular Microbiology. LC 99-44931. (Illus.). 388p. 2000. text 75.95 (*1-55581-157-4*) ASM Pr.

Cossart, V., et al. Resolution of Surface Singularities. (Lecture Notes in Mathematics Ser.: Vol. 1101). vii, 132p. 1985. 29.95 (*0-387-13904-4*) Spr-Verlag.

Cosse, Laurence. A Corner of the Veil. Asher, Linda, tr. from FRE. LC 98-50059. 272p. 1999. 23.00 (*0-684-84667-5*) Scribner.

Cosse, Rene. Basics of Reservoir Engineering. (Illus.). 372p. 1993. 75.00 (*0-88415-184-0*, 5184) Gulf Pub.

Cosse, Rene, jt. auth. see Leblond, A.

Cossec, F. & Dolgachev, I. V. Enriques Surfaces I. (Progress in Mathematics Ser.: No. 76). (SPA.). 400p. 1988. 54.50 (*0-8176-3417-7*) Birkhauser.

Cossen, Richard. Power Block Ideas for Teachers. (Illus.). 87p. (Orig.). 1993. pap. 4.50 (*0-9614646-3-1*) Ctr Innovation.

Cossentino, F., et al. Local & Regional Response to Global Pressure: The Case of Italy & Its Industrial Districts. LC 97-120558. (Research Ser.: Vol. 103). x,206p. 1996. pap. 22.50 (*92-9014-568-4*) Intl Labour Office.

Cossery, Albert. Les Faineants Dans la Vallee Fertile. (FRE.). 212p. 1977. pap. 10.95 (*0-7859-1852-3*, 2070369498) Fr & Eur.

— Mendiants et Orgueilleux. (FRE.). 1979. pap. 10.95 (*0-7859-1894-9*, 2070371190) Fr & Eur.

— Proud Beggars. Cushing, Thomas, tr. from FRE. LC 81-1095. 200p. (Orig.). 1981. 14.00 (*0-87685-451-X*); pap. 10.00 (*0-87685-450-1*) Black Sparrow.

— Proud Beggars, signed ed. deluxe ed. Cushing, Thomas, tr. from FRE. LC 81-1095. 200p. (Orig.). 1981. 20.00 (*0-87685-452-8*) Black Sparrow.

Cosset, J. M., et al. Interstitial, Endocavitary & Perfusional Hyperthermia. (Clincial Thermology Ser.: Vol. 5). (Illus.). 120p. 1990. 125.00 (*0-387-50983-6*) Spr-Verlag.

***Cossetat, Graham W.** Modern Auditing. LC 99-40990. 1999. write for info. (*0-471-81058-4*) Wiley.

Cossette, Claude. La Preparation du Bois les Pates Mechaniques. (FRE., Illus.). 242p. 1991. pap. text (*2-9801486-5-2*) CA66.

Cossey, Betty & Harrington, Lucille. The Rose Quilts: The Portable Wrap-Around Method. LC 93-21684. (Illus.). 1994. pap. 24.95 (*1-884209-99-8*) Small Change.

Cossey, John. Geometric Group Theory down Under: Proceedings of a Special Year in Geometric Group Theory, Canberra, Australia, 1996. LC 98-53281. 332p. 1999. 129.95 (*3-11-016366-7*) De Gruyter.

Cossi, Gabriella, jt. auth. see Evans, Matthew.

Cossi, Olga. Edna Hibel: Her Life & Art. Weisman, JoAnne B., ed. LC 94-70009. (Picture-Book Biography). (Illus.). 128p. (YA). 1994. lib. bdg. 14.95 (*1-878668-31-5*) Disc Enter Ltd.

— Fire Mate. rev. ed. LC 94-66085. (Council for Indian Education Ser.). 100p. (J). (gr. 4-8). 1994. pap. 7.95 (*1-879373-87-4*) Roberts Rinehart.

— Harp Seals. (Nature Watch Bks.). (Illus.). 48p. (J). (gr. 2-5). 1991. lib. bdg. 19.95 (*0-87614-437-7*, Carolrhoda) Lerner Pub.

— Harp Seals. (Illus.). 48p. (J). (gr. 2-5). 1992. pap. 6.95 (*0-87614-567-5*, Carolrhoda) Lerner Pub.

Cossi, Olga. The Magic Box. LC 89-8461. 192p. (YA). 1990. pap. 12.95 (*1-56554-381-5*) Pelican.

Cossi, Olga. The Magic Box. LC 89-8461. 192p. (YA). (gr. 12). 1990. 12.95 (*0-88289-748-9*) Pelican.

— Think Pink. LC 93-5556. (Illus.). 32p. (J). (ps-3). 1994. 10.95 (*0-88289-995-3*) Pelican.

— Water Wars: The Fight to Control & Conserve Nature's Most Precious Resource. LC 92-43968. (Earthcare Bks.). (Illus.). 128p. (J). (gr. 6-7). 1993. lib. bdg. 13.95 (*0-02-724595-0*, New Dscvry Bks) Silver Burdett Pr.

Cossick, Vicky, ed. AIDS: Meeting the Community Challenge. 190p. 1989. pap. 27.00 (*0-86217-288-8*, Pub. by Veritas Pubns) St Mut.

***Cossin.** Advanced Credit Risk Analysis. LC 99-57861. 400p. 2000. text 95.00 (*0-471-98723-9*) Wiley.

Cossins, A. R., ed. Temperature Adaptation of Biological Membranes. LC 95-140747. (Portland Press Proceedings Ser.: Vol. 7). (Illus.). 240p. (C). 1994. text 110.50 (*1-85578-062-3*, Pub. by Portland Pr Ltd) Ashgate Pub Co.

Cossins, A. R. & Bowler, K. Temperature Biology of Animals. 300p. 1987. text 57.50 (*0-412-15900-7*) Chapman & Hall.

Cossins, Anne. Annotated Freedom of Information Act NSW. 540p. 1997. pap. 65.00 (*0-455-21500-6*, Pub. by LawBk Co) Gaunt.

***Cossins, Anne.** Masculinities, Sexualities & Child Sexual Abuse. 316p. 2000. 93.00 (*90-411-1355-X*) Kluwer Law Intl.

***Cossio, Alicia Y.** Bruna & Her Sisters in the Sleeping City. Wishnia, Kenneth J., tr. from SPA. LC 99-39373. 240p. 1999. 24.95 (*0-8101-1408-9*, Hydra Bks) Northwestern U Pr.

Cossio, Aluigi. The Canzoniere of Dante: A Contribution to Its Critical Edition. 1977. lib. bdg. 59.95 (*0-8490-1569-3*) Gordon Pr.

Cossio del Pomar, Felipe. Mundo de los Incas. (SPA.). pap. 6.99 (*968-16-0563-2*, Pub. by Fondo) Continental Bk.

Cossio, Jane & Young, J. Cuban Home Cooking. 118p. 1989. pap. 11.95 (*0-942084-37-3*) SeaSide Pub.

Cossio, Jorge. SSM-ALG COLL STUD 3/E (KOLMAN) 3rd ed. 119p. (C). 1991. pap. text, student ed. 24.50 (*0-15-502164-8*) SCP.

Cossio, Jose M. Los Toros: Tratado Tecnico e Historico, 11 vols., Set. 1989. 3250.00 (*84-239-6008-0*) Elliots Bks.

Cossio, Jose Maria de, ed. see Antonio De Guevara, Fray.

Cossio, Manuel B. El Greco. 2nd ed. (Illus.). 312p. 1989. 295.00 (*84-239-4284-8*) Elliots Bks.

Cossitt, P. S. & White, F. H. Cossit Family: Genealogical History of Rene Cossitt, a Frenchman Who Settled in Granby, Ct., a.d. 1717, & His Descendants. (Illus.). 220p. 1995. reprint ed. pap. 35.00 (*0-8328-4760-7*); reprint ed. lib. bdg. 45.00 (*0-8328-4759-3*) Higginson Bk Co.

Cosslett, Tess. Victorian Women Poets. LC 96-23025. (C). 1996. text 50.95 (*0-582-27650-0*) Longman.

— Victorian Women Poets. LC 96-23025. 286p. (C). 1996. pap. 35.66 (*0-582-27649-7*) Longman.

— Women Writing Childbirth: Modern Discourses on Motherhood. LC 93-45572. (Illus.). 204p. 1994. text 27.95 (*0-7190-4324-7*, Pub. by Manchester Univ Pr) St Martin.

***Cosslett, Tess, et al.** Feminism & Autobiography: Texts, Theories, Methods. LC 00-32842. (Transformations Ser.). 2000. pap. write for info. (*0-415-23202-3*) Routledge.

Cosslett, Tess, et al. Women, Power & Resistance: An Introduction to Women's Studies. LC 96-22705. 301p. 1996. 90.95 (*0-335-19391-9*); pap. 26.95 (*0-335-19390-0*) OpUniv Pr.

Cossman, Brenda & Kapur, Ratna. Secularism's Last Sigh: Hindutva & the (Mis) Rule of Law. LC 99-938561. (Law in India Ser.). 212p. 2000. text 22.00 (*0-19-564813-7*) OUP.

Cossman, Brenda, et al. Bad Attitude's on Trial: Pornography, Feminism, & the Butler Decision. (Illus.). 272p. 1997. text 55.00 (*0-8020-0687-6*); pap. text 18.95 (*0-8020-7643-2*) U of Toronto Pr.

Cossman, Brenda, jt. auth. see Kapur, Ratna.

Cossman, E. Joseph. How I Made One Million Dollars in Mail Order-And You Can Too! rev. ed. 2725p. 1993. pap. 13.00 (*0-671-87276-1*, Fireside) S&S Trade Pap.

Cossolotto, Matthew. The Almanac of European Politics, 1994. LC 94-32762. 340p. (C). 1995. pap. text 36.95 (*0-87187-913-1*) Congr Quarterly.

— The Almanac of European Politics, 1994. LC 94-32762. 340p. (C). 1995. text 56.95 (*0-87187-914-X*) Congr Quarterly.

Cosson, Annie, ed. see McDowell, Josh.

Cosson, Annie L., ed. see Lundstrom, Lowell.

Cosson, Annie L., ed. see Robertson, Pat.

Cosson, Emilius A. De, see De Cosson, Emilius A.

Cosson, M. J. The Elephant's Ancestors. LC 98-196545. (Cover-To-Cover Bks.). 56 p. 1997. write for info. (*0-7807-6683-0*, Covercraft) Perfection Learn.

Cosstick, Vicky, ed. AIDS: Meeting the Community Challenge. (C). 1988. 39.00 (*0-85439-264-5*, Pub. by St Paul Pubns) St Mut.

Cossu, Raffaello, jt. ed. see Carra, Joseph S.

Cost. Desktop Publisher's Desktop Companion. (Graphic Communications Ser.). 1997. pap. 29.95 (*0-8273-7125-X*) Delmar.

Cost, Bruce. Asian Ingredients: A Guide to the Foodstuffs of China, Japan, Korea, Thailand & Vietnam. rev. ed. LC 99-86440. (Illus.). 352p. 2000. pap. 18.00 (*0-06-093204-X*, Quil) HarperTrade.

— Big Bowl Noodles & Rice: Fresh Asian Cooking from the Renowned Restaurant. LC 00-25543. (Illus.). 224p. 2000. 25.00 (*0-06-019420-0*, HarpCollins) HarperTrade.

— Ginger East to West. 2nd rev. ed. 1989. pap. 14.00 (*0-201-51798-1*) Addison-Wesley.

— Ginger East to West: A Cook's Tour with Recipes, Techniques & Lore. LC 84-2842. (Illus.). 192p. (Orig.). 1984. 17.95 (*0-943186-13-7*); pap. 10.95 (*0-943186-06-4*) Aris Bks.

Cost, Curtis. Vaccines Are Dangerous: A Warning to the Black Community. 160p. 1992. pap. text 9.95 (*1-881316-08-4*) A&B Bks.

Cost, Frank. Pocket Guide to Digital Printing. (Graphic Communications Ser.). (Illus.). 228p. 1996. mass mkt. 17.95 (*0-8273-7592-1*) Delmar.

Cost, March. A Key to Laurels. large type ed. 1982. 27.99 (*0-7089-0775-X*) Ulverscroft.

Cost, Marco T. El Mago Desinventor (The Magic Dis-inventor) Mansour, Monica, tr. (SPA., Illus.). (J). (gr. 5-6). 1994. pap. 5.99 (*968-16-4240-6*, Pub. by Fondo) Continental Bk.

Cost, Neil D., et al. Making Turkey Callers in the Gobbler's Shop: The Gobbler's Shop. LC 99-90184. (Illus.). 132p. 1999. write for info. (*0-9671259-0-1*) B Berryhill.

Costa. American Short Stories. 2nd ed. (C). 1998. pap. text 20.50 (*0-03-021334-7*, Pub. by Harcourt Coll Pubs) Harcourt.

An Asterisk (*) at the beginning of an entry indicates that the title is appearing for the first time.

Costa. New Trends in Nuclear Neurology & Psychiatry. 192p. 42.00 (*0-86196-401-2*, Pub. by J Libbey Med) Bks Intl VA.

Costa. Pulmonary Function Testing. 1995. write for info. (*0-8493-8859-7*) CRC Pr.

— Shape Analysis & Recognition: Theory & Practice. (Image Processing Ser.). 1999. ring bd. 89.95 (*0-8493-3493-4*) CRC Pr.

Costa, ed. Seneca: Four Dialogues. 1995. 59.99 (*0-85668-560-7*, Pub. by Aris & Phillips); pap. 28.00 (*0-85668-561-5*, Pub. by Aris & Phillips) David Brown.

Costa & Gold Country Enterprises Staff, ed. see Costa, Eric J.

Costa, Adrian, jt. auth. see Gonzales, Dario Angel.

Costa, Albert H. The California Directory of Experts: A Master Reference Guide. (Illus.). 235p. 1989. reprint ed. pap., ring bd. 120.00 (*0-922784-00-0*) AC Enterprises.

— Child Support: An American Dilemma. 60p. 1988. write for info. (*0-318-64261-1*) AC Enterprises.

Costa, Angela. 1000 Reasons You Might Think She Is My Lover. (Illus.). 180p. 1997. pap. 10.95 (*1-886383-21-9*) Pride & Imprints.

Costa, Annie. The Feel Good Handbook: A Survival Guide for Anyone Sensitive to MSG & Other Food Additives. (Illus.). 120p. 1998. pap. 14.95 (*0-9662169-9-7*) LightHse Pr.

In easy-to-understand layman's terms, THE FEEL GOOD HANDBOOK identifies common reactions, HIDDEN SOURCES, & provides a simple plan to help eliminate MSG & other substances in your diet. Written using information supplied from consumer advocacy groups, THE FEEL GOOD HANDBOOK weaves into its informative text anecdotal stories of personal experiences & success stories of suffers on file at the FDA. The appendices are loaded with reference materials, web sites, recommended reading, medical references, related subjects & recipes. THE FEEL GOOD HANDBOOK is the ultimate guide to improving your health if you suffer from chronic illness: migraine headaches, asthma, chronic fatigue syndrome, mitral valve prolapse, digestive or intestinal distress, heart, lung, skin. To Order: call The LightHouse Press at 888-298-5100 or write us at 3555 South El Camino Real #301, San Mateo, CA 94403. Soft cover only. See our WEB site for more details & related information - www.MSGFREE.com or www.thelighthousepress.com. *Publisher Paid Annotation.*

Costa, Arthur, et al, eds. If Minds Matter: A Foreword to the Future, 2 vols., Vol. I. (Illus.). 304p. (Orig.). 1992. pap. 43.95 (*0-932935-36-2*) SkyLght.

— If Minds Matter: A Foreword to the Future, 2 vols., Vol. II. (Illus.). 368p. (Orig.). 1992. pap. 43.95 (*0-932935-40-0*) SkyLght.

Costa, Arthur L. The School As a Home for the Mind: A Collection of Articles by Arthur L. Costa. LC 91-61609. 176p. 1991. pap. 24.95 (*0-932935-33-8*) SkyLght.

Costa, Arthur L., intro. Developing Minds Vol. 1: A Resource Book for Teaching Thinking. LC 91-3069. (Illus.). 400p. (Orig.). 1991. pap. 29.95 (*0-87120-180-1*, 611-91026) ASCD.

Costa, Arthur L. & Garmston, Robert J. Cognitive Coaching: A Foundation for Renaissance Schools. (Illus.). 256p. (Orig.). (C). 1994. text 39.95 (*0-926842-37-4*) CG Pubs Inc.

***Costa, Arthur L. & Kallick, Bena O.** Activating & Engaging Habits of Mind. LC 00-9346. 2000. write for info. (*0-87120-369-3*) ASCD.

Costa, Arthur L. & Kallick, Bena O., eds. Assessment in the Learning Organization: Shifting the Paradigm. LC 95-32492. 1995. pap. 25.95 (*0-87120-250-6*) ASCD.

***Costa, Arthur L. & Kallick, Bena O., eds.** Discovering & Exploring Habits of Mind. LC 99-50943. (Habits of Mind - A Developmental Ser.). (Illus.). 108p. 2000. pap. 20.95 (*0-87120-368-5*) ASCD.

Costa, Arthur L. & Liebmann, Rosemarie M. The Process-Centered School: Sustaining a Renaissance Community. (Illus.). 264p. 1997. 69.95 (*0-8039-6313-0*); pap. 32.95 (*0-8039-6314-9*) Corwin Pr.

— Supporting the Spirit of Learning: When Process Is Content. LC 96-10144. 264p. 1997. 69.95 (*0-8039-6311-4*); pap. 32.95 (*0-8039-6312-2*) Corwin Pr.

Costa, Arthur L. & Liebmann, Rosemarie M., eds. Envisioning Process As Content: Toward a Renaissance Curriculum. 280p. 1996. 69.95 (*0-8039-6309-2*); pap. 32.95 (*0-8039-6310-6*) Corwin Pr.

Costa, Bill. Bill Costa Icons. 1997. pap. 39.95 (*3-86187-091-6*) B Gmunder.

Costa, Bill. Costa. 1995. text 13.00 (*0-312-11809-0*, Stonewall Inn) St Martin.

Costa, C. A. Bana E, see Bana e Costa, C. A., ed.

Costa, C. D., ed. see Lucretius.

Costa, C. D. N., ed. see Seneca, Lucius Annaeus.

Costa, Carlos A. & Cabral, Joaquim S., eds. Chromatographic & Membrane Processes in Biotechnology. 488p. (C). 1991. text 229.00 (*0-7923-1417-4*) Kluwer Academic.

Costa, Catherine R. Puffins & Pine Trees: Maine Designs for Machine Knitters. LC 91-117128. (Illus.). 142p. 1990. spiral bd. 14.95 (*0-89272-277-0*) Down East.

Costa, Corrado. The Complete Films of Corrado Costa. Vangelisti, Paul, tr. from ITA. LC 83-60077. 64p. (Orig.). 1983. pap. 4.00 (*0-88031-063-4*) Invisible-Red Hill.

— Complete Plays of Corrado Costa. Vangelisti, Paul, tr. (Littoral Bks.). 144p. 1999. pap. 11.95 (*1-928801-01-3*, Pub. by Sun & Moon CA) Consort Bk Sales.

— Our Positions. Vangelisti, Paul, tr. from ITA. 1975. 2.50 (*0-88031-021-9*) Invisible-Red Hill.

Costa Cruises, Inc. Staff. Cooking & Cruising Italian Style: Light & Healthy Cuisine. Cooper, Lucy, ed. (Illus.). 150p. (Orig.). 1989. pap. 16.95 (*0-942084-89-6*) SeaSide Pub.

Costa, D. C., et al. Thallium Myocardial Perfusion Tomography in Clinical Cardiology. (Illus.). 240p. 1994. 242.00 (*0-387-19675-7*) Spr-Verlag.

Costa, D. Margaret & Guthrie, Sharon R., eds. Women & Sport: Interdisciplinary Perspectives. LC 93-50167. (Illus.). 416p. 1994. text 47.00 (*0-87322-686-0*, BCOS0686) Human Kinetics.

Costa, Da, see Da Costa.

Costa, Dan, jt. ed. see Langendoen, David.

Costa de Beauregard, Diane. Animals in Jeopardy. Bogard, Vicki, tr. from FRE. LC 90-50779. (Young Discovery Library). (Illus.). 38p. (J). (gr. k-5). 1991. 5.95 (*0-944589-37-5*, 375) Young Discovery Lib.

Costa de Beauregard, Olivier. Time, the Physical Magnitude. 344p. (C). 1987. text 176.50 (*90-277-2444-X*, D Reidel) Kluwer Academic.

Costa, Denise De, see De Costa, Denise.

Costa, Dennis. Irenic Apocalypse: Some Uses of Apocalyptic in Dante, Petrarch & Rabelais. (Stanford French & Italian Studies: Vol. 21). vi, 143p. 1981. pap. 56.50 (*0-915838-18-4*) Anma Libri.

Costa, Dolores Guiral de, see Guiral de Costa, Dolores, intro.

Costa, Dora L. The Evolution of Retirement: An American Economic History, 1880-1990. LC 97-29755. (National Bureau of Economic Research Monographs). 240p. 1998. 40.00 (*0-226-11608-5*) U Ch Pr.

***Costa, Dora L.** Evolution of Retirement: An American Economic History, 1880-1990. (NBER Series on Long-Term Factors in Economic Development). 2000. pap. text 19.00 (*0-226-11609-3*) U Ch Pr.

Costa, E., ed. New Directions for Intelligent Tutoring Systems. (NATO ASI Series F: Computer & Systems Science: Vol. 91). x, 396p. 1992. 84.00 (*0-387-55754-7*) Spr-Verlag.

Costa, E. & Racagni, Giorgio, eds. Typical & Atypical Antidepressants: Molecular Mechanisms. fac. ed. LC 81-23409. (Advances in Biochemical Psychopharmacology Ser.: No. 31). 415p. pap. 128.70 (*0-7837-7202-5*, 204709700005) Bks Demand.

Costa, E. & Sandler, M., eds. Monoamine Oxidases - New Vistas. fac. ed. LC 72-192861. (Advances in Biochemical Psychopharmacology Ser.: No. 5). (Illus.). 464p. pap. 143.90 (*0-7837-7537-7*, 204696700005) Bks Demand.

Costa, E. & Trabucchi, Marco, eds. Regulatory Peptides, from Molecular Biology to Function. fac. ed. LC 81-40857. (Advances in Biochemical Psychopharmacology Ser.). (Illus.). 587p. pap. 182.00 (*0-7837-7213-0*, 204708500005) Bks Demand.

Costa, E., jt. ed. see Biggio, Giovanni.

Costa, Eduardo, tr. see Barreneche, Raul.

Costa, Edward J. Tales by the Dozen. LC 97-92665. i, 126p. 1997. pap. 4.99 (*0-9661274-0-4*) Q-Wax Pr.

Costa, Emilia V. Da, see Da Costa, Emilia V.

Costa, Eric J. Old Vines, a History of Wine Growing in Amador County (CA) Costa & Gold Country Enterprises Staff, ed. (Illus.). 86p. (Orig.). 1994. pap. 9.95 (*0-938121-08-1*) Cenotto Pubns.

Costa, Erminio. The Benzodiazepines: From Molecular Biology to Clinical Practice. LC 83-9706. (Illus.). 446p. 1983. reprint ed. pap. 138.30 (*0-7837-9550-5*, 206029900005) Bks Demand.

Costa, Erminio, ed. Neurochemical Pharmacology: A Tribute to B. B. Brodie. LC 89-3846. (Fidia Research Foundation Symposium Ser.: No. 2). (Illus.). 393p. 1989. reprint ed. pap. 121.90 (*0-608-00677-7*, 206126400007) Bks Demand.

Costa, Erminio & Gessa, Gian L., eds. Nonstriatal Dopaminergic Neurons. LC 76-5661. (Advances in Biochemical Psychopharmacology Ser.: No. 16). (Illus.). 728p. pap. 200.00 (*0-7837-7543-1*, 204696100005) Bks Demand.

Costa, Erminio & Trabucchi, Marco, eds. Neural Peptides & Neuronal Communication. fac. ed. LC 79-66738. (Advances in Biochemical Psychopharmacology Ser.: No. 22). (Illus.). 677p. pap. 200.00 (*0-7837-7245-9*, 204706000005) Bks Demand.

Costa, Erminio, jt. ed. see Biggio, Giovanni.

Costa, Erminio, jt. ed. see Greengard, Paul.

Costa, Ernesto, et al, eds. Progress in Artificial Intelligence: 8th Portuguese Conference on Artificial Intelligence, EPIA '97, Coimbra, Portugal, October 6-9, 1997 : Proceedings. LC 97-40472. (Lecture Notes in Computer Science Ser.: Vol. 1323). xiv, 388p. 1997. pap. 67.00 (*3-540-63586-6*) Spr-Verlag.

Costa, F. J., et al. Asian Urbanization Problems & Processes. (Urbanization of the Earth Ser.: Vol. 5). (Illus.). 165p. 1988. lib. bdg. 63.00 (*3-443-37007-1*) Lubrecht & Cramer.

Costa, Fernando De la, see De la Costa, Fernando.

Costa Fontes, Manuel da, see Da Costa Fontes, Manuel.

Costa, Francis D., ed. see Hopko, Thomas, et al.

Costa, Francisco Da, see Mickle, M. M. & Da Costa, Francisco.

Costa, Frank J., jt. ed. see Dutt, Ashok K.

Costa, Frank J., jt. ed. see Noble, Allen G.

Costa, G. Trends in Electrochemical Biosensors: Proceedings of the Conference. 216p. 1993. text 95.00 (*981-02-1247-X*) World Scientific Pub.

Costa, G. & Calucci, G. Conceptual Tools for Understanding Nature: Proceedings of the 3rd International Symposium, University of Trieste, Italy, 21-23 June 1995. Giorgi, M., ed. 300p. 1997. 78.00 (*981-02-3173-3*) World Scientific Pub.

Costa, G., et al. Conceptual Tools for Understanding Nature. 296p. 1995. text 97.00 (*981-02-2144-4*) World Scientific Pub.

— Conceptual Tools for Understanding Nature: Proceedings of the International Symposium. 260p. 1993. text 67.00 (*981-02-1564-9*) World Scientific Pub.

Costa, Gino F. Brazil's Foreign Policy: Toward Regional Dominance, Vol. 7. (Foreign Relations of Latin America Ser.). 175p. (C). 1989. pap. text 37.50 (*0-8133-7693-9*) Westview.

Costa, Giovanna F., jt. ed. see Costa, Mariarosa D.

Costa, Giovanna F. Dalla, see Dalla Costa, Mariarosa & Dalla Costa, Giovanna F., eds.

Costa, Giovanni. Behavioural Adaptations of Desert Animals. LC 94-41930. (Adaptations of Desert Organisms Ser.). 1995. write for info. (*0-387-58578-8*) Spr-Verlag.

Costa, Greg. American Short Stories: Exercises in Reading & Writing. 142p. (C). 1983. pap. text 15.50 (*0-15-502391-8*, Pub. by Harcourt Coll Pubs) Harcourt.

Costa, Grovann. Behavioural Adaptations of Desert Animals. Cloudsley-Thompson, J. L., ed. LC 94-41930. (Adaptations of Desert Organisms Ser.). (Illus.). 232p. 1995. 157.95 (*3-540-58578-8*) Spr-Verlag.

Costa, Gwen, ed. see Barry, Helen B.

Costa, Gwen, ed. see Bell, Addie.

Costa, Gwen, ed. see Brashear, William.

Costa, Gwen, ed. see Byers, Louise.

Costa, Gwen, ed. see Demay, Sally.

Costa, Gwen, ed. see Donovan, Timothy O.

Costa, Gwen, ed. see Eveland, Edward M.

Costa, Gwen, ed. see Gregory, Rex O.

Costa, Gwen, ed. see Hankins, Richard J.

Costa, Gwen, ed. see Harris, Y. L.

Costa, Gwen, ed. see Hassman, Mina.

Costa, Gwen, ed. see Higgins, Clay.

Costa, Gwen, ed. see Judge, Vincent.

Costa, Gwen, ed. see Locke, Norton.

Costa, Gwen, ed. see Manes, Rose T.

Costa, Gwen, ed. see Marchese, Raymond.

Costa, Gwen, ed. see McField, R. C.

Costa, Gwen, ed. see Meyer, Frank.

Costa, Gwen, ed. see Miller, Leo.

Costa, Gwen, ed. see Napora, Paul E.

Costa, Gwen, ed. see Noble, Nathaniel N.

Costa, Gwen, ed. see Nordquist, Kay.

Costa, Gwen, ed. see Parry, Joan & Freudenberg, Marie.

Costa, Gwen, ed. see Remakus, Bernard L.

Costa, Gwen, ed. see Stoltz, Donald R.

Costa, Gwen, ed. see Stover, Richard L.

Costa, Gwen, ed. see Thomas, Stephen.

Costa, Gwen, ed. see Vitolo, Sheri J.

Costa, Gwen, ed. see Weite, Rose.

Costa, Gwen, ed. see Windward, Shirley.

Costa, H. & Herrmann, P., eds. Training in Medical Psychotherapy: Cross-Cultural Diversity. (Psychotherapy & Psychosomatics Ser.: Vol. 53, No. 1-4, 1990) (Illus.). 208p. 1990. pap. 150.50 (*3-8055-5321-8*) S Karger.

Costa, Helena R. Bibliographical Supplement to Liberty of Conscience. 105p. 1986. pap. 10.00 (*0-916617-03-3*) J C Brown.

Costa, Hippolyto J. Da, see Da Costa, Hippolyto J.

Costa, Horacio de la, see De la Costa, Horacio, ed.

Costa, J. Almeida. Diccionario de Lingua Portuguesa. 7th ed. (POR.). 1995. 125.00 (*0-7859-9771-7*) Fr & Eur.

— Dicionario Da Lingua Portuguesa. 6th ed. (POR.) 1811p. 1992. 95.00 (*0-8288-8536-2*) Fr & Eur.

Costa, J. E. & Fleisher, p. J., eds. Developments & Applications of Geomorphology. (Illus.). 300p. 1984. 152.95 (*0-387-13457-3*) Spr-Verlag.

Costa, J. M., ed. see Mercer, A. D.

Costa, J. R. Da, see Loucks, Daniel P. & Da Costa, J. R., eds.

Costa, Jaki Da, see Da Costa, Jaki.

Costa, Janeen A., ed. Gender Issues & Consumer Behavior. LC 94-11313. 240p. 1994. 52.00 (*0-8039-5323-2*); pap. 24.00 (*0-8039-5324-0*) Sage.

Costa, Janeen A. & Bamossy, Gary J. Marketing in a Multicultural World: Ethnicity, Nationalism & Cultural Identity. (Illus.). 352p. 1995. text 58.00 (*0-8039-5327-5*); pap. text 26.95 (*0-8039-5328-3*) Sage.

Costa, Jim, jt. ed. see Machado, Michael J.

Costa, Joao, ed. Portuguese Syntax: New Comparative Studies. LC 99-28002. 288p. 2000. text 75.00 (*0-19-512575-4*) OUP.

Costa, John D. The Ethical Imperative: Why Moral Leadership Is Good Business. (Illus.). 368p. 1999. pap. text 18.00 (*0-7382-0130-8*, Pub. by Perseus Pubng) HarpC.

Costa, John E., et al, eds. Natural & Anthropogenic Influences in Fluvial Geomorphology. LC 95-19002. (Geophysical Monograph Ser.: Vol. 89). 1995. 50.00 (*0-87590-046-1*) Am Geophysical.

Costa, John E. & Baker, Victor R. Surficial Geology: Building with the Earth. (Illus.). 510p. (C). 1990. reprint ed. text 125.00 (*1-878907-17-4*) TechBooks.

Costa, John E. & Wieczorek, Gerald F., eds. Debris Flows - Avalanches: Process, Recognition, & Mitigation. LC 87-19657. (Reviews in Engineering Geology Ser.: Vol. 7). (Illus.). 245p. 1987. reprint ed. pap. 76.00 (*0-608-07764-X*, 206785200010) Bks Demand.

Costa, Joseph. Primal Legacy: Thinking for the 21st Century. (Illus.). 309p. 1995. lib. bdg. 24.95 (*1-883333-25-3*) Better Lfe Bks.

— Yeshu Hannosri: For God So Loved the World. LC 93-80536. 353p. (Orig.). 1994. pap. 14.95 (*1-883333-10-5*) Better Lfe Bks.

Costa, Joseph E. The Generic Job Search Manual: The One That Really Works! 113p. 1991. student ed. 7.50 (*0-9630256-0-0*) Costa Servs.

***Costa, Juan G., ed.** Portuguese Syntax: New Comparative Studies. LC 99-28002. (Oxford Studies in Comparative Syntax). 288p. 2000. pap. text 45.00 (*0-19-512576-2*) OUP.

Costa, Juan G., tr. see Coelho, Paulo.

Costa, L. G., et al, eds. Toxicology of Pesticides: Experimental, Clinical & Regulatory Perspectives. (NATO ASI Series H: Vol. 13). 335p. 1987. 121.00 (*0-387-16093-0*) Spr-Verlag.

Costa Lima, Luiz. Control of the Imaginary: Reason & Imagination in Modern Times. LC 88-19154. (Theory & History of Literature Ser.: Vol. 50). xxiii, 250p. 1989. pap. 18.95 (*0-8166-1563-2*) U of Minn Pr.

Costa-Lima, Luiz. The Limits of Voice. Britto, Paulo H., tr. LC 95-36712. 375p. 1996. 49.50 (*0-8047-2540-3*) Stanford U Pr.

Costa Lopez, Toni. Diccionari de Tintin. (CAT.). 80p. 1987. pap. 19.95 (*0-7859-5830-4*, 8426122744) Fr & Eur.

Costa, Louis, ed. see Benton, Arthur L.

Costa, Lucio G. & Manzo, Luigi. Occupational Neurotoxicology. LC 98-5973. 296p. 1998. boxed set 139.95 (*0-8493-9231-4*) CRC Pr.

Costa, Luis F., et al, eds. German & International Perspectives on the Spanish Civil War: The Aesthetics of Partisanship. (GERM Ser.). 520p. 1992. 75.00 (*1-879751-09-7*) Camden Hse.

Costa, M., et al, eds. Sensory Nerves & Neuropeptides in Gastroenterology: From Basic Science to Clinical Perspectives. (Advances in Experimental Medicine & Biology Ser.). (Illus.). 318p. (C). 1991. text 126.00 (*0-306-43911-5*, Kluwer Plenum) Kluwer Academic.

Costa, Manuel J. Tackling Life Head On: Lessons for Kids' Lives with Ronnie Lott as "Coach" LC 97-19984. (Illus.). 80p. (J). (gr. 4-12). 1997. pap. 9.95 (*0-917479-17-3*) Guild Psy.

Costa, Manuel L. General Equilibrium Analysis & the Theory of Markets. LC 98-29697. 224p. 1999. 80.00 (*1-85898-958-2*) E Elgar.

Costa, Margaret F., tr. see Lisboa, Eugenio & Macedo, Helder, eds.

Costa, Margaret J. Dedalus Book of Spanish Fantasy. 1999. pap. text 15.99 (*1-873982-18-6*) Dedalus.

Costa, Margaret J., ed. see Mirbeau, Octave.

Costa, Margaret J., ed. & tr. see De Querioz, Eca.

Costa, Margaret J., ed. & tr. see De Sa-Carneiro, Mario.

Costa, Margaret J., tr. see Atxaga, Bernardo.

Costa, Margaret J., tr. see De Sa-Carnejio, Maria.

Costa, Margaret J., tr. see Del Valle-Inclan, Ramon.

Costa, Margaret J., tr. see Marias, Javier.

Costa, Margaret J., tr. see Perez-Reverte, Arturo.

Costa, Margaret J., tr. see Saer, Juan J.

Costa, Margaret J., tr. see Tabucchi, Antonio.

Costa, Margaret Jull, jt. auth. see Eca de Queiroz, Jose Maria.

Costa, Margaret Jull, tr. see Coelho, Paulo.

Costa, Margaret Jull, tr. see Gaite, Carmen Martin.

Costa, Margaret Jull, tr. see Marias, Javier.

Costa, Maria. Abortion: A Reference Handbook. LC 91-15231. 339p. 1991. lib. bdg. 39.50 (*0-87436-602-X*) ABC-CLIO.

Costa, Maria & Grogan, Rob. When the Vows Break: Living Through Separation & Divorce, Vol. 1. LC 96-92843. (Illus.). 176p. (Orig.). 1996. pap. 16.95 (*0-9654990-0-6*) M Costa & Assocs.

Costa, Mariarosa D. & Costa, Giovanna F., eds. Paying the Price: Women & the Politics of International Economic Strategy. LC 95-13679. 112p. (C). 1995. text 19.95 (*1-85649-298-2*, Pub. by Zed Books) St Martin.

Costa, Mariarosa Dalla, see Dalla Costa, Mariarosa, ed.

Costa, Marie. Abortion: A Reference Handbook. 2nd ed. LC 96-12251. (Contemporary World Issues Ser.). 339p. 1996. lib. bdg. 45.00 (*0-87436-827-8*) ABC-CLIO.

— Adult Literacy-Illiteracy in the United States: A Handbook for Reference & Research. LC 87-31696. (Contemporary World Issues Ser.). 167p. 1988. lib. bdg. 39.50 (*0-87436-492-2*) ABC-CLIO.

Costa, Marie, jt. auth. see Grazie, Sol.

Costa, Marithelma. Las Dos Caras de la Escritura. 238p. 1989. 12.00 (*0-8477-3634-2*) U of PR Pr.

Costa, Marithelma & Figueroa, Alvin J. Kaligrafiando. 157p. 1991. pap. 7.95 (*0-8477-3238-X*) U of PR Pr.

Costa, Marithelma, et al. Hispanic Immigrant Writers & the Question of Identity: Escritors Inmigrantes Hispanos y la Identidad. (Literature - Conversation Ser.: Vol. 1). (ENG & SPA.). 88p. (C). 1989. pap. 9.00 (*0-685-30057-9*) Ollantay Pr.

Costa, Michael & Duffy, Mark. Labor Prosperity in the '90's. 180p. 1991. pap. 28.00 (*1-86287-060-8*, Pub. by Federation Pr) Gaunt.

Costa, Michael & Hearn, Mark. Reforming Australia's Unions. 290p. 1997. pap. 29.00 (*1-86287-248-1*, Pub. by Federation Pr) Gaunt.

Costa, Michael J. Master Trust: Simplifying Employee Benefits Trust Fund Administration. LC 80-65872. 221p. reprint ed. pap. 68.60 (*0-608-12158-4*, 202391300034) Bks Demand.

Costa, Nancy, jt. auth. see Quintero, Ana H.

Costa, Natalia, tr. see Jorge, Lidia.

***Costa, Nicholas.** Shattered Illusions: Albania, Greece & Yugoslavia. LC 98-74965. 200p. 1998. 28.00 (*0-88033-418-5*, 520, Pub. by East Eur Monographs) Col U Pr.

C

Costa, Nicoletta. My Poke & Look Busy Book. (Poke & Look Bks.). (Illus.). 44p. (J). (ps-2). 1990. spiral bd. 14.95 (*0-448-21034-7*, G & D) Peng Put Young Read.

Costa Nunez, Ralph Da, see Da Costa Nunez, Ralph.

Costa, Octavio R. Bolivar: Mas Alla del Tiempo y del Espacio. LC 98-86088.Tr. of Bolivar: Further the Time & the Space. (SPA., Illus.). 208p. 1998. pap. 16.00 (*0-89729-856-X*) Ediciones.

— Don Pepe Mora y su Familia. (Coleccion Cuba y sus Jueces). (SPA.). 279p. (Orig.). 1991. 19.95 (*0-89729-600-1*) Ediciones.

— Imagen y Trayectoria del Cubano en la Historia II: La Republica, 1902-1959. LC 93-73803. (Coleccion Cuba y sus Jueces). (SPA., Illus.). 620p. 1998. pap. 39.95 (*0-89729-683-4*, 683-4) Ediciones.

— Imagen y Trayectoria del Cubano en la Historia, 1492-1902. (SPA.). 1994. pap. 29.95 (*0-89729-682-6*) Ediciones.

— El Impacto Creador de Espana En America, 1492-1592. LC 91-71900. (Coleccion de Estudios Hispanicos - Hispanic Studies Collection). (SPA.). 278p. (Orig.). 1992. pap. 19.95 (*0-89729-605-2*) Ediciones.

— Manuel Sanguily: Historia de un Ciudadano. 2nd ed. LC 89-83536. (Coleccion Cuba y sus Jueces). (SPA.). 156p. 1989. pap. 9.95 (*0-89729-532-3*) Ediciones.

— Modesto M. Mora, M. D. La Gesta de un Medico. LC 96-84349. (Coleccion Cuba y sus Jueces). (SPA., Illus.). 430p. 1996. 30.00 (*0-89729-805-5*) Ediciones.

— Perfil y Aventura del Hombre en la Historia (1492-1988) LC 88-82372. (SPA.). 624p. (Orig.). 1988. pap. 30.00 (*0-89729-505-6*) Ediciones.

— Variaciones en Torno a Dios, El Tiempo, la Muerte y Otros Temas. LC 87-81633. (SPA.). 463p. (Orig.). 1987. pap. 20.00 (*0-89729-450-5*) Ediciones.

Costa-Pace, Rosa. The City. LC 93-17918. (Junior Library of Ecology).Tr. of La/Ciudad. (Illus.). 32p. (J). (gr. 4 up). 1994. lib. bdg. 14.95 (*0-7910-2101-7*) Chelsea Hse.

— The Junior Library of Ecology, 5 vols., Set. (Illus.). 32p. (J). (gr. 4 up). 1994. lib. bdg. 74.75 (*0-7910-2100-9*) Chelsea Hse.

— Keeping the Air Clean. (Junior Library of Ecology). (Illus.). 32p. (J). (gr. 4 up). 1994. lib. bdg. 15.95 (*0-7910-2103-3*) Chelsea Hse.

— Protecting Our Forests. (Junior Library of Ecology). (Illus.). 32p. (J). (gr. 4 up). 1994. lib. bdg. 15.95 (*0-7910-2104-1*) Chelsea Hse.

— Protecting Our Rivers & Lakes. (Junior Library of Ecology). (Illus.). 32p. (J). (gr. 4 up). 1994. lib. bdg. 15.95 (*0-7910-2105-X*) Chelsea Hse.

Costa, Pamela K. Publish It Now Vol. 1: Your Complete Guide to Self-Publishing Success & Small Business Expansion. (Illus.). 90p. (Orig.). 1997. pap. 14.95 (*0-9643002-1-4*) Costa Pubng.

— Through the Eyes of a Young Heart. LC 94-93835. 108p. (YA). (gr. 8-12). 1994. pap. 9.95 (*0-9643002-0-6*) Costa Pubng.

Costa, Paolo M. Musandam: Architecture & Material Culture of a Little Known Region of Oman. LC 93-166933. (Illus.). 250p. (C). 1995. 84.00 (*0-907151-37-X*, Pub. by IMMEL Pubng) St Mut.

— Studies in Arabian Architecture. (Collected Studies: No. CS 455). (Illus.). 336p. 1994. 157.95 (*0-86078-436-3*, Pub. by Variorum) Ashgate Pub Co.

Costa-Pau, Rosa. Conservation of the Sea. LC 93-19872. (Junior Library of Ecology). (Illus.). 32p. (J). (gr. 4 up). 1994. lib. bdg. 14.95 (*0-7910-2102-5*) Chelsea Hse.

Costa, Paul, jt. auth. see McCrae, Robert R.

Costa, Paul T. Early Identification of Alzheimer's Disease & Related Dementias 19: Reference for Clinicians. 28p. 1997. pap. 39.00 (*0-16-061552-6*) USGPO.

— Recognition & Initial Assessment of Alzheimer's Disease & Related Dementias, Clinical Practice 19. 151p. 1997. per. 8.00 (*0-16-061553-4*) USGPO.

Costa, Paul T., Jr., et al, eds. Alzheimer's Disease: Abstracts of the Psychological & Behavioral Literature. (Bibliographies in Psychology Ser.: No. 4). 149p. 1989. pap. 25.00 (*1-55798-049-7*) Am Psychol.

Costa, Paul T., Jr. & VandenBos, Gary R., eds. Psychological Aspects of Serious Illness: Chronic Conditions, Fatal Diseases, & Clinical Care. 172p. 1990. pap. text 19.95 (*1-55798-105-1*) Am Psychol.

Costa, Paul T., Jr. & Widiger, Thomas A., eds. Personality Disorders & the Five-Factor Model of Personality. LC 93-26795. 364p. 1994. text 39.95 (*1-55798-214-7*) Am Psychol.

Costa, Peter. Question & Answer: Conversations with Harvard Scholars. (Illus.). 304p. (C). 1991. 18.95 (*0-674-74000-9*) HUP.

Costa, Peter J., ed. Bridging Mind & Model: Papers in Applied Mathematics. LC 93-86932. 325p. 1994. 24.95 (*0-9624229-7-5*) St Thomas Tech.

Costa Picazo, Rolando, tr. see Alvarez, Julia.

Costa-Pierce, B. A. Culture of Common Carp in Floating Net Cages. (ICLARM Education Ser.: No. 7). 1989. pap. write for info. (*971-10-2272-9*, Pub. by ICLARM) Intl Spec Bk.

Costa-Pierce, B. A. & Soemarwoto, O., eds. Reservoir Fisheries & Aquaculture Development for Resettlement in Indonesia. (ICLARM Technical Reports: No. 23). 378p. 1990. per. write for info. (*971-10-2250-8*, Pub. by ICLARM) Intl Spec Bk.

Costa-Pierce, B. A., et al. Growing Fish in Cages. (ICLARM Education Ser.: No. 10). (Illus.). 43p. 1989. write for info. (*971-10-2275-3*, Pub. by ICLARM) Intl Spec Bk.

— Growing Fish in Pen Systems. (ICLARM Education Ser.: No. 9). (Illus.). 40p. 1989. write for info. (*971-10-2274-5*, Pub. by ICLARM) Intl Spec Bk.

— A Small-Scale Hatchery for Common Carp. (ICLARM Education Ser.: No. 8). (Illus.). 42p. 1989. write for info. (*971-10-2273-7*, Pub. by ICLARM) Intl Spec Bk.

Costa-Pierce, B. A., jt. ed. see Msiska, O. V.

Costa-Pierce, Barry A. From Farmers to Fishers: Developing Reservoir Aquaculture for People Displaced by Dams. LC 97-25585. (Technical Paper Ser.: No. 369). 68p. 1997. pap. 22.00 (*0-8213-3995-8*, 13995) World Bank.

Costa-Pierce, Barry A. & Rakocy, James E., eds. Tilapia Aquaculture in the Americas. (Illus.). 258p. (C). 1997. pap. text 60.00 (*1-888807-01-6*) World Aquaculture.

Costa Pinto, Antonio. Salazar's Dictatorship & European Fascism: Problems & Perspectives of Interpretation. (Social Science Monographs). 220p. 1996. 31.00 (*0-88033-968-3*, 382, Pub. by East Eur Monographs) Col U Pr.

Costa Pinto, Antonio, ed. Modern Portugal. LC 97-45654. 332p. 1998. 39.50 (*0-930664-17-5*) SPOSS.

Costa Ramos, S. & Dias de Deus, J., eds. The Physics of the Quark-Gluon Plasma: Proceedings of the IX Autumn School of Physics, Lisbon. 332p. (C). 1988. text 84.00 (*9971-5-0570-3*) World Scientific Pub.

Costa, Ray. How to Be a Male Exotic Dancer. (Illus.). 114p. (Orig.). pap. text 9.95 (*0-686-38733-3*) Costa.

Costa, Rene De, see De Costa, Rene.

Costa, Richard H. Alison Lurie. 160p. (C). 1992. 22.95 (*0-8057-7634-6*, Twyne) Mac Lib Ref.

— An Appointment with Somerset Maugham: And Other Encounters with Literary Life. LC 94-12375. (Illus.). 248p. 1994. 35.00 (*0-89096-618-4*); pap. 18.95 (*0-89096-619-2*) Tex A&M Univ Pr.

— Edmund Wilson: Our Neighbor from Talcottville. LC 80-23453. (New York State Bks.). (Illus.). 192p. 1980. 39.95 (*0-8156-0163-8*) Syracuse U Pr.

*__Costa, Roberto.__ Nonassociative Algebra & Its Applications: The 4th International Conference. LC 00-26394. (Lecture Notes in Pure & Applied Mathematics Ser.). 2000. write for info. (*0-8247-0406-1*) Dekker.

*__Costa, S., et al, eds.__ Measuring the Size of Things in the Universe: HBT Interferometry & Heavy Ion Physics. 500p. 1999. 128.00 (*981-02-4038-4*) World Scientific Pub.

Costa, Shu Shu. Lotus Seeds & Lucky Stars: Asian Myths & Traditions on Pregnancy & Birthing. LC 97-53269. 144p. 1998. 17.45 (*0-684-84397-8*) S&S Trade.

— Wild Geese & Tea: An Asian-American Wedding Planner. 176p. 1998. pap. 15.00 (*1-57322-650-5*, Riverhd Trade) Berkley Pub.

Costa, Susanne. Glossary of Harpsicord Terms. Kellner, Herbert A., tr. (ENG & GER.). 116p. 1980. 34.95 (*0-933224-30-3*, I129) Bold Strummer Ltd.

Costa, Tom. Life! You Wanna Make Something of It? Bayless, Warren, ed. LC 88-82324. 176p. (Orig.). 1988. pap. 8.95 (*0-937611-37-9*, 110) Hay House.

Costa, Tom-Nicholas. Calling All Saints. LC 97-45678. 80p. 1998. pap. 15.95 (*1-56072-534-6*, Nova Troitsa Bks) Nova Sci Pubs.

*__Costa, Tom-Nicholas.__ Calling More Saints. LC 99-52423. 117p. 2000. pap. 15.95 (*1-56072-728-4*, Nova Troitsa Bks) Nova Sci Pubs.

Costa, Uriel Da, see Da Costa, Uriel.

*__Costa, Vanina.__ Musee D'orsay. 1998. pap. text 12.95 (*2-86656-123-6*) Scala Edit.

Costa, Vasco & Frances, Osvald. Diccionario de Unidadaes y Tablas de Conversion. 3rd ed. (SPA.). 168p. 1977. pap. 17.95 (*0-8288-5328-2*, S50579) Fr & Eur.

Costa, Wilson J. Pearl Killifishes: The Cynolebiatinae. (Illus.). 128p. 1996. 23.95 (*0-7938-2089-8*, TS239) TFH Pubns.

Costa, Xavier, jt. text see Hartray, Guido.

Costabel, Martin, et al, eds. Boundary Value Problems & Integral Equations in Nonsmooth Domains. LC 94-32078. (Lecture Notes in Pure & Applied Mathematics Ser.: Vol. 167). (Illus.). 320p. 1994. pap. text 150.00 (*0-8247-9320-X*) Dekker.

Costabel, U. Atlas of Bronchoaveolar Lavage. Mitchell, J., tr. (Illus.). 112p. 1999. text 98.50 (*0-412-79270-2*, Pub. by E A) OUP.

Costabile, G., et al, eds. Nonlinear Superconductive Electronics & Josephson Devices. (Illus.). 456p. (C). 1992. text 162.00 (*0-306-44100-4*, Kluwer Plenum) Kluwer Academic.

Costabile-Heming, Carol A. Intertextual Exile - Volker Braun's Dramatic Re-Vision of GDR Society. LC 97-134992. (Germanistische Texte und Studien: Bd. 54). 264p. 1997. 50.00 (*3-487-10288-9*) G Olms Pubs.

Costaftis, Michel & Vernadat, Francois, eds. Advances in Factories of the Future, CIM & Robotics. LC 93-16288. (Manufacturing Research & Technology Ser.: Vol. 16). xii,538p. 1993. 213.00 (*0-444-89856-5*) Elsevier.

Costain & Coruh. Basic Theory in Reflection Seismology. (Handbook of Geophysical Exploration: Vol. 1). 1995. write for info. (*0-08-037019-5*, Pergamon Pr) Elsevier.

Costain, Anne N. Inviting Women's Rebellion: A Political Process Interpretation of the Women's Movement. 208p. 1992. text 35.00 (*0-8018-4333-2*) Johns Hopkins.

— Inviting Women's Rebellion: A Political Process Interpretation of the Women's Movement. 216p. (C). 1994. reprint ed. pap. text 14.95 (*0-8018-4874-1*) Johns Hopkins.

Costain, Anne N. & McFarland, Andrew S., eds. Social Movements & American Political Institutions. LC 98-13239. (People, Passions, & Power Ser.). (Illus.). 368p. 1998. 65.00 (*0-8476-8357-5*); pap. 22.95 (*0-8476-8358-3*) Rowman.

Costain, Anne N., jt. ed. see Chambers, Simone.

Costain, Lynne R. & Moawad, Karen. Managing Medical Office Personnel: A Comprehensive Guide to Personnel Management in the Medical Office. rev. ed. Rogers, Gregg, ed. 250p. 1994. reprint ed. student ed. 49.95 (*1-57066-006-9*, 5839M) Practice Mgmt Info.

Costain, Lynne R., jt. auth. see Moawad, Karen.

Costain, Meredith. The Mummy's Curse. LC 99-173652. (Brains & Parker McGoohan Ser.). 64 p. 1999. write for info. (*0-7608-1938-6*) Sundance Pub.

*__Costain, Meredith.__ Olympic Summer Games 2000. Puffin Books Staff, ed. (Illus.). 64p. (J). (gr. 3-7). 2000. pap. 3.99 (*0-14-130903-2*, PuffinBks) Peng Put Young Read.

Costain, Meredith. Rock Raps: Five Decades of Popular Music. (True Stories Ser.). (Illus.). 96p. (J). (gr. 3-9). 1998. pap. 6.95 (*1-86448-441-1*) IPG Chicago.

Costain, Thomas B. The Black Rose. 1976. 29.95 (*0-8488-0466-X*) Amereon Ltd.

— The Black Rose. 1998. reprint ed. 45.95 (*1-56849-701-6*) Buccaneer Bks.

— The Conquering Family. 1994. reprint ed. lib. bdg. 41.95 (*1-56849-372-X*) Buccaneer Bks.

— The Last Plantagenets. 1994. reprint ed. lib. bdg. 45.95 (*1-56849-373-8*) Buccaneer Bks.

— The Magnificent Century. 1994. reprint ed. lib. bdg. 41.95 (*1-56849-371-1*) Buccaneer Bks.

— The Silver Chalice. 1998. reprint ed. 49.95 (*1-56849-702-4*) Buccaneer Bks.

— Son of a Hundred Kings. 1994. lib. bdg. 24.95 (*1-56849-467-X*) Buccaneer Bks.

— The Three Edwards. 1994. reprint ed. lib. bdg. 45.95 (*1-56849-370-3*) Buccaneer Bks.

Costalas, Nicholas, tr. see Dowling, David W.

Costales, Bryan & Allman, Eric. Sendmail. 2nd ed. Estabrook, Gigi & O'Reilly, Tom, eds. (Illus.). 1050p. 1997. reprint ed. pap. 44.95 (*1-56592-222-0*) OReilly & Assocs.

— Sendmail Desktop Reference. Estabrook, Gigi, ed. (Illus.). 76p. 1997. reprint ed. pap. 8.95 (*1-56592-278-6*) OReilly & Assocs.

Costales, Bryan, et al. Sendmail. O'Reilly, Tim, ed. (Computer Science). (Illus.). 830p. 1993. pap. 32.95 (*1-56592-056-2*) Thomson Learn.

Costales, S. B. Guide to Understanding Financial Statements. 2nd ed. 208p. 1993. 34.95 (*0-07-013191-0*) McGraw.

— Guide to Understanding Financial Statements. 2nd ed. 170p. 1993. pap. 14.95 (*0-07-013197-X*) McGraw.

Costall. Situating Action. (EOC Ser.: Vol. 8, No. 2). 1997. pap. 20.00 (*0-8058-9888-3*) L Erlbaum Assocs.

Costamiris, Lois K. Windmills, Washboards & Whippersnappers: The Legends Live on in Hamilton County, Indiana, Vol. 3. LC 98-72778. 225p. 1998. 20.00 (*1-57860-067-7*) Guild Pr IN.

Costanso, Miguel. Account of the Portola Expedition Which Discovered San Francisco Bay. 1998. pap. write for info. (*0-87770-673-5*) Ye Galleon.

— The Discovery of San Francisco Bay: The Portola Expedition of 1769-1770, The Diary of Miguel Costanso: El Descubrimiento de la Bahia de San Francisco: La Expedicion de Portola de 1769-1770, Wait, Maria L., tr. from SPA. LC 92-7885. (ENG & SPA.). 256p. (C). 1992. reprint ed. pap. 14.95 (*0-944220-06-1*) Great West Bks.

Costantakos, Chris A. Demetrios Constantine Dounis: His Method in Teaching the Violin. 2nd rev. ed. LC 97-20842. (American University Studies XIV: Vol. 13). 157p. (C). 1997. text 38.50 (*0-8204-3895-2*) P Lang Pubng.

Costantakos, Chrysie M. The American-Greek Subculture: Process of Continuity. Cordasco, Francesco, ed. LC 80-848. (Amercian Ethnic Groups Ser.). 1981. lib. bdg. 78.95 (*0-405-13411-8*) Ayer.

*__Costantini, Costanzo.__ Bird of Paradise. 2000. 18.00 (*88-7301-403-8*) Gremese Intl.

Costantini, Costanzo. Conversations with Fellini. 1996. pap. 16.00 (*0-614-12550-2*, Harvest Bks) Harcourt.

— Conversations with Fellini. Sorooshian, Sohrab, tr. from ITA. (Illus.). 256p. 1996. pap. 16.00 (*0-15-600440-2*, Harvest Bks) Harcourt.

Costantini, Domenico, jt. ed. see Cooke, Roger.

Costantini, Frank & Jaenisch, Rudolf, eds. Genetic Manipulation of the Early Mammalian Embryo. (Banbury Reports: No. 20). (Illus.). 289p. (C). 1985. text 63.00 (*0-87969-220-0*) Cold Spring Harbor.

*__Costantini, Mary Ann.__ Patterns in Life. LC 00-102665. 112p. 2000. 16.95 (*1-56167-612-8*) Noble Hse MD.

Costantini, Paolo & Mossetto, Gianfranco, texts. Venezia-Marghera: Photography & Transformations in the Contemporary City. (Illus.). 208p. 1998. pap. 45.00 (*88-8158-128-0*, 811081, Pub. by Charta) Dist Art Pubs.

Costantino. Moving Don't Be Taken. 1990. pap. 12.95 (*0-945155-04-2*) Trans Pub.

Costantino, Maria. Art Nouveau. (Illus.). 112p. 1999. pap. 19.95 (*1-57715-074-0*) Knckerbocker.

— Fashions of a Decade: The 1930s. Cumming, Valerie & Feldman, Elane, eds. (Illus.). 64p. (J). (gr. 4-9). 1992. 19.95 (*0-8160-2466-9*) Facts on File.

— Impressionists. 1993. 29.98 (*1-55521-931-4*) Bk Sales Inc.

— Klimt. (Illus.). 112p. 1998. pap. 19.95 (*1-57715-053-8*) Knckerbocker.

— The Life & Works of Frank Lloyd Wright. LC 97-77958. (Illus.). 160p. 1998. 19.98 (*0-7624-0378-0*, Courage) Running Pr.

— Men's Fashion in the Twentieth Century: From Frock Coats to Intelligent Fibres. (Illus.). 160p. (Orig.). 1997. pap. 29.95 (*0-89676-225-4*, Costume & Fashion Pr) QSMG Ltd.

Costantino, Mario. Basic Italian Conversation. (ITA., Illus.). 280p. 1995. pap. 19.06 (*0-8442-8055-0*, 80550, Natl Textbk Co) NTC Contemp Pub Co.

— Now You're Talking: Italian in No Time. 3rd ed. (ITA.). 2000. pap. text 14.95 incl. audio (*0-7641-7356-1*) Barron.

Costantino, Mario & Gambella, Lawrence R. The Italian Way: Aspects of Behavior, Attitudes, & Customs of the Italians. LC 96-221220. (Illus.). 128p. 1995. pap. 12.95 (*0-8442-8072-0*, 80720, Passprt Bks) NTC Contemp Pub Co.

Costantino, R. F. & Desharnais, R. A. Population Dynamics & the Tribolium Model: Genetics & Demography. Frankel, R. et al, eds. (Monographs on Theoretical & Applied Genetics: Vol. 13). (Illus.). xii, 258p. 1991. 144.00 (*0-387-97581-0*) Spr-Verlag.

Costanza, Chuck, et al. 1995 Directory of State Toxic Contacts. 74p. 1995. 10.00 (*0-614-10574-9*, 6466) Natl Conf State Legis.

Costanza, John R. Quantum Leap: In Speed to Market. 352p. 1996. 45.00 (*0-9628182-1-6*, Irwn Prfssnl) McGraw-Hill Prof.

— The Quantum Leap . . . In Speed to Market. (Illus.). 336p. 1990. 64.95 (*0-9628182-0-8*) J I T Inst.

Costanza, Mike & Lawrence, Greg. The Real Seinfeld: As Told by the Real Costanza. (Illus.). 128p. 1998. pap. 14.95 (*0-9663298-0-5*) WordWise Lit Servs.

Costanza, Robert. Frontiers in Ecological Economics: Transdisciplinary Essays by Robert Costanza. LC 97-14366. 528p. (C). 1997. text 100.00 (*1-85898-503-X*) E Elgar.

*__Costanza, Robert.__ Institutions, Ecosystems & Sustainability. 1999. 49.95 (*1-56670-389-1*) Lewis Pubs.

Costanza, Robert, ed. Ecological Economics. (Illus.). 555p. 1991. text 73.50 (*0-231-07562-6*) Col U Pr.

— Ecological Economics: The Science & Management of Sustainability. 544p. (C). 1992. pap. text 30.50 (*0-231-07563-4*) Col U Pr.

Costanza, Robert, et al, eds. The Development of Ecological Economics. LC 96-34463. (International Library of Critical Writings in Economics Ser.: No. 75). 816p. 1997. 265.00 (*1-85898-386-X*) E Elgar.

— Ecosystem Health: New Goals for Environmental Management. LC 92-10531. 269p. 1992. pap. 27.00 (*1-55963-140-6*) Island Pr.

Costanza, Robert, et al, eds. Getting down to Earth: Practical Applications of Ecological Economics. 463p. 1996. pap. text 40.00 (*1-55963-503-7*) Island Pr.

Costanza, Robert, et al, eds. Introduction to Ecological Economics. LC 97-204572. 288p. (C). 1997. boxed set 54.95 (*1-884015-72-7*) St Lucie Pr.

Costanza, Robert, jt. auth. see Prugh, Thomas.

Costanzi, John J., ed. Clinical Management of Malignant Melanoma. (Cancer Treatment & Research Ser.). 1984. text 103.50 (*0-89838-656-X*) Kluwer Academic.

Costanzo. Physiology. (Board Review Ser.). 1994. 19.95 (*0-685-75156-2*) Lppncott W & W.

— Psychology Applied to Law. (Psychology Ser.). 2001. pap. 28.00 (*0-534-36629-5*) Brooks-Cole.

Costanzo, Angelo. Surprizing Narrative: Olaudah Equiano & the Beginnings of Black Autobiography, 104. LC 86-25748. (Contributions in Afro-American & African Studies: No. 104). 156p. 1987. 49.95 (*0-313-25633-0*, CZO/, Greenwood Pr) Greenwood.

Costanzo, Charlene A. The Twelve Gifts of Birth. (Illus.). 64p. (J). (ps-3). 1998. 19.95 (*1-891836-12-9*) Featherfew.

Costanzo, Christie. Learning New Roles. LC 91-11572. (Women Today Ser.). 64p. (J). (gr. 6-12). 1991. 12.95 (*0-685-59202-2*) Rourke Corp.

— Learning New Roles. LC 91-11572. (Women Today Ser.). 64p. (YA). (gr. 6-12). 1991. lib. bdg. 17.95 (*0-86593-117-8*) Rourke Corp.

— Scuba Diving & Snorkeling. 1992. pap. text 10.95 (*1-56065-059-1*) Capstone Pr.

— Volleyball. LC 93-27153. (Pro-Am Sports Ser.). 48p. (J). (gr. 3-8). 1993. lib. bdg. 17.95 (*0-86593-344-8*) Rourke Corp.

*__Costanzo, Gerald.__ American Poetry: The Next Generation. 2000. 39.95 (*0-88748-348-8*) Carnegie-Mellon.

— Great Disguise. 50p. (C). 2000. pap. 8.00 (*0-9679429-1-8*) Air & Nothing.

Costanzo, Gerald. Nobody Lives on Arthur Godfrey Boulevard. (American Poets Continuum Ser.: Vol. 24). 77p. 1992. 20.00 (*0-918526-92-2*); pap. 10.00 (*0-918526-93-0*) BOA Edns.

Costanzo, Gerald, ed. The Devins Award Poetry Anthology. LC 97-40959. 264p. 1998. pap. 16.95 (*0-8262-1161-5*) U of Mo Pr.

— Three Rivers Ten Years. LC 83-70363. 1983. 20.95 (*0-915604-84-1*); pap. 11.95 (*0-915604-85-X*) Carnegie-Mellon.

*__Costanzo, Gerald & Daniels, Jim, eds.__ American Poetry: The Next Generation. LC 99-74773. 480p. 2000. 39.95 (*0-88748-337-2*, Pub. by Carnegie-Mellon); pap. 24.95 (*0-88748-343-7*, Pub. by Carnegie-Mellon) CUP Services.

Costanzo, Gerald & Daniels, Jim, eds. Carnegie Mellon Anthology of Poetry. LC 92-74533. 1993. 29.95 (*0-88748-162-0*); pap. 16.95 (*0-88748-163-9*) Carnegie-Mellon.

Costanzo, Linda S. Physiology. Schmitt, William, ed. LC 97-28809. (Text & Review Ser.). (Illus.). 416p. 1998. pap. text 29.95 (*0-7216-6611-6*, W B Saunders Co) Harcrt Hlth Sci Grp.

*__Costanzo, Linda S.__ Physiology. 2nd ed. LC 98-7540. (Board Review Ser.). 326p. 1998. 24.95 (*0-683-30396-1*) Lppncott W & W.

Costanzo, Margot. Legal Writing. (Legal Skills Ser.). 171p. 1994. pap. 22.00 (*1-874241-43-0*, Pub. by Cavendish Pubng) Gaunt.

— Problem Solving. Macfarlane, Julie, ed. LC 95-123406. (Legal Skills Ser.). 254p. 1995. pap. 19.00 (*1-874241-46-5*, Pub. by Cavendish Pubng) Gaunt.

Costanzo, Mariangela, jt. auth. see Sajeva, Maurizio.

Costanzo, Mark. Just Revenge: Costs & Consequences of the Death Penalty. LC 97-17045. 224p. 1997. text 22.95 (*0-312-15559-X*); pap. text 14.95 (*0-312-17945-6*) St Martin.

Costanzo, Mark & Oskamp, Stuart. Violence & the Law. LC 94-19053. (Claremont Symposium on Applied Social Psychology Ser.: Vol. 7). 256p. 1994. 39.95 (*0-8039-5341-0*); pap. 18.95 (*0-8039-5342-9*) Sage.

An Asterisk (*) at the beginning of an entry indicates that the title is appearing for the first time.

Costanzo, Mark, jt. ed. see Oskamp, Stuart.

Costanzo, W. Kenneth. Getting Hired: How to Sell Yourself. (Illus.). 104p. 1987. 12.95 (*0-945490-00-3*) Carolina Pacific.

Costanzo, William V. The Electronic Text: Learning to Write, Read, & Reason with Computers. LC 88-31175. (Illus.). 320p. 1989. 39.95 (*0-87778-208-3*) Educ Tech Pubns.

— Reading the Movies: Twelve Great Films on Video & How to Teach Them. (Illus.). 201p. (C). 1992. pap. 14.95 (*0-8141-3910-8*) NCTE.

***Costar, Brian.** Deadlock or Democracy: The Future of the Senate. (Frontline Ser.). 64p. 1999. pap. 9.95 (*0-86840-570-1*, Pub. by NSW U Pr) Intl Spec Bk.

Costar, Brian, ed. For Better of for Worse: The Federal Coalition. 176p. 1994. pap. 24.95 (*0-522-84617-3*, Pub. by Melbourne Univ Pr) Paul & Co Pubs.

***Costar, Brian & Economou, Nick, eds.** The Kennett Revolution: Victorian Politics in the 1990's. 288p. 1999. pap. 25.00 (*0-86840-545-0*, Pub. by NSW U Pr) Intl Spec Bk.

Costar, James W. Focus on Improving Your Middle School Guidance Program. Romano, Louis G., ed. 50p. 1988. pap. 3.00 (*0-918449-11-1*) MI Middle Educ.

Costarella, Linda, jt. auth. see Bove, Mary.

***Costas, Bob.** Fair Ball: A Fan's Case for Baseball. LC 99-87992. 192p. 2000. 21.95 (*0-7679-0465-6*) Broadway BDD.

Costas, Bob, et al. St. Louis Tapestry. LC 99-36019. (Urban Tapestry Ser.). (Illus.). 512p. 1999. 49.95 (*1-881096-72-6*) Towery Pub.

Costas, Gloria, tr. see Lehman, Yvette K.

Costas, M., jt. auth. see Rodriquez, R.

Costas, Orlando E. Christ Outside the Gate: Mission Beyond Christendom. LC 82-7892. 254p. (Orig.). reprint ed. pap. 78.80 (*0-608-20183-9*, 207144200010) Bks Demand.

— Comunicacion Por Medio de la Predicacion. (SPA.). 255p. 1991. reprint ed. pap. 9.99 (*0-89922-021-5*) Caribe Betania.

Costas, Procope S. An Outline History of the Greek Language. LC 97-177918. 143p. 1997. pap. 20.00 (*0-89005-259-X*) Ares.

Costas, Suzanne, jt. auth. see Bieler, Peter.

Coste, Christine. Lonely Planet Quebec et Ontario. (FRE.). 1998. 24.95 (*2-84070-077-8*) Lonely Planet.

Coste, D., jt. ed. see Galisson, Robert.

Coste, Didier. Narrative As Communication. (Theory & History of Literature Ser.: Vol. 80). 370p. (Orig.). 1989. pap. 19.95 (*0-8166-1720-1*) U of Minn Pr.

Coste, M., et al, eds. Real Algebraic Geometry: Proceedings of the Conference Held in Rennes, France, June 24-28, 1991. LC 92-27019. 1992. 79.95 (*0-387-55992-2*) Spr-Verlag.

Coste, Marion. Honu. LC 93-20745. (Illus.). 32p. (J). (ps-4). 1993. 9.95 (*0-8248-1507-6*, Kolowalu Bk) UH Pr.

— Kolea: The Story of the Pacific Golden Plover. LC 98-7673. (Illus.). 32p. (J). (gr. 2-4). 1998. 14.95 (*0-8248-1961-6*, Kolowalu Bk) UH Pr.

— Nene. LC 92-36543. (Illus.). 32p. (J). (gr. 3-6). 1993. 9.95 (*0-8248-1389-8*, Kolowalu Bk) UH Pr.

Coste, Twila Robar-De, see Hickman, Pamela.

Coste, Warren La, see La Coste, Warren.

***Costeau, Jean-Michel & Richards, Mose.** Cousteau's Great White Shark. LC 94-37477. (Illus.). 176p. 2000. pap. 19.98 (*0-8109-8134-3*, Pub. by Abrams) Time Warner.

Costecalde, Claude B., ed. The DK Illustrated Family Bible: New International Version Bible. LC 97-131843. (Illus.). 384p. (J). (ps up). 1997. 29.95 (*0-7894-1503-8*) DK Pub Inc.

Costecvalde, Claude-Bernard, et al, eds. The Jubilee Illustrated Family Bible. (Illus.). 383p. (J). 1997. 29.95 (*1-57727-100-9*) Jubilee Pub Grp.

Costeel, J. Doyle & Stahl, Robert J. Doorways to Decision Making: A Handbook for Teaching Decision Making Strategies. 280p. 1996. pap. 29.95 (*1-882664-21-3*) Prufrock Pr.

Costello. Controlling Conflict: Alternative Dispute Resolution for Business. LC 96-164544. 512p. 1996. 59.00 (*0-8080-0088-8*, 5057) CCH INC.

— Gendered Voices. LC 94-79795. (C). 1995. pap. text 35.00 (*0-15-501578-8*, Pub. by Harcourt Coll Pubs); pap. text, teacher ed. 30.00 (*0-15-503149-X*) Harcourt Coll Pubs.

Costello, et al. Minnesota Misdemeanor & Moving Traffic Violations, Vol. ISS.11. 328p. 1996. ring bd. 165.00 (*0-86678-933-2*, 81819-15, MICHIE) LEXIS Pub.

— Minnesota Misdemeanors & Moving Traffic Violations. 1998. ring bd. 165.00 (*0-327-00145-3*, 81819-18) LEXIS Pub.

— Minnesota Misdemeanors & Moving Traffic Violations, 2 vols., No. 15. 300p. 1998. ring bd. 165.00 (*0-327-00771-0*, 8181919) LEXIS Pub.

Costello, A. Gemma. In God's Hands: The Story of Sister Mary Consilio & Cuan Mhuire. 90p. 1989. pap. 22.00 (*0-86217-255-1*, Pub. by Veritas Pubns) St Mut.

Costello, Andrew. Down to Earth but Looking Up: Stories to Lift the Spirit. (Illus.). 239p. 1999. pap. 14.95 (*0-88347-429-8*, Pub. by T More) BookWorld.

Costello, Anthony. Improving Newborn Health in Developing Countries. LC 99-30272. 1998. 48.00 (*1-86094-097-8*, Pub. by Imperial College) World Scientific Pub.

Costello, Augustine & Ferdinand, Theodore N. Our Police Protectors: History of the New York Police. 3rd ed. LC 79-129324. (Criminology, Law Enforcement, & Social Problems Ser.: No. 127). (Illus.). 653p. 1972. reprint ed. lib. bdg. 50.00 (*0-87585-127-4*) Patterson Smith.

Costello, Augustine E. Our Firemen: History of the New York Fire Departments. (Illus.). 1112p. 1997. reprint ed. 24.95 (*1-57715-013-9*) Knckerbocker.

Costello, Bagz. Where Have All the Little Girls Gone? 320p. (Orig.). 1987. mass mkt. 3.50 (*0-87067-838-8*) Holloway.

Costello, Bill. Awaken Your Birdbrain: Using Creativity to Get What You Want. LC 98-90139. (Illus.). 166p. 1999. 24.95 (*1-891905-33-3*); pap. 14.95 (*1-891905-34-1*) Thinkorporated.

— Cartooning with Letters, Numbers, & Shapes: Creating Creatures & Critters. (Illus.). 56p. (J). (ps-8). 1995. reprint ed. pap. 8.95 (*1-891905-30-9*) Thinkorporated.

— Cartooning with Math. LC 98-90141. (Illus.). 64p. (J). (ps-8). 1998. pap. 8.95 (*1-891905-31-7*) Thinkorporated.

— Creativity for Kids of All Ages. LC 98-90140. (Illus.). 64p. (J). (gr. 1-12). 1998. pap. 8.95 (*1-891905-32-5*) Thinkorporated.

Costello, Bonnie. Elizabeth Bishop: Questions of Mastery. 280p. (C). 1993. pap. 17.50 (*0-674-24690-X*) HUP.

— Marianne Moore: Imaginary Possessions. LC 81-1133. 281p. 1981. 28.00 (*0-674-54848-5*) HUP.

Costello, Bonnie, et al, eds. The Selected Letters of Marianne Moore. LC 96-52200. (Illus.). 597p. 1997. 35.00 (*0-679-43909-9*) Knopf.

Costello, Brian. Taking Care of Your Money: Multi-Dimensional Investing That Works. 200p. 1997. pap. 19.95 (*1-55022-307-0*, Pub. by ECW) LPC InBook.

Costello, C. G. Symptoms of Psychopathology: A Handbook. LC 78-88309. 693p. (C). 1970. reprint ed. pap. 200.00 (*0-8357-9988-3*, 205518600011) Bks Demand.

Costello, Carol, jt. auth. see Glickstein, Lee.

Costello, Charles G. Anxiety & Depression: The Adaptive Emotions. LC 76-382042. 159p. reprint ed. pap. 49.30 (*0-7837-1036-4*, 204134700020) Bks Demand.

— Symptoms of Depression. LC 92-18109. (Series on Personality Processes). 336p. 1993. 99.95 (*0-471-54304-7*) Wiley.

Costello, Charles G., ed. Basic Issues in Psychopathology. LC 92-48972. 465p. 1993. lib. bdg. 58.00 (*0-89862-139-9*) Guilford Pubns.

— Personality Characteristics of the Personality Disordered. LC 95-7510. 340p. 1995. 75.00 (*0-471-01529-6*) Wiley.

***Costello, Chris.** Lou's on First: A Biography of Lou Costello. 2000. pap. 17.95 (*0-8154-1083-2*) Cooper Sq.

Costello, Chris. Lou's on First: The Biography of Lou Costello. (Illus.). 384p. 1982. pap. 9.95 (*0-312-49914-0*) St Martin.

Costello, Con. Botany Bay: The Story of the Convicts Transported from Ireland to Australia 1791-1853. 176p. 1997. pap. 12.95 (*0-85342-808-5*, Pub. by Mercier Pr) Irish Amer Bk.

— A Most Delightful Station: The British Army on the Curragh of Kildare, Ireland. LC 96-170733. 432p. 1996. 59.95 (*1-898256-08-X*) Dufour.

***Costello, Con.** A Most Delightful Station: The British Army on the Curragh of Kildore, Ireland, 1855-1922. (Illus.). 432p. 1999. pap. 27.95 (*1-898256-73-X*, Pub. by Collins Press) Irish Bks Media.

Costello, Cynthia. The How-to-Make-a-Book Book: Directions for Making More Than Thirty Books. Clark Editorial & Design Staff & Clark, Kimberley, eds. (Illus.). 88p. (J). (gr. 1-6). 1997. pap. 10.95 (*0-88160-277-9*, LW347) Learning Wks.

Costello, Cynthia & Fish-Parcham, Cheryl. One Out of Three: Children Without Health Insurance, 1995-1996. (Illus.). 41p. 1998. pap. text 20.00 (*0-7881-7057-0*) DIANE Pub.

Costello, Cynthia B. We're Worth It! Women & Collective Action in the Insurance Workplace. 168p. 1992. text 23.50 (*0-252-01803-6*) U of Ill Pr.

Costello, D. P., tr. see Hidayat, Sadiq.

Costello, Darby. Astrology. (Pocket Guides Ser.: No. 22). (Illus.). 128p. (J). 1996. pap. 6.95 (*0-7894-1019-2*) DK Pub Inc.

Costello, Elaine. Random House Webster's American Sign Language Dictionary, Concise Edition. LC 95-105155. 1102p. 1994. 55.00 (*0-394-58580-1*) Random.

— Random House Webster's American Sign Language Dictionary, Concise Edition. LC 97-21538. (Illus.). 704p. 1997. pap. 20.00 (*0-679-78011-4*) Random Ref & Info.

***Costello, Elaine.** Random House Webster's American Sign Language Medical Dictionary. (Illus.). 2000. 34.95 (*0-375-42554-3*); pap. 16.95 (*0-375-70927-4*) Random.

Costello, Elaine. Religious Signing. (Illus.). 240p. 1997. pap. 17.95 (*0-553-34244-4*) Bantam.

— Signing: How to Speak with Your Hands. 1995. 23.05 (*0-606-02988-5*, Pub. by Turtleback) Demco.

— Signing: How to Speak with Your Hands. rev. ed. LC 94-46156. (Illus.). 288p. 1995. pap. 17.95 (*0-553-37539-3*) Bantam.

— Webster's Concise American Sign Language Dictionary. LC 98-31262. 1999. pap. 10.95 (*0-375-70352-7*) Random.

***Costello, Elaine.** Webster's Pocket American Sign Language Dictionary. (Illus.). 400p. 1999. pap. 7.99 (*0-375-70700-X*) Random Ref & Info.

Costello, Emily. Against the Rules. (Soccer Stars Ser.: No. 3). 144p. (J). (gr. 3-7). 1998. pap. 3.99 (*0-553-48646-2*) BDD Bks Young Read.

***Costello, Emily.** Animal Emergency: Abandoned Puppy, Vol. 1. (Animal Emergency Ser.: No. 1). 128p. (J). (gr. 3-7). 1999. mass mkt. 3.99 (*0-380-79753-4*, Avon Bks) Morrow Avon.

— Animal Emergency: Bad Luck Lion, Vol. 3. (Animal Emergency Ser.: No. 3). 128p. (J). (gr. 3-7). 1999. mass mkt. 3.99 (*0-380-79755-0*, Avon Bks) Morrow Avon.

— Animal Emergency: Ducks in Danger, Vol. 2. (Animal Emergency Ser.: No. 2). 128p. (J). (gr. 3-7). 1999. mass mkt. 3.99 (*0-380-79754-2*, Avon Bks) Morrow Avon.

— Animal Emergency: Frightened Fawn, Vol. 8. LC 00-100193. (Animal Emergency Ser.: No. 8). 128p. (J). (gr. 3-7). 2000. mass mkt. 3.99 (*0-380-81601-6*) Morrow Avon.

— Animal Emergency: Hit-and-Run Retriever, Vol. 7. LC 99-96358. (Animal Emergency Ser.: No. 7). (Illus.). 128p. (J). (gr. 3-7). 2000. mass mkt. 3.99 (*0-380-81600-8*) Morrow Avon.

— Animal Emergency: Lost Kitten, Vol. 6. LC 99-95487. (Animal Emergency Ser.: No. 6). 128p. (J). (gr. 3-7). 2000. mass mkt. 3.99 (*0-380-81111-1*) Morrow Avon.

— Animal Emergency: Rabbit Rescue, Vol. 5. LC 99-95193. (Animal Emergency Ser.: No. 5). 128p. (J). (gr. 3-7). 2000. mass mkt. 3.99 (*0-380-81110-3*) Morrow Avon.

— Animal Emergency: Runaway Wolf Pups, Vol. 4. (Animal Emergency Ser.: No. 4). (Illus.). 128p. (J). (gr. 3-7). 1999. mass mkt. 3.99 (*0-380-79757-7*) Morrow Avon.

Costello, Emily. Best Friend Face-Off. (Soccer Stars Ser.: No. 4). (J). (gr. 3-7). 1998. pap. 3.99 (*0-553-48647-0*) BDD Bks Young Read.

— Blue Ribbon Christmas. (Full House Stephanie Ser.: Vol. 23). 160p. (J). (gr. 3-6). 1997. per. 3.99 (*0-671-00830-7*) PB.

— Calling the Shots. (Soccer Stars Ser.: No. 7). 160p. (J). (gr. 3-7). 1999. pap. 3.99 (*0-553-48683-7*) BDD Bks Young Read.

— Fireworks & Flamingoes. (Full House Club Stephanie Ser.: Vol. 2). 144p. (J). (gr. 3-6). 1997. per. 3.99 (*0-671-00827-7*) PB.

— Foul Play. (Soccer Stars Ser.: No. 1). 128p. (J). (gr. 3-7). 1998. pap. 3.99 (*0-553-48644-6*, Skylark BDD) BDD Bks Young Read.

— Foul Play, 1. (Soccer Stars Ser.: No. 1). (J). (gr. 3-7). 1998. 9.09 (*0-606-13785-8*, Pub. by Turtleback) Demco.

— Lottery Blues. (Soccer Stars Ser.: No. 5). (J). (gr. 3-7). 1998. pap. 3.99 (*0-553-48648-9*) BDD Bks Young Read.

— On the Sidelines. (Soccer Stars Ser.: No. 2). 128p. (J). (gr. 3-7). 1998. pap. 3.99 (*0-553-48645-4*, Skylark BDD) BDD Bks Young Read.

— On the Sidelines. (Soccer Stars Ser.: No. 2). (J). (gr. 3-7). 1998. 9.09 (*0-606-13786-6*, Pub. by Turtleback) Demco.

***Costello, Emily.** Realm of the Panther: A Story of South Florida's Forests. LC 99-43775. (Habitat Ser.). (Illus.). 36p. (J). (gr. 1-4). 2000. 26.95 (*1-56899-851-I*) Soundprints.

— Realm of the Panther: A Story of South Florida's Forests. LC 99-43775. (Habitat Ser.). (Illus.). 36p. (J). (ps-3). 2000. 15.95 (*1-56899-847-3*); 15.95 incl. audio (*1-56899-849-X*); pap. 5.95 (*1-56899-848-1*) Soundprints.

— Realm of the Panther Included Toy: A Story of South Florida's Forests. LC 99-43775. (Habitat Ser.). (Illus.). 36p. (J). (gr. 1-4). 2000. pap. 16.95 (*1-56899-852-X*) Soundprints.

Costello, Emily. Teaming Up. (Soccer Stars Ser.: No. 8). 144p. (J). (gr. 3-7). 1999. pap. 3.99 (*0-553-48684-5*) BDD Bks Young Read.

— Tournament Trouble. (Soccer Stars Ser.: No. 6). (J). (gr. 3-7). 1998. pap. 3.99 (*0-553-48649-7*) BDD Bks Young Read.

— The Truth about Boys. (Full House Stephanie Ser.: Vol. 20). 144p. (J). (gr. 3-6). 1997. pap. 3.99 (*0-671-00361-5*, Minstrel Bks) PB.

Costello, Emily & Lipinski, Tara. Tara Lipinski: Triumph on Ice: The Official Autobiography of America's Olympic Gold Medalist. (Illus.). 144p. 1998. mass mkt. 4.99 (*0-553-57136-2*) Bantam.

Costello, Emily, jt. auth. see Kinoian, Vartkis.

***Costello, Francis J.** The Irish Revolution & Its Aftermath. (Illus.). 352p. 2000. 54.50 (*0-7165-2633-6*, Pub. by Irish Acad Pr) Intl Spec Bk.

Costello, Frank, ed. Michael Collins: In His Own Words. LC 97-161282. 192p. 1997. pap. 17.95 (*0-7171-2436-3*, Pub. by Gill & MacMill) Irish Bks Media.

Costello, Frank B. The Political Philosophy of Luis de Molina, S. J. 1974. pap. 18.00 (*88-7041-338-1*) Jesuit Hist.

Costello, G. A. Theory of Wire Rope. Ling, Frederick F., ed. (Mechanical Engineering Ser.). 120p. 1990. 69.00 (*0-387-97189-0*) Spr-Verlag.

Costello, George A. Theory of Wire Rope. 2nd ed. Ling, F. F., ed. LC 97-9273. (Mechanical Engineering Ser.). (Illus.). 152p. 1997. 59.00 (*0-387-98202-7*) Spr-Verlag.

Costello, Gerald M. Mission to Latin America: The Successes & Failures of a Twentieth-Century Crusade. LC 78-12974. 319p. reprint ed. pap. 98.90 (*0-8357-8956-X*, 203357000086) Bks Demand.

Costello, Gwen. A Bible Way of the Cross for Children. (Illus.). 32p. (Orig.). (J). (gr. 4-6). 1988. pap. 1.95 (*0-89622-353-1*) Twenty-Third.

— Classroom Prayer Services for the Days of Advent & Lent. LC 97-60728. 144p. (J). (gr. 2-7). 1997. pap. 12.95 (*0-89622-737-5*) Twenty-Third.

— Edna Eagle. Kendzia, Mary C., ed. (Illus.). 32p. (Orig.). (J). 1992. pap. 4.95 (*0-89622-528-3*) Twenty-Third.

— A Prayer Primer for Catechists & Teachers: For Personal & Classroom Use. LC 97-62565. 64p. 1998. pap. 5.95 (*0-89622-922-X*) Twenty-Third.

— Prayer Services for Catechist & Teacher Meetings. LC 96-60347. 72p. (Orig.). 1996. pap. 12.95 (*0-89622-696-4*) Twenty-Third.

— A Prayerbook for Catechists. 41p. 1999. pap. 5.95 (*0-89622-979-3*) Twenty-Third.

— Praying with the Saints: 30 Classroom Services for Children. (Illus.). 95p. (J). (gr. 3-6). 1999. pap. 12.95 (*0-89622-982-3*) Twenty-Third.

— Priscilla Tadpole. Kendzia, Mary C., ed. (Illus.). 32p. (Orig.). (J). 1992. pap. 4.95 (*0-89622-527-5*) Twenty-Third.

— Reconciliation Services for Children: 18 Prayer Services to Celebrate God's Forgiveness. LC 92-60230. 72p. (Orig.). 1992. pap. 9.95 (*0-89622-516-X*) Twenty-Third.

— Stations of the Cross for Teenagers. (Illus.). 32p. (YA). 1988. pap. 1.95 (*0-89622-386-8*) Twenty-Third.

Costello, Gwen & Paprocki, Joe. Seven Steps to Great Religion Classes. LC 98-60622. 80p. 1998. pap. 7.95 (*0-89622-934-3*) Twenty-Third.

Costello, Harry J. A Season of Mists. 422p. mass mkt. 4.99 (*1-55197-052-X*) Picasso Publ.

Costello, Harry T. Josiah Royce's Seminar, 1913-1914: As Recorded in the Notebooks of Harry T. Costello. Smith, Grover C., ed. LC 81-4213. (Illus.). 209p. 1981. reprint ed. lib. bdg. 59.50 (*0-313-23080-3*, COJR) Greenwood.

— Philosophy of the Real & the Possible. LC 72-972. reprint ed. 20.00 (*0-404-01737-1*) AMS Pr.

Costello, Hilary & De-Bhaldraithe, Eoin, trs. The Life of St. Benedict: Text & Commentary. LC 93-420. 186p. 1993. pap. 19.95 (*0-932506-77-1*) St Bedes Pubns.

Costello, Hilary & Holdsworth, Christopher, eds. A Gathering of Friends: Learning & Spirituality in John of Forde. (Cistercian Studies: No. CS161). 214p. Date not set. pap. 21.95 (*0-87907-761-1*) Cistercian Pubns.

Costello, J. A. Indian History of the Northwest: Siwash: The Siwash, Their Life, Legends & Tales. (Illus.). 183p. (C). 1895. reprint ed. pap. text 19.38 (*1-55567-616-2*) Coyote Press.

— The Siwash: Their Life, Legends, & Tales. 178p. 1977. 19.95 (*0-87770-398-1*) Ye Galleon.

Costello, J. F., ed. Sympathomimetic Enantiomers in the Treatment of Asthma: The Proceedings of a Meeting Held by the Section of Respiratory Medicine, the Royal Society of Medicine, London, October 1995. LC 96-44595. (Illus.). 138p. 1997. text 48.00 (*1-85070-776-6*) Prthnon Pub.

Costello, J. F. & Mann, R. D., eds. Beta Agonists in the Treatment of Asthma. LC 92-49662. 158p. 1992. 68.00 (*1-85070-438-4*) Prthnon Pub.

Costello, J. F., et al. An Atlas of Lung Infections. (Encyclopedia of Visual Medicine Ser.). (Illus.). 112p. (C). 1996. 85.00 (*1-85070-456-2*) Prthnon Pub.

Costello, J. P., jt. auth. see Patrick, E. A.

Costello, Jacinta L., jt. auth. see Masterson, James F.

Costello, Jacqueline & Tucker, Amy. A Writing Course by & for ESL Students. 320p. (C). 1984. pap. 29.38 (*0-07-554586-1*) McGraw.

Costello, Jacqueline & Tucker, Amy, eds. Forms of Literature. 1050p. (C). 1988. pap. 49.69 (*0-07-554798-8*) McGraw.

Costello, James A. The Underbelly Poems. 1981. pap. 2.95 (*0-9605098-0-1*) En Passant Poet.

Costello, Jena H. Just the Basics. Goodrich, Leah K., ed. (Illus.). 128p. (Orig.). 1995. pap. 9.95 (*0-9649130-0-3*) J C Pubng.

Costello, Joan, et al. Growing up American: Contemporary Children & Their Society. 206p. 1986. 24.95 (*0-87073-303-6*); pap. 18.95 (*0-87073-304-4*) Schenkman Bks Inc.

Costello, John. The Mask of Treachery. 1990. mass mkt. 5.95 (*0-446-35783-9*, Pub. by Warner Bks) Little.

— Mathematics for the Management, Life & Social Sciences (Custom Pub) (C). 1994. pap. text. write for info. (*0-07-047138-X*) McGraw.

— The Pacific War. LC 82-15054. 800p. 1982. pap. 18.95 (*0-688-01620-0*, Quil) HarperTrade.

— Virginia Criminal Law & Procedure: 1991 Supplement. 122p. 1991. 25.00 (*0-87473-916-0*, 61001-10, MICHIE) LEXIS Pub.

— Virginia Criminal Law & Procedure: 1992 Supplement. 199p. 1992. pap. write for info. (*1-55834-018-1*, 61002-10, MICHIE) LEXIS Pub.

— Virtue under Fire: How World War II Changed Our Social & Sexual Attitudes. 1986. 17.95 (*0-316-73968-5*) Little.

— Virtue under Fire: How World War II Changed Our Social & Sexual Attitudes. LC 87-335. (Illus.). 309p. 1995. reprint ed. pap. 9.95 (*0-88064-070-7*) Fromm Intl Pub.

***Costello, John & Christle, Joe.** Older People: Law & Finance. 150p. 1999. pap. 15.00 (*1-901657-80-9*, 18427, Pub. by Blackhall Pub) Gaunt.

Costello, John F. & Piper, Priscilla J., eds. Methylxanthines & Phosphodiesterase Inhibitors in the Treatment of Airways Disease: The Proceedings of a Meeting Held by the Royal Society of Medicine's Section of Respiratory Medicine, RSM, London, November 1993. LC 94-16137. (Illus.). 200p. (C). 1994. 42.00 (*1-85070-597-6*) Prthnon Pub.

Costello, John L. Virginia Criminal Law & Procedure. 866p. 1990. 110.00 (*0-87473-671-4*, MICHIE) LEXIS Pub.

— Virginia Criminal Law & Procedure. 2nd ed. LC 95-81968. 1281p. 1995. 110.00 (*1-55834-308-3*, 61000-11, MICHIE) LEXIS Pub.

— Virginia Criminal Law & Procedure: 1998 Cumulative Supplement. 2nd ed. 369p. 1998. pap. write for info. (*0-327-00292-1*, 6100215) LEXIS Pub.

— Virginia Criminal Law & Procedure, 1999 Spring Cumulative Edition. 2nd ed. 455p. 1999. pap., suppl. ed. write for info. (*0-327-01191-2*, 6100216) LEXIS Pub.

— Virginia Remedies. LC 97-70688. 1012p. 1997. text 95.00 (*1-55834-474-8*, 67922-10, MICHIE) LEXIS Pub.

***Costello, John L.** Virginia Remedies. 2nd ed. 1000p. 1999. 110.00 (*0-327-04970-7*, 6792211) LEXIS Pub.

Costello, John R. Syntactic Change & Syntactic Reconstruction: A Tagmemic Approach. LC 83-60279. (Publications in Linguistics: No. 68). 78p. (Orig.). 1983. pap. 9.00 (*0-88312-092-5*) S I L Intl.

Costello, Joseph T., jt. auth. see Costello, Timothy W.

Costello, Julia, ed. Documentary Evidence for the Spanish Missions of Alta California. LC 91-45782. (Spanish Borderlands Sourcebooks Ser.: Vol. 14). 565p. 1992. text 30.00 (*0-8240-1953-9*) Garland.

Costello, Julia, jt. ed. see Barker, Leo R.

C

Costello, Kevin S., et al, eds. Sarasota Review of Poetry. 1998. pap. 9.98 (*0-9662719-0-4*) R B Abel.

Costello, Kitty, ed. see Robertson, Eric.

***Costello, Liam.** Through the Veils of Morning: An Inner Journey in the Pathways of Francis & Clare of Assisi. 192p. 2000. pap. 16.95 (*1-85390-500-3*) Veritas Pubns.

Costello, Louisa S. Catherine de Medici. LC 70-162911. (Bentley's Standard Novels Ser.: No. 112). reprint ed. 37.50 (*0-404-54512-2*) AMS Pr.

Costello, M. J. The Greatest Games of All Time. 192p. 1991. pap. 12.95 (*0-471-52975-3*) Wiley.

Costello, M. Rita, jt. auth. see Popovich, Charles J.

Costello, Marian D., et al. Heart Beats. (ECS Intermediate Thematic Unit Ser.). 96p. (Orig.). 1994. pap., teacher ed. 12.95 (*0-944459-98-6*) ECS Lrn Systs.

— Inventions! Inventions! (ECS Intermediate Thematic Unit Ser.). (Illus.). 96p. (Orig.). 1996. pap., teacher ed. 14.95 (*1-57022-051-4*) ECS Lrn Systs.

Costello, Mark. Middle Murphy. (Illinois Short Fiction Ser.). 152p. 1991. 10.95 (*0-252-06319-8*); text 16.95 (*0-252-01795-1*) U of Ill Pr.

— The Murphy Stories. LC 72-86409. (Illinois Short Fiction Ser.). 120p. 1973. 9.95 (*0-252-00309-8*) U of Ill Pr.

Costello, Martin J. Hating the Sin, Loving the Sinner: The Minneapolis Children's Theatre Company Adolescent Sexual Abuse Prosecutions. LC 91-21985. (American Legal & Constitutional History Ser.). 240p. 1991. text 10.00 (*0-8153-0027-1*) Garland.

Costello, Martin J., et al. Minnesota Advising Corporations & Other Business Organizations. 1994. ring bd., suppl. ed. 48.50 (*0-614-03161-3*, MICHIE) LEXIS Pub.

Costello, Martin J., et al. Minnesota Misdemeanors & Moving Traffic Violations, 2 Vols. 3rd ed. 184.00 (*0-327-12457-1*) LEXIS Pub.

— Minnesota Misdemeanors & Moving Traffic Violations, 2 vols. 3rd ed. Incl. Vol. 1. Minnesota Misdemeanors & Moving Traffic Violations. 3rd ed. 600p. 1999. ring bd. (*0-327-04905-7*); Vol. 2. Minnesota Misdemeanors & Moving Traffic Violations. 3rd ed. 600p. 1999. ring bd. (*0-327-04906-5*, 8181820); 1200p. 1999. ring bd. write for info. (*0-327-04904-9*) LEXIS Pub.

Costello, Martin J., et al. Minnesota Misdemeanors & Moving Traffic Violations, 1990-1992, 2 vols. 2nd ed. suppl. ed. write for info. (*0-250-40723-X*, MICHIE) LEXIS Pub.

— Minnesota Misdemeanors & Moving Traffic Violations, 1990-1992, 2 vols., Set. 2nd ed. 700p. 1994. spiral bd. 165.00 (*0-86678-932-4*, 81815-10, MICHIE) LEXIS Pub.

***Costello, Mary.** Titanic Town. 340p. 2000. pap. 10.95 (*0-413-77210-1*, Methuen Drama) Methn.

Costello, Mary, et al, eds. The American Woman 1998-99: A Century of Change-What's Next? LC 99-166526. (Illus.). 416p. 1998. pap. 15.95 (*0-393-31862-1*) Norton.

Costello, Mary C. Between Fixity & Flux: A Study of the Concept of Poetry in the Criticism of T. S. Eliot. LC 47-5815. 128p. reprint ed. pap. 39.70 (*0-8357-7149-0*, 202952100061) Bks Demand.

Costello, Mathew. Magic Everywhere: How to Perform Amazing Magic Using Everyday Household Objects. LC 98-40677. 144p. 1999. pap. 10.00 (*0-609-80357-3*) Crown Pub Group.

Costello, Matthew. Seaquest DSV: Fire Below. (Orig.). 1994. mass mkt. 4.99 (*0-441-00039-8*) Ace Bks.

Costello, Matthew J. The Greatest Puzzles of All Time. unabridged ed. LC 96-14796. 1996. reprint ed. pap. 7.95 (*0-486-29225-8*) Dover.

— How to Write Science Fiction. 144p. 1995. pap. 10.95 (*1-56924-844-3*) Marlowe & Co.

***Costello, Matthew J.** Maelstrom: Poltergeist. (Legacy Ser.). (Illus.). (J). 2000. mass mkt. 5.99 (*0-441-00711-2*) Ace Bks.

Costello, Matthew J. & Gardner, Graig S. The 7th Guest: A Novel. 224p. 1995. boxed set 21.95 (*0-7615-0086-3*) Prima Pub.

Costello, Matthew J., jt. auth. see Kilcommons, Brian.

Costello, Matthew J., jt. auth. see Wilson, F. Paul.

Costello, Melina P. Tutti-Frutti Town: Blinky Blueberry Finds a Friend. (Illus.). 32p. (Orig.). (J). (gr. k-3). 1991. pap. 6.50 (*1-878130-01-3*) Bang A Drum.

Costello, Michael J., Jr. In the Garden of Life. 2nd ed. 105p. 1997. reprint ed. 14.95 (*0-9660326-0-8*) Apollo Pacific.

Costello, Moya. Small Ecstasies. LC 94-136840. 1994. pap. 14.95 (*0-7022-2600-9*, Pub. by Univ Queensland Pr) Intl Spec Bk.

***Costello, Neil.** Stability & Change in High-Tech Enterprises: Organisational Practices in SMES. LC 00-38249. 2000. pap. write for info. (*0-415-23121-3*) Routledge.

Costello, Neil & Richardson, Michael, eds. Continuing Education for the Post-Industrial Society. 160p. 1982. pap. 29.00 (*0-335-10186-0*) OpUniv Pr.

Costello-Nickitas, Donna. Quick Reference to Nursing Leadership. (Professional Reference - Nursing Ser.). 240p. 1996. mass mkt. 41.95 (*0-8273-6997-2*) Delmar.

Costello, Pat, et al. Sharing Maths Learning with Children. (C). 1990. 65.00 (*0-86431-101-X*, Pub. by Aust Council Educ Res) St Mut.

Costello, Patricia. Female Fitness Stars of T. V. & the Movies. (Legends of Health & Fitness Ser.). (Illus.). 128p. (YA). (gr. 6-12). 2000. lib. bdg. 24.95 (*1-58415-050-5*) M Lane Pubs.

Costello, Patrick J. Liberating Children's Minds: Education, Citizenship & Critical Thinking. 1999. write for info. (*1-85359-382-6*, Pub. by Multilingual Matters); pap. write for info. (*1-85359-381-8*, Pub. by Multilingual Matters) Taylor & Francis.

Costello, Patrick J. & Mitchell, Sally, eds. Competing & Consensual Voices: The Theory & Practice of Argument. LC 95-6553. (Language & Education Library: Vol. 8). 1995. write for info. (*1-85359-277-3*, Pub. by Multilingual Matters); pap. write for info. (*1-85359-276-5*, Pub. by Multilingual Matters) Taylor & Francis.

Costello, Paul. World Historians & Their Goals: Twentieth-Century Answers to Modernism. 307p. 1993. lib. bdg. 30.00 (*0-87580-173-0*) N Ill U Pr.

— World Historians & Their Goals: Twentieth-Century Answers to Modernism. LC 94-15134. 325p. 1995. pap. 18.00 (*0-87580-564-7*) N Ill U Pr.

Costello, Peter. Dublin[0012]s Literary Pubs. 2nd ed. 1998. 12.95 (*0-7735-1814-2*) McG-Queens Univ Pr.

— The Irish Too: A Ranking of the Most Influential Irish Men & Women of All Time. LC 99-25960. (Illus.). 336p. 1999. 27.50 (*0-8065-2061-2*, Citadel Pr) Carol Pub Group.

— James Joyce. 2nd ed. (Gill's Irish Lives Ser.). (Illus.). 132p. 1998. reprint ed. pap. 13.95 (*0-7171-2687-0*, Pub. by Gill & MacMill) Irish Bks Media.

— Liam O'Flaherty's Ireland. LC 97-116148. (Illus.). 127p. 1997. 29.95 (*0-86327-550-8*) Irish Bks Media.

— The Life of Leopold Bloom: A Novel. LC 92-61909. 197p. (Orig.). 1993. pap. 9.95 (*1-879373-34-3*) Roberts Rinehart.

— The Real World of Sherlock Holmes: The True Crimes Investigated by Arthur Conan Doyle. (Illus.). 256p. 1993. pap. 10.95 (*0-7867-0020-3*) Carroll & Graf.

Costello, Peter, jt. auth. see Jackson, John W.

Costello, Peter, ed. see Verne, Jules.

Costello, R. M. & Schneider, S. L., eds. Forensic Psychology for the Journeyman Clinician. 350p. (C). 1991. pap. text. write for info. (*0-9630867-0-7*) TX Psych Found.

Costello, Rick & Roberts, K. K. The Lemming Shepherds Vol. 1: Symphony for the Census. (Illus.). 40p. (J). (gr. 4-12). 1997. pap. 5.00 (*0-9655201-0-2*, EMCD9904-96); pap. 29.95 incl. cd-rom (*0-9655201-2-9*, EMCD9904-96); cd-rom 24.95 (*0-9655201-1-0*, EMCD9904-96) Exzel Music.

Costello, Robert, ed. Macmillan Dictionary for Children. LC 97-12732. (Illus.). 896p. (J). (gr. 3-7). 1997. per. 16.95 (*0-689-81384-8*) S&S Childrens.

Costello, Robert B. American Heritage Dictionary. 3rd ed. (Delta Bks.). 1994. 18.05 (*0-606-01307-5*, Pub. by Turtleback) Demco.

Costello, S. & Johnstone, T. Famous Last Words: Obituaries from the Scotsman, 1817-1996. LC 97-174844. 176p. 1996. pap. 40.00 (*1-873644-63-9*, Pub. by Mercat Pr Bks) St Mut.

Costello, Sharon, ed. see Smith, Carol.

Costello, Sharon, ed. see Teague, Jan.

Costello, Sheila. Managing Change at Work. 128p. 1994. text 10.95 (*0-7863-0162-7*, Irwn Prfssnl) McGraw-Hill Prof.

Costello, Sheila J. Effective Performance Management. LC 93-21873. (Business Skills Express Ser.). 144p. 1993. pap. 10.95 (*1-55623-867-3*, Irwn Prfssnl) McGraw-Hill Prof.

— Managing Change at Work. LC 93-40306. 1994. write for info. (*0-7863-0104-X*, Irwn Prfssnl) McGraw-Hill Prof.

Costello, T. Mark. Confessions of a Special Eddie: Reflections in Appreciation of Human Difference. LC 94-237522. 190p. (Orig.). 1994. pap. write for info. (*1-881135-04-7*) Wizard Pr.

Costello, Thomas. Gut-Level Management: Developing People Skills for Food Service Managers. Carter, Jacqueline, ed. (Illus.). 150p. 17.95 (*0-9616814-0-3*) Gut Level Pub.

Costello, Thomas G. FAA-PMA: The Parts Manufacturer's Approval Process. 1999. write for info. (*0-7680-0051-3*, R-179) Soc Auto Engineers.

Costello, Tim, jt. auth. see Brecher, Jeremy.

Costello, Tim, jt. ed. see Brecher, Jeremy.

Costello, Timothy W. & Costello, Joseph T. HCO Abnormal Psychol. LC 90-56016. (College Outline Ser.). (Illus.). 448p. (C). 1992. pap. 16.00 (*0-06-467121-6*, Harper Ref) HarpC.

Costello, Tom. Gut-Level Management: Dealing with Situations That Can Make or Break Your Foodservice Business. (Illus.). 184p. (Orig.). 1993. pap. 19.95 (*1-883800-02-1*) C P Pub.

Costello, Tom, jt. ed. see Univ. of Liverpool Staff.

Costello, William. The Performance Process & Performance Audit Findings: An Explanation of Terms. LC 97-61110. (Illus.). 75p. 1997. pap. 22.00 (*1-882194-31-4*) TN Valley Pub.

Costello, William T. Poems of William T. Costello, SJ. 2nd ed. 128p. 1993. pap. 7.95 (*0-9629578-3-6*) Intl Long WA.

Costello, William T., jt. auth. see Parsons, Robert.

Costelloe, M. Joseph, tr. see Ricciotti, Abbot G.

Costelloe, M. Joseph, tr. & intro. see Xavier, Francis.

Costelloe, Morgan. Matt Talbot: Hope for Addicts. 1989. pap. 25.00 (*0-86217-229-2*, Pub. by Veritas Pubns) St Mut.

Costelloe, Peter. Waterford: A Celebration of Fine Crystal. (Illus.). 160p. 1997. 35.00 (*1-85793-905-0*, Pub. by Pavilion Bks Ltd) Trafalgar.

Costelloe, Stephen J. Basil Hume: Builder of Community. 1989. pap. 22.00 (*1-85390-061-3*, Pub. by Veritas Pubns) St Mut.

Costeloe, Michael P. The Central Republic in Mexico, 1835-1846: Hombres de Bien in the Age of Santa Anna. LC 92-33950. (Cambridge Latin American Studies: No. 73). 340p. (C). 1993. text 74.95 (*0-521-44121-8*) Cambridge U Pr.

Costen. Cathars & Albigensian Crusade. LC 97-6133. 1997. text 29.95 (*0-7190-4332-8*, Pub. by Manchester Univ Pr) St Martin.

Costen, James H., et al. Reclamation of Black Prisoners: A Challenge to the African American Church. Askew, Gloria & Wilmore, Gayraud, eds. (Black Church Scholars Ser.: Vol. 3). 134p. (C). 1992. pap. 8.95 (*0-614-08301-X*) Jrnl Interdenom.

Costen, Melva W. African American Christian Worship. LC 93-13826. 144p. (Orig.). 1993. pap. 13.95 (*0-687-00931-6*) Abingdon.

Costenbader, Carol W. The Big Book of Preserving the Harvest. Lappies, Pamela, ed. LC 97-22704. (Illus.). 352p. 1997. 27.95 (*0-88266-800-5*, Storey Pub); pap. 18.95 (*0-88266-978-8*, Storey Pub) Storey Bks.

***Costenbader, Carol W.** Food Drying Techniques. LC 99-34999. 1999. pap. 3.95 (*1-58017-218-0*) Random.

Costenbader, Carol W. Mustards, Ketchups & Vinegars: Making the Most of Seasonal Abundance. LC 95-42378. (Well Stocked Pantry Ser.). (Illus.). 96p. 1996. 16.95 (*0-88266-813-7*, 813-7, Storey Pub) Storey Bks.

— Preserving Fruits & Vegetables: Making the Most of Seasonal Abundance. LC 95-42379. (Well Stocked Pantry Ser.). (Illus.). 96p. 1996. 16.95 (*0-88266-852-8*, 852-8, Storey Pub) Storey Bks.

***Costenbader, Jan.** Get Ready for Shell. 372p. 1999. pap. 69.95 incl. cd-rom (*0-9671012-0-4*) Electric Tours.

Costenoble, Steven R., jt. auth. see Waner.

Costenoble, Steven R., jt. auth. see Waner, Stefan.

Coster, C. H. Iudicium Quinquevirale. (Mediaeval Academy of America Publications: Vol. 22). 1935. 30.00 (*0-527-01694-2*) Periodicals Srv.

Coster, Patience. Farming & Industry. LC 97-13567. (Step-by-Step Geography Ser.). (Illus.). 32p. 1998. lib. bdg. 17.70 (*0-516-20354-1*) Childrens.

— Towns & Cities. LC 97-16182. (Step-by-Step Geography Ser.). (Illus.). 32p. (J). 1998. 18.00 (*0-516-20355-X*) Childrens.

Costermans, Jean & Fayol, Michael, eds. Processing Interclausal Relationships in the Production & Comprehension of Text: Studies in the Production & Comprehension of Text. 344p. 1996. 59.95 (*0-8058-1846-4*); pap. 29.95 (*0-8058-1847-2*) L Erlbaum Assocs.

Costerton. Biofilm Microbiology. 256p. 1997. write for info. (*0-12-191540-9*) Acad Pr.

Costerton, J. W. & Colwell, R. R., eds. Native Aquatic Bacteria: Enumeration, Activity & Ecology - STP 695. 219p. 1979. 25.00 (*0-8031-0526-6*, STP695) ASTM.

Costerton, J. William, jt. ed. see Lappin-Scott, Hilary M.

Costigan, Lucy. Bullying & Harrasment in the Workplace: A Guide for Employees, Managers & Employers. LC 98-166558. 142 p. 1998. write for info. (*1-85607-237-1*) Intl Scholars.

Costigan, Daniel M. & Szabocsik, Paul M. Showplace. LC 92-61773. v, 80 p. 1993. write for info. (*0-9625524-1-0*) D M Costigan.

***Costigan, Fran.** Great Good Desserts: Secrets of Sensational Sin-Free Sweets. 144p. 1999. pap. 15.95 (*0-9673108-0-6*, Pub. by Good Cakes Prodns) Book Pub Co.

Costigan, Sean, jt. auth. see Callan, Benedicte.

Costigan, Sean S., jt. ed. see Markusen, Ann R.

Costigan, Shirleyann. Dede & the Dinosaur: Big Book. (Wonders! Ser.: Level 1). (Illus.). 24p. (Orig.). (J). (gr. 1-3). 1992. pap. text 29.95 (*1-56334-174-3*) Hampton-Brown.

— Dede & the Dinosaur: Small Book. (Wonders! Ser.: Level 1). (Illus.). 24p. (Orig.). (J). (gr. 1-3). 1992. pap. text 6.00 (*1-56334-176-X*) Hampton-Brown.

— Just One Seed: Big Book. (Illus.). 16p. (Orig.). (J). (ps-1). 1992. pap. text 29.95 (*1-56334-180-8*) Hampton-Brown.

— Just One Seed: Small Book. (ESL Theme Links Ser.). (Illus.). 16p. (Orig.). 1992. pap. text 6.00 (*1-56334-183-2*) Hampton-Brown.

— The Little Ant: Big Book. (ESL Theme Links Ser.). (Illus.). 16p. (Orig.). (J). (gr. 1-3). 1992. pap. text 29.95 (*1-56334-066-6*) Hampton-Brown.

— The Little Ant: Small Book. (ESL Theme Links Ser.). (Illus.). 16p. (Orig.). (J). (gr. 1-3). 1992. pap. text 6.00 (*1-56334-072-0*) Hampton-Brown.

Costigan, Shirleyann, et al. El Sabelotodo: The Bilingual Teacher's Best Friend. (ENG & SPA., Illus.). 176p. (Orig.). 1988. pap. 21.95 (*0-917837-01-0*) Hampton-Brown.

Costiglia, Paul, jt. ed. see Gorelick, Victor.

Costigliola, Frank. Awkward Dominion: American Political, Economic, & Cultural Relations with Europe 1919-1933. LC 84-45150. 376p. 1984. text 47.50 (*0-8014-1679-5*); pap. text 24.95 (*0-8014-9505-9*) Cornell U Pr.

— France & the United States: The Cold Alliance since World War II. (Twayne's International History Ser.: No. 9). 200p. (C). 1992. pap. 15.95 (*0-8057-9205-8*); text 27.95 (*0-8057-7902-7*) Macmillan.

Costik, Sally. Around Bradford. (Images of America Ser.). 1997. pap. 16.99 (*0-7524-0502-0*) Arcadia Publng.

— Around Bradford, Vol. II. LC 98-85886. (Images of America Ser.). (Illus.). 128p. 1998. pap. 16.99 (*0-7524-1215-9*) Arcadia Publng.

Costikyan, Edward N. & Lehman, Maxwell. New Strategies for Regional Cooperation: A Model for the Tri-State New York-New Jersey-Connecticut Area. LC 73-9388. (Special Studies in U. S. Economic, Social & Political Issues). 1973. 32.50 (*0-275-28777-7*) Irvington.

Costikyan, Edward N & Lehman, Maxwell. Re-Structuring the Government of New York City: Report of the Scott Commission Task Force on Jurisdiction & Structure. LC 72-86838. (Special Studies in U. S. Economic, Social & Political Issues). 1972. 27.50 (*0-275-06320-8*) Irvington.

Costikyan, Greg. By the Sword. (Magic of the Plains Ser.: Vol. 1). 256p. 1994. mass mkt. 4.99 (*0-8125-2268-0*, Pub. by Tor Bks) St Martin.

***Costikyan, Greg.** First Contract. LC 00-26243. 288p. 2000. 23.95 (*0-312-87396-4*, Pub. by Tor Bks) St Martin.

Costikyan, Greg. One Quest, Hold the Dragons No. 2: Cups & Sorcery. (Cups & Sorcery Ser.: No. 2). 384p. (Orig.). 1995. mass mkt. 4.99 (*0-8125-2269-9*) Tor Bks.

Costill, David L. Inside Running. LC 85-73461. (Illus.). 198p. (C). 1986. reprint ed. pap. text 20.00 (*1-884125-18-2*) Cooper Pubng.

Costill, David L., jt. auth. see Wilmore, Jack H.

Costillo, Roger, ed. see Ludlum, James S.

Costin. Classic Readings in Strategy. (C). 1997. pap. text 51.50 (*0-03-017983-1*) Harcourt Coll Pubs.

Costin, Carolyn. The Eating Disorder Sourcebook. 2nd ed. 304p. 1997. reprint ed. pap. 15.00 (*1-56565-853-1*, Anodyne) Lowell Hse.

— Eating Disorder Sourcebook: A Comprehensive Guide to the Causes, Treatments & Prevention. 2nd ed. LC 99-37565. 320p. 1999. pap. 16.95 (*0-7373-0102-3*, 01023W) NTC Contemp Pub Co.

— The Eating Disorder Sourcebook: Everything You Need to Know about Anorexia, Bulimia, & Other Eating Disorders. 304p. 1996. 17.00 (*1-56565-463-3*) Lowell Hse.

— Your Dieting Daughter: Is She Dying for Attention? LC 96-38423. 240p. 1996. pap. 19.95 (*0-87630-836-1*) Brunner-Mazel.

***Costin, Cathy Lynne, et al.** Craft & Social Identity. LC 98-50642. (Archeological Papers of the American Anthropological Association). 1998. write for info. (*0-913167-90-8*) Am Anthro Assn.

Costin, Glynis, jt. auth. see Ashwell, Rachel.

Costin, Harry. Managing in the Global Economy: The European Union. 384p. (C). 1995. text 55.00 (*0-03-015347-6*) Dryden Pr.

Costin, Harry & Vanolli, Hector. Economic Reform in Latin America. LC 97-73493. (C). 1997. pap. text 50.00 (*0-03-017987-4*) Dryden Pr.

Costin, Harry I. Readings in Total Quality Management. 2nd ed. 1999. pap. text 53.50 (*0-03-024611-3*, Pub. by Harcourt Coll Pubs) Harcourt.

Costin, L., et al, eds. Arms Control & Verification. 81p. 1992. pap. 29.95 (*0-9627451-1-1*) TSI Pr.

Costin, Lela B. Two Sisters for Social Justice: A Biography of Grace & Edith Abbott. LC 82-21790. (Illus.). 336p. 1983. text 29.95 (*0-252-01013-2*) U of Ill Pr.

Costin, Lela B. & Gruener, Jennette R. Licensing of Family Homes in Child Welfare: A Guide for Instructors & Trainees. LC 65-12939. 160p. reprint ed. pap. 49.60 (*0-608-16615-4*, 202767900055) Bks Demand.

Costin, Lela B., et al. The Politics of Child Abuse in America. (Child Welfare: A Series in Child Welfare Practice, Policy, & Research). (Illus.). 208p. 1997. reprint ed. pap. 17.95 (*0-19-511668-2*) OUP.

Costin, M. Georgia. Priceless Spirit: A History of the Sisters of the Holy Cross, 1841-1893. LC 93-23642. (C). 1994. text 29.00 (*0-268-03804-X*) U of Notre Dame Pr.

Costinett, Sandra. Language of Accounting in English. (English for Careers Ser). 104p. (YA). (gr. 10-12). 1994. pap. text 20.40 (*0-13-523226-0*, 18512) Prentice ESL.

Costingan, Shirleyann. The Little Ant. (ESL Theme Links Ser.). (Illus.). (J). (gr. k-3). 1993. 35.00 (*1-56334-316-9*); audio 10.50 (*1-56334-315-0*) Hampton-Brown.

— The Little Ant Theme Link. (ESL Theme Links Ser.). (Illus.). (J). (gr. k-3). 1993. 99.50 (*1-56334-317-7*) Hampton-Brown.

Costley, Alex W., ed. see Hawkeswood, William G.

Costley, Dan L., et al. Human Relations in Organizations. 5th ed. Fenton, ed. LC 93-35451. 680p. (C). 1993. mass mkt. 57.00 (*0-314-02689-4*) West Pub.

Costley, Dan L., jt. auth. see Howell, Jon P.

Costley, Sarah & Kightly, Charles. Celtic Book of Days. LC 97-61661. (Illus.). 208p. 1998. 12.95 (*0-500-01835-9*, Pub. by Thames Hudson) Norton.

Costlow, Jane, tr. see Zinovieva-Annibal, Lydia.

Costlow, Jane T., et al, eds. Sexuality & the Body in Russian Culture. LC 92-47410. 372p. 1993. 49.50 (*0-8047-2113-0*) Stanford U Pr.

— Sexuality & the Body in Russian Culture. (Illus.). 372p. 1997. pap. 19.95 (*0-8047-3155-1*) Stanford U Pr.

Costlow, Judy, et al. Menopause: A Self-Care Manual. rev. ed. (Illus.). 72p. 1989. 5.00 (*0-9622933-1-8*) Santa Fe Health.

Costner, Herbert L. The Changing Folkways of Parenthood: A Content Analysis. Zuckerman, Harriet & Merton, Robert K., eds. LC 79-8987. (Dissertations on Sociology Ser.). 1980. lib. bdg. 39.95 (*0-405-12960-2*) Ayer.

Costner, Kevin, et al. Dances with Wolves: The Illustrated Story of the Epic Film. LC 90-13429. (Illus.). 160p. 1990. pap. 16.95 (*1-55704-088-5*, Pub. by Newmarket) Norton.

— Dances with Wolves: The Illustrated Story of the Epic Film. rev. ed. LC 91-20284. (Illus.). 160p. 1991. 29.95 (*1-55704-101-6*, Pub. by Newmarket) Norton.

Costo, Jeannette H., jt. auth. see Costo, Rupert.

Costo, Rupert & Costo, Jeannette H. The Missions of California: A Legacy of Genocide. 248p. (C). 1987. pap. 11.50 (*0-317-64539-0*) Indian Hist Pr.

Costomiris, Lois. More Rail Fences, Rolling Pins & Rainbows. 1995. 20.00 (*1-878208-72-1*) Guild Pr IN.

— Rail Fences, Rolling Pins & Rainbows: Hamilton County Bygone Days. LC 94-77599. 300p. 1994. 20.00 (*1-878208-25-X*) Guild Pr IN.

Coston, Henry, ed. Dictionnaire des Dynasties Bourgecises et du Monde des Affaires. (FRE.). 599p. 1975. 75.00 (*0-8288-5850-0*, M6617) Fr & Eur.

Coston, John. Sleep My Child, Forever. 320p. (Orig.). 1995. mass mkt. 5.99 (*0-451-40335-5*, Onyx) NAL.

***Coston, Stephen A., Sr.** King James VI & I & Papal Opposition. (Illus.). 90p. 1998. pap. 14.95 (*0-9656777-4-5*) KonigsWort.

— King James VI & I Innocent until Proven Guilty. (Illus.). 98p. 1998. pap. 14.95 (*0-9656777-5-3*) KonigsWort.

Coston, Stephen A., Sr. King James VI of Scotland & I of England Unjustly Accused? LC 95-69081. (Illus.). 448p. (Orig.). 1996. pap. 14.95 (*0-9656777-3-7*) KonigsWort.

Coston, William H. The Spanish-American War Volunteer. 2nd enl. rev. ed. LC 75-164384. (Black Heritage Library Collection). 1977. reprint ed. 29.95 (*0-8369-8843-4*) Ayer.

Costonis, John J. Icons & Aliens: Law, Aesthetics, & Environmental Change. (Illus.). 152p. 1989. text 24.95 (*0-252-01553-3*) U of Ill Pr.

— Space Adrift: Landmark Preservation & the Marketplace. fac. ed. LC 73-5405. (Illus.). 227p. 1974. pap. 70.40 (*0-7837-7617-9*, 204736900007) Bks Demand.

Costonis, John J. & DeVoy, Robert S. The Puerto Rico Plan: Environmental Protection Through Development Rights Transfer. LC 75-15460. 64p. reprint ed. pap. 30.00 (*0-608-12219-X*, 202388300034) Bks Demand.

Costonis, Maureen N., ed. Therapy in Motion. LC 77-9077. 298p. 1977. text 29.95 (*0-252-00586-4*) U of Ill Pr.

Costopoulos, William. The White Lady War. LC 89-328. 1990. 21.95 (*0-87949-301-1*) Ashley Bks.

Costopoulos, William C. Guilty of Innocence. LC 99-36755. 224p. 1999. 22.00 (*0-940159-57-0*) Camino Bks.

— Principal Suspect: The True Story of Dr. Jay Smith & the Main Line Murders. LC 96-5989. (Illus.). 312p. 1996. 22.00 (*0-940159-36-8*) Camino Bks.

Costouros, George J. & Seventer, Van A. Contemporary Accounting Issues. LC 79-54304. 1979. 16.40 (*0-9602956-3-1*) Bay Books.

Costume Society of America Staff, jt. auth. see Ordodnez, Margaret T.

Cosulich, Bernice. Tucson. (Illus.). (Orig.). 1987. reprint ed. pap. 8.00 (*0-918080-36-3*) Treas Chest Bks.

Cosway, Ted, et al. Design & Make It! Resistant Materials Technology. 144p. 1998. pap. 30.00 (*0-7487-2470-2*) St Mut.

***Cota-Cardenas, Margarita.** Puppet: A Chicano Novella. LC 00-8469. 2000. pap. write for info. (*0-8263-2229-8*) U of NM Pr.

Cota-Robles, Patricia D. The Awakening...Eternal Youth, Vibrant Health, Radiant Beauty. (Illus.). 194p. (Orig.). 1993. pap. 14.00 (*0-9615287-3-7*) New Age Study Human.

— It Is Time for You to Be Financially Free. 51p. 1997. pap. text 7.00 (*0-9615287-6-1*) New Age Study Human.

— The Next Step . . . Re-Unification with the Presence of God Within Our Hearts. 2nd ed. Picas & Points, eds. (Illus.). 369p. 1989. 17.00 (*0-9615287-1-0*) New Age Study Human.

— Stargate of the Heart. 263p. 1989. pap. 14.00 (*0-9615287-4-5*) New Age Study Human.

— Take Charge of Your Life. 4th ed. Dunlap, Elvira & Meyer, Kay, eds. (Illus.). 179p. 1983. reprint ed. pap. 12.00 (*0-9615287-0-2*) New Age Study Human.

— What on Earth Is Going On? 447p. (Orig.). 1997. pap. text 22.00 (*0-9615287-5-3*) New Age Study Human.

Cota, Sancho. Memorias de Sancho Cota. Keniston, Hayward, ed. LC 64-16064. (Studies in Romance Languages: No. 28). 269p. 1964. 15.00 (*0-674-56600-9*) HUP.

Cotarelo y Mori, E., et al, intros. Obras de Lope de Vega: Segunda Serie: Obras Dramaticas del Fenix, 13 vols. (Real Academia Ser.). (SPA.). 1968. 1000.00 (*0-614-00128-5*) Elliots Bks.

***Cotbe, William E. & Simpson, Roger.** Covering Violence: A Guide to Ethical Reporting about Victims & Trauma. LC 00-34627. (Illus.). 2000. pap. 17.50 (*0-231-11451-6*) Col U Pr.

Cotchett, Joseph. Federal Courtroom Evidence. 4th rev. ed. LC 98-67059. 1001p. 1998. ring bd. 130.00 (*0-327-00131-3*, 80456-11) LEXIS Pub.

Cotchett, Joseph W. & Elkind, Arnold B. Federal Courtroom Evidence. 3rd ed. 550p. 1994. ring bd. 115.00 (*0-250-40714-0*, 80456, MICHIE) LEXIS Pub.

Cotchett, Joseph W. & Haight, Fulton. California Courtroom Evidence. 4th ed. 1995. spiral bd. 135.00 incl. cd-rom (*1-55834-261-3*) LEXIS Pub.

— California Courtroom Evidence, Issue 4. 500p. 1999. ring bd. write for info. (*0-327-01046-0*, 8022614) LEXIS Pub.

— California Courtroom Evidence, 1988-93. 3rd ed. 670p. 1994. ring bd. 115.00 (*1-55943-122-9*, MICHIE) LEXIS Pub.

Cotchett, Joseph W. & Pizzo, Stephen P. The Ethics Gap. LC 91-61484. 220p. 1991. pap. 19.95 (*1-55943-113-X*, MICHIE) LEXIS Pub.

Cotchett, Joseph W. & Rothman, Frank. Persuasive Opening Statements & Closing Arguments. 375p. 1988. 80.00 (*0-88124-165-2*, CP-39650) Cont Ed Bar-CA.

Cotchett, Joseph W. & Uelman, Gerald F. California Courtroom Evidence Foundations. 220p. 1994. spiral bd. 39.50 (*0-250-47229-5*, MICHIE) LEXIS Pub.

Cotchett, Joseph W., jt. auth. see Rothman, Frank.

Cote. Arrested Adulthood. pap. text 18.50 (*0-8147-1599-0*) NYU Pr.

Cote, tr. Letters from Kartini. pap. 5.99 (*0-7326-0267-X*, Pub. by Jarrold Pub) Seven Hills Bk.

Cote, A. E., jt. auth. see Bugbee, Percy.

Cote, Anne. Les Malheurs de Sophie.Tr. of Sophie's Misfortune. (FRE.). 1998. boxed set 12.95 incl. audio (*2-921997-47-9*, Pub. by Coffragants) Penton Overseas.

***Cote, Anne.** Les Malheurs de Sophie.Tr. of Sophie's Misfortune. (FRE.). 1998. pap., boxed set 16.95 incl. audio compact disk (*2-921997-46-0*, Pub. by Coffragants) Penton Overseas.

Cote, Bernard, tr. see Sionneau, Philippe.

***Cote, Charles J., et al.** A Practice Anesthesia for Infants & Children. 3rd ed. (Illus.). 605p. (C). 1999. text. write for info. (*0-7216-7286-8*, W B Saunders Co) Harcrt Hlth Sci Grp.

Cote, Charles J., et al. A Practice of Anesthesia for Infants & Children. 2nd ed. (Illus.). 558p. 1992. text 96.00 (*0-7216-3198-3*, W B Saunders Co) Harcrt Hlth Sci Grp.

Cote, Charlotte. Olympia Brown: The Battle for Equality. LC 88-60777. 200p. 1989. pap. 9.95 (*0-941300-09-9*); text 16.95 (*0-941300-11-0*) Mother Courage.

Cote, Daniel, jt. auth. see St. Pierre, Maurice.

Cote, Daniel, jt. auth. see St-Pierre, Maurice.

Cote, Denis. L' Arrivee des Inactifs. (Novels in the Roman Plus Ser.). (FRE.). 160p. (YA). (gr. 8 up). 1993. pap. 8.95 (*2-89021-191-6*, Pub. by La Courte Ech) Firefly Bks Ltd.

— Aux Portes de L'Horreur. (Novels in the Roman Plus Ser.). (FRE., Illus.). 160p. (YA). (gr. 8 up). 1994. pap. 8.95 (*2-89021-228-9*, Pub. by La Courte Ech) Firefly Bks Ltd.

— Descente Aux Enfers. (Novels in the Roman Plus Ser.). (FRE.). 160p. (YA). (gr. 8 up). 1994. pap. 8.95 (*2-89021-208-4*, Pub. by La Courte Ech) Firefly Bks Ltd.

— Les Geants de Blizzard. (Novels in the Roman Jeunesse Ser.). (FRE.). 96p. (J). (gr. 4-7). 1985. pap. 7.95 (*2-89021-126-6*, Pub. by La Courte Ech) Firefly Bks Ltd.

— L' Idole Des Inactifs. (Novels in the Roman Plus Ser.). (FRE., Illus.). 160p. (YA). (gr. 8 up). 1989. pap. 7.95 (*2-89021-106-1*, Pub. by La Courte Ech) Firefly Bks Ltd.

— La Nuit du Vampire. (Novels in the Roman Jeunesse Ser.). (FRE.). 96p. (J). (gr. 4-7). 1990. pap. 7.95 (*2-89021-117-7*, Pub. by La Courte Ech) Firefly Bks Ltd.

— Le Parc aux Sortileges. (Novels in the Roman Jeunesse Ser.). (FRE.). 96p. (J). (gr. 4-7). 1994. pap. 8.95 (*2-89021-210-6*, Pub. by La Courte Ech) Firefly Bks Ltd.

— Les Prisonniers du Zoo. (Novels in the Roman Jeunesse Ser.). (FRE.). 96p. (J). (gr. 4-7). 1988. pap. 8.95 (*2-89021-074-X*, Pub. by La Courte Ech) Firefly Bks Ltd.

— Le Retour des Inactifs. (Novels in the Roman Plus Ser.). (FRE.). 160p. (YA). (gr. 8 up). 1998. pap. 8.95 (*2-89021-142-8*, Pub. by La Courte Ech) Firefly Bks Ltd.

— La Revolte des Inactifs. (Novels in the Roman Jeunesse Ser.). (FRE.). 160p. (YA). (gr. 8 up). 1990. pap. 8.95 (*2-89021-127-4*, Pub. by La Courte Ech) Firefly Bks Ltd.

— Terminus Cauchemar. (Novels in the Roman Plus Ser.). (FRE.). 160p. (YA). (gr. 8 up). 1991. pap. 8.95 (*2-89021-149-5*, Pub. by La Courte Ech) Firefly Bks Ltd.

— La Trahison du Vampire. (Novels in the Roman Jeunesse Ser.). (FRE., Illus.). 96p. (J). (gr. 4-7). 1995. pap. 8.95 (*2-89021-238-6*, Pub. by La Courte Ech) Firefly Bks Ltd.

— Viaje en el Tiempo (Voyage in Time) Peyron, Gabriela, tr. (SPA., Illus.). 64p. (J). (gr. 5-6). 1992. reprint ed. pap. 5.99 (*968-16-3536-1*, Pub. by Fondo) Continental Bk.

— Le Voyage dans le Temps. (Novels in the Roman Jeunesse Ser.). (FRE.). 96p. (J). (gr. 4-7). 1989. pap. 8.95 (*2-89021-095-2*, Pub. by La Courte Ech) Firefly Bks Ltd.

— Les Yeux d'Emeraude. (Novels in the Roman Jeunesse Ser.). (FRE.). 96p. (J). (gr. 4-7). 1991. pap. 8.95 (*2-89021-165-7*, Pub. by La Courte Ech) Firefly Bks Ltd.

Cote, Doc, ed. see Barnum, William J.

Cote, Elizabeth. Hans Christian Andersen. (Reaching Your Goal Ser.: Set II). (Illus.). 24p. (J). (gr. 1-4). 1989. lib. bdg. 18.60 (*0-86592-430-9*) Rourke Enter.

— Hans Christian Andersen, Reading Level 2. (Reaching Your Goal Bks.: Set II). (Illus.). 24p. (J). (gr. 1-4). 1989. 10.95 (*0-685-58798-3*) Rourke Corp.

— Hans Christian Andersen, Vida de Cuento de Hadas. LC 92-9534. (Biografias de Triunfadores Ser.). (SPA., Illus.). (YA). 1992. 10.95 (*0-685-59299-5*) Rourke Corp.

— Hans Christian Andersen, Vida de Cuento de Hadas. LC 92-9534. (Biografias de Triunfadores Ser.). (SPA., Illus.). 24p. (J). (gr. 1-4). 1992. lib. bdg. 13.95 (*0-86593-186-0*) Rourke Corp.

Cote, Gerry. The Five Minute Citizen. 216p. 1992. pap. 9.95 (*0-9634352-0-5*) Publius OR.

Cote, J. M. General Technical-Engineering Lexicon: Lexique Technique General. 262p. 1983. 95.00 (*0-8288-2101-1*, M9873) Fr & Eur.

Cote, James E. Adolescent Storm & Stress: An Evaluation of the Mead-Freeman Controversy. (Research Monographs in Adolescence). 200p. 1994. text 49.95 (*0-8058-1506-6*) L Erlbaum Assocs.

Cote, James E. & Allahar, Anton L. Generation on Hold: Coming of Age in the Late Twentieth Century. 220p. (C). 1995. text 45.00 (*0-8147-1531-1*); pap. text 18.50 (*0-8147-1532-X*) NYU Pr.

Cote, Jim, jt. auth. see Hendricks, William.

Cote, Joseph & Siew Meng Leong, eds. Asia Pacific Advances in Consumer Research, Vol. 1. 323p. 1995. 49.00 (*0-915552-33-7*) Assn Consumer Res.

Cote, Lucian, et al, eds. Parkinson's Disease & Quality of Life. LC 00-28034. 223p. 2000. 49.95 (*0-7890-0763-0*) Haworth Pr.

***Cote, Lucien A., et al, eds.** Parkinson's Disease & Quality of Life. LC 00-28034. 223p. 2000. pap. text 19.95 (*0-7890-0810-6*) Haworth Pr.

***Cote, Lyn.** Echoes of Mercy. (Blessed Assurance Ser.: No. 3). 256p. 2000. pap. 12.99 (*0-8054-1969-1*) Broadman.

— Hope's Garden. (Love Inspired Ser.). 2000. mass mkt. 4.50 (*0-373-87117-1*, 1-87117-7, Steeple Hill) Harlequin Bks.

— Lost in His Love. LC 99-45167. (Blessed Assurance Ser.: No. 2). 256p. 2000. pap. 12.99 (*0-8054-1968-3*) Broadman.

Cote, Lyn. Never Alone. (Love Inspired Ser.). 1998. per. 4.50 (*0-373-87030-2*, 1-87030-2) Harlequin Bks.

— New Man in Town. No. 66. 1999. per. 4.50 (*0-373-87066-3*, 1-87066-6, Harlequin) Harlequin Bks.

***Cote, Lyn.** Whispers of Love. LC 99-26539. 1999. 9.99 (*0-8054-1967-5*) Broadman.

Cote, Lynne D., ed. see Nelsson, James & Riedel, Susan A.

Cote, Lynne D., ed. see Ramos, Emilio, et al.

Cote, M., ed. see Larouche, L. & Pilon, J.

Cote, Marc-Yvan. The Policy on Health & Well-Being (In Canada) 170p. 1999. reprint ed. pap. text 35.00 (*0-7881-8018-5*) DIANE Pub.

Cote, Maureen. Russian Psychology in Transition: Interviews with Moscow Psychologists. LC 98-29055. 1998. 75.00 (*1-56072-601-6*) Nova Sci Pubs.

Cote, Maureen, tr. & selected by see Tolstoy, Leo.

Cote, Nancy. Flip-Flops. LC 97-33143. (Illus.). 24p. (J). (gr. k-3). 1998. lib. bdg. 13.95 (*0-8075-2504-9*) A Whitman.

— Palm Trees. LC 92-18938. (Illus.). 40p. (J). (ps-2). 1993. lib. bdg. 14.95 (*0-02-724760-0*, Four Winds P) S&S Childrens.

Cote, Normand. English - French Vocabulary of Automobile Mechatronics. (ENG & FRE.). 35p. 1992. pap. 19.95 (*0-8288-9395-0*) Fr & Eur.

— Paper & Carton Vocabulary: Vocabulaire des Papiers et des Cartons. (ENG & FRE.). 77p. 1983. pap. 5.95 (*0-8288-1429-5*, M6650) Fr & Eur.

— Vocabulaire de la Mechatronique Automobile, la Transmission Vol. 2: Vocabulary of Automobile Mechatronics, English - French. (ENG & FRE.). 32p. 1993. pap. 19.95 (*0-7859-3640-8*, 2551155150) Fr & Eur.

Cote, Normand & Gaumond, J. Nomenclature des Appelations d'emploi dans L' Industrie Papetiere Quebecoise: Anglais-Francais. (ENG & FRE.). 114p. 1977. pap. 9.95 (*0-7859-0652-5*, M9234) Fr & Eur.

Cote, Oliver. Going Down. LC 78-70409. 1979. pap. 6.95 (*0-917300-08-4*) Singlejack Bks.

Cote, Owen R., jt. ed. see Brown, Michael E.

Cote, Paul R., jt. auth. see Mitchell, Constantina T.

Cote, Paul R., tr. see Laborit, Emmanuelle.

Cote, Pierre & Gilliam, T. Michael, eds. Environmental Aspects of Stabilization & Solidification of Hazardous & Radioactive Wastes, STP 1033. LC 89-17761. (Special Technical Publication Ser.). (Illus.). 450p. 1989. text 64.00 (*0-8031-1261-0*, STP1033) ASTM.

Cote, Raymond. Business Math Concepts. rev. ed. 408p. (C). 1986. student ed. 22.50 (*0-89702-047-2*, Irwn McGrw-H) McGrw-H Hghr Educ.

— Business Math Concepts. 4th rev. ed. 408p. (C). 1988. 33.50 (*0-89702-045-6*, Irwn McGrw-H) McGrw-H Hghr Educ.

— Understanding Hospitality Accounting I. LC 97-23155. 452p. 1997. pap. write for info. (*0-86612-154-4*) Educ Inst Am Hotel.

— Understanding Hospitality Accounting II. 3rd ed. LC 96-35894. 1996. pap. write for info. (*0-86612-135-8*) Educ Inst Am Hotel.

Cote, Raymond P. & Wells, Peter G., eds. Controlling Chemical Hazards: Fundamentals of the Management of Toxic Chemicals. (Illus.). 288p. (C). 1991. pap. 142.95 (*0-04-604002-1*) Thomson Learn.

Cote, Remy, et al. Driving a Passenger Vehicle: Driving Techniques. (Illus.). 237p. 1998. reprint ed. pap. text 30.00 (*0-7881-7166-6*) DIANE Pub.

Cote, Richard G. Re-Visioning Mission: The Catholic Church & Culture in Postmodern America. (Isaac Hecker Studies in Religion & American Culture). 224p. 1996. pap. 14.95 (*0-8091-3645-7*, 3645-7) Paulist Pr.

Cote, Richard N. The Genealogists Guide to Charleston County, South Carolina. (Illus.). 52p. 1982. reprint ed. pap. 10.00 (*0-89308-245-7*) Southern Hist Pr.

— Love by Mail: The International Guide to Personal Advertising. LC 92-28035. 1992. pap. 9.95 (*0-910155-22-4*, Enigma Bks) Bartleby Pr.

***Cote, Richard N.** Mary's World: Love, War & Family Ties in Nineteenth-Century Charleston. Burnett, Elizabeth, ed. (Illus.). 352p. 2000. 29.95 (*1-929175-19-1*, Corinthian Bks) Cote Lit Grp.

Cote, Richard N. & Williams, Patricia H., eds. The Dictionary of South Carolina Biography, Vol. 1. (Illus.). 404p. 1985. 30.00 (*0-89308-275-9*) Southern Hist Pr.

Cote, Richard N., ed. see Heitzler, Michael J.

Cote, Richard N., ed. see Wilcox, Dorris R.

Cote, Ron. Life Safety Code Handbook. (Illus.). 1997. 89.50 (*0-87765-425-5*, 101HB97) Natl Fire Prot.

Cote, Thelma D., jt. auth. see Nacke, Judy.

Cote, Wilfred A., ed. Papermaking Fibers: A Photomicrographic Atlas. LC 80-131975. (Renewable Materials Institute Ser.: No. 1). (Illus.). 196p. reprint ed. pap. 60.80 (*0-8357-3122-7*, 203938300012) Bks Demand.

Cote, Wilfred A., jt. auth. see Nanko, Heroki.

Cote, Wilfred A., Jr., ed. see Advanced Science Seminar (1964: Pinebrook Conferen.

Cotela, Antonino. The Book for Better Results & the Best Employees. 20p. 1994. pap. 12.95 (*0-9642375-0-4*) Cotela Enter.

Cotelingam, James D., jt. auth. see Schumacher, Harold R.

Cotera, Maria, ed. see Gonzalez, Jovita & Raleigh, Eve.

Cotera, Martha P., tr. see Hazen, Nancy.

Cotera, Olga. Nursing Case Management. 131p. 1998. spiral bd. 125.00 (*1-879575-94-9*) Acad Med Sys.

— Preadmissions Policy & Procedures. 1993. 70.00 (*1-879575-32-9*) Acad Med Sys.

— Quality Management Policy & Procedures. 1993. 90.00 (*0-685-66663-8*) Acad Med Sys.

— Utilization Case Management. 121p. 1997. spiral bd. 110.00 (*1-879575-77-9*) Acad Med Sys.

Cotes, Mrs. Everard, see Duncan, Sara Jeannette, pseud.

Cotes, Peter. Thinking Aloud: Fragments of Autobiography. (Illus.). 208p. 1994. 35.00 (*0-7206-0900-3*, Pub. by P Owen Ltd) Dufour.

Cotgrave, Randle. A Dictionary of the French & English Tongues. (Anglistica & Americana Ser.: No. 77). (ENG & FRE.). 1970. reprint ed. 210.00 incl. 3.5 hd (*0-685-66455-4*, 05103206) G Olms Pubs.

Cotham, Edward T., Jr. Battle on the Bay: The Civil War Struggle for Galveston. LC 97-4835. 252p. 1998. 37.50 (*0-292-71204-9*, COTBAT); pap. 16.95 (*0-292-71205-7*, COTBAP) U of Tex Pr.

Cotham, Perry C. The Heart & Soul of Business: A Christian Perspective. LC 98-66609. 320p. 1998. pap. 19.95 (*1-57736-105-9*) Providence Hse.

— Toil, Turmoil, & Triumph: A Portrait of the Tennessee Labor Movement. LC 95-71978. 352p. (C). 1995. 29.95 (*1-881576-64-7*, Hillsboro Pr) Providence Hse.

Cothen, Grady C. The New SBC: Fundamentalism's Impact on the Southern Baptist Convention. LC 95-2441. 232p. 1995. pap. 18.00 (*1-57312-025-1*) Smyth & Helwys.

Cothen, Joe H. Pulpit Is Waiting: A Guide for Pastoral Preaching. LC 97-53291. 304p. 1998. 22.50 (*1-56554-301-7*) Pelican.

Cothen, Joseph H. Equipped for Good Work: A Guide for Pastors. LC 80-37964. 352p. 1981. 22.95 (*0-88289-271-1*) Pelican.

Cothera, Richard, et al, eds. Risk Assessment & Risk Management of Industrial & Envrionmental Chemicals. (Advances in Modern Envrionmental Toxicology Ser.: Vol. 15). (Illus.). 246p. 1988. 65.00 (*0-911131-16-7*) Specialist Journals.

Cothern, C. R. & Smith, J. E. Environmental Radon. LC 87-29108. (Environmental Science Research Ser.: Vol. 35). (Illus.). 378p. (C). 1988. text 95.00 (*0-306-42707-9*, Kluwer Plenum) Kluwer Academic.

Cothern, C. Richard, ed. Comparative Environmental Risk Assessment. 336p. 1992. lib. bdg. 95.00 (*0-87371-605-1*, L605) Lewis Pubs.

— Handbook for Environmental Risk Decision Making: Values, Perceptions, & Ethics. LC 95-16857. 432p. 1995. lib. bdg. 85.00 (*1-56670-131-7*, L1131) Lewis Pubs.

Cothern, C. Richard & Rebers, Paul A., eds. Radon, Radium, & Uranium in Drinking Water. (Illus.). 296p. 1990. lib. bdg. 99.95 (*0-87371-207-2*, L207) Lewis Pubs.

Cothern, C. Richard & Ross, N. Phillip, eds. Environmental Statistics, Assessment, & Forecasting. LC 93-25598. 432p. 1993. lib. bdg. 104.95 (*0-87371-936-0*, GE45) Lewis Pubs.

Cothern, C. Richard, jt. auth. see Byrd, Daniel M., III.

Cothern, Clark. At the Heart of Every Great Father: The Heart of Jesus. LC 97-32501. 1998. pap. 6.99 (*1-57673-213-4*) Multnomah Pubs.

— Detours: Sometimes Rough Roads Lead to Right Place. LC 98-37402. 1999. pap. 10.99 (*1-57673-286-X*) Multnomah Pubs.

***Cothern, Clark.** Spirit Controlled Living: Turning Negative Impulses into Positive Thoughts, Feelings & Actions. LC 00-8305. (Illus.). 192p. 2000. pap. 10.99 (*1-57673-639-3*, Pub. by Multnomah Pubs) GL Services.

Cothon, et al. Science Experiments 100's Middle School. 160p. (C). 1996. pap., per. 18.95 (*0-7872-1574-0*) Kendall-Hunt.

Cothran, Bettina, ed. Handbook for German in Business & Technology. (GER., Illus.). 167p. (C). 1994. pap. text 5.00 (*0-942017-16-1*) Amer Assn Teach German.

Cothran, Betty. Destinations, Detours & Diversions: A Guide to Family Outings & Good Times. (Illus.). 75p. (Orig.). (YA). 1989. pap. 2.50 (*0-9625229-0-2*) Seaworthy Pubns.

Cothran, Christel M. 1994-95 International Registry of Certified Corporate Wildlife Habitats. 120p. 1994. write for info. (*0-9646852-5-6*) Wildlife Habitat.

— 1993 International Registry of Certified Corporate Wildlife Habitats. 102p. 1993. write for info. (*0-9646852-4-8*) Wildlife Habitat.

Cothran, Christel M. & Hendey, Dan. Wildlife at Work: Team Kit. 1995. suppl. ed. write for info. (*0-9646852-7-2*) Wildlife Habitat.

Cothran, Dan A. Political Stability & Democracy in Mexico: The Perfect Dictatorship? LC 93-23679. 272p. 1994. 65.00 (*0-275-94345-3*, Praeger Pubs) Greenwood.

Cothran, Dan A., tr. see Schmidt, Samuel.

Cothran, Frank, jt. illus. see Hoch, George.

***Cothran, Helen.** Endangered Species: Opposing Viewpoints. LC 99-85752. (Opposing Viewpoints Ser.). 2000. pap. write for info. (*0-7377-0506-X*) Greenhaven.

— Nuclear Security. LC 00-30904. (At Issue Ser.). (Illus.). 2001. lib. bdg. write for info. (*0-7377-0478-0*) Greenhaven.

— Police Brutality: Opposing Viewpoints. LC 00-32996. (Opposing Viewpoints Ser.). 2001. lib. bdg. write for info. (*0-7377-0515-9*) Greenhaven.

Cothran, James R. Gardens of Historic Charleston. LC 94-18769. 188p. 1995. 39.95 (*1-57003-004-9*) U of SC Pr.

Cothran, John C. African-American Culture & Life Search. LC 92-61350. (Illus.). 400p. 1999. lib. bdg. 24.95 (*0-9634002-1-5*) Stardate Pub.

Cothren, Paige. Walk Carefully Around the Dead. 252p. 1998. pap. write for info. (*0-9667072-0-6*) P Cothren.

Cothron, Julia, et al. Pak: Science Experiments by the Hundreds. 224p. 1996. teacher ed. 26.95 (*0-7872-2140-6*) Kendall-Hunt.

— Science Experiments & Projects for Students. 198p. (C). 1996. pap., per. 18.95 (*0-7872-1590-2*) Kendall-Hunt.

Cothron, Julia, et al. Science Experiments & Projects for Students. 3rd ed. 208p. (C). per. 25.95 (*0-7872-6478-4*) Kendall-Hunt.

C

An Asterisk (*) at the beginning of an entry indicates that the title is appearing for the first time.

— Students & Research: Practical Strategies for Science Classrooms & Competitions. 3rd ed. 304p. (C). per. 30.95 (*0-7872-6477-6*) Kendall-Hunt.

Cothron, Julia H. Students & Research: Practical Strategies for Science Classrooms & Competitions. 2nd ed. 304p. 1995. per. 25.95 (*0-8403-7766-5*) Kendall-Hunt.

Cothrun, Bettina & Karottki, Hartmut. Vier Plus: Ubungsmaterial Zur Vorbereitung Auf die "Prufung Wirtschaftsdeutsch International" (GER.). 155p. (C). 1994. pap. 15.00 (*0-942017-24-2*) Amer Assn Teach German.

***Coti, William & Simpson, Roger.** Covering Violence: A Guide to Ethical Reporting About Victims & Trauma. 288p. 2000. text 49.50 (*0-231-11450-8*) Col U Pr.

Cotic, Meir. The Prague Trial: The First Anti-Zionist Show Trial in the Communist Bloc. LC 87-47555. 288p. 1987. 19.50 (*0-317-59699-3*, Cornwall Bks) Assoc Univ Prs.

Coticchia, Mark E., et al. Cad/Cam/Cae Systems: Justification, Implementation, Productivity Measurement. 2nd ed. LC 92-22195. (Computer-Aided Engineering Ser.: Vol. 2). (Illus.). 352p. 1993. text 89.75 incl. disk (*0-8247-8961-X*) Dekker.

Cotich, Felicia, et al. Primavera V. Heller, Janet R. et al, eds. LC 76-647540. (Illus.). (C). 1979. pap. 4.00 (*0-916980-05-7*) Primavera.

Cotillon, Pierre. Stratigraphy. Noble, James P., tr. LC 92-19762. (ENG & FRE., Illus.). 200p. 1992. 54.95 (*0-387-54675-8*) Spr-Verlag.

Cotiviela, A., tr. see Schrolder, A. & Bonnet, L.

Cotkin, George. Reluctant Modernism: American Thought & Culture, 1880-1900. (American Thought & Culture Ser.). 250p. (C). 1992. 28.95 (*0-8057-9054-3*, Twyne) Mac Lib Ref.

***Cotkin, George.** Reluctant Modernism: American Thought & Culture, 1880-1900. 188p. 1999. reprint ed. text 29.00 (*0-7881-6245-4*) DIANE Pub.

Cotkin, George. William James, Public Philosopher. LC 89-33036. (New Studies in American Intellectual & Cultural History). 272p. 1989. text 38.00 (*0-8018-3878-9*) Johns Hopkins.

— William James, Public Philosopher. LC 93-36078. 232p. 1994. pap. text 17.95 (*0-252-06392-9*) U of Ill Pr.

Cotler. Surgery of Spinal Trauma. 175.00 (*0-683-18108-4*) Lppncott W & W.

Cotler, Amy. One-Pot Vegetarian Dishes. 1996. write for info. (*0-614-96292-7*) HarpC.

— Wrap It Up: 100 Fresh, Bold & Bright Sandwiches with a Twist. LC 97-31689. 208p. 1998. pap. 14.95 (*0-609-80236-4*) Crown Pub Group.

Cotler, Amy & Burnett, Frances Hodgson. The Secret Garden Cookbook: Recipes Inspired by Frances Hodgson Burnett's The Secret Garden. LC 98-22437. (Secret Garden Ser.). (Illus.). 128p. (J). (gr. 3-7). 1999. 17.95 (*0-06-027740-8*) HarpC Child Bks.

Cotler, Gordon. Artist's Proof: A Mystery. LC 97-15631. 272p. 1997. text 21.95 (*0-312-16831-4*) St Martin.

— Prime Candidate. 1996. mass mkt. 5.99 (*0-312-96072-7*) St Martin.

Cotler, H. B., jt. auth. see Cotler, J. M.

Cotler, Irwin, ed. Nuremberg Forty Years Later: The Struggle against Injustice in Our Time. LC 95-191527. 304p. 1995. 65.00 (*0-7735-1239-X*, Pub. by McG-Queens Univ Pr); pap. 22.95 (*0-7735-1250-0*, Pub. by McG-Queens Univ Pr) CUP Services.

Cotler, Irwin & Marx, Herbert, eds. The Law & the Poor in Canada. LC 78-305100. 144p. 1977. reprint ed. pap. 44.70 (*0-608-00459-6*, 206127800007) Bks Demand.

Cotler, J. M. & Cotler, H. B. Spinal Fusion: Science & Technique. (Illus.). xvi, 407p. 1990. 298.00 (*0-387-97054-1*) Spr-Verlag.

Cotler, Stephen R. Removing the Barriers: Accessibility Guidelines & Specifications. (Illus.). 125p. 1991. pap. 55.00 (*0-913359-59-9*) APPA VA.

Cotliar, William & Bauer, Lawrence, eds. Complying with FDA Good Manufacturing Practice Requirements: How to Develop Your Quality System Manual. LC 97-209936. (Orig.). 1996. pap. 195.00 (*1-57020-077-7*) Assn Adv Med Instrn.

Cotliar, William, jt. auth. see Riordan, John.

Cotliar, William, jt. auth. see Riordan, John J.

Cotman. Bake the Scottish Way. (Illus.). 32p. pap. 3.95 (*0-7117-0228-4*, Pub. by JARR UK) Seven Hills Bk.

Cotman, Carl W., ed. Neuronal Plasticity. fac. ed. LC 77-72807. 349p. pap. 108.20 (*0-7837-7259-9*, 204704600005) Bks Demand.

Cotman, Carl W., et al, eds. The Neuro-Immune Endocrine Connection. LC 86-26037. (Illus.). 166p. 1987. reprint ed. pap. 51.50 (*0-608-07201-X*, 206742600009) Bks Demand.

Cotman, Carl W., jt. auth. see Angevine, Jay B., Jr.

Cotman, Jacqueline N., ed. see Cotman, Sochitl S.

Cotman, Jacqueline N., ed. & photos by see Cotman, Sochitl S.

Cotman, John W. Birmingham, JFK & the Civil Rights Act of 1963: Implications for Elite Theory. (American University Studies: Political Science: Ser. X, Vol. 17). XII, 211p. (C). 1988. text 32.60 (*0-8204-0806-9*) P Lang Pubng.

— The Gorrion Tree: Cuba & the Grenada Revolution. LC 92-29573. (American University Studies: Political Science: Ser. X, Vol. 38). XVI, 272p. (C). 1993. text 48.95 (*0-8204-2026-3*) P Lang Pubng.

Cotman, Robert J., et al, eds. Sponsors Report Almanac, 1992 Edition: Exposure Analysis, Trends & Projections. LC 91-1164. 175p. 1992. pap. 87.50 (*0-9630140-0-5*) J Julius Assocs.

Cotman, Sochitl S. The Holy Land. Cotman, Jacqueline N., ed. & photos by by. (Luxury Paradise Ser.: Vol. 3). (Illus.). 50p. 1998. pap. 10.00 (*0-9652390-4-7*, 999997577) J N Cotman.

— Luxury Paradise: Brazil Our Love, Vol. 2. Cotman, Jacqueline N. & Peterman, Peggy M., eds. LC 97-92167. (Illus.). 40p. (Orig.). 1997. pap. 10.00 (*0-9652390-3-9*) J N Cotman.

— Luxury Paradise Vol. 1: Cayman Islands. Cotman, Jacqueline N., ed. & photos by by. (Illus.). 32p. (Orig.). 1995. pap. text 13.09 (*0-9652390-0-4*) J N Cotman.

— Snow How: St. Moritz, Switzerland. Cotman, Jacqueline N., ed. & photos by by. LC 96-96409. (Illus.). 26p. (Orig.). (J). 1996. pap. 9.00 (*0-9652390-1-2*) J N Cotman.

***Cotner.** Bedside Prayers: Prayers & Poems for When You Rise & Go to Sleep. large type ed. 192p. 1999. pap. 16.00 (*0-06-093319-4*) HarpC.

Cotner. Graces. Date not set. pap. 13.00 (*0-06-061561-3*) HarpC.

Cotner, June. Amazing Graces. LC 99-29158. (J). 2000. write for info. (*0-688-15566-9*, Wm Morrow) Morrow Avon.

***Cotner, June.** Animal Blessings: Prayers & Poems Celebrating Our Pets. 176p. 2000. 19.00 (*0-06-251645-0*) Harper SF.

Cotner, June. Bedside Prayers: Prayers & Poems for When You Rise & Go to Sleep. LC 97-19818. 176p. 1997. 16.00 (*0-06-251529-2*, Pub. by Harper SF) HarpC.

— Bless the Day: Prayers & Poems to Nurture Your Soul. LC 98-21401. 224p. 1998. 16.00 (*1-56836-251-X*) Kodansha.

— Family Celebrations: Prayers, Poems & Toasts for Every Occasion. LC 98-48036. xxi, 195p. 1999. 16.95 (*0-8362-7856-9*) Andrews & McMeel.

***Cotner, June.** Get Well Wishes: Prayers, Poems & Blessings. large type ed. 192p. 2000. 19.00 (*0-06-019705-6*) HarpC.

— Get Well Wishes: Prayers, Poems to Wish You Well. LC 99-87900. 176p. 2000. 19.00 (*0-06-251646-9*, Pub. by Harper SF) HarpC.

Cotner, June. Graces: Prayers for Everyday Meals & Special Occasions. LC 94-8034. (Illus.). 208p. 1994. 18.00 (*0-06-065956-4*, Pub. by Harper SF) HarpC.

Cotner, Robert & Baillie, Kenneth. Survivors: Faces of Those in Need. (Illus.). 52p. (Orig.). 1997. pap. 25.00 (*0-9657275-0-5*) Slvation Army.

Cotner, Sam. McMillen's Texas Gardening: Vegetables. (Illus.). 160p. 1998. pap. 15.95 (*0-88415-895-0*, 5895) Gulf Pub.

— The Vegetable Book: A Texan's Guide to Gardening. (Illus.). 422p. 1985. 26.95 (*0-914641-01-8*) TX Gardener Pr.

— The Vegetable Book: A Texan's Guide to Gardening. rev. ed. (Illus.). 400p. 1996. pap. 24.95 (*0-914641-15-8*) TX Gardener Pr.

Cotner, Thomas E. Military & Political Career of Jose Joaquin de Herrera, 1792-1854, 7--7. LC 69-19007. 336p. 1970. reprint ed. lib. bdg. 69.50 (*0-8371-1018-1*, TICH, Greenwood Pr) Greenwood.

***Coto-Millan, P.** Utility & Production: Theory & Applications. LC 99-49525. (Contributions to Economics Ser.). xii, 147p. 1999. pap. 56.00 (*3-7908-1153-X*) Spr-Verlag.

Cotolo, F. M. Pony Player. Taylor, Chuck, ed. 175p. (Orig.). 1989. 16.95 (*0-941720-54-3*); pap. 8.95 (*0-941720-55-1*) Slough Pr TX.

Cotoner, Luisa, tr. & intro. see Riera, Carmen.

Cotran & Mallet. Yearbook of Islamic & Middle Eastern Law, Vol. 2, 1995. 1997. 276.00 (*90-411-0257-4*) Kluwer Law Intl.

Cotran, E., jt. ed. see Rubin, N. N.

Cotran, Eugene, et al, eds. The Arab-Israeli Accords: Legal Perspective. LC 96-1100. (CIMEL Book Ser.: No. 1). 303p. 1996. 117.00 (*90-411-0902-1*) Kluwer Law Intl.

Cotran, Eugene & Amissah, Austin. Arbitration in Africa. LC 96-36768. (London Court of International Arbitration Ser.: Vol. 2). 1997. 182.00 (*90-411-0294-9*) Kluwer Law Intl.

***Cotran, Eugene & Mallat, Chibli, eds.** Yearbook of Islamic & Middle Eastern Law Vol. 4: 1997-1998. 676p. 1998. 270.00 (*90-411-0593-X*) Kluwer Law Intl.

Cotran, Eugene & Mallat, Chibli, eds. Yearbook of Islamic & Middle Eastern Law 1998, Vol. 3. 584p. 1998. text 245.00 (*90-411-0443-7*) Kluwer Law Intl.

Cotran, Eugene & Sherif, Adel O., eds. The Role of the Judiciary in the Protection of Human Rights. LC 97-35079. (Cimel Book Ser.). 492p. 1998. 190.00 (*90-411-0512-3*) Kluwer Law Intl.

***Cotran, Eugene & Sherif, Adel Omar.** Democracy: The Rule of Law & Islam. LC 99-29150. (Centre of Islamic & Middle Eastern Law Ser.: Vol. 6). 600p. 1999. 225.00 (*90-411-1185-9*) Kluwer Law Intl.

Cotran, Ramzi, jt. auth. see Leaf, Alexander.

Cotran, Ramzi S., et al. Robbins Pathologic Basis of Disease. 5th ed. LC 94-2629. (Illus.). 1414p. (C). 1994. text 75.00 (*0-7216-5032-5*, W B Saunders Co) Harcrt Hlth Sci Grp.

— Robbin's Pathologic Basis of Disease. 6th ed. Schmitt, Bill, ed. LC 98-36022. (Illus.). 1472p. (C). 1998. text 75.00 (*0-7216-7335-X*, W B Saunders Co) Harcrt Hlth Sci Grp.

Cotrell, Georgia. Shoulders. LC 87-7413. 258p. (Orig.). 1987. pap. 9.95 (*0-932379-25-7*); lib. bdg. 20.95 (*0-932379-26-5*) Firebrand Bks.

Cotroneo, George V. & Rumer, Ralph R., eds. Hydraulic Engineering '94: Proceedings of the 1994 Conference Sponsored by the Hydraulics Division of the ASCE, Buffalo, NY, August 1-5, 1994, 2 vols. 1408p. 1994. 140.00 (*0-7844-0037-7*) Am Soc Civil Eng.

Cotroneo, Ross R. History of the Northern Pacific Land Grant, 1900-1952. Bruchey, Stuart, ed. LC 78-56728. (Management in Public Lands in the U. S. Ser.). (Illus.). 1979. lib. bdg. 34.95 (*0-405-11329-3*) Ayer.

Cotruvo, Joseph A., jt. ed. see Rice, Rip G.

***Cotsakis, Spiro & Gibbons, G. W., eds.** Mathematical & Quantum Aspects of Relativity & Cosmology: Proceedings of the Second Samos Meeting on Cosmology, Geometry & Relativity, Held at Pythagoreon, Samos, Greece, 31 August-4 September 1998. LC 99-59222. (Lecture Notes in Physics Ser.). xii, 251p. 2000. 58.00 (*3-540-66865-9*) Spr-Verlag.

Cotsakis, Spiros & Gibbons, Gary W., eds. Global Structure & Evolution in General Relativity: Proceedings of the First Samos Meeting on Cosmology, Geometry & Relativity, Held at Karlovassi, Samos, Greece, September 5-7, 1994. LC 95-50353. (Lecture Notes in Physics Ser.: Vol. 460). 182p. 1996. 67.00 (*3-540-60751-X*) Spr-Verlag.

***Cotsakos, Christos M.** The ARE E*Trade Guide to Online Investing. 2000. pap. 15.00 (*0-06-095741-7*) HarpC.

— It's Your Money: E*TRADE Step by Step Guide to Online Investing. (Illus.). 128p. 2000. pap. 15.00 (*0-06-662003-1*, HarpBusn) HarpInfo.

— Management. 2001. write for info. (*0-06-662008-2*, HarpBusn) HarpInfo.

Cotsell. Dickens a Tale of Two Cities. large type ed. LC 98-21418. (Critical Essays Ser.). 226p. 1998. 49.00 (*0-7838-0072-X*, G K Hall Lrg Type) Mac Lib Ref.

Cotsell, Michael. Critical Essays on Charles Dickens' "Great Expectations" Bowen, Zack R., ed. (Critical Essays on British Literature Ser.). 248p. (C). 1990. 49.00 (*0-8161-8852-1*, G K Hall & Co) Mac Lib Ref.

Cotsell, Michael, ed. Creditable Warriors: 1830-1876, Vol. 3. LC 88-7489. (English Literature & the Wider World Ser.). (Illus.). 328p. (C). 1990. text 55.00 (*0-948660-10-4*, Pub. by Ashfield Pr) Humanities.

Cotsell, Michael, ed. & intro. see Dickens, Charles.

***Cotsen, Lloyd, et al.** Japanese Bamboo Baskets: Masterworks of Form & Texture. (Illus.). 391p. 1999. 800.00 (*1-878529-59-5*) Art Media Resources.

Cotsforde, Thomas, tr. see Zwingli, Ulrich.

Cotsonis, John A. Byzantine Figural Processional Crosses. LC 94-29675. (Byzantine Collection Publications: 10). (Illus.). 1994. pap. 20.00 (*0-88402-228-5*) Dumbarton Oaks.

***Cotsonitia, Nicholas J.** Century of Champions: One Hundred Years of Michigan Memories. Myers, Gene, ed. (Illus.). 336p. 1999. 49.95 (*0-937247-29-4*) Detroit Pr.

Cott, Allan. Fasting: The Ultimate Diet. 280p. 1996. pap. 14.95 (*0-8038-9382-5*, Pub. by Hastings) Midpt Trade.

***Cott, Ann.** A Century in the Shadow of Pikes Peak: Don Lawrie, His Mountain, His Life. xvi, 141p. 1999. pap. 14.95 (*0-9674709-0-0*) Ann Cott.

Cott, Donna L. Van, see Van Cott, Donna L.

Cott, Gary A. Van, see Van Cott, Gary A.

Cott, Jonathan. Conversations with Glenn Gould. 160p. 1984. reprint ed. 15.95i (*0-316-15777-5*) Little.

Cott, Jonathan. The Search for Omm Sety: A Story of Eternal Love. 288p. 1989. mass mkt. 9.95 (*0-446-39040-2*, Pub. by Warner Bks) Little.

Cott, Jonathan. Wandering Ghost: The Odyssey of Lafcadio Hearn. (Illus.). 464p. 1992. reprint ed. pap. 14.95 (*4-7700-1659-X*) Kodansha.

Cott, Jonathan, ed. Beyond the Looking Glass: Extraordinary Works of Fairy Tale & Fantasy. LC 84-22675. (Illus.). 519p. 1985. 30.00 (*0-87951-995-9*, Pub. by Overlook Pr) Penguin Putnam.

— Beyond the Looking Glass: Extraordinary Works of Fairy Tale & Fantasy. (Illus.). 519p. 1988. pap. 15.95 (*0-87951-238-5*, Pub. by Overlook Pr) Penguin Putnam.

Cott, Nancy, ed. A Woman Making History: Mary Ritter Beard Through Her Letters. 400p. (C). 1991. 50.00 (*0-300-04825-4*) Yale U Pr.

Cott, Nancy F. The Bonds of Womanhood: "Woman's Sphere" in New England, 1780-1835. LC 76-49728. 1978. pap. 14.00 (*0-300-02289-1*) Yale U Pr.

— Bonds of Womanhood: "Woman's Sphere" in New England, 1780-1835. 2nd ed. LC 97-60429. 256p. 1997. pap. 15.00 (*0-300-07298-8*) Yale U Pr.

— The Grounding of Modern Feminism. LC 87-10642. 384p. 1987. 50.00 (*0-300-03892-5*) Yale U Pr.

— The Grounding of Modern Feminism. LC 87-10642. 384p. (C). 1989. reprint ed. pap. 17.00 (*0-300-04228-0*) Yale U Pr.

***Cott, Nancy F.** No Small Courage: A History of Women in the United States. (Illus.). 768p. 2000. 35.00 (*0-19-513946-0*) OUP.

— Public Vows: A History of Marriage & the Nation. 288p. 2001. 27.95 (*0-674-00320-9*) HUP.

— Young Oxford History of Women in the United States, 11 vols., Set. (Illus.). 1998. pap., boxed set 122.45 (*0-19-512398-0*) OUP.

Cott, Nancy F., et al, eds. Root of Bitterness: Documents of the Social History of American Women. 2nd ed. LC 95-44965. 448p. (C). 1996. text 47.50 (*1-55553-255-1*) NE U Pr.

— Root of Bitterness: Documents on the Social History of American Women. 2nd ed. LC 95-44965. 448p. (C). 1996. pap. text 16.95 (*1-55553-256-X*) NE U Pr.

Cott, Nancy F., intro. History of Women in the United States: Topically Arranged Articles on the Evolution of Women's History in the United States, 20 Vols., Set. Incl. Industrial Wage Work Vol. 7, Pts. I & II. LC 92-16765. 336p. 1993. lib. bdg. 240.00 (*3-598-41461-7*); Vol. 1. Theory & Method in Women's History. LC 92-16765. 326p. 1992. lib. bdg. 240.00 (*3-598-41455-2*); Vol. 2. Household Constitution & Family Relationships Vol. 2. LC 92-16765. 442p. 1992. lib. bdg. 120.00 (*3-598-41456-0*); Vol. 3. Domestic Relations & Law. LC 92-16765. 461p. 1992. lib. bdg. 120.00 (*3-598-41457-9*); Vol. 4, Pts. I & II. Domestic Ideology & Domestic Work. LC 92-16765. 320p. 1992. lib. bdg. 240.00 (*3-598-41458-7*); Vol. 5, Pts. I & II. Intersection of Work & Family Life. LC 92-16765. 1992. lib. bdg. 240.00 (*3-598-41459-5*); Vol. 6. Working on the Land. LC 92-16765. 1993. lib. bdg. 120.00 (*3-598-41460-9*); Vol. 8, Pts. I & II. Professional & White Collar Employment. LC 92-16765. 348p. 1993. lib. bdg. 240.00 (*3-598-41462-5*); Vol. 9. Prostitution. LC 92-16765. 393p. 1993. lib. bdg. 120.00 (*3-598-41463-3*); Vol. 10. Sexuality & Sexual Behavior Vol. 10. LC 92-16765. 591p. 1993. lib. bdg. 120.00 (*3-598-41464-1*); Vol. 11. Women's Bodies Vol. 11: Health & Childbirth. LC 92-16765. 406p. 1993. lib. bdg. 120.00 (*3-598-41465-X*); Vol. 12. Education Vol. 12. 481p. 1993. lib. bdg. 120.00 (*3-598-41466-8*); Vol. 13. Religion. 499p. 1993. 120.00 (*3-598-41467-6*); Vol. 14. Intercultural & Interracial Relations. LC 92-16765. 442p. 1993. lib. bdg. 120.00 (*3-598-41468-4*); Vol. 15. Women & War. LC 92-16765. 518p. 1993. lib. bdg. 120.00 (*3-598-41469-2*); Vol. 16. Women Together Vol. 16: Organizational Life. LC 92-16765. 350p. 1994. lib. bdg. 120.00 (*3-598-41470-6*); Vol. 17, Pt. 1. Social & Moral Reform. LC 92-16765. 275p. 1994. lib. bdg. 120.00 (*3-598-41471-4*); Vol. 17, Pt. 2. Social. LC 92-16765. 275p. 1994. lib. bdg. 120.00 (*3-598-41695-4*); Vol. 18, Pt. 1. Women & Politics. LC 92-16765. 275p. 1994. lib. bdg. 120.00 (*3-598-41472-2*); Vol. 18, Pt. 2. Women & Politics. LC 92-16765. 275p. 1994. lib. bdg. 120.00 (*3-598-41697-0*); Vol. 19, Part 1. Woman Suffrage Vol. 19, Pt. I. LC 92-16765. 275p. 1994. lib. bdg. 120.00 (*3-598-41473-0*); Vol. 19, Part 2. Woman Suffrage Vol. 19, Pt. II. LC 92-16765. 275p. 1994. lib. bdg. 120.00 (*3-598-41696-2*); Vol. 20. Feminist Struggles for Sex Equality. LC 92-16765. 350p. 1994. lib. bdg. 120.00 (*3-598-41474-9*); LC 92-16765. 1994. Set lib. bdg. 3055.00 (*3-598-41454-4*) K G Saur Verlag.

Cott, Nancy F. & Pleck, Elizabeth H. A Heritage of Her Own: Families, Work & Feminism in America. 1980. pap. 17.95 (*0-671-25068-X*, Touchstone) S&S Trade Pap.

Cotta, Alain. Dictionnaire de la Science Economique. 3rd ed. (FRE.). 448p. pap. 39.95 (*0-7859-0740-8*, M-6092) Fr & Eur.

Cotta, John. A Short Discoverie of the Dangers of Ignorant Practisers of Physicke. LC 72-38168. (English Experience Ser.: No. 445). 144p. 1972. reprint ed. 21.00 (*90-221-0445-1*) Walter J Johnson.

Cotta, M., jt. ed. see Blondel, Jean.

Cotta, Maurizio, jt. auth. see Blondel, Jean.

Cotta, Maurizio, jt. ed. see Best, Heinrich.

Cotta, Maurizio, jt. ed. see Liebert, Ulrike.

Cotta, Renato M. The Integral Transform Method in Thermal & Fluids Sciences & Engineering. LC 98-22155. 430p. 1998. 87.50 (*1-56700-120-3*) Begell Hse.

— Integral Transforms in Computational Heat & Fluid Flow. 352p. 1993. boxed set 94.95 (*0-8493-8665-9*, TJ260) CRC Pr.

Cotta, Renato M., et al. Computational & Analytical Heat Conduction. LC 97-7327. 366p. 1997. 155.00 (*0-471-95648-1*) Wiley.

Cotta, Sergio. Montesquieu e la Scienza Della Societa. Mayer, J. P., ed. LC 78-67343. (European Political Thought Ser.). (ITA.). 1979. reprint ed. lib. bdg. 53.95 (*0-405-11688-8*) Ayer.

— Why Violence? A Philosophical Interpretation. LC 84-25779. Orig. Title: Perche la Violenza? Una Interpretazione Filosofica. 164p. 1985. reprint ed. pap. 50.90 (*0-608-04511-X*, 206525600001) Bks Demand.

Cottam, Angela, jt. auth. see Mudie, Peter.

Cottam, Calvin. Cranial & Facial Adjusting Step-by-Step: Twenty-Two Lessons. (Illus.). 439p. 1985. 144.00 (*0-917628-12-8*); ring bd. 88.00 (*0-917628-07-1*) Coraco.

— How to Be Positive in Negative Situations. 44p. 1997. pap. write for info. (*0-917628-16-0*) Coraco.

— Secret, Sacred, Symbolic Story Revealing Hidden Meanings of Our Journey Through This Life & the Rest of Eternity. 44p. 1996. pap. 10.00 (*0-917628-14-4*) Coraco.

Cottam, Chris, jt. auth. see Hughes, James.

Cottam, Christine M., ed. Women, Aid & Development: Essays in Honour of Professor T. Scarlett Epstein. (C). 1993. 28.00 (*81-7075-026-1*, Pub. by Hindustan) S Asia.

Cottam, K. J., ed. The Girl from Kashin: Soviet Women in Resistance in World War II. (Illus.). 230p. 1984. pap. text 36.95 (*0-89126-128-1*) MA-AH Pub.

— The Golden-Tressed Soldier. 287p. 1983. pap. 43.95 (*0-89126-119-2*) MA-AH Pub.

— In the Sky above the Front. (Illus.). 270p. 1984. pap. text 36.95 (*0-89126-126-5*) MA-AH Pub.

Cottam, K. J., tr. Soviet Airwomen in Combat in World War II. 141p. 1983. pap. 30.95 (*0-89126-118-4*) MA-AH Pub.

Cottam, Kazimiera J. Boleslaw Limanowski, (1835-1935) (East European Monographs: No. 41). 365p. 1978. text 75.50 (*0-914710-34-6*, Pub. by East Eur Monographs) Col U Pr.

Cottam, M. G. Linear & Nonlinear Spin Waves in Magnetic Films & Superlattices. 400p. 1994. text 106.00 (*981-02-1006-X*) World Scientific Pub.

Cottam, M. G. & Tilley, D. R. Introduction to Surface & Superlattice Excitations. (Illus.). 352p. 1989. text 115.00 (*0-521-32154-9*) Cambridge U Pr.

Cottam, Martha L. Images & Intervention: U. S. Policies in Latin America. (Latin American Ser.). 240p. (Orig.). (C). 1994. pap. 19.95 (*0-8229-5526-1*); text 49.95 (*0-8229-3797-2*) U of Pittsburgh Pr.

***Cottam, Martha L. & Cottam, Richard W.** Nationalism & Politics: The Political Behavior of Nation States. 330p. 2000. lib. bdg. 59.95 (*1-55587-919-5*) L Rienner.

Cottam, Martha L. & Shih, Chih-Yu, eds. Contending Dramas: A Cognitive Approach to International Organization. LC 91-30947. 280p. 1992. 65.00 (*0-275-93526-4*, C3526, Praeger Pubs) Greenwood.

An Asterisk (*) at the beginning of an entry indicates that the title is appearing for the first time.

Cottam, Michael G. & Lockwood, David J. Light Scattering in Magnetic Solids. 264p. (C). 1986. reprint ed. text 41.95 (*0-471-81701-5*) Krieger.
Cottam, Peter F. Ghost Flyers. (C). 1989. 39.00 (*0-86303-456-X*) St Mut.
Cottam, Richard. Understanding Negotiation: The Academic Contribution. (Pew Case Studies in International Affairs). 50p. (C). 1993. pap. text 3.50 (*1-56927-413-4*) Geo U Inst Dplmcy.
Cottam, Richard W. Competitive Interference & Twentieth Century Diplomacy. LC 67-13925. 251p. reprint ed. pap. 77.90 (*0-608-12638-1*, 202543500043) Bks Demand.
— Foreign Policy Motivation: A General Theory & a Case Study. LC 76-6659. 384p. 1977. text 49.95 (*0-8229-3323-3*) U of Pittsburgh Pr.
— Iran & the United States: A Cold War Case Study. LC 88-1340. (Series in Policy & Institutional Studies). 298p. (Orig.). 1988. text 15.95 (*0-8229-3588-0*) U of Pittsburgh Pr.
— Nationalism in Iran: Updated Through 1978. LC 78-12302. 384p. (C). 1979. pap. 17.95 (*0-8229-5299-8*) U of Pittsburgh Pr.
Cottam, Richard W., jt. auth. see Cottam, Martha L.
Cottam, S. Barry & National Archives of Canada Staff. Aboriginal Peoples & Archives: A Brief History of Aboriginal & European Relations in Canada. LC 98-230985. ii, 23p. 1997. write for info. (*0-662-25560-7*, Pub. by Can7 Govern Pub) Intl Spec Bk.
Cottam, Sally, et al, eds. TrAC 94: Theoretical Roman Archaeology. 150p. 1995. pap. 18.00 (*0-946897-86-7*, Pub. by Oxbow Bks) David Brown.
Cottam, Sue. Life Around Longreach. 64p. (C). 1990. pap. 50.00 (*0-646-08772-X*, Pub. by Boolarong Pubns) St Mut.
Cottam, Walter P., et al. Oak Hybridization at the University of Utah. (State Arboretum of Utah Ser.: Publication No. 1, 1982). (Illus.). 96p. 1982. 15.00 (*0-942830-00-8*); pap. 10.00 (*0-942830-01-6*) State Arbor.
*__Cottar, Charles.__ Cottar: The Exception Was the Rule. LC 99-62677. (Illus.). 343p. 1999. 135.00 (*1-882458-23-0*) Trophy Rm Bks.
Cottarelli, Carlo. Limiting Central Bank Credit to the Government: Theory & Practice. LC 93-42537. (Occasional Papers: No. 110). 57p. 1993. pap. 15.00 (*1-55775-358-X*) Intl Monetary.
Cottarelli, Carlo & International Monetary Fund Staff. Hungary, Economic Policies for Sustainable Growth. LC 98-130240. (Occasional Paper Ser.). ix, 99 p. 1998. write for info. (*1-55775-709-7*) Intl Monetary.
Cottarelli, Carlo, et al. Moderate Inflation: The Experience of Transition Economies. LC 98-24879. 1998. write for info. (*1-55775-699-6*) Intl Monetary.
Cottarelli, Carlo, jt. ed. see Balino, Thomas J.
Cottart, Nicole, ed. see Vajda, Georges.
Cotte, Carlos. Chumba la Cachumba. (SPA.). 24p. (J). (ps-1). pap. 6.95 (*980-257-114-8*, Pub. by Ediciones Ekare) Kane-Miller Bk.
Cotte, John, ed. The Shell Guide to Yacht Navigation. 128p. (C). 1987. 115.00 (*0-571-14691-0*, Pub. by Laurie Norie & Wilson Ltd) St Mut.
Cottell & Olarewaju. Tropical Refrigeration & Air Conditioning. 1984. pap. text, write for info. (*0-582-65803-9*, Pub. by Addison-Wesley) Longman.
Cottell, Beryl, jt. auth. see Smith, Ernest.
Cottell, Philip G., Jr. & Perlin, Terry M. Accounting Ethics: A Practical Guide for Professionals. LC 89-24368. 184p. 1990. 59.95 (*0-89930-401-X*, CTF/, Quorum Bks) Greenwood.
Cottell, Philip G., Jr., jt. auth. see Millis, Barbara J.
*__Cotten, Cynthia S.__ Snow Ponies. 1999. text 16.95 (*0-8050-6063-4*) St Martin.
Cotten, Cynthia S., jt. auth. see Silverstein, Alan J.
Cotten, Doyice, jt. auth. see Wilde, T. Jesse.
Cotten, Doyice J. & Cotten, Mary B. Legal Aspects of Waivers in Sport, Recreation & Fitness Activities. 200p. 1997. pap. 39.95 (*0-944183-25-5*) PRC Pub.
Cotten, Emmi. Clothes Make Magic. 2nd rev. ed. Rateaver, Bargyla & Rateaver, Gylver, eds. LC 79-55932. (Conservation Gardening & Farming Ser. The Home). (Illus.). 223p. (gr. 9-10). 1980. reprint ed. pap. 35.00 (*0-915966-00-X*) Rateavers.
Cotten, Jerry W. & Wootten, Bayard M. Light & Air: The Photography of Bayard Wootten. LC 98-3421. (Illus.). 272p. 1998. 37.50 (*0-8078-2445-3*) U of NC Pr.
Cotten, Joseph. Vanity Will Get You Somewhere. 256p. 1988. mass mkt. 4.50 (*0-380-70534-6*, Avon Bks) Morrow Avon.
Cotten, Lee. All Shook Up: Elvis Day-by-Day, 1954-1977. 2nd ed. (Rock & Roll Reference Ser.: No. 13). (Illus.). 528p. 1998. lib. bdg. 55.00 (*1-56075-046-4*) Popular Culture.
— Did Elvis Sing in Your Hometown? (Illus.). 280p. 1995. 26.95 (*0-9646588-0-1*); pap. 14.95 (*0-9646588-1-X*) High Sierra Bks.
— Did Elvis Sing in Your Hometown, Too? (Illus.). 316p. 1997. 28.95 (*0-9646588-2-8*); pap. 17.95 (*0-9646588-3-6*) High Sierra Bks.
— Reelin' & Rockin' Vol. 2: The Golden Age of American Rock & Roll, Vol. II: 1956-1959. Schultheiss, Thomas, ed. (Rock & Roll Reference Ser.: No. 39). (Illus.). 300p. 1995. lib. bdg. 55.00 (*1-56075-039-1*) Popular Culture.
— Shake, Rattle, & Roll Vol. 1: The Golden Age of American Rock 'n Roll, 1952-1955. Schultheiss, Thomas, ed. (Rock & Roll Reference Ser.: No. 31). (Illus.). 390p. 1990. reprint ed. lib. bdg. 45.00 (*1-56075-017-0*) Popular Culture.
— Twist & Shout Vol. 3: The Golden Age of American Rock 'n Roll, 1960-1963. (Rock & Roll Reference Ser.: Vol. 41). (Illus.). 550p. 2001. lib. bdg. 65.00 (*1-56075-047-2*) Popular Culture.
Cotten, Lee & DeWitt, Howard. Jailhouse Rock: The Bootleg Records of Elvis Presley, 1970-1983. (Rock & Roll Reference Ser.: No. 8). (Illus.). 412p. 1993. reprint ed. 34.50 (*1-56075-034-0*) Popular Culture.
Cotten, Martha L. Cotten Tales. Christian, Robert, ed. LC 93-83379. (Illus.). 111p. 1993. 12.95 (*0-9635907-9-0*) Parvenir Pr.
Cotten, Mary B., jt. auth. see Cotten, Doyice J.
Cotten, Michelle. Reach & Teach Your Peers. Kirby, Judy, ed. 24p. (YA). 1995. pap. 5.95 (*0-934513-60-0*, MCI) Natl Crime DC.
Cotten, Patricia M. Laid Back in Hollywood: Remembering. Burk, Margaret & Slater, Heather, eds. LC 97-77221. (Illus.). 256p. 1998. 24.95 (*0-9649635-1-5*); pap. 16.95 (*0-9649635-2-3*) Belle Pubng CA.
*__Cotter.__ Hematology. (Quick Look Veterinary Ser.). 2000. 23.95 (*1-889325-46-5*, Pub. by Fence Crk Pubng) Blackwell Sci.
Cotter. Homeopathic Teachings from a Master. 107p. 1987. pap. 7.95 (*0-85207-183-3*, Pub. by C W Daniel) Natl Bk Netwk.
*__Cotter, Arlene.__ From This Moment On: A Guide for Those Recently Diagnosed with Cancer. LC 99-31658. 384p. 1999. 24.95 (*0-375-50309-9*) Random.
Cotter, Arundel. Fool's Profits. Brief, Richard P., ed. LC 80-1481. (Dimensions of Accounting Theory & Practice Ser.). 1980. reprint ed. lib. bdg. 21.95 (*0-405-13511-4*) Ayer.
Cotter, Barry. Cotter: Defective & Unsafe Products - Law & Practice. Williams, John M., ed. 1996. pap. write for info. (*0-406-00248-7*, CPL, MICHIE) LEXIS Pub.
Cotter, Betty. Peace Dale. LC 98-87322. (Images of America Ser.). (Illus.). 128p. 1998. pap. 16.99 (*0-7524-1296-5*) Arcadia Publng.
*__Cotter, Betty.__ South Shore. (Images of America Ser.). 128p. 1999. pap. 18.99 (*0-7524-1295-7*) Arcadia Publng.
*__Cotter, Betty J.__ Kingston. (Images of America Ser.). 128p. 1999. pap. 18.99 (*0-7524-1294-9*) Arcadia Publng.
Cotter, Betty J. Wakefield. (Images of America Ser.). 1996. pap. 16.99 (*0-7524-0863-1*) Arcadia Publng.
Cotter, C. H. The Atlantic Ocean. (C). 1987. 35.00 (*0-85174-212-2*) St Mut.
— The Elements of Navigation & Nautical Astronomy. enl. rev. ed. (C). 1987. 100.00 (*0-85174-270-X*) St Mut.
— History of the Navigator's Sextant. (C). 1987. 175.00 (*0-85174-427-3*) St Mut.
Cotter, C. H., rev. The Docks Regulations Nineteen Thirty-Four Explained. rev. ed. (C). 1987. 40.00 (*0-85174-122-3*) St Mut.
Cotter, Carolyn, jt. auth. see Green, George H.
Cotter, Chris, ed. see Balmer, Alden J.
Cotter, Cornelius P. Party Organizations in American Politics. LC 89-40205. (Pitt Series in Policy & Institutional Studies). 230p. 1989. pap. 71.30 (*0-608-05084-9*, 206563800005) Bks Demand.
— Political Science Annual: An International Review, Vol. 5. annuals LC 66-29710. 1974. write for info. (*0-672-61318-2*, Bobbs) Macmillan.
Cotter, Cornelius P., ed. Political Science Annual: An International Review, Vol. 4. annuals LC 66-29710. 1973. 16.25 (*0-672-51808-2*, Bobbs) Macmillan.
— Political Science Annual: An International Review, Vol. 6. annuals LC 66-29710. 352p. 1975. text 20.85 (*0-672-61319-0*, Bobbs) Macmillan.
*__Cotter, Craig.__ Chopstix Numbers. Trusky, Tom, ed. 60p. 2000. pap. 6.95 (*0-916272-68-0*) Ahsahta Pr.
Cotter, Craig. There's Something Seriously Wrong with Me. LC 91-13176. 68p. (Orig.). 1991. pap. 10.50 (*0-941749-27-4*) Black Tie Pr.
Cotter, David, et al. Nonlinear Optics of Free Atoms & Molecules. MacAdam, David L., ed. (Optical Sciences Ser.: Vol. 17). (Illus.). 1980. 78.95 (*0-387-09628-0*) Spr-Verlag.
Cotter, David, jt. auth. see Butcher, Paul N.
Cotter, David J. Biology: A Human Endeavor. 216p. (C). 1992. write for info. (*1-880161-01-X*) Bookmark Pubs.
*__Cotter, David W.__ Exodus. (Berit Olam (The Everlasting Covenant) Ser.). 2000. 0.00 (*0-8146-5041-4*) Liturgical Pr.
— Genesis. (Berit Olam (The Everlasting Covenant) Ser.). 2000. 0.00 (*0-8146-5040-6*) Liturgical Pr.
— Isaiah 40-55. (Berit Olam (The Everlasting Covenant) Ser.). 2000. 0.00 (*0-8146-5058-9*) Liturgical Pr.
Cotter, Donald R., et al. The Nuclear "Balance" in Europe: Status, Trends, Implications. (USSI Report Ser.: No. 83-1). (Illus.). 48p. (Orig.). 1983. pap. 5.00 (*0-913187-01-1*) U S Strat Inst.
Cotter, Doris D. Walking--The Principle Science & Exercise of Life: Index of New Information. (Illus.). 160p. Date not set. 47.50 (*0-7883-1934-5*); pap. 44.50 (*0-7883-1935-3*) ABBE Pubs Assn.
Cotter, Finbarr, ed. Molecular Diagnosis of Cancer. (Methods in Molecular Medicine Ser.: Vol. 6). (Illus.). 236p. 1996. 79.50 (*0-89603-341-4*) Humana.
Cotter, Francis. Friars Minor in Ireland from Their Arrival to 1400. (History Ser.). 271p. 1994. pap. 20.00 (*1-57659-083-6*) Franciscan Inst.
Cotter, George. Proverbs & Sayings of the Oromo People of Ethiopia & Kenya with English Translations. LC 92-4367. (African Studies: Vol. 25). (Illus.). 612p. 1992. lib. bdg. 129.95 (*0-7734-9695-5*) E Mellen.
Cotter, George, jt. auth. see Aubin, Pierre.
Cotter, Geraldine. Traditional Irish Tin Whistle Tutor. LC 87-753556. 102p. Date not set. 14.95 (*0-946005-12-5*, OS 10116, Pub. by Ossian) Music Sales.
Cotter, Gerry. The Curlew. (Natural History Ser.: No. 55). (Illus.). 24p. 1989. pap. 5.25 (*0-7478-0090-1*, Pub. by Shire Pubns) Parkwest Pubns.
Cotter, Holland. Matt Mullican: Banners, Monuments, & the City: An Exhibition of Work for Public Spaces. Longhauser, Elsa, ed. LC 89-84230. (Illus.). 24p. 1987. pap. 25.00 (*1-58442-032-4*) Galleries at Moore.
*__Cotter, Holland, et al.__ Traveler's Guide to Art Museum Exhibitions 2001: The New York Times. Shortz, Will & Roberts, Fletcher, eds. (Illus.). 500p. 2000. pap. 16.95 (*0-8109-6724-3*, Pub. by Abrams) Time Warner.
Cotter, James F. Inscape: The Christology & Poetry of Gerald Manley Hopkins. LC 73-189857. 369p. reprint ed. pap. 114.40 (*0-608-12640-3*, 202543600043) Bks Demand.
Cotter, James F., tr. see Dante Alighieri.
Cotter, Jerome M., jt. auth. see An, Howard S.
*__Cotter, Jim.__ Brainsquall: Soundings from a Deep Depression. 176p. 1999. 60.00 (*0-85305-422-3*, Pub. by Arthur James) St Mut.
— Dazzling Darkness. 80p. 1999. pap. 22.00 (*0-85305-461-4*, Pub. by Arthur James) St Mut.
— Love Re-Membered: Resources for a House Eucharist. 64p. 1999. pap. 24.00 (*0-85305-347-2*, Pub. by Arthur James) St Mut.
— Love Rekindled: Practising Hospitality. 64p. 1999. pap. 24.00 (*0-85305-348-0*, Pub. by Arthur James) St Mut.
— Prayer at Day's Dawning. 208p. 1999. 40.00 (*0-85305-459-2*, Pub. by Arthur James) St Mut.
— Prayer at Night's Approaching. 1999. 40.00 (*0-85305-419-3*, Pub. by Arthur James) St Mut.
Cotter, Jim. Prayer at Night's Approaching. 208p. 1998. 16.95 (*0-8192-1772-7*) Morehouse Pub.
— Psalms for a Pilgrim People. LC 98-42301. 336p. 1998. pap. 17.95 (*0-8192-1778-6*) Morehouse Pub.
*__Cotter, Jim.__ Through the Year with Alan Ecclestone. 160p. 1999. pap. 48.00 (*0-85305-421-5*, Pub. by Arthur James) St Mut.
Cotter, Jim, ed. Credit pour Petites et Miro Enterprises: Recommendations et Etudes des Cas Presentes au Cours de l'Atelier "Meilleurres Pratiques" 156p. (Orig.). 1994. pap. text 25.00 (*0-9637044-6-X*) PACT Pubns.
*__Cotter, Jim & Yerrell, Stuart.__ No Thank You, I'm 1662. 1999. pap. 22.00 (*0-85305-458-4*, Pub. by Arthur James) St Mut.
Cotter, Jim, jt. auth. see Community Economics Corporation Staff.
Cotter, Joan A. Activities for the Abacus: A Hands on Approach to Arithmetic. 2nd ed. (Illus.). 152p. 1988. pap. 18.00 (*0-9609636-4-2*) Activities Learning.
— Math Card Games: 340 Games for Learning & Enjoying Math. 2nd ed. (Illus.). 156p. 1987. pap. 18.00 (*0-9609636-3-4*) Activities Learning.
— Worksheets for the Abacus, Complete Volume. (Illus.). 320p. (J). (gr. k-4). 1988. pap. 25.00 (*0-9609636-6-9*) Activities Learning.
Cotter, John J. The 20Solution: Using Rapid Redesign to Create Tomorrow's Organization Today. 2nd ed. LC 95-36689. 230p. 1995. 24.95 (*0-471-13278-0*) Wiley.
— The Twenty-Percent Solution: Using Rapid Redesign to Create Tomorrow's Organizations - Today. 288p. 1995. 25.00 (*0-939246-80-5*) Wiley.
Cotter, John L. Archeological Excavations at Jamestown, Virginia, Vol. 32. rev. ed. (Illus.). 299p. (C). 1994. pap. 37.00 (*1-884626-23-8*) Archeolog Soc.
Cotter, John L., et al. The Buried Past: An Archaeological History of Philadelphia. LC 92-10736. (Illus.). 568p. (C). 1992. 41.95 (*0-8122-3142-2*) U of Pa Pr.
— Walnut Street Prison Workshop. (Illus.). 1988. pap. 7.50 (*0-916530-12-4*) Athenaeum Phila.
Cotter, John L., jt. auth. see Boldurian, Anthony T.
Cotter, Joseph S. Caleb, the Degenerate: A Play in Four Acts. LC 72-1045. reprint ed. 31.50 (*0-404-00024-X*) AMS Pr.
Cotter, Joseph S., Sr. Collected Poems of Joseph S. Cotter, Sr. LC 75-179298. (Black Heritage Library Collection). 1977. reprint ed. 16.95 (*0-8369-8919-8*) Ayer.
Cotter, Joseph S. Negro Tales. LC 75-83923. (Black Heritage Library Collection). 1977. 22.95 (*0-8369-8548-6*) Ayer.
— A White Song & a Black One. LC 73-18568. reprint ed. 19.50 (*0-404-11382-6*) AMS Pr.
Cotter, Kelly & Cotter, Maury. Kids with Courage Thoughts & Stories about Growing up with Cancer. Barnes, P. T. et al, eds. (Illus.). xvii, 99p. 1998. pap. 14.95 (*1-882145-05-4*) U WI Clearinghse.
*__Cotter, Liller Burk.__ On the River of Grace: A Spiritual Journey in the Alaskan Wilderness. LC 99-57087. 157p. 2000. pap. 12.95 (*1-887400-21-4*, EVB-1022) Earthen Vessel Prodns.
Cotter, Louise. Milady's for Men Only: Styling & Techniques. LC 93-39834. 160p. 1994. pap. 34.95 (*1-56253-203-0*) Thomson Learn.
— Milady's Hair Coloring Techniques. LC 92-34815. (HAIR). 114p. 1993. pap. 27.75 (*1-56253-116-6*) Thomson Learn.
Cotter, Louise. Salon Solutions. LC 92-13681. (HAIR). 206p. 1992. pap. 17.95 (*1-56253-115-8*) Milady Pub.
Cotter, Louise. Salonovations' Beautiful Black Styles. (HAIR). 160p. 1995. mass mkt. 33.95 (*1-56253-222-7*) Delmar.
Cotter, Louise & DuBose, Frances L. The Transition: How to Become a Salon Professional. (Career Development Ser.). 352p. 1996. pap. 23.95 (*1-56253-263-4*) Thomson Learn.
Cotter, Louise, jt. auth. see Ekstrom, Candi.
Cotter, Louise, jt. auth. see Getschel, Beverly.
Cotter, Louise, jt. auth. see Ringler, Sara.
Cotter, Maria W. & Cotter, Patrick J. The Secondhand Basenji Handbook: The Guide to Adopting & Loving with a "Rescued" Basenji. (Illus.). xii, 218p. 1996. spiral bd. 12.00 (*0-9658488-0-9*) Windigo.
— The Secondhand Basenji Handbook: The Guide to Adopting & Living with a "Rescued" Basenji. 2nd rev. ed. (Illus.). 1999. pap. write for info. (*0-9658488-1-7*) Windigo.
Cotter, Maury & Seymour, Daniel T. Kidgets: And Other Insightful Stories about Quality in Education. LC 93-27803. (Illus.). 105p. 1993. 17.00 (*0-87389-248-8*, H0795) ASQ Qual Pr.
Cotter, Maury, jt. auth. see Cheaney, Lee.
Cotter, Maury, jt. auth. see Cotter, Kelly.
Cotter, Noreen. Definitely Different. LC 93-133. (Illus.). (J). 1994. write for info. (*0-383-03685-2*) SRA McGraw.
Cotter, Patrick, jt. auth. see Swihart, Ernest W.
Cotter, Patrick J., jt. auth. see Cotter, Maria W.
Cotter, Richard V. & Fritzsche, David J. The Business Policy Game: An International Simulation: Player's Manual. 4th ed. LC 94-44025. (Illus.). 304p. 1995. pap. text 42.00 (*0-13-339144-2*) P-H.
Cotter, Robert J. Engineering Plastics: A Handbook of Polyarylethers. 357p. 1995. text 132.00 (*2-88449-112-0*) Gordon & Breach.
— Time-of-Flight Mass Spectrometry: Instrumentation & Applications in Biological Research. LC 97-3734. (Professional Reference Bks.). 350p. 1997. text 125.00 (*0-8412-3474-4*, Pub. by Am Chemical) OUP.
Cotter, Robert J., ed. Time-of-Flight Mass Spectrometry. LC 93-23638. 233p. 1994. text 65.00 (*0-8412-2771-3*, Pub. by Am Chemical) OUP.
Cotter, Susan, ed. Clinical Uses of Prism: A Spectrum of Applications. (Illus.). 320p. (C). (gr. 13). 1995. pap. text 39.95 (*0-8151-1810-4*, 24310) Mosby Inc.
Cotter, Susan, jt. ed. see Campbell, Dennis.
Cotter, T. G. & Martin, S. J. Techniques in Apoptosis: A User's Guide. (Illus.). 344p. (Orig.). (C). 1996. text 89.50 (*1-85578-076-3*, Pub. by Portland Pr Ltd) Ashgate Pub Co.
— Techniques in Apoptosis: A User's Guide. (Illus.). 344p. (Orig.). (C). 1997. pap. text 67.50 (*1-85578-129-8*, Pub. by Portland Pr Ltd) Ashgate Pub Co.
Cotter, Theresa. Called to Preside: A Handbook for Laypeople. LC 97-219071. (Illus.). 160p. 1997. pap. 12.95 (*0-86716-232-5*, B2325) St Anthony Mess Pr.
— Christ Is Risen: Celebrating Lent, Easter & Pentecost. 238p. 1994. pap. 9.95 (*0-86716-200-7*) St Anthony Mess Pr.
— Daily Meditations (with Scripture) for Busy Grandmas. 368p. (Orig.). 1996. pap. 8.95 (*0-87946-148-9*, 251) ACTA Pubns.
Cotter, Wendy. Miracles in Greco-Roman Antiquity: A Sourcebook. LC 98-19320. 1999. write for info. (*0-415-11863-8*); pap. 23.99 (*0-415-11864-6*) Routledge.
Cotter, William R. & Russell, John. Alex Katz at Colby College. (Illus.). 116p. 1997. pap. 35.00 (*0-910394-80-6*) Dist Art Pubs.
Cotterall, J. E. West Lancashire Railway. 54p. (C). 1985. 39.00 (*0-85361-288-9*) St Mut.
*__Cotterall, Sara & Crabbe, David, eds.__ Learner Autonomy in Language Learning: Defining the Field & Effecting Change. (Bayreuth Contributions to Glottodidactics Ser.). x, 184p. 1999. 37.95 (*3-631-34890-8*) P Lang Pubng.
Cotterall, Sara & Crabbe, David, eds. Learner Autonomy in Language Learning: Defining the Field & Effecting Change. LC 99-34316. (Bayreuth Contributions to Glottodidactics Ser.: Vol. 8). (Illus.). x, 184p. 1999. pap. text 37.95 (*0-8204-4337-9*) P Lang Pubng.
*__Cotterell, Arthur.__ Ancient China. (Eyewitness Books). (Illus.). (J). (gr. 4-7). 2000. 19.99 (*0-7894-6604-X*) DK Pub Inc.
— Ancient China. (Eyewitness Books). (J). (gr. 4-7). 2000. 15.95 (*0-7894-5866-7*) DK Pub Inc.
Cotterell, Arthur. Celtic Mythology: The Fairytale Myths of the Celtic World. 1999. 12.95 (*1-85967-954-4*) Anness Pub.
*__Cotterell, Arthur.__ Classical Mythology. (Illustrated Encyclopedias Ser.). (Illus.). 2000. pap. 14.95 (*0-7548-0510-7*, Lorenz Bks) Anness Pub.
Cotterell, Arthur. Diccionario de Mitologia Universal. (SPA.). 288p. 1988. pap. 24.95 (*0-7859-5926-2*, 8434410826) Fr & Eur.
— A Dictionary of World Mythology. (Oxford Paperback Reference Ser.). (Illus.). 320p. 1990. pap. 12.95 (*0-19-217747-8*) OUP.
— East Asia: From Chinese Predominance to the Rise of the Pacific Rim. LC 93-26263. (Illus.). 368p. 1995. reprint ed. pap. 14.95 (*0-19-508841-7*) OUP.
— From Aristotle to Zoroaster: An A-to-Z Companion to the Classical World. LC 98-21729. 448p. 1998. 30.00 (*0-684-85596-8*) Free Pr.
— The Macmillan Illustrated Encyclopedia of Myths & Legends. (Illus.). 256p. 1995. 24.95 (*0-02-860851-8*) Macmillan.
— Mythology: Classical. 1999. 12.95 (*1-85967-993-5*, Lorenz Bks) Anness Pub.
— Norse Mythology: The Stormy Myths of the Nordic Gods. 1999. 12.95 (*1-85967-998-6*) Anness Pub.
Cotterell, Arthur, ed. The Penguin Encyclopedia of Ancient Civilizations. (Illus.). 384p. 1989. pap. 21.95 (*0-14-011434-3*, Penguin Bks) Viking Penguin.
— The Penguin Encyclopedia of Classical Civilizations. (Illus.). 320p. 1996. pap. 19.99 (*0-14-051344-2*, Penguin Bks) Viking Penguin.
Cotterell, Brian & Kamminga, Johan. Mechanics of Pre-Industrial Technology: An Introduction to the Mechanics of Ancient & Traditional Material Culture. (Illus.). 341p. (C). 1991. text 59.95 (*0-521-34194-9*) Cambridge U Pr.
Cotterell, Brian, jt. auth. see Mai, Yiu-Wing.
Cotterell, John. Social Networks & Social Influences in Adolescence. (Adolescence & Society Ser.). (Illus.). 256p. (C). 1996. pap. 25.99 (*0-415-10974-4*) Routledge.

An Asterisk (*) at the beginning of an entry indicates that the title is appearing for the first time.

Cotterell, M. Software Project Planning. 1995. mass mkt. 27.50 (*0-412-60400-0*) Chapman & Hall.

Cotterell, Mabel, tr. see Steiner, Rudolf.

***Cotterell, Maurice M.** The Supergods: They Came on a Mission to Save Mankind. (Illus.). 256p. 1998. pap. 14.95 (*0-7225-3463-9*, Pub. by Thorsons MD) Natl Bk Netwk.

Cotterell, Mike & Hughes, Robert. Software Project Management. (Illus.). 336p. 1995. mass mkt. 31.95 (*1-85032-190-6*) ITCP.

Cotterell, Peter, jt. auth. see Turner, Max.

***Cotterell, Robert.** POW. LC 00-190157. 2000. 25.00 (*0-7388-1538-1*); pap. 18.00 (*0-7388-1539-X*) Xlibris Corp.

Cotterell, Yong Y. Chinese Cooking for Pleasure. LC 88-33014. (Illus.). 252p. (C). 1989. 18.95 (*0-941533-62-X*, NAB) I R Dee.

Cotteret & Moreau, Josephine. Recherches Sur le Vocabulaire du General de Gaulle: Analyse Statistique des Allocutions Radiodiffusees (1958-1965) 23.65 (*0-685-33949-1*, F101840) Fr & Eur.

Cotterill. Serge Trotsky Papers: Correspondence & Other Writings. LC 93-51068. (FRE.). (C). 76.00 (*0-7453-0515-6*) Pluto GBR.

Cotterill, Charles H. Investment Performance Mathematics: Time Weighted & Dollar Weighted Rates of Return. LC 96-95098. (Illus.). xxx, 755p. (Orig.). 1996. pap. text 85.00 (*0-9655074-0-8*) Metri-Star Pr.

Cotterill, H. B., ed. see Elton, J. F.

Cotterill, Lesley. The Social Integration of People with Schizophrenia. (Studies of Care in the Community). 154p. 1994. 69.95 (*1-85628-841-2*, Pub. by Avebry) Ashgate Pub Co.

Cotterill, Owen J., jt. auth. see Stadelman, William J.

Cotterill, Pamela. Friendly Relations? Mothers & Their Daughters-in-Law. LC 93-35799. 1994. 65.00 (*0-7484-0150-4*, Pub. by Tay Francis Ltd); pap. 25.00 (*0-7484-0151-2*, Pub. by Tay Francis Ltd) Taylor & Francis.

Cotterill, R. S. The Southern Indians: The Story of the Civilized Tribes Before Removal. LC 54-5931. (Civilization of the American Indian Ser.: Vol. 38). 259p. 1954. pap. 13.95 (*0-8061-1171-2*) U of Okla Pr.

Cotterill, Robert S. History of Pioneer Kentucky. viii, 262p. 1997. reprint ed. pap. text 21.50 (*0-7884-0754-6*, C577) Heritage Bk.

Cotterill, Rodney. Enchanted Looms: Conscious Networks in Brains & Computers. LC 98-20548. (Illus.). 400p. (C). 1998. 24.95 (*0-521-62435-5*) Cambridge U Pr.

***Cotterill, Rodney.** Enchanted Looms: Conscious Networks in Brains & Computers. (Illus.). 526p. 2000. pap. text 16.95 (*0-521-79462-5*) Cambridge U Pr.

Cotterill, Rodney M., ed. Computer Simulation in Brain Science. (Illus.). 584p. 1989. text 110.00 (*0-521-34179-5*) Cambridge U Pr.

— Models of Brain Function. (Illus.). 590p. (C). 1990. text 100.00 (*0-521-38503-2*) Cambridge U Pr.

Cotterill, Rowland. Wagner. 160p. 1997. 60.00 (*1-873376-63-4*, Pub. by Spellmnt Pubs) St Mut.

Cotterill, Sarah. In the Nocturnal Animal House. LC 90-26544. 74p. 1991. pap. 14.95 (*1-55753-009-2*) Purdue U Pr.

Cotterill, Sue, ed. Eukaryotic DNA Replication: A Practical Approach. LC 98-39019. (Illus.). 304p. 1999. text 115.00 (*0-19-963681-8*); pap. text 49.95 (*0-19-963680-X*) OUP.

Cotterman, Sandra K. Y's Way to Weight Management. 152p. (Orig.). 1985. pap. text 15.00 (*0-87322-032-3*, LCOT4725, YMCA USA) Human Kinetics.

Cotterrell, R. B. The Politics of Jurisprudence: A Critical Introduction to Legal Philosophy. 255p. 1989. pap. 34.00 (*0-406-50088-6*, UK, MICHIE) LEXIS Pub.

***Cotterrell, Roger.** Emile Durkheim: Law in A Moral Domain. LC 99-71076. (Jurists). 276p. 1999. 55.00 (*0-8047-3808-4*) Stanford U Pr.

— Emile Durkheim: Law in A Moral Domain. 1999. pap. text 19.95 (*0-8047-3823-8*) Stanford U Pr.

Cotterrell, Roger. Law's Community: Legal Theory in Sociological Perspective. (Oxford Socio-Legal Studies). 400p. 1997. pap. text 38.00 (*0-19-826490-9*) OUP.

Cotterrell, Roger. The Politics of Jurisprudence: A Critical Introduction to Legal Philosophy. LC 91-40233. 296p. (C). 1992. pap. text 18.95 (*0-8122-1393-9*) U of Pa Pr.

Cottes, A. La Mission Cottes au Sud-Cameroun (1905-1908) (B. E. Ser.: No. 145). (FRE.). 30.00 (*0-8115-3066-3*) Periodicals Srv.

Cottet, Georges-Henri & Koumoutsakos, Petros D. Vortex Methods: Theory & Applications. 2nd ed. LC 99-12277. (Illus.). 300p. (C). 2000. text 59.95 (*0-521-62186-0*) Cambridge U Pr.

Cottey, Andrew. Subregional Cooperation in the New Europe: Building Security, Prosperity & Solidarity from the Barents to the Black Sea LC 98-37391. 1999. text 69.95 (*0-312-22072-3*) St Martin.

Cottez, H. Dictionnaire des Structures de Vocabulaire Savant. 4th rev. ed. (FRE.). 515p. 1988. 75.00 (*0-7859-4865-1*, M9516) Fr & Eur.

Cottier, Cynthia, et al. Functional AAC Intervention: A Team Approach. Drolet, Cindy, ed. (Illus.). 152p. 1997. spiral bd. 41.00 (*1-883315-22-0*, 7203) Imaginart Intl.

Cottier, Edward. Homeopathic Teachings from a Master. 88p. (Orig.). pap. 11.95 (*0-8464-4230-2*) Beekman Pubs.

Cottier, H. & Kraft, R., eds. Gut-Derived Infectious-Toxic Shock (GITS) A Major Variant of Septic Shock. (Current Studies in Hematology & Blood Transfusion: No. 59). (Illus.). x, 370p. 1991. 301.00 (*3-8055-5435-4*) S Karger.

Cottier, H., jt. ed. see Studer, A.

Cottier, Randy L., et al. Selected Bibliography of Missouri Archaeology. Wood, W. Raymond, ed. LC 72-619659. (Research Ser.: No. 10). (Illus.). 34p. (Orig.). 1973. pap. 2.00 (*0-943414-11-3*) MO Arch Soc.

Cottier, Thomas. Regulatory Barriers, Vol. 2. (World Trade Forum Ser.). 472p. 2000. text 65.00 (*0-472-11100-0*, 11100) U of Mich Pr.

Cottier, Thomas, jt. ed. see Mavroidis, Petros.

Cottin, Paul & Henault, Maurice. Memoirs of Sergeant Bourgogne, 1812-1813. 356p. 1998. pap. 19.95 (*0-09-477230-4*, Pub. by Constable & Co) Trafalgar.

Cottingham, Carl D., et al. General John A. Logan: His Life & Times. Otterson, Lynn, ed. (Illus.). 30p. 1989. pap. 5.95 (*0-913415-06-5*) Am Kestrel Pr.

Cottingham, Carl D., et al. General John Logan: His Life & Times. pap. 6.95 (*0-913415-11-1*, Pub. by Amer Kestrel) Booksource.

Cottingham, Clive, Jr. Billiards: Pocket-Carom-Three Cushion. 1976. reprint ed. pap. 10.00 (*0-87980-317-7*) Wilshire.

Cottingham, John. Healing Through Touch. 1985. pap. 8.95 (*0-930385-01-2*) Rolf Inst.

— Philosophy & the Good Life: Reason & the Passions in Greek, Cartesian & Psychoanalytic Ethics. LC 97-27898. (Illus.). 172p. (C). 1998. pap. 17.95 (*0-521-47890-1*); text 54.95 (*0-521-47310-1*) Cambridge U Pr.

— Rationalism. (Key Texts Ser.). 187p. 1984. pap. 19.00 (*1-85506-524-X*) Thoemmes Pr.

Cottingham, John, ed. Descartes. LC 98-2535. (Oxford Readings in Philosophy Ser.). 334p. 1998. text 62.00 (*0-19-875183-4*); pap. text 19.95 (*0-19-875182-6*) OUP.

— Reason, Will, & Sensation: Studies in Descartes' Metaphysics. (Illus.). 344p. 1994. text 59.00 (*0-19-824083-X*) OUP.

Cottingham, John, ed. Western Philosophy: An Anthology. 704p. (C). 1996. pap. 33.95 (*0-631-18627-1*) Blackwell Pubs.

Cottingham, John, ed. see Descartes, Rene.

Cottingham, John E., ed. see Descartes, Rene.

Cottingham, John G. Descartes. 224p. 1986. pap. text 24.95 (*0-631-15046-3*) Blackwell Pubs.

— The Rationalists. (History of Western Philosophy Ser.: No. 4). 246p. (C). 1988. pap. text 17.95 (*0-19-289190-1*) OUP.

Cottingham, John G., ed. The Cambridge Companion to Descartes. (Companions to Philosophy Ser.). 455p. (C). 1992. text 69.95 (*0-521-36623-2*); pap. text 22.95 (*0-521-36696-8*) Cambridge U Pr.

Cottingham, John G., tr. see Descartes, Rene, et al.

Cottingham, Laura. Linda Matalon: Sculpture. (Illus.). 8p. (Orig.). 1993. pap. 5.00 (*0-9626731-5-3*) Yoshii Gallery.

Cottingham, Laura, jt. auth. see Lipparo, Lucy.

Cottingham, Leslie & Timblin, Carol L. Bard of Ottaray: Life, Letters & Documents of S. M. Dugger. (Illus.). 1980. 7.00 (*0-686-27987-5*) Puddingstone.

Cottingham, Marian. Excel 2000 Developer's Handbook. LC 99-62859. (Developer's Handbks.). (Illus.). 896p. 1999. pap. text 49.99 (*0-7821-2328-7*) Sybex.

***Cottingham, Marion.** Auto CAD VBA Handbook. (Illus.). 896p. 2000. pap. text 49.99 (*0-7821-2743-6*) Sybex.

Cottingham, Marion & Davis, Harold. Visual Basic 6 for Windows: Visual QuickStart Guide. 288p. (C). 1999. pap. text 18.99 (*0-201-35383-0*) Addson-Wesley Educ.

Cottingham, W. M & Greenwood, D. A. An Introduction to Nuclear Physics. (Illus.). 160p. 1986. pap. text 24.95 (*0-521-31960-9*, Pub. by Sterling Pubs) Cambridge U Pr.

Cottingham, W. N. & Greenwood, D. A. Electricity & Magnetism. (Illus.). 215p. (C). 1991. text 64.95 (*0-521-36229-6*); pap. text 24.95 (*0-521-36803-0*) Cambridge U Pr.

— An Introduction to the Standard Model of Particle Physics. LC 98-14144. (Illus.). 260p. (C). 1998. 74.95 (*0-521-58191-5*); pap. text 29.95 (*0-521-58832-4*) Cambridge U Pr.

Cottington, David. Cubism. LC 98-20439. (Movements in Modern Art Ser.). (Illus.). 96p. (C). 1998. pap. 13.95 (*0-521-64610-3*) Cambridge U Pr.

— Cubism in the Shadow of War: The Avant-Garde & Politics in Paris, 1905-1914. LC 98-15163. (Illus.). 256p. 1998. 45.00 (*0-300-07529-4*) Yale U Pr.

Cottington, Jack & Akenhead, Robert. Site Investigation & the Law. 184p. 1984. 34.00 (*0-7277-0188-6*, Pub. by T Telford) RCH.

Cottino-Jones. Italia: Tutto in Italiano, Pt. 1. 96p. 1991. pap. text. write for info. (*0-8403-4913-0*) Kendall-Hunt.

Cottino-Jones, Marga & Pucciani, Oreste. Italia: Lingua e Cultura. 2nd ed. (ITA.). 462p. (C). 1996. pap. text, per. 58.95 (*0-7872-3237-8*, 41323701) Kendall-Hunt.

***Cottis, Bob, et al, eds.** Corrosion Testing Made Easy Vol. 7: Impedance & Noise Analysis. (Illus.). 200p. 2000. 127.00 (*1-57590-067-X*, 37565) NACE Intl.

Cottis, David R. Highway to Happiness: Understanding Your Life & Transforming Your Consciousness. LC 94-92309. 297p. (Orig.). 1994. pap. 7.00 (*0-9642583-0-7*) D R Cottis.

***Cottle.** 2000 Target Marketing for Professional. 350p. 1999. pap. text 74.00 (*0-15-607051-0*) Harcourt.

Cottle, Charles M. Options: Perception & Deception: Superior Results Through Position Analysis & Risk Control. 308p. 1996. text 60.00 (*1-55738-907-1*, Irwn Prfssnl) McGraw-Hill Prof.

Cottle, David W. Managing by the Numbers: Monitoring Your Firm's Profitability. LC 92-38936. 1992. 30.00 (*0-87051-127-0*) Am Inst CPA.

— Managing for Profitability: How Winning Professionals Earn What They're Worth. 210p. 1993. 99.00 (*1-883711-00-2*) Hightower Pub.

Cottle, Gordon W., ed. see Clawson, Jeff J. & Dernocoeur, Kate B.

Cottle, Joan. Emily's Shoes. LC 98-53054. (Rookie Readers Ser.). 32p. (J). (gr. 1-2). 1999. 17.50 (*0-516-21585-X*) Childrens.

***Cottle, Joan.** Emily's Shoes. (Rookie Readers Ser.). (J). 2000. pap. text 4.95 (*0-516-26544-X*) Childrens.

— Miles Away from Home. LC 99-50609. (Illus.). (J). 2001. write for info. (*0-15-202212-0*) Harcourt.

Cottle, John & Fairley, Judith. New Zealand Administrative Reports. ring bd. 351.00 (*0-614-05552-0*, NZ, MICHIE) LEXIS Pub.

Cottle, Joseph, ed. see Chatterton, Thomas.

Cottle, R. W., ed. Mathematical Programming Essays in Honor of George B. Dantzig, 2 pts., Set. 1985. pap. 50.00 (*0-317-44633-9*, North Holland) Elsevier.

Cottle, Rex L., et al. Labor & Property Rights in California Agriculture: An Economic Analysis of the CALRA. LC 82-40318. (Economics Ser.: No. 6). 136p. 1982. 24.95 (*0-89096-132-8*) Tex A&M Univ Pr.

Cottle, Richard W., et al, eds. Variational Inequalities & Complementarity Problems: Theory & Applications. LC 79-40108. 426p. reprint ed. pap. 132.10 (*0-608-17431-9*, 202985600066) Bks Demand.

Cottle, Richard W & Lemke, C. E., eds. Nonlinear Programming: Proceedings of the SIAM-AMS Symposia, New York, March, 1975, Vol. 9. LC 75-45471. 200p. 1980. reprint ed. pap. 27.00 (*0-8218-1329-3*, SIAMS/9) Am Math.

Cottle, Richard W., et al. The Linear Complementarity Problem. (Computer Science & Scientific Computing Ser.). (Illus.). 762p. 1992. text 74.95 (*0-12-192350-9*) Acad Pr.

Cottle, S., et al. Security Analysis. 5th ed. 658p. 1988. 59.95 (*0-07-013235-6*) McGraw.

Cottle, Sidney, et al. Security Analysis. 5th ed. 1990. pap. 9.95 incl. audio (*0-07-013238-0*) McGraw.

Cottle, Simon. Television & Ethnic Minorities: Producers' Perspectives: A Study of BBC In-House & Independent Producers of Minority Ethnic Programmes. LC 96-79841. 246p. 1997. 72.95 (*1-85972-502-3*, Pub. by Avebry) Ashgate Pub Co.

— TV News, Urban Conflict & the Inner City. (Studies in Communication & Society). 266p. 1993. pap. 29.95 (*0-7185-1462-9*) Bks Intl VA.

— TV News, Urban Conflict & the Inner City. (Leicester University Press Book). 266p. 1993. 85.00 (*0-7185-1447-5*) Bks Intl VA.

Cottle, Simon, jt. auth. see Battie, David.

Cottle, T. Jeffery, ed. see B. Y. U. Religious Studies Center Staff.

***Cottle, Thomas J.** At Peril: Stories of Injustice. 2000. 29.95 (*1-55849-278-X*) U of Mass Pr.

Cottle, Thomas J. College: Reward & Betrayal. LC 76-57922. 1982. pap. text 8.00 (*0-226-11598-4*) U Ch Pr.

— Divorce & the Jewish Child. 28p. 1981. pap. 2.50 (*0-87495-034-1*) Am Jewish Comm.

***Cottle, Thomas J.** Hardest Times: The Trauma of Long Term Unemployment. LC 00-32373. 306p. 2000. 40.00 (*0-275-96984-3*, C6984, Praeger Pubs) Greenwood.

Cottle, Thomas J. Like Fathers, Like Sons: Portraits of Intimacy & Strain. LC 81-2171. (Modern Sociology Ser.). 140p. 1981. pap. 39.50 (*0-89391-087-2*); text 73.25 (*0-89391-054-6*) Ablx Pub.

— Perceiving Time: A Psychological Investigation with Men & Women. LC 76-18768. 283p. reprint ed. pap. 87.80 (*0-8357-9950-6*, 201188300080) Bks Demand.

— Private Lives & Public Accounts. LC 77-73476. 208p. 1977. 27.50 (*0-87023-240-1*) U of Mass Pr.

Cottler, Irv. I've Got You under My Skins. 1986. pap. 19.95 incl. audio (*0-7390-0772-6*, 173) Alfred Pub.

Cottler, Joseph. Champions of Democracy. LC 78-128229. (Essay Index Reprint Ser.). 1977. 21.95 (*0-8369-1826-6*) Ayer.

Cottler, Marty. Come Quickly, My Darling Children! Stories by Western Devotees of Mata Amritanandamayi. (Illus.). 160p. (Orig.). 1996. pap. 15.00 (*0-9641040-0-8*) Sierra Vsta Pubng.

Cottman, Evans W. Out-Island Doctor. 1999. lib. bdg. 23.95 (*1-56723-200-0*) Yestermorrow.

Cottman, Evans W. & Blassingame, Wyatt. Out Island Doctor. LC 63-8607. 264p. 1988. pap. 8.95 (*0-913428-18-3*) Landfall Pr.

Cottman, Gwen. Traveling in Africa. 36p. 1982. pap. 3.50 (*0-912444-24-X*) DARE Bks.

***Cottman, Michael H.** Spirit Dive: An African American's Journey to Uncover a Sunken Slave Ship's Past. 1999. pap. 14.00 (*0-609-80552-5*) Harmony Bks.

Cottman, Michael H. The Wreck of the Henrietta Marie: An African American's Journey to Uncover a Sunken Slave Ship's Past. LC 98-29574. (Illus.). 288p. 1998. 23.00 (*0-517-70328-9*) Harmony Bks.

Cottmon, Ronald J. Total Engineering Quality Management: The Care & Feeding of the Engineering Process. LC 92-25552. (Quality & Reliability Ser.: Vol. 37). (Illus.). 152p. 1992. text 59.75 (*0-8247-8740-4*) Dekker.

Cotto, Deborah B. On the Write Track Teacher's Guide: Beginning Literacy for Secondary Students. (Illus.). 122p. (YA). (gr. 6-12). 1997. teacher ed. 14.50 (*1-882483-39-1*) Alta Bk Ctr.

Cotto, Deborah Becker, see Becker Cotto, Deborah.

Cotto-Falcon, Hector M. Poesias para Recordar un Pasado. (SPA.). 16p. (Orig.). 1996. pap. 4.95 (*0-9652064-0-8*) Edit Naboria.

Cottom, jt. auth. see Mudie.

Cottom, Daniel. Abyss of Reason: Cultural Movements, Revelations & Betrayals. (Illus.). 320p. 1991. text 65.00 (*0-19-506857-2*) OUP.

***Cottom, Daniel.** Cannibals & Philosophers: Bodies of Enlightenment. LC 00-40562. 2001. write for info. (*0-8018-6551-4*) Johns Hopkins.

Cottom, Daniel. Ravishing Tradition: Cultural Forces & Literary History. 240p. 1996. text 39.95 (*0-8014-3245-6*); pap. text 16.95 (*0-8014-8324-7*) Cornell U Pr.

— Social Figures: George Eliot, Social History & Literary Representation. LC 86-19249. (Theory & History of Literature Ser.: Vol. 44). 265p. 1987. pap. 17.95 (*0-8166-1548-9*) U of Minn Pr.

— Text & Culture: The Politics of Interpretation. LC 88-17341. (Theory & History of Literature Ser.: Vol. 62). 177p. (Orig.). 1989. pap. 14.95 (*0-8166-1763-5*) U of Minn Pr.

Cottom, Robert I. & Hayward, Mary E. Maryland in the Civil War. (Illus.). 128p. 1996. pap. text 24.95 (*0-938420-51-8*) MD Hist.

Cottom, Robert I., jt. ed. see Bailey, Judith A.

Cottom-Winslow, Margaret. Environmental Design. LC 95-13983. (Illus.). 160p. 1995. 32.50 (*0-86636-430-7*) PBC Intl Inc.

Cotton. Astronomy Lab. (C). 1998. pap. text, lab manual ed. 9.00 (*0-471-32744-1*) Wiley.

— Basic Inorganic Chemistry Solutions. 3rd ed. text. write for info. (*0-471-37197-1*) Wiley.

— International Business Topics. 1991. pap. text. write for info. (*0-17-555822-1*) Addison-Wesley.

— Keys to Management. 1991. pap. text, student ed. write for info. (*0-17-555825-6*) Addison-Wesley.

— World of Business. 1991. pap. text, student ed. write for info. (*0-17-555855-8*) Addison-Wesley.

Cotton & Robbins. Business Class. Date not set. pap. text, student ed. write for info. (*0-17-556337-3*) Addison-Wesley.

Cotton, jt. ed. see Harris.

Cotton & Oliver Staff. Understanding Hypermedia. 1997. pap. text 39.95 (*0-7148-3740-7*) Phaidon Press.

Cotton, Albert, et al. Basic Inorganic Chemistry. 3rd ed. LC 94-20754. 856p. 1994. text 111.95 (*0-471-50532-3*) Wiley.

Cotton, Andrew, jt. auth. see Franceys, Richard.

Cotton, Ann, et al. Charleston Entertains: Season by Season. (Illus.). 208p. 1991. 29.95 (*0-933101-15-5*) Legacy Pubns.

Cotton, Bernard D. The English Regional Chair. (Illus.). 512p. 1990. 99.50 (*1-85149-023-X*) Antique Collect.

Cotton, Bob. New Guide to Graphic Design. 1990. 25.98 (*1-55521-508-4*) Bk Sales Inc.

Cotton, Bob & Oliver, Richard. The Cyberspace Lexicon: An Illustrated Dictionary of Terms from Multimedia to Virtual Reality. LC 96-154523. (Illus.). 224p. (C). 1994. pap. 29.95 (*0-7148-3267-7*, Pub. by Phaidon Press) Phaidon Pr.

Cotton, C. M. Ethnobotany: Principles & Applications. LC 95-52721. 434p. 1996. pap. 69.95 (*0-471-95537-X*) Wiley.

Cotton, Charles, jt. auth. see Walton, Izaak.

Cotton, Charles S. Forest Service Decision-Making: A Framework for Improving Performance. (Illus.). 146p. (C). 1998. pap. text 30.00 (*0-7881-3846-4*) DIANE Pub.

***Cotton, Charlotte, ed.** Imperfect Beauty: The Making of Contemporary Fashion Photography. (Illus.). 160p. 2000. pap. 45.00 (*1-85177-320-7*, Pub. by V & A) Antique Collect.

***Cotton, Cynthia.** At the Edge of the Woods. 2001. text 16.95 (*0-8050-6354-4*) St Martin.

Cotton, D. B., ed. see Hankins, Gary D., et al.

Cotton de Bennetot, Arlette. Petit Dictionnaire des Rues de Blaye. (FRE.). 160p. 1983. 32.95 (*0-7859-8075-X*, 2852760185) Fr & Eur.

Cotton, Deborah & Watts, D. H., eds. Medical Management of AIDS in Women. LC 95-48022. 488p. 1996. 119.95 (*0-471-07674-0*) Wiley.

Cotton, Deborah J., ed. see Hecht, Frederick M. & Soloway, Bruce.

Cotton, Delores & Metta, Vito. Type Right! A Complete Program for Business Typewriting. 2nd ed. LC 78-73160. 1986. text 32.24 (*0-02-830550-7*) Glencoe.

— Type Right! A Complete Program for Business Typewriting. 2nd ed. LC 78-73160. 1986. teacher ed., ring bd. 23.80 (*0-02-830560-4*) Glencoe.

Cotton, Dennis W. A Synopsis of General Pathology for Surgeons. LC 97-938. 174p. 1997. pap. text 37.50 (*0-7506-3592-4*) Buttrwrth-Heinemann.

Cotton, Dorothy H. Stress Management: An Integrated Approach. LC 89-38991. (Psychosocial Stress Ser.: No. 17). 288p. 1990. text 38.95 (*0-87630-557-5*) Brunner-Mazel.

Cotton, Edward H., ed. Has Science Discovered God: A Symposium of Modern Scientific Opinion. LC 68-8452. (Essay Index Reprint Ser.). 1977. 23.95 (*0-8369-0340-4*) Ayer.

Cotton, Eileen G. The Online Classroom: Teaching with the Internet. 4th ed. Essex, Christopher, ed. LC 97-33875. (Illus.). 253p. (J). (gr. 1-12). 2000. pap. 29.95 (*1-883790-29-8*, EDINFO Pr) Grayson Bernard Pubs.

Cotton, Eleanor G. & Sharp, John M. Spanish in the Americas. LC 87-12005. (Romance Languages & Linguistics Ser.). (Illus.). 399p. (Orig.). reprint ed. pap. 123.70 (*0-608-08046-2*, 206901100002) Bks Demand.

Cotton, F. Albert. Chemical Applications of Group Theory. 3rd ed. LC 89-16434. 480p. 1990. 79.95 (*0-471-51094-7*) Wiley.

Cotton, F. Albert & Walton, Richard A. Multiple Bonds Between Metal Atoms. LC 88-91. 480p. (C). 1988. reprint ed. lib. bdg. 62.50 (*0-89464-291-X*) Krieger.

— Multiple Bonds Between Metal Atoms. 2nd ed. LC 92-15945. (Illus.). 816p. 1993. 125.00 (*0-19-855649-7*, Clarendon Pr) OUP.

***Cotton, F. Albert, et al.** Advanced Inorganic Chemistry. 6th ed. LC 98-8020. 1376p. 1999. 89.95 (*0-471-19957-5*, Wiley-Interscience) Wiley.

Cotton, F. Albert, jt. ed. see Adams, Richard D.

***Cotton, Gordon.** Vicksburg, MS. LC 99-61641. (Images of America Ser.). (Illus.). 128p. 1999. pap. 18.99 (*0-7385-0155-7*) Arcadia Publng.

Cotton, H. India in Transition. 1985. 44.95 (*0-318-36970-2*) Asia Bk Corp.

C

An Asterisk (*) at the beginning of an entry indicates that the title is appearing for the first time.

Cotton, Hannah & Yardeni, Ada, eds. Aramaic, Hebrew & Greek Documentary Texts from Nahal Hever & Other Sites No. II: With an Appendix Containing Alleged Qumran Texts: The Seiyal Collection II. LC 98-100002. (Discoveries in the Judaean Desert Ser.: No. XXVII). (Illus.). 408p. 1997. text 175.00 (*0-19-826395-3*) OUP.

Cotton, Hazel S. Precious Memories. 90p. (Orig.). 1996. pap. write for info. (*1-57502-255-9*, P0937) Morris Pubng.

Cotton, Helen S. A Few Miles above Shanklin Alley. LC 95-39925. 1995. write for info. (*0-916078-40-X*) Iris Pr.

Cotton, Henry. The Typographical Gazetteer. 1975. reprint ed. 40.00 (*1-55888-238-3*) Omnigraphics Inc.

Cotton, Henry A. The Defective Delinquent & Insane. Grob, Gerald N., ed. LC 78-22557. (Historical Issues in Mental Health Ser.). (Illus.). 1980. reprint ed. lib. bdg. 19.95 (*0-405-11911-9*) Ayer.

Cotton, Hope D., ed. see Brooke, Frances.

Cotton, Ian. The Hallelujah Revolution: The Rise of the New Christians. LC 96-2658. 262p. 1996. 26.95 (*1-57392-055-X*) Prometheus Bks.

Cotton Incorporated Staff. Cotton Dyeing & Finishing: A Technical Guide. viii, 230p. 1997. write for info. (*0-9653358-0-1*) Cotton Inc.

Cotton, Irene, ed. see McCann, Michael L.

Cotton, James. James Harrington's Political Thought & Its Context. LC 91-11109. (Political Theory & Political Philosophy Ser.). 256p. 1991. text 10.00 (*0-8153-0130-8*) Garland.

— Politics & Policy in the New Korean State: From Roh Tae-Woo to Kim Young-Sam. 232p. 1995. text 59.95 (*0-312-12549-6*) St Martin.

Cotton, James, ed. Korea under Roh Tae-Woo: Democratization, Northern Policy & Inter-Korean Relations. 364p. (Orig.). 1993. pap. text 24.95 (*1-86373-397-3*, Pub. by Allen & Unwin Pty) Paul & Co Pubs.

Cotton, James & Australian National University Staff. State Determination & State Autonomy in Theories of Regime Maintenance & Regime Change. LC 98-137119. (Discussion Paper Series/Political & Social Change). 14p. 1991. write for info. (*0-7315-1250-2*, Pub. by Aust Nat Univ) UH Pr.

Cotton, James, jt. ed. see Harris, Stuart.

Cotton, Jane. Wall-Eyed Caesar's Ghost & Other Sketches. LC 77-106281. (Short Story Index Reprint Ser.). 1977. 18.95 (*0-8369-3315-X*) Ayer.

Cotton, Jane B., ed. The Maryland Calendar of Wills: Wills from 1635-1743; Vol. I: 1635-1685; Vol. II: 1685-1702; Vol. III: 1703-1713; Vol. IV: 1713-1720; Vol. V: 1720-1726; Vol. VI: 1726-1732; Vol. VII: 1732-1738: Vol. VIII: 1738-1743, 8 vols. in 4. 2583p. 1997. reprint ed. pap. 175.00 (*0-8063-4744-9*) Clearfield Co.

Cotton, John. Bloudy Tenent, Washed, & Made White in the Bloud of the Lambe. LC 78-141105. (Research Library of Colonial Americana). 1972. reprint ed. 33.95 (*0-405-03319-2*) Ayer.

— Brief Exposition with Practical Observation upon the Whole Book of Canticles. LC 71-141106. (Research Library of Colonial Americana). 1972. reprint ed. 26.95 (*0-405-03320-6*) Ayer.

— Christ the Fountaine of Life, Or, Sundry Choyce Sermons on Part of the Fifth Chapter of the First Epistle of St. John. LC 75-141107. (Research Library of Colonial Americana). 1972. reprint ed. 26.95 (*0-405-03321-4*) Ayer.

***Cotton, John.** Elements of Astronomy: Physics 1311. 1999. pap. text 14.70 (*1-56870-357-0*) RonJon Pub.

Cotton, John. God's Mercie Mixed with His Justice. LC 58-5651. 160p. 1977. reprint ed. 50.00 (*0-8201-1242-9*) Schol Facsimiles.

— Gods Promise to His Plantation. (Works of John Cotton Ser.). 1990. reprint ed. lib. bdg. 90.00 (*0-7812-2315-6*) Rprt Serv.

— The Keyes of the Kingdom of Heaven. (Works of John Cotton Ser.). 1990. reprint ed. lib. bdg. 79.00 (*0-7812-2316-4*) Rprt Serv.

— Milk for Babes. (Works of John Cotton Ser.). 1990. reprint ed. lib. bdg. 79.00 (*0-7812-2318-0*) Rprt Serv.

— Survey of the Summe of Church-Discipline, Bk. II. (Works of John Cotton Ser.). 1990. reprint ed. lib. bdg. 79.00 (*0-7812-2320-2*) Rprt Serv.

— Two Sermons. LC 79-141108. (Research Library of Colonial Americana). 1972. reprint ed. 24.95 (*0-405-03322-2*) Ayer.

— The Way of the Churches of Christ in New England. (Works of John Cotton Ser.). 1990. reprint ed. lib. bdg. 90.00 (*0-7812-2317-2*) Rprt Serv.

— The Way of the Congregational Churches Clearde. (Works of John Cotton Ser.). 1990. reprint ed. lib. bdg. 79.00 (*0-7812-2319-9*) Rprt Serv.

— The Works of John Cotton. 1990. reprint ed. lib. bdg. 63.00 (*0-685-27666-X*) Rprt Serv.

Cotton, John L. Employee Involvement: Methods for Improving Performance & Work Attitudes. (Illus.). 320p. (C). 1993. text 48.00 (*0-8039-4532-9*); pap. text 23.50 (*0-8039-4533-7*) Sage.

Cotton, John W. Analyzing Within-Subjects Experiments. LC 97-8624. 1997. write for info. (*0-8058-2804-4*) L Erlbaum Assocs.

Cotton, Joseph P., ed. The Constitutional Decisions of John Marshall, 2 vols. LC 67-25445. (Law, Politics & History Ser.). 1969. reprint ed. lib. bdg. 75.00 (*0-306-70947-3*) Da Capo.

Cotton, Julie. The Theory of Learning: An Introduction. (The Theory of Training & Assessment Ser.). 128p. 1995. pap. 29.95 (*0-7494-1479-0*); pap. 29.95 (*0-7494-1480-4*) Taylor & Francis.

Cotton, K. C. Evaluating & Improving Steam Turbine Performance. (Illus.). 500p. (C). 1998. text 125.00 (*0-9639955-0-2*) Cotton Fact.
This book is an excellent example of the practical application of thermodynamics & fluid flow fundamentals to the solution of performance problems in power plants. Current design practices & methods for testing steam turbines & interpreting the test results are presented. This book concentrates on measuring turbine & cycle-component performance & on calculating the effects that measured deviations from design values (e.g. increased steam-path clearances, blade deposits, or solid particle erosion) have on turbine efficiency. In an impressive array of examples, measured performance & current design data are compared to quantify performance losses. Then, using these measurements & deductive reasoning, the book pinpoints problem areas that help identify the nature of the deficiency & proposes remedial action. This book develops a better appreciation for optimum turbine design which enables the evaluation of proposed efficiency improvements. It also quantifies the effect of power plant operation (abnormal conditions) on turbine efficiency, throttle flow, & stage pressures. This book was written for engineers responsible for the efficient operation of electric utilities, power plants, & cogeneration plants. Review questions have been provided so that this material may be used as a textbook or reference book in colleges & universities. To order: Cotton Fact Inc., 346 Kingsley Rd., Burnt Hills, NY 12027. Phone: 518-384-7885. www.cottonfact.com. *Publisher Paid Annotation.*

Cotton, Katherine. Smart Guide to Healing Foods. LC 99-17880. 192p. 1999. pap. 10.95 (*0-471-31860-4*) Wiley.

Cotton, Kathleen L. & Webber, Ellen J. Financial Planning from We to Me: Divorce Strategies to Help You Get More of What You Want. 132p. (Orig.). 1996. pap. 9.95 (*0-9618700-2-8*) Wealth Bks.

Cotton, Kenneth C. Evaluating & Improving Steam Turbine Performance: Includes Cogeneration & Combined Cycles. 2nd rev. ed. (Illus.). 535p. (C). 1998. 145.00 (*0-9639955-1-0*) Cotton Fact.

Cotton, Leo. Old Mr. Boston's Bartender's Guide. 1974. 7.95 (*0-685-22064-8*) Wehman.

Cotton, Leonard, jt. auth. see Ham, Rosalind.

Cotton, Lin, jt. auth. see Horton, Alvin.

Cotton, M. A. Late Republican Villa at Posto, Francolise. (Illus.). 200p. 1979. 30.00 (*0-904152-03-0*, Pub. by British Schl Rome) David Brown.

Cotton, M. A. & Metraux, G. San Rocco Villa at Francolise. (Illus.). 277p. 1985. 30.00 (*0-904152-08-1*, Pub. by British Schl Rome) David Brown.

Cotton, M. C. Hurricanes over Burma. 1996. 34.95 (*1-898697-40-X*, Pub. by Grub St) Seven Hills Bk.

Cotton, M. Jeanne. Getting It Together: You, Life & Living. 110p. (Orig.). (C). 1995. pap. text 19.50 (*0-8191-9806-4*); lib. bdg. 39.00 (*0-8191-9805-6*) U Pr of Amer.

Cotton, Maggie. Agogo Bells to Xylophone. (J). pap. 16.95 (*0-7136-4314-5*, Pub. by A & C Blk) Midpt Trade.

Cotton, Marjorie, jt. auth. see Saxby, H. M.

Cotton, Martha. Dinner Dates: A Cookbook for Couples Cooking Together. LC 98-45202. 144p. 1999. pap. 12.00 (*0-380-79881-6*, Avon Bks) Morrow Avon.

Cotton, Maureen K. & American Society of Civil Engineers Staff. Civil Engineers Influencing Public Policy: Proceedings of the Sessions Sponsored by the Construction Division of the American Society of Civil Engineers in Conjunction with the ASCE National Convention in Washington, D. C., November 10-14, 1996. LC 96-36639. 144p. 1996. 25.00 (*0-7844-0204-3*) Am Soc Civil Eng.

Cotton, Michael. Classic Porsche Racing Cars LC 89-200101. 152p. 1988. write for info. (*0-85059-947-4*) P Stephenson.

Cotton, Michael. Porsche 911 & Derivatives Vol. 1: A Collector's Guide, 1963-1980. (Illus.). 128p. 1994. 19.98 (*0-947981-90-X*, Pub. by Motor Racing) Motorbooks Intl.

— Porsche 911 & Derivatives Vol. 2: 1981-1994: A Collector's Guide. (Illus.). 128p. 2000. pap. 19.95 (*1-899870-49-0*, 130539AE, Pub. by Motor Racing) Motorbooks Intl.

— Porsche 924, 944 & 968: A Collector's Guide. (Illus.). 144p. 2000. pap. 19.95 (*1-899870-47-4*, 130540AE, Pub. by Motor Racing) Motorbooks Intl.

Cotton, Michael. Porsche Progress: Stuttgart's Modern Development Story LC 88-175132. 200p. 1988. write for info. (*0-85059-928-8*) P Stephenson.

Cotton, Michael, jt. auth. see Frankenberg, Richard A.

***Cotton, Michael H.** The Slobber-Giggle Roundup: A Collection of Tales from the Funny Farm. (Illus.). 79p. 2000. pap. 9.95 (*0-9961949-3-2*) Harrah Hse.

— The Slobber-Giggle Roundup: A Collection of Tales from the Funny Farm. (Illus.). 87p. 2000. pap. 9.99 (*0-9661949-3-4*) Harrah Hse.

Cotton, Michelle & Modglin, Terry. Teens, Crime, & the Community: A Program for Community-Based Organizations. Kirby, Judy, ed. LC 98-149690. 53p. 1997. pap. 9.95 (*0-934513-13-9*, M49) Natl Crime DC.

Cotton, Nancy S. Lessons from the Lion's Den: Therapeutic Management of Children in Psychiatric Hospitals & Treatment Centers. LC 93-3623. (Social & Behavioral Sciences Ser.). 345p. 1993. text 36.95 (*1-55542-575-5*) Jossey-Bass.

Cotton, Nero A., jt. auth. see British Library, Manuscript Staff.

Cotton, Ottis L. Poems That Warm Your Heart. 256p. 1998. write for info. (*0-933380-44-5*) Olive Pr Pubns.

Cotton, P. B. & Williams, C. B., eds. Practical Gastrointestinal Endoscopy. 3rd ed. (Illus.). 288p. 1990. 54.95 (*0-632-02435-6*) Mosby Inc.

Cotton, Peter B. & Williams, Christopher B. Practical Gastrointestinal Endoscopy. 4th ed. LC 95-25737. (Illus.). 352p. 1996. 145.00 (*0-86542-851-4*) Blackwell Sci.

Cotton, R. E. Lecture Notes on Pathology. 4th ed. (Lecture Notes Ser.). (Illus.). 448p. 1992. pap. 34.95 (*0-632-03355-X*) Blackwell Sci.

Cotton, Ralph. Badlands. (Cotton's Big Iron Ser.: Bk. 2). 1998. mass mkt. 5.99 (*0-451-19495-0*, Sig) NAL.

— Border Dogs. 320p. 1999. mass mkt. 5.99 (*0-451-19815-8*) NAL.

***Cotton, Ralph.** Hangman's Choice. 2000. mass mkt. 5.99 (*0-451-20143-4*, Sig) NAL.

Cotton, Ralph. Justice. 320p. 1999. mass mkt. 5.99 (*0-451-19496-9*, Sig) NAL.

***Cotton, Ralph.** Misery Express. 2000. mass mkt. 5.99 (*0-451-19999-5*, Sig) NAL.

Cotton, Ralph. Price of a Horse. 1996. mass mkt. 5.99 (*0-312-95793-9*, Pub. by Tor Bks) St Martin.

Cotton, Ralph W. Cost of a Killing. 1996. mass mkt. 5.99 (*0-671-57032-3*) PB.

— Powder River. large type ed. LC 96-19595. 570p. 1996. lib. bdg. 22.95 (*0-7862-0794-9*) Thorndike Pr.

Cotton, Ray, jt. auth. see Durey, David D.

Cotton, Richard, jt. ed. see Sawhill, John C.

Cotton, Richard G. Mutation Detection. (Illus.). 216p. 1997. text 85.00 (*0-19-854888-5*); pap. text 45.00 (*0-19-854889-3*) OUP.

Cotton, Richard T., ed. Ace Lifestyle & Weight Management Consultant Manual. (Illus.). 330p. 1996. text 34.95 (*0-9618161-5-5*) Am Coun Exer.

Cotton, Richard T., ed. Ace Personal Trainer Manual: The Resource for Fitness Professionals. 2nd ed. (Illus.). 501p. (C). 1997. text 44.95 (*0-9618161-6-3*) Am Coun Exer.

Cotton, Richard T., et al, eds. Exercises for Older Adults: ACE's Guide for Fitness Professionals. LC 97-7816. (Illus.). 248p. 1998. pap. text 25.00 (*0-88011-942-X*, BACE0942) Human Kinetics.

Cotton, Richard T. & Goldstein, Robert L., eds. Ace Aerobics Instructor Manual: The Resource for Fitness Professionals. (Illus.). 536p. (C). 1993. text 39.95 (*0-9618161-3-9*) Am Coun Exer.

Cotton, Richard T., ed. see Andrews, Guy.

Cotton, Richard T., ed. see Seibert, Richard J.

Cotton, Robert B. The Danger Wherein the Kingdome Now Standeth, & the Remedie, No. 721. LC 74-28839. 1975. reprint ed. 15.00 (*90-221-0721-3*) Walter J Johnson.

Cotton, Robert C., tr. see Ardant Du Picq, Charles J.

Cotton, Robin T. & Myer, Charles M., 3rd, eds. Practical Pediatric Otolaryngology. LC 98-17722. (Illus.). 900p. 1998. text 245.00 (*0-397-51720-3*) Lppncott W & W.

***Cotton, S.** Advertising The $100 Billion Dollar Misunderstanding. 167p. 1998. pap. 19.95 (*0-9660411-1-9*) Back II Basics.

Cotton, S. J. Stories of Nehalem. 160p. 1998. reprint ed. pap. 12.95 (*0-89288-264-6*) Maverick.

Cotton, Samuel. Silent Terror: A Journey into Contemporary African Slavery. 240p. 1998. pap. 15.95 (*0-86316-259-2*) Writers & Readers.

Cotton, Sidney & Barker, Ralph. Aviator Extraordinary: The Sidney Cotton Story. LC 72-386287. 297p. 1969. write for info. (*0-7011-1334-0*, Pub. by Chatto & Windus) Trafalgar.

Cotton, Simon A., ed. Chemistry of Precious Metals. 392p. 1997. write for info. (*0-7514-0413-6*) Kluwer Academic.

Cotton, Stan. Anybody Can Be in Advertising... It Beats Working for a Living: 12 Easy Steps. (Illus.). 174p. 1997. pap. 19.95 (*0-9660411-0-0*) Back II Basics.

Cotton, William D. The Cottons of Catahoula & Related Families. Cotton-Winn, Carole & Gorman, Carolyn P., eds. (Illus.). 300p. 1987. text 35.00 (*0-961846-0-2*) Wm Davis Cotton.

Cotton, William R. & Anthes, Richard A. Storm & Cloud Dynamics. (International Geophysics Ser.). 900p. 1989. text 82.00 (*0-12-192530-7*) Acad Pr.

— Storm & Cloud Dynamics. (International Geophysics Ser.: Vol. 44). (Illus.). 883p. 1992. pap. text 82.00 (*0-12-192531-5*) Acad Pr.

Cotton, William R. & Pielke, Roger A. Human Impacts on Weather & Climate. (Geophysical Science Ser.: Vol. 2). (Illus.). 288p. (Orig.). (C). 1992. pap. 39.95 (*0-9625986-1-5*) Aster Pr.

— Human Impacts on Weather & Climate. (Illus.). 296p. (Orig.). (C). 1995. pap. text 27.95 (*0-521-49929-1*) Cambridge U Pr.

— Human Impacts on Weather & Climate. (Illus.). 296p. (Orig.). (C). 1995. text 74.95 (*0-521-49592-X*) Cambridge U Pr.

Cotton-Winn, Carole, ed. see Cotton, William D.

Cottone, G., jt. ed. see Hebel, W.

Cottone, James A. & Standish, S. Miles, eds. Outline of Forensic Dentistry. LC 81-24081. 179p. reprint ed. pap. 55.50 (*0-608-15905-0*, 203084000071) Bks Demand.

Cottone, James A., et al. Practical Infection Control in Dentistry. LC 90-5643. (Illus.). 286p. 1990. pap. 36.95 (*0-8121-1326-8*) Lppncott W & W.

— Practical Infection Control in Dentistry. 2nd ed. LC 95-2678. (Illus.). 456p. 1996. pap. 37.50 (*0-683-02138-9*) Lppncott W & W.

Cottone, James A., jt. auth. see Bernstein, Mark L.

Cottone, Rocco R. & Tarvydas, Vilia M. Ethical & Professional Issues in Counseling. LC 97-28262. 444p. 1997. pap. text 45.00 (*0-13-569138-9*) P-H.

Cottone, Vince. Good Beer Guide: Breweries & Pubs of the Pacific Northwest. Chieger, Bob, ed. (Poor Man's Guide Ser.). (Illus.). 192p. (Orig.). 1986. pap. 8.95 (*0-930180-09-7*) Homestead Bk.

Cottonwood, Joe. The Adventures of Boone Barnaby. 240p. (J). (gr. 7-9). 1992. pap. 3.50 (*0-590-43547-7*, Apple Paperbacks) Scholastic Inc.

— Adventures of Boone Barnaby. (Apple Paperbacks (Turtleback) Ser.). (J). 1992. 9.20 (*0-606-02471-9*, Pub. by Turtleback) Demco.

— Babcock. LC 95-15549. 240p. (YA). (gr. 4-7). 1996. 15.95 (*0-590-22221-X*) Scholastic Inc.

— Danny Ain't. LC 91-46240. 304p. (YA). (gr. 4-7). 1992. 13.95 (*0-590-45067-0*, 026, Scholastic Hardcover) Scholastic Inc.

— Quake! LC 94-18193. (J). 1995. 13.95 (*0-614-32018-6*) Scholastic Inc.

— Quake! A Novel. LC 94-18193. (J). (gr. 5 up). 1996. pap. 3.50 (*0-590-22233-3*) Scholastic Inc.

Cottonwood, Joe. Quake! A Novel. 1995. 8.60 (*0-606-09773-2*, Pub. by Turtleback) Demco.

Cottral, George E., ed. see National Research Council, Subcommittee on Metabolism Staff.

Cottrel, Leonard. The Lost Pharaohs. 23.95 (*0-88411-523-2*) Amereon Ltd.

***Cottrel, Pamela.** Green Saxon Darkness. 300p. 1999. pap. 19.95 (*1-58444-001-5*, Looking Glass Pr) DiscUs Bks.

Cottrell. Business & Accounting Research. 1997. pap., student ed. 20.94 (*0-07-292989-8*) McGraw.

— Creative Drama in the Classroom: Primary Grades 1-3. (Illus.). 256p. (J). (gr. 1-3). 1987. 28.19 (*0-8442-5496-7*) NTC Contemp Pub Co.

— Creative Drama in the Classroom: Primary Grades 4-6. (Illus.). 288p. (J). (gr. 4-6). 1987. 28.19 (*0-8442-5497-5*) NTC Contemp Pub Co.

— Health Education & Health Promotion. LC 98-38235. 306p. 1998. pap. text 38.00 (*0-205-27365-3*) Allyn.

Cottrell. Industrial Finance 1830-1914. 320p. 1993. 61.95 (*0-7512-0229-0*) Ashgate Pub Co.

Cottrell. Skiing Everyone. 3rd ed. 112p. 1998. pap. text 15.95 (*0-88725-226-5*) Hunter Textbks.

Cottrell & Cassis. Private Banking in Europe. 68.95 (*1-85928-432-9*) Ashgate Pub Co.

Cottrell, A. H. Theory of Crystal Dislocations. (Documents on Modern Physics Ser.). x, 94p. 1964. pap. text 129.00 (*0-677-00175-4*) Gordon & Breach.

Cottrell, A. H., jt. auth. see Pettifor, D. G.

Cottrell, Alan. Chemical Bonding in Transition Metal Carbides. 99p. 1995. 36.00 (*0-901716-68-5*, Pub. by Inst Materials) Ashgate Pub Co.

— Concepts in the Electron Theory of Alloys. (Illus.). 136p. 1998. 40.00 (*1-86125-075-4*, Pub. by Inst Materials) Ashgate Pub Co.

— An Introduction to Metallurgy. 2nd ed. 548p. 1995. reprint ed. pap. 25.00 (*0-901716-93-6*, Pub. by Inst Materials) Ashgate Pub Co.

— Introduction to the Modern Theory of Metals. 272p. 1988. text 70.00 (*0-904357-97-X*, Pub. by Inst Materials) Ashgate Pub Co.

Cottrell, Alan P., tr. see Steiner, Rudolf.

Cottrell, Allin, jt. auth. see Cockshott, W. Paul.

Cottrell, Allin F., et al, eds. The Causes & Costs of Depository Institution Failures. LC 95-34988. (Innovations in Financial Markets & Institutions Ser.). 264p. (C). 1995. lib. bdg. 109.00 (*0-7923-9634-0*) Kluwer Academic.

Cottrell, Allin F. & Lawlor, Michael S., eds. New Perspectives on Keynes. 320p. 1995. text 49.95 (*0-8223-1705-2*) Duke.

Cottrell, Alvin J. The United States & the Persian Gulf Crisis. 45p. 1982. pap. 24.95 (*0-87855-909-4*) Transaction Pubs.

Cottrell, Alvin J., et al, eds. The Persian Gulf States: A General Survey. LC 79-19452. 736p. 1980. reprint ed. pap. 200.00 (*0-608-03679-X*, 206450500009) Bks Demand.

Cottrell, Alvin J. & Dougherty, James E. Iran's Quest for Security: U. S. Arms Transfers & the Nuclear Option. LC 77-80298. (Foreign Policy Reports). 59p. 1977. 7.50 (*0-89549-004-8*) Inst Foreign Policy Anal.

Cottrell, Alvin J. & Hahn, Walter F. Naval Race or Arms Control in the Indian Ocean? Some Problems for Negotiating Naval Limitations. 78p. 1978. pap. text 17.95 (*0-87855-799-7*) Transaction Pubs.

Cottrell, Alvin J., et al. The Sea Power & Strategy in the Indian Ocean. LC 80-28415. 148p. reprint ed. pap. 45.90 (*0-8357-8450-9*, 203471400091) Bks Demand.

Cottrell, Alvin J., jt. auth. see Adams, Thomas W.

Cottrell, Anna M. Walk in the Light. Wilkingstad, Nancy, ed. LC 87-15821. (Illus.). 128p. (Orig.). 1987. pap. 9.95 (*0-931892-12-0*) B Dolphin Pub.

Cottrell, Arlene F. Visual Aid Calorie Counter. 246p. 1993. ring bd. write for info. (*0-9642419-0-0*) Seven-Shooter.

— Visual Calorie Counter. 2nd ed. (Illus.). 246p. spiral bd. 35.95 (*0-9642419-1-9*) Seven-Shooter.

Cottrell, Barbara J., jt. auth. see Larsen, Lawrence H.

Cottrell, C. L., ed. Welding Cast Irons. (Illus.). 32p. 1986. pap. 55.00 (*0-85300-176-6*, Pub. by Woodhead Pubng) Am Educ Systs.

Cottrell, Calvert B., jt. auth. see Schneider, David M.

C

An Asterisk (*) at the beginning of an entry indicates that the title is appearing for the first time.

Cottrell, Clayton. The Thirty-Fourth World's Fair Exposition Scrapbook. Nord, Barry M., ed. (Illus.). 55p. (Orig.). 1982. pap. 10.95 (*0-935656-06-5*, 101F) Nords Studio.

Cottrell, Cletus S. Poems from the Heart: Intimate Thoughts of Life & My Faith. (Illus.). 32p. 1999. pap. 8.00 (*0-8059-4601-2*) Dorrance.

Cottrell, Dana. The Seven Days of Creation: A Study Guide to Genesis. LC 95-61623. 142p. 1995. pap. 10.50 (*0-7880-0634-7*, Fairway Pr) CSS OH.

Cottrell, David. Birdies, Pars, Bogies: Leadership Lessons from the Links. 112p. 1998. pap. 12.95 (*0-9658788-2-1*) CornerStone Leader.

— Leadership . . . Biblically Speaking: The Power of Principle-Based Leadership. Coffman, Sue, ed. (Illus.). ix, 210p. 1998. 17.95 (*0-9658788-1-3*) CornerStone Leader.

Cottrell, Debbie M. Pioneer Woman Educator: The Progressive Spirit of Annie Webb Blanton. LC 93-9375. (Centennial Series of the Association of Former Students: No. 48). (Illus.). 208p. 1993. 28.50 (*0-89096-543-9*); pap. 12.95 (*0-89096-555-2*) Tex A&M Univ Pr.

Cottrell, Dennis M. The Law of Gravity. Wyrick, Charles L., Jr., ed. 329p. 1995. 21.95 (*0-941711-25-0*) Wyrick & Co.

Cottrell, Donald P. Instruction & Instructional Facilities in the Colleges of the United Lutheran Church in America. LC 79-176672. (Columbia University. Teachers College. Contributions to Education Ser.: No. 376). reprint ed. 37.50 (*0-404-55376-1*) AMS Pr.

Cottrell, Edyth Y. Mrs. Cottrell's Stretching-the-Food-Dollar Cookbook. LC 80-36894. (Illus.). 128p. (Orig.). 1982. pap. 4.95 (*0-912800-80-1*) Woodbridge Pr.

— The Oats, Peas, Beans, & Barley Cookbook: A Complete Vegetarian Cookbook Using Nature's Most Economical Foods. rev. ed. LC 80-80794. (Illus.). 283p. (Orig.). 1989. pap. 12.95 (*0-912800-85-2*) Woodbridge Pr.

— Sugar-Coated Teddy: A Children's Book about Good Health. LC 75-37441. (Illus.). 80p. (J). 1976. pap. 4.95 (*0-912800-25-9*) Woodbridge Pr.

Cottrell, Elizabeth H., ed. see Maggiolo, Paulette B.

Cottrell, Fred W. The Railroader. (Russell Sage Foundation Reprint Ser.). 1971. reprint ed. lib. bdg. 22.00 (*0-697-00210-1*) Irvington.

Cottrell, Garrison W. A Connectionist Approach to Word Sense Disambiguation. (Research Notes in Artificial Intelligence Ser.). (Illus.). 230p. (Orig.). (C). 1989. pap. text 34.95 (*0-934613-61-3*) Morgan Kaufmann.

***Cottrell, Glenn R.** From Hell to Heaven. 147p. 2000. 19.95 (*0-7541-1130-X*) Minerva Pr.

Cottrell, Gregory P. Pharmacology for Respiratory Care Practitioners. LC 94-41358. 414p. 1995. 37.95 (*0-8036-1989-8*) Davis Co.

Cottrell Houle, Marcy. Wings for My Flight: The Peregrine Falcons of Chimney Rock. LC 99-27068. 187p. 1999. pap. 14.95 (*0-87108-897-5*) Pruett.

Cottrell, J. D., et al. Teaching of Public Health in Europe. (Monographs: No. 58). 246p. 1969. pap. text 36.00 (*92-4-140058-7*, 1140058) World Health.

Cottrell, J. E., tr. see Popescu, Dumitru R.

Cottrell, Jack. God the Redeemer. LC 87-70449. (What the Bible Says Ser.). 598p. 1991. pap. text 12.99 (*0-89900-368-0*) College Pr Pub.

— His Truth. LC 79-67437. 106p. (Orig.). 1989. pap. 6.99 (*0-89900-328-1*) College Pr Pub.

— Romans, Vol. 2. (NIV Commentary Ser.). 580p. 1998. 21.99 (*0-89900-647-7*) College Pr Pub.

***Cottrell, Jack.** 13 Lessons on Grace. 104p. 1999. pap. 14.00 (*1-57910-269-7*) Wipf & Stock.

Cottrell, James E. Anesthesia & Neurosurgery. 3rd ed. Smith, David S., ed. (Illus.). 704p. (C). (gr. 13). 1994. text 134.00 (*0-8016-6573-6*, 06573) Mosby Inc.

***Cottrell, James E. & Golden, Stephanie.** Under the Mask: A Guide to Feeling Secure & Comfortable During Anesthesia & Surgery. LC 00-34202. (Illus.). 256p. 2001. pap. 20.00 (*0-8135-2878-X*); text 39.00 (*0-8135-2877-1*) Rutgers U Pr.

Cottrell, James E., jt. auth. see Newfield, Phillippa.

Cottrell, Jill. Law of Defamation in Commonwealth Africa. LC 97-38535. (Law, Social Change & Development Ser.). 327p. 1998. 82.95 (*1-84014-092-5*, KQC237.L53C68, Pub. by Ashgate Pub) Ashgate Pub Co.

— Legal Research: A Guide for Hong Kong Students. 320p. (Orig.). 1997. pap. 42.50 (*962-209-430-9*, Pub. by HK Univ Pr) Coronet Bks.

Cottrell, Jim. Skiing Everyone. rev. ed. 116p. 1998. pap. text 12.76 (*0-88725-243-5*) Hunter Textbks.

***Cottrell, Jim.** Skiing Everyone. 4th ed. (Illus.). 150p. 2000. pap. text 17.95 (*0-88725-265-6*) Hunter Textbks.

Cottrell, L., jt. auth. see Bierce, T. H.

Cottrell, Leonard. The Bull of Minos. 24.95 (*0-88411-469-4*) Amereon Ltd.

— Hannibal: Enemy of Rome. (Illus.). 287p. 1992. pap. 13.95 (*0-306-80498-0*) Da Capo.

— Lost Civilizations. LC 73-15299. (International Library Ser.). 128 p. 1974. write for info. (*0-531-02119-X*) Watts.

***Cottrell, Leonard.** Seeing Roman Britain. (Illus.). 295p. 2000. reprint ed. 25.00 (*0-7881-9421-6*) DIANE Pub.

Cottrell, Leonard. Up in a Balloon. LC 69-17423. (Illus.). (J). (gr. 8 up). 1970. 29.95 (*0-87599-142-4*) S G Phillips.

Cottrell, Leonard B. The Lost Pharaohs: The Romance of Egyptian Archaeology. LC 72-90140. 256p. 1969. reprint ed. lib. bdg. 35.00 (*0-8371-2260-0*, COLP, Greenwood Pr) Greenwood.

Cottrell, Leonard S. American Opinion on World Affairs in the Atomic Age. (History - United States Ser.). 152p. 1993. reprint ed. lib. bdg. 69.00 (*0-7812-4919-8*) Rprt Serv.

Cottrell, Leonard S. & Eberhart, Sylvia. American Opinion on World Affairs in the Atomic Age. LC 69-13867. 152p. 1969. reprint ed. lib. bdg. 38.50 (*0-8371-0361-4*, COAO, Greenwood Pr) Greenwood.

Cottrell, Leonard S., Jr., jt. auth. see Foote, Nelson N.

Cottrell, Martha C., jt. auth. see Kushi, Michio.

Cottrell, Michael H. Baby Jesus. LC 98-93143. (Footsteps to Follow Ser.: Vol. 3). (Illus.). 32p. (J). (gr. k-4). 1998. 14.95 (*0-9657091-4-0*) Christian Soldiers.

Cottrell, P. L., et al, eds. European Industry & Banking Between the Wars: A Review of Bank-Industry Relations. 1992. write for info. (*0-318-69326-7*) St Martin.

Cottrell, P. L., jt. ed. see Hearnshaw, J. B.

Cottrell, Philip, et al, eds. Finance in the Age of the Corporate Economy: The Third Anglo-Japanese Business History Conference. LC 96-26138. (Studies in Banking History). 288p. (C). 1996. text 83.95 (*1-85928-342-X*, Pub. by Scolar Pr) Ashgate Pub Co.

Cottrell, Philip L. Rebuilding the Financial System in Central & Eastern Europe, 1918-1994. LC 96-40378. (European Banking History Association Ser.). 192p. 1997. text 74.95 (*1-85928-413-2*, Pub. by Scolar Pr) Ashgate Pub Co.

Cottrell, Randall. Wellness: Stress Management. 160p. (C). 1991. text 13.50 (*0-87967-872-0*, Dshkn McG-Hill) McGrw-H Hghr Educ.

— Wellness: Weight Control. 176p. (C). 1991. text 13.50 (*0-87967-878-X*, Dshkn McG-Hill) McGrw-H Hghr Educ.

Cottrell, Randall R., et al, des. Program Evaluation: A Compilation of Articles from the Journal of Health Education. (Illus.). 124p. 1997. pap. 15.95 (*0-88314-607-X*) AAHPERD.

***Cottrell, Rita P.** Proactive Approaches in Psychosocial Occupational Therapy. (Illus.). 516p. 2000. pap. text 42.00 (*1-55642-455-8*) SLACK Inc.

Cottrell, Rita P. Psychosocial Occupational Therapy: Proactive Approaches. 600p. (C). 1993. pap. text 60.00 (*0-910317-96-8*) Am Occup Therapy.

Cottrell, Robert. The End of Hong Kong: The Secret Diplomacy of Imperial Retreat. (Illus.). 256p. 1993. pap. 22.95 (*0-7195-5291-5*, Pub. by John Murray) Trafalgar.

— Golfer's Performance Analyzer. 120p. (Orig.). 1988. pap. 19.95 (*0-937313-21-1*) Ogden Shepard Pub.

***Cottrell, Robert.** Roger Nash Baldwin & the American Civil Liberties Union. 2001. 34.50 (*0-231-11972-0*) Col U Pr.

Cottrell, Robert. Write Your Own Contracts: Business. 350p. (Orig.). 1987. pap. 14.95 (*0-937313-13-0*) Ogden Shepard Pub.

— Write Your Own Contracts: Family - Personal. 256p. (Orig.). 1987. pap. 14.95 (*0-937313-17-3*) Ogden Shepard Pub.

— Write Your Own Contracts: Real Estate & Leases. 320p. (Orig.). 1987. pap. 14.95 (*0-937313-33-5*) Ogden Shepard Pub.

Cottrell, Robert, ed. see Fathers, Michael & Higgins, Andrew.

Cottrell, Robert C. Izzy: A Biography of I. E. Stone. (C). 1992. 35.00 (*0-8135-1847-4*) Rutgers U Pr.

— Izzy: A Biography of I. F. Stone. 388p. (C). 1994. reprint ed. pap. 16.95 (*0-8135-2008-8*) Rutgers U Pr.

***Cottrell, Robert C.** Roger Nash Baldwin & the American Civil Liberties Union. LC 00-43129. (Illus.). 2000. pap. write for info. (*0-231-11973-9*) Col U Pr.

Cottrell, Robert C. The Social Gospel of E. Nicholas Comfort: Founder of the Oklahoma School of Religion. LC 96-36293. (Illus.). 360p. 1997. 34.95 (*0-8061-2931-X*) U of Okla Pr.

Cottrell, Robert D. The Grammar of Silence: A Reading of Marguerite de Navarre's Poetry. LC 85-12734. 350p. 1986. reprint ed. pap. 108.50 (*0-7837-9197-6*, 204989900004) Bks Demand.

Cottrell, Roger. The Orpheus Programme. 515p. (Orig.). (YA). (gr. 10). 1995. pap. 21.00 (*1-85863-203-X*) AK Pr Dist.

Cottrell, Roger, ed. Law & Society. LC 94-10239. (International Library of Essays in Law & Theory, Areas Ser.: Vol. 13). 500p. (C). 1994. lib. bdg. 150.00 (*0-8147-1461-7*) NYU Pr.

Cottrell, Steve. Civil War in Texas & New Mexico Territory. LC 97-6464. 112p. 1997. pap. 9.95 (*1-56554-253-3*) Pelican.

— Civil War in the Indian Territory. LC 95-2484. (Illus.). 112p. 1995. pap. 9.95 (*1-56554-110-3*) Pelican.

Cottrell, Steve, jt. auth. see Steele, Phillip W.

Cottrell, Susan C. But Listen! 1976. 3.50 (*0-87129-405-2*, B35) Dramatic Pub.

Cottrell, Tony. Evolving Stages. (Illus.). 198p. 1991. text 35.00 (*0-312-04747-9*) St Martin.

Cottrell, Valerie H., tr. see Becher, Peter.

Cottrell, W. F. Death by Dieselization: A Case Study in the Reaction to Technological Change. (Reprint Series in Social Sciences). (C). 1993. reprint ed. pap. text 1.00 (*0-8290-3794-2*, S-53) Irvington.

— Of Time & the Railroader. (Reprint Series in Social Sciences). (C). 1993. reprint ed. pap. text 5.00 (*0-8290-2794-7*, S-54) Irvington.

Cottrell, W. Frank. Better Born Lucky. 416p. 1984. 59.00 (*0-7212-0689-1*, Pub. by Regency Pr GBR) St Mut.

Cottrell, William F. Energy & Society: The Relation Between Energy, Social Change & Economic Development. LC 75-100152. 330p. 1970. reprint ed. lib. bdg. 35.00 (*0-8371-3679-2*, COES, Greenwood Pr) Greenwood.

Cottrell, William H. Born of Fire: The Volcanic Origins of Yellowstone National Park. 64p. (Orig.). (J). (gr. 3 up). 1987. pap. 11.95 (*0-911797-35-1*) Roberts Rinehart.

— Rock Climbs of Cosumnes River Gorge. 1997. (Illus.). 50p. (Orig.). 1997. pap. 13.95 (*1-891119-03-6*) El Dorado Publ.

***Cottret, Bernard.** Calvin: A Biography. LC 00-37142. 2000. 28.00 (*0-8028-4289-5*) Eerdmans.

Cottret, Bernard, ed. Bolingbroke's Political Writings: The Conservative Enlightenment. LC 94-17767. 270p. 1997. text 65.00 (*0-312-12322-1*) St Martin.

Cottridge, D. & Vinicombe, K. Collins Birding World: Rare Birds in Britain & Ireland: A Photographic Record. 192p. 1996. 45.00 (*0-00-219976-9*, Pub. by HarpC) Trafalgar.

Cottridge, David, jt. auth. see Rosair, David.

***Cottridge, David M.** A Photographic Guide to Birds of Israel & the Middle East. (Illus.). 144p. 2000. pap. 15.95 (*0-88359-055-7*, RCB-0557, R Curtis Bk) R Curtis Pubng.

Cottril, C. General Biology Lab. 1996. 12.25 (*0-07-013400-6*) McGraw.

Cottrill, Dick, et al, eds. A Practical Guide to the Employment Function. 112p. 1988. 15.00 (*0-910402-80-9*) Coll & U Personnel.

Cottrill, Judith E. Dog Bones. 105p. 1997. pap. 14.95 (*0-9654867-3-7*) Bennington NY.

Cottrill, Tim, et al. Science Fiction & Fantasy Series & Sequels: A Bibliography. LC 85-45121. (Garland Reference Library of the Humanities). 1986. 28.00 (*0-8240-8671-6*) Garland.

Cottringer, Anne. Ella & the Naughty Lion. LC 95-53271. (Illus.). 32p. (J). (ps-3). 1996. 14.95 (*0-395-79753-5*) HM.

***Cottringer, Anne.** Movie Magic. LC 98-53325. (Eyewitness Readers). 48p. (J). (gr. 2-3). 1999. 12.95 (*0-7894-4009-1*); pap. 3.95 (*0-7894-4008-3*) DK Pub Inc.

Cottrol, Robert J. The Afro-Yankees: Providence's Black Community in the Antebellum Era, 68. LC 81-23717. (Contributions in Afro-American & African Studies: No. 68). (Illus.). 200p. 1982. 52.95 (*0-313-22936-8*, CBL/, Greenwood Pr) Greenwood.

Cottrol, Robert J., ed. Gun Control & the Constitution: Sources & Explorations on the Second Amendment. LC 92-42633. (Controversies in Constitutional Law Ser.: Vol. 1). 352p. 1993. text 72.00 (*0-8153-1269-5*) Garland.

— Gun Control & the Constitution: Sources & Explorations on the Second Amendment. LC 94-15079. 480p. 1994. reprint ed. pap. text 24.95 (*0-8153-1666-6*) Garland.

— Gun Control & the Constitution: Special Topics on Gun Control. LC 92-42633. (Controversies in Constitutional Law Ser.). 328p. 1993. reprint ed. text 66.00 (*0-8153-1271-7*) Garland.

— Gun Control & the Constitution Vol. 3: Sources & Explorations on the Second Amendment: Advocates & Scholars: The Modern Debate on Gun Control. LC 92-42633. (Controversies in Constitutional Law Ser.). 392p. 1993. reprint ed. text 77.00 (*0-8153-1270-9*) Garland.

Cottrol, Robert J., ed. From African to Yankee: Narratives of Slavery & Freedom in Antebellum New England. LC 97-41904. 248p. (C). (gr. 13). 1998. text 72.95 (*0-7656-0110-9*); pap. text 24.95 (*0-7656-0111-7*) M E Sharpe.

Cotts, D. & Reyes, Z. Electrically Conductive Organic Polymers for Advanced Applications. LC 86-18053. (Illus.). 212p. 1987. 69.00 (*0-8155-1094-2*) Noyes.

Cotts, David G. The Facility Management Handbook. 2nd rev. ed. LC 98-12400. 432p. 1997. 69.95 (*0-8144-0380-8*) AMACOM.

Cotts, David G. & Lee, Michael. The Facility Management Handbook. 432p. 1992. 69.95 (*0-8144-0117-1*) AMACOM.

Cotts, David G., jt. auth. see Friday, Stormy.

Cottu, Charles. De l'administration de la Justice Criminelle en Angleterre, et de l'esprit du Gouvernement Anglais. Mayer, J. P., ed. LC 78-67348. (European Political Thought Ser.). (FRE.). 1980. reprint ed. lib. bdg. 25.95 (*0-405-11689-6*) Ayer.

Cotugna, Nancy, jt. auth. see Vickery, Connie E.

Coty, F. Tearing Away the Veils: The Financiers Who Control the World. 1987. lib. bdg. 79.95 (*0-8490-3948-7*) Gordon Pr.

Coty, Francois. Tearing Away the Veils of International Finance. 1979. lib. bdg. 69.95 (*0-8490-3011-0*) Gordon Pr.

Couani, Anna & Lyssiotis, Peter. The Harbour Breathes. 64p. (C). 1990. 150.00 (*0-908152-14-0*, Pub. by Pascoe Pub) St Mut.

Couat, A. Alexandrian Poetry under the First Three Ptolemies, 324-222 B. C. Loeb, James, tr. from FRE. xx, 638p. (C). 1993. reprint ed. pap. text 30.00 (*0-89005-500-9*) Ares.

Coubertin, Pierre De, see De Coubertin, Pierre.

Couch. City of Change & Challenge. 63.95 (*1-84014-857-8*) Ashgate Pub Co.

— Digital & Analog Communication Systems. 6th ed. 750p. 2000. 105.00 (*0-13-081223-4*) P-H.

Couch. Reteaching Worksheet, Skills for Life. (CA - Career Development Ser.). 1997. mass mkt. 13.95 (*0-314-20337-0*) S-W Pub.

— Skills for Life. (CA - Career Development Ser.). 1997. mass mkt., wbk. ed. 13.95 (*0-314-20332-X*) S-W Pub.

Couch. Skills for Life: Scans Act. Book. 1996. text 24.00 (*0-314-09790-2*, Pub. by West Pub) Thomson Learn.

Couch. Skills Life Academics. (Skills Life & Living Now Ser.). 1996. mass mkt. write for info. (*0-314-09789-9*) West Pub.

— Skills Life Careers. (Skills Life & Living Now Ser.). 1996. mass mkt. write for info. (*0-314-09787-2*) West Pub.

— Skills Life Health. (Skills Life & Living Now Ser.). Date not set. write for info. (*0-314-09788-0*) West Pub.

— Skills Life Work & Family. (Skills Life & Living Now Ser.). 1996. mass mkt. 24.00 (*0-314-09791-0*) West Pub.

Couch & Felstehausen. Resolving Conflicts: Let's Work It Out:Skills for Life. (Unknown Planning Family Ser.). 1996. text 99.00 (*0-314-09814-3*) West Pub.

Couch, et al. Health & Hygiene: Skills for Life. 1996. pap. 24.00 (*0-314-20343-5*) Thomson Learn.

Couch, Bob E. "Can Do" Thoughts in a "Can't Do" World Vol. 1: Ideas of Leaders. LC 93-192737. (Illus.). 160p. (Orig.). 1993. pap. 15.95 (*1-882555-00-7*) Town Creek Pubns.

— "Can Do" Thoughts in a "Can't Do" World Vol. 3: Leadership Ideas. LC 93-192737. 160p. (Orig.). 1997. pap. 15.95 (*1-882555-13-9*) Town Creek Pubns.

— "Can Do" Thoughts in a "Can't Do" World Vol. 3: Leadership Ideas. LC 93-94097. (Illus.). 160p. (Orig.). 1999. pap. 15.95 (*1-882555-07-4*) Town Creek Pubns.

Couch, Carl J. Constructing Civilizations. LC 83-48084. (Contemporary Studies in Sociology: Vol. 5). 401p. 1984. 78.50 (*0-89232-438-4*) Jai Pr.

— Constructing Civilizations. LC 90-26539. 401p. 1991. pap. 25.75 (*1-55938-299-6*) Jai Pr.

— Information Technologies & Social Orders. Maines, David R. & Chen, Shing-Ling, eds. (Communication & Social Order Ser.). 291p. 1996. pap. text 24.95 (*0-202-30516-3*); lib. bdg. 49.95 (*0-202-30515-5*) Aldine de Gruyter.

— Researching Social Processes in the Laboratory. LC 87-2758. (Contemporary Studies in Sociology: Vol. 6). 198p. 1987. 78.50 (*0-89232-823-1*) Jai Pr.

Couch, Chris, ed. see Eisner, William.

Couch, Chris, ed. see Geissman, Grant.

Couch, Chris, ed. see Shepard, Jewel.

Couch, Dennis, ed. see Rand, Melroe & Rand, Ingersoll.

Couch, Dick. Rising Wind. LC 95-49583. 432p. 1998. mass mkt. 6.99 (*0-380-72978-4*, Avon Bks) Morrow Avon.

— Rising Wind. LC 95-49583. 352p. 1996. 24.95 (*1-55750-133-5*) Naval Inst Pr.

Couch, Donna E. The Photograph. (Illus.). 40p. (J). (gr. 1-6). 1992. 10.00 (*0-9634359-0-6*) Seabright Pr.

Couch, Ernie. Country Music Trivia & Fact Book. rev. ed. LC 93-20504. (Illus.). 288p. (Orig.). 1996. pap. 9.95 (*1-55853-423-7*) Rutledge Hill Pr.

— Michigan Trivia. rev. ed. LC 95-5333. 192p. 1995. pap. 6.95 (*1-55853-344-3*) Rutledge Hill Pr.

— Missouri Trivia. LC 92-32523. 192p. (Orig.). 1992. pap. 6.95 (*1-55853-203-X*) Rutledge Hill Pr.

— Oklahoma Trivia. LC 99-13904. 192p. 1999. pap. 6.95 (*1-55853-732-5*) Rutledge Hill Pr.

— Presidential Trivia. LC 96-2523. 192p. 1996. pap. text 6.95 (*1-55853-412-1*) Rutledge Hill Pr.

Couch, Ernie & Couch, Jill. Florida Trivia. rev. ed. LC 94-32152. 192p. 1994. pap. 6.95 (*1-55853-316-8*) Rutledge Hill Pr.

— Georgia Trivia. rev. ed. LC 86-15423. 160p. (Orig.). 1993. pap. 6.95 (*1-55853-228-5*) Rutledge Hill Pr.

— Indiana Trivia. 2nd rev. ed. LC 97-30811. 192p. 1997. pap. 6.95 (*1-55853-551-9*) Rutledge Hill Pr.

— Kentucky Trivia. LC 91-15368. 192p. (Orig.). 1991. pap. 6.95 (*1-55853-095-9*) Rutledge Hill Pr.

— North Carolina Trivia. rev. ed. LC 91-2463. 192p. (Orig.). 1991. pap. 6.95 (*1-55853-112-2*) Rutledge Hill Pr.

— Ohio Trivia. rev. ed. LC 88-4979. 192p. 1992. pap. 6.95 (*1-55853-207-2*) Rutledge Hill Pr.

— Pennsylvania Trivia. rev. ed. LC 95-24376. 192p. 1995. pap. 6.95 (*1-55853-356-7*) Rutledge Hill Pr.

— Tennessee Trivia. rev. ed. LC 91-8994. 192p. (Orig.). 1991. pap. 6.95 (*1-55853-109-2*) Rutledge Hill Pr.

— Virginia Trivia. rev. ed. LC 91-36309. 192p. (Orig.). 1991. pap. 6.95 (*1-55853-139-4*) Rutledge Hill Pr.

Couch, Ernie, jt. auth. see Couch, Jill.

Couch, F. Hill: Genealogy of the Hill, Dean, Pinckney, Austin, Barker, Anderson, Rhoades & Finch Families. (Illus.). 124p. 1991. reprint ed. pap. 22.00 (*0-8328-1733-3*); reprint ed. lib. bdg. 32.00 (*0-8328-1732-5*) Higginson Bk Co.

Couch, Gordon. Access in London: A Guide for Those Who Have Problems Getting Around. (Illus.). 340p. 1996. pap. text 11.95 (*1-899163-18-2*) Cimino Pub Grp.

— Access in Paris: A Guide fo Those Who Have Problems Getting Around. (Illus.). 1994. pap. 30.00 (*1-870948-62-9*, Pub. by Quiller Pr) St Mut.

Couch, Graeme, intro. Electric Energy Conference, 1992: Driving Systems Harder. (Illus.). 411p. (Orig.). 1992. pap. text 110.50 (*0-85825-560-X*, Pub. by Inst Engrs Aust-EA Bks) Accents Pubns.

Couch, Greg, jt. illus. see Anderson, Stephen A.

Couch, Herbert N. Classical Civilization: Greece. LC 76-156186. (Illus.). 622p. 1973. reprint ed. lib. bdg. 35.00 (*0-8371-6129-0*, COCC, Greenwood Pr) Greenwood.

Couch, Houston B. Diseases of Turfgrasses. 3rd ed. (Illus.). 434p. (C). 1995. 94.50 (*0-89874-211-0*) Krieger.

— The Turfgrass Disease Handbook. LC 99-53330. (Illus.). 220p. 2000. 42.50 (*1-57524-076-9*) Krieger.

Couch, J. Hudson. The Braves First Fifteen Years in Atlanta. LC 84-81647. 436p. (Orig.). 1984. pap. 9.95 (*0-931083-00-1*) Other Alligator.

Couch, J. N., jt. auth. see Coker, W. C.

Couch, James B. The Health Care Professional's Guide to Disease Management. LC 98-27918. 400p. 1998. pap. 49.00 (*0-8342-1166-1*, 11661) Aspen Pub.

— The Physician's Guide to Disease Management: Patient-Centered Care for the 21st Century. LC 97-18244. 368p. 1997. pap. 49.00 (*0-8342-1003-7*) Aspen Pub.

Couch, James E. The Fuji Agenda. ix, 328p. (Orig.). 1995. pap. 6.00 (*1-888929-00-6*) Ridge Pub FL.

Couch, James H., et al. Una Vez Mas. (gr. 4-12). 1982. 4.25 (*0-317-02593-7*) Longman.

An Asterisk (*) at the beginning of an entry indicates that the title is appearing for the first time.

— Una Vez Mas. (gr. 4-12). 1989. pap. 13.95 (*0-88334-164-6*) Longman.

— Una Vez Mas. 240p. 1993. student ed. 17.33 (*0-8013-0973-5*, 79254) Longman.

— Una Vez Mas. 2nd ed. 240p. 1992. text, student ed. write for info. (*0-8013-0972-7*, 79253) Longman.

— Una Vez Mas. 2nd ed. 240p. 1993. pap., student ed. 25.33 (*0-8013-0971-9*, 79252) Longman.

Couch, James R., Jr., jt. ed. see Good, David C.

***Couch, Jane.** Jane Couch: Fleetwood Assassin. (Illus.). 2000. 24.95 (*1-85782-435-0*) Blake Publng.

Couch, Janet. Generation K: The Kvechies. LC 97-93082. (Illus.). 110p. (Orig.). 1997. pap. 10.00 (*0-9657088-0-2*, 1001) Bim Bks.

***Couch, Janet.** Generation K: The Kvechies: God's Revenge on the 60s Generation. 2nd rev. ed. LC 97-93082. (Illus.). 112p. 1999. pap. 10.00 (*0-9657088-9-6*, 2001) Bim Bks.

***Couch-Jareb, Annette L.** Cyber Bride. LC 99-94441. 184p. 1999. 18.95 (*0-8034-9364-9*, Avalon Bks) Bouregy.

Couch, Jean. Yoga Book. (Runner's World Ser.). 1982. pap. 9.95 (*0-02-499670-X*, Macmillan Coll) P-H.

— Yoga Book, No. 2. (Runner's World Ser.). 1983. pap. 9.95 (*0-02-499680-7*, Macmillan Coll) P-H.

Couch, Jean & Weaver, Nell. Runner's World Yoga Book. LC 78-68619. (Runner's World Instructional Ser.). (Illus.). 228p. 1982. reprint ed. spiral bd. 11.95 (*0-89037-206-3*) Anderson World.

Couch, Jill & Couch, Ernie. Alabama Trivia. LC 87-4491. 192p. (Orig.). 1987. pap. 5.95 (*0-934395-44-6*) Rutledge Hill Pr.

— Texas Trivia. rev. ed. LC 91-9502. 192p. (Orig.). 1991. pap. 6.95 (*1-55853-114-9*) Rutledge Hill Pr.

Couch, Jill, jt. auth. see Couch, Ernie.

Couch, Jim F. & Shughart, William F., II. The Political Economy of the New Deal. LC 98-27149. (Locke Institute Ser.). 264p. 1998. 85.00 (*1-85898-899-3*) E Elgar.

Couch, John A. Pathobiology of Marine & Estuarine Organisms. 576p. 1992. lib. bdg. 95.00 (*0-8493-8662-4*, SF997) CRC Pr.

Couch, John N., jt. auth. see Coker, William C.

Couch, Jonathan. The History of Polperro. (C). 1989. 35.00 (*1-85022-013-1*, Pub. by Dyllansow Truran) St Mut.

Couch, Justin. Advanced Java Network Programming. (Java Masters Ser.). 1998. pap. text 44.95 (*0-07-913741-5*) McGraw.

— Real-World Java 1.2 Networking. (Java Masters Ser.). 488p. 1999. pap. text 44.99 incl. cd-rom (*0-07-134813-1*) McGraw.

Couch, Justin, jt. auth. see Murdock, Kelly.

Couch, Justin, jt. auth. see Roehl, Bernie.

Couch, Larry. Dada Dog. Strahan, Bradley R., ed. (Black Buzzard Illustrated Poetry Chapbook Ser.). (Illus.). 24p. 1983. pap. text 5.50 (*0-938872-04-4*) Black Buzzard.

Couch, Larry, ed. Let Us Serve Them All Their Days: Young Volunteers Serving Homebound Elderly Persons. 170p. 1992. pap. 15.00 (*0-910883-66-1*, 2051) Natl Coun Aging.

Couch, Lee, jt. auth. see Wright.

Couch, Leon W., II. Digital & Analog Communication Systems. 5th ed. LC 96-26985. 742p. (C). 1996. 105.00 (*0-13-522583-3*) P-H.

Couch, Mal. Biblical Handbook to the Acts of the Apostles. 464p. 1998. 25.99 (*0-8254-2360-0*) Kregel.

— Dictionary of Premillennial Theology: A Practical Guide to the People, Viewpoints, & History of Prophetic Studies. LC 96-22346. 448p. 1996. 23.99 (*0-8254-2351-1*) Kregel.

***Couch, Mal.** Fundamentals for the Twenty-First Century: Examining the Crucial Issues of the Christian Faith. LC 99-43086. 2000. 29.99 (*0-8254-2368-6*) Kregel.

***Couch, Mal, ed.** A Biblical Theology of the Church. LC 99-33785. 336p. 1999. 17.99 (*0-8254-2361-9*) Kregel.

— Issues 2000: Evangelical Faith & Cultural Trends in a New Millennium. LC 99-19008. 160p. 1999. pap. 9.99 (*0-8254-2363-5*) Kregel.

***Couch, Mal & Penney, Russell.** Classical Evangelical Hermeneutics: A Guide to the History & Practice of Biblical Interpretation. LC 99-33767. 376p. 1999. pap. 15.99 (*0-8254-2367-8*) Kregel.

Couch, Malcolm. Creative Calligraphy, 1. 1998. 16.98 (*1-880908-99-9*) Todtri Prods.

***Couch, Malcolm.** Greek & Roman Mythology, 1. 1998. pap. text 14.98 (*1-57717-064-4*) Todtri Prods.

Couch, Malcolm. Greek & Roman Mythology: Malcolm Couch. (Mythology Bks.). (Illus.). 128p. 1998. 9.99 (*1-56799-657-4*, Thunder Bay) Advantage Pubs.

Couch, Margaret Z. There's an Elephant in the Copy Room: Bold Remedies for Resolving Workplace Dilemmas. LC 98-67491. 256p. 1998. pap. 16.95 (*0-9666165-5-3*) Perelandra.

Couch, Martha. Fantase. 200p. 1996. pap. text 3.95 (*0-9654286-0-5*) M Couch.

Couch, Marvin. Jesus My Father. 1992. pap. 9.95 (*0-938645-65-X*) In His Steps.

— Jesus My Lord. 1990. pap. 5.95 (*0-938645-40-4*) In His Steps.

Couch, N. C. Christopher. Faces of Eternity: A Unique Exhibition. Eckman, Joanna et al, eds. (Illus.). 90p. 1991. pap. 15.00 (*1-879128-03-9*) Americas Soc.

Couch, N. C. Christopher, ed. see Capp, Al.

Couch, N. C. Christopher, ed. see O'Barr, J., et al.

Couch, Nena. The Humanities & the Library. 2nd ed. Allen, Nancy, ed. LC 92-32610. 338p. reprint ed. pap. 104.80 (*0-608-06020-8*, 206634800008) Bks Demand.

Couch, Nena, ed. see Kingsley, Sidney.

Couch, Ruth. This Land of Legend. LC 90-62573. 71p. 1992. per. 18.00 (*0-914546-88-0*) Rose Pub.

Couch, Stephen R. & Kroll-Smith, J. Stephen. Communities at Risk: Collective Responses to Technical Hazards. LC 89-13557. (Worcester Polytechnic Institute Studies in Science, Technology, & Culture: Vol. 3). (Illus.). VI, 320p. (C). 1991. text 50.95 (*0-8204-0712-7*) P Lang Pubng.

Couch, Sue, et al. Couch Skills for Life. LC 96-232416. 1996. pap. 45.50 (*0-314-05109-0*) West Pub.

Couch, Sue, jt. auth. see Felstehausen, Ginny.

***Couch, Tiffany.** Rosemary Rose: Discovering Balance & Joy. (Illus.). 32p. 2000. pap. 14.95 (*1-885473-43-5*) Wood N Barnes.

Couch, Tony. Watercolor: You Can Do It! (Illus.). 176p. 1996. pap. 24.99 (*0-89134-697-X*, North Lght Bks) F & W Pubns Inc.

Couch, Warrick J., jt. ed. see Morganti, Rafaella O.

Couch, William, Jr., ed. New Black Playwrights: An Anthology. LC 68-31137. 282p. reprint ed. pap. 87.50 (*0-608-14359-6*, 201957400013) Bks Demand.

Couchenour-Chrisman. Families Schools & Communities. LC 99-49260. (Early Childhood Education Ser.). (C). 1999. pap. 43.95 (*0-7668-0257-4*) Delmar.

Couchenour, Donna. Learning All Day: Curriculum for Infants & Toddlers. (Bright Ideas Ser.). 20p. (Orig.). (C). 1994. pap. text 3.00 (*0-942388-14-3*) So Early Chldhood Assn.

Coucher, Mimi. Hugs & Kisses. 1998. 11.95 (*0-7892-0361-8*) Abbeville Pr.

Couchman, Donald H. Cooke's Peak - Pasaron Por Aqui: A Focus on United States History in Southwestern New Mexico. (Cultural Resources Ser.: No. 7). (Illus.). 268p. (Orig.). 1990. pap. write for info. (*1-878178-08-3*) Bureau of Land Mgmt NM.

Couchman, Gordon W. This Our Caesar: A Study of Bernard Shaw's "Ceasar & Cleopatra" 1973. pap. text 36.95 (*90-279-2601-8*) Mouton.

Couchman, Jason S. Oracle 8 Certified Professional DBA Certification Exam Guide. (Illus.). 1187p. 1999. 99.99 incl. cd-rom (*0-07-212087-8*) Osborne-McGraw.

— Oracle Certified Professional DBA Certification Exam Guide. 1257p. 1998. pap. 99.99 (*0-07-882549-0*) Osborne-McGraw.

***Couchman, Jason S.** Oracle Certified Professional DBO Certification Exam Guide. 543p. 2000. 59.99 (*0-07-212361-3*) McGraw.

Couchman, Jason S., et al. Oracle Certified Professional Application Developer Exam Guide. (Illus.). 1351p. 1999. pap. 99.99 incl. cd-rom (*0-07-211975-6*) McGraw.

Couchman, Judith. Breakfast for the Soul: Spiritual Nourishment to Start Your Day. 208p. 1998. 14.99 (*1-56292-531-8*) Honor Bks OK.

— Designing a Woman's Life: Discovering Your Unique Purpose & Passion. LC 96-109282. 166p. 1995. 12.99 (*0-88070-837-9*) Multnomah Pubs.

— Designing a Woman's Life Bible Study: A Practical Guide to Discovering Your Unique Purpose & Passion. 126p. 1996. pap. 6.99 (*0-88070-887-5*, Multnomah Bks) Multnomah Pubs.

— A Garden's Promise: Spiritual Reflections on Growing from the Heart. 1998. 135.60 (*1-57856-062-4*) Waterbrook Pr.

***Couchman, Judith.** A Garden's Promise: Spiritual Reflections on Growing from the Heart. LC 98-218565. 144p. 1998. 16.95 (*1-57856-010-1*) Waterbrook Pr.

Couchman, Judith. His Gentle Voice. LC 98-13887. (Listening Ser.). 176p. 1998. 14.99 (*1-57673-076-X*, Multnomah Bks) Multnomah Pubs.

— Shaping a Woman's Soul: Daily Devotions to Calm Your Spirit & Lead You into God's Presence. 160p. 1996. pap. 10.99 (*0-310-20517-4*) Zondervan.

— Voices of Faith for a New Millennium: 365 Daily Reminders. 196p. 1999. 14.99 (*1-56955-162-6*, Vine Bks) Servant.

— Woman Behind the Mirror. LC 97-6535. 1997. pap. 10.99 (*0-8054-6077-2*) Broadman.

Couchman, Judith, compiled by. One Holy Passion: Growing Deeper in Your Walk with God. LC 98-229071. 256p. 1998. 16.95 (*1-57856-038-1*) Waterbrook Pr.

Couchman, Judith & Chambers, Oswald. Growing Deeper with God. LC 97-7890. (Life Messages of Great Christians Ser.). 180p. 1997. pap. 10.99 (*1-56955-007-7*, Vine Bks) Servant.

Couchman, Judith, ed. see Wigglesworth, Smith.

***Couchman, Judy, compiled by.** The Way of Faith: Martin Luther. LC 99-37123. (Life Messages of Great Christians Ser.). 185p. 1999. pap. 10.99 (*1-56955-115-4*, Vine Bks) Servant.

***Couchman, Ken, ed.** Through His Eyes: The Story of Youth in Mission. 88p. 1999. pap. 6.75 (*0-8341-1768-1*) Beacon Hill.

Couchman, Robert, ed. see Dawson, Louis W., II.

Couchman, Robert, ed. see Dawson, Louis W., 2nd.

Couchman, Robert, ed. see Geiman, Ric.

***Couchman, Vicki.** A Trail of Visions: Route One: India, Sri Lanka, Thailand, Sumatra. Hiscocks, Dan, ed. (Illus.). 128p. 2000. 19.95 (*1-871349-33-8*, Pub. by Travellerseye Ltd) Midpt Trade.

— Trail of Visions: Route One: India, Sri Lanka, Thailand, Sumatra. (Illus.). 2000. 19.95 (*1-903070-03-1*) Travellerseye Ltd.

— A Trail of Visions: Route Two: Peru, Bolivia, Ecuador, Columbia. Hiscocks, Dan, ed. (Illus.). 110p. 2000. 19.95 (*0-9530575-0-X*, Pub. by Travellerseye Ltd) Midpt Trade.

Couchot, Lise. Thin Scars - Purple Leaves. (Rockbook Ser.: No. 10). 24p. (Orig.). 1981. pap. 3.00 (*0-930012-40-2*) J Mudfoot.

Couchot, Virginia. Davis - Woodruff Families of Western Kentucky. (Illus.). 74p. 1993. reprint ed. pap. 15.00 (*0-8328-3070-4*); reprint ed. lib. bdg. 25.00 (*0-8328-3069-0*) Higginson Bk Co.

Coude, C., et al. L' Anglais Medical: Spoken & Written Medical English. (ENG & FRE.). 272p. 1983. pap. 79.95 (*0-8288-0561-X*, M14533) Fr & Eur.

Couderc, Jean-Mary, text. A Village in France: Louis Clergeau's Photographic Portrait of Daily Life in Pontlevoy, 1902-1936. LC 96-84380. (Illus.) 140p. 1996. 45.00 (*0-8109-3747-6*, Pub. by Abrams) Time Warner.

Coudert, Allison, et al. Leibniz, Mysticism & Religion. LC 98-27908. (International Archives of the History of Ideas Ser.). 1998. write for info. (*0-7923-5223-8*) Kluwer Academic.

Coudert, Allison P. The Impact of the Kabbalah in the Seventeenth Century: The Life & Thought of Francis Mercury van Helmont (1614-1698) LC 98-4716. (Series in Jewish Studies: Vol. 9). xx, 418p. 1998. 147.00 (*90-04-09844-5*) Brill Academic Pubs.

— Leibniz & the Kabbalah, 142. LC 94-32967. (International Archives of the History of Ideas Ser.). 1995. lib. bdg. 121.50 (*0-7923-3114-1*) Kluwer Academic.

Coudert, Allison P., ed. see Conway, Anne.

Coudert, Frederic R., Jr. Marriage & Divorce Laws in Europe: A Study in Comparative Legislation. 1993. reprint ed. 32.50 (*0-8377-2021-4*, Rothman) W S Hein.

Coudert, Jo. The Alcoholic in Your Life. LC 70-185955. 264p. 1987. pap. 9.95 (*0-8128-6121-3*, Scrbrough Hse) Madison Bks UPA.

— Seven Cats & the Art of Living. 208p. 1998. mass mkt. 12.00 (*0-446-67444-3*, Pub. by Warner Bks) Little.

Coudert, Jo, jt. auth. see Thornton, Yvonne S.

Coudris, Manuel D. Diary of an Unborn Child: A Baby Speaks from Its Mother's Womb. (Illus.). 192p. 1992. pap. write for info. (*0-946551-80-4*) ACCESS Pubs Network.

Coudron, Jill M. Alphabet Activities. (J). (ps-3). 1982. pap. 12.99 (*0-8224-0297-1*) Fearon Teacher Aids.

— Alphabet Fun & Games. LC 83-62563. 1984. pap. 12.99 (*0-8224-0295-5*) Fearon Teacher Aids.

— Alphabet Puppets. LC 78-72077. (J). (gr. k-3). 1979. pap. 9.99 (*0-8224-0298-X*) Fearon Teacher Aids.

— Alphabet Stories. (J). (ps-3). 1982. pap. 12.99 (*0-8224-0299-8*) Fearon Teacher Aids.

Coudurier, L., et al. Fundamentals of Metallurgical Processes. (International Series of Monographs on Materials Science & Technology: Vol. 27). (Illus.). 400p. 1985. text 187.00 (*0-08-032536-X*, Pub. by PPL); pap. text 44.00 (*0-08-032537-8*, Pub. by PPL) Franklin.

Coue, Emile. How to Practice Suggestion & Autosuggestion. 128p. 1993. pap. 12.00 (*0-89540-197-5*, SB-197) Sun Pub.

— How to Practice Suggestion & Autosuggestion. 128p. 1996. reprint ed. spiral bd. 11.00 (*0-7873-0225-2*) Hlth Research.

— My Method. 97p. 1983. pap. 10.00 (*0-89540-147-9*, SB-147) Sun Pub.

— Self Mastery Through Conscious Autosuggestion. 93p. 1981. pap. 10.00 (*0-89540-095-2*, SB-095) Sun Pub.

— Self Mastery Through Conscious Autosuggestion. 94p. 1996. reprint ed. spiral bd. 11.00 (*0-7873-0226-0*) Hlth Research.

— Self Mastery Through Conscious Autosuggestion (1922) 93p. 1996. reprint ed. pap. 9.95 (*1-56459-721-0*) Kessinger Pub.

Coue, Stephanie. Hagiographie im Kontext: Schreibanlass & Funktion von Bischofsviten aus dem 11. & vom Anfang des 12. Jahr-hunderts. (Arbeiten zur Fruehmittelalterforschung Ser.: Vol. 24). (GER.). xi, 203p. (C). 1996. lib. bdg. 117.05 (*3-11-014825-0*) De Gruyter.

Couer, Robert M. & Fiss, Owen M. The Structure of Procedure. (University Textbook Ser.). 560p. (C). 1992. reprint ed. pap. text 21.00 (*0-88277-499-9*) Foundation Pr.

Coues, Elliot, compiled by. Ornithological Bibliography. 859p. 1995. reprint ed. 95.00 (*1-57898-023-2*) Martino Pubng.

Coues, Elliot, ed. see Fowler, Jacob.

Coues, Elliot, ed. see Lewis, Meriwether & Clark, William.

Coues, Elliott. Birds of the Colorado Valley: A Repository of Scientific & Popular Information Concerning North American Ornithology, Vol. 11. LC 73-17814 (Natural Sciences in America Ser.). 820p. 1974. reprint ed. 59.95 (*0-405-05730-X*) Ayer.

— Birds of the Northwest: A Handbook of the Ornithology of the Region Drained by the Missouri River & Its Tributaries. LC 73-17815. (Natural Sciences in America Ser.). 808p. 1974. reprint ed. 58.95 (*0-405-05731-8*) Ayer.

— Fur-Bearing Animals of North America. LC 79-125735. (American Environmental Studies). (Illus.). 1976. reprint ed. 40.95 (*0-405-02660-9*) Ayer.

— Key to North American Birds: Containing a Concise Account of Every Species of Living & Fossil Bird at Present Known from the Continent North of the Mexican & the United States Boundary, Inclusive of Greenland & Lower California, 2 vols., Set. 5th ed. LC 73-17816. (Natural Sciences in America Ser.). (Illus.). 1189p. 1974. reprint ed. 84.95 (*0-405-05732-6*) Ayer.

— Key to North American Birds: Containing a Concise Account of Every Species of Living & Fossil Bird at Present Known from the Continent North of the Mexican & the United States Boundary, Inclusive of Greenland & Lower California, 2 vols., Vol. 1. 5th ed. LC 73-17816. (Natural Sciences in America Ser.). (Illus.). 1189p. 1974. reprint ed. 42.95 (*0-405-05774-1*) Ayer.

— Key to North American Birds: Containing a Concise Account of Every Species of Living & Fossil Bird at Present Known from the Continent North of the Mexican & the United States Boundary, Inclusive of Greenland & Lower California, 2 vols., Vol. 2. 5th ed. LC 73-17816. (Natural Sciences in America Ser.). (Illus.). 1189p. 1974. reprint ed. 42.95 (*0-405-05775-X*) Ayer.

— War & Christianity. 1973. 250.00 (*0-8490-1276-7*) Gordon Pr.

Coues, Elliott, jt. auth. see Fowler, Jacob.

Couet, Alain. Traditional, Regional & Special Breads. (Special & Decorative Breads Ser.). 304p. 1997. text 69.95 (*0-470-25006-2*) Halsted Pr.

Couey. Play Golf Effectively. (Adaptable Courseware-Softside). 1993. mass mkt. 16.75 (*0-314-02912-5*) West Pub.

Couey, Dick. Nutrition for God's Temple. LC 93-20409. (Studies in Health & Human Services: Vol. 22). 664p. 1993. pap. 109.95 (*0-7734-9288-7*); text 129.95 (*0-7734-9286-0*) E Mellen.

Couey, Robin, ed. see Nelson, Bobbe.

Couey, Stanley D. A Couey Genealogy: Some Descendants of Joseph Couey (1764-1844) 244p. (Orig.). 1988. pap. write for info. (*0-318-63231-4*) S Couey.

Coufal, H., jt. ed. see Luscher, E.

***Coufal, Hans J., et al, eds.** Holographic Data Storage. (Series in Optical Sciences: Vol. 76). (Illus.). xxiv, 469p. 2000. 165.00 (*3-540-66691-5*) Spr-Verlag.

Coufal, James E., jt. auth. see Allen, Douglas C.

Couffer, Jack. Bat Bomb: World War II's Other Secret Weapon. LC 92-11888. (Illus.). 284p. 1992. 24.95 (*0-292-70790-8*) U of Tex Pr.

— The Cats of Lamu. LC 97-43247. (Illus.). 160p. 1998. pap. 24.95 (*1-55821-675-8*) Lyons Pr.

Couffignal, L. Quelques Notions de Base pour l'Economie. (Economies et Societes Series N: No. 4). 1962. pap. 11.00 (*0-8115-0768-8*) Periodicals Srv.

Coufoudakis, Van. Essays on the Cyprus Conflict. LC 76-10112. 53p. 1976. text 9.00 (*0-918618-01-0*); pap. text 6.00 (*0-918618-00-2*) Pella Pub.

Coufoudakis, Van, et al, eds. Greece & the New Balkans: Challenges & Opportunities. LC 99-70137. (Modern Greek Research Ser.: Vol. VII). 500p. (C). 1999. pap. 30.00 (*0-918618-72-X*) Pella Pub.

C

Couger, Daniel J. & Zawacki, Robert A. Motivating & Managing Computer Personnel. 232p. 1980. 25.95 (*0-318-17053-1*); 27.95 (*0-318-17054-X*) AITP.

Couger, J. Daniel & Zawacki, Robert A. Motivating & Managing Computer Personnel. 213p. 1980. 101.95 (*0-471-08485-9*) Wiley.

Couger, J. Daniel, et al. Advanced System Development - Feasibility Techniques. LC 82-2818. 522p. reprint ed. pap. 161.90 (*0-7837-2371-7*, 204005700006) Bks Demand.

Coughanower, Donald R. Process Systems Analysis & Control. 2nd ed. 640p. (C). 1991. 92.50 (*0-07-013212-7*) McGraw.

***Coughenour, C. Milton & Chamala, Shankariah.** Conservation Tillage & Cropping Innovation: Constructing the New Culture of Agriculture. (Illus.). 420p. 2000. 59.95 (*0-8138-1947-4*) Iowa St U Pr.

Coughlan. Value Judgements. text. write for info. (*0-471-49128-4*) Wiley.

Coughlan & Carnegie. Pride of the River: The Forceful Story. (Illus.). (YA). 1990. pap. 30.00 (*0-86439-046-7*, Pub. by Boolarong Pubns) St Mut.

Coughlan, Andrew & Miller, Andrew, eds. BSAVA Manual of Small Animal Fracture Repair & Management. (Illus.). 200p. 1997. pap. 94.95 (*0-8138-2794-9*, Pub. by BSAVA) Iowa St U Pr.

***Coughlan, Anne T.** Marketing Channels. 6th ed. LC 00-55058. 2000. write for info. (*0-13-012772-8*) P-H.

Coughlan, Cheryl. Ants. 1999. 13.25 (*0-516-21822-0*) Capstone Pr.

— Beetles. 1999. 13.25 (*0-516-21823-9*) Capstone Pr.

— Bumble Bees. 1999. 13.25 (*0-516-21824-7*) Capstone Pr.

— Crickets. 1999. 13.25 (*0-516-21825-5*) Capstone Pr.

— Dragonflies. 1999. 13.25 (*0-516-21826-3*) Capstone Pr.

— Fireflies. 1999. 13.25 (*0-516-21827-1*) Capstone Pr.

— Flies. 1999. 13.25 (*0-516-21828-X*) Capstone Pr.

— Grasshoppers. 1999. 13.25 (*0-516-21829-8*) Capstone Pr.

Coughlan, Cheryl. Insects. Saunders-Smith, Gail, ed. (Illus.). 24p. 99.50 (*0-7368-0265-7*) Capstone Pr.

Coughlan, Cheryl. Ladybugs. 1999. 13.25 (*0-516-21830-1*) Capstone Pr.

— Mosquitoes. 1999. 13.25 (*0-516-21831-X*) Capstone Pr.

Coughlan, Cheryl, jt. auth. see Peterson, Cheryl.

Coughlan, G. D. & Dodd, J. E. The Ideas of Particle Physics: An Introduction for Scientists. 2nd ed. (Illus.). 256p. (C). 1991. text 85.00 (*0-521-38506-7*); pap. text 42.95 (*0-521-38677-2*) Cambridge U Pr.

***Coughlan, Geoff.** World War 2 Luftwaffe Fighter Modelling. (Illus.). 128p. 2000. 29.95 (*1-84176-060-9*, 130579AE, Pub. by Osprey) Motorbooks Intl.

Coughlan, James E. & McNamara, Deborah J. Asians in Australia: Patterns of Migration & Settlement LC 98-170581. 1997. write for info. (*0-7329-4562-3*) Macmill Educ.

Coughlan, James E. & McNamara, Deborah J., eds. Asians in Australia: Patterns of Migration & Settlement. LC 98-170581. 344p. 1998. 64.95 (*0-7329-4561-5*, Pub. by Macmill Educ) Paul & Co Pubs.

Coughlan, John. Experimental & Concept Cars. (Wheels Ser.). (Illus.). 48p. (J). (gr. 3-6). 1994. 19.00 (*0-516-35210-5*); pap. 5.95 (*0-516-40210-2*) Childrens.

Coughlan, John, jt. auth. see Toth, Susan A.

Coughlan, Joseph D. & Strand, William K. Depreciation: Accounting, Taxes & Business Decisions. LC 69-12971. (Illus.). 356p. reprint ed. pap. 110.40 (*0-608-30129-9*, 201241000081) Bks Demand.

Coughlan, Kathryn I. Rokeby, a Page in History: The Archives Revisited. (Illus.). 48p. (Orig.). (C). 1993. pap. 9.95 (*0-9637161-0-7*) K&D Ltd.
Coughlan, M. P. & Hazlewood, G. P., eds. Hemicellulose & Hemicellulases. (Portland Press Research Monographs: Vol. 4). 156p. (C). 1993. text 85.00 (*1-85578-036-4*, Pub. by Portland Pr Ltd) Ashgate Pub Co.
***Coughlan, Margaret N.** Folklore from Africa to the United States: An Annotated Bibliography. LC 99-23245. 1999. 40.00 (*0-7808-0314-0*) Omnigraphics Inc.
Coughlan, Patricia B. Facing Alzheimer's: Family Caregivers Speak. 1993. mass mkt. 4.99 (*0-345-37549-1*) Ballantine Pub Grp.
— Modernism & Ireland: The Poetry of the 1930's. 1995. pap. text 24.00 (*1-85918-061-2*) Intl Spec Bk.
Coughlan, Reed, jt. ed. see De A Samarasinghe, S. W.
Coughlan, Ronan. Irish Myth & Legend. (Appletree Pocket Guides Ser.). (Illus.). 72p. (Orig.). 1985. pap. 7.95 (*0-86281-152-X*, Pub. by Appletree Pr) Irish Bks Media.
***Coughlan, William D.** Legacy or Love. 240p. 2000. pap. 15.00 (*0-9678341-0-4*) Coughlan & Assocs.
Coughli. CALCULUS WITH APPLICATIONS 2E. 2nd ed. (C). 1993. text 91.00 (*0-03-055757-7*) Harcourt Coll Pubs.
— Graphing Calculator Supplement. 2nd ed. (C). 1993. pap. text 7.00 (*0-03-097367-8*) Harcourt Coll Pubs.
Coughlin. Brief Calculus with Applications: Prep Tests. (C). 1990. pap. text 40.50 (*0-03-033122-6*, Pub. by Harcourt Coll Pubs) Harcourt.
— Calculus with Applications. 2nd ed. (C). 1993. pap. text, teacher ed. 15.00 (*0-03-072868-1*); pap. text, teacher ed., suppl. ed. 21.50 (*0-03-072871-1*, Pub. by Harcourt Coll Pubs) Harcourt.
— Father Coughlin on Money & Gold. Carpenter, Kenneth E., ed. LC 74-368. (Gold Ser.: Vol. 4). 1974. reprint ed. 26.95 (*0-405-05929-9*) Ayer.
— SSM T/A BRIEF CALC 2E AND CAL. 2nd ed. (C). 1993. pap. text, student ed. 24.50 (*0-03-072869-X*) Harcourt Coll Pubs.
***Coughlin.** Surgery: Foot & Ankle. 7th ed. LC 99-20312. 1605p. 1999. text 295.00 (*0-323-00327-3*) Mosby Inc.
— Surgery of the Foot & Ankle. 7th ed. (C). 1999. text 295.00 (*0-323-00899-2*) Mosby Inc.
Coughlin. Trigonometry. (C). 1998. text 53.25 (*0-03-093715-9*) Harcourt Coll Pubs.
Coughlin, Ann, et al. You Know You're a Peace Officer's Wife When . . . 56p. (Orig.). 1978. pap. 7.95 (*1-56325-016-0*, DH016) Davis Pub Law.
Coughlin, C. E. A Series of Lectures on Social Justice. LC 71-173652. (FDR & the Era of the New Deal Ser.). 242p. 1971. reprint ed. lib. bdg. 32.50 (*0-306-70373-4*) Da Capo.
Coughlin, Carol M. Good News about Good Food: A Practical Guide to Healthy Vegetarian Meals. 63p. 1997. 17.00 (*1-892014-02-5*) Integrative Med.
Coughlin, Carol M. & DeBusk, Ruth M. Integrative Medicine: Your Quick Reference Guide. 292p. 1998. ring bd. 70.00 (*1-892014-00-9*) Integrative Med.
— Integrative Medicine: Your Quick Reference Guide: Supplement, 1998. 150p. 1998. suppl. ed. 45.00 (*1-892014-03-3*) Integrative Med.
Coughlin, Caroline M. & Gertzog, Alice. Lyle's Administration of the College Library. LC 97-8758. 208p. 1997. 38.00 (*0-8108-3333-6*); pap. 29.50 (*0-8108-3330-1*) Scarecrow.
— Lyle's Administration of the College Library. 5th ed. LC 92-6328. (Illus.). 621p. 1992. 61.00 (*0-8108-2552-X*); 73.00 (*0-8108-2578-3*) Scarecrow.
Coughlin, Charles E. Father Coughlin's "Last Testament", 4 vols., Set. 1991. lib. bdg. 179.95 (*0-8490-4409-X*) Gordon Pr.
***Coughlin, Charles E.** Money! Questions & Answers. 192p. 1998. pap. 7.00 (*0-944379-24-9*) CPA Bk Pub.
Coughlin, Charles E. Sermons, 2 vols., Set. 1972. 250.00 (*0-8490-1025-X*) Gordon Pr.
Coughlin, Dan. Inside Out: A Catalyst for Conscious Living. 128p. (Orig.). 1995. pap. 10.00 (*0-9648770-0-7*) Pos Pubng.
***Coughlin, Deborah.** The Mainstreaming Handbook: Legal Guidance & Classroom Strategies. LC 99-55088. 144p. 2000. pap. text 15.00 (*0-325-00226-6*) Heinemann.
Coughlin, Edward V. Adelardo Lopez de Ayala. LC 77-5670. (Twayne's World Authors Ser.). 152p. (C). 1977. 17.95 (*0-8057-6303-1*) Irvington.
Coughlin, Edward V., ed. from SPA. Poems by Roberto Sosa. LC 83-72296. 119p. 1984. 14.00 (*0-938972-06-5*) Spanish Lit Pubns.
Coughlin, Eileen V., ed. Successful Drug & Alcohol Prevention Programs. LC 85-644751. (New Directions for Student Services Ser.: No. SS 67). 97p. (Orig.). 1994. pap. 22.00 (*0-7879-9996-2*) Jossey-Bass.
Coughlin, F. Edward, ed. Selected Works of Spiritual Theology. (Works of Saint Bonaventure: No. 7). 275p. Date not set. pap. write for info. (*1-57659-162-X*) Franciscan Inst.
Coughlin, George G. Will Requirements of Various States. 40p. 1984. write for info. (*0-318-59084-0*) Am Coll Trust & Est.
Coughlin, George G., Jr. Your Handbook of Everyday Law: Fifth Edition. 5th rev. ed. LC 93-25283. Orig. Title: Your Introduction to Law. 464p. 1993. pap. 16.00 (*0-06-273240-4*, Harper Ref) HarpC.
Coughlin, James, jt. auth. see LaRocco, Christine.
Coughlin, James P. Diary of a County Executive. 160p. 1991. 15.95 (*0-938627-14-7*) New Past Pr.
— Fifty Years of Village Service. Goc, Michael J., ed. (Illus.). 256p. 1996. 29.95 (*0-938627-31-7*) New Past Pr.
Coughlin, James P. & Baran, Robert H. Neural Computation in Hopfield Networks & Boltzmann Machines. LC 94-23048. (Illus.). 296p. 1995. 38.50 (*0-87413-464-1*) U Delaware Pr.
Coughlin, Kari. Rhyolite Activity Book. 48p. 1994. pap. 3.00 (*1-885770-02-2*) Frnds Rhyolite.
— Rhyolite Activity Book. rev. ed. (Illus.). 80p. 1994. pap. 10.00 (*1-885770-03-0*) Frnds Rhyolite.
Coughlin, Kari, jt. auth. see Graves, Kate.
Coughlin, Katie. Semi-Analytic Methods for the Navier-Stokes Equations. LC 99-14403. (CRM Proceedings & Lecture Notes). xiv, 119p. 1999. write for info. (*0-8218-0878-8*) Am Math.
Coughlin, Ken, ed. 1998 Medicaid Managed Behavioral Care Sourcebook. (Illus.). 495p. 1997. pap. text 195.00 (*1-57987-008-2*) Faulkner & Gray.
— 1999 Medicaid Managed Behavioral Care Sourcebook: Strategies & Opportunities for Providers & Purchasers. LC 99-192066. (Illus.). 560p. 1998. pap. 225.00 (*1-57987-047-3*) Faulkner & Gray.
— 1999 Medical Quality Management Sourcebook: A Comprehensive Guide to Measuring Quality & Applying the Results. rev. ed. 608p. 1998. pap. 250.00 (*1-57987-087-2*) Faulkner & Gray.
— 1997 Behavioral Outcomes & Guidelines Sourcebook. (Illus.). 575p. 1996. pap. text 295.00 (*1-881393-93-3*) Faulkner & Gray.
Coughlin, Ken & Youngs, Maralee, eds. 1997 Medical Quality Management Sourcebook. 524p. 1996. 275.00 (*1-881393-85-2*) Faulkner & Gray.
Coughlin, Kenneth, jt. ed. see Levy, Eric.
Coughlin, Kenneth M., ed. 1998 Behavioral Outcomer & Guideliner Sourcebook: A Practical Guide to Measuring, Managing & Standardizing Mental Health & Substance Abuse Treatment. 672p. 1997. pap. 295.00 (*1-57987-030-9*) Faulkner & Gray.
— 1999 Behavioral Outcomes & Guidelines Sourcebook. 736p. 1998. pap. 295.00 (*1-57987-091-0*) Faulkner & Gray.
— 1999 Medicaid Managed Care Sourcebook. 560p. 1998. pap. 265.00 (*1-57987-105-4*) Faulkner & Gray.
— 1997 Guide to Behavioral Resources on the Internet: A Review of Mental Health & Substance Abuse Web Sites, Mailing Lists & Support Forms. (Illus.). 519p. (Orig.). 1997. pap. text 245.00 (*1-881393-99-2*) Faulkner & Gray.
***Coughlin, Kenneth M., ed.** 2000 Post Acute Outcomes Sourcebook: A Guide to Methods, Measures & Strategies in Post Acute Care. (Illus.). 545p. 1999. pap. 265.00 (*1-57987-112-7*) Faulkner & Gray.
***Coughlin, Kenneth M. & Trabin, Tom, eds.** Behavioral Outcomes & Guidelines Sourcebook 2000: A Practical Guide to Measuring, Managing & Standardizing Mental Health & Substance Abuse Treatment. (Illus.). 774p. 1999. pap. 295.00 (*1-57987-122-4*) Faulkner & Gray.
Coughlin, Kenneth M. & Wingerson, Lois, eds. 1998 Medicaid Managed Care Sourcebook. 558p. 1997. pap. 245.00 (*1-57987-041-4*) Faulkner & Gray.
Coughlin, Mary Ann & Pagano, Marian. Case Study Applications of Statistics in Institutional Research. No. 10. 66p. (C). 1997. pap. text 15.25 (*1-882393-06-6*) Assn Instl Res.
Coughlin, Michael E., et al, eds. Benjamin R. Tucker & the Champions of Liberty: A Centenary Anthology. LC 86-11647. (Illus.). 228p. (Orig.). 1986. 15.00 (*0-9602574-4-6*); pap. 7.95 (*0-9602574-5-4*) M E Coughlin.
Coughlin, Pam, jt. auth. see Dratfield, Jim.
Coughlin, Patricia. The Awakening. 1993. mass mkt. 3.39 (*0-373-09804-9*, 5-09804-1) Silhouette.
— The Bargain. (Men Made in America Ser.). 1995. mass mkt. 3.59 (*0-373-45189-X*, 1-45189-7) Harlequin Bks.
— Borrowed Bride. (Intimate Moments Ser.: No. 722). 242p. 1996. per. 3.99 (*0-373-07722-X*, 1-07722-1) Silhouette.
— Her Brother's Keeper. (Special Edition Ser.: No. 726). 1992. mass mkt. 3.29 (*0-373-09726-3*, 5-09726-6) Harlequin Bks.
— Joyride. (Congratulations Ser.). 1995. per. 3.75 (*0-373-09982-7*) Harlequin Bks.
— The Last Frontier. (Men Made in America Ser.). 1995. mass mkt. 3.59 (*0-373-45190-3*, 1-45190-5) Harlequin Bks.
— Lord Savage. 448p. 1996. mass mkt. 5.50 (*0-553-57520-1*, Fanfare) Bantam.
— Love Child. (Silhouette Ser.: No. 245). 1992. mass mkt. 4.99 (*0-373-48245-0*) Silhouette.
— Love in the First Degree: Romantic Traditions. (Intimate Moments Ser.). 1995. per. 3.75 (*0-373-07632-0*, 1-07632-2) Silhouette.
— Mail Order Cowboy. large type ed. (Silhouette Romance Ser.). 1995. 18.95 (*0-373-59639-1*) Harlequin Bks.
— Merely Married. 327p. 1998. mass mkt. 5.99 (*0-553-57521-X*) BDD Bks Young Read.
— My Sweet Baby. 1993. per. 3.50 (*0-373-09837-5*, 5-09837-1) Silhouette.
— When Stars Collide. (Special Edition Ser.). 1994. per. 3.50 (*0-373-09867-7*, 5-09867-8) Silhouette.
Coughlin, Paul. Timeless New York: A Literary & Photographic Tribute. (Illus.). 80p. 1998. 19.95 (*0-7893-0240-3*, Pub. by Universe) St Martin.
Coughlin, Paul, jt. auth. see Dratfield, Jim.
Coughlin, Paul T. Secrets, Plots & Hidden Agendas: What You Don't Know about Conspiracy Theories. LC 98-29822. 228p. 1999. pap. 12.99 (*0-8308-1624-0*, 1624) InterVarsity.
Coughlin, Peter & Ikiara, Gerrishon K., eds. Industrialization in Kenya: In Search of a Strategy. 328p. (Orig.). (C). 1989. pap. text 22.50 (*0-435-08033-4*, 08033) Heinemann.
Coughlin, Peter J. Probabilistic Voting Theory. (Illus.). 266p. (C). 1992. text 69.95 (*0-521-36052-8*) Cambridge U Pr.
Coughlin, R. E., et al. Urban Analysis for Branch Library System Planning. 1. LC 71-133496. (Contributions in Librarianship & Information Science Ser.: No. 1). 167p. (C). 1972. 45.00 (*0-8371-5161-9*, CLP/, Greenwood Pr) Greenwood.
Coughlin, Ramona, tr. see Green, Krister.
Coughlin, Raymond F., jt. auth. see Zitarelli, David E.
Coughlin, Richard J. Double Identity: The Chinese in Modern Thailand. LC 76-42298. (Illus.). 222p. 1977. reprint ed. lib. bdg. 35.00 (*0-8371-9292-7*, CODI, Greenwood Pr) Greenwood.
Coughlin, Richard M., ed. Morality, Rationality, & Efficiency: New Perspectives on Socio-Economics. LC 90-19137. (Studies in Socio-Economics). 432p. (gr. 13). 1991. pap. text 42.95 (*0-87332-822-1*) M E Sharpe.
— Morality, Rationality, & Efficiency: New Perspectives on Socio-Economics. LC 90-19137. (Studies in Socio-Economics). 432p. (C). (gr. 13). 1991. text 87.95 (*0-87332-821-3*) M E Sharpe.
Coughlin, Robert D. A Storybook Site: The Early History & Construction of Buford Dam. LC 97-77681. (Illus.). vi, 390p. 1998. 59.95 (*0-9662245-0-7*) R D Coughlin.
Coughlin, Robert E. Agricultural Land Conversion in the Urban-Rural Fringe. Stevens, Benjamin H., ed. (Discussion Papers: No. 111). 39p. 1979. pap. 10.00 (*1-55869-139-1*) Regional Sci Res Inst.
— Criteria for Open Space System Planning: An Exploratory Survey & Synthesis. (Discussion Papers: No. 83). 1975. pap. 10.00 (*1-55869-021-2*) Regional Sci Res Inst.
— Goal Attainment Levels in One Hundred & One Metropolitan Areas. (Discussion Papers: No. 41). 1970. pap. 10.00 (*1-55869-050-6*) Regional Sci Res Inst.
— The Perception & Valuation of Water Quality: A Review of Research Method & Findings. (Discussion Papers: No. 80). 1975. pap. 10.00 (*1-55869-091-3*) Regional Sci Res Inst.
— State Standards & Local Planning Regulation for Farmland Preservation in Oregon. Stevens, Benjamin H., ed. (Discussion Papers: No. 124). 67p. (Orig.). 1981. pap. 10.00 (*1-55869-001-8*) Regional Sci Res Inst.
— The Transfer of Development Rights: Buckingham Township (Bucks County, PA) & Other Experiences. Stevens, Benjamin H., ed. (Discussion Papers: No. 126). 61p. (Orig.). 1981. pap. 10.00 (*1-55869-003-4*) Regional Sci Res Inst.
Coughlin, Robert E. & Fritz, James. Land Values & Environmental Characteristics in the Rural-Urban Fringe. (Discussion Papers: No. 45). 1971. pap. 10.00 (*1-55869-066-2*) Regional Sci Res Inst.
Coughlin, Robert E. & Goldstein, Karen A. The Extent of Agreement among Observers on Environmental Attractiveness. (Discussion Papers: No. 37). 1970. pap. 10.00 (*1-55869-045-X*) Regional Sci Res Inst.
— The Public's View of the Outdoor Environment As Interpreted by Magazine Ad-Makers. (Discussion Papers: No. 25). 1968. pap. 10.00 (*1-55869-102-2*) Regional Sci Res Inst.
Coughlin, Robert E. & Isard, Walter. Planning Efficient Hospital Systems. (Discussion Papers: No. 1). 1963. pap. 10.00 (*1-55869-094-8*) Regional Sci Res Inst.
Coughlin, Robert E. & Kawashima, Tatsuhiko. Property Values & Open Space in Northwest Philadelphia: An Empirical Analysis. (Discussion Papers: No. 64). 1973. pap. 10.00 (*1-55869-101-4*) Regional Sci Res Inst.
Coughlin, Robert E. & Plaut, Thomas. The Use of Less-Than-Fee Acquisition for the Preservation of Open Space. (Discussion Papers: No. 101). 1977. pap. 10.00 (*1-55869-131-6*) Regional Sci Res Inst.
Coughlin, Robert E. & Scherer, Ursala. A Pilot Household Survey of Perception & Use of a Large Urban Park. (Discussion Papers: No. 59). 1972. pap. 10.00 (*1-55869-093-X*) Regional Sci Res Inst.
Coughlin, Robert E., et al. The Activity Structure & Transportation Requirements of a Major University Hospital. (Discussion Papers: No. 4). 1964. pap. 10.00 (*1-55869-007-7*) Regional Sci Res Inst.
— Agricultural Land Evaluation & Site Assessment: Status of State & Local Programs. 397p. 1991. spiral bd. 45.00 (*1-884320-01-5*) ASU Herberger Ctr.
— Differential Assessment of Real Property As an Incentive to Open Space Preservation & Farmland Retention, No. 102. 1978. pap. 10.00 (*1-55869-025-5*) Regional Sci Res Inst.
— The Distribution of Social Service Facilities Within the City of Philadelphia. (Discussion Papers: No. 93). 1976. pap. 10.00 (*1-55869-027-1*) Regional Sci Res Inst.
— The Intensity of Development along Small & Medium Sized Streams in Suburban Philadelphia. (Discussion Papers: No. 50). 1971. pap. 10.00 (*1-55869-060-3*) Regional Sci Res Inst.
— An Investigation of Location Factors Influencing the Economy of the Philadelphia Region. (Discussion Papers: No. 12). 1967. pap. 10.00 (*1-55869-064-6*) Regional Sci Res Inst.
— Perception & Use of Streams in Suburban Areas: Effects of Water Quality & of Distance from Residence to Stream. (Discussion Papers: No. 53). 1972. pap. 10.00 (*1-55869-090-5*) Regional Sci Res Inst.
— Perceptions of Landfill Operations Held by Nearby Residents. (Discussion Papers: No. 65). 1973. pap. 10.00 (*1-55869-092-1*) Regional Sci Res Inst.
Coughlin, Robert E., jt. auth. see Berry, David.
Coughlin, Robert E., jt. auth. see Rabinowitz, Carla B.
Coughlin, Robert E., jt. auth. see Rosenberger, Lisa.
Coughlin, Robert E., jt. auth. see Stevens, Benjamin H.
Coughlin, Robert F. & Driscoll, Fred F. Operational Amplifiers & Linear Intergrated Circuits. 5th ed. LC 97-14621. 515p. (C). 1997. 97.00 (*0-13-206541-X*) P-H.
***Coughlin, Robert F. & Driscoll, Frederick F.** Operational Amplifiers & Linear Intergrated Circuits. 6th ed. LC 00-40633. 2001. write for info. (*0-13-014991-8*) P-H.
Coughlin, Robert F., jt. auth. see Driscoll, Frederick F., Jr.
Coughlin, Robert W., see Caldwell, John, pseud.
Coughlin, Robert W., ed. see Caldwell, John, pseud.
Coughlin, Roberta. The Gardener's Companion: A Book of Lists & Lore. LC 89-45643. (Illus.). 448p. 1990. reprint ed. pap. 12.95 (*0-00-001516-4*) HarperTrade.
Coughlin, Ruth. Grieving: A Love Story. large type ed. LC 94-918. 192p. 1994. lib. bdg. 21.95 (*0-8161-5962-9*, G K Hall Lrg Type) Mac Lib Ref.
Coughlin, Sally. Health Care for the Medically Indigent. (Orig.). 1986. pap. text 1.00 (*0-915757-10-9*) League Women Voters TX.
Coughlin, Sean T. Storming the Desert: A Marine Lieutenant's Day-by-Day Chronicle of the Persian Gulf War. LC 96-27287. (Illus.). 176p. 1996. pap. 19.95 (*0-7864-0195-8*) McFarland & Co.
Coughlin, Steven S. Ethics in Epidemiology & Public Health Practice: Collected Works. 232p. 1997. pap., per. 19.95 (*0-9661520-0-X*) S S Coughlin.
Coughlin, Steven S., ed. Ethics in Epidemiology & Clinical Research: Annotated Readings. LC 95-7873. 272p. (C). 1995. pap. text 35.00 (*0-917227-08-5*) Epidemiology.
Coughlin, Steven S., et al, eds. Case Studies in Public Health Ethics. LC 97-76770. 182p. (Orig.). 1997. pap., teacher ed. 37.00 (*0-87553-232-2*) Am Pub Health.
Coughlin, Steven S. & Beauchamp, Thomas L., eds. Ethics & Epidemiology. 320p. (C). 1996. text 52.50 (*0-19-510242-8*) OUP.
***Coughlin, T. Glen.** Steady Eddie. 2001. 23.00 (*1-56947-221-1*) Soho Press.
Coughlin, Teresa A., et al. Medicaid since 1980: Cost, Coverage, & the Shifting Alliance Between the Federal Government & the States. 200p. 1994. pap. text 23.00 (*0-87766-618-0*); lib. bdg. 49.00 (*0-87766-617-2*) Urban Inst.
***Coughlin, Thomas E.** Maggie May's Diary, 1. LC 98-73598. 1998. pap. 13.95 (*0-9666202-0-8*) Fitzgerald & LaChapelle.
Coughlin, William. The Heart of Justice, Vol. 1. 1995. mass mkt. 6.99 (*0-312-95551-0*, Pub. by Tor Bks) St Martin.
Coughlin, William J. The Court. 384p. 2000. mass mkt. 6.99 (*0-312-97027-X*, St Martins Paperbacks) St Martin.
— Day of Wrath. 1994. lib. bdg. 45.95 (*1-56849-409-2*) Buccaneer Bks.
— Death Penalty. 432p. 1993. mass mkt. 5.99 (*0-06-109053-0*, Harp PBks) HarpC.
— The Destruction Committee. 1994. lib. bdg. 37.95 (*1-56849-408-4*) Buccaneer Bks.
— Her Father's Daughter. 1994. lib. bdg. 39.95 (*1-56849-406-8*) Buccaneer Bks.
— Her Honor. 1994. lib. bdg. 39.95 (*1-56849-405-X*) Buccaneer Bks.
— In the Presence of Enemies. 1994. mass mkt. 6.99 (*0-312-95164-7*) St Martin.
— The Judgement. LC 97-13265. 352p. 1997. text 24.95 (*0-312-15558-1*) St Martin.
— The Judgement. abr. large type ed. 352p. 1995. lib. bdg. 27.00 incl. audio (*1-57490-025-0*, Beeler LP Bks) T T Beeler.
— The Judgment. large type ed. LC 97-36861. (CD Ser.). 613p. 1997. 26.95 (*0-7862-1243-8*) Thorndike Pr.
— The Judgment, Vol. 1. 424p. 1999. mass mkt. 6.99 (*0-312-96244-4*, St Martins Paperbacks) St Martin.
— Shadow of a Doubt. 1993. mass mkt. 6.99 (*0-312-92745-2*) St Martin.
— Shadow of a Doubt. large type ed. (General Ser.). 562p. 1992. 18.95 (*0-8161-5346-9*, G K Hall Lrg Type); lib. bdg. 21.95 (*0-8161-5345-0*, G K Hall Lrg Type) Mac Lib Ref.
— The Stalking Man, Vol. 1. 345p. 1998. mass mkt. 6.99 (*0-312-96487-0*, St Martins Paperbacks) St Martin.
— The Twelve Apostles. 1994. lib. bdg. 41.95 (*1-56849-407-6*) Buccaneer Bks.
Coughran, Jane, jt. auth. see Botkin, Jana.
Coughran, Mabel H. Horas Encantadas. (SPA., Illus.). 128p. 1994. pap. 9.06 (*0-8442-7656-1*, 76561, Natl Textbk Co) NTC Contemp Pub Co.
Coughran, Mabel H. Horas Encantadas: Playlets, Poems, Songs, & Word Games. (ENG & SPA.). (J). 1977. 13.05 (*0-606-01282-6*, Pub. by Turtleback) Demco.
Coughran, W. M., Jr., et al, eds. Semiconductors, Pt. I. LC 93-50622. (IMA Volumes in Mathematics & Its Applications Ser.: Vol. 58). (Illus.). xxiv, 154p. 1994. 65.95 (*0-387-94250-5*) Spr-Verlag.
— Semiconductors, Pt. II. LC 93-50622. (IMA Volumes in Mathematics & Its Applications Ser.: Vol. 59). (Illus.). xxii, 408p. 1994. 89.95 (*0-387-94251-3*) Spr-Verlag.
Coughtrey, P. J., et al. Radionuclide Distribution & Transport in Terrestrial & Aquatic Ecosystems: A Critical Review of Data, 6 vols. 2544p. 1983. 1106.00 (*90-6191-277-6*, Pub. by A A Balkema) Ashgate Pub Co.
Coughtry, Jamie, ed. George L. Ullom: Politics & Development in Las Vegas, 1930s-1970s. (Illus.). 152p. 1989. lib. bdg. 37.50 (*1-56475-342-5*); fiche. write for info. (*1-56475-343-3*) U NV Oral Hist.
— Woodrow Wilson: Race, Community & Politics in Las Vegas, 1940s-1980s. (Illus.). 1989. fiche. write for info. (*1-56475-345-X*) U NV Oral Hist.
— Woodrow Wilson: Race, Community & Politics in Las Vegas, 1940s-1980s. (Illus.). 160p. 1990. lib. bdg. 37.50 (*1-56475-344-1*) U NV Oral Hist.
Coughtry, Jamie & King, R. T., eds. Lubertha Johnson: Civil Rights Efforts in Las Vegas, 1940s-1960s. (Illus.). 88p. 1988. write for info. (*1-56475-334-4*); lib. bdg. 32.50 (*1-56475-333-6*); fiche. write for info. (*1-56475-335-2*) U NV Oral Hist.
Coughtry, Jamie, jt. ed. see Blue, Helen M.
Coughtry, Jamie, jt. ed. see King, R. T.
Coughtry, Jay, et al. Papers of the American Slave Trade. LC 97-46700. (Black Studies Research Sources). 1997. pap. text 3170.00 (*1-55655-650-0*); pap. text 4135.00 (*1-55655-651-9*) U Pubns Amer.

An Asterisk (*) at the beginning of an entry indicates that the title is appearing for the first time.

Cougias, Dorian, et al. Designing Appletalk Network Architectures. (Network Frontiers Field Manual Ser.). (Illus.). 389p. 1996. pap. text 34.95 (*0-12-192566-8*) Acad Pr.

Cougill, Wynne, ed. see Green, Marshall.

Cougny, Gaston, jt. auth. see Robert, Adolphe.

Couhig, Mark S. Environmental Health & Safety Manager's Guide to the Internet. rev. ed. 1995. ring bd. 99.95 (*0-614-08831-3*, 170006) Busn Legal Reports.

Couillard, Mike, et al. Miracle on the Mountain: A True Tale of Faith & Survival. LC 97-29978. 256p. 1998. mass mkt. 20.00 (*0-380-97392-8*, Avon Bks) Morrow Avon.

— Miracle on the Mountain: A True Tale of Faith & Survival. LC 97-29978. 256p. 1999. mass mkt. 5.99 (*0-380-78979-5*, Avon Bks) Morrow Avon.

Coukoulis, Peter P. Guru, Psychotherapist & Self: A Comparative Study of the Guru-Disciple Relationship & the Jungian Analytic Process. 1977. 14.00 (*0-87516-222-3*); pap. 8.90 (*0-87516-221-5*) DeVorss.

Coulabin, H. Dictionnaire des Locutions Populaires du Bon Pays de Rennes en Bretagne. (FRE.). 392p. 1978. 85.00 (*0-7859-7989-1*, 2734802961) Fr & Eur.

Coulam, Robert F. & Smith, Richard A., eds. Managerial Cognition & Organizational Information Vol. 2: Research on Public Organizations. 311p. 1985. 73.25 (*0-89232-425-2*) Jai Pr.

Coulange, Bernard. Software Reuse. Craig, I., tr. from FRE. LC 97-29212. (Illus.). xiii, 293p. 1997. pap. 74.95 (*3-540-76084-9*) Spr-Verlag.

Coulanges, Claudine & Daniel, Flake. Un Coup d'Oeil sur la France. 2nd ed. (FRE.). 144p. (C). 1991. pap. 15.45 (*0-8442-1235-0*, VF1235-0) NTC Contemp Pub Co.

Coulanges, Numa D. De, see De Coulanges, Numa D.

Coulbourn, John. Selection of Teachers in Large City School Systems. LC 72-176673. (Columbia University. Teachers College. Contributions to Education Ser.: No. 740). reprint ed. 37.50 (*0-404-55740-6*) AMS Pr.

Coulbourn, Keith & O'Barry, Richard. Behind the Dolphin Smile. 288p. pap. 15.95 (*1-58063-101-0*) Renaissance.

Coulbourn, Keith, jt. auth. see O'Barry, Richard.

***Coulby, David.** World Yearbook of Education: Education of Times of Crisis, 2000. 2000. 69.95 (*0-7494-2504-0*) Kogan Page Ltd.

Coulby, David & Bash, Leslie. The Education Reform Act: Competition & Control. 144p. 1989. pap. text 29.95 (*0-304-31768-3*) Continuum.

Coulby, David & Ward, Stephen, eds. The Primary Core National Curriculum: Policy into Practice. 2nd ed. (Education Ser.). (Illus.). 160p. 1996. pap. 29.95 (*0-304-33804-4*) Continuum.

Coulby, David, jt. ed. see Booth, Tony.

Couldery, Fred. Understanding Accounts. 2nd ed. 100p. 1998. pap. 44.00 (*0-85297-483-3*, Pub. by Chartered Bank) St Mut.

Couldrette 14th/15th Century & Skeat, Walter W. The Romans of Partenay, or of Lusignen: Otherwise Known as the Tale of Melusine. LC 78-9953. (Early English Text Society [publications]). 287 p. 1969. write for info. (*0-8371-1783-6*, Greenwood Pr) Greenwood.

Couldrey, V. Art of Louis Comfort Tiffany. 192p. 1996. 24.98 (*1-55521-447-9*) Bk Sales Inc.

***Couldry, Nick.** Place of Media Power. (Comedia Ser.). 240p. 2000. pap. 27.99 (*0-415-21315-0*); text 75.00 (*0-415-21314-2*) Routledge.

Coulehan, Jack. First Photographs of Heaven. Zarucchi, Roy & Page, Carolyn, eds. (Poetry Ser.). (Illus.). 60p. (Orig.). 1994. pap. 9.95 (*1-879205-49-1*) Nightshade Pr.

Coulehan, Jack, jt. ed. see Belli, Angela.

Coulehan, John L. & Block, Marian R. The Medical Interview: Mastering Skills for Clinical Practice. 3rd ed. LC 97-6737. (Illus.). 287p. (C). 1997. pap. text 29.95 (*0-8036-0267-7*) Davis Co.

Coules, Victoria. Forces of the Wild. LC 99-474912. 1999. 29.95 (*0-7137-2745-4*) Blandford Pr.

Coulet, Henri, ed. see Marivaux, A.

Coulet, Pierre R., jt. ed. see Blum, Loic J.

Coulette, Henri. The Collected Poems of Henri Coulette. Justice, Donald & Mezey, Robert, eds. 270p. 1990. pap. 18.00 (*1-55728-145-9*) U of Ark Pr.

Couliano, Ioan P. Eros & Magic in the Renaissance. Cook, Margaret, tr. (Illus.). 296p. (Orig.). 1987. pap. text 15.00 (*0-226-12316-2*) U Ch Pr.

— Eros & Magic in the Renaissance. Cook, Margaret, tr. (Illus.). 296p. (Orig.). 1998. lib. bdg. 42.00 (*0-226-12315-4*) U Ch Pr.

Coulibaly, Modibo D. & Green, Rodney. Segregation in Federally Subsidized Low-Income Housing in the United States. LC 97-23347. (Praeger Series in Political Economy). 168p. 1998. 65.00 (*0-275-94820-X*, Praeger Pubs) Greenwood.

Coulie, Bernard. Role of 5-Hydroxytryptamine-1 Receptors in the Regulation of Gastrointestinal Motility. (Acta Biomedica Lovaniensia Ser.: No. 129). (Illus.). 141p. (Orig.). 1996. pap. 42.50 (*90-6186-742-8*, Pub. by Leuven Univ) Coronet Bks.

Couling, Della, ed. Dutch Plays. LC 97-160285. (International Collection). 256p. (Orig.). 1997. pap. 25.95 (*1-85459-289-0*, Pub. by N Hern Bks) Theatre Comm.

Couling, Della, tr. see Meulenbelt, Anja, et al, eds.

Coull, Alex, jt. auth. see Stafford-Smith, Bryan S.

Coull, Cheryl. A Traveller's Guide to Aboriginal B. C. (Illus.). 280p. 1996. pap. 15.95 (*1-55110-402-4*) Whitecap Bks.

Coull, David C. The Law of Bankruptcy in Scotland. 395p. 1989. boxed set 114.00 (*0-406-10170-1*, U.K., MICHIE) LEXIS Pub.

Coull, James R. Sea Fisheries in Scotland. 336p. 1996. 90.00 (*0-85976-410-9*, Pub. by J Donald) St Mut.

***Coull, Sam.** Nothing But My Sword: The Life of James Keith. 224p. 2000. pap. 19.95 (*1-84158-024-4*, Pub. by Birlinn Ltd) Dufour.

Coullet, P. & Huerre, P., eds. New Trends in Nonlinear Dynamics & Pattern-Forming Phenomena: The Geometry of Nonequilibrium. (NATO ASI Ser.: Vol. 231). (Illus.). 368p. (C). 1990. text 144.00 (*0-306-43692-2*, Kluwer Plenum) Kluwer Academic.

Coulling, Kate, jt. auth. see Brophy, Peter.

Coulling, Mary P. The Lee Girls. (Illus.). 242p. (Orig.). 1996. pap. 12.95 (*0-89587-147-5*) Blair.

Coulmas, Florian. The Blackwell Encyclopedia of Writing Systems. (Illus.). 640p. 1996. text 88.95 (*0-631-19446-0*) Blackwell Pubs.

— The Blackwell Encyclopedia of Writing Systems. 640p. 1999. reprint ed. pap. 34.95 (*0-631-21481-X*) Blackwell Pubs.

— A Festschrift for Native Speaker. (Janua Linguarum, Series Major: No. 97). 406p. 1981. 88.50 (*90-279-3498-3*) Mouton.

— The Handbook of Sociolinguistics. LC 95-47148. (Handbooks in Linguistics Ser.: Vol. 4). (Illus.). 544p. (C). 1996. 99.95 (*0-631-19339-1*) Blackwell Pubs.

— The Handbook of Sociolinguistics. LC 98-26119. (Blackwell Handbooks in Linguistics). 544p. 1998. reprint ed. pap. 34.95 (*0-631-21193-4*) Blackwell Pubs.

— The Writing Systems of the World. (Language Library). 1993. pap. 28.95 (*0-631-18028-1*) Blackwell Pubs.

Coulmas, Florian, ed. Conversational Routine. (Janua Linguarum, Series Major: Vol. 2). 1980. text 70.80 (*90-279-3098-8*) Mouton.

— Direct & Indirect Speech. (Trends in Linguistics, Studies & Monographs: No. 31). (Illus.). x, 370p. 1986. text 130.80 (*0-89925-176-5*) Mouton.

— Journal of Asian Pacific Communication Vol. 2: The Economics of Language in the Pacific. 200p. 1991. pap. 100.00 (*0-685-52424-8*, Pub. by Multilingual Matters) Taylor & Francis.

— A Language Policy for the European Community: Prospects & Quandries. LC 91-32522. (Contributions to the Sociology of Language Ser.: No. 61). x, 311p. (C). 1991. lib. bdg. 113.85 (*3-11-012869-1*) Mouton.

— Linguistic Minorities & Literacy: Language Policy Issues in Developing Countries. LC 84-14746. (Trends in Linguistics, Studies & Monographs: No. 26). (Illus.). x, 133p. 1984. 40.00 (*3-11-009867-9*) Mouton.

Coulmas, Florian & Ehlich, Konrad, eds. Writing in Focus. LC 83-13095. (Trends in Linguistics, Studies & Monographs: No. 24). viii, 405p. 1983. 126.95 (*90-279-3359-6*) Mouton.

Coulmas, Florian, et al. Small Japanese-German Form Lexicon: Kleines Formlexikon Japanisch-Deutsch. (GER & JPN.). 216p. 1983. 59.95 (*0-8288-1017-6*, M15780) Fr & Eur.

Coulomb, J. Sea Floor Spreading & Continental Drift. Tanner, R. W., tr. from FRE. LC 79-179891. (Geophysics & Astrophysics Monographs: No. 2). 184p. 1972. pap. text 70.50 (*90-277-0238-1*); lib. bdg. 82.50 (*90-277-0232-2*) Kluwer Academic.

Coulombe, Charles A. Everyman Today Call Rome. 2nd rev. ed. LC 87-72184. 144p. (Orig.). 1988. pap., student ed. 7.95 (*0-944455-00-X*) Charlemagne Pr.

— The White Cockade: A Book of Poetry & Verse. Farrell, J. Fred, ed. (Illus.). 100p. (Orig.). (C). 1990. pap. text 10.00 (*0-685-45128-3*) Charlemagne Pr.

Coulombe, Deborah, ed. Flippers & Flukes Marine Mammals Coloring Book. (Illus.). 16p. (J). (ps-3). 1996. pap. 3.95 (*1-878244-14-0*) Monterey Bay Aquarium.

Coulombe, Deborah A. The Seaside Naturalist: A Guide to Study at the Seashore. (Illus.). 256p. 1990. per. 15.00 (*0-671-76503-5*) S&S Trade Pap.

Coulombe, Pierre A. Language Rights in French Canada. 2nd ed. (Francophone Cultures & Literatures Ser.: Vol. 2). VIII, 183p. (C). 1997. reprint ed. pap. text 32.95 (*0-8204-3938-X*) P Lang Pubng.

***Coulombe, Raymond M.** Transdimensional Blues: A Science Fiction Tale. LC 99-91545. 1999. 25.00 (*0-7388-0868-7*); pap. 18.00 (*0-7388-0869-5*) Xlibris Corp.

Coulombre, Rich. FILEMAKR PRO 2 0 MAC: 480p. 1992. pap. text 36.95 (*0-201-62212-2*) Addison-Wesley.

***Coulombre, Rich.** Special Edition Using Filemaker Pro 5. (Illus.). 700p. 2000. 39.99 (*0-7897-2201-1*) Que.

Coulombre, Rich & Price, Jonathan. Filemaker Pro 2.0 WIN. LC 93-7002. 464p. 1993. pap. text 34.95 (*0-201-62213-0*) Addison-Wesley.

Coulon, A., ed. Inventaire des Sceaux de la Bourgogne. 1990. reprint ed. 110.00 (*3-262-00239-9*) Periodicals Srv.

Coulon, Alain. Ethnomethodology, Vol. 36. (Qualitative Research Methods Ser.). 96p. 1995. 24.00 (*0-8039-4776-3*); pap. 10.50 (*0-8039-4777-1*) Sage.

Coulon, Christian, jt. auth. see Boillot, Gilbert.

Coulon, Christian, jt. ed. see O'Brien, Donal B.

Coulon, Frederic De, see De Coulon, Frederic.

Coulon, Jenny, tr. see Laidi, Zaki.

Coulon, Jocelyn. Soldiers of Diplomacy (Les Casques Bleus) The United Nations, Peacekeeping & the New World Order. Aronoff, Phyllis & Scott, Howard, trs. from FRE. LC 98-229699. 272p. 1998. text 35.00 (*0-8020-0899-2*) U of Toronto Pr.

Coulonges, Georges. La Madelon de l'An 40. large type ed. 1996. pap. 25.99 (*2-84011-145-4*) Ulverscroft.

Coulont-Henderson, Francoise. Le Desir de la Voix Vive: Etude du "Ton" Chez Stendhal. LC 90-70980. (FRE.). 176p. 1990. lib. bdg. 28.95 (*0-917786-79-3*) Summa Pubns.

Couloumbis, Audrey. Getting Near to Baby. LC 99-18191. 224p. (J). (gr. 5-9). 1999. 17.99 (*0-399-23389-X*, G P Putnam) Peng Put Young Read.

***Couloumbis, Audrey.** Getting near to Baby. LC 00-34375. (Illus.). (J). 2000. write for info. (*0-7862-2765-2*) Thorndike Pr.

Couloumbis, Theodore A. Greek Political Reaction to American & NATO Influences. LC 66-12491. 260p. reprint ed. pap. 80.60 (*0-608-14186-0*, 202199100024) Bks Demand.

Couloumbis, Theodore A., et al, eds. Foreign Interference in Greek Politics. LC 76-45495. 171p. 1976. text 12.00 (*0-918618-03-7*); pap. text 7.00 (*0-918618-02-9*) Pella Pub.

Couloumbis, Theodore A. & Iatrides, John O., eds. Greek American Relations: A Critical Review. LC 80-80007. 263p. 1980. pap. text 10.00 (*0-918618-17-7*) Pella Pub.

Couloumbis, Theodore A. & Wolfe, James H. Introduction to International Relations. 4th ed. 448p. (C). 1989. pap. text 37.60 (*0-13-484684-2*) P-H.

***Coulouris, George.** Distributed Systems. 3rd ed. 672p. (C). 2000. text 70.00 (*0-201-61918-0*) Addison-Wesley.

Coulouris, George. Distributed Systems: Concepts & Design. 2nd ed. LC 94-153222. 644p. (C). 1994. 60.00 (*0-201-62433-8*) Addison-Wesley.

Coulouris, George & Dollimore, Jean. Distributed Systems: Concepts & Design. (International Computer Science Ser.). (Illus.). 320p. (C). 1988. text 43.25 (*0-201-18059-6*) Addison-Wesley.

Coulson. Future of the Organisation: Achieving Excellence. pap. 75.00 (*0-8464-4880-7*) Beekman Pubs.

Coulson, Andrew. Tanzania: A Political Economy. (Illus.). 410p. 1982. reprint ed. pap. 28.00 (*0-19-828293-1*) OUP.

Coulson, Andrew, ed. Local Government in Eastern Europe: Establishing Democracy at the Grassroots. (Studies of Communism in Transition). 304p. 1995. 95.00 (*1-85278-798-8*) E Elgar.

Coulson, Andrew J. Market Education: The Unknown History. LC 98-44583. 430p. 1999. 54.95 (*1-56000-408-8*); pap. 24.95 (*0-7658-0496-4*) Transaction Pubs.

Coulson, Andy. The White Gull Inn Centenniel Cookbook: More Favorite Recipes from Our Kitchen. 2nd ed. LC 97-73879. (Illus.). 152p. 1997. pap. 21.95 (*0-942495-74-8*) Palmer Pubns Inc.

Coulson, Anthony, ed. Exiles & Migrants: Crossing Thresholds in European Culture & Society. LC 97-26462. 224p. 1997. 59.95 (*1-898723-69-9*, Pub. by Sussex Acad Pr) Intl Spec Bk.

Coulson, Anthony J. A Bibliography of Design in Britain, 1851-1970. 292p. (C). 1979. text 110.00 (*0-85072-091-5*) St Mut.

Coulson, Arlene & Lewis, Noreen. Atlas of Interpretive Radiographic Anatomy of the Dog & Cat. (Illus.). 672p. (C). 1998. text 154.95 (*0-632-04078-5*, Pub. by Blckwell Science) Iowa St U Pr.

Coulson, Arline, ed. see Coulson, John G.

Coulson, Brent. Not Exactly Rocket Science. LC 98-90529. (Illus.). 112p. 1998. pap. 10.00 (*0-9665637-0-0*) Smirk Prods.

Coulson, Charles A. Coulson's Valence. 3rd ed. McWeeny, Roy, ed. (Oxford Chemistry Ser.). (Illus.). 446p. 1980. pap. 50.00 (*0-19-855145-2*) OUP.

Coulson, Charles A. & Boyd, T. J. Electricity. 2nd ed. LC 78-40510. (Longman Mathematical Texts Ser.). (Illus.). 406p. reprint ed. pap. 125.90 (*0-8357-6103-7*, 203450900090) Bks Demand.

Coulson, Christopher J. Molecular Mechanisms of Drug Action. 2nd ed. LC 93-32329. 300p. 1993. 99.00 (*0-7484-0068-0*, Pub. by Tay Francis Ltd); pap. 39.95 (*0-7484-0078-8*, Pub. by Tay Francis Ltd) Taylor & Francis.

Coulson, Danelle, jt. auth. see Henderson, Pauline.

Coulson, Danny O. No Heroes: Inside the FBI's Secret Counter-Terror Force. 2000. mass mkt. 7.99 (*0-671-02062-5*) S&S Trade.

Coulson, Danny O. & Shannon, Elaine. No Heroes: Inside the FBI's Secret Counter-Terror Force. LC 99-204502. 608p. 1999. 25.00 (*0-671-02061-7*, PB Hardcover) PB.

***Coulson, David, photos by.** African Rock Art: Paintings & Engravings on Stone. (Illus.). 224p. 2000. 60.00 (*0-8109-4363-8*, Pub. by Abrams) Time Warner.

Coulson, G., jt. ed. see Sventek, Joseph.

Coulson, Gail V., et al. The Enduring Church: Christians in China & Hong Kong. 1995. 8.95 (*0-377-00306-9*) Friendship Pr.

Coulson, Herbert H., jt. auth. see Cave, Roy C.

***Coulson, Ian.** Archives in Education. 1999. 26.00 (*1-873162-24-3*, Pub. by PRO Pubns) Midpt Trade.

Coulson, J. & Richardson, J. Chemical Engineering Vol. 6: Design, Vol. 6. 2nd rev. ed. LC 95-23187. (Illus.). 976p. 1996. pap. text 59.95 (*0-7506-2558-9*) Buttrwrth-Heinemann.

Coulson, J. M. Chemical Engineering: An Introduction to Design, Vol. 6. (Illus.). 720p. 1983. text 125.00 (*0-08-022969-7*, Pergamon Pr); pap. text 44.00 (*0-08-022970-0*, Pergamon Pr) Elsevier.

— Chemical Engineering: Particle Technology & Separation Processes, Vol. 2. 4th ed. Richardson, J. F., ed. 982p. 1990. pap. text 59.95 (*0-7506-2942-8*, Prgamon Press) Buttrwrth-Heinemann.

***Coulson, J. M. & Richardson, J. F.** Coulson & Richardson's Chemical Engineering 6th ed. LC 99-36977. 895p. 1999. pap. text 59.95 (*0-7506-4444-3*) Buttrwrth-Heinemann.

Coulson, J. M., et al. Chemical Engineering: Solutions to the Problems in Volume Two, Vol. 5. 3rd ed. LC 78-40923. (Chemical Engineering Technical Ser.). (Illus.). 255p. 1979. pap. text 39.95 (*0-08-022952-2*, Prgamon Press) Buttrwrth-Heinemann.

— Chemical Engineering Vol. 1: Fluid Flow, Heat Transfer & Mass Transfer, Vol. 1. 5th ed. LC 95-23187. (Illus.). 732p. 1996. pap. text 59.95 (*0-7506-2557-0*) Buttrwrth-Heinemann.

Coulson, J. R. Chemical Engineering, Vol. 3. 2nd ed. (Chemical Engineering: Concepts & Reviews Ser.: No. 3). 1979. text 190.00 (*0-08-023818-1*, Pergamon Pr); pap. text 54.00 (*0-08-023819-X*, Pergamon Pr) Elsevier.

Coulson, Jessie. Dostoevsky: A Self Portrait. LC 75-26212. (Illus.). 279p. 1975. reprint ed. lib. bdg. 49.50 (*0-8371-8405-3*, CODO, Greenwood Pr) Greenwood.

Coulson, Jessie, et al, eds. The Oxford Russian Dictionary: Russian-English, English-Russian. (ENG & RUS.). 1360p. (C). 1994. 55.00 (*0-19-864189-3*) OUP.

***Coulson, Jessie, et al, eds.** The Pocket Oxford Russian Dictionary. 636p. 2000. pap. 11.95 (*0-19-860150-6*) OUP.

Coulson, Jessie, et al, eds. The Pocket Oxford Russian Dictionary. 2nd ed. LC 99-176653. 636p. 1995. pap. 11.95 (*0-19-864526-0*) OUP.

Coulson, Jessie, tr. see Dostoyevsky, Fyodor.

***Coulson, Jo, ed.** Living with a Labrador Retriever. (Living with a Pet Ser.). (Illus.). 128p. 2000. 14.95 (*0-7641-5260-2*) Barron.

Coulson, John. Exploring Essex by Wheel. unabridged ed. (Illus.). 128p. 1996. pap. 15.00 (*0-86025-471-2*, Pub. by I Henry Pubns) Empire Pub Srvs.

— Religion & Imagination. 1981. 49.95 (*0-19-826656-1*) OUP.

Coulson, John, ed. see Newman, John Henry.

Coulson, John G. T. I. P. Thoughts in Passing. Coulson, Arline, ed. LC 96-90882. 136p. (Orig.). 1997. pap. 10.95 (*0-533-12203-1*) Vantage.

Coulson, Joseph. A Measured Silence. LC 86-82129. 68p. 1986. pap. 5.00 (*0-939483-00-9*) Hundred Pound Pr.

Coulson, Juanita. The Death God's Citadel. 400p. (Orig.). 1984. mass mkt. 2.95 (*0-345-31789-0*) Ballantine Pub Grp.

— The Web of Wizardry. 1984. mass mkt. 2.95 (*0-345-31788-2*, Ballantine) Ballantine Pub Grp.

Coulson, Kinsell L. Polarization & Intensity of Light in the Atmosphere. LC 88-25698. 596p. 1988. 105.00 (*0-937194-12-3*) A Deepak Pub.

Coulson, Margaret & Riddell, Carol. Approaching Sociology. rev. ed. 144p. 1980. pap. 12.95 (*0-7100-0575-X*) Routledge.

Coulson, Mark, jt. auth. see Greene, Judith.

Coulson, Michael. Teach Yourself Sanskrit. (Teach Yourself Ser.). 1992. 25.95 (*0-8288-8389-0*) Fr & Eur.

— Teach Yourself Sanskrit: A Complete Course for Beginners. (ENG & SAN., Illus.). 544p. 1995. pap. 17.95 (*0-8442-3825-2*, Teach Yrslf) NTC Contemp Pub Co.

Coulson, Michael, ed. see Bhavabhuti.

Coulson, N. J. History of Islamic Law. 270p. 1996. pap. 19.95 (*0-614-21149-2*, 443); pap. 19.95 (*0-614-21197-2*, 443) Kazi Pubns.

Coulson, Noel. Commercial Law in the Gulf States: The Islamic Legal Tradition. 128p. 1984. lib. bdg. 96.50 (*0-86010-574-1*) Kluwer Law Intl.

Coulson, Noel J. Conflicts & Tensions in Islamic Jurisprudence. Polk, William R., ed. LC 79-80433. (Publications of the Center for Middle Eastern Studies: No. 5). 1969. lib. bdg. 12.00 (*0-226-11610-7*) U Ch Pr.

— History of Islamic Law. (Islamic Surveys Ser.). 272p. 1994. pap. 25.00 (*0-7486-0514-2*, Pub. by Edinburgh U Pr) Col U Pr.

Coulson, Robert. ADR in America. 128p. 1993. pap. 19.95 (*0-943001-53-6*) Am Arbitration.

— Arbitration in the Schools. LC 85-73739. 152p. 1986. pap. 8.95 (*0-318-43192-0*) Am Arbitration.

— Business Arbitration - What You Need to Know. 4th ed. LC 85-48286. 180p. 1991. pap. 10.00 (*0-943001-25-0*) Am Arbitration.

— Business Mediation - What You Need to Know. LC 87-70084. 128p. 1987. pap. 8.00 (*0-943001-07-2*) Am Arbitration.

— Family Mediation: Managing Conflict, Resolving Disputes. 2nd ed. LC 96-25262. 288p. 1996. 32.95 (*0-7879-0312-4*) Jossey-Bass.

— How to Stay out of Court. LC 83-73660. 200p. 1984. pap. 7.95 (*0-943001-04-8*) Am Arbitration.

— Labor Arbitration - What You Need to Know. 3rd rev. ed. LC 81-66912. 176p. 1986. pap. 8.00 (*0-943001-05-6*) Am Arbitration.

— Police under Pressure: Resolving Disputes, 40. LC 92-35551. (Criminology & Crime Control Policy Ser.: No. 40). 176p. 1993. 47.95 (*0-313-28791-0*, GM8791, Greenwood Pr) Greenwood.

— Professional Mediation of Civil Disputes. LC 84-72418. 62p. 1984. pap. 7.50 (*0-943001-18-8*) Am Arbitration.

Coulson, Robert & Goldberg, Mitchell. Alcohol, Drugs & Arbitration. LC 87-71691. 200p. 1987. pap. 9.95 (*0-943001-20-X*) Am Arbitration.

Coulson, Robert & Singer, David. Family Mediation: Resolving Crisis. rev. ed. 1994. write for info. (*0-318-72532-0*) Am Arbitration.

Coulson, Robert N. & Witter, John A. Forest Entomology: Ecology & Management. LC 83-23492. 688p. 1984. 135.00 (*0-471-02573-9*) Wiley.

Coulson, Roland A. Why David Was a Threat to Goliath: Engineering Limitations to Enzyme Kinetics in Vivo. LC 96-90991. 150p. (Orig.). 1997. pap. 14.95 (*0-533-12240-6*) Vantage.

Coulson, Ruth. Growing African Violets. 2nd ed. (Growing Ser.). (Illus.). 96p. 1993. pap. 13.95 (*0-86417-509-4*, Pub. by Kangaroo Pr) Seven Hills Bk.

***Coulson, Seana.** Semantic Leaps: Frame-Shifting & Conceptual Blending in Meaning Construction. (Illus.). 320p. 2000. write for info. (*0-521-64361-9*) Cambridge U Pr.

Coulson, Sheila. Making Your Own Cross Stitch Gifts: Creative Ideas for Giving. LC 94-23178. (Illus.). 96p. 1995. pap. 16.95 (*0-88266-892-7*, Storey Pub) Storey Bks.

C

An Asterisk (*) at the beginning of an entry indicates that the title is appearing for the first time.

Coulson, Sheila, jt. auth. see Brown, Tessa.

Coulson-Thomas, Colin. Business Process Re-Engineering. LC 95-177022. 1997. 19.95 (*0-7494-1442-1*) Kogan Page Ltd.

— Creating Excellence in the Boardroom: A Guide to Shaping Directorial Competence & Board Effectiveness. LC 93-892. (Henley Management Ser.). 1993. write for info. (*0-07-707796-2*) McGraw.

— Creating the Global Company: Successful Internationalization. LC 92-16115. (Henley Management Ser.). 1992. 29.95 (*0-07-707599-4*) McGraw.

— Future of the Organization. (Business & Management Ser.). 1997. 24.95 (*0-7494-1935-0*) Kogan Page Ltd.

Coulson, Walter F. Atlas of Normal Histology. 500p. 1997. text 125.00 (*0-397-51419-0*) Lppncott W & W.

— Surgical Pathology, 2 vols. 2nd ed. LC 65-7743. (Illus.). 1824p. 1988. text 245.00 (*0-397-50609-0*, Lippncott) Lppncott W & W.

Coulson, William. Ancient Naukratis Vol. II: Survey at Naukratis & Environs, Pt. 1. (Monographs in Archaeology: Vol. 60). (Illus.). 220p. 1996. 48.00 (*1-900188-05-8*, Pub. by Oxbow Bks) David Brown.

— Ancient Naukratis Vol. II: Survey at Naukratis & Environs, Pt. 1: The Survey at Naukratis. (Oxbow Monographs in Archaeology: No. 60). (Illus.). 240p. 1996. 48.00 (*1-900188-22-8*, Pub. by Oxbow Bks) David Brown.

Coulson, William & Kyrieleis, H. Proceedings of an International Symposium of the Olympic Games. (Illus.). 190p. 1992. pap. 50.00 (*0-946897-53-0*) David Brown.

Coulson, William, jt. ed. see Palagia, Olga.

Coulson, William D. The Dark Age Pottery of Messenia. (Studies in Mediterranean Archaeology & Literature: No. 43). (Illus.). 146p. (Orig.). 1986. pap. 42.50 (*91-86098-46-2*, Pub. by P Astroms) Coronet Bks.

Coulson, William D., jt. ed. see Vaughan, Sarah J.

Coulstock, Patricia H. Collegiate Church of Wimborne Minster. LC 93-31431. (Studies in the History of Medieval Religion: Vol. V). (Illus.). 279p. 1993. 75.00 (*0-85115-339-9*, Boydell Pr) Boydell & Brewer.

Coulston, Frederick & Shubik, Philippe, eds. Human Epidemiology & Animal Laboratory Correlations in Chemical Carcinogens. LC 79-25466. (Current Topics Biomedical Research Ser.). 1980. text 73.25 (*0-89391-026-0*) Ablx Pub.

Coulston, J. C. & Phillips, E. J. Hadrian's Wall West of the North Tyne, & Carlisle, Fascicule 6, Vol. I, Fascicule 6. (Corpus Signorum Imperii Romani, Great Britain: Vol. I). (Illus.). 326p. 1988. 225.00 (*0-19-726058-6*) OUP.

Coultard-Clark, Chris. The Shame of Savo: Anatomy of a Naval Disaster. LC 94-66596. (Illus.). 346p. 1994. 35.00 (*1-55750-763-5*) Naval Inst Pr.

Coultard-Clark, Chris, jt. auth. see Loxton, Bruce.

Coultas, Barbara. Business French: A Complete Course for Beginners. (Teach Yourself Ser.). (FRE., Illus.). 296p. 1995. pap. 12.95 (*0-8442-3774-4*, Teach Yrslf) NTC Contemp Pub Co.

— Teach Yourself Business French, Set. (Teach Yourself Ser.). (FRE.). 296p. 1995. pap. 24.95 incl. audio (*0-8442-3890-2*, Teach Yrslf) NTC Contemp Pub Co.

Coultas, Brenda. Early Films. 75p. (Orig.). 1996. pap. 10.00 (*1-887289-15-1*) Rodent Pr.

Coultass, Clive. Images for Battle: British Film & the Second World War, 1939-1945. LC 87-40355. (Illus.). 224p. 1989. 50.00 (*0-87413-334-3*) U Delaware Pr.

Coultate, T. Food: The Chemistry of Its Components. 1988. 20.00 (*0-85186-483-X*) CRC Pr.

Coultate, T. P. Food: The Chemistry of Its Components. 1996. pap. 31.00 (*0-85404-513-9*) Am Chemical.

Coultate, T. P., ed. Food: The Chemistry of Its Components. 2nd ed. 250p. 1989. 39.00 (*0-85186-433-3*) CRC Pr.

Coultate, Tom & Davies, Jill. Food: The Definitive Guide. 167p. 1994. 47.00 (*0-85186-431-7*) CRC Pr.

Coulter. Entrepreneurship: In Action. 350p. (C). 2000. pap. 56.00 (*0-13-946088-8*) P-H.

***Coulter, Angela & Ham, Chris.** The Global Challenge of Health Care Rationing. LC 99-32133. (State of Health Ser.). 2000. 34.95 (*0-335-20463-5*) OpUniv Pr.

Coulter, Angela, jt. auth. see Singer, Ron.

Coulter, Angela, jt. ed. see Roland, Martin.

Coulter, Ann. High Crimes & Misdemeanors: The Case Against Bill Clinton. 1998. 24.95 (*0-89526-360-2*) Regnery Pub.

— High Crimes & Misdemeanors: The Case Against Bill Clinton. large type ed. LC 98-48560. (Thorndike Americana Ser.). 1999. 27.95 (*0-7862-1756-1*) Thorndike Pr.

***Coulter, Anne A.** Hidden Lives & Unhistoric Acts. (Illus.). 140p. 1999. pap. write for info. (*0-9662621-1-5*) W Shore Pr.

Coulter, Bill. Stock Car Model Kit Encyclopedia & Price Guide. LC 99-61254. 208p. 1999. pap. 19.95 (*0-87341-732-1*) Krause Pubns.

Coulter, Bill, jt. auth. see Bongard, Tim.

Coulter, C. Brewster & Webber, Bert. The Pig War & Other Experiences of William A. Peck, Soldier, 1858-1862: The Journal of William A. Peck, Jr. LC 93-26331. (Illus.). 224p. 1993. pap. 12.95 (*0-936738-17-0*) Webb Research.

Coulter, Carleton, III. Profitable Estimating for Constructions Firms: A Guide for Contractors, Subcontractors, Builders, & Developers. (Illus.). 120p. (C). 1986. 37.50 (*1-55538-012-3*) Pract Mgmt Assocs.

Coulter, Carol. The Hidden Tradition. 64p. 1993. pap. 18.95 (*0-902561-72-3*, Pub. by Cork Univ) Stylus Pub VA.

Coulter, Carol. Ireland: Between the First & the Third Worlds. (C). 1989. 35.00 (*0-946211-93-0*) St Mut.

Coulter, Catherine. Afterglow. 1998. per. 5.50 (*1-55166-472-0*, 1-66472-1, Mira Bks) Harlequin Bks.

— Afterglow. 1993. mass mkt. 4.50 (*0-373-48260-4*, 5-48260-9) Silhouette.

— Aftershocks. (Mira Bks.). 1998. per. 5.50 (*1-55166-443-7*, 1-66443-2, Mira Bks) Harlequin Bks.

— The Aristocrat. 1993. per. 4.50 (*0-373-48261-2*, 5-48261-7) Harlequin Bks.

— The Aristocrat. 251p. 1999. mass mkt. 6.99 (*1-55166-513-1*, Mira Bks) Harlequin Bks.

— Beyond Eden. 448p. 1993. mass mkt. 7.50 (*0-451-40339-8*, Onyx) NAL.

***Coulter, Catherine.** Beyond Eden. 2000. mass mkt. 7.50 (*0-451-20231-7*, Sig) NAL.

Coulter, Catherine. Beyond Eden. large type ed. LC 98-35884. 1998. 25.95 (*1-56895-658-4*) Wheeler Pub.

— Calypso Magic. 412p. 1999. mass mkt. 7.50 (*0-451-40877-2*, Topaz) NAL.

***Coulter, Catherine.** Calypso Magic. 416p. 1999. 26.00 (*0-7278-2247-0*, Pub. by Severn Hse) Chivers N Amer.

— Calypso Magic. LC 99-56258. (Thorndike Romance Ser.). 2000. 28.95 (*0-7862-2347-2*) Thorndike Pr.

Coulter, Catherine. Chandra. (Scarlet Ribbons Ser.). 352p. 1985. mass mkt. 7.50 (*0-451-15881-4*, Onyx) NAL.

***Coulter, Catherine.** Chandra. LC 99-55836. (Medieval Song Quartet Ser.). 2000. write for info. (*0-7862-2354-5*) Thorndike Pr.

Coulter, Catherine. Circule de Enganis. 1998. pap. 6.95 (*84-01-50703-0*) Lectorum Pubns.

***Coulter, Catherine.** The Countess. 416p. 1999. mass mkt. 7.50 (*0-451-19850-6*, Sig) NAL.

— The Courtship. 352p. 2000. mass mkt. 7.50 (*0-515-12721-3*, Jove) Berkley Pub.

— The Courtship. large type ed. LC 00-27585. (Core Ser.). 448p. 2000. 31.95 (*0-7838-9032-X*, G K Hall Lrg Type) Mac Lib Ref.

— The Courtship. large type ed. LC 00-27585. (Core Ser.). 2001. pap. 29.95 (*0-7838-9033-8*, G K Hall Lrg Type) Mac Lib Ref.

Coulter, Catherine. The Cove. large type ed. 366p. 1996. mass mkt. 7.50 (*0-515-11865-6*, Jove) Berkley Pub.

— Deception. 1998. mass mkt. 7.50 (*0-451-40858-6*, Topaz) NAL.

— Deception. large type ed. LC 98-42683. 1999. 29.95 (*0-7862-1730-8*, G K Hall Lrg Type) Mac Lib Ref.

— The Deception. large type ed. LC 98-42683. (Paperback Bestsellers Ser.). 1999. pap. 27.95 (*0-7862-1731-6*) Thorndike Pr.

— Devil's Daughter. 416p. 1985. mass mkt. 7.50 (*0-451-15863-6*, Onyx) NAL.

— Devil's Embrace. 1985. mass mkt. 7.50 (*0-451-14198-9*, Onyx) NAL.

***Coulter, Catherine.** Devil's Embrace. 416p. 2000. mass mkt. 7.50 (*0-451-20026-8*, Sig) NAL.

Coulter, Catherine. The Duke. LC 96-43099. (Star-Romance Ser.). 328p. 1997. 23.95 (*0-7862-0914-3*) Five Star.

— The Duke. 384p. 1995. mass mkt. 7.50 (*0-451-40617-6*, Topaz) NAL.

— The Duke. large type ed. LC 97-714. 1997. 25.56 (*1-56895-416-6*) Wheeler Pub.

— El Duque. 1998. pap. 6.95 (*84-01-50704-9*) Lectorum Pubns.

— Earth Song. 1990. mass mkt. 7.50 (*0-451-40206-5*, Onyx) NAL.

***Coulter, Catherine.** Earth Song. large type ed. LC 99-56259. (Basic Ser.). 539p. 2000. 29.95 (*0-7862-2356-1*) Thorndike Pr.

Coulter, Catherine. The Edge. LC 99-21347. 388p. 1999. 21.95 (*0-399-14506-0*) Peng Put Young Read.

***Coulter, Catherine.** Edge. 2000. mass mkt. 7.99 (*0-515-12860-0*) Berkley Pub.

— The Edge. large type ed. LC 99-46182. 1999. 30.95 (*0-7862-2240-9*) Thorndike Pr.

— The Edge. large type ed. LC 99-46182. 2000. pap. 28.95 (*0-7862-2241-7*) Thorndike Pr.

Coulter, Catherine. Evening Star. LC Onyx. 1996. mass mkt. 6.99 (*0-451-40709-1*, Topaz) NAL.

***Coulter, Catherine.** Evening Star. large type ed. LC 99-59453. 2000. 25.95 (*1-56895-836-6*) Wheeler Pub.

— False Pretenses. 393p. 2000. mass mkt. 7.50 (*0-451-19968-5*, Sig) NAL.

— False Pretenses. large type ed. LC 98-49020. (Large Print Book Ser.). 1998. 25.95 (*1-56895-594-4*) Wheeler Pub.

Coulter, Catherine. Fire Song. 1985. mass mkt. 7.50 (*0-451-40238-3*, Onyx) NAL.

***Coulter, Catherine.** Fire Song. LC 99-55822. 2000. 29.95 (*0-7862-2355-3*) Thorndike Pr.

Coulter, Catherine. The Heir. large type ed. 384p. 1996. mass mkt. 7.50 (*0-451-18861-6*, Topaz) NAL.

— The Heir. large type ed. LC 96-52538. 525p. 1997. 27.95 (*0-7862-1041-9*) Thorndike Pr.

— The Heiress Bride. 416p. 1993. mass mkt. 7.50 (*0-515-11131-7*, Jove) Berkley Pub.

— The Hellion Bride. 384p. 1992. mass mkt. 7.50 (*0-515-10974-6*, Jove) Berkley Pub.

— Impulse. 400p. 1991. mass mkt. 7.50 (*0-451-40250-2*, Onyx) NAL.

— Impulse. large type ed. LC 98-24434. 1998. 25.95 (*1-56895-611-8*) Wheeler Pub.

— Jade Star. 1987. mass mkt. 7.50 (*0-451-40448-3*, Onyx) NAL.

— Jade Star. 416p. 1999. 26.00 (*0-7278-2291-8*, Pub. by Severn Hse) Chivers N Amer.

— Lord Harry. 1995. mass mkt. 7.50 (*0-451-40591-9*, Topaz) NAL.

— Lord Harry. large type ed. LC 96-38767. (ROMC-Hall Ser.). 424p. 1997. lib. bdg. 27.95 (*0-7838-2001-1*, G K Hall Lrg Type) Mac Lib Ref.

— Lord of Falcon Ridge. (Orig.). 1995. mass mkt. 6.99 (*0-515-11584-3*, Jove) Berkley Pub.

— Lord of Falcon Ridge. large type ed. (Large Print Bks.). (Orig.). 1995. pap. 20.95 (*1-56895-253-8*) Wheeler Pub.

— Lord of Hawkfell Island. 416p. 1993. mass mkt. 6.99 (*0-515-11230-5*, Jove) Berkley Pub.

— Lord of Hawkfell Island. large type ed. LC 95-17031. (Large Print Bks.). 1995. pap. 20.95 (*1-56895-235-X*) Wheeler Pub.

— Lord of Raven's Peak. 400p. (Orig.). 1994. mass mkt. 6.99 (*0-515-11351-4*, Jove) Berkley Pub.

— Lord of Raven's Peak. large type ed. LC 95-10893. (Large Print Bks.). (Orig.). 1995. 23.95 (*1-56895-223-6*) Wheeler Pub.

***Coulter, Catherine.** Mad Jack. 352p. 1999. mass mkt. 7.50 (*0-515-12420-6*, Jove) Berkley Pub.

— Mad Jack. LC 99-46172. 1999. 26.95 (*1-56895-784-X*, Wheeler) Wheeler Pub.

Coulter, Catherine. The Maze. 1997. mass mkt. 7.50 (*0-515-12249-1*, Jove) Berkley Pub.

— The Maze. large type ed. LC 98-26429. (Large Print Book Ser.). 1998. 26.95 (*1-56895-578-2*) Wheeler Pub.

— Midnight Star. 1986. mass mkt. 7.50 (*0-451-40446-7*, Onyx) NAL.

***Coulter, Catherine.** Midnight Star. large type ed. LC 00-22867. 2000. 25.95 (*1-56895-862-5*) Wheeler Pub.

Coulter, Catherine. Midsummer Magic. 1999. 26.00 (*0-7278-5468-2*, Pub. by Severn Hse) Chivers N Amer.

— Midsummer Magic. (Historical Romance Ser.). 412p. 1998. reprint ed. mass mkt. 7.50 (*0-451-40870-5*, Topaz) NAL.

— Moonspun Magic. 1999. mass mkt. 7.50 (*0-451-40884-5*, Topaz) NAL.

***Coulter, Catherine.** Moonspun Magic. large type ed. LC 99-56260. 2000. 28.95 (*0-7862-2348-0*) Thorndike Pr.

— Nature & Human Personality: Homeopathic Archetypes. 250p. 2000. 18.50 (*1-57626-117-4*) Quality Med Pub.

Coulter, Catherine. Night Fire. large type ed. LC 97-15890. (Wheeler Large Print Book Ser.). 1997. 23.95 (*1-56895-457-3*) Wheeler Pub.

— Night Fire. 400p. 1989. reprint ed. mass mkt. 6.99 (*0-380-75620-X*, Avon Bks) Morrow Avon.

— Night Fire. 392p. 1995. reprint ed. 18.00 (*0-7278-4787-2*) Severn Hse.

— Night Shadow. 400p. 1989. mass mkt. 6.99 (*0-380-75621-8*, Avon Bks) Morrow Avon.

— Night Shadow. large type ed. LC 97-34584. (Large Print Bks.). 1997. 24.95 (*1-56895-499-9*) Wheeler Pub.

— Night Storm. 400p. 1990. mass mkt. 6.99 (*0-380-75623-4*, Avon Bks) Morrow Avon.

— Night Storm. large type ed. LC 98-6712. 1998. 25.95 (*1-56895-558-8*, Wheeler) Wheeler Pub.

— The Nightingale Legacy. 464p. 1995. mass mkt. 6.99 (*0-515-11624-6*, Jove) Berkley Pub.

***Coulter, Catherine.** Novia de Sherbrooke. (SPA.). 1998. pap. 10.95 (*84-01-50700-6*) Plaza.

— La Novia Maliciosa. (SPA.). 368p. 2000. pap. 9.50 (*0-553-06126-7*) Bantam.

Coulter, Catherine. The Offer. 1997. mass mkt. 7.50 (*0-451-40794-6*, Topaz) NAL.

— The Rebel Bride. 384p. 1994. mass mkt. 7.50 (*0-451-40432-7*, Topaz) NAL.

— The Rebel Bride. large type ed. LC 96-43098. (Star-Romance Ser.). 405p. 1997. 23.95 (*0-7862-0915-1*) Five Star.

— The Rebel Bride. large type ed. LC 96-35470. (Romance-Hall Ser.). 530p. 1997. lib. bdg. 27.95 (*0-7838-2002-X*, G K Hall Lrg Type) Mac Lib Ref.

***Coulter, Catherine.** Riptide. LC 00-35248. 384p. 2000. 23.95 (*0-399-14616-4*) Putnam Pub Group.

— Riptide. large type ed. LC 00-33753. 2000. write for info. (*0-7862-2642-0*) Thorndike Pr.

Coulter, Catherine. Rosehaven. large type ed. LC 96-49134. (Large Print Bks.). 1997. 26.95 (*1-56895-405-0*) Wheeler Pub.

— Rosehaven. 384p. 1997. reprint ed. mass mkt. 6.99 (*0-515-12088-X*, Jove) Berkley Pub.

— Season of the Sun. 384p. 1991. mass mkt. 7.50 (*0-451-40262-6*, Onyx) NAL.

Coulter, Catherine. Season of the Sun. 416p. 26.00 (*0-7278-5544-1*) Severn Hse.

Coulter, Catherine. Secret Song. 1991. mass mkt. 7.50 (*0-451-40234-0*, Onyx) NAL.

***Coulter, Catherine.** Secret Song. LC 99-55837. (Medieval Song Quartet Ser.). 2000. write for info. (*0-7862-2357-X*) Thorndike Pr.

Coulter, Catherine. The Sherbrooke Bride. 1992. mass mkt. 6.99 (*0-515-10766-2*, Jove) Berkley Pub.

— The Sherbrooke Bride. large type ed. LC 95-9761. 465p. 1995. 23.95 (*0-7838-1293-0*, G K Hall Lrg Type) Mac Lib Ref.

***Coulter, Catherine.** The Target. 387p. 1999. mass mkt. 7.50 (*0-515-12562-8*, Jove) Berkley Pub.

— The Target. LC 98-10563. 384p. 1998. 15.95 (*0-399-14395-5*, G P Putnam) Peng Put Young Read.

— The Target. large type ed. LC 98-29236. (Large Print Book Ser.). 1998. 26.95 (*1-56895-586-3*) Wheeler Pub.

Coulter, Catherine. The Valentine Legacy. 432p. 1996. mass mkt. 6.99 (*0-515-11836-2*, Jove) Berkley Pub.

— The Valentine Legacy. large type ed. 573p. 1995. 25.95 (*0-7838-1497-6*, G K Hall Lrg Type) Mac Lib Ref.

— The Wild Baron. 376p. 1997. mass mkt. 6.99 (*0-515-12044-8*, Jove) Berkley Pub.

— The Wild Baron. large type ed. LC 97-17236. 1997. 24.95 (*0-7862-1117-2*) Thorndike Pr.

— Wild Star. 1986. mass mkt. 7.50 (*0-451-40447-5*, Onyx) NAL.

***Coulter, Catherine.** Wild Star. large type ed. LC 00-39862. 2000. write for info. (*1-56895-915-X*) Wheeler Pub.

Coulter, Catherine. Wild Star. 1994. reprint ed. lib. bdg. 22.00 (*0-7278-4687-6*) Severn Hse.

— The Wyndham Legacy. 400p. 1994. reprint ed. mass mkt. 6.99 (*0-515-11449-9*, Jove) Berkley Pub.

Coulter, Catherine, jt. auth. see Albom, Mitch.

Coulter, Catherine R. Portraits in Homoeopathic Medicines Vol. 3: Expanding Views of the Materia Medica. LC 97-30347. 338p. 1998. 33.00 (*1-57626-091-7*, QMP) Quality Med Pub.

— Portraits of Homoeopathic Medicines Vol. 1: Psychophysical Analyses of Selected Constitutional Types. LC 97-30347. 422p. 1997. 33.00 (*1-57626-089-5*) Quality Med Pub.

— Portraits of Homoeopathic Medicines Vol. 2: Psychophysical Analyses of Selected Constitutional Types. LC 97-30347. 300p. 1997. 33.00 (*1-57626-090-9*) Quality Med Pub.

Coulter, Charles R. & Turner, Patricia. Encyclopedia of Ancient Dieties. LC 97-40330. 605p. 1999. lib. bdg. 75.00 (*0-7864-0317-9*) McFarland & Co.

Coulter, Charles W., jt. auth. see Creamer, Daniel.

***Coulter, Colin.** Contemporary Northern Irish Society: An Introduction. LC 99-28413. (Contemporary Irish Studies). 288p. 2000. 69.95 (*0-7453-1254-3*, Pub. by Pluto GBR); pap. 25.00 (*0-7453-1244-6*, Pub. by Pluto GBR) Stylus Pub VA.

Coulter, Doug. Digital Audio Processing. 432p. 2000. pap. 54.95 incl. cd-rom (*0-87930-566-5*, Pub. by C M P Books) Publishers Group.

***Coulter, Douglass.** Chiropractic: A Philosophy for Alternative Health Care. LC 99-27299. 117p. 1999. pap. text 39.95 (*0-7506-4006-5*) Buttrwrth-Heinemann.

Coulter, E. Merton. Abraham Baldwin: Patriot, Educator, & Founding Father. LC 87-10486. 304p. 1987. 24.95 (*0-918339-06-5*) Vandamere.

— The Civil War & Readjustment in Kentucky. 1926. 16.50 (*0-8446-1131-X*) Peter Smith.

— The Confederate States of America 1861-1865. LC 50-6319. (History of the South Ser.: No. VII). (Illus.). 644p. 1950. text 60.00 (*0-8071-0007-2*) La State U Pr.

— South During Reconstruction, 1865-1877. LC 48-5161. (History of the South Ser.: Vol. 8). (Illus.). 426p. 1947. text 50.00 (*0-8071-0008-0*) La State U Pr.

— Travels in the Confederate States: A Bibliography. LC 94-17847. 304p. 1994. pap. 14.95 (*0-8071-1952-0*) La State U Pr.

— Travels in the Confederate States: A Bibliography. xiv, 289p. 1981. reprint ed. 30.00 (*0-916107-02-7*) Broadfoot.

— William G. Brownlow: Fighting Parson of the Southern Highlands. LC 71-136309. (Tennesseana Editions Ser.). (Illus.). 458p. reprint ed. pap. 142.00 (*0-8357-9767-8*, 201617300001) Bks Demand.

Coulter, E. Merton, ed. Confederate Receipt Book: A Compilation of Over One Hundred Receipts, Adapted to the Times. LC 60-9896. 38p. 1981. pap. 5.95 (*0-8203-0561-8*) U of Ga Pr.

Coulter, E. Merton & Saye, Albert B. A List of the Early Settlers of Georgia. LC 83-80998. 111p. 1998. reprint ed. pap. 15.00 (*0-8063-1031-6*) Clearfield Co.

Coulter, Edwin M. Principles of Politics & Government. 5th ed. LC 92-74917. 320p. (C). 1993. text. write for info. (*0-697-12697-8*) Brown & Benchmark.

— Principles of Politics & Government. 6th ed. LC 96-84171. 320p. (C). 1996. text. write for info. (*0-697-23762-1*) Brown & Benchmark.

***Coulter, Elizabeth & Dey-Bergmoser, Olga.** Artists 2000: Expressions of Beauty on the Dawning of a New Age. 360p. 2000. 19.95 (*0-88962-701-0*, Pub. by Mosaic) Midpt Trade.

Coulter, Ellis M. Civil War & Readjustment in Kentucky. (History - United States Ser.). 468p. 1992. reprint ed. lib. bdg. 99.00 (*0-7812-6185-6*) Rprt Serv.

***Coulter, Fred R.** The Christian Passover: What Does It Mean? When Should It Be Observed the 14th or the 15th. 2nd rev. ed. 500p. 1999. 35.95 (*0-9675479-0-3*) York Pubng Co.

Coulter, Fredrick L., jt. auth. see Ornelas-Struve, Carole M.

Coulter, George & Coulter, Shirley. Bicycles. LC 96-7516. (You Make It Work Ser.). (Illus.). 32p. (J). (gr. 3-6). 1996. lib. bdg. 18.60 (*0-86625-587-7*) Rourke Pubns.

— Computers. LC 96-3905. (You Make It Work Ser.). (Illus.). 32p. (J). (gr. 3-6). 1996. lib. bdg. 17.27 (*0-86625-585-0*) Rourke Pubns.

— Movies. LC 96-11643. (You Make It Work Ser.). (Illus.). 32p. (J). (gr. 3-6). 1996. lib. bdg. 17.27 (*0-86625-586-9*) Rourke Pubns.

— Radio. LC 96-3906. (You Make It Work Ser.). (Illus.). 32p. (J). (gr. 3-6). 1996. lib. bdg. 23.93 (*0-86625-584-2*) Rourke Pubns.

— Science in Art. LC 94-49347. (Science Projects Ser.). (Illus.). 32p. (J). (gr. 3-6). 1994. lib. bdg. 23.93 (*0-86625-519-2*) Rourke Pubns.

— Science in Food. LC 94-49348. (Science Projects Ser.). 32p. (J). (gr. 3-6). 1994. lib. bdg. 23.93 (*0-86625-518-4*) Rourke Pubns.

— Science in History. LC 95-7209. (Science Projects Ser.). 32p. (J). (gr. 3-6). 1994. lib. bdg. 23.93 (*0-86625-521-4*) Rourke Pubns.

— Science in Math. LC 95-6591. (Science Projects Ser.). 32p. (J). (gr. 3-6). 1994. lib. bdg. 23.93 (*0-86625-522-2*) Rourke Pubns.

— Science in Nature. LC 95-2399. (Science Projects Ser.). 32p. (J). (gr. 3-6). 1994. lib. bdg. 23.93 (*0-86625-520-6*) Rourke Pubns.

— Science in Sports. LC 94-43479. (Science Projects Ser.). 32p. (J). (gr. 3-6). 1994. lib. bdg. 23.93 (*0-86625-517-6*) Rourke Pubns.

— Television. LC 95-51374. (You Make It Work Ser.). (Illus.). 32p. (J). (gr. 3-6). 1995. lib. bdg. 17.27 (*0-86625-583-4*) Rourke Pubns.

— Video. LC 96-15474. (You Make It Work Ser.). (Illus.). 32p. (J). (gr. 3-6). 1995. lib. bdg. 23.93 (*0-86625-588-5*) Rourke Pubns.

An Asterisk (*) at the beginning of an entry indicates that the title is appearing for the first time.

Coulter, Harris L. AIDS & Syphilis: The Hidden Link. LC 87-21961. 132p. (Orig.). 1987. 20.00 (*1-55643-025-6*); pap. 8.95 (*1-55643-021-3*) North Atlantic.

— The Controlled Clinical Trial: An Analysis. LC 91-8016. 176p. (Orig.). 1991. pap. 12.00 (*0-916386-04-X*) Ctr Emp Med.

— Divided Legacy, 4 vols., Set. 1973. 200.00 (*0-916386-00-7*) Ctr Emp Med.

— Divided Legacy: A History of the Schism in Medical Thought. The Patterns Emerge: Hippocrates to Paracelsus, 4 vols. LC 73-75718. 537p. 1994. 50.00 (*0-916386-01-5*) Ctr Emp Med.

— Divided Legacy: The Conflict Between Homoeopathy & the American Medical Association. LC 73-75718. (Science & Ethics in American Medicine 1800-1910 Ser.: Vol. III). 552p. (Orig.). 1973. reprint ed. pap. 20.00 (*0-913028-96-7*) North Atlantic.

— Divided Legacy: The Conflict Between Homoeopathy & the American Medical Association. LC 73-75718. (Science & Ethics in American Medicine 1800-1910 Ser.: Vol. III). 552p. (Orig.). 1982. reprint ed. 50.00 (*0-938190-57-1*) North Atlantic.

— Divided Legacy Vol. II: A History of the Schism in Medical Thought. The Origins of Modern Western Medicine: J.B. Van Helmont to Claude Bernard, 4 vols. LC 73-75718. 1973. 50.00 (*0-916386-02-3*) Ctr Emp Med.

— Divided Legacy Vol. 2: The Origins of Modern Medicine: J. B. Van Helmont to Claude Bernard. 785p. 1988. 50.00 (*1-55643-035-3*) North Atlantic.

— Divided Legacy: A History of the Schism in Medical Thought Vol. 4: The Bacteriological Age: Twentieth Century Medicine. LC 73-75718. 776p. 1994. 50.00 (*1-55643-170-8*) North Atlantic.

— Homoeopathic Influences in Nineteenth-Century Allopathic Therapeutics. LC 73-75139. 1973. pap. 2.50 (*0-685-64858-3*) Formur Intl.

— Homoeopathic Medicine. LC 74-190020. 1972. pap. 2.50 (*0-89378-072-3*) Formur Intl.

— Vaccination, Social Violence & Criminality: The Medical Assault on the American Brain. LC 90-7991. 300p. (Orig.). 1990. 25.00 (*1-55643-103-1*); pap. 14.95 (*1-55643-084-1*) Ctr Emp Med.

Coulter, Harris L. & Fisher, Barbara L. A Shot in the Dark: Why the P In DPT Vaccination May Be Hazardous to Your Child's Health. LC 91-21991. 256p. (Orig.). pap. 10.95 (*0-89529-463-X*, Avery) Penguin Putnam.

Coulter, Hope N. Uncle Chuck's Truck. LC 91-42638. (Illus.). 32p. (J). (ps-1). 1993. lib. bdg. 13.95 (*0-02-724825-9*, Bradbury S&S) S&S Childrens.

Coulter, J. Liberalization of Cereals Marketing in Sub-Saharan Africa: Lessons from Experience. 1994. pap. 30.00 (*0-85954-368-4*, Pub. by Nat Res Inst) St Mut.

Coulter, J. & Compton, J. A. Liberalization of Cereals Marketing in Sub-Saharan Africa: Implementation Issues. 1992. pap. 35.00 (*0-85954-280-7*, Pub. by Nat Res Inst) St Mut.

Coulter, J. W. Land Utilization in American Samoa. (BMB Ser.: Vol. 170). 1969. reprint ed. pap. 25.00 (*0-527-02278-0*) Periodicals Srv.

— Population & Utilization of Land & Sea in Hawaii. (BMB Ser.: No. 88). 1974. reprint ed. pap. 25.00 (*0-527-02194-6*) Periodicals Srv.

Coulter, Jeff. Mind in Action. LC 89-11106. 200p. (C). 1989. pap. 17.50 (*0-391-03657-2*) Humanities.

Coulter, Jeremy. Lotus 7: A Collector's Guide. (Collector's Guide Ser.). (Illus.). 128p. 1995. 19.98 (*0-947981-71-3*, Pub. by Motor Racing) Motorbooks Intl.

Coulter, Jeremy, ed. see Williams, Paul O.

Coulter, Jerry. Beholding & Becoming. LC 94-69043. 140p. (Orig.). 1995. pap. 8.95 (*0-940232-51-0*) Seedsowers.

Coulter, John C., jt. auth. see Simpson, Patricia R.

Coulter, John S. Physical Therapy. LC 75-23658. (Clio Medica Ser.: 8). (Illus.). reprint ed. 29.50 (*0-404-58908-1*) AMS Pr.

Coulter, Julie M., tr. see Cavalletti, Sofia.

Coulter, Kathryn A. Does Cupid Do Takeout? large type ed. 211p. 1995. per. 20.95 (*0-7838-1518-2*, G K Hall Lrg Type) Mac Lib Ref.

Coulter, Lane, et al. Ann Orr: Silversmith, Goldsmith & Enamelist. Eiland, William U., ed. LC 94-16290. (Illus.). 69p. 1994. pap. 20.00 (*0-915977-15-X*) Georgia Museum of Art.

***Coulter, Laurie.** When John & Caroline Lived in the White House. (Illus.). 64p. (J). (gr. 3-7). 2000. 19.99 (*0-7868-0624-9*, Pub. by Disney Pr) Time Warner.

Coulter, Laurie, jt. auth. see Brewster, Hugh.

***Coulter, Linda.** Memories from My Heart: A Journal. LC 99-75573. 128p. 1999. pap. 9.95 (*1-58597-003-4*) Leathers Pub.

Coulter, Lisa O., jt. auth. see Williams, Gareth.

Coulter Martens, Anne. Professor, How Could You! 96p. 1939. pap. 5.25 (*0-87129-874-0*, P39) Dramatic Pub.

Coulter, Mary. Strategic Management in Action. LC 97-36849. 383p. (C). 1997. pap. text 56.00 (*0-13-606773-5*) P-H.

Coulter, Mary K., jt. auth. see Robbins, Stephen P.

Coulter, Matthew W. The Senate Munitions Inquiry of the 1930s: Beyond the Merchants of Death, 177. LC 97-1692. (Contributions in American History Ser.: Vol. 177). 200p. 1997. 59.95 (*0-313-30394-0*, Greenwood Pr) Greenwood.

Coulter, Merle C. The Story of the Plant Kingdom. rev. ed. Dittmer, Howard J., ed. LC 64-10093. 480p. (C). 1992. pap. text 4.95 (*0-226-11611-5*, P494) U Ch Pr.

Coulter, Page P. The Cowbridge at Dawn: Poems. LC 92-44221. 64p. 1993. pap. 12.95 (*0-7734-2764-3*) E Mellen.

— New England Weather: Poems. LC 97-11767. 68p. 1997. pap. 14.95 (*0-7734-2822-4*, Mellen Poetry Pr) E Mellen.

Coulter, Patricia M., tr. see Cavalletti, Sofia.

Coulter, Philip, jt. ed. see Busson, Terry.

Coulter, Philip B. Political Voice: Citizen Demand for Urban Public Services. LC 86-14617. (University of Alabama, Institute for Social Science Research Ser.: No. 1). 123p. reprint ed. pap. 38.20 (*0-608-09219-3*, 205272300005) Bks Demand.

Coulter, Phillip, jt. ed. see Busson, Terry.

Coulter, Sara. Introductory Bibliography for Curriculum Transformation. LC 98-226662. (Women in the Curriculum Ser.: Vol. 2). 15p. (Orig.). 1997. pap. 7.00 (*1-885303-32-7*) Towson St Univ.

Coulter, Shirley. Chemistry. (Science Fair Ser.). 48p. (J). (gr. 3-6). Date not set. lib. bdg. 22.60 (*1-57103-427-7*) Rourke Pr.

Coulter, Shirley, jt. auth. see Coulter, George.

Coulter, Silvia. Climb to the Top: Client Development for Lawyers. 49p. 1994. 195.00 incl. audio (*0-9650920-0-3*) Coulter Legal.

Coulter, Silvia L. It Takes Balls to Stay in Business. (Illus.). ii, 48p. (Orig.). 1996. pap. 8.95 (*0-9650920-1-1*) Coulter Legal.

Coulter, Tony. Jacques Cartier, Samuel de Champlain, & the Explorers of Canada. Goetzmann, William H., ed. (World Explorers Ser.). (Illus.). 120p. (YA). (gr. 5 up). 1993. lib. bdg. 19.95 (*0-7910-1298-0*) Chelsea Hse.

Coulter, Willa M. Some Families of Revolutionary War Patriots from Virginia, Maryland, Pennsylvania, South Carolina & Kentucky: Duncan, Miller, Coulter, Fleming, Pomeroy, Junkin, Harned, Galloway, Hartley, Weatherholt, Crawford, Mason, Pate, Moorman, Adams, Lewis, Johnston, Clark, Walker, Martin, Reynolds, Head, Long, Seaton, Kenner, Thompson, Greenwell, Bonum, Philpot... unabridged ed. LC 93-73281. 860p. 1993. lib. bdg. 48.00 (*0-9654367-0-5*) W Coulter.

Coulter, William. Building & Detailing Scale Model Stock Cars. LC 98-144183. (Illus.). 112p. 1998. pap. 17.95 (*0-89024-285-2*, 12172, Kalmbach Books) Kalmbach.

***Coulter, William.** Celtic Crossing - Guitar: Intermediate Level. 88p. 1998. pap. 14.95 (*0-7866-2487-6*, 96316) Mel Bay.

— Celtic Crossing - Guitar CD Package. 88p. 1998. pap. 29.95 incl. cd-rom (*0-7866-2764-6*, 96316CDP) Mel Bay.

— Celtic Crossing-Guitar. 88p. 1998. pap. 24.95 incl. audio (*0-7866-2763-8*, 96316P) Mel Bay.

Coulter, William & Banks, Michael. Second Stage: Advanced Model Rocketry. 2nd unabridged ed. Van Milligan, Tim, ed. (Illus.). 72p. (Orig.). 1998. pap. 15.95 (*0-89024-212-7*, 12140, Kalmbach Books) Kalmbach.

Coulter, William, et al. Building & Detailing Scale Model Pickup Trucks. (Illus.). 88p. (Orig.). 1997. pap. 14.95 (*0-89024-267-4*, 12164, Kalmbach Books) Kalmbach.

***Coulthard-Clark, C. D.** Australia's Military Map-Makers: The Royal Australian Survey Corps 1915-1996. (Australian Army History Ser.). (Illus.). 352p. 2000. text 35.00 (*0-19-551343-6*) OUP.

Coulthard-Clark, Chris. The RAAF in Vietnam Vol. 4: Australian Air Operations in the Vietnam War 1962-1975. (Illus.). 352p. 1995. 59.95 (*1-86373-305-1*) Paul & Co Pubs.

— Soldiers in Politics: The Impact of the Military on Australian Political Life & Institutions. (Illus.). 256p. 1997. pap. 29.95 (*1-86448-185-4*, Pub. by Allen & Unwin Pty) Paul & Co Pubs.

Coulthard-Clark, Chris, ed. The Diggers: Makers of the Australian Military Tradition. (Illus.). 384p. 1993. 44.95 (*0-522-84470-7*, Pub. by Melbourne Univ Pr) Paul & Co Pubs.

Coulthard, Glen, et al. Windows 3.1. (C). 1994. text 22.50 (*0-256-18653-7*, Irwn McGrw-H) McGrw-H Hghr Educ.

Coulthard, Glen, jt. auth. see Hutchinson-Clifford, Sarah.

Coulthard, Glen, jt. auth. see Hutchinson, Sarah E.

Coulthard, Glen J., jt. auth. see Hutchinson, Sarah E.

Coulthard, John. A Game That Never Ends. 257p. (Orig.). (C). 1990. pap. 17.50 (*971-10-0272-8*, Pub. by New Day Pub) Cellar.

Coulthard, Joseph, tr. see von Humboldt, Wilhelm.

Coulthard, Malcolm, ed. Advances in Spoken Discourse Analysis. LC 91-40402. 288p. (C). 1992. pap. 29.99 (*0-415-06687-5*, A7481) Routledge.

— Advances in Written Text Analysis. LC 93-25182. 352p. (C). 1994. pap. 27.99 (*0-415-09520-4*) Routledge.

— Advances in Written Text Analysis. LC 93-25182. 1994. write for info. (*0-04-150519-0*) Routledge.

Coulthard, Malcolm & De Baubeta, Pat O., eds. Theoretical Issues & Practical Cases in Portuguese-English Translations. LC 95-26635. 144p. 1996. text 69.95 (*0-7734-8806-5*) E Mellen.

Coulthard, Malcolm & Odber de Baubeta, Patricia A., eds. The Knowledges of the Translator: From Literary Interpretation to Machine Classification. LC 96-84. (Illus.). 336p. 1996. text 99.95 (*0-7734-8826-X*) E Mellen.

Coulthard, Malcolm, jt. auth. see Sarangi, Srikant.

Coulthard, Malcolm, jt. compiled by see Caldas-Coulthard, Carmen R.

Coulthard, Malcolm, jt. ed. see Montgomery, Martin.

Coulthard, Max, et al. Business Planning: The Key to Success. 368p. 1997. 79.95 (*0-7329-3061-8*, Pub. by Macmill Educ); pap. 39.95 (*0-7329-3062-6*, Pub. by Macmill Educ) Paul & Co Pubs.

***Coulthard, Phil & Farr, George.** Java for S/390 & AS/400 Cobol Programmers. (Illus.). 832p. 2000. pap. 79.00 (*1-58347-011-5*, 5202, IBM) Midrange Comput.

Coulthard, Phil, jt. auth. see Farr, George.

Coulthart, Gordon, jt. auth. see Waisglass, David.

***Coultoff, Eric.** Thinking Your Way Around the Golf Course: Solid Decision Making to Lead to Better Scoring. Peters, James, ed. (Illus.). 40p. 2000. pap. write for info. (*0-9678513-1-9*) Go Low Golf.

***Coulton, A.** Our Farm of Four Acres & the Money We Made by It. Griffith, Nathan, ed. LC 99-80033. (Illus.). 101p. 2000. pap. 10.00 (*0-9665103-2-1*) Cobblemead Publications.

Coulton, Gary. In Situ Hybridization. 1998. pap. text 64.95 (*3-540-57119-1*) Spr-Verlag.

Coulton, Bill. The Labyrinth Bk. 1: The Sea Siren. LC 98-87152. 325p. 1998. 25.00 (*0-7388-0077-5*); pap. 15.00 (*0-7388-0078-3*) Xlibris Corp.

— The Labyrinth Bk. 2: The Minotaur. LC 98-87152. 325p. 1998. 25.00 (*0-7388-0075-9*); pap. 15.00 (*0-7388-0076-7*) Xlibris Corp.

Coulton, Claudia J. Social Work Quality Assurance Programs: A Comparative Analysis. LC 79-64947. 112p. reprint ed. pap. 34.80 (*0-7837-5362-4*, 204512500005) Bks Demand.

***Coulton, G.** Medieval Scene: An Informal Introduction to the Middle Ages. 2000. pap. 7.95 (*0-486-40963-5*) Dover.

Coulton, G. G. Infant Perdition in the Middle Ages. 1977. lib. bdg. 59.95 (*0-8490-2058-1*) Gordon Pr.

— Inquisition & Liberty. 1990. 16.50 (*0-8446-0560-3*) Peter Smith.

— The Medieval Village. 1989. pap. 13.95 (*0-486-26002-X*) Dover.

— Some Problems in Medieval Historiography. 1974. lib. bdg. 59.95 (*0-8490-1079-9*) Gordon Pr.

Coulton, G. R. & De Belleroche, J., eds. In Situ Hybridization: Medical Applications. (C). 1992. text 90.50 (*0-7923-8989-1*) Kluwer Academic.

Coulton, J. J. Ancient Greek Architects at Work: Problems of Structure & Design. 208p. 1982. pap. text 17.95 (*0-8014-9234-3*) Cornell U Pr.

Coulton, Mia, jt. auth. see Oppenlander, Meredith.

Coultrap, M. W. Coultrap-Cramblit. Data Concerning the Coultrap-Cramblit Lineage, Including Eichors, Randals, Simms & Their Descendants; Also the Wilson-Hardesty Descendants. 133p. 1997. reprint ed. pap. 21.50 (*0-8328-8078-7*); reprint ed. lib. bdg. 31.50 (*0-8328-8077-9*) Higginson Bk Co.

Coultrap-McQuin, Susan. Doing Literary Business: American Women Writers in the Nineteenth Century. LC 90-12006. (Gender & American Culture Ser.). (Illus.). xviii, 254p. (C). 1990. 34.95 (*0-8078-1914-X*); pap. 14.95 (*0-8078-4284-2*) U of NC Pr.

Coultrap-McQuin, Susan, jt. ed. see Cole, Eve B.

Coultrap-McQuin, Susan M. Doing Literary Business: American Women Writers in the Nineteenth Century. LC 90-12006. (Gender & American Culture Ser.). 271p. reprint ed. pap. 84.10 (*0-608-08613-4*, 206913600003) Bks Demand.

Coultras, Barbara. Teach Yourself French Business. (Teach Yourself Ser.). 1992. 19.95 (*0-8288-8324-6*); 45.00 incl. audio (*0-8288-8325-4*) Fr & Eur.

Coumbs, Jennifer L. Creative Achievement Days: Fast, an Activity Book for Primary Leaders. 40p. (J). 1998. pap. 9.98 (*0-88290-632-1*, 2074) Horizon Utah.

***Counce, Jacqueline A.** Attitudes of Life. 143p. 2000. pap. 12.95 (*1-891429-09-4*) Armadillo Pubng.

Councell, Ruth T. Once upon a Bedtime Story: Classic Tales. LC 96-80397. 96p. (J). (ps-1). 1997. 17.95 (*1-56397-484-3*) Boyds Mills Pr.

Council, Aaron, jt. auth. see Bohm, Kristie.

Council District Columbia Staff. District of Columbia Practice Manual. 6th ed. 1997. ring bd. 165.00 (*0-944694-14-4*) DC Bar.

Council for Advancement & Support of Education Staff. Higher Education in the News. 20p. 1998. pap. 44.95 (*0-89964-337-X*) Coun Adv & Supp Ed.

***Council for Advancement & Support of Education Staff, ed.** Donor Relations: The Essential Guide To Stewardship Policies, Procedures & Protocol. 80p. 1998. pap. 52.00 (*0-89964-339-6*) Coun Adv & Supp Ed.

Council for Advancement and Support of Education. CASE Guide to Advancing Education: Giving Opportunities at Colleges & Universities : a Gift Planning Guide for Attorneys, Financial Advisors, & Supporters of U.S. Higher Education. LC 98-124557. (Illus.). 1997. write for info. (*0-89964-318-3*) Coun Adv & Supp Ed.

Council for Agricultural Science & Technology Staf. Agriculture & Ground Water Quality. annot. ed. (Illus.). (C). 1988. 100.00 (*81-85046-66-2*, Pub. by Scientific) St Mut.

— Food Safety, Sufficiency, & Security. LC 98-23078. (Special Publication Ser.). 1998. 26.00 (*1-887383-13-1*) CAST.

— Foodborne Pathogens: Review of Recommendations. LC 98-35835. (Special Publication Ser.). 1998. 15.00 (*1-887383-14-X*) CAST.

***Council for Agricultural Science & Technology Staff.** Benefits of Biodiversity. LC 98-50296. (Task Force Report Ser.: No. 133). (Illus.). vi, 33 p. 1999. write for info. (*1-887383-15-8*) CAST.

Council for Basic Education Staff. Renewal & Recognition of Teachers: Fellowships for Independent Study. 22p. 1985. pap. 4.95 (*0-931989-26-4*) Coun Basic Educ.

Council for Continuous Improvement Staff. Basic Continuous Improvement Tools Handbook. (Illus.). 64p. 1994. pap. text 11.95 (*0-527-76233-4*, 762334) Productivity Inc.

— Design of Experiments Overview Handbook. (Illus.). 30p. 1994. pap. text 11.95 (*0-527-76236-9*, 762369) Productivity Inc.

— New Continuous Improvement Tools Handbook. (Illus.). 58p. 1994. pap. text 11.95 (*0-527-76234-2*, 762342) Productivity Inc.

— QFD Overview Handbook. (Illus.). 29p. 1994. pap. text 11.95 (*0-527-76235-0*, 762350) Productivity Inc.

— Team Facilitator's Handbook. (Illus.). 119p. 1992. pap. text 20.00 (*0-527-91702-8*, 917028) Productivity Inc.

— Team Leader's Handbook. (Illus.). 148p. 1992. pap. text 20.00 (*0-527-91701-X*, 91701X) Productivity Inc.

— Team Member's Handbook. (Illus.). 113p. 1992. pap. text 20.00 (*0-527-91700-1*, 917001) Productivity Inc.

Council for Court Excellence Staff. A Citizen's Guide to the Courts in the Washington Region. (Illus.). 32p. (Orig.). 1990. pap. text 5.00 (*0-940259-01-X*, TXU 399-229) Council Ct Excell.

Council for Exceptional Children Staff. IEP Team Guide. 115p. (C). 1999. pap. 29.95 (*0-86586-320-2*, P5274) Coun Exc Child.

— Publish & Flourish: A Guide for Writing in Education. Algozzine, Bob et al, eds. LC 98-44123. 1998. pap. text 24.95 (*0-86586-319-9*, P5273) Coun Exc Child.

— What Every Special Educator Must Know: The International Standards for the Preparation & Licensure of Special Educators. 3rd ed. 1998. pap. 16.00 (*0-86586-323-7*) Coun Exc Child.

Council for Exceptional Children Staff, jt. auth. see Bootel, Jaclyn A.

Council for Exceptional Children Staff, jt. auth. see Brolin, Donn E.

Council for Exceptional Children Staff, jt. auth. see Field, Sharon.

Council for Exceptional Children Staff, jt. auth. see West, Lynda L.

Council for National Cooperation in Aquatics Staff. Action in Aquatics: CNCA Eighteenth National Aquatic Conference: Phoenix, AZ, Del Webb's Towne House, November 22-26, 1974. Empleton, Bernard E., ed. LC 77-358552. (Illus.). 238p. reprint ed. pap. 73.80 (*0-8357-3833-7*, 203655800004) Bks Demand.

— Aquatics for All: The Next Quarter Century, 1976-CNCA 19th National Aquatic Conference, Urbana-Champaign, IL. Empleton, Bernard E., ed. LC GV0770.5.C6x. (Illus.). 116p. reprint ed. pap. 36.00 (*0-8357-3834-5*, 203655900004) Bks Demand.

— Aquatics in the Eighty's: The Conservation, Education, & Research: CNCA 21st National Aquatic Conference, November 20-23, 1980, Atlanta Biltmore Hotel, Georgia Institute of Technology. Priest, E. Louise, ed. LC GV0770.5.C66. (Illus.). 164p. reprint ed. pap. 50.90 (*0-8357-3836-1*, 203656100004) Bks Demand.

— Diving Injuries: A Critical Insight & Recommendations. Clayton, Robert D., ed. LC 84-198346. (Illus.). 204p. reprint ed. pap. 63.30 (*0-7837-5567-8*, 204534200005) Bks Demand.

— Lifeguard Training: Principles & Administration. 2nd rev. ed. LC 68-9312. (Illus.). 223p. reprint ed. pap. 69.20 (*0-8357-3831-0*, 203655500004) Bks Demand.

— New Horizons in Aquatics: CNCA Twentieth National Aquatic Conference, Town & Country Inn, San Diego, CA, November 13-17, 1978. Empleton, Bernard E., ed. LC GV0770.3.C68. (Illus.). 114p. reprint ed. pap. 35.40 (*0-8357-3835-3*, 203656000004) Bks Demand.

— Opportunities in Aquatics: A Report of the 1984 National Conference, Fort Worth, TX, November 8-11, 1984. Priest, Louise & Crowner, Ann, eds. LC GV0770.. (Illus.). 137p. reprint ed. pap. 42.50 (*0-8357-3837-X*, 203656300004) Bks Demand.

— A Practical Guide for Teaching the Mentally Retarded to Swim. LC 74-9727. (Illus.). 160p. reprint ed. pap. 49.60 (*0-7837-5568-6*, 204534300005) Bks Demand.

Council for Scholarly Evaluation of Gaelic Gotham. The Gaelic Gotham Report: Analysis of a Controversial Exhibition at the Museum of the City of New York. LC 97-66733. (Illus.). 160p. (Orig.). 1997. pap. 25.00 (*0-9657397-0-8*) NY Irish Hist.

Council for Science & Society Staff. Benefits & Risks of Knowledge-Based Systems. 88p. 1989. pap. 16.95 (*0-19-854743-9*) OUP.

— Companion Animals in Society. 94p. 1988. pap. text 15.95 (*0-19-857697-8*) OUP.

— Human Procreation: Ethical Aspects of the New Techniques. (Illus.). 96p. 1984. pap. 12.95 (*0-19-857608-0*) OUP.

— U. K. Military R & D. (Illus.). 90p. 1986. pap. 9.95 (*0-19-859930-7*) OUP.

Council-George, Marian, jt. auth. see Ayum, Evelyn.

Council History Task Force Staff & Sturrock, James P. Scouting in the Santa Clara Valley: The Seventy Year Adventure, 1920-1990. Bennett, Mardi, ed. (Illus.). 232p. 1990. 29.95 (*0-9628133-0-3*) Santa Clara Cnty BSA.

***Council Library & Info Resources Staff.** Innovative Use of Information Technology by Colleges. 87p. 1999. 20.00 (*1-887334-70-X*) Coun Lib & Info.

Council, Mildred. Mama Dip's Kitchen. LC 99-19973. (Illus.). 230p. 1999. 27.50 (*0-8078-2508-5*); pap. 15.95 (*0-8078-4790-9*) U of NC Pr.

Council of American Building Officials Staff. You Can Build It! 58p. 1989. pap. 4.70 (*1-884590-31-4*, 223S00) Intl Conf Bldg Off.

Council of Community Services Staff. Directory of Licensed Mental Health Care Providers, 1995-1996: Middle Tennessee Edition. 120p. 1996. spiral bd. 8.00 (*1-888334-00-2*) Coun Commun Serv.

— Directory of Nashville Area Support Groups. 125p. 1996. spiral bd. 8.00 (*1-888334-01-0*) Coun Commun Serv.

Council of Educators in Landscape Architecture Sta. Continuing Education in Landscape Architecture. Burkart, M. et al, eds. LC 80-621598. (Illus.). 103p. reprint ed. pap. 32.00 (*0-8357-3043-3*, 203929800012) Bks Demand.

— Environmental Ethics: Values & Obligations in the Landscape. LC SB0469. (CELA Forum Ser.: Vol. 1, No. 4). 45p. reprint ed. pap. 30.00 (*0-608-12786-8*, 202348300033) Bks Demand.

C

An Asterisk (*) at the beginning of an entry indicates that the title is appearing for the first time.

— The Landscape: Critical Issues & Resources: Proceedings of the 1983 Conference of Educators in Landscape Architecture, August 6-10, 1983, Utah State University, Logan, Utah. LC SB0469.. 310p. reprint ed. pap. 96.10 (*0-608-14470-3*, 202108100020) Bks Demand.

— Landscape & Architecture: Sharing Common Ground, Defining Turf, Charting New Paths: Proceedings. McAvin, Margaret, ed. LC 88-71962. (Illus.). 853p. reprint ed. pap. 200.00 (*0-8357-6182-7*, 203461500090) Bks Demand.

— The Rural Landscape: Abstracts of Papers Presented at the Annual Meeting of CELA, October 23-27, 1982. LC SB0469.4. 127p. reprint ed. pap. 39.40 (*0-608-14341-3*, 201963400013) Bks Demand.

— Teaching on the Crest of the Third Wave: Proceedings CELA '84. LC SB0469.4.A3. 471p. reprint ed. pap. 146.10 (*0-608-12784-1*, 202348200033) Bks Demand.

— Teaching, Research, & Community Service - Paradigms for Success in the 1990's: Proceedings. Westphal, Joanne M., ed. LC SB0469.23.C6. (CELA Conference Proceedings Ser.: No. 1). 188p. reprint ed. pap. 58.30 (*0-7837-1135-2*, 204166500022) Bks Demand.

***Council of Europe, ed.** Yearbook of the European Convention on Human Rights (Annuaire de la Convention Europeenne des Droits de l'Homme) Vol. 41A: Key Extracts from a Selection of Judgements of the European Court of Human Rights & Decisions & Reports of the European Commission of Human Rights. 448p. 1999. 225.00 (*90-411-1245-6*) Kluwer Law Intl.

Council of Europe - Conseil de l'Europe Staff, ed. Yearbook of the European Convention on Human Rights - Annuaire de la Convention Europeenne des Droit de l'Homme, Vol. 1: 1955-1956-1957 (Documents & - et Decisions) (European Commission of Human Rights) 276p. (C). 1959. lib. bdg. 223.50 (*0-7923-2571-0*) Kluwer Academic.

— Yearbook of the European Convention on Human Rights - Annuaire de la Convention Europeenne des Droits de l'Homme, Vol. 30, 1987. 704p. (C). 1992. lib. bdg. 286.50 (*0-7923-1575-8*) Kluwer Academic.

Council of Europe, Directorate of Education, Cultu, ed. EUDISED: European Educational Research Yearbook. 480p. 1995. 175.00 (*3-598-23460-0*) K G Saur Verlag.

— EUDISED European Educational Research Yearbook, 1997: Project Reports - People - Contacts. 516p. 1998. 185.00 (*3-598-23464-3*) K G Saur Verlag.

— EUDISED European Educational Research Yearbook, 1997: Project Reports - People - Contacts. 4th ed. 516p. 1997. 185.00 (*3-598-23463-5*) K G Saur Verlag.

— EUDISED European Educational Yearbook 1996: Project Reports - People - Contacts. 516p. 1996. 185.00 (*3-598-23462-7*) K G Saur Verlag.

Council of Europe-Directorate of Human Rights Staf, ed. Collected Edition of the "Travaux Preparatoires" of the European Convention on Human Rights, Vol. VI. 1985. lib. bdg. 195.00 (*90-247-2230-6*) Kluwer Academic.

Council of Europe Staff. Abuse of Rights & Equivalent Concepts: The Principle & Its Present Day Application (Proceedings of the 19th Colloquy on European Law, Luxembourg, 1989) 1990. 21.00 (*92-871-1868-X*, Pub. by Council of Europe) Manhattan Pub Co.

— Adapting Social Security to the Emering Needs of a Changing Society. 1989. 21.00 (*92-871-1758-6*, Pub. by Council of Europe) Manhattan Pub Co.

— Additional Protocol to the Agreement on the Temporary Importation, Free of Duty, of Medical, Surgical & Laboratory Equipment for Use on Free Loan in Hospitals & Other Medical Institutions for Purposes of Diagnosis or Treatment. (Conventions & Agreements Ser.: No. 110). (ENG & FRE.). 1983. 12.00 (*92-871-0195-7*, Pub. by Council of Europe) Manhattan Pub Co.

— Additional Protocol to the European Agreement on the Exchange of Tissue-Typing Reagents. (Conventions & Agreements Ser.: No. 89). (ENG & FRE.). 1976. 12.00 (*92-871-0135-3*, Pub. by Council of Europe) Manhattan Pub Co.

— Additional Protocol to the European Agreement on the Exchanges of Blood-Grouping Regeants. (Conventions & Agreements Ser.: No. 111). (ENG & FRE.). 1983. 12.00 (*92-871-0196-5*, Pub. by Council of Europe) Manhattan Pub Co.

— Additional Protocol to the European Agreement on the Protection of Television Broadcasts. (Conventions & Agreements Ser.: No. 113). (ENG & FRE.). 1983. 12.00 (*92-871-0234-1*, Pub. by Council of Europe) Manhattan Pub Co.

— Additional Protocol to the European Convention on Extradition. (Conventions & Agreements Ser.: No. 86). (ENG & FRE.). 1980. 12.00 (*92-871-0132-9*, Pub. by Council of Europe) Manhattan Pub Co.

— Additional Protocol to the European Convention on Information on Foreign Law. (Conventions & Agreements Ser.: No. 97). (ENG & FRE.). 1978. 12.00 (*92-871-0141-8*, Pub. by Council of Europe) Manhattan Pub Co.

— Additional Protocol to the European Convention on Mutual Assistance in Criminal Matters. (Conventions & Agreements Ser.: No. 99). (ENG & FRE.). 1983. 12.00 (*92-871-0284-8*, Pub. by Council of Europe) Manhattan Pub Co.

— Advanced Information Technologies: The Impact on Training. (Congress of Local & Regional Authorities of Europe Ser.: No. 26). 1992. 15.00 (*92-871-2156-7*, Pub. by Council of Europe) Manhattan Pub Co.

— Agreement Between the Member States of the Council of Europe on the Issue to Military & Civilian War-Disabled of an International Book of Vouchers for the Repair of Prosthetic & Orthopaedic Appliances. (Conventions & Agreements Ser.: No. 40). (ENG & FRE.). 1976. 12.00 (*92-871-0092-6*, Pub. by Council of Europe) Manhattan Pub Co.

— Agreement on the Exchange of War Cripples Between Member Countries of the Council of Europe with a View to Medical Treatment. (Conventions & Agreements Ser.: No. 20). (ENG & FRE.). 1976. 12.00 (*92-871-0076-4*, Pub. by Council of Europe) Manhattan Pub Co.

— Agreement on the Temporary Importation, Free of Duty, of Medical, Surgical & Laboratory Equipment for Use on Free Loan in Hospitals & Other Medical Institutions for Purposes of Diagnosis or Treatment. (Conventions & Agreements Ser.: No. 33). (ENG & FRE.). 1976. 12.00 (*92-871-0086-1*, Pub. by Council of Europe) Manhattan Pub Co.

— Agreement on the Transfer of Corpses. (Conventions & Agreements Ser.: No. 80). (ENG & FRE.). 1973. 12.00 (*92-871-0127-2*, Pub. by Council of Europe) Manhattan Pub Co.

— Agreement Relating to the Application of the European Convention on International Commercial Arbitration. (Conventions & Agreements Ser.: No. 42). (ENG & FRE.). 1983. 12.00 (*92-871-0282-1*, Pub. by Council of Europe) Manhattan Pub Co.

— Agriculture & the Environment: Technical & Vocational Education. (Nature & Environment Ser.: No. 52). 1991. 12.00 (*92-871-1927-9*, Pub. by Council of Europe) Manhattan Pub Co.

— Album Praw Czlowieka. (POL.). (J). (gr. 1-7). 1992. 15.00 (*92-871-2096-X*, Pub. by Council of Europe) Manhattan Pub Co.

— Annexes to the European . . . (Conventions & Agreements Ser.: No. 78a). (ENG & FRE.). 1978. 18.00 (*92-871-0125-6*, Pub. by Council of Europe) Manhattan Pub Co.

— Annexes to the European . . . (Conventions & Agreements Ser.: No. 14a). (ENG & FRE.). 1983. 12.00 (*92-871-0281-3*, Pub. by Council of Europe) Manhattan Pub Co.

— Annexes to the European . . . (Conventions & Agreements Ser.: No. 12a). (ENG & FRE.). 1984. 12.00 (*92-871-0066-7*, Pub. by Council of Europe) Manhattan Pub Co.

— Annexes to the European . . . (Conventions & Agreements Ser.: No. 13a). (ENG & FRE.). 1984. 12.00 (*92-871-0068-3*, Pub. by Council of Europe) Manhattan Pub Co.

— Anti-Doping Convention. (Conventions & Agreements Ser.: No. 135). (ENG & FRE.). 1989. 12.00 (*92-871-1782-9*, Pub. by Council of Europe) Manhattan Pub Co.

— Arbitral Tribunals under the Laundering Convention (Recommendation), No. R(91)12. 1992. 12.00 (*92-871-2041-2*, Pub. by Council of Europe) Manhattan Pub Co.

— Archaeological Sites in Europe: Conservation, Maintenance & Enhancement (Conimbriga, 1990) (Cultural Heritage Ser.: No. 22). 1992. 21.00 (*92-871-2047-1*, Pub. by Council of Europe) Manhattan Pub Co.

— Architectural Heritage, New Technologies in Documentation - Report of the London Round Table. (Cultural Heritage Ser.: No. 19). 1990. 21.00 (*92-871-1839-6*, Pub. by Council of Europe) Manhattan Pub Co.

— Arrangement for the Application of the European Agreement of 17 October, 1980 Concerning the Provision of Medical Care to Persons During Temporary Residence. (Conventions & Agreements Ser.: No. 129). (ENG & FRE.). 1988. 12.00 (*92-871-1594-X*, Pub. by Council of Europe) Manhattan Pub Co.

— Art & the Media (Colloquy Organised by Eighty, the Dernieres Nouvelles d'Alsace & the Council of Europe) 1990. 18.00 (*92-871-1794-2*, Pub. by Council of Europe) Manhattan Pub Co.

— Assessment of Damage to the Environment. 1992. 12.00 (*92-871-2098-6*, Pub. by Council of Europe) Manhattan Pub Co.

— Atalase Maila (The Threshold Level for Basque) (BAQ.). 1988. 21.00 (*92-871-1545-1*, Pub. by Council of Europe) Manhattan Pub Co.

— Balanced Development of the Countryside in Western Europe. (Nature & Environment Ser.: No. 58). 1992. 12.00 (*92-871-2113-3*, Pub. by Council of Europe) Manhattan Pub Co.

— The Bern Convention on Nature Conservation. 1991. 15.00 (*92-871-1947-3*, Pub. by Council of Europe) Manhattan Pub Co.

— Die Berner Konvention Uber die Erhaltung der Natur. (GER.). 1992. 15.00 (*92-871-2140-0*, Pub. by Council of Europe) Manhattan Pub Co.

— The Biological Significance & Conservation of Hymenoptera in Europe. (Nature & Environment Ser.: No. 44). 12.00 (*92-871-1831-0*, Pub. by Council of Europe) Manhattan Pub Co.

— The Biology, Status & Conservation of the Monk Seal (Monachus Monachus) (Nature & Environment Ser.: No. 41). 1989. 12.00 (*92-871-1662-8*, Pub. by Council of Europe) Manhattan Pub Co.

— Blood Transfusion: 2nd European Course (Madrid, 1990) (ENG & FRE.). 1992. 21.00 (*92-871-2063-3*, Pub. by Council of Europe) Manhattan Pub Co.

— Borrowing by Local & Regional Authorities. (Local & Regional Authorities in Europe Ser.: No. 47). 1992. 12.00 (*92-871-2073-0*, Pub. by Council of Europe) Manhattan Pub Co.

— Case-Law of the European Commission of Human Rights: Decisions & Reports: Summaries & Indexes, Nos. 1-20. 1981. 25.00 (*92-871-0941-9*, Pub. by Council of Europe) Manhattan Pub Co.

— Case-Law of the European Commission of Human Rights: Decisions & Reports: Summaries & Indexes, Nos. 21-40. 1987. 25.00 (*92-871-1541-9*, Pub. by Council of Europe) Manhattan Pub Co.

— Case-Law on the European Social Charter. 1982. 21.00 (*92-871-0165-5*, Pub. by Council of Europe) Manhattan Pub Co.

— Case-Law on the European Social Charter. 1986. suppl. ed. 21.00 (*92-871-0847-1*, Pub. by Council of Europe) Manhattan Pub Co.

— Case-Law on the European Social Charter. 1987. 21.00 (*92-871-1093-X*, Pub. by Council of Europe) Manhattan Pub Co.

— Certificate of the Secretary General Containing the Revised Text of the Protocol to the European Agreement on the Exchange of Therapeutic Substances of Human Origin & Annexes to the Said Protocol. (Conventions & Agreements Ser.: No. 26a). (ENG & FRE.). 1982. 12.00 (*92-871-0050-0*, Pub. by Council of Europe) Manhattan Pub Co.

— The Challenges Facing European Society with the Approach of the Year 2000: Strategies for Sustainable Quality Tourism. (European Regional Planning Ser.: No. 53). 1992. 18.00 (*92-871-2133-8*, Pub. by Council of Europe) Manhattan Pub Co.

— Chart Showing Signatures & Ratifications of Council of Europe Conventions & Agreements. (Conventions & Agreements Ser.). (ENG & FRE.). 1988. ring bd. 38.00 (*92-871-1520-6*, Pub. by Council of Europe) Manhattan Pub Co.

— A Coherent Policy for the Rehabilitation of People with Disabilities. 1992. 12.00 (*92-871-2147-8*, Pub. by Council of Europe) Manhattan Pub Co.

— Cohort Fertility in Member States of the Council of Europe. (Population Studies: No. 21). 1990. 21.00 (*92-871-1790-X*, Pub. by Council of Europe) Manhattan Pub Co.

— Colloquy on the Berne Convention Invertebrates & Their Conservation. (Environmental Encounters Ser.: No. 10). (ENG & FRE.). 1990. 15.00 (*92-871-1881-7*, Pub. by Council of Europe) Manhattan Pub Co.

— Communication to Third Parties of Personal Data Held by Public Bodies (Recommendation), No. R(91)10. 1993. 12.00 (*92-871-2119-2*, Pub. by Council of Europe) Manhattan Pub Co.

— Comparative Study of the Organisation & Functioning of Emergency Medical Assistance Services. 1990. 21.00 (*92-871-1727-6*, Pub. by Council of Europe) Manhattan Pub Co.

— Computer-Related Crime. 1990. 25.00 (*92-871-1792-6*, Pub. by Council of Europe) Manhattan Pub Co.

— Computerisation of Medical Data in Hospital Services Including University Hospitals. 1989. 21.00 (*92-871-1602-4*, Pub. by Council of Europe) Manhattan Pub Co.

— The Conceptual Framework of the International Classification of Impairments, Disabilities & Handicaps (ICIDH) 1992. 12.00 (*92-871-1972-4*, Pub. by Council of Europe) Manhattan Pub Co.

— Conference of European Mountain Regions (Trento, 1988) Working Documents & Conclusions. (Congress of Local & Regional Authorities of Europe Ser.: No. 9). 1988. 21.00 (*92-871-1642-3*, Pub. by Council of Europe) Manhattan Pub Co.

— Conference on Free Local Government: Deregulation, Efficiency, Democracy (Ostersund, 1988) Working Documents & Conclusions. (Congress of Local & Regional Authorities of Europe Ser.: No. 11). 1989. 21.00 (*92-871-1723-3*, Pub. by Council of Europe) Manhattan Pub Co.

— Conference on Improving Traffic & Quality of Life in Metropolitan Areas (Goteborg, 1990) Working Documents & Conclusions. (Congress of Local & Regional Authorities of Europe Ser.: No. 16). 1990. 21.00 (*92-871-1860-4*, Pub. by Council of Europe) Manhattan Pub Co.

— Conference on Regional Transport (Cologne, 1989) Working Documents & Conclusions. (Congress of Local & Regional Authorities of Europe Ser.: No. 13). 1990. 21.00 (*92-871-1754-3*, Pub. by Council of Europe) Manhattan Pub Co.

— Conscientious Objection to Compulsory Military Service (Recommendation), No. R(87)8. 12.00 (*92-871-1568-0*, Pub. by Council of Europe) Manhattan Pub Co.

— The Conservaiton of European Orchids. (Nature & Environment Ser.: No. 57). 1992. 15.00 (*92-871-2011-0*, Pub. by Council of Europe) Manhattan Pub Co.

— Conservation of Natural Habitats Outside Protected Areas - Legal Analysis. (Nature & Environment Ser.: No. 56). 1992. 15.00 (*92-871-1997-X*, Pub. by Council of Europe) Manhattan Pub Co.

— Conservation of the Mediterranean Monk Seal - Technical & Scientific Aspects. (Environmental Encounters Ser.: No. 13). (ENG & FRE.). 1992. 21.00 (*92-871-2009-9*, Pub. by Council of Europe) Manhattan Pub Co.

— Conservation of Threatened Freshwater Fish in Europe. (Nature & Environment Ser.: No. 46). 1991. 12.00 (*92-871-1884-1*, Pub. by Council of Europe) Manhattan Pub Co.

— The Conservation of Wild Progenitors of Cultivate Plants. (Environmental Encounters Ser.: No. 8). 1991. 21.00 (*92-871-1929-5*, Pub. by Council of Europe) Manhattan Pub Co.

— Conserving & Managing Wetlands for Invertebrates (Vaduz, 1991) (Environmental Encounters Ser.: No. 14). (ENG & FRE.). 1992. 21.00 (*92-871-2031-5*, Pub. by Council of Europe) Manhattan Pub Co.

— Contributions Following Divorce (Recommendation & Explanatory Memorandum), No. R(89)1. 1989. 12.00 (*92-871-1731-4*, Pub. by Council of Europe) Manhattan Pub Co.

— El Convenio de Berna para la Conservacion de la Naturaleza. (SPA.). 1992. 15.00 (*92-871-2141-9*, Pub. by Council of Europe) Manhattan Pub Co.

— Convention for the Protection of Human Rights & Fundamental Freedoms & Protocols to the Said Convention: (Includes Nos. 9, 44, 45, 46, 55, 114, 117, 118, 140) (Conventions & Agreements Ser.: No. 5). (ENG & FRE.). 1991. 12.00 (*92-871-1961-9*, Pub. by Council of Europe) Manhattan Pub Co.

— Convention for the Protection of Individuals with Regard to Automatic Processing of Personal Data. (Conventions & Agreements Ser.: No. 108). (ENG & FRE.). 1982. 12.00 (*92-871-0022-5*, Pub. by Council of Europe) Manhattan Pub Co.

— Convention for the Protection of the Architectural Heritage of Europe. (Conventions & Agreements Ser.: No. 121). (ENG & FRE.). 1985. 12.00 (*92-871-0799-8*, Pub. by Council of Europe) Manhattan Pub Co.

— Convention on Certain International Aspects of Bankruptcy. (Conventions & Agreements Ser.: No. 136). (ENG & FRE.). 1990. 12.00 (*92-871-1842-6*, Pub. by Council of Europe) Manhattan Pub Co.

— Convention on Insider Trading & Additional Protocol. (Conventions & Agreements Ser.: Nos. 130 & 133). (ENG & FRE.). 1989. 12.00 (*92-871-1853-1*, Pub. by Council of Europe) Manhattan Pub Co.

— Convention on Laundering, Search, Seizure & Confiscation of the Proceeds from Crime (Strasbourg, 1990) (Conventions & Agreements Ser.: No. 141). (ENG & FRE.). 1991. 12.00 (*92-871-1905-8*, Pub. by Council of Europe) Manhattan Pub Co.

— Convention on Mutual Administrative Assistance in Tax Matters. (Conventions & Agreements Ser.: No. 127). (ENG & FRE.). 1988. 12.00 (*92-871-1571-0*, Pub. by Council of Europe) Manhattan Pub Co.

— Convention on the Conservation of European Wildlife & Natural Habitats. (Conventions & Agreements Ser.: No. 104). (ENG & FRE.). 1982. 12.00 (*92-871-0020-9*, Pub. by Council of Europe) Manhattan Pub Co.

— Convention on the Establishment of a Scheme of Registration of Wills. (Conventions & Agreements Ser.: No. 77). (ENG & FRE.). 1976. 12.00 (*92-871-0124-8*, Pub. by Council of Europe) Manhattan Pub Co.

— Convention on the Liability of Hotel-Keepers Concerning the Property of Their Guests. (Conventions & Agreements Ser.: No. 41). (ENG & FRE.). 1978. 12.00 (*92-871-0093-4*, Pub. by Council of Europe) Manhattan Pub Co.

— Convention on the Participation of Foreigners in Public Life at Local Level (Strasbourg, 1992) (Conventions & Agreements Ser.: No. 144). (ENG & FRE.). 1992. 12.00 (*92-871-2061-7*, Pub. by Council of Europe) Manhattan Pub Co.

— Convention on the Reduction of Cases of Multiple Nationality & Military Obligations in Cases of Multiple Nationality, Protocol Amending the Convention & Additional Protocol to the Convention. (Conventions & Agreements Ser.: No. 43). (ENG & FRE.). 1978. 12.00 (*92-871-0095-0*, Pub. by Council of Europe) Manhattan Pub Co.

— Convention on the Transfer of Sentenced Persons. (Conventions & Agreements Ser.: No. 112). (ENG & FRE.). 1983. 12.00 (*92-871-0233-3*, Pub. by Council of Europe) Manhattan Pub Co.

— Convention on the Unification of Certain Points of Substantive Law on Patents for Inventions. (Conventions & Agreements Ser.: No. 47). (ENG & FRE.). 1978. 12.00 (*92-871-0096-9*, Pub. by Council of Europe) Manhattan Pub Co.

— Convention Relating to Stops on Bearer Securities in International Circulation. (Conventions & Agreements Ser.: No. 72). (ENG & FRE.). 1979. 12.00 (*92-871-0119-1*, Pub. by Council of Europe) Manhattan Pub Co.

— The Council of Europe & Child Welfare: The Need for a European Convention on Children's Rights. (Human Rights Files Ser.: No. 10). 1989. 18.00 (*92-871-1609-1*, Pub. by Council of Europe) Manhattan Pub Co.

— The Council of Europe's Work on Sport, 1967-71, Vol. I. 1992. 18.00 (*92-871-2102-8*, Pub. by Council of Europe) Manhattan Pub Co.

— The Council of Europe's Work on Sport, 1967-71, Vol. II. 1992. 18.00 (*92-871-2104-4*, Pub. by Council of Europe) Manhattan Pub Co.

— Cultural Policy in France No. 1: European Programme for the Appraisal of Cultural Policies. 1991. 25.00 (*92-871-1923-6*, Pub. by Council of Europe) Manhattan Pub Co.

— Culture & Regions of Europe. 1993. 25.00 (*92-871-2159-1*, Pub. by Council of Europe) Manhattan Pub Co.

— Data Protection & the Media. 1991. 12.00 (*92-871-1937-6*, Pub. by Council of Europe) Manhattan Pub Co.

— Datasheets of Flora Species for Revision of Appendix I of the Bern Convention, Vol. II. (Nature & Environment Ser.: No. 61). 1992. 15.00 (*92-871-2088-9*, Pub. by Council of Europe) Manhattan Pub Co.

— Datasheets of Flora Species for Revision of Appendix I of the Bern Convention, Vol. III. (Nature & Environment Ser.: No. 62). 1992. 15.00 (*92-871-2089-7*, Pub. by Council of Europe) Manhattan Pub Co.

— Datasheets of Flora Species for Revision of Appendix I of the Bern Convention, Vol. IV. (Nature & Environment Ser.: No. 63). 1992. 15.00 (*92-871-2090-0*, Pub. by Council of Europe) Manhattan Pub Co.

— Datasheets of the Flora Species for Revision of Appendix I of the Bern Convention, Vol. I. (Nature & Environment Ser.: No. 60). 1992. 15.00 (*92-871-2087-0*, Pub. by Council of Europe) Manhattan Pub Co.

— Decentralisation & the Strengthening of Local Self-Government. (Local & Regional Authorities in Europe Ser.: No. 48). 1992. 18.00 (*92-871-2127-3*, Pub. by Council of Europe) Manhattan Pub Co.

— Delays in the Criminal Justice System: (Reports Presented

An Asterisk (*) at the beginning of an entry indicates that the title is appearing for the first time.

at the 9th Criminological Colloquy, 1989) (Collected Studies in Criminological Research: Vol. XXVIII). 1991. 12.00 (*92-871-1846-9*, Pub. by Council of Europe) Manhattan Pub Co.

— The Democratic Principle of Equal Representation - Forty Years of Council of Europe Activity: (Proceedings of the Seminar, Strasbourg, 1989) (Equality of the Sexes Ser.). 1992. 12.00 (*92-871-2049-8*, Pub. by Council of Europe) Manhattan Pub Co.

— Development of the Pont du Gard Site: Technical Assistance Report. (Cultural Heritage Ser.: No. 17). 1989. 12.00 (*92-871-1748-9*, Pub. by Council of Europe) Manhattan Pub Co.

— Developments in National Social Security Legislation: (Period from 1 July, 1988 to 30 June, 1989) 1990. 12.00 (*92-871-1825-6*, Pub. by Council of Europe) Manhattan Pub Co.

— Disparities in Sentencing: Causes & Solutions. (Collected Studies in Criminological Research: Vol. XXVI). 25.00 (*92-871-1621-0*, Pub. by Council of Europe) Manhattan Pub Co.

— Drempelniveau (The Threshold Level for Dutch) (DUT.). 1985. 25.00 (*92-871-0817-X*, Pub. by Council of Europe) Manhattan Pub Co.

— Education in Prison (Recommendation & Explanatory Memorandum), No. R(89)12. 1990. 21.00 (*92-871-1816-7*, Pub. by Council of Europe) Manhattan Pub Co.

— The Elimination of Sexism from Language (Recommendation), No. R(90)4. (Equality of the Sexes Ser.). 1991. 12.00 (*92-871-1955-4*, Pub. by Council of Europe) Manhattan Pub Co.

— Environment in Europe: Co-Operation Between Local & Regional Authorities (Siofok, 1991) Working Documents & Conclusions. (Congress of Local & Regional Authorities of Europe Ser.: No. 21). 1992. 21.00 (*92-871-2058-7*, Pub. by Council of Europe) Manhattan Pub Co.

— Equalisation of Resources Between Local Authorities (Recommendation), No. R(91)4. 1992. 12.00 (*92-871-2078-1*, Pub. by Council of Europe) Manhattan Pub Co.

— Equivalence of Professional & Technical Qualifications (Recommendation & Commentaries), No. R(89)10. 1990. 12.00 (*92-871-1849-3*, Pub. by Council of Europe) Manhattan Pub Co.

— Et Taerskelniveau for Dansk - Appendix-Annexe-Appendiks. (DAN.). 1983. 18.00 (*92-871-0293-7*, Pub. by Council of Europe) Manhattan Pub Co.

— Et Taerskelniveau for Dansk (The Threshold Level for Danish) (DAN.). 1983. 18.00 (*92-871-0250-3*, Pub. by Council of Europe) Manhattan Pub Co.

— Et Terskelniva for Norsk (The Threshold Level for Norwegian) (NOR.). 1988. 21.00 (*92-871-1542-7*, Pub. by Council of Europe) Manhattan Pub Co.

— The Ethical Issues of HIV Infection in the Health Care & Social Settings (Recommendation), No. R(89)14. 1990. 15.00 (*92-871-1780-2*, Pub. by Council of Europe) Manhattan Pub Co.

— Europe, 1990-2000: Multiculturalism in the City: The Integration of Immigrants. (Congress of Local & Regional Authorities of Europe Ser.: No. 25). 1992. 18.00 (*92-871-2109-5*, Pub. by Council of Europe) Manhattan Pub Co.

— European Agreement Concerning Programme Exchanges by Means of Television Films. (Conventions & Agreements Ser.: No. 27). (ENG & FRE.). 1980. 12.00 (*92-871-0081-0*, Pub. by Council of Europe) Manhattan Pub Co.

— European Agreement for the Prevention of Broadcasts Transmitted from Stations Outside National Territories. (Conventions & Agreements Ser.: No. 53). (ENG & FRE.). 1976. 12.00 (*92-871-0102-7*, Pub. by Council of Europe) Manhattan Pub Co.

— European Agreement on Au Pair Placement. (Conventions & Agreements Ser.: No. 68). (ENG & FRE.). 1979. 12.00 (*92-871-0115-9*, Pub. by Council of Europe) Manhattan Pub Co.

— European Agreement on Continued Payment of Scholarships to Students Studying Abroad. (Conventions & Agreements Ser.: No. 69). (ENG & FRE.). 1979. 12.00 (*92-871-0116-7*, Pub. by Council of Europe) Manhattan Pub Co.

— European Agreement on Mutual Assistance in the Matter of Special Medical Treatments & Climatic Facilities. (Conventions & Agreements Ser.: No. 38). (ENG & FRE.). 1977. 12.00 (*92-871-0090-X*, Pub. by Council of Europe) Manhattan Pub Co.

— European Agreement on Regulations Governing the Movement of Persons Between Member States of the Council of Europe. (Conventions & Agreements Ser.: No. 25). (ENG & FRE.). 1984. 12.00 (*92-871-0079-9*, Pub. by Council of Europe) Manhattan Pub Co.

— European Agreement on the Abolition of Visas for Refugees. (Conventions & Agreements Ser.: No. 31). (ENG & FRE.). 1981. 12.00 (*92-871-0084-5*, Pub. by Council of Europe) Manhattan Pub Co.

— European Agreement on the Exchange of Blood-Grouping Reagents. (Conventions & Agreements Ser.: No. 39). (ENG & FRE.). 1978. 12.00 (*92-871-0091-8*, Pub. by Council of Europe) Manhattan Pub Co.

— European Agreement on the Exchange of Therapeutic Substances of Human Origin (1983) & Additional Protocol (1990) (Conventions & Agreements Ser.: Nos. 26 & 109). (ENG & FRE.). 1990. 12.00 (*92-871-1799-3*, Pub. by Council of Europe) Manhattan Pub Co.

— European Agreement on the Exchange of Tissue-Typing Reagents. (Conventions & Agreements Ser.: No. 84). (ENG & FRE.). 1987. 12.00 (*92-871-0130-2*, Pub. by Council of Europe) Manhattan Pub Co.

— European Agreement on the Instruction & Education of Nurses. (Conventions & Agreements Ser.: No. 59). (ENG & FRE.). 1978. 12.00 (*92-871-0106-X*, Pub. by Council of Europe) Manhattan Pub Co.

— European Agreement on the Protection of Television Broadcasts, Protocol to the European Agreement & Additional Protocol to the Protocol to the European Agreement. (Conventions & Agreements Ser.: No. 34). (ENG & FRE.). 1977. 12.00 (*92-871-0087-X*, Pub. by Council of Europe) Manhattan Pub Co.

— European Agreement on the Restriction of the Use of Certain Detergents in Washing & Cleaning Products. (Conventions & Agreements Ser.: No. 64). (ENG & FRE.). 1984. 12.00 (*92-871-0111-6*, Pub. by Council of Europe) Manhattan Pub Co.

— European Agreement on the Transmission of Applications for Legal Aid. (Conventions & Agreements Ser.: No. 92). (ENG & FRE.). 1986. 12.00 (*92-871-0138-8*, Pub. by Council of Europe) Manhattan Pub Co.

— European Agreement on Transfer of Responsibility for Refugees. (Conventions & Agreements Ser.: No. 107). (ENG & FRE.). 1980. 12.00 (*92-871-0149-3*, Pub. by Council of Europe) Manhattan Pub Co.

— European Agreement on Travel by Young Persons on Collective Passports Between Member Countries of the Council of Europe. (Conventions & Agreements Ser.: No. 37). (ENG & FRE.). 1985. 12.00 (*92-871-0089-6*, Pub. by Council of Europe) Manhattan Pub Co.

— European Agreement Relating to Persons Participating in Proceedings of the European Commission & Court of Human Rights. (Conventions & Agreements Ser.: No. 67). (ENG & FRE.). 1979. 12.00 (*92-871-0114-0*, Pub. by Council of Europe) Manhattan Pub Co.

— European Campaign for the Countryside: Conclusions & Declarations. 1989. 18.00 (*92-871-1769-1*, Pub. by Council of Europe) Manhattan Pub Co.

— European Charter for Local Self-Government. (Conventions & Agreements Ser.: No. 122). (ENG & FRE.). 1985. 12.00 (*92-871-0804-8*, Pub. by Council of Europe) Manhattan Pub Co.

— European Co-Operation Concerning Epidemiological Studies in the Field of Mental Health. 1993. 12.00 (*92-871-2100-1*, Pub. by Council of Europe) Manhattan Pub Co.

— European Code of Social Security, & Protocol to the European Code of Social Security. (Conventions & Agreements Ser.: No. 48). (ENG & FRE.). 1986. write for info. (*92-871-0097-7*, Pub. by Council of Europe) Manhattan Pub Co.

— European Code of Social Security (Rome, 1990) rev. ed. (Conventions & Agreements Ser.: No. 139). (ENG & FRE.). 1991. 12.00 (*92-871-1919-8*, Pub. by Council of Europe) Manhattan Pub Co.

— European Convention for the Peaceful Settlement of Disputes. (Conventions & Agreements Ser.: No. 23). (ENG & FRE.). 1981. 12.00 (*92-871-0078-0*, Pub. by Council of Europe) Manhattan Pub Co.

— European Convention for the Prevention of Torture & Inhuman or Degrading Treatment or Punishment. (Conventions & Agreements Ser.: No. 126). (ENG & FRE.). 1987. 12.00 (*92-871-1526-5*, Pub. by Council of Europe) Manhattan Pub Co.

— European Convention for the Protection of Animals During International Transport & Protocol. (Conventions & Agreements Ser.: Nos. 65 & 103). (ENG & FRE.). 1979. 12.00 (*92-871-1810-8*, Pub. by Council of Europe) Manhattan Pub Co.

— European Convention for the Protection of Animals for Slaughter. (Conventions & Agreements Ser.: No. 102). (ENG & FRE.). 1979. 12.00 (*92-871-0146-9*, Pub. by Council of Europe) Manhattan Pub Co.

— European Convention for the Protection of Animals Kept for Farming Purposes. (Conventions & Agreements Ser.: No. 87). (ENG & FRE.). 1985. 12.00 (*92-871-0133-7*, Pub. by Council of Europe) Manhattan Pub Co.

— European Convention for the Protection of Vertebrate Animals Used for Experimental & Other Scientific Purposes. (Conventions & Agreements Ser.: No. 123). (ENG & FRE.). 1986. 12.00 (*92-871-0868-4*, Pub. by Council of Europe) Manhattan Pub Co.

— European Convention on Civil Liability for Damage by Motor Vehicles. (Conventions & Agreements Ser.: No. 79). (ENG & FRE.). 1984. 12.00 (*92-871-0126-4*, Pub. by Council of Europe) Manhattan Pub Co.

— European Convention on Compulsory Insurance Against Civil Liability in Respect of Motor Vehicles. (Conventions & Agreements Ser.: No. 29). (ENG & FRE.). 1982. 12.00 (*92-871-0082-9*, Pub. by Council of Europe) Manhattan Pub Co.

— European Convention on Consular Functions. (Conventions & Agreements Ser.: No. 61). (ENG & FRE.). 1976. 12.00 (*92-871-0108-6*, Pub. by Council of Europe) Manhattan Pub Co.

— European Convention on Establishment. (Conventions & Agreements Ser.: No. 19). (ENG & FRE.). 1977. 12.00 (*92-871-0075-6*, Pub. by Council of Europe) Manhattan Pub Co.

— European Convention on Extradition. (Conventions & Agreements Ser.: No. 24). (ENG & FRE.). 1982. write for info. (*92-871-0018-7*, Pub. by Council of Europe) Manhattan Pub Co.

— European Convention on Foreign Money Liabilities. (Conventions & Agreements Ser.: No. 60). (ENG & FRE.). 1981. 12.00 (*92-871-0107-8*, Pub. by Council of Europe) Manhattan Pub Co.

— The European Convention on Human Rights & Property Rights. (Human Rights Files Ser.: No. 11). 1992. 12.00 (*92-871-1841-8*, Pub. by Council of Europe) Manhattan Pub Co.

— European Convention on Information on Foreign Law. (Conventions & Agreements Ser.: No. 62). (ENG & FRE.). 1984. 12.00 (*92-871-0109-4*, Pub. by Council of Europe) Manhattan Pub Co.

— European Convention on Mutual Assistance in Criminal Matters. (Conventions & Agreements Ser.: No. 30). (ENG & FRE.). 1987. 12.00 (*92-871-0083-7*, Pub. by Council of Europe) Manhattan Pub Co.

— European Convention on Offences Relating to Cultural Property. (Conventions & Agreements Ser.: No. 119). (ENG & FRE.). 1985. 12.00 (*92-871-0798-X*, Pub. by Council of Europe) Manhattan Pub Co.

— European Convention on Products Liability in Regard to Personal Injury & Death. (Conventions & Agreements Ser.: No. 91). (ENG & FRE.). 1986. 12.00 (*92-871-0137-X*, Pub. by Council of Europe) Manhattan Pub Co.

— European Convention on Recognition & Enforcement of Decisions Concerning Custody of Children & on Restoration of Custody of Children. (Conventions & Agreements Ser.: No. 105). (ENG & FRE.). 1980. 12.00 (*92-871-0148-5*, Pub. by Council of Europe) Manhattan Pub Co.

— European Convention on Social & Medial Assistance, & Protocol. (Conventions & Agreements Ser.: No. 14). (ENG & FRE.). 1984. 12.00 (*92-871-0069-1*, Pub. by Council of Europe) Manhattan Pub Co.

— European Convention on Social Security & Supplementary Agreement for the Application of the European Convention on Social Security. (Conventions & Agreements Ser.: No. 78). (ENG & FRE.). 1982. 18.00 (*92-871-0019-5*, Pub. by Council of Europe) Manhattan Pub Co.

— European Convention on Spectator Violence & Misbehaviour at Sports Events & in Particular at Football Matches. (Conventions & Agreements Ser.: No. 120). (ENG & FRE.). 1987. 12.00 (*92-871-0796-3*, Pub. by Council of Europe) Manhattan Pub Co.

— European Convention on State Immunity & Additional Protocol. (Conventions & Agreements Ser.: No. 74). (ENG & FRE.). 1981. 12.00 (*92-871-0121-3*, Pub. by Council of Europe) Manhattan Pub Co.

— European Convention on the Abolition of Legalisation of Documents Executed by Diplomatic Agents or Consular Officers. (Conventions & Agreements Ser.: No. 63). (ENG & FRE.). 1968. 12.00 (*92-871-0110-8*, Pub. by Council of Europe) Manhattan Pub Co.

— European Convention on the Academic Recognition of University Qualifications. (Conventions & Agreements Ser.: No. 32). (ENG & FRE.). 1987. 12.00 (*92-871-0085-3*, Pub. by Council of Europe) Manhattan Pub Co.

— European Convention on the Adoption of Children. (Conventions & Agreements Ser.: No. 58). (ENG & FRE.). 1980. 12.00 (*92-871-0105-1*, Pub. by Council of Europe) Manhattan Pub Co.

— European Convention on the Calculation of Time-Limits. (Conventions & Agreements Ser.: No. 76). (ENG & FRE.). 1977. 12.00 (*92-871-0123-X*, Pub. by Council of Europe) Manhattan Pub Co.

— European Convention on the Compensation of Victims of Violent Crimes. (Conventions & Agreements Ser.: No. 116). (ENG & FRE.). 1983. 12.00 (*92-871-0302-X*, Pub. by Council of Europe) Manhattan Pub Co.

— European Convention on the Control of the Acquisition & Possession of Firearms by Individuals. (Conventions & Agreements Ser.: No. 101). (ENG & FRE.). 1987. 12.00 (*92-871-0145-0*, Pub. by Council of Europe) Manhattan Pub Co.

— European Convention on the Equivalence of Diplomas Leading to Admission to Universities. (Conventions & Agreements Ser.: No. 15). (ENG & FRE.). 1987. 12.00 (*92-871-0071-3*, Pub. by Council of Europe) Manhattan Pub Co.

— European Convention on the Establishment of Companies. (Conventions & Agreements Ser.: No. 57). (ENG & FRE.). 1975. 12.00 (*92-871-0104-3*, Pub. by Council of Europe) Manhattan Pub Co.

— European Convention on the General Equivalence of Periods of University Study (Rome, 1990) (Conventions & Agreements Ser.: No. 138). (ENG & FRE.). 1991. 12.00 (*92-871-1918-X*, Pub. by Council of Europe) Manhattan Pub Co.

— European Convention on the International Classification of Patents for Inventions: (Including Annex As Amended) (Conventions & Agreements Ser.: No. 17). (ENG & FRE.). 1966. 12.00 (*92-871-0073-X*, Pub. by Council of Europe) Manhattan Pub Co.

— European Convention on the International Effects of Deprivation of the Right to Drive a Motor Vehicle. (Conventions & Agreements Ser.: No. 88). (ENG & FRE.). 1985. 12.00 (*92-871-0283-X*, Pub. by Council of Europe) Manhattan Pub Co.

— European Convention on the International Validity of Criminal Judgments. (Conventions & Agreements Ser.: No. 70). (ENG & FRE.). 1985. 12.00 (*92-871-0117-5*, Pub. by Council of Europe) Manhattan Pub Co.

— European Convention on the Legal Status of Children Born Out of Wedlock. (Conventions & Agreements Ser.: No. 85). (ENG & FRE.). 1980. 12.00 (*92-871-0131-0*, Pub. by Council of Europe) Manhattan Pub Co.

— European Convention on the Legal Status of Migrant Workers. (Conventions & Agreements Ser.: No. 93). (ENG & FRE.). 1985. 12.00 (*92-871-0139-6*, Pub. by Council of Europe) Manhattan Pub Co.

— European Convention on the Non-Applicability of Statutory Limitation to Crimes Against Humanity & War Crimes. (Conventions & Agreements Ser.: No. 82). (ENG & FRE.). 1984. 12.00 (*92-871-0128-0*, Pub. by Council of Europe) Manhattan Pub Co.

— European Convention on the Obtaining Abroad of Information & Evidence in Administrative Matters. (Conventions & Agreements Ser.: No. 100). (ENG & FRE.). 1978. 12.00 (*92-871-0144-2*, Pub. by Council of Europe) Manhattan Pub Co.

— European Convention on the Place of Payment of Money Liabilities. (Conventions & Agreements Ser.: No. 75). (ENG & FRE.). 1977. 12.00 (*92-871-0122-1*, Pub. by Council of Europe) Manhattan Pub Co.

— European Convention on the Protection of the Archaeological Heritage. (Conventions & Agreements Ser.: No. 66). (ENG & FRE.). 1979. 12.00 (*92-871-0113-2*, Pub. by Council of Europe) Manhattan Pub Co.

— European Convention on the Punishment of Road Traffic Offences. (Conventions & Agreements Ser.: No. 52). (ENG & FRE.). 1979. 12.00 (*92-871-0101-9*, Pub. by Council of Europe) Manhattan Pub Co.

— European Convention on the Recognition of the Legal Personality of International Non-Governmental Organisations. (Conventions & Agreements Ser.: No. 124). (ENG & FRE.). 1986. 12.00 (*92-871-0869-2*, Pub. by Council of Europe) Manhattan Pub Co.

— European Convention on the Repatriation of Minors. (Conventions & Agreements Ser.: No. 71). (ENG & FRE.). 1979. 12.00 (*92-871-0118-3*, Pub. by Council of Europe) Manhattan Pub Co.

— European Convention on the Service Abroad of Documents Relating to Administrative Matters. (Conventions & Agreements Ser.: No. 94). (ENG & FRE.). 1985. 12.00 (*92-871-0140-X*, Pub. by Council of Europe) Manhattan Pub Co.

— European Convention on the Social Protection of Farmers. (Conventions & Agreements Ser.: No. 83). (ENG & FRE.). 1976. 12.00 (*92-871-0129-9*, Pub. by Council of Europe) Manhattan Pub Co.

— European Convention on the Supervision of Conditionally Sentenced or Conditionally Released Offenders. (Conventions & Agreements Ser.: No. 51). (ENG & FRE.). 1984. write for info. (*92-871-0100-0*, Pub. by Council of Europe) Manhattan Pub Co.

— European Convention on the Suppression of Terrorism. (Conventions & Agreements Ser.: No. 90). (ENG & FRE.). 1986. 12.00 (*92-871-0136-1*, Pub. by Council of Europe) Manhattan Pub Co.

— European Convention on the Transfer of Proceedings in Criminal Matters. (Conventions & Agreements Ser.: No. 73). (ENG & FRE.). 1984. 12.00 (*92-871-0120-5*, Pub. by Council of Europe) Manhattan Pub Co.

— European Convention on Transfrontier Television. (Conventions & Agreements Ser.: No. 132). (ENG & FRE.). 1989. 12.00 (*92-871-1715-2*, Pub. by Council of Europe) Manhattan Pub Co.

— European Convention Providing a Uniform Law on Arbitration. (Conventions & Agreements Ser.: No. 56). (ENG & FRE.). 1984. 12.00 (*92-871-0103-5*, Pub. by Council of Europe) Manhattan Pub Co.

— European Convention Relating to the Formalities Required for Patent Applications. (Conventions & Agreements Ser.: No. 16). (ENG & FRE.). 1983. 12.00 (*92-871-0072-1*, Pub. by Council of Europe) Manhattan Pub Co.

— European Cultural Convention. (Conventions & Agreements Ser.: No. 18). (ENG & FRE.). 1982. 12.00 (*92-871-0074-8*, Pub. by Council of Europe) Manhattan Pub Co.

— European Interim Agreement on Social Security Schemes Relating to Old Age, Invalidity & Survivors, & Protocol Thereto. (Conventions & Agreements Ser.: No. 12). (ENG & FRE.). 1975. 12.00 (*92-871-0065-9*, Pub. by Council of Europe) Manhattan Pub Co.

— European Outline Convention on Transfrontier Co-Operation Between Territorial Communities or Authorities. (Conventions & Agreements Ser.: No. 106). (ENG & FRE.). 1982. 12.00 (*92-871-0021-7*, Pub. by Council of Europe) Manhattan Pub Co.

— European Regional Planning Strategy. 1992. 50.00 (*92-871-1995-3*, Pub. by Council of Europe) Manhattan Pub Co.

— European Social Charter: Addendum to Conclusions IX-2: Second Report of Spain. 1987. 15.00 (*92-871-0989-3*, Pub. by Council of Europe) Manhattan Pub Co.

— European Social Charter: Addendum to Conclusions VI: Iceland's First Report. 1983. 12.00 (*92-871-0228-7*, Pub. by Council of Europe) Manhattan Pub Co.

— European Social Charter: Addendum to Conclusions VIII: First Report of the Kingdom of the Netherlands. 1985. 12.00 (*92-871-0786-6*, Pub. by Council of Europe) Manhattan Pub Co.

— European Social Charter: Addendum to Conclusions X-1. 1990. 12.00 (*92-871-1837-X*, Pub. by Council of Europe) Manhattan Pub Co.

— European Social Charter: Addendum to Conclusions XI-2: Ireland's Eleventh Report. 1991. 21.00 (*92-871-1943-0*, Pub. by Council of Europe) Manhattan Pub Co.

— European Social Charter: Conclusions of the Committee of Independent Experts of the European Social Charter, Vol. XI-1. 1989. 25.00 (*92-871-1742-X*, Pub. by Council of Europe) Manhattan Pub Co.

— European Social Charter: Conclusions of the Committee of Independent Experts of the European Social Charter, Vol. XI-2. 1991. 25.00 (*92-871-1904-X*, Pub. by Council of Europe) Manhattan Pub Co.

— European Social Charter: Conclusions of the Committee of Independent Experts of the European Social Charter, Vol. XII-1. 1992. 25.00 (*92-871-2067-6*, Pub. by Council of Europe) Manhattan Pub Co.

— European Social Charter: Governmental Committee: 11th Report (II) (1987-88) & Addendum to the 10th Report (I) 1992. 15.00 (*92-871-2030-7*, Pub. by Council of Europe) Manhattan Pub Co.

— European Social Charter: Third Report on Certain Provisions of the Charter Which Have Not Been Accepted. 1989. 12.00 (*92-871-1744-6*, Pub. by Council of Europe) Manhattan Pub Co.

— European Social Charter & Additional Protocol.

C

(Conventions & Agreements Ser.: Nos. 35 & 128). (ENG & FRE.). 1990. 12.00 (*92-871-1811-6*, Pub. by Council of Europe) Manhattan Pub Co.

— Evaluation of the Use of the International Classification of Impairments, Disabilities & Handicaps (ICIDH) in Surveys & Health-Related Statistics. 1990. 12.00 (*92-871-1852-3*, Pub. by Council of Europe) Manhattan Pub Co.

— Evergreen Forests in the Macaronesian Region. (Nature & Environment Ser.: No. 49). 1990. 18.00 (*92-871-1876-0*, Pub. by Council of Europe); 18.00 (*92-871-1877-9*, Pub. by Council of Europe) Manhattan Pub Co.

— Explanatory Report Concerning the Convention on the Conservation of European Wildlife & Natural Habitats. (Conventions & Agreements Ser.: No. 104). (ENG & FRE.). 1979. 12.00 (*92-871-0479-4*, Pub. by Council of Europe) Manhattan Pub Co.

— Explanatory Report on Protocol to the Convention for the Protection of Human Rights & Fundamental Freedoms, No. 7. (Conventions & Agreements Ser.: No. 117). (ENG & FRE.). 1985. 12.00 (*92-871-0759-9*, Pub. by Council of Europe) Manhattan Pub Co.

— Explanatory Report on Protocol to the Convention for the Protection of Human Rights & Fundamental Freedoms, No. 8. (Conventions & Agreements Ser.: No. 118). (ENG & FRE.). 1985. 12.00 (*92-871-0709-2*, Pub. by Council of Europe) Manhattan Pub Co.

— Explanatory Report on Protocol to the Convention for the Protection of Human Rights & Fundamental Freedoms, No. 9. (Conventions & Agreements Ser.: No. 140). (ENG & FRE.). 1992. 12.00 (*92-871-2008-0*, Pub. by Council of Europe) Manhattan Pub Co.

— Explanatory Report on Protocol to the Convention for the Protection of Human Rights & Fundamental Freedoms Concerning the Abolition of the Death Penalty, No. 6. (Conventions & Agreements Ser.: No. 114). (ENG & FRE.). 1983. 12.00 (*92-871-0216-3*, Pub. by Council of Europe) Manhattan Pub Co.

— Explanatory Report on the Additional Protocol to the European Convention on Extradition. (Conventions & Agreements Ser.: No. 86). (ENG & FRE.). 1975. 12.00 (*92-871-0464-6*, Pub. by Council of Europe) Manhattan Pub Co.

— Explanatory Report on the Additional Protocol to the European Convention on Information on Foreign Law. (Conventions & Agreements Ser.: No. 97). (ENG & FRE.). 1978. 12.00 (*92-871-0473-5*, Pub. by Council of Europe) Manhattan Pub Co.

— Explanatory Report on the Additional Protocol to the European Convention on Mutual Assistance in Criminal Matters. (Conventions & Agreements Ser.: No. 99). (ENG & FRE.). 1978. 12.00 (*92-871-0475-1*, Pub. by Council of Europe) Manhattan Pub Co.

— Explanatory Report on the Agreement on the Transfer of Corpses. (Conventions & Agreements Ser.: No. 80). (ENG & FRE.). 1975. 12.00 (*92-871-0462-X*, Pub. by Council of Europe) Manhattan Pub Co.

— Explanatory Report on the Anti-Doping Convention. (Conventions & Agreements Ser.: No. 135). (ENG & FRE.). 1990. 18.00 (*92-871-1821-3*, Pub. by Council of Europe) Manhattan Pub Co.

— Explanatory Report on the Convention for the Protection of Individual with Regard to Automatic Processing of Personal Data. (Conventions & Agreements Ser.: No. 108). (ENG & FRE.). 1981. 12.00 (*92-871-0482-4*, Pub. by Council of Europe) Manhattan Pub Co.

— Explanatory Report on the Convention for the Protection of the Architectural Heritage of Europe. (Conventions & Agreements Ser.: No. 121). (ENG & FRE.). 1986. 12.00 (*92-871-0830-7*, Pub. by Council of Europe) Manhattan Pub Co.

— Explanatory Report on the Convention on Insider Trading & Additional Protocol. (Conventions & Agreements Ser.: Nos. 130 & 133). (ENG & FRE.). 1989. 12.00 (*92-871-1698-9*, Pub. by Council of Europe) Manhattan Pub Co.

— Explanatory Report on the Convention on Laundering, Search, Seizure & Confiscation of the Proceeds from Crime. (Conventions & Agreements Ser.: No. 141). (ENG & FRE.). 1991. 21.00 (*92-871-1933-3*, Pub. by Council of Europe) Manhattan Pub Co.

— Explanatory Report on the European Agreement on the Transmission of Applications for Legal Aid. (Conventions & Agreements Ser.: No. 92). (ENG & FRE.). 1977. 12.00 (*92-871-0469-7*, Pub. by Council of Europe) Manhattan Pub Co.

— Explanatory Report on the European Agreement on Transfer of Responsibility for Refugees. (Conventions & Agreements Ser.: No. 107). (ENG & FRE.). 1980. 12.00 (*92-871-0481-6*, Pub. by Council of Europe) Manhattan Pub Co.

— Explanatory Report on the European Charter of Local Self-Government. (Conventions & Agreements Ser.: No. 122). (ENG & FRE.). 1986. 12.00 (*92-871-0860-9*, Pub. by Council of Europe) Manhattan Pub Co.

— Explanatory Report on the European Convention for the Prevention of Torture & Inhuman or Degrading Treatment or Punishment. (Conventions & Agreements Ser.: No. 126). (ENG & FRE.). 1989. 15.00 (*92-871-1678-4*, Pub. by Council of Europe) Manhattan Pub Co.

— Explanatory Report on the European Convention for the Protection of Animals During International Transport. (Conventions & Agreements Ser.: No. 65). (ENG & FRE.). 1969. 12.00 (*92-871-0929-X*, Pub. by Council of Europe) Manhattan Pub Co.

— Explanatory Report on the European Convention for the Protection of Animals for Slaughter. (Conventions & Agreements Ser.: No. 102). (ENG & FRE.). 1979. 12.00 (*92-871-0478-6*, Pub. by Council of Europe) Manhattan Pub Co.

— Explanatory Report on the European Convention for the Protection of Pet Animals. (Conventions & Agreements Ser.: No. 125). (ENG & FRE.). 1987. 12.00 (*92-871-1525-7*, Pub. by Council of Europe) Manhattan Pub Co.

— Explanatory Report on the European Convention for the Protection of Vertebrate Animals Used for Experimental & Other Scientific Purposes. (Conventions & Agreements Ser.: No. 123). (ENG & FRE.). 1986. 21.00 (*92-871-0863-3*, Pub. by Council of Europe) Manhattan Pub Co.

— Explanatory Report on the European Convention on Au Pair Placement. (Conventions & Agreements Ser.: No. 68). (ENG & FRE.). 1972. 12.00 (*92-871-0456-5*, Pub. by Council of Europe) Manhattan Pub Co.

— Explanatory Report on the European Convention on Civil Liability for Damage by Motor Vehicles. (Conventions & Agreements Ser.: No. 79). (ENG & FRE.). 1973. 12.00 (*92-871-0461-1*, Pub. by Council of Europe) Manhattan Pub Co.

— Explanatory Report on the European Convention on Consular Functions & Its Protocols. (Conventions & Agreements Ser.: No. 61). (ENG & FRE.). 1968. 12.00 (*92-871-0445-X*, Pub. by Council of Europe) Manhattan Pub Co.

— Explanatory Report on the European Convention on Extradition. (Conventions & Agreements Ser.: No. 24). 1985. 12.00 (*92-871-0766-1*, Pub. by Council of Europe) Manhattan Pub Co.

— Explanatory Report on the European Convention on Foreign Money Liabilities. (Conventions & Agreements Ser.: No. 60). 1968. 12.00 (*92-871-0444-1*, Pub. by Council of Europe) Manhattan Pub Co.

— Explanatory Report on the European Convention on Information on Foreign Law. (Conventions & Agreements Ser.: No. 62). (ENG & FRE.). 1968. 12.00 (*92-871-0446-8*, Pub. by Council of Europe) Manhattan Pub Co.

— Explanatory Report on the European Convention on International Validity of Criminal Judgments. (Conventions & Agreements Ser.: No. 70). (ENG & FRE.). 1970. 12.00 (*92-871-0453-0*, Pub. by Council of Europe) Manhattan Pub Co.

— Explanatory Report on the European Convention on Mutual Assistance in Criminal Matters. (Conventions & Agreements Ser.: No. 30). 1969. 12.00 (*92-871-0448-4*, Pub. by Council of Europe) Manhattan Pub Co.

— Explanatory Report on the European Convention on Offences Relating to Cultural Property. (Conventions & Agreements Ser.: No. 119). (ENG & FRE.). 1985. 12.00 (*92-871-0795-5*, Pub. by Council of Europe) Manhattan Pub Co.

— Explanatory Report on the European Convention on Products Liability in Regard to Personal Injury & Death. (Conventions & Agreements Ser.: No. 91). (ENG & FRE.). 1977. 12.00 (*92-871-0468-9*, Pub. by Council of Europe) Manhattan Pub Co.

— Explanatory Report on the European Convention on Providing a Uniform Law on Arbitration. (Conventions & Agreements Ser.: No. 56). 1967. 12.00 (*92-871-0443-3*, Pub. by Council of Europe) Manhattan Pub Co.

— Explanatory Report on the European Convention on Recognition & Enforcement of Decisions Concerning Custody of Children & on Restoration of Custody of Children. (Conventions & Agreements Ser.: No. 105). (ENG & FRE.). 1980. 12.00 (*92-871-0480-8*, Pub. by Council of Europe) Manhattan Pub Co.

— Explanatory Report on the European Convention on Social Security & on the Supplementary Agreement for the Application of the European Convention on Social Security. (Conventions & Agreements Ser.: No. 78). (ENG & FRE.). 1978. 21.00 (*92-871-0460-3*, Pub. by Council of Europe) Manhattan Pub Co.

— Explanatory Report on the European Convention on State Immunity & the Additional Protocol. (Conventions & Agreements Ser.: No. 74). (ENG & FRE.). 1985. 12.00 (*92-871-0730-0*, Pub. by Council of Europe) Manhattan Pub Co.

— Explanatory Report on the European Convention on the Abolition of Legalisation of Documents Executed by Diplomatic Agents or Consular Officers. (Conventions & Agreements Ser.: No. 63). (ENG & FRE.). 1968. 12.00 (*92-871-0447-6*, Pub. by Council of Europe) Manhattan Pub Co.

— Explanatory Report on the European Convention on the Adoption of Children. (Conventions & Agreements Ser.: No. 58). 1969. 12.00 (*92-871-0449-2*, Pub. by Council of Europe) Manhattan Pub Co.

— Explanatory Report on the European Convention on the Calculation of Time-Limits. (Conventions & Agreements Ser.: No. 76). (ENG & FRE.). 1973. 12.00 (*92-871-0458-1*, Pub. by Council of Europe) Manhattan Pub Co.

— Explanatory Report on the European Convention on the Compensation of Victims of Violent Crimes. (Conventions & Agreements Ser.: No. 116). (ENG & FRE.). 1984. 12.00 (*92-871-0306-2*, Pub. by Council of Europe) Manhattan Pub Co.

— Explanatory Report on the European Convention on the Control of the Acquisition & Possession of Firearms by Individuals. (Conventions & Agreements Ser.: No. 101). (ENG & FRE.). 1979. 12.00 (*92-871-0477-8*, Pub. by Council of Europe) Manhattan Pub Co.

— Explanatory Report on the European Convention on the Establishment of a Scheme of Registration of Wills. (Conventions & Agreements Ser.: No. 77). (ENG & FRE.). 12.00 (*92-871-0459-X*, Pub. by Council of Europe) Manhattan Pub Co.

— Explanatory Report on the European Convention on the International Effects of Deprivation of the Right to Drive a Motor Vehicle. (Conventions & Agreements Ser.: No. 88). (ENG & FRE.). 1976. 12.00 (*92-871-0466-2*, Pub. by Council of Europe) Manhattan Pub Co.

— Explanatory Report on the European Convention on the Legal Status of Children Born Out of Wedlock. (Conventions & Agreements Ser.: No. 85). (ENG & FRE.). 1975. 12.00 (*92-871-0463-8*, Pub. by Council of Europe) Manhattan Pub Co.

— Explanatory Report on the European Convention on the Legal Status of Migrant Workers. (Conventions & Agreements Ser.: No. 93). (ENG & FRE.). 1985. 12.00 (*92-871-0472-7*, Pub. by Council of Europe) Manhattan Pub Co.

— Explanatory Report on the European Convention on the Obtaining Abroad of Information & Evidence in Administrative Matters. (Conventions & Agreements Ser.: No. 100). (ENG & FRE.). 1978. 12.00 (*92-871-0476-X*, Pub. by Council of Europe) Manhattan Pub Co.

— Explanatory Report on the European Convention on the Place of Payment of Money Liabilities. (Conventions & Agreements Ser.: No. 75). (ENG & FRE.). 1972. 12.00 (*92-871-0457-3*, Pub. by Council of Europe) Manhattan Pub Co.

— Explanatory Report on the European Convention on the Protection of Animals Kept for Farming Purposes. (Conventions & Agreements Ser.: No. 87). (ENG & FRE.). 1976. 12.00 (*92-871-0465-4*, Pub. by Council of Europe) Manhattan Pub Co.

— Explanatory Report on the European Convention on the Protection of the Archaeological Heritage. (Conventions & Agreements Ser.: No. 66). (ENG & FRE.). 1970. 12.00 (*92-871-0452-2*, Pub. by Council of Europe) Manhattan Pub Co.

— Explanatory Report on the European Convention on the Punishment of Road Traffic Offences. (Conventions & Agreements Ser.: No. 52). 1970. 12.00 (*92-871-0451-4*, Pub. by Council of Europe) Manhattan Pub Co.

— Explanatory Report on the European Convention on the Recognition of the Legal Personality of International Non-Governmental Organisations. (Conventions & Agreements Ser.: No. 124). (ENG & FRE.). 1986. 12.00 (*92-871-0897-8*, Pub. by Council of Europe) Manhattan Pub Co.

— Explanatory Report on the European Convention on the Repatriation of Minors. (Conventions & Agreements Ser.: No. 71). (ENG & FRE.). 1971. 12.00 (*92-871-0455-7*, Pub. by Council of Europe) Manhattan Pub Co.

— Explanatory Report on the European Convention on the Service Abroad of Documents Relating to Administrative Matters. (Conventions & Agreements Ser.: No. 94). (ENG & FRE.). 1977. 12.00 (*92-871-0470-0*, Pub. by Council of Europe) Manhattan Pub Co.

— Explanatory Report on the European Convention on the Supervision of Conditionally Sentenced or Conditionally Released Offenders. (Conventions & Agreements Ser.: No. 51). 1970. 12.00 (*92-871-0450-6*, Pub. by Council of Europe) Manhattan Pub Co.

— Explanatory Report on the European Convention on the Suppression of Terrorism. (Conventions & Agreements Ser.: No. 90). (ENG & FRE.). 1977. 12.00 (*92-871-0467-0*, Pub. by Council of Europe) Manhattan Pub Co.

— Explanatory Report on the European Convention on the Transfer of Proceedings in Criminal Matters. (Conventions & Agreements Ser.: No. 73). (ENG & FRE.). 1985. 12.00 (*92-871-0764-5*, Pub. by Council of Europe) Manhattan Pub Co.

— Explanatory Report on the European Convention on Transfrontier Television. (Conventions & Agreements Ser.: No. 132). (ENG & FRE.). 1990. 21.00 (*92-871-1819-1*, Pub. by Council of Europe) Manhattan Pub Co.

— Explanatory Report on the European Outline Convention on Transfrontier Co-Operation Between Territorial Communities or Authorities. (Conventions & Agreements Ser.: No. 106). (ENG & FRE.). 1980. 12.00 (*92-871-0062-4*, Pub. by Council of Europe) Manhattan Pub Co.

— Explanatory Report on the Protection of the Archaeological Heritage. (Conventions & Agreements Ser.: No. 143). (ENG & FRE.). 1993. 12.00 (*92-871-2125-7*, Pub. by Council of Europe) Manhattan Pub Co.

— Explanatory Report on the Protocol Amending the Convention on Reduction of Cases of Multiple Nationality & Military Obligations in Cases of Multiple Nationality & on the Additional Protocol to the Convention. (Conventions & Agreements Ser.: Nos. 43, 95, 96). (ENG & FRE.). 1978. 12.00 (*92-871-0471-9*, Pub. by Council of Europe) Manhattan Pub Co.

— Explanatory Report on the Protocol of Amendment to the European Convention for the Protection of Animals Kept for Farming Purposes. (Conventions & Agreements Ser.: No. 145). (ENG & FRE.). 1993. 12.00 (*92-871-2117-6*, Pub. by Council of Europe) Manhattan Pub Co.

— Explanatory Report on the Second Additional Protocol to the European Convention on Extradition. (Conventions & Agreements Ser.: No. 98). (ENG & FRE.). 1978. 12.00 (*92-871-0474-3*, Pub. by Council of Europe) Manhattan Pub Co.

— Extraterritorial Criminal Jurisdiction. 1990. 18.00 (*92-871-1786-1*, Pub. by Council of Europe) Manhattan Pub Co.

— Fifth Protocol to the General Agreement on Privileges & Immunities of the Council of Europe. (Conventions & Agreements Ser.: No. 137). (ENG & FRE.). 1990. 12.00 (*92-871-1843-4*, Pub. by Council of Europe) Manhattan Pub Co.

— The Flexibility of Retirement Age. 1989. 18.00 (*92-871-1725-X*, Pub. by Council of Europe) Manhattan Pub Co.

— General Agreement on Privileges & Immunities of the Counil of Europe: (Including the Supplementary Agreement & the Four Protocols) (Conventions & Agreements Ser.: No. 2). (ENG & FRE.). 1983. 12.00 (*92-871-0280-5*, Pub. by Council of Europe) Manhattan Pub Co.

— Guide of Cultural Centres in Europe (Guide des Centres Cultùrels Europeens) (ENG & FRE.). 1990. 25.00 (*92-871-1880-9*, Pub. by Council of Europe) Manhattan Pub Co.

— Heritage & Successful Town Regeneration: Report of the Halifax Colloquy. (Cultural Heritage Ser.: No. 14). 1989. 18.00 (*92-871-1710-1*, Pub. by Council of Europe) Manhattan Pub Co.

— Higher Education & Research: Student Handbook. 1991. 25.00 (*92-871-1960-0*, Pub. by Council of Europe) Manhattan Pub Co.

— Historic Towns & Tourism: 6th European Symposium (Cambridge, 1989) Working Documents & Conclusions. (Congress of Local & Regional Authorities of Europe Ser.: No. 19). 1991. 21.00 (*92-871-1978-3*, Pub. by Council of Europe) Manhattan Pub Co.

— Household Structures in Europe. (Population Studies: No. 22). 1990. 18.00 (*92-871-1796-9*, Pub. by Council of Europe) Manhattan Pub Co.

— Human Artificial Procreation. (Bioethics Ser.). 1989. 18.00 (*92-871-1676-8*, Pub. by Council of Europe) Manhattan Pub Co.

— The Human Rights Album. (J). (gr. 1-7). 1992. 15.00 (*92-871-2095-1*, Pub. by Council of Europe) Manhattan Pub Co.

— Impact of the Aids Epidemic on Health Care Services & Planning in Europe. 1992. 12.00 (*92-871-2060-9*, Pub. by Council of Europe) Manhattan Pub Co.

— The Impact of the Completion of the Internal Market on Local & Regional Autonomy. (Congress of Local & Regional Authorities of Europe Ser.: No. 12). 1990. 18.00 (*92-871-1829-9*, Pub. by Council of Europe) Manhattan Pub Co.

— The Incidence of "Crack" in North American & European Cities. (Congress of Local & Regional Authorities of Europe Ser.: No. 18). 1992. 12.00 (*92-871-2123-0*, Pub. by Council of Europe) Manhattan Pub Co.

— Information & Education in Demography. (Population Studies: No. 24). 1993. 12.00 (*92-871-2111-7*, Pub. by Council of Europe) Manhattan Pub Co.

— Integrated Work Stations in the Legal Sector & Decision Support Systems: (Proceedings of the 7th Colloquy on the Use of Computers in the Administration of Justice, Lisbon, 1988) 1989. 25.00 (*92-871-1788-8*, Pub. by Council of Europe) Manhattan Pub Co.

— International Aspects of Bankruptcy: Explanatory Report on the Istanbul Convention. (Conventions & Agreements Ser.: No. 136). (ENG & FRE.). 1990. 21.00 (*92-871-1914-7*, Pub. by Council of Europe) Manhattan Pub Co.

— International Conference On: "European Towns: Strategies & Programmes" (Strasbourg, 1990) Working Documents & Conclusions. (Congress of Local & Regional Authorities of Europe Ser.: No. 17). 1991. 21.00 (*92-871-1901-5*, Pub. by Council of Europe) Manhattan Pub Co.

— The Introduction & Use of Personal Identification Numbers: The Data Protection Issues. 1991. 12.00 (*92-871-1935-X*, Pub. by Council of Europe) Manhattan Pub Co.

— Language Learning in Europe: The Challenge of Diversity (Final Conference of the Modern Languages Project No. 12, Strasbourg, 1988) 1989. 21.00 (*92-871-1696-2*, Pub. by Council of Europe) Manhattan Pub Co.

— Legislation on the Rehabilitation of Disabled People in Sixteen Member States of the Council of Europe. 4th ed. 1990. 25.00 (*92-871-1870-1*, Pub. by Council of Europe) Manhattan Pub Co.

— Liability of Enterprises for Offences (Recommendation & Explanatory Memorandum), No. R(88)16. 1990. 12.00 (*92-871-1750-0*, Pub. by Council of Europe) Manhattan Pub Co.

— Livello Soglia (The Threshold Level for Italian) (ITA.). 1982. 25.00 (*92-871-0000-4*, Pub. by Council of Europe) Manhattan Pub Co.

— Local & Regional Authorities & the Challenge of Unemployment: Action of the CLRAE, 1983-88. (Congress of Local & Regional Authorities of Europe Ser.: No. 10). 1988. 12.00 (*92-871-1640-7*, Pub. by Council of Europe) Manhattan Pub Co.

— Local Strategies for the Reduction of Urban Insecurity in Europe (Barcelona, 1987) (Urban Renaissance in Europe Ser.: No. 35). 1989. 42.00 (*92-871-1691-1*, Pub. by Council of Europe) Manhattan Pub Co.

— Long-Term Unemployed & the Elderly in Migrant Communities in Europe. 1992. 12.00 (*92-871-2019-6*, Pub. by Council of Europe) Manhattan Pub Co.

— Management of Public Access to the Heritage Landscape. (Cultural Heritage Ser.: No. 24). 1992. 15.00 (*92-871-2145-1*, Pub. by Council of Europe) Manhattan Pub Co.

— Management of the Mediterranean Wetlands. (Environmental Encounters Ser.: No. 12). 1992. 15.00 (*92-871-2033-1*, Pub. by Council of Europe) Manhattan Pub Co.

— Manual on Information Technology Applications in Correctional Administration. LC 98-220024. 27p. 1998. write for info. (*92-871-3617-3*) Council of Europe.

— Marine Reserves & Conservation of Mediterranean Coastal Habitats. (Nature & Environment Ser.: No. 50). 1990. 18.00 (*92-871-1889-2*, Pub. by Council of Europe) Manhattan Pub Co.

— Marine Turtles in the Mediterranean: Distribution,

An Asterisk (*) at the beginning of an entry indicates that the title is appearing for the first time.

Population Status, Conservation. (Nature & Environment Ser.: No. 48). 1990. 18.00 (*92-871-1864-7*, Pub. by Council of Europe) Manhattan Pub Co.
— Measures to Combat Piracy in the Field of Copyright & Neighbouring Rights (Recommendation & Explanatory Memorandum), No. R(88)2. 1989. 12.00 (*92-871-1674-1*, Pub. by Council of Europe) Manhattan Pub Co.
— Mining Engineering Monuments As a Cultural Heritage: Report of the Bochum Colloquy (Federal Republic of Germany) (Cultural Heritage Ser.: No. 15). 1989. 18.00 (*92-871-1740-3*, Pub. by Council of Europe) Manhattan Pub Co.
— The Multidisciplinary Care of Cancer Patients. 1992. 21.00 (*92-871-2043-9*, Pub. by Council of Europe) Manhattan Pub Co.
— Nature Museums: Tools for Learning about, Promoting & Protecting the Natural Heritage of Europe. (Environmental Encounters Ser.: No. 9). 1990. 15.00 (*92-871-1823-X*, Pub. by Council of Europe) Manhattan Pub Co.
— Nature Tomorrow. (Environmental Encounters Ser.: No. 7). 1989. 12.00 (*92-871-1684-9*, Pub. by Council of Europe) Manhattan Pub Co.
— New Social Strategies & the Criminal Justice System. (Collected Studies in Criminological Research: Vol. XXIX). 1994. 15.00 (*92-871-2024-2*, Pub. by Council of Europe) Manhattan Pub Co.
— New Technologies: A Challenge to Privacy Protection? 1989. 15.00 (*92-871-1617-2*, Pub. by Council of Europe) Manhattan Pub Co.
— Nivel Limiar (The Threshold Level for Portuguese) (POR.). 1988. 25.00 (*92-871-1554-0*, Pub. by Council of Europe) Manhattan Pub Co.
— Un Nivel Umbral (The Threshold Level for Spanish) (SPA.). 1980. 18.00 (*92-871-0746-7*, Pub. by Council of Europe) Manhattan Pub Co.
— The Parliamentary Assembly: Procedure & Practice. 9th ed. (Parliamentary Assembly Ser.). 1990. 45.00 (*92-871-1801-9*, Pub. by Council of Europe) Manhattan Pub Co.
— Participation of Foreigners in Public Life at a Local Level: Explantory Report on the Convention Opened for Signature on 5 February, 1992. (Conventions & Agreements Ser.: No. 144). (ENG & FRE.). 1993. 12.00 (*92-871-2084-6*, Pub. by Council of Europe) Manhattan Pub Co.
— People on the Move - New Migration Flows in Europe. 1992. 21.00 (*92-871-2021-8*, Pub. by Council of Europe) Manhattan Pub Co.
— Pesticides: Advice & Recommendations to Be Used by National & Other Authorities As Well As Manufacturers Concerned with the Registration of Agricultural & Non-Agricultural Pesticides. 7th ed. 1992. 21.00 (*92-871-1958-9*, Pub. by Council of Europe) Manhattan Pub Co.
— Plasma Products & European Self-Sufficiency: Collection, Preparation & Use. 1992. 12.00 (*92-871-1925-2*, Pub. by Council of Europe) Manhattan Pub Co.
— Privatisation of Crime Control. (Collected Studies in Criminological Research: Vol. XXVII). 1990. 25.00 (*92-871-1737-3*, Pub. by Council of Europe) Manhattan Pub Co.
— Proceedings of the 3rd Round Table with European Ombudsmen (Florence, 1991) (Human Rights & Democracy Ser.). 1992. 18.00 (*92-871-2153-2*, Pub. by Council of Europe) Manhattan Pub Co.
— Profiles & Training for Senior Officials of Local & Regional Authorities (Barcelona, 1990) (Congress of Local & Regional Authorities of Europe Ser.: No. 20). 1991. 15.00 (*92-871-1983-X*, Pub. by Council of Europe) Manhattan Pub Co.
— Programme Sponsorship & New Forms of Commercial Promotion on Television. (Mass Media Files Ser.: No. 9). 1991. 18.00 (*92-871-1879-5*, Pub. by Council of Europe) Manhattan Pub Co.
— Protection of Personal Data Used for Employment Purposes (Recommendation), No. R(89)2. 1990. 18.00 (*92-871-1714-4*, Pub. by Council of Europe) Manhattan Pub Co.
— Protection of Personal Data Used for Payment & Other Related Operations (Recommendation), No. R(90)19. 1993. 12.00 (*92-871-1922-8*, Pub. by Council of Europe) Manhattan Pub Co.
— The Protection of Persons Working at Home. 1989. 21.00 (*92-871-1718-7*, Pub. by Council of Europe) Manhattan Pub Co.
— The Protection of the Architectural Heritage Against Natural Disasters. (Cultural Heritage Ser.: No. 21). 1992. 12.00 (*92-871-2005-6*, Pub. by Council of Europe) Manhattan Pub Co.
— The Protection of Youth Against Physical & Moral Danger. 1990. 21.00 (*92-871-1835-3*, Pub. by Council of Europe) Manhattan Pub Co.
— Protocol Amending the European Social Charter (Turin, 1991) (Conventions & Agreements Ser.: No. 142). (ENG & FRE.). 1991. 12.00 (*92-871-2014-5*, Pub. by Council of Europe) Manhattan Pub Co.
— Protocol of Amendment to the European Convention for the Protection of Animals Kept for Farming Purposes (Strasbourg, 1992) (Conventions & Agreements Ser.: No. 145). (ENG & FRE.). 1992. 12.00 (*92-871-2062-5*, Pub. by Council of Europe) Manhattan Pub Co.
— Protocol to the Convention for the Protection of Human Rights & Fundamental Freedoms (Strasbourg, 1992), No. 10. (Conventions & Agreements Ser.: No. 146). (ENG & FRE.). 1992. 12.00 (*92-871-2093-5*, Pub. by Council of Europe) Manhattan Pub Co.
— Protocol to the Convention on the Elaboration of a European Pharmacopoeia. (Conventions & Agreements Ser.: No. 134). (ENG & FRE.). 1989. 12.00 (*92-871-1781-0*, Pub. by Council of Europe) Manhattan Pub Co.
— Protocol to the European Convention on the Equivalence of Diplomas Leading to Admission to Universities. (Conventions & Agreements Ser.: No. 49). (ENG & FRE.). 1981. 12.00 (*92-871-0098-5*, Pub. by Council of Europe) Manhattan Pub Co.
— Provisional Court Protection in Administrative Matters (Recommendation & Explanatory Memorandum), No. R(89)8. 1990. 12.00 (*92-871-1807-8*, Pub. by Council of Europe) Manhattan Pub Co.
— Rehabilitation of Natural Habitats in Rural Areas. (Nature & Environment Ser.: No. 59). 1992. 12.00 (*92-871-2115-X*, Pub. by Council of Europe) Manhattan Pub Co.
— Report on the Integration of Disabled Children into Their Family & Society: (Steering Committee on Social Policy (CDPS), 1989) 1989. 18.00 (*92-871-1756-X*, Pub. by Council of Europe) Manhattan Pub Co.
— Responsibilities of Health Authorities in the Field of Blood Transfusion (Recommendation), No. R(88)4. 1989. 12.00 (*92-871-1688-1*, Pub. by Council of Europe) Manhattan Pub Co.
— Revised Protocol to the European Agreement on the Exchange of Tissue-Typing Reagents. (Conventions & Agreements Ser.: No. 84a). (ENG & FRE.). 1985. 12.00 (*92-871-0767-X*, Pub. by Council of Europe) Manhattan Pub Co.
— Revitalisation of the Countryside: Local & Regional Government Action (Proceedings, Vila Real, 1989) (Congress of Local & Regional Authorities of Europe Ser.: No. 8). 1991. 15.00 (*92-871-1916-3*, Pub. by Council of Europe) Manhattan Pub Co.
— The Role of Employment & Training Services in Fighting Long-Term Unemployment. 1992. 12.00 (*92-871-2106-0*, Pub. by Council of Europe) Manhattan Pub Co.
— Roles in the Organisation of Legal Data Processing Systems: (Proceedings of the 8th Colloquy on Legal Data Processing in Eruope, Malta, 1990) 1992. 21.00 (*92-871-2017-X*, Pub. by Council of Europe) Manhattan Pub Co.
— The Santiago de Compostela Pilgrim Routes: Report of the Bamberg Congress. (Cultural Heritage Ser.: No. 16). 1989. 21.00 (*92-871-1746-2*, Pub. by Council of Europe) Manhattan Pub Co.
— Saproxylic Invertebrates & Their Conservation. (Nature & Environment Ser.: No. 42). 1989. 18.00 (*92-871-1680-6*, Pub. by Council of Europe) Manhattan Pub Co.
— School Exchanges: The Role of Local & Regional Authorities. (Congress of Local & Regional Authorities of Europe Ser.: No. 23). 1992. 15.00 (*92-871-2075-7*, Pub. by Council of Europe) Manhattan Pub Co.
— School Health Education & the Role & Training of Teachers (Recommendation), No. R(88)7. 1989. 18.00 (*92-871-1682-2*, Pub. by Council of Europe) Manhattan Pub Co.
— Schooling for Gypsies' & Travellers' Children - Evaluating Innovation: (Report of the 35th European Seminar, Donaueschingen, Federal Republic of Germany, 1987) 1992. 21.00 (*92-871-2037-4*, Pub. by Council of Europe) Manhattan Pub Co.
— Second Additional Protocol to the European Convention on Extradition. (Conventions & Agreements Ser.: No. 98). (ENG & FRE.). 1985. 12.00 (*92-871-0442-6*, Pub. by Council of Europe) Manhattan Pub Co.
— The Second Demographic Transition: Fact or Fiction? (Population Studies: No. 23). 1991. 18.00 (*92-871-1963-5*, Pub. by Council of Europe) Manhattan Pub Co.
— Seminar for Managers of Diploma-Holding Areas. (Environmental Encounters Ser.: No. 15). 1992. 12.00 (*92-871-2143-5*, Pub. by Council of Europe) Manhattan Pub Co.
— Seminar on Present Demographic Trends & Lifestyles in Europe: Proceedings of the Seminar (Strasbourg, 1990) 1991. 25.00 (*92-871-1945-7*, Pub. by Council of Europe) Manhattan Pub Co.
— Seminar on "The Effects of 1992 on the Triaining of European Local & Regional Authority Staff" (Montpellier, 1989) Working Documents & Conclusions. (Congress of Local & Regional Authorities of Europe Ser.: No. 15). 1990. 18.00 (*92-871-1805-1*, Pub. by Council of Europe) Manhattan Pub Co.
— Sexual Exploitation, Pornography, & Prostitution of, & Trafficking in, Children & Young Adults (Recommendation & Report of the European Committee on Crime Problems), No. R(91)11. 56p. 1993. 12.00 (*92-871-2035-8*, Pub. by Council of Europe) Balogh.
— Share Borne by the Beneficiary of the Cost of Medical Care & of Medical Rehabilitation Supplies: (Situation at 1 July, 1988) 2nd ed. 1990. 15.00 (*92-871-1858-2*, Pub. by Council of Europe) Manhattan Pub Co.
— The Situation, Conservation Needs & Reintroduction of Lynx in Europe. (Environmental Encounters Ser.: No. 11). 1992. 18.00 (*92-871-1970-8*, Pub. by Council of Europe) Manhattan Pub Co.
— Social Development Fund: Collection of Statutory Texts. (ENG & FRE.). 1991. 12.00 (*92-871-1974-0*, Pub. by Council of Europe) Manhattan Pub Co.
— Sound & Audiovisual Private Copying (Recommendation & Explanatory Memorandum), No. R(88)1. 1989. 12.00 (*92-871-1669-5*, Pub. by Council of Europe) Manhattan Pub Co.
— Sport & the Law: (Proceedings of the 18th Colloquy on European Law, Maastricht, 1988) 1989. 21.00 (*92-871-1708-X*, Pub. by Council of Europe) Manhattan Pub Co.

***Council of Europe Staff.** Standard Terms, 2000: Pharmaceutical Dosage Forms - Routes of Administration - Containers. 350p. 2000. 56.00 (*0-11-986041-4*, Pub. by Statnry Office) Balogh.
Council of Europe Staff. Status & Conservation Needs of the Wolf (Canis Lupus) in the Council of Europe Member States. (Nature & Environment Ser.: No. 47). 1990. 12.00 (*92-871-1863-9*, Pub. by Council of Europe) Manhattan Pub Co.
— Status & Conservation of the Pardel Lynx (Lynx Pardina) in the Iberian Peninsula. (Nature & Environment Ser.: No. 55). 1992. 12.00 (*92-871-1991-0*, Pub. by Council of Europe) Manhattan Pub Co.
— Status & Working Conditions of Local & Regional Elected Representatives: Basic Principles. (Local & Regional Authorities in Europe Ser.: No. 46). 1992. 12.00 (*92-871-2071-4*, Pub. by Council of Europe) Manhattan Pub Co.
— Status, Conservation Needs & Reintroduction of the Lynx (Lynx Lynx) in Europe. (Nature & Environment Ser.: No. 45). 1990. 12.00 (*92-871-1845-0*, Pub. by Council of Europe) Manhattan Pub Co.
— Statute of the Council of Europe: (Including Amendments & Additions) (Conventions & Agreements Ser.: No. 1). (ENG & FRE.). 1995. 12.00 (*92-871-0017-9*, Pub. by Council of Europe) Manhattan Pub Co.
— Systems Based on Artificial Intelligence in the Legal Field: Proceedings of the 9th Symposium on Legal Data Processing in Europe, Bonn, 1989. 1991. 21.00 (*92-871-1952-X*, Pub. by Council of Europe) Manhattan Pub Co.
— Technical Assistance for a Computerised Heritage Documentation Centre in Malta. (Cultural Heritage Ser.: No. 23). 1992. 12.00 (*92-871-2139-7*, Pub. by Council of Europe) Manhattan Pub Co.
— Third Additional Protocol to the European Agreement on the Protection of Television Broadcasts. (Conventions & Agreements Ser.: No. 131). (ENG & FRE.). 1989. 12.00 (*92-871-1706-3*, Pub. by Council of Europe) Manhattan Pub Co.
— 3rd Conference of European Island Regions (Mariehamn, Aland Islands, 1991) (Congress of Local & Regional Authorities of Europe Ser.: No. 22). 1992. 18.00 (*92-871-2056-0*, Pub. by Council of Europe) Manhattan Pub Co.
— Threatened Non-Marine Molluscs of Europe. (Nature & Environment Ser.: No. 64). 1992. 18.00 (*92-871-2107-9*, Pub. by Council of Europe) Manhattan Pub Co.
— Threshold Level, 1990. 1991. 25.00 (*92-871-2003-X*, Pub. by Council of Europe) Manhattan Pub Co.
— Tourism & Integrated Planning Policy: (Proceedings of the Limassol Seminar, 1989) (Congress of Local & Regional Authorities of Europe Ser.: No. 14). 1990. 12.00 (*92-871-1784-5*, Pub. by Council of Europe) Manhattan Pub Co.
— Towards the Conservation of Aculeate Hymenoptera in Europe. (Nature & Environment Ser.: No. 51). 1991. 15.00 (*92-871-1911-2*, Pub. by Council of Europe) Manhattan Pub Co.
— Town Planning Assistance to Dalt Vila, Ibiza: Technical Assistance Report. (Cultural Heritage Ser.: No. 18). 1989. 12.00 (*92-871-1765-9*, Pub. by Council of Europe) Manhattan Pub Co.
— Training Functions in Europe (Grenaa, 1991) (Congress of Local & Regional Authorities of Europe Ser.: No. 24). 1992. 15.00 (*92-871-2092-7*, Pub. by Council of Europe) Manhattan Pub Co.
— Training of Staff, Other Than Health Care Staff, Concerned with Rehabilitation. 1992. 12.00 (*92-871-1966-X*, Pub. by Council of Europe) Manhattan Pub Co.
— Trends in the Establishment & Composition of Remunderation in Employment Contracts: (Report Prepared by the Study Group of the 1989-90 Co-Ordinated Research Programme in the Social Field) 1991. 18.00 (*92-871-1941-4*, Pub. by Council of Europe) Manhattan Pub Co.
— The Unemployment Trap - Long-Term Unemployment & Low Educational Attainment in Six Countries. 1992. 12.00 (*92-871-2054-4*, Pub. by Council of Europe) Manhattan Pub Co.
— The Use of Analysis of Deoxyribonucleic Acid (DNA) Within the Framework of the Criminal Justice System (Recommendation), No. R(92)1. 1993. 12.00 (*92-871-2131-1*, Pub. by Council of Europe) Manhattan Pub Co.
— The Use of the International Classification of Impairments, Disabilities & Handicaps (ICIDH) in Mental Health. 1991. 18.00 (*92-871-1939-2*, Pub. by Council of Europe) Manhattan Pub Co.
— The Use of the International Classification of Impairments, Disabilities & Handicaps (ICIDH) in Rehabilitation. 1989. 12.00 (*92-871-1767-5*, Pub. by Council of Europe) Manhattan Pub Co.
— Use of the International Classification of Impairments, Disabilities & Handicaps (ICIDH) in the Assessment of Technical Aids. 1992. 12.00 (*92-871-2137-0*, Pub. by Council of Europe) Manhattan Pub Co.
— Watercourses (Conservation, Maintenance & Management) (Planning & Management Ser.: No. 2). 1994. 21.00 (*92-871-1894-9*, Pub. by Council of Europe) Manhattan Pub Co.
— Waystage, 1990. 1991. 25.00 (*92-871-2002-1*, Pub. by Council of Europe) Manhattan Pub Co.
— Wild Mink (Mustela Lutreola) in Europe. (Nature & Environment Ser.: No. 54). 1991. 21.00 (*92-871-1986-4*, Pub. by Council of Europe) Manhattan Pub Co.
— Workshop on the Situation & Protection of the Brown Bear (Ursus Arctos) in Europe. (Environmental Encounters Ser.: No. 6). 1989. 15.00 (*92-871-1660-1*, Pub. by Council of Europe) Manhattan Pub Co.
— Yearbook of the European Convention on Human Rights, Vol. 21. 1979. lib. bdg. 327.00 (*90-247-2215-2*) Kluwer Academic.
— Yearbook of the European Convention on Human Rights Colloquy, Vol. 38A, ECHR. 1997. 244.00 (*90-411-0367-8*) Kluwer Law Intl.
— Youth Employment: (Proceedings of the Conference of Saarbrucken, 1986) (Congress of Local & Regional Authorities of Europe Ser.: No. 6). 1988. 15.00 (*92-871-1539-7*, Pub. by Council of Europe) Manhattan Pub Co.
Council of Europe Staff, ed. Collected Edition of the "Travaux Preparatoires" of the European Convention on Human Rights Vol. V: Legal Committee-Ad Hoc Joint Committee-Committee of Ministers-Consultative Assembly 23 June - 28 August 1950. 356p. 1979. lib. bdg. 277.50 (*90-247-1970-4*) Kluwer Academic.
— Collected Edition of the "Travaux Preparatories" of the European Convention on Human Rights, Vol. 6. 1978. lib. bdg. 195.00 (*90-247-1969-0*) Kluwer Academic.
— European Convention on Human Rights: Collected Texts. 1986. lib. bdg. 134.00 (*90-247-3266-2*) Kluwer Academic.
— Freedom of Association: Seminar Organized by the Secretariat General of the Council of Europe in Co-Operation with the Ministery of Justice of Iceland, Reykjavik. LC 94-22419. (Yearbook of European Convention of Human Rights Ser.). 472p. (C). 1994. lib. bdg. 222.50 (*0-7923-3001-3*, Pub. by M Nijhoff) Kluwer Academic.
— Human Rights of Aliens in Europe. 1985. lib. bdg. 195.00 (*90-247-3215-8*) Kluwer Academic.
— Yearbook of the European Convention on Human Rights. (European Convention on Human Rights Ser.: No. 22). 688p. 1980. lib. bdg. 327.00 (*90-247-2383-3*) Kluwer Academic.
— Yearbook of the European Convention on Human Rights. (C). 1990. lib. bdg. 299.00 (*0-7923-0207-9*) Kluwer Academic.
— Yearbook of the European Convention on Human Rights. (C). 1993. lib. bdg. 269.50 (*0-7923-1787-4*) Kluwer Academic.
— Yearbook of the European Convention on Human Rights, Vol. 36, 1993. 1076p. 1996. 385.00 (*90-411-0151-9*) MNP-G&T.
— Yearbook of the European Convention on Human Rights: Annuaire De la Convention Europeenne Des Droit De l'Homme, 1990, Vol. 33. 748p. (C). 1994. lib. bdg. 286.00 (*0-7923-2572-9*) Kluwer Academic.
***Council of Europe Staff, ed.** Yearbook of the European Convention on Human Rights Vol. 40: 1997.Tr. of Annuaire de la Convention Europeenne des Droits de L'Homme. 1744p. 1998. 375.00 (*90-411-1103-4*) Kluwer Law Intl.
Council of Europe Staff, ed. Yearbook of the European Convention on Human Rights, 1982, Vol. 25. 1986. lib. bdg. 328.00 (*90-247-3262-X*) Kluwer Academic.
— Yearbook of the European Convention on Human Rights, 1985, Vol. 28. 656p. 1991. lib. bdg. 290.50 (*0-7923-0652-X*) Kluwer Academic.
— Yearbook of the European Convention on Human Rights, 1986: Annuaire de la Convention Europeenne de l'Homme, Vol. 29. 624p. (C). 1991. lib. bdg. 273.50 (*0-7923-1109-4*) Kluwer Academic.
— Yearbook of the European Convention on Human Rights, 1989, Vol. 32. 660p. (C). 1993. lib. bdg. 269.50 (*0-7923-2132-4*) Kluwer Academic.
Council of Europe Staff & Project Group on Data Protection Staff. The Protection of Medical Data: Recommendation No. R (97) 5 LC 98-136807. (Legal Issues Ser.). 65p. 1997. write for info. (*92-871-3334-4*) Council of Europe.
Council of Europe Staff, jt. auth. see Colloquy on Legal Data Processing in Europe Staff.
Council of European Communities Staff. European Communities Glossary. 8th ed. (ENG & FRE.). 1589p. 1984. 49.95 (*0-8288-0967-4*, M6546) Fr & Eur.
Council of European Publishing Staff. The Human Rights, Ethical & Moral Dimensions of Health Care: 120 Practical Case Studies. 485p. 1998. pap. 60.00 (*92-871-3055-8*, Pub. by Statnry Office) Balogh.
Council of Independent Black Institutions Staff. Positive African Images for Children: CIBI: Social Studies Curriculum. LC 90-60173. (Illus.). 64p. 1990. pap. 7.95 (*0-932415-48-2*) Red Sea Pr.
Council of Law Reporting of Victoria, Australia St. Victorian Law Reports: Australia, 138 vols. 4279.00 (*0-409-49004-0*, MICHIE) LEXIS Pub.
***Council of Literary Magazines & Presses Staff.** Directory of Literary Magazines 2001. 2000. pap. 12.95 (*1-55921-288-8*) Moyer Bell.
Council of Literary Magazines Staff. Directory of Literary Magazines, 1999. 301p. 1999. pap. 12.95 (*1-55921-269-1*) Moyer Bell.
— Directory of Literary Magazines, 2000. 302p. 2000. pap. 12.95 (*1-55921-239-X*) Moyer Bell.
Council of Medical Specialty Societies Task Force & Eddy, David M. A Manual for Assessing Health Practices & Designing Practice Policies: The Explicit Approach. 144p. 1992. pap. 34.00 (*0-943126-18-5*, MAH91) Amer Coll Phys.
Council of National Library & Information Associat & American National Standards Committee on Library W. American National Standard for Patent Documents-Identification of Bibliographic Data, Z39.46. 1983. 6.00 (*0-685-07730-6*) ANSI.
Council of New York Law Associates Staff. Should You Incorporate? (ENG & SPA.). 24p. 1977. 3.00 (*0-685-08021-8*) Coun NY Law.
Council of New York Law Associates Staff, ed. By-Laws: A Guide for Not-for-Profit Organizations & Their Lawyers. 20p. 1984. pap. 6.00 (*0-318-03105-1*) Coun NY Law.

C

— Legal Handbook for Community Development Organizations. 67p. 1983. pap. 25.00 (*0-318-03110-8*) Coun NY Law.

Council of New York Law Associates Staff, et al, eds. Practicing Law in New York City. 195p. 1975. pap. 3.75 (*0-318-03111-6*) Coun NY Law.

Council of New York Law Associates Staff & Community Law Offices Staff, eds. New York Not-for-Profit Organization Manual. rev. ed. 190p. 1985. reprint ed. pap. 25.00 (*0-686-37424-X*) Coun NY Law.

***Council of School Attorneys Members.** The 1999 Idea Regulations: A Practical Analysis. 90p. 1999. pap. 25.00 (*0-88364-225-5*, 06-170, Pub. by Natl Sch Boards) PMDS-AACRAO.

— A School Law Primer, Pt. I. 125p. 1999. ring bd. 400.00 (*0-88364-224-7*, 06-169, Pub. by Natl Sch Boards) PMDS-AACRAO.

— A School Law Retreat 1999. 412p. 1999. ring bd. 200.00 (*0-88364-228-X*, 06-172, Pub. by Natl Sch Boards) PMDS-AACRAO.

Council of School Attorneys Members. Student-to-Student Sexual Harassment: A Legal Guide for Schools. 186p. 1998. pap. 35.00 (*0-88364-216-6*, 06-166) Natl Sch Boards.

***Council of School Attorneys Staff.** A School Law Retreat, 1998. 545p. 1998. ring bd. 200.00 (*0-88364-218-2*, 06-167) Natl Sch Boards.

Council of State Government Staff. Book of States. (Book of the States (paper) Ser.). 1998. pap. text 79.00 (*0-87292-948-5*) Coun State Govts.

— Book of the States. 1998. 99.00 (*0-87292-947-7*) Coun State Govts.

***Council of State Government Staff.** Book of the States 2000 -2001, Vol. 33. 2000. 99.00 (*0-87292-877-2*) Coun State Govts.

— Book of the States 2000-2001, Vol. 33. 2000. pap. 79.00 (*0-87292-878-0*) Coun State Govts.

Council of State Government Staff. Directory II Legislative Leaders, 1999 ed. 1998. pap. text 49.99 (*0-87292-853-5*) Coun State Govts.

***Council of State Government Staff.** Directory III Administrative, 1999 ed. 1998. 49.99 (*0-87292-854-3*) Coun State Govts.

Council of State Government Staff. Directory of Elective Officials, 1999. 1998. 49.99 (*0-87292-852-7*) Coun State Govts.

— State Elective Officials, 1995. 1995. 59.50 (*0-87292-998-1*) Coun State Govts.

— State Legislative Leaders, 1996. 1996. pap. text 59.50 (*0-87292-905-1*) Coun State Govts.

***Council of State Government Staff.** State Legislative Leaders 2000. 2000. pap. 49.99 (*0-87292-874-8*) Coun State Govts.

Council of State Government Staff, contrib. by. The Book of the States, 1962-1963, Vol. 14. LC 35-11433. 626p. 1962. pap. 194.10 (*0-608-07494-2*, 206771700014) Bks Demand.

Council of State Governments Staff. The Book of the States: 1992-1993 Edition, Vol. 29. 720p. 1992. 79.00 (*0-87292-963-9*, C-024-91) Coun State Govts.

— Drug Testing: Protection for Society or a Violation of Civil Rights? LC 88-143569. (Publication Ser.: No. C86). 95p. reprint ed. pap. 30.00 (*0-7837-2659-7*, 204301900006) Bks Demand.

— Federal Grants-in-Aid. LC 77-74937. (American Federalism-the Urban Dimension Ser.). (Illus.). 1978. reprint ed. lib. bdg. 29.95 (*0-405-10484-7*) Ayer.

— Federal-State Relations. LC 77-74938. (American Federalism-the Urban Dimension Ser.). (Illus.). 1978. reprint ed. lib. bdg. 29.95 (*0-405-10485-5*) Ayer.

— The Lieutenant Governor: The Office & Its Powers. White, Keith C., ed. 68p. pap. 20.00 (*0-87292-954-X*, C-89) Coun State Govts.

— The New Domestic Agenda: A Strengthened American Family, a Strengthened Economy. LC 89-168361. (Publication Ser.: No. C135). 96p. reprint ed. pap. 30.00 (*0-7837-2657-0*, 204301600006) Bks Demand.

— Secretary of State: The Office & Duties. 3rd ed. 105p. 1991. pap. 30.00 (*0-87292-964-7*, D-009-91) Coun State Govts.

— State Administrative Officials Classified by Function, 1991-1992. 300p. 1992. pap. 30.00 (*0-87292-962-0*, D-003-91) Coun State Govts.

— State & Local Government Purchasing. LC 83-621513. (Publication Ser.: No. C3). 295p. (Orig.). reprint ed. pap. 91.50 (*0-7837-2661-9*, 204302300006) Bks Demand.

— State Credentialing of the Health Occupations & Professions. LC KF2905.1.Z95. (Publication Ser.: No. C40). 244p. reprint ed. pap. 75.70 (*0-7837-2656-2*, 204301400006) Bks Demand.

— State Elective Officials & the Legislatures 1991-92. 176p. 1991. pap. 30.00 (*0-87292-960-4*, D-001-91) Coun State Govts.

***Council of State Governments Staff.** State Elective Officials 2000. 2000. pap. 49.99 (*0-87292-873-X*) Coun State Govts.

Council of State Governments Staff. State Leadership Directory Vol. 1: Elective Officials, 1997. 300p. pap. 45.00 (*0-87292-923-X*) Coun State Govts.

— State Leadership Directory Vol. 2: Legislative Leadership, Committees & Staff, 1997. 325p. pap. 45.00 (*0-87292-924-8*) Coun State Govts.

— State Leadership Directory Vol. 3: Administrative Officials, 1997. 445p. pap. 45.00 (*0-87292-925-6*) Coun State Govts.

— State Legislative Leadership, Committees & Staff, 1991-92. 290p. 1991. pap. 30.00 (*0-87292-961-2*, D-002-91) Coun State Govts.

— The State of the States: Current Conditions, Future Directions. rev. ed. Hersman, Frank, ed. 1986. pap. 22.50 (*0-87292-064-X*, C-33) Coun State Govts.

— State Personnel Office: Roles & Functions. Carroll, Linda, ed. 39p. (Orig.). 1987. pap. 20.00 (*0-87292-072-0*, C-74) Coun State Govts.

— State Regulation of the Health Occupations & Professions, 1985-86: Final Report, March 10, 1987. LC KF2905.1.S73. (Publication Ser.: No. C76). 249p. reprint ed. pap. 77.20 (*0-7837-2654-6*, 204300900006) Bks Demand.

— Suggested State Legislation, Vol. 47. LC 87-642172. 340p. reprint ed. pap. 105.40 (*0-608-07515-9*, 206773800047) Bks Demand.

— Suggested State Legislation, Vol. 48. LC 87-642172. 201p. reprint ed. pap. 62.40 (*0-608-07516-7*, 206773800048) Bks Demand.

— Suggested State Legislation, Vol. 49. LC 87-642172. 179p. reprint ed. pap. 55.50 (*0-608-07517-5*, 206773800049) Bks Demand.

— Suggested State Legislation, Vol. 50. LC 87-642172. 168p. 1946. pap. 52.10 (*0-608-07518-3*, 206773800050) Bks Demand.

— Suggested State Legislation, Vol. 51. LC 87-642172. 192p. 1946. pap. 59.60 (*0-608-07519-1*, 206773800051) Bks Demand.

— Suggested State Legislation, Vol. 52. LC 87-642172. 191p. 1946. pap. 59.30 (*0-608-07520-5*, 206773800052) Bks Demand.

— Suggested State Legislation, Vol. 53. LC 87-642172. 216p. 1946. pap. 67.00 (*0-608-07521-3*, 206773800053) Bks Demand.

— Suggested State Legislation, Vol. 54. LC 87-642172. 188p. 1946. pap. 58.30 (*0-608-07522-1*, 206773800054) Bks Demand.

Council of State Governments Staff, ed. Suggested State Legislation, 1941-1995, 54 vols., Set. LC 72-81556. 1995. reprint ed. lib. bdg. 2500.00 (*0-912004-05-3*) Gaunt.

Council of State Governments Staff, jt. auth. see National Clearinghouse on Licensure, Enforcement,.

Council of Superior Court Judges of Georgia Commit. Suggested Pattern Jury Instructions: Civil Cases, Vol. I. 3rd ed. 379p. 1994. ring bd. 65.00 (*0-89854-152-2*) U of GA Inst Govt.

— Suggested Pattern Jury Instructions, Vol. II: Criminal Cases, Vol. II. 2nd ed. Institute of Government Staff, ed. 201p. 1994. ring bd. 65.00 (*0-89854-153-0*) U of GA Inst Govt.

Council of the Great City Schools Staff. Special Education in America's Cities: A Descriptive Study. 121p. 1988. pap. 21.95 (*1-56602-022-0*) Research Better.

***Council of Tree & Landscape Appraisers Staff, et al.** Guide for Plant Appraisal. 9th rev. ed. (Illus.). 144p. 2000. pap. 125.00 (*1-881956-25-3*) Int Soc Arboricult.

Council of Trent Staff. The Catechism of the Council of Trent. LC 82-50588. 603p. 1992. reprint ed. pap. 24.00 (*0-89555-185-3*) TAN Bks Pubs.

Council on Accreditation of Services for Families. Manual for Agency Accreditation. rev. ed. LC 91-77835. 1080p. 1991. disk 90.00 (*0-685-59101-8*) Coun Accred Srvs Fam & Child.

— Manual for Agency Accreditation, Set. rev. ed. LC 91-77835. 1080p. 1991. per. 75.00 (*1-880853-01-9*) Coun Accred Srvs Fam & Child.

— Standards for Agency Management & Service Delivery. LC 91-77979. 232p. 1991. per. 50.00 (*1-880853-00-0*); disk 60.00 (*0-685-59102-6*) Coun Accred Srvs Fam & Child.

Council on Aging Staff. Directory of Services for Senior Citizens. 200p. 1995. pap. text 3.00 (*1-888334-03-7*) Coun Commun Serv.

Council on Civil Society Staff, et al, eds. A Call to Civil Society: Why Democracy Needs Moral Truths. (Illus.). 32p. 1998. 7.00 (*0-9659841-2-5*) Inst for Am Val.

Council on Competitiveness Staff. Going Global: The New Shape of American Innovation. (Illus.). 75p. 1998. pap. 45.00 (*1-889866-21-0*) Coun on Competitiveness.

— Winning the Skills Race. (Illus.). 94p. 1998. pap. 25.00 (*1-889866-19-9*) Coun on Competitiveness.

Council on Economic Priorities, jt. auth. see Marlin, A. Tepper.

Council on Economic Priorities Staff, et al. Hazardous Waste Management: Reducing the Risk. Marlin, Alice T. & Ross, Steven S., eds. LC 36-2748. (Illus.). 316p. 1986. text 75.00 (*0-933280-30-0*); pap. text 45.00 (*0-933280-31-9*) Island Pr.

— Rating America's Corporate Conscience. LC 86-8064. 499p. 1987. 21.95 (*0-201-15886-8*); pap. 14.95 (*0-201-15879-5*) Addison-Wesley.

Council on Foreign & Defense Policy Staff, jt. ed. see Carnegie Endowment for International Peace Staff.

Council on Foreign Affairs. Democracy. 1998. pap. 11.95 (*0-87609-240-7*) Coun Foreign.

***Council on Foreign Affairs Staff.** Asia: Rising or Falling? 1999. pap. 11.95 (*0-87609-265-2*) Coun Foreign.

— A New Europe. 1999. pap. 11.95 (*0-87609-266-0*) Coun Foreign.

Council on Foreign Affairs Staff. The Rise of China. 1998. pap. 11.95 (*0-87609-242-3*) Coun Foreign.

Council on Foreign Relations, Inc. Staff. Catalog of the Foreign Relations Library, First Supplement. 1980. 435.00 (*0-8161-0306-2*, G K Hall & Co) Mac Lib Ref.

Council on Foundations Staff, jt. auth. see Freeman, David F.

Council on Governmental Ethics Laws. Campaign Finance 1991: Legislation & Litigation. 120p. 1991. 20.00 (*0-685-60082-3*) Coun State Govts.

— Ethics & Lobbying 1991: Legislation & Litigation. 92p. 1991. 20.00 (*0-685-60025-4*) Coun State Govts.

Council on Governmental Ethics Laws & Council of S. Cogel Blue Book: Campaign Finance, Ethics & Lobby Law. 9th ed. 1992. 59.00 (*0-87292-968-X*) Coun State Govts.

Council on Health Care Technology Institute of Med. Improving Consensus Development for Health Technology Assessment: An International Perspective. Goodman, Clifford & Baratz, Sharon R., eds. 176p. 1990. pap. text 15.00 (*0-309-04239-9*) Natl Acad Pr.

***Council on Hotel, Restaurant & Institutional Educa.** A Guide to Collelge Programs in Culinary Arts, Hospitality, & Tourism. 6th ed. 376p. 1999. pap. 29.95 (*0-471-32942-8*) Wiley.

Council on International Educational Exchange Staf. Work, Study, Travel Abroad, 1994-1995: The Whole World Handbook. 12th ed. Hernandez, Lazaro & Terry, Max, eds. (Illus.). 600p. (Orig.). (C). 1994. pap. 13.95 (*0-312-10578-9*) St Martin.

Council on Keying Education Staff. Keyboarding Toolbox: Teaching Methods for Keyboarding Technique, Accuracy, & Speed. (Illus.). 32p. 1993. spiral bd. 9.95 (*1-56484-049-2*) Intl Society Tech Educ.

Council on Library & Information Resources Staff, et al. The Mirage of Continuity: Reconfiguring Academic Information Resources for the 21st Century. Hawkins, Brian L. & Battin, Patricia, eds. LC 98-28434. 301p. 1998. 25.00 (*1-887334-59-9*) Coun Lib & Info.

***Council on Social Work Education Staff.** Statistics on Social Work Education in the United States, 1998. 126p. 1999. pap. 16.00 (*0-87293-073-4*) Coun Soc Wk Ed.

Council on Social Work Education Staff. Summary Information on Master of Social Work Programs, 1997-98. 96p. 1998. pap. 11.00 (*0-87293-065-3*) Coun Soc Wk Ed.

***Council on Social Work Education Staff.** Summary Information on Master of Social Work Programs, 1998-99. 90p. 1999. pap. 11.00 (*0-87293-071-8*) Coun Soc Wk Ed.

Council on Tall Buildings & Urban Habitat. High-Rise Buildings: Recent Progress. (Monograph on the Planning & Design of Tall Buildings). (Illus.). 310p. 1986. 25.00 (*0-939493-00-4*) Coun Tall Bldg.

Council on Tall Buildings & Urban Habitat Staff. Second Conference on Tall Buildings in Seismic Regions, Proceedings. (Illus.). 436p. 1991. text 55.00 (*0-939493-07-1*, 903.409) Coun Tall Bldg.

Council on Tall Buildings & Urban Habitats Staff. Fire Safety in Tall Buildings. Sfintesco, Duiliu et al, eds. LC 92-14561. (Tall Buildings & Urban Environment Ser.). 348p. 1992. 35.00 (*0-07-012531-7*) McGraw.

— First Conference on Tall Buildings in Seismic Regions. (Illus.). 427p. (C). 1986. pap. text 10.00 (*0-939493-04-7*, 903.377) Coun Tall Bldg.

— Tall Building Criteria & Loading. (Monograph on Tall Buildings Ser.: Vol. CL). 909p. 1980. text 50.00 (*0-87262-237-1*) Am Soc Civil Eng.

— Tall Building Systems & Concepts. (Monograph on Tall Buildings Ser.: Vol. SC). 550p. 1980. 50.00 (*0-87262-239-8*) Am Soc Civil Eng.

— Tall Buildings: 2000 & Beyond: Proceedings of Fourth World Congress, Hong Kong. Rice, Dolores B., ed. (Illus.). 1192p. (C). 1990. 30.00 (*0-939493-05-5*, 903.390) Coun Tall Bldg.

Council on Tall Buildings & Urban Habitats Staff, ed. Structural Design, Codes, & Special Building Projects. (Illus.). 119p. 1997. text 25.00 (*0-939493-16-0*) Coun Tall Bldg.

Council on Tall Buildings & Urban Habitats Staff, et al, eds. Architecture of Tall Buildings. LC 94-47110. (Tall Buildings & Urban Environment Ser.). 750p. 1995. text 75.00 (*0-07-012540-6*) McGraw.

Council on Tall Buildings Staff. Tall Buildings: 2000 & Beyond - Collected Papers: Fourth World Congress, Hong Kong. (Illus.). 800p. (C). 1991. text 24.00 (*0-939493-06-3*, 903.407) Coun Tall Bldg.

Council on Technology Teacher Education Staff. Conducting Technical Research: 36th Yearbook. Isreal & Wright, eds. 1999. 18.96 (*0-02-677113-6*) Glencoe.

— Construction in Technology Education: 43rd Yearbook. Wescott, Jack W. & Henak, Richard M., eds. 1999. 18.96 (*0-02-677141-1*) Glencoe.

— Diversity in Technology Education: 47th Yearbook. 1999. 18.96 incl. cd-rom (*0-02-831274-0*) Glencoe.

— Elementary School Technology Education: 46th Yearbook. Kirkwood, R. C. & Foster, eds. 1999. 18.96 (*0-02-677152-7*) Glencoe.

— Foundations of Technology Education: 44th Yearbook. Martin, ed. 1999. 18.96 (*0-02-677149-7*) Glencoe.

— Instructional Strategies for Technology Education: 37th Yearbook. Kemp, William H. & Schwaller, Anthony E., eds. 1999. 18.96 (*0-02-677114-4*) Glencoe.

— Manufacturing in Technology Education: 42nd Yearbook. Seymour, R. B. & Shackelford, eds. 1999. 18.96 (*0-02-677140-3*) Glencoe.

— Technology & the Quality of Life: 45th Yearbook. Custer, Rodney & Wiens, Emerson, eds. 1999. 18.96 (*0-02-838638-8*) Glencoe.

— Transportation in Technology Education: 41st Yearbook. Wright & Komacek, Stanley A., eds. 1999. 18.96 (*0-02-677127-6*) Glencoe.

Council, R. Bruce, et al. Industry & Technology in Antebellum Tennessee: The Archaeology of Bluff Furnace. LC 91-32554. (Illus.). 248p. (Orig.). 1992. pap. text 18.95 (*0-87049-744-8*); lib. bdg. 42.50 (*0-87049-743-X*) U of Tenn Pr.

Council Soil Testing & Plant Staff. Handbook of Reference Methods for Soil Analysis. rev. ed. 200p. 1998. boxed set 39.95 (*1-57444-178-7*) St Lucie Pr.

Cound, Dana M. A Leader's Journey to Quality. (Quality & Reliability Ser.: Vol. 31). (Illus.). 208p. 1991. text 65.00 (*0-8247-8574-6*) Dekker.

Cound, John J., et al. Cases & Materials on Civil Procedure. 6th ed. (American Casebook Ser.). 1353p. (C). 1993. text 56.00 (*0-314-02219-8*) West Pub.

— Cases & Materials on Civil Procedures. 7th ed. LC 97-22403. (Paralegal). 1327p. (C). 1997. text 49.25 (*0-314-21115-2*) West Pub.

— Civil Procedure Supplement for Use with All Pleading & Procedure Casebooks, 1994. (American Casebook Ser.). 475p. 1994. pap. text. write for info. (*0-314-04282-2*) West Pub.

— 1998 Civil Procedure Supplement for Use with All Pleading & Procedure Casebooks. (American Casebook Ser.). 500p. 1998. pap. 20.50 (*0-314-23248-6*) West Pub.

— 1996 Civil Procedure Supplement for Use with All Pleading & Procedure Casebooks. (American Casebook Ser.). 478p. 1996. pap. text, suppl. ed. write for info. (*0-314-20239-0*) West Pub.

***Coundouriotis, Eleni.** Claiming History: Colonialism, Ethnography, & the Novel. LC 98-34458. 256p. 1998. pap. 16.50 (*0-231-11351-X*); lib. bdg. 49.50 (*0-231-11350-1*) Col U Pr.

Counhaye, Guy. The Chilly Bear. (Child's World Library). (Illus.). 32p. (J). (gr. k-5). 1992. lib. bdg. 18.50 (*0-89565-740-6*) Childs World.

Counihan, Carole. Anthropology of Food & Body: Gender, Meaning & Power. LC 98-49970. 1999. write for info. (*0-415-92192-9*) Routledge.

Counihan, Carole & Van Esterik, Penny. Food & Culture: A Reader. LC 96-46430. (Illus.). 432p. 1997. pap. 25.99 (*0-415-91710-7*) Routledge.

— Food & Culture: A Reader. LC 96-46430. (Illus.). 432p. (C). 1997. 80.00 (*0-415-91709-3*) Routledge.

Counihan, Carole M. Anthropology of Food & Body: Gender, Meaning & Power. 1999. pap. 19.99 (*0-415-92193-7*) Routledge.

Counihan, Carole M. & Kaplan, Steven L. Food & Gender: Identity & Power. (Food in History & Culture Ser.: Vol. 1). 157p. 1998. text 48.00 (*90-5702-573-6*, ECU38); pap. text 16.00 (*90-5702-568-X*, ECU21) Gordon & Breach.

Counihan, Martin. FORTRAN 95. 2nd ed. 320p. 1997. pap. 37.95 (*1-85728-367-8*, Pub. by UCL Pr Ltd) Taylor & Francis.

***Counsel, J.** But Martin! 2000. pap. 6.95 (*0-552-52312-7*, Pub. by Transworld Publishers Ltd) Trafalgar.

Counseling & Career Center Staff. STFF Survival Tips for Freshmen. 352p. (C). 1999. spiral bd. 88.95 (*0-7872-5358-8*, 41535801) Kendall-Hunt.

Counsell, Christine & Howe, Kate. Life in Tudor Times. LC 97-158699. (Primary History Ser.). (Illus.). 49p. (C). 1997. pap. 9.95 (*0-521-55758-5*) Cambridge U Pr.

Counsell, Christine & Steer, Chris. Industrial Britain: The Workshop of the World. (Cambridge History Programme Ser.). 96p. (C). 1993. pap. 14.95 (*0-521-42494-1*) Cambridge U Pr.

Counsell, Colin. Signs of Performance: A Student's Guide. LC 95-37692. (Illus.). 256p. (C). 1996. pap. 20.99 (*0-415-10643-5*) Routledge.

— Signs of Performance: A Student's Guide. LC 95-37692. (Illus.). 256p. (C). 1996. 85.00 (*0-415-10642-7*) Routledge.

Counsell, Lynne, jt. auth. see Asbe, Michael.

***Counsell, Michael.** Every Pilgrim's Guide to Oberammergau & Its Passion Play. 124p. 1999. 8.95 (*1-85311-213-5*, 6111, Pub. by Canterbury Press Norwich) Morehouse Pub.

Counsell, Michael. 2000 Years of Prayer. LC 99-33794. 644p. 1999. 35.95 (*0-8192-1825-1*) Morehouse Pub.

Counselman, Mary E. Half in Shadow. LC 77-78597. 1978. 12.95 (*0-87054-081-5*) Arkham.

Counselors of Real Estate Staff. Real Estate Issues. 56p. 33.00 (*0-318-13259-1*) Couns Real Estate.

Counsilman, Brian E., jt. auth. see Counsilman, James E.

Counsilman, James E. & Counsilman, Brian E. The New Science of Swimming. 2nd ed. LC 93-29229. 432p. 1994. pap. text 53.00 (*0-13-099888-5*) P-H.

Count, Alice, jt. auth. see Count, Earl W.

Count, Cynthia G. Le, see Le Count, Cynthia G.

***Count, Earl W.** 4000 Years of Christmas: A Gift from the Ages. (Illus.). 112p. 2000. pap. 9.95 (*1-56975-235-4*) Ulysses Pr.

Count, Earl W. & Bowles, Gordon T., eds. Fact & Theory in Social Science. LC 64-16921. 1964. 44.95 (*0-8156-2063-2*) Syracuse U Pr.

Count, Earl W. & Count, Alice. 4,000 Years of Christmas: A Gift from the Ages. LC 97-36946. 112p. 1997. 16.00 (*1-56975-087-4*) Ulysses Pr.

Count of Clandemond, jt. auth. see MacCarthy, Mor.

Count of Clandermond, ed. Links in a Golden Chain: Essays on the History of the Niadh Nask. (Illus.). 225p. 1998. 40.00 (*0-9654220-2-X*) Gryfons Pubs & Dist.

***Counter, C. & Tani, Karl, compiled by.** Palette in the Kitchen. anniversary rev. ed. (Illus.). 64p. 1999. pap. 10.95 (*0-86534-283-0*) Sunstone Pr.

Counter, W. Charles. Counter. Genealogy of the Counter Family, Primarily of Chas. Counter, Son of George & Alice Caunter, from 1819 to 1955. 94p. 1997. reprint ed. pap. 18.50 (*0-8328-8080-9*); reprint ed. lib. bdg. 28.50 (*0-8328-8079-5*) Higginson Bk Co.

Countess, Imani, et al. Making Connections for Africa: Report from a Constituency Builders' Dialogue. LC 97-37593. 94p. 1997. pap. 8.95 (*0-9634238-4-3*) Africa Policy Info.

***Countess of Ranfurly Hermione.** The Ugly One. large type unabridged ed. 1999. 25.95 (*0-7531-5095-6*, 150956, Pub. by ISIS Lrg Prnt) ISIS Pub.

Countess of Romanones, Aline. The Spy Went Dancing. 1991. mass mkt. 5.95 (*0-515-10507-4*, Jove) Berkley Pub.

— The Spy Wore Red. 1990. mass mkt. 5.99 (*0-515-10653-4*, Jove) Berkley Pub.

— The Spy Wore Silk. 1992. mass mkt. 5.99 (*0-515-10876-6*, Jove) Berkley Pub.

— The Well-Mannered Assassin. 368p. 1995. pap. text 5.99 (0-515-11533-9, Jove) Berkley Pub.

Countess of Romanones, Aline. The Well-Mannered Assassin. large type ed. LC 94-20267. 584p. 1994. lib. bdg. 24.95 (0-8161-7447-4, G K Hall Lrg Type) Mac Lib Ref.

Country Dance & Song Society Staff, ed. Gems: The Best of the Country Dance & Song Society Diamond Jubilee Music, Dance & Song Contest. LC 93-70628. (Illus.). 94p. 1993. spiral bd. 16.00 (0-917024-09-5) Country Dance and Song.

***Country Home Staff, contrib. by.** Country Home Quick Country Decorating. (Illus.). 216p. 2000. 34.95 (0-696-21179-3, Better Homes) Meredith Bks.

***Country Homes & Garden Staff, ed.** Decorating Country Style: A Complete Guide to Paint Effects & Stencilling. (Illus.). 192p. 2000. pap. 24.99 (1-55870-574-0, Betrwy Bks) F & W Pubns Inc.

— Decorating with Color: Inspired Ideas for Your Home. (Illus.). 192p. 2000. pap. 24.99 (1-55870-573-2, Betrwy Bks) F & W Pubns Inc.

***Country Homes and Gardens Staff.** The Decorated Home: Imaginative Designs & Painting Techniques. (Illus.). 192p. 2000. pap. 24.99 (1-55870-572-4) F & W Pubns Inc.

Country Life Magazine Staff. Living National Treasures: A Celebration of British Craftsmanship Through the Eyes of Country Life. (Illus.). 144p. 1998. 75.00 (1-86205-032-5, Pub. by Pavilion Bks Ltd) Trafalgar.

Country Living. Country Living Handmade Frames: Decorating Throughout Your Home. LC 98-32090. 1999. 19.95 (0-688-16773-X, Hearst) Hearst Commns.

— Fabric, a Seasonal Guide. LC 97-21899. 1998. 30.00 (0-688-15499-9, Hearst) Hearst Commns.

— Handmade Halloween. LC 99-23394. 1999. 19.95 (0-688-16775-6, Hearst) Hearst Commns.

Country Living, ed. Decorating II. LC 99-42886. 192p. 1999. 30.00 (0-688-16752-7, Wm Morrow) Morrow Avon.

Country Living Editors. Country Living Handmade Country. (Illus.). 224p. 1997. 29.95 (0-688-14470-5, Hearst) Hearst Commns.

Country Living Gardener Staff. Gardener's Latin. LC 98-43254. 80p. 1999. write for info. (0-688-16779-9, Hearst) Hearst Commns.

***Country Living Gardener Staff.** Irish Gardens. LC 99-33713. 224p. 1999. 40.00 (0-688-16885-X, Wm Morrow) Morrow Avon.

Country Living Magazine Editors. Country Living Colors. LC 96-42686. 1997. 27.50 (0-688-15094-2, Hearst) Hearst Commns.

— Country Living Country Christmas. LC 90-80313. (Illus.). 176p. 1990. 21.95 (0-688-09738-3, Hearst) Hearst Commns.

Country Living Magazine Staff. Peaceful Home-Country Living. LC 97-21898. 1998. 30.00 (0-688-15618-5, Hearst) Hearst Commns.

Country Living Magazine Staff, contrib. by. Christmas with Country Living, Vol. 2. 1999. 29.95 (0-8487-1845-3) Oxmoor Hse.

Country Living Staff. Candles. LC 97-41039. 1998. 19.95 (0-688-15563-4, Hearst) Hearst Commns.

***Country Living Staff.** Christmas Ornaments. LC 99-23396. (Illus.). 112p. 1999. 19.95 (0-688-16776-4, Hearst) Hearst Commns.

Country Living Staff. Christmas with Country Living. Vol. 99. (Illus.). 160p. 1999. 29.95 (0-8487-1880-1) Oxmoor Hse.

***Country Living Staff.** Country Living Decorating with Baskets. LC 00-20495. (Illus.). 112p. 2000. 23.00 (0-688-17503-1, Hearst) Hearst Commns.

— Country Living Garden Decorating. 2000. write for info. (0-688-17504-X, Hearst) Hearst Commns.

— The Country Living Country Look. 2000. pap. 22.00 (0-688-17767-0) Morrow Avon.

— Country Living Decorating with Candles: Accents Throughout the Home. LC 99-36437. (Illus.). 112p. 2000. 23.00 (0-688-17502-3) Morrow Avon.

— Living with Folk Art: Ethnic Styles from Around the World. (Illus.). 160p. 2000. pap. 22.00 (0-688-17769-7) Morrow Avon.

Country Living Staff, ed. Tranquil Garden: Creating Peaceful Spaces Outdoors. LC 98-8318. (Country Living Gardner Ser.). 192p. 1999. 30.00 (0-688-16407-2, Hearst) Hearst Commns.

Country Miniature Staff. Medieval Britain. (Weidenfeld Country Miniature Ser.). (Illus.). 64p. 1995. 9.95 (0-297-83489-4, Pub. by Orion Publng Grp) Trafalgar.

Country Music Foundation Staff. Country: The Music & the Musicians. exp. rev. ed. LC 95-147475. (Illus.). 432p. 1994. 45.00 (1-55859-879-0) Abbeville Pr.

— The Country Music Hall of Fame & Museum Book. rev. ed. 56p. 1995. 4.50 (0-915608-12-X) Country Music Found.

Country Music Foundation Staff, ed. Cooking with Country Music Stars. LC 89-49642. (Illus.). 224p. 1990. reprint ed. 19.95 (0-88289-793-4) Pelican.

Country Music Magazine Editors. Comprehensive Country Music Encyclopedia. (Illus.). 688p. 1994. 25.00 (0-8129-2247-6, Times Bks) Crown Pub Group.

Country Threads Staff, et al, des. Quilted for Christmas: A Collection of Festive Quilts for the Holidays. LC 93-44135. (Illus.). 120p. 1998. reprint ed. pap. 22.95 (1-56477-054-0, B176, That Patchwrk Pl) Martingale & Co.

Countryman. Beginnings of Slavery. LC 98-87525. 1999. pap. 11.95 (0-312-18261-9) St Martin.

— How Did American Slavery Begin? LC 98-87525. 120p. 1999. text 35.00 (0-312-21820-6) St Martin.

— Meaning of Constitution. LC 98-87526. 1999. pap. 11.95 (0-312-18262-7) St Martin.

Countryman, Alvin. Countryman Genealogy. (Illus.). 364p. 1997. reprint ed. pap. 55.00 (0-8328-8082-5); reprint ed. lib. bdg. 65.00 (0-8328-8081-7) Higginson Bk Co.

***Countryman, Beckie.** Miss Millie. (Illus.). 12p. (J). 2000. pap. 3.00 (0-9650312-7-6) Cosmo Starr.

Countryman, David W. & Sofranko, Denise M., eds. Guiding Land Use Decisions: Planning & Management for Forests & Recreation. LC 81-14281. 264p. 1982. reprint ed. pap. 81.90 (0-608-05939-0, 206627600008) Bks Demand.

Countryman, Edward. The American Revolution. Foner, Eric, ed. 288p. 1985. pap. 10.00 (0-8090-0162-4) Hill & Wang.

— Americans: A Collision of Histories. 1959p. 1997. pap. 13.00 (0-8090-1598-6) Hill & Wang.

— Did the American People Create the Constitution. LC 98-87526. 120p. 1999. text 35.00 (0-312-21821-4) St Martin.

— In Their Own Words: Robber Barons & Radicals. Stiles, T. J., ed. & compiled by by. 464p. 1997. pap. 16.00 (0-399-52279-4, Perigee Bks) Berkley Pub.

***Countryman, Edward & Von Heusen-Countryman, Evonne.** Shane. 1999. pap. 10.95 (0-85170-732-7, Pub. by British Film Inst) Ind U Pr.

Countryman, J. Christian Daily Planner, 1. 1999. 17.99 (0-8499-5518-1) Word Pub.

— Christian Daily Planner, 1. 2000th ed. 1999. 17.99 (0-8499-5516-5); 17.99 (0-8499-5517-3) Word Pub.

— Christian Daily Planner: 1999 Ed. 1998. bond lthr. 17.99 (0-8499-5389-8) Word Pub.

— Christian Daily Planner: 1999 Edition. 1998. bond lthr. write for info. (0-8499-5393-6) Word Pub.

— Christian Daily Planner 1999: Pocket Edition. 1998. lthr. 9.99 (0-8499-5396-0) Word Pub.

— Christian Pocket Planner, 1. 2000th ed. 1999. 9.99 (0-8499-5513-0); 9.99 (0-8499-5514-9); 9.99 (0-8499-5515-7) Word Pub.

— Gods Answers for Your Life, 1. 1999. pap. text 2.97 (90-71676-25-0) Word Pub.

— God's Best for a Father's Success, 1. 1999. pap. 3.99 (0-8499-5491-6) Word Pub.

— God's Promise for Your Every Need, 1. 1999. pap. text 2.97 (90-71676-23-4) Word Pub.

***Countryman, J.** God's Promises for Singles. 2000. pap. 3.99 (0-8499-5675-7) J Countryman.

Countryman, J. God's Tender Promises for Mothers, 1. 1999. pap. 3.99 (0-8499-5490-8) Word Pub.

***Countryman, J.** Joy for the Journey, 1. (Illus.). 208p. 2000. write for info. (0-8499-5587-4) J Countryman.

Countryman, J. Leather Christian Planner 1999: Pocket Edition. 1998. lthr. 9.99 (0-8499-5395-2) Word Pub.

Countryman, J., jt. auth. see Lucado, Max.

Countryman, J., ed. see Word Publishing Staff.

Countryman, Jack. Deeper Than Tears: Promises of Comfort & Hope. Gibbs, Terry, ed. LC 98-116128. (Illus.). 96p. 1997. 9.99 (0-8499-1496-5) Word Pub.

***Countryman, Jack.** God's Promises for Men, 1. 1999. mass mkt. 3.99 (0-8499-5619-6); mass mkt. 2.97 (0-8499-5621-8) J Countryman.

— God's Promises for Women, 1. 1999. mass mkt. 3.99 (0-8499-5620-X); mass mkt. 3.99 (0-8499-5622-6) J Countryman.

Countryman, Jack. God's Promises for Your Every Need. deluxe ed. 334p. 1981. emb. lthr. 14.95 (0-937347-00-0) C & D Intl.

— Heartstrings of Laughter & Love: A Tribute to Mothers. 1999. 12.99 (0-8499-5492-4) Word Pub.

— Joy for the Journey: A Woman's Book of Joyful Promise, Superspecial ed., 1. 1999. 7.99 (0-8499-5488-6) Word Pub.

— Refresh My Heart in Spring. Gibbs, Terry, ed. (Illus.). 148p. 1998. 12.99 (0-8499-5337-5) Word Pub.

Countryman, Jack D. Where Eagles Fly. (Illus.). 20p. 1992. pap. 4.00 (1-878149-13-X) Counterpoint Pub.

Countryman, Joan. Writing to Learn Mathematics: Strategies that Work, K-12. LC 91-38215. 101p. (C). (gr. k). 1992. pap. text 18.00 (0-435-08329-5, 08329) Heinemann.

Countryman, L. William. Biblical Authority or Biblical Tyranny? Scripture & the Christian Pilgrimage. rev. ed. LC 93-43184. 144p. (C). 1994. reprint ed. pap. 13.00 (1-56338-085-4) TPI PA.

— Biblical Authority or Biblical Tyranny: Scripture & the Christian Pilgrimage. rev. ed. LC 93-43184. 125p. 1994. pap. 11.95 (1-56101-088-X) Cowley Pubns.

— Dirt, Greed, & Sex: Sexual Ethics in the New Testament & Their Implications for Today. LC 88-45235. 292p. 1988. pap. 22.00 (0-8006-2476-9, 1-2476, Fortress Pr) Augsburg Fortress.

— Forgiven & Forgiving. LC 97-50258. 144p. 1998. pap. 10.95 (0-8192-1734-4) Morehouse Pub.

— Good News of Jesus: Reintroducing the Gospel. LC 92-33566. 112p. 1993. pap. 9.95 (1-56101-068-5) Cowley Pubns.

— Good News of Jesus: Reintroducing the Gospel. LC 92-33566. 96p. 1993. pap. 10.00 (1-56338-050-1) TPI PA.

— The Language of Ordination: Ministry in an Ecumenical Context. LC 92-21970. 112p. 1992. pap. 12.00 (1-56338-046-3) TPI PA.

— Living on the Border of the Holy: Renewing the Priesthood of All. LC 98-42777. 224p. 1999. pap. 17.95 (0-8192-1773-5) Morehouse Pub.

— The Mystical Way in the Fourth Gospel: Crossing over into God. LC 94-40675. 176p. 1995. pap. 16.00 (1-56338-103-6) TPI PA.

— Read It in Greek: A Short Course for Exegetes. 208p. (Orig.). (C). 1992. pap. text 15.00 (0-8028-0665-1) Eerdmans.

— The Rich Christian in the Church of the Early Empire: Contradictions & Accommodations. LC 80-81884. (Texts & Studies in Religion: Vol. 7). viii, 248p. 1980. lib. bdg. 89.95 (0-88946-970-9) E Mellen.

Countryman, M. God Does Care. deluxe ed. 324p. 1987. ring bd. 14.95 (0-937347-09-4) C & D Intl.

— God's Answers for Your Life. deluxe ed. 320p. 1988. lthr. 14.95 (0-937347-15-9) C & D Intl.

— God's Gift for Mothers. deluxe ed. 202p. 1989. ring bd. 12.95 (0-937347-23-X) C & D Intl.

— God's Power for Fathers. deluxe ed. 288p. 1989. emb. lthr. 14.95 (0-937347-27-2) C & D Intl.

— God's Promises for the Golden Years. deluxe ed. 288p. 1989. ring bd. 14.95 (0-937347-29-9) C & D Intl.

— God's Promises for Your Every Need: Simple English Edition. deluxe ed. 368p. 1988. ring bd. 12.95 (0-937347-18-3) C & D Intl.

— God's Wisdom for Business Success. deluxe ed. 304p. 1989. emb. lthr. 14.95 (0-937347-21-3) C & D Intl.

— Golden Verses. deluxe ed. 350p. 1988. ring bd. 12.95 (0-937347-26-4) C & D Intl.

— Hebrew Honey. 322p. 1987. write for info. (0-937347-08-6) C & D Intl.

— Prayers for Prisoners. 224p. 1989. pap. 12.95 (0-937347-30-2) C & D Intl.

— Promises de Dios. (SPA.). 320p. 1987. pap. 3.95 (0-937347-12-4) C & D Intl.

— Respuestas de Dios. deluxe ed. (SPA.). 328p. 1989. ring bd. 12.95 (0-937347-35-3) C & D Intl.

— Thanksgiving & Praise. deluxe ed. 336p. 1989. ring bd. 14.95 (0-937347-22-1) C & D Intl.

— Word of God for All Occasions & Traditional Catholic Prayers. 334p. 1987. ring bd. 12.95 (0-937347-13-2) C & D Intl.

Countryman, Marsha, ed. see Wilkerson, Ralph.

Countryman, Rachel, jt. auth. see Jamison, Patricia P.

Countryman, Ruth & Hopper, Elizabeth W. Women's Wear of the 20's. unabridged ed. Landes, William-Alan, ed. LC 97-41614. (Illus.). 208p. 1997. pap. 57.00 (0-88734-654-5) Players Pr.

Countryman, Ruth, jt. auth. see Hopper, Elizabeth.

Countryman Staff. Father's Legacy. 1998. 7.99 (0-8499-5415-0) Word Pub.

— Forever in Love: Valentines Edition. deluxe ed. (Illus.). 350p. 1996. 9.99 (0-8499-5217-4) Word Pub.

— Forever in Love: Wedding Edition. deluxe ed. LC 95-18138. (Illus.). 350p. 1995. 19.99 (0-8499-5153-4) Word Pub.

— God's Promises for the Graduate. 352p. 1998. 14.99 (0-8499-5372-3) Word Pub.

— Quiet Places of the Heart in Winter: Meditations for Women. Gibbs, Terry, ed. LC 98-109800. (Illus.). 148p. 1997. 12.99 (0-8499-1498-1) Word Pub.

— Touch My Heart in Summer: Meditations for Women. Gibbs, Terri, ed. (Illus.). 144p. 1998. 12.99 (0-8499-5355-3) Word Pub.

Countryman, Vern. Cases & Materials on Debtor & Creditor. 2nd ed. 1974. 30.00 (0-316-15803-8, Aspen Law & Bus) Aspen Pub.

— The Judicial Record of Justice William O. Douglas. LC 74-76655. 426p. reprint ed. pap. 132.10 (0-7837-2242-7, 205733000004) Bks Demand.

Countryman, Vern, ed. Discrimination & the Law: Papers. LC 65-24422. 184p. reprint ed. pap. 57.10 (0-608-12554-7, 202403900035) Bks Demand.

Countryman, Vern, et al. Commercial Law: Cases & Materials. 2nd ed. LC 81-81533. 1326p. (C). 1982. 50.00 (0-316-15796-1) Little.

— Commercial Law: Selected Statutes. 2nd ed. 1980. pap. 23.00 (0-316-15813-5, Aspen Law & Bus) Aspen Pub.

Countryman, Vern, ed. see Douglas, William O.

***Countryman, William L.** The Poetic Imagination: An Anglican Spiritual Tradition. LC 99-49300. (Traditions of Christian Spirituality Ser.). 214p. 2000. pap. 16.00 (1-57075-307-5) Orbis Bks.

Countryside Books Staff. Home Landscaping. rev. ed. (Illus.). 144p. 1997. pap. 16.95 (0-8134-3068-2) Interstate.

Countrysport Inc. Staff. A Breed Apart: A Tribute to the Hunting Dogs That Own Our Souls. LC 96-84191. 374p. 1996. pap. 18.00 (0-924357-61-4, 51215-A) Countrysport Pr.

Counts, Alex. Banking on the Poor. LC 95-40251. 1996. write for info. (0-614-08615-9, Times Bks) Crown Pub Group.

Counts, Angela. Hedy Understands Anxiety. 1995. 5.60 (0-87129-567-9, H67) Dramatic Pub.

Counts, Anna B. Gifts of Power. 1989. pap. 6.95 (0-89137-450-7) Quality Pubns.

Counts, David & Counts, Dorothy, eds. Coping with the Final Tragedy: Dying & Grieving in Cross Cultural Perspective. (Perspectives on Death & Dying Ser.). 366p. 1991. text 45.95 (0-89503-082-9); pap. text 34.47 (0-89503-081-0) Baywood Pub.

Counts, David R., jt. auth. see Counts, Dorothy A.

Counts, David R., jt. ed. see Counts, Dorothy A.

Counts, Dorothy, jt. ed. see Counts, David.

Counts, Dorothy A., ed. Domestic Violence in Oceania. (Special Issue of the Journal Pacific Studies: Vol. 13, No. 3). 312p. 1990. pap. text 10.00 (0-939154-59-5) Inst Polynesian.

Counts, Dorothy A. & Counts, David R. Over the Next Hill: RVing Seniors in North America. 240p. 1996. pap. 16.95 (1-55111-116-0) Broadview Pr.

Counts, Dorothy A. & Counts, David R., eds. Aging & Its Transformations: Moving Toward Death in Pacific Societies. LC 91-38834. (Association for Social Anthropology in Oceania Monographs). 352p. (Orig.). 1992. reprint ed. pap. 19.95 (0-8229-5477-X) U of Pittsburgh Pr.

Counts, Dorothy A., jt. ed. see Rodman, William L.

***Counts, Dorothy Ayers.** To Have & to Hit: Cultural Perspectives on Wife Beating. 2nd ed. LC 98-58070. 344p. 1999. 42.50 (0-252-02481-8) U of Ill Pr.

Counts, Elizabeth. Buffy Visits the Beach. (Illus.). 24p. (J). (gr. k-2). 1998. pap. 7.00 (0-8059-4472-9) Dorrance.

Counts, George S. American Road to Culture: A Social Interpretation of Education in the United States. LC 70-165736. (American Education Ser.: No.2).). 1978. reprint ed. 17.95 (0-405-03605-1) Ayer.

— Country of the Blind: The Soviet System of Mind Control. LC 79-100153. 1970. reprint ed. lib. bdg. 75.00 (0-8371-3680-6, CCOB, Greenwood Pr) Greenwood.

— Dare the School Build a New Social Order? LC 78-18895. (Arcturus Books Paperbacks). 68p. 1978. reprint ed. pap. 9.95 (0-8093-0878-9) S Ill U Pr.

— Dare the Schools Build a New Social Order. LC 71-89165. (American Education: Its Men, Institutions, & Ideas Series 1). 1974. reprint ed. 17.95 (0-405-01496-1) Ayer.

— School & Society in Chicago. LC 71-165715. (American Education Ser., No. 2). 1975. reprint ed. 30.95 (0-405-03704-X) Ayer.

— Selective Character of American Secondary Education. LC 75-89166. (American Education: Its Men, Institutions, & Ideas. Series 1). 1975. reprint ed. 17.95 (0-405-01404-X) Ayer.

— Social Composition of Boards of Education. LC 79-89167. (American Education: Its Men, Institutions, & Ideas. Series 1). 1975. reprint ed. 12.95 (0-405-01405-8) Ayer.

Counts, I. Wilmer & Dilts, Jon. The Magnificent 92 Indiana Courthouses. rev. ed. LC 99-28355. 1999. write for info. (0-253-33638-4) Ind U Pr.

Counts, M. Reid, jt. auth. see Crews, Gordon A.

***Counts, Will, photos by.** A Life Is More Than a Moment: The Desegregation of Little Rock's Central High. (Illus.). 1999. 29.95 (0-253-33637-6) Ind U Pr.

***Counts, Wilma.** My Lady Governess. (Regency Romance Ser.). 2000. mass mkt. 4.99 (0-8217-6483-7, Zebra Kensgtn) Kensgtn Pub Corp.

Counts, Wilma. Willed to Wed, 1. 224p. 1999. mass mkt. 4.99 (0-8217-6323-7) Kensgtn Pub Corp.

***Counts, Wilma.** Willful Miss Winthrop. (Regency Romance Ser.). 256p. 2000. mass mkt. 4.99 (0-8217-6706-2, Zebra Kensgtn) Kensgtn Pub Corp.

County, Jane & Smith, Rupert. Man Enough to Be a Woman: The Autobiography of Jayne County. LC 95-68386. (Illus.). 184p. (Orig.). 1996. pap. 17.99 (1-85242-338-2) Serpents Tail.

Coupar, Mike, jt. auth. see Coupar, Pat.

Coupar, Pat & Coupar, Mike. Flying Colours: Common Butterflies, Moths, Caterpilars of Southeastern Australia. 1992. pap. 22.95 (0-86840-021-1, Pub. by New South Wales Univ Pr) Intl Spec Bk.

Coupe, B. E. Regional Economic Structure & Environmental Pollution. (Studies in Applied Regional Science: No. 5). 1977. pap. text 72.50 (90-207-0646-2) Kluwer Academic.

Coupe, Judith & Goldbart, Juliet, eds. Communication Before Speech: Normal Development & Impaired Communication. 128p. 1988. text 45.00 (0-7099-4841-7) Routledge.

***Coupe, Laurence.** The Green Studies Reader: From Romanticism to Ecocriticism. LC 00-28064. 2000. write for info. (0-415-20407-0) Routledge.

Coupe, Laurence. Myth. LC 97-7292. (New Critical Idiom Ser.). 240p. (C). 1997. pap. 12.99 (0-415-13494-3) Routledge.

— Myth. LC 97-7292. (New Critical Idiom Ser.). 240p. (C). 1998. 50.00 (0-415-13493-5) Routledge.

Coupe, Nez. Free Radical. LC 92-70130. 240p. 1992. 12.95 (0-9632124-0-0); pap. 8.95 (0-9632124-1-9) Croomia Bks.

Coupe-Okane, Judith. Taking Control: Enabling People with Learning Difficulties. LC 94-210853. 1994. 29.95 (1-85346-230-6, Pub. by David Fulton) Taylor & Francis.

Coupe, Ray & Parish, Roberta. Plants of Southern Interior British Columbia. Lloyd, Dennis, ed. LC 97-193096. (Illus.). 464p. 1996. pap. 19.95 (1-55105-057-9) Lone Pine.

***Coupe, Robert.** Magnificent Australia. 1998. 49.95 (1-86436-221-9) New Holland.

Coupe, Robert, photos by. Australia: The Photographer's View from the 1850's to the Bicentenary. (Illus.). 1988. 19.95 (0-582-66357-1) Longman.

Coupe, Sheena. History Begins. 2nd ed. (J). 1993. pap. text 29.36 (0-8013-1044-X) Addison-Wesley.

— Sharks. (Great Creatures of the World Ser.). (Illus.). 72p. (J). (gr. 4-9). 1990. 17.95 (0-8160-2270-4) Facts on File.

— Threads of Time. 2nd ed. (J). 1992. pap. text 26.60 (0-8013-1041-5) Addison-Wesley.

Coupe, Sheena & Scanlan, Barbara. History Begins: A Global History of the Ancient World. 2nd ed. 1993. pap. text 26.76 (0-8013-1040-7) Longman.

— Threads of Time. 1985. pap. text 16.65 (0-582-66342-3, 74669) Longman.

Coupe, Stuart, et al, eds. Crosstown Traffic. 229p. (Orig.). 1993. pap. 12.95 (1-875604-15-4, Pub. by Five Isl Pr) Firebird Dist.

Couper. Activities for Developing People Skills. 1993. 253.95 (1-85904-003-9) Ashgate Pub Co.

Couper & Stewart. Twenty-Five Roleplays of Developing Counselling Skills. 216p. 1995. pap. 131.95 (0-566-07663-2) Ashgate Pub Co.

Couper, A. D. New Cargo-Handling Techniques: Implications for Port Employment & Skills. xii, 172p. 1986. 36.00 (92-2-105420-9); pap. 27.00 (92-2-105419-5) Intl Labour Office.

C

*Couper, A. D. Voyages of Abuse: Seafarers, Human Rights & International Shipping. 1999. pap. 29.95 (0-7453-1540-2) Pluto GBR.

Couper, Alastair. Development & Social Change in the Pacific Islands. (Croom Helm Maritime Ser.). 176p. (C). 1989. lib. bdg. 55.00 (0-415-00917-0) Routledge.

Couper, Alastair, et al, eds. The Marine Environment & Sustainable Development: Law, Policy, & Science, 25th Annual Conference Proceedings. 688p. 1993. 58.00 (0-911189-25-4) Law Sea Inst.

Couper, Alastair, jt. ed. see Gardiner, Robert.

Couper, Benita, ed. see Rahming, D'Arcy.

Couper, D. P. Aging & Our Families: Handbook for Family Caregivers. (Illus.). 120p. 1989. pap. 18.95 (0-89885-441-5, Kluwer Acad Hman Sci) Kluwer Academic.

— Aging & Our Families: Leader's Guide to Caregiver Programs. (Illus.). 140p. 1989. pap. 20.95 (0-89885-440-7, Kluwer Acad Hman Sci) Kluwer Academic.

Couper, Dave. Storylines Level 1: George Sees Stars. (Illus.). 24p. 1996. pap. text 4.95 (0-19-421931-3) OUP.

Couper, David & Stewart, Jacqueline. Twenty-Five Role Plays for Counselling Skills Training. 216p. 1993. ring bd. 125.95 (0-566-07341-2, Pub. by Gower) Ashgate Pub Co.

Couper, David, jt. auth. see Stewart, Jacqueline.

Couper, David C. How to Rate Your Local Police. 26p. (Orig.). 1983. pap. 3.00 (1-878734-15-6) Police Exec Res.

— Quality Policing: The Madison Experience. LC 90-61772. 100p. (C). 1991. pap. 11.00 (1-878734-22-9) Police Exec Res.

Couper, Greta E. An American Sculptor on the Grand Tour: The Life & Works of William Couper (1853-1942) Calcott, M. V., ed. LC 88-50666. (Illus.). 188p. 1988. 34.95 (0-9620635-4-1) TreCavalli Pr.

Couper, H. & Henbest, Nigel. The Space Atlas: A Pictorial Guide to Our Universe. (Illus.). 64p. (J). (gr. 3-7). 1992. 19.00 (0-15-200598-6, Gulliver Bks) Harcourt.

Couper, Heather & Henbest, Nigel. Big Bang: The Story of the Universe. LC 96-30995. (Illus.). 48p. (YA). (gr. 6-9). 1997. 16.95 (0-7894-1484-8) DK Pub Inc.

— Black Holes: A Journey to the Heart of a Black Hole. LC 95-44391. (Illus.). 48p. (J). (gr. 4-6). 1996. 16.95 (0-7894-0451-6) DK Pub Inc.

*Couper, Heather & Henbest, Nigel. DK Space Encyclopedia. LC 99-25468. 304p. (YA). (gr. 6-10). 1999. 29.95 (0-7894-4708-8) DK Pub Inc.

Couper, Heather & Henbest, Nigel. How the Universe Works: Fascinating Ways Parents & Kids Can Share the Secrets of the Universe. LC 93-21345. (Illus.). 160p. 1994. 24.00 (0-89577-576-X, Pub. by RD Assn) Penguin Putnam.

— Is Anyone Out There? The Search for Life Beyond Our Planet... LC 97-35398. (Illus.). 48p. (J). (gr. 4-6). 1998. pap. 16.95 (0-7894-2798-2) DK Pub Inc.

Couper-Kuhlen, Elizabeth. English Speech Rhythm: Form & Function in Everyday Verbal Interaction. LC 93-6530. (Pragmatics & Beyond New Ser.: No. 25). x, 346p. 1993. 76.00 (1-55619-293-2) J Benjamins Pubng Co.

*Couper-Kuhlen, Elizabeth & Kortmann, Bernd. Cause, Condition, Concession, Contrast: Cognitive & Discourse Perspectives. LC 00-33563. (Topics in English Linguistics Ser.). 2000. write for info. (3-11-016690-9) De Gruyter.

Couper-Kuhlen, Elizabeth & Selting, Margret, eds. Prosody in Conversation: Interactional Studies. (Studies in International Sociolinguistics: No. 12). 480p. (C). 1996. text 74.95 (0-521-46075-1) Cambridge U Pr.

Couper, Mick P. Computer Assisted Survey Information Collection. LC 98-11963. (Series in Probability & Statistics). 653p. 1998. 94.95 (0-471-17848-9) Wiley.

Couper, Mick P., jt. auth. see Groves, Robert M.

Couper, W. J., et al. Scotland Saw His Glory: A History of Revivals in Scotland. Roberts, Richard O., ed. LC 95-78264. (Illus.). 351p. 1995. lib. bdg. 21.95 (0-940033-51-8) R O Roberts.

Couperie, Pierre, et al. Encyclopedie de la Bande Dessinee, 3 vols., Set. pap. 85.00 (0-7859-0741-6, M-6093) Fr & Eur.

Couperin, Francois. L' Art de Toucher le Clavecin. fac. ed. (Monuments of Music & Music Literature in Facsimile Ser., Series II: Vol. 23). (Illus.). 1969. lib. bdg. 50.00 (0-8450-2223-7) Broude.

— Keyboard Works, Ser. I, Ordres I-XIII. 1988. pap. 10.95 (0-486-25795-9) Dover.

— Keyboard Works, Ser. 2, Ordres XIV-XXVII & Misc. Pieces. 1988. pap. 11.95 (0-486-25796-7) Dover.

Couperin, Francois. Pieces de Clavecin: Premier, Second, Troisieme et Quatrieme Livres. fac. ed. (Monuments of Music & Music Literature in Facsimile Ser., Series I: Vol. 9). 1974. lib. bdg. 125.00 (0-8450-2009-9) Broude.

Couperin, Francois. Two Masses for Organ. 96p. 1994. pap. 8.95 (0-486-28285-6) Dover.

Couperus, L. The Hidden Force. Teixeira de Mattos, Alexander, tr. from DUT. LC 84-16208. (Library of the Indies). 272p. (C). 1990. reprint ed. pap. 17.95 (0-87023-715-2) U of Mass Pr.

Couperus, Louis. Ecstasy. de Mattos, A. Teixeira & Gray, John, trs. from DUT. 157p. 2000. pap. 12.95 (1-885586-12-4, Pub. by Turtle Point Pr) Dist Art Pubs.

— Psyche. de Mattos, A. Teixeira & Gray, John, trs. from DUT. 150p. 1999. pap. 12.95 (1-885586-10-8, Pub. by Turtle Point Pr) Dist Art Pubs.

Coupey, Philip, ed. see Deshmaru, Taisen.

*Coupey, Susan M., ed. Primary Care of Adolescent Girls. LC 99-47482. (Illus.). 376p. 1999. 36.00 (1-56053-369-2, Pub. by Hanley & Belfus) Mosby Inc.

Coupier, J. Dictionary French to Provencal. (FRE & PRO.). 1998. 69.95 (0-320-00377-9) Fr & Eur.

— Little Dictionary French to Provencal. (FRE & PRO.). 1998. 69.95 (0-320-00187-3) Fr & Eur.

Couplan, Francois. The Encyclopedia of Edible Plants of North America. LC 98-23434. (Illus.). 570p. 1998. pap. 19.95 (0-87983-821-3, 38213K, Keats Publng) NTC Contemp Pub Co.

Coupland. Multimedia: The Creators. 1995. 24.95 (1-56276-296-6, Ziff-Davis Pr) Que.

— Sociolinguistics: A Reader. LC 97-11315. 560p. 1997. text 59.95 (0-312-17572-8) St Martin.

Coupland, A., ed. Reclaiming the City. (Illus.). 304p. (C). 1996. pap. 49.99 (0-419-21360-0, E & FN Spon) Routledge.

Coupland, Beth, tr. see Allard, Michel, et al.

Coupland, Douglas. Generation X: Tales for an Accelerated Culture. write for info. (0-06-039250-9) HarpC.

— Generation X: Tales for an Accelerated Culture. 1991. pap. 14.95 (0-312-05436-X) St Martin.

*Coupland, Douglas. Girlfriend in a Coma. 284p. 2000. pap. 18.00 (0-00-638542-7) HarpC.

Coupland, Douglas. Girlfriend in a Coma. LC 97-49961. 288p. 1998. 24.00 (0-06-039178-2, ReganBks) HarperTrade.

— Girlfriend in a Coma. LC 97-49961. 288p. 1999. pap. 13.00 (0-06-098732-4, ReganBks) HarperTrade.

*Coupland, Douglas. Girlfriend in a Coma: Leonard,&Robert Sean, Set. abr. ed. 1998. audio 18.00 (0-694-51951-0, Caedmon) HarperAudio.

Coupland, Douglas. Life after God. Einhorn, Amy, ed. 368p. 1995. per. 10.00 (0-671-87434-9) PB.

— Microserfs. 384p. 1996. pap. 13.00 (0-06-098704-9) HarpC.

— Microserfs. 371p. Date not set. 21.00 (0-614-32429-7) HarperTrade.

— Microserfs. 1996. pap. 12.00 (0-614-97780-0, Perennial) HarperTrade.

*Coupland, Douglas. Miss Wyoming. LC 99-15212. 320p. 1999. 23.00 (0-375-40734-0) Pantheon.

— Miss Wyoming. 2001. pap. 13.00 (0-375-70723-9) Vin Bks.

Coupland, Douglas. Polaroids from the Dead. (Illus.). 208p. 1997. pap. 15.00 (0-06-098721-9, ReganBks) HarperTrade.

— Shampoo Planet. Regan, Judith, ed. 312p. 1993. reprint ed. per. 14.00 (0-671-75506-4) PB.

Coupland, Douglas & Ward, Kip. Lara's Book: Lara Croft & the Tomb Raider Phenomenon. LC 98-65455. 200p. 1998. per. 19.99 (0-7615-1580-1) Prima Pub.

Coupland, Gary. Prehistoric Cultural Change at Kitselas Canyon, No. 138. (Mercury Ser.: ASC No. 138). (Illus.). 400p. 1996. pap. 24.95 (0-660-10781-3, Pub. by CN Mus Civilization) U of Wash Pr.

Coupland, Gary, jt. auth. see Matson, R. G.

Coupland, J. W., ed. Concurrent Engineering: An Information Pack. 111p. 1992. 55.50 (0-85296-499-4, BI029) INSPEC Inc.

Coupland, J. W. & Fountain, P. D., eds. Electromagnetic Compatibility: Bibliography & Information Pack. 98p. 1993. 57.00 (0-85296-450-1, BI030) INSPEC Inc.

*Coupland, Justine. Small Talk. LC 00-27545. (Language in Social Life Ser.). 2000. pap. write for info. (0-582-41426-1) Pearson Educ.

Coupland, Justine, jt. ed. see Nussbaum, Jon F.

Coupland, Ken. Web Design Now. (Illus.). 240p. 1997. 69.95 (1-888001-36-4) Graphis US.

*Coupland, Ken. Webworks: Navigation. 2000. pap. 40.00 (1-56496-662-3) Rockport Pubs.

*Coupland, Ken, ed. Design.com. (Illus.). 208p. 1999. text 70.00 (1-888001-83-6) Graphis US.

Coupland, N. & Giles, Howard. Language: Contexts & Consequences. Manstead, Anthony S., ed. (Mapping Social Psychology Ser.). 264p. 1991. pap. 28.95 (0-335-09872-X) OpUniv Pr.

Coupland, Nicholas, jt. auth. see Tracy, Karen.

Coupland, Nikolas. Sociolinguistics: A Reader. Jaworski, Adam, ed. LC 97-11315. 560p. 1997. pap. 24.95 (0-312-17573-6) St Martin.

Coupland, Nikolas, et al, eds. Miscommunication & Problematic Talk. (Illus.). 432p. 1991. 55.00 (0-8039-4032-7); pap. 26.95 (0-8039-4033-5) Sage.

— Miscommunication & Problematic Talk. LC 90-22484. (Illus.). 384p. 1991. reprint ed. pap. 119.10 (0-608-01715-9, 206237000003) Bks Demand.

Coupland, Nikolas & Nussbaum, Jon F. Discourse & Lifespan Development. (Language & Language Behaviors Ser.: Vol. 4). (Illus.). 320p. (C). 1993. text 55.00 (0-8039-5105-1); pap. text 26.00 (0-8039-5106-X) Sage.

Coupland, Nikolas & Thomas, Alan R., eds. English in Wales: Diversity, Conflict & Change. (Multilingual Matters Ser.: No. 52). 210p. 1989. 99.00 (1-85359-032-0, Pub. by Multilingual Matters); pap. 44.95 (1-85359-031-2, Pub. by Multilingual Matters) Taylor & Francis.

Coupland, Nikolaus, ed. Styles of Discourse. 240p. 1988. lib. bdg. 82.50 (0-7099-4852-2, Pub. by C Helm) Routldge.

Coupland, R. T. Natural Grasslands. (Ecosystems of the World Ser.: Vol. 8A). xiv,470p. 1992. 265.50 (0-444-88264-2) Elsevier.

Coupland, R. T., ed. Natural Grasslands: Eastern Hemisphere & Resume. (Ecosystems of the World Ser.: Vol. 8B). xvi,556p. 1993. 276.50 (0-444-89557-4) Elsevier.

Coupland, Reginald. The Exploitation of East Africa. 507p. 1967. 35.00 (0-89771-008-8) St Mut.

— The Quebec Act: A Study in Statesmanship. (BCL1 - History - Canada Ser.). 224p. 1991. reprint ed. lib. bdg. 79.00 (0-7812-6357-3) Rprt Serv.

Coupland, Reginald, ed. The American Revolution & the British Empire: The Sir George Watson Lectures for 1928, Delivered Before the University of London in the Winter of 1928-9. (BCL1 - U. S. History Ser.). 331p. 1991. reprint ed. lib. bdg. 89.00 (0-7812-6104-X) Rprt Serv.

Couples, Fred & Andrisani, John. Total Shotmaking: The Golfer's Guide to Par Shooting. (Illus.). 192p. 1995. pap. 16.00 (0-06-272060-0, Harper Ref) HarpC.

*Cour, Jean-Marie & Snrech, Serge, eds. Preparing for the Future: A Vision of West Africa in the Year 2020. (West Africa Long-Term Perspective Study Ser.). 156p. 1998. pap. 27.00 (92-64-15407-8, 44 98 01 1 P, Pub. by Org for Econ) OECD.

Cour, Marshall La, see La Cour, Marshall.

Courage Books Staff. Cherubs: A Joyous Celebration. LC 98-70168. (Illus.). 128p. 1998. 19.98 (0-7624-0344-6, Courage) Running Pr.

— Chicago: A Photographic Celebration. LC 98-70511. (Illus.). 128p. 1998. 13.98 (0-7624-0386-1, Courage) Running Pr.

Courage Books Staff. A Christmas Treasury: The Children's Classic Edition. LC 96-71141. (Illus.). 48p. (J). 1997. 14.95 (0-7624-0075-7, Courage) Running Pr.

Courage Books Staff. Empress. 160p. 1997. 5.98 (0-7624-0230-X, Courage) Running Pr.

— Horse Plaid. 160p. 1997. 5.98 (0-7624-0229-6, Courage) Running Pr.

— Leopard Lounge. 160p. 1997. 5.98 (0-7624-0226-1, Courage) Running Pr.

— Mothers: A Loving Celebration. LC 96-71607. (Illus.). 128p. 1997. 19.98 (0-7624-0050-1, Courage) Running Pr.

— New York City: A Photographic Celebration. LC 97-66816. (Illus.). 128p. 13.98 (0-7624-0284-9, Courage) Running Pr.

— Pantry Print. 160p. 1997. 5.98 (0-7624-0222-9, Courage) Running Pr.

— Purple Vineyard. 160p. 1997. 5.98 (0-7624-0221-0, Courage) Running Pr.

— San Francisco: A Photographic Celebration. LC 98-70512. (Illus.). 128p. 1998. 13.98 (0-7624-0387-X, Courage) Running Pr.

— Shamrock. 160p. 1997. 5.98 (0-7624-0225-3, Courage) Running Pr.

— Washington D. C. A Photographic Celebration. LC 97-66806. (Illus.). 128p. 1998. 13.98 (0-7624-0285-7, Courage) Running Pr.

Courage Promotional Books Staff. Angels: A Joyous Celebration. LC 96-67156. (Illus.). 128p. 1996. 19.98 (1-56138-743-6, Courage) Running Pr.

Courakis, Anthony & Taylor, Mark P., eds. Policy Issues for Interdependent Economics. (Illus.). 456p. 1991. pap. text 32.50 (0-19-828325-3) OUP.

Courakis, Anthony S., ed. Inflation, Depression & Economic Policy in the West. LC 79-55497. 376p. 1981. text 50.00 (0-389-20144-8, N6410) B&N Imports.

Courant, Paul N., jt. auth. see Lipsey, Richard G.

Courant, Paul N., ed. see De Beaumarchais, Pierre-Augustin C.

*Courant, R. & John, F. Introduction to Calculus & Analysis. (Classics in Mathematics Ser.: Vol. II-1 Chapters 1-4). xvi, 558p. 2000. 39.95 (3-540-66569-2) Spr-Verlag.

— Introduction to Calculus & Analysis. (Classics in Mathematics: Vol. II-2, Chapters 5-8). xxviii, 412p. 2000. pap. 40.00 (3-540-66570-6) Spr-Verlag.

Courant, Richard. Differential & Integral Calculus, 2 vols. 1298p. 1992. pap. 160.00 (0-471-58881-4) Wiley.

— Differential & Integral Calculus, Vol. 1. (Classics Library). 640p. 1988. pap. 120.00 (0-471-60842-4) Wiley.

— Differential & Integral Calculus, Vol. 2. (Classics Library). 694p. 1988. 120.00 (0-471-60840-8) Wiley.

Courant, Richard & Friedrichs, K. O. Supersonic Flow & Shock Waves. (Applied Mathematical Sciences Ser.: Vol. 21.). 1992. 89.95 (0-387-90232-5) Spr-Verlag.

Courant, Richard & Fritz, John. Introduction to Calculus & Analysis. LC 98-32314. (Classics in Mathematics Ser.). 1998. 45.00 (3-540-65058-X) Spr-Verlag.

Courant, Richard & Hilbert, D. Methods of Mathematical Physics, 2 vols. (Classics Library). 1390p. 1989. pap. 135.00 (0-471-55760-9) Wiley.

— Methods of Mathematical Physics, Vol. 1. (Classics Library). 560p. 1989. pap. 79.95 (0-471-50447-5) Wiley.

— Methods of Mathematical Physics, Vol. 2. (Classics Library). 856p. 1989. pap. 84.95 (0-471-50439-4) Wiley.

Courant, Richard & John, F. Introduction to Calculus & Analysis, Vol. I. (Illus.). xxiii, 661p. 1993. 59.95 (0-387-97151-3) Spr-Verlag.

— Introduction to Calculus & Analysis, Vol. II. (Illus.). xxv, 954p. 1993. 64.95 (0-387-97152-1) Spr-Verlag.

Courant, Richard, et al. What Is Mathematics? An Elementary Approach to Ideas & Methods. 2nd ed. (Illus.). 592p. (C). 1996. pap. 19.95 (0-19-510519-2) OUP.

Courant, Richard, jt. ed. see Behnke, H.

Courau, A. & Kessler, P., eds. Photon-Photon Collision: Proceedings of the VII International Workshop, Paris, France 1-5 April 1986. 500p. 1987. text 114.00 (9971-5-0138-4) World Scientific Pub.

Couraud, Louis, jt. ed. see Patterson, Alec.

Couraud, Pierre-Olivier & Scherman, Daniel, eds. Biology & Physiology of the Blood-Brain Barrier: Transport, Cellular Interactions & Brain Pathologies. LC 96-34815. (Advances in Behavioral Biology Ser.: Vol. 46). (Illus.). 403p. (C). 1996. text 107.00 (0-306-45362-2, Kluwer Plenum) Kluwer Academic.

Courbage & Fargues, Phillipe. Christians & Jews under Islam. 256p. 1998. pap. 22.50 (1-86064-285-3, Pub. by I B T) St Martin.

Courbaud, Edmond. Horace, Sa Vie et Sa Pensee a l'Epoque des Epitres. (GER.). viii, 368p. 1973. reprint ed. lib. bdg. 95.00 (3-487-05052-8) G Olms Pubs.

Courbet, Gustave. Letters of Gustave Courbet. LC 91-21917. (Illus.). 738p. 1992. 63.50 (0-226-11653-0) U Ch Pr.

Courbin, Paul. What Is Archaeology? An Essay on the Nature of Archaeological Research. Bahn, Paul, tr. (Illus.). 224p. 1988. 29.95 (0-226-11656-5) U Ch Pr.

*Courbis, Raymond & Welfe, Wladyslaw, eds. Central & Eastern Europe on Its Way to European Union: Simulation Studies Based on Macromodels. 608p. 1999. pap. 68.95 (3-631-32383-2) P Lang Pubng.

— Central & Eastern Europe on Its Way to European Union: Simulation Studies Based on Macromodels. LC 99-58040. 608p. (C). 1999. pap. text 68.95 (0-8204-3520-1) P Lang Pubng.

Courbon, Paul, et al. Atlas of the Great Caves of the World. LC 89-15722. (Illus.). 369p. 1989. pap. 20.00 (0-939748-21-5) Cave Bks MO.

Courcelle-Seneuil, J. G. Traite Elementaire de Comptabilite: Elementary Treatise on Accounting. Brief, Richard P., ed. (Dimensions of Accounting Theory & Practice Ser.). (FRE.). 1980. reprint ed. lib. bdg. 24.95 (0-405-13513-0) Ayer.

Courcelles, M. Extract from the Despatches of Courcelles. Bell, Robert, ed. LC 72-1015. (Bannatyne Club, Edinburgh. Publications: No. 22). reprint ed. 37.50 (0-404-52728-0) AMS Pr.

Courcey, Philip De, see De Courcey, Philip.

Courchene, Thomas J. No Place to Stand? Abandoning Monetary Targets: An Evaluation. LC 83-136524. 120p. 1983. reprint ed. pap. 37.20 (0-608-01378-1, 206212600002) Bks Demand.

Courchene, Thomas J., ed. The Nation State in a Global/Information Era: Policy Challenges. 375p. 1997. text 55.00 (0-88911-766-7, Pub. by McG-Queens Univ Pr); pap. text 24.95 (0-88911-770-5, Pub. by McG-Queens Univ Pr) CUP Services.

Courchene, Thomas J. & Neave, Edwin H., eds. Reforming the Canadian Financial Sector: Canada in Global Perspective. 300p. 1997. text 49.95 (0-88911-768-3, Pub. by McG-Queens Univ Pr); pap. text 18.95 (0-88911-688-1, Pub. by McG-Queens Univ Pr) CUP Services.

*Courchene, Thomas J. & Wilson, Thomas A., eds. Fiscal Targets & Economic Growth. 375p. 1999. pap. 24.95 (0-88911-778-0) Que6ens U Study Econ.

Courcoubetis, C., ed. Computer Aided Verification: Proceedings of the 5th International Conference, CAV 93, Elounda, Crete, Greece, June 28-July 1, 1993. (Lecture Notes in Computer Science Ser.: Vol. 697). ix, 504p. 1993. 73.95 (0-387-56922-7) Spr-Verlag.

Courcy, G. De, see Revesz, Geza.

Courcy, Pol Potier De, see Potier De Courcy, Pol.

Coureas, Nicholas. The Latin Church in Cyprus, 1195-1312. LC 97-23242. 376p. 1997. text 83.95 (1-85928-447-7, Pub. by Ashgate Pub) Ashgate Pub Co.

Couret, Jacques, ed. see Dunklin, Philip I.

Couret, Jacques, jt. ed. see Smith, L. Dennis.

Couret Klein, Victor. Soul Shadows. LC 96-68269. (Illus.). 144p. 1997. pap. 9.95 (1-57087-248-1, 02) Lycanthrope Pr.

Courgeau, Daniel & Lelievre, Eva. Event History Analysis in Demography. (Illus.). 236p. 1993. text 58.00 (0-19-828738-0) OUP.

*Couri, Kathy. Goodnight Bear! (Illus.). 12p. (J). 1999. bds. 10.98 (1-58048-063-2) Sandvik Pub.

Couri, Kathy. Goodnight Bear! A Book & Night Light. (Illus.). 12p. (J). (ps-k). 1999. 11.95 (1-58117-059-9) Intervisual Bks.

— Tinytown Ball. LC 98-221237. (Jewel Sticker Stories Ser.). (Illus.). 24p. 1998. pap. text 3.99 (0-448-41836-3, G & D) Peng Put Young Read.

Couric, Emily. The Trial Lawyers: The Nation's Top Litigators Tell How They Win. 5th ed. 384p. 1990. pap. 16.95 (0-312-05172-7) St Martin.

Couric, Emily, ed. The Business of Law: A Handbook on How to Manage Law Firms. LC 84-11258. 470p. 1984. 55.00 (0-15-004290-6) Harcourt.

*Couric, Katie. The Brand New Kid. 32p. (YA). 2000. 15.95 (0-385-50030-0) Doubleday.

Courier. Oeuvres Completes. (Pleiade Ser.). (FRE.). 1951. 85.00 (0-8288-3469-5, F59620) Fr & Eur.

Courier, Herb, jt. auth. see Likely, Newt A.

Courington, Rebecca. Personal Productivity Tools. 334p. (C). 1994. text 37.40 (0-536-58704-3) Pearson Custom.

Courjon, Daniel, jt. ed. see Pohl, Dieter W.

Courlander. People of Short Blue Corn. (J). 1996. 9.95 (0-8050-4585-6) H Holt & Co.

Courlander, Harold. The African. LC 93-13923. 320p. 1995. pap. 14.95 (0-8050-3000-X) H Holt & Co.

— Cow-Tail Switch: And Other West African Stories. 1986. 15.05 (0-606-01318-0, Pub. by Turtleback) Demco.

— The Fourth World of the Hopis: The Epic Story of the Hopi Indians As Preserved in Their Legends & Traditions. LC 70-168320. (Illus.). 239p. 1987. reprint ed. pap. 13.95 (0-8263-1011-7) U of NM Pr.

— Negro Folk Music U. S. A. LC 92-35475. (Illus.). xi, 324p. 1998. reprint ed. pap. text 9.95 (0-486-27350-4) Dover.

— People of the Short Blue Corn: Tales & Legends of the Hopi Indians. LC 95-37318. (Illus.). 160p. (J). (gr. 5-9). 1995. pap. 9.95 (0-8050-3511-7, Owlet BYR) H Holt & Co.

— People of the Short Blue Corn, Tales & Legends fo the Hopi Indians. LC 95-37318. 1996. 15.05 (0-606-10282-5, Pub. by Turtleback) Demco.

— Tales of Yoruba Gods & Heroes. 256p. 1995. pap. 11.95 (0-942272-40-4) Original Pubns.

An Asterisk (*) at the beginning of an entry indicates that the title is appearing for the first time.

— The Tiger's Whisker: And Other Tales from Asia, the Pacific, & the Middle East. LC 95-15322. (Illus.). (J). (gr. 5-9). 1995. pap. 10.95 (*0-8050-3512-5*) H Holt & Co.

— Tiger's Whisker, & Other Tales from Asia & the Pacific. 1995. 16.05 (*0-606-09962-X*, Pub. by Turtleback) Demco.

— A Treasury of African-American Folklore: The Oral Literature, Traditions, Recollections. (Illus.). 618p. (Orig.). 1995. pap. 14.95 (*1-56924-811-7*) Marlowe & Co.

— A Treasury of African Folklore: The Oral Literature, Traditions, Myths, Legends, Epics, Tales, Recollections, Wisdom, Sayings, & Humor of Africa. (Illus.). 617p. 1995. pap. 15.95 (*1-56924-816-8*) Marlowe & Co.

*__Courlander, Harold.__ A Treasury of Afro-American Folklore: The Oral Literature, Traditions, Recollections, Legends, Tales, Songs, Religious Beliefs, Customs, Sayings & Humor of Peoples of African Descents in the Americas. (Illus.). 618p. 1999. reprint ed. text 25.00 (*0-7881-6560-7*) DIANE Pub.

Courlander, Harold & Herzog, George. The Cow-Tail Switch & Other West African Stories. LC 47-30108. 160p. (J). (gr. 2-4). 1995. pap. 7.95 (*0-8050-0298-7*) H Holt & Co.

Courlander, Harold & Leslau, Wolf. The Fire on the Mountain: And Other Stories from Ethiopia & Eritrea. (Illus.). 144p. (J). (gr. 4-7). 1995. pap. 7.95 (*0-8050-3652-0*, Owlet BYR) H Holt & Co.

Courlander, Harold & Sako, Ousmane. The Heart of the Ngoni: Heroes of the African Kingdom of Segu. LC 94-236. 192p. (C). 1994. reprint ed. pap. 15.95 (*0-87023-929-5*) U of Mass Pr.

Courmel, Katie & Goldstein, Jay A. A Companion Volume to Dr. Jay A. Goldstein's Betrayal by the Brain: A Guide for Patients & Their Physicians. LC 96-20456. 98p. 1996. pap. 14.95 (*0-7890-0119-5*) Haworth Pr.

Cournand, Andre & Meyer, Michael. From Roots...to Late Budding: The Intellectual Adventures of a Medical Scientist. 1986. 29.95 (*0-89876-105-5*) Gardner Pr.

Cournand, Marie-Claire, tr. see Danielou, Alain.

*__Courneya, Dennis.__ Sudden Death, Overtime. LC 00-190838. 2000. 25.00 (*0-7388-1991-3*); pap. 18.00 (*0-7388-1992-1*) Xlibris Corp.

*__Cournos, Francine.__ City of One: A Memoir. 2000. pap. 12.95 (*0-452-28181-4*, Plume) Dutton Plume.

Cournos, Francine. City of One: A Memoir. LC 98-48136. 224p. 1999. text 23.95 (*0-393-04731-8*) Norton.

Cournos, Francine & Bakalar, Nicholas, eds. AIDS & People with Severe Mental Illness: A Handbook for Mental Health Professionals. LC 96-10948. 384p. 1996. 40.00 (*0-300-06757-7*) Yale U Pr.

Cournos, John. Autobiography. LC 78-64010. (Des Imagistes: Literature of the Imagist Movement Ser.). (Illus.). 368p. reprint ed. 35.00 (*0-404-17084-6*) AMS Pr.

— In Exile. LC 78-64011. (Des Imagistes: Literature of the Imagist Movement Ser.). reprint ed. 29.50 (*0-404-17085-4*) AMS Pr.

— The Mask. LC 74-26098. (Labor Movement in Fiction & Non-Fiction Ser.). reprint ed. 47.50 (*0-404-58416-0*) AMS Pr.

Cournos, John, tr. from RUS. Short-Story Masterpieces Vol. 3: Russian. LC 79-179299. (Short Story Index Reprint Ser.). 1977. reprint ed. 18.95 (*0-8369-4038-5*) Ayer.

Cournos, John, tr. see Biely, Andrei.

Cournot, Antoine A. An Essay on the Foundations of Our Knowledge. Moore, M. H., tr. 1956. pap. 3.95 (*0-672-60400-0*, Bobbs) Macmillan.

Cournot, Augustin. Researches into the Mathematical Principles of the Theory of Wealth. LC 73-28986. (Reprints of Economic Classics Ser.). xxv, 213p. 1971. reprint ed. 35.00 (*0-678-00066-2*) Kelley.

— Revue Sommaire le Doctrines Economiques. LC 68-22372. (Reprints of Economic Classics Ser.). viii, 339p. 1968. reprint ed. 49.50 (*0-678-00377-7*) Kelley.

Cournoyer. Hotel, Restaurant & Travel Law. 4th ed. (Food & Hospitality Ser.). 1993. teacher ed. 16.95 (*0-8273-5290-5*) Delmar.

— Hotel, Restaurant & Travel Law. 5th ed. (Hospitality, Travel & Tourism Ser.). 128p. 1998. pap. text, teacher ed. 19.95 (*0-8273-7537-9*) Delmar.

— Hotel, Restaurant & Travel Law CTB. 4th ed. (Hospitality, Travel & Tourism Ser.). 1994. pap. 64.95 (*0-8273-5404-5*) Delmar.

— The Social Work Skills Workbook. 3rd ed. 1999. pap., wbk. ed. 50.95 (*0-534-35678-8*) Thomson Learn.

— Talking Social Work. (Social Work Ser.). 2000. mass mkt. 24.00 (*0-534-34305-8*) Brooks-Cole.

Cournoyer & Marshall. Hotel, Restaurant & Travel Law. 5th ed. (C). 1997. pap. text 49.95 (*0-8273-7790-8*) Delmar.

Cournoyer, Barry. The Social Work Skills Workbook. 384p. (C). 1991. pap. 24.75 (*0-534-14730-5*) Brooks-Cole.

— The Social Work Skills Workbook. 2nd ed. LC 95-12973. 464p. 1995. pap. 31.25 (*0-534-33875-5*) Brooks-Cole.

Cournoyer, Carmelle P. The Nurse Manager & the Law. 388p. (C). 1989. 69.00 (*0-8342-0049-X*) Aspen Pub.

Cournoyer, Cynthia. What about Immunizations: Exposing the Vaccine Philosophy. 200p. (Orig.). 1995. pap. 12.95 (*0-9612188-5-1*) Nelsons Bks.

Cournoyer, David E. Research Methods for Social Work. LC 99-18625. 274p. 1999. 44.00 (*0-205-28741-7*) Allyn.

Cournoyer, Jill, et al. Make Way for the Automobile: The History of the Maine Automobile Association, 1910-1997. LC 98-30596. (Illus.). 96p. 1998. pap. write for info. (*1-892168-00-6*) Custom Communs.

Cournoyer, Jill, jt. auth. see Dudley Gold, Susan.

Cournoyer, Norman G. Hotel, Restaurant & Travel Law. 5th ed. LC 97-13961. (Hospitality, Travel & Tourism Ser.). 592p. (C). 1998. 74.95 (*0-8273-7536-0*) Delmar.

Cournoyer, Norman G., et al. Hotel, Restaurant, & Travel Law: A Preventive Approach. 4th ed. LC 92-42471. 644p. (C). 1993. mass mkt. 71.95 (*0-8273-5289-1*) Delmar.

Couro, Ted. San Diego County Indians As Farmers & Wage Earners. reprint ed. pap. 2.00 (*0-686-69102-4*) Acoma Bks.

Couro, Ted & Hutcheson, Christina. Dictionary of Mesa Grande Diegueno. 1973. pap. 7.50 (*0-939046-14-8*) Malki Mus Pr.

Courot, M., ed. The Male in Farm Animal Reproduction. (Current Topics in Veterinary Medicine & Animal Science Ser.). 1984. text 247.50 (*0-89838-682-9*) Kluwer Academic.

Courrege, Beverly. Answers to WWJD. 160p. 1998. pap. 6.99 (*1-56292-462-1*) Honor Bks OK.

*__Courrege, Beverly.__ The Joy of Resurrection. LC 99-48410. (Illus.). 144p. 2000. 14.99 (*0-7852-6932-0*) Nelson.

Courrege, Beverly. What Would Jesus Do? Think about It. LC 98-7202. 96p. 1998. pap. 6.99 (*0-7852-8212-2*) Nelson.

— Y2J Yield to Jesus. LC 99-39346. 192p. 1999. 10.99 (*0-7852-6852-9*) Nelson.

*__Courrier, Dinah W.__ Potomac State College. (College History Ser.). (Illus.). 128p. 2000. pap. 19.99 (*0-7385-0621-4*) Arcadia Publng.

Courrier, Kevin & Green, Susan. Law & Order: The Unofficial Companion. LC 98-7012. (Illus.). 256p. 1998. pap. 16.95 (*1-58063-022-7*) Renaissance.

*__Courrier, Kevin & Green, Susan.__ Law & Order: The Unofficial Companion. rev. ed. 1999. pap. 17.95 (*1-58063-108-8*) Renaissance.

Coursault, Jesse H. The Learning Process: Educational Theory Implied in Theory of Knowledge. LC 76-176674. (Columbia University. Teachers College. Contributions to Education Ser.: No. 16). reprint ed. 37.50 (*0-404-55016-9*) AMS Pr.

Course, A. G. & Oram, R. B. Glossary of Cargo Handling Terms. (C). 1989. 50.00 (*0-85174-080-4*) St Mut.

Course, Charles, jt. auth. see Noble, David.

Course, Charles, jt. ed. see Noble, David.

Course, John. The Bedside Guardian Forty-One 1992. (Illus.). 384p. 1993. 29.95 (*1-85702-057-X*) Trafalgar.

Course, John E. Speech & Response: A Rhetorical Analysis of the Introductions of Speeches of the Book of Job, Chapters 4-24. LC 94-26566. (Catholic Biblical Quarterly Monographs: Vol. 25). 1994. 8.50 (*0-915170-24-8*) Catholic Bibl Assn.

*__Course Technology Incorporated Staff.__ Managing & Maintaining Your PC Marketing Piece. (Programming Ser.). (C). 1999. pap. write for info. (*0-619-01560-8*) Course Tech.

Course Technology Incorporated Staff, ed. Outlook 2000 Expert. (C). 1999. 15.00 (*0-619-00128-3*) Course Tech.

*__Course Technology Staff.__ Freight: Overnight. 1999. write for info. (*0-619-02343-0*) Course Tech.

— Freight: Standard Ground. 1999. write for info. (*0-619-02341-4*) Course Tech.

— Freight: 2nd Day. 1999. write for info. (*0-619-02342-2*) Course Tech.

Course Technology Staff. Lab Manual for Ms Windows 2000 Professional. (C). 2000. pap. 15.00 (*0-619-01512-8*) Thomson Learn.

— Lab Manual Networking Essentials. (C). 2000. pap. 15.00 (*0-619-01508-X*) Thomson Learn.

— Lab Manual Windows 2000 Advanced Server. (C). 2000. pap. 15.00 (*0-619-01504-7*) Thomson Learn.

— Managing & Maintaining PCs. 2nd ed. (C). 1998. pap. 35.00 (*0-7600-5073-2*) Course Tech.

*__Course Technology Staff.__ MCSE Guide to Internet Explorer 5.0. (Networking Ser.). (C). 2000. text 45.00 (*0-7600-1146-X*) Course Tech.

— Microsoft Access 2000. (SAM's License Card for Course CBT Ser.). (C). 2000. text. write for info. (*0-619-00930-6*) Course Tech.

— Microsoft Access 2000 Expert. (SAM's License Card for Course CBT Ser.). (C). 2000. text. write for info. (*0-619-00931-4*) Course Tech.

— Microsoft Excel 2000. (SAM's License Card for Course CBT Ser.). (C). 2000. text. write for info. (*0-619-00928-4*) Course Tech.

— Microsoft Excel 2000 Expert. (SAM's License Card for Course CBT Ser.). (C). 2000. text. write for info. (*0-619-00929-2*) Course Tech.

— Microsoft NT Workstation 4.0 for End Users: Basic. (SAM's License Card for Course CBT Ser.). (C). 2000. text. write for info. (*0-619-00945-4*) Course Tech.

— Microsoft Office 2K Certified with Window 98 Expert. (SAM's License Card for Course CBT Ser.). (C). 2000. text 25.00 (*0-619-00935-7*) Course Tech.

— Microsoft Powerpoint 2000. (SAM's License Card for Course CBT Ser.). (C). 2000. text. write for info. (*0-619-00932-2*) Course Tech.

— Microsoft Windows 98 for End Users: Advance. (SAM's License Card for Course CBT Ser.). (C). 2000. text. write for info. (*0-619-00943-8*) Course Tech.

— Microsoft Word 2000. (SAM's License Card for Course CBT Ser.). (C). 2000. text. write for info. (*0-619-00926-8*) Course Tech.

— Sam 2000 Student Tutorial. 2nd ed. (C). 2000. 11.50 (*0-619-00147-X*) Course Tech.

— Shelly Cashman Web. (C). 2000. 1.00 (*0-7895-2832-0*) Course Tech.

Coursen, H. R. After the War: An Illustrated Novel about Rittmeister Manfred Frhr, Von Richthofen, The Red Baron. LC 81-4241. (Illus.). 190p. 1981. 13.95 (*0-918606-06-3*); pap. 8.95 (*0-918606-05-5*) Heidelberg Graph.

— The Golden Haze: A Story of the Future. 163p. (Orig.). 1995. pap. 15.95 (*1-880664-12-7*) E M Pr.

— The Outfielder. LC 91-38244. (Illus.). 270p. 1993. 19.95 (*0-918606-10-1*) Heidelberg Graph.

Coursen, H. R. Penelope. 304p. mass mkt. 5.99 (*1-55197-031-7*) Picasso Publ.

— Pim Pim the Mouse. 1999. text 15.95 (*0-8050-6095-2*) St Martin.

Coursen, H. R. Reading Shakespeare on Stage. LC 94-39270. (Illus.). 304p. 1995. 45.00 (*0-87413-538-9*) U Delaware Pr.

— Recalling August. LC 95-2044. 56p. 1996. pap. 10.00 (*1-880664-11-9*) E M Pr.

— Return to Archerland: Sequel to the Search for Archerland. LC 99-34054. 224p. 1999. pap. 16.95 (*0-918606-14-4*) Heidelberg Graph.

— Rewinding the Reel. St. Cyr, Napoleon, ed. 80p. (Orig.). 1989. pap. 7.50 (*0-910380-07-4*) Cider Mill.

— Rewriting the Book. St. Cyr, Napoleon, ed. 48p. (Orig.). 1987. pap. 4.50 (*0-910380-06-6*) Cider Mill.

— The Search for Archerland. (Illus.). 245p. (Orig.). (YA). (gr. 8 up). 1993. pap. 12.50 (*1-880664-02-X*) E M Pr.

— Shakespeare: The Two Traditions. LC 98-23511. (Illus.). 272p. 1999. 42.50 (*0-8386-3774-4*) Fairleigh Dickinson.

— Shakespeare in Production: Whose History? LC 95-34091. (Illus.). 301p. (C). 1996. text 39.95 (*0-8214-1140-3*) Ohio U Pr.

— Teaching Shakespeare with Film & Television: A Guide. LC 96-49732. 208p. 1997. lib. bdg. 49.95 (*0-313-30066-6*, Greenwood Pr) Greenwood.

— The Thirteen Greatest Love Songs. LC 98-61470. 375p. 1999. pap. 14.95 (*1-881636-26-7*) Windsor Hse Pub Grp.

— War Stories: Poems. Turco, Lewis, ed. LC 84-72827. (Illus.). 48p. 1984. 4.00 (*0-910380-05-8*) Cider Mill.

— Winter Dreams. St. Cyr, Napoleon, ed. LC 82-4152. (Illus.). (Orig.). 1982. pap. 4.00 (*0-910380-04-X*) Cider Mill.

Coursen, Herbert M. New & Collected Poems, 1966-1996. LC 96-28680. 155p. 1996. pap. 17.50 (*1-880664-17-8*) E M Pr.

Coursen, Herbert R., Jr. Christian Ritual & the World of Shakespeare's Tragedies. 441p. 1976. 45.00 (*0-8387-1518-4*) Bucknell U Pr.

Coursen, Herbert R. Macbeth: A Guide to the Play. LC 96-49733. (Greenwood Guides to Shakespeare Ser.). 224p. 1997. lib. bdg. 49.95 (*0-313-30047-X*, Greenwood Pr) Greenwood.

Coursen, Herbert R., Jr. Shakespearean Performance As Interpretation. LC 90-50933. 280p. 1992. 42.50 (*0-87413-432-3*) U Delaware Pr.

*__Coursen, Herbert R.__ The Tempest: A Guide to the Play. LC 99-51320. (Greenwood Guides to Shakespeare Ser.). 256p. 2000. lib. bdg. 65.00 (*0-313-31191-9*, Greenwood Pr) Greenwood.

Coursen, Herbert R. Watching Shakespeare on Television. LC 92-55123. 1993. 34.50 (*0-8386-3521-0*) Fairleigh Dickinson.

*__Coursen, Valerie.__ Inspirations: Poems: A Book & a Journal. 2000. 12.95 (*0-7624-0810-3*) Running Pr.

Coursen, Valerie. Mordant's Wish. LC 96-44210. (Illus.). 32p. (J). (ps-2). 1995. 15.95 (*0-8050-4374-8*) H Holt & Co.

— Smiles Notes. (Notes Ser.). (Illus.). 80p. 1996. pap. text 4.95 (*1-56138-757-6*) Running Pr.

*__Coursesmith Staff.__ Coursesmith - Education from the Newspaper. 50p. (C). 2000. pap., wbk. ed. 35.95 (*1-890928-63-1*) Frieda Carrol.

— Coursesmith - Education from Travel Guides, Etc. 51p. (C). 2000. pap., wbk. ed. 35.95 (*1-890928-65-8*) Frieda Carrol.

— Coursesmith - History Education from Museums, Societies, Etc. 52p. (C). 2000. pap., wbk. ed. 35.95 (*1-890928-67-4*) Frieda Carrol.

— Coursesmith - Math Education from the Grocery Ads. 70p. (C). 2000. pap., wbk. ed. 35.95 (*1-890928-64-X*) Frieda Carrol.

— Coursesmith - Recycling Courses. 63p. (C). 2000. pap., wbk. ed. 35.95 (*1-890928-66-6*) Frieda Carrol.

Coursey, Cameron K. Understanding Digital PCS: The TDMA Standard. 382p. 1998. 89.00 (*0-89006-362-1*) Artech Hse.

*__Coursey, Denise Hawkins.__ Frommer's Maryland & Delaware. 4th ed. (Illus.). 336p. 2000. pap. 15.99 (*0-02-863707-X*, Frommer) Macmillan Gen Ref.

Coursey, Josephine & Stewart, Jeanette. Microbiology Lab Notebook. 112p. (C). 1995. ring bd. 13.95 (*0-7872-1889-8*) Kendall-Hunt.

Courson, Bruce, ed. Summering on Nantucket. (Illus.). 49p. 1986. 9.50 (*0-9607340-6-6*) Nantucket Hist Assn.

Courson, Diana. Let's Learn about Safety. (Illus.). 64p. (J). (ps-2). 1987. pap. 7.99 (*0-86653-382-6*, GA1011) Good Apple.

Courson, Diana F. & Foster, Tom. The Arts & Sciences. (Focus On...Ser.). 96p. teacher ed. 7.99 (*0-86653-750-3*, GA1465) Good Apple.

Courson, J. The Tree of Life: Matthew. 1993. pap. 19.95 (*1-882743-00-8*) Tree Life OR.

*__Courson, Jon.__ A Future & a Hope: Sermons of Comfort in Seasons of Change. 183p. 1999. pap. 5.99 (*0-9676661-0-4*) Calvary Dist.

Court, Brian, jt. auth. see Steele, Paul T.

Court-Brown, C. M. An Atlas of Closed Nailing of the Tibia & Femur. (Illus.). 240p. 1991. 130.00 (*0-387-91396-3*) Spr-Verlag.

Court-Brown, Charles & Pennig, Dietmar, eds. Tibia & Fibula. (Musculoskeletal Trauma Ser.). (Illus.). 288p. 1997. text 130.00 (*0-7506-0529-4*) Buttrwrth-Heinemann.

Court, David, jt. auth. see Coleman, James S.

Court, Deborah, jt. ed. see Riecken, Ted.

Court, Donald P. Van, see Van Court, Donald P.

Court, Doreen. Succulent Flora of Southern Africa: A Comprehensive & Authoritative Guide to the Indigenous Succulents of S Africa, Botswana, S-W Africa, Namibia, Angola, Zambia, Zimbabwe, Rhodesia & Mozambique Incorporating the Latest Research & Changes in Nomenclature. 240p. (C). 1981. text 95.00 (*90-6191-091-9*, Pub. by A A Balkema) Ashgate Pub Co.

Court, Franklin E. Institutionalizing English Literature: The Culture & Politics of Literary Study, 1750-1900. LC 91-43364. 224p. (C). 1992. 35.00 (*0-8047-2043-6*) Stanford U Pr.

Court, Franklin E., ed. Walter Pater: An Annotated Bibliography of Writings about Him. LC 78-56125. (Annotated Secondary Bibliography Series on English Literature in Transition, 1880-1920). 411p. 1980. 55.00 (*0-87580-072-6*) N Ill U Pr.

Court, Gil. The Third Secret. 613p. mass mkt. 5.99 (*1-55197-408-8*) Picasso Publ.

Court, Jamie & Smith, Francis. Making a Killing: HMOs & the Threat to Your Health. LC 99-37783. 1999. 29.95 (*1-56751-169-4*) Common Courage.

— Making a Killing: HMOs & the Threat to Your Health. LC 99-37783. 224p. 1999. pap. 12.71 (*1-56751-168-6*, Pub. by Common Courage) SPD-Small Pr Dist.

Court, John. Hypnosis Healing & the Christian. xii, 162p. 1997. reprint ed. pap. 16.99 (*0-85364-802-6*, Pub. by Paternoster Pub) OM Literature.

Court, John. The Puberty Game: A Guide to Help Parents Get Ready to Play. 224p. 1998. pap. 13.95 (*0-7322-5786-7*) HarpC.

*__Court, John M.__ The Book of Revelation & the Johannine Apocalyptic Tradition. (Journal for the Study of the New Testament, Supplement Ser.: No. 190). 192p. 2000. 57.50 (*1-84127-073-3*, Pub. by Sheffield Acad) CUP Services.

Court, John M. Reading the New Testament. LC 96-33159. (New Testament Readings Ser.). (Illus.). 192p. (C). 1997. 60.00 (*0-415-10367-3*); pap. 17.99 (*0-415-10368-1*) Routledge.

— Revelation. (New Testament Guides Ser.). 134p. 1994. pap. 12.50 (*1-85075-705-4*, Pub. by Sheffield Acad) CUP Services.

Court, John M., jt. auth. see Werther, George A.

Court, L. & Bodet, B., eds. Transmissible Subacute Spongiform Encephalopathies: Prion Diseases. 508p. 1996. pap. 139.00 (*2-906077-91-7*) Elsevier.

Court, Nathan A. Modern Pure Solid Geometry. 2nd ed. LC 64-18134. 1979. text 27.50 (*0-8284-0147-0*) Chelsea Pub.

Court, Pieter De La, see De La Court, Pieter.

Court, S. & Lamb, B. Childhood & Adolescent Diabetes. LC 97-3042. 384p. 1997. 120.00 (*0-471-97003-4*) Wiley.

*__Court, Sally.__ Modern Garden Makers. (Illus.). 2000. 34.95 (*0-304-35325-6*) Continuum.

*__Court, Sharon.__ Nurse in Need. large type ed. 336p. 1999. pap. 20.99 (*1-85389-944-5*, Dales) Ulverscroft.

Court Statistics Project Staff. State Court Caseload Statistics, 1995: Supplement to Examining the Work of State Courts, 1995. (Illus.). 252p. 1996. pap. 12.00 (*0-89656-173-9*, R-192) Natl Ctr St Courts.

Court TV Staff & American Lawyer Staff, eds. Court TV's Cradle-to-Grave Legal Survival Guide: A Complete Resource for Any Question You Might Have about the Law. 528p. 1995. pap. 19.95 (*0-316-03663-3*, Back Bay) Little.

Court, William H. Scarcity & Choice in History. LC 74-113460. viii, 256p. 1970. lib. bdg. 39.50 (*0-678-08017-8*) Kelley.

Courtalon, Corinne. On the Banks of the Pharaoh's Nile. LC 87-37195. (Illus.). 38p. (J). (gr. k-5). 1988. 5.95 (*0-944589-07-3*, 073) Young Discovery Lib.

Courtauld, Caroline. Burma (Myanmar) 2nd ed. (Odyssey Passport Ser.). 1999. pap. text 19.95 (*962-217-608-9*) Norton.

— Fujian. (Illus.). 144p. 1994. pap. 9.95 (*0-8442-9821-2*, Passprt Bks) NTC Contemp Pub Co.

— Nanjing Wuxi, Suzhou & Jiangsu Province. (Illus.). 160p. 1995. pap. 8.95 (*0-8442-9818-2*, Passprt Bks) NTC Contemp Pub Co.

Courtauld, Caroline & Holdsworth, May. The Hong Kong Story. LC 97-19191. (Illus.). 176p. (C). 1997. text 29.95 (*0-19-590353-6*) OUP.

Courtauld, Caroline & Hunt, Jill. Hong Kong. 3rd ed. LC 90-63334. (China Guides Ser.). (Illus.). 208p. 1994. reprint ed. pap. 11.95 (*0-8442-9807-7*, Passprt Bks) NTC Contemp Pub Co.

Courtauld Institute of Art, London Staff & Troutman, Philip. The Painting Collections of the Courtauld Institute of Art. LC 78-13168. 128p. 1995. lib. bdg. 96.00 (*0-226-68904-2*, CVL 24) U Ch Pr.

Courtauld, Pari. A Persian Childhood. (Illus.). 148p. 1990. pap. 17.95 (*0-948695-19-6*, Pub. by Rubicon Pr) David Brown.

Courtault, Martine. Going West: Cowboys & Pioneers. Bogard, Vicki, tr. from FRE. LC 89-5365. (Young Discovery Library). (Illus.). 38p. (J). (gr. k-5). 1989. 5.95 (*0-944589-21-9*, 021) Young Discovery Lib.

*__Courtaway, Robbi.__ Spirits of St. Louis. 208p. 1999. pap. write for info. (*1-891442-07-4*, Pub. by VA Pub Corp) Booksource.

Courteau, E. Coins & Tokens of Nova Scotia. (Illus.). 1982. reprint ed. pap. 8.00 (*0-942666-09-7*) S J Durst.

Courteau, Joanna. The Poetics of Rasalia De Castro's Sombra Negra. LC 94-36502. (Hispanic Literature Ser.: No. 23). 136p. 1995. text 69.95 (*0-7734-9055-8*) E Mellen.

Courtecuisse, R. & Duhem, B. Collins Field Guide: Mushrooms & Toadstools. 480p. 1995. 29.95 (*0-00-220025-2*, Pub. by HarpC) Trafalgar.

*__Courtecuisse, Regis.__ Mushrooms of Britain & Europe. (Collins Wild Guide Ser.). (Illus.). 904p. 2000. pap. 29.95 (*0-00-220012-0*, Pub. by HarpC) Trafalgar.

C

Courteline, Georges. Les Balances. (FRE.). 34p. 1946. 10.95 (*0-7859-1160-X*, 2080501429) Fr & Eur.
— Les Gaites de l'Escadron. (FRE.). 1990. pap. 10.95 (*0-7859-2966-5*) Fr & Eur.
— Messieurs les Ronds-de-Cuir. (FRE.). 1990. pap. 10.95 (*0-7859-2960-6*) Fr & Eur.
— La Paix Chez Soi. 40p. 1966. 8.95 (*0-7859-0694-0*, F97610) Fr & Eur.
— Theatre: Avec: Boubouroche, la Peur des Coups. (FRE.). 253p. 1965. 10.95 (*0-7859-1168-5*, 2080700650) Fr & Eur.
— Theatres: Romans et Nouvelles, Philosophie, Ecrits Divers. (FRE.). 1990. pap. 48.95 (*0-7859-3030-2*) Fr & Eur.
— Le Train de 8h 47. 256p. 1959. 14.95 (*0-7859-0695-9*, F97630) Fr & Eur.
Courtenay, Anthea. The Sleep Technique: Simple Secrets for a Deep, Restorative Night's Sleep. 175p. 1999. pap. 8.00 (*0-7225-3793-X*) Thorsons PA.
Courtenay, Anthea, jt. auth. see La Tourelle, Maggie.
Courtenay, Bryce. April Fool's Day. 1996. pap. 14.95 (*0-433-39848-5*) Buttrwrth-Heinemann.
Courtenay, Bryce. April Fool's Day. 674p. 1997. 24.95 (*0-433-39710-1*) Buttrwrth-Heinemann.
— The Power of One. LC 96-96683. 518p. 1996. pap. 12.95 (*0-345-41005-X*) Ballantine Pub Grp.
— Tandia. 1992. write for info. (*0-316-15828-3*) Little.
***Courtenay, Bryce.** Tommo & Hawk. LC 98-193830. 1998. write for info. (*0-14-027156-2*) Penguin Books.
Courtenay, John. A Poetical Review of the Literary & Moral Character of the Late Samuel Johnson. 3rd rev. ed. LC 92-22689. (Augustan Reprints Ser.: No. 133). 1969. reprint ed. 14.50 (*0-404-70133-7*, PR4508) AMS Pr.
Courtenay, Lynn T., ed. Engineering of Medieval Cathedrals. LC 97-29054. (Studies in the History of Civil Engineering: Vol. 1). 400p. 1997. text 157.95 (*0-86078-750-8*, Pub. by Ashgate Pub) Ashgate Pub Co.
Courtenay, P. P. The Rice Sector of Peninsular Malaysia: A Rural Paradox. (ASAA Southeast Asia Publications Ser.). (Illus.). 208p. 1996. 29.95 (*1-86373-991-2*, Pub. by Allen & Unwin Pty) Paul & Co Pubs.
Courtenay, Thomas P. Commentaries on the Historical Plays of Shakspeare, 2 vols. LC 72-1030. reprint ed. 115.00 (*0-404-01781-9*) AMS Pr.
Courtenay-Thompson, Fiona, jt. ed. see Liddiard, Nicola.
Courtenay, Walter R., Jr. & Stauffer, Jay R., Jr., eds. Distribution, Biology, & Management of Exotic Fishes. LC 83-18723. (Illus.). 448p. 1984. reprint ed. pap. 138.90 (*0-608-05940-4*, 206627700008) Bks Demand.
Courtenay, William J. Covenant & Causality in Medieval Thought: Studies in Philosophy, Theology & Economic Practice. (Collected Studies: No. CS206). 164p. (C). 1984. reprint ed. text 117.95 (*0-86078-154-2*, Pub. by Variorum) Ashgate Pub Co.
— Parisian Scholars in the Early Fourteenth Century: A Social Portrait. LC 98-34292. (Cambridge Studies in Medieval Life & Thought: No. 41). (Illus.). 285p. (C). 1999. text 64.95 (*0-521-64212-4*) Cambridge U Pr.
— Schools & Scholars in Fourteenth-Century England. LC 87-14808. 456p. 1987. reprint ed. 141.40 (*0-608-04592-6*, 206536200006) Bks Demand.
Courteney, Hazel. Body & Beauty Foods: More Than 100 Delicious Recipes to Improve You Health, Boost Your Immune System. (Foods That Heal Cookbook Ser.). 1998. 24.95 (*0-7621-0103-2*, Pub. by RD Assn) Penguin Putnam.
Courter, Eileen, et al. A Lending Hand: Credit Union Executives Share Loan-Generating Success Stories. 91p. (Orig.). 1994. pap. 79.00 (*1-889394-14-9*) Credit Union Execs.
Courter, Gay. The Midwife. 536p. 1985. mass mkt. 6.99 (*0-451-15623-4*, Sig) NAL.
Courter, Gini. Mastering Microsoft Office 2000: Premium Edition. (Mastering Ser.). 1488p. 1999. 49.99 (*0-7821-2312-0*) Sybex.
— Mastering Microsoft Outlook 98. LC 98-85470. (Illus.). 816p. 1998. pap. text 34.99 (*0-7821-2276-0*) Sybex.
***Courter, Gini.** Mastering Microsoft Outlook 2000: Premium Edition. (Illus.). 1104p. 2000. 44.99 (*0-7821-2676-6*) Sybex.
— Mastering Microsoft Project 2000. (Mastering Ser.). 2000. pap. 34.99 (*0-7821-2656-1*) Sybex.
Courter, Gini. Microsoft Office 97 User Certification: Study Guide. LC 97-81080. 864p. 1998. student ed. 39.99 incl. cd-rom (*0-7821-2263-9*) Sybex.
— Professional Guide to Office 97. 1997. pap. text 39.99 (*0-7821-2062-8*) Sybex.
Courter, Gini & Marquis, Annette. Mastering Microsoft Office 2000 Professional Edition. LC 98-88950. (Mastering Ser.). (Illus.). 1200p. 1999. 39.99 (*0-7821-2313-9*) Sybex.
***Courter, Gini & Marquis, Annette.** Mastering Office 2000 with CD-ROM. 2nd ed. (Mastering Ser.). 1456p. 2000. pap. 39.99 incl. cd-rom (*0-7821-2823-8*) Sybex.
Courter, Gini & Marquis, Annette. Microsoft Office 2000: No Experienced Required. 2nd ed. LC 99-60014. (No Experience Required Ser.). (Illus.). 742p. 1999. pap. 24.99 (*0-7821-2293-0*) Sybex.
Courter, Gini Marquis, see Marquis Courter, Gini.
Courter, J. W. Aladdin Electric Lamps. (Illus.). (C). 1987. 24.95 (*0-9618879-0-7*) J W Courter.
Courtes, J., jt. auth. see Greimas, A. J.
Courteult, Pascal. Automotives Voisin, 1919-1958, 2 vols. Hull, Peter, tr. (Illus.). 374p. 1992. boxed set 195.00 (*0-904568-72-5*) Pincushion Pr.
Courthion, Pierre. Impressionism. Shepley, John, tr. (Illus.). 206p. 1971. 49.50 (*0-8109-0202-8*); pap. 14.95 (*0-685-00034-6*) Abrams.
— Impressionism. 1989. 14.98 (*0-88365-740-6*) Galahad Bks.
— Manet. (Masters of Art Ser.). (Illus.). 1984. 24.95 (*0-8109-1318-6*, Pub. by Abrams) Time Warner.
— Seurat. (Illus.). 128p. 1988. 24.95 (*0-8109-1519-7*, Pub. by Abrams) Time Warner.
Courthope, William J. Addison. Morley, John, ed. LC 68-58375. (English Men of Letters Ser.). reprint ed. lib. bdg. 41.50 (*0-404-51707-2*) AMS Pr.
— Liberal Movement in English Literature. LC 72-458. reprint ed. 38.50 (*0-404-01784-3*) AMS Pr.
— Life in Poetry. LC 72-992. reprint ed. 49.50 (*0-404-01785-1*) AMS Pr.
Courti, jt. auth. see Chisholm.
Courtice, Katie, jt. auth. see Powell, Lenore S.
Courtie, Brenda. Christianity Explored. 1990. pap. 16.95 (*0-7459-1800-X*, Pub. by Lion Pubng) Trafalgar.
***Courtier, Jane.** Container Gardening. LC 99-40071. (Time-Life Garden Factlife Ser.). 112p. 2000. spiral bd. 12.95 (*0-7370-0606-4*) T-L Custom Pub.
Courtier, Jane. Gardener. (Infatuation Ser.). 1998. 12.95 (*1-897954-86-7*, Pub. by Mus Quilts Pub) Sterling.
— Growing Indoor Plants. (Ward Lock Master Gardener Ser.). (Illus.). 96p. 1993. pap. 10.95 (*0-7063-7106-2*, Pub. by WrLock) Sterling.
***Courtier, Jane.** The Time-Life Book of Garden Improvement Techniques. 256p. 2001. pap. 29.95 (*0-7370-0630-7*) Time-Life Educ.
Courtier, Jane & Rogers Clausen, Ruth. No Garden Gardener: The Essential Guide to Gardening in Small Spaces. LC 98-30453. 1999. 29.95 (*0-7621-0127-X*, Pub. by RD Assn) Penguin Putnam.
Courtier, Jane, et al. Indoor Plants: The Essential Guide to Choosing & Caring for Houseplants. LC 96-42046. (Illus.). 240p. 1997. 30.00 (*0-89577-921-8*, Pub. by RD Assn) Penguin Putnam.
Courtiere, Miles. Celtic Music for Piano. Gordon, Andrew D., ed. 45p. 1998. pap. 12.95 (*1-882146-60-3*) A D G Prods.
Courtiess, Thomas F. Corrections in the Criminal Justice System: Law, Policies & Practice. LC 96-26551. 450p. 1997. 76.95 (*0-314-20187-4*) West Pub.
Courtillon, Janine & De Salins, Genevieve-Dominique. Libre Echange, No. 1. 2nd ed. (FRE., Illus.). 255p. 1995. pap. text 23.95 (*2-278-04461-3*, Pub. by Edns Didier) Hatier Pub.
— Libre Echange, No. 2. (FRE., Illus.). 271p. 1991. pap. text 23.95 (*2-278-04022-7*, Pub. by Edns Didier) Hatier Pub.
— Libre Echange, No. 3. (FRE., Illus.). 255p. 1993. pap. text 24.95 (*2-278-04026-X*, Pub. by Edns Didier) Hatier Pub.
Courtillot, Vincent. Evolutionary Catastrophes: The Science of Mass Extinction. McClinton, Joe, tr. from FRE. LC 98-32169. (Illus.). 200p. (C). 1999. 24.95 (*0-521-58392-6*) Cambridge U Pr.
Courtin, Jean, jt. auth. see Clottes, Jean.
Courtin, Robina, ed. see McDonald, Kathleen.
Courtin, Robina, ed. see Rinpoche, Lama Thubten Zopa.
Courtin, Robina, ed. see Yeshe, Lama Thubten.
Courtin, Thierry. Daddy & Me. LC 96-78083. (Lift & Look Board Bks.). (Illus.). 12p. (J). (ps). 1997. bds. 4.95 (*0-448-41617-4*, G & D) Peng Put Young Read.
Courtin, Thierry. Peek-a-Boo Moon. LC 95-77543. (Lift & Look Board Bks.). 12p. (J). (ps-3). 1996. bds. 4.95 (*0-448-41282-9*, G & D) Peng Put Young Read.
***Courtine-Denamy, Sylvie.** Three Women in Dark Times: Edith Stein, Hannah Arendt, Simone Weil. Goshgarian, G. M., tr. from FRE. 2000. 29.95 (*0-8014-3572-2*) Cornell U Pr.
Courtine, Jean, jt. auth. see Janicaud, Dominique.
Courtine, R. J. The New Larousse of Gastronomy: Nouveau Larousse Gastronomique. (ENG & FRE.). 1152p. 1984. 150.00 (*0-8288-0157-6*, M6433) Fr & Eur.
Courtine, Robert H. Dictionnaire des Fromages.Tr. of Cheese Dictionary. (FRE.). 250p. 1972. pap. 17.95 (*0-8288-6374-1*, F83160) Fr & Eur.
***Courtis, John.** The Bluffer's Guide to Management: Bluff Your Way in Management. (Bluffer's Guides Ser.). 64p. 1999. pap. 5.95 (*1-902825-52-7*) Oval Bks.
— Getting a Better Job. 96p. 2000. pap. 17.95 (*0-8464-5065-8*) Beekman Pubs.
Courtis, John. Getting a Better Job. 144p. (C). 1993. pap. 30.00 (*0-85292-512-3*, Pub. by IPM Hse) St Mut.
— Interviews: Skill & Strategy. 96p. (C). 1988. 55.00 (*0-85292-406-2*) St Mut.
— The IPM Guide to Cost Effective Recruitment. 99p. (C). 1985. 70.00 (*0-85292-340-6*, Pub. by IPM Hse) St Mut.
***Courtis, John.** Recruitment Advertising: Right First Time. 104p. 2000. pap. 32.95 (*0-8464-5138-7*) Beekman Pubs.
Courtis, John, ed. Recruiting for Profit. 128p. (C). 1989. pap. 60.00 (*0-85292-427-5*, Pub. by IPM Hse) St Mut.
Courtis, Stuart A., jt. auth. see Caldwell, Otis W.
Courtivron, Isabelle De, see Chadwick, Whitney & De Courtivron, Isabelle, eds.
Courtless. Corrections & the Criminal Justice System. (Criminal Justice Ser.). 1997. mass mkt. 13.00 (*0-314-20747-3*) West Pub.
Courtmanche, John, ed. see De la Cruz, Ben.
Courtnail, Ray. Making Master Guitars. (Illus.). 1993. 124.95 (*0-7090-4809-2*, I330) Bold Strummer Ltd.
***Courtnay, Eileen.** Rheumatoid Arthritis: A Separate World: A Personal Account of Living with Rheumatoid Arthritis. Caso, Adolph, ed. (Illus.). 146p. 2000. pap. 19.95 (*0-8283-2058-6*) Branden Bks.
Courtnay, Jack. Theatre Organ World. (Illus.). 230p. 1946. pap. 38.00 (*0-913746-33-9*) Organ Lit.
Courtney. Mechanical Behavior of Material. 2nd ed. LC 99-31791. (Series in Materials Science & Engineering). 752p. 1999. 108.44 (*0-07-028594-2*) McGraw.
Courtney, ed. Nationalism & War in the Near East. LC 79-135800. (Eastern Europe Collection). 1971. reprint ed. 28.95 (*0-405-02742-7*) Ayer.
Courtney, jt. auth. see Andrews.
Courtney, jt. auth. see Briggs.
Courtney, jt. auth. see Olson.
Courtney, B., jt. auth. see Harrington, J.
Courtney, Brian. Butterworths Trust Taxation Manual. 3rd ed. 176p. (Orig.). 1993. pap. text 60.00 (*0-406-02176-7*, UK, MICHIE) LEXIS Pub.
Courtney, C. P., ed. Constant: Adolphe. (Bristol French Texts Ser.). (FRE.). 224p. 1989. pap. 15.95 (*0-631-16205-4*) Blackwell Pubs.
Courtney, Caroline. Libertine in Love. 224p. 1984. mass mkt. 2.25 (*0-446-32591-0*, Pub. by Warner Bks) Little.
Courtney, Cathy. Speaking of Book Art: Interviews with British & American Book Artists. (Illus.). 241p. 1999. pap. 29.95 (*0-9626372-5-4*, Pub. by Anderson-Lovelace Pubs) SPD-Small Pr Dist.
Courtney, Cathy, ed. Jocelyn Herbert: A Theatre Workbook. (Illus.). 240p. 1995. 59.95 (*1-55783-218-8*) Applause Theatre Bk Pubs.
— Jocelyn Herbert: A Theatre Workbook. (Illus.). 256p. 1998. pap. text 35.00 (*1-55783-326-5*) Applause Theatre Bk Pubs.
Courtney, Chandrakantha, jt. auth. see Courtney, David.
Courtney, Charles, ed. East Wind: Taoist & Cosmological Implications of Christian Theology. LC 97-27213. 192p. (C). 1997. 46.00 (*0-7618-0860-4*); pap. 26.50 (*0-7618-0861-2*) U Pr of Amer.
Courtney, Charles, tr. see Dumery, Henry.
Courtney-Clark, Margaret. Ndebele: The Art of an African Tribe. LC 85-4382. (Illus.). 208p. 1990. 60.00 (*0-8478-0685-5*, Pub. by Rizzoli Intl) St Martin.
Courtney-Clarke, Margaret. African Canvas: The Art of West African Women. LC 89-24037. (Illus.). 204p. 1990. 60.00 (*0-8478-1166-2*, Pub. by Rizzoli Intl) St Martin.
***Courtney-Clarke, Margaret.** Maya Angelou: The Poetry of Living. LC 99-34225. 132p. 1999. 22.50 (*0-609-60458-9*) C Potter.
Courtney-Clarke, Margaret. Places in the Sand. LC 97-28067. (Illus.). 128p. 1997. 45.00 (*1-885254-76-8*, Pub. by Monacelli Pr) Penguin Putnam.
Courtney-Clarke, Margaret & Brooks, Geraldine. Imazighen: The Vanishing Traditions of North African Women. 1996. 55.00 (*0-614-20393-7*) C Potter.
Courtney, Claudia. Barns of Barley: The Parable of the Rich Fool. (Phonetic Bible Stories). (Illus.). 16p. (ps-1). 1998. pap. 2.59 (*0-570-05095-2*) Concordia.
— Bleat: The Parable of the Lost Sheep. (Phonetic Bible Stories). (Illus.). 16p. (ps-1). 1998. pap. 2.59 (*0-570-05092-8*) Concordia.
— Blow: Jesus Calms the Storm. (Illus.). 16p. (J). (ps-1). 1998. pap. 2.59 (*0-570-05093-6*) Concordia.
***Courtney, Claudia.** Choose! (Phonetic Bible Stories Ser.). (Illus.). 16p. (J). (ps-1). 1999. pap. text 2.59 (*0-570-07003-1*) Concordia.
— Daniel Blessed Daniel & the Lion's Den, Vol. 1. (Heartland Ser.). 1999. pap. 3.00 (*0-570-05560-1*) Concordia.
— Defiant Giant The Story of David & Goliath. (Heartland Ser.). 1999. pap. 3.00 (*0-570-05561-X*) Concordia.
— Jesus Is Born! The Story of Christmas. (Phonetic Bible Stories Ser.). (Illus.). 16p. (J). (ps-1). 1998. pap. 2.59 (*0-570-05462-1*, 56-1925GJ) Concordia.
Courtney, Claudia. Little Is Big: Jesus Feeds the Crowd. (Phonetic Bible Stories). (Illus.). 16p. (J). (ps-1). 1998. pap. 2.59 (*0-570-05094-4*) Concordia.
***Courtney, Claudia.** Modest King. (Phonetic Bible Stories Ser.). (Illus.). 16p. (J). (ps-1). 1999. pap. text 2.59 (*0-570-07001-5*) Concordia.
— Rise & Shine. (Phonetic Bible Stories Ser.). (Illus.). 16p. (J). (ps-1). 1999. pap. text 2.59 (*0-570-07002-3*) Concordia.
— Saved by Faith: Noah & the Ark. (Phonetic Bible Stories Ser.). (Illus.). 16p. (J). (ps-1). 1998. pap. 2.59 (*0-570-05461-3*, 56-1924GJ) Concordia.
— Tan Man The Parable of the Good Samaritan, Vol. 1. (Phonetic Bible Stories Ser.). 1999. pap. 3.00 (*0-570-05559-8*) Concordia.
Courtney, D. G. King's Cross: A Story of Regicide. 384p. 1993. pap. 14.95 (*1-55082-082-6*, Pub. by Quarry Pr) LPC InBook.
Courtney, David & Courtney, Chandrakantha. Elementary North Indian Vocal. 5th expanded rev. ed. LC 95-68751. (Illus.). 174p. 1995. spiral bd. 34.95 (*0-9634447-4-3*) Sur Sangeet.
Courtney, David R. Fundamentals of Tabla. 3rd rev. ed. LC 98-160377. (Complete Reference for Tabla Ser.). (Illus.). 272p. 1998. spiral bd. 34.95 (*0-9634447-8-6*) Sur Sangeet.
Courtney, Don. Divine Healing. 1997. pap. 7.95 (*0-9656180-1-3*) D Courtney.
— In the Beginning: Evolution, Science, & the Bible. 89p. (Orig.). 1996. pap. 7.95 (*0-9656180-0-5*) D Courtney.
— 2000 A. D. 1998. pap. 7.95 (*0-9656180-2-1*) D Courtney.
Courtney, Don, jt. auth. see Madgwick, Wendy.
Courtney, E. A Commentary on the Satires of Juvenal. (Illus.). 650p. (C). 1980. text 110.00 (*0-485-11190-X*, Pub. by Athlone Pr) Humanities.
— Musa Lapidaria: A Selection of Latin Verse Inscriptions. LC 95-30859. (American Philological Association American Classical Studies: No. 36). 457p. (C). 1995. pap. 27.95 (*0-7885-0142-9*, 400436) OUP.
— The Poems of Petronius. 86p. 1991. pap. 13.95 (*1-55540-588-6*, 40 04 25) OUP.
Courtney, E., ed. Silvae. (Oxford Classical Texts Ser.). 198p. 1990. text 60.00 (*0-19-814683-3*) OUP.
Courtney, E., jt. auth. see Rudd, Niall.
Courtney, E. C., jt. auth. see Rudd, Niall.
Courtney, E. Wayne. Under the Winds of Yaquina. Orig. Title: Dunlins & Sanderlings: Under the Winds of Yaquina. (Illus.). 66p. (Orig.). 1988. pap. text 3.95 (*0-9616063-5-5*) Sanderling Pr.
Courtney, Edith. Love Me Never. 256p. 25.00 (*0-7278-5213-2*) Severn Hse.
— My Feet Are Killing Me. 203p. (C). 1977. 30.00 (*0-85088-416-0*, Pub. by Gomer Pr) St Mut.
Courtney, Edward. Archaic Latin Prose. LC 99-12849. (American Philological Association American Classical Studies). 164p. 1999. pap. 12.95 (*0-7885-0545-9*, 40 04 42) OUP.
***Courtney, Edward.** Archaic Latin Prose. LC 99-12849. (American Philological Association American Classical Studies). 164p. 1999. text 19.95 (*0-7885-0544-0*, 40 04 42) OUP.
Courtney, Edward, comment. The Fragmentary Latin Poets. LC 92-12387. 530p. (C). 1993. text 89.00 (*0-19-814775-9*, Clarendon Pr) OUP.
Courtney, Elise & Celeste, Emily. How to Find Music Easily for Good Times in Harmony. LC 80-51888. (Illus.). 317p. (Orig.). 1980. pap. 6.00 (*0-686-28899-8*) Merk.
Courtney, Gary, et al, eds. Residential Sprinklers: A Primer. (Illus.). 16p. 1986. pap. text 6.00 (*0-685-59454-8*) IFSTA.
Courtney-Green, P. R. Ammunition for the Land Battle. Lee, R. G. & Hartley, Frank, eds. (Brassey's Battlefield Weapons Systems & Technology Ser.: Vol. 4). 300p. 1991. 40.00 (*0-08-035821-7*, Pub. by Brasseys); 25.00 (*0-08-035807-1*, Pub. by Brasseys) Brasseys.
Courtney, Gregory W. Biosystematics of the Nymphomyiidae: Insecta: Diptera: Life History, Morphology, & Phylogenetic Relationships. LC 93-40217. (Smithsonian Contributions to Zoology Ser.: No. 550). (Illus.). 45p. reprint ed. pap. 30.00 (*0-7837-6893-1*, 204672300003) Bks Demand.
Courtney, Gretchen. Story Dramas: A New Literature Experience for Children. LC 99-176676. 1998. pap. 9.95 (*0-673-36374-0*, GoodYrBooks) Addson-Wesley Educ.
Courtney, Gretchen, jt. auth. see Jossart, Sarah.
Courtney, J. W. Conquest of Nerves (1914) 280p. 1998. reprint ed. pap. 17.95 (*0-7661-0500-8*) Kessinger Pub.
Courtney, Jane. Where Have All the Colours Gone? (Illus.). (J). 1990. 29.00 (*0-85439-407-9*, Pub. by St Paul Pubns) St Mut.
Courtney, Janet E. Adventurous Thirties: A Chapter in the Women's Movement. LC 67-26728. (Essay Index Reprint Ser.). 1977. 20.95 (*0-8369-0341-2*) Ayer.
— Freethinkers of the Nineteenth Century. LC 67-30182. (Essay Index Reprint Ser.). 1977. 23.95 (*0-8369-0342-0*) Ayer.
Courtney, John C. Do Conventions Matter? Choosing National Party Leaders in Canada. 432p. 1995. text 65.00 (*0-7735-1357-4*) McG-Queens Univ Pr.
— Do Conventions Matter? Choosing National Party Leaders in Canada. LC 96-153762. 432p. (C). 1995. pap. text 24.95 (*0-7735-1358-2*, Pub. by McG-Queens Univ Pr) CUP Services.
Courtney, Julie, ed. Fumio Yoshimura. (Illus.). 32p. 1987. pap. 5.00 (*0-939351-04-8*) Temple U Tyler Gal.
Courtney, Julie, et al. Philadelphia Art Now: Artists Choose Artists. (Illus.). 126p. 1991. pap. 15.00 (*0-88454-075-8*) U of Pa Contemp Art.
Courtney, Julie, jt. auth. see Muchnic, Suzanne.
Courtney, Kent. Returning to the Civil War: Grand Reenactments of an Anguished Time. LC 96-41231. (Illus.). 96p. 1997. pap. 21.95 (*0-87905-783-1*) Gibbs Smith Pub.
***Courtney, Kent.** Returning to the Civil War: Grand Reenactments of an Anguished Time. (Illus.). 96p. 1999. reprint ed. pap. text 22.00 (*0-7881-6716-2*) DIANE Pub.
Courtney, Leanna. New Life in Christ: Christ My Hope of Glory. 188p. (Orig.). 1997. pap. 10.00 (*1-57502-378-4*, PO1202) Morris Pubng.
Courtney, Linda J. The TBI Tool Kit. Burns, Pamela G., ed. 224p. (Orig.). 1994. pap. 24.95 (*1-882855-07-8*) HDI Pubs.
Courtney, Linda J., ed. Integrating Community Resources. 284p. (Orig.). 1994. pap. 16.50 (*1-882855-30-2*) HDI Pubs.
— Social Security Benefits - A Guide to Accessing Services for Persons with Traumatic Brain Injury. 40p. 1994. pap. 6.50 (*1-882855-28-0*) HDI Pubs.
Courtney, Lisa. A Coming of Age. LC 78-54786. (Illus.). 1978. 10.95 (*0-932464-01-7*) Trek-CIR.
Courtney, Mark E., jt. auth. see Specht, Harry.
Courtney, Mary. Financial Management in Health Services. 453p. 1997. pap. 80.00 (*0-8036-0338-X*) Davis Co.
Courtney, Max. Investigation of Clandestine Amphetamine Laboratories. (Illus.). 250p. 1989. pap. text 32.50 (*0-685-27232-X*) Spotlight Pub.
Courtney, Max & Hueske, Edward E. A Study of the Management, Deployment & Utilization of Crime Labs in Texas. 92p. 1984. 3.75 (*0-936440-58-9*) U TX SUPA.
Courtney, Nicholas. Five Rounds Rapid: The Autobiography of Nicholas Courtney. (Illus.). 1999. text 24.95 (*1-85227-782-3*, Pub. by Virgin Bks) London Brdge.
— Princess Anne: A Biography. large type ed. (Illus.). 256p. 1987. 17.95 (*0-7089-8409-6*, Charnwood) Ulverscroft.
— The Tiger: Symbol of Freedom. (Illus.). 128p. 1981. 25.00 (*0-7043-2245-5*, Pub. by Quartet) Charles River Bks.
Courtney, Pat. Per-sist-ent Ster-e-o-types. 1988. pap. 10.00 (*0-932526-19-5*) Nexus Pr.
Courtney, Paul. Medieval & Later USK: Report on the Excavations at USK, 1965-1976. 165p. 1994. 60.00 (*0-7083-1245-4*, Pub. by Univ Wales Pr) Paul & Co Pubs.
***Courtney, Philippa.** 4 Steps to Bring the Right Person into Your Life Right Now! deluxe ed. LC 99-66552. xix, 215p. 2000. pap. 14.95 (*1-58639-000-7*) MeanttwoBe.
Courtney, Richard. The Birth of God: The Moses Play & Monotheism in Ancient Israel. LC 95-43349. (American University Studies XXVI: Vol. 26). (Illus.). XIV, 235p. (C). 1997. 44.95 (*0-8204-3055-2*) P Lang Pubng.
— Buyers Are Liars & Sellers Are Too! 1992. pap. 4.95 (*0-9635026-0-3*) Picasso Publ.

C

An Asterisk (*) at the beginning of an entry indicates that the title is appearing for the first time.

— Drama & Feeling: An Aesthetic Theory. 248p. 1994. 60.00 (*0-7735-1228-4*, Pub. by McG-Queens Univ Pr) CUP Services.

— Drama & Intelligence: A Cognitive Theory. 208p. (C). 1990. text 60.00 (*0-7735-0766-3*, Pub. by McG-Queens Univ Pr) CUP Services.

— The Quest: Research & Inquiry in Arts Education. 2nd ed. LC 97-9478. 160p. 1997. 40.00 (*0-7618-0773-X*) U Pr of Amer.

Courtney, Richard, jt. auth. see Maccarone, Grace.

Courtney, Richard, jt. ed. see Schattner, Gertrud.

Courtney, Richard D. Normandy to the Bulge: An American Infantry GI in Europe During World War II. LC 96-7731. (Illus.). 208p. (C). 1996. 29.95 (*0-8093-2084-3*) S Ill U Pr.

***Courtney, Richard D.** Normandy to the Bulge: An American Infantry GI in Europe During World War II. (Illus.). 181p. 2000. pap. 19.95 (*0-8093-2102-5*) S Ill U Pr.

***Courtney, Susan J. & Allen, James E.** Long Term Care Administration State Licensure Requirements & College Directory. 191p. 1999. pap. write for info. (*0-9635064-5-5*) Nat Assn Bds Exam.

Courtney, Thomas H. Mechanical Behavior of Materials. (Electrical Engineering Ser.). 710p. (C). 1990. 101.56 (*0-07-013265-8*); pap. text 23.75 (*0-07-013266-6*) McGraw.

Courtney, Vincent. Goblins. 416p. 1994. mass mkt. 4.50 (*0-8217-4630-8*, Zebra Kensgtn) Kensgtn Pub Corp.

***Courtney, Vincent.** Goblins. 2000. mass mkt. 5.99 (*0-7860-1240-4*, Pinncle Kensgtn) Kensgtn Pub Corp.

Courtney, Vincent. Let's Pretend You're Dead. 1991. mass mkt. 4.50 (*1-55817-557-1*, Pinncle Kensgtn) Kensgtn Pub Corp.

— Virtual Fred & the Big Dip. (Stepping Stone Bks.). (J). 1997. 9.19 (*0-606-12840-9*, Pub. by Turtleback) Demco.

— Wake up Screaming. 384p. 1992. mass mkt. 4.50 (*1-55817-605-5*, Pinncle Kensgtn) Kensgtn Pub Corp.

Courtney, W. & Auld, J. W. Memoir on the Sawunt Waree State. (C). 1995. reprint ed. 64.00 (*81-206-1016-4*, Pub. by Asian Educ Servs) S Asia.

Courtney, W. Keith. Bud: A New Home. Acker, Chris & Acker, Jorge, eds. (Bud Bk.). (Illus.). 32p. (J). (ps-3). 1996. 14.95 incl. audio (*1-888133-00-7*) Bud Pubs.

Courtney, W. L. The Life of J. S. Mill: 1888 Edition. 212p. 1996. reprint ed. 58.00 (*1-85506-358-1*) Bks Intl VA.

Courtney, William L. Old Saws & Modern Instances. LC 69-18924. (Essay Index Reprint Ser.). 1977. 20.95 (*0-8369-0039-1*) Ayer.

Courtney, William P. & Smith, David N. A Bibliography of Samuel Johnson. With Johnson Bibliography, a Supplement to Courtney. Chapman, R. W., ed. 246p. 1984. reprint ed. 55.00 (*0-938768-11-5*) Oak Knoll.

***Courtois, B.** Microelectronics Education: Proceedings of the 3rd European Workshop on Microelectronics Workshop Hosted by St. University, France, May 18 & 19, 2000. European Workshop on Microelectronics Education Staff, ed. LC 00-41592. 2000. write for info. (*0-7923-6456-2*) Kluwer Academic.

***Courtois, Bernard & Demidenko, Serge, eds.** Design, Characterization & Packaging for MEMS & Microelectronics. 1999. pap. text 103.00 (*0-8194-3494-9*) SPIE.

***Courtois, Christine.** Complex Posttraumatic Stress Disorder & Incest/Child Sexual Abuse: Approaches to Treatment. (LEA/DLN Mental Health Professionals Video Reference Library). 1999. VHS 129.95 (*0-8058-3302-1*) L Erlbaum Assocs.

Courtois, Christine A. Adult Survivors of Child Sexual Abuse. LC 93-18434. (Workshop Models for Family Life Education Ser.). 144p. 1993. pap. 18.95 (*0-87304-247-6*) Manticore Pubs.

— Healing the Incest Wound: Adult Survivors in Therapy. (Professional Bks.). 1988. 34.95 (*0-393-70051-8*) Norton.

— Healing the Incest Wound: Adult Survivors in Therapy. 416p. 1996. pap. 19.95 (*0-393-31356-5*) Norton.

— Recollections of Sexual Abuse: Treatment Principles & Guidelines. LC 98-42100. 1999. text 45.00 (*0-393-70281-2*) Norton.

***Courtois, Stephane, et al.** The Black Book of Communism: Crimes, Terror, Repression. Murphy, Jonathan & Kramer, Mark, trs. from FRE. LC 99-29758. (Illus.). 1120p. 1999. 37.50 (*0-674-07608-7*) HUP.

Courtois, Todd. Java Communications. LC 97-22731. 352p. (C). 1997. pap. text 39.95 (*0-13-850454-7*) P-H.

— Java Networking & Communications. 1997. pap. 39.95 incl. cd-rom (*0-614-28518-6*) P-H.

Courtois, Y., et al. Modern Trends in Aging Research. (Colloque de L'INSERM Ser.). (ENG & FRE.). 620p. 1987. lib. bdg. 85.00 (*2-85598-309-6*) S M P F Inc.

Courton, ed. see Moliere.

Courtot, M. E. & Nier, M., eds. Standards for Electronic Imaging Systems: Critical Reviews. 1991. pap. 20.00 (*0-8194-0567-1*, VOL. CR37) SPIE.

Courtot, Marilyn, ed. Ballet & Other Forms of Dance: Book Reviews. (Illus.). 40p. (Orig.). (J). 1997. pap. 14.99 (*1-890920-06-1*) Childrens Lit.

— Board & Interactive Books: Book Reviews. (Illus.). 44p. (J). 1997. pap. 14.99 (*1-890920-07-X*) Childrens Lit.

— Children's Literature Choice List 1996. (Illus.). 40p. (Orig.). (J). 1996. pap. 14.99 (*1-890920-02-9*) Childrens Lit.

— Children's Literature Choice List 1997. (Illus.). 36p. (Orig.). (J). 1997. pap. 14.99 (*1-890920-05-3*) Childrens Lit.

— The Children's Literature Compendium: Reviews of over 500 Books. (Illus.). 114p. (Orig.). (J). 1995. pap. 10.99 (*1-890920-00-2*) Childrens Lit.

— Children's Multimedia: In Good, Bad, & the Ugly of Children's Software & Multimedia. (Illus.). 66p. (Orig.). (J). 1996. pap. 14.99 (*1-890920-03-7*) Childrens Lit.

— Far Eastern Cultures: East of the Urals. (Illus.). 48p. (Orig.). (J). 1998. pap. 14.99 (*1-890920-09-6*) Childrens Lit.

— Hispanic Peoples of North, Central, South America & the Caribbean. (Illus.). 44p. (Orig.). (J). 1998. pap. 14.99 (*1-890920-08-8*) Childrens Lit.

— Native Americans: From the Arctic to the Rainforest. (Illus.). 44p. (Orig.). (J). 1996. pap. 14.95 (*1-890920-04-5*) Childrens Lit.

— Twins: A Compilation of Book Reviews. (Illus.). 40p. (Orig.). (J). 1997. pap. 14.99 (*1-890920-10-X*) Childrens Lit.

Courtoy, Pierre J., et al, eds. Endocytosis: From Cell Biology to Health, Disease & Therapy. LC 92-2176. (NATO ASI Series H: Cell Biology: Vol. 62). (Illus.). 530p. 1992. 318.95 (*0-387-53146-7*) Spr-Verlag.

***Courtright, Mark A.** God Wrote It, I Just Took Dictation: Inspirational Poetry for Ordinary Folks. 2000. 6.00 (*0-9700177-0-7*) M A Courtright.

Courtright, Alan M. The Six-Twelve Plan: Reslicing the Work Pie. 168p. (Orig.). 1989. pap. 9.95 (*0-9624078-0-1*) Sharebooks Pub.

Courtright, Dudley V. Courtright. History of the Van Kortryks or Courtrights, Also Families Staud, Vattier, Moore. 105p. 1997. reprint ed. pap. 17.50 (*0-8328-8090-6*); reprint ed. lib. bdg. 27.50 (*0-8328-8089-2*) Higginson Bk Co.

Courtright, Gordon. Trees & Shrubs for Temperate Climates. 3rd ed. (Illus.). 250p. 1998. pap. 29.95 (*0-88192-415-6*) Timber.

— Tropicals. (Illus.). 155p. 1995. pap. 24.95 (*0-88192-332-X*) Timber.

Courtright, John & Perse, Elizabeth. Communicating Online: A Brief Guide to the Internet. x, 150p. 1998. pap. 16.95 (*0-7674-0246-4*, 0246-4) Mayfield Pub.

***Courtright, John A. & Perse, Elizabeth M.** The Mayfield Quick Guide to the Internet for Communication Students. LC 99-187313. (Illus.). iv, 84p. (C). 1998. pap. text 7.95 (*0-7674-0029-1*, 0029-1) Mayfield Pub.

***Courtright, Karen.** Entertaining with Kern. (Illus.). 44p. 2000. 10.95 (*1-57377-099-X*, 0-19884-02336-4) Easl Pubns.

Courtright, Nicola. Northern Travelers to Sixteenth-Century Italy: Drawings from New England Collections. (Illus.). 1990. pap. 5.00 (*0-914337-14-9*) Mead Art Mus.

Courtright, Paul & Lewallen, Susan. Guide to Ocular Leprosy for Health Workers. 52p. 1993. pap. text 33.00 (*981-02-1328-X*) World Scientific Pub.

— Training Health Workers to Recognize, Treat, Refer & Educate. 60p. 1993. pap. text 23.00 (*981-02-1329-8*) World Scientific Pub.

Courtright, Paul, ed. see Harlan, Lindsey.

Courtright, Paul B. Ganesa: Lord of Obstacles, Lord of Beginnings. 296p. (C). 1989. pap. text 23.95 (*0-19-505742-2*) OUP.

***Courtright, Paul B.** Ganesa: Lord of Obstacles Lord of Beginnings. 274p. 1999. 150.00 (*81-208-1604-8*, Pub. by Motilal Bnarsidass); pap. 75.00 (*81-208-1610-2*, Pub. by Motilal Bnarsidass) St Mut.

Courtright, Richard D., jt. ed. see Gallagher, James J.

Courts, Kitty. Down the Old Spanish Trail Vol. I: The Histories of the Plantations from Mintmere to Gravier. (Illus.). 301p. 1997. 85.00 (*0-9658756-0-1*) Res Servs.

— Down the Old Spanish Trail Vol. II: The Histories of the Plantations from Rosedale to Bayside. (Illus.). 506p. 1997. 85.00 (*0-9658756-1-X*) Res Servs.

Courts, Mark A. Thirty-Six Americans, Vol. 1. 49p. (YA). 1997. spiral bd. 10.00 (*0-9659934-0-X*) B H Communs.

— Thirty-Six More Americans, Vol. 2. 1998. spiral bd. 10.00 (*0-9659934-1-8*) B H Communs.

Courts, Patrick L. Literacy & Empowerment: The Meaning Makers. LC 91-2267. (Language & Ideology Ser.). 216p. 1991. 57.95 (*0-89789-260-7*, H260, Bergin & Garvey); pap. 22.95 (*0-89789-261-5*, G261, Bergin & Garvey) Greenwood.

— Multicultural Literacies: Dialect, Discourse & Diversity. LC 96-42973. (Counterpoints Ser.: No. 45). VIII, 196p. (C). 1997. pap. 29.95 (*0-8204-3675-5*) P Lang Pubng.

Courts, Patrick L. & McInerney, Kathleen H. Assessment in Higher Education: Politics, Pedagogy, & Portfolios. LC 92-41612. 208p. 1993. 59.95 (*0-275-94426-3*, C4426, Praeger Pubs); pap. 19.95 (*0-275-94427-1*, B4427, Praeger Pubs) Greenwood.

Courts, Randy & St. Germain, Mark. Jack's Holiday: A Musical LC 98-131018. (French's Musical Library). 127 p. 1997. write for info. (*0-573-69584-9*) French.

Courts, Randy, jt. auth. see St. Germain, Mark.

Courtwright, David T. Dark Paradise: Opiate Addiction in America before 1940. LC 81-6958. (Illus.). 280p. 1982. 37.95 (*0-674-19261-3*) HUP.

— Violent Land: Single Men & Social Disorder from the Frontier to the Inner City. LC 96-9277. (Illus.). 416p. 1996. 32.00 (*0-674-27870-4*) HUP.

— Violent Land: Single Men & Social Disorder from the Frontier to the Inner City. (Illus.). 400p. 1998. pap. text 17.95 (*0-674-27871-2*) HUP.

Courtwright, David T., et al. Addicts Who Survived: An Oral History of Narcotic Use in America, 1923-1965. LC 88-20583. (Illus.). 416p. 1989. 34.00 (*0-87049-587-9*) U of Tenn Pr.

Courville, Jacques, et al, eds. The Inferior Olivary Nucleus: Anatomy & Physiology. fac. ed. LC 76-63918. (Illus.). 408p. pap. 126.50 (*0-7837-7252-1*, 204705300005) Bks Demand.

Courville, Serge, jt. ed. see Boucher, Philip P.

Courvisanos, Jerry. Investment Cycles in Capitalist Economies: A Kaleckian Behavioural Contribution. LC 96-14167. (New Directions in Modern Economics Ser.). (Illus.). 288p. (C). 1996. text 95.00 (*1-85898-410-6*) E Elgar.

Courvoisier, T. J. & Blecha, A., eds. Multi-Wavelength Continuum Emission of AGN: Proceedings of the 159th Symposium of the International Astronomical Union Held in Geneva, Switzerland, August 30-September 3, 1993. LC 94-4220. (International Astronomical Union Symposia Ser.). 564p. (C). 1994. lib. bdg. 183.00 (*0-7923-2744-6*) Kluwer Academic.

Coury, Elaine. Terence's Bembine Phormio: A Palaeographic Examination. LC 81-71636. (Illus.). 150p. 1982. 59.00 (*0-86516-011-2*) Bolchazy-Carducci.

Coury, Elaine, ed. see Terence.

Coury, John E., jt. auth. see Adler, Andrew.

Coury, Ralph M. Making of an Egyptian Arab Nationalist: The Early Years of Azzam Pasha, 1893-1936. 250p. 1998. 45.00 (*0-86372-233-4*, Pub. by Garnet-Ithaca) LPC InBook.

Cous, Hippocrates. Hippocratis Qui Fertur De Morbis Mulierum Liber Primus. Plieninger, Helga, ed. write for info. (*0-318-70940-6*) G Olms Pubs.

Cousain, Hattie M. When I Was Little. (J). 8.95 (*0-9640459-0-7*) C Coles Cnslt.

Cousar, Charles B. Galatians. LC 81-82354. (Interpretation: A Bible Commentary for Teaching & Preaching Ser.). 168p. (C). 1986. 21.00 (*0-8042-3138-9*) Westminster John Knox.

— A Theology of the Cross: The Death of Jesus in the Pauline Letters. LC 90-31424. (Overtures to Biblical Theology Ser.). 208p. (Orig.). 1990. pap. 17.00 (*0-8006-1558-1*, 1-1558) Augsburg Fortress.

Cousar, Charles B., et al. Texts for Preaching: A Lectionary Commentary Based on the NRSV - Year C. 624p. 1994. 33.00 (*0-664-22000-2*) Westminster John Knox.

Cousar, Charles B., jt. ed. see Tucker, Gene M.

Cousar, Jane. Affirm Your Life: Life-Affirming Statements for Everyone. LC 98-116460. (Illus.). 140p. (Orig.). 1996. pap. 9.95 (*0-9653195-0-4*) Hearts Content.

Cousar, Robert M., ed. Digest of the Laws & Decisions Relating to the Appointment, Salary, & Compensation of the Officials of the United States Courts: With the Instructions of the Attorney-General to United States District Attorneys, Clerks, & Marshals. 300p. 1991. reprint ed. 42.50 (*0-8377-2018-4*, Rothman) W S Hein.

***Cousens, Elizabeth M. & Cater, Charles K.** Toward Peace in Bosnia: Implementing the Dayton Accords. (IPA Occasional Paper Ser.). 110p. 2000. pap. 9.95 (*1-55587-942-X*) L Rienner.

***Cousens, Elizabeth M. & Kumar, Chetan, eds.** Peacebuilding as Politics: Cultivating Peace in Fragile Societies. (Project of the International Peace Academy Ser.). 220p. 2000. 45.00 (*1-55587-921-7*); pap. 16.95 (*1-55587-946-2*) L Rienner.

Cousens, Gabriel. Conscious Eating. 2nd ed. LC 98-50038. 450p. 2000. pap. 35.00 (*1-55643-285-2*) North Atlantic.

— Spiritual Nutrition & the Rainbow Diet. 239p. 1986. 13.95 (*0-9615875-2-0*) Cassandra Pr.

Cousens, Gabriel & Mayell, Mark. Depression-Free for Life: An All-Natural, Five-Step Plan to Reclaim Your Zest for Living. LC 99-40101. 288p. 2000. 23.00 (*0-688-16500-1*, Wm Morrow) Morrow Avon.

Cousens, Gabriel & Wagner, David. Tachyon Energy: A New Paradigm in Holistic Healing. (Illus.). 120p. 1999. pap. 12.95 (*1-55643-310-7*) North Atlantic.

Cousens, H. The Architectural Antiquities of Western India. (Illus.). 1983. text 34.00 (*0-685-14107-1*) Coronet Bks.

Cousens, Michael & Blair, Ruth M., eds. Butterworths Police & Criminal Evidence Act Cases. ring bd. write for info. (*0-406-99649-0*, BPCEASET, MICHIE) LEXIS Pub.

Cousens, Mildred. Time to Consider. 1990. 12.95 (*0-87233-099-0*) Bauhan.

Cousens, Roger & Mortimer, Martin. Dynamics of Weed Populations. (Illus.). 346p. (C). 1995. text 80.00 (*0-521-49649-7*); pap. text 30.95 (*0-521-49669-0*) Cambridge U Pr.

Couser, G. Thomas. Altered Egos: Authority in American Autobiography. 304p. 1989. text 65.00 (*0-19-505833-X*) OUP.

— Recovering Bodies: Illness, Disability, & Life-Writing. LC 97-11952. (Wisconsin Studies in American Autobiography). 334p. 1997. 55.00 (*0-299-15560-9*); pap. 24.95 (*0-299-15564-1*) U of Wis Pr.

Couser, G. Thomas & Fichtelberg, Joseph, eds. True Relations: Essays on Autobiography & the Postmodern. 85. LC 97-9384. (Contributions to the Study of World Literature Ser.: Vol. 85). 184p. 1998. 55.00 (*0-313-30509-9*, Greenwood Pr) Greenwood.

Couser, Richard B. Ministry & the American Legal System: A Guide for Clergy, Lay Workers, & Congregations. LC 92-34214. 360p. 1993. 42.00 (*0-8006-2603-5*, 1-2603, Fortress Pr) Augsburg Fortress.

Couser, Thomas. Real Men Pray Vol. 28, No. 2: Prayer Thoughts for Husbands & Fathers. LC 95-53687. Vol. 2. 304p. 1996. pap. 13.99 (*0-570-04849-4*) Concordia.

Cousin Alice, ed. see Bradley, Mary E.

***Cousin, Evelyn.** That Saved a Wretch Like Me. 113p. 1999. pap. 11.95 (*1-881524-65-5*, Prof Busn) Mill gan Bks.

Cousin, Geraldine. Churchill the Playwright. (Modern Theatre Profiles Ser.). (Illus.). 135p. (C). 1989. pap. write for info. (*0-413-14790-8*, A0051, Methuen Drama) Methn.

— King John. LC 93-49013. (Shakespeare in Performance Ser.). 1994. text 69.95 (*0-7190-2753-5*) Manchester Univ Pr.

***Cousin, Geraldine.** Recording Women: A Documentation of Six Theatre Productions. (Contemporary Theatre Studies: Vol. 34). (Illus.). 180p. 2000. text 36.00 (*90-5755-092-X*, Harwood Acad Pubs) Gordon & Breach.

Cousin, Geraldine. Women in Dramatic Place & Time: Contemporary Female Characters on Stage. 224p. (C). 1996. 85.00 (*0-415-06733-2*); pap. 25.99 (*0-415-06734-0*) Routledge.

Cousin, Margaret J., ed. see African Methodist Episcopal Church, First Episcopa.

Cousin, Michelle. Writing a Television Play. 2nd rev. ed. xiii, 202p. 1986. pap. 18.95 (*0-931642-18-3*) Lintel.

Cousin, Patricia T., et al. All Dressed Up. (Visions: African-American Experiences: Vol. 1). (Illus.). 8p. (Orig.). (J). (gr. k-1). 1996. pap. text 3.00 (*1-57518-043-X*) Arborlake.

— The Alphabet Race. (Visions: African-American Experiences: No. 31). (Illus.). 8p. (Orig.). (J). (gr. k-1). 1996. pap. text 3.00 (*1-57518-030-8*) Arborlake.

— At Christmas Time. (Visions: African-American Experiences: No. 2). (Illus.). 8p. (Orig.). (J). (gr. k-1). 1995. pap. text 3.00 (*1-57518-001-4*) Arborlake.

— At the Playground. (Visions: African-American Experiences: No. 32). (Illus.). 8p. (Orig.). (J). (gr. k-1). 1996. pap. text 3.00 (*1-57518-031-6*) Arborlake.

— At the Store. (Visions: African-American Experiences: No. 1). (Illus.). 8p. (Orig.). (J). (gr. k-1). 1995. pap. text 3.00 (*1-57518-000-6*) Arborlake.

— Bare Feet. (Visions: African-American Experiences: No. 3). (Illus.). 8p. (Orig.). (J). (gr. k-1). 1995. pap. text 3.00 (*1-57518-002-2*) Arborlake.

— Big Sister. (Visions: African-American Experiences: No. 4). (Illus.). 8p. (Orig.). (J). (gr. k-1). 1995. pap. text 3.00 (*1-57518-003-0*) Arborlake.

— Church. (Visions: African-American Experiences: No. 6). (Illus.). 8p. (Orig.). (J). (gr. k-1). 1995. pap. text 3.00 (*1-57518-005-7*) Arborlake.

— The City Bus. (Visions: African-American Experiences: No. 23). (Illus.). 8p. (Orig.). (J). (gr. k-1). 1995. pap. text 3.00 (*1-57518-022-7*) Arborlake.

— City Lights. (Visions: African-American Experiences: No. 33). (Illus.). 8p. (Orig.). (J). (gr. k-1). 1996. pap. text 3.00 (*1-57518-032-4*) Arborlake.

— Dancing. (Visions: African-American Experiences: No. 7). (Illus.). 8p. (Orig.). (J). (gr. k-1). 1995. pap. text 3.00 (*1-57518-006-5*) Arborlake.

— First Day of School. (Visions: African-American Experiences: No. 24). (Illus.). 8p. (Orig.). (J). (gr. k-1). 1996. pap. text 3.00 (*1-57518-023-5*) Arborlake.

— Fly High. (Visions: African-American Experiences: No. 34). (Illus.). 8p. (Orig.). (J). (gr. k-1). 1996. pap. text 3.00 (*1-57518-033-2*) Arborlake.

— Football. (Visions: African-American Experiences: No. 25). (Illus.). 8p. (Orig.). (J). (gr. k-1). 1996. pap. text 3.00 (*1-57518-024-3*) Arborlake.

— For Breakfast. (Visions: African-American Experiences: No. 35). (Illus.). 8p. (Orig.). (J). (gr. k-1). 1996. pap. text 3.00 (*1-57518-034-0*) Arborlake.

— Fruit Trees. (Visions: African-American Experiences: No. 36). (Illus.). 8p. (Orig.). (J). (gr. k-1). 1996. pap. text 3.00 (*1-57518-035-9*) Arborlake.

— Going to the Park with Granddaddy. (Visions: African-American Experiences: No. 26). (Illus.). 8p. (Orig.). (J). (gr. k-1). 1996. pap. text 3.00 (*1-57518-025-1*) Arborlake.

— I Can. (Visions: African-American Experiences: No. 5). (Illus.). 8p. (Orig.). (J). (gr. k-1). 1995. pap. text 3.00 (*1-57518-004-9*) Arborlake.

— I Could Be. (Visions: African-American Experiences: No. 8). (Illus.). 8p. (Orig.). (J). (gr. k-1). 1995. pap. text 3.00 (*1-57518-007-3*) Arborlake.

— I Dress up Like Mama. (Visions: African-American Experiences: No. 9). (Illus.). 8p. (Orig.). (J). (gr. k-1). 1995. pap. text 3.00 (*1-57518-008-1*) Arborlake.

— I Get Ready for School. (Visions: African-American Experiences: No. 27). (Illus.). 8p. (Orig.). (J). (gr. k-1). 1996. pap. text 3.00 (*1-57518-026-X*) Arborlake.

— I Have Shoes. (Visions: African-American Experiences: No. 10). (Illus.). 8p. (Orig.). (J). (gr. k-1). 1995. pap. text 3.00 (*1-57518-009-X*) Arborlake.

— I Like Fruit. (Visions: African-American Experiences: No. 37). (Illus.). 8p. (Orig.). (J). (gr. k-1). 1996. pap. text 3.00 (*1-57518-036-7*) Arborlake.

— I Like Me. (Visions: African-American Experiences: No. 11). (Illus.). 8p. (Orig.). (J). (gr. k-1). 1995. pap. text 3.00 (*1-57518-010-3*) Arborlake.

— I Thought I Couldn't. (Visions: African-American Experiences: No. 12). (Illus.). 8p. (Orig.). (J). (gr. k-1). 1995. pap. text 3.00 (*1-57518-011-1*) Arborlake.

— I Want My Own Room. (Visions: African-American Experiences: No. 13). (Illus.). 8p. (Orig.). (J). (gr. k-1). 1995. pap. text 3.00 (*1-57518-012-X*) Arborlake.

— I'm Hungry. (Visions: African-American Experiences: No. 14). (Illus.). 8p. (Orig.). (J). (gr. k-1). 1995. pap. text 3.00 (*1-57518-013-8*) Arborlake.

— In My Backyard. (Visions: African-American Experiences: No. 38). (Illus.). 8p. (Orig.). (J). (gr. k-1). 1995. pap. text 3.00 (*1-57518-037-5*) Arborlake.

— The Laundromat. (Visions: African-American Experiences: No. 28). (Illus.). 8p. (Orig.). (J). (gr. k-1). 1996. pap. text 3.00 (*1-57518-027-8*) Arborlake.

— Love Is. (Visions: African-American Experiences: No. 15). (Illus.). 8p. (Orig.). (J). (gr. k-1). 1995. pap. text 3.00 (*1-57518-014-6*) Arborlake.

— My Apartment. (Visions: African-American Experiences: No. 16). (Illus.). 8p. (Orig.). (J). (gr. k-1). 1995. pap. text 3.00 (*1-57518-015-4*) Arborlake.

— My Big Wheel. (Visions: African-American Experiences: No. 17). (Illus.). 8p. (Orig.). (J). (gr. k-1). 1995. pap. text 3.00 (*1-57518-016-2*) Arborlake.

C

— My Birthday Party. (Visions: African-American Experiences: No. 18). (Illus.). 8p. (Orig.). (J). (gr. k-1). 1995. pap. text 3.00 (*1-57518-017-0*) Arborlake.
— My Friend at School. (Visions: African-American Experiences: No. 29). (Illus.). 8p. (Orig.). (J). (gr. k-1). 1996. pap. text 3.00 (*1-57518-028-6*) Arborlake.
— My Mama. (Visions: African-American Experiences: No. 19). (Illus.). 8p. (Orig.). (J). (gr. k-1). 1995. pap. text 3.00 (*1-57518-018-9*) Arborlake.
— My Uncle's Truck. (Visions: African-American Experiences: No. 20). (Illus.). 8p. (Orig.). (J). (gr. k-1). 1995. pap. text 3.00 (*1-57518-019-7*) Arborlake.
— Shapes. (Visions: African-American Experiences: No. 39). (Illus.). 8p. (Orig.). (J). (gr. k-1). 1995. pap. text 3.00 (*1-57518-038-3*) Arborlake.
— Sometimes I'm Silly. (Visions: African-American Experiences: No. 21). (Illus.). 8p. (Orig.). (J). (gr. k-1). 1995. pap. text 3.00 (*1-57518-020-0*) Arborlake.
— Spots. (Visions: African-American Experiences: No. 40). (Illus.). 8p. (Orig.). (J). (gr. k-1). 1995. pap. text 3.00 (*1-57518-039-1*) Arborlake.
— The Train. (Visions: African-American Experiences: No. 30). (Illus.). 8p. (Orig.). (J). (gr. k-1). 1996. pap. text 3.00 (*1-57518-029-4*) Arborlake.
— Visions: African-American Experiences, 40 vols. (Young Readers Ser.). (Illus.). (Orig.). (J). (gr. k-1). 1995. pap. text 125.00 (*1-57518-040-5*) Arborlake.
— Visions: Early Emergent Teacher's Resource Guide. (Visions: African-American Experiences). (Illus.). (Orig.). 1995. pap. text 14.50 (*1-57518-041-3*) Arborlake.
— What's under My Bed? (Visions: African-American Experiences: No. 22). (Illus.). 8p. (Orig.). (J). (gr. k-1). 1995. pap. text 3.00 (*1-57518-021-9*) Arborlake.

Cousin, Patricia T., jt. ed. see Poplin, Mary S.

***Cousin, Pierre & Lee, Wendy.** The Oxford Easy French Grammar. 128p. 2000. pap. 7.95 (*0-19-860341-X*) OUP.
— The Oxford Easy Spanish Grammar. 128p. 2000. pap. 7.95 (*0-19-860343-6*) OUP.

Cousin, Pierre-Henri. Dictionnaire Collins Francais-Anglais, Anglais-Francais. (ENG & FRE.). 1990. write for info. (*0-7859-7893-3*, 2-501-01445-6) Fr & Eur.

***Cousin, Pierre-Henri.** French Concise Dictionary Plus Grammar. rev. ed. 255p. 2000. reprint ed. pap. 15.00 (*0-7881-9345-7*) DIANE Pub.

Cousin, Pierre-Henry. Dictionnaire Francais-Anglais, Anglais-Francais. (ENG & FRE.). 1988. write for info. (*0-7859-7602-7*, 2010095804) Fr & Eur.

***Cousin, Pierre Jean.** Aromatherapy Facial Massage. LC 99-46586. 128p. 2000. pap. 16.95 (*1-58017-242-3*) Storey Bks.

Cousin, Victor, ed. see Diadochus, Proclus.

Cousineau. Art of the Pilgrimage. 288p. 1999. 7.98 (*1-56731-351-5*, MJF Bks) Fine Comms.

Cousineau, Alain, ed. see American Marketing Association.

Cousineau, Diane. Letters & Labyrinths: Women Writing/Cultural Codes. LC 96-53198. 232p. 1997. 36.50 (*0-87413-627-X*) U Delaware Pr.

Cousineau, G. & Mauny, M. The Functional Approach to Programming. LC 97-42892. (Illus.). 460p. (C). 1998. text 85.00 (*0-521-57183-9*); pap. text 39.95 (*0-521-57681-4*) Cambridge U Pr.

Cousineau, Jacques G. Methode de Harpe. fac. ed. (Monuments of Music & Music Literature in Facsimile Ser., Series II: Vol. 86). 1968. lib. bdg. 45.00 (*0-8450-2286-5*) Broude.

Cousineau, Leslie & Miura, Nobuyasu. Construction Robots: The Search for New Building Technology in Japan. LC 97-46869. (Illus.). 144p. 1998. pap. 39.00 (*0-7844-0317-1*) Am Soc Civil Eng.

Cousineau, Madeleine, ed. Religion in a Changing World: Comparative Studies in Sociology. LC 98-15658. (Religion in the Age of Transformation Ser.). 256p. 1998. 65.00 (*0-275-96078-1*, Praeger Pubs); pap. 22.95 (*0-275-96079-X*, Praeger Pubs) Greenwood.

Cousineau, Paul, ed. The Hero's Journey: The Life & Work of Joseph Campbell. 256p. 1999. text 29.95 (*1-86204-598-4*, Pub. by Element MA) Penguin Putnam.

Cousineau, Phil. The Art of Pilgrimage: A Seeker's Guide to Making Travel Sacred. LC 98-39639. (Illus.). 300p. 1998. 20.00 (*1-57324-080-X*) Conari Press.

***Cousineau, Phil.** The Art of Pilgrimage: The Seekers Guide to Making Travel Sacred. (Illus.). 288p. 2000. reprint ed. pap. 16.95 (*1-57324-509-7*) Conari Press.
— Riddle Me This: A World Treasury of Word Puzzles, Folk Wisdom, & Literary Conundrums. LC 98-54332. 200p. 1999. 13.13 (*1-57324-145-8*) Conari Press.

Cousineau, Phil. Soul Moments: Marvelous Stories of Synchroncidy - Meaning Coincidences from a Seemingly Random World. LC 97-1301. 224p. (Orig.). 1997. pap. 14.95 (*1-57324-079-6*) Conari Press.
— UFOs: A Manual for the Millenium. LC 95-7239. 272p. 1995. mass mkt. 5.99 (*0-06-258638-6*) HarpC.

Cousineau, Phil, ed. The Soul of the World: A Modern Book of Hours. LC 92-53902. (Illus.). 1993. pap. 15.00 (*0-06-251004-5*, Pub. by Harper SF) HarpC.

Cousineau, Phil & Lawton, Eric. The Soul Aflame: A Modern Book of Hours. LC 99-58207. 128p. 1999. pap. 18.95 (*1-57324-186-5*) Conari Press.

Cousineau, Phil, jt. ed. see Zelov, Chris.

Cousineau, Robert H. Zarathustra & the Ethical Ideal: Timely Meditations on Philosophy. LC 91-21726. x, 224p. 1991. 76.00 (*1-55619-114-6*) J Benjamins Pubng Co.

Cousineau, Ruth. Country Suppers: Simple, Hearty Fare for Family & Friends. Hoenig, Pamela, ed. LC 97-7232. (Illus.). 288p. 1997. 24.00 (*0-688-15223-6*, Wm Morrow) Morrow Avon.

Cousineau, Thomas J. After the Final No: Samuel Beckett's Trilogy. LC 98-33979. 168p. 1999. 32.50 (*0-87413-662-8*) U Delaware Pr.

Cousins. Pain: Scientific Basis & Clin. 2000. text. write for info. (*0-7216-6220-X*, W B Saunders Co) Harcrt Hlth Sci Grp.

***Cousins, A. D.** Shakespeare: The Sonnets & Narrative Poems. LC 99-16779. (Medieval & Renaissance Library Ser.). 240p. (C). 1999. pap. 31.80 (*0-582-21512-9*) Longman.
— Shakespeare: The Sonnets & Narrative Poems. LC 99-16779. (Medieval & Renaissance Library Ser.). 240p. 2000. 85.95 (*0-582-21513-7*) Longman.

Cousins, A. D. & Grace, Damian, eds. More's Utopia & Utopian Inheritance. LC 95-9779. 159p. 1995. lib. bdg. 37.50 (*0-8191-9915-X*) U Pr of Amer.

Cousins, A. D., jt. auth. see Condren, Conal.

***Cousins, Barbara.** Cooking Without: Recipes Free from Added Gluten, Sugar, Dairy Products, Yeast, Salt & Saturated Fat. (Illus.). (J). 2000. pap. 16.95 (*0-7225-4022-1*) Thorsons.

Cousins, Bill, jt. auth. see Cousins, Jean.

Cousins, Christine. Society, Work & Welfare in Europe. LC 98-35436. 224p. 1999. text 55.00 (*0-312-21889-3*) St Martin.

Cousins, Colleen C., jt. auth. see Reynolds, Tonga.

Cousins, Don & Poling, Judson. Amistad Con Dios. (Serie Caminemos Con Dios).Tr. of Friendship with God. (SPA.). 1994. 6.99 (*0-89922-484-9*, C014-4849) Caribe Betania.
— Building Your Church. (Walking with God Ser.). 96p. 1992. pap. 5.99 (*0-310-59183-X*) Zondervan.
— El Cristo Incomparable. (Serie Caminemos Con Dios).Tr. of Incomparable Christ. (SPA.). 1999. 6.99 (*0-89922-485-7*, C014-4857) Caribe Betania.
— Desarrollemos Nuestra Iglesia. (Serie Caminemos Con Dios).Tr. of Building Your Church. (SPA.). 1995. 5.99 (*0-89922-507-1*, C014-5071) Caribe Betania.
— Discovering the Church. (Walking with God Ser.). 96p. 1992. pap. 5.99 (*0-310-59173-2*) Zondervan.
— Follow Me. (Walking with God Ser.). 96p. 1992. pap. 5.99 (*0-310-59163-5*) Zondervan.
— Friendship with God. (Walking with God Ser.). 96p. 1992. pap. 5.99 (*0-310-59143-0*) Zondervan.
— La Iglesia: Un Concepto Mejor. (Serie Caminemos con Dios).Tr. of Discovering the Church. (SPA.). 1995. 6.99 (*0-89922-506-3*, C014-5063) Caribe Betania.
— Impacte Al Mundo. (Serie Caminemos con Dios).Tr. of Impacting the World. (SPA.). 1995. 6.99 (*0-89922-508-X*, C014-508X) Caribe Betania.
— Impacting Your World. (Walking with God Ser.). 96p. 1992. pap. 5.99 (*0-310-59193-7*) Zondervan.
— The Incomparable Jesus. (Walking with God Ser.). 96p. 1992. pap. 5.99 (*0-310-59153-8*) Zondervan.
— Serie Caminemos Con Dios Tutor, No. 1.Tr. of Walking with God Series Leaders' Guide. (SPA.). 1994. teacher ed. 12.99 (*0-89922-482-2*, C014-4822) Caribe Betania.
— Serie Caminemos Con Dios Tutor, No. 2.Tr. of Walking with God Series Leaders' Guide. (SPA.). 1995. teacher ed. 12.99 (*0-89922-500-4*, C014-5004) Caribe Betania.
— Sigueme! (Serie Caminemos Con Dios).Tr. of Follow Me!. (SPA.). 1999. 6.99 (*0-89922-486-5*, C014-4865) Caribe Betania.
— Walking with God: Leaders Guide, Vol. I. 500p. 1992. pap., teacher ed. 22.99 (*0-310-59203-8*) Zondervan.
— Walking with God: Leaders Guide, Vol. II. 500p. 1992. pap., teacher ed. 22.99 (*0-310-59213-5*) Zondervan.

Cousins, E. F. & Anthony, R. Pease & Chitty's Law of Markets & Fairs. 500p. 1993. 60.00 (*0-85314-534-2*, Pub. by Tolley Pubng) St Mut.

Cousins, Eleanor. Caring for the Healing Heart: An Eating Plan for Recovery from Heart Attack. 160p. 1989. pap. 3.95 (*0-380-70744-6*, Avon Bks) Morrow Avon.

Cousins, Ewert, ed. Bonaventure: The Soul's Journey into God: the Tree of Life, the Life of Francis. LC 78-60723. (Classics of Western Spirituality Ser.). 380p. 1978. pap. 19.95 (*0-8091-2121-2*) Paulist Pr.

Cousins, Ewert, ed. see Green, Arthur.

Cousins, Ewert H. Bonaventure & the Coincidence of Opposites: The Theology of Bonaventure. 316p. 1978. 12.95 (*0-8199-0580-1*, Frncscn Herld) Franciscan Pr.
— Christ of the Twenty-First Century. 224p. 1994. reprint ed. pap. 15.95 (*0-8264-0699-8*) Continuum.

Cousins, Frank & Riley, Phil M. The Colonial Architecture of Salem. (Illus.). 282p. 1989. reprint ed. lib. bdg. 39.00 (*0-8328-1400-8*) Higginson Bk Co.
— Wood Carver of Salem: Samuel McIntire, His Life & Work. LC 74-119649. (BCL Ser. II). reprint ed. 39.50 (*0-404-01786-X*) AMS Pr.
— The Wood-Carver of Salem: Samuel McIntire, His Life & Work. (Illus.). 168p. 1989. reprint ed. lib. bdg. 39.00 (*0-8328-1399-0*) Higginson Bk Co.

Cousins, J. Bradley & Earl, Lorna M., eds. Participatory Evaluation in Education: Studies in Evaluation Use & Organizational Learning. LC 95-7253. 224p. 1995. 79.95 (*0-7507-0402-0*, Falmer Pr); pap. 34.95 (*0-7507-0403-9*, Falmer Pr) Taylor & Francis.

Cousins, Jean. Nature Walks Around Vancouver. LC 96-910831. 1997. pap. write for info. (*1-55054-562-0*) DGL.

Cousins, Jean. The Shiftwork Swindle. (C). 1988. 21.00 (*0-901108-81-2*, Pub. by NCCL) St Mut.

Cousins, Jean & Cousins, Bill. Tales from Wide Ruins: Jean & Bill Cousins, Traders. Engels, Mary T., ed. LC 96-2260. (Illus.). 264p. 1996. 29.95 (*0-89672-368-2*) Tex Tech Univ Pr.

Cousins, Jill & Robinson, Lesley. The Online Manual: A Practical Guide to Business Databases. 2nd ed. 837p. 1993. 238.95 (*0-631-18931-9*) Blackwell Pubs.

Cousins, John, et al. Food & Beverage Management. 288p. (Orig.). 1995. pap. 47.50 (*0-582-27543-1*) Trans-Atl Phila.

Cousins, John, jt. auth. see Durkin, Andrew.

Cousins, Kelley, ed. see Woods, Debby.

Cousins, L., et al, eds. Buddhist Studies in Honour of I. B. Horner. LC 74-77963. 275p. 1974. lib. bdg. 148.50 (*90-277-0473-2*) Kluwer Academic.

Cousins, Linda. Caribbean Bound! Culture Roots, Places, & People. 160p. (Orig.). 1994. pap. 9.95 (*0-930569-02-4*) Univ Black Pr.
— Monica Made Me Promise. (Illus.). 32p. (J). (gr. 5-8). 1994. pap. 3.99 (*0-912444-39-8*) DARE Bks.

Cousins, Linda, ed. Ancient Black Youth & Elders Reborn. LC 84-50898. (Illus.). 252p. (Orig.). 1985. pap. 10.00 (*0-930569-00-8*) Univ Black Pr.

Cousins, Lucy. El Arca De Noe Noah's Ark. 1998. 10.95 (*84-88061-66-8*) Lectorum Pubns.
— Count with Maisy. LC 96-85446. (Maisy Bks.). (Illus.). 24p. (J). (ps). 1997. 8.99 (*0-7636-0156-X*) Candlewick Pr.
— Count with Maisy. LC 96-85446. (Maisy Bks.). (Illus.). 24p. (J). (ps). 1999. bds. 5.99 (*0-7636-0234-5*, Pub. by Candlewick Pr) Penguin Putnam.
— Country Animals. LC 98-73055. (Illus.). 14p. (J). (ps). 1999. bds. 3.99 (*0-7636-0609-X*, Pub. by Candlewick Pr) Penguin Putnam.

***Cousins, Lucy.** Dress Maisy Sticker Book. (Illus.). 16p. (ps-k). 1999. pap. text 3.99 (*0-7636-0749-5*) Candlewick Pr.

Cousins, Lucy. Farm Animals. LC 98-73056. (Illus.). 14p. (J). (ps). 1999. bds. 3.99 (*0-7636-0610-3*, Pub. by Candlewick Pr) Penguin Putnam.
— Flower in the Garden. LC 91-71854. (Illus.). 8p. (J). (ps). 1992. 5.95 (*1-56402-029-0*) Candlewick Pr.
— Garden Animals. LC 98-73053. (Illus.). 14p. (J). (ps). 1999. bds. 3.99 (*0-7636-0611-1*, Pub. by Candlewick Pr) Penguin Putnam.
— Happy Birthday Maisy. LC 97-75274. (Maisy Bks.). (Illus.). 16p. (J). (ps). 1998. 12.99 (*0-7636-0577-8*) Candlewick Pr.

***Cousins, Lucy.** Feliz Cumpleanos, Maisy. (Maisy Bks.). (Illus.). (J). (ps). 1999. 16.95 (*84-88061-96-X*) SL Ed Serres.

Cousins, Lucy. Hen on the Farm. LC 91-71849. (Illus.). 8p. (J). (ps). 1992. 5.95 (*1-56402-032-0*) Candlewick Pr.
— Katy Cat & Beaky Boo. LC 95-71374. (Illus.). 24p. (J). (ps). 1996. 14.99 (*1-56402-884-4*) Candlewick Pr.
— Katy Cat & Beaky Boo's Play Set. LC 98-102723. (Illus.). (J). (ps-2). 1997. 22.99 (*0-7636-0345-7*) Candlewick Pr.
— Kite in the Park. LC 91-71842. (Illus.). 8p. (J). (ps). 1992. 5.95 (*1-56402-031-2*) Candlewick Pr.
— Little Miss Muffet. LC 97-150996. (J). 1997. pap. 5.99 (*0-525-45749-6*) NAL.
— The Lucy Cousins Book of Nursery Rhymes. 64p. (ps-k). 1999. 16.99 (*0-525-46133-7*, Dutton Child) Peng Put Young Read.
— The Lucy Cousins Book of Nursery Rhymes. 32p. (J). (ps-1). 1999. pap. 5.99 (*0-14-056495-0*, PuffinBks) Peng Put Young Read.
— Lucy Cousins Book of Nursery Rhymes & Beanbag. (Illus.). (J). (ps up). 2000. 14.99 (*0-525-46081-0*, Dutton Child) Peng Put Young Read.
— Maisy & Her Friends. 1999. pap. text. write for info. (*0-7636-0821-1*) Candlewick Pr.
— Maisy at the Farm. LC 97-92360. (Maisy Bks.). (Illus.). 16p. (J). (ps). 1998. 12.99 (*0-7636-0576-X*) Candlewick Pr.

***Cousins, Lucy.** Maisy en la Granja. (Maisy Bks.). (Illus.). (J). (ps). 1999. 16.95 (*84-88061-97-8*) SL Ed Serres.

Cousins, Lucy. Maisy Dresses Up. LC 98-43219. (Maisy Bks.). (Illus.). 24p. (J). (ps). 1999. 10.99 (*0-7636-0885-8*) Candlewick Pr.

***Cousins, Lucy.** Maisy Dresses Up. LC 98-43219. (Maisy Bks.). (Illus.). 24p. (J). (ps). 1999. pap. 3.29 (*0-7636-0909-9*) Candlewick Pr.
— Maisy Drives the Bus. LC 99-54075. (Maisy Bks.). (Illus.). 24p. (J). (ps). 2000. 3.29 (*0-7636-1085-2*) Candlewick Pr.
— Maisy Drives the Bus. LC 99-54075. (Maisy Bks.). (Illus.). 24p. (J). (ps-k). 2000. 9.99 (*0-7636-1083-6*) Candlewick Pr.

Cousins, Lucy. Maisy Goes Swimming. (Maisy Bks.). 14p. (J). (ps). 1990. 13.95 (*0-316-15834-8*) Little.
— Maisy Goes to Bed. LC 89-43577. (Maisy Bks.). (Illus.). 14p. (J). (ps). 1990. 13.95 (*0-316-15832-1*) Little.
— Maisy Goes to School. LC 91-58743. (Maisy Bks.). (Illus.). 16p. (J). (ps). 1992. 12.95 (*1-56402-085-1*) Candlewick Pr.
— Maisy Goes to the Playground. LC 91-58742. (Maisy Bks.). (Illus.). 16p. (J). (ps). 1992. 12.95 (*1-56402-084-3*) Candlewick Pr.

Cousins, Lucy. Maisy Se Va al Parque. (Maisy Bks.). (SPA., Illus.). (J). (ps). 1997. 16.95 (*84-88061-45-5*) SL Ed Serres.

Cousins, Lucy. Maisy Makes Gingerbread. LC 98-53909. (Maisy Bks.). (Illus.). 24p. (J). (ps). 1999. 10.99 (*0-7636-0887-4*) Candlewick Pr.

***Cousins, Lucy.** Maisy Makes Gingerbread. LC 98-53909. (Maisy Bks.). (Illus.). 24p. (J). (ps). 1999. pap. 3.29 (*0-7636-0910-2*) Candlewick Pr.
— Maisy Takes a Bath. LC 99-53240. (Maisy Bks.). (Illus.). 24p. (J). (ps). 2000. 9.99 (*0-7636-1082-8*); pap. 3.29 (*0-7636-1084-4*) Candlewick Pr.
— Maisy y Sus Amigos. (SPA., Illus.). (J). (ps-k). 1999. 16.95 (*84-95040-02-6*) SL Ed Serres.

Cousins, Lucy. Maisy's Bedtime. LC 98-49555. (Maisy Bks.). (Illus.). 24p. (J). (ps). 1999. 10.99 (*0-7636-0884-X*); pap. 3.29 (*0-7636-0908-0*) Candlewick Pr.

***Cousins, Lucy.** Maisy's Busy Book. (Maisy Bks.). (Illus.). (J). (ps). 1999. pap. text 4.99 (*0-7636-0927-7*) Candlewick Pr.

Cousins, Lucy. Maisy's Colors. LC 96-85451. (Maisy Bks.). (Illus.). 24p. (J). (ps). 1997. 8.99 (*0-7636-0159-4*) Candlewick Pr.
— Maisy's Colors. 2nd ed. LC 96-85451. (Maisy Bks.). (Illus.). 24p. (J). (ps). 1999. bds. 5.99 (*0-7636-0237-X*, Pub. by Candlewick Pr) Penguin Putnam.
— Maisy's Day. (Illus.). (ps-k). 1999. pap. text 3.99 (*0-7636-0750-9*) Candlewick Pr.
— Maisy's Favorite Things. (Illus.). 24p. (ps-1). 1999. pap. text 1.49 (*0-7636-0820-3*) Candlewick Pr.
— Maisy's Mix-and-Match Mousewear. LC 00-265158. (Maisy Bks.). (Illus.). 12p. (J). (ps). 1999. 6.99 (*0-7636-0751-7*) Candlewick Pr.
— Maisy's Party Book. (Maisy Bks.). (Illus.). 16p. (J). (ps). 1999. pap. text 4.99 (*0-7636-0926-9*) Candlewick Pr.
— Maisy's Pool. LC 99-14585. (Maisy Bks.). (Illus.). 24p. (J). (ps). 1999. 10.99 (*0-7636-0886-6*); pap. 9.99 (*0-7636-0907-2*) Candlewick Pr.
— Maisy's Pop-Up Playhouse. LC 96-124605. (Maisy Bks.). (Illus.). (J). (ps). 1995. 19.99 (*1-56402-635-3*) Candlewick Pr.

***Cousins, Lucy.** Merry Christmas, Maisy. LC 99-88331. (Maisy Bks.). (Illus.). 24p. (J). (ps). 2000. 12.99 (*0-7636-1279-0*) Candlewick Pr.

Cousins, Lucy. Noah's Ark. LC 92-54589. (Illus.). 24p. (J). (ps-k). 1997. bds. 6.99 (*0-7636-0250-7*) Candlewick Pr.
— Noah's Ark. 1995. 11.19 (*0-606-07957-2*, Pub. by Turtleback) Demco.
— Pet Animals. LC 98-73057. (Illus.). 14p. (J). (ps). 1999. bds. 3.99 (*0-7636-0612-X*, Pub. by Candlewick Pr) Penguin Putnam.
— Teddy in the House. LC 91-71821. (Illus.). 8p. (J). (ps). 1992. 5.95 (*1-56402-030-4*) Candlewick Pr.
— Wee Willie Winkie. LC 97-150457. (J). 1997. pap. 6.99 (*0-525-45751-8*) NAL.
— What Can Pinky Hear? LC 96-85090. (Illus.). 16p. (J). (ps). 1997. reprint ed. pap. 5.99 (*0-7636-0109-8*) Candlewick Pr.
— What Can Pinky See? LC 96-85057. (Illus.). 16p. (J). (ps up). 1997. reprint ed. pap. 5.99 (*0-7636-0110-1*) Candlewick Pr.

***Cousins, Lucy.** Where Are Maisy's Friends? (Maisy Bks.). (Illus.). 12p. (J). (ps). 2000. bds. 4.99 (*0-7636-1119-0*, Pub. by Candlewick Pr) Penguin Putnam.
— Where Does Maisy Live? (Maisy Bks.). (Illus.). 12p. (J). (ps). 2000. bds. 4.99 (*0-7636-1163-8*, Pub. by Candlewick Pr) Penguin Putnam.
— Donde Se Esconde Maisy? (Maisy Bks.). (SPA., Illus.). (J). (ps-k). 1999. 13.50 (*84-95040-05-0*) SL Ed Serres.
— Where Is Maisy? LC 98-86846. (Maisy Bks.). (Illus.). 14p. (J). (ps). 1999. bds. 4.99 (*0-7636-0752-5*) Candlewick Pr.

Cousins, Lucy. Where Is Maisy's Panda? LC 98-86847. (Maisy Bks.). (Illus.). 14p. (J). (ps). 1999. bds. 4.99 (*0-7636-0753-3*) Candlewick Pr.

***Cousins, Lucy.** Donde Esta el Panda de Maisy? (Maisy Bks.). (SPA., Illus.). (J). (ps-k). 1999. 13.50 (*84-95040-07-7*) SL Ed Serres.

Cousins, Lucy. Za-Za's Baby Brother. LC 94-47190. (Illus.). 32p. (J). (ps-3). 1995. 16.95 (*1-56402-582-9*) Candlewick Pr.
— Za-Za's Baby Brother. LC 94-47190. (Illus.). 32p. (J). (ps-3). 1997. reprint ed. pap. 7.99 (*0-7636-0337-6*) Candlewick Pr.

Cousins, Lucy. Jack & Jill: And Other Nursery Rhymes. LC 96-217756. 14p. (J). (ps). 1996. pap. 6.99 (*0-525-45676-7*) NAL.

Cousins, Lucy. Noah's Ark. LC 92-54589. 40p. (J). (ps up). 1993. 15.99 (*1-56402-213-7*) Candlewick Pr.

Cousins, Lucy, retold by. Noah's Ark. LC 92-54589. (Illus.). 32p. (J). (ps-k). 1993. pap. 5.99 (*1-56402-515-2*) Candlewick Pr.

Cousins, M. F. Engineering Drawing from the Beginning, Vol. 2. 1970. 86.00 (*0-08-006853-7*, Pub. by Pergamon Repr); text 29.00 (*0-08-006854-5*, Pub. by Pergamon Repr) Franklin.

Cousins, Margaret. Ben Franklin of Old Philadelphia. Date not set. lib. bdg. 18.95 (*0-8488-2182-3*) Amereon Ltd.
— Ben Franklin of Old Philadelphia. (Landmark Bks.). 1981. 11.09 (*0-606-02039-X*, Pub. by Turtleback) Demco.
— Ben Franklin of Old Philadelphia. LC 81-806. (Landmark Ser.: No. 10). 160p. (J). (gr. 5-9). 1981. reprint ed. pap. 5.99 (*0-394-84928-0*, Pub. by Random Bks Yng Read) Random.
— The Boy in the Alamo. LC 83-72585. (Illus.). 180p. (J). (gr. 5-7). 1983. reprint ed. pap. 8.95 (*0-931722-26-8*) Corona Pub.
— Christmas Keepers: 8 Memorable Stories from the 40s & 50s. LC 96-85581. 1996. 18.00 (*0-931722-55-1*) Corona Pub.
— The Story of Thomas Alva Edison. (Landmark Bks.). (J). 1981. 11.09 (*0-606-11922-1*, Pub. by Turtleback) Demco.

Cousins, Michael. English Matters, Vol. 3. 96p. (J). (gr. 8-10). 1985. pap. 8.95 (*0-7175-1201-0*) Dufour.

Cousins, Michael J., ed. Neural Blockage in Clinical Anesthesia & Management of Pain. 3rd ed. LC 97-26333. 1,200p. 1997. text 169.00 (*0-397-51159-0*) Lppncott W & W.

Cousins, Michael J. & Phillips, Garry D., eds. Acute Pain Management. LC 85-22382. (Clinics in Critical Care Medicine Ser.). (Illus.). 318p. reprint ed. pap. 98.60 (*0-7837-6822-2*, 204665400003) Bks Demand.

Cousins, Michael J., jt. ed. see Tiengo, Mario.

Cousins, Norman. Anatomy of an Illness: As Perceived by the Patient. 20th anniversary ed. 176p. 1995. 18.95 (*0-393-03887-4*) Norton.

An Asterisk (*) at the beginning of an entry indicates that the title is appearing for the first time.

— Anatomy of an Illness As Perceived by the Patient. 176p. 1991. pap. 13.95 (*0-553-34365-3*) Bantam.

— Head First: The Biology of Hope. large type ed. 565p. 1991. reprint ed. lib. bdg. 13.95 (*1-56054-090-7*) Thorndike Pr.

— Head First: The Biology of Hope & the Healing Power of the Human Spirit. 380p. 1990. pap. 19.99 (*0-14-013965-6*, Penguin Bks) Viking Penguin.

— Healing & Belief. LC 82-81098. 64p. 1982. 72.00 (*0-88014-041-0*) Mosaic Pr OH.

— The Healing Heart. 240p. 1984. mass mkt. 4.95 (*0-380-69245-7*, Avon Bks) Morrow Avon.

Cousins, Norman, ed. see Saturday Review Staff.

Cousins, Peter, ed. see Fudge, Edward W.

Cousins, Ronald B. The Effects of Task & Sex of Co-Actor on Female Expectancy Level & Performance. LC 84-22857. (Landmark Dissertations in Women's Studies). 128p. 1984. 47.95 (*0-275-91142-X*, C1142, Praeger Pubs) Greenwood.

Cousins, Russell, et al. Studying & Working in France: A Student Guide. LC 94-12626. 1994. pap. 18.95 (*0-7190-4220-8*, Pub. by Manchester Univ Pr) St Martin.

Cousins, S., ed. Integrating the Automated Factory. 280p. 1988. 8.75 (*0-87263-298-9*) SME.

Cousins, Sandra O'Brien & Horne, Tammy. Active Living among Older Adults: Health Benefits & Outcomes. LC 97-38963. 1997. pap. 29.95 (*1-56032-817-7*) Hemisp Pub.

Cousins, Sandra O'Brien, see O'Brien Cousins, Sandra.

***Cousins, Steven.** Frankenbug. LC 00-35104. 80p. (J). (gr. 3-7). 2000. 15.95 (*0-8234-1496-5*) Holiday.

Cousins, Stewart, jt. auth. see Bell, Brian.

Cousot, Patrick, et al. Static Analysis: Third International Workshop, WSA '93, Padova, Italy, September 1993: Proceedings. LC 93-23377. (Lecture Notes in Computer Science Ser.: Vol. 724). 1993. 44.95 (*0-387-57264-3*) Spr-Verlag.

Cousot, Radhia & Schmidt, David A. Static Analysis: Third International Symposium, SAS '96, Aachen, Germany, September 24-26, 1996 - Proceedings, Vol. 114. LC 96-35936. (Lecture Notes in Computer Science Ser.). ix, 389p. 1996. 62.00 (*3-540-61739-6*) Spr-Verlag.

Coussa, Zaki. Practical Arabic-French Dictionary: Dictionnaire Pratique Arabe-Francais. (ARA & FRE.). 440p. 1986. pap. 26.95 (*0-8288-0997-6*, M15721) Fr & Eur.

— Practical French-Arabic Dictionary (Dictionnaire Pratique Francais-Arabe) 440p. 1986. 24.95 (*0-7859-4851-1*) Fr & Eur.

Coussemaker, Charles E. Scriptorum de Musica Medii Aevi Novam Seriem a Gerbertina Alteram Collegit Nuncque Primum Edidit, 4 vols., Set. 1988. reprint ed. 560.00 (*3-487-05126-5*) G Olms Pubs.

Coussemaker, Charles, pseud. L' Art Harmonique aux Douzieme et Treizieme Siecles. cxvii, 415p. 1964. reprint ed. 160.00 (*0-318-71332-2*) G Olms Pubs.

— Chants Populaires des Flamands de France. xxvi, 419p. 1971. reprint ed. 3.5 hd 130.00 (*3-487-04162-6*) G Olms Pubs.

— Histoire de l'Harmonie au Moyen-Age. lvii, 374p. 1966. reprint ed. 145.00 (*0-318-71333-0*) G Olms Pubs.

— Notice sur les Collections Musicales de la Bibliotheque de Cambrai. 180p. 1975. reprint ed. 50.00 (*3-487-05857-X*) G Olms Pubs.

Coussemaker, Edmond, see Coussemaker, Charles, pseud.

Coussens, Penrhyn. Poems Children Love. LC 72-98078. (Granger Index Reprint Ser.). 1977. 20.95 (*0-8369-6073-4*) Ayer.

Coussins, Jean. The Equality Report. (C). 1988. 30.00 (*0-901108-61-8*, Pub. by NCCL) St Mut.

— Shift Work Swindle. 1979. 25.00 (*0-7855-1468-6*, Pub. by NCCL) St Mut.

Coussirat-Coustere, Vincent, ed. Repertoire de la Jurisprudence Arbitrale Internationale-Repertory of International Arbitral Jurisprudence, Vol. 3, No. 3. (C). 1990. lib. bdg. 585.00 (*0-7923-1083-7*) Kluwer Academic.

Coussirat-Coustere, Vincent & Eisemann, Pierre M., eds. Repertory of International Arbitral Jurisprudence. 1989. lib. bdg. 301.50 (*90-247-3762-1*) Kluwer Academic.

Coussirat-Coustere, Vincent & Eismann, Pierre M., eds. Repertory of International Arbitral Jurisprudence, 2 vols., Vol. 1. (ENG & FRE.). 1989. lib. bdg. 279.50 (*90-247-3761-3*) Kluwer Academic.

— Repertory of International Arbitral Jurisprudence, 2 vols., Vol. 2. (ENG & FRE.). 1991. 287.00 (*0-318-68291-5*) Kluwer Academic.

— Repertory of International Arbitral Jurisprudence, 2 vols., Vol. 3. (ENG & FRE.). 1990. lib. bdg. 663.50 (*0-7923-1090-X*) Kluwer Academic.

Coussons, R. Timothy. Manual of Medical Care. 4th ed. 1990. 34.95 (*0-316-77493-6*, Little Brwn Med Div) Lppncott W & W.

— Manual of Medical Care Asia, No. 4. 1990. 10.95 (*0-316-77490-1*, Little Brwn Med Div) Lppncott W & W.

Coussot, Philippe. Mudflow Rheology & Dynamics. (IAHR Monograph Ser.). (Illus.). 272p. (C). 1997. text 95.00 (*90-5410-693-X*, Pub. by A A Balkema) Ashgate Pub Co.

Coussy, Olivier. Mechanics of Porous Continua. LC 96-110649. 472p. 1995. 160.00 (*0-471-95267-2*) Wiley.

Coustan, Donald R., et al, eds. Human Reproduction: Growth & Development. LC 94-22477. 512p. 1995. pap. text 39.95 (*0-316-15827-5*) Lppncott W & W.

Coustan, Donald R. & Mochizuki, Tara K. Handbook for Prescribing Medications During Pregnancy. 3rd ed. LC 98-17363. 510p. 1998. pap. text 24.95 (*0-316-15826-7*) Lppncott W & W.

Coustan, Donald R., jt. ed. see Reece, E. Albert.

Coustan, Donald R., jt. ed. see Weiss, P. A.

Cousteau, Jacques. A Bill of Rights for Future Generations. 33p. (Orig.). (gr. 8-12). 1980. pap. 1.50 (*0-913098-29-9*) Orion Society.

— Dolphins. 1987. 16.98 (*0-88486-015-9*) Arrowood Pr.

Cousteau, Jacques. Jacques Cousteau: The Ocean World. (Illus.). 446p. 1985. pap. 34.98 (*0-8109-8068-1*, Pub. by Abrams) Time Warner.

Cousteau, Jacques. Undersea Discoveries of Jacques-Yves Cousteau, Set. 1989. boxed set 49.98 (*0-88486-017-5*) Arrowood Pr.

Cousteau Society Staff. Adventure in New Zealand. LC 91-3292. (Cousteau Nature Adventure Bks.). (J). (gr. 4-7). 1992. pap. 14.00 (*0-671-77072-1*) S&S Bks Yung.

— Penguins. (J). 1998. 3.95 (*0-87628-987-1*) Ctr Appl Res.

— Penguins. LC 91-35229. (Illus.). 24p. (J). (ps-1). 1992. 3.95 (*0-671-77058-6*) Litle Simon.

— Seals. LC 91-34459. (Illus.). 24p. (J). (ps-3). 1992. pap. 4.95 (*0-671-77061-6*) Litle Simon.

Cousteix, J., jt. auth. see Cebeci, Tuncer.

Coustenis, Athena & Taylor, Fred. Titan. 400p. 1999. 38.00 (*981-02-3921-1*) World Scientific Pub.

Coustillas, Pierre, ed. London & the Life of Literature in Late Victorian England: The Diary of George Gissing, Novelist. LC 77-72970. 617p. 1978. 85.00 (*0-8387-2145-1*) Bucknell U Pr.

Coustillas, Pierre & Bridgewater, Patrick. George Gissing at Work: A Study of His Notebook "Extracts from My Readin" LC 87-82529. (1880-1920 British Authors Ser.: No. 2). (Illus.). 192p. (C). 1988. lib. bdg. 30.00 (*0-944318-01-0*) ELT Pr.

Coustillas, Pierre & Partridge, Colin, eds. Gissing: The Critical Heritage. (Critical Heritage Ser.). 1972. 69.50 (*0-7100-7367-4*, Routledge Thoemms) Routledge.

Coustillas, Pierre, ed. see Kipling, Rudyard.

***Cousto.** The Cosmic Octave: Origin of Harmony. 144p. 2000. pap. 16.95 (*0-940795-20-5*) LifeRhythm.

Coustols, E., ed. Turbulence Control by Passive Means. (C). 1990. lib. bdg. 124.50 (*0-7923-1020-9*) Kluwer Academic.

Cousy, Bob. Cousy on the Celtic Mystique. 1990. mass mkt. 3.95 (*0-8217-3007-X*, Zebra Kensgtn) Kensgtn Pub Corp.

Cousy, H., jt. ed. see Fredericq, S.

Coutagne, Denis. Cezanne in Provence. (Illus.). 80p. 1996. text 18.95 (*0-7893-0059-1*) St Martin.

Coutanceau, Maurice. Encyclopedie des Jardins: Gardening Encyclopedia. (FRE.). 556p. 1973. 75.00 (*0-8288-6284-2*, M-6198) Fr & Eur.

Coutanche, A. M., jt. auth. see Anspach, L. E.

Coutard, Olivier. The Governance of Large Technical Systems. LC 98-33941. 1999. write for info. (*0-415-19603-5*) Routledge.

Coutaz, Joelle, jt. ed. see Taylor, Richard M.

Coutchie, MariAnn. Jewelry on Display. 3rd ed. 120p. 1989. 9.95 (*0-911380-82-5*) ST Pubns.

Coute, A. & Tell, Guillermo. Ultrastructure de la Paroi Cellulaire des Desmidiacees au Microscope Electronique a Balayage. (Nova Hedwigia Beiheft Ser.: No. 68). (FRE., Illus.). 228p. 1982. lib. bdg. 96.00 (*3-7682-5468-2*) Lubrecht & Cramer.

Coute, A., jt. auth. see Bourrelly, Pierre.

Coute, Gaston. Les Mangeux D'Terre. (FRE.). 1995. pap. 49.95 (*2-86808-041-3*) Intl Scholars.

Couteau, Jean, jt. auth. see Darling, Diana.

Coutelle, Louis, et al. A Greek Diptych: Dionysios Solomos & Alexandros Papadiamantis. LC 86-61637. (Modern Greek History & Culture Ser.). 128p. 1986. 25.00 (*0-932963-03-X*) Nostos Bks.

***Coutellier, Connie L. & Henchey, Kathleen.** Camp Is for the Camper: A Counselor's Guide to Youth Development. 64p. 2000. pap. 9.95 (*0-87603-168-8*, Pub. by Am Camping) IPG Chicago.

Couth, Bill. Brant Broughton in the Nineteenth Century. (C). 1984. text 40.00 (*0-7855-3209-9*, Pub. by Univ Nottingham) St Mut.

Couth, Bill, ed. Grantham During the Interregnum: The Hallbook of Grantham 1641-1649. (Publications of the Lincoln Record Society: Vol. 83). 159p. 1995. 45.00 (*0-901503-56-8*) Boydell & Brewer.

Coutie, M. G. & Davies, G., eds. Tubular Structures, No. 5. LC 93-33027. (Illus.). 800p. (C). 1993. 180.00 (*0-419-18770-7*, E & FN Spon) Routledge.

Coutifaris, Cristos & Mastroianni, Luigi. New Horizons in Reproductive Medicine. LC 96-37080. (International Congress, Symposium & Seminar Ser.: Vol. 12). (Illus.). 620p. 1997. text 98.00 (*1-85070-793-6*) Prthnon Pub.

***Coutin, Susan Bibler.** Legalizing Moves: Salvadoran Immigrants' Struggle for U.S. Residency. LC 99-6550. 248p. (C). 2000. text 44.50 (*0-472-11012-8*, 11012) U of Mich Pr.

Coutinho, Antonio & Kazatchkine, Michel D., eds. Autoimmunity: Physiology & Disease. 474p. 1993. 149.95 (*0-471-59227-7*, Wiley-Interscience) Wiley.

Coutinho, E., et al, contrib. by. Latin America As Its Literature: Selected Papers of the XIVth Congress of ICLA. (CNL/World Report Ser.: Vol. XIII). 220p. 1995. pap. 4.95 (*0-918680-55-7*) Griffon House.

***Coutinho, E. M. & Spinola, P., eds.** Reproductive Medicine: A Millennium Review: Proceedings of the 10th World Congress on Human Reproduction. LC 99-26999. (Illus.). 316p. 1999. 110.00 (*1-85070-088-5*) Prthnon Pub.

Coutinho, Edilberto. Bye-Bye, Soccer. Loria, Wilson, tr. from POR. (Illus.). 135p. (Orig.). 1994. pap. 9.95 (*0-924047-10-0*) Host Pubns.

Coutinho, Eduardo De Faria, see De Faria Coutinho, Eduardo.

Coutinho, Elsimar M. & Segal, Sheldon J. The Trouble with Menstruation. LC 99-17765. 208p. 1999. 24.00 (*0-19-513021-9*) OUP.

Coutinho-Filho, Mauricio D. & Rezende, Sergio M., eds. New Trends in Magnetism. 336p. (C). 1990. text 151.00 (*981-02-0013-7*) World Scientific Pub.

***Coutinho, Joao D., ed.** A Kind of Absence. LC 97-61544. 128p. 1998. pap. 9.95 (*0-938999-10-9*) Yuganta Pr.

Coutinho, Martha J. & Repp, Alan C. Inclusion: The Integration of Students with Disabilities. LC 98-17646. 1998. pap. 66.95 (*0-534-56718-5*) Wadsworth Pub.

Coutinho, S. C. The Mathematics of Ciphers: Number Theory & RSA Cryptography. LC 98-49611. Orig. Title: Numeros Inteiros e Criptografia. (Illus.). 198p. 1998. 30.00 (*1-56881-082-2*) AK Peters.

— A Primer of Algebraic D-Modules. (London Mathematical Society Student Texts Ser.: No. 33). 219p. (C). 1995. text 69.95 (*0-521-55119-6*); pap. text 25.95 (*0-521-55908-1*) Cambridge U Pr.

Coutlas, Charles L. & Hsieh, Yuch P., eds. Ecology & Management of Tidal Marshes: A Model from the Gulf of Mexico. LC 97-116846. (Illus.). 352p. 1996. lib. bdg. 69.95 (*1-57444-026-8*) St Lucie Pr.

Couto, Armando. Florisardo, el Septimo Elegido. LC 87-82705. (Coleccion Caniqui). (SPA.). 112p. (Orig.). 1988. pap. 9.95 (*0-89729-465-3*) Ediciones.

— La Triste Historia de Mi Vida Oscura: A Peticion Popular. LC 78-70332. 1978. pap. 5.95 (*0-89729-196-4*) Ediciones.

Couto, C. Guillermo, jt. auth. see Nelson, Richard W.

Couto, Mia. Every Man Is a Race. (African Writers Ser.). 160p. 1994. pap. 9.95 (*0-435-90982-7*, 90982) Heinemann.

— Voices Made Night. (African Writers Ser.). 115p. (Orig.). (C). 1990. pap. 9.95 (*0-435-90570-8*, 90570) Heinemann.

Couto, Nancy V. The Face in the Water. LC 90-33960. (Poetry Ser.). 64p. 1990. pap. 10.95 (*0-8229-5440-0*); text 19.95 (*0-8229-3652-6*) U of Pittsburgh Pr.

Couto, Richard, et al. Transformational Leadership Working Papers. Webster, Scott & Adams, Bruce, eds. (Kellogg Leadership Studies Project). 180p. 1997. pap. text. write for info. (*1-891464-02-7*) J M Burns Academy.

Couto, Richard A. Ain't Gonna Let Nobody Turn Me Round: The Pursuit of Racial Justice in the Rural South. 310p. 1991. 59.95 (*0-87722-806-X*) Temple U Pr.

— Ain't Gonna Let Nobody Turn Me Round: The Pursuit of Racial Justice in the Rural South. 421p. 1992. pap. 22.95 (*1-56639-004-4*) Temple U Pr.

— Lifting the Veil: A Political History of Struggles for Emancipation. LC 93-23842. (Illus.). 368p. (C). 1993. pap. 18.00 (*0-87049-808-8*); text 40.00 (*0-87049-807-X*) U of Tenn Pr.

***Couto, Richard A.** Making Democracy Work Better: Mediating Structures, Social Capital, & the Democratic Prospect: Mediating Structures, Social Capital, & the Democratic Prospect. LC 98-53439. (Illus.). 384p. 1999. 49.95 (*0-8078-2488-7*); pap. 19.95 (*0-8078-4824-7*) U of NC Pr.

Couto, Richard A. Streams of Idealism & Health Care Innovation: An Assessment of Service-Learning & Community Mobilization. LC 82-10240. 189p. reprint ed. pap. 58.60 (*0-8357-3030-1*, 203927700011) Bks Demand.

Couto, Richard A., jt. ed. see Becker, Theodore L.

***Couto-Stutts.** Mending Broken Promises: Justice for Children at Risk. 152p. (C). 2000. per. 15.95 (*0-7872-7124-1*) Kendall-Hunt.

Couton, Georges, jt. auth. see Corneille, Pierre.

Couton, Georges, ed. see Corneille, Pierre.

Couton, Georges, ed. see Moliere.

Coutouvidis, John & Reynolds, Jaime. Poland, 1935 to 1947. Warner, Geoffrey & Ellwood, David M., eds. LC 86-14814. (Politics of Liberation Ser.). (Illus.). 393p. 1986. 65.00 (*0-8419-1093-6*) Holmes & Meier.

Coutouvidis, John, ed. see Garlicki, Andrej.

Coutts, Alfred. Hans Denck, Fourteen Ninety-Five to Fifteen Twenty-Seven: Humanistic & Heretic. LC 83-45607. reprint ed. 32.00 (*0-404-19825-2*) AMS Pr.

Coutts, Ben. Auld Acquaintance. 128p. 1996. pap. 32.00 (*1-873644-30-2*, Pub. by Mercat Pr Bks) St Mut.

— Bothy to Big Ben: An Autobiography. (Illus.). 200p. 1988. pap. 14.00 (*0-08-036396-2*, Pub. by Aberdeen U Pr) Macmillan.

— Bred in the Highlands: Ponies, Cattle & Folk. LC 98-187775. 144p. 1996. pap. 40.00 (*1-873644-68-X*, Pub. by Mercat Pr Bks) St Mut.

— Highland Air: A Farmer's Diary. (Illus.). 126p. 1990. pap. 9.95 (*0-08-037976-1*, Pub. by Aberdeen U Pr) Macmillan.

— A Scotsman's War. 128p. 1989. pap. 36.00 (*1-873644-47-7*, Pub. by Mercat Pr Bks) St Mut.

Coutts, Fred. History of the Salvation Army, Vol. 7. 348p. 1988. pap. 9.95 (*0-86544-048-4*) Salv Army Suppl South.

Coutts, J. & Meakin, J. O., eds. Current Topics in Photovoltaics, Vol. 4. 191p. 1990. text 110.00 (*0-12-153414-6*) Acad Pr.

Coutts, J., et al. Encyclopaedia of Horticulture, 2 vols., Set. 1992. reprint ed. pap. 145.50 (*81-7158-015-7*, Pub. by Anmol) S Asia.

Coutts, John J. How the Christian Faith Began: A Commentary on the Gospel According to St. Luke & the Acts of the Apostles. LC 74-6967. 256p. 1973. pap. 79.40 (*0-608-05248-5*, 206578500002) Bks Demand.

Coutts, Kenneth, et al. Industrial Pricing in the United Kingdom. LC 77-8976. (University of Cambridge, Dept. of Applied Economics, Occasional Papers: No. 26). 155p. reprint ed. pap. 44.20 (*0-608-17578-1*, 2030586) Bks Demand.

Coutts, Lorne. The Naked Drawings. (Illus.). 80p. 1994. 25.00 (*0-88962-193-4*) Mosaic.

— The Naked Drawings of Lorne Coutts. (Illus.). 80p. 1995. pap. 9.95 (*0-88962-223-X*) Mosaic.

Coutts, Lyn & Hardy, Leslie K. Teaching for Health. 2nd ed. 1995. write for info. (*0-443-04126-1*) Church.

Coutts, Lyn C. & Hardy, Leslie K. Teaching for Health: The Nurse As Health Educator. LC 84-11365. (Illus.). 225p. 1989. pap. text 28.00 (*0-443-02751-X*) Church.

Coutts, M. P. & Grace, J., eds. Wind & Trees. (Illus.). 501p. (C). 1995. text 100.00 (*0-521-46037-9*) Cambridge U Pr.

Coutts, Mary C., jt. ed. see Nolen, Anita L.

Coutts, Peter J. An Archaeological Perspective of Panay Island, Philippines. (San Carlos Humanities Ser.: No. 13). (Illus.). 342p. (Orig.). 1983. pap. 27.50 (*971-10-0043-1*, Pub. by San Carlos Univ) Cellar.

Coutts, Robert, jt. ed. see Beardy, Flora.

***Coutts, Russell & Larsen, Paul.** America's Cup - Challenge 2000. LC 99-41410. (Illus.). 192p. 1999. 34.95 (*0-7370-0059-7*) T-L Custom Pub.

Coutts, T. J. & Meakin, J. D., eds. Current Topics in Photovoltaics, Vol. 1. 1985. text 159.00 (*0-12-193860-3*) Acad Pr.

— Current Topics in Photovoltaics, Vol. 2. 208p. 1987. text 145.00 (*0-12-153412-X*) Acad Pr.

— Current Topics in Photovoltaics, Vol. 3. 350p. 1988. text 145.00 (*0-12-153413-8*) Acad Pr.

Coutts, Timothy J. The First NREL Conference on Thermophotovoltaic Generation of Electricity. (AIP Conference Proceedings Ser.: No. 321). 600p. 1994. text 110.00 (*1-56396-353-1*) Am Inst Physics.

Coutts, Timothy J., et al, eds. Thermophotovoltaic Generation of Electricity: 4th NREL Conference. (AIP Conference Proceedings Ser.). (Illus.). 570p. 1999. 150.00 (*1-56396-828-2*) Am Inst Physics.

Coutu, Albert C. Hispanism in France from Morel-Fatio to the Present. LC 70-94187. (Catholic University of America. Studies in Romance Languages & Literatures: No. 49). reprint ed. 37.50 (*0-404-50349-7*) AMS Pr.

Couturat, Louis. L' Algebre de la Logique. 100p. 1965. reprint ed. 25.00 (*0-318-71334-9*) G Olms Pubs.

— La Logique de Leibniz. xiv, 608p. 1985. reprint ed. 120.00 (*3-487-00098-9*); reprint ed. pap. 65.00 (*3-487-02381-4*) G Olms Pubs.

— Les Principes des Mathematiques. viii, 310p. 1979. reprint ed. 55.00 (*3-487-00847-5*) G Olms Pubs.

Couturat, Louis & Leau, Leopold. Histoire de la Langue Universelle. (Documenta Semiotica, Ser. Linguistica). xxx, 576p. 1979. reprint ed. 160.00 (*3-487-06885-0*) G Olms Pubs.

***Couture, Alain & Veyrac, C.** Transfontanellar Doppler Imaging in Neonates. LC 00-38812. (Medical Radiology Ser.). (Illus.). 2000. write for info. (*3-540-64463-6*) Spr-Verlag.

Couture, Barbara. Toward a Phenomenological Rhetoric: Writing, Profession & Altruism. LC 97-25211. (Shawnee Classics Ser.). 368p. (C). 1995. reprint ed. 29.95 (*0-8093-2033-9*) S Ill U Pr.

Couture, Barbara & Farr, Marcia, eds. Functional Approaches to Writing Research. (Writing Research Ser.: Vol. 9). 288p. (C). 1986. text 73.25 (*0-89391-375-8*) Ablx Pub.

Couture, Dawn. Essentials of Mass Law. (C). 1998. 30.59 (*1-56870-281-7*) RonJon Pub.

Couture, E. T., jt. auth. see Edelstein, B. A.

Couture, Faye, jt. ed. see Reams, Bernard D., Jr.

***Couture, Jackie.** Madison County, Kentucky Court Order Bk. B: 1791-1801. 319p. 2000. pap. 28.00 (*0-7884-1463-1*, 1463) Heritage Bk.

Couture, Jackie. Madison County, Kentucky, Court Order Book A, 1787-1791. v, 152p. (Orig.). 1996. pap. 20.00 (*0-7884-0594-2*, C587) Heritage Bk.

Couture, Jacqueline A. & Dimitrou, Jerry P. Richmond Remembered: A Bicentennial History of Richmond, Kentucky. LC 98-5274. (Illus.). 150p. 1998. pap. 20.00 (*0-9615162-4-0*) Madison Cty KY Hist.

***Couture, Jacqueline Ann & Dimitrou, Jerry Parrish.** Inventory of Burials: Richmond, Kentucky Cemetery Inc. LC 99-47899. (Illus.). 550p. 2000. 30.00 (*0-9615162-5-9*) Madison Cty KY Hist.

Couture-Lafleur, Raymonde, jt. auth. see Beall, Julianne.

Couture, Larry, jt. ed. see Rossi, John J.

Couture, Pamela D. Blessed Are the Poor? LC 91-15985. 1991. pap. 19.95 (*0-687-03615-1*) Abingdon.

Couture, Pascale. Guadeloupe. 3rd ed. (Ulysses Travel Guide Ser.). (Illus.). 224p. 1998. pap. 17.95 (*2-89464-135-4*) Ulysses Travel.

— Ontario: Ulysses Travel Guide. Ulysses Travel Guide Staff, ed. (Ulysses Travel Guide Ser.). (Illus.). 1999. 19.95 (*2-89464-119-2*) Ulysses Travel.

***Couture, Pascale.** Ontario's Best Hotels & Restaurants. 2000. pap. 12.95 (*2-89464-303-9*, Pub. by Ulysses Travel) Globe Pequot.

— Ottawa. 2nd ed. (Travel Guide Ser.). (Illus.). 2001. pap. 12.95 (*2-89464-331-4*) Ulysses Travel.

Couture, Pascale. Ottawa: Ulysses Travel Guide. Ulysses Travel Guide Staff, ed. (Ulysses Travel Guide Ser.). (Illus.). 192p. pap. 12.95 (*2-89464-170-2*, 862588Q) Ulysses Travel.

— Puerto Plata, Sosua, Cabarete: Ulysses Due South Guide. (Illus.). 80p. 1994. pap. 5.95 (*2-921444-91-7*) Ulysses Travel.

***Couture, Pascale.** Ulysses Due South Saint Martin-Saint Barts. 3rd ed. (Due South Guide Ser.). (Illus.). 192p. 1999. pap. 12.95 (*2-89464-212-1*, Pub. by Ulysses Travel) Globe Pequot.

Couture, Pascale & Prieur, Benoit. Ulysses Travel Guide: Dominican Republic. 5th ed. (Illus.). 276p. 1999. pap. 17.95 (*2-89464-209-1*, Pub. by Ulysses Travel) Globe Pequot.

Couture, Susan A. Alfonso's Dream. LC 93-5784. (J). 1996. text. write for info. (*0-02-724827-5*, Mac Bks Young Read) S&S Childrens.

C

An Asterisk (*) at the beginning of an entry indicates that the title is appearing for the first time.

— The Biggest Horse I Ever Did See. LC 95-23470. (Laura Geringer Bks.). (Illus.). 32p. (J). (ps-2). 1997. 14.95 (*0-06-023467-9*) HarpC Child Bks.

— The Block Book. LC 89-34504. (Illus.). 32p. (J). (ps-3). 1990. 12.95 (*0-06-020523-7*) HarpC Child Bks.

— Melanie Jane. LC 94-18699. (Illus.). 32p. (J). (ps-1). 1996. lib. bdg. 14.89 (*0-06-023392-3*) HarpC Child Bks.

Couture, Teri. The Birthday Surprise. LC 97-61042. (Aesop's Fables Running Start Ser.). (Illus.). 32p. (J). (gr. 1-3). 1997. pap. 4.95 (*1-890570-43-5*) Huckleberry CT.

— The Fortune Teller. LC 97-61031. (Aesop's Fables Running Start Ser.). (Illus.). 32p. (J). (gr. 1-3). 1997. pap. 4.95 (*1-890570-12-5*) Huckleberry CT.

— Hare Say. LC 97-61029. (Aesop's Fables Running Start Ser.). (Illus.). 32p. (J). (gr. 1-3). 1997. pap. 4.95 (*1-890570-07-9*) Huckleberry CT.

— Too Many Promises. LC 97-61030. (Aesop's Fables Running Start Ser.). (Illus.). (J). (gr. 1-3). 1997. pap. 4.95 (*1-890570-08-7*) Huckleberry CT.

Couture, Thomas & Springfield Museum of Fine Arts Staff. Enrollment of the Volunteers: Thomas Couture & the Painting of History. LC 80-80318. (Illus.). 92p. 1980. pap. 10.00 (*0-916746-02-X*) Springfield Lib & Mus.

***Couturie, Sylvia.** No Tears in Ireland: A Memoir. 2001. 24.00 (*0-7432-0193-0*) Free Pr.

***Couturier, Alain J.** Occupational & Environmental Infectious Diseases: Epidemiology, Prevention & Clinical Management. LC 00-37443. 2000. write for info. (*1-883595-27-4*, OEM Pr) OEM Health.

Couturier, M. A. Sacred Art. Ryant, Granger, tr. from FRE. LC 89-12869. Orig. Title: Art Sacre. (Illus.). 159p. 1983. 35.00 (*0-292-77639-X*) Menil Found.

Couvalis, George. Feyerbend's Critique of Foundationalism. (Avebury Series in Philosophy). 176p. 1989. text 78.95 (*0-566-07043-X*, Pub. by Avebry) Ashgate Pub Co.

— The Philosophy of Science: Science & Objectivity. 224p. 1997. 69.95 (*0-7619-5100-8*); pap. 24.95 (*0-7619-5101-6*) Sage.

***Couvares, Francis G.** Patterns & Perspectives: Vol. 1 Through Reconstruction. 7th ed. (Interpretations of American History Ser.). 448p. 2000. 17.95 (*0-684-86773-7*) Free Pr.

— Patterns & Perspectives: Vol. 2 from Reconstruction, Vol. 2. 7th ed. (Interpretations of American History Ser.). 464p. 2000. 17.95 (*0-684-87118-1*) Free Pr.

Couvares, Francis G. The Remaking of Pittsburgh: Class & Culture in an Industrializing City, 1877-1919. LC 83-5044. 187p. (C). 1984. pap. text 19.95 (*0-87395-779-2*) State U NY Pr.

Couvares, Francis G., ed. Movie Censorship & American Culture. (Studies in the History of Film & Television). (Illus.). 256p. 1996. text 45.00 (*1-56098-668-9*); pap. text 17.95 (*1-56098-669-7*) Smithsonian.

Couver, Maria Von, see Von Couver, Maria.

Couvering, David Van, see Van Couvering, David.

Couvering, John A. Van, see Van Couvering, John A., ed.

Couvillon, Alice & Moore, Elizabeth. Mimi's First Mardi Gras. LC 91-24006. (Illus.). 32p. (J). (ps-3). 1992. 14.95 (*0-88289-840-X*) Pelican.

***Couvillon, Alice, et al.** Evangeline for Children. LC 99-57101. (Illus.). (J). 2000. write for info. (*1-56554-709-8*) Pelican.

Couvillon, Alice W. & Moore, Elizabeth. Mimi & Jean-Paul's Cajun Mardi Gras. LC 95-31612. (Illus.). 32p. (J). (ps-3). 1996. 14.95 (*1-56554-069-7*) Pelican.

Couvillon, Arthur R. The Complete Firefighter Candidate. LC 89-81738. 150p. (Orig.). 1990. pap. 12.95 (*0-938329-58-8*) Info Guides.

— Emergencies in the Home. (Orig.). 1991. pap. text 16.95 (*0-938329-74-X*) Info Guides.

Couvillon, Arthur R. Fire Captain Oral Exam Study Guide. Information Guides Staff, ed. 228p. pap. 18.95 (*0-938329-57-X*) Info Guides.

Couvillon, Arthur R. Fire Captain Written Exam Study Guide. 2nd ed. Information Guides Staff, ed. 320p. pap. 18.95 (*0-938329-66-9*) Info Guides.

— Fire Engineer Oral Exam Study Guide. 2nd rev. ed. Information Guides Staff, ed. LC 88-80888. 192p. 1988. pap. 15.95 (*0-938329-53-7*) Info Guides.

— Fire Engineer Written Exam Study Guide. 2nd rev. ed. Information Guides Staff, ed. LC 86-81299. 180p. 1988. pap. 15.95 (*0-938329-52-9*) Info Guides.

Couvillon, Arthur R. Firefighter Oral Exam Study Guide. 226p. pap. text 15.95 (*0-938329-60-X*) Info Guides.

Couvillon, Arthur R. Firefighter Written Exam Study Guide. 2nd ed. 368p. pap. 19.95 (*0-938329-65-0*) Info Guides.

— A System for Advancement in the Fire Service. LC 88-83385. 130p. 1990. pap. 9.95 (*0-938329-56-1*) Info Guides.

Couvillon, Arthur R. & Stein, Paul H. Fire Service Entrance Exam Preparation. LC 91-92875. 1991. pap. text, teacher ed. 35.00 (*0-938329-72-3*) Info Guides.

— Fire Service Entrance Exam Preparation. 2nd ed. 400p. pap. 39.00 (*0-938329-73-1*) Info Guides.

Couvin, jt. auth. see Baker.

Couvreur, P., ed. see Von Alexandreia, Hermeias.

***Couvreur, Patrick & Malvy, Claude.** Pharmaceutical Aspects of Oligonucleotides LC 99-34210. (Series in Pharmaceutical Sciences). 2000. write for info. (*0-7484-0841-X*, Pub. by Tay Francis Ltd) Taylor & Francis.

Couvreur, Patrick, jt. ed. see Guiot, Pierre.

***Couwenberghe, Aaron & Camou, Mario.** Debian GNU/Linux 2.1 Unleashed. 1100p. 1999. 49.99 (*0-672-31700-1*) Sams.

Couzens, Dominic. Collins Wings Guide to British Birds. (Illus.). 252p. 1997. pap. 24.95 (*0-00-220069-4*, Pub. by HarpC) Trafalgar.

Couzens, Gerald S., jt. auth. see Hogshead, Nancy.

Couzens, Gerald S., jt. auth. see Lamm, Steven.

Couzens, Gerald Secor, jt. auth. see Lamm, Steven.

***Couzens, J. Richard.** The California Three Strikes Sentencing Law. 1999. write for info. (*1-58012-044-X*) James Pub Santa Ana.

Couzens, Reginald C. The Stories of the Months & Days. LC 89-43348. (Illus.). 160p. 1990. reprint ed. lib. bdg. 38.00 (*1-55888-881-0*) Omnigraphics Inc.

Couzens, Tim. Tramp Royal: The True Story of Trader Horn. LC 93-219090. (Illus.). 624p. (C). 1993. pap. text 19.95 (*0-86975-416-5*, Pub. by Ravan Pr) Ohio U Pr.

Couzens, Tim & Patel, Essop, eds. The Return of the Amasi Bird: Black South African Poetry, 1891-1981. 411p. 1982. pap. text 12.95 (*0-86975-195-6*, Pub. by Ravan Pr) Ohio U Pr.

Couzens, Tim, jt. auth. see Rive, Richard.

Couzereau, B. Fachworterbuch der Zweiradtechnik: Two-Wheeler Technical Dictionary. (ENG, FRE & GER.). 450p. 1990. lib. bdg. 95.00 (*0-8288-3842-9*, F50302) Fr & Eur.

— Two-Wheeler Technology, Dictionary of German, French, & English. 432p. 1990. 79.00 (*3-87073-054-4*) IBD Ltd.

Couzins-Scott, Elizabeth. Papermaking: The New Crafts Collection. (Illus.). 96p. 1999. 16.95 (*1-85967-892-0*) Anness Pub.

Couzinte, J. P. Dictionnaire de la Langue Romano-Castraise et des Contrees Limitrophes. (FRE.). 563p. 1976. 125.00 (*0-7859-7990-5*, 2734803003) Fr & Eur.

Couzn, Jeni. In the Skin House. 80p. 1994. pap. 14.95 (*1-85224-254-X*, Pub. by Bloodaxe Bks) Dufour.

Couzyn, Jeni. Life by Drowning. 1985. pap. 17.95 (*0-906427-73-8*, Pub. by Bloodaxe Bks) Dufour.

— Life by Drowning: Selected Poems. 174p. (Orig.). 1983. pap. 8.95 (*0-88784-098-1*, Pub. by Hse of Anansi Pr) Genl Dist Srvs.

Couzyn, Jeni, ed. Singing down the Bones: An Invitation to Poetry. (Livewire Ser.). (YA). (gr. 6-9). pap. 6.95 (*0-7043-4913-2*, Pub. by Womens Press) Trafalgar.

Couzzens, Veronica. Expressions. unabridged ed. 25p. 1998. pap. 8.95 (*0-9665678-9-7*) Buy Books.

Cova, Antonio De La, see De La Cova, Antonio.

Cova, J. L. & Maingon, Charles. One Hundred One Problematic Phrases in Translating from English to French: Clearing up Misleading Meanings. LC 90-25039. 124p. 1991. lib. bdg. 59.95 (*0-88946-496-0*) E Mellen.

Covach, John & Boone, Graeme, eds. Understanding Rock Music: Essays in Musical Analysis. LC 96-53475. (Illus.). 240p. 1997. pap. 19.95 (*0-19-510005-0*) OUP.

***Covach, John & Everett, Walter, eds.** American Rock & the Classical Music Tradition. (Illus.). 88p. 1999. pap. text 21.00 (*90-5755-119-5*, Harwood Acad Pubs) Gordon & Breach.

— Traditions, Institutions & American Popular Tradition. (Illus.). 88p. 1999. pap. text 21.00 (*90-5755-120-9*, Harwood Acad Pubs) Gordon & Breach.

Covachev, V., jt. auth. see Bainov, Drumi D.

Covachev, V., jt. ed. see Bainov, D.

***Covaci, Stefan, ed.** Active Networks: Proceedings, 1st International Workshop, IWAN'99, Berlin, Germany, June 30-July 2, 1999. LC 99-34030. (Lecture Notes in Computer Science Ser.: Vol. 1653). xiii, 346p. 1999. pap. 62.00 (*3-540-66238-3*) Spr-Verlag.

Coval, S. C. & Campbell, P. G. Agency in Action: The Practical Rational Agency Machine. (Studies in Cognitive Systems). 224p. 1992. lib. bdg. 141.50 (*0-7923-1661-4*, Pub. by Kluwer Academic) Kluwer Academic.

Coval, S. C. & Smith, J. C. Law & Its Presuppositions: Actions, Agents & Rules. (International Library of Philosophy). 134p. 1986. lib. bdg. 35.00 (*0-7102-0446-9*, Routledge Thoemms) Routledge.

Covalioff, Anatoly A., tr. see Braginsky, Vladimir I. & Dyakonova, Yelena M., eds.

Covalt, Isabel J. My Name Is Izzy. LC 99-24091. (Illus.). 192p. 1999. pap. 14.95 (*0-89407-128-9*) Strawberry Hill.

Covalt, Jeanie, jt. auth. see Braddock, Betty.

Covan, Frederick L. & Kahn, Carol. Crazy All the Time: Life, Lessons, & Insanity on the Psych Ward of Bellevue Hospital. 1994. 23.00 (*0-671-79159-1*) S&S Trade.

— Crazy All the Time: On the Psyche Ward of Bellevue Hospital. 1995. mass mkt. 5.99 (*0-449-22366-3*) Fawcett.

CoVan, James. Safety Engineering. LC 93-27077. (New Dimensions in Engineering Ser.). 256p. 1995. 110.00 (*0-471-55612-2*) Wiley.

Covan, Jennie, tr. see Gorky, Maxim.

Covan, Jenny, jt. auth. see Gorky, Maksim.

***Covan, Penney.** From Patiant to Person: First Steps: A Workbook for People with Chronic Pain. Carington, Edward & Lan, Darna, eds. Orig. Title: ACPA Wrokbook Manual. (Illus.). 195p. 2000. pap. 25.00 (*0-9673878-3-3*, 13300) Amer Chronic.

Covarrubias, Alvaro J. & World Bank Staff. Lending for Electric Power in Sub-Saharan Africa. LC 96-1958. (Operations Evaluation Studies). 120p. 1996. pap. 22.00 (*0-8213-3644-4*) World Bank.

Covarrubias, Consuelo, ed. see Tarango, Yolanda, et al.

Covarrubias Horozco, Sebastian De, see De Covarrubias Horozco, Sebastian.

Covarrubias, Jorge. Manual de Tecnicas de Redaccion Periodistica. Abreu, Jose, ed. LC 96-84354. (SPA.). 233p. (Orig.). 1996. pap. text 13.95 (*0-917360-13-3*) Assoc Pr.

Covarrubias, Miguel. Island of Bali. 430p. 1994. pap. 31.00 (*0-7103-0134-0*) Routledge.

— Island of Bali. 1999. pap. 19.95 (*962-593-060-4*) Tuttle Pubng.

— Mexico South: The Isthmus of Tehuantepec. (Illus.). 400p. 1986. pap. text 19.95 (*0-7103-0184-7*) Routledge.

Covas, J. A., et al, eds. Rheological Fundamentals of Polymer Processing: Proceedings of the NATO Advanced Study Institute, Alvor, Portugal, September 16 - October 8, 1994. (NATO Advanced Science Institutes Ser.: Series E). 463p. (C). 1995. text 239.50 (*0-7923-3792-1*) Kluwer Academic.

Covault, Ruth M. Pablo & Pimienta (Pablo y Pimienta) LC 94-25445. (ENG & SPA., Illus.). 32p. (J). (gr. 1-3). 1994. lib. bdg. 14.95 (*0-87358-588-7*, Rising Moon Bks) Northland AZ.

— Pablo & Pimienta (Pablo y Pimienta) (ENG & SPA., Illus.). 32p. (J). (gr. 1-3). 1998. pap. 7.95 (*0-87358-708-1*, Rising Moon Bks) Northland AZ.

Cove, Arthur. My Way with Trout. (Illus.). 186p. 1993. pap. 24.95 (*1-85223-680-9*, Pub. by Crolwood) Trafalgar.

Cove, D. J. Genetics. LC 75-160089. 221p. reprint ed. pap. 63.00 (*0-608-12222-0*, 2024430) Bks Demand.

Cove, David, jt. auth. see Russo, Enzo.

Cove, Emile. How to Practice Suggestion & Autosuggestion (1923) 128p. 1996. reprint ed. pap. 16.95 (*1-56459-937-X*) Kessinger Pub.

— My Method: Including American Impressions. 221p. 1996. reprint ed. pap. 19.95 (*1-56459-622-2*) Kessinger Pub.

Cove, Gordon. Revival Now Through Prayer & Fasting. 1988. pap. 9.99 (*0-88019-227-5*) Schmul Pub Co.

Cove, John J., jt. ed. see MacDonald, George F.

Cove, Margaret, jt. intro. see Sarfati, Hady.

Cove-Smith, Chris. London's Waterway Guide. 2nd rev. ed. (Illus.). 200p. (C). 1986. pap. 125.00 (*0-85288-104-5*, Pub. by Laurie Norie & Wilson Ltd) St Mut.

— The River Thames Book: Including the River Wey, Basingstoke Canal & Kennel & Avon Canal. (Illus.). 180p. 1996. pap. 125.00 (*0-85288-286-6*, Pub. by Laurie Norie & Wilson Ltd) St Mut.

— The River Thames Book: Including the River Wey, Basingstoke Canal & Kennet & Avon Canal. 220p. 1998. pap. 150.00 (*0-85288-399-4*) Laurie Norie & Wilson Ltd.

Covel, Betsey B. Women's Studies Manuscript Collections from the Schlesinger Library, Radcliffe College: Papers of Mary Ware Dennett . . . LC 94-17171. (Research Collections in Women's Studies). 1994. 4965.00 (*1-55655-510-5*) U Pubns Amer.

Covel, Paul F. Beacons along a Naturalist's Trail: California Naturalists & Innovators. LC 87-34691. (Illus.). xii, 153p. (Orig.). 1988. pap. 10.95 (*0-931430-01-1*) Western Interp.

Covel, William. William Covel's a Just & Temperate Defence of the Five Books of Ecclesiastical Polity Written by Richard Hooker. Taylor, John A., ed. LC 98-44216. (Texts & Studies in Religion: Vol. 79). 208p. 1998. text 89.95 (*0-7734-8243-1*) E Mellen.

Covell. A Coding Workbook for the Physician's Office 1998. 5th ed. 112p. (C). 1998. pap., wbk. ed. 21.95 (*0-7668-0080-6*) Delmar.

— A Coding Workbook for the Physician's Office - IML, 1998. 10p. 1998. teacher ed. 4.95 (*0-7668-0082-2*) Delmar.

— 1999 Coding Workbook: Physician's Office. 6th ed. (C). 1999. pap., wbk. ed. 25.95 (*0-7668-0853-X*) Thomson Learn.

— Physicians Office 97: Coding Workbook. 4th ed. (Medical Assisting Ser.). (C). 1997. text 17.50 (*0-7668-0081-4*) Delmar.

Covell, A. T. Old Chatham & Neighboring Dwellings South of the Berkshires, Vol. 5, No. 5. 1993. reprint ed. lib. bdg. 89.00 (*0-7812-5322-5*) Rprt Serv.

Covell, Alan, jt. auth. see Covell, Jon C.

Covell, Alan C. Folk Art & Magic: Shamanism in Korea. LC 86-82713. (Illus.). 216p. 1993. 46.95 (*0-930878-57-4*) Hollym Intl.

Covell, Alice. A Coding Workbook for the Physician's Office. (Medical Assisting Ser.). 96p. (C). 1996. wbk. ed. 19.95 (*0-8273-8074-7*) Delmar.

Covell, Andy. Digital Convergence: How the Merging of Computers, Communications & Multimedia Is Transforming Our Lives. LC 99-37431. (Illus.). 220p. 1999. pap. 14.95 (*1-890154-16-4*) Aegis Pub Grp.

***Covell, Charles V., Jr.** The Butterflies & Moths (Lepidoptera) of Kentucky: An Annotated Checklist. unabridged ed. LC 99-64169. (Scientific & Technical Ser.). 220p. 1999. pap. 15.00 (*0-9673646-5-5*) KY State Nature.

Covell, Ian, ed. J. T. McIntosh: Memoir & Bibliography. (Drumm Booklet Ser.: No. 25). 32p. (Orig.). 1987. 5.00 (*0-936055-29-4*); pap. 2.00 (*0-936055-28-6*) C Drumm Bks.

Covell, Joan, jt. compiled by see Kennedy, Pamela.

Covell, John E. Joyce Kilmer: A Literary Biography. (Illus.). Date not set. write for info. (*0-615-11175-0*) Write-Fit.

Covell, Jon C. Korea's Cultural Roots. LC 83-81319. (Illus.). 132p. 1992. 27.95 (*0-930878-32-9*) Hollym Intl.

Covell, Jon C. & Covell, Alan. Korean Impact on Japanese Culture: Japan's Hidden History. LC 83-81484. (Illus.). 112p. 1998. 27.95 (*0-930878-34-5*) Hollym Intl.

***Covell, Karen, et al.** How to Talk about Jesus Without Freaking Out: An Easy to Use Practical Guide to Relationship Witnessing. LC 00-8423. 256p. 2000. pap. 10.99 (*1-57673-737-3*) Multnomah Pubs.

Covell, L. T. A Digest of English Grammar, Synthetical & Analytical. LC 89-24052. 224p. 1989. reprint ed. 50.00 (*0-8201-1441-3*) Schol Facsimiles.

Covell, Lauren K., jt. auth. see Covell, Stephen E.

Covell, Maureen. Historical Dictionary of Madagascar. LC 94-45309. (African Historical Dictionaries Ser.: No. 50). (Illus.). 408p. 1995. 73.50 (*0-8108-2973-8*) Scarecrow.

— Madagascar: Politics, Economics & Society. (Marxist Regimes Ser.). 225p. 1987. text 49.00 (*0-86187-428-5*); text 17.50 (*0-86187-429-3*) St Martin.

Covell, Ralph. Pentecost of the Hills in Taiwan: The Christian Faith among the Original Inhabitants. LC 97-27762. (Illus.). 320p. 1997. pap. 15.95 (*0-932727-90-5*) Hope Pub Hse.

— W. A. P Martin: Pioneer of Progress in China. LC 77-13321. 311p. reprint ed. 96.50 (*0-8357-9133-5*, 201272300083) Bks Demand.

Covell, Ralph R. The Liberating Gospel in China: The Christian Faith among China's Minority Peoples. LC 94-42375. (Illus.). 320p. 1995. pap. 17.99 (*0-8010-2595-8*) Baker Bks.

— Mission Impossible: The Unreached Nosu on China's Frontier. LC 89-19918. (Illus.). 310p. 1990. pap. 12.95 (*0-932727-35-2*); lib. bdg. 17.95 (*0-932727-38-7*) Hope Pub Hse.

Covell, Scott F., jt. ed. see Murray, Patricia Y.

Covell, Stephen E. & Covell, Lauren K. The Louisiana Legal Advisor. 3rd ed. LC 93-70673. 302p. 1993. pap. 11.95 (*0-935773-23-1*) Charleston Pr.

Covell, Stephen E. & Lauren, Covell K. Your Louisiana Legal Advisor. rev. ed. LC 85-733336. 297p. (Orig.). 1989. pap. 9.95 (*0-685-21019-7*) Charleston Pr.

***Covell, Victoria.** Spirit Animals. LC 00-8828. 2000. pap. write for info. (*1-58469-010-0*) Dawn CA.

Covell, W. & Lupton, K. Principles of Remedies. LC 96-150595. 320p. 1995. pap. write for info. (*0-409-30777-7*, MICHIE) LEXIS Pub.

Covella, Francis, tr. see Fowler, David C., ed.

Covelle, Cristobal, tr. see Zook, Mollie.

Covello, A. New Perspectives in Nuclear Structure. 650p. 1996. text 148.00 (*981-02-2359-5*) World Scientific Pub.

***Covello, Aldo.** Highlights of Modern Nuclear Structure: Proceedings of the 6th International Spring Seminar on Nuclear Structure. 1999. 125.00 (*981-02-3708-1*) World Scientific Pub.

Covello, Aldo. Understanding the Variety of Nuclear Excitations: Third International Spring Seminar on Nuclear Physics. 788p. 1991. text 147.00 (*981-02-0401-9*) World Scientific Pub.

Covello, Aldo, ed. Shell Model & Nuclear Structure: Where Do We Stand? 668p. (C). 1989. text 131.00 (*9971-5-0757-9*) World Scientific Pub.

Covello, Charles J. Real Estate Buying & Selling Guide for Washington. 4th rev. ed. (Legal Ser.). (Illus.). 96p. 1991. pap. 8.95 (*0-88908-747-4*) Self-Counsel Pr.

Covello, Joseph & Hazelgren, Brian. Your First Business Plan: Learn the Critical Steps to Writing a Winning Business Plan. 3rd rev. ed. LC 97-51869. 160p. 1997. pap. 12.95 (*1-57071-219-0*) Sourcebks.

Covello, Joseph A. & Hazelgren, Brian J. The Complete Book of Business Plans: Simple Steps to Writing a Powerful Business Plan. LC 93-41064. (Small Business Sourcebooks Ser.). (Illus.). 317p. 1993. pap. 19.95 (*0-942061-41-1*) Sourcebks.

Covello, S. Glad Rags & All That Jazz: Early Intermediate Piano Solos. 16p. 1991. pap. 4.95 (*0-7935-0610-7*, 00290307) H Leonard.

— The Little Avant Garde: Piano for Pre-Schoolers. 3rd rev. ed. 40p. 1986. pap. 4.95 (*0-7935-3981-1*) H Leonard.

— Winning Solos: Early Intermediate Piano Solos. 24p. 1991. pap. 4.95 (*0-7935-0632-8*) H Leonard.

— Winning Solos: Late Elementary Piano. 24p. 1991. pap. 4.95 (*0-7935-0631-X*) H Leonard.

— Winning Solos: Late Intermediate. 28p. 1992. pap. 4.95 (*0-7935-1846-6*) H Leonard.

Covello, V. T., et al. Effective Risk Communication: The Role & Responsibility of Government & Nongovernment Organizations. (Contemporary Issues in Risk Analysis Ser.: Vol. 4). (Illus.). 366p. (C). 1989. 110.00 (*0-306-43075-4*, Plenum Trade) Perseus Pubng.

Covello, V. T., et al. Risk Evaluation & Management. (Contemporary Issues in Risk Analysis Ser.: Advances in Risk Analysis Ser. vol. 1). (Illus.). 556p. (C). 1986. 140.00 (*0-306-41978-5*, Plenum Trade) Perseus Pubng.

Covello, Vincent, ed. Poverty & Public Policy: An Evaluation of Social Science Research. 314p. 1980. pap. text 13.95 (*0-87073-355-9*) Schenkman Bks Inc.

Covello, Vincent T. Japanese Art of Stone Appreciation: Suiseki & Its Use with Bonsai. 166p. 1995. pap. 19.95 (*0-8048-2047-3*) Tuttle Pubng.

Covello, Vincent T., et al, eds. The Analysis of Actual Versus Perceived Risks. LC 83-11071. (Advances in Risk Analysis Ser.: Vol. 1). (Illus.). 387p. (C). 1983. 138.00 (*0-306-41397-3*, Plenum Trade) Perseus Pubng.

Covello, Vincent T. & Merkhoher, Miley W. Risk Assessment Methods: Approaches for Assessing Health & Environmental Risks. (Illus.). 334p. (C). 1994. 83.00 (*0-306-44382-1*, Plenum Trade) Perseus Pubng.

Covello, Vincent T. & Tinker, Tim L. Scientific Uncertainty & Its Influence on the Public Communication Process: Proceedings of the NATO Advanced Research Workshop, Paris, France, September 8-10, 1994. Sublet, Virginia H., ed. LC 96-28467. (NATO ASI Series D: Behavioural & Social Sciences). 248p. (C). 1996. text 144.00 (*0-7923-4180-5*) Kluwer Academic.

Covello, Vincent T., et al. Environmental Impact Assessment, Technology Assessment & Risk Analysis. (NATO ASI Series G: No. 4). x, 1068p. 1986. 350.95 (*0-387-15684-4*) Spr-Verlag.

Covello, Vincent T., jt. auth. see Cohrssen, John J.

Covello, Vincent T., jt. ed. see Fiksel, J.

Covello, Vincent T., jt. ed. see Lave, Lester B.

Covello, Vincent T., jt. ed. see Shipple, Chris.

Coven, Brenda. American Women Dramatists of the Twentieth Century: A Bibliography. LC 82-5942. 244p. 1982. 26.50 (*0-8108-1562-1*) Scarecrow.

Coven, Brenda, et al. David Merrick & Hal Prince: An Annotated Bibliography. LC 93-20378. 248p. 1993. text 20.00 (*0-8240-3041-9*, H883) Garland.

Coven, Brenda, jt. auth. see King, Christine E.

An Asterisk (*) at the beginning of an entry indicates that the title is appearing for the first time.

Coven, Ellen. Seniorobics: The Fitness Guide for People 55 Plus. LC 92-70482. (Illus.). 96p. (Orig.). 1992. pap. 14.95 (*0-9631945-7-7*) FitWise Progs.

Covenant Communications Staff, ed. see Stansfield, Anita.

Covenant House Texas Guild Staff. Loving Spoonfuls. (Illus.). 224p. 1995. 15.50 (*0-9648928-2-0*) Covenant House TX.

Coveney & Moore. Dictionary of Management Terms. (ARA, ENG & FRE.). 109p. 1990. pap. 19.95 (*0-86685-505-X*, LDL505X, Pub. by Librairie du Liban) Intl Bk Ctr.

***Coveney, Aidan.** Contemporary French Pronunciation. 100p. 1999. pap. 17.95 (*1-902454-02-2*, Pub. by Elm Bank Pubns) Intl Spec Bk.

Coveney, J., et al. Glossary of Spanish & English Management Terms. 2nd rev. ed. 1980. pap. 14.95 (*0-8288-0126-6*, S 39784) Fr & Eur.

***Coveney, John.** Food, Morals & Meaning: The Pleasure & Anxiety of Eating. LC 99-33642. 232p. 2000. text. write for info. (*0-415-20748-7*) Routledge.

— Food, Morals & Meaning: The Pleasure & Anxiety of Eating. 232p. 2000. pap. 25.99 (*0-415-20749-5*) Routledge.

Coveney, Michael. The World According to Mike Leigh. (Illus.). 260p. 1998. pap. 11.95 (*0-00-638339-4*, Pub. by HarpC) Trafalgar.

Coveney, Patrick & Moore, Karl. Business Angels: Securing Start up Finance. LC 97-31197. 244p. 1998. 79.50 (*0-471-97718-7*) Wiley.

Coveney, Peter & Highfield, Roger. Frontiers of Complexity: The Search for Order in a Chaotic World. (Illus.). 408p. 1996. pap. 15.00 (*0-449-91081-4*) Fawcett.

Coveney, Stephen R. & Pain, Andrew J. Interests in Land: A Practical Guide to Effective Protection at the Land Registry. 313p. 1995. pap. 125.00 (*0-85459-949-5*, Pub. by Tolley Pubng) St Mut.

Coveney, V. A., jt. ed. see Boast, D.

Coventry, Eng. Staff. The Coventry Leet Book: Parts I & II, Set. (EETS, OS Ser.: Nos. 134-35). 1972. reprint ed. 80.00 (*0-527-00132-5*) Periodicals Srv.

— The Coventry Leet Book: Parts III & IV, Set. (EETS, OS Ser.: Nos. 138 & 146). 1972. reprint ed. 72.00 (*0-527-00133-3*) Periodicals Srv.

Coventry, F., tr. see Grotius, Hugo.

Coventry, John. Faith in Jesus Christ. 54p. 1981. 3.95 (*0-86683-620-9*) Harper SF.

Coventry, Lucinda & Nixon, Martin, eds. The Oxford English Minidictionary. 5th ed. LC PE1628.O868 1999. 632p. 1999. pap. 6.95 (*0-19-860255-3*) OUP.

— Oxford Minireference Thesaurus. 2nd ed. LC 98-51864. 640p. 1999. pap. 7.95 (*0-19-860256-1*) OUP.

Coventry Pool & Garden Houses, Inc., Staff. Coventry Pool & Garden Houses. 1995. pap. 19.95 (*0-9645844-0-9*) Manor Hse.

Coventry, W. & Burstinger, Irving. Management: A Basic Handbook. 1977. 12.95 (*0-13-549188-6*, Spectrum IN) Macmillan Gen Ref.

Coventry, W. B. Notes on the Construction of the Violin, 1902. 75p. 1899. pap. 15.00 (*0-87556-358-9*) Saifer.

Cover & Garns. Theories of Knowledge & Reality. 2nd ed. (C). 1994. pap. 26.88 (*0-07-013269-0*) McGraw.

Cover, Arthur B. Autumn Angels. Krever, A. J., ed. 1999. pap. write for info. (*1-893475-01-8*) Alexander Pubg.

— An East Wind Coming. Date not set. write for info. (*1-893475-02-6*) Alexander Pubg.

— Infocom, No. 4: Stationfall. 304p. (Orig.). 1989. pap. 3.95 (*0-380-75387-1*, Avon Bks) Morrow Avon.

— Planetfall: In Search of Floyd. (INFOCOM Ser.: No. 1). 304p. 1988. pap. 3.95 (*0-380-75384-7*, Avon Bks) Morrow Avon.

— The Platypus of Doom (And Other Nihilists) Krever, A. J., ed. 1999. pap. write for info. (*1-893475-03-4*) Alexander Pubg.

— The Sound of Winter. Date not set. pap. write for info. (*1-893475-04-2*) Alexander Pubg.

Cover, Arthur B., ed. see Blaylock, James P.

Cover, Arthur B., ed. see Effinger, George A.

Cover, Arthur B., ed. see McEnroe, Richard.

Cover, Arthur B., ed. see Nolan, William F.

Cover, Arthur B., ed. see Schow, David J.

Cover, Arthur B., ed. see Shirley, John.

Cover, Arthur B., ed. see Somtow, S. P.

Cover, Arthur Byron. Night of the Living Rerun. (Buffy the Vampire Slayer Ser.: No. 4). 178p. (YA). (gr. 7-12). 1998. pap. 4.50 (*0-671-01715-2*) PB.

Cover, Dan. Sociological Investigations. 2nd ed. (C). 1997. spiral bd. 15.31 (*0-697-35634-5*) McGraw.

— Sociological Investigations. 2nd ed. LC 96-84718. 240p. 1993. 14.95 (*0-697-31043-4*, Dshkn McG-Hill) McGrw-H Hghr Educ.

Cover, Fred, jt. auth. see Pritchett, Price.

Cover, J. A. & O'Leary-Hawthorne, John. Substance & Individuation in Leibniz. LC 98-37115. 331p. 1999. 59.95 (*0-521-59394-8*) Cambridge U Pr.

Cover, Jan & Kulstad, Mark, eds. Central Themes in Early Modern Philosophy: Essays Presented to Jonathan Bennett. LC 90-44730. 350p. (C). 1990. pap. text 16.95 (*0-87220-109-0*); lib. bdg. 37.95 (*0-87220-110-4*) Hackett Pub.

Cover, Jan A., jt. auth. see Curd, Martin.

Cover, Jeanne. Love - The Driving Force: Mary Ward's Spirituality: Its Significance for Moral Thought. LC 96-51198. (Studies in Theology: No. 13). 217p. (Orig.). 1997. pap. 25.00 (*0-87462-637-4*) Marquette.

Cover, John H. Neighborhood Distribution & Consumption of Meat in Pittsburgh: As Related to Other Social & Economic Factors. LC 75-39353. (Getting & Spending: The Consumer's Dilemma Ser.). 1976. reprint ed. 23.95 (*0-405-08017-4*) Ayer.

Cover, Kathi & Chisum, Donald S. Acquiring & Protecting Intellectual Property Rights. Vol. IP3. text 82.00 (*0-8205-2399-2*) Bender.

Cover, Robert. Justice Accused: Antislavery & the Judicial Process. LC 74-19573. 334p. 1984. reprint ed. pap. 20.00 (*0-300-03252-8*, Y-509) Yale U Pr.

Cover, Rose M., et al. A Ministry of Consolation: Involving Your Parish in the Order of Christian Funerals. LC 96-36774. 136p. (Orig.). 1997. pap. text 14.95 (*0-8146-2460-X*, Liturg Pr Bks) Liturgical Pr.

Cover, T. M. & Gopinath, B., eds. Open Problems in Communication & Computation. (Illus.). 230p. 1987. 58.95 (*0-387-96621-8*) Spr-Verlag.

Cover, Thomas M. & Thomas, Joy A. Elements of Information Theory. 9th ed. LC 90-45484. (Series in Telecommunications). 576p. 1991. 79.95 (*0-471-06259-6*) Wiley.

Coverdale, Andrew. Football's Quick Passing Game Vol. 1: Fundamentals & Techniques. LC 97-69611. (Illus.). 164p. 1998. pap. 17.95 (*1-57167-155-2*) Coaches Choice.

— Football's Quick Passing Game Vol. 2: More Advanced Routes. LC 97-69611. (Illus.). 150p. 1998. pap. 17.95 (*1-57167-156-0*) Coaches Choice.

— Football's Quick Passing Game Vol. 3: Implementing the Package. LC 97-69611. (Illus.). 264p. 1998. pap. 19.95 (*1-57167-192-7*) Coaches Choice.

Coverdale, Andrew & Robinson, Dan. The Bunch Attack: Using Compressed Formations in the Passing Game. LC 96-69210. (Art & Science of Coaching Ser.). (Illus.). 260p. 1996. pap. 19.95 (*1-57167-044-0*) Coaches Choice.

Coverdale, John F. The Basque Phase of Spain's First Carlist War. LC 83-43068. (Illus.). 349p. reprint ed. pap. 108.20 (*0-8357-3843-4*, 203657600004) Bks Demand.

— The Political Transformation of Spain after Franco. LC 78-19777. (Praeger Special Studies). 150p. 1979. 45.00 (*0-275-90343-5*, C0343, Praeger Pubs) Greenwood.

Coverdale, Linda, tr. see Barthes, Roland.

Coverdale, Linda, tr. see Bianciotti, Hector.

Coverdale, Linda, tr. see Bontempelli, Bruno.

Coverdale, Linda, tr. see Carrere, Emmanuel.

Coverdale, Linda, tr. see Chamoiseau, Patrick.

Coverdale, Linda, tr. see Confiant, Raphael.

Coverdale, Linda, tr. see Darrieussecq, Marie.

Coverdale, Linda, tr. see Gille, Elizabeth.

Coverdale, Linda, tr. see Guibert, Herve.

Coverdale, Linda, tr. see Japrisot, Sebastien.

Coverdale, Linda, tr. see Labro, Philippe.

Coverdale, Linda, tr. see Manea, Norman.

Coverdale, Linda, tr. see Steinberg, Paul.

Coverdale, Linda, tr. see Szymusiak, Molyda.

Coverdale, Linda, tr. see Volodine, Antoine.

Coverdale, M., tr. from DUT. The Original & Sprynge of All Sectes & Orders by Whome, Wha or Where (Sic) They Beganne. LC 79-84127. (English Experience Ser.: No. 946). 140p. 1979. reprint ed. lib. bdg. 20.00 (*90-221-0946-1*) Walter J Johnson.

Coverdale, Myles. A Confutation of That Treatise Which One John Standish Made Agaynst the Protestacion of D. Barnes. LC 79-84096. (English Experience Ser.: No. 917). 212p. 1979. reprint ed. lib. bdg. 30.00 (*90-221-0917-8*) Walter J Johnson.

Coverdale, Myles, tr. see Bullinger, Heinrich.

Coverey, P. & Highfield, R. The Secret Art: Beyond Chaos. Date not set. pap. write for info. (*0-449-90833-X*) Fawcett.

Coverly, Carol J., ed. & compiled by see Macewen, Florence L.

***Coverly, Dave.** Speed Bump: Collection of Cartoon Skidmarks. LC 99-68669. (Illus.). 144p. 2000. pap. 9.95 (*0-7407-0599-7*) Andrews & McMeel.

Coverman, Sidney H., jt. auth. see Clarke, Antony B.

Covert, Alice L. What Price Love? (Orig.). 1979. mass mkt. 2.25 (*0-89083-491-1*, Zebra Kensgtn) Kensgtn Pub Corp.

Covert, Alice L. & O'More, Peggy. The Alien Heart. 1982. mass mkt. 2.50 (*0-451-11893-6*, AE1893, Sig) NAL.

Covert, Angela & Fredericks, H. D., eds. Transitions for Persons with Deaf-Blindness & Other Profound Handicaps: State of the Art. 180p. (Orig.). 1987. 10.00 (*0-944232-00-0*) Teaching Res.

Covert, Catherine L. & Stevens, John D., eds. Mass Media Between the Wars: Perceptions of Cultural Tension, 1918-1941. LC 83-20329. 240p. 1984. text 39.95 (*0-8156-2307-0*) Syracuse U Pr.

Covert, Catherine L., jt. auth. see Christians, Clifford G.

Covert, Eugene E., et al, eds. Thrust & Drag: Its Prediction & Verification. LC 85-18681. (PAAS Ser.: Vol. 98). (Illus.). 346p. 1985. 69.95 (*0-930403-00-2*, V-98) AIAA.

Covert, Henry G. Ministry to the Incarcerated. LC 95-8780. 185p. (Orig.). 1995. pap. 16.95 (*0-8294-0860-6*) Loyola Pr.

Covert, James T., ed. A Victorian Family As Seen Through the Letters of Louise Creighton to Her Mother, 1872-1880. LC 97-47571. 352p. 1998. text 99.95 (*0-7734-8500-7*) E Mellen.

Covert, Kim. The Coast Miwok Indians. LC 98-20013. (J). 1998. 14.00 (*0-7368-0077-8*, Bridgestone Bks) Capstone Pr.

— Miwok Indians. (Native Peoples Ser.). (J). 1998. 14.00 (*0-516-21355-5*) Childrens.

— The Powhatan People. LC 98-7269. (Native Peoples Ser.). (J). 1998. 14.00 (*0-7368-0078-6*, Bridgestone Bks) Capstone Pr.

***Covert, Kim.** U.S. Air Force Special Forces: Combat Controllers. LC 99-27334. (Warfare & Weapons Ser.). 1999. 19.93 (*0-7368-0334-3*) Capstone Pr.

— U.S. Air Force Special Forces: Pararescue. LC 99-14618. (Warfare & Weapons Ser.). (Illus.). 48p. (gr. 4-7). 1999. 19.93 (*0-7368-0335-1*) Capstone Pr.

Covert, Kim, et al. Warfare & Weapons. (Illus.). 48p. 127.60 (*0-7368-0465-X*, Capstone Bks) Capstone Pr.

Covert, Mary L., jt. auth. see Covert, William

Covert, Mildred L. & Gerson, Sylvia. Kosher Cajun Cookbook. LC 87-21110. (Illus.). 256p. 1987. pap. 17.95 (*0-88289-651-2*) Pelican.

Covert, Mildred L. & Gerson, Sylvia P. Kosher Creole Cookbook. LC 81-15841. (Illus.). 224p. 1982. spiral bd. 17.95 (*0-88289-775-6*) Pelican.

— Kosher Southern-Style Cookbook. LC 92-15413. (Illus.). 256p. 1992. 17.95 (*0-88289-850-7*) Pelican.

Covert, Nadine, et al, eds. Films & Videos on Photography. 132p. 1991. pap. 14.95 (*0-87099-573-1*) OUP.

Covert, Nadine & Wick, Vivian, compiled by. Films on Art Bibliography. 40p. 1994. pap. 15.00 (*0-87099-704-1*) J P Getty Trust.

Covert, Nadine & Wick, Vivian, eds. Architecture on Screen: Films & Videos on Architecture, Landscape Architecture, Historic Preservation, City & Regional Planning. LC 93-36811. 300p. 1994. 75.00 (*0-8161-0593-6*, G K Hall & Co); pap. 45.00 (*0-8161-0625-8*, G K Hall & Co) Mac Lib Ref.

Covert, Pat. Basics of Scale Automotive Modeling: Getting Started in the Hobby. LC 99-186287. 1999. pap. text 15.95 (*0-89024-320-4*) Kalmbach.

— Building Better Scale Model Cars & Trucks: Detailing Tips & Techniques. LC 98-206286. 1998. pap. text 14.95 (*0-89024-288-7*) Kalmbach.

— The Modeler's Guide to Scale Automotive Finishes. unabridged ed. LC 97-152892. (Illus.). 88p. (Orig.). 1997. pap. 17.95 (*0-89024-265-8*, 12162, Kalmbach Books) Kalmbach.

Covert, Paul. Cages. (New Writers Ser.). 1971. 3.95 (*0-87140-531-8*, Pub. by Liveright) Norton.

Covert, Rosemary, jt. auth. see Comeau, Gilles.

Covert, Susan B. Whatever It Takes! Excellence in Family Support: When Families Experience a Disability. LC 95-7831. (Illus.). 89p. (Orig.). 1995. pap. 2?.00 (*1-883302-08-0*) Trning Res.

Covert, William & Covert, Mary L. Home Tweet Home: The Bird Lover's Housebuilding Guide for Feathered Friends. (Illus.). 64p. 1999. pap. 19.95 (*1-885221-21-5*) BookPartners.

Covert, William V. & Patterson, Maurice, eds. The Covert Family. (Illus.). 600p. 1989. lib. bdg. 35.00 (*0-9622056-0-5*) Interlaken Hist.

Coverte, Robert. A True & Almost Incredible Report of an Englishman That Travelled by Land Through Many Kingdoms. LC 72-186. (English Experience Ser.: No. 302). 1971. reprint ed. 20.00 (*90-221-0302-1*) Walter J Johnson.

Covesdale, Linda, tr. see Ernaux, Annie.

Covey, jt. auth. see Cavalier.

***Covey, Anne.** The Workplace Law Advisor: From Harassment & Discrimination Policies to Hiring & Firing Guidelines--What Every Manager & Employee Needs to Know. 256p. 2000. pap. text 17.00 (*0-7382-0374-2*, Pub. by Perseus Pubng) HarpC.

Covey, Barbara L., jt. auth. see Sivertsen, Barbara J.

Covey, Bruce. The Greek Gods As Telephone Wires. LC 92-71048. (Orig.). 1992. pap. 6.95 (*0-9628759-1-8*) Front Rm.

Covey-Crump, W. W. The Hiramic Tradition: A Survey of Hypotheses Concerning It. 120p. 1992. reprint ed. pap. 16.00 (*1-56459-294-4*) Kessinger Pub.

Covey, Cyclone, tr. see Nunez Cabeza de Vaca, Alvar.

Covey, Elizabeth, jt. auth. see Ingham, Rosemary.

Covey, Ellen, et al, eds. Neural Representation of Temporal Patterns: Proceedings of a Symposium Held in Durham, North Carolina, April 29-May 2, 1993. 274p. (C). 1996. text 95.00 (*0-306-45199-9*, Kluwer Plenum) Kluwer Academic.

Covey, Ellen, tr. see Neuweiler, Gerhard.

Covey, Herbert C. Images of Older People in Western Art & Society. LC 90-38714. 216p. 1991. 55.00 (*0-275-93435-7*, C3435, Praeger Pubs) Greenwood.

Covey, Herbert C., et al. Juvenile Gangs. 2nd ed. LC 96-30243. (Illus.). 374p. 1996. text 69.95 (*0-398-06716-3*); pap. text 49.95 (*0-398-06717-1*) C C Thomas.

Covey, Herbert C., jt. auth. see Mercer, Blaine.

Covey, Herbert S. Social Perceptions of People with Disabilities in History. LC 97-38919. (Illus.). 324p. 1998. text 62.95 (*0-398-06837-2*); pap. text 49.95 (*0-398-06838-0*) C C Thomas.

Covey, Karen J. The Complete First Kitchen Handbook: A Complete Guide to Setting up Your First Kitchen Including over a Hundred Quick & Easy Recipes for Both the New & More Experienced Cook. (Illus.). 176p. (Orig.). 1996. pap. 16.95 (*0-9646880-0-X*) Fiyah Pubng.

Covey Leadership Center, Inc Staff. Quotes & Quips. pap. 8.95 (*1-883219-12-4*) Franklin Covey.

Covey, Lirio S., jt. ed. see Seldman, Daniel F.

Covey, Liz, jt. auth. see Ingham, Rosemary.

***Covey, Mary M.** A Snowman's Family Album Quilt. LC 00-33932. (Illus.). 2000. write for info. (*1-56477-318-3*) Martingale & Co.

Covey, R. O. Probing Our Problems. 176p. (Orig.). 1986. pap. 5.95 (*0-934942-59-5*, 3950) White Wing Pub.

Covey, S. N., jt. auth. see Grierson, Donald.

***Covey, Sean.** Daily Reflections for Highly Effective Teens. LC 99-43820. 384p. 1999. per. 11.00 (*0-684-87060-6*) S&S Trade.

— 7 Habits of Highly Effective Teens. 1999. pap., wbk. ed. 5.00 (*1-929494-17-3*) Franklin Covey.

Covey, Sean. The 7 Habits of Highly Effective Teens: The Ultimate Teenage Success Guide. LC 98-38031. 288p. (YA). 1998. per. 14.00 (*0-684-85609-3*) S&S Trade Pap.

Covey, Sean & Harris-Johnson, Debrah. The 7 Habits of Highly Effective Teens Journal. 1999. 14.95 (*1-883219-85-X*) Franklin Covey.

Covey, Stephen R. Aura of the Cause. 206p. 1997. text 49.95 (*0-252-02377-3*) U of Ill Pr.

— Before I Do Math: Discovering First Number Skills. (Illus.). 32p. (J). (ps-3). 1991. pap. 2.09 (*0-307-03597-2*, 03597, Goldn Books) Gldn Bks Pub Co.

— Cursive Writing. (Step Ahead Plus Workbooks). (Illus.). 64p. (J). (gr. 1-6). 1997. pap., wbk. ed. 3.49 (*0-307-03660-X*, 03660) Gldn Bks Pub Co.

— Daily Reflections for Highly Effective People: Living the Seven Habits Everyday. 384p. 1994. per. 11.00 (*0-671-88717-3*, Fireside) S&S Trade Pap.

— The Divine Center. 1982. 16.95 (*0-88494-471-9*) Bookcraft Inc.

— How to Succeed with People. 141p. 1993. reprint ed. pap. 12.95 (*0-87579-681-8*) Deseret Bk.

— I Can Read. (Step Ahead Workbooks Ser.). (Illus.). 32p. (J). (ps-3). 1985. pap. 2.09 (*0-307-03588-3*, 03588, Goldn Books) Gldn Bks Pub Co.

— I Know the Alphabet. (Step Ahead Plus Ser.). (Illus.). 64p. (J). (ps-3). 1993. pap., wbk. ed. 3.50 (*0-307-03669-3*, 03669) Gldn Bks Pub Co.

— Kindergarten Skills. (Step Ahead Plus Workbks.). (Illus.). 64p. (J). (ps-k). 1997. pap., wbk. ed. 3.49 (*0-307-03673-1*, 03673) Gldn Bks Pub Co.

— Learn with Dots & Mazes. (Step Ahead Plus Ser.). (Illus.). 64p. (J). (ps-3). 1995. pap., wbk. ed. 3.49 (*0-307-03648-0*, 03648, Goldn Books) Gldn Bks Pub Co.

Covey, Stephen R. Living the 7 Habits. abr. ed. audio 12.00 (*0-671-51994-8*, 390132, Pub. by S&S Audio) Lndmrk Audiobks.

— Living the Seven Habits: Applications & Insights. 368p. 1999. 12.00 incl. audio (*0-671-04567-9*) S&S Audio.

— Living the 7 Habits: Stories of Courage & Inspiration. 336p. 2000. per. 14.00 (*0-684-85716-2*, Fireside) S&S Trade Pap.

Covey, Stephen R. Living the 7 Habits: Understanding, Using, Succeeding. LC 99-28061. 336p. 1999. 26.00 (*0-684-84664-0*) S&S Trade.

***Covey, Stephen R.** Los 7 Habitos De La Familias Altamente Efectivas. 1999. pap. 23.95 (*970-05-1004-2*) Distribks Inc.

Covey, Stephen R. Math Skillbuilders. (Step Ahead Plus Workbooks). (Illus.). 64p. (J). (gr. 3-4). 1995. pap., wbk. ed. 3.50 (*0-307-03657-X*, 03657) Gldn Bks Pub Co.

***Covey, Stephen R.** The Portable 7 Habits: Choice: Choosing the Proactive Life You Want to Live. 128p. 1999. 10.95 (*1-929494-02-5*) Franklin Covey.

Covey, Stephen R. Precious Moments: Little Blessings. (Super Shape Bks.). (Illus.). 24p. (J). (ps-3). 1996. pap. text 3.29 (*0-307-10001-4*, 10001, Goldn Books) Gldn Bks Pub Co.

— Principle-Centered Leadership. 336p. 1991. 24.50 (*0-671-74910-2*) Summit Bks.

— Principle-Centered Leadership: Strategies for Personal & Professional Effectiveness. 336p. 1992. per. 14.00 (*0-671-79280-6*) S&S Trade.

— Quotes & Quips: Insights on Living the 7 Habits. 1998. 12.95 (*1-883219-93-0*) Franklin Covey.

***Covey, Stephen R.** Renewal: Nourishing Mind, Body, Heart & Soul. (Portable 7 Habits Ser.). 128p. 1999. 10.95 (*1-929494-03-3*) Franklin Covey.

Covey, Stephen R. 7 Habits Family Journal. 1998. 14.95 (*1-883219-57-4*); pap. 14.95 (*1-883219-58-2*) Franklin Covey.

— The 7 Habits of Highly Effective Families. 3rd unabridged ed. 400p. 1998. pap. 15.00 (*0-307-44085-0*, Whitman Coin) St Martin.

— The 7 Habits of Highly Effective Families: Building a Beautiful Family Culture in a Turbulent World. unabridged ed. LC 97-23152. (Illus.). 390p. 1997. text 25.00 (*0-307-44008-7*, Whitman Coin) St Martin.

— The Seven Habits of Highly Effective Families. 1996. 25.00 (*0-684-82608-9*) S&S Trade.

— The 7 Habits of Highly Effective People. large type ed. LC 97-4210. 585p. 1997. 27.95 (*0-7838-8115-0*, G K Hall Lrg Type) Mac Lib Ref.

— The Seven Habits of Highly Effective People: Powerful Lessons in Personal Change. 352p. 1989. 24.50 (*0-671-66398-4*) S&S Trade.

— Seven Habits of Highly Effective People: Powerful Lessons in Personal Change. 368p. 1990. per. 14.00 (*0-671-70863-5*) S&S Trade.

— Shapes & Colors. (Step Ahead Plus Ser.). (Illus.). 64p. (J). (ps-3). 1995. pap., wbk. ed. 3.49 (*0-307-03649-9*, 03649, Goldn Books) Gldn Bks Pub Co.

— Los Siete Habitos de la Gente Altamente Effectiva: The Seven Habits of Highly Effective People. 448p. 1997. pap. text 14.00 (*0-684-84344-7*) Simon & Schuster.

— Spiritual Roots of Human Relations. 2nd ed. LC 93-2875. 326p. 1993. pap. 14.95 (*0-87579-705-9*) Deseret Bk.

— Splash & Play: Super Paint with Water. (Little Mermaid Ser.). (J). 1997. pap. text 2.99 (*0-307-02708-2*, 02708, Goldn Books) Gldn Bks Pub Co.

— 360 Words I Know. (Step Ahead Plus Workbks.). (Illus.). 64p. (J). (gr. k-2). 1997. pap., wbk. ed. 3.49 (*0-307-03672-3*, 03672) Gldn Bks Pub Co.

— What a Wonderful World: Precious Moments. (Super Shape Bks.). (Illus.). 24p. (J). (ps). 1992. 3.29 (*0-307-10022-7*, 10022) Gldn Bks Pub Co.

Covey, Stephen R., et al, contrib. by. Power Talk, unabridged ed. (Professional Ser.). 1993. text 48.85 incl. audio (*1-55927-254-6*) Audio Renaissance.

Covey, Stephen R. & Merrill, A. Roger. First Things First. (Illus.). 384p. 1996. per. 14.00 (*0-684-80203-1*, Fireside) S&S Trade Pap.

— First Things First: A Principle-Centered Approach to Time & Life Management. (Illus.). 384p. 1994. 22.50 (*0-671-86441-6*) S&S Trade.

Covey, Stephen R., et al. First Things First. 1995. pap. 14.00 (*0-668-48020-3*) S&S Trade.

C

— First Things First Everyday. LC 97-9970. 1997. pap. 11.00 (0-684-84240-8, Fireside) S&S Trade Pap.
***Covey, Stephen R., et al.** The Nature of Leadership. 1998. 37.95 (1-883219-90-6) Franklin Covey.
***Covey, Steven R.** The 7 Habits of Highly Effective People. 2000. 4.95 (0-7624-0833-2) Running Pr.
Covi, Madeline C., jt. auth. see Knoefel, Peter K.
Covian, F. Grande. Nutricion y Salud. 1999. pap. text 10.95 (84-7880-758-6) Planeta.
Covich, Alan P., jt. ed. see Thorp, James H.
Covici, Pascal, Jr. Humor & Revelation in American Literature: The Puritan Connection. LC 96-43457. 248p. (C). 1997. 39.95 (0-8262-1095-3) U of Mo Pr.
Covici, Pascal, Jr., jt. auth. see Crane, Stephen.
Covici, Pascal, Jr., ed. see Steinbeck, John.
Coviello, Carole, ed. see Huber, Helen & Spatz, Audree.
Covill, Dave, jt. auth. see Mitchler, John D.
Covill, Randall. Migrating to the Intranet & Microsoft Exchange. LC 96-29966. 223p. 1997. pap. text 29.95 (1-55558-172-2) Buttrwrth-Heinemann.
Covill, Randall J. Implementing Extranets. LC 98-23427. 204p. 1998. pap. text 32.95 (1-55558-197-8) DEC.
Coville. Aliens Stole My Body Bruce Covilles Alien Adventures. (J). 1998. per. 3.99 (0-671-79835-9) PB.
— My Teacher Fried My Brains. (J). 1991. per. 2.99 (0-671-74610-3) PB.
Coville, Alfred, et al, eds. Studies in Anglo-French History During the Eighteenth, Nineteenth & Twentieth Centuries. LC 67-23197. (Essay Index Reprint Ser.). 1977. 19.95 (0-8369-0343-9) Ayer.
Coville, Bruce. Aliens Ate My Homework. 179p. (J). (gr. 4-6). pap. 3.99 (0-8072-1503-1) Listening Lib.
Coville, Bruce. Aliens Ate My Homework. (Illus.). 160p. (J). (gr. 3-6). 1993. 14.00 (0-671-87249-4, Minstrel Bks); per. 3.99 (0-671-72712-5, Minstrel Bks) PB.
Coville, Bruce. Aliens Ate My Homework. (J). 1993. 9.09 (0-606-05111-2, Pub. by Turtleback) Demco.
Coville, Bruce. Aliens Stole My Body. (Illus.). (J). (gr. 3-7). 1997. write for info. (0-614-29159-3, Minstrel Bks) PB.
— Aliens Stole My Body. (Bruce Coville's Alien Adventures Ser.). (J). (gr. 3-7). 1998. 9.09 (0-606-13115-9, Pub. by Turtleback) Demco.
Coville, Bruce. Amulet of Doom. (Bruce Coville's Chamber of Horrors Ser.). (J). 1996. 9.09 (0-606-09111-4, Pub. by Turtleback) Demco.
Coville, Bruce. Amulet of Doom: Bruce Coville's Chamber of Horrors. (Chamber of Horrors Ser.: No. 1). (YA). (gr. 6 up). 1996. mass mkt. 3.99 (0-671-53637-0, Archway) PB.
— Angells Players. (J). 1999. pap. 3.50 (0-14-036884-1, Viking) Viking Penguin.
— The Attack of the Two-Inch Teacher. 165p. (J). (gr. 3-6). 1999. per. 3.99 (0-671-02651-8) S&S Trade.
***Coville, Bruce.** Attack of the Two-Inch Teacher. (Illus.). (J). 1999. 9.34 (0-606-18374-4) Turtleback.
Coville, Bruce. Blork's Evil Twin. (Space Brat Ser.: No. 2). (Illus.). 80p. (J). (gr. 4-7). 1993. 12.00 (0-671-87038-6, Minstrel Bks); pap. 3.99 (0-671-77713-0, Minstrel Bks) PB.
— Blork's Evil Twin. (Space Brat Ser.: No. 2). (J). (gr. 4-7). 1993. 9.09 (0-606-05616-5, Pub. by Turtleback) Demco.
Coville, Bruce. Bruce Coville, 4 bks. (YA). 1996. pap., boxed set 15.96 (0-590-67593-1) Scholastic Inc.
— Bruce Coville's Book of Aliens: More Tales to Warp Your Mind. 1996. 9.09 (0-606-10765-7, Pub. by Turtleback) Demco.
Coville, Bruce. Bruce Coville's Book of Aliens: Tales to Warp Your Mind. 160p. (J). (gr. 4-7). 1994. pap. 3.99 (0-590-46162-1) Scholastic Inc.
Coville, Bruce. Bruce Coville's Book of Aliens: Tales to Warp Your Mind. (J). 1994. 9.09 (0-606-05771-4, Pub. by Turtleback) Demco.
Coville, Bruce. Bruce Coville's Book of Aliens II. LC 49-242560. (Illus.). (J). (gr. 5-7). 1996. pap. 3.99 (0-590-85293-0) Scholastic Inc.
— Bruce Coville's Book of Ghosts: Tales to Haunt You. LC 94-231878. 160p. (J). (gr. 5-7). 1994. pap. 3.99 (0-590-46160-5) Scholastic Inc.
— Bruce Coville's Book of Ghosts 2: More Tales to Haunt You. LC 97-140290. 1997. pap. text 3.99 (0-590-85294-9) Scholastic Inc.
— Bruce Coville's Book of Magic: Tales to Cast a Spell on You. (J). (gr. 3-7). 1996. pap. 3.99 (0-614-15769-2, Apple Paperbacks) Scholastic Inc.
— Bruce Coville's Book of Magic II. LC 97-205626. 165p. (J). (gr. 3-7). 1997. pap. text 3.99 (0-590-85297-3) Scholastic Inc.
— Bruce Coville's Book of Magic Tales to Cast a Spell on You. (J). (gr. 3-7). 1996. pap. 3.99 (0-590-25931-8) Scholastic Inc.
— Bruce Coville's Book of Monsters, No. 2. LC 96-201792. (Illus.). (J). (gr. 3-7). 1996. pap. text 3.99 (0-590-85292-2) Scholastic Inc.
— Bruce Coville's Book of Monsters: Tales to Give You the Creeps. (Illus.). 176p. (J). (gr. 4-7). 1993. pap. 3.99 (0-590-46159-1) Scholastic Inc.
Coville, Bruce. Bruce Coville's Book of Monsters: Tales to Give You the Creeps. 1993. 9.09 (0-606-05173-2, Pub. by Turtleback) Demco.
Coville, Bruce. Bruce Coville's Book of Nightmares: More Tales to Make You Scream. 1997. 9.09 (0-606-11170-0, Pub. by Turtleback) Demco.
— Bruce Coville's Book of Nightmares: Tales to Make You Scream. 160p. (J). (gr. 4-7). 1995. pap. 3.99 (0-590-46161-3) Scholastic Inc.
— Bruce Coville's Book of Nightmares II: More Tales to Make You Scream. (J). (gr. 3-7). 1997. pap. 3.99 (0-614-29023-6, Apple Classics) Scholastic Inc.
— Bruce Coville's Book of Spine Tinglers. 1997. 9.09 (0-606-11171-9, Pub. by Turtleback) Demco.
— Bruce Coville's Book of Spine Tinglers: Tales to Make You Shiver. (Illus.). (J). (gr. 4-7). 1996. pap. text 3.99 (0-590-25930-X) Scholastic Inc.
— Bruce Coville's Book of Spine Tinglers: Tales to Make You Shiver. (J). (gr. 3-7). 1996. pap. 3.99 (0-614-15768-4, Apple Paperbacks) Scholastic Inc.
***Coville, Bruce.** Bruce Coville's Strange Worlds. LC 98-94952. (Illus.). 208p. (J). (gr. 3-7). 2000. mass mkt. 4.99 (0-380-80256-2, Avon Bks) Morrow Avon.
— Bruce Coville's Strange Worlds. (Illus.). (J). 2000. 10.34 (0-606-17960-7) Turtleback.
— Bruce Coville's UFOs. (Illus.). (J). 2000. 10.34 (0-606-18679-4) Turtleback.
— Bruce Coville's Ufos. LC 99-96357. (Illus.). 224p. (J). (gr. 3-7). 2000. mass mkt. 4.99 (0-380-80257-0) Morrow Avon.
— The Dinosaur That Followed Me Home. (Camp Haunted Hills Ser.). (J). 1990. 8.60 (0-606-03212-6, Pub. by Turtleback) Demco.
Coville, Bruce. The Dinosaur That Followed Me Home, No. 3. (Camp Haunted Hills Ser.). (Illus.). 160p. (J). (gr. 3-6). 1990. mass mkt. 3.50 (0-671-64750-4, Minstrel Bks) PB.
— Don't Fry My Veeblax Vol. 6: I Was a Sixth Grade Alien. Vol. 6. (Illus.). 208p. (J). (gr. 3-6). 2000. per. 3.99 (0-671-02655-0, Minstrel Bks) PB.
— The Dragonslayers. MacDonald, Patricia, ed. LC 93-40194. (Illus.). 128p. (J). (gr. 3-6). 1994. 14.00 (0-671-89036-0, Minstrel Bks); per. 3.99 (0-671-79832-4, Minstrel Bks) PB.
— The Dragonslayers. LC 93-40194. (J). 1994. 9.09 (0-606-06337-4, Pub. by Turtleback) Demco.
— Eyes of the Tarot. LC 49-118050. (Bruce Coville's Chamber of Horrors Ser.: No. 3). 160p. (J). (gr. 7 up). 1996. per. 3.99 (0-671-53639-7) S&S Trade.
— Eyes of the Tarot. 1996. 9.09 (0-606-10150-0, Pub. by Turtleback) Demco.
— Forever Begins Tomorrow. (A. I. Gang Ser.: No. 3). (J). (gr. 3-6). 1995. pap. 3.99 (0-671-89253-3, Minstrel Bks) PB.
— Forever Begins Tomorrow. (A.I. Gang Ser.). 1995. 9.09 (0-606-07168-7, Pub. by Turtleback) Demco.
— Fortune's Journey. LC 94-38121. 224p. (YA). (gr. 5 up). 1997. 13.95 (0-8167-3650-2) BrdgeWater.
— Fortune's Journey. (J). 1997. pap. 4.95 (0-8167-3651-0) Troll Communs.
— Ghost in the Big Brass Bed. 192p. (J). (gr. 4-7). 1991. pap. 3.99 (0-553-15827-9) Bantam.
— Ghost in the Big Brass Bed. (J). 1991. 9.09 (0-606-00467-X, Pub. by Turtleback) Demco.
— Ghost in the Third Row. 144p. (J). 1987. pap. 4.50 (0-553-15646-2, Skylark BDD) BDD Bks Young Read.
— Ghost in the Third Row. (J). 1987. 9.09 (0-606-01903-0, Pub. by Turtleback) Demco.
— The Ghost Saw Red. (J). 1998. write for info. (0-385-32215-1) BDD Bks Young Read.
— The Ghost Wore Grey. 160p. (Orig.). (J). 1988. pap. 4.50 (0-553-15610-1, Skylark BDD) BDD Bks Young Read.
— A Glory of Unicorns. LC 97-13689. (J). 1998. pap. write for info. (0-590-95582-9) Scholastic Inc.
***Coville, Bruce.** A Glory of Unicorns. (Illus.). 208p. (J). (gr. 4-9). 2000. mass mkt. 5.50 (0-439-06628-X, Apple Paperbacks) Scholastic Inc.
Coville, Bruce. A Glory of Unicorns. LC 97-13689. (Illus.). 198p. (J). (gr. 4-9). 1998. 16.95 (0-590-95943-3) Scholastic Inc.
***Coville, Bruce.** Glory of Unicorns. (Illus.). (J). 1998. 9.85 (0-606-18551-8) Turtleback.
Coville, Bruce. Goblins in the Castle. MacDonald, Pat, ed. LC 94-134074. (Illus.). 176p. (J). (gr. 4-7). 1992. pap. 3.99 (0-671-72711-7, Minstrel Bks) PB.
— Goblins in the Castle. (J). 1992. 9.09 (0-606-02190-6, Pub. by Turtleback) Demco.
— How I Survived My Summer Vacation. (Camp Haunted Hills Ser.). (J). 1988. 9.09 (0-606-03819-1, Pub. by Turtleback) Demco.
— How I Survived My Summer Vacation, No. 1. (Camp Haunted Hills Ser.). (Illus.). 96p. (J). (gr. 3-5). 1988. mass mkt. 3.99 (0-671-68176-1, Minstrel Bks) PB.
— I Left My Sneakers in Dimension X. MacDonald, Pat, ed. 160p. (J). (gr. 3-6). 1994. 14.00 (0-671-89072-7, Minstrel Bks); pap. 3.99 (0-671-79833-2, Minstrel Bks) PB.
Coville, Bruce. I Left My Sneakers in Dimension X. 1994. 9.09 (0-606-07008-7, Pub. by Turtleback) Demco.
— I Lost My Grandfather's Brain. (Illus.). (J). 1999. 9.34 (0-606-18306-X) Turtleback.
— I Was a Sixth Grade Alien. 170p. (J). (gr. 4-6). pap. 3.99 (0-8072-8202-2) Listening Lib.
— I Was a 6th Grade Alien. LC 99-23229. 1999. 16.00 (0-671-03651-3); per. 3.99 (0-671-02650-X) S&S Trade.
Coville, Bruce. Into the Land of the Unicorns. LC 94-16892. (Unicorn Chronicles Ser.: Bk. 1). 176p. (J). (gr. 3-7). 1994. 12.95 (0-590-45955-4) Scholastic Inc.
— Into the Land of the Unicorns. (Unicorn Chronicles Ser.: Bk. 1). 176p. (J). (gr. 3-7). 1995. pap. 4.50 (0-590-45956-2) Scholastic Inc.
— Into the Land of the Unicorns. (Unicorn Chronicles). 1994. 9.60 (0-606-07710-3, Pub. by Turtleback) Demco.
— Into the Land of the Unicorns, 2. unabridged ed. (Unicorn Chronicles: Bk. 1). (J). (gr. 3-6). 1998. audio 16.98 (0-8072-7962-5, YA952CX) Listening Lib.
Coville, Bruce. Into the Land of the Unicorns: The Unicorn Chronicles Book One. 159p. pap. 4.50 (0-8072-1518-X) Listening Lib.
Coville, Bruce. Is Your Teacher an Alien? 1997. mass mkt. 3.50 (0-671-01184-7) PB.
— Jennifer Murdley's Toad. LC 91-33811. (Illus.). 160p. (J). (ps-3). 1992. 16.95 (0-15-200745-8, Gulliver Bks) Harcourt.
Coville, Bruce. Jennifer Murdley's Toad. 159p. pap. 3.99 (0-8072-1483-3) Listening Lib.
Coville, Bruce. Jennifer Murdley's Toad. (Magic Shop Bks.). (J). 1992. 9.09 (0-606-05382-4, Pub. by Turtleback) Demco.
— Jennifer Murdley's Toad. MacDonald, Pat, ed. (Illus.). 176p. (J). (gr. 4-7). 1993. reprint ed. pap. 3.99 (0-671-79401-9, Minstrel Bks) PB.
— Jeremy Thatcher, Dragon Hatcher. Yolen, Jane, ed. LC 90-5101. (Illus.). 160p. (J). (gr. 4-7). 1991. 16.95 (0-15-200748-2, Harcourt Child Bks) Harcourt.
Coville, Bruce. Jeremy Thatcher, Dragon Hatcher. 148p. (J). (gr. 4-6). pap. 4.50 (0-8072-1471-X) Listening Lib.
Coville, Bruce. Jeremy Thatcher, Dragon Hatcher. (Magic Shop Bks.). (J). 1991. 9.09 (0-606-00886-1, Pub. by Turtleback) Demco.
— Jeremy Thatcher, Dragon Hatcher. MacDonald, Patricia, ed. LC 90-5101. (Illus.). 64p. (J). (ps-3). 1992. reprint ed. pap. 3.99 (0-671-74782-7, Minstrel Bks) PB.
Coville, Bruce. Jeremy Thatcher, Dragon Hatcher. unabridged ed. (J). (gr. 3-6). 1995. pap. 21.98 incl. audio (0-8072-7532-8) Listening Lib.
Coville, Bruce. The Lapsnatcher. LC 96-21611. (Illus.). 32p. (J). 1997. 15.95 (0-8167-4233-2) BrdgeWater.
— Monster of the Year. (J). (gr. 3-6). 1990. pap. 3.50 (0-671-73147-5, Minstrel Bks) PB.
— Monster of the Year. (J). 1989. 9.09 (0-606-01968-5, Pub. by Turtleback) Demco.
— The Monster's Ring. (Magic Shop Bks.). (J). (gr. 3-6). 1989. mass mkt. 3.99 (0-671-69389-1, Minstrel Bks) PB.
Coville, Bruce. Monster's Ring. (J). 1982. 9.09 (0-606-03620-2, Pub. by Turtleback) Demco.
Coville, Bruce. My Grandfather's House. LC 95-3630. (Illus.). 32p. (J). (gr. k-3). 1996. 14.95 (0-8167-3804-1) BrdgeWater.
— My Grandfather's House. (Illus.). (J). (gr. 3 up). 1997. pap. 4.95 (0-8167-3805-X) Troll Communs.
— My Teacher Flunked the Planet. (J). 1992. per. 3.99 (0-671-79199-0) PB.
— My Teacher Flunked the Planet. MacDonald, Pat, ed. (Illus.). 176p. (J). (gr. 3-8). 1992. pap. 3.99 (0-671-75081-X, Minstrel Bks) PB.
— My Teacher Flunked the Planet. (My Teacher Is an Alien Ser.). (J). 1992. 8.60 (0-606-02087-X, Pub. by Turtleback) Demco.
— My Teacher Fried My Brains. MacDonald, Patricia, ed. 128p. (J). (gr. 3-7). 1991. per. 3.99 (0-671-72710-9, Minstrel Bks) PB.
— My Teacher Fried My Brains. (J). 1991. 9.09 (0-606-04984-3, Pub. by Turtleback) Demco.
— My Teacher Glows in the Dark. MacDonald, Patricia, ed. (Illus.). 144p. (J). (gr. 4-7). 1991. per. 3.99 (0-671-72709-5, Minstrel Bks) PB.
— My Teacher Glows in the Dark. (J). 1991. 9.09 (0-606-04985-1, Pub. by Turtleback) Demco.
Coville, Bruce. My Teacher Is an Alien. 123p. (J). (gr. 3-6). pap. 4.50 (0-8072-1528-7) Listening Lib.
— My Teacher Is an Alien. (Camp Haunted Hills Ser.). (Illus.). 123p. (J). (gr. 3-7). 1989. pap. 3.99 (0-671-73729-5, Minstrel Bks) PB.
Coville, Bruce. My Teacher Is an Alien. (J). 1997. per. 3.99 (0-671-31189-1) PB.
— My Teacher Is an Alien. 1997. cd-rom 34.95 (0-671-57662-3) S&S Childrens.
***Coville, Bruce.** My Teacher Is an Alien. (J). 1999. pap. 16.00 (0-671-03571-1) S&S Trade.
Coville, Bruce. My Teacher Is an Alien. (J). 1989. 9.09 (0-606-04280-6, Pub. by Turtleback) Demco.
Coville, Bruce. Night. LC 97-155113. (J). 1997. mass mkt. 3.99 (0-590-85295-7) Scholastic Inc.
— Odder Than Ever. LC 98-51102. 160p. (YA). (gr. 7 up). 1998. 16.00 (0-15-201747-X, Harcourt Child Bks) Harcourt.
— Odder Than Ever. 144p. (YA). (gr. 8-12). 2000. pap. 6.00 (0-15-202465-4, Harcourt Child Bks) Harcourt.
Coville, Bruce. Oddly Enough. LC 94-16286. (Illus.). 176p. (YA). (gr. 7 up). 1994. 15.95 (0-15-200093-3, Harcourt Child Bks) Harcourt.
— Oddly Enough. (YA). 1997. per. 3.99 (0-671-51693-0) PB.
Coville, Bruce. Oddly Enough. LC 94-16286. 1997. 9.09 (0-606-11695-8, Pub. by Turtleback) Demco.
Coville, Bruce. Operation Sherlock. MacDonald, Pat, ed. (A. I. Gang Ser.). 224p. (J). 1995. pap. 3.99 (0-671-89249-5, Minstrel Bks) PB.
— Operation Sherlock. (A.I. Gang Ser.). 1995. 9.09 (0-606-07169-5, Pub. by Turtleback) Demco.
***Coville, Bruce.** Peanut Butter Lover Boy. (I Was a Sixth Grade Alien Ser.: Vol. 4). (Illus.). 192p. (J). 2000. per. 3.99 (0-671-02653-4, Minstrel Bks) PB.
— Peanut Butter Lover Boy. (Illus.). (J). 2000. 9.34 (0-606-18307-8) Turtleback.
Coville, Bruce. Planet of the Dips. LC 95-69331. (Space Brat Ser.: No. 4). (Illus.). 71p. (J). (gr. 4-7). 1995. 14.00 (0-671-50090-2, Minstrel Bks); pap. 3.99 (0-671-50092-9, Minstrel Bks) PB.
— Planet of the Dips. (Space Brat Ser.: No. 4). (J). (gr. 4-7). 1995. 9.19 (0-606-08188-7, Pub. by Turtleback) Demco.
***Coville, Bruce.** The Prince of Butterflies. LC 99-50811. (Illus.). (J). 2002. write for info. (0-15-201454-3, Harcourt Child Bks) Harcourt.
Coville, Bruce. Robot Trouble. MacDonald, Pat, ed. (A. I. Gang Ser.). 224p. (J). 1995. pap. 3.99 (0-671-89252-5, Minstrel Bks) PB.
— Robot Trouble. (A.I. Gang Ser.). 1995. 9.09 (0-606-07170-9, Pub. by Turtleback) Demco.
— The Saber-Toothed Poodnoobie. (Space Brat Ser.: No. 5). (Illus.). (J). (gr. 4-7). 1984. per. 1.50 (0-671-00870-6, Minstrel Bks) PB.
— The Saber-Toothed Poodnoobie. (Space Brat Ser.: No. 5). (Illus.). 80p. (J). (gr. 4-7). 1997. 14.00 (0-671-00871-4, Minstrel Bks) PB.
— The Saber-Toothed Poodnoobie. (Space Brat Ser.: No. 5). (J). (gr. 4-7). 1997. 9.09 (0-606-12817-4, Pub. by Turtleback) Demco.
— Sarah & the Dragon. LC 83-48447. (Illus.). 48p. (J). (gr. k-3). 1984. lib. bdg. 12.89 (0-397-32070-1) HarpC Child Bks.
— Sarah's Unicorn. (Illus.). (J). (ps-2). 1979. 7.66 (0-397-31872-3, 246042) Lppncott W & W.
— Sarah's Unicorn. (J). 1985. 11.15 (0-606-00441-6, Pub. by Turtleback) Demco.
— The Search for Snout: Bruce Coville's Alien Adventures. 192p. (J). (gr. 3-6). 1995. per. 3.99 (0-671-79834-0) PB.
— The Search for Snout: Bruce Coville's Alien Adventures. (Bruce Coville's Alien Adventures Ser.). (J). (gr. 3-6). 1995. 14.00 (0-671-89073-5) PB.
Coville, Bruce. The Search for Snout: Bruce Coville's Alien Adventures. 1995. 9.09 (0-606-09107-6, Pub. by Turtleback) Demco.
Coville, Bruce. The Skull of Truth. LC 97-9264. (Illus.). 195p. (J). (gr. 3-7). 1997. 17.00 (0-15-275457-1) Harcourt.
Coville, Bruce. The Skull of Truth. 208p. (J). (gr. 5-7). pap. 3.99 (0-8072-1538-4) Listening Lib.
Coville, Bruce. The Skull of Truth. (J). 1999. pap. 3.99 (0-671-02343-8) S&S Trade.
— Some of My Best Friends Are Monsters. (Camp Haunted Hills Ser.). (J). 1988. 8.60 (0-606-03925-2, Pub. by Turtleback) Demco.
— Some of My Best Friends Are Monsters, No. 2. (Camp Haunted Hills Ser.). (J). 1989. mass mkt. 3.99 (0-671-70652-7, Minstrel Bks) PB.
***Coville, Bruce.** Song of the Wanderer. LC 98-40760. (J). 1999. pap. 20.01 (0-590-45954-6) Scholastic Inc.
— Song of the Wanderer. LC 98-40760. (Unicorn Chronicles Ser.: Bk. 2). 330p. (J). (gr. 3-7). 1999. 16.95 (0-590-45953-8) Scholastic Inc.
— Space Brat. MacDonald, Patricia, ed. (Space Brat Ser.: No. 1). (Illus.). 80p. (J). (gr. 4-7). 1992. pap. 3.99 (0-671-74567-0, Minstrel Bks) PB.
Coville, Bruce. Space Brat. MacDonald, Patricia, ed. (Space Brat Ser.: No. 1). (Illus.). 80p. (J). (gr. 4-7). 1993. 12.00 (0-671-87059-9, Minstrel Bks) PB.
— Space Brat. MacDonald, Patricia, ed. (Space Brat Ser.: No. 1). (J). (gr. 4-7). 1992. 9.09 (0-606-02099-3, Pub. by Turtleback) Demco.
— Space Station Ice-3. 1996. 9.09 (0-606-10938-2, Pub. by Turtleback) Demco.
— Space Station Ice-3, No. 3. 192p. (YA). (gr. 6 up). 1996. per. 3.99 (0-671-53641-9) PB.
— Spine Tinglers - More Tales to Make You Shiver. (Coville Anthologies Ser.: No. 11). (J). 1997. mass mkt. 3.99 (0-590-85296-5, Apple Paperbacks) Scholastic Inc.
— Spirits & Spells. (Chamber of Horrors Ser.: No. 2). (YA). (gr. 6 up). 1996. mass mkt. 3.99 (0-671-53638-9, Archway) PB.
Coville, Bruce. Spirits & Spells. (Bruce Coville's Chamber of Horrors Ser.). 1996. 9.09 (0-606-09112-2, Pub. by Turtleback) Demco.
— Too Many Aliens. (Sixth Grade Alien Ser.: Vol. 7). (Illus.). 176p. (YA). (gr. 3-6). 2000. per. 3.99 (0-671-02656-9, Minstrel Bks) PB.
— The Unicorn Chronicles, Book One: Into the Land of the Unicorns. rev. ed. 1999. mass mkt. 4.50 (0-439-10838-1) Scholastic Inc.
Coville, Bruce. Waiting Spirits. (Chamber of Horrors Ser.: No. 4). (Orig.). (YA). (gr. 6 up). 1996. mass mkt. 3.99 (0-671-53640-0) PB.
— William Shakespeare's The Tempest. 1996. 12.19 (0-606-12100-5, Pub. by Turtleback) Demco.
— The World's Worst Fairy Godmother. (Illus.). 128p. (J). (gr. 3-6). 1996. pap. 3.99 (0-671-00228-7) PB.
— The World's Worst Fairy Godmother. (J). (gr. 3-6). 1997. 14.00 (0-671-00229-5, PB Hardcover) PB.
— The World's Worst Fairy Godmother. (J). 1996. 9.09 (0-606-12116-1, Pub. by Turtleback) Demco.
— The Wrath of Squat. (Space Brat Ser.: No. 3). (J). (gr. 4-7). 1994. 14.00 (0-671-89198-7, Minstrel Bks) PB.
— The Wrath of Squat. LC 93-50602. (Space Brat Ser.: No. 3). (Illus.). (J). (gr. 4-7). 1994. pap. 3.99 (0-671-86844-6, Minstrel Bks) PB.
Coville, Bruce. The Wrath of Squat. (Space Brat Ser.: No. 3). (J). (gr. 4-7). 1994. 8.60 (0-606-06756-6, Pub. by Turtleback) Demco.
— Zombies of the Science Fair. (Illus.). (J). 2000. 9.34 (0-606-18308-6) Turtleback.
— Zombies of the Science Fair. 5th ed. (I Was a Sixth Grade Alien Ser.: Vol. 5). (Illus.). 160p. (J). (gr. 3-6). 2000. per. 3.99 (0-671-02654-2, Minstrel Bks) PB.
***Coville, Bruce, compiled by.** Bruce Coville's Alien Visitors. 208p. (J). (gr. 3-7). 1999. mass mkt. 4.99 (0-380-80254-6, Avon Bks) Morrow Avon.
— Bruce Coville's Shapeshifters. 192p. (J). (gr. 3-7). 1999. mass mkt. 4.99 (0-380-80255-4, Avon Bks) Morrow Avon.
Coville, Bruce, ed. Aliens Ate My Homework, Set. unabridged ed. (YA). 1997. 21.98 incl. audio (0-8072-7832-7, YA928SP) Listening Lib.
Coville, Bruce & Coville, Katherine. The Foolish Giant. LC 77-18522. (Illus.). (J). (gr. k-2). 1978. lib. bdg. 13.89 (0-397-31800-6) HarpC Child Bks.
— Sarah's Unicorn. LC 79-2408. (Lippincott-I-Like-to-Read Bks.). (Illus.). 48p. (J). (ps-2). 1979. lib. bdg. 14.89 (0-397-31873-1) HarpC Child Bks.
— Sarah's Unicorn. LC 85-42749. (Trophy Picture Bk.). (Illus.). 48p. (J). (gr. 1-4). 1985. pap. 5.95 (0-06-443084-7, HarpTrophy) HarpC Child Bks.

C

An Asterisk (*) at the beginning of an entry indicates that the title is appearing for the first time.

Coville, Bruce & Lee, Artis. Read On! Two, Bk. 4. Lawson, V. K., ed. (Illus.). 1987. pap. text 3.75 (*0-930713-05-2*); audio 8.00 (*0-930713-18-4*) Lit Vol Am.

— Read On! Two, Bk. 6. Lawson, V. K., ed. (Illus.). 48p. 1987. pap. text 3.75 (*0-930713-07-9*); audio 10.00 (*0-930713-34-6*) Lit Vol Am.

— Read On! Two, Wkbk. 4. Lawson, V. K., ed. (Illus.). 56p. 1987. pap. text 2.75 (*0-930713-14-1*) Lit Vol Am.

— Read On! Two, Wkbk. 6. Lawson, V. K., ed. (Illus.). 48p. 1987. pap. text 2.75 (*0-930713-16-8*) Lit Vol Am.

Coville, Bruce, et al. Sophisticated Leisure: Travel Directory, 1986. (Illus.). 348p. 1986. pap. 8.95 (*0-9614965-4-1*) Schueler Comm.

— Sophisticated Leisure: Travel Directory, 1987. (Illus.). 348p. 1986. pap. 8.95 (*0-9614965-5-X*) Schueler Comm.

Coville, Bruce, jt. auth. see Abbott, Tony.

Coville, Bruce, jt. auth. see Yolen, Jane.

Coville, Gary & Lucanio, Patrick. Jack the Ripper: His Life & Crimes in Popular Entertainment. LC 99-24751. (Illus.). 203p. 1999. lib. bdg. 29.95 (*0-7864-0616-X*) McFarland & Co.

Coville, Gary, jt. auth. see Lucanio, Patrick.

Coville, Katherine. Aliens Stole My Body: Bring Back My Body! (J). (gr. 3-9). 1998. 14.00 (*0-671-02414-0*) S&S Trade.

Coville, Katherine, jt. auth. see Coville, Bruce.

Coville, Rollin E. Wasps of the Genus Trypoxylon Subgenus Trypargilum in North America (Hymenoptera: Sphecidae) LC 81-16395. (University of California Publications in Entomology: No. 97). 155p. 1981. pap. 48.10 (*0-7837-7476-1*, 204919800010) Bks Demand.

Covin, Carol. Covin's New England Computer Job Guide. 2nd ed. 320p. Date not set. 13.95 (*0-918339-40-5*) Vandamere.

Covin, Carol L. Covin's Mid-West Computer Job Guide. (Covin's Computer Professional Job Guide Ser.). 364p. (Orig.). 1994. pap. 13.95 (*0-918339-34-0*) Vandamere.

— Covin's Southeast Computer Job Guide. 322p. 1998. 13.95 (*0-918339-39-1*) Vandamere.

— Covin's Washington Area Computer Job Guide. 2nd ed. (Covin's Computer Professional Job Guide Ser.). 320p. 1993. pap. 10.95 (*0-918339-20-0*) Vandamere.

Covin, David. Brown Sky. 1987. 16.95 (*0-910671-11-7*) Path Pr Chicago.

Covina, Gina. The City of Hermits. LC 82-74335. 232p. (Orig.). 1983. 14.95 (*0-9609626-2-X*) Barn Owl Bks.

Covina, Gina & Galana, Laurel, eds. Lesbian Reader. 1975. pap. 8.95 (*0-9609626-0-3*, Amazon Pr) Barn Owl Bks.

***Covington.** Cleaving Reader's Edition. 1999. pap. text. write for info. (*0-86547-568-7*) N Point Pr.

Covington. Digital Reveue. (Business Technology Ser.). (C). 1998. pap. 34.95 (*0-442-02623-4*, VNR) Wiley.

Covington, A. Ion-Selective Electrodes. 1981. 40.00 (*0-85186-398-1*) St Mut.

Covington, A. K., ed. Ion Selective Electrode Methodology, 2 vols., Vol. 1. 272p. 1979. 81.50 (*0-8493-5247-9*, CRC Reprint) Franklin.

— Ion Selective Electrode Methodology, 2 vols., Vol. 2. 144p. 1979. 68.00 (*0-8493-5248-7*, CRC Reprint) Franklin.

Covington, Cary R., et al. Dynamics of Democracy. 2nd ed. 720p. (C). 1996. text. write for info. (*0-697-32752-3*) Brown & Benchmark.

Covington, Dennis. Lasso the Moon. (J). 1996. 20.95 (*0-385-30991-0*) BDD Bks Young Read.

— Lasso the Moon. LC 94-26073. 1996. 9.60 (*0-606-09526-8*, Pub. by Turtleback) Demco.

— Lizard. 208p. (YA). 1993. mass mkt. 4.50 (*0-440-21490-4*) Dell.

— Lizard. (J). 1991. 9.09 (*0-606-02725-4*, Pub. by Turtleback) Demco.

— Salvation on Sand Mountain: Snake Handling & Redemption in Southern Appalachia. (Illus.). 256p. 1996. pap. 12.95 (*0-14-025458-7*) Viking Penguin.

Covington, Dennis & Covington, Vicki. Cleaving: The Story of a Marriage. LC 98-51173. 224p. 1999. 22.00 (*0-86547-548-2*) N Point Pr.

***Covington, Dennis & Covington, Vicki.** Cleaving: The Story of a Marriage. 224p. 2000. pap. 13.00 (*0-86547-589-X*) N Point Pr.

Covington, Donald P. Burlingame Vol. 1: The Tract of Character 1912-1929. LC 97-66951. (Illus.). 100p. (Orig.). 1997. pap. 15.00 (*0-9657837-0-7*) Park Villa.

Covington, George A. & Hannah, Bruce. Access by Design. (Interior Design Ser.). 240p. 1996. 59.95 (*0-471-28726-1*, VNR) Wiley.

Covington, George A. & Hannah, Bruce. Access by Design: A Review of Universal Products. LC 96-3175. (Interior Design Ser.). (Illus.). 240p. 1996. text 49.95 (*0-442-02126-7*, VNR) Wiley.

Covington, Howard E. & Ellis, Marion A. The Story of NationsBank: Changing the Face of American Banking. LC 92-50814. (Illus.). 346p. reprint ed. pap. 107.30 (*0-608-06018-6*, 206634600008) Bks Demand.

***Covington, Howard E., Jr. & Ellis, Marion A.** Terry Sanford: Politics, Progress & Outrageous Ambitions. LC 99-26289. 608p. 1999. text 34.95 (*0-8223-2356-7*) Duke.

Covington, J. S., Jr. Basic Law of Corporations, Cases, Text & Analyses. LC 89-80347. 643p. 1989. boxed set 48.00 (*0-916081-14-1*) J Marshall Pub Co.

— Beginning Accounting in Law: Text, Problems & Workbook. 3rd ed. LC 90-60701. 190p. 1990. pap. text 29.50 (*0-916081-24-9*) J Marshall Pub Co.

— The Structure of Legal Argument & Proof: Cases, Materials & Analyses. LC 93-79684. 415p. 1993. pap. 36.60 (*0-916081-09-5*) J Marshall Pub Co.

Covington, J. S., Jr. & Evans, Susanne W. Law of Business Organizations. LC 91-60808. (Undergraduate & Paralegal Studies). 303p. 1991. pap. 32.40 (*0-916081-22-2*) J Marshall Pub Co.

Covington, James W. The Seminoles of Florida. LC 92-40978. (Illus.). 416p. 1993. 49.95 (*0-8130-1196-5*); pap. 18.95 (*0-8130-1204-X*) U Press Fla.

Covington, John. Applying the Theory of Constraints to Supply Chain Management. (APICS Series on Constraints Management). 250p. 1993. lib. bdg. 42.50 (*1-57444-107-8*, SL1078) St Lucie Pr.

— Tough Fabric: The Domestic Apparel & Textile Chain Regain Market Share. 63p. 1995. pap. text 13.00 (*0-9647126-0-1*) Chesapke Cnslting.

Covington-Jones, Barbara, ed. see American Trucking Association Staff.

Covington, Kae. Gathered in Time: Utah Quilts & Their Makers, Settlement to 1950. LC 97-4034. 168p. 1997. pap. 24.95 (*0-87480-541-4*) U of Utah Pr.

***Covington, Karen.** Creators: Artists, Designers & Craftswomen. LC 99-15958. (Remarkable Women--Past & Present Ser.). (Illus.). 80p. (gr. 4-7). 2000. lib. bdg. 28.55 (*0-8172-5725-X*) Raintree Steck-V.

— Performers: Actors, Directors, Dancers & Musicians. LC 00-26831. (Remarkable Women Ser.). (Illus.). (J). 2000. pap. 27.12 (*0-8172-5727-6*) Raintree Steck-V.

Covington, Karen, jt. auth. see Benedict, Kitty.

Covington, Kentucky City & Zoning Commission. Comprehensive Plan for Covington, Kentucky & Environs. LC 73-2904. (Metropolitan America Ser.). 144p. 1974, reprint ed. 27.95 (*0-405-05393-2*) Ayer.

Covington, Lee. How to Dump Your Wife. LC 94-70591. 160p. 1996. reprint ed. pap. 14.95 (*0-9640354-7-2*) Fender Pubng.

Covington, Linda. Liberty's Flame. 432p. 1994. mass mkt. 4.50 (*0-8217-4699-5*, Zebra Kensgtn) Kensgtn Pub Corp.

Covington, Marilyn. A Texas Christmas. LC 99-23652. (Illus.). 128p. 1999. 39.95 (*1-56579-344-7*) Westcliffe Pubs.

Covington, Martin V. Making the Grade: A Self-Worth Perspective on Motivation & School Reform. (Illus.). 361p. (C). 1992. text 64.95 (*0-521-34261-9*); pap. text 21.95 (*0-521-34803-X*) Cambridge U Pr.

— The Will to Learn: A Guide for Motivating Young People. LC 97-21296. 328p. (C). 1998. text 59.95 (*0-521-55353-9*); pap. text 19.95 (*0-521-55679-1*) Cambridge U Pr.

Covington, Martin V. & Manheimteel, Karen. Overcoming Student Failure: Changing Motives & Incentives for Learning. LC 95-39473. (Psychology in Classroom Ser.). 131p. (Orig.). 1996. pap. text, teacher ed. 17.95 (*1-55798-343-7*) Am Psychol.

***Covington, Melanie.** Step by Step Computer Keyboarding. 3rd ed. 2000. pap. 16.95 (*0-7641-1270-8*) Barron.

Covington, Michael. Computer Science. (Barron's EZ-101 Study Keys Ser.). 144p. 1991. pap. 5.95 (*0-8120-4586-6*) Barron.

Covington, Michael A. Astrophotography for the Amateur. 2nd expanded rev. ed. LC 98-20464. (Illus.). 380p. (C). 1999. pap. 34.95 (*0-521-62740-0*); text 80.00 (*0-521-64133-0*) Cambridge U Pr.

— Natural Language Processing for Prolog Programmers. 348p. (C). 1993. 51.00 (*0-13-629213-5*) P-H.

Covington, Michael A. & Nute, Donald. Prolog Programming in Depth. LC 96-1642. 516p. (C). 1996. pap. 36.80 (*0-13-138645-X*) P-H.

Covington, Michael A., et al. Prolog Programming in Depth. LC 96-1642. 1997. write for info. (*0-614-12747-5*) P-H.

Covington, Michael A., jt. auth. see Pasachoff, Jay M.

Covington, Paula, ed. Latin American Frontiers, Borderlands, & Hinterlands: Research Needs & Resources. (Papers of the Seminar on the Acquisition of Latin American Library Materials: No. 33). xv, 494p. (Orig.). 1990. pap. 50.00 (*0-917617-24-X*) SALALM.

Covington, Paula H., et al, eds. Latin America & the Caribbean: A Critical Guide to Research Sources, 2. LC 91-34622. (Bibliographies & Indexes in Latin American & Caribbean Studies: No. 2). 960p. 1992. lib. bdg. 145.00 (*0-313-26403-1*, CVL/, Greenwood Pr) Greenwood.

Covington, Phillip A. Computers the Plain English Guide: Almost Everything You Need to Know about Computers, Even If You Don't Know Anything about Computers. 3rd ed. LC 88-92376. (Illus.). 295p. 1991. pap. 19.95 (*0-942059-01-8*) QNS Pub.

Covington, Robert L. The War Diaries of Sgt. Robert L. Covington: 60th Fighter Squadron, 33rd Fighter Group, U. S. Army Air Corps, November, 1942-February, 1945. LC 97-50207. 1998. 24.95 (*0-936015-76-4*) Pocahontas Pr.

Covington, Sally. Community Foundations & Citizen Empowerment: Limited Support for Democratic Renewal. 16p. 1994. pap. 5.00 (*1-891465-03-1*) Natl Comm Philan.

— Community Foundations & the Disenfranchised: A Report on Ten Top Community Foundations' Responsiveness to Low Income & Other Historically Disenfranchised. 62p. 1997. pap. 20.00 (*1-891465-02-3*) Natl Comm Philan.

— Foundations in the New Era. 52p. 1995. pap. 25.00 (*1-891465-06-6*) Natl Comm Philan.

— Moving a Public Policy Agenda: The Strategic Philanthropy of Conservative Foundations. 54p. 1997. pap. 25.00 (*1-891465-07-4*) Natl Comm Philan.

— The New Age of Nonprofit Accountability. 24p. 1997. pap. 25.00 (*1-891465-05-8*) Natl Comm Philan.

Covington, Sharon N., jt. auth. see Burns, Linda H.

***Covington, Stephanie.** Helping Women Recover A Program for Treating Substance Abuse. 1999. 149.95 (*0-7879-4609-5*) Jossey-Bass.

Covington, Stephanie. Leaving the Enchanted Forest: The Path from Relationship Addiction. LC 88-45130. 208p. 1988. pap. 14.00 (*0-06-250163-1*, Perennial) HarperTrade.

Covington, Stephanie S. Helping Women Recover: A Program for Treating Substance Abuse. LC 98-40164. 1999. 149.95 (*0-7879-4580-3*) Jossey-Bass.

— Helping Women Recover: A Woman's Journal. 1999. pap. 19.95 (*0-7879-4430-0*) Jossey-Bass.

— A Woman's Way Through the Twelve Steps. (Illus.). 228p. pap. 10.00 (*0-89486-993-0*) Hazelden.

***Covington, Stephanie S.** A Woman's Way Through the Twelve Steps. 64p. 2000. pap. 9.00 (*1-56838-522-6*) Hazelden.

***Covington, Stephanie S., contrib. by.** Awakening Your Sexuality: A Guide for Recovering Women/Stephanie S. Covington. LC 99-58065. 286p. 2000. 15.00 (*1-56838-360-6*) Hazelden.

Covington, Tim R., ed. Nonprescription Drug Therapy: Guiding Patient Self-Care. (Illus.). 1008p. 1999. ring bd. write for info. (*1-57439-048-1*) Facts & Comparisons.

Covington, Timothy R. & Walker, J. Ingram. Current Geriatric Therapy. (Illus.). 463p. 1984. text 49.00 (*0-7216-2743-9*, W B Saunders Co) Harcrt Hlth Sci Grp.

Covington, Vicki. Bird of Paradise. LC 98-51108. (Voices of the South Ser.). 216p. 1999. pap. 14.95 (*0-8071-2386-2*) La State U Pr.

— Gathering Home. LC 99-20122. 240p. 1999. pap. 14.95 (*0-8173-1002-9*) U of Ala Pr.

— The Last Hotel for Women. 304p. 1996. 23.00 (*0-684-81111-1*) S&S Trade.

***Covington, Vicki.** The Last Hotel for Women. LC 99-20121. 304p. 1999. pap. 16.95 (*0-8173-1003-7*) U of Ala Pr.

Covington, Vicki. Night Ride Home. LC 92-15507. 1992. 20.00 (*0-671-74345-7*) S&S Trade.

— Night Ride Home. large type ed. (Americana Series). 385p. 1993. reprint ed. lib. bdg. 19.95 (*1-56054-672-7*) Thorndike Pr.

Covington, Vicki, jt. auth. see Covington, Dennis.

Covington, W. A. History of Colquitt County, Georgia. 365p. 1997. reprint ed. pap. 30.00 (*0-8063-4741-4*, Pub. by Clearfield Co) ACCESS Pubs Network.

Covington, Wallace & Wagner, Pamela K., eds. Conference on Adaptive Ecosystem Restoration & Management: Restoration of Cordilleran Conifer Landscapes of North America. (Illus.). 91p. (C). 1998. reprint ed. pap. text 30.00 (*0-7881-3986-X*) DIANE Pub.

***Covington, William G., Jr.** Creativity in TV & Cable Managing & Producing. LC 99-29353. 160p. 1999. pap. 25.50 (*0-7618-1436-1*) U Pr of Amer.

Covington, William G., Jr. Systems Theory Applied to Television Station Management in the Competitive Marketplace. LC 97-25128. 181p. (C). 1997. pap. 27.50 (*0-7618-0824-8*) U Pr of Amer.

Covington, William S. Covington: The Covingtons: Being a Collection of Family Information. (Illus.). 201p. 1992. reprint ed. pap. 32.00 (*0-8328-2483-6*); reprint ed. lib. bdg. 42.00 (*0-8328-2482-8*) Higginson Bk Co.

Covino, Benjamin G., et al. Handbook of Spinal Anaesthesia & Analgesia. (Illus.). 168p. 1994. text 94.50 (*0-7216-5606-4*, W B Saunders Co) Harcrt Hlth Sci Grp.

Covino, Joseph, Jr. Berkeley Bashed: Student Guide to the Backward, Barbaric, Butt-Ugly Bog. LC 97-76438. 150p. 1998. 11.95 (*0-943283-03-5*) New Human Pr.

— Celestial Verses: The Lost Tale of the Arabian Nights. LC 91-72214. 300p. (Orig.). 1992. pap. 14.95 (*0-943283-01-9*) New Human Pr.

— Lab Animal Abuse: Vivisection Exposed! LC 87-61519. 533p. (Orig.). 1990. pap. 19.95 (*0-943283-00-0*) New Human Pr.

Covino, Michael. Off-Season. 224p. 1985. 14.95 (*0-89255-099-6*) Persea Bks.

— Unfree Associations. 64p. (Orig.). 1982. pap. 9.95 (*0-917658-17-5*) BPW & P.

Covino, Paul, ed. Celebrating Marriage: Preparing the Wedding Liturgy - A Workbook for the Engaged Couple. 1987. pap. 10.95 (*1-56929-026-1*, Pastoral Press) OR Catholic.

Covino, William A. The Art of Wondering: A Revisionist Return to the History of Rhetoric. LC 87-31561. 141p. (Orig.). (C). 1988. pap. text 21.50 (*0-86709-193-2*, 0193, Pub. by Boynton Cook Pubs) Heinemann.

Covino, William A. Elements of Persuasion. LC 97-13582. 165p. (C). 1997. pap. text 15.00 (*0-205-19661-6*) P-H.

Covino, William A. Forms of Wondering: A Dialogue on Writing, for Writers. LC 90-4417. 310p. (Orig.). (C). 1990. pap. text 25.00 (*0-86709-259-9*, 0259, Pub. by Boynton Cook Pubs) Heinemann.

— Magic, Rhetoric, & Literacy: An Eccentric History of the Composing Imagination. LC 93-41344. (SUNY Series, Literacy, Culture, & Learning: Theory & Practice). 189p. (C). 1994. pap. text 16.95 (*0-7914-2084-1*) State U NY Pr.

— Magic, Rhetoric, & Literacy: An Eccentric History of the Composing Imagination. LC 93-41344. (SUNY Series, Literacy, Culture, & Learning: Theory & Practice). 189p. (C). 1994. text 49.50 (*0-7914-2083-3*) State U NY Pr.

Covino, William A. & Jolliffe, David A. Rhetoric. rev. ed. 1995. pap. text 58.00 (*0-205-18462-6*) P-H.

Covino, William A. & Orton, Peter Z. Verbal Review for Standardized Tests. (Cliffs Test Preparation Ser.). (Illus.). 376p. 1986. pap. text 7.95 (*0-8220-2034-3* Cliff) IDG Bks.

Covino, William A., et al. GRE Preparation Guide: Graduate Record Examination. rev. ed. (Cliffs Test Preparation Ser.). (Illus.). 456p. 1980. pap. text 9.95 (*0-8220-2073-4*, Cliff) IDG Bks.

Covins. Law of Federal Taxation. (Paralegal Ser.). 1995. pap., teacher ed. 10.00 (*0-8273-5989-6*) Delmar.

Covins, Susan. Federal Taxation. 576p. (C). 1995. mass mkt. 77.95 (*0-8273-5988-8*) Delmar.

***Covita, Joel.** Visions in the Night: Jungian & Ancient Dream Interpretation. 128p. 2000. pap. 16.00 (*0-919123-92-9*, 012/142, Pub. by Inner City Bks) BookWorld.

***Covitz, Akiba.** Sams Teach Yourself E-Personal Law Today: Using the Internet to Research & Resolve Your Common. (Illus.). 300p. 2000. pap. 17.99 (*0-672-31982-9*) Sams.

Covitz, Barbara, tr. see Muro, Ernest A.

***Covitz, Carl D., ed.** Of the People, by the People: Principles for Cooperative Civil Service Reform (in California) (Illus.). 103p. (C). 1999. pap. text 25.00 (*0-7881-8313-3*) DIANE Pub.

Covitz, Frank H., jt. auth. see Rifi, M. R.

Covitz, Howard. Oedipal Paradigms in Collision: A Centennial Emendation of a Piece of Freudian Canon (1897-1997) LC 97-31584. (Reshaping of Psychoanalysis: Vol. 9). XVI, 385p. (C). 1998. text 59.95 (*0-8204-3921-5*) P Lang Pubng.

Covitz, Joel D. Emotional Child Abuse: The Family Curse. LC 85-26050. 162p. (Orig.). 1986. 24.95 (*0-938434-22-5*); pap. 14.95 (*0-938434-23-3*) Sigo Pr.

Cowan. I/M Writing. 3rd ed. (C). 1997. text, teacher ed. 24.00 (*0-673-47864-5*) Addison-Wesley.

— Rebecca West Revisited. 1998. 22.95 (*0-8057-4606-4*, Twyne) Mac Lib Ref.

— You Can Take Care of Yourself. 1989. 60.00 (*0-295-96838-9*) U of Wash Pr.

Cowan, jt. auth. see Glenn.

Cowan, A. M. The Tree of Northern Bengal. 178p. 1979. 125.00 (*0-7855-6657-0*, Pub. by Intl Bk Distr) St Mut.

— The Trees of Northern Bengal. 178p. (C). 1979. text 125.00 (*0-89771-589-6*, Pub. by Intl Bk Distr) St Mut.

— The Trees of Northern Bengal. 178p. 1993. pap. 175.00 (*81-7089-188-4*, Pub. by Intl Bk Distr) St Mut.

Cowan, Alan & Lewis, John W., eds. Buprenorphine: Combatting Drug Abuse with a Unique Opioid. LC 94-28470. (Illus.). 326p. 1995. 124.95 (*0-471-56198-3*, Wiley-Liss) Wiley.

Cowan, Alan, jt. auth. see sawynod, jana.

Cowan, Alexander. Urban Europe, 1500-1700. 256p. pap. text. write for info. (*0-7131-6529-4*, Pub. by E A) Routldge.

— Urban Europe, 1500-1700. LC 98-19577. 240p. (C). 1998. text 75.00 (*0-340-66324-3*, Pub. by E A) OUP.

— Urban Europe, 1500-1700. LC 98-19577. (Illus.). 240p. 1998. pap. text 19.95 (*0-340-71981-8*, Pub. by E A) St Martin.

Cowan, Alexander, ed. Mediterranean Urban Culture 1400-1700. (Illus.). 240p. 1999. text 60.00 (*0-85989-578-5*, Pub. by Univ Exeter Pr) Northwestern U Pr.

Cowan, Andrew. Common Ground. LC 97-11307. 1997. 22.00 (*0-15-100265-7*) Harcourt.

— Pig. LC 96-19123. 224p. 1996. 21.00 (*0-15-100218-5*) Harcourt.

— Pig. 224p. (YA). 1997. pap. 12.00 (*0-15-600545-X*, Harcourt Child Bks) Harcourt.

Cowan, Anita P., jt. auth. see Stettner, Allison G.

Cowan, Anthony. Good-Bye, Yellow Brick Road: A Memoir of the Sexual Revolution in the Seventies. LC 96-77707. (Illus.). 168p. (Orig.). 1996. pap. 9.95 (*1-881147-23-1*) Lowell Print.

Cowan, Ari & Paterson, Lee T. Managing Section 89: The Complete Compliance Guide. 1989. ring bd. 195.00 (*0-932823-00-9*) Am Somerset.

Cowan, Ari & Paterson, Lee T., eds. The Section Eighty-Nine Companion. (Orig.). 1989. pap. 38.00 (*0-932823-01-7*) Am Somerset.

Cowan, Art. Executive's & Professional Employment Contracts. 120p. 1990. pap. 39.50 (*1-55943-072-9*, MICHIE) LEXIS Pub.

Cowan, Bainard & Humphries, Jefferson, eds. Poetics of the Americas: Race, Founding, & Textuality. LC 96-52687. (Horizons in Theory & American Culture Ser.). (Illus.). 240p. 1997. text 35.00 (*0-8071-2142-8*); pap. text 12.95 (*0-8071-2181-9*) La State U Pr.

Cowan, Bainard & Kronick, Joseph G., eds. Theorizing American Literature: Hegel, the Sign, & History. LC 90-49723. 320p. 1991. text 45.00 (*0-8071-1628-9*) La State U Pr.

***Cowan, Bianca.** Monster is Hiding, 1vol. (Illus.). (J). 1999. pap. text 7.95 (*0-9669645-3-5*) OHollow.

Cowan, Bianca, jt. auth. see Scott, R. James.

Cowan, Bill. Computer Basics. (Illus.). 48p. 1996. pap., teacher ed. 7.95 (*1-55734-999-1*, TCM999) Tchr Create Mat.

Cowan, Brian. Classical Mechanics. (Student Physics Ser.). (Illus.). 128p. (Orig.). 1984. pap. 12.95 (*0-7102-0280-6*, Routledge Thoemms) Routledge.

— Nuclear Magnetic Resonance & Relaxation. LC 96-46614. 457p. 1997. text 99.95 (*0-521-30393-1*) Cambridge U Pr.

***Cowan, Brian, et al, eds.** Directory of Northridge Earthquake Research. (Illus.). 160p. (C). 2000. reprint ed. pap. text 30.00 (*0-7881-8740-6*) DIANE Pub.

Cowan, Bryan D., ed. Reproductive Endocrinology. LC 96-28717. 448p. 1996. text 83.00 (*0-397-51186-8*) Lppncott W & W.

***Cowan, C. Chancelor.** Through My Eyes: Love, Sex, Lies, Poetry & Scandal. x, 270p. 2001. 20.00 (*0-9677385-0-4*); pap. 15.00 (*0-9677385-1-2*) Exqsit Thought.

Cowan, C. Wesley & Watson, Patty J., eds. The Origins of Agriculture: An International Perspective. LC 91-32767. (Series in Archaeological Inquiry). (Illus.). 250p. (C). 1992. pap. text 21.95 (*0-87474-991-3*) Smithsonian.

***Cowan, Carolyn P. & Cowan, Philip A.** When Partners Become Parents: The Big Life Change for Couples. LC 99-40499. 1999. pap. write for info. (*0-8058-3559-8*) L Erlbaum Assocs.

Cowan, Carolyn P., jt. ed. see Bronstein, Phyllis.

Cowan, Catherine. My Friend the Piano. LC 93-37437. (Illus.). 32p. (J). (gr. k-3). 1998. 16.00 (*0-688-13239-1*, Wm Morrow) Morrow Avon.

***Cowan, Catherine.** My Friend the Piano. LC 93-37437. (Illus.). 32p. (J). (gr. k-3). 1998. 15.89 (*0-688-13240-5*, Wm Morrow) Morrow Avon.

— My Life with the Wave: Based on the Story by Octavio Paz. 2000. pap. write for info. (*0-688-17524-4*, Wm Morrow) Morrow Avon.

Cowan, Catherine & Paz, Octavio. My Life with the Wave: Based on the Story by Octavio Paz. LC 93-33625. (Illus.). 32p. (J). (gr. k-3). 1997. 16.00 (*0-688-12660-X*) Lothrop.

Cowan, Catherine & Paz, Octavio. My Life with the Wave: Based on the Story by Octavio Paz. LC 93-33625. (Illus.). 32p. (J). (gr. k-3). 1997. lib. bdg. 15.93 (*0-688-12661-8*) Lothrop.

Cowan, Cathy, ed. see Jackson, Carla.

Cowan, Charles. How to Dwell in the Fire of God. Trent, Rhonda, ed. 16p. 1999. pap. 1.50 (*0-943109-00-0*) Faith is Victory Church Pubns.

— What Determines Your Desire? Mini-Book. Trent, Rhonda, ed. 13p. 1999. pap. 1.50 (*0-943109-01-9*) Faith is Victory Church Pubns.

Cowan, Charles D. Southeast Asian History & Historiography: Essays Presented to D. G. E. Hall. LC 75-18726. (Illus.). 437p. reprint ed. pap. 135.50 (*0-608-08088-8*, 206904700002) Bks Demand.

Cowan, Chris, jt. auth. see Beck, Don.

Cowan, Christina E., ed. see Society of Environmental Toxicology & Chemistry (S.

Cowan, Christine, ed. see Saint-Julien, Derrick J.

Cowan, Colin F., jt. auth. see Mulgrew, Bernard.

Cowan, Connell & Kinder, Melvyn. Smart Women, Foolish Choices. 1986. mass mkt. 6.99 (*0-451-15885-7*, Sig) NAL.

— Women Men Love - Women Men Leave. 1988. mass mkt. 6.99 (*0-451-16641-8*, Sig) NAL.

Cowan, Connell & Parent, Gail. The Art of War for Lovers. 224p. 1998. pap. 12.00 (*0-671-70210-6*); per. 12.00 (*0-671-00063-2*, PB Trade Paper) PB.

Cowan, Craig. Cowan. 1995. text 13.00 (*0-312-11810-4*, Stonewall Inn) St Martin.

Cowan, Dale H. Preferred Provider Organizations: Planning, Structure & Operation. 320p. 1984. 87.00 (*0-89443-593-0*) Aspen Pub.

Cowan, Daniel. Mind Underlies Spacetime: The Infinite-System Model of Connected Existence. 2nd ed. 1988. 17.00 (*0-915878-08-9*); pap. 12.00 (*0-915878-07-0*) Joseph Pub Co.

— Practical Guide to Clinical Laboratory Testing. LC 96-46197. 356p. (Orig.). 1997. pap. 34.95 (*0-86542-470-5*) Blackwell Sci.

Cowan, Daniel A. Language & Negation: The Two-Level Structure That Prevents Paradox. LC 76-21954. 112p. 1980. pap. 6.00 (*0-915878-03-8*) Joseph Pub Co.

Cowan, David. Homelessness: The (In-)Appropriate Applicant. LC 97-24586. (Socio-Legal Studies). (Illus.). 272p. 1997. text 77.95 (*1-85521-531-4*, Pub. by Ashgate Pub) Ashgate Pub Co.

— Introduction to Modern Literary Arabic. 218p. (C). 1958. pap. text 27.95 (*0-521-09240-X*) Cambridge U Pr.

— Taking Charge of Organizational Conflict: A Guide to Handling the Demands of Human Interactions. Schilling, Dianne, ed. 165p. (Orig.). 1995. pap., teacher ed. 16.95 (*1-56499-019-2*, IP9019) Innerchoice Pub.

Cowan, David, ed. Housing: Participation & Exclusion: Collected Papers from the Socio-Legal Studies Annual Conference, 1997, University of Wales, Cardiff. LC 98-3166. (Socio Legal Studies). (Illus.). 260p. 1998. text 77.95 (*1-84014-415-7*, HD7333.A3S62, Pub. by Ashgate Pub) Ashgate Pub Co.

Cowan, David & Kuenster, John. To Sleep with the Angels: The Story of a Fire. (Illus.). 320p. 1998. pap. 14.95 (*1-56663-217-X*, Pub. by I R Dee) Natl Bk Netwk.

Cowan, David, et al. Conflict Resolution Skills for Teens. (Illus.). 181p. (Orig.). (YA). (gr. 7-12). 1994. pap. text 21.95 (*1-56499-023-0*, IP9023) Innerchoice Pub.

— Teaching the Skills of Conflict Resolution: Activities & Strategies for Counseling & Teaching. (Illus.). 186p. 1992. pap. text 19.95 (*1-56499-009-5*); pap. text 21.95 (*1-56499-008-7*, IP9008) Innerchoice Pub.

Cowan, David, jt. auth. see Palomares, Susanna.

Cowan, Debra. Dare to Remember. (Intimate Moments Ser.). 1997. per. 3.99 (*0-373-07774-2*, 1-07774-2) Silhouette.

— For Pete's Sake. 288p. (Orig.). 1996. mass mkt. 5.99 (*0-515-11863-X*, Jove) Berkley Pub.

— One Silent Night: Men in Blue. (Intimate Moments Ser.: No. 899). 1998. per. 4.25 (*0-373-07899-4*, 1-07899-7) Silhouette.

— Plus Fort Que la Peur. (Amours d'Aujourd'Hui Ser.: Vol. 322). (FRE.). 1999. mass mkt. 4.99 (*0-373-38322-3*, 1-38322-3) Harlequin Bks.

— The Rescue of Jenna West. 1998. per. 4.25 (*0-373-07858-7*, 1-07858-3) Silhouette.

Cowan, Debra S. The Matchmaker. 272p. (Orig.). 1995. mass mkt. 4.99 (*0-515-11711-0*, Jove) Berkley Pub.

Cowan, Donald. Unbinding Prometheus: Education for the Coming Age. 223p. 1988. 17.00 (*0-911005-12-9*); pap. 15.00 (*0-911005-33-1*) Dallas Inst Pubns.

Cowan, Donald & Cowan, Louise, eds. Classic Texts & the Nature of Authority: An Account of a Principals' Institute Conducted by the Dallas Institute of Humanities & Culture on the Campus of the University of Dallas, June 22-July, 8, 1990. LC 93-34910. 1993. pap. 19.95 (*0-911005-23-4*) Dallas Inst Pubns.

Cowan, Donna M. The Single Solution: A Survival Guide for Today's Single Christian Woman, Vol. 1. LC 97-73131. 192p. 1996. pap. 9.95 (*0-89221-319-1*) New Leaf.

Cowan, Dorothy. Make Me a Zoo. (Illus.). 64p. (Orig.). (J). (ps-1). 1991. pap. text 8.95 (*0-86530-177-8*, IP 194-5) Incentive Pubns.

Cowan, Douglas, et al. Defending DUIs in Washington. LC 98-67072. 801p. 1998. lib. bdg. 135.00 (*0-327-00905-5*, 8280811) LEXIS Pub.

Cowan, Douglas E. A Nakid Entent unto God: A Source-Commentary on the Cloud of Unknowing. LC 90-19810. 400p. (C). 1992. text 40.00 (*0-89341-645-2*, Longwood Academic) Hollowbrook.

Cowan, Douglas L. & Hayne, Stephen W. Defending DWIs in Washington. 470p. Date not set. 115.00 (*0-614-10383-5*, 301850, MICHIE) LEXIS Pub.

— Defending DWIs in Washington. 470p. 1987. ring bd. 115.00 (*0-409-20028-X*, MICHIE) LEXIS Pub.

Cowan, E. W. The Polar Twins: Scottish History & Scottish Literature. 230p. 1998. pap. 45.00 (*0-85976-494-X*, Pub. by J Donald) St Mut.

Cowan, Edward J. Montrose: For Covenant & King. 326p. 1998. pap. 14.95 (*0-86241-556-X*) Interlink Pub.

Cowan, Edward J., ed. The People's Past. 1991. 11.95 (*0-7486-6157-3*, Pub. by Polygon) Subterranean Co.

Cowan, Eliot. Plant Spirit Medicine: Healing with the Power of Plants. 154p. 1991. pap. 13.95 (*1-893183-11-4*, Pub. by Granite Pub) ACCESS Pubns Network.

— Plant Spirit Medicine: The Healing Power of Plants. 175p. 1995. pap. 13.95 (*0-926524-09-7*) Granite WI.

Cowan, Elisabeth, ed. see Bell, George E.

Cowan, Elizabeth W., ed. Either Way Will Hurt & Other Essays on English 1975: A Selection of Outstanding Essays from the ADE Bulletin. LC 75-35280. 92p. 1976. reprint ed. pap. 30.00 (*0-608-05663-4*, 206603700007) Bks Demand.

— The Undergraduate Curriculum. LC 74-31961. (Options for the Teaching of English Ser.: No. 1). 127p. 1975. pap. 39.40 (*0-608-05577-8*, 206603800006) Bks Demand.

Cowan, Frank. Revi-Lona: A Romance of Love in a Marvelous Land. Reginald, R. & Melville, Douglas, eds. LC 77-84216. (Lost Race & Adult Fantasy Ser.). 1978. reprint ed. lib. bdg. 24.95 (*0-405-10971-7*) Ayer.

Cowan, Frank, Jr., jt. auth. see Moak, Lennox L.

Cowan, Fred F. Dental Pharmacology. 2nd ed. LC 90-13637. (Illus.). 1991. text 39.50 (*0-8121-1385-3*) Lppncott W & W.

— Pharmacology for the Dental Hygienist: For Students & Practitioners. LC 77-17477. (Illus.). 419p. reprint ed. pap. 129.90 (*0-8357-7643-3*, 205696800096) Bks Demand.

Cowan, G., tr. see Brandt, S.

***Cowan, George A., et al, eds.** Complexity: Metaphors, Models & Reality. 752p. 1999. pap. text 39.00 (*0-7382-0232-0*, Pub. by Perseus Pubng) HarpC.

Cowan, George S. & Scheetz, Walter L., eds. Intravenous Hyperalimentation. LC 70-170734. (Illus.). 249p. reprint ed. pap. 77.20 (*0-608-30498-0*, 201453600092) Bks Demand.

Cowan, George W., et al. Complexity: Metaphors, Models & Reality. 752p. (C). 1994. pap. 40.00 (*0-201-62606-3*) Addison-Wesley.

Cowan, Georgianne, jt. ed. see Tobias, Michael.

Cowan, Glen. Statistical Data Analysis. LC 98-14554. (Illus.). 212p. 1998. text 65.00 (*0-19-850156-0*); pap. text 35.00 (*0-19-850155-2*) OUP.

Cowan, Gregory, jt. auth. see McPherson, Elizabeth.

Cowan, Helen I. Charles Williamson: Genesee Promoter, Friend of Anglo-American Rapprochement. LC 68-55516. (Library of Early American Business & Industry: No. 45). xx, 387p. 1973. reprint ed. 49.50 (*0-678-00862-0*) Kelley.

Cowan, Henry. John Knox: The Hero of the Scottish Reformation. LC 70-133817. (Illus.). reprint ed. 49.50 (*0-404-01788-6*) AMS Pr.

— Landmarks of Church History to the Reformation. enl. rev. ed. LC 70-144590. reprint ed. 39.50 (*0-404-01787-8*) AMS Pr.

Cowan, Henry J. Dictionary of Architectural & Building Technology. 3rd ed. LC 98-34257. 1998. pap. 25.99 (*0-419-22280-4*, E & FN Spon) Routledge.

***Cowan, Henry J.** From Wattle & Daub to Concrete & Steel: The Engineering Heritage of Australia's Buildings. 248p. 1999. 49.95 (*0-522-84730-7*, Pub. by Melbourne Univ Pr) Paul & Co Pubs.

Cowan, Henry J. The Master Builders. LC 84-19400. 314p. (C). 1986. reprint ed. lib. bdg. 42.50 (*0-89874-804-6*) Krieger.

— Predictive Methods for the Energy Conserving Design of Buildings. (Illus.). 128p. 1983. text 37.00 (*0-08-029838-9*, Pergamon Pr) Elsevier.

Cowan, Henry J., ed. Solar Energy Applications in the Design of Buildings. (Illus.). x, 325p. 1980. 88.25 (*0-85334-883-9*) Elsevier.

Cowan, I. B., ed. Blast & Counterblast: Contemporary Writings on the Scottish Reformation. 76p. 1986. 20.00 (*0-85411-008-9*, Pub. by Saltire Soc) St Mut.

Cowan, Ian B. Mary Queen of Scots. 31p. 1986. 30.00 (*0-85411-037-2*, Pub. by Saltire Soc) St Mut.

Cowan, Ian B. & Easson, David E. Medieval Religious Houses, Scotland: With an Appendix on the Houses in the Isle of Man. 2nd ed. LC 75-42083. 288p. reprint ed. pap. 89.30 (*0-7837-1596-X*, 204188800024) Bks Demand.

Cowan, J. A. Inorganic Biochemistry: An Introduction. 2nd ed. 456p. 1997. 76.95 (*0-471-18895-6*, Wiley-VCH) Wiley.

Cowan, J. A., ed. The Biological Chemistry of Magnesium. 254p. 1995. 110.00 (*0-471-18583-3*) Wiley.

Cowan, J. D., ed. Some Mathematical Questions in Biology, Pt. II. (Lectures on Mathematics in the Life Sciences: Vol. 3). 121p. 1972. 27.00 (*0-8218-1153-3*, LLSCI/3) Am Math.

— Some Mathematical Questions in Biology, Pt. III. (Lectures on Mathematics in the Life Sciences: Vol. 4). 151p. 1972. pap. 31.00 (*0-8218-1154-1*, LLSCI/4) Am Math.

— Some Mathematical Questions in Biology, Pt. V. (Lectures on Mathematics in the Life Sciences: Vol. 6). 141p. 1975. pap. 30.00 (*0-8218-1156-8*, LLSCI/6) Am Math.

Cowan, J. D., et al, eds. Some Mathematical Questions in Biology, Pt. IV. (Lectures on Mathematics in the Life Sciences: Vol. 5). 150p. 1973. pap. 38.00 (*0-8218-1155-X*, LLSCI/5) Am Math.

Cowan, J. Milton, ed. see Wehr, Hans.

Cowan, J. Milton, tr. see Wehr, Hans.

Cowan, J. Ronayne & Schuh, Russell G. Spoken Hausa. LC 75-15184. (Spoken Language Ser.). 350p. 1976. pap. text 15.00 (*0-87950-401-3*) Spoken Lang Serv.

Cowan, J. Ronayne, et al. Spoken Hausa, Vol. 1. LC 75-15184. (Spoken Language Ser.). 350p. 1976. pap. text 90.00 incl. audio (*0-87950-403-X*) Spoken Lang Serv.

Cowan, J. Ronayne, et al. Spoken Hausa, Vol. 1. LC 75-15184. (Spoken Language Ser.). 350p. 1976. audio 75.00 (*0-87950-402-1*) Spoken Lang Serv.

— Spoken Hausa, Vol. 2. LC 75-15184. (Spoken Language Ser.). 350p. 1976. audio 105.00 (*0-87950-404-8*) Spoken Lang Serv.

Cowan, J. S., ed. The Biological Chemistry of Magnesium. LC 94-26741. (Illus.). xvi, 266p. 1995. 59.95 (*1-56081-627-9*, Wiley-VCH) Wiley.

Cowan, Jack. Nothing Serious...The Best of Jack Cowan. LC 87-91343. 200p. 1987. 12.95 (*0-9617335-2-7*); pap. write for info. (*0-9617335-3-5*) San Angelo Standard Times.

Cowan, Jack C. & Weintritt, Donald J. Water-Formed Scale Deposits. LC 75-5089. (Illus.). 606p. reprint ed. pap. 187.90 (*0-8357-8371-5*, 203417300088) Bks Demand.

Cowan, Jack D., et al, eds. Advances in Neural Information Processing Systems, Vol. 6. 1203p. 1994. text 56.95 (*1-55860-322-0*) Morgan Kaufmann.

Cowan, Jack D. & Giles, C. Lee, eds. Advances in Neural Information Processing Systems, Vol. 5. 1049p. (C). 1993. text 56.95 (*1-55860-274-7*) Morgan Kaufmann.

Cowan, Jack D., ed. see Symposium on Mathematical Biology (5th, 1970, Chicago) Staff.

***Cowan, James.** Architectural Acoustics Design Guide. (Time-Saver Standards Ser.). (Illus.). 352p. 2000. 59.95 (*0-07-135938-9*) McGraw-Hill Prof.

— Balgo: New Directions. (Illus.). 144p. 1999. text 42.00 (*90-5703-611-8*, Harwood Acad Pubs) Gordon & Breach.

Cowan, James. Daybreak: A Romance of an Old World. 2nd ed. LC 72-154436. (Utopian Literature Ser.). (Illus.). 1976. reprint ed. 28.95 (*0-405-03519-5*) Ayer.

— Element Classics: Rum's Divan of Shems of Tabriz. LC 96-49589. (Element Classics of World Spirtuality Ser.). 144p. 1997. pap. 16.95 (*1-85230-919-9*, Pub. by Element MA) Penguin Putnam.

— Elements of the Aborigine Tradition. (Elements of...Ser.). 144p. (Orig.). 1997. pap. 9.95 (*1-86204-144-X*, Pub. by Element MA) Penguin Putnam.

— Fairy Folk Tales of the Maori. 2nd ed. LC 75-35246. reprint ed. 39.50 (*0-404-14420-9*) AMS Pr.

— A Mapmaker's Dream: The Meditations of Fra Mauro, Cartographer to the Court of Venice. LC 96-7439. 208p. 1996. 18.00 (*1-57062-196-9*, Pub. by Shambhala Pubns) Random.

Cowan, James. A Mapmaker's Dream: The Meditations of Fra Mauro, Cartographer to the Court of Venice. LC 97-26164. 176p. 1997. mass mkt. 10.99 (*0-446-67338-2*, Pub. by Warner Bks) Little.

Cowan, James. Mysteries of the Dreamtime: The Spiritual Life of the Australian Aborigine. 192p. (Orig.). 1990. pap. write for info. (*1-85327-038-5*, Pub. by Prism Pr) Assoc Pubs Grp.

— New Zealand Wars. 2 vols. LC 76-100514. (BCL Ser. II). reprint ed. 64.00 (*0-404-00600-0*) AMS Pr.

— Tales of the Maori Bush. LC 75-35248. reprint ed. 49.50 (*0-404-14422-5*) AMS Pr.

— Troubadour's Testament. LC 97-29650. 208p. 1998. 20.00 (*1-57062-339-2*, Pub. by Shambhala Pubns) Random.

— Where Two Oceans Meet. 1992. pap. 13.95 (*1-85230-330-1*, Pub. by Element MA) Penguin Putnam.

— Wirrimanu: Aboriginal Art from the Balgo Hills. (Illus.). 180p. 1994. text 35.00 (*976-8097-75-2*) Gordon & Breach.

***Cowan, James, ed.** The Fantastic Art of H. R. Giger, 1971-1980. (Morpheus Masters Series Portfolio). (Illus.). 48p. 2000. pap. 19.95 (*1-883398-48-7*, Pub. by Morpheus Intl) Publishers Group.

Cowan, James & Cowan, Lois. Lights & Sirens. LC 97-48735. (Behind the Scenes Ser.). (Illus.). 272p. 1998. pap. 16.99 (*0-89879-806-X*, Wrtrs Digest Bks) F & W Pubns Inc.

Cowan, James, ed. see Plinius Secundus, C.

Cowan, James A. Inorganic Biochemistry: An Introduction. LC 93-10766. 1993. 49.95 (*1-56081-537-X*, Wiley-VCH) Wiley.

— Inorganic Biochemistry: An Introduction. 2nd ed. 400p. 1996. 55.00 (*1-56081-923-5*, Wiley-VCH) Wiley.

Cowan, James C. D. H. Lawrence & the Trembling Balance. 312p. 1990. lib. bdg. 35.00 (*0-271-00692-7*) Pa St U Pr.

Cowan, James C., ed. D. H. Lawrence: An Annotated Bibliography of Writings about Him, Vol. I. LC 80-8664. (Annotated Secondary Bibliography Series on English Literature in Transition, 1880-1920). 612p. 1982. 55.00 (*0-87580-077-7*) N Ill U Pr.

— D. H. Lawrence: An Annotated Bibliography of Writings about Him, Vol. II. LC 80-8664. (Annotated Secondary Bibliography Series on English Literature in Transition, 1880-1920). 768p. 1985. 55.00 (*0-87580-105-6*) N Ill U Pr.

Cowan, James G. Mysteries of the Dreamtime: The Spiritual Life of Australian Aborigines. (Illus.). 164p. (Orig.). 1989. pap. 11.95 (*1-85327-077-6*, Pub. by Prism Pr) Assoc Pubs Grp.

— Myths of the Dreaming: Interpreting Aboriginal Legends. (Illus.). 192p. (Orig.). (C). 1994. pap. 14.95 (*1-85327-085-7*, Pub. by Prism Pr) Assoc Pubs Grp.

Cowan, James P. Handbook of Environmental Acoustics. (Industrial Health & Safety Ser.). 283p. 1993. 90.00 (*0-471-28584-6*, VNR) Wiley.

Cowan, James P. Handbook of Environmental Acoustics. (Illus.). 304p. 1994. text 68.95 (*0-442-01644-1*, VNR) Wiley.

Cowan, Jane, jt. auth. see Waiters, Tony.

Cowan, Jessica & Gold, Steve, eds. The Stimulation Effect: Proceedings of a National Conference on the Uses of Government Procurement Leverage to Benefit Taxpayers, Consumers & the Environment. 302p. (Orig.). 1990. pap. write for info. (*0-936758-28-7*) Ctr Responsive Law.

Cowan, Jim. Holy Is the Lord: Lyric Booklet. 1990. pap. 4.50 (*0-940535-10-6*, UP904) Franciscan U Pr.

— Holy Is the Lord Complete Melody & Chords Book. 19p. 1988. pap. 19.95 (*0-940535-57-2*, UP915) Franciscan U Pr.

Cowan, John. The Common Table: Reflections & Meditations on Community & Spirituality in the Workplace. LC 92-56235. 160p. 1993. 17.50 (*0-88730-649-7*, HarpBusn) HarpInfo.

— On Becoming an Innovative University Teacher: Reflection in Action. LC 98-9787. 173p. 1998. 85.00 (*0-335-19994-1*); pap. 29.95 (*0-335-19993-3*) OpUniv Pr.

— Small Decencies: Reflections & Meditations on Being Human at Work. LC 91-58502. 144p. 1992. 15.00 (*0-88730-559-8*, HarpBusn) HarpInfo.

***Cowan, John.** XML: A Developer's Guide. 1999. pap. 54.99 incl. cd-rom (*0-07-135124-8*) McGraw.

Cowan, John, jt. auth. see George, Judith.

***Cowan, John D.** The Indian Princess & the Great Storm. (Illus.). 1999. write for info. (*1-929282-01-X*, Desmond Pub) J D Cowan Assoc Inc.

— Requiem for the Aviators. 2000. write for info. (*1-929282-03-6*, Desmond Pub) J D Cowan Assoc Inc.

— The Seven Deadly Sins of Selling. 120p. 1999. 19.95 (*1-929282-00-1*, Desmond Pub) J D Cowan Assoc Inc.

— Stuff. 2001. write for info. (*1-929282-05-2*, Desmond Pub) J D Cowan Assoc Inc.

— $385.00 a Month & Free Bullets. 2000. write for info. (*1-929282-04-4*, Desmond Pub) J D Cowan Assoc Inc.

— Winning Attitudes for Selling Success. 1999. write for info. (*1-929282-02-8*, Desmond Pub) J D Cowan Assoc Inc.

Cowan, John W. The Complete Lojban Language. 630p. 1997. text 48.00 (*0-9660283-0-9*) Logical Lang Grp.

Cowan, Joseph L., ed. Studies in Thought & Language. LC 75-89620. 232p. reprint ed. pap. 72.00 (*0-608-30770-X*, 202275500029) Bks Demand.

Cowan, Judith, tr. see Prefontaine, Yves.

Cowan, K. C., et al. Portland: The Riches of a City. LC 98-35379. (Illus.). 304p. 1998. 45.00 (*1-885352-70-0*) Community Comm.

Cowan, Kristen T., jt. auth. see Manasevit, Leigh M.

Cowan, L. Gray. Privatization in the Developing World. LC 90-7573. 160p. 1990. pap. 14.95 (*0-275-93631-7*, B3631, Praeger Pubs) Greenwood.

— Privatization in the Developing World, 112. LC 90-32461. (Contributions in Economics & Economic History Ser.: No. 112). 160p. 1990. 59.95 (*0-313-27330-8*, CPK/, Greenwood Pr) Greenwood.

Cowan, Laing G. France & the Saar, 1680-1948. LC 50-3112. (Columbia University. Studies in the Social Sciences: No. 561). reprint ed. 32.50 (*0-404-51561-4*) AMS Pr.

— Local Government in West Africa. LC 75-110429. (BCL Ser. I). reprint ed. 36.00 (*0-404-00144-0*) AMS Pr.

Cowan, Laura, ed. T. S. Eliot: Man & Poet, 2 vols. (Man & Poet Ser.). 1990. 45.00 (*0-943373-09-3*); pap. 25.00 (*0-943373-10-7*) Natl Poet Foun.

Cowan, Lee D. The Little Green Mountain Fire. LC 98-86879. 192p. 1999. pap. 12.95 (*1-56167-506-7*, Five Star Spec Ed) Am Literary Pr.

Cowan, Leo. It Was This Way. 140p. 1998. pap. 10.95 (*1-57502-998-7*, PO2721) Morris Pubng.

Cowan, Les. CD-ROM Book: Using CD-ROM as a Publishing Medium & a Publishing Tool. 224p. 1995. pap. 27.95 (*0-941845-12-5*) Micro Pub Pr.

Cowan, Linda, ed. see DeVours, Lanier.

Cowan, Lois, jt. auth. see Cowan, James.

Cowan, Louise. The Southern Critics: An Introduction to the Criticism of John Crow Ransom, Allen Tate, Donald Davidson, Robert Penn Warren, Cleanth Brooks, & Andrew Lytle. LC 73-186934. 84p. 1971. 3.95 (*0-911005-35-8*) Dallas Inst Pubns.

Cowan, Louise, ed. The Terrain of Comedy. LC 84-22667. 259p. (Orig.). 1984. pap. 16.00 (*0-911005-05-6*) Dallas Inst Pubns.

Cowan, Louise & Guinness, Os, eds. Invitation to the Classics. LC 97-43058. (Masterworks Ser.). (Illus.). 384p. (gr. 11 up). 1998. 34.99 (*0-8010-1156-6*) Baker Bks.

Cowan, Louise, et al. The Twelve Olympians. (Entities Trilogy Ser.). 160p. (Orig.). 1995. pap. 20.00 (*0-911005-28-5*) Dallas Inst Pubns.

Cowan, Louise, jt. ed. see Cowan, Donald.

An Asterisk (*) at the beginning of an entry indicates that the title is appearing for the first time.

Cowan, Lyn Barrett. Masochism: A Jungian View. rev. ed. LC 82-16957. 138p. (Orig.). (C). 1998. pap. 15.00 (*0-88214-367-0*) Spring Pubns.
Cowan, M. & Spielman, R. B., eds. Megagauss Magnetic Field Generation & Pulsed Power Applications. (Illus.). 1097p. (C). 1994. lib. bdg. 295.00 (*1-56072-160-X*) Nova Sci Pubs.
Cowan, Marian & Futrell, John C. Companions in Grace: A Handbook for Directors of the Spiritual Exercises of St. Ignatius of Loyola. LC 93-6194. 256p. (Orig.). 1993. pap. 14.95 (*1-55612-667-0*) Sheed & Ward WI.
Cowan, Marti, jt. auth. see Helfand, Margaret.
***Cowan, Marvin W.** What Every Mormon Should Ask. 32p. 2000. pap. 4.99 (*0-7369-0231-7*) Harvest Hse.
Cowan, Mary M. Ice Country. (Illus.). (J). (gr. 6-8). 1995. 18.95 (*0-89725-220-9*, 1597, Cricketfld Pr) Picton Pr.
— Ice Country: One Boys Adventure in the Arctic with Commander Donald MacMillan. LC 95-68744. (Illus.). 150p. 1995. pap. 8.95 (*0-89725-340-X*, 1597S) Picton Pr.
Cowan, Maxine, jt. auth. see Rutledge, Margie.
Cowan, Maxwell W., et al, eds. Annual Review of Neuroscience, Vol. 8. 500p. 1985. 24.00 (*0-318-18123-1*) Soc Neuroscience.
Cowan, Michael, jt. auth. see Lee, Bernard J.
Cowan, Michael A. & Lee, Bernard J. Conversation, Risk, & Conversion: The Inner & Public Life of Small Christian Communities. LC 97-18566. 160p. (Orig.). 1997. pap. 15.00 (*1-57075-149-8*) Orbis Bks.
Cowan, Mike. The Practice Pro. 98p. (C). 1996. spiral bd. 18.95 (*0-7872-2449-9*, 41244901) Kendall-Hunt.
Cowan-Neeld, Elizabeth. Writing: Brief. 2nd ed. (C). 1986. pap. text 12.66 (*0-673-18151-0*, Scott Frsmn) Addson-Wesley Educ.
Cowan-Neeld, Elizabeth & Kiefer, Kathleen E. Writing: Brief. 3rd ed. 362p. (C). 1991. pap. text 56.00 (*0-673-38383-0*) Addson-Wesley Educ.
Cowan, Neil M. & Cowan, Ruth S. Our Parents' Lives: Jewish Assimilation in Everyday Life. LC 96-19113. (Illus.). 330p. (Orig.). 1996. pap. text 16.95 (*0-8135-2296-X*) Rutgers U Pr.
Cowan, Nell B., jt. auth. see Parker, Emma.
Cowan, Nelson. Attention & Memory: An Integrated Framework. (Oxford Psychology Ser.: No. 26). (Illus.). 344p. 1995. text 70.00 (*0-19-506760-6*) OUP.
— Attention & Memory: An Integrated Framework. (Oxford Psychology Ser.: No. 26). (Illus.). 344p. 1998. pap. text 27.50 (*0-19-511910-X*) OUP.
— The Development of Memory in Childhood. LC 97-202137. (Studies in Developmental Psychology). (Illus.). viii, 392p. 1997. write for info. (*0-86377-495-4*, Pub. by Psychol Pr) Taylor & Francis.
***Cowan, Nelson, ed.** The Development of Memory in Childhood. (Studies in Developmental Psychology). 400p. 1998. pap. 27.95 (*0-86377-496-2*, Pub. by Psychol Pr) Taylor & Francis.
Cowan, Paul. Only Yesterday: A Quiz on the Sixties. 160p. (Orig.). 1990. mass mkt. 7.95 (*0-446-39036-4*, Pub. by Warner Bks) Little.
Cowan, Paul & Cowan, Rachel. Mixed Blessings: Overcoming the Stumbling Blocks in an Interfaith Marriage. 288p. 1988. pap. 13.95 (*0-14-011189-1*, Penguin Bks) Viking Penguin.
Cowan, Penney. American Chronic Pain Association Family Manual: A Manual for Families of Persons with Pain. Kelly, Nicole et al, eds. (Illus.). 145p. 1997. pap. 25.00 (*0-9673878-2-5*, 13350) Amer Chronic.
— American Chronic Pain Association Staying Well: Advanced Pain Management for ACPA Members. Lidz, Charles et al, eds. (Illus.). 157p. 1994. pap. 25.00 (*0-9673878-1-7*, 13310) Amer Chronic.
Cowan, Penney. Patient or Person: Living with Chronic Pain. 196p. 1992. pap. 21.95 (*0-89876-186-7*) Gardner Pr.
Cowan, Penney, et al. American Chronic Pain Association Workbook Manual. 3rd ed. Lidz, Charles et al, eds. (Illus.). 117p. 1987. pap., wbk. ed. 20.00 (*0-9673878-0-9*, 13300) Amer Chronic.
Cowan, Peter. A Unique Position: A Biography of Edith Dircksey Cowan, 1861-1932. 1979. 29.75 (*0-85564-135-5*, Pub. by Univ of West Aust Pr) Intl Spec Bk.
Cowan, Peter, ed. The Future of Planning. LC 73-80439. (Centre for Environmental Studies Ser.: Vol. 1). 190p. reprint ed. pap. 58.90 (*0-608-14196-8*, 202188200026) Bks Demand.
Cowan, Philip, et al, eds. Family, Self & Society: Towards a New Agenda for Family Research. 504p. 1993. text 99.95 (*0-8058-0999-6*) L Erlbaum Assocs.
Cowan, Philip A. & Hetherington, E. Mavis, eds. Family Transitions. 328p. 1991. 69.95 (*0-8058-0784-5*) L Erlbaum Assocs.
Cowan, Philip A., jt. auth. see Cowan, Carolyn P.
Cowan, R. E. A Bibliography of the History of California, 1510-1930, 3 vols. 825p. 1997. reprint ed. 75.00 (*1-57898-057-7*) Martino Pubng.
Cowan, R. S. & Lindeman, J. C. Phanerogams: Caesalpiniaceae. Goerts-van-Rijn, A. R. A., ed. (Flora of the Guianas Ser.: Series A, Fascicle 7). (Illus.). 166p. 1989. pap. 66.00 (*3-87429-287-8*, 036890, Pub. by Koeltz Sci Bks) Lubrecht & Cramer.
Cowan, R. S., jt. auth. see Stafleu, F. A.
Cowan, Rachel, jt. auth. see Cowan, Paul.
Cowan, Rich, jt. ed. see Massachi, Dalya.
Cowan, Richard A. Campus Organizing Guide for Peace & Justice Groups. (Study War No More Guidebook Ser.: No. 2). (Illus.). 6p. 1994. pap. 2.95 (*0-945210-04-3*) Public Search.
Cowan, Richard O. Answers to Your Questions about the Doctrine & Covenants. LC 96-27337. viii, 167p. 1996. 16.95 (*1-57345-201-7*) Deseret Bk.
Cowan, Richard O. Temples to Dot the Earth. pap. 14.95 (*1-55517-339-X*) CFI Dist.
Cowan, Richard O., et al, eds. California Saints: A 150-Year Legacy. 1996. 15.95 (*1-57008-200-6*) Bookcraft Inc.
Cowan, Richard O., jt. auth. see Backman, Milton V., Jr.
Cowan, Richard S. Swartzia (Leguminosae, Caesalpinioideae, Swartzieae) LC 67-14268. (Flora Neotropica Monographs: No. 1). (Illus.). 228p. 1987. reprint ed. pap. text 15.00 (*0-89327-320-1*) NY Botanical.
Cowan, Richard S., ed. Emerging Technologies for Machinery Health Monitoring & Prognosis: ASME International Mechanical Engineering Congress & Exposition, Dallas, TX, 1997. LC 97-76705. (TRIB Ser.: Vol. 7). 75p. 1997. pap. 64.00 (*0-7918-1826-8*, TJ148) ASME Pr.
Cowan, Robert. London after Dark. (Illus.). 128p. (C). 1993. text 35.00 (*0-7148-2870-X*, Pub. by Phaidon Press) Phaidon Pr.
Cowan, Robert D. The Theory of Atomic Structure & Spectra. LC 81-4578. (Los Alamos Series in Basic & Applied Sciences: No. 3). 650p. 1981. 75.00 (*0-520-03821-5*, Pub. by U CA Pr) Cal Prin Full Svc.
Cowan, Robert E. A Bibliography of the History of California, 3 vols. 1992. reprint ed. lib. bdg. 225.00 (*0-7812-5019-6*) Rprt Serv.
— A Bibliography of the History of California & the Pacific Coast, 1510-1906. 380p. 1997. reprint ed. 60.00 (*1-57898-037-2*) Martino Pubng.
— Forgotten Characters of Old San Francisco. 1992. reprint ed. lib. bdg. 75.00 (*0-7812-5018-8*) Rprt Serv.
Cowan, Robin & Rizzo, Mario J., eds. Profits & Morality. (Illus.). 192p. 1995. 27.50 (*0-226-11632-8*) U Ch Pr.
Cowan, Ruth S. More Work for Mother: The Ironies of Household Technology from the Open Hearth to the Microwave. LC 83-70759. 272p. 1985. pap. 17.00 (*0-465-04732-7*, Pub. by Basic) HarpC.
— A Social History of American Technology. (Illus.). 352p. 1997. pap. 23.95 (*0-19-504605-6*) OUP.
Cowan, Ruth S., jt. auth. see Cowan, Neil M.
Cowan, S. D., jt. auth. see Orr, William I.
Cowan, Sada. Pomp & Other Plays. LC 79-50024. (One-Act Plays in Reprint Ser.). 1980. reprint ed. 25.00 (*0-8486-2048-8*) Roth Pub Inc.
Cowan, Sally. Left-Handed Sewing. (Illus.). 64p. 1994. reprint ed. pap. text 2.95 (*0-486-27752-6*) Dover.
— Left-Handed Stitchery. LC 85-31175. (Illus.). 64p. 1986. pap. 9.95 (*0-671-61393-6*) P-H.
— Left-Handed Stitchery. LC 87-61438. (Illus.). 64p. 1987. pap. 9.95 (*0-88740-110-4*) Schiffer.
***Cowan, Sally.** Sew a Beautiful Home: Quick & Easy Home Decorating Projects. LC 99-64192. (Illus.). 160p. 2000. pap. 24.95 (*0-87341-804-2*) Krause Pubns.
Cowan, Sam. Handbook of Modern Electronics Math. 1987. 29.95 (*0-317-59840-6*, Busn); pap. 12.95 (*0-13-380452-6*, Busn) P-H.
Cowan, Simon & Armstrong, Mark. Regulatory Reform: Economic Analysis & British Experience. 1994. pap. text 21.50 (*0-262-51079-0*) MIT Pr.
***Cowan, Steven.** Five Views of Apologetics. (Counterpoints Ser.). 2000. pap. 17.99 (*0-310-22476-4*) Zondervan.
Cowan, Stuart, jt. auth. see Orr, William I.
Cowan, Stuart D. & Orr, William I. All about Cubical Quad Antennas. (Illus.). 112p. pap. 13.95 (*0-8230-8703-4*, RAC Bks) Watsn-Guptill.
Cowan, Stuart D., jt. auth. see Orr, William I.
Cowan, Sweby. The Guide to European Property Investment, 2 vols., Vol. 1. (Waterlow Publications). 160p. 1990. 81.00 (*0-685-29309-2*); pap. 45.00 (*0-685-29310-6*) Macmillan.
— The Guide to European Property Investment, 2 vols., Vol. 2. (Waterlow Publications). 144p. 1990. pap. 50.00 (*0-08-040125-2*) Macmillan.
Cowan, T. The Clearing Banks & the Trade Unions. 1984. 70.00 (*0-85297-116-8*, Pub. by Chartered Bank) St Mut.
— Personnel Management & Banking. 1985. 50.00 (*0-85297-077-3*, Pub. by Chartered Bank) St Mut.
Cowan, T., jt. auth. see Popoff, B.
Cowan, T. K., jt. auth. see Popoff, B.
Cowan, Thomas. Dallas Darts: An Alternative Fiction. LC 97-91537. 150p. (Orig.). 1997. pap. 9.95 (*0-9643885-8-8*) Personal Profiles.
Cowan, Thomas, jt. auth. see Norman, Laura.
Cowan, Tom. The Book of Seance. 208p. 1994. pap. 9.95 (*0-8092-3733-4*, 373340, Contemporary Bks) NTC Contemp Pub Co.
— Fire in the Head: Shamanism & the Celtic Spirit. LC 92-53909. 240p. 1993. pap. 17.00 (*0-06-250174-7*, Pub. by Harper SF) HarpC.
— Gay Men & Women Who Enriched the World. 2nd rev. ed. LC 96-44992. (Illus.). 256p. 1996. reprint ed. pap. 10.95 (*1-55583-391-8*) Alyson Pubns.
— Pocket Guide to Shamanism. LC 97-9449. (Crossing Press Pocket Ser.). (Illus.). 128p. 1997. pap. 6.95 (*0-89594-845-1*) Crossing Pr.
— Shamanism As a Spiritual Practice for Daily Life. (Illus.). 224p. (Orig.). 1996. pap. 16.95 (*0-89594-838-9*) Crossing Pr.
— Timelines of African-American History: Five Hundred Years of Black Achievement. Maguire, Jack et al, eds. 368p. (Orig.). 1994. pap. 16.95 (*0-399-52127-5*, Perigee Bks) Berkley Pub.
***Cowan, Tom.** The Way of the Saints: Prayers, Practices & Meditations. LC 98-14924. 451p. 1998. 30.00 (*0-399-14416-1*, G P Putnam) Peng Put Young Read.
— The Way of the Saints: Prayers, Practices & Meditations. 1999. reprint ed. pap. 16.00 (*0-399-52544-0*, Perigee Bks) Berkley Pub.
Cowan, Tom, jt. auth. see Cabot, Laurie.
Cowan, Tom, jt. auth. see Stanton, Gary.
Cowan, Tony, jt. auth. see McKenna, Megan.
***Cowan, W. Maxwell.** Synapses. (Illus.). 656p. 2000. 69.95 (*0-8018-6498-4*) Johns Hopkins.
Cowan, W. Maxwell, ed. Annual Review of Neuroscience, Vol. 10. (Illus.). 1987. text 40.00 (*0-8243-2410-2*) Annual Reviews.
— Annual Review of Neuroscience, Vol. 20. 1997. text 60.00 (*0-8243-2420-X*) Annual Reviews.
— Annual Review of Neuroscience, Vol. 21. 1998. text 60.00 (*0-8243-2421-8*) Annual Reviews.
— Annual Review of Neuroscience, 1995, Vol. 18. 550p. 1995. text 47.00 (*0-8243-2418-8*) Annual Reviews.
Cowan, W. Maxwell, et al, eds. Annual Review of Neuroscience, Vol. 1. (Illus.). 1978. text 40.00 (*0-8243-2401-3*) Annual Reviews.
— Annual Review of Neuroscience, Vol. 2. (Illus.) 1979. text 40.00 (*0-8243-2402-1*) Annual Reviews.
— Annual Review of Neuroscience, Vol. 3. (Illus.) 1980. text 40.00 (*0-8243-2403-X*) Annual Reviews.
— Annual Review of Neuroscience, Vol. 4. (Illus.) 1981. text 40.00 (*0-8243-2404-8*) Annual Reviews.
— Annual Review of Neuroscience, Vol. 5. (Illus.) 1982. text 40.00 (*0-8243-2405-6*) Annual Reviews.
— Annual Review of Neuroscience, Vol. 6. (Illus.) 1983. text 40.00 (*0-8243-2406-4*) Annual Reviews.
— Annual Review of Neuroscience, Vol. 7. (Illus.) 1984. text 40.00 (*0-8243-2407-2*) Annual Reviews.
— Annual Review of Neuroscience, Vol. 9. (Illus.) 1986. text 40.00 (*0-8243-2409-9*) Annual Reviews.
— Annual Review of Neuroscience, Vol. 12. (Illus.). 1989. text 40.00 (*0-8243-2412-9*) Annual Reviews.
— Annual Review of Neuroscience, Vol. 13. 1990. text 40.00 (*0-8243-2413-7*) Annual Reviews.
— Annual Review of Neuroscience, Vol. 14. 1991. text 40.00 (*0-8243-2414-5*) Annual Reviews.
— Annual Review of Neuroscience, Vol. 15. 1992. text 44.00 (*0-8243-2415-3*) Annual Reviews.
— Annual Review of Neuroscience, Vol. 16. (Illus.). 1993. text 44.00 (*0-8243-2416-1*) Annual Reviews.
— Annual Review of Neuroscience, Vol. 17. (Illus.). 1994. text 47.00 (*0-8243-2417-X*) Annual Reviews.
— Annual Review of Neuroscience, Vol. 19. (Illus.). 1996. text 52.00 (*0-8243-2419-6*) Annual Reviews.
— Annual Review of Neuroscience Vol. 22: 1999. 652p. 1999. 120.00 (*0-8243-2422-6*) Annual Reviews.
— Molecular & Cellular Approaches to Neural Development. LC 96-38648. (Illus.). 576p. 1998. text 68.50 (*0-19-511166-4*) OUP.
Cowan, Walter G., et al. New Orleans, Yesterday & Today: A Guide to the City. LC 83-772. (Illus.). xiv, 272p. 1983. 14.95 (*0-8071-1108-2*); pap. 11.95 (*0-8071-1109-0*) La State U Pr.
Cowan, Wayne H., ed. Witness to a Generation: Significant Writings from Christianity & Crisis, 1941-1966. LC 66-29152. (Orig.). 1966. 6.55 (*0-672-50852-4*, Bobbs) Macmillan.
Cowan, William. Source Book for Linguistics. 3rd ed. (Paperbacks Ser.). 1998. 19.95 (*90-272-2162-5*) J Benjamins Pubng Co.
Cowan, William, et al, eds. New Perspectives in Language, Culture & Personality: Proceedings of the Edward Sapir Centenary Conference (Ottawa, 1-3 October 1984) LC 86-26834. (Studies in the History of the Language Sciences: No. 41). xiv, 627p. 1986. 110.00 (*90-272-4522-3*) J Benjamins Pubng Co.
Cowan, William & Foster, Michael K., eds. E. F. Konrad Koerner Bibliography. vii, 85p. 1989. 24.00 (*0-931922-36-4*) Eurolingua.
***Cowan, William & Rakusan, Jaromira, eds.** Sourcebook for Linguistics. 3rd rev. ed. LC 98-41604. xii 250p. 1999. pap. 19.95 (*1-55619-516-8*) J Benjamins Pubng Co.
Cowan, William & Rakusan, Jeromira. Source Book for Linguistics. LC 85-26862. (Paperbacks Ser.: No. 5). xxvi, 338p. 1985. pap. 19.95 (*0-915027-82-8*) J Benjamins Pubng Co.
Cowan, William, ed. see Day, Gordon M.
Cowan, Zachary S. & Cowans, Martha W. Cowan. History of the Cowan Family, with List of Descendants of Dr. James Jones Cowan & Sarah Ann Cook Cowan. (Illus.). 71p. 1997. reprint ed. pap. 14.50 (*0-8328-8094-9*); reprint ed. lib. bdg. 24.50 (*0-8328-8093-0*) Higginson Bk Co.
Cowans & Phelan. Bankruptcy Law & Practice, 4 vols. 6th ed. LC 93-60288. Date not set. text 485.00 (*0-314-02339-9*, 63370, MICHIE) LEXIS Pub.
Cowans, Daniel R. Bankruptcy Law & Practice, Index. 7th ed. 3600p. 1998. write for info. (*0-327-00857-1*) LEXIS Pub.
— Bankruptcy Law & Practice, Vol. 1. 7th ed. 3600p. 1998. write for info. (*0-327-00840-7*, 6337111) LEXIS Pub.
— Bankruptcy Law & Practice, Vol. 2. 7th ed. 3600p. 1998. write for info. (*0-327-00841-5*, 6337211) LEXIS Pub.
— Bankruptcy Law & Practice, Vol. 3. 7th ed. 3600p. 1998. write for info. (*0-327-00842-3*, 6337311) LEXIS Pub.
— Bankruptcy Law & Practice, Vol. 4. 7th ed. 3600p. 1998. write for info. (*0-327-00843-1*, 6337411) LEXIS Pub.
— Bankruptcy Law & Practice, Vol. 5. 7th ed. 3600p. 1998. write for info. (*0-327-00844-X*, 6337511) LEXIS Pub.
— Bankruptcy Law & Practice, 6 vols., Vols. 1-5 & Index. 7th ed. LC 98-89493. 3600p. 1998. 485.00 (*0-327-00839-3*, 6337011) LEXIS Pub.
— Cowans Bankruptcy Law & Practice. 1986. 180.00 (*0-685-43635-7*) West Pub.
Cowans, Daniel R. & Phelan, Robin E. Bankruptcy Law & Practice. 6th ed. 1994. im. lthr. write for info. (*0-327-00054-6*); im. lthr. write for info. (*0-327-00055-4*); im. lthr. write for info. (*0-327-00057-0*) LEXIS Pub.
— Bankruptcy Law & Practice. 6th ed. 1994. im. lthr. write for info. (*0-327-00056-2*) LEXIS Pub.
Cowans, Martha W., jt. auth. see Cowan, Zachary S.
Coward, Barry. Social Change & Continuity: England, 1550-1750. 2nd ed. LC 97-4237. (Seminar Studies in History). 160p. (C). 1997. pap. 16.80 (*0-582-29442-8*) Addison-Wesley.
Coward, Barry. The Stuart Age. LC 79-42887. (History of England Ser.). (Illus.). 493p. (C). 1980. pap. text 28.50 (*0-582-48833-8*, 73385) Longman.
— The Stuart Age. 2nd ed. LC 93-26405. (History of England Ser.). 496p. (C). 1995. pap. text 36.56 (*0-582-06722-7*, 76265, Pub. by Addison-Wesley) Longman.
Coward, D., jt. auth. see Ince, D.
Coward, David. L' Eau des Collines, Pagnol: Critical Monographs in English. 96p. 1993. pap. 45.00 (*0-85261-391-1*, Pub. by Univ of Glasgow) St Mut.
Coward, David, ed. The Count of Monte Cristo. (Oxford World's Classics Ser.). 1,162p. 1998. pap. 12.95 (*0-19-283395-2*) OUP.
Coward, David, ed. see Diderot, Denis.
Coward, David, ed. & intro. see Dumas, Alexandre.
Coward, David, tr. see Dumas, Alexandre.
Coward, David, tr. see Maupassant, Guy de.
Coward, David, tr. see Sade, Marquis de.
Coward, David, tr. & intro. see Cohen, Albert.
Coward, David, tr. & intro. see Maupassant, Guy de.
Coward, David G. Manufacturing Management: Learning Through Case Studies. (Illus.). 204p. (C). 1998. pap. text 30.00 (*0-333-64777-7*, Pub. by Macmillan Ed) Scholium Intl.
Coward, E. Walter, ed. Irrigation & Agricultural Development in Asia: Perspectives from the Social Sciences. LC 79-24319. (Illus.). 368p. 1980. pap. text 27.50 (*0-8014-9871-6*) Cornell U Pr.
Coward, Harold. Derrida & Indian Philosophy. LC 90-32875. 256p. (C). 1990. text 54.50 (*0-7914-0499-4*); pap. text 18.95 (*0-7914-0500-1*) State U NY Pr.
— Hindu-Christian Dialogue Perspectives & Encounters. LC 89-29673. (Faith Meets Faith Ser.). 272p. 1989. 40.00 (*0-88344-634-0*); pap. 18.00 (*0-88344-633-2*) Orbis Bks.
***Coward, Harold, ed.** Experiencing Scripture in World Religions. LC 99-58570. (Faith Meets Faith Ser.). 176p. 2000. pap. 16.00 (*1-57075-298-2*) Orbis Bks.
Coward, Harold, ed. Hindu-Christian Dialogue: Perspectives & Encounters. LC 89-29673. (Faith Meets Faith Ser.). 303p. reprint ed. pap. 94.00 (*0-608-20244-4*, 207150300012) Bks Demand.
— Life after Death in the World Religions. LC 96-51083. (Faith Meets Faith Ser.). 125p. (Orig.). 1997. pap. 15.00 (*1-57075-119-6*) Orbis Bks.
— Modern Indian Responses to Religious Pluralism. LC 87-1943. 340p. (C). 1987. pap. text 18.95 (*0-88706-572-4*) State U NY Pr.
— Population, Consumption, & the Environment: Religious & Secular Responses. LC 95-81019. 319p. (C). 1995. pap. text 21.95 (*0-7914-2672-6*) State U NY Pr.
— Revelation in Indian Thought: A Festschrift in Honor of Professor T. R. V. Murti. LC 77-71192. 1977. 30.00 (*0-913546-52-6*) Dharma Pub.
— Traditional & Modern Approaches to the Environment on the Pacific Rim: Tensions & Values. LC 98-9800. 240p. (C). 1998. text 59.50 (*0-7914-3845-7*); pap. text 19.95 (*0-7914-3846-5*) State U NY Pr.
Coward, Harold, et al, eds. The South Asian Religious Diaspora in Britain, Canada & the United States. LC 99-39476. (C). 2000. text 62.50 (*0-7914-4509-7*); pap. text 20.95 (*0-7914-4510-0*) State U NY Pr.
Coward, Harold & Cook, Philip, eds. Religious Dimensions of Child & Family Life: Reflections on the UN Convention on the Rights of the Child. LC 96-910613. 203p. 1996. pap. 17.95 (*1-55058-104-X*) W Laurier U Pr.
Coward, Harold & Foshay, Toby, eds. Derrida & Negative Theology. LC 91-9956. 349p. (C). 1992. pap. text 21.95 (*0-7914-0964-3*) State U NY Pr.
— Derrida & Negative Theology. LC 91-9956. 349p. (C). 1992. text 64.50 (*0-7914-0963-5*) State U NY Pr.
Coward, Harold & Hurka, Thomas, eds. Ethics & Climate Change: The Greenhouse Effect. 224p. (C). 1993. text 35.00 (*0-88920-233-8*) W Laurier U Pr.
***Coward, Harold & Maguire, Daniel C., eds.** Visions of a New Earth: Religious Perspectives on Population, Consumption, & Ecology. LC 99-24398. (C). 1999. text 54.50 (*0-7914-4457-0*); pap. text 17.95 (*0-7914-4458-9*) State U NY Pr.
Coward, Harold, jt. ed. see McLaren, John.
Coward, Harold, ed. see Murty, T. R.
Coward, Harold G. Jung & Eastern Thought. LC 85-2784. (SUNY Series in Transpersonal & Humanistic Psychology). 218p. (C). 1985. text 54.50 (*0-88706-052-8*); pap. text 19.95 (*0-88706-051-X*) State U NY Pr.
— Sacred Word & Sacred Text: Scripture in World Religions. LC 87-31321. 232p. 1988. reprint ed. pap. 72.00 (*0-7837-9857-1*, 206058600005) Bks Demand.
— Sphota Theory of Language. 1981. 16.00 (*0-8364-0692-3*) S Asia.
— The Sphota Theory of Language: A Philosophical Analysis. xx, 158p. 1986. 14.00 (*81-208-0181-4*, Pub. by Motilal Bnarsidass) S Asia.
Coward, Harold G., ed. Studies in Indian Thought: Collected Papers of Professer T. R. V. Murti. (C). 1996. 42.00 (*81-208-1310-3*, Pub. by Motilal Bnarsidass) S Asia.
Coward, Harold G., et al, eds. Hindu Ethics: Purity, Abortion, & Euthanasia. LC 87-18075. (McGill Studies in the History of Religions). 139p. (C). 1988. text 64.50 (*0-88706-763-8*) State U NY Pr.

— Hindu Ethics: Purity, Abortion, & Euthanasia. LC 87-18075. (McGill Studies in the History of Religions). 139p. (C). 1988. pap. text 21.95 (*0-88706-764-6*) State U NY Pr.

Coward, Harold G. & Goa, David J. Mantra: Hearing the Divine in India. LC 96-28527. 1996. 15.50 (*0-231-10783-8*) Col U Pr.

***Coward, Harold G. & Ratanakul, Pinit, eds.** A Cross-Cultural Dialogue on Health Care Ethics. LC 99-930548. 274p. 1999. pap. 29.95 (*0-88920-325-3*) Wilfrid Laurier.

Coward, Harold G., ed. see Wiebe, Rudy, et al.

Coward, Henry. Choral Technique & Interpretation. LC 72-1254. (Select Bibliographies Reprint Ser.). 1977. reprint ed. 23.95 (*0-8369-6824-7*) Ayer.

Coward, Joan W. Kentucky in the New Republic: The Process of Constitution Making. LC 77-92920. (Illus.). 232p. 1979. 29.95 (*0-8131-1380-6*) U Pr of Ky.

Coward, John M. The Newspaper Indian: Native American Identity in the Press, 1820-90. LC 98-19663. (History of Communication Ser.). 264p. 1998. text 39.95 (*0-252-02432-X*) U of Ill Pr.

— The Newspaper Indian: Native American Identity in the Press, 1820-90. LC 98-19663. (The History of Communication Ser.). 264p. 1999. pap. 18.95 (*0-252-06738-X*) U of Ill Pr.

Coward, L. Andrew. Pattern Thinking. LC 89-16377. 192p. 1990. 57.95 (*0-275-93427-6*, C3427, Greenwood Pr) Greenwood.

Coward, M. P., et al, eds. Structural Geology in Reservoir Characterization. (Geological Society Special Publication Ser.: No. 127). (Illus.). 290p. 1998. 115.00 (*1-897799-94-2*, Pub. by Geol Soc Pub Hse) AAPG.

Coward, M. P. & Ries, A. C., eds. Early Precambrian Processes. (Geological Society Special Publication Ser.: No. 95). (Illus.). 308p. 1995. 112.00 (*1-897799-36-5*, 338, Pub. by Geol Soc Pub Hse) AAPG.

***Coward, Mat.** Up & Down, 1. (Five Star Mysteries Ser.). 246p. 2000. 21.95 (*0-7862-2541-6*) Mac Lib Ref.

Coward, Noel. Blithe Spirit, Hay Fever, Private. LC 98-47414. 1999. pap. 13.00 (*0-679-78179-X*) Vin Bks.

— Brief Encounter. (Illus.). 96p. (Orig.). 1999. pap. 14.00 (*0-571-19680-2*) Faber & Faber.

***Coward, Noel.** Coward on Film. 1999. 40.00 (*1-84002-055-5*, Pub. by Theatre Comm) Consort Bk Sales.

Coward, Noel. The Lyrics of Noel Coward. 1978. pap. 6.95 (*0-670-44470-7*, Viking) Viking Penguin.

— The Lyrics of Noel Coward. LC 73-77884. 432p. 1973. reprint ed. 25.00 (*0-87951-197-4*, Pub. by Overlook Pr) Penguin Putnam.

— The Lyrics of Noel Coward. LC 73-77884. 432p. 1983. reprint ed. pap. 12.95 (*0-87951-187-7*, Pub. by Overlook Pr) Penguin Putnam.

***Coward, Noel.** Noel Coward: Collected Revue Sketches & Parodies. Day, Barry, ed. (Illus.). 282p. 2000. pap. text 14.95 (*0-413-73390-4*) Methn.

— Noel Coward: Collected Short Stories. 630p. 2000. pap. 17.95 (*0-413-59970-1*) Methn.

— Noel Coward: Collected Verse. Tickner, Martin & Payn, Graham, eds. 212p. 2000. pap. 14.95 (*0-413-55150-4*) Methn.

— Noel Coward Autobiography. (Illus.). 514p. 2000. pap. text 16.95 (*0-413-73380-7*) Methn.

— Noel Coward Collected Plays: Blithe Spirit; Present Laughter; This Happy Breed, Vol. 4. 496p. 2000. pap. 14.95 (*0-413-46120-3*, Methuen Drama) Heinemann.

— Noel Coward Collected Plays: Design for Living; Cavalcade;Conversation Piece, Vol. 3. 432p. 2000. pap. text 16.95 (*0-413-46100-9*, Methuen Drama) Methn.

— Noel Coward Collected Plays: Hay Fever; The Vortex, Fallen Angels; Easy Virtue, Vol. 1. 384p. 2000. pap. 16.95 (*0-413-46060-6*) Methn.

— Noel Coward Collected Plays: Private Lives; Bitter Sweet; The Marquise; Post Mortem, Vol. 2. 384p. 2000. pap. 16.95 (*0-413-46080-0*) Methn.

— Noel Coward Collected Plays: Quadrille; "Peace in Our Time";, Vol. 7. (Methuen World Classics: The Noel Coward Collection Ser.). 416p. 2000. pap. 16.95 (*0-413-73400-5*) Methn.

— Noel Coward Collected Plays: Relative Values; Look After Lulu; Waiting in the Wings; Suite in Three Keys, Vol. 5. 560p. 2000. pap. text 16.95 (*0-413-51740-3*, Methuen Drama) Methn.

— Noel Coward Collected Plays: Semi Monde; Point Valaine; South Sea Bubble; Nude with Violin, Vol. 6. (Methuen World Classics: The Noel Coward Collection Ser.). 448p. 2000. pap. 16.95 (*0-413-73410-2*) Methn.

Coward, Noel. Pomp & Circumstance. 24.95 (*0-89190-219-8*) Amereon Ltd.

***Coward, Noel.** Pomp & Circumstance: Novel. 304p. 2000. pap. 12.95 (*0-413-56370-7*) Methn.

Coward, Noel. Spangled Unicorn. LC 82-83582. (Illus.). 101p. 1982. reprint ed. 12.50 (*0-910638-00-4*) Frisch H.

***Coward, Noel.** Unknown Noel. 1999. 40.00 (*1-84002-056-3*, Pub. by Theatre Comm) Consort Bk Sales.

Coward, Noel, ed. The Noel Coward Songbook. (Illus.). 304p. 1984. pap. 15.95 (*0-416-00961-1*, NO. 9205) Routledge.

Coward, Raymond T., et al, eds. Health Services for Rural Elders. LC 93-33551. 304p. 1994. 39.95 (*0-8261-8340-9*) Springer Pub.

Coward, Raymond T. & Krout, John A., eds. Aging in Rural Settings: Life Circumstances & Distinctive Features. LC 97-49348. (Illus.). 320p. 1998. 49.95 (*0-8261-9720-5*) Springer Pub.

Coward, Raymond T. & Smith, William M., Jr., eds. Family Services: Issues & Opportunities in Contemporary Rural America. LC 83-1267. 226p. 1983. reprint ed. pap. 70.10 (*0-608-01849-X*, 206249900003) Bks Demand.

Coward, Raymond T., jt. auth. see Dwyer, Jeffrey W.

Coward, Raymond T., jt. ed. see Dwyer, Jeffrey W.

Coward, Rosalind. Female Desires. LC 84-73207. 253p. 1985. pap. 10.95 (*0-8021-5033-0*, Grove) Grove-Atltic.

— Patriarchal Precedents: Sexuality & Social Relations. 280p. (Orig.). 1983. pap. 14.95 (*0-7100-9324-1*, Routledge Thoemms) Routledge.

Coward, Rosalind & Ellis, John A. Language & Materialism: Developments in Semiology & the Theory of the Subject. 1977. pap. 13.95 (*0-7100-8627-X*, Routledge Thoemms) Routledge.

Coward, Sylvia. The Complete Book of Cake Decorating with Sugarpaste. 176p. (C). 1988. 110.00 (*1-85368-000-1*, Pub. by New5 Holland) St Mut.

— The Complete Book of Cake Decorating with Sugarpaste. LC 95-105760. (Illus.). 176p. 1994. pap. 19.95 (*1-85368-242-X*, Pub. by New5 Holland) Sterling.

— Wedding Cakes: Exciting Designs with Full Step-by-Step Instructions. LC 95-178425. (Illus.). 80p. 1995. pap. 14.95 (*1-85368-293-4*, Pub. by New5 Holland) Sterling.

Coward, Sylvia & Birnie, Shelley. Birthday Cakes. (C). 1989. 35.00 (*1-85368-042-7*, Pub. by New5 Holland) St Mut.

Cowardin, Lewis M., et al. Classification of Wetlands & Deepwater Habitats of the U. S. (Illus.). 131p. (Orig.). (C). 1994. pap. text 50.00 (*0-7881-1416-6*) DIANE Pub.

***Cowart, Bob.** Special Edition Using Microsoft Windows 2000 Professional, 1. 1400p. 2000. pap. 39.99 (*0-7897-2125-2*) Que.

Cowart, David. History & the Contemporary Novel. LC 88-18230. (Crosscurrents-Modern Critiques, Third Ser.). 256p. (C). 1989. text 31.95 (*0-8093-1479-7*) S Ill U Pr.

— Thomas Pynchon: The Art of Allusion. LC 79-20157. (Crosscurrents-Modern Critiques, New Ser.). 168p. 1980. 21.95 (*0-8093-0944-0*) S Ill U Pr.

Cowart, David, ed. Twentieth-Century American Science Fiction Writers, 2 vols., Set. (Dictionary of Literary Biography Ser.: Vol. 8). 688p. 1981. text 296.00 (*0-8103-0918-1*) Gale.

Cowart, Georgia. The Origins of Modern Musical Criticism: French & Italian Music, 1600-1750. LC 81-641. (Studies in Musicology: No. 38). 228p. reprint ed. pap. 70.70 (*0-8357-1166-8*, 207026500065) Bks Demand.

Cowart, Georgia, ed. French Musical Thought, 1600-1800. LC 88-38521. (Illus.). 266p. 1991. 50.00 (*0-8357-1882-4*) Univ Rochester Pr.

Cowart, J. B., jt. auth. see Osmond, J. K.

Cowart, Jack, intro. Proof Positive: Forty Years of Contemporary American Printmaking at Ulae, 1957-1997. (Illus.). 272p. 1998. pap. 60.00 (*0-8109-6351-5*, Pub. by Abrams) Time Warner.

Cowart, Jack & Hamilton, Juan. Georgia O'Keefe: Arts & Letters. Greenough, Sarah, ed. 1989. 29.95 (*0-318-41640-9*) Little.

Cowart, Jack, et al. Georgia O'Keeffe: Art & Letters. (Illus.). 1989. pap. 29.95 (*0-8212-1767-4*) Bulfinch Pr.

— Manuel Neri: Early Work, 1953-1978. LC 96-11220. (Illus.). 424p. 1997. 65.00 (*0-88675-046-6*, Pub. by Hudson Hills) Natl Bk Netwk.

— Matisse in Morocco: Paintings & Drawings, 1912-1913. LC 89-13676. (Illus.). 300p. 1990. pap. 11.99 (*0-89468-140-0*) Natl Gallery Art.

Cowart, Jack, et al. Proof Positive: Forty Years of Contemporary American Printmaking at ULAE, 1957-1997. LC 98-155075. (Illus.). 1997. write for info. (*0-88675-049-0*) Corcoran.

Cowart, Jack, et al. Rauschenberg Overseas Culture Interchange (ROCI) (Illus.). 199p. 1991. 65.00 (*3-7913-1147-6*, Pub. by Prestel) te Neues.

Cowart, Jim F., jt. auth. see Lieberman, Lauren J.

Cowart, John L. Prison Minister's Handbook: Volunteer Ministry to the Forgotten Christian. LC 95-44869. 192p. 1996. pap. 17.95 (*0-89390-338-8*) Resource Pubns.

Cowart, John W. Why Don't I Get What I Pray For? LC 93-3527. 180p. (Orig.). 1993. pap. 8.99 (*0-8308-1344-6*, 1344, Saltshaker Bk) InterVarsity.

Cowart, Lynette, ed. see Dawson United Methodist Women's Staff.

Cowart, Marie E. Lifestyles & Housing of Older Adults: The Florida Experience. LC 88-32230. (Journal of Housing for the Elderly: Vol. 5, No. 1). (Illus.). 114p. 1989. text 3.95 (*0-86656-872-7*) Haworth Pr.

Cowart, Marie E. & Quadagno, Jill S., eds. From Nursing Homes to Home Care. LC 96-14870. (Journal of Aging & Social Policy: Vol. 7, Nos. 3/4). 214p. 1996. 49.95 (*1-56024-826-2*) Haworth Pr.

Cowart, Marie E. & Serow, William J., eds. Nurses in the Workplace. (Illus.). 304p. 1992. 39.95 (*0-8039-4313-X*) Sage.

Cowart, Mark C. How to Build Firm Foundations in Your Life. rev. ed. 46p. 1996. wbk. ed. write for info. (*0-9644803-1-X*) Dominion Prodns.

Cowart, Robert. Bob Cowart's Windows NT 4.0 Unleashed: Professional Reference Edition. LC 96-70402. 1400p. 1997. 59.99 incl. cd-rom (*0-672-31001-5*) Sams.

— Grampop IBM: Writer's Handbook. (C). 1991. 97.50 (*0-15-597654-0*) Harcourt Coll Pubs.

— Mastering Windows 98. 2nd ed. LC 98-84008. (Illus.). 1200p. 1996. 34.99 (*0-7821-1961-1*) Sybex.

***Cowart, Robert.** Mastering Windows 98. 2nd ed. (Mastering Ser.). 928p. 1999. pap. 39.99 (*0-7821-2618-9*) Sybex.

Cowart, Robert. Mastering Windows 98 - Premium Edition. LC 98-84032. 1664p. 1998. 59.99 (*0-7821-2186-1*) Sybex.

— Mastering Windows 95: Special Edition. 3rd ed. LC 95-67727. 1216p. 1995. 34.99 (*0-7821-1413-X*) Sybex.

— Windows 95 Quick & Easy. 2nd ed. LC 95-69863. 272p. 1995. 22.99 (*0-7821-1511-X*) Sybex.

— Windows NT Server 4: No Experience Required. 1997. pap. 29.99 (*0-614-28533-X*) Sybex.

— Windows NT Server 4.O Administrator's Guide. LC 96-78236. (Illus.). 1000p. 1996. pap. 49.99 (*0-7645-8009-4*) IDG Bks.

— Windows X Quick & Easy. (Illus.). 272p. 1996. 24.99 (*0-7821-1954-9*) Sybex.

Cowart, Robert, et al. Windows NT 4 Administrator's Handbook, Option Pack Edition. LC 99-11587. (Administrator's Handbook). (Illus.). 544p. 1999. pap. 29.99 (*0-7645-3287-1*) IDG Bks.

— Windows NT 3.51 Unleashed. 3rd ed. LC 95-72342. (Illus.). 1031p. 1996. 55.00 incl. cd-rom (*0-672-30902-5*) Sams.

Cowart, Robert, jt. auth. see Cummings, Steve.

Cowart, Ross P. An Outline of Swine Diseases: A Handbook. LC 95-22163. 152p. 1995. pap. text 24.95 (*0-8138-2899-6*) Iowa St U Pr.

Cowart, Samuel. Old Mules, New Ground & Cotton Blooms. 1991. pap. 9.95 (*0-938645-52-8*) In His Steps.

Cowart, Virginia S., jt. auth. see Yesalis, Charles E.

Cowart, Wayne. Experimental Syntax: Applying Objective Methods to Sentence Judgements. LC 96-35620. 197p. 1996. 46.00 (*0-7619-0042-X*); pap. 21.95 (*0-7619-0043-8*) Sage.

Cowasjee, Saros. Assistant Professor. LC 97-180291. 160p. 1996. pap. text 11.95 (*0-920661-50-5*, Pub. by TSAR Pubns) LPC InBook.

— Studies in Indian & Anglo-Indian Fiction. (C). 1993. 18.00 (*81-7223-072-9*, Pub. by Indus Pub) S Asia.

Cowasjee, Saros, ed. The Best Short Stories of Flora Anne Steel. (C). 1995. 26.50 (*81-7223-175-X*) S Asia.

***Cowasjee, Saros, ed.** The Oxford Anthology of Raj Stories. LC 98-909291. 360p. 1999. text 29.95 (*0-19-564279-1*) OUP.

Cowasjee, Saros & Duggal, K. S., eds. Orphans of the Storm: Stories on the Partition of India. LC 94-906939. (C). 1995. text 28.00 (*81-7476-017-2*, Pub. by UBS Pubs Dist); pap. text 12.00 (*81-85944-92-X*, Pub. by UBS Pubs Dist) S Asia.

Cowasjee, Saros & Theroux, Paul. Stories from the Raj: From Kipling to Independence LC 82-104722. 271p. 1982. 7.50 (*0-370-30456-X*) Bodley Head.

Cowboy Artists of America Staff. Cowboy Artists of America: Thirty-Second Annual Exhibition. 1997. pap. text 19.95 (*1-890752-00-2*) Cowboy Art Am.

***Cowboy Artists of America Staff.** 1999 Cowboy Artists of America: Thirty-Fourth Annual Exhibition Catalog. (Illus.). 1999. pap. write for info. (*1-890752-06-1*) Cowboy Art Am.

Cowburn, Will. Class Ideology & Community Action. Campling, Jo, ed. (Radical Forum on Adult Education Ser.). 192p. 39.95 (*0-7099-3497-1*, Pub. by C Helm) Routldge.

Cowcher, Helen. Antarctica. (Illus.). 1990. text 15.00 (*0-374-30368-1*) FS&G.

— Antarctica. LC 89-45911. (Illus.). 32p. (J). (gr. k-3). 1991. pap. 5.95 (*0-374-40371-6*, Sunburst Bks) FS&G.

Cowcher, Helen. Antarctica. Erdogan, Fatih, tr. (Illus.). 33p. (ps-3). 1997. 16.95 (*1-84059-004-1*) Milet Ltd.

Cowcher, Helen. El Bosque Tropical. 1996. 11.15 (*0-606-10798-3*, Pub. by Turtleback) Demco.

— El Bosque Tropical: Rain Forest. LC 91-34047. (SPA.). 32p. (YA). (ps-3). 1992. 15.00 (*0-374-30900-0*) FS&G.

— El Bosque Tropical - Rain Forest. LC 49-242890. (SPA.). 32p. (J). (ps-3). 1996. pap. 5.95 (*0-374-42043-2*) FS&G.

— Jaguar. LC 96-52956. (Illus.). 32p. (J). (ps-5). 1997. 15.95 (*0-590-29937-9*) Scholastic Inc.

Cowcher, Helen. Kaplan. (Illus.). (J). 1997. 16.95 (*1-84059-031-9*) Milet Ltd.

Cowcher, Helen. Rain Forest. LC 88-45178. (Illus.). 32p. (J). (ps up). 1988. 15.00 (*0-374-36167-3*) FS&G.

— Rain Forest. 1998. 10.15 (*0-606-04780-8*, Pub. by Turtleback) Demco.

— La Tigresa. Marcuse, Aida E., tr. LC 92-54836. (SPA.). 32p. (J). (ps-3). 1993. pap. 5.95 (*0-374-47779-5*) FS&G.

— La Tigresa. LC 92-54836. (SPA.). (J). 1993. 11.15 (*0-606-05902-4*, Pub. by Turtleback) Demco.

— Tigress. 1993. 11.15 (*0-606-06060-X*, Pub. by Turtleback) Demco.

Cowcher, Helen. Whistling Thorn. 1997. 16.95 (*1-84059-039-4*) Milet Ltd.

Cowcher, Helen. Whistling Thorns. LC 92-39533. (J). (gr. 6 up). 1993. 14.95 (*0-590-47299-2*) Scholastic Inc.

Cowcher, Helen. Tigress. LC 91-12513. 32p. (J). (ps-3). 1991. bds. 14.95 (*0-374-37567-4*) FS&G.

— Tigress. LC 91-12513. 32p. (J). (ps-3). 1993. pap. 5.95 (*0-374-47781-7*) FS&G.

Cowdell, C. Banking in the European Community after 1992. (Occasional Papers). (C). 1989. 115.00 (*0-85297-302-0*, Pub. by Chartered Bank) St Mut.

Cowdell, Jane. Investment. 523p. 2000. pap. 120.00 (*0-85297-553-8*, Pub. by Chartered Bank) St Mut.

Cowdell, Jane & Farrance, Christ. Marketing of Financial Services. 465p. 1990. pap. 125.00 (*0-85297-337-3*, Pub. by Chartered Bank) St Mut.

Cowdell, Jane, jt. auth. see Cowdell, Paul.

Cowdell, Paul. Banking Law & Practice. 1997. pap. 90.00 (*0-85297-411-6*, Pub. by Chartered Bank) St Mut.

Cowdell, Paul & Cowdell, Jane. Law Relating to Banking Services. 484p. 1990. pap. 125.00 (*0-85297-357-8*, Pub. by Chartered Bank) St Mut.

Cowdell, Scott. Is Jesus Unique? The Christological Debate Today. LC 95-47055. (Theological Inquiries Ser.). 320p. 1996. pap. 24.95 (*0-8091-3628-7*, 3628-7) Paulist Pr.

Cowdell, Theo, jt. auth. see Chapman, David.

Cowden, Diane, jt. auth. see Preece, Alison.

Cowden, Dudley J. Measures of Exports of the United States. LC 68-58561. (Columbia University. Studies in the Social Sciences: No. 356). reprint ed. 20.00 (*0-404-51356-5*) AMS Pr.

Cowden, Frances & Hatchett, Eve B. Of Butterflies & Unicorns: And Other Wonders of the Earth. LC 94-75436. (Illus.). 68p. (J). (gr. 2-12). 1994. pap. 8.95 (*1-884289-04-5*) Grandmother Erth.

Cowden, Frances, ed. see Benedict, Burnette B.

Cowden, Frances, ed. see Boren, Blanche.

Cowden, Frances, ed. see Crow, Geraldine.

Cowden, Frances, ed. see Hatchett, Eve B.

Cowden, Frances, jt. ed. see Smith, Patricia.

Cowden, Frances B. Angels: Messengers of Love & Grace. 80p. 1998. pap. 9.95 (*1-884289-18-5*) Grandmother Erth.

— View from A Mississippi River Cotton Sack. Zarshenas, Marcelle B., ed. (Illus.). 68p. (Orig.). 1993. spiral bd. 10.95 (*1-884289-01-0*) Grandmother Erth.

— View from A Mississippi River Cotton Sack. 2nd ed. Zarshenas, Marcelle B., ed. LC 93-80265. (Illus.). 80p. (Orig.). 1994. 15.00 (*1-884289-03-7*) Grandmother Erth.

Cowden, Frances B., ed. Grandmother Earth I: Prize-Winning Poems. (Illus.). 111p. (Orig.). 1995. pap., per. 10.00 (*1-884289-09-6*) Grandmother Erth.

— To Love a Whale: Learning about Endangered Animals from the Young & Young-at-Heart. LC 95-76847. (Illus.). 116p. (J). (gr. 3-9). 1995. pap. 8.00 (*1-884289-06-1*) Grandmother Erth.

Cowden, Frances B. & Abbott, Barbara, eds. Grandmother Earth's Healthy & Wise Cookbook: Easy & Healthy Recipes. (Illus.). 192p. 1998. pap. 12.95 (*1-884289-13-4*) Grandmother Erth.

Cowden, Frances B. & Zarshenas, Marcelle, eds. Grandmother Earth II 1996: Prize Winning Poems. LC 96-147800. (Illus.). 134p. 1996. pap., per. 10.00 (*1-884289-14-2*) Grandmother Erth.

Cowden, Frances B., ed. see Schirz, Shirley R.

Cowden, J. E. & Duffy, J. O. The Elder Dempster Fleet History 1852-1985. 1990. 90.00 (*0-9509453-2-3*, Pub. by Ship Pictorial Pubng) St Mut.

Cowden, Jim. The Field Sales Handbook: Checklists, Summaries & Case Studies. (Institute of Management Ser.). 256p. (Orig.). 1994. pap. 47.50 (*0-273-60716-2*, Pub. by Pitman Pub) Trans-Atl Phila.

Cowden, Jo E., et al. Pediatric Adapted Motor Development & Exercise: An Innovative Multisystem Approach for Professionals & Families. LC 97-46392. (Illus.). 346p. 1998. text 66.95 (*0-398-06848-8*); pap. text 53.95 (*0-398-06849-6*) C C Thomas.

Cowden, John B. Cowden. Southern Cowdens. (Illus.). 112p. 1997. reprint ed. pap. 19.00 (*0-8328-8100-7*); reprint ed. lib. bdg. 29.00 (*0-8328-8099-X*) Higginson Bk Co.

***Cowden, Lisa.** Ladle, Leaf & Loaf: Soup, Salad & Bread for Every Season. (Illus.). 256p. 2000. pap. 16.00 (*0-395-96715-5*) HM.

Cowden, Morton. Russian Bolshevism & British Labor, 1917-1921. 238p. 1984. text 55.50 (*0-88033-045-7*, Pub. by East Eur Monographs) Col U Pr.

Cowden, R. Cowden - Gilliland. 179p. 1991. reprint ed. pap. 27.50 (*0-8328-2022-9*); reprint ed. lib. bdg. 37.50 (*0-8328-2021-0*) Higginson Bk Co.

Cowden, Robert. A Brief Sketch of the Organization & Services of the Fifty-Ninth Regiment of United States Colored Infantry. LC 74-168514. (Black Heritage Library Collection). 1977. reprint ed. 29.95 (*0-8369-8866-3*) Ayer.

Cowden, Robert H. Classical Singers of the Opera & Recital Stages: A Bibliography of Biographical Materials, 42. LC 94-6329. (Music Reference Collection). 528p. 1994. lib. bdg. 79.50 (*0-313-29332-5*, Greenwood Pr) Greenwood.

— Concert & Opera Conductors: A Bibliography of Biographical Materials, 14. LC 87-11821. (Music Reference Collection). 301p. 1987. lib. bdg. 65.00 (*0-313-25620-9*, Greenwood Pr) Greenwood.

— Opera Companies of the World: Selected Profiles. LC 91-24186. 368p. 1992. lib. bdg. 85.00 (*0-313-26220-9*, CPC, Greenwood Pr) Greenwood.

— Popular Singers of the Twentieth Century: A Bibliography of Biographical Materials, 78. LC 99-22691. (Music Reference Collection: No. 78). 520p. 1999. lib. bdg. 85.00 (*0-313-29333-3*, GR9333, Greenwood Pr) Greenwood.

Cowden, Robert H., compiled by. Concert & Opera Singers: A Bibliography of Biographical Materials, 5. LC 85-12717. (Music Reference Collection: No. 5). 278p. 1985. lib. bdg. 57.95 (*0-313-24828-1*, CCT/, Greenwood Pr) Greenwood.

— Instrumental Virtuosi: A Bibliography of Biographical Materials, 18. LC 88-34816. (Music Reference Collection: No. 18). 366p. 1989. lib. bdg. 59.95 (*0-313-26075-3*, CDU/, Greenwood Pr) Greenwood.

Cowden, Robert L. & Klotman, Robert H. Administration & Supervision of Music. 2nd rev. ed. (Illus.). 328p. 1991. reprint ed. 45.00 (*0-02-871211-0*, Schirmer Books) Mac Lib Ref.

Cowden, Steve, jt. auth. see Lloyd, Tanya.

***Cowden, Tami D., et al.** Complete Writer's Guide to Heroes & Heroines: 16 Master Archetypes. (Illus.). 300p. 2000. pap. text 17.95 (*1-58065-024-4*) Lone Eagle Pub.

Cowder, Frances, ed. Person to Person to God: The Power of Prayer. 2000. pap. 10.00 (*1-884289-19-3*) Grandmother Erth.

Cowdery, Charles K. Blues Legends. LC 95-13142. (Illus.). 96p. 2000. reprint ed. 19.95 incl. audio compact disk (*0-87905-688-6*) Gibbs Smith Pub.

Cowdery, James. The Melodic Tradition of Ireland. LC 89-24436. (World Music Ser.). 215p. 1990. 24.00 (*0-87338-407-5*) Kent St U Pr.

Cowdery, Josephine, jt. tr. see Cowdery, Ray.

Cowdery, Josephine N., jt. auth. see Cowdery, Ray R.

An Asterisk (*) at the beginning of an entry indicates that the title is appearing for the first time.

Cowdery, Lauren T. The Nouvelle of Henry James in Theory & Practice. LC 85-24619. (Studies in Modern Literature: No. 47). 146p. reprint ed. pap. 45.30 (*0-8357-1623-6*, 207048000096) Bks Demand.

Cowdery, Ray. All-American Wonder: The Military Jeep 1941-1945, Vol. 1. (Illus.). 144p. 1993. reprint ed. pap. text 25.00 (*0-910667-10-1*) Victory WW Two.

Cowdery, Ray & Cowdery, Josephine, trs. from GER. Katyn, an Examination of the Evidence. (Illus.). 48p. 1995. pap. 10.00 (*0-910667-43-8*) USM.

Cowdery, Ray & Robinson, George C. Nazi Para-Military Organizations & Their Badges. LC 83-60048. (Illus.). 142p. 1985. pap. 20.00 (*0-910667-05-5*) USM.

Cowdery, Ray R. All-American Wonder Vol. 2: The Military Jeep 1941-1945. (Illus.). 132p. 1990. pap. text 25.00 (*0-910667-20-9*) Victory WW Two.

— Grossdeutschland: Guidebook to the Third Reich. (GER., Illus.). 24p. (Orig.). 1992. reprint ed. pap. 10.00 (*0-910667-23-3*) USM.

— Hitler's New German Reichschancellery in Berlin, 1938-1945. LC 86-5082. (Illus.). 64p. 1987. 50.00 (*0-910667-12-8*) USM.

— Nazi Militaria - Fake or Real? (Illus.). 144p. (Orig.). 1992. pap. 10.00 (*0-910667-08-X*) USM.

Cowdery, Ray R., tr. from GER. I Fight: Ich Kampfe. LC 82-61240. (Illus.). 144p. (Orig.). 1992. pap. 20.00 (*0-910667-01-2*) USM.

Cowdery, Ray R. & Cowdery, Josephine N. Masters of Ceremony. (Illus.). 128p. 1998. reprint ed. pap. 20.00 (*0-910667-38-1*) USM.

— Papers Please! Identity Documents, Permits & Authorizations of the Third Reich. (Illus.). 144p. 1996. 29.95 (*0-910667-36-5*) USM.

Cowdery, Ray R. & Vodenka, Peter. Reinhard Heydrich: Assassination! (Illus.). 96p. (Orig.). 1994. pap. 15.00 (*0-910667-42-X*) USM.

Cowdery, Ray R., ed. see Enright, R. T.

Cowdery, Ray R., tr. see Siegmann, Hermann.

Cowdrey, Albert E. Fighting for Life: American Military Medicine in World War II. LC 94-8280. 392p. 1994. 29.95 (*0-02-906835-5*) Free Pr.

— This Land, This South: An Environmental History. LC 82-20154. (New Perspectives on the South Ser.). 250p. reprint ed. pap. 77.50 (*0-7837-5807-3*, 204547300006) Bks Demand.

— This Land, This South: An Environmental History. rev. ed. LC 95-36831. (New Perspectives on the South Ser.). (Illus.). 256p. 1995. pap. 17.00 (*0-8131-0851-9*) U Pr of Ky.

— United States Army in the Korean War: Medic's War. (Center for Military History Publication German Report Series, DA Pam: No. 20-5). (Illus.). 409p. 1987. text 27.00 (*0-16-001949-4*, 008-029-00147-1) USGPO.

— War & Healing: Stanhope Bayne-Jones & the Maturing of American Medicine. Cooper, William J., Jr., ed. LC 91-32513. (Southern Biography Ser.). (Illus.). 264p. (C). 1992. text 42.50 (*0-8071-1717-X*) La State U Pr.

Cowdrey, Albert E., jt. auth. see Crabb, Cecil V., Jr.

Cowdrey, Albert L., jt. auth. see Condon-Rall, Mary Ellen.

Cowdrey, H. E. The Age of Abbot Desiderius: Montecassino, the Papacy & the Normans in the Eleventh & Early Twelfth Centuries. 1983. 69.00 (*0-19-821939-3*) OUP.

***Cowdrey, H. E.** The Crusades & Latin Monasticism, 11th-12th Centuries. LC 99-29850. (Variorum Collected Studies Ser.). 1999. 97.95 (*0-86078-795-8*, Pub. by Ashgate Pub) Ashgate Pub Co.

— Pope Gregory VII, 1073-1085. 760p. 1998. text 150.00 (*0-19-820646-1*) OUP.

— Popes & Church Reform in the 11th Century. 101.95 (*0-86078-797-4*) Ashgate Pub Co.

Cowdrey, H. E. Popes, Monks & Crusaders. 400p. (C). 1983. 60.00 (*0-907628-34-6*) Hambledon Press.

Cowdrey, H. E., ed. see Gregory VII.

Cowdrey, Michael L. & Drew, Melinda. Basic Law for the Allied Health Professions. 2nd ed. LC 94-38115. 336p. 1995. pap. 40.00 (*0-86720-710-8*) Jones & Bartlett.

***Cowdrey, Mike.** Arrows Elk Society Ledger. Delisi-Holmes, Lesa & Chiasson, Joan, eds. 1999. pap. 35.00 (*0-9617085-3-0*) Morning Star Gal.

Cowdrey, Peter A., Jr., jt. auth. see St. Claire, Dana.

Cowdrey, Peter R. The Kamikaze Virus. 184p. 1996. pap. 19.00 (*0-8059-3952-0*) Dorrance.

Cowdrey, Richard, jt. illus. see Brett, Jessica.

Cowdry, E. V. & Kastenbaum, Robert J., eds. Problems of Aging: Biological & Medical Aspects. LC 78-22196. (Aging & Old Age Ser.). (Illus.). 1979. reprint ed. lib. bdg. 52.95 (*0-405-11813-9*) Ayer.

Cowdry, Mary B., ed. see Woodward, Mary D.

Cowe, Ian A., jt. ed. see Murray, Ian.

Cowe, Roger. Handbook of Management Accounting. 2nd ed. 500p. 1988. text 96.95 (*0-566-02615-5*, Pub. by Gower) Ashgate Pub Co.

Cowe, Roger, ed. The Guardian Guide to the U. K.'s Top Companies, 1995. 480p. 1995. 55.00 (*1-85702-239-4*) Fourth Estate.

Cowe, Roger, jt. auth. see Brummer, Alex.

Cowe, S. Peter, jt. ed. see Parlakian, Nishan.

Cowe, S. Peter, tr. see Oghlukian, Abel.

Cowee, William. Bones Set Against the Drift. xii, 89p. 1997. pap. 12.00 (*1-891033-09-3*, Rainshadow Editns) Black Rock Pr.

Cowell, A. T. Tactics at Gettysburg. 81p. 1987. reprint ed. 9.00 (*0-942211-05-7*) Olde Soldier Bks.

***Cowell, Adrian.** The Decade of Destruction: The Crusade to Save the Amazon Rain Forest. (Illus.). 215p. 1999. reprint ed. text 20.00 (*0-7881-6688-3*) DIANE Pub.

Cowell, Adrian. The Tribe That Hides from Man. LC 74-152872. 251 p. 1973. write for info. (*0-370-01379-4*) Bodley Head.

— The Tribe That Hides from Man. (Illus.). 265p. 1996. pap. 16.95 (*0-7126-5959-5*, Pub. by Pimlico) Trafalgar.

Cowell, Andrew. At Play in the Tavern: Signs, Coins & Bodies in the Middle Ages. LC 98-40266. (Stylus Ser.). 280p. 1999. text 47.50 (*0-472-11007-1*, 11007) U of Mich Pr.

Cowell, Barbara, jt. auth. see Wilson, John.

Cowell, Benjamin. Spirit of '76 in Rhode Island. 560p. 1996. reprint ed. lib. bdg. 55.00 (*0-8328-5115-9*) Higginson Bk Co.

***Cowell, C. Mark, et al.** The Physical Environment: Laboratory Exercises for Geo 111l. 116p. (C). 1999. per. 18.95 (*0-7872-6097-5*, 41609701) Kendall-Hunt.

Cowell, Christopher T., ed. Growth & Sexual Development. 288p. 1993. text 92.00 (*3-7186-5403-2*, Harwood Acad Pubs) Gordon & Breach.

***Cowell, Cressida.** Don't Do That, Kitty Kilroy. LC 99-25546. (Illus.). 32p. (J). (ps-2). 1999. 15.95 (*0-531-30209-1*) Orchard Bks Watts.

Cowell, Cressida. Little Bo Peep's Library Book. LC 98-42424. (Illus.). 32p. (J). (ps-2). 1999. 14.95 (*0-531-30179-6*) Orchard Bks Watts.

***Cowell, Cressida & Godon, Ingrid.** What Shall We Do with the Boo-Hoo Baby? LC 99-52907. (J). 2000. pap. write for info. (*0-439-15312-3*) Scholastic Inc.

Cowell, David, jt. auth. see Stenson, Kevin.

Cowell, E. B. The Jataka or Stories of the Buddha's Former Births, 6 vols. in 3 bks., Set. (C). 1994. reprint ed. text 88.00 (*81-208-0725-1*, Pub. by Motilal Bnarsidass) S Asia.

Cowell, E. B., ed. The Jataka or Stories of the Buddha's Former Births, 6 vols., Set. (C). 1990. reprint ed. 149.00 (*0-86013-260-9*) Wisdom MA.

— The Jataka or Stories of the Buddha's Former Births, Vol. 3 & 4. (C). 1990. reprint ed. 52.50 (*0-86013-054-1*) Wisdom MA.

— The Jataka or Stories of the Buddha's Former Births, Vols. 1 & 2. (C). 1990. reprint ed. 52.50 (*0-86013-053-3*) Wisdom MA.

— The Jataka or Stories of the Buddha's Former Births, Vols. 5 & 6. (C). 1990. reprint ed. 52.50 (*0-86013-055-X*) Wisdom MA.

Cowell, E. B., et al, eds. Buddhist Mahayana Texts. 448p. 1987. reprint ed. pap. 9.95 (*0-486-25552-2*) Dover.

Cowell, Eileen, ed. see Calciano, Joan.

Cowell, F. A. & Champernowne, David G. Economic Inequality & Income Distribution. 480p. (C). 1997. pap. text 29.95 (*0-521-58959-2*) Cambridge U Pr.

— Economic Inequality & Income Distribution. 432p. (C). 1999. 74.95 (*0-521-58055-2*) Cambridge U Pr.

Cowell, F. R. Daily Life in Ancient Greece & Rome. rev. ed. (Illus.). 64p. (C). 1991. pap. text 2.00 (*1-877891-10-X*) Paperbook Pr Inc.

— Life in Ancient Rome. 1976. pap. 12.95 (*0-399-50328-5*, Perigee Bks) Berkley Pub.

Cowell, Frank & Amiel, Yoram. Thinking about Inequality: Personal Judgment & Income Distributions. LC 99-13081. (Illus.). 196p. 2000. 64.95 (*0-521-46131-6*); pap. 24.95 (*0-521-46696-2*) Cambridge U Pr.

Cowell, Glynis S. & Turner, Joan F. Tapices Literarios: Stories for Building Language Skills & Cultural Awareness. (C). 1996. pap. text 24.00 (*0-07-912039-3*) McGraw.

***Cowell, Henry.** Essential Cowell: Selected Writings on Music. Higgins, Dick, ed. 2000. 35.00 (*0-929701-63-1*) McPherson & Co.

Cowell, Henry. New Musical Resources. 195p. (C). 1996. text 59.95 (*0-521-49651-9*); pap. text 21.95 (*0-521-49974-7*) Cambridge U Pr.

Cowell, Henry, ed. American Composers on American Music: A Symposium. LC 33-13037. (Illus.). 238p. 1933. reprint ed. pap. 30.00 (*0-8357-5358-1*, 205632000058) Bks Demand.

Cowell, Henry & Cowell, Sidney. Charles Ives & His Music. (Music Reprint Ser.). x, 253p. 1981. reprint ed. 35.00 (*0-306-76125-4*) Da Capo.

Cowell, Ian G. & Austin, Caroline A., eds. cDNA Library Protocols. (Methods in Molecular Biology Ser.: Vol. 69). (Illus.). 336p. 1996. 79.50 (*0-89603-383-X*) Humana.

Cowell, J. Essential Delphi 2.0 Fast: How to Develop Applications in Delphi 2.0. LC 96-33758. 184p. 1996. pap. 26.95 (*3-540-76026-1*) Spr-Verlag.

***Cowell, J.** Essential Java 2 - Fast: How to Develop Applications & Applets with Java 2. LC 99-25430. (Essential Ser.). ix, 240p. 1999. pap. 29.95 (*1-85233-071-6*) Spr-Verlag.

Cowell, John. Dublin's Famous People & Where They Lived: And Where They Lived. LC 96-161830. (Illus.). 192p. 1997. pap. 14.95 (*0-86278-468-9*) Irish Amer Bk.

— Essential Delphi 3 Fast: Includes ActiveX Control Development. LC 97-40559. (Essential Fast Ser.). (Illus.). x, 188p. 1997. pap. 29.95 (*3-540-76150-0*) Spr-Verlag.

— Essential Java with Latte Fast. LC 97-5550. 200p. 1997. pap. text 24.95 incl. cd-rom (*3-540-76052-0*) Spr-Verlag.

***Cowell, John.** Essential Visual Basic 6.0 Fast. LC 99-46242. (Essential Ser.). 235p. 2000. 29.95 (*1-85233-207-7*, Pub. by Spr-Verlag) Spr-Verlag.

Cowell, John. Essential Visual BASIC 4.0 Fast: How to Develop Applications in Visual Basic. LC 96-10945. 186p. 1996. pap. 24.95 (*3-540-19998-5*) Spr-Verlag.

— Essential Visual Basic 5.0 Fast. LC 97-17622. (Essential Ser.). 200p. 1997. pap. 24.95 (*3-540-76148-9*) Spr-Verlag.

— The Interpreter: Or, Book Containing the Signification of Words. LC 76-25757. (English Experience Ser.: No. 231). 584p. 1970. reprint ed. 75.00 (*90-221-0231-9*) Walter J Johnson.

Cowell, John & Keynes, Milton. Essential Visual J++ Fast: How to Develop Applications & Applets in Java. LC 98-7024. 220p. 1998. pap. 29.95 (*1-85233-013-9*) P-H.

***Cowell, John K.** Molecular Genetics of Cancer. 245p. 1999. 105.00 (*0-12-220441-7*) Acad Pr.

Cowell, Mark W. A Reference Grammar of Syrian Arabic. (Richard Slade Harrell Arabic Ser.). 579p. 1964. pap. 16.95 (*0-87840-009-5*); audio 20.00 (*0-87840-019-2*) Georgetown U Pr.

Cowell, Michael. Song for the Navigator. 1993. pap. 5.50 (*0-87129-185-1*, S37) Dramatic Pub.

***Cowell, R. G., et al.** Probabilistic Networks & Expert Systems. Jordan, M. et al, eds. LC 99-13242. (Statistics for Engineering Information Science Ser.). (Illus.). 368p. 1999. 69.95 (*0-387-98767-3*) Spr-Verlag.

Cowell, R. W. & Innes, J. B. The Wetlands of Merseyside. (North West Wetlands Survey 1; Lancaster Imprints Ser.: No. 2). (Illus.). 258p. 1995. pap. 45.00 (*0-901800-40-6*, Pub. by Lancaster U Archaeol) David Brown.

Cowell, Raymond, ed. Critics on Yeats. LC 78-143725. (Readings in Literary Criticism Ser.: No. 10). 1979. pap. 19.95 (*0-87024-200-8*) U of Miami Pr.

Cowell, Rick L., et al. Diagnostic Cytology of the Dog & Cat. 2nd ed. LC 98-14959. (Illus.). 352p. (C). (gr. 13). 1998. text 89.95 (*0-8151-0362-X*, 31755) Mosby Inc.

Cowell, Sidney, jt. auth. see Cowell, Henry.

Cowell, Stephanie. The Players: A Novel of the Young Shakespeare. LC 96-34987. 352p. (C). 1997. 24.00 (*0-393-04060-7*) Norton.

Cowell, W. James. Incorporating New Members: Bonds of Believing, Belonging, & Becoming. LC 91-71727. 96p. 1992. pap. 8.95 (*0-88177-112-0*, DR112) Discipleship Res.

Cowell, W. R., et al. Toolpack 1: Introductory Guide. (Orig.). 1985. pap. 4.20 (*0-317-52233-7*, Pub. by Numer Algo) Princeton Bk Co.

Cowen. Linear Algebra for Engineer. 1999. pap. text 64.95 (*0-7167-3207-6*) W H Freeman.

***Cowen.** Matrix Analysis. 1999. pap. text. write for info. (*0-7167-3206-8*) W H Freeman.

Cowen, Anne & Cowen, Roger. Victorian Jews Through British Eyes. LC 99-170246. (Illus.). 224p. 1998. 39.95 (*1-874774-29-3*, Pub. by Littman Lib) Intl Spec Bk.

Cowen, Ari. 50 Ways to Stop Violence. Date not set. pap. 56.00 (*0-393-31411-1*) Norton.

Cowen, Ari & Washington Physicians for Social Responsibility St. 50 Ways to Stop the Violence Now: In the World, in Our Country, in Your Workplace, in Our Schools, in Your Home, in Yourself. 150p. (Orig.). 1996. pap. 7.00 (*0-393-31357-3*, Norton Paperbks) Norton.

Cowen, Carl C. Introduction to Matrix Analysis for Engineering & Science. 5th ed. (Illus.). viii, 428p. 1997. pap. text 32.00 (*0-9650717-6-6*) West Pickle.

— Linear Algebra for Engineering & Science: Preliminary Edition. 2nd ed. (Illus.). viii, 462p. 1997. pap. text 40.00 (*0-9650717-4-X*) West Pickle.

Cowen, Carl C., Jr. & MacCluer, Barbara I. Composition Operators on Spaces of Analytic Functions. 400p. 1995. boxed set 79.95 (*0-8493-8492-3*, 8492) CRC Pr.

Cowen, Cynthia. A Christmas Gift: A Christmas Eve Worship Service. 16p. 1998. pap. 3.95 (*0-7880-1288-6*) CSS OH.

— Creating God's Family in Christmas: An Advent Service for All Ages. LC 98-167598. 24p. (Orig.). 1997. pap. 5.25 (*0-7880-1053-0*) CSS OH.

***Cowen, Cynthia.** Hear the Bells Ring: A Service of Carols for Christmas Day. 28p. 1998. pap. 4.50 (*0-7880-1287-8*) CSS OH.

Cowen, Cynthia. It's Jesus' Birthday! A Christmas Eve Service. LC 98-167600. 20p. (Orig.). 1997. pap. 5.25 (*0-7880-1063-8*) CSS OH.

***Cowen, Cynthia.** Lights, Symbols & Angels: Six Worship Resources for Advent/Christmas. LC 99-37622. 100p. 1999. pap. 10.75 (*0-7880-1517-6*) CSS OH.

Cowen, Cynthia E. Bread & Broth: A Bible Study for Lent. LC 95-39881. 73p. (Orig.). 1996. pap. 8.50 (*0-7880-0710-6*) CSS OH.

— Christians, Christians, Everywhere, How Do Your Gardens Grow? A Stewardship Service for Youth. (Orig.). 1994. pap. 5.50 (*0-7880-0115-9*) CSS OH.

— Christmas Preparations: A Christmas Pageant for Youth. (YA). 1994. pap. 4.95 (*0-7880-0098-5*) CSS OH.

— Eighteen Special Worship Celebrations! Worship Services for Congregational Use. LC 93-37990. 112p. 1994. pap. 10.95 (*1-55673-830-7*) CSS OH.

— Search, Journey, Discovery. 1992. pap. 6.95 (*1-55673-571-5*, 9257) CSS OH.

— This Is the King! A Service for Palm-Passion Sunday. 1992. pap. 3.25 (*1-55673-568-5*, 9315) CSS OH.

— The Weaving of Hearts. 1991. pap. 6.95 (*1-55673-392-5*, 9210) CSS OH.

— Who - Me? Do a Program? Vol. 2: Program Resources for Congregational Events. 232p. 1999. pap. 19.95 (*0-7880-1342-4*) CSS OH.

— Who-Me? Do a Program? LC 95-12243. 167 p. 1995. 14.95 (*0-7880-0590-1*) CSS OH.

Cowen, Cynthia E. & Cowen, Stephen. Holy Week Confessions: Twelve Worship Resources for Holy Week. LC 92-36162. 1992. pap. 6.95 (*1-55673-566-9*, 9313) CSS OH.

Cowen, D. V. & Gering, Leonard. Cowen on the Law of Negotiable Instruments in South Africa Vol. 1: General Principles. 5th ed. 612p. 1985. 59.00 (*0-7021-1570-3*, 15606, Pub. by Juta & Co) Gaunt.

***Cowen, David Jack.** The Origins & Economic Impact of the First Bank of the United States, 1791-1797. LC 00-39315. (Financial Sector of the American Economy Ser.). (Illus.). 2000. write for info. (*0-8153-3837-6*) Garland.

Cowen, David L. & Bowers, Roy A. The Rutgers University College of Pharmacy: A Centennial History. LC 90-39149. (Illus.). 175p. (C). 1991. text 35.00 (*0-8135-1634-X*) Rutgers U Pr.

Cowen, David L. & Helfand, William H. Pharmacy: An Illustrated History. (Illus.). 272p. (gr. 13). 1990. 85.00 (*0-8109-1498-0*) Mosby Inc.

Cowen, David L. & Segelman, Alvin B. Antibiotics in Historical Perspective. 238p. 1981. write for info. (*0-911910-71-9*) Merck-Sharp-Dohme.

Cowen, Deborah, ed. The Year of Grace of the Lord. 254p. (Orig.). 1980. pap. 11.95 (*0-913836-68-0*) St Vladimirs.

Cowen, Emory L., et al. School-Based Prevention for Children at Risk: The Primary Mental Health Project. LC 96-23913. 356p. 1996. 39.95 (*1-55798-353-4*); pap. 29.95 (*1-55798-374-7*) Am Psychol.

Cowen, Eve. Catch the Sun. (Sportellers Ser.). 1981. 15.27 (*0-606-02379-8*, Pub. by Turtleback) Demco.

Cowen, Eve. High Escape. (Sportellers Ser.). (J). 1981. 15.27 (*0-606-02394-1*, Pub. by Turtleback) Demco.

— Race to Win. (Sportellers Ser.). 1981. 15.27 (*0-606-02426-3*, Pub. by Turtleback) Demco.

Cowen-Fletcher, Jane. Baby Angels. LC 95-19911. (Illus.). 24p. (J). (ps-1). 1996. 15.99 (*1-56402-666-3*) Candlewick Pr.

— Baby Angels. LC 95-19911. (Illus.). 24p. (J). (ps). 1998. reprint ed. bds. 5.99 (*0-7636-0414-3*) Candlewick Pr.

***Cowen-Fletcher, Jane.** Farmer Will. LC 99-57127. (Illus.). (J). 2001. write for info. (*0-7636-0988-9*) Candlewick Pr.

Cowen-Fletcher, Jane. It Takes a Village. LC 92-32324. (ITA.). 32p. (J). (ps-3). 1994. 15.95 (*0-590-46573-2*) Scholastic Inc.

— Mama Zooms. (J). (ps-3). 1993. 19.95 (*0-590-72848-2*) Scholastic Inc.

— Mama Zooms. 32p. (J). (ps-3). 1994. pap. 3.95 (*0-590-45775-6*) Scholastic Inc.

— Mama Zooms. 1995. 10.19 (*0-606-11593-5*, Pub. by Turtleback) Demco.

Cowen, Harry. Community Care, Ideology, & Social Policy. LC 98-5599. (Contemporary Social Policy Ser.). 1998. write for info. (*0-13-727843-8*) P-H.

— The Human Nature Debate. 240p. (C). 1994. 49.95 (*0-7453-0740-X*, Pub. by Pluto GBR); pap. 19.95 (*0-7453-0741-8*, Pub. by Pluto GBR) Stylus Pub VA.

Cowen, Janet, ed. see Chaucer, Geoffrey.

Cowen, Janet, ed. see Malory, Thomas.

Cowen, Jim. Live Events Promotional Graphics. (Illus.). 160p. 1994. 34.99 (*1-56496-082-X*) Rockport Pubs.

Cowen, Joel M. & Peterson, Robert D. The Cal/OSHA Source. LC 98-233119. 350p. 1998. pap. 55.00 (*0-9663378-0-8*) CA Safety.

Cowen, John E. English Teacher's Portfolio of Multicultural Activities: Ready-to-Use Lessons & Cooperative Activities for Grades 7-12. LC 95-25860. 288p. 1996. pap. text, teacher ed. 28.95 (*0-87628-300-8*) Ctr Appl Res.

Cowen, John E., ed. Teaching Reading Through the Arts. LC 82-12755. 118p. reprint ed. pap. 36.60 (*0-8357-2635-5*, 204012300014) Bks Demand.

Cowen-Karp, Regina, ed. Central & Eastern Europe: The Challenge of Transition. (SIPRI Publication). (Illus.). 336p. 1994. text 55.00 (*0-19-829169-8*) OUP.

***Cowen, Lauren.** Girlfriends: A Celebration. 2000. 4.95 (*0-7624-0845-6*) Running Pr.

Cowen, Lauren & Wexler, Jayne. Daughters & Mothers. LC 96-86295. (Illus.). 128p. 1997. 19.98 (*0-7624-0110-9*, Courage) Running Pr.

Cowen, M. P. & Shenton, Robert W. Doctrines of Development. LC 95-5870. (Illus.). 576p. (C). (gr. 13). 1995. 100.00 (*0-415-12515-4*) Routledge.

— Doctrines of Development. LC 95-5870. (Illus.). 576p. (C). 1996. pap. 29.99 (*0-415-12516-2*) Routledge.

Cowen, P. J., jt. ed. see Idzikowski, C.

Cowen, P. N. & Smiddy, F. G. Pocket Examiner in Pathology. 2nd ed. LC 95-33681. 148p. 1996. pap. text 22.00 (*0-443-05418-5*) Church.

Cowen, Philip. Memories of an American Jew. LC 74-27974. (Modern Jewish Experience Ser.). (Illus.). 1975. reprint ed. 41.95 (*0-405-06703-8*) Ayer.

Cowen, Philip, jt. auth. see Thompson, Chris.

Cowen, Philip, jt. ed. see Hawton, Keith E.

Cowen, Richard. History of Life. 2nd ed. (Illus.). 512p. 1994. pap. 44.95 (*0-86542-354-7*) Blackwell Sci.

***Cowen, Richard.** History of Life. 3rd ed. LC 99-16542. (Illus.). 1999. pap. 49.95 (*0-632-04444-6*) Blackwell Sci.

Cowen, Richard W. Papa Raker's Dream: A Loving History of Good Shepherd. (Illus.). 318p. 1988. 15.00 (*0-9620808-0-2*) Good Shepherd.

Cowen, Rick. The Next Marketing Handbook for Independent Schools. 1991. 27.00 (*0-934338-75-2*) NAIS.

Cowen, Roger, jt. auth. see Cowen, Anne.

Cowen, Ron. The Book of Murder. 1974. pap. 5.25 (*0-8222-0133-X*) Dramatists Play.

— Saturday Adoption. 1969. pap. 5.25 (*0-8222-0987-X*) Dramatists Play.

— Summertree. 1968. pap. 5.25 (*0-8222-1099-1*) Dramatists Play.

Cowen, Shimon D., tr. see Zalman, Schneur.

Cowen, Stephen, jt. auth. see Cowen, Cynthia E.

Cowen, Stuart, jt. auth. see Van der Ryn, Sim.

Cowen, Tyler. In Praise of Commercial Culture. LC 97-40445. 288p. 1999. text 27.95 (*0-674-44591-0*) HUP.

***Cowen, Tyler.** In Praise of Commercial Culture. 2000. pap. 14.95 (*0-674-00188-5*) HUP.

— What Price Fame? LC 99-45903. 208p. 2000. 22.00 (*0-674-00155-9*) HUP.

Cowen, Tyler, ed. Public Goods & Market Failures: A Critical Examination. 384p. (C). 1999. pap. text 24.95 (*1-56000-570-X*) Transaction Pubs.

— The Theory of Market Failure: A Critical Examination. 410p. (C). 1988. lib. bdg. 72.50 (*0-913969-13-3*) Univ Pub Assocs.

C

*__Cowen, Tyler, et al, eds.__ Economic Welfare. LC 99-56208. (Critical Ideas in Economics Ser.). 624p. 2000. 230.00 (*1-85898-931-0*) E Elgar.

Cowen, Tyler & Kroszner, Randall. Explorations in the New Monetary Economics. LC 93-22618. (Illus.). 224p. 1994. 61.95 (*1-55786-071-8*) Blackwell Pubs.

Cowen, Tyler & Parker, David. Markets in the Firm: A Market-Process Approach to Management. (Hobart Paper Ser.: No. 134). 95p. 1997. pap. 22.50 (*0-255-36405-9*, Pub. by Inst Economic Affairs) Coronet Bks.

Cowen, Tylor. Risk & Business Cycles: New & Old Austrian Perspectives. LC 97-13794. (Foundations of the Modern Economy Ser.). 240p. (C). 1998. write for info. (*0-415-16919-4*) Routledge.

Cowen, William. Central African Odyssey. 1995. text 45.00 (*1-85043-923-0*, Pub. by I B T) St Martin.

Cowen, Zelman. British Commonwealth of Nations in a Changing World: Law, Politics & Prospects. LC 65-12096. (Julius Rosenthal Memorial Lecture: 1964). 127p. reprint ed. pap. 39.40 (*0-8357-9448-2*, 201529200001) Bks Demand.

— Reflections on Medicine, Biotechnology & the Law. LC 86-1492. 68p. reprint ed. pap. 30.00 (*0-7837-1818-7*, 204201800001) Bks Demand.

Cowens, Deborah & Monte, Tom. A Gift for Healing. (Illus.). 256p. 1996. 17.00 (*0-517-88651-0*) Crown Pub Group.

Cowern, Nicholas E., et al, eds. Silicon Front-End Technology Vol. 532: Materials Processing & Modelling. (Symposium Proceedings Ser.). 228p. 1998. 84.00 (*1-55899-438-6*) Materials Res.

Cowes, B. The America's Cup. 200p. 2000. 65.00 (*1-86046-304-5*, Pub. by Harvill Press) FS&G.

Cowett, Mark. Birmingham's Rabbi: Morris Newfield & Alabama, 1895-1940. LC 85-20897. (Judaic Studies Ser.). (Illus.). 238p. reprint ed. pap. 73.80 (*0-608-09220-7*, 205272400005) Bks Demand.

Cowett, R. M., ed. Principles of Perinatal-Neonatal Metabolism. (Illus.). xxi, 774p. 1991. 240.00 (*0-387-97499-7*) Spr-Verlag.

Cowett, Richard M., ed. Diabetes, No. 35. LC 95-810. (Nestle Nutrition Workshop Ser.: Vol. 35). (Illus.). 320p. 1995. text 69.00 (*0-7817-0324-7*) Lppncott W & W.

— Principles of Perinatal-Neonatal Metabolism. 2nd ed. LC 97-24816. (Illus.). 1088p. 1998. 250.00 (*0-387-94965-8*) Spr-Verlag.

Cowey, C. B. Nutritional Strategies & Management of Aquaculture Waste, Vol. 10. (Water Science & Technology Ser.: Vol. 31). 262p. 1995. pap. write for info. (*0-08-042662-X*, Pergamon Pr) Elsevier.

Cowger, Barry D. Applying Astrology to Family Psychology. Christy, Martha M., ed. 225p. (Orig.). 1992. pap. 12.95 (*0-9632091-0-8*) Wishland Inc.

Cowger, J. F. Friction Ridge Skin: Comparison & Identification of Fingerprints. (Practical Aspects of Criminal & Forensic Investigations Ser.: Vol. 2). 220p. 1992. 64.95 (*0-444-00770-9*, HV6094) CRC Pr.

Cowger, James F. Friction Ridge Skin: Comparison & Identification of Fingerprints. LC 93-24980. 232p. (YA). (gr. 7 up). 1992. per. 94.95 (*0-8493-9502-X*) CRC Pr.

Cowger, Thomas, contrib. by. The National Congress of American Indians: The Founding Years. LC 99-17940. (Illus.). 1999. text 45.00 (*0-8032-1502-9*) U of Nebr Pr.

Cowgill, Allison A., jt. auth. see Mirkovich, Thomas R.

*__Cowgill, Bob.__ Kiawah's Wild Side: Wildlife on a Barrier Island on the Carolina Coast. unabridged ed. (Illus.). 148p. 2000. pap. 13.50 (*0-9661595-1-9*) Bobcat Pr.

Cowgill, Carol & Campbell, James P. Christ Yesterday & Today. 141p. (Orig.). 1986. student ed. 8.95 (*1-55588-125-4*) St Michael Guild.

Cowgill, George L., jt. ed. see Yoffee, Norman.

*__Cowgill, J., et al.__ Knives & Scabbards. 2nd ed. (Illus.). 180p. 2000. 45.00 (*0-85115-805-6*) Boydell & Brewer.

Cowgill, Joy. Wagon Train, 1958. (Illus.). 78p. 1980. pap. 5.00 (*0-916552-21-7*) Acoma Bks.

Cowgill, Judy. Kentucky's Parks (Kentucky State Parks) Butler, William & Strode, William, eds. (Illus.). 112p. 1991. 35.00 (*1-56469-000-8*) Harmony Hse Pub.

Cowgill, Kent. The Cranberry Trail: Misfits, Dreamers & Drifters on the Heartland Road. LC 95-81507. (Illus.). 208p. (Orig.). 1996. pap. 11.95 (*1-883477-09-3*) Lone Oak MN.

Cowgill, Linda. Secrets of Screenplay Structure. LC 98-45740. 318p. 1998. pap. 16.95 (*1-58065-004-X*) Lone Eagle Pub.

— Writing Short Films: Structure & Content for Screenwriters. LC 97-2155. 256p. (Orig.). 1997. pap. 19.95 (*0-943728-80-0*) Lone Eagle Pub.

Cowgill, Robert W. Nature's Way on Kiawah: A Barrier Island on the Carolina Coast. (Illus.). 150p. 1998. pap. 12.00 (*0-9661595-0-0*) Bobcat Pr.

Cowgill, U. M. & Williams, L. R., eds. Aquatic Toxicology & Hazard Assessment, Vol. 12. (Special Technical Publication Ser.: No. STP 1027). (Illus.). 445p. 1989. text 65.00 (*0-8031-1253-X*, STP1027) ASTM.

Cowgill, Ursula M. Soil Fertility & the Ancient Maya. (Connecticut Academy of Arts & Sciences Ser., Trans.: Vol. 42). 1961. pap. 49.50 (*0-685-22891-6*) Elliots Bks.

Cowgill, Ursula M., et al. The History of Laguna de Petenxil: A Small Lake in Northern Guatemala. (Connecticut Academy of Arts & Sciences Ser., Trans.: Vol. 17). 1966. pap. 75.00 (*0-685-22854-1*) Elliots Bks.

Cowherd, Carrie. Persius Saturae. (Latin Commentaries Ser.). 129p. (Orig.). (C). 1986. pap. text 7.00 (*0-929524-48-9*) Bryn Mawr Commentaries.

Cowherd, Kevin. Last Call at the 7-Eleven: Fine Dining at 2 a.m., the Search for Spandex People, & Other Reasons to Go on Living. Bortz, Bruce, ed. LC 96-163549. 243p. 1995. 19.95 (*0-9635376-3-6*) Bancroft MD.

— When I Was Your Age, We Didn't Even HAVE Church: Chronicles of a Catholic Parent. LC 95-68833. 144p. 1995. pap. 7.95 (*0-87973-672-0*) Our Sunday Visitor.

Cowherd, Raymond G. The Humanitarians & the Ten Hour Movement in England. (Kress Library of Business & Economics Publication: No. 10). (Illus.). 27p. 1956. pap. 9.95 (*0-678-09905-7*) Kelley.

Cowhey, Dennis R. What Does That Mean? The Personal Stories Behind Vanity License Plates. Cowhey, Julie A., ed. 221p. 1994. 19.95 (*0-9642823-1-3*); pap. 9.95 (*0-9642823-0-5*) Key Answer Prods.

Cowhey, Julie A., ed. see Cowhey, Dennis R.

Cowhey, Peter, et al, eds. Changing Networks: Mexico's Telecommunications Options. (Monographs: No. 32). 126p. (Orig.). (C). 1989. 12.95 (*0-935391-86-X*, MN32C) UCSD Ctr US-Mex.

Cowhey, Peter F. & Aronson, Jonathan. Managing the World Economy: The Consequences of Corporate Alliances. LC 92-42450. 363p. 1993. reprint ed. pap. 112.60 (*0-608-02009-5*, 206266500003) Bks Demand.

Cowhey, Peter F. & McCubbins, Mathew D., eds. Structure & Policy in Japan & the United States. (Political Economy of Institutions & Decisions Ser.). (Illus.). 308p. (C). 1995. text 64.95 (*0-521-46151-0*); pap. text 20.95 (*0-521-46710-1*) Cambridge U Pr.

Cowhey, Peter F, jt. auth. see Aronson, Jonathan D.

*__Cowie & Aalsvoort.__ Social Interaction in Learning & Instruction. (Advances in Learning & Instruction Ser.: Vol. 9). 2000. 50.00 (*0-08-043597-1*, Pergamon Pr) Elsevier.

Cowie, A. P. English Dictionaries for Foreign Learners: A History. LC 99-21395. (Oxford Studies in Lexicography & Lexicology). (Illus.). 240p. 2000. text 72.00 (*0-19-823506-2*) OUP.

— Phraseology: Theory, Analysis, & Applications. 272p. 1998. text 82.00 (*0-19-829425-5*) OUP.

Cowie, A. P., ed. see Hornby, A. S.

Cowie, Alexander. John Trumbull, Connecticut Wit. (BCL1-PS American Literature Ser.). 230p. 1993. reprint ed. lib. bdg. 79.00 (*0-7812-6941-5*) Rprt Serv.

Cowie, Colin. Effortless Elegance with Colin Cowie: Menus, Tips, Strategies & More Than 200 Recipes for Easy Entertaining. LC 96-11108. (Illus.). 272p. 1996. 47.50 (*0-06-270152-5*, HarperStyle) HarpC.

*__Cowie, Colin.__ For the Bride. LC 99-55635. (Illus.). 160p. 2000. 24.95 (*0-385-33442-7*) Delacorte.

— For the Groom. LC 99-55634. (Illus.). 144p. 2000. 24.95 (*0-385-33443-5*) Delacorte.

Cowie, E. E. The English Spa, 1815 to Present Day. (C). 1997. text 95.00 (*0-485-11502-6*) Humanities.

Cowie, Elizabeth. Representing the Woman: Cinema & Psychoanalysis. LC 96-20752. 416p. (C). 1996. pap. 19.95 (*0-8166-2913-7*) U of Minn Pr.

Cowie, Evelyn E., jt. auth. see Cowie, Leonard W.

Cowie, Fiona. What's Within? Nativism Reconsidered. LC 98-5364. (Philosophy of Mind Ser.). (Illus.). 352p. 1998. 35.00 (*0-19-512384-0*) OUP.

Cowie, Fiona, jt. ed. see Bradney, Anthony.

Cowie, Harrie. Venture Capital in Europe. 1999. pap. text 25.00 (*0-901573-86-8*, Kogan Pg Educ) Stylus Pub VA.

Cowie, Helen & Pecherek, Andrea. Counselling: Approaches & Issues in Education. 176p. 1994. pap. 27.00 (*1-85346-293-4*, Pub. by David Fulton) Taylor & Francis.

Cowie, Helen & Sharp, Sonia, eds. Peer Counselling in Schools: A Time to Listen. 160p. 1996. pap. 24.95 (*1-85346-367-1*, Pub. by David Fulton) Taylor & Francis.

Cowie, Helen, et al. Cooperation in the Multi-Ethnic Classroom: The Impact of Cooperative Group Work on Social Relationships in Middle Schools. 144p. 1994. pap. 27.00 (*1-85346-284-5*, Pub. by David Fulton) Taylor & Francis.

Cowie, Helen, jt. auth. see Sharp, Sonia.

Cowie, Isaac. The Company of Adventurers: A Narrative of Seven Years in the Service of the Hudson's Bay Company During 1867-1874. LC 92-37703. (Illus.). iv, 555p. 1993. pap. 15.95 (*0-8032-6350-3*, Bison Books); text 50.00 (*0-8032-1464-2*) U of Nebr Pr.

Cowie, J. M. Polymers: Chemistry & Physics of Modern Materials. 2nd enl. rev. ed. 448p. 1991. pap. 39.95 (*0-412-03121-3*, A6369, Chap & Hall NY) Chapman & Hall.

Cowie, J. M., ed. see Plate, N. A. & Shibaev, V. P.

*__Cowie, Jefferson.__ Capital Moves: RCA's Seventy-Year Quest for Cheap Labor. LC 98-49784. (Illus.). 288p. 1999. 29.95 (*0-8014-3525-0*) Cornell U Pr.

Cowie, Jefferson R. Capital Moves: RCA's Seventy-Year Quest for Cheap Labor. LC 98-49784. 1999. write for info. (*0-8014-8522-3*) Cornell U Pr.

Cowie, Jonathan. Climate & Human Change: Disaster or Opportunity. LC 97-24533. (Illus.). 384p. 1998. 34.50 (*1-85070-971-8*) Prthnon Pub.

Cowie, Leonard W. Edmund Burke, 1729-1797: A Bibliography, Vol. 19. LC 93-45955. (Bibliographies of British Statesmen Ser.: No. 19). 146p. 1994. lib. bdg. 69.50 (*0-313-28710-4*, Greenwood Pr) Greenwood.

Cowie, Leonard W. Lord Nelson, 1758-1805: A Bibliography, 7. LC 89-12756. (Bibliographies of British Statesmen Ser.: No. 7). 200p. 1990. lib. bdg. 65.00 (*0-313-28082-7*, CBK/, Greenwood Pr) Greenwood.

— William Wilberforce, 1759-1833: A Bibliography, 17. LC 92-5351. (Bibliographies of British Statesmen Ser.: No. 17). 160p. 1992. lib. bdg. 59.95 (*0-313-28283-8*, CWW, Greenwood Pr) Greenwood.

Cowie, Leonard W., compiled by. Sir Robert Peel, 1788-1850: A Bibliography, 13. LC 95-41985. (Bibliographies of British Statesmen Ser.: No. 13). 152p. 1996. lib. bdg. 69.50 (*0-313-29447-X*, Greenwood Pr) Greenwood.

Cowie, Leonard W. & Cowie, Evelyn E. British Spas: From 1815 to the Present Day. LC 96-43104. (Illus.). 240p. 1997. 48.50 (*0-8386-3748-5*) Fairleigh Dickinson.

Cowie, Marian L., ed. see Schott, Peter.

Cowie, Murray A., ed. see Schott, Peter.

Cowie, Peter. Annie Hall. (BFI Film Classics Ser.). (Illus.). 72p. 1996. pap. 10.95 (*0-85170-580-4*, Pub. by British Film Inst) Ind U Pr.

— Coppola: A Biography. LC 94-16270. (Illus.). 352p. 1994. reprint ed. pap. 16.00 (*0-306-80598-7*) Da Capo.

— The Godfather Book, 1. 272p. 1999. pap. text 20.00 (*0-8133-3723-2*) Westview.

— Ingmar Bergman: A Critical Biography. LC 91-43134. (Illus.). 404p. 1992. reprint ed. pap. 17.95 (*0-87910-155-5*) Limelight Edns.

— International Film Guide, 1992. (Illus.). 496p. 1992. pap. 16.95 (*0-233-98720-7*) S French Trade.

Cowie, Peter. International Film Guide, 1995. 1995. pap. text 18.95 (*0-600-58516-6*) Hamlyn Publishing Group Ltd.

Cowie, Peter. Scandinavian Cinema. 1992. pap. 24.95 (*0-573-69911-9*) French.

— Variety International Film Guide, 1996. (Illus.). 448p. 1995. pap. 18.95 (*0-240-80253-5*, Focal) Buttrwrth-Heinemann.

— World Filmography, Vol.1. 35.00 (*0-8453-1565-X*, Cornwall Bks) Assoc Univ Prs.

— World Filmography, Vol.2. 35.00 (*0-8453-1569-2*, Cornwall Bks) Assoc Univ Prs.

Cowie, Peter, ed. International Film Guide, 1989. (Illus.). 496p. 1989. pap. 15.95 (*0-900730-30-7*); pap. 15.95 (*0-685-70311-8*) S French Trade.

— International Film Guide, 1991. (Illus.). 504p. 1991. pap. 16.95 (*0-233-98613-8*) S French Trade.

— International Film Guide, 1993. (Illus.). 528p. 1993. pap. 17.95 (*0-685-70310-X*) S French Trade.

— International Film Guide, 1993. (Illus.). 528p. 1993. pap. 17.95 (*0-233-98807-6*) S French Trade.

— International Film Guide, 1994. (Illus.). 448p. 1994. pap. 18.95 (*0-600-58005-9*) S French Trade.

— International Film Guide, 1999 (Variety) 36th ed. (Illus.). 416p. 1998. pap. 23.95 (*1-879505-47-9*) Silman James Pr.

*__Cowie, Peter, ed.__ The Variety Almanac, 2000. (Illus.). 416p. 2000. 37.50 (*0-7522-7159-8*, Pub. by Boxtree) Trans-Atl Phila.

— Variety International: Film Guide 2000. (Illus.). 416p. 2000. pap. 23.95 (*1-879505-52-5*, Pub. by Silman James Pr) SCB Distributors.

Cowie, Peter & Scorsese, Martin. World Cinema: Diary of a Day. LC 94-28116. (Illus.). 400p. 1995. 29.95 (*0-87951-573-2*, Pub. by Overlook Pr) Penguin Putnam.

Cowie, R. H., et al. Catalog of the Native Land & Freshwater Molluscs of the Hawaiian Islands. (Illus.). 254p. 1995. pap. 52.00 (*90-73348-43-9*, Pub. by Backhuys Pubs) Balogh.

Cowie, Robert H. Catalog of the Nonmarine Snails & Slugs of the Samoan Islands. (Bulletin in Zoology Ser.: Vol. 3). (Illus.). 122p. (C). 1998. pap. 29.95 (*0-930897-99-4*) Bishop Mus.

Cowie, Roddy & Douglas-Cowie, Ellen. Postlingually Acquired Deafness: Speech Deterioration & the Wider Consequences. LC 92-12793. (Trends in Linguistics, Studies & Monographs: Vol. 62). x, 304p. (C). 1992. lib. bdg. 106.15 (*3-11-012575-7*, 105-92) Mouton.

Cowie, Scott, jt. auth. see Gordon, Rodney.

Cowie, Valerie, jt. ed. see Roth, Martin.

Cowie, Vera. Designing Woman. 192p. 1999. 25.00 (*0-7278-5421-6*, Pub. by Severn Hse) Chivers N Amer.

*__Cowie, Vera.__ Designing Woman. 288p. 2000. 31.99 (*0-7505-1556-2*) Ulverscroft.

Cowie, Vera. A Girl's Best Friend. large type ed. (Black Satin Romance Ser.). 476p. 1997. 27.99 (*1-86110-019-1*) Ulverscroft.

*__Cowie, Vera.__ Shades of Love. 1999. 26.00 (*0-7278-5484-4*, Pub. by Severn Hse) Chivers N Amer.

Cowie, Vera. Unsentimental Journey. large type ed. (Black Satin Romance Ser.). 501p. 1996. 27.99 (*1-86110-020-5*) Ulverscroft.

Cowie, Victor & Davies, Victor. The Magic Trumpet. (J). 1997. pap. 4.95 (*0-88801-094-X*, Pub. by Turnstone Pr) Genl Dist Srvs.

*__Cowin, Dana & Hill, Judith, eds.__ Food & Wine Magazine's 2000 Annual Cookbook. (Food & Wine Bks.). (Illus.). 464p. 2000. 25.95 (*0-916103-60-9*) Am Express Food.

*__Cowin, Hugh.__ German & Austrian Aviation of World War I. (Illus.). 96p. 2000. pap. 15.95 (*1-84176-069-2*, 130031AE, Pub. by Ospry) Motorbooks Intl.

Cowin, Hugh. X-Planes Research Aircraft, 1911-1969: A Unique Pictorial Record of Flying Prototypes, Their Designers & Pilots. (Illus.). 96p. 1999. pap. 15.95 (*1-85532-876-3*, 128407AE) Motorbooks Intl.

Cowin, Hugh W. Racing & Record Setting Aircraft 1908-1968. (Aviation Pioneers Ser.: Vol. 1). (Illus.). 96p. 1999. pap. 15.95 (*1-85532-904-2*, 129052AE, Pub. by Ospry) Motorbooks Intl.

Cowin, Pamela & Klymkowsky, Michael. Cytoskeletal-Membrane Interactions & Signal Transduction. LC 97-19386. (Molecular Biology Intelligence Unit Ser.). 225p. 1997. 99.00 (*1-57059-455-4*) Landes Bioscience.

Cowin, Stephen C., ed. Bone Mechanics. 320p. (C). 1988. boxed set 249.00 (*0-8493-4562-6*, QP303) CRC Pr.

Cowin, Stephen C., ed. see ASME Applied Mechanics Summer Conference Staff.

Cowing, Cedric B. The Saving Remnant: Religion & the Settling of New England. 320p. 1995. 19.95 (*0-252-06440-2*); text 39.95 (*0-252-02138-X*) U of Ill Pr.

Cowing, Janet McKay, see McKay Cowing, Janet.

Cowing, Renee. The Complete Book of Pet Names. 8.95 (*0-9626950-1-7*) Fireplug CA.

— The Complete Book of Pet Names. LC 90-81851. 112p. (YA). 1990. 8.95 (*0-9626950-2-5*) Fireplug CA.

*__Cowing, Sheila.__ Stronger in the Broken Places. LC 99-19033. (Illus.). 72p. 1999. pap. 12.00 (*1-890932-06-X*) Sherman Asher Pub.

Cowing, Sue, selected by. Fire in the Sea: An Anthology of Poetry & Art. (Illus.). 152p. (J). 1996. 29.95 (*0-8248-1649-8*) UH Pr.

Cowing, Susan B., tr. see Coedes, G.

Cowing, T. G. & Stevenson, R. E., eds. Productivity Measurement in Regulated Industries. LC 80-1685. (Economic Theory, Econometrics & Mathematical Economics Ser.). 1981. text 119.95 (*0-12-194080-2*) Acad Pr.

Cowitt, Philip, ed. World Currency Yearbook, 1986-1987: International Currency Analysis. 25th ed. 1984. 250.00 (*0-917645-02-2*) Currency Data & Intell.

Cowitt, Philip, ed. see International Currency Analysis Staff.

Cowitt, Philip P. World Currency Yearbook, 1988-1989: International Currency Analysis. 26th ed. 900p. 1991. 250.00 (*0-917645-03-0*) Currency Data & Intell.

Cowl, Richard P. Theory of Poetry in England: From the 16th to the 19th Century. 1972. 59.95 (*0-8490-1190-6*) Gordon Pr.

Cowlard, Keith A., jt. auth. see Panton, Kenneth J.

Cowler, Rosemary, ed. The Prose Works of Alexander Pope Vol. II: The Major Works, 1725-1744. LC 86-3625. xv, 529p. (C). 1986. lib. bdg. 57.50 (*0-208-02059-4*, Archon Bks) Shoe String.

Cowles, Ben T. Free to Be Responsible: How to Assume Response-Ability. LC 90-36177. 397p. 1991. pap. 12.95 (*0-932727-27-1*); text 19.95 (*0-932727-28-X*) Hope Pub Hse.

— Through the Dragon's Mouth: Journeys in the Yangzi Gorges. LC 98-33984. (Illus.). 320p. 1999. 24.95 (*1-56474-294-6*) Fithian Pr.

Cowles, C. McKeen. Nursing Homes Statistical Yearbook, 1997. 260p. text 50.00 (*0-8018-5802-X*) Johns Hopkins.

Cowles, C. McKeen, ed. Nursing Home Statistical Yearbook, 1995. 256p. (C). 1996. text 45.00 (*0-8018-5378-8*) Johns Hopkins.

— Nursing Home Statistical Yearbook, 1996. 256p. 1997. text 50.00 (*0-8018-5638-8*) Johns Hopkins.

Cowles Creative Pub. Staff. Built-In Essentials. LC 97-145171. (Black & Decker Quick Steps Ser.). (Illus.). 80p. (Orig.). 1997. pap. 9.95 (*0-86573-644-8*) Creat Pub Intl.

— Door & Window Essentials. LC 97-145555. (Black & Decker Quick Steps Ser.). (Illus.). 80p. (Orig.). 1997. pap. 9.95 (*0-86573-648-0*) Creat Pub Intl.

— Kitchen Planner. LC 97-11856. (Home Project Manager Ser.). (Illus.). 144p. 1997. spiral bd. 24.95 (*0-86573-641-3*) Creat Pub Intl.

— Roof & Siding Essentials. LC 97-145181. (Black & Decker Quick Steps Ser.). (Illus.). 80p. (Orig.). 1997. pap. 9.95 (*0-86573-649-9*) Creat Pub Intl.

— Traditional Christmas Two: Cooking, Crafts & Gifts. LC 97-9479. (Illus.). 320p. 1997. 32.95 (*0-86573-899-8*) Creat Pub Intl.

*__Cowles Creative Publishing, Inc. Staff.__ Curtains for Beginners. LC 98-19091. (Seams Sew Easy Ser.). (Illus.). 128p. 1998. pap., spiral bd. 17.95 (*0-86573-325-2*) Creat Pub Intl.

Cowles Creative Publishing, Inc. Staff. Halloween Decorating. LC 98-4402. (Arts & Crafts for Holiday Decorating Ser.). (Illus.). 130p. 1998. 18.95 (*0-86573-414-3*); pap. 16.95 (*0-86573-415-1*) Creat Pub Intl.

— Pillows: For Beginners. LC 98-18266. (Seams Sew Easy Ser.). (Illus.). 128p. 1998. 17.95 (*0-86573-324-4*) Creat Pub Intl.

— A Portfolio of Home Spa Ideas. LC 98-17225. (Illus.). 96p. 1998. pap. 10.95 (*0-86573-890-4*) Creat Pub Intl.

— Tis the Season: Creative Christmas Decorating. LC 98-20187. (Arts & Crafts for Home Decorating Ser.). (Illus.). 1998. 18.95 (*0-86573-416-X*); pap. 16.95 (*0-86573-417-8*) Creat Pub Intl.

Cowles Creative Publishing, Inc. Staff & Black & Decker Staff. A Portfolio of Home Entertainment Ideas. LC 98-7293. (Illus.). 96p. 1998. pap. 10.95 (*0-86573-891-2*) Creat Pub Intl.

Cowles Creative Publishing, Inc. Staff & Hearst Corp. (House Beautiful) Staff. How to Paint: A Complete Guide to Painting Your Home. LC 98-19866. (Illus.). 1998. pap. 16.95 (*0-86573-190-X*) Creat Pub Intl.

Cowles Creative Publishing, Inc. Staff & Times Mirror Magazines, Inc. Staff. Essential Home Tips: 500 Solutions for Problems Around Your Home. LC 98-19038. (Illus.). 160p. 1998. 24.95 (*0-86573-758-4*) Creat Pub Intl.

— Field & Stream - The World of Whitetail Hunting. LC 98-19054. (Illus.). 1998. 24.95 (*0-86573-083-0*); pap. 19.95 (*0-86573-084-9*) Creat Pub Intl.

Cowles Creative Publishing Staff. Advanced Home Plumbing. LC 97-1176. (Black & Decker Home Improvement Library). (Illus.). 120p. 1997. 16.95 (*0-86573-750-9*) Creat Pub Intl.

— All-Time Favorite Fish Recipes. LC 98-223127. (Freshwater Angler Ser.). 160p. 1998. pap. 16.95 (*0-86573-078-4*) Creat Pub Intl.

— Bathroom Planner: A Step-by-Step Planning Workbook for Bathroom Remodeling. LC 98-10905. (Home Project Manager Ser.). (Illus.). 150p. 1998. ring bd. 34.95 (*0-86573-640-5*) Creat Pub Intl.

— Create Custom Curtains. (Illus.). 18p. 1995. pap. text 4.49 (*0-86573-913-7*) Creat Pub Intl.

— Creative Floral Arranging. LC 97-22203. (Illus.). 224p. 1997. 29.95 (*0-86573-197-7*) Creat Pub Intl.

— Decorative Accessories. LC 97-24170. (Portable Workshop Ser.). (Illus.). 96p. 1997. spiral bd. 14.95 (*0-86573-643-X*) Creat Pub Intl.

C

An Asterisk (*) at the beginning of an entry indicates that the title is appearing for the first time.

— Fabric Artistry. LC 97-48864. (Singer Design Ser.). (Illus.). 1998. 18.95 (*0-86573-323-6*); pap. 16.95 (*0-86573-326-0*) Creat Pub Intl.

— A Festive Christmas: Wonderful Ideas for Decorating, Cooking & Gift Giving. LC 97-13374. (Illus.). 224p. 1997. write for info. (*0-86573-198-5*) Creat Pub Intl.

— Floor Finishes Etc. LC 96-37444. (Creative Touches Ser.). (Illus.). 64p. (Orig.). 1997. pap. 9.95 (*0-86573-878-5*) Creat Pub Intl.

— Fly Fishing for Trout in Streams. LC 97-32138. (Hunting & Fishing Library). (Illus.). 175p. 1998. 19.95 (*0-86573-073-3*) Creat Pub Intl.

— Game Bird Cookery. LC 97-24704. (Hunting & Fishing Library). (Illus.). 128p. 1997. 19.95 (*0-86573-070-9*) Creat Pub Intl.

— Great Decks & Furnishings: A Step-by-Step Guide. LC 98-19927. (Black & Decker Portable Workshop Ser.). (Illus.). 112p. 1998. spiral bd. 16.95 (*0-86573-656-1*) Creat Pub Intl.

***Cowles Creative Publishing Staff.** Grilling with Flavor! 150 Recipes to Mix & Match. (Illus.). 2000. 19.95 (*0-86573-593-X*) Creat Pub Intl.

Cowles Creative Publishing Staff. Halloween Costumes. LC 97-3875. (Singer Sewing Reference Library). (Illus.). 128p. 1997. 18.95 (*0-86573-316-3*); pap. 16.95 (*0-86573-317-1*) Creat Pub Intl.

— Holiday Projects. LC 96-48294. (Singer Sewing Reference Library). (Illus.). 128p. 1997. 18.95 (*0-86573-314-7*); pap. 16.95 (*0-86573-315-5*) Creat Pub Intl.

— Kitchen Accessories. LC 97-20287. (Portable Workshop Ser.). (Illus.). 1997. spiral bd. 16.95 (*0-86573-642-1*) Creat Pub Intl.

— Landscape Essentials. (Black & Decker Quick Steps Ser.). (Illus.). 80p. (Orig.). 1996. pap. 9.95 (*0-86573-654-5*) Creat Pub Intl.

***Cowles Creative Publishing Staff.** Memory Albums by Design. (Illus.). 80p. 1999. 12.95 (*0-86573-183-7*) Creat Pub Intl.

Cowles Creative Publishing Staff. Painting Essentials. (Black & Decker Quick Steps Ser.). (Illus.). 80p. (Orig.). 1996. pap. 9.95 (*0-86573-655-3*) Creat Pub Intl.

— Plumbing Essentials. (Black & Decker Quick Steps Ser.). (Illus.). 80p. (Orig.). 1996. pap. 9.95 (*0-86573-651-0*) Creat Pub Intl.

— Porch & Patio Essentials. (Black & Decker Quick Steps Ser.). (Illus.). 80p. (Orig.). 1997. pap. 9.95 (*0-86573-645-6*) Creat Pub Intl.

— Slipcovers. LC 97-14622. (Creative Textiles Ser.). (Illus.). 112p. 1997. pap. 16.95 (*0-86573-411-9*) Creat Pub Intl.

— Upholstery Basics. LC 97-14879. (Singer Sewing Reference Library). (Illus.). 128p. 1997. 18.95 (*0-86573-318-X*); pap. 16.95 (*0-86573-319-8*) Creat Pub Intl.

— Venison Cookery. LC 97-8256. (Hunting & Fishing Library). (Illus.). 128p. 1997. 19.95 (*0-86573,068-7*) Creat Pub Intl.

— Wall Finishes Etc. LC 96-37445. (Creative Touches Ser.). (Illus.). 64p. (Orig.). 1997. pap. 9.95 (*0-86573-882-3*) Creat Pub Intl.

— Wiring Essentials. (Black & Decker Quick Steps Ser.). (Illus.). 80p. (Orig.). 1996. pap. 9.95 (*0-86573-650-2*) Creat Pub Intl.

Cowles Creative Publishing Staff & Hearst Corporation (Popular Mechanics) Staff. Houseworks: Guide to Understanding Your Home. LC 97-49057. (Illus.). 1998. 24.95 (*0-86573-752-5*) Creat Pub Intl.

Cowles Creative Publishing Staff & Home Decorating Institute Staff. Low Sew Window Treatments. LC 97-37376. (Creative Textiles Ser.). (Illus.). 112p. 1997. pap. 16.95 (*0-86573-413-5*) Creat Pub Intl.

Cowles Creative Publishing Staff & Outdoor Life (Times Mirror Magazine, Inc.) Staff. The Best of Outdoor Life: One Hundred Years of Classic Stories. LC 97-44258. 224p. 1998. 34.95 (*0-86573-076-8*) Creat Pub Intl.

Cowles Creative Publishing Staff & Sports Afield Staff. Hunting Today's Whitetail: Strategies for Success. LC 97-47033. 160p. 1998. 24.95 (*0-86573-077-6*) Creat Pub Intl.

***Cowles Creative Publishing Staff, et al.** Outdoor Life: 100 Years in Pictures. LC 97-49710. 224p. 1998. 34.95 (*0-86573-075-X*) Creat Pub Intl.

Cowles Creative Publishing Staff, jt. auth. see Brossard, Judith.

Cowles Creative Publishing Staff, jt. auth. see Howe, Deborah.

Cowles Creative Staff. Ceramic Tile Essentials. LC 97-196891. (Black & Decker Quick Steps Ser.). (Illus.). 1997. pap. text 9.95 (*0-86573-873-4*) Creat Pub Intl.

Cowles, David. Complete Guide to Winning Keno. LC 95-68285. (Illus.). 272p. 1996. pap. 14.95 (*0-940685-62-0*) Cardoza Pub.

Cowles, David, et al. The Critical Experience. 352p. (C). 1995. pap. text, per. 18.95 (*0-7872-0012-3*) Kendall-Hunt.

Cowles, David L. & Cowles, Delys. Miracle Victory over the Flesh-Eating Bacteria. LC 96-39228. 160p. 1997. pap. 10.95 (*0-87905-809-9*) Gibbs Smith Pub.

Cowles, Delys, jt. auth. see Cowles, David L.

Cowles, Ernest L., jt. auth. see Gransky, Laura.

Cowles, Fleur. The Best of Flair. (Illus.). 336p. 1999. 250.00 (*0-8478-2229-X*, Pub. by Rizzoli Intl) St Martin.

***Cowles, Frederick.** The Night Wind Howls: The Complete Supernatural Stories. Lamb, Hugh, ed. xx, 400p. 1999. 50.00 (*1-899562-66-4*) Ash-Tree.

Cowles, George W., et al, eds. Landmarks of Wayne County: With Biographical & Family Sketches. (Illus.). 821p. 1997. reprint ed. lib. bdg. 92.00 (*0-8328-6273-8*) Higginson Bk Co.

Cowles, H. Robert. Holiness Voices. 1995. mass mkt. 5.99 (*0-87509-576-3*) Chr Pubns.

— Prime Time: Three Hundred Sixty-Five Devotions for Seniors. LC 91-73585. 366p. 1991. kivar 10.99 (*0-87509-468-6*) Chr Pubns.

Cowles, H. Robert, ed. Questions & Answers for Young Disciples: Truth for Children Straight from Scripture. 46p. 1993. pap. 1.49 (*0-87509-466-X*) Chr Pubns.

Cowles, H. Robert & Foster, K. Neill. Missionary Voices. 272p. 1996. mass mkt. 5.99 (*0-87509-682-4*) Chr Pubns.

— Prayer Voices. 308p. 1996. mass mkt. 5.99 (*0-87509-677-8*) Chr Pubns.

Cowles, Harry. Art of Squash Racquets: Playing Squash. (Illus.). 88p. 1998. reprint ed. pap. text 25.00 (*0-87556-854-8*) Saifer.

Cowles History Group, Inc. Staff. American History Illustrated: Twenty-Seven Year Cumulative Index, Volume 1, no. 1 (April 1966) through volume 27, no. 6 (January/February 1993). LC 98-176837. 183 p. 1993. write for info. (*0-9639479-1-5*) Cowles Mag.

— Best of the Wild West. LC 96-36889. 300p. 1996. write for info. (*0-86573-859-9*) Creat Pub Intl.

— Great Commanders in Action. LC 96-36890. 300p. 1996. write for info. (*0-86573-860-2*) Creat Pub Intl.

Cowles, Jane. Pain Relief: How to Say No to Acute, Chronic & Cancer Pain. 416p. 1994. 22.95 (*0-942361-77-6*) MasterMedia Pub.

Cowles, Julia. The Robinson Crusoe Reader. (Illus.). 106p. (J). (gr. 2). 1992. pap. text 4.00 (*1-930092-32-6*, CLP29525) Christian Liberty.

Cowles, Luther E. Civil War Infantry, History of the Fifth Massachusetts Battery, Organized Oct. 3, 1861, Mustered Out June 12, 1865. (Illus.). 991p. 1995. reprint ed. lib. bdg. 99.00 (*0-8328-4635-X*) Higginson Bk Co.

***Cowles, Maria Green & Smith, Michael, eds.** The State of the European Union: Risks, Reforms, Renewals, & Revival. 400p. 2000. pap. 29.95 (*0-19-829757-2*); text 85.00 (*0-19-829752-1*) OUP.

Cowles, Michael. Statistics in Psychology: An Historical Perspective. 224p. (C). 1989. text 49.95 (*0-8058-0031-X*) L Erlbaum Assocs.

***Cowles, Michael.** Statistics in Psychology: An Historical Perspective. 2nd ed. 336p. 2000. write for info. (*0-8058-3509-1*); pap. 24.95 (*0-8058-3510-5*) L Erlbaum Assocs.

Cowles, Milly & Aldridge, Jerry. Activity-Oriented Classrooms, K-3. 80p. 1992. pap. 8.95 (*0-8106-0352-7*) NEA.

Cowles, Milly, jt. auth. see Walsh, Kevin.

Cowles, Raymond B., et al. Desert Journal: A Naturalist Reflects on Arid California. LC 74-22959. (Illus.). 279p. reprint ed. pap. 86.50 (*0-7837-4809-4*, 204445600003) Bks Demand.

Cowles, Rose, jt. auth. see Swanson, Diane.

Cowles, Roy T. The Cantonese Speaker's Dictionary. LC 66-808. 1574p. reprint ed. pap. 200.00 (*0-608-01386-2*, 206214700002) Bks Demand.

Cowles, Russell. Russell Cowles: American Autobiography. 53p. 1995. lib. bdg. 69.00 (*0-7812-8490-2*) Rprt Serv.

Cowles, Toy T. Pocket Dictionary of Cantonese. 3rd ed. 448p. 1986. pap. 29.50 (*962-209-122-9*, Pub. by HK Univ Pr) Coronet Bks.

Cowles, Virginia, jt. auth. see Gellhorn, Martha E.

Cowley. Balancing Act. 1998. 55.00 (*0-7616-6400-9*) Acad Pr.

Cowley. Science of Powder Coatings. text 125.00 (*0-471-97899-X*) Wiley.

Cowley, A. E. The Hittites. (British Academy, London; Schweich Lectures on Biblical Archaeology Series, 1918). 1969. reprint ed. pap. 25.00 (*0-8115-1260-6*) Periodicals Srv.

Cowley, Abraham. Essays, Plays & Sundry Verses. reprint ed. lib. bdg. 79.00 (*0-7812-0102-0*) Rprt Serv.

— Essays, Plays & Sundry Verses. 499p. reprint ed. 69.00 (*0-403-04057-4*) Somerset Pub.

— Poetry & Prose, with Thomas Sprat's Life, & Observations by Dryden, Addison, Johnson & Others. 1988. reprint ed. lib. bdg. 49.00 (*0-7812-0276-0*) Rprt Serv.

Cowley, Alan H., ed. Inorganic Syntheses, Vol. 31. LC 39-23015. 347p. 1996. 84.95 (*0-471-15288-9*) Wiley.

— Rings, Clusters, & Polymers of the Main Group Elements. LC 83-15462. (ACS Symposium Ser.: No. 232). 192p. 1983. lib. bdg. 36.95 (*0-8412-0801-8*) Am Chemical.

— Rings, Clusters, & Polymers of the Main Group Elements. LC 83-15462. (ACS Symposium Ser.: Vol. 232). 192p. 1983. reprint ed. pap. 59.60 (*0-608-03081-3*, 206353400007) Bks Demand.

Cowley, Alan H., jt. ed. see Sykes, Geoff.

Cowley, Allen W., Jr., et al, eds. Vasopressin: Cellular & Integrative Functions. LC 87-43176. 542p. 1988. reprint ed. pap. 168.10 (*0-608-04722-8*, 206544300004) Bks Demand.

Cowley, Arthur E., ed. The Samaritan Liturgy, 2 vols., Set. LC 77-87608. reprint ed. 87.50 (*0-404-16430-7*) AMS Pr.

Cowley, C. R., et al, eds. Upper Main Sequence Stars with Anomalous Abundances. 1986. text 221.50 (*90-277-2296-X*) Kluwer Academic.

Cowley, Charles. Famous Divorces of All Ages. LC 91-73011. xl, 292p. 1991. reprint ed. 42.00 (*0-89941-771-X*, 305990) W S Hein.

— Illustrated History of Lowell, Massachusetts. (Illus.). 235p. 1993. reprint ed. lib. bdg. 29.50 (*0-8328-3136-0*) Higginson Bk Co.

Cowley, Charles R. An Introduction to Cosmochemistry. (Illus.). 502p. (C). 1995. pap. text 36.95 (*0-521-45920-6*) Cambridge U Pr.

— An Introduction to Cosmochemistry. (Illus.). 502p. (C). 1995. text 85.00 (*0-521-41538-1*) Cambridge U Pr.

— Theory of Stellar Spectra. (Topics in Astrophysics & Space Physics Ser.). xii, 260p. 1970. text 306.00 (*0-677-02400-2*) Gordon & Breach.

Cowley, Clifford, intro. West Wind Review: Reality. 192p. (C). 1992. write for info. (*0-9630694-1-1*) So Oregon.

Cowley, Con, ed. Understanding Brands: Ten Experts Who Do. (Marketing & Sales Ser.). 224p. 1996. pap. 25.00 (*0-7494-2110-X*) Kogan Page Ltd.

Cowley, Deborah & Serour, Aleya. Cairo 1997: The Practical Guide. 7th ed. Francy, Claire E. et al, eds. (Illus.). 452p. 1996. pap. 18.95 (*977-424-394-3*, Pub. by Am Univ Cairo Pr) Col U Pr.

Cowley, Deborah & Serour, Aleya, eds. Cairo: A Practical Guide with Directory & Maps. 5th ed. 1987. pap. 15.00 (*977-424-136-3*, Pub. by Am Univ Cairo Pr) Col U Pr.

Cowley, Elizabeth. A Tender Contempt: A Career in British Television. (Illus.). 126p. 1998. 42.50 (*1-85776-291-6*, Pub. by Book Guild Ltd) Trans-Atl Phila.

Cowley, Fraser. Metaphysical Delusion. LC 91-16767. 200p. (C). 1991. 33.95 (*0-87975-669-1*) Prometheus Bks.

Cowley, J. M., et al, eds. Modulated Structures - 1979. LC 79-53846. (AIP Conference Proceedings Ser.: No. 53). (Illus.). 1979. lib. bdg. 22.00 (*0-88318-152-5*) Am Inst Physics.

Cowley, Jean, jt. auth. see University of the Witwatersrand.

Cowley, Jill. Beds & Borders. (Illus.). 128p. 1997. pap. 16.95 (*0-7063-7576-9*, Pub. by WrLock) Sterling.

Cowley, John. Carnival, Canboulay & Calypso: Caribbean Traditions in the Making. (Illus.). 309p. (C). 1996. text 59.95 (*0-521-48138-4*) Cambridge U Pr.

***Cowley, John.** Carnival, Canboulay & Calypso: Traditions in the Making. (Cambridge Companions to Music Ser.). (Illus.). 293p. (C). 1999. pap. text 19.95 (*0-521-65389-4*) Cambridge U Pr.

Cowley, John. The Victorian Encounter with Marx: A Study of Ernest Belfort Bax. 224p. (C). 1993. text 59.50 (*1-85043-601-0*, Pub. by I B T) St Martin.

Cowley, John & Oliver, Paul. The New Blackwell Guide to Recorded Blues. (Illus.). 448p. 1996. 55.95 (*0-631-20163-7*); pap. 22.95 (*0-631-19639-0*) Blackwell Pubs.

Cowley, John D. Bibliography of Abridgments, Digests, Dictionaries & Indexes of English Law to the Year Eighteen Hundred. LC 79-54119. (Illus.). 196p. 1979. reprint ed. lib. bdg. 125.00 (*0-912004-15-0*) Gaunt.

Cowley, John M. Diffraction Physics. 2nd rev. ed. (North-Holland Personal Library: Vol. 1). 430p. 1985. reprint ed. pap. 72.50 (*0-444-86925-5*, North Holland) Elsevier.

— Diffraction Physics. 3rd rev. ed. LC 95-38709. (Illus.). 496p. 1995. pap. 89.00 (*0-444-82218-6*, North Holland) Elsevier.

Cowley, John M., ed. Electron Diffraction Techniques. (International Union of Crystallography Monographs on Crystallography: No. 4, Vol. 2). (Illus.). 432p. 1993. text 90.00 (*0-19-855733-7*) OUP.

— Electron Diffraction Techniques, Vol. 1. (International Union of Crystallography Monographs on Crystallography: No. 3, Vol. 1). (Illus.). 596p. 1992. text 110.00 (*0-19-855558-X*) OUP.

Cowley, Joseph G. The Stargazers: An Historical Drama in Two Acts. 100p. (Orig.). 1996. pap. 11.95 (*1-57502-259-1*, P0941) Morris Pubng.

Cowley, Joy. Agapanthus Hum & the Eyeglasses. LC 97-38404. (Illus.). 48p. (J). (gr. k-3). 1999. 13.99 (*0-399-23211-7*) Putnam Pub Group.

— Big Moon Tortilla. LC 97-77902. (Illus.). 32p. (J). (gr. 1-4). 1998. 14.95 (*1-56397-601-3*) Boyds Mills Pr.

— Garcias, The Thanksgiving Turkey. 1998. pap. 5.99 (*0-590-46977-0*) Scholastic Inc.

— Gracias, the Thanksgiving Turkey. LC 95-25063. (Illus.). 32p. (J). (ps-3). 1996. 15.95 (*0-590-46976-2*, Scholastic Hardcover) Scholastic Inc.

— Hitchhikers: Stories from Joy Cowley. (J). 1997. mass mkt. 3.99 (*0-590-73904-2*, Apple Paperbacks) Scholastic Inc.

— Hitchhikers, Stories from Joy Cowley. 1997. 9.60 (*0-606-11463-7*, Pub. by Turtleback) Demco.

— Mrs. Wishy-Washy. LC 98-67176. (Illus.). 16p. (ps-k). 1999. 5.99 (*0-399-23391-1*) Putnam Pub Group.

***Cowley, Joy.** Mrs. Wishy-Washy. 1998. write for info. (*0-7802-7466-0*) Wright Group.

Cowley, Joy. Nicketty-Nacketty, Noo-Noo-Noo. LC 98-17759. (J). (ps-2). 1999. pap. 4.95 (*1-57255-558-0*) Mondo Pubng.

— The Red-Eyed Tree Frog. LC 98-15674. (J). 1999. pap. write for info. (*0-590-87176-5*) Scholastic Inc.

***Cowley, Joy.** The Red-Eyed Tree Frog. LC 98-15674. (Illus.). 32p. (J). (ps-2). 1999. 16.95 (*0-590-87175-7*) Scholastic Inc.

Cowley, Joy. The Rusty, Trusty Tractor. LC 97-77970. (Illus.). 32p. (J). (ps-3). 1999. 14.95 (*1-56397-565-3*) Boyds Mills Pr.

***Cowley, Joy.** The Rusty, Trusty Tractor. LC 97-77970. (Illus.). 32p. (J). (ps-3). 2000. pap. 7.95 (*1-56397-873-3*) Boyds Mills Pr.

Cowley, Joy. Screaming Mean Machine. (J). (gr. 4-7). 1994. pap. 4.95 (*0-590-48013-8*) Scholastic Inc.

— Singing down the Rain. LC 96-43055. (Illus.). 32p. (J). (gr. 1-4). 1997. lib. bdg. 14.89 (*0-06-027603-7*) HarpC Child Bks.

— Singing down the Rain. LC 96-10179. (Illus.). (J). 1997. write for info. (*0-590-52701-0*) Scholastic Inc.

— Singing Down the Rain. LC 96-43055. (Illus.). 32p. (J). (gr. k-4). 1997. 14.95 (*0-06-027602-9*) HarpC Child Bks.

— Starbright & the Dream Eater. LC 99-48094. 208p. (J). (gr. 4 up). Date not set. pap. 4.95 (*0-06-440791-8*) HarpC Child Bks.

— Starbright & the Dream Eater. LC 99-48094. (Illus.). 208p. (YA). (gr. 4-7). 2000. 14.95 (*0-06-028419-6*); lib. bdg. 14.89 (*0-06-028420-X*) HarpC Child Bks.

***Cowley, Joy.** The Video Shop Sparrow. (Illus.). 32p. (YA). (gr. 1-4). 1999. 15.95 (*1-56397-826-1*) Boyds Mills Pr.

Cowley, Joy. Whole Learning - Whole Child. 58p. (Orig.). 1994. pap. 4.95 (*0-7802-1484-6*) Wright Group.

— Wild West Gang. 1999. pap. text 5.95 (*1-86950-285-X*, Pub. by HarpC) Consort Bk Sales.

Cowley, Joy, et al. Gracias, El Pavo de Thanksgiving, 1. (J). (ps-3). 1998. pap. 5.99 (*0-590-39964-0*) Scholastic Inc.

***Cowley, Ken.** Miscellany Macabre: Tales of the Unknown. (Illus.). 75p. 1999. pap. 14.95 (*0-9524153-6-4*, Pub. by BFS) Firebird Dist.

Cowley, Malcolm. After the Genteel Tradition: American Writers since 1910. (BCL1-PS American Literature Ser.). 270p. 1993. reprint ed. lib. bdg. 79.00 (*0-7812-6579-7*) Rprt Serv.

— Exile's Return: A Literary Odyssey of the 1920s. 1983. 23.75 (*0-8446-6053-1*) Peter Smith.

— Exile's Return: A Literary Odyssey of the 1920s. LC 94-12846. 352p. 1994. pap. 14.95 (*0-14-018776-6*, Penguin Classics) Viking Penguin.

— Unshaken Friend: A Profile of Maxwell Perkins. (Illus.). 48p. 1985. 14.50 (*0-911797-15-7*) Roberts Rinehart.

Cowley, Malcolm & Smith, Bernard, eds. Books That Changed Our Minds. LC 72-128230. (Essay Index Reprint Ser.). 1977. 23.95 (*0-8369-1912-2*) Ayer.

Cowley, Malcolm, ed. see Emerson, Ralph Waldo.

Cowley, Malcolm, ed. see Faulkner, William.

Cowley, Malcolm, ed. see Hawthorne, Nathaniel.

Cowley, Malcolm, ed. & intro. see Whitman, Walt.

Cowley, Malcolm, tr. see Bibesco, Marthe.

Cowley, Marjorie. Anooka's Answer. LC 98-4800. (Illus.). (J). (gr. 4-9). 1999. 16.00 (*0-395-88530-2*, Clarion Bks) HM.

— Dar & the Spear Thrower. 128p. (J). (gr. 4-7). 1994. 14.00 (*0-395-68132-4*, Clarion Bks) HM.

— Dar & the Spear Thrower. LC 93-17200. 160p. (gr. 4-7). 1996. pap. 5.95 (*0-395-79725-X*) HM.

Cowley, Marjorie. Dar & the Spear-Thrower. 1994. 11.05 (*0-606-10778-9*, Pub. by Turtleback) Demco.

Cowley, Mert. Growing up with Joey: A Fishing Trip for Joey - Joey & the Cabin in the Woods. LC 91-70217. (Illus.). 40p. (Orig.). (J). (ps-2). pap. 3.29 (*0-9627867-2-1*) Banksiana.

— A Hundred Hunts Ago: Seasons of the Past. LC 94-74347. (Illus.). 518p. (Orig.). 1996. pap. 17.95 (*0-9627867-4-8*) Banksiana.

— In Camps of Orange: Poetic Tales of Deer Hunting from the Pearly Swamp Camp, II. LC 93-90585. (Illus.). 265p. (Orig.). 1993. pap. 13.95 (*0-9627867-3-X*) Banksiana.

— The Ultimate Stand Vol. I: Poetic Tales of Deer Hunting from the Pearly Swamp Camp. LC 90-84001. (Illus.). 157p. (Orig.). 1990. pap. text 11.95 (*0-9627867-0-5*) Banksiana.

Cowley, Michael & Domb, Ellen. Beyond Strategic Vision: Effective Corporate Action with Hoshin Planning. LC 96-46662. 240p. 1997. pap. text 17.95 (*0-7506-9843-8*) Buttrwrth-Heinemann.

Cowley, Philip, ed. Conscience & Parliament. LC 97-49298. (Library of Legislative Studies). 224p. 1998. 52.50 (*0-7146-4836-1*, Pub. by F Cass Pubs); pap. 22.50 (*0-7146-4388-2*) F Cass Pubs.

Cowley, R. Adams, jt. ed. see Dunham, C. Michael.

Cowley, Rich. Bang! Bang! Toot Toot. (Snappy Sounds Ser.: No. 3). (Illus.). 24p. (YA). (ps up). 1996. bds. 3.95 (*1-55209-034-5*, Pub. by Annick) Firefly Bks Ltd.

— BRRRM! Woosh. (Snappy Sounds Ser.: No. 4). (Illus.). 24p. (YA). (ps up). 1996. 3.95 (*1-55209-038-8*, Pub. by Annick) Firefly Bks Ltd.

— Ring! Tick Tock. (Snappy Sounds Ser.). (Illus.). 24p. (YA). (ps up). 1996. 3.95 (*1-55209-036-1*) Firefly Bks Ltd.

— Snap! Snap! Buzz Buzz. (Snappy Sounds Ser.). (Illus.). 24p. (YA). (ps up). 1996. 3.95 (*1-55209-032-9*, Pub. by Annick) Firefly Bks Ltd.

Cowley, Richard J., Jr. Eshopper: A Consumer's Guide to Shopping the Internet. xvi, 399p. 1999. pap. 11.95 (*0-9663243-1-5*) James Publ.

Cowley, Robert. Journey on the Western Front. Date not set. write for info. (*0-465-03694-5*) Basic.

— On the Western Front. 1999. write for info. (*0-201-62639-X*) Addison-Wesley.

***Cowley, Robert.** What If? The World's Foremost Military Historians Imagine What Might Have Been. (Illus.). 2000. pap. 13.95 (*0-425-17642-8*) Berkley Pub.

***Cowley, Robert, ed.** What If? The World's Foremost Military Historians Imagine What Might Have Been. LC 99-32215. 336p. 1999. 27.95 (*0-399-14576-1*, G P Putnam) Peng Put Young Read.

Cowley, Robert, et al. The Reader's Companion to Military History. LC 96-8577. (Illus.). 608p. 1996. 45.00 (*0-395-66969-3*) HM.

Cowley, Robert L. Hogarth's "Marriage A-la-mode" LC 82-70749. (Illus.). 192p. 1983. text 62.50 (*0-8014-1525-X*) Cornell U Pr.

Cowley, Sarah. The Changing Nature of Nursing in a Managerial Age. LC 99-17633. 1999. pap. text 29.95 (*0-632-04252-4*) Blackwell Sci.

Cowley, Stewart. Dalmatian Dot. (Waggy Tales Ser.: No. 2). (Illus.). 10p. (J). (gr. k-3). 1998. bds. 4.99 (*1-57584-217-3*, Pub. by Rdrs Digest) Random.

— From My Window. (Tiny Magic Window Bks.). (Illus.). 14p. (J). (ps). 1994. 2.99 (*0-89577-595-6*) RD Assn.

***Cowley, Stewart.** Ginger Kitten. (Waggy Tales x 2 Ser.). (Illus.). 10p. (gr. k-3). 2000. bds. 4.99 (*1-57584-349-8*) Rdrs Digest.

Cowley, Stewart. Little Chick. LC 95-80204. (Fluffy Tales Ser.). (Illus.). 10p. (J). (gr. k-3). 1996. bds. 4.99 (*1-57584-007-3*, Pub. by Rdrs Digest) Random.

C

An Asterisk (*) at the beginning of an entry indicates that the title is appearing for the first time.

— Molly Collie. (Waggy Tales Ser.: Vol. 4). (Illus.). 10p. (J). (gr. k-3). 1998. bds. 4.99 (*1-57584-246-7*, Pub. by Rdrs Digest) Random.

*__Cowley, Stewart.__ Pepper. (Illus.). 10p. (gr. k-3). 2000. bds. 4.99 (*1-57584-350-1*) Rdrs Digest.

Cowley, Stewart. Santa's Littlest Helper (Mouse) (Fluffy Tales Christmas Ser.). (Illus.). 10p. (J). (gr. k-3). 1996. bds. 4.99 (*0-88705-964-3*) Rdrs Digest.

— Speedie Scottie. (Waggy Tales Ser.: Vol. 3). (Illus.). 10p. (J). (gr. k-3). 1998. bds. 4.99 (*1-57584-245-9*, Pub. by Rdrs Digest) Random.

*__Cowley-Taylor, Elizabeth.__ Murder at Les Halles. 157p. 2000. 21.95 (*0-7541-0980-1*, Pub. by Minerva Pr) Unity Dist.

Cowley, William H. Presidents, Professors & Trustees: The Evolution of American Academic Government. Williams, Donald T., Jr., ed. LC 79-92461. (Jossey-Bass Series in Higher Education). 280p. reprint ed. pap. 86.80 (*0-8357-4937-1*, 203786700009) Bks Demand.

Cowlin, Matthew. Poems of a Civil War Veteran. LC 91-73855. (Illus.). 35p. (Orig.). 1991. pap. 5.00 (*0-9633524-2-3*) JB Press.

Cowling. Delmar Radiographic Positioning & Procedures Vol. II: Slides. 32p. 1998. 575.00 (*0-8273-6995-6*) Delmar.

— The Editorial Eye. 2nd ed. 2000. pap., wbk. ed. write for info. (*0-312-15756-8*) St Martin.

— Radiographic Positioning, Vol. II. LC 97-43449. (Radiographic Technology Ser.). 1998. mass mkt. 69.95 (*0-8273-6317-6*) Delmar.

— Radiographic Positioning, Vol. II. (Radiographic Technology Ser.). 1998. teacher ed. 14.00 (*0-8273-6994-8*) Delmar.

— Radiographic Positioning CTB, Vol. II. (Radiographic Technology Ser.). 1998. 49.95 (*0-8273-6996-4*) Delmar.

Cowling & Wilde. Approaches to Marx. 1989. 110.00 (*0-335-15622-3*); pap. 35.95 (*0-335-15621-5*) OpUniv Pr.

Cowling, Adams. Delmar Radiographic Positioning & Procedures Vol. II: Workbook, Vol. 1. (Radiographic Technology Ser.). 275p. 1998. wbk. ed. 29.95 (*0-8273-6993-X*) Delmar.

Cowling, Alan. The Essence of Industrial Relations & Personnel Management. 192p. (C). 1994. pap. text 19.95 (*0-13-131848-9*) P-H.

Cowling, Alan & Lundy, Olive. Strategic Human Resource Management. LC 95-19819. 224p. (C). 1995. pap. 17.99 (*0-415-09989-7*) Thomson Learn.

Cowling, Alan, jt. auth. see Lundy, Olive.

Cowling, Anthony J. An Introduction to Software Engineering & Systems Analysis. 192p. 1996. pap. 39.95 (*1-85554-764-3*) Blackwell Pubs.

Cowling, David. Building the Text: Architecture As Metaphor in Late Medieval & Early Modern France. LC 97-44261. (Oxford Modern Languages & Literature Monographs). (Illus.). 254p. 1998. text 75.00 (*0-19-815959-5*) OUP.

Cowling, Dorothy N., jt. auth. see Binford, Virgie M.

Cowling, Elizabeth. Dada & Surrealist Art & Their Inheritors: The Gabrielle Keiller Bequest. (Illus.). 160p. 1997. pap. 39.95 (*0-903598-68-X*, Pub. by Natl Galleries) Antique Collect.

— On Classic Ground: Picasso, Leger, De Chirico & the New Classicism, 1910-1930. 1991. pap. text 39.95 (*1-85437-043-X*) Tate Gallery.

Cowling, George H. Chaucer. LC 74-150179. (Select Bibliographies Reprint Ser.). 1977. reprint ed. 18.95 (*0-8369-5692-3*) Ayer.

— Music on the Shakespearian Stage. LC 74-24063. reprint ed. 27.50 (*0-404-12889-0*) AMS Pr.

— Shelley, & Other Essays. LC 67-23198. (Essay Index Reprint Ser.). 1977. 19.95 (*0-8369-0344-7*) Ayer.

Cowling, Graham J., ed. Apoptosis & Programmed Cell Death (PCD) Protocols. (Methods in Molecular Medicine Ser.: No. 22). 1999. 79.50 (*0-89603-557-3*) Humana.

Cowling, Keith & Sugden, Roger. A New Economic Policy for Britain: Essays on the Development of Industry LC 90-5573. 217 p. 1990. write for info. (*0-7190-3271-7*) Manchester Univ Pr.

Cowling, Keith & Sugden, Roger, eds. Current Issues in Industrial Economic Strategy. 288p. 1992. text 79.95 (*0-7190-3811-1*, Pub. by Manchester Univ Pr) St Martin.

*__Cowling, Keith, et al.__ Industrial Policy in Europe: Theoretical Perspectives & Practical Proposals. LC 98-37406. 1999. write for info. (*0-415-20493-3*); pap. write for info. (*0-415-20494-1*) Routledge.

Cowling, M., jt. auth. see Milton, J. R.

Cowling, Mark. Date Rape & Consent. LC 98-72629. 176p. 1998. 55.95 (*1-85972-509-0*) Ashgate Pub Co.

*__Cowling, Mark & Reynolds, Paul.__ Marxism, the Millenium & Beyond. LC 00-42062. .p. 2000. write for info. (*0-312-23597-6*) St Martin.

Cowling, Mark, ed. see Marx, Karl & Engels, Friedrich.

Cowling, Maurice. The Impact of Hitler: British Politics & British Policy, 1933-1940. 1995. reprint ed. pap. text 10.00 (*0-226-11660-3*, P747) U Ch Pr.

— The Nature & Limits of Political Science. LC 85-12591. 214p. 1985. reprint ed. lib. bdg. 65.00 (*0-313-24949-0*, CNLI, Greenwood Pr) Greenwood.

— Religion & Public Doctrine in Modern England, Vol. 2. (Cambridge Studies in the History & Theory of Politics). 403p. 1985. text 69.95 (*0-521-25959-2*) Cambridge U Pr.

Cowling, R. M., et al, eds. Vegetation of Southern Africa. LC 96-13572. (Illus.). 680p. (C). 1997. text 225.00 (*0-521-57142-1*) Cambridge U Pr.

Cowling, Tania K. Shake, Tap, & Play a Merry Tune. 1992. pap. 9.99 (*0-86653-949-2*) Fearon Teacher Aids.

*__Cowling, Vicki.__ Children of Parents with Mental Illness. 200p. 1999. pap. 15.95 (*0-86431-282-2*, Pub. by Aust Council Educ Res) Stylus Pub VA.

*__Cowlishaw, Gillian K.__ Rednecks, Eggheads & Blackfellas: A Study of Racial Power & Intimacy in Australia. LC 99-36477. 388p. (C). 1999. pap. text 26.95 (*0-472-08648-0*, 08648) U of Mich Pr.

*__Cowlishaw, Guy.__ Primate Conservation Biology. 1999. pap. text 27.00 (*0-226-11637-9*); lib. bdg. 70.00 (*0-226-11636-0*) U Ch Pr.

Cowlishaw, Michael F. The Net REXX Language. LC 96-45703. 208p. (C). 1996. pap. 50.00 (*0-13-806332-X*) P-H.

Cowlishaw, Mike. REXX Language: A Practical Approach to Programming. 2nd ed. 203p. 1990. pap. 68.00 (*0-13-780651-5*) P-H.

Cowman. Manantiales en el Desierto (Streams in the Desert) (SPA.). 1998. 10.99 (*0-88113-022-2*, B000-0222) Caribe Betania.

Cowman, Charles E. Devotions for Morning & Evening. 768p. 1999. 14.99 (*0-88486-249-6*) Galahad Bks.

— Manantiales en el Desierto, No. 2. Vol. 2.Tr. of Streams in the Dessert. (SPA.). 304p. 1989. pap. 6.99 (*0-945792-51-4*, 498521) Editorial Unilit.

— Manantiales en el Desierto: Streams in the Desert. rev. ed. Luis, Jose & Martinez, Violeta, eds. Serrano, Antonio, tr. from ENG. (SPA.). 368p. 1992. pap. 12.50 (*0-311-40055-8*) Casa Bautista.

*__Cowman, Charles E.__ Stream in the Desert. (Devotion Ser.). 370p. 1999. 10.00 (*1-885216-26-2*) Evan Formosan.

Cowman, Charles E. Traveling Toward Sunrise. 1988. 10.95 (*0-310-35390-4*, 6812) Zondervan.

— Words of Comfort & Cheer. 1988. 10.99 (*0-310-35400-5*, 6815) Zondervan.

Cowman, Charles E. & Serrano, Antonio. Manantiales en el Desierto: Streams in the Desert. 1973. reprint ed. pap. 10.50 (*0-311-40028-0*, Edit Mundo) Casa Bautista.

Cowman, Greg. Secrets of a New Orleans Chef: Recipes from Tom Cowman's Cookbook. LC 99-31340. (Illus.). 250p. 1999. 25.00 (*1-57806-179-2*) U Pr of Miss.

Cowman, Ian. Dominion or Decline: Anglo-American Naval Relations in the Pacific, 1937-1941. 300p. 1997. 65.00 (*1-85973-111-2*, Pub. by Berg Pubs); pap. 19.50 (*1-85973-116-3*, Pub. by Berg Pubs) NYU Pr.

Cowman, L. B. Manantiales en el Desierto. rev. ed. (SPA.). 480p. 1998. pap. 12.50 (*0-311-40056-6*) Baptist Spanish.

Cowman, Lettie B. Cumbres de Inspiracion: Mountain Trailways for Youth. Robleto, Adolfo, tr. 1974. reprint ed. pap. 12.99 (*0-311-40026-4*) Casa Bautista.

— Streams in the Desert, 5 vols. 1984. 47.25 (*0-310-37668-8*, 6882) Zondervan.

— Streams in the Desert. anniversary ed. (Zondervan Classics Ser.). 384p. 1996. 15.99 (*0-310-48400-6*) Zondervan.

— Streams in the Desert. large type ed. 128p. 1983. pap. 5.99 (*0-310-37651-3*, 6881P) Zondervan.

— Streams in the Desert, Vol. 1. 384p. 1984. 14.99 (*0-310-22420-9*, 6901) Zondervan.

— Streams in the Desert, Vol. 3. 1984. 10.45 (*0-310-22440-3*, 6903) Zondervan.

— Streams in the Desert, Vol. 4. 1984. 10.45 (*0-310-22470-5*, 6904) Zondervan.

— Streams in the Desert, 5 vols., Vol. 5. 1984. 10.45 (*0-310-22480-2*, 6905) Zondervan.

— Streams in the Desert: 366 Daily Devotional Readings. large type ed. Reimann, James, ed. 512p. 1997. reprint ed. pap. 22.99 (*0-310-22129-3*) Zondervan.

— Streams in the Desert: 366 Daily Devotional Readings. rev. ed. Reimann, James, ed. LC 96-48454. 464p. 1997. 14.99 (*0-310-21006-2*) Zondervan.

— Streams in the Desert Daybreak. (Daybreaks Ser.). 1996. 9.99 (*0-310-96769-4*) Zondervan.

Cowman, Lettie B., ed. Springs in the Valley. 2nd ed. 384p. 1980. pap. 7.95 (*0-310-22511-6*, 6806P) Zondervan.

Cowman, Mrs. Charles. Streams in the Desert: A Daily Devotional Journal. unabridged ed. 384p. 1998. reprint ed. lthr. 19.97 (*1-57748-340-5*) Barbour Pub.

Cowmeadow, Oliver. A Practical Introduction: Shiatsu. LC 98-4676. 1998. pap. 14.95 (*1-86204-162-8*, Pub. by Element MA) Penguin Putnam.

Cowne, Elizabeth. The SENCO Handbook: Working Within a Whole-School Approach. 160p. 1996. pap. 24.95 (*1-85346-413-9*) Taylor & Francis.

Cownie, Emma. Religious Patronage in Anglo-Norman England, 1066-1135. LC 98-9940. (Studies in History, New Ser.: Vol. 7). 272p. 1998. 60.00 (*0-86193-232-3*, Royal Historical Soc) Boydell & Brewer.

Cownie, Emma, ed. see Lewis, C. P.

Cownie, Emma, jt. ed. see Lewis, C. P.

Cownie, Fiona. The English Legal System in Context. 1995. pap. text 26.00 (*0-406-51181-0*, UK, MICHIE) LEXIS Pub.

Cownie, Fiona, ed. The Law School: Global Issues, Local Questions. LC 98-47262. 280p. (C). 1999. text 78.95 (*1-85521-856-9*, K100.L39, Pub. by Ashgate Pub) Ashgate Pub Co.

Cownie, Fiona, jt. auth. see Bradney, Anthony.

Cowper, et al. World War I & Its Consequences. 1990. pap. 34.95 (*0-335-09306-X*) OpUniv Pr.

Cowper, A. D., tr. see Einstein, Albert.

Cowper, C. J. & Derose, A. J. The Analysis of Gases by Chromatography. LC 83-6207. (Pergamon Series on Analytical Chemistry: Vol. 7). (Illus.). 159p. 1983. text 77.00 (*0-08-024027-5*, Pub. by Pergamon Repr) Franklin.

*__Cowper, D.__ Breakthrough: Take Your Business & Sales to the Top. 1998. pap. write for info. (*0-9682030-0-0*) DNA Creative.

Cowper, David S. Northwest Passage Solo. LC 93-34441. (Illus.). 244p. 1994. 23.95 (*0-924486-65-1*) Sheridan.

*__Cowper, David S. & Haynes, Andrew.__ Mega-Selling: Secrets of a Master Salesman. 256p. 2000. pap. 24.95 (*0-471-64529-X*) Wiley.

Cowper, Elizabeth A. A Concise Introduction to Syntactic Theory: The Government-Binding Approach. 218p. 1992. pap. text 18.50 (*0-226-11646-8*) U Ch Pr.

— A Concise Introduction to Syntactic Theory: The Government-Binding Approach. 240p. 1995. lib. bdg. 69.00 (*0-226-11644-1*) U Ch Pr.

Cowper, H. Through Turkish Arabia. 512p. 1987. 350.00 (*1-85077-170-7*, Pub. by Darf Pubs Ltd) St Mut.

Cowper, H. W. The Hill of the Graces. 392p. 1990. 140.00 (*1-85077-003-4*, Pub. by Darf Pubs Ltd) St Mut.

Cowper, J. M., ed. Meditacyuns on the Soper of Our Lord. (EETS, OS Ser.: No. 60). 1969. reprint ed. 30.00 (*0-527-00054-X*) Periodicals Srv.

Cowper, J. M., ed. see Crowley, Robert.

Cowper, J. M., ed. see Starkey, Thomas.

Cowper-Thomas, Wendy, jt. auth. see Tomarelli, Patti Rae.

*__Cowper, William.__ The Centenary Letters. Malpas, Simon, ed. 256p. 2000. pap. 24.95 (*1-85754-463-3*, Pub. by Carcanet Pr) Paul & Co Pubs.

Cowper, William. Correspondence of William Cowper, 4 Vols. LC 68-24904. (English Biography Ser.: No. 31). 1969. reprint ed. lib. bdg. 199.00 (*0-8383-0156-8*) M S G Haskell Hse.

— Correspondence of William Cowper, 4 vols., Set. Wright, Thomas, ed. (Illus.). 1970. reprint ed. 49.00 (*0-403-00203-6*) Scholarly.

— The Correspondence of William Cowper, 4 vols., Set. (BCL1-PR English Literature Ser.). 1992. reprint ed. lib. bdg. 300.00 (*0-7812-7337-4*) Rprt Serv.

— The Letters & Prose Writings of William Cowper, 5 vols. King, James & Ryskamp, Charles, eds. (Illus.). 640p. 1979. text 115.00 (*0-19-811863-5*) OUP.

— The Letters & Prose Writings of William Cowper, 5 vols., Vol. II: Letters, 1782-1786. King, James & Ryskamp, Charles, eds. (Illus.). 680p. 1981. text 155.00 (*0-19-812607-7*) OUP.

— The Letters & Prose Writings of William Cowper: Letters, 1792-1799, Vol. 4. Ryskamp, Charles & King, James, eds. (Illus.). 532p. 1984. text 175.00 (*0-19-812681-6*) OUP.

— The Letters & Prose Writings of William Cowper Vol. 3: Letters, 1787-1791. King, James & Ryskamp, Charles, eds. (Illus.). 664p. 1983. text 110.00 (*0-19-812608-5*) OUP.

— The Letters & Prose Writings of William Cowper Vol. 5: Prose, 1756-1798 & Cumulative Index. King, James & Ryskamp, Charles, eds. 272p. (C). 1986. text 72.00 (*0-19-812690-5*) OUP.

— Letters of William Cowper, 2 Vols, Set. Frazer, James George, ed. LC 70-103647. (Select Bibliographies Reprint Ser.). 1977. 60.95 (*0-8369-5147-6*) Ayer.

— The Poems of William Cowper, 1782-1785 Vol. 2, Vol. 2. Baird, John D. & Ryskamp, Charles, eds. (Oxford English Texts Ser.). (Illus.). 484p. (C). 1996. text 120.00 (*0-19-812339-6*) OUP.

— The Poems of William Cowper, 1785-1800 Vol. 3, Vol. 3. Baird, John D. & Ryskamp, Charles, eds. (Oxford English Texts Ser.). (Illus.). 466p. 1996. text 98.00 (*0-19-818296-1*) OUP.

— The Poems of William Cowper, 1748-1782 Vol. I, Vol. 1. Baird, John D. & Ryskamp, Charles, eds. (Oxford English Texts Ser.). (Illus.). 642p. 1980. text 115.00 (*0-19-811875-9*) OUP.

— The Poetical Works of William Cowper. 4th ed. Milford, H. S., ed. LC 75-41066. (BCL Ser. II). reprint ed. 49.50 (*0-404-14525-6*) AMS Pr.

— Unpublished & Uncollected Letters. (BCL1-PR English Literature Ser.). 85p. 1992. reprint ed. lib. bdg. 59.00 (*0-7812-7338-2*) Rprt Serv.

— William Cowper: Selected Letters. King, James & Ryskamp, Charles, eds. (Illus.). 268p. 1989. text 59.00 (*0-19-818596-0*) OUP.

— William Cowper (1731-1800) Selected Poems. Rhodes, Nick, ed. 1984. pap. 7.50 (*0-85635-414-7*) Carcanet Pr.

— Works of William Cowper, 15 vols. Southey, Robert, ed. LC 71-18097. reprint ed. 1140.00 (*0-404-01840-8*) AMS Pr.

Cowper, William, tr. see Homer.

Cowrie, Judy. Children's Stages of Development. (C). 1993. pap. text. write for info. (*0-201-53945-4*) Addison-Wesley.

Cowsik, R. Nonaccelerator Particle Physics: Proceedings of the International Conference. 600p. 1995. text 109.00 (*981-02-1811-7*) World Scientific Pub.

Cowsik, R., ed. see COSPAR, Twenty-Second Plenary Meeting Staff.

Cowsjee, S. & Shahane, V., eds. Modern Indian Fiction. 195p. 1981. 18.50 (*0-7069-1051-6*) Asia Bk Corp.

Cowton, Christopher & Crisp, Roger, eds. Business Ethics: Perspectives on the Practice of Theory. 224p. 1999. text 55.00 (*0-19-829031-4*) OUP.

Cowx, I. Rehabilitation of Freshwater Fisheries. 1994. 95.00 (*0-85238-195-6*) Blackwell Sci.

Cowx, I. G. Stocking & Introduction of Fish. LC 97-12908. 1997. 125.00 (*0-85238-239-1*) Blackwell Sci.

Cowx, Ian G. Catch Effort Sampling Strategies: Their Application in Freshwater Fisheries Management. (Illus.). 432p. 1991. 115.00 (*0-85238-177-8*) Blackwell Sci.

Cowx, Ian G., ed. Stock Assessment in Inland Fisheries. 288p. 1996. 99.95 (*0-85238-224-3*) Blackwell Sci.

Cowx, Ian G., ed. see United Nations Food & Agriculture Organization Staff.

Cowxm, Ian G. & Welcomme, Robin L., eds. Rehabilitation of Rivers for Fish. LC 98-226171. 296p. 1998. pap. 82.00 (*92-5-104018-4*, F40184, Pub. by FAO) Bernan Associates.

Cox. Aging. 9th ed. 1993. 12.74 (*1-56134-254-8*) McGraw.

*__Cox.__ Aryan Mythology, the Mythology of the Aryan Nations. 1999. 88.00 (*81-7020-917-X*, Pub. by Cosmo Pubn) S Asia.

Cox. Coal Industry. LC 95-77027. 1995. 125.00 (*0-316-24650-6*) Little.

— Conservation Biology. 2nd ed. 1996. 13.75 (*0-697-21815-5*, WCB McGr Hill) McGrw-H Hghr Educ.

— Conservation Ecology. 1992. 13.75 (*0-697-16539-6*, WCB McGr Hill) McGrw-H Hghr Educ.

*__Cox.__ Conservative Biology. 3rd ed. 2001. 46.00 (*0-07-012198-2*) McGraw.

Cox. Corporation, 2 vols. 1995. 150.00 (*0-316-65110-9*, Aspen Law & Bus) Aspen Pub.

— Corporation, Vol. 2. 1995. 150.00 (*0-316-65106-0*, Aspen Law & Bus) Aspen Pub.

— Corporation, Vol. 3. 1995. 150.00 (*0-316-65105-2*, Aspen Law & Bus) Aspen Pub.

— Crafting Prose. (C). 1991. pap. text, teacher ed. 3.00 (*0-15-515631-4*) Harcourt Coll Pubs.

— Employment Discrimination, 2 vols., Issue 6. 2nd ed. 501p. 1998. ring bd. write for info. (*0-327-00506-8*, 8039616) LEXIS Pub.

— Family Living. annot. ed. Date not set. text, teacher ed. 50.95 (*0-314-93495-2*) West Pub.

— Human Intimacy. 6th ed. Date not set. pap. text, student ed. 19.00 (*0-314-01890-5*) West Pub.

— Immunology of the Fungal Diseases. 264p. 1989. lib. bdg. 169.00 (*0-8493-6153-2*, QR245) CRC Pr.

— Introduction to the Criminal Justice Network. 4th ed. 2000. 28.50 (*0-07-232148-2*) McGraw.

— Jeannie. 1999. pap. write for info. (*0-312-18730-0*) St Martin.

— Labor Law: Adaptable to Courses Utilizing Materials by Cox. 7th ed. LC 87-114965. (Legalines Ser.). 248p. 11.50 (*0-685-18531-1*) Harcourt.

— Lifepoints. 1996. mass mkt. write for info. (*0-312-95783-1*) St Martin.

— Linear Electronics: Integrated & Discrete. 2nd abr. rev. ed. (Electronics Technology Ser.). 1998. text, teacher ed. 14.00 (*0-8273-6852-6*) Delmar.

— New Realism. LC 96-17550. 304p. 1997. text 55.00 (*0-312-16234-0*) St Martin.

— Nursing Education. (International Journal of Nursing Studies). 1985. pap. 30.00 (*0-08-031849-5*, Pergamon Pr) Elsevier.

— Police: Practices, Perspectives, Problems. LC 95-684. 300p. 1995. 72.00 (*0-205-16198-7*) Allyn.

— Poor Black Welfare. (C). Date not set. write for info. (*0-415-03238-5*) Routledge.

— Sales & Sales Management. 240p. 1998. pap. text 34.95 (*0-7506-2849-9*) Buttrwrth-Heinemann.

*__Cox.__ Secret Ingredients. 2000. pap. 12.95 (*0-553-50554-8*, Pub. by Transworld Publishers Ltd) Trafalgar.

Cox. Sport Psychology. 3rd ed. 1993. teacher ed. 9.68 (*0-697-12622-6*) McGraw.

— Sport Psychology. 5th ed. 2000. 33.50 (*0-07-232914-9*) McGraw.

— Technical Guide to Program Controllers. 3rd ed. (Electrical Trades Ser.). 144p. 1995. mass mkt., lab manual ed. 20.00 (*0-8273-7151-9*) Delmar.

— Theoretical Statistics. 2nd ed. (C). (gr. 13). 1997. text. write for info. (*0-412-42860-1*) Chapman & Hall.

Cox & Fitzgerald. Police in the Community. 3rd ed. 1995. teacher ed. 7.81 (*0-697-27548-5*, WCB McGr Hill) McGrw-H Hghr Educ.

Cox & Haskins. African American Healers. LC 99-29978. (Black Stars Ser.). 164p. (YA). (gr. 6-9). 1999. 22.95 (*0-471-24650-6*) Wiley.

Cox & Hill. Securities Regulation: Cases & Materials. 1991. 57.00 (*0-316-15865-8*, Aspen Law & Bus) Aspen Pub.

Cox & Ridenour. Fundamentals of Nursing Care. 3rd ed. 1997. pap. write for info. (*0-614-26985-7*, Little Brwn Med Div) Lppncott W & W.

Cox & Rosenfeld. State & Local Politics. (Political Science Ser.). 2000. pap. text 37.00 (*0-534-55539-X*) Wadsworth Pub.

Cox & Wilton. Liquid Crystal Polymers. (Rapra Review Reports: Vol. 1). 1992. pap. 115.00 (*0-08-035923-X*, Pergamon Pr) Elsevier.

Cox & Zarrillo. Teaching Reading with Children's Literature. 448p. (C). 1997. pap. text 46.60 (*0-13-640012-4*) P-H.

Cox, et al. Business - auf Deutsch: Kopiervorlagen. (GER.). 40p. (C). 1991. pap. text 19.25 (*3-12-675213-6*, Pub. by Klett Edition) Intl Bk Import.

— Business - auf Deutsch: Lehrbuch. (GER.). 272p. (C). 1990. pap. text 36.00 (*3-12-675210-1*, Pub. by Klett Edition) Intl Bk Import.

— 1993 Statutory Supplement to Labor Law. 1993. pap. text 10.25 (*1-56662-056-2*) Foundation Pr.

Cox, jt. auth. see Conolly.

Cox, jt. auth. see Ramp.

Cox, A., ed. see Dickens, Charles.

Cox, A. B. New Light on the Strength of Gear Teeth. (Technical Papers: Vol. P70A). (Illus.). 36p. 1932. pap. text 30.00 (*1-55589-264-7*) AGMA.

Cox, A. J. The Making of the Book. Koda, Paul S., ed. LC 85-28384. (History of the Book: Vol. 3). 88p. 1986. reprint ed. 25.00 (*0-938768-10-7*) Oak Knoll.

Cox, A. N., et al, eds. Stellar Pulsation. (Lecture Notes in Physics Ser.: Vol. 274). xii, 422p. 1987. 59.95 (*0-387-17668-3*) Spr-Verlag.

Cox, Adele, jt. auth. see Beardsmore, Valerie.

Cox, Adrian. The Universe of Adrian Cox. (Little Book Ser.). 1998. 7.00 (*0-7117-0977-7*, Pub. by JARR UK) Seven Hills Bk.

*__Cox, Aidan.__ European Development Cooperate. 2000. text 65.00 (*0-312-23054-0*) St Martin.

An Asterisk (*) at the beginning of an entry indicates that the title is appearing for the first time.

Cox, Allan & Hart, Brian R. Plate Tectonics: How It Works. LC 86-6138. (Illus.). 400p. 1986. pap. text 52.95 (*0-86542-313-X*) Blackwell Sci.

Cox, Allen D., jt. ed. see Streng, William P.

Cox, Alwyn. The Flying Spy. (American Structural Readers Ser.: Stage 1). (Illus.). 16p. 1989. pap. text 6.31 (*0-582-79882-5*, 75121) Longman.

Cox, Ana M., jt. ed. see Anuff, Joey.

Cox, Andrew & Furlong, Paul. A Modern Companion to the European Community: A Guide to Key Facts, Institutions & Terms. 336p. 1992. text 95.00 (*1-85278-516-0*) E Elgar.

Cox, Andrew, et al. Classification of Hazardous Locations. 201p. 1990. pap. 95.00 (*0-85295-258-9*, 9CH54) Gulf Pub.

— The Political Economy of Modern Britain. LC 96-48952. 288p. 1997. 90.00 (*1-85278-411-3*) E Elgar.

— The Political Economy of Modern Britain. LC 96-48952. 288p. 1998. pap. text 30.00 (*1-85898-616-8*) E Elgar.

Cox, Andrew W., et al. Privatisation & Supply Chain Management: On the Effective Alignment of Purchasing & Supply after Privatisation. LC 98-38317. (Studies in Business Organization & Networks Ser.). 1999. write for info. (*0-415-17300-0*) Routledge.

***Cox, Angela.** And Then My Soul Spoke: A Soulful Poetic Experience. 2000. pap. write for info. (*1-930183-10-0*, POE-0001) Anyanwu.

Cox, Ann. Autumn Dawn: Triumph over Eating Disorders. 194p. 1995. pap. 22.50 (*1-85776-155-3*, Pub. by Book Guild Ltd) Trans-Atl Phila.

— Beginner's Guide to Silk Ribbon Embroidery. (Illus.). 48p. 1998. pap. 14.95 (*0-85532-835-5*, 8355, Pub. by Srch Pr) A Schwartz & Co.

Cox, Annette. Art-as-Politics: The Abstract Expressionist Avant-Garde & Society. Foster, Stephen, ed. LC 82-4760. (Studies in the Fine Arts: The Avant-Garde: No. 26). 216p. reprint ed. pap. 67.00 (*0-8357-1908-1*, 207062100008) Bks Demand.

Cox, Archibald. The Court & the Constitution. (C). 1989. 80.00 (*0-7855-3717-1*) St Mut.

Cox, Archibald, et al. Civil Rights, the Constitution, & the Courts. LC 67-20874. 84p. reprint ed. pap. 30.00 (*0-7837-1686-9*, 205721600024) Bks Demand.

— Labor Law. 12th ed. LC 96-20608. (Paralegal). 1194p. 1996. text 42.00 (*1-56662-347-2*) Foundation Pr.

— Statutory Supplement to Cases & Materials on Labor Law. 12th ed. LC 96-20608. (University Casebook Ser.). 130p. pap. text, suppl. ed. write for info. (*1-56662-437-1*) Foundation Pr.

Cox, Archibald S. Freedom of Expression. LC 81-4374. 96p. 1981. pap. text 7.00 (*0-674-31913-3*) HUP.

— Law & the National Labor Policy. LC 82-20930. 111p. 1983. reprint ed. lib. bdg. 45.00 (*0-313-23794-8*, COLN, Greenwood Pr) Greenwood.

— Warren Court: Constitutional Decision As an Instrument of Reform. LC 68-21971. 144p. 1968. pap. 18.50 (*0-674-94740-1*) HUP.

Cox, Archibald S., et al. Labor Law, Cases & Materials On. 11th ed. (University Casebook Ser.). 1249p. 1990. text 44.95 (*0-88277-829-3*) Foundation Pr.

— Labor Law, 1993, Statutory Supplement to Cases & Material On. 11th ed. 130p. (C). 1992. write for info. (*0-318-70006-9*) Foundation Pr.

Cox, Art, ed. see Antonson, Belinda.

Cox, Arthur B., Jr. Escape Through Enemy Territory. McCormack, Michael, ed. (Illus.). 48p. (Orig.). 1988. pap. 3.95 (*0-942459-01-6*) McCormack Co.

Cox, Arthur J., jt. ed. see Hudson, Christopher G.

Cox, Arthur N., ed. Allen's Astrophysical Quantities. 4th ed. LC 98-53154. 736p. 2000. 79.95 (*0-387-98746-0*) Spr-Verlag.

Cox, Arthur N., et al, eds. Solar Interior & Atmosphere. LC 91-34154. (Space Science Ser.). (Illus.). 1416p. 1992. 82.00 (*0-8165-1229-9*) U of Ariz Pr.

***Cox, B.** Measurement Uncertainty for Pitch & Runout Artifacts. (Technical Papers: Vol. 99FTM3). 14p. 1999. pap. 30.00 (*1-55589-741-X*) AGMA.

Cox, B., ed. QCD Hard Hadronic Processes. (NATO ASI Series B, Physics: Vol. 197). (Illus.). 566p. 1988. 140.00 (*0-306-43204-8*, Plenum Trade) Perseus Pubng.

Cox, B., et al, eds. Thermoregulatory Mechanisms & Their Therapeutic Implications: Symposium, 4th, Oxford, July-August, 1979. (Illus.). 1979. 56.75 (*3-8055-0277-X*) S Karger.

***Cox, B., et al.** Calibration of Master Gears on Coordinate Measurement Machines. (Technical Papers: Vol. 98FTM6). 18p. 1998. pap. 30.00 (*1-55589-724-X*) AGMA.

Cox, B. G. Modern Liquid Phase Kinetics. (Oxford Chemistry Primers Ser.: Vol. 21). (Illus.). 96p. 1994. 31.95 (*0-19-855745-0*); pap. text 12.95 (*0-19-855744-2*) OUP.

***Cox, Barbara.** Internet Marketing in Real Estate. (Illus.). 264p. 2000. pap. 19.33 (*0-13-011547-9*) P-H.

— Language of Real Estate. 2000. pap. text. write for info. (*0-13-016843-2*) P-H.

Cox, Barbara. Vocabulary Basics. 160p. (C). 1993. pap. text 13.95 (*1-56118-175-7*) Paradigm MN.

— Vocabulary Basics. 1993. text 36.00 incl. audio (*1-56118-177-3*) Paradigm MN.

— Vocabulary Basics. 160p. (C). 1993. pap. text, teacher ed. 8.00 (*1-56118-176-5*) Paradigm MN.

***Cox, Barbara, et al.** Prentice Hall Dictionary of Real Estate: A Complete Reference. 2000. pap. text. write for info. (*0-13-020832-9*) P-H.

— Prentice Hall Dictionary of Real Estate: A Handy Reference Pocket Edition. (Illus.). 256p. 2000. pap. text 16.00 (*0-13-020835-3*) P-H.

***Cox, Barbara G. & Koelzer, William.** Web Marketing for the Real Estate Professional. LC 00-25018. 64p. 2000. pap. 9.33 (*0-13-088060-4*) P-H.

Cox, Barbara G., et al. Living with Lung Cancer: A Guide for Patients & Their Families. 4th rev. ed. LC 97-50581. 144p. 1998. pap. 14.95 (*0-937404-53-5*) Triad Pub FL.

Cox, Barbara J., jt. auth. see Barnard-Ray, Mary.

Cox, Barbara J., jt. auth. see Ray, Mary B.

Cox, Barry. Collins Illustrated Encyclopedia of Dinosaurs & Prehistoric Animals. LC 89-185354. 312p. 1989. write for info. (*0-7322-0051-2*) Consort Bk Sales.

Cox, Barry. The History of the Planet Earth: From the Dawn of Time to the Modern Age & Beyond. (Illus.). 336p. 1991. 32.00 (*0-614-95660-9*) RD Assn.

Cox, Barry, jt. auth. see Vale, Janet.

Cox, Barry A. Establishing Your Course Through the Prophetic Ancrotine. large type ed. LC 99-220523. 1998. pap. 10.00 (*1-890820-03-2*) Battlecry Pr.

Cox, Benita & Saunders, Peter. The International Simulation & Gaming Yearbook, Vol. 5. write for info. (*0-7494-2174-6*, Kogan Pg Educ) Stylus Pub VA.

***Cox, Bert.** Find the Gold Mine in Your Business: Marketing Secrets for Optimum Profits. 1999. 49.95 (*1-930717-00-8*) Advantg Busn.

Cox, Bertha M. True Tales of Texas. LC 87-12091. (Illus.). 292p. (J). (gr. 3-8). 1987. reprint ed. 16.95 (*0-937460-28-1*) Hendrick-Long.

Cox, Bertram, ed. see Smart, George.

Cox, Bette Y. Central Avenue Its Rise & Fall 1890-c. 1955 Including the Musical Renaissance of Black Los Angeles. rev. ed. Butler, David, ed. LC 96-83001. (Illus.). 380p. 1996. pap. write for info. (*0-9650783-1-0*); text. write for info. (*0-9650783-0-2*) BEEM.

Cox, Betty, jt. auth. see Clipp, Katherine.

Cox, Betty, ed. see Carter, Robert F.

Cox, Betty E. Simply Following: In All My Journeying God Went Before. Runyon, Daniel V., ed. (Illus.). 224p. 1998. pap. 15.00 (*1-878559-05-2*) Saltbox Pr.

Cox, Betty W. Liz Carpenter: Girl from Salado. 144p. (J). (gr. 7-8). 1994. 14.95 (*0-89015-940-8*) Sunbelt Media.

Cox, Betty W., ed. see Stewart, Ozella T.

Cox, Betty W., ed. see Wood, John M.

Cox, Beverly. Spirit of the Harvest: North American Indian Cooking. LC 91-12119. (Illus.). 256p. 1991. 35.00 (*1-55670-186-1*) Stewart Tabori & Chang.

— Spirit of the West: Cooking from Ranch House & Range. LC 96-21063. (Illus.). 224p. 1996. 35.00 (*1-885183-21-6*) Artisan.

***Cox, Beverly & Jacobs, Martin.** Spirit of the Earth. LC 00-22480. 2000. write for info. (*1-58479-024-5*) Stewart Tabori & Chang.

Cox, Bill. The Cameron Aurameter in Action: Step-by-Step Method for Use of the Aurameter in Dowsing. (Illus.). 48p. 1982. per. 12.00 (*0-88234-008-5*) Life Understanding.

— The Psychology of Treasure Dowsing. (Illus.). 96p. 1989. pap. 12.75 (*0-88234-010-7*) Life Understanding.

— Techniques of Pendulum Dowsing: Step by Step Method for Use of the Pendulum in Dowsing. (Illus.). 38p. 1977. 8.75 (*0-88234-006-9*) Life Understanding.

— Techniques of Swing-Rod Dowsing: Step-by-Step Method for Use of the Pendulum in Dowsing. (Illus.). 38p. 1977. 8.75 (*0-88234-007-7*) Life Understanding.

— Unseen Kingdoms: UFOs & Invisible Elemental Forces. (Illus.). 72p. 1983. pap. 15.00 (*0-938294-14-8*) Inner Light.

Cox, Bill, jt. auth. see Verne L., Cameron.

Cox, Bill, ed. see Cameron, Verne L., et al.

Cox, Bill G. Born Bad. 1996. mass mkt. 5.99 (*0-7860-0274-3*, Pinncle Kensgtn) Kensgtn Pub Corp.

***Cox, Bill G.** No Safe Place: A Husband's Sick Demands Were a Prelude to Murder. (Pinnacle True Crime Ser.). 2000. mass mkt. 6.50 (*0-7860-1037-1*, Pinncle Kensgtn) Kensgtn Pub Corp.

Cox, Bill G. Over the Edge. LC 97-210558. 320p. 1997. mass mkt. 5.99 (*0-7860-0430-4*, Pinncle Kensgtn) Kensgtn Pub Corp.

— Shop of Horrors. 320p. 1998. pap. 5.99 (*0-7860-0500-9*, Pinncle Kensgtn) Kensgtn Pub Corp.

Cox, Bill J. & Horsley, F. William. Square Foot Estimating. 2nd ed. LC 96-168632. 1996. 69.95 (*0-87629-418-2*, 67145A) R S Means.

Cox, Birck, jt. ed. see Barnes, Robert W.

Cox, Blackstone & Spencer Staff. APICS Dictionary 1995. 8th ed. LC 95-79477. 102p. 1995. pap. 10.00 (*1-55822-123-9*) Am Prod & Inventory.

***Cox, Bo Don.** God Is Not in the Thesaurus: Stories from an Oklahoma Prison. (Illus.). 160p. 1999. pap. 8.95 (*0-88028-214-2*) Forward Movement.

Cox, Bobbi & Flanagan, Beth. Cape Cod Bed & Breakfast Guide & Innkeepers' Recipes Including Martha's Vineyard & Nantucket. Shortsleeve, Brian F. & McEwen, Colleen M., eds. 225p. (Orig.). 1989. pap. 12.95 (*0-9622782-0-3*) Cape Cod Life Mag.

Cox, Bonnie J., jt. ed. see Pattie, Ling-Yuh W.

Cox, Brad C. Object-Oriented Programming: An Evolutionary Approach. LC 85-22921. 300p. 1986. text 31.25 (*0-201-10393-1*) Addison-Wesley.

Cox, Brad J. Programacion Orientada a Objectos. (SPA.). 384p. (C). 1993. pap. text 17.00 (*0-201-60112-5*) Addison-Wesley.

— Superdistribution: Objects As Property on the Electronic Frontier. (Illus.). 224p. (C). 1996. pap. text 32.95 (*0-201-50208-9*) Addison-Wesley.

Cox, Brad J. & Novobilski, Andrew. Object-Oriented Programming: An Evolutionary Approach. 2nd ed. (Illus.). 320p. (C). 1991. pap. 44.95 (*0-201-54834-8*) Addison-Wesley.

Cox, Brenda G., et al, eds. Business Survey Methods. (Series in Probability & Mathematical Statistics). 752p. 1995. 198.00 (*0-471-59852-6*) Wiley.

Cox, Brenda S. Who Talks Funny? A Book about Languages for Kids. LC 94-5379. xii, 202p. 1995. lib. bdg. 25.00 (*0-208-02378-X*, Linnet Bks) Shoe String.

Cox, Brent A. Heart of the Eagle: Dragging Canoe & the Emergence of the Chickamauga Confederacy. LC 98-93649. (Illus.). 314p. 1999. pap. text 20.00 (*0-9667177-0-8*) Chenanee Pubs.

Cox, Brett E., ed. Basin Analysis & Paleontology of the Paleocene & Eocene Goler Formation, El Paso Mountains California. (Illus.). 67p. (Orig.). 1987. pap. 8.00 (*1-878861-12-3*) Pac Section SEPM.

Cox, Brian. The Lear Diaries: The Story of the Royal National Theatre's Productions of Richard III & King Lear. 224p. 1996. pap. 19.95 (*0-413-69880-7*) Heinemann.

— Literacy Is Not Enough: Essays on the Importance of Reading. 208p. 1999. pap. 19.95 (*0-7190-5669-1*) Manchester Univ Pr.

— Salem to Moscow: An Actor's Odyssey. (Illus.). 181p. (C). 1991. write for info. (*0-413-62820-5*, A0545, Methuen Drama); pap. 17.95 (*0-413-66450-3*, A0644, Methuen Drama) Methn.

Cox, Brian D., ed. The Health & Lifestyle Survey: Seven Years On. 412p. 1993. 87.95 (*1-85521-410-5*, Pub. by Dartmth Pub) Ashgate Pub Co.

Cox, Brian D. & Lightfoot, Cynthia, eds. Sociogenetic Perspectives on Internalization. LC 96-39146. 264p. 1997. 49.95 (*0-8058-1708-5*) L Erlbaum Assocs.

Cox, Brneda G. & Cohen, Steven. Methodological Issues for Health Care Surveys. (Statistics: Textbooks & Monographs: Vol. 61). (Illus.). 480p. 1985. text 175.00 (*0-8247-7323-3*) Dekker.

Cox, Bruce A., ed. Native People, Native Lands: Canadian Indians, Inuit & Metis. 300p. 1988. pap. 18.95 (*0-88629-062-7*) OUP.

Cox, Bruce L. & Smith, Robert E. Calibration of Gear Measuring Instruments & Their Application to the Inspection of Product Gears. (Technical Papers: Vol. 97FTM1). (Illus.). 67p. 1997. pap. text 30.00 (*1-55589-695-2*) AGMA.

Cox, C. A., jt. auth. see Ross, Turchaninov.

Cox, C. B. The Free Spirit: A Study of Liberal Humanism in the Novels of George Eliot, Henry James, E. M. Forster, Virginia Woolf, Angus Wilson. LC 80-13281. 195p. 1980. reprint ed. lib. bdg. 49.75 (*0-313-22449-8*, COFS, Greenwood Pr) Greenwood.

— Joseph Conrad, the Modern Imagination. LC 74-186948. 191 p. 1974. write for info. (*0-460-10574-4*) J M Dent & Sons.

Cox, C. B. & Cox, Dyson. Modern Poetry: Studies in Practical Criticism. 1988. reprint ed. lib. bdg. 49.00 (*0-7812-0131-4*) Rprt Serv.

Cox, C. B. & Dyson, A. E. Modern Poetry: Studies in Practical Criticism. LC 78-158904. 1971. reprint ed. 45.00 (*0-403-01306-2*) Scholarly.

Cox, C. B. & Moore, P. D. Biogeography: An Ecological & Evolutionary Approach. 5th ed. (Illus.). 320p. 1993. pap. text 44.95 (*0-632-02967-6*) Blackwell Sci.

***Cox, C. Barry & Moore, Peter D.** Biogeography: An Ecological & Evolutionary Approach. 2nd ed. LC 99-14649. (Illus.). 1999. pap. 49.95 (*0-86542-778-X*) Blackwell Sci.

Cox, C. L., ed. see Smart, George.

Cox, C. R. Operation & Control of Water Treatment Processes. (Monographs: No. 49). (ENG, FRE, RUS & SPA., Illus.). 390p. 1964. pap. text 52.00 (*92-4-140049-8*, 1140049) World Health.

Cox, C. S. The Aerobiological Pathway of Microorganisms. LC 86-15710. (Wiley-Interscience Publications). 305p. reprint ed. pap. 94.60 (*0-7837-3229-5*, 204324700007) Bks Demand.

Cox, C. S. & Wathes, C. M. Bioaerosols: Handbook of Samplers & Sampling. LC 94-44749. 656p. 1995. lib. bdg. 95.00 (*0-87371-615-9*, L615) Lewis Pubs.

Cox, Carol. The Water in the Pearl. 1982. pap. 6.50 (*0-914610-28-7*) Hanging Loose.

— Woodworking & Places Nearby. 1979. pap. 5.00 (*0-914610-13-9*) Hanging Loose.

***Cox, Carol, et al.** Resolutions. 352p. 1999. pap. 4.97 (*1-57748-639-0*) Barbour Pub.

Cox, Carol, jt. auth. see Jeavons, John.

Cox, Carol, jt. auth. see Rivlin, Alice.

Cox, Carol, ed. see Hightower, Sheree & Stanga, Cathie.

Cox, Carol T., jt. auth. see Cohen, Barry M.

Cox, Carole. The Frail Elderly: Problems, Needs & Community Responses. LC 92-38000. 224p. 1993. 59.95 (*0-86569-031-6*, T031, Auburn Hse); pap. 19.95 (*0-86569-228-9*, R228, Auburn Hse) Greenwood.

***Cox, Carole.** Teaching Language Arts. 3rd ed. LC 98-24552. 558p. 1998. 73.33 (*0-205-28137-0*) P-H.

Cox, Carole, ed. To Grandmother's House We Go & Stay: A Subjective Experience of Homelessness. LC 99-15737. (Series on Life Styles & Issues in Aging). (Illus.). 288p. 1999. text 38.95 (*0-8261-1286-2*) Springer Pub.

Cox, Carole & Ephross, Paul H. Ethnicity & Social Work Practice. LC 96-34098. 192p. (C). 1997. text 44.95 (*0-19-509930-3*); pap. text 21.95 (*0-19-509931-1*) OUP.

Cox, Carole, et al. Crossroads: Literature & Language in Culturally & Linguistically Diverse Classrooms. LC 96-30761. 201p. 1996. pap. text 42.00 (*0-13-191578-9*, Merrill Coll) P-H.

Cox, Carole, jt. auth. see Monk, Abraham.

Cox, Carole, jt. ed. see Many, Joyce.

Cox, Caroline & Scruton, Roger, eds. Peace Studies: A Critical Survey. (C). 1990. 35.00 (*0-907967-15-9*, Pub. by Inst Euro Def & Strat) St Mut.

Cox, Catharine M. The Early Mental Traits of Three Hundred Geniuses. (Genetic Studies of Genius: Vol. II). xxiii, 842p. 1926. 85.00 (*0-8047-0010-9*) Stanford U Pr.

Cox, Catherine S. Gender & Language in Chaucer. LC 97-9730. 240p. 1997. 49.95 (*0-8130-1519-7*) U Press Fla.

Cox, Catherine S., jt. ed. see Shoaf, R. A.

Cox, Celestina M. Emotions of Time. 26p. (Orig.). 1996. pap. 9.95 (*1-885206-39-9*, Iliad Pr) Cader Pubng.

Cox, Chana B. A River Went Out of Eden. (Illus.). 208p. (Orig.). 1992. 24.95 (*0-938530-57-7*); pap. 14.95 (*0-938530-56-9*) Lexikos.

Cox-Chapman, Mally. The Case for Heaven: Messages of Hope from People Who Touched Eternity. 224p. 1996. reprint ed. pap. 12.00 (*0-425-15401-7*) Berkley Pub.

Cox, Charles, jt. ed. see Beck, John E.

Cox, Charles B., ed. Dylan Thomas: A Collection of Critical Essays. (Illus.). 1966. 12.95 (*0-13-919381-2*, Spectrum IN) Macmillan Gen Ref.

***Cox, Charlie C.** The Web We Weave. (Illus.). 288p. 2000. pap. write for info. (*1-57197-232-3*) Pentland Pr.

***Cox, Cheryl A.** Household Interests: Property, Marriage Strategies & Family Dynamics in Ancient Athens. LC 97-11775. 304p. 1998. text 45.00 (*0-691-01572-4*, Pub. by Princeton U Pr) Cal Prin Full Svc.

Cox, Cheryl A., jt. ed. see Dye, David H.

Cox, Chris. Waking up in a Cornfield: Selected Columns. LC 98-43949. 150p. 1999. 14.95 (*1-887905-13-8*) Pkway Pubs.

Cox, Christine, ed. see Dalai Lama XIV.

Cox, Christopher. A Key West Companion: Views of Six Nobel Laureates. 7th ed. (Illus.). 224p. 1983. pap. 15.95 (*0-312-45183-0*) St Martin.

— Nietzsche: Naturalism & Interpretation. LC 99-30107. 241p. 1999. text 45.00 (*0-520-21553-2*, Pub. by U CA Pr) Cal Prin Full Svc.

***Cox, Christopher, ed.** U. S. National Security & Military/Commercial Concerns with the People's Republic of China: The Cox Report. (Illus.). 901p. (C). 1999. pap. text 95.00 (*0-7881-8207-2*) DIANE Pub.

Cox, Christopher R. Chasing the Dragon. 352p. 1997. pap. 12.95 (*0-8050-5507-X*) H Holt & Co.

***Cox, Cindy.** Stand for Your Man. 1999. pap. 6.99 (*1-891774-12-3*) Path Pubng.

Cox, Clarice. Instant Teaching Skills for Adult Education. 64p. 1996. pap. text 17.95 (*1-889373-01-X*) Prof Trning.

Cox, Clarice R., jt. auth. see Brown, Jerrold G.

Cox, Claude E., ed. The Campbell-Stone Movement in Ontario: Christian Church (Disciples of Christ), Churches of Christ, Independent Christian Churches-Churches of Christ. LC 93-45602. (Illus.). 484p. 1994. 109.95 (*0-7734-9421-9*) E Mellen.

Cox, Claudie. Petit Lexique de la France Contemporaine: A Concise Dictionary of Contemporary France. LC 87-18226. 117p. 1988. pap. 13.00 (*0-85496-534-3*) Berg Pubs.

Cox, Clif, ed. see Goebel, Wales & Buck, Janie.

***Cox, Clinton.** African American Teachers. (Black Stars Ser.). 176p. (YA). (gr. 5-9). 2000. pap. text 22.95 (*0-471-24649-2*) Wiley.

Cox, Clinton. Come All You Brave Soldiers: Blacks in the Revolutionary War. LC 97-44198. (Illus.). 208p. (YA). (gr. 5-9). 1999. 15.95 (*0-590-47576-2*, Pub. by Scholastic) Scholastic Inc.

— Fiery Vision: The Life & Death of John Brown. (J). (gr. 4-7). 1997. 15.95 (*0-614-29010-4*) Scholastic Inc.

— Firey Vision: The Life & Death of John Brown. LC 96-21368. 240p. (J). (gr. 7-12). 1997. 15.95 (*0-590-47574-6*) Scholastic Inc.

— The Forgotten Heroes: The Story of the Buffalo Soldiers. LC 92-36622. 192p. (J). (gr. 3-9). 1996. pap. 3.99 (*0-590-45122-7*) Scholastic Inc.

— The Forgotten Heroes: The Story of the Buffalo Soldiers. LC 92-36622. 1993. 9.09 (*0-606-09292-7*, Pub. by Turtleback) Demco.

— Mark Twain - America's Humorist, Dreamer, Prophet: A Biography. LC 94-18624. 240p. (J). (gr. 3-9). 1995. 14.95 (*0-590-45642-3*, Scholastic Hardcover) Scholastic Inc.

***Cox, Clinton.** Mark Twain - America's Humorist, Dreamer, Prophet: A Biography. 1999. pap. text 4.50 (*0-590-45641-5*) Scholastic Inc.

Cox, Clinton. The Undying Glory: The Story of the Massachusetts 54th Regiment. 176p. (YA). (gr. 4-7). 1993. pap. 3.99 (*0-590-44171-X*, Pub. by Scholastic) Scholastic Inc.

— Undying Glory: The Story of the Massachusetts 54th Regiment. (Scholastic Biography Ser.). (J). 1991. 9.09 (*0-606-02957-5*, Pub. by Turtleback) Demco.

Cox, Clyde, ed. Corrugator Major Components: Maintenance & Operating Guidelines. 93p. 1993. pap. 75.00 (*0-89852-319-2*, 0101R226) TAPPI.

Cox, Connie. Maternity Massage: A Healthy Indulgence a Welcome Relief. LC 94-66358. 98p. 1994. pap. 12.95 (*1-885044-01-1*) Stress Less.

— Simply Organized: How to Simplify Your Complicated Life. 1991. pap. 4.99 (*0-425-13088-6*) Berkley Pub.

Cox, Connie & Evatt, Cris. Simply Organized! How to Simplify Your Complicated Life. 128p. (Orig.). 1988. pap. 8.95 (*0-399-51451-1*, Perigee Bks) Berkley Pub.

— Simply Organized! How to Simplify Your Complicated Life. pap. 4.50 (*0-425-13108-4*) Berkley Pub.

***Cox, Connie & Evatt, Cris.** 30 Days to a Simpler Life. LC 98-18436. 240p. 1998. pap. 11.95 (*0-452-28013-3*, Plume) Dutton Plume.

Cox-Conrad. Juvenile Justice. 4th ed. 1995. teacher ed. 6.25 (*0-697-12701-X*, WCB McGr Hill) McGrw-H Hghr Educ.

Cox, Craig. Storefront Revolution: Food Co-Ops & the Counterculture. LC 93-45522. (Perspectives on the Sixties Ser.). 170p. (C). 1994. pap. 16.00 (*0-8135-2102-5*); text 37.00 (*0-8135-2101-7*) Rutgers U Pr.

C

*Cox, Crystal L. Edible & Medical Plants of Northwest Montana. 114p. 1999. pap. 12.00 (1-892930-01-3) Nakaii Pubg.

Cox, D., et al, eds. Novel Forms of Carbon. (Materials Research Society Symposium Proceedings Ser.: Vol. 270). 521p. 1992. text 30.00 (1-55899-165-4) Materials Res.

Cox, D., et al. Processing & Utilization of Sorghum: Selected Bibliographical Reference (with Abstracts) from 1990 to 1996. 98p. 1997. pap. 75.00 (0-85954-477-X, Pub. by Nat Res Inst) St Mut.

Cox, D. A., et al. Using Algebraic Geometry, Vol. 185. Axler, S. et al, eds. LC 98-11964. (Graduate Texts in Mathematics Ser.). (Illus.). 496p. 1998. 59.95 (0-387-98487-9); pap. 34.95 (0-387-98492-5) Spr-Verlag.

Cox, D. H. A Third Century Hoard of Tetradrachms from Gordion. (University Museum Monographs: No. 9). (Illus.). vi, 20p. 1953. pap. 6.00 (0-934718-01-6) U Museum Pubns.

Cox, D. June. The Way It Was. (Illus.). 124p. (Orig.). 1989. pap. 23.20 (0-685-44898-3) D J Cox.

Cox, D. R. Applied Statistics: Some Principles & Examples. 192p. (gr. 13). 1981. per. 52.95 (0-412-16570-8, NO.6548, Chap & Hall CRC) CRC Pr.

— Multidimensional Scaling. 216p. 1994. ring bd. 68.95 (0-412-49120-6, Chap & Hall CRC) CRC Pr.

Cox, D. R. Multivariate Dependencies, 1 vol. LC 98-48949. 272p. 1996. boxed set 64.95 (0-412-75410-X) CRC Pr.

Cox, D. R., et al, eds. Genetic Analysis Workshop Seven: Issues in Gene Mapping & Detection of Major Genes Held at Bergamo Conference Center, Dayton, Ohio, October 1990. (Journal: Cytogenetics & Cell Genetics: Vol. 59, No. 2-3, 1992). (Illus.). 176p. 1992. pap. 62.75 (3-8055-5578-4) S Karger.

Cox, D. R. & Isham, V. Point Processes. (Monographs on Statistics & Applied Probability). 200p. 1980. boxed set 19.95 (0-412-21910-7, NO. 2962) Chapman & Hall.

Cox, D. R. & Oakes, D. O. Analysis of Survival Data. LC 83-20882. (Monographs on Statistics & Applied Probability). 208p. (C). (gr. 13). 1984. boxed set 73.95 (0-412-24490-X, NO. 6810, Chap & Hall CRC) CRC Pr.

*Cox, D. R. & Reid, N. The Theory of the Design of Experiments, Vol. 86. LC 00-29529. (Monographs on Statistics & Applied Probability). 336p. (C). 2000. boxed set 69.95 (1-58488-195-X, Chap & Hall CRC) CRC Pr.

Cox, D. R. & Snell, E. Joyce. Applied Statistics: A Handbook of BMDP Analysis. 120p. 1987. mass mkt. 29.95 (0-412-28410-3, 9985) Chapman & Hall.

Cox, D. R., jt. auth. see Barndorff-Nielsen, O. E.

Cox, D. R., jt. ed. see Hawkes, A. J.

Cox, Daniel J. Black Bear. LC 90-40768. (Illus.). 96p. 1990. 22.95 (0-87701-727-1) Chronicle Bks.

— Mountain Lion. LC 98-3760. (Illus.). 120p. 1999. pap. 18.95 (0-8118-1930-2) Chronicle Bks.

*Cox, Daniel J., photos by. Bear: A Celebration of Power & Beauty. (Illus.). 176p. 2000. 50.00 (0-609-60795-2) Sierra.

Cox, Danny. There Are No Limits: Breaking the Barriers in Personal High Performance. LC 98-16985. 256p. 1998. pap. 24.99 (1-56414-340-6) Career Pr Inc.

Cox, Danny & Hoover, John. Leadership When the Heat's On. 200p. 1992. 24.99 (0-07-013267-4) McGraw.

*Cox, Danny & Hoover, John. Leadership When the Heat's On. 200p. 1999. reprint ed. text 25.00 (0-7881-6826-6) DIANE Pub.

Cox, Danny, et al. Leadership When the Heat's On. 200p. 1993. pap. 14.95 (0-07-013312-3) McGraw.

Cox, Danny, jt. auth. see Hoover, John.

*Cox, Dave. The Sailing Handbook. LC 99-38471. 160p. 2000. pap. 21.95 (0-8117-2922-2) Stackpole.

*Cox, David. Close Protection: The Politics of Guarding Russia's Rulers. LC 00-29850. 2000. write for info. (0-275-96688-7) Greenwood.

Cox, David. Planning of Experiments. LC 92-7007. (Classics Library). 320p. 1992. pap. 64.95 (0-471-57429-5) Wiley.

— Retreating from the Cold War: Germany, Russia, & the Withdrawal of the Western Group of Forces. 160p. (C). 1996. text 40.00 (0-8147-1528-1) NYU Pr.

Cox, David, ed. The Walden Interviews. (C). 1990. 75.00 (1-85283-104-9, Pub. by Boxtree) St Mut.

Cox, David, et al. Ideals, Varieties, & Algorithms: An Introduction to Computational Algebraic Geometry & Commutative Algebra. Ewing, J. H. et al, eds. LC 92-13290. (Undergraduate Texts in Mathematics Ser.). (Illus.). 513p. 1995. reprint ed. 39.95 (0-387-97847-X) Spr-Verlag.

Cox, David, jt. auth. see Bramham, John.

Cox, David, jt. ed. see Goldblat, Jozef.

Cox, David, jt. ed. see Leaver, Richard.

Cox, David A. Primes of the Form x2 + ny2: Fermat, Class Field Theory & Complex Multiplication. LC 89-5555. (Pure & Applied Mathematics Ser.). 351p. 1997. pap. 59.95 (0-471-19079-9, Wiley-Interscience) Wiley.

*Cox, David A. & Katz, Sheldon. Mirror Symmetry & Algebraic Geometry. LC 98-55564. (Mathematical Surveys & Monographs). xxi, 469p. 1999. write for info. (0-8218-1059-6) Am Math.

Cox, David A., ed. see Manocha, Dinesh N.

Cox, David F. Starting a Small Business of Your Own - With "No" Money. LC 89-82744. 83p. 1990. pap. 14.95 (0-9616213-1-1) Empire Pub.

*Cox, David Harold. Irwin Bazelon: A Bio-Bibliography, 80. (Bio-Bibliographies in Music Ser.: Vol. 80). 176p. 2000. lib. bdg. 66.00 (0-313-30550-1, Greenwood Pr) Greenwood.

Cox, David L. Albanian-Newspaper Reader. 1997. write for info. (1-881265-51-X) Dunwoody Pr.

Cox, David N., jt. auth. see Wilson, Glenn D.

Cox, David R. & Snell, E. Joyce. Analysis of Binary Data. 2nd ed. 200p. (gr. 13). 1988. pap. 59.95 (0-412-30620-4, A2799, Chap & Hall CRC) CRC Pr.

*Cox, David S. John Quincy Adams: Character in Time: The U. S. Presidents. Cox, R. David & Kuhens, Brian, eds. 40p. 1998. 5.95 (1-929403-04-6) History Proj.

Cox, Davina, ed. see Cameron, Verne L., et al.

Cox, Deborah L., et al. Clinical, Developmental Perspectives on Women's Anger: A Potion Strong & Good. LC 99-29693. 1999. boxed set 24.95 (0-87630-946-5) Brunner-Mazel.

Cox, Debra, jt. auth. see Curry, Linda.

Cox, Dee. Cook Gourmet Everyday. LC 85-80696. (Illus.). 74p. (Orig.). 1985. pap. 5.95 (0-9615184-0-5) Lifestyle Systems.

Cox, Dennis, photos by. Michigan: Photos of Dennis Cox. (Illus.). 144p. 1993. 39.95 (1-55868-099-3) Gr Arts Ctr Pub.

Cox, Derek. Facing the Future: Issues for Industrial Adult Education. (C). 1992. 39.00 (1-85041-064-X, Pub. by Univ Nottingham) St Mut.

Cox, Dermot. The Psalms in the Life of God's People. (C). 1988. 60.00 (0-85439-237-8, Pub. by St Paul Pubns) St Mut.

Cox, Dermot & Board of St. Paul Editorial Staff. Man's Anger & God's Silence: The Book of Job. 144p. (C). 1996. pap. 39.95 (0-85439-316-1, Pub. by St Paul Pubns) St Mut.

Cox, Desiree. An Introduction to Office Management for Secretaries. LC 96-33110. 133p. 1997. pap. 29.95 (0-304-70072-X, HF5382, Pub. by Cassell) LPC InBook.

Cox, Dian, ed. see Cassell, Jenna.

*Cox, Diane. Occupational Therapy & Chronic Fatigue Syndrome. 2000. pap. 34.95 (1-86156-155-5) Whurr Pub.

Cox, Diane, et al. Our Corner of the World: Seventeen Illinois Artists. (Illus.). 32p. 1989. 7.00 (0-945558-05-8) ISU Univ Galls.

Cox, Dianne L., ed. see Faulkner, William.

*Cox, Don. Stories from the Sagebrush: Celebrating Northern Nevada at the Millennium. Dixon, Jean, tr. (Halcyon Imprint Ser.). (Illus.). 319p. 1999. 50.00 (1-890591-05-X) NV Humanities.

Cox, Don, tr. see Dabrowski, Hans-Peter & Koos, Volker.

Cox, Don, tr. see Dressel, Joachim & Griehl, Manfred.

Cox, Don, tr. see Elfrath, Ulrich.

Cox, Don, tr. see Engelmann, Joachim.

Cox, Don, tr. see Frank, Reinhard.

Cox, Don, tr. see Held, Werner & Obermaier, Ernst.

Cox, Don, tr. see Nowarra, Heinz J.

Cox, Don, tr. see Scheibert, Horst.

Cox, Don, tr. see Spielberger, Walter J.

Cox, Don R. The Mystery of Edwin Drood: An Annotated Bibliography. (Dickens Bibliographies Ser.: Vol. 11). 400p. 74.00 (0-8240-8511-6, H707) Garland.

Cox, Don R., ed. Sexuality & Victorian Literature. LC 83-21655. (Tennessee Studies in Literature: Vol. 27). (Illus.). 278p. 1984. reprint ed. pap. 86.20 (0-608-07988-X, 206795300012) Bks Demand.

Cox, Don R. & Dickens, Charles. Charles Dickens's the Mystery of Edwin Drood: An Annotated Bibliography. LC 97-36302. (Studies in the Nineteenth Century: 17). 1997. 124.50 (0-404-61497-3) AMS Pr.

Cox, Donald D. Seaway Trail Wildguide to Natural History. Dunn, Kara L., ed. LC 96-69011. (Illus.). 178p. (Orig.). 1996. pap. 7.95 (0-943689-04-X) Seaway Trail Inc.

Cox, Donald H., Sr. Beekeeper Ugli, Bk. One. LC 88-70542. (Illus.). 56p. 1988. pap. write for info. (0-9620307-0-8) D H Cox.

— Beekeeper Ugli, Bk. Two: My Visit to Li'l Pinch. LC 88-70543. (Illus.). 60p. 1988. pap. write for info. (0-9620307-1-6) D H Cox.

Cox, Donald W. The Doomsday Asteroid. 337p. 1998. pap. text 17.95 (1-57392-271-4) Prometheus Bks.

— Hemlock's Cup: The Struggle for Death with Dignity. LC 93-20382. 311p. 1993. 26.95 (0-87975-808-2) Prometheus Bks.

Cox, Donald W. & Chestek, James H. Doomsday Asteroid: Can We Survive? LC 96-27159. (Illus.). 338p. 1996. 26.95 (1-57392-066-5) Prometheus Bks.

Cox, Dorothy G. The Dreamer. 1998. pap. write for info. (1-57553-851-2) Watermrk Pr.

Cox, Doug. Blues Dobro. (Illus.). 96p. 1998. pap. 19.95 incl. audio compact disk (1-57424-055-2) Centerstream Pub.

*Cox, Doug. Introduction to Roots Guitar Book/CD Package: An Overview of North American Folk Styles. (Illus.). 56p. 2000. 17.95 incl. audio compact disk (1-57424-085-4) Centerstream Pub.

Cox, Doug. Slide Guitar & Open Tunings: Book & CD Package. (Illus.). 56p. 1999. pap. 19.95 incl. audio compact disk (1-57424-068-4) Centerstream Pub.

Cox, Douglas C. & Tanner, Wilmer W. Snakes of Utah. LC 95-50195. (Illus.). iv, 92p. 1995. pap. 18.95 (0-8425-2331-6, Friends of the Library) Brigham.

*Cox, Dwayne & Morison, William J. The University of Louisville. LC 99-28299. (Illus.). 256p. 1999. 30.00 (0-8131-2142-6) U Pr of Ky.

Cox, Dyson, jt. auth. see Cox, C. B.

Cox, E. Celebrate Jesus Activity Book. 1995. 3.99 (1-85792-133-X, Pub. by Christian Focus) Spring Arbor Dist.

Cox, E. & Ravthon, H. New York Times Cryptic Handbook. 224p. 1996. pap. 14.00 (0-8129-2621-8) Random.

Cox, E. J. Identification of Freshwater Diatoms from Live Material. (Illus.). 128p. 1996. write for info. (0-412-49380-2) Kluwer Academic.

Cox, E. L., ed. see Fielder, Barbara L.

Cox, E. M. H. Farrer's Last Journey. LC 76-48121. (Illus.). 1977. reprint ed. write for info. (0-913728-16-0) Theophrastus.

Cox, E. Sam. The P. S. Roadtripper: Electronic Field Trips for Public Speakers. 128p. (C). 1998. per. 19.95 (0-7872-5420-7, 41542001) Kendall-Hunt.

*Cox, Earl. Fuzzy Modeling Tools for Data Mining & Knowledge Discovery. 500p. 1999. 49.95 (0-12-194275-9) Morgan Kaufmann.

Cox, Earl, et al. The Fuzzy Systems Handbook: A Practioner's Guide to Building, Using, & Maintain Fuzzy Systems. 2nd ed. LC 98-23214. (Illus.). 716p. (C). 1998. pap. text 59.95 incl. cd-rom (0-12-194455-7) Morgan Kaufmann.

Cox, Earl, jt. auth. see Paul, Gregory S.

Cox, Earl D. Fuzzy Logic Applications in Business & Industry. (Illus.). 450p. (Orig.). 1995. pap. 44.95 (1-886801-01-0) Thomson Learn.

— Fuzzy Models Using Java. (Illus.). 650p. (Orig.). 1997. pap. 49.95 (1-886801-31-2) Thomson Learn.

Cox, Edward G. Reference Guide to the Literature of Travel, 3 vols. 1727p. 1992. reprint ed. 195.00 (1-57898-024-0) Martino Pubng.

Cox, Edward L. Free Coloreds in the Slave Societies of St. Kitts & Grenada, 1763-1833. LC 83-14646. 212p. reprint ed. pap. 65.80 (0-7837-1315-0, 204146300020) Bks Demand.

Cox, Edwin B., et al. The Bank Director's Handbook. 2nd ed. LC 86-3592. (Illus.). 317p. 1986. 65.00 (0-86569-145-2, Auburn Hse) Greenwood.

Cox, Eileen. Dynamic Positioning Treatment. 112p. 1987. pap. write for info. (0-88144-117-1) Christian Pub.

Cox, Elenor R. & Bold, Harold C. Phycological Studies Vol. 7: Taxonomic Investigations of Stigeoclonium. (University Texas Publication: No. 6618). (Illus.). 167p. 1977. reprint ed. pap. 52.70 (3-87429-130-8, 007825, Pub. by Koeltz Sci Bks) Lubrecht & Cramer.

*Cox, Elizabeth. Bargains in the Real World: 13 Stories. LC 00-41741. 2001. write for info. (0-679-46329-1) Random.

Cox, Elizabeth. Familiar Ground. 240p. 1986. pap. 3.95 (0-380-69978-8, Avon Bks) Morrow Avon.

— Japan Inc. in Latin America: A Status Report on Aid, Trade, Debt & Investment. Werrett, Rosemary, ed. 103p. 1989. 125.00 (0-923351-01-9) Latin Am Info.

— Night Talk. LC 97-71190. 267p. 1997. 23.95 (1-55597-267-5) Graywolf.

— Night Talk. LC 98-36888. 272p. 1998. pap. 13.95 (0-312-19516-8) St Martin.

Cox, Elizabeth M. Women in Modern American Politics: A Bibliography, 1900-1995. LC 96-38898. 414p. (YA). (gr. 11). 1997. text 130.00 (1-56802-133-X) Congr Quarterly.

*Cox, Elizabeth M. Women State & Territorial Legislators, 1895-1995. (Illus.). 398p. 1999. reprint ed. text 30.00 (0-7881-6734-0) DIANE Pub.

Cox, Elizabeth M. Women State & Territorial Legislators, 1895-1995: A State-by-State Analysis, with Rosters of 6,000 Women. LC 95-32652. (Illus.). 408p. 1995. lib. bdg. 55.00 (0-7864-0078-1) McFarland & Co.

Cox, Emily. Boston Globe Crossword Puzzle, Vol. 7. 1998. pap. 9.00 (0-8129-3023-1, Times Bks) Crown Pub Group.

Cox, Emma. Idaho Mountains, Our Home: The Life Story of Lafe & Emma Cox. LC 97-199912. (Illus.). 248p. 1997. pap. 18.95 (0-9658635-0-6) VO Ranch.

Cox, Emma D., jt. auth. see Smith, Angel.

Cox, Ethelyn. Historic Alexandria, Virginia, Street by Street. LC 76-1042. (Illus.). 216p. 1976. pap. 12.95 (0-939009-18-8, EPM) Howell Pr VA.

Cox, Eunice, jt. ed. see Winters, Stanley A.

Cox, Eve & Leonard, Helen. Recognising Women's Skill. 1996. pap. 59.95 (0-7300-1804-0, Pub. by Deakin Univ) St Mut.

Cox, F. Topley & Wilson's Microbiology & Microbial Infections: Parasitology, Vol. 5. 9th ed. (Illus.). 750p. 1998. text 195.00 (0-340-66320-0, Pub. by E A) OUP.

Cox, F. E., ed. Modern Parasitology: A Textbook of Parasitology. (Illus.). 358p. (C). 1982. pap. text 35.00 (0-632-00612-9) Blackwell Sci.

Cox-Fill, Olivia. For Our Daughters: How Outstanding Women Worldwide Have Balanced Home & Career. LC 94-34412. 312p. 1996. 45.00 (0-275-95199-5, Praeger Pubs) Greenwood.

Cox, Fiona. Aeneas Takes the Metro: The Presence of Virgil in Twentieth Century French Literature. (Legenda Ser.: Vol. 3). 238p. 1999. pap. 49.50 (1-900755-10-6, Pub. by E H R C) David Brown.

Cox, Fran, jt. auth. see Cox, Louis.

Cox, Francis A. The Life of Philip Melanchthon. LC 83-45641. reprint ed. 72.50 (0-404-19824-4) AMS Pr.

*Cox, Frank. Trusting God's Heart: Finding Peace in Times of Sorrow. (Illus.). 272p. 2000. 17.95 (1-888237-33-3) Baxter Pr.

Cox, Frank, rev. The Enlisted Soldier's Guide. 3rd ed. LC 92-45037. (Illus.). 240p. 1993. pap. 12.95 (0-8117-2540-5) Stackpole.

— The Enlisted Soldier's Guide. 4th ed. (Illus.). 240p. 1996. pap. 12.95 (0-8117-3008-5) Stackpole.

— The NCO Guide. 5th ed. (Illus.). 336p. 1995. pap. 18.95 (0-8117-2563-4) Stackpole.

Cox, Frank D. The AIDS Booklet. 4th ed. 67p. (C). 1995. text 6.59 (0-697-26261-8, WCB McGr Hill) McGrw-H Hghr Educ.

— The AIDS Booklet. 6th ed. 96p. 1999. pap. 8.44 (0-697-29428-5) McGraw.

— Family Living: Relationships & Decisions. LC 93-27762. 1994. pap. 52.00 (0-314-91536-2) West Pub.

— Human Intimacy: Marriage, the Family, & Its Meaning. 6th ed. Perlee, Clyde & Simon, eds. LC 92-35570. 670p. (C). 1993. text 55.25 (0-314-01067-X) West Pub.

— Human Intimacy: Marriage, the Family & Its Meaning. 8th ed. LC 98-12807. 625p. 1998. pap. 73.95 (0-534-55251-X) Brooks-Cole.

— Human Intimacy:marriage,the Family & Its Meaning. 7th ed. LC 95-33305. (Sociology-Upper Level). 575p. (C). 1996. pap. 47.00 (0-314-06455-9) West Pub.

Cox, Frank E., jt. ed. see Fee Yow Liew.

Cox, Frank L. According to Luke. 1941. pap. 2.75 (0-88027-030-6) Firm Foun Pub.

— One Hundred One Sermon Outlines. 1971. 4.95 (0-88027-028-4) Firm Foun Pub.

Cox, Frank L., jt. auth. see Showalter, G. H.

Cox, Frank W., III. I Bleed Maroon. (Illus.). 100p. (Orig.). 1992. pap. 9.95 (0-9626069-6-0) Insite Pub.

Cox, Fred M. & Hesslegrave, Barbara L. Pharmacoeconomics: Unique Perspectives on Cost, Outcomes & Value. (Illus.). 225p. 1998. 55.00 (0-07-013404-9) McGraw.

Cox, Freda. Seasons in a Country Garden. (Illus.). 160p. 1995. 27.95 (1-55591-233-8) Fulcrum Pub.

Cox, G., ed. Combustion Fundamentals of Fire. (Combustion Treatise Ser.). (Illus.). 476p. 1995. text 137.00 (0-12-194230-9) Acad Pr.

Cox, G., et al. Echoes. (Star Trek: No. 15). 1998. per. 5.99 (0-671-00200-7, Star Trek) PB.

Cox, Gail, ed. see Flores, Kathy.

Cox, Gale, jt. auth. see Chesser, Beverly.

Cox, Gale, ed. see Bond, Mel.

Cox, Gale R., jt. auth. see Price, Ray B.

Cox, Gary. Crime & Punishment: A Mind to Murder. (Twayne's Masterwork Studies). 168p. 1990. 23.95 (0-8057-7993-0, Twyne) Mac Lib Ref.

— Tyrant & Victim in Dostoevsky. 119p. 1984. pap. 15.95 (0-89357-125-3) Slavica.

Cox, Gary C. An Integrated Children's Mental Health System: Coordinating the Needs of Children with Multiple Problems. (Illus.). 114p. (Orig.). (C). 1994. pap. text 35.00 (0-7881-0747-X) DIANE Pub.

Cox, Gary W. Making Votes Count: Strategic Coordination in the World's Electoral System. (Political Economy of Institutions & Decisions Ser.). 354p. 1997. text 59.95 (0-521-58516-3); pap. text 18.95 (0-521-58527-9) Cambridge U Pr.

Cox, Gary W. & McCubbins, Mathew D. Legislative Leviathan: Party Government in the House. 289p. 1993. pap. 17.95 (0-520-07220-0, Pub. by U CA Pr) Cal Prin Full Svc.

— Legislative Leviathan: Party Government in the House. 289p. 1994. 55.00 (0-520-07219-7, Pub. by U CA Pr) Cal Prin Full Svc.

Cox, Gene. The Multiple Offense. (Illus.). vi, 172p. 1997. pap. 18.95 (0-9669672-0-8) G Cox.

— The Sunset Lounge. 276p. 1997. pap. 6.99 (0-9649791-2-8) Riverrun Ent.

Cox, Geof & Dufault, Chuch. 25 Roleplays for Interview Training. 216p. 1997. pap. 131.95 (0-566-07903-8, Pub. by Gower) Ashgate Pub Co.

*Cox, Geoffrey. Eyewitness: A Memoir of 1930s Europe. 288p. 1999. pap. 39.95 (1-877133-70-1, Pub. by Univ Otago Pr) Intl Spec Bk.

Cox, Geoffrey & Francis, Malcom. Sharks & Rays of New Zealand. (Illus.). 68p. (Orig.). (YA). 1997. pap. 29.95 (0-908812-60-4, Pub. by Canterbury Univ) Accents Pubns.

*Cox, George W. Alien Species in North America & Hawaii: Impacts on Natural Ecosystems. LC 99-16652. 344p. 2000. 60.00 (1-55963-679-3) Island Pr.

Cox, George W. Conservation Biology: Concepts & Applications. 2nd ed. LC 96-60380. 368p. (C). 1996. text. write for info. (0-697-21814-7, WCB McGr Hill); per. write for info. (0-07-114298-3, WCB McGr Hill) McGrw-H Hghr Educ.

— Conservation Ecology: Biosphere & Biosurvival. 368p. (C). 1992. text. write for info. (0-697-14046-6, WCB McGr Hill) McGrw-H Hghr Educ.

— General Ecology. 7th ed. 288p. (C). 1995. text, lab manual ed. write for info. (0-697-24365-6, WCB McGr Hill) McGrw-H Hghr Educ.

— General Ecology. 8th ed. 2001. lab manual ed. 36.50 (0-07-290974-9) McGraw.

— Laboratory Manual of General Ecology. 6th ed. 272p. (C). 1989. text. write for info. (0-697-05138-2, WCB McGr Hill) McGrw-H Hghr Educ.

Cox, Gerald. Mountain Signs/Mountain Life. (Illus.). 96p. 1990. 5.95 (0-935576-35-5) Kesend Pub Ltd.

— Pond Life. (Illus.). 88p. (Orig.). 1988. pap. 5.95 (0-935576-24-X) Kesend Pub Ltd.

— Springsigns. (Illus.). 80p. 1987. pap. 5.95 (0-935576-20-7) Kesend Pub Ltd.

— Wintersigns in the Snow. (Illus.). 80p. 1989. pap. 5.95 (0-935576-11-8) Kesend Pub Ltd.

Cox, Gerry R. & Fundis, Ronald J., eds. Spiritual, Ethical & Pastoral Aspects of Death & Bereavement. (Death, Value & Meaning Ser.). 289p. 1992. text 40.95 (0-89503-100-0); pap. text 30.72 (0-89503-101-9) Baywood Pub.

Cox, Gerry R. & MacDaniels, Carol. Guide to Nebraska Authors, Vol. 1. LC 98-36889. (Illus.). 272p. 1998. pap. 16.98 (1-886225-35-4, 1000) Dageforde Pub.

*Cox, Gerry R., et al. Complicated Grieving & Bereavement: Understanding & Treating People Experiencing Loss. LC 00-41426. (Death, Value & Meaning Ser.). 2000. write for info. (0-89503-213-9) Baywood Pub.

Cox, Gertrude M., jt. auth. see Cochran, William G.

Cox, Gloria A. There Is Peace, There Is Hope. 1998. pap. write for info. (1-58235-025-6) Watermrk Pr.

Cox, Goef, et al. Fifty Activities on Creativity & Problem Solving. 200p. 1993. text 229.95 (0-566-02980-4, Pub. by Gower) Ashgate Pub Co.

Cox, Gordon. A History of Music Education in England, 1872-1928. LC 93-1811. 196p. 1993. 69.95 (0-85967-978-0, Pub. by Scolar Pr) Ashgate Pub Co.

Cox, Graham, et al. The Voluntary Principles in Conservation. 180p. (C). 1991. text 129.00 (*1-85341-041-1*, Pub. by Surrey Beatty & Sons) St Mut.

Cox, Gray. Bearing Witness: Quaker Process & a Culture of Peace. LC 85-61133. 32p. (Orig.). 1985. pap. 4.00 (*0-87574-262-9*) Pendle Hill.

Cox, Greg. Assignment Eternity. (Star Trek: No. 85). 1998. per. 5.99 (*0-671-00117-5*) PB.

***Cox, Greg.** Battle On! An Unauthorized, Irreverent Look at Xena, Warrior Princess. LC 98-8451. 1998. pap. 11.95 (*0-451-45731-5*, ROC) NAL.

Cox, Greg. Black Shore, Vol. 13. (Star Trek). 1997. per. 5.99 (*0-671-56061-1*, Star Trek) PB.

— Iron Man: The Armor Trap. (Orig.). 1995. mass mkt. 6.50 (*1-57297-008-1*) Blvd Books.

— The Klingon Way: A Warriors Guide. (Star Trek Ser.). 1996. mass mkt. 5.99 (*0-671-00257-0*) PB.

— Operation A. I. M. (Iron Man Ser.: No. 2). (J). 1996. mass mkt. 5.99 (*1-57297-195-9*) Blvd Books.

— The Q-Continuum No. 1: Q-Space. (Star Trek: The Next Generation Ser.: No. 47). 271p. 1998. per. 6.50 (*0-671-01915-5*, Star Trek) PB.

— The Q Continuum No. 2: Q-Zone. (Star Trek: The Next Generation Ser.: No. 48). 270p. 1998. per. 6.50 (*0-671-01921-X*, Star Trek) PB.

— The Q Continuum No. 3: Q-Strike. (Star Trek: The Next Generation Ser.: Vol. 49). 272p. 1998. per. 6.50 (*0-671-01922-8*, Star Trek) PB.

— Star Trek Deep Space Nine. (Star Trek: No. 11). (Illus.). (J). 1995. mass mkt. 5.50 (*0-671-88114-0*) PB.

— X-Men & the Avengers. (Gamma Quest Trilogy : Vol. 1). (Illus.). 278p. 1999. mass mkt. 6.99 (*0-425-16973-1*) Blvd Books.

— X-Men & the Avengers Bk. I: Gamma Quest Trillogy, 1 vol. 224p. 1999. mass mkt. 6.99 (*0-425-17038-1*) Blvd Books.

— X-Men & the Avengers Bk. II: Gamma Quest. Vol. 2. 304p. 1999. mass mkt. 6.99 (*0-425-16989-8*) Blvd Books.

Cox, Greg & Weisskopf, T. K. Tomorrow Bites. 1995. mass mkt. 5.99 (*0-671-87691-0*) Baen Bks.

— Tomorrow Sucks: SF Vampire Stories. 304p. (Orig.). 1994. mass mkt. 4.99 (*0-671-87626-0*) Baen Bks.

***Cox, Gregory S.** St. Peter Port, Guernsey, 1680-1831: The History of an International Entrepot. LC 99-47697. (Illus.). 288p. 2000. 63.00 (*0-85115-758-0*, Suffolk Records Soc) Boydell & Brewer.

Cox, H. & Bisplinghoff, R. Design of Structures of Least Weight. LC 65-14782. (International Series of Monographs in Aeronautics & Astronautics: Vol. 8). 1965. 65.00 (*0-08-011165-3*, Pub. by Pergamon Repr) Franklin.

Cox, H. Keith. Management Issues in Application Program Maintenance. 68p. 1993. ring bd. 160.00 (*1-56909-002-5*) Info Systs Mgmt.

Cox, H. M. Cox Family in America: History & Genealogy of the Older Branches of the Family from the Appearance of Its First Representative in This Country in 1610. (Illus.). 325p. 1993. reprint ed. pap. 51.00 (*0-8328-3287-1*); reprint ed. lib. bdg. 61.00 (*0-8328-3286-3*) Higginson Bk Co.

Cox, Halley J. & Stasack, Edward. Hawaiian Petroglyphs. LC 78-111491. (Special Publications: No. 60). (Illus.). 108p. 1970. pap. 15.00 (*0-910240-09-4*) Bishop Mus.

***Cox, Harold.** Aging 2000-2001. (Annual Editions Ser.). 240p. (C). 1999. pap. 16.56 (*0-07-233950-0*) McGrw-H Hghr Educ.

Cox, Harold. Annual Editions: Aging. annuals 10th rev. ed. (Annual Ser.). (Illus.). 256p. (C). 1995. text 12.95 (*1-56134-342-0*, Dshkn McG-Hill) McGrw-H Hghr Educ.

— Annual Editions: Aging. 11th ed. 256p. (C). 1996. text 12.25 (*0-697-36328-7*) Brown & Benchmark.

***Cox, Harold.** Later Life: The Realities of Aging. 5th ed. LC 00-27203. (Illus.). 432p. 2000. pap. 57.33 (*0-13-013831-2*) P-H.

Cox, Harold E. Diamond State Trolleys: Electric Railways of Delaware. (Illus.). 88p. (Orig.). 1991. pap. 14.00 (*0-911940-49-9*) Cox.

— Early Electric Cars of Baltimore. (Illus.). 92p. (Orig.). 1979. pap. 11.00 (*0-911940-31-6*) Cox.

— Hill City Trolleys: Street Railways of Lynchburg, Virginia. (Illus.). (Orig.). 1977. pap. 11.00 (*0-911940-27-8*) Cox.

— Wyoming Valley Trolleys: Street Railways of Wilkes-Barre, Nanticoke & Pittston, Pennsylvania. (Illus.). 100p. (Orig.). 1988. pap. 15.00 (*0-911940-45-6*) Cox.

Cox, Harold E., ed. The Electric Railway Snow Plows Made by the Taunton Locomotive Manufacturing Company. (Illus.). 11p. (Orig.). 1990. reprint ed. pap. 4.00 (*0-911940-47-2*) Cox.

Cox, Harold E., jt. auth. see Hudson, Alvin W.

Cox, Harold E., jt. auth. see Hupchick, Dennis P.

Cox, Harold E., jt. auth. see Schieck, Paul J.

Cox, Harold E., jt. auth. see Steinmetz, Richard H.

Cox, Harold G. Later Life: The Realities of Aging. 4th ed. LC 95-19675. 386p. 1995. 72.00 (*0-13-409707-6*) P-H.

Cox, Harvey. Feast of Fools: A Theological Essay on Festivity & Fantasy. LC 75-75914. (William Belden Noble Lectures). 216p. 1969. 24.50 (*0-674-29525-0*) HUP.

— Fire from Heaven: Pentecostalism, Spirituality & the Reshaping of Religion in the Twenty-First Century. LC 94-18640. 368p. 1995. 24.00 (*0-201-62656-X*) Addison-Wesley.

— Fire from Heaven: The Rise of Pentecostal Spirituality & the Reshaping of Religion in the Twenty-first Century. 368p. 1996. pap. 15.00 (*0-201-48931-7*) Addison-Wesley.

— Many Mansions: A Christian's Encounter with Other Faiths. 2nd ed. LC 91-28603. 240p. 1992. pap. 13.00 (*0-8070-1213-0*) Beacon Pr.

Cox, Heather. Problems & Solutions to Accompany McQuarrie - Simon Physical Chemistry: A Molecular Approach. (Illus.). 956p. (C). 1997. pap. text 52.00 (*0-935702-43-1*) Univ Sci Bks.

Cox, Heather & McQuarrie, Carole. Problems & Solutions to Accompany Molecular Thermodynamics. (Illus.). 528p. (C). 1999. pap. text, student ed. 52.00 (*1-891389-07-6*) Univ Sci Bks.

Cox, Heather & Rickard, Garth. Carols to Sing, Clap & Play: A Companion to the Soprano Recorder Tuition Books. (Illus.). 48p. 1984. pap. 6.50 (*0-918812-36-4*) MMB Music.

— Sing, Clap, & Play the Recorder, Vol. 1. (Illus.). 1983. pap. 6.50 (*0-918812-29-1*, SE 0883) MMB Music.

— Sing, Clap, & Play the Recorder, Vol. 2. (Illus.). 1983. pap. 6.50 (*0-918812-30-5*, SE 0884) MMB Music.

Cox, Helen. Silver Flatware: An Illustrated Guide to Pieces, Manufacturers & Care. Cox, Tracy, ed. (Illus.). 133p. (Orig.). 1994. pap. 12.95 (*0-9643982-0-6*) As You Like It.

Cox, Helen C., et al. Clinical Applications of Nursing Diagnosis: Adult, Child, Women's, Psychiatric, Gerontic, & Home Health Considerations. 3rd ed. LC 96-34957. (Illus.). 800p. (C). 1997. pap. text 36.95 (*0-8036-0177-8*) Davis Co.

Cox, Henry B., jt. auth. see American Bar Association Staff.

Cox, Homer T. Henry Seton Merriman. LC 66-21746. (English Authors Ser.). 1967. pap. text 9.95 (*0-89197-992-1*); lib. bdg. 20.95 (*0-89197-785-6*) Irvington.

Cox, Howard. The Global Cigarette: Origins & Evolution of British American Tobacco, 1880-1945. LC 99-86915. (Illus.). 300p. 2000. text 60.00 (*0-19-829221-X*) OUP.

Cox, Howard, et al, eds. The Growth of Global Business. LC 93-7245. (International Business Ser.). 256p. (C). (gr. 13). 1993. pap. 74.95 (*0-415-09062-8*) Thomson Learn.

Cox, Howard H., ed. see Bach, Johann Sebastian.

Cox, I. J. & Wilfong, G. T., eds. Autonomous Robot Vehicles. (Illus.). xxvi, 462p. 1990. 113.95 (*0-387-97240-4*) Spr-Verlag.

Cox, Ignatius W. Liberty Vol. 2: Its Use & Abuse. LC 36-23289. 280p. reprint ed. pap. 86.80 (*0-7837-5581-3*, 204536900002) Bks Demand.

Cox, Ingemar J., et al, eds. Partitioning Data Sets: DIMACS Workshop, April 19-21, 1993. LC 94-25120. (DIMACS Series in Discrete Mathematics & Theoretical Computer Science: Vol. 19). 408p. 1995. text 85.00 (*0-8218-6606-0*, DIMACS/19) Am Math.

Cox, Isaac J. Louisiana-Texas Frontier. 1993. reprint ed. lib. bdg. 75.00 (*0-7812-5871-5*) Rprt Serv.

— The West Florida Controversy, 1798-1813: A Study in American Diplomacy. (BCL1 - United States Local History Ser.). 699p. 1991. reprint ed. lib. bdg. 109.00 (*0-7812-6301-8*) Rprt Serv.

Cox, Isaac J, ed. The Journeys of Rene Robert Cavelier, 2 vols., Set. LC 72-2828. (American Explorers Ser.). (Illus.). reprint ed. 105.00 (*0-404-54917-9*) AMS Pr.

Cox, J. Erte's Costumes & Sets for "Der Rosenkavalier" (C). 1990. 100.00 (*0-7855-4467-4*, Pub. by Collets) St Mut.

— Erte's Theatrical Costumes. (C). 1990. pap. 100.00 (*0-685-34366-9*, Pub. by Collets) St Mut.

Cox, J. & Tait, N. Reliability, Safety & Risk Management. (Illus.). 256p. 1991. pap. 82.95 (*0-7506-1073-5*) Buttrwrth-Heinemann.

Cox, J., jt. auth. see Cocks, G. W.

Cox, J. E. Five Years in the United States Army. 1976. 21.95 (*0-8488-0228-4*, J M C & Co) Amereon Ltd.

Cox, J. Halley & Davenport, William H. Hawaiian Sculpture. rev. ed. LC 88-10714. (Illus.). 224p. 1988. pap. 27.95 (*0-8248-1069-4*) UH Pr.

Cox, J. I. What Is a Horoscope? 166p. 1985. 15.50 (*0-86690-238-4*, C2332-014) Am Fed Astrologers.

Cox, J. Lamarr. The Sun Shines at Midnight Too. LC 95-76784. (Illus.). 315p. (Orig.). 1995. pap. 13.95 (*0-9646440-0-2*) Aureole Pub.

Cox, J. P., ed. Principle of Stellar Structure, 2 vols., Vol. 2. LC 68-26755. (Illus.). L, 1328p. (C). 1968. text 1063.00 (*0-677-01950-5*) Gordon & Breach.

***Cox, J. Randolph.** The Dime Novel Companion: A Source Book. 376p. 2000. lib. bdg. 79.50 (*0-313-25674-8*, Greenwood Pr) Greenwood.

Cox, J. Randolph. Man of Magic & Mystery: A Guide to the Work of Walter B. Gibson. LC 88-31917. (Illus.). 416p. 1989. 41.50 (*0-8108-2192-3*) Scarecrow.

— Masters of Mystery & Detective Fiction. (Magill Bibliographies Ser.). 281p. 1989. 42.00 (*0-8108-2804-9*) Scarecrow.

— TAD-Schrift: Twenty Years of Mystery Fandom in The Armchair Detective. LC 87-36810. viii, 111p. (C). 1987. reprint ed. pap. 17.00 (*0-941028-05-4*) Millefleurs.

Cox, J. Randolph, jt. auth. see Scheick, William J.

Cox, Jack. Beyond Basic Turning: Off-Center Coopered & Laminated Work. LC 93-27393. (Illus.). 256p. 1993. pap. 28.95 (*0-941936-25-2*) Linden Pub Fresno.

— Decorative Routing: Jigs & Techniques. LC 97-36114. (Illus.). 192p. 1998. pap. 25.95 (*0-941936-44-9*) Linden Pub Fresno.

***Cox, Jack F.** The 1850 Census of Georgia Slave Owners. LC 99-199887. 348p. 2000. reprint ed. pap. 27.50 (*0-8063-4837-2*, Pub. by Clearfield Co) ACCESS Pubs Network.

Cox, Jack R. Advanced Cabochon Cutting: A Gemcutter's Handbook. (Illus.). 64p. 1986. pap. 4.50 (*0-910652-14-7*) Gembooks.

— Cabochon Cutting: Gemcutter's Handbook. (Illus.). 64p. 1986. pap. 4.50 (*0-910652-12-0*) Gembooks.

Cox, Jack R., ed. see Soukup, Edward J.

Cox, Jacob D. Atlanta. (Illus.). 300p. 1987. 20.00 (*0-89029-089-X*) Morningside Bkshop.

— Sherman's Battle for Atlanta. LC 94-11264. Orig. Title: Atlanta. (Illus.). 294p. 1994. reprint ed. pap. 12.95 (*0-306-80588-X*) Da Capo.

— Sherman's March to the Sea: Hood's Tennessee Campaign & the Carolina Campaigns of 1865. LC 94-1263. Orig. Title: The March to the Sea: Franklin & Nashville. (Illus.). 289p. 1994. reprint ed. pap. 12.95 (*0-306-80587-1*) Da Capo.

Cox, James. Executive's Guide to Information Technology: Shrinking the IT Gap. LC 99-29007. 304p. 1999. text 39.95 (*0-471-35668-9*) Wiley.

— Journey Through My Years: American Autobiography. 463p. 1995. lib. bdg. 99.00 (*0-7812-8491-0*) Rprt Serv.

— Your Opinion, Please! How to Build the Best Questionnaires in the Field of Education. LC 96-27821. (1-Off Ser.). (Illus.). 112p. 1996. pap. 24.95 (*0-8039-6523-0*) Corwin Pr.

— Your Opinion, Please! How to Build the Best Questionnaires in the Field of Education. LC 96-27821. (Illus.). 112p. 1996. 55.95 (*0-8039-6522-2*) Corwin Pr.

Cox, James, ed. Corporations. 2nd rev. ed. (Quick Review Ser.). 203p. (C). 1996. pap. text 18.95 (*1-57793-004-5*) Sum & Substance.

Cox, James, et al. Low Back Pain. 5th ed. (Illus.). 645p. 1990. 100.00 (*0-683-02152-4*) Lppncott W & W.

Cox, James, jt. auth. see Goodheart, Berny.

Cox, James A. Savannah Tour of Homes & Gardens. Miller, Sheryl Krieger, ed. (Illus.). 80p. 1996. 39.95 (*0-9610106-0-6*) Historic Sav.

***Cox, James A. D.** Savannah Hidden & Public Gardens. (Illus.). 127p. 2000. 44.95 (*0-9610106-2-2*) Historic Sav.

Cox, James B. Becoming One with Christ. 170p. 1990. student ed. 8.00 (*0-9646887-1-9*); audio 41.95 (*0-9646887-2-7*) Natl Mrkting.

— How to Qualify for the Celestial Kingdom, Today. 234p. 1984. pap. text 8.95 (*0-9646887-0-0*) Natl Mrkting.

Cox, James C., et al. Patterson's German-English Dictionary for Chemists, 4E. 4th ed. LC 90-45365. 944p. 1991. 129.00 (*0-471-66991-1*) Wiley.

Cox, James D. Financial Information, Accounting & the Law: Cases & Materials. 1980. 49.00 (*0-316-15861-5*, Aspen Law & Bus) Aspen Pub.

— Moss' Radiation Oncology: Rationale, Technique & Results. 7th ed. LC 93-34732. (Illus.). 1040p. (C). (gr. 13). 1993. text 155.00 (*0-8016-6940-5*, 06940) Mosby Inc.

Cox, James D., ed. Moss' Radiation Oncology: Rationale, Technique & Results. 7th rev. ed. LC 93-34732. 1992. 40.00 (*0-8016-6906-5*) Mosby Inc.

Cox, James D., et al. Corporations, 3 vols. 1744p. 1998. ring bd. 425.00 (*0-316-65111-7*, 51117, Aspen Law & Bus) Aspen Pub.

Cox, James D., et al. Corporations. LC 97-15595. 700p. 1997. pap. text 34.95 (*1-56706-553-8*, 65538) Panel Pubs.

Cox, James D., et al. Securities Regulation: Cases & Materials. 2nd ed. LC 96-79068. 1500p. 1997. teacher ed., boxed set 62.00 (*1-56706-513-9*, 65139) Panel Pubs.

***Cox, James D., et al.** Securities Regulation: Cases & Materials, 2000 Case Supplement. 2nd ed. 130p. 2000. pap. text 20.95 (*0-7355-1324-4*, 13244) Panel Pubs.

Cox, James E. Nondestructive Testing Eddy Current, 3 pts. Pherigo, George, ed. Incl. Classroom Training Handbook. (Illus.). 177p. (C). 1997. reprint ed. pap. text 17.50 (*1-886630-17-8*); Vol. I. Basic Principles. (Illus.). 377p. (C). 1997. reprint ed. pap. text 32.25 (*1-886630-07-0*); Vol. II. Applications Vol. II rev. ed. (Illus.). (C). 1997. pap. text (*1-886630-19-4*); write for info. (*1-886630-21-6*) PH Diversified.

Cox, James F. Fundamentals of Linear Electronics: Integrated & Discrete. LC 96-13896. (Illus.). 800p. (C). 1997. mass mkt. 93.95 (*0-8273-6851-8*) Delmar.

Cox, James F., et al. Apics Dictionary. 9th ed. LC 98-231689. 104 p. 1998. write for info. (*1-55822-162-X*) Am Prod & Inventory.

Cox, James F., jt. auth. see Crawford, Karlene M.

Cox, James F., jt. auth. see Finch, Byron J.

Cox, James F., III, jt. auth. see Lockamy, Archie, III.

Cox, James F., III, jt. auth. see Spencer, Michael S.

Cox, James H. The Great Radio Soap Operas. LC 99-29045. (Illus.). 341p. 1999. boxed set 55.00 (*0-7864-0589-9*) McFarland & Co.

Cox, James L. The Impact of Christian Missions on Indigenous Cultures: The Real People & the Unreal Gospel. LC 91-3306. (Studies in the History of Missions: Vol. 4). 260p. 1991. lib. bdg. 89.95 (*0-88946-072-8*) E Mellen.

— Mississippi Almanac: The Ultimate Reference on the State of Mississippi. 560p. (Orig.). 1995. pap. 25.00 (*0-9643545-0-0*) Comp Search & Res.

Cox, James M. Low Back & Leg Pain. 5th ed. (Illus.). 20p. 1988. write for info. (*0-9616488-3-X*) Alef Bet Comns.

— Low Back Pain: Mechanisms, Diagnosis & Treatment. 6th ed. LC 98-17984. 736p. 1998. 89.00 (*0-683-30358-9*) Lppncott W & W.

— Mark Twain: The Fate of Humor. LC 66-11966. 331p. reprint ed. pap. 102.70 (*0-7837-1938-8*, 204215300001) Bks Demand.

— Neck, Upper Back, Shoulder & Arm Pain. (Illus.). 11p. (Orig.). (C). 1992. pap. text 2.00 (*0-9616488-9-9*) Alef Bet Comns.

Cox, James M., ed. Robert Frost: A Collection of Critical Essays. 1962. 12.95 (*0-13-331512-6*, Spectrum IN) Macmillan Gen Ref.

Cox, James P. Harrison on Wills & Administration for Virginia & West Virginia, 1998 Cumulative Supplement, 4 vols. 442p. 1998. pap. write for info. (*0-327-00812-1*, 6277916) LEXIS Pub.

Cox, James W. Ministers Manual: 1999 Edition. 1998. 19.95 (*0-7879-4250-2*) Jossey-Bass.

— The Minister's Manual: 2000 Edition. 448p. 1999. 21.00 (*0-7879-4546-3*) Jossey-Bass.

***Cox, James W.** Minister's Manual 2001. 448p. 2000. 21.00 (*0-7879-5002-5*) Jossey-Bass.

Cox, James W., ed. The Ministers Manual, 1988. 73rd ed. LC 25-21658. (Religion in Practice Ser.). 1997. 19.95 (*0-7879-0882-7*) Jossey-Bass.

***Cox, Jamie.** Talking Turkey: And Other Stories of North Carolina's Oddly Named Places. (Illus.). 184p. 2000. 14.95 (*1-878086-82-0*, Pub. by Down Home NC) Blair.

Cox, Jane. London's East End (Life & Traditions) LC 98-195964. (Illus.). 160p. 1998. pap. (*1-85799-956-8*) Phoenix Hse.

***Cox, Jane.** Never Been Here Before? A Genealogists' Guide to the Family Records Centre. 2nd rev. ed. LC 98-161164. 119p. 1999. pap. 10.95 (*1-873162-41-3*) PRO Pubns.

— New to Kew? 1999. pap. 12.95 (*1-873162-40-5*) PRO Pubns.

Cox, Janet, jt. auth. see L'Abate, Luciano.

Cox, Janice. Natural Beauty at Home. 1995. pap. 15.95 (*0-8050-3313-0*) H Holt & Co.

— Natural Beauty for All Seasons: 250 Simple Recipes & Gift Giving Ideas for Year-Round Beauty. (Illus.). 288p. 1995. pap. 16.95 (*0-8050-4655-0*) H Holt & Co.

— Natural Beauty from the Garden: More Than 200 Do-It-Yourself Beauty Recipes & Garden Ideas. LC 98-19042. (Natural Beauty Ser.: Bk. 3). (Illus.). 274p. 1999. pap. 16.95 (*0-8050-5781-1*, Pub. by H Holt & Co) VHPS.

Cox, Janice H., ed. Nutrition Manual for At-Risk Infants & Toddlers. rev. ed. LC 96-49613. 248p. 1997. 59.95 (*0-944496-47-4*) Precept Pr.

Cox, Jann, ed. see Wood, Eugene & Pinto, Lawrence.

***Cox, Jeanette M.** The Gospel Truth. 32p. 2000. pap. 4.95 (*1-886895-21-X*) Poetry Harbor.

— War & Peace. 32p. 1996. pap. 3.95 (*1-886895-20-1*) Poetry Harbor.

Cox, Jeff. Creating a Garden for the Senses. LC 93-3281. (Illus.). 192p. 1939. 39.95 (*1-55859-329-2*) Abbeville Pr.

— Decorating Your Garden. LC 98-40477. (Illus.). 192p. 1999. 39.95 (*0-7892-0229-8*) Abbeville Pr.

— From Vines to Wines. 3rd ed. LC 98-39860. 1999. pap. 18.95 (*1-58017-105-2*) Storey Bks.

— From Vines to Wines: The Complete Guide to Growing Grapes & Making Your Own Wine. Clarkson, Sarah M., ed. LC 88-42898. (Illus.). 288p. 1989. reprint ed. pap. 14.95 (*0-88266-528-6*, Garden Way Pub) Storey Bks.

— Landscaping with Nature: Using Nature's Designs to Plan Your Yard. LC 90-45938. 352p. 1991. 26.95 (*0-87857-911-7*, 01-357-0) Rodale Pr Inc.

— Landscaping with Nature: Using Nature's Designs to Plan Your Yard. 1996. pap. 16.95 (*0-87596-742-6*) Rodale Pr Inc.

— The Venture: A Novel for Entrepreneurs. 352p. 1998. mass mkt. 14.99 (*0-446-67407-9*, Pub. by Warner Bks) Little.

Cox, Jeff & Cox, Marilyn. Effective Evaluation & Project Evaluation Set. (Illus.). 320p. 1995. 98.00 (*0-614-04997-0*, EVPJ) Capitol Publns.

— The Perennial Garden: Color Harmonies Through the Seasons. LC 85-14192. (Illus.). 320p. 1992. pap. 16.95 (*0-87596-123-1*, 01-644-1) Rodale Pr Inc.

Cox, Jeff & Rodale Press Garden Books Editors. Your Organic Garden with Jeff Cox. LC 93-21061. (Illus.). 352p. 1994. pap. 16.95 (*0-87596-624-1*) Rodale Pr Inc.

***Cox, Jeff & Stevens, Howard.** Selling the Wheel: Choosing the Best Way to Sell for You, Your Company, Your Customers. 2001. pap. 12.00 (*0-684-85601-8*, Touchstone) S&S Trade Pap.

— Selling the Wheel: Choosing the Best Ways to Sell for You, Your Company & Your Customers. LC 99-38449. 256p. 2000. 20.50 (*0-684-85600-X*) S&S Trade.

Cox, Jeff, jt. auth. see Byham, William C.

Cox, Jeff, jt. auth. see Goldratt, Eliyahu M.

Cox, Jeff, ed. see Byham, William C.

Cox, Jeffrey & Reynolds, Larry, eds. New Historical Literary Study: Essays on Reproducing Texts, Representing History. (Illus.). 344p. (C). 1993. text 57.50 (*0-691-06990-5*, Pub. by Princeton U Pr) Cal Prin Full Svc.

Cox, Jeffrey & Stromquist, Shelton, eds. Contesting the Master Narrative: Essays in Social History. LC 98-24439. 296p. 1998. text 32.95 (*0-87745-624-0*) U of Iowa Pr.

Cox, Jeffrey N. Poetry & Politics in the Cockney School: Keats, Shelley, Hunt & Their Circle. LC 98-12838. (Studies in Romanticism: No. 31). (Illus.). 250p. (C). 1999. text 59.95 (*0-521-63100-9*) Cambridge U Pr.

Cox, Jeffrey N., ed. Seven Gothic Dramas, 1789-1825. LC 91-31262. 425p. (C). 1994. pap. text 24.95 (*0-8214-1065-2*) Ohio U Pr.

Cox, Jewel R. A Guide to Peer Counseling. LC 97-45908. 1998. pap. 30.00 (*0-7657-0153-7*) Aronson.

Cox, Jim. The Concise Guide to Economics. 2nd ed. LC 96-70958. 167p. 1997. pap. 10.00 (*1-57087-292-9*) Prof Pr NC.

— Electric Motors in the Home Workshop: A Practical Guide to Methods of Utilising Readily Available Electric Motors in Typical Small Workshop Applications. (Workshop Practice Ser.: No. 24). (Illus.). 133p. (Orig.). 1996. pap. 19.95 (*1-85486-133-6*, Pub. by Nexus Special Interests) Trans-Atl Phila.

***Cox, Jim.** The Methodists at Middletown, 1800-2000: A Bicentennial History of Middletown United Methodist Church. Strode, William H., ed. LC 99-73603. (Illus.). 214p. 1999. write for info. (*1-56469-063-6*) Harmony Hse Pub.

C

An Asterisk (*) at the beginning of an entry indicates that the title is appearing for the first time.

Cox, John. Cambridge Pocket Star Atlas. LC 96-226102. (Illus.). 48p. (C). 1996. pap. 7.95 (*0-521-58992-4*) Cambridge U Pr.

— Cambridge Pocket Star Finder: A Month-by-Month Guide to the Night Sky. (Illus.). 56p. (C). 1996. pap. 7.95 (*0-521-58993-2*) Cambridge U Pr.

— Keyguide to Information Sources in Online & CD-ROM Database Searching. (Illus.). 272p. 1991. text 110.00 (*0-7201-2093-4*) Continuum.

— Overkill: Weapons of the Nuclear Age. LC 77-27663. (Illus.). (YA). (gr. 7 up). 1978. lib. bdg. 12.89 (*0-690-03857-7*) HarpC Child Bks.

Cox, John & Kaston, David. A New History of Early English Drama. LC 96-29670. (Illus.). 384p. (C). 1997. 25.00 (*0-231-10243-7*) Col U Pr.

Cox, John, Jr., jt. auth. see Cocks, George W.

Cox, John, jt. auth. see Monkhouse, Richard.

Cox, John, Jr., ed. see Cherry, Lina V.

Cox, John B. & American Society of Association Executives Staff. Professional Practices in Association Management. LC 98-106191. vi, 352 p. 1997. 49.95 (*0-88034-113-0*) Am Soc Assn Execs.

Cox, John C. & Cox, Pamela. Best Seat in the House - DFW. rev. ed. (Illus.). 36p. (C). pap. text 8.95 (*1-883949-00-9*) Best Seat Hse.

Cox, John C. & Rubinstein, Mark. Options Markets. (Illus.). 432p. (C). 1985. 66.00 (*0-13-638205-3*, Pub. by P-H) S&S Trade.

Cox, John D. Shakespeare & the Dramaturgy of Power. LC 88-29311. 300p. reprint ed. pap. 93.00 (*0-608-06436-X*, 206664900008) Bks Demand.

***Cox, John D.** Weather for Dummies. (For Dummies (Lifestyles) Ser.). (Illus.). 384p. 2000. pap. 19.99 (*0-7645-5243-0*) IDG Bks.

Cox, John D. & Kastan, David S. A New History of Early English Drama. LC 96-29670. 1997. 52.00 (*0-231-10242-9*) Col U Pr.

Cox, John F., ed. see Shakespeare, William.

Cox, John H. Cox Genealogy: Some Materials Towards a History of the Early Cox Families of New England. (Illus.). 143p. 1995. reprint ed. pap. 25.00 (*0-8328-4904-9*); reprint ed. lib. bdg. 35.00 (*0-8328-4903-0*) Higginson Bk Co.

Cox, John Harrington. Folk-Songs Mainly from West Virginia. Herzog, George & Halpert, Herbert, eds. LC 76-58548. (Music Reprint Ser.). 1977. reprint ed. lib. bdg. 32.50 (*0-306-70786-1*) Da Capo.

Cox, John S., jt. auth. see Theoharis, Athan G.

***Cox, Johnny D.** Nomadic Nature: A New Gate. (Illus.). 90p. (YA). 2000. pap. 19.95 (*0-9679972-0-8*) Servano.

Cox-Johnson, Phillip J. Hosanna! We Cry. 1.50 (*0-687-06197-0*) Abingdon.

Cox, Joseph A., et al. New York Civil Practice: SCPA, 6 vols. 1970. ring bd. 1380.00 (*0-8205-1808-5*) Bender.

Cox, Joseph T. The Written Wars: American War Prose Through the Civil War. LC 95-32374. xviii, 282p. (C). 1996. lib. bdg. 39.50 (*0-208-02344-5*, Archon Bks) Shoe String.

Cox, Josephine. Born to Serve. large type ed. 528p. 32.99 (*0-7089-8860-1*) Ulverscroft.

— The Devil You Know. large type ed. 464p. 1997. 27.99 (*0-7089-8931-4*) Ulverscroft.

***Cox, Josephine.** The Gilded Cage. abr. ed. 1999. pap. 16.85 (*1-84032-137-7*, Pub. by HOD2) Ulverscroft.

— The Gilded Cage. large type ed. 424p. 2000. write for info. (*0-7089-9141-6*) Ulverscroft.

Cox, Josephine. Her Father's Sins. large type ed. 528p. 1989. 17.95 (*0-7089-2036-5*) Ulverscroft.

— A Little Badness. large type ed. 560p. 1997. 27.99 (*0-7089-8888-1*) Ulverscroft.

— Living a Lie. large type ed. (Charnwood Large Print Ser.). 528p. 1997. 27.99 (*0-7089-8905-5*, Charnwood) Ulverscroft.

***Cox, Josephine.** Love Me or Leave Me. large type ed. 400p. 1999. 31.99 (*0-7089-9077-0*) Ulverscroft.

Cox, Josephine. More Than Riches. large type ed. 544p. 1997. 27.99 (*0-7089-8865-2*) Ulverscroft.

— Nobody's Darling. large type ed. 640p. 32.99 (*0-7089-8827-X*) Ulverscroft.

— A Time for Us. large type ed. (Charnwood Large Print Ser.). 496p. 1997. 27.99 (*0-7089-8960-8*, Charnwood) Ulverscroft.

— Vagabonds. large type ed. 608p. 1994. 27.99 (*0-7089-3073-5*) Ulverscroft.

Cox, Joyce. One-Day Quick Course in Microsoft Windows 98: Education - Training Edition. Dudley, Christina, ed. LC 98-66726. (One-Day Quick Course). (Illus.). 128p. 1998. pap. text 10.95 (*1-879399-90-3*) Online Training.

***Cox, Joyce.** Quick Course in Creating a Web Site Using Microsoft FrontPage 2000: Education/Training Edition. LC 99-70322. (Quick Course Ser.). 160p. 1999. pap. text 15.95 (*1-58278-008-0*) Online Training.

— Quick Course in Microsoft Access 2000: Education/Training Edition. LC 99-70319. (Quick Course Ser.). 1999. pap. text 14.95 (*1-58278-005-6*) Online Training.

Cox, Joyce. Quick Course in Microsoft Excel 2000: Education/Training Edition. LC 99-70317. (Quick Course Ser.). 1999. pap. text 15.95 (*1-58278-003-X*) Online Training.

***Cox, Joyce.** Quick Course in Microsoft Outlook 2000: Education/Training Edition. LC 99-70321. (Quick Course Ser.). 1999. pap. text 15.95 (*1-58278-006-4*) Online Training.

— Quick Course in Microsoft PowerPoint 2000: Education/Training Edition. LC 99-70318. (Quick Course Ser.). (Illus.). 176p. 1999. pap. text 15.95 (*1-58278-004-8*) Online Training.

— Quick Course in Microsoft Publisher 2000: Education/Training Edition. LC 99-70320. (Quick Course Ser.). 178p. 1999. pap. text 15.95 (*1-58278-007-2*) Online Training.

Cox, Joyce. Quick Course in Microsoft Windows 98: Education/Training Edition. Dudley, Christina, ed. (Quick Course Ser.). (Illus.). 208p. 1998. pap. text 15.95 (*1-879399-81-4*) Online Training.

***Cox, Joyce.** Quick Course in Microsoft Word 2000: Education/Training Edition. LC 99-70316. (Quick Course Ser.). 1999. pap. text 15.95 (*1-58278-002-1*) Online Training.

— Quick Course in the Internet Using Internet Explorer 5: Education/Training Edition. LC 99-70323. (Quick Course Ser.). 1999. pap. text 15.95 (*1-879399-91-1*) Online Training.

Cox, Joyce. Quick Course in the Internet Using Netscape Navigator, Versions 2 & 3: Education/Training Edition. LC 96-68408. (Quick Course Ser.). (Illus.). 138p. 1996. pap. text 14.95 (*1-879399-67-9*) Online Training.

— Quick Course in Windows 95: Education/Training Edition. LC 95-71904. (Quick Course Ser.). (Illus.). 172p. 1995. pap. text 14.95 (*1-879399-34-2*) Online Training.

***Cox, Joyce.** Workbook for Quick Course in Microsoft Windows 98: Education - Training Edition. Dudley, Christina, ed. (Workbook Quick Course). (Illus.). 60p. 1998. pap. text 12.95 (*1-879399-88-1*) Online Training.

Cox, Joyce & Cox, Ted. Quick Course in Microsoft Works 3 for Windows: Education/Training Edition. LC 93-86356. (Quick Course Ser.). (Illus.). 170p. 1995. pap. text 14.95 (*1-879399-42-3*) Online Training.

Cox, Joyce & Dudley, Christina. Quick Course in Microsoft Outlook 98: Education/Training Edition. LC 98-163922. (Quick Course Ser.). (Illus.). 160p. 1998. pap. text 14.95 (*1-879399-80-6*) Online Training.

Cox, Joyce & Dudley, Christina/. Quick Course in Word 7 for Windows 95: Education/Training Edition. LC 96-67884. (Quick Course Ser.). (Illus.). 156p. 1996. pap. text 14.95 (*1-879399-50-4*) Online Training.

Cox, Joyce & Dudley, Nathan. Quick Course in Access 7 for Windows 95: Education/Training Edition. LC 96-70855. (Quick Course Ser.). (Illus.). 172p. (Orig.). 1996. pap. text 14.95 (*1-879399-52-0*) Online Training.

Cox, Joyce & Elison, Mike. Quick Course in Access 2 for Windows: Education/Training Edition. LC 93-84869. (Quick Course Ser.). (Illus.). 172p. 1994. pap. text 14.95 (*1-879399-32-6*) Online Training.

Cox, Joyce & Kervran, Patrick. Quick Course in Windows for Workgroups: Education/Training Edition. LC 92-62065. (Quick Course Ser.). (Illus.). 151p. 1992. pap. text 14.95 (*1-879399-22-9*) Online Training.

Cox, Joyce & Lambert, Steve. Quick Course in Word 6 for Windows: Education/Training Edition. LC 93-86381. (Quick Course Ser.). (Illus.). 164p. (Orig.). 1993. pap. text 14.95 (*1-879399-27-X*) Online Training.

Cox, Joyce & Urban, Polly. Quick Course in Microsoft Office for Windows Version 4.3: Education/Training Edition. LC 95-68957. (Quick Course Ser.). (Illus.). 268p. 1995. pap. text 24.95 (*1-879399-39-3*) Online Training.

— Quick Course in Microsoft Office for Windows 95 & Windows NT: Education/Training Edition. LC 95-72653. (Quick Course Ser.). (Illus.). 284p. 1996. pap. text 24.95 (*1-879399-54-7*) Online Training.

— Quick Course in PowerPoint 4 for Windows: Education/Training Edition. LC 94-66495. (Quick Course Ser.). (Illus.). 164p. (Orig.). 1994. pap. text 14.95 (*1-879399-33-4*) Online Training.

Cox, Joyce, et al. Quick Course in Excel 5 for Windows: Education/Training Edition. LC 93-86431. (Quick Course Ser.). (Illus.). 164p. 1994. pap. text 14.95 (*1-879399-28-8*) Online Training.

— Quick Course in Excel 7 for Windows 95: Education/Training Edition. LC 96-67883. (Quick Course Ser.). (Illus.). 163p. (Orig.). 1996. pap. text 14.95 (*1-879399-51-2*) Online Training.

Cox, Joyce, et al. Quick Course in Microsoft Office 97: Education/Training Edition. LC 96-71317. (Quick Course Ser.). (Illus.). 300p. (C). 1997. pap. text 24.95 (*1-879399-69-5*) Online Training.

— Quick Course in Microsoft Office 2000: Education/Training Edition. LC 99-70315. (Quick Course Ser.). (Illus.). 416p. 1999. pap. text 25.95 (*1-58278-001-3*) Online Training.

Cox, Joyce, et al. Quick Course in Windows NT Workstation 4: Education/Training Edition. LC 97-69952. (Quick Course Ser.). (Illus.). 204p. 1997. pap. text 16.95 (*1-879399-64-4*) Online Training.

Cox, Joyce, jt. auth. see Urban, Polly.

Cox, Joyce K. & Dudley, Christina. A Quick Course in Word 97: Education/Training Edition. LC 97-66249. (Quick Course Ser.). 164p. 1997. pap. text 14.95 (*1-879399-70-9*) Online Training.

Cox, Joyce K. & Dudley, Nathan. Quick Course in Access 97: Education/Training Edition. LC 97-66247. (Quick Course Ser.). (Illus.). 172p. 1997. pap. text 14.95 (*1-879399-73-3*) Online Training.

Cox, Joyce K. & Urban, Polly. Quick Course in PowerPoint 97: Education/Training Edition. LC 97-66248. (Quick Course Ser.). (Illus.). 163p. 1997. pap. text 14.95 (*1-879399-72-5*) Online Training.

Cox, Joyce K., et al. Quick Course in Excel 97: Education/Training Edition. LC 96-72484. (Quick Course). (Illus.). 170p. (Orig.). 1997. pap. text 14.95 (*1-879399-71-7*) Online Training.

— Quick Course in the Internet Using Internet Explorer 4: Education/Training Edition. LC 97-69953. (Quick Course Ser.). (Illus.). 168p. 1997. pap. text 14.95 (*1-879399-68-7*) Online Training.

Cox, Judith. Mud on My Feet. 140p. 1992. pap. 9.95 (*0-9634536-0-2*, TXU 367-733) Healing Design.

— The Wellness Tree. LC 95-76782. (Illus.). 32p. (J). (gr. k-4). 1995. 19.95 (*1-878044-29-X*) Mayhaven Pub.

— The Wellness Tree Activity Book. (Illus.). 32p. (Orig.). (J). (gr. k-4). 1995. pap. 2.95 (*1-878044-35-4*) Mayhaven Pub.

***Cox, Judy.** Mean, Mean Maureen Green. LC 99-11935. (Illus.). 80p. (J). (gr. 1-5). 1999. 15.95 (*0-8234-1502-3*) Holiday.

Cox, Judy. My Family Plays Music. LC 96-35009. (Illus.). (J). 2001. lib. bdg. write for info. (*0-8234-1285-7*) Holiday.

— Now We Can Have a Wedding! LC 97-11103. (Illus.). 32p. (J). (ps-3). 1998. lib. bdg. 15.95 (*0-8234-1342-X*) Holiday.

— Rabbit Pirates: A Tale of the Spinach Main. LC 98-17481. 32p. (J). (ps-3). 1999. 16.00 (*0-15-201832-8*, Harcourt Child Bks) Harcourt.

***Cox, Judy.** Third Grade Pet. (Illus.). 112p. (J). 2000. pap. 4.50 (*0-440-41628-0*, Yearling) BDD Bks Young Read.

Cox, Judy. Third Grade Pet. LC 98-6896. (Illus.). 80p. (J). (gr. k-5). 1998. 15.95 (*0-8234-1379-9*) Holiday.

— Weird Stories from the Lonesome Cafe. LC 98-56016. (Illus.). 80p. (J). (gr. 2-5). 2000. 15.00 (*0-15-202134-5*, Harcourt Child Bks) Harcourt.

— The West Texas Chili Monster. LC 97-34303. (Illus.). 32p. (J). (gr. 1-4). 1998. 15.95 (*0-8167-4546-3*) BrdgeWater.

Cox, Julia. The Adventures of Boo, Vol. 2: Circus. (Illus.). 32p. (J). 1992. write for info. (*0-9627586-2-0*) Mango Entrps.

Cox, Julie. The Adventures of Boo: The Journey Begins. LC 90-62757. (Illus.). 32p. (J). 1990. write for info. (*0-9627586-0-4*); audio. write for info. (*0-9627586-1-2*) Mango Entrps.

Cox, June. Comprehensive Programming: Handbook for Planning, Developing, Evaluating Educational Programs for Specially-Gifted. 1989. pap. 14.99 (*0-89824-506-0*) Trillium Pr.

Cox, June, et al. Educating Able Learners: Programs & Promising Practices. LC 85-7405. (Illus.). 261p. 1985. pap. 13.95 (*0-292-70387-2*) U of Tex Pr.

Cox, Karen Q. Just Dried Tomatoes! (Illus.). 109p. 1989. spiral bd. 9.95 (*1-886501-00-9*) Tomato Press.

— A Little Bit(e) of Dried Tomatoes. (Illus.). 13p. (Orig.). 1991. pap. text 3.00 (*1-886501-01-7*) Tomato Press.

***Cox, Kathleen M.** Vastu Living: Creating a Home for the Soul. (Illus.). 272p. 2000. pap. 16.95 (*1-56924-644-0*, Pub. by Marlowe & Co) Publishers Group.

Cox, Kathryn. Pocket Guide to Wild Edible & Medicinal Plants. (Illus.). 80p. (Orig.). 1996. spiral bd. 12.95 (*0-9651749-0-5*) Motherlove Herbal.

Cox, Kay. Being a Health Unit Coordinator. 2nd ed. LC 83-15824. (Illus.). 368p. (C). 1984. teacher ed. 9.95 (*0-89303-329-4*) P-H.

Cox, Kay & Hospital Research & Educational Trust Staff. Being a Health Unit Coordinator. 4th ed. LC 97-34711. 512p. 1998. pap. text 51.00 (*0-8359-5158-8*) P-H.

Cox, Kay, ed. see McBrien, Marianne.

Cox, Kay, ed. see Virgilio, Mary.

Cox, Keith K., jt. auth. see Kotler, Philip.

Cox, Keith K., jt. ed. see Higginbotham, James B.

Cox, Keller & Frazier, Raymond L. Buck: A Tennessee Boy in Korea. 1982. 9.95 (*0-9610818-0-5*); pap. 4.95 (*0-9610818-1-3*) Chogie Pubs.

***Cox, Ken.** Doctor & Patient: Exploring Clinical Thinking. 288p. 1999. pap. 29.95 (*0-86840-505-1*, Pub. by NSW U Pr) Intl Spec Bk.

Cox, Kenneth. Rhododendrons, 6 vols. LC 98-18555. (Care Manual Ser.). (Illus.). 128p. 1998. 19.95 (*1-57145-620-1*, Laurel Glen Pub) Advantage Pubs.

Cox, Kenneth E., jt. auth. see Cox, Peter A.

Cox, Kenyon. Classic Point of View: Six Lectures on Painting. LC 68-22907. (Essay Index Reprint Ser.). 1977. 20.95 (*0-8369-0345-5*) Ayer.

— Old Masters & New. LC 74-90627. (Essay Index Reprint Ser.). 1977. 23.95 (*0-8369-1403-1*) Ayer.

— Painters & Sculptors. LC 70-105006. (Essay Index Reprint Ser.). 1977. 23.95 (*0-8369-1458-9*) Ayer.

— What Is Painting? "Winslow Homer" & Other Essays. (Classical America Series in Art & Architecture). (Illus.). 1988. pap. 12.50 (*0-393-30545-7*) Norton.

Cox, Kerry, jt. auth. see Wolff, Jurgen.

Cox, Kevin. Hooked On Earth Science! 101 Ready-to-Use Crossword Puzzles Featuring Vocabulary, Concepts & Fun of Earth Science, Grades 5-12. LC 96-19279. 228p. 1996. pap. text 28.95 (*0-87628-416-0*) Ctr Appl Res.

— Hooked on Earth Science! 101 Ready-to-Use Crossword Puzzles Featuring Vocabulary, Concepts & Fun Of Earth Science, Grades 5-12. LC 96-19279. 228p. 1996. pap. 28.50 (*0-87628-420-9*) Ctr Appl Res.

Cox, Kevin & Jones, William. The Administrator's Guide to Microsoft SQL Server 6.5. LC 97-4755. (Illus.). 469p. (Orig.). 1997. pap. 39.95 (*1-882419-53-7*) News Four-Hund.

Cox, Kevin R. Spaces of Globalization: Reasserting the Power of the Local. LC 96-30010. (Perspectives on Economic Change Ser.). 292p. 1997. lib. bdg. 44.95 (*1-57230-196-1*, 0196) Guilford Pubns.

Cox, Kevin R., ed. Spaces of Globalization: Reasserting the Power of the Local. LC 96-30010. (Perspectives on Economic Change Ser.). 292p. 1997. pap. text 23.95 (*1-57230-199-6*, 0199) Guilford Pubns.

Cox, Kevin R. & Johnston, R. J., eds. Conflict, Politics & the Urban Scene. LC 86-672522. (Illus.). 271p. reprint ed. pap. 84.10 (*0-8357-6072-3*, 203448200090) Bks Demand.

Cox, Kris, jt. auth. see Cox, Mike.

Cox, Kristoffer. Gen X & God: A Gen X Perspective. LC 98-90387. 134p. 1998. pap. 10.99 (*0-9664413-0-3*) Tekna Bks.

Cox, Kurt H. & Langellier, John P. Longknives: The U. S. Cavalry & Other Mounted Forces, 1845-1942. (GI: The Illustrated History of the American Soldier, His Uniform, & His Equipment Ser.). (Illus.). 80p. 1996. pap. 12.95 (*1-85367-233-5*, Pub. by Greenhill Bks) Stackpole.

Cox, Kurt Hamilton. Custer & His Commands: From West Point to Little Bighorn. LC 98-49438. (G. I. Ser.). 1999. pap. 13.95 (*1-85367-358-7*) Stackpole.

— Longknives: The U.S. Cavalry & Other Mounted Forces, 1845-1942. LC 99-20252. (G.I. Ser.). (Illus.). 84p. 1999. 19.95 (*0-7910-5367-9*) Chelsea Hse.

Cox, L. A. New Risks: Issues & Management. Ricci, Paolo F., ed. LC 90-7162. (Advances in Risk Analysis Ser.: Vol. 6). (Illus.). 728p. (C). 1990. text 210.00 (*0-306-43537-3*, Kluwer Plenum) Kluwer Academic.

Cox, L. S. Cox: The Cox Families of Holderness. 235p. 1991. reprint ed. pap. 37.00 (*0-8328-2216-7*); reprint ed. lib. bdg. 47.00 (*0-8328-2215-9*) Higginson Bk Co.

— New Hampshire Branch of the Pease Family, Being the Results of a Search for the Ancestors of Patty Pease Who Married John Pivkering of Barnstead, N. H. 64p. 1993. reprint ed. pap. 13.00 (*0-8328-3775-X*); reprint ed. lib. bdg. 23.00 (*0-8328-3774-1*) Higginson Bk Co.

Cox, Larry. Book of Tucson Firsts, 1. LC 98-96671. 1998. pap. text 14.95 (*0-9667658-0-X*) Javalina Pr.

Cox, LaWanda. Lincoln & Black Freedom: A Study in Presidential Leadership. LC 84-16445. (Blacks in the New World Ser.). 272p. 1985. reprint ed. pap. 10.95 (*0-252-01173-2*) U of Ill Pr.

— Lincoln & Black Freedom: A Study in Presidential Leadership. rev. ed. LC 93-37859. 270p. (C). 1994. reprint ed. pap. 12.95 (*0-87249-997-9*) U of SC Pr.

Cox, Leona D. Secret of the 2 Bar 4 Ranch. LC 93-81079. (Illus.). 153p. (J). (gr. 4-12). 1994. pap. 11.95 (*0-9627680-6-5*) Inkwell CA.

— Single Woman Homesteader. rev. ed. LC 90-89552. (Illus.). 214p. 1991. 21.95 (*0-9627680-7-3*) Inkwell CA.

Cox, Leonard. Arte or Crafte of Rhethoryke. Carpenter, Frederic I., ed. LC 73-136371. (Chicago. University. English Studies: No. 5). reprint ed. 29.50 (*0-404-50265-2*) AMS Pr.

Cox, Linda. Guided Meditation Scripts, Vol. I. 74p. (Orig.). 1997. pap., spiral bd. 15.00 (*1-890272-00-0*) Purple Pr.

Cox, Lindsay. Kotahitanga: The Search for Maori Political Unity. (Illus.). 250p. 1994. text 38.00 (*0-19-558280-2*) OUP.

Cox, Lloyd M. In the Days When the Rivers Ran Backwards. 64p. 1995. pap. 12.75 (*0-9646353-3-X*) L M Cox.

Cox, Loren, et al. Powering Asia: Is Gas the Answer?: 14th Annual Pacific Rim Workshop. LC 98-191720. iii, 23 p. 1998. 8.00 (*0-89843-231-6*) The Aspen Inst.

Cox, Louis & Cox, Fran. A Conscious Life: Cultivating the Seven Qualities of Authentic Adulthood. (Illus.). 225p. 1996. pap. 12.95 (*0-943233-76-3*) Conari Press.

***Cox, Lynn & Lubbers, Terry.** Make It Take It! Creating Movement Challenge Kits for Play at Home or School. LC 99-64342. (Illus.). 159p. 2000. pap. 19.99 (*0-9664413-4-6*) Tekna Bks.

Cox, Lynne. Sea Zoo: Sea Creatures. (Illus.). 20p. (J). (ps-6). 1997. 5.95 (*1-891258-04-4*, LCPSZ) L Cox Pubns.

— The Singing Rainbow. (Illus.). 16p. (J). (ps-6). 1996. 8.00 (*1-891258-01-X*, LCP2) L Cox Pubns.

Cox, M. G. & Hammarling, S., eds. Reliable Numerical Computation. (Illus.). 368p. 1991. 75.00 (*0-19-853564-3*) OUP.

Cox, M. G., jt. auth. see Mason, J. C.

Cox, M. G., jt. ed. see Mason, J. C.

Cox, M. Jerel, et al. A Photographic Guide to Snakes & Other Reptiles of Thailand, Singapore & Peninsular Malaysia. (Photographic Wildlife Pocket Guide Ser.). (Illus.). 144p. 1998. pap. 15.95 (*0-88359-043-3*, Pub. by R Curtis Pubng) Chelsea Green Pub.

***Cox, M. L.** Advances in Chrysomelidae Biology. (Illus.). 671p. 1999. 160.00 (*90-5782-028-5*, Pub. by Backhuys Pubs) Balogh.

Cox, M. L., jt. ed. see Jolivet, P. H.

Cox, Madison. Gardening Is in the Details. 1995. 45.00 (*0-8050-4615-1*) H Holt & Co.

Cox, Madison, ed. Artists' Gardens: From Claude Monet to Jennifer Bartlett. LC 93-7307. (Illus.). 208p. 1993. 49.50 (*0-8109-1931-1*, Pub. by Abrams) Time Warner.

Cox, Madison, jt. auth. see Berge, Pierre.

Cox, Marcelion. Second Class Suburbanites: White Blue-Collar Suburbs & Black White-Collar Suburbs, No. 739. 1975. 6.00 (*0-686-20337-2*, Sage Prdcls Pr) Sage.

Cox, Margie & Randolph, Jewell, eds. 1880 McDowell County, North Carolina Census. LC 96-229719. 197p. (Orig.). (C). 1996. lib. bdg. write for info. (*1-888549-02-5*) Appalachan Pr.

Cox, Marilyn, jt. auth. see Cox, Jeff.

Cox, Mark. Smoulder. 96p. 1989. pap. 9.95 (*0-87923-814-3*) Godine.

Cox, Mark. Thirty-Seven Years from the Stone. LC 97-45365. (Pitt Poetry Ser.). 58p. 1998. pap. 12.95 (*0-8229-5669-1*); text 25.00 (*0-8229-4065-5*) U of Pittsburgh Pr.

Cox, Mark, jt. auth. see Richmond, Alan.

Cox, Martha J., et al, eds. Foster Care: Current Issues, Policies & Practices. LC 84-20482. (Child & Family Policy Ser.: Vol. 4). 264p. (C). 1985. text 73.25 (*0-89391-228-X*) Ablx Pub.

Cox, Martha J. & Brooks-Gunn, Jeanne, eds. Conflict & Cohesion in Families: Causes & Consequences. LC 98-28381. (Advances in Family Research Ser.). 372p. 1999. 79.95 (*0-8058-2410-3*) L Erlbaum Assocs.

Cox, Marvel Kohlhof, jt. auth. see Damon, Lisa M.

***Cox, Marvell.** The Hurried Household Cookbook. deluxe ed. 2000. write for info. (*0-9679691-0-7*) Franklin Enter.

An Asterisk (*) at the beginning of an entry indicates that the title is appearing for the first time.

***Cox, Mary, ed.** Artist's & Graphic Designer's Market. 720p. 2000. pap. 24.99 (*0-89879-979-1*) F & W Pubns Inc.

— 2000 Artist's & Graphic Designer's Market: 2,500 Places to Sell Your Art & Design. LC 95-640723. (Illus.). 720p. 1999. pap. 24.99 (*0-89879-913-9*, 10611, Wrtrs Digest Bks) F & W Pubns Inc.

Cox, Mary, ed. see Rosemond, John.

Cox, Mary-Lea & Kruger, Eric J. The Politics & Economics of the Internet & Cyberspace. 192p. 1998. 39.00 (*1-883223-13-X*) Pacific NY.

Cox, Maureen. Blast Off with Music Theory! LC 99-189126. 72 p. 1998. write for info. (*1-56939-084-3*) FJH Music Co Inc.

— The Child's Point of View. 2nd ed. LC 91-6691. 256p. 1991. reprint ed. pap. text 24.00 (*0-89862-471-1*) Guilford Pubns.

Cox, Maureen, jt. ed. see Cooke, Grant.

Cox, Maureen V. Children's Drawings of the Human Figure. Bryant, Peter et al, eds. (Essays in Developmental Psychology Ser.). 168p. 1993. 39.95 (*0-86377-268-4*) L Erlbaum Assocs.

— Drawings of People by the Under-5s. LC 97-126098. 160p. 1996. pap. 24.95 (*0-7507-0584-1*, Falmer Pr) Taylor & Francis.

Cox, Meg. The Heart of a Family: Searching America for New Traditions That Fulfill Us. LC 98-9585. 320p. 1998. 24.95 (*0-679-44863-2*) Random.

Cox, Melissa, ed. see Wilson, Archie W.

Cox, Merel J. The Snakes of Thailand & Their Husbandry. 564p. (C). 1991. 82.50 (*0-89464-437-8*) Krieger.

Cox, Meridith B. The Court System. 2nd ed. (Introduction to the Law, Legal System & Legal Liability Ser.: Vol. II). (Illus.). (C). 1988. pap. text 35.00 (*0-912665-19-X*) BusinessWatch.

— The Legal System. 2nd ed. (Introduction to the Law, Legal System & Legal Liability Ser.: Vol. I). (Illus.). (C). 1988. pap. text 35.00 (*0-912665-18-1*) BusinessWatch.

— Monitoring Patient Care: Are Your Patients Safe? (Risk Management Ser.). (Orig.). (C). 1999. pap. text 30.00 (*0-912665-23-8*) BusinessWatch.

— Presenting Evidence in Court: It's the Way You Do It That Counts. (Risk Management Ser.). (Illus.). (C). 1999. pap. text 25.00 (*0-912665-27-0*) BusinessWatch.

— Risk Management for the Department Head: An Integrated Approach. (Illus.). 200p. (Orig.). (C). 1991. spiral bd. 55.00 (*0-912665-37-8*); ring bd. 75.00 (*0-912665-30-0*) BusinessWatch.

— Risks in Labor & Delivery & Pediatrics. (Risk Management Ser.). (C). 1997. pap. text, wbk. ed. 20.00 (*0-912665-25-4*) BusinessWatch.

— Risks in O. R. & Post-Op Care. (Risk Management Ser.). (Orig.). (C). 1997. pap. text, wbk. ed. 25.00 (*0-912665-26-2*) BusinessWatch.

— Safety & Equipment Risks: Do You Prevent Injuries? (Orig.). (C). 1991. pap. text 55.00 (*0-912665-24-6*) BusinessWatch.

— Special Report on Medical Records. (Risk Management Ser.). 1999. pap. 50.00 (*0-912665-29-7*) BusinessWatch.

— Standards of Care for the Health Care Professional. (Legal Aspects of Medical & Health Records Ser.). (Illus.). xiii, 130p. (C). 1984. pap. 40.00 (*0-912665-05-X*) BusinessWatch.

— Standards of Care for the Health Care Professional. 2nd ed. (Illus.). xiii, 130p. 1999. spiral bd. 65.00 (*0-912665-53-X*) BusinessWatch.

Cox, Merry L. Death by Bookbag: A Collection of Middle School Stories. 64p. (J). (gr. 6 up). 1998. pap. 7.00 (*1-884416-27-6*) A Press.

***Cox, Michael.** Gluten-Free: More Than 100 Delicious Recipes Your Family Will Love. LC 00-24511. (Illus.). 2000. pap. 18.00 (*0-684-87251-X*, Fireside) S&S Trade Pap.

— Oxford Book of Twentieth-Century Ghost Stories. 446p. 1997. pap. 12.95 (*0-19-288038-1*) OUP.

Cox, Michael. Twelve Tales of the Supernatural. LC 98-129986. (Oxford Twelves). 198p. 1997. pap. 9.95 (*0-19-288027-6*) OUP.

— U. S. Foreign Policy after the Cold War: Superpower Without a Mission? (Chatham House Papers). 160p. 1995. 44.95 (*1-85567-220-0*) Bks Intl VA.

— U. S. Foreign Policy after the Cold War: Superpower Without a Mission? LC 97-120950. (Chatham House Papers). 160p. 1995. pap. 16.95 (*1-85567-221-9*, Pub. by Cassell) LPC InBook.

Cox, Michael, ed. Beyond the Cold War: Superpowers at the Crossroads. (Exxon Education Foundation Series on Rhetoric & Political Discourse: Vol. 14). 258p. (C). 1990. pap. text 26.00 (*0-8191-7865-9*); lib. bdg. 46.00 (*0-8191-7864-0*) U Pr of Amer.

— Bone to His Bone: The Stoneground Ghost Tales of E. G. Swain. large type ed. (Lythway Ser.). 248p. 1990. 19.95 (*0-7451-1203-X*, G K Hall Lrg Type) Mac Lib Ref.

— Exploring Scottish History: Resource Centers for Local & National History. 120p. 1991. pap. write for info. (*0-08-041214-9*, Pub. by Aberdeen U Pr) Macmillan.

— The Oxford Book of Spy Stories. 376p. (C). 1996. 30.00 (*0-19-214242-9*) OUP.

— The Oxford Book of Spy Stories. 376p. 1997. reprint ed. pap. 14.95 (*0-19-283267-0*) OUP.

— Rethinking the Soviet Collapse: Sovietology, the Death of Communism & the New Russia. LC 98-30260. 288p. (C). 1999. 79.50 (*1-85567-321-5*) Bks Intl VA.

— Rethinking the Soviet Collapse: Sovietology, the Death of Communism & the New Russia. LC 98-30260. ix, 294 p. (C). 1999. pap. 24.95 (*1-85567-322-3*) Continuum.

— Twelve Victorian Ghost Stories. LC 97-2624. (Oxford Twelves). 224p. 1997. pap. 9.95 (*0-19-288026-8*) OUP.

— Victorian Detective Stories: An Oxford Anthology. 606p. (C). 1993. pap. 16.95 (*0-19-283150-X*, 12242) OUP.

***Cox, Michael, et al, eds.** American Democracy Promotion: Impulses, Strategies, & Impacts. 320p. 2000. pap. 22.00 (*0-19-924097-3*); text 74.00 (*0-19-829678-9*) OUP.

— The Interregnum: Controversies in World Politics 1989-1999. LC 99-87292. 290p. (C). 2000. pap. 24.95 (*0-521-78509-X*) Cambridge U Pr.

Cox, Michael, et al, eds. The Language of Biotechnology: A Dictionary of Terms. 2nd ed. LC 94-23812. (Professional Reference Book). (Illus.). 300p. 1995. pap. text 32.00 (*0-8412-2982-1*, Pub. by Am Chemical) OUP.

Cox, Michael, selected by. Twelve English Detective Stories. LC 98-30773. (Oxford Twelves Ser.). 266p. 1999. pap. 9.95 (*0-19-288096-9*) OUP.

Cox, Michael & Adrian, Jack, eds. The Oxford Book of Historical Stories. 464p. 1995. 35.00 (*0-19-214219-4*) OUP.

Cox, Michael & Gilbert, R. A., eds. Victorian Ghost Stories: An Oxford Anthology. 518p. 1993. reprint ed. pap. 16.95 (*0-19-282999-8*) OUP.

Cox, Michael & Walker, John M., eds. The Language of Biotechnology: A Dictionary of Terms. 2nd ed. LC 94-23812. (Professional Reference Book). (Illus.). 300p. 1995. text 55.00 (*0-8412-2957-0*, Pub. by Am Chemical) OUP.

Cox, Michael, et al. The Subversive Vegetarian. LC 80-635. (Illus.). 129p. (Orig.). 1980. pap. 3.95 (*0-912800-83-6*) Woodbridge Pr.

Cox, Michael, jt. auth. see Walker, John M.

Cox, Michael, ed. & intro. see James, Montague Rhodes.

Cox, Michael A. Oxycal vs. Arthritis. 171p. (Orig.). 1984. pap. 5.95 (*0-942078-07-1*) R Tanner Assocs Inc.

Cox, Michael J. Static Corrections for Seismic Reflection Surveys. LC 98-30018. (Geophysical Reference Ser.: Vol. 9). 531p. 1999. 122.00 (*1-56080-080-1*) Soc Expl Geophys.

Cox, Michael T. & Freed, Michael, eds. Representing Mental States & Mechanisms: Papers from the 1995 Spring Symposium. (Technical Reports). (Illus.). 141p. 1995. spiral bd. 25.00 (*0-929280-88-1*) AAAI Pr.

Cox, Michele L., ed. see Popkin, Michael H.

***Cox, Mike.** Historic Amarillo: An Illustrated History. (Illus.). 208p. 2000. 34.95 (*1-893619-05-2*) Hist Pub Network.

Cox, Mike. Historic Austin: An Illustrated History. (Illus.). 160p. 1998. 49.95 (*0-9654999-8-7*) Hist Pub Network.

— Stand-Off in Texas: "Just Call Me a Spokesman for DPS . . ." LC 98-204456. (Illus.). 308p. 1998. 22.95 (*1-57168-231-7*, Eakin Pr); pap. 16.95 (*1-57168-246-5*, Eakin Pr) Sunbelt Media.

— Texas Ranger Tales. LC 97-6899. 248p. 1997. pap. 16.95 (*1-55622-537-7*, Rep of TX Pr) Wordware Pub.

***Cox, Mike.** Texas Ranger Tales: Stories That Need Telling. 1999. 27.95 (*1-55622-732-9*, Rep of TX Pr) Wordware Pub.

Cox, Mike. Texas Ranger Tales Ii. LC 99-27602. 1998. pap. text 16.95 (*1-55622-640-3*) Wordware Pub.

***Cox, Mike.** Texas Ranger Tales II. 1999. 27.95 (*1-55622-740-X*, Rep of TX Pr) Wordware Pub.

Cox, Mike. The Texas Rangers: Men of Valor & Action. (Illus.). 144p. (J). (gr. 6-9). 1994. 14.95 (*0-89015-818-5*) Sunbelt Media.

— Texas Standoff: Media Relations in a Crisis. 1998. pap. text 16.95 (*1-55622-621-7*, Seaside Pr) Wordware Pub.

Cox, Mike & Cork. Flowers. (First Nature Bks.). (Illus.). 24p. (J). (gr. k-3). 1980. lib. bdg. 12.95 (*0-88110-074-9*, Usborne) EDC.

Cox, Mike & Cox, Kris. Flowers. Wasserman, Dan, ed. (Ten Word Book Ser.). (Illus.). (J). 1979. 9.95 (*0-89868-076-X*); pap. 3.95 (*0-89868-087-5*) ARO Pub.

Cox, Mike, et al. Fire Drill. Wasserman, Dan, ed. (Ten Word Book Ser.). (Illus.). (J). (gr. k-1). 1979. 9.95 (*0-89868-071-9*); pap. 3.95 (*0-89868-082-4*) ARO Pub.

Cox, Miles, ed. Why People Drink: Parameters of Alcohol As a Reinforcer. LC 87-19775. 336p. 1991. text 34.95 (*0-89876-132-8*) Gardner Pr.

Cox, Montagu H., ed. The Parish of St. Margaret, Westminster, Pt. 1. LC 70-138272. (London County Council. Survey of London Ser.: No. 10). (Illus.). reprint ed. 84.50 (*0-404-51660-2*, DA685) AMS Pr.

Cox, Montagu H. & Forrest, G. Topham. The Parish of St. Margaret, Westminster Vol. 1: Neighbourhood of Whitehall, Pt. 2. LC 70-138272. (London County Council. Survey of London Ser.: No. 13). reprint ed. 84.50 (*0-404-51663-7*, NA995) AMS Pr.

Cox, Murray. Coding the Therapeutic Process: Emblems of Encounter, A Manual for Counsellors & Therapists. 1978. pap. 21.00 (*1-85302-029-X*) Taylor & Francis.

— The Group As Poetic Play-Ground: From Metaphor to Metamorphosis. 1993. 29.00 incl. audio (*1-85302-203-9*) Taylor & Francis.

— Structuring the Therapeutic Process: Compromise with Chaos - a Therapist's Response to the Individual & the Group. 1978. pap. 27.00 (*1-85302-028-1*) Taylor & Francis.

Cox, Murray, ed. Remorse & Reparation. LC 98-41231. (Forensic Focus Ser.: Vol. 7). 300p. 1997. 80.00 (*1-85302-451-1*, Pub. by Jessica Kingsley); pap. 29.95 (*1-85302-452-X*, Pub. by Jessica Kingsley) Taylor & Francis.

— Shakespeare Comes to Broadmoor: "The Actors Are Come Hither" 200p. 1992. 49.50 (*1-85302-135-0*); pap. 24.95 (*1-85302-121-0*) Taylor & Francis.

Cox, Murray & Theilgaard, Alice. Mutative Metaphors in Psychotherapy. 280p. (C). 1987. pap. 18.95 (*0-422-61810-1*, Pub. by Tavistock); lib. bdg. 49.50 (*0-422-61800-4*, Pub. by Tavistock) Routldge.

— Mutative Metaphors in Psychotherapy: The Aeolian Mode. 308p. 1997. reprint ed. pap. write for info. (*1-85302-459-7*, Pub. by Jessica Kingsley) Taylor & Francis.

— Shakespeare As Prompter: The Amending Imagination in Theatre & Therapy. LC 94-223496. 328p. 1994. pap. 34.95 (*1-85302-159-8*) Taylor & Francis.

Cox Murray, Margaret, ed. Reflections on Maine. (Illus.). 100p. 1998. pap. write for info. (*0-9665140-0-9*) Rainbow Pr ME.

Cox, Nancy. Building & Managing a Web Services Team. LC 96-41389. (Communications Ser.). (Illus.). 300p. (C). 1997. pap. 32.95 (*0-442-02274-3*, VNR) Wiley.

***Cox, Nancy.** Electronic Messaging. LC 99-44881. (Best Practices Ser.). 672p. 1999. boxed set 79.95 (*0-8493-9825-8*) CRC Pr.

Cox, Nancy. Why Don't Teenagers Come with a Manual? Keeping It Simple & Sane. 45p. 1997. pap., per. 10.00 (*0-9661958-0-9*) NKC Ent.

Cox, Nancy A. Building & Managing a Web Services Organization. 1996. 29.95 incl. disk (*0-442-02273-5*, VNR) Wiley.

— Building & Managing a Web Services Team. 384p. 1996. pap. 32.95 (*0-471-28766-0*, VNR) Wiley.

— Handbook of Electronic Messaging 1999. 99th ed. LC 99-160116. 732p. 1998. boxed set 95.00 (*0-8493-9969-6*) CRC Pr.

Cox, Nancy A., et al. LAN Times Guide to Multimedia Networking. (Lan Times Ser.). 400p. 1995. pap. text 29.95 (*0-07-882114-2*) Osborne-McGraw.

Cox, Naomi I., jt. auth. see Daniels, Teresa.

Cox, Neil D. How to Perform Statistical Tolerance Analysis, Vol. 11. 55p. 1986. pap. 27.00 (*0-87389-010-8*, T3511) ASQ Qual Pr.

Cox, Neil H. Diagnostic Picture Tests in Clinical Dermatology. 1995. write for info. (*0-7234-2193-5*) Martin Dunitz.

Cox, Neil H. & Lawrence, Clifford M. Diagnostic Problems in Dermatology. 1998. write for info. (*0-7234-2790-9*, Pub. by Martin Dunitz) Mosby Inc.

Cox, Nicola. Bridge Player's Supper Book. 96p. 1995. pap. 13.95 (*0-575-05945-1*, Pub. by V Gollancz) Trafalgar.

— Country Cooking from Farthinghoe. (Illus.). 156p. 1984. 29.95 (*0-575-03504-8*, Pub. by V Gollancz) Trafalgar.

Cox, Nigel. Lambretta: An Illustrated History. (Illus.). 96p. 1996. 29.95 (*0-85429-963-7*, Pub. by GT Foulis) Haynes Manuals.

Cox, Nonie. Christopher Columbus. (Illus.). 48p. (J). (ps-1). 1992. pap. 9.95 (*1-55799-240-1*, EMC 271) Evan-Moor Edu Pubs.

***Cox, Nora.** Egungun Youth Festival: A Celebration of Empowerment for Children of African Descent. large type ed. (Illus.). 44p. 1999. pap. 15.00 (*1-930183-00-3*, ED-0001-99) Anyanwu.

Cox, Oliver Cromwell. Caste, Class, & Race. LC 59-8866. 624p. 1970. pap. 22.00 (*0-85345-116-8*, Pub. by Monthly Rev) NYU Pr.

— Race: A Study in Social Dynamics. LC 98-48876. 340p. 1999. 48.00 (*0-85345-941-X*, Pub. by Monthly Rev) NYU Pr.

***Cox, Oliver Cromwell.** Race: A Study in Social Dynamics. LC 98-48876. 1999. pap. text 21.00 (*1-58367-006-8*, Pub. by Monthly Rev) NYU Pr.

Cox, Oliver Cromwell. Race Relations: Elements & Social Dynamics. LC 75-38572. 354p. reprint ed. pap. 109.80 (*0-608-14450-9*, 202502200040) Bks Demand.

Cox, P. Radiopharmacy & Radiopharmacology: Yearbook 3. xii, 348p. 1988. kivar 282.00 (*2-88124-670-2*) Gordon & Breach.

Cox, P., ed. see Hussey, Jill.

Cox, P. A. The Electronic Structure & Chemistry of Solids. (Illus.). 270p. 1987. pap. text 45.00 (*0-19-855204-1*) OUP.

— The Elements: Their Origin, Abundance, & Distribution. (Illus.). 216p. 1989. pap. text 29.95 (*0-19-855298-X*) OUP.

— The Elements on Earth: Inorganic Chemistry in the Environment. (Illus.). 296p. 1995. pap. text 45.00 (*0-19-855903-8*) OUP.

***Cox, P. A.** Inorganic Chemistry. LC 00-39829. (Instant Notes Ser.). 2000. write for info. (*0-387-91604-0*) Spr-Verlag.

Cox, P. A. Introduction to Quantum Theory & Atomic Structure. (Oxford Chemistry Primers Ser.). (Illus.). 96p. (C). 1996. pap. text 12.95 (*0-19-855916-X*) OUP.

— Transition Metal Oxides: An Introduction to Their Electronic Structure & Properties. (International Series of Monographs on Chemistry: Vol. 27). (Illus.). 294p. 1995. pap. text 45.00 (*0-19-855925-9*) OUP.

Cox, P. A., ed. Civil Engineering Project Procedure in the EC. 214p. 1991. text 76.00 (*0-7277-1639-5*, Pub. by T Telford) RCH.

Cox, P. A., jt. auth. see Henrich, Victor H.

Cox, P. H. & Touja, E. New Perspectives in Nuclear Medicine Vol. 1: Clinical in Vitro Studies. xxx, 394p. 1986. write for info. (*2-88124-129-8*) Gordon & Breach.

— New Perspectives in Nuclear Medicine Vol. 2: Instrumentation, Laboratory Investigations & in Vitro Studies. 1986. write for info. (*2-88124-130-1*) Gordon & Breach.

Cox, P. Roxbee. Prisoner of Portcullis Castle. (Solve It Yourself Ser.). (Illus.). 48p. (YA). (gr. 7-12). 1997. pap. 7.95 (*0-7460-2697-8*, Usborne); lib. bdg. 15.95 (*0-88110-948-7*, Usborne) EDC.

Cox, P. Roxbee & Heath, R. The Second Usborne Book of Solve It Yourself Mysteries. (Solve It Yourself Ser.). 66p. (Orig.). (J). (gr. 7 up). 1997. pap. 15.95 (*0-7460-2701-X*, Usborne) EDC.

Cox, P. Roxbee & Stewart, Paul. Spine Chillers. (Illustrated Spinechillers Ser.). (Illus.). 48p. (J). (gr. 4 up). 1996. pap. 11.95 (*0-7460-2069-4*, Usborne) EDC.

Cox, Palmer. Brownies: Their Book. (Illus.). 1995. reprint ed. lib. bdg. 24.95 (*1-56849-662-1*) Buccaneer Bks.

Cox, Pamela, jt. auth. see Cox, John C.

***Cox, Pat M., et al.** Child Sexual Assault: Feminist Perspectives. LC 00-42077. 2000. write for info. (*0-312-23526-7*) St Martin.

Cox, Patrick. Patrick Cox: Wit, Irony & Footwear. (Cutting Edge Ser.). 1998. pap. text 16.95 (*0-8230-1148-8*) Watsn-Guptill.

Cox, Patsi B., jt. auth. see Emery, Ralph.

Cox, Patsi B., jt. auth. see Tucker, Tanya.

Cox, Patsi Bale, jt. auth. see Emery, Ralph.

Cox, Paul. Case of the Botched Book. LC 91-3853. (Adventures of Archibald the Koala on Rastepappe Island Ser.). (J). (ps-3). 1992. pap. 16.00 (*0-671-77586-3*, Green Tiger S&S) S&S Childrens.

— Great Eucalyptus Mystery. LC 91-3853. (Adventures of Archibald the Koala on Rastepappe Island Ser.). (J). (ps-3). 1992. pap. 16.00 (*0-671-77574-X*, Green Tiger S&S) S&S Childrens.

— The Law of Employment Discrimination: Cases & Commentary. 720p. 1999. ring bd. 67.00 (*1-879581-67-1*) Lupus Pubns.

— Reflections: An Autobiographical Journey. (Illus.). 1998. pap. 29.95 (*0-86819-549-9*, Pub. by Currency Pr) Accents Pubns.

— Riddle of the Floating Island. LC 91-3853. (Adventures of Archibald the Koala on Rastepappe Island Ser.). (J). (ps-3). 1992. pap. 16.00 (*0-671-77579-0*, Green Tiger S&S) S&S Childrens.

— Three Screenplays: Lonely Hearts, My First Wife & a Woman's Tale. 1998. pap. 24.95 (*0-86819-547-2*, Pub. by Currency Pr) Accents Pubns.

Cox, Paul & Banack, Sandra A., eds. Islands, Plants, & Polynesians. LC 90-19562. (Illus.). 240p. 1991. text 34.95 (*0-931146-18-6*, Dioscorides) Timber.

Cox, Paul, jt. auth. see Rae, Scott.

Cox, Paul A. Nafanua: Saving the Samoan Rain Forest. 238p. 1999. pap. text 14.95 (*0-7167-3563-6*) W H Freeman.

Cox, Paul A., jt. auth. see Balick, Michael J.

Cox, Paul Alan. Nafanua: Saving the Samoan Rain Forest. LC 97-37379. 226p. 1997. pap. text 23.95 (*0-7167-3116-9*) W H Freeman.

Cox-Paul, Lori & Wengert, James, eds. Frontier Army Christmas. LC 96-70900. 148p. 1996. pap. 12.95 (*0-933307-02-0*) Nebraska Hist.

***Cox, Paul N.** Employment Discrimination, 2 vols. 3rd ed. 800p. 1999. ring bd. 185.00 (*0-327-04956-1*, 8039211) LEXIS Pub.

Cox, Paul N. Employment Discrimination, 1987-1993, 2 vols. 2nd ed. 1480p. 1993. ring bd. 180.00 (*0-8240-7303-7*, MICHIE) LEXIS Pub.

— Employment Discrimination, 1987-1993, 2 vols. 2nd ed. 1480p. 1993. spiral bd., suppl. ed. 185.00 (*1-56257-260-1*, MICHIE) LEXIS Pub.

Cox, Paul W. & Leslie, Patty. Texas Trees: A Friendly Guide. LC 87-72604. (Illus.). 260p. 1988. pap. 14.95 (*0-931722-67-5*) Corona Pub.

Cox, Penny. Honda CBR900RR. LC 96-79565. (Service & Repair Manual Ser.). 1997. write for info. (*1-85960-350-5*) Haynes Manuals.

Cox, Penny. Triumph Triples & Fours: Service & Repair Manual. (Service & Repair Manual Ser.). 1996. pap. 23.95 (*1-56392-162-6*) Haynes Manuals.

Cox, Penny & Coombs, Matthew. Honda CBR900RR Owners Workshop Manual. LC 95-80720. (Owners Workshop Manual Ser.). 1995. write for info. (*1-56392-161-8*) Haynes Manuals.

Cox, Penny, jt. auth. see Darlington, Mansur.

Cox, Perry. Beatles Records & Memorabilia. 1999. pap. write for info. (*0-676-60181-2*) Hse Collectbls.

Cox, Peter. Two Youths & Other Stories. (C). 1990. 29.00 (*0-7223-2500-2*, Pub. by A H S Ltd) St Mut.

— Writing Specifications for Construction. LC 93-12838. 1993. write for info. (*0-07-707803-9*) McGraw.

Cox, Peter & Brusseau, Peggy. Lifepoints. 1997. 23.00 (*0-614-20669-3*) P-H.

Cox, Peter, jt. auth. see Brusseau, Peggy.

Cox, Peter A. The Smaller Rhododendrons. (Illus.). 295p. 1985. 29.95 (*0-88192-014-2*) Timber.

Cox, Peter A. & Cox, Kenneth E. Cox's Guide to Choosing Rhododendrons. (Illus.). 176p. 1995. pap. 19.95 (*0-88192-323-0*) Timber.

Cox, Peter Alfred. Dwarf Rhododenrons. 1985. 17.95 (*0-02-528560-2*) Macmillan.

Cox, Peter H. Cholescintigraphy: Developments in Nuclear Medicine, No. 1. 250p. 1981. text 149.50 (*90-247-2524-0*) Kluwer Academic.

— Progress in Radiopharmacology 3. 1982. text 141.50 (*90-247-2768-5*) Kluwer Academic.

Cox, Peter H., ed. The Clinical Applications of SPET. LC 94-37462. (Developments in Nuclear Medicine Ser.: Vol. 25). 288p. (C). 1995. text 121.50 (*0-7923-3187-7*) Kluwer Academic.

— Radiopharmacy & Radiopharmacology: Yearbook 2. xii, 434p. (C). 1987. text 190.00 (*2-88124-167-0*); pap. text 74.00 (*2-88124-168-9*) Gordon & Breach.

Cox, Peter H., et al, eds. Progress in Radiopharmacology, 1985. LC 85-13774. (Developments in Nuclear Medicine Ser.). 1985. text 191.00 (*0-89838-745-0*) Kluwer Academic.

— Progress in Radiopharmacy. (Developments in Nuclear Medicine Ser.). 1986. lib. bdg. 314.00 (*0-89838-823-6*) Kluwer Academic.

Cox, Peter H. & Buscombe, John R. The Imaging of Infection & Inflammation. LC 98-21151. (Developments in Nuclear Medicine Ser.). 240p. 1998. 146.00 (*0-7923-5087-1*) Kluwer Academic.

Cox, Peter H. & King, Christine M. Radiopharmacy & Radiopharmacology: Yearbook 1. xii, 376p. 1985. text 157.00 (*2-88124-114-X*); pap. text 58.00 (*2-88124-113-1*) Gordon & Breach.

C

An Asterisk (*) at the beginning of an entry indicates that the title is appearing for the first time.

Cox, Peter H. & Touja, E., eds. New Perspectives in Nuclear Medicine. (Monographs in Nuclear Medicine: Vol. 2). xxviii, 414p. 1986. text 489.00 (*2-88124-131-X*) Gordon & Breach.

Cox, Peter H., jt. ed. see Biersack, Hans J.

Cox, Peter H., jt. ed. see Deckhart, H.

Cox, Phil. Fragment of a Sidewalk. (Illus.). 24p. 1986. boxed set 5.00 (*0-934714-12-6*) Swamp Pr.

Cox, Phil R. Ghost Train to Nowhere. (Spinechillers Ser.). (Illus.). 48p. (J). (gr. 4 up). 1994. lib. bdg. 13.95 (*0-88110-519-8*, Usborne) EDC.

Cox, Phil R. Ghost Train to Nowhere. (Spinechillers Ser.). (Illus.). 48p. (J). (gr. 4 up). 1994. pap. 5.95 (*0-7460-0677-2*, Usborne) EDC.

— Haunting of Dungeon Creek. (Spinechillers Ser.). (Illus.). 48p. (J). (gr. 4-7). 1995. pap. 5.95 (*0-7460-2085-6*, Usborne) EDC.

Cox, Phil R. Haunting of Dungeon Creek. (Spinechillers Ser.). (Illus.). 48p. (J). (gr. 4 up). 1995. lib. bdg. 13.95 (*0-88110-756-5*, Usborne) EDC.

— Teddyland. (Spot the Differences Ser.). (Illus.). 32p. (ps-3). 1999. pap. text 6.95 (*0-7460-3316-8*, Usborne) EDC.

— Whatever Happened to Professor Potts? (Solve It Yourself Ser.). 48p. (J). (gr. 7 up). 1995. pap. 7.95 (*0-7460-2051-1*, Usborne); lib. bdg. 15.95 (*0-88110-780-8*, Usborne) EDC.

— Who Shot the Sheriff. (Solve It Yourself Ser.). (Illus.). 48p. (YA). (gr. 7 up). 1997. pap. 7.95 (*0-7460-2695-1*, Usborne) EDC.

— Who Shot the Sheriff? (Solve It Yourself Ser.). (Illus.). 48p. (J). (gr. 7 up). 1997. lib. bdg. 15.95 (*0-88110-912-6*, Usborne) EDC.

— Who Were the Vikings? (Starting Point History Ser.). (Illus.). 32p. (J). (gr. 1 up). 1995. pap. 4.95 (*0-7460-2038-4*, Usborne); lib. bdg. 12.95 (*0-88110-770-0*, Usborne) EDC.

Cox, Phil R. & Healh, Rupert. The Usborne Book of Solve It Yourself Mysteries: Follow the Clues to Unravel Three Mysteries. 144p. 1996. pap. 15.95 (*0-7460-2057-0*, Usborne) EDC.

Cox, Phil R. & Heath, Rupert. The Second Usborne Book of Solve It Yourself Mysteries. 144p. (YA). (gr. 7 up). 1997. lib. bdg. 23.95 (*0-88110-949-5*, Usborne) EDC.

***Cox, Phil Roxbee.** Ositolandia - Teddyland. (Illus.). 32p. (YA). (ps up). 2000. pap. 6.95 (*0-7460-3892-5*, Usborne) EDC.

— Sam Sheep Can't Sleep. (Easy Words to Read Ser.). (Illus.). 16p. (J). (ps up). 2000. pap. 7.95 (*0-7460-3861-5*, Usborne) EDC.

Cox, Phil Roxbee. Teddyland. (Illus.). 32p. (ps-3). 1999. 14.95 (*1-58086-186-5*) EDC.

***Cox, Phil Roxbee.** Toad Makes a Road. (Easy Words to Read Ser.). (Illus.). 16p. (J). (ps up). 2000. pap. 7.95 (*0-7460-3859-3*, Usborne) EDC.

***Cox, Phil Roxbee, ed.** Fat Cat on a Mat. (Easy Words to Read Ser.). (Illus.). 16p. (J). (ps-3). 2000. pap. 7.95 (*0-7460-3025-8*, Pub. by Usbrne Pbng UK) EDC.

— Find the Duck. (Find It Board Bks.). (Illus.). 10p. (ps up). 2000. bds. 3.95 (*0-7460-3821-6*, Pub. by Usbrne Pbng UK) EDC.

— Mystery Files. (Puzzle Adventure Kits Ser.). (Illus.). (J). (gr. 4-7). 2000. 15.95 (*0-7460-3677-9*, Pub. by Usbrne Pbng UK) EDC.

Cox, Philip. Gender, Genre & the Romantic Poets: An Introduction. LC 95-41314. 176p. 1996. text 69.95 (*0-7190-4263-1*) Manchester Univ Pr.

— Gender Genre & the Romantic Poets: An Introduction. LC 95-41314. 176p. 1996. text 24.95 (*0-7190-4264-X*, Pub. by Manchester Univ Pr) St Martin.

***Cox, Philip.** Reading Adaptations: Novels & Verse Narratives on the Stage 1790. 224p. 2000. pap. 24.95 (*0-7190-5341-2*, Pub. by Manchester Univ Pr); text 69.95 (*0-7190-5340-4*, Pub. by Manchester Univ Pr) St Martin.

Cox, R. & Brittain, P. Retail Management. 305p. (Orig.). (C). 1988. 90.00 (*0-7855-5661-3*, Pub. by Inst Pur & Supply) St Mut.

Cox, R. A., ed. Mathematics in Major Accident Risk Assessment. (Institute of Mathematics & Its Applications Conference Series, New Ser.: New Series 19). (Illus.). 272p. 1989. text 75.00 (*0-19-853616-X*) OUP.

— Offshore Medicine. 2nd ed. (Illus.). 280p. 1986. 102.00 (*0-387-16201-1*) Spr-Verlag.

Cox, R. A., et al, eds. Fitness for Work: The Medical Aspects. 2nd ed. (Illus.). 562p. 1995. pap. text 55.00 (*0-19-262345-1*) OUP.

***Cox, R. David.** Adams: Character in Time: The U. S. Presidents. Kuhens, Brian, ed. 36p. 1999. 5.95 (*1-929403-08-9*) History Proj.

— Bond & Covenant: A Perspective on Holy Matrimony from the Book of Common Prayer. LC 99-53176. 1999. pap. write for info. (*0-89869-325-X*) Church Pub Inc.

— Jefferson: Character in Time: The U. S. Presidents. 32p. 1997. 5.95 (*1-929403-02-X*) History Proj.

— Madison: Character in Time: The U. S. Presidents. 40p. 1998. 5.95 (*1-929403-10-0*) History Proj.

— Washington: Character in Time: The U. S. Presidents. 32p. 1998. 5.95 (*1-929403-00-3*) History Proj.

Cox, R. David, ed. see Ash, Lorraine.

Cox, R. David, ed. see Cox, David S.

Cox, R. H. Cellular & Molecular Mechanisms in Hypertension. (Advances in Experimental Medicine & Biology Ser.: Vol. 308). (Illus.). 264p. (C). 1992. text 95.00 (*0-306-44084-9*, Kluwer Plenum) Kluwer Academic.

Cox, R. H., jt. auth. see Arnstein, H. R.

Cox, R. Merritt. Tomas de Iriarte. LC 79-169629. (Twayne's World Authors Ser.). 161p. (C). 1972. lib. bdg. 20.95 (*0-8290-1736-4*) Irvington.

Cox, R. R. Schutz's Theory of Relevance: A Phenomenological Critique. (Phaenomenologica Ser.: Vol. 77). 246p. 1978. lib. bdg. 162.50 (*90-247-2041-9*, Pub. by M Nijhoff) Kluwer Academic.

Cox, Rachel T., ed. Vital Records of Bowdoin to the Year 1892: Volume I, Births; Volume II, Births & Deaths; Volume III, Marriages. (Illus.). 583p. 1997. reprint ed. lib. bdg. 57.50 (*0-8328-5814-5*) Higginson Bk Co.

Cox, Ralph. God Is, God Spoke, God Came. Martin, Carol, ed. 160p. 1997. write for info. (*1-879908-10-7*) Milton Pub.

Cox, Randall T. Birder's Dictionary. LC 96-15363. (Illus.). 186p. 1996. pap. text 8.95 (*1-56044-423-1*) Falcon Pub Inc.

Cox, Raymond A., et al. Financial Administration & Control. LC 93-78971. 374p. 1993. pap. text 50.95 (*1-878975-34-X*) Blackwell Pubs.

Cox, Raymond W., III, et al. Public Administration in Theory & Practice. LC 93-5592. 281p. (C). 1993. 48.00 (*0-13-739384-9*) P-H.

Cox-Rearick, Janet. Bronzino's Chapel of Eleonora in the Palazzo Vecchio. (California Studies in the History of Art: No. XXIX). (C). 1992. 90.00 (*0-520-07480-7*, Pub. by U CA Pr) Cal Prin Full Svc.

— The Collection of Francis I: Royal Treasures. (Illus.). 432p. 1995. 145.00 (*0-8109-4038-8*, Pub. by Abrams) Time Warner.

***Cox-Rearick, Janet, et al.** Giulio Romano, Master Designer: An Exhibition of Drawings in Celebration of the 500th Anniversary of His Birth. LC 99-73766. (Illus.). 168p. 1999. pap. 40.00 (*1-885998-21-X*) Hunter College.

Cox, Reavis. Competition in the American Tobacco Industry, 1911-1932. LC 68-58562. (Columbia University. Studies in the Social Sciences: No. 381). reprint ed. 84.50 (*0-404-51381-6*) AMS Pr.

***Cox, Reg.** Ancient World. (Wonders of the World Ser.). (Illus.). (J). 2000. 16.95 (*0-7910-6046-2*) Chelsea Hse.

— Medieval World. (Wonders of the World Ser.). (Illus.). (J). 2000. 16.95 (*0-7910-6047-0*) Chelsea Hse.

— Modern World. (Wonders of the World Ser.). (Illus.). (J). 2000. 16.95 (*0-7910-6048-9*) Chelsea Hse.

— Natural World. (Wonders of the World Ser.). (Illus.). (J). 2000. 16.95 (*0-7910-6049-7*) Chelsea Hse.

Cox, Reg & Morris, Neil. The Seven Wonders of the Ancient World. LC 95-30827. (Wonders of the World Ser.). (Illus.). 32p. (J). (gr. 4 up). 1996. pap. 7.95 (*0-382-39267-1*); lib. bdg. 14.95 (*0-382-39266-3*) Silver Burdett Pr.

— The Seven Wonders of the Historic World. (Illus.). 32p. (J). (gr. 5). 1996. pap. 7.95 (*0-382-39270-1*) Silver.

— The Seven Wonders of the Historic World. (Wonders of the World Ser.). (Illus.). 32p. (J). (gr. 4 up). 1996. lib. bdg. 14.95 (*0-382-39269-8*, Dillon Silver Burdett) Silver Burdett Pr.

— The Seven Wonders of the Modern World. (Wonders of the World Ser.). (Illus.). 32p. (J). (gr. 4 up). 1996. pap. 7.95 (*0-382-39272-8*, Dillon Silver Burdett); lib. bdg. 14.95 (*0-382-39271-X*, Dillon Silver Burdett) Silver Burdett Pr.

— The Seven Wonders of the Natural World. LC 95-42387. (Wonders of the World Ser.). (Illus.). 32p. (J). (gr. 4 up). 1996. pap. 7.95 (*0-382-39274-4*, Dillon Silver Burdett); lib. bdg. 14.95 (*0-382-39273-6*, Dillon Silver Burdett) Silver Burdett Pr.

Cox, Reva, ed. see Cox, Tom & Franz, G. Kim.

Cox, Rhonda. Andi's Wool. (Books for Young Learners). (Illus.). 12p. (J). (gr. k-2). 1997. pap. text 5.00 (*1-57274-110-4*, A2420) R Owen Pubs.

— At the Horse Show. (Books for Young Learners). (Illus.). 8p. (J). (gr. k-2). 1997. pap. text 5.00 (*1-57274-075-2*, A2425) R Owen Pubs.

— Best Friends. (Books for Young Learners). (Illus.). 16p. (J). (gr. k-2). 1999. pap. text 5.00 (*1-57274-237-2*) R Owen Pubs.

— Los Cerdos Espian! Torres, Raquel, tr. (Books for Young Learners).Tr. of Pigs Peek. (SPA., Illus.). 12p. (J). (gr. k-2). 1996. pap. text 5.00 (*1-57274-036-1*, A2836) R Owen Pubs.

— Chickens. (Books for Young Learners). (Illus.). 8p. (J). (gr. k-2). 1997. pap. text 5.00 (*1-57274-069-8*, A2437) R Owen Pubs.

— Clic! Romo, Alberto, tr. (Books for Young Learners).Tr. of Click!. (SPA., Illus.). 8p. (J). (gr. k-2). 1997. pap. text 5.00 (*1-57274-186-4*, A2839) R Owen Pubs.

— Click! (Books for Young Learners). (Illus.). 8p. (J). (gr. k-2). 1997. pap. text 5.00 (*1-57274-076-0*, A2439) R Owen Pubs.

***Cox, Rhonda.** I Ride the Waves. (Books for Young Learners). (Illus.). 8p. (J). (gr. k-2). 1999. pap. text 5.00 (*1-57274-335-2*, A2464) R Owen Pubs.

Cox, Rhonda. La Lana de Andi. Romo, Alberto, tr. (Books for Young Learners).Tr. of Andi's Wool. (SPA., Illus.). 12p. (J). (gr. k-2). 1999. pap. text 5.00 (*1-57274-296-8*) R Owen Pubs.

— Pigs Peek. (Books for Young Learners). (Illus.). 12p. (J). (gr. k-2). 1996. pap. text 5.00 (*1-57274-030-2*, A2180) R Owen Pubs.

***Cox, Rhonda.** Watermelon. (Books for Young Learners). (Illus.). 12p. (J). (gr. k-2). 1999. pap. text 5.00 (*1-57274-236-4*, A2540) R Owen Pubs.

Cox, Richard. The Columbus Option. large type ed. 544p. 1988. 27.99 (*0-7089-1845-X*) Ulverscroft.

— Program Controllers. 4th ed. (Electrical Trades Ser). (C). 2000. pap. 43.50 (*0-7668-1427-0*) Thomson Learn.

— Singing in English: A Manual of English Diction for Singers & Choral Directors. (Monograph Ser.: No. 5). 109p. 1988. 10.00 (*0-614-05592-X*) Am Choral Dirs.

— Singing in English: A Manual of English Diction for Singers & Choral Directors. (Monographs: No. 5). 109p. (C). 1990. pap. 10.00 (*1-882648-04-8*) Am Choral Dirs.

— Technical Guide to Program Controllers. 3rd ed. (Electrical Trades Ser.). 32p. 1996. teacher ed. 16.00 (*0-8273-6239-0*) Delmar.

Cox, Richard & Overland, Carlton. Warrington Colescott: Forty Years of Printmaking: A Retrospective, 1948-1988. (Illus.). (Orig.). (C). 1988. pap. 19.95 (*0-932900-19-4*) Elvejhem Mus.

***Cox, Richard, et al.** Encyclopedia of British Sport. 2000. lib. bdg. write for info. (*1-85109-344-3*) ABC-CLIO.

Cox, Richard, jt. auth. see Laudet, Claire.

Cox, Richard, ed. see Evy & Chick Staff.

Cox, Richard, jt. ed. see Laudet, Claire.

Cox, Richard A. Technicians Guide to Programmable Controllers. 2nd ed. (C). 1988. pap., teacher ed. 15.00 (*0-8273-2831-1*) Delmar.

— Technicians Guide to Programmable Controllers. 2nd ed. (C). 1989. pap. 31.95 (*0-8273-2830-3*) Delmar.

— Technician's Guide to Programmable Controllers. 3rd ed. LC 94-24400. 320p. 1995. mass mkt. 68.95 (*0-8273-6238-2*) Delmar.

***Cox, Richard A.** Technician's Guide to Programmable Controllers. 4th ed. LC 00-43131. (Illus.). 2000. pap. write for info. (*0-7668-1428-9*) Delmar.

Cox, Richard D. Singer's Manual of German & French Diction. 80p. 1970. 15.00 (*0-02-870650-1*, Schirmer Books) Mac Lib Ref.

Cox, Richard E., ed. Atchison, Topeka & Santa Fe Railway. (Illus.). 40p. (Orig.). 1984. pap. 5.97 (*0-912935-00-6*) Vanishing Vistas.

— Norfolk & Western Railway. (Illus.). 40p. (Orig.). 1985. pap. 5.97 (*0-912935-01-4*) Vanishing Vistas.

Cox, Richard H. Four Pillars of Constitutionalism: The Organic Laws of the United States. LC 98-18635. 142p. 1998. pap. text 12.95 (*1-57392-215-3*) Prometheus Bks.

***Cox, Richard H.** Issues of the Soul: Core & Ethic of Some of the Most Important Aspects of Living. 250p. 2000. pap. 19.95 (*0-9673439-9-2*, Synch Pr) InSync Commn.

Cox, Richard H. Sport Psychology: Concepts & Applications. 3rd ed. 464p. (C). 1993. text. write for info. (*0-697-12621-8*) Brown & Benchmark.

Cox, Richard H., jt. ed. see Cole, Richard J.

Cox, Richard H., ed. see Locke, John.

Cox, Richard J. American Archival Analysis: The Recent Development of the Archival Profession in the United States. 363p. 1990. 41.50 (*0-8108-2338-1*) Scarecrow.

***Cox, Richard J.** Closing an Era: Historical Perspectives on Modern Archives & Records Management, 35. LC 99-89071. (New Directions in Information Management Ser.: Vol. 35). 2000. write for info. (*0-313-31331-8*, Greenwood Pr) Greenwood.

Cox, Richard J. Documenting Localities: A Practical Model for American Archivists & Manuscript Curators. (Society of American Archivists Ser.). 224p. 1996. 37.50 (*0-8108-3043-4*) Scarecrow.

— The First Generation of Electronic Records Archivists in the United States: A Study in Professionalization. LC 94-17961. (Primary Sources & Original Works: Vol. 3, Nos. 3-4). 220p. 1995. 49.95 (*1-56024-644-8*) Haworth Pr.

— Managing Institutional Archives: Foundational Principles & Practices. LC 91-34470. (Library Management Collection). 324p. 1992. lib. bdg. 65.00 (*0-313-27251-4*, CIG/, Greenwood Pr) Greenwood.

***Cox, Richard J.** Managing Records as Evidence & Information. 2000. write for info. (*1-56720-231-4*, Quorum Bks) Greenwood.

Cox, Richard J., ed. A Name Index to the Baltimore City Tax Records: 1798-1808 of the Baltimore City Archives. 229p. (Orig.). 1981. pap. 6.50 (*0-916623-01-7*) City Baltimore.

Cox, Richard L. & Sullivan, Larry E. Guide to the Research Collection of the Maryland Historical Society. (Illus.). 354p. 1981. 22.00 (*0-938420-01-1*) MD Hist.

Cox, Richard T. Time, Space, & Atoms. LC 33-6773. 170p. reprint ed. pap. 52.70 (*0-608-18650-3*, 205596200041) Bks Demand.

Cox, Robert. The Pillar of Celestial Fire. Stanley, Tom, ed. LC 97-66694. (Illus.). 230p. 1997. pap. 18.95 (*1-887472-30-4*) Sunstar Pubng.

Cox, Robert, jt. auth. see Utz, James.

Cox, Robert D. David. 189p. 1989. pap. 5.95 (*0-9621663-0-8*) Robair Pub.

Cox, Robert G., jt. auth. see Wixon, Rufus.

Cox, Robert H., ed. Acute Myocardial Infarction: Emerging Concepts of Pathogenesis & Treatment. LC 88-27576. 218p. 1989. 69.50 (*0-275-92438-6*, C2438, Praeger Pubs) Greenwood.

Cox, Robert W. Approaches to World Order. LC 96-33161. 571p. 1996. pap. text 27.95 (*0-521-46651-2*) Cambridge U Pr.

— Approaches to World Order. LC 96-33161. (Studies in International Relations: No. 40). (Illus.). 571p. (C). 1996. text 74.95 (*0-521-46114-6*) Cambridge U Pr.

— Power, Production & World Order: Social Forces in the Making of History. (Political Economy of International Change Ser.). 392p. 1987. text 80.00 (*0-231-05808-X*) Col U Pr.

— Production, Power, & World Order: Social Forces in the Making of History. Ruggie, John G., ed. (Political Economy of International Change Ser.). 301p. 1989. pap. text 23.00 (*0-231-05809-8*) Col U Pr.

Cox, Robert W. & Jacobson, Harold K. The Anatomy of Influence: Decision Making in International Organization. LC 72-75188. 511p. reprint ed. pap. 158.50 (*0-7837-4553-2*, 208034400005) Bks Demand.

***Cox, Robin, et al, eds.** Fitness for Work: The Medical Aspects. 3rd ed. (Illus.). 736p. 2000. pap. text 69.50 (*0-19-263043-1*) OUP.

Cox, Roger. Best Places to Stay in the Rocky Mountain Region. 2nd rev. ed. (Best Places to Stay Ser.). (Illus.). 352p. 1994. pap. 16.95 (*0-395-66619-8*) HM.

— Shaping Childhood: Themes of Uncertainty in the History of Adult-Child Relationships. 248p. (C). 1996. 85.00 (*0-415-11044-0*) Routledge.

Cox, Roger, jt. auth. see Pascall, Gillian.

Cox, Ronald J., Sr. Roadside Ron. LC 97-95324. 376p. 1998. 23.95 (*0-9662586-0-6*) Cox CA.

Cox, Ronald W. Power & Profits: U. S. Policy Toward Central America. LC 93-41718. 200p. 1994. 29.95 (*0-8131-1865-4*) U Pr of Ky.

Cox, Ronald W., ed. Business & the State in International Relations. (Interventions). 288p. (C). 1996. pap. 75.00 (*0-8133-8949-6*, Pub. by Westview) HarpC.

Cox, Ronald W. & Skidmore-Hess, Daniel. U. S. Politics & the Global Economy: Corporate Power, Conservative Shift. LC 98-29595. 250p. 1999. lib. bdg. 49.95 (*1-55587-771-0*) L Rienner.

Cox, Rosamund & Cork. Birds. (First Nature Bks.). (Illus.). (J). (gr. k-3). 1980. lib. bdg. 12.95 (*0-88110-072-2*, Usborne) EDC.

— Butterflies & Moths. (First Nature Bks.). (J). (gr. k up). 1980. lib. bdg. 12.95 (*0-88110-073-0*) EDC.

Cox, Rosamund K. Birds. (First Nature Bks.). (Illus.). 24p. (J). (gr. k-3). 1980. pap. 4.50 (*0-86020-475-8*, Usborne) EDC.

— Butterflies & Moths. (First Nature Bks.). (Illus.). 24p. (J). (gr. k-3). 1980. pap. 4.50 (*0-86020-477-4*) EDC.

— The Usborne Complete First Book of Nature. (Illus.). 168p. (J). (gr. k up). 1990. lib. bdg. 24.95 (*1-58086-027-3*, Usborne) EDC.

Cox, Rosamund K. & Cork, Patrick. Flowers. (First Nature Bks.). (Illus.). 24p. (J). (gr. k-3). 1980. pap. 4.50 (*0-86020-479-0*, Usborne) EDC.

Cox, Rosemary C., jt. auth. see Cox, Willis F.

Cox, Roxbee. Who Were the Romans? (Starting Point History Ser.). (Illus.). 24p. (J). (gr. 1-4). 1994. pap. 4.95 (*0-7460-1339-6*, Usborne) EDC.

— Who Were the Romans? (Starting Point History Ser.). (Illus.). 24p. (J). (gr. 1 up). 1994. lib. bdg. 12.95 (*0-88110-669-0*, Usborne) EDC.

Cox, S. F., jt. ed. see Davis, E. A.

Cox, S. W. Measurement & Control in Agriculture. LC 98-55556. 1997. 99.95 (*0-632-04114-5*) Blackwell Sci.

— Microelectronics in Agriculture & Horticulture: Electronics & Computers in Farming. 240p. (C). 1982. pap. text 44.00 (*0-86598-087-X*) Rowman.

Cox, S. W. & Filby, D. E. Instrumentation in Agriculture. (Illus.). 160p. 1972. 22.00 (*0-8464-0519-9*) Beekman Pubs.

Cox, Sally, ed. see Bailey, Joanne I. & Nyberg, Carl O.

Cox, Sam D., jt. auth. see Hayes, A. B.

***Cox, Samuel H. & Hall, Dale.** Exercises for the Society of Actuaries Textbook Acturial Mathematics: Course 3. 333p. 1998. spiral bd. 34.80 (*0-87563-959-3*) Stipes.

Cox, Samuel S. Orient Sunbeams: From the Porte to the Pyramids, by Way of Palestine. Davis, Moshe, ed. LC 77-70665. (America & the Holy Land Ser.). (Illus.). 1977. reprint ed. lib. bdg. 36.95 (*0-405-10238-0*) Ayer.

— Three Decades of Federal Legislation, 1855 to 1885. LC 75-114870. (Select Bibliographies Reprint Ser.). 1977. 58.95 (*0-8369-5275-8*) Ayer.

— Why We Laugh. 2nd enl. ed. LC 67-13325. 1972. reprint ed. 29.95 (*0-405-08379-3*, Pub. by Blom Pubns) Ayer.

Cox, Sandford C. Recollections of the Early Settlement of the Wabash Valley. LC 78-117870. (Select Bibliographies Reprint Ser.). 1977. 24.95 (*0-8369-5323-1*) Ayer.

Cox, Sandra, jt. auth. see Davies, Nicola.

Cox, Sarah, jt. auth. see Alonso, Andres R.

Cox, Sebastian, ed. The Strategic War Against Germany: The British Bombing Survey Unit. LC 97-22017. (Studies in Air Power: No. 4). (Illus.). 195p. 1998. 59.50 (*0-7146-4722-5*, Pub. by F Cass Pubs) Intl Spec Bk.

Cox, Sebastian, ed. see Ritchie, Sebastian.

Cox, Shelley. A Personal Name Index to "New Directions", Vols. 1-35. LC 37-1751. vi, 167p. 1980. 42.00 (*0-87875-180-7*) Whitston Pub.

Cox, Sherri, jt. auth. see Cox, Tom.

Cox, Sophie O. Yewka & the Two Pear Trees: A Family Story. (Illus.). 24p. (YA). (gr. 7-12). 1995. spiral bd. 15.00 (*0-9641138-1-3*) Beach Pebbles.

Cox Staff. Diccionario Castella-Catala, Catala-Castella Vox Compacte. (SPA.). 608p. 1989. 14.95 (*0-7859-6484-3*) Fr & Eur.

Cox, Stanley M. Cox. Joseph Cox, Ancestors & Descendants. 144p. 1997. reprint ed. pap. 24.00 (*0-8328-8112-0*); reprint ed. lib. bdg. 34.00 (*0-8328-8111-2*) Higginson Bk Co.

Cox, Stefanie O., tr. see Martinson, Paul V., ed.

Cox, Stephen. The Addams Chronicles: An Altogether Ooky Look at the Addams Family. 2nd rev. ed. LC 98-30015. (Illus.). 240p. 1998. pap. 18.95 (*1-888952-91-1*) Cumberland Hse.

— Dreaming of Jeannie: TV's Prime Time in a Bottle. 2000. pap. 14.95 (*0-312-15517-4*) St Martin.

***Cox, Stephen.** Dreaming of Jeannie: TV's Prime Time in a Bottle. LC 99-89790. (Illus.). 288p. 2000. pap. 15.95 (*0-312-20417-5*) St Martin.

Cox, Stephen. The Hooterville Handbook: A Viewer's Guide to Green Acres. LC 92-44422. 1993. pap. 12.95 (*0-312-08811-6*) St Martin.

— Managing the Pressure in Teaching: Practical Ideas for Tutors & Their Students. LC 99-167510. 1998. 79.00 (*0-7507-0836-0*); pap. text 22.95 (*0-7507-0835-2*, Falmer Pr) Taylor & Francis.

— The Munchkins of Oz. rev. ed. Orig. Title: The Munchkins Remember. (Illus.). 256p. 1996. pap. 18.95 (*1-888952-04-0*) Cumberland Hse.

***Cox, Stephen.** The Titanic Story: Hard Choices, Dangerous Decisions. (Illus.). 120p. 1999. pap. 16.95 (*0-8126-9396-5*) Open Court.

An Asterisk (*) at the beginning of an entry indicates that the title is appearing for the first time.

Cox, Stephen, intro. The God of the Machine. rev. ed. LC 92-32935. (Library of Conservative Thought). 292p. (C). 1999. pap. text 24.95 (*1-56000-666-8*) Transaction Pubs.

Cox, Stephen & Lofflin, John. The Abbott & Costello Story: Sixty Years of "Who's on First?" 2nd rev. ed. LC 97-24295. (Illus.). 256p. 1997. pap. 22.95 (*1-888952-61-X*) Cumberland Hse.

Cox, Stephen, jt. auth. see Kelley, David.

Cox, Steve & Carey, Peter. Generations of Resistance: East Timor. LC 96-145114. Date not set. pap. 21.95 (*0-304-33252-6*, Pub. by Cassell) LPC InBook.

Cox, Steve, tr. see Anissimov, Myriam.

Cox, Steve, tr. see Clement, Catherine.

Cox, Steven. Big Machines in the Farm. (Illus.). 24p. (J). pap. 7.95 (*0-14-056209-5*, Pub. by Pnguin Bks Ltd) Trafalgar.

Cox, Steven & Lasiecka, Irena, eds. Optimization Methods in Partial Differential Equations: Proceedings from the 1996 Joint Summer Research Conference, June 16-20, 1996, Mt. Holyoke College. LC 97-22252. (Contemporary Mathematics Ser.: Vol. 209). 349p. 1997. pap. 69.00 (*0-8218-0604-1*) Am Math.

Cox, Steven, ed. see Ebsen, Buddy.

Cox, Steven L. Essentials of New Testament Greek: A Student's Guide. rev. ed. 288p. (C). 1999. pap. text 17.99 (*0-8054-2029-0*) Broadman.

— A History & Critique of Scholarship Concerning the Markan Endings. LC 93-33176. (Biblical Press Ser.: Vol. 17). 290p. 1993. text 89.95 (*0-7734-2380-X*, Mellen Biblical Pr) E Mellen.

Cox, Steven M. Annual Editions: Aging. 12th ed. 1997. pap. 16.56 (*0-697-39296-1*) McGraw.

— Human Sexuality. 2001. pap. text 20.00 (*0-697-12011-2*); pap. text, student ed. 12.00 (*0-697-12013-9*) McGraw.

— Police: Practices, Perspectives, Problems. (C). 1995. teacher ed. write for info. (*0-205-18480-4*, H8480-9) Allyn.

— Sport Psychology. 4th ed. LC 97-34896. 480p. 1997. pap. 44.06 (*0-697-29507-9*) McGraw.

Cox, Steven M. & Conrad, John J. Juvenile Justice. 4th ed. LC 94-72872. 320p. (C). 1995. text. write for info. (*0-697-12700-1*) Brown & Benchmark.

— Juvenile Justice. 4th ed. 320p. (C). 1996. student ed., per. write for info. (*0-07-114135-9*) Brown & Benchmark.

— Juvenile Justice. 5th ed. 2000. pap. text 30.74 (*0-697-35617-5*) McGraw.

Cox, Steven M. & Fitzgerald, Jack D. Police & Community Relations: Critical Issues. 208p. (C). 1983. pap. write for info. (*0-697-08219-9*) Brown & Benchmark.

— Police in Community Relations: Critical Issues. 3rd ed. LC 94-73759. 240p. (C). 1995. text. write for info. (*0-697-25119-5*) Brown & Benchmark.

— Police in Community Relations: Critical Issues. 3rd ed. 240p. (C). 1997. student ed., per. write for info. (*0-07-114136-7*) Brown & Benchmark.

— Police in Community Relations: Critical Issues. 4th ed. 1999. pap. text 25.00 (*0-697-35610-8*) McGraw.

Cox, Steven M. & Wade, John. The Criminal Justice Network: An Introduction. 3rd ed. LC 96-85978. 336p. (C). 1997. text. write for info. (*0-697-12699-4*, WCB McGr Hill) McGrw-H Hghr Educ.

Cox-Stevens, Kay, ed. see Garber, Debra.

Cox-Stevens, Kay, ed. see Marshall, Jacquelyn R.

Cox-Stevens, Kay, ed. see Marshburn, Beverly.

***Cox-Stubblefield, Deborah.** Anna's Testimony: A Woman's Journey to Holiness. 32p. 1998. pap. 12.00 (*1-930183-01-1*, DR-0001-99) Anyanwu.

— A Cry from Hell. 25p. 1998. pap. 13.00 (*1-930183-08-9*, DR-0002E-99) Anyanwu.

— A Cry from Hell, Pt. I. 1998. pap. 10.00 (*1-930183-06-2*, DR-0002C-99) Anyanwu.

— A Cry from Hell, Pt. II. 1998. pap. 10.00 (*1-930183-07-0*, DR-0002D-99) Anyanwu.

— Let the Healing Begin. 26p. 1998. pap. 12.00 (*1-930183-04-6*, DR-0002A-99) Anyanwu.

— Letters from the Grave. 2000. pap. 12.00 (*1-930183-09-7*, DR-0004-99) Anyanwu.

— The Live-Ins. Date not set. pap. write for info. (*1-930183-03-8*, DR-0003-99) Anyanwu.

— The Murder of Woodworm. 1998. pap. 8.00 (*1-930183-05-4*, DR-0002B-99) Anyanwu.

Cox, Sue, ed. Female Psychology: The Emerging Self. 2nd ed. 480p. (C). 1981. pap. text 20.00 (*0-312-28743-7*) St Martin.

Cox, Sue & Cox, Tom. Safety, Systems & People. (Illus.). 256p. 1996. 65.00 (*0-7506-2089-7*) Buttrwrth-Heinemann.

Cox, Sue, jt. auth. see Tait, N. R.

Cox, Susan M. & Budeit, Janice L., compiled by. Early English Newspapers, Bibliography & Guide to the Microfilm Collection (Cumulative Units 1-24), Units 1-24. 106p. 1983. 95.00 (*0-89235-076-8*) Primary Srce Media.

Cox, Susan N., ed. 20th Century American Ceramics Price Guide: Collectible Pottery & Porcelain Wares Produced since the Turn of the Century. LC 95-76097. (Illus.). 256p. 1996. pap. 14.95 (*0-930625-42-0*, Antique Trader) Krause Pubns.

Cox, Susan N., jt. ed. see Husfloen, Kyle.

***Cox, Susan Soon-Keum, ed.** Voices from Another Place: A Collection of Works from a Generation Born in Korea. 152p. (J). 1999. pap. 12.00 (*0-9638472-4-4*) Yeong & Yeong.

Cox, Susie. International Directory of Astrologers. 150p. 1992. pap. 19.95 (*0-9634178-4-3*) S Cox.

— International Directory of Astrologers, 1995-96. 150p. (Orig.). 1995. pap. 20.00 (*0-9634178-8-6*) S Cox.

Cox, Suzy. Diary of a Secretary: Humility & Pain. 1997. 13.25 (*0-9645042-1-9*) Suzy Cox.

— Suzanne's 10th Birthday. 64p. (Orig.). (J). (gr. 1-6). 1995. per. 9.95 (*0-9645042-0-0*) Suzy Cox.

Cox, Sylvia. Younger People with Dementia: Planning, Practice & Development. LC 99-171530. 328p. 1998. 29.95 (*1-85302-588-7*) Taylor & Francis.

Cox, T., jt. auth. see Brearley, A.

Cox, Taylor, Jr. Cultural Diversity in Organizations: Theory, Research, & Practice. LC 93-17920. (Illus.). 314p. 1994. pap. 19.95 (*1-881052-43-5*) Berrett-Koehler.

Cox, Taylor, Jr. & Beale, Ruby L. Developing Competency to Manage Diversity: Readings, Cases, & Activities. LC 97-19978. 376p. (Orig.). 1997. pap. 29.95 (*1-881052-96-6*) Berrett-Koehler.

Cox, Ted. Emmitt Smith: Finding Daylight. LC 93-43837. (Sports Stars Ser.). (Illus.). 48p. (J). (gr. 2-8). 1994. lib. bdg. 19.00 (*0-516-04383-8*) Childrens.

— Emmitt Smith: Finding Daylight. (Sports Stars Ser.). (J). (gr. 3-6). 1994. pap. 5.95 (*0-516-44383-6*) Childrens.

— Football. LC 96-7514. (Successful Sports Ser.). (J). 1998. (*1-57572-067-1*) Heinemann Lib.

— Frank Thomas: The Big Hurt. LC 94-9914. (Sports Stars Ser.). (Illus.). 48p. (J). (gr. 2-8). 1994. pap. 5.95 (*0-516-44386-0*) Childrens.

— Greg Maddux: Pitching Ace. LC 94-36915. (Sports Stars Ser.). 48p. (J). (gr. 3-4). 1995. lib. bdg. 19.00 (*0-516-04389-7*) Childrens.

— Greg Maddux: Pitching Ace. (Sports Stars Ser.). (J). (gr. 3-4). 1995. pap. 5.95 (*0-516-44389-5*) Childrens.

— The Temptations. LC 97-5278. (African-American Achievers Ser.). 124p. (YA). (gr. 5 up). 1997. pap. 8.95 (*0-7910-2588-8*) Chelsea Hse.

— The Temptations. LC 97-5278. (African-American Achievers Ser.). 124p. (YA). (gr. 5 up). 1997. lib. bdg. 19.95 (*0-7910-2587-X*) Chelsea Hse.

— Whitney Houston: Singer/Actress. LC 97-38158. (Black Americans of Achievement Ser.). (Illus.). 124p. (YA). (gr. 5 up). 1997. lib. bdg. 19.95 (*0-7910-4455-6*) Chelsea Hse.

— Whitney Houston: Singer/Actress. LC 97-38158. (Black Americans of Achievement Ser.). (Illus.). 124p. (YA). (gr. 5 up). 1997. pap. 8.95 (*0-7910-4456-4*) Chelsea Hse.

Cox, Ted, jt. auth. see Cox, Joyce.

Cox, Terry. Peasants, Class & Capitalism: The Rural Research of L. N. Kritsman & His School. 280p. 1986. 49.95 (*0-19-878014-1*) OUP.

***Cox, Terry.** You Can Write Song Lyrics. 112p. 2000. pap. 14.99 (*0-89879-989-9*) F & W Pubns Inc.

Cox, Terry, ed. From Perestroika to Privatisation. 176p. 1996. 69.95 (*1-85972-198-2*, Pub. by Avebry) Ashgate Pub Co.

— Hungary 1956 - Forty Years On. LC 97-18278. 162p. 1997. 45.00 (*0-7146-4766-7*, Pub. by F Cass Pubs); pap. 24.00 (*0-7146-4309-2*, Pub. by F Cass Pubs) Intl Spec Bk.

Cox, Terry & Furlong, Andy, eds. Hungary: The Politics of Transition. LC 95-6650. (Illus.). 196p. 1995. pap. 22.50 (*0-7146-4167-7*, Pub. by F Cass Pubs) Intl Spec Bk.

Cox, Terry & Littlejohn, Gary, eds. Kritsman & the Agrarian Marxists. LC 83-25225. (Library of Peasant Studies: No. 7). (Illus.). 150p. 1984. 35.00 (*0-7146-3237-6*, BHA-03237, Pub. by F Cass Pubs) Intl Spec Bk.

***Cox, Terry & Mason, Bob.** Social & Economic Transformation in East Central Europe: Institutions, Property Relations & Social Interests. LC 98-55209. 256p. 1999. 85.00 (*1-85898-427-0*) E Elgar.

Cox, Theo, ed. Combating Educational Disadvantage: Meeting the Needs of Vulnerable Children. LC 99-39563. 240p. 1999. 71.00 (*0-7507-0901-4*, Pub. by Falmer Pr UK); pap. 32.95 (*0-7507-0900-6*, Pub. by Falmer Pr UK) Taylor & Francis.

— The National Curriculum & the Early Years: Challenges & Opportunities. 192p. 1997. pap. 27.95 (*0-7507-0601-5*, Falmer Pr) Taylor & Francis.

Cox, Theo & Sanders, Susan. The Impact of the National Curriculum on the Teaching of Five-Year-Olds. LC 93-48764. 152p. 1994. 85.00 (*0-7507-0250-8*, Falmer Pr) Taylor & Francis.

***Cox, Theodore O.** Mission to Japan: Travels Through a Missionary Career LC 99-180084. 187 p. 1998. write for info. (*1-55630-874-4*) Brentwood Comm.

Cox, Thomas. French Grammar. LC 86-16417. (College Outline Ser.). 253p. (C). 1986. pap. text 10.25 (*0-15-601611-7*) Harcourt Coll Pubs.

Cox, Thomas C. Blacks in Topeka, Kansas, 1865-1915: A Social History. LC 81-14310. 248p. 1982. pap. 76.90 (*0-7837-8527-5*, 204933600011) Bks Demand.

Cox, Thomas J. For Freedom's Battle: An Historical Documentary in the Form of a Filmplay. (Illus.). 1995. vinyl bd. 17.50 (*1-879710-09-9*) Riverside FL.

— For You & for Many: A Filmplay. 111p. (Orig.). 1992. vinyl bd. 14.50 (*1-879710-06-4*) Riverside FL.

— Leaflets of the White Rose: A Filmplay. 119p. (Orig.). (YA). 1991. pap. 14.50 (*1-879710-02-1*) Riverside FL.

— Palm Ninety. 20p. 1993. vinyl bd. 7.45 (*1-879810-07-7*) Riverside FL.

— Secretary to the Delegation: A Filmplay. 119p. (Orig.). 1991. pap. 14.50 (*1-879710-01-3*) Riverside FL.

Cox, Thomas J., ed. The Trial of the IRA Five: Documentary. (Illus.). 363p. (Orig.). (C). 1992. vinyl bd. 27.50 (*1-879710-05-6*) Riverside FL.

Cox, Thomas R. The Park Builders: A History of State Parks in the Pacific Northwest. LC 88-5462. (Illus.). 280p. 1988. pap. 14.95 (*0-295-96620-3*) U of Wash Pr.

Cox, Thomas R., et al. This Well-Wooded Land: Americans & Their Forests from Colonial Times to the Present. LC 85-1141. (Illus.). 365p. reprint ed. pap. 113.20 (*0-7837-7048-0*, 204685900004) Bks Demand.

Cox, Thomas S. Civil-Military Relations in Sierra Leone: A Case Study of African Soldiers in Politics. 283p. 1976. 37.95 (*0-674-13290-4*) HUP.

***Cox, Thomas S.** Civil-Military Relations in Sierra Leone: A Case Study of African Soldiers in Politics. 286p. 1999. 27.95 (*0-7351-0180-9*) Replica Bks.

Cox, Timothy M. & Sinclair, John. Molecular Biology in Medicine. LC 96-21997. (Illus.). 384p. 1997. pap. text 68.95 (*0-632-02785-1*) Blackwell Sci.

Cox, Tom. Power for Yachts. (Illus.). 1975. 29.95 (*0-8464-0739-6*) Beekman Pubs.

Cox, Tom, ed. Women & Work. (Work & Stress Ser.: Vol. 1, No. 3). 122p. 1988. pap. 29.00 (*0-85066-906-5*) Taylor & Francis.

Cox, Tom & Cox, Sherri. School Records: Kindergarten-12 Grade. (Illus.). 27p. (J). (gr. k-12). 1990. spiral bd. 9.95 (*0-9626932-0-0*) TCA Pub.

Cox, Tom & Franz, G. Kim. The Day Is Such a Lady. Cox, Reva, ed. 124p. (Orig.). 1994. pap. write for info. (*0-9644276-0-5*) Cox-Franz Pr.

Cox, Tom, jt. auth. see Cox, Sue.

***Cox, Tracey.** Hot Relationships: How to Know What You Want, Get What You Want & Keep It Red Hot. 432p. 2000. pap. 12.95 (*0-553-38033-8*, Spectra) Bantam.

Cox, Tracey. Hot Sex: How to Do It. LC 98-43546. 400p. 1999. reprint ed. pap. 12.95 (*0-553-38032-X*, Fanfare) Bantam.

Cox, Tracy, ed. see Cox, Helen.

Cox, Trenchard. Jehan Foucquet, Native of Tours. LC 72-7072. (Select Bibliographies Reprint Ser.). 1977. reprint ed. 20.95 (*0-8369-6926-X*) Ayer.

Cox, V. J. Electric Motors. (Workshop Practice Ser.: No. 16). (Illus.). 136p. (Orig.). 1987. pap. 19.95 (*0-85242-914-2*, Pub. by Nexus Special Interests) Trans-Atl Phila.

Cox, Verna. Illustrated Braiding Guide. (Illus.). 1995. pap. text 9.95 (*1-883830-06-0*) Cox Enterprises.

Cox, Vic. The Challenge of Immigration. LC 94-34645. (Multicultural Issues Ser.). (Illus.). 128p. (YA). (gr. 6 up). 1995. lib. bdg. 20.95 (*0-89490-628-3*) Enslow Pubs.

— Guns, Violence & Teens. LC 96-36365. (Issues in Focus Ser.). 112p. (YA). (gr. 6 up). 1997. lib. bdg. 20.95 (*0-89490-721-2*) Enslow Pubs.

***Cox, Vicki.** Diana, Princess of Wales. LC 00-26847. (They Died Too Young Ser.). (Illus.). 2000. 16.95 (*0-7910-5854-9*) Chelsea Hse.

— Rising Stars & Ozark Constellations: Faces of Courage, Ingenuity & Success. LC 00-38787. (Illus.). 2000. pap. write for info. (*1-881554-07-4*) Skyward Pub.

Cox, Virginia, tr. see Fonte, Moderata.

Cox, Virginia, tr. see Gramsci, Antonio.

Cox, Virginia D. & Weathers, Willie. Old Houses of King & Queen County Virginia. LC 73-89225. (Illus.). 404p. 1998. 22.00 (*0-9664788-0-0*) King & Queen.

— Old Houses of King & Queen County Virginia. LC 73-89225. (Illus.). 404p. 1998. reprint ed. 25.00 (*0-9664788-2-7*) King & Queen.

Cox, W. If Any Man's Work Abides by God's Rules. 1995. pap. 5.95 (*0-9617286-3-9*) Today Bible & You.

Cox, W. E. Cox. Descendants of Solomon Cox of Cole Creek, Virginia, & Other Early Cox Ancestry of the Cole Creek Coxes. (Illus.). 89p. 1997. reprint ed. pap. 17.50 (*0-8328-8114-7*); reprint ed. lib. bdg. 27.50 (*0-8328-8113-9*) Higginson Bk Co.

Cox, W. Eugene. Great Smoky Mountains: The Story Behind the Scenery. 2nd rev. ed. LC 98-65024. (Illus.). 48p. 1998. pap. 7.95 (*0-88714-137-4*) KC Pubns.

— Great Smoky Mountains: The Story Behind the Scenery. 2nd rev. ed. Morales, Brigitte, tr. (GER., Illus.). 48p. 1998. pap. 8.95 (*0-88714-823-9*) KC Pubns.

— In Pictures Everglades: The Continuing Story. LC 89-80844. (Illus.). 48p. (Orig.). 1989. pap. 7.95 (*0-88714-040-8*) KC Pubns.

— In Pictures Everglades: The Continuing Story. (GER., Illus.). 48p. (Orig.). 1990. pap. 8.95 (*0-88714-713-5*) KC Pubns.

— In Pictures Everglades: The Continuing Story. Le Bras, Yvon, tr. (FRE., Illus.). 48p. (Orig.). 1990. pap. 8.95 (*0-88714-714-3*) KC Pubns.

— In Pictures Everglades: The Continuing Story. Marapodi, Carlos, tr. (SPA., Illus.). 48p. (Orig.). 1990. pap. 8.95 (*0-88714-715-1*) KC Pubns.

— In Pictures Everglades: The Continuing Story. Comollo, Adriano, tr. (ITA., Illus.). 48p. (Orig.). 1997. pap. 8.95 (*0-88714-814-X*) KC Pubns.

Cox, W. Michael & Alm, Richard. Myths of Rich & Poor: Why We're Better off Than We Think. LC 99-177815. (Illus.). 256p. 1998. 25.00 (*0-465-04784-X*, Pub. by Basic) HarpC.

***Cox, W. Michael & Alm, Richard.** Myths of Rich & Poor: Why We're Better Off Than We Think. 1999. pap. 14.00 (*0-465-04783-1*, Pub. by Basic) HarpC.

Cox, W. Michael & Fox, Beverly J. What's Happening to Americans' Income?, BG138. 11p. 1996. pap. 5.00 (*1-56808-069-7*) Natl Ctr Pol.

Cox, W. Miles. The Addictive Personality. (Encyclopedia of Psychoactive Drugs Ser.: No. 1). (Illus.). 124p. (YA). (gr. 7 up). 1987. lib. bdg. 19.95 (*0-87754-773-4*) Chelsea Hse.

— Treatment & Prevention of Alcohol Problems. (Personality, Psychopathology & Psychotherapy Ser.). 1986. text 53.00 (*0-12-194470-0*) Acad Pr.

Cox, W. Robert, jt. auth. see Utz, James.

Cox, W. W. History of Seward County, Nebraska. 290p. 1993. reprint ed. lib. bdg. 35.00 (*0-8328-2939-0*) Higginson Bk Co.

Cox, Wayne, tr. see Marti i Pol, Miguel.

Cox, Wayne S., jt. auth. see Sjolander, Claire T.

Cox, Wendell & Love, Jean. The Best Investment a Nation Ever Made: A Tribute to the Dwight D. Eisenhower System of Interstate & Defense Highways. (Illus.). 41p. 1998. pap. text 20.00 (*0-7881-4186-4*) DIANE Pub.

Cox, Willard. Between March & May. LC 97-77476. 680p. 1997. 21.95 (*1-56883-073-4*) Colonial Pr AL.

***Cox, William.** Guide to the Best European Business Schools. (Illus.). 256p. 2000. pap. 18.95 (*0-07-135720-3*) McGraw.

Cox, William E. Amillennialism Today. LC 66-28450. 1972. pap. 6.99 (*0-87552-151-7*) P & R Pubng.

— Biblical Studies in Final Things. LC 67-11794. 1967. pap. 9.99 (*0-87552-152-5*) P & R Pubng.

— Life on the New River: A Pictorial History of the New River Gorge. (Illus.). 66p. 1984. pap. 5.25 (*0-915992-45-0*) Eastern National.

***Cox, William E.** Life on the New River: A Pictorial History of the New River Gorge. rev. ed. (Illus.). 72p. 1999. pap. 9.95 (*1-888213-51-5*) Eastern National.

Cox, William E. Why I Left Scofieldism. 1975. pap. 1.50 (*0-87552-154-1*) P & R Pubng.

Cox, William J. Designing a Single Adult Ministry. 56p. 1996. pap. 9.95 (*0-88177-150-3*, DR150) Discipleship Res.

— Knowledge of Life: Applying Leadership. 64p. (Orig.). 1994. pap. 6.95 (*0-9638471-1-2*) WJC Pr.

— The Oracle of Leadership, 2 Bk. Kit. 128p. (Orig.). 1995. pap. 12.95 (*0-9638471-4-7*) WJC Pr.

— The Path: A Philosophy of Leadership. 64p. (Orig.). 1993. pap. 6.95 (*0-9638471-0-4*) WJC Pr.

Cox, William N. A Guide to Effective Employee Relations for the Nineties. (Illus.). 245p. 1991. student ed. 53.50 (*1-880429-00-4*) CR & Assocs.

— How to Administer an Effective Human Resources Program. (Illus.). 235p. 1996. wbk. ed. 59.95 (*1-880429-05-5*) CR & Assocs.

— How to Administer an Effective Safety Program & Assure Compliance with OSHA. (Illus.). 293p. 1996. wbk. ed. 69.95 (*1-880429-06-3*) CR & Assocs.

— How to Get a Job & Keep It. (Illus.). 200p. (Orig.). 1992. pap. 8.95 (*1-880429-03-9*) CR & Assocs.

— How to Prepare a Personnel Policy Manual. rev. ed. 145p. 1989. student ed. 53.50 (*1-880429-02-0*) CR & Assocs.

— Retirement Life Planning: A Home Seminar for Husbands & Wives. rev. ed. 82p. 1989. student ed. 59.95 (*1-880429-01-2*) CR & Assocs.

Cox, William R. Cemetery Jones & Maverick Kid. large type ed. (Linford Western Library). 1990. pap. 16.99 (*0-7089-6805-8*, Linford) Ulverscroft.

— Cemetery Jones & the Dancing Guns. large type ed. 1990. pap. 16.99 (*0-7089-6857-0*, Linford) Ulverscroft.

— Cemetery Jones & the Gungslingers. large type ed. 1990. pap. 16.99 (*0-7089-6944-5*, Linford) Ulverscroft.

— Comanche Moon. 224p. 1989. pap. 2.95 (*0-380-70830-2*, Avon Bks) Morrow Avon.

— Gunfight at Razor Edge. large type ed. 1998. 19.95 (*1-57490-160-5*, Sagebrush LP West) T T Beeler.

— The Gunsharp. 1996. 17.50 (*0-7451-4678-3*, Gunsmoke) Chivers N Amer.

— The Gunsharp. large type ed. (Linford Western Library). 304p. 1988. pap. 16.99 (*0-7089-6528-8*, Linford) Ulverscroft.

— Moon of Cobre. 224p. 1989. pap. 2.95 (*0-380-70832-9*, Avon Bks) Morrow Avon.

— Navajo Blood. 240p. 1989. pap. 2.95 (*0-380-70831-0*, Avon Bks) Morrow Avon.

***Cox, William Robert.** Bigger Than Texas. large type ed. LC 99-43652. 1999. 20.95 (*1-57490-234-2*) T T Beeler.

Cox, William T. Fearsome Creatures of the Lumberwoods. (Illus.). 47p. (Orig.). 1984. reprint ed. pap. 5.00 (*0-9618946-0-1*) Bishop Publishing.

Cox, Willis F. Conversations about God from the Journal of Willis F. Cox. LC 85-91148. (Illus.). (Orig.). 1985. 11.95 (*0-9610758-2-1*); pap. 6.95 (*0-9610758-3-X*); pap. text 6.95 (*0-9610758-1-3*) W F Cox.

— Tidbits for Thought: From the Journal of Willis F. Cox. LC 83-90752. (Illus.). (Orig.). 1983. pap. 6.95 (*0-9610758-0-5*) W F Cox.

Cox, Willis F. & Cox, Rosemary C. Phillip's Daffodil. (Orig.). (J). (gr. k-8). 1987. pap. 2.95 (*0-9610758-4-8*) W F Cox.

***Cox-Wood, Deborah.** Settling with Power: 3 Steps to Mastering Life. LC 99-51906. 2000. 19.95 (*1-888426-13-6*) Pisces Press.

Coxall, Michelle & Singh, Sarina. Lonely Planet Rajasthan. (Illus.). 352p. 1997. pap. 15.95 (*0-86442-470-1*) Lonely Planet.

Coxall, Michelle, jt. auth. see Singh, Sarina.

Coxe, Anthony H. & Coxe, Araminda H. The Great Book of Sausages. 252p. 1996. pap. 15.95 (*0-87951-682-8*, Pub. by Overlook Pr) Penguin Putnam.

Coxe, Anthony H., tr. see Liksen, H. J.

Coxe, Antony & Coxe, Araminta H. The Great Book of Sausages. 252p. 1992. 22.95 (*0-87951-464-7*, Pub. by Overlook Pr) Penguin Putnam.

Coxe, Araminda H., jt. auth. see Coxe, Anthony H.

Coxe, Araminta H., jt. auth. see Coxe, Antony.

Coxe, Brinton, tr. see Gutterbock, Carl.

Coxe, Daniel. A Description of the English Province of Carolana, by the Spaniards Call'd Florida, & by the French la Louisiane. LC 76-18184. (Floridiana Facsimile & Reprint Ser.). (Illus.). 122p. 1976. reprint ed. 24.95 (*0-8130-0402-0*) U Press Fla.

Coxe, Dees. Before You Landscape. 80p. (Orig.). 1990. pap. 6.95 (*0-930401-39-5*) Artex Pub.

Coxe, Francis. A Short Treatise Declaringe the Detestable Wickednesse of Magicall Sciences. LC 72-5971. (English Experience Ser.: No. 501). 32p. 1972. reprint ed. 20.00 (*90-221-0501-6*) Walter J Johnson.

Coxe, George H. The Inside Man. large type ed. 376p. 1977. 27.99 (*0-85456-517-5*) Ulverscroft.

Coxe, George H., ed. Stories by Members of the Mystery Writers of America. 350p. Date not set. 25.95 (*0-8488-2239-0*) Amereon Ltd.

C

Coxe, H. O., ed. Roger of Wendover: Chronica Sive Flores Historiarum, 4 vols. (English Historical Society Publications: Vol. 12). 1974. reprint ed. 250.00 (*0-8115-1537-0*) Periodicals Srv.

Coxe, Louis O. Edwin Arlington Robinson. LC 62-62785. (University of Minnesota Pamphlets on American Writers Ser.: No. 17). 48p. (Orig.). reprint ed. pap. 30.00 (*0-7837-2893-X*, 205756200006) Bks Demand.

— Edwin Arlington Robinson: The Life of Poetry. LC 69-15698. 1969. 30.50 (*0-672-53528-9*) Irvington.

— The Second Man, & Other Poems. LC 55-9369. 72p. reprint ed. pap. 30.00 (*0-608-18630-9*, 20558510039) Bks Demand.

— The Wilderness, & Other Poems. LC 58-59912. 74p. reprint ed. pap. 30.00 (*0-608-18629-5*, 205585200039) Bks Demand.

Coxe, Louis O., jt. auth. see Chapman, Robert.

Coxe, Molly. Big Egg. LC 96-31978. (Early Step into Reading Ser.). (J). (ps-1). 1997. lib. bdg. 11.99 (*0-679-98126-8*, Pub. by Random Bks Yng Read) Random.

— Big Egg. (Early Step into Reading Ser.). (Illus.). (J). (ps-k). 1997. pap. 3.99 (*0-614-28932-7*) Random Bks Yng Read.

— Big Egg. LC 96-31978. (Early Step into Reading Ser.). (Illus.). 32p. (J). (ps-1). 1997. pap. 3.99 (*0-679-88126-3*, Pub. by Random Bks Yng Read) Random.

— Big Egg. (Early Step into Reading Ser.). (J). (ps-k). 1997. 9.19 (*0-606-11124-7*, Pub. by Turtleback) Demco.

***Coxe, Molly.** Bookworm. LC 99-87822. (Road to Reading Mile Ser.). (Illus.). (J). 2000. pap. 3.99 (*0-307-26112-3*) Gldn Bks Pub Co.

— Bookworm. LC 99-87822. (Road to Reading Ser.). (J). 2000. pap. 10.99 (*0-307-46112-2*) Gldn Bks Pub Co.

Coxe, Molly. Cat Traps. LC 94-34989. (Early Step into Reading Ser.). (Illus.). (J). (ps-3). 1996. pap. 3.99 (*0-679-86441-5*) Random.

— Cat Traps. LC 94-34989. (Early Step into Reading Ser.). (Illus.). (J). (ps-3). 1996. lib. bdg. 11.99 (*0-679-96441-X*) Random.

— Cat Traps. (Early Step into Reading Ser.). (J). (ps-k). 1996. 9.19 (*0-606-08711-7*, Pub. by Turtleback) Demco.

***Coxe, Molly.** Fox Trot. (Road to Reading Ser.). (Illus.). 32p. (J). (gr. 1-2). 1999. 10.99 (*0-307-46209-9*, Goldn Books) Gldn Bks Pub Co.

Coxe, Molly. Fox Trot. LC 98-38485. (Road to Reading Ser.). (Illus.). 32p. (J). (gr. 1-2). 1999. pap. text 3.99 (*0-307-26209-X*, Goldn Books) Gldn Bks Pub Co.

***Coxe, Molly.** Fox Trot. LC 98-38485. (Road to Reading Ser.). (J). 1999. lib. bdg. write for info. (*0-03-074629-9*, W B Saunders Co) Harcrt Hlth Sci Grp.

Coxe, Molly. The Great Snake Escape. LC 92-26528. (I Can Read Bks.). (Illus.). 48p. (J). (ps-3). 1994. lib. bdg. 15.89 (*0-06-022869-5*) HarpC Child Bks.

— The Great Snake Escape. LC 92-26528. (I Can Read Bks.). (Illus.). 48p. (J). (ps-3). 1996. pap. 3.95 (*0-06-444208-X*, HarpTrophy) HarpC Child Bks.

— The Great Snake Escape. (I Can Read Bks.). (J). (gr. 1-3). 1996. 8.95 (*0-606-09360-5*, Pub. by Turtleback) Demco.

— Hot Dog. LC 98-12021. (Road to Reading Ser.). 32p. (J). 1998. pap. 3.99 (*0-307-26101-8*, 26101) Gldn Bks Pub Co.

***Coxe, Molly.** Hot Dog. (Road to Reading Ser.). (Illus.). (J). 1999. 10.44 (*0-606-16255-0*, Pub. by Turtleback) Demco.

Coxe, Molly. R Is for Radish. LC 97-10046. (Step into Reading Ser.: A Step 2 Book). (Illus.). 32p. (J). (gr. k-3). 1997. pap. 3.99 (*0-679-88574-9*); lib. bdg. 11.99 (*0-679-98574-3*) Random.

Coxe, Molly. R Is for Radish. (Step into Reading Ser.: A Step 2 Book). (J). (gr. 1-3). 1997. 9.19 (*0-606-13020-9*, Pub. by Turtleback) Demco.

— 6 Sticks. LC 97-7972. (Early Step into Reading Ser.). (Illus.). 32p. (J). (ps-3). 1999. pap. 3.99 (*0-679-88689-3*) Random.

Coxe, Molly. 6 Sticks. LC 97-7972. (Early Step into Reading Ser.). (J). (ps-3). 1999. lib. bdg. 11.99 (*0-679-98689-8*) Random.

— Whose Footprints? LC 89-70850. (Illus.). 40p. (J). (ps-1). 1990. 14.95 (*0-690-04835-1*); lib. bdg. 14.89 (*0-690-04837-8*) HarpC Child Bks.

***Coxe, Molly & Silin-Palmer, Pamela.** Bunny & the Beast. LC 99-48621. (J). 2001. 12.00 (*0-375-80468-4*) Random.

Coxe, Nicholas. The Falconer. LC 91-76501. 105p. 1992. 19.00 (*0-685-55192-X*) Chalidze.

***Coxe, Paula Peisner.** Finding Peace: Letting Go & Liking It. 2nd ed. 352p. 2000. pap. 9.95 (*1-57071-533-5*) Sourcebks.

— Finding Time: Breathing Space for Women Who Do Too Much. 2nd ed. 306p. 2000. pap. 9.95 (*1-57071-532-7*) Sourcebks.

Coxe, Tench. A View of the United States of America in a Series of Papers Written Between the Years 1787 & 1794. LC 64-24342. (Reprints of Economic Classics Ser.). 512p. 1965. reprint ed. 75.00 (*0-678-00070-0*) Kelley.

Coxe, Weld. Marketing Architectural & Engineering Services. 2nd ed. LC 89-31795. (Illus.). 310p. (C). 1990. reprint ed. lib. bdg. 39.50 (*0-89464-377-0*) Krieger.

Coxe, William. Anecdotes of George Frederick Handel & John Christopher Smith. LC 79-15128. (Music Reprint Ser.). 1979. reprint ed. 29.50 (*0-306-79512-4*) Da Capo.

— History of the House of Austria: From the Foundation of the Monarchy by Rhodolph of Hapsburgh to the Death of Leopold the Second, 1218-1792, 3 vols., Set. LC 72-135801. (Eastern Europe Collection). 1971. reprint ed. 116.95 (*0-405-02743-5*) Ayer.

— History of the House of Austria: From the Foundation of the Monarchy by Rhodolph of Hapsburgh to the Death of Leopold the Second, 1218-1792, 3 vols., Vol. 1. LC 72-135801. (Eastern Europe Collection Ser.). 1971. reprint ed. 39.95 (*0-405-02790-7*) Ayer.

— History of the House of Austria: From the Foundation of the Monarchy by Rhodolph of Hapsburgh to the Death of Leopold the Second, 1218-1792, 3 vols., Vol. 2. LC 72-135801. (Eastern Europe Collection). 1971. reprint ed. 39.95 (*0-405-02791-5*) Ayer.

— History of the House of Austria: From the Foundation of the Monarchy by Rhodolph of Hapsburgh to the Death of Leopold the Second, 1218-1792, 3 vols., Vol. 3. LC 72-135801. (Eastern Europe Collection). 1971. reprint ed. 39.95 (*0-405-02792-3*) Ayer.

— Memoirs of the Administration of the Right Honourable Henry Pelham, 2 vols. LC 74-130626. reprint ed. 135.00 (*0-404-01794-0*) AMS Pr.

— Travels in Poland & Russia. LC 73-115524. (Russia Observed Ser.). 1970. reprint ed. 58.95 (*0-405-03017-7*) Ayer.

— Travels into Poland. LC 76-135802. (Eastern Europe Collection). (Illus.). 226p. 1971. reprint ed. 18.95 (*0-405-02744-3*) Ayer.

Coxeter, H. S. Introduction to Geometry. 2nd ed. 496p. 1989. pap. 67.95 (*0-471-50458-0*) Wiley.

— Non-Euclideon Geometry. 6th ed. LC 98-85640. 320p. 1998. pap. text 30.95 (*0-88385-522-4*) Math Assn.

— Projective Geometry. 2nd ed. (Illus.). xii, 162p. 1994. reprint ed. 52.95 (*0-387-96532-7*) Spr-Verlag.

— The Real Projective Plane: With an Appendix for Mathematics by George Beck. 3rd ed. LC 92-22637. (Illus.). 232p. 1992. reprint ed. 64.95 incl. disk (*0-387-97890-9*) Spr-Verlag.

— The Real Projective Plane: With an Appendix for Mathematics by George Beck. 3rd ed. LC 92-22637. (Illus.). 232p. 1995. reprint ed. 67.95 incl. disk (*0-387-97889-5*) Spr-Verlag.

— Regular Complex Polytopes. 2nd ed. (Illus.). 224p. (C). 1991. text 69.95 (*0-521-39490-2*) Cambridge U Pr.

— Regular Polytopes. (Illus.). 321p. 1973. reprint ed. pap. 9.95 (*0-486-61480-8*) Dover.

— Twisted Honeycombs. LC 75-145638. (CBMS Regional Conference Series in Mathematics: Vol. 4). 47p. 1971. pap. 16.00 (*0-8218-1653-5*, CBMS/4C) Am Math.

Coxeter, H. S., et al, eds. M. C. Escher: Art & Science. xiv,402p. 1986. 133.50 (*0-444-70011-0*, North Holland) Elsevier.

Coxeter, H. S. & Greitzer, S. L. Geometry Revisited. LC 67-20607. (New Mathematical Library: No. 19). 193p. 1967. pap. text 18.95 (*0-88385-619-0*, NML-19) Math Assn.

Coxeter, H. S. & Moser, W. O. Generators & Relations for Discrete Groups. 3rd rev. ed. LC 72-79063. (Ergebnisse der Mathematik und Ihrer Grenzgebiete Ser.: Vol. 14). (Illus.). ix, 169p. 1986. 79.95 (*0-387-09212-9*) Spr-Verlag.

Coxeter, H. S., et al. The Fifty-Nine Icosahedra. (Illus.). 30p. 1982. reprint ed. 38.95 (*0-387-90770-X*) Spr-Verlag.

Coxeter, H. S. M. Beauty of Geometry: Twelve Essays. LC 99-35678. 1999. pap. text 9.95 (*0-486-40919-8*) Dover.

***Coxeter, H. S. M.** The Fifty-Nine Icosahedra. 3rd ed. (Illus.). 1999. pap. 18.95 (*1-899618-32-5*, Pub. by Tarquin Pubns) Parkwest Pubns.

Coxeter, H. S. M., jt. auth. see Ball, W. W. Rouse.

Coxeter, Harold & Macdonald, Scott. The Real Projective Plane. 2nd ed. LC 60-3540. 238p. reprint ed. pap. 67.90 (*0-608-10294-6*, 2050796) Bks Demand.

Coxford. Algebra 1. 1990. student ed. 52.50 incl. reel tape (*0-15-353640-3*) Harcourt Schl Pubs.

— Algebra 1. 1990. pap. text, teacher ed. 53.25 (*0-15-353664-0*) Holt R&W.

— Algebra 1: Practice Book. 1990. pap. text, student ed., wbk. ed. 12.50 (*0-15-353652-7*) Holt R&W.

— Algebra 1: Tests. 1990. pap. text 12.50 (*0-15-353648-9*) Holt R&W.

— Algebra 2 with Trigonometry. 1990. pap. text, teacher ed., wbk. ed. 9.00 (*0-15-353695-0*) Holt R&W.

— Algebra 2 with Trigonometry. (YA). 1990. pap. text, student ed. 56.25 (*0-15-353665-9*) Holt R&W.

— Algebra 2 With Trigonometry. 1990. teacher ed. 91.00 (*0-15-353645-4*); student ed. 54.50 (*0-15-353641-1*) Harcourt Schl Pubs.

— Algebra 2 with Trigonometry: Practice Book. 90th ed. 1990. pap. text, student ed., wbk. ed. 14.25 (*0-15-353653-5*) Holt R&W.

— Algebra 2 with Trigonometry: Tests. 1990. pap. text 13.00 (*0-15-353649-7*) Holt R&W.

— HBJ Advanced Math: A Preparation for Calculus. rev. ed. 1988. text 67.20 (*0-15-353803-1*) Harcourt.

— Resource Guide for Trigonometry, 1987. 1987. pap., teacher ed. 57.00 (*0-15-359371-7*) Harcourt Schl Pubs.

Coxford & Hirsch. Exploring Circles: Teacher's Edition. (Mathematics Replacement Units Ser.). 1996. teacher ed. 11.46 (*0-02-824220-3*) Glencoe.

— Exploring Data: Teacher's Edition. (Mathematics Replacement Units Ser.). 1995. teacher ed. 14.79 (*0-02-824207-6*) Glencoe.

Coxford, jt. auth. see Hirsch.

Coxford, Arthur. Trigonometry, 1987. 1987. text 57.00 (*0-15-359370-9*) Holt R&W.

Coxford, Arthur F., ed. The Ideas of Algebra, K-12: 1988 Yearbook. (Illus.). 248p. 1988. 22.95 (*0-87353-250-3*, 380E1) NCTM.

Coxford, Arthur F. & Core-Plus Mathematics Project Staff. Contemporary Mathematics in Context: A Unified Approach. LC 96-29041. 1997. text 34.95 (*0-939765-92-6*); pap. text 22.95 (*0-939765-93-4*) Janson Pubns.

Coxford, Arthur F., Jr., et al. Geometry from Multiple Perspectives. Hirsch, Christian R., ed. LC 91-16636. (Curriculum & Evaluation Standards for School Mathematics Addenda Ser.: Grades 9-12). (Illus.). 72p. 1991. pap. text 15.95 (*0-87353-330-5*) NCTM.

Coxford, Arthur F., ed. see NCTM Staff.

Coxford, Lola M. Resume Writing Made Easy. 6th ed. LC 97-22038. 147p. (C). 1997. pap. text 15.40 (*0-13-679853-5*) P-H.

Coxhead, David & Hiller, Susan. Dreams: Visions of the Night. LC 88-51555. (Art & Imagination Ser.). (Illus.). 96p. 1989. reprint ed. pap. 15.95 (*0-500-81012-5*, Pub. by Thames Hudson) Norton.

Coxhead, Elizabeth. Daughters of Erin. 236p. 1979. pap. 15.95 (*0-901072-60-5*, Pub. by Smyth) Dufour.

Coxhead, Peter & Foster, Martin. The Kitcar Builders Manual. 2nd ed. (Illus.). 192p. 1994. 29.95 (*1-85010-898-6*, Pub. by J H Haynes & Co) Motorbooks Intl.

Coxhill, Deidre C., frwd. see Bamburak, Gary P.

Coxo, jt. auth. see Davies.

Coxon, Anthony P. Between the Sheets: Sexual Diaries & Gay Men's Sex in the Era of AIDS. (Illus.). 224p. 1996. 69.95 (*0-304-33198-8*) Continuum.

Coxon, James Morriss, ed. Advances in Carbocation Chemistry, Vol. 3. Date not set. 109.50 (*0-7623-0345-X*) Jai Pr.

— Advances in Detailed Reaction Mechanisms, Vol. 5. Date not set. 109.50 (*0-7623-0061-2*) Jai Pr.

— Advances in Detailed Reaction Mechanisms Vol. 1: Radical, Single Electron Transfers & Concerted Reactions. 186p. 1991. 109.50 (*1-55938-164-7*) Jai Pr.

— Advances in Detailed Reaction Mechanisms Vol. 2: Mechanisms of Biological Importance. 292p. 1992. 109.50 (*1-55938-505-7*) Jai Pr.

— Advances in Detailed Reaction Mechanisms Vol. 3: Reactions of Importance in Synthesis. 289p. 1994. 109.50 (*1-55938-741-6*) Jai Pr.

— Advances in Detailed Reaction Mechanisms Vol. 4: Synthetically Useful Reactions. 222p. 1995. 109.50 (*1-55938-787-4*) Jai Pr.

Coxon, James Morriss & Creary, Xavier, eds. Advances in Carbocation Chemistry, Vol. 2. 273p. 1995. 109.50 (*0-89232-952-1*) Jai Pr.

Coxon, James Morriss, et al. Worked Solutions in Organic Chemistry. LC 97-74038. xxi, 516 p. 1998. write for info. (*0-7514-0422-5*) B Acad & Prof.

Coxon, Lucinda. Waiting at the Water's Edge. 116p. 1996. pap. 13.95 (*1-85411-149-3*) Dufour.

***Coxon, Michele.** The Cat Who Found His Way Home. (Illus.). 32p. (J). (ps-k). 2000. 13.95 (*1-899248-88-9*, Pub. by Happy Cat) Star Brght Bks.

Coxon, Michele. The Cat Who Found His Way Home. LC 99-70743. (Illus.). 32p. (J). 1999. pap. 5.95 (*1-887734-67-8*) Star Brght Bks.

— The Cat Who Lost His Purr. (Illus.). 32p. (J). 1996. pap. 5.99 (*0-14-055608-7*, PuffinBks) Peng Put Young Read.

***Coxon, Michele.** The Cat Who Lost His Purr. (Illus.). 32p. (YA). (ps-3). 2000. 7.95 (*1-887734-77-5*) Star Brght Bks.

— The Cat Who Lost His Purr. LC 90-14412. (J). 1996. 10.19 (*0-606-09135-1*, Pub. by Turtleback) Demco.

— Catch up, Little Cheetah: A Lift-the-Flap Book. (Illus.). 32p. (J). (ps-k). 2000. 13.95 (*1-899248-23-4*, Pub. by Happy Cat) Star Brght Bks.

Coxon, Michele. Catch up, Little Cheetah: A Lift-the-Flap Book. LC 99-70741. (Illus.). 16p. (J). 1999. pap. 6.95 (*1-887734-63-5*) Star Brght Bks.

— Kitten Finds a Home. (Illus.). 16p. (J). (ps-1). 1998. pap. 5.99 (*0-14-056377-6*) Viking Penguin.

***Coxon, Michele.** Kitten's Adventure. (Illus.). 32p. (J). 2000. 13.95 (*1-899248-01-3*, Pub. by Happy Cat) Star Brght Bks.

Coxon, Michele. Kitten's Adventure. LC 98-60804. (Illus.). 32p. (J). (ps). 1998. pap. 5.50 (*1-887734-38-4*) Star Brght Bks.

— Look Out, Lion Cub! LC 99-70740. (Lift-the-Flap Bks.). (Illus.). 16p. (J). (ps). 1998. pap. 6.95 (*1-887734-39-2*) Star Brght Bks.

***Coxon, Michele.** Too Big! LC 00-100128. (Illus.). 16p. (J). (ps-k). 2000. 13.70 (*1-899248-64-1*, Pub. by Happy Cat) Star Brght Bks.

— Too Big! (Lift-the-Flap Bks.). (Illus.). 16p. (J). (ps-3). 2000. pap. 6.95 (*1-887734-78-3*) Star Brght Bks.

Coxon, Michele. Where's My Kitten? 16p. (J). 1996. pap. 6.99 (*0-14-055907-8*, PuffinBks) Peng Put Young Read.

***Coxson, Lorraine, et al.** Cooking to Learn. 290p. 1999. 59.95 (*1-884074-86-3*) PCI Educ Pubg.

Coxwell, C. Fillingham, tr. see Krylov, Ivan H.

Coxwell, Charles F. Siberian & Other Folk-Tales: Primitive Literature from the Empire of the Tsars. LC 78-67702. (Folktale Ser.). 1056p. reprint ed. 87.50 (*0-404-16076-X*) AMS Pr.

Coy, Ed. D., et al. ESLOA Test: English Second Language Oral Assessment. (Illus.). 75p. 1980. pap. 6.00 (*0-930713-29-X*) Lit Vol Am.

Coy, Fred E., Jr. Rock Art of Kentucky. LC 96-20466. (Perspectives on Kentucky's Past Ser.). (Illus.). 192p. 1996. 34.95 (*0-8131-1986-3*) U Pr of Ky.

Coy, Harold. Man Comes to America. LC 76-189260. x, 150p. 1973. write for info. (*0-316-15906-9*) Little.

Coy, James W., ed. The Ministers Manual: 1999 Edition. 74th ed. (Religion in Practice Ser.). 375p. 1998. 19.95 (*0-7879-4205-7*) Jossey-Bass.

Coy, Javier. Touching Extremes. 1992. pap. 7.00 (*84-87467-16-4*, Pub. by Zasterle Pr) SPD-Small Pr Dist.

Coy, Jimmie D., ed. A Gathering of Eagles: Advice on Leadership, Success & Significance. 224p. 1999. pap. 11.95 (*1-58169-024-X*) Genesis Comm Inc.

***Coy, Jimmie Dean, ed.** A Gathering of Eagles: Advice on Leadership, Success & Significance. 2nd ed. 320p. 2000. 24.95 (*1-58169-053-3*, Evergrn Pr AL) Genesis Comm Inc.

— A Gathering of Eagles: Advice on Leadership, Success & Significance. 2nd ed. (Illus.). 320p. 2000. pap. 14.95 (*1-58169-049-5*, Evergrn Pr AL) Genesis Comm Inc.

Coy, John. Night Driving. LC 95-6063. (Illus.). 32p. (J). (ps-2). 1995. 14.95 (*0-8050-2931-1*, B Martin BYR) H Holt & Co.

— Night Driving. (Illus.). (J). 1996. 14.95 (*0-8050-4586-4*) H Holt & Co.

— La Shonda's Ride. (J). 1999. 17.00 (*0-517-80009-8*, Pub. by Crown Bks Yng Read); lib. bdg. 18.99 (*0-517-80010-1*, Pub. by Crown Bks Yng Read) Random.

— Strong to the Hoop. LC 98-33264. (Illus.). 32p. (YA). (gr. 1 up). 1999. 16.95 (*1-880000-80-6*, Pub. by Lee & Low Bks) Publishers Group.

Coy, John, ed. A Special Stretch of Sky. (Illus.). 134p. 1997. pap. 10.00 (*0-927663-30-9*) COMPAS.

Coy, John, jt. auth. see Davies, J. Alans.

Coy, Joye J., et al. ESL Oral Assessment (ESLOA) 1989. pap. text 6.00 (*0-318-41219-5*) Lit Vol Am.

— ESLOA Trainer's Kit. 1989. student ed. 20.00 incl. audio (*0-930713-41-9*) Lit Vol Am.

Coy, Larry. A Passenger's Guide to Airline Flying. LC 98-65643. (Illus.). 144p. 1998. pap. 15.95 (*1-57197-123-8*) Pentland Pr.

Coy, Michael W., ed. Apprenticeship: From Theory to Method & Back Again. LC 88-8550. (SUNY Series in Anthropology of Work). 310p. (C). 1989. pap. text 24.95 (*0-7914-0061-1*) State U NY Pr.

Coy, Michael W., Jr. & Plotnicov, Leonard, eds. Africa in World History: Old, New, Then, & Now. LC 94-62224. (Ethnology Monographs: No. 16). x, 164p. (Orig.). (C). 1995. pap. text 10.00 (*0-945428-09-X*) Ethnology Monographs.

— African & African-American Sensibility. LC 94-62223. (Ethnology Monographs: No. 15). (Illus.). xiv, 122p. (Orig.). (C). 1995. pap. 10.00 (*0-945428-08-1*) Ethnology Monographs.

Coy, Patrick G., ed. A Revolution of the Heart: Essays on the Catholic Worker. LC 83-34910. (Illus.). 408p. (C). 1988. 39.95 (*0-87722-531-1*) Temple U Pr.

***Coy, Patrick G. & Woehrle, Lynne M., eds.** Social Conflicts & Collective Identities. 224p. 2000. 65.00 (*0-7425-0050-0*); pap. 25.95 (*0-7425-0051-9*) Rowman.

Coy, Stanley C. Beaufort County: "Queen of the Carolina Sea Islands" Activity Book. 21p. (J). (gr. 3-5). 1992. pap. 3.95 (*1-881459-00-4*) Eagle Pr SC.

— First Steps: Your Child from Birth to Starting School. (Illus.). 40p. (Orig.). 1994. pap. 5.95 (*1-881459-14-4*) Eagle Pr SC.

— Surviving the One Computer Classroom: A Handbook for Classroom Teachers. 39p. (Orig.). (C). 1992. pap. 6.50 (*1-881459-01-2*) Eagle Pr SC.

Coy, Stanley C., ed. see Baldwin, Barbara.

Coy, Stanley C., ed. see Barra, Paul A.

Coy, Stanley C., ed. see Broome, Betsy & Cummings, Cynthia.

Coy, Stanley C., ed. see Harding, Deborah C.

Coy, Stanley C., ed. see Jones, Deborah E.

Coy, Stanley C., ed. see Kozak, Ginnie.

Coy, Stanley C., ed. see Phiffer, Cynthia L.

Coy, Stanley C., ed. see Quinn, Christopher.

Coy, Stanley C., ed. see Warren, Deanna.

Coy, Stanley C., ed. see Whitten, William H.

Coy, Stanley C., ed. see Wilson, Lynne.

Coydon, Bernard. AS/400 Programming. LC 94-20005.Tr. of AS/400 Systeme d'Exploitation et Programmation. 1994. write for info. (*0-07-707745-8*) McGraw.

Coye, Beth F. My Navy Too. LC 97-92277. 432p. (Orig.). 1997. pap. 16.95 (*0-9658578-0-8*) Cedar Hollow.

Coye, Dale F. Pronouncing Shakespeare's Words: A Guide from A to Zounds. LC 97-44868. 744p. 1998. lib. bdg. 99.50 (*0-313-30655-9*, Greenwood Pr) Greenwood.

***Coye, Dale F., ed.** Pronouncing Shakespeare's Words: A Guide from A to Zounds. 744p. 1998. pap. text 100.00 (*1-57958-081-5*) Fitzroy Dearborn.

Coye, Jennifer Marmaduke, jt. auth. see Cooper-Mullin, Alison.

Coye, Molly J., ed. see Institute of Medicine Staff & National Research Council Staff.

Coyer & Smith. Power, Choice, Governing: A Reader. 2nd ed. (C). 1994. pap. text 17.25 (*0-07-011406-4*) McGraw.

Coyet, Wilsun. Light Visions: A Collection of Poetry & Prose. (Illus.). 70p. 1998. pap. text. write for info. (*0-9644611-0-2*) Sonset Prod.

Coyhis, Don. Fall. LC 95-79098. (Meditations with Native American Elders Ser.). 112p. 1995. reprint ed. pap. 9.95 (*1-887874-02-X*) Moh-He-Con-Nuck.

— Meditations with Native American Elders, 4 bks., Set. 1995. pap. 31.00 (*1-887874-04-6*) Moh-He-Con-Nuck.

— Spring. LC 95-79096. (Meditations with Native American Elders Ser.). 112p. 1995. reprint ed. pap. 9.95 (*1-887874-00-3*) Moh-He-Con-Nuck.

— Summer Meditations with Native American Elders. LC 95-79099. (Meditations with Native American Elders Ser.). 106p. 1995. reprint ed. pap. 9.95 (*1-887874-01-1*) Moh-He-Con-Nuck.

— Winter. LC 95-79100. (Meditations with Native American Elders Ser.). 112p. 1995. reprint ed. pap. 9.95 (*1-887874-03-8*) Moh-He-Con-Nuck.

Coyier, Duane L. & Roane, Martha K., eds. Compendium of Rhododendron & Azalea Diseases. LC 86-72873. (Disease Compendium Ser.). (Illus.). 88p. (Orig.). 1986. pap. 42.00 (*0-89054-075-6*) Am Phytopathol Soc.

An Asterisk (*) at the beginning of an entry indicates that the title is appearing for the first time.

Coykendall, Ralf, Jr. Coykendall's Complete Guide to Sporting Collectibles. LC 95-53850. (Illus.). 304p. 1996. pap. 22.95 (*0-87069-736-6*, Wllce-Homestd) Krause Pubns.
— Duck Decoys: And How to Rig Them. (Illus.). 136p. 1989. pap. 14.95 (*1-55821-039-3*) Lyons Pr.
Coykendall, Ralf W., ed. The Golden Age of Fly-Fishing: The Best of the Sportsman, 1927-1937. LC 97-10387. (Illus.). 240p. 1997. 32.50 (*0-88150-398-3*, Pub. by Countryman) Norton.
Coyle. Mathematics for Business Decisions. 1971. 50.95 (*0-442-30727-6*, VNR) Wiley.
Coyle, et al, eds. Benefits of Therapeutic Recreation: A Consensus View. 424p. (C). 1991. pap. text 32.00 (*1-882883-06-3*, 241) Idyll Arbor.
Coyle, Anne F. Leadership: ASTD Trainer's Sourcebook. LC 96-78874. 210p. 1996. pap. 39.95 (*0-07-053439-X*) McGraw.
Coyle, Berniece D., compiled by. Census of Leake County, Mississippi, 1840. 17p. 1989. pap. text 5.00 (*1-882111-86-9*) Coyle Data Co.
— Census of Yazoo County, Mississippi, 1840. 1990. pap. text 10.00 (*1-56088-001-5*) Coyle Data Co.
— Eighteen Forty Census of Tallahatchie Co., Mississippi. 15p. 1989. pap. text 5.00 (*1-882111-87-7*) Coyle Data Co.
— Newton Co., Ms. Census, 1840. 19p. 1989. pap. text 10.00 (*1-882111-85-0*) Coyle Data Co.
Coyle, Berniece D., ed. Census of Madison County, Mississippi, 1840. 40p. 1990. pap. text 10.00 (*1-882111-94-X*) Coyle Data Co.
Coyle, Berniece D. & Coyle, Thomas E., compiled by. Arkansas Eighteen Forty Census: Surnames in Census Order, Vol. 2. 278p. 1994. pap. text 35.00 (*1-56088-055-4*) Coyle Data Co.
— Arkansas Eighteen Forty Census Alphabetically Listed by Surname, Vol. 1. 252p. 1994. pap. text 35.00 (*1-56088-054-6*) Coyle Data Co.
Coyle, Berniece D., jt. auth. see Coyle, Thomas E.
Coyle, Betsy & Bakst, Daren L., eds. Virtual Learning Environments: Implications for the 21st Century. 272p. 1998. pap., per. 28.00 (*1-57858-015-3*, 3010) Am Assn Coll Registrars.
Coyle, Beverly. In Troubled Waters. 336p. 1994. pap. 12.95 (*0-14-023301-6*, Penguin Bks) Viking Penguin.
— In Troubled Waters. large type ed. LC 93-1597. 1993. lib. bdg. 23.95 (*0-8161-5821-5*) Thorndike Pr.
— The Kneeling Bus. 192p. 1992. pap. 10.95 (*0-14-014898-1*, Penguin Bks) Viking Penguin.
— Taken In. LC 98-2804. 305p. 1998. 24.95 (*0-670-86398-X*) Viking Penguin.
— Taken In. 320p. 1999. pap. 12.95 (*0-14-025030-1*) Viking Penguin.
— A Thought to Be Rehearsed: Aphorism in Wallace Steven's Poetry. LC 83-5778. (Studies in Modern Literature: No. 9). (Illus.). 130p. reprint ed. pap. 40.30 (*0-8357-1414-4*, 207054100001) Bks Demand.
Coyle, Beverly & Filreis, Alan, eds. Secretaries of the Moon: The Letters of Wallace Stevens & Jose Rodriguez Feo. LC 86-16835. x, 202p. 1986. text 32.95 (*0-8223-0670-0*) Duke.
Coyle, C., et al. The Management of Business Logistics. 631p. (C). 1988. 180.00 (*0-7855-5731-8*, Pub. by Inst Pur & Supply) St Mut.
Coyle, Carolyn. Designing with Tile. (Architecture Ser.). 193p. 1995. 80.00 (*0-471-28603-6*, VNR) Wiley.
Coyle, Carolyn. Designing with Tile. (Illus.). 208p. 1995. text 69.95 (*0-442-01731-6*, VNR) Wiley.
Coyle, Chester. Coyle: King of the Road. (Illus.). 248p. (Orig.). 1993. pap. 12.50 (*0-9625423-6-9*) Four-G Pubs.
Coyle, David C. Irrepressible Conflict: Business vs. Finance. LC 73-103648. (Select Bibliographies Reprint Ser.). 1977. 17.95 (*0-8369-5148-4*) Ayer.
— Ordeal of the Presidency. LC 72-10691. (Illus.). 408p. 1973. reprint ed. lib. bdg. 35.00 (*0-8371-6612-8*, COOP, Greenwood Pr) Greenwood.
— Roads to a New America. LC 77-103649. (Select Bibliographies Reprint Ser.). 1977. 35.95 (*0-8369-5149-2*) Ayer.
Coyle, David C., et al. American Way. LC 68-58781. (Essay Index Reprint Ser.). 1977. 19.95 (*0-8369-0107-X*) Ayer.
Coyle, Debbie. Everybody Sings! 3rd rev. ed. Orig. Title: Did You Ever Sing a Mooley Cow?. (Illus.). 90p. (J). (ps). 1994. reprint ed. pap. text 18.95 (*0-9626801-0-9*) D K Coyle.
Coyle, Dennis J. Property Rights & the Constitution: Shaping Society Through Land Use Regulation. LC 92-16680. (SUNY Series in the Constitution & Economic Rights). 382p. (C). 1993. text 64.50 (*0-7914-1443-4*); pap. text 21.95 (*0-7914-1444-2*) State U NY Pr.
***Coyle, Diane.** Governing the World Economy. 2000. 56.95 (*0-7456-2363-8*, Pub. by Polity Pr); pap. 21.95 (*0-7456-2364-6*, Pub. by Polity Pr) Blackwell Pubs.
Coyle, Diane. The Weightless World: Strategies for Managing the Digital Economy. LC 98-24518. (Illus.). 272p. 1998. 25.00 (*0-262-03259-7*) MIT Pr.
— The Weightless World: Strategies for Managing the Digital Economy. (OBEX Ser.). (Illus.). 272p. 1999. pap. 13.95 (*0-262-53166-6*) MIT Pr.
Coyle, Dominick J. Minorities in Revolt. LC 81-65866. (Illus.). 256p. 1983. 38.50 (*0-8386-3120-7*) Fairleigh Dickinson.
Coyle, Douglas, jt. ed. see Lunt, Neil.
Coyle, Eveleen. Irish Potato Cookbook. (Illus.). 96p. 1997. pap. 7.95 (*0-7171-2539-4*, Pub. by Gill & MacMill) Irish Bks Media.
Coyle, F. T., ed. Chemical Analysis of Metals, STP 944. LC 86-32130. (Special Technical Publication Ser.). (Illus.). 140p. 1986. text 27.00 (*0-8031-0942-3*, STP944) ASTM.
Coyle, Frank P., jt. auth. see Arranga, Edmund C.
Coyle, Gary. Progressive Socialism. 56p. (Orig.). (C). 1984. pap. 2.50 (*0-9591792-1-6*) Proutist Universal.
Coyle, Gary, ed. see Prabhat Rainjan Sarkar.
Coyle, Harold. Bright Star. 1990. 239.40 (*0-671-94300-6*) S&S Trade.
— Bright Star. McCarthy, Paul, ed. 512p. 1991. reprint ed. mass mkt. 6.99 (*0-671-68543-0*, Pocket Star Bks) PB.
— Code of Honor. 480p. 1995. mass mkt. 6.99 (*0-671-51029-0*) PB.
— Code of Honor. 1994. 23.00 (*0-671-77801-3*) S&S Trade.
***Coyle, Harold.** God's Children. LC 99-59570. 320p. 2000. 24.95 (*0-312-86296-2*, Pub. by Forge NYC) St Martin.
— God's Children. 2000. mass mkt. 7.99 (*0-8125-7538-5*) Tor Bks.
Coyle, Harold. Look Away. 1996. mass mkt. 6.99 (*0-671-52819-X*) PB.
— Look Away. 1997. per. 3.99 (*0-671-00991-5*) PB.
— Savage Wilderness. 1998. pap. 6.99 (*0-671-00387-9*) PB.
— Savage Wilderness. LC 97-13257. 1997. 25.50 (*0-684-83433-2*) S&S Trade.
— Sword Point. 1990. mass mkt. 6.99 (*0-671-73712-0*, Pocket Star Bks) PB.
— Team Yankee. 352p. 1988. pap. 6.99 (*0-425-11042-7*) Berkley Pub.
— The Ten Thousand. McCarthy, Paul, ed. xvi, 592p. 1994. reprint ed. mass mkt. 6.99 (*0-671-88565-0*) PB.
— Trial by Fire. McCarthy, Paul, ed. 544p. 1993. reprint ed. mass mkt. 6.99 (*0-671-79658-5*) PB.
— Until the End. 1997. per. 6.99 (*0-671-89017-4*) PB.
Coyle-Hennessey, Bobbi. Once More with Love: A Guide to Marrying Again. LC 92-74312. 192p. 1993. pap. 11.95 (*0-87793-498-3*) Ave Maria.
Coyle, J. D. Introduction to Organic Photochemistry. LC 85-29593. 184p. 1988. pap. 78.00 (*0-471-90975-0*) Wiley.
Coyle, J. D., et al, eds. Light, Chemical Change & Life. 420p. 1982. pap. 38.00 (*0-335-16100-6*) OpUniv Pr.
Coyle, J. D., jt. auth. see Barltrop, J. A.
Coyle, J. Kevin & Muir, Steven C., eds. Healing in Religion & Society, from Hippocrates to the Puritans: Selected Studies. LC 98-53715. (Studies in Religion & Society: Vol. 43). 212p. 1999. text 89.95 (*0-7734-8145-1*) E Mellen.
Coyle, Jean M. Handbook on Women & Aging. LC 96-32414. 504p. 1997. lib. bdg. 95.00 (*0-313-28857-7*) Greenwood.
Coyle, Jean M., compiled by. Families & Aging: A Selected, Annotated Bibliography, 14. LC 91-29593. (Bibliographies & Indexes in Gerontology Ser.: No. 14). 240p. 1991. lib. bdg. 49.95 (*0-313-27211-5*, CFB/, Greenwood Pr) Greenwood.
— Women & Aging: A Selected Annotated Bibliography, 9. LC 88-28975. (Bibliographies & Indexes in Gerontology Ser.). 163p. 1989. lib. bdg. 49.95 (*0-313-26021-4*, CWA, Greenwood Pr) Greenwood.
Coyle, Joe, jt. auth. see Enna, Sam J.
Coyle, John. James Joyce, Ulysses, a Portrait of the Artist As a Young Man. LC 98-39510. (Columbia Critical Guides Ser.). 186p. 1998. 39.50 (*0-231-11530-X*); pap. 14.50 (*0-231-11531-8*) Col U Pr.
— Narrative. 200p. (C). 1998. 50.00 (*0-415-13479-X*) Routledge.
Coyle, John J. Business Logistics: Independent Study Manual. 2nd ed. 272p. (C). 1994. pap. text, per. 21.95 (*0-8403-8836-5*) Kendall-Hunt.
Coyle, John J. & Bardi. The Management of Business Logistics. 7th ed. (SWC-Management Ser.). 2001. pap. 52.00 (*0-324-00751-5*) Thomson Learn.
Coyle, John J. & Bardi, Edward J. Transportation. 5th ed. LC 99-16907. 512p. (C). 1999. pap. 87.95 (*0-538-88180-1*) S-W Pub.
Coyle, John J., et al. Business Logistics. 5/e. 5th ed. Fenton & Craig, eds. (SWC-General Business). 580p. (C). 1992. mass mkt. 63.25 (*0-314-93364-6*) West Pub.
— The Management of Business Logistics. 6th ed. LC 95-39258. 650p. (C). 1996. mass mkt. 95.95 (*0-314-06507-5*) West Pub.
— Transportation. 4th ed. Fenton, ed. LC 93-23611. 550p. (C). 1993. pap. 62.50 (*0-314-02853-6*) West Pub.
Coyle, Joseph. Read English, Bk. 2. (Speak English Ser.). (Illus.). 80p. (Orig.). 1991. pap. 7.95 (*0-8325-0508-0*, Natl Textbk Co) NTC Contemp Pub Co.
Coyle, Joseph M. & Corley, Mary A. Speak English, Text 1. (Illus.). 80p. (Orig.). 1992. pap. text 7.95 (*0-8325-0501-3*, Natl Textbk Co) NTC Contemp Pub Co.
Coyle, Joseph S. How to Retire Young & Rich. (America's Financial Advisor Ser.). 208p. (Orig.). 1996. reprint ed. mass mkt. 12.95 (*0-446-67164-9*, Pub. by Warner Bks) Little.
Coyle, Joseph T. & Enna, Sam J., eds. Neuroleptics: Neurochemical, Behavioral, & Clinical Perspectives. LC 81-40892. (Central Nervous System Pharmacology Ser.). (Illus.). 341p. 1983. reprint ed. pap. 105.80 (*0-7837-9519-X*, 206026800005) Bks Demand.
Coyle, Karen. Coyle's Information Highway Handbook: A Practical File on the New Information Order. LC 97-16838. 297p. 1997. 30.00 (*0-8389-0708-3*) ALA.
Coyle, Kathleen. The Magical Realm: An Irish Childhood. (Illus.). 272p. (J). (gr. 4-7). 1998. pap. 14.95 (*0-86327-548-6*, Pub. by Wolfhound Press) Irish Amer Bk.
— Mary in the Christian Tradition. LC 95-78539. 152p. (Orig.). 1996. pap. 12.95 (*0-89622-672-7*) Twenty-Third.
Coyle, Lee P. George Ade. LC 64-20713. (Twayne's United States Authors Ser.). 1964. pap. text 7.95 (*0-8290-1933-2*); lib. bdg. 20.95 (*0-8057-0004-8*) Irvington.
Coyle, Lester N., jt. auth. see Lawler, Gregory F.
Coyle, Martin. William Shakespeare, Richard II. LC 98-39520. (Critical Guides Ser.). 192p. 1999. pap. 14.50 (*0-231-11537-7*) Col U Pr.
***Coyle, Martin.** William Shakespeare, Richard II. LC 98-39520. (Critical Guides Ser.). 192p. 1999. 39.50 (*0-231-11536-9*) Col U Pr.
Coyle, Martin, ed. Niccolo Machiavelli's The Prince: New Interdisciplinary Essays. LC 95-910. (Texts in Culture Ser.). 224p. 1995. text 69.95 (*0-7190-4195-3*, Pub. by Manchester Univ Pr); text 26.95 (*0-7190-4196-1*, Pub. by Manchester Univ Pr) St Martin.
Coyle, Martin & Garside, Peter, eds. Encyclopedia of Literature & Criticism. 1264p. (C). 1993. 165.00 (*0-415-02065-4*) Routledge.
Coyle, Martin, ed. see Shakespeare, William.
Coyle, Matthew, jt. auth. see Lamb, Peter.
Coyle, Michael. Ezra Pound & the Career of Modern Criticism. (LCENG Ser.). 2001. write for info. (*1-57113-192-2*) Camden Hse.
— Ezra Pound, Popular Genres & the Discourse of Culture. LC 94-31113. 264p. 1995. 40.00 (*0-271-01421-0*) Pa St U Pr.
Coyle, Neva. All New Free to Be Thin Lifestyle Plan: The Successful Weight-Management Plan That Links How To. 288p. 1993. pap. 9.99 (*1-55661-343-1*) Bethany Hse.
— Answering God's Call to Quiet: Finding Strength & Peace for a Pressured Life. LC 97-4735. (Devotional Daybook Ser.). 192p. 1997. pap. 8.99 (*1-55661-938-3*) Bethany Hse.
— Close to a Father's Heart. 256p. 1996. pap. 8.99 (*1-55661-548-5*) Bethany Hse.
— A Door of Hope. LC 95-485. (Summerwind Ser.: Bk. 1). 272p. 1995. pap. 8.99 (*1-55661-475-6*) Bethany Hse.
— The Free to Be Thin Cookbook. 16p. (Orig.). 1982. pap. 9.99 (*0-87123-255-3*) Bethany Hse.
— Free to Be Thin Daily Planner. 144p. (Orig.). 1983. pap. 7.99 (*0-87123-284-7*) Bethany Hse.
— Free to Dream. 16p. (Orig.). 1990. pap. 8.99 (*0-87123-997-3*) Bethany Hse.
— Inside the Private Hedge. LC 95-45869. (Summerwind Ser.: Vol. 2). 256p. (Orig.). 1996. pap. 8.99 (*1-55661-547-7*) Bethany Hse.
— Learning to Know God: And to Love His Friends. 16p. 1993. pap. 8.99 (*1-55661-339-3*) Bethany Hse.
— Living Free. LC 81-3811. 128p. 1981. pap. 6.99 (*0-87123-346-0*) Bethany Hse.
— Making Sense of Pain & Struggle: Finding the Strength to Go On. (Devotional Daybook Ser.). 16p. (Orig.). 1992. pap. 8.99 (*1-55661-276-1*) Bethany Hse.
— Meeting the Challenges of Change. 176p. (Orig.). 1993. pap. 8.99 (*1-55661-278-8*) Bethany Hse.
— A New Heart - A New Start: Discovering the Promise of Restoration. (Devotional Daybook Ser.: Vol. 2). 16p. (Orig.). 1992. pap. 8.99 (*1-55661-277-X*) Bethany Hse.
— Overcoming the Diet Dilemma. LC 91-24062. 92p. (Orig.). 1991. pap. 8.99 (*1-55661-232-X*) Bethany Hse.
— Sharon's Hope. 288p. (J). 1996. pap. 10.99 (*0-7852-7660-2*) Nelson.
***Coyle, Neva.** What Does God Want Anyway? Finding the Tender Heart of God Toward Me. 214p. 1999. pap. 10.99 (*1-56955-104-9*, Vine Bks) Servant.
Coyle, Neva. Whatever Happened to the Real Me? The Joy of Finding Your True Self--The Person God Made You to Be. LC 99-23193. 214p. 1999. pap. 10.99 (*1-56955-103-0*, Vine Bks) Servant.
— When Life Takes More Than It Gives: A Devotional Daybook. 16p. 1996. pap. 8.99 (*1-55661-589-2*) Bethany Hse.
— Woman of Strength: Reclaim Your Past, Seize Your Present, & Secure Your Future. LC 97-24505. 220p. 1997. pap. text 10.99 (*1-56955-036-0*) Servant.
Coyle, Neva & Anderson, Zane. Living by Chance or by Choice: Replacing Choices You Can't Change with Decisions Only You Can Make. LC 94-38360. 224p. 1995. pap. 8.99 (*1-55661-486-1*) Bethany Hse.
Coyle, Neva & Chapian, Marie. The All-New Free to Be Thin: The Successful Weight-Management Plan That Links How to Eat with How... 224p. 1994. pap. 9.99 (*1-55661-534-5*) Bethany Hse.
— Libre para Ser Delgado.Tr. of Free to Be Thin. (SPA.). 176p. (Orig.). 1992. pap. 8.99 (*0-88113-247-0*) Caribe Betania.
Coyle, Neva, jt. auth. see Chapian, Marie.
***Coyle, P. Allan.** Roy Rogers & Dale Evans Toys & Memorabilia: Identification & Values. (Illus.). 240p. 2000. pap. 24.95 (*1-57432-181-1*) Collector Bks.
Coyle, Patrick G., Jr. Understanding the Life of Birds. 1987. 21.95 (*0-939423-02-7*) Summit Publns.
Coyle, Petah, et al. Petah Coyne. LC 96-31061. 1996. pap. write for info. (*0-88675-048-2*) Corcoran.
Coyle, R. G. Decision Analysis. LC 74-163046. 122 p. 1972. write for info. (*0-17-761017-4*) ITP Nelson.
Coyle, R. G. Management System Dynamics. LC 76-40144. (Illus.). 475p. reprint ed. pap. 147.30 (*0-8357-5597-5*, 203523600093) Bks Demand.
Coyle, R. G. System Dynamics Modelling: A Practical Approach. 1996. ring bd. 89.95 (*0-412-61710-2*) Chapman & Hall.
Coyle, Rena. My First Baking Book. LC 87-40645. (Bialosky & Friends Bks.). (Illus.). 144p. (J). (gr. 1-5). 1988. pap. 9.95 (*0-89480-579-7*, 1579) Workman Pub.
— My First Cookbook. LC 84-40683. (Bialosky & Friends Bks.). (Illus.). 128p. (J). (gr. 1-5). 1985. pap. 10.95 (*0-89480-846-X*, 846) Workman Pub.
Coyle, Rena & Messing, Patricia. Baby Let's Eat! LC 86-40548. (Illus.). 128p. 1987. pap. 9.95 (*0-89480-300-X*, 1300) Workman Pub.
Coyle, Richard, jt. auth. see Mulder, Mary J.
Coyle, Richard J., ed. The McGraw-Hill Handbook of American Depository Receipts. 392p. 1995. 59.95 (*0-07-013333-6*) McGraw.
Coyle, Robert, Jr. The Lost in Space Yearbook. 100p. 1992. pap. 9.95 (*1-880417-06-5*) Star Tech.
Coyle, Rosemary. In His Love. 196p. 1991. pap. 6.95 (*0-9631545-0-8*) Cath Charismatic.
Coyle, Shawn C. Art & Science of Flying Helicopters. (Illus.). 238p. 1996. pap. 36.95 (*0-8138-2169-X*, Pub. by E A) Iowa St U Pr.
Coyle, Susan L. Between Shadows & Light: Poetry of Suzy Coyle. (Illus.). 85p. 1999. text 10.00 (*0-9668903-9-6*) Wildflower Progs.
Coyle, Susan L., ed. see National Research Council Staff.
Coyle, Terence, jt. auth. see Hale, Robert B.
Coyle, Terence, jt. auth. see Hale, Robert Beverly.
Coyle, Thomas. This Is Our Mass. LC 89-50155. 160p. 1989. pap. 7.95 (*0-89622-394-9*) Twenty-Third.
Coyle, Thomas E., ed. Mississippi 1840 Census Vol. 1: Alphabetically Listed by Surnames. 551p. 1990. pap. text 60.00 (*1-56088-011-2*) Coyle Data Co.
— Ms. Eighteen Forty Census Vol. 2: Surnames in Census Order. 652p. 1992. pap. text 60.00 (*1-56088-053-8*) Coyle Data Co.
Coyle, Thomas E. & Coyle, Berniece D. Denton County, Texas Census with Index, 1860. 151p. 1991. pap. text 25.00 (*1-56088-017-1*) Coyle Data Co.
— Denton County, Texas Census with Index, 1870. 233p. 1990. pap. text 35.00 (*1-56088-014-7*) Coyle Data Co.
Coyle, Thomas E., jt. compiled by see Coyle, Berniece D.
Coyle, Virginia, jt. auth. see Zimmerman, Jack.
Coyle, Wendy & Shortland, Sue. International Relocation: A Global Perspective. LC 92-227667. (Illus.). 274p. reprint ed. pap. 85.00 (*0-608-09703-9*, 206986900007) Bks Demand.
Coyle, William. Firestorm. large type ed. (General Ser.). 463p. 1989. lib. bdg. 19.95 (*0-8161-4800-7*, G K Hall Lrg Type) Mac Lib Ref.
— Research Papers. 11th ed. LC 98-5504. 322p. 1998. spiral bd. 29.00 (*0-205-28725-5*) Allyn.
Coyle, William, ed. Aspects of Fantasy: Selected Essays from the Second International Conference on the Fantastic in Literature & Film, 19. LC 84-12787. (Contributions to the Study of Science Fiction & Fantasy Ser.: No. 19). (Illus.). 259p. 1986. 59.95 (*0-313-24608-4*, CAF/) Greenwood.
Coyle, William J. Libraries in Prisons: A Blending of Institutions, 15. LC 86-25719. (New Directions in Information Management Ser.: No. 15). 153p. 1987. 49.95 (*0-313-24769-2*, CRO/, Greenwood Pr) Greenwood.
Coyle, William P. & Haman, Edward A. New York Power of Attorney Handbook. LC 97-40127. (Legal Survival Guides Ser.). 144p. 1997. pap. 12.95 (*1-57071-188-7*) Sourcebks.
Coyne. Crowded Prairie: American National Identity in the Hollywood Western. 264p. 1998. pap. 18.95 (*1-86064-259-4*, Pub. by I B T) St Martin.
— Intro to Soil Microbiology. (Agriculture Ser.). (C). 1999. pap. 16.00 (*0-8273-8435-1*, AutoDesk Pr) Delmar.
— To Match a Dream. LC 99-161726. 1999. pap. 19.99 (*0-7710-2277-8*) McCland & Stewart.
Coyne, Andre. Biography of Cesar Moro: Signatary of the Surrealist Manifesto. 1990. write for info. (*0-318-67003-8*) Extramares Edit.
— The Life of Cesar Moro: A Latinamerican Signer of the Surrealist Manifesto. Bustamante, Cecilia, ed. (Illus.). (C). 1989. write for info. (*0-318-66713-4*) Extramares Edit.
Coyne, Anthony M. Introduction to Inductive Reasoning. LC 84-3560. 294p. (Orig.). 1984. pap. text 24.00 (*0-8191-3883-5*) U Pr of Amer.
Coyne, Edward J., Sr. Targeting the Foreign Direct Investor: Strategic Motivation, Investment Size, & Developing Country Investment-Attraction Packages. LC 95-37845. 224p. (C). 1995. lib. bdg. 103.00 (*0-7923-9638-3*) Kluwer Academic.
Coyne, Erwin, contrib. by. Additives to Blood Collective Devices: EDTA; Tentative Guideline (1992) 1992. 75.00 (*1-56238-162-8*, H35-T) NCCLS.
Coyne, Gary S. The Laboratory Companion: A Practical Guide to Materials, Equipment & Techniques. rev. ed. LC 97-16689. 552p. 1997. 64.95 (*0-471-18422-5*) Wiley.
Coyne, George V., et al, eds. Polarized Radiation of Circumstellar Origin. 795p. 1989. pap. 48.00 (*0-8165-1120-9*) U of Ariz Pr.
Coyne, George V., tr. see Fantoli, Annibale.
Coyne, George V., tr. see Heller, Michael.
Coyne, James C., ed. Essential Papers on Depression. (Essential Papers in Psychoanalysis). 496p. (C). 1986. pap. text 27.50 (*0-8147-1399-8*) NYU Pr.
Coyne, James C., jt. auth. see Lakoff, Robin T.
Coyne, James C., jt. ed. see Joiner, Thomas.
Coyne, James K. & Fund, John H. Cleaning House: America's Campaign for Term Limits. LC 92-19278. 352p. 1992. 21.95 (*0-89526-516-8*) Regnery Pub.
Coyne, James P. Airpower in the Gulf. 2nd ed. (Illus.). 224p. 1992. pap. 12.60 (*0-9608492-1-1*) Aero Ed Found.
— A Visual Novel of the War of Tomorrow Vol. 1: Strike Eagles. 224p. 1990. pap. 6.95 (*0-380-75845-8*, Avon Bks) Morrow Avon.
Coyne, Jan, ed. see Henry, James A., et al.
Coyne, Jim. Avid Reader's Bookmark. 12p. (C). 1995. pap. 2.50 (*0-9648228-0-6*) Elysium Pubng.
— Fast Adult Education Series. Dec, Maryann, ed. 320p. (Orig.). (YA). 1996. pap. 25.00 (*0-9648228-2-2*) Elysium Pubng.
— The Repugnant Warehouse: An Expose of the Federal Prison System. Dec, Maryann, ed. 212p. (Orig.). 1995. pap. 12.95 (*0-9648228-1-4*) Elysium Pubng.
— 3 to 1. Dec, Maryann, ed. (Jim Coyne Ser.). 215p. (Orig.). (YA). 1996. pap. 11.00 (*0-9648228-3-0*) Elysium Pubng.
Coyne, John. Child of Shadows. 336p. 1991. mass mkt. 4.99 (*0-446-36124-0*, Pub. by Warner Bks) Little.

C

— Hobgoblin. 1990. mass mkt. 4.95 (0-446-35921-1, Pub. by Warner Bks) Little.

— The Hunting Season. 1988. mass mkt. 4.50 (0-446-34321-8, Pub. by Warner Bks) Little.

Coyne, John, ed. Living on the Edge: Fiction by Peace Corps Writers. LC 98-17464. 320p. 1999. pap. 17.95 (1-880684-57-8, Pub. by Curbstone) SPD-Small Pr Dist.

— The Penland School of Crafts Book of Jewelry Making. LC 74-31333. (Illus.). 192p. 1975. 12.95 (0-672-51967-4, Bobbs) Macmillan.

Coyne, John & Miller, Jerry L. How to Make Upside-Down Dolls. LC 76-4086. (Illus.). 1977. 12.95 (0-672-52157-1, Bobbs) Macmillan.

Coyne, John & Wright, Mike, eds. Divestment & Strategic Change. LC 84-24456. 224p. 1986. 53.00 (0-389-20547-8, 08111) B&N Imports.

Coyne, John, jt. auth. see Hebert, Tom.

Coyne, John J., tr. see Schutte, Josef F.

Coyne, K. R. & Hiskey, J. B. In-Situ Recovery of Minerals. LC 89-85005. 380p. 1989. 50.00 (0-939204-37-1, 88-03) Eng Found.

Coyne, K. R., ed. see Engineering Foundation U. S. Conferences Staff.

Coyne Kelley, Kathleen. A. S. Byatt. LC 96-23773. 1996. 32.00 (0-8057-7043-7, Twyne) Mac Lib Ref.

***Coyne, Kevin.** Best Years of Our Lives. 304p. 2001. 24.95 (0-670-87150-8, Viking) Viking Penguin.

Coyne, Kevin. A Day in the Night of America. LC 90-53139. 320p. 1992. 20.00 (0-685-48008-9) Random.

— Day in the Night of America. 336p. 1995. pap. 14.95 (0-8050-2874-9) H Holt & Co.

— Domers: A Year at Notre Dame. 336p. 1996. pap. 12.95 (0-14-017898-8, Penguin Bks) Viking Penguin.

— The Party Dress. LC 90-60286. 192p. 1991. pap. 13.95 (1-85242-197-5) Serpents Tail.

— Show Business. (Masks Ser.). 176p. 1993. pap. 14.99 (1-85242-251-3) Serpents Tail.

Coyne, Lelia M., et al, eds. Spectroscopic Characterization of Minerals & their Surfaces. (ACS Symposium Ser.: No. 415). (Illus.). 492p. 1989. text 105.00 (0-8412-1716-5, Pub. by Am Chemical) OUP.

Coyne, Mark. Soil Microbiology: An Exploratory Approach. 2nd rev. abr. ed. LC 98-39580. 480p. (C). 1999. pap. 63.95 (0-8273-8434-3) Delmar.

Coyne, Mark, jt. ed. see Allin, Craig.

Coyne, Michael. The Crowded Prairie: American National Identity in Hollywood Western. LC 96-181893. (Illus.). 264p. 1997. text 29.95 (1-86064-040-0, Pub. by I B T) St Martin.

Coyne, Patricia, tr. from LAT. Priscian of Caesares's "De Laude Anastasii Imperatoris" LC 91-20935. (Studies in Classics: Vol. 1). 248p. 1991. lib. bdg. 89.95 (0-7734-9772-2) E Mellen.

***Coyne, Philip.** Motorcycle Roadcraft: The Police Rider's Handbook to Better Motorcycling. 178p. 2000. pap. 24.00 (0-11-341143-X, Pub. by Statnry Office) Balogh.

Coyne, Philip. Roadcraft: The Police Driver's Handbook. 177p. 2000. pap. 20.00 (0-11-340858-7, HM08587, Pub. by Statnry Office) Balogh.

***Coyne, Philip.** Towing Roadcraft: The Essential Towing Handbook. (Illus.). xii, 196p. 2000. pap. 20.00 (0-11-552022-8, Pub. by Statnry Office) Balogh.

***Coyne, Phyllis, et al.** Developing Leisure Time Skills for Persons with Autism: A Practical Approach for Home, School & Community. (Illus.). 228p. 1999. spiral bd. 39.95 (1-885477-56-2) Fut Horizons.

Coyne, Rachel. Daughter, Have I Told You? LC 97-13723. (Illus.). 32p. (J). (gr. k-3). 1998. 15.95 (0-8050-5301-8) H Holt & Co.

Coyne, Randall & Entzeroth, Iyn. Capital Punishment & the Judicial Process. 188p. 1996. pap. text, suppl. ed. 15.00 (0-89089-007-2) Carolina Acad Pr.

Coyne, Randall & Entzeroth, Lyn. Capital Punishment & the Judicial Process: Cases & Materials. LC 94-70568. 754p. 1994. lib. bdg. 75.00 (0-89089-581-3) Carolina Acad Pr.

Coyne, Richard. Designing Information Technology in the Postmodern Age: From Method to Metaphor. LC 95-8253. (Leonardo Book Ser.). 399p. 1995. 44.00 (0-262-03228-7) MIT Pr.

— Technoromanticism: Digital Narrative, Holism, & the Romance of the Real. LC 99-21241. (Illus.). 384p. 1999. 40.00 (0-262-03260-0) MIT Pr.

Coyne, Robert, jt. ed. see Levin, Bruce A.

Coyne, Tami. Your Life's Work: A Guide to Creating a Spiritual & Successful Work Life. LC 98-163042. 256p. 1998. pap. 12.95 (0-425-16162-5) Berkley Pub.

Coyne, Thomas A. Federal Rules of Civil Procedure. 2nd ed. LC 81-18095. (Federal Court Rules Ser.). 1994. ring bd. 145.00 (0-87632-063-9) West Group.

Coyne, Thomas J. Readings in Managerial Economics. 5th ed. 465p. (C). 1992. pap. text 34.50 (0-9633192-0-5) Coyne Pub.

Coyne, Thomas Joseph. Readings in Managerial Economics. 4th ed. (C). 1984. pap. text 25.95 (0-256-03056-1, Irwn McGrw-H) McGrw-H Hghr Educ.

Coyner, Dale. Motorcycle Journeys Through the Appalachians. (Motorcycle Journeys Ser.). (Illus.). 320p. 1995. pap. 19.95 (1-884313-02-7) Whitehorse NH.

Coyner, David H. The Lost Trappers. Weber, David J., ed. & afterword by by. LC 94-36584. (Illus.). 232p. 1995. pap. 12.95 (0-8061-2725-2) U of Okla Pr.

— The Lost Trappers. 1992. reprint ed. lib. bdg. 75.00 (0-7812-5020-X) Rprt Serv.

Coyningham, Melosina Lenox, ed. Diaries of Ireland: From Ludolf von Munchhausen to Lady Gregory. LC 98-147644. 256p. 1998. pap. 22.95 (1-874675-78-3, Pub. by Lilliput Pr) Irish Bks Media.

Coyote, Bertha L. & Giglio, Virginia. Leaving Everything Behind: The Songs & Memories of a Cheyenne Woman. LC 97-11270. (Illus.). xix, 166p. 1997. 29.95 (0-8061-2984-0); 40.00 incl. disk (0-8061-2987-5) U of Okla Pr.

***Coyote, Ivan.** Close to Spider Man. 2000. pap. 13.95 (1-55152-086-9) Arsenal Pulp.

Coyote, Lloyd M., jt. auth. see Smith, Helene.

Coyote, Peter. Sleeping Where I Fall: A Chronicle. LC 97-47740. (Illus.). 368p. 1998. 26.00 (1-887178-67-8, Pub. by Counterpt DC) HarpC.

— Sleeping Where I Fall: A Chronicle. (Illus.). 384p. 1999. pap. text 14.00 (1-58243-011-X, Pub. by Counterpt DC) HarpC.

Coysh. The Dictionary of Picture Postcards in Britain, 1894-1939. (Illus.). 312p. 1996. 39.50 (1-85149-231-3) Antique Collect.

Coysh, A. W. & Henrywood, R. K. The Dictionary of Blue & White Printed Pottery, 1780-1880, Vol. I. (Illus.). 424p. 1982. 59.50 (0-907462-06-5) Antique Collect.

— The Dictionary of Blue & White Printed Pottery, 1780-1880, Vol. II. (Illus.). 240p. 1989. 49.50 (1-85149-093-0) Antique Collect.

Coyte, Rodney, jt. auth. see Barbera, Maria.

Cozarinsky, Edgardo. Borges in & on Film. Waldman, Gloria & Christ, Ronald J., trs. from SPA. 117p. (Orig.). 1988. pap. 10.95 (0-930829-08-5) Lumen Inc.

— Urban Voodoo.Tr. of Vudu Urbano. 127p. (Orig.). 1991. pap. 9.95 (0-930829-15-8) Lumen Inc.

Cozart, Carol, jt. auth. see Foehner, Charlotte.

Cozart, Cheryl A. & Harper, John A. Oil & Gas Developments in Pennsylvania in 1991. (Progress Reports: No. 205). (Illus.). 96p. (Orig.). 1993. pap. 4.10 (0-8182-0178-9) Commonweal PA.

Cozart, Cheryl L., jt. auth. see Harper, John A.

Cozart, Cheryl L., jt. auth. see Heyman, Louis.

Cozby, Paul C. Methods in Behavioral Research. 6th rev. ed. LC 96-12005. (Illus.). xii, 335p. (C). 1996. pap. text 39.95 (1-55934-659-0, 1659) Mayfield Pub.

***Cozby, Paul C.** Methods in Behavioral Research. 7th ed. LC 00-21365. (Illus.). 2000. write for info. (0-7674-1063-7) Mayfield Pub.

Cozby, Paul C. Methods in Behavioral Research: Test Bank, Testbank. 6th ed. (C). 1997. disk. write for info. (0-318-69287-2) Mayfield Pub.

— Methods in Behavioral Research: Transparencies, Masters. 6th ed. 1997. trans. write for info. (0-614-02717-9) Mayfield Pub.

Cozby, Paul C., et al. Research Methods in Human Development. 2nd ed. LC 98-16053. 416p. 1998. text 47.95 (1-55934-875-5, 1875) Mayfield Pub.

Cozen, Lewis. Children with Deformities. (Illus.). 112p. 1999. pap. 14.00 (0-8059-4571-7) Dorrance.

Cozen, Lewis, ed. The Natural History of Orthopaedic Disease: A Gatekeeper's Guide. (Illus.). 600p. (Orig.). 1993. 20.00 (0-9637929-0-3) Dr L Cozen Pub.

Cozen, Stephen A., et al. Insuring Real Property, 3 vols. 1989. ring bd. 370.00 incl. cd-rom (0-8205-1315-6) Bender.

Cozens, Bronwyn. Color Crazy: The Complete Color Guide for Cosmetologists. LC 91-3556. (Illus.). 184p. (C). 1991. pap. 15.95 (1-56253-034-8) Milady Pub.

— Science in Your Salon. LC 91-3555. (Illus.). 220p. (C). 1991. pap. 17.50 (1-56253-035-6) Milady Pub.

Cozens, Frederick W. & Stumpf, Florence S. Sports in American Life. LC 75-22810. (America in Two Centuries Ser.). 1976. reprint ed. 31.95 (0-405-07681-9) Ayer.

***Cozens, Simon.** Beginning Perl. 700p. 2000. pap. 39.99 (1-86100-314-5) Wrox Pr Inc.

***Cozens, Simon, et al.** Professional Perl Programming. 1100p. 2000. pap. 59.99 (1-86100-449-4) Wrox Pr Inc.

Cozic, Charles P. The Information Highway. (Current Controversies Ser.). 208p. (J). (gr. 5-12). 1996. pap. text 16.20 (1-56510-374-2); lib. bdg. 26.20 (1-56510-375-0) Greenhaven.

Cozic, Charles P., ed. An Aging Population: Opposing Viewpoints. LC 95-49646. (Opposing Viewpoints Ser.). 1996. pap. 16.20 (1-56510-394-7); lib. bdg. 26.20 (1-56510-395-5) Greenhaven.

— America's Prisons. LC 96-47990. (Opposing Viewpoints Ser.). (Illus.). (J). (gr. 5-12). 1997. pap. 16.20 (1-56510-549-4) Greenhaven.

— Civil Liberties: Opposing Viewpoints. rev. ed. LC 93-16419. 240p. (YA). 1994. pap. 16.20 (1-56510-057-3) Greenhaven.

— Education in America: Opposing Viewpoints. LC 91-42495. (Opposing Viewpoints Ser.). (Illus.). 288p. (YA). (gr. 10 up). 1992. pap. text 16.20 (0-89908-163-0) Greenhaven.

— Ethnic Conflict. (At Issue Ser.). 107p. 1995. lib. bdg. 18.70 (1-56510-298-3) Greenhaven.

Cozic, Charles P., ed. Ethnic Conflict. (At Issue Ser.). 107p. (C). 1995. pap. text 11.20 (1-56510-265-7) Greenhaven.

Cozic, Charles P., ed. The Future of the Internet. LC 97-22. (At Issue Ser.). (YA). (gr. 9 up). 1997. pap. 11.20 (1-56510-658-X); lib. bdg. 18.70 (1-56510-659-8) Greenhaven.

Cozic, Charles P., ed. Gangs: Opposing Viewpoints. LC 95-9015. (Opposing Viewpoints Ser.). (Illus.). 191p. 1996. lib. bdg. 26.20 (1-56510-363-7) Greenhaven.

Cozic, Charles P., ed. Gangs: Opposing Viewpoints. LC 95-9015. (Opposing Viewpoints Ser.). (Illus.). 191p. (J). (gr. 5-12). 1996. pap. text 22.45 (1-56510-362-9) Greenhaven.

— Garbage & Waste. LC 97-23. (Current Controversies Ser.). (J). (gr. 5-12). 1997. pap. 16.20 (1-56510-565-6); lib. bdg. 26.20 (1-56510-566-4) Greenhaven.

Cozic, Charles P., ed. Global Resources. LC 97-19698. (Opposing Viewpoints Ser.). (Illus.). (YA). (gr. 5-12). 1997. lib. bdg. 26.20 (1-56510-673-3) Greenhaven.

Cozic, Charles P., ed. Illegal Drugs. LC 97-29281. (Current Controversies Ser.). (YA). (gr. 5-12). 1997. lib. bdg. 26.20 (1-56510-683-0) Greenhaven.

Cozic, Charles P., ed. Illegal Drugs. LC 97-29281. (Current Controversies Ser.). (YA). (gr. 5-12). 1997. pap. 16.20 (1-56510-682-2) Greenhaven.

Cozic, Charles P., ed. Illegal Immigration. LC 96-22686. (Opposing Viewpoints Ser.). (Illus.). (J). (gr. 5-12). 1996. lib. bdg. 26.20 (1-56510-514-1) Greenhaven.

Cozic, Charles P., ed. Illegal Immigration. LC 96-22686. (Opposing Viewpoints Ser.). (Illus.). (J). (gr. 5-12). 1996. pap. 16.20 (1-56510-513-3) Greenhaven.

Cozic, Charles P., ed. The Militia Movement. LC 96-44910. (At Issue Ser.). (J). (gr. 5-12). 1996. pap. 11.20 (1-56510-541-9) Greenhaven.

Cozic, Charles P., ed. The Militia Movement. LC 96-44910. (At Issue Ser.). (J). (gr. 5-12). 1996. lib. bdg. 18.70 (1-56510-542-7) Greenhaven.

Cozic, Charles P., ed. Nationalism & Ethnic Conflict. LC 93-19854. (Current Controversies Ser.). 288p. (YA). 1994. pap. 16.20 (1-56510-079-4); lib. bdg. 26.20 (1-56510-080-8) Greenhaven.

Cozic, Charles P., ed. Politicians & Ethics. LC 96-11848. (Current Controversies Ser.). 208p. (J). (gr. 5-12). 1996. pap. text 16.20 (1-56510-406-4); lib. bdg. 26.20 (1-56510-407-2) Greenhaven.

Cozic, Charles P., ed. Pollution. LC 93-4552. (Current Controversies Ser.). 224p. 1994. pap. 16.20 (1-56510-075-1); lib. bdg. 26.20 (1-56510-076-X) Greenhaven.

— Rainforests. LC 97-38571. (At Issue Ser.). 120p. (J). (gr. 5-12). 1997. lib. bdg. 18.70 (1-56510-695-4) Greenhaven.

— Rainforests. LC 97-38571. (At Issue Ser.). 120p. (YA). (gr. 5-12). 1997. pap. 11.20 (1-56510-694-6) Greenhaven.

— Space Exploration: Opposing Viewpoints. LC 92-8149. (Illus.). 192p. (YA). (gr. 10 up). 1992. lib. bdg. 26.20 (0-89908-197-5) Greenhaven.

— U. S. Policy Toward China. (At Issue Ser.). 96p. 1996. pap. text 11.20 (1-56510-388-2) Greenhaven.

— Welfare Reform. LC 96-33567. (At Issue Ser.). (J). (gr. 5-12). 1996. pap. 11.20 (1-56510-545-1) Greenhaven.

Cozic, Charles P., ed. Welfare Reform. LC 96-33567. (At Issue Ser.). (J). (gr. 5-12). 1996. lib. bdg. 18.70 (1-56510-546-X) Greenhaven.

Cozic, Charles P. & Petrikin, Jonathan S., eds. The Abortion Controversy. (Current Controversies Ser.). 288p. 1995. pap. text 16.20 (1-56510-228-2, 2282); lib. bdg. 26.20 (1-56510-229-0, 2290) Greenhaven.

Cozic, Charles P. & Winters, Paul A., eds. Gambling. LC 94-43378. (Current Controversies Ser.). 208p. 1995. pap. text 16.20 (1-56510-234-7, 2347); lib. bdg. 26.20 (1-56510-235-5, 2355) Greenhaven.

Cozic, Charles P. & Winters, Paul A., eds. Welfare. LC 96-31261. (Opposing Viewpoints Ser.). (Illus.). (J). (gr. 5-12). 1997. lib. bdg. 26.20 (1-56510-520-6) Greenhaven.

Cozic, Charles P. & Winters, Paul A., eds. Welfare. LC 96-31261. (Opposing Viewpoints Ser.). (Illus.). (J). (gr. 5-12). 1997. pap. 16.20 (1-56510-519-2) Greenhaven.

Cozic, Charles P., jt. ed. see Biskup, Michael D.

Cozic, Charles P., jt. ed. see Roleff, Tamara L.

Cozic, Charles P., jt. ed. see Weksesser, Carol.

Cozier, Tony, jt. auth. see Holding, Michael.

Cozijnsen, Anton & Vrakking, Willem, eds. Handbook on Innovation Management. LC 92-29861. 1993. 58.95 (0-631-17616-0) Blackwell Pubs.

Cozort, Daniel. Highest Yoga Tantra: An Introduction to the Esoteric Buddhism of Tibet. 200p. (C). 1994. pap. 14.95 (1-55939-036-0) Snow Lion Pubns.

— The Sand Mandala of Vajrabhairava. (Illus.). 40p. 1995. pap. 8.95 (1-55939-056-5) Snow Lion Pubns.

— Unique Tenets of the Middle Way Consequence School. LC 97-37351. 632p. 1998. 45.00 (1-55939-059-X); pap. 29.95 (1-55939-077-8) Snow Lion Pubns.

Cozta, Margaret J., tr. see Eca de Queiroz, Jose Maria.

Cozyris, George A. Christian Metz & the Reality of Film. Jowett, Garth S., ed. LC 79-6670. (Dissertation on Film, Ser.). 1980. lib. bdg. 15.95 (0-405-12904-1) Ayer.

Cozza, Carm & Ordermatt, Rick. True Blue: The Carm Cozza Story. LC 99-24185. (Illus.). 224p. 1999. 29.95 (0-300-08099-9) Yale U Pr.

***Cozzani, Giuseppe.** Garden of Orthodontics: Thoughts, Suggestions, Errors. LC 00-27503. (Illus.). 432p. 2000. 180.00 (0-86715-388-1) Quintessence.

Cozzarelli, Francis A., jt. auth. see Shames, Irving H.

Cozzarelli, Nicholas R. & Wang, James C., eds. DNA Topology & Its Biological Effects. (Monographs: No. 20). (Illus.). 480p. (C). 1990. text 97.00 (0-87969-348-7) Cold Spring Harbor.

Cozzarini, Christian, jt. auth. see Lenz, Hans Peter.

Cozzens. Writing Links. (C). 1998. pap. text 28.00 (0-15-505324-8) Harcourt Coll Pubs.

***Cozzens, Donald B.** The Changing Face of the Priesthood: A Reflection on the Priest's Crisis of Soul. LC 99-34368. 160p. 2000. pap. 14.95 (0-8146-2504-5) Liturgical Pr.

Cozzens, Donald B. The Spirituality of the Diocesan Priest. LC 96-51709. 200p. (Orig.). 1997. pap. text 14.95 (0-8146-2421-9, Liturg Pr Bks) Liturgical Pr.

Cozzens, Frederic S. Sparrowgrass Papers. LC 72-76922. (American Fiction Reprint Ser.). 1977. 18.95 (0-8369-7001-2) Ayer.

***Cozzens, Gary.** Adult Agencies: Linkages for Adolescents in Transition. LC 98-49957. 1999. pap. write for info. (0-89079-815-X) PRO-ED.

Cozzens, James G. By Love Possessed. LC 57-10062. 1957. 8.50 (0-15-115113-X) Harcourt.

— By Love Possessed. 1994. reprint ed. lib. bdg. 21.95 (1-56849-549-8) Buccaneer Bks.

— A Flower in Her Hair. limited ed. 1974. 55.00 (0-89723-011-6) Bruccoli.

— Guard of Honor. LC 97-39459. 1998. 22.00 (0-679-60305-0) Modern Lib NY.

— The Just & the Unjust. LC 42-17992. 444p. 1965. pap. 12.95 (0-15-646578-7, Harvest Bks) Harcourt.

— A Rope for Dr. Webster. limited ed. 1976. boxed set 55.00 (0-89723-010-8) Bruccoli.

— Selected Notebooks, 1960-1967. Bruccoli, Matthew J., ed. 1984. 25.00 (0-89723-042-6) Bruccoli.

— The Son of Perdition. LC 83-45738. reprint ed. 29.00 (0-404-20069-9) AMS Pr.

— A Time of War: Air Force Diaries & Pentagon Memos, 1943-45. Bruccoli, Matthew J., ed. 1984. 45.00 (0-89723-043-4) Bruccoli.

Cozzens, James Gould. By Love Possessed. LC 97-27582. 570p. 1998. pap. 13.95 (0-7867-0503-5) Carroll & Graf.

Cozzens, Margaret & Porter, Richard. Recurrence Relations - Counting Backwards. 2nd ed. (Hi Map Ser.: No. 2). (Illus.). 60p. pap. text 9.99 (0-614-05323-4, HM 5602) COMAP Inc.

***Cozzens, Margaret B.** The Challenge & Promise of K-8 Science Education Reform. 99p. (C). 1999. reprint ed. pap. text 20.00 (0-7881-7258-1) DIANE Pub.

Cozzens, Margaret B. & Porter, Richard. Problem Solving Using Graphs. (Hi Map Ser.). (Illus.). 9.99 (0-614-05321-8, HM 5606) COMAP Inc.

Cozzens, Margaret B. & Porter, Richard D. Mathematics with Calculus & Its Applications to Management, Life & Social Sciences. LC 86-81262. 893p. (C). 1987. text 77.96 (0-669-09366-1) HM Trade Div.

Cozzens, Peter. The Battle of Stones River. (Civil War Ser.). (Illus.). 52p. 1995. pap. 4.95 (0-915992-67-1) Eastern National.

— The Battles for Chattanooga. (National Park Civil War Ser.). (Illus.). 55p. 1996. pap. 4.95 (0-915992-95-7) Eastern National.

— The Civil War in the West: From Stones River to Chattanooga. (Illus.). 1,528p. 1996. 49.95 (0-252-02236-X) U of Ill Pr.

— The Darkest Days of the War: The Battles of Iuka & Corinth. LC 96-9613. (Civil War America Ser.). 448p. (C). (gr. 13). 1997. 45.00 (0-8078-2320-1) U of NC Pr.

***Cozzens, Peter.** General John Pope: A Life for the Nation. LC 99-6848. 2000. 39.95 (0-252-02363-3) U of Ill Pr.

Cozzens, Peter. No Better Place to Die: The Battle of Stones River. LC 89-30577. (Illus.). 304p. 1990. 29.95 (0-252-01652-1) U of Ill Pr.

— No Better Place to Die: The Battle of Stones River. (Illus.). 304p. 1991. 15.95 (0-252-06229-9) U of Ill Pr.

— The Shipwreck of Their Hopes: The Battles for Chattanooga. LC 94-6269. (Illus.). 536p. 1994. pap. 34.95 (0-252-01922-9) U of Ill Pr.

— The Shipwreck of Their Hopes: The Battles for Chattanooga. (Illus.). 536p. 1998. 18.95 (0-252-06595-6) U of Ill Pr.

— This Terrible Sound: The Battle of Chickamauga. (Illus.). 688p. (C). 1992. 39.95 (0-252-01703-X) U of Ill Pr.

— This Terrible Sound: The Battle of Chickamauga. (Illus.). 688p. 1998. 21.95 (0-252-06594-8) U of Ill Pr.

Cozzens, Peter & Girardi, Robert, eds. The Military Memoirs of General John Pope. LC 98-13801. (Civil War America Ser.). (Illus.). 320p. 1998. 34.95 (0-8078-2444-5) U of NC Pr.

Cozzens, Samuel W. Marvelous Country: Three Years in Arizona & New Mexico, the Apaches Home. 1967. reprint ed. 20.00 (0-87018-011-8) Ross.

Cozzens, Susan, jt. ed. see Bud, Robert F.

Cozzens, Susan E. & Gieryn, Thomas F., eds. Theories of Science in Society. LC 89-45476. (Science, Technology, & Society Ser.). (Illus.). 272p. 1990. pap. 84.40 (0-608-05013-X, 205967400004) Bks Demand.

***Cozzens, Tracy.** Arabian Knight. 2000. pap. 9.95 (1-893896-15-3) Ima Jinn.

— Only in Your Arms. 2000. mass mkt. 4.99 (0-8217-6530-2, Zebra Kensgtn) Kensgtn Pub Corp.

— Prince's Bride, Vol. 16. (Zebra Bouquet Ser.). 1999. mass mkt. 3.99 (0-8217-6351-2, Zebra Kensgtn) Kensgtn Pub Corp.

— Seducing Alicia. (Zebra Bouquet Ser.: No. 48). 2000. mass mkt. 3.99 (0-8217-6606-6, Zebra Kensgtn) Kensgtn Pub Corp.

Cozzi, Cirro. Ciro's Provincetown Kitchen: Italian Cooking by the Sea. 2nd ed. 250p. 1995. pap. 16.95 (0-9635257-5-1) Mt Ivy Pr.

Cozzi, Elbio P., jt. auth. see Zancolli, Eduardo A.

Cozzi, Robert, Jr. Introduction to RPG IV. LC 99-189928. (Illus.). 320p. 1998. pap. 59.00 (1-883884-46-2, 577) Midrange Comput.

— Introduction to RPG with Interactive Programming. 300p. (Orig.). 1993. pap. 65.00 (0-9621825-5-9) Cozzi Research.

— The Modern RPG IV Language. LC 97-196973. (Illus.). 570p. 1996. pap. 99.00 (1-883884-31-4, 546) Midrange Comput.

***Cozzi, Robert, Jr.** The Modern RPG IV Language. 2nd ed. (Illus.). 576p. 1999. pap. 99.00 (1-58347-002-6) Midrange Comput.

Cozzi, Robert, Jr. The Modern RPG IV Language Reference Summary. 2nd ed. (Illus.). 95p. 1997. reprint ed. pap. 29.00 (1-883884-38-1, 545) Midrange Comput.

— The Modern RPG Language Reference Summary. 60p. 1992. 24.95 (0-9621825-3-2) Cozzi Research.

— The Modern RPG Language with Structured Programming. 4th ed. King, Theresa & Veal, Greg, eds. (Illus.). 500p. (C). 1993. pap. text 65.00 (0-9621825-0-8) Cozzi Research.

Cozzi, Robert, Jr., ed. see Bains, Richard & Chakravarti, Robin.

Cozzi, Robert, Jr., ed. see Veal, Greg.

Cozzi, Steve. Planets in Locality. LC 88-45190. (Modern Astrology Library). (Illus.). 320p. (Orig.). 1997. pap. 20.00 (*0-87542-098-2*) Am Fed Astrologers.

***Cozzi, Terenzio & Marchionatti, Roberto.** Piero Sraffa's Political Economy: A Centenary Estimate. LC 00-30515. 2000. write for info. (*0-415-22424-1*) Routledge.

Cozzillio, Michael J. & Levinstein, Mark S. Sports Law: Cases & Materials. LC 97-22517. 1088p. (C). 1997. boxed set 80.00 (*0-89089-835-9*) Carolina Acad Pr.

Cozzo, Cesare. Meaning & Argument: A Theory of Meaning Centered on Immediate Argumental Role. LC 96-141811. (Stockholm Studies in Philosophy: Vol. 17). 208p. 1994. pap. 46.50 (*91-22-01648-1*, Pub. by Almqvist Wiksell) Coronet Bks.

Cozzo, Gayle, see Cunningham, Jill, pseud.

Cozzo, Joseph. The Money Swallow. 287p. 1996. write for info. (*1-85863-726-0*, Pub. by Minerva Pr) Unity Dist.

***Cozzola.** Corel Wordperfect 8 Illustrated Standard. (C). 1998. pap. text 21.95 (*0-7600-5948-9*) Thomson Learn.

Cozzola & Bunin. Corel Wordperfect 8. (Illustrated Ser.). (Illus.). 1998. mass mkt. 16.00 (*0-7600-6125-4*) Course Tech.

Cozzola, Mary-Terese. Lotus WordPro 96 for Windows 95: Illustrated Brief Edition. 10th ed. (Illustrated Ser.). (Illus.). 96p. (C). 1996. pap. 12.95 (*0-7600-4700-6*) Course Tech.

Cozzolani, Chiara M. Chiara Margarita Cozzolani: Motets. Kendrick, Robert L., ed. (Recent Researches in Music of the Baroque Era Ser.: No. RRB87). (Illus.). xxxii, 271p. 1998. pap. 100.00 (*0-89579-402-0*) A-R Eds.

Cozzolino, John M., jt. auth. see Gupta, Shiv K.

CPB Netherlands Bureau for Economic Policy Analysis, ed. Challenging Neighbours: Rethinking German & Dutch Economic Institutions. LC 97-29384. (Illus.). xi, 592p. 1998. pap. text 52.95 (*3-540-63501-7*) Spr-Verlag.

CPIM Staff. Ssqd Eng. Voc: Home. (C). 1995. pap. text 26.25 (*0-15-599844-7*) Harcourt Coll Pubs.

Cpmpans, Richard W., jt. ed. see Mahy, Brian W.J.

CPP Belwin Staff. Beach Boys Compilation Vol. 1. 1993. pap. 19.95 (*0-89898-688-5*, P0413SMX) Wrner Bros.

— Best of Garth Brooks: Greatest Hits Tabulation. 1992. pap. 16.95 (*0-89898-632-X*, P0942GTX) Wrner Bros.

— Best of the 90's So Far/Country. rev. ed. 356p. (YA). 1995. pap. 16.95 (*0-89724-661-6*, F3416SMA) Wrner Bros.

— Best of 90's Popular. 1994. pap. text 18.95 (*0-89724-463-X*, F3415SMA) Wrner Bros.

— Bette Midler Greatest Hits. 1993. pap. 16.95 (*0-89898-668-0*, P0129SMX) Wrner Bros.

— Bing Crosby LPs, Vol. 3. 1984. pap. 11.95 (*0-89898-612-5*, TPF0132) Wrner Bros.

— Christmas, Popular & Traditional. 1990. pap. 12.95 (*0-89898-930-2*, F3027SMX) Wrner Bros.

— Comprehensive Guitar Methods. 1985. pap. 10.00 (*0-89898-701-6*, EL02287) Wrner Bros.

— Creedence Clearwater Complete. 1982. pap. 18.95 (*0-89898-156-5*, P0408SMX) Wrner Bros.

— Creedence Clearwater Greatest Anthology. 1991. pap. 19.95 (*0-89898-671-0*, P0890GTX) Wrner Bros.

— The Doors Complete. 1993. pap. 18.95 (*0-89898-180-8*, P0443SMX) Wrner Bros.

— Everly Brothers LPs, Vol. 7. 1988. pap. 14.95 (*0-89898-615-X*, TPF0147) Wrner Bros.

— The Great Music of Duke Ellington. 1985. pap. 16.95 (*0-89898-634-6*, 11632) Wrner Bros.

— Hank Williams: Complete Works. 1989. pap. 19.95 (*0-89898-574-9*, P0765SMX) Wrner Bros.

— Movie Songs of the 80's. 1993. pap. 12.95 (*0-89898-686-9*, F3317SMX) Wrner Bros.

— Nat King Cole LPs, Vol. 9. 1989. pap. text 14.95 (*0-89724-590-3*, TPF0150) Wrner Bros.

— New Home Library Vol. 5: PV the Greatest Sons of 1975-1990. 1994. pap. text 12.95 (*0-89898-986-8*) Wrner Bros.

— Otis Redding, Vol. 8. (Legendary Performer Ser.). 1989. pap. 14.95 (*0-89898-617-6*, TPF0149) Wrner Bros.

— Phil Spector Back to Mono. 1993. pap. 24.95 (*0-89898-564-1*, P0966SMX) Wrner Bros.

— Ray Charles LPs, Vol. 5. 1993. pap. text 13.95 (*0-89724-518-0*, TPF0144) Wrner Bros.

— Ricky Nelson, Vol. 11. (Legendary Performer Ser.). 1990. pap. 14.95 (*0-89898-620-6*, TPF0153) Wrner Bros.

— Rolling Stones Singles Guitar. 1993. pap. 29.95 (*0-89898-639-7*) Wrner Bros.

— Roy Orbison LPs, Vol. 6. 1988. pap. 13.95 (*0-89898-618-4*, TPF0146) Wrner Bros.

— RRL Hot Country Guitar. 1993. pap. 12.95 (*0-89898-568-4*, F3714GTX) Wrner Bros.

— Showstoppers '90s. 1995. pap. text 18.95 (*0-89724-979-8*, F3223SMA) Wrner Bros.

— Showstoppers Ragtime. 1987. pap. 17.95 (*0-89898-674-5*, F2867SMX) Wrner Bros.

— That's Entertainment. 1994. pap. 22.50 (*0-89898-979-5*) Wrner Bros.

— Top 50 BMI Motion Picture Songs & Themes. 1994. pap. 14.95 (*0-89898-757-1*, F3406SMX) Wrner Bros.

— Wizard of Oz Movie Selections. 1993. pap. 12.95 (*0-89898-623-0*, TSF0038) Wrner Bros.

— The World's Greatest Fake Book. rev. ed. 1996. pap. 39.95 (*0-89898-814-4*, F3287FBA) Wrner Bros.

— Yip Harburg Songbook. 1994. pap. 16.95 (*0-89898-555-2*, P1024SMX) Wrner Bros.

CPR-I Consulting Staff. Year 2000 Contingency & Business Resumption Plan: Y2KCP Model. (Contingency Planning & Business Continuity Ser.). (Illus.). 200p. 1998. ring bd. write for info. (*0-940706-43-1*) Management Advisory Pubns.

***CPR-I Consulting Staff.** Y2K Zero Hour Contingency Action Plan. (Contingency Planning & Business Continuity Ser.). (Illus.). 175p. 1999. ring bd. 295.00 (*0-940706-44-X*) Management Advisory Pubns.

CPRI Researchers Staff & Alock, Norman Z. Global Models & Projections of Arms, War & Development 1982. 1978. 4.00 (*0-933061-05-6*) Lentz Peace Res.

CPSB (Isaksen) Staff. Facilitative Leadership: Making a Difference with Creative Problem Solving. 212p. text. write for info. (*0-7872-6703-1*) Kendall-Hunt.

CPUSA Staff. The People vs. Monopoly: Nineteen Eighty Draft Program of the Communist Party, U. S. A. 62p. (Orig.). 1980. pap. 0.50 (*0-87898-142-X*) New Outlook.

CQ Inc. Staff. Congressional Roll Call, 1988. 250p. 1989. 33.95 (*0-87187-504-7*) Congr Quarterly.

— Congressional Roll Call, 1989. 300p. 1990. 33.95 (*0-87187-548-9*) Congr Quarterly.

— Congressional Roll Call, 1990. 1991. 33.95 (*0-87187-564-0*) Congr Quarterly.

— Congressional Roll Call, 1991. 1992. 33.95 (*0-87187-698-1*) Congr Quarterly.

— Guide to the U. S. Supreme Court. 2nd ed. 1060p. 1989. 239.00 (*0-87187-502-0*) Congr Quarterly.

— Historic Documents of 1988. 1000p. 1989. 125.00 (*0-87187-493-8*) Congr Quarterly.

— Historic Documents of 1989. 900p. 1990. 125.00 (*0-87187-535-7*) Congr Quarterly.

— Historic Documents on the Presidency. LC 88-37588. 528p. 1989. text 95.00 (*0-87187-518-7*) Congr Quarterly.

— Historic Documents 1990. 1991. 125.00 (*0-87187-563-2*) Congr Quarterly.

— Historic Documents 1991. 800p. 1992. 125.00 (*0-87187-665-5*) Congr Quarterly.

— Politics in America 1992. Duncan, Phil, ed. 1991. 79.95 (*0-87187-599-3*); pap. 49.95 (*0-87187-641-8*) Congr Quarterly.

CQ Inc. Staff & Nelson, Michael. Guide to the Presidency. 1521p. 1989. 199.95 (*0-87187-500-4*) Congr Quarterly.

CRA (Miller) Staff. Finance Your Small Business. 128p. 1995. pap. text, per. 16.95 (*0-7872-1570-8*) Kendall-Hunt.

CRA Staff. Communicate! A Workbook for Interpersonal Communication. 6th ed. 300p. 1997. 29.95 (*0-7872-4510-0*) Kendall-Hunt.

***Craats, Rennay.** For the Love of Baseball. (For the Love of Sports Ser.). (Illus.). 24p. (J). (gr. k-3). 2000. write for info. (*1-930954-00-X*) Weigl Pubs.

— For the Love of Basketball. (For the Love of Sports Ser.). (Illus.). 24p. (J). (gr. k-3). 2000. write for info. (*1-930954-05-0*) Weigl Pubs.

Craats, Rennay, ed. see Booth, Tanis.

Crabb. Understanding People. 1995. 10.99 (*0-310-22609-0*) Zondervan.

Crabb & Gagne. Database Design & Publishing with Filemaker Pro 4 for Mac & Windows. 1997. 39.95 (*0-8055-1514-3*, M&T Bks) IDG Bks.

Crabb, Jr & Lawrence, J. Encouragement. 1986. 14.99 (*0-88469-199-3*) BMH Bks.

— The Marriage Builder. 1986. 12.99 (*0-88469-185-3*) BMH Bks.

Crabb, A. L., et al. Seven Early Churches of Nashville. (Illus.). 1972. 35.00 (*0-918450-07-1*) C Elder.

Crabb, A. Richard. Radio's Beautiful Day: Memoirs of Everett Mitchell, Pioneer Radio Announcer. LC 82-73438. (Illus.). 1984. 19.95 (*0-916445-06-2*) Crossroads Comm.

Crabb, Arthur. Samuel Lyle Criminologist. LC 74-121531. (Short Story Index Reprint Ser.). (Illus.). 1977. 23.95 (*0-8369-3487-3*) Ayer.

Crabb, Bart. The Quest for the World Record Bass. 1997. 14.95 (*1-57785-016-5*, Lghthse Pr) ProStar Pubns.

Crabb, Cecil V., Jr. The American Approach to Foreign Policy: A Pragmatic Perspective. LC 84-29087. (Credibility of Institutions, Policies & Leadership Ser.: Vol. 2). 102p. (Orig.). 1985. pap. text 14.00 (*0-8191-4423-1*) U Pr of Amer.

— The American Approach to Foreign Policy: A Pragmatic Perspective. LC 84-29087. (Credibility of Institutions, Policies & Leadership Ser.: Vol. 2). 102p. (Orig.). 1985. lib. bdg. 35.50 (*0-8191-4422-3*, Pub. by White Miller Center) U Pr of Amer.

— Policy Makers & Critics: Conflicting Theories of American Foreign Poilicy. rev. ed. LC 86-16901. 311p. 1986. pap. 18.95 (*0-275-92210-3*, B2210, Praeger Pubs) Greenwood.

— Policy Makers & Critics: Conflicting Theories of American Foreign Poilicy. rev. ed. LC 86-16901. 311p. 1986. 69.50 (*0-275-92209-X*, C2209, Praeger Pubs) Greenwood.

Crabb, Cecil V., Jr. & Cowdrey, Albert E. The Doctrines of American Foreign Policy: Their Meaning, Role & Future. LC 81-20846. 446p. (C). 1982. pap. 24.95 (*0-8071-1060-4*) La State U Pr.

Crabb, Cecil V. & Mulcahy, Kevin V. Presidents & Foreign Policy Making: From FDR to Reagan. LC 86-7508. (Political Traditions in Foreign Policy Ser.). 375p. 1986. pap. 106.90 (*0-7837-8530-5*, 2049339) Bks Demand.

Crabb, Cecil V., Jr., et al. Congress & the Foreign Policy Process: Modes of Legislative Behavior. LC 99-16518. (Political Traditions in Foreign Policy Ser.). 280p. 2000. text 39.95 (*0-8071-2444-3*); pap. text 24.95 (*0-8071-2510-5*) La State U Pr.

Crabb, Cecil Van, see Van Crabb, Cecil.

Crabb, Daniel M. Comparative Study of Word Order in Old Spanish & Old French Prose Works. LC 78-94189. (Catholic University of America. Studies in Romance Languages & Literatures: No. 51). reprint ed. 37.50 (*0-404-50351-9*) AMS Pr.

Crabb, Don. Guide to Macintosh System 7.5.5. LC 94-75945. (Illus.). 400p. 1994. 25.00 (*1-56830-109-X*) Hayden.

— MACSpeed. (Illus.). (Orig.). 1995. pap. 40.00 (*1-56830-227-4*) Hayden.

— MacWeek Guide to System 7. (Guide to...Ser.). (Illus.). 296p. (Orig.). 1991. pap. 24.95 (*1-56276-029-7*, Ziff-Davis Pr) Que.

— Running UNIX So It Doesn't Run You. 1993. pap. 29.95 (*1-56276-061-0*, Ziff-Davis Pr) Que.

Crabb, George. History of English Law: An Attempt to Trace the Rise, Progress & Successive Changes of the Common Law; from the Earliest Period to the Present Time. vii, 595p. 1987. reprint ed. 58.50 (*0-8377-2013-3*, Rothman) W S Hein.

Crabb, Howard C. The Virtual Engineer: 21st Century Product Development. LC 97-61866. 166p. 1998. 39.00 (*0-7918-0066-0*, TS170) ASME Pr.

— The Virtual Engineer TM: 21st Century Product Development. LC 97-61866. (Illus.). 166p. 1998. 39.00 (*0-87263-491-4*, PI2640) SME.

Crabb, John H. The Constitution of Belgium & the Belgian Civil Code. 448p. 106.50 (*90-6544-062-3*) Kluwer Academic.

Crabb, John H., tr. The French Civil Code (as Amended to July 1, 1976) xx, 443p. 1977. text 60.00 (*0-8377-0531-2*, Rothman) W S Hein.

Crabb, John H., tr. from FRE. Constitution of Belgium & the Belgian Civil Code. LC 82-18059. ix, 428p. 1982. reprint ed. 65.00 (*0-8377-0438-3*, Rothman) W S Hein.

— French Business Enterprises: Basic Legislative Texts. viii, 355p. 1979. 45.00 (*0-8377-0425-1*, Rothman) W S Hein.

— French Civil Code. rev. ed. LC 94-11035. xxxiii 460p. 1995. 95.00 (*0-8377-0467-7*, Rothman) W S Hein.

— The French Civil Code. rev. ed. LC 94-11035. 1994. write for info. (*90-6544-797-0*) W S Hein.

Crabb, John W. Techniques in Protein Chemistry VI. (Illus.). 585p. 1995. pap. text 58.00 (*0-12-194713-0*) Acad Pr.

Crabb, John W., ed. Techniques in Protein Chemistry V. (Illus.). 1994. spiral bd. 62.00 (*0-12-194711-4*) Acad Pr.

— Techniques in Protein Chemistry VI. (Illus.). 585p. 1995. text 116.00 (*0-12-194712-2*) Acad Pr.

Crabb, Katherine S. Hardin County, Kentucky 1850 Census. 250p. 1987. pap. 23.00 (*1-889221-11-2*) Ancestral Trails.

— Hart County, Kentucky 1850 Census. 140p. 1990. pap. 15.00 (*1-889221-22-8*) Ancestral Trails.

Crabb, L. De Adentro Hacia Afuera.Tr. of Inside Out. (SPA.). 6.99 (*1-56063-128-7*, 498472) Editorial Unilit.

***Crabb, Larry.** Bring Home the Joy. 2000. pap. 12.99 (*0-310-23448-4*) Zondervan.

Crabb, Larry. Connecting. LC 97-26524. 240p. 1997. 19.99 (*0-8499-1413-2*) Word Pub.

— Finding God. LC 96-164970. 240p. 1995. pap. 12.99 (*0-310-20544-1*) Zondervan.

Crabb, Larry, Jr. Finding God. large type ed. LC 94-15735. 240p. 1994. pap. 12.95 (*0-8027-2684-4*) Walker & Co.

Crabb, Larry. Hombres y Mujeres: Disfrutando la Diferencia.Tr. of Men & Women: Enjoying the Difference. (SPA.). 243p. 1991. pap. write for info. (*0-614-27063-4*) Editorial Unilit.

— Hombres y Mujeres (Men & Women) Disfrutando la Diferencia (Enjoying the Difference) (SPA.). 1993. 6.99 (*1-56063-168-6*, 498419) Editorial Unilit.

— How to Deal with Anger. 1991. pap. 2.50 (*0-89109-526-8*) NavPress.

— Inside Out. LC 87-63399. 225p. 1991. pap. 12.00 (*0-89109-643-4*) NavPress.

— Inside Out: Real Change is Possible If You're Willing to Start from the Beginning. 10th ed. LC 98-11353. 224p. 1998. pap. 12.00 (*1-57683-082-9*) NavPress.

— Inside Out-Study Guide. 108p. 1989. pap. 7.00 (*0-89109-281-1*) NavPress.

— Men & Women. 256p. 1991. 15.99 (*0-310-33830-1*) Zondervan.

— Men & Women: Enjoying the Difference. 240p. 1993. pap. 12.99 (*0-310-33831-X*) Zondervan.

— Safest Place in the World. LC 99-38663. 240p. 1999. 19.99 (*0-8499-1456-6*) Word Pub.

***Crabb, Larry.** Safest Place in the World. 240p. 1999. 16.99 (*0-8499-6286-2*) Word Pub.

Crabb, Larry. Understanding Who You Are: What Your Relationships Tell You about Yourself. rev. ed. LC 96-6536. Orig. Title: Who We Are & How We Relate. 78p. (Orig.). 1997. pap. 7.00 (*1-57683-014-4*) NavPress.

Crabb, Larry & Allender, Dan. Encouragement: Key to Caring. 144p. 1990. pap. 12.99 (*0-310-22591-4*) Zondervan.

Crabb, Larry & Allender, Dan B. Hope When You're Hurting: Answers to Four Questions Hurting People Ask. 208p. 1997. pap. 12.99 (*0-310-21930-2*) Zondervan.

— Hope When You're Hurting: Answers to Four Questions Hurting People Ask. large type ed. LC 99-31850. 320p. 2000. pap. 15.95 (*0-8027-2744-1*) Walker & Co.

***Crabb, Larry, et al.** Joy Breaks for Couples. 2000. 14.99 (*0-310-23122-1*) Zondervan.

Crabb, Lawrence J., Jr. Basic Principles of Biblical Counseling. 1986. 16.99 (*0-88469-186-1*) BMH Bks.

— Basic Principles of Biblical Counseling. 112p. 1975. 18.99 (*0-310-22560-4*, 10159) Zondervan.

— Effective Biblical Counseling: A Model for Helping Caring Christians Become Capable Counselors. 208p. 1977. 18.99 (*0-310-22570-1*, 10173) Zondervan.

— How to Become One with Your Mate. 1986. 5.59 (*0-88469-184-5*) BMH Bks.

— Understanding People: Deep Longings for Relationship. 224p. 1987. 16.99 (*0-310-22600-7*, 10171) Zondervan.

Crabb, Lawrence J., Jr. & Allender, Dan B. Encouragement: The Key to Caring. 144p. 1984. 12.95 (*0-310-22590-6*, 10182) Zondervan.

Crabb, Lawrence J., Jr. & Lawrence, J. Effective Biblical Counseling. 1986. 16.99 (*0-88469-187-X*) BMH Bks.

Crabb, M. C. Fibrewise Homotopy Theory. LC 98-7022. (Springer Monographs In Mathematics). 1998. 79.95 (*1-85233-014-7*) Spr-Verlag.

***Crabb, Martha L.** All Afire to Fight: The Untold Tale of the Civil War's Ninth Texas Cavalry. LC 99-42903. 464p. 2000. 30.00 (*0-380-97794-X*, Avon Bks) Morrow Avon.

Crabb, Rachael & Hart, Raeann. The Personal Touch: Encouraging Others Through Hospitality. LC 90-63217. 132p. (Orig.). 1991. pap. 8.00 (*0-89109-607-8*) NavPress.

Crabb, Richard, jt. auth. see Moore, Jean.

Crabb, S. Chats on Old Pewter. 1998. mass mkt. 6.95 (*1-56333-611-1*) Masquerade.

Crabbae, P., jt. auth. see NATO Advanced Research Workshop on Implementing Ecological Integrity: Restoring Regional & Global Environmental & Human Health Staff.

Crabbe. Metals Trading Handbook. 1998. ring bd. 99.95 (*0-8493-0518-7*) CRC Pr.

***Crabbe, Anne B.** Strozzi of Florence: Widowhood & Family Solidarity in the Renaissance. LC 99-6805. 390p. (C). 1999. text 49.50 (*0-472-10912-X*, 10912) U of Mich Pr.

Crabbe, David, jt. ed. see Cotterall, Sara.

Crabbe, George. George Crabbe: The Complete Poetical Works, Vol. 1. Dalrymple-Champneys, Norma & Pollard, Arthur, eds. (Oxford English Texts Ser.). (Illus.). 872p. 1988. text 155.00 (*0-19-811882-1*) OUP.

— George Crabbe: The Complete Poetical Works, Vol. 2. Dalrymple-Champneys, Norma & Pollard, Arthur, eds. (Oxford English Texts Ser.). (Illus.). 1024p. 1988. 180.00 (*0-19-812787-1*) OUP.

— George Crabbe: The Complete Poetical Works, Vol. 3. Dalrymple-Champneys, Norma & Pollard, Arthur, eds. (Oxford English Texts Ser.). (Illus.). 552p. 1988. text 140.00 (*0-19-812788-X*) OUP.

— George Crabbe (1754-1832) Selected Poems. Poster, Jem, ed. 1986. pap. 7.50 (*0-85635-621-2*) Carcanet Pr.

— New Poems. LC 85-30523. (Illus.). 198p. 1986. reprint ed. lib. bdg. 55.00 (*0-313-25046-4*, CRNE, Greenwood Pr) Greenwood.

— Peter Grimes from the Borough. 1993. 90.00 (*0-907664-07-5*, Pub. by Old Stiles) St Mut.

— Poems, 3 vols., Vols. 1 - 3. Ward, Adolphus W., ed. LC 75-41067. (BCL Ser. II). reprint ed. 210.00 (*0-404-14860-3*) AMS Pr.

— Poetical Works of George Crabbe. Carlyle, A. J., ed. reprint ed. lib. bdg. 79.00 (*0-7812-0304-X*) Rprt Serv.

— Selected Letters & Journals of George Crabbe. Faulkner, Thomas C. & Blair, Rhonda L., eds. (Illus.). (C). 1985. 74.00 (*0-19-812570-4*) OUP.

— Tales, Eighteen Twelve, & Other Selected Poems. Mills, Howard, ed. LC 67-10348. 483p. reprint ed. pap. 137.70 (*0-608-12080-4*, 2024577) Bks Demand.

Crabbe, J. C., Jr. & Harris, R. A. The Genetic Basis of Alcohol & Drug Actions. (Illus.). 400p. (C). 1991. text 110.00 (*0-306-43868-2*, Kluwer Plenum) Kluwer Academic.

Crabbe, James C., jt. auth. see Mann, John.

Crabbe, Justice. Legislative Precedents, Vol. II. 268p. 1998. 117.00 (*1-85941-421-4*) Gaunt.

— Understanding Statutes. 260p. 1995. pap. 50.00 (*1-85941-138-X*, Pub. by Cavendish Pubng) Gaunt.

Crabbe, Matthew, jt. auth. see French, Paul.

Crabbe, P. D. LME Metals Trading Manual. 288p. 1998. 120.00 (*1-85573-347-1*, Pub. by Woodhead Pubng) Am Educ Systs.

***Crabbe, Richard E.** Suspension. 480p. 2000. 27.95 (*0-312-20371-3*, Thomas Dunne) St Martin.

Crabbe, V. C. Legislative Drafting. 318p. 1994. 60.00 (*1-874241-15-5*, Pub. by Cavendish Pubng) Gaunt.

Crabbere, Edna D. Curriculum Ideas for Young Children. Crabbere, Peter E., ed. 23p. 1999. pap. text 20.00 (*0-9667830-2-6*, 0043) Early Lrning Assessmnt.

— Emotional Security for the Millennium Child & Child Development Student Observations. Crabbere, Peter E., ed. LC 98-93414. (Illus.). 69p. 1998. pap. text 20.00 (*0-9667830-0-X*, 0043) Early Lrning Assessmnt.

— Friendly Discipline for Young Children, Vol. 2. Crabbere, Peter E., ed. 23p. (Orig.). 1999. pap. text 20.00 (*0-9667830-3-4*, 0043) Early Lrning Assessmnt.

— Friendly Discipline 0-7 Years, No. 1. Crabbere, Peter E., ed. 3p. 1999. pap. text 3.00 (*0-9667830-1-8*) Early Lrning Assessmnt.

Crabbere, Peter E., ed. see Crabbere, Edna D.

Crabble, M. James C. From Soul to Self: Post-Colonial Theory, India & the Mystic East's. LC 98-41840. 1999. pap. 21.99 (*0-415-17118-0*) Routledge.

Crabbs, Lelah M., jt. auth. see McCall, William A.

Crabill, Calvin D., jt. auth. see Stein, Sherman K.

Crabill, Delmar. Statistical Theory: An Introduction. 296p. (Orig.). (C). 1984. pap. text 24.00 (*0-8191-3796-0*) U Pr of Amer.

Crabill, Janice, et al. Multidisciplinary Competency Assessment: Ensuring Staff Performance. Jaeger, Joseph, ed. LC 95-60800. (Illus.). 320p. 1995. pap. 85.00 (*1-880254-30-1*) Vista.

Crabill, Paula. Colours in Verse. unabridged ed. (Illus.). 68p. 1997. pap. 22.95 (*1-890644-05-6*) Union Cnty.

Crabites, Pierre. Gordon, the Sudan & Slavery. LC 72-88999. 334p. 1970. reprint ed. lib. bdg. 35.00 (*0-8371-1764-X*, CRS&) Greenwood.

Crable, John V., jt. ed. see Kneip, Theodore J.

Crable, Richard E. & Vibbert, Steven L. Public Relations As Communication Management. (Illus.). 436p. (C). 1986. text. write for info. (*0-8087-4878-5*) Pearson Custom.

Crabtree. Archaeology & Prehistory. 2000. 43.74 (*0-07-840516-5*) McGraw.

Crabtree. Precalcus. 34.21 (*0-673-23434-7*, Scott Frsmn) Addson-Wesley Educ.

C

Crabtree, Adam. Trance Zero: Breaking the Spell of Conformity. 288p. pap. 24.95 (*1-894042-04-2*) Somerville Hse.

Crabtree, Adam. Trance Zero: The Psychology of Maximum Experience. LC 99-40428. 288p. 1999. text 23.95 (*0-312-24425-8*) St Martin.

Crabtree, Alfred B. & Martin, Hattie B. Hancock, 1828-1928. (Illus.). 90p. 1997. reprint ed. pap. 18.00 (*0-8328-5853-6*) Higginson Bk Co.

Crabtree, Benjamin F., et al, eds. Developing Collaborative Research in Primary Care. 340p. 1994. 58.00 (*0-8039-5489-1*); pap. 26.50 (*0-8039-5490-5*) Sage.

Crabtree, Benjamin F. & Miller, William L. Doing Qualitative Research: Multiple Strategies. (Research Methods for Primary Care Ser.: Vol. 3). 272p. (C). 1992. text 58.00 (*0-8039-4311-3*) Sage.

***Crabtree, Benjamin F. & Miller, William L., eds.** Doing Qualitative Research. 2nd ed. LC 99-6645. 406p. 1999. 65.95 (*0-7619-1497-8*) Sage.

Crabtree, Beth G. & Langston, Ruth C., eds. The North Carolina Historical Review: Fifty-Year Index, 1924-1973. vi, 534p. 1984. pap. 30.00 (*0-86526-211-X*) NC Archives.

Crabtree, Beth G. & Patton, James W., eds. Journal of a Secesh Lady: The Diary of Catherine Ann Devereux Edmondston, 1860-1866. (Illus.). xxxviii, 850p. (C). 1999. reprint ed. 35.00 (*0-86526-047-8*) NC Archives.

Crabtree, Bob, jt. ed. see Brouwer, Floor.

Crabtree, Catherine G. A la Aspen, Restaurant Recipes. (Illus.). 190p. (Orig.). 1978. pap. 17.95 (*0-937070-00-9*) Crabtree.

— A la San Francisco, Restaurant Recipes. (Illus.). 240p. (Orig.). 1980. pap. 17.95 (*0-937070-01-7*) Crabtree.

— A la Texas, Restaurant Recipes. 1986. spiral bd. 17.95 (*0-937070-04-1*) Crabtree.

— Seattle Lite: Lite Recipes from Seattle's Top Restaurants. Grady, Michael, ed. (Cookbook Ser.). (Illus.). 150p. (Orig.). 1998. pap. 17.95 (*0-937070-11-4*) Crabtree.

Crabtree, Cathy L. & Fowler, Joanne. Poor Me & the Magic of Christmas. rev. ed. LC 89-84463. (Poor Me Collections). (Illus.). 20p. (J). (gr. 2-3). 1989. pap. text 5.95 (*0-9622719-0-X*) Lavender Pr.

Crabtree, Charles T. This I Believe. LC 81-84913. 160p. (Orig.). 1982. pap. 4.95 (*0-88243-758-5*, 02-0758) Gospel Pub.

***Crabtree, Charlotte A. & Nash, Gary B., eds.** National Standards for History for Grades K-4: Expanding Children[0012]s World in Time & Space (rev. ed.) rev. ed. (Illus.). 78p. (C). 2000. pap. text 25.00 (*0-7567-0001-9*) DIANE Pub.

Crabtree, Cheryl & Bridgers, Karen. The Insiders' Guide to Santa Barbara. (Insiders' Guide Travel Ser.). (Illus.). 416p. 1999. pap. 16.95 (*1-57380-071-6*, The Insiders Guide) Falcon Pub Inc.

Crabtree, David J., jt. auth. see Glaser, Barney G.

Crabtree, Davida F. The Empowering Church: How One Congregation Supports Lay People's Ministries in the World. LC 89-85376. 86p. (Orig.). 1989. pap. 10.25 (*1-56699-034-3*, AL115) Alban Inst.

Crabtree, Dennis R., et al, eds. Astronomical Data Analysis Software & Systems III, No. 61. 576p. 1994. 34.00 (*0-937707-80-5*) Astron Soc Pacific.

Crabtree, Derek & Thirlwall, A. P., eds. Keynes & the Bloomsbury Group. 100p. 1980. 36.00 (*0-8419-5066-0*) Holmes & Meier.

— Keynes & the Role of the State: The Tenth Keynes Seminar Held at the University of Kent at Canterbury, 1991. LC 92-24794. 240p. 1993. text 69.95 (*0-312-08979-1*) St Martin.

Crabtree, Evelyn. Business Is Business...Right? 150p. (Orig.). 1996. pap. 5.95 (*0-945969-06-6*) Kohinoor Bks.

Crabtree, Helen. Hold Your Horse. (Illus.). 288p. 1997. text 29.95 (*0-9655501-1-7*) Saddle & Bridle.

Crabtree, Helen K. Saddle Seat Equitation: The Definitive Guide. rev. ed. (Illus.). 380p. 1999. pap. 29.95 (*0-9665194-0-X*) Wstrn Intl.

***Crabtree, Howard.** When Pigs Fly. 112p. 1998. otabind 16.95 (*0-7935-9484-7*) H Leonard.

Crabtree, J., jt. auth. see Romain, R.

Crabtree, J. C., ed. Visual Display Units: An Information Pack. 60p. 1994. 58.50 (*0-85296-963-5*, BI032) INSPEC Inc.

Crabtree, Jack. Better Safe Than Sued: Keeping Out of Trouble in Youth Ministry. Buller, Bob, ed. LC 98-9995. (Illus.). 240p. (YA). 1998. per. 16.99 (*0-7644-2053-4*, Vital Ministry) Group Pub.

Crabtree, James. On Air Defense. LC 94-8639. (Military Profession Ser.). 256p. 1994. pap. 21.95 (*0-275-94939-7*, Praeger Pubs) Greenwood.

Crabtree, James D. On Air Defense. LC 94-8639. (Military Profession Ser.). 256p. 1994. 69.50 (*0-275-94792-0*, Praeger Pubs) Greenwood.

Crabtree, Jeanne L., ed. see Shaw, John R.

Crabtree, Karen, jt. auth. see Crabtree, Trevor.

Crabtree, Karen, jt. auth. see Wishon, Philip M.

Crabtree, Kristen M., jt. auth. see Morrison, Ann M.

Crabtree, Lou V. The River Hills & Beyond: Poems. (Illus.). 72p. 1998. pap. 12.00 (*1-885912-19-6*) Sows Ear Pr.

Crabtree, Lucille. Basic Intarsia: With Lucille Crabtree. LC 94-37135. (Illus.). 64p. (Orig.). 1995. pap. 12.95 (*0-88740-727-7*) Schiffer.

— Intarsia. LC 95-5475. (Illus.). 64p. (Orig.). 1995. pap. 12.95 (*0-88740-728-5*) Schiffer.

***Crabtree, Margaret.** Growing up in North Ockendon & Upminster. (Illus.). 80p. 1999. pap. 14.00 (*0-86025-475-5*, Pub. by I Henry Pubns) Empire Pub Srvs.

Crabtree, Paul. I Sincerely Doubt That This Old House Is Very Haunted: Musical. (J). 1968. 6.00 (*0-87602-142-9*) Anchorage.

Crabtree, Phillip D. Sourcebook for Research in Music. 1999. pap. text 14.95 (*0-253-21323-1*) Ind U Pr.

Crabtree, Phillip D. & Foster, Donald H. Sourcebook for Research in Music. LC 92-32038. 260p. (C). 1993. text 25.00 (*0-253-31476-3*) Ind U Pr.

Crabtree, Robbin & Goss, Blain. Principles of Human Communication. 2nd ed. 62p. (C). 1996. pap. text, student ed., spiral bd. 15.95 (*0-7872-2724-2*, 41272401) Kendall-Hunt.

***Crabtree, Robert.** The Organometallic Chemistry of the Transition Metals. 3rd ed. 500p. 2001. 69.95 (*0-471-18423-3*) Wiley.

Crabtree, Robert H. The Organometallic Chemistry of the Transition Metals. 2nd ed. LC 93-9498. 512p. 1994. 74.95 (*0-471-59240-4*) Wiley.

Crabtree, Ronald. On Wings of Healing. 80p. 1986. 40.00 (*0-7223-2002-7*, Pub. by A H S Ltd) St Mut.

***Crabtree, Sally.** One Spinning Spider. (Illus.). (J). 2000. 10.95 (*1-86233-167-7*) Levinson Bks.

— Ten Buzzy Bees. (Illus.). (J). 2000. 10.95 (*1-86233-162-6*) Levinson Bks.

Crabtree, Sam. Lifestyle with Meaning. (Discipleship Ser.). 118p. (Orig.). 1993. pap. 2.75 (*0-89827-118-5*, BKO91) Wesleyan Pub Hse.

— Spiritual Life Disciplines: A Four Week Study to Help Teenagers Understand & Develop Spiritual Disciplines. Swyers, Gary et al, eds. (Bible Basics Ser.). (Illus.). 32p. (Orig.). (YA). (gr. 6-12). 1992. pap., wbk. ed. 8.95 (*0-89827-093-6*, BKW13) Wesleyan Pub Hse.

Crabtree, Sam, ed. People Just Like Us: Leader's Book. (Illus.). 80p. 1994. teacher ed., spiral bd., wbk. ed. 14.95 (*0-89827-128-2*, BKR11) Wesleyan Pub Hse.

Crabtree, Susan & Beudert, Peter. Scenic Art for the Theatre. LC 97-34534. 272p. 1998. pap. text 36.95 (*0-240-80187-3*, Focal) Buttrwrth-Heinemann.

Crabtree, T. T. Guia Pastoral (Pastor Guide), Vol. IV. (SPA.). 4.95 (*0-685-74942-8*, 540253) Editorial Unilit.

— The Zondervan 1999 Pastor's Annual: An Idea & Resource Book. 448p. 1998. pap. 15.99 (*0-310-22215-X*) Zondervan.

***Crabtree, T. T.** Zondervan Pastor's Annual: An Idea & Resource Book 2001. (Ideas Library). 2000. pap. 18.99 (*0-310-23273-2*) Zondervan.

Crabtree, T. T. The Zondervan Pastor's Annual, 1989. 384p. 1988. pap. 12.95 (*0-310-61311-6*, 11386P) Zondervan.

— The Zondervan Pastor's Annual, 1990. 400p. 1989. pap. 12.95 (*0-310-22221-4*) Zondervan.

— The Zondervan Pastor's Annual, 1992. 400p. 1991. pap. 14.99 (*0-310-52161-0*) Zondervan.

— The Zondervan Pastor's Annual, 1993. 416p. 1992. pap. 14.99 (*0-310-54291-X*) Zondervan.

— The Zondervan Pastor's Annual, 1991: An Idea & Resource Book. 400p. 1990. pap. 12.95 (*0-310-52121-1*) Zondervan.

Crabtree, T T. Zondervan 2000 Pastor's Annual: An Idea & Resource Book. annuals 448p. 1999. pap. 18.99 (*0-310-22657-0*) Zondervan.

Crabtree, T. T., ed. The Zondervan Pastor's Annual, 1995: An Idea & Resource Book. 400p. 1994. pap. 14.99 (*0-310-42931-5*) Zondervan.

Crabtree, Tracy, jt. auth. see Jones, Russell K.

Crabtree, Traves. BRS Surgery. 350p. 25.95 (*0-683-30636-7*) Lppncott W & W.

Crabtree, Traves D. BRS Surgical Specialties. 300p. pap. text 25.95 (*0-7817-2771-5*) Lppncott W & W.

Crabtree, Trevor & Crabtree, Karen. Parenting in the '90s: Where Have We Gone Wrong? 286p. 1998. pap. 13.00 (*1-887827-04-8*) New Authors Pubns.

Cracas, David J. 1001 Visual Basic Secrets: Shortcuts & Tricks Every Visual Basic Programmer Should Know. LC 95-61395. 280p. (Orig.). 2000. pap. 24.95 (*0-9640945-9-2*) Pierpoint-Martin.

***Cracchiolo, Barbara.** Learning Through Movement: Alphabet & Numbers. 112p. 2000. pap. 12.95 (*1-57690-646-9*) ISI Books.

— Learning Through Movement: Monthly Activities. 112p. 2000. pap. 12.95 (*1-57690-647-7*) Tchr Create Mat.

Cracchiolo, Edith, ed. see Khalsa, Guru K.

Crace, J. Quarantine Reader's Guide. 1997. text. write for info. (*0-374-95783-5*) FS&G.

Crace, Jim. Arcadia. 320p. 1992. 20.00 (*0-689-12158-X*) Atheneum Yung Read.

— Arcadia. LC 96-42026. 311p. 1997. pap. 13.00 (*0-88001-530-6*) HarpC.

***Crace, Jim.** Being Dead. LC 99-45082. 224p. 2000. 23.00 (*0-374-11013-1*) FS&G.

Crace, Jim. Continent. 2nd ed. LC 96-43869. 160p. 1996. reprint ed. pap. 12.00 (*0-88001-498-9*) HarpC.

— The Gift of Stones. 176p. 1989. 16.95 (*0-684-19070-2*, Scribners Ref) Mac Lib Ref.

— The Gift of Stones. large type ed. LC 89-5066. 230p. 1989. lib. bdg. 16.95 (*0-89621-914-3*) Thorndike Pr.

— Gift Of Stones. 170p. 1996. reprint ed. pap. 13.00 (*0-88001-450-4*) HarpC.

— Quarantine. LC 97-61489. 256p. 1998. 23.00 (*0-374-23962-2*) FS&G.

— Quarantine. LC 98-51205. 256p. 1999. pap. 13.00 (*0-312-19951-1*, Picador USA) St Martin.

— Quarantine. large type ed. LC 98-12779. (Core Ser.). 308p. 1998. 28.95 (*0-7838-0113-0*, G K Hall & Co) Mac Lib Ref.

— Signals of Distress. LC 95-10100. 277p. 1995. 22.00 (*0-374-26379-5*) FS&G.

— Signals Of Distress. 2nd ed. LC 96-47426. 288p. 1996. reprint ed. pap. 15.00 (*0-88001-486-5*) HarpC.

***Craciun, Adriana & Lokke, Kari E., eds.** Rebellious Hearts: British Women Writers & the French Revolution. (C). 2001. pap. text 20.95 (*0-7914-4970-X*) State U NY Pr.

— Rebellious Hearts: British Women Writers & the French Revolution. (C). 2001. text 62.50 (*0-7914-4969-6*) State U NY Pr.

Craciun, Adriana, ed. see Dacre, Charlotte.

Crackanthorpe, Hubert. Collected Stories, 1893-1897., 4 Vols. in 1. LC 74-75379. 866p. 1969. 90.00 (*0-8201-1056-6*) Schol Facsimiles.

***Cracken, L. William.** Between the Lines: Reflections on War & Peacetime. (Illus.). 235p. 1998. 19.95 (*0-9668794-0-6*) J R W Cracken.

Crackenell, D. G. & Wilson, C. H. Roman Law: Origins & Influence. 200p. (C). 1990. pap. 60.00 (*1-85352-823-4*, Pub. by HLT Pubns) St Mut.

Cracknell, A. Applied Group Theory. LC 67-18948. 1968. reprint ed. 193.00 (*0-08-103190-4*, Pub. by Pergamon Repr) Franklin.

— Physical Processes in the Coastal Zone: Computer Modelling & Remote Sensing. (Scottish Universities Summer School in Physics Ser.: No. 49). 389p. 1998. 240.00 (*0-7503-0563-0*) IOP Pub.

Cracknell, A. P. Remote Sensing in Meteorology, Oceanography & Hydrology. LC 81-4151. (Environmental Sciences Ser.). 542p. 1981. text 139.00 (*0-470-27183-3*) P-H.

Cracknell, A. P. & Vaughan, R. A. Magnetism in Solids: Some Current Topics. (Scottish Universities Summer School in Physics, a NATO Advanced Study Institute Ser.: No. 22). (Illus.). 490p. 1981. 189.00 (*0-905945-05-0*) IOP Pub.

Cracknell, A. P., jt. auth. see Kondratyev, K. Ya.

Cracknell, Arthur P. The Advanced Very High Resolution Radiometer. LC 97-171558. 500p. 1996. 126.00 (*0-7484-0209-8*) Taylor & Francis.

— Space Oceanography - An Intensive Course. 550p. 1992. pap. 41.00 (*981-02-0507-4*); text 151.00 (*981-02-0506-6*) World Scientific Pub.

Cracknell, Arthur P., ed. Remote Sensing Applications in Marine Science & Technology. 1983. text 255.50 (*90-277-1608-0*) Kluwer Academic.

Cracknell, Arthur P. & Clark, J. L. Ultrasonics. LC 79-26250. (Wykeham Science Ser.: No. 55). 200p. (C). 1980. pap. 18.00 (*0-8448-1330-3*, Crane Russak) Taylor & Francis.

Cracknell, Arthur P. & Hayes, L. W. Introduction to Remote Sensing. 304p. 1991. 99.95 (*0-85066-409-8*); pap. 39.95 (*0-85066-335-0*) Taylor & Francis.

Cracknell, Arthur P. & Hayes, L. W., eds. Remote Sensing Yearbook, 1987, Vol. 2. 690p. 1987. 231.00 (*0-85066-378-4*) Taylor & Francis.

Cracknell, Arthur P., jt. ed. see Vaughan, Robin A.

Cracknell, D. G., ed. English Legal System. 250p. (C). 1991. pap. 75.00 (*1-85352-367-4*, Pub. by HLT Pubns) St Mut.

— General Paper, No. 1. 360p. (C). 1991. 80.00 (*1-85352-879-X*, Pub. by HLT Pubns) St Mut.

— General Paper, No. 2. 360p. (C). 1991. 80.00 (*1-85352-889-7*, Pub. by HLT Pubns) St Mut.

Cracknell, H. L. & Kaufmann, R. J., trs. Escoffier: The Complete Guide to the Art of Modern Cookery. 646p. 1983. 64.95 (*0-471-29016-5*, VNR) Wiley.

Cracknell, H.L. & Kaufmann, R.J. Practical Professional Cookery. 3rd ed. 908p. 1994. pap. 49.95 (*0-470-23411-3*) Wiley.

Cracknell, Ian D. & Mead, Michael. Atlas of Minor Surgery. LC 96-26057. (C). 1998. text 29.95 (*0-443-05304-9*) Church.

Cracknell, Kenneth. Justice, Courtesy & Love: Theologians & Missionaries Encountering World Religions, 1846-1914. 1995. pap. 35.00 (*0-7162-0501-7*) Epworth Pr.

Cracknell Long, Vera A. From Britain with Love: World War II Pilgrim Brides Sail to America. rev. ed. LC 99-94615. (Illus.). 248p. 1999. write for info. (*0-9645977-1-3*); pap. write for info. (*0-9645977-0-5*) Denecroft.

Cracknell, Robert. The Psychic Reality: Developing Your Natural Abilities. LC 99-71618. 200p. 1999. pap. 12.95 (*1-57174-132-1*) Hampton Roads Pub Co.

Cracknell, Stephen. Roman Alcester Defences & Defended Area: Gateway Supermarket & Gas House Lane. LC 97-138702. xix, 162 p. 1996. write for info. (*1-872414-77-X*) Council for British Archeology.

Crackower, Sydney H., et al. Two M. D.'s & a Pharmacist Ask, "Are You Getting It 5 Times a Day?" Fruits & Vegetables : Enzymes, Antioxidants & Fiber. LC 99-26939. 1999. 6.95 (*0-9644958-2-1*) One Wrld Press.

Craco, Catherine. By Invitation Only. 352p. 1990. mass mkt. 4.95 (*0-445-21061-3*, Pub. by Warner Bks) Little.

Cracraft, James. The Petrine Revolution in Russian Imagery. LC 97-6309. 416p. 1997. 50.00 (*0-226-11665-4*) U Ch Pr.

Cracraft, James, ed. For God & Peter the Great. (East European Monographs: No. 96). 461p. 1982. text 56.50 (*0-914710-90-7*, Pub. by East Eur Monographs) Col U Pr.

— Major Problems in the History of Imperial Russia. LC 93-70549. 661p. (C). 1994. pap. text 29.96 (*0-669-21497-3*) HM Trade Div.

— The Soviet Union Today: An Interpretive Guide. 2nd ed. (Illus.). 396p. 1987. pap. text 14.95 (*0-226-11663-8*) U Ch Pr.

— The Soviet Union Today: An Interpretive Guide. 2nd ed. (Illus.). 400p. 1996. lib. bdg. 46.50 (*0-226-11661-1*) U Ch Pr.

Cracraft, James, intro. From Kievan Rus' to Modern Ukraine: The Formation of the Ukrainian Nation. 40p. 1994. write for info. (*0-9609822-2-1*) Ukrainian Studies Fund.

Cracraft, James E. The Petrine Revolution in Russian Architecture. (Illus.). 408p. 1988. 54.00 (*0-226-11664-6*) U Ch Pr.

Cracraft, James E., ed. Peter the Great Transforms Russia. 3rd ed. LC 90-81300. (Problems in European Civilization Ser.). 305p. (C). 1991. pap. text 20.36 (*0-669-21674-7*) HM Trade Div.

***Cracraft, Joel.** Living Planet in Crisis: Biodiversity Science & Policy. LC 98-31465. 1999. 60.00 (*0-231-10864-8*); pap. text 25.00 (*0-231-10865-6*) Col U Pr.

Cracraft, Joel, jt. ed. see Miyamoto, Michael M.

Cracroft, Richard. Washington Irving: The Western Works. LC 74-1973. (Western Writers Ser.: No. 14). 48p. 1974. pap. 4.95 (*0-88430-013-7*) Boise St U W Writ Ser.

Cradall, Melissa. Earth 2. 272p. (Orig.). 1994. pap. text 5.50 (*0-441-00146-7*) Ace Bks.

Cradden, Terry, jt. auth. see Collins, Neil.

Craddock, jt. auth. see Visible Ink Press Staff.

Craddock, Betty K., ed. see Dilley, James P.

Craddock, C. H., ed. see Virgil.

Craddock, Campbell, ed. see Symposium on Antarctic Geology & Geophysics Staff.

Craddock, Clare E. Style Theories as Found in Stylistic Studies of Romance Scholars - 1900-1950. LC 70-94184. (Catholic University of America. Studies in Romance Languages & Literatures: No. 43). reprint ed. 37.50 (*0-404-50343-8*) AMS Pr.

Craddock, Curtis. Sparrow's Flight. 376p. 2000. pap. 18.99 (*1-885173-40-7*, Pub. by Write Way) Midpt Trade.

***Craddock, Curtis.** Sparrow's Flight. 376p. 2000. pap. 18.99 (*1-885173-85-7*, Pub. by Write Way) Midpt Trade.

***Craddock, Fran, et al.** In the Fullness of Time: A History of Women in the Christian Church (Disciples of Christ) LC 99-43443. 1999. pap. 14.99 (*0-8272-1618-1*) Chalice Pr.

Craddock, Fred B. As One Without Authority. 1979. reprint ed. pap. 7.95 (*0-687-01930-3*) Abingdon.

— First & Second Peter & Jude. Bartlett, David L. & Miller, Patrick D., eds. (Westminster Bible Companion Ser.). 160p. 1995. pap. 15.00 (*0-664-25265-6*) Westminster John Knox.

— Luke. (Interpretation: a Bible Commentary for Preaching & Teaching Ser.). 300p. 1990. text 27.00 (*0-8042-3123-0*) Westminster John Knox.

— Philippians. LC 84-47797. (Interpretation: A Bible Commentary for Teaching & Preaching Ser.). 96p. 1987. 20.00 (*0-8042-3140-0*) Westminster John Knox.

— Preaching. 1990. pap. 14.95 (*0-687-33648-1*) Abingdon.

Craddock, Fred B., et al. Preaching Through the Christian Year: Year A - A Comprehensive Commentary on the Lectionary. LC 92-25860. 576p. 1992. pap. 30.00 (*1-56338-054-4*) TPI PA.

— Preaching Through the Christian Year: Year B - A Comprehensive Commentary on the Lectionary. LC 92-25860. 544p. (Orig.). (C). 1993. pap. 30.00 (*1-56338-068-4*) TPI PA.

— Preaching Through the Christian Year: Year C - A Comprehensive Commentary on the Lectionary. LC 92-25860. 544p. (Orig.). (C). 1994. pap. 30.00 (*1-56338-100-1*) TPI PA.

Craddock, Gerard, jt. auth. see Hayes, Susan C.

Craddock, Jerry R., jt. ed. see Bares, Kathryn.

Craddock, Jim & Connors, Martin, eds. Golden Movie Retriever. 7th rev. ed. (VideoHound Ser.). 1711p. 1997. pap. 19.95 (*1-57859-024-8*) Visible Ink Pr.

Craddock, Jim & Roberts, Renee. Be Transformed: Biblical Solutions to Life's Problems. LC 98-61073. (Illus.). 256p. 1998. pap. 23.95 (*0-934426-85-6*) NAPSAC Reprods.

Craddock, Jim, jt. ed. see Connors, Martin.

***Craddock, John.** The Buzz on Finance. 224p. 2000. pap. 16.95 (*0-86730-818-4*) Lebhar Friedman.

Craddock, M. K., jt. auth. see Dutto, G.

Craddock, Mary. A North Country Maid. large type unabridged ed. (Reminiscence Ser.). 240p. 1998. 24.95 (*0-7531-5072-7*, 150727) ISIS Pub.

Craddock, P. T., jt. contrib. by see Ramage, Andrew.

Craddock, Patricia B. Young Edward Gibbon: Gentleman of Letters. LC 81-13726. 399p. 1982. reprint ed. pap. 123.70 (*0-608-03654-4*, 206448000009) Bks Demand.

Craddock, Patricia B. & Hay, Carla H., eds. Studies in Eighteenth-Century Culture, Vol. 21. 320p. 1991. 35.00 (*0-937191-42-6*) Mich St U Pr.

— Studies in Eighteenth-Century Culture, Vol. 22. 360p. 1992. 35.00 (*0-937191-46-9*) Mich St U Pr.

Craddock, Patricia B. & Huff, Margaret C. Edward Gibbon. 475p. 1987. 55.00 (*0-8161-8217-5*, Hall Reference) Macmillan.

Craddock, Patricia B., jt. ed. see Brown, Leslie E.

Craddock, Paul, jt. ed. see Neice, Susan L.

Craddock, Paul T. Early Metal Mining & Production. (Illus.). 320p. 1995. text 65.00 (*1-56098-535-6*) Smithsonian.

Craddock, Percy. In Pursuit of British Interests: Reflections on Foreign Policy under Margaret Thatcher & John Major. LC 98-179595. (Illus.). 240p. 1998. 40.00 (*0-7195-5464-0*, Pub. by John Murray) Trafalgar.

Craddock, Rosemary. The Abbey Governess. large type ed. (Dales Large Print Ser.). 272p. 1996. pap. 18.99 (*1-85389-670-5*, Dales) Ulverscroft.

Craddock, Sacha & Pringle, Alexander. Gillian Ayres. (Illus.). 48p. 1997. pap. 24.95 (*0-900946-54-7*, Pub. by Art Bks Intl) Partners Pubs Grp.

Craddock, Sally. Retired Except on Demand: The Life of Dr. Cicely Williams. 1984. 29.95 (*0-19-520446-8*) OUP.

Craddock, Sonia. The Secret of the Cards. (J). 1990. pap. 4.99 (*0-590-73662-0*) Scholastic Inc.

— Sleeping Boy. LC 98-19066. (Illus.). 40p. (J). 1999. 16.95 (*0-689-81763-0*) Atheneum Yung Read.

Craddock, Valda M. Cancer of the Esophagus: Approaches to the Etiology. (Cambridge Monographs on Cancer Research). (Illus.). 296p. (C). 1993. text 110.00 (*0-521-37393-X*) Cambridge U Pr.

Cradic, Amy, jt. auth. see Gruzlovic, Hope.

An Asterisk (*) at the beginning of an entry indicates that the title is appearing for the first time.

Cradler, Dan. Hacker's Guide to Navigator. LC 97-3256. 300p. 1997. 24.99 (*1-57169-094-8*) Sams.

Cradock, Percy. Experiences of China. (Illus.). 277p. 1995. 39.95 (*0-7195-5349-0*, Pub. by John Murray) Trafalgar.

***Cradock, Percy.** Experiences of China: New Edition. (Illus.). 320p. 2000. pap. 24.95 (*0-7195-6042-X*, Pub. by John Murray) Trafalgar.

Craemer-Ruegenberg, I. & Zimmermann, Albert, eds. Orientalische Kultur und Europaisches Mittelalter. (Miscellanea Mediaevalia Ser.: Band 17). ix, 440p. 1985. 203.85 (*3-11-010531-4*) De Gruyter.

Craemer-Ruegenberg, Ingrid & Speer, Andreas, eds. Scientia & Ars im Hoch- & Spaetmittelalter, Pts. 1-2. (Miscellanea Mediavalia Ser.: Band 22). (GER.). (C). 1993. lib. bdg. 446.15 (*3-11-014058-6*) De Gruyter.

Craemer, Willy De, see De Craemer, Willy.

Craen, Pete Van de, see Wodak, Ruth & Van de Craen, Pete, eds.

Craeybeckx, A. S. Elsevier's Dictionary of Photography. (ENG, FRE & GER.). 672p. 1965. 237.00 (*0-444-40146-6*) Elsevier.

— Elsevier's Dictionary of Photography in English, French & German. (ENG, FRE & GER.). 660p. 1965. 325.00 (*0-8288-9272-5*, M7946) Fr & Eur.

Craford, Johnathan. The World Toy Soldier Directory & Compendium: Everything Imaginable about Collecting Toy Soldiers, All in One Place. (Illus.). 214p. 1998. pap. 21.95 (*0-9668863-0-5*) Cullen & Coolidge.

Craft. Desktop Publishing, Techknowledge Reference Series. (TP - Technology Education Ser.). (J). (gr. k-12). 1998. pap. 18.95 (*0-538-66138-0*) S-W Pub.

Craft & Godfrey. American Electronic Media. (Radio/TV/Film Ser.). 2000. mass mkt. 48.95 (*0-534-19566-0*) Wadsworth Pub.

Craft, Cassady. Weapons for Peace, Weapons for War. LC 98-49428. 1999. pap. 20.99 (*0-415-92259-3*) Routledge.

— Weapons for Peace, Weapons for War: The Effect of Arms Transfers on War Outbreak, Involvement & Outcomes. LC 98-49428. 1999. write for info. (*0-415-92258-5*) Routledge.

Craft, Alma, ed. International Developments in Assuring Quality in Higher Education: Selected Papers from an International Conference, Montreal, 1993. LC 94-16435. 200p. 1994. 95.00 (*0-7507-0314-8*, Falmer Pr); pap. 34.95 (*0-7507-0315-6*, Falmer Pr) Taylor & Francis.

— Quality Assurance in Higher Education. 238p. 1992. 79.95 (*0-7507-0070-X*, Falmer Pr) Taylor & Francis.

Craft, Ann, jt. auth. see Brown, Hilary.

***Craft, Anna.** Continuing Professional Development: A Practical Guide for Teachers & Schools. 2nd ed. LC 00-30825. 2000. write for info. (*0-415-23770-X*) Routledge.

Craft, Anna. Creativity Across Primary Curriculum: Framing & Developing Practice. LC 99-26795. 1999. pap. write for info. (*0-415-20095-4*) Routledge.

***Craft, Anna.** Teaching Creativity: Philosophy & Practice. LC 99-26795. 168p. (C). 1999. text. write for info. (*0-415-20094-6*) Routledge.

Craft, Anna & Bollington, Rob. Continuing Professional Development: Practical Guide for Teachers in Schools. (Educational Management Ser.). 224p. (C). 1996. pap. 24.99 (*0-415-13533-8*) Routledge.

***Craft, Barry.** Thy Father Is a Gorbellied Codpiece! Create over 100,000 of Your Own Shakespearean Insults! LC 97-62149. (Illus.). 60p. 1998. 7.98 (*0-7651-9148-2*) Smithmark.

Craft, Benjamin C., et al. Well Design: Drilling & Production. 1962. text 72.00 (*0-13-950022-7*) P-H.

Craft, Berniece R. An Introduction to Legal Typing. LC 78-2421. 1978. teacher ed. 3.71 (*0-672-97313-8*, Bobbs); pap. 12.19 (*0-672-97097-X*, Bobbs) Macmillan.

— Speedwriting Legal Dictionary. 170p. 1972. pap. write for info. (*0-672-96142-3*) Macmillan.

Craft, Berniece R., et al. Speedwriting for the Legal Secretary. LC 78-10833. 1979. pap. write for info. (*0-672-97013-9*) Macmillan.

Craft, Berniece Roninette. Speedwriting for the Legal Secretary. 1984. pap. 18.80 (*0-02-679670-8*) Macmillan.

Craft, Billy, et al. Mayhaws. 125p. (Orig.). 1996. pap. 12.95 (*1-57502-235-4*, P0906) Morris Pubng.

Craft, C. H. & Kirk-Greene, Anthony H. Teach Yourself Hausa. (HAU., Illus.). 400p. 1995. pap. 17.95 (*0-8442-3791-4*, Teach Yrslf) NTC Contemp Pub Co.

Craft, Catherine & Kluver, Billy. Robert Rauschenberg: Haywire. LC 98-100549. (Illus.). 120p. 1997. 39.95 (*3-7757-0686-0*) Dist Art Pubs.

***Craft, Charlotte.** King Midas & the Golden Touch. LC 98-24035. (Illus.). 32p. (YA). (gr. k up). 1999. 15.89 (*0-688-13166-2*, Wm Morrow) Morrow Avon.

***Craft, Charlotte, as told by.** King Midas & the Golden Touch. LC 98-24035. 32p. (J). (gr. 1-6). 1999. 15.95 (*0-688-13165-4*, Wm Morrow) Morrow Avon.

Craft, Christopher. Another Kind of Love: Male Homosexual Desire in English Discourse, 1850-1920. LC 93-25759. (C). 1994. 35.00 (*0-520-08492-6*, Pub. by U CA Pr) Cal Prin Full Svc.

***Craft, David.** Great Moments in Baseball. 80p. 2000. text 20.00 (*0-7881-9059-8*) DIANE Pub.

Craft, David. Great Moments in Baseball. LC 96-48672. 80p. 1997. 11.98 (*1-56799-418-0*, Friedman-Fairfax) M Friedman Pub Grp Inc.

— Rookies of the Year: New Kids Who Took the Field. LC 94-27732. (Illus.). 80p. 1995. 11.98 (*1-56799-143-2*, MetroBooks) M Friedman Pub Grp Inc.

Craft, David & Owens, Tom. Redbirds Revisited: Great Memories & Stories from St. Louis Cardinals. LC 89-81939. (Illus.). 246p. 1990. 19.95 (*0-929387-12-0*) Bonus Books.

Craft, David, et al. History of Scranton, Pennsylvania. (Illus.). 583p. 1996. pap. 38.00 (*0-7884-0588-8*, C602) Heritage Bk.

Craft-Denehy. Nursing Interventions for Infants & Children. (Illus.). 416p. 1989. text 58.00 (*0-7216-2129-5*, W B Saunders Co) Harcrt Hlth Sci Grp.

Craft, Diane H., jt. auth. see McCall, Renee M.

Craft, Elisabeth. Cafe 2: I'll Have What He's Having. (J). 1997. per. 3.99 (*0-671-00446-8*) PB.

Craft, Elisabeth R. A Spy for Hannibal: A Novel of Carthage. LC 95-13835. 290p. 1996. 21.95 (*0-910155-33-X*) Bartleby Pr.

Craft, Elizabeth. Flavor of the Day. (@Cafe Ser.: No. 4). (J). 1998. per. 3.99 (*0-671-00448-4*, Archway) PB.

***Craft, Elizabeth.** Jake & Christy. (Love Stories Ser.). 192p. (YA). (gr. 7-12). 2000. mass mkt. 4.50 (*0-553-49320-5*, Skylark BDD) BDD Bks Young Read.

— Justin & Nicole. (Love Stories Ser.). 192p. (YA). (gr. 7-12). 2000. mass mkt. 4.50 (*0-553-49319-1*) BDD Bks Young Read.

Craft, Elizabeth. Love Bytes: Cafe 1. 224p. (J). (gr. 7). 1997. per. 3.99 (*0-671-00445-X*, Archway) PB.

— Make Mine to Go. (@Cafe Ser.: No. 3). (YA). 1998. per. 3.99 (*0-671-00447-6*, Archway) PB.

***Craft, Elizabeth.** Max & Jane. (Love Stories Ser.). 192p. (YA). (gr. 7-12). 2000. mass mkt. 4.50 (*0-553-49318-3*) BDD Bks Young Read.

— Turning Seventeen: Show Me Love, No. 4. LC 00-100945. (Turning Seventeen Ser.: No. 4). 208p. (YA). (gr. 7 up). 2000. mass mkt. 4.95 (*0-06-447240-X*, HarpTrophy) HarpC Child Bks.

Craft, Elizabeth. What We Did Last Summer. (Love Stories Ser.: V). 192p. (YA). (gr. 7-12). 1998. mass mkt. 3.99 (*0-553-49255-1*) Bantam.

Craft, Ellen, jt. auth. see Craft, William.

Craft-Fairchild, Catherine. Masquerade & Gender: Disguise & Female Identity in Eighteenth-Century Fictions by Women. LC 92-30851. 184p. 1993. 30.00 (*0-271-00918-7*); pap. 17.95 (*0-271-00919-5*) Pa St U Pr.

Craft, Francine. Arabesque: Still in Love. 1999. pap. 4.99 (*1-58314-005-0*) BET Bks.

— The Black Pearl. 352p. 1996. mass mkt. 4.99 (*0-7860-0236-0*, Pinncle Kensgtn) Kensgtn Pub Corp.

— Devoted. 256p. 1995. mass mkt. 4.99 (*0-7860-0094-5*, Pinncle Kensgtn); mass mkt. 4.99 (*0-8217-0094-4*, Zebra Kensgtn) Kensgtn Pub Corp.

— Lyrics of Love. 320p. 1998. pap. 4.99 (*0-7860-0531-9*) Kensgtn Pub Corp.

***Craft, Francine.** Star Crossed. 2000. mass mkt. 5.99 (*1-58314-099-9*) BET Bks.

Craft, George S. California State University, Sacramento: The First Forty Years. Welch, Geri M., ed. (Illus.). 280p. (Orig.). 1987. write for info. (*0-9619307-0-5*) CA State Univ.

Craft, Hazel S. Jesus: God's Gift of Peace to You. 100p. (Orig.). 1983. pap. 5.95 (*0-88144-013-2*, CPS-013) Christian Pub.

Craft, J. L., ed. see Bouwsma, O. K.

Craft, Jerry. Mama's Boyz: As American As Sweet Potato Pie. LC 97-94046. (Illus.). 96p. (Orig.). 1997. pap. 9.95 (*0-9656967-0-7*) American Pub Co.

Craft, John. The Anatomy & Development of the Stock Car. (Anatomy & Development Ser.). (Illus.). 160p. 1993. pap. 21.95 (*0-87938-800-5*) MBI Pubg.

— Boss & Cobra Jet Mustangs: 302, 351, 428, & 429. LC 96-717. (Muscle Car Color History Ser.). (Illus.). 128p. 1996. pap. 21.95 (*0-7603-0050-X*) MBI Pubg.

— Chrysler Plymouth, Dodge Stock Cars. LC 97-13563. (Enthusiast Color Ser.). (Illus.). 96p. 1997. pap. 13.95 (*0-7603-0357-6*) MBI Pubg.

— Classic Stock Cars. LC 97-18635. (Illus.). 128p. 1997. pap. 19.95 (*0-7603-0298-7*, 125119AP) MBI Pubg.

— Ford Lincoln & Mercury Stock Cars. LC 98-49598. (Enthusiast Color Ser.). (Illus.). 96p. 1999. pap. 13.95 (*0-7603-0487-4*) MBI Pubg.

— Legends of Stock Car Racing. (Illus.). 160p. 1995. pap. 19.95 (*0-7603-0144-1*) MBI Pubg.

— Vintage & Historic Stock Cars. (Enthusiast Color Ser.). (Illus.). 96p. 1994. pap. 13.95 (*0-87938-898-6*) MBI Pubg.

***Craft, John A.** Chevy Stock Cars. LC 99-44191. (Enthusiast Color Ser.). (Illus.). 96p. 2000. pap. 13.95 (*0-7603-0587-0*, 129000AP, Pub. by MBI Pubg) Motorbooks Intl.

Craft, John L. Statistics & Data Analysis for Social Workers. 2nd ed. LC 89-63450. 194p. (C). 1990. pap. text 30.00 (*0-87581-343-7*, DASW2) F E Peacock Pubs.

Craft, Julian. The Life & Opinion of Tom Collins: A Study of the Works of Joseph Furphy. 1991. pap. 14.95 (*0-7022-2364-6*, Pub. by Univ Queensland Pr) Intl Spec Bk.

Craft, Kenneth F. Ohio County (WV) Index Vol. 1: Index to County Court Order Books, Pt. 1 - 1777. LC 97-219683. 224p. 1998. pap. 39.00 (*0-7884-0797-X*, C603) Heritage Bk.

— Ohio County (WV) Index Vol. 2: Index to County Court Order Books (Part 2) 1777-1881 Plus Gazetteer & Map Book. (Illus.). 501p. 1998. pap. 69.00 (*0-7884-1023-7*, C702) Heritage Bk.

Craft, Kenneth F., Jr. Ohio County (WV) Index Vol. 3, Pt. 3: Index to County Court Order Books, 1777-1881. 396p. 1999. pap. 55.00 (*0-7884-1134-9*, C703) Heritage Bk.

***Craft, Kenneth Fischer, Jr.** Ohio County (West Virginia) Index Vol. 4: Index to County Court Order Books 1777-1881. 401p. 1999. pap. 57.00 (*0-7884-1318-X*, C704) Heritage Bk.

— Ohio County (WV) Index Vol. 5: Index to County Court Order Books, 1777-1881. 387p. 2000. pap. 40.00 (*0-7884-1469-0*, C705) Heritage Bk.

***Craft, Kinukó.** Cinderella. (Illus.). (J). 2000. 15.95 (*1-58717-004-3*) SeaStar.

***Craft, Kinuko.** Cinderella. LC 00-24540. (J). 2000. lib. bdg. write for info. (*1-58717-005-1*) SeaStar.

Craft, Linda J. Novels of Testimony & Resistance from Central America. LC 96-45381. 240p. 1997. 39.95 (*0-8130-1508-1*) U Press Fla.

Craft, Louise, jt. auth. see Harrast, Tracy L.

Craft, Louise, jt. auth. see Mateer, Charlotte F.

Craft, Lucille, jt. auth. see Maeda, Misayo G.

Craft, Malee V. White Supremacist Activity in Montana. (Illus.). 57p. (C). 1998. reprint ed. pap. text 20.00 (*0-7881-7480-0*) DIANE Pub.

Craft, Marie. Cupid & Psyche. LC 95-14895. (Illus.). 40p. (J). 1996. lib. bdg. 15.93 (*0-688-13164-6*, Wm Morrow) Morrow Avon.

— Cupid & Psyche. LC 95-14895. (Illus.). (J). (ps-3). 1996. 16.00 (*0-688-13163-8*, Wm Morrow) Morrow Avon.

Craft, Mary. Hali: Ventana Wilderness Sanctuary, Eaglet. (Illus.). 18p. (Orig.). 1990. pap. 4.00 (*0-9624842-1-0*) M Craft.

— Sea Otters Cruz & Slick. (Illus.). 24p. (Orig.). (J). (ps-3). 1991. pap. 4.00 (*0-9624842-2-9*) M Craft.

Craft, Mary B. Many Happy Returns. LC 96-86072. 38p. (Orig.). 1996. pap. 4.95 (*1-56883-065-3*) Colonial Pr AL.

— Where Do I Put My Purse While I Preach? LC 88-64024. (Miss Father Ser.). (Illus.). 64p. (Orig.). 1990. pap. 6.00 (*0-938991-40-X*) Colonial Pr AL.

— Would Somebody Hold My Purse While I Preach: A Collection of Miss Father Cartoons. LC 89-82713. (Miss Father Ser.). (Orig.). 1990. pap. 6.00 (*0-938991-44-2*) Colonial Pr AL.

Craft, Mary Beth. Goldengrove. 183p. 1999. 16.95 (*1-885478-97-6*, Pub. by Genesis Press) BookWorld.

Craft, Maurice, ed. Teacher Education in Plural Societies: An International Review. LC 95-47193. 177p. 1996. 79.95 (*0-7507-0519-1*, Falmer Pr); pap. 27.95 (*0-7507-0520-5*, Falmer Pr) Taylor & Francis.

Craft, Maurice, jt. ed. see Tomlinson, Sally.

Craft, Melanie. A Hard-Hearted Man. (Intimate Moments Ser.). 1998. per. 4.25 (*0-373-07870-6*, 1-07870-8) Silhouette.

***Craft, Melissa, et al.** Network+ Exam Prep. LC 99-31053. (Exam Prep (Coriolis' Certification Insider Press) Ser.). (Illus.). 695p. 1999. pap. 44.99 incl. cd-rom (*1-57610-412-5*) Coriolis Grp.

Craft, Michael. Alien Impact, Vol. 1. Vol. 1. 352p. 1997. mass mkt. 6.99 (*0-312-96287-8*) St Martin.

— Body Language. 288p. 1999. text 22.00 (*1-57565-419-4*) Kensgtn Pub Corp.

***Craft, Michael.** Body Language. (Mark Manning Mystery Ser.). 273p. 2000. pap. text 13.00 (*1-57566-554-9*, Knsington) Kensgtn Pub Corp.

Craft, Michael. Eye Contact. LC 97-74365. 352p. 1998. 21.95 (*1-57566-292-2*, Knsington) Kensgtn Pub Corp.

— Eye Contact. 352p. 1999. pap. 12.00 (*1-57566-425-9*) Kensgtn Pub Corp.

— Flight Dreams. LC 96-79076. 224p. 1997. 19.95 (*1-57566-174-8*, Knsington) Kensgtn Pub Corp.

— Flight Dreams. Vol. 1. 256p. 1998. pap. 10.95 (*1-57566-294-9*, Knsington) Kensgtn Pub Corp.

***Craft, Michael.** Name Games: A Mark Manning Mystery. 320p. 2000. 23.95 (*0-312-24552-1*, Minotaur) St Martin.

Craft, Michael. Rehearsing. LC 92-70179. 120p. (Orig.). 1993. pap. 9.95 (*1-879603-09-8*) Los Hombres.

Craft, Michael, et al. Mental Handicap: A Multi-Disciplinary Approach. 1985. text 115.00 (*0-7020-1085-5*) Bailliere Tindall.

***Craft, Naomi, et al.** The Good Health Directory. (Illus.). 208p. 2000. spiral bd. 18.95 (*0-7641-5314-5*) Barron.

Craft, Nina. Think It, Do It! Eliminating Fears. 60p. (Orig.). 1997. pap. 10.00 (*0-9652087-2-9*) VisionFocus.

— Think It, Do It! The Procrastinator's Guide to Action. 50p. 1993. pap. 10.00 (*0-9652087-0-2*) VisionFocus.

— Think It, Do It! The Procrastinator's Guide to Action. 2nd rev. ed. 1999. pap. 10.00 (*0-9652087-3-7*) VisionFocus.

Craft, Page, ed. see Roach, Margaret J.

Craft, Ralph & Dobson, Eric N. Truck & Bus Accidents: Getting the Facts. 62p. (Orig.). 1992. pap. text 15.00 (*1-55877-132-8*) Natl Governor.

Craft, Ralph, et al. Metropolitan Mobility & Air Quality. Feinstein, Gerry R. & Glass, Karen, eds. 60p. (Orig.). 1992. pap. text 15.00 (*1-55877-173-5*) Natl Governor.

Craft, Robert. The Moment of Existence: Music, Literature & the Arts, 1990-1995. LC 95-52713. 336p. 1996. 28.95 (*0-8265-1276-3*) Vanderbilt U Pr.

***Craft, Robert.** Places: A Travel Companion for Music & Art Lovers. LC 99-66974. (Illus.). 2000. 29.95 (*0-500-01990-8*, Pub. by Thames Hudson) Norton.

Craft, Robert. Stravinsky: Chronicle of a Friendship. LC 94-12666. (Illus.). 608p. 1996. pap. 24.95 (*0-8265-1285-2*) Vanderbilt U Pr.

— Stravinsky: Chronicle of a Friendship. rev. ed. LC 94-12666. (Illus.). 608p. (C). 1994. 39.95 (*0-8265-1258-5*) Vanderbilt U Pr.

— Stravinsky: Chronicle of a Friendship, 1948-1971. 424p. reprint ed. lib. bdg. 59.00 (*0-685-14852-1*) Rprt Serv.

Craft, Robert, jt. auth. see Chambers, Harry.

Craft, Robert, jt. auth. see Stravinsky, Igor.

***Craft-Rosenberg, Martha & Denehy, Janice Ann.** Nursing Interventions for Infants, Children & Families. LC 00-8361. (Illus.). 2000. write for info. (*0-7619-0725-4*) Sage.

Craft, Sarah S. Mother Beluga Whales & Their Babies. LC 98-18931. (Zoo Life Book Ser.). 24p. (J). (gr. k-4). 1999. 17.27 (*0-8239-5315-7*, PowerKids) Rosen Group.

— Mother Giraffes & Their Babies. LC 98-23985. (Zoo Life Book Ser.). 24p. (J). (gr. k-4). 1999. 18.60 (*0-8239-5316-5*, PowerKids) Rosen Group.

— Mother Gorillas & Their Babies. LC 98-23986. (Zoo Life Book Ser.). 24p. (J). (gr. k-4). 1999. 18.60 (*0-8239-5313-0*, PowerKids) Rosen Group.

— Mother Indian Rhinos & Their Babies. LC 98-7668. (Zoo Life Book Ser.). 24p. (J). (gr. k-4). 1999. 18.60 (*0-8239-5318-1*, PowerKids) Rosen Group.

— Mother Snow Leopards & Their Babies. LC 98-23987. (Zoo Life Book Ser.). 24p. (J). (gr. k-4). 1999. 18.60 (*0-8239-5317-3*, PowerKids) Rosen Group.

— Mother Wallabies & Their Babies. LC 98-23982. (Zoo Life Book Ser.). 24p. (J). (gr. k-4). 1999. 18.60 (*0-8239-5314-9*, PowerKids) Rosen Group.

Craft, Sharon. The Other Victims of Suicide. 115p. (Orig.). 1998. pap. 9.50 (*1-879366-18-5*) Hearthstone OK.

Craft-Tripp, Marsha, jt. auth. see Glatthorn, Allan A.

Craft, W. Bert. Agony of Hell. LC 94-60251. 142p. 1994. 24.95 (*1-56311-139-X*) Turner Pub KY.

Craft, W. J. & Achgill, D. M., eds. Space Exploration Science & Technologies Research. (AD Ser.: Vol. 31). 160p. 1993. 45.00 (*0-7918-1106-9*, G00750) ASME.

Craft, William. Labyrinth of Desire: Invention & Culture in the Work of Sir Philip Sidney. LC 93-39886. (C). 1994. 33.50 (*0-87413-522-2*) U Delaware Pr.

— Running a Thousand Miles for Freedom: Or, the Escape of William & Ellen Craft from Slavery. LC 77-89417. (Black Heritage Library Collection). 1977. 22.95 (*0-8369-8549-4*) Ayer.

***Craft, William.** Running a Thousand Miles for Freedom: or The Escape of William & Ellen Craft from Slavery. Ernest, John, ed. LC 99-66365. (Emergent Texts in American Literature Ser.). 81p. (C). 2000. pap. text 6.95 (*1-58390-011-X*, Copley Editions) Copley Pub.

Craft, William & Craft, Ellen. Running a Thousand Miles for Freedom: The Escape of William & Ellen Craft from Slavery. LC 98-35264. (Illus.). 136p. 1999. pap. 14.95 (*0-8071-2320-X*) La State U Pr.

— Running a Thousand Miles for Freedom: The Escape of William & Ellen Craft from Slavery. LC 98-41981. (Illus.). 144p. 1999. reprint ed. pap. 12.00 (*0-8203-2104-4*) U of Ga Pr.

Crafter, Helen. Health Promotion in Midwives: Principles & Practice. (Illus.). 160p. (Orig.). 1997. pap. 39.95 (*1-56593-756-2*, 1470) Singular Publishing.

Craftman. Contractor's Index to the 1997 Uniform Building Code for Vol. 1. 192p. 1998. ring bd. 29.00 (*1-57218-068-4*) Craftsman.

Crafton, Barbara. The Sewing Room: Uncommon Reflections on Life, Love & Work. LC 97-35126. 200p. 1997. pap. 12.95 (*0-8192-1723-9*) Morehouse Pub.

***Crafton, Barbara C.** Blessed Paradoxes: The Beatitudes As Painted Prayer. LC 98-28299. (Illus.). 48p. 1998. 14.95 (*0-8192-1763-8*) Morehouse Pub.

Crafton, Barbara C. Finding Time for Serenity: Every Woman's Book of Days. 416p. (Orig.). 1994. pap. 9.00 (*0-345-38134-3*) Ballantine Pub Grp.

— Let Every Heart Prepare: Meditations for Advent & Christmas. LC 98-27850. 96p. 1998. pap. 7.95 (*0-8192-1755-7*) Morehouse Pub.

***Crafton, Barbara C.** Living Lent: Meditations for These Forty Days. 112p. 1998. pap. 8.95 (*0-8192-1756-5*) Morehouse Pub.

Crafton, Barbara C. Meditations on the Book of Psalms: A Guide to the Care & Feeding of the Spirit. 448p. 1996. pap. 10.00 (*0-345-39738-X*) Ballantine Pub Grp.

— The Sewing Room. large type ed. LC 93-37650. 282p. 1994. lib. bdg. 21.95 (*0-8161-5910-6*, G K Hall Lrg Type) Mac Lib Ref.

Crafton, Don. History of the American Cinema 1926-1930, Vol. 4. LC 97-40474. 639p. 1997. 85.00 (*0-684-19585-2*) S&S Trade.

Crafton, Donald. Before Mickey: The Animated Film, 1898-1928. (Illus.). 436p. 1993. pap. 20.00 (*0-226-11667-0*) U Ch Pr.

— Emile Cohl, Caricature, & Film. (Illus.). 430p. 1990. pap. text 29.95 (*0-691-00881-7*, Pub. by Princeton U Pr) Cal Prin Full Svc.

— The Talkies: American Cinema's Transition to Sound, 1926-1931. LC 99-20221. Vol. 4. 650p. 1999. pap. 24.95 (*0-520-22128-1*, Pub. by U CA Pr) Cal Prin Full Svc.

Crafton, Helen & Lindgren, Dorothy. The Elsah Landing Restaurant Cookbook. WB Design & Development, Inc. Staff, ed. LC 81-43379. (Illus.). 224p. 1981. 14.95 (*0-9606150-0-8*) Elsah Landing.

Crafton, Jeffrey A. The Agency of the Apostle: A Dramatic Analysis of Paul's Response to Conflict in 2 Corinthians. (Journal for the Study of the New Testament, Supplement Ser.: Vol. 51). 188p. 1991. 57.50 (*1-85075-268-0*, Pub. by Sheffield Acad) CUP Services.

Crafton, Linda. Challenges of Holistic Teaching: Answering the Tough Questions. (Illus.). 232p. (Orig.). 1994. pap. text 28.95 (*0-926842-34-X*) CG Pubs Inc.

Crafton, Linda K. Standards in Practice: Grades K-2. LC 95-26593. (Illus.). 121p. 1996. pap., teacher ed. 15.95 (*0-8141-4691-0*) NCTE.

— Whole Language: Getting Started . . . Moving Forward. LC 90-7977. 336p. (Orig.). (C). 1991. pap. text 24.95 (*0-913461-19-9*, 39) R Owen Pubs.

Crafton, Lisa P., ed. The French Revolution Debate in English Literature & Culture, 87. LC 97-13719. (Contributions to the Study of World Literature Ser.: Vol. 87). 176p. 1997. 55.00 (*0-313-30496-3*, Greenwood Pr) Greenwood.

Crafton, Steven M. & Brinig, Margaret F. Quantitative Methods for Lawyers. LC 94-72118. 1192p. (C). 1994. pap. 65.00 (*0-89089-604-6*) Carolina Acad Pr.

Crafts & Arts Publishing Company Staff, ed. see Hoyt, Homer L.

Crafts, George R., ed. Mysteries of Freemasonry (The Morgan Espose) 206p. 1993. reprint ed. pap. 17.95 (*1-56459-342-8*) Kessinger Pub.

Crafts, James M. History of the Town of Whately, Mass., Including Events from the First Planting of Hatfield, 1661-1899 with Genealogies. rev. ed. (Illus.). 636p. 1989. reprint ed. lib. bdg. 64.00 (*0-8328-0919-5*, MA0107) Higginson Bk Co.

C

Crafts, James M. & Crafts, W. F. The Crafts Family: A Genealogical & Biographical History of the Descendants of Griffin & Alice Craft of Roxbury, Mass., 1630-1890. (Illus.). 807p. 1989. reprint ed. pap. 99.00 (0-8328-0435-5); reprint ed. lib. bdg. 109.00 (0-8328-0434-7) Higginson Bk Co.

Crafts Magazine Staff. Dozens of Dolls. 1992. pap. 19.95 (0-9621148-8-X) PRMDIA Spcl Intrst.

Crafts Magazine Staff, jt. auth. see Creative Publishing International Staff.

Crafts, N. F., et al, eds. Quantitative Economic History. (Oxford Economic Papers Special Issue). (Illus.). 280p. 1991. pap. 24.95 (0-19-828310-5) OUP.

Crafts, N. F. & Woodward, Nicholas W., eds. The British Economy since 1945. (Illus.). 560p. 1991. pap. 32.00 (0-19-877273-4); text 85.00 (0-19-877274-2, 12227) OUP.

Crafts, N. F., jt. ed. see Broadberry, S. N.

Crafts, Nicholas. The Conservative Government's Economic Record: The End of Term Report. (Occasional Papers: No. 104). 45p. 1998. pap. 11.95 (0-255-36413-X, Pub. by Inst Economic Affairs) Coronet Bks.

Crafts, Nicholas, jt. auth. see Van Ark, Bart.

Crafts, Nick & Toniolo, Gianni, eds. Economic Growth in Post-1945 Europe. (Illus.). 623p. (C). 1996. pap. text 33.95 (0-521-49964-X) Cambridge U Pr.

Crafts, Prescott C. Duval: Genealogy & History of a Branch of the Duval Family: Peter (Pierre) Duval (I) & His Descendants. (Illus.). 100p. 1997. reprint ed. pap. 18.00 (0-8328-8398-0); reprint ed. lib. bdg. 28.00 (0-8328-8397-2) Higginson Bk Co.

Crafts, W. F., jt. auth. see Crafts, James M.

Crafts, Wilbur F. Successful Men of To-Day: And What They Say of Success. LC 73-2500. (Big Business; Economic Power in a Free Society Ser.). 1973. reprint ed. 20.95 (0-405-05081-X) Ayer.

Craftsman. Permanent Wood Foundation. 1995. 35.00 (0-9694527-0-5) J E Traister.

***Craftsman Book Co. Staff.** Building News Electrical Costbook 2000. 7th ed. 350p. 1999. pap. text 59.95 (1-55701-293-8) BNI Pubns.

— Building News Facilities Manager's Costbook 2000. 5th ed. 1999. pap. text 89.95 (1-55701-295-4) BNI Pubns.

— Building News General Construction Costbook 2000. 10th ed. 525p. 1999. pap. text 74.95 (1-55701-289-X) BNI Pubns.

— Building News Home Builder's Costbook 2000. 8th ed. 1999. pap. text 49.95 (1-55701-292-X) BNI Pubns.

— Building News Home Remodeler's Costbook 2000. 6th ed. 350p. 1999. pap. text 49.95 (1-55701-296-2) BNI Pubns.

— Building News Mechanical/Electrical Costbook 2000. 10th ed. 1999. pap. text 74.95 (1-55701-291-1) BNI Pubns.

— Building News Public Works Costbook 2000. 7th ed. 525p. 1998. pap. text 74.95 (1-55701-294-6) BNI Pubns.

— Building News Remodeling Costbook 2000. 10th ed. 500p. 1999. pap. text 74.95 (1-55701-290-3) BNI Pubns.

Cragan & Shields. Understanding Communication Theory. LC 97-28099. 422p. 1997. 60.00 (0-205-19587-3) P-H.

Cragan & Wright. Theory & Research in Small Group Communication: A Reader. 2nd ed. 1996. write for info. (0-8087-7286-4) Pearson Custom.

Cragan, John F. Communication in Small Groups: Theory, Process, Skills. 5th ed. LC 98-16391. 1998. 53.95 (0-534-54549-1) Wadsworth Pub.

Cragan, John F. & Shields, Donald C. Symbolic Theories in Applied Communication Research: Bormann, Burke & Fisher. Kreps, Gary L., ed. LC 94-49142. (Speech Communication Association Applied Communication Ser.). 368p. 1995. text 72.50 (1-881303-77-2); pap. text 28.50 (1-881303-78-0) Hampton Pr NJ.

Cragan, John F. & Shields, Donald S. Understanding Communication Theory: The Communicative Forces for Human Action: Instructor's Manual & Test Bank. 224p. (C). 1997. pap. text, teacher ed. write for info. (0-205-27975-9, T7975-0) Allyn.

Cragan, John F. & Wright, David W. Communications in Small Groups: Theory, Process & Skills. 4th ed. LC 94-33080. 330p. (C). 1995. pap. 34.00 (0-314-04226-1) West Pub.

***Cragan, Wright.** Communication in Small Groups: Theory, Process, Skills. 6th ed. 2001. text 36.75 (0-534-54551-3) Thomson Learn.

Cragen, Dorothy C. The Boys in the Sky Blue Pants. (Illus.). 1975. 15.00 (0-914330-07-1) Linrose Pub.

Crager, Wendy. More Than a Recycling Directory for More Than Atlanta. 44p. 1991. pap. text 2.75 (0-9629951-0-X) Atlanta Sierra.

Cragg. House of Islam. 2nd ed. (Religion Ser.). 1975. pap. 11.50 (0-8221-0139-4) Wadsworth Pub.

Cragg, jt. auth. see Sherman.

Cragg, Anthony. Anthony Cragg. (Illus.). 160p. 1999. 35.00 (3-89322-955-8) Edition Cantz.

Cragg, Cecil. Spring of Criticism. (C). 1989. 60.00 (0-86303-481-0, Pub. by Merlin Bks) St Mut.

Cragg, Cecil, tr. see Lefranc, Abel.

Cragg, D. & Cragg, Sherman D. Starfist: School of Fire. 1998. mass mkt. 5.99 (0-345-40623-0, Del Rey) Ballantine Pub Grp.

Cragg, D. & Sherman, D. First to Fight, Bk. 1. 1997. mass mkt. 5.99 (0-345-40622-2) Ballantine Pub Grp.

Cragg, Dan. Guide to Military Installations. 4th ed. 480p. 1994. pap. 18.95 (0-8117-3023-9) Stackpole.

— Guide to Military Installations. 5th ed. LC 96-53964. (Illus.). 416p. 1997. pap. 19.95 (0-8117-2484-0) Stackpole.

***Cragg, Dan & Sherman, David.** Starfist Bk. 5: Technokill. 352p. 2000. mass mkt. 6.50 (0-345-43591-5, Del Rey) Ballantine Pub Grp.

Cragg, Dan, jt. auth. see Grose, Francis.

Cragg, Dan, jt. auth. see Lanning, Michael L.

Cragg, Dan, jt. auth. see Sherman, David.

Cragg, F. W., jt. auth. see Patton, W. S.

Cragg, Gerald R. Church & the Age of Reason, 1648-1789. 1990. pap. 13.95 (0-14-013761-0, Penguin Bks) Viking Penguin.

Cragg, Gordon M. Organoboranes in Organic Synthesis. LC 72-90962. (Studies in Organic Chemistry: No. 1). (Illus.). 438p. reprint ed. pap. 135.80 (0-7837-0726-6, 204105000019) Bks Demand.

Cragg, J. B., ed. Advances in Ecological Research, Vol. 12. (Serial Publication Ser.). 1982. text 104.00 (0-12-013912-X) Acad Pr.

Cragg, John G. & Malkiel, Burton Gordon. Expectations & the Structure of Share Prices. LC 82-8388. (National Bureau of Economic Research Monographs). 184p. 1996. lib. bdg. 29.00 (0-226-11668-9) U Ch Pr.

***Cragg, Kenneth.** Call of the Minaret. 2000. pap. 25.95 (1-85168-210-4, Pub. by Onewrld Pubns) Penguin Putnam.

— The Education of Christian Faith: Critical & Literary Encounters with the New Testament. LC 99-48132. 252p. 2000. 65.00 (1-902210-49-2, Pub. by Sussex Acad Pr) Intl Spec Bk.

Cragg, Kenneth. The Event of the Quran. 208p. 1996. pap. 13.95 (0-614-21053-4, 274) Kazi Pubns.

— The Event of the Qur'an: Islam in Its Scripture. 208p. 1995. pap. 13.95 (1-85168-067-5, Pub. by Onewrld Pubns) Penguin Putnam.

— Faith & Life Negotiate: A Christian Story-Study. 1995. pap. 25.95 (1-85311-088-4, 6337, Pub. by Canterbury Press Norwich) Morehouse Pub.

— Jesus & the Muslim: An Exploration. 352p. 1999. pap. 22.95 (1-85168-180-9, Pub. by Onewrld Pubns) Penguin Putnam.

— Muhammad & the Christian: A Question of Response. 180p. 1996. pap. 18.00 (0-614-21675-3, 808) Kazi Pubns.

— Muhammad & the Christian: A Question of Response. 192p. 1999. pap. 17.95 (1-85168-179-5, Pub. by Onewrld Pubns) Penguin Putnam.

— Palestine: The Prize & Price of Zion. LC 98-109158. 224p. 1997. pap. 24.95 (0-304-70075-4) Continuum.

— The Pen & the Faith: Eight Modern Muslim Writers & the Qur'an. 188p. (C). 1985. text 24.95 (0-04-297044-X) Routledge.

— Readings in the Qur'an. LC 87-24981. 392p. 1995. reprint ed. pap. 18.00 (0-00-627959-7, Pub. by Fount) Harper SF.

— The Secular Experience of God. LC 97-41102. (Christian Mission & Modern Culture Ser.). 80p. (Orig.). 1998. pap. 8.00 (1-56338-223-7) TPI PA.

— Troubled by Truth. 319p. (C). 1989. text 60.00 (1-872795-71-4, Pub. by Pentland Pr) St Mut.

***Cragg, Kenneth.** The Weight in the Word: Prophethood: Biblical & Quranic. LC 99-20796. 216p. 1999. 65.00 (1-902210-27-1, Pub. by Sussex Acad Pr) Intl Spec Bk.

Cragg, Kenneth. With God in Human Trust: Christian Faith & Contemporary Humanism: A Meeting of Minds. LC 98-46428. 288p. 1999. 69.50 (1-902210-15-8) Intl Spec Bk.

Cragg, Kenneth, ed. Common Prayer: A Muslim-Christian Spiritual Anthology. (Illus.). 160p. 1999. 14.95 (1-85168-181-7, Pub. by Onewrld Pubns) Penguin Putnam.

***Cragg, Kenneth, ed.** Readings on the Qurr'an. LC 99-24296. 389p. 1999. 29.95 (1-902210-31-X) Intl Spec Bk.

Cragg, Kenneth & Speight, R. Marston. The House of Islam. 3rd ed. 152p. (C). 1987. 22.00 (0-534-08736-1) Wadsworth Pub.

Cragg, Kenneth, jt. auth. see Husayn, Taha.

***Cragg, Richard.** The Demographic Investor: Strategies for Surviving the Pensions Crisis. (Illus.). 287p. 1998. 52.50 (0-273-63736-3, Pub. by Pitman Pbg) Trans-Atl Phila.

Cragg, Roger. Civil Engineering Heritage: Wales & West Central England. 316p. 1997. 26.00 (0-7277-2576-9) Am Soc Civil Eng.

Cragg, Sarah. What Do You Sacrifice Now? A Thought Provoking Message for God-Fearing Jews. 104p. 1997. pap. write for info. (1-57502-647-3, PO 1831) Morris Pubng.

***Cragg, Sheila.** Near to the Heart of God: Scripture Prayer Journal. 384p. 2000. 14.99 (1-58134-226-8) Crossway Bks.

Cragg, Sheila. A Woman's Journey Toward Holiness: A Daily Guide for Prayer & Godly Living. LC 97-8087. 272p. 1997. pap. 11.99 (0-89107-960-2) Crossway Bks.

— A Woman's Pilgrimage of Faith: A Daily Guide for Prayer & Spiritual Renewal. LC 98-55706. 254p. 1999. pap. 11.99 (1-58134-050-8) Crossway Bks.

Cragg, Shelia. A Woman's Walk with God: A Daily Guide for Prayer & Spiritual Growth. LC 95-46385. 256p. 1996. pap. 11.99 (0-89107-875-4) Crossway Bks.

Cragg, Sherman D., jt. auth. see Cragg, D.

Cragg, Tony. Tony Cragg: Writings (1981-1992) (Illus.). 25p. 1992. pap. 17.50 (2-903004-24-2, Pub. by Galerie Isy Brachot) Dist Art Pubs.

Craggs, J. D., jt. auth. see Meek, J. M.

Craggs, Stewart R. Alun Hoddinott: A Bio-Bibliography, 44. LC 92-38456. (Bio-Bibliographies in Music Ser.: No. 44). 256p. 1993. lib. bdg. 65.00 (0-313-27321-9, CGH/) Greenwood.

— Arthur Bliss: A Bio-Bibliography, 13. LC 88-10975. (Bio-Bibliographies in Music Ser.: No. 13). 192p. 1988. lib. bdg. 55.00 (0-313-25739-6, CSB/, Greenwood Pr) Greenwood.

— Arthur Bliss: A Source Book. LC 95-35103. 384p. 1996. 113.95 (0-85967-940-3, Pub. by Scolar Pr) Ashgate Pub Co.

— John McCabe: A Bio-Bibliography, 32. LC 90-20135. (Bio-Bibliographies in Music Ser.: No. 32). 296p. 1991. lib. bdg. 69.50 (0-313-26445-7, CJM/, Greenwood Pr) Greenwood.

***Craggs, Stewart R.** Lennox Berkeley: A Source Book. LC 99-36002. 300p. 1999. text 70.95 (0-85967-933-0) Ashgate Pub Co.

Craggs, Stewart R. Soundtracks: An International Dictionary of Film Music Composers. LC 97-19854. 345p. 1997. text 83.95 (1-85928-189-3, ML102.M68C73, Pub. by Scolar Pr) Ashgate Pub Co.

— William Mathias: A Bio-Bibliography, 58. LC 95-21758. (Bio-Bibliographies in Music Ser.: Vol. 58). 264p. 1995. lib. bdg. 69.50 (0-313-27865-2, Greenwood Pr) Greenwood.

— William Walton: A Source Book. 300p. 1993. 104.95 (0-85967-934-9, Pub. by Scolar Pr) Ashgate Pub Co.

Craggs, Stewart R., compiled by. Richard Rodney Bennett: A Bio-Bibliography, 24. LC 89-23674. (Bio-Bibliographies in Music Ser.: No. 24). 262p. 1990. lib. bdg. 57.95 (0-313-26179-2, CGB/, Greenwood Pr) Greenwood.

Craggs, Stewart R., ed. William Walton: Music & Literature. LC 98-42921. 330p. 1999. text 96.95 (1-85928-190-7, ML410.W292W53, Pub. by Scolar Pr) Ashgate Pub Co.

Craghan, John. Psalms for All Seasons. 192p. (Orig.). 1993. pap. 6.95 (0-8146-2205-4) Liturgical Pr.

Craghan, John & McGrath, Elsie H. Journey of Faith: Occasional Sundays with the Easter Triduum: A Supplement. 24p. 1994. pap. 1.95 (0-89243-699-9) Liguori Pubns.

Craghan, John, et al. Journey of Faith Cycle C: Leader's Book. 128p. 1994. pap. 3.95 (0-89243-558-5) Liguori Pubns.

— Journey of Faith Cycle C: Participant's Book. 64p. 1994. pap. 1.95 (0-89243-561-5) Liguori Pubns.

Craghan, John F. Exodus. (Collegeville Bible Commentary - Old Testament Ser.). 112p. 1985. pap. 4.95 (0-8146-1371-3) Liturgical Pr.

***Craghan, John F., et al.** The Word into Life Cycle B: A Guide for Group Reflection on Sunday Scripture. LC 99-71831. (Journey of Faith Ser.). 176p. 1999. pap. 7.95 (0-7648-0513-4) Liguori Pubns.

Craghead, Richard, ed. see Stafford, Gilbert W.

Craghead, Richard, ed. see Swoope, Diana.

Cragie. The Mysterious Mask. Date not set. pap. text. write for info. (0-17-556001-3) Addison-Wesley.

Cragin, George, tr. see Steffen, Albert.

Cragin, Murray, et al. The Deep-Sky Field Guide to Uranometria 2000.0. LC 92-27060. 1993. 49.95 (0-943396-38-7) Willmann-Bell.

Craglia, Massimo. Geographic Information Research: Transatlantic Perspectives. LC 99-217534. 607p. 1998. 89.95 (0-7484-0801-0) Taylor & Francis.

Cragnolino, Gustavo & Sribhar, Narasu, eds. Application of Accelerated Corrosion Tests to Service Life Prediction of Materials. LC 93-47376. (Special Technical Publication: No. 1194). (Illus.). 405p. 1994. 61.00 (0-8031-1853-8, STP1194) ASTM.

***Crago, Hugh.** A Circle Unbroken: The Hidden Emotional Patterns That Shape Our Lives. 232p. 2000. pap. 16.95 (1-86448-813-1, Pub. by Allen & Unwin Pty) IPG Chicago.

Crago, Hugh, jt. auth. see Crago, Maureen.

Crago, James D. Background Investigations Made Easy for the General Public by Examining Public Records: Public Records. 2nd rev. ed. Kaploff, Corey, ed. LC 97-222997. (Illus.). 128p. 1996. pap. text 19.95 (0-9616336-1-1) Invest USA.

Crago, Marjorie, jt. ed. see Beutler, Larry E.

Crago, Martha B. & Pickering, Marisue, eds. Supervision in Human Communication Disorders: Perspectives on a Process. LC 87-3757. (Illus.). 250p. (Orig.). (C). 1987. pap. 39.95 (1-56593-562-4, 0017) Singular Publishing.

Crago, Maureen & Crago, Hugh. Prelude to Literacy: A Preschool Child's Encounter with Picture & Story. LC 82-19235. (Illus.). 320p. 1983. 20.95 (0-8093-1077-5) S Ill U Pr.

Crago, Patrick E., jt. ed. see Winters, Jack M.

Crago, Tracey, jt. auth. see Adams, Steve.

Crago, Tracey, jt. ed. see Adams, Steve.

Cragoe, Edward J., Jr., ed. Diuretic Agents: Based on a Symposium. LC 78-23405. (ACS Symposium Ser.: No. 83). (Illus.). 248p. 1978. reprint ed. pap. 76.90 (0-608-04343-5, 206512300001) Bks Demand.

Cragoe, Edward J., Jr., et al, eds. Amiloride & Its Analogs: Unique Cation Transport Inhibitors. LC 92-24492. 1992. 115.00 (1-56081-056-4, Wiley-VCH) Wiley.

Cragoe, Matthew. An Anglican Aristocracy: The Moral Economy of the Landed Estate in Carmarthenshire, 1832-1895. LC 95-30138. (Historical Monographs). (Illus.). 292p. (C). 1996. text 74.00 (0-19-820594-5, Clarendon Pr) OUP.

Cragon, Harvey. Computer Architecture & Implementation. LC 99-16243. (Illus.). 400p. (C). 2000. 44.95 (0-521-65168-9) Cambridge U Pr.

— Memory Systems & Pipeline Processors. (Computer Science Ser.). 592p. 1996. 70.00 (0-86720-474-5) Jones & Bartlett.

Crahall, Joseph. The Completest Angling Booke That Ever Was Writ. (Illus.). 256p. 1970. boxed set 27.50 (0-88395-007-3) Freshet Pr.

Crahan, Margaret E., ed. Human Rights & Basic Needs in the Americas. LC 82-6211. 357p. reprint ed. pap. 110.70 (0-7837-6312-3, 204602700010) Bks Demand.

Crahan, Margaret E. & Knight, Franklin W., eds. Africa & the Caribbean: The Legacies of a Link. LC 78-20531. (Johns Hopkins Studies in Atlantic History & Culture Ser.). 173p. reprint ed. pap. 53.70 (0-8357-5222-4, 202789800057) Bks Demand.

Crahan, Margaret E. & Vourvoulias-Bush, Alberto. The City & the World: New York's Global Future. LC 97-31556. 202p. 1997. 17.95 (0-87609-208-3) Coun Foreign.

Craib, Ian. Classical Social Theory: An Introduction to the Thought of Marx, Weber, Durkheim & Simmel. LC 96-24111. (Illus.). 326p. (C). 1997. text 79.95 (0-19-878116-4); pap. text 27.95 (0-19-878117-2) OUP.

— The Importance of Disappointment. LC 94-5593. 256p. (C). 1994. pap. 24.99 (0-415-09383-X, B4585) Routledge.

— Psychoanalysis & Social Theory: The Limits of Sociology. LC 89-20163. 224p. (C). 1989. pap. 15.95 (0-87023-702-0); lib. bdg. 35.00 (0-87023-701-2) U of Mass Pr.

Craies, William F., jt. auth. see Eversley, William P.

Craievich, A., et al, eds. Microlithography: High Integration in Microelectronics. 192p. (C). 1990. text 81.00 (981-02-0137-0) World Scientific Pub.

Craievich, Aldo F. Synchrotron Light: Applications & Related Instrumentation II. 312p. (C). 1990. text 92.00 (981-02-0088-9) World Scientific Pub.

— Synchrotron Light, Applications & Related Instrumentation: Proceedings of the lst Workshop. 320p. 1989. text 108.00 (9971-5-0843-5) World Scientific Pub.

Craig. Automation. (C). 1999. pap. 59.95 (0-12-194860-9) Acad Pr.

Craig. Britain Votes. 1989. 72.95 (0-900178-22-1) Ashgate Pub Co.

— British Parliamentary Election Results 1832-1885. 746p. 1989. 133.95 (0-900178-26-4) Ashgate Pub Co.

— British Parliamentary Election Results 1885-1918. 676p. 1989. 122.95 (0-900178-27-2) Ashgate Pub Co.

Craig. Group G: Computer Aided Design - Engineering Graphics Workbook - Intro to Engineering Design. 676p. (Orig.). (C). 1995. pap. text. write for info. (1-887503-21-8) Schroff Dev Corp.

— Heritage, Vol. A & Map. 3rd ed. 1994. 47.00 (0-02-325524-2) S&S Trade.

— Human Development. 8th ed. 1998. pap. text, student ed. 20.00 (0-13-923830-1) P-H.

— Introduction to Art Custom. 3rd ed. 1999. 14.74 (0-07-235463-1) McGraw.

Craig. Materiales Dentales. 6th ed. (C). 1996. text 29.42 (84-8174-188-4) Mosby Inc.

Craig. Modern Pharmacology: International. 3rd ed. 1990. 30.00 (0-316-15929-8, Little Brwn Med Div) Lppncott W & W.

— Modern Pharmacology with Clinical Applications. 5th ed. LC 96-23366. 848p. 1997. pap. text 51.95 (0-316-15934-4) Lppncott W & W.

***Craig.** Norwegian-English Dictionary. (ENG & NOR.). 420p. 1999. 195.00 (0-320-01674-9) Fr & Eur.

Craig. Nuclear Arms Race. 2nd ed. 1989. teacher ed. 25.62 (0-07-013348-4) McGraw.

***Craig.** Online Journalism. 2002. pap. 35.00 (0-534-53146-6) Thomson Learn.

Craig. Pilot in Command. 268p. 1999. 29.95 (0-07-134844-1) McGraw.

— Primary Headship in 1990s. 1989. pap. text. write for info. (0-582-04007-8, Pub. by Addison-Wesley) Longman.

Craig. Quattro Pro: Concepts & Applications. (C). 1992. 35.25 (0-538-70723-2); 35.25 (0-538-70724-0) Thomson Learn.

Craig & Kelly. Sales Training Handbook. (C). 1989. text 69.95 (0-13-788175-4) S&S Trade.

Craig & Sathianathan, Dhushy. Group B: Computer Aided Design - Engineering Graphics Workbook. 596p. (Orig.). (C). 1995. pap. text. write for info. (1-887503-16-1) Schroff Dev Corp.

Craig, et al. Human Development. 8th ed. LC 98-28291. 691p. (C). 1998. 78.00 (0-13-922774-1) P-H.

Craig, jt. auth. see Schroff Dev. Staff.

Craig, ed. see Coyle, John J., et al.

Craig, ed. see Daft, Richard L.

Craig, ed. see Hellriegel, Don, et al.

Craig, ed. see Madura, Jeff.

Craig, ed. see Smith, Len Y., et al.

Craig, A. & Rosney, C. Science Encyclopedia. (Encyclopedias Ser.). (Illus.). 128p. (J). 1989. pap. 14.95 (0-7460-0419-2); lib. bdg. 22.95 (0-88110-390-X) EDC.

Craig, A., tr. see Dautray, R. & Lions, J. L.

Craig, A. H. & Gunnison, Binney, eds. Pieces for Prize Speaking. LC 75-5592. (Granger Index Reprint Ser.). 1977. reprint ed. 25.95 (0-8369-6371-7) Ayer.

Craig, Aaron. Time Wasted . . . But Not a Lifetime! unabridged ed. (Illus.). 49p. 1998. pap. 8.95 (1-892651-09-2) Columbia Pubns.

Craig, Adam & Brownlee, Keith. Picture Tests for the MRCP (Paediatrics) (Illus.). 235p. 1997. pap. text 45.00 (0-7020-2163-6, Pub. by W B Saunders) Saunders.

Craig, Adrian, jt. auth. see Feare, Chris.

Craig, Alan, jt. auth. see Sherman, William.

Craig, Alan K. Geography of Fishing in British Honduras & Adjacent Coastal Waters. LC 66-64636. (Louisiana State University Studies, Coastal Studies Ser.: No. 14). 159p. reprint ed. pap. 49.30 (0-608-13750-2, 205163800004) Bks Demand.

— Gold Coins of the Seventeen Fifteen Spanish Plate Fleet: A Numismatic Study of the State of Florida Collection. (Florida Archaeology Ser.: No. 4). (Illus.). 99p. 1988. 22.00 (0-923308-04-0) FL Bur Archaeol.

***Craig, Alan K.** Spanish Colonial Gold Coins in the Florida Collection. LC 00-42310. (Florida History & Culture Ser.). (Illus.). 2000. write for info. (0-8130-1802-1) U Press Fla.

— Spanish Colonial Silver Coins in the Florida Collection. LC 00-24588. (Florida Heritage Publications). (Illus.). 240p. 2000. 49.95 (0-8130-1748-3) U Press Fla.

An Asterisk (*) at the beginning of an entry indicates that the title is appearing for the first time.

Craig, Alan K. & West, Robert C., eds. In Quest of Mineral Wealth: Aboriginal & Colonial Mining in Spanish America. LC 94-19560. (Geoscience & Man Ser.: Vol. 33). (Illus.). 364p. (C). 1995. pap. text 25.00 (*0-938909-57-6*) Geosci Pubns LSU.

Craig, Albert M. & Shively, Donald H., eds. Personality in Japanese History. LC 94-43147. (Michigan Classics in Japanese Studies: No. 13). x, 481p. 1995. reprint ed. pap. 18.95 (*0-939512-67-X*) U MI Japan.

***Craig, Albert M., et al.** The Heritage of World Civilization: To 1650, Vol. I 5th ed. 559p. (C). 1999. pap. text 61.00 (*0-13-012453-2*) P-H.

Craig, Albert M., et al. The Heritage of World Civilizations Combined. (Illus.). 1252p. (C). 1993. write for info. (*0-318-69916-8*) Macmillan.

— The Heritage of World Civilizations, Combined, 5 vols., Vol. A. 3rd ed. (Illus.). 538p. (C). 1993. pap. text 47.00 (*0-02-325509-9*, Macmillan Coll) P-H.

— The Heritage of World Civilizations, Combined, 5 vols., Vol. B. 3rd ed. (Illus.). 402p. (C). 1993. pap. text 45.00 (*0-02-325511-0*, Macmillan Coll) P-H.

Craig, Albert M., jt. auth. see Reischauer, Edwin O.

Craig, Alec. Above All Liberties. LC 70-37839. (Essay Index Reprint Ser.). 1977. reprint ed. 18.95 (*0-8369-2587-4*) Ayer.

— The Banned Books of England & Other Countries: A Study of the Conception of Literary Obscenity. LC 77-9968. 243p. 1977. reprint ed. lib. bdg. 35.00 (*0-8371-9709-0*, CRBB, Greenwood Pr) Greenwood.

Craig, Alexander. Ionia: Land of Wise Men & Fair Women. LC 76-154437. (Utopian Literature Ser.). (Illus.). 1976. reprint ed. 25.95 (*0-405-03520-9*) Ayer.

Craig, Alisa, pseud. A Dismal Thing to Do. 400p. 1988. mass mkt. 4.99 (*0-380-70338-6*, Avon Bks) Morrow Avon.

— The Grub & Stakers House a Haunt. 224p. 1994. mass mkt. 4.99 (*0-380-71044-7*, Avon Bks) Morrow Avon.

— The Grub-&-Stakers Pinch a Poke. (Illus.). 208p. (Orig.). 1988. pap. 3.50 (*0-380-75538-6*, Avon Bks) Morrow Avon.

— The Grub-&-Stakers Quilt a Bee. 192p. 1987. pap. 3.50 (*0-380-70337-8*, Avon Bks) Morrow Avon.

— The Grub-&-Stakers Spin a Yarn. 224p. 1990. pap. 3.50 (*0-380-75540-8*, Avon Bks) Morrow Avon.

— Murder Goes Mumming. 192p. 1989. mass mkt. 3.99 (*0-380-70335-1*, Avon Bks) Morrow Avon.

— A Pint of Murder. 192p. 1988. mass mkt. 3.99 (*0-380-70334-3*, Avon Bks) Morrow Avon.

— The Terrible Tide. 192p. 1987. mass mkt. 3.99 (*0-380-70336-X*, Avon Bks) Morrow Avon.

— Trouble in the Brasses. 224p. 1989. mass mkt. 4.50 (*0-380-75539-4*, Avon Bks) Morrow Avon.

— The Wrong Rite. 288p. 1993. mass mkt. 4.99 (*0-380-71043-9*, Avon Bks) Morrow Avon.

Craig, Alix, jt. auth. see Gadd, Toby.

Craig, Allen T., jt. auth. see Hogg, Robert V.

Craig, Ann. Encyclopedie de la Femme, 1: Les Secrets de la Beaute. (FRE.). 144p. 11.95 (*0-7859-0742-4*, M-6096) Fr & Eur.

Craig, Ann L. Mexican Immigration: Changing Terms of the Debate in the United States & Mexico. (Research Reports: No. 4). 29p. (Orig.). (C). 1981. pap. 5.00 (*0-935391-03-7*, RR-04) UCSD Ctr US-Mex.

Craig, Ann L., jt. ed. see Foweraker, Joe.

Craig, Annabel & Rosney, Cliff. Science Encyclopedia. (Encyclopedias Ser.). (Illus.). 128p. (J). (gr. 3-7). 1998. lib. bdg. 22.95 (*0-88110-964-9*, Usborne) EDC.

— Science Enclyclopedia. rev. ed. (Illus.). 128p. (J). (gr. 3-7). 1998. pap. 14.95 (*0-7460-3052-5*, Usborne) EDC.

Craig, Austin. Lineage, Life & Labors of Jose Rizal: The Phillippine Patriot, a Study of the Growth of Free Ideas in the Transpacific American Territory. 1977. lib. bdg. 59.95 (*0-8490-2168-5*) Gordon Pr.

Craig, B. D. Fundamental Aspects of Corrosion Films in Corrosion Science. (Illus.). 206p. (C). 1991. text 65.00 (*0-306-43623-X*, Kluwer Plenum) Kluwer Academic.

Craig, B. D. & Anderson, H. D., eds. Handbook of Corrosion Data. 2nd ed. LC 94-73644. (Illus.). 1000p. 1995. 213.00 (*0-87170-518-4*, 6407) ASM.

Craig, Barbara & James, Peter D. A Guide to the Fonds D'Archives & Collections in the Holdings of the York University Archives: Th Wide Opn Look Uv the Eyez. (Illus.). 600p. 1995. 70.00 (*1-55022-229-5*, Pub. by ECW) LPC InBook.

Craig, Barbara H. Chadha: The Story of an Epic Constitutional Struggle. LC 89-29841. 1990. pap. 15.95 (*0-520-06955-2*, Pub. by U CA Pr) Cal Prin Full Svc.

Craig, Barbara H. & O'Brien, David M. Abortion & American Politics. LC 92-41395. (Illus.). 398p. (C). 1993. pap. text 26.95 (*0-934540-89-6*, Chatham House Pub) Seven Bridges.

Craig, Barbara L. Archival Appraisal: Theory & Practice. 240p. 2000. 60.00 (*1-85739-009-1*) Bowker-Saur.

Craig, Barry. Art & Decoration of Central New Guinea. (Ethnography Ser.: No. 5). (Illus.). 64p. 1989. pap. 10.50 (*0-85263-941-4*, Pub. by Shire Pubns) Parkwest Pubns.

***Craig, Barry, et al.** Art & Performance in Oceania. LC 99-39638. 1999. 48.00 (*0-8248-2283-8*) UH Pr.

Craig, Bette & Kornbluh, Joyce L. I Just Wanted Someone to Know. LC 81-85377. 1981. pap. 3.95 (*0-918266-16-5*) Smyrna.

Craig, Betty L. & Miles, Joyce B. Careers in Home Economics: Teacher's annotated edition. 49.00 (*0-8219-0769-7*) EMC-Paradigm.

— Carreers in Home Economics: Workbook teacher's edition. 10.95 (*0-8219-0768-9*) EMC-Paradigm.

Craig, Beverly, ed. see Viglione, Steve.

***Craig, Brian.** The Wine of Chaeron. 2000. per. 6.95 (*0-7434-1158-7*) PB.

Craig, Brian, ed. see Corbin, B. J., et al.

***Craig, Bruce.** A 19th Century Friend: A Narrative in Verse. 70p. 1999. pap. 10.00 (*0-9665614-0-6*) SkylondaWorks.

Craig, Bruce D. Practical Oil-Field Metallurgy & Corrosion. 2nd ed. LC 92-33961. 270p. 1993. 35.00 (*0-87814-388-2*) PennWell Bks.

Craig, C., ed. Advances in Site Investigation Practice: Proceedings of the International Conference Organized by the Institution of Civil Engineers, London, March 30-31, 1995. LC 96-170507. 958p. 1996. 154.00 (*0-7277-2513-0*) Am Soc Civil Eng.

— The History of Scottish Literature: Twentieth Century, Vol. 4. 400p. 1987. text 39.95 (*0-08-035057-7*, Pub. by Aberdeen U Pr) Macmillan.

— The History of Scottish Literature, Vol. 4: The Twentieth Century. 414p. 1989. pap. text 25.00 (*0-08-037728-9*, Pub. by Aberdeen U Pr) Macmillan.

Craig, C. & Hook, Andrew, eds. The History of Scottish Literature, 1660-1800, Vol. 2. 320p. 1987. text 39.95 (*0-08-035055-0*, Pub. by Aberdeen U Pr) Macmillan.

Craig, C. Samuel, jt. auth. see Douglas, Susan P.

***Craig, Cairns.** The Modern Scottish Novel: Narrative & the National Imagination. 256p. 1998. pap. 26.00 (*0-7486-0893-1*, Pub. by Edinburgh U Pr) Col U Pr.

Craig, Cairns. Out of History. 1996. 24.00 (*0-7486-6082-8*, Pub. by Polygon) Subterranean Co.

Craig, Cairns, jt. auth. see Stevenson, Randall.

Craig, Cairns, jt. ed. see Gifford, D. J.

Craig, Campbell. Destroying the Village: The Prospect of Thermonuclear War in American Security Policy. LC 98-11023. 240p. 1998. 50.00 (*0-231-11122-3*); pap. 20.50 (*0-231-11123-1*) Col U Pr.

Craig, Charlene, ed. see Kopperfield, Antoinette.

Craig, Charles R. & Stitzel, Robert E., eds. Modern Pharmacology. 2nd ed. 1115p. (C). 1986. 44.50 (*0-316-15925-5*, Little Brwn Med Div) Lppncott W & W.

— Modern Pharmacology. 4th ed. LC 93-35535. 1994. 49.95 (*0-316-15932-8*, Little Brwn Med Div) Lppncott W & W.

Craig, Charlotte, ed. see Fry, Harold P.

Craig, Charlotte M., ed. Lichtenberg: Essays Commemorating the 250th Anniversary of His Birth. LC 93-19264. (Enlightenment Ser.: Vol. 4). XV, 152p. (C). 1993. text 47.95 (*0-8204-2132-4*) P Lang Pubng.

Craig, Chris. Call for Fire. large type ed. (Charnwood Large Print Ser.). (Illus.). 496p. 1997. 27.99 (*0-7089-8927-6*, Charnwood) Ulverscroft.

Craig, Christine. Mint Tea. (Caribbean Writers Ser.). 144p. 1993. pap. 9.95 (*0-435-98932-4*, 98932) Heinemann.

Craig, Christine, jt. ed. see Watson, Dennis.

Craig, Christopher. Call for Fire: Sea Combat in the Falklands & the Gulf War. (Illus.). 320p. 1996. 45.00 (*0-7195-5453-5*, Pub. by John Murray) Trafalgar.

Craig, Christopher P. Form As Argument in Cicero's Speeches: A Study of Dilemma. LC 93-4254. (American Philological Association, American Classical Studies: Vol. 31). 266p. 1993. pap. 19.95 (*1-55540-879-6*, 400431) OUP.

Craig, Christy, ed. see Lichten, Joanne V.

Craig-Claar, Deborah. What to Do with the Second Shepherd on the Left: Staging the Seasonal Musical. 269p. 1992. 19.99 (*0-8341-9734-0*, MP-671) Nazarene.

Craig-Claar, Deborah & Hayes, Mark. Four Tickets to Christmas. 1996. pap. 6.99 (*0-8341-9480-5*, MC-96) Nazarene.

— Four Tickets to Christmas: Director's Guide. 1996. pap. 34.99 (*0-8341-9481-3*) Nazarene.

— Four Tickets to Christmas: Dramascript. 1996. pap. 3.99 (*0-8341-9482-1*, MC-96S) Nazarene.

Craig, Claire. Incredible Creatures. LC 96-12344. (Nature Company Young Discoveries Ser.). (Illus.). 32p. (J). 1999. 10.00 (*0-7835-4840-0*) Time-Life.

Craig, Claire & Discoveries Library Staff. Explorers & Traders. LC 95-32624. (Nature Company Discoveries Library). (Illus.). 64p. (J). (gr. 4-7). 1999. 16.00 (*0-8094-9373-X*) Time-Life.

Craig, Claire & Young Discoveries Staff. Animal Babies. LC 96-16965. (Nature Company Young Discoveries Ser.). (Illus.). 32p. (J). 1999. 10.00 (*0-7835-4839-7*) Time-Life.

Craig, Clarence T., ed. Challenge of Our Culture. LC 70-167331. (Essay Index Reprints - Interseminary Ser.: Vol. 1). 1977. reprint ed. 20.95 (*0-8369-2765-6*) Ayer.

Craig-Clear, Deborah. Season Tickets: Christian Drama-Three Musical Plays. 1997. pap. 8.99 (*0-8341-9745-6*) Lillenas.

Craig, Clifford B. Utah: A Geography. 1996. text 35.00 (*0-86531-076-9*) Westview.

— Utah: A Geography. (C). 1996. pap. text 20.00 (*0-86531-473-X*) Westview.

Craig, Colette, ed. Noun Classes & Categorization: Proceedings of a Symposium on Categorization & Noun Classification, Eugene, Oregon, October 1983. LC 86-3651. (Typological Studies in Language: Vol. 7). vii, 481p. 1986. 115.00 (*0-915027-33-X*) J Benjamins Pubng Co.

Craig, Colette G. The Structure of Jacaltec. LC 76-27109. 444p. reprint ed. pap. 137.70 (*0-8357-7734-0*, 203609100002) Bks Demand.

Craig County Heritage Association Staff, ed. The Story of Craig County, Oklahoma: It's People & Places, Vol. II. (Illus.). 325p. 1991. 65.00 (*0-88107-181-1*) Curtis Media.

Craig, D. & Chaves, Antonia. Managing the Corporate Legal Function. Vol. C1. text 82.00 (*0-8205-2398-4*) Bender.

Craig, D. P. & Thirunamachandran, T. Molecular Quantum Electrodynamics: An Introduction to Radiation-Molecule Interactions. unabridged ed. LC 98-12709. 324p. 1998. pap. 12.95 (*0-486-40214-2*) Dover.

Craig, Dale. Quattro Pro: Concepts & Applications. LC 92-29442. (C). 1992. mass mkt. 27.95 (*0-538-70720-8*) S-W Pub.

Craig, Dana. Paper Mache. (Art for Children's Ser.). 96p. 1992. 12.98 (*1-55521-773-7*) Bk Sales Inc.

Craig, Darrell. IAI: The Art of Drawing the Sword. 4th ed. LC 83-193519. (Illus.). 258p. 1988. reprint ed. pap. 14.95 (*0-8048-7023-3*) Tuttle Pubng.

— Japan's Ultimate Martial Art: Jujitsu Before 1882. (Illus.). 224p. (Orig.). 1995. pap. 24.95 (*0-8048-3027-4*) Tuttle Pubng.

Craig, Darrell Max. Heart of Kendo. LC 98-40527. 1999. 35.00 (*1-57062-407-0*, Pub. by Shambhala Pubns) Random.

Craig, David. Landmarks: An Exploration of Great Rocks. (Illus.). 334p. 1996. pap. 19.95 (*0-7126-7320-2*, Pub. by Jonathan Cape) Trafalgar.

— Like Taxes: Marching Through Gaul. 1990. 21.50 (*0-916379-65-5*) Scripta.

— Luggage Labels: Mementos from the Golden Age of Travel. (Illus.). 120p. 1988. pap. 14.95 (*0-87701-531-7*) Chronicle Bks.

— On Singing Onstage. 2nd rev. ed. (Acting Ser.). 296p. 1990. pap. 12.95 (*1-55783-043-6*) Applause Theatre Bk Pubs.

— A Performer Prepares: A Guide to Song Preparation for Actors, Singers & Dancers. (Acting Ser.). 324p. 1993. 21.95 (*1-55783-133-5*) Applause Theatre Bk Pubs.

— A Performer Prepares: A Guide to Song Preparation for Actors, Singers & Dancers. 324p. 1999. pap. 18.95 (*1-55783-395-8*) Applause Theatre Bk Pubs.

— Peter Maurin & Other Poems. (Cleveland Poets Ser.: No. 40). 60p. (Orig.). 1985. pap. 5.00 (*0-914946-54-4*) Cleveland St Univ Poetry Ctr.

***Craig, David.** What Christians Believe. 2000. pap. 14.95 (*1-85168-218-X*, Pub. by Onewrld Pubns) Penguin Putnam.

Craig, David & Egan, Michael. Extreme Situations: Literature & Crisis from the Great War to the Atom Bomb. LC 79-54651. 1980. text 44.00 (*0-06-491305-8*, N6411) B&N Imports.

***Craig, David & McCann, Janet, eds.** Place of Passage: Contemporary Catholic Poetry. LC 00-27109. 288p. 2000. pap. 18.95 (*1-885266-86-3*, Pub. by Story Line) Consort Bk Sales.

Craig, David, et al. Tales from the Steep: John Long's Favorite Climbing Literature. Long, John, ed. LC 92-45869. 184p. (Orig.). 1993. pap. 14.95 (*0-934802-92-0*) Globe Pequot.

Craig, David, jt. auth. see Goldsworthy, Andy.

***Craig, David M.** Tilting at Mortality: Narrative Strategies in Joseph Heller's Fiction. (Humor in Life & Letters Ser.). 2000. pap. 19.95 (*0-8143-2912-8*) Wayne St U Pr.

Craig, Deborah. How to Use Microsoft Excel 97 for Windows. LC 98-159766. 240p. 1996. pap. text 24.99 (*1-56276-469-1*, Ziff-Davis Pr) Que.

— Quattro Pro 5 Made Easy. 512p. 1993. pap. 24.95 (*0-07-881963-6*) McGraw.

Craig, Deborah & Kunkel, Gerard. PC Magazine Guide to Persuasion. (Guide to...Ser.). (Illus.). 582p. (Orig.). 1992. pap. 27.95 (*1-56276-015-7*, Ziff-Davis Pr) Que.

Craig, Deborah, et al. How to Use Microsoft Excel 2000. LC 98-88497. (How to Use ... (Que) Ser.). (Illus.). 199p. 1999. pap. 24.99 (*0-672-31538-6*) Sams.

Craig, Deborah, jt. auth. see Davis, Phyllis.

Craig, Dennis. Horse-Racing. 286p. 1990. 52.00 (*0-85131-357-4*, Pub. by J A Allen) St Mut.

Craig, Diana. Art for Children: Draw Perfect Pets, Sketch the Great Outdoors, & Fantastic Face Painting Techniques. 1998. pap. 19.99 (*0-7858-0516-8*) Bk Sales Inc.

— How to Draw & Paint Pets. 96p. (J). 1991. 12.98 (*1-55521-716-8*) Bk Sales Inc.

— Making Models. (Crafts for Children Ser.). (Illus.). 32p. (YA). (gr. 3 up). 1997. pap. 4.95 (*1-56010-217-9*, CC07) W Foster Pub.

— Making Models: Three-D Creations from Paper & Clay. LC 92-18413. (First Guide Ser.). (Illus.). 96p. (J). (gr. 3-6). 1993. pap. 9.95 (*1-56294-710-9*) Millbrook Pr.

Craig, Diana, jt. auth. see Harris, Sarah.

Craig, Diane. Images of Impressionism. LC 99-23575. (Images of Ser.). (Illus.). 96p. 1999. 22.00 (*1-57145-643-0*, Laurel Glen Pub) Advantage Pubs.

Craig-Dodd. Peter Schaufuss - Dancer. 1987. 69.00 (*1-869828-00-3*, Pub. by Moonstone Bks) St Mut.

Craig, Don. Economic Justice: Political & Economic Changes Crucial to Mankind's Survival. LC 90-64076. (Illus.). 507p. (Orig.). 1991. pap. 21.95 (*0-9628488-0-8*) Sawyer Bks.

Craig, Doris, compiled by. Catch Phrases, Cliches & Idioms: A Dictionary of Familiar Expressions. LC 89-43644. 238p. 1990. lib. bdg. 38.50 (*0-89950-467-1*) McFarland & Co.

Craig, Dorothy. Sustainable Communities: A Community Action Guide. Boyd, Susan & Lapham, Burks, eds. (Community Action Guides Ser.). (Illus.). (Orig.). (YA). (gr. 6-12). 1997. pap. 4.00 (*0-937345-09-1*) CONCERN.

Craig, Dorothy, ed. see Tobias, Cindy U. & Guild, Pat B.

Craig, Dorothy P., ed. see Nilson, Donald E. & Kroenke, David M.

Craig, Douglas B. After Wilson: The Struggle for the Democratic Party, 1920-1934. LC 92-53629. xviii, 406p. (C). 1993. 59.95 (*0-8078-2058-X*) U of NC Pr.

***Craig, Douglas B.** Fireside Politics: Radio & Political Culture in the United States, 1920-1940. (Reconfiguring American Political History Ser.). (Illus.). 368p. 2000. 45.00 (*0-8018-6439-9*) Johns Hopkins.

Craig, Douglas B., jt. auth. see Elson, Mark D.

Craig, Drew. Joy in Shared Tears. 1997. pap. 9.99 (*1-898787-55-7*) Emerald House Group Inc.

Craig, Drew, jt. auth. see Beckwith, Bob.

Craig, Duane. BODYBASEX Personal Fitness Guide. Groesbeeck, Christi et al, eds. (Illus.). 156p. 1999. pap. 14.95 (*0-9672869-1-3*) BODYBASEX.

— BODYBASEX Personal Fitness Guide & Personal Fitness Planner, 2 vols., Set. Groesbeeck, Christi et al, eds. (Illus.). 257p. 1999. pap. 39.95 (*0-9672869-2-1*) BODYBASEX.

— BODYBASEX Personal Fitness Planner. Groesbeeck, Christi, ed. (Illus.). 101p. 1999. 24.95 (*0-9672869-0-5*) BODYBASEX.

Craig, Duncan. Dielectric Analysis of Pharmaceutical Systems. (Pharmaceutical Sciences Ser.). 240p. 1996. 125.00 (*0-13-210279-X*, Pub. by Tay Francis Ltd) Taylor & Francis.

Craig, E. C. Laboratory Manual for Electronics via Waveform Analysis. (Illus.). 144p. 1993. 19.95 (*0-387-94136-3*) Spr-Verlag.

Craig, E. Gordon. Gordon Craig on Movement & Dance. 288p. 1977. 29.95 (*0-903102-37-4*, Pub. by Dance Bks) Princeton Bk Co.

Craig, E. Quita. Black Drama of the Federal Theatre Era: Beyond the Formal Horizons. LC 79-22924. (Illus.). 256p. 1980. lib. bdg. 30.00 (*0-87023-294-0*) U of Mass Pr.

Craig, Edith, ed. see Terry, Ellen.

Craig, Edward. Hume on Religion. LC 97-913659. 78p. 1997. pap. 8.00 (*81-85952-42-6*, Pub. by Indian Inst) Nataraj Bks.

— Knowledge & the State of Nature: An Essay in Conceptual Synthesis. 182p. 1991. text 65.00 (*0-19-824243-3*) OUP.

— Knowledge & the State of Nature: An Essay in Conceptual Synthesis. 169p. 1999. pap. 19.95 (*0-19-823879-7*) OUP.

— The Mind of God & the Works of Man. LC 87-1514. 362p. 1987. text 69.00 (*0-19-824933-0*) OUP.

— The Mind of God & the Works of Man. 364p. 1997. reprint ed. pap. text 21.00 (*0-19-823682-4*) OUP.

Craig, Edward, ed. Routledge Encyclopedia of Philosophy, 10 vols. LC 97-4549. (Illus.). 8361p. (C). 1998. 2995.00 (*0-415-07310-3*) Routledge.

— Routledge Encyclopedia of Philosophy, 10 vols. 8136p. (C). 1998. text 3495.00 incl. cd-rom (*0-415-16917-8*) Routledge.

Craig, Edward G. Books & Theatres. LC 67-26729. (Essay Index Reprint Ser.). 1977. 22.95 (*0-8369-0346-3*) Ayer.

— Henry Irving. LC 79-91486. (Illus.). 1972. 24.95 (*0-405-08380-7*, Pub. by Blom Pubns) Ayer.

— The Mask, Vol. 6. LC 65-27911. 1972. 52.95 (*0-405-08388-2*) Ayer.

— The Mask, Vol. 16. LC 65-27911. 1972. 30.95 (*0-405-08398-X*) Ayer.

— Scene. LC 65-20498. (Illus.). 1972. reprint ed. 20.95 (*0-405-08381-5*, Pub. by Blom Pubns) Ayer.

— The Theatre Advancing. 1980. 34.95 (*0-405-09144-3*, 1708) Ayer.

— Toward a New Theatre. LC 68-56531. (Illus.). 106p. 1972. 38.95 (*0-405-08399-8*, Pub. by Blom Pubns) Ayer.

Craig, Edward G., ed. The Mask. 1972. 52.95 (*0-405-08394-7*) Ayer.

— The Mask, 16 vols., 14 bks., Set. LC 65-27911. 1965. reprint ed. 674.95 (*0-405-08382-3*, Pub. by Blom Pubns) Ayer.

— The Mask, Vol. 2. LC 65-27911. 1972. 52.95 (*0-405-08383-1*); 52.95 (*0-405-08384-X*) Ayer.

— The Mask, Vol. 3. LC 65-27911. 1972. 52.95 (*0-405-08385-8*) Ayer.

— The Mask, Vol. 4. LC 65-27911. 1972. 52.95 (*0-405-08386-6*) Ayer.

— The Mask, Vol. 5. LC 65-27911. 1972. 52.95 (*0-405-08387-4*) Ayer.

— The Mask, Vol .11. LC 65-27911. 1972. 52.95 (*0-405-08393-9*) Ayer.

— The Mask, Vol. 13. LC 65-27911. 1972. 52.95 (*0-405-08395-5*) Ayer.

— The Mask, Vol. 14. LC 65-27911. 1972. 52.95 (*0-405-08396-3*) Ayer.

— The Mask, Vol. 15. LC 65-27911. 1972. 52.95 (*0-405-08397-1*) Ayer.

— The Mask, vols. 7 & 8. LC 65-27911. 1972. 52.95 (*0-405-08389-0*) Ayer.

— The Mask, vols. 9 & 10. LC 65-27911. 1972. 52.95 (*0-405-08391-2*) Ayer.

Craig, Edward V. Orthopaedics: A Review Book. Date not set. write for info. (*0-683-30243-4*) Lppncott W & W.

— Textbook of Orthopaedic Surgery. LC 98-15922. 1000p. 1998. write for info. (*0-683-02180-X*) Lppncott W & W.

Craig, Edward V., ed. The Shoulder (Master Techniques in Orthopaedic Surgery) Master Techniques in Orthopaedic Surgery. (Master Techniques in Orthopaedic Surgery Ser.). (Illus.). 496p. 1995. text 189.00 (*0-7817-0035-3*) Lppncott W & W.

Craig, Edwin C. Electronics via Waveform Analysis. LC 92-43410. (Illus.). 432p. 1993. 59.95 (*0-387-94015-4*) Spr-Verlag.

Craig, Eleanor. Como Escuchar a los Ninos (How to Listen to Children) (SPA.). 290p. 1987. pap. 8.99 (*968-16-2505-6*, Pub. by Fondo) Continental Bk.

— The Moon Is Broken. 1999. pap. 9.00 (*0-452-26990-3*, Plume) Dutton Plume.

Craig, Elizabeth. Don't Slurp Your Soup: A Basic Guide to Business Etiquette. 2nd rev. ed. LC 96-11547. 224p. 1996. pap. 13.95 (*0-918420-26-1*) Brighton Pubns.

— English Royal Cookbook: Favorite Court Recipes. 187p. 1998. reprint ed. pap. 11.95 (*0-7818-0583-X*) Hippocrene Bks.

Craig, Elvira. Rapture 2000 Party over Out of Time 00:01. 1997. pap. 12.00 (*1-891680-00-5*) End Times.

Craig, Emma. Christmas Pie. 320p. (Orig.). 1997. mass mkt. 4.99 (*0-8439-4331-9*, Leisure Bks) Dorchester Pub Co.

C

— Enchanted Christmas. 400p. 1998. mass mkt. 5.99 (*0-505-52287-X*, Love Spell) Dorchester Pub Co.

***Craig, Emma.** A Gambler's Magic. 368p. (Orig.). 2000. pap. 5.50 (*0-505-52358-2*, Love Spell) Dorchester Pub Co.

Craig, Emma. Gentle Magic, 1 vol. (Love Spell Ser.). 368p. 1999. mass mkt. 5.50 (*0-505-52321-3*) Dorchester Pub Co.

— Rosamunda's Revenge. 368p. (Orig.). 1997. mass mkt. 5.50 (*0-505-52213-6*, Love Spell) Dorchester Pub Co.

Craig, Emma, et al. The Magic of Christmas. 400p. 1998. mass mkt. 5.99 (*0-505-52283-7*, Love Spell) Dorchester Pub Co.

— Midsummer Night's Magic. 368p. (Orig.). 1997. mass mkt. 5.50 (*0-505-52209-8*, Love Spell) Dorchester Pub Co.

***Craig, Emma, et al.** Winter Wonderland. 400p. 1999. mass mkt. 5.99 (*0-505-52339-6*, Love Spell) Dorchester Pub Co.

Craig, Emma-Lou, ed. see Hanson, Bertha.

Craig, F. F., Jr. Aspectos de Ingenieria de la Inyeccion de Agua. 132p. 1982. 10.00 (*0-89520-313-8*, EORMONO0035P) Soc Petrol Engineers.

— Reservoir Engineering Aspects of Water Flooding. 134p. 1976. 30.00 (*0-89520-202-6*, EORMONO003) Soc Petrol Engineers.

Craig, F. Franklin. Mustang, Fury over Europe: Fury over Europe. LC 95-13108. (Illus.). 104p. (Orig.). 1995. pap. 9.95 (*1-878815-07-5*) Reflected Images.

***Craig, F. Franklin.** Mustang: Fury Over Europe: 8th Air Force Fighter Command, World War II. large type ed. Webber, Bert, ed. LC 95-13108. Orig. Title: Mustang: Fury Over Europe. (Illus.). 104p. 2000. pap. Price not set. (*1-878815-14-8*) Reflected Images.

Craig, F. W. Britain Votes 4: British Parliamentary Election Results, 1983-87. 4th ed. 256p. 1989. 61.95 (*0-900178-25-6*, Pub. by Dartmth Pub) Ashgate Pub Co.

— British Electoral Facts, 1832-1987. 210p. 1989. text 82.95 (*0-900178-30-2*, Pub. by Dartmth Pub) Ashgate Pub Co.

— British General Election Manifestos 1959-1987. (Parliamentary Research Services Ser.). 516p. 1990. text 101.95 (*0-900178-34-5*, Pub. by Dartmth Pub) Ashgate Pub Co.

Craig, Freeman. Coinage of El Peru No. 7: Handbook. 24p. 1988. 9.50 (*0-685-72025-X*) Am Numismatic.

— Coinage of El Peru No. 7: Handbook, 36 slides, Set. 24p. 1988. boxed set 30.00 incl. sl. (*0-685-72026-8*) Am Numismatic.

Craig, G. & Hull, J., eds. James Hutton - Present & Future. (Geological Society Special Publication Ser.: No. 150). 208p. 1999. 99.00 (*1-86239-026-6*, Pub. by Geol Soc Pub Hse) AAPG.

Craig, G. M. The Agriculture of the Sudan. (Centre for Agricultural Strategy Ser.: No. 1). (Illus.). 488p. 1991. 125.00 (*0-19-859210-8*) OUP.

Craig, G. Y., ed. Geology of Scotland. (Illus.). 628p. (C). 1991. 109.00 (*0-903317-63-X*, 271, Pub. by Geol Soc Pub Hse); pap. 49.00 (*0-903317-64-8*, 272, Pub. by Geol Soc Pub Hse) AAPG.

Craig, G. Y. & Jones, E. J., eds. A Geological Miscellany. LC 84-42952. (Illus.). 211p. 1985. pap. text 15.95 (*0-691-02389-1*, Pub. by Princeton U Pr) Cal Prin Full Svc.

Craig, G. Y., ed. see Schafer, Wilhelm.

Craig, Gale M. Stop Abusing Bernoulli! How Airplanes Really Fly. LC 97-91991. (Illus.). 160p. (YA). (gr. 12). 1998. pap. 17.00 (*0-9646806-2-9*); text 29.00 (*0-9646806-1-0*) Regen Pr.

Craig, George & McGowan, Margaret, eds. Moy Qui Me Voy: The Writer & the Self from Montaiqne to Leiris. 240p. 1989. 70.00 (*0-19-815153-5*) OUP.

Craig, George B. & Sesnic, Steve S. Investigations of Field Effect Transistors at Cryogenic Temperatures. LC 75-139809. 85p. 1970. 19.00 (*0-403-04491-X*) Scholarly.

Craig, George D. The Modernist Trend in Spanish American Poetry. LC 78-131249. 347p. 1971. reprint ed. 50.00 (*0-87752-129-8*) Gordian.

Craig, George D., ed. The Modernist Trend in Spanish American Poetry. 1977. lib. bdg. 59.95 (*0-8490-2273-8*) Gordon Pr.

Craig, Georgia. Come Home Holly Lowman. large type ed. (Linford Romance Library). 320p. (Orig.). 1995. pap. 16.99 (*0-7089-7785-5*, Linford) Ulverscroft.

— The Girl Outside. large type ed. (Linford Romance Library). 304p. 1997. pap. 16.99 (*0-7089-5113-9*, Linford) Ulverscroft.

— No Part of Marriage! large type ed. (Linford Romance Library). 304p. 1993. pap. 16.99 (*0-7089-7330-2*, Linford) Ulverscroft.

— Nurse at Guale Farms. large type ed. (Romance Ser.). 288p. 1992. 27.99 (*0-7089-2709-2*) Ulverscroft.

Craig, Gerald M. The United States & Canada. LC 67-30826. (American Foreign Policy Library). 376p. reprint ed. pap. 116.60 (*0-7837-4459-5*, 205798900012) Bks Demand.

Craig, Gerald S. Certain Techniques Used in Developing a Course of Study in Science for the Horace Mann Elementary School. LC 77-176677. (Columbia University. Teachers College. Contributions to Education Ser.: No. 276). reprint ed. 37.50 (*0-404-55276-5*) AMS Pr.

Craig, Gillian M., ed. The Agriculture of Egypt. (Centre for Agricultural Strategy Ser.: No. 3). (Illus.). 536p. 1993. text 110.00 (*0-19-859203-5*) OUP.

Craig, Glen K. U. S. Army Special Forces Medical Handbook. (Illus.). 608p. 1988. pap. 27.00 (*0-87364-454-9*) Paladin Pr.

Craig, Gloria. Clinical Calculations Using Dimensional Analysis. LC 96-13233. 352p. 1996. pap. text 24.95 (*0-397-55320-X*) Lppncott W & W.

Craig, Gordon A. The Battle of Koniggratz: Prussia's Victory over Austria, 1866. LC 75-35334. (Illus.). 211p. 1976. reprint ed. lib. bdg. 35.00 (*0-8371-8563-7*, CRBK, Greenwood Pr) Greenwood.

— Diplomats, 1919-1939. 712p. (C). pap. text 24.95 (*0-691-03660-8*, Pub. by Princeton U Pr) Cal Prin Full Svc.

— Diplomats, 1939-1979. 725p. (C). 1994. text 49.50 (*0-691-03613-6*, Pub. by Princeton U Pr) Cal Prin Full Svc.

— The End of Prussia. LC 83-40261. (Curti Lectures, 1982). 109p. reprint ed. pap. 33.80 (*0-608-20419-6*, 207167200002) Bks Demand.

— Europe Since Nineteen Fourteen. 3rd ed. LC 77-140148. (Orig.). (C). 1972. pap. text 51.00 (*0-03-089193-0*, Pub. by Harcourt Coll Pubs) Harcourt.

— Europe, 1815-1914, Vol. 1. 3rd ed. LC 77-140148. (C). 1972. pap. text 53.00 (*0-03-089194-9*, Pub. by Harcourt Coll Pubs) Harcourt.

— From Bismarck to Adenau: Aspects of German Statecraft. LC 78-10800. (Albert Shaw Lectures on Diplomatic History). 156p. 1979. reprint ed. lib. bdg. 49.75 (*0-313-21233-3*, CRFB, Greenwood Pr) Greenwood.

— The Germans. 368p. 1991. pap. 15.95 (*0-452-01085-3*, Mer) NAL.

— Germany, Eighteen Sixty-Six to Nineteen Forty-Five. (History of Modern Europe Ser.). 825p. 1980. pap. text 31.95 (*0-19-502724-8*) OUP.

— Politics of the Prussian Army, 1640-1945. 556p. 1964. reprint ed. pap. text 25.95 (*0-19-500257-1*) OUP.

— The Politics of the Unpolitical: German Writers & the Problem of Power, 1770-1871. 208p. 1995. text 45.00 (*0-19-509499-9*) OUP.

— Theodor Fontane: Literature & History in the Bismarck Reich. LC 98-47520. 256p. 1999. 35.00 (*0-19-512837-0*) OUP.

Craig, Gordon A. & George, Alexander L. Force & Statecraft: Diplomatic Problems of Our Time. 3rd ed. (Illus.). 320p. (C). 1995. pap. text 24.95 (*0-19-509244-9*) OUP.

***Craig, Gordon Alexander.** Politics & Culture in Modern Germany: Essays from the New York Review of Books. LC 99-45708. 400p. 2000. pap. 24.50 (*0-930664-22-1*) SPOSS.

***Craig, Grace J. & Kermis, Marguerite D.** Children Today: Canadian Edition. 2nd ed. 1019p. 2000. pap. write for info. (*0-13-087003-X*) P-H.

Craig, Grace J. & Kermis, Marguerite D. Children Today. LC 94-13293. (Illus.). 686p. (C). 1994. 82.00 (*0-13-146275-X*) P-H.

Craig-Green, Laurence. The Christmas Book. (Illus.). 48p. 1985. pap. 12.50 (*0-916922-13-8*) Poet Tree Pr.

— For... rev. ed. (Illus.). 48p. 1984. pap. 8.25 (*0-916922-07-3*) Poet Tree Pr.

— The Honeymoon. (Illus.). 48p. 1984. pap. 8.25 (*0-916922-06-5*) Poet Tree Pr.

— To a Friend. (Illus.). 16p. 1985. pap. 6.50 (*0-916922-10-3*) Poet Tree Pr.

Craig, H., ed. Two Coventry Corpus Christi Plays. (EETS Extra Ser.: Vol. 87). 1966. reprint ed. 20.00 (*0-19-722577-2*, Pub. by EETS) Boydell & Brewer.

Craig, H., ed. see Metham, John.

Craig, H. A. Bilal. 160p. 1994. pap. 6.95 (*0-7043-3160-8*, Pub. by Quartet) Interlink Pub.

Craig, H. L., ed. Stress Corrosion - New Approaches - STP 610. 429p. 1976. 43.00 (*0-8031-0580-0*, STP610) ASTM.

Craig, H. Stanley. Clark - Dixon Family: The Ancestry & Descendants of James Clark & His Wife Jane (Dixon) Clark of Fairton, Cumberland County, New Jersey. (Illus.). 141p. 1997. reprint ed. pap. 22.00 (*0-8328-7938-X*); reprint ed. lib. bdg. 32.00 (*0-8328-7937-1*) Higginson Bk Co.

— Genealogical Data from Cumberland County Wills. (Illus.). 157p. 1997. reprint ed. pap. 21.00 (*0-8328-6046-8*) Higginson Bk Co.

***Craig, H. Stanley.** South Jersey Marriages, Supplementing the Cape May, Cumberlandum Gloucester & Salem County Marriage Records. 164p. 1999. reprint ed. pap. 21.50 (*0-8328-9814-7*) Higginson Bk Co.

Craig, H. Stanley, compiled by. Burlington County Marriages. 339p. 1997. reprint ed. lib. bdg. 37.50 (*0-8328-6044-1*) Higginson Bk Co.

— Cumberland County Genealogical Data: Records Pertaining to Persons Residing in Cumberland County Prior to 1800. (Illus.). 248p. 1996. reprint ed. pap. 27.00 (*0-8328-5066-7*) Higginson Bk Co.

— Cumberland County Marriages. 333p. 1997. reprint ed. lib. bdg. 37.00 (*0-8328-6047-6*) Higginson Bk Co.

Craig, H. Stanley, contrib. by. Salem County Wills Recorded in the Office of the Surrogate at Salem, 1804-1830. 214p. 1995. reprint ed. pap. 21.00 (*0-8328-4706-2*) Higginson Bk Co.

— Salem County Wills Recorded in the Office of the Surrogate at Salem, 1804-1830. 417p. 1998. reprint ed. pap. 39.50 (*0-8328-9614-4*) Higginson Bk Co.

Craig, Hardin. The Enchanted Glass: The Elizabethan Mind in Literature. LC 75-11492. 293p. 1975. reprint ed. lib. bdg. 41.50 (*0-8371-8200-X*, CREG, Greenwood Pr) Greenwood.

— Literary Study & the Scholarly Profession. LC 72-84303. (Essay Index Reprint Ser.). 1977. 19.95 (*0-8369-1079-6*) Ayer.

Craig, Hardin & Thomas, J. M., eds. English Prose of the Nineteenth Century. 1929. 59.50 (*0-89197-147-5*) Irvington.

Craig, Hardin, ed. see Shakespeare, William.

Craig, Hardin, ed. see Stanford University, School of Letters Staff.

Craig, Hazel T. Thresholds to Adult Living. rev. ed. 1978. teacher ed. 18.21 (*0-02-665950-6*) Glencoe.

— Thresholds to Adult Living. rev. ed. (YA). (gr. 9-12). 1982. text 34.99 (*0-02-665940-9*) Glencoe.

Craig, Helen. Charlie & Tyler at the Seashore. LC 94-24620. (Illus.). 24p. (J). (ps-3). 1996. pap. 5.99 (*1-56402-595-0*) Candlewick Pr.

— Charlie & Tyler at the Seashore. LC 94-24620. 1996. 11.19 (*0-606-09136-X*, Pub. by Turtleback) Demco.

— I See the Moon & the Moon Sees Me. LC 92-18996. (Willa Perlman Bks.). (Illus.). 48p. (J). (ps-2). 1993. 16.00 (*0-06-021453-8*) HarpC Child Bks.

— The Night of the Paper Bag Monsters. LC 92-44610. (Illus.). 32p. (J). (ps up). 1994. reprint ed. pap. 4.95 (*1-56402-120-3*) Candlewick Pr.

***Craig, Helen.** Random House Book of Nursery Songs. LC 99-41658. (Illus.). 96p. (J). (gr. 4-7). 2000. 19.95 (*0-375-80586-9*, Pub. by Random Bks Yng Read) Random.

— Random House Book of Nursery Stories. LC 99-41658. (Illus.). 96p. (J). (ps-3). 2000. lib. bdg. 21.99 (*0-375-90586-3*) Random Bks Yng Read.

Craig, Helen. A Welcome for Annie. LC 92-43770. (Illus.). 32p. (J). (ps up). 1994. pap. 4.99 (*1-56402-144-0*) Candlewick Pr.

***Craig, Helen.** Foggy Friday. LC 99-47079. 24p. (J). (ps up). 2001. 10.99 (*0-7636-0777-0*) Candlewick Pr.

— Meow Monday. LC 99-47078. 24p. (J). (ps up). 2000. 10.99 (*0-7636-0832-7*) Candlewick Pr.

Craig, Helen & Aesop. The Town Mouse & the Country Mouse. 1995. 11.19 (*0-606-08890-3*, Pub. by Turtleback) Demco.

***Craig, Helen & Holabird, Katharine.** Angelina & Alice. LC 00-41660. (Illus.). (J). 2001. write for info. (*1-58485-130-9*) Pleasant Co.

— Angelina on Stage. LC 00-41661. (Illus.). 2001. write for info. (*1-58485-150-3*) Pleasant Co.

Craig, Helen, jt. auth. see Dunbar, Joyce.

Craig, Helen, jt. auth. see Heneveld, Ward.

Craig, Helen, jt. auth. see Holabird, Katharine.

Craig, Helen, jt. auth. see Root, Phyllis.

Craig, Henry A. The Delinquents. 170p. mass mkt. 4.99 (*1-55197-770-2*) Picasso Publ.

— The Wire Fence. 160p. mass mkt. 4.95 (*1-896329-18-7*) Picasso Publ.

Craig, Horace. Fort Worth Stockyards National Historic District: Illustrated History & Guide. 90p. (Orig.). 1995. pap. write for info. (*1-57502-005-X*) Morris Pubng.

***Craig, I.** The Interpretation of Object-Oriented Programming Languages. LC 99-43762. (Illus.). 270p. 2000. 69.95 (*1-85233-159-3*, Pub. by Spr-Verlag) Spr-Verlag.

Craig, I. & Rawlings, C., eds. Human Gene Mapping 10.5: Update to the Tenth International Workshop on Human Gene Mapping, Oxford 1990. (Journal: Cytogenetics & Cell Genetics: Vol. 55, No. 1-4). (Illus.). viii, 786p. 1991. pap. 191.50 (*3-8055-5381-1*) S Karger.

Craig, I., tr. see Coulange, Bernard.

Craig, I. D. Programming in Dylan, Vol. XI. LC 96-36945. (Illus.). 254p. 1996. pap. 34.95 (*3-540-76053-9*) Spr-Verlag.

Craig, I. J. & Brown, J. C. Inverse Problems in Astronomy: A Guide to Inversion Strategies for Remotely Sensed Data. (Illus.). 160p. 1986. 86.00 (*0-85274-369-6*) IOP Pub.

Craig, Iain D. The Cassandra Architecture: Distributed Control in a Blackboard System. 1989. text 75.00 (*0-470-21353-1*) P-H.

Craig, Ian, ed. Managing Primary Classrooms. 1997. pap. 54.50 (*0-273-62712-0*, Pub. by F T P-H) Trans-Atl Phila.

Craig, J. F. & Kemper, J. B., eds. Regulated Streams. LC 87-16596. (Advances in Ecology Ser.). (Illus.). 444p. 1987. 120.00 (*0-306-42674-9*, Plenum Trade) Perseus Pubng.

Craig, James. Basic Typography: A Design Manual. (Illus.). 192p. 1990. pap. 19.95 (*0-8230-0451-1*) Watsn-Guptill.

— Designing with Type: A Basic Course in Typography. LC 70-159564. 175 p. 1971. write for info. (*0-8230-1320-0*) Watsn-Guptill.

— Designing with Type: A Basic Course in Typography. 3rd ed. (Illus.). 176p. 1992. 24.95 (*0-8230-1305-7*) Watsn-Guptill.

— Production for the Graphic Designer. (Illus.). 208p. 1990. 29.95 (*0-8230-4416-5*) Watsn-Guptill.

Craig, James & Bevington, William. Designing with Type: A Basic Course in Typography. 4th rev. ed. LC 98-53402. (Illus.). 176p. 1999. text 24.95 (*0-8230-1347-2*) Watsn-Guptill.

— Working with Graphic Designers. (Illus.). 160p. 1999. reprint ed. pap. text 22.00 (*0-7881-6011-7*) DIANE Pub.

Craig, James, jt. auth. see Grant, Robert M.

Craig, James B. Craig. The Craigs of Goulbourn & N. Gower. (Illus.). 220p. 1997. reprint ed. pap. 33.50 (*0-8328-8120-1*); reprint ed. lib. bdg. 43.50 (*0-8328-8119-8*) Higginson Bk Co.

Craig, James H. & Craig, Marguerite. Synergic Power: Beyond Domination, Beyond Permissiveness. 2nd ed. LC 79-67184. (Illus.). 164p. 1979. pap. 6.95 (*0-914158-28-7*) ProActive Pr.

Craig, James R. & Vaughan, David. Ore Microscopy & Ore Petrography. 2nd ed. 448p. 1994. 140.00 (*0-471-55175-9*) Wiley.

Craig, James R., et al. Resources of the Earth. 2nd ed. 472p. (C). 1996. 84.00 (*0-13-457029-4*) P-H.

Craig, James T. Gibson, see Gibson Craig, James T.

Craig, Jane M. Craig. Samuel Craig, Sr., Pioneer to Western Pennsylvania, & His Descendants. 143p. 1997. reprint ed. pap. 23.00 (*0-8328-8118-X*); reprint ed. lib. bdg. 33.00 (*0-8328-8117-1*) Higginson Bk Co.

Craig, Jane M., jt. auth. see Kloser, Patricia.

Craig, Jane MacLean, see Feder, Lewis M. & MacLean Craig, Jane.

Craig, Jane MacLean, see Warren, Kaile R. & MacLean Craig, Jane.

Craig, Janet. Amazing World of Night Creatures. LC 89-5002. (Illus.). 32p. (J). (gr. 2-4). 1990. lib. bdg. 17.25 (*0-8167-1749-4*) Troll Communs.

— Amazing World of Spiders. LC 89-5005. (Illus.). 32p. (J). (gr. 2-4). 1990. lib. bdg. 17.25 (*0-8167-1751-6*) Troll Communs.

— Amazing World of Spiders. LC 89-5005. (Illus.). 32p. (J). (ps-3). 1997. pap. 3.50 (*0-8167-1752-4*) Troll Communs.

— Apple Picking. (Illus.). 32p. (J). (gr. k-2). pap. 2.95 (*0-8167-4249-9*) Troll Communs.

— Bubble Trouble Ghost. LC 94-12894. (Illus.). 32p. (J). (gr. k-2). 1994. pap. text 3.95 (*0-8167-3587-5*) Troll Communs.

— Candytown. 1999. pap. text 2.95 (*0-8167-4914-0*) Troll Communs.

— Descubriendo Ballenas & Delfines. (SPA.). (J). 1992. pap. 3.50 (*0-8167-3044-X*) Troll Communs.

— Discovering Prehistoric Animals. LC 89-4973. (Illus.). 32p. (J). (gr. 2-4). 1990. pap. 3.50 (*0-8167-1756-7*); lib. bdg. 17.25 (*0-8167-1755-9*) Troll Communs.

— Discovering Whales & Dolphins. LC 89-5004. (Illus.). 32p. (J). (gr. 2-4). 1989. pap. 3.50 (*0-8167-1760-5*) Troll Communs.

— Discovering Whales & Dolphins. LC 89-5004. (Illus.). 32p. (J). (gr. 2-4). 1990. lib. bdg. 17.25 (*0-8167-1759-1*) Troll Communs.

— Good Luck Clover. 1999. pap. text 2.50 (*0-8167-4540-4*) Troll Communs.

— Here Comes Winter. LC 87-13738. (Illus.). 32p. (J). (gr. k-2). 1988. lib. bdg. 13.05 (*0-8167-1225-5*) Troll Communs.

— Here Comes Winter. LC 87-13738. (Illus.). 32p. (J). (gr. k-2). 1997. pap. 2.50 (*0-8167-1226-3*) Troll Communs.

— Homer the Beachcomber. LC 87-10913. (Giant First Start Reader Ser.). (Illus.). 32p. (J). (gr. k-2). 1988. lib. bdg. 17.25 (*0-8167-1085-6*) Troll Communs.

— Homer the Beachcomber. LC 87-10913. (Giant First Start Reader Ser.). (Illus.). 32p. (J). (ps-3). 1996. pap. 3.95 (*0-8167-1086-4*) Troll Communs.

— Hugs All Around. LC 94-43061. (Giant First-Start Reader Ser.). (Illus.). 32p. (J). (gr. k-2). 1995. pap. text 3.95 (*0-8167-3704-5*); lib. bdg. 17.25 (*0-8167-3703-7*) Troll Communs.

— Little Danny Dinosaur. LC 87-16228. (Illus.). 32p. (J). (gr. k-2). 1997. pap. 2.50 (*0-8167-1230-1*) Troll Communs.

— Little Danny Dinosaur. 1999. pap. text 2.50 (*0-8167-3286-8*) Troll Communs.

— Little Danny Dinosaur. enl. ed. 1999. pap. text 16.95 (*0-8167-4091-7*) Troll Communs.

***Craig, Janet.** Little Groundhog's Shadow. LC 98-122860. (First Start Easy Reader Ser.). 1998. pap. text 2.95 (*0-8167-4519-6*) Troll Communs.

Craig, Janet. Las Maravillas de la Selva. (SPA.). (J). 1997. pap. 3.50 (*0-8167-3258-2*) Troll Communs.

— Max & Maggie in Spring. (Nice Mice Ser.). (J). 1995. 7.70 (*0-606-07848-7*, Pub. by Turtleback) Demco.

— Max & Maggie in Winter. LC 94-34183. (Illus.). 32p. (J). (ps-3). 1996. pap. 3.50 (*0-8167-3355-4*) Troll Communs.

— Max & Maggie in Winter. (Nice Mice Ser.). (J). 1995. 7.70 (*0-606-07849-5*, Pub. by Turtleback) Demco.

— Muffy & Fluffy: The Kittens Who Didn't Agree. 1999. pap. text 2.50 (*0-8167-3109-8*); pap. text 16.95 (*0-8167-6282-1*) Troll Communs.

***Craig, Janet.** 100 Days of Fun at School. LC 98-208163. (First Start Easy Reader Ser.). 1998. pap. text 2.95 (*0-8167-4541-2*) Troll Communs.

Craig, Janet. Red Fox in Winter. 1999. pap. text 2.95 (*0-8167-4324-X*) Troll Communs.

— Santa's Cookie Surprise. LC 88-19997. (First-Start Easy Readers Ser.). (Illus.). 32p. (J). (gr. k-2). 1989. lib. bdg. 13.05 (*0-8167-1538-6*) Troll Communs.

— Santa's Cookie Surprise. LC 88-19997. (First-Start Easy Readers Ser.). (Illus.). 32p. (J). (gr. k-2). 1997. pap. 2.50 (*0-8167-1539-4*) Troll Communs.

***Craig, Janet.** Three Little Pilgrims. LC 98-119810. (First Start Easy Reader Ser.). 1998. pap. text 2.95 (*0-8167-4520-X*) Troll Communs.

Craig, Janet. Thump, Bump. LC 87-10933. (Illus.). 32p. (J). (gr. k-2). 1988. lib. bdg. 17.25 (*0-8167-1077-5*) Troll Communs.

— Thump, Bump. LC 87-10933. (Illus.). 32p. (J). (gr. k-2). 1997. pap. 3.95 (*0-8167-1078-3*) Troll Communs.

— Tiniest Pumpkin. 1999. pap. text 2.95 (*0-8167-4925-6*) Troll Communs.

— Tortugas (Turtles) (J). 1996. pap. 2.95 (*0-8167-3039-3*) Troll Communs.

— Turtles. LC 81-11448. (Now I Know Ser.). (Illus.). 32p. (J). (gr. k-2). 1982. lib. bdg. 17.25 (*0-89375-664-4*) Troll Communs.

— Turtles. LC 81-11448. (Now I Know Ser.). (Illus.). 32p. (J). (gr. k-2). 1997. pap. 3.50 (*0-89375-665-2*) Troll Communs.

— Viene el Invierno.Tr. of Here Comes Winter. (SPA., Illus.). 32p. (gr. k-2). 1999. pap. text 1.95 (*0-8167-3727-4*) Troll Communs.

— Welcome, Little Chick. (Illus.). 32p. (J). (gr. k-2). pap. 2.95 (*0-8167-4325-8*) Troll Communs.

— What's under the Ocean. LC 81-11425. (Now I Know Ser.). (Illus.). 32p. (J). (gr. k-2). 1996. pap. 3.50 (*0-89375-653-9*) Troll Communs.

— Windy Day. LC 87-10909. (Illus.). 32p. (J). (gr. k-2). 1997. pap. 2.50 (*0-8167-0983-1*) Troll Communs.

— Windy Day. 1999. pap. text 2.50 (*0-8167-3116-0*) Troll Communs.

— Windy Day. enl. ed. 1999. pap. text 16.95 (*0-8167-6283-X*) Troll Communs.

— Wonders of the Rain Forest. LC 89-5001. (Illus.). 32p. (J). (gr. 2-4). 1997. pap. 3.50 (*0-8167-1764-8*) Troll Communs.

C

An Asterisk (*) at the beginning of an entry indicates that the title is appearing for the first time.

Craig, Janet A. Amazing World of Night Creatures. LC 89-5002. (Illus.). 32p. (J). (gr. 2-4). 1997. pap. 3.50 (*0-8167-1750-8*) Troll Communs.
— A Letter to Santa. LC 93-2214. (Let's Celebrate Holidays Library). (Illus.). 32p. (J). (gr. k-2). 1993. lib. bdg. 17.25 (*0-8167-3252-3*, BL025) Troll Communs.
— A Letter to Santa. LC 93-2214. (Giant First Start Reader Ser.). (Illus.). 32p. (J). (gr. k-2). 1997. pap. 3.95 (*0-8167-3253-1*) Troll Communs.
— Valentine's Day Mess. LC 93-2211. (Giant First Start Reader Ser.). (Illus.). 32p. (J). (gr. k-2). 1993. lib. bdg. 17.25 (*0-8167-3254-X*) Troll Communs.
— Valentine's Day Mess. LC 93-2211. (Giant First Start Reader Ser.). (Illus.). 32p. (J). (gr. k-2). 1997. pap. 3.95 (*0-8167-3255-8*) Troll Communs.
Craig, Jean. Between Hello & Goodbye. Rubenstein, Julie, ed. 416p. 1992. reprint ed. mass mkt. 5.99 (*0-671-75039-9*) PB.
Craig, Jeanne. Fishing Fame! How to Catch World-Record Fish. LC 98-51699. (Illus.). 128p. 1999. pap. 15.95 (*0-07-013457-X*, Ragged Mntain) McGraw-Hill Prof.
Craig, Jenny. The Jenny Craig Cookbook: Cutting Through the Fat. 1997. pap. text 18.95 (*0-8487-1592-6*) Oxmoor Hse.
— The Jenny Craig Cookbook: Cutting Through the Fat. (Illus.). 224p. 1997. 24.95 (*0-8487-1496-2*) Oxmoor Hse.
— Jenny Craig Little Survival Guide. LC 96-70024. 160p. 1996. pap. 6.95 (*0-8487-1552-7*, 102586) Oxmoor Hse.
— Jenny Craig No Diet Required. LC 97-65133. 224p. 1997. 24.95 (*0-8487-1600-0*) Oxmoor Hse.
— Jenny Craig's Simple Pleasures Recipes to Nourish Body & Soul. LC 98-66931. (Illus.). 224p. 1998. 24.95 (*0-8487-1838-0*) Oxmoor Hse.
— Jenny Craig's What Have You Got to Lose? LC 92-39917. 384p. 1993. pap. 14.00 (*1-55958-301-0*) Prima Pub.
— Jenny Craig's What Have You Got to Lose? (Illus.). 384p. 1996. per. 14.00 (*0-7615-0786-8*) Prima Pub.
Craig, Jerry W. Group H: Engineering Graphics Workbook & Introduction to Engineering Design. 512p. (C). Date not set. pap. text. write for info. (*1-887503-24-2*) Schroff Dev Corp.
— An Introduction to Engineering Design. 80p. (Orig.). (C). 1995. pap. text. write for info. (*1-887503-01-3*) Schroff Dev Corp.
Craig, Jerry W. & Craig, Orval B. Engineering Graphics Workbook. 432p. (C). 1994. pap. text. write for info. (*1-887503-00-5*) Schroff Dev Corp.
Craig, Jo & Harries, Kerenza. Book of Chicken Dishes. (Illus.). 120p. 1993. pap. 12.00 (*1-55788-075-1*, HP Books) Berkley Pub.
Craig, Joan L. Mama Fanelli's Secret Italian Recipes. (Illus.). 105p. (Orig.). 1992. pap. text 11.95 (*0-9632570-1-3*) J&W Craig Ent.
Craig, Joann M. Culture Shock! Singapore. LC 92-81939. (Illus.). 296p. 1992. pap. 12.95 (*1-55868-108-6*) Gr Arts Ctr Pub.
Craig, Joe M. & Craig, Mary. John Toole & Ruth Ann Rankin & Their Descendants. (Illus.). 358p. (Orig.). 1984. pap. text 25.00 (*0-910513-03-1*) Mayfield Printing.
Craig, John. Introduction to Robotics. 3rd ed. 480p. (C). 2000. text 95.00 (*0-201-54361-3*) Addison-Wesley.
— Remarks on Some Fundamental Doctrines of Political Economy. LC 70-121321. (Reprints of Economic Classics Ser.). xi, 244p. 1970. reprint ed. lib. bdg. 39.50 (*0-678-00684-9*) Kelley.
Craig, John & Davison, Tim. Racing: A Beginner's Manual. 64p. (C). 1990. text 59.00 (*0-906754-37-2*) Fernhurst Bks.
Craig, John & Webb, Jeff. Microsoft Visual Basic 5.0 Developer's Workshop: With CD-ROM. 4th ed. LC 97-837. 700p. 1997. pap. text 44.99 (*1-57231-436-2*) Microsoft.
Craig, John, jt. auth. see Collinson, Patrick.
Craig, John C. True BASIC: Programs & Subroutines. (Illus.). 256p. (Orig.). 1985. 24.95 (*0-8306-0990-3*, 1990) McGraw-Hill Prof.
Craig, John C. & Breta, Jeff. IBM PC Graphics. 1991. 24.95 (*0-8306-6618-4*) McGraw-Hill Prof.
Craig, John C. & Bretz, Jeff. IBM-PC Graphics. LC 84-8893. (Illus.). 250p. (Orig.). 1984. pap. 16.95 (*0-8306-1860-0*, 1860) McGraw-Hill Prof.
— One Hundred Ready-to-Run Programs. 1991. 29.95 (*0-8306-1049-9*) McGraw-Hill Prof.
— Programs & Subroutines for the IBM. 1991. 19.95 (*0-8306-6619-2*) McGraw-Hill Prof.
Craig, John C. & Webb, Jeff. Microsoft Visual Basic 6.0 Developer's Workshop: Developer's Workshop. 5th ed. LC 98-34255. 750p. 49.99 incl. cd-rom (*1-57231-883-X*) Microsoft.
***Craig, John D. R.** Privacy & Employment Law. 320p. 1999. 54.00 (*1-84113-059-1*, Pub. by Hart Pub) Intl Spec Bk.
Craig, John E. Scholarship & Nation Building: The Universities of Strasbourg & Alsatian Society, 1871-1939. LC 83-24341. 528p. (C). 2000. 36.00 (*0-226-11670-0*) U Ch Pr.
Craig, John G. The Nature of Co-Operation. 254p. (Orig.). 1993. text 48.99 (*1-895431-69-7*, Pub. by Black Rose); pap. text 19.99 (*1-895431-68-9*, Pub. by Black Rose) Consort Bk Sales.
Craig, John J. Introduction to Robotics. LC 85-13527. (Illus.). 128p. (C). 1985. teacher ed. 4.00 (*0-201-10327-3*) Addison-Wesley.
— Introduction to Robotics: Mechanics & Control. LC 85-13527. (Illus.). 400p. (C). 1985. write for info. (*0-201-10326-5*) Addison-Wesley.
— Introduction to Robotics: Mechanics & Control. 2nd ed. (A-W Series in Electrical & Computer Engineering - Control Engineering). (Illus.). 450p. (C). 1989. 105.00 (*0-201-09528-9*) Addison-Wesley.
Craig, John M. Lucia Ames Mead (1856-1936) & the American Peace Movement. LC 89-12887. (Studies in World Peace: Vol. 4). 232p. 1990. lib. bdg. 89.95 (*0-88946-094-9*) E Mellen.
Craig, John M., jt. auth. see Potter, Edith L.
Craig, John R. Dating: (How to Pick & Choose Your Date) 144p. (Orig.). 1992. pap. text 5.95 (*0-9614423-0-1*) Rite Bks Pub.
— Don't Marry a Friend: Escape This Divorce Trap... Friends Can Ruin Your Life. LC 85-60318. 144p. (Orig.). 1985. pap. text 2.95 (*0-9614423-5-2*) Rite Bks Pub.
— Ranching with Lords & Commons: or Twenty Years on the Range. LC 79-132387. reprint ed. 45.00 (*0-404-01798-3*) AMS Pr.
— Smarte Date Pak. 144p. (Orig.). 1992. pap. text 5.95 (*0-9614423-1-X*) Rite Bks Pub.
Craig, John R. & Benavidez, Roy P. Medal of Honor: A Vietnam Warrior's Story. LC 94-27283. (Illus.). 240p. 1995. 26.95 (*0-02-881098-8*) Brasseys.
Craig, John R. & Rogers, Phillip A. The Man on the Grassy Knoll. 312p. (Orig.). 1992. mass mkt. 4.50 (*0-380-77127-6*, Avon Bks) Morrow Avon.
Craig, Jordan. Felicity Pilot. 192p. (J). 1998. pap. 3.99 (*0-7868-4309-8*, Pub. by Hyprn Ppbks) Little.
Craig, Judith E. Handling the Everyday Hassles of Childrearing: A Practical Guide for Parents. LC 84-80449. 80p. (Orig.). 1984. pap. 8.00 (*0-934955-07-7*) Watercress Pr.
— You're Grounded Till You're Thirty! What Works & What Doesn't in Parenting Teens Today. LC 95-33480. 1996. pap. 12.00 (*0-688-13196-4*, Hearst) Hearst Commns.
Craig, Karen. Matin Latin, Vol. I. (Illus.). 144p. (J). (gr. 3-6). 1998. pap. text 25.00 (*1-885767-46-3*) Canon Pr ID.
— Matin Latin, Vol. II. (Illus.). 144p. (J). (gr. 3-6). 1998. pap. text 30.00 (*1-885767-48-X*) Canon Pr ID.
Craig, Karen, jt. auth. see Santomero, Angela C.
Craig, Karen, jt. auth. see Wilson, Douglas.
***Craig, Karen L.** Latin Grammar 2: Student Edition. (Mars Hill Textbook Ser.). 250p. (YA). 1999. pap., student ed. 23.00 (*1-885767-61-7*) Canon Pr ID.
— Latin Grammar 2: Student Edition. (Mars Hill Textbook Ser.). 250p. (YA). (gr. 7). 1999. student ed., spiral bd. 23.00 (*1-885767-60-9*) Canon Pr ID.
— Matin Latin 1: Teacher's Edition. (Mars Hill Textbook Ser.). 144p. 1998. teacher ed., spiral bd. 28.00 (*1-885767-47-1*) Canon Pr ID.
— Matin Latin 2. (Mars Hill Textbook Ser.). 208p. 1999. teacher ed., spiral bd. 33.00 (*1-885767-49-8*) Canon Pr ID.
Craig, Katherine T. The Stars of Destiny: The Ancient Science of Astrology & How to Make Use of it Today. 312p. 1981. pap. 27.00 (*0-89540-115-0*, SB-115) Sun Pub.
Craig, Katrina G., jt. ed. see Lugowski, Marek.
Craig, Katrina Grace, ed. see Lugowski, Marek.
Craig, Katrina Grace, jt. ed. see Lugowski, Marek.
Craig, Kenneth. Reading Esther: A Case for the Literary Carnivalesque. (Literary Currents in Biblical Interpretation Ser.). 144p. (Orig.). 1995. pap. 22.95 (*0-664-25518-3*) Westminster John Knox.
***Craig, Kenneth, et al.** Lee's North Carolina Family Law, Vol. 2. 5th ed. 800p. 1999. write for info. (*0-327-04937-5*, 6427211) LEXIS Pub.
Craig, Kenneth, jt. auth. see Reynolds, Suzanne.
Craig, Kenneth D. & Dobson, Keith S., eds. Anxiety & Depression in Adults & Children. (Banff International Conference Ser.: Vol. 1). 296p. 1994. 35.00 (*0-8039-7020-X*); pap. 15.99 (*0-8039-7021-8*) Sage.
Craig, Kenneth D., jt. auth. see Dobson, Keith S.
Craig, Kenneth D., jt. ed. see Dobson, Keith S.
Craig, Kenneth M., Jr. A Poetics of Jonah: Art in the Service of Ideology. LC 99-19934. 208p. 1999. pap. 19.95 (*0-86554-614-2*) Mercer Univ Pr.
Craig, Kit. Gone: A Novel. large type ed. LC 92-44608. (General Ser.). 396p. 1993. lib. bdg. 22.95 (*0-8161-5708-1*, G K Hall Lrg Type) Mac Lib Ref.
— Gone: A Novel. large type ed. LC 92-44608. (General Ser.). 396p. 1993. pap. 17.95 (*0-8161-5709-X*, G K Hall Lrg Type) Mac Lib Ref.
— Twice Burned. 352p. 1995. mass mkt. 5.99 (*0-425-14877-7*) Berkley Pub.
***Craig, Lawrence H.** Surviving in a Cordless World: Gospel Sermons for Sundays after Pentecost (Middle Third), Cycle B. LC 99-33001. 80p. 1999. pap. 8.50 (*0-7880-1500-1*) CSS OH.
Craig, Lee A. To Sow One Acre More: Childbearing & Farm Productivity in the Antebellum North. LC 92-40483. (Studies in Historical & Political Science). 168p. (C). 1993. text 30.00 (*0-8018-4529-7*) Johns Hopkins.
***Craig, Lee A. & Fisher, Douglas.** The European Macroeconomy: Growth Integration & Cycles, 1500-1913. LC 99-31597. 416p. 2000. 120.00 (*1-85278-643-4*) E Elgar.
Craig-lees. Consumer Behaviour. 528p. 1997. write for info. (*0-471-33518-5*) Wiley.
Craig, Leon H. The War Lover: A Study of Plato's Republic. 504p. (C). 1994. text 78.00 (*0-8020-0586-1*) U of Toronto Pr.
— The War Lover: A Study of Plato's Republic. LC 96-187300. 440p. 1997. reprint ed. pap. text 34.75 (*0-8020-7942-3*) U of Toronto Pr.
Craig, Linda & Praytor, Phyllis. Criterion Referenced Test Kit: Math. (Criterion Reference Tests Ser.). (Illus.). 54p. (J). (gr. 4). 1978. write for info. (*0-936394-01-3*) Education Serv.
Craig, Linda, ed. see Lucia, Tina.
Craig, Lyda J. & Dobkin, David S. Community Dynamics of Small Mammals in Mature & Logged Atlantic White Cedar Swamps of the New Jersey Pine Barrens. (Bulletin Ser.: No. 487). (Illus.). 32p. 1994. 8.95 (*1-55557-229-4*) NYS Museum.
Craig, Lynn. Collinsville High. (Forever Friends Ser.: No. 04). (YA). 1994. pap. 5.99 (*0-8407-9242-5*) Nelson.
— Friends Make the Difference. LC 94-2938. (Forever Friends Ser.: Bk. 2). (J). 1994. pap. 5.99 (*0-8407-9240-9*) Nelson.
Craig, Lynn & Kusminak, Mike. Millennium Countdown: A Practical Guide to Preparing Your Business for the Year 2000. 150p. 1998. pap. 14.95 (*0-7494-2887-2*) Kogan Page Ltd.
Craig, M. Jean. The Donkey Prince. 1977. 7.95 (*0-385-11294-7*) Doubleday.
— Questions about Weather. (Illus.). (J). (gr. 2-5). 1996. pap. 4.95 (*0-614-15762-5*) Scholastic Inc.
— Questions & Answers about Weather. (Illus.). 64p. (J). (gr. k-3). 1977. pap. 5.99 (*0-590-41142-X*) Scholastic Inc.
— The Three Wishes. (Easy-to-Read Folktales Ser.). (Illus.). 32p. (Orig.). (J). (gr. k-3). 1986. pap. 2.99 (*0-590-41744-4*) Scholastic Inc.
Craig, Maggie. Damn' Rebel Bitches: The Women of the '45. (Illus.). 192p. 1998. 35.00 (*1-85158-962-7*, Pub. by Mainstream Pubng) Trafalgar.
***Craig, Maggie.** The River Flows On. large type ed. 480p. 1999. 31.99 (*0-7089-4155-9*) Ulverscroft.
Craig, Malcolm. Analyzing Learning Needs. 160p. 1994. 74.95 (*0-566-07448-6*, Pub. by Gower) Ashgate Pub Co.
— How to Invest in Gold. 160p. 1991. 69.95 (*1-85573-062-6*, Pub. by Woodhead Pubng) Am Educ Systs.
***Craig, Malcolm.** Investing in Options: For the Private Investor. 128p. 1999. 24.95 (*1-873668-59-7*, Pub. by Take That Bks) Trafalgar.
Craig, Marguerite, jt. auth. see Craig, James H.
Craig, Marion S. Early Arkansas Residents, 1814-1816. 50p. 1992. reprint ed. pap. 10.00 (*0-941765-76-8*) Arkansas Res.
— Lawrence County, Arkansas, Loose Probate Papers, 1815-1890. 300p. 1992. reprint ed. pap. 28.00 (*0-941765-81-4*) Arkansas Res.
— Montgomery County, Arkansas, Loose Probate Records, 1842-1930. Allen, Desmond W., ed. 65p. (Orig.). 1996. pap. 15.00 (*1-56546-098-7*) Arkansas Res.
Craig, Marjorie R. Poems about Little Angels: A Precious Child I Am. 1998. pap. 6.95 (*0-533-12699-1*) Vantage.
***Craig, Marva E. & Carruthers, William L.** The Mediator's Guidebook: A Guide to Successful Mediations. 24p. (YA). (gr. 6-10). 1999. pap. 5.95 (*0-932796-97-4*) Ed Media Corp.
Craig, Marveen. Introduction to Ultrasonography & Patient Care. (Illus.). 229p. 1992. pap. text 32.50 (*0-7216-4229-2*, W B Saunders Co) Harcrt Hlth Sci Grp.
— Introduction to Ultrasonography & Patient Care. (Illus.). 1993. pap., teacher ed. write for info. (*0-7216-3777-9*, W B Saunders Co) Harcrt Hlth Sci Grp.
Craig, Marveen, et al. Diagnostic Medical Sonography Vol. II: Echocardiography. (Illus.). 461p. 1991. text 99.00 (*0-397-50953-7*) Lppncott W & W.
— Ultrasound Examination Review: Sonographer's Self-Assessment Guide. 2nd ed. LC 93-41354. (Illus.). 400p. 1994. pap. text 38.00 (*0-397-55021-9*) Lppncott W & W.
***Craig, Mary.** Blessings: A Heartwarming Classic of Hope. LC 00-103187. 160p. 2000. pap. 12.95 (*1-893732-19-3*) SORIN BKS.
Craig, Mary. Kundun: A Biography of the Family of the Dalai Lama. (Illus.). 416p. 1998. reprint ed. pap. 23.50 (*1-887178-91-0*, Pub. by Counterpt DC) HarpC.
***Craig, Mary.** Tears of Blood. 2000. pap. 16.00 (*1-58243-102-7*, Pub. by Counterpt DC) HarpC.
— Tears of Blood: A Cry for Tibet. LC DS786.C7 1999. 384p. 1999. text 26.00 (*1-58243-025-X*, Pub. by Counterpt DC) HarpC.
Craig, Mary, jt. auth. see Craig, Joe M.
***Craig, Mary Dale.** Fear of Crime among the Elderly: A Multi-Method Study of the Small Town Experience. LC 00-35349. (Studies on the Elderly in America) 2000. write for info. (*0-8153-3784-1*) Garland.
Craig, Mary R. The Parents' Preschool Primer. 34p. 1989. pap. 2.00 (*0-923672-03-6*) Hearth Pubns.
Craig, Maurice. Classic Irish Houses of the Middle Size. 1977. 18.95 (*0-8038-0044-4*) Archit CT.
Craig, Maurice, jt. auth. see Knight of Glin Staff.
***Craig, Michael.** The 50 Best (and Worst) Business Deals of All Time. 256p. 2000. 21.99 (*1-56414-477-1*) Career Pr Inc.
Craig, Mickey G. Defending the Reagan Legacy: Rejecting Revisionist History. (Essay Ser.: No. 7). 28p. 1993. pap. text 3.00 (*1-878802-17-8*) J M Ashbrook Ctr Pub Affairs.
Craig, M.J. Questions & Answers about Weather. (J). 1996. 11.19 (*0-606-09774-0*, Pub. by Turtleback) Demco.
Craig, N. C. Entropy Analysis: An Introduction to Chemical Thermodynamics Reviews. 220p. 1992. pap. 54.95 (*0-471-18578-7*) Wiley.
Craig, Nancy. Reckless Breeding: A Voice on the Road Between Adoption, Choice, Family Secrets & Open Records. 65p. (Orig.). 1997. pap. 10.95 (*0-9657876-0-5*) Super Ego.
Craig, Neil. Black Watch, Red Dawn: The Hong Kong Handover to China. 1998. 27.95 (*1-85753-266-0*, Pub. by Brasseys) Brasseys.
***Craig, Neil.** From Here on In. (Illus.). 164p. 2000. 24.95 (*1-58320-011-8*) Lifestyles.
Craig, Neville B. History of Pittsburgh, with a Brief Notice of Its Facilities of Communication & Other Advantages. (Illus.). 312p. 1997. reprint ed. lib. bdg. 39.00 (*0-8328-6441-2*) Higginson Bk Co.
Craig, Norman C. Entropy Analysis: An Introduction to Chemical Thermodynamics. 208p. 1992. pap. text 29.95 (*1-56081-599-X*, Wiley-VCH) Wiley.
Craig, Oman. Childhood Diabetes: The Facts. (Facts Ser.). (Illus.). 178p. 1982. 17.50 (*0-19-261330-8*) OUP.
Craig, Orval B., jt. auth. see Craig, Jerry W.
Craig, P. & MacPherson, C. N. L., eds. Parasitic Helminths & Zoonoses in Africa. (Illus.). 308p. (C). 1990. text 82.00 (*0-04-445565-8*) Routledge.
Craig, P. J., ed. Organometallic Compounds in the Environment: Principles & Reactions. 368p. 1986. 265.00 (*0-471-84727-5*) Wiley.
Craig, P. P. & Harlow, Carol. Lawmaking in the European Union. LC 98-29114. (W. G. Hart Legal Workshop Ser.). 1998. 111.00 (*90-411-9683-8*) Kluwer Law Intl.
Craig, P. P. & Jungerman, J. A. Nuclear Arms Race: Technology & Society. 2nd ed. 576p. (C). 1990. pap. 50.94 (*0-07-013347-6*) McGraw.
Craig, Patricia. The Oxford Book of Travel Stories. 458p. 1996. 35.00 (*0-19-214253-4*) OUP.
— The Rattle of the North: An Anthology of Ulster Prose. 464p. 1995. pap. 24.95 (*0-85640-464-0*, Pub. by Blackstaff Pr) Dufour.
***Craig, Patricia, ed.** The Oxford Book of Detective Stories. LC 99-45926. 587p. 2000. pap. 18.95 (*0-19-288067-5*) OUP.
Craig, Patricia, ed. The Oxford Book of English Detective Stories. 576p. 1990. 35.00 (*0-19-214187-2*) OUP.
— The Oxford Book of English Detective Stories. 576p. 1992. pap. 14.95 (*0-19-282968-8*) OUP.
— The Oxford Book of Ireland. (Illus.). 530p. 1998. 35.00 (*0-19-214261-5*) OUP.
— The Oxford Book of Ireland. (Oxford Books of Verse Ser.). (Illus.). 536p. 1999. pap. 17.95 (*0-19-288112-4*) OUP.
— The Oxford Book of Modern Women's Stories. 544p. 1994. 30.00 (*0-19-214232-1*) OUP.
— The Oxford Book of Modern Women's Stories. 538p. 1995. pap. 13.95 (*0-19-283204-2*) OUP.
— The Oxford Book of Travel Stories. 458p. 1997. pap. 14.95 (*0-19-288031-4*) OUP.
Craig, Patricia, intro. Twelve Irish Ghost Stories. (Oxford Twelves Ser.). 156p. 1998. pap. 9.95 (*0-19-288070-5*) OUP.
Craig, Patricia B. Power Discipleship. LC 98-90516. 1999. pap. 12.95 (*0-533-12828-5*) Vantage.
Craig, Paul. Be a Better Pilot: Making the Right Decisions. LC 91-11564. 240p. 1992. pap. 18.95 (*0-07-157664-9*) McGraw.
— Public Law & Democracy in the United Kingdom & the United States of America. (Clarendon Law Ser.). 454p. 1991. text 95.00 (*0-19-825637-X*) OUP.
— Stalls & Spins. 336p. 1993. 26.95 (*0-07-013421-9*) McGraw.
Craig, Paul & De Burca, Grainne. EC Law: Text, Cases & Materials. 1288p. 1995. text 89.00 (*0-19-876272-0*) OUP.
— EU Law: Text, Cases & Materials. 2nd ed. LC 98-18233. 1,324p. 1998. pap. text 45.00 (*0-19-876509-6*) OUP.
Craig, Paul & De Burca, Grainne, eds. The Evolution of EU Law. LC 98-50347. 938p. 1999. text 115.00 (*0-19-826481-X*); pap. text 55.00 (*0-19-876508-8*) OUP.
Craig, Paul A. Be A Better Pilot: Making the Right Decisions. 224p. 1991. 24.95 (*0-8306-2053-2*); pap. 15.95 (*0-8306-2047-8*) McGraw-Hill Prof.
***Craig, Paul A.** Killing Zone: How & Why Pilots Die. (Illus.). 2000. 29.95 (*0-07-136269-X*) McGraw.
Craig, Paul A. Light Airplane Navigation Essentials. LC 97-819. (Practical Flying Ser.). (Illus.). 256p. 1997. 34.95 (*0-07-013454-5*); pap. 24.95 (*0-07-013456-1*) McGraw.
— Multi-Engine Flying. LC 93-46034. (Illus.). 212p. 1994. pap. 19.95 (*0-07-013423-5*) McGraw-Hill Prof.
— Multiengine Flying. 2nd ed. LC 96-44272. 1996. write for info. (*0-07-870624-6*) McGraw.
— Multiengine Flying. 2nd ed. LC 96-44272. (Illus.). 362p. 1997. 44.95 (*0-07-013452-9*) McGraw.
— Multiengine Flying. 2nd ed. LC 96-44272. (Illus.). 362p. 1997. pap. 34.95 (*0-07-013453-7*) McGraw.
— Stalls & Spins. (Illus.). 304p. 1993. 24.95 (*0-8306-4019-3*, 4174); pap. 16.95 (*0-8306-4020-7*, 4174) McGraw-Hill Prof.
***Craig, Paula M.** Mr. Wiggle's Book. LC 00-22243. (Illus.). (J). 2000. write for info. (*1-56822-975-5*) Instruct Fair.
***Craig, Peter.** The Martini Shot: A Hollywood Novel. LC 97-41898. 288p. 2000. pap. 12.00 (*0-688-17581-3*, Quil) HarperTrade.
— The Martini Shot: A Hollywood Novel. LC 97-41898. 256p. 1998. 22.00 (*0-688-15658-4*, Wm Morrow) Morrow Avon.
Craig, Peter M. Accounting & Finance for Magazine Publishers. 3rd rev. ed. 300p. 1991. pap. 69.95 (*0-918110-27-0*) Primedia Intertec.
Craig, Peter M., ed. Financial & Accounting Management for Magazine Publishing. 2nd ed. 500p. (C). 1993. 69.95 (*0-918110-20-3*) Primedia Intertec.
Craig, Peter S. The Census of the Swedes on the Delaware, 1693: Family Histories of the Swedish Lutheran Church Members Residing in Pennsylvania, Delaware, West New Jersey & Cecil County, Md., 1638-1693. LC 92-82858. (Studies in Swedish American Genealogy: Vol. 3). (Illus.). 224p. 1993. lib. bdg. 37.50 (*0-9616105-1-4*) SAG Pubns.
Craig, Petra. Winnie the Pooh Mask Book. LC 94-71798. (Illus.). 26p. (J). (ps-3). 1995. pap. 12.95 (*0-7868-4033-1*, Pub. by Disney Pr) Time Warner.
***Craig, Philip A.** Vineyard Blues: A Martha's Vineyard Mystery. LC 99-58385. 224p. 2000. 23.00 (*0-684-83455-3*) Scribner.

C

An Asterisk (*) at the beginning of an entry indicates that the title is appearing for the first time.

Craig, Philip R. A Beautiful Place to Die: A Martha's Vineyard Mystery. 224p. 1991. mass mkt. 5.50 (*0-380-71155-9*, Avon Bks) Morrow Avon.

— Case of Vineyard Poison. 1996. mass mkt. 5.99 (*0-380-72679-3*, Avon Bks) Morrow Avon.

— Cliff Hanger: A Martha's Vineyard Mystery. 224p. 1994. mass mkt. 4.99 (*0-380-72240-2*, Avon Bks) Morrow Avon.

— Deadly Vineyard Holiday. LC 97-4487. (Martha's Vineyard Mystery Ser.). 240p. 1998. mass mkt. 5.99 (*0-380-73110-X*, Avon Bks) Morrow Avon.

— A Deadly Vineyard Holiday: A Martha's Vineyard Mystery. LC 97-4487. 1997. 20.50 (*0-684-19718-9*) S&S Trade.

— A Deadly Vineyard Holiday: A Martha's Vineyard Mystery. large type ed. LC 97-18108. (Core Ser.). 344p. 1997. lib. bdg. 24.95 (*0-7838-8278-5*, G K Hall Lrg Type) Mac Lib Ref.

— Death on Vineyard Beach. 224p. 1997. mass mkt. 5.99 (*0-380-72873-7*, Avon Bks) Morrow Avon.

— The Double Minded Men: A Martha's Vineyard Mystery. (Martha's Vineyard Mystery Ser.: No. 3). 256p. 1992. text 20.00 (*0-684-19396-5*, Scribners Ref) Mac Lib Ref.

— The Double Minded Men: A Martha's Vineyard Mystery. 256p. 1993. mass mkt. 4.99 (*0-380-71973-8*, Avon Bks) Morrow Avon.

***Craig, Philip R.** A Fatal Vineyard Season: A Martha's Vineyard Mystery. (Martha's Vineyard Mystery Ser.). 224p. 2000. mass mkt. 5.99 (*0-380-73289-0*, Avon Bks) Morrow Avon.

Craig, Philip R. A Fatal Vineyard Season: A Martha's Vineyard Mystery. LC 98-54710. (Martha's Vineyard Mystery Ser.). 224p. 1999. 21.50 (*0-684-85544-5*) Scribner.

***Craig, Philip R.** A Fatal Vineyard Season: A Martha's Vineyard Mystery. large type ed. LC 99-43300. (Thorndike Mystery Ser.). 1999. 27.95 (*0-7862-2207-7*) Thorndike Pr.

Craig, Philip R. Off Season: A Martha's Vineyard Mystery. 256p. 1994. 20.00 (*0-684-19617-4*, Scribners Ref) Mac Lib Ref.

Craig, Philip R. Off Season: A Martha's Vineyard Mystery. (Martha's Vineyard Ser.: No. 5). 224p. 1996. mass mkt. 5.99 (*0-380-72588-6*, Avon Bks) Morrow Avon.

Craig, Philip R. A Shoot on Martha's Vineyard: A Martha's Vineyard Mystery. 256p. 1999. mass mkt. 5.99 (*0-380-73201-7*, Avon Bks) Morrow Avon.

— A Shoot on Martha's Vineyard: A Martha's Vineyard Mystery. LC 97-51141. 288p. 1998. 22.00 (*0-684-83454-5*) S&S Trade.

***Craig, Philip R.** A Shoot on Martha's Vineyard: A Martha's Vineyard Mystery. large type ed. LC 98-34902. 388p. 1999. 26.95 (*0-7862-1614-X*) Thorndike Pr.

— Vineyard Blues: A Martha's Vineyard Mystery. LC 00-33757. 2000. write for info. (*0-7862-2591-2*) Thorndike Pr.

Craig, Philip R. The Woman Who Walked into the Sea: A Martha's Vineyard Mystery. 224p. 1993. reprint ed. mass mkt. 4.99 (*0-380-71536-8*, Avon Bks) Morrow Avon.

Craig, Philip R., jt. auth. see Clayton, Tim.

Craig, R. Contributions Agency Customer Satisfaction Survey, 1994. (DSS Research Report Ser.). 1995. write for info. (*0-11-762339-3*, Pub. by Statnry Office) Bernan Associates.

— Norwegian-English Contract Law Dictionary. (ENG & NOR.). 150p. 1992. 69.00 (*0-7859-8909-9*) Fr & Eur.

Craig, R. & Hussey, R. Keeping Employees Informed. 1982. pap. 50.00 (*0-409-30943-5*, AT, MICHIE) LEXIS Pub.

Craig, R. & Tippett, M. Questions on Management Accounting. 1984. pap. 63.00 (*0-409-49252-3*, AT, MICHIE) LEXIS Pub.

Craig, R., et al. Contributions Agency Customer Satisfaction Survey, 1992. (DSS Research Report Ser.). 1993. write for info. (*0-11-762064-5*, Pub. by Statnry Office) Bernan Associates.

— Contributions Agency Customer Satisfaction Survey, 1993. (DSS Research Report Ser.). 1994. write for info. (*0-11-762220-6*, Pub. by Statnry Office) Bernan Associates.

Craig, R. F. Soil Mechanics. 496p. (C). (gr. 13). 1997. pap. 32.99 (*0-419-22450-5*); pap. 19.99 (*0-419-22460-2*) Routledge.

Craig, R. P., jt. auth. see Hopper, Vincent F.

Craig, Randall. Promising Language: Betrothal in Victorian Law & Fiction. LC 99-22478. (C). 1999. text 71.50 (*0-7914-4425-2*); pap. text 23.95 (*0-7914-4426-0*) State U NY Pr.

— The Tragicomic Novel: Studies in a Fictional Mode from Meredith to Joyce. LC 87-40544. 192p. 1989. 32.50 (*0-87413-339-4*) U Delaware Pr.

***Craig, Raymond A.** A Concordance to the Complete Works of Anne Bradstreet Vol. 1: Special Edition of Puritan American Spirituality. LC 99-462312. 636p. 2000. text 129.95 (*0-7734-7812-4*) E Mellen.

— A Concordance to the Complete Works of Anne Bradstreet Vol. 2: Special Edition of Puritan American Spirituality. LC 99-462312. 648p. 2000. text 129.95 (*0-7734-7814-0*) E Mellen.

Craig, Raymond A., ed. A Concordance to the Minor Poetry of Edward Taylor (1642? - 1729) American Colonial Poet, 2 vols. LC 92-3910. 596p. 1992. lib. bdg. 119.95 (*0-7734-9632-7*); lib. bdg. 109.95 (*0-7734-9633-5*) E Mellen.

Craig, Raymond C., ed. The Humor of H. E. Taliaferro. LC 86-27251. (Illus.). 272p. 1987. text 32.00 (*0-87049-528-3*) U of Tenn Pr.

Craig, Rebecca T. & Bryant, Lucinda L. HIV-Infected Health Workers: Debating the Issues. (State Legislative Reports: Vol. 17, No. 18). 11p. 1992. pap. text 15.00 (*1-55516-290-8*, 7302-1718) Natl Conf State Legis.

Craig, Rebecca T. & Wright, Barbara. Mental Health Financing & Programming a Legislator's Guide. Michaels, Shirley, ed. (Illus.). 135p. (Orig.). 1988. pap. 15.00 (*1-55516-679-2*, 6619) Natl Conf State Legis.

Craig, Reginald S. Fighting Parson: A Biography of Col. John M. Chivington. 284p. 1994. 24.95 (*0-87026-082-0*) Westernlore.

Craig, Richard A., jt. auth. see Evered, Roger.

Craig, Richard D., et al. Oklahoma Limited Liability Company Forms & Practice Manual. LC 99-42622. 440p. 1999. ring bd. 219.90 (*1-57400-027-6*) Data Trace Pubng.

Craig, Robert. Derek Jeter: A Biography. 160p. (J). (gr. 4-7). 1999. mass mkt. 4.99 (*0-671-02808-1*, Archway) PB.

— The New River Company: Mining Coal & Making History, 1906-1976. (Illus.). 111p. 1991. reprint ed. pap. 10.00 (*1-881413-06-3*) Thomas In-Prints.

Craig, Robert, et al. Essays in Academic Ethics. (SPE Monograph Ser.). 1992. 10.00 (*0-685-62308-4*) Soc Profs Ed.

Craig, Robert C., et al. Contemporary Educational Psychology: Concepts, Issues, Applications. LC 74-13462. (Illus.). 570p. reprint ed. pap. 176.70 (*0-7837-3436-0*, 205775800008) Bks Demand.

Craig, Robert D. Captain Cook in the Pacific. (Pamphlets Polynesia Ser.: No. 1). (Illus.). 1978. pap. 3.50 (*0-939154-00-5*) Inst Polynesian.

— Dictionary of Polynesian Mythology. LC 89-7479. 456p. 1989. lib. bdg. 65.00 (*0-313-25890-2*, Greenwood Pr) Greenwood.

— Historical Dictionary of Polynesia. LC 93-4745. (Oceanian Historical Dictionaries Ser.: No. 2). 326p. 1993. 39.50 (*0-8108-2706-9*) Scarecrow.

Craig, Robert D. & Clement, Russell T., compiled by. Who's Who In Oceania: 1980-1981. 1981. 12.95 (*0-939154-13-7*); pap. 7.95 (*0-939154-14-5*) Inst Polynesian.

Craig, Robert D. & King, Frank P., eds. Historical Dictionary of Oceania. LC 80-24779. (Illus.). 392p. 1981. lib. bdg. 125.00 (*0-313-21060-8*, KHD/, Greenwood Pr) Greenwood.

Craig, Robert D. & Pere, Vernice W. Tapa Samples from Polynesia. 1980. pap. 5.00 (*0-939154-06-4*) Inst Polynesian.

Craig, Robert F. Soil Mechanics. 5th ed. (Illus.). 440p. (Orig.). (C). (gr. 13). 1995. mass mkt. 38.50 (*0-412-39590-8*, Chap & Hall NY) Chapman & Hall.

— Soil Mechanics: Solutions Manual. 5th ed. (Illus.). 88p. (Orig.). (C). (gr. 13). 1992. mass mkt. 20.50 (*0-412-47230-9*, Chap & Hall NY) Chapman & Hall.

Craig, Robert G. Restorative Dental Materials. 10th ed. (Illus.). 608p. (C). (gr. 13). 1996. pap. text 60.00 (*0-8151-1920-8*, 25552) Mosby Inc.

Craig, Robert G. & O'Brien, William J. Dental Materials: Properties & Manipulation. 6th ed. (Illus.). 304p. (C). (gr. 13). 1995. pap. text 35.00 (*0-8151-1919-4*, 25195) Mosby Inc.

***Craig, Robert G., et al.** Dental Materials: Properties & Manipulation. 7th ed. (Illus.). 1999. teacher ed. write for info. (*0-323-00521-7*); text 37.00 (*0-323-00512-8*) Mosby Inc.

Craig, Robert H. Religion & Radical Politics: An Alternative Christian Tradition in the United States. (Illus.). 320p. (C). 1992. 49.95 (*0-87722-973-2*) Temple U Pr.

— Religion & Radical Politics: An Alternative Christian Tradition in the United States. (Illus.). 320p. (C). 1995. pap. text 22.95 (*1-56639-335-3*) Temple U Pr.

Craig, Robert H. & Worley, Robert C. Dry Bones Live: Helping Congregations Discover New Life. LC 92-28535. 128p. (Orig.). 1993. pap. 13.95 (*0-664-25316-4*) Westminster John Knox.

Craig, Robert J. Interpreting Personality Tests: A Clinical Manual for the MMP1-2, MCMI-III, CPI-R, & 16PF. LC BF698.5.C73 1999. 268p. 1999. 55.00 (*0-471-34818-X*) Wiley.

— The No-Nonsense Guide to Achieving ISO 9000 Registration. 200p. 1994. 39.95 (*0-7918-0032-6*, 800326) ASME Pr.

— Psychological Assessment with the Millon Clinical Multiaxial Inventory (II) No. II: An Interpretive Guide. LC 93-11583. 120p. 1993. pap. 26.00 (*0-911907-10-6*) Psych Assess.

Craig, Robert J., ed. Clinical & Diagnostic Interviewing. LC 89-29. 355p. 1989. 55.00 (*0-87668-848-2*) Aronson.

— Clinical & Diagnostic Interviewing. LC 89-29. 380p. 1995. reprint ed. pap. 40.00 (*1-56821-526-6*) Aronson.

— The Million Clinical Multiaxial Inventory: A Clinical Research Information Synthesis. 312p. 1993. text 69.95 (*0-8058-1145-1*) L Erlbaum Assocs.

Craig, Robert L. The Alaska Pololini: Vicarious Extortion of the Northern Extreme. Elder, Lorraine, ed. (Illus.). 220p. 1989. 9.95 (*0-685-24274-9*) AK-Gastineau.

— Training & Development Handbook. 4th ed. 1088p. 1996. 89.50 (*0-07-013359-X*) McGraw.

Craig, Robert M. Atlanta Architecture Vol. I: Art Deco to Modern Classic, 1929-1959. LC 94-2732. (Illus.). 160p. 1995. 29.95 (*0-88289-961-9*) Pelican.

Craig, Robert P., ed. Issues in Philosophy & Education. 128p. 1973. pap. text 8.95 (*0-8422-0372-9*) Irvington.

Craig, Robert S. The Virginia Updikes-Updykes. 1050p. 1985. 40.00 (*0-9615135-0-0*) Craig Pub Hse.

Craig, Robert S., et al. Microsoft Data Warehousing: Building Distributed Decision Support Systems. LC 99-21793. 384p. 1999. pap. 39.99 (*0-471-32761-1*) Wiley.

Craig, Robert T. & Tracy, Karen, eds. Conversational Coherence: Form, Structure, & Strategy. LC 83-13856. (Sage Series in Interpersonal Communication: No. 2). (Illus.). 344p. 1983. reprint ed. pap. 106.70 (*0-608-01121-5*, 20594250001) Bks Demand.

***Craig, Ronald J.** Stor norsk engelsk juridisk ordbok/Norwegian English Law Dictionary. 323p. 1999. 49.00 (*82-00-12923-3*) Scandnvan Univ Pr.

Craig, Ronald J. Where Could a Color Hide? (Illus.). 64p. (J). (gr. 3-6). 2000. pap. 16.95 (*1-57532-223-4*) Press-Tige Pub.

Craig, Roy. UFOs: An Insider's View of the Official Quest for Evidence. LC 95-10882. (Illus.). 276p. 1995. pap. 19.95 (*0-929398-94-7*) UNTX Pr.

Craig, Roy C. Mechanics of Deformable Bodies. LC 95-34726. 752p. 1996. text 109.95 (*0-471-50284-7*) Wiley.

Craig, Roy R. An Introduction to Structural Dynamics. LC 80-39798. 544p. (C). 1981. text 114.95 (*0-471-04499-7*) Wiley.

***Craig, Roy R.** Mechanics of Materials. 2nd ed. LC 99-43425. 804p. (C). 1999. text 113.95 incl. cd-rom (*0-471-33176-7*) Wiley.

***Craig, Royal L.** Bedside Manor: Poetry & Prose to Dream By. LC 00-190188. 206p. 2000. 25.00 (*0-7388-1536-5*); pap. 18.00 (*0-7388-1537-3*) Xlibris Corp.

Craig, Russell L. & Rausch, David A. A Historical, Philosophical, & Pragmatic Approach to Penology. LC 94-49062. 216p. 1995. 89.95 (*0-7734-8977-0*) E Mellen.

Craig, Ruth. Malu's Wolf. LC 95-6031. 192p. (J). (gr. 3-7). 1995. 15.95 (*0-531-09484-7*); lib. bdg. 16.99 (*0-531-08784-0*) Orchard Bks Watts.

Craig, R.W. Procurement Law for Construction & Engineering Works & Services. LC 98-52407. 1999. write for info. (*0-632-04927-8*) Blackwell Sci.

Craig, Sally, jt. auth. see Carnes, Robin.

Craig, Samuel C. International Marketing Research. LC 99-25240. 448p. 1999. pap. 39.95 (*0-471-98322-5*) Wiley.

Craig, Selene, et al. The Complete Book of Alternative Nutrition: Powerful New Ways to Use Foods, Herbs, Supplements & Special Diets to Prevent & Cure Disease. LC 96-27098. 464p. 1997. text 27.95 (*0-87596-322-6*) Rodale Pr Inc.

Craig, Sharyn S. Design Challenge: Northwind Quilts. Roberts, Nancy & Libal, Joyce, eds. LC 97-17299. (Illus.). 16p. 1997. pap. 7.95 (*1-885588-17-8*) Chitra Pubns.

— Design Challenge: Pyramids Plus. Roberts, Nancy & Libal, Joyce, eds. LC 97-17382. (Illus.). 16p. (Orig.). 1997. pap. 7.95 (*1-885588-16-X*) Chitra Pubns.

— Designing New Traditions in Quilts. Braunstein, Jack, ed. LC 91-14621. (Illus.). 96p. (Orig.). 1991. pap. 24.95 (*0-9622565-1-X*) Chitra Pubns.

— LeMoyne Stars Made Easy. Roberts, Nancy et al, eds. LC 97-48541. (Illus.). 32p. 1998. pap. 12.95 (*1-885588-19-4*) Chitra Pubns.

— Twist 'n Turn: A Fun Way to Frame Quilt Blocks. Roberts, Nancy, ed. LC 96-23733. (Illus.). 32p. (Orig.). 1996. pap. 11.95 (*1-885588-10-0*, 800-628-8244) Chitra Pubns.

Craig, Sharyn S., jt. auth. see Hargrave, Harriet.

Craig, Shawn. Between Sundays: A Year of Transforming Devotionals for the Toughest Days of Your Week. LC 98-40524. 320p. 1998. 14.99 (*1-878990-92-6*) Howard Pub LA.

Craig-Smith, Stephen J. & Fagence, Michael, eds. Recreation & Tourism As a Catalyst for Urban Waterfront Redevelopment: An International Survey. LC 95-3329. 192p. 1995. 59.95 (*0-275-94550-2*, Praeger Pubs) Greenwood.

Craig, Stephanie, tr. see Reboul, Antoine.

Craig, Stephen C. & Bennett, Stephen E., eds. After the Boom: The Politics of Generation X. LC 96-51719. (People, Passions, & Power Ser.). (Illus.). 212p. 1997. pap. 20.95 (*0-8476-8360-5*); text 68.50 (*0-8476-8359-1*) Rowman.

Craig, Stephen C. & Dodd, Lawrence C., eds. Broken Contract? Changing Relationships Between Americans & Their Government. LC 95-18230. (Transforming American Politics). 352p. (C). 1995. 30.00 (*0-8133-2263-4*, Pub. by Westview) HarpC.

Craig, Stephen R. Housekeeping Management in the Hospitality Industry. 125p. (Orig.). 1988. pap. text 12.95 (*0-935920-65-X*, Ntl Pubs Blck) P-H.

Craig, Steve, ed. Men, Masculinity & the Media. (Research on Men & Masculinities Ser.: Vol. 2). (Illus.). 280p. 1992. 58.00 (*0-8039-4162-5*) Sage.

— Men, Masculinity & the Media, No. 2. (Research on Men & Masculinities Ser.: Vol. 2). (Illus.). 280p. 1992. pap. 26.00 (*0-8039-4163-3*) Sage.

Craig, Sue. Make Your Mark! Influencing Across Your Organization. LC 97-9738. (Illus.). 254p. 1998. pap. 19.95 (*0-07-709159-0*) McGraw.

Craig, Sue, jt. auth. see Jassim, Hadi.

Craig, Susan & Johnson, Ken. The Softball Handbook. LC 84-12253. (Illus.). 160p. (Orig.). 1985. pap. 16.95 (*0-88011-260-3*, PCRA0260) Human Kinetics.

— Softball's Power Offense. (Illus.). 112p. 1997. pap. 16.95 (*1-57167-141-2*) Coaches Choice.

Craig, Suze. Tails & Tales: Small Farming in New England. LC 93-79739. (Illus.). 224p. (Orig.). 1993. pap. 15.00 (*1-883977-05-3*) Lind Hill Pr.

Craig, T. K., jt. ed. see Davies, T.

Craig, Terrence. Racial Attitudes in English-Canadian Fiction, 1905-1980. 163p. (C). 1987. 29.95 (*0-88920-952-9*) W Laurier U Pr.

Craig, Terrence L. The Missionary Lives: A Study in Canadian Missionary Biography & Autobiography. LC 97-8352. (Studies in Christian Mission: Vol. 19). 152p. 1997. text 68.50 (*90-04-10815-7*) Brill Academic Pubs.

Craig, Terry L. Gatekeeper, 01. LC 98-44579. 1999. pap. 12.99 (*0-88419-597-X*) Creation House.

— Swordsman. 304p. (Orig.). 1987. pap. 7.95 (*0-9618852-0-3*) Berachah Pub.

Craig, Teruko, tr. & intro. see Shiba, Goro.

Craig, Teruko, tr. & intro. see Shiba, Goro, et al.

Craig, Theresa & Wharton, Edith. Edith Wharton: A House Full of Rooms: Architecture, Interiors, & Gardens. LC 96-22036. (Illus.). 208p. 1996. 60.00 (*1-885254-42-3*, Pub. by Monacelli Pr) Penguin Putnam.

Craig, Thomas L., jt. ed. see Jacobs, Joshua J.

***Craig, Timothy J., ed.** Japan Pop! Inside the World of Japanese Popular Culture. LC 00-21812. (Illus.). 2000. pap. write for info. (*0-7656-0561-9*, East Gate Bk) M E Sharpe.

***Craig, Timothy J., ed.** Japan Pop! Inside the World of Japanese Popular Culture. LC 00-21812. (Illus.). 360p. 2000. text 64.95 (*0-7656-0560-0*, East Gate Bk) M E Sharpe.

Craig, Trevor J. Village Health Care Manual: An Approach to Patient Care in Places with Limited Medical Resources. 130p. 1997. pap. text 9.99 (*0-9661484-1-X*) Stony Pt Christian.

Craig, Vernal. Answers to My "Why Lord?" 1986. write for info. (*0-935087-14-1*) Wright Pub Co.

Craig, Victor. Smart Choices. LC 81-70755. (Illus.). 112p. 1982. pap. 9.95 (*0-941156-00-1*) Clear View Pubns.

Craig, W. H., et al, eds. Centrifuges in Soil Mechanics. 244p. (C). 1988. text 155.00 (*90-6191-800-6*, Pub. by A A Balkema) Ashgate Pub Co.

Craig, W. J., ed. see Shakespeare, William.

Craig, W. Laurence, et al. Annotated Guide to the 1998 Arbitration Rules: With Commentary. (International Court of Arbitration Ser.). 236p. 1998. text 125.00 (*92-842-1252-9*, 595) ICC Pub.

— Craig, Park & Paulsson's Annotated Guide to the 1998 ICC Arbitration Rules with Commentary. LC 97-52688. 236p. 1998. text 100.00 (*0-379-21391-5*) Oceana.

— International Chamber of Commerce Arbitration. 3rd ed. LC 97-47674. 2000. 125.00 (*0-379-21392-3*) Oceana.

Craig, W. Lawrence, et al. International Commercial Arbitration: International Chamber of Commerce Arbitration. 2nd ed. 1984. ring bd. 325.00 (*0-379-10160-2*) Oceana.

Craig, Warren. Sweet & Lowdown: America's Popular Song Writers. LC 77-20223. 1978. 47.50 (*0-8108-1089-1*) Scarecrow.

Craig, Wendy, ed. Childhood Social Development. LC 99-47285. (Essential Readings in Developmental Psychology Ser.). 256p. 2000. pap. 24.95 (*0-631-21741-X*) Blackwell Pubs.

— Childhood Social Development: The Essential Readings. LC 99-47285. (Essential Readings in Developmental Psychology Ser.). 256p. 1999. 59.95 (*0-631-21740-1*) Blackwell Pubs.

Craig, William. Fall of Japan: A Chronicle of the End of an Empire. 416p. 1997. 10.99 (*0-88365-985-9*) Galahad Bks.

Craig, William B. Mediation Book, Childhood Sexual Abuse, Repressed Memory. 238p. 1994. student ed. 125.00 (*1-885689-05-5*) Spread the Wrd.

— Mediator Book, Childhood Sexual Abuse, Repressed Memory. 61p. 1994. student ed. 125.00 (*1-885689-04-7*) Spread the Wrd.

— Trial Book, Childhood Sexual Abuse, Repressed Memory. 275p. 1994. student ed. 125.00 (*1-885689-03-9*) Spread the Wrd.

Craig, William L. Assessing the New Testament Evidence for the Historicity of the Resurrection of Jesus. LC 88-25838. (Studies in Bible & Early Christianity: Vol. 16). 462p. 1989. lib. bdg. 109.95 (*0-88946-616-5*) E Mellen.

— Divine Foreknowledge & Human Freedom: The Coherence of Theism: Omniscience. LC 90-42346. (Brill's Studies in Intellectual History: Vol. 19). xiii, 360p. 1990. 119.50 (*90-04-09250-1*) Brill Academic Pubs.

— Enemy at the Gates. 1974. mass mkt. 1.95 (*0-345-25885-1*) Ballantine Pub Grp.

— The Historical Argument for the Resurrection of Jesus. LC 85-21570. (Texts & Studies in Religion: Vol. 23). 696p. 1985. lib. bdg. 129.95 (*0-88946-811-7*) E Mellen.

— Reasonable Faith: Christian Truth & Apologetics. rev. ed. LC 94-21577. 350p. 1994. pap. 20.00 (*0-89107-764-2*) Crossway Bks.

Craig, William L. & McLeod, Mark S., eds. The Logic of Rational Theism: Exploratory Essays. LC 90-39313. (Problems in Contemporary Philosophy Ser.: Vol. 24). 260p. 1990. lib. bdg. 89.95 (*0-88946-369-7*) E Mellen.

***Craig, William L. & Moreland, James P.** Naturalism: A Critical Analysis. LC 00-25324. 2000. write for info. (*0-415-23524-3*) Routledge.

Craig, William L. & Smith, Quentin. Theism, Atheism, & Big Bang Cosmology. (Illus.). 352p. 1995. pap. text 21.00 (*0-19-826383-X*) OUP.

Craig, William L., jt. auth. see Crossan, John Dominic.

***Craig, William Lane.** The Only Wise God: The Compatibility of Divine Foreknowledge & Human Freedom. 157p. 2000. pap. 17.00 (*1-57910-316-2*) Wipf & Stock.

Craig, William T. Team Sergeant. 1998. mass mkt. 6.99 (*0-8041-1714-4*) Ivy Books.

Craig, Yvonne. Advocacy, Counselling & Mediation in Casework: Processes of Empowerment. 1998. pap. 29.95 (*1-85302-564-X*, Pub. by Jessica Kingsley) Taylor & Francis.

— Peacemaking for Churches. 1999. pap. text 17.95 (*0-281-05177-1*) Society Prom Christ Know.

Craig, Yvonne J. Elder Abuse & Mediation: Exploratory Studies in America, Britain & Europe. 230p. 1997. text 64.95 (*1-85972-615-1*, Pub. by Avebry) Ashgate Pub Co.

Craige, Betty J. American Patriotism in a Global Society. LC 95-44254. 198p. (C). 1996. text 54.50 (*0-7914-2959-8*); pap. text 17.95 (*0-7914-2960-1*) State U NY Pr.

— Laying the Ladder Down: The Emergence of Cultural

C

An Asterisk (*) at the beginning of an entry indicates that the title is appearing for the first time.

Holism. LC 92-10934. (Critical Perspectives on Modern Culture Ser.). 176p. 1992. 30.00 (*0-87023-805-1*); pap. 15.95 (*0-87023-806-X*) U of Mass Pr.
— Literary Relativity: An Essay on Twentieth Century Narrative. LC 81-69634. (Illus.). 136p. 1982. 26.50 (*0-8387-5034-6*) Bucknell U Pr.
— Lorca's Poet in New York: The Fall into Consciousness. LC 76-24339. (Studies in Romance Languages: No. 15). 106p. reprint ed. pap. 32.90 (*0-7837-5818-9*, 204548500006) Bks Demand.
Craige, Betty J., tr. The Poetry of Gabriel Celaya. LC 83-45367. 160p. 1984. 29.50 (*0-8387-5062-1*) Bucknell U Pr.
Craige, Betty J., jt. auth. see Asbury, Herbert.
Craige, Betty J., jt. auth. see Mantero, Manuel.
Craige, Patricia V. Born to Win: Bred to Succeed. Luther, Luana & Ross, Nina P., eds. LC 96-84690. (Illus.). 289p. 1997. 39.95 (*0-944875-40-8*, Pub. by Doral Pub) Natl Bk Netwk.
Craigen, D. & Summerskill, K., eds. Formal Methods for Trustworthy Computer Systems (FM89) Report from FM89: A Workshop on the Assessment of Formal Methods for Trustworthy Computer Systems, Halifax, Nova Scotia, Canada, 23-27 July 1989. (Workshops in Computing Ser.). x, 248p. 1990. pap. 49.00 (*0-387-19635-8*) Spr-Verlag.
Craigen, Dan, et al. Industrial Applications of Formal Methods to Model, Design & Analyze Computer Systems: An International Survey. LC 94-23432. (Advanced Computing & Telecommunications Ser.). (Illus.). 306p. 1995. 54.00 (*0-8155-1362-3*) Noyes.
Craigen, Heather. Simple Pleasures: Recipes for Gourmet Entertaining When You're Short of Time. Craigen, Robin, ed. (Illus.). 144p. 1998. 22.95 (*1-928661-20-3*) Moving Mtns Inc.
Craigen, Robin, ed. see Craigen, Heather.
Craighead, Alice M., ed. see Foust, Steve D.
Craighead, Charles. The Eagle & the River. LC 92-23240. (Illus.). 32p. (J). 1994. mass mkt. 16.00 (*0-02-762265-7*, Mac Bks Young Read) S&S Childrens.
Craighead, Charlie. Who Ate the Backyard? Living with Wildlife on Private Land. 1997. pap. text 14.95 (*0-931895-48-0*) Grand Teton NHA.
Craighead, Charlie, ed. see Exum, Glen.
Craighead, David. Financial Analysis of a Reinsurance Office. (DYP Textbook Ser.). 212p. 1989. pap. 155.00 (*1-870255-20-8*) LLP.
— Financial Analysis of a Reinsurance Office. (C). 1989. 350.00 (*0-7855-4172-1*, Pub. by Witherby & Co) St Mut.
Craighead, Ernest S. Fulton Family of Westmoreland County, Pennsylvania, 1712-1772-1940: Account of the Descendants of Abraham Fulton & Margaret Guthry, Who Emigrated from Articlave, Londonderry County, Ireland, & Settled in Westmoreland County, Pennsylvania, Together with Genealogical Notes on Intermarried Families. 216p. 1997. reprint ed. pap. 33.50 (*0-8328-8674-2*); reprint ed. lib. bdg. 43.50 (*0-8328-8673-4*) Higginson Bk Co.
Craighead, F. C., jt. auth. see Boeving, A. G.
Craighead, Frank, Jr., jt. auth. see Craighead, John.
Craighead, Frank C. For Everything There Is a Season. LC 93-33281. (Illus.). 208p. (Orig.). 1994. pap. 16.95 (*1-56044-187-9*) Falcon Pub Inc.
Craighead, Frank C., Jr. Track of the Grizzly. LC 78-8563. (Sierra Club Guides Ser.). (Illus.). 272p. 1982. reprint ed. pap. 16.00 (*0-87156-322-3*, Pub. by Sierra) Random.
Craighead, Frank C., Jr. & Craighead, John J. How to Survive on Land & Sea. 4th rev. ed. LC 84-4879. (Illus.). 412p. 1984. 28.95 (*0-87021-278-8*) Naval Inst Pr.
Craighead, Geoff. High Rise Security & Fire Life Safety. LC 95-34538. 360p. 1995. 64.95 (*0-7506-9576-5*) Buttrwrth-Heinemann.
Craighead, J. J., et al. A Definitive System for Analysis of Grizzly Bear Habitat & Other Wilderness Resources Utilizing LANDSAT Multispectral Imagery & Computer Technology. Peterson, C. et al, eds. (Illus.). 279p. (Orig.). (C). 1982. pap. text 12.00 (*0-910439-01-X*) Wildlife-Wildlands.
Craighead, John & Craighead, Frank, Jr. Hawks in the Hand: Adventures in Photography & Falconry. LC 97-420. (Illus.). 384p. 1997. reprint ed. 40.00 (*1-55821-560-3*) Lyons Pr.
Craighead, John E. Pathology & Pathogenesis of Human Viral Disease. 600p. 1999. 99.95 (*0-12-195160-X*) Acad Pr.
Craighead, John J., et al. The Grizzly Bears of Yellowstone: Their Ecology in the Yellowstone Ecosystem, 1959-1992. 560p. (C). 1995. text 115.00 (*1-55963-456-1*) Island Pr.
Craighead, John J., jt. auth. see Craighead, Frank C., Jr.
Craighead, Joni. First Impressions: Tips to Enhance Your Image. Colvin, Rod & Adams, Susan, eds. LC 96-30554. (Illus.). 200p. (Orig.). 1996. pap. 14.95 (*1-886039-26-7*) Addicus Bks.
Craighead, Karen. Large Mammals of Yellowstone & Grand Teton National Parks. LC 79-65734. (Illus.). 31p. 1999. 2.50 (*0-934948-00-3*, 10247) Yellowstone Assn.
***Craighead, Lance.** Bears of the World. LC 00-27759. (Illus.). 132p. 2000. 29.95 (*0-89658-503-4*) Voyageur Pr.
Craighead, Linda, et al, eds. Cognitive & Behavioral Interventions: An Empirical Approach to Mental Health Problems. LC 93-31930. 464p. (C). 1993. 68.00 (*0-205-14586-8*) Allyn.
Craighead, Linda, jt. auth. see Gagnier de Mendoza, Mary Jane.
Craighead, Linda, ed. see Mayfield, Signe.
Craighead, Meinrad. Liturgical Art. LC 88-61723. (Illus.). 34p. 1988. pap. 24.95 (*1-55612-069-9*, LL1069) Sheed & Ward WI.
— The Mother's Songs: Images of God the Mother. LC 85-50408. 96p. (Orig.). 1985. pap. 17.95 (*0-8091-2716-4*) Paulist Pr.
Craighead, Nancy A., jt. ed. see Ripich, Danielle N.
Craighead, Tom. Skydivers, Flying with Their Pants on Fire. (Illus.). xviii, 327p. 1999. pap. 19.95 (*0-9670990-0-5*, 001) Crunk Pubg.
Craighead, W. E., jt. auth. see Meyers, A. W.
***Craighead, W. Edward & Nemeroff, Charles B.** The Corsini Encyclopedia of Psychology & Behavioral Science, Set. 3rd ed. LC 99-58006. 2700p. 2000. text 450.00 (*0-471-23949-6*) Wiley.
Craighill Handy, E. S. & Pukui, Mary K. The Polynesian Family System in Ka'u, Hawai'i. 288p. 1999. mass mkt. 7.95 (*1-56647-232-6*) Mutual Pub HI.
Craighill, Nancy L. OpenStep for Enterprises. LC 96-1798. 245p. 1996. pap. text 34.95 incl. cd-rom, disk (*0-471-30859-5*) Wiley.
Craighill, Peyton G., ed. Diaconal Ministry-Past, Present, & Future: Essays from Philadelphia Symposium, 1992. 139p. (Orig.). 1994. pap. 10.00 (*1-886136-00-9*) N Am Assn Diaconate.
Craigie, E. Horne, ed. see Bensley, Benjamin A.
Craigie, E. Horne, tr. see Cajal, Santiago R.
Craigie, Edward H. A Laboratory Guide to the Anatomy of the Rabbit. 2nd ed. LC 70-358625. 123p. reprint ed. pap. 38.20 (*0-608-15657-4*, 203191700077) Bks Demand.
Craigie, Eric. An Irish Sporting Life. 192p. 1994. pap. 14.95 (*1-874675-40-6*) Dufour.
Craigie, John D., jt. auth. see Marks, James R.
Craigie, N. S., et al, eds. Monopoles in Quantum Field Theory: Proceedings of the Monopole Meeting, Trieste, Italy, Dec. 11-15, 1981. 461p. 1982. 78.00 (*9971-950-28-6*); pap. 33.00 (*9971-950-29-4*) World Scientific Pub.
Craigie, Peter C. Deuteronomy. (New International Commentary on the Old Testament Ser.). 424p. 1976. 36.00 (*0-8028-2524-9*) Eerdmans.
— Ezekiel. 332p. 1993. pap. 22.00 (*0-7152-0530-7*) St Mut.
— Psalms 1-50. (Biblical Commentary Ser.: Vol. 19). 1983. 29.99 (*0-8499-0218-5*) Word Pub.
— Twelve Prophets, Vol. 1. LC 84-2372. 256p. 1993. pap. text 22.00 (*0-7152-0534-X*, Pub. by St Andrew) St Mut.
— Twelve Prophets, Vol. 2. LC 84-2372. 260p. 1993. pap. text 22.00 (*0-7152-0538-2*) St Mut.
Craigie, Peter C., et al. Ascribe to the Lord: Biblical & Other Essays in Memory of Peter C. Craigie LC 99-203713. xv, 633 p. 1988. write for info. (*1-85075-189-7*, Pub. by Sheffield Acad) CUP Services.
Craigie, Peter C., et al. Jeremiah 1-25. (Biblical Commentary Ser.: Vol. 26). 29.99 (*0-8499-0225-8*) Word Pub.
Craigie, W. A. Scandinavian Folklore. 1973. 59.95 (*0-8490-0996-0*) Gordon Pr.
Craigie, William A. Religion of Ancient Scandinavia. LC 74-99657. (Select Bibliographies Reprint Ser.). 1977. 18.95 (*0-8369-5086-0*) Ayer.
Craigin, Elisabeth. Either Is Love. LC 75-12311. (Homosexuality Ser.). 1975. reprint ed. 13.95 (*0-405-07379-8*) Ayer.
Craigmill, Arthur L., et al. Handbook of Comparative Pharmacokinetics: Residues of Veterinary Therapeutic Drugs. LC 93-40739. 676p. 1994. lib. bdg. 152.95 (*0-8493-3212-5*, SF917) CRC Pr.
Craigmyle, Lord. John Marshall in Diplomacy & in Law. 158p. 1996. reprint ed. 45.00 (*1-56169-200-X*) Gaunt.
— John Marshall in Diplomacy & in Law. LC 95-80914. viii,145p. 1995. reprint ed. 50.00 (*0-89941-998-4*, 309030) W S Hein.
Craigmyle, Marshall B. The Apocrine Glands & the Breast. LC 84-7567. (Wiley Medical Publications). (Illus.). 92p. reprint ed. pap. 30.00 (*0-8357-4547-3*, 203744600008) Bks Demand.
Craik. The Little Lame Prince. 1997. pap. 2.95 (*0-89375-710-1*) Troll Communs.
***Craik, Anne.** Cottage Country. (Illus.). 168p. 2000. pap. 13.95 (*1-55046-276-8*) Boston Mills.
Craik, D. J. Magnetism & Electricity: A Unified Text. LC 98-27221. 324p. 1999. 185.00 (*0-471-98639-9*) Wiley.
Craik, D. J. & Tebble, Robert S. Magnetic Materials. LC 71-80119. 740p. reprint ed. pap. 200.00 (*0-608-10028-5*, 205124500005) Bks Demand.
Craik, David J., ed. NMR in Drug Design. LC 95-34213. (Analytical Biotechnology Ser.). 496p. 1995. boxed set 209.95 (*0-8493-7824-9*, 7824) CRC Pr.
Craik, Derek. Magnetism: Principles & Applications. 3rd ed. LC 93-38155. 468p. 1995. pap. 74.95 (*0-471-95417-9*) Wiley.
Craik, Derek J. Magnetism: Principles & Applications. LC 93-38155. (Illus.). 467p. 1995. reprint ed. pap. 144.80 (*0-608-03998-5*, 206473500011) Bks Demand.
Craik, Derek J., ed. Magnetic Oxides, 2 pts., Pt. 1. LC 73-14378. 504p. 1975. reprint ed. pap. 156.30 (*0-608-08263-5*, 202667300001) Bks Demand.
Craik, Derek J., ed. see Drake, William.
Craik, Dinah. Olive & the Half-Caste. Kaplan, Cora, ed. & intro. by. LC 95-25866. (Oxford Popular Fiction Ser.). 398p. 1996. pap. 10.95 (*0-19-289262-2*) OUP.
Craik, Dinah M. Unkind Word & Other Stories. LC 70-101278. (Short Story Index Reprint Ser.). 1977. 23.95 (*0-8369-3215-3*) Ayer.
Craik, Dinah M., jt. auth. see Rossetti, Christina Georgina.
***Craik, Edna Emma.** How Beautiful upon the Mountain. LC 99-63248. 160p. 1999. pap. 9.95 (*1-57258-150-6*) Teach Servs.
Craik, Elizabeth, ed. see Euripides.
Craik, Elizabeth M., ed. Marriage & Property. (SWSS Ser.). 202p. 1991. pap. text 13.90 (*0-08-041205-X*, Pub. by Aberdeen U Pr) Macmillan.
— Marriage & Property. 208p. 1984. text 31.00 (*0-08-028448-5*, Pergamon Pr) Elsevier.
— Owls to Athens: Essays on Classical Culture Presented to Sir Kenneth Dover. (Illus.). 430p. 1990. text 98.00 (*0-19-814478-4*) OUP.
Craik, Elizabeth M., ed. & tr. see Hippocrates.
Craik, F. I., jt. ed. see Roediger, H. L., III.
Craik, Fergus & Trehub, Sandra E., eds. Aging & Cognitive Processes. LC 82-18129. (Advances in the Study of Communication & Affect Ser.: Vol. 8) 396p. 1982. 80.00 (*0-306-40946-1*, Plenum Trade) Perseus Pubng.
Craik, Fergus I., et al, eds. Expertise & Technology: Issues in Cognition & Human-Computer Cooperation. (Expertise Ser.). 312p. 1994. text 59.95 (*0-8058-1511-2*) L Erlbaum Assocs.
***Craik, Fergus I. & Salthouse, Timothy A.** The Handbook of Aging & Cognition. 2nd ed. LC 99-31065. 755p. 1999. write for info. (*0-8058-2966-0*) L Erlbaum Assocs.
Craik, Fergus I. & Salthouse, Timothy A., eds. The Handbook of Aging & Cognition. 600p. 1992. text 120.00 (*0-8058-0713-6*) L Erlbaum Assocs.
Craik, Fergus M., jt. ed. see Tulving, Endel.
Craik, George L. Spenser & His Poetry, 3 vols. in 1. rev. ed. LC 74-99247. reprint ed. 76.50 (*0-404-01826-2*) AMS Pr.
Craik, Henry. The Life of Jonathan Swift, Dean of St. Patrick's Dublin. (BCL1-PR English Literature Ser.). 576p. 1992. reprint ed. lib. bdg. 99.00 (*0-7812-7412-5*) Rprt Serv.
Craik, Henry, ed. English Prose, 5 vols. reprint ed. 395.00 (*0-404-01860-2*) AMS Pr.
Craik, Jennifer. The Face of Fashion: Cultural Studies in Fashion. LC 93-10546. (Illus.). 304p. (C). (gr. 13). 1994. pap. 22.99 (*0-415-05262-9*, B0843) Routledge.
— Identity Gender & Culture. 224p. (C). 1998. 75.00 (*0-415-11714-3*) Routledge.
— Resorting to Tourism: Cultural Policies for Tourist Development in Australia LC 92-205826. xii, 281p. 1991. write for info. (*1-86373-040-0*, Pub. by Allen & Unwin Pty) IPG Chicago.
Craik, Jennifer, et al. Public Voices, Private Interests: Australia's Media Policy. 296p. 1996. pap. 29.95 (*1-86373-628-X*, Pub. by Allen & Unwin Pty) Paul & Co Pubs.
Craik, K. H., et al. Fifty Years of Personality Psychology. (Perspectives on Individual Differences Ser.). (Illus.). 324p. (C). 1993. 59.50 (*0-306-44291-4*, Plenum Trade) Perseus Pubng.
Craik, Kenneth H. & McKechnie, George E., eds. Personality & the Environment. LC 77-94068. (Sage Contemporary Social Science Issues Ser.: Vol. 42). 128p. reprint ed. pap. 39.70 (*0-608-30798-X*, 202188300026) Bks Demand.
Craik, Kenneth J. The Nature of Psychology: A Selection of Papers Essays, & Other Writings. LC 65-14851. 204p. reprint ed. pap. 58.20 (*0-608-11273-9*, 2051423) Bks Demand.
Craik, Maria M. Little Lame Prince & the Adventures of a Brownie. Date not set. lib. bdg. 25.95 (*0-8488-2095-9*) Amereon Ltd.
Craik, R. J. Sir Thomas Urquhart of Cromarty (1611-1660), Adventurer, Polymath, & Translator of Rabelais. LC 93-15151. 248p. 1993. text 89.95 (*0-7734-9269-0*) E Mellen.
Craik, Rebecca L. & Oatis, Carol A. Gait Analysis: Theory & Application. (Illus.). 432p. (C). (gr. 13). 1994. text 53.95 (*0-8016-6964-2*, 06964) Mosby Inc.
Craik, Robert J. Sound Transmission Through Buildings: Using Statistical Energy Analysis. (Illus.). 280p. 1996. 96.95 (*0-566-07572-5*, Pub. by Gower) Ashgate Pub Co.
***Craik, T. W., ed.** The Maid's Tragedy: Francis Beaumont & John Fletcher. (Revels Plays Ser.). 212p. 1999. pap. 19.95 (*0-7190-3098-6*, Pub. by Manchester Univ Pr) St Martin.
Craik, T. W., ed. see Beaumont, Francis & Fletcher, John.
Craik, T. W., ed. see Shakespeare, William.
Craik, Thomas, et al. The Revels History of Drama in English, 1500-1576, Vol. 2. 1980. 59.95 (*0-416-13030-5*, NO. 6365) Routledge.
Crain. Development. (LAN Ser.: Vol. 2, No. 4). 1993. 24.50 (*0-8058-9993-6*) L Erlbaum Assocs.
— Introduction To Texas Politics. 3rd ed. (Political Science). 1999. pap. 15.95 (*0-534-56970-6*) Wadsworth Pub.
— Theories of Development. 4th ed. LC 99-45003. 400p. 1999. pap. text 35.00 (*0-13-955402-5*) P-H.
Crain, Ada E. The Deacon. 180p. 1995. 13.95 (*0-9643286-0-7*) A E Crain.
Crain, Bill. The Little Planet & the Magic Hats. Zark, T. J., ed. (Little Planet Literacy Ser.). (Illus.). 48p. (Orig.). (J). (gr. k-5). 1995. pap. write for info. (*0-9644866-4-4*) App Learn Tech.
Crain, Caleb, tr. see Kriseova, Eda.
Crain, Cynthia D. Movement & Rhythmic Activities for the Mentally Retarded. (Illus.). 136p. 1981. 26.95 (*0-398-04174-1*) C C Thomas.
Crain, Dale, ed. see Byrne, John.
Crain, DeLoris. Saved by the Judge. (Judge Ser.). 132p. (Orig.). 1995. pap. 8.99 (*0-9627099-4-8*) Zephyr Pub Corp.
Crain, Duran, ed. see Becht, Kenneth R.
Crain, E. R. The Log Analysis Handbook. 684p. 1986. 35.00 (*0-87814-298-3*, P4407) PennWell Bks.
Crain, Edward E. Historic Architecture in the Caribbean Islands. LC 94-3870. (Illus.). 304p. 1994. 60.00 (*0-8130-1293-7*) U Press Fla.
Crain, Ellen & Gershel, Jeffrey C. Clinical Manual of Emergency Pediatrics. 3rd ed. LC 96-23809. (Illus.). 592p. 1996. text 35.00 (*0-07-013429-4*) McGraw-Hill HPD.
Crain, Elley. Deep in the Heart. (Intimate Moments Ser.). 1993. mass mkt. 3.39 (*0-373-07478-6*, 5-07478-6) Silhouette.
— New Year's Resolution. (Intimate Moments Ser.). 1993. per. 3.50 (*0-373-07533-2*, 5-07533-8) Silhouette.
Crain, Ernest & Perkins, James. Introduction to Texas Politics. LC 94-42150. 177p. (C). 1995. pap. 11.00 (*0-314-05590-8*) West Pub.
— Introduction To Texas Politics. 2nd ed. LC 97-21793. (Political Science). (C). 1997. 9.50 (*0-534-54207-7*) Wadsworth Pub.
Crain, Ernest, jt. auth. see Maxwell, William E.
***Crain, Frances Utterback.** Of Weeds & Views. 2000. pap. 9.75 (*1-892343-10-X*, Oak Tree Bk) Oak Tree Pub.
Crain, Jean, jt. auth. see Crain, Jim.
Crain, Jeffrey S. & Morrow, Roy W., eds. Applications of Inductively Coupled Plasma-Mass Spectrometry to Radionuclide Determinations. LC 95-47789. (STP, Special Technical Publication Ser.: No. 1291). (Illus.). 150p. 1995. text 59.00 (*0-8031-2034-6*, STP1291) ASTM.
Crain, Jeffrey S., jt. ed. see Morrow, Roy W.
Crain, Jeremy. Writing the Novel - Craft & Style. 136p. (Orig.). 1997. pap. 13.95 (*0-9657212-7-2*) Trail Rdge.
Crain, Jim & Crain, Jean. How to Cook Cajun & Other Recipes. 144p. 1993. pap. 7.95 (*0-9636307-0-9*) Levee Pr LA.
Crain, John A., jt. auth. see Kemerer, Frank R.
Crain, Madeleine. Medical Decision-Making among Chinese-Born & Euro-American Elderly: A Comparative Study of Values. LC 97-33211. (Studies on the Elderly in America). 123p. 1997. text 41.00 (*0-8153-3003-0*) Garland.
Crain, Mark. Comeback Man. LC 94-71433. 1994. 21.00 (*0-9641608-8-9*) F E A Laser.
Crain, Mary B., jt. auth. see Edelman, Joel.
Crain, Mary B., jt. auth. see Taylor, Terry L.
***Crain, Mary Beth.** A Widow, a Chihuahua & Harry Truman: A Story of Love, Loss & Love Again. LC 00-27732. 2000. pap. write for info. (*0-06-251673-6*) Harper SF.
— A Widow, a Chihuahua, & Harry Truman: A Story of Love, Loss, & Love Again. LC 00-27732. 224p. 2000. 22.00 (*0-06-251672-8*, Pub. by Harper SF) HarpC.
Crain, Mary Beth, jt. auth. see Taylor, Terry L.
Crain, Mary Beth, jt. auth. see Taylor, Terry Lynn.
Crain, Mary M., jt. ed. see Hughes-Freeland, Felicia.
Crain, Paulette. Delore's Confession. LC 98-18982. 387p. 1998. 24.95 (*1-892343-00-2*) Oak Tree Pub.
Crain, Ray. The Land Beyond the Mountains. (Illus.). 346p. (C). 1994. 35.00 (*0-9641149-0-9*) Main Graphics.
— The Land Beyond the Mountains. 2nd ed. (Illus.). 393p. 1996. reprint ed. 35.00 (*0-9641149-7-6*) Main Graphics.
— The Long Green Valley. (Illus.). 372p. 1996. 35.00 (*0-9641149-1-7*) Main Graphics.
— Simon Kenton: The Great Frontiersman. (Illus.). 52p. (Orig.). 1992. 18.00 (*0-9641149-4-1*); pap. 12.00 (*0-9641149-5-X*) Main Graphics.
Crain, Rickey D. Crain's Muscle World: Workout Training Log. (Illus.). 125p. 1995. pap. 12.00 (*0-929994-00-0*) Crains Muscle.
— To Squat or Not to Squat . . . That Is the Question? (Illus.). 140p. (Orig.). 1994. pap. text 16.95 (*0-929994-06-X*) Crains Muscle.
— To Squat or Not to Squat . . . That Is the Question? (Illus.). 140p. (Orig.). (C). 1994. text 29.95 (*0-929994-07-8*) Crains Muscle.
Crain, Robert L. Politics of School Desegregation: Comparative Case Studies of Community Structure & Policy-Making. LC 67-27390. (Monographs in Social Research: No. 14). (Illus.). 1968. 15.00 (*0-202-30033-1*) Natl Opinion Res.
— Southern Schools: An Evaluation of the Emergency School Assistance Program (EASP) & of School Desegregation, Set. (Report Ser.: Nos. 124A-124B). 1973. 30.00 (*0-932132-21-9*) Natl Opinion Res.
Crain, Robert L., et al. The Politics of Community Conflict: The Fluoridation Decision. LC 68-31777. 1969. pap. text 6.95 (*0-672-60840-5*) Irvington.
— The Politics of Community Conflict: The Fluoridation Decision. LC 68-31777. 1969. 7.50 (*0-672-51164-9*, Bobbs) Macmillan.
Crain, Robert L., jt. auth. see Wells, Amy S.
Crain, Ronald D., jt. ed. see Havlicek, Larry L.
Crain, Sharon S., jt. auth. see Goosens, Carl.
Crain, Stanley M. Neurophysiologic Studies in Tissue Culture. fac. ed. LC 75-14567. (Illus.). 292p. pap. 90.60 (*0-7837-7541-5*, 204696300005) Bks Demand.
***Crain, Stephen.** Lighting for People Photography. 2nd ed. (Illus.). 128p. 2000. pap. 29.95 (*1-58428-016-6*) Amherst Media.
Crain, Stephen & Lillo-Martin, Diane. Language & Mind. LC 98-34401. (Blackwell Textbooks in Linguistics). 1999. 69.95 (*0-631-19535-1*); pap. 34.95 (*0-631-19536-X*) Blackwell Pubs.
Crain, Stephen & Thornton, Rosalind. Investigations in Universal Grammar: A Guide to Experiments on the Acquisition of Syntax & Semantics. LC 97-44971. (Language, Speech & Communication Ser.). (Illus.). 368p. 1998. 55.00 (*0-262-03250-3*, Bradford Bks) MIT Pr.
***Crain, Stephen & Thornton, Rosalind.** Investigations in Universal Grammar: A Guide to Experiments on the Acquisition of Syntax & Semantics. (Language, Speech & Communication Ser.). (Illus.). 360p. (C). 2000. reprint ed. pap. 37.00 (*0-262-53180-1*) MIT Pr.
Crain, Thomas. Schlecter's Chess Games. (Great Masters Ser.). (Illus.). 288p. 1998. 30.00 (*0-939433-53-2*) Caissa Edit.

C

— Shades of Injustice: Uncovering the Collapse of Hennepin County Detox Center. 175p. (Orig.). 1997. pap. 12.99 (*0-9627099-7-2*) Zephyr Pub Corp.

— Touching Thomas. 130p. (Orig.). 1996. pap. 8.99 (*0-9627099-6-4*) Zephyr Pub Corp.

Crain, Thomas L., compiled by. Night Voices. (Illus.). 164p. 1991. pap. text 12.95 (*0-9627099-0-5*) Zephyr Pub Corp.

Crain, W. Mark. Televised Legislatures: Political Information Technology & Public Choice. (C). 1988. lib. bdg. 69.00 (*0-89838-262-9*) Kluwer Academic.

Craine. Money & Banking. (C). 1998. text 61.50 (*0-03-096959-X*) Harcourt Coll Pubs.

***Craine, Debra & Mackrell, Judith.** The Oxford Dictionary of Dance. (Illus.). 512p. 2000. 39.95 (*0-19-860106-9*) OUP.

Craine, E. R., jt. auth. see Rossano, G. S.

***Craine, Eric, et al, eds.** CCD Precision Photometry Workshop. LC 99-67173. (Conference Series Proceedings: Vol. 189). 274p. 1999. text 52.00 (*1-58381-015-3*) Astron Soc Pacific.

Craine, Eric R. Burma Roadsters: The 464th in China-Burma-India. LC 92-33293. 1992. write for info. (*0-934525-21-8*) West Research.

— A Handbook of Quasistellar & BL Lacertae Objects. (Astronomy & Astrophysics Ser.: Vol. 4). 292p. 1977. pap. 19.00 (*0-912918-23-3*, 0923) Pachart Pub Hse.

— Log of the Near Infrared Photographic Sky Survey. (Astronomy & Astrophysics Ser.). (Illus.). 168p. 1988. pap. 40.00 (*0-934525-04-8*); disk 50.00 (*0-934525-09-9*) West Research.

Craine, Eric R. & Wemple, Neil T. Astronomical Image Comparator: An Astronomical Video Image Comparator System. (Astronomy & Astrophysics Ser.). (Illus.). 26p. 1988. pap. 20.00 (*0-934525-07-2*); student ed. 225.00 incl. disk (*0-934525-08-0*) West Research.

Craine, Eric R., jt. auth. see Engel, John R.

Craine, Eric R., jt. auth. see Wemple, Neil T.

Craine, Fynlo. Designing Real-Time Systems. (C). 1998. text. write for info. (*0-201-87715-5*) Addison-Wesley.

Craine, J. F. & Martin, G. R. Microcomputers in Engineering & Science. (C). 1985. pap. text 34.50 (*0-201-14217-1*) Addison-Wesley.

Craine, James F. & Gudeman, Howard E. The Rehabilitation of Brain Functions: Principles, Procedures & Techniques of Neurotraining. (Illus.). 358p. (C). 1981. spiral bd. 56.95 (*0-398-04605-0*) C C Thomas.

Craine, Lyle E. Water Management Innovations in England. LC 70-75182. 135p. reprint ed. pap. 41.90 (*0-7837-3136-1*, 205210900034) Bks Demand.

Craine, Michael F. Hear Well Again: A Step by Step Program to Better Hearing. 144p. (Orig.). 1994. pap. 19.00 (*1-880365-76-6*) Prof Pr NC.

Craine, Naomi. A Packinghouse Worker's Fight for Justice: The Mark Curtis Story. (FRE.). 83p. pap. 6.00 (*0-87348-817-2*) Pathfinder NY.

— A Packinghouse Worker's Fight for Justice: The Mark Curtis Story. (Illus.). 83p. 1996. pap. 6.00 (*0-87348-844-X*) Pathfinder NY.

— Por Que Sigue Preso Mark Curtis? (Why Is Mark Cortis Still in Prison?) El Caso Fabricado Contra un Sindicalista y Socialista y la Campana Por Su Libertad. (SPA.). 86p. 1995. pap. 6.00 (*0-87348-809-1*) Pathfinder NY.

Craine, Nick. Portrait of a Thousand Punks: Hard Core Logo. LC 99-192475. (Illus.). 128p. 1998. pap. 14.95 (*0-88784-606-8*, Pub. by Hse of Anansi Pr) Genl Dist Srvs.

Craine, Renate. Hildegard: Prophet of the Cosmic Christ. LC 97-14702. (Crossroad Spiritual Legacy Ser.). (Illus.). 163p. 1997. pap. 14.95 (*0-8245-2510-8*) Crossroad NY.

Crainer, Stuart. Business the Jack Welch Way: Ten Secrets of the World's Greatest Turnaround King. LC 98-50489. (Business Way Ser.). 137p. 1999. pap. 14.95 (*0-8144-7033-5*) AMACOM.

— Business the Rupert Murdoch Way: Ten Secrets of the World's Greatest Deal Maker. LC 98-50488. (Business Way Ser.). 160p. 1999. pap. 14.95 (*0-8144-7034-3*) AMACOM.

— The Financial Times Handbook of Management. 1000p. 1995. 75.00 (*0-273-60694-8*) F T P-H.

— Key Management Ideas. 3rd ed. (Illus.). 320p. 1999. pap. 21.99 (*0-273-63808-4*) Pitman Pbg.

***Crainer, Stuart.** Key Management Ideas: Thinkers That Changed the Management World. 3rd ed. 320p. 1998. 24.99 (*0-273-64114-X*, Pub. by F T P H) Trans-Atl Phila.

— The Management Century: A Critical Review of 20th Century Thought & Practice. LC 99-56006. (Strategy & Business Book Ser.: No. 5). 304p. 2000. 28.00 (*0-7879-5224-9*, Pfffr & Co) Jossey-Bass.

— The 75 Greatest Management Decisions Ever Made ... & 21 of the Worst. LC 99-30611. 256p. 1999. 24.95 (*0-8144-0491-X*) AMACOM.

Crainer, Stuart. The Ultimate Book of Business Gurus: 100 Thinkers Who Have Really Made a Difference. LC 98-7432. 288p. 1998. 35.95 (*0-8144-0448-0*) AMACOM.

— The Ultimate Book of Business Quotations. LC 97-53258. 358p. 1998. 35.95 (*0-8144-0447-2*) AMACOM.

— The Ultimate Business Library: 50 Books That Shaped Management Thinking. LC 97-20779. 352p. 1997. 35.95 (*0-8144-0395-6*) AMACOM.

***Crainer, Stuart, ed.** Financial Times Handbook of Management: Concise Edition. rev. ed. (Illus.). 974p. 1999. pap. 59.50 (*0-273-63943-9*, Pub. by Pitman Pbg) Trans-Atl Phila.

Crainer, Stuart & Dearlove, Des. Gravy Training: Inside the Shadowy World of Business Schools. 288p. 1998. 24.95 (*1-900961-68-7*) Capstone Pub NH.

Crainer, Stuart & Dearlove, Des. Gravy Training: Inside the Business of Business Schools. LC 99-6683. 352p. 1999. 25.00 (*0-7879-4931-0*) Jossey-Bass.

Crainic, Teodor G. & Laporte, Gilbert. Fleet Management & Logistics. LC 98-6780. (Center for Research on Transportation 25th Anniversary Series, 1971-1996). (FRE.). 1998. 115.00 (*0-7923-8161-0*) Kluwer Academic.

***Crainshaw, Jill Y.** Wise & Discerning Hearts: An Introduction to a Wisdom Liturgical Theology. LC 99-54882. 296p. 2000. pap. 32.95 (*0-8146-6182-3*) Liturgical Pr.

Crais, Clifton, jt. ed. see Worden, Nigel.

Crais, Clifton C. White Supremacy & Black Resistance in Pre-Industrial South Africa: The Making of the Colonial Order in the Eastern Cape, 1770-1865. (African Studies: No. 72). (Illus.). 302p. (C). 1992. text 85.00 (*0-521-40479-7*) Cambridge U Pr.

***Crais, Robert.** Demolition Angel. LC 00-29054. 384p. 2000. 24.95 (*0-385-49584-6*) Doubleday.

— The Devil's Cantina. LC 98-33499. 288p. 1999. 22.45 (*0-7868-6355-2*, Pub. by Hyperion) Little.

Crais, Robert. Free Fall. LC 93-18361. 304p. 1994. mass mkt. 6.50 (*0-553-56509-5*) Bantam.

***Crais, Robert.** Indigo Slam. 2001. mass mkt. 6.99 (*0-345-43564-8*) Ballantine Pub Grp.

— Indigo Slam. LC 97-966. 304p. 1997. 22.45 (*0-7868-6261-0*, Pub. by Hyperion) Time Warner.

Crais, Robert. Indigo Slam. 384p. 1999. mass mkt. 5.99 (*0-7868-8929-2*) Hyperion.

***Crais, Robert.** L. A. Requiem. LC 99-91176. 391p. 2000. mass mkt. 6.99 (*0-345-43447-1*) Ballantine Pub Grp.

Crais, Robert. L. A. Requiem. LC 98-52921. 400p. 1999. 23.95 (*0-385-49583-8*) Broadway BDD.

***Crais, Robert.** L. A. Requiem. large type ed. LC 00-39858. 2000. write for info. (*1-56895-881-1*) Wheeler Pub.

Crais, Robert. Lullaby Town. 352p. 1993. mass mkt. 6.50 (*0-553-29951-4*) Bantam.

— The Monkey's Raincoat. 201p. 1992. reprint ed. mass mkt. 6.50 (*0-553-27585-2*) Bantam.

— Stalking the Angel. LC 89-6805. 288p. 1992. mass mkt. 6.50 (*0-553-28644-7*) Bantam.

— Sunset Express. (Elvis Cole Ser.). 288p. 1996. 21.95 (*0-7868-6096-0*, Pub. by Hyperion) Time Warner.

— Sunset Express. 416p. 1997. mass mkt. 5.99 (*0-7868-8915-2*, Pub. by Hyperion) Time Warner.

— Voodoo River. 304p. 1995. 21.95 (*0-7868-6076-6*, Pub. by Hyperion) Time Warner.

— Voodoo River. LC 94-32389. (Elvis Cole Ser.). 416p. 1996. mass mkt. 5.99 (*0-7868-8905-5*, Pub. by Hyperion) Time Warner.

Craissata, Jackie. Child Sexual Abusers: A Community Treatment Approach. LC 99-171027. 152p. 1999. 29.95 (*0-86377-734-1*) Taylor & Francis.

***Craissati, Jackie.** Child Sexual Abusers: A Community Treatment Approach. 1999. pap. 24.95 (*0-86377-735-X*) Psychol Pr.

Crakanthorp, Richard. Defensio Ecclesiae Anglicanae. LC 72-1027. (Library of Anglo-Catholic Theology: No. 6). reprint ed. 65.00 (*0-404-52087-1*) AMS Pr.

***Craker, Lorilee.** A Is for Adam: Biblical Bible Names. 160p. 2000. pap. 7.95 (*1-57856-324-0*) Waterbrook Pr.

Craker, Lyle E. & Dinda, Kara M. Exercises in Herb Science. (Illus.). 120p. (C). 1997. spiral bd., lab manual ed. write for info. (*0-9629868-2-8*) HSMP Pr.

Craker, Lyle E. & Simon, James E., eds. Herbs, Spices, & Medicinal Plants: Recent Advances in Botany, Horticulture, & Pharmacology. 242p. 1995. 95.00 (*1-56022-857-1*) Haworth Jrnl Co-Edits.

— Herbs, Spices & Medicinal Plants: Recent Advances in Botany, Horticulture & Pharmacology, Vol. 1. LC 85-11551. (Illus.). 368p. 1986. lib. bdg. write for info. (*0-89774-143-9*) Haworth Pr.

— Herbs, Spices, & Medicinal Plants: Recent Advances in Botany, Horticulture, & Pharmacology, Vol. 1. 345p. 1992. 95.00 (*1-56022-043-0*) Haworth Jrnl Co-Edits.

— Herbs, Spices & Medicinal Plants: Recent Advances in Botany, Horticulture, & Pharmacology, Vol. 2. (Illus.). 272p. 1987. write for info. (*0-89774-332-6*) Haworth Pr.

— Herbs, Spices, & Medicinal Plants: Recent Advances in Botany, Horticulture, & Pharmacology, Vol. 2. 255p. 1991. 95.00 (*1-56022-018-X*) Haworth Jrnl Co-Edits.

Craker, Lyle E., jt. auth. see Halva, Seija.

Craker, Lyle E., jt. auth. see Morris, Karen S.

Cralle, Harry. Agronomy: From World Hunger to Biotechnology. 1991. spiral bd. 34.70 (*0-88252-130-6*) Paladin Hse.

— Agronomy: Science & Technology of Crop Growth, Breeding & Production. 1986. spiral bd. 37.00 (*0-88252-128-4*) Paladin Hse.

***Cralle, Trevor.** The Surfin'ary: A Dictionary of Surfing Terms & Surf Speak. rev. ed. (Illus.). 256p. 2000. pap. 19.95 (*1-58008-193-2*) Ten Speed Pr.

Cralle, Trevor, ed. Flinging Monkeys at the Coconuts: A Traveler's Companion of Quotations. LC 93-8992. (Illus.). 160p. 1993. pap. 9.95 (*0-89815-575-4*) Ten Speed Pr.

Cralley, Lester V., et al, eds. Health & Safety Beyond the Workplace. 336p. 1990. 325.00 (*0-471-50452-1*) Wiley.

— In-Plant Practices for Job Related Health Hazards Control, 2 vols., Set. 1510p. 1989. 375.00 (*0-471-51097-1*) Wiley.

— In-Plant Practices for Job Related Health Hazards Control, Vol. 1, Production Processes. LC 88-17200. 938p. 1989. 215.00 (*0-471-61975-2*) Wiley.

— In-Plant Practices for Job Related Health Hazards Control: Engineering Aspects, Vol. 2, Engineering Aspects. LC 88-17200. 578p. 1989. 215.00 (*0-471-50121-2*) Wiley.

Cralley, Lester V., ed. see Cralley, Lewis J.

Cralley, Lewis J. Industrial Hygiene Aspects of Plant Operations: Engineering Considerations in Equipment Selection, Layout, & Building Design, II. Cralley, Lester V., ed. 552p. (C). 1986. text 77.50 (*0-471-62492-6*) Krieger.

— Industrial Hygiene Aspects of Plant Operations: Engineering Considerations in Equipment Selection, Layout, & Building Design, III. Cralley, Lester V., ed. 800p. (C). 1985. 89.50 (*0-02-949370-6*) Free Pr.

Cralley, Lewis J., et al, eds. Patty's Industrial Hygiene & Toxicology, Vol. 3, 2 Pt. Set. 3rd ed. 1649p. 1995. 435.00 (*0-471-58677-3*) Wiley.

— Patty's Industrial Hygiene & Toxicology: Theory & Rationale of Industrial Hygiene Practice, Vol. 3, Pt. B, Theory and Rationale of Industrial. 3rd ed. LC 93-23747. 784p. 1995. 249.00 (*0-471-53065-4*) Wiley.

— Patty's Industrial Hygiene & Toxicology: Theory & Rationale of Industrial Hygiene Practice-Biological Responses, Vol. 3. 3rd ed. 864p. 1994. 225.00 (*0-471-53066-2*, Pub. by Interscience) Wiley.

Cram, Bob. Ms Office 2000 Ill Projects. (C). 1999. pap. text 19.95 (*0-7600-6159-9*) Course Tech.

***Cram, Carol M.** Adobe Pagemaker 6.5. (C). 1998. pap. 24.95 (*0-7600-5844-X*) Course Tech.

Cram, Carol M. Applying Harvard Graphics. LC 94-164378. (C). 1993. pap. 32.36 (*0-395-66220-6*) HM.

— Applying Harvard Graphics. (C). 1994. pap., teacher ed. 5.96 (*0-395-66221-4*) HM.

— Applying Lotus 1-2-3 for Windows, Release 5: A Project Approach. (C). 1995. text, teacher ed. 11.96 (*0-395-73634-X*) HM.

— Applying Microsoft Excel 5.0 for Windows: A Project Approach. (C). 1995. text, teacher ed. 4.47 (*0-395-73637-4*) HM.

— Applying Microsoft Word 6.0 for Windows: A Project Approach. 529p. (C). 1994. spiral bd. 35.16 (*0-395-71769-8*) HM.

— Applying Microsoft Word 6.0 for Windows: A Project Approach. (C). 1995. text, teacher ed. 11.96 (*0-395-72115-6*) HM.

— Applying WordPerfect 6.0: A Project Approach. (C). 1994. spiral bd. 35.96 incl. 3.5 hd (*0-395-69264-4*) HM.

— Applying WordPerfect 6.0 for Windows: A Project Approach. 563p. (C). 1995. spiral bd. 33.96 (*0-395-70685-8*) HM.

— Corel WordPerfect 7 for Windows 95: Illustrated Projects. 10th ed. (Illustrated Ser.). (Illus.). 160p. (C). 1997. pap. 19.95 (*0-7600-5196-8*) Course Tech.

— CRAM APPLY EXCEL 5.0 WIND W/IB. 416p. (C). 1995. spiral bd. 35.16 (*0-395-73635-8*) HM.

— CRAM APPLY LOTUS 5.0 WIND W/IB. 448p. (C). 1995. spiral bd. 35.16 (*0-395-73632-3*) HM.

— CRAM WORDPERF 6.0DOS W/IBM5" (C). 1994. spiral bd. 35.96 incl. 5.25 hd (*0-395-69263-6*) HM.

— Excel 2000 Expert. (C). 1999. pap. 20.00 (*0-619-00104-6*) Course Tech.

— Excel 5.0 for Windows. LC 96-130249. (C). 1995. pap. text 31.16 (*0-395-73636-6*) HM.

— Microsoft Excel 5/7 for Windows 95: Illustrated Projects. 10th ed. (Illustrated Ser.). (Illus.). 160p. (C). 1997. pap. 19.95 (*0-7600-4661-6*) Course Tech.

— Microsoft Excel 97: Illustrated Projects. (Illustrated Ser.). (Illus.). (C). 1997. pap., teacher ed. 18.50 (*0-7600-5126-7*) Course Tech.

— Microsoft Excel 97: Illustrated Projects. 10th ed. (Illustrated Ser.). (Illus.). 160p. (C). 1997. pap. 19.95 (*0-7600-5125-9*) Course Tech.

— Microsoft Office for Windows 95: Professional Edition - Illustrated Projects. 10th ed. (Illustrated Ser.). (Illus.). 192p. (C). 1996. pap. 19.95 (*0-7600-4675-1*) Course Tech.

— Microsoft Office 97: Illustrated Projects. 10th ed. (Illustrated Ser.). (Illus.). 184p. (C). 1997. pap. 19.95 (*0-7600-5133-X*) Course Tech.

— Microsoft Word 97: Illustrated Projects. 10th ed. (Illustrated Ser.). (Illus.). 160p. (C). 1997. pap. 19.95 (*0-7600-5123-2*) Course Tech.

— Microsoft Word 7 for Windows 95: Illustrated Projects. 10th ed. (Illustrated Ser.). (Illus.). 160p. (C). 1996. pap. 19.95 (*0-7600-4678-6*) Course Tech.

***Cram, Carol M.** MOUS Word 2000 Exam Prep. (Exam Prep Ser.). 2000. pap. text 29.99 (*1-57610-481-8*) Coriolis Grp.

Cram, Carol M. Powerpoint 2000 Expert. (C). 1999. 15.00 (*0-619-00124-0*) Course Tech.

— WordPerfect for Windows. (C). 1995. pap., teacher ed. 11.96 (*0-395-69266-0*) HM.

— WordPerfect 6.0 for DOS. (C). 1994. pap., teacher ed. 4.76 (*0-395-69265-2*) HM.

— The World Wide Web: Illustrated Projects. 10th ed. (Illustrated Ser.). (Illus.). 160p. (C). 1997. pap. 19.95 (*0-7600-5127-5*) Course Tech.

***Cram, Carol M. & Hirsch.** Microsoft Publisher 97 Illustrated Project. (C). 1998. pap. 23.95 (*0-7600-5843-1*) Thomson Learn.

Cram, Carol M. & Hirschl, Meta Chaya. Creating Web Sites. (C). 1997. pap. 19.95 (*0-7600-5802-4*) Course Tech.

Cram, Carol M., et al. Microsoft Word 2000: Certified Course CBT. 26.95 (*0-619-00112-7*, Pub. by Course Tech) Thomson Learn.

***Cram, David, et al, eds.** History of Linguistics 1996 Vol. 2: From Classical to Contemporary Linguistics: Selected Papers from the 7th International Conference on the History of the Language Sciences, Oxford, 12-17 September, 1996. LC 99-55069. (Studies in the History of the Language Sciences: Vol. 95). x, 390p. 1999. 95.00 (*1-55619-214-2*, JB3395) J Benjamins Pubng.

— History of Linguistics 1996: Traditions in Linguistics Worldwide: Selected Papers from the 7th International Conference on the History of the Language Sciences, Oxford, 12-17 September, 1996, Vol. 1. LC 99-55069. (Studies in the History of the Language Sciences: Vol. 94). xx, 341p. 1999. 90.00 (*1-55619-213-4*, JB3394) J Benjamins Pubng.

Cram, David, jt. ed. see Reed, T. J.

***Cram, David L.** Coping with Psoriasis: A Patient's Guide to Treatment. 152p. 2000. pap. 14.95 (*1-886039-47-X*, Pub. by Addicus Bks) LPC Group.

Cram, David L. The Healing Touch: Keeping the Doctor-Patient Relationship Alive under Managed Care. Colvin, Rod, ed. LC 97-17574. 127p. (Orig.). 1997. pap. 9.95 (*1-886039-31-3*) Addicus Bks.

— Understanding Parkinson's Disease: A Self-Help Guide. LC 99-17981. (Illus.). 184p. 1999. pap. 14.95 (*1-886039-40-2*) Addicus Bks.

Cram, Donald J. From Discovery to Design in Organic Chemistry. (Illus.). 146p. 1990. text 36.00 (*0-8412-1768-8*, Pub. by Am Chemical) OUP.

Cram, Donald J. & Cram, Jane M., eds. Container Molecules & Their Guests: Monographs in Supramolecular Chemistry. (Monographs in Supramolecular Chemistry). 223p. 1994. 100.00 (*0-85186-972-6*, R6972) CRC Pr.

Cram, Donald J., jt. auth. see Cram, Jane M.

Cram, Henry, jt. auth. see Germinario, Vito.

***Cram, Henry G.** Leading & Learning in Schools: Brain-Based Practices. LC 99-57352. 216p. 2000. pap. 29.95 (*0-8108-3755-2*) Scarecrow.

Cram, Ire H., ed. Future Petroleum Provinces of the United States: Their Geology & Potential, 2 vols., Vol. 1. LC 73-165867. (American Association of Petroleum Geologists. Memoir Ser.: No. 15). 811p. reprint ed. pap. 200.00 (*0-608-11133-3*, 205002400057) Bks Demand.

— Future Petroleum Provinces of the United States: Their Geology & Potential, 2 vols., Vol. 2. LC 73-165867. (American Association of Petroleum Geologists. Memoir Ser.: No. 15). 701p. reprint ed. pap. 200.00 (*0-608-11134-1*, 205002400058) Bks Demand.

Cram, J. S. Water: Canadian Needs & Resources. 3rd ed. LC 74-171154. (Environment Ser.). 220p. reprint ed. pap. 68.20 (*0-608-13581-X*, 202229000026) Bks Demand.

Cram, Jane M. & Cram, Donald J. Essence of Organic Chemistry. LC 77-73957. (Chemistry Ser.). 1978. text. write for info. (*0-201-01031-3*); student ed. write for info. (*0-201-01032-1*) Addison-Wesley.

Cram, Jane M., jt. ed. see Cram, Donald J.

Cram, Jeffrey R., ed. Clinical Emg for Surface Recordings, Vol. 2. 408p. (C). 1990. text 50.00 (*1-878701-00-2*) Clinical Resc.

Cram, Jeffrey R. & Kasman, Glenn S. Introduction to Surface Electromyography. LC 97-21523. 560p. 1997. 55.00 (*0-8342-0751-6*, 20751) Aspen Pub.

Cram, L. E. & Millar, D. D. Living with the Environment. (Illus.). 210p. 1991. pap. text 22.00 (*0-08-041574-1*) Elsevier.

***Cram, Laura.** Developments in The European Union. LC 99-22005. 1999. text 55.00 (*0-312-22532-6*) St Martin.

Cram, Laura. Policy Making in the European Union: Conceptual Lenses & the Integration Process. LC 98-108264. (European Public Policy Ser.). 200p. (C). 1997. pap. 27.99 (*0-415-14626-7*) Routledge.

— Policy Making in the European Union: Conceptual Lenses & the Integration Process. 2nd ed. LC 98-108264. (European Public Policy Ser.). 200p. (C). 1997. 90.00 (*0-415-14625-9*) Routledge.

Cram, Laura, et al. Developments in the European Union LC 99-22005. 1999. pap. 21.95 (*0-312-22533-4*) St Martin.

Cram, Lillian. Left-Handed. Lane, Barry, ed. (Opening Doors Ser.: No. 1). (Illus.). 32p. (Orig.). 1989. pap. 4.00 (*1-877829-06-4*) Homegrown Bks.

Cram, Mary F. Chautauqua Salute: A Memoir of the Bestor Years. 160p. (Orig.). 1990. pap. 9.95 (*0-941149-01-3*) Chautauqua Inst.

Cram, Micheal A. The Cram Sourcebook, Vol. 2. 524p. (Orig.). 1996. pap. 69.00 (*0-7884-0459-8*, C606) Heritage Bk.

— The Cram Sourcebook, Vol. 3. 216p. (Orig.). 1996. pap. 34.00 (*0-7884-0458-X*, C605); pap. 27.00 (*0-7884-0460-1*, C607) Heritage Bk.

Cram, Mildred. Stranger Things. LC 78-121532. (Short Story Index Reprint Ser.). 1977. 19.95 (*0-8369-3488-1*) Ayer.

Cram, R. A. The Cathedral of Palma de Mallorca, Vol. 14. 1932. 40.00 (*0-527-01687-X*) Periodicals Srv.

Cram, Ralph A. Black Spirits & White: A Book of Ghost Stories. LC 70-167445. (Short Story Index Reprint Ser.). 1977. reprint ed. 17.95 (*0-8369-3971-9*) Ayer.

— The Catholic Church & Art. 1972. 59.95 (*0-87968-817-3*) Gordon Pr.

— Convictions & Controversies. LC 74-121460. (Essay Index Reprint Ser.). 1977. 21.95 (*0-8369-1704-9*) Ayer.

— Ministry of Art. LC 67-30203. (Essay Index Reprint Ser.). 1977. 19.95 (*0-8369-0347-1*) Ayer.

— Walled Towns. 1973. 59.95 (*0-8490-1271-6*) Gordon Pr.

— Walled Towns. LC 19-18459. 107p. 1987. reprint ed. pap. 10.00 (*0-942153-15-4*) Entropy Conserv.

Cram, Ralph A., et al. Six Lectures on Architecture. LC 68-57314. (Essay Index Reprint Ser.). 1977. 18.95 (*0-8369-0348-X*) Ayer.

Cram, Ronald H., ed. Understanding Trends in Protestant Education in the Twentieth Century. LC 97-44739. 244p. (C). 1998. 52.00 (*0-7618-0987-2*); pap. 32.50 (*0-7618-0988-0*) U Pr of Amer.

Cram, Roy. Gamesmen of Kasar. (Illus.). 1982. 5.95 (*0-940244-17-9*) Flying Buffalo.

— Wilderness Encounters, Bk. 1. Stackpole, Michael A., ed. (Illus.). 74p. 1991. pap. 9.95 (*0-940244-85-3*) Flying Buffalo.

Cram, Thomas J. Topographical Memoir. 126p. 1978. 18.95 (*0-87770-193-8*) Ye Galleon.

C

Cram, W. J., et al. Sulphur Metabolism in Higher Plants: Molecular, Ecophysiological & Nutritional Aspects. (Illus.). 367p. 1997. 98.00 (*90-73348-13-7*, Pub. by Backhuys Pubs) Balogh.

Crama, Yves, et al. Production Planning in Automated Manufacturing. LC 94-11600. (Lecture Notes in Economics & Mathematical Systems Ser.: Vol. 414). 1994. 49.95 (*0-387-58082-4*) Spr-Verlag.

— Production Planning in Automated Manufacturing. 2nd ed. LC 96-28430. 239p. 1996. 84.95 (*3-540-61359-5*) Spr-Verlag.

Cramb, Auslan. Who Owns Scotland Now? The Use & Abuse of Private Land. LC 97-186651. (Illus.). 208p. 1996. pap. 22.95 (*1-85158-964-3*, Pub. by Mainstream Pubng) Trafalgar.

Cramb, Ian. Art of the Stonemason. (Illus.). 176p. 1992. pap. 17.99 (*1-55870-225-3*, Betrwy Bks) F & W Pubns Inc.

Crambari, I., intro. Technology Transfer to Developing Nations. (Illus.). 198p. (C). 1995. pap. text. write for info. (*1-885778-04-X*) Seaburn.

Cramberg, JoAnne, jt. auth. see Trowbridge, Helen.

Cramberg, JoAnne, ed. see Bristen, Darryl.

Cramberg, JoAnne, ed. see Filkey, Mark S.

Cramberg, JoAnne, ed. see Fruga, Alvin D.

Cramberg, JoAnne, ed. see Kayatin, Louis F.

Cramberg, JoAnne, ed. see Trowbridge, Helen.

Crame, Jim. Buick Technical Tips. 325p. 1993. 19.95 (*0-9636866-0-7*) W MI Buick.

Crame, Kathleen T. Pennsauken. LC 97-191401. (Images of America Ser.). 1997. pap. 16.99 (*0-7524-0550-0*) Arcadia Publng.

Cramer. Prentice Hall Federal Taxation 2000: Comprhn. 1456p. (C). 1999. pap. text 90.00 (*0-13-020357-2*) P-H.

Cramer, jt. auth. see Bulow.

Cramer & Hurst. How to Find a Teaching Job. 96p. 1999. pap. 15.93 (*0-13-013605-0*) S&S Trade.

Cramer-Azima, Fern J. & Grizenko, Natalie, eds. Immigrant & Refugee Children & Their Families: Clinical, Research & Training Issues. 300p. 2000. write for info. (*0-8236-2535-4*) Intl Univs Pr.

Cramer, B. C., jt. auth. see Parfrey, P. S.

Cramer, Bertrand G. The Scripts Parents Write & the Roles Babies Play: The Importance of Being Baby. Gill, Gillian, tr. from FRE. LC 97-35914. 216p. 1997. pap. 30.00 (*0-7657-0136-7*) Aronson.

Cramer, Betty, jt. auth. see Blackford, Barbara J.

Cramer, Cahroul. Twisted. LC 97-42995. 196p. 1998. pap. 9.95 (*1-881164-82-9*) Intercont VA.

Cramer, Cathleen. The Legend of the Eagle Clan. 281p. (Orig.). 1995. pap. 12.95 (*0-929385-68-3*) Light Tech Pubng.

Cramer, Christopher J. & Truhlar, Donald G., eds. Structure & Reactivity in Aqueous Solution: Characterization of Chemical & Biological Systems. LC 94-29430. (Symposium Ser.: No. 568). (Illus.). 448p. 1994. text 110.00 (*0-8412-2980-5*, Pub. by Am Chemical) OUP.

Cramer, Clayton E. Black Demographic Data, 1790-1860: A Sourcebook. LC 96-38833. 176p. 1997. lib. bdg. 59.95 (*0-313-30243-X*, Greenwood Pr) Greenwood.

Cramer, Clayton E. Concealed Weapon Laws of the Early Republic: Dueling, Southern Violence & Moral Reform. LC 99-18014. 192p. 1999. 55.00 (*0-275-96615-1*, Praeger Pubs) Greenwood.

— For the Defense of Themselves & the State: The Original Intent Judicial Interpretation of the Right to Keep & Bear Arms. LC 94-13728. 304p. 1994. 55.00 (*0-275-94913-3*, Praeger Pubs) Greenwood.

Cramer, Clayton E., intro. By the Dim & Flaring Lamps: The Civil War Diaries of Samuel McIlvaine. LC 89-12579. (Illus.). 157p. 1990. 28.95 (*0-912526-46-7*) Lib Res.

Cramer, Clayton E. & Kopel, David B. Shall Issue: The New Wave of Concealed Handgun Permit Laws. 38p. 1993. pap. text 8.00 (*1-57655-105-9*) Independ Inst.

Cramer, Colleen. Gifts on a Shoestring. 1996. pap. 10.95 (*0-9632481-3-8*) Shoestring.

Cramer, Colleen S. Romance on a Shoestring: Cheap Dates in & Around Seattle & Puget Sound from Bellingham to Tacoma. 2nd ed. Fry, Ted, ed. LC 92-61650. 176p. 1995. pap. 9.95 (*0-9632481-2-X*) Shoestring.

Cramer, D. L. Craniofacial Morphology of Pan Paniscus. Szalay, F. S., ed. (Contributions to Primatology Ser.: Vol. 10). (Illus.). 1977. 41.75 (*3-8055-2391-2*) S Karger.

Cramer, Daniel. Octoginta Emblemata Moralia Nova e Sacris Literis Petita, Formandis Ad Veram Pietatem Accomodata Et Elegantibus Picturis. (GER.). xxxii, 317p. 1981. reprint ed. 80.00 (*3-487-05356-X*) G Olms Pubs.

— The Rosicrucian Emblems of Daniel Cramer. Tait, Fiona, tr. from LAT. LC 90-47420. (Magnum Opus Hermetic Sourceworks Ser.: No. 4). (Illus.). 80p. (Orig.). 1991. 27.00 (*0-933999-87-9*); pap. 15.00 (*0-933999-88-7*) Phanes Pr.

Cramer, Denise, ed. see Eastman, Mark & Missler, Chuck.

Cramer, Dennis. Mara: Celtic Shamaness, Vol. 2. 36. pap. 19.95 (*1-56097-294-7*, Pub. by Fantagraph Bks) Seven Hills Bk.

Cramer, Dennis. Mara of the Celts. (Eros Graphic Novel Ser.: No. 17). 136p. 1995. pap. 16.95 (*1-56097-215-7*) Fantagraph Bks.

Cramer, Diane L. How to Give an Astrological Health Reading. LC 88-70458. 122p. 1986. 14.95 (*0-86690-332-1*, C2803-014) Am Fed Astrologers.

Cramer, Don. Collector's Encyclopedia of Toys & Banks. 208p. 1978. pap. 16.95 (*0-89145-256-7*) L-W Inc.

Cramer, Donnie. No Need to Panic. (Illus.). 170p. (Orig.). 1995. pap. 9.95 (*0-938711-27-X*) Tecolote Pubns.

Cramer, Duncan. Basic Statistics for Social Research: Step-by-Step Calculations & Computer Techniques Using Minitab. 424p. (C). 1997. pap. 29.99 (*0-415-12005-5*) Routledge.

— Basic Statistics for Social Research: Step-by-Step Calculations & Computer Techniques Using Minitab. (Illus.). 424p. (C). 1997. 90.00 (*0-415-12004-7*) Routledge.

— Close Relationships: The Study of Love & Friendship. LC 98-13915. (Arnold Publication). (Illus.). 224p. 1998. text 75.00 (*0-340-62533-3*); pap. text 24.95 (*0-340-62534-1*) OUP.

— Fundamental Statistics for Social Research: Step-by-Step Calculations & Computer Techniques Using SPSS for Windows. LC 97-12951. (Illus.). 480p. (C). 1998. 100.00 (*0-415-17203-9*); pap. 32.99 (*0-415-17204-7*) Routledge.

— Introducing Statistics for Social Research: Step-by-Step Calculations & Computer Techniques using SPSS. LC 93-4071. 336p. (C). 1994. text 69.95 (*0-415-07514-9*) Routledge.

Cramer, Duncan, jt. auth. see Bryman, Alan.

Cramer, Duncan, jt. auth. see Howitt, Dennis.

Cramer, E. Victoria Officim Hebdomadae Sanctae, Two Vol. 31/2, Pt. 1: Maunday Thursday. (Wissenschaftliche Abhandlungen - Musicological Studies). 1996. 4.00 (*0-931902-05-3*) Inst Mediaeval Mus.

— Victoria Officium Hebdomadae Sanctae Pt. 1: Introduction. 1979. lib. bdg. 40.00 (*0-931902-04-5*) Inst Mediaeval Mus.

— Victoria Officium Hebdomadae Sanctae Vol. III, Pt. 2: Good Friday. 1979. lib. bdg. 40.00 (*0-931902-06-1*) Inst Mediaeval Mus.

— Victoria Officium Hebdomadae Sanctae Vol. IV, Pt. 4: Holy Saturday. 1979. lib. bdg. 40.00 (*0-931902-07-X*) Inst Mediaeval Mus.

Cramer, Earl H., jt. auth. see Doane, Doris C.

Cramer, Esther, jt. ed. see Milkovich, Barbara A.

Cramer, Esther R. Brea: The City of Oil, Oranges, & Opportunity. 384p. 1992. 32.27 (*0-9632638-0-3*); boxed set 112.60 (*0-9632638-1-1*) City Brea.

Cramer, Eugene C. Tomas Luis de Victoria: A Guide to Research. Marco, Guy A., ed. LC 97-44502. (Composer Resource Manuals: Vol. 43). (Illus.). 403p. 1998. 76.00 (*0-8153-2096-5*, H1931) Garland.

Cramer, Eugene H. & Castle, Marrietta, eds. Fostering the Love of Reading: The Affective Domain in Reading Education. 288p. 1994. pap. 22.95 (*0-87207-125-1*) Intl Reading.

Cramer, F. Chaos & Order: The Complex Structure of Living Systems. Loewus, D. I., tr. LC 93-32939. 249p. 1993. 64.95 (*3-527-29067-2*, Wiley-VCH) Wiley.

Cramer, F. H., jt. auth. see Eisenack, A.

Cramer, Frederick, jt. auth. see Donaldson, Ivan.

Cramer, Frederick H. Astrology in Roman Law & Politics. 1996. 35.00 (*0-89005-560-2*) Ares.

— Astrology in Roman Law & Politics. LC 54-6119. (American Philosophical Society, Philadelphia. Memoirs Ser.: Vol. 37). 303p. reprint ed. pap. 94.00 (*0-8357-5821-4*, 200035200025) Bks Demand.

Cramer, Frederick S., jt. ed. see Li, Wen-Ren.

Cramer, Frederick S., jt. ed. see Unsworth, Ian P.

***Cramer, Gail L., et al.** Agricultural Economics & Agribusiness. 576p. (C). 2000. write for info. (*0-471-38847-5*) Wiley.

Cramer, Gail L., et al. Agricultural Economics & Agribusiness. 7th ed. LC 96-29529. 576p. 1997. text 95.95 (*0-471-17376-2*) Wiley.

Cramer, Gerald. Chagall's Monotypes, 1966-1975. (FRE.). 104p. 1976. 175.00 (*1-55660-114-X*) A Wofsy Fine Arts.

Cramer, Gerald & Cramer, Patrick. Henry Moore: Complete Graphic Work, 4 vols., Set. (Illus.). 1986. 1500.00 (*1-55660-066-6*) A Wofsy Fine Arts.

Cramer, Gregory D. & Darby, Susan A. Spinal Anatomy. (Illus.). 448p. (C). (gr. 13). 1995. text 99.95 (*0-8016-6467-5*, 06467) Mosby Inc.

Cramer, H. Mathematical Methods of Statistics. (Mathematical Ser.: Vol. 9). 592p. 1946. text 89.50 (*0-691-08004-6*, Pub. by Princeton U Pr) Cal Prin Full Svc.

Cramer, Harald. Harald Cramer: Selected Works. Martin-Lof, Anders, ed. 1410p. 1993. write for info. (*3-540-56671-6*) Spr-Verlag.

***Cramer, Harald.** Mathematical Methods of Statistics. LC 99-12516. 1999. pap. text 24.95 (*0-691-00547-8*, Pub. by Princeton U Pr) Cal Prin Full Svc.

Cramer, Harold. Elements of Probability Theory & Some of Its Applications. 2nd ed. LC 73-90331. 282p. 1974. reprint ed. pap. text 22.50 (*0-88275-144-1*) Krieger.

***Cramer, Harriet L.** A Garden in the Shade. LC 99-54626. (Illus.). 144p. 2000. 20.00 (*1-56799-963-8*, Friedman-Fairfax) M Friedman Pub Grp Inc.

Cramer, Harriet L. Great Gardens in the Shade. LC 97-13043. 1997. write for info. (*1-56799-534-9*) M Friedman Pub Grp Inc.

Cramer, Hinrich & Schultz, Joachim, eds. Cyclic 3', 5'-Nucleotides: Mechanisms of Action. fac. ed. LC 76-45361. (Illus.). 568p. pap. 176.10 (*0-7837-7360-9*, 204716900005) Bks Demand.

Cramer, J. A. Anecdota Graeca e Codicibus Manuscriptis Bibliothecae Regiae Parisiensis, 4 vols., Set. vi, 1802p. 1967. reprint ed. 400.00 (*0-318-70903-1*) G Olms Pubs.

Cramer, J. A., tr. see Nucius, Nicander.

Cramer, J. B. Fifty Selected Studies for Piano. Von Bulow, Hans, ed. (Carl Fischer Music Library: No. 525). 116p. (J). 1946. pap. 12.00 (*0-8258-0138-9*, L 525) Fischer Inc NY.

Cramer, J. S. The Logit Model: An Introduction for Economists. (Illus.). 120p. 1991. text 39.95 (*0-340-54111-3*, A6423, Pub. by E A) Routldge.

Cramer, James & Johnson, Dean. Window Boxes, Indoors & Out. LC 98-50970. (Illus.). 176p. 1999. 27.50 (*1-57965-124-0*, 85124) Artisan.

Cramer, James A., ed. Courts & Judges. LC 81-5611. (Sage Criminal Justice System Annuals Ser.: No. 15). 280p. reprint ed. pap. 86.80 (*0-8357-4779-4*, 203771600009) Bks Demand.

— Preventing Crime. LC 78-8400. (Sage Criminal Justice System Annuals Ser.: No. 10). 255p. reprint ed. pap. 79.10 (*0-8357-8451-7*, 203471500091) Bks Demand.

Cramer, James Edward, ed. Military Marching: A Pictorial History. 172p. (C). 1992. 110.00 (*0-946771-79-3*, Pub. by Spellmnt Pubs) St Mut.

Cramer, James P. Design Plus Enterprise. 120p. 1994. 19.95 (*1-55835-131-0*) AIA Press.

Cramer, Jeffrey S. Robert Frost among His Poems: A Literary Companion to the Poet's Own Biographical Contexts & Associations. LC 95-39536. 304p. 1995. lib. bdg. 42.50 (*0-7864-0079-X*) McFarland & Co.

Cramer, Joe J., Jr., jt. auth. see Nelson, G. Kenneth.

Cramer, Johann U. Von, see Von Cramer, Johann U.

Cramer, John. Einstein's Bridge. LC 96-3072. 368p. 1997. 23.00 (*0-380-97510-6*, Avon Bks) Morrow Avon.

— Einstein's Bridge M. LC 96-30722. 310p. 1998. mass mkt. 3.99 (*0-380-78831-4*, Avon Bks) Morrow Avon

— Einstein's Bridge T. LC 96-3072. 368p. 1997. pap. 13.00 (*0-380-79279-6*, Avon Bks) Morrow Avon.

— Twistor. 352p. 1991. mass mkt. 5.99 (*0-380-71027-7*, Avon Bks) Morrow Avon.

Cramer, John A., ed. Catenae Graecorum Patrum in Novum Testamentum, 8 vols., Set. lxxviii, 4039p. 1967 reprint ed. 865.00 incl. 3.5 hd (*0-318-70890-6*) G Olms Pubs.

Cramer, John E. No Man's a Mountain. LC 96-76312. 276p. 1996. 19.95 (*1-878044-48-6*) Mayhaven Pub.

Cramer, Joyce. Quality of Life & Pharmacoeconomics in Clinical Trials. 2nd abr. ed. LC 97-37999. 190p. 1997. pap. text 45.00 (*0-397-51845-5*) Lppncott W & W.

Cramer, Joyce A. & Spilker, Bert, eds. Patient Compliance in Medical Practice & Clinical Trials. 432p. 1991. text 83.00 (*0-88167-735-3*) Lppncott W & W.

Cramer, Joyce A., jt. auth. see Spilker, Bert.

Cramer, Kathleen, et al. Rational Number Project: Fraction Lessons for the Middle Grades, Level 1. 228p. (C). 1997. pap. text, spiral bd. 32.95 (*0-7872-3464-8*, 41346401) Kendall-Hunt.

— Rational Number Project: Fraction Lessons for the Middle Grades, Level 2. 230p. (C). 1997. pap. text, spiral bd. 32.95 (*0-7872-3470-2*, 41347001) Kendall-Hunt.

Cramer, Kathryn. Forty Get Set Grow. 1999. pap. 8.95 (*0-14-015442-6*, Viking) Viking Penguin.

— Staying on Top When Your World Turns Upside Down. 1994. 11.00 incl. audio (*0-671-51074-6*) S&S Trade.

Cramer, Kathryn & Hartwell, David G., eds. The Ascent of Wonder: The Evolution of Hard Science Fiction. 992p. 1994. 35.00 (*0-312-85062-X*, Pub. by Tor Bks) St Martin.

Cramer, Kathryn, jt. ed. see Hartwell, David G.

Cramer, Kathryn D. Forty Get Set Grow. 1999. pap. 20.00 (*0-670-83978-7*) Viking Penguin.

— Roads Home: Seven Pathways to Midlife Wisdom. (Illus.). 368p. 1997. reprint ed. pap. 12.00 (*0-688-15122-1*, Quil) HarperTrade.

Cramer, Kathryn D., ed. Walls of Fear. 400p. 199_. mass mkt. 4.99 (*0-380-70789-6*, Avon Bks) Morrow Avon.

Cramer, Kathryn D. & Pautz, Peter D., eds. The Architecture of Fear. 288p. 1989. pap. 3.95 (*0-380-70553-2*, Avon Bks) Morrow Avon.

Cramer, Kathy, jt. auth. see Hein, Peg.

Cramer, Lenox. Slow Dance on the Killing Ground. LC 89-81582. (Illus.). 274p. 1990. 19.95 (*0-939427-57-5*, 14001) Alpha Pubns OH.

— Slow Dance on the Killing Ground. 272p. 1991. pap. 3.95 (*0-380-71445-0*, Avon Bks) Morrow Avon.

— War with Empty Hands: Self-Defense Against Aggression. 2nd ed. (Illus.). 209p. (Orig.). 1991. pap. 16.95 (*0-939427-41-9*, 05017) Alpha Pubns OH.

— War with Empty Hands Suppl. 1: Advanced Training. LC 91-73340. (Shadow Warrior Ser.). (Illus.). 96p. (Orig.). 1991. pap. 10.00 (*0-939427-42-7*, 05055) Alpha Pubns OH.

— War with Empty Hands Suppl. 2: Field Craft. LC 91-73340. (Shadow Warrior Ser.). (Illus.). 82p. 1991. pap. 14.00 (*0-939427-43-5*, 05056) Alpha Pubns OH.

Cramer, Lina. Parent Time Curriculum Guide: A Learning Activities Guide for the PACE Family Literacy Program. 188p. 1991. ring bd. 35.00 (*1-885429-02-9*) Family Resource.

Cramer, Lina, jt. auth. see Ahsan, Nilofer.

Cramer, Lorraine, ed. see Nelson-Erichsen, Jean & Erichsen, Heino R.

Cramer, M. L. Facing Adversity with Faith. 1997. 17.95 (*0-87306-847-5*) Feldheim.

Cramer, Malinda E. The Christ. McCrary, Joan C., ed. LC 89-50609. (Come Unto Me Ser.: Vol. 3). 220p. (Orig.). 1994. pap. (*0-9617598-6-0*) Divine Sci Fed.

Cramer, Malinda E. Divine Science & Healing. 1988. 12.95 (*0-9617598-0-1*) Divine Sci Fed.

Cramer, Malinda E. Job. McCrary, Joan C., ed. LC 89-50609. (Come Unto Me Ser.: Vol. 2). 115p. (Orig.). 1989. pap. (*0-9617598-5-2*) Divine Sci Fed.

— The Light. McCrary, Joan C., ed. LC 89-50609. (Come Unto Me Ser.: Vol. 1). 103p. (Orig.). 1989. pap. (*0-9617598-4-4*) Divine Sci Fed.

***Cramer, Marc.** Imperial Mongolian Cooking: Recipes from the Kingdom of Genghis Khan. 275p. 2000. 24.95 (*0-7818-0827-8*) Hippocrene Bks.

Cramer, Marianne, jt. auth. see Putnam, Karen.

***Cramer, Mark.** Barcelona at Your Door. (Culture Shock! Ser.). 2000. pap. 12.95 (*1-55868-537-5*) Gr Arts Ctr Pub.

Cramer, Mark. Culture Shock! Cuba. LC 98-70217. (Culture Shock! Ser.). 1998. pap. 12.95 (*1-55868-411-5*) Gr Arts Ctr Pub.

— Culture shock! Mexico. LC 97-74477. (Culture Shock). 222 p. 1998. pap. text 12.95 (*1-55868-399-2*) Gr Arts Ctr Pub.

— Culture Shock! Bolivia. LC 96-77213. (Culture Shock Ser.). 1996. pap. 12.95 (*1-55868-298-8*) Gr Arts Ctr Pub.

***Cramer, Mark.** Culture Shock-New York at Your Door: New York at Your Door. 1999. pap. 12.95 (*1-55868-502-2*) Gr Arts Ctr Pub.

Cramer, Mark. Fast Track to Thoroughbred Profits. 184p. 1984. pap. 8.95 (*0-89746-025-1*) Gambling Times.

— Funkytowns U. S. A. The Best Alternative, Eclectic, Irreverent & Visionary Places. LC 95-90413. (Illus.). 180p. (Orig.). 1995. pap. 11.95 (*0-9646815-0-1*) TBS Pub.

***Cramer, Mark.** Havana at Your Door. (Culture Shock! Ser.). (Illus.). 2000. pap. 12.95 (*1-55868-531-6*) Gr Arts Ctr Pub.

Cramer, Mark. The Odds on Your Side: The Logic of Racetrack Investing. 240p. (Orig.). 1987. pap. 24.95 (*0-9614168-4-X*) Cynthia Pub Co.

— Scared Money. LC 94-68302. 134p. 1994. 19.95 (*0-933944-15-2*) City Miner Bks.

— Value Handicapping: The Art of Making Your Own Line & Identifying Overlays. 150p. 1998. per. 25.00 (*0-933944-22-5*) City Miner Bks.

Cramer, Martin R. & Ruden, Sanford I. Survival Guide for Older Americans. LC 94-218332. 188p. pap. text 17.95 (*0-9640843-0-9*) Camco Enter.

Cramer, P. The Development of Defense Mechanisms: Theory, Research & Assessment. 352p. 1990. 105.00 (*0-387-97298-6*) Spr-Verlag.

Cramer, Patricia, jt. auth. see Barrett, Eileen.

Cramer, Patricia, jt. auth. see Bollinger, Theresa.

Cramer, Patricia, jt. ed. see Barrett, Eileen.

Cramer, Patrick. Chagall's Illustrated Books: Catalogue Raisonne. (Illus.). 310p. 1995. 275.00 (*1-55660-144-1*) A Wofsy Fine Arts.

— Meckseper's Etchings, 1956-1990: Catalogue Raisonne. (GER., Illus.). 292p. 1993. 195.00 (*1-55660-156-5*) A Wofsy Fine Arts.

— Miro Lithographs, 1976-1981, Vol. 6. (Illus.). 292p. 1992. 270.00 (*1-55660-190-5*) A Wofsy Fine Arts.

— Miro Lithographs, 1972-1975, Vol. 5. (Illus.). 192p. 1992. 250.00 (*1-55660-189-1*) A Wofsy Fine Arts.

— Miro's Illustrated Books. (Illus.). 680p. 1989. boxed set 395.00 (*1-55660-102-6*) A Wofsy Fine Arts.

Cramer, Patrick, jt. auth. see Cramer, Gerald.

Cramer, Patrick, ed. see Miro, Joan.

***Cramer, Pauline E.** Meet Me in the Garden. 2000. 15.99 (*1-56292-816-3*) Honor Bks OK.

Cramer, Peggy C. Complete Records of St. Matthew's Lutheran Church 1844-1932, McVille, Armstrong Co., PA. 175p. 1991. per. 16.95 (*1-55856-064-5*, 089) Closson Pr.

— Emmanuel Evangelical Lutheran Church Freeport. 152p. 1991. per. 12.95 (*1-55856-062-9*, 058) Closson Pr.

— Index to Marriage Notices, 1843-1899 from the Norristown Herald, Montgomery County, Pa. 1989. pap. text 24.95 (*1-55856-010-6*, 248) Closson Pr.

— Records of Clinton Lutheran Church, South Buffalo Township, Armstrong County, PA. 17p. 1990. per. 5.00 (*1-55856-063-7*, 359) Closson Pr.

Cramer, Peter. Baptism & Change in the Early Middle Ages, c. 200-c. 1150. LC 92-17489. (Cambridge Studies in Medieval Life & Thought: No. 20). 378p. (C). 1993. text 74.95 (*0-521-35163-4*) Cambridge U Pr.

Cramer, Phebe. Storytelling, Narrative & the Thematic Apperception Test. LC 96-5520. (Assessment of Personality & Psychopathology Ser.). 374p. 1996. lib. bdg. 45.00 (*1-57230-094-9*) Guilford Pubns.

Cramer, Phil, jt. auth. see Winer, Ethan.

Cramer, Phillip F. Deep Environmental Politics: The Role of Radical Environmentalism in Crafting American Environmental Policy. LC 97-34749. 256p. 1998. 55.00 (*0-275-96051-X*, Praeger Pubs) Greenwood.

***Cramer, Phillip F.** Rethinking Environmental Protection: A Natural Approach to Nature. 240p. 2000. 60.00 (*0-7391-0115-3*) Lxngtn Bks.

Cramer, Rebecca. Mission to Sonora. 298p. 1998. pap. 10.95 (*1-881542-50-5*) Book World Inc.

— View from Frog Mountain. Date not set. 10.95 (*1-881542-63-7*) Book World Inc.

Cramer, Reid, jt. auth. see Wilson, Robert H.

Cramer, Richard B. What It Takes: The Way to the White House. LC 92-50848. 1051p. 1993. pap. 19.00 (*0-679-74649-8*) Vin Bks.

Cramer, Richard Ben. Joe DiMaggio: The Hero's Life. (Illus.). 480p. 1999. 24.50 (*0-684-85391-4*) Simon & Schuster.

Cramer, Robert. Vergils Weltsicht: Optimismus und Pessimus in Vergils Georgica. 288p. 1998. 113.00 (*3-11-015728-4*) De Gruyter.

Cramer, Ronald L. The Spelling Connection: Integrating Reading, Writing & Spelling Instruction. LC 97-47395. 216p. 1998. pap. text 24.95 (*1-57230-329-8*, C0329); lib. bdg. 42.95 (*1-57230-328-X*, C0328) Guilford Pubns.

Cramer, Rose F. Wayne County, Missouri. (Illus.). 734p. 1972. 11.00 (*0-911208-22-4*) Ramfre.

Cramer, Sharon F. Collaboration. LC 97-4245. 304p. 1997. pap. text 51.00 (*0-205-18511-8*) P-H.

Cramer, Sharon F. Collaboration: A Success Strategy for Special Educators. 144p. (C). 1997. pap. text, teacher ed. write for info. (*0-205-27385-8*, T7385-2) Allyn.

Cramer, Shirley C. & Ellis, William, eds. Learning Disabilities: Lifelong Issues. 352p. (Orig.). 1996. pap. text 36.00 (*1-55766-240-1*, 2401) P H Brookes.

Cramer, Stanley, jt. auth. see Herr, Edwin L.

Cramer, Stanley H, jt. auth. see Herr, Edwin L.

C

An Asterisk (*) at the beginning of an entry indicates that the title is appearing for the first time.

Cramer, Steven. Dialogue for the Left & Right Hand. LC 97-247. 98p. 1997. pap. 13.95 (*1-57129-033-8*) Brookline Bks.
— The Eye That Desires to Look Upward. LC 86-82444. 66p. (Orig.). 1987. 12.95 (*0-913123-10-2*); pap. text 6.95 (*0-913123-11-0*) Galileo.
— The World Book. LC 92-6797. 63p. (Orig.). 1992. pap. 9.95 (*0-914278-59-2*) Copper Beech.
Cramer, Steven A. Conquering Your Own Goliaths. 106p. 1988. pap. 9.95 (*1-55517-122-2*) CFI Dist.
— Great Shall Be Your Joy. 211p. 1992. pap. 12.95 (*1-55517-097-8*) CFI Dist.
***Cramer, Steven A.** In His Image: Finding Courage, Hope & Confidence to Become More Christlike. LC 99-33930. 1999. 17.95 (*1-57734-583-5*, 01114263) Covenant Comms.
— In the Arms of His Love. 1991. 14.95 (*1-57734-662-9*) Covenant Comms.
— Putting on the Armor of God. pap. 14.98 (*1-55517-283-0*) CFI Dist.
Cramer, Steven A. The Worth of a Soul. 127p. 1995. pap. 10.95 (*1-55517-171-0*) CFI Dist.
Cramer, Stuart. The Tom Peters Phenomenon: Corporate Man to Corporate Skunk. 320p. 1998. pap. 15.95 (*1-84112-013-8*) Capstone Pub NH.
Cramer, T. Dudley. The Pecos Ranchers in the Lincoln County War. Bohn, Dave, ed. LC 96-8559. (Illus.). 216p. (Orig.). 1996. 40.00 (*0-9653183-0-3*); pap. 22.95 (*0-9653183-1-1*) Branding Iron.
Cramer, Thomas, tr. see Hartmann Von Aue.
Cramer, Tim. The Life of Other Days. 172p. 1991. pap. 14.95 (*0-9516036-6-3*) Dufour.
Cramer, W. A. & Knaff, D. B. Energy Transduction in Biological Membranes. (Advanced Texts in Chemistry Ser.). (Illus.). 544p. 1989. 108.00 (*0-387-96761-3*) Spr-Verlag.
— Energy Transduction in Biological Membranes. (Advanced Texts in Chemistry Ser.). (Illus.). 592p. 1991. teacher ed. 47.95 (*0-387-97533-0*) Spr-Verlag.
Cramer, William J., Jr. Air Combat with the Mighty 8th: A Teenage Warrior in World War II. (Illus.). 166p. 1993. 19.95 (*0-89015-939-4*) Sunbelt Media.
***Crameri, Kathryn.** Language, the Novelist & National Identity in Post-Franco Catalonia. (Legenda Ser.). 200p. (C). 2000. pap. 49.50 (*1-900755-37-8*, Pub. by E H R C) David Brown.
Crames, Michael J., et al. The Fundamentals of Bankruptcy & Corporate Reorganization. LC 98-21662. 1998. 95.00 (*1-57823-054-3*) Juris Pubng.
Cramez, C. Glossaire de Stratigraphie Sequentielle. (ENG & FRE.). 1990. lib. bdg. 29.95 (*0-8288-3186-6*) Fr & Eur.
— Glossary of Sequence Stratigraphy: English-French. (French Oil & Gas Industry Association Publications). 22p. (C). 1990. pap. 70.00 (*2-7108-0596-0*, Pub. by Edits Technip) Enfield Pubs NH.
Cramm, Dagmar Von, see Von Cramm, Dagmar.
Cramm, Joetta. Historical Ellicott City: A Walking Tour. 2nd rev. ed. LC 96-77542. (Illus.). 104p. 1996. pap. 9.95 (*0-9637161-1-5*) K&D Ltd.
Cramm, R. H. & Sibbach, W. R., eds. Coextrusion Coating & Film Fabrication. (Illus.). 251p. 1983. 37.00 (*0-89852-412-1*, 0101R112) TAPPI.
Crammatte, Alan B. Meeting the Challenge: Hearing-Impaired Professionals in the Workplace. fac. ed. LC 87-118. 258p. 1994. pap. 80.00 (*0-7837-7690-X*, 204744600007) Bks Demand.
Crammer, John L., ed. Asylum History: Buckinghamshire County Pauper Lunatic Asylum - St. John's. 195p. 1990. pap. text 27.50 (*0-902241-34-6*, 4134, Pub. by Royal Coll Psych) Parkwest Pubns.
Crammer, John L., et al. The Use of Drugs in Psychiatry. 2nd ed. LC RC0483.C88. 268p. reprint ed. pap. 83.10 (*0-8357-7775-8*, 203613500002) Bks Demand.
Cramp, Adrian, et al, eds. Geological Evolution of Ocean Basins: Results from the Ocean Drilling Program. LC 99-203355. (Geological Society Special Publication: No. 131). 336p. 1998. 115.00 (*1-86239-003-7*, Pub. by Geol Soc Pub Hse) AAPG.
Cramp, D. G., ed. Quantitative Approaches to Metabolism: The Role of Tracers & Models in Clinical Medicine. LC 81-21992. 402p. reprint ed. pap. 124.70 (*0-608-15666-3*, 203193600077) Bks Demand.
Cramp, D. G., jt. ed. see Carson, Ewart R.
Cramp, Derek & Carson, Ewart R., eds. Liver Function Vol. 3: Measurement in Medicine. 300p. 1990. 74.95 (*0-412-33950-1*, A4470) Chapman & Hall.
Cramp, Leonard G. Cosmic Matrix: Piece for a Jig-Saw. (Piece). (Illus.). 364p. 1998. pap. 16.00 (*0-932813-64-X*) Adventures Unltd.
— UFOs & Anti-Gravity: Piece for a Jig-Saw. 1997. pap. text 16.95 (*0-932813-43-7*) Adventures Unltd.
Cramp, Rosemary. Grammar of Anglo-Saxon Ornament: A General Introduction to the Corpus of Anglo-Saxon Stone Sculpture. (Corpus of Anglo-Saxon Stone Sculpture British Academy Ser.). (Illus.). 52p. 1991. pap. text 19.95 (*0-19-726098-5*) OUP.
Cramp, Rosemary, jt. auth. see Bailey, Richard N.
Cramp, Stanley, ed. Handbook of the Birds of Europe, the Middle East, & North America, 9 vols. Incl. Vol. I. Handbook of the Birds of Europe, the Middle East & North Africa: The Birds of the Western Palaearctic: Ostriches to Ducks. Ferguson-Lees, James & Simmons, K. E., eds. (Illus.). 732p. 1978. text 165.00 (*0-19-857358-8*); Vol. II. Handbook of the Birds of Europe, the Middle East & North Africa: The Birds of the Western Palaearctic: Hawks to Bustards. (Illus.). 696p. 1980. text 165.00 (*0-19-857505-X*); Vol. III. Handbook of the Birds of Europe, the Middle East & North Africa: The Birds of the Western Palaearctic: Waders to Gulls. (Illus.). 1,000p. 1983. text 165.00 (*0-19-857506-8*); Vol. IV. Handbook of the Birds of Europe, the Middle East & North Africa: The Birds of the Western Palaearctic: Terns to Woodpeckers. (Illus.). 970p. 1986. text 165.00 (*0-19-857507-6*); Vol. V. Handbook of the Birds of Europe, the Middle East & North Africa: The Birds of the Western Palaearctic: Tyrant Flycatchers to Thrushes. (Illus.). 1,084p. 1988. text 165.00 (*0-19-857508-4*); Vol. VI. Handbook of the Birds of the Middle East & North Africa: The Birds of the Western Palaearctic: Warblers. (Illus.). 736p. (C). 1993. 165.00 (*0-19-857509-2*); Vol. VII. Handbook of the Birds of Europe, the Middle East & North Africa: The Birds of the Western Palaearctic: Old World Flycatchers to Shrikes. Perrins, Christopher M., ed. (Illus.). 584p. 1993. 165.00 (*0-19-857510-6*); Vol. VIII. Handbook of the Birds of Europe, the Middle East & North Africa: The Birds of the Western Palaearctic: Crows to Finches. Perrins, Christopher M., ed. (Illus.). 906p. 1994. 165.00 (*0-19-854679-3*); Vol. IX. Handbook of the Birds of Europe, the Middle East & North Africa: The Birds of the Western Palaearctic: Buntings & New World Warblers. Perrins, Christopher M., ed. (Illus.). 496p. 1994. 165.00 (*0-19-854843-5*); 7200p. 1995. Set text 1350.00 (*0-19-854890-7*) OUP.
Cramp, Stephen, ed. Handbook of the Birds of Europe, the Middle East, & North Africa, Set, Vols. 1-7. 1994. 1010.00 (*0-19-521067-0*) OUP.
Crampa, Jonas. Labraunda: Swedish Excavations & Researches - The Greek Inscriptions, Pt. II: 13-133. (Acta Instituti Atheniensis Regni Sueciae Ser.: Vol. V,III:2). (Illus.). 225p. 1972. pap. 79.95 (*91-85086-07-X*, Pub. by P Astroms) Coronet Bks.
Crampagne, R., jt. auth. see Bialko, Michal.
Crampsey, Bob. Aberdeen - Final Edition. 200p. (C). 1990. pap. text 65.00 (*1-870978-30-7*) St Mut.
— Now You Know about . . . Celtic. 160p. 1994. pap. write for info. (*0-7855-2704-4*, Pub. by Argyll Pubng) St Mut.
— Now You Know about . . . Rangers. 160p. 1994. pap. write for info. (*1-874640-11-4*, Pub. by Argyll Pubng) St Mut.
Crampton, Beecher. Grasses in California. (California Natural History Guides Ser.: No. 33). (Illus.). (Orig.). 1974. pap. 13.95 (*0-520-02507-5*, Pub. by U CA Pr) Cal Prin Full Svc.
Crampton, Ben, jt. auth. see Crampton, Richard.
Crampton, Ben, jt. auth. see Crampton, Richard J.
Crampton, C. Gregory. Ghosts of Glen Canyon. rev. ed. (Illus.). 136p. 1997. pap. 19.95 (*0-9656645-0-3*) Tower Prods.
— Ghosts of Glen Canyon: History Beneath Lake Powell. (Illus.). 136p. (Orig.). 1986. pap. text 14.95 (*0-939771-00-4*) Pubs Place UT.
— Historical Sites in Cataract & Narrow Canyons & in Glen Canyon to California Bar. (Glen Canyon Ser.: No. 24). reprint ed. 28.00 (*0-404-60672-5*) AMS Pr.
— Historical Sites in Glen Canyon, Mouth of Hansen Creek to Mouth of San Juan River. (Glen Canyon Ser.: No. 17). reprint ed. 30.00 (*0-404-60661-X*) AMS Pr.
— Historical Sites in Glen Canyon, Mouth of San Juan River to Lees Ferry. (Glen Canyon Ser.: No. 12). reprint ed. 30.00 (*0-404-60646-6*) AMS Pr.
— Outline History of the Glen Canyon Region, 1776-1922. (Glen Canyon Ser.: No. 9). reprint ed. 32.50 (*0-404-60642-3*) AMS Pr.
— The San Juan Historical Sites. (Glen Canyon Ser.: No. 22). reprint ed. 24.50 (*0-404-60709-8*) AMS Pr.
— Standing up Country: The Canyon Lands of Utah & Arizona. (Illus.). 128p. 2000. pap. 16.95 (*1-887896-15-5*, Rio Nuevo) Treas Chest Bks.
Crampton, C. Gregory & Madsen, Steven K. In Search of the Spanish Trail: Santa Fe to Los Angeles, 1829-1848. LC 94-18621. (Illus.). 144p. 1994. pap. 29.95 (*0-87905-614-2*) Gibbs Smith Pub.
Crampton, C. Gregory, ed. see Eccleston, Robert.
Crampton, C. Gregory, ed. see Hall, Sharlot M.
Crampton, Charles G. The Zunis of Cibola. LC 77-72586. (Illus.). 216p. reprint ed. pap. 67.00 (*0-8357-7080-X*, 203336000085) Bks Demand.
Crampton, D., ed. The Space Distribution of Quasars. (ASP Conference Series Proceedings: Vol. 21). 401p. 1991. 34.00 (*0-937707-40-6*) Astron Soc Pacific.
Crampton, Faith E., jt. auth. see Bauman, Paul.
Crampton, Faith E., jt. auth. see Whitney, Terry N.
Crampton, Frank A. Deep Enough: A Working Stiff in the Western Mine Camps. LC 81-43639. (C). 1993. pap. 17.95 (*0-8061-2529-2*) U of Okla Pr.
Crampton, George H., ed. Motion & Space Sickness. 496p. 1990. lib. bdg. 219.00 (*0-8493-4703-3*, RC103) CRC Pr.
Crampton, Georgia R. The Condition of Creatures: Suffering & Action in Chaucer & Spenser. LC 73-93281. 218p. reprint ed. pap. 67.60 (*0-608-10705-0*, 202199200024) Bks Demand.
Crampton, Georgia R., ed. Shewings of Julian of Norwich. (Teams Middle English Text Ser.). 1998. pap. 10.00 (*1-879288-45-1*) Medieval Inst.
Crampton, Gertrude. Scuffy the Tugboat. (Little Golden Storybks.). (J). 1997. 3.99 (*0-307-16059-9*, 16059, Goldn Books) Gldn Bks Pub Co.
Crampton, Gertrude. Scuffy the Tugboat. deluxe ed. (Illus.). (J). (ps-2). Date not set. reprint ed. write for info. (*1-929566-59-X*) Cronies.
— Scuffy the Tugboat: Classic Edition. (Illus.). (J). Date not set. reprint ed. write for info. (*1-929566-52-2*) Cronies.
Crampton, Gertrude. Tootle. (Little Golden Storybks.). (J). 1997. 3.99 (*0-307-16044-0*, 16044, Goldn Books) Gldn Bks Pub Co.
Crampton, Gertrude. Tootle. deluxe ed. (Illus.). (J). (ps-2). Date not set. reprint ed. write for info. (*1-929566-58-1*) Cronies.
— Tootle: Classic Edition. (Illus.). 21p. (J). (ps-1). Date not set. write for info. (*1-929566-53-0*) Cronies.
Crampton, J. M., et al, eds. Molecular Biology of Insect Disease Vectors: A Methods Manual. LC 96-70874. (Illus.). 416p. 1996. pap. write for info. (*0-412-73660-8*) Kluwer Academic.
Crampton, Julian M. & Eggleston, Paul, eds. Insect Molecular Science. (Illus.). 270p. 1992. text 83.00 (*0-12-195210-X*) Acad Pr.
Crampton, Luke, jt. auth. see Rees, Dafydd.
Crampton, Norm. Complete Trash: The Best Way to Get Rid of Practically Everything Around the House. LC 89-1516. (Illus.). 144p. (Orig.). 1989. pap. 8.95 (*0-87131-572-6*) M Evans.
Crampton, Norman. The 100 Best Small Towns in America. 2nd ed. LC 95-42820. 400p. 1995. 13.95 (*0-02-860577-2*, Arco) Macmillan Gen Ref.
Crampton, Norman J. Preventing Waste at the Source. LC 98-29657. 220p. 1998. lib. bdg. 49.95 (*1-56670-317-4*) Lewis Pubs.
Crampton, P. & Whittome, S. The Domestic Central Heating Market in Great Britain. 1992. 1580.00 (*0-86022-351-5*, Pub. by Build Servs Info Assn) St Mut.
— The U. K. Market for Commercial Boilers. 1991. 1280.00 (*0-86022-277-2*, Pub. by Build Servs Info Assn) St Mut.
Crampton, P., et al. In-Depth Country Appraisal - EC Countries. 1991. 500.00 (*0-86022-272-1*, Pub. by Build Servs Info Assn) St Mut.
Crampton, P., jt. auth. see Pavey, N. L.
Crampton, P. R., jt. auth. see Gregory, D. P.
Crampton, Patricia, ed. see Prelovsek, Damjan.
Crampton, Patricia, tr. see Bjork, Christina.
Crampton, Patricia, tr. see Gyllenskold, Karin.
Crampton, Patricia, tr. see Hofer, Angelika & Ziesler, Gunter.
Crampton, Patricia, tr. see Kalas, Sybille.
Crampton, Patricia, tr. see Pausewang, Gudrun.
Crampton, Patricia, tr. see Somme, Lauritz.
Crampton, R. J. A Concise History of Bulgaria. (Cambridge Concise Histories Ser.). (Illus.). 274p. (C). 1997. pap. 17.95 (*0-521-56719-X*); text 54.95 (*0-521-56183-3*) Cambridge U Pr.
— Eastern Europe in the Twentieth Century & After. 2nd ed. LC 97-665. (Illus.). 560p. (C). 1997. pap. 27.99 (*0-415-16423-0*) Routledge.
— Eastern Europe in the Twentieth Century & After. 2nd ed. LC 97-665. 560p. (C). 1997. write for info. (*0-415-16422-2*) Routledge.
Crampton, Richard & Crampton, Ben. Atlas of Eastern Europe in the Twentieth Century. (Illus.). 320p. (C). 1997. pap. 27.99 (*0-415-16461-3*) Routledge.
Crampton, Richard J. Bulgaria, Eighteen Seventy-Eight to Nineteen Eighteen: A History. (East European Monographs: No. 138). 580p. 1983. text 79.00 (*0-88033-029-5*, Pub. by East Eur Monographs) Col U Pr.
Crampton, Richard J., ed. Bulgaria. annot. ed. LC 90-182068. (World Bibliographical Ser.: No. 107). 268p. 1989. lib. bdg. 65.00 (*1-85109-104-1*) ABC-CLIO.
Crampton, Richard J. & Crampton, Ben. Atlas of Eastern Europe in the Twentieth Century. LC 95-4172. 336p. (C). (gr. 13). 1995. 90.00 (*0-415-06689-1*) Routledge.
Crampton, Stephen. Eurospeak Explained, 1992. 157p. (C). 1990. text 32.00 (*1-85631-001-9*, Pub. by Rosters Ltd) St Mut.
***Crampton, W. Gary.** The Scripturalism of Gordon H. Clark. 100p. 1999. pap. 9.95 (*0-940931-53-2*) Trinity Found.
Crampton, W. Gary. Study Guide to the Westminster Confession. 112p. 1998. reprint ed. pap. text, student ed. 10.95 (*0-940931-79-6*) Trinity Found.
— What Calvin Says: An Introduction to the Theology of John Calvin. Robbins, John W., ed. & intro. by. 160p. 1992. pap. 7.95 (*0-940931-35-4*) Trinity Found.
***Crampton, William.** Flag. (Eyewitness Books). (Illus.). (J). (gr. 4-7). 2000. 19.99 (*0-7894-6565-5*) DK Pub Inc.
— Flag. (Eyewitness Books). (J). (gr. 4-7). 2000. 15.95 (*0-7894-5824-1*) DK Pub Inc.
Crampton, William G. The World of Flags. LC 94-3493. (Illus.). 48p. 1994. 12.95 (*0-528-83720-6*) Rand McNally.
Cramton, Roger C. Conflict of Laws: Adaptable to Courses Utilizing Materials by Cramton. LC 87-114670. (Legalines Ser.). 132p. 9.95 (*0-685-18524-9*) Harcourt.
Cramton, Roger C., et al. Conflict of Law: Cases - Comments - Questions. 4th ed. 876p. (C). 1993. reprint ed. text 41.95 (*0-314-39866-X*) West Pub.
— Conflict of Laws: Cases - Comments - Questions. 5th ed. (American Casebook Ser.). 280p. 1993. pap. text, teacher ed. write for info. (*0-314-03249-5*) West Pub.
— Conflict of Laws: Cases, Comments, Questions. 5th ed. (American Casebook Ser.). 743p. (C). 1993. 57.50 (*0-314-02015-2*) West Pub.
Cramton, Roger C., jt. auth. see Barcelbo, John J.
Cramton, Roger C., ed. see Hazard, Geoffrey C., Jr., et al.
Cran, Angela & Robertson, James, compiled by. A Dictionary of Scottish Quotations. 448p. 1997. 39.95 (*1-85158-812-4*, Pub. by Mainstream Pubng) Trafalgar.
Cranach, M., et al, eds. Social Representation & the Social Bases of Knowledge. (Illus.). 290p. 1992. pap. text 36.00 (*0-88937-070-2*) Hogrefe & Huber Pubs.
Cranach, Mario Von, see Von Cranach, Mario.
Cranach, Michael Von, see Mezzich, Juan E. & Von Cranach, Michael, eds.
Cranberries. The Best of the Cranberries for Guitar. 80p. 1997. otabind 19.95 (*0-7935-6053-5*) H Leonard.
— To the Faithful Departed. 64p. 1997. otabind 16.95 (*0-7935-6663-0*) H Leonard.
Cranberry, Nola, tr. see Shely, Patricia.
Cranberry, Nola, tr. see Woggon, Guillermo.
Cranbrook Academy of Art, Architecture Studio Staf. Plus Text. 63p. 1991. pap. 6.00 (*1-880337-02-9*) Cranbrook Acad.
Cranch, Christopher P. The Bird & the Bell, with Other Poems. LC 72-4960. (Romantic Tradition in American Literature Ser.). 344p. 1978. reprint ed. 28.95 (*0-405-04632-4*) Ayer.
— Collected Poems, 1835-1892. DeFalco, Joseph, ed. LC 70-161930. 744p. 1971. 90.00 (*0-8201-1091-4*) Schol Facsimiles.
— The Life & Letters of Christopher Pearse Cranch. LC 72-90096. (Illus.). reprint ed. 52.50 (*0-404-05641-5*) AMS Pr.
— The Life & Letters of Christopher Pearse Cranch. (American Biography Ser.). 395p. 1991. reprint ed. lib. bdg. 79.00 (*0-7812-8093-1*) Rprt Serv.
— The Life & Letters of Christopher Pearse Cranch, by His Daughter Lenora Cranch Scott. (BCL1-PS American Literature Ser.). 395p. 1992. reprint ed. lib. bdg. 89.00 (*0-7812-6695-5*) Rprt Serv.
***Crancher, Steve.** Uncle Fred's History of Westcliffe. unabridged ed. (Illus.). 80p. 2000. pap. 15.00 (*0-86025-478-X*, Pub. by I Henry Pubns) Empire Pub Srvs.
Crandall. Contracts. 2nd ed. 1168p. 1993. 54.00 (*0-316-16016-4*, Aspen Law & Bus) Aspen Pub.
— 1995 Supplement to UCC One to Five. 1995. 150.00 (*0-316-16029-6*, Aspen Law & Bus) Aspen Pub.
— UCC Law. 1993. 135.00 (*0-316-16010-5*, Aspen Law & Bus); 595.00 (*0-316-16026-1*, Aspen Law & Bus) Aspen Pub.
— UCC Law, Vol. 2. 1993. 135.00 (*0-316-16022-9*, Aspen Law & Bus) Aspen Pub.
— UCC Law, Vol. 3. 1993. 135.00 (*0-316-16023-7*, Aspen Law & Bus) Aspen Pub.
— UCC Law, Vol. 4. 1993. 135.00 (*0-316-16024-5*, Aspen Law & Bus) Aspen Pub.
— UCC Law, Vol. 5. 1993. 135.00 (*0-316-16025-3*, Aspen Law & Bus) Aspen Pub.
Crandall, et al. An Agenda for Federal Regulatory Reform. LC 98-118406. 1997. pap. 9.95 (*0-8447-7104-X*) Am Enterprise.
Crandall, Alan S., jt. ed. see Masket, Samuel.
Crandall, Alissa. Along the Alaska Marine Highway. Bovy, Edward, ed. (Mini-Book Ser.). (Illus.). 24p. 1994. pap. 5.95 (*0-936425-27-X*) Greatland Graphics.
Crandall, B. C., ed. Nanotechnology: Molecular Speculations on Global Abundance. (Illus.). 224p. 1996. 35.00 (*0-262-03237-6*, Bradford Bks); pap. text 18.50 (*0-262-53137-2*, Bradford Bks) MIT Pr.
— Nanotechnology: Research & Perspectives. (Illus.). 480p. 1992. 50.00 (*0-262-03195-7*) MIT Pr.
Crandall, B. J. Morphology & Development of Branches in the Leafy Hepaticae. (Illus.). 1970. 80.00 (*3-7682-5430-5*) Lubrecht & Cramer.
Crandall, Barbara, jt. auth. see Crandall, Chuck.
Crandall, Bonnie. Abolish Anxiety: Discover Inner Peace in a Stressed Out World. 128p. 1999. pap. 14.95 (*0-9663946-1-5*) Hatch Creek.
— PanicBuster: Learn to Conquer Panic Attacks & Agoraphobia. 67p. 1995. spiral bd., wbk. ed. 12.95 (*0-9663946-0-7*) Hatch Creek.
Crandall, Cass. Bed & Breakfast Alaska Style. (Illus.). 158p. (Orig.). 1990. 12.95 (*0-9626071-0-X*) Kachemak Pub.
— Bed & Breakfast Alaska Style. 3rd ed. LC 92-81933. (Illus.). 250p. (Orig.). 1993. pap. 14.95 (*0-9626071-4-2*) Kachemak Pub.
— Bed & Breakfast Alaska Style! 4th ed. (Illus.). 16.95 (*0-9626071-5-0*) Kachemak Pub.
Crandall, Cass, jt. auth. see Doogan, Kathy.
Crandall, Cass, ed. see Gerkin, Mary.
Crandall, Chuck. Gardener's Guide to Planters Containers & Raised Beds. (Illus.). 144p. 1998. 17.95 (*0-8069-4243-6*) Sterling.
Crandall, Chuck & Crandall, Barbara. All about Landscape Plans. LC 98-66907. (Illus.). 96p. 1998. pap. 11.95 (*0-89721-433-1*, Ortho Bks) Meredith Bks.
— Courtyards & Patios: Creating Elegant Outdoor Spaces. LC 97-36152. 1998. write for info. (*1-56799-554-3*, Friedman-Fairfax) M Friedman Pub Grp Inc.
***Crandall, Chuck & Crandall, Barbara.** Courtyards & Patios: Designing & Landscaping Elegant Outdoor Spaces. LC 00-28800. (Illus.). 2000. write for info. (*1-58663-010-5*) M Friedman Pub Grp Inc.
Crandall, Chuck & Crandall, Barbara. Creating Privacy in the Garden. LC 96-44264. 1997. 29.95 (*0-8478-2003-3*, Pub. by Rizzoli Intl) St Martin.
— Flowering, Fruiting & Foliage Vines: A Gardener's Guide. LC 94-37154. (Illus.). 192p. (Orig.). 1996. pap. 19.95 (*0-8069-0727-4*) Sterling.
— Movable Harvests: The Simplicity & Bounty of Container Gardens. (Illus.). 128p. 1995. pap. 19.95 (*1-881527-70-0*, Chapters Bks) HM.
Crandall, Clifford C., Jr. The American Eagle Style Instructional Textbook. (Illus.). 294p. 1996. pap. text 19.95 (*0-9636605-3-5*) Tonfa Mstr.
Crandall, Clifford C., Jr. Best Handbook to Secure Living. 2nd ed. (Illus.). 43p. (Orig.). (YA). (ps). 1993. pap. 9.95 (*0-9636605-0-0*) Tonfa Mstr.
— The Crandall System "Children's Self-Defense & Awareness" 10p. (Orig.). 1998. pap. 3.00 (*0-9636605-2-7*) Tonfa Mstr.
***Crandall, David.** Fly Free As Easy As 1-2-3. Terra, Jean, ed. Terra, Richard, tr. LC 98-92066. (Illus.). 128p. 1998. pap. 11.95 (*1-887747-21-4*, San 297-321-X) Legendary Pub.
***Crandall, David P.** The Place of Stunted Ironwood Trees: A Year in the Lives of the Cattle-Herding Himba of Namibia. LC 00-34065. 2000. write for info. (*0-8264-1270-X*) Continuum.
Crandall, Diane M. Violent Crime: I Never Thought It Would Happen to Me, but It Did. LC 94-90566. 44p. (Orig.). 1994. pap. 10.95 (*0-9642965-0-0*) For-giving Pr.

An Asterisk (*) at the beginning of an entry indicates that the title is appearing for the first time.

Crandall, Earl. Power Supply Testing: A Handbook for Making Strategic Choices. 1990. text 89.95 (*0-442-23845-2*, VNR) Wiley.

Crandall, Earl P. Bliven, Five Families of Charlestown, R. I. Bliven, Crandall, Macomber, Money & Taylor, with Appendix. 285p. 1993. pap. 29.00 (*0-8328-3217-0*); lib. bdg. 39.00 (*0-8328-3216-2*) Higginson Bk Co.

— Congdon. Great Grandma Was a Congdon: Some Lines of Descent of John Congdon of Wales. (Illus.). 462p. 1995. pap. 69.50 (*0-8328-4677-5*); lib. bdg. 79.50 (*0-8328-4676-7*) Higginson Bk Co.

— Kenfield History: Some Lines of Descent from William Canfield of Northampton, Massachusetts. 125p. 1993. reprint ed. pap. 19.50 (*0-8328-3358-4*); reprint ed. lib. bdg. 29.50 (*0-8328-3357-6*) Higginson Bk Co.

— Saunders. "Old Tobe" Some Lines of Descent of Tobias Saunders of Westerly, Rhode Island. (Illus.). 334p. 1995. pap. 48.00 (*0-8328-4675-9*); lib. bdg. 58.00 (*0-8328-4674-0*) Higginson Bk Co.

Crandall, Earl P., ed. Charlestown in the Mid-19th Century, As Seen Through the Eyes of "Uncle Phineas" (Nelson Byron Vars) (Illus.). 79p. 1995. pap. 16.00 (*0-8328-5117-5*); lib. bdg. 26.00 (*0-8328-5116-7*) Higginson Bk Co.

Crandall-Frazier, Cindy. Sock Doll Workshop: 30 Delightful Dolls to Create & Cherish. Needham, Bobbe, ed. (Illus.). 112p. 1995. 19.95 (*0-937274-94-1*) Lark Books.

— Sock Doll Workshop: 30 Delightful Dolls to Create & Cherish. (Illus.). 112p. 1996. pap. 12.95 (*1-887374-08-6*) Lark Books.

Crandall, George W. Tennessee Williams: A Descsriptive Bibliography. (Series in Bibliography). (Illus.). 704p. (C). 1993. text 195.00 (*0-8229-3769-7*) U of Pittsburgh Pr.

Crandall, Hugh. Grand Teton: The Story Behind the Scenery. LC 78-57539. (Illus.). 48p. (Orig.). 1978. pap. 7.95 (*0-916122-22-0*) KC Pubns.

Crandall, Hugh & Engle, Reed. Shenandoah: The Story Behind the Scenery. rev. ed. LC 88-82821. (Illus.). 48p. (Orig.). 1990. pap. 7.95 (*0-88714-027-0*) KC Pubns.

Crandall, J. C. Crandall: Elder John Crandall of Rhode Island & His Descendants. 797p. 1991. reprint ed. pap. 129.00 (*0-8328-1807-0*); reprint ed. lib. bdg. 119.00 (*0-8328-1806-2*) Higginson Bk Co.

Crandall, James E. Theory & Measurement of Social Interest. LC 81-9973. 224p. 1981. text 56.00 (*0-231-05256-1*) Col U Pr.

***Crandall, Jennette.** Along the Way: Selected Poems, Photos & Lyrics by Jennette Crandall. large type ed. LC 98-92128. (Illus.). ix, 55p. 1999. 19.00 (*0-9676387-0-4*) L Kayle.

Crandall, Jerry C. Doras of the Galland Circus. (Library of Eagles: Vol. 1). (Illus.). 60p. 1999. pap., per. 25.00 (*0-9660706-2-3*) Eagle Edtns.

***Crandall, Jerry C.** Yellow 10. (Library of Eagles: Vol. 2). (Illus.). 80p. 1999. pap. 30.00 (*0-9660706-3-1*) Eagle Edtns.

Crandall, Jo Ann. Directions in Vocational Education for Limited English-Proficient Students & Adults. 30p. 1985. 3.50 (*0-318-22076-8*, OC109) Ctr Educ Trng Employ.

Crandall, JoAnn, ed. see Dale, Theresa C., et al.

Crandall, Joann, ed. see Rigg, Pat, et al.

Crandall, Joanne. Self-Transformation Through Music. (Illus.). 165p. 1988. pap. 7.50 (*0-8356-0608-2*, Quest) Theos Pub Hse.

Crandall, John G., jt. auth. see Keller, Howard.

Crandall, Joseph, tr. see Yonghui, Fu.

Crandall, Judith, et al, eds. What Works in Education. LC 98-203033. (Behavior Monographs). (Illus.). 64p. 1998. pap. 12.95 (*1-881317-05-6*) Cambdge Ctr Behav.

Crandall, Judith A. How to Write Tutorial Documents. (Illus.). 208p. (C). 1987. text 21.95 (*0-13-467820-6*) P-H.

Crandall, Judy. Cowgirls: Early Images & Collectibles. (Illus.). 112p. (Orig.). 1994. pap. 19.95 (*0-88740-646-7*) Schiffer.

Crandall, Katherine. The Fine Old Town of Stonington. 2nd ed. LC 95-104911. (Illus.). 151p. (J). 1994. pap. 20.00 (*0-910258-22-8*) Book & Tackle.

***Crandall, Keith A.** Evolution of HIV. 1999. write for info. (*0-8018-6150-0*) Johns Hopkins.

Crandall, Keith A. Evolution of HIV. LC 98-45736. (Illus.). 462p. 1999. pap. text 34.95 (*0-8018-6151-9*) Johns Hopkins.

Crandall, Lee S. Management of Wild Mammals in Captivity. LC 64-10498. (Illus.). 1993. lib. bdg. 40.00 (*0-226-11758-8*) U Ch Pr.

— The Management of Wild Mammals in Captivity. LC 64-10498. (Illus.). 785p. reprint ed. pap. 200.00 (*0-608-09290-8*, 205416400004) Bks Demand.

Crandall, Melissa. Earth 2. 1994. mass mkt. 5.50 (*1-57297-170-3*) Blvd Books.

— Quantum Leap: Search & Rescue, No. 5. 240p. (Orig.). 1994. pap. text 4.99 (*0-441-00122-X*) Ace Bks.

— Shell Game. Stern, Dave, ed. (Star Trek Ser.: No. 63). 288p. 1993. mass mkt. 5.50 (*0-671-79572-4*) PB.

Crandall, N. Fredric & Wallace, Marc J. Work & Rewards in the Virtual Workplace: A "New Deal" for Organizations & Employees. LC 98-17092. 288p. 1998. 27.95 (*0-8144-0375-1*) AMACOM.

Crandall, Perry C. Bramble Production: The Marketing & Management of Raspberries & Blackberries. LC 93-43912. 1995. pap. 19.95 (*1-56022-853-9*) Haworth Pr.

Crandall, Perry C. Bramble Production: The Marketing & Management of Raspberries & Blackberries. LC 93-43912. (Illus.). 219p. 1995. lib. bdg. 49.95 (*1-56022-852-0*) Haworth Pr.

Crandall, R. Introduction to Scientific Computation: A Primer. 256p. 1997. pap. text 29.95 (*0-387-94840-6*) Spr-Verlag.

— Projects in Scientific Computation. 470p. 1996. 54.95 incl. disk (*3-540-97808-9*) Spr-Verlag.

Crandall, R. & Levich, M. The Virtual Goliath: Logic & Responsibility in the Computer Age. LC 97-33271. 256p. 1997. 29.95 (*0-387-94647-0*) Spr-Verlag.

Crandall, Ralph. Shaking Your Family Tree. (Illus.). 256p. 1988. reprint ed. pap. 10.95 (*0-89909-148-2*, 80-551-6) Yankee Bks.

Crandall, Ralph J., jt. ed. see Taylor, Robert M., Jr.

***Crandall, Richard.** Primes: A Computational Perspective. 2000. 49.95 (*0-387-94777-9*) Spr-Verlag.

— Projects in Scientific Computation. (Illus.). 496p. 2000. pap. 39.95 incl. disk (*0-387-95009-5*, Telos) Spr-Verlag.

Crandall, Richard & Levich, Marvin. The Virtual Goliath. 1996. 29.95 (*0-614-14503-1*) Spr-Verlag.

Crandall, Richard C. Gerontology: A Behavioral Science Approach. 2nd ed. 576p. (C). 1991. 68.13 (*0-07-013446-4*) McGraw.

***Crandall, Richard C.** Inuit Art: A History. LC 99-48304. 427p. 1999. lib. bdg. 55.00 (*0-7864-0711-5*) McFarland & Co.

Crandall, Richard E. Mathematica for the Sciences. (Illus.). 320p. (C). 1991. 40.95 (*0-201-51001-4*) Addison-Wesley.

— Topics in Advanced Scientific Computation. (Electronic Library of Science). 340p. 1995. 53.95 (*0-387-94473-7*) Spr-Verlag.

Crandall, Richard E. & Colgrove, Marianne M. Scientific Applications for the Next Computer System: Technical Examples & Methodology. 300p. 1989. pap. 22.95 (*0-201-51732-9*) Addison-Wesley.

Crandall, Richard L. & Robins, Sam. The Incorruptible Cashier: The Brass Era, Vol. 2. LC 88-135. (Illus.). 408p. 1999. pap. 49.95 (*0-911572-95-3*, Pub. by Madison Bks UPA) Natl Bk Netwk.

Crandall, Rick. Break-Out Creativity. LC 98-135828. 180p. (Orig.). 1997. pap. 14.95 (*0-9644294-7-0*) Select Pr.

***Crandall, Rick.** Celebrate Customer Service. 185p. 1998. pap. 14.95 (*1-890777-06-4*) Select Pr.

— Celebrate Marketing. (Illus.). 230p. 1999. pap. 14.95 (*1-890777-07-2*) Select Pr.

— How to Exploit Your Children for Fun & Profit. 100p. 1998. pap. 9.95 (*1-890777-05-6*) Select Pr.

— How to Really Run a Successful Business. 220p. 2000. pap. 16.95 (*1-890777-11-0*) Select Pr.

Crandall, Rick. Marketing Your Services: For People Who Hate to Sell. 320p. 1996. pap. 16.95 (*0-8092-3157-3*, 315730, Contemporary Bks) NTC Contemp Pub Co.

— Marketing Your Services: For People Who Hate to Sell. LC 94-74836. 149p. 1995. pap. 15.95 (*0-9644294-0-3*) Select Pr.

— 1001 Ways to Market Your Services. LC 97-41744. 384p. 1997. pap. 16.95 (*0-8092-3158-1*, 315810, Contemporary Bks) NTC Contemp Pub Co.

Crandall, Rick, ed. Celebrate Selling the Relationship - Consultative Way. 185p. 1998. pap. 14.95 (*1-890777-04-8*) Select Pr.

— Marketing for People Not in Marketing. 180p. (Orig.). 1997. pap. 14.95 (*0-9644294-8-9*) Select Pr.

— Thriving on Change. 380p. 1997. pap. 7.95 (*0-9644294-5-4*) Select Pr.

Crandall, Rick & Perrewe, Pamela L., eds. Occupational Stress: A Handbook. 2nd ed. (Health Psychology & Behavioral Medicine Ser.). 280p. 1995. pap. 39.95 (*1-56032-367-1*) Taylor & Francis.

Crandall, Rick, jt. auth. see Diener, Edward.

Crandall, Robert W. After the Breakup: U.S. Telecommunications in a More Competitive Era. 180p. 1991. 31.95 (*0-8157-1606-0*); pap. 12.95 (*0-8157-1605-2*) Brookings.

— Controlling Industrial Pollution: The Economics & Politics of Clean Air. LC 82-45982. (Studies on the Regulation of Economic Activity). 199p. 1983. 34.95 (*0-8157-1604-4*); pap. 14.95 (*0-8157-1603-6*) Brookings.

— Manufacturing on the Move. 111p. (C). 1993. 32.95 (*0-8157-1598-6*) Brookings.

Crandall, Robert W. Manufacturing on the Move. LC 92-43320. 111p. (C). 1993. pap. 12.95 (*0-8157-1597-8*) Brookings.

Crandall, Robert W. The U. S. Steel Industry in Recurrent Crisis: Policy Options in a Competitive World. LC 81-4642. 184p. 1981. 26.95 (*0-8157-1602-8*); pap. 9.95 (*0-8157-1601-X*) Brookings.

***Crandall, Robert W.** Who Pays for Universal Service? When Telephone Subsidies Become Transparent. 2000. pap. 16.95 (*0-8157-1611-7*) Brookings.

Crandall, Robert W. & Flamm, Kenneth, eds. Changing the Rules: Technological Change, International Competition, & Regulation in Communications. 450p. 1989. 52.95 (*0-8157-1596-X*); pap. 24.95 (*0-8157-1595-1*) Brookings.

Crandall, Robert W. & Furchtgott-Roth, Harold. Cable TV: Regulation or Competition? 160p. (C). 1996. 34.95 (*0-8157-1610-9*); pap. 14.95 (*0-8157-1609-5*) Brookings.

Crandall, Robert W. & Lave, Lester B., eds. The Scientific Basis of Health & Safety Regulation. LC 81-10227. (Studies in the Regulation of Economic Activity). 309p. 1981. 34.95 (*0-8157-1600-1*); pap. 14.95 (*0-8157-1599-4*) Brookings.

Crandall, Robert W. & Waverman, Leonard. Talk Is Cheap: Declining Costs, New Competition, & Regulatory Reform in Telecommunications. (Integrating National Economies: Promise & Pitfalls Ser.). 294p. (C). 1995. 42.95 (*0-8157-1608-7*); pap. 18.95 (*0-8157-1607-9*) Brookings.

Crandall, Robert W., et al. Regulating the Automobile. LC 85-48171. (Studies in the Regulation of Economic Activity). 202p. 1986. 29.95 (*0-8157-1594-3*) Brookings.

Crandall, Robert W., jt. auth. see Barnett, Donald F.

Crandall, Robert W., jt. auth. see Nivola, Pietro S.

Crandall, Ronald. Turnaround Strategies for the Small Church. (Effective Church Ser.). 176p. (Orig.). 1995. pap. 12.95 (*0-687-00467-5*) Abingdon.

Crandall, Samuel B. Treaties, Their Making & Enforcement. LC 74-76672. (Columbia University. Studies in the Social Sciences: No. 54). reprint ed. 42.50 (*0-404-51054-X*) AMS Pr.

Crandall, Sandra G. Avoiding the "Ms"conceptions of Aging. (Illus.). 32p. 1994. pap. 10.00 (*0-9636792-4-4*) Ctr Nursing Excell.

Crandall, Sharon Olexa, jt. auth. see Baker, Lynda A.

Crandall, Stephen H., et al. Dynamics of Mechanical & Electromechanical Systems. LC 82-9890. 478p. 1982. reprint ed. lib. bdg. 53.50 (*0-89874-529-2*) Krieger.

— An Introduction to the Mechanics of Solids. 2nd ed. (Illus.). 640p. (C). 1972. text 82.50 (*0-07-013436-7*) McGraw.

Crandall-Stotler, Barbara & Stotler, Raymond E. Plants: Evolution & Diversity. 3rd ed. 212p. 1995. spiral bd. 28.95 (*0-7872-1965-7*) Kendall-Hunt.

Crandall, Thomas D. & Whaley, Douglas J. Cases, Problems, & Materials on Contracts. 2nd ed. 1168p. 1993. teacher ed. write for info. (*0-316-16028-8*, 60288) Aspen Law.

— Cases, Problems & Materials on Contracts. 3rd ed. LC 98-43617. 1008p. 1999. boxed set 58.00 (*0-7355-0027-4*) Panel Pubs.

Crandell. Automotive Painting for Collision Repair. LC 98-34630. (C). 1998. pap. 41.95 (*0-7668-0905-6*) Delmar.

***Crandell.** Classroom Acoustics for Normal & Hearing Impaired Children. 2001. pap. 69.95 (*0-7693-0074-X*) Singular Publishing.

Crandell & Beiger. Human Development. 6th ed. (C). 1994. pap. text 16.25 (*0-07-048761-8*) McGraw.

Crandell, Carl C., et al. Sound-Field FM Amplification: Theory & Practical Applications. (Illus.). 246p. (C). 1995. pap. text 45.00 (*1-56593-450-4*, 1066) Thomson Learn.

Crandell, George W. The Critical Response to Tennessee Williams, 24. LC 96-18345. (Critical Responses in Arts & Letters Ser.). 352p. 1996. lib. bdg. 65.00 (*0-313-29372-4*) Greenwood.

— Ogden Nash: A Descriptive Bibliography. LC 90-33726. 482p. 1990. 50.00 (*0-8108-2332-2*) Scarecrow.

Crandell, Gina. Nature Pictorialized: The View in Landscape History. (Illus.). 240p. 1993. text 35.95 (*0-8018-4397-9*) Johns Hopkins.

Crandell, Jay H. Design Guide for Frost-Protected Shallow Foundations. (Illus.). 42p. (Orig.). (C). 1995. pap. text 40.00 (*0-7881-1611-8*) DIANE Pub.

Crandell, John S. Moving Psychotherapy: Theory & Application of Pesso System- Psychomotor Therapy. Pesso, Albert, ed. LC 90-1623. 306p. 1990. text 39.95 (*0-914797-72-7*) Brookline Bks.

Crandell, Michael. Estimating for Collision Repair. LC 98-22159. 368p. 1998. 41.95 (*0-7668-0891-2*) Delmar.

Crandell, Susan. Snippets. Crowe, Robert L., ed. 96p. (Orig.). 1995. pap. write for info. (*0-9644681-1-5*) Consortium IL.

Crandell, Susan, ed. see Finney, Paul B.

Crandell, Tom. Victory Through Fire. (Illus.). 136p. (Orig.). (J). 1996. pap. text 10.00 (*0-9652105-0-2*) Quintastar.

Crandell, Tom, jt. auth. see Gibbs, David.

Crandjean, P., tr. see Rebreanu, Liviu.

Crandon-Malamud, Libbet. From the Fat of Our Souls: Social Change, Political Process, & Medical Pluralism in Bolivia. LC 90-37178. (Comparative Studies of Health Systems & Medical Care: Vol. 26). (Illus.). 368p. 1991. 55.00 (*0-520-07011-9*, Pub. by U CA Pr); pap. 18.95 (*0-520-08430-6*, Pub. by U CA Pr) Cal Prin Full Svc.

Crane. Act 1. (New Readers Ser.). 1994. pap. text 12.95 (*0-15-599434-4*) Harcourt Schl Pubs.

— Act 2. (New Readers Ser.). 1994. pap. text 12.95 (*0-15-599428-X*) Harcourt Schl Pubs.

— Brotherhood. 1983. 2.25 (*0-671-53597-8*) S&S Trade.

— Contemporary Reading for General Biology 1998. 5th ed. (Biology Ser.). 1998. 14.00 (*0-534-51633-5*) Wadsworth Pub.

— Divided Lives. 1999. text 26.95 (*0-312-21953-9*) St Martin.

— Global Financial Systems. 1995. 37.50 (*0-07-103626-1*) McGraw.

— Mental Retardation:a Community Integration. (Special Education). 1999. pap. 48.95 (*0-534-33923-9*) Brooks-Cole.

Crane & Zief, Morris. Chromatographic Chiral Separations. (Chromatographic Science Ser.: Vol. 40). (Illus.). 432p. 1987. text 210.00 (*0-8247-7786-7*) Dekker.

Crane, et al. Filters & Power Conditioning. LC 83-81460. (Electromagnetic Interference & Compatibility Ser.: Vol. 4). (Illus.). 323p. 1988. 50.00 (*0-944916-04-X*) emf-emi Control.

***Crane, Stephen.** Maggie: A Girl of the Streets. (Norton Critical Editions Ser.). (C). 1999. pap. text 30.00 (*0-393-98960-7*) Norton.

— The Open Boat. (Short Stories Ser.). 22p. 2000. pap. 3.95 (*1-86092-025-X*, Pub. by Travelman Pub) IPG Chicago.

— Red Badge of Courage. (Library Classics). 336p. 2000. pap. 8.95 (*0-679-78320-2*) Modern Lib NY.

Crane, Virginia Glenn. The Oshkosh Woodworkers' Strike of 1898: A Wisconsin Community in Crisis. (Illus.). xi, 569p. 1998. pap. 15.00 (*0-9669195-0-5*) Virginia Crane.

Crane, Alfred V. The Law of Unlawful Possession. xxi, 169p. 1999. reprint ed. 65.00 (*1-56169-505-X*) Gaunt.

Crane, Allen & Crane, Virginia. Buzzards to Bluebirds: Improve Your Child's Learning & Behavior in 6 Weeks: Help Stop Dyslexia, School Dropouts & School Failures. LC 97-44508. 1997. 19.95 (*0-943599-87-3*) OEPF.

***Crane, Amy.** Rejoice in the Light: A Woman's Journey Out of the Mystery of Epilepsy. LC 99-95323. (Illus.). 330p. 2000. per. 21.95 (*0-9669786-0-9*) Agape Pub.

***Crane, Andrew.** Marketing, Morality & the Natural Environment. LC 00-35310. (Advances in Management & Business Studies). 2001. write for info. (*0-415-21382-7*) Routledge.

Crane, Anita L. Making Adorable Teddy Bears: From Anita Louise's Bearlace Cottage. (Illus.). 144p. (Orig.). 1996. pap. 14.95 (*0-8069-0993-5*, Chapelle) Sterling.

— Teddy Bear Magic: Making Adorable Teddy Bears from Anita Louise's Bearlace Cottage. LC 94-23433. (Illus.). 144p. 1995. 27.95 (*0-8069-0992-7*, Chapelle) Sterling.

***Crane, Anita Louise.** Adorable Furniture for Dolls & Teddy Bears. LC 00-28511. (Illus.). 2000. write for info. (*0-8069-4493-5*) Sterling.

Crane, Anita Louise. Two-Hour Dolls' Clothes. LC 99-14088. 128p. 1999. 27.95 (*0-8069-3889-7*) Sterling.

***Crane, Anita Louise.** Two-Hour Scrap Crafts. LC 00-33900. (Illus.). 2000. write for info. (*0-8069-8783-9*) Sterling.

— Two-Hour Teddy Bears. LC 98-26734. 1998. 27.95 (*0-8069-3800-5*) Sterling.

***Crane, Anita Louise.** Two-Hour Teddy Bears. (Two-Hour Crafts Bks.). (Illus.). 2000. pap. 14.95 (*0-8069-4327-0*) Sterling.

Crane, Anson. Uncertain Light. 320p. (Orig.). 1994. pap. 7.85 (*0-9639069-5-X*) Desert Low.

Crane, Arnold. On the Other Side of the Camera. (ENG, FRE & GER., Illus.). 240p. 1997. 39.95 (*3-89508-093-4*, 810045) Konemann.

Crane, Arthur G. Education for the Disabled in War & Industry: Army Hospital Schools. LC 70-176678. (Columbia University. Teachers College. Contributions to Education Ser.: No. 110). reprint ed. 37.50 (*0-404-55110-6*) AMS Pr.

Crane, Barbara J. Apple & the Ax. (Crane Reading System-English Ser.). (Illus.). (gr. k-2). 1977. pap. text 5.15 (*0-89075-097-1*) Bilingual Ed Serv.

— As I Skillbooklet. (Crane Reading System-English Ser.). (Illus.). (gr. k-2). 1982. pap. text 2.49 (*0-89075-027-0*) Bilingual Ed Serv.

— AS2 Skillbooklet. (Crane Reading System-English Ser.). (Illus.). (gr. k-2). 1982. pap. text 2.49 (*0-89075-029-7*) Bilingual Ed Serv.

— The Baby Jay. (Crane Reading System-English Ser.). (Illus.). (J). (gr. k-2). 1977. pap. 4.85 (*0-89075-095-5*) Bilingual Ed Serv.

— The Bee Book. (Crane Reading System-English Ser.). (Illus.). (gr. k-2). 1977. pap. text 4.85 (*0-89075-094-7*) Bilingual Ed Serv.

— BS 1 Skillbooklet, No. I. (Crane Reading System-English Ser.). (Illus.). (J). (gr. k-2). 1982. pap. text 2.49 (*0-89075-031-9*) Bilingual Ed Serv.

— Crane Reading System, Practice Bks, A-J. Incl. Practice Book A. (Illus.). 1977. pap. text 4.75 (*0-89075-052-1*); Practice Book B. (Illus.). 1977. pap. text 4.75 (*0-89075-054-8*); Practice Book C. (Illus.). 1977. pap. text 4.75 (*0-89075-055-6*); Practice Book D. (Illus.). 1977. pap. text 4.75 (*0-89075-056-4*); Practice Book E. (Illus.). 1977. pap. text 4.75 (*0-89075-057-2*); Practice Book F. (Illus.). 1977. pap. 4.95 (*0-89075-058-0*); Practice Book G. (Illus.). 1977. pap. 4.95 (*0-89075-059-9*); Practice Book H. (Illus.). 1977. pap. 4.95 (*0-89075-060-2*); Practice Book I. (Illus.). 1977. pap. 4.95 (*0-89075-061-0*); Practice Book J. (Illus.). 1977. pap. 4.95 (*0-89075-062-9*); (Illus.). (gr. k-2). 1977. pap. text. write for info. (*0-318-51460-5*) Bilingual Ed Serv.

— CS 1 Skillbooklet. (Crane Reading System-English Ser.). (Illus.). (gr. k-2). 1982. pap. text 2.49 (*0-89075-033-5*) Bilingual Ed Serv.

— DS 1 Skill Booklet. (Crane Reading System-English Ser.). (Illus.). (gr. k-2). 1982. pap. text 2.49 (*0-89075-035-1*) Bilingual Ed Serv.

— ES 1 Skillbooklet. (Crane Reading System-English Ser.). (Illus.). (gr. k-2). 1978. pap. text 2.49 (*0-89075-038-6*) Bilingual Ed Serv.

— GS 1 Skill Booklet. (Crane Reading System-English Ser.). (Illus.). (J). (gr. k-2). 1982. pap. text 2.49 (*0-89075-042-4*) Bilingual Ed Serv.

— A Head Start Through Reading. (Crane Reading System-English Ser.). (Illus.). (gr. k-2). 1977. pap. text 26.55 (*0-89075-135-8*) Bilingual Ed Serv.

— I'm Late. (Crane Reading System-English Ser.). (Illus.). (gr. k-2). 1977. pap. text 5.15 (*0-89075-099-8*) Bilingual Ed Serv.

— Me. (Crane Reading System-English Ser.). (Illus.). (gr. k-2). 1977. pap. text 4.85 (*0-89075-092-0*) Bilingual Ed Serv.

— My New Friends. (Crane Reading System-English Ser.). (gr. k-2). 1977. pap. text 5.15 (*0-89075-102-1*) Bilingual Ed Serv.

— Only for a Day. (Crane Reading System-English Ser.). (Illus.). (gr. k-2). 1977. pap. text 5.15 (*0-89075-101-3*) Bilingual Ed Serv.

— Over the Top. (Crane Reading System-English Ser.). (Illus.). (gr. k-2). 1977. pap. text 5.15 (*0-89075-100-5*) Bilingual Ed Serv.

— Playmates. (Crane Reading System-English Ser.). (Illus.). (gr. k-2). 1977. pap. text 4.85 (*0-89075-096-3*) Bilingual Ed Serv.

— The Queen & I. (Crane Reading System-English Ser.). (Illus.). (gr. k-2). 1977. pap. text 4.85 (*0-89075-093-9*) Bilingual Ed Serv.

Crane, Basil K. Dust from an Alkali Flat: A Forest Ranger Remembers Central Nevada. LC 83-27330. (Bristlecone Paperback Ser.). (Illus.). 166p. 1984. reprint ed. pap. 51.50 (*0-608-01264-5*, 206201300001) Bks Demand.

Crane, Ben. The Before & after Trade Card. (Illus.). 136p. (Orig.). 1995. pap. 20.00 (*0-9657480-0-6*) B Crane.

C

Crane, Beryl. Reflexology: Guide to Herbalism. LC 98-41259. (Illustrated Guide Ser.). (Illus.). 144p. 1999. pap. 19.95 (*1-86204-169-5*, Pub. by Element MA) Penguin Putnam.

— Reflexology: The Definitive Practitioner's Manual: Recommended by the International Therapy Examination Council for Students & Practitioners. LC 97-29169. 448p. 1998. 59.95 (*1-86204-125-3*, Pub. by Element MA) Penguin Putnam.

Crane, Bo. Of Heaven & Earth. LC 92-36831. 232p. 1992. text 89.95 (*0-7734-9869-9*) E Mellen.

Crane, Bob, jt. auth. see Golant, Mitch.

Crane, Bonnie L. Blanche Ames: Artist & Activist. (Illus.). 40p. (Orig.). 1982. pap. 4.95 (*0-934358-10-9*) Fuller Mus Art.

Crane, Brian. Pickles. LC 98-66374. (Illus.). 96p. 1998. pap. 7.95 (*1-56352-510-0*) Longstreet.

***Crane, Brian.** Pickles Mixed Counter Display. 1999. pap. text 95.40 (*1-56352-591-7*) Longstreet.

— Pickles, Too: The Older I Get, the Better I Was. LC 99-61758. (Illus.). 96p. 1999. pap. 7.95 (*1-56352-583-6*) Longstreet.

Crane, Brian A., et al. Supreme Court of Canada Practice, 1994 LC 93-222531. xxxii, 290 p. 1993. write for info. (*0-459-55760-2*) Carswell.

Crane, Carl D., III & Duffy, Joseph. Kinematic Analysis of Robot Manipulators. LC 97-13161. (Illus.). 456p. (C). 1998. text 90.00 (*0-521-57063-8*) Cambridge U Pr.

Crane, Carla, ed. see Butts, Laurie, et al.

Crane, Carla, ed. see Clark, Lea, et al.

Crane, Carla J., ed. see Cooper, Robin S., et al.

Crane, Charles & Crane, Diane. The Clergy Search Dilemma: Pastors & Lay People Reflect on the Crisis of Clergy Deployment. LC 90-22731. 220p. 1991. pap. 11.95 (*1-56101-019-7*) Cowley Pubns.

Crane, Charles & Crane, Steven. Ashamed of Joseph: Mormon Foundations Crumble. 270p. 1993. 10.99 (*0-89900-615-9*) College Pr Pub.

Crane, Cheri J. Following Kate: A Novel. LC 98-215129. 281 p. (J). 1998. pap. 12.95 (*1-57734-319-0*, 01113585) Covenant Comms.

— Forever Kate. LC 97-26015. (J). 1997. pap. 12.95 (*1-57734-127-9*, 01112902) Covenant Comms.

— Kate's Return. LC 96-24829. (J). 1996. pap. 13.95 (*1-55503-982-0*, 01112457) Covenant Comms.

— Kate's Turn: A Novel. LC 94-31946. 1994. pap. 11.95 (*1-55503-715-1*, 019404) Covenant Comms.

Crane, Cheryl & Jahr, Cliff. Detour: A Hollywood Story. 1989. mass mkt. 4.50 (*0-380-70580-X*, Avon Bks) Morrow Avon.

Crane, Chilton & Warren, Richard. Procedures in Vascular Surgery. 2nd ed. LC 75-22597. 1976. 47.00 (*0-316-16014-8*, Little Brwn Med Div) Lppncott W & W.

Crane, Conrad C. American Airpower Strategy in Korea, 1950-1953. LC 99-35874. (Modern War Studies). (Illus.). 248p. 2000. 35.00 (*0-7006-0991-1*) U Pr of KS.

— Bombs, Cities, & Civilians: American Airpower Strategy in World War II. LC 92-28141. (Modern War Studies). (Illus.). 208p. 1993. 29.95 (*0-7006-0574-6*) U Pr of KS.

Crane, D. Russell. Fundamentals of Marital Therapy. LC 96-34763. (Basic Principles into Practice Ser.: Vol. 14). 192p. 1996. pap. 23.95 (*0-87630-801-9*) Brunner-Mazel.

***Crane, Dale.** Airframe Vol. 1: Structures. 2nd ed. Michmerhuizen, Terry et al, eds. LC 94-22063. (Aviation Maintenance Technician Ser.). (Illus.). 536p. 1999. pap. 29.95 (*1-56027-339-9*) ASA Inc.

— Airframe Vol. 2: Systems. 2nd ed. Michmerhuizen, Terry et al, eds. LC 94-22063. (Illus.). 480p. 1999. pap. 29.95 (*1-56027-340-2*) ASA Inc.

Crane, Dale. AMT Series Curriculum Guide: #ASA-AMT-CG. (Illus.). 482p. 1998. ring bd. 149.95 (*1-56027-238-4*, ASA-AMT-CG) ASA Inc.

— Aviation Maintenance Technician Oral & Practical Exam Guide ASA-OEG-AMT: #ASA-OEG-AMT. LC 94-33147. (Illus.). 176p. 1994. pap. 10.95 (*1-56027-199-X*, ASA-OEG-AMT) ASA Inc.

— Aviation Maintenance Technician Series General: #ASA-AMT-G. LC 93-1292. (Illus.). 772p. 1993. pap. 44.95 (*1-56027-336-4*, ASA-AMT-G) ASA Inc.

— Aviation Maintenance Technician Series Powerplant: #ASA-AMT-D. LC 95-50012. (Illus.). 760p. 1996. pap. 44.95 (*1-56027-154-X*, ASA-AMT-P) ASA Inc.

— Aviation Mechanic Handbook: #ASA-M-HB1. LC 92-34331. 1992. pap. 12.95 (*1-56027-132-9*, ASA-M-HB1) ASA Inc.

— Dictionary of Aeronautical Terms: #ASA-DAT-3. 3rd ed. LC 97-29690. (Illus.). 1997. pap. 19.95 (*1-56027-287-2*) ASA Inc.

— Inspection Authorization Test Prep: Test Preparation & Study References for the FAA Inspection Authorization Knowledge Test. 2nd ed. LC 96-45676. (Fast-Track Series Guide). (Illus.). 400p. 1998. pap. 24.95 (*1-56027-367-4*, ASA-IA-2) ASA Inc.

— Physics: A Basic Course, High School Sophomore Level (Grade 10) LC 86-22225. (ABC (A Basic Course) Ser.). (Illus.). (Orig.). (C). 1986. pap. text 12.95 (*0-914565-23-0*) Capstan Pubns.

Crane, Dale, ed. see FAA Staff.

Crane, Dale, ed. see Siegel, Jerry.

***Crane, Danford L.** The Other Simon: An Eye Witness Account by the Man Who Carried the Cross. 192p. 1998. pap. 9.95 (*1-57636-062-8*) SunRise Pbl.

— Son of Simon: Sequel to "The Other Simon" Larsen, Dawnie, ed. 264p. 1999. pap. text 12.95 (*1-57636-076-8*, Pub. by SunRise Pbl) Granite UT.

Crane, Daniel M. & Breslin, Thomas A. An Ordinary Relationship: American Opposition to Republican Revolution in China. LC 85-26452. 256p. 1986. 32.95 (*0-8130-0800-X*) U Press Fla.

Crane, David. The Canadian Dictionary of Business & Economics. 416p. 1993. 45.00 (*0-7737-2691-8*) Genl Dist Srvs.

— Lord Byron's Jackal: The Life of Edward John Trelawny. LC 99-16413. (Illus.). 408p. 1999. 30.00 (*1-56858-143-2*) FWEW.

— The Next Canadian Century. 224p. 1992. 26.95 (*0-7737-2569-5*) Genl Dist Srvs.

Crane, David, jt. auth. see Coen, Larry.

Crane, David, ed. see Dryden, John.

Crane, David, jt. ed. see Morwood, James.

Crane, David, ed. see Shakespeare, William.

Crane, Denis, jt. auth. see Masters, Colin.

Crane, Diana. Invisible Colleges: Diffusion of Knowledge in Scientific Communities. 224p. 1995. pap. text 14.95 (*0-226-11856-8*, Midway Reprint) U Ch Pr.

— The Production of Culture: Media & the Urban Arts, No. 1. (Foundations of Popular Culture Ser.: Vol. 1). 220p. (C). 1992. text 42.00 (*0-8039-3693-1*) Sage.

— The Sanctity of Social Life: Physicians' Treatment of Critically Ill Patients. LC 74-15510. 186p. 1975. 30.00 (*0-87154-209-9*) Russell Sage.

— The Sanctity of Social Life: Physician's Treatment of Critically Ill Patients. LC 74-15510. (Illus.). 286p. 1977. reprint ed. pap. text 21.95 (*0-87855-648-6*) Transaction Pubs.

— The Transformation of the Avant-Garde: The New York Art World, 1940-1985. LC 87-5013. (Illus.). x, 204p. (C). 1989. pap. text 13.95 (*0-226-11790-1*) U Ch Pr.

— The Transformation of the Avant-Garde: The New York Art World, 1940-1985. LC 87-5013. (Illus.). x, 194p. (C). 1994. 24.95 (*0-226-11789-8*) U Ch Pr.

Crane, Diana, ed. The Sociology of Culture: Emerging Theoretical Perspectives. LC 93-34717. (Illus.). 352p. 1994. pap. 29.95 (*1-55786-463-2*) Blackwell Pubs.

Crane, Diane & Scholastic, Inc. Staff, eds. Artfully Easy. 1983. pap. 12.95 (*0-590-49019-2*, Scholastic Hardcover) Scholastic Inc.

Crane, Diane, jt. auth. see Crane, Charles.

Crane, Dick. A Wonderful Journey: The Autobiography of Dick Crane. Ryan, Susan & O'Keefe, Peggy, eds. Johnson, Debbie & Grant, Susan, trs. (Illus.). 188p. 1996. reprint ed. pap. 9.95 (*0-9641092-1-2*) Wrds In Motion.

Crane, Donald P. Personnel: Management Of Human Resources. 3rd ed. LC 81-19295. (SWC-Management). 752p. (C). 1982. mass mkt. 28.25 (*0-534-01070-9*) PWS Pubs.

— Personnel Mgt Situational Apprch. (SWC-Management). 1974. pap. 15.75 (*0-534-00356-7*) PWS Pubs.

Crane, Donald P., jt. auth. see Miner, John B.

Crane, Dwight B., et al. The Global Financial System: A Functional Perspective. 288p. 1995. 35.00 (*0-87584-622-X*) Harvard Busn.

Crane, E. B. Genealogy of the Crane Family, 2 vols. (Illus.). 839p. 1989. reprint ed. pap. 115.00 (*0-8328-0439-8*); reprint ed. lib. bdg. 123.00 (*0-8328-0438-X*) Higginson Bk Co.

— The Rawson Family: A Revised Memoir of Edward Rawson, Secretary of the Colony of Mass. Bay, from 1650 to 1686. (Illus.). 350p. 1989. reprint ed. pap. 52.00 (*0-8328-1005-3*); reprint ed. lib. bdg. 60.00 (*0-8328-1004-5*) Higginson Bk Co.

Crane, Edgar. Marketing Communications. 2nd ed. LC 72-4505. (Marketing Ser.). 510p. (C). reprint ed. 158.10 (*0-8357-9929-8*, 201311600084) Bks Demand.

Crane, Edward H. & Boaz, David, eds. An American Vision: Policies for the '90s. LC 88-35280. 358p. 1989. pap. 3.00 (*0-932790-73-9*) Cato Inst.

— Cato Handbook for Congress: Policy Recommendations for the 106th Congress. LC 98-55951. 618p. 1999. pap. 18.95 (*1-882577-80-9*) Cato Inst.

— Cato Handbook for Congress: 106th Congress. 550p. 1999. pap. 25.00 (*1-882577-73-6*, Pub. by Cato Inst) Natl Bk Netwk.

Crane, Edward H., jt. ed. see Boaz, David.

Crane, Elaine F. A Dependent People: Newport, Rhode Island in the Revolutionary Era. rev. ed. LC 92-6806. (Illus.). 196p. 1992. pap. 19.95 (*0-8232-1112-6*) Fordham.

— The Diary of Elizabeth Drinker: The Life Cycle of an Eighteenth-Century Woman. abr. ed. LC 94-4525. 320p. 1994. text 47.50 (*1-55553-190-3*); pap. text 17.95 (*1-55553-191-1*) NE U Pr.

— Ebb Tide in New England: Women, Seaports, & Social Change, 1630-1800. LC 97-43479. 333p. 1998. pap. 17.95 (*1-55553-336-1*); text 50.00 (*1-55553-337-X*) NE U Pr.

Crane, Elaine F., ed. The Diary of Elizabeth Drinker, 3 vols., Set. 2400p. 1991. text 250.00 (*1-55553-093-1*) NE U Pr.

Crane, Elizabeth. Time Remembered. 448p. (Orig.). 1997. mass mkt. 5.50 (*0-505-52223-3*, Love Spell) Dorchester Pub Co.

Crane, Ellery Bicknell, see Bicknell Crane, Ellery.

Crane, Eva. The Archaeology of Beekeeping. LC 82-74021. (Illus.). 320p. 1983. text 52.50 (*0-8014-1609-4*) Cornell U Pr.

— Bees & Beekeeping: Science, Practice, & World Resources. LC 89-17477. (Illus.). 640p. 1990. text 115.00 (*0-8014-2429-1*) Cornell U Pr.

— The World History of Beekeeping & Honey Hunting. LC 99-25816. 682p. 1999. 125.00 (*0-415-92467-7*) Routledge.

Crane, F. G. Professional Services Marketing: Strategy & Tactics. LC 91-36043. 131p. 1993. pap. 14.95 (*1-56024-241-8*) Haworth Pr.

— Professional Services Marketing: Strategy & Tactics. LC 91-36043. (Illus.). 142p. 1993. lib. bdg. 39.95 (*1-56024-240-X*) Haworth Pr.

Crane, F. L., et al, eds. Plasma Membrane Oxidoreductases in Control of Animal & Plant Growth. (NATO ASI Series A, Life Sciences: Vol. 157). (Illus.). 460p. 1988. 125.00 (*0-306-43092-4*, Plenum Trade) Perseus Pubng.

Crane, Frank. Four Minute Essays (1919) 140p. 1998. reprint ed. pap. 16.95 (*0-7661-0630-6*) Kessinger Pub.

Crane, Frank, intro. The Lost Books of the Bible & the Forgotten Books of Eden. LC 98-18468. 269p. 1994. pap. text 11.95 (*1-881316-63-7*) A&B Bks.

Crane, Frasier & Crane, Niles. Frasier, Cafe Nervosa: The Connoisseur's Cookbook. LC 96-69578. 108p. 1996. 14.95 (*0-8487-1550-0*, 102584) Oxmoor Hse.

Crane, Frederick. Materials for the Study of the 15th-Century Basse Danse. (Wissenschaftliche Abhandlungen-Musicological Studies: Vol. 16). 128p. 1970. lib. bdg. 40.00 (*0-912024-86-0*) Inst Mediaeval Mus.

Crane, Frederick & Grant, Stephen. Marketing: Insights & Applicatons. 512p. (C). 1997. per. 47.96 (*0-256-19520-X*, Irwn McGrw-H) McGrw-H Hghr Educ.

Crane, Frederick L., et al. Oxidoreduction at the Plasma Membrane Vol. 1: Relation to Growth & Transport: Animals. 328p. 1990. lib. bdg. 230.00 (*0-8493-6937-1*, QP602) CRC Pr.

— Oxidoreduction at the Plasma Membrane Vol. 2: Relation to Growth & Transport: Plants. 264p. 1991. lib. bdg. 225.00 (*0-8493-6938-X*, QP602) CRC Pr.

Crane, Gene A., jt. auth. see Kojima, Setsuko.

Crane, George & Tsai, Tsung. Bones of the Master: A Buddhist Monk's Search for the Lost Heart of China. LC 99-37868. 304p. 2000. 25.95 (*0-553-10650-3*) Bantam.

Crane, George T. The Political Economy of China's Special Economic Zones. LC 89-10759. (Studies on Contemporary China). 206p. (C). (gr. 13). 1990. text 70.95 (*0-87332-514-1*, East Gate Bk) M E Sharpe.

Crane, Gergory. The Blinded Eye: Thucydides & the New Written Word. (Greek Studies: Interdisciplinary Approaches). 294p. (C). 1996. lib. bdg. 64.00 (*0-8476-8129-7*) Rowman.

Crane, Geroge T. & Amawi, Abla M., eds. The Theoretical Evolution of International Political Economy: A Reader. 2nd ed. LC 96-8401. 352p. (C). 1997. pap. text 23.95 (*0-19-509443-3*) OUP.

Crane, Gregory. The Blinded Eye: Thucydides & the New Written Word. (Greek Studies). 288p. 1995. pap. text 22.95 (*0-8476-8130-0*) Littlefield.

— Thucydides & the Ancient Simplicity: The Limits of Political Realism. LC 96-29615. 330p. 1997. 45.00 (*0-520-20789-0*, Pub. by U CA Pr) Cal Prin Full Svc.

Crane, Gregory, ed. Perseus 1.0 Manual: Interactive Sources & Studies on Ancient Greece. (Illus.). (Orig.). 1992. 25.00 (*0-300-05088-7*); vdisk 200.00 (*0-300-05086-0*); cd-rom 125.00 (*0-300-05087-9*) Yale U Pr.

Crane, H. Richard. How Things Work. (Illus.). 114p. (Orig.). (C). 1992. reprint ed. per. 29.00 (*0-917853-44-X*, OP-60) Am Assn Physics.

Crane, Hamilton. Bonjour, Miss Seeton. LC 96-53661. 272p. 1997. pap. 21.95 (*0-425-15968-X*, Prime Crime) Berkley Pub.

— Bonjour, Miss Seeton. (Heron Carvic's Miss Seeton Ser.: Vol. 21). 272p. 1998. reprint ed. mass mkt. 5.99 (*0-425-16534-5*) Berkley Pub.

— Hands up, Miss Seeton. 1992. mass mkt. 5.50 (*0-425-13132-7*) Berkley Pub.

***Crane, Hamilton.** Miss Seeton by Moonlight. large type ed. LC 99-462229. (Mystery Ser.). 336p. 2000. 27.95 (*0-7862-2481-9*) Thorndike Pr.

Crane, Hamilton. Miss Seeton Cracks the Case. 1991. mass mkt. 4.99 (*0-425-12676-5*) Berkley Pub.

— Miss Seeton Goes to Bat. LC 99-32537. 1999. 26.95 (*0-7862-2065-1*) Thorndike Pr.

— Miss Seeton Rocks the Cradle. 208p. (Orig.). 1992. mass mkt. 4.99 (*0-425-13400-8*) Berkley Pub.

— Miss Seeton Rules. 272p. 1995. mass mkt. 4.99 (*0-425-15006-2*, Prime Crime) Berkley Pub.

— Miss Seeton's Finest Hour, 1 vol. 259p. 1999. mass mkt. 5.99 (*0-425-17026-8*, Prime Crime) Berkley Pub.

— Sold to Miss Seeton. LC 95-6298. (Heron Carvic's Miss Seeton Ser.). 272p. 1995. pap. 19.95 (*0-425-14936-6*, Prime Crime) Berkley Pub.

— Sweet Miss Seeton. (Heron Carvic's Miss Seeton Ser.). 272p. 1996. pap. 21.95 (*0-425-15471-8*, Prime Crime) Berkley Pub.

— Sweet Miss Seeton. 256p. 1997. reprint ed. mass mkt. 5.99 (*0-425-15962-0*, Prime Crime) Berkley Pub.

Crane, Hamilton & Carvic, Heron. Miss Seeton Goes to Bat. 208p. 1993. mass mkt. 4.99 (*0-425-13576-4*) Berkley Pub.

Crane, Hart. The Bridge. LC 72-131277. 112p. 1992. reprint ed. pap. 10.95 (*0-87140-225-4*) Norton.

***Crane, Hart.** Complete Poems of Hart Crane: Centennial Edition. 288p. 2000. 29.95 (*0-87140-656-X*, Pub. by Liveright) Norton.

Crane, Hart. Letters of Hart Crane & His Family. Lewis, Thomas S., ed. LC 73-21675. 699p. reprint ed. pap. 200.00 (*0-8357-4575-9*, 203748400008) Bks Demand.

— O My Land, My Friends: The Selected Letters of Hart Crane. Weber, Brom & Hammer, Langdon, eds. LC 88-21303. 562p. 1997. 35.00 (*0-941423-18-2*) FWEW.

— White Buildings. 1986. pap. 3.95 (*0-87140-272-6*, Pub. by Liveright) Norton.

Crane, Hewitt D. New Social Marketplace: Notes on Effecting Social Change in America's 3rd Century. LC 80-11674. (Communication & Information Science Ser.). (Illus.). 136p. 1980. text 73.25 (*0-89391-063-5*) Ablx Pub.

Crane, Howard. Risale-i Mi'mariyye: An Early-Seventeenth Century Ottoman Treatise on Architecture. (Muquarnas Supplements Studies in Islamic Architecture Ser.: Vol. 1). (Illus.). x, 126 , 85 facp. 1987. 89.50 (*90-04-07846-0*) Brill Academic Pubs.

Crane, Howard, tr. see Hafz Hhuseyin Ayvansarayc Staff.

Crane, J. The Synoptics. 1990. pap. 32.00 (*0-7220-8711-X*) St Mut.

Crane, J., et al, eds. Materials Issues for Advanced Electronic & Opto-Electronic Connectors. LC 91-61921. (Illus.). 157p. 1991. pap. 48.70 (*0-608-04891-7*, 206558300004) Bks Demand.

Crane, J. D. Manual para Predicadores Laicos: Manual for the Lay Preachers Student. 122p. 1967. reprint ed. pap. 9.99 (*0-311-42039-7*) Casa Bautista.

Crane, J. L., et al. An Annotated Catalogue of Types of the University of Illinois Mycological Collections. LC 96-2752. (Illinois Biological Monographs). (Illus.). 376p. 1997. text 35.00 (*0-252-02319-6*) U of Ill Pr.

Crane, James D. Bosquejos para Sermones Biblicos.Tr. of Sermon Outlines for Biblical Messages. (SPA.). 128p. 1996. pap. text 6.99 (*0-311-43048-1*) Casa Bautista.

Crane, James D. La Oracion Cristiana - Privilegio y Responsabilidad: The Christian Prayer - Privilege & Responsibility. (SPA.). 96p. (Orig.). 1991. pap. 7.50 (*0-311-40048-5*) Casa Bautista.

— El Sermon Eficaz: Effective Preaching. (SPA.). 308p. 1962. reprint ed. pap. 9.50 (*0-311-42032-X*) Casa Bautista.

— Timoteo y Tito: Obreros Aprobados. (Estudios Biblicos Basicos Ser.).Tr. of Studies in Timothy & Titus. (SPA.). 160p. 1990. pap. 7.99 (*0-311-04364-X*) Casa Bautista.

Crane, Janet. French Guiana. (World Bibliographical Ser.). 198p. 1999. lib. bdg. 59.00 (*1-85109-241-2*) ABC-CLIO.

Crane, Janet, compiled by. Martinique. LC 96-192593. (World Bibliographical Ser.: Vol. 175). 174p. 1995. lib. bdg. 55.00 (*1-85109-151-3*) ABC-CLIO.

Crane, Joan. Guy Davenport: A Descriptive Bibliography 1947-1995. (Illus.). 296p. 1996. 75.00 (*0-9622236-1-1*) J S Jaffe.

Crane, Joan S., jt. auth. see Clifton Waller Barrett Library Staff.

***Crane, John.** A Traders Handbook: The Reversal Day Phenomenon. (Illus.). 181p. 1998. 175.00 (*1-883272-28-9*) Traders Lib.

Crane, John, et al. Biological Investigation. 144p. (C). 1990. 19.95 (*0-89863-108-4*) Star Pub CA.

Crane, John A. The Evaluation of Social Policies. (International Series in Social Welfare). 1982. lib. bdg. 66.50 (*0-89838-075-8*) Kluwer Academic.

Crane, John B. Ray Dream 3D Design Solutions. 1997. 45.00 (*1-56205-763-4*) New Riders Pub.

Crane, John K. The Yoknapatawpha Chronicle of Gavin Stevens. LC 87-42809. 312p. 1988. 42.50 (*0-941664-90-2*) Susquehanna U Pr.

Crane, John O. & Crane, Sylvia. Czechoslovakia: Anvil of the Cold War. LC 90-39146. 384p. 1990. 65.00 (*0-275-93577-9*, C3577, Praeger Pubs) Greenwood.

Crane, John W. Contemporary Readings for General Biology. 4th ed. (Biology Ser.). 1995. 14.00 (*0-534-21087-2*) Wadsworth Pub.

— Contemporary Readings for General Biology. 5th ed. (Biology Ser.). 144p. 1996. 14.00 (*0-534-51632-7*) Wadsworth Pub.

Crane, John W., ed. Contemporary Readings for General Biology. 154p. (C). 1987. pap. 8.00 (*0-534-06931-2*) Wadsworth Pub.

— Contemporary Readings for General Biology. 2nd ed. 152p. (C). 1989. pap. 9.50 (*0-534-09188-1*) Wadsworth Pub.

— Contemporary Readings for General Biology. 3rd ed. 146p. (C). 1991. mass mkt. write for info. (*0-534-13376-2*) Wadsworth Pub.

Crane, Jonathan. Social Programs That Work. LC 97-44908. (Illus.). 314p. 1998. 42.50 (*0-87154-173-4*) Russell Sage.

Crane, Jonathan L. Terror & Everyday Life: Singular Moments in the History of the Horror Film. 235p. 1994. 42.00 (*0-8039-5848-X*); pap. 19.50 (*0-8039-5849-8*) Sage.

Crane, Joseph. Blessings, Gifts & Deeds: Building Your Celestial Mansion. 180p. 1996. pap. 14.95 (*1-890613-00-2*) West Coast Media.

Crane, Judy B. How to Survive Your Hospital Stay. LC 97-26727. 128p. 1997. pap. 11.95 (*1-889198-02-1*) Ctr Pr CA.

— How to Survive Your Hospital Stay. LC 97-26727. (Illus.). 128p. 1997. spiral bd. 11.95 (*1-889198-05-6*) Ctr Pr CA.

Crane, Julia & Angrosino, Michael. Field Projects in Anthropology: A Student Handbook. 3rd rev. ed. (Illus.). 200p. (Orig.). (C). 1992. pap. text 11.95 (*0-88133-685-8*) Waveland Pr.

Crane, Julia G. Statia Silhouettes. LC 97-91263. 1998. 29.95 (*0-533-12612-6*) Vantage.

Crane, Julianne, jt. auth. see Israel, Richard.

Crane, K., jt. auth. see Crane, R.

Crane, Karen, jt. auth. see Bean, Richard.

Crane, Keith, tr. see Pecsi, Kalman.

Crane, Kitty, ed. see Saban, Vera.

***Crane, Larry.** Tape Op: The Book about Creative Music Recording. 2000. pap. 19.95 (*0-922915-60-1*) Feral Hse.

Crane, Loren D. Executive Functions of the Brain. 3rd ed. 148p. (C). 1992. text 27.00 (*0-536-58193-2*) Pearson Custom.

Crane, Loren D. The Public Speaker's Bible: How to Capitolize on Your Personal Style- Avoid the 9 Myths.' LC 98-87547. (Illus.). 192p. 2000. pap. 20.00 (*0-9667330-0-2*) Brain Research.

Crane, Louise. The Land & People of the Congo. LC 79-141447. (Portraits of the Nations Ser.). (Illus.). 144p. (J). (gr. 5-9). 1971. lib. bdg. 11.89 (*0-397-31172-9*) HarpC Child Bks.

Crane, Lucy, tr. see Grimm, Jacob W. & Grimm, Wilhelm K.

An Asterisk (*) at the beginning of an entry indicates that the title is appearing for the first time.

Crane, Lynette. Psychology of Stress: From Distress to Eustress. 2nd ed. 144p. 1996. ring bd. 46.95 (*0-7872-1980-0*) Kendall-Hunt.

***Crane, M. E.** Prince William: A Birthday Scrapbook. Orig. Title: Prince William Bio, Prince William Comes of Age. (J). (gr. 4-6). 2000. per. 6.99 (*0-689-83532-9*) Aladdin.

Crane, M. F. & Fischer, William C. Fire Ecology of the Forest Habitat Types of Central Idaho. (Illus.). 92p. 1997. reprint ed. 17.40 (*0-89904-631-2*); reprint ed. pap. 12.40 (*0-89904-632-0*) Crumb Elbow Pub.

Crane, Madge L. & Crane, Phillip L. Most Distinguished Characters on the American Frontier, Robert Looney (B. 1692-1702, D. 1770) of Augusta (Now Botetourt) County, Virginia, & Some of His Descendants, with Histories of the Great Road, Looney's Ferry, Crow's Ferry, Anderson's Ferry, Boyd's Ferry, & Beale's Bridge. LC 98-72164. (Illus.). 442p. 1998. 40.00 (*0-9664321-1-8*) P L Crane.

Crane, Margaret, ed. Rooms of Our Own: More Stories for Young Feminists. (Illus.). 192p. (YA). (gr. 8 up). 1995. 15.95 (*0-8050-1616-3*, Bks Young Read) H Holt & Co.

Crane, Margaret, jt. auth. see Buchholz, Barbara B.

Crane, Margaret, jt. auth. see Bucholz, Barbara B.

Crane, Mary T. Framing Authority: Sayings, Self & Society in Sixteenth-Century England. LC 92-19878. 291p. 1993. reprint ed. pap. 90.30 (*0-608-02563-1*, 206320800004) Bks Demand.

***Crane, Mary Thomas.** Shakespeare's Brain: Reading with Cognitive Theory. LC 00-39143. 288p. 2000. pap. 19.95 (*0-691-06992-1*) Princeton U Pr.

— Shakespear's Brain: Reading with Cognitive Theory. 288p. 2000. 49.50 (*0-691-05087-2*) Princeton U Pr.

Crane, Mary Thomas, ed. see Lewalski, Barbara Kiefer.

Crane, Maureen K. Understanding Older Homeless People Their Circumstances, Problems & Needs. LC 98-45150. 1999. 85.00 (*0-335-20187-3*) Taylor & Francis.

***Crane, Maureen K.** Understanding Older Homeless People: Their Circumstances, Problems, & Needs. LC 98-45150. 224p. 1999. pap. 27.95 (*0-335-20186-5*) OpUniv Pr.

Crane, Maureen K., ed. Artists' & Writers' Market List: A Guide to Greeting Card Publishers' Submission Criteria for Art, Photography & Editorial Entries. 2nd rev. ed. 130p. 1997. pap. 49.95 (*0-938369-29-6*) Grtng Card Creat Netwk.

Crane, Milton, ed. Fifty Great American Short Stories. 512p. 1984. mass mkt. 5.99 (*0-553-27294-2*, Bantam Classics) Bantam.

— Fifty Great Short Stories. 480p. 1983. mass mkt. 5.99 (*0-553-27745-6*, Bantam Classics) Bantam.

Crane, Milton G. Plugged Arteries & a Clogged Immune System. LC 98-88032. (Illus.). 110p. 1998. per. 18.95 (*1-57258-145-X*) Teach Servs.

— Preparacion Para la Traslacion (Preparation for Translation) rev. ed. LC 93-61527. (SPA.). 272p. 1995. per. 8.95 (*0-945383-66-5*) Teach Servs.

— Preparation for Translation, Ver. 3. rev. ed. LC 88-50091. 229p. 1992. pap. 7.95 (*0-945383-33-9*, 945-5818) Teach Servs.

— Subtle Challenge to God's Authority. LC 88-50302. 144p. 1988. per. 5.50 (*0-945383-03-7*) Teach Servs.

— Such a Cloud of Witnesses. rev. ed. LC 91-65119. 80p. 1995. per. 4.95 (*1-57258-045-3*) Teach Servs.

Crane, Nancy, jt. auth. see Li, Xia.

Crane, Nancy B., jt. auth. see Li, Xia.

Crane, Nicholas. Clear Waters Rising: A Mountain Walk Across Europe. LC 98-148806. (Illus.). 1997. write for info. (*0-14-024332-1*) Penguin Books.

Crane, Nicholas, jt. auth. see Crane, Richard.

Crane, Niles, jt. auth. see Crane, Frasier.

Crane, P., jt. ed. see Duric, N.

Crane, P., jt. ed. see Meylan, G.

Crane, P., jt. ed. see Tinney, Chris G.

Crane, P. W. Worked Examples in Basic Electronics. 1967. 128.00 (*0-08-012217-5*, Pub. by Pergamon Repr) Franklin.

Crane, Patricia, ed. see Crawford, James.

Crane, Paul & Crane, Sophie. North Carolina Taproots: Courthouses of North Carolina. LC 97-75414. (Illus.). 144p. 1997. 19.95 (*1-57736-042-7*, Hillsboro Pr) Providence Hse.

Crane, Paul, jt. auth. see Crane, Sophie.

Crane, Paula, jt. auth. see Brown, Dave.

Crane, Peter R. & Blackmore, Stephen, eds. Evolution, Systematics, & Fossil History of the Hamamelidae, Vol. 1. (Systematics Association Special Volume Ser.: Vol. 40A). (Illus.). 305p. 1990. text 90.00 (*0-19-857711-7*) OUP.

— Evolution, Systematics, & Fossil History of the Hamamelidae, Vol. 2. (Systematics Association Special Volume Ser.: Vol. 40B). (Illus.). 368p. 1990. text 105.00 (*0-19-857726-5*) OUP.

Crane, Peter R., jt. auth. see Kenrick, Paul.

***Crane, Philip, ed.** U. S. - China Trade Relations & Renewal of China's Most-Favored-Nation Status: Congressional Hearing. 221p. (C). 1999. reprint ed. pap. text 40.00 (*0-7881-8442-3*) DIANE Pub.

Crane, Philippe, ed. see ESO/EIPC Workshop on the Light Element Abundances.

Crane, Phillip L., jt. auth. see Crane, Madge L.

Crane, R., et al, eds. Materials for Optical Limiting, Vol. 374. (MRS Symposium Proceedings Ser.). 390p. 1995. 81.00 (*1-55899-276-6*) Materials Res.

Crane, R. & Crane, K. Aikido in Training: A Manual of Traditional Aikido Practice & Principles. LC 93-71042. 336p. 1993. 34.95 (*0-9636429-5-2*) Cool Rain Prods.

Crane, R. H. Crossed Silver: Poems in Poetry, Drawing, & Geometry. 68p. 1993. 16.95 (*0-9631041-0-1*) M M & C.

Crane, R. L., et al, eds. Nondestructive Characterization of Materials in Aging Systems Vol. 503: Materials Research Society Symposium Proceedings. LC 98-28359. 342p. 1998. text 71.00 (*1-55899-408-4*) Materials Res.

Crane, R. S. Critical & Historical Principles of Literary History. LC 75-159832. 1971. pap. text 1.75 (*0-226-11826-6*, P442) U Ch Pr.

Crane, Ralph & Livett, Anne. Troubled Pleasures: The Fiction of J. G. Farrell. LC 98-115348. 240p. 1997. 50.00 (*1-85182-310-7*, Pub. by Four Cts Pr) Intl Spec Bk.

Crane, Ralph J. Ruth Prawer Jhabvala. LC 92-11257. (English Authors Ser.: No. 494). 160p. 1992. 32.00 (*0-8057-7030-5*, Twyne) Mac Lib Ref.

Crane, Ralph J., ed. J. G. Farrell: The Critical Grip. 208p. 1998. boxed set 55.00 (*1-85182-421-9*, Pub. by Four Cts Pr) Intl Spec Bk.

— Nayantara Sahgal's India: Passion, Politics & History. LC 98-909223. xiv, 178p. 1998. write for info. (*81-207-2009-1*) Sterling Pub.

Crane, Randall, jt. auth. see Boarnet, Marlon.

Crane, Randy. Image Processing. 336p. (C). 1996. pap. text 77.00 incl. disk (*0-13-226416-1*) P-H.

Crane, Randy & Naqui, Shaz. Introduction Volume Rendering. LC 98-12074. 256p. (C). 1998. text 68.00 incl. cd-rom (*0-13-861683-3*) P-H.

Crane, Rhonda J. Politics of International Standards: France & the Color TV War. LC 79-4231. (Communication & Information Science Ser.). 124p. 1979. text 73.25 (*0-89391-019-8*) Ablx Pub.

Crane, Richard & Crane, Nicholas. Journey to the Centre of the Earth. large type ed. (Illus.). 619p. 1989. 27.99 (*0-7089-1928-6*) Ulverscroft.

Crane, Richard F. A French Conscience in Prague: Louis Eugene Faucher & the Abandonment of Czechoslovakia. LC 96-61467. 187p. 1996. 31.00 (*0-88033-350-2*, 453, Pub. by East Eur Monographs) Col U Pr.

***Crane, Robert.** European Business Culture. LC 99-42593. 240p. 2000. pap. 34.67 (*0-13-574559-4*) P-H.

Crane, Robert D. Shaping the Future: Challenge & Response. LC 97-28694. 1997. write for info. (*1-56888-242-4*); pap. write for info. (*1-56888-246-7*) Tapestry Pr.

Crane, Robert G., jt. ed. see Hewitson, Bruce C.

Crane, Robert K. Electromagnetic Wave Propagation Through Rain. LC 95-20817. 273p. 1996. 98.95 (*0-471-61376-2*) Wiley.

Crane, Robert T. The State in Constitutional & International Law. LC 78-63921. (Johns Hopkins University. Studies in the Social Sciences. Thirtieth Ser. 1912: 6-7). reprint ed. 37.50 (*0-404-61172-9*) AMS Pr.

Crane, Robin. Indoor Sports Spaces. 1990. pap. 36.95 (*0-442-30525-7*, VNR) Wiley.

Crane, Robin & Dixon, Malcolm. The Shape of Space: Indoor Sports Spaces. 1991. pap. 49.95 (*0-471-29386-5*) Wiley.

Crane, Rochelle, jt. auth. see Pierangelo, Roger.

Crane, Ronald S. The Languages of Criticism & the Structure of Poetry. LC PN1042.C7. (University of Toronto, Alexander Foundation, the Alexander Lectures: 1951-52). 236p. 1964. reprint ed. pap. 73.20 (*0-608-16159-4*, 203671000005) Bks Demand.

— The Languages of Criticism & the Structure of Poetry. LC 86-11387. xviii, 234p. (C). 1996. reprint ed. pap. text 19.50 (*0-226-11797-9*) U Ch Pr.

Crane, Ronald S., et al, compiled by. English Literature, Sixteen Sixty to Eighteen Hundred: A Bibliography of Modern Studies (Volume 2 1939-1950) LC 73-19999. 715p. 1974. reprint ed. 75.00 (*0-87752-163-8*) Gordian.

Crane, Ronald S., ed. see Goldsmith, Oliver.

Crane-Ross, Dushka. Reducing Stigma Through Education: Post Traumatic Stress Disorder. Keane, Terence M., ed. 1998. 175.00 (*1-889022-06-3*) Mental Hlth KY.

Crane, Sarah S. Crane Family History. (Illus.). 67p. 1997. reprint ed. pap. 13.50 (*0-8328-8122-8*); reprint ed. lib. bdg. 23.50 (*0-8328-8121-X*) Higginson Bk Co.

Crane, Sophie & Crane, Paul. Tennessee Taproots: Courthouses of Tennessee. rev. ed. LC 96-75691. (Illus.). 144p. 1996. 19.95 (*1-881576-26-4*, Hillsboro Pr) Providence Hse.

Crane, Sophie, jt. auth. see Crane, Paul.

Crane, Sophie M. A Legacy Remembered: One Hundred Years of Medical Missions. LC 98-65983. (Illus.). 512p. 1998. 34.95 (*1-57736-091-5*) Providence Hse.

Crane, Stephen. Active Service. (Works of Stephen Crane). 1990. reprint ed. lib. bdg. 79.00 (*0-7812-2432-2*) Rprt Serv.

— The Black Riders: The Original Version. unabridged ed. Pastore, Stephen, ed. (Illus.). 160p. 1998. 68.00 (*1-893173-02-X*) YaleBooks.

— The Black Riders & Other Lines. (Works of Stephen Crane). 1990. reprint ed. lib. bdg. 79.00 (*0-7812-2427-6*) Rprt Serv.

— The Bride Comes to Yellow Sky. 1970. pap. 3.25 (*0-8222-0152-6*) Dramatists Play.

— The Complete Poems of Stephen Crane. Katz, Joseph, ed. & intro. by. 191p. 1972. pap. text 13.95 (*0-8014-9130-4*) Cornell U Pr.

— La Conquete Du Courage. (FRE.). 1982. pap. 10.95 (*0-7859-1950-3*, 2070373517) Fr & Eur.

— The Correspondence of Stephen Crane, 2 vols., Set. Wertheim, Stanley & Sorrentino, Paul, eds. (Illus.). 1988. text 139.00 (*0-231-06002-5*) Col U Pr.

— Drawn from Life. 1995. 8.95 (*0-912756-17-9*) Union Coll.

— George's Mother. (Works of Stephen Crane). 1990. reprint ed. lib. bdg. 79.00 (*0-7812-2428-4*) Rprt Serv.

— Great Short Works Cran. 384p. 1942. pap. 8.50 (*0-06-083032-8*) HarperTrade.

— Little Regiment: And Other Episodes of the American Civil War. LC 70-150471. (Short Story Index Reprint Ser.). 1977. reprint ed. 15.95 (*0-8369-3811-9*) Ayer.

— "The Little Regiment" & Other Civil War Stories. LC 96-43701. (Thrift Editions Ser.). (Illus.). 80p. (Orig.). 1997. pap. 1.00 (*0-486-29557-5*) Dover.

— The Little Regiment & Other Episodes of the Civil War. (Works of Stephen Crane). 1990. reprint ed. lib. bdg. 79.00 (*0-685-44796-0*) Rprt Serv.

— Maggie. (Classics Library). 1998. pap. 3.95 (*1-85326-559-4*, 5594WW, Pub. by Wrdsworth Edits) NTC Contemp Pub Co.

***Crane, Stephen.** Maggie: A Girl of the Streets: And Other Tales of New York. (Penguin Classics Ser.). 2000. pap. 8.95 (*0-14-043797-5*) Viking Penguin.

Crane, Stephen. Maggie, a Girl of the Streets. 166p. 1985. mass mkt. 5.99 (*0-449-30024-2*, Prem) Fawcett.

— Maggie, a Girl of the Streets. Gullason, Thomas A., ed. (Critical Editions Ser.). (C). 1979. pap. text 12.50 (*0-393-95024-7*) Norton.

— Maggie, a Girl of the Streets. LC 95-9642. (Literary Classics Ser.). 90p. 1995. pap. 5.95 (*1-57392-037-1*) Prometheus Bks.

— Maggie, a Girl of the Streets. LC 98-86156. xvii, 374p. 1999. pap. 11.95 (*0-312-15266-3*) St Martin.

— Maggie, a Girl of the Streets. 1989. pap. 6.50 (*0-685-26534-X*) Vin Bks.

— Maggie, a Girl of the Streets. (Works of Stephen Crane). 1990. reprint ed. lib. bdg. 79.00 (*0-685-44763-4*) Rprt Serv.

— Maggie, a Girl of the Streets: A Story of New York. Hayes, Kevin J., ed. LC 98-86156. 384p. 1999. text 39.95 (*0-312-21824-9*) St Martin.

— Maggie, a Girl of the Streets: A Story of New York. LC 66-20867. 192p. 1978. reprint ed. 50.00 (*0-8201-1268-2*) Schol Facsimiles.

— Maggie, a Girl of the Streets: And Selected Stories. Kazin, Alfred, ed. 224p. 1991. mass mkt. 4.95 (*0-451-52552-3*, Sig Classics) NAL.

— Maggie, a Girl of the Streets & George's Mother: Two Novels. 1983. 11.09 (*0-606-02532-4*, Pub. by Turtleback) Demco.

— Maggie, a Girl of the Streets & Other Short Fiction. 208p. 1986. mass mkt. 4.95 (*0-553-21355-5*, Bantam Classics) Bantam.

— Maggie & Other Stories. (Airmont Classics Ser.). (YA). (gr. 11 up). 1968. mass mkt. 3.25 (*0-8049-0166-X*, CL-166) Airmont.

— Maggie & Other Stories. 26.95 (*0-88411-572-0*) Amereon Ltd.

— Men, Women & Boats. LC 70-113652. (Short Story Index Reprint Ser.). 1977. 21.95 (*0-8369-3381-8*) Ayer.

Crane, Stephen. Men, Women & Boats. (Works of Stephen Crane). 1990. reprint ed. lib. bdg. 79.00 (*0-7812-2438-1*) Rprt Serv.

Crane, Stephen. Men, Women & Boats. 247p. 1998. reprint ed. lib. bdg. 79.00 (*0-7812-4802-7*) Rprt Serv.

— The Monster & Other Stories. (Works of Stephen Crane). 1990. reprint ed. lib. bdg. 79.00 (*0-685-44792-8*) Rprt Serv.

— The Open Boat. 1999. pap. write for info. (*0-451-52646-5*, Sig Classics) NAL.

— The Open Boat & Other Stories. LC 93-12734. (Thrift Editions Ser.). 112p. 1993. reprint ed. pap. 1.50 (*0-486-27547-7*) Dover.

— The Open Boat & Other Tales of Adventure. LC 06-30865. 65.00 (*0-403-00012-2*) Scholarly.

— The Open Boat & Other Tales of Adventure. (Works of Stephen Crane). 1990. reprint ed. lib. bdg. 79.00 (*0-685-44794-4*) Rprt Serv.

— The O'Ruddy. (Works of Stephen Crane). 1990. reprint ed. lib. bdg. 79.00 (*0-685-44788-X*) Rprt Serv.

— The Portable Stephen Crane. Katz, Joseph, ed. & intro. by. LC 77-8036. (Portable Library: No. 68). 576p. 1977. pap. 15.95 (*0-14-015068-4*, Penguin Bks) Viking Penguin.

— Prose & Poetry. Levenson, J. C., ed. LC 83-19908. 1379p. 1984. 35.00 (*0-940450-17-8*, Pub. by Library of America) Penguin Putnam.

— Prose & Poetry: Maggie: A Girl of the Streets; The Red Badge of Courage; George's Mother; The Third Violet; Journalism, Poetry, Tales, & Sketches. Levenson, J. C., ed. (Library of America College Editions). 1379p. (C). 1996. pap. text 15.95 (*1-883011-39-6*, Pub. by Library of America) Penguin Putnam.

— The Red Badge of Courage. (Classics Illustrated Study Guides Ser.). (Illus.). 1997. mass mkt. 4.99 (*1-57840-040-6*, Pub. by Acclaim Bks) Penguin Putnam.

— The Red Badge of Courage. (Illustrated Classics Collection 1). 64p. 1994. pap. 4.95 (*0-7854-0669-7*, 40352) Am Guidance.

— The Red Badge of Courage. 17.95 (*0-89190-118-3*) Amereon Ltd.

— The Red Badge of Courage. 1998. pap. text 14.95 (*1-55701-230-X*) BNI Pubns.

— The Red Badge of Courage. 160p. (gr. 7-12). 1981. mass mkt. 3.95 (*0-553-21011-4*, Bantam Classics) Bantam.

— The Red Badge of Courage. Green, Frank & Seely, John, eds. LC 99-25633. (Classic Novels). 200p. 1999. pap. text 8.95 (*0-7641-1145-0*) Barron.

— The Red Badge of Courage. (Dover Thrift Editions Ser.). (Illus.). 112p. 1991. pap. 1.00 (*0-486-26465-3*) Dover.

— The Red Badge of Courage. (Cloth Bound Pocket Ser.). 1998. 7.95 (*3-89508-686-X*) Konemann.

— The Red Badge of Courage. 187p. (C). 1951. pap. 5.00 (*0-07-555608-1*) McGraw.

— The Red Badge of Courage. LC 42-36053. 251p. 1980. pap. 4.00 (*0-685-03394-5*) Modern Lib NY.

— The Red Badge of Courage. 1998. 15.50 (*0-679-60296-8*) Modern Lib NY.

— The Red Badge of Courage. Binder, Henry, ed. 208p. 1987. mass mkt. 3.50 (*0-380-70432-3*, Avon Bks) Morrow Avon.

— The Red Badge of Courage. Shefter, Harry, ed. (Enriched Classics Edition Ser.). 224p. 1990. mass mkt. 4.99 (*0-671-74081-4*, WSP) PB.

— The Red Badge of Courage. 1996. per. 5.99 (*0-671-00275-9*) PB.

***Crane, Stephen.** The Red Badge of Courage. LC 99-36549. (Masterpiece Series Access Editions). (J). 1999. write for info. (*0-8219-1981-4*) Paradigm MN.

Crane, Stephen. The Red Badge of Courage. Shapiro, Irwin, ed. LC 73-75464. (Now Age Illustrated Ser.). (Illus.). 64p. (J). (gr. 5-10). 1973. pap. 2.95 (*0-88301-101-8*) Pendulum Pr.

— The Red Badge of Courage. (Puffin Classics Ser.). (Illus.). 224p. (YA). (gr. 5 up). 1995. pap. 3.99 (*0-14-036710-1*, PuffinBks) Peng Put Young Read.

— The Red Badge of Courage. Hanft, Joshua, ed. (Great Illustrated Classics Ser.: Vol. 27). (Illus.). 240p. (J). (gr. 3-6). 1993. 9.95 (*0-86611-978-7*) Playmore Inc.

— The Red Badge of Courage. 32p. (J). (gr. 4-7). 1993. pap. 4.95 (*0-8114-6837-2*) Raintree Steck-V.

— The Red Badge of Courage. (C). 1951. pap. write for info. (*0-318-54362-1*, T45) Random.

— The Red Badge of Courage. Green, Frank, ed. (Thornes Classic Novels Ser.). (Illus.). 194p. 1996. pap. 16.75 (*0-7487-2423-0*, Pub. by S Thornes Pubs) Trans-Atl Phila.

— The Red Badge of Courage. (YA). 1990. pap. 2.50 (*0-8125-0479-8*, Pub. by Tor Bks) St Martin.

— The Red Badge of Courage. 1997. pap. 2.95 (*0-89375-606-7*) Troll Communs.

— The Red Badge of Courage. Bradbury, Malcolm, ed. 140p. 1993. pap. 2.50 (*0-460-87381-4*, Everyman's Classic Lib) Tuttle Pubng.

— The Red Badge of Courage. LC 90-50273. (Vintage-Library of America Ser.). 160p. 1990. pap. 9.50 (*0-679-73223-3*) Vin Bks.

***Crane, Stephen.** The Red Badge of Courage. 1999. pap. 2.99 (*0-14-130548-7*, PuffinBks) Peng Put Young Read.

— Red Badge of Courage. (Wordsworth Classics). 1999. pap. 3.95 (*1-85326-084-3*) Wrdsworth Edits.

Crane, Stephen. The Red Badge of Courage. large type ed. (Large Print Heritage Ser.). 233p. 1997. lib. bdg. 28.95 (*1-58118-019-5*, 21491) LRS.

— The Red Badge of Courage. large type ed. LC 97-12339. 190p. 1997. 22.95 (*1-56000-528-9*) Transaction Pubs.

— The Red Badge of Courage. large type ed. reprint ed. 10.00 (*0-89064-053-X*) NAVH.

***Crane, Stephen.** The Red Badge of Courage. (Twelve-Point Ser.). 155p. 2000. reprint ed. lib. bdg. 22.00 (*1-58287-123-X*) North Bks.

Crane, Stephen. The Red Badge of Courage. (Works of Stephen Crane). 1990. reprint ed. lib. bdg. 79.00 (*0-7812-2426-8*) Rprt Serv.

— The Red Badge of Courage. LC 67-26616. 1967. reprint ed. 40.00 (*0-8201-1010-8*) Schol Facsimiles.

— The Red Badge of Courage. 180p. (YA). (gr. 7-12). 1972. reprint ed. pap. 2.25 (*0-590-02117-6*) Scholastic Inc.

***Crane, Stephen.** The Red Badge of Courage. large type ed. 250p. 2000. reprint ed. lib. bdg. 24.00 (*0-939495-99-6*) North Bks.

Crane, Stephen. The Red Badge of Courage. unabridged ed. 135p. 1997. reprint ed. pap. 9.95 (*1-57002-051-5*) Univ Publng Hse.

— The Red Badge of Courage. unabridged ed. (Classics Ser.). (YA). (gr. 7 up). 1962. mass mkt. 2.50 (*0-8049-0003-5*, CL-3) Airmont.

— The Red Badge of Courage. unabridged ed. (Wordsworth Classics). (YA). (gr. 6-12). 1998. 5.27 (*0-89061-567-5*, R5675WW, Jamestwn Pub) NTC Contemp Pub Co.

— The Red Badge of Courage. 3rd ed. Pizer, Donald, ed. LC 93-9918. (Critical Text Ser.). (C). 1993. pap. text 12.50 (*0-393-96430-2*) Norton.

— The Red Badge of Courage: An Episode of the American Civil War. 1993. write for info. (*0-318-69700-9*) Modern Lib NY.

— The Red Badge of Courage: An Episode of the American Civil War. 192p. 1999. pap. 10.00 (*0-393-31954-7*) Norton.

Crane, Stephen. The Red Badge of Courage: An Episode of the American Civil War. 1987. 8.60 (*0-606-03448-X*, Pub. by Turtleback) Demco.

Crane, Stephen. The Red Badge of Courage: An Historically Annotated Edition. LaRocca, Charles J., ed. LC 95-22834. (Illus.). 212p. 1995. pap. 18.00 (*0-935796-68-1*) Purple Mnt Pr.

— The Red Badge of Courage: And Four Stories. rev. ed. Stallman, R. W., ed. & notes by. (Signet Classics Ser.). 226p. 1997. mass mkt. 3.95 (*0-451-52647-3*, Sig Classics) NAL.

— The Red Badge of Courage: And Selected Stories. (Signet Classics). 1960. 9.05 (*0-606-00225-1*, Pub. by Turtleback) Demco.

***Crane, Stephen.** The Red Badge of Courage: The Comprehensive Edition: The December 1894 Newspaper Serial & the Novel. LC 98-73948. 189p. (Orig.). 1999. pap. 10.95 (*0-9655309-2-2*) Ironweed Pr.

Crane, Stephen. The Red Badge of Courage & Other Stories. Robertson, Fiona & Mellors, Anthony, eds. LC 98-10535. (Oxford World's Classics Ser.). 308p. 1998. pap. 7.95 (*0-19-283315-4*) OUP.

Crane, Stephen. The Red Badge of Courage & Other Writings, 001. Chase, Richard, ed. (YA). (gr. 9 up). 1972. pap. 13.16 (*0-395-05143-6*, RivEd) HM.

Crane, Stephen. The Red Badge of Courage & Selected Stories. 224p. 1987. reprint ed. lib. bdg. 21.95 (*0-89966-620-5*) Buccaneer Bks.

An Asterisk (*) at the beginning of an entry indicates that the title is appearing for the first time.

— The Red Badge of Courage Readalong. (Illustrated Classics Collection 1). 64p. 1994. pap. 14.95 incl. audio (*0-7854-0710-3*, 40354) Am Guidance.

— RED BADGE OF COURAGE 3/E *47* 3rd ed. Gibson, William M., ed. 652p. (C). 1968. pap. text 26.50 (*0-03-073360-X*, Pub. by Harcourt Coll Pubs) Harcourt.

— Sullivan County Sketches of Stephen Crane. (BCL1-PS American Literature Ser.). 85p. 1993. reprint ed. lib. bdg. 59.00 (*0-7812-6954-7*) Rprt Serv.

— Sullivan County Tales & Sketches. Stallman, R. W., ed. LC 95-11021. (Illus.). 151p. 1995. pap. 15.00 (*0-935796-64-9*) Purple Mnt Pr.

— The Third Violet. (Works of Stephen Crane). 1990. reprint ed. lib. bdg. 79.00 (*0-685-44795-2*) Rprt Serv.

— The University of Virginia Edition of the Works of Stephen Crane, Vol. 5: Tales of Adventure. Bowers, Fredson, ed. LC 68-8536. 440p. reprint ed. pap. 136.40 (*0-7837-2432-2*, 204258000005) Bks Demand.

— War Is Kind. (Works of Stephen Crane). 1990. reprint ed. lib. bdg. 79.00 (*0-7812-2434-9*) Rprt Serv.

— War Is Kind, & Other Poems. LC 98-41719. (Thrift Editions Ser.). 64p. 1998. pap. 1.00 (*0-486-40424-2*) Dover.

— Whilomville Stories. 1991. 65.00 (*0-403-00013-0*) Scholarly.

— Whilomville Stories. (Works of Stephen Crane). 1990. reprint ed. lib. bdg. 79.00 (*0-7812-0378-3*) Rprt Serv.

Crane, Stephen. Wishbone Classic: The Red Badge of Courage, No. 10. LC 95-77839. (Wishbone Classics Ser.: No. 10). 128p. (J). (gr. 5-7). 1996. mass mkt. 3.99 (*0-06-106497-1*, Harp PBks) HarpC.

Crane, Stephen. The Works of Stephen Crane. 1990. reprint ed. lib. bdg. 63.00 (*0-685-27798-4*) Rprt Serv.

— The Works of Stephen Crane Vol. 1: Bowery Tales; Maggie & George's Mother. Bowers, Fredson, ed. LC 68-8536. (Illus.). 184p. (C). 1969. 35.00 (*0-8139-0258-4*) U Pr of Va.

— The Works of Stephen Crane Vol. 2: The Red Badge of Courage. Bowers, Fredson, ed. LC 68-8536. 420p. 1975. text 35.00 (*0-8139-0514-1*) U Pr of Va.

— The Works of Stephen Crane Vol. 3: The Third Violet & the Active Service. Bowers, Fredson, ed. LC 68-8536. 492p. 1976. 35.00 (*0-8139-0666-0*) U Pr of Va.

— The Works of Stephen Crane Vol. 4: The O'Ruddy. Bowers, Fredson, ed. LC 68-8536. (Illus.). 362p. 1971. text 35.00 (*0-8139-0341-6*) U Pr of Va.

— The Works of Stephen Crane Vol. 6: Tales of War. Bowers, Fredson, ed. LC 68-8536. (Illus.). 400p. 1970. text 35.00 (*0-8139-0294-0*) U Pr of Va.

— The Works of Stephen Crane Vol. 7: Tales of Whilomville, the Monster, His New Mittens. Bowers, Fredson, ed. LC 68-8536. (Illus.). 277p. (C). 1969. 35.00 (*0-8139-0259-2*) U Pr of Va.

— The Works of Stephen Crane Vol. 8: Tales, Sketches, & Reports. Bowers, Fredson, ed. LC 68-8536. (Illus.). 1183p. 1973. text 47.50 (*0-8139-0405-6*) U Pr of Va.

— The Works of Stephen Crane Vol. 9: Reports of War. Bowers, Fredson, ed. LC 68-8536. (Illus.). 678p. 1971. text 37.50 (*0-8139-0342-4*) U Pr of Va.

— The Works of Stephen Crane Vol. 10: Poems & Literary Remains. Bowers, Fredson, ed. LC 68-8536. 1975. text 35.00 (*0-8139-0610-5*) U Pr of Va.

— Wounds in the Rain. LC 72-3294. (Short Story Index Reprint Ser.). 1977. reprint ed. 26.95 (*0-8369-4145-4*) Ayer.

— Wounds in the Rain. (Works of Stephen Crane). 1990. reprint ed. lib. bdg. 79.00 (*0-7812-2435-7*) Rprt Serv.

Crane, Stephen & Covici, Pascal, Jr. The Red Badge of Courage & Other Stories. 304p. 1991. pap. 8.95 (*0-14-039081-2*, Penguin Classics) Viking Penguin.

Crane, Stephen, jt. auth. see Center for Learning Network Staff.

***Crane, Stephen L.** Survivor from an Unknown War. (Illus.). 333p. 1999. text 28.00 (*0-7881-8270-6*) DIANE Pub.

***Crane, Stephen Lee.** Survivor from an Unknown War: The Life of Isak Jan Narzikul. LC 99-94704. (Illus.). 333p. (C). 1999. pap. text 14.95 (*0-7881-7730-3*) DIANE Pub.

Crane, Stephen W., jt. ed. see Betts, C. W.

Crane, Steven, jt. auth. see Crane, Charles.

***Crane, Susan.** Collecting & Historical Consciousness: New Forms for Collective Memory in Early Nineteenth-Century. 2000. write for info. (*0-8014-3752-0*) Cornell U Pr.

Crane, Susan. Gender & Romance in Chaucer's Canterbury Tales. LC 93-32421. 248p. 1994. pap. text 16.95 (*0-691-01527-9*, Pub. by Princeton U Pr) Cal Prin Full Svc.

Crane, Susan, jt. auth. see Berrigan, Philip.

***Crane, Susan A.** Museums & Memory. LC 99-89384. (Cultural Sitings Ser.). (Illus.). 2000. 55.00 (*0-8047-3564-6*) Stanford U Pr.

— Museums & Memory. LC 99-89384. (Cultural Sitings Ser.). (Illus.). 2000. pap. 19.95 (*0-8047-3565-4*) Stanford U Pr.

Crane, Sylvia, jt. auth. see Crane, John O.

Crane, T. D., jt. auth. see Hails, M. R.

Crane, Teresa. Darling Kate. large type ed. LC 96-53157. 198p. 1997. pap. 20.95 (*0-7862-1022-2*) Thorndike Pr.

— Icon of Gold. large type ed. LC 97-52111. 1998. 21.95 (*0-7862-1395-7*) Thorndike Pr.

***Crane, Teresa.** Siena Summer. large type ed. LC 99-25638. 299p. 1999. 21.95 (*0-7862-1982-3*) Mac Lib Ref.

Crane, Thomas E. The Message of St. John: The Spiritual Teachings of the Beloved Disciple. LC 80-11779. 184p. 1980. pap. 5.95 (*0-8189-0402-X*) Alba.

Crane, Thomas F. The Exempla or Illustrative Stories from the Sermones: Vulgares off Jacques de Vitry. (Folk-Lore Society, London Monographs: Vol. 26). 1972. reprint ed. pap. 40.00 (*0-8115-0512-X*) Periodicals Srv.

Crane, Thomas G. The Heart of Coaching: Using Transformational Coaching to Create a High-Performance Culture. Patrick, Lerissa, ed. LC 97-78150. (Illus.). 224p. 1998. pap. 18.95 (*0-9660874-0-2*) FTA Pr.

Crane, Tim, ed. The Contents of Experience: Essays on Perception. (Illus.). 287p. (C). 1992. text 64.95 (*0-521-41727-9*) Cambridge U Pr.

Crane, Tim, jt. auth. see Bannister, Hank.

Crane, Tim, ed. & intro. see Armstrong, D. M., et al.

Crane, Tom, jt. auth. see Moss, Roger W.

Crane, Valerie, et al. Informal Science Learning: What the Research Says about Television, Science Museums, & Community-Based Projects. Research Communications Ltd. Staff, ed. (Illus.). 280p. (Orig.). 1994. pap. 9.95 (*0-9640423-0-4*) Res Communs.

Crane, Virginia, jt. auth. see Crane, Allen.

Crane, Walter. The Decorative Illustration of Books. (Illus.). 243p. 1998. reprint ed. pap. text 10.00 (*0-7881-5193-2*) DIANE Pub.

***Crane, Walter.** Illustrations & Ornamentation from the Faerie Queene. LC 99-12167. (Illus.). 1999. pap. text 11.95 (*0-486-40274-6*) Dover.

Crane, Walter. Favorite Poems of Childhood. LC 92-42770. (J). 1993. 14.00 (*0-671-86614-1*, Green Tiger S&S) S&S Childrens.

Crane, Walter & Caldecott, Randolph. Mother Goose & Other Nursery Songs. 32p. (J). (ps up). 1997. 16.95 incl. audio (*0-930647-03-3*) Lancaster Prodns.

***Crane, Walter Sanger, IV.** Sheba Vol. 1: The Sands of Seth. (Illus.). 192p. 2000. pap. 17.95 (*0-9701814-0-X*) Sick Mind Pr.

Crane, William C. Life & Select Literary Remains of Sam Houston of Texas, 2 vols in 1. LC 74-38348. (Select Bibliographies Reprint Ser.). 1977. reprint ed. 37.95 (*0-8369-6765-8*) Ayer.

— Life & Select Literary Remains of Sam Houston of Texas. 1993. reprint ed. lib. bdg. 75.00 (*0-7812-5872-3*) Rprt Serv.

Cranefield, Paul, jt. ed. see Brooks, Chandler.

Cranefield, Paul F. Born Wanderer: The Life of Stanley Portal Hyatt. LC 94-5304. 1994. 20.00 (*0-913848-01-8*, Futura Media) Futura Pub.

— Science & Empire: East Coast Fever in Rhodesia & the Transvaal. (Cambridge History of Medicine Ser.). (Illus.). 403p. (C). 1991. text 85.00 (*0-521-39253-5*) Cambridge U Pr.

Cranefield, Paul F. & Hoffman, Brian F., eds. Paired Pulse Stimulation of the Heart. (Illus.). 224p. 1968. 7.50 (*0-87470-009-4*) Rockefeller.

Cranefield, Paul F., tr. see Du Bois-Reymond, Emil H.

Craner, Kathy. Nibbles the Rabbit Has a Good Habit. (Illus.). (Orig.). (J). (ps-2). 1998. pap. 12.95 (*0-7880-1404-8*, Fairway Pr) CSS OH.

***Craney, Linda D.** Happiness Is Wholesome Foods. LC 98-91002. 1999. pap. 15.95 (*0-533-13009-3*) Vantage.

***Cranfield.** Marketing Management: A Relationship to Marketing Perspective. LC 00-21419. 370p. 2000. text 79.95 (*0-312-23186-5*) St Martin.

***Cranfield, Arthur.** Essential Pool: A Complete Course from a World Champion. (Illus.). 2000. pap. 12.95 (*1-55821-995-1*) Lyons Pr.

***Cranfield, Arthur & Moy, Laurence S.** The Straight Pool Bible. LC 00-20307. 2000. pap. 19.95 (*1-58574-025-X*) Lyons Pr.

Cranfield, C. E. The Apostle's Creed: A Faith to Live By. 80p. 1998. pap. 14.95 (*0-567-29227-4*, Pub. by T & T Clark) Bks Intl VA.

— Commentary on Romans. abr. ed. 320p. 1985. pap. 20.00 (*0-8028-0012-2*) Eerdmans.

— The Gospel According to St. Mark. 480p. 1959. pap. text 34.95 (*0-521-09204-3*) Cambridge U Pr.

— On Romans: And Other New Testament Essays. 192p. 1998. 44.95 (*0-567-08624-0*, Pub. by T & T Clark) Bks Intl VA.

Cranfield, C. E., et al. Christians in the Public Square: Law, Gospel, & Public Policy. 391p. 1996. pap. 20.00 (*1-896363-05-9*) CN Inst for Law.

Cranfield, Charles E. The Bible & Christian Life. 256p. 1985. pap. 27.95 (*0-567-29125-1*, Pub. by T & T Clark) Bks Intl VA.

— If God Be for Us: A Collection of Sermons. 192p. pap. 25.95 (*0-567-29126-X*, Pub. by T & T Clark) Bks Intl VA.

— Romans: Critical & Exegetical Commentary, 2 vols., Vol. I. Emerton, John A., ed. (International Critical Commentary Ser.). 472p. 49.95 (*0-567-05040-8*, Pub. by T & T Clark) Bks Intl VA.

— Romans: Critical & Exegetical Commentary, 2 vols., Vol. II. Emerton, John A., ed. (International Critical Commentary Ser.). 496p. 49.95 (*0-567-05041-6*, Pub. by T & T Clark) Bks Intl VA.

Cranfield, Charles E., ed. see McKane, William.

Cranfield, Geoffrey A. The Press & Society: From Caxton to Northcliffe. LC 77-21904. (Themes in British Social History). 250p. reprint ed. pap. 77.50 (*0-8357-3502-8*, 203448800090) Bks Demand.

Cranfield, Ingrid. The Archaeology Kit: Science Action Book. (Illus.). 20p. (J). (gr. 4-7). 1998. pap. 19.95 (*0-7624-0366-7*) Running Pr.

— Georgian House Style: An Architectural & Interior Design. LC 98-155851. (Illus.). 192p. 1998. 34.95 (*0-7153-0553-0*, Pub. by D & C Pub) Sterling.

Cranfield, Ingrid, tr. see Hoang, Michel.

Cranfield, Steve & Humphries, Martin. Salt & Honey. 1995. per. 7.95 (*0-85449-101-5*, Pub. by Gay Mens Pr) LPC InBook.

Cranfield, Tom. Alaska Statutes 1998 Advance Legislative Service. 900p. 1998. pap. 57.00 (*0-327-05396-8*, 40345-15) LEXIS Pub.

Cranfield, Tom, ed. Alaska Statutes: 1998 Replacement Volumes, Vol. 13. 140p. 1998. write for info. (*0-327-06089-1*, 40236-11) LEXIS Pub.

— Alaska Statutes, 1998 Replacement Volumes, 13 vols. Incl. Vol. 1. Alaska Statutes: 1998 Replacement Volumes. 670p. 1998. (*0-327-06077-8*, 40222-11); Vol. 2. Alaska Statutes: 1998 Replacement Volumes. 670p. 1998. (*0-327-06078-6*, 40223-11); Vol. 3. Alaska Statutes: 1998 Replacement Volumes. 680p. 1998. (*0-327-06079-4*, 40224-11); Vol. 4. Alaska Statutes: 1998 Replacement Volumes. 630p. 1998. (*0-327-06080-8*, 40226-11); Vol. 5. Alaska Statutes: 1998 Replacement Volumes. 610p. 1998. (*0-327-06081-6*, 40227-11); Vol. 6. Alaska Statutes: 1998 Replacement Volumes. 770p. 1998. (*0-327-06082-4*, 40228-11); Vol. 7. Alaska Statutes: 1998 Replacement Volumes. 810p. 1998. (*0-327-06083-2*, 40229-11); Vol. 8. Alaska Statutes: 1998 Replacement Volumes. 780p. 1998. (*0-327-06084-0*, 40231-11); Vol. 9. Alaska Statutes: 1998 Replacement Volumes. 750p. 1998. (*0-327-06085-9*, 40232-11); Vol. 10. Alaska Statutes: 1998 Replacement Volumes. 850p. 1998. (*0-327-06086-7*, 40233-11); Vol. 11. Alaska Statutes: 1998 Replacement Volumes. 740p. 1998. (*0-327-06087-5*, 40234-11); Vol. 12. Alaska Statutes: 1998 Replacement Volumes. 1180p. 1998. (*0-327-06088-3*, 40237-11); write for info. (*0-327-06076-X*) LEXIS Pub.

— Georgia Rules of Court Annotated, August 1998 Supplement. annot. ed. 50p. 1998. pap., suppl. ed. write for info. (*0-327-06091-3*, 42074-16) LEXIS Pub.

Cranfill, J. B., ed. see Truett, George W.

Cranfill, Ray. Ferns & Fern Allies of Kentucky. unabridged ed. (Kentucky Nature Preserves Commission Scientific & Technical Ser.: Vol. 1). (Illus.). 284p. 1980. pap. 6.27 (*0-9673646-0-4*) KY State Nature.

Cranfill, S. A. They Came from Babel: Meet the Ancient Advanced Civilization That Dispersed to the Americas in 2000 B. C. (Biblical History of the Americas Ser.: Vol. 1). 256p. 1999. pap. 14.99 (*0-9639202-1-9*) Dake Pub.

Cranfill, Thomas M. & Clark, Robert L., Jr. Anatomy of the Turn of the Screw. LC 78-159037. 195p. (C). 1971. reprint ed. 50.00 (*0-87752-151-4*) Gordian.

Cranford, Carolyn E., ed. see American Automobile Association Staff.

Cranford, Clarence W. Cups of Light & Other Illustrations For Sermons & Meditations. 160p. (Orig.). 1988. pap. 12.00 (*0-8170-1142-0*) Judson.

Cranford, J. C. Zion National Park: An Illustrated History. (Illus.). 48p. 1989. pap. 6.95 (*0-917859-26-X*) Sunrise SBCA.

Cranford, James B. Selecting the Landscape Maintenance Contractor: Selecting the Landscape Maintenance Contractor. 3rd ed. (GAP Reports: Vol. 12). (C). 1996. pap. 17.50 (*0-944715-26-5*) CAI.

— Selecting the Landscape Maintenance Contractor No. 12: GAP Reports. 4th ed. 32p. 1996. pap. 17.50 (*0-944715-43-5*) CAI.

***Cranford, Marti.** Travels: A Personal Journey Through the United Kindom, France & Switzerland, 1. LC 98-93222. 1998. 20.00 (*0-9665141-0-6*) Informative Pubns.

Cranford, Mary C. The Racehorse Caper. LC 98-226344. 100p. (Orig.). (J). (gr. 4-6). 1997. pap. 5.00 (*0-88092-068-8*) Royal Fireworks.

Cranford, Paul Stewart, ed. Winston Fitzgerald: A Collection of Fiddle Tunes. 104p. 1997. 16.95 (*0-7866-3498-7*, 97122) Mel Bay.

Cranford, Peter G. How to Be Your Own Psychologist: The Art of Irresistible Influence--Compossibility! 223p. 1981. 14.95 (*0-9605822-0-7*) Great Pyramid.

— Zen in Golf & Life. 76p. (Orig.). 1995. pap. text 22.50 (*0-9605822-3-1*) Great Pyramid.

Cranford, Peter G., ed. Whatever Happened to Peter Downstairs? (Illus.). 400p. (Orig.). 1991. pap. 12.95 (*0-9605822-2-3*) Great Pyramid.

Cranford, Ron. Farewell Fidel, Hello Santa Anna. unabridged ed. Pechstein, Cricket, ed. 304p. (Orig.). 1996. pap. 10.95 (*0-9653856-0-4*) Shining Sea Pr.

Cranford, William. Consorts of Five Parts. Brookes, Virginia, ed. (Viol Consort Ser.: Vol. 31). ii, 44p. (Orig.). 1997. pap. 19.00 (*1-56571-147-5*) PRB Prods.

— Six Fantasias for Six Viols. Brookes, Virginia, ed. (Viol Consort Ser.: Vol. VC027). v, 71p. (Orig.). 1996. pap. text 28.00 (*1-56571-128-9*) PRB Prods.

Crang, Jeremy A. The British Army & the Peoples War 1939-1945. text. write for info. (*0-7190-4741-2*, Pub. by Manchester Univ Pr) St Martin.

Crang, Mike. Cultural Geography. LC 97-45070. (Routledge Contemporary Human Geography Ser.). 256p. (C). 1998. pap. 17.99 (*0-415-14083-8*) Routledge.

— Cultural Geography. LC 97-45070. (Routledge Contemporary Human Geography Ser.). (Illus.). 224p. (C). 1998. 60.00 (*0-415-14082-X*) Routledge.

— The Virtual Geographies: Bodies, Space & Relations. LC 98-30450. 1999. pap. 25.99 (*0-415-16828-7*) Routledge.

***Crang, Mike.** Virtual Geographies: Bodies, Space & Relations. LC 98-30450. 1999. 85.00 (*0-415-16827-9*) Routledge.

***Crang, Mike & Thrift, N. J.** Thinking Space. LC 99-52190. (Critical Geographies Ser.). 352p. 2000. pap. write for info. (*0-415-16016-2*) Routledge.

Crang, Philip. Displacement. 224p. text. write for info. (*0-340-65304-3*, Pub. by E A); pap. text. write for info. (*0-340-57214-0*, Pub. by E A) Routldge.

Crang, R. F. & Klomparens, K. L. Artifacts in Biological Electron Microscopy. LC 88-15217. (Illus.). 254p. (C). 1988. text 79.50 (*0-306-42863-6*, Kluwer Plenum) Kluwer Academic.

Crangle, Colleen & Suppes, Patrick C. Language & Learning for Robots. LC 93-43516. (CSLI Lecture Notes Ser.: Vol. 41). 1995. 54.95 (*1-881526-20-8*); pap. 21.95 (*1-881526-19-4*) CSLI.

Crangle, John. Solid State Magnetism. (Illus.). 324p. (gr. 13). 1991. mass mkt. 48.95 (*0-442-30856-6*) Chapman & Hall.

Crangle, Richard. Invention Works Vol. I: Success: Develop, Protect & Make Money with Your Invention. (Illus.). 116p. 1999. pap. 14.95 (*0-9664835-1-0*) Crantec Research.

— Invention Works Vol. II: Piracy: Understand Piracy & Protect your Inventions, Copyrights, Trademarks & Trade Secrets. (Illus.). 171p. 1999. 19.95 (*0-9664835-2-9*) Crantec Research.

— Technology Innovation Vol. 1: Research, Development & the Patent Process. unabridged ed. (Illus.). 110p. 1998. 19.95 (*0-9664835-0-2*) Crantec Research.

Craniford, Ada. Fiction & Fact in Mordecai Richler's Novels. LC 92-46177. 180p. 1993. text 79.95 (*0-88946-018-3*) E Mellen.

Cranin, A. N., et al, eds. Atlas of Oral Implantology. LC 93-781. (Illus.). 342p. 1993. text 189.00 (*0-86577-449-8*) Thieme Med Pubs.

***Cranin, A. Norman, et al.** Atlas of Oral Implantology. 2nd ed. (Illus.). 416p. (C). 1999. text. write for info. (*1-55664-552-X*) Mosby Inc.

Craninckx, J. & Steyaert, Michiel. Wireless CMOS Frequency Synthesizer Design. LC 98-14445. (International Series in Engineering & Computer Science). 1998. 115.00 (*0-7923-8138-6*) Kluwer Academic.

Cranitch, Ellen. Thirty Popular Tunes Easy Rec. 2. 20p. 1987. pap. 8.75 (*0-7866-1586-9*, 95171WW) Mel Bay.

Cranitch, Matt. Irish Fiddle Book. 1988. pap. 29.95 (*0-85342-803-4*) Dufour.

Cranitch, Matt. Irish Fiddle Book: The Art of Traditional Fiddle-Playing. (Illus.). 1988. pap. 24.95 (*1-900428-90-3*) Ossian.

Crank, David. Freedom from Fear & Anxiety. LC 96-114529. 112p. (Orig.). 1995. pap. 5.99 (*0-89274-926-1*, HH-926) Harrison Hse.

— Godly Finances: The Bible Way to Pay off Your Home. 50p. (Orig.). 1986. pap. 4.95 (*0-936437-00-6*) D Crank Pubns.

— Samson - A Type of the Church. 64p. (Orig.). 1991. pap. 5.99 (*0-89274-864-8*, HH-864) Harrison Hse.

Crank, Gretchen, ed. Reflections of the Florissant Valley, Missouri. (Illus.). 120p. 1990. reprint ed. text 40.00 (*0-88107-173-0*) Curtis Media.

Crank, John. Free & Moving Boundary Problems. (Illus.). 424p. 1987. pap. text 45.00 (*0-19-853370-5*) OUP.

— The Mathematics of Diffusion. 2nd ed. (Illus.). 424p. 1980. pap. text 65.95 (*0-19-853411-6*) OUP.

Crank, John P. Understanding Police Culture. LC 97-28123. 348p. (C). 1997. pap. 32.95 (*0-87084-203-X*) Anderson Pub Co.

***Crank, John P. & Caldero, Michael A.** Police Ethics: The Corruption of Noble Cause. LC 99-38850. 275p. 1999. pap. 32.95 (*1-58360-504-5*) Anderson Pub Co.

Crank, T. Seeking the Lord, the Real Key to Success. 1995. pap. 6.00 (*0-927936-56-9*) Vincom Pubng Co.

Crank, Val, et al, eds. Key Maths: Special Resource 7 Teacher File. 336p. 1998. pap. 99.50 (*0-7487-2974-7*, Pub. by S Thornes Pubs) Trans-Atl Phila.

Crank, Val, et al. Key Maths 7: Paced for Slower Learners. (Illus.). 320p. (J). (gr. 6-9). 1998. pap. 24.00 (*0-7487-2975-5*, Pub. by S Thornes Pubs) Trans-Atl Phila.

Cranker, Lyle E., jt. auth. see Dinda, Kara M.

Crankshaw, Edward. The Forsaken Idea: A Study of Viscount Milner. LC 73-17918. 178p. 1974. reprint ed. lib. bdg. 55.00 (*0-8371-7278-0*, CRFI, Greenwood Pr) Greenwood.

— Gestapo: Instrument of Tyranny. 276p. 1991. 35.00 (*1-85367-077-4*, 5513) Stackpole.

— Gestapo: Instrument of Tyranny. LC 93-33616. (Illus.). 281p. 1994. reprint ed. pap. 13.95 (*0-306-80567-7*) Da Capo.

— Memoir. 1999. pap. write for info. (*0-670-80405-3*) Viking Penguin.

— New Cold War: Moscow vs. Peking. LC 79-133518. (Select Bibliographies Reprint Ser.). 1980. 18.95 (*0-8369-5550-1*) Ayer.

***Crankshaw, Edward.** Shadow of the Winter Palace: Russia's Drift to Revolution, 1825-1917. 440p. 2000. pap. text 18.00 (*0-306-80940-0*) Da Capo.

Crankshaw, Owen. Race, Class, & the Changing Division of Labour under Apartheid. 224p. (C). 1996. 80.00 (*0-415-14613-5*) Routledge.

Cranley, John J. Atlas of Duplex Scanning: Extremities. (Illus.). 426p. 1992. text 185.00 (*0-7216-3466-4*, W B Saunders Co) Harcrt Hlth Sci Grp.

Cranley, Paul, ed. see Najvar, Daniel.

Cranmer & Richerson, eds. Mechanical Testing Methodology for Ceramic Design & Reliability. (Illus.). 448p. 1998. text. write for info. (*0-8247-9567-9*) Dekker.

Cranmer-Byng, J. L. Patee Byng's Journal. (C). 1987. 135.00 (*0-7855-3953-0*) St Mut.

Cranmer-Byng, J. L., ed. Chinese Buddhist Verse. Robinson, Richard H., tr. from CHI. LC 79-8725. 85p. 1980. reprint ed. lib. bdg. 35.00 (*0-313-22189-8*, ROCB, Greenwood Pr) Greenwood.

Cranmer-Byng, J. L., ed. see Murray, Margaret A.

Cranmer-Byng, Launcelot A. A Lute of Jade: Selections from the Classical Poets of China. LC 77-26072. 112p. 1978. reprint ed. lib. bdg. 45.00 (*0-313-20080-7*, CBLJ, Greenwood Pr) Greenwood.

Cranmer, D. & Laroy, C. Musical Openings: Using Music in the Language Classroom. 111p. 1995. audio 28.00 (*0-582-07503-3*, 79846) Longman.
Cranmer, David. Motivating High Level Learners. (Pilgrims Longman Resource Bks.). 1996. pap. 21.32 (*0-582-20976-5*) Addison-Wesley.
Cranmer, David J. & Woolston, Valerie A. Southern Africa: A Study of the Educational Systems of Botswana, Lesotho, South Africa, Southwest Africa - Namibia, & Swaziland with an Addendum on Zimbabwe-Rhodesia: A Guide to the Academic Placement of Students in Educational Institutions of the United States. LC 80-14066. (World Education Ser.). 264p. reprint ed. pap. 81.90 (*0-8357-7533-X*, 203624600001) Bks Demand.
Cranmer, H. Jerome. The New Jersey Canals: State Policy & Private Enterprise, 1820-1832. LC 77-14768. (Dissertations in American Economic History Ser.). 1978. 37.95 (*0-405-11030-8*) Ayer.
Cranmer, Jeff & Martin, Steven. The Rough Guide to Laos. (Illus.). 352p. 2000. 17.95 (*1-85828-447-3*, Pub. by Rough Guides) Penguin Putnam.
***Cranmer, Kathy & Seed, Jennifer, eds.** Annotated Bibliography. 96p. 1999. pap., teacher ed. 28.50 (*1-881678-58-X*) CSEE.
Cranmer, Leon E., et al. Cushnoc: The History & Archaeology of Plymouth Colony Traders on the Kennebec. (Occasional Publications in Maine Archaeology). (Illus.). 125p. (Orig.). (C). 1990. pap. 10.00 (*0-935447-06-7*) ME Hist Preserv.
Cranmer, Steven R., jt. auth. see Kohl, John L.
Cranna, Michael, ed. The True Cost of Conflict: Seven Recent Wars & Their Effects on Society. 240p. 1995. pap. 16.00 (*1-56584-268-5*, Pub. by New Press NY) Norton.
Crannell. Voice & Articulation. 2nd ed. (Speech & Theater Ser.). 1991. mass mkt., teacher ed. write for info. (*0-534-14113-7*) Wadsworth Pub.
— Voice & Articulation. 4th ed. LC 99-33073. (Speech & Theater Ser.). 1999. pap. 50.95 (*0-534-52354-4*) Wadsworth Pub.
Crannell, Annalisa, jt. auth. see Bennett, Curtis D.
Crannell, Kenneth C. Voice & Articulation. 369p. (C). 1987. pap. write for info. (*0-534-07164-3*) Wadsworth Pub.
— Voice & Articulation. 2nd ed. 428p. (C). 1990. mass mkt. 27.25 (*0-534-14112-9*) Wadsworth Pub.
***Cranny.** Crossroads to Social Studies. 1999. text. write for info. (*0-13-786807-3*, Prentice Hall) P-H.
Cranny & Gerrod. Pacific Rim Discovery Student Resource Guide. (HA - Social Studies Ser.). 1995. mass mkt. 41.95 (*0-538-66135-6*) S-W Pub.
Cranny, Charles J., et al. Job Satisfaction: How People Feel about Their Jobs, & How It Affects Their Performance. 296p. 1992. 30.95 (*0-669-21289-X*) Lxngtn Bks.
Cranny-Francis, Anne. The Body in the Text. LC 96-139405. (Interpretations Ser.). 136p. 1995. pap. 14.95 (*0-522-84575-4*, Pub. by Melbourne Univ Pr) Paul & Co Pubs.
— Engendered Fictions: Analyzing Gender in the Production & Reception of Texts. (C). 1992. pap. 27.95 (*0-86840-165-X*, Pub. by New South Wales Univ Pr) Intl Spec Bk.
Cranny-Francis, Anne. Feminist Fiction: Feminist Uses of Generic Fiction LC 92-114207. 228 p. 1990. write for info. (*0-7456-0528-1*, Pub. by Polity Pr) Blackwell Pubs.
Cranny-Francis, Anne, jt. ed. see Threadgold, Terry.
Crano, J. C. & Guglielmetti, R., eds. Organic Photochromic & Thermochromic Compounds, Vol. 2. LC 98-31170. (Topics in Applied Chemistry Ser.). (Illus.). 450p. (C). 1998. text. write for info. (*0-306-45883-7*, Kluwer Plenum) Kluwer Academic.
Crano, John C. & Guglielmetti, Robert, eds. Organic Photochromic & Thermochromic Compounds Vol. 1: Photochromic Families. (Topics in Applied Chemistry Ser.). (Illus.). 400p. (C). 1998. text 125.00 (*0-306-45882-9*, Kluwer Plenum) Kluwer Academic.
Crano, William D., jt. auth. see Selnow, Gary W.
Cranor, Carl F. Regulating Toxic Substances: A Philosophy of Science & the Law. (Environmental Ethics & Science Policy Ser.). (Illus.). 272p. 1993. text 75.00 (*0-19-507436-X*) OUP.
— Regulating Toxic Substances: A Philosophy of Science & the Law. (Environmental Ethics & Science Policy Ser.). (Illus.). 272p. 1997. reprint ed. pap. 22.00 (*0-19-511378-0*) OUP.
Cranor, Carl F., ed. Are Genes Us? The Social Consequences of the New Genetics. LC 94-14617. 260p. (C). 1994. pap. text 21.00 (*0-8135-2124-6*) Rutgers U Pr.
Cranor, Henry D. Marriage Licenses of Caroline County, Maryland, 1774-1815. LC 75-986. 62p. 1998. reprint ed. pap. 12.50 (*0-8063-0667-X*) Clearfield Co.
Cranor, Phoebe. Ranch Life. (Illus.). 173p. (Orig.). 1996. pap. 10.00 (*0-9655322-0-8*) Davidson Pub.
Cranor, Rosalind. You Name It Company. 1996. text 60.00 (*0-07-013466-9*) McGraw.
Cranor, Rosalind & Templeton, Steve. Updated Price Guide to Elvis Collectibles. 48p. 1992. pap. 4.95 (*0-932807-81-X*) Overmountain Pr.
Crans, Berend J. Aircraft Finance: Recent Developments & Prospects. LC 95-44238. 164p. 1996. 59.50 (*90-411-0141-1*) Kluwer Law Intl.
Crans, Debbie C., jt. ed. see Tracey, Alan S.
Cranshaut, Kate. Art of Good Food: Pasta Sauces. 80p. 1996. 7.98 (*0-7858-0375-0*) Bk Sales Inc.
***Cranshaw, Alwyn.** You Can Paint Watercolors. (Illus.). 96p. 2000. pap. 9.95 (*0-8230-5989-8*) Watsn-Guptill.
Cranshaw, Florence. Bearing Up: Teddy Bears As Catalysts in Caring Relationships. LC 97-60035. (Illus.). 96p. 1997. pap. 8.95 (*0-932796-80-X*) Ed Media Corp.
Cranshaw, Kate. Little Book of Desserts. 1994. 4.98 (*0-7858-0140-5*) Bk Sales Inc.
— Little Book of Herbs & Spices. 1994. 4.98 (*0-7858-0144-8*) Bk Sales Inc.
Cranshaw, Whitney. Pests of the West: Prevention & Control for Today's Garden & Small Farm. LC 98-29636. (Illus.). 224p. (Orig.). 1998. pap. 19.95 (*1-55591-401-2*) Fulcrum Pub.
Cranshaw, Whitney & Kondratieff, Boris C. Bagging Big Bugs: How to Identify, Collect & Display the Largest & Most Colorful Insects of the Rocky Mountain Region. LC 94-34085. 1995. pap. 16.95 (*1-55591-178-1*) Fulcrum Pub.
Cranshaw, Whitney & Ward, Charles R. Turf Insects of Colorado & New Mexico. Weitzel, Debby, ed. (Illus.). 40p. (Orig.). 1996. pap. 8.00 (*1-889143-00-6*, 560A) CO St U Coop.
Cranston, Alan, et al. Report on the Mongolian Presidential Elections: June 6, 1993. ii, 42p. 1993. pap. 6.00 (*1-879720-71-X*) Intl Fndt Elect.
Cranston, C. The Legal Implications for Banking, 1992. Cranston, Ross, ed. 188p. (C). 1990. 150.00 (*0-85297-243-1*, Pub. by Chartered Bank) St Mut.
— Legal Issues of Cross Border Banking. Cranston, Ross, ed. 158p. (C). 1990. 150.00 (*0-85297-232-6*, Pub. by Chartered Bank) St Mut.
Cranston-Cuebas, Meg & Cranston-Cuebas, Todd. Molokai Notes Vol. 1: Meg & Todd's Portable Guide. (Illus.). 144p. (Orig.). 1996. pap. 9.95 (*0-9655141-0-2*) Sticky Monkey.
Cranston-Cuebas, Todd, jt. auth. see Cranston-Cuebas, Meg.
Cranston, Edwin A., tr. A Waka Anthology: The Gem-Glistening Cup, Vol. 1. 1016p. 1993. 119.50 (*0-8047-1922-5*) Stanford U Pr.
Cranston, Edwina A., tr. A Waka Anthology Vol. 1: The Gem-Glistening Cup. (Waka Anthology Ser.: Vol. 1). 1016p. 1997. pap. 34.95 (*0-8047-3157-8*) Stanford U Pr.
Cranston, Fumiko E., jt. auth. see Rosenfield, John M.
Cranston, Jerneral W. Transformations Through Drama: A Teacher's Guide to Educational Drama, Grads K-8. 335p. (C). 1995. pap. text 21.00 (*0-9648006-0-8*) Jenfred Pr.
***Cranston, Jodi.** The Poetics of Portraiture in the Italian Renaissance. LC 99-59861. (Illus.). 304p. 2000. write for info. (*0-521-65324-X*) Cambridge U Pr.
Cranston, Maurice. Noble Savage: Jean-Jacques Rousseau, 1754-1762: Jean-Jacques Rousseau, 1754-1762. LC 90-28111. (Illus.). 400p. 1999. pap. 20.00 (*0-226-11864-9*) U Ch Pr.
— The Romantic Movement. (Making of Europe Ser.). 194p. 1994. 48.95 (*0-631-17399-4*); pap. 24.95 (*0-631-19471-1*) Blackwell Pubs.
— The Solitary Self: Jean-Jacques Rousseau in Exile & Adversity. LC 96-12922. (Illus.). 264p. 1997. 29.95 (*0-226-11865-7*) U Ch Pr.
— The Solitary Self: Jean-Jacques Rousseau in Exile & Adversity. 1999. pap. 20.00 (*0-226-11866-5*) U Ch Pr.
Cranston, Maurice & Boralevi, Lea C., eds. Culture & Politics. (European University Institute, Series C (Political & Social Science): No. 12). 137p. (C). 1988. lib. bdg. 46.95 (*3-11-011527-1*) De Gruyter.
Cranston, Maurice, tr. see Hartnack, Justus.
Cranston, Maurice, tr. & anno. see Rousseau, Jean-Jacques.
Cranston, Maurice, tr. & intro. see Rousseau, Jean-Jacques.
Cranston, Maurice W. Jean-Jacques: The Early Life & Work of Jean-Jacques Rousseau, 1712-1754. LC 90-45994. (Illus.). 382p. 1991. pap. 21.95 (*0-226-11862-2*) U Ch Pr.
— John Locke: A Biography. Mayer, J. P., ed. LC 78-67349. (European Political Thought Ser.). 1980. reprint ed. lib. bdg. 37.95 (*0-405-11690-X*) Ayer.
— The Noble Savage: Jean-Jacques Rousseau, 1754-1762. (Illus.). 414p. 1991. 37.50 (*0-226-11863-0*) U Ch Pr.
Cranston, Maurice W. & Mair, Peter. Ideology & Politics. 168p. 1980. lib. bdg. 52.00 (*90-286-0770-6*) Kluwer Academic.
Cranston, Mechthild. Beyond the Book: Marguerite Duras, "Infans" 140p. 59.00 (*1-882528-21-2*) Scripta.
— Laying Ways. 1990. 26.50 (*0-916379-77-9*) Scripta.
Cranston, Mechthild, ed. In Language & in Love Marguerite Duras: The Unspeakable, Essays for Marguerite Duras. LC 92-16717. 1992. 46.50 (*0-916379-97-3*) Scripta.
Cranston, Meg & Mann, Jeff, eds. TV Generations. (Illus.). 71p. (Orig.). (C). 1986. pap. 10.00 (*0-937335-00-2*) LA Contemp Exhib.
Cranston, Michael C., et al, eds. Stochastic Analysis, 57. LC 94-27794. (Proceedings of Symposia in Pure Mathematics Ser.: Vol. 57). 621p. 1994. text 129.00 (*0-8218-0289-5*, PSPUM/57) Am Math.
Cranston, P. S., ed. Chironomids: From Genes to Ecosystems. (Illus.). 496p. 1995. 120.00 (*0-643-05656-4*, Pub. by CSIRO) Accents Pubns.
***Cranston, Patty.** The Best on Ice: The World's Top Figure Skaters. (Illus.). 32p. (J). (gr. 2-5). 1999. pap. text 6.95 (*1-55074-581-6*) Kids Can Pr.
Cranston, Patty. Magic on Ice: Figure Skating Stars, Tips & Facts. (Illus.). 48p. (J). (gr. 4-8). 1998. pap. 6.95 (*1-55074-455-0*, Pub. by Kids Can Pr) Genl Dist Srvs.
Cranston, Patty. Superstars on Ice: Figure Skating Champions. (Illus.). 40p. (Orig.). (J). 1996. pap. 6.95 (*1-55074-303-1*) Kids Can Pr.
Cranston, Patty. Superstars on Ice: Figure Skating Champions. unabridged ed. (Illus.). 40p. (Orig.). (YA). (gr. 3 up). 1997. pap. 5.95 (*1-55074-400-3*, Pub. by Kids Can Pr) Genl Dist Srvs.
Cranston, Peter S., jt. auth. see Gullan, P. J.
Cranston, Philip. Naissances-Births. 99p. 35.00 (*0-916379-92-2*) Scripta.
Cranston, R. & Goode, R. M., eds. New Directions in Commercial Law. LC 92-24004. (Illus.). 450p. 1993. text 95.00 (*0-19-825714-7*, Clarendon Pr) OUP.
Cranston, Ross. Banks, Liability & Risk. 1990. 110.00 (*1-85044-311-4*) LLP.
— Consumers & the Law. 2nd ed. (Law in Context Ser.). xxxvi, 503p. 1984. reprint ed. 38.50 (*0-297-78272-X*) W S Hein.
— Legal Foundations of the Welfare State. (Law in Context Ser.). 490p. (C). 1994. pap. text 33.95 (*0-297-78534-6*) Northwestern U Pr.
— Legal Foundations of the Welfare State. (Law in Context Ser.). (Illus.). xxxiv, 453p. 1985. 26.00 (*0-297-78487-0*) W S Hein.
— Principles of Banking Law. LC 96-40367. (Illus.). 568p. 1997. text 120.00 (*0-19-876484-7*) OUP.
Cranston, Ross. Principles of Banking Law. (Illus.). 568p. 1997. pap. text 47.00 (*0-19-876483-9*) OUP.
Cranston, Ross. The Single Market & the Law of Banking. 2nd ed. 350p. 1995. 110.00 (*1-85044-552-4*) LLP.
Cranston, Ross, ed. Banks & Remedies. 294p. 1992. 105.00 (*1-85044-447-1*) LLP.
— Banks, Liability & Risk. 2nd ed. 450p. 1995. 110.00 (*1-85044-843-4*) LLP.
— Commercial Law. LC 92-36315. (International Library of Essays in Law & Legal Theory: Vol. 16). (C). 1993. lib. bdg. 150.00 (*0-8147-1472-2*) NYU Pr.
— European Banking Law: The Banker-Customer Relationship. 358p. 1993. 110.00 (*1-85044-459-5*) LLP.
— Legal Ethics & Professional Responsibility. LC 95-39861. 242p. 1996. text 65.00 (*0-19-825931-X*) OUP.
— Making Commercial Law: Essays in Honour of Roy Goode. LC 97-7395. (Illus.). 616p. 1997. text 115.00 (*0-19-826081-4*) OUP.
Cranston, Ross & Zuckerman, Adrian A., eds. Reform of Civil Procedure: Essays on "Access to Justice" (Illus.). 470p. 1996. text 90.00 (*0-19-826092-X*); pap. text 38.00 (*0-19-826093-8*) OUP.
Cranston, Ross, ed. see Cranston, C.
Cranston, Ruth. World Faith. LC 68-58782. (Essay Index Reprint Ser.). 1977. 19.95 (*0-8369-0108-8*) Ayer.
Cranston, S. L., jt. ed. see Head, Joseph.
Cranston, Sylvia. H. P. B. The Extraordinary Life & Influence of Helena Blavatsky. (Illus.). 672p. 1998. pap. 24.95 (*0-9662115-1-0*) Path Pub Hse.
— Reincarnation: The Phoenix Fire Mystery. LC 93-43965. 640p. 1998. reprint ed. pap. 22.95 (*1-55700-026-3*) Theos U Pr.
Cranston, Sylvia & Williams, Carey. Reincarnation: A New Horizon in Science, Religion & Society. LC 93-30942. 399p. (C). 1999. reprint ed. pap. 17.95 (*1-55700-025-5*) Theos U Pr.
Cranston, Toller & Kimball, Martha. Zero Tolerance: An Intimate Memoir by the Man Who Revolutionized Figure Skating. LC 98-124127. (Illus.). 320p. 1997. 24.95 (*0-7710-2334-0*) McCland & Stewart.
Cranston, Toller & Kimball, Martha L. Zero Tollerance: An Intimate Memoir by the Man Who Revolutionized Figure Skating. (Illus.). 320p. 1998. pap. 15.95 (*0-7710-2335-9*) McCland & Stewart.
Crant, Phillip A. Herve Bazin: His Fiction. 218p. 1995. pap. text 21.95 (*1-886935-11-4*) New Prdigm Pr.
Cranton, Elmer M. Bypassing Bypass: The New Technique of Chelation Therapy. 272p. 1990. pap. 12.95 (*0-9624375-1-4*) Hampton Roads Pub Co.
Cranton, Elmer M., ed. Chelation Therapy, Vol 2, No. 1 - 2: Special Issue of Journal of Advancement in Medicine. (Illus.). 280p. 1989. pap. 21.95 (*0-89885-480-6*, Kluwer Acad Hman Sci) Kluwer Academic.
Cranton, Elmer M. & Fryer, William. Resetting the Clock: 5 Anti-Aging Hormones That Are Revolutionizing the Quality & Length of Life. LC 96-23750. 272p. 1996. 21.95 (*0-87131-801-6*) M Evans.
— Resetting the Clock: 5 Anti-Aging Hormones That Improve & Extend Life. 2nd ed. 270p. 1997. reprint ed. pap. 14.95 (*0-87131-823-7*) M Evans.
***Cranton, Patricia.** Becoming an Authentic Teacher in Higher Education. LC 00-37118. (Professional Practices in Adult Education & Human Resource Development Ser.). (Illus.). (C). 2000. text. write for info (*1-57524-119-6*) Krieger.
Cranton, Patricia. Personal Empowerment Through Type. (Illus.). viii, 220p. 1997. pap. 19.95 (*0-9661480-0-2*) Psychol Type Pr.
— Professional Development As Transformative Learning: New Perspectives for Teachers of Adults. LC 95-36272. (Higher & Adult Education Ser.). 226p. 1996. 34.95 (*0-7879-0197-0*) Jossey-Bass.
— Understanding & Promotion Transformative Learning: A Guide for Educators of Adult. LC 94-21300. (Higher & Adult Education Ser.). 272p. 1994. text 34.95 (*0-7879-0017-6*) Jossey-Bass.
Cranton, Patricia, ed. Psychological Type in Action. (Illus.). 200p. 1998. pap. 19.95 (*0-9661480-1-0*) Psychol Type Pr.
Cranwell, Barry. Planet Boys: The Most Beautiful Boys on the Planet. 1996. pap. text 30.00 (*0-9524667-1-3*, Pub. by Prowler Pr) LPC InBook.
Cranwell, John P. Spoilers of the Sea. LC 78-93331. (Essay Index Reprint Ser.). 1977. 30.95 (*0-8369-1563-1*) Ayer.
Cranwell-Ward, Jane. Thriving on Stress. 2nd ed. (Self-Development for Managers Ser.). 128p. (C). 1990. pap. 17.95 (*0-415-04465-0*, A6319) Thomson Learn.
Cranz, David. Quellen zur Missionsgeschichte der Herrnhuter Brudergemeine, 2 vols. (GER.). 1995. reprint ed. write for info. (*3-487-09992-6*) G Olms Pubs.
Cranz, F. Edward. Luther's Thought: Essay on the Development of Luther's Thought on Justice, Law, & Society. 210p. 1998. reprint ed. pap. 19.00 (*1-888961-01-5*, 1015) Sigler Pr.
— Nicholas of Cusa & the Renaissance. Izbicki, Thomas M. & Christianson, Gerald, eds. (Variorum Collected Studies Ser.: Vol. CS654). 280p. 1999. text 97.95 (*0-86078-801-6*, Pub. by Ashgate Pub) Ashgate Pub Co.
Cranz, F. Edward & Brown, Virginia, eds. Catalogus Translationum et Commentariorum: Mediaeval & Renaissance Latin Translations & Commentaries, Annotated Lists & Guides, Vol. 6. LC 60-4006. 204p. 1986. 54.95 (*0-8132-0618-9*) Cath U Pr.
Cranz, F. Edward & Kristeller, Paul O., eds. Catalogus Translationum et Commentariorum: Medieval & Renaissance Latin Translations & Commentaries, Vol. 5. 448p. 1984. pap. 54.95 (*0-8132-0580-8*) Cath U Pr.
Cranz, F. Edward, jt. auth. see Fuermann, George M.
Cranz, Galen. The Chair. 288p. 2000. pap. 13.95 (*0-393-31955-5*) Norton.
— The Chair: Rethinking Culture, Body, & Design. LC 97-43898. (Illus.). 288p. 1998. 27.50 (*0-393-04655-9*) Norton.
Crapanzano, Vincent. The Hamadsha: A Study in Moroccan Ethnopsychiatry. LC 72-75529. 1973. pap. 17.95 (*0-520-04510-6*, Pub. by U CA Pr) Cal Prin Full Svc.
— Serving the Word: Literalism in America from the Pulpit to the Bench. LC 99-22220. 448p. 2000. 25.00 (*1-56584-412-2*, Pub. by New Press NY) Norton.
— Tuhami: Portrait of a Moroccan. LC 79-24550. 204p. (C). 1986. reprint ed. pap. text 12.00 (*0-226-11871-1*) U Ch Pr.
Crapanzano, Vincent, tr. see Leenhardt, Maurice.
Crapanzo, Vincent. Hermes' Dilemma & Hamlet's Desire: On the Epistemology of Interpretation. 400p. (C). 1992. pap. 19.95 (*0-674-38981-6*) HUP.
Craparo, John S. TrunKalculator (Version 1.0) The Telecommunications Management Tool. 1989. 69.95 (*0-685-74155-9*); 69.95 incl. disk (*0-685-74156-7*, CR1001) Wynnewood Rsch.
Crapo. Course Integrator - Cultural Anthropology. 4th ed. 1996. 14.06 (*0-697-34973-X*, WCB McGr Hill) McGrw-H Hghr Educ.
***Crapo.** Cultural Anthropology. 5th ed. 2001. 33.75 (*0-07-238152-3*) McGraw.
Crapo. Cultural Anthropology: Test Item File. 4th ed. 1996. teacher ed. 14.06 (*0-697-33615-8*, WCB McGr Hill) McGrw-H Hghr Educ.
— Webquester: Anthropology. 2nd ed. 150p. 1999. spiral bd. 13.13 (*0-07-235612-X*) McGraw.
— Webquester: Cultural Anthroplgy. 1998. 10.00 (*0-07-365792-1*) McGraw.
Crapo, C., et al. Recoveries & Yields from Pacific Fish & Shellfish. 2nd rev. ed. (Marine Advisory Bulletin Ser.: No. 37). 36p. 1993. pap. 5.00 (*1-56612-012-8*) AK Sea Grant CP.
Crapo, Chuck & Paust, Brian C. Air Shipment of Fresh Fish: A Primer for Shippers & Cargo Handlers. rev. ed. (Marine Advisory Bulletin Ser.: No. 32). 32p. 1991. reprint ed. pap. 3.00 (*1-56612-001-2*) AK Sea Grant CP.
Crapo, H. H. Crapo Certain Comeovers, 2 vols. 1044p. 1989. reprint ed. pap. 139.00 (*0-8328-0441-X*); reprint ed. lib. bdg. 147.00 (*0-8328-0440-1*) Higginson Bk Co.
Crapo, Richley. Cultural Anthropology: Understanding Ourselves & Others. 3rd ed. 448p. (C). 1993. text 25.95 (*1-56134-222-X*, Dshkn McG-Hill) McGrw-H Hghr Educ.
Crapo, Richley & Angeloni, Elvio. Course Kit: Cultural Anthropology: Understanding Ourselves & Others/Annual Editions: Anthropology 95/96. 3rd ed. (C). 1996. text. write for info. (*0-697-29667-9*) Brown & Benchmark.
Crapol, Edward P. America for Americans: Economic Nationalism & Anglophobia in the Late Nineteenth Century, 28. LC 71-176287. (Contributions in American History Ser.: No. 28). 248p. 1973. 59.95 (*0-8371-6273-4*, CRA/, Greenwood Pr) Greenwood.
— James G. Blaine: Architect of Empire. Fry, Joseph A., ed. LC 99-25105. (Biographies in American Foreign Policy Ser.: No. 4). 220p. 1999. pap. 17.95 (*0-8420-2605-3*) Scholarly Res Inc.
***Crapol, Edward P.** James G. Blaine: Architect of Empire. Fry, Joseph A., ed. LC 99-25105. (Biographies in American Foreign Policy Ser.: No. 4). 220p. 1999. 50.00 (*0-8420-2604-5*) Scholarly Res Inc.
Crapol, Edward P., ed. Women & American Foreign Policy: Lobbyists, Critics, & Insiders. 2nd rev. ed. LC 91-46045. (America in the Modern World Ser.). 200p. (C). 1992. reprint ed. 45.00 (*0-8420-2431-X*, SR Bks) Scholarly Res Inc.
— Women & American Foreign Policy: Lobbyists, Critics, & Insiders, 76. LC 86-22798. (Contributions in Women's Studies: No. 76). 213p. 1987. 55.00 (*0-313-24636-X*, CWF/, Greenwood Pr) Greenwood.
Crapotta. Facetas. (College Spanish Ser.). (C). 1993. text, teacher ed. 21.95 (*0-8384-4651-5*) Heinle & Heinle.
Crapotta, James. Facetas. (Bridging the Gap Ser.). (C). 1994. text, student ed. 36.95 (*0-8384-4650-7*) Heinle & Heinle.
— Kingship & Tyranny in the Theatre of Guillen de Castro. (Monagrafias A Ser.). 188p. (C). 1984. 51.00 (*0-7293-0163-X*, Pub. by Tamesis Bks Ltd) Boydell & Brewer.
Crapper, G. D. Introduction to Waterwaves. (Mathematics & Its Applications Ser.). 224p. 1984. text 68.95 (*0-470-20122-3*) P-H.
Crapps, Robert W. An Introduction to the Psychology of Religion. LC 86-8586. 408p. (C). 1995. pap. text 24.95 (*0-86554-195-7*, P021) Mercer Univ Pr.
Crapser, William. Remains: Stories of Vietnam. LC 88-6667. 175p. 1988. pap. 9.95 (*0-937584-14-2*) Sachem Pr.
Crapsey, Edward. Nether Side of New York. LC 69-14919. (Criminology, Law Enforcement, & Social Problems Ser.: No. 46). 1969. reprint ed. 26.50 (*0-87585-046-4*) Patterson Smith.
Crapuchettes, Bruce, ed. see Beauvoir, Francine C.

***Crary, Alice Marguerite & Read, Rupert J., eds.** The New Wittgenstein. LC 99-48803. 416p. (C). 2000. pap. write for info. (0-415-17319-1) Routledge.
— New Wittgenstein. LC 99-48803. 416p. (C). 2000. text 90.00 (0-415-17318-3) Routledge.

***Crary, Dan.** Dan Crary "Guitar" 88p. 1998. pap. 16.95 (0-7866-3547-9) Mel Bay.

Crary, Dan. Dan Crary, the Flatpickers Guide. 112p. 1986. pap. text 19.95 incl. audio compact disk (0-931759-12-9) Centerstream Pub.

Crary, Dan. Dan Crary/Jammed If I Do. Libertine, Dan, tr. 100p. 1996. 16.95 (0-7866-1786-1, 95733) Mel Bay.
— Jammed If I Do: Intermediate Level. 100p. 1996. spiral bd. 31.95 (0-7866-1788-8, 95733CDP) Mel Bay.

Crary, David T. & Pfahl, John K. Personal Finance. 7th ed. LC 79-27578. (Illus.). 734p. reprint ed. pap. 200.00 (0-608-10695-X, 202150100021) Bks Demand.

Crary, Elbert P. The Children of God: A Metaphysical Interpretation of the Gospel of St. John. LC 91-73347. 104p. (Orig.). 1991. pap. 18.00 (0-9629950-0-2) Ashbrook Pub.

***Crary, Elizabeth.** Amor y Limites: Una Guia para Ser Padres Creativos. Patrino de McVittie, Marina, tr. from ENG.Tr. of Love & Limits: Guidance Tools for Creative Parenting. (SPA.). 48p. 1999. pap. 8.95 (1-884734-51-0); lib. bdg. 18.95 (1-884734-52-9) Parenting Pr.

Crary, Elizabeth. Finders, Keepers? LC 87-60369. (Decision Is Yours Ser.). (Illus.). 64p. (Orig.). (J). (gr. 2-6). 1987. pap. 5.95 (0-943990-38-6); lib. bdg. 16.95 (0-943990-39-4) Parenting Pr.
— Help! The Kids Are at It Again: Using Kids' Quarrels to Teach "People" Skills. LC 96-32502. (Illus.). 96p. (Orig.). 1997. pap. 11.95 (1-884734-08-1); lib. bdg. 18.95 (1-884734-09-X) Parenting Pr.
— I Can't Wait. 2nd rev. ed. LC 96-21278. (Children's Problem Solving Bk.). (Illus.). 32p. (Orig.). (J). (ps-3). 1996. pap. 6.95 (1-884734-22-7); lib. bdg. 16.95 (1-884734-23-5) Parenting Pr.
— I Want It. 2nd rev. ed. LC 96-21575. (Children's Problem Solving Bk.). (Illus.). 32p. (Orig.). (J). (ps-3). 1996. pap. 6.95 (1-884734-14-6); lib. bdg. 16.95 (1-884734-15-4) Parenting Pr.
— I Want to Play. 2nd rev. ed. LC 96-21284. (Children's Problem Solving Bk.). (Illus.). 32p. (Orig.). (J). (ps-3). 1996. pap. 6.95 (1-884734-18-9); lib. bdg. 16.95 (1-884734-19-7) Parenting Pr.
— I'm Excited. LC 93-85378. (Dealing with Feelings Ser.). (Illus.). 32p. (J). (ps-4). 1994. pap. 6.95 (0-943990-91-2); lib. bdg. 16.95 (0-943990-92-0) Parenting Pr.
— I'm Frustrated. LC 90-63870. (Illus.). 32p. (J). (ps-3). 1992. pap. 6.95 (0-943990-64-5); lib. bdg. 16.95 (0-943990-65-3) Parenting Pr.
— I'm Furious. LC 93-79529. (Dealing with Feelings Ser.). (Illus.). 32p. (J). (ps-4). 1994. pap. 6.95 (0-943990-93-9); lib. bdg. 16.95 (0-943990-94-7) Parenting Pr.
— I'm Lost. 2nd rev. ed. LC 96-21283. (Children's Problem Solving Bk.). (Illus.). 32p. (Orig.). (J). (ps-3). 1996. pap. 6.95 (1-884734-24-3); lib. bdg. 16.95 (1-884734-25-1) Parenting Pr.
— I'm Mad. LC 90-63869. (Illus.). 32p. (J). (ps-3). 1992. pap. 6.95 (0-943990-62-9) Parenting Pr.
— I'm Proud. LC 90-63871. (Illus.). 32p. (J). (ps-3). 1992. pap. 6.95 (0-943990-66-1); lib. bdg. 16.95 (0-943990-67-X) Parenting Pr.
— I'm Scared. LC 93-85377. (Dealing with Feelings Ser.). (Illus.). 32p. (Orig.). (J). (ps-4). 1994. pap. 6.95 (0-943990-89-0); lib. bdg. 16.95 (0-943990-90-4) Parenting Pr.
— Kids Can Cooperate. LC 84-60587. (Illus.). 104p. 1984. pap. 12.95 (0-943990-04-1); lib. bdg. 19.95 (0-943990-05-X) Parenting Pr.
— Love & Limits: Guidance Tools for Creative Parenting. LC 93-49556. (Star Parenting Bk.). 48p. (Orig.). 1994. pap. 6.95 (1-884734-04-9); lib. bdg. 16.95 (1-884734-05-7) Parenting Pr.
— Magic Tools for Raising Kids. (Tools for Everyday Parenting Ser.). (Illus.). 128p. (Orig.). 1995. pap. 9.95 (0-943990-77-7); lib. bdg. 18.95 (0-943990-78-5) Parenting Pr.
— Mommy, Don't Go. 2nd rev. ed. LC 96-23352. (Children's Problem Solving Bk.). (Illus.). 32p. (J). (ps-3). 1996. pap. 6.95 (1-884734-20-0); lib. bdg. 16.95 (1-884734-21-9) Parenting Pr.
— My Name Is Not Dummy. 2nd rev. ed. LC 96-20259. (Children's Problem Solving Bk.). (Illus.). 32p. (Orig.). (J). (ps-3). 1996. pap. 6.95 (1-884734-16-2); lib. bdg. 16.95 (1-884734-17-0) Parenting Pr.
— Pick up Your Socks... And Other Skills Growing Children Need! A Practical Guide to Raising Responsible Children. LC 89-62656. (Illus.). 112p. 1990. pap. 14.95 (0-943990-52-1); lib. bdg. 19.95 (0-943990-53-X) Parenting Pr.
— Three Hundred Sixty-Five Wacky, Wonderful Ways to Get Your Children to Do What You Want. (Tools for Everyday Parenting Ser.). (Illus.). 104p. (Orig.). 1995. pap. 9.95 (0-943990-79-3); lib. bdg. 18.95 (0-943990-80-7) Parenting Pr.
— Without Spanking or Spoiling: A Practical Approach to Toddler & Preschool Guidance. 2nd rev. ed. LC 92-83497. (Illus.). 128p. (Orig.). 1993. pap. 14.95 (0-943990-74-2); lib. bdg. 19.95 (0-943990-87-4) Parenting Pr.
— Without Spanking or Spoiling: Leader's Guide. 1996. spiral bd. 22.95 (0-943990-86-6) Parenting Pr.

Crary, Elizabeth, ed. Historical Activity Guide. (Illus.). 88p. (J). (gr. 2-6). 1993. spiral bd. 24.95 (0-943990-47-5) Parenting Pr.

Crary, Elizabeth & Steelsmith, Shari. When You're Happy. LC 96-68715. (Feelings for Little Children Ser.). (Illus.). 10p. (J). (ps-1). 1997. bds. 5.95 (1-884734-12-X) Parenting Pr.
— When You're Mad. LC 96-68717. (Feelings for Little Children Ser.). (Illus.). 10p. (J). (ps-1). 1997. bds. 5.95 (1-884734-10-3) Parenting Pr.
— When You're Shy. LC 96-68716. (Feelings for Little Children Ser.). (Illus.). 10p. (J). (ps-1). 1997. bds. 5.95 (1-884734-11-1) Parenting Pr.
— When You're Silly. LC 96-68714. (Feelings for Little Children Ser.). (Illus.). 10p. (J). (ps-1). 1997. bds. 5.95 (1-884734-13-8) Parenting Pr.

Crary, Elizabeth & Whitney, Jean. I'm Mad. LC 90-63869. (Illus.). 32p. (J). (ps-3). 1992. lib. bdg. 16.95 (0-943990-63-7) Parenting Pr.

Crary, Frances E. People of the Valley: Awakening & Journey, 2 vols. LC 91-73346. (Orig.). 1992. pap. 14.95 (0-9629950-3-7) Ashbrook Pub.
— People of the Valley Bk. 1: The Awakening. LC 91-73346. 702p. (Orig.). 1992. pap. 14.95 (0-9629950-1-0) Ashbrook Pub.
— People of the Valley Bk. 2: The Journey. LC 91-73346. 645p. (Orig.). 1992. pap. 14.95 (0-9629950-2-9) Ashbrook Pub.
— We Who Live in the Castle: An Allegorical Novel. LC 91-75127. 310p. (Orig.). 1991. pap. 11.95 (0-9629950-4-5) Ashbrook Pub.

***Crary, Jonathan.** Suspensions of Perception: Attention, Spectacle & Modern Culture. LC 99-26071. (Illus.). 340p. 1999. 37.50 (0-262-03265-1) MIT Pr.

Crary, Jonathan. Techniken des Betrachters Sehen und Moderne Im 19. Jahrhundert. (GER., Illus.). 192p. 1996. text 37.00 (3-364-00359-9) Gordon & Breach.
— Techniques of the Observer: On Vision & Modernity in the Nineteenth Century. (Illus.). 200p. 1990. 33.00 (0-262-03169-8) MIT Pr.
— Techniques of the Observer: On Vision & Modernity in the Nineteenth Century. (Illus.). 184p. 1992. reprint ed. pap. text 16.50 (0-262-53107-0) MIT Pr.

Crary, Jonathan & Kwinter, Sanford. Incorporations: Zone Six. LC 88-51439. (Illus.). 634p. 1992. pap. 34.95 (0-942299-29-9) Zone Bks.

Crary, Jonathan & Kwinter, Sanford, eds. Incorporations: Zone Six. LC 88-51439. (Illus.). 634p. 1992. 65.00 (0-942299-30-2) Zone Bks.

Crary, Jonathan & Levin, Kim. Eleanor Antin: The Angel of Mercy. (Illus.). 28p. 1977. pap. 2.00 (0-934418-02-0) Mus Contemp Art.

Crary, Michael A. Developmental Motor Speech Disorders. LC 93-3711. (Illus.). 298p. (Orig.). (C). 1993. pap. text 42.50 (1-879105-92-6, 0356) Thomson Learn.

Crary, Michael A., jt. auth. see Groher, Michael E.

Crary, Robert W. The Still Small Voice. LC 92-82655. 210p. (Orig.). 1993. pap. 9.95 (0-914711-06-7) Rishis Inst.
— The Voice from Within. LC 95-70819. 336p. (Orig.). 1996. pap. 12.95 (0-914711-12-1) Rishis Inst.

Crary, Robert W., jt. auth. see Lorr, Regina E.

Crary, Robert Wall. The Way to Spiritual Mastery. LC 91-60438. 208p. (Orig.). 1991. pap. 10.95 (0-914711-02-4) Rishis Inst.

Crase, Dixie R. How to Answer Big Questions from Little Children. 48p. 1990. 3.95 (0-936625-83-X) New Hope AL.

Crase, Douglas. Amerifil.Txt: A Commonplace Book. 160p. 1996. pap. 13.95 (0-472-06636-6, 06636); text 39.50 (0-472-09636-2, 09636) U of Mich Pr.

Crasemann, Bernd, ed. Atomic Inner-Shell Physics. LC 85-12357. (Physics of Atoms & Molecules Ser.). 770p. 1985. 145.00 (0-306-41847-9, Plenum Trade) Perseus Pubng.
— X-Ray & Atomic Inner-Shell Physics, 1982. LC 82-74075. (AIP Conference Proceedings Ser.: No. 94). 802p. 1982. lib. bdg. 44.50 (0-88318-193-2) Am Inst Physics.

Crasemann, Bernd, jt. auth. see Powell, John L.

***Crash Course.** Gastroenterology. 1999. text. write for info. (0-7234-3153-1) Harcourt.
— Neurology. 1999. text. write for info. (0-7234-3141-8) Harcourt.

Crashaw, Richard. The Complete Works of Richard Crashaw, 2 vols., Set. LC 73-21062. (Fuller Worthies' Library). (Illus.). reprint ed. 153.00 (0-404-11479-2) AMS Pr.

Crashaw, W., tr. see Balbani, Niccolo.

Crask & Fox. Marketing Research Reprint. 1997. pap. text 40.00 (0-13-911025-9) P-H.

Craske, Jacqueline. Prayers & Thoughts for Peace. 60p. 1986. pap. 5.95 (0-900125-67-5) Bahai.

Craske, Margaret. The Dance of Love: My Life with Meher Baba. LC 80-53859. 193p. (Orig.). 1980. pap. 10.00 (0-913078-40-9) Sheriar Pr.
— Still Dancing with Love: More Stories of Life with Meher Baba. LC 89-78069. 104p. (Orig.). 1990. pap. 8.95 (0-913078-64-6) Sheriar Pr.

Craske, Matthew. Art in Europe 1700-1830. (Oxford History of Art). (Illus.). 320p. 1997. pap. 15.95 (0-19-284206-4) OUP.
— Art in Europe 1700-1830. (Oxford History of Art). (Illus.). 320p. (C). 1997. 39.95 (0-19-284246-3) OUP.
— William Hogarth. (British Artists Ser.). (Illus.). 80p. 2000. pap. 14.95 (0-691-07067-9) Princeton U Pr.

Craske, Michelle. Anxiety Disorders: Psychological Approaches to Theory & Treatment. LC 98-19027. (Perspectives in Clinical Psychology Ser.). 448p. 1998. text 65.00 (0-8133-3250-8, Pub. by Westview) HarpC.

***Craske, Michelle G.** Mastery of Your Anxiety & Panic: Therapist Guide. 3rd ed. 2000. pap. text 35.00 (0-12-784464-3) Acad Pr.

Craske, Michelle G. Mastery of Your Specific Phobia Client Workbook. 1998. pap. text 40.00 (0-12-785034-1) Acad Pr.
— Mastery of Your Specific Phobia Therapist Guide. 1999. pap. text 35.50 (0-12-785033-3) Acad Pr.

Craske, Nikki. Women & Politics in Latin America. LC 98-51550. 272p. (C). 1999. text 50.00 (0-8135-2692-2); pap. text 20.00 (0-8135-2693-0) Rutgers U Pr.

Crasnaru, Daniela. Sea Level Zero. Sorkin, Adam J., tr. from ROM. (New American Translations Ser.: Vol. 12). 100p. 1999. pap. 13.50 (1-880238-79-9, Pub. by BOA Edns) Consort Bk Sales.

Crasnow, Ellman, ed. Walt Whitman. (Everyman's Poetry Ser.). 116p. 1997. pap. 1.95 (0-460-87825-5, Everyman's Classic Lib) Tuttle Pubng.

Crass, David C., et al, eds. The Southern Colonial Backcountry: Interdisciplinary Perspectives on Frontier Communities. LC 98-8978. (Illus.). 288p. 1998. text 38.00 (1-57233-019-8) U of Tenn Pr.

Crass, John, ed. Pocket Guide to U. S. Electric Utilities. 4th rev. ed. 400p. 1996. pap. 110.00 (1-56760-039-5) Utility Data Inst.

Crass, M. F. Calcium Regulating Hormones & Cardiovascular Function. 352p. 1994. boxed set 168.95 (0-8493-8661-6) CRC Pr.

Crasselame, Marc-Antonio. A Light from Out of the Darkness: On the Composition of the Stone of the Philosophers. Smith, Patrick, ed. Smith, Patrick J., tr. from FRE. (Alchemical Studies Ser.: No. 1). (Illus.). (Orig.). 1997. pap. 8.95 (1-55818-356-6, Alchemical) Holmes Pub.

Crassweller, Robert O. Peron & the Enigmas of Argentina. (Illus.). 1988. pap. 16.95 (0-393-30543-0) Norton.

Craster, H. H., ed. see Halifax, Edward F.

Crastes de Paulet, C., et al, eds. Free Radicals, Lipoproteins & Membrane Lipids. LC 90-7159. (NATO ASI Ser.: Vol. 189). (Illus.). 430p. (C). 1990. text 150.00 (0-306-43580-2, Kluwer Plenum) Kluwer Academic.

Craswell, Allan. For Your Freedom & Ours: Polish Forces in Scotland, 1940-1946. (Illus.). 36p. 1995. pap. 4.95 (0-948636-54-8, 6548, Pub. by Natl Mus Scotland) A Schwartz & Co.

Craswell, E. T. & Pushparajah, E., eds. Management of Acid Soils in the Humid Tropics of Asia. 118p. 1989. pap. 75.00 (1-86320-001-0) St Mut.

Craswell, E. T. & Simpson, J. R. Soil Fertility & Climatic Conditions in Dryland Agriculture. 137p. 1994. pap. 90.00 (1-86320-122-X, Pub. by ACIAR) St Mut.

Craswell, Richard & Schwartz, Alan, eds. Foundations of Contract Law. LC 93-43175. (Interdisciplinary Readers in Law Ser.). (Illus.). 368p. (C). 1994. text 59.95 (0-19-509035-7); pap. text 27.95 (0-19-507940-X) OUP.

Crate, Joan. Pale As Real Ladies: Poems for Pauline Johnson. 76p. 1989. pap. 11.95 (0-919626-43-2, Pub. by Brick Bks) Genl Dist Srvs.

Crater, Don R. Cone Crafting. (Illus.). 52p. (Orig.). 1980. pap. 6.95 (0-940654-00-8) Tribune Pub.
— The Dried Guide. LC 81-52464. (Illus.). 56p. (Orig.). 1981. pap. 7.95 (0-940654-01-6) Tribune Pub.

Crater, Flora. Almanac of Virginia Politics: 1990 Supplement. 1990. pap. 11.95 (0-917560-50-7) Woman Activist.
— Woman Activist Guide to Precinct Politics. 3rd ed. 1997. pap. 5.00 (0-685-38090-4) Woman Activist.

Crater, Flora, et al. Almanac of Virginia Politics: 1986 Supplement. 1989. write for info. (0-917560-21-3) Woman Activist.
— Almanac of Virginia Politics: 1987 Regular. 1989. 13.95 (0-917560-22-1) Woman Activist.
— Almanac of Virginia Politics: 1988 Supplement. 1989. pap. 5.95 (0-917560-23-X) Woman Activist.
— Almanac of Virginia Politics: 1989 Regular. 1990. pap. 17.95 (0-917560-24-8) Woman Activist.
— Almanac of Virginia Politics: 1991 Regular. 1990. 19.95 (0-917560-25-6) Woman Activist.
— Almanac of Virginia Politics: 1992 Supplement. 1993. 13.95 (0-917560-26-4) Woman Activist.
— Almanac of Virginia Politics: 1993 Regular. 1993. 21.95 (0-917560-27-2) Woman Activist.
— Almanac of Virginia Politics: 1994 Supplement. 1995. pap. 15.95 (0-917560-28-0) Woman Activist.

***Crater, Flora, et al.** Almanac of Virginia Politics, 1999 Regular. 1999. pap. 25.95 (0-917560-33-7) Woman Activist.
— Almanac of Virginia Politics, 2000 Regular. 2000. pap. 25.95 (0-917560-34-5) Clark Pub.

Crater, Mark, et al. Carter House Cookbook. LC 95-7447. (Illus.). 144p. 1995. pap. 8.95 (0-89815-773-0) Ten Speed Pr.

Crater, Timothy & Hunsicker, Ranelda. A Christian Heritage Treasury. LC 97-29943. (Illus.). 96p. (J). (gr. 2-7). 1997. 16.99 (0-7814-0014-7, Chariot Bks) Chariot Victor.

Crathorne, James. Cliveden: The Place & the People. (Illus.). 240p. 1995. 55.00 (1-85585-223-3, Pub. by Collins & Br) Trafalgar.

Craton, Michael. Empire, Enslavement & Freedom in the Caribbean. LC 97-12391. 544p. (C). 1997. text 44.95 (1-55876-158-6); pap. text 24.95 (1-55876-159-4) Wiener Pubs Inc.

Craton, Michael & Saunders, Gail. Islanders in the Stream: A History of the Bahamian People, from Aboriginal Times to the End of Slavery, Vol. 1 LC 91-21737. (Illus.). 480p. 1999. pap. text 24.95 (0-8203-2122-2) U of Ga Pr.
— Islanders in the Stream Vol. 2: A History of the Bahamian People: From the Ending of Slavery to the Twenty-First Century. 608p. 1998. text 75.00 (0-8203-1926-0) U of Ga Pr.

Craton, Michael M. Searching for the Invisible Man: Slaves & Plantation Life in Jamaica. LC 76-48281. 448p. 1978. 45.00 (0-674-79629-2) HUP.

Cratsley, Bruce, photos by. Bruce Cratsley: White Light, Silent Shadows. (Illus.). 170p. 1998. text 60.00 (0-9657280-5-6, 810312) Arena Editions.

Cratty, Bryant J. Adapted Physical Education in the Mainstream. 2nd ed. LC 86-82896. (Illus.). 574p. 1989. text 48.00 (0-89108-130-5) Love Pub Co.
— Clumsy Child Syndromes: Descriptions, Evaluation, & Remediation. LC 92-34999. 649p. 1993. text 81.00 (3-7186-0548-1); pap. text 57.00 (3-7186-0575-9) Gordon & Breach.
— Coding Games: Active Ways to Enhance Reading & Thinking: Grades k-5. 1981. pap. 7.95 (0-89108-101-1, 8106) Love Pub Co.
— Motor Activity & the Education of Retardates. LC 73-23008. (Lea & Febiger Health, Physical Education & Recreation Ser.). (Illus.). 312p. reprint ed. 96.80 (0-8357-9411-3, 201453700093) Bks Demand.
— Movement Behavior & Motor Learning. 3rd ed. LC 73-1938. (Health Education, Physical Education, & Recreation Ser.). 530p. reprint ed. pap. 164.30 (0-608-17778-4, 205656800074) Bks Demand.
— Remedial Motor Activity for Children. LC 74-26973. 335p. reprint ed. pap. 103.90 (0-7837-1484-X, 205717900023) Bks Demand.

Cratty, Bryant J. & Goldman, Richard L. Learning Disabilities: Contemporary Viewpoints. 248p. 1996. pap. text 25.00 (3-7186-0623-2, Harwood Acad Pubs) Gordon & Breach.

Cratty, Bryant J. & Hutton, Robert S. Experiments in Movement Behavior & Motor Learning. LC 72-85840. (Illus.). 223p. reprint ed. pap. 69.20 (0-608-30628-2, 201453800096) Bks Demand.

Crauder. Functions & Their Uses. 2000. pap. text 30.57 (0-395-91158-3) HM.

Crauderueff, Elaine J. War Taxes. LC 89-61822. (Orig.). 1989. pap. 1.00 (0-87574-286-6) Pendle Hill.

Crauel, H. & Gundlach, Matthias, eds. Stochastic Dynamics. LC 98-43868. (Illus.). 440p. 1999. 59.95 (0-387-98512-3) Spr-Verlag.

Crauford, Emma, tr. see Marcel, Gabriel.

Crauford, Lane. Acting: Its Theory & Practice. LC 75-84510. 1972. 23.95 (0-405-08400-5, Pub. by Blom Pubns) Ayer.

Craufurd, Emma, tr. see Walter, Gerard.

Craufurd-Smith, Rachael. Broadcasting Law & Fundamental Rights. LC 97-10246. 294p. 1997. text 89.00 (0-19-826221-3) OUP.

***Craughwell, Thomas J.** Alligators in the Sewer & 222 Other Urban Legends: Absolutely True Stories That Happened to a Friend of a Friend of a Friend. LC 98-50123. 240p. 1999. 8.98 (1-57912-061-X) Blck Dog & Leventhal.
— Baby on the Car Roof & 222 Other Urban Legends: Absolutely True Stories That Happened to a Friend of a Friend of a Friend. 240p. 2000. 8.98 (1-57912-147-0) Blck Dog & Leventhal.
— Every Eye Beholds You: A World Treasury of Prayer. 2001. pap. write for info. (0-15-600707-X) Harcourt.

Craughwell, Thomas J. Great Books for Every Book Lover: 2002 Great Reading Suggestions for the Discriminating Bibiliophile. (Illus.). 704p. 1998. 14.98 (1-57912-044-X) Blck Dog & Leventhal.

***Craughwell, Thomas J.** Wisdom of The Popes. LC 99-89733. 256p. 2000. text 23.95 (0-312-25356-7) St Martin.

Craughwell, Thomas J., ed. Every Eye Beholds You: A World Treasury of Prayer. LC 99-29111. 344p. (C). 1999. 25.00 (0-15-100483-8, Harvest Bks) Harcourt.

Craughwell, Tom. Fifty States. LC 99-182087. (Fandex Family Field Guide Ser.). (Illus.). 1998. pap. 9.95 (0-7611-1399-1) Workman Pub.

Craul, Philip J. Urban Soils: Applications & Practices. LC 98-38197. 366p. (C). 1999. 79.95 (0-471-18903-0) Wiley.

Craul, Phillip J. Urban Soil in Landscape Design. LC 91-36557. 416p. 1992. 120.00 (0-471-80598-X) Wiley.

Craumer, Paul. Rural & Agricultural Development in Ukbekistan. (Former Soviet-South Papers). 60p. (C). 1995. pap. 12.95 (1-899658-02-5) Brookings.

Craun, Edwin D. Lies, Slander & Obscenity in Medieval English Narrative: Pastoral Rhetoric & the Deviant Speaker. LC 96-20416. (Cambridge Studies in Medieval Literature: No. 31). 270p. (C). 1997. text 64.95 (0-521-49690-X) Cambridge U Pr.

Craun, Gunther, ed. Safety of Water Disinfection: Balancing Chemical & Microbial Risks. LC 93-61033. (Illus.). 690p. 1993. pap. 52.50 (0-944398-11-1) ILSI.

Craun, G.unther, ed. Water Quality in Latin America: Balancing the Microbial & Chemical Risks in Drinking Water Disinfection. 211p. 1996. pap. 52.50 (0-944398-48-0) ILSI.

Craun, Gunther, ed. Water Quality in Latin America: Balancing the Microbial & Chemical Risks in Drinking Water Disinfection. (SPA.). 211p. 1996. pap. 52.50 (0-944398-49-9) ILSI.

Craun, Gunther F., ed. Waterborne Diseases in the United States. 336p. 1986. 173.00 (0-8493-5937-6, RA642, CRC Reprint) Franklin.

Craun, Gunther F., jt. ed. see Talbott, Evelyn O.

Craun, Guther, jt. ed. see Kopfler, Frederick C.

Craun, Victor S. Craun Family in America, & Its Connections with Other Families. (Illus.). 354p. 1997. reprint ed. pap. 55.00 (0-8328-8126-0); reprint ed. lib. bdg. 65.00 (0-8328-8125-2) Higginson Bk Co.

Crausaz, Winston. Pico de Orizaba: or Citlaltepetl: Geology, Archaeology, History, Natural History, & Mountaineering Routes: With Additional Material on the High Mexican Volcanoes. LC 93-80607. (Illus.). xiv, 594p. 1993. 125.00 (1-884681-50-6) Geopress Intl.

 An Asterisk (*) at the beginning of an entry indicates that the title is appearing for the first time.

***Crause, Gayle.** Red Roots. 1999. pap. 14.95 (*0-9676010-0-2*) Fire Horse AL.

Crauzat, E. De, see De Crauzat, E.

Cravalho, Ernest G. Critical Issues in Medical Technology. McNeil, Barbara J., ed. LC 81-7900. 447p. 1981. 28.00 (*0-86569-070-7*, Auburn Hse) Greenwood.

***Cravat, Victor.** Suzette. 2000. mass mkt. 7.95 (*1-56201-207-X*) Blue Moon Bks.

Cravath, Lynne. Over the River & Through the Woods Board Book. (Illus.). 12p. (J). (ps up). 1998. 6.95 (*0-694-01218-1*) HarpC.

***Cravath, Lynne W.** My First Action Rhymes. LC 99-69949. (Illus.). 24p. (J). (ps). 2000. pap. 9.95 (*0-694-01418-4*, HarpFestival) HarpC Child Bks.

Cravath, Lynne Woodcock, jt. illus. see Hayles, Marsha.

Cravath, Lynne Woodcock, jt. illus. see Whelan, Gloria.

Cravath, Prosper & Steele, Spencer. Early Annals of Whitewater, 1837-1867. Salisbury, Albert, ed. (Illus.). 283p. 1995. reprint ed. lib. bdg. 37.50 (*0-8328-4602-3*) Higginson Bk Co.

Crave, R., ed. see Moore, George.

Craven. Diego Rivera As Epic Modernist. 1997. 30.00 (*0-8161-0762-9*, G K Hall Lrg Type) Mac Lib Ref.

— Diego Rivera As Epic Modernist. LC 97-24321. 1997. 55.00 (*0-8161-0537-5*, G K Hall Lrg Type) Mac Lib Ref.

— Surgical MCQS. 3rd ed. 1993. pap. 26.95 (*0-443-04702-2*, W B Saunders Co) Harcrt Hlth Sci Grp.

Craven & Mason. Strategic Marketing Cases. 5th ed. 1996. 67.00 (*0-256-24803-6*) McGraw.

Craven, A. J., ed. Electron Microscopy & Analysis 1993: Proceedings of the Institute of Physics Electron Microscopy & Analysis Group Conference, University of Liverpool, 14-17 September 1993. (Institute of Physics Conference Ser.: No. 138). (Illus.). 546p. 1994. 236.00 (*0-7503-0321-2*) IOP Pub.

Craven, A. J., jt. ed. see Chapman, J. N.

Craven, Alana. The Old Wood Burning Cook Stove: Heart of My Farmhouse Kitchen. Wightman, Heather A., ed. (Illus.). 40p. (Orig.). 1997. pap. 5.50 (*1-888911-02-6*) Benson Smythe.

Craven, Amanda. Sex Magic: Casting a Spell in the Bedroom. 224p. (Orig.). 2000. pap. text, wbk. ed. 14.95 (*0-7535-0324-7*) Virgin Bks.

Craven, Arthur. The Borzoi As I Know It. deluxe ed. (Illus.). 80p. 1995. 20.00 (*0-614-04528-2*) Donald R Hoflin.

Craven, Arthur, et al. 4 Dada Suicides. LC 95-219590. (Atlas Anti-Classics Ser.). 256p. (Orig.). 1995. pap. 14.99 (*0-947757-74-0*, Pub. by Atlas Pr) Serpents Tail.

Craven, Avery O. Civil War in the Making, 1815-1860. LC 59-7943. (Walter Lynwood Fleming Lectures). xiv, 116p. 1968. pap. text 12.95 (*0-8071-0131-1*) La State U Pr.

— Coming of the Civil War. 2nd ed. LC 57-8572. 508p. 1966. pap. text 18.95 (*0-226-11894-0*, P210) U Ch Pr.

— Edmund Ruffin, Southerner: A Study in Secession. LC 64-11059. x, 284p. 1966. pap. text 19.95 (*0-8071-0104-4*) La State U Pr.

— Growth of Southern Nationalism, 1848-1861. LC 53-11470. (History of the South Ser.: Vol. 6). (Illus.). x, 434p. 1953. text 50.00 (*0-8071-0006-4*) La State U Pr.

— An Historian & the Civil War. LC 64-15802. (Phoenix Bks.). 239p. reprint ed. pap. 74.10 (*0-608-11494-4*, 202004900016) Bks Demand.

Craven, Avery O. Rachel of Old Louisiana. LC 74-15921. (Illus.). 122p. 1995. pap. 11.95 (*0-8071-2016-2*) La State U Pr.

Craven, Avery O. The Repressible Conflict, 1830-1861. LC 83-45425. reprint ed. 39.50 (*0-404-20070-2*) AMS Pr.

— The Repressible Conflict, 1830-1861. (History - United States Ser.). 97p. 1993. reprint ed. lib. bdg. 59.00 (*0-7812-4904-X*) Rprt Serv.

— Soil Exhaustion As a Factor in the Agricultural History of Virginia & Maryland, 1606-1860. 1926. 16.50 (*0-8446-1136-0*) Peter Smith.

Craven, B. D. Control & Optimization. (Illus.). 208p. 1998. lib. bdg. 54.95 (*0-412-55890-4*, Chap & Hall CRC) CRC Pr.

Craven, Bryan M., ed. Proceedings of the Symposium on "Neutron Diffraction," University of Texas, Austin, March 16, 1987. (Transactions of the American Crystallographic Association Ser.: Vol. 23). 104p. 1988. pap. 25.00 (*0-937140-31-7*) Polycrystal Bk Serv.

Craven, Carolyn. What the Mailman Brought. (J). 1999. pap. 4.95 (*0-399-21307-4*) Putnam Pub Group.

Craven, Charles E. History of Mattituck, Long Island. (Illus.). 400p. 1997. reprint ed. lib. bdg. 42.00 (*0-8328-6173-1*) Higginson Bk Co.

— History of Mattituck, Long Island, New York. Date not set. lib. bdg. 27.95 (*0-8488-0777-4*) Amereon Ltd.

Craven, Claudia. CADKEY 97 Quick Reference. LC 98-7292. (CAD/CAM Ser.). 288p. 1998. 33.95 (*0-7668-0144-6*) Delmar.

Craven, David. Abstract Expressionism as Cultural Critique: Dissent During the McCarthy Period. LC 98-35100. (Studies in American Visual Culture). (Illus.). 256p. (C). 1999. text 65.00 (*0-521-43415-7*) Cambridge U Pr.

— The New Concept of Art & Popular Culture in Nicaragua since the Revolution in 1979: An Analytical Essay & Compendium of Illustrations. LC 88-9350. (Latin American Studies: Vol. 1). (Illus.). 450p. 1988. lib. bdg. 109.95 (*0-88946-489-8*) E Mellen.

— Poetics & Politics in the Art of Rudolf Baranik. LC 96-18347. (Illus.). 224p. (C). 1996. text 49.95 (*0-391-03988-1*) Humanities.

Craven, David, et al. Norman Lewis: Black Paintings, 1946-1977. Salomon, Stephanie, ed. LC 98-60258. (Illus.). 124p. 1998. pap. 29.95 (*0-942949-14-5*) Studio Mus Harlem.

Craven, Elizabeth. Journey Through the Crimea to Constantinople in a Series of Letters. LC 73-115525. (Russia Observed, Series I). 1970. reprint ed. 25.95 (*0-405-03018-5*) Ayer.

Craven, George F. & Skedd, Richard F. Evanescent Mode: Microwave Components. LC 87-70485. (Artech House Microwave Library). 179p. reprint ed. pap. 55.50 (*0-7837-3019-5*, 204292100006) Bks Demand.

Craven, Gregory, ed. Australian Federation: Towards the Second Century. 258p. 1992. 49.95 (*0-522-84416-2*, Pub. by Melbourne Univ Pr) Paul & Co Pubs.

Craven, Helena. A Bluebird's First Summer. 16th ed. (Illus.). 14p. (Orig.). (J). (gr. k-6). 1996. pap. 6.95 (*0-9653954-0-5*) H Craven.

Craven, Henry & Barfield, John. English-Congo & Congo-English Dictionary. LC 75-157365. (Black Heritage Library Collection). 1977. 28.95 (*0-8369-8803-5*) Ayer.

***Craven, Ian.** Australian Cinema in the 1990s. (Illus.). 192p. 1999. 45.00 (*0-7146-4974-0*); pap. 24.50 (*0-7146-8034-6*) F Cass Pubs.

Craven, Ian, ed. Australian Popular Culture. 234p. (C). 1994. pap. text 21.95 (*0-521-46667-9*) Cambridge U Pr.

Craven, Ian, jt. auth. see Maltby, Richard.

Craven, J. B. Count Michael Maier: Life & Writings. 165p. 1992. reprint ed. pap. 17.95 (*0-922802-92-0*) Kessinger Pub.

— Doctor Robert Fludd: The English Rosicrucian. 260p. 1992. reprint ed. pap. 19.95 (*0-922802-96-3*) Kessinger Pub.

Craven, J. L., jt. auth. see Lumley, J. S.

Craven, Jerry. Aikido. LC 94-4093. (Illustrated History of Martial Arts Ser.). 32p. (J). (gr. 3-8). 1994. lib. bdg. 14.95 (*0-86593-364-2*) Rourke Corp.

— Celebrations. LC 96-8229. (Customs, Costumes, & Cultures Ser.). 32p. (J). (gr. 3-6). 1996. lib. bdg. 18.60 (*0-86625-595-8*) Rourke Pubns.

— Festivals. LC 96-11395. (Customs, Costumes, & Cultures Ser.). 32p. (J). (gr. 3-6). 1996. lib. bdg. 18.60 (*0-86625-594-X*) Rourke Pubns.

— Folk Pageants. LC 96-19233. (Customs, Costumes, & Cultures Ser.). 32p. (J). (gr. 3-6). 1996. lib. bdg. 18.60 (*0-86625-593-1*) Rourke Pubns.

— Japanese Sports Cars: Speed & Style, LC 93-14917. (Car Classics Ser.). (Illus.). 32p. (YA). (gr. 5-12). 1993. lib. bdg. 15.95 (*0-86593-256-5*) Rourke Corp.

— Ninja. LC 94-2528. (Illustrated History of Martial Arts Ser.). (Illus.). 32p. (J). (gr. 3-8). 1994. lib. bdg. 14.95 (*0-86593-365-0*) Rourke Corp.

— Rolls-Royce: Leader in Luxury, Set I. (Car Classics Ser.). 32p. (YA). (gr. 5-12). 1991. lib. bdg. 15.95 (*0-86593-147-X*) Rourke Corp.

***Craven, Jerry.** Snake Mountain: A Novel. LC 99-57781. 272p. 2000. 24.50 (*0-87565-221-2*, Pub. by Tex Christian) Tex A&M Univ Pr.

Craven, Jerry. Tae Kwon Do. LC 94-4086. (Illustrated History of Martial Arts Ser.). 32p. (J). (gr. 3-8). 1994. lib. bdg. 14.95 (*0-86593-367-7*) Rourke Corp.

— Tickling Catfish: A Texan Looks at Culture from Amarillo to Borneo. LC 96-25540. (Illus.). 160p. (Orig.). 1996. pap. 14.95 (*0-89096-728-8*) Tex A&M Univ Pr.

Craven, Joan. Help! School Starts in September. 127p. (Orig.). 1993. pap. 13.95 (*1-55059-064-2*) Temeron Bks.

Craven, John. Psychiatric Aspects of Organ Transplantation. Rodin, Gary M., ed. (Illus.). 256p. 1992. text 55.00 (*0-19-262073-8*) OUP.

— Social Choice: A Framework for Collective Decisions & Individual Judgements. (Illus.). 162p. (C). 1992. text 59.95 (*0-521-32536-6*); pap. text 18.95 (*0-521-31051-2*) Cambridge U Pr.

Craven, John P., et al, eds. International Implications of Extended Maritime Jurisdiction in the Pacific, 21st Annual Conference Proceeding. 471p. 1989. 42.50 (*0-911189-19-X*) Law Sea Inst.

Craven, John P., jt. ed. see Allen, Scott.

Craven, John V. Industrial Organization, Anti-Trust & Public Policy. (Middlebury College Conference Series on Economic Issues). 1982. lib. bdg. 73.50 (*0-89838-103-7*) Kluwer Academic.

Craven, Kenneth A. Programming in Q-Basic for Engineering Technology. LC 98-9672. 451p. (C). 1998. pap. text 86.00 (*0-13-622748-1*) P-H.

Craven, Leonard S., jt. auth. see Hall, Betty L.

Craven, Linda. Jaguar: The King of the Cats. (Car Classics Ser.). 32p. (YA). (gr. 5-12). 1991. lib. bdg. 15.95 (*0-86593-144-5*) Rourke Corp.

— Mustang: Ford's Wild Pony, LC 93-20243. (Car Classics Ser.). 32p. (YA). (gr. 5-12). 1993. lib. bdg. 15.95 (*0-86593-255-7*) Rourke Corp.

— Thunderbird: The High-Flying Ford, LC 93-219. (Car Classics Ser.). 32p. (YA). (gr. 5-12). 1993. lib. bdg. 15.95 (*0-86593-254-9*) Rourke Corp.

Craven, Margaret. Again Calls the Owl. 128p. 1983. mass mkt. 5.99 (*0-440-30074-6*) Dell.

— I Heard the Owl Call My Name. 160p. (YA). (gr. 7 up). 1979. mass mkt. 6.50 (*0-440-34369-0*, LE) Dell.

— I Heard the Owl Call My Name. 1973. 11.09 (*0-606-03572-9*, Pub. by Turtleback) Demco.

— I Heard the Owl Call My Name. 250p. 1991. reprint ed. lib. bdg. 25.95 (*0-89966-854-2*) Buccaneer Bks.

— Walk Gently This Good Earth. 1995. reprint ed. lib. bdg. 21.95 (*1-56849-646-X*) Buccaneer Bks.

Craven, Marilyn, jt. auth. see Kates, Nick.

Craven, Mary-Louise, et al, eds. Call: Papers & Reports. LC 89-82446. (Illus.). 1990. pap. 14.95 (*0-940753-01-4*) Athelstan Pubns.

Craven, Matthew C. The International Covenant on Economic, Social & Cultural Rights: A Perspective on Its Development. (Oxford Monographs on International Law). 480p. 1998. reprint ed. pap. text 39.95 (*0-19-826788-6*) OUP.

Craven, Paul. An Impartial Umpire: Industrial Relations & Canadian State 1900-1911. LC 81-116206. (State & Economic Life Ser.: No. 3). 396p. reprint ed. pap. 122.80 (*0-608-16914-5*, 202641600049) Bks Demand.

Craven, Paul, ed. Labouring Lives: Work & Workers in Nineteenth-Century Ontario. (Ontario Historical Studies). (Illus.). 640p. 1995. text 65.00 (*0-8020-0641-8*); pap. text 29.95 (*0-8020-7594-0*) U of Toronto Pr.

Craven, Peter, ed. Great Books That Shaped Australia. 350p. 1996. 59.95 (*0-522-84678-5*, Pub. by Melbourne Univ Pr) Paul & Co Pubs.

Craven, Peter & Rutherford, Andrew, eds. Scripsi, Vol. 7, No. 2. (Illus.). 250p. 1992. pap. 14.95 (*0-19-553383-6*) OUP.

Craven, Richard C. Poems by Richard C. 1987. pap. 4.00 (*0-932526-15-2*) Nexus Pr.

Craven, Robert M., jt. auth. see Andersen, Barry W.

Craven, Robert R. Guide to Fishing: Westchester & Putnam Counties. 96p. 1982. pap. 4.95 (*0-939166-03-8*) Outdoor Pubns.

— Symphony Orchestras of the World. LC 86-29452. 491p. 1987. lib. bdg. 115.00 (*0-313-24073-6*, CRW, Greenwood Pr) Greenwood.

Craven, Robert R., compiled by. Billiards, Bowling, Table Tennis, Pinball & Video Games: A Bibliographic Guide. LC 82-21077. 163p. 1983. lib. bdg. 52.95 (*0-313-23462-0*, CBB/, Greenwood Pr) Greenwood.

Craven, Robert R., ed. Symphony Orchestras of the United States: Selected Profiles. LC 85-7637. 544p. 1986. lib. bdg. 65.00 (*0-313-24072-8*, CRU/, Greenwood Pr) Greenwood.

Craven, Roberta Jill, jt. auth. see Basch, Linda G.

Craven, Roy C. Ceremonial Centers of the Maya. LC 74-2016. 160p. reprint ed. pap. 49.60 (*0-8357-6918-6*, 203797700009) Bks Demand.

— Indian Art. 2nd rev. ed. LC 97-60255. (World of Art Ser.). (Illus.). 256p. 1997. pap. 14.95 (*0-500-20302-4*, Pub. by Thames Hudson) Norton.

Craven, Roy C., Jr., ed. Ramayana Pahari Paintings. 106p. (C). 1993. 150.00 (*81-85026-11-4*, Pub. by Marg Publns) Art Media Resources.

Craven, Roy C., jt. ed. see Chandler, Vishwa.

Craven, Ruth F. & Hirnle, Constance J. Fundamentals of Nursing: Human Health & Function. 2nd ed. LC 95-32206. 1,728p. 1996. text 58.95 (*0-397-55169-X*) Lppncott W & W.

Craven, Ruth F. & Hirnle, Constance J. Study Guide to Accompany Fundamentals of Nursing: Human Health & Function. 3rd ed. 400p. pap. text 18.95 (*0-7817-1911-9*) Lppncott W & W.

Craven, Sara. Les Amants de Toscane. (Azur Ser.: No. 712). (FRE.). 1998. pap. 3.50 (*0-373-34712-X*, 1-34712-9) Harlequin Bks.

— Un Amour Orageux. (Azur Ser.: No. 728). (FRE.). 1998. mass mkt. 3.50 (*0-373-34728-6*, 1-34728-5) Harlequin Bks.

— Un Ano y un Dia Juntos: A Year & a Day Together.Tr. of A Year & A Day Together. (SPA.). 1999. per. 3.50 (*0-373-33503-2*, 1-33503-3) Harlequin Bks.

***Craven, Sara.** Atrapado en la Mentira (Caught Him in a Lie) (Bianca Ser.). (SPA.). 2000. mass mkt. 3.50 (*0-373-33581-4*, 1-33581-9) Harlequin Bks.

Craven, Sara. Bajo Sospecha: Marriage under Suspicion. (Bianca Ser.: No. 175).Tr. of Under Suspicion. (SPA.). 1999. per. 3.50 (*0-373-33525-3*, 1-33525-6) Harlequin Bks.

***Craven, Sara.** Bartaldi's Bride. 288p. 2000. 26.99 (*0-263-16368-7*) Mills & Boon.

— Bartaldi's Bride: Wedlocked. 2000. mass mkt. 3.99 (*0-373-12119-9*, 121193) Harlequin Bks.

Craven, Sara. Dark Apollo. LC 95-22377. (Presents Ser.). 189p. 1996. per. 3.25 (*0-373-11786-8*, 1-11786-0) Harlequin Bks.

— Dark Apollo. large type ed. (Harlequin Romance Ser.). 1995. lib. bdg. 18.95 (*0-263-14073-3*) Mac Lib Ref.

— Dark Ransom. (Presents Ser.). 1993. pap. 2.89 (*0-373-11549-0*, 1-11549-2) Harlequin Bks.

— Dawn Song. large type ed. (Harlequin Ser.). 1994. lib. bdg. 19.95 (*0-263-13766-X*) Thorndike Pr.

— Deceived. 1997. per. 3.50 (*0-373-11901-1*, 1-11901-5) Harlequin Bks.

— Deceived. large type ed. 288p. 1997. 20.95 (*0-263-14797-5*) Thorndike Pr.

— Desperate Measures. large type ed. 1992. reprint ed. 18.95 (*0-263-13026-6*) Mac Lib Ref.

— Devil & the Deep Sea. large type ed. 254p. 1992. 27.99 (*0-7505-0435-8*) Ulverscroft.

— Engano. (SPA.). 1997. per. 3.50 (*0-373-33408-7*, 1-33408-5) Harlequin Bks.

— Enganos del Pasado: One Reckless Night. (Bianca Ser.: Vol. 126).Tr. of Past Deceit. (SPA.). 1998. per. 3.50 (*0-373-33476-1*, 1-33476-2) Harlequin Bks.

— A High Price to Play. large type ed. LC 94-9520. 219p. 1994. lib. bdg. write for info. (*0-8161-5979-3*, G K Hall Lrg Type) Mac Lib Ref.

— Irresistible Temptation. (Presents Ser.: Bk. 2077). 184p. 2000. per. 3.75 (*0-373-12077-X*, 1-12077-3) Harlequin Bks.

***Craven, Sara.** Irresistible Temptation. large type ed. 288p. 2000. 25.99 (*0-263-16283-4*, Pub. by Mills & Boon) Ulverscroft.

— Marriage at a Distance. (Presents Ser.). 2000. per. 3.99 (*0-373-12093-1*) Harlequin Bks.

Craven, Sara. Marriage under Suspicion. (Presents Ser.: No. 2058). 1999. per. 3.75 (*0-373-12058-3*, 1-12058-3) Harlequin Bks.

— A Nanny for Christmas: (Nanny Wanted!) (Presents Ser.: No. 1999). 1998. per. 3.75 (*0-373-11999-2*, 1-11999-9) Harlequin Bks.

— A Nanny for Christmas: (Nanny Wanted!) large type ed. (Mills & Boon Large Print Ser.). 288p. 1998. 24.99 (*0-263-15513-7*, Pub. by Mills & Boon) Ulverscroft.

***Craven, Sara.** Ningun Hombre para Ella (No Man for Her) The Seduction Game. (Bianca Ser.: No. 187). 1999. per. 3.50 (*0-373-33537-7*, 1-33537-1) Harlequin Bks.

Craven, Sara. One Reckless Night. (Presents Ser.). 1998. per. 3.75 (*0-373-11944-5*, 1-11944-5) Harlequin Bks.

— The Seduction Game. (Presents Ser.: No. 2030). 1999. per. 3.75 (*0-373-12030-3*, 1-12030-2) Harlequin Bks.

***Craven, Sara.** The Seduction Game. large type ed. 1999. 21.95 (*0-263-16135-8*) P-H.

Craven, Sara. Thunder on the Reef. (Presents Plus Ser.). 1995. per. 3.25 (*0-373-11761-2*) Harlequin Bks.

— Thunder on the Reef. large type ed. 288p. 1995. 23.99 (*0-263-14210-8*, Pub. by Mills & Boon) Ulverscroft.

— Tower of Shadows. large type ed. (Harlequin Ser.). 1994. lib. bdg. 18.95 (*0-263-13648-5*) Thorndike Pr.

— Tower of Shadows: (Postcards from Europe) (Presents Ser.). 1994. per. 2.99 (*0-373-11708-6*, 1-11708-4) Harlequin Bks.

— Ultimate Temptation. (Presents Ser.). 1998. per. 3.75 (*0-373-11963-1*, 1-11963-5) Harlequin Bks.

— Ultimate Temptation. large type ed. 1997. 20.95 (*0-263-15121-2*) Mac Lib Ref.

Craven, Sue, jt. auth. see Newman, Phyllis E.

Craven, Thomas. Modern Art: The Men, the Movements, the Meaning. LC 40-7043. 1940. reprint ed. 59.00 (*0-403-03081-1*) Somerset Pub.

Craven, Toni. Ezekiel, Daniel. (Collegeville Bible Commentary - Old Testament Ser.). 144p. 1986. pap. 4.95 (*0-8146-1423-X*) Liturgical Pr.

Craven, Wayne. American Art: History & Culture. 688p. (C). 1993. text. write for info. (*0-697-16763-1*) Brown & Benchmark.

— Sculpture in America. 2nd ed. LC 82-40439. (Illus.). 808p. 1984. 60.00 (*0-8453-4776-4*, Cornwall Bks) Assoc Univ Prs.

— Sculpture in America. 2nd ed. LC 82-40439. (Illus.). 808p. 1984. 60.00 (*0-87413-225-8*) U Delaware Pr.

***Craven, Wes.** Fountain Society. LC 99-23455. 352p. 1999. 24.50 (*0-684-84660-8*) S&S Trade.

— Fountain Society. large type ed. LC 99-47940. (Basic Ser.). 596p. 1999. 26.95 (*0-7862-2270-0*) Thorndike Pr.

— Fountain Society. 464p. 2000. reprint ed. 6.99 (*0-671-01724-1*, Pocket Star Bks) PB.

Craven, Wes & Wagner, Bruce. The Dream Warriors. New Line Cinema Staff, ed. LC 92-502. (Nightmare on Elm Street Ser.). 1992. lib. bdg. 13.95 (*1-56239-158-5*) ABDO Pub Co.

Craven, Wes, jt. auth. see Williamson, Kevin.

Craven, Wesley F. The Legend of the Founding Fathers. LC 82-25241. (New York University, Stokes Foundation, Anson G. Phelps Lectureship on Early American History Ser.). 222p. 1983. reprint ed. lib. bdg. 59.50 (*0-313-23840-5*, CRLE) Greenwood.

— Southern Colonies in the Seventeenth Century, 1607-1689. LC 49-3595. (History of the South Ser.: Vol. 1). (Illus.). xvi, 452p. 1949. text 50.00 (*0-8071-0001-3*) La State U Pr.

— The Virginia Company of London, 1606-1624. (Illus.). 70p. 1997. reprint ed. pap. 10.00 (*0-8063-4555-1*, 9069) Clearfield Co.

Craven, Wesley F., intro. Early Accounts of Life in Colonial Virginia 1609-1613. LC 75-42069. 136p. 1976. reprint ed. lib. bdg. 50.00 (*0-8201-1165-1*) Schol Facsimiles.

Craven, Wesley F. & Cate, James L. The Army Air Forces in World War II, 7 vols., Set. Gilbert, James B., ed. LC 79-7244. (Flight: Its First Seventy-Five Years Ser.). (Illus.). 1979. reprint ed. lib. bdg. 294.00 (*0-405-12135-0*) Ayer.

— The Army Air Forces in World War II, 7 vols., Vol. 1. Gilbert, James B., ed. LC 79-7244. (Flight: Its First Seventy-Five Years Ser.). (Illus.). 1980. reprint ed. lib. bdg. 46.95 (*0-405-12136-9*) Ayer.

— The Army Air Forces in World War II, 7 vols., Vol. 2. Gilbert, James B., ed. LC 79-7244. (Flight: Its First Seventy-Five Years Ser.). (Illus.). 1980. reprint ed. lib. bdg. 46.95 (*0-405-12137-7*) Ayer.

— The Army Air Forces in World War II, 7 vols., Vol. 3. Gilbert, James B., ed. LC 79-7244. (Flight: Its First Seventy-Five Years Ser.). (Illus.). 1979. reprint ed. lib. bdg. 46.95 (*0-405-12138-5*) Ayer.

— The Army Air Forces in World War II, 7 vols., Vol. 4. Gilbert, James B., ed. LC 79-7244. (Flight: Its First Seventy-Five Years Ser.). (Illus.). 1979. reprint ed. lib. bdg. 46.95 (*0-405-12139-3*) Ayer.

— The Army Air Forces in World War II, 7 vols., Vol. 5. Gilbert, James B., ed. LC 79-7244. (Flight: Its First Seventy-Five Years Ser.). (Illus.). 1979. reprint ed. lib. bdg. 46.95 (*0-405-12140-7*) Ayer.

— The Army Air Forces in World War II, 7 vols., Vol. 6. Gilbert, James B., ed. LC 79-7244. (Flight: Its First Seventy-Five Years Ser.). (Illus.). 1979. reprint ed. lib. bdg. 46.95 (*0-405-12141-5*) Ayer.

— The Army Air Forces in World War II, 7 vols., Vol. 7. Gilbert, James B., ed. LC 79-7244. (Flight: Its First Seventy-Five Years Ser.). (Illus.). 1979. reprint ed. lib. bdg. 46.95 (*0-405-12142-3*) Ayer.

Craven, Wesley F., jt. auth. see Woodward, Ruth L.

Cravens, Alice I. Comforted of God. 1985. pap. 4.75 (*0-89137-454-X*) Quality Pubns.

— A New Song. 1988. pap. 3.85 (*0-89137-445-0*) Quality Pubns.

— Ways Which Be in Christ. 1990. pap. 4.75 (*0-89137-449-3*) Quality Pubns.

Cravens, David. Strategic Marketing, International. 3rd ed. (C). 1991. student ed., per. 30.95 (*0-256-11405-6*, Irwn McGrw-H) McGrw-H Hghr Educ.

C

Cravens, David W. Strategic Marketing. 5th ed. (Irwin Series in Marketing). 704p. (C). 1996. text 70.95 (*0-256-21438-7*, Irwn Prfssnl) McGraw-Hill Prof.

***Cravens, David W.** Strategic Marketing. 6th ed. LC 99-10060. (Illus.). 2000. write for info. (*0-07-027543-2*) McGraw-Hill Prof.

Cravens, David W. Strategic Marketing Management Cases. 6th ed. 1998. pap., student ed. 64.69 (*0-07-561887-7*) McGraw.

Cravens, David W. & Woodruff, Robert B. Marketing. LC 84-24357. 800p. (C). 1986. text 29.56 (*0-201-10840-2*); pap. text 80.00 (*0-201-10842-9*); student ed. 15.16 (*0-201-10843-7*) Addison-Wesley.

— Marketing Management. LC 84-24357. 800p. (C). 1986. pap. text 16.00 (*0-201-10853-4*) Addison-Wesley.

Cravens, David W., et al. Strategic Marketing Management Cases. 5th ed. LC 95-12120. (Series in Marketing). 608p. (C). 1995. text 53.50 (*0-256-13689-0*, Irwn McGrw-H) McGrw-H Hghr Educ.

— Strategic Marketing Management Cases. 6th ed. LC 98-3555. (Series in Marketing). 1998. 66.00 (*0-256-26125-3*, Irwn Prfssnl) McGraw-Hill Prof.

Cravens, Dick. ACT 3.0 Fast & Easy. LC 97-67399. 352p. 1997. per. 16.99 (*0-7615-1175-X*) Prima Pub.

Cravens El At. Strategies to Marketing & Management Cases. 6th ed. 1999. teacher ed. 48.50 (*0-256-26126-1*) McGraw.

Cravens, Gwyneth. The Gates of Paradise. 208p. 1992. mass mkt. 4.99 (*0-446-36261-1*, Pub. by Warner Bks) Little.

Cravens, Hamilton. Before Head Start: The Iowa Station & America's Children. LC 92-44806. xx, 328p. 1993. 49.95 (*0-8078-2092-X*) U of NC Pr.

— The Triumph of Evolution: The Heredity-Environment Controversy, 1900-1941. LC 88-45394. 376p. 1988. pap. 16.95 (*0-8018-3742-1*) Johns Hopkins.

Cravens, Hamilton, ed. Ideas in America's Cultures from Republic to Mass Society. LC 81-15577. 225p. 1982. reprint ed. pap. 69.80 (*0-608-00155-4*, 206093600006) Bks Demand.

Cravens, Hamilton, et al, eds. Technical Knowledge in American Culture: Science, Technology, & Medicine since the Early 1800s. LC 95-19084. (History of American Science & Technology Ser.). (FRE & GER.). 280p. (Orig.). (C). 1996. pap. text 24.95 (*0-8173-0793-1*) U of Ala Pr.

Cravens, Hamilton, jt. ed. see Marcus, Alan I.

Cravens, R. H. Edward Weston. 2nd ed. (Masters of Photography Ser.). (Illus.). 76p. 1997. reprint ed. 18.95 (*0-89381-747-3*) Aperture.

Cravens, R. H., jt. auth. see Desikachar, T. K.

Cravens, Richard. ACT! 4.0 Fast & Easy. LC 98-65967. (Illus.). 350p. 1998. per. 16.99 (*0-7615-1412-0*) Prima Pub.

***Cravens, Richard.** ACT! 2000 Fast & Easy. (Fast & Easy Ser.). 2000. pap. 16.99 (*0-7615-1987-4*) Prima Pub.

Cravens, Richard. The Essential Windows NT 4 Book. LC 96-70099. 448p. 1996. per. 24.99 (*0-7615-0752-3*) Prima Pub.

Cravens, Richard & Koers, Diane. Office 2000 Fast & Easy. LC 98-68147. (Fast & Easy Ser.). (Illus.). 435p. 1999. pap. 16.99 (*0-7615-1762-6*, Prima Tech) Prima Pub.

***Cravens, Richard, et al.** Create Frontpage 98 Web Pages in a Weekend. LC 97-76505. 384p. 1998. per. 24.99 (*0-7615-1348-5*) Prima Pub.

Cravens, Richard, jt. auth. see James, Phil.

Cravens, Richard, jt. auth. see Wempen, Faithe.

Cravens, Richard, jt. auth. see Witherspoon, Coletta.

Cravens, Sydney P., jt. ed. see Aycock, Wendell M.

Cravens, T. E. & Kivelson, Margaret G. Planetary Ionospheres & Magnetospheres. (Advances in Space Research Ser.: Vol. 20). 184p. 1997. pap. 100.50 (*0-08-043297-2*, Pergamon Pr) Elsevier.

Cravens, Thomas D., jt. ed. see Harris-Northall, Raymond.

Cravens, Thomas E. Physics of Solar System Plasmas. LC 96-48929. (Atmospheric & Space Science Ser.). (Illus.). 493p. (C). 1997. text 90.00 (*0-521-35280-0*) Cambridge U Pr.

Cravens, Thomas F. Exploring Human Society: An Introduction to Sociology. 256p. 1995. per. 34.95 (*0-8403-8506-4*) Kendall-Hunt.

***Craver.** An Introduction to Found American Education. 2001. 39.00 (*0-07-239071-9*) McGraw.

Craver, Charles B. Can Unions Survive? The Rejuvenation of the American Labor Movement. LC 92-40980. 224p. (C). 1993. text 45.00 (*0-8147-1498-6*) NYU Pr.

— Can Unions Survive? The Rejuvenation of the American Labor Movement. LC 92-40980. 224p. (C). 1995. pap. text 17.50 (*0-8147-1512-5*) NYU Pr.

Craver, Charles B. Effective Legal Negotiation & Settlement. 3rd ed. 486p. 55.00 (*0-327-01958-1*) LEXIS Pub.

Craver, Charles B., et al. Hornbook on Employment Law. Rothstein, Mark A., ed. (Hornbook Ser.). 738p. 1994. 41.00 (*0-314-03527-3*) West Pub.

— Labor Relations Law: Cases & Materials. 10th ed. LC 99-60689. 1200p. 1999. text 56.00 (*0-327-00929-2*, 1311712) LEXIS Pub.

— Labor Relations Law, Selected Federal Statutes & Sample Bargaining Agreement, 1999 Edition: Selected Federal Statutes & Sample Bargaining Agreement. LC 99-60690. 150p. (Orig.). 1999. pap. 15.00 (*0-327-00936-5*, 1311812) LEXIS Pub.

Craver, Charles B., jt. auth. see Brunet, Edward.

Craver, Clara D., ed. Polymer Characterization: Spectroscopic, Chromatographic & Physical Instrumental Methods. LC 82-24496. (Advances in Chemistry Ser.: Vol. 203). 808p. 1983. reprint ed. pap. 200.00 (*0-608-03508-4*, 206422700008) Bks Demand.

— Polymer Characterization, Spectroscopic, Chromatographic, & Physical Instrumental Methods. LC 82-24496. (Advances in Chemistry Ser.: No. 203). 791p. 1982. lib. bdg. 38.95 (*0-8412-0700-3*, Pub. by Am Chemical) OUP.

Craver, Clara D. & Provder, Theodore, eds. Polymer Characterization: Physical Property, Spectroscopic, & Chromatographic Methods Developed from a Symposium Sponsored by the Division of Polymeric Materials: Science & Engineering at the 196th National Meeting of the American Chemical Society, Los Angeles, CA, September 25-30, 1988. LC 90-47157. (Advances in Chemistry Ser.: No. 227). (Illus.). 536p. 1990. reprint ed. pap. 166.20 (*0-608-06792-X*, 206698900009) Bks Demand.

Craver, Clara D., jt. ed. see Urban, Marek W.

Craver, John S. Graph Paper from Your Computer or Copier. 3rd ed. LC 96-5298. (Illus.). 256p. 1996. pap. 24.95 incl. disk (*1-55561-076-5*) Fisher Bks.

Craver, Kathleen. School Library Media Centers in the 21st Century: Changes & Challenges. LC 94-5146. 216p. 1994. 39.95 (*0-313-29100-4*) Greenwood.

Craver, Kathleen W. Teaching Electronic Literacy: A Concepts-Based Approach for School Library Media Specialists. LC 96-53844. (Greenwood Professional Guides in School Librarianship Ser.). 208p. 1997. 39.95 (*0-313-30220-0*, Greenwood Pr) Greenwood.

***Craver, Kathleen W.** Using Internet Primary Sources to Teach Critical Thinking Skills in History. LC 99-17841. (Professional Guides in School Librarianship Ser.). 280p. 1999. 39.95 (*0-313-30749-0*) Greenwood.

Craver, Lionel, et al. Introduction to Engineering. (Illus.). 608p. 1995. text 79.95 (*0-19-510725-X*) OUP.

Craver, Mark. The Problem of Grace. LC 85-81601. (Lost Roads Ser.: No. 29). 64p. (Orig.). (C). 1986. pap. 6.95 (*0-918786-33-9*) Lost Roads.

— Seven Crowns for the White Lady of the Other World & Blood Poems. LC 91-27166. 80p. (Orig.). 1992. pap. 10.00 (*0-914061-25-9*) Orchises Pr.

— They Come for What You Love. LC 97-37575. 80p. 1998. pap. 12.95 (*0-914061-64-X*) Orchises Pr.

Craver, Rebecca & Margo, Adair, eds. Tom Lea: An/Oral History. LC 94-61797. (Illus.). 185p. 1995. 50.00 (*0-87404-234-8*) Tex Western.

Craves, Julie A. Birds of Southeastern Michigan: Dearborn. LC 96-85802. (Bulletin Ser.: No. 62). (Illus.). 168p. (Orig.). 1996. pap. 8.00 (*0-87737-041-9*) Cranbrook.

Cravey, Altha J. Women & Work in Mexico's Maquiladoras. LC 98-36864. (Illus.). 176p. 1998. 52.00 (*0-8476-8885-2*); pap. 19.95 (*0-8476-8886-0*) Rowman.

Cravey, Charles E. Diamonds in the Rough. 64p. (Orig.). 1986. pap. 9.95 (*0-938645-00-5*) In His Steps.

— Fruits from the Vineyard. 1990. pap. 10.00 (*0-938645-30-7*) In His Steps.

— Lord, Teach Us to Pray. 1989. pap. 9.95 (*0-938645-16-1*) In His Steps.

— Memories, Reflections & Words of Hope. 1991. pap. 9.95 (*0-938645-63-3*) In His Steps.

— Pen & Ink. 1990. pap. 9.95 (*0-938645-33-1*) In His Steps.

— Poems, Prayers & Promises. (Illus.). 120p. (Orig.). 1988. pap. 9.95 (*0-938645-02-1*) In His Steps.

— The Poet's Pen, Vol. 4, No. 3. 1992. 10.00 (*0-938645-64-1*) In His Steps.

— Pot-Liquor Hill. 1989. pap. 9.95 (*0-938645-27-7*) In His Steps.

— Prepared for Battle: A Guide for the Christian Journey. (Illus.). 48p. (Orig.). 1988. pap. 4.95 (*0-938645-01-3*) In His Steps.

— Tapestries. 1992. 15.95 (*0-938645-67-6*) In His Steps.

Cravey, Charles E., ed. Boundless Treasures. 1991. pap. 10.95 (*0-938645-48-X*) In His Steps.

— Christmas Memories. 1992. pap. 9.95 (*0-938645-80-3*) In His Steps.

— From the Poet's Pen, Vol. 1. 1989. pap. 10.00 (*0-938645-15-3*) In His Steps.

— From the Poet's Pen, Vol. 2. 1991. 10.00 (*0-938645-62-5*) In His Steps.

— From the Poet's Pen, Vol. 3. 1992. pap. 10.00 (*0-938645-74-9*) In His Steps.

— From the Poet's Pen, Vol. 4. 1993. pap. 10.95 (*0-938645-85-4*) In His Steps.

***Cravey, Charles E., ed.** From the Poet's Pen, Vol. 5. (Illus.). 68p. 2000. pap. 10.95 (*1-58535-016-8*) In His Steps.

Cravey, Charles E., ed. Georgia Rhymes. 1992. pap. 14.95 (*0-938645-77-3*) In His Steps.

— Gossamer Threads & Weavings. 1992. pap. 9.95 (*0-938645-69-2*) In His Steps.

— Heart of Gold. 1993. pap. 9.95 (*0-938645-94-3*) In His Steps.

— In Search of New Beginnings. 1993. pap. 12.95 (*0-938645-96-X*) In His Steps.

— Poems from the Heartland. 1993. pap. 9.95 (*0-938645-87-0*) In His Steps.

— Poetic Journeys of the Heart. 1990. pap. 9.95 (*0-938645-44-7*) In His Steps.

— The Poet's Choice, Vol. 1, No. 1. 1993. pap. 12.95 (*0-938645-98-6*) In His Steps.

— The Poet's Pen, Vol. 4, No. 4. 1992. 10.00 (*0-938645-70-6*) In His Steps.

— The Poet's Pen, Vol. 5, No. 1. 1992. 10.00 (*0-938645-76-5*) In His Steps.

— The Poet's Pen, Vol. 5, No. 2. 1992. 10.00 (*0-938645-81-1*) In His Steps.

— The Poet's Pen, Vol. 5, No. 3. 1993. 10.00 (*0-938645-86-2*) In His Steps.

— The Poet's Pen, Vol. 5, No. 4. 1993. 10.00 (*0-938645-88-9*) In His Steps.

— The Poet's Pen, Vol. 6, No. 1. 1993. 10.00 (*0-938645-92-7*) In His Steps.

— The Poet's Pen, Vol. 6, No. 2. 1993. 10.00 (*0-938645-97-8*) In His Steps.

— Seasons of the Wind. 1990. pap. 10.95 (*0-938645-35-8*) In His Steps.

— Seize the Moment. 1993. pap. 12.95 (*0-938645-90-0*) In His Steps.

— Standing on the Promises. 1990. pap. 9.95 (*0-938645-36-6*) In His Steps.

Cravey, Robert H., jt. auth. see Baselt, Randall C.

***Cravitz, Mike.** ILE by Example. 250p. 2000. pap. 69.95 (*1-58304-032-3*) News Four-Hund.

Cravitz, Mike. Introduction to SQL/400: Database Design & Programming for DB2 UDB for AS/400. Orig. Title: Database Design & Programming for DB2/400. 330p. 2000. pap. text 55.00 (*1-882419-70-7*) News Four-Hund.

Craw, H. Allen, ed. see Dussek, Jan L.

Craw, R. Andy, ed. & illus. see Roos, Roy E.

***Craw, R. C.** Molytini: (Insecta: Coleoptera: Curculionidae: Molytinae) (Fauna of New Zealand Ser.: No. 39). 68p. 1999. pap. 29.50 (*0-478-09325-X*, Pub. by Manaaki Whenua) Balogh.

Craw, Robin C., et al. Panbiogeography: Tracking the History of Life. (Oxford Biogeography Ser.: No. 11). (Illus.). 240p. 1999. text 65.00 (*0-19-507441-6*) OUP.

Craw, William. France Free & Unfree: The Literary & Sociological Image. 128p. 1993. 59.00 (*0-85261-369-5*, Pub. by Univ of Glasgow) St Mut.

Crawcour. An Introduction to Kambun. pap. 4.95 (*0-939512-00-9*, Pub. by B G Teubner) MBIPubg.

Crawford. American Musical Life. LC 99-47565. (Illus.). 704p. 2000. text 39.95 (*0-393-04810-1*) Norton.

— Current Diagnosis & Treatment in Cardiology. 2nd ed. (C). 1999. 45.00 (*0-8385-1473-1*) Appleton & Lange.

— Deadly Fighting Skills. 1999. pap. 17.95 (*0-312-20262-8*) St Martin.

***Crawford.** General Biology 1 & 2. 8th ed. 294p. 1999. pap. text 31.40 (*0-536-02798-6*) Pearson Custom.

Crawford. Genral Biology 1 & 2. 3rd ed. 1991. pap. text, lab manual ed. 43.00 (*0-536-58036-7*) S&S Trade.

— Music in American Life. Date not set. write for info. (*0-393-04736-9*) Norton.

***Crawford.** New Product Management. 6th ed. LC 99-34882. 560p. 1999. 86.25 (*0-07-027552-1*) McGraw.

— Statehood & Recognition. 203.95 (*1-84014-076-3*) Ashgate Pub Co.

— Unwise Passions. 2000. write for info. (*0-684-83474-X*) Simon & Schuster.

Crawford & Croot. General Biology 1 & 2. 6th ed. 238p. (C). 1998. pap. text, lab manual ed. 25.75 (*0-536-01522-8*) Pearson Custom.

Crawford & Erickson. Century 21 Keyboarding, Instructional Chart. 4th ed. (TA - Typing/Keyboarding Ser.). 1987. 903.95 (*0-538-20577-6*) S-W Pub.

— Century 21 Keyboarding, Instructional Charts. 4th ed. (TA - Typing/Keyboarding Ser.). 1987. 1097.95 (*0-538-20578-4*) S-W Pub.

— Century 21 Keyboarding, Keyboard Chart. 4th ed. (TA - Typing/Keyboarding Ser.). 1987. 76.95 (*0-538-20566-0*) S-W Pub.

***Crawford & Siano.** Journey to Perfection: The Agricultural Art of Ross Butler. LC 98-177119. (Heritage Bks.). (Illus.). 176p. 1999. pap. 21.95 (*1-55082-212-8*) Quarry Pr.

Crawford, et al. BCCTA Notebook, 1998. (Illus.). 200p. (C). 1998. text. write for info. (*0-938541-10-2*) Origins Program.

— Bookstand. 3rd ed. (TA - Typing/Keyboarding Ser.). 1970. 10.75 (*0-538-24126-8*) S-W Pub.

— Century 21 Keyboarding. 4th ed. (Keyboarding/Typesetting-1St Yr Ser.). 1986. teacher ed. 10.75 (*0-538-27903-6*) S-W Pub.

— Century 21 Keyboarding. 4th ed. (Keyboarding/Typesetting-1St Yr). 1987. teacher ed. 8.95 (*0-538-27905-2*) S-W Pub.

— Century 21 Keyboarding Placement Test 2. 4th ed. (TA - Typing/Keyboarding Ser.). 1987. 2.95 (*0-538-20557-1*) S-W Pub.

— Century 21 Keyboarding Problem Solutions. 4th ed. (Keyboarding/Typesetting-1St Yr Ser.). 1986. 19.95 (*0-538-27902-8*) S-W Pub.

— Century 21 Typewriting. 3rd ed. (Typing/Keyboarding Ser.). 1982. pap., lab manual ed. 9.95 (*0-538-20511-3*) S-W Pub.

— Century 21 Typing Gold Charm. 3rd ed. (TA - Typing/Keyboarding Ser.). 1972. 3.75 (*0-538-24215-9*) S-W Pub.

— Century 21 Typing Roll of Honor. 3rd ed. (TA - Typing/Keyboarding Ser.). 1973. mass mkt. 3.75 (*0-538-29087-0*) S-W Pub.

— Century 21 Keyboarding Placement Test 1. 4th ed. (TA - Typing/Keyboarding Ser.). 1987. 2.50 (*0-538-20556-3*) S-W Pub.

— Century 21 Keyboarding Typewriting Style. 4th ed. (TA - Typing/Keyboarding Ser.). 1987. 3.25 (*0-538-20561-X*) S-W Pub.

— Table Formatting, Microcomputer - Keyboarding - Formatting Applications. (TA - Typing/Keyboarding Ser.). 1986. pap. 13.95 (*0-538-26130-7*) S-W Pub.

Crawford, jt. auth. see Das, Sakti.

Crawford, jt. auth. see Klotz.

Crawford, jt. auth. see Preston, Edward J.

Crawford, jt. ed. see Crosbie.

Crawford, A. Reminiscences of a Naval Officer: A Quarter-Deck View of the War Against Napoleon. 1999. pap. text 21.95 (*1-86176-109-0*) Chatham Pr.

Crawford, A. Berry & Peterson, Dean F., eds. Environmental Management in the Colorado River Basin. LC 74-12364. (Illus.). 325p. reprint ed. pap. 100.80 (*0-7837-6212-7*, 204593600009) Bks Demand.

Crawford, A. Berry, jt. ed. see Peterson, Dean F.

Crawford, A. F., ed. see Brooks, Rebecca.

Crawford, A. J., ed. Boninites. 353p. 1989. text 231.00 (*0-04-445003-6*) Kluwer Academic.

Crawford, Adam. The Local Governance of Crime: Appeals to Community & Partnerships. LC 97-5572. (Clarendon Studies in Criminology). (Illus.). 384p. 1997. text 69.00 (*0-19-826253-1*, Clarendon Pr) OUP.

— The Local Governance of Crime: Appeals to Community & Partnerships. (Illus.). 384p. 1999. pap. text 29.95 (*0-19-829845-5*) OUP.

***Crawford, Adam & Goodey, Jo, eds.** Integrating a Victim Perspective Within Criminal Justice: International Debates. (Advances in Criminology Ser.). 300p. 2000. text 70.95 (*1-84014-486-6*, Pub. by Ashgate Pub) Ashgate Pub Co.

Crawford, Adam, jt. auth. see Wood, James.

Crawford, Alan. C. R. Ashbee. LC 85-40459. (Illus.). 416p. 1986. 80.00 (*0-300-03467-9*) Yale U Pr.

— Charles Rennie Mackintosh. LC 94-62072. (World of Art Ser.). (Illus.). 216p. (Orig.). 1995. pap. 14.95 (*0-500-20283-4*, Pub. by Thames Hudson) Norton.

Crawford, Albert G. & Monson, Rela G. Academy & Community: A Study of the Jewish Identity & Involvement of Professors. LC 80-68432. 40p. 1980. pap. 2.00 (*0-685-00263-2*) Am Jewish Comm.

Crawford, Alice. Paradise Pursued: The Novels of Rose Macaulay. LC 94-30239. 1995. 36.50 (*0-8386-3573-3*) Fairleigh Dickinson.

Crawford, Alistair, jt. auth. see Woollen, Hilary.

Crawford, Amanda M. The Herbal Menopause Book: Herbs, Nutrition & Other Natural Therapies. (Illus.). 224p. (Orig.). 1996. pap. 16.95 (*0-89594-799-4*) Crossing Pr.

Crawford, Amanda M. Herbal Remedies for Women. LC 97-7653. 304p. 1997. pr. 18.00 (*0-7615-0980-1*) Prima Pub.

— Licorice Root. (Keats Good Herb Guide Ser.). 1998. mass mkt. 4.95 (*0-87983-930-9*, Keats Publng) NTC Contemp Pub Co.

Crawford, Amber, ed. see Engelsman, Alan & Engelsman, Penny.

Crawford, Amber, ed. see Engelsman, Penny & Engelsman, Alan.

Crawford, Andrew. Fine Decorative Boxes: Designing & Making Original Works of Art. LC 98-4281. (Illus.). 144p. 1998. pap. 19.95 (*0-8069-9862-8*) Sterling.

Crawford, Andy. Fun with Opposites. (Illus.). (J). 9.99 (*0-590-24640-2*) Scholastic Inc.

Crawford, Andy, jt. auth. see Langley, Andrew.

Crawford, Ann. New Life, New Land. (Illus.). 48p. (J). 1997. 8.95 (*1-57168-004-7*, Eakin Pr) Sunbelt Media.

Crawford, Ann, ed. see Bierhorst, John & Olive Natural Heritage Society Staff.

Crawford, Ann C. & Crawford, William R. Military Space-A Air Basic Training & Reader Trip Reports. Russell, Donna L., ed. LC 97-29517. 1995. pap. write for info. (*0-914862-66-9*) Military Living Pubns.

Crawford, Ann C., et al. Military Living's: Temporary Military Lodging Around the World. LC 97-17542. 1997. pap. write for info. (*0-914862-67-7*) Military Living Pubns.

— Military Living's Temporary Military Lodging Around the World. LC 98-25190. 1998. 18.45 (*0-914862-72-3*) Military Living Pubns.

Crawford, Ann C., jt. auth. see Crawford, William R.

***Crawford, Ann Caddell & Crawford, William R.** U. S. Forces Travel Guide to U. S. Military Installations. LC 99-56743. 1999. write for info. (*0-914862-81-2*) Military Living Pubns.

***Crawford, Ann Caddell & Crawford, William Roy.** Military Living's Space-A Air Opportunities Around the World. LC 99-59039. 2000. write for info. (*0-914862-87-1*) Military Living Pubns.

Crawford, Ann Caddell, jt. auth. see Crawford, William Roy.

Crawford, Ann F. Jane Long - Frontier Woman. (Texas Pioneers Ser.). (Illus.). 64p. (J). (gr. 4-7). 1990. lib. bdg. 12.95 (*0-87443-090-9*) Benson.

— Lizzie - Queen of the Cattle Trails. (Texas Pioneers Ser.). (Illus.). 64p. (J). (gr. 4-7). 1990. lib. bdg. 12.95 (*0-87443-091-7*) Benson.

— Sam Houston: American Hero. LC 93-77618. (Illus.). 64p. (J). (gr. 2 up). 1993. reprint ed. 15.95 (*0-937460-88-5*) Hendrick-Long.

— Women in Texas Study Guide. 64p. 1993. pap. 6.95 (*1-880510-03-0*) State House Pr.

Crawford, Ann F. & Ragsdale, Crystal S. Texas Women: From Frontier to Future. LC 98-10698. (Illus.). 382p. 1998. 24.95 (*1-880510-52-9*) State House Pr.

— Texas Women: Frontier to Future. LC 98-10698. (Illus.). 382p. 1998. pap. 17.95 (*1-880510-53-7*) State House Pr.

— Women in Texas: Their Lives, Their Experiences, Their Accomplishments. rev. ed. LC 91-29391. (Illus.). 445p. 1992. reprint ed. pap. 16.95 (*0-938349-73-2*) State House Pr.

Crawford, Ann F., ed. see Anna, Santa.

Crawford, Ann F., ed. see Brooks, Rebecca, et al.

***Crawford, Ann Fears.** Frankie: Mrs. R. D. Randolph & Texas Liberal Politics. LC 99-52369. 1999. write for info. (*1-57168-351-8*, Eakin Pr) Sunbelt Media.

***Crawford, Ann Fears & Ragsdale, Crystal Sasse.** Texas Women: Frontier to Future. LC 98-10698. (Illus.). 392p. 1998. 60.00 (*1-880510-54-5*) State House Pr.

Crawford, Ann Fears & Ragsdale, Crystal Sasse. Women in Texas: Their Lives, Their Experiences, Their Accomplishments. limited rev. ed. LC 91-29391. (Illus.). 445p. 1992. reprint ed. 60.00 (*0-938349-74-0*) State House Pr.

Crawford, Anne, ed. The Letters of the Queens of England, 1100-1547. LC 93-33709. 250p. 1994. 33.95 (*0-86299-726-7*, Pub. by Sutton Pub Ltd) Intl Pubs Mktg.

An Asterisk (*) at the beginning of an entry indicates that the title is appearing for the first time.

— The Letters of the Queens of England, 1100-1547. (Illus.). 256p. 1997. pap. 22.95 (*0-7509-1606-0*, Pub. by Sutton Pub Ltd) Intl Pubs Mktg.

Crawford, Anne & Von Rable, Baroness. A Shadow on a Wave. Moran, John C. & Knight, Jesse F., eds. (Worthies Library: No. 5). (Illus.). 75p. 1988. 7.50 (*0-317-01471-4*) F M Crawford.

Crawford, Arthur. History of Poona & Deccan in a Perspective. 1987. 28.50 (*81-212-0123-3*, Pub. by Gian Publng Hse) S Asia.

— The Legends of Konkan. 1986. reprint ed. 20.00 (*0-8364-1740-2*, Pub. by Manohar) S Asia.

Crawford, Ashley & Edgar, Ray. Spray: The Work of Howard Arkley. (Illus.). 156p. 1997. text 72.00 (*976-641-028-3*) Gordon & Breach.

Crawford, Ashley & Edgar, Ray, eds. Transit Lounge: Wake-Up Calls & Travelers' Tales from the Future. 192p. (Orig.). 1998. pap. text 28.00 (*90-5704-111-1*) Gordon & Breach.

Crawford, B. E. St. Magnus Cathedral: Orkney's Twelfth-Century Renaissance. (Illus.). 400p. 1989. text 25.00 (*0-08-036580-9*, Pergamon Pr) Elsevier.

Crawford, Barbara. Beatles: A Reference & Value Guide. 2nd ed. 1998. pap. text 19.95 (*1-57432-036-X*) Collector Bks.

— Scotland in Dark Age Britain. 172p. 1990. pap. 27.00 (*1-898218-61-7*) St Mut.

Crawford, Barbara, ed. Scandinavian Settlement in Northern Britain: Place-Name Studies in Their Historical Context. LC 95-10299. 1995. 79.95 (*0-7185-1923-X*) St Martin.

Crawford, Barbara & Lyle, Royster, Jr. Rockbridge County Artists & Artisans. LC 95-18877. (Illus.). 272p. (C). 1995. text 62.50 (*0-8139-1638-0*) U Pr of Va.

Crawford, Barrie & Reeves, Kay. The Gardens of Two Sisters. (Illus.). 276p. 1992. 24.95 (*0-9615559-1-2*) Buckeye Pr.

Crawford, Barrie F. For the Love of Wildflowers. Bell, Ritchie, ed. LC 85-90688. (Illus.). 125p. 1986. 27.95 (*0-9615559-0-4*) Buckeye Pr.

Crawford, Benny. Book for Every Body. LC 78-55792. 240p. 1979. pap. 7.95 (*0-89037-132-6*) Anderson World.

Crawford, Beverly. Economic Vulnerability in International Relations: East-West Trade, Investment & Finance. 334p. 1993. 67.00 (*0-231-08296-7*); pap. 22.00 (*0-231-08297-5*) Col U Pr.

— NATO Alliances Negotiations over the Soviet Pipeline Sanctions. (Pew Case Studies in International Affairs). 50p. (C). 1993. pap. text 3.50 (*1-56927-101-1*) Geo U Inst Dplmcy.

Crawford, Beverly, ed. The Future of European Security. LC 92-6706. (Research Ser.: No. 84). xii, 408p. (Orig.). (C). 1992. pap. text 23.50 (*0-87725-184-3*) U of Cal IAS.

Crawford, Beverly & Lipschutz, Ronnie D., eds. The Myth of "Ethnic Conflict" Politics, Economics & "Cultural" Violence. LC 98-28697. (Research Ser.). vii, 580p. 1998. pap. text 28.50 (*0-87725-198-3*) U of Cal IAS.

Crawford, Beverly & Schulze, Peter W., eds. European Dilemmas after Maastricht. LC 93-14443. (Research Ser.: No. 89). 1993. pap. text 22.95 (*0-87725-189-4*) U of Cal IAS.

— The New Europe Asserts Itself: A Changing Role in International Relations. LC 90-43505. (Research Ser.: No. 77). x, 448p. (Orig.). (C). 1990. pap. text 19.95 (*0-87725-177-0*) U of Cal IAS.

Crawford, Beverly, jt. auth. see Adler, Emanuel.

Crawford, Beverly, jt. auth. see Weber, Valerie.

***Crawford, Bill.** Adam Sandler. LC 00-35271. (Illus.). 192p. 2000. pap. 11.95 (*0-312-26282-5*, St Martin Griffin) St Martin.

Crawford, Bill. All Stressed up, & Nowhere to Go! A Guide to Dealing with Stress & Creating a Purposeful Life. Rombakis, Efthemia, ed. (Illus.). 150p. (Orig.). 1996. pap. 12.95 (*0-9653461-0-2*) Florence Pub.

— Assault on Gravelly Point. unabridged ed. LC 97-93351. 500p. 1998. 24.95 (*0-9657463-0-5*) Kilduck Station.

***Crawford, Bill.** Democrats Do the Dumbest Things. 160p. 2000. pap. text 9.95 (*1-58063-112-6*) Renaissance.

— From Chaos to Calm: Dealing with Difficult People vs. Them Dealing with You! Rombakis, Efthemia, ed. (Illus.). 150p. 1999. pap. 12.95i (*0-9653461-1-0*) Florence Pub.

— Republicans Do the Dumbest Things. 160p. 2000. pap. text 9.95 (*1-58063-111-8*) Renaissance.

Crawford, Bill, jt. auth. see Moser, Margaret.

Crawford, Bill, jt. auth. see Wray, Bill.

Crawford, Bob. Walking Trails of Eastern & Central Wisconsin. LC 97-6432. (North Coast Bks.). (Illus.). 200p. 1997. pap. 16.95 (*0-299-15574-9*) U of Wis Pr.

***Crawford, Bob.** Walking Trails of Southern Wisconsin. 2nd ed. 2000. pap. 16.95 (*0-299-16974-X*) U of Wis Pr.

Crawford, Bonnie, ed. see Crawford, Wesley G.

Crawford-Brown, Douglas. Principles of Environmental Health Science. 350p. 1998. 49.95 (*0-8342-0656-0*) Aspen Pub.

***Crawford-Brown, Douglas J.** Risk-Based Environmental Decisions: Culture & Methods. LC 99-40710. 1999. write for info. (*0-7923-8624-8*) Kluwer Academic.

Crawford-Brown, Douglas J. Theoretical & Mathematical Foundations of Human Health Risk Analysis: Biophysical Theory of Environmental Health Science. LC 97-2501. 1997. text 109.50 (*0-7923-9898-X*) Kluwer Academic.

Crawford, Burt. Getting Results in Accident Prevention. (Illus.). 136p. (Orig.). 1994. pap. text 14.95 (*0-9641522-0-7*) Crawford Safety.

Crawford, C. Merle. New Products Management. 3rd ed. 592p. (C). 1990. text 66.95 (*0-256-08207-3*, 09-1566-03, Irwn McGrw-H) McGrw-H Hghr Educ.

— New Products Management. 4th ed. LC 93-20131. (Marketing Ser.). (Illus.). 528p. (C). 1993. text 69.95 (*0-256-12152-4*, Irwn McGrw-H) McGrw-H Hghr Educ.

— New Products Management, International. 3rd ed. (C). 1991. text, student ed. 30.95 (*0-256-11406-4*, Irwn McGrw-H) McGrw-H Hghr Educ.

Crawford, C. Price. Price Crawford's Official Las Vegas Bartender's Guide. 58p. 1996. pap. 6.95 (*0-9659986-0-6*) T Zimmerman.

Crawford, Campbell, ed. see Gillespie, Hugh M.

Crawford, Caroline. Prague. LC 95-94140. 160p. 1995. pap. 12.50 (*0-9645891-0-9*) Green Trees CA.

Crawford, Catherine, jt. ed. see Clark, Michael.

***Crawford, Charles.** An Essay on the Propagation of the Gospel: In Which There Are Numerous Facts & Arguments Adduced to Prove That Many of the Indians in America Are Descended from the Ten Tribes. (LC History-America-E). 154p. 1999. reprint ed. lib. bdg. 69.00 (*0-7812-4319-X*) Rprt Serv.

Crawford, Charles. Split Time. LC 87-184. (Charlotte Zolotow Bk.). 224p. (YA). (gr. 7 up). 1987. 12.95 (*0-06-021324-8*) HarpC Child Bks.

Crawford, Charles, et al, eds. Sociobiology & Psychology: Ideas, Issues & Applications. LC 87-6783. 446p. 1987. 89.95 (*0-89859-580-0*) L Erlbaum Assocs.

Crawford, Charles & Krebs, Dennis. Handbook of Evolutionary Psychology: Ideas, Issues, & Applications. LC 97-16301. 1997. 150.00 (*0-8058-1666-6*) L Erlbaum Assocs.

Crawford, Charles A. The Writings of a Battle Fatigued Teacher. (Orig.). 1997. pap. write for info. (*1-57553-479-7*) Watermrk Pr.

***Crawford, Charles H.** Scenes of Earlier Days in Crossing the Plains to Oregon & Experiences of Western Life. LC 99-29862. 186p. 1999. pap. 11.95 (*0-87770-696-4*) Ye Galleon.

***Crawford, Charles Howard.** Scenes of Earlier Days in Crossing the Plains to Oregon & Experiences of Western Life. LC 99-29862. 186p. 1999. reprint ed. 16.95 (*0-87770-697-2*) Ye Galleon.

Crawford, Charles O. Rural Community Services. (WVSS Social, Political, & Economic Development Ser.). (C). 1996. pap. text 26.50 (*0-8133-7842-7*) Westview.

Crawford, Charles W., ed. see Church, Roberta & Walter, Ronald.

Crawford, Chauncey E. Crawford. Partial Record of the Descendants of James Crawford & His Wife Huldah Thompson Crawford, of Brunswick Maine. 315p. 1997. reprint ed. pap. 46.00 (*0-8328-8136-8*); reprint ed. lib. bdg. 56.00 (*0-8328-8135-X*) Higginson Bk Co.

Crawford, Chris. How to Program: The Skill that Will Sharpen Your Thinking. 97p. 1991. pap. 5.95 (*0-935166-04-1*) Storm King Pr.

Crawford, Chris, jt. auth. see Brungardt, Curtis.

Crawford, Christina. Mommie Dearest. anniversary ed. (Illus.). 1997. pap. 16.95 (*0-9663369-0-9*) Seven Sprngs Pr.

Crawford, Christina. No Safe Place: The Legacy of Family Violence. LC 94-17737. 176p. 1994. 12.95 (*0-88268-184-2*) Station Hill Pr.

— No Safe Place: The Legacy of Family Violence. 1994. 24.95 (*0-88268-190-7*) Station Hill Pr.

***Crawford, Cindy.** Maquillajo Basico. 1998. 34.95 (*84-08-01907-4*) Planeta.

Crawford, Clan, Jr. Michigan Zoning & Planning. LC 87-83703. 550p. 1993. suppl. ed. 35.00 (*0-685-22741-3*, 93-007) U MI Law CLE.

— Michigan Zoning & Planning. 3rd ed. LC 87-83703. 550p. 1988. 95.00 (*0-685-22740-5*, 88-009) U MI Law CLE.

***Crawford-Clark, Brenda.** Body Sense: Balancing Your Weight & Emotions. 2000. pap. 14.95 (*1-58270-037-0*) Beyond Words Pub.

Crawford, Claud C. The End of the Rope. rev. ed. LC 85-90684. 96p. 1985. pap. 9.95 (*0-933697-00-7*) Claud Crawford.

— The Escape to Love: God's Playing Field. 160p. (Orig.). 1997. pap. 9.95 (*0-933697-08-2*) Claud Crawford.

— Freedom. LC 86-70455. 106p. (Orig.). 1986. pap. 9.95 (*0-933697-05-8*) Claud Crawford.

— Giants, Lovers & Seekers. 96p. (Orig.). 1983. pap. 9.95 (*0-933697-02-3*) Claud Crawford.

— Integrity: The Other Side of Mental Health. rev. ed. LC 86-70145. 102p. 1986. pap. 9.95 (*0-933697-04-X*) Claud Crawford.

— The Really Final Solution. 160p. (Orig.). 1997. pap. 9.95 (*0-933697-07-4*) Claud Crawford.

— Sometimes Giant. 96p. (Orig.). 1984. pap. 9.95 (*0-933697-03-1*) Claud Crawford.

— Why This Skeptic Is a Christian. LC 88-92019. 100p. (Orig.). 1989. pap. 9.95 (*0-933697-06-6*) Claud Crawford.

Crawford, Claudia. The Beginnings of Nietzsche's Theory of Language. (Monographien und Texte zur Nietzscge-Forschung Ser.: No. 19). 412p. (C). 1988. lib. bdg. 123.10 (*3-11-011336-8*) De Gruyter.

— To Nietzsche - Dionysus, I Love You! Ariadne. LC 93-50892. 308p. (C). 1994. text 59.50 (*0-7914-2149-X*); pap. text 19.95 (*0-7914-2150-3*) State U NY Pr.

Crawford, Clinton. Recasting Ancient Egypt in the African Context. 200p. 1995. pap. text 18.95 (*0-86543-381-X*) Africa World.

— Recasting Ancient Egypt in the African Context: Toward a Model Curriculum Using Art & Language. LC 95-51262. 200p. 1996. 59.95 (*0-86543-380-1*) Africa World.

***Crawford, Colin.** Defenders or Criminals? Loyalist Prisoners & Criminalisation. LC 99-196663. (Orig.). 1999. pap. 28.95 (*0-85640-649-X*, Pub. by Blackstaff Pr) Dufour.

Crawford, Colin. Forbidden Femininity: Child Sexual Abuse & Female Sexuality. LC 97-72665. (Illus.). 128p. 1997. text 55.95 (*1-85972-679-8*, Pub. by Ashgate Pub) Ashgate Pub Co.

Crawford, Connie. With the Ups Comes the Downs. (Illus.). 104p. (Orig.). 1986. pap. 2.95 (*0-936369-01-9*) Son-Rise Pubns.

Crawford, Connie A. Art of Fashion Draping. 2nd ed. (Illus.). 396p. (C). 1995. text 53.00 (*1-56367-017-8*) Fairchild.

— Guide to Fashion Sewing. 2nd ed. LC 93-70714. (Illus.). 411p. 1994. 45.00 (*0-87005-748-0*) Fairchild.

Crawford, Constance. The Muse of Menus: Stories from Life & Cooking. LC 88-7100. (Illus.). 160p. (Orig.). 1988. pap. 9.95 (*0-936784-64-4*) J Daniel.

Crawford, Courtnie D. Breaking Free from the Shackles. 1994. pap. text 10.95 (*0-9639904-0-3*) Precious Pubng.

Crawford, Craig, et al. Index. Rosenstein, Julius et al, eds. (Rifts Index Ser.: Vol. 1). (Illus.). 96p. (Orig.). (YA). (gr. 8 up). 1996. pap. 12.95 (*0-916211-95-9*, 823) Palladium Bks.

Crawford, D. The City of London: Its Architectural Heritage. 1977. pap. 45.00 (*0-85941-043-9*); boxed set 40.00 (*0-85941-049-8*) St Mut.

Crawford, D., ed. Light Pollution, Radio Interference, & Space Debris. (ASP Conference Series Proceedings: Vol. 17). 331p. 1991. 34.00 (*0-937707-36-8*) Astron Soc Pacific.

Crawford, D. Boyd. History of Ogden, Utah in Old Post Cards. (Illus.). 124p. 1991. pap. write for info. (*0-9629191-0-1*) Crawford Pub.

Crawford, D. G., ed. Roll of the Indian Medical Service, 1615-1930. (C). 1987. 336.00 (*0-7855-2226-3*, Pub. by Picton) St Mut.

Crawford, Dan. Rouse a Sleeping Cat. 256p. (Orig.). 1993. mass mkt. 4.99 (*0-441-73553-3*) Ace Bks.

— Sure Death of a Mouse. 256p. (Orig.). 1994. mass mkt. 4.99 (*0-441-00024-X*) Ace Bks.

— A Wild Dog & Loan. 368p. (Orig.). 1995. mass mkt. 5.50 (*0-441-00183-1*) Ace Bks.

Crawford, Dan R. Connecting with God: The Priority of Communication in Prayer. 138p. (Orig.). 1994. pap. 13.67 (*1-889730-00-9*, SPI0035) Scripta Pubng.

— Discipleshape: Twelve Weeks to Spiritual Fitness. LC 98-14225. 252p. 1998. 16.95 (*1-56563-370-9*) Hendrickson MA.

— The Prayer-Shaped Disciple: Learn How Prayer Can Enrich Your Spiritual Life. 230p. 1999. 17.95 (*1-56563-092-0*) Hendrickson MA.

***Crawford, Dan R., et al.** Night of Tragedy, Dawning of Light: The Wedgwood Baptist Shootings. LC 00-26551. 180p. 2000. 14.99 (*0-87788-585-0*, H Shaw Pubs) Waterbrook Pr.

***Crawford, Daniel J.** First Marine Division & Its Regiments. 79p. 1999. pap. 8.00 (*0-16-050131-6*) USGPO.

Crawford, Daniel J. Plant Molecular Systematics: Macromolecular Approaches. LC 89-16702. 400p. 1990. 110.00 (*0-471-80760-5*) Wiley.

Crawford, David. Tangled Garden. LC 93-28929. 1995. pap. 6.00 (*0-88734-276-0*) Players Pr.

Crawford, David & Khoo, Chris. Practical Minor Surgery. (Illus.). 1996. audio compact disk 350.00 (*90-5702-006-8*); audio compact disk 70.00 (*90-5702-007-6*) Gordon & Breach.

Crawford, David L., et al, eds. Symposium on Support & Testing of Large Astronomical Mirrors: Proceedings Held in Tuscon, Arizona, December 4-6, 1966. LC QB0088.S96. (Arizona University, Optical Sciences Center, Technical Report Ser.: Vol. 30). 260p. reprint ed. pap. 80.60 (*0-608-13645-X*, 205525300011) Bks Demand.

Crawford, David W. Barren Fields. Landes, William-Alan, ed. LC 99-26182. 20p. 1999. pap. 5.00 (*0-88734-838-6*) Players Pr.

— Borrowed Plumage: A Play in One Act. LC 93-28939. 22p. (Orig.). 1994. pap. 5.00 (*0-88734-343-0*) Players Pr.

Crawford, David W. & Landes, William-Alan. Moments: A Collection of Acting Workshop & Audition Scenes. LC 99-19177. 64p. 1999. pap. 10.00 (*0-88734-664-2*) Players Pr.

Crawford, Debi Dietz. Advice for a Happy Marriage. 1997. 47.70 (*0-446-16450-X*, Pub. by Warner Bks) Little.

Crawford, Dennis, jt. auth. see Horne, Paul.

***Crawford, Dianna.** Freedom's Hope, Vol. 2. (Reardon Brothers Ser.). 2000. pap. text 9.99 (*0-8423-1917-4*) Tyndale Hse.

— Freedom's Promise. (Heart Quest Ser.). 2000. pap. 7.99 (*0-8423-1916-6*) Tyndale Hse.

Crawford, Dianna, jt. auth. see Laity, Sally.

Crawford, Doc. Driftboater's Guide to the Upper McKenzie. (Illus.). 86p. 1986. pap. 8.95 (*0-936608-55-2*) F Amato Pubns.

— North Umpqua Angler's Guide. (Illus.). 96p. 1989. pap. 9.95 (*0-936608-84-6*) F Amato Pubns.

Crawford, Don L., ed. Microbial Transformation of Low Rank Coals. 240p. 1992. lib. bdg. 179.00 (*0-8493-4551-0*, QR53) CRC Pr.

Crawford, Don L., jt. ed. see Crawford, Ronald L.

Crawford, Donald. Airplane Design: A Series of Articles Printed First in Kitplanes Magazine. LC 86-72617. (Illus.). 1986. pap. 25.00 (*0-9603934-1-2*) Crawford Aviation.

***Crawford, Donald.** Michael & Natasha: The Life & Love of Michael II, the Last of the Romanov Tsars. 464p. 2000. pap. 15.00 (*0-380-73191-6*, Avon Bks) Morrow Avon.

Crawford, Donald, jt. auth. see Crawford, Rosemary.

Crawford, Donald R. Practical Guide to Airplane Performance & Design. LC 81-67801. (Illus.). 200p. 1981. pap. text 18.95 (*0-9603934-0-4*) Crawford Aviation.

Crawford, Donald W. Kant's Aesthetic Theory. LC 73-15259. 200p. reprint ed. pap. 62.00 (*0-608-11833-8*, 201781900009) Bks Demand.

Crawford, Donna & Bodine, Richard. Conflict Resolution Education: A Guide to Implementing Programs in Schools, Youth-Serving Organizations, & Community & Juvenile Justice Settings. (Illus.). 138p. (Orig.). (C). 1997. pap. text 40.00 (*0-7881-4027-2*) DIANE Pub.

Crawford, Donna & Bodine, Richard J. The Handbook of Conflict Resolution Education: A Guide to Building Quality Programs in Schools. LC 97-33873. 208p. 1997. 34.95 (*0-7879-1096-1*) Jossey-Bass.

Crawford, Donna K., et al. The School for Quality Learning: Managing the School & Classroom the Deming Way. LC 93-84097. 296p. (Orig.). 1993. pap. text 21.95 (*0-87822-341-X*, 4674) Res Press.

Crawford, Donna K., jt. auth. see Bodine, Richard J.

Crawford, Doreen & Morris, Maryke, eds. Neonatal Nursing. 400p. 1994. pap. 37.50 (*0-412-48730-6*) Chapman & Hall.

***Crawford, Dorothy.** The Invisible Enemy: A Natural History of Viruses. (Illus.). 288p. 2001. 25.00 (*0-19-850332-6*) OUP.

Crawford, Dorothy B., tr. Easy Search For Milam Ancestors: Milam Co. TX Censuses for 1850, 1860 & 1870. (Illus.). 322p. 1994. reprint ed. pap. 32.50 (*0-8328-4426-8*); reprint ed. lib. bdg. 42.50 (*0-8328-4425-X*) Higginson Bk Co.

Crawford, Dorothy L. Evenings on & off the Roof: Pioneering Concerts in Los Angeles, 1939-1971. LC 94-33945. (Illus.). 335p. 1995. 39.95 (*0-520-08891-3*, Pub. by U CA Pr) Cal Prin Full Svc.

Crawford, Dorothy L., jt. auth. see Crawford, John C.

Crawford, Douglas R. & Mannion, Michael T. Psycho-Spiritual Healing after Abortion. LC 88-63847. 104p. (Orig.). 1989. pap. 6.95 (*1-55612-246-2*) Sheed & Ward WI.

Crawford, E., et al. Leadership & Teams Education Management. LC 96-42218. (Leadership & Management in Education Ser.). 1997. 108.00 (*0-335-19842-2*); pap. 32.95 (*0-335-19841-4*) OpUniv Pr.

Crawford, E. David & Das, Sakti. Genitourinary Cancer Surgery. 2nd ed. LC 96-8186. (Illus.). 916p. 1996. write for info. (*0-683-02185-0*) Lppncott W & W.

Crawford, E. David, jt. ed. see Das, Sakti.

Crawford, E. David, jt. ed. see Schulman, Claude C.

Crawford, E. Margaret, ed. Famine: The Irish Experience, 900-1900. 250p. (C). 1989. 75.00 (*0-7855-6975-8*, Pub. by J Donald) St Mut.

Crawford, E. Stanley, jt. auth. see Svensson, Lars G.

***Crawford, Earle W.** Samuel Doak: Pioneer Missionary in East Tennessee. 64p. 1999. reprint ed. pap. 5.95 (*1-57072-096-7*) Overmountain Pr.

Crawford, Ed. The Search for Common Ground in Sex Education: A Call for Community Action. (Illus.). 85p. (Orig.). 1996. pap. 11.00 (*0-9644389-2-5*) Smoky Water Pr.

Crawford, Edward K. A Management Guide to Leveraged Buyouts. LC 86-32390. (Professional Banking & Finance Ser.). 272p. 1987. 110.00 (*0-471-83232-4*) Wiley.

Crawford, Elaine, ed. see Montgomery, L. M.

Crawford, Elisabeth. Arrhenius: From Ionic Theory to the Greenhouse Effect. LC 96-6025. (Uppsala Studies in the History of Science: No. 23). 344p. 1996. 49.95 (*0-88135-166-0*, Sci Hist) Watson Pub Intl.

— Nationalism & Internationalism in Science, 1880-1939: Four Studies of the Nobel Population. (Illus.). 169p. (C). 1992. text 54.95 (*0-521-40386-3*) Cambridge U Pr.

Crawford, Elisabeth, et al, compiled by. The Nobel Population, 1901-1937: A Census of the Nominators & Nominees for the Prizes in Physics & Chemistry. LC 87-60004. (Berkeley Papers in History of Science: No. 11). 337p. 1987. pap. 20.00 (*0-918102-15-4*) U Cal Hist Sci Tech.

Crawford, Elisabeth, et al, eds. Denationalizing Science: The Contexts of International Scientific Practice. LC 92-19396. (Sociology of the Science Yearbook Ser.: Vol. 16). 304p. (C). 1993. lib. bdg. 213.50 (*0-7923-1855-2*) Kluwer Academic.

***Crawford, Elizabeth.** The Women's Suffrage Movement: A Reference Guide, 1866-1928. (Women's & Gender History Ser.). (Illus.). 800p. 1999. 140.00 (*1-84142-031-X*, Pub. by UCL Pr Ltd) Taylor & Francis.

Crawford, Elizabeth D., jt. ed. see De Montreville, Doris.

Crawford, Elizabeth D., tr. see Grimm, Jacob W. & Grimm, Wilhelm K.

Crawford, Elizabeth D., tr. see Handschmann, Johanna.

Crawford, Elizabeth D., tr. see Hartling, Peter.

Crawford, Elizabeth D., tr. see Hegler, Monika.

Crawford, Elizabeth D., tr. see Holub, Josef.

Crawford, Elizabeth D., tr. see Huth, Gunter.

Crawford, Elizabeth D., tr. see Ludwig, Gerd & Steimer, Christine.

Crawford, Elizabeth D., tr. see Pressler, Mirjam.

Crawford, Elizabeth D., tr. see Schinharl, Cornelia.

Crawford, Elizabeth D., tr. see Simon, Herta, et al.

Crawford, Elizabeth D., tr. see Szwillus, Marlisa.

Crawford, Elizabeth D., tr. see Van Dijk, Lutz.

Crawford, Eric W., jt. auth. see Colin, Jean Phillipe.

Crawford, Evans. The Hum: Call & Response in African American Preaching. Troeger, Thomas H., ed. (Preacher's Library). 112p. (Orig.). 1995. pap. 9.95 (*0-687-18020-1*) Abingdon.

Crawford, Evelyn M. Personal Data Directory. 56p. (Orig.). 1982. pap. 5.95 (*0-9608966-0-0*) WY Specialties.

C

An Asterisk (*) at the beginning of an entry indicates that the title is appearing for the first time.

Crawford, F. C. Coolidge: One Branch of the Coolidge Family, 1427-1963. (Illus.). 91p. 1991. reprint ed. pap. 17.50 (0-8328-2125-X) Higginson Bk Co.

Crawford, F. Marion. For the Blood Is the Life & Other Stories. 1996. pap. text 5.99 (1-56504-854-7, Borealis) White Wolf.

***Crawford, F. Marion, et al.** Uncanny Tales; A Werewolf of the Campagna; A Mystery of the Campagna. 270p. 1999. reprint ed. 54.95 (1-872621-37-6, Pub. by Tartarus Pr) Firebird Dist.

Crawford, Finla G. Continuing Education. 1958. 2.50 (0-87060-087-7, PUC 7) Syracuse U Cont Ed.

Crawford Flitch, J. E., tr. see Duret, Theodore.

Crawford, Francis M. American Politician. LC 32-33609. 1967. 8.00 (0-403-00034-3) Scholarly.

— American Politician. LC 73-111088. (BCL Ser. I). reprint ed. 29.50 (0-404-01828-9) AMS Pr.

— Ave Roma Immortalis. (Works of Francis Marion Crawford). 1990. reprint ed. lib. bdg. 79.00 (0-7812-2565-5) Rprt Serv.

— Bar Harbor. (Works of Francis Marion Crawford). 1990. reprint ed. lib. bdg. 79.00 (0-7812-2564-7) Rprt Serv.

— Casa Braccio. (Works of Francis Marion Crawford). 1990. reprint ed. lib. bdg. 79.00 (0-7812-2544-2) Rprt Serv.

— Cecilia. (Works of Francis Marion Crawford). 1990. reprint ed. lib. bdg. 79.00 (0-7812-2553-1) Rprt Serv.

— A Cigarette Makers Romance. (Works of Francis Marion Crawford). 1990. reprint ed. lib. bdg. 79.00 (0-7812-2537-X) Rprt Serv.

— Constantinople. (Works of Francis Marion Crawford). 1990. reprint ed. lib. bdg. 79.00 (0-7812-2563-9) Rprt Serv.

— Coreone. (Works of Francis Marion Crawford). 1990. reprint ed. lib. bdg. 79.00 (0-7812-2549-3) Rprt Serv.

— Dr. Claudius. (Works of Francis Marion Crawford). 1990. reprint ed. lib. bdg. 79.00 (0-7812-2526-4) Rprt Serv.

— Don Orsino. (Works of Francis Marion Crawford). 1990. reprint ed. lib. bdg. 79.00 (0-7812-2541-8) Rprt Serv.

— Fair Margaret. (Works of Francis Marion Crawford). 1990. reprint ed. lib. bdg. 79.00 (0-7812-2556-6) Rprt Serv.

— Francesca Da Rimini. Moran, John C., ed. (Worthies Library: No. 2). (Illus.). 1980. 5.00 (0-318-20643-9) F M Crawford.

— Francesca da Rimini. (Works of Francis Marion Crawford). 1990. reprint ed. lib. bdg. 79.00 (0-7812-2567-1) Rprt Serv.

— Greifenstein. (Works of Francis Marion Crawford). 1990. reprint ed. lib. bdg. 79.00 (0-7812-2535-3) Rprt Serv.

— In the Palace of the King. (Works of Francis Marion Crawford). 1990. reprint ed. lib. bdg. 79.00 (0-7812-2551-5) Rprt Serv.

— Katharine Lauderdale, 2 vols., Set. (BCL1-PS American Literature Ser.). 1992. reprint ed. lib. bdg. 150.00 (0-7812-6697-1) Rprt Serv.

— Katharine Lauderdale, 2 vols., Set. LC 06-30895. 1968. reprint ed. 49.00 (0-403-00099-8) Scholarly.

— Kathreen Lauderdale. (Works of Francis Marion Crawford). 1990. reprint ed. lib. bdg. 79.00 (0-7812-2545-0) Rprt Serv.

— Khaled. (Works of Franics Marion Crawford). 1990. reprint ed. lib. bdg. 79.00 (0-7812-2538-8) Rprt Serv.

— A Lady of Rome. (Works of Francis Marion Crawford). 1990. reprint ed. lib. bdg. 79.00 (0-7812-2557-4) Rprt Serv.

— The Life of Pope Leo XIII. (Works of Francis Marion Crawford). 1990. reprint ed. lib. bdg. 79.00 (0-7812-2568-X) Rprt Serv.

— The Little City of Hope. (Works of Francis Marion Crawford). 1990. reprint ed. lib. bdg. 79.00 (0-7812-2558-2) Rprt Serv.

— Man Overboard. (Works of Francis Marion Crawford). 1990. reprint ed. lib. bdg. 79.00 (0-7812-2554-X) Rprt Serv.

— Marietta. (Works of Francis Marion Crawford). 1990. reprint ed. lib. bdg. 79.00 (0-7812-2552-3) Rprt Serv.

— Marzio's Crucifix. LC 04-15090. 1887. 9.00 (0-403-00014-9) Scholarly.

— Marzio's Crucifix. LC 79-80626. (BCL Ser. I). reprint ed. 31.50 (0-404-01829-7) AMS Pr.

— Marzio's Crucifix. (Works of Francis Marion Crawford). 1990. reprint ed. lib. bdg. 79.00 (0-7812-2532-9) Rprt Serv.

— Mister Isaacs. LC 71-92607. (BCL Ser. I). 1969. reprint ed. 37.50 (0-404-01835-1) AMS Pr.

— Mr. Isaacs. (Works of Francis Marion Crawford). 1990. reprint ed. lib. bdg. 79.00 (0-685-44767-7) Rprt Serv.

— Mister Isaacs: A Tale of Modern India. 1882. 9.00 (0-403-00015-7) Scholarly.

— The Novel: What It Is. LC 79-75506. (Select Bibliographies Reprint Ser.). 1977. 18.95 (0-8369-5003-8) Ayer.

— The Novel: What It Is. LC 73-98831. 108p. 1971. reprint ed. lib. bdg. 49.50 (0-8371-2924-9, CRTN, Greenwood Pr) Greenwood.

— The Novel: What It Is. LC 76-104434. reprint ed. pap. text 10.50 (0-89197-869-0); reprint ed. lib. bdg. 16.75 (0-8398-0280-3) Irvington.

— The Novel: What It Is. (Works of Francis Marion Crawford). 1990. reprint ed. lib. bdg. 79.00 (0-7812-2562-0) Rprt Serv.

— Paul Patoff. (Works of Francis Marion Crawford). 1990. reprint ed. lib. bdg. 79.00 (0-7812-2533-7) Rprt Serv.

— The Primadonna. (Works of Francis Marion Crawford). 1990. reprint ed. lib. bdg. 79.00 (0-7812-2559-0) Rprt Serv.

— A Roman Singer. (Works of Francis Marion Crawford). 1990. reprint ed. lib. bdg. 79.00 (0-7812-2543-4) Rprt Serv.

— A Rose of Yesterday. (Works of Francis Marion Crawford). 1990. reprint ed. lib. bdg. 79.00 (0-7812-2548-5) Rprt Serv.

— The Rulers of the South. (Works of Francis Marion Crawford). 1990. reprint ed. lib. bdg. 79.00 (0-7812-2566-3) Rprt Serv.

— The Rulers of the South, 2 vols., Set. 1972. 250.00 (0-8490-0979-0) Gordon Pr.

— Salve Venetia. (Works of Francis Marion Crawford). 1990. reprint ed. lib. bdg. 79.00 (0-685-44768-5) Rprt Serv.

— Sant' Ilario. (Works of Francis Marion Crawford). 1990. reprint ed. lib. bdg. 79.00 (0-7812-2536-1) Rprt Serv.

— Saracinesca. (Works of Francis Marion Crawford). 1990. reprint ed. lib. bdg. 79.00 (0-7812-2531-0) Rprt Serv.

— A Tale of a Lonely Parish. (Works of Francis Marion Crawford). 1990. reprint ed. lib. bdg. 79.00 (0-7812-2530-2) Rprt Serv.

— Taquisara. (Works of Francis Marion Crawford). 1990. reprint ed. lib. bdg. 79.00 (0-7812-2547-7) Rprt Serv.

— The Three Fates. (Works of Francis Marion Crawford). 1990. reprint ed. lib. bdg. 79.00 (0-7812-2540-X) Rprt Serv.

— To Leeward. (Works of Francis Marion Crawford). 1990. reprint ed. lib. bdg. 79.00 (0-7812-2527-2) Rprt Serv.

— The Upper Berth. (Works of Francis Marion Crawford). 1990. reprint ed. lib. bdg. 79.00 (0-7812-2546-9) Rprt Serv.

— El Via Crucis. (Works of Francis Marion Crawford). 1990. reprint ed. lib. bdg. 79.00 (0-7812-2550-7) Rprt Serv.

— Wandering Ghosts. (Works of Francis Marion Crawford). 1990. reprint ed. lib. bdg. 79.00 (0-7812-2561-2) Rprt Serv.

— The White Sister. (Works of Francis Marion Crawford). 1990. reprint ed. lib. bdg. 79.00 (0-7812-2560-4) Rprt Serv.

— Whosoever Shall Offend. (Works of Francis Marion Crawford). 1990. reprint ed. lib. bdg. 79.00 (0-7812-2555-8) Rprt Serv.

— The Witch of Prague. (Works of Francis Marion Crawford). 1990. reprint ed. lib. bdg. 79.00 (0-7812-2539-6) Rprt Serv.

— With the Immortals. Reginald, R. & Menville, Douglas A., eds. LC 75-46264. (Supernatural & Occult Fiction Ser.). 1976. reprint ed. lib. bdg. 25.95 (0-405-08122-7) Ayer.

— With the Immortals. (Works of Francis Marion Crawford). 1990. reprint ed. lib. bdg. 79.00 (0-7812-2534-5) Rprt Serv.

— The Works of Francis Marion Crawford. 1990. reprint ed. lib. bdg. 79.00 (0-685-44769-3) Rprt Serv.

— Zoroaster. LC 06-30882. 1885. 11.00 (0-403-00100-5) Scholarly.

— Zoroaster. LC 74-126704. (BCL Ser. I). reprint ed. 34.50 (0-404-01836-X) AMS Pr.

— Zoroaster. (Works of Francis Marion Crawford). 1990. reprint ed. lib. bdg. 79.00 (0-7812-2528-0) Rprt Serv.

Crawford, Fred D. Mixing Memory & Desire: The Waste Land & Modern British Novels. LC 82-477. 170p. 1982. 28.50 (0-271-00308-1) Pa St U Pr.

— Richard Aldington & Lawrence of Arabia: A Cautionary Tale. LC 97-25418. 1998. 39.95 (0-8093-2166-1) S Ill U Pr.

Crawford, Fred D., ed. Shaw Offstage: The Nondramatic Writings. LC 88-19770. (Annual of Bernard Shaw Studies: Vol. 9). (Illus.). 243p. 1989. lib. bdg. 35.00 (0-271-00652-8) Pa St U Pr.

— Shaw 12. (Annual of Bernard Shaw Studies). (Illus.). 368p. 1992. text 65.00 (0-271-00811-3) Pa St U Pr.

— Shaw 15. (The Annual of Bernard Shaw Studies). 256p. 1995. 40.00 (0-271-01422-9) Pa St U Pr.

Crawford, Fred D., jt. ed. see Weintraub, Stanley.

Crawford, Fred E. Crawford. Early Ancestors of the Crawfords in America: An Introduction to Genealogies of American Families of the Name. 81p. 1997. reprint ed. pap. 16.00 (0-8328-8132-5); reprint ed. lib. bdg. 26.00 (0-8328-8131-7) Higginson Bk Co.

Crawford, G. E., jt. auth. see Birnbaum, S. L.

Crawford, Gary W. In Shadow Lands: Poems. Boston, Bruce, ed. (Blue Meadow Poets Ser.: No. 4). (Illus.). 29p. 1998. pap. 6.00 (0-910151-05-9) Nashville Hse.

— J. Sheridan Le Fanu: A Bio-Bibliography, 3. LC 94-38419. (Bio-Bibliographies in World Literature Ser.: Vol. 3). 168p. 1995. lib. bdg. 59.95 (0-313-28515-2, Greenwood Pr) Greenwood.

— Paleoethnobotany of the Kameda Peninsula Jomon. (Anthropological Papers Ser.: No. 73). (Illus.). 200p. 1983. pap. 8.00 (0-932206-95-6) U Mich Mus Anthro.

— Poems of the Divided Self. (Blue Meadow Poets Ser.: No. 3). (Illus.). 12p. (Orig.). 1992. pap. 3.00 (0-910151-04-0) Nashville Hse.

— Ramsey Campbell. Schlobin, Roger C., ed. LC 87-16030. (Starmont Reader's Guide Ser.: Vol. 48). vi, 74p. 1988. pap. 15.00 (1-55742-036-X) Millefleurs.

Crawford, Gary W., ed. Supernatural Poetry. (Illus.). 55p. (Orig.). 1995. reprint ed. pap. 4.00 (0-913045-04-7) Gothic Pr.

Crawford, Gary W., ed. see Eng, Steve.

Crawford, Gary William. Gothic Fevers: Selected by Bruce Boston. unabridged ed. (Illus.). 47p. 2000. pap. 8.00 (0-910151-06-7, 0910151067) Nashville Hse.

***Crawford, George & Nicklaus, Janice.** Philosophical & Cultural Values: Applying Ethics in Schools. LC 99-47167. 2000. 29.95 (1-883001-82-X) Eye On Educ.

Crawford, George & Sen, Bidyut. Derivatives for Decision Makers: Strategic Management Issues. 2nd ed. LC 96-17187. 240p. 1996. 29.95 (0-471-12994-1) Wiley.

Crawford, George W. Prince Hall & His Followers. LC 74-144591. reprint ed. 32.50 (0-404-00145-9) AMS Pr.

Crawford, Gerald. The Magic in the Mud. (Illus.). 48p. (J). (gr. 1-4). Date not set. 14.95 (0-9672996-0-8) Red Mud Pr.

***Crawford, Gladys.** General Biology 2080 Lab Manual. 1999. pap. text 22.57 (1-56870-359-7) RonJon Pub.

Crawford, Greg. The Internet & Public Libraries. Shoop, Diane, ed. (Illus.). 52p. 1999. pap. 20.00 (1-58036-132-3) Penn State Data Ctr.

Crawford, Gregory A., et al. Using Microsoft Powerpoint: A How-To-Do-It Manual for Librarians. LC 98-33771. (How-to-Do-It Manual Ser.). 13p. 1998. pap. 38.50 (1-55570-341-0) Neal-Schuman.

Crawford, Gregory P. & Zumer, Slobodan, eds. Liquid Crystals in Complex Geometries Formed by Polymer & Porous Networks. 584p. 1996. 110.00 (0-7484-0464-3) Taylor & Francis.

Crawford, H. Marjorie. Crawford. The Crawfords of Adams County, Ohio. 110p. 1997. reprint ed. pap. 18.50 (0-8328-8134-1); reprint ed. lib. bdg. 28.50 (0-8328-8133-3) Higginson Bk Co.

Crawford, H. W., jt. auth. see McDowell, M. C.

Crawford, Harriet. Dilmun & Its Gulf Neighbours. LC 97-9527. (Illus.). 186p. (C). 1998. text 59.95 (0-521-58348-9); pap. text 23.95 (0-521-58679-8) Cambridge U Pr.

— Sumer & the Sumerians. (Illus.). 192p. (C). 1991. pap. text 19.95 (0-521-38850-3) Cambridge U Pr.

Crawford, Harriet, et al. The Dilmun Temple at Saar: Bahrain & Its Archaeological Inheritance. LC 95-15529. 1995. write for info. (0-7103-0487-0) Routledge.

Crawford, Helen J. & Christensen, Larry B. Developing Research Skills Lab. 3rd ed. 1994. pap. text, lab manual ed. 24.00 (0-205-15569-3) Allyn.

Crawford, Hester M., ed. Herbs & Their Ornamental Uses. (Plants & Gardens Ser.). (Illus.). 1993. per. 7.95 (0-945352-07-7) Bklyn Botanic.

Crawford, Hollie W., jt. auth. see McDowell, Milton C.

Crawford, Ilse. Sensual Home. LC 97-69575. (Illus.). 1998. 39.95 (0-8478-2079-3, Pub. by Rizzoli Intl) St Martin.

Crawford, Ingrid, tr. see Schissel, Robert F.

Crawford, Isabel. Kiowa: A Woman Missionary in Indian Territory. LC 97-49932. (Illus.). xxx, 241p. 1998. pap. 12.00 (0-8032-6387-2, Bison Books) U of Nebr Pr.

Crawford, Isabella. Collected Poems. LC 72-91689. (Literature of Canada, Poetry & Prose in Reprint Ser.). 352p. reprint ed. pap. 109.20 (0-608-12843-0, 202360700033) Bks Demand.

Crawford, Isiah, jt. auth. see Fishman, Baruch.

***Crawford, Isom & Wadleigh, Kevin.** Software Optimization for High Performance Computers. 377p. (C). 2000. pap. 45.00 (0-13-017008-9) P-H.

Crawford, J., et al. Century Twenty-One Typewriting: Complete Course, 2 vols., Set. 3rd large type ed. 1008p. (YA). (gr. 9-12). 1982. 125.00 (0-317-01878-7, J-03580-00) Am Printing Hse.

Crawford, J. B. Getting Started with Micro Focus Personal COBOL 2.0. LC 94-235392. 96p. 1994. pap. 20.95 (0-471-30680-0) Wiley.

***Crawford, J. H.** Car-Free Cities. (Illus.). 2000. pap. 37.95 (0-7506-4788-4) Buttrwrth-Heinemann.

— Carfree Cities. (Illus.). 324p. 2000. 29.95 (90-5727-037-4, Pub. by Intl Bks) Paul & Co Pubs.

Crawford, J. L. Zion Album: A Nostalgic History of Zion Canyon. LC 85-51614. (Illus.). 87p. 1986. pap. text 6.95 (0-915630-21-4) Zion.

Crawford, J. M., jt. auth. see Quinn, John.

Crawford, J. Marshall. Mosby & His Men. 375p. 1987. reprint ed. 30.00 (0-942211-02-2) Olde Soldier Bks.

Crawford, J. R. Lovely Peggy: A Play in Three Acts Based on the Love Romance of Margaret Woffington & David Garrick. 1911. 49.50 (0-686-51412-2) Elliots Bks.

Crawford, J. R. & Parker, D. M., eds. Developments in Clinical & Experimental Neuropsychology. (Illus.). 346p. 1989. 85.00 (0-306-43244-7, Plenum Trade) Perseus Pubng.

Crawford, J. Stephens. The Byzantine Shops at Sardis. (Archaeological Exploration of Sardis Monograph: No. 9). (Illus.). 358p. 1991. 50.00 (0-674-08968-5, CRABYZ) HUP.

Crawford, Jackie, et al. Please! Teach ALL of Me: Multisensory Activities for Preschoolers. (Illus.). 182p. 1994. pap. text, teacher ed. 19.50 (1-57035-001-9, 52ALL) Sopris.

Crawford, Jamarhl Carlton. Prophecy: Reflections on Life & Love from a Black Perspective. v, 127p. 1997. pap. 10.00 (0-9678559-0-X) Prophecy Comns.

Crawford, James. Bilingual Education: History, Politics, Theory, & Practice. 3rd rev. ed. Crane, Patricia et al, eds. LC 89-60152. 313p. (Orig.). (C). 1989. pap. text 24.95 (0-89075-556-6, CPC29) Bilingual Ed Serv.

— The Creation of States in International Law. rev. ed. (Illus.). 526p. 2000. pap. text 39.95 (0-19-825402-4) OUP.

— Language Loyalties: A Source Book on the Official English Controversy. LC 91-29445. (Illus.). 532p. 1992. pap. 17.95 (0-226-12016-3) U Ch Pr.

— Language Loyalties: A Source Book on the Official English Controversy. LC 91-29445. (Illus.). 536p. 1995. lib. bdg. 45.95 (0-226-12015-5) U Ch Pr.

Crawford, James, ed. The Rights of Peoples. 246p. 1992. pap. text 26.00 (0-19-825804-6) OUP.

***Crawford, James & Lowe, Vaughn, eds.** British Year Book of International Law 1999, Vol. 70. 650p. 2000. text 190.00 (0-19-829914-1) OUP.

Crawford, James & Rothwell, Donald R., eds. The Law of the Sea in the Asian Pacific Region: Developments & Prospects. LC 94-4409. (Publications on Ocean Development: Vol. 21). 284p. (C). 1994. lib. bdg. 124.00 (0-7923-2742-X) Kluwer Academic.

Crawford, James, jt. ed. see Alston, Philip.

Crawford, James, jt. ed. see Browlie, Ian.

Crawford, James, jt. ed. see Brownlie, Ian.

Crawford, James, jt. ed. see Onuma, Yasuaki.

Crawford, James A. Frequency Synthesizer Design Handbook. LC 94-7655. 1994. 110.00 (0-89006-440-7) Artech Hse.

Crawford, James E. Officer in Trouble: The Detroit Cop Who Refused to Play the Game. 218p. (Orig.). 1992. pap. 8.95 (0-9625423-5-0) Four-G Pubs.

Crawford, James E. & Martin, Neil B. California Commercial Law: June 1992 Update, 2 vols., Set. Dworin, Christopher D., ed. LC 65-63004. 261p. 1992. pap. 43.00 (0-88124-513-5, BU-30044) Cont Ed Bar-CA.

Crawford, James M. Cocopa Dictionary. LC 89-5151. (University of California Publications in Entomology: No. 114). 546p. 1989. pap. 169.30 (0-7837-7477-X, 204919900010) Bks Demand.

— Cocopa Texts. LC 81-24046. (University of California Publications in Entomology: No. 100). 618p. 1983. pap. 191.60 (0-7837-7478-8, 204920000010) Bks Demand.

— The Mobilian Trade Language. LC 78-13149. 150p. reprint ed. pap. 46.50 (0-608-11957-1, 202316700032) Bks Demand.

Crawford, Jane. Money, Grades 1-2. (Math by All Means Ser.). (Illus.). 182p. 1996. pap. text 23.95 (0-941355-17-9, 00825) Math Solns Pubns.

Crawford, Jane Diehl. Veterinary Medical School Admissions Requirements. 12th ed. 1997. pap. text 14.95 (0-683-30099-7) Lppncott W & W.

Crawford, Jay B. Credit Mobilier of America. LC 75-155099. reprint ed. 37.50 (0-404-01837-8) AMS Pr.

Crawford, Jean, ed. Amazing Facts. LC 93-11599. (Child's First Library of Learning). (Illus.). 88p. (J). (gr. k-3). 1994. lib. bdg. write for info. (0-8094-9459-0) Time-Life.

Crawford, Jean, ed. see Daniels, Patricia S.

Crawford, Jean, ed. see Time-Life Books Editors.

Crawford, Jean B., ed. see Quattlebaum, Mary A.

Crawford, Jean B., ed. see Time-Life Books Editors.

Crawford, Jeanne R., ed. Wheels Led the Way: Horse-Drawn Vehicles, Plain & Fancy 1820-1920. (Illus.). 87p. 1973. pap. 5.00 (1-928707-00-9) Yakima Valley Mus.

Crawford, Jeanne R. & Kime, Kay, eds. As the Valley Was: A Pictorial View of the Community Life in the Yakima River Valley from the Yakima River's Origin at Cle Elem to Its Junction with the Columbia River During the Era 1900-1915. (Illus.). 70p. 1976. pap. 5.00 (1-928707-01-7) Yakima Valley Mus.

Crawford, Jearn, ed. Ecology. LC 93-28657. (Child's First Library of Learning). (Illus.). 88p. (J). (gr. k-3). 1994. lib. bdg. write for info. (0-8094-9467-1) Time-Life.

Crawford, Jenny. Through the Eyes of Spirit: As a Bridge Between This World & the Spirit World, Jenny Brings Us Proof of Life Beyond Death. LC 96-30461. 128p. (Orig.). 1996. pap. 11.00 (0-931892-32-5) B Dolphin Pub.

Crawford, Jerry L., et al. Acting in Person & in Style. 5th ed. LC 94-72076. 384p. (C). 1994. text. write for info. (0-697-20133-3) Brown & Benchmark.

Crawford, Jim. Salmon to a Fly: Fly Fishing for a Pacific Salmon in the Open Ocean. (Illus.). 176p. 1995. pap. 19.95 (1-57188-034-8) F Amato Pubns.

***Crawford, Joanne Sneed.** Respectfully Yours Buford: Program on Respect. (Illus.). 32p. 1999. pap. 6.95 (1-57543-076-2) Mar Co Prods.

Crawford, John. St. Catherine's Parish, Dublin, 1840-1900: A Portrait of a Church of Ireland Community. 64p. 1996. pap. 9.95 (0-7165-2593-3, Pub. by Irish Acad Pr) Intl Spec Bk.

***Crawford, John.** Stars Fall. LC 99-91955. 2000. 25.00 (0-7388-1404-0); pap. 18.00 (0-7388-1405-9) Xlibris Corp.

***Crawford, John, ed.** Kia Kaha: New Zealand in the Second World War. (Illus.). 336p. 2000. text 45.00 (0-19-558438-4) OUP.

Crawford, John C. & Crawford, Dorothy L. Expressionism in Twentieth-Century Music. LC 92-35291. (Illus.). 358p. 1993. 42.00 (0-253-31473-9) Ind U Pr.

Crawford, John G., et al. Wartime Agriculture in Australia & New Zealand, 1939-50. (Illus.). xiii, 354p. 1954. 47.50 (0-8047-0455-4) Stanford U Pr.

Crawford, John J. The Negotiable Instruments Law: From the Draft Prepared for the Commissioners on Uniformity of Laws, & Enacted in New York, Massachusetts, Rhode Island, Connecticut, Pennsylvania, District of Columbia, Maryland, Virginia, North Carolina, Tennessee, Florida, Wisconsin, North Dakota, Colorado, Utah, Oregon & Washington. 2nd ed. xxiv, 173p. 1997. reprint ed. 65.00 (1-56169-307-3, 14591) Gaunt.

Crawford, John L. Zion National Park: Towers of Stone. Tripp, Angela & Vandrame, Carey, eds. Belliston, Scott, tr. (ENG & GER., Illus.). 55p. (Orig.). 1995. pap. 10.95 (0-915630-38-9) Zion.

— Zion National Park: Towers of Stone. 2nd rev. ed. Vandrame, Carey & Tripp, Angela, eds. (Illus.). 55p. (Orig.). 1988. pap. 9.50 (0-915630-33-8) Zion.

Crawford, John R. A Christian & His Money: Earning & Spending in the Light of the Gospel. 2nd rev. ed. 192p. 1988. reprint ed. pap. 5.95 (0-944990-00-2) Medcor.

Crawford, John S., et al. Pediatric Ophthalmology & Strabismus. LC 86-553. (Transactions of the New Orleans Academy of Ophthalmology Ser.). 560p. 1986. reprint ed. pap. 173.60 (0-608-03400-2, 206409700008) Bks Demand.

Crawford, John T., III & Hustrulid, William A., eds. Open Pit Mine Planning & Design. LC 79-52269. (Illus.). 373p. reprint ed. pap. 115.70 (0-8357-6644-6, 203531100094) Bks Demand.

Crawford, John W. Early Shakespearean Actresses. LC 84-47691. (American University Studies: English Language & Literature: Ser. IV, Vol. 8). 205p. (Orig.). (C). 1984. text 36.90 (0-8204-0099-8) P Lang Pubng.

An Asterisk (*) at the beginning of an entry indicates that the title is appearing for the first time.

— I Have Become Familiar with the Rain. LC 92-44222. 64p. 1995. pap. 14.95 (*0-7734-2762-7*, Mellen Poetry Pr) E Mellen.

— The Learning, Wit, & Wisdom of Shakespeare's Renaissance Women. LC 96-51541. (Studies in Renaissance Literature: Vol. 14). 392p. 1997. text 99.95 (*0-7734-8737-9*) E Mellen.

— Making the Connection. Schultz, Patricia, ed. LC 89-12527. (Poetry Ser.: Vol. 2). 64p. 1989. pap. 12.95 (*0-88946-887-7*) E Mellen.

Crawford, John W., ed. Risks of Labour. LC 84-25653. (Wiley Series on Perinatal Practice: No. 2). (Illus.). 226p. reprint ed. pap. 70.10 (*0-8357-4548-1*, 203744700008) Bks Demand.

Crawford, Jon G. Anglicizing the Government of Ireland: The Irish Privy Council & the Expansion of Tudor Rule, 1556-78. (Illus.). 524p. 1993. 52.50 (*0-7165-2498-8*, Pub. by Irish Acad Pr) Intl Spec Bk.

Crawford, Joseph H., et al. Three Hundred Thirty-Three: A Bibliography of the Science Fantasy Novel. LC 74-15959. (Science Fiction Ser.). 82p. 1975. reprint ed. 17.95 (*0-405-06324-5*) Ayer.

Crawford, Joy. If Love Should Come. LC 98-194495. 447p. 1994. write for info. (*976-625-038-3*) Kingston Pub.

— Mom Come Quick. (Illus.). 8p. (Orig.). (J). (ps up). 1997. pap. 4.50 (*0-9652368-3-8*) Wright Pub Co.

Crawford, Judith, ed. see De LaFayette, Jean M.

***Crawford, Julia.** Bernese Mountain Dog: An Owner's Guide to a Happy Healthy Pet. (Guide to a Happy Healthy Pet Ser.). (Illus.). 160p. 2000. 12.95 (*1-58245-162-1*) Howell Bks.

Crawford, June. Cambridge Stratford Study Skills Course, 10 Hour Edition: A College Study Skills Manual: Ten Tips for Academic Success. (Illus.). 98p. (Orig.). 1988. teacher ed. 64.95 (*0-935637-11-7*); student ed. 12.95 (*0-935637-12-5*); audio 40.00 (*0-935637-14-1*); trans. 85.00 (*0-935637-13-3*) Cambridge Strat.

— Emotion & Gender. (Gender & Psychology Ser.: Vol. 5). 226p. (C). 1992. text 69.95 (*0-8039-8309-3*); pap. text 14.99 (*0-8039-8310-7*) Sage.

Crawford, K. Michael. Chicken Little. (J). (ps-3). 1999. 6.95 (*1-57102-150-7*, Ideals Child) Hambleton-Hill.

Crawford, Karen & Heaton, Alan. Problem Solving in Analytical Chemistry. Rafferty, Denise & Sleigh, Sara, eds. 159p. 1999. pap. 29.00 (*1-870343-46-8*) Royal Soc Chem.

Crawford, Karis & Walters, Johanne. Natural Childbirth after Cesarean: A Practical Guide. (Illus.). 218p. (Orig.). 1996. pap. 14.95 (*0-86542-490-X*) Blackwell Sci.

Crawford, Karlene M. & Cox, James F. Management & Technological Changes to Improve Competitiveness: Case Studies of Small to Medium Sized Apparel Industries. 50p. 1988. pap. text 16.00 (*1-55822-002-X*) Am Prod & Inventory.

Crawford, Karlene M., et al. Performance Measurement Systems & the JIT Philosophy. LC 88-72100. (Illus.). 123p. 1988. text 20.00 (*1-55822-011-9*) Am Prod & Inventory.

Crawford, Kathleen & Witcher, Geraldine. Abingdon Book of Bible Stories: Selected for Ages 3-4. (Illus.). 48p. (J). (ps). 1995. 7.95 (*0-687-01496-4*) Abingdon.

Crawford, Kathleen, jt. auth. see Engstrand, Iris H.

Crawford, Kathleen, ed. see O'Grady, Tom.

Crawford, Kathleen, jt. ed. see Taylor, James.

Crawford, Keith. East Central European Politics Today. LC 96-27172. (Politics Today Ser.). 336p. 1997. text 69.95 (*0-7190-4621-1*); text 19.95 (*0-7190-4622-X*, Pub. by Manchester Univ Pr) St Martin.

Crawford, Kelly, ed. see Montgomery, L. M.

Crawford, Ken. Yuki. LC 95-26202. 92p. (YA). (gr. 4-7). 1996. pap. 7.99 (*0-8280-1052-8*) Review & Herald.

Crawford, Kenneth, jt. auth. see Simmons, Paul D.

Crawford, Kenneth C. Yuki. 96p. (J). (gr. 4-7). 1998. pap. 7.99 (*0-8280-1051-X*) Review & Herald.

Crawford, Kenneth G. The Pressure Boys: The Inside Story of Lobbying in America. LC 73-19139. (Politics & People Ser.). 320p. 1974. reprint ed. 23.95 (*0-405-05864-0*) Ayer.

Crawford, L. Ann & Crawford, William R., Sr. U. S. Forces Travel Guide to U. S. Military Installations. Clark, Nicole, ed. LC 97-28319. 1997. pap. write for info. (*0-914862-63-4*) Military Living Pubns.

Crawford, L. Ann, jt. auth. see Crawford, William R.

Crawford, Lee. The Mumwalds. (Illus.). 200p. (Orig.). 1994. pap. 12.99 (*0-8272-2322-6*) Chalice Pr.

Crawford, Lela A. & Crawford, William R. FarmStay U. S. A. pap. write for info. (*0-914862-39-1*) Military Living Pubns.

Crawford, Lela A., jt. auth. see Crawford, William R.

Crawford, Lester M. & Franco, Donald A., eds. Animal Drugs & Human Health. LC 93-61759. 345p. 1994. pap. text 84.95 (*1-56676-102-6*) Technomic.

Crawford, Lewis. The Medora Deadwood Stageline. (Shorey Historical Ser.). 26p. reprint ed. pap. 10.00 (*0-8466-0036-6*, S36) Shoreys Bkstore.

***Crawford, Lewis F.** Exploits of Ben Arnold Vol. 64: Indian Fighter, Gold Miner, Cowboy, Hunter & Army Scout. (Western Frontier Library : Vol. 64). (Illus.). 352p. 2000. pap. text. write for info. (*0-8061-3141-1*) U of Okla Pr.

Crawford, Lewis F. History of North Dakota, 3 vols., Set. 1996. reprint ed. lib. bdg. 195.00 (*0-8328-5216-3*) Higginson Bk Co.

— History of North Dakota, Vol. 1. (Illus.). 641p. 1994. reprint ed. lib. bdg. 64.00 (*0-8328-3858-6*) Higginson Bk Co.

— History of North Dakota, Vol. 2. (Illus.). 653p. 1994. reprint ed. lib. bdg. 66.00 (*0-8328-3859-4*) Higginson Bk Co.

— History of North Dakota, Vol. 3. (Illus.). 617p. 1994. reprint ed. lib. bdg. 62.00 (*0-8328-3860-8*) Higginson Bk Co.

Crawford, Lillian R., ed. see Brown, Raven M.

Crawford, Linda. In a Class by Herself: A Novel LC 76-16561. 243p. 1976. write for info. (*0-684-14759-9*) Free Pr.

Crawford, Linda, ed. The Elders: Passing It On. (Illus.). 31p. (Orig.). 1989. pap. 5.95 (*0-938541-09-9*) Origins Program.

Crawford, Linda, et al. To Hold Us Together: Seven Conversations for Multicultural Understanding. (Illus.). 133p. (Orig.). 1990. pap. 8.95 (*0-938541-07-2*) Origins Program.

***Crawford, Linda L. & O'Donnell, Edward J.** Florida Real Estate Broker's Guide. LC 98-48416. 528p. 1999. 74.95 (*0-7931-2713-0*) Dearborn.

Crawford, Lisa. 101 Creative Ways to Ask & Answer That Date. (Illus.). (Orig.). pap. 8.95 (*0-9651163-4-4*) Harkness Pubng.

Crawford-Lloyd, Melanie. The Woman's Book of Promise, Purpose, & Love. 190p. (Orig.). 1996. pap. write for info. (*0-9652796-0-X*) Crawford-Lloyd.

Crawford, Louellen. Dependent Care & the Employee Benefits Package: Human Resource Strategies for the 1990s. LC 90-32724. 184p. 1990. 55.00 (*0-89930-465-6*, CNC, Quorum Bks) Greenwood.

Crawford, Louis & Farber, Glyn. Louisiana Trade Tokens. 2nd ed. Schenkman, David E., ed. & photos by by. LC 96-61243. (Illus.). 559p. 1997. 44.95 (*0-918492-11-4*) TAMS.

Crawford, Lucy. History of the White Mountains. Mudge, John T., ed. (Illus.). 232p. 1999. reprint ed. 15.95 (*0-9633560-8-9*) Durand Pr.

— The History of the White Mountains from the First Settlement of Upper Coos & Pequaket. (Illus.). 230p. 1992. reprint ed. lib. bdg. 30.00 (*0-8328-2241-8*) Higginson Bk Co.

— History of the White Mountains, from the First Settlement of Upper Coos & Pequaket. 205p. 1997. reprint ed. lib. bdg. 29.50 (*0-8328-5971-0*) Higginson Bk Co.

— Supervisory Skills in Marketing. Dorr, Eugene L., ed. (Occupational Manuals & Projects in Marketing Ser.). (Illus.). (J). (gr. 9-10). 1977. text 12.28 (*0-07-013471-5*) McGraw.

Crawford, Lucy & Lynch, Richard L. Finance & Credit. (Career Competencies in Marketing Ser.). (Illus.). (YA). (gr. 11-12). 1978. text 12.04 (*0-07-013481-2*) McGraw.

Crawford, Lucy C., jt. auth. see Rich, Chris.

***Crawford, Lynn.** Blow. LC 98-42686. (Lingo Magazine Ser.). 96p. 1998. pap. text 12.95 (*1-889097-17-9*, Pub. by Hard Pr MA) Consort Bk Sales.

Crawford, Lynn. Solow. (House of Outsider Ser.: Vol. 1). 72p. 1995. pap. 10.00 (*0-9638433-3-8*) Hard Pr MA.

Crawford, Lynne & Taylor, Linda. Element Guide to Shyness: Your Questions Answered. LC 97-43907. 128p. 1998. pap. 9.95 (*1-86204-183-0*, Pub. by Element MA) Penguin Putnam.

Crawford, M., jt. ed. see Vergroesen, A. J.

Crawford, M. E., jt. ed. see Metzger, D. E.

Crawford, Malcolm. One Money for Europe? The Economics & Politics of EMU. 2nd ed. LC 96-2809. 380p. 1996. text 45.00 (*0-312-16115-8*) St Martin.

Crawford, Margaret. Building the Workingman's Paradise: The Design of American Company Towns. LC 95-37264. (Haymarket Ser.). 160p. (C). 1996. 65.00 (*0-86091-421-6*, Pub. by Verso); pap. 22.00 (*0-86091-695-2*, Pub. by Verso) Norton.

Crawford, Margaret, ed. The Hungry Stream: Essays on Famine & Emigration. LC 97-226155. 215p. 1997. pap. 19.95 (*0-85389-674-7*, Pub. by Inst Irish Studies) Irish Bks Media.

Crawford, Margaret & Kaliski, John. Everyday Urbanism. LC 99-23898. (Illus.). 256p. 1999. 35.00 (*1-885254-81-4*, Pub. by Monacelli Pr) Penguin Putnam.

Crawford, Marion A., tr. see Balzac, Honore de.

Crawford, Mark. Encyclopedia of the Mexican-American War. LC 99-21177. 400p. 1999. lib. bdg. 75.00 (*1-57607-059-X*) ABC-CLIO.

— Habitats & Ecosystems: An Encyclopedia of Endangered America. 398p. 1999. lib. bdg. 75.00 (*0-87436-997-5*) ABC-CLIO.

— Toxic Waste Sites: An Encyclopedia of Endangered America. LC 97-17303. (Illus.). 324p. 1997. lib. bdg. 65.00 (*0-87436-934-7*, FN-1722) ABC-CLIO.

***Crawford, Mark J.** Confederate Courage on Other Fields: Four Lesser Known Accounts of the War Between the States. LC 99-50233. (Illus.). 189p. 2000. boxed set 35.00 (*0-7864-0720-4*) McFarland & Co.

Crawford, Mark J. Physical Geology Quick Review. LC 98-216148. (Cliffs Quick Reviews Ser.). (Illus.). 242p. 1998. pap. text 9.95 (*0-8220-5335-7*, Cliff) IDG Bks.

Crawford, Martin, jt. ed. see Rice, Alan J.

Crawford, Mary. Mystery at Witch Creek. (J). (gr. 3-6). 1995. pap. 9.99 (*0-88092-177-3*) Royal Fireworks.

Crawford, Mary. Talking Difference: On Gender & Language. (Gender & Psychology Ser.: Vol. 7). (Illus.). 224p. 1995. 45.00 (*0-8039-8827-3*); pap. 14.99 (*0-8039-8828-1*) Sage.

Crawford, Mary & Unger, Rhoda K. In Our Own Words: Readings on the Psychology of Women & Gender. LC 96-38653. 350p. (C). 1996. pap. 29.38 (*0-07-065929-X*) McGraw.

— Women & Gender: A Feminist Psychology. 2nd ed. (C). 1995. pap. text 36.50 (*0-07-065942-7*) McGraw.

Crawford, Mary, jt. auth. see Unger, Rhoda K.

Crawford, Mary, jt. ed. see Kimmel, Ellen B.

Crawford, Mary, ed. see Tippitt, John Allen.

Crawford, Mary C. Goethe & His Woman Friends. LC 72-1563. (Studies in German Literature: No. 13). (Illus.). 1972. reprint ed. lib. bdg. 75.00 (*0-8383-1448-1*) M S G Haskell Hse.

***Crawford, Mary C.** The Hundred Dollar Mystery. 126p. 1999. pap. 9.99 (*0-88092-420-9*) Royal Fireworks.

Crawford, Mary C. Little Pilgrimages among Old New England Inns: Being an Account of Little Journeys to Various Quaint Inns & Hotelries of Colonial New England. (Illus.). 381p. 1998. reprint ed. pap. 30.00 (*0-7884-0873-9*, C608) Heritage Bk.

— Romance of the American Theatre. LC 70-144957. 1971. reprint ed. 59.00 (*0-403-00909-X*) Scholarly.

— The Romance of the American Theatre. 508p. 1998. reprint ed. lib. bdg. 120.00 (*0-7812-4790-X*) Rprt Serv.

Crawford, Mary E., jt. auth. see Dockery, Gary L.

Crawford, Mary M. Student Folkways & Spending at Indiana University, 1940-1941. LC 68-58563. (Columbia University. Studies in the Social Sciences: No. 499). reprint ed. 34.50 (*0-404-51499-5*) AMS Pr.

Crawford-Mason, Clare, jt. auth. see Dobyns, Lloyd.

Crawford, Matsu. My Head Is Bloody but Unbowed. 111p. (Orig.). 1983. pap. 5.00 (*0-9612862-0-2*) R E F Typesetting Pub.

Crawford, Maureen. Handmade Greeting Cards. LC 90-28753. (Illus.). 128p. (YA). (gr. 6 up). 1992. pap. 10.95 (*0-8069-8327-2*) Sterling.

Crawford, Max. Lords of the Plains: A Novel. LC 96-41322. 320p. 1997. 14.95 (*0-8061-2908-5*) U of Okla Pr.

Crawford, Medorem. Journal of Medorem Crawford. 26p. 1987. reprint ed. pap. 6.95 (*0-87770-041-9*) Ye Galleon.

Crawford, Megan. Illusions, Delusions, & Other Real Things. LC 96-84394. 83p. (Orig.). 1996. pap. 9.95 (*1-883033-03-9*) Flats Pub.

Crawford, Megan, et al. Taking Issue: Debates in Guidance & Counselling in Learning. LC 98-17804. (Illus.). 224p. (C). 1998. pap. 24.99 (*0-415-19667-1*) Routledge.

Crawford, Meodrem. Journal of Medorem Crawford: An Account of His Trip Across the Plains with the Oregon Pioneers in 1842. 26p. 1986. reprint ed. pap. 10.00 (*0-8466-0141-9*, S-141, Shorey Pubns) Shoreys Bkstore.

***Crawford, Michael.** Parcel Arrived Safely: Tied with String: My Autobiography. (Illus.). 384p. 2000. 24.95 (*0-7126-8440-9*, Pub. by CEN3) Trafalgar.

Crawford, Michael. The Roman Republic. 2nd ed. LC 93-1102. (Illus.). 264p. 1993. pap. 16.00 (*0-674-77927-4*) HUP.

— Roman Republican Coinage. LC 77-164450. (Illus.). 944p. 1975. text 300.00 (*0-521-07492-4*) Cambridge U Pr.

Crawford, Michael & Whitehead, David, eds. Archaic & Classical Greece: A Selection of Ancient Sources in Translation. LC 82-4355. 660p. 1983. text 100.00 (*0-521-22775-5*); pap. text 39.95 (*0-521-29638-2*) Cambridge U Pr.

Crawford, Michael, jt. auth. see Turner, Dennis.

Crawford, Michael E., jt. auth. see Austin, David R.

Crawford, Michael E., jt. auth. see Kays, William M.

Crawford, Michael H. Current Diagnosis & Treatment in Cardiology. 900p. (C). 1995. pap. text 54.95 (*0-8385-1444-8*, A1444-7, Apple Lange Med) McGraw.

— The Origins of Native Americans: Evidence from Anthropological Genetics. LC 97-7474. (Illus.). 326p. (C). 1998. text 64.95 (*0-521-59280-1*) Cambridge U Pr.

— Unstable Angina: Diagnosis & Management: Commentary on the Agency for Health Care Policy & Research Clinical Practice Guidelines. LC 96-26865. 225p. 1997. pap. text 36.95 (*0-412-09771-0*, Pub. by E A) OUP.

Crawford, Michael H., ed. Atlas of Heart Disease: Heart Diseases in the Presence of Disorders of Other Organ Systems. (Atlas of Heart Diseases Ser.: Vol 6). (Illus.). 264p. 1995. text 134.00 (*1-878132-28-8*) Current Med.

— Current Developments in Anthropological Genetics, Black Caribs Vol. 3: A Case Study in Biocultural Adaptation. 412p. 1984. 95.00 (*0-306-41308-6*, Plenum Trade) Perseus Pubng.

Crawford, Michael H. & Mielke, James H., eds. Current Developments in Anthropological Genetics Vol. 2: Ecology & Population Structure. LC 79-24900. (Illus.). 542p. 1982. 95.00 (*0-306-40842-2*, Plenum Trade) Perseus Pubng.

Crawford, Michael H., jt. ed. see Kennedy, Gemma T.

***Crawford, Michael J.** Spanish American War: Historical Overview & Select Bibliography. 138p. 1998. per. 9.00 (*0-16-061430-X*) USGPO.

Crawford, Michael J., ed. Naval Documents of the American Revolution Vol. 10: American Theater: October 1, 1777-December 31, 1777; European Theater: October 1, 1777-December 31, 1777. 1374p. 1996. boxed set 61.00 (*0-16-045286-4*, Defense Dept) USGPO.

Crawford, Michael J. & Hughes, Christine F. The Reestablishment of the Navy, 1787-1801: Historical Overview & Select Bibliography. (Naval History Bibliogrpahies Ser.: No. 4). 1995. pap. text 3.50 (*0-945274-32-7*) Naval Hist Ctr.

Crawford, Michael J., et al. The Spanish-American War: Historical Overview & Select Bibliography. LC 98-39710. (Naval History Bibliogrpahies Ser.). 1998. 9.00 (*0-945274-40-8*) Naval Hist Ctr.

Crawford, Michael J., jt. ed. see Dudley, William S.

***Crawford, Mimi.** Psalms from My Soul. LC 99-66345. 58p. 1999. pap. 7.99 (*1-891774-11-5*) Path Pubng.

Crawford, Moira. Natural Way: Allergies: Your Guide to Complementary Therapies, Alternative Techniques & Conventional Treatments. LC 97-45049. (Natural Way Ser.). (Illus.). 128p. 1998. pap. 5.95 (*1-86204-114-8*, Pub. by Element MA) Penguin Putnam.

Crawford, Muriel L. CPS - Law & the Life Insurance Contract Appendix. 7th ed. 72p. (C). 1995. text 4.50 (*0-256-20251-6*, Irwn McGrw-H) McGrw-H Hghr Educ.

— Law & the Life Insurance Contract. 7th ed. LC 93-29937. (Series in Finance). 720p. (C). 1993. text 57.50 (*0-256-13566-5*, Irwn Prfssnl) McGraw-Hill Prof.

— Law & the Life Insurance Contract. 8th ed. LC 97-20964. 624p. 1997. 88.44 (*0-256-16699-4*) McGraw.

— Life & Health Insurance Law. 7th rev. ed. LC 93-29936. (Series in Finance). 720p. (C). 1993. text 19.40 (*0-256-13567-3*, Irwn Prfssnl) McGraw-Hill Prof.

Crawford, Muriel L. & Beadles, William T. Life & Health Insurance Law. 6th ed. (C). 1988. text 21.00 (*0-256-07121-7*, Irwn McGrw-H) McGrw-H Hghr Educ.

Crawford, N. & Taylor, D. E., eds. Interaction of Cells with Natural & Foreign Surfaces. LC 86-16953. 344p. 1986. 79.50 (*0-306-42373-1*, Plenum Trade) Perseus Pubng.

***Crawford, Natalie W. & Moon, Chung-In.** Emerging Threats, Force Structures & the Role of Air Power in Korea. 372p. (C). 2000. pap. 30.00 (*0-8330-2830-8*, CF-152-AF) Rand Corp.

Crawford, Nelson A. Ethics of Journalism. 1988. reprint ed. lib. bdg. 79.00 (*0-7812-0269-8*) Rprt Serv.

— Ethics of Journalism. LC 71-131676. 1970. reprint ed. 55.00 (*0-403-00563-9*) Scholarly.

— We Liberals. LC 68-22908. (Essay Index Reprint Ser.). 1977. 18.95 (*0-8369-0349-8*) Ayer.

Crawford, Neta C. & Klotz, Audie, eds. How Sanctions Work: Lessons from South Africa. LC 98-38459. 277p. 1999. text 59.95 (*0-312-21854-0*) St Martin.

Crawford, Nigel, et al. Key Moments in Fashion: The Evolution of Style. (Illus.). 176p. 1999. 29.95 (*0-600-59396-7*, Pub. by Hamlyn Publishing Group Ltd) Sterling.

Crawford, O. G. The Eye Goddess. (Illus.). 168p. 1991. reprint ed. pap. 19.95 (*1-878980-04-1*) Delphi IL.

Crawford, Osbert G. The Fung Kingdom of Sennar: With a Geographical Account of the Middle Nile Region. LC 74-15021. (Illus.). reprint ed. 84.50 (*0-404-12019-9*) AMS Pr.

Crawford, Patricia. Women & Religion in England, 1500-1750. (Christianity & Society in the Modern World Ser.). (Illus.). 280p. (C). 1996. pap. 27.99 (*0-415-01697-5*) Routledge.

Crawford, Patricia & Tonkinson, Myrna. The Missing Chapters: Women Staff at the University of Western Australia 1963-1987. pap. 9.95 (*0-86422-073-1*, Pub. by Univ of West Aust Pr) Intl Spec Bk.

Crawford, Patricia, jt. auth. see Mendelson, Sara.

Crawford, Patricia M. & Gowing, Laura. Women's Worlds in Seventeenth-Century England, 1580-1720: Sourcebook. LC 99-24671. 272p. 1999. pap. 24.99 (*0-415-15638-6*) Routledge.

***Crawford, Patricia M. & Gowing, Laura, eds.** Women's Worlds in Seventeenth-Century England, 1580-1720: Sourcebook. LC 99-24671. 272p. (C). 1999. text 85.00 (*0-415-15637-8*) Routledge.

Crawford, Paul, et al. Communicating Care: Nursing Language in Action. (Illus.). 1998. pap. 39.50 (*0-7487-3306-X*, Pub. by S Thornes Pubs) Trans-Atl Phila.

Crawford, Peter. Nomads of the Wind: A Natural History of Polynesia. (Illus.). 272p. 1994. 32.95 (*0-563-36707-5*, BBC-Parkwest) Parkwest Pubns.

Crawford, Peter & Hafsteinsson, Sigurjon B., eds. Construction of the Viewer: Media Ethnography & the Anthropology of Audiences. (Nordic Anthropological Film Association Ser.: Vol. 3). 270p. (Orig.). (C). 1996. pap. text 35.00 (*87-89825-06-3*) Smyrna.

Crawford, Peter I., ed. The Nordic Eye: Proceedings from NAFA I. 128p. 1993. 22.00 (*87-89825-00-4*) Smyrna.

Crawford, Peter I. & Turton, David, eds. Film As Ethnography. LC 92-387. 1992. text 35.00 (*0-7190-3683-6*) Manchester Univ Pr.

Crawford, Peter I., ed. see Simonsen, Jan K.

Crawford, Phyllis, jt. auth. see Sears, Minnie E.

Crawford, R., ed. Major Employers of Europe 1999: The Job Finders Directory. 1100p. 1999. 270.00 (*1-86099-155-6*, Pub. by G & W) Gale.

Crawford, R., ed. see Blake, P.

Crawford, R. D., ed. Poultry Breeding & Genetics. (Developments in Animal & Veterinary Science Ser.: No. 22). 1123p. 1990. 205.00 (*0-444-88557-9*) Elsevier.

Crawford, R. H. Fifty - Fifty: The Misadventures of the Judge, the Jaguar & the Jordan Girl. (Illus.). 256p. (Orig.). 1995. 17.95 (*0-9643695-5-9*); pap. 9.95 (*0-9643695-4-0*) DOBO Bks.

— The Witches Three. LC 97-155475. (Illus.). 272p. 1997. 17.95 (*0-9643695-0-8*, Green Jaguar) DOBO Bks.

Crawford, R. J. Plastics Engineering. (Illus.). 360p. 1981. text 91.00 (*0-08-026262-7*, Pergamon Pr) Elsevier.

— Plastics Engineering. (Illus.). 360p. 1981. pap. text 32.00 (*0-08-026263-5*, Pergamon Pr) Elsevier.

— Plastics Engineering. 3rd ed. LC 97-36604. 352p. 1998. pap. text 49.95 (*0-7506-3764-1*) Buttrwrth-Heinemann.

Crawford, R. J., jt. ed. see Crawford, William R., Sr., et al.

Crawford, R. M. Disturbance & Recovery in Arctic Lands: An Ecological Perspective: Proceedings of the NATO Advanced Research Workshop on Disturbance & Recovery of Arctic Terrestrial Ecosystems, Rovaniemi, Finland, 24-30 Sept. 1995. LC 96-51038. (NATO ASI Series Partnership Subseries 2, Environment: Vol. 2). 632p. (C). 1997. text 311.00 (*0-7923-4418-9*) Kluwer Academic.

— Studies in Plant Survival: An Ecophysiological Examination of Plant Distribution. (Illus.). 300p. (C). 1988. pap. text 49.95 (*0-632-01477-6*) Blackwell Sci.

Crawford, Ralston. Music in the Street: Photographs of New Orleans by Ralston Crawford. Lawrence, John H., ed. & intro. by. LC 83-80537. (Illus.). xii, 36p. (Orig.). 1983. pap. 10.00 (*0-917860-14-4*) Historic New Orleans.

***Crawford, Randy.** Tangrams Pack: The Ancient Chinese Puzzle of Mystery & Challenge. 1999. pap. text 29.95 (*0-8048-3209-9*) Tuttle Pubng.

Crawford, Ray, ed. World Record Game Fishes, 1996. (Illus.). 354p. 1996. pap. 11.75 (*0-935217-22-3*) Intl Game Fish.

— World Record Game Fishes, 1997. 22nd rev. ed. (Illus.). 352p. 1997. pap. 11.75 (*0-935217-23-1*) Intl Game Fish.

C

— World Record Game Fishes 1998. 23rd rev. ed. (Illus.). 352p. 1999. pap. 12.95 (*0-935217-24-X*) Intl Game Fish.

Crawford, Ray, ed. see IGFA Staff.

Crawford, R.D.L., jt. auth. see Rich C & Crawford,R.D.L, C.

Crawford, Richard. The American Musical Landscape. LC 92-11237. (Ernest Bloch Lectures). 390p. (C). 1993. 55.00 (*0-520-07764-4*, Pub. by U CA Pr) Cal Prin Full Svc.

***Crawford, Richard.** American Musical Landscape. rev. ed. (Ernest Bloch Lectures Ser.: Vol. 8). (Illus.). 390p. 2000. pap. 19.95 (*0-520-22482-5*, Pub. by U CA Pr) Cal Prin Full Svc.

Crawford, Richard. American Studies & American Musicology: A Point of View & a Case in Point. LC 75-874. (I.S.A.M. Monographs: No. 4). 34p. 1975. pap. 10.00 (*0-914678-03-5*) Inst Am Music.

***Crawford, Richard.** The Clermont County, Ohio Bicentennial Book of Days. (Illus.). 152p. 1999. pap. 20.00 (*1-890538-24-8*) Rhiannon Pubns.

Crawford, Richard. Lightening Across the River: The Story of Gen. John Hunt Morgan's Raid on Clermont County, Ohio - U. S. Grant Clermont County's Most Noted Son. Spafford, John M., ed. (Illus.). 120p. (Orig.). 1997. pap. 15.00 (*1-890538-18-3*) Rhiannon Pubns.

— Music in American Life. (C). pap. text. write for info. (*0-393-97410-3*) Norton.

— Music in American Life. (C). 2000. pap. text. write for info. (*0-393-97409-X*) Norton.

— Studying American Music. (I.S.A.M. Special Publications: No. 3). 24p. (Orig.). 1985. pap. 4.00 (*0-914678-25-6*) Inst Am Music.

— Thunder Before the Dawn: Stories of the Early Settlers & Warriors in Clermont County, Ohio. Spafford, John M., ed. (Illus.). 154p. (Orig.). 1995. pap. 15.00 (*1-890538-17-5*) Rhiannon Pubns.

— Uneasy Spirits: Ghost Stories & Haunted Places of Clermont County, Ohio. 1997. pap. 15.00 (*1-890538-19-1*) Rhiannon Pubns.

Crawford, Richard, ed. Civil War Songbook. 157p. 1977. pap. 9.95 (*0-486-23422-3*) Dover.

Crawford, Richard, et al, eds. A Celebration of American Music: Word & Music in Honor of H. Wiley Hitchcock. (Illus.). 536p. 1990. text 54.50 (*0-472-09400-9*, 09400) U of Mich Pr.

Crawford, Richard & Magee, Jeffrey. Jazz Standards on Record, 1900-1942: A Core Repertory. (CBMR Monographs: No. 4). 1992. pap. text 10.00 (*0-929911-03-2*) CCCBMR.

Crawford, Richard, jt. auth. see McKay, David P.

Crawford, Richard, ed. see Billings, William.

Crawford, Richard, ed. see Billings, William, et al.

Crawford, Richard D. In the Era of Human Capital: The Emergence of Talent, Intelligence, & Knowledge As the Worldwide Economic Force & What It Means to Managers & Investors. 256p. 1991. 22.95 (*0-88730-506-7*, HarpBusn) HarpInfo.

— In the Era of Human Capital: The Emergence of Talent, Intelligence, & Knowledge As the Worldwide Economic Force & What It Means to Managers & Investors. LC 91-58514. 208p. 1992. reprint ed. pap. 12.00 (*0-88730-535-0*, HarpBusn) HarpInfo.

Crawford, Richard D. & Sihler, William W. The Troubled Money Business: The Death of the Old Order & the Rise of the New Order. LC 92-54591. 304p. 1992. pap. 12.00 (*0-88730-573-3*, HarpBusn) HarpInfo.

Crawford, Richard L. Andrew Law, American Psalmodist. LC 81-1509. (Music Ser.). (Illus.). xix, 424p. 1981. reprint ed. lib. bdg. 42.50 (*0-306-76090-8*) Da Capo.

***Crawford, Richard L., ed.** Selected Web Sites for Biomedical, Pharmaceutical, Veterinary & Animal Sciences. 53p. (C). 2000. pap. text 20.00 (*0-7881-8905-0*) DIANE Pub.

Crawford, Richard W. A Guide to the San Diego Historical Society Public Records Collection. (Illus.). 86p. (Orig.). 1987. pap. 9.95 (*0-918740-11-8*) San Diego Hist.

— Stranger Than Fiction: Vignettes of San Diego History. (Illus.). vii, 72p. (Orig.). 1995. pap., mass mkt. 9.95 (*0-918740-19-3*) San Diego Hist.

Crawford, Robert. Avoiding Counselor Malpractice. LC 93-33194. (ACA Legal Ser.: No. 12). 102p. 1994. pap. text 18.95 (*1-55620-130-3*, 72312) Am Coun Assn.

— Devolving English Literature. 336p. 1992. pap. text 27.00 (*0-19-811955-0*) OUP.

***Crawford, Robert.** The God Man World Triangle: A Dialogue Between Science & Religion. 2000. pap. 22.95 (*0-312-23238-1*) St Martin.

Crawford, Robert. Identifying Poets: Self & Territory in 20th-Century Poetry. 256p. (C). 1994. 55.00 (*0-7486-0409-X*, Pub. by Edinburgh U Pr) Col U Pr.

— Masculinity. 68p. 1997. pap. 14.95 (*0-224-04371-4*, Pub. by Jonathan Cape) Trafalgar.

— The Savage & the City in the Work of T. S. Eliot. (Oxford English Monographs). (Illus.). 264p. 1988. 65.00 (*0-19-812869-X*) OUP.

— The Savage & the City in the Work of T. S. Eliot. (Oxford English Monographs). (Illus.). 264p. 1991. reprint ed. pap. text 21.00 (*0-19-812251-9*) OUP.

— A Scottish Assembly. (Illus.). 64p. 1992. pap. 15.95 (*0-7011-3595-6*, Pub. by Chatto & Windus) Trafalgar.

— The Shroud Society. 192p. 1993. 19.50 (*0-7451-8620-3*, Black Dagger) Chivers N Amer.

***Crawford, Robert.** Spirit Machines. 1999. pap. 17.95 (*0-224-05901-7*, Pub. by Random) Trafalgar.

Crawford, Robert. Talkies. 80p. 1992. pap. 15.95 (*0-7011-3928-5*, Pub. by Chatto & Windus) Trafalgar.

***Crawford, Robert, ed.** Robert Burns & Cultural Authority. 240p. 1999. pap. 27.00 (*0-7486-1295-5*, Pub. by Edinburgh U Pr) Col U Pr.

Crawford, Robert, ed. Robert Burns & Cultural Authority. LC 96-61362. 256p. 1997. text 29.95 (*0-87745-578-3*) U of Iowa Pr.

— The Scottish Invention of English Literature. LC 97-27464. 290p. (C). 1998. 59.95 (*0-521-59038-8*) Cambridge U Pr.

***Crawford, Robert.** Tom Sawyer. 32p. (J). (gr. 1-3). 1998. 12.99 (*1-929174-00-4*) Oshkosh BGosh.

Crawford, Robert & Kinloch, David, eds. Reading Douglas Dunn. (Modern Scottish Writers Ser.). 256p. 1993. pap. text 27.50 (*0-7486-0369-7*, Pub. by Edinburgh U Pr) Col U Pr.

Crawford, Robert & Nairn, Thom, eds. The Arts of Alasdair Gray. (Illus.). 200p. 1992. pap. text 29.00 (*0-7486-0294-1*, Pub. by Edinburgh U Pr) Col U Pr.

Crawford, Robert F. Walking Trails of Southern Wisconsin. LC 93-39165. 1994. 35.00 (*0-299-13840-2*); pap. 16.95 (*0-299-13844-5*) U of Wis Pr.

Crawford, Robert L. Crawford. "Laurus Crawfurdiana" Memorials of That Branch of the Crawford Family, Which Comprises the Descendants of John Crawford of Virginia, 1660-1883, with Notices of the Allied Families. (Illus.). 185p. 1995. reprint ed. pap. 28.50 (*0-8328-4762-3*); reprint ed. lib. bdg. 38.50 (*0-8328-4761-5*) Higginson Bk Co.

— The Lost Hardys a Concordance. 2nd rev. ed. (Illus.). 96p. 1996. spiral bd. 17.95 (*0-9639949-6-4*) SynSine Pr.

***Crawford, Robert M.** Idealism & Realism in International Relations. LC 99-54968. (Advances in International Relations & Politics Ser.). 224p. 2000. 85.00 (*0-415-15473-1*) Routledge.

Crawford, Robert M. Regime Theory in the Post-Cold War World: Rethinking Neoliberal Approaches to International Relations. (Illus.). 250p. 1996. text 77.95 (*1-85521-848-8*, Pub. by Dartmth Pub) Ashgate Pub Co.

***Crawford, Robert M. A. & Jarvis, Darryl S. L., eds.** International Relations--Still an American Social Science? Toward Diversity in International Thought. LC 99-88338. (C). 2000. text 88.50 (*0-7914-4703-0*) State U NY Pr.

Crawford, Robert P. The Techniques of Creative Thinking: How to Use Your Ideas to Achieve Success. LC 54-6456. 287p. 1964. reprint ed. pap. 19.00 (*0-87034-010-7*) Fraser Pub Co.

— Think for Yourself. LC 64-8498. 250p. 1979. reprint ed. pap. 17.00 (*0-87034-011-5*) Fraser Pub Co.

Crawford, Robert W. On Board: Guiding Principles for Trustees of Not-for-Profit Organizations. LC 90-50992. (Illus.). (Orig.). 1991. pap. 7.50 (*0-9611710-5-7*) Western States.

Crawford, Roberta. The Iron Elephant: What You Should Know about the Dangers of Excess Body Iron. LC 92-60466. 172p. (Orig.). 1992. pap. 12.95 (*0-9632547-0-7*) Vida Pub.

— Tick . . . Tick . . . Tick . . . Suspenseful Tale of Outrageous Medical Ignorance. Britt, Alan, ed. LC 94-61928. 375p. 1995. 16.95 (*0-9632547-2-3*) Vida Pub.

Crawford, Roger. Concepts & Problems in Physics, Pt. 1. 168p. 1996. pap. text, spiral bd. 21.95 (*0-7872-2005-1*) Kendall-Hunt.

— How High Can You Bounce: Turn Setbacks into Comebacks. 256p. 1999. reprint ed. pap. 13.95 (*0-553-37856-2*) Bantam.

— Managing Information Technology in Secondary Schools. LC 96-40270. 240p. (C). 1997. 75.00 (*0-415-10734-2*); pap. 25.99 (*0-415-10735-0*) Routledge.

***Crawford, Roger.** Playing from the Heart: A Portrait in Courage. rev. ed. LC 97-26575. (Illus.). 224p. 1998. pap., per. 14.00 (*0-7615-0440-0*) Prima Pub.

Crawford, Roger & Bowker, Michael. Playing from the Heart. 200p. 1994. 17.95 (*1-55958-018-6*) Prima Pub.

Crawford, Ronald, tr. see Weissweiler, Eva, ed.

Crawford, Ronald L. Lignin Biodegradation & Transformation. LC 80-39557. 170p. 1981. 37.50 (*0-471-05743-6*) Krieger.

Crawford, Ronald L. & Crawford, Don L., eds. Bioremediation: Principles & Applications. LC 95-51193. (Biotechnology Research Ser.: No. 5). (Illus.). 412p. (C). 1997. text 110.00 (*0-521-47041-2*) Cambridge U Pr.

Crawford, Ronald L., ed. see International Symposium on Microbial Growth on C1.

Crawford, Ronald L., tr. see Weissweiler, Eva, ed.

Crawford, Rosemary & Crawford, Donald. Michael & Natasha: The Life & Love of Michael II, the Last of the Romanov Tsars. LC 97-22550. (Illus.). 433p. 1997. 29.50 (*0-684-83430-8*) S&S Trade.

Crawford, Roy E., III, et al. California Taxes: June 1993 Update, Vol. 1. 2nd ed. Gamble, Carol E., ed. LC 88-70962. 368p. 1993. 59.00 (*0-88124-648-4*, TX-30944) Cont Ed Bar-CA.

— California Taxes: June 1993 Update, Vol. 2. 2nd ed. Gamble, Carol E., ed. LC 88-70962. 278p. 1993. 59.00 (*0-88124-656-5*, TX-30954) Cont Ed Bar-CA.

— California Taxes, Vol. 1: May 1991 Update. 2nd ed. Gamble, Carol E., ed. LC 88-70962. 325p. 1991. ring bd. 55.00 (*0-88124-405-8*, TX-30942) Cont Ed Bar-CA.

— California Taxes, Vol. 2: May 1991 Update. 2nd ed. Gamble, Carol E., ed. LC 88-70962. 334p. 1991. ring bd. 55.00 (*0-88124-406-6*, TX-30952) Cont Ed Bar-CA.

Crawford, Russell E. Florida Criminal Practice & Procedure, 2 vols. 2nd ed. LC 99-63512. 1750p. 1999. 180.00 (*0-327-01417-2*, 6871011) LEXIS Pub.

— Florida Criminal Practice & Procedure, Vol. 1. 2nd ed. LC 99-63512. 1750p. 1999. write for info. (*0-327-01418-0*, 6871011) LEXIS Pub.

— Florida Criminal Practice & Procedure, Vol. 2. 2nd ed. LC 99-63512. 1750p. 1999. write for info. (*0-327-01419-9*, 6871011) LEXIS Pub.

— Florida Criminal Practice & Procedure: 1998 Cumulative Supplement, Vols. 1 & 2. 1998. 80.00 (*0-327-00138-0*, 68717-11) LEXIS Pub.

Crawford, Ruth. Ruth Crawford: Music for Small Orchestra (1926) & Suite #2 for 4 Strings & Piano (1929) 2nd rev. ed. Tick, Judith & Schneider, Wayne, eds. (Music of the U. S. A. - Recent Researches in American Music Ser.: Vol. MUSA1). xxvi, 63p. 1993. pap. 45.00 (*0-89579-326-1*) A-R Eds.

Crawford, Ruth B. The Woods Afire: The Memories of a Georgia Teacher Before & After Desegregation. LC 96-26366. 1996. pap. 15.00 (*0-916147-98-3*) Regent Pr.

Crawford, S. Cosmeceuticals. 100p. 2000. 1995.00 (*0-614-10253-7*) Lead Edge Reports.

— Gift Wrap & Accessories. 150p. 1999. 1995.00 (*0-614-06124-5*, LE503) Lead Edge Reports.

— The U. S. Greeting Cards Market. 210p. 1998. 1995.00 (*0-318-00525-5*) Lead Edge Reports.

Crawford, S. & Sullivan, G. The Power of Birthdays, Stars & Numbers. LC 98-13941. 1998. pap. 0.24 (*0-345-41819-0*) Ballantine Pub Grp.

Crawford, S. Cromwell. Dilemmas of Life & Death: Hindu Ethics in a North American Context. LC 93-50087. 233p. (C). 1994. text 57.50 (*0-7914-2165-1*); pap. text 19.95 (*0-7914-2166-X*) State U NY Pr.

Crawford, S. J. The Old English Heptateuch, Ms Cott. (EETS, OS Ser.: Vol. 160). 1974. reprint ed. 65.00 (*0-8115-3417-0*) Periodicals Srv.

Crawford, S. J., ed. Byrthferth's Manual Vol. I: Text, Translation, Sources, & Appendices, Vol. I. (EETS Original Ser.: Vol. 177). 1966. reprint ed. 30.00 (*0-19-722177-7*, Pub. by EETS) Boydell & Brewer.

Crawford, Sally S. Childhood in Anglo-Saxon England. 1999. 36.00 (*0-7509-1918-3*) Bks Intl VA.

***Crawford, Sammie.** Gourd Fun for Everyone. LC 99-87186. (Illus.). 128p. 2000. pap. 22.99 (*0-89134-993-6*) F & W Pubns Inc.

Crawford, Samuel J. Kansas in the Sixties. (Illus.). 441p. (C). 1995. pap. 22.95 (*1-878882-08-2*) KS Heritage Pr.

Crawford, Scott, ed. see DeThomas, Art.

Crawford, Shane, et al. Extreme Student Life: Student Discipleship. 38p. (YA). (gr. 9-12). 1996. 7.00 (*1-888220-01-5*) Reality Living.

Crawford, Sharon. The ABCs of Windows 98. 2nd ed. LC 98-84013. 384p. 1998. 19.99 (*0-7821-1953-0*) Sybex.

— Running Microsoft Windows NT Server for Small Businesses. LC 98-9358. 1997. pap. text 39.99 (*1-57231-688-8*) Microsoft.

— Windows 98 No Experience Required. LC 98-84015. (No Experience Required Ser.). 544p. 1998. 24.99 (*0-7821-2128-4*) Sybex.

***Crawford, Sharon.** Windows 2000. (Missing Manuals Ser.). (Illus.). 2000. pap. 19.95 (*1-56592-865-2*) OReilly & Assocs.

— Windows 2000 Pro: The Missing Manual. 2000. 19.95 (*1-58780-025-X*) Carew.

Crawford, Sharon, jt. auth. see Russell, Charlie.

Crawford, Sheryl. Psalms for a Child's Heart. (Illus.). 64p. (J). (ps-2). 1997. 11.99 (*0-7814-3004-6*, Chariot Bks) Chariot Victor.

Crawford, Sheryl Ann. Psalms for a Child's Heart. LC 97-7407. 64p. (J). (ps-2). 1997. write for info. (*0-7814-0022-8*, Chariot Bks) Chariot Victor.

Crawford, Shirley A. Science & Society 10th ed. 202p. (C). 1994. text 37.40 (*0-536-58555-5*) Pearson Custom.

— Science & Society 11th ed. 202p. (C). 1995. text 37.40 (*0-536-58990-9*) Pearson Custom.

***Crawford, Sidnie White.** The Temple Scroll & Related Texts. (Companion to the Qumran Scrolls Ser.: No. 2). 100p. 2000. pap. 14.95 (*1-84127-056-3*, Pub. by Sheffield Acad) CUP Services.

Crawford, Stanley. Log of the S. S. the Mrs. Unguentine. 110p. 1988. pap. 9.95 (*0-945953-02-X*) Living Batch Bks.

— Mayordomo: Chronicle of an Acequia in Northern New Mexico. LC 87-24487. (Illus.). 231p. (C). 1993. reprint ed. pap. 13.95 (*0-8263-1445-7*) U of NM Pr.

— Some Instructions to My Wife: Concerning the Upkeep of the House & Marriage & to My Son & Daughter Concerning the Conduct of Their Childhood. LC 85-72645. 176p. 1985. reprint ed. 20.00 (*0-916583-14-7*) Dalkey Arch.

— Some Instructions to My Wife: Concerning the Upkeep of the House & Marriage & to My Son & Daughter Concerning the Conduct of Their Childhood. LC 85-72645. 176p. 1996. reprint ed. pap. 11.95 (*0-916583-15-5*) Dalkey Arch.

Crawford, Stanley G. A Garlic Testament: Seasons on a Small New Mexico Farm. LC 97-51535. 241p. 1998. reprint ed. pap. 14.95 (*0-8263-1960-2*) U of NM Pr.

Crawford, Stella & Vandivier, Phillip L. Our Schools: What Happened? How to Fix Them. 236p. 1998. pap. 26.50 (*1-57502-693-7*, PO1958) Morris Pubng.

Crawford, Steve. The SAS Encyclopedia. Brown Packaging Books, Ltd. Staff, ed. 288p. 1998. 29.95 (*0-9666771-0-2*) Lewis Intl Inc.

— SAS Gulf Warriors: The Story Behind Bravo Two Zero. (Illus.). 192p. 1999. reprint ed. pap. text 21.00 (*0-7881-6280-2*) DIANE Pub.

***Crawford, Steve.** Unarmed Combat. 2000. text 22.95 (*0-312-26436-4*) St Martin.

Crawford, Susan H. Beyond Dolls & Guns: 101 Ways to Help Children Avoid Gender Bias. LC 95-31952. 212p. 1995. pap. 9.95 (*0-435-08129-2*, 08129) Heinemann.

Crawford, Susan Y., et al. From Print to Electronic: The Transformation of Scientific Communication. LC 96-26791. 118p. 1997. 39.50 (*1-57387-030-7*) Info Today Inc.

Crawford, Sybil. Saline County, Arkansas, Probate Book D: March 25, 1862 to September 8, 1865. 165p. 1988. ring bd. 14.00 (*0-945183-07-0*) Saline Cnty Hist Heritage Soc.

— Saline County, Arkansas, Will & Probate Records, 1842-1905. 291p. 1987. ring bd. 27.00 (*0-945183-08-9*) Saline Cnty Hist Heritage Soc.

— Saline County Arkansas Will Book A-1: September 15, 1842 to December 27, 1861. 54p. 1987. pap. 10.00 (*0-945183-04-6*) Saline Cnty Hist Heritage Soc.

Crawford, T. Hugh. Modernism, Medicine & William Carlos Williams. LC 93-19161. (Series for Science & Culture of the Oklahoma Project for Discourse & Theory: Vol. 1). (Illus.). 208p. 1995. pap. 12.95 (*0-8061-2588-8*) U of Okla Pr.

Crawford, Tad. Business & Legal Forms for Authors & Self-Publishers. 2nd rev. ed. LC 96-84613. 192p. 1996. pap. 19.95 (*1-880559-50-1*) Allworth Pr.

— Business & Legal Forms for Authors & Self-Publishers: With Forms on CD-ROM. rev. ed. LC 99-52297. (Business & Legal Forms Ser.). 192p. 1999. pap. 22.95 incl. cd-rom (*1-58115-039-3*, Pub. by Allworth Pr) Watsn-Guptill.

— Business & Legal Forms for Crafts. LC 97-72221. 144p. 1998. pap. 19.95 (*1-880559-87-0*) Allworth Pr.

— Business & Legal Forms for Fine Artists. LC 95-76695. 144p. 1995. reprint ed. pap. 16.95 (*1-880559-30-7*) Allworth Pr.

— Business & Legal Forms for Fine Artists. rev. ed. LC 98-74528. 144p. 1999. pap. 19.95 incl. audio compact disk (*1-58115-031-8*) Allworth Pr.

— Business & Legal Forms for Illustrators. LC 89-80741. 160p. (Orig.). 1990. pap. 15.95 (*0-927629-02-X*) Allworth Pr.

— Business & Legal Forms for Illustrators. rev. ed. LC 98-72756. (Business & Legal Forms Ser.). 176p. (Orig.). 1998. pap. 24.95 (*1-58115-008-3*) Allworth Pr.

— Business & Legal Forms for Photographers. LC 90-85554. 192p. (Orig.). 1991. pap. 18.95 (*0-9607118-2-1*) Allworth Pr.

— Business & Legal Forms for Photographers. 2nd rev. ed. LC 97-72216. 224p. (Orig.). 1997. pap. 24.95 (*1-880559-82-X*) Allworth Pr.

— Legal Guide for the Visual Artist. 3rd ed. LC 94-72263. 256p. 1994. pap. 19.95 (*0-927629-11-9*) Allworth Pr.

— Legal Guide for the Visual Artist. 4th ed. LC 98-72761. (Illus.). 256p. 1999. pap. 19.95 (*1-58115-003-2*) Allworth Pr.

— The Secret Life of Money: How Money Can Be Food for the Soul. LC 96-84662. Orig. Title: The Secret Life of Money: Teaching Tales of Spending, Receiving, Saving, & Owing. 304p. 1996. reprint ed. pap. 14.95 (*1-880559-51-X*) Allworth Pr.

— The Writer's Legal Guide. 2nd ed. LC 98-72758. 320p. 1998. 19.95 (*1-58115-004-0*) Allworth Pr.

Crawford, Tad & Bruck, Eva D. Business & Legal Forms for Graphic Designers. 224p. 1999. text 24.95 (*1-58115-030-X*) Allworth Pr.

— Business & Legal Forms for Graphic Designers. rev. ed. LC 95-75287. 224p. 1995. pap. 22.95 (*1-880559-26-9*) Allworth Pr.

Crawford, Tad & Lyons, Tony. The Writer's Legal Guide. rev. ed. LC 95-83301. 304p. 1996. pap. 19.95 (*0-927629-13-5*) Allworth Pr.

Crawford, Tad & Mellon, Susan. The Artist-Gallery Partnership: A Practical Guide to Consigning Art. 2nd rev. ed. LC 98-70405. 128p. 1998. pap. 16.95 (*1-880559-92-7*) Allworth Pr.

Crawford, Tad, ed. see American Institute of Graphic Arts Staff.

Crawford, Ted, jt. auth. see Ellis, Albert.

Crawford, Terry & Bertucci, Bob. Winning Track & Field Drills for Women. LC 81-85973. (Illus.). 128p. 1985. reprint ed. pap. 39.70 (*0-608-07063-7*, 206726900009) Bks Demand.

Crawford, Thomas. Burns: A Study of the Poems & Songs. xv, 400p. 1960. pap. 16.95 (*0-8047-0056-7*) Stanford U Pr.

— Burns & the French Revolution. (C). 1993. pap. 21.00 (*0-85411-046-1*, Pub. by Saltire Soc) St Mut.

— Puzzling Optical Illusions. LC 99-42487. 1999. pap. text 1.00 (*0-486-40151-0*) Dover.

Crawford, Thomas, ed. The Correspondence of James Boswell & William Johnson Temple, 1756-1795, Vol. 1. LC 97-60371. 544p. 1997. 80.00 (*0-300-07197-3*) Yale U Pr.

Crawford, Tim & Goy, Francois-Pierre, eds. The St. Petersburg "Swan" Manuscript. fac. ed. (Monuments of the Luetnist Art Ser.: Vol. II). (Illus.). 280p. (Orig.). 1994. pap. 98.00 (*0-936186-82-8*, LUTE-2) Edit Orphee.

Crawford, Tim R. Flute Magic: An Introduction to the Native American Flute. Joyce, Kathleen, ed. (Illus.). 80p. 1997. pap. 19.95 (*0-9659110-0-4*) RainDance Pubns.

***Crawford, Tim R.** Flute Magic: An Introduction to the Native American Flute. 2nd unabridged ed. Joyce-Grendahl, Kathleen, ed. (Illus.). 100p. 1999. pap. 24.95 (*0-9659110-1-2*) RainDance Pubns.

Crawford, Timothy G. Blessing & Curse in Syro-Palestinian Inscriptions of the Iron Age. LC 91-19608. (American University Studies: Theology & Religion: Ser. VII). 259p. (C). 1992. text 46.95 (*0-8204-1662-2*) P Lang Pubng.

Crawford, Todd V., jt. auth. see Cairns, John, Jr.

Crawford, Tom. If It Weren't for Trees. LC 86-20078. 65p. 1986. 15.95 (*0-89924-050-X*) Lynx Hse.

— The Story of King Arthur. LC 94-3363. (Children's Thrift Classics Ser.). (Illus.). 96p. (Orig.). (J). (gr. 4 up). 1994. pap. text 1.00 (*0-486-28347-X*) Dover.

Crawford, Tom, ed. & intro. see Gibbon, Lewis G.

Crawford, Vaughn E. Sumerian Economic Texts from the First Dynasty of Isin. LC 78-63528. (Babylonian Inscriptions in the Collection of James B. Nies Ser.: No. 9). reprint ed. 38.00 (*0-404-60139-1*) AMS Pr.

An Asterisk (*) at the beginning of an entry indicates that the title is appearing for the first time.

Crawford, Verlaine. Daughter of God: Angelic Messages of Wisdom & Love. 1998. pap. text 12.00 (*0-9641854-1-5*) High Castle.
— Ending the Battle Within: How to Create a Harmonious Life Work with Your Sub-Personalities. 197p. 1994. 14.95 (*0-9641854-0-7*) High Castle.
Crawford, Vicki L., et al, eds. Women in the Civil Rights Movement: Trailblazers & Torchbearers, 1941-1965. LC 93-2727. (Blacks in the Diaspora Ser.). (Illus.). 320p. 1993. 14.95 (*0-253-20832-7*) Ind U Pr.
Crawford, Vincent P. International Lending, Long-Term Credit Relationships, & Dynamic Contract Theory. LC 86-33743. (Studies in International Finance: No. 59). 34p. 1987. pap. text 13.50 (*0-88165-231-8*) Princeton U Int Finan Econ.
***Crawford, W. H. & Foy, R. H., eds.** Townlands in Ulster: Local History Studies. LC 99-175798. 239p. 1998. 29.95 (*0-901905-84-4*, Pub. by Ulster Hist Fnd) Irish Bks Media.
Crawford, W. J. The Reality of Psychic Phenomena. 1991. lib. bdg. 83.00 (*0-8490-4527-4*) Gordon Pr.
Crawford, W. Rex, tr. see Vasconcelos, Jose.
Crawford, Walt. Being Analog: Creating Tomorrow's Libraries. LC 98-40764. 264p. 1999. 28.00 (*0-8389-0754-7*) ALA.
— Common Sense Personal Computing: A Handbook for Professionals. LC 86-15074. (Common Sense Computing Ser.: No. 1). 1986. pap. 30.00 (*0-87650-218-4*) Pierian.
— Current Technologies in the Library: An Informal Overview. (Professional Librarian Ser.). 300p. 1988. 30.00 (*0-8161-1888-4*, Hall Reference) Macmillan.
— Desktop Publishing for Librarians. (Professional Librarian Ser.). 1990. 40.00 (*0-8161-1929-5*, Hall Reference); 30.00 (*0-8161-1930-9*, Hall Reference) Macmillan.
— MARC for Library Use: Understanding Integrated USMARC. 2nd ed. (Professional Librarian Ser.). 376p. 1989. 45.00 (*0-8161-1887-6*, Hall Reference) Macmillan.
— The Master's Plan: As the Artist Sees It. (Illus.). 128p. (Orig.). 1989. pap. 6.95 (*0-317-93462-7*) HEPC Inc.
— The Online Catalog Book: Essays & Examples. LC 92-13843. (Professional Librarian Ser.). 230p. 1992. 60.00 (*0-8161-1996-1*, Hall Reference); 35.00 (*0-8161-1995-3*, Hall Reference) Macmillan.
— Patron Access: Issues for Online Catalogs. (Professional Librarian Ser.). 258p. 1987. 40.00 (*0-8161-1850-7*, Hall Reference); 30.00 (*0-8161-1852-3*, Hall Reference) Macmillan.
— Technical Standards: An Introduction for Librarians. 2nd ed. (Professional Librarian Ser.). 220p. 1991. 45.00 (*0-8161-1950-3*, Hall Reference); 30.00 (*0-8161-1951-1*, Hall Reference) Macmillan.
— The Ultimate Gift: As the Artist Sees It. (Illus.). 176p. (Orig.). 1989. pap. 7.95 (*0-927277-00-X*) HEPC Inc.
Crawford, Walt & Gorman, Michael. Future Libraries: Dreams, Madness & Reality. LC 94-43760. 198p. (Orig.). 1995. pap. 28.00 (*0-8389-0647-8*, 0647-8-2045) ALA.
Crawford, Walt, et al. Bibliographic Displays in the Online Catalog. LC 86-15348. (Professional Librarian Ser.). 359p. 1986. 35.00 (*0-86729-198-2*, Hall Reference) Macmillan.
— Libraries in the Age of Automation: A Reader for the Professional Librarian. LC 86-2724. (Professional Librarian Ser.). 160p. 1986. 40.00 (*0-86729-194-X*, Hall Reference); 30.00 (*0-86729-193-1*, Hall Reference) Macmillan.
Crawford, Walter B. Reading Coleridge: Approaches & Applications. LC 79-7616. 288p. reprint ed. pap. 89.30 (*0-608-08089-6*, 206904800002) Bks Demand.
— Samuel Taylor Coleridge: Annotated Bibliography Criticism & Scholarship, Vol. 3. 1996. 60.00 (*0-8161-8727-4*, Hall Reference) Macmillan.
Crawford, Wesley G. Construction Layout: A Step-by-Step Field Engineering Methods Manual. Switzer, Sharyn L. & Crawford, Bonnie, eds. (Illus.). 700p. (C). 1994. text 65.00 (*0-9624124-3-0*) Busn News.
— Construction Surveying & Layout: A Step-by-Step Field Engineering Methods Manual. 2nd ed. (Illus.). 734p. (C). 1995. text 65.00 (*0-9647421-0-1*) Creat Construct Pub.
Crawford, William. The Keepers of Light: A History & Working Guide to Early Photographic Processes. LC 79-88815. 324p. 1979. pap. 35.00 (*0-87100-158-6*, 2158) Morgan.
— Report on the Penitentiaries of the United States: With Introduction Added. LC 69-16235. (Criminology, Law Enforcement, & Social Problems Ser.: No. 97). 1969. reprint ed. 50.00 (*0-87585-097-9*) Patterson Smith.
Crawford, William & Hunter, Jason. Java Servlet Programming. Ferguson, Paula, ed. (Illus.). 528p. 1998. reprint ed. pap. 36.95 (*1-56592-391-X*) OReilly & Assocs.
Crawford, William, et al. Java Enterprise in a Nutshell. Ferguson, Paula, ed. (Illus.). 622p. 1999. pap. 29.95 (*1-56592-483-5*) OReilly & Assocs.
Crawford, William A. My Search for the Real Killer: Not by OJ Simpson. large type ed. LC 97-164616. (Illus.). 120p. (Orig.). 1997. pap. 10.95 (*0-9657235-0-X*) Windfall Pr.
Crawford, William E., ed. Louisiana Code of Civil Procedure: As Amended Through the 1983 Regular Session of the Legislature. LC 84-131708. 1983. pap. 24.00 (*0-317-13475-2*) West Pub.
Crawford, William P. Mariner's Celestial Navigation. (Illus.). 1979. 19.95 (*0-393-60003-3*) Norton.
— Mariner's Weather. (Illus.). 312p. 1992. pap. 22.00 (*0-393-30884-7*) Norton.
***Crawford, William R.** Military RV, Camping & Outdoor Recreation Around the World Including Golf Courses & Marinas. LC 98-31698. 1998. write for info. (*0-914862-74-X*) Military Living Pubns.
Crawford, William R. & Crawford, Ann C. Military Living's Assignment, Washington: A Guide to Washington Area Military Installations. LC 84-9111. vi, 122p. 1984. write for info. (*0-914862-06-5*) Military Living Pubns.
— Military Space-A: Air Opportunities Around the World. Russell, Donna L., ed. LC 98-10819. 1998. pap. 19.95 (*0-914862-69-3*) Military Living Pubns.
Crawford, William R. & Crawford, L. Ann. Military Living's California State Military Road Map. 1994. pap. write for info. (*0-914862-45-6*) Military Living Pubns.
— Military Living's Florida State Military Road Map. 1994. pap. write for info. (*0-914862-46-4*) Military Living Pubns.
— Military Living's Mid-Atlantic United States Military Road Map. 1994. pap. write for info. (*0-914862-47-2*) Military Living Pubns.
— Military Living's Texas State Military Road Map. 1994. pap. write for info. (*0-914862-48-0*) Military Living Pubns.
Crawford, William R. & Crawford, Lela A. Military Living's Desert Shield Commemorative Maps. 1991. pap. write for info. (*0-914862-27-8*) Military Living Pubns.
— Military Space - Air Opportunities Air Route Map. 1995. pap. write for info. (*0-914862-52-9*) Military Living Pubns.
— United States Forces Travel Guide to Overseas U. S. Military Installations. Russell, Donna L., ed. LC 96-21223. 1996. pap. write for info. (*0-914862-43-X*) Military Living Pubns.
— United States Military Medical Facilities Map. 1994. pap. write for info. (*0-914862-54-5*) Military Living Pubns.
Crawford, William R., et al. Assignment Washington Military Road Atlas. Camp, John R., ed. LC 97-42188. 1998. pap. 11.95 (*0-914862-68-5*) Military Living Pubns.
— Military Living, Military RV, Camping & Recreation Areas Around the World. LC 97-10747. 1997. pap. write for info. (*0-914862-65-0*) Military Living Pubns.
Crawford, William R., Sr., et al. United States Military Road Atlas. Crawford, R. J., ed. LC 97-46037. 1995. pap. 19.95 (*0-914862-70-7*) Military Living Pubns.
Crawford, William R., jt. auth. see Crawford, Ann C.
Crawford, William R., jt. auth. see Crawford, Ann Caddell.
Crawford, William R., Sr., jt. auth. see Crawford, L. Ann.
Crawford, William R., jt. auth. see Crawford, Lela A.
***Crawford, William Roy & Crawford, Ann Caddell.** Military Space-A Air Basic Training & Reader Trip Reports. LC 00-31891. 2000. write for info. (*0-914862-89-8*) Military Living Pubns.
Crawford, William Roy, jt. auth. see Crawford, Ann Caddell.
Crawfrod. King Arthur Coloring Book. (Illus.). (J). pap. 2.95 (*0-486-28887-0*) Dover.
Crawfurd, John. History of Indian Archipelago, 3 vols. (C). 1993. text 48.00 (*81-85557-30-6*, Pub. by Low Price) S Asia.
Crawfurd, Martin D., et al, eds. Advances in the Treatment of Inborn Errors of Metabolism: Proceedings of the 2nd Clinical Research Centre Symposium Held in September, 1981. LC 82-1897. (Illus.). 383p. reprint ed. pap. 118.80 (*0-8357-5187-2*, 202963300062) Bks Demand.
Crawfurd, Raymond H. The King's Evil. LC 75-23701. reprint ed. 32.50 (*0-404-13251-0*) AMS Pr.
Crawley. Sonar Performance. (Illus.). 448p. 1999. pap. 138.00 (*0-419-21550-6*) Thomson Learn.
— What's Wrong with My Mouse? Behavioral Phenotyping of Transgenic & Knockout Mic. LC 99-28955. 2000. 79.95 (*0-471-31639-3*) Wiley.
Crawley, Amy & O'Keafe, Cynthia. The Nursing Home Handbook: North Central Texas Region, 1992-1993 Edition. 300p. 1992. pap. 19.95 (*0-9634276-0-1*) Smart Choices.
Crawley, Angela, ed. The Kingfisher Illustrated Pocket Dictionary. LC 95-52440. (Illus.). 236p. (J). (gr. 4-8). 1996. pap. 10.95 (*1-85697-672-6*) LKC.
— Oxford Elementary Learner's Dictionary. 2nd ed. (Illus.). 430p. (J). 1994. pap. text 13.95 (*0-19-431275-5*) OUP.
Crawley, Angela, jt. ed. see Grisewood, John.
Crawley, C. W. The Question of Greek Independence: A Study of British Policy in the Near East, 1821-1833. LC 74-144130. 272p. 1973. reprint ed. 40.00 (*0-86527-161-5*) Fertig.
Crawley, Connie, jt. auth. see Stanley, Kathleen.
Crawley, Drury, jt. ed. see Vine, Edward.
Crawley, Ernest. Studies of Savages & Sex. Besterman, Theodore, ed. LC 77-102231. (Select Bibliographies Reprint Ser.). 1977. 29.95 (*0-8369-5116-6*) Ayer.
***Crawley, Francis, et al, eds.** Nations & Cultures in European Higher Education: Universities Remembering Europe. LC 99-45863. 256p. 2000. 69.95 (*1-57181-957-6*) Berghahn Bks.
Crawley, Harriet. Painted Lady. large type ed. 480p. 1996. 27.99 (*0-7089-3513-3*) Ulverscroft.
Crawley, Jacqueline N. Current Protocols in Neuroscience. LC 97-14252. 700p. 1997. cd-rom 395.00 (*0-471-16359-7*) Wiley.
Crawley, Jacqueline N. & McLean, Stafford, eds. Neuropeptides: Basic & Clinical Advances. LC 96-6767. (Annals of the New York Academy of Sciences Ser.: No. 780). 255p. 1996. 100.00 (*0-89766-989-4*) NY Acad Sci.
Crawley, Jacyntha. The Biorhythm Kit: Plan for the ups & downs in Your Life. 112p. 1996. boxed set 24.95 (*1-885203-33-0*) Jrny Editions.
Crawley, John. Constructive Conflict Management: Managing to Make a Difference. (People Skills for Professionals Ser.). (Illus.). 284p. 1995. reprint ed. pap. 19.95 (*1-85788-014-5*) Nicholas Brealey.
Crawley, John, jt. auth. see Van de Graaff, Kent.
Crawley, John, ed. see Sutherland, Jock.
Crawley, John L., jt. auth. see Van De Graaff, Kent M.
Crawley, M. J. Natural Enemies: The Population Biology of Predators, Parasites & Diseases. (Illus.). 584p. 1992. pap. 75.00 (*0-632-02698-7*) Blackwell Sci.
Crawley, M. J., ed. Plant Ecology. 2nd ed. LC 96-23347. 500p. 1997. pap. 54.95 (*0-632-03639-7*) Blackwell Sci.
Crawley, Michael J. GLIM for Ecologists. LC 92-39214. (Methods in Ecology Ser.). 1993. pap. 55.00 (*0-632-03156-5*) Blackwell Sci.
Crawley, Peter, ed. A Descriptive Bibliography of the Mormon Church, 1830-1847. 1998. 21.95 (*1-57008-395-9*) Bookcraft Inc.
Crawley, Sharon J. & Merritt, King. Remediating Reading Difficulties. 2nd ed. 224p. (C). 1995. text. write for info. (*0-697-24130-0*) Brown & Benchmark.
— Remediating Reading Difficulties. 2nd ed. 240p. (C). 1997. student ed., spiral bd. write for info. (*0-07-114459-5*) McGraw.
Crawley, Sharon J. & Mountain, Lee. Strategies for Guiding Content Reading. 2nd ed. LC 94-42835. 316p. (C). 1995. 49.00 (*0-205-14886-7*) Allyn.
Crawley, Stanley W. & Dillon, Robert M. Steel Buildings: Analysis & Design. 4th ed. LC 92-27769. 736p. 1993. 120.00 (*0-471-84298-2*) Wiley.
Crawley, Stanley W. & Ward, Delbert B. Seismic & Wind Loads in Architectural Design. 2nd ed. 308p. pap. 50.00 (*1-55835-030-6*) AIA Press.
Crawley, Stella T. In Honor of Women: A Revolutionary Approach to Preventing Breast Cancer. LC RC280.B6C73 1998. 320p. 1998. pap. 13.95 (*0-345-42513-8*) Ballantine Pub Grp.
Crawley, Thomas, ed. Four Makers of the American Mind: Emerson, Thoreau, Whitman & Melville, a Bicentennial Tribute. LC 76-24188. 106p. reprint ed. pap. 32.90 (*0-608-15090-8*, 202619400048) Bks Demand.
Crawley, Tim, jt. auth. see Stephens, Paul.
Crawley, Tony. The Films of Brigitte Bardot. rev. ed. LC 93-45772. (Illus.). 1994. 16.95 (*0-8065-1477-9*, Citadel Pr) Carol Pub Group.
— The Films of Sophia Loren. 256p. 1976. 14.00 (*0-8065-0512-5*, Citadel Pr) Carol Pub Group.
Crawley, William B. Bill Tuck: A Political Life in Harry Byrd's Virginia. LC 78-16751. 293p. reprint ed. pap. 90.90 (*0-8357-7210-1*, 202481700038) Bks Demand.
Crawshaw, Alwyn. Acrylics. (Learn to Paint Ser.). (Illus.). 1999. pap. 15.95 (*0-00-413336-6*, Pub. by HarpC) Trafalgar.
— Landscapes. (Learn to Paint Ser.). (Illus.). 1999. pap. 15.95 (*0-00-413342-0*, Pub. by HarpC) Trafalgar.
***Crawshaw, Alwyn.** Oils for Beginners. 1998. pap. 15.95 (*0-00-413344-7*, Pub. by HarpC) Trafalgar.
Crawshaw, Alwyn. Oils for the Beginner. (Learn to Paint Ser.). (Illus.). 1999. pap. 15.95 (*0-00-413345-5*, Pub. by HarpC) Trafalgar.
— Watercolours. (Learn to Paint Ser.). (Illus.). 1999. pap. 15.95 (*0-00-413348-X*, Pub. by HarpC) Trafalgar.
Crawshaw, Dale. Reluctant Rainbows: A Personal Journey from Failure to Freedom. 2nd rev. ed. Lawrence, Gordon, ed. (Illus.). 1999. 15.00 (*1-928554-00-8*) Wisdom Pr GA.
Crawshaw, Fred D. Spinning Metal Made Easy. (Illus.). 72p. 1991. reprint ed. pap. 6.00 (*1-877767-36-0*) Univ Publng Hse.
Crawshaw, G. H. & Ince, J. Textile Floorcoverings. 84p. 1977. 110.00 (*0-7855-7229-5*) St Mut.
Crawshaw, Gerry. Switzerland. (Essential Guides Ser.). (Illus.). 128p. 1994. pap. 7.95 (*0-8442-8934-5*, 89345, Passprt Bks) NTC Contemp Pub Co.
— Turkey. 2nd ed. (Passport's Essential Travel Guides Ser.). (Illus.). 128p. 1998. pap. text 7.95 (*0-8442-0073-5*) NTC Contemp Pub Co.
Crawshaw, J. & Chambers, J. A Concise Course in A-Level Statistics: With Worked Examples. 3rd ed. 752p. (C). 1994. pap. 42.50 (*0-7487-1757-9*, Pub. by S Thornes Pubs) Trans-Atl Phila.
***Crawshaw, J. & Chambers, J.** A Concise Course in Advanced Level Statistics. 4th ed. (Illus.). 768p. (YA). 2000. pap. 49.50 (*0-7487-5475-X*, Pub. by S Thornes Pubs) Trans-Atl Phila.
Crawshaw, Janet & Langley, Paul. Intermediate Maths. (GCSE Ser.). (Illus.). 528p. (YA). (gr. 9-11). 1998. pap. 32.50 (*0-7487-3674-3*, Pub. by S Thornes Pubs) Trans-Atl Phila.
***Crawshaw, Ralph.** Police & Human Rights. LC 99-29580. 1999. 72.00 (*90-411-1209-X*) Kluwer Law Intl.
Crawshaw, Ralph, et al. Human Rights & Policing: Standards for Good Behaviour & a Strategy for Change. LC 98-202657. 312p. 1998. pap. 65.00 (*90-411-1015-1*) Kluwer Law Intl.
Crawshaw, Robert. Stylistics of Contemporary French. 208p. (C). 1999. 65.00 (*0-415-11543-4*) Routledge.
Crawshaw, Robert, ed. The European Business Environment: France. 240p. 1996. pap. 77.95 (*0-415-12855-2*) Thomson Learn.
— The European Business Environment: France. LC 97-5334. 240p. 1997. pap. 19.99 (*0-415-10535-8*) Thomson Learn.
Crawshaw, Robert, et al. Entrepreneurship & Management Education in the New Europe: Issues of Content & Process. 256p. 1996. pap. 59.00 (*0-415-10012-7*); pap. 18.99 (*0-415-10013-5*) Thomson Learn.
***Crawshaw, Robert H. & Tusting, Karin.** Introduction to French Text Analysis. LC 99-53738. 272p. 2000. pap. 27.99 (*0-415-18408-8*) Routledge.
— Introduction to French Text Analysis: Interpretations of National Identity. LC 99-53738. 240p. (C). 2000. text. write for info. (*0-415-18407-X*) Routledge.
Crawshaw, S. L. Application Factors for Helical & Herringbone Speed Reducers. (Technical Papers: Vol. P148). (Illus.). 37p. 1937. pap. text 30.00 (*1-55589-202-7*) AGMA.
— The Selection of Bearings for Gear Drives. (Technical Papers: Vol. P200). (Illus.). 18p. (Orig.). 1940. pap. text 30.00 incl. audio compact disk (*1-55589-364-3*) AGMA.
Crawshay-William, Rupert. Comforts of Unreason: A Study of the Motives Behind Irrational Thought. LC 71-98217. 206p. 1970. reprint ed. lib. bdg. 59.50 (*0-8371-3398-X*, CRUN, Greenwood Pr) Greenwood.
Craxford, S. R. & Suess, Michael J., eds. Manual on Urban Air Quality Management. (WHO Regional Publications). 1976. pap. text 36.00 (*92-9020-101-0*, 1310001) World Health.
Cray-Andrews, Martha, jt. auth. see Baum, Susan E.
Cray, David. Keeplock: A Novel of Crime. 1995. 21.00 (*1-883402-97-2*) S&S Trade.
— Keeplock: A Novel of Crime. large type ed. (Niagara Large Print Ser.). 411p. 1995. 29.50 (*0-7089-5817-6*) Ulverscroft.
Cray, David & Mallory, Geoffrey R. Making Sense of Managing Culture. (Illus.). 224p. 1997. mass mkt. 29.95 (*0-415-07382-0*) Routledge.
— Making Sense of Managing Culture. LC 98-164549. 224p. 1998. pap. 40.00 (*1-86152-177-4*) Thomson Learn.
— Making Sense of Managing Culture. LC 98-164549. (Illus.). 224p. 1998. pap. 13.99 (*1-86152-178-2*) Thomson Learn.
Cray, Dorothy M. House Divided. large type ed. 368p. 1984. 27.99 (*0-7089-1199-4*) Ulverscroft.
— Place for Claire. large type ed. 336p. 1985. 27.99 (*0-7089-1252-4*) Ulverscroft.
Cray, Ed. Chief Justice: A Biography of Earl Warren. LC 97-2984. 592p. 1997. 29.50 (*0-684-80852-8*) S&S Trade.
— Erotic Muse: American Bawdy Sings. 2nd ed. 480p. 1999. pap. text 24.95 (*0-252-06789-4*) U of Ill Pr.
— The Erotic Muse: American Bawdy Songs. 2nd ed. (Illus.). 435p. 1998. text 30.00 (*0-7881-5510-5*) DIANE Pub.
— The Erotic Muse: American Bawdy Songs. 2nd ed. (Music in American Life Ser.). 480p. 1992. 34.95 (*0-252-01781-1*) U of Ill Pr.
***Cray, Ed.** General of the Army: George C. Marshall, Soldier & Statesman. (Illus.). 2000. pap. write for info. (*0-8154-1042-5*, Pub. by Cooper Sq) Natl Bk Netwk.
Cray, Ed, et al. American Datelines. LC 90-33247. 382p. 1990. reprint ed. pap. 118.50 (*0-608-03567-X*, 205965200009) Bks Demand.
Cray, Evelyn S., jt. auth. see Donnelly, Loraine B.
Cray, Jordan. Bad Intent. (Danger.com Ser.: No. 6). 208p. (YA). (gr. 6 up). 1998. per. 3.99 (*0-689-81477-1*) Aladdin.
— Bad Intent, 6. (Danger.com Ser.: No. 6). (YA). (gr. 6 up). 1998. 9.09 (*0-606-13310-0*, Pub. by Turtleback) Demco.
***Cray, Jordan.** Dead Man's Hand. LC 98-25238. (Danger.com Ser.: No. 8). 224p. (YA). (gr. 6 up). 1998. per. 3.99 (*0-689-82383-5*) Aladdin.
Cray, Jordan. Firestorm. (Danger.com Ser.: No. 2). (YA). (gr. 6 up). 1997. 9.09 (*0-606-13306-2*, Pub. by Turtleback) Demco.
— Firestorm, No. 2. LC 96-37898. (Danger.com Ser.: No. 2). 192p. (YA). (gr. 6 up). 1997. mass mkt. 3.99 (*0-689-81431-3*) Aladdin.
— Gemini 7. LC 97-5112. (Danger.com Ser.: No. 1). 192p. (YA). (gr. 6 up). 1997. per. 3.99 (*0-689-81432-1*) Aladdin.
Cray, Jordan. Gemini 7. (Danger.com Ser.: No. 1). (YA). (gr. 6 up). 1997. 11.15 (*0-606-13305-4*, Pub. by Turtleback) Demco.
— Hot Pursuit. (Danger.com Ser.: No. 4). (YA). (gr. 6 up). 1997. 9.09 (*0-606-13308-9*, Pub. by Turtleback) Demco.
Cray, Jordan. Hot Pursuit, No. 4. LC 97-23503. (Danger.com Ser.: No. 4). 192p. (YA). (gr. 6 up). 1997. per. 3.99 (*0-689-81434-8*) Aladdin.
— Most Wanted. LC 97-52648. (Danger.com Ser.: No. 7). 208p. (YA). (gr. 6 up). 1998. mass mkt. 3.99 (*0-689-82040-2*) Aladdin.
— Most Wanted, 7. (Danger.com Ser.: No. 7). (YA). (gr. 6 up). 1998. 9.09 (*0-606-13311-9*, Pub. by Turtleback) Demco.
— Shadow Man, No. 3. LC 97-3173. (Danger.com Ser.: No. 3). 192p. (YA). (gr. 6 up). 1997. per. 3.99 (*0-689-81433-X*) Aladdin.
— Shiver. LC 98-42123. (Danger.com Ser.: No. 9). 224p. (YA). (gr. 6 up). 1998. per. 3.99 (*0-689-82384-3*) Aladdin.
— Stalker. LC 97-30888. (Danger.com Ser.: No. 5). (Illus.). 192p. (YA). (gr. 6 up). 1998. mass mkt. 3.99 (*0-689-81476-3*) Aladdin.
— Stalker. (Danger.com Ser.: No. 5). (YA). (gr. 6 up). 1998. 9.09 (*0-606-13309-7*, Pub. by Turtleback) Demco.
Craycraft, Kenneth & Warner, Laverne. What If . . . Themes. 144p. teacher ed. 13.99 (*0-86653-717-1*, GA1434) Good Apple.
Craycraft, Kenneth, jt. auth. see Warner, Laverne.
Craycraft, Kenneth R., Jr. The American Myth of Religious Freedom. LC 98-43797. 226p. 1999. 27.95 (*1-890626-13-9*) Spence Pub.
Craycroft, Robert & Fazio, Michael W., eds. Change & Tradition in the American Small Town. LC 83-14638. (Small Town Ser.). 122p. 1983. pap. text 12.95 (*0-87805-194-5*) U Pr of Miss.
Crayhon, Robert. The Carnitine Miracle. LC 98-9723. 192p. 1998. 19.95 (*0-87131-825-3*) M Evans.

C

An Asterisk (*) at the beginning of an entry indicates that the title is appearing for the first time.

— The Health Benefits of FOS (Fructooligosaccharides) Bensen, Don R., ed. (Good Health Guides Ser.). 48p. 1995. pap. 3.95 (0-87983-693-8, 36938K, Keats Publng) NTC Contemp Pub Co.
— Robert Crayhon's Nutrition Made Simple: A Comprehensive Guide to the Latest Findings in Optimal Nutrition. LC 95-43216. 320p. 1996. pap. 12.95 (0-87131-796-6) M Evans.
Craymer, Sally. There's a Blue Square on My Brother's School Bus. LC 92-61768. (Illus.). 59p. (Orig.). (J). (gr. k-12). 1992. pap. 4.95 (0-931563-12-7) Wishing Rm.
Craypo, Charles. The Economics of Collective Bargaining: Case Studies in the Private Sector. LC 85-28373. (Illus.). 273p. reprint ed. pap. 84.70 (0-7837-4599-0, 204431800002) Bks Demand.
— The Impact on Organized Labor of Changing Corporate Structure & Technology. 112p. 1979. pap. text 19.95 (0-87855-766-0) Transaction Pubs.
Craypo, Charles & Nissen, Bruce, eds. Grand Designs: The Impact of Corporate Strategies on Workers, Unions, & Communities. LC 93-13434. 296p. 1993. text 47.50 (0-87546-309-6, ILR Press); pap. text 18.95 (0-87546-310-X, ILR Press) Cornell U Pr.
Craythorn, Dennis. Ultimate Guide to Marathons. 2nd ed. 1998. pap. 19.95 (0-9655187-2-8) Marathon Pubs Inc.
— Ultimate Runner's Journal: Your Daily Training Partner & Log. 2nd ed. 1998. pap. text 19.95 (0-9655187-3-6) Marathon Pubs Inc.
Craythorn, Dennis & Hanna, Rich. The Ultimate Guide to International Marathons. LC 98-91304. (Illus.). 352p. 1998. pap. 19.95 (0-9655187-1-X) Marathon Pubs Inc.
Craythorne, D. L. Municipal Administration - A Handbook. 4th ed. LC 98-218203. 530p. 1998. pap. 85.00 (0-7021-4206-9, Pub. by Juta & Co) Intl Spec Bk.
Crayton, John, jt. auth. see Schiller, Eric.
Crayton, Luanne, ed. Construction Robotics & Automation, & Foundations Engineering. (Transportation Research Record Ser.: No. TRR1406). (Illus.). 148p. 1994. pap. text 24.00 (0-309-05553-9) Transport Res Bd.
— Innovations in Travel Behavior Analysis, Demand Forecasting, & Modeling Networks (TRR 1413) (Transportation Research Record Ser.). (Illus.). 156p. 1994. pap. text 31.00 (0-309-05560-1) Natl Res Coun.
— Pavement Surface Courses, Stone Mastic Asphalt Pavements, & Asphalt Concrete Recycling (TRR 1427) (Transportation Research Record Ser.). (Illus.). 68p. 1994. pap. text 22.00 (0-309-05500-8) Natl Res Coun.
— Railroad Freight Transportation Research Needs (CP 2) LC 94-215070. (Conference Proceedings Ser.). (Illus.). 160p. 1994. pap. text 29.00 (0-309-05503-2) Transport Res Bd.
— Structures (TRR 1393) (Transportation Research Record Ser.). (Illus.). 208p. 1993. pap. text 41.00 (0-309-05466-4) Transport Res Bd.
— Transportation System Management, Parking & Travel Demand Management (TRR 1404) (Transportation Research Record Ser.). (Illus.). 1100p. 1993. pap. text 25.00 (0-309-05550-4) Transport Res Bd.
Crayton, Luanne & Solomon, Norman, eds. Innovations in Instrumentation & Data Acquisition Systems (TRR 1432) (Transportation Research Record Ser.). (Illus.). 112p. 1994. pap. text 25.00 (0-309-05514-8, R1432) Transport Res Bd.
Crayton, Spurgeon E. Screams of Protest. (Illus.). 1982. 10.00 (0-8315-0188-X) Speller.
Crayton, Tabatha. The African-American Address Book. LC 94-30205. 304p. (Orig.). 1995. pap. 14.00 (0-399-52148-8, Perigee Bks) Berkley Pub.
Craz, Albert G. & Mavragis, Edward P. Writing: The Business Letter. 68p. 1988. student ed. 3.95 (0-560-78025-7) Comp Pr.
— Writing: The Report. (Writing Ser.). 66p. 1981. student ed. 3.95 (0-9602800-2-2) Comp Pr.
Craze, Galaxy. By the Shore. LC 98-50520. 224p. 1999. 24.00 (0-87113-746-1, Atlntc Mnthly) Grove-Atltic.
***Craze, Galaxy.** By the Shore. 240p. 2000. pap. 12.00 (0-8021-3687-7, Pub. by Grove-Atltic) Publishers Group.
Craze, Richard. Alexander Technique. (Teach Yourself Ser.). (Illus.). 160p. 1996. pap. 14.95 (0-8442-3103-7, Teach Yrslf) NTC Contemp Pub Co.
— The Art of Seduction. LC 98-47762. 1999. pap. 16.95 (0-8069-7074-X) Sterling.
— Astral Projection: A Beginner's Guide. 96p. 1997. pap. 11.95 (0-340-67418-0, Pub. by Headway) Trafalgar.
***Craze, Richard.** Be Better in Bed. (Illus.). 128p. 2000. pap. 16.95 (0-8069-2771-2) Sterling.
Craze, Richard. Beginners Feng Shui: A Complete Guide. (Illus.). 200p. 1997. pap. 17.95 (0-340-69708-3, Pub. by Hodder & Stought Ltd) Trafalgar.
— Chinese Astrology: A Unique Flip Guide to Discover Compatibility in Romance, Friendship, Family & Work. 128p. 1999. spiral bd. 24.95 (0-7641-5158-4) Barron.
— Chinese Astrology Handbook: A Complete Guide to the Chinese Horoscope. (New Life Library). (Illus.). 64p. 1998. 9.95 (1-85967-627-8, Lorenz Bks) Anness Pub.
— Feng Shui: Book & Card Pack. LC 97-592. (Illus.). 64p. 1997. 19.95 (1-57324-082-6) Conari Press.
— Feng Shui Game Pack. (Illus.). 64p. 1998. boxed set 22.95 (1-55670-614-6) Stewart Tabori & Chang.
***Craze, Richard.** Feng Shui Made Easy: An Introduction to the Basics of the Ancient Art of Feng Shui. LC 99-20804. 64p. 1999. 7.95 (0-8069-9855-5) Sterling.
Craze, Richard. Graphology for Beginners. (Headway Guide for Beginners Ser.). 112p. 1995. pap. 11.95 (0-340-60625-8, Pub. by Headway) Trafalgar.
***Craze, Richard.** Guide For Life: Chinese Astrology. 64p. 2000. pap. 6.95 (1-84215-064-2) Anness Pub.
Craze, Richard. Hell: An Illustrated History of the Netherworld. (Illus.). 96p. 1996. 12.95 (1-57324-059-1) Conari Press.
***Craze, Richard.** I Ching. 2000. 19.95 (0-8069-3621-5) Sterling.
— Meditation Made Easy: An Introduction to the Basics of the Ancient Art of Meditation. LC 99-20346. 64p. 1999. pap. text 7.95 (0-8069-9909-8) Sterling.
— Mix & Match Animal & Star Signs. (Illus.). 128p. 2000. spiral bd. 24.95 (0-7641-5302-1) Barron.
— Mix & Match Sun & Moon Signs. (Illus.). 128p. 2000. spiral bd. 24.95 (0-7641-5304-8) Barron.
Craze, Richard. The Pocket Book of Foreplay: The Art of Sexual Excitement Explained. (Illus.). 96p. 1999. pap. 10.95 (0-89793-252-8) Hunter Hse.
***Craze, Richard.** Pocket Book of Sexual Fantasy: The Art of Sexual Excitement Explained. 2000. pap. 10.95 (0-89793-294-3) Hunter Hse.
Craze, Richard. Practical Feng Shui: The Chinese Art of Living in Harmony with Your Surroundings. (New Life Library). (Illus.). 64p. 1997. 9.95 (1-85967-510-7, Lorenz Bks) Anness Pub.
— Relaxation. (Teach Yourself Ser.). 192p. 1998. pap. 11.95 (0-8442-0176-6, 01766, Teach Yrslf) NTC Contemp Pub Co.
— Sextasy Ecstasy Book & Card Pack: Relationships & Sensuality. (Illus.). 64p. 1998. 19.95 (1-885203-52-7) Jmy Editions.
— Shamanism: A Beginner's Guide. (Beginner's Ser.). (Illus.). 96p. 1997. pap. 11.95 (0-340-68010-5, Pub. by Headway) Trafalgar.
— Tantric Sexuality: A Beginner's Guide. 96p. 1997. pap. 11.95 (0-340-68349-X, Pub. by Headway) Trafalgar.
***Craze, Richard.** Zen Meditations on Being a Friend. 2000. 15.00 incl. audio compact disk (1-57071-645-5) Sourcebks.
— Zen Meditations on Being in Love. 2000. 15.00 incl. audio compact disk (1-57071-646-3) Sourcebks.
Craze, Richard & Dixon, Mike. The Illustrated Encyclopedia of Well-Being: For Mind, Body & Spirit. LC 99-30041. (Illus.). 1999. 29.95 (0-8069-2061-0) Sterling.
Craze, Richard & Fou, Jen T. Traditional Chinese Medicine. (Teach Yourself Ser.). (Illus.). 190p. 1998. pap. 9.95 (0-8442-0019-0, 00190, Teach Yrslf) NTC Contemp Pub Co.
Craze, Richard & Jay, Roni. Feng Shui. 192p. 1999. pap. 9.95 (0-8442-1586-4, Natl Textbk Co) NTC Contemp Pub Co.
— The Tao of Food. LC 98-48683. (Illus.). 128p. 1999. 24.95 (0-8069-7075-8) Sterling.
Craze, Richard & Lee, Billy. Chinese Astrology. (Teach Yourself Ser.). (Illus.). 224p. 1998. pap. 10.95 (0-8442-0017-4, 00174, Teach Yrslf) NTC Contemp Pub Co.
Craze, Richard & Ling, Shen. Beginners Feng Shui. (For Beginners Ser.). (Illus.). 112p. 1996. mass mkt. 11.95 (0-340-62079-X, Pub. by Headway) Trafalgar.
Craze, Richard & People's Medical Society Staff. The Spice Companion: The Culinary, Cosmetic & Medicinal Uses of Spices. LC 97-8032. (Illus.). 192p. 1997. 16.95 (1-882606-35-3) Peoples Med Soc.
Craze, Richard, jt. auth. see Jay, Roni.
Craze, Richard, jt. auth. see Tang, Stephen.
Craze, Sophia. Charles Russell. (Illus.). 112p. 1999. pap. 19.95 (1-57715-080-5) Knckerbocker.
— Frederic Remington. (Illus.). 112p. 1999. pap. 19.95 (1-57715-079-1) Knckerbocker.
Craze, Tony, et al. The Verity Bargate Award Plays, 1983: Shona, Lunch Girls & Shelter. Keeffe, Barrie, ed. (Methuen New Theatrescripts Ser.). 128p. (C). 1988. pap. write for info. (0-413-53850-8, A0262, Methuen Drama) Methn.
Crazzolara, J. Pasquale. A Study of the Acooli Language: Grammar & Vocabulary. rev. ed. LC 39-14126. 455p. reprint ed. pap. 141.10 (0-8357-6948-8, 203900700009) Bks Demand.
— A Study of the Logbara (Ma'di) Language: Grammar & Vocabulary. LC 60-2046. 392p. reprint ed. pap. 121.60 (0-8357-6949-6, 203900800009) Bks Demand.
CRC Publications Staff. Authentic Worship in a Changing Culture. LC 97-35035. 1997. pap. 4.45 (1-56212-257-6) CRC Pubns.
— First Steps: Guidelines for New Christians. 15p. 1999. pap. 0.95 (1-56212-432-3, 1920-0200) CRC Pubns.
— Songs for Life. LC 94-40068. 1994. spiral bd. 9.95 (1-56212-070-0) CRC Pubns.
CRC Staff. Composite Index - CRC Handbook, 1991 Supplement 3. 3rd ed. 432p. 1991. boxed set, suppl. ed. 350.00 (0-8493-0285-4) CRC Pr.
Creach, Jerome F. Yahweh As Refuge & the Editing of the Hebrew Psalter. (JSOT Supplement Ser.: No. 217). 156p. 1996. 52.50 (1-85075-601-5, Pub. by Sheffield Acad) CUP Services.
Creach, Jerome F. D. Psalms. LC 98-48124. (Interpretation Bible Studies). 112p. 1998. pap. 7.95 (0-664-50021-8) Geneva Press.
***Creach, Page L. D.** Life in Balance. LC 99-59483. (Real Faith, Real Life Ser.). 64p. 2000. 5.95 (1-57895-077-5) Curriculm Presbytrn KY.
Creadick, Jean P. & Cammack, Nell. Childhood Cancer: The Challenge to Hawaii's Healthcare System. 55p. (Orig.). (C). 1994. pap. text 25.00 (0-7881-0663-5) DIANE Pub.
Cready, Bonnie & Brough, Peggy. Calico Kitchen Muffins. large type ed. 48p. 3.95 (0-9613908-0-8) Bennett Enter.
Creager. Caroline Creager's Airobic Ball Strengthening Workout. 1994. pap. 7.95 (0-9641153-1-X) Exec Phys Therapy.
— Caroline Creager's Airobic Ball Stretching Workout. 1995. pap. 7.95 (0-9641153-2-8) Exec Phys Therapy.
***Creager, Angela.** Science Medicine & Technology. 1999. pap. text 25.00 (0-226-12024-4); lib. bdg. 55.00 (0-226-12023-6) U Ch Pr.
Creager, Joan G. Basic Health Science Chemistry: A Review & Workbook. 192p. (C). 1993. text, wbk. ed. write for info. (0-697-15276-6) Brown & Benchmark.
— Human Anatomy & Physiology. 2nd ed. 960p. (C). 1991. text, student ed. write for info. (0-697-12844-X, WCB McGr Hill) McGrw-H Hghr Educ.
Creager, John A. Theodynamics: NeoChristian Perspectives for the Modern World. 452p. (Orig.). (C). 1994. lib. bdg. 59.00 (0-8191-9363-1) U Pr of Amer.
Creager, Leone R. It's My Life & I'm Going to Live It: The Inspiring True Story of a Remarkable Young Man. rev. ed. (Illus.). 215p. 1990. reprint ed. pap. 7.95 (0-9624638-1-7) L R Creager.
— Let's Go: Creative Ways to Ask - Dates & Proposals - Illustrated. (Illus.). (Orig.). 1990. pap. write for info. (0-9624638-2-5) L R Creager.
Creager, Mark, ed. Vascular Disease, Vol. VII. LC 95-24438. (Atlas of Heart Diseases Ser.: Vol. 7). (Illus.). 232p. 1996. 134.00 (1-878132-26-1) Current Med.
Creager, Mark A., jt. ed. see Braunwald, Eugene.
Creager, William P., et al. Engineering for Dams: Concrete Dams, Vol. II. LC TC0547.C86. 416p. reprint ed. pap. 129.00 (0-608-11493-6, 201262500082) Bks Demand.
Creagh, Carson. Reptiles. LC 95-24477. (Nature Company Discoveries Library). (Illus.). 64p. (J). (gr. 3 up). 1999. 16.00 (0-8094-9247-4) Time-Life.
Creagh, Carson & Discoveries Library Staff. Mammals. LC 95-32820. (Nature Company Discoveries Library). (Illus.). 64p. (J). (gr. 4-7). 1999. 16.00 (0-8094-9372-1) Time-Life.
Creagh, Carson & Young Discoveries Staff. Things with Wings. LC 96-15736. (Young Discoveries Ser.). (Illus.). 32p. (J). 1999. 10.00 (0-7835-4838-9) Time-Life.
***Creagh, D. C. & Bradley, David A.** Radiation in Art & Archeometry. LC 00-34746. 2000. write for info. (0-444-50487-7) Elsevier.
Creagh, Milton. Masquerade: Unveiling Our Deadly Dance with Drugs & Alcohol. 32p. 1996. 28.99 incl. VHS (1-56179-500-3, VI190) Focus Family.
Creagh, Patrick, tr. see Bufalino, Gesualdo.
Creagh, Patrick, tr. see Calvino, Italo.
Creagh, Patrick, tr. see Cassell, Anthony K.
Creagh, Patrick, tr. see Leopardi, Giacomo.
Creagh, Patrick, tr. see Magris, Claudio.
Creagh, Patrick, tr. see Ortese, Anna M.
Creagh, Patrick, tr. see Simonelli, Maria P.
Creagh, Patrick, tr. see Tabucchi, Antonio.
Creagh, Patrick, tr. see Vassalli, Sebastiano.
Creaghead. Assessment & Remediation of Articulatory & Phonological Disorders. 3rd ed. (C). 1999. pap. text 57.00 (0-205-19883-X, Macmillan Coll) P-H.
Creaghead, Nancy, et al. Assessment & Remediation of Articulatory & Phonological Disorders. 2nd ed. 448p. (C). 1990. 84.00 (0-675-20653-7, Merrill Coll) P-H.
Creal, Margaret. Singing Sky. 156p. 1995. pap. 12.95 (1-55050-076-7, Pub. by Coteau) Genl Dist Srvs.
Creal, Margaret. Singing Sky. large type ed. 288p. 1995. pap. 17.95 (1-55050-091-0, Pub. by Coteau) Genl Dist Srvs.
Cream, Penelope. Babies Names. (Select Pocket Library). 96p. 1997. 4.98 (0-7858-0449-8) Bk Sales Inc.
Creamer, Daniel. Personal Income During Business Cycles. LC 84-10763. 166p. 1984. reprint ed. lib. bdg. 69.50 (0-313-24421-9, CRPI, Greenwood Pr) Greenwood.
Creamer, Daniel & Bernstein, Martin. Behavior of Wage Rates During Business Cycles. (Occasional Papers: No. 34). 74p. 1950. reprint ed. 20.00 (0-87014-349-2) Natl Bur Econ Res.
— Capital & Output Trends in Manufacturing Industries, 1880-1948. (Occasional Papers: No. 41). 112p. 1954. reprint ed. 29.20 (0-87014-355-7) Natl Bur Econ Res.
Creamer, Daniel & Coulter, Charles W. Labor & the Shut-Down of the Amoskeag Textile Mills: WPA, National Research Report No. L-5. LC 78-156410. (American Labor Ser., No. 2). (Illus.). 1971. reprint ed. 24.95 (0-405-02919-5) Ayer.
Creamer, Daniel, et al. Capital in Manufacturing & Mining: Its Formation & Financing. (Studies in Capital Formation & Financing: No. 6). 398p. 1960. reprint ed. 103.50 (0-87014-104-X) Natl Bur Econ Res.
Creamer, David G. Guides for the Journey. LC 95-45294. 234p. (C). 1996. pap. text 29.50 (0-7618-0182-0); lib. bdg. 48.00 (0-7618-0181-2) U Pr of Amer.
Creamer, Don G., jt. auth. see Winston, Roger B.
Creamer, Elizabeth G. Assessing Faculty Publication Productivity: Issues of Equity. Fife, Jonathan D., ed. LC 98-84365. (ASHE-ERIC Higher Education Reports: Vol. 26-2). 117p. 1998. pap. 24.00 (1-878380-82-6, 26-2) GWU Grad Schl E&HD.
Creamer, Kitty, ed. see Alexander, Marianne.
Creamer, Lyle R. Computer Applications in Psychology. (C). 1984. spiral bd. 17.50 (0-318-02994-4) L R Creamer.
Creamer, Robert H. Machine Design: A Solution Manual. 3rd ed. LC 83-2567. 540p. 1984. pap. text, teacher ed. 1.50 (0-201-11281-7) Addison-Wesley.
Creamer, Robert W. Babe: The Legend Comes to Life. 448p. 1992. pap. 13.00 (0-671-76070-X, Fireside) S&S Trade Pap.
***Creamer, Robert W.** Baseball (And Other Matters) in 1941. LC 99-48662. (Illus.). 348p. 2000. pap. 17.95 (0-8032-6406-2) U of Nebr Pr.
Creamer, Robert W. Stengel: His Life & Times. LC 95-40143. 349p. 1996. pap. 15.00 (0-8032-6367-8, Bison Books) U of Nebr Pr.
Creamer, Robert W., jt. auth. see Barber, Red.
Creamer, Robert W., jt. auth. see Conlan, Jocko.
Creamer, Robert W., jt. auth. see Mantle, Mickey.
Creamer, Thomas. Tibetan New Words Dictionary. 1996. write for info. (1-881265-30-7) Dunwoody Pr.
Creamer, Thomas, ed. Dictionary of New Chinese Words. LC 89-81269. 86p. 1989. pap. 8.00 (0-931745-69-1) Dunwoody Pr.
— A Dictionary of New Chinese Words. 2nd enl. rev. ed. LC 94-69489. 320p. 1994. 59.00 (1-881265-08-0) Dunwoody Pr.
Creamer, Thomas, et al, eds. A Chinese-English Dictionary of the Wu Dialect (Featuring the Dialect of the City of Shanghai) Wu Ying et al, trs. LC 91-70271. (CHI & ENG.). xi, 192p. 1992. 42.00 (0-931745-81-0) Dunwoody Pr.
Creamer, Winifred. The Architecture of Arroyo Hondo Pueblo, New Mexico. (Illus.). 219p. 1993. pap. 35.00 (0-933452-35-7) Schol Am Res.
Crean, jt. auth. see Kome.
Crean, Catherine. Violence & the Media. 176p. 1998. pap. 31.00 (1-901657-08-6) Gaunt.
Crean, David, et al, eds. Living Simply: An Examination of Christian Lifestyles. 128p. (Orig.). 1984. 5.95 (0-8164-2340-7) Harper SF.
Crean, David & Bastian, Geoff. Sheep & Wool Production. (Illus.). 144p. 1998. pap. text 36.95 (0-7506-8915-3) Buttrwrth-Heinemann.
Crean, G. M., et al, eds. Diagnostic Techniques for Semiconductor Materials Processing Vol. 324: Materials Research Society Symposium Proceedings. LC 94-20397. 503p. 1994. text 17.50 (1-55899-223-5) Materials Res.
Crean, Hugh & Miller, Samuel. Bruce Kurland: Watercolors & Paintings. LC 85-63887. (Illus.). 40p. 1986. pap. 12.00 (0-936827-00-9) C Bernard Gallery Ltd.
Crean, John & Scott, Marilyn. Deutsche Sprache Und Landeskunde, (Tapescript) 4th ed. (C). 1993. pap. text 14.68 (0-07-013517-7) McGraw.
Crean, John, et al. Deutsche Sprache und Landeskunde. 4th ed. (C). 1993. pap., wbk. ed. 27.50 (0-07-013514-2) McGraw.
— Deutsche Sprache und Landeskunde. 4th ed. (C). 1993. pap., lab manual ed. 25.94 (0-07-013515-0) McGraw.
Crean, John E., Jr., et al. Deutsche Sprache und Landeskunde. 4th ed. LC 92-30218. (ENG & GER.). 524p. (C). 1992. 69.69 (0-07-013512-6) McGraw.
— Deutsche Sprache und Landeskunde. 4th ed. LC 92-30218. (ENG & GER.). (C). 1992. text, teacher ed. 64.37 (0-07-013513-4) McGraw.
Crean, Kevin & Symes, David. Fisheries Management in Crisis: A Social Science Perspective. 288p. 1996. text 99.95 (0-85238-231-6) Blackwell Sci.
Crean, Michelle, jt. auth. see Perkins, Paul.
Crean, P. B., et al. Mathematical Modelling of Tides & Estuarine Circulation. (Lecture Notes on Coastal & Estuarine Studies: Vol. 30). xv, 471p. 1988. pap. 65.00 (0-387-96897-0) Spr-Verlag.
Crean, Susan. Grace Hartman: A Woman for Her Time. (Illus.). 248p. 1995. pap. 19.00 (0-921586-47-7, Pub. by New Star Bks) Genl Dist Srvs.
Crean, Susan. Newsworthy: The Lives of Media Women. 350p. 1985. mass mkt. 5.95 (0-88780-150-1, Pub. by Formac Publ Co) Formac Dist Ltd.
Crean, Susan. Newsworthy: The Lives of Media Women. (Illus.). 350p. 1985. 24.95 (0-7737-0081-1) Genl Dist Srvs.
Crean, Susan, ed. Twist & Shout: A Decade of Feminist Writing in "This Magazine" 296p. pap. 14.95 (0-929005-27-9, Pub. by Sec Story Pr) LPC InBook.
Crean, Thomas. Macmillan Atlas of Irish History. LC 97-28623. 144p. 1997. 27.50 (0-02-862011-9) Macmillan.
Creaney, N., jt. ed. see McTear, M.
Creary, Xavier, ed. Advances in Carbocation Chemistry, Vol. 1. 253p. 1989. 109.50 (0-89232-860-6) Jai Pr.
Creary, Xavier, jt. ed. see Coxon, James Morriss.
***Crease, Gail.** Dream Spinner. (Magical Love Ser.). 2000. mass mkt. 5.99 (0-515-12929-1, Jove) Berkley Pub.
Crease, J., et al, eds. Essays on Oceanography: A Tribute to John Swallow. (Illus.). 578p. 1984. 180.00 (0-08-032339-1, Pergamon Pr) Elsevier.
Crease, Robert, jt. auth. see Serber, Robert.
Crease, Robert P. Making Physics: A Biography of Brookhaven National Laboratory, 1946-1972. LC 98-30327. 1999. 38.00 (0-226-12017-1) U Ch Pr.
— Making Physics: A Biography of Brookhaven National Laboratory, 1946-1972. LC 98-30327. (Illus.). 434p. 2000. pap. text 22.50 (0-226-12019-8) U Ch Pr.
— The Play to Nature: Experimentation As Performance. LC 93-2735. (Indiana Series in the Philosophy of Technology). 228p. 1993. 12.95 (0-253-31474-7) Ind U Pr.
Crease, Robert P., ed. Hermeneutics & the Natural Sciences. LC 98-103982. 160p. 1998. text 80.00 (0-7923-4810-9) Kluwer Academic.
Crease, Robert P. & Mann, Charles C. The Second Creation: Makers of the Revolution in Twentieth-Century Physics. 491p. 1995. pap. text 21.95 (0-8135-2177-7) Rutgers U Pr.
Crease, Skid. In the Great Meadow. (Illus.). 32p. (J). (gr. k-3). 1994. pap. 5.95 (1-55037-998-4, Pub. by Annick); lib. bdg. 15.95 (1-55037-999-2, Pub. by Annick) Firefly Bks Ltd.
Creaser, jt. auth. see Davies.
Creasey, see Ashe, pseud.
Creasey, ed. see Ashe, pseud.
Creasey, D. J., et al, eds. Advanced Signal Processing. (Telecommunications Ser.: No. 13). 300p. 1985. boxed set 99.00 (0-86341-037-5, TE013) INSPEC Inc.
Creasey, George W. City of Newburyport, Massachusetts, in the Civil War from 1861 to 1865, with Individual Records of the Soldiers & Sailors Who Served to Its

C

An Asterisk (*) at the beginning of an entry indicates that the title is appearing for the first time.

Credit, Also the War Records of Many Natives & Residents of the City, Credited to Other Places. (Illus.). 539p. 1998. reprint ed. lib. bdg. 57.00 (*0-8328-7122-2*) Higginson Bk Co.

Creasey, John. The Baron on Board. large type ed. LC 91-33571. 274p. 1991. reprint ed. lib. bdg. 18.95 (*1-56054-265-9*) Thorndike Pr.

— Death on Demand. (Black Dagger Crime Ser.). 184p. 1997. 19.50 (*0-7451-8704-8*, Black Dagger) Chivers N Amer.

— The Mists of Fear. large type ed. 436p. 1973. 27.99 (*0-85456-161-7*) Ulverscroft.

— The Plague of Silence. large type ed. 1990. 12.00 (*0-85456-191-9*) Ulverscroft.

— Salute the Toff. LC 75-142845. 143p. (J). 1971. write for info. (*0-8027-5225-X*) Walker Pub Co.

— Stars for the Toff. LC 74-406345. (King Crime Ser.). 192p. (J). 1968. write for info. (*0-340-02945-5*) St Martin.

— The Toff among the Millions. LC 76-13798. 172 p. (J). 1976. write for info. (*0-8027-5349-3*) Walker Pubng.

— The Toff & Old Harry. LC 73-126117. 190p. 1970. write for info. (*0-8027-5217-9*) Walker Pub Co.

— The Toff & the Fallen Angels. LC 73-487417. (King Crime Ser.). 191p. (J). 1970. write for info. (*0-340-10620-4*) St Martin.

— The Toff & the Golden Boy. LC 75-395562. (King Crime Ser.). 158p. (J). 1969. write for info. (*0-340-10977-7*) St Martin.

— The Toff & the Lady. LC 75-24718. 189p. (J). 1975. write for info. (*0-8027-5336-1*) Walker Pubng.

— The Toff & the Sleepy Cowboy: The 56th Book of the Toff. LC 74-21731. 191 p. (J). 1975. write for info. (*0-8027-5313-2*) Walker Pubng.

***Creasey, John.** The Toff & the Stolen Tresses. LC 97-36723. 245p. 1998. write for info. (*0-7540-3124-1*) Chivers N Amer.

Creasey, John. The Toff & the Stolen Tresses. large type ed. LC 97-36723. 268p. 1998. 18.95 (*0-7838-8318-8*, G K Hall Lrg Type) Mac Lib Ref.

— The Toff & the Terrified Taxman. LC 73-83307. 192p. (J). 1973. write for info. (*0-8027-5281-0*) Walker Pub Co.

— The Toff & the Terrified Taxman: The 55th Book of the Toff. LC 73-175107. 192p. (J). 1973. write for info. (*0-340-16487-5*) St Martin.

— The Toff & the Trip-Trip-Triplets. LC 73-167371. (King Crime Ser.). 190p. (J). 1972. write for info. (*0-340-15234-6*) St Martin.

— The Toff & the Trip-Trip-Triplets. LC 72-80532. 190p. (J). 1972. write for info. (*0-8027-5264-0*) Walker Pub Co.

— The Toff in Town. LC 77-80630. 157 p. (J). 1977. write for info. (*0-8027-5380-9*) Walker Pubng.

— The Toff on Board. LC 72-95759. 158p. (J). 1973. write for info. (*0-8027-5270-5*) Walker Pub Co.

— Vote for the Toff. LC 78-161112. 189p. (J). 1971. write for info. (*0-8027-5236-5*) Walker Pub Co.

***Creasey, Malcolm.** The Complete Rock Climber. (Illus.). 2856p. 1999. 30.00 (*1-85967-908-0*, Lorenz Bks) Anness Pub.

Creasey, Pauline. Structural Adjustment in Europe. 280p. 1988. 35.00 (*0-86187-902-3*) St Martin.

Creasey, Pauline & May, Simon. The European Armaments Market & Procurement Cooperation LC 88-202605. x, 201p. 1988. write for info. (*0-333-45905-9*) Mac Bks.

Creasey, Robert K. & Boylan, Peter. Management of Labor & Delivery. LC 96-39912. (Illus.). 593p. 1997. 99.95 (*0-86542-416-0*) Blackwell Sci.

Creasey, William A. Diet & Cancer. LC 84-21845. 231p. reprint ed. pap. 71.70 (*0-7837-2696-1*, 204307400006) Bks Demand.

Creasia, Joan L. & Parker, Barbara J. Conceptual Foundations of Professional Nursing Practice. (Illus.). 1996. teacher ed. write for info. (*0-8151-1921-6*) Mosby Inc.

Creasia, Joan L. & Parker, Barbara J., eds. Conceptual Foundations of Professional Nursing Practice. 2nd ed. (Illus.). 528p. (C). (gr. 13). 1996. pap. text 37.00 (*0-8151-1406-0*, 24506) Mosby Inc.

Creason, Pam, jt. auth. see Sullivan, Wilma.

Creasy, Cathy. Spanish Walking with Jesus.Tr. of Caminando Con Jesus. (SPA., Illus.). 160p. 1998. pap. write for info. (*1-889505-28-5*) White Wing Pub.

Creasy, Donna N. Food Careers. (Home Economics Careers Ser.). (gr. 10-12). 1977. pap. 8.68 (*0-13-392704-0*) P-H.

Creasy, Edward S. Fifteen Decisive Battles of the Western World: From Marathon to Waterloo. (Illus.). 420p. 1994. reprint ed. pap. 15.95 (*0-306-80559-6*) Da Capo.

— First Platform of International Law. xv, 710p. 1998. reprint ed. 180.00 (*1-56169-435-5*) Gaunt.

***Creasy, Edward S.** The Rise & Progress of the English Constitution. xi, 340p. 1999. reprint ed. 107.00 (*1-56169-589-0*, 18453) Gaunt.

Creasy, Edward S. The Rise & Progress of the English Constitution. 16th ed. xii, 400p. 1986. reprint ed. 47.50 (*0-8377-0450-2*, Rothman) W S Hein.

Creasy, Robert K. & Resnick, Robert. Maternal-Fetal Medicine. 4th ed. Bralow, Lisette, ed. LC 98-12044. (Illus.). 1152p. (C). 1998. text 139.00 (*0-7216-7605-7*, W B Saunders Co) Harcrt Hlth Sci Grp.

Creasy, Robert K. & Resnik, Robert, eds. Maternal-Fetal Medicine: Principles & Practice. 3rd ed. LC 92-48215. (Illus.). 1168p. (C). 1993. text 135.00 (*0-7216-6590-X*, W B Saunders Co) Harcrt Hlth Sci Grp.

Creasy, Rosalind. Blue Potatoes, Orange Tomatoes: How to Grow a Rainbow Garden. (Illus.). 48p. (J). (gr. k-3). 1997. pap. 6.95 (*0-87156-919-1*, Pub. by Sierra Club Childrens) Little.

— Blue Potatoes, Orange Tomatoes: How to Grow a Rainbow Garden. (Sierra Club Bks.). 1997. 12.15 (*0-606-11143-3*, Pub. by Turtleback) Demco.

— The Complete Book of Edible Landscaping: Home Landscaping with Food-Bearing Plants & Resource-Saving Techniques. LC 81-14465. (Illus.). 400p. (Orig.). 1982. pap. 25.00 (*0-87156-278-2*, Pub. by Sierra) Random.

— Cooking from the Garden. LC 88-3117. (Illus.). 560p. 1988. 35.00 (*0-87156-731-8*, Pub. by Sierra) Random.

— The Edible Flower Garden. LC 98-36999. (Edible Garden Ser.). (Illus.). 112p. 1999. pap. 12.95 (*962-593-293-3*) Periplus.

— The Edible French Garden. LC 98-41026. (Edible Garden Ser.). (Illus.). 112p. 1999. pap. 12.95 (*962-593-292-5*) Periplus.

— The Edible Heirloom Garden. LC 98-41027. (Edible Garden Ser.). (Illus.). 112p. 1999. pap. 12.95 (*962-593-294-1*) Periplus.

— The Edible Herb Garden. LC 98-34729. (Edible Garden Ser.). (Illus.). 112p. 1999. pap. 9.95 (*962-593-291-7*) Periplus.

Creasy, Rosalind. The Edible Italian Garden. (Edible Garden Ser.). (Illus.). 112p. pap. 12.95 (*1-58017-287-3*) Storey Bks.

Creasy, Rosalind. The Edible Italian Vegetable Garden. LC 98-37000. (Edible Garden Ser.). (Illus.). 112p. 1999. pap. 12.95 (*962-593-295-X*) Periplus.

***Creasy, Rosalind.** The Edible Mexican Garden. LC 99-50250. (Illus.). 112p. 2000. pap. 14.95 (*962-593-297-6*) Periplus.

— The Edible Pepper Garden. LC 99-36394. (Illus.). 112p. 2000. pap. 14.95 (*962-593-296-8*) Periplus.

— The Edible Rainbow Garden. LC 99-36395. (Illus.). 112p. 2000. pap. 14.95 (*962-593-299-2*) Periplus.

Creasy, Rosalind. The Edible Salad Garden. LC 98-38174. (Edible Garden Ser.). (Illus.). 112p. 1999. pap. 12.95 (*962-593-290-9*) Periplus.

Creasy, Rosalind & Saville, Carole. Herbs: A Country Garden Cookbook. 96p. 1995. 15.95 (*0-00-255453-4*) Collins SF.

Creasy, William C. & Thomas, a Kempis. The Imitation of Christ: A New Reading of the 1441 Latin Autograph Manuscript. LC 89-2263. 210p. (C). 1989. 35.00 (*0-86554-339-9*, MUPH281) Mercer Univ Pr.

Creasy, William C., tr. see Thomas, a Kempis.

Creatchman, Marsha, jt. ed. see Landsberger, Sheldon.

Creates, Marlene. Places of Presence. (Illus.). 64p. 1997. pap. 12.95 (*1-895387-87-6*) Creative Bk Pub.

***Creath, Richard & Maienschein, Jane, eds.** Biology & Epistemology. LC 99-22990. (Studies in Philosophy & Biology). (Illus.). 240p. 1999. 59.95 (*0-521-59290-9*); pap. 19.95 (*0-521-59701-3*) Cambridge U Pr.

Creath, Wilgus, jt. auth. see Whitener, Angela.

Creation Enterprises International Staff, ed. see Thompson, Walter C.

Creation Enterprises Staff, ed. see Thompson, Walter C.

Creation House Staff, contrib. by. Iglesia para Ninos Vol. 2: Canas de Pescar y Vides Fructiteras - Extra Leader's Manual. 160p. 1999. teacher ed. 15.00 (*1-57405-454-6*) CharismaLife Pub.

Creation House Staff, ed. Iglesia para Ninos Vol. 2: Canas de Pescar y Vides Fructiferas. 160p. (J). (gr. 1-6). 1999. 129.95 (*1-57405-445-7*) CharismaLife Pub.

Creative & Co. Staff, ed. see Perkins-Carpenter, Betty.

Creative Colleagues Staff. Reading, Rhymes & Recipes: Stories & Recipes Just for Kids. (Illus.). 72p. (J). (gr. 2-6). 1994. pap. 9.00 (*0-9647181-0-3*) Sunshine Herit Pr.

Creative Company Staff, jt. auth. see Beattie, Laura C.

Creative Concepts Publishing Staff. How to Get Real with a Fake Book: A Guide for the Piano Arranger. 1998. 12.95 (*1-56922-121-9*, 07-2047) Creat Cncpts.

— Joy, Joy, Joy, Famous Hymns & Sacred Songs for Easy Piano. 1997. pap. 14.95 (*1-56922-167-7*) Creat Cncpts.

— Ragtime Revival: Original Piano Solos. (All-American Ragtime). 1997. pap. text 14.95 (*1-56922-163-4*) Creat Cncpts.

— Special Wedding. 1998. pap. 12.95 (*1-56922-112-X*); pap. text 12.95 (*1-56922-110-3*) Creat Cncpts.

Creative Editors. Basic Wiring. 3rd rev. ed. Homeowner Press Staff, ed. LC 95-83623. (Illus.). 160p. 1996. pap. 14.95 (*1-880029-79-0*) Creative Homeowner.

Creative Encouragers Staff. The Prayer Organizer: Making a Difference Through Personal Prayer. unabridged ed. 110p. 1996. reprint ed. ring bd. 24.95 (*1-890533-00-9*, Prayer Organizer) Creat Encouragers.

— The Prayer Organizer: Making a Difference Through Personal Prayer. 2nd rev. ed. (Illus.). xii, 116p. 1999. ring bd. 24.95 (*1-890533-03-3*); ring bd. 24.95 (*1-890533-04-1*) Creat Encouragers.

— The Prayer Organizer: Making a Difference Through Personal Prayer Adult Edition. 2nd abr. rev. ed. (Illus.). 110p. ring bd. 24.95 (*1-890533-02-5*, Prayer Organizer) Creat Encouragers.

— The Prayer Organizer: Making a Difference Through Personal Prayer Youth Edition. rev. ed. (Illus.). 110p. (YA). (gr. 7-12). 1997. ring bd. 24.95 (*1-890533-01-7*, Prayer Organizer) Creat Encouragers.

Creative Findings Ltd. Staff. Creative Findings Ltd. 120p. 1990. 25.00 (*0-9643145-0-9*) Creat Fndings.

Creative Homeowner Press Editors. Fences, Gates & Trellises: Plan, Design, Build. LC 97-68496. (Illus.). 160p. 1997. pap. 14.95 (*1-880029-96-0*) Creative Homeowner.

— Quick Guide: Ceramic Tile. Barrett, Jim, ed. LC 93-71661. (Quick Guide Ser.). (Illus.). 80p. 1993. pap. 7.95 (*1-880029-21-9*) Creative Homeowner.

— 600 Most Popular Home Plans. LC 98-85181. (Illus.). 480p. 1999. pap. 9.95 (*1-58011-023-1*) Creative Homeowner.

— Smart Approach to Home Decorating. Robitz, Kathie & Elliott, Lynn, eds. LC 98-84952. (Illus.). 256p. 1998. pap. 24.95 (*1-58011-050-9*) Creative Homeowner.

— 380 Country & Farmhouse Home Plans. LC 98-87397. (Illus.). 352p. 1999. pap. 9.95 (*1-58011-060-5*) Creative Homeowner.

Creative Homeowner Press Editors, ed. Planning a Better Kitchen. 2nd rev. ed. LC 96-84701. (Illus.). 96p. 1996. pap. 10.95 (*1-880029-90-1*) Creative Homeowner.

Creative Homeowner Press Editors, jt. auth. see Beall, Christine.

Creative Homeowner Press Editors, ed. see Feirer, Mark.

Creative Media Applications Staff, ed. see Quin-Hamlin, Janet.

Creative Needle Magazine. A Creative Needle Christmas. Henderson, Ann, ed. (Illus.). 208p. 1997. pap. 34.50 (*0-9660674-0-1*) Needle Pub.

Creative Nursing Management Staff, ed. One Nurse's Notes: A Personal Journal. 78p. (Orig.). 1988. pap. 5.00 (*0-9621520-6-4*) Creative Nursing.

Creative Press. El Expreso Preescolar: Numeros. (J). (ps). 1985. pap. text 3.00 (*0-201-58062-4*) Addison-Wesley.

Creative Products International Staff. Home Buddy: The Essential Family & Home Care Organizer. (Illus.). 44p. 1990. 12.95 (*0-9626775-0-7*) Creative Prods Intl.

Creative Publications Staff. MathTivities! Classroom Activities for Grades One Through Six. LC 97-104172. 240p. 1996. 27.95 (*0-534-52740-X*) Wadsworth Pub.

Creative Publishing Concepts Staff, ed. see Loriuar, Audrea.

***Creative Publishing International, Inc. Staff.** Best Wishes: Gifts for Special Occasions. LC 99-49669. (Illus.). 176p. 2000. 24.95 (*0-86573-864-5*); pap. 19.95 (*0-86573-865-3*) Creat Pub Intl.

— Big Bass Secrets: Catch Trophy Largemouth & Smallmouth with Experts of Outdoor Life. LC 99-56908. (Outdoor Life Ser.). 224p. 2000. pap. 14.95 (*0-86573-111-X*) Creat Pub Intl.

— Black & Decker The Complete Guide to Creative Landscapes. (Complete Guide Ser.). (Illus.). 320p. 2000. pap. 24.95 (*0-86573-579-4*) Creat Pub Intl.

— Building Garden Ornaments: 24 Do-It-Yourself Projects to Accent Any Setting. LC 99-55662. (Outdoor Home Ser.). 112p. 2000. 18.95 (*0-86573-587-5*) Creat Pub Intl.

— Building Garden Ornaments: 24 Do-It-Yourself Projects to Accent Any Setting. LC 99-55662. (Outdoor Home Ser.). (Illus.). 112p. 2000. pap. 14.95 (*0-86573-590-5*) Creat Pub Intl.

— Color & Design on Fabric. LC 99-54247. (Singer Design Ser.). (Illus.). 128p. 2000. write for info. (*0-86573-869-6*) Creat Pub Intl.

— Color & Design on Fabric: Paint, Dye, Stitch, Print. (Singer Design Ser.). (Illus.). 112p. 2000. pap. 18.95 (*0-86573-870-X*) Creat Pub Intl.

— The Complete Guide to Creative Landscapes: Designing, Building & Decorating Your Outdoor Home. (Complete Guide Ser.). (Illus.). 320p. 2000. 24.95 (*0-86573-578-6*) Creat Pub Intl.

— The Complete Guide to Home Masonry: Step-by-Step Projects & Repairs Using Concrete, Brick, Block & Stone. LC 99-57797. (Illus.). 288p. 2000. 24.95 (*0-86573-592-1*) Creat Pub Intl.

— Complete Photo Guide to Home Repair. (Illus.). 2000. 34.95 (*0-86573-543-3*) Creat Pub Intl.

Creative Publishing International, Inc. Staff. Crafts in a Flash: Quick, Quicker & Quickest Projects. (Illus.). 160p. 1998. pap. text 19.95 (*0-86573-186-1*) Creat Pub Intl.

— Creative Floral Arranging. (Arts & Crafts for Home Decorating Ser.). (Illus.). 224p. 1998. pap. text 19.95 (*0-86573-191-8*) Creat Pub Intl.

— Creative Room Styles: Room-by Room Guide to Interior Decorating. 144p. 1998. pap. text 17.95 (*0-86573-194-2*) Creat Pub Intl.

— Deck the Halls: A Treasury of Christmas Crafts. 160p. 1998. pap. text 19.95 (*0-86573-187-X*) Creat Pub Intl.

***Creative Publishing International, Inc. Staff.** Dinner Tonight: Pasta, Chicken, Grilling. LC 99-47730. (Land O'Lakes Ser.). (Illus.). 224p. 2000. 24.95 (*0-86573-871-8*) Creat Pub Intl.

Creative Publishing International, Inc. Staff. Fast & Easy Decorating Ideas: Hundreds of Inspiring Ideas. LC 98-45292. (Illus.). 144p. 1999. pap. text 17.95 (*0-86573-333-3*) Creat Pub Intl.

— Festive Christmas. 224p. 1998. pap. text 24.95 (*0-86573-192-6*) Creat Pub Intl.

***Creative Publishing International, Inc. Staff.** Fishing North America: How to Locate & Catch Popular Freshwater Species. (Freshwater Angler Ser.). 192p. 2000. pap. 12.95 (*0-86573-114-4*) Creat Pub Intl.

Creative Publishing International, Inc. Staff. Garments for Beginners. (Seams Sew Easy Ser.). (Illus.). 128p. 1998. spiral bd. 17.95 (*0-86573-328-7*) Creat Pub Intl.

— Guide to Pattern & Color: Decorating Ideas for Your Home. 144p. 1998. pap. text 17.95 (*0-86573-193-4*) Creat Pub Intl.

— Interior Accents: Over 25 Step-by-Step Decorating Projects. LC 98-44470. (Illus.). 144p. 1999. pap. text 17.95 (*0-86573-334-1*) Creat Pub Intl.

— Joy to the World. 160p. 1998. pap. text 19.95 (*0-86573-188-8*) Creat Pub Intl.

***Creative Publishing International, Inc. Staff.** Kitchen Remodeling: Planning & Reference Guide. LC 99-87082. (Today's Homeowner Ser.). (Illus.). 160p. 2000. 24.95 (*0-86573-589-1*); pap. 19.95 (*0-86573-588-3*) Creat Pub Intl.

— Luring Largemouth Bass: Sure-Fire Strategies for Catching More & Bigger Bass. LC 99-59734. (Freshwater Angler Ser.). (Illus.). 192p. 2000. pap. 12.95 (*0-86573-117-9*) Creat Pub Intl.

— The New Everyday Home Repairs: Simple, Effective Solutions to Your Home's Most Common Problems. (Home Improvement Library). (Illus.). 160p. 2000. pap. 16.95 (*0-86573-591-3*) Creat Pub Intl.

— Nursery Decor for Beginners. LC 99-88292. (Coats & Clark Ser.). (Illus.). 128p. 2000. 17.95 (*0-86573-866-1*) Creat Pub Intl.

Creative Publishing International, Inc. Staff. Quilting for Beginners. LC 98-28530. (Seams Sew Easy Ser.). (Illus.). 128p. 1998. spiral bd. 17.95 (*0-86573-327-9*) Creat Pub Intl.

— Sewing with a Serger. rev. ed. (Singer Sewing Reference Library). Orig. Title: Sewing with an Overlock. (Illus.). 128p. 1998. pap. text 16.95 (*0-86573-330-9*) Creat Pub Intl.

***Creative Publishing International, Inc. Staff.** Striped Bass Fishing: Salt Water Strategies. LC 99-59350. (Salt Water Sportsman Ser.). (Illus.). 144p. 2000. 21.95 (*0-86573-113-6*) Creat Pub Intl.

Creative Publishing International, Inc. Staff. Today's Homeowner: Essential Home Tips. 160p. 1998. pap. text 19.95 (*0-86573-774-6*) Creat Pub Intl.

***Creative Publishing International, Inc. Staff & Black & Decker Manufacturing Company Staff.** The Complete Guide to Home Carpentry. LC 00-31539. (Complete Guide Ser.). (Illus.). 288p. 2000. pap. 24.95 (*0-86573-577-8*) Creat Pub Intl.

Creative Publishing International, Inc. Staff & Black & Decker Staff. The Complete Guide to Home Plumbing. LC 98-34999. (Illus.). 256p. 1998. pap. 19.95 (*0-86573-775-4*) Creat Pub Intl.

***Creative Publishing International Staff.** Amazing Animals. (Illus.). 2000. 16.95 (*1-55971-752-1*) Creat Pub Intl.

Creative Publishing International Staff. Around the Yard: 750 Essential Tips & Projects for Improving Your Landscape. LC 98-53679. (Today's Homeowner Ser.). (Illus.). 160p. 1999. 24.95 (*0-86573-634-0*) Creat Pub Intl.

— Black & Decker Easy Wood Furniture Projects: 32 Step-by-Step Projects for the Home. LC 99-24778. (Black & Decker Home Improvement Library). (Illus.). 158p. 1999. pap. 16.95 (*0-86573-630-8*) Creat Pub Intl.

***Creative Publishing International Staff.** Black & Decker Stonework & Masonry Projects. LC 00-22691. (Black & Decker Home Improvement Library). (Illus.). 128p. 2000. pap. 16.95 (*0-86573-582-4*) Creat Pub Intl.

Creative Publishing International Staff. Building Your Outdoor Home: 30 Easy, Essential Landscaping Projects. LC 98-49605. (Black & Decker Outdoor Home Ser.). 112p. 1999. pap. text 14.95 (*0-86573-756-8*) Creat Pub Intl.

***Creative Publishing International Staff.** Catching Catfish: The Ultimate Guide: Blues, Flatheads, Channels. LC 99-52586. (Freshwater Angler Ser.). (Illus.). 192p. 2000. pap. 12.95 (*0-86573-115-2*) Creat Pub Intl.

— Catfish Identification. (Fisherman's Pocket Guides Ser.). (Illus.). 2000. pap. 4.99 (*0-86573-478-X*) Creat Pub Intl.

— Christmas Classics: Projects, Gifts & Recipes for a Festive Holiday. (Illus.). 320p. 2000. write for info. (*0-86573-544-1*) Creat Pub Intl.

Creative Publishing International Staff. Christmas Crafts & Entertaining. LC 99-24590. (Illus.). 320p. 1999. 24.95 (*0-86573-178-0*) Creat Pub Intl.

***Creative Publishing International Staff.** Christmas Traditions: Gifts, Recipes for a Festive Family Holiday. 320p. 2000. write for info. (*0-86573-545-X*) Creat Pub Intl.

— Christmas Treasures: Projects, Gifts & Recipes for a Festive Family Holiday. (Illus.). 320p. 2000. write for info. (*0-86573-546-8*) Creat Pub Intl.

— Classic Stories. (Outdoor Life Ser.). (Illus.). 224p. 2000. pap. 14.95 (*0-86573-122-5*) Creat Pub Intl.

— Cleaning Fish. (Fisherman's Pocket Guides Ser.). (Illus.). 2000. pap. 4.99 (*0-86573-473-9*) Creat Pub Intl.

Creative Publishing International Staff. The Complete Guide to Decks. LC 98-49169. (Black & Decker Ser.). (Illus.). 288p. 1998. pap. text 19.95 (*0-86573-181-0*) Creat Pub Intl.

***Creative Publishing International Staff.** The Complete Hunter Hunting in North America: Big Game - Small Game - Upland Birds - Waterfowl - Wild Turkey. (Complete Hunter Ser.). (Illus.). 192p. 2000. pap. 12.95 (*0-86573-120-9*) Creat Pub Intl.

Creative Publishing International Staff. The Complete Photo Guide to Home Repair: 2000 Color How-To Photos. LC 99-26355. (Black & Decker Ser.). (Illus.). 512p. 1999. 34.95 (*0-86573-753-3*) Creat Pub Intl.

— Curtains. LC 97-29097. (Creative Textiles Ser.). (Illus.). 112p. 1997. pap. 16.95 (*0-86573-412-7*) Creat Pub Intl.

***Creative Publishing International Staff.** Decoying Ducks. (Hunter's Pocket Guides Ser.). (Illus.). 2000. pap. 4.99 (*0-86573-483-6*) Creat Pub Intl.

— Deer Stand Locations. (Hunter's Pocket Guides Ser.). (Illus.). 2000. pap. 4.99 (*0-86573-481-X*) Creat Pub Intl.

Creative Publishing International Staff. Designer Projects for Bed & Bath. LC 98-49789. (Singer Sewing Reference Library). (Illus.). 128p. 1999. 18.95 (*0-86573-331-7*); pap. text 16.95 (*0-86573-332-5*) Creat Pub Intl.

— Designing Your Outdoor Home: Landscape Planning Made Easy. LC 98-49604. (Black & Decker Outdoor Home Ser.). (Illus.). 112p. 1999. pap. text 14.95 (*0-86573-755-X*) Creat Pub Intl.

***Creative Publishing International Staff.** Designing Your Outdoor Home: Landscape Planning Made Easy. LC 98-53679. (Today's Homeowner Ser.). (Illus.). 112p. 1999. pap. text 14.95 (*0-86573-635-9*) Creat Pub Intl.

— Diving Duck Identification. (Hunter's Pocket Guides Ser.). (Illus.). 2000. pap. 4.99 (*0-86573-482-8*) Creat Pub Intl.

— Do-It-Yourself Fabric Decor: Pillows, Window Treatments & Slipcovers for Home. (Illus.). 320p. 2000. pap. 24.95 (*0-86573-345-7*) Creat Pub Intl.

Creative Publishing International Staff. Fantastic Frames. LC 98-49400. (Illus.). 64p. 1999. pap. text 9.95 (*0-86573-418-6*) Creat Pub Intl.

C

***Creative Publishing International Staff.** Field-Dressing Deer. (Hunter's Pocket Guides Ser.). (Illus.). 2000. pap. 4.99 (*0-86573-472-0*) Creat Pub Intl.

— Finishing Basements & Attics: Ideas & Projects for Expanding Your Living Space. (Black & Decker Home Improvement Library). (Illus.). 160p. 2000. pap. 16.95 (*0-86573-583-2*) Creat Pub Intl.

— Fishing with Artificial Lures: The Complete Guide to Catching Fish on Spinners, Plugs, Soft Plastics, Jigs, Spoons & Flies. LC 99-44755. (Freshwater Angler Ser.). (Illus.). 128p. 1999. 19.95 (*0-86573-110-1*) Creat Pub Intl.

— Forest Animals: Explore the Fascinating Worlds Of...Wolves - Moose - Deer - Black Bear. (Illus.). 2000. 14.95 (*1-55971-708-4*) Creat Pub Intl.

Creative Publishing International Staff. Frame It Yourself: Matting & Framing Step-by-Step. LC 98-43513. (Illus.). 64p. 1999. pap. text 9.95 (*0-86573-419-4*) Creat Pub Intl.

***Creative Publishing International Staff.** Gamefish Identification. (Fisherman's Pocket Guides Ser.). (Illus.). 2000. pap. 4.99 (*0-86573-475-5*) Creat Pub Intl.

Creative Publishing International Staff. Hand-Crafted Weddings: Over 100 Projects & Ideas for Personalizing Your Wedding. LC 99-23625. (Illus.). 192p. 1999. 24.95 (*0-86573-177-2*) Creat Pub Intl.

***Creative Publishing International Staff.** Holiday Theme Parties: Entertaining Ideas, Decorations & Recipes for Nine Unique Parties. LC 00-29500. (Illus.). 144p. 2000. 24.95 (*0-86573-342-2*) Creat Pub Intl.

— Home Decor for Beginners. (Seams Sew Easy Ser.). (Illus.). 128p. 2000. 17.95 (*0-86573-343-0*) Creat Pub Intl.

Creative Publishing International Staff. Hunter's Field Guide. 1999. pap., wbk. ed. write for info. (*0-86573-088-1*) Creat Pub Intl.

***Creative Publishing International Staff.** Knots. (Fisherman's Pocket Guides Ser.). (Illus.). 2000. pap. 4.99 (*0-86573-474-7*) Creat Pub Intl.

Creative Publishing International Staff. The New Kitchen Remodeling. LC 98-49173. (Black & Decker Home Improvement Library). (Illus.). 160p. 1999. pap. text 16.95 (*0-86573-638-3*) Creat Pub Intl.

— The New Quilting by Machine. LC 98-49890. (Singer Sewing Reference Library). (Illus.). 128p. 1999. pap. text 16.95 (*0-86573-335-X*) Creat Pub Intl.

— On the Edge: True Tales of High Adventures from Outdoor Life's Best Storytellers. LC 99-32155. (Times Mirror - Outdoor Life Ser.). (Illus.). 224p. 1999. pap. write for info. (*0-86573-105-5*) Creat Pub Intl.

— Outdoor Wood Furnishing: 35 Easy Projects for Your Yard. LC 98-49168. (Black & Decker Outdoor Home Ser.). (Illus.). 160p. 1998. pap. text 16.95 (*0-86573-633-2*) Creat Pub Intl.

***Creative Publishing International Staff.** Panfish Identification. (Fisherman's Pocket Guides Ser.). (Illus.). 2000. pap. 4.99 (*0-86573-476-3*) Creat Pub Intl.

Creative Publishing International Staff. Pillows. LC 97-7673. (Creative Textiles Ser.). (Illus.). 112p. (Orig.). 1997. pap. 16.95 (*0-86573-410-0*) Creat Pub Intl.

— A Portfolio of Home Office Ideas. LC 98-7294. (Illus.). 96p. 1998. pap. 10.95 (*0-86573-889-0*) Creat Pub Intl.

***Creative Publishing International Staff.** Puddle Duck Identification. (Hunter's Pocket Guides Ser.). (Illus.). 2000. pap. 4.99 (*0-86573-484-4*) Creat Pub Intl.

— Quartering Deer. (Hunter's Pocket Guides Ser.). (Illus.). 2000. pap. 4.99 (*0-86573-477-1*) Creat Pub Intl.

Creative Publishing International Staff. Saltwater Fishing Tactics: Learn from the Experts at Saltwater. LC 98-49172. (Illus.). 176p. 1999. pap. text 21.95 (*0-86573-085-7*) Creat Pub Intl.

— Sewing for Children. LC 99-34194. (Singer Sewing Reference Library). (Illus.). 128p. 1999. pap. 16.95 (*0-86573-174-8*) Creat Pub Intl.

***Creative Publishing International Staff.** Shot Placement. (Hunter's Pocket Guides Ser.). (Illus.). 2000. pap. 4.99 (*0-86573-480-1*) Creat Pub Intl.

Creative Publishing International Staff. Singer. LC 99-29394. (Singer Ser.). (Illus.). 320p. 1999. text 24.95 (*0-86573-173-X*) Creat Pub Intl.

***Creative Publishing International Staff.** Skinning Deer. (Hunter's Pocket Guides Ser.). (Illus.). 2000. pap. 4.99 (*0-86573-479-8*) Creat Pub Intl.

Creative Publishing International Staff. Small Engine Care & Repair. LC 98-42057. (Illus.). 128p. 1998. pap. text 14.95 (*0-86573-180-2*) Creat Pub Intl.

— Successful Walleye Fishing. LC 99-11918. (Illus.). 128p. 1999. 19.95 (*0-86573-095-4*) Creat Pub Intl.

— This Happened to Me. LC 99-27765. (Times Mirror - Outdoor Life Ser.). (Illus.). 224p. 1999. pap. 14.95 (*0-86573-107-1*) Creat Pub Intl.

— Trophy Whitetails. LC 99-33020. (Illus.). 224p. 1999. pap. 14.95 (*0-86573-104-7*) Creat Pub Intl.

***Creative Publishing International Staff.** Trout & Salmon Identification. (Fisherman's Pocket Guides Ser.). (Illus.). 2000. pap. 4.99 (*0-86573-471-2*) Creat Pub Intl.

— Turkey Season: Outdoor Life's Experts Share Their Tips, Techniques & Classic Stories. LC 99-49668. (Outdoor Life Ser.). (Illus.). 224p. 2000. pap. 14.95 (*0-86573-112-8*) Creat Pub Intl.

Creative Publishing International Staff. Weekend Projects: Easy Ways to Improve Your Home. LC 99-33032. (Today's Homeowner Ser.). (Illus.). 160p. 1999. 24.95 (*0-86573-778-9*) Creat Pub Intl.

— The World Incredible Outdoor Adventures. LC 98-54429. (Field & Stream Ser.). (Illus.). 160p. 1999. 24.95 (*0-86573-092-X*); pap. text 19.95 (*0-86573-093-8*) Creat Pub Intl.

***Creative Publishing International Staff.** The World of Big Game Hunting. LC 99-38861. (Field & Stream Ser.). (Illus.). 160p. 1999. 24.95 (*0-86573-098-9*) Creat Pub Intl.

Creative Publishing International Staff. The World of Big Game Hunting. LC 99-38861. (Field & Stream Ser.). (Illus.). 160p. 1999. pap. 19.95 (*0-86573-099-7*) Creat Pub Intl.

— The World of Fishing for Large Mouth Bass. LC 98-48228. (Illus.). 160p. 1999. 24.95 (*0-86573-090-3*); pap. text 19.95 (*0-86573-091-1*) Creat Pub Intl.

***Creative Publishing International Staff, ed.** Today's Homeowner: Around the Home & Yard. LC 00-25701. (Illus.). 2000. 24.95 (*0-86573-586-7*) Creat Pub Intl.

Creative Publishing International Staff & Crafts Magazine Staff. Make It Merry: A Medley of Christmas Crafts. LC 99-23412. 176p. 1999. 24.95 (*0-86573-175-6*) Creat Pub Intl.

— Make it Merry: A Medley of Christmas Crafts. LC 99-23412. (Illus.). 176p. 1999. pap. 19.95 (*0-86573-176-4*) Creat Pub Intl.

***Creative Publishing International Staff & Pillsbury Company Staff.** Pillsbury: All Time Favorite Sweets & Treats. LC 99-26467. (Illus.). 96p. 1999. pap. 14.95 (*0-86573-541-7*) Creat Pub Intl.

Creative Publishing International Staff & Today's Homeowner. Weekend Projects: Easy Ways to Improve Your Home. LC 99-33032. (Today's Homeowner Ser.). (Illus.). 160p. 1999. pap. 19.95 (*0-86573-779-7*) Creat Pub Intl.

Creative Publishing International Staff, jt. auth. see Land O Lakes Staff.

Creative Publishing International Staff, jt. auth. see McManus, Patrick F.

Creative Street, Inc. Staff. Living with High Blood Pressure. 1988. 34.95 incl. VHS (*0-929079-01-9*) Creative Street.

Creaton, Heather, compiled by. London. LC 96-223555. (World Bibliographical Ser.: Vol. 189). 200p. 1996. lib. bdg. 67.00 (*1-85109-248-X*, DA679) ABC-CLIO.

Creaton, Heather, jt. auth. see Gibson, J. S. W.

Creators of the Unofficial Guide. The Eclectic Gourmet Guide to Orlando. LC 99-13544. 256p. 1999. pap. 11.95 (*0-89732-291-6*) Menasha Ridge.

Creatsas, G. & European Society of Contraception Staff. Contraception Today: The Proceedings of the 4th Congress of the European Society of Contraception. Capdevila, C. Coll & Cortit, L. Iglesias, eds. LC 97-48549. (International Congress, Symposium & Seminar Ser.: Vol. 14). (Illus.). 294p. 1998. 78.00 (*1-85070-767-7*) Prthnon Pub.

***Creatsas, G., et al.** The Young Woman at the Rise of the 21st Century: Gynecological & Reproductive Issues in Health & Disease. LC 00-23979. (Annals of the New York Academy of Science Ser.). 2000. pap. write for info. (*1-57331-227-4*) NY Acad Sci.

Creatsas, George. Adolescent Gynecology & Endocrinology. 1999. pap. text 24.95 (*0-8018-6215-9*) Johns Hopkins.

Creatsas, George, et al, eds. Update on Adolescent Gynecology & Endocrinology: Basic & Clinical Aspects. LC 97-13702. (Annals of the New York Academy of Sciences Ser.: Vol. 816). 1997. pap. 140.00 (*1-57331-039-5*) NY Acad Sci.

— Update on Adolescent Gynecology & Endocrinology: Basic & Clinical Aspects, Vol. 816. LC 97-13702. 1997. 140.00 (*1-57331-038-7*) NY Acad Sci.

Creavalle, Laura. The Lite Lifestyle. 126p. 1999. pap. 19.95 (*0-9669168-4-0*) Club Creavalle.

— A Taste of Club Creavalle. 6th ed. 156p. 1998. reprint ed. 24.95 (*0-9669168-1-6*) Club Creavalle.

Creavalle, Laura, jt. auth. see Aceto, Chris.

Creaven, Fintan. The Stepping Stone of God: Creation: Earth Bound Spirituality. 122p. 1996. pap. 39.95 (*0-85439-497-4*, Pub. by St Paul Pubns) St Mut.

Creazza, G. & Mele, M., eds. Advanced Problems in Bridge Construction. (CISM International Centre for Mechanical Sciences Ser.: Vol. 316). (Illus.). vi, 296p. 1991. 86.95 (*0-387-82318-2*) Spr-Verlag.

Crebbin, June. Cows in the Kitchen. LC 97-40960. (Illus.). 32p. (J). (ps-k). 1998. 15.99 (*0-7636-0645-6*) Candlewick Pr.

Crebbin, June. Cows Moo, Cars Toot. (Illus.). 96p. 1996. pap. 7.95 (*0-14-036959-7*, Pub. by Pnguin Bks Ltd) Trafalgar.

Crebbin, June. Danny's Duck. LC 94-10434. (Illus.). (J). 1995. 13.95 (*1-56402-536-5*) Candlewick Pr.

— Danny's Duck. 1996. 11.19 (*0-606-09181-5*, Pub. by Turtleback) Demco.

Crebbin, June. Finder's Keepers. (J). 1991. pap. 7.95 (*0-14-034073-4*, Pub. by Pnguin Bks Ltd) Trafalgar.

Crebbin, June. Fly by Night. LC 92-53140. (Illus.). 32p. (J). (ps up). 1993. 14.95 (*1-56402-149-1*) Candlewick Pr.

— Fly by Night. LC 92-53140. (Illus.). 1995. pap. 5.99 (*1-56402-508-X*) Candlewick Pr.

— Into the Castle. LC 95-38197. (Illus.). 32p. (J). (ps up). 1997. reprint ed. pap. 5.99 (*0-7636-0120-9*) Candlewick Pr.

— The Train Ride. LC 94-15156. (Illus.). (J). (ps up). 1995. 14.95 (*1-56402-546-2*) Candlewick Pr.

— Train Ride. 1996. 11.19 (*0-606-09985-9*, Pub. by Turtleback) Demco.

— The Train Ride. LC 94-15156. (Illus.). 32p. (J). 1996. reprint ed. pap. 5.99 (*1-56402-842-9*) Candlewick Pr.

— The Train Ride: Level Two, Yellow. LC 98-88096. (Reading Together Ser.). (Illus.). (J). 1999. pap. write for info. (*0-7636-0866-1*) Candlewick Pr.

— El Viaje en Tren. Roehrich-Rubio, Esther, tr.Tr. of Train Ride. (SPA., Illus.). 32p. (J). (ps-k). 1998. 14.95 (*1-880507-36-6*) Lectorum Pubns.

Crebbin, June & Vulliamy, Clara. Danny's Duck. LC 94-10434. (Illus.). 32p. (J). 1996. reprint ed. pap. 5.99 (*1-56402-813-5*) Candlewick Pr.

Creber, Ann. Little Book of Vinegars. (Illus.). 114p. 1991. 11.95 (*0-685-41000-5*) HarpC.

— Mustards. LC 94-66. (Williams-Sonoma Essentials Ser.). (Illus.). 1994. 9.95 (*1-875137-19-X*) Weldon Owen.

— Oils. LC 94-4155. (Williams-Sonoma Essentials Ser.). (Illus.). 1994. 9.95 (*1-875137-21-1*) Weldon Owen.

— Vinegars. LC 94-4154. (Williams-Sonoma Essentials Ser.). (Illus.). 1994. 9.95 (*1-875137-20-3*) Weldon Owen.

Creber, Ann & King, Elisabeth. The World's Finest Food: 180 Classic Recipes from Around the World. Olds, Margaret, ed. LC 94-17050. (Illus.). 304p. 45.00 (*1-55670-374-0*) Stewart Tabori & Chang.

Creber, Diane. Crystalline Glazes. (Illus.). 96p. 1997. text. write for info. (*90-5703-881-1*, Harwood Acad Pubs) Gordon & Breach.

Creber, Diane. Crystalline Glazes. (Illus.). 104p. 1998. pap. 24.95 (*0-8122-1648-2*) U of Pa Pr.

Creber, G., jt. auth. see Wrobel, M.

Creber, Geoffrey, jt. compiled by see Wrobel, Murray.

Crebillion, Fils. Egarements du Coeur et de L'Esprit. (Folio Ser.: No. 891). (FRE.). pap. 8.95 (*2-07-036891-2*) Schoenhof.

Crebillon, Claude. Zadig: Or the Book Fate, 1749. Incl. Amours of Zeokinizal King of the Kofirans, 1749. 1975. (Flowering of the Novel, 1740-1775 Ser.: Vol. 25). 1975. Set lib. bdg. 61.00 (*0-8240-1124-4*) Garland.

Crebillon, Claude P. The Wayward Head & Heart. Bray, Barbara, tr. LC 78-16439. 221p. 1978. reprint ed. lib. bdg. 59.50 (*0-313-20578-7*, CRWH, Greenwood Pr) Greenwood.

Crebillon Fils. Les Egarements Du Coeur et De l'Esprit. (FRE.). 309p. 1977. pap. 10.95 (*0-7859-1838-8*, 2070368912) Fr & Eur.

Crebillon, M. De, see De Crebillon, M.

Crecelius, Allan M. & Comrie, Sandra M. Strategic Management: Creating Your Credit Union's Future. 257p. (Orig.). 1994. pap. 99.00 (*1-889394-22-X*) Credit Union Execs.

Crecelius, Allan M., jt. auth. see Comrie, Sandra M.

Crecelius, Daniel. The Roots of Modern Egypt: A Study of the Regimes of Ali Bey al-Kabir & Muhammad Bey Abu al-Dhahab, 1760-1775. LC 81-65972. (Middle Eastern History Studies: No. 6). 300p. (C). 1982. 30.00 (*0-88297-029-1*) Bibliotheca.

Crecelius, Daniel, ed. Eighteenth Century Egypt: The Arabic Manuscript Sources. xiv, 143p. 1991. 26.95 (*0-941690-42-3*) Regina Bks.

Crecelius, Daniel & Al-Wahhab Bakr, 'Abd. Al-Damurdashi's Chronicle of Egypt 1688-1755: Al-Durra al-Musana fi Akhbar al-Kinana. LC 91-10886. (Arab History & Civilization, Studies & Texts: Vol. 2). (Illus.). xii, 425p. 1991. 176.00 (*90-04-09408-3*) Brill Academic Pubs.

Crecelius, Kathryn J. Family Romances: George Sand's Early Novels. LC 86-43051. 191p. 1987. reprint ed. pap. 59.30 (*0-608-01056-1*, 205936400001) Bks Demand.

Crecine, John P., ed. Financing the Metropolis: Public Policy in Urban Economies. LC 72-103479. (Urban Affairs Annual Reviews Ser.: Vol. 4). 632p. reprint ed. pap. 196.00 (*0-608-14195-X*, 202188400026) Bks Demand.

Crecine, John P., jt. ed. see Nagel, Stuart S.

Crecraft, Earl W. Freedom of the Seas. LC 70-102232. (Select Bibliographies Reprint Ser.). 1977. 29.95 (*0-8369-5117-4*) Ayer.

Crecy, M. Vocabulaire Litteraire du Moyen Age. (FRE.). 1997. 49.95 (*0-320-00881-9*) Fr & Eur.

Crede, Andreas. Las Sociedades de Conocimiento... En Sintesis: Tecnologia de la Informacion para un Desarrollo Sustentable. LC 98-702657. (SPA & ENG., Illus.). 50p. 1988. pap. 9.95 (*0-88936-860-0*, Pub. by IDRC Bks) Stylus Pub VA.

***Crede, Andreas & Mansell, Robin.** Knowledge Societies... In a Nutshell: Information Technology for Sustainable Development. 40p. 1998. pap. 9.95 (*0-88936-858-9*) IDRC Bks.

— Les Societes du Savoir... En Bref: La Technologie de l'Information au Service du Developpement Durable. (FRE.). 1998. pap. 9.95 (*0-88936-859-7*, Pub. by IDRC Bks) Stylus Pub VA.

***Credentialing & E Center Staff.** Official Study Course for the National Counselor Examination for Licensure & Certification (NC), 1. 1999. pap. text. write for info. (*1-56032-882-7*) Hemisp Pub.

Credidio, Scott. Guide to Owning a Shetland Sheepdog: AKC Rank #14. (Guide to Owning Ser.). (Illus.). 64p. 1995. pap. 6.95 (*0-7938-1869-9*, RE-319) TFH Pubns.

***Credit, Larry, et al.** Relieving Sciatica: Using Complementary Medicine to Overcome the Pain of Sciatica. LC 99-32978. 224p. 2000. pap. 10.95 (*0-89529-921-6*, Avery) Penguin Putnam.

Credit, Larry, et al. Your Guide to Complementary Medicine: Everything You Need to Know about Choosing. LC 98-9175. 224p. 1998. pap. 10.95 (*0-89529-831-7*, Avery) Penguin Putnam.

Credit Research Foundation. Credit Management Reports. 18p. 1975. 40.00 (*0-939050-14-5*) Credit Res NYS.

— Failure Probability Factors. 12p. 1979. 40.00 (*0-939050-26-9*) Credit Res NYS.

Credit Research Foundation Staff. Accounts Receivable Information System. 12p. 1974. 40.00 (*0-939050-02-1*) Credit Res NYS.

— Allocating Credit & Receivable Costs. 16p. 1984. 40.00 (*0-939050-03-X*) Credit Res NYS.

— Cash Application from Regional Locations. 11p. 1975. 40.00 (*0-939050-04-8*) Credit Res NYS.

— Compensation of Credit Executives Study. 64p. 1999. pap. 20.00 (*0-614-06133-4*) NACM.

— Credit Analysis Method. 1989. 40.00 (*0-939050-58-7*) Credit Res NYS.

— Credit Department Primer for Small Business. 34p. 1985. 40.00 (*0-939050-12-9*) Credit Res NYS.

— Credit Executives Handbook. 650p. 1986. 49.50 (*0-939050-01-3*) Credit Res NYS.

— Credit File Storage & Retrieval. 15p. 1983. 40.00 (*0-939050-13-7*) Credit Res NYS.

— Credit Policy of the Firm & Issues in Cost of Financing Accounts Receivable - Another Look. 11p. 1986. 40.00 (*0-939050-45-5*) Credit Res NYS.

— Customer Deductions Impact on Receivables. 1988. 40.00 (*0-939050-56-0*) Credit Res NYS.

— Deduction Codes for Electronic Payments. 7p. 1977. 40.00 (*0-939050-18-8*) Credit Res NYS.

— A Dynamic Credit Granting System. 1989. 40.00 (*0-939050-59-5*) Credit Res NYS.

— Electronic Business Data Interchange. 5p. 1985. 40.00 (*0-939050-21-8*) Credit Res NYS.

— Electronic Payments in Receivables & Payables Systems. 13p. 1987. 40.00 (*0-939050-49-8*) Credit Res NYS.

— Financial Modeling by Computer. 23p. 1980. 40.00 (*0-939050-27-7*) Credit Res NYS.

— The Future Role of the Credit Function. 19p. 1985. 40.00 (*0-939050-29-3*) Credit Res NYS.

— Guide for Career Development. 11p. 1987. 40.00 (*0-939050-51-X*) Credit Res NYS.

— How to Evaluate Changes in Credit Policy. 1989. 125.00 (*0-939050-60-9*) Credit Res NYS.

— Incentive Pay Programs. 4p. 1982. 40.00 (*0-939050-31-5*) Credit Res NYS.

— Investment & Capital Structure Decision Making in Small Business. 19p. 1974. 40.00 (*0-939050-32-3*) Credit Res NYS.

— Managing the Credit Function. 40p. 1984. 40.00 (*0-939050-33-1*) Credit Res NYS.

— Marginal Account Profile. 8p. 1983. 40.00 (*0-939050-34-X*) Credit Res NYS.

— Operating Criteria for Credit Departments. 52p. 1989. 40.00 (*0-939050-57-9*) Credit Res NYS.

— Personal Computer Use in Credit & Finance. 18p. 1986. 40.00 (*0-939050-53-6*) Credit Res NYS.

— Planning Your Future. 64p. 1963. 40.00 (*0-939050-36-6*) Credit Res NYS.

— Setting Credit Lines. 17p. 1982. 40.00 (*0-939050-39-0*) Credit Res NYS.

— Tasks of Business Credit Personnel. 14p. 1985. 40.00 (*0-939050-40-4*) Credit Res NYS.

Credit Research Staff. Credit Management Handbook. 2nd ed. (C). 1965. 20.00 (*0-256-00085-9*, Irwn McGrw-H) McGrw-H Hghr Educ.

Credit Valley Conservation Foundation Staff & DeVisser, John. Credit River Valley. Hudson, Noel, ed. (Illus.). 120p. 1992. 40.00 (*1-55046-072-2*, Pub. by Boston Mills) Genl Dist Srvs.

***Credland, Arthur G.** The Wilson Line. (Illus.). 128p. 2000. pap. 18.99 (*0-7524-1728-2*, Pub. by Tempus Pubng) Arcadia Publng.

Credsa Staff. Diccionario Basico Ilustrado Espanol English Catalan, 6 vols., Set. (CAT, ENG & SPA.). 1242p. 1990. 595.00 (*0-7859-3359-X*, 8470592797) Fr & Eur.

— Diccionario Basico Ilustrado Espanol-Euskera, 6 vols., Set. (SPA.). 1220p. 1988. 450.00 (*0-7859-6479-7*) Fr & Eur.

— Diccionario Basico Ilustrado Espanol-Euskera, 6 vols., Set. (SPA.). 1989. 395.00 (*0-7859-6100-3*, 8470563335) Fr & Eur.

— Diccionario Basico Ilustrado Espanol-Euskera, Vol. 1. (SPA.). 200p. 1988. 75.00 (*0-7859-6094-5*, 8470562878) Fr & Eur.

— Diccionario Basico Ilustrado Espanol-Euskera, Vol. 1. (SPA.). 200p. 1989. 75.00 (*0-7859-6101-1*, 8470563343) Fr & Eur.

— Diccionario Basico Ilustrado Espanol-Euskera, Vol. 2. (SPA.). 212p. 1988. 75.00 (*0-7859-6095-3*, 8470562886) Fr & Eur.

— Diccionario Basico Ilustrado Espanol-Euskera, Vol. 3. (SPA.). 196p. 1988. 75.00 (*0-7859-6096-1*, 8470562894) Fr & Eur.

— Diccionario Basico Ilustrado Espanol-Euskera, Vol. 3. (SPA., Illus.). 196p. 1989. 75.00 (*0-7859-6480-0*) Fr & Eur.

— Diccionario Basico Ilustrado Espanol-Euskera, Vol. 4. (SPA.). 212p. 1989. 75.00 (*0-7859-6103-8*, 8470563378) Fr & Eur.

— Diccionario Basico Ilustrado Espanol-Euskera, Vol. 5. (SPA.). 196p. 1988. 75.00 (*0-7859-6098-8*, 8470562916) Fr & Eur.

— Diccionario Basico Ilustrado Espanol-Euskera, Vol. 5. (SPA.). 196p. 1989. 75.00 (*0-7859-6104-6*, 8470563386) Fr & Eur.

— Diccionario Basico Ilustrado Espanol-Euskera, Vol. 6. (SPA.). 204p. 1988. 75.00 (*0-7859-6099-6*, 8470562924) Fr & Eur.

— Diccionario Basico Ilustrado Espanol-Euskera, Vol. 6. (SPA.). 228p. 1989. 75.00 (*0-7859-6105-4*, 8470563394) Fr & Eur.

— Diccionario Basico Ilustrado Espanol-Ingles-Catalan, 6 vols., Set. (CAT, ENG & SPA.). 1990. 595.00 (*0-7859-6087-2*, 8470562797) Fr & Eur.

— Diccionario Basico Ilustrado Espanol-Ingles-Catalan, Vol. 1. (CAT, ENG & SPA.). 200p. 1990. 105.00 (*0-7859-6088-0*, 8470562800) Fr & Eur.

— Diccionario Basico Ilustrado Espanol-Ingles-Catalan, Vol. 2. (SPA.). 212p. 1990. 105.00 (*0-7859-6089-9*, 8470562819) Fr & Eur.

— Diccionario Basico Ilustrado Espanol-Ingles-Catalan, Vol. 3. (CAT, ENG & SPA.). 196p. 1990. 105.00 (*0-7859-6090-2*, 8470562827) Fr & Eur.

— Diccionario Basico Ilustrado Espanol-Ingles-Catalan, Vol. 4. (CAT, ENG & SPA.). 212p. 1990. 105.00 (*0-7859-6091-0*, 8470562835) Fr & Eur.

— Diccionario Basico Ilustrado Espanol-Ingles-Catalan, Vol. 5. (CAT, ENG & SPA.). 196p. 1990. 105.00 (*0-7859-6092-9*, 8470562843) Fr & Eur.

An Asterisk (*) at the beginning of an entry indicates that the title is appearing for the first time.

— Diccionario Basico Ilustrado Espanol-Ingles-Catalan, Vol. 6. (CAT, ENG & SPA.). 204p. 1990. 105.00 (*0-7859-6093-7*, 8470562851) Fr & Eur.

— Diccionario Enciclopedia Universal, 13 vols., Set. (ENG, FRE, GER, ITA & SPA.). 5036p. 650.00 (*0-7859-0423-9*, S12271) Fr & Eur.

Cree. Science in Nursing. 3rd rev. ed. 1995. pap. text 54.00 (*0-7295-1422-6*, W B Saunders Co) Harcrt Hlth Sci Grp.

Cree, L. A. Pathology. (Illus.). 608p. 1997. pap. text 32.95 (*0-412-47200-7*, Pub. by E A) OUP.

***Cree, Ann E.** A Bargain with Fate. large type ed. 1999. 25.99 (*0-263-15995-7*, Pub. by Mills & Boon) Ulverscroft.

Cree, Carolyn. Beyond the Golden Door: A Layman's Ministry with Internationals. 95p. (Orig.). 1988. pap. 2.78 (*0-685-29348-3*) Baptist Literacy.

Cree, John. Training the German Shepherd Dog. (Illus.). 192p. 1997. 39.95 (*1-85223-955-7*, Pub. by Cro1wood) Trafalgar.

— Your Dog: A Guide to Solving Behaviour Problems. (Illus.). 160p. 1997. 35.00 (*1-85223-954-9*, Pub. by Cro1wood) Trafalgar.

Cree, Viviene. From Public Streets to Private Lives: The Changing Task of Social Work. 187p. 1995. 70.95 (*1-85628-847-1*, Pub. by Avebry) Ashgate Pub Co.

Cree, Viviene, jt. auth. see Cavanagh, Kate.

***Cree, Viviene E.** Sociology for Social Workers & Probation Officers. LC 99-31463. 232p. (C). 1999. text. write for info. (*0-415-15015-9*) Routledge.

— Sociology for Social Workers & Probation Officers. LC 99-31463. 232p. (C). 2000. pap. 25.99 (*0-415-15016-7*) Routledge.

***Cree, Viviene E. & MaCaulay, Cathlin.** Transfer of Learning in Professional & Vocational Education. LC 00-32170. 2000. write for info. (*0-415-20419-4*) Routledge.

Creeber. Dennis Potter Between Two Worlds: A Critical Reassessment. LC 97-26514. 212p. 1998. text 49.95 (*0-312-17774-7*) St Martin.

Creech, Bill. The Five Pillars of TQM: How to Make Total Quality Management Work for You. 560p. 1995. pap. 16.95 (*0-452-27102-9*, Plume) Dutton Plume.

Creech, D. W. Flight Training Academic Enhancer: A Useful Guide to Preventing Retreating Blade Stall. 2nd ed. LC 97-206915. 1997. write for info. (*0-89826-072-8*) Natl Paperback.

Creech, Dennis B. Homeowner's Guide to Energy Efficient & Passive Solar Homes. (Illus.). 53p. 1996. reprint ed. pap. 20.00 (*0-7881-3310-1*) DIANE Pub.

Creech, Heather. A Guide to Legal Research in Papua New Guinea. vii, 226p. 1990. pap. 39.50 (*0-455-20922-7*, Pub. by LawBk Co) Gaunt.

Creech, James. Closet Writing - Gay Reading: The Case of Melville's Pierre. LC 93-11176. (Illus.). 216p. 1993. pap. text 14.95 (*0-226-12022-8*) U Ch Pr.

— Closet Writing - Gay Reading: The Case of Melville's Pierre. LC 93-11176. (Illus.). 216p. 1997. lib. bdg. 36.00 (*0-226-12020-1*) U Ch Pr.

— Diderot: Thresholds of Representation. LC 85-25881. 225p. 1986. reprint ed. pap. 69.80 (*0-608-00913-X*, 206170700011) Bks Demand.

Creech, Kenneth C. Electronic Media Law & Regulation. 2nd ed. LC 95-24522. (Illus.). 526p. 1995. pap. 39.95 (*0-240-80216-0*, Focal) Buttrwrth-Heinemann.

***Creech, Kenneth C.** Electronic Media Law & Regulation. 3rd ed. LC 99-31485. 336p. 1999. pap. text 44.95 (*0-240-80359-0*) Buttrwrth-Heinemann.

Creech, Linda. Lost in Time. unabridged ed. (Illus.). 20p. (Orig.). 1997. pap. 5.00 (*1-929326-60-2*) Hal Bar Pubg.

Creech, Linda, et al. Four Part Harmony: Selections from the Works of Four of Today's Poets. (Illus.). 48p. 1997. pap. 4.50 (*1-886467-20-X*) WJM Press.

Creech, Margaret. Three Centuries of Poor Law Administration: A Study of Legislation in Rhode Island. 21.95 (*0-405-19031-X*) Ayer.

Creech, Nancy. Cooking for Someone Special...Yourself. LC 85-1494. 208p. 1985. pap. 7.95 (*0-88266-375-5*) Storey Bks.

Creech, Richard D. Reflections from a Unicorn. 1992. pap. 12.95 (*0-9632333-0-0*) RC Pub.

Creech, Sharon. Absolutely Normal Chaos. LC 95-22448. 240p. (J). (gr. 4-7). 1995. 15.95 (*0-06-026989-8*) HarpC Child Bks.

— Absolutely Normal Chaos. LC 95-22448. 240p. (J). (gr. 4 up). 1995. lib. bdg. 15.89 (*0-06-026992-8*, HarpTrophy) HarpC Child Bks.

— Absolutely Normal Chaos. LC 95-22448. (Illus.). 240p. (J). (gr. 4-7). 1997. mass mkt. 4.95 (*0-06-440632-6*, HarpTrophy) HarpC Child Bks.

— Absolutely Normal Chaos. 1997. 10.05 (*0-606-10734-7*, Pub. by Turtleback) Demco.

— Bloomability. LC 98-14601. (Illus.). 288p. (J). (gr. 3-7). 1999. mass mkt. 5.95 (*0-06-440823-X*) HarpC.

— Bloomability. LC 98-14601. 288p. (J). (gr. 3-7). 1998. 15.95 (*0-06-026993-6*, J Cotler) HarpC Child Bks.

— Bloomability. LC 98-14607. 288p. (J). (gr. 3-7). 1998. 15.89 (*0-06-026994-4*, J Cotler) HarpC Child Bks.

— Chasing Redbird. LC 96-44128. (Joanna Cotler Bks.). 272p. (J). (gr. 3-7). 1997. 15.95 (*0-06-026987-1*); 15.89 (*0-06-026988-X*) HarpC Child Bks.

— Chasing Redbird. LC 96-44128. 272p. (J). (gr. 3-7). 1998. mass mkt. 4.95 (*0-06-440696-2*) HarpC Child Bks.

Creech, Sharon. Chasing Redbird. 261p. (J). (gr. 4-6). pap. 4.95 (*0-8072-1532-5*) Listening Lib.

Creech, Sharon. Chasing Redbird. (J). 1998. 10.05 (*0-606-13265-1*, Pub. by Turtleback) Demco.

***Creech, Sharon.** A Fine, Fine School. (J). 2001. 15.95 (*0-06-027736-X*); lib. bdg. 15.89 (*0-06-027737-8*) HarpC Child Bks.

— Fishing in the Air. LC 99-35538. (Illus.). 32p. (J). (ps-3). 2000. 15.95 (*0-06-028111-1*); lib. bdg. 15.89 (*0-06-028112-X*) HarpC Child Bks.

Creech, Sharon. Pleasing the Ghost. LC 95-52280. (Illus.). 96p. (J). (gr. 4-7). 1996. 14.95 (*0-06-026985-5*); lib. bdg. 14.89 (*0-06-026986-3*) HarpC Child Bks.

— Pleasing the Ghost. (J). 1997. 9.70 (*0-606-11757-1*, Pub. by Turtleback) Demco.

— Pleasing the Ghost. LC 95-52280. (Trophy Bk.). (Illus.). 96p. (J). (gr. 2-5). 1997. reprint ed. mass mkt. 4.95 (*0-06-440686-5*, HarpTrophy) HarpC Child Bks.

Creech, Sharon. Ruby Holler. (J). write for info. (*0-06-027732-7*); lib. bdg. write for info. (*0-06-027733-5*) HarpC Child Bks.

Creech, Sharon. Walk Two Moons. LC 93-31277. 288p. (YA). (gr. 4-7). 1994. 15.95 (*0-06-023334-6*); lib. bdg. 15.89 (*0-06-023337-0*) HarpC Child Bks.

— Walk Two Moons. LC 93-31277. (Trophy Bk.). 288p. (YA). (gr. 3-7). 1996. mass mkt. 5.95 (*0-06-440517-6*, HarpTrophy) HarpC Child Bks.

Creech, Sharon. Walk Two Moons. 280p. (J). (gr. 4-6). pap. 4.95 (*0-8072-1509-0*) Listening Lib.

Creech, Sharon. Walk Two Moons. (Pathways to Critical Thinking Ser.). 32p. (YA). (gr. 5 up). 1997. pap. text 19.95 (*1-58303-030-1*) Pthways Pubng.

— Walk Two Moons. (Assessment Packs Ser.). 15p. (YA). (gr. 5 up). 1998. pap. text 15.95 (*1-58303-067-0*) Pthways Pubng.

***Creech, Sharon.** Walk Two Moons. LC 00-41181. (Illus.). 2000. write for info. (*0-7862-2773-7*) Thorndike Pr.

Creech, Sharon. Walk Two Moons. LC 93-31277. (YA). (gr. 5 up). 1996. 10.05 (*0-606-10018-0*, Pub. by Turtleback) Demco.

Creech, Sharon. The Wanderer. LC 99-42699. 320p. (J). (gr. 3-7). 2000. lib. bdg. 15.89 (*0-06-027731-9*) HarpC Child Bks.

***Creech, Sharon.** The Wanderer. LC 99-42699. (Illus.). 320p. (J). (gr. 3-7). 2000. 15.95 (*0-06-027730-0*) HarpC Child Bks.

Creech, Wilbur L. The Scapel & the Cross. (Illus.). 270p. (Orig.). 1993. pap. 19.95 (*1-880994-08-9*) Mt Olive Coll Pr.

Creech, William. Letters, Addressed to Sir John Sinclair, Bart. LC 78-67652. (Scottish Enlightenment Ser.). reprint ed. 39.50 (*0-404-17187-7*) AMS Pr.

Creechan, Jim, jt. auth. see Creechan, Mary L.

***Creechan, Mary L. & Creechan, Jim.** Beginning with Chiles. (Illus.). 188p. 2000. pap. 22.95 (*0-9685066-0-7*) T Norte Pub.

Creecy, James R. Scenes in The South, & Other Miscellaneous Pieces. 1977. 20.95 (*0-8369-9186-9*, 9055) Ayer.

Creecy, John H. Virginia Antiquary Vol. 1: Princess Anne County Loose Papers, 1700-1789. xvi, 221p. 1997. reprint ed. pap. 20.00 (*0-7884-0614-0*, C611) Heritage Bk.

Creecy, John H., ed. Princess Anne County Loose Paper, 1700-89. (Vol. I of "Virginia Antiquary") 221p. 1997. reprint ed. lib. bdg. 37.50 (*0-8328-6519-2*) Higginson Bk Co.

— Princesss Anne County Loose Paper, 1700-89, Vol. 1. 221p. 1997. reprint ed. pap. 27.50 (*0-8328-6520-6*) Higginson Bk Co.

Creed, Alexander. Dominican Republic: Major World Nations. LC 99-19264. (Major World Nations Ser.). (Illus.). 144p. 1999. 19.95 (*0-7910-5382-2*) Chelsea Hse.

— Uganda: Major World Nations. (Major World Nations Ser.). (Illus.). 144p. (YA). (gr. 5 up). 1999. lib. bdg. 19.95 (*0-7910-4770-9*) Chelsea Hse.

Creed, Barbara. The Monstrous Feminine: Film, Feminism, Psychoanalysis. LC 93-445. (Popular Fiction Ser.). 192p. (C). (gr. 13). 1993. pap. 22.99 (*0-415-05259-9*, B2278) Routledge.

Creed, Charles. The Art of the Affair. 80p. (Orig.). 1980. pap. 3.95 (*0-933180-10-1*) Ellis Pr.

— Jubilee College State Park: Retrospective by Way of Explanation. 20p. 1980. pap. 2.50 (*0-933180-11-X*) Spoon Riv Poetry.

Creed, Francis, jt. ed. see Tyrer, Peter.

Creed, Gerald. Domesticating Revolution: From Socialist Reform to Ambivalent Transition in a Bulgarian Village. LC 96-46712. 1997. 50.00 (*0-271-01712-0*); pap. 18.95 (*0-271-01713-9*) Pa St U Pr.

Creed, Gerald, jt. auth. see Ching, Barbara.

Creed, J. L., ed. see Lactantius.

Creed, Jack. Capturing the Magic of Fiction Writing. LC 90-80208. 305p. 1991. 24.95 (*0-944435-10-6*) Glenbridge Pub.

Creed, John, jt. auth. see Andrews, Susan B.

Creed, John, jt. ed. see Andrews, Susan B.

Creed, Robert P. Reconstructing the Rhythm of Beowulf. LC 89-29252. (Illus.). 232p. 1990. text 42.50 (*0-8262-0722-7*) U of Mo Pr.

Creed, Roscoe. How to Build Plastic Models. (Illus.). 10.95 (*0-614-13181-2*, 21-37714) EAA Aviation.

Creed, Ruppert & Hawkins, Jim. The Northern Trawl. 77p. 1986. 35.00 (*0-907033-44-X*) St Mut.

Creede, Gerald. Ambit. 64p. 1993. pap. 8.95 (*0-921331-19-3*, Pub. by Tsunami Edits) Barnholden.

Creeden, Sharon. Fair Is Fair: World Folktales of Justice. (American Storytelling Ser.). (Illus.). 192p. 1995. 19.95 (*0-87483-400-7*) August Hse.

— Fair Is Fair: World Folktales of Justice. (Story Collections). 1997. pap. text 12.95 (*0-87483-477-5*) August Hse.

— In Full Bloom: Tales of Women in Their Prime. LC 99-32891. 212p. 1999. 21.95 (*0-87483-576-3*) August Hse.

Creedman, Michael, jt. auth. see O'Rear, Charles.

Creedman, Theodore S. Historical Dictionary of Costa Rica. 2nd ed. LC 89-6210. (Latin American Historical Dictionaries Ser.: No. 16). (Illus.). 362p. 1991. 50.00 (*0-8108-2215-6*) Scarecrow.

Creedon, Conal. Pancho & Lefty Ride Out. LC 96-157003. 98p. 1995. pap. 12.95 (*1-898256-06-3*) Dufour.

***Creedon, David M.** Kill Me While I Cry. 134p. 2000. pap. 12.95 (*1-878647-72-5*) APU Pub Grp.

Creedon, Michael, jt. auth. see Lechner, Viola M.

Creedon, Pamela J., ed. Women in Mass Communication. 2nd ed. LC 93-20782. 1993. 58.00 (*0-8039-5386-0*); pap. 26.50 (*0-8039-5387-9*) Sage.

— Women, Media & Sport: Challenging Gender Values. LC 93-41211. 320p. (C). 1994. text 55.00 (*0-8039-5233-3*) Sage.

Creedon, Pamela J., ed. Women, Media & Sport: Challenging Gender Values. LC 93-41211. 320p. (C). 1994. pap. text 26.00 (*0-8039-5234-1*) Sage

Creedon, Sharon. A Look over the Edge. (Illus.). 16p. (J). (gr. k-4). 1987. pap. 5.95 (*0-9620446-0-1*) Sunset Mktg.

Creedy. The Economics of Unemployment in Britain. 288p. 1981. pap. text 14.95 (*0-408-10703-0*) Buttrwrth-Heinemann.

Creedy. Edgeworth & the Development of Neo-classical Economy. 1993. 61.95 (*0-7512-0109-X*) Ashgate Pub Co.

Creedy, J., jt. auth. see O'Brien, D. P.

Creedy, John. Demand & Exchange in Economic Analysis: A History from Cournot to Marshall. 224p. 1992. 95.00 (*1-85278-530-6*) E Elgar.

Creedy, John. Development of the Theory of Exchange. LC 98-31082. 208p. 1999. 85.00 (*1-85898-920-5*) E Elgar.

— Dynamics of Income Distribution. (Modern Revivals in Economics Ser.). 184p. 1993. 61.95 (*0-7512-0195-2*, Pub. by Gregg Revivals) Ashgate Pub Co.

— The Dynamics of Inequality & Poverty: Comparing Income Distributions. LC 97-39371. 328p. 1998. 95.00 (*1-85898-801-2*) E Elgar.

— The Economics of Higher Education: An Analysis of Taxes vs. Fees. 168p. 1995. 90.00 (*1-85278-935-2*) E Elgar.

— Fiscal Policy & Social Welfare: An Analysis of Alternative Tax & Transfer Systems. (Illus.). 272p. 1995. 95.00 (*1-85898-246-4*) E Elgar.

— General Equilibrium & Welfare. LC 95-46985. (Illus.). 176p. 1996. 80.00 (*1-85898-418-1*) E Elgar.

— The History of Economic Analysis: Selected Essays by John Creedy. LC 98-29698. 384p. 1999. 95.00 (*1-85898-908-6*) E Elgar.

— Income, Inequality & the Life Cycle. 272p. 1992. 95.00 (*1-85278-609-4*) E Elgar.

***Creedy, John.** Labour Mobility, Earnings & Unemployment: Selected Papers. LC 99-21906. 320p. 1999. 95.00 (*1-84064-137-1*) E Elgar.

Creedy, John. Measuring Welfare Changes & Tax Burdens. LC 98-17082. 221p. 1998. 80.00 (*1-85898-921-3*) E Elgar.

***Creedy, John.** Modelling Indirect Taxes & Tax Reform. LC 99-45040. 232p. 2000. 80.00 (*1-84064-264-5*) E Elgar.

Creedy, John. Pensions & Population Ageing: An Economic Analysis. LC 97-39374. 256p. 1998. 85.00 (*1-85898-802-0*) E Elgar.

Creedy, John. Statics & Dynamics of Income Distribution in New Zealand. LC 97-198346. (Illus.). 1997. write for info. (*0-908935-17-X*) Vict U Well IPS.

***Creedy, John, ed.** Economic Welfare: Concepts & Measurement, 2 vols. LC 99-17565. (International Library of Critical Writings in Economics). 952p. 1999. 370.00 (*1-84064-136-3*) E Elgar.

Creedy, John, ed. The Economics of Aging. LC 94-49066. (International Library of Critical Writings in Economics: Vol. 51). 656p. 1995. 255.00 (*1-85278-827-5*) E Elgar.

— Taxation, Poverty, & Income Distribution. 272p. 1994. 95.00 (*1-85278-913-1*) E Elgar.

Creedy, John & Disney, Richard. Social Insurance in Transition. (Illus.). (Orig.). 1985. 39.95 (*0-19-877228-9*) OUP.

Creedy, John & Martin, Vance L., eds. Chaos & Non-Linear Models in Economics: Theory & Applications. (Illus.). 240p. 1994. 90.00 (*1-85278-722-8*) E Elgar.

— Nonlinear Economic Models: Cross-Sectional, Time Series & Neural Network Applications. LC 97-23224. 304p. (C). 1997. text 95.00 (*1-85898-637-0*) E Elgar.

Creedy, John, jt. auth. see Alvarado, Jose.

Creedy, John, jt. auth. see Cornwell, Antonia.

Creedy, John, jt. ed. see Casson, Mark.

Creedy, John, ed. see Laonhardt, W.

Creeff, K., ed. Cardiac Glycosides, Pt. 1: Experimental Pharmacology of Cardiac Glycosides. (Handbook of Experimental Pharmacology Ser.: Vol. 56-). (Illus.). 682p. 1981. 287.00 (*0-387-10917-X*) Spr-Verlag.

Creegan, Charles C. & Goodnow, Josephine A. Great Missionaries of the Church. LC 73-37522. (Essay Index Reprint Ser.). 1977. reprint ed. 26.95 (*0-8369-2541-6*) Ayer.

Creegan, Charles L. Wittgenstein & Kierkegaard. 176p. 1989. 45.00 (*0-415-00066-1*) Routledge.

Creegan, Patrick J. & Monismith, Carl L. Asphalt Concrete Water Barriers for Embankment Dams. LC 96-3139. 304p. 1996. 52.00 (*0-7844-0141-1*) Am Soc Civil Eng.

Creeger, Catherine, tr. see Steiner, Rudolf.

Creeger, Catherine E., tr. see Koepke, Hermann.

Creeger, Catherine E., tr. see Steiner, Rudolf.

***Creehan, Dennis.** The Wing-T from A-Z Vol. 1: The Base Plan. (Illus.). 224p. 1999. pap. 19.95 (*1-57167-426-8*) Coaches Choice.

— The Wing-T from A-Z Vol. 2: Installing the System. (Illus.). 229p. 2000. pap. 19.95 (*1-57167-427-6*) Coaches Choice.

Creehan, Patricia A., jt. auth. see Simpson, Kathleen R.

Creehan, Patricia A., jt. ed. see Simpson, Kathleen R.

Creek. Occupational Therapy & Mental Health: Principles, Skills & Practice. 2nd ed. 1996. pap. text 58.00 (*0-443-05202-6*, C8637) Church.

Creek, E. J., jt. auth. see Smith, J. Richard.

Creek, Hilary, tr. see Fortunati, Leopoldina.

Creek, Jennifer, ed. Occupational Therapy & Mental Health: Principles, Skills & Practice. (Illus.). 569p. 1990. pap. text 49.95 (*0-443-03758-2*) Church.

Creek, Robert, jt. auth. see Lassetter, Stuart.

Creekmore, Betsey B. Knoxville. LC 66-21195. (Illus.). 379p. reprint ed. pap. 117.50 (*0-608-17424-6*, 202984600066) Bks Demand.

— Tennessee: A Celebration of 200 Years of the University. Baumann, J. Bruce, ed. LC 94-65024. (Illus.). 128p. 1994. 19.94 (*1-884850-00-6*) Scripps Howard.

Creekmore, Donna. The Silver Shroud. large type ed. (Linford Mystery Library). 448p. 1992. pap. 16.99 (*0-7089-7224-1*) Ulverscroft.

Creekmore, Pollyanna. Early East Tennessee Taxpayers (1778-1839) (Illus.). 328p. 1988. 38.50 (*0-89308-145-0*, TN 25) Southern Hist Pr.

Creekmur, Corey K. & Doty, Alexander, eds. Out in Culture: Gay, Lesbian, & Queer Essays on Popular Culture. LC 94-29810. (Series Q). (Illus.). 568p. 1995. text 64.95 (*0-8223-1532-7*); pap. text 22.95 (*0-8223-1541-6*) Duke.

Creel, Ann H. Water at the Blue Earth. LC 98-25018. (Illus.). 148p. (J). (gr. 5-9). 1998. pap. 8.95 (*1-57098-224-4*) Roberts Rinehart.

Creel, Ann Howard. A Ceiling of Stars. LC 99-27129. (American Girl Fiction Ser.). 85p. (J). (gr. 5-7). 1999. text 9.95 (*1-56247-848-6*) Pleasant Co.

***Creel, Ann Howard.** A Ceiling of Stars. LC 99-27129. 96p. (J). (gr. 5-7). 1999. pap. text 5.95 (*1-56247-753-6*) Pleasant Co.

— Ceiling of Stars. (Illus.). (J). 2000. 11.35 (*0-606-18354-X*) Turtleback.

— Nowhere, Now Here. LC 99-86219. (J). 2000. pap. write for info. (*1-58485-200-3*) Pleasant Co.

Creel, Austin B., jt. ed. see Narayanan, Vasudha.

Creel, Bryant L. The Religious Poetry of Jorge de Montemayor. (Monagrafias A Ser.: Vol. LXXVIII). (Illus.). 270p. (C). 1981. 72.00 (*0-7293-0103-6*, Pub. by Tamesis Bks Ltd) Boydell & Brewer.

Creel, Catherine. Texas Flame. 1981. mass mkt. 2.75 (*0-89083-797-X*, Zebra Kensgtn) Kensgtn Pub Corp.

— Texas Torment. 1985. mass mkt. 3.95 (*0-8217-1622-0*, Zebra Kensgtn) Kensgtn Pub Corp.

Creel, G. Mexico: The People Next Door. 1976. lib. bdg. 59.95 (*0-8490-2251-7*) Gordon Pr.

Creel, George. How We Advertised America. LC 72-4664. (International Propaganda & Communications Ser.). (Illus.). 467p. 1978. reprint ed. 35.95 (*0-405-04745-2*) Ayer.

— Rebel at Large: American Autobiography. 384p. 1995. lib. bdg. 89.00 (*0-7812-8492-9*) Rprt Serv.

— Rebel at Large: Recollections of Fifty Crowded Years. (History - United States Ser.). 384p. 1993. reprint ed. lib. bdg. 89.00 (*0-7812-4921-X*) Rprt Serv.

— Sons of the Eagle. LC 79-117778. (Essay Index Reprint Ser.). 1977. 23.95 (*0-8369-1797-9*) Ayer.

Creel, George, ed. The German - Bolshevik Conspiracy. unabridged ed. 30p. 1918. reprint ed. pap. 5.00 (*0-945001-37-1*) GSG & Assocs.

Creel, George, jt. auth. see Sisson, Edgar.

Creel, Herlee G., et al. Literary Chinese by the Inductive Method. Incl. Selections from the Lun Yu. 1994. lib. bdg. 14.00 (*0-226-12032-5*); pap. write for info. (*0-318-56056-9*) U Ch Pr.

Creel, Herrlee G. Chinese Thought from Confucius to Mao Tse-Tung. LC 53-10054. 304p. 1971. reprint ed. pap. text 15.00 (*0-226-12030-9*, P394) U Ch Pr.

— Origins of Statecraft in China: The Western Chou Empire, Vol. 1. LC 73-110072. (Illus.). xiv, 560p. 1995. pap. text 14.50 (*0-226-12044-9*) U Ch Pr.

— Shen Pu-Hai: A Chinese Political Philosopher of the Fourth Century, B. C. LC 73-77130. x, 446p. 1994. lib. bdg. 20.00 (*0-226-12027-9*) U Ch Pr.

— What Is Taoism? And Other Studies in Chinese Cultural History. LC 77-102905. (Midway Reprint Ser.). viii, 200p. (C). 1982. pap. text 20.00 (*0-226-12047-3*) U Ch Pr.

Creel, Herrlee G., et al. Literary Chinese by the Inductive Method: The Mencius, Vol. 3. enl. rev. ed. LC 48-8466. 340p. reprint ed. pap. 105.40 (*0-608-18227-3*, 205663500078) Bks Demand.

Creel, Margaret W. A Peculiar People: Slave Religion & Community Culture among the Gullah. (American Social Experience Ser.: No. 7). (Illus.). 416p. (C). 1989. pap. text 18.50 (*0-8147-1422-6*) NYU Pr.

Creel, Mike & Kelley, Russell L. The Boykin Spaniel: South Carolina's Dog: A Crackerjack Retriever, Trick Artist & Family Favorite. (Illus.). 200p. 1997. 35.00 (*1-887714-21-9*) Summerhse Pr.

Creel, Richard E. Religion & Doubt: Toward a Faith of Your Own. 2nd ed. 176p. (C). 1990. pap. text 22.40 (*0-13-772286-9*) P-H.

Creel, Thomas L., ed. Guide to Patent Arbitration. LC 87-18394. 253p. 1987. reprint ed. pap. 78.50 (*0-608-04272-2*, 206502400012) Bks Demand.

Creel, Von R., jt. auth. see Burke, Bob.

Creeland, Hokulani. Olelo O'iwi ke Kahua: He Puke A'o 'Olelo Hawai'i. (ENG & HAW.). xi, 439p. (YA). (gr. 10 up). 1994. pap. 16.95 (*1-58191-013-4*) Aha Punana Leo.

Creeley, Robert. Autobiography. (Illus.). 115p. (Orig.). 1990. pap. 5.95 (*0-937815-42-X*) Hanuman Bks.

— The Collected Essays of Robert Creeley. 603p. 1989. 55.00 (*0-520-06150-0*, Pub. by U CA Pr) Cal Prin Full Svc.

C

— The Collected Poems of Robert Creeley, 1945-1975. LC 81-19668. 576p. 1982. pap. 17.95 (*0-520-04244-1*, Pub. by U CA Pr) Cal Prin Full Svc.
— The Collected Prose of Robert Creeley. 518p. 1984. 26.00 (*0-7145-2792-0*) M Boyars Pubs.
***Creeley, Robert.** Day Book of a Virtual Poet. LC 98-26145. 122p. 1999. pap. 12.00 (*1-881471-28-4*) S Duyvil.
— Day Book of a Virtual Poet. LC 98-26145. 122p. (YA). 2000. 27.95 (*1-881471-29-2*) S Duyvil.
Creeley, Robert. Echoes. LC 81-23284. 13p. (Orig.). 1982. pap. 12.00 (*0-915124-59-9*) Coffee Hse.
— Echoes. LC 93-46674. 128p. (Orig.). 1994. 17.95 (*0-8112-1263-7*, Pub. by New Directions) Norton.
***Creeley, Robert.** Edges. 56p. 1999. 48.00 (*0-935875-17-4*) P Blum Edit.
— En Famille. LC 99-34342. (Illus.). 80p. 1999. 19.95 (*1-887123-26-1*, Pub. by Granary Bks) DAP Assocs.
Creeley, Robert. Gnomic Verses. 1991. pap. 8.00 (*84-87467-12-1*, Pub. by Zasterle Pr) SPD-Small Pr Dist.
— Jane Hammond. (Illus.). 10p. (Orig.). 1989. pap. 10.00 (*0-913263-26-5*) Exit Art.
— Life & Death. LC 97-45805. 87p. 1998. 19.95 (*0-8112-1384-6*, Pub. by New Directions) Norton.
***Creeley, Robert.** Life & Death. 2000. pap. 9.95 (*0-8112-1449-4*, Pub. by New Directions) Norton.
Creeley, Robert. Ligeia: A Libretto. (Illus.). 40p. 1996. 400.00 (*1-887123-11-3*) Granary Bks.
— Memory Gardens. LC 85-29723. 96p. 1986. pap. 7.95 (*0-8112-0974-1*, NDP613, Pub. by New Directions) Norton.
— Mirror. (Illus.). 24p. (Orig.). (C). 1988. pap. 20.00 (*0-922668-01-9*) SUNYB Poetry Rare Bks.
— Mirror. deluxe limited ed. (Illus.). 24p. (Orig.). (C). 1988. 35.00 (*0-922668-02-7*) SUNYB Poetry Rare Bks.
— Places. (Illus.). 16p. 1990. 7.50 (*0-9628035-1-0*) Shuffaloff Bks.
— A Poetry Anthology. LC 92-74507. (Illus.). 118p. 1992. pap. 14.00 (*1-879003-07-4*) Edmundson.
— Selected Poems. 366p. 1991. 45.00 (*0-520-06935-8*, Pub. by U CA Pr) Cal Prin Full Svc.
— Selected Poems. LC 91-7152. 366p. (C). 1996. pap. 16.95 (*0-520-06936-6*, Pub. by U CA Pr) Cal Prin Full Svc.
— So There: Poems 1976-83. LC 98-35576. 256p. 1998. pap. 14.95 (*0-8112-1397-8*, NDP870, Pub. by New Directions) Norton.
— Tales out of School: Selected Interviews. (Poets on Poetry Ser.). 208p. (C). 1994. pap. 13.95 (*0-472-06536-X*, 06536); text 39.50 (*0-472-09536-6*, 09536) U of Mich Pr.
— Window. (Illus.). 22p. (Orig.). (C). 1988. pap. text 40.00 (*0-685-44373-6*) SUNYB Poetry Rare Bks.
— Windows. LC 89-13345. 160p. 1990. 19.95 (*0-8112-1122-3*, Pub. by New Directions); pap. 10.95 (*0-8112-1123-1*, NDP687, Pub. by New Directions) Norton.
Creeley, Robert, ed. Essential Burns, Vol. 11. 1989. pap. 6.00 (*0-88001-194-7*) HarpC.
Creeley, Robert, intro. Tim Prythero. LC 90-62109. (Illus.). 16p. 1990. pap. 7.00 (*0-935037-34-9*) G Peters Gallery.
Creeley, Robert, et al. Indiana: Les Livres de Peintres. limited ed. (Illus.). 1997. boxed set, lthr. 3500.00 (*0-9632328-3-5*) Marco Fine Arts.
Creeley, Robert, jt. auth. see Bunnell, Peter.
Creeley, Robert, jt. auth. see Ginsberg, Allen.
Creeley, Robert, jt. auth. see Layton, Irving.
Creeley, Robert, jt. auth. see Olson, Charles.
Creeley, Robert, ed. see Olson, Charles.
Creeley, Robert, jt. frwd. see Novik, Mary.
Creelman, Paul. Circle of Ice. (Illus.). 1980. 2.00 (*0-940244-63-2*) Flying Buffalo.
Creelman, W. G., jt. auth. see Gardner, A. C.
Creemers, ed. School Improvement. LC 96-232379. 168p. (C). 1996. 75.00 (*0-415-13023-9*); pap. 22.99 (*0-415-13024-7*) Routledge.
Creemers, B. P., ed. Evaluation Research in Education. (Selecta Reeks Ser.: Vol. 52). 120p. 1985. 15.00 (*90-6472-064-9*) Taylor & Francis.
Creemers, B. P. & Verloop, N., eds. Educational Evaluation in the Netherlands. 100p. 1985. pap. 33.00 (*0-08-032340-5*, Pergamon Pr) Elsevier.
Creemers, H. M., et al, eds. School Effectiveness & School Improvement. xii, 384p. 1989. 70.00 (*90-265-1008-X*) Swets.
Creen, Linette. A Taste of Cuba: Recipes from the Cuban-American Community. (Illus.). 336p. 1994. pap. 17.95 (*0-452-27089-8*, Plume) Dutton Plume.
Creer, Leland H. Mormon Towns in the Region of the Colorado. Incl. Activities of Jacob Hamblin in the Region of the Colorado. (Glen Canyon Ser.: Nos. 3-4). reprint ed. 20.00 (*0-404-60633-4*) AMS Pr.
Creer, Margaret & Cornelia, William. Discovering Hilton Head Island: A View of Nature's Wonders. LC 87-60225. (Illus.). 72p. 1987. 16.95 (*0-9610698-1-3*) SouthArt Inc.
Creer, Thomas L. Psychology of Adjustment. 374p. (C). 1996. pap. text 63.00 (*0-13-254863-1*) P-H.
Creery, Anna. The Donvier Ice Cream Dessert Book. (Illus.). 112p. 1995. reprint ed. pap. 7.95 (*0-89865-627-3*) Donning Co.
Creery, Ian, et al. Polar Peoples: Native Inhabitants of the Far North. LC 94-204813. (Orig.). pap. 24.95 (*1-873194-51-X*, Pub. by Minority Rts Pubns) Paul & Co Pubs.
— Polar Peoples: Native Inhabitants of the Far North. (Illus.). 250p. (Orig.). 1994. text 49.95 (*1-873194-55-2*, Pub. by Minority Rts Pubns); pap. text 19.95 (*1-873194-50-1*, Pub. by Minority Rts Pubns) Paul & Co Pubs.
Creery, Katherine W., jt. auth. see Creery, Presley T.
Creery, Presley T. & Creery, Katherine W. Reducing Labor Turnover in Financial Institutions. LC 87-37572. (Illus.). 186p. 1988. 57.95 (*0-89930-296-3*, CYR/, Quorum Bks) Greenwood.
Creery, Walter E., ed. George Berkeley: Critical Assessments, 3 vols., Set. 1152p. (C). (gr. 13). 1991. text, boxed set 575.00 (*0-415-02092-1*, A5758) Routledge.
Crees, James. George Meredith. LC 67-30812. (Studies in Fiction: No. 34). 1969. reprint ed. lib. bdg. 75.00 (*0-8383-0712-4*) M S G Haskell Hse.
— Meredith Revisited & Other Essays. LC 67-30813. (Studies in Fiction: No. 34). 1969. reprint ed. lib. bdg. 75.00 (*0-8383-0713-2*) M S G Haskell Hse.
Creese & Strong-Boag, Veronica, eds. British Columbia Reconsidered: Essays on Women. 452p. 1992. pap. 21.95 (*0-88974-038-0*, Pub. by Press Gang Pubs) LPC InBook.
Creese, A. & Parker, D., eds. Cost Analysis in Primary Health Care: A Training Manual for Programme Managers. LC 95-202639. (ENG, FRE & SPA.). x, 147p. 1994. pap. text 25.00 (*92-4-154470-8*, 1150415) World Health.
Creese, A., jt. ed. see Tarimo, E.
Creese, Gillian. Contracting Masculinity: Gender, Class & Race in a White-Collar Union, 1944-1994. (Canadian Social History Ser.). (Illus.). 272p. 1999. pap. text 21.95 (*0-19-541454-3*) OUP.
Creese, Helen. Peartheayarna: The Journeying of Partha--An Eighteen-Century Balenese Kalzawin. LC 98-214792. (Bibliotheca Indonesica Ser.). xi, 504 p. 1998. pap. write for info. (*90-6718-117-X*, Pub. by KITLV Pr) Book Bin.
Creese, Ian, jt. ed. see Breese, George R.
Creese, Mary R. Ladies in the Laboratory? American & British Women in Science, 1800-1900: A Survey of Their Contributions to Research. LC 97-1125. (Illus.). 800p. 1998. 98.50 (*0-8108-3287-9*) Scarecrow.
***Creese, Michael & Earley, Peter.** Improving Schools & Governing Bodies: Making Difference. LC 99-20332. 184p. (C). 1999. text. write for info. (*0-415-20510-7*) Routledge.
— Improving Schools & Governors: Making a Difference. LC 99-20332. 1999. pap. write for info. (*0-415-20511-5*) Routledge.
Creese, Robert C. Estimating & Costing for the Metal Manufacturing Industries. (Cost Engineering Ser.: Vol. 18). (Illus.). 288p. 1992. text 135.00 (*0-8247-8712-9*) Dekker.
— Introduction to Manufacturing Processes & Materials. LC 99-18809. (Illus.). 416p. 1999. text 150.00 (*0-8247-9914-3*) Dekker.
Creese, Robert C. & Ganga Rao, Hota, eds. A Conference on Polymer Composites: Infrastructure Renewal & Economic Development. LC 99-61903. 192p. 1999. text 74.95 (*1-56676-802-0*) Technomic.
Creese, Walter L. The Crowning of the American Landscape: Eight Great Spaces & Their Buildings. LC 84-26243. 318p. reprint ed. pap. 98.60 (*0-608-02934-3*, 206400000008) Bks Demand.
— The Search for Environment: The Garden City, Before & After. 2nd ed. (Illus.). 420p. 1992. reprint ed. pap. text 29.95 (*0-8018-4363-4*) Johns Hopkins.
— TVA's Public Planning: The Vision, the Reality. LC 89-28129. 304p. 1990. text 40.00 (*0-87049-638-7*) U of Tenn Pr.
Creevey, Lucy. Changing Women's Lives & Work: An Analysis of the Impact of Eight Microenterprise Projects. LC 96-210705. 304p. 1996. pap. 30.00 (*1-85339-319-3*, Pub. by Intermed Tech) Stylus Pub VA.
Creevey, Lucy, jt. auth. see Callaway, Barbara.
Creevey, Lucy E., ed. Women Farmers in Africa: Rural Development in Mali & the Sahel. LC 85-27771. (Illus.). 232p. 1986. text 39.95 (*0-8156-2358-5*) Syracuse U Pr.
— Women Farmers in Africa: Rural Development in Mali & the Sahel. LC 85-27771. (Contemporary Issues in the Middle East Ser.). (Illus.). 231p. 1986. reprint ed. pap. 71.70 (*0-608-06982-5*, 206719000009) Bks Demand.
Creevy, Bill. The Oil Painting Book: Materials & Techniques for Today's Artist. LC 94-26964. (Illus.). 176p. 1994. 35.00 (*0-8230-3273-6*) Watsn-Guptill.
— The Oil Painting Book: Materials & Techniques for Today's Artist. (Illus.). 176p. 1999. pap. text 19.95 (*0-8230-3274-4*) Watsn-Guptill.
— The Pastel Book. (Illus.). 176p. 1999. pap. 19.95 (*0-8230-3905-6*) Watsn-Guptill.
— The Pastel Book: Materials & Techniques for Today's Artist. (Illus.). 176p. 1991. 32.50 (*0-8230-3902-1*) Watsn-Guptill.
Creevy, Patrick. Lake Shore Drive. 384p. 1994. mass mkt. 4.99 (*0-8125-1279-0*) Tor Bks.
— Tyrus. 1995. write for info. (*0-312-85664-4*) Tor Bks.
Creevy, S. & Hakanson, A. Bites from Boulder Cookbook. (Illus.). 160p. (Orig.). 1987. pap. write for info. (*0-9619649-0-1*) Hakanson-Creevy.
Creff, Albert-Francois. Dictionnaire de la Nouvelle Dietetique. (FRE.). 607p. 1984. 69.95 (*0-7859-8631-6*, 222104276x) Fr & Eur.
Creffield, J. W. Wood-Destroying Insects. 2nd ed. (Illus.). 52p. (Orig.). 1996. pap. 29.95 (*0-643-05151-1*, Pub. by CSIRO) Accents Pubns.
Cregan, Conor. With Extreme Prejudice. 389p. 1996. mass mkt. 10.95 (*0-340-62305-5*, Pub. by Hodder & Stought Ltd) Trafalgar.

Cregan, George R., ed. Through My Monocle. (Illus.). 480p. 1991. pap. 24.95 (*0-87012-636-9*) McClain. Memoirs of the Famous Basso, Andreas Perello de Segurola. Early in this century before television, movies, radio or even recordings, there was indeed a Golden Age of Opera. It is gone now, those days when opera singers dominated our world of entertainment. Progress (so called) changed all that, & the rest is history. This book introduces Count Andreas Perello de Segurola, whose life was a panorama of gaiety, glory & gallantry. Indexed.
Publisher Paid Annotation.

Cregan, Perry B., jt. auth. see Keister, Donald L.
Cregar, Elyse. Gettysburg: By the Third Sun Setting. (Illus.). (Orig.). (YA). (gr. 6-12). 1988. pap. 5.95 (*0-9621292-0-8*) Tamerac Pub.
Cregar, William F. Haines. Ancestry of William Shipley Haines, with Some Account of the Descendants of John & Joseph Haines & Colonel Cowperthwait. (Illus.). 85p. 1997. reprint ed. pap. 16.50 (*0-8328-8890-7*); reprint ed. lib. bdg. 26.50 (*0-8328-8889-3*) Higginson Bk Co.
Creger, Ralph. It's Never Too Late. LC 91-28345. 1992. pap. 9.95 (*0-942637-41-0*) Barricade Bks.
Creger, William P., et al, eds. Annual Review of Medicine: Selected Topics in the Clinical Sciences, Vol. 9. LC 51-1659. 1958. text 40.00 (*0-8243-0509-4*) Annual Reviews.
— Annual Review of Medicine: Selected Topics in the Clinical Sciences, Vol. 18. LC 51-1659. 1967. text 40.00 (*0-8243-0518-3*) Annual Reviews.
— Annual Review of Medicine: Selected Topics in the Clinical Sciences, Vol. 19. 1968. text 40.00 (*0-8243-0519-1*) Annual Reviews.
— Annual Review of Medicine: Selected Topics in the Clinical Sciences, Vol. 20. LC 51-1659. 1969. text 40.00 (*0-8243-0520-5*) Annual Reviews.
— Annual Review of Medicine: Selected Topics in the Clinical Sciences, Vol. 21. LC 51-1659. 1970. text 40.00 (*0-8243-0521-3*) Annual Reviews.
— Annual Review of Medicine: Selected Topics in the Clinical Sciences, Vol. 22. LC 51-1659. 1971. text 40.00 (*0-8243-0522-1*) Annual Reviews.
— Annual Review of Medicine: Selected Topics in the Clinical Sciences, Vol. 23. LC 51-1659. (Illus.). 1972. text 40.00 (*0-8243-0523-X*) Annual Reviews.
— Annual Review of Medicine: Selected Topics in the Clinical Sciences, Vol. 24. LC 51-1659. (Illus.). 1973. text 40.00 (*0-8243-0524-8*) Annual Reviews.
— Annual Review of Medicine: Selected Topics in the Clinical Sciences, Vol. 25. LC 51-1659. (Illus.). 1974. text 40.00 (*0-8243-0525-6*) Annual Reviews.
— Annual Review of Medicine: Selected Topics in the Clinical Sciences, Vol. 26. LC 51-1659. (Illus.). 1975. text 40.00 (*0-8243-0526-4*) Annual Reviews.
— Annual Review of Medicine: Selected Topics in the Clinical Sciences, Vol. 27. LC 51-1659. (Illus.). 1976. text 40.00 (*0-8243-0527-2*) Annual Reviews.
— Annual Review of Medicine: Selected Topics in the Clinical Sciences, Vol. 28. LC 51-1659. (Illus.). 1977. text 40.00 (*0-8243-0528-0*) Annual Reviews.
— Annual Review of Medicine: Selected Topics in the Clinical Sciences, Vol. 29. LC 51-1659. (Illus.). 1978. text 40.00 (*0-8243-0529-9*) Annual Reviews.
— Annual Review of Medicine: Selected Topics in the Clinical Sciences, Vol. 30. LC 51-1659. (Illus.). 1979. text 40.00 (*0-8243-0530-2*) Annual Reviews.
— Annual Review of Medicine: Selected Topics in the Clinical Sciences, Vol. 31. LC 51-1659. (Illus.). 1980. text 40.00 (*0-8243-0531-0*) Annual Reviews.
— Annual Review of Medicine: Selected Topics in the Clinical Sciences, Vol. 32. LC 51-1659. (Illus.). 1981. text 40.00 (*0-8243-0532-9*) Annual Reviews.
— Annual Review of Medicine: Selected Topics in the Clinical Sciences, Vol. 33. LC 51-1659. (Illus.). 1982. text 40.00 (*0-8243-0533-7*) Annual Reviews.
— Annual Review of Medicine: Selected Topics in the Clinical Sciences, Vol. 34. LC 51-1659. (Illus.). 1983. text 40.00 (*0-8243-0534-5*) Annual Reviews.
— Annual Review of Medicine: Selected Topics in the Clinical Sciences, Vol. 35. LC 51-1659. (Illus.). 1984. text 40.00 (*0-8243-0535-3*) Annual Reviews.
— Annual Review of Medicine: Selected Topics in the Clinical Sciences, Vol. 36. LC 51-1659. (Illus.). 1985. text 40.00 (*0-8243-0536-1*) Annual Reviews.
— Annual Review of Medicine: Selected Topics in the Clinical Sciences, Vol. 37. LC 51-1659. (Illus.). 1986. text 40.00 (*0-8243-0537-X*) Annual Reviews.
— Annual Review of Medicine: Selected Topics in the Clinical Sciences, Vol. 38. LC 51-1659. (Illus.). 1987. text 40.00 (*0-8243-0538-8*) Annual Reviews.
— Annual Review of Medicine: Selected Topics in the Clinical Sciences, Vol. 39. 1988. text 40.00 (*0-8243-0539-6*) Annual Reviews.
— Annual Review of Medicine: Selected Topics in the Clinical Sciences, Vol. 40. LC 51-1659. (Illus.). 1989. text 40.00 (*0-8243-0540-X*) Annual Reviews.
— Annual Review of Medicine: Selected Topics in the Clinical Sciences, Vol. 41. LC 51-1659. 1990. text 40.00 (*0-8243-0541-8*) Annual Reviews.
— Annual Review of Medicine: Selected Topics in the Clinical Sciences, Vol. 42. LC 51-1659. 1991. text 40.00 (*0-8243-0542-6*) Annual Reviews.
— Annual Review of Medicine: Selected Topics in the Clinical Sciences, Vol. 43. LC 51-1659. 1992. text 44.00 (*0-8243-0543-4*) Annual Reviews.
— Annual Review of Medicine: Selected Topics in the Clinical Sciences, Vol. 44. LC 51-1659. (Illus.). 1993. text 44.00 (*0-8243-0544-2*) Annual Reviews.
Cregg, James, jt. ed. see Higgins, David R.
Crego, Roy. A Selective History of the Crego Family. LC 92-76117. ix, 127p. 1993. 29.95 (*0-9657133-0-X*) Crego Pubng.
Crehan, Diane. Stories to Tell & How to Tell Them: I Remember Jesus. (Illus.). 104p. 1999. pap. 12.95 (*0-89622-981-5*) Twenty-Third.
Crehan, Herbert F. & Ryan, James W. Lightning in a Bottle - The Sox of '67. (Illus.). 1993. 19.95 (*0-8283-1967-7*); pap. 13.95 (*0-8283-1968-5*) Branden Bks.
Crehan, J. H., ed. see Thurston, Herbert.
Crehan, Kate A. The Fractured Community: Landscapes of Power & Gender in Rural Zambia. LC 96-51849. (Perspectives on Southern Africa Ser.). 277p. 1997. pap. 22.50 (*0-520-20660-6*, Pub. by U CA Pr) Cal Prin Full Svc.
— The Fractured Community: Landscapes of Power & Gender in Rural Zambia. LC 96-51849. (Perspectives on Southern Africa Ser.: Vol. 54). (Illus.). 277p. 1997. 55.00 (*0-520-20659-2*, Pub. by U CA Pr) Cal Prin Full Svc.
Creider, Jane T. The Shrunken Dream. (International Connections Ser.). 360p. pap. 15.95 (*0-88961-175-0*, Pub. by Womens Pr) LPC InBook.
Creifeld, C. Rechtsworterbuch. 14th ed. (GER.). 1598p. 1997. 80.00 (*3-406-42429-5*, Pub. by Beckscshe Verlag) IBD Ltd.
Creifelds, Carl. Creifelds' Law Dictionary: Creifelds' Rechtswoerterbuch. 8th ed. (GER.). 1413p. 1986. 95.00 (*0-8288-1522-4*, M6529) Fr & Eur.
— Creifelds Rechtsworterbuch: Legal Dictionary. 12th ed. 1491p. 1994. 70.00 (*0-7859-8754-1*) Fr & Eur.
Creigh, Alfred. History of Washington County, Pennsylvania. 386p. 1993. reprint ed. lib. bdg. 52.00 (*0-8328-3121-2*) Higginson Bk Co.
Creigh, Dorothy W. Adams County, 2 vols., Set. Incl. People. LC 73-176266. 1971. 10.00 (*0-934858-01-2*); Story of Adams County, Nebraska. LC 73-176266. 1972. 40.00 (*0-934858-00-4*); LC 73-176266. (Illus.). 32.50 (*0-934858-02-0*) Adams County.
— Nebraska, Where Dreams Grow. LC 80-84238. (Illus.). 160p. (Orig.). 1990. reprint ed. pap. 12.95 (*0-934904-15-4*) J & L Lee.
— A Primer for Local Historical Societies. 2nd expanded rev. ed. LC 91-14071. (American Association for State & Local History Book Ser.). (Illus.). 132p. 1991. reprint ed. pap. 19.95 (*0-942063-12-0*) AltaMira Pr.
— Tales from the Prairie, 3 vols., Set. Incl. Vol. 2. LC 74-157038. 1973. pap. 6.95 (*0-934858-04-7*); Vol. 3. LC 74-157038. 1976. pap. 7.95 (*0-934858-05-5*); Vol. 4. LC 74-157038. 1996. pap. 9.95 (*0-934858-06-3*); LC 74-157038. (Illus.). reprint ed. Set pap. 6.95 (*0-934858-09-8*) Adams County.
— Tales from the Prairie, 3 vols., Vols. 1-4. LC 74-157038. (Illus.). reprint ed. write for info. (*0-934858-10-1*) Adams County.
Creigh, S. W., jt. ed. see Evans, Eric W.
***Creighton.** Other Gettysberg. 2000. 27.50 (*0-465-01456-9*, Pub. by Basic) HarpC.
— Other Gettysburg. 2000. pap. 16.00 (*0-465-01457-7*, Pub. by Basic) HarpC.
Creighton, Allan & Kivel, Paul. Helping Teens Stop Violence: A Practical Guide for Counselors, Educators, & Parents. LC 92-23349. (Illus.). 168p. (Orig.). 1992. pap. 14.95 (*0-89793-116-5*); spiral bd. 17.95 (*0-89793-115-7*) Hunter Hse.
Creighton, Andrew J. Kingdoms of Experience: Everest, the Unclimbed Ridge. 288p. 1999. pap. 15.00 (*0-86241-881-X*, Pub. by Canongate Books) Interlink Pub.
Creighton, Andrew J., ed. see Ellebaut.
Creighton, Ann & Adelson-Goldstein, Jayme. Listen First. (Illus.). 64p. 1991. pap. text, teacher ed. 10.95 (*0-19-434423-1*) OUP.
Creighton, B., tr. see Junger, Ernst.
Creighton, Barry. Orthopedic, Neurological & Chiropractic Physical Examinations. (Illus.). 80p. 1986. pap. 39.50 (*0-911110-57-7*, MICHIE) LEXIS Pub.
— Understanding Laboratory Values. 60p. 1988. pap. 39.50 (*0-911110-58-5*, MICHIE) LEXIS Pub.
Creighton, Barry, et al. Attorneys' Medical Reference. 4th ed. 270p. 1984. ring bd. 85.00 (*0-9614995-0-8*, 80163-10, MICHIE) LEXIS Pub.
Creighton, Basil, tr. see Junger, Ernst.
Creighton, Breen & Rozen, Peter. Occupational Health & Safety Law in Victoria. 2nd ed. 213p. 1996. pap. 49.00 (*1-86287-239-2*, Pub. by Federation Pr) Gaunt.
***Creighton, Breen & Stewart, Andrew.** Labour Law: An Introduction. 3rd ed. 500p. 2000. pap. 55.00 (*1-86287-231-7*, 18629, Pub. by Federation Pr) Gaunt.
Creighton, Christopher, jt. auth. see Hynd, Noel.
Creighton, Colin & Omari, C. K. Gender Family & Work in Tanzania. 63.95 (*1-84014-100-X*) Ashgate Pub Co.
Creighton, Colin & Omari, C. K., eds. Gender, Family & Household in Tanzania. 336p. 1995. 84.95 (*1-85628-651-7*, Pub. by Avebry) Ashgate Pub Co.
Creighton, Donald G. Harold Adams Innis: Portrait of a Scholar. LC 58-854. 154p. reprint ed. pap. 47.80 (*0-8357-3659-8*, 203638600003) Bks Demand.
— John A. MacDonald: The Young Politician & the Old Chieftain. LC 98-147627. (Reprints in Canadian History Ser.). 1216p. 1998. reprint ed. pap. text 45.00 (*0-8020-7164-3*) U of Toronto Pr.
— The Road to Confederation: The Emergence of Canada, 1863-1867. LC 75-27652. (Illus.). 489p. 1976. reprint ed. lib. bdg. 35.00 (*0-8371-8435-5*, CRRC, Greenwood Pr) Greenwood.
Creighton, Donald G., et al. Minorities, Schools, & Politics: Essays. LC 76-436561. (Canadian Historical Readings Ser.: No. 7). 123p. reprint ed. pap. 38.20 (*0-8357-6374-9*, 203572800096) Bks Demand.
Creighton, Douglas G. Jacques-Francois DeLuc of Geneva & His Friendship with Jean-Jacques Rousseau. LC 82-5332. (Romance Monographs: No. 42). 128p. 1983. 22.00 (*84-499-5926-8*) Romance.

An Asterisk (*) at the beginning of an entry indicates that the title is appearing for the first time.

Creighton, Gilbert. Seventeenth Century Paintings from the Low Countries. (Illus.). 1966. 10.50 (*0-8079-0117-2*) October.

Creighton, H. C., tr. see Gladkov, K. A.

Creighton, Helen. Law Every Nurse Should Know. 5th ed. (Illus.). 335p. 1986. pap. text 39.50 (*0-7216-1832-4*, W B Saunders Co) Harcrt Hlth Sci Grp.

— Songs & Ballads from Nova Scotia. xxvi, 334p. 1992. pap. 9.95 (*0-486-21703-5*) Dover.

Creighton, Helen & MacLeod, Calum. Gaelic Songs in Nova Scotia. (Illus.). 320p. 1979. pap. 19.95 (*0-660-00144-6*, Pub. by CN Mus Civilization) U of Wash Pr.

Creighton, Helen & Peacock, Kenneth. Folksongs from Southern New Brunswick. (Publications in Folk Culture Ser.: No. 1). (Illus.). 248p. 1971. pap. 8.50 (*0-660-00045-8*, Pub. by CN Mus Civilization) U of Wash Pr.

Creighton, J., tr. see Wundt, Wilhelm M.

Creighton, J. D. & Wilson, R. J., eds. Roman Germany: Studies in Cultural Interaction. (Journal of Roman Archaeology Supplementary Ser.: No. 32). (Illus.). 248p. 1999. pap. 34.95 (*1-887829-32-6*) Jour Roman Arch.

Creighton, James & Simonton, Carl. Getting Well Again. 304p. 1992. mass mkt. 6.99 (*0-553-28033-3*) Bantam.

Creighton, James H. An Introduction to Probability Models & Statistical Inference. LC 93-25369. (Texts in Statistics Ser.). 717p. 1994. 67.95 (*0-387-94114-2*) Spr-Verlag.

Creighton, James L. Discopaedia of the Violin, 1889-1971. LC 79-185708. 1003p. reprint ed. pap. 200.00 (*0-608-16693-6*, 205611600050) Bks Demand.

— How Loving Couples Fight: 12 Essential Tools for Working Through the Hurt. LC 98-19882. 304p. 1998. pap. 16.95 (*0-944031-71-4*) Aslan Pub.

Creighton, James L. & Adams, James W. CyberMeeting: How to Link People & Technology in Your Organization. LC 97-22979. 208p. 1997. 27.95 (*0-8144-0352-2*) AMACOM.

***Creighton, Jayne, contrib. by.** Boomerangs, Blades & Basketballs: The Science of Sports. LC 99-12288. (Science at Work Ser.). (Illus.). 48p. (J). (gr. 4-6). 2000. lib. bdg. write for info. (*0-7398-0132-5*) Princeton U Pr.

Creighton, Jeff J. Combines & Harvesters: Photographic History. LC 96-719. (Illus.). 160p. 1996. pap. 19.95 (*0-7603-0125-5*) MBI Pubg.

— Ford Tractor Data Book. LC 96-8849. (Fordson to the Hundred Ser.). (Illus.). 128p. 1996. pap. 11.95 (*0-7603-0240-5*) Motorbooks Intl.

***Creighton, Jeff J.** Indian Summers: Washington State College & the Nespelem Art Colony, 1937-41. (Illus.). 144p. 2000. 35.95 (*0-87422-191-9*); pap. 22.95 (*0-87422-192-7*) Wash St U Pr.

Creighton, Jennifer, ed. see Islip, Tim, et al.

Creighton, Jill. Au Bout Du Ciel (Where the Sky Begins) (FRE., Illus.). (J). 1996. pap. 6.95 (*1-55037-371-4*, Pub. by Annick) Firefly Bks Ltd.

— 8 O'Cluck. 32p. (J). (ps-2). 1997. mass mkt. 4.99 (*0-590-93568-2*) Scholastic Inc.

— 8 O'Cluck. 1997. 10.19 (*0-606-11014-3*, Pub. by Turtleback) Demco.

— The Great Blue Grump. LC 96-990068. (Illus.). 32p. (J). (ps-2). 1997. 15.95 (*1-55037-433-8*, Pub. by Annick); pap. 5.95 (*1-55037-432-X*, Pub. by Annick) Firefly Bks Ltd.

— One Day There Was Nothing to Do. (Illus.). 24p. (J). (ps-3). 1990. pap. 4.95 (*1-55037-090-1*, Pub. by Annick); lib. bdg. 14.95 (*1-55037-091-X*, Pub. by Annick) Firefly Bks Ltd.

— Where the Sky Begins. (Illus.). 94p. (J). (gr. 4-6). 1996. pap. 4.95 (*1-55037-270-X*, Pub. by Annick) Firefly Bks Ltd.

Creighton, Jill & Creighton, Robert. The Weaver's Horse. (Illus.). 32p. (J). (ps-2). 1991. 15.95 (*1-55037-181-9*, Pub. by Annick); pap. 5.95 (*1-55037-178-9*, Pub. by Annick) Firefly Bks Ltd.

Creighton, Joanne V. William Faulkner's Craft of Revision: The Snopes Trilogy, The Unvanquished, & Go Down, Moses. LC 76-51441. 183p. reprint ed. pap. 56.80 (*0-608-17740-7*, 203204000077) Bks Demand.

***Creighton, John.** Coins & Power in Late Iron-Age Britain. (New Studies in Archaeology). (Illus.). 266p. 2000. 69.95 (*0-521-77207-9*) Cambridge U Pr.

Creighton, John. Fire Engines of Yesterday. (Illus.). (Orig.). 1991. pap. 17.00 (*0-86025-878-5*, Pub. by I Henry Pubns) Empire Pub Srvs.

— G.C.S.E. French: Writing a Letter. 2nd ed. (Illus.). 92p. (Orig.). (C). 1991. pap. 12.00 (*0-86025-911-0*, Pub. by I Henry Pubns) Empire Pub Srvs.

Creighton, John. Oil on Troubled Waters: Gulf Wars 1980-91. 1992. text 70.00 (*1-873395-45-0*) St Martin.

***Creighton, Kathleen.** L'Amour Sans Compromis. (FRE.). 2000. mass mkt. 5.50 (*0-373-38351-7*) Harlequin Bks.

— The Cowboy's Hidden Agenda. 249p. 2000. mass mkt. 4.50 (*0-373-27074-7*) Harlequin Bks.

— Eve's Wedding Knight: The Sisters Waskowitz. (Intimate Moments Ser.: No. 963). 1999. per. 4.25 (*0-373-07963-X*, 1-07963-1) Silhouette.

Creighton, Kathleen. Eyewitness. (Intimate Moments Ser.). 1995. per. 3.50 (*0-373-07616-9*, 1-07616-5) Silhouette.

— Le Fugitif. (Rouge Passion Ser.: No. 484). (FRE.). 1998. mass mkt. 3.50 (*0-373-37484-4*, 1-37484-2) Harlequin Bks.

***Creighton, Kathleen.** L'Etoile de la Chance. (Amours d'Aujourd'Hui Ser.: No. 348). (FRE.). 2000. mass mkt. 5.50 (*0-373-38348-7*, 1-38348-8, Harlequin French) Harlequin Bks.

Creighton, Kathleen. Man of Steel: (Into the Heartland) 1995. mass mkt. 3.75 (*0-373-07677-0*, 1-07677-7) Silhouette.

— Never Trust a Lady. 1997. per. 3.99 (*0-373-07800-5*, 1-07800-5) Silhouette.

— One Christmas Knight. (Intimate Moments Ser.: No. 825). 1997. per. 3.99 (*0-373-07825-0*, 1-07825-2) Harlequin Bks.

— One Good Man. (Intimate Moments Ser.). 1995. per. 3.75 (*0-373-07639-8*, 1-07639-7) Silhouette.

— One More Knight. (Intimate Moments Ser.: No. 890). 1998. per. 4.25 (*0-373-07890-0*, 0-07890-7) Silhouette.

— One Summer's Knight: The Sisters Waskowitz. (Intimate Moments Ser.: No. 944). 1999. per. 4.25 (*0-373-07944-3*, 1-07944-1) Silhouette.

— Rogue's Valley. (Men Made in America Ser.). 1994. per. 3.59 (*0-373-45162-8*, 1-45162-4) Silhouette.

— A Wanted Man: (American Heroes) (Intimate Moments Ser.). 1994. mass mkt. 3.50 (*0-373-07547-2*, 5-07547-8) Silhouette.

— Wolf & the Angel. (Intimate Moments Ser.: No. 417). 1992. per. 3.29 (*0-373-07417-4*, 5-07417-4) Harlequin Bks.

Creighton, Kathleen, et al. In Defense of Love; Her Special Angel; Daddy Christmas; Home for Christmas, 4 bks. in 1. (Romance Digest Ser.: Vol. 9, No. 3). 1999. mass mkt. 3.50i (*0-373-82751-2*, 1-82751-8) Harlequin Bks.

Creighton, Kathleen, jt. auth. see Lebenson, Richard.

Creighton, Kathleen, jt. ed. see Lebenson, Richard.

Creighton, L., ed. see Creighton, Mandell.

Creighton, Linn. Beyond This Darkness. LC 93-533. 176p. 1993. pap. 7.99 (*0-8361-3642-X*) Herald Pr.

***Creighton, Linn.** Beyond This Darkness. large type ed. LC 00-25968. (Christian Fiction Ser.). 2000. 23.95 (*0-7862-2516-5*) Thorndike Pr.

Creighton, Linn. Plays of the Passion. LC 98-15539. 124p. 1998. 13.95 (*1-57895-053-8*) Bridge Resources.

Creighton, Mandell. Historical Lectures & Addresses. Creighton, L., ed. LC 67-26730. (Essay Index Reprint Ser.). 1977. 23.95 (*0-8369-0350-1*) Ayer.

— History of the Papacy from the Great Schism to the Sack of Rome, 6 vols. rev. ed. LC 74-77897. reprint ed. 165.00 (*0-404-01870-X*) AMS Pr.

Creighton, Margaret & Norling, Lisa, eds. Iron Men, Wooden Women: Gender & Seafaring, 1700-1920. LC 95-30921. (Gender Relations in the American Experience Ser.). 304p. (C). 1996. text 48.00 (*0-8018-5159-9*); pap. text 17.95 (*0-8018-5160-2*) Johns Hopkins.

Creighton, Margaret S. Rites & Passages: The Experience of American Whaling, 1830-1870. (Illus.). 249p. (C). 1995. pap. 18.95 (*0-521-48448-0*); text 64.95 (*0-521-43336-3*) Cambridge U Pr.

Creighton, Robert, jt. auth. see Creighton, Jill.

Creighton, Sarah H. Greening the Ivory Tower: Improving the Environmental Track Record of Universities, Colleges, & Other Institutions. LC 97-39382. (Urban & Industrial Environments Ser.). (Illus.). 372p. 1998. pap. text 25.00 (*0-262-53151-8*) MIT Pr.

Creighton, T. E., ed. Protein Function: A Practical Approach. 2nd ed. LC 97-6741. (The Practical Approach Ser.: No. 175). (Illus.). 360p. 1997. text 105.00 (*0-19-963616-8*); pap. text 55.00 (*0-19-963615-X*) OUP.

— Protein Structure: A Practical Approach. 2nd ed. LC 97-162964. (The Practical Approach Ser.: No. 174). (Illus.). 408p. 1997. text 105.00 (*0-19-963619-2*); pap. text 55.00 (*0-19-963618-4*) OUP.

— Protein Structure & Protein Function: A Practical Approach, Two. 2nd ed. LC 97-6741. (Practical Approach Ser.: No. 174, 175). 1997. text 190.00 (*0-19-963617-6*); pap. text 95.00 (*0-19-963620-6*) OUP.

Creighton, T. E., jt. auth. see Darby, N. J.

***Creighton, Theodore B.** Schools & Data: The Educator's Guide to Using Data to Improve Decision-Making. LC 00-8771. 2000. pap. write for info. (*0-7619-7717-1*) Corwin Pr.

Creighton, Thomas E. Proteins: Structures & Molecular Properties. 2nd ed. LC 92-6664. 512p. (C). 1992. pap. text 80.95 (*0-7167-7030-X*) W H Freeman.

Creighton, Thomas E., ed. Encyclopedia of Molecular Biology, 4 vols. LC 99-11575. 2878p. 1999. 1500.00 (*0-471-15302-8*) Wiley.

— Protein Folding. LC 92-10475. 547p. (C). 1992. pap. text 73.95 (*0-7167-7027-X*) W H Freeman.

Creighton, Thomas H., ed. Building for Modern Man. LC 74-80385. (Essay Index Reprint Ser.). 1977. 20.95 (*0-8369-1029-X*) Ayer.

Creighton, W. B., et al. Labour Law: Text & Materials. 2nd ed. 1993. pap. 125.00 (*0-455-21137-X*, Pub. by LawBk Co) Gaunt.

Creighton, W. Breen & Stewart, Andrew. Labour Law. 2nd ed. 375p. 1994. pap. 49.00 (*1-86287-134-5*, Pub. by Federation Pr) Gaunt.

— Labour Law: An Introduction. xxx, 306p. 1990. pap. 43.00 (*1-86287-031-4*, Pub. by Federation Pr) Gaunt.

Creighton, W. Breen, et al. Labour Law: Text & Materials. 2nd ed. 1993. 165.00 (*0-455-21136-1*, Pub. by LawBk Co) Gaunt.

Creighton-Zollar, Ann. The Social Correlates of Infant & Reproductive Mortality in the United States: A Reference Guide. LC 92-41215. 224p. 1993. text 41.00 (*0-8153-0221-5*, SS766) Garland.

Creignou, M. & De Meurville, E. La France Gourmande a Domicile, 1995. 320p. 1995. 49.95 (*0-7859-9038-0*) Fr & Eur.

Creith, Elaine. Undressing Lesbian Sex. 1996. pap. 21.95 (*0-304-32849-9*, Pub. by Cassell) LPC InBook.

Creizenach, W. English Drama in the Age of Shakespeare. LC 65-15873. (Studies in Drama: No. 39). 1969. reprint ed. lib. bdg. 75.00 (*0-8383-0533-4*) M S G Haskell Hse.

Creizenach, Wilhelm. Geschichte des Neureren Dramas, 3 vols., Set. LC 64-14696. 1972. reprint ed. 145.95 (*0-405-08402-1*, Pub. by Blom Pubns) Ayer.

— Geschichte des Neureren Dramas, 3 vols., Vol. 1. LC 64-14696. 1972. reprint ed. 48.95 (*0-405-08403-X*, Pub. by Blom Pubns) Ayer.

— Geschichte des Neureren Dramas, 3 vols., Vol. 2. LC 64-14696. 1972. reprint ed. 48.95 (*0-405-08404-8*, Pub. by Blom Pubns) Ayer.

— Geschichte des Neureren Dramas, 3 vols., Vol. 3. LC 64-14696. 1972. reprint ed. 48.95 (*0-405-08405-6*, Pub. by Blom Pubns) Ayer.

Creleri, Guiliano. Le Corbusier: Les Voyages d'Allemagne, Carnets, 5 vols., Set. LC 95-37459. (Illus.). 500p. 1995. boxed set 250.00 (*1-885254-15-6*, Pub. by Monacelli Pr) Penguin Putnam.

Crelin, Edmund S. Functional Anatomy of the Newborn. LC 72-91292. 99p. reprint ed. pap. 30.70 (*0-8357-8723-0*, 203369800087) Bks Demand.

Crelinsten, J. To the Limit. (Illus.). 64p. (J). (gr. 3 up). 1993. 17.95 (*0-15-200616-8*, Gulliver Bks) Harcourt.

***Crelinsten, Jeffrey.** To the Limit: The Extraordinary Workings of the Human Body. (Illus.). 64p. 1998. 17.95 (*0-921051-55-7*) Somerville Hse.

— To the Limit: The Marvel of Human Performance. (Illus.). 64p. 1999. reprint ed. text 20.00 (*0-7881-6473-2*) DIANE Pub.

Crelinsten, Ronald D., jt. ed. see Schmid, Alex P.

Crellin, J. K. & Philpott, Jane. A Reference Guide to Medicinal Plants: Herbal Medicine Past & Present. LC 97-17089. 1997. pap. write for info. (*0-8223-2068-1*) Duke.

Crellin, John K. Home Medicine: The Newfoundland Experience. (McGill-Queen's Studies in the History of Religion Ser.). (Illus.). 288p. 1994. 65.00 (*0-7735-1196-2*, Pub. by McG-Queens Univ Pr); pap. 22.95 (*0-7735-1197-0*, Pub. by McG-Queens Univ Pr) CUP Services.

— Medical Care in Pioneer Illinois. LC 82-81512. (Illus.). 128p. 1982. 15.95 (*0-931369-19-3*) Southern IL Univ Sch.

Crellin, John K., ed. Plain Southern Eating: Reminiscences of A. L. "Tommie" Bass, Herbalist. LC 87-31765. (Illus.). xii, 130p. 1988. text 19.95 (*0-8223-0828-2*) Duke.

Crellin, John K. & Philpott, Jane. Herbal Medicine Past & Present: A Reference Guide to Medicinal Plants, 2. LC 97-17089. 560p. (Orig.). 1989. text 69.95 (*0-8223-0879-7*) Duke.

— Herbal Medicine Past & Present, Vol. 1: Trying to Give Ease. LC 97-15490. 347p. 1989. text 39.95 (*0-8223-0877-0*) Duke.

— A Reference Guide to Medicinal Plants. LC 97-17089. (Illus.). 560p. (Orig.). 1997. pap. 22.95 (*0-8223-1019-8*) Duke.

— Trying to Give Ease Vol. 1: Tommie Bass & the Story of Herbal Medicine. LC 97-15490. 335p. 1997. pap. 16.95 (*0-8223-2017-7*) Duke.

Crellin, John K., jt. auth. see Crellin, Paul I.

Crellin, M., jt. auth. see Forst, G.

Crellin, Paul I. & Crellin, John K. By the Patient & Not by the Book: Constancy & Change in Small Town Doctoring, 1893-1987. (Illus.). xi, 76p. (Orig.). 1988. pap. 12.95 (*0-89386-021-2*) Acorn NC.

Crelling, John C., jt. auth. see Winans, Randall E.

Crelling, John C., jt. ed. see Anderson, Ken B.

Crelling, John C., jt. ed. see Winans, Randall E.

Crelly, William R. Marcello Giovanetti (1598-1631) A Poet of the Early Roman Baroque. LC 89-9418. (Illus.). 456p. 1989. lib. bdg. 109.95 (*0-88946-146-5*) E Mellen.

Cremades, Bernardo M. Arbitration in Spain. 1650p. 1991. boxed set 96.00 (*0-406-00192-8*, U.K., MICHIE) LEXIS Pub.

Cremades, Bernardo M. & Cabiedes, E. G. Litigating in Spain: Considerations for Foreign Practitioners; Including International Judicial Assistance, Enforcement of Foreign Judgments, Bankruptcy, Arbitration & Other Civil Proceedings. 580p. 1989. 108.00 (*90-6544-377-0*) Kluwer Law Intl.

Cremaldi, Catherine T. The Cremaldi Cookbook: Traditional Italian Recipes & Innovative Tastes for Contemporary Cooks. rev. ed. LC 97-77571. (Illus.). xii, 260p. 1997. pap. 19.95 (*0-9661501-0-4*) Figaro Pr.

Creme, Benjamin. The Ageless Wisdom Teaching LC 99-166741. 62p. 1996. write for info. (*90-71484-13-0*) Share Intl.

— Maitreya's Mission, Vol. 1. 3rd ed. LC 97-222727. 411p. (Orig.). 1993. pap. 13.00 (*90-71484-08-4*) Share Intl.

— Maitreya's Mission, Vol. 2. LC 97-222727. (Illus.). 718p. (Orig.). 1993. pap. 18.00 (*90-71484-11-4*) Share Intl.

— Maitreya's Mission, Vol. 3. LC 97-222727. 704p. (Orig.). 1997. pap. 18.00 (*90-71484-15-7*) Share Intl.
Britain's Benjamin Creme is today's most powerful voice challenging the millennial "prophets of doom" with his compelling & detailed vision of the future - what he calls a "brilliant new civilization in the making." This sweeping transformation is now possible, Creme writes, because a group of extraordinary spiritual teachers are living in the everyday world, ready to begin their open mission of inspiring & guiding humanity. At their head, says Creme, is Maitreya, the World Teacher, the one awaited under different names by people of all spiritual traditions. Creme covers topics both profound & practical, ranging from mankind's origin to the principle of sharing as the first step toward global peace; from meditation & service to the technology of light; from reincarnation & karma to a pollution-free environment. A section on miracles explains the source & purpose of weeping Madonnas, crosses of light, healing waters, "milk-drinking" statues, crop circles & more. Benjamin Creme's message holds a unique place in today's world. It offers a practical application of the ancient wisdom underlying all faiths. It provides the blueprint for a society that offers the basic necessities of life to all. It is the assurance of a hard-won but glorious future for humanity. *Publisher Paid Annotation.*

–The Reappearance of the Christ & the Masters of Wisdom. LC 80-50639. 253p. (Orig.). 1980. pap. 7.00 (*0-936604-00-X*) Tara Ctr.
In this first of six books on the subject, British artist & lecturer Benjamin Creme made the startling announcement that the Christ, as World Teacher for the coming age, is already among us -- gradually emerging into full public recognition. Known at this time as Maitreya, but expected by various religions under different names. He is here to promote cooperation among the many ideological factions, galvanize world goodwill & sharing, & inspire sweeping political, social, economic & environmental reforms. Creme puts the most profound event of the last 2,000 years into its correct historical & esoteric context & describes what effect the World Teacher's presence will have on both the world's institutions & the average person. Through his telepathic contact with a Master of Wisdom, Creme answers a myriad of questions well beyond the scope of his personal knowledge. New insights are offered on such subjects as the soul & reincarnation, telepathy, nuclear energy, ancient civilizations, problems of the developing world & a new economic order -- & he clarifies misunderstandings about the anti-Christ & the Last Judgement. Creme delivers his extraordinary message of hope through lectures & media interviews worldwide. His books are available in eight languages. Distributed by DeVorss, New Leaf, Dempsey. *Publisher Paid Annotation.*

— Transmission: A Meditation for the New Age. 4th rev. ed. (Illus.). 204p. 1998. pap. 11.00 (*90-71484-17-3*) Share Intl.

Creme, Benjamin, intro. A Master Speaks. 2nd ed. 256p. (Orig.). 1994. pap. 11.00 (*90-71484-10-6*) Share Intl.

— Messages from Maitreya the Christ. 2nd ed. 283p. 1992. pap. 9.00 (*0-936604-11-5*) Tara Ctr.

Creme, P. Writing into Higher Education: A Guide for Students. LC 97-16321. 152p. 1997. pap. 79.00 (*0-335-19643-8*) OpUniv Pr.

Creme, Phyllis & Lea, Mary R. Writing for a University: A Guide for Students. LC 97-16321. 160p. 1997. pap. 19.95 (*0-335-19642-X*) OpUniv Pr.

Cremean, D. Brooking on Building Contracts. 3rd ed. LC 96-157361. 320p. 1995. write for info. (*0-409-30065-9*, MICHIE) LEXIS Pub.

Cremean, Damien J. Admiralty Jurisdiction: Law & Practice in Australia. LC 99-160100. 238p. 1997. 79.00 (*1-86287-254-6*, Pub. by Federation Pr) Gaunt.

Cremeans, Charles D. The Reception of Calvinistic Thought in England. LC 83-45578. reprint ed. 41.50 (*0-404-19896-1*) AMS Pr.

Cremeans, Jack E. Handbook of North American Industry. 2nd rev. ed. (Illus.). 600p. 1999. 89.00 (*0-89059-157-1*, BP1571) Bernan Pr.

Cremeens, David L., et al, eds. Whole Regolith Pedology. LC 93-47659. (Special Publications: No. 34). 136p. 1994. pap. 15.00 (*0-89118-805-3*) Soil Sci Soc Am.

Crement, Xavier. A**hole No More! A Self-Help Guide for Recovering Assholes---& Their Victims. 192p. 1990. pap. 11.95 (*0-89804-804-4*, Pub. by Ariel GA) Alliance Bk Co.

— Assholes Forever: How to Spot 'Em, How to Stop 'Em. 192p. 1992. pap. 11.95 (*0-89804-807-9*, Pub. by Ariel GA) Alliance Bk Co.

Cremer, Charles F. Television News & the New Technology. 3rd ed. 441p. (C). 1995. pap. 45.94 (*0-07-013530-4*) McGraw.

Cremer, Charles F., jt. auth. see Yoakam, Richard D.

Cremer, Drutmar. Sing Me the Song of My World. (C). 1988. 39.00 (*0-85439-191-6*, Pub. by St Paul Pubns) St Mut.

Cremer, Herbert W. & Davies, Trefor, eds. Chemical Engineering Practice, 12 vols., Set. Incl. Vol. 1. General. LC 56-58716. 524p. pap. 162.50 (*0-608-04749-X*, 202576300001); Vol. 2. Solid State. LC 56-58716. 669p. pap. 200.00 (*0-608-04750-3*, 202576300002); Vol. 3. Solid Systems. LC 56-58716. 574p. pap. 178.00 (*0-608-04751-1*, 202576300003); Vol. 4. Fluid State. LC 56-58716. 649p. pap. 200.00 (*0-608-04752-X*, 202576300004); Vol. 5. Fluid Systems I. LC 56-58716. 732p. pap. 200.00 (*0-608-04753-8*, 202576300005); Vol. 6. Fluids Systems II. LC 56-58716. 638p. pap. 197.80 (*0-608-04754-6*, 202576300006); Vol. 8. Chemical Kinetics. LC 56-58716. 630p. pap. 195.30 (*0-608-04756-2*, 202576300008); Vol. 9. Design & Construction. LC 56-58716. 476p. pap. 147.60 (*0-608-04757-0*, 202576300009); Vol. 10. Ancillary Services. LC 56-58716. 630p. pap. 195.30 (*0-608-04758-9*, 202576300010); Vol. 11. Work Design.

C

LC 56-58716. 414p. pap. 128.40 (*0-608-04759-7*, 202576300011); Vol. 12: Index. LC 56-58716. pap. 76.30 (*0-608-16088-1*); LC 56-58716. reprint ed. pap. write for info. (*0-608-18691-0*, 2025763) Bks Demand.

— Heat Transfer, Vol. 7. LC 56-58716. 479p. pap. 148.50 (*0-608-04755-4*, 202576300007) Bks Demand.

Cremer, Holger. The Diatom Flora of the Laptev Sea, Arctic Ocean. (Bibliotheca Diatomologica Ser.: Band 40). (Illus.). 170p. 1998. 72.00 (*3-443-57031-3*, Pub. by Gebruder Borntraeger) Balogh.

Cremer, J. Records of the Dorland Family in America: Including Principal Branches Dorland, Dorlon, Dorlan, Durland, Daarling in the U. S. & Canada. 320p. 1989. reprint ed. pap. 48.00 (*0-8328-0487-8*); reprint ed. lib. bdg. 56.00 (*0-8328-0486-X*) Higginson Bk Co.

Cremer, Jacques. Models of the Oil Market, Vol. 44. (Fundamentals of Pure & Applied Economics Ser.). ix, 106p. 1991. pap. text 62.00 (*3-7186-5072-X*, Harwood Acad Pubs) Gordon & Breach.

Cremer, John. Testament of Cremer, the English Alchemist. 1984. pap. 3.95 (*0-916411-96-6*) Holmes Pub.

Cremer, L. & Heckl, M. A. Structure-Borne Sound. (Illus.). 550p. 1988. 142.95 (*0-387-18241-1*) Spr-Verlag.

Cremer, Lothar. The Physics of the Violin. Allen, John S., tr. from GER. 472p. 1984. 55.00 (*0-262-03102-7*) MIT Pr.

Cremer, Marion, jt. auth. see Warfel, M. C.

Cremer, Marion L. Quality Food in Quantity: Management & Science. LC 97-84186. (Illus.). 370p. 1998. 60.00 (*0-8211-0232-X*) McCutchan.

Cremer, Peter. U-Boat Commander: A Periscope View of the Battle of the Atlantic. LC 84-61243. 244p. 1984. 27.95 (*0-87021-969-3*) Naval Inst Pr.

Cremer, Roel, jt. ed. see Snel, Jan.

Cremer, Stephane. Trivial Pursuit Encyclopedie Junior: Dictionnaire. (FRE.). 558p. 1989. 75.00 (*0-7859-8135-7*, 2863913247) Fr & Eur.

Cremers, A. B. & Kriegel, H. P., eds. Theoretical Computer Science: Proceedings, Dortmund, FRG, 1983. (Lecture Notes in Computer Science Ser.: Vol. 145). 367p. 1983. 35.00 (*0-387-11973-6*) Spr-Verlag.

Cremers, C. & Hogland, G., eds. Pediatric Otology. (Advances in OtoRhinoLaryngology Ser.: Vol. 40). (Illus.). viii, 168p. 1988. 129.75 (*3-8055-4726-9*) S Karger.

Cremers, C. J. & Hine, H. A., eds. Thermal Conductivity, Vol. 21. LC 90-45242. (Illus.). 728p. (C). 1990. text 198.00 (*0-306-43672-8*, Kluwer Plenum) Kluwer Academic.

Cremers, David A., jt. auth. see Radziemski, Leon J.

Cremers, G., et al. Ferns & Fern Allies: Dennstaeditaceae & Hymenophyllopsidacae. Goerts-van-Rijn, A. R. A., ed. (Flora of the Guianas Ser.: Series B, Fascicle 4). (Illus.). 48p. 1990. pap. 35.00 (*3-87429-305-X*, 041499, Pub. by Koeltz Sci Bks) Lubrecht & Cramer.

Cremin, Aedeen. The Celts. LC 97-76002. (Illus.). 160p. 1998. 19.95 (*0-8478-2105-6*, Pub. by Rizzoli Intl) St Martin.

Cremin, Aedeen, ed. The Enduring Past: Archaeology of the Ancient World for Australians. 230p. pap. 22.95 (*0-86840-114-5*, Pub. by New South Wales Univ Pr) Intl Spec Bk.

Cremin, Aedeen, jt. auth. see Jack, Ian.

Cremin, Bryan J. Childhood Tuberculosis: Modern Imaging & Clinical Concepts. Jamieson, Douglas H., ed. LC 95-7046. (Illus.). 122p. 1995. 108.00 (*3-540-19925-X*) Spr-Verlag.

Cremin, Joan. Selfhood, Fiction, & Desire in Stendhal's "Vie de Henry Brulard" & "Armance" LC 96-18971. (Age of Revolution & Romanticism: Vol. 21). (Illus.). 116p. (C). 1998. text 36.95 (*0-8204-3369-1*) P Lang Pubng.

Cremin, Lawrence. The Genius of American Education. LC 65-28146. (Horace Mann Lectures: 1965). 132p. reprint ed. pap. 41.00 (*0-608-12760-4*, 202433000037) Bks Demand.

Cremin, Lawrence A. Transformation of the School: Progressivism in American Education, 1876-1957. 1964. pap. text 5.95 (*0-07-553704-4*) McGraw.

Cremin, Lawrence A., ed. Republic & the School: Horace Mann on the Education of Free Men. 7th ed. LC 57-9102. (Classics in Education Ser.). 112p. (Orig.). 1957. pap. text 7.00 (*0-8077-1206-X*) Tchrs Coll.

Cremin, Lawrence A. & Barnard, Frederick A., eds. American Education: Its Men, Ideas, & Institutions, Series 1-2, 92 vols., Set. 1972. 984.00 (*0-405-01497-X*) Ayer.

Cremin, Lawrence A., ed. see American Unitarian Association Staff.

Cremin, Lawrence A., ed. see Campbell, Thomas M.

Cremin, Pedar, jt. auth. see Regan, Colm.

***Cremins, Robert.** A Sort of Homecoming: A Novel. LC 99-89011. 304p. 2000. pap. 13.95 (*0-393-32023-5*, Norton Paperbks) Norton.

Cremins, Robert. Animal Acrobats: A National Geographic Pop-Up Book. LC 93-9768. (Pop-Up Bks.). 10p. (YA). (ps up). 1995. 16.00 (*0-87044-955-9*, Pub. by Natl Geog) Publishers Group.

Cremlyn, R. J. Agrochemicals: Preparation & Mode of Action. 2nd ed. LC 90-2242. 406p. 1991. pap. 98.00 (*0-471-92992-1*) Wiley.

— An Introduction to Organosulfur Chemistry. LC 96-25732. 262p. 1996. 175.00 (*0-471-95512-4*) Wiley.

Cremmins, Edward T. The Art of Abstracting. 2nd ed. LC 95-82341. 230p. 1996. pap. text 34.95 (*0-87815-066-8*) Info Resources.

Cremo, Michael. Forbidden Archeology's Impact: How a Controversial New Book Shocked the Scientific Community & Became an Underground Classic. LC 97-42314. xxxiv, 569p. (C). 1998. 35.00 (*0-89213-283-3*) Bhaktivedanta.

Cremo, Michael & Thompson, Richard. Forbidden Archeology: The Hidden History of the Human Race. LC 92-76168. (Illus.). 960p. (C). 1993. 44.95 (*0-9635309-8-4*) Govardhan Hill.

Cremo, Michael A. & Goswami, Mukunda D. Divine Nature: A Spiritual Perspective on the Environmental Crisis. LC 95-5867. (Illus.). 108p. 1995. pap. 9.95 (*0-89213-297-3*, DN) Bhaktivedanta.

Cremo, Michael A. & Thompson, Richard L. Forbidden Archeology: The Hidden History of the Human Race. rev. ed. LC 92-76168. (Illus.). xxxviii, 914p. (C). 1994. 44.95 (*0-89213-294-9*, Pub. by Bhaktivedanta) Torchlght Pub.

— The Hidden History of the Human Race: Major Scientific Coverup Exposed. abr. ed. LC 94-15720. (Illus.). 352p. 1994. 22.95 (*0-9635309-6-8*, HH) BBT Sci Bks.

— The Hidden History of the Human Race: The Condensed Edition of Forbidden Archeology. 2nd ed. LC 94-15720. (Illus.). 322p. 1999. reprint ed. pap. 15.95 (*0-89213-325-2*, Pub. by Bhaktivedanta) Torchlght Pub.

Cremona. French Grammar. (Grammar Card Guides Ser.). (ENG & FRE.). 1977. pap. 3.50 (*0-8120-5042-8*) Barron.

Cremona, Candida H. Access Travel U. S. A. A Directory for People with Disabilities. LC 94-79131. 176p. (Orig.). 1994. pap. text 19.95 (*0-9642279-0-8*) Creat Hosp Concepts.

Cremona, Carlo. Saint Paul. Duggan, Paul, tr. from ITA. 228p. 1995. pap. 14.95 (*0-8198-6974-0*) Pauline Bks.

Cremona, Carolus A., ed. Phaedrus - Lexicon Phaedrianum. (Alpha-Omega, Reihe A Ser.: Bd. XV). xxxiv, 663p. 1980. 150.00 (*3-487-06970-9*) G Olms Pubs.

Cremona, J. E. Algorithms for Modular Elliptic Curves. 2nd ed. (Illus.). 377p. (C). 1997. 74.95 (*0-521-59820-6*) Cambridge U Pr.

Cremona, Joseph. Buongiorno Italia: Teacher's guide. text 4.90 (*0-8219-0242-3*) EMC-Paradigm.

— Buongiorno Italia! Text workbook. 19.95 (*0-8219-0146-X*) EMC-Paradigm.

— Buongiorno Italia: Textbook. text 14.50 (*0-8219-0241-5*) EMC-Paradigm.

Cremona, Joseph, jt. auth. see EMC Publishing Company Staff.

Cremona, Julian. Handbook of Off-Road Driving. 2nd ed. 1994. pap. text 30.00 (*1-85253-285-8*, Pub. by Quiller Pr) St Mut.

Cremony, John C. Life among the Apaches. LC 82-16106. 322p. 1983. reprint ed. pap. 13.95 (*0-8032-6312-0*, Bison Books) U of Nebr Pr.

Crena De Iongh, Daniel. Byzantine Aspects of Italy. LC 67-19211. (Illus.). 1967. 7.50 (*0-393-04134-4*) Norton.

Crenne, Helisenne D. A Renaissance Woman: Helisenne's Personal & Invective Letter. Mustacchi, Marianna M. & Archambault, Paul J., eds. LC 85-20812. (Illus.). 149p. 1986. reprint ed. pap. 46.20 (*0-608-06973-6*, 206718100009) Bks Demand.

Crenner, James. My Hat Flies on Again. LC 79-25793. 62p. (Orig.). 1980. pap. 4.25 (*0-934332-23-1*) LEpervier Pr.

Crensham, Curtis I. & Gunn, Grover E., III. Dispensationalism Today, Yesterday, & Tomorrow. 350p. (Orig.). 1994. pap. 12.95 (*1-877818-01-1*) Footstool Pubns.

Crenshaw. Human Sexuality: HP 615 Course. 100p. (C). 1991. 69.95 incl. audio (*0-933195-65-6*) CA College Health Sci.

— Human Sexuality CEU Course: 30 CEUs. 100p. (C). 1991. student ed. 49.95 incl. audio (*0-933195-79-6*) CA College Health Sci.

Crenshaw, A. W. Operative Orthopaedics Cd-Rom Library Institutional. 1996. text 495.95 (*0-8151-1901-1*) Mosby Inc.

Crenshaw, Betsy, compiled by. No Crystal Stair: An African American Booklist. 40p. 1996. pap. 8.00 (*0-87104-736-5*) NY Pub Lib.

Crenshaw, Curtis I. Keeping Covenant & Educating Our Children. 125p. pap. 3.00 (*1-877818-09-7*) Footstool Pubns.

— Lordship Salvation: The Only Kind There Is. 250p. (Orig.). 1994. pap. 10.95 (*1-877818-12-7*) Footstool Pubns.

— Man As God: The Word of Faith Movement. 450p. (Orig.). 1994. pap. 14.95 (*1-877818-11-9*) Footstool Pubns.

Crenshaw, Curtis I., tr. see Boston, Thomas.

Crenshaw, David A. Bereavement: Counseling the Grieving Throughout the Life Cycle. 228p. 1995. pap. 13.95 (*0-8245-1291-X*) Crossroad NY.

Crenshaw, Floyd D. & Flanders, John A., eds. Christian Values & the Academic Disciplines. 224p. (Orig.). 1985. pap. text 22.00 (*0-8191-4307-3*) U Pr of Amer.

Crenshaw, George. Belvedere: Beware - Obedience School Dropout. 128p. 1991. pap. 3.50 (*0-8125-1449-1*, Pub. by Tor Bks) St Martin.

— Belvedere: Bone Pie. (Illus.). 128p. 1992. pap. 3.50 (*0-8125-1554-4*, Pub. by Tor Bks) St Martin.

— Belvedere: Fine Jewelry. (Illus.). 128p. 1988. pap. 1.95 (*0-8125-6210-0*, Pub. by Tor Bks) St Martin.

— Belvedere: Flapjacks. (Illus.). 128p. (Orig.). 1990. pap. 2.95 (*0-8125-0607-3*, Pub. by Tor Bks) St Martin.

— Belvedere: How Was That for a Karate Chop? (Illus.). 128p. (Orig.). 1991. pap. 3.50 (*0-8125-1552-8*, Pub. by Tor Bks) St Martin.

— Belvedere: I Said I'm Not Ready to Get up Yet! (Illus.). 128p. (Orig.). 1991. pap. 3.50 (*0-8125-1553-6*, Pub. by Tor Bks) St Martin.

— Belvedere: Next Time I'll Pack the Food. (Illus.). 1991. pap. 3.50 (*0-8125-1549-8*, Pub. by Tor Bks) St Martin.

— Belvedere: Now Just One Minute! (Illus.). 128p. 1990. pap. 2.95 (*0-8125-0806-8*, Pub. by Tor Bks) St Martin.

— Belvedere: Now Just One Minute! 128p. 1987. reprint ed. pap. 1.95 (*0-8125-6205-4*, Pub. by Tor Bks) St Martin.

— Belvedere & Friend. 1990. pap. 2.95 (*0-8125-1015-1*, Pub. by Tor Bks) St Martin.

— Belvedere V. 256p. 1984. pap. 2.50 (*0-8125-6220-8*) Tor Bks.

— Don't Push Your Luck! (Belvedere Ser.: No. 3). (Illus.). 128p. pap. 2.95 (*0-8125-6212-7*, Pub. by Tor Bks) St Martin.

Crenshaw, Gwendolyn J. Bury Me in a Free Land: The Abolitionist Movement in Indiana, 1816-1865. 69p. 1993. pap. 6.25 (*1-885323-48-4*) IN Hist Bureau.

Crenshaw, Gwendolyn J., jt. auth. see AESOP Enterprises, Inc. Staff.

Crenshaw, Harry M., jt. auth. see Hoyle, John.

Crenshaw, Hatcher. Funny Bone: Amusing Stories - Short & Sassy. (Illus.). 190p. 1999. 19.95 (*0-9673102-0-2*) Five Star Pr.

***Crenshaw, Jack.** Math Toolkit for Real-Time Development. 416p. 2000. pap. 44.95 incl. cd-rom (*1-929629-09-5*, Pub. by C M P Books) Publishers Group.

Crenshaw, James. Telephone Between Worlds. 233p. 1996. reprint ed. pap. 12.95 (*0-87516-692-X*) DeVorss.

Crenshaw, James, ed. see VanderKam, James C.

Crenshaw, James F. Across This Doctor's Horizons: My Own Mission Field. (Illus.). 176p. (Orig.). 1995. pap. text 9.95 (*0-87651-937-0*) Southern U Pr.

Crenshaw, James L. Ecclesiastes, a Commentary. LC 87-16053. (Old Testament Library). 192p. (C). 1987. 22.00 (*0-664-21295-6*) Westminster John Knox.

— Education in Ancient Israel: Across the Deadening Silence. LC 97-33440. (Anchor Bible Reference Library Ser.). 320p. 1998. 34.95 (*0-385-46891-1*) Doubleday.

— Hymnic Affirmation of Divine Justice. LC 75-22349. (Society of Biblical Literature. Dissertation Ser.: No. 24). 190p. reprint ed. pap. 58.90 (*0-8357-9571-3*, 201752300007) Bks Demand.

— Joel: A New Translation with Introduction & Commentary. LC 94-34473. (Bible Ser.). 272p. 1995. 34.95 (*0-385-41205-3*) Doubleday.

— Old Testament Wisdom: An Introduction. LC 80-82183. 262p. (C). 1981. pap. 18.95 (*0-8042-0142-0*) Westminster John Knox.

— Old Testament Wisdom: An Introduction. enl. rev. ed. LC 98-7520. xv, 255p. 1998. pap. 20.00 (*0-664-25462-4*) Westminster John Knox.

— Prophetic Conflict: Its Effect upon Israelite Religion. (Beiheft zur Zeitschrift fuer die Alttestamentliche Wissenschaft Ser.: No. 124). 134p. (C). 1971. 66.15 (*3-11-003363-1*) De Gruyter.

— Samson: A Secret Betrayed, a Vow Ignored. LC 77-15748. 173p. 1981. text 9.95 (*0-8042-0170-6*, MUP-H001) Mercer Univ Pr.

— Urgent Advice & Probing Question: Collected Writings on Old Testament: Wisdom. LC 95-13926. 620p. (C). 1995. text 45.00 (*0-86554-483-2*, MUP/H379) Mercer Univ Pr.

Crenshaw, James L. & Sandmel, Samuel. The Divine Helmsman: Studies on God's Control of Human Events. 1979. 35.00 (*0-87068-700-X*) Ktav.

***Crenshaw, Janice.** Spiritual Ejaculation - The Final Hours of Great Deception. 1999. pap. text 15.00 (*0-9676714-0-X*) J C Pubng FL.

Crenshaw, Kimberle, et al, eds. Critical Race Theory: The Key Writings that Formed the Movement. 520p. 1996. 60.00 (*1-56584-270-7*, Pub. by New Press NY); pap. 30.00 (*1-56584-271-5*, Pub. by New Press NY) Norton.

Crenshaw, Larry, ed. The Outward Bound EarthBook. (Illus.). 128p. 1995. pap. 14.95 (*0-89732-195-2*) Menasha Ridge.

Crenshaw, Laura. The Bill & Hillary Joke Book. (Illus.). 64p. (Orig.). 1995. pap. 5.95 (*0-9632280-1-3*) Peroxide Pr.

Crenshaw, Laura & Stokes, April. The World's Best Blonde Jokes. 56p. 1992. pap. 4.95 (*0-9632280-0-5*) Peroxide Pr.

Crenshaw, Martha, ed. Terrorism in Africa. LC 93-38368. (International Library of Terrorism: No. 4). 535p. 1994. 50.00 (*0-8161-7336-2*, G K Hall & Co) Mac Lib Ref.

— Terrorism in Context. LC 93-13785. 656p. 1995. 85.00 (*0-271-01014-2*); pap. 25.00 (*0-271-01015-0*) Pa St U Pr.

— Terrorism, Legitimacy, & Power: The Consequences of Political Violence: Essays. LC 82-23756. 174p. 1983. reprint ed. pap. 54.00 (*0-608-02317-5*, 206295800004) Bks Demand.

Crenshaw, Martha & Pimlott, John, eds. Encyclopedia of World Terrorism, 3 vols., Set. LC 96-9913. 768p. (C). (gr. 13). 1996. text 299.00 (*1-56324-806-9*, Sharpe Ref) M E Sharpe.

— International Encyclopedia of Terrorism. 1997. lib. bdg. 175.00 (*1-57958-022-X*) Fitzroy Dearborn.

Crenshaw, Mary Ann, jt. auth. see Dibra, Bash.

Crenshaw, Nadine. The Art of Living: Simple Wisdom for the Self. LC 97-53265. 224p. 1998. 18.00 (*0-7615-1236-5*) Prima Pub.

— Buffy X-Posed: The Unauthorized Biography of Sarah Michelle Gellar & Her On-Screen Character. LC 98-19144. 256p. 1998. per. 16.00 (*0-7615-1368-X*) Prima Pub.

— Celtic Tales: Balor of the Evil Eye: A Novel. LC 95-71554. 264p. 1995. mass mkt. 5.99 (*0-7615-0247-5*) Prima Pub.

***Crenshaw, Nadine.** Extraordinary Women: Women Leaders Past & Present. LC 99-55509. 384p. 2000. 14.95 (*1-58062-301-8*) Adams Media.

Crenshaw, Nadine. Fields of the Sun. 384p. 1997. mass mkt. 4.99 (*0-8217-5606-0*, Zebra Kensgtn) Kensgtn Pub Corp.

— Scully X-Posed: The Unauthorized Biography of Gillian Anderson & Her On-Screen Character. LC 97-19730. 272p. 1997. per. 16.00 (*0-7615-1111-3*) Prima Pub.

— Xena X-Posed: The Unauthorized Biography of Lucy Lawless & Her On-Screen Character. LC 97-40183. 256p. 1997. per. 16.95 (*0-7615-1265-9*) Prima Pub.

Crenshaw, Ollinger. The Slave States in the Presidential Election of 1860. 1990. 16.50 (*0-8446-1138-7*) Peter Smith.

— The Slave States in the Presidential Election of 1860. LC 78-64199. (Johns Hopkins University. Studies in the Social Sciences. Thirtieth Ser. 1912: 3). reprint ed. 37.50 (*0-404-61305-5*) AMS Pr.

— The Slave States in the Presidential Election of 1860. (History - United States Ser.). 332p. 1993. reprint ed. lib. bdg. 89.00 (*0-7812-4824-8*) Rprt Serv.

Crenshaw, R. The Battle of Tassafaronga. (Illus.). 224p. 1995. 29.95 (*1-877853-37-2*) Nautical & Aviation.

Crenshaw, R. S., Jr. Naval Shiphandling. 4th ed. LC 74-26360. (Illus.). 479p. 1975. text, suppl. ed. 45.00 (*0-87021-474-8*) Naval Inst Pr.

Crenshaw, Raymond. Never Been Kissed. 256p. 1999. mass mkt. 5.99 (*0-06-102013-3*) HarpC.

Crenshaw, Richard, jt. auth. see Arkin, Lois.

Crenshaw, Russell S., Jr. South Pacific Destroyer: The Battle for the Solomons from Savo Island to Vella Gulf. LC 98-14265. (Illus.). 336p. 1998. 32.95 (*1-55750-136-X*) Naval Inst Pr.

Crenshaw, Ruth, et al. Lights along the Way. Gray, Jim, ed. LC 97-69698. (Illus.). 248p. 1997. pap. 12.95 (*0-9652829-2-9*) Creekwood Pr TN.

Crenshaw, Theresa. Beyond Aphrodisiacs. Date not set. write for info. (*0-393-03462-3*) Norton.

— Sex Rx. 288p. 1998. pap. 12.00 (*0-06-272052-X*, Perennial) HarperTrade.

Crenshaw, Theresa L. The Alchemy of Love & Lust: How Our Sex Hormones Influence Our Relationships. 368p. 1997. per. 14.00 (*0-671-00444-1*) PB.

Crenshaw, Theresa L. & Goldberg, James P. Sexual Pharmacology: Drugs That Affect Sexual Function. 500p. (C). 1996. 75.00 (*0-393-70144-1*) Norton.

Crenshaw, Vernita Y. Black Girl. Aqu, Dr., ed. 290p. (Orig.). pap. 19.95 (*0-9635763-0-5*) V Crenshaw.

Crenson, Matthew A. Building the Invisible Orphanage: A Prehistory of the American Welfare State. LC 98-26789. 384p. 1998. 45.00 (*0-674-46591-1*) HUP.

— The Federal Machine: Beginnings of Bureaucracy in Jacksonian America. LC 74-6818. 200p. reprint ed. pap. 62.00 (*0-7837-2185-4*, 204252300004) Bks Demand.

— Neighborhood Politics. (Illus.). 352p. (C). 1983. 43.00 (*0-674-60785-6*) HUP.

Crenson, Victoria. The Nutcracker. (Classic Christmas Sticker Storybook Ser.). (Illus.). 16p. (J). (ps-3). 1996. 3.50 (*0-689-80257-9*) Aladdin.

Crenson, Victoria, jt. auth. see Smith, Kathie B.

Creo, Robert A., jt. auth. see Celmer, Al.

Creoghegan, Tighe. El Desarrollo Rural Atraves del Turismo de Patrimonio Natural y Cultural: Lineamientos para el Caribe. (Canari Serie Lineamientos). Orig. Title: Rural Development Through Heritage Tourism: Guidelines for the Caribbean. (SPA., Illus.). 28p. 1998. pap. 5.00 (*1-890792-02-0*) Caribbean Nat Res.

Creore, JoAnn, jt. auth. see Anderson, James M.

Crepaldi, G., et al, eds. Diabetes, Obesity & Hyperlipidemias: The Plurimetabolic Syndrom; Proceedings of the European Symposium on Metabolism, Padova, 24-26 May, 1993. LC 93-38467. (International Congress Ser.: No. 1039). 310p. 1993. 206.50 (*0-444-81639-9*, Excerpta Medica) Elsevier.

— Microvascular & Neurological Complication of Diabetes. (FIDIA Research Ser.: Vol. 10). 325p. 1988. 162.00 (*0-387-96619-6*) Spr-Verlag.

***Crepaldi, Gabriele & Renoir, Auguste.** Renoir. LC 00-8296. 2000. write for info. (*0-7894-6126-9*) DK Pub Inc.

Crepaldi, Gaetano, et al, eds. Arteriosclerotic Brain Disease. fac. ed. LC 83-2910. (Illus.). 285p. pap. 88.40 (*0-7837-7198-3*, 204710100005) Bks Demand.

Crepax, Guido. Anita, Vol. 2. Gaudiano, Stefano, tr. from ITA. 48p. 1992. pap. 4.99 (*1-56163-044-6*, Eurotica) NBM.

— Emmanuelle, Vol. 1. Gaudiano, Stefano, tr. from ITA. Vol. 1. 80p. 1990. pap. 4.99 (*0-918348-87-0*, Eurotica) NBM.

***Crepax, Guido.** Emmanuelle, Bianca & Venus in Furs. (Illus.). 2000. 39.99 (*3-8228-6301-7*) Taschen Amer.

Crepax, Guido. Emmanuelle Three: Anti-Virgin. Gaudiano, Stefano, tr. from ITA. 88p. 1992. pap. 4.99 (*1-56163-057-8*, Eurotica) NBM.

***Crepax, Guido.** Jusine & the Story of O. 2000. 39.99 (*3-8228-6302-5*) Taschen Amer.

Crepax, Guido. Justine Two. Gaudiano, Stefano, tr. from ITA. 96p. 1993. pap. 4.99 (*1-56163-079-9*, Eurotica) NBM.

Crepax, Guido, jt. auth. see James, Henry.

Crepaz, Markus M., et al, eds. Democracy & Institutions: The Life Work of Arend Lijphart. (Illus.). 260p. (C). text 49.50 (*0-472-11126-4*, 11126) U of Mich Pr.

Crepeau, Elizabeth Blesedell, jt. auth. see Neistadt, Maureen E.

Crepeau, P. A. & Macpherson, C. B., eds. The Future of Canadian Federalism: L'Avenir Du Federalisme. LC 65-8930. 202p. reprint ed. pap. 62.70 (*0-8357-4152-4*, 203692600007) Bks Demand.

Crepeau, Pierre. Playing with the Wind: The Whirligig Collection of the Canadian Museum of Civilization. (Illus.). 55p. 1991. pap. 9.95 (*0-660-12923-X*, Pub. by CN Mus Civilization) U of Wash Pr.

***Crepeau, Richard C.** Baseball: America's Diamond Mind. LC 99-56234. (Illus.). 240p. 2000. pap. 13.95 (*0-8032-6408-9*, Bison Books) U of Nebr Pr.

Crepeau, Richard C. Baseball: America's Diamond Mind, 1919-1941. LC 79-16237. (Illus.). xii, 228p. 1980. 34.95 (*0-8130-0645-7*) U Press Fla.

An Asterisk (*) at the beginning of an entry indicates that the title is appearing for the first time.

— Melbourne Village: The First 25 Years (1946-1971) LC 87-16205. (Illus.). 215p. 1988. 34.95 (*0-8130-0867-0*) U Press Fla.

Crepet. Suicidal Behaviour in Europe. 328p. 52.00 (*0-86196-356-3*, Pub. by J Libbey Med) Bks Intl VA.

Crepin, F. Primitiae Monographiae Rosarum: Meteriaux Pour Servir a L'Histoire Des Roses, 6 pts. in 1 vol. 1972. reprint ed. 60.00 (*3-7682-0759-5*) Lubrecht & Cramer.

Crepin, Joseph. La Chevre. Colfax, David & Colfax, Micki, eds. Culver, Will & Lipmanson, Don, trs. from FRE. (Illus.). 168p. (C). 1990. pap. 12.95 (*0-939665-04-2*) Mountain Hse Pr.

Crepon, Pierre. Dictionnaire Pratique de l'Acupuncture et de l'Acupressure.Tr. of Practical Dictionary of Acupuncture & Accupressure. (FRE.). 192p. 1980. 39.95 (*0-8288-1797-9*, M8979) Fr & Eur.

— Dictionnaire Pratique de l'Acupuncture et de L'Acupressure. (FRE.). 1980. write for info. (*0-7859-7968-9*, 2-7256-1308-6) Fr & Eur.

Creps, Bob, jt. auth. see Caplan.

Creps, David B. Randy Roy Persnazznur. LC 80-51270. (Orig.). 1980. pap. 4.95 (*0-930830-32-6*) Great Basin.

Creps, Earl G., III. One for the Lord: Insights for Singles. LC 97-122117. 112p. 1997. pap., student ed. 4.95 (*0-88243-117-X*, 02-217) Gospel Pub.

Creps, Earl G., 3rd. One for the Lord: Insights for Singles. LC 97-122117. (Spiritual Discovery Ser.). 128p. 1996. pap., teacher ed. 9.95 (*0-88243-217-6*, 02-0217) Gospel Pub.

Crerar, David A., jt. auth. see Anderson, Greg M.

Crerar, Duff. Padres in No Man's Land: Canadian Chaplains & the Great War. LC 95-181165. (McGill-Queen's Studies in the History of Religion Ser.: No. 16). (Illus.). 440p. 1995. 55.00 (*0-7735-1230-6*, Pub. by McG-Queens Univ Pr) CUP Services.

Crerar, John, Library Staff. Author-Title Catalog, 35 Vols, Set. 1970. 3955.00 (*0-8161-0728-9*, G K Hall & Co) Mac Lib Ref.

Crerar, Lorne D. Crerar: Banking Law in Scotland. 1997. pap. write for info. (*0-406-05458-4*, CBLS, MICHIE) LEXIS Pub.

Crerend, William J. & Jaeger, Robert A. Fundamentals of Hedge Fund Investing: A Professional Investor's Guide. LC 97-43914. 250p. 1998. 55.00 (*0-07-013522-3*) McGraw-Hill Prof.

Cresanta, Judy & Ludke, Jill B. Nevada's Health: An Analysis of Health Care Options for Nevada's Working Uninsured. 20p. 1993. 10.00 (*1-886306-04-4*) Nevada Policy.

Cresanta, Judy M. Designing a Public School Choice Program That Can Pay for Itself. 12p. 1993. 10.00 (*1-886306-03-6*) Nevada Policy.

— The Instruction Gap: A Ten Year Study of Education Spending in Nevada. 36p. 1995. pap. text 10.00 (*1-886306-13-3*) Nevada Policy.

Crescas, Hasdai. The Refutation of the Christian Principles. Lasker, Daniel J., tr. LC 91-15118. (SUNY Series in Jewish Philosophy). 156p. (C). 1992. text 59.50 (*0-7914-0965-1*); pap. text 19.95 (*0-7914-0966-X*) State U NY Pr.

Crescent Family. Origin & History of the Name of Bennett. (Illus.). 112p. 1988. reprint ed. pap. 20.00 (*0-8328-0239-5*); reprint ed. lib. bdg. 28.00 (*0-8328-0238-7*) Higginson Bk Co.

Crescenti, Peter. Official Honeymooners Treasury. 1989. 8.98 (*0-88365-739-2*) Galahad Bks.

Crescenz, Rose, ed. see Flaws, Bob & Finney, Daniel.

Crescenz, Rose, jt. tr. see Wolfe, Honora L.

Crescenzi, G. Serlupi, ed. A Multidisciplinary Approach to Myelin Diseases. LC 87-29227. (NATO ASI Series A, Life Sciences: Vol. 142). (Illus.). 416p. 1987. 110.00 (*0-306-42776-1*, Plenum Trade) Perseus Pubng.

Crescenzi, M. De, see De Crescenzi, M.

Crescenzi, V., et al, eds. New Developments in Industrial Polysaccharides. x, 386p. 1985. text 274.00 (*2-88124-032-1*) Gordon & Breach.

Crescenzo, Casimiro Di, see Di Crescenzo, Casimiro.

Cresci, Giovanni F. A Renaissance Alphabet: Il Perfetto Scrittore, Parte Seconda. LC 77-121765. 80p. 1971. reprint ed. pap. 30.00 (*0-608-01937-2*, 206259200003) Bks Demand.

Cresci, Martha W. Complete Book of Model Business Letters. 298p. (C). 1979. pap. text 11.95 (*0-13-157412-4*) P-H.

— Complete Book of Model Business Letters. 298p. 1986. 21.95 (*0-13-157438-8*) P-H.

Cresci, Maureen M. Creative Dramatics for Children. (Illus.). 56p. (Orig.). (J). (gr. 3-6). 1989. pap. 7.95 (*0-673-38464-0*, GoodYrBooks) Addson-Wesley Educ.

***Cresci, Monica.** Creative Mosaics. (Illus.). 2000. 27.95 (*0-8069-7140-1*) Sterling.

Creson, Steve, ed. see Jones, Jim.

***Cresp, Gael.** The Tale of Gilbert Alexander Pig. (Illus.). 32p. (J). (ps-3). 2000. 15.95 (*1-84148-215-3*) Barefoot Bks NY.

Crespi. Bonsai Complete Illustrated Guide. 1995. write for info. (*0-7858-0215-0*) Bk Sales Inc.

Crespi, Bernard J., jt. ed. see Choe, Jae C.

Crespi, Bernard J., jt. ed. see Elgar, Mark A.

Crespi, Camilla T. The Trouble with a Bad Fit. 320p. 1997. mass mkt. 4.99 (*0-06-109408-0*, Harp PBks) HarpC.

— The Trouble with a Small Raise. 288p. 1991. mass mkt. 3.95 (*0-8217-3274-9*, Zebra Kensgtn) Kensgtn Pub Corp.

— The Trouble with Going Home. 304p. 1996. mass mkt. 4.99 (*0-06-109153-7*) HarpC.

— The Trouble with Too Much Sun. (Simona Griffo Mystery Ser.). 1992. mass mkt. 3.99 (*0-8217-3776-7*, Zebra Kensgtn) Kensgtn Pub Corp.

Crespi, F. A Walk in Monet's Garden. 1998. pap. 60.00 (*0-7112-0961-8*, Pub. by F Lincoln) St Mut.

***Crespi, Francesca.** A Christmas Carousel. 5p. 1999. pap. 12.95 (*0-8118-2614-7*) Chronicle Bks.

Crespi, Francesca. Make a Joyful Noise: A Pop-Up Book of Christmas Carols. (Illus.). 5p. (J). (ps up). 1997. per. 14.95 (*0-689-81526-3*) Aladdin.

Crespi, Francesca. Make a Joyful Noise: A Pop-Up Book of Christmas Carols. (J). 1997. write for info. (*0-614-29304-9*) Litle Simon.

Crespi, Francesca. Little Box of Ballet Stories, 3 vols. Incl. Coppelia. LC 86-930. (Illus.). 1986. Fire Bird. LC 86-930. (Illus.). 1986. Petrushka. LC 86-930. (Illus.). 1986. LC 86-930. (Illus.). 28p. (J). (ps-3). 1986. 8.95 (*0-8037-0265-5*, Dial Yng Read) Peng Put Young Read.

— A Walk in Monet's Garden: A Pop-Up Book. 24p. 1995. 19.95 (*0-8212-2195-7*, Pub. by Bulfinch Pr) Little.

Crespi, Francesca, jt. auth. see Jones, Olive.

Crespi, Irving. Pre-Election Polling: Sources of Accuracy & Error. LC 88-15770. 208p. 1988. 24.95 (*0-87154-208-0*) Russell Sage.

— The Public Opinion Process: How the People Speaks. LC 97-1381. 1997. 49.95 (*0-8058-2664-5*); pap. 22.50 (*0-8058-2665-3*) L Erlbaum Assocs.

Crespi, Juan. Fray Juan Crespi, Missionary Explorer on the Pacific Coast, 1769-1774. (BCL1 - United States Local History Ser.). 402p. 1991. reprint ed. lib. bdg. 99.00 (*0-7812-6339-5*) Rprt Serv.

Crespi, R. S. Patenting in the Biological Sciences: A Practical Guide for Research Scientists in Biotechnology & the Pharmaceutical & Agrochemical Industries. LC 81-19771. (Illus.). 217p. 1982. reprint ed. pap. 67.30 (*0-7837-8870-3*, 204958100001) Bks Demand.

Crespi, R. Stephen & Straus, Joseph. Intellectual Property, Technology Transfer & Genetic Resources: An OECD Study of Current Practices & Policies. 88p. (C). 1998. reprint ed. pap. text 25.00 (*0-7881-7474-6*) DIANE Pub.

Crespi, Tony D. Licensure in Professional Psychology: Preparatory Techniques. LC 94-14145. 1994. 39.95 (*1-56032-310-8*) Taylor & Francis.

Crespin, Regine. On Stage, off Stage: A Memoir. Bourdain, G. S., tr. LC 97-19907. (Illus.). 256p. 1997. text 29.95 (*1-55553-328-0*) NE U Pr.

Crespo, A. & De La Puente, J. A. Real-Time Programming, 1988. (IFAC Proceedings Ser.: 83). 97p. 1989. 50.00 (*0-08-036236-2*, Pergamon Pr) Elsevier.

Crespo, A. & IFAC Symposium on Artificial Intelligence in Real, eds. Artificial Intelligence in Real Time Control 1994: A Postprint Volume from the IFAC Symposium, Valencia, Spain, 3-5 October 1994. LC 95-7031. (IFAC Postprint Volume Ser.). 400p. 1995. pap. 90.00 (*0-08-042236-5*, Pergamon Pr) Elsevier.

Crespo, Ana M. & Brambila, Rosa, eds. Queretaro Prehispanico. 206p. 1991. pap. 15.00 (*968-29-3492-3*, IN023) UPLAAP.

Crespo, Ana M. & Viramontes, Carlos, eds. Tiempo y Territorio en Arqueologia: El Centro-Norte de Mexico. (SPA., Illus.). 192p. 1996. pap. 13.00 (*968-29-9048-3*, IN80, Pub. by Dir Gen Pubicaiones) UPLAAP.

Crespo, Angel. Juan Ramon Jimenez y la Pintura. (UPREX, Humanidades Ser.: No. 26). (Illus.). 309p. (C). 1974. pap. 1.50 (*0-8477-0026-7*) U of PR Pr.

Crespo, Angel, ed. & tr. see Pessoa, Fernando.

Crespo, Angel, tr. see Dante Alighieri.

Crespo, Angel, tr. see Gomez Bedate, Pilar.

Crespo, Angel, tr. & intro. see Petratca, Francesco.

Crespo, Beverly. Melanin 'n Me. Taylor, Maxwell, ed. LC 96-3487. (Illus.). 32p. (J). (gr. 1-3). 1996. pap. 6.95 (*1-881316-46-7*) A&B Bks.

***Crespo, C., et al.** Manual de Gerencia para una Escuela de Calidad. 102p. 1999. write for info. (*92-806-3515-8*) U N I C E.

Crespo, George. Maria Ceniczienta. 1999. 15.99 (*0-525-45346-6*) NAL.

Crespo, Joao G. & Boddekker, Karl W., eds. Membrane Processes in Separation & Purification. LC 94-17901. (NATO ASI Series E, Applied Sciences: Vol. 272). 1994. text 326.50 (*0-7923-2929-5*) Kluwer Academic.

Crespo, Michael. Watercolor Class: An Innovative Course in Transparent Watercolor. (Illus.). 256p. 1994. pap. 24.95 (*0-8230-5659-7*, Watson-Guptill Bks) Watsn-Guptill.

Crespo, Noberto Gonzalez, see Gonzalez Crespo, Noberto.

Crespo, Patria C. De, see Falcon, Luis N. & De Crespo, Patria C.

Crespo, Rafael. Como Yo Te Amo. (Romance Real Ser.). (SPA.). 192p. 1981. pap. 1.50 (*0-88025-003-8*) Roca Pub.

— Siempre Junto a Ti. (Romance Real Ser.). (SPA.). 192p. 1981. pap. 1.50 (*0-88025-004-6*) Roca Pub.

Crespo, Victoria, ed. see Hessen, Johannes.

***Cress.** Handbook of Geriatric Care Management. 2000. 49.00 (*0-8342-1667-1*) Aspen Pub.

Cress, Alan, tr. see Cavaliere, Barbara.

Cress, Donald, tr. see Descartes, Rene.

Cress, Donald A., jt. ed. see Cress, Elizabeth J.

Cress, Donald A., ed. & tr. see Rousseau, Jean-Jacques.

Cress, Donald A., tr. see Descartes, Rene.

Cress, Donald A., tr. see Rousseau, Jean-Jacques.

Cress, Elizabeth J. & Cress, Donald A., eds. A Guide to Rare & Out-of-Print Books in the Vatican Film Library: An Author List. LC 85-9085. 280p. 1985. lib. bdg. 49.50 (*0-8191-4726-5*) U Pr of Amer.

***Cress, Eric.** Your Potential Is Huge! Roberts, Cathy et al, eds. (Illus.). 24p. (YA). (gr. 7-10). 1999. pap. text 2.95 (*1-929488-19-X*) Cress Co.

***Cress, James A.** Common Sense Ministry: A Blueprint for Successful Laity & Pastoral Leadership. 96p. 1999. pap. 8.95 (*1-57847-059-5*) Genl Conf Svnth-day.

Cress, Joseph N. & Berlowe, Burt. Peaceful Parenting in a Violent World. 275p. 1995. pap. 14.95 (*0-9645335-0-2*) Perspect Pubns.

***Cress, Michelle.** Annie the Astronaut Meets Gussie the Green Man. large type ed. (LB Ser.). (Illus.). 8p. (J). (ps-1). 1999. pap. text 10.95 (*1-57332-153-2*); pap. text 10.95 (*1-57332-152-4*) HighReach Lrning.

***Cress, Sharon, ed.** Seasoned with Laughter. (Illus.). 106p. 1999. pap. 8.95 (*1-57847-057-9*) Genl Conf Svnth-day.

***Cresse, Gina.** A Deadly Change of Course - Plan B. LC 98-96073. 192p. 1998. 18.95 (*0-8034-9299-3*, Avalon Bks) Bouregy.

Cressell, H. B. The Honeywood File. LC 99-10243. 230p. 1999. pap. 14.95 (*0-89733-473-6*) Academy Chi Pubs.

Cresser. Annual Reports on Analytical Atomic Spectroscopy, Vol. 13. 1987. 148.00 (*0-85186-687-5*) CRC Pr.

Cresser, M. S. Annual Reports on Analytical Atomic Spectroscopy, Vol. 14. 1987. 156.00 (*0-85186-677-8*) CRC Pr.

Cresser, Malcom S. Flame Spectrometry in Environmental Chemical Analysis: A Practical Guide. Barnett, Neil, ed. (Royal Society of Chemistry Analytical Spectroscopy Monographs). 118p. 1994. 58.00 (*0-85186-734-0*, R6734) CRC Pr.

Cressey, Donald R. Other People's Money: A Study in the Social Psychology of Embezzlement (With New Intro. by Author Added) LC 73-7907. (Criminology, Law Enforcement, & Social Problems Ser.: No. 202). 204p. 1973. reprint ed. lib. bdg. 26.50 (*0-87585-202-5*) Patterson Smith.

Cressey, Donald R., jt. auth. see Coleman, James W.

Cressey, Ernest W. Cressey. Story of Your Ancestors: Cressey, 286 Years in America. 155p. 1998. reprint ed. pap. 24.00 (*0-8328-9649-7*); reprint ed. lib. bdg. 34.00 (*0-8328-9648-9*) Higginson Bk Co.

Cressey, George B. Soviet Potentials: A Geographic Appraisal. LC 62-8478. (Illus.). (C). 1962. pap. 12.95 (*0-8156-2034-9*) Syracuse U Pr.

Cressey, Paul G. The Taxi-Dance Hall: A Sociological Study in Commercialized Recreation & City Life. LC 69-16236. (Criminology, Law Enforcement, & Social Problems Ser.: No. 76). (Illus.). 1969. reprint ed. 12.00 (*0-87585-076-6*) Patterson Smith.

Cressey, Peter & Jones, Bryn, eds. Work & Employment in Europe: A New Convergence? LC 95-7768. 272p. (C). (gr. 13). 1997. 80.00 (*0-415-12532-4*) Routledge.

Cressey, Roger F. Parasitic Copepods from the Gulf of Mexico & Caribbean Sea Pt. 2: Part 2, Bomolochidae. LC 81-9055. (Smithsonian Contributions to Zoology Ser.: No. 389). 40p. reprint ed. pap. 30.00 (*0-608-14276-X*, 202219900024) Bks Demand.

— Parasitic Copepods from the Gulf of Mexico & Caribbean Sea Pt. 3: Caligus. LC 81-9055. (Smithsonian Contributions to Zoology Ser.: No. 497). 57p. reprint ed. pap. 30.00 (*0-7837-0270-1*, 204057900003) Bks Demand.

Cressey, William W. Spanish Phonology & Morphology: A Generative View. LC 78-23327. 184p. 1978. reprint ed. pap. 12.00 (*0-87840-045-1*) Georgetown U Pr.

Cressey, William W., et al. Expanding the Curriculum in Foreign Language Classes: Spanish & Contemporary Affairs: a Report on the Humanities Institute Held at Georgetown University, Summer of 1980. Addison, Alice A., ed. LC PC4068.U5E96. (Illus.). 66p. reprint ed. pap. 30.00 (*0-7837-6313-1*, 204602800010) Bks Demand.

Cressey, William W., jt. auth. see Diaz-Plaja, Fernando.

Cressie, N., jt. auth. see Read, T. R.

Cressman, J. Michael, jt. auth. see Cressman, Robert J.

Cressman, L. S., et al. Archaeological Researches in the Northern Great Basin. (Carnegie Institution of Washington, Washington, D. C. Ser.: No. 538). (Illus.). 269p. (C). 1942. reprint ed. pap. text 28.13 (*1-55567-606-5*) Coyote Press.

— Early Man in Oregon: Archaeological Studies in the Northern Great Basin. fac. ed. (University of Oregon Monographs, Studies in Anthropology: No. 3). (Illus.). 92p. 1940. reprint ed. pap. text 10.31 (*1-55567-554-9*) Coyote Press.

Cressman, Luther S. A Golden Journey: Memoirs of an Archaeologist. LC 87-30286. 524p. 1988. pap. 162.50 (*0-7837-8562-3*, 204937700011) Bks Demand.

— Prehistory of the Far East: Homes of Vanished Peoples. LC 75-30153. (Illus.). 269p. reprint ed. pap. 83.40 (*0-8357-6849-X*, 203554400095) Bks Demand.

— The Sandal & the Cave: The Indians of Oregon. LC 81-915. (Illus.). 96p. 1981. reprint ed. pap. 9.95 (*0-87071-078-8*) Oreg St U Pr.

Cressman, R. The Stability Concept of Evolutionary Game Theory: A Dynamic Approach. Levin, S. A., ed. (Lecture Notes in Biomathematics Ser.: Vol. 94). viii, 128p. 1992. 39.95 (*0-387-55419-X*) Spr-Verlag.

Cressman, Robert J. A Magnificent Fight: Marines in the Battle for Wake Island. (Illus.). 37p. (C). 1996. reprint ed. pap. text 25.00 (*0-7881-3523-6*) DIANE Pub.

— A Magnificent Fight: The Battle for Wake Island. LC 94-32013. (Illus.). 352p. 1995. 32.95 (*1-55750-140-8*) Naval Inst Pr.

— Official Chronology of the U.S. Navy in World War II. LC 99-39136. (Illus.). 400p. 1999. 49.95 (*1-55750-149-1*) Naval Inst Pr.

— That Gallant Ship USS Yorktown (CV-5) LC 84-62874. (Illus.). 196p. 1985. pap. 14.95 (*0-933126-57-3*) Pictorial Hist.

Cressman, Robert J. & Cressman, J. Michael. Steady Nerves & Stout Hearts: The Enterprise (CVG) Air Group & Pearl Harbor, 7 December, 1941. LC 90-60875. (Illus.). 80p. (Orig.). 1990. pap. 9.95 (*0-929521-25-0*) Pictorial Hist.

Cressman, Robert J. & Ewing, Steve. A Glorious Page in Our History: The Battle of Midway, 4-6 June 1942. LC 90-63323. (Illus.). 226p. (Orig.). 1990. pap. text 14.95 (*0-929521-40-4*) Pictorial Hist.

Cressman, Robert J. & Wenger, J. Michael. Infamous Day: Marines at Pearl Harbor, 7 December 1941. (Illus.). 33p. 1996. reprint ed. pap. text 20.00 (*0-7881-3526-0*) DIANE Pub.

Cresson, B. Introduction au Francais Commercial. (FRE.). pap. 24.95 (*0-7859-7568-3*) Fr & Eur.

— Introduction au Francais Economique. (FRE.). pap. 24.95 (*0-7859-7569-1*) Fr & Eur.

Cresson, Edith & European Commission. Research & Technological Development in Europe: 36 Examples of Projects. LC 98-196895. 79 p. 1998. 13.00 (*92-828-1057-7*, Pub. by Comm Europ Commun) Intl Pubns Serv.

Cresson, Ezra T., Jr., et al. Yale North India Expedition. (Connecticut Academy of Arts & Sciences Ser., Trans.: Vol. 10, Articles 1-9). 1934. pap. 200.00 (*0-685-44365-5*) Elliots Bks.

Cresson, H. T. Report upon Pile-Structures in Naaman's Creek, Near Claymont, Delaware. (Harvard University Peabody Museum of Archaeology & Ethnology Papers: HU. PMP Vol. 1, No. 4). 1974. reprint ed. pap. 25.00 (*0-527-01186-X*) Periodicals Srv.

Cresson, Warder. The Key of David: David the True Messiah. Davis, Moshe, ed. LC 77-70671. (America & the Holy Land Ser.). (Illus.). 1977. reprint ed. lib. bdg. 29.95 (*0-405-10239-9*) Ayer.

Cresson, William P. The Cossacks: Their History & Country. LC 77-87541. reprint ed. 55.00 (*0-404-16608-3*) AMS Pr.

Cresson, Wood C. Effective Information Security Management. xii, 236p. 1991. 195.00 (*1-85617-070-5*, Pub. by Elsvr Adv Tech) Elsevier.

Cresswell & Winte. Gift From Winklesea. (J). 1996. text 19.95 (*0-340-10472-4*, Pub. by Hodder & Stought Ltd) Trafalgar.

Cresswell, Don. The Laughable, Loveable, Little Give-Me-As-a-Gift Book, No. 1. (Illus.). 24p. (Orig.). 1983. pap. 2.95 (*0-930943-00-7*) Cresswell Ent.

— The Laughable, Loveable, Little Give-Me-As-a-Gift Book, No. 2. (Illus.). 24p. (Orig.). 1984. pap. 2.95 (*0-930943-01-5*) Cresswell Ent.

Cresswell, Donald H., ed. see Lane, Christopher W.

Cresswell, H. Bag of Bones. (J). 1997. mass mkt. 8.95 (*0-340-67302-8*, Pub. by Hodder & Stought Ltd) Trafalgar.

— Sea Piper. 1998. mass mkt. 7.95 (*0-340-68285-X*, Pub. by Hodder & Stought Ltd) Trafalgar.

— Story Book & Gift from Winklesea. 1996. mass mkt. 7.95 (*0-340-64642-X*, Pub. by Hodder & Stought Ltd) Trafalgar.

— Story Book Mystery at Winklesea. (J). 1996. mass mkt. 6.95 (*0-340-64643-8*, Pub. by Hodder & Stought Ltd) Trafalgar.

Cresswell, Helen. The Little Sea Pony. (Chapter Bks.). (Illus.). 304p. (J). (gr. 3-7). 1997. pap. 3.95 (*0-614-19173-4*, HarpTrophy) HarpC Child Bks.

— The Little Sea Pony. (Trophy Picture Bk.). (Illus.). 80p. (J). (gr. 2-5). 1997. pap. 3.95 (*0-06-442059-0*, HarpTrophy) HarpC Child Bks.

— Posy Bates, Again! LC 93-5789. (Illus.). 112p. (J). (gr. k-4). 1994. mass mkt. 13.95 (*0-02-725372-4*, Mac Bks Young Read) S&S Childrens.

Cresswell, Helen. Sophie & the Sea Wolf. (Illus.). (J). text 22.95 (*0-340-65608-5*, Pub. by Hodder & Stought Ltd) Trafalgar.

Cresswell, Helen. Time Out. 1997. 14.95 (*0-7188-2658-2*, Lutterworth-Parkwest) Parkwest Pubns.

— The Watchers: A Mystery at Alton Towers. LC 93-41683. 160p. (J). (gr. 3-7). 1994. mass mkt. 15.95 (*0-02-725371-6*, Mac Bks Young Read) S&S Childrens.

— The Watchers: A Mystery at Alton Towers, Set. unabridged ed. (J). (gr. 5 up). 1996. audio 29.98 (*0-8072-7565-4*, YA881CX) Listening Lib.

Cresswell, Helen & Winte. Whatever Happened in Winklesea? (J). 1996. text 19.95 (*0-340-64648-9*, Pub. by Hodder & Stought Ltd) Trafalgar.

Cresswell, Jasmine. Caroline. large type ed. (Nightingale Ser.). 282p. 1990. pap. 14.95 (*0-8161-5043-5*, G K Hall Lrg Type) Mac Lib Ref.

— Charades. (Mira Bks.). 1996. per. 5.50 (*1-55166-154-3*, 1-66154-5, Mira Bks) Harlequin Bks.

— Chase the Past. 251p. 1995. per. 4.99 (*1-55166-040-7*, Mira Bks) Harlequin Bks.

— The Daughter. (Mira Bks.). 1998. per. 5.99 (*1-55166-425-9*, 1-66425-9, Mira Bks) Harlequin Bks.

— Desires & Deceptions. 400p. 1995. per. 4.99 (*1-55166-036-9*, 1-66036-4, Mira Bks) Harlequin Bks.

***Cresswell, Jasmine.** The Disappearance. 408p. 1999. per. 5.99 (*1-55166-486-0*, 1-66486-1, Mira Bks) Harlequin Bks.

Cresswell, Jasmine. Edge of Eternity. 1994. per. 2.99 (*0-373-22297-1*, 1-22297-5) Harlequin Bks.

— Forgotten Marriage. large type ed. (Linford Romance Library). 304p. 1996. pap. 16.99 (*0-7089-7840-1*, Linford) Ulverscroft.

— House Guest. (Intrigue Ser.: No. 182). 1992. per. 2.89 (*0-373-22182-7*, 1-22182-9) Harlequin Bks.

— I Do, Again. (Weddings by DeWilde Ser.). 256p. 1997. per. 4.50 (*0-373-82548-X*, 1-82548-8) Harlequin Bks.

***Cresswell, Jasmine.** The Inheritance. 408p. 2000. per. 5.99 (*1-55166-511-5*, 1-66511-6, Mira Bks) Harlequin Bks.

Cresswell, Jasmine. Love for Hire. (Romance Ser.: No. 176). 1992. per. 2.79 (*0-373-03176-9*, 1-03176-4) Harlequin Bks.

— Midnight Fantasy. LC 96-2429. (Temptation Ser.). 219p. 1996. per. 3.50 (*0-373-25674-4*, 1-25674-2) Harlequin Bks.

— No Sin Too Great. (Mira Bks.). 408p. 1996. per. 5.99 (*1-55166-147-0*, 1-66147-9, Mira Bks) Harlequin Bks.

— Nowhere to Hide. (Intrigue Ser.). 1992. per. 2.89 (*0-373-22194-0*, 1-22194-4) Harlequin Bks.

C

An Asterisk (*) at the beginning of an entry indicates that the title is appearing for the first time.

— Paternity. 1997. per. 4.50 (0-373-82561-7, 1-82561-1) Harlequin Bks.
— The Perfect Bride. (Romance Ser.). 1993. per. 2.99 (0-373-03270-6, 1-03270-5) Harlequin Bks.
— Rakes & Rascals. LC 96-458. 440p. 1995. per. 4.99 (0-373-31219-9, 1-31219-8) Harlequin Bks.
*Cresswell, Jasmine. The Refuge. 2000. mass mkt. 6.50 (1-55166-608-1, 1-66608-0, Mira Bks) Harlequin Bks.
Cresswell, Jasmine. The Rossiter Arrangement. large type ed. (Linford Romance Library). 304p. 1996. pap. 16.99 (0-7089-7901-7) Ulverscroft.
— Secret Sins. (Mira Bks.). 408p. 1997. per. 5.99 (1-55166-261-2, 1-66261-8, Mira Bks) Harlequin Bks.
— Shattered Vows. (Weddings by DeWilde Ser.). 1996. per. 4.50 (0-373-82537-4, 1-82537-1, Wrldwide Lib) Harlequin Bks.
— The Substitute Bride. large type ed. (Linford Romance Large Print Ser.). 304p. 1996. pap. 16.99 (0-7089-7958-0, Linford) Ulverscroft.
— Tarrisbroke Hall. large type ed. 1995. 27.99 (0-7089-3373-4) Ulverscroft.
— Undercover. (Men at Work Ser.: Vol. 10). 1998. mass mkt. 4.50 (0-373-81022-9, 1-81022-5) Harlequin Bks.
Cresswell, Jasmine & St. George, Margaret. He Said, She Said. 1997. per. 5.99 (0-373-83330-X, 1-83330-0) Harlequin Bks.
Cresswell, John. Teach Yourself Esperanto. (Teach Yourself Ser.). 1992. 14.95 (0-8288-8314-9); 45.00 incl. audio (0-8288-8315-7) Fr & Eur.
Cresswell, John & Hartley, John. Teach Yourself Esperanto: A Complete Course for Beginners. (Teach Yourself Ser.). (ESP.). 260p. 1995. pap. 16.95 (0-8442-3763-9, Teach Yrslf) NTC Contemp Pub Co.
— Teach Yourself Esperanto Complete Course. rev. ed. (Teach Yourself Ser.). (ESP.). 260p. 1994. pap. 27.95 incl. audio (0-8442-3858-9, Teach Yrslf) NTC Contemp Pub Co.
***Cresswell, Julia.** Babies' Names. (Collins Gem Ser.). (Illus.). 256p. 2000. pap. 7.95 (0-00-472291-4, Pub. by HarpC) Trafalgar.
Cresswell, Julia. Irish First Names. LC 96-230653. (Collins Gem Ser.). 1998. pap. 6.95 (0-00-470942-X) Collins SF.
***Cresswell, Julia.** Irish First Names. (Collins Gem Ser.). (Illus.). 256p. 2000. 7.95 (0-00-472347-3, Pub. by HarpC) Trafalgar.
— Scottish First Names. (Scottish Collection Ser.). (Illus.). 64p. 2000. 8.95 (0-00-472259-0, Pub. by HarpC) Trafalgar.
Cresswell, M. J. Language in the World: A Philosophical Enquiry. (Cambridge Studies in Philosophy). 170p. (C). 1994. text 54.95 (0-521-44562-0) Cambridge U Pr.
— Semantic Indexicality. LC 95-52126. (Studies in Linguistics & Philosophy: Vol. 60). 228p. (C). 1996. text 98.00 (0-7923-3914-2) Kluwer Academic.
— Die Sprachen der Logik und die Logik der Sprache. (Grundlagen der Kommunikation De Gruyter Studienbuch Ser.). (C). 1979. 33.85 (3-11-004923-6) De Gruyter.
Cresswell, M. J., jt. auth. see Hughes, G. E.
Cresswell, Maxwell J. Adverbial Modification. 232p. 1985. lib. bdg. 122.00 (90-277-2059-2, D Reidel) Kluwer Academic.
— Entities & Indices. (Studies in Linguistics & Philosophy). 288p. 1990. pap. text 36.00 (0-7923-0967-7, Pub. by Kluwer Academic); lib. bdg. 107.00 (0-7923-0966-9, Pub. by Kluwer Academic) Kluwer Academic.
— Semantical Essays. (C). 1988. text 145.50 (1-55608-061-1) Kluwer Academic.
— Structured Meanings: The Semantics of Propositional Attitudes. 1985. 27.50 (0-262-03108-6) MIT Pr.
Cresswell, Maxwell J., jt. auth. see Hughes, G. E.
Cresswell, Maxwell J., jt. auth. see Hughes, George E.
Cresswell, Ned. Hollywood Conscience. 1995. pap. 14.95 (1-873741-19-7, Pub. by Millvres Bks) LPC InBook.
Cresswell, O. D. Chinese Cash. (Illus.). 1980. reprint ed. pap. 12.00 (0-915262-41-X) S J Durst.
— Tibetan Coins. 67p. 1977. pap. 4.00 (1-889172-08-1) Numismatic Intl.
Cresswell, Oliver D. Early Coinage of South East Asia. 64p. 1974. pap. 3.00 (1-889172-03-0) Numismatic Intl.
Cresswell, Peter, et al, eds. Encyclopedia of Banking Law. 1995. ring bd. write for info. (0-406-99810-8, EBLASET, MICHIE) LEXIS Pub.
Cresswell, Peterjon. European Football: A Fan's Handbook, Updated Edition. 688p. 1998. pap. 23.95 (1-85828-472-4, Pub. by Rough Guides) Penguin Putnam.
Cresswell, Rachel L., jt. auth. see Fry, Elizabeth.
Cresswell, Roy, ed. Urban Planning & Public Transport. (Illus.). 172p. 1980. text 38.00 (0-86095-849-3) Longman.
Cresswell, Roy, jt. ed. see Young, Tony.
Cresswell, Stephen. Multiparty Politics in Mississippi, 1877-1902. LC 94-44902. (Illus.). 240p. 1995. text 40.00 (0-87805-770-6) U Pr of Miss.
Cresswell, Stephen E. Homemade Root Beer, Soda, & Pop. LC 97-49254. 128p. 1998. pap. 14.95 (1-58017-052-8) Storey Bks.
Cresswell, Tim. In Place-Out of Place: Geography, Ideology, & Transgression. 1996. pap. 18.95 (0-8166-2389-9); text 47.95 (0-8166-2388-0) U of Minn Pr.
Cressy, Clive. Swedish-English, English-Swedish Medical Dictionary. 2nd ed. (ENG & SWE.). 547p. 1988. lib. bdg. 195.00 (0-8288-3312-5, F136120) Fr & Eur.
Cressy, Clive K. Swedish-English - English-Swedish Medical & Pharmaceutical Dictionary. 3rd ed. (ENG & SWE.). 682p. 1992. 248.00 (0-7859-8923-4) Fr & Eur.
Cressy, David. Birth, Marriage, & Death: Ritual, Religion, & the Life Cycle in Tudor & Stuart England. (Illus.). 658p. 1997. 39.95 (0-19-820168-0) OUP.
***Cressy, David.** Birth, Marriage & Death: Ritual, Religion & the Life Cycle in Tudor & Stuart England. (Illus.). 658p. 1999. pap. 19.95 (0-19-820788-3) OUP.
Cressy, David. Travesties & Transgressions in Tudor & Stuart England: Tales of Discord & Dissension. LC 99-16110. (Illus.). 368p. 2000. 35.00 (0-19-820781-6) OUP.
Cressy, David & Ferrell, Lori A., eds. Religion & Society in Early Modern England: A Sourcebook. LC 95-38690. 224p. (C). 1996. 70.00 (0-415-11848-4); pap. 20.99 (0-415-11849-2) Routledge.
Cressy, Judith. Near-Death Experience: Mysticism or Madness. LC 92-74362. 1994. 14.95 (0-8158-0490-3) Chris Mass.
***Crestani, Fabio & Pasi, Gabriella, eds.** Soft Computing in Information Retrieval: Techniques & Applications. LC 00-38555. (Studies in Fuzziness & Soft Computing: Vol. 50). (Illus.). xii, 393p. 2000. 102.00 (3-7908-1299-4, Pub. by Physica-Verlag) Spr-Verlag.
Crestel, Jack, et al. The Consolidated Tax Return. 1056p. 1993. 215.00 (0-7913-1629-7, 5) Warren Gorham & Lamont.
Cresti, M., et al. Fertilization in Higher Plants: Molecular & Cytological Aspects. LC 98-39228. 1999. write for info. (3-540-64879-8) Spr-Verlag.
Cresti, Mauro, et al, eds. Sexual Reproduction in Higher Plants. (Illus.). 530p. 1989. 152.95 (0-387-18673-5) Spr-Verlag.
Cresti, Mauro & Tiezzi, Antonio, eds. Sexual Plant Reproduction. LC 92-25601. (Illus.). 253p. 1992. 118.95 (0-387-55746-6) Spr-Verlag.
Cresti, Mauro, et al. Atlas of Sexual Plant Reproduction. (Illus.). 253p. 1996. 149.50 (0-387-54904-8) Spr-Verlag.
Crestin-Billet, Frederique, jt. auth. see Mantoux, Marie-Laure.
Crestohl, Robert. The Baseball & Sports Publications Price Guide. 2nd ed. Alexander, David T., ed. (Illus.). 244p. 1997. pap. 25.00 (0-9647400-1-X) Century Sports.
Crestol, Jack & Schneider, Herman M. Tax Planning for Investors: The 90's Guide to Securities & Commodities Investments. 296p. 1993. 35.00 (0-318-37891-4, 4906) CCH INC.
Crestol, Jack, et al. The Consolidated Tax Return. 4th ed. 1990. ring bd. 190.00 (0-7913-0083-8) Warren Gorham & Lamont.
— The Consolidated Tax Return, No. 1. 4th ed. 1991. suppl. ed. 65.00 (0-7913-0894-4) Warren Gorham & Lamont.
— The Consolidated Tax Return: Principles, Practice, Planning. 4th ed. 1988. text 190.00 (0-685-69542-5, CTR) Warren Gorham & Lamont.
Crestol, Jack, jt. auth. see McQueen, C. Richard.
Creston, P. Concertino for Marimba. 36p. 1986. pap. 18.00 (0-7935-5535-3, 50337080) H Leonard.
— Fantasy for Trombone: Piano/Redorig for Orchestra. 28p. 1986. pap. 12.00 (0-7935-4945-0, 50285630) H Leonard.
Creswell, Dennis R. St. Augustine's Dilemma: Grace & Eternal Law in the Major Works of Augustine of Hippo. LC 96-1623. (Studies in Church History: Vol. 5). XV, 159p. (C). 1997. 39.95 (0-8204-2843-4) P Lang Pubng.
Creswell, Jeff. Creating Worlds, Constructing Meaning: The Scottish Storyline Method. LC 97-30219. 1997. pap. text 20.00 (0-435-07244-7) Heinemann.
Creswell, John. Generals & Admirals: The Story of Amphibious Command. LC 75-8486. (Illus.). 1977. reprint ed. lib. bdg. 85.00 (0-8371-8151-8, CRGAD, Greenwood Pr) Greenwood.
Creswell, John W. Faculty Research Performance: Lessons from the Sciences & the Social Sciences. Fife, Jonathan D., ed. LC 85-103507. (ASHE-ERIC Higher Education Reports: No. 85-4). 76p. (Orig.). 1985. pap. 24.00 (0-913317-23-3) GWU Grad Schl E&HD.
— Qualitative Inquiry & Research Design: Choosing among 5 Traditions. LC 97-4820. 430p. 1997. text 62.00 (0-7619-0143-4); pap. text 28.95 (0-7619-0144-2) Sage.
— Research Design: Qualitative & Quantitative Approaches. 200p. (C). 1994. text 49.95 (0-8039-5254-6); pap. text 21.00 (0-8039-5255-4) Sage.
Creswell, John W., et al. The Academic Chairperson's Handbook. LC 90-30548. xiv, 128p. 1990. text 30.00 (0-8032-1450-2) U of Nebr Pr.
Creswell, K. A. Muslim Architecture of Egypt, 2 vols. LC 75-11056. (Illus.). 1978. reprint ed. lib. bdg. 500.00 (0-87817-175-4) Hacker.
— Short Account of Early Muslim Architecture. 1968. 22.00 (0-86685-010-4) Intl Bk Ctr.

Creswell, Thomas J. Usage in Dictionaries & Dictionaries of Usage. (Publications of the American Dialect Society: Nos. 63 & 64). (Illus.). 213p. 1975. pap. text 18.80 (0-8173-0662-5) U of Ala Pr.
Creswick, Paul. Robin Hood. LC 84-10662. (Illus.). 362p. 1984. 28.00 (0-684-18162-2) Scribner.
Creswl, J. Caroline. large type ed. 1990. pap. 5.00 (0-7451-1281-1, Pub. by Chivers N Amer) Chivers N Amer.
Cret, Rene P. Du, see Kuni, Christopher C.
Cret, Rene P. Du, see Kuni, Christopher C. & Du Cret, Rene P.
Cretcher, Dorothy. Steering Clear: Helping Your Child Through the High-Risk Drug Years. 112p. (Orig.). 1984. 4.95 (0-86683-689-6) Harper SF.
Crete, Liliane. Daily Life in Louisiana, 1815-1830. LC 81-8315. 327p. 1981. pap. 101.40 (0-7837-8525-9, 204933400011) Bks Demand.
Crete, Liliane, jt. auth. see Olivera, Ruth R.
Creteau, Paul G. Principles of Real Estate Law. LC 76-52549. (Illus.). 1977. 22.00 (0-9603372-0-2) Castle Pub Co.
— Real Estate Appraising (Step-by-Step) 2nd ed. LC 73-90006. 1974. 18.00 (0-9603372-1-0) Castle Pub Co.
Cretella, Louis A. Italo-British Relations in the Eastern Mediterranean, 1919-1923: The View from Rome. LC 91-25713. (Modern European History Outstanding Studies & Dissertations). 464p. 1991. text 25.00 (0-8153-0476-5) Garland.
Creth, Sheila D., jt. ed. see Dewey, Barbara I.
Creth, Sheila D., jt. ed. see Lipow, Anne G.
Creth, Shiela & Duda, Frederick. Personnel Administration in Libraries. 2nd ed. 353p. 1989. pap. text 55.00 (1-55570-036-5) Neal-Schuman.
Creti, Antonio & Marafotti, Salvatore. In This Corner: Anectodes, Testimonies & Fighting Words from Annals of the Boxing World. (Illus.). 128p. 1996. 24.95 (88-7301-048-2, Pub. by Gremese Intl) Natl Bk Netwk.
Cretin, E. The Angler's Handbook for India. 332p. 1984. 175.00 (81-7089-950-8, Pub. by Intl Bk Distr) St Mut.
— The Angler's Handbook for India. 332p. (C). 1984. 250.00 (0-7855-6889-1, Pub. by Intl Bk Distr) St Mut.
— The Angler's Handbook for India. 332p. 1985. pap. 425.00 (81-7089-095-0, Pub. by Intl Bk Distr) St Mut.
— The Angler's Handbook for India. 332p. 1984. reprint ed. 175.00 (0-7855-6656-2, Pub. by Intl Bk Distr) St Mut.
Cretion, Pam, ed. see Sulivan, Wilma.
Cretney, Antonia & Davis, Gwynn. Punishing Violence. LC 95-8208. (Illus.). 248p. (C). (gr. 13). 1995. 85.00 (0-415-09839-4, C0341) Routledge.
Cretney, Antonia, jt. auth. see Davis, Gwynn.
Cretney, Stephen M. Enduring Powers of Attorney: A Practitioner's Guide. 160p. 1986. 50.00 (0-85308-103-4) Jordan Pubng.
***Cretney, Stephen Michael.** Law, Law Reform & the Family. LC 98-38625. 420p. 1999. 80.00 (0-19-826871-8) OUP.
Cretser, Gary A. & Leon, Joseph J., eds. Intermarriage in the United States. LC 82-6213. (Marriage & Family Review Ser.: Vol. 5, No. 1). 111p. 1982. text 32.95 (0-917724-60-7) Haworth Pr.
Crett, John. Colorado Gardener's Guide: The What, Where, When, How & Why of Gardening in Colorado. (Illus.). 400p. 1998. pap. 19.95 (1-888608-48-X) Cool Springs Pr.
Cretzianu, Alexandru. Relapse into Bondage: Political Memoirs of a Romanian Diplomat, 1918-1947. Spector, Sherman D., ed. LC 99-168115. 352p. 1998. 50.00 (973-98091-8-9, Pub. by Ctr Romanian Studies) Intl Spec Bk.
Cretzmeyer, Stacy. Your Name Is Renee: Ryth Kapp Hartz's Story As a Hidden Child in Nazi-Occupied France. LC 98-56108. (Illus.). 240p. (YA). 1999. 17.95 (0-19-513259-9) OUP.
Creurer, Michael, jt. auth. see Bissell, Dee.
Creus, Ricard, jt. auth. see Boix, Esther.
Creutz, M. Quantum Fields on the Computer. (Advanced Series on "Directions in High Energy Physics": No. 11). 444p. 1992. text 121.00 (981-02-0939-8) World Scientific Pub.
Creutz, M., ed. Quantum Fields on the Computer. (Advanced Series on Directions in High Energy Physics": Vol. 11). 444p. 1992. pap. 67.00 (981-02-0940-1) World Scientific Pub.
Creutz, Michael. Quarks, Gluons & Lattices. LC 83-2089. (Cambridge Monographs on Mathematical Physics). 176p. 1985. pap. text 29.95 (0-521-31535-2) Cambridge U Pr.
Creutzfedt, W. & Stoeckmann, F., eds. Eighth International Symposium on Gastrointestinal Hormones, Timmendorfer Strand, Baltic Sea, September 1990, Abstracts. (Journal: Digestion: Vol. 46, Suppl. 1, 1990). (Illus.). ii, 138p. 1990. pap. 42.75 (3-8055-5291-2) S Karger.
Creutzfeldt, Mary, tr. see Creutzfeldt, O.
Creutzfeldt, O. Cortex Cerebri: Performance, Structural & Functional Organisation of the Cortex. Creutzfeldt, Mary, tr. (Illus.). 672p. 1995. text 129.50 (0-19-852324-6) OUP.
Creutzfeldt, O., jt. auth. see Eccles, John C.
Creutzfeldt, O., jt. ed. see Eccles, John C.
Creutzfeldt, W., ed. Acarbose for the Treatment of Diabetes Mellitus. (Illus.). 210p. 1989. 58.00 (0-387-19145-3) Spr-Verlag.
— The Entero-Insular Axis. (Frontiers of Hormone Research Ser.: Vol. 7). (Illus.). x, 310p. 1980. 100.00 (3-8055-0795-X) S Karger.
Creutzfeldt, W. & Lefebvre, Pierre J., eds. Diabetes Mellitus: Pathophysiology & Therapy. (Illus.). xxvi, 358p. 1989. 116.95 (0-387-50506-7) Spr-Verlag.
Creux, Francois Du, see Du Creux, Francois.
***Creuze, Aude & Habegre, Veronique.** Porcelain Painter's Handbook. (Illus.). 80p. 2000. pap. 19.95 (0-233-99550-1, Pub. by Andre Deutsch) Trafalgar.
Creuzer, Georg F. Symbolik und Mythologie der Alten Volker, 4 vols. in 2. (Volkskundliche Quellen, Reihe V Ser.). (GER.). xvi, 3022p. 1990. reprint ed. 800.00 (3-487-04371-8) G Olms Pubs.
— Symbolik und Mythologie der Alten Volker Besonders der Griechen, 6 vols. Bolle, Kees W., ed. LC 77-79119. (Mythology Ser.). (GER., Illus.). 1978. reprint ed. lib. bdg. 357.95 (0-405-10531-2) Ayer.
Creuziger, Clementine G. Childhood in Russia: Representation & Reality. (C). 1996. pap. text 39.00 (0-7618-0289-4); lib. bdg. 58.00 (0-7618-0288-6) U Pr of Amer.
Crevacoeur, Michel G. Sketches of Eighteenth Century America: More Letters from an American Farmer. Bourdin, Henri L. et al, eds. (BCL1 - U. S. History Ser.). 342p. 1991. reprint ed. lib. bdg. 89.00 (0-7812-6005-1) Rprt Serv.
Crevar-Donaldson, Donna, jt. auth. see Gould, David.
Crevea, Rafael A. History of Spanish Civilization. Volkov, P., tr. LC 77-22622. reprint ed. 52.50 (0-404-16030-1) AMS Pr.
Crevecoeur, E. E. Old Settlers' Tales, Pottawatamie & Nemaha Counties: Historical & Biographical Sketches of the Early Settlement & Settlers of Northeastern Pottawatomie & Southwestern Nemaha Counties, from Earliest Settlement to the Year 1877. (Illus.). 162p. 1995. reprint ed. pap. 17.00 (0-8328-5031-4); reprint ed. lib. bdg. 25.00 (0-8328-5030-6) Higginson Bk Co.
Crevel, Rene. Babylon. Boyle, Kay, tr. from FRE. & afterword by by. (Classics Ser.: No. 148).Tr. of Babylone. (Illus.). 170p. (Orig.). 1996. pap. 12.95 (1-55713-196-1) Sun & Moon CA.
— 1830. Waldrop, Keith, tr. from FRE. (Illus.). 22p. 1996. 950.00 (0-9640399-6-6) Elysium Pr.
— Putting My Foot in It. Buckley, Thomas, tr. from FRE. LC 92-504. 200p. 1993. reprint ed. pap. 9.95 (1-56478-017-1) Dalkey Arch.
Creveld, Marijke. Epilithic Lichen Communities in the Alpine Zone of Southern Norway. (Bibliotheca Lichenologica Ser.: Vol. 17). (Illus.). 288p. 1981. text 80.00 (3-7682-1313-7) Lubrecht & Cramer.
Creveld, Martin L. Van, see Van Creveld, Martin L.
Creveld, Martin Van. Command in War. LC 84-12934. (Illus.). 352p. 1987. pap. text 18.50 (0-674-14441-4) HUP.
Creveling, C. M. Tolerance Design: A Handbook for Developing Optimum Specifications. LC 96-37196. 448p. 1996. 70.00 (0-201-63473-2) Addison-Wesley.
Creveling, Clyde M., jt. auth. see Fowlkes, William Y.
Crevello, Paul D., ed. see SEPM Core Workshop Staff.
Crevelt, Dwight. Slot Machine Mania. 243p. 1989. pap. 6.99 (0-914839-13-6) Gollehon Pr.
Crevelt, Dwight & Crevelt, Louise. Video Poker Mania. 160p. 1991. pap. 6.99 (0-914839-20-9) Gollehon Pr.
Crevelt, Louise, jt. auth. see Crevelt, Dwight.
Creviere, Paul J., Jr. Wild Gales & Tattered Sails: The Shipwrecks of Northwest Lake Michigan from Two Creeks, Wisconsin to Dutch Johns Point, Michigan & All of the Bay of Green Bay. (Illus.). xii, 340p. 1997. 44.95 (0-9660328-0-2); pap. 24.95 (0-9660328-1-0) Paul J Creviere.
Creviston, J. Contemporary Personal Finance. 1984. teacher ed. write for info. (0-318-59422-6, H83678) P-H.
Crew, David. Nazism & German Society, 1933-1945. LC 93-47053. (Rewriting Histories Ser.). 336p. (C). 1994. pap. 17.95 (0-415-08240-4, B4251) Routledge.
Crew, David F. From Weimar to Hitler: Germans on Welfare, 1919-1933. 336p. Date not set. pap. 19.95 (0-19-511878-2) OUP.
— Germans on Welfare: From Weimar to Hitler, 1919-1933. LC 97-8445. (Illus.). 304p. (C). 1998. text 19.95 (0-19-505311-7) OUP.
***Crew, Edna.** Money Talk: Finance & Investment Terms for Busy People. 128p. 2000. pap. 7.95 (1-86508-087-X, Pub. by Allen & Unwin Pty) Paul & Co Pubs.
Crew, Gary. Angel's Gate. LC 95-4047. 256p. (YA). (gr. 4-7). 1995. pap. 16.00 (0-689-80166-1) S&S Bks Yung.
Crew, Gary. Bright Star. LC 97-16260. (Illus.). 32p. (J). (ps-3). 1997. 13.95 (0-916291-75-8, Cranky Nell Bks) Kane-Miller Bk.
— First Light. LC 96-31213. (Quality Time Picture Bks.). (Illus.). 32p. (YA). (gr. 3 up). 1996. lib. bdg. 19.93 (0-8368-1664-1) Gareth Stevens Inc.
— No Such Country. LC 93-17619. 192p. (J). (gr. 5-9). 1994. pap. 15.00 (0-671-79760-3) S&S Bks Yung.
— The Watertower. 32p. (J). (gr. 2-9). 1999. pap. 7.95 (1-56656-331-3) Interlink Pub.
Crew, Henry, tr. from LAT. The Photismi de Lumine of Maurolycus: A Chapter in Late Medieval Optics. 1940. 30.00 (0-686-30225-7) R S Barnes.
Crew, Henry, tr. see Galilei, Galileo.
***Crew, Hilary.** Is It Really Mommy Dearest? LC 99-48315. (Illus.). 296p. (YA). 1999. 48.00 (0-8108-3692-0) Scarecrow.
Crew, Keith & Heck, Douglas. Prairie Homestead: Meet the Browns & Their Neighbors. (Illus.). 40p. (Orig.). 1996. mass mkt. 3.95 (0-9651386-0-7) Prairie Homestead.
Crew, Linda. Brides of Eden. 160p. (gr. 5 up). mass mkt. 4.95 (0-06-447217-5) HarpC.
— Brides of Eden. 160p. (YA). (gr. 5 up). 2001. 15.95 (0-06-028750-0); lib. bdg. 15.89 (0-06-028751-9) HarpC Child Bks.
Crew, Linda. Children of the River. 224p. (YA). (gr. 7 up). 1991. mass mkt. 5.50 (0-440-21022-4, LLL BDD) BDD Bks Young Read.
— Children of the River. (Laurel-Leaf Contemporary Fiction Ser.). 1989. 10.09 (0-606-04891-X, Pub. by Turtleback) Demco.
— Children of the River. large type ed. 1993. 58.00 (0-614-09874-2, L-05042-00) Am Printing Hse.

C

— Fire on the Wind. (J). 1995. 20.95 (*0-385-31003-X*) BDD Bks Young Read.
— Fire on the Wind. 208p. (YA). 1997. mass mkt. 3.99 (*0-440-21961-2*, YB BDD) BDD Bks Young Read.
— Fire on the Wind. 1997. 9.09 (*0-606-11326-6*, Pub. by Turtleback) Demco.
— Long Time Passing. LC 96-54715. 208p. (YA). (gr. 5-9). 1997. 15.95 (*0-385-32496-0*) Delacorte.
— Nekomah Creek. (Illus.). 192p. (J). (gr. 4-7). 1993. pap. 3.99 (*0-440-40788-5*) Dell.
Crew, Linda. Nekomah Creek. 1991. 9.09 (*0-606-05506-1*, Pub. by Turtleback) Demco.
Crew, Linda. Nekomah Creek Christmas. (Illus.). 160p. (J). (gr. 4-7). 1995. pap. 3.99 (*0-440-41099-1*, YB BDD) BDD Bks Young Read.
— Nekomah Creek Christmas. (J). 1995. 9.34 (*0-606-07940-8*) Turtleback.
***Crew, Linda.** Nekomah Creek Christmas. (Illus.). 147p. (YA). (gr. 6-9). 1999. reprint ed. text 15.00 (*0-7881-6628-X*) DIANE Pub.
Crew, Louie, ed. A Book of Revelations: Lesbian & Gay Episcopalians Tell Their Own Stories. 224p. (Orig.). 1991. pap. 9.95 (*0-9629506-0-2*) Integrity DC.
— The Gay Academic. LC 75-37780. 1978. 24.95 (*0-88280-036-1*) ETC Pubns.
Crew, Michael A. Incentive Regulation for Public Utilities. LC 94-22634. (Topics in Regulatory Economics & Policy Ser.: Vol. 18). 224p. (C). 1994. lib. bdg. 98.50 (*0-7923-9495-X*) Kluwer Academic.
— Pricing & Regulatory Innovations under Increasing Competition. LC 96-36206. (Topics in Regulatory Economics & Policy Ser.). 216p. (C). 1996. lib. bdg. 91.00 (*0-7923-9810-6*) Kluwer Academic.
— Regulation under Increasing Competition. LC 98-45039. 1998. 95.00 (*0-7923-8367-2*) Kluwer Academic.
Crew, Michael A., ed. Competition & Innovation in Postal Services. (C). 1991. lib. bdg. 139.50 (*0-7923-9147-0*) Kluwer Academic.
— Competition & the Regulation of Utilities. (Topics in Regulatory Economics & Policy Ser.). 224p. 1990. lib. bdg. 113.50 (*0-7923-9083-0*) Kluwer Academic.
— Economic Innovations in Public Utility Regulation. LC 92-26307. (Topics in Regulatory Economics & Policy Ser.: Vol. 10). 172p. (C). 1992. lib. bdg. 78.00 (*0-7923-9269-8*) Kluwer Academic.
Crew, Michael A. & Kleindorfer, Paul R. The Economics of Postal Service: A Research Study Supported by WIK. LC 92-23471. (Topics in Regulatory Economics & Policy Ser.). (C). 1992. lib. bdg. 94.00 (*0-7923-9274-4*) Kluwer Academic.
— Emerging Competition in Postal & Delivery Services LC 99-11330. (Topics in Regulatory Economics & Policy Ser.). 9p. 1999. write for info. (*0-7923-8454-7*) Kluwer Academic.
Crew, Michael A. & Kleindorfer, Paul R., eds. Commercialization of Postal & Delivery Services: National & International Perspectives. (Topics in Regulatory Economics Ser.: Vol. 19). 304p. (C). 1994. lib. bdg. 113.00 (*0-7923-9514-X*) Kluwer Academic.
— Regulation & the Nature of Postal & Delivery Services. LC 92-34657. (C). 1992. lib. bdg. 125.00 (*0-7923-9301-5*) Kluwer Academic.
Crew, Michael A., ed. see Kleindorfer, Paul R.
Crew, P. Mack. The Cambridge Ancient History Vols. 1-2: Volume of Plates: Illustrating. (Illus.). 181p. 1977. text 80.00 (*0-521-20571-9*) Cambridge U Pr.
Crew, R. Thomas, Jr. & Trask, Benjamin H. Grimes' Battery, Grandy's Battery & Huger's Battery Virginia Artillery. (Virginia Regimental Histories Ser.). (Illus.). 118p. 1995. 19.95 (*1-56190-080-X*) H E Howard.
Crew, Randolph E. A Killing Shadow. Parker, Nancy, ed. 369p. 1996. 23.95 (*0-9651430-8-2*) Artec Pubng.
Crewdson, Joan O. Christian Doctrine in the Light of Michael Polanyi's Theory of Personal Knowledge: A Personalist Theology. LC 94-38970. (Toronto Studies in Theology: Vol. 66). 464p. 1994. text. write for info. (*0-7734-9150-3*) E Mellen.
Crewdson, Michael, jt. auth. see Mittelbach, Margaret.
***Crewdson, Richard.** Apollo's Swan & Lyre: Five Hundred Years of the Musician's Company. (Illus.). 298p. 2000. 60.00 (*0-85115-766-1*, Suffolk Records Soc) Boydell & Brewer.
Crewe & Wells. Liaison Tonight's the Night. 1997. mass mkt. 6.95 (*0-7472-5626-8*, Pub. by Headline Bk Pub) Trafalgar.
— Satin by Night. mass mkt. 6.95 (*0-7472-5509-1*) Headline Bk Pub.
— Seeing Double. 1998. mass mkt. 6.95 (*0-7472-5857-0*, Pub. by Headline Bk Pub) Trafalgar.
— Sleepless Nights. mass mkt. 6.95 (*0-7472-5055-3*, Pub. by Headline Bk Pub) Trafalgar.
Crewe, jt. auth. see Wells.
Crewe, Albert V. & Katz, Joseph J. Nuclear Research U. S. A. Knowledge for the Future. (Illus.). 1990. 13.00 (*0-8446-0564-6*) Peter Smith.
***Crewe, Candida.** The Last to Know. large type unabridged ed. 1999. 25.95 (*0-7531-5973-2*, 159732, Pub. by ISIS Lrg Prnt) ISIS Pub.
Crewe, Emma. Whose Develpoment? An Ethnography of Aid. 256p. 1999. text 55.00 (*1-85649-605-8*) St Martin.
Crewe, Ivor, et al, eds. Political Communications: Why Labour Won the General Election of 1997. 288p. 1998. 49.50 (*0-7146-4923-6*, Pub. by F Cass Pubs) Intl Spec Bk.
— Political Communications: Why Labour Won the General Election of 1997. LC 98-38304. 288p. 2000. pap. 22.50 (*0-7146-4482-X*, Pub. by F Cass Pubs) Intl Spec Bk.
Crewe, Ivor & Gosschalk, Brian, eds. Political Communications: The General Election Campaign of 1992. LC 93-47235. (Illus.). 292p. (C). 1995. text 64.95 (*0-521-45396-8*); pap. text 24.95 (*0-521-46964-3*) Cambridge U Pr.
Crewe, Ivor & King, Anthony. SDP: The Birth, Life & Death of the Social Democratic Party. (Illus.). 652p. 1996. 49.95 (*0-19-828050-5*) OUP.
— SDP: The Birth, Life & Death of the Social Democratic Party. (Illus.). 636p. 1998. reprint ed. pap. text 32.00 (*0-19-829313-5*) OUP.
Crewe, Ivor, et al. The British Electorate, 1963-1992: A Compendium of Data from the British Election Studies. 2nd ed. 511p. (C). 1996. text 140.00 (*0-521-49646-2*); pap. text 49.95 (*0-521-49965-8*) Cambridge U Pr.
Crewe, Jonathan. Hidden Designs: The Critical Profession & Renaissance Literature. 192p. 1987. 35.00 (*0-416-92350-X*, 1030) Routledge.
— Trials of Authorship: Anterior Forms & Poetic Reconstruction from Wyatt to Shakespeare. 1990. 45.00 (*0-520-06693-6*, Pub. by U CA Pr) Cal Prin Full Svc.
Crewe, Jonathan, ed. Reconfiguring the Renaissance: Essays in Critical Materialism. LC 91-55211. (Bucknell Review Ser.: Vol. 35, No. 2). (Illus.). 176p. 1992. 21.00 (*0-8387-5223-3*) Bucknell U Pr.
***Crewe, Jonathan, ed.** Twelfth Night. (Shakespeare Ser.). 128p. (C). 2000. pap. 4.95 (*0-14-071489-8*) Penguin Putnam.
Crewe, Jonathan, ed. see Shakespeare, William.
Crewe, Jonathan V. Unredeemed Rhetoric: Thomas Nashe & the Scandal of Authorship. LC 82-6554. 135p. reprint ed. pap. 41.90 (*0-8357-6608-X*, 203525300094) Bks Demand.
Crewe, Lindy. Spindle Whorls: A Study of Form, Function & Decoration in Prehistoric Bronze Age Cyprus. (Illus.). 125p. 1998. pap. 49.50 (*91-7081-176-8*, Pub. by P Astroms) Coronet Bks.
Crewe, Nancy M. & Athelstan, Gary T. Functional Assessment Inventory Manual. rev. ed. (Illus.). 96p. 1984. pap. 12.00 (*0-916671-53-4*) TRR.
Crewe, Nancy M., et al. Independent Living for Physically Disabled People: Developing, Implementing, & Evaluating Self-Help Rehabilitation Programs. LC 82-48067. (Jossey-Bass Social & Behavioral Science Ser.). 432p. reprint ed. pap. 134.00 (*0-7837-2534-5*, 204269300006) Bks Demand.
Crewe, Quentin. Crewe House - The Royal Embassy of Saudi Arabia. (Illus.). 88p. 1995. boxed set 34.95 (*0-905743-78-4*, Pub. by Stacey Intl) Intl Bk Ctr.
Crewe, S. Stained Glass in England. (C). 1990. 75.00 (*0-7855-7551-0*) St Mut.
Crewe, Sabrina. The Alligator. LC 96-53250. (Life Cycles Bks.). (Illus.). 32p. (J). (ps-4). 1998. lib. bdg. 21.40 (*0-8172-4375-5*) Raintree Steck-V.
— The Bear. LC 96-4845. (Life Cycles Bks.). (Illus.). 32p. (J). (ps-4). 1997. lib. bdg. 21.40 (*0-8172-4367-4*) Raintree Steck-V.
— The Beaver. LC 96-40496. (Life Cycles Bks.). (Illus.). 32p. (J). (ps-4). 1998. lib. bdg. 21.40 (*0-8172-4376-3*) Raintree Steck-V.
— The Bee. LC 96-4833. (Life Cycles Bks.). (Illus.). 32p. (J). (ps-4). 1997. lib. bdg. 21.40 (*0-8172-4362-3*) Raintree Steck-V.
— The Buffalo. LC 96-40494. (Life Cycles Bks.). (Illus.). 32p. (J). (ps-4). 1998. lib. bdg. 21.40 (*0-8172-4377-1*) Raintree Steck-V.
Crewe, Sabrina. The Butterfly. LC 96-4844. (Life Cycles Bks.). (Illus.). 32p. (J). (ps-4). 1997. lib. bdg. 21.40 (*0-8172-4364-X*) Raintree Steck-V.
Crewe, Sabrina. The Chimpanzee. LC 96-4826. (Life Cycles Bks.). (Illus.). 32p. (J). (ps-4). 1997. lib. bdg. 21.40 (*0-8172-4368-2*) Raintree Steck-V.
Crewe, Sabrina. The Frog. LC 96-4831. (Life Cycles Bks.). (J). (gr. 2-5). 1997. pap. 4.95 (*0-8172-6232-6*) Raintree Steck-V.
Crewe, Sabrina. The Frog. LC 96-4831. (Life Cycles Bks.). (Illus.). 32p. (J). (ps-4). 1997. lib. bdg. 21.40 (*0-8172-4369-0*) Raintree Steck-V.
— The Kangaroo. LC 96-4829. (Life Cycles Bks.). (Illus.). 32p. (J). (ps-4). 1997. lib. bdg. 21.40 (*0-8172-4370-4*) Raintree Steck-V.
— The Ladybug. LC 96-4830. (Life Cycles Bks.). (Illus.). 32p. (J). (gr. 2-5). 1997. lib. bdg. 21.40 (*0-8172-4366-6*) Raintree Steck-V.
***Crewe, Sabrina.** Life Cycle of the Alligator. (Life Cycles Ser.). 1998. pap. 5.95 (*0-8172-6245-8*) Raintree Steck-V.
— Life Cycle of the Bear. LC 96-4845. (Life Cycles Bks.). (Illus.). (J). (gr. 2-5). 1997. pap. 5.95 (*0-8172-6230-X*) Raintree Steck-V.
Crewe, Sabrina. Life Cycle of the Beaver. 1999. pap. text 5.95 (*0-8172-4249-X*) Raintree Steck-V.
Crewe, Sabrina. Life Cycle of the Bee. LC 96-4833. (Life Cycles Bks.). 32p. (J). (gr. 2-5). 1997. pap. 5.95 (*0-8172-6225-3*) Raintree Steck-V.
— Life Cycle of the Buffalo. 1999. pap. text 5.95 (*0-8172-6238-5*) Raintree Steck-V.
— Life Cycle of the Kangaroo. LC 96-4829. (Life Cycles Bks.). (J). (gr. 2-5). 1997. pap. 5.95 (*0-8172-6233-4*) Raintree Steck-V.
Crewe, Sabrina. Life Cycle of the Mountain Lion. (Life Cycles Ser.). 1998. pap. 5.95 (*0-8172-6239-3*) Raintree Steck-V.
***Crewe, Sabrina.** Life Cycle of the Penguin. (Life Cycles Ser.). (Illus.). 32p. (J). (gr. 2-5). 1998. pap. 5.95 (*0-8172-6240-7*) Raintree Steck-V.
Crewe, Sabrina. Life Cycle of the Snake. LC 96-4827. (Life Cycles Bks.). (Illus.). (J). 1997. pap. 5.95 (*0-8172-6235-0*) Raintree Steck-V.
***Crewe, Sabrina.** Life Cycle of the Spider. (Life Cycles Ser.). 1998. pap. 5.95 (*0-8172-6241-5*) Raintree Steck-V.
— Life Cycle of the Whale. LC 96-4846. (Life Cycles Bks.). (Illus.). 32p. (J). (gr. 2-5). 1997. pap. 5.95 (*0-8172-6226-1*) Raintree Steck-V.
Crewe, Sabrina. The Mountain Lion. LC 96-53251. (Life Cycles Bks.). (Illus.). 32p. (J). (ps-4). 1998. lib. bdg. 21.40 (*0-8172-4378-X*) Raintree Steck-V.
— The Penguin. LC 96-53248. (Life Cycles Bks.). (Illus.). 32p. (J). (gr. 2-5). 1998. lib. bdg. 21.40 (*0-8172-4379-8*) Raintree Steck-V.
— The Prairie Dog. LC 96-4828. (Life Cycles Bks.). (Illus.). 32p. (J). (ps-4). 1996. lib. bdg. 21.40 (*0-8172-4365-8*) Raintree Steck-V.
— The Salmon. LC 96-4834. (Life Cycles Bks.). (Illus.). 32p. (J). (gr. 2-5). 1996. lib. bdg. 21.40 (*0-8172-4371-2*) Raintree Steck-V.
— The Snake. LC 96-4827. (Life Cycles Bks.). (Illus.). 32p. (J). (ps-4). 1996. lib. bdg. 21.40 (*0-8172-4372-0*) Raintree Steck-V.
— The Spider. LC 96-40493. (Life Cycles Bks.). (Illus.). 32p. (J). (ps-4). 1998. lib. bdg. 21.40 (*0-8172-4380-1*) Raintree Steck-V.
— The Swallow. LC 96-4832. (Life Cycles Bks.). (Illus.). 32p. (J). (ps-4). 1996. lib. bdg. 21.40 (*0-8172-4373-9*) Raintree Steck-V.
— The Whale. LC 96-4846. (Life Cycles Bks.). (Illus.). 32p. (J). (ps). 1997. lib. bdg. 21.40 (*0-8172-4363-1*) Raintree Steck-V.
***CREWRT-L Member Staff.** Radio! Radio! 40p. 2000. pap. 7.00 (*1-877603-70-8*, Pub. by Pecan Grove) Herveys Bklink.
Crews, C. Daniel, tr. see Rican, Rudolf.
Crews, Clyde. American & Catholic: A Popular History of Catholicism in the United States. 168p. 1994. pap. 11.95 (*0-86716-175-2*) St Anthony Mess Pr.
— English Catholic Modernism: Maude Petre's Way of Faith. LC 83-50747. 156p. 1984. text 25.50 (*0-268-00912-0*) U of Notre Dame Pr.
Crews, Clyde F. An American Holy Land: A History of the Archdiocese of Louisville. (Illus.). 421p. reprint ed. pap. 24.95 (*0-932244-22-X*) Ikonographics.
— English Catholic Modernism: Maude Petre's Way of Faith. 168p. 1994. pap. 36.00 (*0-86012-136-4*, Pub. by Srch Pr) St Mut.
Crews, Clyde F., ed. Mike Barry & the Kentucky Irish American: An Anthology. LC 95-7902. (Illus.). 184p. 1995. text 25.00 (*0-8131-1898-0*) U Pr of Ky.
Crews, Clyde R. Ultimate Questions: A Theological Primer. 176p. 1986. pap. 11.95 (*0-8091-2774-1*) Paulist Pr.
Crews, David, jt. ed. see Gans, Carl.
Crews, Diane. Dust Rag Stone. 22p. (J). (gr. k-6). 1997. pap. 3.00 (*1-57514-186-8*, 3083) Encore Perform Pub.
— Hunters, Hooma & Huckleberry Bread. 23p. (J). (gr. 4-10). 1957. pap. 3.00 (*1-57514-187-6*, 3084) Encore Perform Pub.
Crews, Donald. Award Puzzles: Freight Train. (Caldecott Collection). (J). 1991. 6.95 (*0-938971-70-0*) JTG Nashville.
Crews, Donald. Bicycle Race. LC 84-27912. (Illus.). 32p. (J). (ps-1). 1985. 15.93 (*0-688-05172-3*, Grenwillow Bks) HarpC Child Bks.
Crews, Donald. Bicycle Race. LC 84-27912. (Illus.). 32p. (J). (ps-3). 1985. 16.00 (*0-688-05171-5*, Grenwillow Bks) HarpC Child Bks.
— Bigmama's. LC 90-33142. (Illus.). 32p. (J). (ps-3). 1991. 16.00 (*0-688-09950-5*, Grenwillow Bks) HarpC Child Bks.
Crews, Donald. Bigmama's. LC 90-33142. (Illus.). 32p. (J). (ps-3). 1991. 15.89 (*0-688-09951-3*, Grenwillow Bks) HarpC Child Bks.
— Bigmama's. 32p. (J). (ps up). 1998. mass mkt. 5.95 (*0-688-15842-0*, Wm Morrow) Morrow Avon.
Crews, Donald. Bigmama's. 1998. 10.15 (*0-606-12890-5*, Pub. by Turtleback) Demco.
Crews, Donald. Carousel. LC 82-3062. (Illus.). 32p. (J). (ps-3). 1982. 15.93 (*0-688-00909-3*, Grenwillow Bks) HarpC Child Bks.
Crews, Donald. Cloudy Day Sunny Day. LC 98-3847. (Green Light Readers Ser.). (Illus.). 24p. (J). 1999. pap. 3.95 (*0-15-201997-9*) Harcourt.
***Crews, Donald.** Cloudy Day Sunny Day. (Green Light Readers Ser.). (Illus.). 24p. (J). (gr. k-3). 2000. 10.95 (*0-15-202357-7*) Harcourt.
Crews, Donald. Flying. LC 85-27022. (Illus.). 32p. (J). (ps-3). 1986. 16.00 (*0-688-04318-6*, Grenwillow Bks) HarpC Child Bks.
Crews, Donald. Flying. LC 85-27022. (Illus.). 32p. (J). (ps-3). 1986. 15.93 (*0-688-04319-4*, Grenwillow Bks) HarpC Child Bks.
— Flying. LC 85-27022. (Illus.). 32p. (J). (ps up). 1989. reprint ed. mass mkt. 5.95 (*0-688-09235-7*, Wm Morrow) Morrow Avon.
— Freight Train. LC 78-2303. (Illus.). 32p. (J). (gr. k-3). 1978. 15.95 (*0-688-80165-X*, Grenwillow Bks) HarpC Child Bks.
Crews, Donald. Freight Train. LC 78-2303. (Illus.). 26p. (J). 1996. pap. 6.95 (*0-688-14900-6*, Grenwillow Bks) HarpC Child Bks.
Crews, Donald. Freight Train. LC 78-2303. (Illus.). 24p. (J). (ps up). 1992. mass mkt. 4.95 (*0-688-11701-5*, Wm Morrow) Morrow Avon.
Crews, Donald. Freight Train. 1992. 9.15 (*0-606-01356-3*, Pub. by Turtleback) Demco.
Crews, Donald. Freight Train Lf. LC 78-2303. (Illus.). 32p. (J). (gr. k-3). 1978. 15.93 (*0-688-84165-1*, Grenwillow Bks) HarpC Child Bks.
— Freight Train Big Book. (J). (ps up). 1993. pap. 18.95 (*0-688-12940-4*, Wm Morrow) Morrow Avon.
Crews, Donald. Freight Train Sliding. (J). 200_. bds. 9.95 (*0-688-17087-0*, Wm Morrow) Morrow Avon.
Crews, Donald. Harbor. LC 81-6607. (Illus.). 32p. (J). (ps-3). 1982. 15.93 (*0-688-00862-3*, Grenwillow Bks) HarpC Child Bks.
Crews, Donald. Harbor. LC 81-6607. (J). (ps up). 1987. reprint ed. mass mkt. 4.95 (*0-688-07332-8*, Wm Morrow) Morrow Avon.
— Night at the Fair. LC 96-48780. (Illus.). 24p. (J). (ps-3). 1998. 15.00 (*0-688-11483-0*, Grenwillow Bks) HarpC Child Bks.
***Crews, Donald.** Night at the Fair. LC 96-48780. (Illus.). 24p. (J). (ps-3). 1998. 14.93 (*0-688-11484-9*, Grenwillow Bks) HarpC Child Bks.
Crews, Donald. Parade. LC 82-20927. (Illus.). 32p. (J). (gr. k-3). 1983. 16.00 (*0-688-01995-1*, Grenwillow Bks); lib. bdg. 15.93 (*0-688-01996-X*, Grenwillow Bks) HarpC Child Bks.
— Parade. LC 82-20927. (Illus.). (J). (ps-3). 1986. mass mkt. 4.95 (*0-688-06520-1*, Wm Morrow) Morrow Avon.
— Sail Away. LC 94-6004. (Illus.). 40p. (J). (ps-3). 1995. 16.00 (*0-688-11053-3*, Grenwillow Bks) HarpC Child Bks.
— Sail Away. LC 94-6004. (Illus.). 32p. (J). (ps up). 1995. lib. bdg. 15.93 (*0-688-11054-1*, Grenwillow Bks) HarpC Child Bks.
***Crews, Donald.** Sail Away. LC 94-6004. (Illus.). 32p. (J). (ps up). 2000. pap. 5.95 (*0-688-17517-1*, Grenwillow Bks) HarpC Child Bks.
— School Bus. LC 83-18681. (Illus.). 32p. (J). (gr. k-3). 1984. 15.89 (*0-688-02808-X*, Grenwillow Bks) HarpC Child Bks.
Crews, Donald. School Bus. LC 83-18681. (Illus.). 32p. (J). (ps-3). 1984. 16.00 (*0-688-02807-1*, Grenwillow Bks) HarpC Child Bks.
— School Bus. LC 92-43766. (Illus.). 32p. (J). (ps up). 1993. mass mkt. 5.95 (*0-688-12267-1*, Wm Morrow) Morrow Avon.
— School Bus. 1993. 10.15 (*0-606-05992-X*, Pub. by Turtleback) Demco.
— Shortcut. LC 91-36312. (Illus.). 32p. (J). (ps-3). 1992. 16.00 (*0-688-06436-1*, Grenwillow Bks) HarpC Child Bks.
Crews, Donald. Shortcut. LC 91-36312. (Illus.). 32p. (J). (ps-3). 1992. 15.93 (*0-688-06437-X*, Grenwillow Bks) HarpC Child Bks.
Crews, Donald. Shortcut. LC 91-36312. (Illus.). 40p. (J). 1996. mass mkt. 5.95 (*0-688-13576-5*, Wm Morrow) Morrow Avon.
Crews, Donald. Shortcut. 1996. 11.40 (*0-606-11840-3*) Turtleback.
— Ten Black Dots. LC 85-14871. (Illus.). 32p. (J). (ps up). 1995. mass mkt. 4.95 (*0-688-13574-9*, Wm Morrow) Morrow Avon.
Crews, Donald. Ten Black Dots. (J). 1994. 10.15 (*0-606-08275-1*, Pub. by Turtleback) Demco.
— Ten Black Dots. rev. ed. LC 85-14871. (Illus.). 32p. (J). (ps-3). 1986. 16.00 (*0-688-06067-6*, Grenwillow Bks) HarpC Child Bks.
Crews, Donald. Ten Black Dots. rev. ed. LC 85-14871. (Illus.). 32p. (J). (ps-3). 1986. 15.89 (*0-688-06068-4*, Grenwillow Bks) HarpC Child Bks.
Crews, Donald. Truck. LC 79-19031. (Illus.). 32p. (J). (ps-3). 1980. 16.00 (*0-688-80244-3*, Grenwillow Bks) HarpC Child Bks.
— Truck. LC 79-19031. (Illus.). 36p. 1997. pap. 6.95 (*0-688-15597-9*, Hearst) Hearst Commns.
— Truck. LC 79-19031. (Illus.). 32p. (J). (ps-3). 1991. reprint ed. mass mkt. 4.95 (*0-688-10481-9*, Wm Morrow) Morrow Avon.
Crews, Donald. Truck: By Donald Crews. LC 79-19031. (Illus.). 32p. (J). (ps-3). 1980. 15.89 (*0-688-84244-5*, Grenwillow Bks) HarpC Child Bks.
— Truck Big Book. (Illus.). 32p. (J). (ps-3). 1993. reprint ed. mass mkt. 18.95 (*0-688-12611-1*, Wm Morrow) Morrow Avon.
— UPC Freight Train. 1999. pap. 6.95 (*0-688-16808-6*) HarpC.
Crews, Dougalas E. & Garruto, Ralph M., eds. Biological Anthropology & Aging: Perspectives on Human Variation over the Span. (Illus.). 472p. 1994. text 100.00 (*0-19-506829-7*) OUP.
Crews, Ed. Virginia: The Enterprising Dominion Enters the Twenty-First Century. (Illus.). 356p. 1999. write for info. (*1-882933-27-3*) Cherbo Pub Grp.
Crews, Edward R. & Parrish, Timothy A. Fourteenth Virginia Infantry. (Virginia Regimental Histories Ser.). (Illus.). 161p. 1995. 19.95 (*1-56190-077-X*) H E Howard.
Crews, Ethel Maxam, ed. see Matos, Candi & Matos, Chris.
Crews, Freda F. Get Off Your Own Back: Confront Your Myths with Reality. LC 97-195475. 180p. 1997. pap. 12.99 (*1-56043-292-6*, Treasure Hse) Destiny Image.
Crews, Frederick C. Borzoi Handbook for Writers, 2 vols., Set. 3rd ed. 672p. (C). 1992. 34.06 (*0-07-911401-6*) McGraw.
— Outright Freud. LC 98-11418. 301p. 1998. 24.95 (*0-670-87221-0*) Viking Penguin.
— Pooh Perplexed. (Winnie-the-Pooh Collection). 1999. 19.99 (*0-525-45602-3*) NAL.
— The Random House Handbook. 6th ed. 800p. (C). 1991. 40.31 (*0-07-013636-X*) McGraw.
— Random House Handbook. 6th ed. 1992. teacher ed. 9.06 (*0-07-013642-4*) McGraw.
— The Random House Handbook: Diagnostic Tests. 4th ed. Date not set. pap. text. write for info. (*0-07-013643-2*) McGraw.
— The Sins of the Fathers: Hawthorne's Psychological Themes. 1989. pap. 16.95 (*0-520-06817-3*, Pub. by U CA Pr) Cal Prin Full Svc.

C

— The Sins of the Fathers: Hawthorne's Psychological Themes. 1989. 45.00 (*0-520-06834-3*, Pub. by U CA Pr) Cal Prin Full Svc.

— Unauthorized Freud: Doubters Confront a Legend. 336p. 1999. pap. 13.95 (*0-14-028017-0*, PuffinBks) Peng Put Young Read.

Crews, Frederick C. & Schor, Sandra. The Borzoi Handbook for Writers. 3rd ed. 352p. (C). 1992. pap. 34.06 (*0-07-013648-3*) McGraw.

Crews, Frederick C., et al. The Borzoi Handbook for Writers. LC 92-33521. (C). 1993. 12.81 (*0-07-040497-6*) McGraw.

— The Borzoi Handbook for Writers. LC 92-33521. (C). 1994. 20.93 (*0-07-040494-1*) McGraw.

— The Borzoi Handbook for Writers. 3rd ed. LC 92-33521. 1994. 21.95 (*0-07-013638-6*) McGraw.

— The Memory Wars: Freud's Legacy in Dispute. 300p. 1995. 22.95 (*0-940322-04-8*) NY Rev Bks.

— The Memory Wars: Freud's Legacy in Dispute. LC 95-37847. 300p. 1997. pap. 12.95 (*0-940322-07-2*) NY Rev Bks.

Crews, Gordon A. & Counts, M. Reid. The Evolution of School Disturbance in America: Colonial Times to Modern Day. LC 97-5582. 168p. 1997. 49.95 (*0-275-95842-6*, Praeger Pubs) Greenwood.

Crews, Gordon A., jt. auth. see Garris, William R.

Crews, Gordon A., jt. auth. see Montgomery, Reid H.

Crews, Harry. Celebration: A Novel. 272p. 1999. pap. 13.00 (*0-684-84810-4*) S&S Trade.

— Celebration: A Novel. LC 97-33368. 256p. 1998. 22.50 (*0-684-83758-7*) Simon & Schuster.

— A Childhood: The Biography of a Place. LC 95-14557. 1995. 24.95 (*0-8203-1759-4*) U of Ga Pr.

— Classic Crews: A Harry Crews Reader. 448p. 1993. per. 16.00 (*0-671-86527-7*) S&S Trade.

— A Feast of Snakes. LC 86-47945. 177p. 1987. pap. 10.00 (*0-689-70715-0*, 350) Macmillan.

— A Feast of Snakes. LC 97-31155. 192p. 1998. per. 11.00 (*0-684-84248-3*, Scribner Pap Fic) S&S Trade Pap.

— Florida Frenzy. LC 82-1997. vii, 138p. 1982. pap. 16.95 (*0-8130-0726-7*) U Press Fla.

— The Mulching of America. 272p. 1996. per. 11.00 (*0-684-82541-4*) S&S Trade.

— The Mulching of America: A Novel. LC 95-11358. 256p. 1995. 22.00 (*0-684-80934-6*) Simon & Schuster.

— Realm of Chaos. Gascoigne, Marc & Jones, Andy, eds. 288p. mass mkt. 6.95 (*0-671-78405-6*, Pocket Books) PB.

— Where Does One Go When There's No Place Left to Go? deluxe limited ed. 105p. 1998. 75.00 (*0-940941-09-0*) Blood & Guts Pr.

Crews, Helen M. & Hanley, A. Bryan, eds. Biomarkers in Food Chemical Risk Assessment. 138p. 1995. 70.00 (*0-85404-790-5*, TX531) CRC Pr.

Crews, James. The Heart of the Preacher. (Illus.). 78p. 1998. pap. 5.99 (*0-89114-291-6*) Baptist Pub Hse.

***Crews, John.** California Virtual Image Map. (Illus.). 2000. 40.00 (*1-929444-00-1*) GeoWare.

***Crews, John & Whittington, Frank J., eds.** Vision Loss in an Aging Society: A Multidisciplinary Perspective. LC 99-57908. 224p. 1999. pap. 27.95 (*0-89128-307-2*) Am Foun Blind.

Crews, Judith, ed. see Mays, Carl.

Crews, Judson. Against All Wounds. (Backpocket Poets Ser.). 36p. (Orig.). 1987. pap. 2.50 (*0-916155-06-4*) Trout Creek.

— The Clock of Moss. Berge, Carol & Boyer, Dale, eds. LC 82-73828. (Ahsahta Press Modern & Contemporary Poets of the West Ser.). 60p. (Orig.). 1983. pap. 6.95 (*0-916272-21-4*) Ahsahta Pr.

— A Fragment from a Memoir: Big Sur Days 1945. (Illus.). 28p. 1995. 5.95 (*1-878116-39-8*) JVC Bks.

— Henry Miller & My Big Sur Days: Vignettes from Memory. Subraman, Belinda, ed. 52p. (C). 1992. text 5.95 (*0-935839-15-1*) Virgin Press.

— Henry Miller & My Big Sur Days: Vignettes from Memory. LC PS3525.I5454. 58p. 1992. reprint ed. pap. 30.00 (*0-7837-9062-7*, 204981100003) Bks Demand.

— Nolo Contendere. LC 78-73263. 1978. 25.00 (*0-930324-08-0*); pap. 15.00 (*0-930324-09-9*) Wings Pr.

Crews, Judson, ed. see Greasybear, Charley J.

***Crews, June T.** Can Anyone Fix My Broken Heart? 2000. pap. 6.99 (*1-57921-228-X*, Pub. by WinePress Pub) BookWorld.

Crews, Kenneth D. Copyright, Fair Use, & the Challenge for Universities: Promoting the Progress of Higher Education. LC 93-3839. (Illus.). 262p. 1993. 22.50 (*0-226-12055-4*) U Ch Pr.

— Edward S. Corwin & the American Constitution: A Bibliographical Analysis, 2. LC 84-19185. (Bibliographies & Indexes in Law & Political Science Ser.: No. 2). (Illus.). 226p. 1985. lib. bdg. 59.95 (*0-313-24233-X*, CRE/) Greenwood.

Crews, Kenneth D., jt. auth. see Corwin, Edward S.

Crews, Lary. Novel Secrets: Ten Secrets Novelists Need to Know. Haborak, George J., ed. 80p. (Orig.). 1996. pap. 9.95 (*0-9656132-0-8*) Sarasota Bay Pub.

Crews, Laura E. Crews. My Kinsfolk: Story & Genealogy of the Crews, Sampson, Wilber & Waddel Families. (Illus.). 169p. 1997. reprint ed. pap. 24.50 (*0-8328-8140-6*); reprint ed. lib. bdg. 34.50 (*0-8328-8139-2*) Higginson Bk Co.

Crews, Leon A. Roulette Recorder. (Roulette Recorders Ser.). (Illus.). 24p. 1979. pap. 3.99 (*1-929707-00-2*) LA Crews.

— Roulette Recorder: By the Numbers. (Roulette Recorders Ser.). (Illus.). 1999. pap. 3.99 (*1-929707-02-9*) LA Crews.

— Roulette Recorder: Single 0. (Roulette Recorders Ser.). (Illus.). 24p. 1999. pap. 3.99 (*1-929707-01-0*) LA Crews.

Crews, Mickey. The Church of God: A Social History. LC 89-38121. (Illus.). 272p. 1990. text 36.00 (*0-87049-634-4*) U of Tenn Pr.

Crews, Monica & McLaughlin, Louise, eds. Searching for Success. 200p. (Orig.). 1996. pap. 15.00 (*0-9653446-0-6*) Results Pr.

***Crews, Nina.** Ghost Story. (J). 2001. 15.95 (*0-688-17673-9*, Grenwillow Bks); lib. bdg. 15.89 (*0-688-17674-7*, Grenwillow Bks) HarpC Child Bks.

Crews, Nina. A High, Low, Near, Far, Loud, Quiet Story. LC 98-33273. (Illus.). 24p. (J). (ps-3). 1999. 16.00 (*0-688-16794-2*, Grenwillow Bks) HarpC Child Bks.

***Crews, Nina.** A High, Low, Near, Far, Loud, Quiet Story. LC 98-33273. (Illus.). 24p. (J). (ps-3). 1999. 15.93 (*0-688-16795-0*, Grenwillow Bks) HarpC Child Bks.

Crews, Nina. I'll Catch the Moon. LC 95-12346. (Illus.). 32p. (J). (ps-3). 1996. 15.00 (*0-688-14134-X*, Grenwillow Bks) HarpC Child Bks.

Crews, Nina. I'll Catch the Moon. LC 95-12346. (Illus.). 32p. (J). (ps-3). 1996. 14.89 (*0-688-14135-8*, Grenwillow Bks) HarpC Child Bks.

Crews, Nina. One Hot Summer Day. LC 94-6268. (Illus.). 32p. (J). (ps-3). 1995. 15.00 (*0-688-13393-2*, Grenwillow Bks) HarpC Child Bks.

Crews, Nina. One Hot Summer Day. LC 94-6268. (Illus.). 32p. (J). (ps-3). 1995. 14.89 (*0-688-13394-0*, Grenwillow Bks) HarpC Child Bks.

Crews, Nina. Snowball. LC 96-48180. (Illus.). 24p. (J). (ps-3). 1997. 15.00 (*0-688-14928-6*, Grenwillow Bks) HarpC Child Bks.

Crews, Nina. Snowball. LC 96-48180. (Illus.). 24p. (J). (ps-3). 1997. 14.89 (*0-688-14929-4*, Grenwillow Bks) HarpC Child Bks.

Crews, Nina. You Are Here. LC 97-36312. (Illus.). 32p. (J). (gr. k-3). 1998. 16.00 (*0-688-15753-X*, Grenwillow Bks) HarpC Child Bks.

***Crews, Nina.** You Are Here. LC 97-36312. (Illus.). 32p. (J). (gr. k-3). 1998. 15.93 (*0-688-15754-8*, Grenwillow Bks) HarpC Child Bks.

Crews, Patricia C. & Naugle, Ronald C., eds. Nebraska Quilts & Quiltmakers. LC 90-41995. x, 245p. 1991. text 60.00 (*0-8032-1452-9*) U of Nebr Pr.

***Crews, Patricia Cox, ed.** A Flowering of Quilts. 2001. 35.00 (*0-8032-1513-4*) U of Nebr Pr.

Crews, Paul, Sr., jt. auth. see Wilson, Rodman.

Crews, Paul B. Early Hiking in the Olympics 1922-1942. Markham, Kathy, ed. LC 95-74834. 192p. (Orig.). 1996. pap. 14.95 (*0-89716-602-7*, Peanut Btr Pubng) Elton-Wolf Pub.

Crews, Phillip, et al. Organic Structure Analysis. LC 97-31686. (Topics in Organic Chemistry). (Illus.). 576p. (C). 1998. text 89.00 (*0-19-510102-2*) OUP.

Crews, Richard. Foods & Moods. 88p. (Orig.). 1993. pap. 8.95 (*0-945864-47-7*) Columbia Pacific U Pr.

— From Textbook to Pocketbook: Making Your Education Pay Off. (Illus.). 8.95 (*0-945864-46-9*) Columbia Pacific U Pr.

— Modern Higher Education: A Wholistic View. 89p. (Orig.). (C). 1993. pap. text 11.95 (*0-945864-48-5*) Columbia Pacific U Pr.

Crews, Richard L. Independent Study - Foundational Competence for Lifelong Learning: Guidelines. 56p. (C). 1988. student ed. write for info. (*0-945864-15-9*); pap. text. write for info. (*0-945864-14-0*) Columbia Pacific U Pr.

— Materials & Methods Researching Information Resources & Developing a Learning Plan: Guidelines. 110p. (C). 1988. student ed. write for info. (*0-945864-01-9*); pap. text. write for info. (*0-945864-00-0*) Columbia Pacific U Pr.

— The Mind Alone & in Groups: Archetypes, Myths & Rituals: The Deepest Patterns of the Mind. 46p. (C). 1988. pap. text. write for info. (*0-945864-05-1*) Columbia Pacific U Pr.

— The Mind Alone & in Groups: Individuality in a Cultural Context: The Culmination of Mental Activities. 28p. (C). 1988. pap. text. write for info. (*0-945864-07-8*) Columbia Pacific U Pr.

— The Mind Alone & in Groups: Psychology & Semantics: The Causes & Mechanisms of Mental Function. 67p. (C). 1988. pap. text. write for info. (*0-945864-06-X*) Columbia Pacific U Pr.

— Our Context: The Cosmos & the Flow of History: Measurement & Uncertainty: Perspectives on the Present. 43p. (C). 1988. pap. text. write for info. (*0-945864-03-5*) Columbia Pacific U Pr.

— Our Context: The Cosmos & the Flow of History: Origins: Perspectives on the Past. 70p. (C). 1988. pap. text. write for info. (*0-945864-02-7*) Columbia Pacific U Pr.

— Our Context: The Cosmos & the Flow of History: Probabilities & Possibilities: Perspectives on the Future. 62p. (C). 1988. pap. text. write for info. (*0-945864-04-3*) Columbia Pacific U Pr.

— Personal Choices & Goals: Guidelines. 66p. (C). 1988. student ed. write for info. (*0-945864-12-4*); pap. text. write for info. (*0-945864-11-6*) Columbia Pacific U Pr.

— Wholism & Wholistic Health: The Individual in a Personal Context - Ecology - Our Home & Heritage Held in Trust. 40p. (C). 1988. pap. text. write for info. (*0-945864-09-4*) Columbia Pacific U Pr.

— Wholism & Wholistic Health: The Individual in a Personal Context - Health & Healing - Ultimate Perspectives & Practicalities. 45p. (C). 1988. pap. text. write for info. (*0-945864-10-8*) Columbia Pacific U Pr.

— Wholism & Wholistic Health: The Individual in a Personal Context - Wholism - The Concept, Its Origins & Implications. 29p. (C). 1988. pap. text. write for info. (*0-945864-08-6*) Columbia Pacific U Pr.

Crews, Richard L. & Kozlenko, Richard L. Nutrition & Health Habits: Discussion. 80p. (C). 1988. student ed. write for info. (*0-945864-20-5*); pap. text. write for info. (*0-945864-13-2*) Columbia Pacific U Pr.

Crews, Richard L., jt. auth. see Columbia Pacific University Faculty Staff.

***Crews, Robin J.** Oryx Higher Education Service Learning Source Book. (Illus.). 240p. 2001. boxed set 64.50 (*1-57356-253-X*) Oryx Pr.

Crews, Tuda Libby. Wild, Wild 1950s Cookies. LC 98-45263. (Illus.). 48p. 1999. 12.95 (*0-87905-893-5*) Gibbs Smith Pub.

— Wild, Wild West Cowboy Cookies. LC 96-50416. (Illus.). 48p. 1997. 12.95 (*0-87905-808-0*) Gibbs Smith Pub.

***Crews, Wanda J.** The Story of L'Alouette As Told by Genevieve. (Illus.). 2000. mass mkt. 19.95 (*0-9675825-1-2*) W J Crews.

***Crews, Wayne, Jr.** Electricity Reform in Colorado: A Resource Guide for Citizens & Policymakers. 1999. pap. write for info. (*1-57655-182-2*) Independ Inst.

Crews, William C. Creating Your Personal Plan for Financial Success. 167p. (Orig.). pap. text 19.95 (*0-9615787-0-X*) Creative Intl.

Crewz, David W., jt. ed. see Barnett, Michael R.

Creyghton, Edward J. New Applications of Zeolite Beta in Selective Catalytic Hydrogenations. (Illus.). 157p. (Orig.). 1996. pap. 43.50 (*90-407-1382-0*, Pub. by Delft U Pr) Coronet Bks.

Criado, Frank J., ed. Endovascular Intervention: Basic Concepts & Techniques. LC 99-29255. (Illus.). 208p. 1999. 79.00 (*0-87993-415-8*) Futura Pub.

Criado, Isabel, ed. see Unamuno, Miguel de.

Criag. Norwegian-English Contract Law Dictionary. (ENG & NOR.). 150p. 1992. 69.95 (*0-7859-7481-4*, 8200213277) Fr & Eur.

Cribb. Values & Comparative Politics. 1991. 82.95 (*1-85628-230-9*) Ashgate Pub Co.

Cribb, A., jt. auth. see Tingle, John.

Cribb, Alan. Health Promotion: Concepts & Practice. Dines, Alison, ed. LC 93-1873. 192p. 1993. pap. 24.95 (*0-632-03543-9*) Blackwell Sci.

Cribb, Alan, jt. ed. see Seedhouse, David.

Cribb, C. C. Armageddon-Dead Ahead. LC 77-70212. pap. 2.95 (*0-932046-03-7*) Manhattan Ltd NC.

— The Coming Kingdom. LC 77-70213. pap. 2.95 (*0-932046-04-5*) Manhattan Ltd NC.

— The Devil's Empire. LC 77-70211. pap. 2.95 (*0-932046-02-9*) Manhattan Ltd NC.

— Digging Diamonds Daily, 1. LC 77-70215. 12.95 (*0-932046-07-X*) Manhattan Ltd NC.

— Digging Diamonds Daily, 2. LC 77-70215. 12.95 (*0-932046-08-8*) Manhattan Ltd NC.

— Digging Diamonds Daily, Set. LC 77-70215. write for info. (*0-932046-09-6*) Manhattan Ltd NC.

— Flying High Against the Sky: If God Has It I Want It! LC 79-84881. pap. 2.95 (*0-932046-16-9*) Manhattan Ltd NC.

— From Now till Eternity. LC 76-21571. 12.95 (*0-932046-00-2*) Manhattan Ltd NC.

— Getting Ready for Heaven. LC 78-60614. (If God Has It I Want It! Ser.). 1979. pap. 2.95 (*0-685-96444-2*) Manhattan Ltd NC.

— The Horrified & the Glorified. LC 77-70214. pap. 2.95 (*0-932046-05-3*) Manhattan Ltd NC.

— Man's Earth-Lease Is about to Expire. LC 77-70210. pap. 2.95 (*0-932046-01-0*) Manhattan Ltd NC.

— Spinning Straw into Gold. LC 79-84880. (If God Has It I Want It! Ser.). pap. 2.95 (*0-932046-15-0*) Manhattan Ltd NC.

— Staking Your Claim on Healing. LC 79-83919. (If God Has It I Want It! Ser.). 1979. pap. 2.95 (*0-932046-14-2*) Manhattan Ltd NC.

***Cribb, Joe.** Money. (Eyewitness Books). (Illus.). (J). (gr. 4-7). 2000. 19.99 (*0-7894-6567-1*) DK Pub Inc.

— Money. (Eyewitness Books). (J). (gr. 4-7). 2000. 15.95 (*0-7894-5822-5*) DK Pub Inc.

Cribb, Joe, ed. see Lowic, Nicholas.

Cribb, Joe, ed. see Lowick, Nicholas.

Cribb, John. A Field Guide to Interstate 95: The Traveler's Companion to the History, Geography & Trivia That Lie Beneath the Nation's Busiest Highway. 243p. 1989. pap. 9.95 (*0-8191-7010-0*) Madison Bks UPA.

Cribb, Larry. How You Can Make $25,000 a Year with Your Camera. (Illus.). 224p. (Orig.). 1991. pap. 15.99 (*0-89879-445-5*, 10211, Wrtrs Digest Bks) F & W Pubns Inc.

Cribb, P. J. A Revision of the Antelope & "Latourea" Dendrobiums. (Illus.). 144p. 1989. pap. 24.00 (*1-878762-62-1*, Pub. by Royal Botnic Grdns) Balogh.

***Cribb, P. J. & Butterfield, I.** The Genus Pleione. (Illus.). x, 165p. 1999. write for info. (*983-812-022-7*, Pub. by Royal Botnic Grdns) Balogh.

Cribb, P. J. & Fay, J. M. Orchids of the Central African Republic: A Provisional Checklist. 26p. 1987. reprint ed. 10.00 (*1-878762-56-7*, Pub. by Royal Botnic Grdns) Balogh.

Cribb, P. J. & Whistler, W. Arthur. Orchids of Samoa. (Illus.). vii, 144p. 1996. pap. 40.00 (*1-900347-01-6*, Pub. by Royal Botnic Grdns) Balogh.

Cribb, P. J., jt. auth. see Lewis, B. A.

Cribb, P. J., jt. auth. see Wood, J. J.

***Cribb, Phillip.** Genus Paphiopendium. 2nd ed. (Illus.). 427p. 1998. 85.00 (*983-812-023-5*, Pub. by Royal Botnic Grdns) Balogh.

Cribb, Phillip, et al. The Genus Cypripedium. LC 96-30083. (Illus.). 358p. 1997. 39.95 (*0-88192-403-2*) Timber.

Cribb, Phillip J. & Bell, Sandra. Thesaurus Woolwardiae Pt. 1: Orchids of the Marquis of Lothian: The Slipper Orchids. Luer, Carlyle A., ed. & frwd. by. (Thesaurus Woolwardiae Ser.). (Illus.). 78p. 1993. pap. 60.00 (*0-915279-14-2*) Miss Botan.

Cribb, Phillip J., ed. see Chase, Mark W.

Cribb, Phillip J., ed. see Stewart, Joyce.

Cribb, Phillip J., ed. see Wood, Jeffrey J.

Cribb, Phillip J., ed. see Wood, Jeffrey J., et al.

Cribb, R. B. Gangsters & Revolutionaries: The Jakarta People's Militia & the Indonesian Revolution 1945-1949. LC 90-27543. (Illus.). 244p. 1991. reprint ed. pap. 69.60 (*0-608-04377-X*, 2065158) Bks Demand.

Cribb, Robert. Historical Atlas of Indonesia. (Illus.). 240p. 2000. text 100.00 (*0-8248-2111-4*) UH Pr.

— Historical Dictionary of Indonesia. LC 92-19210. (Asian Historical Dictionaries Ser.: No. 9). (Illus.). 688p. 1992. 79.00 (*0-8108-2542-2*) Scarecrow.

Cribb, Robert & Brown, Colin. Modern Indonesia: A History since 1945. LC 94-48236. (Postwar World Ser.). (C). 1995. text 44.75 (*0-582-05712-4*, Pub. by Addison-Wesley) Longman.

Cribb, Roger. Nomads in Archaeology. (New Studies in Archaeology). (Illus.). 267p. (C). 1991. text 74.95 (*0-521-32881-0*) Cambridge U Pr.

Cribb, T. J. Imagined Commonwealths: Cambridge Essays on Commonwealth & International Literature in English. LC 98-38109. (Cambridge Commonwealth Ser.). 304p. 1999. text 55.00 (*0-312-21666-1*) St Martin.

Cribben, Larry D. & Ungar, Irwin A. River Birch (Betula Nigra L.) Communities of Southeastern Ohio. (Biological Notes Ser.: No. 8). 1974. pap. text 3.00 (*0-86727-076-4*) Ohio Bio Survey.

Cribbet, John E. & Johnson, Corwin W. Property, Cases On. 5th ed. (University Casebook Ser.). 32.00 (*0-685-08785-9*) Foundation Pr.

— Property, Principles of the Law Of. 3rd ed. (University Textbook Ser.). 481p. 1991. reprint ed. text 27.50 (*0-88277-718-1*) Foundation Pr.

Cribbet, John E., et al. Property: Manual to Accompany Cases & Materials. 6th ed. 268p. 1990. pap. text, teacher ed. write for info. (*0-88277-849-8*) Foundation Pr.

— Property: Teacher's Manual to Accompany Cases & Materials on. 7th ed. (University Casebook Ser.). 252p. (C). 1996. pap. text, student ed. write for info. (*1-56662-352-9*) Foundation Pr.

— Property, Cases & Materials On. 6th ed. 1441p. 1991. reprint ed. text 46.95 (*0-88277-782-3*) Foundation Pr.

— PROPERTY 7E. 7th ed. LC 96-3610. (Paralegal). 1345p. (C). 1996. text 45.00 (*1-56662-334-0*) Foundation Pr.

Cribbin, James, jt. auth. see Hanan, Mack.

Cribbin, James J. Effective Managerial Leadership. LC 71-166554. 172p. reprint ed. pap. 53.40 (*0-608-11914-8*, 202356400033) Bks Demand.

— Leadership: Strategies for Organizational Effectiveness. LC 81-12722. 304p. reprint ed. pap. 94.30 (*0-7837-4241-X*, 204393000012) Bks Demand.

Cribbins, Laurette S. . . . Regret to Inform You. . . A Reflection on the Noble Children of the Depression. (Illus.). 88p. 1998. pap. 12.00 (*0-9663211-0-3*) L S Cribbins.

Cribbins, Paul D. Civil Engineering: CE2 - Transportation Engineering. (Professional Engineering Exam Review Ser.). (Illus.). 100p. (Orig.). (C). 1983. pap. text 30.00 (*1-56049-048-9*) NCSU CE IES.

— Civil Engineering No. CE2A: Transportation Engineering: Highway Capacity Manual. (Professional Engineering Exam Review Ser.). (Illus.). 100p. (Orig.). (C). 1983. pap. text 20.00 (*1-56049-049-7*) NCSU CE IES.

Cribbs, Dianna G. A Kid's Guide to Fishing & Fun Things to Do! (Illus.). 113p. (J). (gr. 1-5). 1990. pap. 6.95 (*0-943487-27-7*) Sevgo Pr.

Cribbs, Gillian, jt. auth. see Burks, Eddie.

Cribier, Michel, jt. ed. see Berthomieu, Gabrielle.

***Criblez, Lucien, et al.** Eine Schule fur die Demokratie: Zur Entwicklung der Volksschule in der Schweiz im 19. Jahrhundert. (Explorationen. Studien zur Erziehungswissenschaft Ser.). (GER.). 471p. 1999. 24.95 (*3-906763-77-3*) P Lang Pubng.

Crich, D., jt. auth. see Motherwell, W. B.

Crichett, Jan. Our Land Till We Die. 2nd rev. ed. (Illus.). 112p. 1992. pap. 30.00 (*0-949823-24-4*, Pub. by Deakin Univ) St Mut.

***Crichlow, Joel M.** The Essence of Distributed Systems. LC 99-41802. (Essence of Computing Ser.). 1999. write for info. (*0-13-015167-X*) P-H.

Crichlow, Michaeline A., jt. auth. see Tabak, Faruk.

Crichlow, Warren, jt. ed. see McCarthy, Cameron.

Crichton. America 1900: The Turning Point. Date not set. pap. 17.50 (*0-8050-5435-9*) H Holt & Co.

Crichton, Alexander. An Inquiry into the Nature & Origin of Mental Derangement, 2 vols. in 1. LC 75-14763. (Language, Man & Society Ser.). reprint ed. 94.50 (*0-404-08212-2*) AMS Pr.

Crichton, Anne & Neuhauser, Duncan, eds. The New Epidemiology: A Challenge to Health Administration. LC 82-82961. (Illus.). 133p. (Orig.). (C). 1982. pap. text 12.95 (*0-914904-84-1*) AUPHA Pr.

Crichton, Charles, jt. auth. see Cleese, John.

Crichton, David R., jt. auth. see Seidel, Arthur H.

***Crichton, Elizabeth G. & Krutzsch, Philip H., eds.** Reproductive Biology of Bats. 500p. 2000. 85.00 (*0-12-195670-9*) Acad Pr.

***Crichton, Iain.** A Country for Old Men & My Canadian Uncle. 128p. 2000. pap. 14.95 (*1-85754-474-9*, Pub. by Carcanet Pr) Paul & Co Pubs.

Crichton, J. D. Celebrating the Word. pap. text 14.95 (*1-85607-123-5*) Intl Scholars.

Crichton, J. D. The Dedication of a Church. 82p. 1989. 60.00 (*0-905092-84-8*, Pub. by Veritas Pubns) St Mut.

— The Once & Future Liturgy. 143p. 1989. pap. 22.00 (*0-905092-40-6*, Pub. by Veritas Pubns) St Mut.

— Our Lady in the Liturgy. LC 97-13583. 1997. pap. 9.95 (*0-8146-2493-6*) Liturgical Pr.

Crichton, James. Mixed Company. 160p. (C). 1988. pap. text 29.00 (*0-7152-0626-5*) St Mut.

Crichton, Jennifer. Family Reunion Planner. LC 97-53256. 320p. 1998. pap. 13.95 (*0-7611-0585-9*) Workman Pub.

Crichton, Judy. America 1900: The Turning Point. LC 98-19909. (Illus.). 288p. 1998. 29.95 (0-8050-5365-4) H Holt & Co.
***Crichton, Judy.** America 1900: The Turning Point. large type ed. LC 99-40173. (American History Ser.). 1999. 26.95 (0-7838-8764-7, G K Hall & Co) Mac Lib Ref.
Crichton, Kyle. The Happiest Millionaire. 1957. pap. 5.25 (0-8222-0496-7) Dramatists Play.
Crichton, Kyle S. Law & Order LTD: The Rousing Life of Elfego Baca of New Mexico. LC 73-14200. (Mexican American Ser.). (Illus.). 258p. 1977. reprint ed. 21.95 (0-405-05674-5) Ayer.
Crichton, Michael. Airframe. (YA). 1997. mass mkt. 7.99 (0-345-40287-1) Ballantine Pub Grp.
— Airframe. LC 96-39154. 351p. (YA). 1996. 26.00 (0-679-44648-6) Knopf.
— Airframe. large type ed. (YA). 1996. pap. 26.00 (0-679-75898-4) Random Hse Lrg Prnt.
— Airframe. limited ed. 352p. 1996. boxed set 150.00 (0-9631925-7-4) B E Trice.
— The Andromeda Strain. 288p. 1992. mass mkt. 6.99 (0-345-37848-2) Ballantine Pub Grp.
— The Andromeda Strain. 1997. pap. 12.00 (0-345-41898-0) Ballantine Pub Grp.
— The Andromeda Strain. 1969. 25.00 (0-394-41525-6) Knopf.
— The Andromeda Strain. large type ed. 608p. 1997. 34.50 (0-7089-8937-3) Ulverscroft.
— The Andromeda Strain. 1991. reprint ed. lib. bdg. 21.95 (1-56849-066-6) Buccaneer Bks.
— A Case of Need. 416p. 1994. mass mkt. 7.99 (0-451-18366-5, Sig) NAL.
— Congo. 1993. mass mkt. 6.99 (0-345-37849-0) Ballantine Pub Grp.
Crichton, Michael. Congo. 1985. pap. 11.95 (84-01-49234-3) Plaza.
Crichton, Michael. Congo. 1993. reprint ed. lib. bdg. 27.95 (1-56849-126-3) Buccaneer Bks.
— Disclosure. 512p. 1994. mass mkt. 6.99 (0-345-39105-5) Ballantine Pub Grp.
— Disclosure. 1994. 24.00 (0-679-41945-4) Random.
— Eaters of the Dead. 1988. mass mkt. 5.99 (0-345-90229-7) Ballantine Pub Grp.
— Eaters of the Dead. 1998. mass mkt. 7.99 (0-345-91283-7) Ballantine Pub Grp.
— Eaters of the Dead. 1999. pap. 7.99 (0-345-91474-0) Ballantine Pub Grp.
Crichton, Michael. Eaters of the Dead. large type ed. 240p. 31.99 (0-7089-9063-0) Ulverscroft.
Crichton, Michael. Eaters of the Dead: The Manuscript of Ibn Fadlan, Relating His Experiences with the Northmen in A. D. 922. 224p. 1993. pap. 10.00 (0-345-38324-9) Ballantine Pub Grp.
— Eaters of the Dead: The Manuscript of Ibn Fadlan, Relating His Experiences with the Northmen in A. D. 922. 1976. 25.00 (0-394-49400-8) Knopf.
***Crichton, Michael.** Esfera. (SPA.). 1998. pap. 6.95 (84-01-49231-9) Plaza.
Crichton, Michael. Five Patients. 384p. 1989. mass mkt. 6.99 (0-345-35464-8) Ballantine Pub Grp.
— The Great Train Robbery. 281p. 1994. mass mkt. 6.99 (0-345-39092-X) Ballantine Pub Grp.
— The Great Train Robbery. 1975. 25.00 (0-394-49401-6) Knopf.
— The Great Train Robbery. large type ed. 384p. 1997. 34.50 (0-7089-8928-4) Ulverscroft.
— The Great Train Robbery. 1994. reprint ed. lib. bdg. 29.95 (1-56849-268-5) Buccaneer Bks.
— Great Train Robbery Trade. 1997. pap. 12.00 (0-345-41899-9) Ballantine Pub Grp.
— Jasper Johns. rev. ed. LC 93-12278. (Illus.). 296p. 1994. 60.00 (0-8109-3515-5, Pub. by Abrams) Time Warner.
— Jurassic Park. LC 90-52960. (Illus.). 416p. (YA). 1991. mass mkt. 6.99 (0-345-37077-5) Ballantine Pub Grp.
— Jurassic Park. LC 90-52960. 399p. 1990. 26.95 (0-394-58816-9) Knopf.
— Jurassic Park. (YA). 1991. 12.09 (0-606-01181-1, Pub. by Turtleback) Demco.
— The Lost World: A Novel. (YA). 1996. mass mkt. 7.99 (0-345-40288-X) Ballantine Pub Grp.
— The Lost World: A Novel. (YA). 1997. pap. 12.00 (0-345-41900-6); mass mkt. 7.99 (0-345-91166-0) Ballantine Pub Grp.
— The Lost World: A Novel, 4 vols. 1995. audio 27.50 (0-679-44763-6) Discovery.
— The Lost World: A Novel. (YA). 1997. 14.95 (0-679-45540-X) Knopf.
— The Lost World: A Novel. large type ed. 640p. (YA). 1995. 25.95 (0-7838-1589-1, G K Hall Lrg Type) Mac Lib Ref.
— Michael Crichton's Jurassic World. LC 97-73821. 1997. 14.95 (0-375-40107-5) Knopf.
— El Mundo Perdido, 1. 1998. pap. text 6.95 (84-01-49240-8) Lectorum Pubns.
— A New Collection. LC 93-40887. 720p. 1994. 13.99 (0-517-10135-1) Random Hse Value.
— Parque Jurasico, 1. 1998. pap. text 6.95 (84-01-49236-X) Lectorum Pubns.
— Punto Critico. 1998. pap. text 6.95 (84-01-46683-0) Lectorum Pubns.
— Rising Sun. 384p. 1993. mass mkt. 7.99 (0-345-38037-1) Ballantine Pub Grp.
— Rising Sun. 1997. pap. 12.00 (0-345-41896-4) Ballantine Pub Grp.
— Rising Sun. LC 91-53173. 355p. 1992. 26.00 (0-394-58942-4) Knopf.
— Sphere. 1988. mass mkt. 7.99 (0-345-35314-5, Del Rey) Ballantine Pub Grp.
— Sphere. 1997. pap. text 6.99 (0-345-91174-1) Ballantine Pub Grp.
— Sphere. LC 86-46321. 1987. 27.50 (0-394-56110-4) Knopf.
— Sphere. 1987. 17.95 (5-551-88083-4) Knopf.
— Sphere. large type ed. 638p. 1989. 17.95 (0-7089-1941-3) Ulverscroft.
— Sphere. 1996. reprint ed. mass mkt. 6.99 (0-345-91067-2) Ballantine Pub Grp.
— Sphere. 1993. reprint ed. lib. bdg. 29.95 (1-56849-127-1) Buccaneer Bks.
— The Terminal Man. 1988. mass mkt. 6.99 (0-345-35462-1, Del Rey) Ballantine Pub Grp.
— The Terminal Man. LC 97-93310. 1997. pap. 12.00 (0-345-41901-4) Ballantine Pub Grp.
— The Terminal Man. 1972. 23.00 (0-394-44768-9) Knopf.
— The 13th Warrior. Orig. Title: Eaters of the Dead. 1988. mass mkt. 7.99 (0-345-35461-3) Ballantine Pub Grp.
— Three Complete Novels. LC 92-38676. 688p. 1993. 13.99 (0-517-08479-1) Random Hse Value.
***Crichton, Michael.** Timeline. 512p. 2000. mass mkt. 7.99 (0-345-41762-3) Ballantine Pub Grp.
Crichton, Michael. Timeline. 449p. 1999. 26.95 (0-679-44481-5) Knopf.
***Crichton, Michael.** Timeline. large type ed. 2000. pap. 14.95 (0-375-70416-7) Random.
— Timeline. large type ed. LC 99-37040. 1999. 26.95 (0-375-40873-8) Random Hse Lrg Prnt.
Crichton, Michael. Travels. 1989. mass mkt. 6.99 (0-345-35932-1) Ballantine Pub Grp.
— Travels. 400p. 1993. pap. 10.00 (0-345-37966-7) Ballantine Pub Grp.
— Travels. LC 87-46040. 1988. 25.50 (0-394-56236-4) Knopf.
***Crichton, Michael.** Turbulences. 1999. pap. 14.95 (2-266-08515-8) Distribks Inc.
Crichton, Robert. The Secret of Santa Vittoria. 1993. reprint ed. lib. bdg. 21.95 (1-56849-149-2) Buccaneer Bks.
Crichton-Smith, I. Selected Poems. LC 74-135657. 1970. 14.95 (0-8023-1160-1) Dufour.
Crichton-Stuart, John P., tr. see Coptic Church Staff.
Crick, Bernard. The American Science of Politics: Its Origin & Conditions. LC 82-15829. 252p. 1982. lib. bdg. 49.75 (0-313-23696-8, CRAS, Greenwood Pr) Greenwood.
— Essays on Politics & Literature. 259p. 1990. pap. 30.00 (0-7486-0105-8, Pub. by Edinburgh U Pr) Col U Pr.
— In Defence of Politics. rev. ed. LC 72-86545. 1993. pap. text 9.95 (0-226-12065-1, P492) U Ch Pr.
— In Defence of Politics. 4th ed. LC 93-12889. 272p. 1993. pap. text 14.00 (0-226-12067-8) U Ch Pr.
— In Defense of Politics. 1994. 25.75 (0-8446-6735-8) Peter Smith.
— In Defense of Politics. 2nd ed. LC 72-86545. 1993. lib. bdg. 15.00 (0-226-12064-3) U Ch Pr.
— Political Thoughts & Polemics. 238p. 1990. 70.00 (0-7486-0120-1, Pub. by Edinburgh U Pr) Col U Pr.
— Political Thoughts & Polemics. 238p. 1991. pap. text 30.00 (0-7486-0145-7, Pub. by Edinburgh U Pr) Col U Pr.
— Socialism. Parkin, Frank, ed. (Concepts in the Social Sciences Ser.). 136p. (Orig.). 1987. 32.50 (0-335-15388-7); pap. 9.99 (0-335-15387-9) OpUniv Pr.
Crick, Bernard, ed. see Machiavelli, Niccolo.
Crick, Bernard, jt. ed. see Robson, William A.
Crick, Bernard R. In Defence of Politics. 2nd ed. LC 72-86545. (Nature of Human Society Ser.). 204p. reprint ed. pap. 63.30 (0-608-09291-6, 205416500004) Bks Demand.
Crick, Brian. Love & the Intellectual: A Pair of Blue Eyes. (C). 1989. 35.00 (0-907839-20-7, Pub. by Brynmill Pr Ltd) St Mut.
Crick, Brian & Ferns, John, selected by. George Whalley: Studies in Literature & the Humanities. 200p. 1985. 60.00 (0-7735-0535-0, Pub. by McG-Queens Univ Pr) CUP Services.
Crick, Debbie, jt. auth. see Hathaway, Susan.
Crick, Francis Harry Compton. The Astonishing Hypothesis: The Scientific Search for the Soul. Grossman, B., ed. (Illus.). 317p. 1994. 25.00 (0-684-19431-7, Scribners Ref) Mac Lib Ref.
— The Astonishing Hypothesis: The Scientific Search for the Soul. 1995. per. 14.00 (0-684-80158-2, Touchstone) S&S Trade Pap.
Crick, Joe E. & Stolurow, Lawrence M. The Use of Computers in High Schools. LC 74-121200. 172p. 1965. 25.00 (0-403-04492-8) Scholarly.
Crick, Joyce, tr. see Freud, Sigmund.
Crick, Julia. The Historia Regum Britannie of Geoffrey of Monmouth IV: Dissemination & Reception in the Later Middle Ages. (Historia Regum Britannie Ser.). 368p. (C). 1991. 75.00 (0-85991-215-9) Boydell & Brewer.
— Historia Regum Brittanie of Geoffrey of Monmouth III: A Summary Catalogue of the Manuscripts. 400p. (C). 1989. 75.00 (0-85991-213-2) Boydell & Brewer.
Crick, Malcolm. Resplendent Sites, Discordant Voices: Sri Lankans & International Tourism. LC 94-1708. (Studies in Anthropology & History: Vol.8). x, 237p. 1994. text 71.00 (3-7186-5564-0) Gordon & Breach.
Crick, Malcolm, jt. auth. see Geddes, Bill.
Crick, Malcoln & Geddes, Bill, eds. Research Methods in the Fields: Ten Anthropological Accounts. 263p. (C). 1995. pap. 54.00 (0-949823-31-7, Pub. by Deakin Univ) St Mut.
***Crick, Michael.** Michael Heseltine. 496p. 1998. pap. 19.95 (0-14-025969-4, Pub. by Pnguin Bks Ltd) Trafalgar.
Crick, R. E., ed. Origin, Evolution & Modern Aspects of Biomineralization in Plants & Animals. (Illus.). 548p. (C). 1990. text 180.00 (0-306-43498-9, Kluwer Plenum) Kluwer Academic.
Crick, Ronald P. & Khaw, Peng. Textbook of Clinical Ophthalmology. 2nd ed. 500p. 1997. text 99.00 (981-02-2262-9); pap. text 48.00 (981-02-2373-0) World Scientific Pub.
Crickard, Fred W., et al, eds. Multinational Naval Cooperation & Foreign Policy into the 21st Century. LC 97-50012. (Illus.). 305p. 1998. text 72.95 (1-85521-997-2, VA40.M85, Pub. by Ashgate Pub) Ashgate Pub Co.
Cricket Magazine Staff. Best Ever Crossbird Puzzle Book. (J). 1998. pap. text 5.95 (0-8126-0077-0) Open Court.
— Crazy (about Crossbirds) Puzzle Book. 1998. pap. text 5.95 (0-8126-0085-1) Open Court.
— Treasure Chest of Crossbird Puzzles. (J). 1998. pap. text 5.95 (0-8126-0084-3) Open Court.
Crickhowell, Nicholas. Opera House Lottery: Zaha Hadid & the Cardiff Bay Project. LC 98-109784. (Illus.). xi, 175p. 1997. 34.50 (0-7083-1442-2, Pub. by Univ Wales Pr) Paul & Co Pubs.
Crickmay, Chris, jt. auth. see Tufnell, Miranda.
Crickmer, Douglas F. & Zegeer, David A., eds. Elements of Practical Coal Mining. 2nd ed. LC 79-57346. (Illus.). 855p. 1981. reprint ed. pap. 200.00 (0-7837-9170-4, 204987000003) Bks Demand.
Crickmore, Alice, jt. auth. see Crickmore, Paul.
Crickmore, Paul. The Concorde Story: British Airways. (Illus.). 168p. 1997. pap. 21.95 (1-85532-667-1, Pub. by Osprey) Motorbooks Intl.
***Crickmore, Paul.** Lockheed SR-71: The Secret Missions Exposed. (Illus.). 262p. 2000. pap. 26.95 (1-84176-098-6, 130578AE, Pub. by Osprey) Motorbooks Intl.
Crickmore, Paul. Lockheed SR-71 the Secret Missions Exposed. rev. ed. (Illus.). 280p. 1997. 34.95 (1-85532-681-7, Pub. by Osprey) Motorbooks Intl.
***Crickmore, Paul.** Lockheed's Blackworld Skunkworks: U2, SR-71, F-117. (Aviation Pioneers Ser.: Vol. 4). (Illus.). 112p. 2000. pap. 16.95 (1-84176-059-5, 130580AE, Pub. by Osprey) Motorbooks Intl.
Crickmore, Paul & Crickmore, Alice. F-117 Nighthawk. LC 99-12320. (Illus.). 192p. 1999. 29.95 (0-7603-0585-4, 128071AP, Pub. by MBI Pubg) Motorbooks Intl.
Crickmore, Paul F. Lockheed SR-71: The Mach 3 Blackbird. (Color Classics Ser.). (Illus.). 128p. 1997. pap. 10.95 (1-85532-712-0, Pub. by Osprey) Stackpole.
***Crico, Giandonato.** Maria Callas. 2000. pap. 12.95 (88-7301-394-5) Gremese Intl.
Criddle, Byron, jt. auth. see Bell, D. S.
Criddle, Byron, jt. auth. see Bell, David S.
Criddle, JoAn D. Bamboo & Butterflies: From Refugee to Citizen. LC 92-70276. 224p. (Orig.). 1992. pap. 12.95 (0-9632205-0-0) East West Bdg.
— To Destroy You Is No Loss: The Odyssey of a Cambodian Family. rev. ed. LC 97-219592. 294p. 1998. pap. 16.95 (0-9632205-1-9) East West Bdg.
Criddle, W. J. & Ellis, G. P. Spectral & Chemical Characterization of Organic Compounds: A Laboratory Handbook. 2nd ed. LC 80-40497. (Illus.). 127p. reprint ed. pap. 39.40 (0-8357-5563-0, 203519200093) Bks Demand.
— Spectral & Chemical Characterization of Organic Compounds: A Laboratory Handbook. 3rd ed. LC 89-21467. 132p. 1990. pap. 98.00 (0-471-92715-5) Wiley.
Crider, Abraham. Garling. Genealogy of the Garling Family. (Illus.). 183p. 1997. reprint ed. pap. 16.00 (0-8328-8704-8); reprint ed. lib. bdg. 26.00 (0-8328-8703-X) Higginson Bk Co.
Crider, Andrew B., et al. Psychology & Practice. 4th ed. LC 92-30213. (C). 1997. pap. text 93.00 (0-673-46835-6) Addson-Wesley Educ.
Crider, Barbara. Traveling with Tangerines: Refreshing Biblical Truths for Women Journeying Through Family Life. Hansen, Susan, ed. 64p. 1996. pap. text 5.95 (1-56309-166-6, W964103) Womans Mission Union.
Crider, Bill. A Dangerous Thing. 1996. per. 4.99 (0-373-26216-7, 1-26216-1, Wrldwide Lib) Harlequin Bks.
— A Dangerous Thing. 200p. 1994. 19.95 (0-8027-3187-2) Walker & Co.
— Dead on the Island. 193p. 1991. 18.95 (0-8027-5787-1) Walker & Co.
***Crider, Bill.** Death by Accident. 2000. per. 4.99 (0-373-26343-0) Harlequin Bks.
Crider, Bill. Death by Accident. LC 98-35883. (Large Print Book Ser.). 1998. 28.69 (1-56895-663-0) Wheeler Pub.
— Death by Accident: A Sheriff Dan Rhodes Mystery. LC 97-35452. 1998. text 22.95 (0-312-18080-2) St Martin.
— Death on the Move. 204p. 1989. 17.95 (0-8027-5730-8) Walker & Co.
— Gator Kill: A Truman Smith. 202p. 1992. 18.95 (0-8027-3213-5) Walker & Co.
***Crider, Bill.** Ghost of a Chance. 2000. text 23.95 (0-312-20889-8) St Martin.
Crider, Bill. Medicine Show. large type ed. 311p. 1991. reprint ed. lib. bdg. 16.95 (1-56054-142-3) Thorndike Pr.
— Mike Gonzo & the Almost Invisible Man. (J). (gr. 2-4). 1996. mass mkt. 3.99 (0-671-53652-4) PB.
— Mike Gonzo & the Sewer Monster. (J). (gr. 2-4). 1996. mass mkt. 3.99 (0-671-53651-6) PB.
— Mike Gonzo & the UFO Terror. (YA). 1997. mass mkt. 3.99 (0-671-53653-2) PB.
— Murder Is an Art. LC 98-41786. 256p. 1999. text 21.95 (0-312-19927-9) St Martin.
— Murder Takes a Break: A Truman Smith Mystery. LC 97-19939. 246p. 1997. 21.95 (0-8027-3308-5) Walker & Co.
— Muttketeer! LC 97-73288. (Adventures of Wishbone Ser.: No. 8). (Illus.). 144p. (J). (gr. 3-6). 1997. mass mkt. 3.99 (1-57064-272-9, Big Red) Lyrick Pub.
— One Dead Dean. 208p. 1988. 17.95 (0-8027-5711-1) Walker & Co.
— Outrage at Blanco. 1998. mass mkt. 5.99 (0-440-23454-9) Dell.
— The Prairie Chicken Kill: A Truman Smith Mystery. (Truman Smith Mystery Ser.). 216p. 1996. 20.95 (0-8027-3282-8) Walker & Co.
— Shotgun Saturday Night. 1987. 16.95 (0-8027-5684-0) Walker & Co.
— A Time for Hanging. large type ed. LC 90-34619. 339p. 1990. lib. bdg. 14.95 (1-56054-002-8) Thorndike Pr.
— Too Late to Die. 192p. 1986. 14.95 (0-8027-5650-6) Walker & Co.
— When Old Men Die. LC 94-15356. 192p. 1994. 19.95 (0-8027-3195-3) Walker & Co.
***Crider, Bill.** Winning Can Be Murder. (WWL Mystery Ser.: Bk. 354). 256p. 2000. mass mkt. 5.99 (0-373-26354-6, 1-26354-0, Wrldwide Lib) Harlequin Bks.
Crider, Bill. Winning Can Be Murder. 240p. 1996. 21.95 (0-312-14072-X) St Martin.
Crider, Bill, et al. White House Horrors. Greenberg, Martin H., ed. 1996. pap. 5.99 (0-88677-659-7, Pub. by DAW Bks) Penguin Putnam.
Crider, Bill, jt. auth. see Scott, Willard.
Crider, Tom. Give Sorrow Words: A Father's Passage Through Grief. 192p. 1996. 16.95 (1-56512-116-3, 72116) Algonquin Bks.
***Crider, Tom, ed.** A Nature Lover's Book of Quotations. (Illus.). xiv, 271p. 2000. 29.00 (0-9679430-0-0) Birch Tree Pub.
Crider, Virginia. Answering the Cry. (Northland Ser.). 116p. 1976. pap. 3.25 (0-87813-510-3) Christian Light.
— Life with an Alcoholic. 94p. (Orig.). 1996. pap. 5.95 (0-87813-563-4) Christian Light.
***Cridland, Arthur.** I'll Take It: A Down-to-Earth Guide to Running Fine Retail Stores. LC 99-23. (Illus.). 484p. 1999. per. 60.00 (1-55212-254-9) Trafford Pub.
Cridland, Nancy C., jt. auth. see Wiltz, John E.
Crido de Val, M. Diccionario del Espanol Equivoco: Spanish Dictionary of Ambiguities. (SPA.). 122p. 1981. pap. 12.95 (0-8288-2041-4, S38322) Fr & Eur.
Crieger, Axel. American Night. (Illus.). 156p. 1991. 40.00 (0-9627387-1-9) Seven Wolves.
Crielaard, Jan P., ed. Homeric Questions: The Proceedings of a Colloquium organized by the Netherlands Institute at Athens, May 15, 1993. LC 95-214591. (Publications of the Netherlands Institute at Athens: No. 2). (Illus.). 328p. 1995. lib. bdg. 94.00 (90-5063-095-2, Pub. by Gieben) J Benjamins Pubng Co.
***Crielaard, Jan P., et al, eds.** The Complex Past of Pottery: Circulation & Consumption of Mycenaean & Greek Pottery 1600-500 B C. 327p. 1999. 78.00 (90-5063-327-7, Pub. by Gieben) J Benjamins Pubng Co.
Crifo, J. F., et al. Molecular Complexes in Earth's, Planetary & Cometary Atmospheres. LC 98-6454. 300p. 1997. text 68.00 (981-02-3211-X) World Scientific Pub.
Crigger. Cases in Bioethics. LC 97-65208. 304p. 1998. pap. 26.95 (0-312-15269-8) St Martin.
Crigger, David. How to Make Your Drum Machine Sound Like a Drummer. (C). 1987. pap. 21.95 (0-939067-30-7) Alexander Pub.
Crighton, D. G., et al. Modern Methods in Analytical Acoustics: Lecture Notes. (Illus.). 680p. 1994. 54.95 (0-387-19737-0) Spr-Verlag.
Crighton, David A., jt. auth. see Towl, Graham J.
Crighton, James. Buchner & Madness: Schizophrenia in Georg Buchner's Lenz & Woyzeck. LC 98-39783. (Bristol German Publications: Vol. 9). 318p. 1998. text 99.95 (0-7734-1352-9) E Mellen.
Crighton, John C. The History of Health Services in Missouri. (Illus.). 278p. 1993. text 34.95 (0-9639699-0-0) J C Crighton Pub.
Crighton, Noel P. Why Do We Say That: An Exercise in Etymology. 1998. pap. text 12.95 (0-7981-3743-6) Human & Rousseau.
Crigler, Ann N., ed. The Psychology of Political Communication. LC 96-10324. 280p. (C). 1996. text 49.50 (0-472-10641-4, 10641) U of Mich Pr.
— The Psychology of Political Communication. 280p. 1998. pap. text 19.95 (0-472-08579-4, 08579) U of Mich Pr.
Crile, G. W. Bipolar Theory of Living Processes: How to Treat Chronic Fatigue, Exhaustion & Death from an Electrical Energy Standpoint. 1991. lib. bdg. 88.95 (0-8490-4933-4) Gordon Pr.
Crile, George, Jr. The Way It Was: Sex, Surgery, Treasure, & Travel, 1907-1987. LC 92-2971. (Illus.). 432p. 1992. 35.00 (0-87338-465-2) Kent St U Pr.
Criley, J. Michael. Physiological Origins of Heart Sounds & Murmurs CD-ROM. 1995. 149.95 (0-316-16154-3, Little Brwn Med Div) Lppncott W & W.
Criley, Richard. "The FBI vs. the First Amendment" "How the FBI Attempted to 'Neutralize' the National Committee Against Repressive Legislation (NCARL) - Founded in 1960 As the National Committee to Abolish HUAC (House Committee on Un-American Activities)" LC 90-83117. (Illus.). 96p. 1990. pap. 10.00 (0-9627705-0-7) Frst Amendment.
Crill, Hildred, jt. auth. see Agran, Rick.
***Crill, Rosemary.** Indian Embroidery. (Illus.). 144p. 2000. 45.00 (1-85177-310-X) V & A.
Crill, Rosemary. Indian Ikat Textiles. (Illus.). 76p. 1998. 45.00 (0-8348-0451-4) Weatherhill.
Crill, Rosemary, jt. auth. see Askari, Nasreen.
Crilley, Mark. Akiko, Vol. 1. (Illus.). 160p. 1997. pap. 14.95 (1-57989-009-1) Sirius Ent.
— Akiko, Vol. 2. (Illus.). 128p. 1998. pap. 11.95 (1-57989-019-9) Sirius Ent.
— Akiko, Vol. 3. (Illus.). 104p. 1999. pap. 11.95 (1-57989-023-7) Sirius Ent.
— Akiko, Vol. IV. (Illus.). 144p. 2000. pap. 14.95 (1-57989-034-2) Sirius Ent.
— Akiko & Great Wall of Trudd. 2001. mass mkt. (0-385-32727-7) BDD Bks Young Read.

C

— Akiko in the Sprubly Islands. (Illus.). 176p. (J). (ps up). 2000. 9.95 (*0-385-32726-9*) Delacorte.

— Akiko on the Planet Smoo. LC 99-32522. 176p. (J). (gr. 3-5). 2000. 9.95 (*0-385-32724-2*) Delacorte.

— Akiko On The Planet Smoo. 176p. 2001. pap. 4.99 (*0-440-41648-5*) BDD Bks Young Read.

Crilley, Raymond E., Sr. International Directory of Model Construction Equipment: Featuring Caterpillar. (Illus.). 210p. 1992. pap. 27.95 (*0-9625212-2-1*) Intl Farm Model.

Crilley, Raymond E., Sr. & Burkholder, Charles E. International Directory of Model Farm Toys Featuring John Deere. (Illus.). 500p. 1993. pap. 35.95 (*0-9625212-3-X*) Intl Farm Model.

Crilley, Raymond E. & Burkholder, Charles E. International Directory of Model Farm Tractors. LC 85-61520. (Illus.). 356p. 1985. pap. 39.95 (*0-88740-030-2*) Schiffer.

— International Directory of Model Farm Tractors Featuring Allis-Chalmers, Deutz, Deutz-Allis, Deutz-Fahr, Fahr, LaCrosse, Monarch, Rumely, Simplicity & Vendeuvre. (Illus.). 150p. (Orig.). 1990. pap. 17.95 (*0-9625212-0-5*) Intl Farm Model.

Crillis, Carla. I Can Help. 14p. (J). (ps). 1991. reprint ed. bds. 5.50 (*0-86315-123-X*, Pub. by Floris Bks) Gryphon Hse.

Crilly, A. J., et al, eds. Applications of Fractals & Chaos. LC 93-8105. 1993. 78.95 (*0-387-56492-6*) Spr-Verlag.

— Applications of Fractals & Chaos: The Shape of Things. (Illus.). vii, 311p. 1993. write for info. (*3-540-56492-6*) Spr-Verlag.

Crilly, Donna M., jt. ed. see Hamma, Robert M.

Crilly, Eileen & Morris, Stephanie. Get Ready, Set, Grow. LC 84-60318. (J). (ps). 1984. pap. 12.99 (*0-8224-5858-6*) Fearon Teacher Aids.

Crilly, William M. Due Diligence Handbook. LC 97-39711. 1400p. 1997. spiral bd. 695.00 (*0-8144-0407-3*) AMACOM.

— Due Diligence Handbook. LC 93-92762. 790p. 1993. ring bd. 295.00 (*0-9637605-0-5*) Newport Pacific.

Crim, D., jt. auth. see Cohn, Alvin.

***Crim, Julia H. & Crim, Keith R.** Abound with Blessings: A Month of Poems & Prayers. 144p. 2000. pap. 8.95 (*0-8091-3970-7*) Paulist Pr.

Crim, Julia R., et al. Imaging of the Foot & Ankle. LC 95-33415. 244p. 1996. text 131.00 (*0-397-51463-8*) Lppncott W & W.

Crim, K. R., tr. see Westermann, Claus.

Crim, Keith. The Perennial Dictionary of World Religions. LC 89-45260. 848p. 1990. pap. 36.00 (*0-06-061613-X*, Pub. by Harper SF) HarpC.

Crim, Keith R., et al, eds. The Interpreter's Dictionary of the Bible. LC 62-9387. (Illus.). 998p. 1976. suppl. ed. 44.95 (*0-687-19269-2*) Abingdon.

Crim, Keith R., jt. auth. see Crim, Julia H.

Crim, Keith R., jt. ed. see Buttrick, George A.

Crim, Keith R., tr. see Kraus, Hans-Joachim.

Crim, Lottie & McAlister, Katsy. Missions Events with a Sizable Difference: Ning Events for Small & Large Churches. Nelson, Becky, ed. 35p. 1993. pap. text 4.95 (*1-56309-073-2*, W933122) Womans Mission Union.

Crim, Mort. Good News for a Change! Touching Your Heart, Increasing Your Hope. LC 99-32752. 192p. 1999. pap. 10.99 (*1-56955-182-0*, Vine Bks) Servant.

— Mort Crim's Second Thoughts: One Hundred Upbeat Messages for Beat up Americans. unabridged ed. 1997. audio 14.95 (*1-55874-570-X*) Health Comm.

Crim, Mort. Second Thoughts: One Hundred Upbeat Messages for Beat-Up Americans. LC 97-36854. 200p. 1997. pap. 12.95 (*1-55874-566-1*) Health Comm.

— Second Thoughts On: How to Be as Terrific as Your Dog Thinks You Are! LC 00-25331. 200p. 2000. pap. 12.95 (*1-55874-784-2*) Health Comm.

Crim, Mort & VanDeRyt, Susan. Greater Detroit: Renewing the Dream. LC 96-37664. (Urban Tapestry Ser.). (Illus.). 368p. 1997. 44.95 (*1-881096-37-8*) Towery Pub.

Crim, Sarah & Moulton, Gwen. Washington Frugal Mania: A Money Saving Guide to the National Capital Area. LC 96-85487. 181p. 1996. pap. 12.95 (*0-9653092-0-7*) Capital Frugalist.

Crimando, William & Riggar, T. F. Handbook for In-Service Training in Human Services. LC 87-36967. (Illus.). 200p. (Orig.). (C). 1988. pap. text 17.95 (*0-8093-1402-9*) S Ill U Pr.

— Staff Training: An Annotated Review of the Literature, 1980-1988. LC 90-3254. (Research & Information Guides in Business, Industry & Economic Institutions Ser.: Vol. 3). 358p. 1990. text 15.00 (*0-8240-7385-1*, SS662) Garland.

Crimando, William & Riggar, T. F., eds. Utilizing Community Resources: An Overview of Human Services. 370p. 1996. lib. bdg. 37.00 (*1-57444-020-9*) St Lucie Pr.

Crime Time Publishing Co. Staff. The Investigator's Little Black Book: Hundreds & Hundreds & Hundreds of Inside Sources. LC 96-85004. 110p. 1997. pap. 21.95 (*0-9652369-0-0*) Crime Time.

Crimi, Alfred D. A Look Back - A Step Forward. LC 86-33228. (Illus.). 242p. 1987. 19.95 (*0-934733-13-9*) CMS.

***Crimi, Carolyn.** Don't Need Friends. LC 98-29883. (Illus.). 32p. (J). (gr. k-2). 1999. 15.95 (*0-385-32643-2*) Doubleday.

— Kidding Around Chicago: What to Do, Where to Go & How to Have Fun in Chicago. 2nd ed. (Kidding Around Ser.). (Illus.). 144p. (J). (gr. 1-5). 2000. pap. 8.95 (*1-56261-587-4*) Avalon Travel.

Crimi, Carolyn. Outside, Inside. LC 93-46897. (Illus.). 40p. (J). (ps-2). 1995. 15.00 (*0-671-88688-6*) S&S Bks Yung.

Criminale, Ulrike, jt. auth. see American Cultural Exchange, Language School Staff.

Criminology Review Yearbook Staff. Criminology Review Yearbook, Vol. 1. Messinger, Sheldon L. & Bittner, Egon, eds. LC 79-642873. 767p. pap. 200.00 (*0-8357-8497-5*, 203477300001) Bks Demand.

Crimm. 1993 Tax: Chapter One. 1993. 20.00 (*0-316-16113-6*, Aspen Law & Bus) Aspen Pub.

— 1993 Tax: Chapter 2. 1993. 30.00 (*0-316-16116-0*, Aspen Law & Bus) Aspen Pub.

— Tax Literature, 1995. 1995. suppl. ed. 105.00 (*0-316-16106-3*, Aspen Law & Bus) Aspen Pub.

Crimm, Nina J. Tax Court Litigation: Practice & Procedure. 848p. 1992. ring bd. 145.00 (*0-316-16109-8*, Aspen Law & Bus) Aspen Pub.

Crimmel, Henry H. The Liberal Arts College & the Ideal of Liberal Education: The Case of Radical Reform. LC 93-11066. 390p. (Orig.). (C). 1993. pap. text 37.50 (*0-8191-9174-4*); lib. bdg. 64.00 (*0-8191-9173-6*) U Pr of Amer.

Crimmens, Paula. Storymaking & Creative Groupwork with Elderly People. LC 96-48680. 1997. pap. write for info. (*1-85302-440-6*, Pub. by Jessica Kingsley) Taylor & Francis.

Crimmins. Lethal Losses. 1999. pap. 60.00 (*0-8133-3352-0*) Westview.

***Crimmins, C. E.** The Quotable Cat. 2000. pap. 8.95 (*1-887166-73-4*, Hysteria Pubns) Sourcebks.

Crimmins, Cathy. Tamagotchi Egg: The Unofficial Guide to the Complete Care of Your Egg. LC GV1220.8.C75 1997. 1997. mass mkt. 4.99 (*0-8125-6192-9*, Pub. by Forge NYC) St Martin.

— When My Parents Were My Age, They Were Old: Who Are You Calling Middle-Aged? 1995. pap. 10.00 (*0-671-89944-9*, Fireside) S&S Trade Pap.

***Crimmins, Cathy.** Where Is the Mango Princess? LC 00-20917. 272p. 2000. 24.00 (*0-375-40491-0*) Knopf.

Crimmins, Cathy & Maeder, Tom. Seven Habits of Highly Defective People: A Parody. abr. ed. 1996. audio. write for info. (*0-7871-1069-8*, Dove Audio) NewStar Media.

Crimmins, Cathy & O'Leary, Tom. The Gay Man's Guide to Heterosexuality. LC 97-46093. xiii, 155p. 1998. pap. 10.95 (*0-312-18102-7*) St Martin.

Crimmins, Daniel B., jt. auth. see Durand, V. Mark.

Crimmins, Eileen M., jt. auth. see Easterlin, Richard A.

Crimmins, G. Garfield. The Republic of Dreams: A Reverie. LC 98-13791. (Illus.). 96p. 1998. 21.95 (*0-393-04633-8*) Norton.

Crimmins, James & Keil, Mary. Enterprise in the Nonprofit Sector. 144p. 1983. pap. 12.00 (*0-941182-03-7*) Partners Livable.

Crimmins, James, jt. auth. see Rathmann, Charles.

Crimmins, James C. The American Promise: Adventures in Grass-Roots Democracy. LC 95-37518. (Illus.). 224p. 1995. pap. 24.95 (*0-912333-71-5*) BB&T Inc.

— The American Promise: Adventures in Grass-Roots Democracy. (Illus.). 197p. 1999. reprint ed. pap. text 25.00 (*0-7881-6327-2*) DIANE Pub.

Crimmins, James E. Secular Utilitarianism: Social Science & the Critique of Religion in the Thought of Jeremy Bentham. 360p. 1990. text 85.00 (*0-19-827741-5*) OUP.

Crimmins, James E., ed. Utilitarians & Religion. 470p. 1998. 120.00 (*1-85506-570-3*); pap. 35.00 (*1-85506-571-1*) Thoemmes Pr.

Crimmins, J.C., & Company Staff. The Challenge of the Unknown: Teaching Guide. (C). 1986. pap. text, teacher ed. 7.50 (*0-393-95536-2*) Norton.

Crimmins, Jerry. Obits & Murders: A Newspaper Story Set in Chicago. LC 90-91570. 519p. 1992. 20.00 (*0-9626047-0-4*) Ozanam Pr.

Crimmins, Mark. Talk about Beliefs. (Illus.). 224p. 1992. 28.50 (*0-262-03185-X*, Bradford Bks) MIT Pr.

Crimmins, Robert. Cell 17: Interviews with the Imprisoned. LC 96-177583. (Illus.). 160p. (Orig.). 1995. pap. 12.95 (*0-9648513-1-8*) Pond Publng.

Crimmins, Timothy J. & Shumsky, Neil L. American Life, American People, 2 vols., Vol. 1. 298p. (C). 1988. pap. text 34.00 (*0-15-502360-8*, Pub. by Harcourt Coll Pubs) Harcourt.

— American Life, American People, 2 vols., Vol. 2. 323p. (C). 1988. pap. text 34.00 (*0-15-502361-6*, Pub. by Harcourt Coll Pubs) Harcourt.

Crimp, Douglas. On the Museum's Ruins. (Illus.). 368p. 1995. pap. text 21.00 (*0-262-53126-7*) MIT Pr.

— Uber die Ruinen des Museums das Museum, die Photographie und die Postmoderne. (Illus.). 440p. 1996. text 51.00 (*3-364-00328-9*) Gordon & Breach.

Crimp, Douglas, ed. AIDS: Cultural Analysis, Cultural Activism. (October Bks.). 275p. 1988. pap. text 18.95 (*0-262-53079-1*) MIT Pr.

Crimp, Douglas & Rolston, Adam. AIDS Demo Graphics. LC 89-81756. (Illus.). 144p. (Orig.). 1990. pap. 13.95 (*0-941920-16-X*) Bay Pr.

Crimp, Douglas, jt. auth. see Marincola, Paula.

Crimp, Margaret, jt. auth. see Wright, Len Tiu.

***Crimp, Martin.** Martin Crimp: Plays 1: Dealing with Clair; Play with Repeats; Getting Attention; The Treatment. 352p. 2000. pap. 17.00 (*0-571-20345-0*) Faber & Faber.

Crimp, Martin. The Treatment. 96p. 1993. pap. 12.95 (*1-85459-240-8*, Pub. by N Hern Bks) Theatre Comm.

Crimp, Martin & Ionesco, Eugene. Chairs. 1998. pap. text 11.95 (*0-571-19451-6*) Faber & Faber.

***Crimp, Susan.** Touched by a Saint: Personal Encounters with Mother Teresa. LC 00-102080. (Illus.). 128p. 2000. pap. 14.95 (*1-893732-22-3*) SORIN BKS.

Crimp, Susan & Burstein, Patricia. The Many Lives of Elton John. (Illus.). 288p. 1992. 19.95 (*1-55972-111-1*, Birch Ln Pr) Carol Pub Group.

Crimson, Harvard. Essays That Worked. LC 99-15304. 192p. 1999. pap. 12.95 (*0-312-20647-X*) St Martin.

Crine, J. P., ed. Hazards, Decontamination, & Replacement of PCB: A Comprehensive Guide. LC 88-31630. (Environmental Science Research Ser.: Vol. 37). (Illus.). 240p. 1989. 75.00 (*0-306-43088-6*, Plenum Trade) Perseus Pubng.

Crinelli, Lorenzo. Treasures from Italy's Great Libraries. LC 97-16448. (Illus.). 288p. 1997. text 65.00 (*0-86565-986-9*) Vendome.

Criner, Calvin L. The Moon Gate. 72p. 1999. pap. 8.00 (*0-8059-4579-2*) Dorrance.

Criner, G. & D'Alonzo, G. Pulmonary Pathophysiology. (Pathophysiology Ser.). 1998. pap. text 24.95 (*1-889325-05-8*) Fence Crk Pubng.

Cringely, Robert X. Accidental Empires. LC 96-34100. 384p. 1996. pap. 14.00 (*0-88730-855-4*) HarpC.

— Accidental Empires: How the Boys of Silicon Valley Make Their Millions, Battle Foreign Competition & Still Can't Get a Date. 320p. 1992. 19.95 (*0-201-57032-7*) Addison-Wesley.

Cringle, Barbara. The Tasty House of Mother Mouse. (Illus.). 32p. (J). 1997. pap. 7.00 (*0-8059-4331-5*) Dorrance.

Crinion, Gregory P., ed. Transnational Dispute Resolution, 1984. (Wisconsin International Law Journal, 1982 Ser.). 300p. (Orig.). 1985. pap. text 8.00 (*0-933431-02-3*) U Wisc Law Madison.

Crinita, Joey. From Chains to Wings, the Journey into Spirit. 192p. (Orig.). 1994. pap. 10.95 (*0-9641254-0-4*) Berkheimer Pr.

Crinnin, Gerry. False Shuffles & the Disappearing Ace. 24p. (Orig.). 1989. pap. 4.00 (*0-945926-08-1*) Paradigm RI.

Crinnion, J. Evolutionary Systems Development: A Practical Guide to the Use of Prototyping Within a Structured Systems Methodology. (Software Science & Engineering Ser.). (Illus.). 384p. (C). 1992. 89.50 (*0-306-44139-X*, Plenum Trade) Perseus Pubng.

Crinson, Mark. Empire Building: Orientalism & Victorian Architecture. LC 95-26418. (Illus.). 304p. (C). 1996. 90.00 (*0-415-13940-6*); pap. 29.99 (*0-415-13941-4*) Routledge.

Crinson, Mark & Lubbock, Jules. Architecture - Art or Profession? Three Hundred Years of Architectural Education in Britain. LC 93-49014. 1994. text 79.95 (*0-7190-4171-6*) Manchester Univ Pr.

Cripe, Clair A. Legal Aspects of Corrections Management. LC 97-1322. 350p. 49.00 (*0-8342-0866-0*, 8660) Aspen Pub.

Cripe, Daniel E. Not Ashamed of the Gospel: A Commentary on St. Paul's Epistle to the Romans. (Historic, Orthodox Exposition of the Bible Ser.: Vol. VI). 684p. (Orig.). 1997. pap. 23.95 (*1-890875-00-7*) Jordan Pub Hse.

Cripe, Donald. The Lonely Christmas Tree. (Illus.). 24p. (Orig.). (J). (gr. k-3). 1995. pap. 6.95 (*0-9649625-0-0*) Buds Pubng.

Cripe, Douglas D. Blueprints for Building Christian Education. 1998. pap. text 9.95 (*0-8272-0224-5*) Chalice Pr.

Cripe, Edward J. & Mansfield, Richard S. Value-Added Employee: 31 Skills to Make Yourself Irresistible to Any Company. LC 99-17265. (Illus.). 196p. 1999. pap. 21.95 (*0-88415-136-0*, 5136) Gulf Pub.

Cripe, Helen & Campbell, Diane. American Manuscripts, 1763-1815: An Index to Documents Described in Auction Records & Dealers' Catalogues. LC 77-2525. 1977. 125.00 (*0-8420-2122-1*) Scholarly Res Inc.

Cripe, Helen, ed. see Becnel, Irwin J., Jr. & Nicholson, Kenneth E.

Cripe, Helen, ed. see Moore, Greg.

Cripe, Helen, ed. see Nicholson, Kenneth E.

Cripe, Juliann J. A Family's Guide to the Individualized Family Service Plan. LC 95-25310. 1995. 44.00 incl. VHS (*1-55766-220-7*) P H Brookes.

Cripe, Juliann J., et al, eds. AEPS Curriculum for Birth to Three Years. (Assessment, Evaluation, & Programming System (AEPS) for Infants & Children Ser.: Vol. 2). 496p. (C). 1992. spiral bd. 59.95 (*1-55766-096-4*) P H Brookes.

— AEPS Family Interest Survey, Family Interest Survey, pkg. of 30. (Assessment, Evaluation, & Programming System (AEPS) for Infants & Children Ser.: Vol. 2). 496p. (C). 1998. 15.00 (*1-55766-098-0*) P H Brookes.

Cripe, Nicholas, jt. auth. see Flood, Royce E.

Crippen. Horizons: Science Activity. (DA - Computer Education Ser.). (J). (gr. k-8). 1995. 36.95 (*0-538-62602-X*) S-W Pub.

— Video Stop: A Computer Applications Simulation. (DF - Computer Applications Ser.). 1994. mass mkt. 22.25 (*0-538-62860-X*) S-W Pub.

Crippen, Alan, ed. Reclaiming the Culture. (Orig.). 1996. pap. 12.99 (*1-56179-440-6*) Focus Family.

Crippen, Dan. Managing County Money: A Cash Flow Problem. 1975. 1.00 (*1-55614-061-4*) U of SD Gov Res Bur.

***Crippen, Dan L., ed.** An Analysis of the President's Budgetary Proposals for Fiscal Year 2000. (Illus.). 85p. (C). 2000. pap. text 25.00 (*0-7881-8675-2*) DIANE Pub.

Crippen, Lee F. Simon Cameron: Ante Bellum Years. LC 76-168674. (American Scene Ser.). 1972. reprint ed. lib. bdg. 39.50 (*0-306-70362-9*) Da Capo.

Crippen, Renae, ed. see Jordan, Don.

Crippen, T. F., jt. auth. see Lynn, I. H.

Crippen, Thomas G. Christmas & Christmas Lore. LC 89-43370. (Illus.). 1990. reprint ed. 42.00 (*1-55888-860-8*) Omnigraphics Inc.

Crippen, Timothy, jt. auth. see Lopreato, Joseph.

Crippen, Waldo. The Kansas Pacific Railroad: A Cross Section of an Age of Railroad Building. Bruchey, Stuart, ed. LC 80-1278. (Railroads Ser.). 1981. lib. bdg. 15.95 (*0-405-13753-2*) Ayer.

Cripps, Arthur S. An Africa for Africans. 1970. reprint ed. lib. bdg. 49.50 (*0-8371-2764-5*) Greenwood.

Cripps, Brian. Llanelli: Postcards of Yesteryear. 105p. 1994. pap. 21.00 (*1-85902-193-X*, Pub. by Gomer Pr) St Mut.

— Pembroke & Pembroke Dock: Postcards of Yesteryear. 116p. 1996. pap. 23.95 (*0-8464-4612-X*) Beekman Pubs.

— St. David's & St. Bride's Bay Postcards of Yesteryear. 1997. pap. 32.00 (*1-85902-492-0*, Pub. by Gomer Pr) St Mut.

— St. David's & St. Bride's Bay: Postcards of Yesteryear. 1997. pap. 23.95 (*0-8464-4583-2*) Beekman Pubs.

— Tenby Postcards of Yesteryear. 124p. 1995. pap. 20.95 (*0-8464-4686-3*) Beekman Pubs.

Cripps, Colin. Drugs: Losing the War. LC 97-223324. (Illus.). 224p. 1996. 45.00 (*1-873797-21-4*, Pub. by New Clarion); pap. 19.95 (*1-873797-20-6*, Pub. by New Clarion) Paul & Co Pubs.

Cripps-Day, Francis H. The History of Tournament in England & in France. LC 78-63490. (Illus.). 264p. reprint ed. 57.50 (*0-404-17138-9*) AMS Pr.

Cripps, Francis. Manifesto: A Radical Strategy for Britain's Future LC 82-101165. (Politics Ser.). 224 p. 1981. write for info. (*0-330-26402-8*) Pan.

Cripps, Francis & Ward, Terry. Europe Can Afford to Work: Strategies for Growth & Employment in the European Community. 60p. 1993. 47.50 (*0-85124-551-X*, Pub. by Spkesman) Coronet Bks.

Cripps, J. C., et al, eds. The Engineering Geology of Weak Rock: Proceedings of the 25th Annual Conference of the Engineering Group of the Geological Society, Leeds, UK, 9-13 September 1990. (Engineering Geology Special Publications: No. 8). (Illus.). 520p. (C). 1993. text 149.00 (*90-6191-167-2*, Pub. by A A Balkema) Ashgate Pub Co.

Cripps, Jeremy, tr. see Pacioli, Luca.

Cripps, L. L. Calamity in the Caribbean: Puerto Rico & the Bomb. LC 87-28887. 185p. 1987. pap. 13.95 (*0-87047-035-3*) Schenkman Bks Inc.

Cripps, Louise. C. L. R. James: Memories & Commentaries. LC 96-43630. (Illus.). 200p. 1997. 18.95 (*0-8453-4865-5*, Cornwall Bks) Assoc Univ Prs.

— Puerto Rico: UNA ISLA que Cristobal Colon Descubrio Hace 500 Anos. (SPA., Illus.). 1989. 3.50 (*0-942423-01-1*) Borinquen Bks.

— Puerto Rico the Island Christopher Columbus Discovered 500 Years. 103p. 1987. pap. 3.65 (*0-942423-00-3*) Borinquen Bks.

Cripps, Louise L. Human Rights in a United States Colony. 200p. 1982. pap. 13.95 (*0-87073-589-6*) Schenkman Bks Inc.

— Lirazel. LC 96-9785. 232p. 1997. 18.95 (*0-8453-4864-7*, Cornwall Bks) Assoc Univ Prs.

Cripps, Michael. Turning Goblets. LC 96-15554. (Illus.). 64p. 1996. pap. 12.95 (*0-7643-0033-4*) Schiffer.

Cripps, Mike. Turning Candlesticks with Mike Cripps. LC 97-80403. (Illus.). 64p. 1998. pap. 14.95 (*0-7643-0469-0*) Schiffer.

— Turning Pens & Other Desk Accessories. (Illus.). 64p. 1996. pap. 12.95 (*0-7643-0051-2*) Schiffer.

Cripps, Mike & Snyder, Jeffrey B. Wood Turning for the Garden with Mike Cripps. LC 96-70409. (Illus.). 64p. 1997. pap. 12.95 (*0-7643-0032-6*) Schiffer.

Cripps, S. Periodontal Disease: Recognition, Interception & Perception. 292p. 1984. text 104.00 (*0-86715-118-8*) Quint Pub Co.

Cripps, Steve C. RF Power Amplifiers for Wireless Communications. LC 99-17792. (Microwave Library). 1999. 95.00 (*0-89006-989-1*) Artech Hse.

Cripps, T. F. & Tarling, R. J. Growth in Advanced Capitalist Economies, 1950-1970. LC 73-84317. (University of Cambridge, Dept. of Applied Economics, Occasional Papers: 40). 64p. reprint ed. pap. 25.00 (*0-608-12228-9*, 2024429) Bks Demand.

Cripps, Thomas. Black Film As Genre. LC 77-23630. 192p. reprint ed. pap. 54.80 (*0-8357-7288-8*, 2056029) Bks Demand.

— Hollywood's High Noon: Moviemaking & Society Before Television. (The American Moment Ser.). (Illus.). 200p. 1996. text 38.50 (*0-8018-5315-X*); pap. text 14.95 (*0-8018-5316-8*) Johns Hopkins.

— Slow Fade to Black: The Negro in American Film, 1900-1942. (Illus.). 464p. 1977. pap. 14.95 (*0-19-502130-4*) OUP.

Cripps, Thomas & Balio, Tino, eds. The Green Pastures. LC 79-3959. (Warner Bros. Screenplay Ser.). (Illus.). 228p. 1979. pap. 9.95 (*0-299-07924-4*) U of Wis Pr.

Cripps, Yvonne M. Controlling Technology: Genetic Engineering & the Law. LC 80-13754. 154p. 1980. 57.95 (*0-275-90465-2*, C0465, Praeger Pubs) Greenwood.

Cripwell. Titantic Is Sinking. Date not set. pap. text. write for info. (*0-17-556580-5*) Addison-Wesley.

Crisafi, Frank J., jt. auth. see Plum, Henry J.

Crisafulli, Alessandro S., ed. Linguistic & Literary Studies in Honor of Helmut A. Hatzfeld. LC 64-55374. 426p. reprint ed. pap. 132.10 (*0-608-17256-1*, 202950800061) Bks Demand.

Crisafulli, Chuck. Teen Spirit. LC 97-160317. 1996. per. 16.00 (*0-684-83356-5*) S&S Trade.

***Crisafulli, Chuck & DiMartino, Dave.** The Doors: Strange Days. (Illus.). 176p. 2000. pap. 22.95 (*1-56025-266-9*, Thunders Mouth) Avalon NY.

Crisafulli, John, et al. Backstage Pass: Cooking for the Stars. LC 98-27719. (Illus.). 304p. 1998. pap. 18.95 (*1-58182-001-1*) Cumberland Hse.

Crisafulli, V. S., tr. The Miracles of St. Artemios: A Collection of Miracle Stories by an Anonymous Author of Seventh Century Byzantium. LC 96-47378. xxii, 319p. 1996. 122.50 (*90-04-10574-3*) Brill Academic Pubs.

Crisan, M. Theory of Superconductivity. 312p. (C). 1989. text 70.00 (*9971-5-0569-X*); pap. text 36.00 (*9971-5-0997-0*) World Scientific Pub.

C

An Asterisk (*) at the beginning of an entry indicates that the title is appearing for the first time.

Crisanti, Andrea, et al. Products of Random Matrices in Statistical Physics. LC 93-15234. (Solid-State Sciences Ser.: Vol. 104). 1993. 75.95 (*0-387-56575-2*) Spr-Verlag.

Criscenti, Joseph T., ed. Sarmiento & His Argentina. LC 92-38372. 216p. 1993. lib. bdg. 35.00 (*1-55587-351-0*) L Rienner.

Criscenzo, Jeeni. Place of Mirrors: Lessons of the Ancient Maya. LC 96-76576. 300p. 1996. 21.95 (*0-9652318-1-X*) Jaguar Books.

Crisci, Elizabeth W. Letters That Help Churches Grow. (Illus.). 160p. 1987. ring bd. 24.95 (*0-89265-113-X*) Randall Hse.

— 100 Publicity Ideas for Local Churches. Spear, Cindy G., ed. 113p. 1997. ring bd. 38.95 (*1-57052-076-3*) Chrch Grwth VA.

Crisci, Jorge V., et al. Order & Diversity in the Living World: Teaching Taxonomy & Systematics in Schools. 1993. 3.00 (*0-941212-11-4*) Natl Assn Bio Tchrs.

Criscito, Pat. Designing the Perfect Resume. LC 95-5699. (Illus.). 304p. 1995. pap. 13.95 (*0-8120-9329-1*) Barron.

***Criscito, Pat.** Designing the Perfect Resume. 2nd ed. LC 99-86610. (Illus.). 304p. 2000. pap. 14.95 (*0-7641-1268-6*) Barron.

— Guide to Distance Learning. LC 98-32255. 512p. 1999. pap. 18.95 (*0-7641-0725-9*) Barron.

— Resumes in Cyberspace. 2nd ed. 300p. 2000. pap. 14.95 (*0-7641-1489-1*) Barron.

Criscito, Pat. Resumes in Cyberspace: Your Complete Guide to a Computerized Job Search. LC 96-49151. 304p. 1997. pap. 14.95 (*0-8120-9919-2*) Barron.

***Crisco, Richard.** The Final Frontier. LC 99-172478. 1998. pap. 10.99 (*0-7684-2003-2*, Revival Pr) Destiny Image.

Crisco, Richard. It's Time: Passing Revival to the Next Generation. LC 97-218795. 140p. 1997. pap. 9.99 (*1-56043-690-5*, Revival Pr) Destiny Image.

Criscoe, Betty L. Award-Winning Books for Children & Young Adults: An Annual Guide, 1989. LC 90-38848. (Illus.). 310p. 1990. 39.50 (*0-8108-2336-5*) Scarecrow.

Criscoe, Betty L. & Lanasa, Philip J., III. Award-Winning Books for Children & Young Adults, 1990-1991. (Illus.). 714p. 1992. 83.50 (*0-8108-2597-X*) Scarecrow.

Criscuolo. Mrs. Morellis Revenge. 1999. text 17.95 (*0-312-08853-1*) St Martin.

Criscuolo, C. Clark. Bank Robbers. 256p. 1996. mass mkt. 5.50 (*1-57566-088-1*, Knsington) Kensgtn Pub Corp.

— Wiseguys in Love. 288p. 1995. mass mkt. 4.99 (*0-8217-4802-5*, Zebra Kensgtn) Kensgtn Pub Corp.

Criscuolo, Claire. Claire's Classic American Vegetarian Cooking. LC 96-34726. 288p. 1997. 24.95 (*0-525-94179-7*, Dutt) Dutton Plume.

— Claire's Classic American Vegetarian Cooking: 225 New & Favorite Homestyle Vegetarian Recipes. 303p. 1999. pap. 17.95 (*0-452-27790-6*, Plume) Dutton Plume.

— Claire's Corner Copia: Two Hundred Twenty Five Homestyle Vegetarian Recipes from Claire's Family to Yours. LC 94-11882. 1994. pap. 15.95 (*0-452-27176-2*, Plume) Dutton Plume.

— Claire's Italian Feast: 165 Vegetarian Recipes from Nonna's Kitchen. LC 98-25758. 224p. 1998. pap. 13.95 (*0-452-27881-3*, Plume) Dutton Plume.

Criscuolo, Nicholas P. & Herman, Barry. Fun With Words. (J). (gr. 2-5). 1988. pap. 8.99 (*0-8224-3172-6*) Fearon Teacher Aids.

***Criscuolo, Santo.** Pacific Northwest & British Columbia. (Ski & Snowboard America Ser.). (Illus.). 2000. pap. 17.95 (*0-7627-0844-1*) Globe Pequot.

***Crise, Martha White.** Two Fast? Having a Second Baby Within Three Years of the First. 160p. 2000. pap. 14.95 (*1-893162-22-2*) Erica Hse.

Crisell, Andrew. An Introductory History of British Broadcasting. LC 97-9354. 296p. (C). 1997. 65.00 (*0-415-12802-1*); pap. 20.99 (*0-415-12803-X*) Routledge.

— Understanding Radio. (Communication Ser.). 256p. 1987. 32.50 (*0-416-38330-0*, 1067); pap. 11.95 (*0-416-38340-8*, 1085) Routledge.

— Understanding Radio. 2nd ed. LC 93-43580. (Studies in Culture & Communication). 256p. (C). 1994. pap. 21.99 (*0-415-10315-0*, B3810) Routledge.

Crisenbery, Miriam. God Made Them All. 1992. pap. 5.95 (*0-87813-534-0*) Christian Light.

Crisfield, D. W. The Complete Idiot's Guide to Soccer. LC 98-87596. 1998. pap. text 16.95 (*0-02-862725-3*) Macmillan Gen Ref.

***Crisfield, D. W.** Louisville Slugger Book of Great Hitters. LC 97-45744. (Louisville Slugger Ser.). 192p. (J). (gr. 4-8). 1998. pap. 12.95 (*0-471-19772-6*) Wiley.

— Pick-Up Games: The Rules, the Players, the Equipment. (Illus.). 192p. (gr. 5-10). 1999. pap. text 13.00 (*0-7881-6481-3*) DIANE Pub.

— Pick-Up Games: The Rules, the Players, the Equipment. 208p. 1999. 22.95 (*0-7351-0196-5*) Replica Bks.

Crisfield, Deborah. Eating Disorders. LC 93-5538. (Update Ser.). (J). 1994. pap. 4.95 (*0-382-24756-6*, Crstwood Hse) Silver Burdett Pr.

Crisfield, Deborah. Eating Disorders. LC 93-5538. (Update Ser.). 1994. 10.15 (*0-606-10351-1*, Pub. by Turtleback) Demco.

— Hernan Cortes. LC 99-54467. (Explorers & Exploration Ser.). (Illus.). 48p. (J). 2000. write for info. (*0-7398-1488-5*) Raintree Steck-V.

Crisfield, Deborah. Pick-Up Games: The Rules, the Players, the Equipment. LC 92-16296. 208p. 1993. reprint ed. pap. 64.50 (*0-608-02833-9*, 206390000007) Bks Demand.

— Travel: Careers in Travel. LC 93-15211. (Now Hiring Ser.). (Illus.). 48p. (J). (gr. 5-6). 1994. lib. bdg. 14.95 (*0-89686-790-0*, Crstwood Hse) Silver Burdett Pr.

Crisfield, Deborah, jt. auth. see Monteleone, John.

Crisfield, Deborah W. Winning Soccer for Girls. LC 95-42612. 160p. 1996. 24.95 (*0-8160-3271-8*) Facts on File.

— Winning Volleyball For Girls. LC 94-27344. (Illus.). 160p. 1995. 24.95 (*0-8160-3033-2*) Facts on File.

— Winning Volleyball For Girls. LC 94-27344. (Illus.). 160p. 1996. pap. 12.95 (*0-8160-3034-0*) Facts on File.

Crisfield, M. A. Non-Linear Finite Element Analysis of Solids & Structures: Advanced Topics, Vol. 2, Advanced Topics. 508p. 1997. 160.00 (*0-471-95649-X*) Wiley.

Crisfield, M. A. Non-Linear Finite Elements Analysis of Solids & Structures: Essentials, Vol. 1, Essentials. 362p. 1996. pap. 49.95 (*0-471-97059-X*) Wiley.

Crisler. Discrete Mathematics. 2nd ed. 1999. teacher ed. write for info. (*0-7167-3656-X*); pap. text 54.95 (*0-7167-3652-7*) St Martin.

Crisler, B. Cobbey. Search the Scriptures - The Complete Cobrey Crisler Talks: Walk to Emmaus. (Search the Scriptures Ser.: Vol. 1). 145p. 1998. pap. 18.00 (*1-891331-08-6*) Nebbadoon Pr.

Crisler, Curtis L., et al. Black: One Man's Mind One Black Man's Mind. White, Rhonda & Tapp-Sanders, Marcia, eds. (C). pap. text 5.95 (*1-883517-12-5*) Alef Bet Comns.

***Crisler, Lois.** Arctic Wild: The Remarkable True Story of One Couple's Adventure Living Among Wolves. LC 99-36157. 1999. pap. text 16.95 (*1-55821-688-X*) Lyons Pr.

— Captive Wild: One Woman's Adventure Living with Wolves. 2000. pap. 16.95 (*1-58574-123-X*) Lyons Pr.

Crisler, Nancy. Discrete Mathematics Through Applications. LC 94-2597. 1994. 35.95 (*0-7167-2427-8*) W H Freeman.

Crisler, Nancy, et al. Discrete Mathematics Through Applications. LC 94-2597. (C). 1994. pap. text 52.95 (*0-7167-2577-0*) W H Freeman.

Crisler, Shirley, jt. auth. see Mosle, Mira.

Crislip, Betty P., ed. see Daniels-Moseley, Julia.

Crisman, Kevin J. & Cohn, Arthur B. When Horses Walked on Water: Horse-Powered Ferries in Nineteenth-Century America. LC 97-26750. (Illus.). 368p. 1998. text 37.50 (*1-56098-843-6*) Smithsonian.

Crisman, Peggy & Worley, Shirley. Bead Talk. (Illus.). 201p. (YA). 1994. pap. text 8.95 (*0-9635501-0-1*) Beads Unique.

Crisman, Ruth. Racing the Iditarod Trail. LC 92-25870. (Illus.). 72p. (J). (gr. 5 up). 1993. lib. bdg. 14.95 (*0-87518-523-1*, Dillon Silver Burdett) Silver Burdett Pr.

— Racing the Iditarod Trail. 72p. (J). 1996. pap. 7.95 (*0-382-39229-9*) Silver Burdett Pr.

Crisman, William. The Crises of "Language & Dead Signs" in Ludwig Tieck's Prose Fiction. LC 95-17122. (GERM Ser.). viii, 202p. (C). 1997. 55.00 (*1-57113-014-4*) Camden Hse.

Crismier, Chuck. Out of Egypt: A Prophetic Call to the End-Time Church. 288p. 1999. pap. 15.99 (*1-57921-196-8*, Pub. by WinePress Pub) BookWorld.

Crismon, Fred. Fire Engines. LC 97-19417. (Junior Crestline Ser.). (Illus.). 160p. 1997. pap. 21.95 (*0-7603-0381-9*) MBI Pubg.

— Modern U. S. Military Vehicles. LC 98-19124. (Junior Crestline Ser.). (Illus.). 160p. 1998. pap. 21.95 (*0-7603-0526-9*) MBI Pubg.

Crismon, Fred W. International Trucks. (Motorbooks International Ser.). (Illus.). 608p. 1995. 49.95 (*0-7603-0069-0*, Crestline Pub) MBI Pubg.

Crismon, Joy. Chinese Brush Painting. 84p. (J). (gr. 1-7). pap. write for info. (*1-56861-049-1*) Swift Lrn Res.

— Start with Art. 339p. (J). (gr. 1-7). pap. 59.95 (*1-56861-046-7*) Swift Lrn Res.

Crismore, Avon. Talking with Readers: Metadiscourse As Rhetorical Act. (American University Studies: Language: Ser. XIV, Vol. 17). 294p. (C). 1989. text 41.95 (*0-8204-0793-3*) P Lang Pubng.

***Crisorio, Mary.** Keys to Achieving Your Goals. 1999. 7.95 (*1-56245-369-6*) Great Quotations.

Crisorio, Mary, ed. Keys to Happiness & Success. 78p. (Orig.). 1990. pap. 7.95 (*0-931089-89-1*) Great Quotations.

Crisostomo, Isabelo T. Cory - Profile of a President. 340p. 1987. reprint ed. 22.95 (*0-8283-1913-8*) Branden Bks.

Crisostomo, Manny. Mainstreet: A Portrait of Small-Town Michigan. 2nd ed. (Illus.). 205p. 1986. 28.95 (*0-9614344-4-9*) Historical Soc MI.

Crisotomo, Isabelo T. Filipino Achievers in the U. S. A. & Canada: Profiles in Excellence. (Illus.). 352p. 1996. 65.00 (*0-931613-11-6*) Bkhaus.

***Crisp.** Introduction to Fiber Optics. 256p. 2001. pap. 32.95 (*0-7506-5030-3*) Buttrwrth-Heinemann.

Crisp, Alan, jt. auth. see Berman, Jude.

Crisp, Arthur H. & Stonehill, E. Sleep, Nutrition & Mood. LC 75-16121. (Illus.). 183p. reprint ed. pap. 56.80 (*0-608-17659-1*, 203037200069) Bks Demand.

Crisp, Barbara. Human Spaces: Life-Enhancing Designs for Healing, Working, & Living. (Illus.). 192p. 1999. 50.00 (*1-56496-432-9*) Rockport Pubs.

***Crisp, Brian F.** Democratic Institutional Design. LC 99-55624. 2000. 55.00 (*0-8047-3570-0*) Stanford U Pr.

Crisp, C. G. Eric Rohmer, Realist & Moralist. LC 86-46378. 151p. 1988. pap. 46.90 (*0-608-05014-8*, 205967500004) Bks Demand.

Crisp, Colin. The Classic French Cinema, 1930-1960. LC 92-21657. (Illus.). 516p. (C). 1994. 59.95 (*0-253-31550-6*) Ind U Pr.

— The Classic French Cinema, 1930-1960. (Illus.). 1997. pap. 16.95 (*0-253-21115-8*) Ind U Pr.

Crisp, D. J., ed. see European Marine Biology Symposium Staff.

Crisp, Debbie, et al. Case Screening by the Crown Prosecution Service: How & Why Cases Are Terminated. LC 95-190162. (Home Office Research Study Ser.). viii, 66 p. 1994. 25.00 (*0-11-341137-5*, Pub. by Statnry Office) Bernan Associates.

Crisp, Extraordinary, ed. see Howard, Joseph J. & Herald, Mallravers.

Crisp, Extraordinary, ed. see Howard, Joseph J. & Herald, Maltravers.

Crisp, F. A., ed. see Howard, Joseph J. & Herald, Mallravers.

Crisp, Frank. Mediaeval Gardens. LC 67-4273. (Illus.). 1979. lib. bdg. 90.00 (*0-87817-007-3*) Hacker.

Crisp, Frederich A., jt. auth. see Howard, Joseph J.

Crisp, Frederick, jt. auth. see Howard, Joseph J.

Crisp, Frederick A. Fragmenta Genealogica, Vol 1. (Illus.). 83p. 1996. pap. 20.00 (*0-7884-0463-6*, C001) Heritage Bk.

— Fragmenta Genealogica, Vol. 2. (Illus.). 93p. 1996. pap. 20.00 (*0-7884-0464-4*, C002) Heritage Bk.

Crisp, Frederick A. Fragmenta Genealogica, Vol. 3. (Illus.). 93p. 1996. pap. 20.00 (*0-7884-0492-X*, C003) Heritage Bk.

— Fragmenta Genealogica, Vol. 4. (Illus.). 97p. 1996. pap. 20.00 (*0-7884-0493-8*, C004) Heritage Bk.

— Fragmenta Genealogica, Vol. 5. vi, 152p. 1996. reprint ed. pap. 22.00 (*0-7884-0545-4*, C005) Heritage Bk.

— Fragmenta Genealogica, Vol. 6. vi, 170p. 1996. reprint ed. pap. 22.00 (*0-7884-0546-2*, C006) Heritage Bk.

— Fragmenta Genealogica, Vol. 7. 180p. 1996. pap. 22.00 (*0-7884-0577-2*, C007) Heritage Bk.

— Fragmenta Genealogica, Vol. 8. 162p. 1996. pap. 22.00 (*0-7884-0578-0*, C008) Heritage Bk.

— Fragmenta Genealogica, Vol. 11. 284p. 1997. reprint ed. pap. 37.00 (*0-7884-0647-7*, CD11) Heritage Bk.

— Fragmenta Genealogica, Vol. 12. 154p. 1997. reprint ed. pap. 22.00 (*0-7884-0648-5*, C012) Heritage Bk.

— Fragmenta Genealogica, Vol. 13. 158p. 1997. pap. 22.00 (*0-7884-0649-3*, C013) Heritage Bk.

— Fragments Genealogica. 166p. 1997. reprint ed. pap. 22.00 (*0-7884-0608-6*, C010) Heritage Bk.

Crisp, Frederick A., ed. List of Parish Registers & Other Genealogical Works. xxx, 343p. 1997. reprint ed. pap. 27.00 (*0-7884-0692-2*, C637) Heritage Bk.

Crisp, Frederick A., et al. Visitation of England & Wales Notes, 1917, Vol. 12. 205p. 1998. reprint ed. pap. 31.00 (*0-7884-0826-7*, HN12) Heritage Bk.

Crisp, Frederick A., jt. auth. see Howard, Joseph J.

Crisp, Frederick A., ed. see Howard, Joseph J.

Crisp, Frederick A., ed. see Howard, Joseph J. & Herald, Maltravers.

Crisp, Frederick A., jt. ed. see Howard, Joseph J.

Crisp, George. Salvador Dali: Spanish Painter. (Hispanics of Achievement Ser.). (Illus.). 120p. (YA). (gr. 5 up). 1993. lib. bdg. 19.95 (*0-7910-1778-8*) Chelsea Hse.

Crisp, George R. Miles Davis. LC 96-26427. (Impact Biographies Ser.). 144p. (YA). (gr. 6 up). 1997. lib. bdg. 23.60 (*0-531-11319-1*) Watts.

— Miles Davis. (Impact Biographies Ser.). 144p. (YA). (gr. 6 up). 1997. pap. text 9.95 (*0-531-15865-9*) Watts.

Crisp, Jane, et al. Child Victims & Witnesses: A Three-State Profile. (Illus.). 190p. (C). 1995. reprint ed. pap. text 40.00 (*0-7881-2437-4*) DIANE Pub.

***Crisp, Jane, et al.** Deciphering Culture: Ordinary Curiosities & Subjective Narratives. LC 00-34473. 2000. pap. write for info. (*0-415-10838-1*) Routledge.

Crisp, Jerry, tr. see Vesaas, Tarjei.

***Crisp, John.** Introduction to Digital Systems. (Illus.). 272p. 2000. pap. 36.95 (*0-7506-4583-0*, Newnes) Buttrwrth-Heinemann.

Crisp, John. Introduction to Fibre Optics. LC 97-121914. 240p. 1999. pap. text 32.95 (*0-7506-2467-1*) Buttrwrth-Heinemann.

— Introduction to Microprocessors. LC 98-229015. (Illus.). 240p. 1998. pap. text 32.95 (*0-7506-3787-0*, Newnes) Buttrwrth-Heinemann.

Crisp, M. D. & Doyle, J. J., eds. Advances in Legume Systematics Pt. 7: Phylogeny. x, 371p. 1995. pap. 36.00 (*0-947643-79-6*, Pub. by Royal Botnic Grdns) Balogh.

***Crisp, Marty.** Black & White. LC 00-21109. (Illus.). (J). (ps-3). 2000. 12.95 (*0-87358-756-1*, Rising Moon Bks) Northland AZ.

Crisp, Marty. Buzzard Breath. LC 94-16664. 140p. (J). (gr. 2-6). 1995. 15.00 (*0-689-31964-9*) S&S Bks Yung.

***Crisp, Marty.** My Dog, Cat. (Illus.). 64p. (J). (gr. 2-5). 2000. 15.95 (*0-8234-1537-6*) Holiday.

— Private Captain. LC 00-25570. (Illus.). (J). 2001. write for info. (*0-399-23577-9*, Philomel) Peng Put Young Read.

Crisp, Marty. Ratzo. LC 98-22089. (J). (gr. 3-7). 1998. 12.95 (*0-87358-722-7*); pap. 8.95 (*0-87358-723-5*) Northland AZ.

Crisp, Michael, ed. see Bone, Diane.

Crisp, Michael, ed. see Brock, Susan L.

Crisp, Michael, ed. see Chapman, E.

Crisp, Michael, ed. see Chapman, Elwood N.

Crisp, Michael, ed. see Conrad, Pam.

Crisp, Michael, ed. see Fritz, Roger.

Crisp, Michael, ed. see Gill, James O.

Crisp, Michael, ed. see Goman, Carol K.

Crisp, Michael, ed. see Haynes, Marion E.

Crisp, Michael, ed. see Johnson, Tom.

Crisp, Michael, ed. see Klosowski, Allen.

Crisp, Michael, ed. see Lengefeld, Uelaine.

Crisp, Michael, ed. see Lloyd, Sam R.

Crisp, Michael, ed. see Maddux, Robert B.

Crisp, Michael, ed. see Mandel, Steve.

Crisp, Michael, ed. see Martin, William.

Crisp, Michael, ed. see Mcardle, G.

Crisp, Michael, ed. see Minor, Marianne.

Crisp, Michael, ed. see Palladino, Connie.

Crisp, Michael, ed. see Pokras, Sandy.

Crisp, Michael, ed. see Raber, Merill F. & Dyck, George.

Crisp, Michael, ed. see Scott, Cynthia D. & Jaffe, Dennis T.

Crisp, Michael, ed. see Simons, George & Zuckerman, Amy J.

Crisp, Michael G. & Burley-Allen, Madelyn. Memory Skills in Business: Basic Techniques for Memory Improvement. LC 88-70089. (Fifty-Minute Ser.). (Illus.). 63p. (Orig.). 1988. pap. 10.95 (*0-931961-56-4*) Crisp Pubns.

Crisp, Michael G. & Paulson, Terry. Making Humour Work: Taking Your Job Seriously & Yourself Lightly. LC 88-72262. (Fifty-Minute Ser.). (Illus.). 77p. (Orig.). 1989. pap. 10.95 (*0-931961-61-0*) Crisp Pubns.

Crisp, Michael G., ed. see Albin, Mel & Johnson, Noel.

Crisp, Michael G., ed. see Cadwell, Charles.

Crisp, Michael G., ed. see Chapman, Edwood N.

Crisp, Michael G., ed. see Chapman, Elwood N.

Crisp, Michael G., ed. see Chapman, Elwood N. & Heim, Pat.

Crisp, Michael G., ed. see Dell, Twyla.

Crisp, Michael G., ed. see Dvorak, Robert R.

Crisp, Michael G., ed. see Finch, Lloyd.

Crisp, Michael G., ed. see Fossum, Lynn.

Crisp, Michael G., ed. see Freestone, Julie & Brusse, Janet.

Crisp, Michael G., ed. see Gelatt, H. G.

Crisp, Michael G., ed. see Hart, Lois B.

Crisp, Michael G., ed. see Haynes, Marion E.

Crisp, Michael G., ed. see Horn, Sam.

Crisp, Michael G., ed. see Jaffee, Dennis & Scott, Cynthia D.

Crisp, Michael G., ed. see Jones, Frederic H.

Crisp, Michael G., ed. see Karlson, David.

Crisp, Michael G., ed. see Kast, Fremont, et al.

Crisp, Michael G., ed. see Klosowski, Allen.

Crisp, Michael G., ed. see Maddux, Robert B.

Crisp, Michael G., ed. see Maddux, Robert B. & Voorhees, Lynda.

Crisp, Michael G., ed. see Mallory, Charles.

Crisp, Michael G., ed. see Manning, Marilyn & Barnes, Carolyn.

Crisp, Michael G., ed. see Martin, Charles L.

Crisp, Michael G., ed. see Morgan, Rebecca.

Crisp, Michael G., ed. see Nothstine, William.

Crisp, Michael G., ed. see Pollar, Odette.

Crisp, Michael G., ed. see Pooser, Doris.

Crisp, Michael G., ed. see Scott, Dru.

Crisp, Michael G., ed. see Timm, Paul R.

Crisp, Michael J., ed. see Decker, Bert.

Crisp, Michale G., ed. see Kindler, Herbert S.

Crisp, Mike. Directing Single Camera Drama. 2nd ed. LC 97-46870. 256p. 1997. pap. text 36.95 (*0-240-51478-5*) Buttrwrth-Heinemann.

— The Practical Director. 2nd ed. LC 97-105432. (Illus.). 224p. 1996. pap. 39.95 (*0-240-51448-3*, Focal) Buttrwrth-Heinemann.

Crisp, N., jt. auth. see Ritter, M.

Crisp, Olga & Edmondson, Linda H., eds. Civil Rights in Imperial Russia. (Illus.). 338p. 1989. 72.00 (*0-19-822867-8*) OUP.

***Crisp, Peter.** Ancient Rome. rev. ed. (My Word Ser.). (Illus.). (J). 2000. 9.95 (*1-58728-062-0*); pap. 5.95 (*1-58728-068-X*) Two Can Pub.

Crisp, Peter. The Parthenon. LC 96-48751. (Great Buildings Ser.). 48p. (J). 1997. lib. bdg. 25.69 (*0-8172-4917-6*) Raintree Steck-V.

***Crisp, Peter.** Romans. (Interfact Ser.). (Illus.). (J). (gr. 2-7). 2000. spiral bd. 14.95 (*1-58728-462-6*) Two Can Pub.

Crisp, Quentin. How to Have a Lifestyle. 200p. 1998. pap. 10.95 (*1-55583-406-X*) Alyson Pubns.

— Naked Civil Servant. 1997. pap. 12.95 (*0-14-118053-6*) Viking Penguin.

— Resident Alien: The New York Diaries. 232p. 1998. pap. 11.95 (*1-55583-466-3*) Alyson Pubns.

— The Wit & Wisdom of Quentin Crisp. 200p. 1998. pap. 10.95 (*1-55583-407-8*) Alyson Pubns.

Crisp, Randall, jt. auth. see Scholder, Fritz.

Crisp, Robert. Feeding a Giant: Advanced Network Marketing. (Illus.). 199p. 1998. pap. 22.95 (*1-892018-01-2*) R Crisp Ent.

— Raising a Giant: A Book about Leadership in Network Marketing. 3rd ed. (Illus.). 180p. 1993. reprint ed. 22.95 (*1-892018-00-4*); reprint ed. pap. 22.95 (*1-892018-02-0*) R Crisp Ent.

— Windows NT Security Unleashed. 700p. 1997. 49.99 (*0-672-31088-0*) Sams.

Crisp, Roger. Routledge Philosophy Guidebook to Mill on Utilitarianism. LC 97-1476. (Routledge Philosophy Guidebooks Ser.). 256p. (C). 1997. 60.00 (*0-415-10977-9*); pap. 12.99 (*0-415-10978-7*) Routledge.

Crisp, Roger, ed. How Should One Live? Essays on the Virtues. 272p. 1998. reprint ed. pap. text 18.95 (*0-19-875234-2*) OUP.

Crisp, Roger & Slote, Michael, eds. Virtue Ethics. (Oxford Readings in Philosophy Ser.). 290p. 1997. pap. text 18.95 (*0-19-875188-5*) OUP.

— Virtue Ethics. LC 97-161358. (Oxford Readings in Philosophy). 290p. (C). 1997. text 65.00 (*0-19-875189-3*) OUP.

Crisp, Roger, jt. auth. see Warner, Martin.

Crisp, Roger, ed. see Aristotle.

Crisp, Roger, jt. ed. see Cowton, Christopher.

Crisp, Roger, ed. see Griffin, James.

Crisp, Roger, ed. see Mill, John Stuart.

***Crisp, Terri.** Emergency Animal Rescue Stories. 4th ed. 2000. 24.95 (*0-7615-1706-5*) Prima Pub.

C

Crisp, Terri. Out of Harm's Way: The Extraordinary True Story of One Woman's Lifelong Devotion to Animals. 416p. 1997. per. 14.00 (*0-671-52278-7*) PB.

***Crisp, Tony.** Coincidences: A Look Beyond Logical Thought. 2000. pap. text 10.95 (*1-902809-17-3*) Allison & Busby.

Crisp, Tony. Dream Dictionary. LC 93-7742. 432p. 1993. 8.99 (*0-517-09331-6*) Random Hse Value.

— Dream Dictionary: A Guide to Dream & Sleep Experiences. 420p. 1991. mass mkt. 6.99 (*0-440-20861-0*) Dell.

— The Instant Dream Book. 224p. (Orig.). pap. 20.95 (*0-8464-4243-4*) Beekman Pubs.

— The Instant Dream Book. 153p. (Orig.). 1989. pap. 13.95 (*0-85435-125-6*, Pub. by C W Daniel) Natl Bk Netwk.

— Mind & Movement. 108p. 1987. pap. 9.95 (*0-85207-182-5*, Pub. by C W Daniel) Natl Bk Netwk.

— Mind & Movement: The Practice of Coex. 200p. (Orig.). pap. 14.95 (*0-8464-4255-8*) Beekman Pubs.

— Super Minds: People with Amazing Mind Power!, 1. 128p. (YA). (gr. 5 up). 1999. pap. 4.95 (*1-901881-03-2*, Pub. by Element MA) Penguin Putnam.

Crisp, Wendy Reid. Do As I Say, Not As I Did. 1997. 15.00 (*0-614-27826-0*, Perigee Bks) Berkley Pub.

— Do As I Say, Not As I Did: Perfect Advice from an Imperfect Mother. 173p. 1999. text 15.00 (*0-7881-6117-2*) DIANE Pub.

— Do As I Say, Not As I Did: 100 Things I'm Telling My Daughter. LC 97-6415. 192p. 1997. pap. 15.00 (*0-399-52334-0*, Perigee Bks) Berkley Pub.

— 100 Things I Am Not Going to Do Now That I'm over 50. LC 94-24657. 224p. 1995. pap. 14.00 (*0-399-51936-X*, Perigee Bks) Berkley Pub.

Crispe, I. Nicholas, ed. Lymphocytes in the Liver: Inmunobiology, Pathology, & Host Defense. LC 98-7962. 256p. 1999. 104.95 (*0-471-19218-X*, Wiley-Liss) Wiley.

Crispe, Thomas E. Reminiscences of A. K. C. 334p. 1996. reprint ed. 85.00 (*1-56169-208-5*) Gaunt.

Crispell, Brian Lewis. Testing the Limits: George Armistead Smathers & Cold War America. LC 98-48350. (Illus.). 234p. 1999. 35.00 (*0-8203-2103-6*) U of Ga Pr.

C

Crispell, Diane. Insider's Guide to Demographic Know-How: Everything You Need to Find, Analyze & Use. 1992. pap. 24.95 (*1-55738-472-X*, Irwn Prfssnl) McGraw-Hill Prof.

Crispell, Kenneth & Gomez, Carlos F. Hidden Illness in the White House. LC 88-7158. (Illus.). xiv, 269p. 1988. text 38.95 (*0-8223-0839-8*) Duke.

Crispell, Kenneth, et al. Papers on Presidential Disability & the Twenty-Fifth Amendment. Thompson, Kenneth W., ed. 144p. 1997. 46.50 (*0-7618-0724-1*); pap. 26.50 (*0-7618-0725-X*) U Pr of Amer.

Crispelli, Paul. Trust Me. 15p. 1993. pap. 2.00 (*1-884047-59-9*) Mass Extinct.

Crispen, Joanne L., ed. The Americans with Disabilities Act: Its Impact on Libraries & the Library's Response in "Doable" Steps. LC 92-37146. 163p. 1993. pap. 28.00 (*0-8389-7636-0*) ALA.

Crispen, P. D. Atlas for the Information Superhighway. (DF - Computer Applications Ser.). 320p. 1996. pap., mass mkt., spiral bd. 41.95 (*0-538-65864-9*) S-W Pub.

***Crispen, Patrick D., et al.** Web Page Design. LC 99-231667. 192p. 1999. pap. 31.95 (*0-538-68997-8*) Sth-Wstrn College.

Crispi, Luca, jt. ed. see Herbert, Stacey.

Crispian Scully. Color Atlas of Oral Pathology. (Illus.). 137p. (C). (gr. 13). 1995. text 71.95 (*0-8151-7590-6*, 21954) Mosby Inc.

Crispin, A. C. Exiles Trilogy, No. 2. Date not set. mass mkt. write for info. (*0-380-78285-5*) Morrow Avon.

Crispin, A. C. The Eyes of the Beholders. Stern, David, ed. (Star Trek: The Next Generation Ser.: No. 13). 256p. 1990. mass mkt. 5.50 (*0-671-70010-3*) PB.

— The Hutt Gambit. (Star Wars: No. 2). 368p. (YA). (gr. 5 up). 1997. mass mkt. 5.99 (*0-553-57416-7*, Spectra) Bantam.

— The Paradise Snare. (Star Wars: No. 1). 336p. (YA). (gr. 5 up). 1997. mass mkt. 5.99 (*0-553-57415-9*, Spectra) Bantam.

— The Paradise Snare. (Star Wars: No. 1). (YA). (gr. 5 up). 1997. 11.09 (*0-606-11896-9*, Pub. by Turtleback) Demco.

— Rebel Dawn. (Star Wars: No. 3). 400p. (YA). (gr. 5 up). 1998. mass mkt. 5.99 (*0-553-57417-5*) Bantam.

***Crispin, A. C.** Rebel Dawn, Set. abr. ed. (Star Wars: No. 3). (YA). (gr. 5 up). 1998. audio 16.99 (*0-553-47746-3*, 395670) BDD Aud Pub.

Crispin, A. C. Resurrection. limited ed. (Alien Ser.). 1997. mass mkt. 134.73 (*0-446-16497-6*, Aspect) Warner Bks.

— Sarek. Ryan, Kevin, ed. (Star Trek Ser.). 416p. 1995. per. 5.99 (*0-671-79562-7*, Star Trek) PB.

***Crispin, A. C.** Sarek. (Star Trek Ser.). 416p. 2000. mass mkt. 3.99 (*0-7434-0374-6*) PB.

Crispin, A. C. Starbridge. 1989. mass mkt. 4.99 (*0-441-78329-5*) Ace Bks.

— Time for Yesterday. (Star Trek Ser.: No. 39). 288p. 1989. mass mkt. 5.50 (*0-671-70094-4*) PB.

— Time for Yesterday. 1999. mass mkt. 3.99 (*0-671-03857-5*) PB.

— Voices of Chaos. (Starbridge Ser.). 1998. mass mkt. 5.99 (*0-441-00516-0*) Ace Bks.

— Yesterday's Son. 1999. mass mkt. 3.99 (*0-671-03851-6*) PB.

Crispin, A. C., contrib. by. Alien: Resurrection. 288p. (Orig.). 1997. mass mkt. 4.99 (*0-446-60229-9*, Pub. by Warner Bks) Little.

Crispin, A. C. & King, T. Jackson. Ancestor's World. (Starbridge Ser.: No. 6). 1996. mass mkt. 5.99 (*0-441-00351-6*) Ace Bks.

Crispin, A. C. & O'Malley, Kathleen. Silent Songs. (Starbridge Ser.: No. 05). 304p. (Orig.). 1994. mass mkt. 4.99 (*0-441-00061-4*) Ace Bks.

Crispin, A. C., jt. auth. see Norton, Andre.

Crispin, Alan J. Programmable Logic Controllers & Their Engineering Applications. 2nd ed. LC 96-27718. 1996. pap. write for info. (*0-07-709317-8*) McGraw.

Crispin, Edmund. Beware of Trains & Other Stories. 1976. 20.95 (*0-8488-0469-4*) Amereon Ltd.

— Buried for Pleasure. 191p. reprint ed. lib. bdg. 20.95 (*0-89190-691-6*, Rivercity Pr) Amereon Ltd.

— Fen Country. 18.95 (*0-89190-694-0*) Amereon Ltd.

— Frequent Hearses. large type ed. LC 93-20751. (General Ser.). 311p. 1994. lib. bdg. 16.95 (*0-8161-5860-6*, G K Hall Lrg Type) Mac Lib Ref.

— The Glimpses of the Moon. 23.95 (*0-89190-695-9*) Amereon Ltd.

— Holy Disorders. 1976. 22.95 (*0-8488-0468-6*) Amereon Ltd.

— Love Lies Bleeding. 20.95 (*0-89190-693-2*) Amereon Ltd.

— The Moving Toy Shop. 20.95 (*0-8488-0104-0*) Amereon Ltd.

Crispin, Edmund. The Moving Toy Shop. LC 99-996984. 208p. 1989. pap. 6.99 (*0-14-008817-2*, Penguin Bks) Viking Penguin.

Crispin, Edmund. Swan Song. LC 80-80453. 192p. 1980. 16.95 (*0-8027-5420-1*) Boulevard.

— Swan Song. large type ed. (Linford Mystery Library). 311p. 1987. pap. 16.99 (*0-7089-6361-7*, Linford) Ulverscroft.

— Swan Song. 1993. reprint ed. lib. bdg. 16.95 (*1-56849-195-6*) Buccaneer Bks.

Crispin, Gerry & Mehler, Mark. Career X Roads: Your Internet Directory for Jobs/Recruiting. 200p. (Orig.). 1996. pap. 19.95 (*0-9652239-6-5*) MMC Grp.

— Career XRoads: 1998 Directory to Jobs, Resumes, & Career Management on the World Wide Web. 3rd rev. ed. 350p. 1998. pap. 19.95 (*0-9652239-4-9*) MMC Grp.

— Careerx Roads: The 2000 Directory to the 500 Best Job Resume & Career Management Senses on the World Wide Web. 5th rev. ed. 416p. 1999. pap. 26.95 (*0-9652239-2-2*, Pub. by MMC Grp) IEEE Comp Soc.

— Careerxroads: The 1999 Directory to the 500 Best Job Resume & Career Management Sites on the World Wide Web. 4th rev. ed. 354p. 1998. 24.95 (*0-9652239-3-0*) MMC Grp.

Crispin, John. Pedor Salinas. LC 73-17149. (Twayne's World Authors Ser.). 180p. (C). 1974. lib. bdg. 20.95 (*0-8057-2784-1*) Irvington.

Crispin, John, tr. see Hiller, Phyllis U.

Crispin-Little, Jan & Ricks, Gary K. Utah's High Technology Directory, 1993. Gillam, Diane, ed. 100p. (Orig.). 1993. pap. 10.00 (*0-942486-09-9*) Univ Utah.

— Utah's High Technology Directory, 1996. Gillam, Diane S., ed. 104p. (Orig.). 1996. pap. 15.00 (*0-942486-12-9*) Univ Utah.

Crispin, M. Jackson & Macary, Leonce. Falaise Roll: Recording Prominent Companions of William Duke of Normandy at the Conquest of England. (Illus.). 258p. 1994. reprint ed. 30.00 (*0-8063-0080-9*, 1210) Genealog Pub.

Crispin, Sheila M., jt. ed. see Petersen-Jones, Simon M.

Crispin, William F. Crispin. Biographical & Historical Sketch of Captain William Crispin of the British Navy . . . Also an Historical Research Concerning the Remote Ancestry of English & American Crispin . . . to Which Is Added a Section on Genealogy & Ancestry. (Illus.). 144p. 1997. reprint ed. pap. 24.00 (*0-8328-8144-9*); reprint ed. lib. bdg. 34.00 (*0-8328-8143-0*) Higginson Bk Co.

Crispino, D. M. & Hooper, John R. The Chevrolet Pace Car Book from 1948-1990. (Illus.). v, 218 p. 1992. pap. text 21.95 (*0-9633802-1-4*) I&D Pubns.

Crispino, Enrica. Van Gogh. LC 97-118073. (Masters of Art Ser.). (Illus.). 64p. (J). (gr. 4-7). 1996. lib. bdg. 22.50 (*0-87226-525-0*, 65250B, P Bedrick Books) NTC Contemp Pub Co.

Crispo, Cassand, jt. auth. see Crispo, Chad.

Crispo, Chad & Crispo, Cassand. Love Ripples of the Sunstar's Tree. LC 91-70114. (Illus.). 75p. (Orig.). 1991. pap. 15.95 (*0-945306-01-6*) W F Garnett.

Crispo, Dorothy. The Story of Our Fruits & Vegetables. pap. 7.95 (*0-8159-6826-4*) Devin.

Crispolti, Enrico & Siligato, Rosella, eds. Lucio Fontana: Catalogue Rome, 1998. (Illus.). 375p. 1998. pap. 65.00 (*88-435-6521-4*) Gingko Press.

Criss, Bilge. Istanbul under Allied Occupation, 1918-1923. LC 98-42291. (Ottoman Empire & Its Heritage Ser.). 1999. 70.00 (*90-04-11259-6*) Brill Academic Pubs.

Criss, Dani. Family in the Making. (Romance Ser.). 1995. per. 2.99 (*0-373-19065-4*, 1-19065-1) Silhouette.

— Family Ties. 1995. per. 2.99 (*0-373-19112-X*, 1-19112-1) Silhouette.

— For Kaitlyn's Sake. 1997. per. 3.99 (*0-373-07822-6*, 1-07822-9) Silhouette.

Criss, Lydia. Sealed with a Kiss - The Lydia Criss KISS Scrapbook. Conte, Robert V., ed. LC 97-62416. (Illus.). 144p. 1998. pap. 29.95 (*1-890313-03-3*, RCTP9803, Silver Skull) Studio Chikara.

***Criss, Robert E.** Principles of Stable Isotope Distribution. LC 98-24609. (Illus.). 264p. 1999. text 65.00 (*0-19-511775-1*) OUP.

Criss, Wayne E., et al, eds. Control Mechanisms in Cancer. LC 75-30234. (Progress in Cancer Research & Therapy Ser.: No. 1). (Illus.). 481p. reprint ed. pap. 149.20 (*0-7837-7102-9*, 204693100004) Bks Demand.

Criss, Wayne E., jt. ed. see Sharma, Rameshwar K.

Crissey, Brian, ed. see Leir, Roger K.

Crissey, Brian L., ed. see Lauck, Joanne E.

Crissey, Harrington E., Jr. Athletes Away. (Illus.). 75p. (Orig.). 1984. pap. 4.00 (*0-9608878-3-0*) H E Crissey.

— Teenagers, Graybeards & 4-F's. Incl. Vol. 2. American League. (Illus.). 179p. 1982. pap. 11.00 (*0-9608878-1-4*); pap. write for info. (*0-9608878-2-2*) H E Crissey.

Crissey, Harrinton, ed. see Tchaikovskaya, Yelena.

Crissey, John T. & Parish, Lawrence C. The Dermatology & Syphilology of the Nineteenth Century. LC 81-1954. 439p. 1981. 115.00 (*0-275-91343-0*, C1343, Praeger Pubs) Greenwood.

Crissey, John T., et al. Manual of Medical Mycology. LC 94-3339. (Illus.). 300p. 1995. 79.95 (*0-86542-363-6*) Blackwell Sci.

Crissey, Theron W., jt. auth. see Eldridge, Joseph T.

Crissman, Charles C., et al, eds. Economic, Environmental, & Health Tradeoffs in Agriculture: Pesticides & the Sustainability of Andean Potato Production. LC 97-41524. (Natural Resource Management & Policy Ser.: No. 12). 408p. 1997. 187.00 (*0-7923-8056-8*) Kluwer Academic.

Crissman, Charles C., et al. Economic, Environmental, & Health Tradeoffs in Agriculture: Pesticides & the Sustainability of Andean Potato Production. LC 97-41524. (Natural Resource Management & Policy Ser.). 1997. pap. text. write for info. (*0-7923-8057-6*) Kluwer Academic.

Crissman, James. Jailbait in Holy Water. 1998. pap. 7.95 (*0-944754-60-0*) Pudding Hse Pubns.

Crissman, James K. Death & Dying in Central Appalachia: Changing Attitudes & Practices. LC 93-23784. (Illus.). 264p. 1994. text 39.95 (*0-252-02061-8*); pap. text 14.95 (*0-252-06355-4*) U of Ill Pr.

Crissman, Randy D., jt. ed. see Caldwell, Stan R.

Crissman, Randy D., jt. ed. see Ryan, William L.

Crisswell, Colin N. The Taipans: Hong Kong's Merchant Princes. (Illus.). 260p. 1991. pap. text 18.95 (*0-19-585373-3*, 12303) OUP.

Crist, jt. auth. see Browne.

Crist, jt. auth. see Krause.

Crist, jt. auth. see Parker.

Crist, Ann D. Love & Libido: Index of Modern Authors & Subjects with Guide for Rapid Research. LC 90-56243. 190p. 1991. 47.50 (*1-55914-236-7*); pap. 44.50 (*1-55914-237-5*) ABBE Pubs Assn.

***Crist, B. Vincent.** Handbook of Monochromatic XPS Spectra, 3 vols. LC 00-32484. 2000. pap. write for info. (*0-471-49266-3*) Wiley.

***Crist, Caroline & Ayers, Becky.** Stones to Bread. 454p. 1999. pap. write for info. (*0-7392-0384-3*, PO3605) Morris Pubng.

Crist, Darlene T. Losing Eubie. (Illus.). 40p. (J). (gr. 3-5). 1998. pap. 9.95 (*0-9665072-0-7*) Red Bird Publ.

Crist, Dean, jt. auth. see Sumichrast, Michael.

Crist, Ed, jt. auth. see Krause, John.

Crist, Edward. Erie Memories. (Illus.). 1994. 39.95 (*0-915276-53-4*) Quadrant Pr.

Crist, Eileen. Images of Animals. LC 98-19425. (Animals, Culture & Society Ser.). (Illus.). 256p. 2000. text 69.50 (*1-56639-656-5*) Temple U Pr.

***Crist, Eileen.** Images of Animals: Anthropomorphism & Animal Mind. (Animals, Culture & Society Ser.). (Illus.). 256p. 2000. pap. 22.95 (*1-56639-788-X*) Temple U Pr.

Crist-Evans, Craig. Moon over Tennessee: A Boy's Civil War Journal. LC 98-11912. (Illus.). 64p. (YA). (gr. 3 up). 1999. 15.00 (*0-395-91208-3*) HM.

Crist, Gary M. In the Zone: A Novel about Championship Golf. 186p. 1998. pap. 11.95 (*0-9664366-1-X*) Down the Middle.

Crist, Harold L. Back to the Alleghenies. large type ed. (Illus.). 281p. (Orig.). 1995. pap. text 8.50 (*0-9621743-2-7*) H L Crist.

— Seven Moons to Texas. (Illus.). 121p. 1997. pap. 8.50 (*0-9621743-3-5*) H L Crist.

— Twice a Hero. 112p. (Orig.). (YA). 1990. pap. 5.95 (*0-9621743-1-9*) H L Crist.

-Where Virgins Abound. LC 88-92740. (Illus.). 106p. 1989. reprint ed. pap. text 7.00 (*0-9621743-0-0*) H L Crist.

Around the turn of he century Pocahontas County & surrounding areas became a mecca for those seeking to reap the stands of virgin timber. The hardwoods of oak, hickory, male & birch grew on the slopes & valleys while the pines & spruce crowned the Appalachians. The saw soon changed the scenic beauty of these towering sentinels top stubble & waste, leaving scars that would take years to heal. Railroad radiating from the main hub into the hollows brought logs to the swollen streams that carried them to the mill where powerful saws ripped them into aromatic slivers to be shipped to the eastern markets. Today, remains of this glorious era can still be seen. WHERE VIRGINS ABOUND is of this era. Fact or fiction, true or make-believe-only the mind needs to make a distinction. Available from author. Call for more information. *Publisher Paid Annotation.*

Crist, J. Take 22. 1999. pap. write for info. (*0-14-009462-8*, Penguin Bks) Viking Penguin.

Crist, James J. ADHD: A Teenagers Guide. 175p. (YA). 1996. pap. 19.95 (*1-882732-41-3*) Childswork.

Crist, Joseph G. Reporting, Recordkeeping & Disclosure Requirements for an Environmental Audit. (Environmental Audit Handbook Ser.: Vol. 2). 1989. pap. 49.95 (*1-55840-064-8*) Exec Ent Pubns.

Crist, Judith, jt. intro. see Vermilye, Jerry.

***Crist, Linda A.** Ballet Barre & Center Combinations: Word Descriptions. 236p. 2000. pap. 34.95 (*0-87127-220-2*) Princeton Bk Co.

— Ballet Barre & Center Combinations Vol. 3: Labanotation. 282p. 2000. pap. 49.95 (*0-87127-222-9*) Princeton Bk Co.

Crist, Linda A. Three-by-Three. LC 92-524579. 41p. (C). 1991. pap. text 25.00 (*0-9620289-1-6*) Crist Pubns.

Crist, Linda A., ed. see Martinet, Francoise.

Crist, Lyle. Afterwords: An English Prof's Reflections on a Campus Career. (Illus.). 198p. (Orig.). 1989. pap. write for info. (*0-9624800-0-2*) Mt Union Coll.

Crist, Lyle, jt. auth. see Bara, Craig.

Crist, Lynda L., ed. see Davis, Jefferson.

Crist, Maria P. The Internet: Strategies for Effective Use in Law Practice. LC 98-85287. (Illus.). 165p. 1998. pap. text 40.00 (*0-9664544-0-5*) OSBACLE Institute.

Crist, Marilyn I., jt. auth. see Parker, Henry H.

Crist, Nancy. Everything's Relative. 82p. 1991. pap. 5.50 (*0-87129-052-9*, E29) Dramatic Pub.

***Crist, Nancy & Sheedy, Rose.** Spin, Say & Do: Includes S, R, L, Blends, CH, SH & TH. (Illus.). 139p. (J). (ps-6). 1998. spiral bd., wbk. ed. 26.95 (*1-58650-069-4*, BK-267) Super Duper.

Crist, Nancy, jt. auth. see Sheedy, Rose.

Crist, Patricia & Royeen, Charlotte B., eds. Infusing Occupation Into Practice: Comparison of Three Clinical Approaches in Occupational Therapy. LC 97-174733. 112p. (Orig.). (C). 1997. pap. text 22.00 (*1-56900-077-8*) Am Occup Therapy.

Crist, Patricia A., ed. Innovations in Occupational Therapy Education (IOTE) (Illus.). 1999. pap. 25.00 (*1-56900-119-7*) Am Occup Therapy.

Crist, Robert, tr. from GRE. Grind the Big Tooth. LC 97-66941. (Illus.). 64p. 1997. pap. 7.99 (*1-56315-075-1*) SterlingHse.

Crist, Robert G., ed. Penn's Example to the Nations: 300 Years of the Holy Experiment. LC 86-63552. (Illus.). 276p. (Orig.). 1987. 18.95 (*0-9618164-0-6*) PA Coun Churches.

Crist Staff. Two Colts. 0.00 (*0-393-02239-0*) Norton.

***Crist, Terry.** Discover the Power of Being Made in His Image. 2000. pap. 12.99 (*0-88419-637-2*) Creation House.

Crist, Terry. Leaving the Comfort Zone. 47p. 1991. pap. 5.99 (*0-88368-221-4*) Whitaker Hse.

— The Meek Shall Inherit the Earth - But Who Wants It? Peacock, Jimmy, ed. 64p. (Orig.). 1990. pap. 4.95 (*0-9623768-9-2*) SpiritBuilder.

— The Power of Praying in Other Tongues: Mini Book. Peacock, Jimmy, ed. (Illus.). (Orig.). (C). 1990. 1.00 (*0-9623768-5-X*) SpiritBuilder.

Crist, Terry M., Jr. Interceding Against the Powers of Darkness. Peacock, Jimmy, ed. (Illus.). 144p. (Orig.). (C). 1990. pap. 5.95 (*0-685-35591-8*) SpiritBuilder.

— Leaving the Comfort Zone: A Call to Cutting Edge Christianity. Peacock, Jimmy, ed. (Illus.). 150p. (Orig.). (C). 1990. pap. 5.95 (*0-9623768-4-1*) SpiritBuilder.

— The Prophetic Church. Mackall, Phyllis, ed. (Illus.). (Orig.). (C). 1989. pap. 5.95 (*0-9623768-0-9*) SpiritBuilder.

— A Time for War. 64p. (Orig.). (C). 1989. student ed. 10.00 (*0-9623768-1-7*) SpiritBuilder.

— Warring According to Prophecy. Peacock, Jimmy, ed. (Illus.). 63p. (Orig.). (C). 1990. pap. 4.95 (*0-9623768-2-5*) SpiritBuilder.

Crist, Vonnie W. & Wasserman, Debra. Leprechaun Cake & Other Tales: A Vegetarian Story-Cookbook. Stahler, Charles, ed. LC 94-61558. (Illus.). 128p. (Orig.). (J). (gr. 1-5). 1995. pap. text 9.95 (*0-931411-13-0*) Vegetarian Resc.

Crist, Vonnie Winslow. Essential Fables: Poems & Art by Vonnie Winslow Crist. (Illus.). 93p. 1996. 9.95 (*0-9641622-0-2*) Lite Circle.

***Crist, Vonnie Winslow & Kriebel, David W., eds.** Lower Than the Angels: Science Fact, Science Fiction & Fantasy. 192p. 1999. pap. 14.95 (*0-9641622-2-9*) Lite Circle.

***Cristaldi, Kathryn.** Around the World in Tweety Time: Tattoo Storybook. (Illus.). 24p. (ps-3). 2000. pap. text 5.99 (*0-439-20282-5*) Scholastic Inc.

Cristaldi, Kathryn. Baseball Ballerina. LC 90-20234. (Step into Reading Ser.: A Step 2 Book). (Illus.). 48p. (J). (gr. 1-3). 1992. pap. 3.99 (*0-679-81734-4*, Pub. by Random Bks Yng Read) Random.

Cristaldi, Kathryn. Baseball Ballerina. (Step into Reading Ser.: A Step 2 Book). (J). (gr. 1-3). 1992. 9.19 (*0-606-01496-9*, Pub. by Turtleback) Demco.

Cristaldi, Kathryn. Christmas in Toyland. (J). 1997. pap. 2.75 (*0-679-88877-2*, Pub. by Random Bks Yng Read) Random.

— Disney's The Hunchback of Notre Dame, Level 3. LC 96-85692. (Disney's First Readers Ser.). (Illus.). 40p. (J). (gr. 2-4). 1997. pap. 3.50 (*0-7868-4106-0*, Pub. by Disney Pr) Time Warner.

— Even Steven & Odd Todd. LC 95-13239. (Hello Math Reader Ser.: Level 3). (Illus.). 32p. (J). (gr. 1-3). 1996. pap. 3.99 (*0-590-22715-7*, Cartwheel) Scholastic Inc.

— Even Steven & Odd Todd. LC 95-13239. (Hello Math Reader Ser.). 1996. 9.19 (*0-606-09244-7*, Pub. by Turtleback) Demco.

— Hide-&-Seek, Level 2. (Disney First Reader Ser.: No. 9). (Illus.). 32p. (J). (ps-1). 1998. pap. 2.95 (*0-7868-4074-9*, Pub. by Disney Pr) Time Warner.

— Princess Lulu Goes to Camp. LC 96-30742. (All Aboard Reading Ser.: Level 2). (Illus.). 48p. (J). (gr. 1-3). 1997. pap. 3.95 (*0-448-41125-3*, G & D) Peng Put Young Read.

— Princess Lulu Goes to Camp. LC 96-30742. (All Aboard Reading Ser.). 1997. 9.15 (*0-606-11764-4*, Pub. by Turtleback) Demco.

— Samantha the Snob. LC 93-19649. (Step into Reading Ser.: A Step 2 Book). (Illus.). 48p. (J). (gr. k-2). 1994. pap. 3.99 (*0-679-84640-9*, Pub. by Random Bks Yng Read) Random.

— Samantha the Snob. LC 93-19649. (Step into Reading Ser.: A Step 2 Book). (Illus.). 48p. (J). (ps-3). 1994. lib. bdg. 11.99 (*0-679-94640-3*, Pub. by Random Bks Yng Read) Random.

Cristaldi, Kathryn. Samantha the Snob. (Step into Reading Ser.: A Step 2 Book). (J). (gr. 1-3). 1994. 9.19 (*0-606-07076-1*, Pub. by Turtleback) Demco.

Cristaldi, Kathryn. The Secret Garden. (Illus.). 32p. (J). (ps-3). 1993. pap. 2.95 (*0-590-47170-8*) Scholastic Inc.

***Cristaldi, Kathryn.** Tweety's High-Flying Adventure. (Illus.). 32p. (J). (ps-3). 2000. pap. text 3.50 (*0-439-20281-7*) Scholastic Inc.

***Cristaldi, Kathryn & Adams, Lynn.** Training Wheels. LC 99-41298. (Hello Reader! Ser.). (Illus.). (J). 2000. write for info. (*0-439-09913-7*) Scholastic Inc.

Cristall, Barbara. Coping When a Parent Has Multiple Sclerosis. Rosen, Ruth C., ed. (Coping Ser.). (YA). (gr. 7-12). 1992. lib. bdg. 17.95 (*0-8239-1406-2*) Rosen Group.

Cristaudo, Wayne. The Metaphysics of Science & Freedom: From Descartes to Kant to Hegel. (Avebury Series in Philosophy). 187p. 1991. text 82.95 (*1-85628-132-9*, Pub. by Avebury) Ashgate Pub Co.

Cristaudo, Wayne, jt. auth. see Catley, Bob.

Cristel, Francine. Skipping a Grade Can Be Fun. 1984. pap. 5.00 (*0-89824-037-9*) Trillium Pr.

Cristescu, N. Rock Rheology. (C). 1988. text 226.50 (*90-247-3660-9*) Kluwer Academic.

Cristescu, N. & Hunsche, U. Time Effects in Rock Mechanics. LC 97-35151. 350p. 1997. 160.00 (*0-471-95517-5*) Wiley.

Cristescu, N. D. & Gioda, G., eds. Visco-Plastic Behaviour of Geomaterials. (CISM International Centre for Mechanical Sciences: Vol. 350). 317p. 1994. 86.95 (*0-387-82586-X*) Spr-Verlag.

Cristescu, Romulus & Marinescu, Gheorgha. Applications of the Theory of Distributions. Teleman, Silviu, tr. from RUM. LC 72-9080. 227p. reprint ed. pap. 70.40 (*0-8357-5673-4*, 201614600098) Bks Demand.

Cristi, Renato. Carl Schmitt & Authoritarian Liberalism: Strong State, Free Economy. LC 98-206620. (Political Philosophy Now Ser.). 192p. 1998. 55.00 (*0-7083-1440-6*, Pub. by Univ Wales Pr); pap. 25.00 (*0-7083-1441-4*, Pub. by Univ Wales Pr) Paul & Co Pubs.

Cristiani, Leon. Evidence of Satan in the Modern World. Rowland, Cynthia, tr. from FRE. LC 62-9278. 1977. reprint ed. pap. 10.00 (*0-89555-032-6*) TAN Bks Pubs.

— St. Bernard of Clairvaux. LC 77-4942. 174p. 1977. 4.50 (*0-8198-0463-0*) Pauline Bks.

— The Village Priest Who Fought God's Battles. 176p. 1977. pap. 4.50 (*0-8198-0481-9*) Pauline Bks.

Cristiani, Therese S., jt. auth. see George, Rickey L.

***Cristianini, Nello & Shawe-Taylor, John.** An Introduction to Support Vector Machines: And Other Kernel-Based Learning Methods. LC 99-54716. (Illus.). 204p. 2000. text 44.95 (*0-521-78019-5*) Cambridge U Pr.

Cristin, Renato. Heidegger & Leibniz: Reason & the Path. LC 98-20769. (Contributions to Phenomenology Ser.). 132p. 1998. 98.00 (*0-7923-5137-1*) Kluwer Academic.

Cristina, George R. di, see di Cristina, George R.

***Cristini, Annalisa.** Unemployment & Primary Commodity Prices: Theory & Evidence in a Global Perspective. LC 98-44643. 176p. 1999. text 69.95 (*0-312-22036-7*) St Martin.

Cristini, Ermanno & Puricelli, Luigi. In My Garden. LC 85-9402. (Illus.). 28p. (J). (ps up). 1991. pap. 12.95 (*0-907234-05-4*, Picture Book Studio) S&S Childrens.

Cristino, Donna M., jt. auth. see Cristino, George.

Cristino, Donna M., ed. see Cristino, George.

Cristino, George. The Anatomy of the Next Century: New Technologies, Materials & Their Applications in Medicine. 200p. 1997. pap. text 640.00 (*1-886974-15-2*) Inst Knowledge.

— Suggested Anatomical Landmarks for Entree Ports in Endoscopy. 2nd ed. Cristino, Donna M., ed. (Illus.). 223p. (C). 1995. text 220.00 (*1-886974-03-9*) Inst Knowledge.

— Trocars & Pneumoperitoneum Needles in Minimally Invasive Surgery: Litigation, Legal, Marketing & Design. 1996. 465.00 (*1-886974-14-4*) Inst Knowledge.

Cristino, George & Cristino, Donna M. Gecris Endoscopy Dictionary. 2nd ed. 172p. (C). 1996. text 85.00 (*1-886974-09-8*) Inst Knowledge.

— History of Endoscopy Developments. 2nd ed. 52p. (C). 1996. text 85.00 (*1-886974-06-3*) Inst Knowledge.

— Medical Research Data: Essential Information for Scientists & Engineers in Medical Devices Industry. 2nd ed. (Illus.). 387p. (C). 1996. text 295.00 (*1-886974-04-7*) Inst Knowledge.

Cristino, George & Zhuk, Yuri N. Worldwide Medical Applications of Shape Memory Alloy Implants & Instrumentation. (Illus.). 56p. (C). 1997. text 625.00 (*1-886974-11-X*) Inst Knowledge.

Cristo, Albert Di, see Hirst, Daniel & Di Cristo, Albert, eds.

Cristofalo, V. & Adelman, Richard C. Handbook of Cell Biology of Aging. LC 84-14312. (Series in Aging). 608p. 1985. lib. bdg. 279.95 (*0-8493-3142-0*, CRC Reprint) Franklin.

Cristofalo, Vincent J., ed. Annual Review of Gerontology & Geriatrics: Biology of Aging, Vol. 10. 240p. (C). 1990. 46.00 (*0-8261-6492-7*) Springer Pub.

Cristofano, Sam M. & Foster, William S., eds. Management of Local Public Works. (Municipal Management Ser.). 448p. 1986. text 41.95 (*0-87326-048-1*) Intl City-Cnty Mgt.

Cristofer, Michael. Black Angel. 1984. pap. 5.25 (*0-8222-0124-0*) Dramatists Play.

— The Lady & the Clarinet. 102p. 1985. pap. 5.25 (*0-8222-0627-7*) Dramatists Play.

Cristoffanini, Pablo R. Dominacion y Legitimidad Politica en Hispanoamerica: Un Estudio de la Historia de las Ideas Politicas en la Experiencia Colonial y la Formacion del Estado Nacional en Chile. 192p. 1996. pap. 23.00 (*87-7288-307-3*, Pub. by Aarhus Univ Pr) David Brown.

Cristofoi, Marilyn, ed. Hanya Holm: A Pioneer in American Dance, Vol. 2, Part 2. 120p. 1992. pap. text 15.00 (*3-7186-5277-3*, Harwood Acad Pubs) Gordon & Breach.

Cristoforo, R. The Table Saw Book. 1991. 23.95 (*0-8306-5304-X*) McGraw-Hill Prof.

Cristol, Gerry. A Light in the Prairie: Temple Emanu-el of Dallas, 1872-1997. LC 97-37503. (Illus.). 296p. 1998. 29.95 (*0-87565-184-4*) Tex Christian.

Cristol, Jaymi. Three Wishes. (Lucky in Love Ser.: No. 28). 304p. 1993. mass mkt. 3.50 (*0-8217-4114-4*, Zebra Kensgtn) Kensgtn Pub Corp.

***Cristol, Steven M. & Sealey, Peter.** Simplicity Marketing: Relieving Customer Stress in the Digital Age. 2000. 26.00 (*0-684-85918-1*) Free Pr.

Cristoloveanu, S., et al, eds. Silicon-on-Insulator Technology & Devices VIII. LC 97-197227. (Proceedings Ser.: Vol. 97-23). 414p. 1997. 73.00 (*1-56677-176-5*) Electrochem Soc.

Cristoloveanu, Sorin & Li, Sheng S. Electrical Characterization of Silicon-on-Insulator Materials & Devices. LC 94-43971. (International Series in Engineering & Computer Science: Vol. 305). 400p. (C). 1995. text 151.50 (*0-7923-9548-4*) Kluwer Academic.

Cristoloveanu, Sorin, ed. see International Symposium on Silicon-on-Insulator Te.

Crisuolo, Claire. Claire's Classic American Vegetarian Cooking. 1996. 24.95 (*0-614-19365-6*) NAL.

Criswell, Ann. Houston Is Cooking! 1993. pap. text 15.95 (*1-882296-01-X*) Houston Gourmet.

— Houston Is Cooking at Home. Steiner, Ann, ed. LC 98-229521. (Illus.). 144p. 1998. pap. 21.95 (*1-882296-04-4*) Houston Gourmet.

— Houston Is Cooking the Best. McDonald, Linda & Moody, Denman, eds. (Illus.). 128p. (Orig.). 1996. pap. 19.95 (*1-882296-03-6*) Houston Gourmet.

***Criswell, Ann.** Houston Is Cooking 2000. (Illus.). 156p. 1999. pap. 21.95 (*1-882296-05-2*) Houston Gourmet.

Criswell, Ann & McDonald, Linda. Houston Gourmet Cooks! Cookbook & Chefs. 112p. (Orig.). 1987. pap. text. write for info. (*0-9613643-3-5*) Houston Gourmet.

— Houston Gourmet Cooks!! Two Cookbooks & Chefs. 112p. (Orig.). 1988. pap. text. write for info. (*0-9613643-5-1*) Houston Gourmet.

— Houston Gourmet Cooks & Caterers: Cookbook, Showcase Chefs & Caterers. 112p. (Orig.). 1990. pap. text. write for info. (*0-9613643-7-8*) Houston Gourmet.

Criswell, Charles. Nobody Knows What the Stork Will Bring. 1958. 11.95 (*0-8392-1076-0*) Astor-Honor.

Criswell, D., jt. auth. see Lunar & Planetary Institute Staff.

Criswell, E. H., et al. Oil Refinery Terms in Oklahoma, Experiment in State-Wide Dialect Collecting, Problems Confronting the Investigator of Gullah. (Publications of the American Dialect Society Ser.: No. 9). 89p. 1948. pap. text 8.90 (*0-8173-0609-9*) U of Ala Pr.

Criswell, Eleanor. Biofeedback & Somatics: Toward Personal Evolution. LC 96-212338. (Illus.). 217p. (Orig.). 1995. pap. 14.95 (*0-918236-06-1*) Freeperson.

— How Yoga Works: An Introduction to Somatic Yoga. (Illus.). 216p. 1987. pap. 14.95 (*0-318-37563-X*); pap. 14.95 (*0-918236-04-5*) Freeperson.

Criswell, Grover. Comprehensive Catalog of Confederate Paper Money. (Illus.). 356p. 1996. 35.00 (*0-931960-47-9*, 47-9) BNR Pr.

Criswell, Joan, et al, eds. Mathematical Methods in Small Group Processes. viii, 361p. 1962. 47.50 (*0-8047-0116-4*) Stanford U Pr.

Criswell, Joan H., ed. see Symposium on Mathematical Methods in Small Group P.

Criswell, John B. Cov: His Bird Dogs, His Field Trials. LC 92-90351. 312p. 1994. 25.00 (*0-9633790-0-3*) Cass Hill.

Criswell, John W. Maintenance Time Management. 132p. 1991. 57.00 (*0-88173-116-1*) Fairmont Pr.

— Planned Maintenance for Productivity & Energy Conservation. 3rd ed. (Illus.). 191p. Date not set. 57.00 (*0-88173-098-X*) Fairmont Pr.

Criswell, M. J., jt. auth. see Hughes, G. E.

Criswell, Millie. Dangerous. 384p. 1998. mass mkt. 5.99 (*0-446-60497-6*, Pub. by Warner Bks); mass mkt. 161.73 (*0-446-16541-7*) Warner Bks.

— Defiant. 368p. 1998. mass mkt. 5.99 (*0-446-60498-4*, Pub. by Warner Bks) Little.

— Desperate. 368p. 1997. reprint ed. mass mkt. 5.99 (*0-446-60415-1*, Pub. by Warner Bks) Little.

***Criswell, Millie.** The Marrying Man. 2000. per. 4.99 (*0-373-29108-6*) Harlequin Bks.

Criswell, Millie. Prim Rose. 352p. (Orig.). 1996. reprint ed. mass mkt. 5.99 (*0-446-60323-6*, Pub. by Warner Bks) Little.

— Sweet Laurel. 352p. (Orig.). 1996. reprint ed. mass mkt. 5.99 (*0-446-60172-1*, Pub. by Warner Bks) Little.

— True Love. 336p. 1999. mass mkt. 6.50 (*0-446-60499-2*, Pub. by Warner Bks) Little.

***Criswell, Millie.** The Wedding Planner. (American Romance Ser.: No. 810). 2000. per. 4.25 (*0-373-16810-1*, 1-16810-3, Harlequin) Harlequin Bks.

Criswell, Millie. Wild Heather. 352p. 1995. reprint ed. mass mkt. 5.99 (*0-446-60171-3*, Pub. by Warner Bks) Little.

Criswell, Robert. Uncle Tom's Cabin Contrasted with Buckingham Hall, the Planter's Home. LC 72-950. reprint ed. 32.50 (*0-404-00254-4*) AMS Pr.

Criswell, Sara D. Homelessness. LC 97-42439. (Overview Ser.). (Illus.). 112p. (YA). (gr. 7 up). 1997. lib. bdg. 22.45 (*1-56006-180-4*) Lucent Bks.

Criswell, Susie G. Nature Through Science & Art. (Illus.). 156p. (J). (gr. 3-6). text 22.95 (*0-8306-4575-6*) TAB Bks.

— Nature Through Science & Art. (Illus.). 156p. (J). (gr. 3-6). 1996. pap. 12.95 (*0-8306-4576-4*) TAB Bks.

Criswell, Susie G. & Gradwohl, Judith. Nature Through Science & Art. LC 93-38579. 1993. 22.95 (*0-07-013782-X*); pap. 12.95 (*0-07-013783-8*) McGraw-Hill Prof.

Criswell, W. A. The Baptism, Filling & Gifts of the Holy Spirit. 192p. 1984. pap. 7.95 (*0-310-22751-8*, 18351P) Zondervan.

— Expository Sermons on the Book of Ezekiel. 272p. 1987. 13.95 (*0-310-23010-1*, 18352) Zondervan.

— Great Doctrines of the Bible, Vol. 1. 144p. 1982. 13.95 (*0-310-43850-0*, 9427) Zondervan.

— Great Doctrines of the Bible, Vol. 5. 144p. 1985. 12.95 (*0-310-43930-2*, 11664) Zondervan.

— Great Doctrines of the Bible Vol. 2: Christology. 192p. (C). 1982. 13.95 (*0-310-43860-8*, 11660) Zondervan.

— Great Doctrines of the Bible Vol. 4: Pneumatology. 112p. 1984. 11.95 (*0-310-43910-8*, 11662) Zondervan.

— Great Doctrines of the Bible Vol. 6: Christian Life & Stewardship. 128p. 1986. 12.95 (*0-310-43950-7*, 11665) Zondervan.

— Great Doctrines of the Bible Vol. 7: Prayer & Angelology. 144p. 1987. 12.95 (*0-310-43960-4*, 11667) Zondervan.

***Criswell, W. A.** El Pastor y Su Ministerio: Una Guia Pratica. Eustache, Alirio, tr. Orig. Title: Criswell's Guidbook for Pastors. (SPA.). 368p. 1998. pap. text 14.99 (*0-311-42102-4*) Casa Bautista.

Critchell, Laurence. Four Stars of Hell. (Airborne Ser.: No. 13). (Illus.). 368p. 1982. reprint ed. 34.95 (*0-89839-059-1*) Battery Pr.

Critchell, Richard A., ed. Roofing Research & Standards Development. (Special Technical Publication Ser.: No. 959). (Illus.). 126p. 1987. text 26.00 (*0-8031-0956-3*, STP959) ASTM.

Critcher, C., et al. Sociology of Leisure: A Reader. (Illus.). 304p. (Orig.). (C). 1994. pap. 29.99 (*0-419-19420-7*, E & FN Spon) Routledge.

Critcher, Harold & Critcher, June, compiled by. Why We Are Happily Married. 1979. pap. 1.95 (*0-89265-054-0*) Randall Hse.

Critcher, Has, et al, eds. Regeneration of the Coalfield Areas: Anglo-German Perspectives. LC 95-3375. 194p. 1995. 69.95 (*1-85567-205-7*) St Martin.

Critcher, June, jt. compiled by see Critcher, Harold.

Critchett, Jan. A Distant Field of Murder: Western District Frontiers 1834-1848. 318p. 1992. pap. 19.95 (*0-522-84527-4*, Pub. by Melbourne Univ Pr) Paul & Co Pubs.

***Critchett, Jan.** Untold Stories: Memories & Lives of Victorian Kooris. 296p. 1999. pap. 29.95 (*0-522-84818-4*, Pub. by Melbourne Univ Pr) Paul & Co Pubs.

Critchett, Jan, ed. Richard Bennett's Early Days of Port Fairy. 92p. 1984. pap. 45.00 (*0-949759-32-5*, Pub. by Deakin Univ) St Mut.

Critchfield, F. & Belcher, R. Organic Functional Group Analysis. LC 62-22068. (International Series of Monographs on Analytical Chemistry: Vol. 8). 1963. 83.00 (*0-08-013500-5*, Pub. by Pergamon Repr) Franklin.

Critchfield, Howard J. General Climatology. 4th ed. (Illus.). 464p. (C). 1982. text 52.60 (*0-13-349217-6*) P-H.

Critchfield, Howard J., ed. Pacific Northwest: Essays in Honor of James W. Scott. 280p. (C). 1993. text 26.00 (*0-930216-06-7*); pap. text 16.00 (*0-930216-05-9*) West Wash Univ.

Critchfield, Margot A., jt. auth. see Dwyer, Thomas A.

Critchfield, Marty. The Art of Hitting: Controlled Insanity. deluxe ed. (Illus.). 22p. 1999. pap. 12.95 (*0-9672945-0-9*) M Critchfield.

Critchfield, Richard. Those Days. 1987. pap. 8.95 (*0-440-58505-8*, LE) Dell.

— Trees, Why Do You Wait? America's Changing Rural Culture. LC 90-20898. 265p. 1991. pap. 17.95 (*1-55963-028-0*); text 38.00 (*1-55963-029-9*) Island Pr.

— When Lucifer Cometh: The Autobiographical Discourse of Writers & Intellectuals Exiled During the Third Reich. LC 93-42551. (Literature & the Sciences of Man Ser.: Vol. 7). VII, 189p. (C). 1994. text 41.95 (*0-8204-2313-0*) P Lang Pubng.

Critchfield, Richard & Koepke, Wulf, eds. Eighteenth Century German Authors & Their Aesthetic Theories: Literature & the Other Arts. LC 87-70863. (GERM Ser.: Vol. 34). x, 230p. 1988. 35.00 (*0-938100-55-6*) Camden Hse.

Critchfield, Sandra, et al. K-8 Building Blocks for Algebra: Patterns, Functions, Relationships. (Illus.). 106p. 1998. teacher ed., spiral bd. 18.00 (*1-891677-04-7*) Appalachia Educ.

Critchley, B. B. Pests of Vegetables: Their Identification & Control in Ghana. 282p. 1997. pap. 90.00 (*0-85954-463-X*, Pub. by Nat Res Inst) St Mut.

Critchley, E., et al, eds. Diseases of the Spinal Cord. (Clinical Medicine & the Nervous System Ser.). (Illus.). xiii, 453p. 1992. 159.00 (*0-387-19684-6*) Spr-Verlag.

***Critchley, E. & Eisen, A., eds.** Spinal Cord Disease: Basic Science, Diagnosis & Management. (Illus.). xxv, 610p. 1999. pap. 89.00 (*1-85233-121-6*, Pub. by Spr-Verlag) Spr-Verlag.

Critchley, E. M. & Eisen, Andrew A., eds. Spinal Cord Disease: Basic Science, Diagnosis & Management, Vol. XIV. 2nd rev. ed. LC 96-24791. (Illus.). 610p. 1996. 169.00 (*3-540-19935-7*) Spr-Verlag.

Critchley, Eileen A., jt. auth. see Critchley, Macdonald.

Critchley, J., jt. auth. see Cartwright, J.

Critchley, J. P., et al, eds. Heat-Resistant Polymers: Technologically Useful Materials. LC 83-3987. 476p. 1983. 110.00 (*0-306-41058-3*, Plenum Trade) Perseus Pubng.

Critchley, Jay. Playing Games: Zoa, the Greek Fertility Goddess, Shoots for the Gold. (Illus.). 40p. (Orig.). 1995. pap. 7.95 (*0-9644145-2-X*) Parfait de Cocoa.

Critchley, John S. Marco Polo's Book. 224p. 1993. 83.95 (*0-86078-361-8*, Pub. by Variorum) Ashgate Pub Co.

Critchley, Julian. Floating Voter. large type ed. (Ulverscroft). 400p. 1994. 27.99 (*0-7089-3021-2*) Ulverscroft.

Critchley, Julian & Halcrow, Morrison. Collapse of Stout Party: The Decline & Fall of the Tories. (Illus.). 256p. 1998. 40.00 (*0-575-06277-0*, Pub. by V Gollancz) Trafalgar.

Critchley, Laurie & Windrath, Helen, eds. Feast! Women Write about Food. 151p. 1998. pap. 13.95 (*0-7043-4500-5*, Pub. by Womens Press) Trafalgar.

Critchley, Macdonald. The Citadel of the Senses & Other Essays. LC 85-2365. (Illus.). 287p. reprint ed. pap. 89.00 (*0-608-07231-1*, 206745600009) Bks Demand.

— The Divine Banquet of the Brain & Other Essays. LC 78-24621. (Illus.). 279p. 1979. reprint ed. pap. 86.50 (*0-608-07206-0*, 206743100009) Bks Demand.

— Language of Gesture. LC 74-122981. (Studies in Language: No. 41). 1970. reprint ed. lib. bdg. 75.00 (*0-8383-1113-X*) M S G Haskell Hse.

Critchley, MacDonald. Mirror Writing. LC 78-72793. reprint ed. 42.50 (*0-404-60857-4*) AMS Pr.

Critchley, Macdonald. The Ventricle of Memory: Personal Recollections of Some Neurologists. LC 89-11003. (Illus.). 223p. 1990. reprint ed. pap. 69.20 (*0-608-07204-4*, 206742900009) Bks Demand.

Critchley, Macdonald, ed. The Trial of August Sangret, No. 1. (Notable British Trials Ser.). xxiv, 233p. 1995. reprint ed. 78.00 (*1-56169-194-1*) Gaunt.

— The Trial of Neville George Clevely Heath. (Notable British Trials Ser.). 239p. 1995. reprint ed. 75.00 (*1-56169-186-0*) Gaunt.

Critchley, Macdonald & Critchley, Eileen A. John Hughlings Jackson: Father of English Neurology. (Illus.). 256p. 1998. text 59.50 (*0-19-512339-5*) OUP.

***Critchley, Simon.** Companion to Continental Philosophy. (Companions to Philosophy Ser.). 704p. 1999. pap. 34.95 (*0-631-21850-5*) Blackwell Pubs.

Critchley, Simon. Ethics - Politics - Subjectivity: Derrida, Levinas & Contemporary French Thought. 240p. 1998. 60.00 (*1-85984-849-4*, Pub. by Verso) Norton.

***Critchley, Simon.** Ethics of Deconstruction. 1999. pap. 24.95 (*1-55753-190-0*) Purdue U Pr.

— The Ethics of Deconstruction: Derrida & Levinas. 2nd ed. LC 99-487855. 312p. 2000. pap. text 25.00 (*0-7486-1217-3*) Col U Pr.

Critchley, Simon. Ethics-Politics-Subjectivity: Essays on Derrida, Levinas, & Contemporary French Thought. (Illus.). 302p. 1999. pap. 20.00 (*1-85984-246-1*, Pub. by Verso) Norton.

— Very Little - Almost Nothing: Death, Philosophy, Literature. LC 96-39076. (Warwick Studies in European Philosophy Ser.). 232p. (C). 1997. 80.00 (*0-415-12821-8*); pap. 22.99 (*0-415-12822-6*) Routledge.

Critchley, Simon & Dews, Peter, eds. Deconstructive Subjectivities. LC 95-10495. (SUNY Series in Contemporary Continental Philosophy). 257p. (C). 1996. text 64.50 (*0-7914-2723-4*); pap. text 21.95 (*0-7914-2724-2*) State U NY Pr.

Critchley, Simon & Schroeder, William, eds. A Companion to Continental Philosophy. LC 97-10146. (Companions to Philosophy Ser.: Vol. 11). 704p. (C). 1999. text 99.95 (*0-631-19013-9*) Blackwell Pubs.

Critchley, Simon, et al. Deconstruction & Pragmatism. Mouffe, Chantal, ed. 88p. 1996. pap. 18.99 (*0-415-12170-1*) Routledge.

— Deconstruction & Pragmatism. Mouffe, Chantal, ed. 112p. (C). 1996. 65.00 (*0-415-12169-8*) Routledge.

Critchley, Simon, jt. ed. see Bernasconi, Robert.

Critchley, T. A., jt. auth. see James, P. D.

Critchley, Will. Looking after Our Land. (FRE., Illus.). 88p. (C). 1991. pap. 25.95 (*0-85598-171-7*, Pub. by Oxfam Pubns) St Mut.

— Looking after Our Land: Environment. (Illus.). 88p. (C). 1991. pap. 14.95 (*0-85598-170-9*, Pub. by Oxfam Pub) Stylus Pub VA.

Critchlow, D. E. Metric Methods for Analyzing Partially Ranked Data. (Lecture Notes in Statistics Ser.: Vol. 34). x, 216p. 1986. 52.95 (*0-387-96288-3*) Spr-Verlag.

Critchlow, Donald E. Dos Amigos Verbal Language Scales: 1996 Edition. rev. ed. Martin, Nancy, ed. 20p. 1996. pap. text, teacher ed. 12.00 (*1-57128-075-8*, 075-8); pap. text, teacher ed. 15.00 (*1-57128-076-6*, 076-6) Acad Therapy.

Critchlow, Donald T. The Brookings Institution, Nineteen Sixteen to Nineteen Fifty-Two: Expertise & the Public Interest in a Democratic Society. LC 84-20699. (Illus.). 247p. 1985. 32.00 (*0-87580-103-X*) N Ill U Pr.

— Intended Consequences: Birth Control, Abortion & the Federal Government in Modern America. LC 98-13691. 320p. 1999. 30.00 (*0-19-504657-9*) OUP.

— Studebaker: The Life & Death of an American Corporation. LC 95-52639. (Midwestern History & Culture Ser.). (Illus.). 288p. (C). 1997. 39.95 (*0-253-33065-3*) Ind U Pr.

Critchlow, Donald T., ed. The Politics of Abortion & Birth Control in Historical Perspective. (Issues in Policy History Ser.: Vol. 5). 184p. 1996. pap. 16.95 (*0-271-01570-5*) Pa St U Pr.

Critchlow, Donald T. & Hawley, Ellis W., eds. Federal Social Policy: The Historical Dimension. LC 87-19395. (Illus.). 192p. 1988. lib. bdg. 40.00 (*0-271-00617-X*) Pa St U Pr.

Critchlow, Donald T. & Parker, Charles H., eds. With Us Always: A History of Private Charity & Public Welfare. LC 97-40121. 276p. 1997. 56.00 (*0-8476-8969-7*); pap. 22.95 (*0-8476-8970-0*) Rowman.

Critchlow, Donald T., jt. auth. see Rorabaugh, William J.

Critchlow, F. L., tr. see Desclot, Bernardo.

***Critchlow, Keith.** Islamic Patterns: An Analytical & Cosmological Approach. LC 99-28364. (Illus.). 192p. 1999. pap. 29.95 (*0-89281-803-4*) Inner Tradit.

Crite, Allan R. Were You There When They Crucified My Lord? A Negro Spiritual in Illustrations. LC 70-84107. (Illus.). 94p. reprint ed. 26.95 (*0-8434-0048-X*) Ayer.

Criteria Committee of the New York Heart Associati. Nomenclature & Criteria for Diagnosis of Diseases of the Heart & Great Vessels. 9th ed. Dolgin, Martin et al, eds. LC 93-43623. 352p. 1994. pap. text 34.95 (*0-316-60538-7*, Little Brwn Med Div) Lppncott W & W.

Crites, John O. Evaluation of Career Guidance Programs: Models, Methods, & Microcomputers. 32p. 1987. 4.75 (*0-317-03313-1*, IN317) Ctr Educ Trng Employ.

Crites, Laura L. & Hepperle, Winifred L. Women, the Courts & Equality. LC 86-15515. (Yearbooks in Women's Policy Studies: Vol. 11). 1987. 44.00 (*0-8039-2811-4*); pap. 21.95 (*0-8039-2812-2*) Sage.

Crites, Laura L. & Hepperle, Winifred L., eds. Women, the Courts & Equality. LC 86-15515. (Sage Yearbooks in Women's Policy Studies: No. 11). 256p. 1987. reprint ed. pap. 79.40 (*0-608-01538-5*, 205958200002) Bks Demand.

Crites, Mitchell. Visual Journeys. LC 94-60283. (Illus.). 256p. 1994. 50.00 (*0-500-97414-4*, Pub. by Thames Hudson) Norton.

Crites, Stephen. Dialectic & Gospel in the Development of Hegel's Thinking. LC 97-39499. 572p. 1998. 65.00 (*0-271-01759-7*) Pa St U Pr.

Crites, Susan. Confederate Ghosts. 48p. 1994. pap. 5.00 (*1-881562-05-0*) Butternut Pubns.

— Lively Ghosts. (Illus.). 43p. pap. 5.00 (*0-681-87306-X*) Butternut Pubns.

— More Lively Ghosts. 48p. 1992. pap. 5.00 (*1-881562-01-8*) Butternut Pubns.

— Murder at Confederate Headquarters. large type ed. 200p. (Orig.). 1994. pap. 9.95 (*1-881562-07-7*) Butternut Pubns.

— Murder at the Fair. 158p. 1993. pap. 10.00 (*1-881562-02-6*) Butternut Pubns.

— Murder in Martinsburg, West Virginia. 160p. 1992. pap. 10.00 (*1-881562-00-X*) Butternut Pubns.

— Union Ghosts. 48p. 1993. pap. 5.00 (*1-881562-06-9*) Butternut Pubns.

Critescu, N. & Suliciu, I. Viscoplasticity. 1982. lib. bdg. 64.40 (*90-247-2592-5*) Kluwer Academic.

Critical Art Ensemble Staff. Electronic Civil Disobedience & Other Unpopular Ideas. 1996. pap. 8.00 (*1-57027-056-2*) Autonomedia.

Critical Arts Ensemble Staff. The Electronic Disturbance. 147p. Date not set. 7.00 (*1-57027-006-6*) Autonomedia.

— Flesy Machine: Cyborgs, Designer Babies, & New Eugenic Consciousness. (New Autonomy Ser.). (Illus.). 160p. 1998. pap. 8.00 (*1-57027-067-8*) Autonomedia.

Critical Mass Energy Project Staff. The Green Buyer's Car Book: Environmental Ratings of 1994 Cars & Light Trucks. (Illus.). 200p. (C). 1994. pap. text 20.00 (*0-937188-92-1*) Pub Citizen.

— The Green Buyer's Car Guide: Environmental Ratings of 1994 Cars & Light Trucks. (Illus.). 50p. (C). 1994. pap. text 5.00 (*0-937188-91-3*) Pub Citizen.

— National Directory of Safe Energy Organizations. 8th ed. 80p. (C). 1994. student ed. 30.00 (*0-937188-90-5*) Pub Citizen.

— A Roll of the Dice: NRC's Efforts to Renew Nuclear Reactor Licenses. (Illus.). 54p. (C). 1995. pap. text 5.00 (*0-937188-89-1*) Pub Citizen.

— Twenty Years after the Embargo: The Costs of U. S. Oil Import Dependence & How They Can Be Reduced. (Illus.). 44p. (C). 1993. pap. text 30.00 (*0-937188-43-3*) Pub Citizen.

Critoph, E., et al. Canada Enters the Nuclear Age: A Technical History of Atomic Energy of Canada Limited as Seen from Its Research Laboratories. LC 99-168721. (Illus.). 448p. 1997. 70.00 (*0-7735-1601-8*, Pub. by McG-Queens Univ Pr) CUP Services.

Crits-Christoph, Paul & Barber, Jacques P., eds. Handbook of Short-Term Dynamic Psychotherapy. LC 91-70846. 368p. (C). 1991. pap. 38.00 (*0-465-02875-6*, Pub. by Basic) HarpC.

Crits-Christoph, Paul, jt. auth. see Luborsky, Lester.

Crits-Christoph, Paul, jt. ed. see Barber, Jacques P.

Critser, John K., jt. ed. see Karow, Armand.

Critten, P. Developing Your Professional Portfolio. (Illus.). 144p. 1995. ring bd. write for info. (*0-443-05170-4*) Church.

Critten, Peter. Investing in People: Towards Corporate Capability. 280p. 1994. pap. text 36.95 (*0-7506-1880-9*) Buttrwrth-Heinemann.

— Investing in People: Towards Corporate Capability. LC 94-66243. 261p. reprint ed. pap. 81.00 (*0-608-06253-7*, 206658200008) Bks Demand.

Crittenden. Bibliography of the First Fleet. (Australian National University Press Ser.). 1982. pap. text 33.00 (*0-08-032979-9*, Pergamon Pr) Elsevier.

Crittenden, B. D., jt. auth. see Thomas, W. J.

Crittenden, Barry, jt. ed. see Bahu, Richard.

***Crittenden, Camille.** Johann Strauss & Vienna: Operetta & the Politics of Popular Culture. LC 99-88871. (Cambridge Studies in Opera). (Illus.). 250p. (C). 2000. text Price not set. (*0-521-77121-8*) Cambridge U Pr.

Crittenden, Catherine, ed. Pennsylvania Law Encyclopedia, Interim Index. 2nd ed. 180p. 1999. pap. write for info. (*0-327-00945-4*, 6368010) LEXIS Pub.

Crittenden, Charles. Unreality: The Metaphysics of Fictional Objects. LC 90-55739. 192p. 1991. text 37.50 (*0-8014-2520-4*) Cornell U Pr.

Crittenden, Danielle. What Our Mothers Didn't Tell Us: Why Happiness Eludes the Modern Woman. 208p. 2000. per. 12.00 (*0-684-85959-9*) S&S Trade.

— What Our Mothers Didn't Tell Us: Why Happiness Eludes the Modern Woman. LC 98-42580. 224p. 1999. 22.50 (*0-684-83219-4*) Simon & Schuster.

Crittenden, Delores, ed. see Chase, Shoddy.

Crittenden, H. Temple. The Comp'ny. (Illus.). 232p. 1967. reprint ed. 25.00 (*0-87012-631-8*) McClain.

Crittenden, James A. Exclusive Production of Neutral Vector Mesons at the Electron-Proton Collider HERA. LC 97-28373. (Tracts in Modern Physics Ser.: Vol. 140). (Illus.). viii, 105p. 1997. 69.00 (*3-540-63261-1*) Spr-Verlag.

Crittenden, Lindsey. The View from Below: Stories by Lindsey Crittenden. LC 98-50586. (First Ser.). 160p. 1999. pap. 14.00 (*0-922811-40-7*) Mid-List.

Crittenden, Mabel. Trees of the West. 220p. 1992. pap. 14.95 (*0-88839-269-9*) Hancock House.

Crittenden, Mabel & Telfer, Dorothy. Wildflowers of the West. 206p. 1992. pap. 14.95 (*0-88839-270-2*) Hancock House.

Crittenden, Mary C. Let's Obraize Our Activities! Faber-Czingula, Linda, ed. 134p. 1996. ring bd. 49.00 (*1-890118-06-0*, QualityCare Pub) Convalescnt Cnslts.

Crittenden, Max D., Jr., et al, eds. Cordilleran Metamorphic Core Complexes. LC 80-67489. (Geological Society of America, Memoir Ser.: No. 153). (Illus.). 496p. reprint ed. pap. 153.80 (*0-7837-5360-8*, 204512300005) Bks Demand.

***Crittenden, Patricia McKinsey & Claussen, Angelika Hartl, eds.** The Organization of Attachment Relationships: Maturation, Culture & Context. (Illus.). 432p. (C). 2000. 69.95 (*0-521-58002-1*) Cambridge U Pr.

Crittenden, Penelope, jt. auth. see North, Barbara.

Crittenden, Robert, jt. auth. see Schieffelin, Edward L.

***Crittenden, Robert N.** Politics of Change: A Brief History. 352p. 2000. pap. 16.95 (*0-9671290-1-X*) Hargrave Pubg.

— Two Studies of Public Policy in Washington State: The Elite Planners & Salmon at Risk. 198p. 1995. 20.00 (*0-9671290-0-1*) Hargrave Pubg.

Crittenden, Roger. La Nuit Americaine. LC 98-215545. (Film Classics Ser.). (Illus.). 80p. 1998. pap. 10.95 (*0-85170-672-X*) Ind U Pr.

Crittenden, Vicky L. Jazz: A Case Study. 48p. (C). 1986. pap. text. write for info. (*0-201-11365-1*) Addison-Wesley.

Crittenden, Victoria L., ed. see Academy of Marketing Science Staff.

Critter Press, jt. auth. see McLennan, Bardi.

Critter Press Staff. Freshwater Aquarium in Your Life. LC 97-31146. 1997. write for info. (*0-87605-433-5*) Critters Pr.

Critter Press Staff, jt. auth. see Pavia, Audrey.

Critter Press Staff, jt. auth. see Rach, Julie.

***Critto, Adolfo.** Choosing Models of Society & Social Norms: Improving Choices & Quality of Life. LC 99-35038. 368p. 1999. pap. 34.50 (*0-7618-1454-X*) U Pr of Amer.

— Consistency: Being Coherent. 136p. 2000. pap. 24.50 (*0-7618-1745-X*) U Pr of Amer.

Critto, Adolfo. Overcoming Modern Confusion: Consistency & Choice. LC 99-18632. 352p. 1999. pap. 34.50 (*0-7618-1361-6*) U Pr of Amer.

Critzer, John W., jt. auth. see Rai, Kul B.

Crivellari, Lucio, et al, eds. Stellar Atmospheres: Beyond Classical Models. (C). 1991. text 225.00 (*0-7923-1343-7*) Kluwer Academic.

Crivellari, Lucio, jt. ed. see Beckman, John E.

Crivelli, A. J., et al. Ecology, Conservation & Management of Colonial Waterbirds in the Mediterranean Region. (Colonial Waterbirds Ser.: Vol. 19, No. 1). (Illus.). 240p. (Orig.). 1996. pap. text 25.00 (*0-9651399-1-3*) Colonial Wtrbird.

Crivelli, Alain J. & Catsadorakis, George, eds. Lake Prespa, North-Western Greece: A Unique Balkan Wetland. LC 97-31472. (Developments in Hydrobiology Ser.: No. 122). 196p. 1997. text 154.00 (*0-7923-4795-1*) Kluwer Academic.

Crivelli, Renzo S. James Joyce: Triestine Itineraries. (Illus.). 254p. 1997. pap. 59.95 (*88-86424-23-X*) Intl Scholars.

***Crivello, J. V. & Dietliker, K. K.** Photoinitiators for Free Radical Cationic & Anionic Photopolymerisation, Vol. 3. Bradley, G., ed. 600p. 1999. 189.95 (*0-471-97892-2*) Wiley.

Crivellone, Donald P. Oberammergau: A Decade of Experiences in a Bavarian Village. 112p. (Orig.). 1994. pap. 9.95 (*0-9643005-0-8*) Dobin Enter.

Crix, Bernard & Ladbrooke, Alan. The School Audit Manual for Primary Schools. 160p. 1996. pap. 162.50 (*0-273-62581-0*, Pub. by F T P-H) Trans-Atl Phila.

— The School Audit Manual for Secondary Schools & Colleges. 160p. 1996. pap. 172.50 (*0-273-62580-2*, Pub. by F T P-H) Trans-Atl Phila.

— The School Development Manual. 200p. 1997. pap. 162.50 (*0-273-63284-1*, Pub. by F T P-H) Trans-Atl Phila.

CRM Staff. The Challenges for the Eighties: Chinese Edition. (CHI.). 77p. 1985. pap. 4.50 (*1-56582-088-6*) Christ Renew Min.

— The Gold Seekers: Chinese Edition. (CHI.). 85p. 1984. pap. 4.50 (*1-56582-082-7*) Christ Renew Min.

— The Human Bondage. (CHI.). 99p. 1984. pap. 4.50 (*1-56582-083-5*) Christ Renew Min.

— In the Newness of Life - Chinese Edition. (CHI.). 113p. 1984. pap. 4.50 (*1-56582-085-1*) Christ Renew Min.

— The Love Story. (CHI.). 111p. 1984. pap. 4.50 (*1-56582-086-X*) Christ Renew Min.

— Metamorphoses: Chinese Edition. (CHI.). 131p. 1984. pap. 4.50 (*1-56582-084-3*) Christ Renew Min.

— The True Freedom: Chinese Edition. (CHI.). 101p. 1987. pap. 4.50 (*1-56582-087-8*) Christ Renew Min.

CRM Staff, tr. Creator or Liar - Chinese Edition. (CHI.). 22p. 1983. pap. 0.50 (*1-56582-072-X*) Christ Renew Min.

— The Fool - Chinese Edition. (CHI.). 22p. 1986. pap. 0.50 (*1-56582-071-1*) Christ Renew Min.

— Frame-Up - Chinese Edition. (CHI.). 22p. 1983. pap. 0.50 (*1-56582-073-8*) Christ Renew Min.

CRM Staff, tr. see Dawson, David.

CRM Staff, tr. see Moody Institute of Science Staff.

CRM Staff, tr. see Murray, Andrew.

Crncic, Tony. How I Became a Health Nut: A Humorous Beginners Guide. LC 98-92707. 160p. 1998. pap. 8.95 (*0-9663383-0-8*) Far North Pub.

Crnkovic, Gordana P. Imagined Dialogues: Eastern European Literature in Conversation with American & English Literature. LC 99-48789. 184p. 1999. 64.95 (*0-8101-1717-7*); pap. 19.95 (*0-8101-1718-5*) Northwestern U Pr.

Crnkovic, Z., tr. see Coric, Simun S.

Crnobrnja, Mihailo. The Yugoslav Drama. 296p. 1994. pap. 19.95 (*0-7735-1213-6*, Pub. by McG-Queens Univ Pr) CUP Services.

— The Yugoslav Drama. 2nd ed. 296p. 1994. 60.00 (*0-7735-1203-9*, Pub. by McG-Queens Univ Pr) CUP Services.

— The Yugoslav Drama. 2nd ed. 312p. 1996. pap. 19.95 (*0-7735-1429-5*, Pub. by McG-Queens Univ Pr) CUP Services.

Cro, Stelio. The Noble Savage: Allegory of Freedom. 184p. (C). 1990. text 29.95 (*0-88920-983-9*) W Laurier U Pr.

Croake, James. Curiosities of Law & Lawyers. enl. ed. viii, 790p. 1988. reprint ed. 65.00 (*0-8377-2304-3*, Rothman) W S Hein.

Croake, James W., jt. auth. see Mays, Mark.

Croaker, John, ed. Molecular Biology in Histopathology. LC 93-50921. (Molecular Medical Science Ser.). 190p. 1994. 135.00 (*0-471-94093-3*) Wiley.

Croal, Melva, jt. auth. see Nugent, Charles.

Croall, C. & Sempler, S. Nuclear Power for Beginners. 1990. pap. 35.00 (*0-7855-7026-8*, Pub. by Northcote House) St Mut.

Croall, Hazel. Crime & Society in Britain. LC 97-46850. viii, 359p. 1998. pap. 31.00 (*0-582-29897-0*, 15739) Gaunt.

— White Collar Crime. 176p. 1992. pap. 34.95 (*0-335-09656-5*) OpUniv Pr.

Croall, I. F. & Mason, J. P., eds. Industrial Applications of Neural Networks: Project ANNIE Handbook. (Research Reports ESPRIT, Project ANNIE, Coed: Commission of the European Communities: Vol. 1). ix, 297p. 1992. 50.95 (*0-387-55875-6*) Spr-Verlag.

Croall, Stephen, tr. see Lindstrom, Eva.

Croally, N. T. Euripidean Polemic: The Trojan Women & the Function of Tragedy. LC 93-44672. (Cambridge Classical Studies). 327p. (C). 1995. text 64.95 (*0-521-46490-0*) Cambridge U Pr.

Croarken, Mary. Early Scientific Computing in Britain. (Illus.). 176p. 1990. 55.00 (*0-19-853748-4*) OUP.

Croasdale, H. & Flint, E. A. Flora of New Zealand: Desmids, Vol. I. 1986. 58.75 (*0-477-02530-7*, Pub. by Manaaki Whenua) Balogh.

— Flora of New Zealand Vol. II: Actinotaenium, Cosmarium, Cosmocladium & Xanthidium. (Illus.). 212p. 1988. 58.75 (*0-477-01353-8*, Pub. by Manaaki Whenua) Balogh.

Croasdale, H., et al. Flora of New Zealand: Desmids, Vol. III. 1994. 60.00 (*0-477-01642-1*, Pub. by Manaaki Whenua) Balogh.

Croasdale, Laurine. Red Golf Balls. LC 98-203250. (J). 1998. pap. 12.95 (*0-7022-2970-9*, Pub. by Univ Queensland Pr) Intl Spec Bk.

— Trivia Man. 130p. (YA). 1997. pap. 12.95 (*0-7022-2920-2*, Pub. by Univ Queensland Pr) Intl Spec Bk.

Croasmun, W. R. & Carlson, R. M., eds. Two-Dimensional NMR Spectroscopy: Applications for Chemists & Biochemists. 2nd ed. (Methods in Stereochemical Analysis Ser.). 958p. 1994. 185.00 (*0-471-18593-0*) Wiley.

Croat, Thomas B. Flora of Barro Colorado Island. LC 76-23371. (Illus.). 953p. 1978. 68.95 (*0-8047-0950-5*) Stanford U Pr.

Croatto, J. Severino. Biblical Hermeneutics: Toward a Theory of Reading as the Production of Meaning. Barr, Robert R., tr. from SPA. LC 87-12314.Tr. of Hermeneutica Biblica, para Una Teoria de la Lectura Como Produccion Sentido. 96p. (Orig.). 1999. reprint ed. pap. 20.00 (*0-88344-582-4*) Orbis Bks.

Croatto, Jose S. Biblical Hermeneutics: Toward a Theory of Reading As the Production of Meaning. Barr, Robert R., tr. from SPA. LC 87-12314. 104p. reprint ed. pap. 32.30 (*0-608-20186-3*, 207144500012) Bks Demand.

Crocco, G., et al. Conditionals: From Philosophy to Computer Science. (Studies in Logic & Computation: No. 5). (Illus.). 376p. 1996. text 95.00 (*0-19-853861-8*) OUP.

Crocco, Margaret Smith, et al. Pedagogies of Resistance: Women Educator Activists, 1880-1960. LC 98-54347. 144p. 1999. 44.00 (*0-8077-6298-9*); pap. 19.95 (*0-8077-6297-0*) Tchrs Coll.

Crocco, Stephen, ed. see Ramsey, Paul.

Croce, Arlene. George Balanchine. text. write for info. (*0-374-29988-9*) FS&G.

Croce, Arlene. Sight Lines. 1988. 19.95 (*0-317-68135-4*) Knopf.

***Croce, Arlene.** Writing in the Dark, Dancing in the New Yorker. LC 00-35448. 720p. 2001. 30.00 (*0-374-10455-7*) FS&G.

Croce, Augusto. Savonarola: or The Unarmed Prophet: An Historical Drama. 72p. (Orig.). 1995. pap. 7.50 (*0-9635358-2-X*) ARS Historica.

Croce, Benedetto. Aesthetic. 536p. 1985. pap. 22.50 (*0-7206-0635-7*, Pub. by P Owen Ltd) Dufour.

— Aesthetic: As Science of Expression & General Linguistic. Ainslie, Douglas, tr. from ITA. LC 94-44020.Tr. of Estetica come Scienza dell'Espressione e Linguistica Generale. 510p. 1995. pap. 29.95 (*1-56000-818-0*) Transaction Pubs.

— The Aesthetic as the Science of Expression & of the Linguistic in General (ESTETICA), Pt. I: Theory. Lyas, Colin, tr. 208p. (C). 1992. pap. text 21.95 (*0-521-35996-1*) Cambridge U Pr.

— Autobiography. Collingwood, Robin George, tr. LC 79-114871. (Select Bibliographies Reprint Ser.). 1977. 16.95 (*0-8369-5276-6*) Ayer.

— Ce qui est vivant et Ce qui est morte De la philosophie De Hegel: Etude Critique Suivie d,un Essai De Bibliographie Hegelienne. Buriot, Henri, tr. from ITA. (Reprints in Philosophy Ser.). (FRE.). reprint ed. lib. bdg. 43.00 (*0-697-00051-6*) Irvington.

— Conduct of Life. Livingston, A., tr. LC 67-30204. (Essay Index Reprint Ser.). 1977. 20.95 (*0-8369-0351-X*) Ayer.

— Croce, the King & the Allies. LC 78-63660. (Studies in Fascism: Ideology & Practice). reprint ed. 22.50 (*0-404-16916-3*) AMS Pr.

— European Literature in the Nineteenth Century. LC 67-30822. (Studies in Comparative Literature: No. 35). 1969. reprint ed. lib. bdg. 75.00 (*0-8383-0735-3*) M S G Haskell Hse.

— Guide to Aesthetics. Romanell, Patrick, tr. from ITA. LC 94-43408. (HPC Classics Ser.).Tr. of Breviario di Estetica. 128p. (C). 1995. pap. text 7.95 (*0-87220-304-2*); lib. bdg. 29.95 (*0-87220-305-0*) Hackett Pub.

— Historical Materialism & the Economics of Karl Marx. LC 78-66239. (Social Science Classics Ser.). 225p. 1981. 39.95 (*0-87855-313-4*); pap. text 24.95 (*0-87855-695-8*) Transaction Pubs.

***Croce, Benedetto.** History as the Story of Liberty. Sprigge, Sylvia, tr. from ITA. LC 99-32048.Tr. of Storia Come Pensiero e Come Ezione. 1999. pap. 9.00 (*0-86597-269-9*) Liberty Fund.

— History as the Story of Liberty. Sprigge, Sylvia, tr. from ITA. LC 99-32048.Tr. of Storia Come Pensiero e Come Ezione. 2000. 17.00 (*0-86597-268-0*) Liberty Fund.

Croce, Benedetto. The History of the Kingdom of Naples. Hughes, H. Stuart, ed. Frenaye, Frances, tr. from ITA. LC 71-113253. (Classic European Historians Ser.). xxiv, 260p. 1972. pap. text 2.95 (*0-226-12081-3*, P377) U Ch Pr.

— My Philosophy & Other Essays on the Moral & Political Problems of Our Time. Caritt, E. F., tr. LC 75-41068. (BCL Ser. II). reprint ed. 37.50 (*0-404-14526-4*) AMS Pr.

— Philosophy of the Practical. Ainslie, Douglas, tr. LC 66-30790. 1913. 32.00 (*0-8196-0192-6*) Biblo.

— The Poetry of Dante (1922) 319p. reprint ed. 15.00 (*0-911858-12-1*) Appel.

— Thought, Action & Intuition As a Symposium on the Philosophy of Benedetto Croce. Palmer, L. M. & Harris, H. S., eds. vii, 363p. 1976. lib. bdg. 70.00 (*3-487-05860-X*) Lubrecht & Cramer.

Croce, Carlo, jt. ed. see Mihich, Enrico.

Croce, Ingrid. Thyme in a Bottle: Recipes from Ingrid Croce's San Diego Cafes. LC 95-48280. (Illus.). 256p. 1996. 25.00 (*0-06-258624-6*, Pub. by Harper SF) HarpC.

***Croce, Julia Della.** Italy. (Vegetarian Table Ser.). 2000. pap. 16.95 (*0-8118-3034-9*) Chronicle Bks.

— Pasta. (Living Ser.). 168p. 2000. pap. text 13.95 (*0-7894-5118-2*, D K Ink) DK Pub Inc.

Croce, N. Della, et al. Coastal Ocean Space Utilization Iii. 688p. (C). (gr. 13). 1995. 200.00 (*0-419-20900-X*) Routledge.

Croce, Nicholas J. & Burke, Susan. Emmett Kelly, Jr. Travels Through American History with the World's Most Famous Hobo Clown. Burke, Thomas, ed. (Illus.). 48p. 1993. 35.00 (*0-9634549-0-0*) NJ Croce.

Croce, Pat. The Baseball Player's Guide to Sports Medicine. LC 82-83936. (Illus.). 120p. (Orig.). 1987. reprint ed. pap. 37.20 (*0-608-04286-2*, 206506500012) Bks Demand.

***Croce, Pat.** I Feel Great & You Will Too! An Inspiring Journey of Success with Practical Tips on How to Score Big in Life. (Illus.). 2000. 24.95 (*0-7624-0807-3*) Running Pr.

— Time Out Management. (YA). 1999. 19.95 incl. audio (*1-893714-02-0*) Moro Mgmt.

Croce, Paul J. Science & Religion in the Era of William James Vol. I: Eclipse of Certainty. LC 94-29749. (Illus.). 380p. 1995. pap. text 19.95 (*0-8078-4506-X*); lib. bdg. 49.95 (*0-8078-2200-0*) U of NC Pr.

***Croce, Pietro.** Vivisection or Science? LC 99-24761. 2000. text 65.00 (*1-85649-732-1*) St Martin.

— Vivisection or Science?, 2nd Ed. 2nd ed. LC 99-24761. 2000. pap. 22.50 (*1-85649-733-X*) St Martin.

Crocetti, Enzo & Giordano, Mario. A Crowd of Witnesses: Interviews with Famous New Testament Men & Women. Maroni, Lisa, tr. from ITA. LC 94-20697.Tr. of Personaggi del Vangelo. (Illus.). 160p. (J). 1994. pap. 9.95 (*0-8198-1531-4*) Pauline Bks.

Crocetta, Lionel, jt. auth. see Menichelli, Edward.

C

An Asterisk (*) at the beginning of an entry indicates that the title is appearing for the first time.

Crocetti, Annemarie F., jt. auth. see Mushak, Paul.

Crocetti, Enzo & Giordano, Mario. A Crowd of Witnesses: Interviews with Famous Old Testament Men & Women. Maroni, Lisa, tr. from ITA. LC 94-17857. (Illus.). 136p. (J). (gr. 4-8). 1995. pap. 9.95 (*0-8198-1530-6*) Pauline Bks.

Crocetti, Gina L. Culture Shock! United Arab Emirates. (Culture Shock Ser.). 1996. pap. text 12.95 (*1-55868-300-3*) Gr Arts Ctr Pub.

Crocetti, Gino, jt. auth. see Martinson, Thomas H.

Crocetti, Guido M., et al. Contemporary Attitudes Toward Mental Illness. LC 73-80071. (Contemporary Community Health Ser.). 262p. reprint ed. 81.30 (*0-8357-9752-X*, 201786400009) Bks Demand.

***Crochemore, M. & Paterson, M. S., eds.** Combinatorial Pattern Matching: 10th Annual Symposium, CPM 99, Warwick University, U. K., July 22-24, 1999 Proceedings. (Lecture Notes in Computer Science Ser.: Vol. 1645). viii, 293p. 1999. pap. 56.00 (*3-540-66278-2*) Spr-Verlag.

Crochemore, Maxime & Gusfield, Dan, eds. Combinatorial Pattern Matching: Proceedings of the 5th Annual Symposium, CPM '94, Asilomar, CA, U. S. A., June 5-8, 1994. LC 94-20069. (Lecture Notes in Computer Science Ser.: Vol. 807). 1994. write for info. (*0-387-58094-8*) Spr-Verlag.

Crochemore, Maxime & Rytter, Wojciech. Text Algorithms. (Illus.). 432p. 1994. text 120.00 (*0-19-508609-0*) OUP.

Crochet, M. J., et al. Numerical Simulation of Non-Newtonian Flow. (Rheology Ser.: Vol. 1). xiv, 352p. 1991. reprint ed. 183.00 (*0-444-42291-9*) Elsevier.

Crochet, Marcel J., jt. ed. see Casey, James.

Crochet, Monique Y. Le Francais des Professions Medicales et Sociales: Textes et Controverses. 352p. (Orig.). (C). 1986. pap. text 29.00 (*0-8191-5085-1*) U Pr of Amer.

Crochet, Treena. Designer's Guide to Furniture Styles. LC 98-19923. 292p. 1998. 61.00 (*0-13-374695-X*) P-H.

Crochiere, ed. see Best, John B.

Crochiere, Ronald E. & Rabiner, Lawrence R. Multirate Digital Signal Processing. (Illus.). 336p. (C). 1983. text 67.51 (*0-13-605162-6*) P-H.

Croci, G. Conservation & Structural Restoration of Architectural Heritage, 2 vols. Incl. Conservation & Structural Restoration of Architectural Heritage: Theory & Practice. LC 96-86036. 272p. 1998. 195.00 (*1-85312-482-6*, 4826, Pub. by WIT Pr); (Advances in Architecture Ser.: Vol. 1). 472p. 1998. (*1-56252-315-5*, 3919) Computational Mech MA.

Crocitti, John J., jt. ed. see Levine, Robert M.

***Crocitto, Frank, ed.** New Suns Will Arise: From the Journals of Henry David Thoreau. 80p. (YA). (gr. 7 up). 2000. 24.99 (*0-7868-0539-0*, Pub. by Hyprn Child) Time Warner.

Crocitto, Jane B., jt. auth. see Bullock, Gloria S.

Crocitto, Madeline, jt. ed. see Betters-Reed, Bonita.

Crocitto, Rosanna, tr. see Borradori, Giovanna.

Crock, Henry V. Practice of Spinal Surgery. (Illus.). 340p. 1983. 153.00 (*0-387-81738-7*) Spr-Verlag.

— A Short Practice of Spinal Surgery. 2nd ed. (Illus.). 319p. 1993. 154.00 (*3-211-82351-4*) Spr-Verlag.

— A Short Practice of Spinal Surgery. 2nd rev. ed. LC 92-48889. (Illus.). 344p. 1993. 169.00 (*0-387-82351-4*) Spr-Verlag.

Crock, Mary, ed. Protection or Punishment: The Detention of Asylum Seekers in Australia. 200p. 1993. pap. 24.00 (*1-86287-125-6*, Pub. by Federation Pr) Gaunt.

***Crockard, Alan, et al.** Neurosurgery. 3rd rev. ed. LC 99-28832. (Illus.). 1301p. 2000. 495.00 (*0-632-04838-7*) Blackwell Sci.

Crockatt, Richard. Fifty Years War. 448p. (C). 1996. pap. 20.99 (*0-415-13554-0*) Routledge.

— The Fifty Years War: The United States & the Soviet Union in World Politics, 1941-1991. LC 94-15096. 352p. (C). (gr. 13). 1994. 75.00 (*0-415-10471-8*, B4148) Routledge.

Crockcroft, James D. Diego Rivera: Mexican Painter. (Illus.). 120p. (YA). (gr. 5 up). 1991. lib. bdg. 19.95 (*0-7910-1252-2*) Chelsea Hse.

— Diego Rivera: Mexican Painter. (Illus.). 120p. (YA). (gr. 5 up). 1992. pap. 8.95 (*0-7910-1279-4*) Chelsea Hse.

Crockem, Linda. Count with Me in Tennessee. 12p. (J). 1997. 14.99 (*1-887637-05-2*) First Bk Prodns.

— Counting from 1-10 in the Lone Star State Texas. 12p. (J). (ps). 1995. 14.99 (*1-887637-02-8*, TX3-993-328) First Bk Prodns.

— Fruits & Veget"bets" 28p. (J). (ps). 1988. 19.99 (*1-887637-00-1*) First Bk Prodns.

— One to Ten We Are Counting Again in Iowa. (Illus.). 12p. (J). (ps-k). 1997. 14.99 (*0-614-29772-9*) First Bk Prodns.

— 123 Louisiana & Me. 12p. (J). (ps). 1989. 14.99 (*1-887637-01-X*, TX378468) First Bk Prodns.

— 1 2 3 North Carolina & Me! 12p. (J). (ps). 1997. 14.99 (*1-887637-04-4*) First Bk Prodns.

— Seven & Three in Mississippi. 12p. (J). 1997. 14.99 (*1-887637-07-9*) First Bk Prodns.

— Ten Peaches Things about Georgia. 12p. (J). 1994. 14.99 (*1-887637-06-0*) First Bk Prodns.

Crocker & Kramsch, C. Reden, Mitreden, Dazwischenreden. 2nd ed. (C). 1990. 41.95 incl. audio (*0-8384-1940-2*) Heinle & Heinle.

Crocker, jt. auth. see Davidson.

Crocker, jt. auth. see Kramsch.

Crocker, Alan. Building Failures: Recovering the Costs. 151p. 1990. 47.00 (*0-614-16812-0*, BSP158) Am Soc Civil Eng.

Crocker, Allen, ed. see Josephson, Gretchen.

Crocker, Allen C., jt. auth. see Rubin, I. Leslie.

Crocker, Betty. Betty Crocker Cookbook. 1994. mass mkt. 8.99 (*0-553-85060-1*) Bantam.

— Betty Crocker Fast & Flavorful 100 Main Dishes You Can Make in 20 Minutes or Less. LC 97-17150. 144p. 1997. 19.95 (*0-02-861985-4*, Betty Crocker) IDG Bks.

— Betty Crocker's Baking with Kids. (Illus.). 112p. (J). 1995. 14.95 (*0-02-860369-9*, Betty Crocker) IDG Bks.

— Betty Crocker's Baking with Kids. LC 94-24258. (J). 1995. 15.00 (*0-671-52284-1*) Macmillan.

— Betty Crocker's Best Bread Machine Cookbook: The Goodness of Homemade Bread the Easy Way. LC 99-12272. (Illus.). 240p. 1999. 19.95 (*0-02-863023-8*, Betty Crocker) IDG Bks.

— Betty Crocker's Best Chicken Cookbook. LC 99-17883. (Illus.). 304p. 1999. 21.95 (*0-02-863155-2*, Betty Crocker) IDG Bks.

***Crocker, Betty.** Betty Crocker's Best Christmas Cookbook. LC 99-35731. 352p. 1999. 21.95 (*0-02-863465-9*) Macmillan.

Crocker, Betty. Betty Crocker's Best Loved Recipes. LC 98-38261. 226p. 1998. 24.95 (*0-02-862450-5*, Betty Crocker) IDG Bks.

— Betty Crocker's Best of Baking. LC 97-22856. 444p. 1997. pap. text 24.95 (*0-02-862066-6*, Betty Crocker) IDG Bks.

— Betty Crocker's Best of Baking. 432p. 1997. 24.95 (*0-02-862219-7*, Pub. by Macmillan) S&S Trade.

— Betty Crocker's Best of Healthy & Hearty Cooking: More than 400 Recipes Your Family Will Love. LC 98-20103. (Illus.). 448p. 1998. 24.95 (*0-02-862452-1*, Betty Crocker) IDG Bks.

— Betty Crocker's Bread Machine Cookbook. LC 95-4973. (Illus.). 96p. 1995. 9.95 (*0-02-860367-2*, Pub. by Macmillan) S&S Trade.

— Betty Crocker's Chinese Low-Fat Cooking. LC 95-35415. (Illus.). 144p. 1996. 16.00 (*0-02-860391-5*) Macmillan Info.

— Betty Crocker's Complete Pasta Cookbook. LC 95-12564. (Illus.). 224p. 1995. 19.95 (*0-02-860374-5*) Macmillan.

— Betty Crocker's Cookbook. 7th ed. 1993. pap. 16.00 (*0-671-85039-3*, B Crocker) Macmillan Gen Ref.

— Betty Crocker's Cookbook. 8th ed. 1996. 24.00 (*0-671-51124-6*) Prntice Hall Bks.

***Crocker, Betty.** Betty Crocker's Cookbook: Everything You Need to Know to Cook. 9th ed. LC 00-27581. (Illus.). 2000. 25.99 (*0-7645-6079-4*) IDG Bks.

Crocker, Betty. Betty Crocker's Cookbook: Fortieth Anniversary Edition. (Illus.). 432p. 1991. 25.00 (*0-13-073768-2*, B Crocker) Macmillan Gen Ref.

— Betty Crocker's Cookie Book: More than 250 of America's Best-Loved Cookies. LC 98-6406. 304p. 1998. 21.95 (*0-02-862603-6*, Betty Crocker) IDG Bks.

— Betty Crocker's Cooking Library: Pasta Favorites & Quick Dinners. 1997. pap. text 19.95 (*0-02-862598-6*, Betty Crocker) IDG Bks.

— Betty Crocker's Cooking with Kids. (Illus.). 144p. 1995. 14.95 (*0-02-860363-X*, Betty Crocker) IDG Bks.

— Betty Crocker's Creative Cookies. LC 95-4981. (Illus.). 96p. 1995. 9.95 (*0-02-860366-4*, Pub. by Macmillan) S&S Trade.

— Betty Crocker's Do-Ahead Cookbook. (Illus.). 1994. 18.00 (*0-671-50124-0*, B Crocker) Macmillan Gen Ref.

— Betty Crocker's Do Ahead Cookbook. 160p. 1995. 19.95 (*0-02-860030-4*, B Crocker) Macmillan Gen Ref.

— Betty Crocker's Easy Everyday Vegetarian. LC 97-32222. 256p. 1998. 19.95 (*0-02-862261-8*) Macmillan.

— Betty Crocker's Easy Low Fat Cooking. 144p. 1995. 15.00 (*0-02-860086-X*, Betty Crocker) IDG Bks.

— Betty Crocker's Easy Low Fat Cooking. 1995. 15.00 (*0-671-52037-7*, B Crocker) Macmillan Gen Ref.

— Betty Crocker's Eat & Lose Weight. (Illus.). 1990. 20.00 (*0-13-074303-8*, B Crocker) Macmillan Gen Ref.

— Betty Crocker's Expressipes! 100 Great Recipes in 30 Minutes or Less. LC 97-17149. 176p. 1997. pap. text 14.95 (*0-02-862027-5*, Betty Crocker) IDG Bks.

— Betty Crocker's Fabulous Fish & Seafood. LC 94-37683. 96p. 1995. 27.00 (*0-02-860281-1*, Betty Crocker) IDG Bks.

— Betty Crocker's Good & Easy. 432p. 1997. pap. 15.95 (*0-02-862288-X*, Betty Crocker) IDG Bks.

— Betty Crocker's Good & Easy - Cookbook. 1997. 29.95 (*0-02-862213-8*, 753202) Macmillan.

— Betty Crocker's Good & Easy Cookbook. (Illus.). 432p. 1999. 25.00 (*0-02-863680-5*, B Crocker) Macmillan Gen Ref.

— Betty Crocker's Good & Easy Cookbook: Sure-fire Recipies that Get Dinner on the Table Every Night. 1997. 29.95 (*0-02-861895-5*) Macmillan.

— Betty Crocker's Great Grilling: 200 Tantalizing, Easy-to-Prepare Recipes for Entertaining. LC 97-4286. (Illus.). 240p. 1997. 19.95 (*0-02-861851-3*, Betty Crocker) IDG Bks.

***Crocker, Betty.** Betty Crocker's Healthy New Choices. LC 98-48797. 432p. 1998. 25.00 (*0-02-862958-2*, Betty Crocker) IDG Bks.

Crocker, Betty. Betty Crocker's Healthy New Choices. 432p. 1999. pap. text 16.95 (*0-02-863717-8*) S&S Trade.

— Betty Crocker's Healthy New Choices: A Fresh Approach to Eating Well, 2 vols. (Illus.). 432p. 1999. 29.95 (*0-02-863358-X*, Betty Crocker) IDG Bks.

— Betty Crocker's Holiday Baking. (Illus.). 88p. (Orig.). 1993. pap. 8.00 (*0-671-86961-2*, B Crocker) Macmillan Gen Ref.

— Betty Crocker's Holiday Baking. LC 92-46360. (Orig.). 1994. 8.00 (*0-671-06961-6*, B Crocker) Macmillan Gen Ref.

— Betty Crocker's Kids Cook. LC 99-40460. (Betty Crocker's Ser.). 160p. 1999. 15.95 (*0-02-863406-3*, B Crocker) Macmillan Gen Ref.

— Betty Crocker's Kitchen Library. Betty Crocker Editors, ed. 304p. 1998. 39.95 (*0-02-862770-9*, Betty Crocker) IDG Bks.

— Betty Crocker's Low Fat Cholesterol Cookbook. 1991. 18.95 (*0-13-084138-2*) P-H.

— Betty Crocker's Low Fat Cooking K-Mart. 1996. 6.99 (*0-02-861623-5*) Macmillan.

— Betty Crocker's New Cake Decorating. LC 99-461778. 160p. 1999. 16.95 (*0-02-862527-7*, Pub. by Macmillan) S&S Trade.

— Betty Crocker's New Cake Decorating. rev. ed. LC 93-51020. 1994. 15.00 (*0-671-89748-9*, B Crocker) Macmillan Gen Ref.

— Betty Crocker's New Chinese Cookbook. (Illus.). 144p. 1990. per. 16.00 (*0-13-083254-5*, B Crocker) Macmillan Gen Ref.

— Betty Crocker's New Choices for Pasta, Grains & Beans: Great Ideas for Healthy Meals. 160p. 1995. 19.95 (*0-02-860362-1*, B Crocker) Macmillan Gen Ref.

— Betty Crocker's New Choices for Pasta, Grains & Beans Cookbook. (Illus.). 1995. 16.00 (*0-671-52285-X*) Macmillan.

— Betty Crocker's New Choices for Two. LC 95-4980. (Illus.). 144p. 1995. 16.00 (*0-02-860368-0*) Macmillan.

— Betty Crocker's New Christmas Cookbook. LC 92-35119. 1993. per. 19.95 (*0-671-79927-4*, B Crocker) Macmillan Gen Ref.

— Betty Crocker's New Cookbook. 1997. 14.95 (*0-614-28089-3*) Macmillan USA.

— Betty Crocker's New Cookbook. 1998. pap. text 29.95 (*0-02-862260-X*) McGraw.

— Betty Crocker's New Cookbook. 8th ed. 448p. 1996. pap. text 14.95 (*0-02-861764-9*) Macmillan.

— Betty Crocker's New Cookbook. 8th ed. 448p. 1998. 25.00 (*0-02-863009-2*, Pub. by Macmillan) S&S Trade.

— Betty Crocker's New Cookbook: Bride's Edition. 320p. 1999. 29.95 (*0-02-862887-X*, Pub. by Macmillan) S&S Trade.

***Crocker, Betty.** Betty Crocker's New Cookbook: Bride's Edition. 480p. 1999. 27.95 (*0-02-863024-6*, Pub. by Macmillan) S&S Trade.

Crocker, Betty. Betty Crocker's New Cookbook: Everything You Need to Know to Cook. 8th ed. LC 95-49105. (Illus.). 448p. 1996. 25.00 (*0-02-860395-8*) Macmillan.

— Betty Crocker's New Cookbook & Betty Crocker's Appetizers. 1997. 29.95 (*0-02-862229-4*) Macmillan.

— Betty Crocker's New Cookbook & Cookie Jar Cookbook. 1996. 29.95 (*0-02-861546-8*, Betty Crocker) IDG Bks.

— Betty Crocker's New Eat & Lose Weight. LC 96-26602. 272p. 1996. 21.95 (*0-02-861500-X*) Macmillan.

— Betty Crocker's New Eat & Lose Weight. 1998. 16.00 (*0-02-862638-9*, Pub. by Macmillan) S&S Trade.

— Betty Crocker's New International Cookbook. LC 96-137110. (Illus.). 384p. 1994. 19.00 (*0-671-88763-7*, B Crocker) Macmillan Gen Ref.

— Betty Crocker's New Italian Cookbook. 176p. 1995. 19.95 (*0-02-860031-2*, B Crocker) Macmillan Gen Ref.

— Betty Crocker's New Italian Cooking. 1995. 18.00 (*0-671-51123-8*, B Crocker) Macmillan Gen Ref.

Crocker, Betty. Betty Crocker's New Lowfat, Low-cholesterol Cookbook. 256p. 1900. 21.95 (*0-02-863762-3*) Macmillan.

Crocker, Betty. Betty Crocker's New Microwaving for One or Two. large type ed. LC 90-45452. 1990. reprint ed. lib. bdg. 19.95 (*1-56054-033-8*) Thorndike Pr.

— Betty Crocker's New Pasta Cookbook. LC 98-53854. (Illus.). 240p. 1999. 19.95 (*0-02-863082-3*, Betty Crocker) IDG Bks.

— Betty Crocker's One Hundred Twenty-Five Low-Calorie Main Dishes. (Illus.). 144p. 1992. 19.95 (*0-13-085531-6*, B Crocker) Macmillan Gen Ref.

— Betty Crocker's Rising to the Occasion. 196p. 1998. 14.95 (*0-02-862262-6*, Pub. by Macmillan) S&S Trade.

— Betty Crocker's Sensational Salads. LC 94-36647. 352p. 1995. pap. 20.00 (*0-02-860280-3*, B Crocker) Macmillan Gen Ref.

***Crocker, Betty.** Betty Crocker's Slow Cooker Cookbook: Delicious, Satisfying Meals You Can Make in a Snap. LC 99-35736. 224p. 1999. pap. 19.95 (*0-02-863469-1*) Macmillan.

Crocker, Betty. Betty Crocker's Soups & Stews. LC 92-44793. (Illus.). 96p. 1993. pap. 8.00 (*0-671-86960-4*, B Crocker) Macmillan Gen Ref.

— Betty Crocker's Southwest Cooking. 222p. 1989. per. 19.95 (*0-671-86818-7*) S&S Trade.

***Crocker, Betty.** Betty Crocker's the Heart of the Kitchen. 700p. 2000. pap. text 27.95 (*0-02-863798-4*) Macmillan.

Crocker, Betty. Betty Crocker's Ultimate Cookie Book. (Illus.). 208p. 1997. per. 19.95 (*0-13-084492-6*, B Crocker) Macmillan Gen Ref.

Crocker, Betty, ed. Betty Crocker's New Low-Fat, Low Cholesterol Cookbook. LC 95-16653. (Illus.) 224p. 1995. 19.95 (*0-02-860388-5*) Macmillan.

Crocker, Betty & Mitchell, Carolyn B. Betty Crocker's Best Barbecue Recipes. LC 92-34873. (Illus.). 80p. 1993. pap. 8.00 (*0-671-86517-X*, B Crocker) Macmillan Gen Ref.

— Betty Crocker's Great Chicken Recipes. LC 92-25398. 1993. pap. 8.00 (*0-671-84689-2*, B Crocker) Macmillan Gen Ref.

— Betty Crocker's It's Chicken Cookbook. LC 93-44974. 1994. 19.95 (*0-671-89243-6*, Betty Crocker) IDG Bks.

— Betty Crocker's Low-Calorie Cooking. LC 92-25397. 1993. per. 8.00 (*0-671-84690-6*, B Crocker) Macmillan Gen Ref.

— Betty Crocker's Low-Fat Cooking. LC 93-38096. 96p. 1994. 9.95 (*0-671-88771-8*, B Crocker) Macmillan Gen Ref.

— Betty Crocker's Pasta Favorites. LC 92-34872. 1993. per. 9.95 (*0-671-86516-1*, B Crocker) Macmillan Gen Ref.

— Betty Crocker's Quick Dinners. LC 92-25396. 1993. pap. 8.00 (*0-671-84692-2*, B Crocker) Macmillan Gen Ref.

— Betty Crocker's Vegetarian Cookbook. LC 93-36694. 96p. 1994. per. 9.95 (*0-671-88770-X*, B Crocker) Macmillan Gen Ref.

Crocker, Bosworth. Humble Folk. LC 77-94338. (One-Act Plays in Reprint Ser.). 1978. reprint ed. 20.00 (*0-8486-2036-4*) Roth Pub Inc.

Crocker, Cedric, ed. see Brandies, Monica.

Crocker, Cedric, ed. see Horton, Alvin & Cotton, Lin.

***Crocker, Chester A., et al.** Herding Cats: Multiparty Mediation in a Complex World. LC 99-35750. 1999. pap. 29.95 (*1-878379-92-5*) US Inst Peace.

Crocker, Chester A., et al. Managing Global Chaos: Sources of & Responses to International Conflict. LC 96-31858. 1996. 55.00 (*1-878379-59-3*); pap. text 29.95 (*1-878379-58-5*) US Inst Peace.

Crocker, Chester A., jt. auth. see Smock, David R.

Crocker, Chris. Cyndi Lauper. Arico, Diane, ed. (Illus.). 64p. (J). (gr. 3-7). 1985. 9.29 (*0-685-09958-X*) S&S Trade.

— Metallica: The Frayed Ends of Metal. LC 92-33808. 1992. pap. 12.95 (*0-312-08635-0*) St Martin.

Crocker, Dan, jt. ed. see Young, Jimmy A.

Crocker, Daniel. Long Live the 2 of Spades. 63p. 1999. pap. 7.00 (*1-891408-10-0*, GBP-11) Green Bean.

— People Everyday & Other Poems. unabridged ed. ii, 92p. 1998. pap. 12.00 (*1-891408-06-2*, GBP-7) Green Bean.

***Crocker, David, ed.** Dictionary of Aeronautical English. 249p. 2000. 45.00 (*1-57958-201-X*) Fitzroy Dearborn.

Crocker, David, et al. Guitars Guitars Guitars: A Pictorial Reference Book. LC 88-70077. 150p. (Orig.). 1988. pap. 14.95 (*0-945706-00-6*) All Amer Music.

Crocker, David A. & Linden, Toby, eds. The Ethics of Consumption: The Good Life, Justice & Global Stewardship. LC 97-14380. (Philosophy & the Global Context Ser.: No. 107). 564p. 1997. 84.50 (*0-8476-8494-6*); pap. 27.95 (*0-8476-8495-4*) Rowman.

Crocker, Douglas C. How to Use Regression Analysis in Quality Control, Vol. 9. rev. ed. 80p. 1990. pap. 20.00 (*0-87389-103-1*, T3509) ASQ Qual Pr.

Crocker, Elizabeth. Baby Moses. (Great Big Bks.). (Illus.). 16p. (J). (ps). 1996. pap. 14.95 (*0-687-06677-8*) Abingdon.

— Good News. (Great Big Bks). (Illus.). 16p. (J). 1995. pap. 14.95 (*0-687-01447-6*) Abingdon.

Crocker, Elizabeth. Good News! Leader's Guide. (J). 1.50 (*0-687-05346-3*) Abingdon.

Crocker, Elizabeth, jt. ed. see Harris, Laura.

Crocker, Emily, ed. see Lavender, Cheryl.

Crocker, George N. Roosevelt's Road to Russia. LC 74-26540. (FDR & the Era of the New Deal Ser.). (Illus.). xvii, 312p. 1975. reprint ed. lib. bdg. 39.50 (*0-306-70714-4*) Da Capo.

Crocker, Glenys. The Gun Powder Industry. (Illus.). 32p. 1989. pap. 6.25 (*0-7478-0393-5*, Pub. by Shire Pubns) Parkwest Pubns.

Crocker, Glenys. The Gunpowder Industry. 1989. pap. 25.00 (*0-85263-780-2*, Pub. by Shire Pubns) St Mut.

Crocker, H. W., III. Robert E. Lee on Leadership: Executive Lessons in Character, Courage & Vision. LC 99-15074. 224p. 1999. 22.00 (*0-7615-1680-8*) Prima Pub.

***Crocker, H. W., III.** Robert E. Lee on Leadership: Executive Lessons in Character, Courage & Vision. 4th ed. 256p. 2000. pap. 14.95 (*0-7615-2554-8*) Prima Pub.

Crocker, Henry G. Crocker: Nathaniel Crocker, His Descendants & Ancestors of the Names of Allen, Blood, Bragg, Brewster, et al, Together with Genealogies of Many of Their Connections. (Illus.). 76p. 1996. reprint ed. pap. 16.00 (*0-8328-5597-9*); reprint ed. lib. bdg. 26.00 (*0-8328-5596-0*) Higginson Bk Co.

— Crocker. Nathaniel Crocker, 1758-1855, His Descendants & Ancestors in the Names of Allen, Blood, Bragg, Brewster, Bursley, Chase, Davis, Etc. 76p. 1996. reprint ed. pap. 15.00 (*0-8328-5236-8*); reprint ed. lib. bdg. 25.00 (*0-8328-5235-X*) Higginson Bk Co.

Crocker, Herbert L., jt. auth. see Ciabotti, Patricia A.

Crocker, J. Cell Proliferation in Lymphomas. (Illus.). 224p. 1993. 145.00 (*0-632-02925-0*) Blackwell Sci.

Crocker, J., jt. auth. see Curran, R. C.

Crocker, J. R., et al. Crocker Genealogy: Descendants of Wm. Crocker of Barnstable MA, 1612-1692. (Illus.). 321p. 1994. reprint ed. pap. 49.00 (*0-8328-4270-2*); reprint ed. lib. bdg. 59.00 (*0-8328-4269-9*) Higginson Bk Co.

Crocker, Jim, et al. Heroic Adventures. Arsenault, Mark, ed. (Illus.). 96p. 1996. pap. 16.00 (*1-890305-00-6*) Gold Rush.

Crocker, John. Bermuda, Bahamas, Hispanola, Puerto Rico & the Virgin Islands. 1968. 25.00 (*0-87556-062-8*) Saifer.

Crocker, John, jt. auth. see Mosley, Pat.

Crocker, Jonathan. Jonathan. 1994. pap. 22.50 (*0-9622885-7-8*) An LaBarre.

Crocker, Jonathan. Jonathan: A Memoir. 341p. 1994. 40.00 (*0-9622885-8-6*) Psyche Pr NY.

Crocker, Lawrence H. Positive Liberty: An Essay in Normative Political Philosophy. (Melbourne International Philosophy Ser.: Vol. 7). 156p. 1980. lib. bdg. 94.00 (*90-247-2291-8*, Pub. by M Nijhoff) Kluwer Academic.

Crocker, Lawrence P. Army Officer's Guide. 46th ed. (Illus.). 624p. 1993. pap. 19.95 (*0-8117-2510-3*) Stackpole.

— Army Officer's Guide. 47th ed. (Illus.). 608p. 1996. pap. 19.95 (*0-8117-2665-7*) Stackpole.

Crocker, Lester G. An Age of Crisis: Man & World in Eighteenth Century French Thought. LC 59-14233. (Goucher College Ser.). 516p. reprint ed. 160.00 (*0-8357-9260-9*, 201198300080) Bks Demand.

Crocker, Lester G., ed. see Rousseau, Jean-Jacques.

Crocker, Lester G., jt. ed. see Seibert, Louise C.

An Asterisk (*) at the beginning of an entry indicates that the title is appearing for the first time.

Crocker, Linda & Algina, James. Introduction to Classical & Modern Test Theory. 512p. (C). 1986. pap. 74.00 (*0-03-061634-4*, Pub. by Harcourt Coll Pubs) Harcourt.

Crocker, Liu H., jt. auth. see Brown, Stephen J.

Crocker, Malcolm. Encyclopedia of Acoustics, 4 vols. LC 96-37424. 2096p. 1997. 650.00 (*0-471-80465-7*) Wiley.

***Crocker, Malcolm.** Handbook of Acoustics. LC 97-41670. 1488p. 1998. 195.00 (*0-471-25293-X*, Wiley-Interscience) Wiley.

— Handbook of Acoustics, 1. 648p. 1997. write for info. (*0-471-17767-9*) Wiley.

Crocker, Malcolm J., ed. Inter-Noise '72: Proceedings of the International Conference on Noise Control Engineering Held in Washington, D. C. October 4-6, 1972. LC 72-91606. (Inter-Noise Ser.). 656p. Date not set. 25.00 (*0-614-11284-2*) Noise Control.

Crocker, Malcolm J. & Kessler, F. M., eds. Noise & Noise Control, Vol. II. 312p. 1982. 175.00 (*0-8493-5094-8*, TD892, CRC Reprint) Franklin.

Crocker, Mark. The Body Atlas. 2nd ed. LC 92-11313. (Illus.). 64p. (J). (gr. 3-6). 1994. 18.95 (*0-19-520963-X*) OUP.

Crocker, Mary C. Schaum's Outline of French Grammar. 3rd ed. (Schaum's Outline Ser.). 340p. (C). 1990. pap. 14.95 (*0-07-013885-0*) McGraw.

— Schaum's Outline of French Grammar. 4th expanded ed. LC 99-32210. (Illus.). 352p. 1999. pap. 15.95 (*0-07-013887-7*, Schaums Outlne) McGraw-Hill Prof.

Crocker, Mary E. Schaum's Outline of French Vocabulary. 2nd ed. LC 97-26860. (Schaum's Ser.). (FRE & ENG., Illus.). 432p. (C). 1997. pap. 15.95 (*0-07-013886-9*) McGraw.

Crocker, Mary E Coffman. French. 1999. pap. text 8.95 (*0-07-052715-6*) McGraw-Hill Pubng.

***Crocker, Matthew H.** Magic of the Many: Josiah Quincy & the Rise of Mass Politics in Boston, 1800-1830. LC 99-15158. 280p. 2000. text 35.00 (*1-55849-222-4*) U of Mass Pr.

Crocker, Matthew W. Computational Psycholinguistics: An Interdisciplinary Approach to the Study of Language. LC 95-43997. (Studies in Theoretical Psycholinguistics: Vol. 20). 260p. (C). 1996. lib. bdg. 112.00 (*0-7923-3802-2*) Kluwer Academic.

— Computational Psycholinguistics: An Interdisciplinary Approach to the Study of Language. (Studies in Theoretical Psycholinguistics). 260p. (C). 1996. pap. text 44.00 (*0-7923-3806-5*) Kluwer Academic.

***Crocker, Matthew W., et al, eds.** Architectures & Mechanisms for Language Processing. LC 99-11605. (Illus.). 400p. 1999. 64.95 (*0-521-63121-1*) Cambridge U Pr.

***Crocker, Michael R.** Children of the Sand: Life & Times of the American Children Who Grew up in Saudi Arabia. (Illus.). 232p. 1999. 30.00 (*1-928991-00-9*) M R Crocker.

Crocker, Pat. The Healing Herbs Cookbook. (Illus.). 192p. 1999. pap. 17.95 (*0-7788-0004-0*, Pub. by R Rose Inc) Firefly Bks Ltd.

— Riversong Recipes. (Illus.). 144p. 1997. pap. 14.95 (*0-9697079-6-7*) Moulin Publ.

***Crocker, Pat & Eagles, Susan.** The Juicing Bible. (Illus.). 224p. 2000. pap. 18.95 (*0-7788-0019-9*, Pub. by R Rose Inc) Firefly Bks Ltd.

Crocker, Richard & Hiley, David, eds. The New Oxford History of Music Vol. 2: The Early Middle Ages to 1300. 2nd ed. (Illus.). 816p. 1990. text 105.00 (*0-19-316329-2*) OUP.

Crocker, Richard L. A History of Musical Style. 576p. 1986. reprint ed. pap. 16.95 (*0-486-25029-6*) Dover.

***Crocker, Richard L.** An Introduction to Gregorian Chant. LC 99-88603. 256p. 2000. pap. 30.00 (*0-300-08310-6*) Yale U Pr.

Crocker, Richard L. Studies in Medieval Music Theory & the Early Sequence. LC 97-3006. (Variorum Collected Studies Ser.: Vol. 580). (Illus.). 352p. 1997. text 97.95 (*0-86078-643-9*, Pub. by Ashgate Pub) Ashgate Pub Co.

Crocker, Ruth, jt. ed. see Altman, Marjorie.

Crocker, Ruth H. Social Work & Social Order: The Settlement Movement in Two Industrial Cities, 1889-1930. 364p. 1992. text 39.95 (*0-252-01790-0*) U of Ill Pr.

Crocker, Thomas D. & Teasley, John L., eds. Economic Perspectives on Acid Deposition Control. (Acid Precipitation Ser.: Vol. 8). 208p. 1984. 69.95 (*0-250-40573-3*) Buttrwrth-Heinemann.

Crocker, W. & Barton, L. V. The Physiology of Seeds: An Introduction to the Study of Seed & Germination Problems. (Illus.). 267p. 1990. reprint ed. text 45.00 (*0-685-41268-7*, Pub. by Mahendra Pal Singh) Lubrecht & Cramer.

Crocker, W. D. Go to Jericho. unabridged ed. LC 98-27019. 55p. 1998. pap. 5.00 (*0-88734-755-X*) Players Pr.

Crocker, Walter R. Nigeria: A Critique of British Colonial Administration. LC 76-160964. (Select Bibliographies Reprint Ser.). 1977. reprint ed. 28.95 (*0-8369-5832-2*) Ayer.

***Crocker-White, Daphne.** Skylark. (Illus.). 128p. 2000. mass mkt. 9.95 (*0-9662719-3-9*) R B Abel.

Crocker, William H. The Canela (Eastern Timbira), No. 1: An Ethnographic Introduction. LC 89-600303. (Smithsonian Contributions to Anthropology Ser.: No. 33). 507p. reprint ed. pap. 157.20 (*0-8357-2753-X*, 203986900013) Bks Demand.

Crocket, Dennis. Schwarzweiss: The Revival of the Print in Germany, 1881-1924. Mitchell, Ben, ed. (Illus.). 1995. 10.00 (*1-880269-11-2*) D H Sheehan.

Crockett. International Money Issues. pap. 17.95 (*0-317-64183-2*, VNR) Wiley.

— Sea Chemical Engineering: Review for the P. E. Exam. 1995. pap. text 110.00 (*0-471-15473-3*) Wiley.

Crockett, et al. Starting Your Own Mediation Practice: A Workbook. rev. ed. (C). 1992. write for info. (*0-9617319-1-5*) CasaMar Ent.

Crockett, Albert S. Peacocks on Parade: A Narrative of a Unique Period in American Social History & Its Most Colorful Figures. LC 75-1836. (Leisure Class in America Ser.). (Illus.). 1975. reprint ed. 24.95 (*0-405-06905-7*) Ayer.

Crockett, Andrew. The Theory & Practice of Financial Stability. LC 97-5227. (Essays in International Finance Ser.: Vol. 203). 52p. 1997. pap. 10.00 (*0-88165-110-9*) Princeton U Int Finan Econ.

— William Taylor Memorial Lecture No. 4: Banking Supervision & Financial Stability. 31p. 1998. pap. 10.00 (*1-56708-107-X*) Grp of Thirty.

Crockett, Art. From the Files of True Detectives: Serial Murders. 1990. mass mkt. 4.95 (*1-55817-432-X*, Pinncle Kensgtn) Kensgtn Pub Corp.

— Spree Killers. 1991. mass mkt. 4.95 (*1-55817-461-3*, Pinncle Kensgtn) Kensgtn Pub Corp.

Crockett, Arthur. Count Saint Germain. 132p. 1990. pap. 21.95 (*0-938294-67-9*) Inner Light.

— Nostradamus' Unpublished Prophecies: The Untold Story. 64p. 1983. 10.00 (*0-938294-16-4*) Hlth Research.

— Three Secret Prophecies of Fatima Revealed. (Illus.). 72p. 1982. pap. 15.00 (*0-938294-13-X*) Inner Light.

Crockett, Arthur & Beckley, Timothy G. Angels of the Lord: Calling upon Your Guardian Angel for Guidance & Protection. 144p. 1993. 15.00 (*0-938294-03-2*) Inner Light.

Crockett, Arthur, jt. auth. see Beckley, Timothy G.

Crockett, Barry G. & Crockett, Lynette B. Family Emergency Plan, Vol. I. LC 89-91819. (Illus.). 80p. 1990. pap. 11.95 (*0-915131-89-7*) Crockett Pub Co.

— Seventy-Two Hour Emergency Preparedness Checklist: Prepare Every Needful Thing. 2nd rev. ed. LC 83-73117. (Illus.). 64p. 1990. pap. 10.95 (*0-915131-06-4*) Crockett Pub Co.

— A Year's Supply: "Take Heed, Prepare, Watch, & Be Ready" LC 88-71201. (Illus.). 117p. 1988. pap. 13.95 (*0-915131-88-9*) Crockett Pub Co.

Crockett, Bryan. The Play of Paradox: The Play of Paradox in Early Modern England: Stage & Sermon in Renaissance England. 240p. 1995. text 32.95 (*0-8122-3316-6*) U of Pa Pr.

Crockett, Candace. Card Weaving. LC 91-24156. (Illus.). 141p. (Orig.). 1991. pap. 19.95 (*0-934026-61-0*) Interweave.

Crockett, David. The Autobiography of David Crockett. LC 80-2887. (BCL Ser.: No. I & II). reprint ed. 42.50 (*0-404-18059-0*) AMS Pr.

— Autobiography of David Crockett. (BCL1 - United States Local History Ser.). 328p. 1991. reprint ed. lib. bdg. 89.00 (*0-7812-6314-X*) Rprt Serv.

— Davy Crockett's Own Story: A Narrative of the Life of David Crockett of the State of Tennessee. LC 93-34222. (Illus.). 128p. (J). 1993. reprint ed. pap. 12.95 (*1-55709-218-4*) Applewood.

— First American Born: The Life & Journal of Jonathan Belcher, the First-Known, American-Born Freemason. x, 267p. (Orig.). 1992. pap. text 22.00 (*1-55613-726-5*) Heritage Bk.

— A Narrative of the Life of David Crockett. Arpad, Joseph J., ed. 1972. pap. 12.95 (*0-8084-0021-5*) NCUP.

— A Narrative of the Life of David Crockett. (American Biography Ser.). 373p. 1991. reprint ed. lib. bdg. 79.00 (*0-7812-8094-X*) Rprt Serv.

— A Narrative of the Life of David Crockett of the State of Tennessee. LC 72-177358. (Tennesseana Editions Ser.). 232p. 1973. pap. 15.95 (*0-87049-533-X*) U of Tenn Pr.

— A Narrative of the Life of David Crockett of the State of Tennessee. LC 87-16226. lvii, 211p. 1987. reprint ed. pap. 10.95 (*0-8032-6325-2*, Bison Books) U of Nebr Pr.

— Sketches & Eccentricities of Colonel David Crockett of West Tennessee. LC 74-15735. (Popular Culture in America Ser.). 214p. 1975. reprint ed. 23.95 (*0-405-06370-9*) Ayer.

Crockett, David R. Saints Find the Place: A Day-by-Day Pioneer Experience. LC 97-92622. (Pioneer Trek Ser.: Vol. 3). (Illus.). 450p. 1997. pap. 19.95 (*0-9656108-4-5*) LDS-Gems Pr.

— Saints in Exile: A Day-by-Day Pioneer Experience. LC 96-95323. (Pioneer Trek Ser.: Vol. 1). (Illus.). x, 448p. 1996. pap. 25.00 (*0-9656108-0-2*) LDS-Gems Pr.

— Saints in the Wilderness: A Day-by-Day Pioneer Experience. LC 97-93244. (Pioneer Trek Ser.: No. 2). (Illus.). x, 450p. 1997. pap. 19.95 (*0-9656108-1-0*) LDS-Gems Pr.

***Crockett, Davy.** Davy Crockett's Own Story. 384p. 1999. reprint ed. 7.98 (*1-56852-243-6*) W S Konecky Assocs.

Crockett, Dennis. German Post-Expressionism: The Art of the Great Disorder, 1918-1924. LC 97-48435. (Illus.). 1140p. 1999. 55.00 (*0-271-01796-1*) Pa St U Pr.

Crockett, Dina B., tr. see Apresjan, Yuri D.

Crockett, Edward S., jt. auth. see Culliney, John L.

Crockett, Eleanor E. Fifty-Three Ford. 1979. pap. 5.00 (*0-930324-14-5*) Wings Pr.

Crockett, Ellen, ed. see Petersen, John L.

Crockett, Frank & Garner, Jocelyn. MFC Developer's Workshop. 2nd ed. 475p. 39.99 incl. cd-rom (*1-57231-859-7*) Microsoft.

Crockett, James E. Your Heart: A Basic Book for Heart Patients. 2nd ed. (Illus.). 216p. 1989. pap. 12.00 (*0-685-44369-8*) Eucalyptus Pr.

— Your Heart: In Sickness & in Health. (Illus.). 176p. (Orig.). 1984. pap. 10.00 (*0-9611980-0-1*) Eucalyptus Pr.

Crockett, James U. Crockett's Flower Garden. 311p. 1981. pap. 24.95 (*0-316-16133-0*) Little.

— Crockett's Victory Garden. (Illus.). 1977. pap. 19.95 (*0-316-16121-7*) Little.

Crockett, Jean B. & Kauffman, James M. The Least Restrictive Environment: Its Origins & Interpretations in Special Education. LC 99-12804. (A Volume in the Special Education & Disability Series). 248p. 1999. 49.95 (*0-8058-3101-0*); pap. 22.50 (*0-8058-3102-9*) L Erlbaum Assocs.

***Crockett, Jim.** The Why-To of Scuba Diving. LC 99-57722. 56p. 2000. pap. 14.95 (*1-881652-21-1*, Pub. by Aqua Quest) Natl Bk Netwk.

Crockett, John, tr. see Vaggioli, Dom Felice.

Crockett, Joseph V. Teaching Scripture from an African-American Perspective. LC 90-82978. 104p. 1990. pap. 7.95 (*0-88177-086-8*, DR086) Discipleship Res.

Crockett, Kent. The 911 Handbook: Biblical Solutions to Everyday Problems. LC 97-23128. 232p. 1997. 16.95 (*1-56563-295-8*) Hendrickson MA.

Crockett, Larry, jt. auth. see Fitz, Robert M.

***Crockett, Laura.** The Booke of Betrothal: Verses, Vows & Etiquette for the Romantic Renaissance Couple. Berkeley, Robert J., ed. (Illus.). 56p. 2000. pap. 24.00 (*0-9701492-3-9*, WCD1) Hist Resour.

— Trippingly on the Tongue: A Booke of Instruction for Speaking Early Modern English. Berkeley, Robert J., ed. 38p. 1997. pap. 16.00 (*0-9701492-1-2*, EME1) Hist Resour.

— Words of Course: A Book of Vocabularies from the 16th & 17th Centuries. 2nd ed. (Illus.). 70p. 1998. pap. 18.00 (*0-9701492-2-0*, EME2) Hist Resour.

Crockett, Laura, ed. see Giles, Paul.

Crockett, Linda. Carousel. 512p. 1995. 5.99 (*0-8125-0830-0*) Forge NYC.

— Dreamwalker. 1995. 21.95 (*0-685-75365-4*) Tor Bks.

Crockett, Lisa J. & Crouter, Ann C., eds. Pathways Through Adolescence: Individual Development in Relation to Social Contexts. (Penn State Series on Child & Adolescent Development). 280p. 1995. 49.95 (*0-8058-1500-7*) L Erlbaum Assocs.

***Crockett, Lisa J. & Silbereisen, Rainier K., eds.** Negotiating Adolescence in Times of Social Change. LC 99-10716. (Illus.). 344p. (C). 1999. 49.95 (*0-521-62389-8*) Cambridge U Pr.

Crockett, Lynette B., jt. auth. see Crockett, Barry G.

Crockett, M. H. & Dease, Barbara C. Through the Years: Light Out of Darkness, 1867-1977. (Illus.). 473p. (Orig.). 1991. pap. 30.00 (*1-882133-03-X*) Barefoot Pr.

Crockett, Marilyn, et al. The Money Club: How We Taught Ourselves the Secret to a Secure Financial Future - And How You Can, Too. 320p. 1998. pap. 13.00 (*0-684-84605-5*) S&S Trade.

— The Money Club: The Park Avenue Women's Guide to Personal Finance. LC 97-23184. 288p. 1997. 24.00 (*0-684-83719-6*) S&S Trade.

Crockett, Marsha. Sanctuary. LC 99-6411. 224p. 1999. pap. text 9.99 (*0-7642-2189-2*) Bethany Hse.

— Weaving a Life of Prayer: A 30 Day Journey. LC 98-16741. 108p. 1998. pap. 8.99 (*0-8308-1949-5*, 1949) InterVarsity.

Crockett, Mary E. Church Laces-Creative Crocheting. (Illus.). 125p. 1980. 9.00 (*0-8187-0037-8*) Harlo Press.

Crockett, Michael, jt. auth. see McClintock, Grant.

Crockett, Michael, jt. auth. see McCloud, Kevin.

Crockett, N., et al. Statpak. 254p. 1988. pap. text 34.95 (*0-471-33435-9*) Wiley.

Crockett, Pat. What's in It for Us? A Guide to Chambers of Commerce. Dawson, David, ed. 56p. (Orig.). 1993. pap. text 10.95 (*1-881096-06-8*) Towery Pub.

Crockett, Peter. Evatt: A Life. (Illus.). 416p. (C). 1994. 49.95 (*0-19-553558-8*) OUP.

***Crockett, Richard D., et al.** British Documents on Foreign Affairs. LC 99-41008. 1999. write for info. (*1-55655-766-3*) U Pubns Amer.

Crockett, Richard F. Angels Twelve. LC 84-90388. 1984. 15.00 (*0-87212-183-6*) Libra.

Crockett, Roger A. Understanding Friedrich Durrenmatt. Hardin, James N., ed. LC 97-33889. (Understanding Modern European & Latin American Literature Ser.). 256p. 1998. lib. bdg. 29.95 (*1-57003-213-0*) U of SC Pr.

***Crockett, S. R.** The Black Douglas. 252p. 2000. pap. 9.95 (*0-594-03061-7*) Eightn Hundrd.

Crockett, S. R. The Grey Man. (C). 1988. 65.00 (*0-907526-15-2*, Pub. by Alloway Pub) St Mut.

— The Grey Man. 1980. pap. 40.00 (*0-907526-14-4*, Pub. by Alloway Publ) St Mut.

***Crockett, S. R.** Maid Margaret. 252p. 2000. pap. 9.95 (*0-594-00477-2*) Eightn Hundrd.

— The Men of the Moss-Hags. 252p. 2000. pap. 9.95 (*0-594-00030-0*) Eightn Hundrd.

Crockett, S. R. The Raiders. 1980. pap. 40.00 (*0-907526-53-5*) Alloway Publ.

***Crockett, S. R.** The Raiders. 252p. 2000. pap. 9.95 (*0-594-00009-2*) Eightn Hundrd.

— The Red Axe. 252p. 2000. pap. 9.95 (*0-594-00036-X*) Eightn Hundrd.

— The Silver Skull. 252p. 2000. pap. 9.95 (*0-594-00069-6*) Eightn Hundrd.

Crockett, Samuel R. Adventurer in Spain. LC 70-106282. (Short Story Index Reprint Ser.). 1977. 21.95 (*0-8369-3319-2*) Ayer.

— Bog-Myrtle & Peat: Being Tales Chiefly of Galloway. LC 72-5909. (Short Story Index Reprint Ser.). 1977. reprint ed. 28.95 (*0-8369-4206-X*) Ayer.

— Love Idylls. LC 73-130055. (Short Story Index Reprint Ser.). 1977. 20.95 (*0-8369-3572-1*) Ayer.

— Stickit Minister, & Some Common Men. 2nd ed. LC 72-163023. (Short Story Index Reprint Ser.). 1977. reprint ed. 20.95 (*0-8369-3937-9*) Ayer.

Crockett, Samuel R., et al. Tales of Our Coast. LC 70-116966. (Short Story Index Reprint Ser.). (Illus.). 1977. 19.95 (*0-8369-3470-9*) Ayer.

Crockett, Silvia. Angels in Traditional Design. (International Design Library). (Illus.). 48p. (Orig.). 1987. pap. 5.95 (*0-88045-086-X*) Stemmer Hse.

Crockett-Smith, D. L. Civil Rites: New & Selected Poems. Chrisman, Robert, ed. & pref. by. (Orig.). 1996. pap. 5.95 (*0-933296-17-7*) Black Scholar Pr.

— Cowboy Amok. 30p. 1987. pap. 6.95 (*0-933296-14-2*) Black Scholar Pr.

***Crockett, Tom.** The Artist Inside: A Spiritual Guide to Cultivating Your Creative Self. LC 99-54388. 272p. 2000. pap. 15.00 (*0-7679-0394-3*) Broadway BDD.

Crockett, Tom. The Portfolio Journey: A Creative Guide to Keeping Student-Managed Portfolios in the Classroom. LC 97-52984. 1998. 25.00 (*1-56308-454-6*) Teacher Ideas Pr.

Crockett, Walter H. Soldiers of the Revolutionary War Buried in Vermont: And Anecdotes & Incidents Relating to Some of Them. 82p. 1998. reprint ed. pap. 10.95 (*0-8063-0534-7*, 1220) Clearfield Co.

Crockett, Wendy. Sweetwater Wisdom: A Native American Spiritual Way. LC 97-4155. 108p. (Orig.). 1997. pap. 13.95 (*0-8245-1485-8*) Crossroad NY.

Crockett, William. The Secrets of a Dynamic Subordinate: That Every Manager Should Know. (Illus.). 200p. (Orig.). (C). 1995. pap. 21.95 (*0-9631994-5-5*) Ctr Appl Behav Sci.

Crockett, William, ed. Four Views on Hell. (Counterpoints Ser.). 192p. 1996. reprint ed. pap. 14.99 (*0-310-21268-5*) Zondervan.

Crockett, William D. A Harmony of Samuel, Kings & Chronicles. LC 53-9880. 376p. 1985. pap. 14.99 (*0-8010-2511-7*) Baker Bks.

Crockett, William E. Chemical Engineering Review for PE Exam. LC 85-5382. 288p. 1985. 120.00 (*0-471-87874-X*) Wiley.

Crockett, William J. Faith: Voices from the Heart. 15p. pap. 3.00 (*0-934383-31-6*) Pride Prods.

— Fiftieth Anniversary "Voices from the Heart" 11p. 1985. pap. text 3.00 (*0-934383-01-4*) Pride Prods.

— Friendship: Voices from the Heart. 15p. 1985. pap. 3.00 (*0-934383-04-9*) Pride Prods.

— God's Way: Voices from the Heart. 15p. 1985. pap. 3.00 (*0-934383-34-0*) Pride Prods.

— Life: Voices from the Heart. 15p. 1985. pap. 3.00 (*0-934383-05-7*) Pride Prods.

— Love-Voices from the Heart. 15p. 1985. pap. text 3.00 (*0-934383-03-0*) Pride Prods.

— Mother's Day: Voices from the Heart. 15p. 1985. pap. 3.00 (*0-934383-33-2*) Pride Prods.

— My Quest: Voices from the Heart. 15p. 1985. pap. 3.00 (*0-934383-32-4*) Pride Prods.

Crockett, William R. Eucharist: Symbol of Transformation. 286p. 1992. pap. 15.95 (*0-8146-6098-3*, Pueblo Bks) Liturgical Pr.

Crockford, H. D., et al. Laboratory Manual of Physical. 2nd ed. 368p. (C). 1976. pap. 62.95 (*0-471-18844-1*) Wiley.

Crockford, N. Introduction to Risk Management. 2nd ed. (C). 1986. 320.00 (*0-7855-4113-6*, Pub. by Witherby & Co) St Mut.

Crockford, Neil. Administration of Insurance. (C). 1987. 250.00 (*0-7855-4324-4*, Pub. by Witherby & Co) St Mut.

— Risk Management. 86p. (C). 1992. 80.00 (*1-85609-024-8*, Pub. by Witherby & Co) St Mut.

Crockford, Neil, jt. auth. see Harrari, Jean-Claude.

***Crockford, Richard E.** The Spillers' Indian Summer. 2000. pap. 18.00 (*0-7388-2151-9*) Xlibris Corp.

Crockin, Susan L., jt. auth. see Seibel, Machelle M.

Crockwell, J. H. Pictures & Biographies of Brigham Young & His Wives. 1980. lib. bdg. 59.95 (*0-8490-3158-3*) Gordon Pr.

Crocomo, O. J., et al, eds. Biotechnology of Plants & Microorganisms. LC 86-23890. 487p. reprint ed. pap. 151.00 (*0-608-09664-4*, 206977900006) Bks Demand.

Croddy, Eric. Chemical & Biological Warfare: An Annotated Bibliography. LC 96-37866. 400p. 1997. 45.00 (*0-8108-3271-2*) Scarecrow.

Croddy, Marshall, et al. The Challenge of Diversity. (Illus.). 1999. teacher ed. 8.95 (*1-886253-11-0*) Constitutional Rights Found.

***Croddy, Marshall, et al.** The Challenge of Diversity. LC 99-49819. (W.M. Keck Foundation Ser.). 1999. pap. write for info. (*1-886253-10-2*) Constitutional Rights Found.

Croddy, Marshall, et al. The Challenge of Violence. (Texts Foundation Ser.). (Illus.). (Orig.). (J). 1997. teacher ed. 8.95 (*1-886253-02-1*) Constitutional Rights Found.

— The Challenge of Violence. (Texts Foundation Ser.). (Illus.). 72p. (Orig.). (YA). (gr. 9-12). 1997. pap. text 9.95 (*1-886253-01-3*) Constitutional Rights Found.

Croel, Thomas E. Maggie, Medworth & Me: How to Cook for Pets. 84p. 1984. write for info. (*0-318-58345-3*) G Whittell Mem.

Croes, Dale R. Cordage from the Ozette Village Archaeological Site: A Technological, Functional, & Comparative Study. fac. ed. (Washington Archaeological Laboratory of Anthropology Ser.: No. 9). (Illus.). 183p. (C). 1980. reprint ed. pap. text 19.38 (*1-55567-505-0*) Coyote Press.

— The Hoko River Archaeological Site Complex: The Wet/Dry Site (45CA213) 3,000-1,700 B. P. (Illus.). 272p. (Orig.). 1996. pap. text 50.00 (*0-87422-117-X*) Wash St U Pr.

Croes, Kathleen. A-Oxidation of 3-Methyl-Branched Fatty Acids: A Revised Pathway. (Acta Biomedica Lovaniensia Ser.). (Illus.). 113p. 1998. pap. 34.50 (*90-6186-869-6*, Pub. by Leuven Univ) Coronet Bks.

Croes, Martin & McNicoll, Andre. Marijuana Reappraised: Two Personal Accounts. LC 77-15695. 20p. 1977. pap. 1.00 (*0-913098-08-6*) Orion Society.

Croese, jt. auth. see Rue.

An Asterisk (*) at the beginning of an entry indicates that the title is appearing for the first time.

C

An Asterisk (*) at the beginning of an entry indicates that the title is appearing for the first time.

Croix, I. F. La, see La Croix, I. F.
Croix, Isobyl La, see La Croix, Isobyl.
Croix, Otto De La, see De La Croix, Otto.
Croix, Richard R. La, see La Croix, Richard R., ed.
Croizat, Victor J. Journey among Warriors: The Memoirs of a Marine. LC 97-11296. (Illus.). 233p. 1996. 30.00 (*1-57249-008-X*) White Mane Pub.
Croke, Brian. Christian Chronicles & Byzantine History, Fifth-Sixth Centuries. (Collected Studies: No. CS386). 352p. 1992. 115.95 (*0-86078-343-X*, Pub. by Variorum) Ashgate Pub Co.
Croke, Brian & Emmett, Edward A., eds. History & Historians in Late Antiquity. 184p. 1984. text 31.00 (*0-08-029840-0*, Pergamon Pr) Elsevier.
Croke, Frank J. & Croke, William F. Family Trusts. LC 98-45094. (Illus.). 307p. 1998. pap. 26.95 (*1-892879-12-3*, 102) Capital Mgmt Pr.
***Croke, Frank J. & Croke, William F.** Family Trusts: Financial Errors in Trusts--How to Avoid & Correct Them, Provide for Your Family, Save Taxes, Protect Your Assests & Avoid Probate. 2nd ed. LC 00-24879. 2000. write for info. (*1-892879-13-1*) Capital Mgmt Pr.
Croke, Vicki. Cats up Close. LC 97-23691. (Tiny Folio Ser.). (Illus.). 288p. 1997. 5.95 (*0-7892-0510-6*) Abbeville Pr.
— The Modern Ark: The Story of Zoos, Past, Present & Future. 272p. 1998. pap. 12.00 (*0-380-73131-2*, Avon Bks) Morrow Avon.
***Croke, Vicki.** The Modern Ark: The Story of Zoos: Past, Present & Future. (Illus.). 272p. 2000. reprint ed. pap. text 26.00 (*0-7881-9169-1*) DIANE Pub.
Croke, Vicki, jt. auth. see Tufts University School of Veterinary Medicine Staff.
Croke, Vickie. The Modern Ark: The History of Zoos: Past, Present & Future. LC 96-48901. 272p. 1997. 25.50 (*0-684-19712-X*) S&S Trade.
Croke, Vicky. Cats up Close. (Illus.). 144p. 1998. 19.98 (*0-89660-092-0*, Artabras) Abbeville Pr.
— Dogs up Close. LC 97-43082. (Tiny Folio Ser.). (Illus.). 288p. 1998. 11.95 (*0-7892-0428-2*) Abbeville Pr.
Croke, William F., jt. auth. see Croke, Frank J.
Croken, Robert C., ed. see Lonergan, Bernard.
Croker, John W. Croker Papers, 3 vols. 2nd rev. ed. Jennings, L. J., ed. LC 77-154125. reprint ed. 225.00 (*0-404-01880-7*) AMS Pr.
— Essays on the Early Period of the French Revolution. LC 78-114146. reprint ed. 57.50 (*0-404-01858-0*) AMS Pr.
Croker, John W., ed. see Pope, Alexander.
Croker, P. F. & Shannon, P. M., eds. The Petroleum Geology of Ireland's Offshore Basins. (Geological Society Special Publication Ser.: No. 93). (Illus.). 504p. 1995. 117.00 (*1-897799-34-9*, 335, Pub. by Geol Soc Pub Hse) AAPG.
Croker, T. Crofton. Irish Folk Stories for Children. (Illus.). 96p. (J). (gr. 4-7). 1991. pap. 10.95 (*0-85342-919-7*) Dufour.
Croker, Thomas C. Fairy Legends & Traditions of the South of Ireland. LC 82-5885. 464p. 1983. 75.00 (*0-8201-1380-8*) Schol Facsimiles.
— Fairy Legends & Traditions of the South of Ireland. 2nd ed. LC 99-173915. 364p. 1998. reprint ed. pap. 15.95 (*1-898256-53-5*, Pub. by Collins Press) Irish Bks Media.
Croker, Thomas C., ed. Narratives Illustrative of the Contests in Ireland in 1641 & 1690. (Camden Society, London. Publications, First Ser.: No. 14). reprint ed. 50.00 (*0-404-50114-1*) AMS Pr.
Crole, Robin. The Pipe: The Art & Love of a Great Tradition. LC 99-32960. (Illus.). 144p. 1998. boxed set 25.00 (*0-7615-1507-0*) Prima Pub.
Crole, Roy L. Categories for Types. (Illus.). 353p. (C). 1994. text 80.00 (*0-521-45092-6*); pap. text 31.95 (*0-521-45701-7*) Cambridge U Pr.
***Crolet, J. M.** Computational Methods for Flow & Transport in Porous Media. LC 00-29618. 2000. write for info. (*0-7923-6263-2*) Kluwer Academic.
Crolet, J. M. Computational Methods for Fluid-Structure Interaction. 1994. pap. 79.95 (*0-582-23691-6*, Pub. by Addison-Wesley) Longman.
Crolet, J. M. & El Hatri, M. Recent Advances in Problems of Flow & Transport in Porous Media. LC 97-48763. (Theory & Applications of Transport in Porous Media Ser.). 247p. 1998. write for info. (*0-7923-4938-5*) Kluwer Academic.
***Croley, Thomas E.** Using Meteorology Probability Forecasts in Operational Hydrology. LC 99-58022. 216p. 2000. 45.00 (*0-7844-0459-3*) Am Soc Civil Eng.
Crolius, Kendall. Knitting with Dog Hair. 112p. 1997. pap. 10.95 (*0-312-15290-6*) St Martin.
Crolius, Peter C., ed. The Rhode Island Scene. (Illus.). 160p. (Orig.). 1986. pap. 10.95 (*0-934881-01-4*) Dutch Island.
— A Wickford Anthology. LC 85-7265. (Illus.). 160p. (Orig.). 1985. pap. 6.95 (*0-934881-00-6*) Dutch Island.
Croll, Alistair & Packman, Eric. Managing Bandwidth: Deploying QOS Across Enterprise Networks. LC 99-35921. 450p. (C). 1999. 49.99 (*0-13-011391-3*, Pub. by P-H) S&S Trade.
Croll, Carolyn. The Little Snowgirl. (Illus.). 32p. (J). (ps-3). 1996. pap. 5.95 (*0-698-11424-8*, PapStar) Peng Put Young Read.
Croll, Carolyn. Little Snowgirl, An Old Russian Tale. LC 88-30667. 1996. 11.15 (*0-606-10254-X*, Pub. by Turtleback) Demco.
Croll, Carolyn. Too Many Babas: Newly Illustrated Edition. LC 92-18779. (I Can Read Bks.). (Illus.). 64p. (J). (ps-3). 1994. lib. bdg. 15.89 (*0-06-021384-1*) HarpC Child Bks.
Croll, Carolyn. The Story of Christmas, Story Book Set & Advent Calendar. 4p. (Orig.). (J). 1994. bds. 17.95 (*1-56305-547-3*, 3547) Workman Pub.
Croll, Carolyn, jt. auth. see Nagel, Karen B.
Croll, Elisabeth. From Heaven to Earth: Images & Experiences of Development in China. LC 93-12543. 272p. (C). 1993. pap. 27.99 (*0-415-10187-5*) Routledge.
— Wise Daughters from Foreign Lands: European Women Writers in China. 252p. 1989. 29.95 (*0-04-440414-X*) Routledge.
Croll, Elisabeth & Parkin, David, eds. Bush Base, Forest Farm: Culture, Environment & Development. (European Inter-University Development Opportunity Study Group Ser.). (Illus.). 288p. (C). 1992. pap. 25.99 (*0-415-06657-3*, A7340) Routledge.
Croll, Elizabeth. Women & Rural Development in China: Production & Reproduction. (Women, Work & Development Ser.: No. 11). viii, 172p. (Orig.). 1985. pap. 18.00 (*92-2-105217-6*) Intl Labour Office.
Croll, John D. Implementing a Trade Secrets Protection Program: A Practical Guide for California Businesses. Woods, Michael L., ed. 56p. 1994. pap. text 20.00 (*0-88124-711-1*, BU-32020) Cont Ed Bar-CA.
Croll, Mike. The History of Landmines. 1998. 39.95 (*0-85052-628-0*, 526280, Pub. by Leo Cooper) Combined Pub.
Croll, Morris W. Style, Rhetoric, & Rhythm. LC 88-19519. xvi, 450p. 1989. reprint ed. 42.00 (*0-918024-66-8*); reprint ed. pap. 17.50 (*0-918024-67-6*) Ox Bow.
— The Works of Fulke Greville. LC 70-100743. (English Literature Ser.). 1979. pap. 39.95 (*0-8383-0019-7*) M S G Haskell Hse.
Croll, Oswald. Basilica Chymica. (GER.). 1997. reprint ed. 248.00 (*3-487-10021-5*) G Olms Pubs.
Croll, P. C. Ancient & Historic Landmarks in the Lebanon Valley. (Illus.). 334p. 1997. reprint ed. lib. bdg. 39.50 (*0-8328-6423-4*) Higginson Bk Co.
***Croll, Paul.** Special Needs in the Primary School: One in Five? 2000. pap. 26.95 (*0-304-70564-0*) Continuum.
— Special Needs in the Primary School: One in Five? (Illus.). 2000. 74.95 (*0-304-70563-2*) Continuum.
Croll, Paul. Systematic Classroom Observation. 2nd ed. 224p. 1997. 75.00 (*0-7507-0711-9*, Falmer Pr); pap. 26.95 (*0-7507-0652-X*, Falmer Pr) Taylor & Francis.
Croll, Paul, ed. Teachers, Pupils & Primary Schooling. (Education Ser.). (Illus.). 176p. 1996. pap. 31.95 (*0-304-33659-9*); text 90.00 (*0-304-33660-2*) Continuum.
Croll, Theodore P. Enamel Microabrasion. (Illus.). 102p. 1991. text 65.00 (*0-86715-243-5*) Quint Pub Co.
Crolley, Jane. Relations in Industry. 464p. (C). 1989. pap. text 74.00 (*0-13-445685-8*) P-H.
Crolley, Liz, jt. auth. see Duke, Vic.
Crolley, Mary J., et al. Machinations: The Writings of Three Generations of Hollingsworth Women Telling of Wealth & Power - The Textile Machinery Empire & the Family Tragedy That Created A Billionaire. (Illus.). 431p. (Orig.). (C). 1988. pap. 19.95 (*0-9621955-0-2*) MJH Crolley.
Crols, J. & Steyaert, Michiel. CMOS Wireless Transceiver Design. LC 97-19895. (International Series in Engineering & Computer Science). 1997. text 126.50 (*0-7923-9960-9*) Kluwer Academic.
Croly, Ralph, et al. Lifelines 3: Letters from Famous People about Their Favourite Poem. LC 97-224487. xv, 291 p. 1997. write for info. (*1-86059-049-7*) Town Hse.
Croly, David. Miscegenation: The Theory of the Blending of the Races. 60p. 1995. pap. 7.50 (*0-88092-199-4*, 1994, Kav Bks) Royal Fireworks.
Croly, David G. Miscegenation. LC 70-104435. reprint ed. lib. bdg. 42.00 (*0-8398-0281-1*) Irvington.
Croly, George. Jerusalem & the Holy Land Rediscovered: The Prints of David Roberts, 1796-1864. (Illus.). 392p. 1997. 89.95 (*0-938989-15-4*) Duke.
Croly, Herbert. The Promise of American Life. LC 92-9926. 502p. (C). 1992. pap. 29.95 (*1-56000-628-5*) Transaction Pubs.
— The Promise of American Life. 468p. 1989. reprint ed. pap. text 18.95 (*1-55553-062-1*) NE U Pr.
Croly, Herbert & Pearson, Sidney A. Progressive Democracy. LC 97-24833. 460p. 1997. pap. text 29.95 (*1-56000-963-2*) Transaction Pubs.
Croly, Herbert D. Marcus Alonzo Hanna. 1993. reprint ed. lib. bdg. 89.00 (*0-7812-5352-7*) Rprt Serv.
— Marcus Alonzo Hanna: His Life & Work. (History - United States Ser.). 495p. 1992. reprint ed. lib. bdg. 99.00 (*0-7812-6197-X*) Rprt Serv.
— Willard Straight. 1977. 48.95 (*0-8369-7107-8*, 7941) Ayer.
Croly, Jane, jt. auth. see Fairfield, Francis G.
Crom, Scott. Encounters with Transcendence: Confessions of a Religious Philosopher. LC 86-60282. (Orig.). 1986. 4.00 (*0-87574-267-X*) Pendle Hill.
— Obstacles to Mystical Experience. LC 63-23067. (C). 1963. pap. 4.00 (*0-87574-132-0*) Pendle Hill.
— On Being Real. LC 67-29811. (Orig.). 1967. pap. 4.00 (*0-87574-155-X*) Pendle Hill.
— Quaker Worship & Techniques of Meditation. LC 74-82795. (C). 1974. pap. 4.00 (*0-87574-195-9*) Pendle Hill.
Crom, Theodore R. Early Lancashire Horological Tools & Their Makers. LC 93-90749. (Illus.). 300p. 1994. boxed set 140.00 (*0-9604888-4-7*) T R Crom.
— An Eighteenth Century English Brass Hardware Catalogue. LC 93-90749. (Illus.). 160p. 1994. boxed set 95.00 (*0-9604888-5-5*) T R Crom.
— Horological & Other Shop Tools, 1700 to 1900: Seventeen Hundred to Nineteen Hundred. LC 87-70330. (Illus.). 388p. 1987. boxed set 105.00 (*0-9604888-2-0*) T R Crom.
— Horological Shop Tools, 1700 to 1900. LC 80-69542. (Illus.). 694p. 1980. boxed set 130.00 (*0-9604888-0-4*) T R Crom.
— Horological Wheel Cutting Engines, 1700 to 1900. LC 76-19334. (Illus.). 150p. 1970. boxed set 25.00 (*0-9604888-1-2*) T R Crom.
— Trade Catalogues, 1542 to 1842. LC 88-93066. (Illus.). 404p. 1989. boxed set 165.00 (*0-9604888-3-9*) T R Crom.
Cromack, Celeste, ed. see Renfro, Nancy.
Croman, Charlotte & Schick, Suzanne C. Speaking for Today's World. 172p. (C). 1994. text 31.20 (*0-536-58630-6*) Pearson Custom.
— Speaking for Today's World 82p. (C). 1995. text, wbk. ed. 11.80 (*0-536-59254-3*) Pearson Custom.
Cromartie, Alan. Sir Matthew Hale, 1609-1676: Law, Religion & Natural Philosophy. (Cambridge Studies in Early Modern British History). 278p. (C). 1995. text 59.95 (*0-521-45043-8*) Cambridge U Pr.
Cromartie, Michael. Might & Right after the Cold War: Can Foreign Policy Be Moral? 146p. (C). 1993. text 18.95 (*0-89633-180-6*) Ethics & Public Policy.
Cromartie, Michael, ed. Evangelicals & Foreign Policy: Four Perspectives. LC 89-39175. 100p. (Orig.). (C). 1989. pap. text 12.75 (*0-89633-140-7*) Ethics & Public Policy.
— Evangelicals & Foreign Policy: Four Perspectives. LC 89-39175. 100p. (Orig.). (C). 1990. lib. bdg. 27.25 (*0-89633-139-3*) Ethics & Public Policy.
— No Longer Exiles: The Religious New Right in American Politics. 164p. 1992. 18.95 (*0-89633-172-5*) Ethics & Public Policy.
— Peace Betrayed: Essays on Pacifism & Politics. 275p. (C). 1990. pap. text 22.75 (*0-89633-144-X*); lib. bdg. 39.50 (*0-89633-143-1*) Ethics & Public Policy.
— A Preserving Grace: Protestants, Catholics, & Natural Law. LC 96-48112. 201p. (Orig.). 1997. pap. 20.00 (*0-8028-4306-9*) Eerdmans.
Cromartie, Michael, jt. ed. see Neuhaus, Richard J.
Cromarty. Book for Family Reading, Vol. 3. 1997. pap. 13.99 (*0-85234-391-4*, Pub. by Evangelical Pr) P & R Pubng.
Cromarty, Jim. Book for Family Reading, Vol. 2. 1996. pap. 13.99 (*0-85234-352-3*, Pub. by Evangelical Pr) P & R Pubng.
— Book for Family Worship. 1997. pap. 13.99 (*0-85234-388-4*, Pub. by Evangelical Pr) P & R Pubng.
— King of the Cannibals. 1998. pap. 13.99 (*0-85234-401-5*) P & R Pubng.
— Mighty Fortress is Our God. 1998. pap. 13.99 (*0-85234-411-2*, Pub. by Evangelical Pr) P & R Pubng.
***Cromarty, Jim.** Take Care in the Bath. 1999. pap. 13.99 (*0-85234-417-1*) Evangelical Pr.
— You Sank My Boat. 1999. pap. text 13.99 (*0-85234-432-5*) Evangelical Pr.
Crombie, A. C. Augustine to Galileo. (Illus.). 728p. 1980. 40.00 (*0-674-05273-0*) HUP.
— The History of Science from Augustine to Galileo. unabridged ed. LC 95-16536. (Illus.). 464p. 1996. reprint ed. pap. text 16.95 (*0-486-28850-1*) Dover.
— Science, Art & Nature in Medieval & Modern Thought. LC 95-49964. 1996. 70.00 (*1-85285-067-1*) Hambledon Press.
— Science, Optics & Music in Medieval & Early Modern Thought. 450p. 1990. 70.00 (*0-907628-79-6*) Hambledon Press.
Crombie, A. C., ed. George Berkeley Bicentenary, Vol. 4, No. 13. (Philosophy of George Berkeley Ser.). 92p. 1988. text 10.00 (*0-8240-2438-9*) Garland.
Crombie, David. Piano: A Photographic History of the World's Most Celebrated Instrument. (Illus.). 112p. 1995. 35.00 (*0-87930-372-7*) Miller Freeman.
Crombie, Deborah. All Shall Be Well. 272p. 1995. mass mkt. 5.99 (*0-425-14771-1*) Berkley Pub.
— All Shall Be Well. large type ed. (Cloak & Dagger Ser.). 351p. 1994. lib. bdg. 20.95 (*0-7862-0298-X*) Thorndike Pr.
— All Shall Be Well: A Superintendent Duncan Kincaid - Sergeant Gemma James Mystery. 256p. 1994. text 20.00 (*0-684-19654-9*, Scribners Ref) Mac Lib Ref.
— Dreaming of the Bones. LC 97-16336. 416p. 1998. mass mkt. 5.99 (*0-553-57931-2*) Bantam.
— Dreaming of the Bones. LC 97-16336. 1997. 21.50 (*0-684-84720-5*); 21.50 (*0-684-80141-8*) S&S Trade.
— Kissed a Sad Goodbye. LC 98-50186. 336p. 1999. 23.95 (*0-553-10943-X*) Bantam.
***Crombie, Deborah.** Kissed a Sad Goodbye. large type ed. LC 99-22158. (Large Print Book Ser.). 1999. 23.95 (*1-56895-731-9*) Wheeler Pub.
Crombie, Deborah. Leave the Grave Green. 304p. 1996. mass mkt. 5.99 (*0-425-15308-8*) Berkley Pub.
***Crombie, Deborah.** Leave the Grave Green. large type ed. LC 00-22864. 2000. pap. 22.95 (*1-56895-846-3*) Wheeler Pub.
Crombie, Deborah. Mourn Not Your Dead. 304p. 1997. reprint ed. mass mkt. 5.99 (*0-425-15778-4*, Prime Crime) Berkley Pub.
— Mourn Not Your Dead: A Duncan Kincaid/Gemma James Crime Novel. large type ed. LC 96-3011. 1996. 24.95 (*1-56895-367-4*, Compass) Wheeler Pub.
— A Share in Death: A Mystery Introducing Superintendent Duncan Kincaid & Sergeant Gemma James. large type ed. LC 93-21675. 316p. 1993. reprint ed. lib. bdg. 20.95 (*0-7862-0012-X*) Thorndike Pr.
— A Share in Death: A Mystery Introducing Superintendent Duncan Kincaid & Sergeant Gemma James. 208p. 1994. reprint ed. pap. 5.99 (*0-425-14197-7*, Prime Crime) Berkley Pub.
Crombie, I. K., ed. The Pocket Guide to Critical Appraisal. 66p. 1996. pap. text 18.00 (*0-7279-1099-X*, Pub. by BMJ Pub) Login Brothers Bk Co.
Crombie, I. K. & Davies, H. T. Research in Health Care: Design, Conduct & Interpretation of Health Services Research. LC 95-42359. 302p. 1996. pap. 59.95 (*0-471-96259-7*) Wiley.
Crombie, I. K., et al. The Audit Handbook: Improving Health Care through Clinical Audit. LC 92-48371. 242p. 1993. 115.00 (*0-471-93766-5*, Wiley-Interscience) Wiley.
Crombie, I. M. Plato: The Midwife's Apprentice. LC 81-6812. 195p. 1981. reprint ed. lib. bdg. 49.75 (*0-313-23243-1*, CRPL, Greenwood Pr) Greenwood.
Crombie, Iain K. & Florey, Charles D., eds. The Pocket Guide to Grant Applications. 68p. 1998. pap. text 29.00 (*0-7279-1219-4*, Pub. by BMJ Pub) Login Brothers Bk Co.
Crombie, Iain K., ed. see Von Korff, Michael.
Crombie, L., ed. Recent Advances in the Chemistry of Insect Control, Vol. 2. (C). 1990. text 132.00 (*0-85186-627-1*) CRC Pr.
Crombie, W. Curriculum Innovation: A Celebration of Classroom Practice. LC 96-33217. 1997. 94.00 (*0-335-19757-4*); pap. 27.95 (*0-335-19756-6*) OpUniv Pr.
Crombleholme, William, jt. auth. see Brown, Jeanette.
Cromby, John, jt. auth. see Nightingale, David J.
Crome, Peter. Drugs & the Older Population. 1998. 58.00 (*1-86094-099-4*, Pub. by Imperial College) World Scientific Pub.
Cromell, Cathy L., et al. Desert Gardening for Beginners: How to Grow Vegetables, Flowers & Herbs in an Arid Climate. LC 99-72759. (Illus.). 102p. (Orig.). 1999. pap. 7.95 (*0-9651987-2-3*, Pub. by AZ Mstr Grdnr) Sunbelt Pubns.
Cromer, Alan. Experiments in Introductory Physics. 177p. (C). 1994. 22.32 (*1-56870-148-9*) RonJon Pub.
— Physics for the Life Sciences. 2nd ed. (C). 1994. text 52.50 (*0-07-014440-0*) McGraw.
— Uncommon Sense: The Heretical Nature of Science. (Illus.). 256p. 1995. pap. 14.95 (*0-19-509636-3*) OUP.
Cromer, Alan H. Connected Knowledge: Science, Philosophy & Education. LC 96-14270. (Illus.). 240p. 1997. 30.00 (*0-19-510240-1*) OUP.
— Uncommon Sense: The Heretical Nature of Science. (Illus.). 256p. (C). 1993. text 27.50 (*0-19-508213-3*, 11091) OUP.
Cromer, Evelyn B. Political & Literary Essays: 1st Series. LC 68-8453. (Essay Index Reprint Ser.). 1977. 26.95 (*0-8369-1058-3*) Ayer.
— Political & Literary Essays: 2nd Series. LC 73-108636. (Essay Index Reprint Ser.). 1977. 23.95 (*0-8369-1564-X*) Ayer.
— Political & Literary Essays: 3rd Series. LC 74-107690. (Essay Index Reprint Ser.). 1977. 23.95 (*0-8369-1494-5*) Ayer.
Cromer, Jim. History, Theory, & Practice of Art Criticism in Art Education. 93p. (C). 1990. pap. 18.00 (*0-937652-50-4*, 242) Natl Art Ed.
Cromer, John, jt. ed. see Bullen, Keith.
Cromer, Marie W. Modern Indians of Alabama: Remnants of the Removal. (Illus.). 388p. (Orig.). 1987. pap. 12.50 (*0-685-19422-1*) Southern U Pr.
Cromer, Mark. Health Care Handbook: A Consumer's Guide to the American Health Care System. LC 97-15262. 256p. (Orig.). 1997. pap. 12.95 (*0-9639946-7-0*, 46-7-0) Snta Monica.
Cromer, Mary L. Stories for Jason. LC 93-37765. 110p. (J). 1993. pap. 9.00 (*0-944350-28-3*) Friends United.
Cromer, Peggy, ed. see Zalm, Bill V.
Cromey, Robert W. In God's Image: Christian Witness to the Need for Gay-Lesbian Equality in the Eyes of the Church. Herrman, Bert, ed. LC 91-70093. (Illus.). 128p. (Orig.). 1991. pap. 9.95 (*0-9624751-2-2*) Alamo Sq Pr.
Cromie, Alice. A Tour Guide to the Civil War. 4th rev. ed. LC 92-22746. (Illus.). 336p. (Orig.). 1992. pap. 12.95 (*1-55853-200-5*) Rutledge Hill Pr.
Cromie, Bob. Illinois Trivia. LC 92-9312. 1992. pap. 6.95 (*1-55853-162-9*) Rutledge Hill Pr.
Cromie, Cynthia. Who Will Educate Your Children? A Family Reading Program. LC 97-192650. (Illus.). 85p. 1997. pap. 4.50 (*0-9661755-0-6*) Pillow Polk.
Cromie, Richard M. Christ Will See You Through. 3rd ed. 36p. 1993. pap. 2.95 (*0-914733-04-4*) Desert Min.
***Cromie, Richard M.** Christ Will See You Through. 5th ed. 68p. 1999. 8.95 (*0-914733-25-7*) Desert Min.
Cromie, Richard M. Como Vivir Con Cancer. 28p. 1991. pap. 2.95 (*0-914733-13-3*) Desert Min.
— How to Live with Cancer. 5th rev. ed. LC 84-72666. 24p. 1992. reprint ed. pap. 2.95 (*0-914733-01-X*) Desert Min.
— The Rhapsody of Scripture. 60p. 1996. pap. 5.95 (*0-914733-20-6*) Desert Min.
— When You Lose Someone You Love. 76p. 1993. pap. 8.95 (*0-914733-18-4*) Desert Min.
Cromie, Robert. The Great Chicago Fire. LC 93-30996. (Illus.). 192p. 1993. reprint ed. 24.95 (*1-55853-264-1*) Rutledge Hill Pr.
Cromie, Robert. The Great Chicago Fire. LC 93-30996. (Illus.). 192p. 1994. reprint ed. pap. 18.95 (*1-55853-265-X*) Rutledge Hill Pr.
— A Short History of Chicago. (Short History Ser.). (Illus.). 160p. (Orig.). 1984. pap. 12.95 (*0-938530-28-3*) Lexikos.
Cromie, Robert & Pinkston, Joseph. Dillinger: A Short & Violent Life. 266p. 1990. reprint ed. pap. text 10.95 (*0-924772-06-9*) CH Bookworks.
Cromie, Robert A. Chicago. pap. 13.95 (*0-528-88061-6*) Rand McNally.
Cromie, Stephen. International Commercial Litigation: 1990 Edition. 622p. 1996. text 125.00 (*0-406-29002-4*, 81216-10, MICHIE) LEXIS Pub.
Cromie, Stephen & Park, William D. International Commercial Litigation. 580p. 1990. 125.00 (*0-88063-706-4*, MICHIE) LEXIS Pub.
Cromley, Elizabeth C. Alone Together: A History of New York's Early Apartments. LC 89-42895. (Illus.). 252p. 1990. text 37.50 (*0-8014-2324-4*) Cornell U Pr.

An Asterisk (*) at the beginning of an entry indicates that the title is appearing for the first time.

— Alone Together: A History of New York's Early Apartments. 1999. 19.95 (*0-8014-8613-0*) Cornell U Pr.

Cromley, Elizabeth C. & Hudgins, Carter L., eds. Gender, Class & Shelter: Perspectives in Venacular Architecture, Vol. V. LC 94-18715. (Illus.). 288p. (C). 1995. pap. text 27.50 (*0-87049-872-X*) U of Tenn Pr.

Cromley, Elizabeth C., jt. ed. see Hudgins, Carter L.

Cromley, Ellen, ed. see Aitken, Stuart C.

Cromley, Ellen, ed. see Griffith, Daniel A.

Cromley, Ellen, ed. see MacEachren, Alan M.

Cromley, Ellen, ed. see Moon, Henry.

Cromley, Ellen K., ed. see McMaster, Robert B. & Shea, K. Stuart.

Cromley, Richard, ed. see Griffith, Daniel A.

Cromley, Robert, ed. see Aitken, Stuart C.

Cromley, Robert, ed. see MacEachren, Alan M.

Cromley, Robert, ed. see Moon, Henry.

Cromley, Robert G., ed. see McMaster, Robert B. & Shea, K. Stuart.

Crommelin. Topics in Pharmaceutical Science, 1991. 1992. 143.00 (*3-88763-016-5*) CRC Pr.

Crommelin, D. J. & Schellekens, H., eds. From Clone to Clinic. (Developments in Biotherapy Ser.). (C). 1990. text 221.50 (*0-7923-0945-6*) Kluwer Academic.

Crommelinck, M., jt. auth. see Roucoux, A.

Crommelynck, Aldo, et al. Picasso: Inside the Image. LC 94-62008. (Illus.). 128p. 1995. 27.50 (*0-500-09251-6*, Pub. by Thames Hudson) Norton.

Cromphout, Gustaaf Van, see Van Cromphout, Gustaaf.

Crompton. Children & Counseling. 256p. 1992. pap. 35.95 (*1-56593-563-2*, 0532) Singular Publishing.

— An Introduction to Housing Studies. 1997. pap. text. write for info. (*0-582-27999-2*, Pub. by Addison-Wesley) Longman.

— Karate Training Methods. pap. write for info. (*0-901764-67-1*, 93221, Pub. by P H Crompton) Midpt Trade.

Crompton, Anne E. Johnny's Trail: Story of Johnny Appleseed. LC 86-60054. 112p. 1986. 6.95 (*0-87785-131-X*) Swedenborg.

— Queen of Swords. LC 79-26496. 1980. 9.95 (*0-416-30611-X*, NO. 0165) Routledge.

— The Rainbow Pony. (J). (gr. 3-6). 1995. pap. 3.99 (*0-671-51121-1*, Minstrel Bks) PB.

— The Snow Pony. (J). (gr. 3-6). 1994. per. 3.99 (*0-671-78507-9*) S&S Trade.

— The Sorcerer. LC 82-61042. 176p. 1982. reprint ed. 22.00 (*0-933256-36-1*) Second Chance.

— The Wildfire Pony. (J). (gr. 3-7). 1996. pap. 3.50 (*0-614-15699-8*, Minstrel Bks) PB.

— The Wildflower Pony. (J). (gr. 3-6). 1996. per. 3.99 (*0-671-51120-3*, Minstrel Bks) PB.

Crompton, Anne Eliot. Percival's Angel. 1999. mass mkt. 5.99 (*0-451-45757-9*) NAL.

Crompton, Anne Eliot. Rainbow Pony. 1995. 9.09 (*0-606-08931-4*, Pub. by Turtleback) Demco.

Crompton, Anne Eliot. Snow Pony. 1991. 9.09 (*0-606-06005-7*, Pub. by Turtleback) Demco.

Crompton, C. W. Pollen Grains of Canadian Honey Plants. (Illus.). 228p. (Orig.). 1993. pap. 51.95 (*0-660-14818-8*, Pub. by Canadian Govt Pub) Accents Pubns.

Crompton, Carrie. Bach Dances for Hammered Dulcimer. 40p. 1997. pap. 11.95 (*0-7866-2879-0*, 96697); pap. 26.92 incl. audio compact disk (*0-7866-2881-2*, 96697CDP) Mel Bay.

Crompton, Charles S., Jr., et al. Corporate & Commercial Practice in the Delaware Court of Chancery. 1997. 105.00 (*1-55834-544-2*, 61110) LEXIS Pub.

Crompton, D. W. & Joyner, S. M. Parasitic Worms. 208p. 1980. pap. 18.00 (*0-85109-830-4*) Taylor & Francis.

Crompton, D. W. & Newton, B. A., eds. Trends & Perspectives in Parasitology, Vol. 2. LC 81-642963. 101p. reprint ed. pap. 28.80 (*0-608-17048-8*, 2027281) Bks Demand.

Crompton, David W., jt. auth. see Coombs, Isabel.

Crompton, Frank. Workhouse Children. 1997. pap. 26.95 (*0-7509-1429-7*, Pub. by Sutton Pub Ltd) Intl Pubs Mktg.

— Workhouse Children: Infant & Child Paupers under the Worchester Poor Law, 1780-1871. LC 97-158877. (Illus.). 224p. 1997. 72.00 (*0-7509-1281-2*, Pub. by Sutton Pub Ltd) Intl Pubs Mktg.

Crompton, Gerald, ed. Canals & Inland Navigation. (Studies in Transport History). 200p. 1996. 61.95 (*1-85928-346-2*, Pub. by Scolar Pr) Ashgate Pub Co.

Crompton, John. The Hunting Wasp. (Illus.). 256p. 1987. reprint ed. pap. 8.95 (*0-941130-49-5*) Lyons Pr.

Crompton, John L. & Havitz, Mark. Financing & Acquiring Park & Recreation Resources. LC 98-8643. (Illus.). 552p. 1998. text 49.00 (*0-88011-806-7*, BCRO0806) Human Kinetics.

Crompton, John L., jt. auth. see Howard, Dennis R.

Crompton, John L., jt. ed. see Witt, Peter A.

Crompton, Louis. Byron & Greek Love: Homophobia in 19th Century England. 429p. 1997. pap. 19.95 (*0-85449-263-1*, Pub. by Gay Mens Pr) LPC InBook.

— Shaw the Dramatist. LC 69-11202. 273p. reprint ed. pap. 84.70 (*0-608-16793-2*, 205617200054) Bks Demand.

— Shaw the Dramatist: A Study of the Intellectual Background of the Major Plays. LC 72-169714. xi, 261p. 1971. write for info. (*0-04-822034-5*) Allen & Unwn AT.

Crompton, Louis, ed. see Shaw, George Bernard.

Crompton, Margaret. Children, Spirituality, Religion & Social Work. LC 98-70340. 280p. 1998. pap. 31.95 (*1-85742-377-1*, Pub. by Ashgate Pub) Ashgate Pub Co.

***Crompton, Paul.** Bruce Lee Anthology: Films & Fighting. (Illus.). 150p. 1999. pap. text 24.95 (*1-874250-90-1*) P H Crompton.

Crompton, Paul. Elements of Tai Chi. 1997. pap. 9.95 (*1-86204-039-7*, Pub. by Element MA) Penguin Putnam.

— Five Steps: Meditative Sensations Walking. 80p. 1996. pap. 19.95 (*1-874250-60-X*) P H Crompton.

— A Practical Introduction: Tai Chi. LC 97-45125. 1998. pap. 14.95 (*1-86204-163-6*, Pub. by Element MA) Penguin Putnam.

— Self Defense for Today. pap. 13.95 (*0-901764-99-X*, 93164, Pub. by P H Crompton) Midpt Trade.

***Crompton, Paul.** Tai Chi: An Introductory Guide to the Chinese Art of Movement. (New Perspectives (Element) Ser.). (Illus.). 128p. 2000. pap. 9.95 (*1-86204-760-X*, Pub. by Onewrld Pubns) Penguin Putnam.

Crompton, Paul. Tai Chi Combat. 136p. 1994. pap. 17.95 (*1-874250-25-1*, 93162, Pub. by P H Crompton) Midpt Trade.

— Tai Chi for Two: The Practice of Push Hands. pap. 17.95 (*1-874250-40-5*, 93306) P H Crompton.

— The T'ai Chi Workbook. LC 87-9736. (Illus.). 157p. 1987. pap. 19.00 (*0-87773-424-0*, Pub. by Shambhala Pubns) Random.

— Walking Meditation: Pakua - The Martial Art of the I Ching. LC 96-17951. (Illus.). 192p. 1997. pap. 14.95 (*1-85230-897-4*, Pub. by Element MA) Penguin Putnam.

Crompton, Paul, ed. & tr. see Frederic, Louis.

Crompton, R. W., et al, eds. Gaseous Electronics & Its Applications. (Advances in Solid State Technology Ser.). 360p. 1991. text 225.00 (*0-7923-1214-7*) Kluwer Academic.

Crompton, R. Z. Dead Tones. LC 97-90968. 400p. 1997. pap. text 15.95 (*0-9649438-2-4*) Zoller Pubng.

— Death by Association. LC 95-71134. 400p. 1995. pap. write for info. (*0-9649438-0-8*) Zoller Pubng.

— Steel Illusions. 400p. 1996. pap. text 15.95 (*0-9649438-1-6*) Zoller Pubng.

***Crompton, Ray.** Determination of Organic Compunds in Soils, Sediments, & Sludges. 560p. 2000. 149.00 (*0-419-25270-3*, E & FN Spon) Routledge.

Crompton, Richard. The Mansion of Magnanimitie: Wherein Is Shewed the Acts of Sundrie English Kings, No. 722. LC 74-28841. 1975. reprint ed. 20.00 (*90-221-0722-1*) Walter J Johnson.

— Star-Chamber Cases, Shewing What Causes Properly Belong to the Cognizance of That Court. LC 74-28842. (English Experience Ser.: No. 723). 1975. reprint ed. 20.00 (*90-221-0723-X*) Walter J Johnson.

Crompton, Rob, ed. Computers & the Primary School Curriculum. 200p. 1989. pap. 34.95 (*1-85000-455-2*, Falmer Pr) Taylor & Francis.

Crompton, Rob & Mann, Philip, eds. IT Across the Primary Curriculum. (Education Ser.). (Illus.). 160p. 1996. pap. 39.95 (*0-304-33290-9*); text 89.50 (*0-304-33288-7*) Continuum.

Crompton, Rosemary. Class & Stratification: An Introduction to Current Debates. LC 92-41451. 1993. pap. 26.95 (*0-7456-0947-3*) Blackwell Pubs.

— Class & Stratification: An Introduction to Current Debates. 2nd rev. ed. LC 98-23965. 240p. 1998. 59.95 (*0-7456-1792-1*); pap. 26.95 (*0-7456-1793-X*) Blackwell Pubs.

— Women & Work in Modern Britain. (Oxford Modern Britain Ser.). (Illus.). 166p. 1998. pap. text 19.95 (*0-19-878097-4*) OUP.

— Women & Work in Modern Britain. (Oxford Modern Britain Ser.). (Illus.). 166p. (C). 1998. text 55.00 (*0-19-878096-6*) OUP.

Crompton, Rosemary, ed. Restructuring Gender Relations & Employment: The Decline of the Male Breadwinner. LC 99-19786. 256p. 1999. 78.00 (*0-19-829469-7*); pap. 29.95 (*0-19-829608-8*) OUP.

Crompton, Rosemary, et al, eds. Changing Forms of Employment: Organizations, Skills, & Gender. LC 95-25433. 296p. (C). 1996. 85.00 (*0-415-13371-8*); pap. 24.99 (*0-415-14116-8*) Routledge.

Crompton, Rosemary & Mann, Michael. Gender & Stratification. 400p. 1986. pap. text 29.95 (*0-7456-0168-5*) Blackwell Pubs.

Crompton, Rosemary & Sanderson, Kay. Gendered Jobs & Social Change. 224p. (C). 1990. text 49.95 (*0-04-445597-6*) Routledge.

Crompton, Samuel. 100 Battles That Shaped World History. 1997. pap. 7.95 (*0-912517-27-1*) Bluewood Bks.

— 100 Wars That Shaped World History. 1997. pap. 7.95 (*0-912517-28-X*) Bluewood Bks.

Crompton, Samuel W. Gods & Goddesses of Classical Mythology. 64p. 1997. 4.98 (*1-889461-01-6*) DoveTail Bks.

— 100 Americans Who Shaped American History. 1998. pap. text 7.95 (*0-912517-32-8*) Bluewood Bks.

— 100 Families Who Shaped World History. 1998. pap. 7.95 (*0-912517-34-4*) Bluewood Bks.

— 100 Leaders Who Shaped Colonial North America. 1998. pap. 7.95 (*0-912517-35-2*) Bluewood Bks.

— 100 Military Leaders Who Shaped World History. 1998. pap. text 7.95 (*0-912517-33-6*) Bluewood Bks.

***Crompton, Samuel Willard.** Altas of Native American History. (Illus.). 1999. 29.99 (*0-7858-1118-4*) Bk Sales Inc.

***Crompton, Samuel Willard & Rhein, Michael J.** The Ultimate Book of Lighthouses. LC 99-87171. 2000. 24.98 (*1-57145-224-9*, Thunder Bay) Advantage Pubs.

***Crompton, Sheila.** All about Your Ferret. 32p. 1999. pap. text 3.50 (*0-7641-1189-2*) Barron.

Crompton, T. R. The Analysis of Natural Waters Vol. 1: Complex-Formation Preconcentration Techniques, 2 vols., Vol. 1. LC 92-23860. (Illus.). 232p. 1993. 75.00 (*0-19-855395-1*) OUP.

— The Analysis of Natural Waters Vol. 2: Direct Preconcentration Techniques, 2 vols., Vol. 2. (Illus.). 264p. 1993. 75.00 (*0-19-855394-3*) OUP.

— Analysis of Seawater. 422p. 1989. text 305.00 (*0-407-01610-4*) Buttrwrth-Heinemann.

— Analysis of Solids in Natural Waters. 307p. 1996. 129.00 (*3-540-60163-5*) Spr-Verlag.

— Analytical Instrumentation for the Water Industry. (Illus.). 272p. 1991. 130.00 (*0-7506-1139-1*) Buttrwrth-Heinemann.

— Battery Reference Book. 750p. 1996. text 79.00 (*1-56091-805-5*, R-167) Soc Auto Engineers.

***Crompton, T. R.** Battery Reference Book. 3rd ed. 800p. 2000. 295.00 (*0-7506-4625-X*, Newnes) Buttrwrth-Heinemann.

Crompton, T. R. Comprehensive Organometallic Analysis. LC 87-13988. (Illus.). 910p. (C). 1988. text 195.00 (*0-306-42593-9*, Kluwer Plenum) Kluwer Academic.

— Determination of Anions. (Illus.). 530p. 1996. 197.00 (*3-540-60162-7*) Spr-Verlag.

— Determination of Organic Compounds in Natural & Treated Waters. LC 98-52383. 1999. text. write for info. (*0-419-24360-7*) Routledge.

— Gas Chromatography of Organometallic Compounds. LC 82-523. 600p. 1982. 115.00 (*0-306-40987-9*, Plenum Trade) Perseus Pubng.

— Manual of Plastics Analysis. LC 98-20244. (Illus.). 524p. (C). 1998. text 135.00 (*0-306-45912-4*, Kluwer Plenum) Kluwer Academic.

— Occurrence & Analysis of Organometallic Compounds in the Environment. LC 97-28546. 248p. 1998. 150.00 (*0-471-97607-5*) Wiley.

— Practical Polymer Analysis. (Illus.). 842p. (C). 1993. text 195.00 (*0-306-44524-7*, Kluwer Plenum) Kluwer Academic.

— Toxicants in the Aqueous Ecosystem. LC 96-37346. 396p. 1997. 185.00 (*0-471-97272-X*) Wiley.

Crompton, Teresa. The Coal Hole Mystery. (J). (gr. 2-5). 1996. 4.99 (*1-85792-217-4*, Pub. by Christian Focus) Spring Arbor Dist.

Crompton, Thomas R. Battery Reference Book. 2nd ed. LC 95-20184. (Illus.). 592p. 1995. pap. text 97.95 (*0-7506-2567-8*) Buttrwrth-Heinemann.

— Determination of Organic Substances in Water, Vol. 1. LC 84-7443. (Illus.). 568p. 1984. reprint ed. pap. 176.10 (*0-8357-3928-7*, 203666300001) Bks Demand.

— Determination of Organic Substances in Water, Vol. 2 - 1985. fac. ed. LC 87-7443. 528p. 1985. pap. 163.70 (*0-7837-8639-5*, 203666300002) Bks Demand.

Cromwall, Liz & Hibner, Dixie. Finger Frolics: Fingerplays for Young Children, No. 19. rev. ed. 1983. pap. 8.95 (*0-933212-10-0*) Partner Pr.

Cromwell, Adelaide, ed. Dynamics of the African-Afro-American Connection: From Dependency to Self-Reliance. 160p. 1987. 21.95 (*0-88258-172-4*) Howard U Pr.

Cromwell, Adelaide M. An African Victorian Feminist: The Life & Times of Adelaide Smith Casely Hayford, 1868-1960. LC 91-30476. 235p. 1992. pap. 18.95 (*0-88258-157-0*) Howard U Pr.

— Afro-Victorian Feminist: The Life & Times of Adelaide Smith Casely Hayford, 1868-1960. (Illus.). 275p. 1986. 38.00 (*0-7146-3226-0*, Pub. by F Cass Pubs) Intl Spec Bk.

— The Other Brahmins: Boston's Black Upper Class, 1750-1950. LC 93-41949. 216p. 1994. text 32.00 (*1-55728-301-X*) U of Ark Pr.

Cromwell, Elizabeth. Government, Farmers & Seeds in a Changing Africa. (Illus.). 192p. 1996. text 60.00 (*0-85198-976-4*) OUP.

***Cromwell, Ellen.** Nurturing Readiness in Early Childhood Education: A Whole-Child Curriculum for Ages 2-5. LC 98-56042. 278p. 1999. pap. text 24.95 (*0-205-28863-4*) Allyn.

Cromwell, Florence, ed. Occupational Therapy Assessment As the Keystone to Treatment Planning. LC 84-697. (Occupational Therapy in Health Care Ser.: Vol. 1, No. 2). 114p. 1984. text 39.95 (*0-86656-305-9*) Haworth Pr.

— Occupational Therapy Assessment As the Keystone to Treatment Planning. LC 84-697. (Occupational Therapy in Health Care Ser.: Vol. 1, No. 2). 114p. 1985. pap. text 19.95 (*0-86656-453-5*) Haworth Pr.

Cromwell, Florence S., ed. The Changing Roles of Occupational Therapists in the 1980s. LC 83-22818. (Occupational Therapy in Health Care Ser.: Vol. 1, No. 1). 99p. 1984. text 29.95 (*0-86656-294-X*) Haworth Pr.

— Computer Applications in Occupational Therapy. 214p. 1986. 49.95 (*0-86656-583-3*) Haworth Pr.

— Occupational Therapy & Adolescents with Disability. LC 85-13954. (Occupational Therapy in Health Care Ser.: Vol. 2, No. 3). 158p. 1985. text 39.95 (*0-86656-447-0*); pap. text 19.95 (*0-86656-455-1*) Haworth Pr.

— Occupational Therapy & the Patient with Pain. LC 84-10496. (Occupational Therapy in Health Care Ser.: Vol. 1, No. 3). 135p. 1984. text 39.95 (*0-86656-306-7*) Haworth Pr.

— Occupational Therapy & the Patient with Pain. LC 84-10496. (Occupational Therapy in Health Care Ser.: Vol. 1, No. 3). 135p. 1985. pap. text 19.95 (*0-86656-454-3*) Haworth Pr.

— Occupational Therapy for People with Eating Dysfunctions. LC 86-12016. (Occupational Therapy in Health Care Ser.: Vol. 3, No. 2). 161p. 1986. text 4.95 (*0-86656-588-4*) Haworth Pr.

— Occupational Therapy for the Energy Deficient Patient. LC 85-27277. (Occupational Therapy in Health Care Ser.: Vol. 3, No. 1). 119p. 1986. text 39.95 (*0-86656-550-7*); pap. text 19.95 (*0-86656-55[illegible]-5*) Haworth Pr.

— Occupational Therapy Strategies & Adaptations for Independent Daily Living. LC 84-19157. (Occupational Therapy in Health Care Ser.: Vol. 1, No. 4). 186p. 1985. text 39.95 (*0-86656-350-4*); pap. text 2.95 (*0-86656-380-6*) Haworth Pr.

— Private Practice in Occupational Therapy. LC 85-5513. (Occupational Therapy in Health Care Ser.: Vol. 2, No. 2). 138p. 1985. text 39.95 (*0-86656-411-X*) Haworth Pr.

— Private Practice in Occupational Therapy. LC 85-5513. (Occupational Therapy in Health Care Ser.: Vol. 2, No. 2). 138p. 1985. pap. text 19.95 (*0-86656-412-8*) Haworth Pr.

— The Roles of Occupational Therapists in Continuity of Care. LC 85-899. (Occupational Therapy in Health Care Ser.: Vol. 2, No. 1). 159p. 1985. text 5.95 (*0-86656-392-X*); pap. text 19.95 (*0-86656-393-8*) Haworth Pr.

— Sociocultural Implications in Treatment Planning in Occupational Therapy. 171p. 1987. 5.95 (*0-86656-612-0*) Haworth Pr.

— Work-Related Programs in Occupational Therapy. LC 85-17690. (Occupational Therapy in Health Care Ser.: Vol. 2, No. 4). 125p. 1985. 3.95 (*0-86656-487-X*); pap. text 14.95 (*0-86656-519-1*) Haworth Pr.

Cromwell, Florence S. & Bear-Lehman, Jane, eds. Hand Rehabilitation in Occupational Therapy. LC 87-32518. (Occupational Therapy in Health Care Ser.: Vol. 4, Nos. 3 & 4). (Illus.). 194p. 1988. text 49.95 (*0-86656-698-8*) Haworth Pr.

Cromwell, Florence S., jt. auth. see Brollier, Chestina.

Cromwell, Harold D. The Bound Boy. 1996. 18.50 (*1-55673-960-5*, Fairway Pr) CSS OH.

Cromwell Hospital International Conference on Mult. Head & Neck Oncology: Cromwell Hospital International Conference on Multidisciplinary Management of Cancer, London, England, 1984. Bloom, H. J. G. et al, eds. LC 86-10176. 381p. 1987. reprint ed. pap. 118.20 (*0-608-00411-1*, 206112500007) Bks Demand.

Cromwell, James White, intro. Agustin De Rojas el Natural Desdichado. (ENG & SPA.). lxxi, 201p. 1939. text 2.60 (*0-318-14233-3*) Hispanic Inst.

***Cromwell, Jason.** Transmen & FTMs: Identities, Bodies, Genders, & Sexualities. LC 99-6186. 264p. 1999. 42.50 (*0-252-02439-7*); pap. text 19.95 (*0-252-06825-4*) U of Ill Pr.

Cromwell, Jeff B., et al, eds. Multivariate Tests for Time Series Models, No. 100. (Quantitative Applications in the Social Sciences Ser.: Vol. 100). 96p. 1994. pap. 10.95 (*0-8039-5440-9*) Sage.

Cromwell, Jeff B. & Labys, Walter C. Univariate Tests for Time Series Models, No. 99. (Quantitative Applications in the Social Sciences Ser.: Vol. 99). (C). 1994. pap. text 10.95 (*0-8039-4991-X*) Sage.

Cromwell, Jerry. Hospital & Physician Rate Setting Systems. 224p. 1996. text 65.00 (*0-7863-1084-7*, Irwn Prfssnl) McGraw-Hill Prof.

Cromwell, John, et al. Managerial Assessment of Water Quality & System Reliability. LC 97-198266. (Illus.). 134p. 1997. pap. 125.00 (*0-89867-905-2*, 90725) Am Water Wks Assn.

Cromwell, Kristi. Time for Tea: A Tea Lover's Journal. 102p. 1998. pap. 12.95 (*0-7392-0028-3*, PO2789) Morris Pubng.

Cromwell-Lacy, Sherry & Rowe, M. Jessica. Iowa Artists, 1991. (Illus.). 44p. 1991. pap. 8.00 (*1-879003-03-1*) Edmundson.

Cromwell, Leslie, et al. Biomedical Instrumentation & Measurements. 2nd ed. (Illus.). 528p. 1980. 110.00 (*0-13-076448-5*) P-H.

Cromwell, Liz. Finger Frolics 2. 1997. pap. 12.95 (*0-933212-11-9*) Partner Prods.

Cromwell, Oliver. Speeches of Oliver Cromwell. 275p. 1989. pap. 8.95 (*0-460-01254-1*, Everyman's Classic Lib) Tuttle Pubng.

Cromwell, Patricia L. Marguerita & Sarabella's Glad Day. large type ed. (Illus.). 16p. (J). (ps-6). 1997. pap. 4.50 (*0-9664794-0-8*, 041998) Patty Cake.

Cromwell, Paul, ed. In Their Own Words: Criminals on Crime (An Anthology) 2nd rev. ed. LC 98-45336. (Illus.). 230p. (C). 1999. pap. text. write for info. (*0-935732-95-0*) Roxbury Pub Co.

Cromwell, Paul E. & Dunham, Roger G. Crime & Justice in America: Realities & Future Prospects. 424p. (C). 1996. pap. text 51.00 (*0-13-228636-X*) P-H.

Cromwell, Paul F. Community-Based Corrections. 4th ed. LC 98-7435. (Criminal Justice Ser.). 1998. pap. 64.95 (*0-534-54639-0*) Wadsworth Pub.

Cromwell, Paul F., et al. Breaking & Entering: An Ethnographic Analysis. (Studies in Crime, Law, & Justice: Vol. 8). (Illus.). 160p. (C). 1990. text 52.00 (*0-8039-4026-2*); pap. text 21.95 (*0-8039-4027-0*) Sage.

— Community-Based Corrections: Probation, Parole & Intermediate Sanctions. 3rd ed. Gill, ed. LC 93-21289. 396p. (C). 1994. pap. 46.50 (*0-314-02570-7*) West Pub.

Cromwell, Peter, jt. auth. see Arvold, Bridget.

***Cromwell, Peter R.** Polyhedra. (Illus.). 465p. (C). 1999. pap. 34.95 (*0-521-66405-5*) Cambridge U Pr.

Cromwell, Richard S. The Rise & Decline of the Late Roman Army Field. LC 97-46692. 79p. 1998. 40.00 (*1-57249-087-X*) White Mane Pub.

Cromwell, Rue L. & Snyder, C. R., eds. Schizophrenia: Origins, Processes, Treatment, & Outcome. LC 92-48996. (Illus.). 384p. (C). 1993. text 115.00 (*0-19-506922-6*) OUP.

Cromwell, Sharon. How Do I Know It's Yucky? And Other Questions about the Senses. LC 97-25180. (Bodywise Ser.). (Illus.). 24p. (J). 1998. 19.95 (*1-57572-160-0*) Heinemann Lib.

— My First Book about the Internet. (Illus.). (J). 1997. pap. 3.50 incl. disk (*0-8167-4320-7*) Troll Communs.

— Why Can't I Breathe Underwater? And Other Questions about the Respiratory System. LC 97-22212. (Bodywise Ser.). (Illus.). (J). 1998. 22.45 (*1-57572-158-9*) Heinemann Lib.

C

An Asterisk (*) at the beginning of an entry indicates that the title is appearing for the first time.

— Why Can't I Fly? And Other Questions about the Motor System. LC 97-22227. (Bodywise Ser.). (Illus.). (J). 1998. 22.45 (*1-57572-159-7*) Heinemann Lib.

— Why Do I Laugh or Cry? And Other Questions about the Nervous System. LC 97-25172. (Bodywise Ser.). (Illus.). 24p. (J). 1998. 19.95 (*1-57572-161-9*) Heinemann Lib.

— Why Do My Feet Fall Asleep? And Other Questions about the Circulatory System. LC 97-22213. (Bodywise Ser.). (Illus.). 24p. (J). 1998. 19.95 (*1-57572-162-7*) Heinemann Lib.

— Why Does My Tummy Rumble When I'm Hungry? And Other Questions about the Digestive System. LC 97-25170. (Bodywise Ser.). (Illus.). (J). 1998. 22.45 (*1-57572-163-5*) Heinemann Lib.

***Cron, Mary.** Dreams: Mind Movies of the Night. LC 00-20885. (Illus.). (J). 2000. lib. bdg. write for info. (*0-7613-1512-8*) Millbrook Pr.

Cron, Mary & Cheney, Martha C. Monster Math Workbook, Bk. 1. 64p. (J). 1995. pap., wbk. ed. 4.95 (*1-56565-307-6*, 03076W, Pub. by Lowell Hse) NTC Contemp Pub Co.

Cron, Mary, et al. Monster Math Super Edition for Ages 6-8. (Monster Math Super Editions Ser.). (Illus.). 256p. (J). (gr. 1-3). 2000. pap. 14.95 (*0-7373-0216-X*, 0216XW) NTC Contemp Pub Co.

Cron, William L., jt. auth. see Dalrymple, Douglas J.

Cronan, Christopher S. Introduction to Ecology & Ecosystems Analysis. LC 95-92667. (Illus.). 256p. (C). 1996. 27.95 (*0-9649337-1-3*) Shaw-Ferguson.

Cronan, David S. Handbook of Marine Mineral Deposits. LC 99-37077. (Marine Science Ser.). 424p. 1999. boxed set 99.95 (*0-8493-8429-X*) CRC Pr.

Cronan, David S., ed. Sedimentation & Mineral Deposits in the Southwestern Pacific Ocean. (Ocean Science, Resources & Technology Ser.). 1986. text 147.00 (*0-12-195870-1*) Acad Pr.

Cronan-Hillix, W. A., jt. auth. see Marx, Melvin H.

Cronan, John, jt. auth. see Maloy, Stanley R.

Cronan, Mary, jt. auth. see Mahoney, Judy.

Cronau, Rudolf. Three Centuries of German Life in America. 1972. 59.95 (*0-8490-1210-4*) Gordon Pr.

Cronauer, Adrian. How to Read Copy: Professionals' Guide to Delivering Voice-Overs & Broadcast Commercials. LC 89-81891. (Illus.). 208p. 1990. 29.95 (*0-929387-14-7*) Bonus Books.

Cronbach, Abraham. The Quest for Peace. LC 79-137533. (Peace Movement in America Ser.). ix, 223p. 1972. reprint ed. lib. bdg. 30.95 (*0-89198-061-X*) Ozer.

Cronbach, Lee J. Designing Evaluations of Educational & Social Programs. LC 81-48664. (Joint Publication in the Jossey-Bass Series in Social & Behavioral Science & in Higher Education). 400p. reprint ed. pap. 124.00 (*0-7837-2538-8*, 204269700006) Bks Demand.

— Essentials of Psychological Testing. 5th ed. 726p. (C). 1997. 113.00 (*0-06-041418-9*) Addson-Wesley Educ.

Cronbach, Lee J. & Snow, Richard E. Aptitudes & Instructional Methods: A Handbook for Research on Interactions. LC 76-5510. (Illus.). 1981. pap. text 27.95 (*0-8290-0103-4*) Irvington.

Cronbach, Lee J., et al. The Dependability of Behavioral Measurements: Theory of Generalizability for Scores & Profiles. LC 70-180269. (Illus.). 430p. reprint ed. pap. 133.30 (*0-8357-6705-1*, AU0038600095) Bks Demand.

— Toward Reform of Program Evaluation. LC 80-8013. (Joint Publication in the Jossey-Bass Series in Social & Behavioral Science & in Higher Education). 462p. reprint ed. pap. 143.30 (*0-8357-4876-6*, 203780800009) Bks Demand.

Cronbach, Steve, jt. auth. see Blacker, Keith.

Cronberg, Gertrud, jt. ed. see Kristiansen, Jorgen.

Crondahl, Judy. Word Processing with IBM's Displaywrite Series. 256p. 1985. pap. 17.95 (*0-317-37789-2*) S&S Trade.

Crone, Anna L. & Chvany, Catherine V., eds. New Studies in Russian Language & Literature. (Illus.). 302p. 1987. 22.95 (*0-89357-168-7*) Slavica.

Crone, Catherine P. & Hunter, Carman S., eds. From the Field: Tested Participatory Activities for Trainers. (Illus.). 148p. 1980. reprint ed. ring bd. 15.50 (*0-914262-19-X*) World Educ.

Crone, Donald K. The ASEAN States: Coping with Dependence. LC 83-2433. 230p. 1983. 31.95 (*0-275-90962-X*, C0962, Praeger Pubs) Greenwood.

Crone, Donald L. GLP - GMP Computer Procedures & Systems. 319p. 1995. ring bd. 247.00 (*0-935184-74-0*) Interpharm.

Crone, F. L. Crone: History of the Crone, Pence, Switzer, Weaver, Heatwole, Stout, Steel & Fissell Families, from Which Are Descended John S. Crone & Ella Weaver Crone. (Illus.). 50p. 1991. reprint ed. pap. 10.00 (*0-8328-1877-1*) Higginson Bk Co.

***Crone-Findlay, Noreen.** Soul Mate Dolls: Dollmaking as a Healing Art. LC 99-66140. (Illus.). 144p. 2000. pap. 21.95 (*0-87341-806-9*, SODO) Krause Pubns.

Crone, G. R. Background to Political Geography. LC 69-14376. (Illus.). 1967. 19.95 (*0-8023-1202-0*) Dufour.

Crone, Hugh D. Banning Chemical Weapons: The Technical Background. (Illus.). 132p. (C). 1992. text 57.95 (*0-521-41699-X*); pap. text 16.95 (*0-521-42711-8*) Cambridge U Pr.

Crone, J. O. The Magnetic Healer's Guide: or Personal Experiences in Magnetic & Suggestive Healing. 1996. reprint ed. spiral bd. 14.00 (*0-7873-1035-2*) Hlth Research.

— The Magnetic Healer's Guide: or Personal Experiences in Magnetic & Suggestive Healing (1903) 127p. 1996. reprint ed. pap. 13.50 (*1-56459-766-0*) Kessinger Pub.

Crone, Jesse E. Getting Started As a Residential Child Care Worker? A Guide for Beginners. 143p. 1984. pap. 12.50 (*0-87868-218-X*, 2180) Child Welfare.

Crone, John, jt. auth. see Auch, Ron.

Crone, Kerry R., jt. auth. see Manwaring, Kim H.

***Crone, Linda.** Fabric Landscapes by Machine: Decorative Stitching Styles for Quilted Scenes. LC 99-68135. (Illus.). 128p. 2000. pap. 19.95 (*0-87341-836-0*, LDMA) Krause Pubns.

Crone, Moira. Dream State. 2nd ed. 189p. 1998. reprint ed. pap. 14.00 (*1-57806-097-4*) U Pr of Miss.

— The Winnebago Mysteries. LC 81-71642. 128p. 1982. 15.95 (*0-914590-68-5*); pap. 6.95 (*0-914590-69-3*) Fiction Coll.

***Crone, Neil & Steen, Brandon.** I Am Dead at Recess. 1999. pap. text 5.95 (*0-9683303-3-9*) TUM.

Crone, Nora. A Portrait of Katherine Mansfield. 348p. 1989. 110.00 (*0-7223-1862-6*, Pub. by A H S Ltd) St Mut.

Crone, Patricia. Meccan Trade & the Rise of Islam. LC 86-42858. 309p. reprint ed. pap. 95.80 (*0-608-06345-2*, 206670700008) Bks Demand.

***Crone, Patricia & Moreh, Shmuel.** The Book of Strangers: Medieval Arabic Graffiti on the Theme of Nostalgia. 200p. 1999. pap. 18.95 (*1-55876-215-9*) Wiener Pubs Inc.

***Crone, Patricia & Moreh, Shmuel, comments.** The Book of Strangers: Medieval Arabic Graffiti on the Theme of Nostalgia. LC 99-16658. 200p. 1999. 49.95 (*1-55876-214-0*) Wiener Pubs Inc.

Crone, Patricia & Zimmermann, Friedrich. The Epistle of Salim Ibn Dhakwan. 350p. 2000. text 95.00 (*0-19-815265-5*) OUP.

Crone, Rainer, et al, eds. Rodin: Eros & Creativity. (Illus.). 236p. 1995. 70.00 (*3-7913-1185-9*, Pub. by Prestel) te Neues.

Crone, Rainer & Moos, David. Kazimir Malevich: The Climax of Disclosure. LC 91-10077. (Illus.). 237p. 1991. pap. text 58.00 (*0-226-12093-7*) U Ch Pr.

Crone, Rainer & Salzmann, Siegfried, eds. Rodin: Eros & Creativity. LC 97-3599. (Illus.). 236p. 1997. pap. 29.95 (*3-7913-1809-8*, Pub. by Prestel) te Neues.

Crone, Rainer & Schaesberg, Petrus Graf. Louise Bourgeois: The Secret of Cells. LC 98-231844. (Illus.). 160p. 1998. 65.00 (*3-7913-1610-9*) te Neues.

Crone, Robert A. A History of Color: The Evolution of Theories of Light & Color. LC 98-51580. 282p. 1999. write for info. (*0-7923-5539-3*) Kluwer Academic.

Crone, Robert W. Covenanters Monuments of Scotland. 96p. 1984. 40.00 (*0-7212-0694-8*, Pub. by Regency Pr GBR) St Mut.

Crone, Tom. Law & the Media. 3rd ed. 214p. 1995. pap. 37.95 (*0-7506-2008-0*) Buttrwrth-Heinemann.

Cronenberg, Allen. Forth to the Mighty Conflict: Alabama & World War II. LC 94-7603. 232p. 1995. text 34.95 (*0-8173-0737-0*) U of Ala Pr.

Cronenberg, David. Crash. (Illus.). 96p. 1997. pap. 12.95 (*0-571-19127-4*) Faber & Faber.

— Existenz: A Graphic Novel. (Illus.). 128p. 1999. pap. 19.95 (*1-55263-027-7*, Pub. by Key Porter) Firefly Bks Ltd.

Cronenberger, Helen J., et al. The IBM-PC in the Clinical Laboratory. 227p. 1985. 41.95 (*0-316-16146-2*, Little Brwn Med Div) Lppncott W & W.

Croner, Don. Travels in Northern Mongolia. 193p. (Orig.). 1999. pap. 12.95 (*0-9669571-0-5*) Polar Star.

Croner, Fritz. Soziologie der Angestellten: Sociology of the White Collar. LC 74-25744. (European Sociology Ser.). 312p. 1975. reprint ed. 25.95 (*0-405-06499-3*) Ayer.

Croner, Helga & Klenicki, Leon, eds. Issues in the Jewish-Christian Dialogue: Jewish Perspectives on Covenant, Mission & Witness. LC 79-88933. (Studies in Judaism & Christianity). 198p. reprint ed. pap. 61.40 (*0-7837-1783-0*, 204198200001) Bks Demand.

Croner, Helga, jt. ed. see Cohen, Martin A.

Croner, Helga B. Stepping Stones to Further Jewish-Christian Relations. LC 78-302169. (Studies in Judaism & Christianity: No. 1). 173p. reprint ed. pap. 53.70 (*0-8357-2703-3*, 203981500013) Bks Demand.

Croner, Herb. Women's Liberation Movement & Pornography. 1970. pap. 3.00 (*0-936128-19-4*) De Young Pr.

Croner, John A. The Basque & the Boy. LC 80-15675. 1982. 21.95 (*0-87949-176-0*) Ashley Bks.

Croner, Marjorie. Fabric Photos. LC 89-24607. (Illus.). 92p. (Orig.). 1990. pap. 14.95 (*0-934026-53-X*) Interweave.

Croney, David & Croney, Paul. Design & Performance of Road Pavements. 3rd rev. ed. LC 97-25155. (Illus.). 528p. 1997. 79.95 (*0-07-014451-6*) McGraw.

Croney, Lionel. Conservative Christianity in Action: An Introduction to Successful Counseling. LC 97-221397. 208p. 1997. pap. write for info. (*1-57502-543-4*, PO1592) Morris Pubng.

Croney, Mary E. Sojourn. LC 93-29800. (Illus.). 214p. (Orig.). 1994. pap. 10.95 (*0-9624209-2-1*) Landmark ID.

— Wait 'til Harvest. 2nd rev. ed. LC 89-63576. (Illus.). 144p. (Orig.). 1996. pap. 10.95 (*0-9624209-5-6*) Landmark ID.

Croney, Paul, jt. auth. see Croney, David.

Cronham, Charles R., ed. see Schreiner, Alexander.

Cronhamar, Ingvar, et al, eds. Cronhammar Vaerker, 1988-1998. (DAN., Illus.). 210p. 1998. 32.95 (*87-89224-44-2*, Pub. by Aarhus Univ Pr) David Brown.

Cronhelm, Frederick W. Double Entry by Single: A New Method of Book-Keeping. Brief, Richard P., ed. LC 77-87267. (Development of Contemporary Accounting Thought Ser.). 1978. reprint ed. lib. bdg. 37.95 (*0-405-10896-6*) Ayer.

Cronin. Critical Essays on Zora Neale Hurston. LC 98-19113. 1998. 49.00 (*0-7838-0021-5*, G K Hall & Co) Mac Lib Ref.

— Government by the People. 18th ed. Burns, James MacGregor, ed. LC 99-15984. 776p. 1999. 60.00 (*0-13-011657-2*) P-H.

— Internet Strategy Handbook. 1996. 39.95 (*0-07-103633-4*) McGraw.

***Cronin.** Introduction to Human Performance Across the Life Span. 2001. pap. 61.50 (*0-7693-0038-3*) Thomson Learn.

Cronin. Mathematics of Cell Electrophysiology. (Lecture Notes in Pure & Applied Mathematics Ser.: Vol. 63). (Illus.). 144p. 1981. pap. text 125.00 (*0-8247-1157-2*) Dekker.

Cronin, jt. auth. see Burns, James MacGregor.

Cronin, jt. auth. see Volpe.

Cronin, A. J. Beyond This Place. 1976. 25.95 (*0-88411-525-9*) Amereon Ltd.

— Beyond This Place. 320p. 1984. reprint ed. 16.45i (*0-316-16195-0*) Little.

— The Citadel. (J). 1983. 16.95 (*0-316-16158-6*) Little.

— Citadel. 1998. lib. bdg. 28.95 (*1-56723-138-1*, 147) Yestermorrow.

— Crusader's Tomb. large type ed. 622p. 1982. 27.99 (*0-7089-8042-2*) Ulverscroft.

— Grand Canary. large type ed. 416p. 1988. 27.99 (*0-7089-8463-0*) Ulverscroft.

— The Judas Tree. large type ed. 1982. 13.95 (*0-7089-8025-2*, Charnwood) Ulverscroft.

— The Keys of the Kingdom. 1979. reprint ed. lib. bdg. 25.95 (*0-89966-431-8*) Buccaneer Bks.

— The Keys of the Kingdom. 352p. 1984. reprint ed. 16.45i (*0-316-16189-6*); reprint ed. pap. 14.95 (*0-316-16184-5*) Little.

— The Northern Light. large type ed. 432p. 1989. 27.99 (*0-7089-8500-9*, Charnwood) Ulverscroft.

— A Pocketful of Rye. 1976. 22.95 (*0-88411-526-7*) Amereon Ltd.

— Shannon's Way. large type ed. 384p. 1984. 27.99 (*0-7089-8182-8*) Ulverscroft.

— Shannon's Way. 1994. reprint ed. lib. bdg. 24.95 (*1-56849-547-1*) Buccaneer Bks.

— Shannon's Way. 320p. 1984. reprint ed. 16.95 (*0-316-16191-8*); reprint ed. mass mkt. 6.95 (*0-316-16185-3*) Little.

— A Song of Sixpence. 21.95 (*0-89190-218-X*) Amereon Ltd.

— A Song of Sixpence. 1992. reprint ed. lib. bdg. 18.95 (*0-89966-965-4*) Buccaneer Bks.

***Cronin, Anne M.** Advertising & Consumer Citizenship: Gender, Images & Rights. LC 00-30518. (Transformations Ser.). 2000. pap. write for info. (*0-415-22324-5*) Routledge.

Cronin, Anthony. Art for the People? 40p. (Orig.). 1988. pap. 6.95 (*1-85186-048-7*) Dufour.

***Cronin, Anthony.** Dead As Doornails. 208p. 2000. reprint ed. pap. 17.95 (*1-901866-42-4*, Pub. by Lilliput Pr) Irish Bks Media.

Cronin, Anthony. No Laughing Matter: The Life & Times of Flann O'Brien. LC 97-40342. (Illus.). 272p. 1998. reprint ed. 29.95 (*0-88064-183-5*) Fromm Intl Pub.

— R. M. S. Titanic. (Raven Long Poems Ser.). 1981. 8.95 (*0-906897-31-9*) Dufour.

— Relationships. LC 94-118019. 48p. 1994. pap. 10.95 (*1-874597-06-5*) Dufour.

— Samuel Beckett: The Last Modernist. LC 98-49249. (Illus.). 672p. 1999. reprint ed. pap. 17.95 (*0-306-80898-6*, Pub. by Da Capo) HarpC.

Cronin, Barbara, ed. see McGee, Frank.

Cronin, Blaise & Davenport, Elisabeth. Elements of Information Management. LC 91-14512. (Illus.). 213p. 1991. 34.50 (*0-8108-2406-X*) Scarecrow.

***Cronin, Bruce.** Community under Anarchy: Transnational Identity & the Evolution of Cooperation. LC 99-10733. 270p. 1999. pap. 18.50 (*0-231-11597-0*) Col U Pr.

— Community under Anarchy: Transnational Identity & the Evolution of Cooperation. LC 99-10733. 270p. 1999. 49.50 (*0-231-11596-2*) Col U Pr.

Cronin, Christopher. Military Psychology: An Introduction. (Illus.). 324p. (C). 1997. text 42.00 (*0-536-00565-6*) Pearson Custom.

Cronin, Christopher, ed. see DeSoto, Richard J. & Bascom, Lionel.

Cronin, Daniel P. Words of Comfort. 208p. (C). 1996. pap. 60.00 (*0-85439-344-7*, Pub. by St Paul Pubns) St Mut.

— Words of Encouragement. 206p. (C). 1996. pap. 60.00 (*0-85439-422-2*, Pub. by St Paul Pubns) St Mut.

— Words of Widsom. 170p. (C). 1996. pap. 60.00 (*0-85439-284-X*, Pub. by St Paul Pubns) St Mut.

Cronin, Deborah. Can Your Dog Hunt? LC 94-61688. 1996. 8.95 (*1-55673-969-9*, Fairway Pr) CSS OH.

Cronin, Deborah K. Holy Ground: Celtic Christian Spirituality. 5 vols. Grana, Janice, ed. LC 98-37058. (Series 2). 112p. 1999. pap. 10.00 (*0-8358-0838-6*, UR838) Upper Room Bks.

Cronin, Denis, et al, eds. Irish Townlands: Essays in Local History. 235p. 1998. boxed set 45.00 (*1-85182-319-0*, Pub. by Four Cts Pr) Intl Spec Bk.

Cronin, Denis A. A Galway Gentleman in the Age of Improvement: Robert French of Monivea, 1716-76. 64p. 1995. pap. 9.95 (*0-7165-2572-0*, Pub. by Irish Acad Pr) Intl Spec Bk.

***Cronin, Doreen.** Click, Clack, Moo: Cows That Type. LC 97-29718. (Illus.). 32p. (J). (ps-2). 2000. per. 15.00 (*0-689-83213-3*) S&S Childrens.

Cronin, Doreen. Cows That Type. LC 97-29718. (Illus.). (J). 1999. 15.99 (*0-525-65239-6*, Dutton Child) Peng Put Young Read.

Cronin, Edward W. Getting Started Birdwatching. (Illus.). 216p. 1999. pap. 9.95 (*0-395-97637-5*) HM.

Cronin, Eileen. Helping Your Dyslexic Child. LC 97-223137. 208p. 1997. per. 13.00 (*0-7615-1004-4*) Prima Pub.

— Helping Your Dyslexic Child: A Step-by-Step Program for Helping Your Child Improve Reading, Writing, Spelling, Comprehension, & Self-Esteem. LC 92-42948. 208p. 1994. 19.95 (*1-55958-290-1*) Prima Pub.

Cronin, Francis R. A Cock for Asclepios, or, Continuing Dialogues with Socrates, in Extremis. LC 91-3331. 1991. write for info. (*0-7734-9916-4*) E Mellen.

Cronin, Gay Lynn. Two Birthdays for Beth. LC 94-39797. (Illus.). 32p. (J). (ps-3). 1995. 14.00 (*0-944934-13-7*) Perspect Indiana.

Cronin, Gaynell. Friend Jesus: Prayers For Children. 96p. 1999. pap. text 9.95 (*0-86716-360-7*) St Anthony Mess Pr.

Cronin, Gaynell B. & Bellina, Joan. Together at Mass. LC 87-70417. (Illus.). 32p. (Orig.). (J). (ps-2). 1987. pap. 3.95 (*0-87793-357-X*) Ave Maria.

Cronin, Gaynell B., jt. auth. see Rathschmidt, Jack.

***Cronin, Gaynell Bordes & Rathschmidt, Jack.** The Blessing Candles: 58 Simple Mealtime Prayer-Celebrations. 2000. pap. 7.95 (*0-86716-379-8*) St Anthony Mess Pr.

***Cronin, Gene & Sherlock, Terence P.** COM Beyond Microsoft: Designing & Implementing COM Servers on Compaq Platforms. 208p. 1999. 29.95 (*1-55558-226-5*, Digital DEC) Buttrwrth-Heinemann.

***Cronin, Gloria L.** A Room of His Own: In Search of the Feminine in the Novels of Saul Bellow. 224p. 2000. 39.95 (*0-8156-2862-5*); pap. 17.95 (*0-8156-2863-3*) Syracuse U Pr.

Cronin, Gloria L. Saul Bellow: An Annotated Bibliography. 2nd ed. LC 87-7607. 496p. 1990. text 10.00 (*0-8240-9421-2*) Garland.

Cronin, Gloria L. & Aharoni, Ada, eds. Saul Bellow: A Mosaic. LC 92-12971. (Twentieth Century American Jewish Writers Ser.: Vol. 3). XIV, 209p. (C). 1993. text 46.95 (*0-8204-1572-3*) P Lang Pubng.

Cronin, Gloria L. & Hall, Blaine H. Jerzy Kosinski: An Annotated Bibliography, 15. LC 91-21555. (Bibliographies & Indexes in American Literature Ser.: No. 15). 128p. 1991. lib. bdg. 49.95 (*0-313-27442-8*, HJO, Greenwood Pr) Greenwood.

Cronin, Gloria L. & Siegel, Ben, eds. Conversations with Saul Bellow. LC 94-19474. (Literary Conversations Ser.). 236p. 1994. pap. 15.95 (*0-87805-718-8*) U Pr of Miss.

Cronin, Gloria L., et al. Jewish American Fiction Writers: An Annotated Bibliography. LC 91-20634. 1250p. 1991. text 50.00 (*0-8240-1619-X*, H972) Garland.

Cronin, Gloria L., jt. ed. see Goldman, L. H.

Cronin, Gloria L., ed. see Moogk, Peter.

Cronin, Grover. Monarch Notes on Fielding's Tom Jones. (Orig.). (C). pap. 2.95 (*0-685-03404-6*, Arco) Macmillan Gen Ref.

Cronin, Harry C. Eugene O'Neill, Irish & American: A Study in Cultural Context. LC 76-6331. (Irish Americans Ser.). 1977. 22.95 (*0-405-09327-6*) Ayer.

Cronin, Irene. South Hadley. LC 98-87330. (Images of America Ser.). 1998. write for info. (*0-7524-1345-7*) Arcadia Publng.

Cronin, Isaac. The International Squid Cookbook. (Illus.). 96p. 1981. pap. 7.95 (*0-943186-07-2*) Aris Bks.

***Cronin, Isaac.** The Mindful Cook: Finding Awareness, Simplicity, & Freedom in the Kitchen. LC 99-20374. (Illus.). 224p. 1999. 19.95 (*0-375-50275-0*) Villard Books.

Cronin, Isaac, et al. The California Seafood Cookbook: A Cook's Guide to the Fish & Shellfish of California, the Pacific Coast & Beyond. LC 82-24450. (Illus.). 288p. 1983. 20.00 (*0-943186-04-8*); pap. 12.95 (*0-943186-03-X*) Aris Bks.

Cronin, Isaac, jt. ed. see Hammer, Dan.

Cronin, James E. Industrial Conflict in Modern Britain. 242p. 1979. 41.00 (*0-8476-6188-1*) Rowman.

— The World the Cold War Made. 256p. (C). 1996. pap. 19.99 (*0-415-90821-3*) Routledge.

Cronin, James E., ed. see Smith, Elihu H.

Cronin, James Wilson. Differential Equations: Introduction & Qualitative Theory. 2nd enl. rev. ed. LC 93-46027. (Pure & Applied Mathematics Ser.: Vol. 180). (Illus.). 392p. 1994. text 135.00 (*0-8247-9189-4*) Dekker.

Cronin, Jane. Fixed Points & Topological Degree in Nonlinear Analysis. 5th ed. LC 62-21550. (Mathematical Surveys & Monographs: Vol. 11). 198p. 1964. reprint ed. pap. 42.00 (*0-8218-1511-3*, SURV/11) Am Math.

— Mathematical Aspects of Hodgkin-Huxley Neural Theory. (Cambridge Studies in Mathematical Biology: NO. 7). (Illus.). 288p. 1987. text 74.95 (*0-521-33482-9*) Cambridge U Pr.

Cronin, Jane & O'Malley, Robert E., Jr. Analyzing Multiscale Phenomena Using Singular Perturbation Methods. LC 99-13036. (Proceedings of Symposia in Pure Mathematics Ser.). 187p. 1999. 44.00 (*0-8218-0929-6*) Am Math.

Cronin, Janet & Vick, Dorothy. Montana's Gallatin Canyon: A Gem in the Treasure State. LC 92-36887. 259p. 1993. 12.00 (*0-87842-277-3*) Mountain Pr.

Cronin, Jeremiah A., et al. University of Chicago Graduate Problems in Physics with Solutions. 272p. 1979. pap. text 17.50 (*0-226-12109-7*, P809) U Ch Pr.

Cronin, Joan. Surgery of the Shoulder. 1992. 495.00 (*0-7216-4891-6*) Harcourt.

***Cronin, Joe.** Walks of Discovery in Cork City & County. (Illus.). 124p. 1999. pap. 15.95 (*1-898256-72-1*, Pub. by Collins Press) Irish Bks Media.

Cronin, John. The Anglo-Irish Novel: The Nineteenth Century, Vol. 1. 1994. 34.99 (*0-904651-33-9*) Ashgate Pub Co.

— The Anglo-Irish Novel, 1900-1940, Vol. 2. 1994. 34.99 (*0-904651-34-7*) Ashgate Pub Co.

Cronin, John. The Anglo-Irish Novel, 1900-1940, Vol. II. 224p. (C). 1990. lib. bdg. 62.00 (*0-389-20918-X*) B&N Imports.

— For the Airline Passenger: Passenger Questions & Pilot Answers. (Illus.). 72p. (Orig.). 1995. pap. 5.50 (*0-9648365-4-8*) J Cronin.

An Asterisk (*) at the beginning of an entry indicates that the title is appearing for the first time.

— Gerald Griffin, 1803-1840: A Critical Biography. LC 77-80831. (Illus.). 187p. reprint ed. pap. 53.30 (*0-608-17579-X*, 2030587) Bks Demand.

— Somerville & Ross. LC 78-126031. (Irish Writers Ser.). 111p. 1975. 8.50 (*0-8387-7767-8*); pap. 1.95 (*0-8387-7698-1*) Bucknell U Pr.

— Your Flight Questions Answered. (Illus.). 100p. 1998. pap. 9.95 (*1-882663-23-3*) Plymouth VT.

Cronin, John, ed. Selected Plays of St. John Ervine. LC 85-31343. (Irish Drama Selections Ser.: No. 5). 387p. 1988. 39.95 (*0-8132-0628-6*); pap. 16.95 (*0-8132-0629-4*) Cath U Pr.

Cronin, John & Kennedy, Robert F., Jr. The Riverkeepers: Two Activists Fight to Reclaim Our Environment As a Basic Human Right. 1997. 26.00 (*0-614-28265-9*, Scribners Ref) Mac Lib Ref.

— The Riverkeepers: Two Activists Fight to Reclaim Our Environment As a Basic Human Right. LC 97-13371. 302p. 1997. 24.50 (*0-684-83908-3*) S&S Trade.

— The Riverkeepers: Two Activists Fight to Reclaim Our Environment As a Basic Human Right. 304p. 1999. per. 14.00 (*0-684-84625-X*) S&S Trade.

Cronin, John, ed. see Weikel, Dana & Krupinski, Eve.

Cronin, Joseph M. The Control of Urban Schools: Perspective on the Power of Educational Reformers. LC 72-78608. 288p. 1973. pap. 18.95 (*0-02-906910-6*) Free Pr.

Cronin, Joseph M. & Simmons, Sylvia Q., eds. Student Loans: Risks & Realities. LC 87-1275. 207p. 1987. 49.95 (*0-86569-165-7*, Auburn Hse) Greenwood.

Cronin, Kevin. Off the Beaten Track: Irish Railway Walks. (Illus.). 190p. 1997. 15.95 (*0-86281-563-0*, Pub. by Appletree Pr) Irish Bks Media.

Cronin, Kevin, ed. The National Book of Lists, 1992. 106p. (Orig.). 1992. pap. 19.95 (*0-9632232-0-8*) Local Know.

Cronin, Kevin M. Kenosis: Emptying Self & the Path of Christian Service. 116p. 1994. reprint ed. pap. 11.95 (*0-8264-0768-4*) Continuum.

Cronin, Kevin M., ed. A Friar's Joy: Magic Moments from Real Life. 144p. 1996. pap. 14.95 (*0-8264-0868-0*) Continuum.

— A Friar's Joy: Magic Moments from Real Life. 156p. 1997. pap. 9.95 (*0-8264-1035-9*) Continuum.

Cronin, L. Eugene, jt. ed. see Neilson, Bruce J.

Cronin, Laura, jt. auth. see Henning, Ann.

Cronin, Laura, jt. auth. see MacUistin, Liam.

Cronin, M. Legal Considerations in Healthcare Delivery. 210p. (C). 1993. spiral bd. write for info. (*0-933195-26-5*) CA College Health Sci.

— Management & Practices for the Health Professional. 176p. (C). 1994. spiral bd. write for info. (*0-933195-64-8*) CA College Health Sci.

— Practicum in Healthcare Management: HSM 489. rev. ed. 10p. (C). 1994. spiral bd. write for info. (*0-933195-71-0*) CA College Health Sci.

— QA-CQI Manual for Clinical Lab. 208p. (C). 1994. 99.95 (*0-933195-67-2*); write for info. (*0-933195-70-2*) CA College Health Sci.

— QA-CQI Manual for Home Care. rev. ed. 122p. (C). 1994. ring bd. 99.95 (*0-933195-39-7*) CA College Health Sci.

— QA-CQI Manual for Physical Therapy. rev. ed. 110p. (C). 1994. ring bd. 99.95 (*0-933195-38-9*) CA College Health Sci.

— QA-CQI Manual for Respiratory Care. rev. ed. 208p. (C). 1994. ring bd. 99.95 (*0-933195-32-X*) CA College Health Sci.

Cronin, M. T. Everything Holy. LC 98-73154. x, 86p. 1998. pap. 12.00 (*1-891811-04-5*) Balcones Intl Pr.

***Cronin Marcello, Patricia.** The Navajo (North America) (Indigenous Peoples Ser.). (Illus.). 144p. (YA). (gr. 6-9). 2000. lib. bdg. 23.70 (*1-56006-619-9*) Lucent Bks.

Cronin, Mary. Performance Measurement for Public Services in Academic & Research Libraries. (Occasional Papers: Vol. 9). 36p. 1985. 25.00 (*0-918006-31-7*, OP09) ARL.

Cronin, Mary E. & Patton, James R. Life Skills Instruction for All Students with Special Needs: A Practical Guide for Integrating Real-Life Content into the Curriculum. LC 92-40196. 171p. (Orig.). (C). 1993. pap. text 29.00 (*0-89079-586-X*, 4048) PRO-ED.

Cronin, Mary J. Banking & Finance on the Internet. 352p. 1997. 45.00 (*0-471-29219-2*, VNR) Wiley.

— Banking & Finance on the Internet. LC 97-20309. (Communications Ser.). 400p. 1998. text 39.95 (*0-442-02468-1*, VNR) Wiley.

— Doing More Business on the Internet. 2nd rev. ed. LC 95-7186. 368p. 1995. pap. 29.95 (*0-442-02047-3*, VNR) Wiley.

Cronin, Mary J. Doing More Business on the Internet: How the Electronic Highway Is Transforming American Companies. 2nd ed. 368p. 1995. pap. 29.95 (*0-471-28701-6*, VNR) Wiley.

— Global Advantage on the Internet: From Corporate Connectivity to International Competitiveness. (Communications Ser.). 358p. 1995. pap. 29.95 (*0-471-28668-0*, VNR) Wiley.

Cronin, Mary J. Global Advantage on the Internet: From Corporate Connectivity to International Competitiveness. (Communications Ser.). 358p. 1996. pap. 29.95 (*0-442-01938-6*, VNR) Wiley.

— Health Care & Medicine on the Internet. 400p. 1997. text 49.95 (*0-442-02560-2*, VNR) Wiley.

— The Internet Strategy Handbook: Lessons from the New Frontier of Business. 320p. 1996. pap. 29.95 (*0-87584-720-X*) Harvard Busn.

Cronin, Mary J., ed. The Internet Strategy Handbook: Lessons from the New Frontier of Business. LC 95-14396. 312p. (C). 1996. 39.95 (*0-87584-631-9*) Harvard Busn.

Cronin, Mary M. & Caplan, Suzanne. Everyone Remembers the Elephant in the Pink Tutu: How to Promote & Publicize Your Business with Impact & Style. LC 98-4096. 192p. 1998. pap. 15.99 (*1-56414-360-0*) Career Pr Inc.

Cronin, Maura. Country, Class or Craft? The Politicisation of the Skilled Artisan in Nineteenth-Century Cork. 1994. 35.95 (*1-85918-027-2*) Cork Univ.

***Cronin, Michael.** Across the Lines: Travel, Language & Translation. 172p. 2000. 19.95 (*1-85918-182-1*, Pub. by Cork Univ); pap. 19.95 (*1-85918-183-X*, Pub. by Cork Univ) Stylus Pub VA.

Cronin, Michael. The Failure of British Fascism: The Far Right & the Fight for Political Recognition. 208p. 1996. text 65.00 (*0-312-15963-3*) St Martin.

— Quality Improvement & Management: HSM 535 Course. 192p. (C). 1993. spiral bd. write for info. (*0-933195-22-2*) CA College Health Sci.

— Translating Ireland: Translation, Languages, Culture. 1996. 46.95 (*1-85918-018-3*, Pub. by Cork Univ); pap. 27.95 (*1-85918-019-1*, Pub. by Cork Univ) Intl Spec Bk.

Cronin, Michael, jt. ed. see Mayall, David.

Cronin, Michael P., ed. Military Operations Research Society Membership Directory. (Orig.). 1996. pap. write for info. (*0-930473-02-7*) Military Opera Res.

Cronin, Mike. The Blueshirts & Irish Politics. (Illus.). 2224p. 1997. boxed set 39.50 (*1-85182-333-6*, Pub. by Four Cts Pr) Intl Spec Bk.

***Cronin, Mike.** A History of Ireland. LC 00-42057. (Essential Histories Ser.). (Illus.). (YA). 2000. write for info. (*0-312-23799-5*) St Martin.

— Sport & Nationalism in Ireland: Gaelic Games, Soccer & Irish Identity since 1870. LC 99-196610. 224p. 1999. pap. 29.50 (*1-85182-456-1*, Pub. by Four Cts Pr) Intl Spec Bk.

***Cronin, Mike.** Sport & Nationalism in Ireland: Gaelic Games, Soccer & Irish Identity since 1870. LC 99-196610. 224p. 1999. 55.00 (*1-85182-408-1*, Pub. by Four Cts Pr) Intl Spec Bk.

***Cronin, Mike & Regan, John.** Ireland. LC 99-40610. 2000. text 59.95 (*0-312-22787-6*) St Martin.

Cronin, N. J. Microwave & Optical Waveguides. (Illus.). 132p. 1995. 90.00 (*0-7503-0215-1*); pap. 34.00 (*0-7503-0216-X*) IOP Pub.

Cronin, Patricia. Writing & Reading the Essay: A Process Approach. LC 93-27123. (Illus.). 229p. 1993. pap. 12.00 (*0-8092-4216-8*) NTC Contemp Pub Co.

***Cronin, Patricia H.** Character Development in the Catholic School. 71p. 1999. pap. 12.00 (*1-55833-224-3*) Natl Cath Educ.

Cronin, Patrick M. Power & Progress, 2015. 173p. 1996. per. 16.00 (*0-16-048752-8*) USGPO.

Cronin, Patrick M., ed. Project 2015: Power & Progress. (Illus.). 157p. (C). 1997. pap. text 30.00 (*0-7881-4646-7*) DIANE Pub.

Cronin, Patrick M. & Green, Michael J. Redefining the U. S. - Japan Alliance: Tokyo's National Defense Program. 61p. (Orig.). (C). 1996. pap. text 25.00 (*0-7881-3281-4*) DIANE Pub.

Cronin, Patrick M., jt. ed. see Green, Michael J.

***Cronin, Richard.** The Politics of Romantic Poetry: In Search of the Pure Commonwealth. LC 99-36364. (Romanticism in Perspective Ser.). 1999. text 59.95 (*0-312-22749-3*) St Martin.

***Cronin, Robert.** Five Minute up Do's: The New Way to Finish Hair, 15 Step by Steps. (Illus.). 64p. 1999. pap. 9.95 (*1-928986-00-5*) Intra Am Beauty.

Cronin, Robert. The Glow of Embers: Fragments with a Twist. (Illus.). 160p. (Orig.). 1996. pap. 9.85 (*0-9653081-0-3*) Kings Crown.

Cronin, Robert C. Youth Environmental Service in Action: Program Summary. (Illus.). 39p. (Orig.). 1996. pap. text 20.00 (*0-7881-3720-4*) DIANE Pub.

Cronin, Sean. Ireland: The Divided Island. 224p. (C). 1999. pap. 36.00 (*0-8133-0709-0*) Westview.

Cronin, Thomas E. Direct Democracy: The Politics of Initiative, Referendum, & Recall. LC 88-14859. (Twentieth Century Fund Study). (Illus.). 289p. 1989. 29.50 (*0-674-21025-5*) HUP.

— Direct Democracy: The Politics of Initiative, Referendum, & Recall. (Twentieth Century Fund Study). 289p. 1990. pap. 18.00 (*0-674-21026-3*) HUP.

Cronin, Thomas E., ed. Inventing the American Presidency. LC 89-16492. (Studies in Government & Public Policy). xii, 404p. 1989. pap. 14.95 (*0-7006-0406-5*) U Pr of KS.

Cronin, Thomas E. & Genovese, Michael A. The Paradoxes of the American Presidency. LC 97-29534. 448p. (C). 1998. pap. text 33.95 (*0-19-511693-3*) OUP.

— The Paradoxes of the American Presidency. LC 97-29534. (Illus.). 448p. (C). 1998. 35.00 (*0-19-511692-5*) OUP.

Cronin, Thomas E. & Greenberg, Sanford D., eds. The Presidential Advisory System. LC 69-18487. 395p. reprint ed. pap. 122.50 (*0-7837-8664-6*, 204906400011) Bks Demand.

Cronin, Thomas E. & Loevy, Robert D. Colorado Politics & Government: Governing the Centennial State. LC 93-6587. (Politics & Governments of the American States Ser.). (Illus.). xxxii, 362p. 1993. pap. text 25.00 (*0-8032-6358-9*) U of Nebr Pr.

— Colorado Politics & Government: Governing the Centennial State. LC 93-6587. (Politics & Governments of the American States Ser.). (Illus.). xxxii, 362p. 1993. text 45.00 (*0-8032-1451-0*) U of Nebr Pr.

Cronin, Thomas E., et al. United States vs. Crime in the Streets. LC 80-8842. 224p. reprint ed. pap. 69.50 (*0-608-17127-1*, 205622100056) Bks Demand.

***Cronin, Thomas M.** Principles of Paleoclimatology. LC 98-48495. (Perspectives in Paleobiology & Earth History Ser.). 1999. 75.00 (*0-231-10954-7*) Col U Pr.

— Principles of Paleoclimatology. LC 98-48495. (Perspectives in Paleobiology & Earth H Ser.). (Illus.). 560p. 1999. pap. 32.00 (*0-231-10955-5*) Col U Pr.

Cronin, Tim. A Century of Golf: The History of the Western Golf Association. LC 98-9688. (Illus.). 224p. 1998. 45.00 (*1-886947-36-8*) Sleepng Bear.

— Purple Roses: Northwestern's Glorious March to Pasadena. (Illus.). 200p. (Orig.). 1996. pap. 19.95 (*1-57167-072-6*) Sports Pub.

Cronin, Xavier. Grave Exodus: Tending to Our Dead in the 21st Century. LC 96-8704. 256p. 1996. 22.50 (*1-56980-095-2*) Barricade Bks.

Croninm. Maximum Digital Value. (Business Technology Ser.). 1998. pap. 29.95 (*0-442-02672-2*, VNR) Wiley.

Cronish, Nettie. Nettie's Vegetarian Kitchen. (Illus.). 200p. 1996. pap. 14.95 (*0-929005-80-5*, Pub. by Sec Story Pr) LPC InBook.

***Cronish, Nettie & Selley, Barbara.** Complete Idiot's Guide to Being Vegetarian. 368p. 2000. pap. 24.95 (*0-13-086723-3*, Prentice Hall) P-H.

Cronister, Amy, jt. ed. see Hagerman, Randi J.

Cronje, D. S. Case Book on the Law of Persons & Family Law. 544p. 1990. pap. 41.00 (*0-409-02080-X*, SA, MICHIE) LEXIS Pub.

— Persone- en Familierreg, Die Suid-Afrikaanse. 3rd ed. (AFR.). 388p. 1994. pap. write for info. (*0-409-04625-6*, MICHIE) LEXIS Pub.

— South African Law of Persons & Family Law. 419p. 1990. pap. 92.00 (*0-409-04622-1*, SA, MICHIE) LEXIS Pub.

— The South African Law of Persons & Family Law. 3rd rev. ed. LC 95-150748. 380p. 1994. pap. write for info. (*0-409-04623-X*, MICHIE) LEXIS Pub.

Cronje, D. S. & Heaton, J. Casebook on the South African Law of Persons & Family Law/Vonnisbundel Oor Die Suid-Afrikaanse Persone- en Familiereg. 2nd ed. LC 95-150790. (AFR & ENG.). 628p. 1994. pap. write for info. (*0-409-02081-8*, MICHIE) LEXIS Pub.

Cronje, Jacobus V. Dionysius of Halicarnassus: De Demosthene. (Spudasmata Ser.: Vol. XXXIX). viii, 295p. 1986. 60.00 (*3-487-07784-1*) G Olms Pubs.

Cronje, M., jt. auth. see Stack, E. M.

Cronje, Ruth, ed. see Almond, Glen, et al.

Cronk, Brian C. How to Use SPSS: A Step-by-Step Guide to Analysis & Interpretation. (Illus.). 120p. (C). 1999. pap. text 23.95 (*1-884585-15-9*) Pyrczak Pub.

Cronk, George. The Message of the Bible: An Orthodox Christian Perspective. LC 82-7355. 293p. (Orig.). 1982. pap. 11.95 (*0-913836-94-X*) St Vladimirs.

Cronk, Kari L. Dear Mr. Sand Man. (Illus.). 16p. (J). (gr. k-3). 1995. pap. 10.95 (*0-8059-3820-6*) Dorrance.

***Cronk, Kelly.** Drug Deal with God. LC 00-190500. (Illus.). 320p. 2000. pap. 17.95 (*0-9700175-7-X*) Skybloom Pubng.

Cronk, Lee. All Covered in Mud: The Dance of Biology & Culture. 208p. 1998. 22.00 (*0-393-04591-9*) Norton.

— That Complex Whole: Culture & the Evolution of Human Behavior. LC 99-28032. 208p. 1999. 50.00 (*0-8133-3704-6*) Westview.

***Cronk, Lee.** That Complex Whole: Culture & the Evolution of Human Behavior. LC 99-28032. 208p. 1999. pap. 20.00 (*0-8133-3705-4*, Pub. by Westview) HarpC.

Cronk, Lee, et al, eds. Adaptation & Human Behavior: An Anthropological Perspective. LC 99-26821. (Evolutionary Foundations of Human Behavior Ser.). 528p. 2000. pap. text 34.95 (*0-202-02044-4*); lib. bdg. 69.95 (*0-202-02043-6*) Aldine de Gruyter.

Cronk, Loren K., ed. Guide to Natural Food Restaurants. 3rd ed. LC 83-51080. Orig. Title: Annual Directory of Vegetarian Restaurants. (Illus.). 209p. 1984. pap. 8.95 (*0-938962-02-7*) Daystar Pub Co.

Cronk, Nicholas, ed. see Voltaire.

Cronk, Sandra. Dark Night Journey: Inward Re-Patterning Toward a Life Centered in God. 182p. (Orig.). 1993. pap. 13.00 (*0-87574-914-3*, 1057) Pendle Hill.

Cronk, Sandra L. Gospel Order: A Quaker Understanding of Faithful Church Community. LC 91-61844. 48p. (Orig.). 1991. pap. 4.00 (*0-87574-297-1*) Pendle Hill.

Cronk, Scott A. Building the E-Motive Industry. 236p. 1995. 29.00 (*1-56091-560-9*, R148) Soc Auto Engineers.

***Cronk, Stephen L., ed.** World's Most Lovable Bears. (Illus.). 2000. 24.95 (*0-942620-36-4*) Portfolio Pr.

Cronkhite, Gary. Persuasion: Speech & Behavioral Change. LC 73-75140. (Speech Communication Ser.). (C). 1969. pap. write for info. (*0-672-61075-2*, SC4, Bobbs) Macmillan.

Cronkite. Genetics Supplement for Biology. 4th ed. (C). 1996. pap. text, teacher ed. 20.50 (*0-03-019089-4*) Harcourt.

Cronkite, E. P. & Carstens, A. L. Diffusion Chamber Culture: Hemopoiesis, Cloning of Tumors, Cytogenetic & Carinogenic Assays. (Illus.). 270p. 1980. 67.95 (*0-387-10064-4*) Spr-Verlag.

Cronkite, Kathy. On the Edge of Darkness: Conversations about Conquering Depression. 368p. 1995. pap. 13.95 (*0-385-31426-4*, Delta Trade) Dell.

Cronkite, Walter. A Reporter's Life. (Illus.). 400p. 1997. pap. 14.00 (*0-345-41103-X*) Ballantine Pub Grp.

— A Reporter's Life. LC 96-21053. (Illus.). 384p. 1996. 6.99 (*0-394-57879-1*) Knopf.

— A Reporter's Life. large type ed. 1996. pap. 26.95 (*0-679-77414-9*) Knopf.

— Walter Cronkite. 1999. text 19.95 (*0-312-00454-0*) St Martin.

***Cronkite, Walter.** Walter Cronkite Remembers. 2000. 23.50 (*0-7435-0632-4*) SimSchuster Interact.

***Cronkite, Walter, narrated by.** The United States Constitution. unabridged ed. 1998. audio 22.00 (*0-671-58079-5*) S&S Audio.

Cronkleton, Robert & Garcia-Ferrer, Frank, eds. Rockhurst Review, 1988: A Fine Arts Journal, Vol. I. 79p. 1988. pap. 5.00 (*1-886761-00-0*) Rockhurst Col.

***Cronley, Connie.** Sometimes a Wheel Falls Off. 2000. 19.95 (*1-930709-13-7*) HAWK Pubng Grp.

Cronly, ed. Binocular Vision - Psychophysics. 1991. 137.00 (*0-8493-7509-6*, QP464) CRC Pr.

Cronly & Mandava. Inherited & Acquired Colour Vision Deficiencies. 1991. 137.00 (*0-8493-7507-X*) CRC Pr.

Cronly-Dillon. Dyslexia. 1991. 137.00 (*0-8493-7513-4*, QP) CRC Pr.

— Evolution of the Eye & Visual System. 1991. 137.00 (*0-8493-7502-9*, QP464) CRC Pr.

— Eye Movements. 1991. 137.00 (*0-8493-7508-8*, QP464) CRC Pr.

— Limits of Visual Perception. 1991. 137.00 (*0-8493-7505-3*, QP464) CRC Pr.

— Man & the Machine Interface. 1991. 137.00 (*0-8493-7515-0*, QP474) CRC Pr.

— Neuroanatomy of the Visual Pathways: Their Retinotopic Organization. 1991. 137.00 (*0-8493-7503-7*) CRC Pr.

— Pattern Recognition by Man & Machine. 1991. 137.00 (*0-8493-7514-2*, QP474) CRC Pr.

— Perceptions of Colour. 1991. 137.00 (*0-8493-7506-1*, QP464) CRC Pr.

— Spatial Vision. 1991. 137.00 (*0-8493-7510-X*, QP474) CRC Pr.

— Vision & Visual Dysfunction, 17 vols. 1991. 2125.00 (*0-8493-7500-2*) CRC Pr.

— Visual Agnosias. 1991. 137.00 (*0-8493-7512-6*) CRC Pr.

Cronly-Dillon, J. Neural Basis/Visual Function. 1991. 137.00 (*0-8493-7504-5*) CRC Pr.

— Susceptible Visual Apparatus. 1991. 137.00 (*0-8493-7516-9*, QP474) CRC Pr.

Cronly-Dillon, John, ed. Vision & Visual Dysfunction Index. 1991. 137.00 (*0-8493-7517-7*) CRC Pr.

Cronly-Dillon, John R. Development & Plasticity of the Visual System. 1991. 137.00 (*0-8493-7511-8*) CRC Pr.

***Cronn-Mills, Daniel.** A Qualitative Analysis of the Jehovah's Witnesses: The Rhetoric, Reality & Religion in the Watchtower Society. LC 99-41403. (Studies in American Religion: Vol. 70). 224p. 1999. text 89.95 (*0-7734-7943-0*) E Mellen.

Cronnet, Lilo G. Pedigree Studies: Index of New Information with Analysis, Research & Results. 160p. 1995. 47.50 (*0-7883-0434-8*); pap. 44.50 (*0-7883-0435-6*) ABBE Pubs Assn.

Cronon, David. The Second World War & the Atomic Age, 1940-1973. LC 74-28589. (Goldentree Bibliographies Series in American History). (C). 1975. pap. text 14.95 (*0-88295-538-1*) Harlan Davidson.

Cronon, E. David. Black Moses: The Story of Marcus Garvey & the Universal Negro Improvement Association. 2nd ed. (Illus.). 302p. 1960. pap. 14.95 (*0-299-01214-X*) U of Wis Pr.

Cronon, E. David & Jenkins, John W. The University of Wisconsin Vol. III: A History: Politics, Depression, & War, 1925-1945. LC 48-4763. (Illus.). 920p. 1994. 40.00 (*0-299-14430-5*) U of Wis Pr.

Cronon, Edmund D. Josephus Daniels in Mexico. LC 60-5672. 391p. 1960. reprint ed. pap. 121.30 (*0-608-01955-0*, 206261000003) Bks Demand.

Cronon, William. Changes in the Land: Indians, Colonists & the Ecology of New England. (American Century Ser.). (Illus.). 242p. (C). 1983. pap. 11.00 (*0-8090-0158-6*) Hill & Wang.

— Nature's Metropolis: Chicago & the Great West. (Illus.). 592p. 1992. pap. 18.95 (*0-393-30873-1*) Norton.

— Uncommon Ground: Rethinking the Human Place in Nature. 562p. 1996. pap. 15.95 (*0-393-31511-8*) Norton.

Cronon, William, ed. Uncommon Ground: Toward Reinventing Nature. LC 95-2147. (Illus.). 544p. 1995. 29.95 (*0-393-03872-6*) Norton.

Cronon, William, et al, eds. Under an Open Sky: Rethinking America's Western Past. 368p. 1993. pap. 12.95 (*0-393-31063-9*) Norton.

Cronon, William, ed. see Muir, John.

Cronquist, A., et al. Intermountain Flora Vol. 4: The Asteridae Except the Asteraceae. LC 73-134298. (Illus.). 573p. 1984. 75.00 (*0-89327-248-5*) NY Botanical.

Cronquist, A., ed. see Barneby, Rupert C.

Cronquist, Arthur. The Evolution & Classification of Flowering Plants. 2nd ed. LC 88-18008. (Illus.). 556p. (C). 1988. text 42.00 (*0-89327-332-5*) NY Botanical.

— An Integrated System of Classification of Flowering Plants. LC 80-39556. (Illus.). 1262p. (C). 1992. text 225.50 (*0-231-03880-1*) Col U Pr.

— Intermountain Flora Vol. 5: The Asteraceae. (Illus.). 1994. 75.00 (*0-89327-375-9*) NY Botanical.

— Vascular Flora of the Southeastern United States Vol. 1: Asteraceae. LC 79-769. (Illus.). 277p. 1980. reprint ed. pap. 85.90 (*0-608-03182-8*, 206363500001) Bks Demand.

Cronquist, Arthur, et al. Compositae (Mutisieae, Senecioneae, Vernoniae) LC 78-17496. (North American Flora Ser.: No. 2, Pt. 10). 245p. 1978. pap. 10.00 (*0-89327-191-8*) NY Botanical.

— Intermountain Flora Vol. 1: Geological & Botanical History, Plant Geography, Vascular Cryptogams, Gymnosperms, Glossary. (Illus.). 270p. 1972. reprint ed. text 32.00 (*0-89327-256-6*) NY Botanical.

— Intermountain Flora Vol. 6: The Monocotyledons. (Illus.). 584p. (C). 1994. reprint ed. text 75.00 (*0-89327-386-4*) NY Botanical.

— Seed Plants. (Pictured Key Nature Ser.). 250p. (C). 1979. text. write for info. (*0-697-04761-X*, WCB McGr Hill) McGrw-H Hghr Educ.

Cronquist, Arthur, jt. auth. see Gleason, Henry Allan.

Cronquist, H. Steven. Insurance: How to Buy It, How to Use It. 60p. 1992. pap. text 9.95 (*0-9634535-0-5*) HSC Pubs.

Cronshaw, Steven F., jt. auth. see Fine, Sidney A.

***Cronstein, B. N., ed.** Methotrexate. (Milestones in Drug Therapy Ser.). 250p. 2000. 159.00 (*3-7643-5959-5*, Pub. by Birkhauser) Spr-Verlag.

C

An Asterisk (*) at the beginning of an entry indicates that the title is appearing for the first time.

Cronwright-Schreiner, S. C., jt. auth. see Findlay, Frederick R. N.

Cronwright-Schreiner, Samuel. The Life of Olive Schreiner. LC 72-2122. (Studies in Women's Rights: No. 51). (Illus.). 1972. reprint ed. lib. bdg. 75.00 (*0-8383-1461-9*) M S G Haskell Hse.

Cronyn, George W. Path on the Rainbow. 4th ed. (Illus.). 360p. 1997. reprint ed. pap. 14.95 (*0-87877-240-5*) Newcastle Pub.

Cronyn, Hume. Bake My Brain. 80p. 1994. pap. 12.95 (*0-88962-543-3*) Mosaic.

Cronyn, J. M. Elements of Archaeological Conservation. (Illus.). 384p. (C). 1990. pap. 32.99 (*0-415-01207-4*, A3491) Routledge.

Croof, V. Impressionist Book of Days. 112p. 1996. 12.98 (*0-7858-0703-9*) Bk Sales Inc.

Croog, Sydney & Levine, Sol. The Heart Patient Recovers: Social & Psychological Factors. LC 77-608112. 432p. 1977. 45.95 (*0-87705-247-6*, Kluwer Acad Hman Sci) Kluwer Academic.

— Life after a Heart Attack: Social & Psychological Factors Eight Years Later. LC 81-6702. 328p. 1982. 45.95 (*0-89885-071-1*, Kluwer Acad Hman Sci) Kluwer Academic.

Crook, A. W., ed. Profiting from Low-Grade Heat: Thermodynamic Cycles for Low-Temperature Heat Sources, Watt Committee on Energy Report. (Energy Ser.: No. 7). 200p. 1993. boxed set 77.00 (*0-85296-835-3*, EN007) INSPEC Inc.

Crook, Alan, et al, eds. Guide to Fisheries Education Resources for Grades K-12. LC 98-86930. 57p. 1998. 16.00 (*1-888569-10-7*, 550.26) Am Fisheries Soc.

Crook, Carol. Colors: In the Scriptures. 37p. 1999. pap. 5.00 (*0-939399-35-0*) Bks of Truth.

— Communion of the Saints. 23p. 1988. pap. 2.50 (*0-939399-02-4*) Bks of Truth.

— Enter-Praise-Worship. (Illus.). 10p. (YA). (gr. 7 up). 1988. pap. 1.75 (*0-939399-03-2*) Bks of Truth.

***Crook, Carol.** The Garments of the Jewish Priests. 87p. 1999. pap. 11.95 (*0-939399-45-8*) Bks of Truth.

Crook, Carol. Gifts of the Holy Spirit Pt. II: The Five-Fold Ministries. Crook, James, ed. (Illus.). 210p. (C). 1998. ring bd. 49.95 (*0-939399-22-9*) Bks of Truth.

— God's Counsel... Being Led by the Spirit. 104p. 1999. ring bd. 25.00 (*0-939399-43-1*) Bks of Truth.

— How to Be Led by God. LC 93-71395. (Illus.). 147p. 1993. pap. 11.25 (*0-939399-19-9*) Bks of Truth.

***Crook, Carol.** How to Be Led by God, 4 vols. 1999. 20.00 incl. audio (*0-939399-25-3*) Bks of Truth.

Crook, Carol. How to Grow a Church. (Illus.). 302p. 1994. student ed., ring bd. 120.36 (*0-939399-20-2*) Bks of Truth.

***Crook, Carol.** The Jewish Prayer Shawl: Banners, Flags & Scarfs. (Illus.). 60p. 1999. pap. 6.95 (*0-939399-29-6*) Bks of Truth.

Crook, Carol. The Masonic Lodge: Where Will It Take You? 1998. pap. 5.25 (*0-939399-23-7*) Bks of Truth.

— Mysteries of God Revealed. 300p. 2001. ring bd. 100.00 (*0-939399-34-2*) Bks of Truth.

— Overflowing with Love. 29p. (YA). (gr. 7 up). 1989. pap. 2.50 (*0-939399-06-7*) Bks of Truth.

***Crook, Carol.** The Prophetic End Time Temple. large type ed. (Illus.). 78p. (C). 1999. ring bd. 22.95 (*0-939399-30-X*) Bks of Truth.

Crook, Carol. Spiritual Warfare. 259p. 1999. ring bd. 50.00 (*0-939399-41-5*) Bks of Truth.

***Crook, Carol.** Spiritual Warfare Manual, 6 vols. 1998. 30.00 incl. audio (*0-939399-26-1*) Bks of Truth.

Crook, Carol. Step Out in Ministry! LC 86-71831. 203p. 1986. pap. 10.95 (*0-939399-07-5*) Bks of Truth.

— Thoughts Turn to Actions. 7p. (YA). (gr. 5 up). 1989. pap. 1.50 (*0-939399-10-5*) Bks of Truth.

— Witchcraft. 23p. 1988. pap. 3.50 (*0-939399-11-3*) Bks of Truth.

Crook, Carol A. & Crook, James A. Gifts of the Holy Spirit Pt. I: The Nine Power Gifts. 225p. 1998. ring bd. 49.95 (*0-939399-21-0*) Bks of Truth.

Crook, Carol A., jt. auth. see Crook, James A.

Crook, Charles. Computers & the Collaborative Experience of Learning. LC 95-50269. (International Library of Psychology). 272p. (C). 1996. pap. 27.99 (*0-415-05360-9*) Routledge.

Crook, Christopher J. Cultural Practices & Socioeconomic Attainment: The Australian Experience, 120. LC 96-53029. (Contributions in Sociology Ser.: Vol. 120). 200p. 1997. 62.95 (*0-313-30340-1*, Greenwood Pr) Greenwood.

***Crook, Connie B.** Maple Moon. (Illus.). 32p. (ps-3). 2000. pap. 6.95 (*0-7737-6098-9*) Stoddart Publ.

Crook, Connie B. Maple Moon. unabridged ed. LC 98-108655. (Illus.). 32p. (YA). (ps-2). 1998. 15.95 (*0-7737-3017-6*) STDK.

— Nellie L. 232p. (Orig.). (YA). (gr. 7-11). 1994. mass mkt. 4.95 (*0-7736-7422-5*) STDK.

— Nellie's Quest. 180p. (YA). (gr. 7-12). 1998. pap. 5.95 (*0-7736-7469-1*) Stoddart Publ.

***Crook, Connie B.** Nellie's Victory. (Illus.). 200p. (J). 2000. mass mkt. 5.95 (*0-7736-7481-0*, Stoddart Kids) Stoddart Publ.

Crook, Cornelia E. Henry Castro - A Story of Early Colonization in Texas. 253p. 1988. write for info. (*0-945632-01-0*) St Marys Univ Pr.

Crook County Historical Society Staff. Echoes from Old Crook County, Vol. II. (Illus.). 288p. 1992. 12.95 (*1-930405-04-9*) Crook County Hist.

Crook County Historical Society Staff & A. R. Bowman Memorial Museum Staff. Echoes from Old Crook County. 176p. 1991. pap. 12.95 (*1-930405-03-0*) Crook County Hist.

***Crook, D., et al.** Lay Taxes in England & Wales, 1188-1688. (PRO Handbks.: No. 31). 371p. 1999. pap. text 49.95 (*1-873162-64-2*, Pub. by PRO Pubns) Midpt Trade.

Crook, David. Orlando di Lasso's Imitation Magnificats for Counter-Reformation Munich. LC 93-33537. 312p. 1994. text 57.50 (*0-691-03614-4*, Pub. by Princeton U Pr) Cal Prin Full Svc.

Crook, David, ed. see Di Lasso, Orlando.

Crook, E. J., tr. see Jordan, Richard.

Crook, Elizabeth. Promised Lands: A Novel of the Texas Rebellion. LC 94-45348. (Southwest Life & Letters Ser.). 528p. 1995. pap. 12.95 (*0-87074-385-6*) SMU Press.

— The Raven's Bride: A Novel of Eliza Allen & Sam Houston. LC 92-35183. (Southwest Life & Letters Ser.). 432p. 1993. reprint ed. pap. 12.95 (*0-87074-348-1*) SMU Press.

Crook, Eugene J., Jr., ed. Fearful Symmetry: Doubles & Doubling in Literature & Film; Selected Papers from the 5th Annual Florida State University Conference on Literature & Film. LC 81-19684. x, 175p. (Orig.). 1981. pap. 19.95 (*0-8130-0723-2*) U Press Fla.

Crook, Eugene J., tr. see Chaucer, Geoffrey.

Crook, G. M., ed. Airports & Automation: Proceedings of the 9th World Airports Conference, Organized by the Institution of Civil Engineers, London, England, September 10-12, 1991. 136p. 1992. 95.00 (*0-7277-1680-8*, Pub. by T Telford) RCH.

Crook-Gandette, Kathy, ed. & illus. see Sandford, Michael.

Crook-Gandette, Kathy, ed. & illus. see Woods, Duanne.

Crook-Gaudette, Kathy, ed. & illus. see Sandford, Michael.

Crook, Geoff, jt. auth. see Waterhouse, Mike.

Crook, George. General George Crook: His Autobiography. LC 85-40938. (Illus.). 368p. (Orig.). 1986. pap. 15.95 (*0-8061-1982-9*) U of Okla Pr.

Crook, Guy & Heinstein, Martin. The Older Worker in Industry. Stein, Leon, ed. LC 79-8664. (Growing Old Ser.). (Illus.). 1980. reprint ed. lib. bdg. 17.95 (*0-405-12782-0*) Ayer.

Crook, H. Clifford. Campanulas. LC 76-46559. (Illus.). 1977. reprint ed. 12.50 (*0-913728-18-7*) Theophrastus.

Crook, J. A. Law & Life of Rome: 90 B. C. to A. D. 212. LC 67-20633. (Aspects of Greek & Roman Life Ser.). 352p. 1984. pap. text 17.95 (*0-8014-9273-4*) Cornell U Pr.

— Legal Advocacy in the Roman World. 224p. 1995. text 52.50 (*0-8014-3158-1*) Cornell U Pr.

Crook, J. A., et al, eds. Last Age of the Roman Republic, 146-43 B. C. 2nd ed. (Ancient History Ser.: Vol. 9). (Illus.). 947p. 1994. text 150.00 (*0-521-25603-8*) Cambridge U Pr.

Crook, J. Mordaunt. The Greek Revival: Neo-Classical Attitudes in British Architecture: New Edition. (Illus.). 368p. 1996. pap. 29.95 (*0-7195-5455-1*, Pub. by John Murray) Trafalgar.

***Crook, J. Mordaunt.** The Rise of the Nouveaux Riches: Style & Status in Victorian & Edwardian Architecture. (Illus.). 354p. 2000. 45.00 (*0-7195-6040-3*, Pub. by John Murray) Trafalgar.

Crook, J. Mordaunt. William Burges & the High Victorian Dream. LC 81-1592. (Illus.). 632p. 1994. 60.00 (*0-226-12117-8*) U Ch Pr.

Crook, James, ed. see Crook, Carol.

***Crook, James A.** Walking with the King. 1999. audio 5.00 (*0-939399-38-5*) Bks of Truth.

— Why Tithe? 41p. (C). 2000. pap. 5.95 (*0-939399-46-6*) Bks of Truth.

— Works. 1999. audio 5.00 (*0-939399-39-3*) Bks of Truth.

Crook, James A. & Crook, Carol A. Relationships. (Illus.). 45p. 1999. pap. 5.95 (*0-939399-40-7*) Bks of Truth.

Crook, James A., jt. auth. see Crook, Carol A.

Crook, James W. German Wage Theories: A History of Their Development. LC 72-77989. (Columbia University. Studies in the Social Sciences: No. 24). 1968. reprint ed. 32.50 (*0-404-51024-8*) AMS Pr.

***Crook, Jeff.** Thieves' Guild, Vol. 2. (Dragonlance Ser.). 2000. mass mkt. 6.99 (*0-7869-1681-8*) Wizards Coast.

Crook, Jo & Learner, Tom. The Impact of Modern Paints. LC 99-55360. (Illus.). 176p. 1999. pap. 35.00 (*0-8230-2543-8*) Watsn-Guptill.

Crook, Joe. Bench Tips. LC 95-83915. (Illus.). 225p. 1996. pap. write for info. (*0-918845-17-3*) Am Watchmakers.

***Crook, John.** The Architectural Setting of the Cult of Saints in the Early Christian West c. 300-1200. (Oxford Historical Monographs). 2000. 85.00 (*0-19-820794-8*) OUP.

Crook, John. Space in Mind: East-West Psychology & Contemporary Buddhism. 1993. pap. 17.95 (*1-85230-154-6*, Pub. by Element MA) Penguin Putnam.

Crook, John, ed. Catching a Feather on a Fan: A Zen Retreat with Master Sheng Yen. 144p. 1993. pap. 12.95 (*1-85230-194-5*, Pub. by Element MA) Penguin Putnam.

Crook, John A. Consilium Principis: Imperial Councils & Counsellors from Augustus to Diocletian. LC 75-7309. (Roman History Ser.). 1978. reprint ed. 23.95 (*0-405-07191-4*) Ayer.

Crook, John H. The Evolution of Human Consciousness. (Illus.). 1980. 42.00 (*0-19-857174-7*) OUP.

Crook, John R., jt. ed. see Caron, David D.

Crook, Joseph R. Labworks: Complete Based Exp Chemistry. (Chemistry Ser.). 1996. pap., teacher ed. 25.00 (*0-7637-0241-2*) Jones & Bartlett.

— Labworks: Complete Based Exp Chemistry, Vol. 1. (Chemistry Ser.). 184p. (C). 1996. pap. 20.75 (*0-7637-0044-4*) Jones & Bartlett.

***Crook, Larry & Johnson, Randal.** Black Brazil: Culture, Identity & Social Mobilization LC 99-33770. (UCLA Latin American Studies). 1999. write for info. (*0-87903-087-9*) UCLA Lat Am Ctr.

Crook, Lydia. Tippy Goes to the Zoo. Mason, Mary J., ed. & photos by by. (Tippy the Turtles' Adventures Ser.). (Illus.). 12p. (J). (ps-6). 1997. pap. 8.00 (*1-890864-03-X*) Breath of Life.

Crook, M. A., ed. see Liquid Scintillation Counting Symposium Staff.

Crook, M. J., jt. auth. see Candlish, J. K.

Crook, Malcolm. Elections in the French Revolution: An Apprenticeship in Democracy, 1789-1799. 235p. (C). 1996. text 54.95 (*0-521-45191-4*) Cambridge U Pr.

— Napoleon Takes Power: Dictatorship & Democracy in France at the Turn of the Nineteenth Century. LC 98-211647. (Past in Perspective Ser.). 128p. 1998. pap. 14.95 (*0-7083-1401-5*, Pub. by Univ Wales Pr) Paul & Co Pubs.

Crook, Marion. The Body Image Trap: Understanding & Rejecting Body Image Myths. (Psychology Ser.). 128p. (Orig.). 1991. pap. 8.95 (*0-88908-975-2*) Self-Counsel Pr.

— Cutting It Close. 93p. (J). (gr. 3-8). 1999. pap. 5.50 (*1-55028-616-1*) Formac Dist Ltd.

***Crook, Marion.** The Face in the Mirror: Teens & Adoption. 2000. pap. 16.95 (*1-55152-079-6*) Arsenal Pulp.

Crook, Marion. Looking Good: Teenagers & Eating Disorders. 128p. (Orig.). 1992. pap. 12.95 (*1-55021-077-7*, Pub. by NC Ltd) U of Toronto Pr.

— Please Listen to Me: Your Guide to Understanding Teenagers & Suicide. 2nd ed. 112p. 1992. pap. 9.95 (*0-88908-544-7*) Self-Counsel Pr.

— Suicide: Teens Talk to Teens. LC 96-910885. 168p. (Orig.). 1997. pap. 12.95 (*1-55180-108-6*) Self-Counsel Pr.

— Summer of Madness. 192p. (Orig.). (YA). 1995. pap. 6.95 (*1-55143-041-X*) Orca Bk Pubs.

— Teenagers Talk about Adoption. 128p. (Orig.). 1987. pap. 12.95 (*0-920053-67-X*, Pub. by NC Ltd) U of Toronto Pr.

— Teenagers Talk about Adoption. 116p. (Orig.). (YA). (gr. 6 up). 1990. pap. 10.95 (*1-55021-047-5*, Pub. by NC Ltd) U of Toronto Pr.

— Teenagers Talk about Suicide. (Teenagers Talk about...Ser.). 128p. (YA). (gr. 7-12). 1988. pap. 12.95 (*1-55021-013-0*, Pub. by NC Ltd) U of Toronto Pr.

— Writing for Kids & Teens. 224p. 1998. pap. 18.95 (*1-55180-191-4*) Self-Counsel Pr.

Crook, Martin. Algorithms in Chemical Pathology. LC 97-26208. (Illus.). 128p. 1997. pap. text 47.00 (*0-7506-2780-8*) Buttrwrth-Heinemann.

Crook, Michael, tr. see Van Buren, Ariane & Pyle, Leo, eds.

Crook, Mordaunt J. The Dilemma of Style: Architectural Ideas from the Picturesque to the Postmodern. LC 87-10821. (Illus.). 340p. 1987. 54.00 (*0-226-12119-4*) U Ch Pr.

Crook, Nigel. India's Industrial Cities: Essays in Economics & Demography. (SOFTS Studies on South Asia). 188p. (C). 1993. 24.00 (*0-19-563172-2*) OUP.

— Principles of Population & Development: With Illustrations from Asia & Africa. Timaeus, Ian M., ed. 1997. 65.00 (*0-614-31301-5*) OUP.

— Principles of Population & Development: With Illustrations from Asia & Africa. Timligus, Ian M., ed. LC 96-28079. (Illus.). 236p. 1997. text 65.00 (*0-19-877489-3*) OUP.

— Principles of Population & Development: With Illustrations from Asia & Africa. Timaeus, Ian M., ed. LC 96-28079. (Illus.). 236p. 1997. pap. text 32.00 (*0-19-877488-5*) OUP.

— The Transmission of Knowledge in South Asia: Essays on Education, Religion, History, & Politics. LC 96-902108. (Studies on South Asia). (Illus.). 346p. (C). 1996. text 29.95 (*0-19-563644-9*) OUP.

Crook, Nigel, jt. auth. see Pryer, Jane.

Crook, Nora, ed. see Shelley, Mary Wollstonecraft.

Crook, Nora, ed. see Shelley, Percy Bysshe.

Crook, Paul. Came the Dawn: Fifty Years an Army Officer. 144p. (C). 1991. 90.00 (*0-946771-21-9*, Pub. by Spellmnt Pubs) St Mut.

— Darwinism, War & History: The Debate over the Biology of War from the "Origin of Species" to the First World War. 318p. (C). 1994. pap. text 29.95 (*0-521-46645-8*) Cambridge U Pr.

Crook, Richard, jt. auth. see Abraham, Anthony L.

Crook, Richard C. & Manor, James. Democracy & Decentralisation in South Asia & West Africa: Participation, Accountability & Performance. LC 97-52669. (Illus.). 352p. (C). 1998. text 64.95 (*0-521-63157-2*); pap. text 24.95 (*0-521-63647-7*) Cambridge U Pr.

Crook, Roger H. An Introduction to Christian Ethics. 3rd ed. LC 98-18579. 290p. (C). 1998. pap. text 33.60 (*0-13-095131-5*) P-H.

— Our Heritage & Our Hope: A History of Pullen Memorial Baptist Church 1884-1984. LC 84-62984. (Illus.). 252p. 1985. 10.00 (*0-9614485-0-4*) Pullen Mem Baptist.

Crook, Sandy. Lop Rabbits As Pets. (Illus.). 128p. 1986. 24.95 (*0-86622-137-9*, PS-809) TFH Pubns.

Crook, Stephen, et al. Postmodernization: Change in Advance Society. 272p. (C). 1992. text 65.00 (*0-8039-8327-1*); pap. text 21.95 (*0-8039-8328-X*) Sage.

Crook, Stephen, ed. see Adorno, Theodor W.

***Crook, Susan.** Fun Food Gourmet Games. 1999. pap. 19.95 (*1-85626-329-0*, Pub. by Cathie Kyle) Trafalgar.

Crook, Thomas H., III & Adderly, Brenda. The Memory Cure: The Safe, Scientifically Proven Breakthrough That Can Slow, Halt, or Even Reverse Age-Related Memory Loss. LC 98-86288. 320p. 1998. 24.00 (*0-671-02642-9*, PB Hardcover) PB.

***Crook, Thomas H., III & Adderly, Brenda.** The Memory Cure: The Safe, Scientifically Proven Breakthrough That Can Slow, Halt, or Even Reverse Age-Related Memory Loss. 1999. reprint ed. mass mkt. 6.99 (*0-671-02643-7*) PB.

Crook, Tim. International Radio Journalism. LC 97-16886. (Communication & Society Ser.). (Illus.). 320p. (C). 1998. 75.00 (*0-415-09672-3*); pap. 24.99 (*0-415-09673-1*) Routledge.

***Crook, Tim.** Radio Drama. LC 99-26899. 1999. pap. write for info. (*0-415-21603-6*) Routledge.

— Radio Drama. LC 99-26899. 304p. (C). 1999. text. write for info. (*0-415-21602-8*) Routledge.

Crook, Vivien. Three-Dimensional Decoupage. (Illus.). 48p. 1996. pap. 11.95 (*0-85532-808-8*, 7936X, Pub. by Srch Pr) A Schwartz & Co.

Crook, Welton J. Abacus Arithmetic. LC 58-7709. (Illus.). 69p. 1958. pap. 2.95 (*0-87015-078-2*) Pacific Bks.

Crook, William. New Hampshire Reports & Current Case Service. 32p. 48.00 (*0-614-03167-2*, MICHIE) LEXIS Pub.

— The Yeast Connection Cookbook. 379p. 1991. 18.95 (*0-933478-17-8*) Prof Bks Future Health.

***Crook, William.** The Yeast Connection Handbook. 2nd ed. (Illus.). 276p. (Orig.). 1999. pap. text 14.95 (*0-933478-24-0*) Prof Bks Future Health.

Crook, William C. Chronic Fatigue Syndrome & the Yeast Connection: A Get-Well Guide for People with this Often Misunderstood Illness & Those Who Care for Them. (Illus.). 400p. (Orig.). 1992. pap. 14.95 (*0-933478-20-8*) Prof Bks Future Health.

Crook, William G. Are You Allergic? rev. ed. 1978. pap. 6.95 (*0-933478-02-X*) Prof Bks Future Health.

— Can Your Child Read? Is He Hyperactive? rev. ed. 1977. pap. 6.95 (*0-933478-01-1*) Prof Bks Future Health.

— Detecting Your Hidden Allergies. (Illus.). 232p. (Orig.). 1988. pap. 11.95 (*0-933478-15-1*) Prof Bks Future Health.

— Help for the Hyperactive Child. (Illus.). 248p. (Orig.). 1991. pap. 14.95 (*0-933478-18-6*) Prof Bks Future Health.

— Tracking down Hidden Food Allergy. 2nd ed. (Illus.). 104p. (Orig.). 1980. pap. 6.95 (*0-933478-05-4*) Prof Bks Future Health.

— The Yeast Connection. 3rd ed. (Illus.). 438p. 1989. reprint ed. pap. 8.95 (*0-933478-11-9*) Prof Bks Future Health.

— The Yeast Connection: A Medical Breakthrough. LC 83-62508. (Illus.). 304p. 1985. 15.95 (*0-933478-10-0*) Prof Bks Future Health.

— The Yeast Connection: A Medical Breakthrough. 1986. pap. 15.00 (*0-394-74700-3*) Vin Bks.

— The Yeast Connection & the Woman. (Illus.). 768p. (Orig.). (C). 1995. pap. 17.95 (*0-933478-22-4*) Prof Bks Future Health.

Crook, William G. & Jones, Marge H. The Yeast Connection Cookbook. (Illus.). 384p. 1989. 12.95 (*0-933478-16-X*) Prof Bks Future Health.

Crookall, David & Arai, K., eds. Global Interdependence - Simulation, Gaming, & Perspectives: Proceedings of the 22nd International Conference of the International Simulation & Gaming Association (ISAGA), Kyoto, Japan, 15-19 July 1991. LC 92-5641. 1992. 148.95 (*0-387-70094-3*) Spr-Verlag.

Crookall, David & Saunders, Danny. Communication & Simulation: From Two Fields to One Theme. 340p. 1989. 99.00 (*0-905028-85-6*, Pub. by Multilingual Matters); pap. 39.95 (*0-905028-84-8*, Pub. by Multilingual Matters) Taylor & Francis.

Crookall, David, et al. Simulation-Gaming in Education & Training: Proceedings of the International Simulation & Gaming Association's 18th International Conference. LC 88-11740. (Illus.). 298p. 1988. 119.95 (*0-08-036465-9*, Prgamon Press) Buttrwrth-Heinemann.

Crookall, David, ed. see International Simulation & Gaming Association, Int.

Crookall, David A. & Arai, Kiyoshi, eds. Simulations & Gaming Across Disciplines & Cultures: ISAGA at a Watershed. LC 95-12230. 288p. (C). 1995. 46.00 (*0-8039-7102-8*); pap. 22.95 (*0-8039-7103-6*) Sage.

Crookall, Robert. Case-Book of Astral Projection, 545-746. 160p. 1980. pap. 3.95 (*0-8065-0730-6*, Citadel Pr) Carol Pub Group.

— Out-of-the-Body Experiences. 224p. 1992. pap. 7.95 (*0-8065-1383-7*, Citadel Pr) Carol Pub Group.

— The Study & Practice of Astral Projection. 1977. pap. 6.95 (*0-8065-0547-8*, Citadel Pr) Carol Pub Group.

Crooke, Carolyn J. Imagine You Are a Race Car Driver. LC 98-26362. (Action Sports Library). 2002. lib. bdg. 21.35 (*1-57765-204-5*) ABDO Pub Co.

— Imagine You Are a Scuba Diver. LC 98-27136. (Action Sports Library). 2002. lib. bdg. 21.35 (*1-57765-201-0*) ABDO Pub Co.

Crooke, Charlotte P. Marklin: Great Toys, 1895-1914. (Illus.). 180p. 1995. pap. text 29.95 (*1-872727-18-2*) Pincushion Pr.

Crooke, H., tr. see Pare, Ambroise.

Crooke, Philip S., jt. auth. see Huang, Cliff J.

Crooke, S. T., jt. auth. see Poste, G.

Crooke, Stanely T. & Poste, George H., eds. Dopamine Receptor Agonists. LC 84-8290. (New Horizons in Therapeutics Ser.). 414p. 1984. 95.00 (*0-306-41654-9*, Plenum Trade) Perseus Pubng.

Crooke, Stanley T. & Agrawal, Sudhir, eds. Antisense Research & Application. LC 97-46586. (Handbook of Experimental Pharmacology Ser.). (Illus.). xxvi, 630p. 1998. 399.00 (*3-540-63833-4*) Spr-Verlag.

An Asterisk (*) at the beginning of an entry indicates that the title is appearing for the first time.

Crooke, Stanley T. & Bradner, W. T. Bleomycin: A Review. 35.00 (*0-915340-05-4*) PJD Pubns.

Crooke, Stanley T. & Lebleu, Bernard, eds. Antisense Research & Applications. 624p. 1993. lib. bdg. 219.00 (*0-8493-4705-X*, RM666) CRC Pr.

Crooke, Stanley T. & Poste, George H., eds. Mechanisms of Receptor Regulation. LC 85-28339. (New Horizons in Therapeutics Ser.). (Illus.). 458p. (C). 1985. text 150.00 (*0-306-42125-9*, Kluwer Plenum) Kluwer Academic.

— New Insights into Cell & Membrane Transport Processes. LC 86-8175. (New Horizons in Therapeutics Ser.). (Illus.). 456p. (C). 1986. text 138.00 (*0-306-42183-6*, Kluwer Plenum) Kluwer Academic.

Crooke, W. Folklore of India. (C). 1993. 44.00 (*81-7305-006-6*, Pub. by Aryan Bks Intl) S Asia.

— Folklore of India. viii, 420p. 1993. 32.95 (*1-881338-26-6*) Nataraj Bks.

— Introduction to the Popular Religion & Folk Lore of Northern India. (C). 1994. reprint ed. text 44.00 (*81-206-0970-0*, Pub. by Asian Educ Servs) S Asia.

— Natives of Northern India. (C). 1995. 36.00 (*81-206-1110-1*, Pub. by Asian Educ Servs) S Asia.

— North-Western Provinces of India: Their History, Ethnology, & Administration. (C). 1994. 42.00 (*81-206-0088-6*, Pub. by Asian Educ Servs) S Asia.

Crooke, William. A Glossary of North Indian Peasant Life. Amin, Shahid, ed. 356p. 1989. 27.50 (*0-19-562209-X*) OUP.

— The North-Western Provinces of India: Their History, Ethnology & Administration. LC 98-906404. x, 361 p. 1998. write for info. (*81-206-1067-9*) Asian Educ Servs.

— Rural & Agricultural Glossary for the NW Provinces & Oudh. (C). 1989. reprint ed. 28.50 (*81-85326-00-2*, Pub. by Usha) S Asia.

Crooke, William, ed. see Ball, V.

Crooke, William, ed. see Tod, James.

Crooke, William, ed. see Yule, Henry & Burnell, A. C.

Crookell, Harold. Canadian-American Trade & Investment under the Free Trade Agreement. LC 90-32922. 240p. 1990. 62.95 (*0-89930-481-8*, CCF/, Quorum Bks) Greenwood.

Crookenden, Julia, tr. see Khazanov, Anatoly M.

Crookenden, Kate, jt. auth. see Willes, Margaret.

Crooker, Barbara. In the Late Summer Garden. 28p. 1998. 5.00 (*0-9620790-3-0*) H & H Pr.

— The Lost Children. 48p. (Orig.). 1989. pap. 17.00 (*0-940592-23-1*) Heyeck Pr.

— Starting from Zero. 28p. 1987. pap. 3.50 (*0-9613465-8-2*) Great Elm.

Crooker, Constance E. The Art of Legal Interpretation: A Guide for Court Interpreters. LC 96-67205. 135p. 1996. 35.00 (*0-87678-116-4*) PSU CE Pr.

Crooker, Judith M. Campus Opportunities. 6th ed. 1999. pap. text 5.00 (*1-57509-052-X*) Octameron Assocs.

Crooker, Nancy, et al, eds. Coronal Mass Ejections: Causes & Consequences. LC 97-26277. (Monograph Ser.: Vol. 99). 1997. 70.00 (*0-87590-081-X*) Am Geophysical.

Crooker, T. W. & Leis, Brian N., eds. Corrosion Fatigue: Mechanics, Metallurgy, Electrochemistry, & Engineering - STP 801. LC 82-83519. 522p. 1983. text 62.00 (*0-8031-0245-3*, STP801) ASTM.

Crooker, T. W., ed. see Conference on Structural Integrity Technology, 197.

Crooker, Thomas W., ed. see Leis, Brian N.

Crooker, William S. Oak Island Gold: One of the World's Most Baffling Mysteries. (Illus.). 228p. 1993. pap. 14.95 (*1-55109-049-X*) Nimbus Publ.

— Tracking Treasure: In Search of East Coast Bounty. 192p. 1998. pap. 16.95 (*1-55109-229-8*) Nimbus Publ.

Crookes. Research into Practice. (C). 1998. pap. text 21.00 (*0-7020-2068-0*, W B Saunders Co) Harcrt Hlth Sci Grp.

Crookes, Graham & Gass, Susan M., eds. Task & Language Learning: Integrating Theory & Practice. LC 92-46197. (Multilingual Matters Ser.). 169p. 1993. 79.00 (*1-85359-185-8*, Pub. by Multilingual Matters); pap. 29.00 (*1-85359-184-X*, Pub. by Multilingual Matters) Taylor & Francis.

— Tasks in a Pedagogical Context: Integrating Theory & Practice. LC 92-45646. 163p. 1993. 79.00 (*1-85359-187-4*, Pub. by Multilingual Matters); pap. 29.00 (*1-85359-186-6*, Pub. by Multilingual Matters) Taylor & Francis.

Crookes, William. Researches in the Phenomena of Spiritualism. 112p. 1996. reprint ed. pap. 9.00 (*0-7873-0228-7*) Hlth Research.

— The Wheat Problem. LC 75-27633. (World Food Supply Ser.). (Illus.). 1976. reprint ed. 25.95 (*0-405-07775-0*) Ayer.

Crooks. Our Sexuality. (Adaptable Courseware Ser.). 1997. 36.25 (*0-534-49830-2*) Brooks-Cole.

— Our Sexuality. 7th ed. (Psychology Ser.). 1998. pap. 29.95 (*0-534-36237-0*); pap., student ed. 20.50 (*0-534-35988-4*) Brooks-Cole.

— Our Sexuality. 7th ed. LC 98-26371. (Health Sciences Ser.). (C). 1998. pap. 46.00 (*0-534-35467-X*) Brooks-Cole.

— Our Sexuality with InfoTrac. 7th ed. (Psychology Ser.). 1998. pap. 46.75 incl. cd-rom (*0-534-36335-0*) Brooks-Cole.

— Salvations Sign & Seal. 1997. pap. 4.99 (*1-85792-316-2*, Pub. by Christian Focus) Spring Arbor Dist.

Crooks & Baur. Our Sexuality. 7th ed. (Psychology Ser.). 1999. pap. text 31.00 (*0-534-76789-3*) Wadsworth Pub.

***Crooks & Baur.** Our Sexuality. 8th ed. (Psychology Ser.). 2001. 52.00 (*0-534-57978-7*) Wadsworth Pub.

Crooks, jt. auth. see Gabler.

Crooks, jt. auth. see Weiten.

Crooks, Alan, jt. auth. see Ball, Terry.

Crooks, Alan F., jt. ed. see Miller, Gilbert H.

Crooks, J. J. History of the Colony of Sierra Leone, Western Africa. 376p. 1972. reprint ed. 49.50 (*0-7146-1646-X*, BHA-01646, Pub. by F Cass Pubs) Intl Spec Bk.

— Records Relating to the Gold Coast Settlements from 1750 to 1874. 576p. 1973. reprint ed. 55.00 (*0-7146-1647-8*, BHA-01647, Pub. by F Cass Pubs) Intl Spec Bk.

Crooks, James B. Jacksonville after the Fire, 1901-1919: A New South City. 208p. 1991. 29.95 (*0-8130-1067-5*) U Press Fla.

— Politics & Progress: The Rise of Urban Progressivism in Baltimore, 1895 to 1911. LC 68-21805. 281p. reprint ed. pap. 87.20 (*0-608-14445-2*, 205187700013) Bks Demand.

Crooks, Lisa. Color Me Learning. (Illus.). 112p. (Orig.). 1997. pap. 4.95 (*1-880505-21-5*, CLC0164) Pieces of Lrning.

Crooks, Lloyd H. Grenada Ghost. LC 98-93701. 422p. 1999. mass mkt. 7.99 (*0-9666296-0-4*) W Brathwaite Pub.

Crooks, Malcolm. Are You Ready to Be Judged by God? 49p. 1999. pap. 8.00 (*0-8059-4423-0*) Dorrance.

Crooks, Robert. Our Sexuality. 5th ed. (Health Sciences Ser.). 1993. text 41.00 (*0-534-33939-5*) Brooks-Cole.

— Our Sexuality. 6th ed. (Health Sciences Ser.). 1995. pap., student ed. 18.25 (*0-534-32096-1*) Brooks-Cole.

— Our Sexuality: Study Guide. 5th ed. (Health Sciences Ser.). 1993. pap., student ed. 17.95 (*0-534-33943-3*) Brooks-Cole.

— Tolley's VAT on Construction, Land & Property. 220p. 1995. 200.00 (*1-86012-045-8*, Pub. by Tolley Pubng) St Mut.

— Tolley's VAT on Construction, Land & Property. 3rd ed. 220p. (C). 1994. 175.00 (*0-85459-700-X*, Pub. by Tolley Pubng) St Mut.

Crooks, Robert & Baur, Karla. Our Sexuality. 5th ed. LC 92-23485. (C). 1993. text 49.50 (*0-8053-0212-3*) Benjamin-Cummings.

— Our Sexuality. 6th ed. LC 95-31922. 680p. 1995. pap. 47.50 (*0-534-32094-5*) Brooks-Cole.

— Our Sexuality. 6th ed. 1995. pap., teacher ed. write for info. (*0-534-34044-X*) Brooks-Cole.

— Our Sexuality: Test Items. 6th ed. 1995. pap. write for info. (*0-534-32097-X*) Brooks-Cole.

Crooks, Robert L., et al. Psychology: Science, Behavior & Life. 3rd ed. (Illus.). 750p. (C). 1993. text 83.50 (*0-15-500998-2*, Pub. by Harcourt Coll Pubs) Harcourt.

Crookshank, Anne. Mildred Anne Butler. (Lives of Irish Artists Ser.). (Illus.). 36p. 1995. 7.95 (*0-948524-37-5*, Pub. by Town Hse) Roberts Rinehart.

Crookshank, Edgar M. History & Pathology of Vaccination, 2 vols. LC 75-23702. reprint ed. write for info. (*0-404-13330-4*) AMS Pr.

***Croom, A. T.** Roman Clothing & Fashion. (Illus.). 176p. 2000. 32.50 (*0-7524-1469-0*, Pub. by Tempus Pubng) Arcadia Publng.

Croom, Emily A. The Genealogist's Companion & Sourcebook. LC 93-46365. 256p. 1994. pap. 16.99 (*1-55870-331-4*, Betrwy Bks) F & W Pubns Inc.

***Croom, Emily A.** The Sleuth Book for Genealogists. LC 99-88395. 192p. 2000. pap. 17.99 (*1-55870-532-5*, Betrwy Bks) F & W Pubns Inc.

Croom, Emily A. Unpuzzling Your Past: A Basic Guide to Genealogy. 3rd ed. LC 95-18210. (Illus.). 180p. 1995. pap. 14.99 (*1-55870-396-9*, Betrwy Bks) F & W Pubns Inc.

— The Unpuzzling Your Past Workbook: Essential Forms & Letters for All Genealogists. 320p. 1996. pap., wbk. ed. 15.99 (*1-55870-423-X*, Betrwy Bks) F & W Pubns Inc.

Croom, Gladys L., jt. ed. see Greene, Beverly.

Croom, Guy. When the Pines Grew Tall. 1991. 12.95 (*1-878096-10-9*) Best E TX Pubs.

Croom, Walt. Overcoming Fear. 170p. 1999. pap. 7.95 (*0-7392-0149-2*, PO3090) Morris Pubng.

Croome, Angela. Hovercraft. (Illus.). (J). (gr. 5 up). 1962. 14.95 (*0-8392-3008-7*) Astor-Honor.

Croome-Gale, Derek J. Creating the Productive Workplace. LC 98-55076. 1999. pap. write for info. (*0-419-23690-2*) Routledge.

Croome, John. Guide to the Urugauy Round Agreements. LC 98-49929. 285p. 1998. 90.00 (*90-411-1125-5*) Kluwer Law Intl.

— Reshaping the World Trading System: A History of the Uruguay Round. (Illus.). 400p. (C). 1996. pap. text 50.00 (*0-7881-3046-3*) DIANE Pub.

— Reshaping the World Trading System: A History of the Uruguay Round. LC 98-49928. 360p. 1998. 90.00 (*90-411-1126-3*) Kluwer Academic.

Croone, Brian, jt. auth. see Harcey, Dennis W.

Croone, E., jt. ed. see Pannekoek, A.

Croopsey. Woman in the Military. 1994. 24.95 (*0-02-906708-1*) Free Pr.

Croot, jt. auth. see Crawford.

Croot, D. G., ed. Glaciotectonics: Proceedings of Various Meetings of the Glaciotectonics Work Group: Field Meeting at Mon, Denmark (1986); INQUA Congress, Ottawa (1987); Field Meeting at Norfolk, U. K. (1988) (Illus.). 220p. (C). 1988. text 85.00 (*90-6191-848-0*, Pub. by A A Balkema) Ashgate Pub Co.

Crop Science Society of America Staff, jt. auth. see Eberhart, Steve A.

Cropanzano, Russell, ed. Justice in the Workplace: Approaching Fairness in Human Resource Management. (Applied Psychology Ser.). 304p. 1993. text 59.95 (*0-8058-1055-2*) L Erlbaum Assocs.

***Cropanzano, Russell, ed.** Justice in the Workplace: From Theory to Practice. 2nd ed. 300p. 2000. write for info. (*0-8058-2694-7*); pap. write for info. (*0-8058-2695-5*) L Erlbaum Assocs.

Cropanzano, Russell, jt. auth. see Folger, Robert.

Cropanzano, Russell S. & Kacmar, K. Michele, eds. Organizational Politics, Justice & Support: Managing the Social Climate of the Workplace. LC 95-7700. 256p. 1995. 65.00 (*0-89930-906-2*, Quorum Bks) Greenwood.

Cropley, A. J. Lifelong Education: A Psychological Analysis. LC 77-5702. 1977. 95.00 (*0-08-021814-8*, Pub. by Pergamon Repr) Franklin.

Cropley, Arthur, jt. auth. see Knapper, Chris.

Cropley, Arthur J. More Ways Than One: Fostering Creativity in the Classroom. LC 92-13362. (Creativity Research Ser.). 144p. 1992. pap. 24.50 (*0-89391-939-X*); text 73.25 (*0-89391-789-3*) Ablx Pub.

Cropley, Arthur J. & Dehn, Detlev, eds. Fostering the Growth of High Ability: European Perspectives. LC 96-15631. (Publications in Creativity Research). 628p. 1996. pap. 39.50 (*1-56750-242-3*); text 78.50 (*1-56750-241-5*) Ablx Pub.

Cropley, J. P., jt. auth. see Gilling, J.

Cropp, M. J., ed. see Euripides.

Cropp, Martin. Euripides Electra. (Greek Commentaries Ser.). 112p. (Orig.). (C). 1989. pap. text 7.00 (*0-929524-57-8*) Bryn Mawr Commentaries.

Cropp, Martin & Hamilton, Richard. Euripides' Heracles. (Greek Commentaries Ser.). 126p. (Orig.). (C) 1987. pap. text 7.00 (*0-929524-09-8*) Bryn Mawr Commentaries.

Cropp, Richard. Writing Magazine & Newspaper Articles. 224p. 1998. pap. 12.95 (*1-55180-193-0*) Self-Counsel Pr.

Cropp, Richard & Braidwood, Barbara. Romantic Days & Nights in Vancouver: Intimate Escapes in Lotus Land. LC 98-14830. (Romantic Days & Nights Ser.). (Illus.). 256p. 1998. pap. 15.95 (*0-7627-0203-6*) Globe Pequot.

Cropp, Richard, et al. Start & Run a Profitable Secondhand Store. (Start & Run Ser.). 216p. (Orig.). 1997. pap. 15.95 (*1-55180-136-1*) Self-Counsel Pr.

Cropp, Richard, jt. auth. see Braidwood, Barbara.

Cropper, Carolyn. ExCet Study Sessions: Early Childhood Education Study Manual for the Texas Teacher ExCET Examination. (C). pap. text, teacher ed. 20.00 (*1-893629-02-3*) ExCET.

— ExCet Study Sessions: Elementary Comprehensive Study Manual for the Texas Teacher ExCET Exam. (C). pap. text 20.00 (*1-893629-07-4*) ExCET.

— ExCet Study Sessions: Generic Special Education Study Manual for the Texas Teacher ExCET Examination. (C). pap. text, teacher ed. 20.00 (*1-893629-06-6*) ExCET.

— ExCet Study Sessions: Practice Questions for the Early Childhood Education Examination for the Texas Teachers ExCET Examination. (C). pap. text, teacher ed. 12.00 (*1-893629-15-5*) ExCET.

— ExCet Study Sessions: Practice Questions for the Elementary Comprehensive Examination for the Texas Teachers ExCET Examination. (C). pap. text, teacher ed. 12.00 (*1-893629-05-8*) ExCET.

— ExCet Study Sessions: Practice Questions for the Generic Special Education Examination for the Texas Teachers ExCET Examination. (C). pap. text, teacher ed. 12.00 (*1-893629-18-X*) ExCET.

— ExCet Study Sessions: Principal (Mid-Management) Study Manual for the Texas Teacher ExCET Examination. (C). pap. text, teacher ed. 20.00 (*1-893629-13-9*) ExCET.

— ExCET Study Sessions: Reading (Secondary) Study Manual for the Texas Teacher ExCET Examination. (C). pap. text 20.00 (*1-893629-00-7*) ExCET.

— ExCet Study Sessions: School Counselor Study Manual for the Texas Teacher ExCET Examination. (C). pap. text 20.00 (*1-893629-14-7*) ExCET.

Cropper, Carolyn & Lara, Susan S. ExCet Study Sessions: Practice Questions for the Bilingual Endorsement Examination for the Texas Teachers ExCET Examination. (C). pap. text, teacher ed. 12.00 (*1-893629-16-3*) ExCET.

Cropper, Charles A., jt. auth. see Triepke, Darryl A.

***Cropper, Elizabeth.** Nicolas Poussin: Friendship & the Love of Painting. 2000. pap. text 35.00 (*0-691-05067-8*, Pub. by Princeton U Pr) Cal Prin Full Svc.

Cropper, Elizabeth. Pontormo: Portrait of a Halberdier. LC 97-19822. (Getty Museum Studies on Art). 133p. 1997. pap. 17.50 (*0-89236-366-5*, Pub. by J P Getty Trust) OUP.

Cropper, Elizabeth, ed. Florentine Drawing at the Time of Lorenzo the Magnificent: Papers from a Colloquium Held at the Villa Spelman, Florence, 1992. (Villa Spelman Colloquium Ser.: No. 4). 350p. (C). 1994. text 49.95 (*88-7779-398-8*) Johns Hopkins.

Cropper, Elizabeth, et al, eds. Documentary Culture: Florence & Rome from Grand-Duke Ferdinand I to Pope Alexander VII. (Villa Spelman Colloquium Ser.: No. 3). (Illus.). 380p. 1992. text 45.00 (*88-7779-327-9*) Johns Hopkins.

Cropper, Elizabeth & Dempsey, Charles. Nicholas Poussin: Friendship & the Love of Painting. LC 95-52-3. 336p. 1996. text 95.00 (*0-691-04449-X*, Pub. by Princeton U Pr) Cal Prin Full Svc.

Cropper, Janet, tr. see Bobrowski, Johannes.

Cropper, Mary, jt. auth. see Martin, Diana.

***Cropper, Maureen.** Valuing Environmental Benefits: Selected Essays of Maureen Cropper. LC 99-12803. (New Horizons in Environmental Economics Ser.). 424p. 1999. 120.00 (*1-85898-737-7*) E Elgar.

Cropper, Maureen L., et al. Public Preferences for Life Saving. (Illus.). 78p. (Orig.). (C). 1993. pap. text 20.00 (*1-56806-370-9*) DIANE Pub.

Cropper, S. Enhancing Health Service Management: The Role of Decision Support Systems. LC 96-51488. (Health Services Management Ser.). 1997. pap. 36.95 (*0-335-19634-9*) OpUniv Pr.

Cropper, Steve & Forte, Paul. Enhancing Decision Making in the National Health Service: The Role of Decision Support Systems. LC 96-51488. (Health Services Management Ser.). 1997. 118.00 (*0-335-19635-7*) OpUniv Pr.

Cropper, Susn, jt. auth. see Stern, Michael.

Cropper, William H. Mathematica Programs for Physical Chemistry. LC 97-34136. (Illus.). 168p. 1998. pap. text 42.00 incl. cd-rom (*0-387-98337-6*) Spr-Verlag.

***Cropsey, Eugene H.** Crosby's Opera House: Symbol of Chicago's Cultural Awakening. LC 99-24104. (Illus.). 456p. 2000. 59.50 (*0-8386-3822-8*) Fairleigh Dickinson.

Cropsey, Joseph. Plato's World. LC 94-34538. 238p. 1995. 29.95 (*0-226-12121-6*) U Ch Pr.

— Plato's World. 1997. pap. text 12.95 (*0-226-12122-4*) U Ch Pr.

— Political Philosophy & the Issues of Politics. LC 76-22960. 340p. 1996. pap. text 9.00 (*0-226-12124-0*) U Ch Pr.

— Polity & Economy: An Interpretation of the Principles of Adam Smith, No. 8-- LC 76-56126. 101p. 1977. reprint ed. lib. bdg. 35.00 (*0-8371-9418-0*, CRPE, Greenwood Pr) Greenwood.

Cropsey, Joseph, jt. ed. see Strauss, Leo.

Cropsey, Joyce M. Register of Revolutionary Soldiers & Patriots Buried in Litchfield County. LC 76-42089. 1976. 9.65 (*0-914016-32-6*) Phoenix Pub.

Cropsey, Karen, et al. A Moment with God for Teachers: Prayers for Every Teacher. LC 97-47068. 64p. 1998. pap. 5.00 (*0-687-07710-9*) Dimen for Liv.

Cropwood Round-Table Conference, jt. auth. see Liebling, Alison.

Cros. Tracheal Intubation. 1992. 70.00 (*0-683-08584-0*) Lppncott W & W.

Cros, Charles & Corbiere, Tristan. Oeuvres Completes. deluxe ed. (Pleiade Ser.). (FRE.). 1512p. 63.95 (*2-07-010155-X*) Schoenhof.

Cros, Didier. Peripheral Neuropathy: A Practical Approach to Diagnosis & Management. 1998. write for info. (*0-397-51781-5*) Lppncott W & W.

Cros, Edmond. Theory & Practice of Sociocriticism. LC 87-21167. (Theory & History of Literature Ser.: Vol. 53). (Illus.). xviii, 275p. 1988. pap. 18.95 (*0-8166-1580-2*) U of Minn Pr.

Cros, J., et al. Progress in Opioid Research. (Advances in the Biosciences Ser.: 75). (Illus.). 812p. 1989. 141.00 (*0-08-037362-3*, Pergamon Pr) Elsevier.

Cros, N. Clayton. A Primer of Biblical Greek. LC 99-34385. 256p. 1999. pap. 18.00 (*0-8028-4628-9*) Eerdmans.

***Cros, Philippe.** The Painters of Provence. (Illus.). 2000. 45.00 (*2-08-013686-0*, Pub. by Flammarion) Abbeville Pr.

Cros, R. Zehn Kleine Zappelmaenner: Handbuch. (GER.). 112p. (J). 1991. pap. text 21.25 (*3-12-675091-5*, Pub. by Klett Edition); audio 27.00 (*3-12-675092-3*, Pub. by Klett Edition) Intl Bk Import.

— Zehn Kleine Zappelmaenner. Deutsch als Fremdsprache fuer Vor- und Grundschulkinder: Heft fuer Kinder. (GER.). 40p. (J). 1991. pap. text 11.00 (*3-12-675090-7*, Pub. by Klett Edition) Intl Bk Import.

Cros, R., et al. Huckepack: Deutsch als Fremdsprache fuer die Grundschule: Handbuch. (GER.). 88p. (J). 1994. pap. text 19.75 (*3-12-675094-X*, Pub. by Klett Edition) Intl Bk Import.

— Huckepack: Materialienbuch. (GER.). 176p. (J). 1994. pap. text 24.00 (*3-12-675096-6*, Pub. by Klett Edition) Intl Bk Import.

Crosbie. Architecture Animals, Architecture Colors, Architecture Counts, Architecture Shapes Set. 90p. 27.80 (*0-471-15289-7*) Wiley.

Crosbie & Crawford, eds. Modeling & Simulation of Embedded Systems. 205p. 1996. pap. 60.00 (*1-56555-048-X*, EMB-95) Soc Computer Sim.

Crosbie, jt. ed. see Hawkins.

Crosbie, A. L., ed. Journal of Thermophysics & Heat Transfer, Vol. 8. 1994. 190.00 (*0-685-30533-3*, JTHT) AIAA.

Crosbie, D., ed. see Cooper, M., et al.

Crosbie, David, et al, eds. Directory of Community Social Work in Scotland: An Initial Appraisal. (C). 1989. 40.00 (*0-7855-5891-8*, Pub. by Natl Inst Soc Work) St Mut.

Crosbie, David, et al. Disseminating Community Social Work in Scotland: An Initial Appraisal. (C). 1989. 50.00 (*0-7855-0091-X*, Pub. by Natl Inst Soc Work) St Mut.

— Disseminating Community Social Work in Scotland: An Intial Appraisal. (C). 1989. 49.00 (*0-902789-65-1*, Pub. by Natl Inst Soc Work) St Mut.

Crosbie, H. The Art & Craftsmanship of French Polishing. 63p. 1989. pap. 35.00 (*0-7223-2102-3*, Pub. by A H S Ltd) St Mut.

Crosbie, John C. No Holds Barred: My Life in Politics. LC 98-107902. (Illus.). 384p. 1998. 27.95 (*0-7710-2427-4*) McCland & Stewart.

Crosbie, John C. & Stevens, Geoffrey. No Holds Barred: My Life in Politics. (Illus.). 512p. 1999. trans. 19.99 (*0-7710-2428-2*) McCland & Stewart.

Crosbie, Karol. Mom & Me. (Illus.). (Orig.). (YA). (gr. 7-12). 1989. pap. 3.95 (*0-945485-13-1*) Comm Intervention.

Crosbie, Lynn. The Gates of Paradise. 704p. Date not set. pap. 19.95 (*0-921912-47-1*) MW&R.

— The Girl Wants To: Women's Representations of Sex & the Body. (Illus.). 224p. 1997. pap. 17.95 (*1-55199-011-3*) MW&R.

— Paul's Case: The Kingston Letters. LC 98-108979. 208p. 1997. pap. text 14.99 (*1-895837-09-X*) Login Pubs Consort.

— Pearl. 62p. (Orig.). 1996. pap. 11.95 (*0-88784-578-9*, Pub. by Hse of Anansi Pr) Genl Dist Srvs.

— Queen Rat: New & Selected Poems. LC 99-185683. 160p. 1999. pap. 14.95 (*0-88784-628-9*) Genl Dist Srvs.

C

***Crosbie, Michael J.** Architecture for the Gods. (Illus.). 192p. 2000. pap. 35.00 (*0-8230-0290-X*) Watsn-Guptill.

Crosbie, Michael J. The Architecture of Frank Williams. (Architecture Today Ser.). (Illus.). 192p. 1996. 39.99 (*1-56496-305-5*) Rockport Pubs.

— Cesar Pelli Recent Themes. LC 98-38515. 1999. 60.00 (*3-7643-5902-1*) Birkhauser.

— Concrete Spirit: The Architecture of Ralph Allen. (Illus.). 128p. 1995. 39.99 (*1-56496-219-9*) Rockport Pubs.

— Green Architecture: A Guide to Sustainable Design. 192p. 1994. 39.99 (*1-56496-096-X*) Rockport Pubs.

Crosbie, Michael J. & Pelli, Cesar. Cesar Pelli: Recent Themes. LC 98-38515. 1998. write for info. (*0-8176-5902-1*) Birkhauser.

Crosbie, Michael J. & Rosenthal, Steve. Architecture: Animals. LC 95-4294. 26p. (J). (ps-2). 1995. 6.95 (*0-471-14358-8*) Wiley.

— Architecture: Colors, Vol. 2. LC 95-50775. (Illus.). 22p. (J). (ps). 1995. 6.95 (*0-471-14359-6*) Wiley.

— Architecture: Count, Vol. 3. LC 95-50573. (Illus.). 22p. (J). (ps). 1995. 6.95 (*0-471-14361-8*) Wiley.

— Architecture: Shapes, Vol. 4. (Illus.). 16p. (J). (ps-2). 1995. 6.95 (*0-471-14366-9*) Wiley.

***Crosbie, Michael J., et al.** Arches to Zigzags: An Architecture Alphabet. LC 99-89643. 48p. (J). 2000. 18.95 (*0-8109-4218-6*, Pub. by Abrams) Time Warner.

Crosbie, Robert. Answers to Questions on the Ocean of Theosophy. 249p. 1933. 6.00 (*0-938998-12-9*) Theosophy.

— The Friendly Philosopher. (Illus.). vii, 415p. 1934. reprint ed. 7.00 (*0-938998-13-7*) Theosophy.

— The Language of the Soul. (Sangam Texts Ser.). 130p. 1986. pap. 12.75 (*0-88695-026-0*) Concord Grove.

— Respuestas a Preguntas Sobre el Oceano de la Teosofia (Answers to Questions on the Ocean of Theosophy) (SPA.). 313p. 1996. pap. 7.50 (*0-938998-37-4*) Theosophy.

— La Teosofia Universal. (SPA., Illus.). 210p. (Orig.). (YA). 1995. pap. 6.50 (*0-938998-36-6*) Theosophy.

— Universal Theosophy. 171p. 1963. pap. 6.00 (*0-938998-31-5*) Theosophy.

Crosbie, Robert, jt. auth. see Judge, William Q.

Crosbie, Steven. Financial Services. 350p. 1990. pap. 125.00 (*0-85297-382-9*, Pub. by Chartered Bank) St Mut.

Crosbie, W. A., et al, eds. Medical Response to Effects of Ionizing Radiation: Proceedings of a Conference on Medical Response to Effects of Ionizing Radiation Held at Queen Elizabeth II Conference Center, London, 28-30 June 1989. 310p. 1989. 81.00 (*1-85166-385-1*) Elsevier.

Crosby. African Experience, Vol. 1. 2nd ed. 344p. (C). 1992. pap. text 46.00 (*0-536-58280-7*) Pearson Custom.

Crosby. Illusion & Disillusion 1st. (Sociology - Introductory Level Ser.). 1973. pap. 4.00 (*0-534-00225-0*) Wadsworth Pub.

***Crosby.** Quality Is Still Free. 1999. write for info. (*0-07-134880-8*) McGraw.

Crosby & Dunn, eds. World Directory of Old Age Organizations. 200p. 1989. 85.00 (*1-55862-023-0*) St James Pr.

Crosby, A. C., jt. auth. see Van Heerden, F. J.

Crosby, Alan. The History of Cheshire & Sullivan Counties, New Hampshire. LC 97-126988. (The Darwen County History Ser.). 144p. 1996. write for info. (*0-85033-932-4*) Phillimore & Co.

— A Society with No Equal: The Chetham Society, 1843-1993 LC 94-212018. (Remains, Historical & Literary, Corrected with the Palatine Counties of Lancaster & & Chester Ser.). ix, 86 p. 1993. write for info. (*1-85936-001-7*) Carnegie Publishing Ltd.

Crosby, Alan, jt. auth. see Levine, Dan.

Crosby, Alan, jt. auth. see Mastrini, John.

Crosby, Alfred W. America's Forgotten Pandemic: The Influenza of 1918. (Illus.). 351p. (C). 1990. pap. text 19.95 (*0-521-38695-0*) Cambridge U Pr.

— The Columbian Exchange: Biological & Cultural Consequences of 1492. LC 73-140916. (Contributions in American Studies: No. 2). 268p. 1973. pap. 14.95 (*0-8371-7228-4*, CCEPB) Greenwood.

— The Columbian Exchange: Biological & Cultural Consequences of 1492, 2. LC 73-140916. (Contributions in American Studies: No. 2). 268p. 1972. 59.95 (*0-8371-5821-4*, CCE/) Greenwood.

— The Columbian Voyages: The Columbian Exchange, & Their Historians. Adas, Michael, ed. LC 87-71265. (Essays on Global & Comparative History Ser.). 29p. 1987. pap. 6.00 (*0-87229-039-5*) Am Hist Assn.

— Ecological Imperialism: The Biological Expansion of Europe, 900-1900. (Studies in Environment & History). (Illus.). 400p. 1986. 44.95 (*0-521-32009-7*) Cambridge U Pr.

— Ecological Imperialism: The Biological Expansion of Europe, 900-1900. (Canto Book Ser.). (Illus.). 384p. (C). 1993. pap. 14.95 (*0-521-45690-8*) Cambridge U Pr.

— Germs, Seeds & Animals: Studies in Ecological History. LC 93-19629. (Sources & Studies in World History). 232p. (C). (gr. 13). 1993. text 70.95 (*1-56324-249-4*); pap. text 31.95 (*1-56324-250-8*) M E Sharpe.

— The Measure of Reality: Quantification & Western Society, 1250-1600. LC 96-3092. (Illus.). 257p. 1996. text 29.95 (*0-521-55427-6*) Cambridge U Pr.

— The Measure of Reality: Quantification & Western Society, 1250-1600. (Illus.). 250p. (C). 1997. reprint ed. pap. 14.95 (*0-521-63990-5*) Cambridge U Pr.

Crosby, Allan J. & Bruce, John, eds. Accounts & Papers Relating to Mary Queen of Scots. (Camden Society, London. Publications, First Ser.: No. 93). reprint ed. 37.50 (*0-404-50193-1*) AMS Pr.

Crosby, Ann D. Dilemmas in Defence Decision-Making: Constructing Canada's Role in Norad, 1958-96. LC 97-38322. (International Political Economy Ser.). 1998. text 69.95 (*0-312-21205-4*) St Martin.

Crosby, Barbara C. Leadership in the Global Commons; Building Transnational Citizenship. LC 98-40149. 1998. pap. 24.95 (*0-7619-1747-0*) Sage.

***Crosby, Barbara C.** Leadership in the Global Commons: Building Transnational Citizenship. LC 98-40149. 4p. 1998. 52.00 (*0-7619-1746-2*) Sage.

Crosby, Barbara C., jt. auth. see Bryson, John M.

Crosby, Benjamin, jt. auth. see Lindenberg, Marc M.

Crosby, Bing & Martin, Pete. Call Me Lucky. (Illus.). 384p. 1993. reprint ed. pap. 13.95 (*0-306-80504-9*) Da Capo.

Crosby, Cathy Lee. Let the Magic Begin. LC 96-49405. 304p. 1997. 22.50 (*0-684-80280-5*) S&S Trade.

Crosby, Charles & Barry, Margaret, eds. Community Care: The Provision of Mental Health Services in North Wales. 288p. 1995. 82.95 (*1-85628-531-6*, Pub. by Avebry) Ashgate Pub Co.

Crosby County Pioneer Memorial Staff. Gone but Not Forgotten: Cemetery Survey of Crosby County, Texas. 1983. pap. 10.00 (*0-9606940-4-8*) Crosby County.

Crosby, Cynthia A. Historical Dictionary of Malawi. 2nd ed. LC 93-15740. (African Historical Dictionaries Ser.: Vol. 54). (Illus.). 243p. 1993. 35.00 (*0-8108-2628-3*) Scarecrow.

Crosby, D'Arcy R. Are You Ready for the Truth? Hart, Glenda & Prothro, Lonnie, III, eds. LC 97-94634. (Illus.). 170p. 1997. pap. 15.95 (*0-9661310-3-7*) Chekmate Pub.

Crosby, David. David Crosby Oh Yes I Can - (Piano - Vocal) (Illus.). 54p. (Orig.). (YA). 1990. pap. text 12.95 (*0-89524-445-4*) Cherry Lane.

***Crosby, David.** Quilts & Quilting in Claiborne County: Tradition & Change in a Rural Southern County. (Illus.). 32p. 1999. pap. 8.00 (*0-9677624-0-5*) Miss Cult Cross.

Crosby, David. Stand & Be Counted. LC 99-45179. 1999. pap. 17.00 (*0-06-251575-6*) HarpC.

Crosby, David, photos by. A Tennessee Christmas. LC 98-18889. (Illus.). 128p. 1998. 39.95 (*1-56579-295-5*) Westcliffe Pubs.

Crosby, David & Bender, David. Stand & Be Counted: Making Music, Making History. LC 99-45179. (Illus.). 256p. 2000. 25.00 (*0-06-251574-8*, Pub. by Harper SF) HarpC.

Crosby, Deb. Victorian Pencils: Tools to Jewels. LC 98-18727. 224p. 1998. 59.95 (*0-7643-0413-5*) Schiffer.

Crosby, Diane. Create Your Own Class Newspaper! A Complete Guide for Planning, Writing, & Publishing a Newspaper. Britt, Leslie, ed. (Illus.). 64p. (Orig.). 1994. pap. text, teacher ed. 8.95 (*0-86530-289-8*, 11-8) Incentive Pubns.

***Crosby, Don & Dale, Jim.** Tiger Woods Made Me Look Like a Genius: 5 Simple Ways to Take 10 Strokes off Your Game. LC 99-42117. (Illus.). 160p. 2000. pap. 12.95 (*0-7407-0472-9*) Andrews & McMeel.

Crosby, Don & Hardwick, Charles, eds. Religious Experience & Ecological Responsibility, Vol. 3. (American Liberal Religious Thought Ser.). X, 652p. (C). 1996. 74.95 (*0-8204-2790-X*) P Lang Pubng.

Crosby, Don, jt. ed. see Hardwick, Charles.

Crosby, Donald A. Interpretive Theories of Religion. (Religion & Reason Ser.: No.20). 335p. 1981. 50.00 (*90-279-3039-2*) Mouton.

— The Specter of the Absurd: Sources & Criticism of Modern Nihilism. LC 87-20917. (SUNY Series in Philosophy). 456p. (C). 1988. text 67.50 (*0-88706-719-0*); pap. text 24.95 (*0-88706-720-4*) State U NY Pr.

Crosby, Donald F. Battlefield Chaplains: Catholic Priests in World War II. LC 93-39804. (Modern War Studies). 328p. 1996. pap. 19.95 (*0-7006-0814-1*) U Pr of KS.

Crosby, Donald G. Environmental Toxicology & Chemistry. LC 97-22438. (Topics in Environmental Chemistry Ser.). (Illus.). 352p. (C). 1998. text 62.95 (*0-19-511713-1*) OUP.

Crosby, Edward, et al, eds. The African Experience in Community Development: The Continuing Struggle in Africa & the Americas, Vol. 1. 420p. (Orig.). (C). 1981. pap. text 18.95 (*0-89894-025-7*) Advocate Pub Group.

Crosby, Edward W. & Hoskins, Linus A., eds. Africa for the Africans: Selected Speeches of Marcus Mosiah Garvey, Malcolm X & Nelson R. Mandela. 115p. (Orig.). (C). 1991. pap. text 9.95 (*0-9613067-4-2*) Imhotep.

Crosby, Eleanor D. Simon Crosby the Emigrant: His English Ancestry & Some of His American Descendents. (Illus.). 195p. 1995. reprint ed. pap. 15.00 (*0-7884-0326-5*) Heritage Bk.

Crosby, Ellen. Hilltop Tennessee: A Woman's Necessity: God's Opportunity. 58p. (Orig.). (YA). 1996. pap. 9.95 (*1-57502-248-6*, P0928) Morris Pubng.

Crosby, Ernest. Garrison the Non-Resistant. LC 72-137534. (Peace Movement in America Ser.). 141p. 1972. reprint ed. lib. bdg. 22.95 (*0-89198-062-8*) Ozer.

Crosby, Ernest H. Captain Jinks, Hero. LC 68-57519. (Muckrakers Ser.). reprint ed. lib. bdg. 21.75 (*0-8398-0282-X*) Irvington.

Crosby, Everett U. Bishop & Chapter in Twelfth-Century England: A Study of the Mensa Episcopalis. LC 93-9580. (Cambridge Studies in Medieval Life & Thought: No. 23). 466p. (C). 1994. text 74.95 (*0-521-44507-8*) Cambridge U Pr.

— Nantucket in Print. 225p. 1997. reprint ed. 19.95 (*1-57898-003-8*) Martino Pubng.

Crosby, Everett U. & Webb, Charles R., Jr., eds. The Past As Prologue: Sources & Studies in European Civilization, 2 vols. (Illus.). (C). 1973. write for info. (*0-318-53721-4*) Irvington.

— The Past As Prologue: Sources & Studies in European Civilization, 2 vols., 1. LC 70-166559. (Illus.). (C). 1973. pap. text 12.95 (*0-89197-331-1*) Irvington.

— The Past As Prologue: Sources & Studies in European Civilization, 2 vols., 2. LC 70-166559. (Illus.). (C). 1973. pap. text 12.95 (*0-89197-332-X*) Irvington.

Crosby, F. J., jt. ed. see Blanchard, F. A.

Crosby, Fanny. This Is My Story This Is My Song. 1997. pap. 7.99 (*1-898787-41-7*) Emerald House Group Inc.

***Crosby, Fanny J.** Fanny J. Crosby: An Autobiography. 270p. 1999. pap. 22.00 (*1-57910-207-7*) Wipf & Stock.

Crosby, Faye J. Juggling: The Unexpected Advantages of Balancing Career & Home for Women & Their Families. 288p. 1993. pap. 14.95 (*0-02-906911-4*) Free Pr.

***Crosby, Faye J. & VanDe Veer, Cheryl, eds.** Sex, Race & Merit: Debating Affirmative Action in Education & Employment. 352p. 2000. text 60.00 (*0-472-09734-2*, 09734); pap. text 22.95 (*0-472-06734-6*, 06734) U of Mich Pr.

Crosby, Faye J., jt. auth. see Clayton, Susan D.

Crosby, George & Crosby, Sue. Crosby's Wedding Invitation & Gift Registry. 46p. 1987. 8.50 (*0-943480-64-7*) Friis-Pioneer Pr.

Crosby, Gerda R. Disarmament & Peace in British Politics, 1914-1919. LC 57-8623. (Historical Monographs: No. 32). 200p. 1957. 20.00 (*0-674-21150-2*) HUP.

***Crosby, Gloria.** What Does God Say? A Biblical Literacy System, Two, One. 144p. 2000. pap. text 5.00 (*1-885504-61-6*) Church Gwth.

Crosby, Greg & McMahon, Brad. Way off Broadway. (Catdog Chapter Bks.: No. 4). 64p. (J). (gr. 4-6). 1999. mass mkt. 3.99 (*0-689-83011-4*, Simon Spot) Little Simon.

Crosby, H. LaMar, tr. Discourses, 5 vols., 4. (Loeb Classical Library: No. 257, 339, 358, 376, 385). 478p. 1946. 18.95 (*0-674-99414-0*) HUP.

— Discourses, 5 vols., 5. (Loeb Classical Library: No. 257, 339, 358, 376, 385). 510p. 1951. 18.95 (*0-674-99424-8*) HUP.

Crosby, Harriet E. "God, Help Me" Short Prayers for Busy Women. LC 98-53693. 1999. pap. text 8.95 (*0-8362-7857-7*) Andrews & McMeel.

— Living Between Jobs: Meditations When You're Looking for Work. LC 96-22559. 128p. 1996. pap. 9.99 (*0-8066-2753-0*, 9-2753, Augsburg) Augsburg Fortress.

Crosby, Harriett, ed. see Hart, David.

Crosby, Harry. Antigua California: Mission & Colony on the Peninsular Frontier, 1697-1768. LC 93-38946. (Illus.). 574p. 1994. reprint ed. pap. 178.00 (*0-608-07272-9*, 206750000009) Bks Demand.

Crosby, Harry. The Cave Paintings of Baja California: Discovering the Great Murals of an Unknown People. Lindsay, Lowell, ed. LC 97-14298. (Natural History Bks.). (Illus.). 256p. 1997. 49.95 (*0-932653-23-5*) Sunbelt Pubns.

***Crosby, Harry.** The Cave Paintings of Baja California; Discovering the Great Murals of an Unknown People. Lindsay, Lowell, ed. Hambleton, Enrique, tr. (Natural History Bks.). (Illus.). 256p. 2000. pap. 34.95 (*0-932653-39-1*) Sunbelt Pubns.

***Crosby, Harry H.** Wing & a Prayer. 336p. 1999. pap. 17.95 (*1-86105-173-5*) Robson.

Crosby, Harry H. & Emery, Robert W. Better Spelling in 30 Minutes a Day. (Better English Ser.). 224p. (Orig.). (YA). 1995. pap. 9.99 (*1-56414-202-7*) Career Pr Inc.

Crosby, Harry W. Antigua California: Mission & Colony on the Peninsular Frontier, 1697-1768. LC 93-38946. (University of Arizona Southwest Center Ser.). 573p. 1994. 35.00 (*0-8263-1495-3*) U of NM Pr.

Crosby, Henry W. Magma: The Indestructible. LC 94-61513. (Illus.). 1994. pap. 9.95 (*0-936029-36-6*) Western Bk Journ.

Crosby, Howard, et al, compiled by. Footprints in Time: A Walk Where New Hampshire Began. LC 95-173521. (Images of America Ser.). 1994. pap. 14.99 (*0-7524-0056-8*) Arcadia Publng.

Crosby, Jack L. Computer Simulation in Genetics. LC 72-5715. 489p. reprint ed. pap. 151.60 (*0-608-13528-3*, 201618200001) Bks Demand.

***Crosby, Janice C.** Cauldron of Changes: Feminist Spirituality in Fantastic Fiction. LC 00-25625. 216p. 2000. pap. 28.50 (*0-7864-0848-0*) McFarland & Co.

Crosby, Jay, jt. auth. see Bruun, Eric A.

***Crosby, Jeff.** Drawing Horses. (Illus.). 32p. (J). (ps-3). 2000. pap. 6.99 (*0-448-41969-6*, G & D) Peng Put Young Read.

Crosby, John, et al. Metaphysics. Marshner, William, tr. from GER. (Aletheia-an International Journal of Philosophy: Vol. 1, Pt. 2). 251p. (Orig.). 1981. reprint ed. pap. 500.00 (*0-86663-784-2*) Ide Hse.

Crosby, John, ed. see Reinach, Adolf, et al.

Crosby, John F. Illusion & Disillusion: The Self in Love & Marriage. 3rd ed. 323p. (C). 1984. pap. write for info. (*0-534-04470-0*) Wadsworth Pub.

***Crosby, John F.** The Legacy of John Paul II: His Contribution to Catholic Thought. LC 99-53600. 2000. write for info. (*0-8245-1850-0*) Crossroad NY.

— Legacy of Pope John Paul II: His Contribution to Catholic Thought. LC 99-53600. 2000. pap. 12.95 (*0-8245-1831-4*, Herdr & Herdr) Crossroad NY.

Crosby, John F. The Selfhood of the Human Person. LC 96-30424. 313p. (C). 1996. text 34.95 (*0-8132-0864-5*); pap. text 19.95 (*0-8132-0865-3*) Cath U Pr.

Crosby, John F., ed. When One Wants Out & the Other Doesn't: Doing Therapy with Polarized Couples. LC 88-7444. 240p. 1989. text 36.95 (*0-87630-527-3*) Brunner-Mazel.

Crosby, John V. Cycles, Trends & Turning Points: Practical Marketing & Sales Forecasting Techniques. LC 98-34338. (Illus.). 288p. 1999. 49.95 (*0-8442-3244-0*, NTC Business Bks) NTC Contemp Pub Co.

— Managing the Big Sale. (Illus.). 256p. 1996. 37.95 (*0-8442-3427-3*, NTC Business Bks) NTC Contemp Pub Co.

Crosby-Jones, Michael, tr. see Kaldhol, Marit.

Crosby, Josiah. Siam: The Crossroads. LC 72-179186. reprint ed. 32.50 (*0-404-54817-2*) AMS Pr.

Crosby, Kate. Buddhism. 288p. 1998. pap. text 14.95 (*1-85168-173-6*, Pub. by Onewrld Pubns) Penguin Putnam.

Crosby, Kate, tr. see Santideva.

Crosby, Kathryn. My Life with Bing. LC 82-74361. (Illus.). 358p. 1983. 29.95 (*0-938728-01-6*) Collage Bks Inc.

Crosby, Kip, jt. auth. see Davis, Fred.

Crosby, Laura S. Art: Ideas for Elementary Classroom Teachers; Bulletin Board Suggestions; Patterns; Ideas for Holidays. (Illus.). 1985. spiral bd. 25.00 (*0-915114-04-6*) Lewis-Sloan.

Crosby, Linda & Bissell, LeClair. Enabling in the Health Professions. 36p. 1989. pap. 5.50 (*1-56246-000-5*, 3290, HazeldenJohnson Inst) Hazelden.

Crosby, Linda R. & Bissell, LeClair. To Care Enough: Intervention with Chemically Dependent Colleagues; a Guide for Healthcare & Other Professionals. 312p. 1989. text 24.95 (*0-935908-49-8*, 6011, HazeldenJohnson Inst) Hazelden.

Crosby, Margaret. Violin Obligato & Other Studies. LC 74-106283. (Short Story Index Reprint Ser.). 1977. 21.95 (*0-8369-3320-6*) Ayer.

***Crosby, Mark.** New York: The Ultimate Photographic Journey. (Illus.). 2000. 29.95 (*0-7893-0504-6*) Universe.

Crosby, Mark, photos by. New York Christmas. (Illus.). 96p. 1999. 20.00 (*0-7893-0370-1*, Pub. by Universe) St Martin.

Crosby, Marshall R. & Magill, Robert E. Index of Mosses, 1990-1992. (Monographs in Systematic Botany from the Missouri Botanical Garden: No. 50). 87p. 1994. pap. 13.95 (*0-915279-25-8*) Miss Botan.

— Index of Mosses, 1993-1995. 106p. 1997. 15.95 (*0-915279-47-9*, MSB-62) Miss Botan.

Crosby, Marshall R., et al. Index of Mosses, 1963-1989. (Monographs in Systematic Botany from the Missouri Botanical Garden: No. 42). 656p. 1992. 38.95 (*0-685-70547-1*) Miss Botan.

***Crosby, Michael.** Solanus Casey: The Official Account of a Virtuous American Life. LC 99-3998. 1999. 19.95 (*0-8245-1835-7*, Pub. by Crossroad NY) Natl Bk Netwk.

Crosby, Michael H. Celibacy: Means of Control or Mandate of the Heart? LC 95-45295. 248p. 1996. pap. 12.95 (*0-87793-569-6*) Ave Maria.

***Crosby, Michael H.** Do You Love Me? Jesus Questions the Church. 250p. 2000. pap. 20.00 (*1-57075-236-2*) Orbis Bks.

Crosby, Michael H. House of Disciples: Church, Economics, & Justice in Matthew. LC 88-5347. 359p. reprint ed. pap. 111.30 (*0-608-20199-5*, 207145800012) Bks Demand.

— The Seven Last Words. LC 93-33911. (Illus.). 112p. (Orig.). 1994. pap. 12.50 (*0-88344-938-2*) Orbis Bks.

— The Spirituality of the Beatitudes: Matthew's Challenge for First World Christians. LC 80-24755. 254p. 1981. pap. 18.50 (*0-88344-465-8*) Orbis Bks.

— Thank God Ahead of Time: The Life & Spirituality of Solanus Casey. 334p. 1998. reprint ed. pap. 10.95 (*0-8199-0879-7*, Frncscn Herld) Franciscan Pr.

Crosby, N. A Crosby Family: Josiah Crosby, Sarah Fitch, & Their Descendants. (Illus.). 143p. 1993. reprint ed. pap. 23.00 (*0-8328-1385-0*); reprint ed. lib. bdg. 33.00 (*0-8328-1384-2*) Higginson Bk Co.

Crosby, Nancy, intro. Gracious Goodness, the Taste of Memphis. LC 87-62419. (Illus.). 384p. 1989. 24.50 (*0-9619131-0-X*) Memphis Symphony.

Crosby, Neil, jt. auth. see Baum, Andrew.

Crosby, Neil T. Determination of Veterinary Residues in Food. 233p. 1991. text 139.95 (*0-7476-0065-1*) Thomson Learn.

Crosby, Neil T. Determination of Veterinary Residues in Food. 240p. 1991. 153.00 (*1-85573-283-1*, Pub. by Woodhead Pubng) Am Educ Systs.

Crosby, Neil T. & Patel, Indu. General Principles of Good Sampling Practice. 68p. 1995. 39.95 (*0-85404-412-4*) CRC Pr.

Crosby, Neil T., jt. auth. see Osborne, Martin R.

***Crosby, Olivia.** Resumes, Applications & Cover Letters. 14p. 1999. pap. 1.50 (*0-16-050224-1*) USGPO.

Crosby, Pamela, jt. auth. see Crosby, Robert C.

Crosby, Peter. A Balance of Risks. Ivery, Martha, ed. Date not set. pap. 12.95 (*1-57532-186-6*) Press-Tige Pub.

Crosby, Philip B. Absolutes of Leadership. 1997. mass mkt. 16.50 (*0-7879-0942-4*) Jossey-Bass.

— Leading: The Art of Becoming an Executive. 214p. 1999. reprint ed. text 20.00 (*0-7881-6189-X*) DIANE Pub.

— Philip Crosby's Reflections on Quality: 295 Inspirations from the World's Foremost Quality Guru. LC 95-37400. 144p. 1995. pap. 10.95 (*0-07-014525-3*) McGraw.

— Quality & Me: Lessons from an Evolving Life. LC 98-58073. (Illus.). 272p. 1999. 30.00 (*0-7879-4702-4*) Jossey-Bass.

— Quality Is Free: The Art of Making Quality Certain. 1980. mass mkt. 6.99 (*0-451-62585-4*, Ment) NAL.

— Quality Is Free: The Art of Making Quality Free. 352p. 1979. 34.95 (*0-07-014512-1*) McGraw.

— Quality Is Still Free: Making Quality Certain in Uncertain Times. LC 95-32400. (Illus.). 288p. 1995. 24.95 (*0-07-014532-6*) McGraw.

— Quality Without Tears. 1985. pap. 12.00 (*0-452-26398-0*, Plume) Dutton Plume.

— Quality Without Tears: The Art of Hassle-Free Management. 205p. 1984. 29.95 (*0-07-014530-X*) McGraw.

— Quality Without Tears: The Art of Hassle-Free Management. 205p. 1995. pap. 11.95 (*0-07-014511-3*) McGraw.

— Running Things: The Art of Making Things Happen. 256p. 1986. 29.95 (*0-07-014513-X*) McGraw.

Crosby, R. W. & Cody, J. Max Brodel: The Man Who Put Art into Medicine. (Illus.). ix, 352p. 1993. 65.00 (*0-387-97563-2*) Spr-Verlag.

C

An Asterisk (*) at the beginning of an entry indicates that the title is appearing for the first time.

Crosby, Robert. More Than a Savior: When Jesus Calls You Friend. LC 99-21883. 230p. 1999. 16.99 (*1-57673-497-8*) Multnomah Pubs.
Crosby, Robert C. Living Life from the Soul: How a Man Unleashes God's Power from the Inside Out. LC 97-21009. 192p. 1997. pap. 9.99 (*1-55661-954-5*) Bethany Hse.
— Now We're Talking: Questions that Bring You Closer to Your Kids. LC 96-21531. 1996. pap. 8.99 (*1-56179-472-4*) Focus Family.
Crosby, Robert C. & Crosby, Pamela. Now We're Talking: Questions to Build Intimacy with Your Spouse. LC 96-21530. 1996. pap. 8.99 (*1-56179-473-2*) Focus Family.
Crosby, Robert P. Living with Purpose When the Gods Are Gone. LC 91-18681. (Illus.). 64p. (Orig.). 1991. pap. 5.95 (*0-87810-038-5*) Times Change.
— Walking the Empowerment Tightrope: Balancing Management Authority & Employee Influence. LC 92-60828. 208p. 1992. pap. 19.95 (*0-925652-15-6*) Orgn Design & Dev.
Crosby, Roberto, tr. see Drury, Keith.
Crosby, Rodney. Ingenious Jigs & Shop Accessories: Clever Ideas for Improving Your Shop & Tools. Vckowski, Andre J, ed. 1999. pap. 17.95 (*1-56158-296-4*) Taunton.
Crosby, Rodney & Fine Woodworking Magazine Editors. The Basics of Craftsmanship: Key Advice on Every Aspect of Woodworking. 1999. pap. 17.95 (*1-56158-297-2*) Taunton.
Crosby, Rodney & Schwartz, Susasn. Cross & Crescent. 1999. pap. 14.95 (*0-312-86807-3*, Pub. by Tor Bks) St Martin.
Crosby, Rodney, jt. auth. see Williams, Tad.
Crosby, Ruthann. Miracle in the Glass. Godfrey, Ellen F. et al, eds. (Illus.). 32p. (Orig.). 1996. pap. 19.95 incl. audio (*0-9649962-0-0*) Gabriels Gthrings.
— Miracle in the Glass: To Save a Life Is to Save the World. large type ed. (Illus.). 48p. (J). (gr. 3-6). 1998. pap. 14.95 (*1-888125-26-8*) Publ Consult.
Crosby, S. S. Early Coins of America. LC 83-71431. 1990. reprint ed. lib. bdg. 50.00 (*0-942666-24-0*) S J Durst.
Crosby, Stanley, ed. see John, Peter Q.
Crosby, Sue, jt. auth. see Crosby, George.
Crosby, Sumner M. The Apostle Bas-Relief at Saint-Denis. LC 71-179471. (Yale Publications in the History of Art: No. 21). (Illus.). 224p. reprint ed. pap. 69.50 (*0-8357-5657-2*, 202199300024) Bks Demand.
— The Royal Abbey of Saint-Denis: From Its Beginnings to the Death of Suger, 475-1151. Blum, Pamela Z., ed. LC 85-26464. (Yale Publications in the History of Art: No. 37). (Illus.). 554p. 1987. reprint ed. pap. 171.80 (*0-608-07884-0*, 205999100010) Bks Demand.
Crosby, Susan. Almost a Honeymoon: Wedding Bells. 1995. per. 3.25 (*0-373-05952-3*) Harlequin Bks.
— Baby Fever. (Desire Ser.). 1996. per. 3.50 (*0-373-76018-3*, 1-76018-0) Silhouette.
***Crosby, Susan.** The Baby Gift. (Desire Ser.: Bk. 1301). 2000. per. 3.99 (*0-373-76301-8*, 1-76301-0) Silhouette.
Crosby, Susan. Bride Candidate, No. 9. 1998. per. 3.75 (*0-373-76131-7*, 1-76131-1) Silhouette.
— Brulant Secret. (Rouge Passion Ser.). 1999. mass mkt. 3.50 (*0-373-37515-8*, 1-37515-3) Harlequin Bks.
— Candidata a Esposa (Wife Candidate) (Bride Candidate Ser.: No. 9). (SPA.). 1999. mass mkt. 3.50 (*0-373-35271-9*, 1-35271-5) Harlequin Bks.
— Casi Luna de Miel - Almost a Honeymoon. (Silhouette Deseo - Silhouette Desire Ser.: Vol. 140).Tr. of Almost a Honeymoon. (ENG & SPA.). 1996. per. 3.50 (*0-373-35140-2*) Harlequin Bks.
— Fiebre de Boda (Wedding Fever) (Deseo Ser.). (SPA.). 1998. per. 3.50 (*0-373-35229-8*, 1-35229-3) Harlequin Bks.
— The Groom's Revenge: Fortune's Children: The Brides. (Desire Ser.: No. 1214). 1999. per. 3.75 (*0-373-76214-3*, 1-76214-5) Silhouette.
— His Most Scandalous Secret. (Desire Ser.). 1998. per. 3.75 (*0-373-76158-9*, 1-76158-4) Silhouette.
— His Seductive Revenge. (Desire Ser.). 1998. per. 3.75 (*0-373-76162-7*, 1-76162-6) Silhouette.
— His Ultimate Temptation: The Lone Wolves. (Desire Ser.: No. 1186). 1998. per. 3.75 (*0-373-76186-4*, 1-76186-5) Silhouette.
— Marriage on His Mind. 1997. per. 3.50 (*0-373-76108-2*, 1-76108-9) Silhouette.
— The Mating Game. 1994. per. 2.99 (*0-373-05888-8*, 1-05888-2) Harlequin Bks.
— Planes de Seduccion - Seduction Plans, Vol. 199. (Silhouette Deseo Ser.).Tr. of Seduction Plans. (SPA.). 1997. per. 3.50 (*0-373-35199-2*, 1-35199-8) Harlequin Bks.
— Su Mas Terrible Secreto: (His Most Scandalous Secret) (Deseo Ser.: Bk. 146). (SPA.). 1999. per. 3.50 (*0-373-35276-X*, 1-35276-4) Harlequin Bks.
— Tentacion Decisiva: His UltimateTemptation. (Deseo Ser.: No. 175).Tr. of Decisive Temptation. (SPA.). 1999. per. 3.50 (*0-373-35305-7*, 1-35305-1) Harlequin Bks.
— Wedding Fever. (Desire Ser.). 1997. per. 3.50 (*0-373-76061-2*, 1-76061-0) Silhouette.
Crosby, Sylvester S. Early Coins of America. rev. ed. LC 77-189168. 1983. 60.00 (*0-88000-137-2*) Quarterman.
Crosby, Tanya A. Angel of Fire. 384p. (Orig.). 1992. mass mkt. 4.50 (*0-380-76773-2*, Avon Bks) Morrow Avon.
***Crosby, Tanya A.** Happily Ever After. 384p. 1999. mass mkt. 5.99 (*0-380-78574-9*, Avon Bks) Morrow Avon.
Crosby, Tanya A. Kissed. 400p. (Orig.). 1995. mass mkt. 5.50 (*0-380-77681-2*, Avon Bks) Morrow Avon.
***Crosby, Tanya A.** Lion Heart. 352p. 2000. mass mkt. 5.99 (*0-380-78575-7*, Avon Bks) Morrow Avon.
Crosby, Tanya A. Lyon's Gift. 384p. 1997. mass mkt. 5.99 (*0-380-78571-4*, Avon Bks) Morrow Avon.
— Mackinnon's Bride. 384p. 1996. mass mkt. 5.99 (*0-380-77682-0*, Avon Bks) Morrow Avon.
— On Bended Knee. 384p. 1999. mass mkt. 5.99 (*0-380-78573-0*, Avon Bks) Morrow Avon.
— Once upon a Kiss. 416p. (Orig.). 1995. mass mkt. 4.99 (*0-380-77680-4*, Avon Bks) Morrow Avon.
— Sagebrush Bride. 368p. (Orig.). 1993. mass mkt. 4.50 (*0-380-77060-1*, Avon Bks) Morrow Avon.
— Viking's Prize. 384p. (Orig.). 1994. mass mkt. 4.50 (*0-380-77457-7*, Avon Bks) Morrow Avon.
Crosby, Tanya Anne. Perfect in My Sight. 384p. 1998. mass mkt. 5.99 (*0-380-78572-2*, Avon Bks) Morrow Avon.
Crosby, Tim, ed. see Richards, H. M. S., Jr.
Crosby, Timothy & Allen, Abigail. Don't You Hate It When. (Illus.). 64p. (Orig.). (J). (gr. 7-8). 1994. pap. 5.00 (*0-9641796-4-4*) Rhed Harering.
Crosby, Timothy & Melashenko, Lonnie. A Passion for Prayer. LC 98-16043. 192p. (Orig.). 1998. pap. 12.99 (*0-8280-1355-1*) Review & Herald.
Crosby, Timothy E., jt. auth. see Melashenko, E. Lonnie.
Crosby, Tony. An Austin Sketchbook. (Illus.). 1978. 22.50 (*0-88426-053-4*) Encino Pr.
Crosby, Travis L. The Impact of Civilian Evacuation in the Second World War. 192p. 1986. 37.50 (*0-7099-3433-5*, Pub. by C Helm) Routldge.
— The Two Mr. Gladstones: A Study in Psychology & History. LC 96-26547. 320p. 1997. 37.00 (*0-300-06827-1*) Yale U Pr.
Crosby, William H., tr. see Baudelaire, Charles.
***Crosdale, Darren.** Dawson's Creek: The Official Companion. (Illus.). (J). 1999. pap. 12.95 (*0-7407-0725-6*) Andrews & McMeel.
— Dawson's Creek Journal. (Illus.). (J). 1999. pap. 9.95 (*0-7407-0733-7*) Andrews & McMeel.
Crose, Mark. Sweet Terror. 224p. 1995. pap. 3.50 (*0-8217-4641-3*) NAL.
Crose, Susan L. Enchantress. 336p. (Orig.). 1993. mass mkt. 4.99 (*0-671-73923-9*) PB.
— Kiss of the Moon. Tolley, Carolyn, ed. 352p. (Orig.). 1994. mass mkt. 5.50 (*0-671-73924-7*) PB.
— Outlaw. 1995. mass mkt. 5.99 (*0-671-88534-0*) PB.
Croser & Chipping. Cross Infection Control in General Dental Practice. LC 93-31256. (Illus.). 118p. 1990. text 34.00 (*0-86715-010-6*) Quint Pub Co.
Croser, J. & Quick, M. Which Way Now? - Small Book. 8p. (J). 1987. 3.95 (*0-88679-539-7*) Educ Insights.
— Which Way Now? - Tall Book. 8p. (J). 1987. 19.95 (*0-88679-538-9*) Educ Insights.
Croser, J. & Vassillou, J. Stuck in the Mud - Small Book. 8p. (J). 1987. 3.95 (*0-88679-543-5*) Educ Insights.
— Stuck in the Mud - Tall Book. 8p. (J). 1987. 19.95 (*0-88679-542-7*) Educ Insights.
Croshaw, Michael. A Harmony of Lights. 156p. pap. write for info. (*3-7052-0633-8*, Pub. by Poetry Salzburg) Intl Spec Bk.
Crosher, Judith. Ancient Egypt. LC 92-80939. (See Through History Ser.). (Illus.). 48p. (J). (gr. 3-7). 1993. 19.99 (*0-670-84755-0*, Viking Child) Peng Put Young Read.
— Technology in the Time of Ancient Egypt. LC 97-13922. (Illus.). 48p. (J). (gr. 3-9). 1998. 25.69 (*0-8172-4875-7*) Raintree Steck-V.
— Technology in the Time of Ancient Greece. LC 97-19067. (J). 1998. 25.69 (*0-8172-4877-3*) Raintree Steck-V.
— Technology in the Time of the Maya. LC 97-24119. (J). 1997. 25.69 (*0-8172-4881-1*) Raintree Steck-V.
Crosher, Patricia. Everlasting Flowers: Making & Arranging Dried, Preserved & Artificial Flowers. LC 96-22859. (Illus.). 128p. (Orig.). 1997. reprint ed. pap. text 14.95 (*0-486-29364-5*) Dover.
***Crosiar, Sally J.** Find the Love of Your Life: A Step-by-Step Guide to Finding a Great Love Relationship. 318p. 2000. pap. 15.95 (*1-930289-00-6*) Hlthy People Pr.
Crosiar, Sally J. Learning about Early Adolescent Development. (Illus.). 196p. 1996. teacher ed., ring bd. 31.50 (*1-57753-098-5*, 109LAD) Corn Coop Ext.
Crosiar, Sally J., et al. Training School-Age Child Care Staff: A Handbook for Workshop Leaders. (Illus.). 704p. 1995. ring bd. 52.50 (*1-57753-009-8*, 321SACC) Corn Coop Ext.
Crosier, Louis M., ed. Casualties of Privilege: Essays on Prep Schools' Hidden Culture. LC 90-84618. 153p. 1991. pap. 14.95 (*0-9627671-0-7*) Avocus Pub.
— Healthy Choices, Healthy Schools: The Residential Curriculum. 2nd ed. LC 92-72463. 201p. (Orig.). 1992. pap. 19.95 (*0-9627671-1-5*) Avocus Pub.
— Losing It: The Virginity Myth. LC 93-71214. 195p. 1993. pap. 12.95 (*0-9627671-2-3*) Avocus Pub.
— Losing It: The Virginity Myth. LC 93-71214. 195p. 1994. 19.95 (*0-9627671-3-1*) Avocus Pub.
Crosier, Louis M., jt. ed. see Bassett, Patrick F.
Crosier, Louis M., jt. ed. see Peter, Jennifer A.
Crosignani, P. G., ed. Women's Health in Menopause: Behaviour, Cancer, Cardiovascular Disease, Vol. 7. 272p. (C). 1994. text 123.00 (*0-7923-3068-4*) Kluwer Academic.
Croskery, Beverly F. Shamir, the White Elephant: A Rain Forest Adventure. LC 97-93252. (Illus.). 128p. (J). (gr. 3-6). 1997. 14.95 (*0-9657619-4-0*) Bell-Forsythe.
Croskey, Mary A. Leukemia: Just a Shadow. LC 97-221872. 80p. (Orig.). 1996. pap. 14.95 (*0-9654678-0-5*) Life Shadows.
Crosland, C., tr. see Hugo, Victor.
Crosland, Charles A. The Future of Socialism. LC 77-4064. 368p. 1977. reprint ed. lib. bdg. 38.50 (*0-8371-9586-1*, CRFS, Greenwood Pr) Greenwood.
Crosland, Jessie. Old French Epic. LC 73-117589. (Studies in French Literature: No. 45). 1970. reprint ed. lib. bdg. 79.95 (*0-8383-1022-2*) M S G Haskell Hse.
Crosland, Jill B. Do Miracles Really Happen Anymore? LC 99-173791. 96 p. 1997. write for info. (*1-55517-338-1*) CFI Dist.
Crosland, Margaret. The Enigma of Giorgio de Chirico. 158p. 2000. 35.95 (*0-7206-1042-7*, Pub. by P Owen Ltd) Dufour.
***Crosland, Margaret.** Madame de Pompadour: Sex, Culture & the Power Game. 2001. 29.95 (*0-7509-2338-5*, Pub. by Sutton Publng) Intl Pubs Mktg.
Crosland, Margaret. Piaf. LC 87-74. (Illus.). 240p. 1987. reprint ed. pap. 8.95 (*0-88064-069-3*) Fromm Intl Pub.
***Crosland, Margaret.** Piaf in Context. 2000. pap. 14.95 (*1-900850-50-8*) Arcadia Bks.
Crosland, Margaret. Sade's Wife: The Woman Behind the Marquis. 192p. 1996. 35.00 (*0-7206-0958-5*, Pub. by P Owen Ltd) Dufour.
— Women of Iron & Velvet & the Books They Wrote in France. LC 77-359824. 255p. reprint ed. pap. 79.10 (*0-608-14384-7*, 201938400011) Bks Demand.
Crosland, Margaret, tr. from FRE. Retreat from Love. 240p. 1996. pap. 23.00 (*0-7206-0954-2*, Pub. by P Owen Ltd) Dufour.
Crosland, Margaret, tr. see Cocteau, Jean.
Crosland, Margaret, tr. see Colette, Sidonie-Gabrielle.
Crosland, Margaret, tr. see Gibran, Kahlil.
Crosland, Margaret, tr. see Guillaumin, Emile.
Crosland, Margaret, tr. see Linhart, Robert.
Crosland, Margaret, tr. see Marquis De Sade, pseud.
Crosland, Margaret, tr. see Piaf, Edith.
Crosland, Margaret, tr. see Wittig, Monique.
Crosland, Margaret, tr. & intro. see De Chirico, Giorgio.
Crosland, Margaret, tr. & intro. see Marquis De Sade, pseud.
Crosland, Maurice, ed. The Emergence of Science in Western Europe. LC 92-35358. (Classics in the History & Philosophy of Science Ser.: Vol. 12). 1993. write for info. (*2-88124-580-3*) Gordon & Breach.
— The Science of Matter: A Historical Survey. LC 92-21727. (Classics in the History & Philosophy of Science Ser.: Vol. 9). 217p. 1992. pap. text 50.00 (*2-88124-570-6*) Gordon & Breach.
Crosland, Maurice P. Science under Control: The French Academy of Sciences, 1795-1914. (Illus.). 474p. (C). 1992. text 130.00 (*0-521-41373-7*) Cambridge U Pr.
Crosland, Patrick D. The Outer Banks. LC 81-132857. (Illus.). 52p. (Orig.). 1981. pap. 6.95 (*0-936478-05-5*) Interpretive Pubns.
Crosley, Clyde. Men or Mules. LC 79-50363. (Illus.). 1979. 14.75 (*0-9603268-1-2*) Crosley.
***Crosley, David.** Common Pediatric Emergencies. (Illus.). 55p. 1999. pap. write for info. (*1-57801-042-X*) Western Schls.
Crosley, David. Pediatric Emergency Nursing. Rodriguez, M. Rosanna, ed. 138p. 1997. pap. write for info. (*1-57801-011-X*) Western Schls.
Crosley, David R., ed. Laser Probes for Combustion Chemistry. LC 80-17137. (ACS Symposium Ser.: No. 134). 1980. 54.95 (*0-8412-0570-1*) Am Chemical.
— Laser Probes for Combustion Chemistry. LC 80-17137. (ACS Symposium Ser.: No. 134). (Illus.). 507p. 1980. reprint ed. pap. 157.20 (*0-608-03236-0*, 206375500007) Bks Demand.
***Crosley, Reginald O.** Voudou Quantum Leap: Alternative Realities, Power & Mysticism. LC 00-28222. 225p. 2000. pap. 12.95 (*1-56718-173-2*) Llewellyn Pubns.
Crosling, G. & Murphy, Herta H. How to Study Business Law: Reading, Writing & Exams. 248p. 1994. pap. 34.00 (*0-409-30847-1*, Austral, MICHIE) LEXIS Pub.
Crosman, Christopher, jt. compiled by see Besemer, Susan P.
Crosman, Coral. Eve of Innocence. 132p. (Orig.). 1984. pap. 6.25 (*0-913884-04-9*) Porphyrion Pr.
— Journey to Middle Grove. 1977. pap. 3.50 (*0-913884-03-0*) Porphyrion Pr.
— Timbered Lives: Selected Poems of 1979-1986. 112p. (Orig.). 1994. pap. text 13.95 (*0-913884-05-7*) Porphyrion Pr.
— Vermont Renaissance. (Illus.). 72p. 1976. pap. 2.50 (*0-913884-01-4*) Porphyrion Pr.
Crosnier, Colette. Branche Entre Nous I. unabridged ed. (FRE.). 48p. (gr. 10 up). 1988. pap. 21.95 incl. audio (*0-88432-256-4*, FRO624) Audio-Forum.
— Branche Entre Nous II. unabridged ed. (FRE.). 48p. (YA). (gr. 10 up). 1992. pap. 21.95 incl. audio (*0-88432-422-2*, FR0625) Audio-Forum.
— French Folk Songs. unabridged ed. (FRE & ENG.). 64p. 1992. pap. 29.95 incl. audio (*0-88432-493-1*, SFR305) Audio-Forum.
Crosnier, Colette & Crosnier, Collette. Entre Nous II. unabridged ed. 49p. 1985. pap. 21.95 incl. audio (*0-88432-130-4*, FR0623) Audio-Forum.
Crosnier, Collette. French, Entre Nous, Vol. 11. 56p. pap. 21.95 incl. audio (*0-88432-140-1*, FR0622) Audio-Forum.
Crosnier, Collette, jt. auth. see Crosnier, Colette.
Croson, David C., jt. auth. see Nolan, Richard L.
Cross. Egypt. 1991. 65.00 (*0-15-145767-0*) Harcourt.
— Electric Utility Regulation in the European Union: A Country by Country Guide. 376p. 1996. text 243.00 (*0-471-95793-3*) Wiley.
Cross. Engineering Design Methods 3rd ed. pap. text. write for info. (*0-471-87250-4*) Wiley.
Cross. Introduction to Critical Thinking & Writing. 2nd ed. (SWC-Business Law Ser.). 1994. 5.00 (*0-314-04984-3*) Sth-Wstrn College.
— Journals of Several Expeditions Made in Western Australia. 262p. 1980. 25.00 (*0-85564-185-1*, Pub. by Univ of West Aust Pr) Intl Spec Bk.
— The Legal Environment of Business. 3rd ed. LC 97-22498. (LA - Business Law Ser.). (C). 1997. mass mkt. 98.95 (*0-538-87965-3*) S-W Pub.
— Legal Environment of Business. 3rd ed. (LA - Business Law Ser.). (C). 1997. mass mkt., student ed. 25.95 (*0-538-87970-X*) S-W Pub.
Cross. Racism & the Colonial Encounter. 59.95 (*1-85628-676-2*) Ashgate Pub Co.
Cross, ed. Anionic Surfactants: Analytical Chemistry. 2nd ed. LC 98-16647. (Illus.). 368p. 1998. text 150.00 (*0-8247-0166-6*) Dekker.
Cross & Anderson. A Guide to Cockatiels & Their Mutations. (Illus.). 95p. 1996. pap. 23.95 (*0-9587455-8-7*) Avian Pubns.
***Cross & Miller.** Legal Environment of Business. 4th ed. (SWC-General Business Ser.). (C). 2000. text, student ed. 23.00 (*0-324-05279-0*) Sth-Wstrn College.
— Web Tutor on Webct to Accompany a West's Legal Environment of Business. 4th ed. 2000. pap. 19.00 (*0-324-06793-3*) Sth-Wstrn College.
Cross & Smiecinsk. Quality Assurance in Microbiology & Biotechnology Research. 128p. 1994. boxed set 73.95 (*0-8493-8693-4*) CRC Pr.
Cross, et al. Guardianship & Conservatorship in Massachusetts, No. 7. 200p. 1998. ring bd. 105.00 (*0-327-00772-9*, 8152415) LEXIS Pub.
Cross, jt. auth. see Clarkson.
Cross, jt. auth. see Ellis.
Cross, jt. auth. see Lamm.
Cross, jt. auth. see Miller.
Cross, A. Trap for Fools. large type ed. 1990. pap. 5.00 (*0-7451-1286-2*, Pub. by Chivers N Amer) Chivers N Amer.
Cross, A. D. & Jones, R. Alan. An Introduction to Practical Infra-Red Spectroscopy. 3rd ed. LC 69-20393. 115p. reprint ed. pap. 35.70 (*0-608-14546-7*, 202471300038) Bks Demand.
Cross, A. G. By the Banks of the Thames: Russians in Eighteenth Century Britain. (Illus.). 356p. 1980. 38.00 (*0-89250-085-9*) Orient Res Partners.
Cross, A. G., ed. Britain & Russia: Contacts & Comparisons, 1700-1800. (Illus.). 1979. 32.00 (*0-89250-109-X*) Orient Res Partners.
— Russia & the West in the Eighteenth Century. (Illus.). 371p. 1983. 36.00 (*0-685-07028-X*) Orient Res Partners.
Cross, A. J. Pilkington's Royal/Ancastrian Pottery & Tiles. (Illus.). 93p. 1980. 75.00 (*0-903685-08-6*, Pub. by R Dennis) Antique Collect.
***Cross, Alan.** Alternative. (20th Century Rock & Roll Ser.). 2000. pap. text 13.95 (*1-896522-19-X*) CN06.
Cross, Alan. Coordinating Design & Technology Across the Primary School. LC 98-190642. (Subject Leaders Handbks.). 215p. 1998. pap. 23.95 (*0-7507-0689-9*, Falmer Pr) Taylor & Francis.
Cross, Alan. The Making of Pretty Hate Machine & the Downward Spiral. 1997. pap. 7.95 (*1-896522-31-9*) CN06.
Cross, Alan J. & Green, A. Richard, eds. International Review of Neurobiology Vol. 40: Neuroprotective Agents & Cerebral Ischaemia. (Illus.). 416p. (C). 1996. text 95.00 (*0-12-366840-9*) Morgan Kaufmann.
— International Review of Neurobiology Vol. 40: Neuroprotective Agents & Cerebral Ischaemia. Vol. 40. (Illus.). 416p. 1996. pap. text 55.00 (*0-12-197880-X*) Morgan Kaufmann.
Cross, Amanda. The Collected Stories. large type ed. LC 97-15301. (Wheeler Large Print Book Ser.). 1997. pap. 22.95 (*1-56895-453-0*) Wheeler Pub.
— Collected Stories of Amanda Cross. LC 97-93906. 192p. 1998. pap. 11.00 (*0-345-42113-2*) Ballantine Pub Grp.
— Death in a Tenured Position. 208p. 1986. mass mkt. 5.99 (*0-345-34041-8*) Ballantine Pub Grp.
— An Imperfect Spy. LC 94-25357. 1996. mass mkt. 5.99 (*0-345-39005-9*) Ballantine Pub Grp.
— In the Last Analysis. 176p. 1981. mass mkt. 5.50 (*0-380-54510-1*, Avon Bks) Morrow Avon.
— The James Joyce Murders. 576p. 1987. mass mkt. 5.99 (*0-345-34686-6*) Ballantine Pub Grp.
— No Word from Winifred. 272p. 1987. mass mkt. 5.99 (*0-345-33381-0*) Ballantine Pub Grp.
— The Players Come Again. 240p. 1991. mass mkt. 5.99 (*0-345-36998-X*) Ballantine Pub Grp.
— The Players Come Again. large type ed. 1991. 27.99 (*0-7089-8615-3*, Charnwood) Ulverscroft.
— Poetic Justice. 176p. 1979. mass mkt. 4.99 (*0-380-44222-1*, Avon Bks) Morrow Avon.
— The Puzzled Heart. 1999. mass mkt. 5.99 (*0-345-41884-0*) Ballantine Pub Grp.
— The Question of Max. 224p. 1987. mass mkt. 5.99 (*0-345-35489-3*) Ballantine Pub Grp.
— Sweet Death, Kind Death. 244p. 1987. mass mkt. 5.99 (*0-345-35254-8*) Ballantine Pub Grp.
— The Theban Mysteries. 192p. 1979. mass mkt. 4.99 (*0-380-45021-6*, Avon Bks) Morrow Avon.
— A Trap for Fools. 224p. 1990. mass mkt. 5.95 (*0-345-35947-X*) Ballantine Pub Grp.
Cross, Andrew. John Philip, 1775-1851. 258p. 1989. pap. 36.00 (*0-08-032467-3*, Pub. by Mercat Pr Bks) St Mut.
Cross, Anita & McCormick, Robert, eds. Technology in Schools. LC 86-12607. (Exploring Curriculum Ser.). 320p. 1986. 113.00 (*0-335-15237-6*) OpUniv Pr.
Cross, Ann, ed. see Trump, Gary D.
Cross, Anthony. By the Banks of the Neva: Chapters from the Lives & Careers of the British in Eighteenth-Century Russia. (Illus.). 489p. (C). 1996. text 85.00 (*0-521-55293-1*) Cambridge U Pr.
— Engraved in Memory: James Walker, Engraver to the Empress Catherine the Great, & His Russian Anecdotes. 200p. 1993. 19.50 (*0-85496-849-0*) Berg Pubs.
Cross, Anthony, jt. ed. see Jones, W. Gareth.
Cross, Anthony, jt. ed. see Waddington, Patrick.
Cross, Anthony R., jt. ed. see Porter, Stanley E.
Cross, Ashton, tr. see Hunter, W. A.

C

Cross, Aureal T., ed. Palynology in Oil Exploration: A Symposium. LC 72-182534. (Society of Economic Paleontologists & Mineralogists, Special Publication Ser.: No. 11). 208p. reprint ed. pap. 64.50 (*0-608-12956-9*, 202473700038) Bks Demand.

Cross, Barrington & Scher, Herbert B., eds. Pesticide Formulations: Innovations & Developments. LC 88-10419. (ACS Symposium Ser.: Vol. 371). 304p. 1988. reprint ed. pap. 94.30 (*0-608-03282-4*, 206380000007) Bks Demand.

Cross, Brad L. Agates of Northern Mexico. 2nd rev. ed. (Illus.). 208p. Date not set. pap. write for info. (*0-945005-31-8*) Geoscience Pr.

***Cross, Burton.** International Business Organization: Subsidiary Management, Entry Strategies, & Emerging Markets. LC 99-18872. (Illus.). 348p. 1999. 69.95 (*0-312-22371-4*) St Martin.

Cross, C. L. The Ascent: Doorway to Eternity. 236p. (Orig.). 1996. pap. 8.95 (*1-881542-27-0*) Blue Star Prodns.

Cross, Carla. Buyer Beware! LC 98-9528. 208p. 1998. pap. text 16.95 (*0-7931-2851-X*) Dearborn.

— How about a Career in Real Estate? 2nd rev. ed. Hogan, Patrick, ed. 175p. (Orig.). 1996. pap. 14.95 (*0-9663614-0-7*) Noteworthy Pub.

— Real Estate Agent's Business Planning Guide. 256p. 1994. pap. 25.95 (*0-7931-0955-8*, 19071101) Dearborn.

— Como Triunfar en la Venta de Propiedades.Tr. of Up & Running in 30 Days. (SPA.). 161p. 1996. pap. 19.95 (*0-7931-2351-8*, 1913-4601) Dearborn.

— Up & Running in 30 Days: Making Money Your First Month in Real Estate. 161p. 1995. pap. 25.95 (*0-7931-1348-2*, 1907-1301, Real Estate Ed) Dearborn.

Cross, Carla M. Crissy Family Encyclopedia with Price Guide. LC 99-200315. 112p. 1998. 24.95 (*0-87588-522-5*) Hobby Hse.

— Modern Doll Rarities. LC 97-72121. (Illus.). 208p. 1997. pap. 24.95 (*0-930625-67-6*, Antique Trader) Krause Pubns.

***Cross, Carla Marie.** Patti Playpal Family: Identification & Price Guide. (Illus.). 160p. 2000. pap. 29.95 (*0-7643-1146-8*) Schiffer.

Cross, Carlene. The Undying West: Stories from Montana's Camas Prairie. LC 99-16314. (Illus.). 176p. 1999. pap. text 16.95 (*1-55591-432-2*) Fulcrum Pub.

Cross, Carol, jt. auth. see Reynolds, Jean E.

Cross, Carole. Look at U. S., Bk. 1. 1989. pap. 11.00 (*0-8092-4387-3*) NTC Contemp Pub Co.

— Look at U. S., Bk. 2. 1989. pap. 11.00 (*0-8092-4386-5*) NTC Contemp Pub Co.

Cross, Caroline. The Baby Blizzard. (Desire Ser.: No. 1079). 1997. per. 3.50 (*0-373-76079-5*, 1-76079-2) Silhouette.

— Cinderella's Tycoon: Texas Cattleman's Club. (Desire Ser.: No. 1238). 1999. mass mkt. 3.75 (*0-373-76238-0*, 1-76238-4) Silhouette.

— Dangerous. (Desire Ser.). 1993. per. 2.99 (*0-373-05810-1*, 5-05810-2) Silhouette.

— Despues del Invierno (After Winter), No. 135. (Harlequin Deseo Ser.). (SPA.). 1998. mass mkt. 3.50 (*0-373-35265-4*, 1-35265-7) Harlequin Bks.

— Gavin's Child. (Desire Ser.: No. 1013). 178p. 1996. per. 3.50 (*0-373-76013-2*, 1-76013-1) Silhouette.

— Gavin's Child. large type ed. 1999. 21.95 (*0-373-59395-3*) Harlequin Bks.

— Un Hombre Atrevido - A Daring Man, Vol. 200. (Silhouette Deseo Ser.).Tr. of A Daring Man. (SPA.). 1997. per. 3.50 (*0-373-35200-X*, 1-35200-4) Harlequin Bks.

***Cross, Caroline.** Husband... Or Enemy? (Desire Ser.: Bk. 1330). 2000. mass mkt. 3.99 (*0-373-76330-1*, 1-76330-9) Silhouette.

Cross, Caroline. The Notorious Groom. (Desire Ser.). 1998. per. 3.75 (*0-373-76143-0*, 0-76143-7) Silhouette.

— Operation Mommy. (Desire Ser.). 1995. per. 3.25 (*0-373-05939-6*, 1-05939-3) Silhouette.

— The Paternity Factor. (Desire Ser.: No. 1173). 1998. per. 3.75 (*0-373-76173-2*, 1-76173-3) Harlequin Bks.

— Rafferty's Angel. (Desire Ser.). 1994. per. 2.99 (*0-373-05851-9*, 5-05851-6) Silhouette.

***Cross, Caroline.** The Rancher & the Nanny. (Desire Ser.: Bk. 1298). 2000. per. 3.99 (*0-373-76298-4*, 1-76298-8) Silhouette.

Cross, Caroline. Truth or Dare. (Desire Ser.). 1995. mass mkt. 3.25 (*0-373-05910-8*, 1-05910-4) Silhouette.

— Una Vida Nueva, Vol. 163. (Silhouette Deseo Ser.). 1999. per. 3.50 (*0-373-35293-X*) Harlequin Bks.

Cross, Caroline J. A Delightful Life. Kellogg, Dimples B., ed. LC 98-73722. (Illus.). 288p. 1998. pap. 22.95 (*1-57736-075-3*) Providence Hse.

Cross, Catherine. Loving Enemy. large type ed. (Dales Large Print Ser.). 124p. 1996. pap. 18.99 (*1-85389-606-3*, Dales) Ulverscroft.

Cross, Cecil M. Development of Self-Government in India, 1858-1914. LC 68-57597. 248p. 1969. reprint ed. lib. bdg. 65.00 (*0-8371-0367-3*, CRSG, Greenwood Pr) Greenwood.

Cross, Charlene. Almost a Whisper. 1994. mass mkt. 5.50 (*0-671-79431-0*) PB.

— Deeper Than Roses. Tolley, Carolyn, ed. 304p. (Orig.). 1992. mass mkt. 5.50 (*0-671-73824-0*) PB.

— Everlasting. 1995. mass mkt. 5.99 (*0-671-79433-7*) PB.

— A Heart So Innocent. Scognamiglio, John, ed. 320p. (Orig.). 1990. mass mkt. 4.50 (*0-671-67700-4*) PB.

— Lord of Legend. 336p. 1993. mass mkt. 5.50 (*0-671-73825-9*) PB.

— Splendor. Tolley, Carolyn, ed. 320p. (Orig.). 1995. mass mkt. 5.99 (*0-671-79432-9*) PB.

Cross, Charles. Will of Instinct: A Biography. (Illus.). 304p. Date not set. 24.95 (*0-7868-6505-9*, Pub. by Hyperion) Time Warner.

***Cross, Charles T.** Born a Foreigner: A Memoir of the American Presence in Asia. LC 99-30232. 304p. 1999. 69.00 (*0-8476-9468-2*); pap. 24.95 (*0-8476-9469-0*) Rowman.

***Cross, Charlotte M.** Schoenberg & Words: The Modernist Years. (Border Crossings Ser.). (Illus.). 2000. 75.00 (*0-8153-2830-3*) Garland.

***Cross, Charlotte M. & Russell, A. Berman, eds.** Political & Religious Ideas in the Works of Arnold Schoenberg. LC 99-31282. (Border Crossings Ser.: Vol. 5). 400p. 1999. 75.00 (*0-8153-2831-1*) Garland.

Cross, Charlotte M., tr. see Schoenberg, Arnold.

Cross, Chodo, jt. tr. see Nishijima, Gudo.

Cross, Christa W. Magister Ludens, der Erzahler in Henrich Wittenweilers Ring. LC 83-16926. (University of North Carolina Studies in the Germanic Languages & Literatures: No. 102). (GER.). 127p. reprint ed. pap. 39.40 (*0-608-20059-X*, 207133100011) Bks Demand.

Cross, Claire. Church & People: England, 1450-1660. LC 99-35404. (Blackwell Classic Histories of England Ser.). 304p. 1999. 59.95 (*0-631-21462-3*); pap. 26.95 (*0-631-21467-4*) Blackwell Pubs.

***Cross, Claire.** Last Highlander. 1998. mass mkt. 5.99 (*0-515-12337-4*, Jove) Berkley Pub.

Cross, Claire. Love Potion #9, 1 vol. (Magical Love Ser.). 309p. 1999. mass mkt. 5.99 (*0-515-12529-6*, Jove) Berkley Pub.

— The Moonstone, Vol. 1. (Time Passages Ser.). 1999. mass mkt. 5.99 (*0-515-12654-3*, Jove) Berkley Pub.

— Once upon a Kiss. (Magical Love Ser.). 1998. mass mkt. 5.99 (*0-515-12300-5*, Jove) Berkley Pub.

***Cross, Claude B.** The American Machine: Perpetual Motion? 170p. 2000. pap. 12.95 (*1-891929-39-9*) Four Seasons.

Cross, Clifton A. Nothing to Lose. 192p. (Orig.). 1995. pap., per. 9.95 (*1-885951-13-2*) Pprbck Writer.

— Santa's Dog & Other Stories. LC 94-93871. 128p. (Orig.). 1994. pap. 5.95 (*1-885951-25-6*) Pprbck Writer.

Cross Communications Staff, ed. FutureSell: Automating Your Sales Force. (Illus.). 309p. 1990. pap. 24.95 (*0-923426-70-1*) Smith Micro.

Cross, Coy F., II. Go West Young Man! Horace Greeley's Vision for America. LC 94-18709. (Illus.). 165p. (C). 1995. 13.95 (*0-8263-1605-0*) U of NM Pr.

***Cross, Coy F., II.** Justin Smith Morrill. LC 99-6502. (Illus.). 159p. 1999. 34.95 (*0-87013-508-2*) Mich St U Pr.

Cross, D. F. Counterurbanisation in England & Wales. 263p. 1990. text 82.95 (*1-85628-024-1*, Pub. by Avebury) Ashgate Pub Co.

Cross, D. T., jt. ed. see Whitehead, C. M.

Cross, Dave, jt. auth. see Kellner, Stan.

***Cross, David.** Data Munging with Perl. 300p. 2000. pap. 36.95 (*1-930110-00-6*, Pub. by Manning Pubns) IPG Chicago.

Cross, David. Large Classes in Action. James, C. Vaughan, ed. LC 95-5585. (International English Language Teaching Ser.). (C). 1998. pap. 18.75 (*0-13-186396-7*) P-H.

— A Practical Handbook of Language Teaching. 296p. (C). 1992. pap. 20.25 (*0-13-380957-9*) P-H.

Cross, David & Morse, Sarah. Easy As One Two Three: Fifty Dulcimer Tunes for Beginners. (Illus.). 32p. (Orig.). (J). (gr. 1-6). 1985. pap. text 4.50 (*0-9614939-4-1*) Backyard Music.

Cross, David & Potter, Joan. The Book of Adirondack Firsts. 2nd ed. LC 92-93333. (Pinto Press Firsts Ser.: Vol. 1). (Illus.). 200p. (Orig.). (YA). (gr. 9-12). 1992. reprint ed. pap. 11.95 (*0-9632476-0-3*) Pinto Pr.

Cross, David & Romney, George. A Striking Likeness: The Life of George Romney. LC 98-53571. (Illus.). 300p. 1999. 61.95 (*1-84014-671-0*) Ashgate Pub Co.

Cross, Derek & Anderson, Brian, eds. Awakening from Nihilism: The 1994 Templeton Prize Awarded to Michael Novak. (Illus.). 115p. (Orig.). 1995. pap. 13.95 (*1-883357-00-4*, Crisis Bks) Dumb Ox Bks.

***Cross, Dolores E.** Breaking Through the Wall: A Marathoner's Story. LC 99-52640. 1999. pap. 14.95 (*0-88378-166-2*) Third World.

Cross, Donna W. Pope Joan. 432p. 1997. pap. 12.95 (*0-345-41626-0*) Ballantine Pub Grp.

— Pope Joan. 432p. 1996. 25.00 (*0-614-18301-4*) Crown Pub Group.

Cross, Doris. Almost Fat Free: Healthy, Heavenly Tasting Food with Just a Touch of Devil in It. LC 98-27194. 272p. 1998. pap. 14.95 (*0-7615-1702-2*) Prima Pub.

— Doris' Fat-Free Homestyle Cooking: Over 175 Fat-Free & Ultra Lowfat Recipes for..., Vol. 3. LC 96-17139. 320p. 1996. pap. 15.00 (*0-7615-0473-7*) Prima Pub.

— Fat Free & Ultra Low Fat Recipes. LC 94-25736. 240p. 1994. spiral bd. 14.95 (*1-55958-584-6*) Prima Pub.

— Fat Free 2. LC 95-23406. 272p. 1995. spiral bd. 15.95 (*0-7615-0129-0*) Prima Pub.

— More Fat Free & Ultra Lowfat Recipes from Doris' Kitchen. (Cookbook Ser.). 215p. 1993. pap. 12.95 (*0-9631490-1-6*) Doris Diet.

— Real Food for People with Diabetes - Mexican. LC 98-28209. 272p. 1998. per. 15.00 (*0-7615-1431-7*) Prima Pub.

— Real Italian Food for People with Diabetes. LC 99-23332. (Illus.). 262p. 1999. pap. 15.00 (*0-7615-1493-7*) Prima Pub.

Cross, Doris & Williams, Alice. Real Food for People with Diabetes. LC 97-23952. 272p. 1997. per. 15.00 (*0-7615-1103-2*) Prima Pub.

Cross, Dorothy. Around the World with Jesus. 1982. 0.60 (*0-88027-102-7*) Firm Foun Pub.

— Movable Property in the Nuzi Documents. (American Oriental Ser.: No. 10). 1937. pap. 25.00 (*0-527-02684-0*) Periodicals Srv.

Cross, Douglas B. Your Opportunities in Computer Programming. (Illus.). 8p. 1994. pap. 2.50 (*0-614-04321-2*) Energeia Pub.

Cross, Edwina P., ed. Motherhood - Journey into Love: An Anthology of Poetry from Welcome Home. LC 97-8268. (Illus.). 102p. 1997. 12.00 (*0-9631188-2-X*) Mothers at Home.

***Cross, Elsie Y.** Managing Diversity--the Courage to Lead. LC 99-40353. 264p. 2000. write for info. (*1-56720-269-1*, Quorum Bks) Greenwood.

Cross, Elsie Y. & White, Margaret B., eds. The Diversity Factor: Capturing the Competitive Advantage of a Changing Workforce. LC 96-3208. 256p. 1996. text 35.00 (*0-7863-0858-3*, Irwn Prfssnl) McGraw-Hill Prof.

Cross, Eric. The Late Operas of Antonio Vivaldi, 1727-1738, Vol. 1. LC 81-77. (Studies in British Musicology). 287p. reprint ed. pap. 89.00 (*0-8357-1185-4*, 207026300001) Bks Demand.

— The Late Operas of Antonio Vivaldi, 1727-1738, Vol. 2. LC 81-77. (Studies in British Musicology). 328p. reprint ed. pap. 101.70 (*0-8357-1186-2*, 207026300002) Bks Demand.

— The Tailor & Ansty. 168p. 1999. reprint ed. pap. 11.95 (*0-85342-050-5*) Irish Bks Media.

Cross, Ernest L. Short Walks in the Cairngorms. 128p. 2000. pap. 9.95 (*0-946487-09-X*, Pub. by Luath Pr Ltd) Midpt Trade.

Cross, F. L. & Livingstone, E. A., eds. The Oxford Dictionary of the Christian Church. 3rd ed. LC 97-165294. 1,824p. (C). 1997. text 125.00 (*0-19-211655-X*) OUP.

Cross, F. L., ed. see Cyril of Jerusalem.

Cross, F. L., ed. see Rashdall, Hastings.

Cross, Faith, ed. see Gadalla, Moustafa.

Cross, Frances. Life Is a Sweeter Song: A Breast Cancer Survivor's Story. 100p. 1995. pap. 9.95 (*1-886979-06-5*) Practicl Pr.

***Cross, Frank.** Vertical Hold One: Connecting with Prayer. (Illus.). 152p. 1998. reprint ed. pap. 9.99 (*1-85078-317-9*, Pub. by O M Pubng) OM Literature.

Cross, Frank B. Environmentally Induced Cancer & the Law: Risks, Regulation, & Victim Compensation. LC 88-38295. 244p. 1989. 69.50 (*0-89930-389-7*, CEM/, Quorum Bks) Greenwood.

— Fishes in Kansas. 2nd ed. Johnston, Richard F., ed. (Public Education Ser.: No. 14). (Illus.). viii, 190p. 1975. pap. 12.95 (*0-89338-004-0*) U KS Nat Hist Mus.

— Legal Responses to Indoor Air Pollution. LC 90-8963. 224p. 1990. 69.50 (*0-89930-519-9*, CAP/, Quorum Bks) Greenwood.

Cross, Frank B. & Collins, Joseph T. Fishes in Kansas. 2nd ed. Johnston, Richard F., ed. (Public Education Ser.: No. 14). (Illus.). 336p. 1975. 35.00 (*0-89338-048-2*) U of KS Pubns.

— Fishes in Kansas. 2nd rev. ed. 336p. 1995. pap. text 19.95 (*0-89338-049-0*) U KS Nat Hist Mus.

— Illustrated Guide to Fishes in Kansas. (Public Education Ser.: No. 4). (Illus.). 14p. (J). (gr. 4-6). 1976. pap. 1.00 (*0-89338-000-8*) U KS Nat Hist Mus.

Cross, Frank B. & Hesketh, Howard E. Engineering Medical Waste-to-Energy Systems. 170p. 1995. text 64.95 (*1-56676-219-7*) Technomic.

Cross, Frank B. & Miller, Roger L. Legal Env Of Bus: Text & Cases. 2nd ed. LC 94-39004. (SWC-Business Law). 1100p. (C). 1994. mass mkt. 58.25 (*0-314-04517-1*) West Pub.

— West's Legal Environment of Business: Text, Cases, Ethical & Regulatory Issues. Perlee, Clyde, ed. 676p. (C). 1992. text 65.25 (*0-314-89333-4*) West Pub.

***Cross, Frank B. & Miller, Roger LeRoy.** West's Legal Environment of Business: Text, Cases, Ethical, Regulatory & International Issues. 5th ed. LC 00-32076. 2000. 99.95 (*0-324-01572-0*) Sth-Wstrn College.

Cross, Frank B., jt. auth. see Miller, Roger L.

Cross, Frank L. & Hesketh, Howard E., eds. Sizing & Selecting Air Pollution Control Systems. LC 93-61892. 170p. 1994. text 84.95 (*1-56676-126-3*) Technomic.

Cross, Frank L., Jr., et al. Environmental Impacts of Hazardous Waste Treatment, Storage & Disposal Facilities. LC 89-50503. 176p. 1989. 29.95 (*0-87762-627-8*) Technomic.

Cross, Frank L., Jr., jt. ed. see Young, Richard A.

Cross, Frank M., Jr. The Ancient Library of Qumran. (Biblical Seminar Ser.: No. 30). 204p. 1995. 57.00 (*1-85075-511-6*, Pub. by Sheffield Acad) CUP Services.

Cross, Frank M. The Ancient Library of Qumran & Modern Biblical Studies. Segovia, Fernando F. & Tolbert, Mary A., eds. LC 95-20117. 232p. 1995. pap. 21.00 (*0-8006-2807-1*, 1-2807) Augsburg Fortress.

— The Ancient Library of Qumran & Modern Biblical Studies, 1956-1957. LC 76-29736. (Haskell Lectures, 1956-57). (Illus.). 196p. 1976. reprint ed. lib. bdg. 41.50 (*0-8371-9281-1*, CRAL, Greenwood Pr) Greenwood.

— Canaanite Myth & Hebrew Epic: Essays in the History of the Religion of Israel. LC 72-76564. 394p. 1973. 46.50 (*0-674-09175-2*) HUP.

— Canaanite Myth & Hebrew Epic: Essays in the History of the Religion of Israel. 400p. 1997. pap. text 19.50 (*0-674-09176-0*) HUP.

— From Epic to Canon: History & Literature in Ancient Israel. LC 98-7322. (Illus.). 304p. 1998. 45.00 (*0-8018-5982-4*) Johns Hopkins.

Cross, Frank M., Jr. & Freedman, David N. Early Hebrew Orthography: A Study of the Epigraphic Evidence. (American Oriental Ser.: Vol. 36). (HEB.). 72p. 1952. pap. 14.00 (*0-940490-36-6*) Am Orient Soc.

— Studies in Ancient Yahwistic Poetry. LC 96-19207. (Biblical Resource Ser.). 143p. 1997. pap. 27.50 (*0-8028-4159-7*) Eerdmans.

Cross, Frank M. & Talmon, Shemaryahu, eds. Qumran & the History of the Biblical Text. LC 75-12529. 413p. 1975. pap. 15.95 (*0-674-74362-8*) HUP.

Cross, Frank M., ed. see Collins, John J.

Cross, Frank M., jt. ed. see Ulrich, Eugene.

Cross, Frank M., Jr., ed. see Zimmerli, Walther.

***Cross, Frank Moore, Jr.** From Epic to Canon: History & Literature in Ancient Israel. (Illus.). 275p. 2000. reprint ed. pap. 17.95 (*0-8018-6533-6*) Johns Hopkins.

Cross, Fredrick T., ed. Indoor Radon & Lung Cancer: Reality or Myth?, 2 vols., Set. (Hanford Symposium on Health & the Environment Ser.: No. 29). 1200p. 1992. pap. 89.95 (*0-935470-69-7*) Battelle.

Cross, G. Folding Napkins. 1997. pap. 12.95 (*1-56799-622-1*, Friedman-Fairfax) M Friedman Pub Grp Inc.

Cross, Gail, ed. see Deuel, Austin.

***Cross, Gary.** An All-Consuming Nation: Why Commercialism Won in Modern America. LC 99-87282. 2000. 27.50 (*0-231-11312-9*) Col U Pr.

Cross, Gary. Kids' Stuff: Toys & the Changing World of American Childhood. LC 97-2655. (Illus.). 352p. 1997. 29.95 (*0-674-89830-3*) HUP.

— Kids' Stuff: Toys & the Changing World of American Childhood. 336p. 1999. pap. 16.95 (*0-674-50335-X*) HUP.

— A Social History of Leisure since 1600. LC 90-70208. (Illus.). 297p. 1990. 27.95 (*0-910251-35-5*) Venture Pub PA.

Cross, Gary & Szostak, Rick. Technology & American Society: A History. LC 94-5332. 352p. 1994. pap. text 42.00 (*0-13-898644-4*) P-H.

Cross, Genevieve. The Engine That Lost Its Whistle. 10th ed. (Illus.). 32p. (J). (gr. 1-3). 1988. reprint ed. pap. 9.00 (*0-9621162-0-3*) Van Buren Cty Hist Soc.

Cross, Geoffrey. Collaboration & Conflict: A Contextual Exploration of Group Writing & Positive Emphasis. Farr, Marcia, ed. LC 93-39852. (Written Language Ser.). 192p. (C). 1994. text 45.00 (*1-881303-16-0*); pap. text 20.95 (*1-881303-17-9*) Hampton Pr NJ.

Cross, George L. Letters to Bill: On University Administration. LC 83-47832. 225p. 1983. 22.95 (*0-8061-1850-4*) U of Okla Pr.

Cross, George L., jt. ed. see Kash, Don.

Cross, George N. Randolph, New Hampshire, Old & New: Its Ways & Its By-Ways. (Illus.). 260p. 1997. reprint ed. lib. bdg. 32.50 (*0-8328-7140-0*) Higginson Bk Co.

Cross, Gilbert B. Next Week East Lynne: Domestic Drama in Performance, 1820-1874. LC 74-25573. (Illus.). 281p. 1976. 38.50 (*0-8387-1646-6*) Bucknell U Pr.

Cross, Gillian. La Cabana En El Arbol.Tr. of Tree House. (Orig.). (J). (gr. 4-7). 1998. pap. text 7.95 (*84-204-4889-3*) Santillana.

— The Dark Behind the Curtain. (Illus.). 160p. (J). (gr. 1-5). 1987. 12.95 (*0-19-271457-0*) OUP.

— The Demon Headmaster. large type ed. 208p. (J). (gr. 3 up). 1990. 16.95 (*0-7451-1150-5*, G K Hall Lrg Type) Mac Lib Ref.

— The Great American Elephant Chase. LC 92-54492. 160p. (J). (gr. 7-12). 1993. 16.95 (*0-8234-1016-1*) Holiday.

— Un Mapa de Ninguna Parte (A Map of Nowhere) (SPA.). (YA). 1997. pap. 6.99 (*968-16-5096-4*, Pub. by Fondo) Continental Bk.

Cross, Gillian. Mysterious Minds. (Illus.). 48p. (J). pap. 7.95 (*0-14-130140-6*, Pub. by Pnguin Bks Ltd) Trafalgar.

Cross, Gillian. New World. (J). 1996. 10.00 (*0-606-11679-6*, Pub. by Turtleback) Demco.

— Pictures in the Dark. LC 96-7660. 208p. (J). (gr. 7-12). 1996. 16.95 (*0-8234-1267-9*) Holiday.

— Pictures in the Dark. 1998. 10.09 (*0-606-13703-3*, Pub. by Turtleback) Demco.

Cross, Gillian. Roman Beanfeast. (Illus.). 96p. (J). 1997. pap. 7.95 (*0-14-037766-2*, Pub. by Pnguin Bks Ltd) Trafalgar.

Cross, Gillian. Roscoe's Leap. LC 87-45328. 160p. (YA). (gr. 7-12). 1987. 15.95 (*0-8234-0669-5*) Holiday.

***Cross, Gillian.** Tightrope. LC 98-55149. 208p. (gr. 7-12). 1999. 16.95 (*0-8234-1512-0*) Holiday.

Cross, Gillian. Wolf. 144p. (J). (gr. 7-9). 1993. pap. 3.25 (*0-590-45608-3*) Scholastic Inc.

Cross, H. J., jt. ed. see Dengerink, H. A.

Cross, H. R. & Overby, A. J., eds. Meat Science, Milk Science & Technology. (World Animal Science Ser.: Vol. B3). xiv,458p. 1988. 344.00 (*0-444-42578-0*) Elsevier.

Cross, H. Russell, jt. ed. see Franklin, Kenneth R.

Cross, Haman, Jr., et al. Wild Thing: Let's Talk about Sex. 76p. Date not set. pap. 6.99 (*1-57902-020-8*) Integrtd Res.

Cross, Hardy. Arches, Continuous Frames, Columns, & Conduits: Selected Papers. LC 63-17046. (Illus.). 275p. reprint ed. pap. 85.30 (*0-8357-5718-8*, 201904400010) Bks Demand.

— Engineers & Ivory Towers. LC 76-99628. (Essay Index Reprint Ser.). 1980. 19.95 (*0-8369-1404-X*) Ayer.

Cross, Harmon S., jt. auth. see Thurston, Florence G.

Cross, Harold L. People's Right to Know. LC 75-170844. reprint ed. 29.50 (*0-404-01859-9*) AMS Pr.

Cross, Harry, et al. Employer Hiring Practices: Differential Treatment of Hispanic & Anglo Job Seekers. LC 90-12115. (Reports: No. 90-4). (Illus.). 110p. (Orig.). (C). 1990. pap. text 18.00 (*0-87766-479-X*) Urban Inst.

Cross, Harry E. & Sandos, James A. Across the Border: Rural Development in Mexico & Recent Migration to the United States. LC 81-6276. 220p. reprint ed. pap. 68.20 (*0-608-20134-0*, 207140600011) Bks Demand.

Cross, Henry & Oliver, William. Study Guide. pap. 14.50 (*0-393-97210-0*) Norton.

Cross, Ian. Music & the Cognitive Sciences, 1990. (Contemporary Music Review Ser.). 320p. 1994. pap. text 44.00 (*3-7186-5420-2*, Harwood Acad Pubs) Gordon & Breach.

C

An Asterisk (*) at the beginning of an entry indicates that the title is appearing for the first time.

C

Cross, Robin. Aftermath of War. LC 93-50154. (World War II Ser.). (Illus.). 48p. (J). (gr. 5-9). 1994. lib. bdg. 24.26 (*1-56847-178-5*) Raintree Steck-V.

— Children & War. (World War II Ser.). (Illus.). 48p. (J). (gr. 5-9). 1994. lib. bdg. 24.26 (*1-56847-180-7*) Raintree Steck-V.

— Cities at War. (World War II Ser.). (Illus.). 48p. (J). (gr. 5-6). 1994. lib. bdg. 24.26 (*1-56847-179-3*) Raintree Steck-V.

— Fallen Eagle: The Last Days of the Third Reich. LC 96-22232. (Illus.). 304p. 1996. 24.95 (*0-471-16408-9*) Wiley.

— Movie Magic: A Behind-the-Scenes Look at Filmmaking. (Illus.). 64p. (J). 1996. pap. 10.95 (*0-8069-1365-7*) Sterling.

— Technology of War. LC 93-48234. (World War II Ser.). (Illus.). 48p. (J). (gr. 5-9). 1994. lib. bdg. 24.26 (*1-56847-177-7*) Raintree Steck-V.

— Victims of War. LC 93-2252. (World War II Ser.). (Illus.). 48p. (J). (gr. 5-9). 1993. lib. bdg. 24.26 (*1-56847-081-9*) Raintree Steck-V.

— Warfare: A Chronological History. 1991. 29.98 (*1-55521-722-2*) Bk Sales Inc.

***Cross, Robin, ed.** True Stories of World War Two. large type unabridged ed. 324p. 1999. 26.95 (*0-7531-5462-5*, 154625, Pub. by ISIS Lrg Prnt) ISIS Pub.

Cross, Robin, ed. Warfare: A Chronological History. (Illus.). 256p. 1997. reprint ed. text 50.00 (*0-7881-5024-3*) DIANE Pub.

Cross, Ronald. Multivalued Linear Operators, Vol. 213. LC 98-24468. (Monographs & Textbooks in Pure & Applied Mathematics). (Illus.). 352p. 1998. text 150.00 (*0-8247-0219-0*) Dekker.

Cross, Ronald A. The Fourth Guardian. 448p. (Orig.). 1994. 21.95 (*0-312-85635-0*) Tor Bks.

— The Fourth Guardian. 448p. (Orig.). 1996. mass mkt. 6.99 (*0-8125-1594-3*, Pub. by Tor Bks) St Martin.

— The Lost Guardian. 1996. mass mkt. 5.99 (*0-8125-1595-1*) Tor Bks.

— The White Guardian. 1999. pap. 14.95 (*0-312-86839-1*, Pub. by Tor Bks) St Martin.

— The White Guardians. LC 98-11421. 432p. 1998. 26.95 (*0-312-85863-9*, Pub. by Tor Bks) St Martin.

Cross, Rosemary E. Midwives & Management. 1996. pap. text 29.00 (*1-898507-20-1*) Buttrwrth-Heinemann.

Cross, Roy, jt. auth. see Green, William.

Cross, Ruth. Big Road. 1993. reprint ed. lib. bdg. 75.00 (*0-7812-5922-3*) Rprt Serv.

Cross, Ruth C. Index to Cambridge Historical Society Publications Proceedings Vols. 1-44: 1905-1979. Roth, Charles, ed. 305p. 1991. 25.00 (*1-878284-45-2*) Cmbrdg Hist.

Cross, S. S. MCQ Companion to General & Systematic Pathology. 2nd ed. 216p. 1998. pap. write for info. (*0-443-05281-6*) Church.

Cross, Samuel H. Mediaeval Russian Churches. (Medieval Academy Bks.: No. 53). 1949. 25.00 (*0-910956-27-8*) Medieval Acad.

Cross, Sharyl & Oborotova, Marina A., eds. The New Chapter in United States-Russian Relations Opportunities. LC 94-16460. 248p. 1994. 59.95 (*0-275-94761-0*, Praeger Pubs) Greenwood.

Cross, Simon S. MCQ Companion to General & Systematic Pathology. 208p. (Orig.). 1992. pap. text 19.95 (*0-443-04367-1*) Church.

Cross, Sir Rupert & Harris, J. W. Precedent in English Law. 4th ed. (Clarendon Law Ser.). 256p. 1991. 75.00 (*0-19-876162-7*); pap. text 28.00 (*0-19-876163-5*) OUP.

Cross, Stephen. Elements of Hinduism. LC 94-28748. (Illus.). 144p. 1997. pap. 9.95 (*1-86204-034-6*, Pub. by Element MA) Penguin Putnam.

Cross, Stephen, compiled by. The Little Book of Hindu Wisdom. LC 97-25236. (Little Bks.). (Illus.). 48p. 1997. 5.95 (*1-86204-109-1*, Pub. by Element MA) Penguin Putnam.

Cross, Stephen M. Economic Decisions under Inflation: The Impact of Accounting Measurement Error. LC 81-81625. (Contemporary Studies in Economic & Financial Analysis: Vol. 40). 170p. 1982. 78.50 (*0-89232-240-3*) Jai Pr.

Cross, Sue, jt. auth. see Cross, Robert.

Cross, Sydney. The Missing Link. 358p. 1994. write for info. (*0-9639626-0-4*) Prescott Png.

***Cross, Tamara E.** Social Security: Capital Markets & Educational Issues Associated with Individual Accounts. 68p. (C). 2000. pap. text 20.00 (*0-7881-8813-5*) DIANE Pub.

Cross, Teresa M., ed. see Trump, Gary D.

***Cross, Terry L. & Powery, Emerson B., eds.** The Spirit & the Mind: Essays in Informed Pentecostalism(to honor Dr. Donald N. Bowdle-Presented on his 65th Birthday) 336p. 2000. 59.00 (*0-7618-1627-5*) U Pr of Amer.

Cross, Terry R., ed. & illus. see Taylor, Charles L. & Udovich, Richard J.

Cross, Thomas B. Centrex II: Strategic Directions. 250p. 1987. 1000.00 (*0-923426-09-4*) Smith Micro.

— Chief Technology Officer. 300p. 1990. 24.95 (*0-685-34871-7*) Smith Micro.

— LanSell: Desktop Guide for Connectivity Sales Professional. 1991. pap. 24.95 (*0-923426-94-9*) Smith Micro.

— Split Second Society. (Illus.). 200p. 1991. pap. 24.95 (*0-685-34872-5*) Smith Micro.

Cross, Thomas B. & Raizman, Marjorie B. Telecommuting: Work Strategies for the Information Organization. 225p. 1986. 32.50 (*0-87094-645-5*, Irwn Prfssnl) McGraw-Hill Prof.

Cross, Thomas S., jt. auth. see Blassingame, Carol.

Cross, Tim, ed. The Lost Voices of World War One: An International Anthology of Writers, Poets & Playwrights. (Illus.). 414p. (Orig.). (C). 1990. pap. text 23.95 (*0-87745-264-4*) U of Iowa Pr.

Cross, Timothy. Comfort from the Bible. 1997. pap. 5.99 (*1-898787-62-X*) Emerald House Group Inc.

— My Father's House. 1997. pap. 5.99 (*0-907927-88-2*) Emerald House Group Inc.

***Cross, Timothy.** A Postcard from Paul: The Letter of Paul to Philemon. 75p. 1999. pap. 8.99 (*1-84030-050-7*) Ambassador Prodns Ltd.

Cross, Timothy. Scent from Heaven. 1997. pap. 6.99 (*1-898787-09-3*) Emerald House Group Inc.

— String of Pearls: Treasures from the Bible. 132p. 1997. pap. 8.99 (*1-898787-95-6*) Emerald House Group Inc.

— Walking with Jesus. 1997. pap. 8.99 (*1-898787-38-7*) Emerald House Group Inc.

Cross, Timothy P. An Oasis of Order: The Core Curriculum at Columbia College. (Illus.). 127p. (Orig.). 1995. pap. 15.00 (*0-9649084-0-9*) Columb Coll.

Cross, Tom. Painting the Warmth of the Sun: St. Ives Artists, 1939-1975. LC 97-66455. 1997. 49.95 (*0-7188-2941-7*, Lutterworth-Parkwest) Parkwest Pubns.

— Painting the Warmth of the Sun: St. Ives Artists, 1939-1975. (Illus.). 208p. 1997. pap. 32.95 (*0-7188-2942-5*, Lutterworth-Parkwest) Parkwest Pubns.

— The Shining Sands: Artists in Newlyn & St. Ives, 1880-1930. LC 95-82207. (Illus.). 1996. 48.95 (*0-7188-2925-5*, Lutterworth-Parkwest) Parkwest Pubns.

— The Shining Sands: Artists in Newlyn & St. Ives, 1880-1930. 1997. pap. text 29.95 (*0-7188-2926-3*, Lutterworth-Parkwest) Parkwest Pubns.

Cross, Tracy L., jt. auth. see Coleman, Laurence J.

Cross, Vince & Sharratt, Nick. Pudding & Pie. (Illus.). 48p. (J). 1994. (*0-19-279988-6*) OUP.

— Ride a Cock Horse. (Illus.). 48p. (J). 1994. (*0-19-279989-4*) OUP.

Cross, Virgil S. The McKennas. LC 97-675. (Orig.). 1997. pap. 22.50 (*1-880664-22-4*) E M Pr.

Cross, W. J., ed. see Jarnigan, Jan G.

Cross, W. J., ed. see Mountain, Rick.

Cross-White, Agnes. African-American Community in Charlottesville, Virginia. (Images of America Ser.). (Illus.). 128p. 1998. pap. 16.99 (*0-7524-0889-5*) Arcadia Publng.

Cross, Wilbur. Amway: The Definitive History of Amway Corporation, 1 vol. 1999. mass mkt. 6.99 (*0-425-17040-3*) Berkley Pub.

***Cross, Wilbur.** Amway: The True Story of the Company That Transformed the Lives of Millions. 2001. pap. 12.95 (*0-425-17646-0*) Berkley Pub.

Cross, Wilbur. Choices with Clout. 224p. (Orig.). 1995. pap. text 5.99 (*0-425-14538-7*) Berkley Pub.

***Cross, Wilbur.** Dictionary of Business Terms. LC 99-218719. 480p. 1999. pap. 20.00 (*0-7352-0099-8*) PH Pr.

— Disaster at the Pole: The Tragedy of the Airship Italia & the 1921 Nobile Expedition to the North Pole. 320p. 2000. 24.95 (*1-58574-049-7*) Lyons Pr.

Cross, Wilbur. First Presbyterian Church, Hilton Head Island, South Carolina: The Authorized History of a Dynamic Community Church. (Illus.). 96p. (Orig.). 1994. pap. 9.95 (*1-881576-33-7*) Providence Hse.

— Legacy of Leadership: The History of Lee Enterprises, Inc. Robbins, Ceila D., ed. (Illus.). 176p. 1990. write for info. (*0-944641-00-8*) Greenwich Pub Group.

— The Prentice Hall Encyclopedia of Model Business Plans. LC 98-15279. 450p. 1998. pap. text 24.95 (*0-7352-0024-6*) PH Pr.

— Prentice Hall Small Business Model Letter Book. 370p. (C). 1992. text 39.95 (*0-13-718602-9*, Busn) P-H.

Cross, Wilbur, jt. auth. see Hausman, Carl.

Cross, Wilbur, jt. auth. see Root, Wayne A.

Cross, Wilbur L. Development of the English Novel. LC 78-90494. 329p. 1969. reprint ed. lib. bdg. 65.00 (*0-8371-2204-X*, CREN, Greenwood Pr) Greenwood.

— Four Contemporary Novelists. LC 67-22087. (Essay Index Reprint Ser.). 1977. 19.95 (*0-8369-0353-6*) Ayer.

— Four Contemporary Novelists. LC 70-136401. (B&cL Ser. I). reprint ed. 20.00 (*0-404-01867-X*) AMS Pr.

— Four Contemporary Novelists. (BCL1-PR English Literature Ser.). 204p. 1992. reprint ed. lib. bdg. 79.00 (*0-7812-7123-1*) Rprt Serv.

— The Life & Times of Laurence Sterne, 2 vols., Set. (BCL1-PR English Literature Ser.). 1992. reprint ed. lib. bdg. 150.00 (*0-7812-7410-9*) Rprt Serv.

— The Modern English Novel: An Address Before the American Academy of Arts & Letters. 1977. 11.95 (*0-8369-6927-8*, 7808) Ayer.

Cross, Wilbur L., ed. see Sterne, Laurence.

Cross, Wilbur L., ed. see Yale Review Staff.

Cross, William, Jr. Endangered Species. (Hands-On Minds-On Science Ser.). (Illus.). 96p. 1994. pap., teacher ed. 11.95 (*1-55734-628-3*) Tchr Create Mat.

Cross, William E. Shades of Black: Diversity in African-American Identity. 1991. pap. 22.95 (*0-87722-949-X*) Temple U Pr.

Crossan. The Birth of Christianity: Discovering What Happened in the Years Immediately after the Execution of Jesus. LC 97-32526. 688p. 1999. pap. 21.00 (*0-06-061660-1*) HarperTrade.

— We Need Not Fear the Truth. 2000. 16.00 (*0-06-069975-2*) HarpC.

Crossan, Dominic J. Essential Jesus. 1998. 7.99 (*0-7858-0901-5*) Bk Sales Inc.

Crossan, John Dominic. The Birth of Christianity: Discovering What Happened in the Years Immediately After the Execution of Jesus. LC 97-32526. 656p. 1998. 30.00 (*0-06-061659-8*, Pub. by Harper SF) HarpC.

— The Birth of Christianity: Discovering What Happened in the Years Immediately after the Execution of Jesus. 653p. 1998. pap. 14.00 (*0-06-061672-5*, Pub. by Harper SF) HarpC.

— The Cross That Spoke: The Origins of the Passion Narrative. LC 87-45696. 452p. 1988. 24.95 (*0-944344-25-9*) Polebridge Pr.

— The Dark Interval: Towards a Theology of Story. LC 88-12471. 128p. 1988. pap. 12.95 (*0-944344-06-2*) Polebridge Pr.

— Finding Is the First Act: Trove Folktales & Jesus' Treasure Parable. LC 79-9898. (Society of Biblical Literature. Semeia Supplements Ser.: No. 9). 149p. (Orig.). reprint ed. pap. 46.20 (*0-7837-5451-5*, 204521600005) Bks Demand.

— Four Other Gospels: Shadows on the Contours of Canon. 2nd ed. LC 92-33028. 160p. 1992. reprint ed. pap. 15.95 (*0-944344-24-0*) Polebridge Pr.

— The Historical Jesus: The Life of a Mediterranean Jewish Peasant. 520p. 1998. pap. 29.95 (*0-567-29229-0*, Pub. by T & T Clark) Bks Intl VA.

— The Historical Jesus: The Life of a Mediterranean Jewish Peasant. LC 90-56451. 544p. 1993. reprint ed. pap. 19.00 (*0-06-061629-6*, Pub. by Harper SF) HarpC.

— In Parables: The Challenge of the Historical Jesus. rev. ed. LC 92-330277. 160p. 1992. reprint ed. pap. 14.95 (*0-944344-22-4*) Polebridge Pr.

— Jesus: A Revolutionary Biography. LC 93-24685. 224p. 1995. pap. 13.00 (*0-06-061662-8*, Pub. by Harper SF) HarpC.

— A Long Way from Tipperary: What a Former Monk Discovered in His Search for the Truth. LC 00-20477. 240p. 2000. 23.00 (*0-06-069974-4*, Pub. by Harper SF) HarpC.

— Religious Worlds: Primary Readings in Comparative Perspective. 624p. (C). 1995. per. 34.95 (*0-8403-6950-6*) Kendall-Hunt.

— Who Killed Jesus: Exposing the Roots of Anti-Semitism in the Gospel Story of the Death of Jesus. LC 95-40200. 256p. 1996. pap. 15.00 (*0-06-061480-3*, Pub. by Harper SF) HarpC.

Crossan, John Dominic & Craig, William L. Will the Real Jesus Please Stand Up? A Debate Between William Lane Craig & John Dominic Crossan. Copan, Paul, ed. LC 98-37884. 186p. (C). 1999. pap. 14.99 (*0-8010-2175-8*) Baker Bks.

Crossan, John Dominic & Watts, Richard G., eds. Who Is Jesus? Answers to Your Questions about the Historical Jesus. LC 99-41130. 160p. 1999. pap. 13.95 (*0-664-25842-5*) Westminster John Knox.

***Crossan, John Dominic, et al.** The Jesus Controversy: Perspectives in Conflict. LC 99-16448. (Rockwell Lecture Ser.). 112p. 1999. 17.00 (*1-56338-289-X*) TPI PA.

Crossan, John Dominic, et al. The Search for Jesus: Modern Scholarship Looks at the Gospels. LC 94-70539. 152p. (Orig.). (C). 1994. pap. text 11.95 (*1-880317-14-1*, 7H44) Biblical Arch Soc.

Crossan, Richard M. & Nance, Harold W. Master Standard Data: The Economic Approach to Work, Measurement. rev. ed. LC 80-11165. 268p. 1980. reprint ed. lib. bdg. 35.50 (*0-89874-133-5*) Krieger.

Crossant, Jeanne. Aristote et les Mysteres. Vlastos, Gregory, ed. LC 78-15863. (Morals & Law in Ancient Greece Ser.). (FRE & GER.). 1979. reprint ed. lib. bdg. 21.95 (*0-405-11534-2*) Ayer.

Crossbie, George F. Bruen Loop: The Jimmy Bruen Story. 1999. 23.95 (*1-85635-068-1*) Mercier Pr.

Crosse, Joanna. Angels to Watch over Me, 1. (Illus.). 96p. (gr. 4). 1999. text 8.95 (*1-901881-04-0*, Pub. by Element MA) Penguin Putnam.

***Crosse, Joanna.** A Child's Book of Angels. (Illus.). 64p. (YA). (gr. 1 up). 2000. 19.99 (*1-84148-082-7*) Barefoot Bks NY.

Crosse, Joanna. The Element Illustrated Encyclopedia of Mind, Body, Spirit & Earth. LC 98-191582. (Illus.). 160p. (J). (gr. 6-10). 1998. 24.95 (*1-901881-10-5*, Pub. by Element MA) Penguin Putnam.

***Crosse, Joanna.** The Pocket Encyclopedia of Mind, Body, Spirit & Earth. (Illus.). 160p. (YA). (gr. 4 up). 1999. pap. 8.95 (*1-902618-10-6*, Pub. by Element Childrns) Penguin Putnam.

Crosse, Marcia, ed. Human Tissue Banks: FDA Taking Steps to Improve Safety, but Some Concerns Remain. (Illus.). 48p. 1999. reprint ed. pap. text 20.00 (*0-7881-8039-8*) DIANE Pub.

***Crosse, Marcia G.** Blood Supply: Transfusion-Associated Risks. (Illus.). 92p. (C). 1999. pap. text 20.00 (*0-7881-7636-6*) DIANE Pub.

Crosse, Marcia G., ed. Blood Supply: FDA Oversight & Remaining Issues of Safety. (Illus.). 153p. (C). 1999. pap. text 35.00 (*0-7881-7635-8*) DIANE Pub.

Crossen, Chaya, ed. see Hecht, Shea & Clorfene, Chaim.

Crossen, Craig & Tirion, Wil. Binocular Astronomy. 1992. 24.95 (*0-943396-36-0*) Willmann-Bell.

***Crossen, Cynthia.** The Rich & How They Got That Way: How the Wealthiest People of All Time - From Genghis Khan to Bill Gates - Made Their Fortunes. LC 99-85978. 320p. 2000. 25.95 (*0-8129-3267-6*, Times Bks) Crown Pub Group.

Crosser, Paul K. Prolegomena to All Future Metaeconomics: Formation & Deformation of Economic Thought. LC 72-13845. (Illus.). 240p. 1974. 10.00 (*0-87527-099-9*) Green.

Crosser, Rick L., ed. see Murphy, Kevin E. & Higgins, Mark.

Crosset, Todd W. Outsiders in the Clubhouse: The World of Women's Professional Golf. LC 94-27916. (SUNY Series on Sport, Culture, & Social Relations). 276p. (C). 1995. pap. text 21.95 (*0-7914-2490-1*) State U NY Pr.

Crossett, John M., jt. tr. see Arieti, James A.

Crossette, Barbara. The Great Hill Stations of Asia. 272p. 1999. pap. 15.00 (*0-465-01488-7*, Pub. by Basic) HarpC.

— The Great Hill Stations of Asia. LC 97-51950. 272p. 1998. text 28.00 (*0-8133-3326-1*, Pub. by Westview) HarpC.

— So Close to Heaven: The Vanishing Buddhist Kingdoms of the Himalayas. (Illus.). 297p. 1995. 25.00 (*0-614-32325-8*) Knopf.

— So Close to Heaven: The Vanishing Buddhist Kingdoms of the Himalayas. 1996. pap. 13.00 (*0-679-74363-4*) Random.

Crossey, Laura J., et al, eds. Siliciclastic Diagenesis & Fluid Flow: Concepts & Applications. (Special Publications: Vol. 55). (Illus.). 220p. (C). 1996. 109.00 (*1-56576-032-8*) SEPM.

Crossfield, A. Scott & Blair, Clay, Jr. Always Another Dawn: The Story of a Rocket Test Pilot. LC 73-169413. (Literature & History of Aviation Ser.). 1972. reprint ed. 43.95 (*0-405-03758-9*) Ayer.

Crossfield, Claire, ed. Kemps Film T. V. & Video Handbook (International) 1997. 1997. 129.95 (*0-611-00928-5*) Intl Spec Bk.

— Kemps North American Production Handbook 1997. 1997. 89.95 (*0-611-00939-0*) Intl Spec Bk.

— Kemps U. K. Production Handbook 1997. 1997. 59.95 (*0-611-00927-7*) Intl Spec Bk.

Crossgrove, David & BDO Consulting Team Staff, eds. In-House Bids in the Context of Competitive Tendering & Market Testing: An Expert Guide. 112p. 1995. pap. 167.50 (*0-582-24658-X*, Pub. by Addison-Wesley) Trans-Atl Phila.

Crossgrove, Hannelore & Crossgrove, William C. Graded German Reader. 2nd ed. (C). 1978. pap. text 29.16 (*0-669-01533-4*) HM Trade Div.

Crossgrove, William C., jt. auth. see Crossgrove, Hannelore.

Crossick, Geoffrey, ed. The Artisan & the European Town, 1500-1900. LC 96-47302. (Historical Urban Studies). 288p. 1997. text 83.95 (*1-85928-232-6*, Pub. by Scolar Pr) Ashgate Pub Co.

Crossick, Geoffrey & Haupt, Heinz-Gerhard. The Petite Bourgeoisie in Europe, 1780-1914. LC 97-21842. 308p. (C). 1997. pap. 25.99 (*0-415-17463-5*) Routledge.

Crossick, Geoffrey & Jaumain, Serge, eds. Cathedrals of Consumption: The European Department Store, 1850-1939. LC 98-19489. (Historical Urban Studies). (Illus.). 384p. 1999. text 96.95 (*1-84014-236-7*, Pub. by Ashgate Pub) Ashgate Pub Co.

Crossin, John W. Friendship: The Key to Spiritual Growth. LC 97-6425. 128p. (Orig.). 1997. pap. 6.95 (*0-8091-3710-0*) Paulist Pr.

— Living Virtuously: Moral Decisions & Spiritual Growth. LC 98-38275. 160p. 1998. pap. 9.95 (*0-8091-3834-4*) Paulist Pr.

Crossin, Kathryn L. Tenascin & Counteradhesive Molecules of the Extracellular Matrix. (Cell Adhesion & Communication Ser.). 176p. 1996. text 57.00 (*3-7186-5841-0*) Gordon & Breach.

Crossing Borders (Program) Staff & Ford Foundation Staff. Crossing Borders: Revitalizing Area Studies. LC 99-13918. 1999. write for info. (*0-916584-53-4*) Ford Found.

***Crossingham, John.** Baseball in Action. (Sports in Action Ser.). (J). 2000. 11.40 (*0-606-18049-4*) Turtleback.

— Basketball in Action. (Sports in Action Ser.). (Illus.). (J). 2000. 11.40 (*0-606-18050-8*) Turtleback.

***Crossingham, John & Dann, Sarah.** Basketball in Action. LC 99-38042. (Sports in Action Ser.). (Illus.). 32p. (J). (gr. 1-4). 1999. pap. 5.95 (*0-7787-0174-3*); lib. bdg. 19.96 (*0-7787-0162-X*) Crabtree Pub Co.

— Volleyball in Action. LC 99-38039. (Sports in Action Ser.). (Illus.). 32p. (J). (gr. 1-4). 1999. pap. 5.95 (*0-7787-0176-X*); lib. bdg. 19.96 (*0-7787-0164-6*) Crabtree Pub Co.

Crossingham, John, jt. auth. see Dann, Sarah.

Crosske, Roger W., jt. ed. see Lane, Richard P.

Crosskey, Roger W. The Natural History of Blackflies. LC 90-12453. 722p. 1990. 560.00 (*0-471-92755-4*) Wiley.

Crosskey, William W. & Jeffrey, William, Jr. Politics & Constitution in the History of the United States, 3 vols. 2040p. 1980. lib. bdg. 168.00 (*0-226-12134-8*) U Ch Pr.

— Politics & the Constitution in the History of the United States Vol. 3: The Political Background of the Federal Convention. LC 53-7433. 608p. 2000. 42.00 (*0-226-12138-0*) U Ch Pr.

Crosskill, W. E. First Beginning. (C). 1989. text 45.00 (*0-948929-08-1*) St Mut.

Crossland, Dennis. The Birthday Directory of Famous & Infamous People. LC 93-91102. 184p. 1994. pap. 16.95 (*0-9639928-3-X*) CAVA Pr.

— The Birthday Directory of Famous & Infamous People. 2nd ed. (Illus.). vi, 243p. 1999. pap. 19.95 (*0-9639928-0-5*) CAVA Pr.

Crossland, Don. A Journey Toward Wholeness. 2nd rev. ed. 157p. 1998. pap. 10.00 (*0-9665252-1-3*) Jrney Pr.

Crossland, Helen. From Pieces to Peace. 144p. 1998. pap. 12.00 (*0-9665252-0-5*) Jrney Pr.

Crossland, Jackie. Collateral Damage: The Tragedy of Medea (A Play) (Illus.). 80p. 1992. pap. 9.95 (*0-88974-042-9*, Pub. by Press Gang Pubs) LPC InBook.

Crossland, John R., ed. The Book of Ballads. LC 72-168779. (Granger Index Reprint Ser.). 1977. reprint ed. 21.95 (*0-8369-6299-0*) Ayer.

Crossland, Paul M., jt. auth. see Cipollaro, Anthony C.

Crossland, Richard B. & Currie, James T. Twice the Citizen: A History of the United States Army Reserve, 1908-1983. (Illus.). 325p. 1999. reprint ed. pap. text 35.00 (*0-7881-7008-2*) DIANE Pub.

C

An Asterisk (*) at the beginning of an entry indicates that the title is appearing for the first time.

Crossley, A. W. & Mahajan, R. P. MCQ Companion to Anaesthesia in Clinical Practice. LC 99-28932. 288p. 2000. pap. write for info. (*0-443-05311-1*, W B Saunders Co) Harcrt Hlth Sci Grp.

Crossley, Alan. Jesus Psychi Super Star. 64p. 1984. 40.00 (*0-7212-0683-2*, Pub. by Regency Pr GBR) St Mut.

Crossley, Alan, ed. A History of Oxfordshire: The City of Oxford, Vol. IV. (Victoria History of the Counties of England Ser.). (Illus.). 526p. 1979. 140.00 (*0-19-722714-7*) OUP.

— A History of the County of Oxford: Wootton Hundred (South) Including Woodstock, Vol. 12. (Victoria History of the Counties of England Ser.). (Illus.). 572p. 1990. 135.00 (*0-19-722774-0*) OUP.

— A History of the County of Oxfordshire: Bampton Hundred, Vol. 13. (Victoria History of the Counties of England Ser.). (Illus.). 248p. 1996. text 155.00 (*0-19-722790-2*) OUP.

Crossley, Alan E., ed. The Story of Helen Duncan. (C). 1990. 50.00 (*0-7223-0840-X*, Pub. by A H S Ltd) St Mut.

Crossley, Ann & Keller, Carol A. The Air Force Wife Handbook: A Complete Social Guide. LC 92-81202. (Illus.). 350p. (Orig.). 1992. pap. 21.95 (*0-9626228-1-8*) ABI Pr.

— The Army Wife Handbook: A Complete Social Guide. 2nd ed. LC 93-73172. (Illus.). 432p. (Orig.). 1994. pap. 21.95 (*0-9626228-2-6*) ABI Pr.

Crossley, Anthony. Training the Young Horse: The First Two Years. (Illus.). 191p. 1994. 14.95 (*0-09-178224-4*, Pub. by S Paul) Trafalgar.

Crossley, B. Alice, jt. auth. see Shapiro, Phyllis P.

Crossley, Ceri. Edgar Quinet (Eighteen Three to Eighteen Seventy-Five) A Study in Romantic Thought. LC 82-82432. (French Forum Monographs: No. 43). 149p. (Orig.). 1983. pap. 12.95 (*0-917058-42-9*) French Forum.

Crossley, Ceri & Small, Ian, eds. The French Revolution & British Culture. 248p. 1989. 49.95 (*0-19-215893-7*) OUP.

Crossley, Ceri, jt. auth. see Cornick, Martyn.

Crossley, D., ed. Earth's Deep Interior: The Doornbos Memorial Volume. (The Fluid Mechanics of Astrophysics & Geophysics Ser.: Vol. 7). 448p. 1997. text 72.00 (*90-5699-032-2*) Gordon & Breach.

Crossley, D. A. & Penman, Sue, eds. Manual of Small Animal Dentistry. 2nd ed. (Illus.). 245p. 1995. pap. text 82.95 (*0-905214-28-5*) Iowa St U Pr.

Crossley, D. A., Jr., jt. auth. see Coleman, David C.

Crossley, D. A., Jr., jt. auth. see Swank, W. T.

Crossley, D. W. Sidney Ironworks Accounts, 1541-73. (Camden Fourth Ser.: No. 15). 27.00 (*0-901050-25-3*) David Brown.

Crossley, Darry, tr. see Reynolds, Ralph V.

Crossley, David. A Guide to Post-Medieval Archaeology in Britain. (Illus.). 288p. 1990. text 55.00 (*0-7185-1285-5*, Pub. by Leicester U Pr) Cassell & Continuum.

— Hide & Seek Peter Cottontail. (Illus.). 12p. (J). (ps-k). 2000. pap. 5.99 (*0-689-83323-7*) S&S Childrens.

— Hide & Seek Puppy. (Illus.). 12p. (J). (ps-k). 2000. pap. 5.99 (*0-689-83324-5*) S&S Childrens.

— Post-Medieval Archaeology in Britain, Vol. 1. rev. ed. 1995. pap. 25.00 (*0-7185-1937-X*) St Martin.

Crossley, David J. & Wilson, Peter A. How to Argue: An Introduction to Logical Thinking. LC 78-25799. 288p. (C). 1979. pap. 27.50 (*0-07-553608-0*) McGraw.

Crossley, E. W., ed. The Parish Registers of Halifax, County York, England Vol. II: Marriages & Burials, 1538-1593. 423p. (Orig.). 1995. reprint ed. pap. text 27.00 (*0-7884-0164-5*) Heritage Bk.

Crossley, Gareth. Everyday Evangelism. 1987. pap. 4.99 (*0-85234-239-X*, Pub. by Evangelical Pr) P & R Pubng.

Crossley, Gary J. Important Bird Areas of Pennsylvania. 1998. pap. 19.95 (*0-8117-2809-9*) Stackpole.

Crossley-Holland, Kevin. Eleanor's Advent. 1993. 90.00 (*0-907664-36-9*, Pub. by Old Stiles) St Mut.

— The Language of Yes: Poems 1990-1995. LC 96-216930. 72p. 1996. pap. 16.95 (*1-870612-37-X*, Pub. by Enitha Pr) Dufour.

— Oenone in January. 1993. 60.00 (*0-907664-17-2*, Pub. by Old Stiles) St Mut.

— The Old Stories: Folk Tales from East Anglia & the Fen Country LC 98-165781. 215 p. 1997. write for info. (*0-905899-51-2*) Colt Bks Ltd.

— Poems from East Anglia. LC 98-143977. 92p. 1998. pap. 18.95 (*1-900564-60-2*, Pub. by Enitha Pr) Dufour.

***Crossley-Holland, Kevin.** The World of King Arthur & His Court: People, Places, Legend & Lore. LC 98-37698. (Illus.). 125p. (YA). (gr. 5 up). 1999. 25.00 (*0-525-46167-1*, Dutton Child) Peng Put Young Read.

Crossley-Holland, Kevin. The Young Oxford Book of Folk-Tales. LC 99-203821. (Illus.). 224p. (YA). 1999. 22.95 (*0-19-278141-3*) OUP.

Crossley-Holland, Kevin, ed. Anglo-Saxon World. (Illus.). 288p. (C). 1994. 55.00 (*0-85115-169-8*, Boydell Pr) Boydell & Brewer.

— The Anglo-Saxon World: An Anthology. (Oxford World's Classics Ser.). 320p. 1999. pap. 8.95 (*0-19-283547-5*) OUP.

— The Norse Myths. 276p. 1981. pap. 16.00 (*0-394-74846-8*) Pantheon.

Crossley-Holland, Kevin, tr. Beowulf. (Illus.). 48p. (YA). 1999. pap. 10.95 (*0-19-272369-3*) OUP.

***Crossley-Holland, Kevin & Sail, Lawrence, eds.** The New Exeter Book of Riddles. 96p. 1999. pap. (*1-900564-31-9*, Pub. by Enitha Pr) Dufour.

Crossley-Holland, Kevin, jt. auth. see Thomas, Gwyn.

Crossley-Holland, Kevin, tr. see O'Donoghue, Heather, ed.

Crossley-Holland, Kevin, jt. tr. see Thomas, Gwyn.

Crossley-Holland, Nicole. Living & Dining in Medieval Paris: The Household of a Fourteenth-Century Knight. LC 97-156005. (Illus.). 224p. 1997. 55.00 (*0-7083-1368-X*, Pub. by Univ Wales Pr) Paul & Co Pubs.

Crossley-Holland, Nicole, tr. from FRE. A Fifteenth Century Franciscan French Office: Translation of "Hours of the Passion" with a Commentary. LC 90-31511. (Medieval Studies: Vol. 4). (Illus.). 240p. 1991. lib. bdg. 89.95 (*0-88946-268-2*) E Mellen.

Crossley-Holland, Peter. Musical Artifacts of Pre-Hispanic West Mexico: Towards an Interdisciplinary Approach. LC 80-50811. (Monograph Series in Ethnomusicology: No. 1). vii, 45p. (Orig.). 1980. pap. text 6.00 (*0-88287-013-0*) UCLA Dept Ethnom.

— Musical Instruments in Tibetan Legend & Folklore. LC 82-50350. (Monograph Series in Ethnomusicology: No. 3). 42p. (Orig.). 1982. pap. text 5.00 (*0-88287-015-7*) UCLA Dept Ethnom.

Crossley-Holland, Peter, ed. Selected Reports in Ethnomusicology Vol. 2, No. 1: The Melograph. LC 73-620035. vii, 125p. (Orig.). 1974. pap. text 7.50 (*0-88287-004-1*) UCLA Dept Ethnom.

Crossley, J. The Emergence of Number. 240p. (C). 1987. text 58.00 (*9971-5-0413-8*); pap. text 33.00 (*9971-5-0414-6*) World Scientific Pub.

Crossley, J. N. What Is Mathematical Logic? x, 82p. 1990. pap. 5.95 (*0-486-26404-1*) Dover.

Crossley, J. N. & Nerode, Anil. Combinatorial Factors. LC 73-10783. (Ergebnisse der Mathematik und Ihrer Grenzgebiete Ser.: Vol. 81). (Illus.). 160p. 1974. 49.95 (*0-387-06428-1*) Spr-Verlag.

Crossley, J. N., tr. see Schuette, K.

Crossley, John C. & Jamieson, Lynn M. Introduction to Commercial & Entrepreneurial Recreation. 2nd rev. ed. (Illus.). 330p. (C). 1997. text 44.95 (*1-57167-130-7*) Sagamore Pub.

Crossley, John N., et al, eds. Logical Methods: In Honor of Anil Nerode's Sixtieth Birthday. LC 93-21451. (Progress in Computer Science & Applied Logic Ser.: Vol. 12). 1993. 115.00 (*0-8176-3690-0*) Birkhauser.

Crossley, Keith, jt. auth. see Von Hassell, Agostino.

Crossley, Kent B. & Archer, Gordon. The Staphylococci in Human Disease. LC 96-49803. 1996. text 115.00 (*0-443-07644-8*) Church.

Crossley, Larry. How to Change Your Life: The Complete Change Manual. 272p. 1995. pap. text 12.95 (*0-9648224-6-6*) Salvtn Army.

Crossley, Louise. Explore Antarctica. (Illus.). 114p. (C). 1995. pap. 21.95 (*0-521-45566-9*); text 48.95 (*0-521-49591-1*) Cambridge U Pr.

Crossley, Louise, ed. Trial by Ice: The Antarctic Journals of John King Davis. 248p. 1998. pap. 125.00 (*1-85297-047-2*, Pub. by Erskine Press) St Mut.

***Crossley, Marie Schlumbrecht.** The Barbour Collection of Connecticut Town Vital Records: Middletown, Part I, A-J 1651-1854. White, Lorraine C., ed. 300p. 2000. pap. 35.00 (*0-8063-1603-9*) Genealog Pub.

Crossley, Michael. Still Life... With Drinks. 40p. 1999. pap. 3.00 (*0-9664124-4-3*) Sweet Lady Moon.

Crossley, Michael, et al, eds. Qualitative Educational Research in Developing Countries: Current Perspectives. LC 96-16786. (Reference Books in International Education: Vol. 35). (Illus.). 328p. 1996. text 65.00 (*0-8153-1494-9*, SS927) Garland.

***Crossley, Michael & Holmes, Keith.** Educational Development in the Small States of the Commonwealth. 112p. 2000. pap. 24.95 (*0-85092-627-0*, Pub. by Comm Sec) Stylus Pub VA.

***Crossley, Michele L.** Introducing Narrative Psychology: Self, Trauma & the Construction of Meaning. LC 99-39403. 2000. pap. 27.95 (*0-335-20290-X*) OpUniv Pr.

— Rethinking Health Psychology. LC 00-35682. (Health Psychology Ser.). 2000. pap. write for info. (*0-335-20431-7*, Pub. by OpUniv Pr) Taylor & Francis.

Crossley, Nick. Intersubjectivity: The Fabric of Social Becoming. (Philosophy & Social Criticism Ser.: Vol. 4). 200p. 1996. 45.00 (*0-8039-7903-7*); pap. 14.99 (*0-8039-7904-5*) Sage.

— The Politics of Subjectivity: Between Foucault & Merleau-Ponty. LC 94-9863. (Avebury Series in Philosophy). 1994. 69.95 (*1-85628-886-2*, Pub. by Avebry) Ashgate Pub Co.

Crossley, P., jt. ed. see Fernie, E.

Crossley, Pamela K. The Manchus. LC 96-17702. (Peoples of Asia Ser.). 1997. 31.95 (*1-55786-560-4*) Blackwell Pubs.

Crossley, Pamela Kyle. A Translucent Mirror: History & Identity in Qing Imperial Ideology. LC 99-11002. 441p. 1999. 45.00 (*0-520-21566-4*, Pub. by U CA Pr) Cal Prin Full Svc.

Crossley, Paul, jt. ed. see Clarke, Georgia.

Crossley, Peter & Kilgour, John. Small Farm Mechanization for Developing Countries. LC 83-5935. (Illus.). 269p. reprint ed. pap. 83.40 (*0-608-18514-0*, 203603400097) Bks Demand.

Crossley, Raymond. Integrated Balance Sheet & Flow Accounts for Insurance Companies & Pension Funds. LC HG8076.. (Bank of England. Discussion Papers. Technical Ser.: No. 17). 382p. reprint ed. pap. 118.50 (*0-7837-2679-1*, 204305600006) Bks Demand.

Crossley, Robert. Olaf Stapledon: Speaking for the Future. (Illus.). 480p. 1994. 45.00 (*0-8156-0281-2*) Syracuse U Pr.

— The Trinity - Chinese Edition. Huang, John, tr. (CHI.). 52p. 1983. pap. 3.00 (*1-56582-094-0*) Christ Renew Min.

Crossley, Robert, ed. An Olaf Stapledon Reader. LC 96-31975. 352p. 1996. 45.00 (*0-8156-2724-6*, CRPP); pap. 19.95 (*0-8156-0430-0*, CRPPP) Syracuse U Pr.

Crossley, Robert, ed. see Stapledon, Olaf & Miller, Agnes.

Crossley, Roger. Chirality & Biological Activity of Drugs. 208p. 1995. boxed set 179.95 (*0-8493-9140-7*, 9140) CRC Pr.

Crossley, Rosemary. And the Walls Came Tumbling Down. 1999. pap. write for info. (*0-452-27667-5*, Plume) Dutton Plume.

— Facilitated Communication Training. LC 93-44306. (Special Education Ser.). 160p. (C). 1994. pap. text 15.95 (*0-8077-3327-X*) Tchrs Coll.

Crosslife Staff. Grace Life Conference Syllabus: The Message of the Exchanged Life. 2nd rev. ed. Orig. Title: The Exchanged Life Conference Syllabus. (Illus.). 45p. 1997. spiral bd. 2.99 (*1-57838-087-1*) CrossLife Express.

— Grace Life Video Conference Leaders Manual. 1997. pap. 2.99 (*1-57838-118-5*) CrossLife Express.

— Grace Life Workshop Syllabus: Discover the Master's Plan for Mastering Life. 4th rev. ed. Orig. Title: The Exchanged Life Workshop Syllabus. (Illus.). 1997. spiral bd. 2.99 (*1-57838-088-X*) CrossLife Express.

— Grace Walk Conference Syllabus French Version. 2nd rev. ed. Orig. Title: The Exchanged Life Conference Syllabus. (FRE., Illus.). 1995. spiral bd. 15.00 (*1-57838-072-3*) CrossLife Express.

— The Grace Walk Workshop Syllabus: Discover the Master's Plan for Mastering Life. 3rd rev. ed. Orig. Title: The Exchanged Life Workshop Syllabus. (Illus.). 59p. 2000. spiral bd. 15.00 (*1-57838-003-0*) CrossLife Express.

Crossman, A. R. & Neary, D. Neuroanatomy: An Illustrated Colour Text. LC 95-6580. (Illus.). 1995. pap. text 28.95 (*0-443-04479-1*) Church.

Crossman, A. R. & Sambrook, M. A. Neural Mechanisms in Disorders of Movement. (Current Problems in Neurology Ser.: Vol. 9). 224p. 1988. 79.95 (*0-86196-164-1*, Pub. by J Libbey Med) Bks Intl VA.

Crossman, Carl L. A Catalogue of Chinese Export Paintings, Furniture, Silver & Other Objects, 1785-1865: 1785-1865. (Illus.). 1970. pap. 4.95 (*0-87577-038-X*, PEMP111, Peabody Museum) Peabody Essex Mus.

— The Decorative Arts of the China Trade. (Illus.). 448p. 1991. 89.50 (*1-85149-096-5*) Antique Collect.

— Design Catalogue of Chinese Export Porcelain for the American Market. (Illus.). 1969. pap. 4.95 (*0-87577-019-3*, PEMP118, Peabody Museum) Peabody Essex Mus.

Crossman, Chris, intro. William Manning: A Ten Year Retrospective, 1984-1994. (Illus.). 24p. (Orig.). 1995. pap. 5.95 (*0-918749-04-2*) W A Farnsworth.

Crossman, David A. Dead of Winter: A Winston Crisp Maine Island Mystery. LC 99-16369. 288p. 1999. 22.95 (*0-89272-445-5*) Down East.

— The Secret of the Missing Grave. LC 99-21629. (Bean & Ab Mystery Ser.). 184p. (YA). (gr. 5-8). 1999. 16.95 (*0-89272-456-0*) Down East.

— The Secret of the Missing Grave: Bean & Ab. LC 99-21629. 192p. (YA). (gr. 4-10). 2000. 16.95 (*0-89272-470-6*) Down East.

— A Show of Hands. LC 96-45604. 288p. 1998. pap. 14.95 (*0-89272-398-X*) Down East.

Crossman, E. C. Military & Sporting Rifle Shooting. (Library Classics). (Illus.). 536p. 1986. reprint ed. 45.00 (*0-935632-34-4*) Wolfe Pub Co.

Crossman, E. J. & Goodchild, Cheryl D. An Annotated Bibliography of the Muskellunge, Esox Masquinongy: Osteichthyes: Salmoniformes. (Illus.). 132p. pap. 20.00 (*0-88854-208-9*) Brill Academic Pubs.

Crossman, E. J., jt. auth. see Mandrak, Nicholas E.

Crossman, Edward J. & Casselman, J. M. An Annotated Bibliography of the Pike, Esox Lucius: Osteichthyes: Salmoniformes. 408p. pap. 23.43 (*0-88854-351-X*) Brill Academic Pubs.

Crossman, Eileen F. Mountain Rain: A Biography of James O. Fraser, Pioneer Missionary to China. LC 93-47631. (Illus.). 256p. 1994. mass mkt. 5.99 (*0-87788-551-6*) OMF Bks.

Crossman, Frank W., ed. see Conference on Failure Modes in Composites Staff.

Crossman, J. R. Surges-McKay: History of the Surges-McKay Families; Also Allied Families, Pflueger, Reibel, Bouville, Beaune. (Illus.). 60p. 1994. reprint ed. pap. 13.50 (*0-8328-4092-0*) Higginson Bk Co.

Crossman, Kelly. Architecture in Transition: From Art to Practice, 1885-1906. 250p. 1987. 65.00 (*0-7735-0604-7*, Pub. by McG-Queens Univ Pr) CUP Services.

Crossman, Meg, ed. Worldwide Perspective: Understanding God's Purposes in the World from Genesis to Revelation. LC 95-7841. 1995. ring bd. 24.95 (*0-87808-765-6*) William Carey Lib.

Crossman, Nancy, ed. see Law, Ruth.

Crossman, Richard C. Paul Tillich: A Comprehensive Bibliography & Keyword Index of Primary & Secondary Writings in English. LC 83-15026. (American Theological Library Association Monograph: No. 9). 193p. 1983. 24.00 (*0-8108-1650-4*) Scarecrow.

Crossman, Richard H. Government & the Governed: A History of Political Ideas & Political Practice. LC 79-15269. 374p. 1980. reprint ed. lib. bdg. 45.00 (*0-313-22015-8*, CRGG, Greenwood Pr) Greenwood.

— Government & the Governed: A History of Political Ideas & Political Practice. LC 77-92506. (Essay Index in Reprint Ser.). 1978. reprint ed. 25.00 (*0-8486-3001-7*) Roth Pub Inc.

— Palestine Mission: A Personal Record. Davis, Moshe, ed. LC 77-70672. (America & the Holy Land Ser.). (Illus.). 1977. reprint ed. lib. bdg. 23.95 (*0-405-10249-2*) Ayer.

Crossman, Richard H., ed. see Koestler, Arthur.

Crossman, Richard H., ed. see Koestler, Arthur, et al.

Crossman, Richard M. Ergonomic Pocket Guide. Gorman, Christine E., ed. (Illus.). 64p. (Orig.). 1993. pap. text 41.80 (*0-931690-60-9*) Genium Pub.

— Office Safety Pocket Guide. Gorman, Christine E., ed. (Illus.). 64p. 1993. pap. 41.80 (*0-931690-51-X*) Genium Pub.

Crossman, Sharyn, jt. auth. see Adams, Gerald.

Crossman, Virginia. Politics, Law & Order in 19th Century Ireland. 300p. 1996. 70.00 (*0-7171-2001-5*, Pub. by Gill & MacMill) Irish Bks Media.

Crossmen, Arthur & Hill, Anthony. Up Against the Wall. 116p. (Orig.). 1995. pap. text 10.00 (*1-887333-00-2*) Touch Down Prodns.

Crosson, Bettie. Beware! Be Wise. 130p. (Orig.). 1984. pap. 4.95 (*0-87508-148-7*) Chr Lit.

Crosson, Bruce. Subcortical Functions in Language & Memory. LC 91-42906. 374p. 1992. lib. bdg. 50.00 (*0-89862-790-7*) Guilford Pubns.

Crosson, Cynthia. Tainted Truth: The Manipulation of Fact in America. 272p. 1996. per. 12.00 (*0-684-81556-7*) S&S Trade.

Crosson, Frederick J., ed. Human & Artificial Intelligence. LC 78-131431. (Orig.). (C). 1970. pap. text 12.95 (*0-89197-220-X*) Irvington.

Crosson, Frederick J., tr. see Lorenzen, Paul.

Crosson, Patricia H. Public Service in Higher Education: Practices & Priorities. Fife, Jonathan D., ed. & frwd. by. LC 84-166237. (ASHE-ERIC Higher Education Reports: No. 83-7). 138p. (Orig.). 1983. pap. 24.00 (*0-913317-06-3*) GWU Grad Schl E&HD.

Crosson, Pierre R. Agricultural Development & Productivity: Lessons from the Chilean Experience. LC 74-128181. (Resources for the Future Ser.). (Illus.). 214p. 1970. 16.50 (*0-8018-1216-X*) Johns Hopkins.

— Agricultural Development & Productivity: Lessons from the Chilean Experience. LC 74-128181. 216p. reprint ed. pap. 67.00 (*0-8357-5268-2*, 203019700067) Bks Demand.

Crosson, Pierre R., ed. The Cropland Crisis: Myth or Reality? LC 81-48216. 250p. 1982. 27.50 (*0-8018-2816-3*); pap. 15.95 (*0-8018-2817-1*) Resources Future.

Crosson, Pierre R., et al, eds. Selected Water Management Issues in Latin American Agriculture. LC 77-10193. (Resources for the Future Ser.). (Illus.). 1978. text 16.50 (*0-8018-2047-2*) Johns Hopkins.

— Selected Water Management Issues in Latin American Agriculture. LC 77-10193. (Illus.). 208p. reprint ed. pap. 64.50 (*0-608-18807-7*, 203019800067) Bks Demand.

Crosson, Pierre R. & Brubaker, Sterling. Resource & Environmental Effects of U. S. Agriculture. LC 82-47984. 255p. 1983. pap. 16.95 (*0-8018-2920-8*) Resources Future.

Crosson, Pierre R. & Frederick, Kenneth D. The World Food Situation: Resource & Environmental Issues in the Developing Countries & the United States. LC 77-90817. (RFF Research Paper Ser.: No. R6). 238p. reprint ed. pap. 73.80 (*0-7837-3135-3*, 204285200006) Bks Demand.

Crosson, Pierre R. & Silvers, Arthur L. Rural Development & Urban Bound Migration in Mexico. LC 80-8024. (Resources for the Future Research Paper: Paper R-17). (Illus.). 160p. (Orig.). 1980. pap. text 11.00 (*0-8018-2493-1*) Johns Hopkins.

Crosson, Pierre R. & Stout, Anthony T. Productivity Effects of Cropland Erosion in the United States. LC 83-19094. 103p. 1983. pap. 11.00 (*0-8018-3207-1*) Resources Future.

Crosson, Robert. Geographies. 80p. (Orig.). 1981. pap. 4.00 (*0-88031-056-1*) Invisible-Red Hill.

Crosson, Robert, et al. Daybook - Division. 128p. 1991. 12.50 (*0-88031-070-7*) Invisible-Red Hill.

***Crosson, Robert S. & Hulme, Ann Ravenscroft.** Vita Sackville-West: A Bibliography. LC 99-32490. (Winchester Bibliographies of 20th Century Writers Ser.). 320p. 1999. 80.00 (*1-58456-004-5*) Oak Knoll.

Crosson-Tower, Cynthia. Exploring Child Welfare: A Practical Perspective. LC 97-28097. 474p. 1997. 64.00 (*0-205-14743-7*) Allyn.

***Crosson-Tower, Cynthia.** Exploring Child Welfare: A Practice Perspective. 2nd ed. 480p. 2000. 56.00 (*0-205-31953-X*) Allyn.

Crosson-Tower, Cynthia. Exploring Child Welfare: A Practice Perspective: Instructor's Manual & Test Bank. 112p. (C). 1997. text, teacher ed. write for info. (*0-205-27963-5*, T7963-6) Allyn.

Crossrig, David H., ed. Diary of the Proceedings in the Parliament & Privy Council of Scotland. LC 72-1026. (Bannatyne Club, Edinburgh. Publications: No. 27). reprint ed. 27.50 (*0-404-52733-7*) AMS Pr.

Crossroad. How to Read the New Testament: Participant's Guide. (Adult Christian Formation Program Ser.). pap. 4.95 (*0-8245-7000-6*) Crossroad NY.

— How to Read the Old Testament: Participant Guide. (Adult Christian Formation Program Ser.). pap. 4.95 (*0-8245-7002-2*) Crossroad NY.

Crossroads Staff, ed. Agriculture & Spirituality. 144p. (Orig.). 1996. pap. 17.50 (*90-6224-980-9*, Pub. by Uitgeverij Arkel) LPC InBook.

Crossroads United Methodist Church Congregation St. What's Cooking in Western Colorado, Vol. 1. Groen, Mildred J. & Holton, Rosalee, eds. LC 89-85767. (Illus.). 300p. (Orig.). 1989. pap. 12.95 (*0-9624514-0-1*) Crossroads United Meth Ch.

Crosswait, C. Bruce, jt. auth. see Wilkes-Hull, Mary.

Crosswait, Helen. Reflections of a Paleface from the Rosebud. 66p. 1992. per. 9.00 (*0-614-24757-8*) Tesseract SD.

— Riot in a Parrot Shoppe. 47p. 1991. pap. 7.50 (*0-614-24756-X*) Tesseract SD.

Crossway Books. The Garden of Love: God's Love Revealed. LC 97-38453. 32p. 1998. 7.99 (*0-89107-991-2*) Crossway Bks.

C

An Asterisk (*) at the beginning of an entry indicates that the title is appearing for the first time.

— More Precious Than Gold: Psalms of Praise & Hope. LC 97-38478. 32p. 1998. 7.99 (*0-89107-988-2*) Crossway Bks.

— Sing to the Lord: Well-Loved Hymns & Choruses. LC 97-38454. 32p. 1998. 7.99 (*0-89107-989-0*) Crossway Bks.

Crossway Books Editors. In the Beginning: The Story of Creation. LC 97-45994. (J). (ps-3). 1998. 14.99 (*0-89107-997-1*) Crossway Bks.

Crossway Books Staff. In the Stillness of the Heart: A Collection of Prayers from the Bible. LC 97-38452. 32p. 1998. 7.99 (*0-89107-990-4*) Crossway Bks.

Crosswell, D. K. The Chief of Staff: The Military Career of General Walter Bedell Smith, 110. LC 90-45328. (Contributions in Military Studies Ser.: No. 106). 464p. 1991. 69.50 (*0-313-27480-0*, CGM, Greenwood Pr) Greenwood.

Crosswhite, H. M., ed. see Dieke, Gerhard H.

Crosswhite, Hazel C. A Prairie Soul: Poems. 136p. 1998. pap. 12.95 (*1-57087-373-9*) Prof Pr NC.

Crosswhite, James. The Rhetoric of Reason: Writing & the Attractions of Argument. LC 95-44286. (Rhetoric of the Human Sciences Ser.). 344p. 1996. 58.00 (*0-299-14950-1*); pap. 24.95 (*0-299-14954-4*) U of Wis Pr.

— The Rhetoric of Reason: Writing & the Attractions of Argument. LC 95-44286. (Rhetoric of the Human Sciences Ser.). 344p. reprint ed. pap. 106.70 (*0-608-20420-X*, 207167300002) Bks Demand.

Crosswy, Tiffany, ed. see Sakach, Deborah & American Historic Inns Incorporated Staff.

Crost, Lyn. Honor by Fire: Japanese Americans at War in Europe & the Pacific. LC 94-16319. (Illus.). 368p. 1996. pap. text 16.95 (*0-89141-608-0*) Presidio Pr.

Crosten, Lesley A. Moonlight in Jungleland. 132p. 1996. pap. 9.95 (*1-888345-03-9*) Paper Jam.

Crosten, William. Boonville & Beyond: An Upstate Sampler. 72p. 1989. 14.95 (*0-932052-82-7*) North Country.

Crosten, William L. French Grand Opera: An Art & a Business. LC 73-171381. 132p. 1972. reprint ed. lib. bdg. 32.50 (*0-306-70405-6*) Da Capo.

Crosthwaite, Elaine. Passing Your IPM Exams. 208p. (C). 1993. pap. 30.00 (*0-85292-515-8*, Pub. by IPM Hse) St Mut.

Crosthwaite, Elaine, jt. ed. see Warner, David.

Crosthwaite, Hugh. KA: A Handbook of Mythology, Sacred Practices, Electrical Phenomena, & their Linguistic Connections in the Ancient Mediterranean World. 225p. 1992. text 40.00 (*0-685-59572-2*) Metron Pubns.

Crosthwaite, Luis H. The Moon Will Forever Be a Distant Love. Nathan, Debbie & Delgadillo, Willivaldo, trs. LC 97-26920.Tr. of La Luna Siempre Sera Un Dificil Amor. 160p. 1997. pap. 12.95 (*0-938317-31-8*) Cinco Puntos.

***Croswell, Katrina.** Long Life Short Stories. 1999. pap. write for info. (*1-58235-006-X*) Watermrk Pr.

Croswell, Ken. The Alchemy of the Heavens: Searching for Meaning in the Milky Way. 352p. 1996. pap. 14.95 (*0-385-47214-5*, Anchor NY) Doubleday.

***Croswell, Ken.** Magnificent Universe. LC 99-23875. (Illus.). 192p. 1999. 60.00 (*0-684-84594-6*) S&S Trade.

— Planet Quest: The Epic Discovery of Alien Solar Systems. (Illus.). 324p. 1999. text 25.00 (*0-7881-6047-8*) DIANE Pub.

Croswell, Ken. Planet Quest: The Epic Discovery of Alien Solar Systems. LC 98-15032. (Illus.). 336p. (C). 1998. pap. 14.00 (*0-15-600612-X*, Harvest Bks) Harcourt.

Croswell, Ken. Planet Quest: The Epic Discovery of Alien Solar Systems. LC 97-27751. 1997. write for info. (*0-19-850198-6*) OUP.

Croswell, Ken. Planet Quest: The Epic Discovery of Alien Solar Systems. LC 97-9473. (Illus.). 336p. 1997. 24.50 (*0-684-83252-6*) S&S Trade.

***Croswell, Ken.** See the Stars: Your First Guide to the Night Sky. (Illus.). 32p. (YA). (gr. 3 up). 2000. 16.95 (*1-56397-757-5*) Boyds Mills Pr.

***Croswell, Peter L., ed.** Spatial Information Technology Standards & System Integration: Tutorial & Annotated Bibliography. annot. ed. (Illus.). ix, 158p. 1998. pap. 55.00 (*0-916848-03-5*) Urban & Regional Information Systems.

Crosweller, David. Reflections of Buddha for Every Day. 1999. pap. 29.95 (*1-885203-86-1*) Jrny Editions.

Crotch, W. J., ed. see Caxton, William.

Crotch, W. Walter. The Pageant of Dickens. LC 72-3293. (Studies in Dickens: No. 52). 1972. reprint ed. lib. bdg. 75.00 (*0-8383-1502-X*) M S G Haskell Hse.

— The Secret of Dickens. LC 72-3292. (Studies in Dickens: No. 52). 1972. reprint ed. lib. bdg. 75.00 (*0-8383-1501-1*) M S G Haskell Hse.

Crotch, Walter. The Soul of Dickens. LC 73-21705. (Studies in Dickens: No. 52). 1974. lib. bdg. 75.00 (*0-8383-1763-4*) M S G Haskell Hse.

Crotchett, Kevin. A Teacher's Project Guide to the Internet. LC 97-4068. 1997. pap. text 26.50 (*0-435-07104-1*, 07104) Heinemann.

Crotean, Marie-Danielle. Fred & the Stinky Cheese. Cummins, Sarah, tr. (First Novels Ser.). (Illus.). 60p. (J). 1996. mass mkt. 3.99 (*0-88780-372-5*, Pub. by Formac Publ Co); bds. 14.95 (*0-88780-373-3*, Pub. by Formac Publ Co) Formac Dist Ltd.

Croteau, Clement. French - English - Latin Lexicon of Fruits. (ENG, FRE & LAT., Illus.). 52p. 1991. pap. 29.95 (*0-8288-9380-2*) Fr & Eur.

Croteau, David. Politics & the Class Divide: Working People & the Middle Class Left. (Labor & Social Change Ser.). 320p. (Orig.). (C). 1994. text 69.95 (*1-56639-254-3*); pap. text 22.95 (*1-56639-255-1*) Temple U Pr.

Croteau, David & Hoynes, William. Media Society: Industries, Images & Audiences. LC 96-45372. 1997. 29.95 (*0-8039-9065-0*) Pine Forge.

Croteau-Fleury, Marie D. & Jorisch, Stephane. Un Reveur Qui Aimait la Mer et les Poissons Dores. 24p. (*2-89021-303-X*) La Courte Ech.

Croteau, James, jt. auth. see Caudill, Gil.

***Croteau, Jan Hellig.** Perform It! The Complete Guide to Young People's Theater. (Illus.). 112p. 2000. pap. 13.95 (*0-325-00230-4*) Heinemann.

Croteau, Marie-Danielle. Le Chat de Mes Reves. (Novels in the Premier Roman Ser.). (FRE.). 64p. (J). (gr. 2-5). 1994. pap. 8.95 (*2-89021-219-X*, Pub. by La Courte Ech) Firefly Bks Ltd.

— Fred & the Flood. (First Novels). 60p. (J). (gr. 1-4). 1998. text 3.99 (*0-88780-430-6*, Pub. by Formac Publ Co) Formac Dist Ltd.

— Fred's Dream Cat. (First Novels Ser.). (Illus.). 61p. (J). (gr. 1-4). 1995. mass mkt. 3.99 (*0-88780-304-0*, Pub. by Formac Publ Co); bds. 14.95 (*0-88780-305-9*, Pub. by Formac Publ Co) Formac Dist Ltd.

— Un Monde a la Derive. (Novels in the Roman Plus Ser.). (FRE., Illus.). 160p. (YA). (gr. 8 up). 1994. pap. 8.95 (*2-89021-218-1*, Pub. by La Courte Ech) Firefly Bks Ltd.

— Le Tresor de Mon Pere. (Novels in the Premier Roman Ser.). (FRE., Illus.). 64p. (J). (gr. 2-5). 1995. pap. 8.95 (*2-89021-246-7*, Pub. by La Courte Ech) Firefly Bks Ltd.

— Un Vent de Liberte. (Novels in the Roman Plus Ser.). (FRE.). 160p. (YA). (gr. 8 up). 1993. pap. 8.95 (*2-89021-204-1*, Pub. by La Courte Ech) Firefly Bks Ltd.

Croteau, Maureen & Worcester, Wayne. The Essential Researcher: A Complete, Up-to-Date, One-Volume Sourcebook for Journalists, Writers, Students, & Everyone Who Needs Facts Fast. LC 91-58264. 624p. 1993. pap. 20.00 (*0-06-273040-1*, Harper Ref) HarpC.

Croteau, Maureen, jt. auth. see Smith, Martha.

Croteau, Rodney, jt. ed. see Parliment, Thomas H.

***Crother, Brian I., ed.** Caribbean Amphibans & Reptiles. (Illus.). 495p. (C). 1999. 99.95 (*0-12-197955-5*) Acad Pr.

Crothers & Sutinen. Conservation Through Compliance. 65.95 (*0-7546-1071-3*) Ashgate Pub Co.

Crothers, Bronson & Paine, Richmond S. The Natural History of Cerebral Palsy. (Classics in Developmental Medicine Ser.: No. 2). (Illus.). 300p. (C). 1991. text 19.95 (*0-521-41327-3*, Pub. by Mc Keith Pr) Cambridge U Pr.

Crothers, Charles. Social Structure. LC 96-14318. 160p. (C). 1996. 80.00 (*0-415-14946-0*) Routledge.

Crothers, Donald M., jt. auth. see Eisenberg, David S.

Crothers, Edward J. Paragraph Structure Inference. LC 78-27307. 124p. 1979. text 73.25 (*0-89391-016-3*) Ablx Pub.

Crothers, J. Frances. The Puppeteer's Library Guide Vol. II: The Bibliographic Index to the Literature of the World Puppet Theatre: The Puppet As an Educator. LC 71-149991. 366p. 1983. 50.00 (*0-8108-1611-3*) Scarecrow.

Crothers, Lane. Culture & Politics: A Reader. write for info. (*0-312-23300-0*) St Martin.

— Rage on the Right: The American Militia Movement. text. write for info. (*0-312-23248-9*) St Martin.

Crothers, Lane & Lockhart, Charles. Culture & Politics: A Reader. 1999. text. write for info. (*0-312-22543-1*) St Martin.

Crothers, Lane, jt. auth. see Vinzant, Janet C.

Crothers, Marta, ed. see Puri, Ishwar C.

Crothers, Nancy, ed. Worker Protection: Private Sector Ergonomics Programs Yield Positive Results. (Illus.). 137p. (C). 1998. pap. text 30.00 (*0-7881-7482-7*) DIANE Pub.

Crothers, Rachel. Susan & God. 1947. pap. 5.25 (*0-8222-1102-5*) Dramatists Play.

Crothers, Samuel M. Cheerful Giver: Essays. LC 73-156634. (Essay Index Reprint Ser.). 1977. reprint ed. 20.95 (*0-8369-2389-8*) Ayer.

— The Children of Dickens. LC 99-10244. (Illus.). 150p. (J). 1999. pap. 16.95 (*0-89733-475-2*) Academy Chi Pubs.

— Dame School of Experience: And Other Papers. LC 77-156635. (Essay Index Reprint Ser.). 1977. reprint ed. 21.95 (*0-8369-2351-0*) Ayer.

— Gentle Reader. LC 71-39162. (Essay Index Reprint Ser.). 1977. reprint ed. 23.95 (*0-8369-2684-6*) Ayer.

— Oliver Wendell Holmes, the Autocrat & His Fellow-Boarders. LC 72-124231. (Select Bibliographies Reprint Ser.). 1977. 12.95 (*0-8369-5420-3*) Ayer.

— Pardoner's Wallet. LC 78-39161. (Essay Index Reprint Ser.). 1977. reprint ed. 23.95 (*0-8369-2685-4*) Ayer.

— Pleasures of an Absentee Landlord: And Other Essays. LC 72-1326. (Essay Index Reprint Ser.). 1977. reprint ed. 20.95 (*0-8369-2844-X*) Ayer.

— Three Lords of Destiny (1913) 130p. 1998. reprint ed. pap. 14.95 (*0-7661-0499-0*) Kessinger Pub.

Crothers, Samuel M., intro. Book of Friendship. LC 76-98079. (Granger Index Reprint Ser.). 1977. 21.95 (*0-8369-6074-2*) Ayer.

Crothers, T. D. Inebriety: A Clinical Treatise on the Etiology, Symptomotology, Neurosis, Psychosis & Treatment & Medico-Legal Relations. Grob, Gerald N., ed. LC 80-1221. (Addiction in America Ser.). 1981. reprint ed. lib. bdg. 33.95 (*0-405-13576-9*) Ayer.

— Morphinism & Narcomanias from Other Drugs: Their Etiology, Treatment, & Medicolegal Relations. Grob, Gerald N., ed. LC 80-1220. (Addiction in America Ser.). 1981. reprint ed. lib. bdg. 31.95 (*0-405-13577-7*) Ayer.

***Crothers, Tim.** Greatest Athletes of the 20th Century. 2000. pap. text 19.95 (*1-892129-18-3*) Total Sprts.

— Sports Illustrated's Greatest Teams. (Illus.). 176p. 2000. 29.95 (*1-892129-91-4*) Total Sprts.

***Crothers, Timothy.** Windows NT Network Security. McKenna, Jill, ed. 1999. pap. write for info. (*1-58143-020-5*, PSG2NTNS) Prosoft I-net.

— Windows NT Network Security: A4, Version 3.07. McKenna, Jill, ed. (CIW Security Professional Track A4 Ser.). (Illus.). 1999. pap. write for info. (*1-58143-090-6*) Prosoft I-net.

***Crothers, Timothy & Jones, Grant.** Windows NT Network Security: Version 3.07. McKenna, Jill, ed. (CIW Security Professional Track Ser.). (Illus.). 1999. pap. write for info. (*1-58143-054-X*) Prosoft I-net.

***Crothers, Timothy & Stanger, James.** Network Security & Firewalls: A4, Version 3.07. McKenna, Jill & Oberman, David, eds. (CIW Security Professional Track A4 Ser.). (Illus.). 1999. pap. write for info. (*1-58143-089-2*) Prosoft I-net.

— Network Security & Firewalls: Version 3.07. (CIW Security Professional Track Ser.). (Illus.). 1999. pap. write for info. (*1-58143-053-1*) Prosoft I-net.

— Security Auditing, Attacks & Threat Analysis: A4, Version 3.07. Lane, Susan M., ed. (CIW Security Professional Track A4 Ser.). (Illus.). 1999. pap. write for info. (*1-58143-091-4*) Prosoft I-net.

— Security Auditing, Attacks & Threat Analysis: Version 3.07. McKenna, Jill, ed. (CIW Security Professional Track Ser.). (Illus.). 1999. pap. write for info. (*1-58143-055-8*) Prosoft I-net.

***Crothers, William L.** American-Built Clipper Ship. 560p. 2000. pap. 39.95 (*0-07-135823-4*) McGraw.

Crots, Marcia. Manners. LC 97-69233. (Illus.). 24p. (J). (gr. k-3). 1998. pap. 6.95 (*1-57197-086-X*) Pentland Pr.

Crotti, A., jt. auth. see Brambilla, R.

Crotti, Renato. Waiting for the Bus: The Private Cold War of Renato Crotti. Rosenthal, Raymond, tr. from ITA. LC 94-5603. 320p. (Orig.). 1994. pap. 14.95 (*0-942963-46-6*) Distinctive Pub.

***Crotts, John C., et al, eds.** Global Alliances in Tourism & Hospitality Management. LC 99-38667. 166p. 1999. pap. text 24.95 (*0-7890-0818-1*) Haworth Pr.

— Global Alliances in Tourism & Hospitality Management. LC 99-38667. 166p. (C). 1999. 39.95 (*0-7890-0783-5*) Haworth Pr.

Crotts, John C. & Ryan, Chris A., eds. Marketing Issues in Pacific Area Tourism. LC 96-52392. (Journal of Travel & Tourism Marketing Monograph Ser.: Vol. 6, No. 1). 136p. (C). 1997. 39.95 (*0-7890-0029-6*); pap. text 14.95 (*0-7890-0310-4*) Haworth Pr.

Crotts, John C. & Van Raaij, W.F., eds. Economic Psychology of Travel & Tourism. (Journal of Travel & Tourism Marketing). (Illus.). 156p. 1995. lib. bdg. 39.95 (*1-56024-705-3*) Haworth Pr.

Crotts, Stephen M. The Beautiful Attitudes: The Wisdom of the Beatitudes. 82p. (Orig.). 1996. pap. 6.25 (*0-7880-0717-3*) CSS OH.

— Saint Nicholas Speaks. 1996. pap. 2.95 (*1-55673-399-2*) CSS OH.

***Crotts, Stephen M.** Wearing the Wind: Sermons for Sundays after Pentecost, Middle Third. LC 99-32681. (First Lessons Ser.). 80p. 1999. pap. 8.50 (*0-7880-1385-8*) CSS OH.

***Crotty.** Americas Choice 2000. 2000. pap. 19.00 (*0-8133-6798-0*, Pub. by Westview) HarpC.

Crotty, ed. Political Parties in the 21st Century. (C). 1998. text. write for info. (*0-321-01354-9*) Addson-Wesley Educ.

Crotty, Cameron, jt. auth. see Seiter, Charles.

Crotty, Daniel. Four Years Campaigning in the Army of the Potomac. (Illus.). 220p. 1995. 24.00 (*1-883926-02-5*) Belle Grv Pub.

Crotty, Gene. Jefferson's Legacy: His Own University. Valenzi, Kathleen D., ed. (Illus.). 96p. 1997. 19.95 (*0-9670312-0-6*) G Crotty.

— Jefferson's Legacy: His Own University. 2nd rev. ed. Valenzi, Kathleen D., ed. (Illus.). 96p. 1998. 19.95 (*0-9670312-1-4*) G Crotty.

Crotty, James & Lan, Michael. Frommer's Monks Guide to New York City. 352p. 1999. 15.95 (*0-02-862755-5*, Pub. by Macmillan) S&S Trade.

Crotty, Jim. How to Talk American: A Guide to Our Native Tongues. LC 97-19794. (Illus.). 256p. 1997. pap. 13.00 (*0-395-78032-2*) HM.

Crotty, Jim & Lane, Michael. California. 384p. 1999. pap. text 19.95 (*0-02-861666-9*, Pub. by Macmillan) S&S Trade.

***Crotty, Kevin.** Dinosongs: Poems to Celebrate a T. Rex Named Sue. (Illus.). 32p. (J). (ps-3). 2000. 12.95 (*0-439-19264-1*) Scholastic Inc.

Crotty, Kevin. The Poetics of Supplication: Homer's "Iliad" & "Odyssey" (Myth & Poetics Ser.). 256p. 1994. text 37.50 (*0-8014-2998-6*) Cornell U Pr.

— Song & Action: The Victory Odes of Pindar. 176p. 1982. text 30.00 (*0-8018-2746-9*) Johns Hopkins.

— Song & Action: The Victory Odes of Pindar. LC 81-48180. 189p. 1982. reprint ed. pap. 58.60 (*0-608-00806-0*, 206159400010) Bks Demand.

Crotty, Lorraine. Days to Remember: An Inspirational Perpetual Calendar & Special Events Record. 372p. 1997. spiral bd. 8.95 (*1-56383-065-5*, 5040) G & R Pub.

Crotty, M. Phenomenology & Nursing Research. 208p. 1996. pap. write for info. (*0-443-05432-0*) Church.

***Crotty, Malcolm, et al, eds.** Termination of Employment Digest. 400p. 2000. pap. 34.95 (*92-2-110842-2*, Pub. by ILO) ILO Pubns Ctr.

***Crotty, Michael.** The Foundations of Social Research. LC 98-202240. 256p. 1998. 74.00 (*0-7619-6105-4*); pap. 24.95 (*0-7619-6106-2*) Sage.

Crotty, Michael. Foundations of Social Research: Meaning & Perspective in the Research Process. 272p. 1998. pap. 39.95 (*1-86448-604-X*, Pub. by Allen & Unwin Pty) Paul & Co Pubs.

Crotty, Patricia M. Family Law in the United States: Changing Perspectives. (Teaching Texts in Law & Politics Ser.: Vol. 7). XII, 165p. (C). 1999. pap. text 24.95 (*0-8204-4183-X*) P Lang Pubng.

— Women & Family Law: Connecting the Public & the Private. (Teaching Texts in Law & Politics Ser.: Vol. 2). XII, 170p. (C). 1998. pap. text 29.95 (*0-8204-3804-9*) P Lang Pubng.

Crotty, Patrick, ed. Modern Irish Poetry: An Anthology. 436p. 1996. pap. 19.95 (*0-85640-561-2*, Pub. by Blackstaff Pr) Dufour.

Crotty, R. Cattle, Economics & Development. 253p. (C). 1996. 40.00 (*0-85198-452-5*) OUP.

Crotty, Raymond. Radical's Response. 170p. 1988. pap. 10.95 (*0-905169-98-0*, Pub. by Poolbeg Pr) Dufour.

Crotty, Robert. The Jew Called Jesus. 1994. pap., teacher ed. 9.95 (*0-85574-165-1*, Pub. by E J Dwyer) Morehouse Pub.

Crotty, Robert B. The Charles Strong Lectures, 1972-1984. (Illus.). xviii, 206p. 1987. pap. 51.50 (*90-04-07863-0*) Brill Academic Pubs.

Crotty, William. America's Choice: The Elections of 1992. 208p. (C). 1993. text 14.95 (*1-56134-252-1*, Dshkn McG-Hill) McGrw-H Hghr Educ.

Crotty, William, ed. Maximizing Voting. (Orig.). 1990. pap. 15.00 (*0-944285-20-1*) Pol Studies.

— Political Participation & American Democracy, 279. LC 91-9175. (Contributions in Political Science Ser.: No. 279). 248p. 1991. 62.95 (*0-313-27652-8*, CPR/, Greenwood Pr) Greenwood.

— Political Parties in Local Areas. LC 86-7093. 272p. 1987. text 34.00 (*0-87049-511-9*) U of Tenn Pr.

Crotty, William, et al, eds. Representing Interests & Interest Group Representation. LC 94-2298. 112p. 1994. 43.50 (*0-8191-9458-1*); pap. 19.00 (*0-8191-9459-X*) U Pr of Amer.

Crotty, William, intro. Political Science Vol. 1: Looking to the Future: The Theory & Practice of Political Science. 237p. (Orig.). 1991. pap. 17.95 (*0-8101-0923-9*) Northwestern U Pr.

— Political Science Vol. 2: Looking to the Future: Comparative Politics, Policy, & International Relations. 294p. (Orig.). 1991. pap. 19.95 (*0-8101-0950-6*) Northwestern U Pr.

— Political Science Vol. 3: Looking to the Future: Political Behavior. 240p. (Orig.). 1991. pap. 17.95 (*0-8101-0952-2*) Northwestern U Pr.

— Political Science Vol. 4: Looking to the Future: American Institutions. 298p. (Orig.). 1991. pap. 19.95 (*0-8101-0954-9*) Northwestern U Pr.

Crotty, William & Jackson, John S., III. Presidential Primaries & Nominations. LC 84-17662. 251p. 1985. pap. 9.95 (*0-87187-260-9*) Congr Quarterly.

Crotty, William & Mileur, Jerome M. America's Choice: The Election of 1996. 2nd ed. LC 97-65305. 224p. 1997. pap. 19.38 (*0-697-36982-X*) McGrw-H Hghr Educ.

Crotty, William J. Decision for the Democrats: Reforming the Party Structure. LC 77-16725. 330p. 1978. reprint ed. pap. 102.30 (*0-608-05941-2*, 206627800008) Bks Demand.

Crotty, William J., jt. auth. see Jackson, John S.

Crotz, D. Keith. Ewaniana: A Bibliography of Joseph & Nesta Ewan. 75p. 1989. 25.00 (*0-929332-01-6*) Amer Botanist.

— Used Book Sales: Less Work & Better Profits. 80p. 1995. pap. 19.00 (*0-917846-32-X*, 95584) Highsmith Pr.

Crotz, D. Keith, ed. see Prentis, Joseph.

***Crouan, Denis.** The Liturgy Betrayed. 125p. 2000. pap. 11.95 (*0-89870-799-4*, Pub. by Ignatius Pr) Midpt Trade.

Crouch, Leanna, ed. One on One: The Imprint Interviews. (Illus.). 219p. 1998. pap. text 13.00 (*0-7881-5937-2*) DIANE Pub.

***Crouch, Alfred.** Design-for-test for Deep Submicron Systems-on-a-chip. 256p. 2000. 75.00 incl. cd-rom (*0-13-089407-9*) P-H.

***Crouch, Alfred, ed.** Design for Test Digital. LC 99-23871. 356p. 1999. 78.00 (*0-13-084827-1*) P-H.

Crouch, Anthony. Inside Counselling: Becoming & Being a Professional Counsellor. 184p. 1997. 55.00 (*0-8039-7528-7*); pap. 19.95 (*0-8039-7529-5*) Sage.

Crouch, Archie R. Christianity in China: A Scholar's Guide to Resources in the Libraries & Archives of the United States. LC 88-18524. 752p. (C). (gr. 13). 1989. text 209.95 (*0-87332-419-6*) M E Sharpe.

Crouch, Barry. The Freedman's Bureau & Black Texans. 216p. 1999. pap. 12.95 (*0-292-71219-7*) U of Tex Pr.

Crouch, Barry A. The Freedmen's Bureau & Black Texans. LC 91-29138. (Illus.). 215p. 1992. 24.95 (*0-292-72475-6*) U of Tex Pr.

Crouch, Barry A. & Brice, Donaly E. Cullen Montgomery Baker, Reconstruction Desperado. LC 97-6677. (Illus.). 240p. 1997. 34.95 (*0-8071-2140-1*) La State U Pr.

Crouch, Barry A., jt. auth. see Van Cleve, John V.

Crouch, Ben M. & Marquart, James W. An Appeal to Justice: Litigated Reform of Texas Prisons. (Illus.). 304p. 1989. 30.00 (*0-292-70407-0*) U of Tex Pr.

Crouch, Bill, Jr., ed. see Gould, Chester.

Crouch, Bradley W. How to Buy & Maintain a Used Car: For the Non-Mechanical Person. LC 86-72180. (Illus.). 162p. (Orig.). 1988. pap. 9.95 (*0-940057-00-X*) Amer Pac Pub.

Crouch, Brodie. Jornada Del Muerto: A Pageant of the Desert. LC 87-90676. (Western Lands & Waters Ser.: Vol. XV). 219p. 1989. 28.50 (*0-87062-180-7*) A H Clark.

Crouch, Bruce R. & Chamala, Shankarish, eds. Extension Education & Rural Development, Vol. 1. LC 79-41221. 397p. 1981. reprint ed. pap. 123.10 (*0-608-08227-9*, 202963000001) Bks Demand.

— Extension Education & Rural Development, Vol. 2. LC 79-41221. 351p. 1981. reprint ed. pap. 108.90 (*0-608-08228-7*, 202963000002) Bks Demand.

An Asterisk (*) at the beginning of an entry indicates that the title is appearing for the first time.

Crouch, Charles E. Principles of New Testament Christianity. 1984. pap. 8.25 (*0-89137-546-5*) Quality Pubns.

— Studies in Galations. 1992. pap. 7.75 (*0-89137-137-0*) Quality Pubns.

***Crouch, Christopher.** Design Culture in Liverpool, 1880-1914: The Origins of the Liverpool School of Architecture. (Illus.). 256p. 1999. 59.95 (*0-85323-884-7*, Pub. by Liverpool Univ Pr); pap. 29.95 (*0-85323-894-4*, Pub. by Liverpool Univ Pr) Intl Spec Bk.

— Modernism in Art, Design, & Architecture. LC 98-28318. 35p. 1999. text 65.00 (*0-312-21830-3*) St Martin.

Crouch, Christopher. Modernism in Art, Design & Architecture. LC 98-28318. viii, 204 p. 1999. pap. 21.95 (*0-312-21832-X*) St Martin.

Crouch, Clifford W. Cuba: Major World nations. LC 97-23543. (Major World Nations Ser.). (Illus.). 144p. (YA). (gr. 5 up). 1999. lib. bdg. 19.95 (*0-7910-4736-9*) Chelsea Hse.

Crouch, Colin. Are Skills the Answer? The Political Economy of Skill Creation in Advanced Industrial Societies. (Illus.). 296p. 1999. text 78.00 (*0-19-829438-7*) OUP.

— Attacking Technique. LC 96-78260. (New American Batsford Chess Library). 112p. (Orig.). 1996. pap. 13.50 (*1-879479-38-9*) ICE WA.

— How to Defend in Chess. 2000. pap. text 19.95 (*1-85744-250-4*) Cadgn Bks.

— Industrial Relations & European State Traditions. (Illus.). 428p. 1994. reprint ed. pap. text 26.00 (*0-19-827974-4*) OUP.

— Social Change in Western Europe. LC 99-32731. (Illus.). 568p. 2000. pap. text 32.00 (*0-19-878068-0*) OUP.

— Social Change in Western Europe. LC 99-32731. (Illus.). 480p. 2000. text 70.00 (*0-19-874275-4*) OUP.

Crouch, Colin, ed. Social Research & Social Reform: Essays in Honour of A. H. Halsey. (Illus.). 420p. 1993. text 85.00 (*0-19-827854-3*) OUP.

Crouch, Colin & Heller, Frank A., eds. Organizational Democracy & Political Processes. LC 83-209112. (International Yearbook of Organizational Democracy Ser.: No. 1). (Illus.). 736p. reprint ed. pap. 200.00 (*0-608-18144-7*, 203283100081) Bks Demand.

Crouch, Colin & Marquand, David, eds. Reinventing Collective Action: From the Global to the Local. (Political Quarterly Ser.). 144p. (Orig.). (C). 1996. pap. text 22.95 (*0-631-19721-4*) Blackwell Pubs.

Crouch, Colin & Pizzorno, Alessandro. Resurgence of Class Conflict in Western Europe since 1968. LC 78-321691. vp. 1977. write for info. (*0-333-19786-0*) Macmillan.

Crouch, Colin & Pizzorno, Alessandro, eds. Resurgence of Class Conflict in Western Europe since 1968, Vol. 1. LC 77-16076. 1983. 49.50 (*0-8419-0355-7*) Holmes & Meier.

— Resurgence of Class Conflict in Western Europe since 1968, Vol. 2. LC 77-16076. 1983. 49.50 (*0-8419-0356-5*) Holmes & Meier.

Crouch, Colin & Streeck, Wolfgang. Political Economy & Modern Capitalism: Mapping Convergence & Diversity. LC 97-68597. 240p. 1997. 79.95 (*0-7619-5652-2*); pap. 26.95 (*0-7619-5653-0*) Sage.

Crouch, Colin & Traxler, Franz. Organized Industrial Relations in Europe: What Future? LC 94-74469. x, 331 p. 1995. 87.95 (*1-85972-061-7*, Pub. by Avebry) Ashgate Pub Co.

Crouch, Colin, jt. auth. see Mednis, Edmar.

Crouch, Colin, jt. ed. see Baglioni, Guido.

Crouch, Colin, ed. see Dore, Ronald.

Crouch, D. History of Architecture. 374p. (C). 1984. pap. 61.25 (*0-07-014524-5*) McGraw.

Crouch, Daniel J. Archaeological Investigations of the Kiowa & Comanche Indian Agency Commissaries 34-Cm 232. (Contributions of the Museum of the Great Plains Ser.: No. 7). (Illus.). 1978. pap. 11.30 (*0-685-91362-7*) Mus Great Plains.

Crouch, Daniel J., et al. Archaeological Investigations along the Waurika Pipeline. (Contributions of the Museum of the Great Plains Ser.: No. 5). (Illus.). 1977. pap. 10.50 (*0-685-88670-0*) Mus Great Plains.

Crouch, David. The Image of Aristocracy: In Britain, 1000-1300. LC 92-1052. (Illus.). 408p. (C). (gr. 13). 1992. 100.00 (*0-415-01911-7*, A6992) Routledge.

***Crouch, David.** Leisure & Tourism Geographies: Practices & Geographical Knowledge. LC 99-45586. (Critical Geographies Ser.). (Illus.). 304p. 1999. pap. 31.99 (*0-415-18109-7*) Routledge.

— The Reign of King Stephen, 1135-1154. LC 99-16588. 384p. 2000. pap. 29.66 (*0-582-22657-0*) Addison-Wesley.

Crouch, David. William Marshal: Court, Career & Chicalry in the Angevin Empire, 1147-1219. (C). 1994. pap. text 21.56 (*0-582-03786-7*, Pub. by Addison-Wesley) Longman.

***Crouch, David, ed.** Leisure & Tourism Geographies: Leisure/Tourism Practices & Geographical Knowledge. LC 99-45586. 304p. (C). 2000. text. write for info. (*0-415-18108-9*) Routledge.

Crouch, David & Ward, Colin. The Allotment: Its Landscape & Culture. 336p. (Orig.). (YA). (gr. 10). 1995. pap. 20.95 (*0-907123-16-3*, Pub. by Five Leaves) AK Pr Dist.

***Crouch, David J. F.** Piety, Fraternity & Power: Religious Gilds in Late Medieval Yorkshire, 1389-1547. LC 99-46618. (Warfare in History Ser.). (Illus.). 288p. 2000. 75.00 (*0-9529734-4-8*, Suffolk Records Soc) Boydell & Brewer.

Crouch, Donia C. Texas Twosomes: Married for Life. LC 98-33589. (Illus.). 104p. 1998. 21.95 (*1-57168-233-3*, Eakin Pr) Sunbelt Media.

***Crouch, Dora P. & Johnson, June G.** Traditions in Architecture: Africa, America, Asia & Oceania. LC 99-39260. 400p. (C). 2000. pap. 35.00 (*0-19-508891-3*) OUP.

— Traditions in Architecture: Africa, America, Asia & Oceania. LC 99-39260. (Illus.). 400p. 2000. text 65.00 (*0-19-508890-5*) OUP.

Crouch, Eleanor & Labbe, Marilyn. Crouch. The Crouches, 1627-1998. 324p. 1998. pap. 48.00 (*0-8328-9569-5*); lib. bdg. 58.00 (*0-8328-9568-7*) Higginson Bk Co.

Crouch, Eleanor M. French Family, 1555-1993: Genealogy of Thomas French & Susan Riddlesdale, Boston, 1629, & Their New Hampshire & Maine Descendants. 100p. 1994. reprint ed. pap. 19.50 (*0-8328-4050-5*); reprint ed. lib. bdg. 29.50 (*0-8328-4049-1*) Higginson Bk Co.

Crouch, Elizabeth. Showcase of Interior Design: Midwest. LC 96-36119. 1996. write for info. (*1-883065-11-9*) Rockport Vitae Pub.

Crouch, Evelyn B., compiled by. History of Montgomery County, Mississippi. 612p. 1993. 70.00 (*0-88107-221-4*) Curtis Media.

Crouch, Evelyn B. & Genola, Christie C. Montgomery County, Mississippi Cemetery Records. 407p. (Orig.). 1996. pap. 42.50 (*1-885480-09-1*) Pioneer Pubng.

Crouch, Gregory. Route Finding: Navigation with a Map & Compass. LC 99-25394. (Illus.). 128p. 1999. pap. 6.95 (*1-56044-820-2*) Falcon Pub Inc.

Crouch, Harold. The Army & Politics in Indonesia. LC 88-47777. (Politics & International Relations of Southeast Asia Ser.). 376p. 1988. reprint ed. pap. text 17.95 (*0-8014-9506-7*) Cornell U Pr.

— Government & Society in Malaysia. 300p. 1997. pap. 34.95 (*1-86448-183-8*, Pub. by Allen & Unwin Pty) Paul & Co Pubs.

— Government & Society in Malaysia. (Asia East by South Ser.). (Illus.). 280p. 1996. text 45.00 (*0-8014-3218-9*); pap. text 17.95 (*0-8014-8310-7*) Cornell U Pr.

Crouch, Holmes. Keeping Good Records. 1998. 72.00 (*90-5704-081-6*, Pub. by IPG Chicago) Gordon & Breach.

Crouch, Holmes F. Being Self-Employed: Understanding the IRS & the Rewards of a Sole Proprietor. 2nd rev. ed. Crouch, Irma J., ed. LC 97-75097. (Series 100 Tax Guides: Vol. 101). (Illus.). 224p. 1998. pap. 19.95 (*0-944817-41-6*, T/G 101) Allyear Tax.

— Citizens Working Abroad: Claiming the "Up to" 80,000 Annual Exclusion for Physical Presence Overseas. Crouch, Irma J., ed. LC 97-75169. (Series 100 Tax Guides: Vol. 105). (Illus.). 224p. 1998. pap. 19.95 (*0-944817-44-0*, T/G 105) Allyear Tax.

***Crouch, Holmes F.** Contesting IRS Penalties: The Role of Reasonable Cause, Adequate Disclosure & Appeals Within the IRS. Crouch, Irma J., ed. LC 99-72408. (Series 500 Tax Guides: ol. 504). (Illus.). 224p. 1999. pap. 19.95 (*0-944817-58-0*) Allyear Tax.

Crouch, Holmes F. Decisions When Retiring: Living Longer with No Safe Haven from Taxation. 2nd rev. ed. Crouch, Irma J., ed. LC 97-73075. (Series 300 Tax Guides: Vol. 301). (Illus.). 224p. 1998. pap. 19.95 (*0-944817-37-8*, T/G 301) Allyear Tax.

— Deducting Job Expenses: Surpassing the 2AGI Floor for Telecommuting & Other Employee Expenses. Crouch, Irma J., ed. LC 97-75163. (Series 100 Tax Guides: Vol. 102). (Illus.). 224p. 1998. pap. 19.95 (*0-944817-42-4*, T/G 102) Allyear Tax.

— Disagreeing with the IRS: How to Stand Your Ground, Reply to Notices & Correct Erroneous Assessments. Crouch, Irma J., ed. LC 97-75302. (Series 500 Tax Guides: Vol. 503). (Illus.). 224p. 1998. pap. 19.95 (*0-944817-47-5*, T/G 503) Allyear Tax.

***Crouch, Holmes F.** Family Tax Strategies: All Exemptions, Credits & Gifts Between Parents, Children & Grandparents. Crouch, Irma J., ed. LC 00-132601. (Series 100 Tax Guides: Vol. 103). (Illus.). 224p. 2000. pap. 19.95 (*0-944817-59-9*, Pub. by Allyear Tax) IPG Chicago.

Crouch, Holmes F. Going into Tax Court: The Role of Timely Petitions, Pretrial Discovery & Being Alert to "Legal Trickery" 2nd rev. ed. Crouch, Irma J., ed. LC 97-75303. (Series 500 Tax Guides: Vol. 505). (Illus.). 224p. 1998. pap. 19.95 (*0-944817-48-3*, T/G 505) Allyear Tax.

— Investor Gains & Losses: Matching Broker Reportings with Cost Basis & Using Preferential Tax Rates. 2nd rev. ed. Crouch, Irma J., ed. LC 98-70244. (Series 200 Tax Guides: Vol. 201). (Illus.). 224p. 1998. pap. 19.95 (*0-944817-49-1*) Allyear Tax.

— Keeping Good Records: How to Distinguish Betwen"Keeping Everything" & "Selective Purging" 2nd rev. ed. Crouch, Irma J., ed. LC 97-75299. (Series 500 Tax Guides: Vol. 501). (Illus.). 224p. 1998. pap. 19.95 (*0-944817-45-9*, T/G 501) Allyear Tax.

— Making Partnerships Work: Importance of Written Agreement for Capital Accounting & Distributive Shore Items. 2nd rev. ed. Crouch, Irma J., ed. LC 98-70247. (Series 200 Tax Guides: Vol. 204). (Illus.). 224p. 1998. pap. 19.95 (*0-944817-52-1*) Allyear Tax.

— Owning Natural Resources: Mining "Tax Gold" (Depletion Allowances) When Extracting from the Earth's Crust. Crouch, Irma J., ed. LC 98-70249. (Series 400 Tax Guides: Vol. 402). (Illus.). 224p. 1998. pap. 19.95 (*0-944817-54-8*) Allyear Tax.

— Rental Real Estate: Reaping the "Tax Blessings" of Depreciation, Passive Losses & Like-Kind Exchanges. 2nd rev. ed. Crouch, Irma J., ed. LC 98-70248. (Series 400 Tax Guides: Vol. 401). (Illus.). 224p. 1998. pap. text 19.95 (*0-944817-53-X*) Allyear Tax.

— Resolving Divorce Issues: Avoiding the "Tax Traps" of Child Support, Alimony & Property Settlement. 2nd rev. ed. Crouch, Irma J., ed. LC 97-75167. (Series 100 Tax Guides: Vol. 104). (Illus.). 224p. 1998. pap. 19.95 (*0-944817-43-2*, T/G 104) Allyear Tax.

— Selling Your Business: Itemizing & Pricing All Tangibles, Intangibles & That "Stickler": Goodwill. 2nd rev. ed. Crouch, Irma J., ed. LC 98-70251. (Series 400 Tax Guides: Vol. 405). (Illus.). 224p. 1998. pap. 19.95 (*0-944817-56-4*, T/G 405) Allyear Tax.

— Selling Your Home: How to Recover All of Your Costs When Claiming the "Up to" 500,000 Capital Gain Exclusion. 2nd rev. ed. Crouch, Irma J., ed. LC 98-70250. (Series 400 Tax Guides: Vol. 404). (Illus.). 224p. 1998. pap. 19.95 (*0-944817-55-6*, T/G 403) Allyear Tax.

— Side Business Ventures: Applying the 10 Profit Motive Tests to Your Entrepreneurial Dreams. 2nd rev. ed. Crouch, Irma J., ed. LC 98-70245. (Series 200 Tax Guides). (Illus.). 224p. 1998. pap. text 19.95 (*0-944817-50-5*) Allyear Tax.

— Simplifying Your Estate: Goals to Pursue for Reducing Attorney Fees & Speeding Distributions to Heirs. Crouch, Irma J., ed. LC 99-72407. (Series 300 Tax Guides: Vol. 303). (Illus.). 224p. 1999. pap. 19.95 (*0-944817-57-2*, Pub. by Allyear Tax) IPG Chicago.

***Crouch, Holmes F.** Small C & S Corporations: Avoiding IRS Suspicions of Improper Personal Gain. Crouch, Irma J., ed. LC 00-132600. (Series 200 Tax Guides: Vol. 205). (Illus.). 224p. 2000. pap. 19.95 (*0-944817-60-2*, Pub. by Allyear Tax) IPG Chicago.

Crouch, Holmes F. Starting Your Business: How Bank Account Discipline, Cost of Goods & Deferred Deductions Affect Choice of Form. 2nd rev. ed Crouch, Irma J., ed. LC 98-70246. (Series 200 Tax Guides: Vol. 203). (Illus.). 224p. 1998. pap. 19.95 (*0-944817-51-3*, T/G 203) Allyear Tax.

— Trusts & Trustees: What Attorneys & Promoters Do Not Explain. Crouch, Irma J., ed. LC 93-72405. (Series 300 Tax Guides: Vol. 305). (Illus.). 224p. 1994. pap. 16.95 (*0-944817-19-X*) Allyear Tax.

— Winning Your Audit: The Magic of Positive Attitude, Good Preparation & Timely Responses to IRS. 2nd rev. ed. Crouch, Irma J., ed. LC 97-75300. (Series 500 Tax Guides: Vol. 502). (Illus.). 224p. 1998. pap. 19.95 (*0-944817-46-7*, T/G 502) Allyear Tax.

— Writing Your Will: Contingency Planning for Executor, Heirs & Property Conveyance. 2nd rev. ed. Crouch, Irma J., ed. LC 97-73079. (Series 300 Tax Guides: Vol. 302). (Illus.). 224p. 1998. pap. 19.95 (*0-944817-38-6*, T/G 302) Allyear Tax.

— Your Executor Duties: The Role of Independent Administration for Inventory, Appraisals & For 706. 2nd rev. ed. Crouch, Irma J., ed. LC 97-73080. (Series 300 Tax Guides: No. 304). (Illus.). 224p. 1998. pap. 19.95 (*0-944817-39-4*, T/G 304) Allyear Tax.

— Your Trustee Duties: How to Dissect a Trust Instrument for Managing an Estate. Crouch, Irma J., ed. LC 97-73081. (Series 300 Tax Guides: No. 305). (Illus.). 224p. 1998. pap. 19.95 (*0-944817-40-8*, T/G 305) Allyear Tax.

Crouch, Howard E. Damien & Dutton, Two Josephs on Molokai. LC 98-93410. 336p. 1998. 18.00 (*0-9606330-4-9*) Damien-Dutton Soc.

Crouch, Howard E. & Augustine, Sister Mary. Once over & Lightly. 2nd ed. LC 94-84819. 239p. 1996. reprint ed. 12.00 (*0-9606330-3-0*) Damien-Dutton Soc.

Crouch, Howard E. & Sr. Mary Augustine. After Damien - Dutton: Yankee Soldier at Molokai. LC 81-67534. (Illus.). 144p. (Orig.). 1981. pap. 5.95 (*0-9606330-0-6*) Damien-Dutton Soc.

— Two Hearts, One Fire: A Glimpse Behind the Mask of Leprosy. LC 89-50271. 240p. (Orig.). 1989. pap. 12.00 (*0-9606330-1-4*) Damien-Dutton Soc.

Crouch, Howard R. Civil War Artifacts: A Guide for the Historian. (Illus.). 238p. 1995. 39.95 (*0-9613541-5-7*) North South Trader.

Crouch, Irma J., ed. see Crouch, Holmes F.

Crouch, Isabel, jt. auth. see Dubois, Betty L.

Crouch, J. Page. Flexography Primer. 2nd rev. ed. LC 97-74132. 192p. (C). 1998. pap. text 25.00 (*0-88362-204-1*, 14302) GATFPress.

Crouch, James E. Functional Human Anatomy. 4th ed. LC 83-24862. (Illus.). 645p. 1985. text 47.50 (*0-8121-0930-9*) Lppncott W & W.

— Text-Atlas of Cat Anatomy. LC 68-25206. 415p. reprint ed. pap. 128.70 (*0-608-13288-8*, 205601600044) Bks Demand.

Crouch, James E. & Carr, Micheline H. Anatomy & Physiology: A Laboratory Manual. LC 76-56507. (Illus.). 369p. (C). 1989. reprint ed. student ed. 25.00 (*0-87484-356-1*) Circle Pr CA.

Crouch, James E., tr. see Becker, Jurgen.

Crouch, James K. & Bachman, Steven B., eds. Tectonics & Sedimentation along the California Margin. (Illus.). 188p. (Orig.). 1984. pap. 7.00 (*1-878861-34-4*) Pac Section SEPM.

Crouch, Leanna. One on One: The Imprint Interviews. (Illus.). 224p. (Orig.). pap. 19.95 (*1-895897-19-X*) Somerville Hse.

Crouch, Leon. Commentary on First & Second Thessalonians. 1993. pap. 8.25 (*0-89137-138-9*) Quality Pubns.

— Deity of Christ. 111p. (Orig.). 1982. pap. 2.50 (*0-933672-43-8*, C-1875) Star Bible.

Crouch, Leroy T. Things My Daddy Said. (Illus.). 192p. 1999. pap. 10.95 (*0-7392-0293-6*, PO3403) Morris Pubng.

— A Tribute to My Mother. 102p. 1999. pap. 6.95 (*0-7392-0279-0*, PO3374) Morris Pubng.

Crouch, M. A. & Roberts, L., eds. The Family in Medical Practice. (Illus.). xiv, 256p. 1986. pap. 37.00 (*0-387-96372-3*) Spr-Verlag.

Crouch, Marcus. Ivan: Stories of Old Russia. (Oxford Myths & Legends Ser.). (Illus.). 80p. (YA). (gr. 5-12). 1989. 20.00 (*0-19-274135-7*) OUP.

Crouch, Margaret, ed. Renewable Energy Dictionary. 500p. 1982. 29.75 (*0-86619-161-5*, 11073-BK) Vols Tech Asst.

— Six Simple Pumps. 94p. 1983. pap. 9.50 (*0-86619-166-6*, E-11075) Vols Tech Asst.

Crouch, Margaret & Doak, Leonard, eds. Village Technology Handbook. rev. ed. 425p. 1987. 19.95 (*0-86619-275-1*) Vols Tech Asst.

Crouch, Margaret, ed. see Baldwin, Sam.

Crouch, Margaret, ed. see Bowman, Thomas.

Crouch, Margaret, ed. see Weber, Fred R. & Stoney, Carol.

Crouch, Margaret, ed. see Wilson, David G.

***Crouch, Margaret A.** Thinking about Sexual Harassment: A Guide for the Perplexed. 336p. 2000. pap. 22.95 (*0-19-514377-9*); text 60.00 (*0-19-514030-3*) OUP.

Crouch, Mark A. The Ugly Truth about Rush Limbaugh: And the Attempted Hijacking of the 1992 Election. 96p. (Orig.). 1996. pap. 10.00 (*1-887934-96-0*) Delmax.

Crouch, Martin & Porter, Robert. Understanding Soviet Politics Through Literature. 300p. 1984. pap. text 16.95 (*0-04-320158-X*) Routledge.

Crouch, Mary A. & Stedman, Jan. Christmas Favorites. 1983. 8.95 (*0-614-29886-5*); pap. text 6.95 (*0-9613770-0-3*) Christmas Favorites.

Crouch, Michael. Relic of Empire: To South Arabia & Beyond. 192p. 1994. text 39.50 (*1-85043-739-4*, Pub. by I B T) St Martin.

***Crouch, Millie.** Me? A Missionary? (Illus.). 123p. 1999. pap. 8.95 (*1-888796-17-0*) ABWE Pubng.

— A Poetic Interlude. 107p. 1999. pap. 5.95 (*1-888796-18-9*) ABWE Pubng.

Crouch, Mira & Manderson, Lenore. New Motherhood: Cultural & Personal Transitions in the 1980's. 222p. 1993. text 61.00 (*2-88124-945-0*) Gordon & Breach.

Crouch, Owen. Expository Preaching & Teaching - Revelation. LC 85-71665. 416p. 1985. pap. 9.99 (*0-89900-207-2*) College Pr Pub.

Crouch, P. E. & Van Der Schaft, A. J. Variational & Hamiltonian Control Systems. (Lecture Notes in Control & Information Sciences: Vol. 101). vi, 121p. 1987. 31.95 (*0-387-18372-8*) Spr-Verlag.

Crouch, Paul F. I Had No Father but God: A Personal Letter to My Two Sons. (Illus.). 263p. (Orig.). 1993. pap. 9.95 (*0-9636407-0-4*) Trinity Broadcast.

— Omega Code: Another Has Risen from The Dead. 1999. 19.99 (*1-888848-35-9*) Western Front.

Crouch, Phoebe F., jt. auth. see Aldridge, Jean P.

Crouch, Richard. Family Law Checklists, 2 vols., Set. LC 90-46750. 1992. 210.00 (*0-685-31928-8*) West Group.

Crouch, Robin. The Americas: A Sticker Atlas of Exploration & Discovery. (Illus.). 21p. (Orig.). (J). (gr. 1-3). 1993. pap. 5.95 (*0-8249-8556-7*, Ideals Child) Hambleton-Hill.

Crouch, Stanley. The All-American Skin Game, or the Decoy of Race: The Long & Short of It, 1990-1994. 267p. 1997. pap. 12.00 (*0-679-77660-5*) Vin Bks.

— Always in Pursuit. 1999. pap. 14.00 (*0-375-70168-0*) Vin Bks.

— Always in Pursuit: Fresh American Perspectives, 1995-1997. LC 97-23796. 321p. 1998. 25.00 (*0-375-40153-9*) Pantheon.

***Crouch, Stanley.** Don't the Moon Look Lonesome? A Novel in Blues & Swing. LC 99-48835. 531p. 2000. 26.95 (*0-375-40932-7*) Pantheon.

Crouch, Stanley R., jt. auth. see Ingle, James D., Jr.

Crouch, Steve. Fog & Sun - Sea & Stone. (Illus.). 160p. 1991. reprint ed. 29.95 (*0-945092-25-3*); reprint ed. pap. 21.95 (*0-945092-26-1*) EZ Nature.

— Steinbeck Country. 192p. 1995. reprint ed. text 35.00 (*0-9645311-0-0*) Pilothse Pub.

Crouch, Steven L. & Starfield, Anthony M. Boundary Element Methods in Solid Mechanics. 322p. (C). 1990. text 49.95 (*0-685-46015-0*); pap. text 34.95 (*0-04-445913-0*) Routledge.

Crouch, Steven L., ed. see Rock Mechanics Symposium Staff.

Crouch, Susan C. Western Responses to Tanzanian Socialism, 1967-83. 300p. 1987. text 77.95 (*0-566-05455-8*, Pub. by Dartmth Pub) Ashgate Pub Co.

Crouch, T. Matrix Methods Applied to Engineering Rigid Body Mechanics. LC 80-41186. 385p. 1981. 159.00 (*0-08-024245-6*, Pub. by Pergamon Repr) Franklin.

Crouch, Tammy. Carpal Tunnel Syndrome & Repetitive Stress Injuries: The Comprehensive Guide to Prevention, Treatment & Recovery. 2nd ed. LC 96-8576. (Illus.). 164p. (Orig.). 1996. pap. 14.95 (*1-883319-50-1*) Frog Ltd CA.

***Crouch, Tanja.** This Joint Is Jumpin' The Illustrated History of Swing. (Illus.). 224p. 2000. 30.00 (*1-57500-133-0*, Pub. by TV Bks) HarpC.

Crouch, Thomas C., ed. A Leader of Volunteers: Frederick Funston & the 20th Kansas in the Philippines. (Illus.). 249p. 1984. 25.00 (*0-87291-167-5*) Coronado Pr.

Crouch, Timothy J. The Book of Offices & Services: After the Usage of the Order of Saint Luke. 92p. (Orig.). 1988. 12.95 (*1-878009-02-8*); pap. 8.95 (*1-878009-01-X*) Order St Luke Pubns.

Crouch, Timothy J. & Babb, Mark R. And Also with You - Year A: Worship Resources Based on the Revised Common Lectionary. 2nd ed. (Illus.). 168p. 1995. reprint ed. spiral bd. 24.95 (*1-878009-26-5*, OSL Pubns) Order St Luke Pubns.

Crouch, Timothy J., et al. And Also with You - Year B: Worship Resources Based on the Revised Common Lectionary, Vol. 2. 2nd rev. ed. (And Also with You Ser.). (Illus.). 168p. 1996. spiral bd. 24.95 (*1-878009-30-3*, 303, OSL Pubns); ring bd. 24.95 (*1-878009-31-1*, 311, OSL Pubns) Order St Luke Pubns.

— And Also with You - Year C: Worship Resources Based on the Revised Common Lectionary. (And Also with You Ser.). (Illus.). 168p. 1994. spiral bd. 24.95 (*1-878009-17-6*, OSL Pubns); ring bd. 24.95 (*1-878009-18-4*, OSL Pubns) Order St Luke Pubns.

Crouch, Timothy J., et al. Worship Resources Based on the Revised Common Lectionary. 2nd ed. (And Also with You Ser.: Vol. 1). 168p. 1995. ring bd. 24.95 (*1-878009-12-5*) Order St Luke Pubns.

Crouch, Timothy J., ed. see O'Donnell, Michael J.

Crouch, Timothy J., ed. see Rattenbury, J. Ernest.

Crouch, Timothy J., ed. see Westerhoff, John H. & Willimon, William H.

Crouch, Timothy J., ed. see Young, Carlton R.

Crouch, Tom D. Aiming for the Stars: The Dreamers & Doers of the Space Age. LC 99-13822. (Illus.). 352p. 1999. 29.95 (*1-56098-386-8*) Smithsonian.

— Bishop's Boys: A Life of Wilbur & Orville Wright. (Illus.). 586p. 1990. pap. 21.95 (*0-393-30695-X*) Norton.

— Bleriot XI: The Story of a Classic Aircraft, Vol. 5. LC 81-607931. (Famous Aircraft of the National Air & Space Museum Ser.). (Illus.). 144p. (Orig.). 1982. pap. 14.95 (*0-87474-345-1*, CRBLP) Smithsonian.

Crouch, Tom D. & Spencer, Alex M., eds. History of Rocketry & Astronautics. (AAS History Ser.: Vol. 14). 222p. 1993. 50.00 (*0-87703-374-9*, Am Astronaut Soc) Univelt Inc.

— History of Rocketry & Astronautics. LC 57-43769. (AAS History Ser.: Vol. 14). (Illus.). 222p. 1993. pap. 35.00 (*0-87703-375-7*, Am Astronaut Soc) Univelt Inc.

Crouch, Tom D. & United States Air Force Academy Staff. The Genesis of Flight: The Aeronautical History Collection of Colonel Richard Gimbel. LC 99-10107. (Illus.). 380p. 2000. 60.00 (*0-295-97811-2*) U of Wash Pr.

Crouch, Tom D., jt. ed. see Goetzmann, William H.

***Crouch, Van.** Dare to Succeed. 1999. 9.99 (*1-57778-045-0*) Albury Pub.

Crouch, Van. Take It Back! What the Enemy Has Stolen God Has Promised to You, Now Is the Time To... 256p. 1998. pap. 9.99 (*1-57778-021-3*, Pub. by Albury Pub) Appalach Bk Dist.

— Winning 101: Insight & Motivation to Help You Achieve Excellence. 1998. 14.99 (*1-56292-457-5*) Honor Bks OK.

— Winning 101. 101. LC 96-123473. 1996. pap. 6.99 (*1-56292-083-9*, HB-083) Honor Bks OK.

Crouch, Viv & Sydenham, Peter, intros. Instrumentation & Measurement, Third Australasian Conference, 1994: Test & Evaluation in the Asia-Pacific Region. (National Conference Publication Ser.: No. 94-5). (Illus.). 536p. (Orig.). 1994. pap. 77.00 (*0-85825-601-0*, Pub. by Inst Engrs Aust-EA Bks) Accents Pubns.

***Crouch, Walter B.** Death & Closure in Biblical Narrative. LC 97-42850. (Studies in Biblical Literature: Vol. 7). 264p. (C). 2000. text 56.95 (*0-8204-3950-9*) P Lang Pubng.

Croucher. We Refuse to Starve in Silence. (C). 1987. pap. 19.50 (*0-85315-681-6*, Pub. by Lawrence & Wishart) NYU Pr.

Croucher, Deborah K., ed. see Croucher, Herman L.

Croucher, Herman L. I Just Want to Play Again. Croucher, Deborah K., ed. (Series of Faith: No. 1). (Illus.). 172p. 1998. pap. 12.95 (*0-9662461-0-1*) H L Croucher.

Croucher, J. H. & Le Gray, Gustave. Plain Directions for Obtaining Photographic Pictures by the Calotype & Energiatype, Also Upon Albumenized Paper & Glass, by Collodion & Albumen, Etc., Etc., Pts. 1[00ad]3. LC 72-9191. (Literature of Photography Ser.). 1979. reprint ed. 17.95 (*0-405-04901-3*) Ayer.

Croucher, John. Exam Scams: Best Cheating Stories & Excuses from Around the World. (Illus.). 168p. 1997. pap. 7.95 (*1-86448-165-X*, Pub. by Allen & Unwin Pty) IPG Chicago.

— Great Frauds & Everyday Scams: True Stories of Adventurers & Innocents. 1998. pap. 8.95 (*1-86448-451-9*, Pub. by Allen & Unwin Pty) IPG Chicago.

Croucher, John S. Operations Research: A First Course. (Illus.). 320p. 1980. pap. text 18.00 (*0-08-024797-0*, Pergamon Pr) Elsevier.

Croucher, Melvin D., jt. ed. see Hair, Michael.

Croucher, Michael, jt. auth. see Reid, Howard.

Croucher, Murlin, ed. Slavic Studies: A Guide to Bibliographies, Encyclopedias, & Handbooks, 2 vols., Set. LC 92-28912. 980p. 1993. 150.00 (*0-8420-2374-7*) Scholarly Res Inc.

Croucher, Norman. High Hopes. large type ed. 288p. 1979. 27.99 (*0-7089-0361-4*) Ulverscroft.

Croucher, Paul. A History of Buddhism in Australia 1848-1988. (Illus.). 160p. 1990. pap. 24.95 (*0-86840-195-1*, Pub. by New South Wales Univ Pr) Intl Spec Bk.

***Croucher, Phil.** The A+ Reference Book: For the Home & Office PC Technician. (Illus.). 2000p. 2000. 25.00 incl. cd-rom (*1-872498-18-3*) Electrocution.

Croucher, Phil. BIOS Companion. 1998. pap. text 29.99 (*0-7897-1825-1*) Que.

***Croucher, Phil.** The Bios Companion: Engineer's Edition. 2nd rev. ed. 550p. 2000. ring bd. 25.00 (*1-872498-10-8*) Electrocution.

Croucher, Phil. Bios Companion: The Book That Doesn't Come with Your Motherboard but Should. 3rd ed. (Companion Ser.). 427p. (gr. 10 up). 1999. pap. 49.95 (*1-889671-20-7*) Advice Pr.

— The Bios Companion: The Book That Should Come with Your Motherboard! (Illus.). 390p. 1993. write for info. (*1-872498-12-4*); pap. text. write for info. (*1-872498-02-7*) Ele4ctrocution.

— Hard Disk Companion. (Companion Ser.). 427p. (gr. 10 up). 1999. pap. 29.95 (*1-889671-21-5*) Advice Pr.

— Motherboard Companion. (Companion Ser.). 427p. 1999. pap. 49.95 (*1-889671-24-X*) Advice Pr.

Croucher, Richard. Engineers at War, 1939-1945. (C). 1982. pap. 9.95 (*0-85036-271-7*, Pub. by MRLN); text 19.95 (*0-85036-270-9*, Pub. by MRLN) Paul & Co Pubs.

Croucher, Rowland. Apart for Busy People. pap. 14.95 (*0-687-05469-9*) Abingdon.

— Delete Title. 384p. 2000. pap. 12.00 (*1-86371-389-1*) Harper SF.

Croucher, Sheila L. Imagining Miami: Ethnic Politics in a Postmodern World. LC 96-41357. (Race, Ethnicity, & Politics Ser.). 250p. 1997. text 45.00 (*0-8139-1704-2*); pap. text 18.00 (*0-8139-1705-0*) U Pr of Va.

Crouchet, Jack. Vietnam Stories: A Judge's Memoir. LC 97-15887. 232p. 1997. 27.50 (*0-87081-453-2*) Univ Pr Colo.

Crouchett, Lawrence P., et al. Visions Toward Tomorrow: A History of the East Bay Afro-American Community, 1852-Present. LC 89-141462. (Illus.). 76p. (Orig.). 1989. pap. 10.00 (*0-9622334-0-4*) N CA Afro-Am Hist.

Crouchley, Arthur Edwin. Investment of Foreign Capital in Egyptian Companies & Public Debt. Wilkins, Mira, ed. LC 76-29989. (European Business Ser.). 1977. reprint ed. lib. bdg. 20.95 (*0-405-09721-2*) Ayer.

***Croue, Jean-Phillipe, et al.** Characterization of Natural Organic Matter in Drinking Water LC 99-41858. 1999. write for info. (*1-58321-015-6*) Am Water Wks Assn.

Croughton, G., et al. Private & Untimetabled Railway Stations: Halts & Stopping Places. 148p. (C). 1985. 75.00 (*0-85361-281-1*) St Mut.

Crouhy. Managing Risk. LC 99-48928. 500p. 2000. 70.00 (*0-07-135731-9*) McGraw.

Crounse, Robert G., jt. ed. see Brown, A. C.

Crous, Ernst. Die Religionsphilosophischen Lehren Lockes und Ihre Stellung zu Dem Deismus Seiner Zeit. (Abhandlungen zur Philosophie und Ihrer Geschichte Ser.: Vol. 34). (GER.). viii, 118p. 1980. reprint ed. write for info. (*3-487-06786-2*) G Olms Pubs.

Crous, Pedro W. Mycospaerella Spp. & Their Anamorphs Associated with Leaf Spot Diseases of Eucalyptus. LC 97-77522. (Mycologia Memoir Ser.: Vol. 21). (Illus.). 170p. 1998. pap. text 49.00 (*0-89054-190-6*) Am Phytopathol Soc.

Crouse. Automobile: Manual Transmission/Power Transmission. 6th ed. 1981. wbk. ed. 25.59 (*0-07-014777-9*) McGraw.

Crouse, Anne, ed. see Taylor, June.

Crouse, Chuck. Reporting for Radio. 205p. 1992. 29.95 (*0-929387-88-0*) Bonus Books.

Crouse, Gloria. Hooking Rugs: New Materials, New Techniques. LC 90-10792. (Illus.). 160p. 1990. 23.95 (*0-942391-41-1*, 070101) Taunton.

Crouse, J. R., III, jt. ed. see Touboul, Pierre-Jean.

Crouse, James & Trusheim, Dale. The Case Against the SAT. xvi, 240p. 1988. 27.00 (*0-226-12142-9*) U Ch Pr.

Crouse, Joan M. The Homeless Transient in the Great Depression: New York State, 1929-1941. LC 86-14451. 319p. (C). 1986. pap. text 24.95 (*0-88706-312-8*) State U NY Pr.

***Crouse, John.** Eventing. 20p. 1999. pap. 6.00 (*1-893541-01-0*, Pub. by Potes Poets) SPD-Small Pr Dist.

Crouse, John. Lapses. LC 94-80137. 69p. 1995. 9.00 (*1-882022-25-4*) O Bks.

Crouse, Kim. The Windows Programming Puzzle Book. 464p. 1993. pap. text 49.95 incl. disk (*0-471-59713-9*) Wiley.

***Crouse, Kristin, photos by.** Uncovering the Mysteries of Your Learning Disability - Discovery, Self-Awareness, Self-Advocacy. (Illus.). iv, 124p. 1999. 15.00 (*0-9701735-0-4*) LDinfo Pubng.

Crouse, Linda J. & Kramer, Paul H., eds. Exercise Echocardiography: A Book & Videotape. (Illus.). 112p. 1991. 95.00 incl. VHS (*0-87993-520-0*) Futura Pub.

Crouse, Richard. A Voice & a Dream. LC ML420.D565C76 1998. 1998. mass mkt. 5.99 (*0-345-42804-8*) Ballantine Pub Grp.

— Who Wrote the Book of Love. 296p. 1998. pap. 14.95 (*0-385-25732-5*) Bantam.

Crouse, Richard J. & Sloyer, Clifford W. Mathematical Questions from the Classroom, Pt. 1 & Pt. 2. rev. ed. LC 86-27502. (Illus.). (Orig.). (C). 1987. pap. text 32.50 (*0-939765-04-7*, G107) Janson Pubns.

— Mathematical Questions from the Classroom, Pts. 1 & 2. rev. ed. LC 86-27502. (Illus.). 208p. (Orig.). (C). 1987. pap. text 18.00 (*0-939765-02-0*, G108); pap. text 18.00 (*0-939765-03-9*, G109) Janson Pubns.

***Crouse, Rodney Ivan.** Wind Song of the Little Smokies. (Illus.). iv, 283p. 1999. write for info. (*0-9677000-0-0*) Foxsong.

Crouse, Roseanna. The Flowering of the Latihan of Subud. (Illus.). 158p. (Orig.). 1990. pap. 8.75 (*0-945126-07-7*) Undiscovd Worlds Pr.

Crouse, Russel, jt. auth. see Lindsay, Howard.

Crouse, Timothy, tr. see Martin du Gard, Roger.

Crouse, Whitney, jt. auth. see Eubanks, Steve.

Crouse, William H. Automotive Engines. 8th ed. 1994. pap. 38.50 (*0-02-801099-X*) Glencoe.

— Automotive Mechanics. 10th ed. 1992. 43.15 (*0-07-015013-3*) McGraw.

— Automotive Tune-up. 3rd ed. 1994. pap. 38.50 (*0-02-801856-7*) Glencoe.

Crouse, William H. & Anglin, Donald L. The Auto Book. 3rd ed. LC 83-16206. 640p. 1984. student ed. 55.00 (*0-07-014573-3*) McGraw.

— The Auto Book. 3rd ed. LC 83-16206. (Illus.). 681p. 1984. text 61.95 (*0-07-014571-7*) McGraw.

— Automotive Air Conditioning. 2nd ed. LC 82-4682. 304p. 1983. text 66.50 (*0-07-014857-0*) McGraw.

— Automotive Automatic Transmissions. 6th ed. LC 81-14262. (Illus.). 314p. 1982. pap. text 61.24 (*0-07-014771-X*) McGraw.

— Automotive Brakes, Suspension & Steering. 6th ed. LC 82-17187. (Automotive Technology Ser.). 1983. text 65.50 (*0-07-014828-7*) McGraw.

— Automotive Electronics & Electrical Equipment. 10th ed. 128p. 1986. text 65.95 (*0-07-014895-3*) McGraw.

— Automotive Engines. 7th ed. 432p. 1986. student ed. 30.50 (*0-07-014958-5*) McGraw.

— Automotive Manual Transmissions & Power Trains. 6th ed. LC 81-17206. (Illus.). 352p. 1982. text 44.34 (*0-07-014776-0*) McGraw.

— Automotive Mechanics. 9th ed. 672p. 1984. text 85.72 (*0-07-014860-0*) McGraw.

— Automotive Mechanics. 9th ed. 672p. 1984. student ed. 41.24 (*0-07-014871-6*) McGraw.

— Automotive Mechanics. 10th ed. LC 92-36588. 1992. write for info. (*0-02-800943-6*) Glencoe.

— Automotive Mechanics. 10th ed. 1999. teacher ed. 11.46 (*0-02-800944-4*) Glencoe.

— Automotive Mechanics. 10th ed. (YA). (gr. 6-12). 1999. student ed. 27.51 (*0-02-800945-2*) Glencoe.

— Automotive Mechanics. 10th ed. (Illus.). (YA). (gr. 6-12). 1999. student ed., wbk. ed. 27.51 (*0-02-800946-0*) Glencoe.

— Small Engine Mechanics. 3rd ed. 304p. 1986. pap. text 45.34 (*0-07-014803-1*) McGraw.

— Small Engine Mechanics. 3rd ed. (Illus.). (gr. 6-12). 1999. student ed., wbk. ed. 22.99 (*0-07-014804-X*) McGraw.

— Small Engine Mechanics: Instructor's Planning Guide. 3rd ed. 1999. teacher ed. 11.62 (*0-07-014805-8*) McGraw.

Crouse, William H., et al. Auto Shop Workbook. 3rd ed. 256p. (C). 1984. pap. text, wbk. ed. 30.87 (*0-07-014572-5*) McGraw.

— General Power Mechanics. 2nd ed. 1976. text 36.32 (*0-07-014697-7*) McGraw.

Crouser, Michael. Saint John's in Pictures. 80p. 1994. 39.00 (*0-9644200-0-7*) Veronica Press.

Crouser, Thomas P. Dead Printer Working: A Printer's Financial Survival Guide. 350p. 1997. 59.95 (*0-9659198-0-3*) Crouser.

Crouset, Francois. Britain, France & International Commerce: From Louis XIV to Victoria. (Collected Studies: No. CS542). 336p. 1996. 109.95 (*0-86078-593-9*, Pub. by Variorum) Ashgate Pub Co.

Croushore, James H., ed. see De Forest, John W.

Crout, Barbara & Flicek, Charles. Nerve Conduction Studies from A to Z. (Illus.). 210p. 1998. spiral bd. 49.95 (*1-57797-032-2*) ASET.

Crout, George C., jt. auth. see Miller, Roger L.

Crout, Robert R., ed. see Lafayette, Le Marquis de.

Crouter, Ann C., jt. ed. see Booth, Alan.

Crouter, Ann C., jt. ed. see Crockett, Lisa J.

Crouter, Ann J., ed. see Shanahan, Michael.

Crouter, Richard, ed. see Schleiermacher, Friedrich Daniel Ernst.

Crouthamel, James L. Bennett's New York Herald & the Rise of the Popular Press. LC 88-34305. (New York State Studies). (Illus.). 217p. 1989. reprint ed. pap. 67.30 (*0-608-06944-2*, 206715200009) Bks Demand.

— James Watson Webb: A Biography. LC 70-82536. 272p. reprint ed. pap. 84.40 (*0-7837-0211-6*, 204051900017) Bks Demand.

Crouthamel, James L., ed. see Edwards, Abial H.

Crouthamel, Thomas G. A History of Trailer Estates. LC 87-30987. (Illus.). (Orig.). 1988. pap. 16.95 (*0-940701-16-2*) Keystone Pr.

Crouthamel, Thomas G., Sr. It's OK. 2nd ed. LC 86-27694. (Illus.). 36p. (YA). (gr. 6 up). 1990. reprint ed. pap. 6.95 (*0-940701-18-9*) Keystone Pr.

Crouthamel, Thomas G. When the Unthinkable Happens: A Father's Journey Through Grief. LC 94-24127. 1995. 19.95 (*0-940701-44-8*) Keystone Pr.

Crouthamel, Thomas G., ed. Blood Bank GMPS. LC 92-81865. (Handi-Regs Ser.: No. 9206). 112p. (Orig.). 1992. pap. 21.95 (*0-940701-26-X*) Keystone Pr.

Croutier, Alev L. Harem: The World Behind the Veil. (Illus.). 224p. 1991. 35.00 (*0-89659-903-5*); pap. 19.95 (*1-55859-159-1*) Abbeville Pr.

***Croutier, Alev Lytle.** The Palace of Tears: A Reverie. LC 00-27921. 2000. write for info. (*0-385-33488-5*) Davies Grp.

Crouwel, Joost. Well Built Mycenae Fasc. 21: Mycenaean Pictorial Pottery. French, E. & Wardle, K., eds. (Illus.). 1991. pap. 15.00 (*0-946897-18-2*, Pub. by Oxbow Bks) David Brown.

Crouzeix, Jean-Pierre, et al. Generalized Convexity, Generalized Monotonicity: Recent Results. LC 98-21024. (Nonconvex Optimization & Its Applications Ser.). 467p. 1998. write for info. (*0-7923-5088-X*) Kluwer Academic.

Crouzeix, M. & Rappaz, J. On Numerical Approximation in Bifurcation Theory. Ciarlet, P. G. & Lions, J. L., eds. (Recherches en Mathematiques Appliquees Ser.: Vol. 13). (Illus.). ix, 165p. 1990. 41.95 (*0-387-51552-6*) Spr-Verlag.

Crouzel, Henri. Les Fins Dernieres Selon Origene. 352p. 1990. text 122.95 (*0-86078-269-7*, Pub. by Variorum) Ashgate Pub Co.

Crouzel, Henri. Origen. 1996. 49.95 (*0-567-09500-2*) Bks Intl VA.

Crouzel, Henri. Origen. Worrall, A. S., tr. 296p. pap. 29.95 (*0-567-08639-9*) T&T Clark Pubs.

Crouzet, ed. see Stendhal, pseud.

Crouzet, F., jt. ed. see Aerts, E.

Crouzet, Francois. Britain Ascendant: Studies in British & Franco-British Economic History. 520p. (C). 1991. text 85.00 (*0-521-34434-4*) Cambridge U Pr.

Crouzet, Francois, ed. The Economic Development of France since 1870, 2 vols. (Economic Development of Modern Europe since 1870 Ser.). 1024p. 1993. 370.00 (*1-85278-700-7*) E Elgar.

Crouzet, Yves. Bamboos. 1998. 19.99 (*3-8228-7759-X*) Taschen Amer.

***Crouzet, Yves.** Bambues. 1998. 25.99 (*3-8228-8034-5*) Benedikt Taschen.

Crovelli, Robert A. Probability & Statistics for Petroleum Resource Assessment. (Illus.). 143p. (C). 1999. reprint ed. pap. text 30.00 (*0-7881-7794-X*) DIANE Pub.

Crovello, T. J., jt. ed. see Nimis, P. L.

Crovetti, A., jt. ed. see Cavalloro, R.

Crovetto, C. Stubble over the Soil: The Vital Role of Plant Residue in Soil Management to Improve Soil Quality. LC 96-85124. 264p. 1996. 40.00 (*0-89118-131-8*) Am Soc Agron.

Crovini, L. & Quinn, T. J., eds. Metrology at the Frontiers of Physics & Technology: Proceedings of the International School of Physics "Enrico Fermi," 27 June-7 July, 1989. LC 92-25710. (Enrico Fermi International School of Physics Ser.: Vol. 110). xxii, 646p. 1992. 304.00 (*0-444-89770-4*, North Holland) Elsevier.

Crovisier, Jacques & Encrenaz, Therese. Comet Science: The Study of Remnants from the Birth of the Solar System. LC 99-19612. (Illus.). 192p. (C). 2000. 54.95 (*0-521-64179-9*) Cambridge U Pr.

***Crovisier, Jacques & Encrenaz, Therese.** Comet Science: The Study of Remnants from the Birth of the Solar System. LC 99-19612. (Illus.). 192p. (C). 2000. pap. 19.95 (*0-521-64591-3*) Cambridge U Pr.

Crovitz, Gordon. Europe's Siberian Gas Line: Economic Lessons & Strategic Implications. (C). 1990. 35.00 (*0-907967-10-8*, Pub. by Inst Euro Def & Strat) St Mut.

Crovo, Bob. Win at Video Poker. (Illus.). 105p. (Orig.). 1994. pap. 12.95 (*0-9644003-0-8*) B Crovo.

Crow. Art of the Sixties: American a European Art. (C). 1996. pap. text 16.40 (*0-13-520784-3*) P-H.

Crow, ed. Human Metabolism of Alcohol, 3 vols., I. 224p. 1989. lib. bdg. 159.00 (*0-8493-4521-9*, QP801) CRC Pr.

— Human Metabolism of Alcohol, 3 vols., Vol. 2. 280p. 1989. boxed set 195.00 (*0-8493-4522-7*, QP801) CRC Pr.

— Human Metabolism of Alcohol, 3 vols., Vol. 3. 248p. 1989. boxed set 195.00 (*0-8493-4523-5*) CRC Pr.

Crow, ed. see Chappuzeau.

Crow, Alice, jt. auth. see Crow, Lester D.

Crow, Amy, ed. Ohio Civil War Genealogy Journal. 1997. 18.00 (*0-935057-87-0*) OH Genealogical.

Crow, Amy Beth, jt. auth. see Thackray, Arnold W.

Crow, Andrew, contrib. by. The Early Years (1910-1912) (Thanhouser Classics Video Collector's Set: Vol. 1). 1998. 24.95 incl. VHS (*0-8108-3457-X*) Scarecrow.

— Edwin Thanhouser Returns. (Thanhouser Classics Video Collector's Set: Vol. 3). 1998. 24.95 incl. VHS (*0-8108-3459-6*) Scarecrow.

***Crow, Andrew, contrib. by.** Thanhouser Classics Video Collector's Set, 3 Vol. 1998. 69.95 incl. VHS (*0-8108-3456-1*) Scarecrow.

Crow, Andrew, contrib. by. Under the Mutual Banner (1912-1914) (Thanhouser Classics Video Collector's Set: Vol. 2). 1998. 24.95 incl. VHS (*0-8108-3458-8*) Scarecrow.

Crow, B., et al. Survival & Change in the Third World. 376p. (C). 1988. pap. text 23.95 (*0-19-520717-3*) OUP.

Crow, Barbara. Coming up for Light & Air. LC 94-67068. (Minnesota Voices Project Ser.: Vol. 67). 72p. 1995. pap. 9.95 (*0-89823-159-0*) New Rivers Pr.

Crow, Barbara A., ed. Radical Feminism. LC 99-44846. 1997. pap. 23.95 (*0-8147-1555-9*); text 60.00 (*0-8147-1554-0*) NYU Pr.

Crow, Ben. Food Question. 1989. 20.00 (*1-85383-063-1*, Pub. by Escan Pubns) Island Pr.

Crow, Ben, et al, eds. Rural Livelihoods: Crises & Responses. (Illus.). 336p. 1992. 69.00 (*0-19-877334-X*); pap. text 21.00 (*0-19-877335-8*) OUP.

Crow, Ben, et al. Sharing the Ganges: The Politics & Technology of River Development. LC 94-32113. 230p. 1995. text 26.00 (*0-8039-9203-3*) Sage.

Crow, Ben, jt. ed. see Thomas, Alan.

Crow, Bill. Jazz Anecdotes. 368p. 1991. reprint ed. pap. 13.95 (*0-19-507133-6*) OUP.

Crow, Brian. An Introduction to Post-Colonial Theatre. (Studies in Modern Theatre). 200p. (C). 1996. text 49.95 (*0-521-49529-6*); pap. text 17.95 (*0-521-56722-X*) Cambridge U Pr.

Crow, Carl. Great American Customer. LC 77-111823. (Essay Index Reprint Ser.). 1977. 23.95 (*0-8369-1645-X*) Ayer.

Crow, Charles L. Janet Lewis. LC 80-69012. (Western Writers Ser.: no. 41). (Illus.). 48p. (Orig.). 1980. pap. 4.95 (*0-88430-065-X*) Boise St U W Writ Ser.

Crow, Charles L., ed. American Gothic: An Anthology, 1787-1916. LC 98-54319. (Anthologies Ser.). 416p. 1999. 74.95 (*0-631-20651-5*) Blackwell Pubs.

***Crow, Charles L., ed.** American Gothic: An Anthology, 1787-1916. LC 98-54319. (Anthologies Ser.). 416p. 1999. pap. 29.95 (*0-631-20652-3*) Blackwell Pubs.

Crow, Charles L., jt. ed. see Kerr, Howard.

Crow, Charles S. Evaluation of English Literature in the High School. LC 74-176679. (Columbia University. Teachers College. Contributions to Education Ser.: No. 141). reprint ed. 37.50 (*0-404-55141-6*) AMS Pr.

Crow, Chizek. Creating the Customer-Driven Retail Bank. 1991. per. 75.00 (*1-55738-732-X*, Irwn Prfssnl) McGraw-Hill Prof.

***Crow, Connie.** Moonlight Fire. 2000. 4.50 (*1-928670-85-7*) Awe Struck E Bks.

An Asterisk (*) at the beginning of an entry indicates that the title is appearing for the first time.

— Teach Yourself the Internet. LC 98-87906. (Teach Yourself Ser.). 400p. 1998. pap. 19.99 (*0-7645-7505-8*) IDG Bks.

***Crowder, David A. & Crowder, Rhonda.** Creating Web Pages with HTML. (Cliffs Notes Ser.). 128p. 1999. pap. text 8.99 (*0-7645-8530-4*) IDG Bks.

Crowder, David A. & Crowder, Rhonda. Mastering Dreamweaver 2. (Mastering Ser.). 912p. 1999. 39.99 (*0-7821-2553-0*) Sybex.

***Crowder, David A. & Crowder, Rhonda.** Mastering Macromedia Dreamweaver 3. (Mastering Ser.). 2000. pap. 39.99 (*0-7821-2624-3*) Sybex.

— Shopping Online with Security. (Cliffs Notes Ser.). 128p. 1999. pap. text 8.99 (*0-7645-8524-X*) IDG Bks.

— Teach Yourself Microsoft FrontPage 2000. LC 99-10958. (Teach Yourself Ser.). (Illus.). 400p. 1999. pap. 19.99 (*0-7645-7523-6*) IDG Bks.

Crowder, Dorothy. In the Land of the Wichitas: Stories about Burkburnett, Texas for the Young Reader. (Illus.). 48p. (Orig.). (J). (gr. 3-4). 1986. pap. text 7.50 (*0-317-91365-4*) Dorthenia Pubs.

— Tales of the Red River Valley. LC 88-72312. (Illus.). 292p. 1988. 24.95 (*0-9621196-1-X*) Dorthenia Pubs.

Crowder, Fred O. Optics in the Health Sciences: Index of New Information for Research & State of Current Progress. 150p. 1997. 47.50 (*0-7883-1380-0*); pap. 44.50 (*0-7883-1381-9*) ABBE Pubs Assn.

— Optometry & the Health Sciences: Index of New Information for Research & Clinical Practice. 150p. 1997. 47.50 (*0-7883-1378-9*); pap. 44.50 (*0-7883-1379-7*) ABBE Pubs Assn.

Crowder, J. P., ed. Flow Visualization VII: Proceedings of the Seventh International Symposium on Flow Visualization. 999p. 1995. 120.00 (*1-56700-036-3*) Begell Hse.

***Crowder, Jack L.** Haskle Runs Away. (SPA, ENG & NAV., Illus.). 64p. (J). (gr. k-3). 1999. pap. 8.95 (*0-9616589-2-4*) J Crowder.

Crowder, Jack L., et al. Stephanie & the Coyote. 3rd rev. ed. Morgan, William, tr. (ENG & NAV., Illus.). 32p. (J). (gr. 3 up). reprint ed. pap. 4.95 (*0-9616589-0-8*) J Crowder.

Crowder, Jerry W., jt. auth. see DePaul, F. Thomas.

Crowder, John. The Birds of Maine: A Coloring-Learning Book. (Adventures in Maine Ser.). (Illus.). 32p. (Orig.). (J). (ps-3). 1995. pap. 2.95 (*1-887487-01-8*) Escapade Games.

— The Birds of New England: A Coloring-Learning Book. (Illus.). 32p. (J). 1997. pap. 2.95 (*1-887487-05-0*) Escapade Games.

— The Wildlife of Maine: A Coloring-Learning Book. (Adventures in Maine Ser.). (Illus.). 32p. (Orig.). (J). (ps-3). 1995. pap. 2.95 (*1-887487-00-X*) Escapade Games.

— The Wildlife of New England. (Illus.). 32p. (J). 1997. pap. 2.95 (*1-887487-06-9*) Escapade Games.

Crowder, John F. Fun Trivia Facts of Boston. (Fun Trivia Facts Ser.). 95p. 1998. pap. 4.95 (*1-887487-10-7*) Escapade Games.

— Fun Trivia Facts of Massachusetts. (Fun Trivia Facts Ser.). 95p. 1998. pap. 4.95 (*1-887487-08-5*) Escapade Games.

Crowder, Julia, jt. auth. see Johnson, Carol.

Crowder, Ken. The Iron Web. 192p. 1985. 14.95 (*0-8027-0846-3*) Walker & Co.

Crowder, Lola F. Early Kaskaskia, Illinois, Newspapers: 1814-1832. 127p. 1994. pap. 19.95 (*0-932231-09-8*) Frontier Pr.

— Early Louisville, Kentucky, Newspaper Abstracts: 1806-1828. 288p. 1995. lib. bdg. 28.00 (*0-932231-10-1*) Frontier Pr.

Crowder, M. J. & Hand, D. J. Analysis of Repeated Measures. 272p. (gr. 13). 1990. boxed set 73.95 (*0-412-31830-X*, A2433, Chap & Hall CRC) CRC Pr.

Crowder, M. J., et al. Statistical Analysis of Reliability Data. 256p. 1991. 49.95 (*0-412-30560-7*, A6119) Chapman & Hall.

Crowder, Martin, jt. auth. see Hand, David.

Crowder, Michael. West Africa: An Introduction to Its History. (Illus.). (C). 1989. pap. 38.00 (*0-582-60003-0*, 74468) Longman.

Crowder, Michael, ed. see Rey, Charles.

***Crowder, Nicholas B., ed.** Spanish Colloquialisms - Ecuador. 1999. 2.95 (*0-9667715-0-8*) Crowder Pubns.

Crowder, Norman K. British Army Pensioners Abroad, 1772-1899. LC 94-73392. 351p. 18.50 (*0-8063-1460-5*) Clearfield Co.

Crowder, R., ed. see Miranda, James.

Crowder, Rhonda, jt. auth. see Crowder, David.

Crowder, Richard. Carl Sandburg. (United States Authors Ser.: No. 47). 176p. 1964. 28.95 (*0-8057-0648-8*, Twyne) Mac Lib Ref.

***Crowder, Richard J.** Back to Basics: A Book of Inspiration & Devotion for Christian Living in the 21st Century. unabridged ed. Urbanska, Wanda, ed. (Illus.). 128p. 1999. 20.00 (*0-9667567-2-X*) Cherry St Bks.

Crowder, Richard M. Electric Drives & Their Controls. (Monographs in Electrical & Electronic Engineering: Vol. 36). (Illus.). 256p. 1998. pap. text 39.95 (*0-19-856565-8*) OUP.

Crowder, Rick. The Travelin' Talk Directory. (Illus.). 530p. (Orig.). 1993. pap. text 35.00 (*0-9635818-4-8*) Travelin Talk.

Crowder, Robert G. & Wagner, Richard K. The Psychology of Reading: An Introduction. 2nd ed. (Illus.). 288p. (C). 1992. text 24.95 (*0-19-506593-X*) OUP.

Crowder, Robert G., jt. ed. see Schab, Frank R.

Crowder, Susan. Daniel au Repaire des Lions. (FRE., Illus.). 36p. (Orig.). (J). 1993. pap. 4.00 (*0-912927-57-7*, D018) St John Kronstadt.

— Le Grand Deluge. Williams, Gregory, tr. (ENG & FRE., Illus.). 28p. (J). 1995. pap. 4.00 (*0-912927-62-3*, D029) St John Kronstadt.

— The Great Flood. (Illus.). 28p. (Orig.). (J). 1988. pap. 2.50 (*0-912927-27-5*, X027) St John Kronstadt.

— The Three Children in the Furnace. (Illus.). 37p. (Orig.). (J). 1984. pap. 2.50 (*0-912927-11-9*, X011) St John Kronstadt.

Crowder, Susan. Daniel in the Lions' Den. 36p. (Orig.). (J). 1984. pap. 3.00 (*0-912927-08-9*, X008) St John Kronstadt.

Crowder, William. Seashore Life Between the Tides. Orig. Title: Between the Tides. (Illus.). 512p. 1991. reprint ed. pap. 10.95 (*0-486-26817-9*) Dover.

Crowdus, Bess. A Garden of Memories: Poems from the Heart. (Illus.). 64p. (Orig.). 1991. pap. 3.95 (*0-918266-24-6*) Smyrna.

Crowdus, Gary, ed. The Political Companion to American Film. 1996. lib. bdg. 95.00 (*1-884964-53-2*) Fitzroy Dearborn.

— The Political Companion to American Film. LC 93-41593. (Illus.). 512p. 1994. 60.00 (*0-941702-37-5*) Lake View Pr.

— The Political Companion to American Film. (Illus.). 512p. 1996. pap. 29.95 (*0-941702-42-1*, 42-1) Lake View Pr.

Crowdus, Gary & Georgakas, Dan, eds. The Cineaste Interview II: Filmmakers on the Art & Politics of the Cinema. (Illus.). 350p. 2000. 29.95 (*0-941702-51-0*, 51-0); pap. 16.95 (*0-941702-50-2*, 50-2) Lake View Pr.

***Crowe.** Biography of Oskar Schindler. 2000. 29.00 (*0-8133-3375-X*, Pub. by Westview) HarpC.

Crowe. Changing Profile Natural. 1978. pap. text 86.50 (*90-247-1992-5*, Pub. by M Nijhoff) Kluwer Academic.

***Crowe.** Preceptor Program. (Illus.). 128p. (C). 2000. pap. text, teacher ed. 62.50 (*0-7637-1222-1*) JB Pubns.

Crowe & Bowen. With Tails We Win. (Illus.). 1954. pap. 5.00 (*0-9600102-5-4*) Shields.

Crowe, A. & Rudge, M., eds. Correlation & Polarization in Electronic & Atomic Collisions: Proceedings of the International Symposium on Queen's Univ., Belfast. 364p. (C). 1988. text 84.00 (*9971-5-0596-7*) World Scientific Pub.

Crowe, Alan J. Inns, Taverns & Pubs of the London Borough of Sutton: Their History & Architecture. 122p. 1988. pap. 30.00 (*0-907335-00-4*, Pub. by Sutton Libs & Arts) St Mut.

Crowe, Alice T. How to Get Black on Track: A Self-Empowerment Guide for People Who Are Ready to Make a Change "Within" Self. LC 94-90916. 160p. 1996. pap. 10.00 (*0-9645984-1-8*) Eye of Atum.

Crowe, Anne. NTC's Dictionary of French Faux Pas. (FRE & ENG., Illus.). 256p. 1994. 14.95 (*0-8442-1465-5*, 14655) NTC Contemp Pub Co.

Crowe, Anne H. Drug Identification & Testing in the Juvenile Justice System. (Illus.). 82p. (C). 1998. pap. text 25.00 (*0-7881-7375-8*) DIANE Pub.

Crowe, Avis & Vermilye, Dyck. Without Agenda: A Sojourn in South Africa. LC 90-62976. 32p. (Orig.). 1990. pap. 1.00 (*0-87574-293-9*) Pendle Hill.

Crowe, Barbara & Reuer, Barbara L. Best Practice in Music Therapy: Utilizing Group Percussion Strategies for Promoting Volunteerism in the Well Older Adult. 88p. (Orig.). 1995. pap. text 25.00 (*1-879167-08-5*) SDSU Coll Hlth Hum Servs.

Crowe, Brian L., jt. auth. see Donner, Ted A.

Crowe, C. Acts. 1989. pap. 30.00 (*0-86217-004-4*, Pub. by Veritas Pubns) St Mut.

Crowe, C. T., et al. Multiphase Flows with Droplets & Particles. LC 97-24341. 496p. 1997. boxed set 79.95 (*0-8493-9469-4*) CRC Pr.

***Crowe, Cameron.** Conversations with Wilder. LC 99-31104. 1999. 35.00 (*0-375-40660-3*) Knopf.

— Untitled. 2000. pap. 14.00 (*0-571-20569-0*) Faber & Faber.

Crowe, Carole. Sharp Horns on the Moon. LC 97-72771. 128p. 1998. 14.95 (*1-56397-671-4*) Boyds Mills Pr.

***Crowe, Carole.** Waiting for Dolphins. LC 99-66548. (Illus.). 144p. (YA). (gr. 5 up). 2000. 14.95 (*1-56397-847-4*) Boyds Mills Pr.

Crowe-Carraco, Carol. The Big Sandy. LC 78-58126. (Kentucky Bicentennial Bookshelf Ser.). 154p. reprint ed. pap. 47.80 (*0-7837-2418-7*, 204256400005) Bks Demand.

— Women Who Made a Difference. LC 89-38085. (New Books for New Readers). (Illus.). 64p. 1989. pap. 5.95 (*0-8131-0901-9*) U Pr of Ky.

Crowe, Catherine. Night-Side of Nature. 1988. pap. 14.95 (*0-85030-519-5*, Pub. by Aqn Pr) HarpC.

Crowe, Chris. Fatherhood, Football & Turning Forty. 1995. 9.95 (*0-88494-989-3*) Bookcraft Inc.

— For the Strength of You. 1997. pap. 8.95 (*1-57008-312-6*) Bookcraft Inc.

***Crowe, Chris.** Presenting Mildred Taylor. LC 99-25527. (United States Authors Ser.). 150p. (YA). 1999. 28.00 (*0-8057-1687-4*, Twyne) Mac Lib Ref.

Crowe, Chris, ed. From the Outside Looking In. LC 98-71544. 1998. pap. 10.95 (*1-57008-412-2*) Bookcraft Inc.

***Crowe, Clayton T., et al.** Engineering Fluid Mechanics. 7th ed. 732p. (C). 2000. write for info. (*0-471-38482-8*) Wiley.

Crowe, Clayton T., jt. auth. see Roberson, John A.

Crowe, D. G., jt. auth. see Dereniak, E. L.

***Crowe, Daniel E.** Prophets of Rage: The Black Freedom Struggle in San Francisco, 1945-1969. LC 00-22424. (Studies in African American History & Culture). 2000. write for info. (*0-8153-3766-3*) Garland.

Crowe, David & Kolsti, John, eds. The Gypsies of Eastern Europe. LC 90-46710. 200p. (gr. 13). 1991. pap. 34.95 (*0-87332-672-5*) M E Sharpe.

— The Gypsies of Eastern Europe. LC 90-46710. 200p. (C). (gr. 13). 1991. 62.95 (*0-87332-671-7*) M E Sharpe.

Crowe, David M. A History of the Gypsies of Eastern Europe & Russia. 336p. 1995. text 49.95 (*0-312-08691-1*) St Martin.

— A History of the Gypsies of Eastern Europe & Russia. 336p. 1996. pap. 14.95 (*0-614-96971-9*) St Martin.

— The Holocaust: Roots, History, & Aftermath. 1999. pap. 35.00 (*0-8133-2913-2*) Westview.

Crowe, Devon G., ed. Selected Papers on Adaptive Optics & Speckle Imaging. LC 93-48071. (Milestone Ser.: Vol. MS93). 1994. 35.00 (*0-8194-1557-X*); pap. 35.00 (*0-8194-1556-1*) SPIE.

Crowe, Donald. Symmetry, Rigid Motion & Patterns. (Hi Map Ser.: No. 4). (Illus.). 92p. pap. text 9.99 (*0-614-05325-0*, HM 5604) COMAP Inc.

Crowe, Donald W., jt. auth. see Washburn, Dorothy K.

***Crowe, Duane E.** Catfish Annie to the Rescue. (Back River Adventures of Catfish Annie Ser.). (Illus.). 48p. (gr. k-5). 2001. write for info. (*0-9672882-0-7*) Back River.

Crowe, Elizabeth, tr. see Mori, Hana, et al.

Crowe, Elizabeth P., jt. auth. see Everett, John H.

Crowe, Elizabeth P., ed. see Peppers, Jerome G.

Crowe, Elizabeth Powell. Genealogy Online: AOL Edition. LC 98-33488. 244p. 1998. pap. 24.99 (*0-07-014755-8*) McGraw.

— Genealogy Online: Millennium Edition. LC 99-39910. 256p. 1999. pap. 19.99 (*0-07-135103-5*) McGraw.

— Genealogy Online: Web Edition. 2nd ed. LC 97-33669. (Illus.). 293p. 1997. pap. 24.95 (*0-07-014722-1*) McGraw.

Crowe, Evelyn A. Amoureux d'une Ombre. (Amours d'Aujourd'Hui Ser.: No. 340). (FRE.). 1999. mass mkt. 5.50 (*0-373-38340-1*, 1-38340-5) Harlequin Bks.

— A Family of His Own. (Superromance Ser.). 1996. per. 3.99 (*0-373-70704-5*, 1-70704-1) Harlequin Bks.

— Fathers & Other Strangers (Family Man) LC 95-21533. 297p. 1995. per. 3.75 (*0-373-70667-7*) Harlequin Bks.

— Legacy of Fear. LC 95-13687. (Superromance Ser.). 297p. 1995. per. 3.75 (*0-373-70646-4*, 1-70646-4) Harlequin Bks.

— Safe Haven: Home on the Ranch. (Superromance Ser.: Bk. 850). 1999. per. 4.25 (*0-373-70850-5*, 1-70850-2) Harlequin Bks.

— So Hard to Forget. 1997. per. 3.99 (*0-373-70745-2*, 1-70745-4) Harlequin Bks.

Crowe, Evelyn A., jt. auth. see Ross, Joann.

Crowe, Frank R., jt. auth. see Sheehan, A. V.

Crowe, Frederick E. Appropriating the Lonergan Idea. Vertin, Michael, ed. LC 87-33855. 424p. 1989. reprint ed. pap. 131.50 (*0-7837-9186-0*, 204988600003) Bks Demand.

— Method in Theology: An Organon for Our Time. LC 80-81015. (Pere Marquette Lectures). 68p. 1980. 15.00 (*0-87462-519-X*) Marquette.

Crowe, Frederick E. & Doran, Robert M., eds. Collected Works of Bernard J. F. Lonergan, Vol. 4. 368p. (C). 1994. pap. text 19.95 (*0-8020-3439-X*) U of Toronto Pr.

Crowe, Frederick E., ed. see Lonergan, Bernard J.

Crowe, Gregory, jt. auth. see Earle, Ralph H.

Crowe, Gregory, tr. see Barabashev, Alexei.

Crowe, Ian, ed. see O'Brien, Conor C., et al.

***Crowe, Ivan.** The Quest for Food: Its Role in Human Evolution & Migration. (History & Archaeology Ser.). (Illus.). 272p. 2000. 37.50 (*0-7524-1462-3*, Pub. by Tempus Pubng) Arcadia Publng.

Crowe, J. O'Beirne, tr. Resurrection of the Dead. 1998. pap. 2.50 (*0-89979-102-6*) British Am Bks.

Crowe, Jerome. From Jerusalem to Antioch: The Gospel Across Cultures. LC 96-51702. 184p. (Orig.). 1997. pap. text 14.95 (*0-8146-2432-4*, Liturg Pr Bks) Liturgical Pr.

Crowe, John. Introduction to Digital Electronics. 224p. 1997. pap. text 19.95 (*0-340-64570-9*, Pub. by E A) Routldge.

Crowe, John H., III. Coming Full Circle. (Illus.). 160p. (Orig.). 1995. pap. 17.95 (*1-887797-00-9*, Pagan Pubng) Tynes Cowan.

— The Realm of Shadows: A Campaign for "Call of Cthulhu" (Illus.). 208p. 1997. pap. 20.95 (*1-887797-10-6*, PAG1006, Pagan Pubng) Tynes Cowan.

Crowe, John H., 3rd, et al. Mortal Coils. (Illus.). 190p. 1998. pap. 19.95 (*1-887797-11-4*, PAG 1007, Pagan Pubng) Tynes Cowan.

Crowe, Joseph A. Raphael, His Life & Works. LC 72-2584. (Select Bibliographies Reprint Ser.). 1977. reprint ed. 52.95 (*0-8369-6852-2*) Ayer.

Crowe, Joseph A. & Cavalcaselle, Giovanni B. History of Painting in Italy, Umbria, Florence, Siena: From the 2nd to the 16th Century, 6 vols. LC 70-154118. (Illus.). reprint ed. 345.00 (*0-404-01920-X*) AMS Pr.

— A History of Painting in North Italy, 3 vols. LC 76-22574. (Illus.). reprint ed. 245.00 (*0-404-09290-X*) AMS Pr.

Crowe, Keith. A History of the Original Peoples of Northern Canada. rev. ed. 264p. 1991. pap. 22.95 (*0-7735-0880-5*, Pub. by McG-Queens Univ Pr) CUP Services.

Crowe, Malcolm, et al. Constructing Systems & Information: A Process View. LC 95-50781. 1996. pap. write for info. (*0-07-707962-0*) McGraw.

Crowe, Michael B. Human Rights. 1989. pap. 15.00 (*0-905092-55-4*, Pub. by Veritas Pubns) St Mut.

Crowe, Michael F. Deco by the Bay: Art Deco Architecture in the San Francisco Bay Area. (Illus.). 128p. 1995. 34.95 (*0-525-93856-7*, Viking Studio) Studio Bks.

Crowe, Michael J. The Extraterrestrial Life Debate, 1750-1900. LC 99-12168. 1999. pap. text 19.95 (*0-486-40675-X*) Dover.

— A History of Vector Analysis: The Evolution of the Idea of a Vectorial System. LC 93-6116. (Illus.). 288p. 1994. reprint ed. pap. 7.95 (*0-486-67910-1*) Dover.

— Modern Theories of the Universe, from Herschel to Hubble. (Illus.). 464p. (Orig.). 1994. pap. text 9.95 (*0-486-27880-8*) Dover.

— Theories of the World from Antiquity to the Copernican Revolution. (Illus.). 256p. 1990. pap. 6.95 (*0-486-26173-5*) Dover.

Crowe, Michael J., et al, eds. A Calendar of the Correspondence of Sir John Herschel. LC 98-22928. 800p. (C). 1998. 150.00 (*0-521-63149-1*) Cambridge U Pr.

Crowe, Norman. Nature & the Idea of a Man-Made World: An Investigation into the Evolutionary Roots of Form & Order in the Built Environment. LC 94-45594. (Illus.). 296p. 1995. 37.50 (*0-262-03222-8*) MIT Pr.

— Nature & the Idea of a Man-Made World: An Investigation into the Evolutionary Roots of Form & Order in the Built Environment. (Illus.). 296p. 1997. reprint ed. pap. text 18.50 (*0-262-53146-1*) MIT Pr.

Crowe, Norman & Laseau, Paul. Visual Notes for Architects & Designers. 224p. 1986. pap. 44.95 (*0-471-28959-0*, VNR) Wiley.

Crowe, Norman & Laseau, Paul. Visual Notes for Architects & Designers. (Illus.). 144p. 1986. pap. text 36.95 (*0-442-29334-8*, VNR) Wiley.

Crowe, Patrick. 24 Ways to Improve Your Self-Serve. 115p. 1997. ring bd. 39.00 (*0-9642640-6-4*) Power Inc.

Crowe, Penelope, tr. from GER. Hamburger Bahnhof, Berlin. LC 97-191. (Museum Guides Ser.). (Illus.). 128p. 1996. pap. 14.95 (*3-7913-1731-8*, Pub. by Prestel) te Neues.

Crowe, Percy R. Concepts in Climatology. LC 72-176213. (Geographies for Advanced Study Ser.). 609p. reprint ed. pap. 188.80 (*0-608-10021-8*, 201960100013) Bks Demand.

Crowe, Richard. Chicago's Streetguide to the Supernatural. (Illus.). 1995. pap., spiral bd. 17.50 (*0-940542-06-4*) Carolando.

Crowe, Robert L. Clyde Monster. (Illus.). 64p. (J). (ps-3). 1993. pap. 5.99 (*0-14-054743-6*, PuffinBks) Peng Put Young Read.

Crowe, Robert L., ed. Courtside Memories. large type ed. 84p. 1998. pap. 9.95 (*0-9644681-3-1*) Creative Ideas.

Crowe, Robert L., ed. see Bradbury, Ken.

Crowe, Robert L., ed. see Crandell, Susan.

Crowe, Robert L., ed. see Crump, Freida M.

Crowe, Robert L., ed. see Klinkerman, O. J.

Crowe, Rosalie & Brinkernoff, Sidney, eds. Early Yuma: A Graphic History of Life on the American Nile. LC 75-27825. 1976. reprint ed. pap. 17.95 (*0-87358-144-X*) Yuma Cnty Hist.

Crowe, Ruth. Experiments with Normal & Transformed Cells: A Laboratory Manual for Working with Cells in Culture. LC QH0583.. 179p. reprint ed. pap. 55.50 (*0-7837-6447-2*, 204644600012) Bks Demand.

Crowe, Sam. Web Wise: A Simplified Management Guide for the Development of a Successful Web Site. (Illus.). 172p. 1999. ring bd. 29.95 (*1-55571-501-X*, Oasis Pr) PSI Resch.

***Crowe, Sam.** Web Wise: A Simplified Management Guide for the Development of a Successful Web Site. (Successful Business Library). (Illus.). 172p. 1999. pap. 19.95 (*1-55571-479-X*, Oasis Pr) PSI Resch.

***Crowe, Sandra A.** Since Strangling Isn't an Option... Dealing with Difficult People - Common Problems & Uncommon Solutions. LC 99-41535. (Illus.). 274p. 1999. pap. 13.95 (*0-399-52540-8*, Perigee Bks) Berkley Pub.

***Crowe, Simon F.** Neuropsychological Effects of the Psychiatric Disorders. 204p. 1998. text 39.00 (*90-5702-289-3*, Harwood Acad Pubs); pap. text 24.00 (*90-5702-377-6*) Gordon & Breach.

Crowe, Suzy & Penney, Elaine. Teachers, Computers & Kids: Recipes for Success in Early Childhood Settings. LC 95-79414. (Kids & Computers Ser.). 200p. 1995. ring bd. 24.95 (*1-887899-00-6*) Bit-By-Bit.

Crowe, Sylvia. Garden Design. LC 94-229860. (Illus.). 296p. 1994. 59.50 (*1-870673-08-5*) Antique Collect.

— Garden Design. 224p. (C). 1991. text 140.00 (*0-906527-05-8*, Pub. by Surrey Beatty & Sons) St Mut.

Crowe, Sylvia & Mitchell, Mary. The Pattern of Landscape. (Illus.). 176p. 1993. pap. 29.50 (*1-85341-020-9*, Pub. by Packard Pubng Ltd) Antique Collect.

Crowe, T. C., ed. Numerical Methods in Multiphase Flows, 1994. LC 90-55409. (Fluids Engineering Division Conference Ser.: Vol. 185). 315p. 1994. pap. text 55.00 (*0-7918-1368-1*) ASME.

Crowe, Thomas A. Applications of Counseling in Speech-Language Pathology & Audiology. LC 96-9331. 392p. 1997. pap. 29.95 (*0-683-02216-4*) Lppncott W & W.

Crowe, Thomas R. Deep Language. limited ed. 40p. 1991. pap. 4.50 (*0-685-64799-4*) New Native Pr.

— The Laugharne Poems. LC 97-183795. 70p. 1997. pap. 10.00 (*0-86381-432-8*) New Native Pr.

— New Native. LC 93-92609. (Night Sun Trilogy Ser.: Bk. 2). 93p. 1993. pap. 9.95 (*1-883197-02-3*) New Native Pr.

— Night Sun: An Initiation Trilogy, 3 vols., Set. LC 93-92604. 250p. (Orig.). 1993. boxed set 24.95 (*1-883197-00-7*) New Native Pr.

— Overpopulation. limited ed. (Illus.). (Orig.). 1995. pap. 1.00 (*0-614-10111-5*, 13) New Native Pr.

— The Personified Street. LC 93-92608. (Night Sun Trilogy Ser.: Bk. 1). 88p. 1993. pap. 9.95 (*1-883197-01-5*) New Native Pr.

— Water from the Moon. LC 93-92605. (Night Sun Trilogy Ser.: Bk. 3). 80p. 1993. pap. 9.95 (*1-883197-03-1*) New Native Pr.

Crowe, Thomas R., et al, eds. Writing the Wind: The New Celtic Poetry: A Celtic Resurgence. LC 97-65729. (Illus.). 365p. (Orig.). 1997. pap. 18.95 (*1-883197-12-0*) New Native Pr.

An Asterisk (*) at the beginning of an entry indicates that the title is appearing for the first time.

Crowe, Thomas R., tr. from PER. In Wineseller's Street (The Poems of Hafez) Renderings by Thomas Rain Crowe. LC 97-43461. (Illus.). 88p. 1997. pap. 12.95 (*0-936347-67-8*) IBEX.

Crowe, Thomas R., ed. see Lane, John.

Crowe, Thomas R., tr. see Dal, Hughes-Alain.

***Crowe, Timothy D.** Crime Prevention Through Environmental Design. 2nd ed. 352p. 2000. 44.95 (*0-7506-7198-X*, BH Security) Buttrwrth-Heinemann.

Crowe, Timothy D. Habitual Juvenile Offenders: Guidelines for Citizen Action & Public Responses. (Illus.). 90p. (Orig.). (C). 1994. pap. text 30.00 (*0-7881-0187-0*) DIANE Pub.

Crowe, Timothy D., jt. auth. see National Crime Prevention Institute Staff.

***Crowe, Tom.** Preceptor Program. (Illus.). 128p. (C). 2000. pap. text, teacher ed. 31.25 (*0-7637-1226-4*) JB Pubns.

— Preceptor Program Intern Manual. (Illus.). 96p. (C). 2000. pap. text 25.00 (*0-7637-1227-2*) JB Pubns.

Crowe, W., et al, eds. Proceedings of the Conference on Groups & Geometry, 2 vols., Set. 350p. 1986. 60.00 (*0-911767-44-4*) Hadronic Pr Inc.

Crowe, W. Houghton. Brontes of Ballynaskeagh. 180p. 1978. 19.95 (*0-85221-100-7*) Dufour.

Crowe, William, Jr. Lewesdon Hill. LC 90-119018. 44p. 1989. reprint ed. 40.00 (*1-85477-005-5*) Continuum.

Crowe, William T., ed. see Jarrett, David L., et al.

Crowed, L., ed. Jason Core Curriculum. LC 95-67944. (Illus.). 212p. 1995. pap. text 8.00 (*0-87355-135-4*, PB110X) Natl Sci Tchrs.

Crowel, H. Crowel History, or "Footprints in the Sands of Times" (Illus.). 55p. 1997. reprint ed. pap. 11.00 (*0-8328-8160-0*); reprint ed. lib. bdg. 21.00 (*0-8328-8159-7*) Higginson Bk Co.

Crowel, Thomas R. Simple Selling: Common Sense That Guarantees Your Success. LC 96-80166. (Illus.). 200p. (Orig.). 1997. pap. 14.95 (*1-884962-09-2*) Success Press.

— Simple Selling: Common Sense That Guarantees Your Success. LC 99-60332. (Illus.). 178p. (Orig.). 1999. reprint ed. pap. 14.95 (*0-9669917-0-2*) Success Press.

***Crowel, Thomas Ray.** Dirty Little Tricks: How Salespeople Are Robbing You Blind. LC 00-90246. 185p. 2000. pap. 14.95 (*0-9669917-2-9*) Success Press.

Crowell & Moring. Civil Use of Government Helicopters. Jensen, Frank L., Jr., ed. 82p. 1994. ring bd. write for info. (*0-9630326-4-X*) Helicopter Assn Intl.

***Crowell, Elizabeth St. Claire.** Acapulco Escapade. LC 00-190543. 2000. 25.00 (*0-7388-1802-X*); pap. 18.00 (*0-7388-1803-8*) Xlibris Corp.

Crowell & Moring Staff. Superfund Manual: Legal & Management Strategies. 6th ed. 470p. 1997. pap. text 115.00 (*0-86587-603-7*, 603) Gov Insts.

Crowell, A. L. Archaeology & the Capitalist World System: A Study from Russian America. LC 97-40644. (Contributions to Global Historical Archaeology Ser.). 308p. (C). 1998. 49.50 (*0-306-45669-9*, Plenum Trade) Perseus Pubng.

Crowell, Al. Love in the Trenches: A Couples Guide to Transforming the Power Struggle. 155p. (Orig.). 1996. pap. 49.95 (*0-9652992-0-1*) A Crowell Publ.

Crowell, Arthur R., Jr. A Handbook for the Special Education Administrator: Organization & Procedures for Special Education. LC 89-48346. (Studies in Education: Vol. 9). 96p. 1990. lib. bdg. 49.95 (*0-88946-922-9*) E Mellen.

Crowell, Benedict & Wilson, Robert F. The Armies of Industry: Our Nation's Manufacture of Munitions for a World in Arms, 1917-1918, 2 vols. in 1. LC 74-75235. (United States in World War I Ser.). (Illus.). xxviii, 738p. 1974. reprint ed. lib. bdg. 72.95 (*0-89198-101-2*) Ozer.

— Demobilization: Our Industrial & Military Demobilization after the Armistice, 1918-1920. LC 74-75236. (United States in World War I Ser.). (Illus.). xvi, 333p. 1974. reprint ed. lib. bdg. 39.95 (*0-89198-102-0*) Ozer.

— The Giant Hand: Our Mobilization & Control of Industry & Natural Resources, 1917-1918. LC 74-75237. (United States in World War I Ser.). (Illus.). xxx, 191p. 1974. reprint ed. lib. bdg. 32.95 (*0-89198-099-7*) Ozer.

— How America Went to War: An Account from Official Sources of the Nation's War Activities, 1917-1920, 4 vols., Set. 1986. reprint ed. 200.00 (*0-89198-098-9*) Ozer.

— The Road to France: The Transportation of Troops & Military Supplies, 1917-1918, 2 vols. in 1. LC 74-75238. (United States in World War I Ser.). (Illus.). xv, 675p. 1974. reprint ed. lib. bdg. 72.95 (*0-89198-100-4*) Ozer.

Crowell, Bill. The Best of Times, the Worst of Times: A Story of World War II. 248p. Date not set. mass mkt. 4.99 (*1-55197-042-2*) Picasso Publ.

Crowell, Caryl G., jt. auth. see Whitmore, Kathryn F.

Crowell, D. H., et al. Childhood Aggression & Violence: Sources of Influence, Prevention, & Control. LC 86-30359. (Applied Clinical Psychology Ser.). (Illus.). 318p. (C). 1987. 65.00 (*0-306-42355-3*, Plenum Trade) Perseus Pubng.

Crowell, David. Exploring Southern California Beaches. (Illus.). 256p. 1999. pap. 18.95 (*1-56044-632-3*) Falcon Pub Inc.

— Mountain Biking: Moab. LC 97-199910. (Illus.). 160p. (Orig.). 1997. pap. 10.95 (*1-56044-530-0*) Falcon Pub Inc.

— Mountain Biking Colorado Springs. (Illus.). 158p. 1998. pap. text 9.95 (*1-56044-822-9*) Falcon Pub Inc.

Crowell, David, tr. see Hutchinson, Anna, ed.

Crowell, David, tr. see Hutchinson, Hanna.

Crowell, Donald R., jt. auth. see Connolly, Walter B., Jr.

Crowell, E. B. Buddhist Mahayana Texts. 1972. lib. bdg. 250.00 (*0-87968-499-2*) Krishna Pr.

Crowell, Haila. The Envelope Mill: Recycle Magazines into Beautiful, New Envelopes. Ford, June, ed. (Illus.). 30p. (Orig.). 1995. pap. 19.95 (*1-56530-149-8*, Pub. by Summit TX) BookWorld.

Crowell, Ivan H. Chip Carving Patterns & Designs. LC 77-78511. (Illus.). 48p. 1977. reprint ed. pap. 4.95 (*0-486-23532-7*) Dover.

Crowell, Jenn. Necessary Madness. 256p. 1998. mass mkt. 6.99 (*0-446-60606-5*, Pub. by Warner Bks) Little.

— Necessary Madness. large type ed. (Niagara Large Print Ser.). 240p. 1997. 29.50 (*0-7089-5889-3*) Ulverscroft.

— Necessary Madness: A Novel. 1998. mass mkt. 251.64 (*0-446-16634-0*) Warner Bks.

Crowell, John, jt. auth. see Sanmann, Stefan.

Crowell, John, ed. see Danford, Heath.

***Crowell, John C.** Pre-Mesozoic Ice Ages: Their Bearing on Understanding the Climate System. (Geological Society of America. Memoir Ser.: Vol. 192). 106p. 1999. 46.00 (*0-8137-1192-4*) Geol Soc.

Crowell, Joseph E. The Young Volunteer: The Everday Experiences of a Soldier Boy in the Civil War. (Illus.). 500p. 1996. reprint ed. pap. 27.95 (*0-9638692-0-5*) NOVA Pubns.

Crowell, Knox, jt. auth. see Mullican, Judy.

Crowell, Krystine. Krystine's Healthy Gourmet Bakery Cookbook: Luscious Guilt-Free Desserts from the Legendary "Baker" LC 97-32732. 256p. 1998. pap. 21.95 (*1-55788-282-7*, HP Books) Berkley Pub.

Crowell, L. Crowe: John Crowe & His Descendants. (Illus.). 109p. 1991. reprint ed. pap. 19.00 (*0-8328-1808-9*) Higginson Bk Co.

Crowell, Linda, ed. Today's Family Guide to Dallas. 1995. 12.95 (*0-938934-27-9*) LCN.

Crowell, Lynda. The Family Guide to Austin. (Illus.). 300p. (Orig.). 1998. pap. 14.95 (*0-938934-40-6*) LCN.

— The Family Guide to Houston. (Illus.). 300p. 1998. pap. 14.95 (*0-938934-41-4*) LCN.

— Today's Family Guide to Austin. rev. ed. 300p. (Orig.). 1993. pap. 12.95 (*0-938934-29-5*) LCN.

— Today's Family Guide to Houston. 400p. (Orig.). 1992. pap. text 12.95 (*0-938934-26-0*) LCN.

— Today's Family Guide to San Antonio. 150p. (Orig.). 1993. pap. 8.95 (*0-938934-28-7*) LCN.

Crowell, Lynda, ed. see Puryear, Kay & Brown, Tracy.

Crowell, Lynda, ed. see Puryear, Kay & Corry, Tracy.

Crowell, Michael, jt. auth. see University of North Carolina at Chapel Hill, Insti.

Crowell, Michael G., jt. auth. see Hook, Julius N.

Crowell, Nancy A. & Leeper, Ethel M., eds. America's Fathers & Public Policy: Report of a Workshop. 51p. (C). 1998. reprint ed. pap. text 25.00 (*0-7881-4872-9*) DIANE Pub.

Crowell, Nancy A., ed. see National Research Council, Panel on Violence Again.

Crowell, Nancy A., jt. ed. see Phillips, Deborah.

Crowell, Norton B. Triple Soul: Browning's Theory of Knowledge. 235p. 1963. text 32.50 (*0-8290-0228-6*) Irvington.

Crowell, Patricia, jt. auth. see Crowell, Peter.

Crowell, Peter & Crowell, Patricia. The Traveler's Radio Guide: Arizona, Utah, Colorado & New Mexico. (Orig.). 1993. pap. text 2.95 (*1-880962-03-9*) TRG Pubns.

— The Traveler's Radio Guide: California & Nevada. 32p. (Orig.). 1992. pap. text 2.95 (*1-880962-00-4*) TRG Pubns.

— The Traveler's Radio Guide: Idaho - Montana - Wyoming. (Orig.). 1993. pap. 2.95 (*1-880962-02-0*) TRG Pubns.

— The Traveler's Radio Guide: Washington & Oregon. 30p. (Orig.). 1992. pap. 2.95 (*1-880962-01-2*) TRG Pubns.

Crowell, Peter M. & Argyle Municipality Historical & Genealogical Society. An Every Name Index to the 1871 Census Returns for Yarmouth County, Nova Scotia: An Every Name Index to the Nominal Return of the Living : Nominal Return of the Deaths Within Last Twelve Months, & the Return of Industrial Establishments. LC 98-177152. ix, 377p. 1997. pap. write for info. (*0-9698298-7-6*) Argyle Muni.

Crowell, Preston R. Stow, Mass. 1683-1933, Compiled in Honor of the 250th Anniversary of the Town. (Illus.). 131p. 1997. reprint ed. pap. 17.50 (*0-8328-5964-8*); reprint ed. lib. bdg. 27.50 (*0-8328-5963-X*) Higginson Bk Co.

Crowell, Richard D., jt. auth. see Dixon, Sheila A.

Crowell, Richard H. & Slesnick, William E. Calculus with Analytic Geometry. (Illus.). (C). 1968. text 50.00 (*0-393-09782-X*) Norton.

Crowell, Richard L., ed. see American Society for Microbiology Staff.

Crowell, Robert M., ed. see Year Book of Neurology & Neurosurgery Staff.

Crowell, Sam, et al. The Re-Enchantment of Learning: A Manual for Teacher Renewal & Classroom Transformation. LC 97-25731. 1997. 32.00 (*1-56976-076-4*) Zephyr Pr AZ.

Crowell, Sandra A. & Asleson, David O. Up the Swiftwater: A Pictorial History of the Colorful Upper St. Joe River Country. (Illus.). 150p. 1995. reprint ed. pap. 19.95 (*0-9643647-3-5*) Mus North Idaho.

Crowell, Sidney R., jt. auth. see Lomax, Alan.

Crowell, Steven G., ed. The Prism of the Self: Philosophical Essays in Honor of Maurice Natanson. (Contributions to Phenomenology Ser.). 372p. (C). 1995. lib. bdg. 166.00 (*0-7923-3546-5*, Pub. by Kluwer Academic) Kluwer Academic.

Crowell, Todd. Farewell My Colony: Last Days in the Life of British Hong Kong. 184p. 1999. pap. 14.00 (*962-7160-54-7*, Pub. by Asia) Weatherhill.

Crowell, Todd & Morimura, Stephanie Forman. Tokyo: City on the Edge. 352p. 1999. pap. 18.00 (*962-7160-80-6*, Pub. by Asia) Weatherhill.

Crowest, F. J. Cherubini. 1988. reprint ed. lib. bdg. 59.00 (*0-7812-0151-9*) Rprt Serv.

— Cherubini. 1976. reprint ed. lib. bdg. 55.00 (*0-403-03761-1*) Scholarly.

Crowest, Frederick. Great Tone-Poets: Being Short Memoirs of the Greater Musical Composers. LC 70-38711. (Essay Index Reprint Ser.). 1977. reprint ed. 28.95 (*0-8369-2641-2*) Ayer.

Crowest, Frederick J. Catechism of Musical History & Biography. 187p. 1991. reprint ed. 69.00 (*0-7812-9312-X*) Rprt Serv.

— Verdi: Man & Musician. LC 74-24065. reprint ed. 39.50 (*0-404-12890-4*) AMS Pr.

Croweyn, Evelyn & Heath, Lorraine. To Tame a Texan. Enderlin, J., ed. 1999. mass mkt. 5.99 (*0-312-96886-8*) St Martin.

Crowfoot, J., jt. ed. see Glebov, O.

Crowfoot, J. W. Early Churches in Palestine. (British Academy, London, Schweich Lectures on Biblical Archaeology Series, 1930). 1972. reprint ed. pap. 35.00 (*0-8115-1279-7*) Periodicals Srv.

Crowfoot, James E., jt. auth. see Lesnick, Michael T.

Crowfoot, John, tr. see Kosals, L.

Crowfoot, John, tr. see Razgon, Lev.

Crowfoot, John, tr. see Shentalinsky, Vitaly.

Crowfoot, John, tr. see Veselakila, Zakilara.

Crowfoot, John W. Early Churches in Palestine. Date not set. write for info. (*0-8434-0127-3*, Pub. by McGrath NH) Ayer.

Crowhurst. ACOL: Complete System. 1996. pap. 17.95 (*1-85744-006-4*, Pub. by Cadgn Bks) Macmillan.

Crowhurst, Eric. ACOL: The Complete System. 1992. 20.00 (*1-85744-506-6*, Maxwell Macmillan) Macmillan.

Crowhurst, Eric & Kambites, Andrew. Understanding ACOL: The Good Bidding Guide. 176p. 1997. pap. 17.95 (*0-575-06457-9*, Pub. by V Gollancz) Trafalgar.

Crowhurst-Lennard, Suzanne H. & Lennard, Henry L. Public Life in Urban Places. LC 83-83342. 80p. (Orig.). 1984. pap. 8.95 (*0-935824-03-0*) Gondolier.

Crowhurst, Megan, ed. Proceedings of the West Coast Conference on Formal Linguistics, Vol. 6. 347p. (Orig.). 1987. pap. 13.95 (*0-937073-31-8*) CSLI.

Crowhurst, Norman H. Basic Electronics Course. 2nd ed. 440p. 1987. pap. 19.95 (*0-07-157487-5*) McGraw.

— Basic Electronics Course. 2nd ed. (Illus.). 400p. 1987. 24.95 (*0-8306-0913-X*, 2613); pap. 18.95 (*0-8306-0413-8*) McGraw-Hill Prof.

— Basic Electronics: Syllabus. 1974. pap. text 11.95 (*0-89420-072-0*, 250111); audio 149.75 (*0-89420-126-3*, 250000) Natl Book.

— English: Syllabus. 138p. 1974. pap. text 10.95 (*0-89420-073-9*, 171050); audio 135.90 (*0-89420-145-X*, 171000) Natl Book.

— Introductory Physics: Syllabus. 1974. pap. text 11.95 (*0-89420-084-4*, 230330); audio 164.70 (*0-89420-158-1*, 230000) Natl Book.

— Mastering Technical Mathematics. 512p. 1991. pap. 29.95 (*0-07-157586-3*) McGraw.

— Mastering Technical Mathematics. (Illus.). 586p. 1991. 34.95 (*0-8306-6438-6*, 3438); pap. 24.95 (*0-8306-3438-X*) McGraw-Hill Prof.

— Problem Solving Arts: Part One Syllabus. 1976. pap. text 12.95 (*0-89420-085-2*, 256040); audio 227.10 (*0-89420-175-1*, 256000) Natl Book.

— Problem Solving Arts: Part Three Syllabus. 1978. pap. text 15.95 (*0-89420-040-2*, 256130); audio 196.20 (*0-89420-177-8*, 256090) Natl Book.

— Problem Solving Arts: Part Two Syllabus. 1977. pap. text 14.95 (*0-89420-029-1*, 256082); audio 195.80 (*0-89420-176-X*, 256050) Natl Book.

— Statistics. 110p. (Orig.). 1981. pap. text 11.95 (*0-89420-111-5*, 413040); audio 103.95 (*0-89420-202-2*, 413000) Natl Book.

— Taking the Mysticism from Mathematics. 2nd ed. 178p. (Orig.). 1981. pap. 9.95 (*0-89420-223-5*, 297020) Natl Book.

Crowl. Educational Psychology. 1996. 11.25 (*0-697-28814-5*, WCB McGr Hill) McGrw-H Hghr Educ.

— Fundamentals of Education. 2nd ed. 1995. teacher ed. 9.06 (*0-697-24134-3*, WCB McGr Hill) McGrw-H Hghr Educ.

Crowl, jt. auth. see Isely, Duane.

Crowl, Christine. The Hunter & the Woodpecker. (American Heritage Ser.). (Illus.). 12p. (Orig.). (J). (ps-6). 1990. pap. 3.95 (*1-877976-09-1*, 406-0015) Tipi Pr.

This children's book describes how the Sioux first discovered the flute, which makes magical music. The Red Headed Woodpecker tells a young brave of its powers to win over a beautiful maiden. A charming story, delightfully illustrated in four colors. A story for children of all ages. *Publisher Paid Annotation.*

–White Buffalo Woman. (American Heritage Ser.). (Illus.). 18p. (Orig.). (YA). (gr. 6 up). 1990. pap. 3.95 (*1-877976-10-5*, 406-0014) Tipi Pr.

This story is a core legend of the Sioux & how the Sioux received the Sacred Prayer Pipe. The pipe was an important religious symbol among the Sioux. It was a "moveable" altar which was used in prayer & ceremony. It was the most cherished thing a man could own. The legend of WHITE BUFFALO WOMEN & the pipe originated with the Brule Sioux & is a story that has been handed down through the centuries. Beautifully told & illustrated in four colors, a charming story for children young & old. *Publisher Paid Annotation.*

Crowl, Daniel A. & Louvar, Joseph F. Chemical Process Safety: Fundamentals with Applications. LC 89-8766. 528p. (C). 1989. 97.00 (*0-13-129701-5*) P-H.

Crowl, Daniel A., et al. Health & Environmental Risk Analysis, Vol. 2. LC 97-34525. Vol. 2. 704p. (C). 1997. 94.00 (*0-13-127739-1*) P-H.

Crowl, Daniel A., jt. auth. see Bollinger, Robert E.

Crowl, Daniel A., jt. ed. see Grossel, Stanley S.

Crowl, Philip A. United States Army in World War 2, War in the Pacific, Campaign in the Marianas. 525p. 1993. per. 41.00 (*0-16-061312-4*) USGPO.

Crowl, Philip A. United States Army in World War 2, War in the Pacific: Campaign in the Marianas. LC 60-60000. (Center for Military History Publication German Report Series, DA Pam: No. 5-7). (Illus.). 505p. 1985. reprint ed. 46.00 (*0-16-001893-5*, S/N 008-029-00040-7) USGPO.

Crowl, Phillip A. Maryland During & after the Revolution: A Political & Economic Study. LC 78-64189. (Johns Hopkins University. Studies in the Social Sciences. Thirtieth Ser. 1912: 1). reprint ed. 37.50 (*0-404-61296-2*) AMS Pr.

Crowl, Samuel. Shakespeare Observed: Studies in Performance on Stage & Screen. LC 92-9364. (Illus.). 208p. (C). 1993. reprint ed. pap. 16.95 (*0-8214-1064-4*); reprint ed. text 35.00 (*0-8214-1034-2*) Ohio U Pr.

Crowl, Susan & King, Roma A., Jr., eds. The Complete Works of Robert Browning: With Variant Readings & Annotations, Vol. 16. 300p. 1998. text 65.00 (*0-8214-1251-5*) Ohio U Pr.

— The Complete Works of Robert Browning with Variant Readings & Annotations, Vol. VIII: The Ring & the Book, Bks. 5-8. 400p. 1988. text 65.00 (*0-8214-0380-X*) Ohio U Pr.

Crowl, Susan, ed. see Browning, Robert.

Crowl, Thomas K. Fundamentals of Educational Research. 2nd ed. LC 95-80771. 443p. (C). 1995. text 42.77 (*0-697-24133-5*) Brown & Benchmark.

Crowl, Thomas K. & Berkowitz, Mina. Educational Psychology. 192p. (C). 1996. text, student ed. 20.62 (*0-697-29467-6*) Brown & Benchmark.

Crowl, Thomas K. & Kaminsky, Sally. Educational Psychology: A Contemporary Perspective. LC 96-83184. 560p. (C). 1996. text. write for info. (*0-697-26816-0*) Brown & Benchmark.

Crowl, Thomas K. & Mendola, Leonard R. Fundamentals of Educational Research. 2nd ed. 304p. (C). 1996. text, student ed. 19.37 (*0-697-29468-4*) Brown & Benchmark.

Crowl, Thomas K., et al. Educational Psychology: Windows on Teaching. 36p. (C). 1996. per. 38.75 (*0-697-38003-3*) Brown & Benchmark.

Crowleigh, Ann. Dead As Dead Can Be. 256p. 1993. mass mkt. 3.99 (*0-8217-4099-7*, Zebra Kensgtn) Kensgtn Pub Corp.

— Wait for the Dark. 256p. 1993. mass mkt. 3.99 (*0-8217-4298-1*, Zebra Kensgtn) Kensgtn Pub Corp.

Crowles, Joseph. Fundamentals of Electrostatics. 1986. text 52.95 (*0-471-80318-9*) Krieger.

Crowley. Clinical Trials in Oncology. 208p. 1997. ring bd. 79.95 (*0-412-99631-6*, Chap & Hall CRC) CRC Pr.

— Introduction to Human Disease. 3rd ed. (Health Science Ser.). 848p. (C). 1992. pap., teacher ed. 10.00 (*0-86720-850-3*) Jones & Bartlett.

Crowley & North. Paleoclimatology. (Series on Geology & Geophysics: No. 18). (Illus.). 360p. 1996. pap. text 43.95 (*0-19-510533-8*) OUP.

Crowley, tr. see Tournay, Raymond J.

Crowley, Aleister. Absinthe: The Green Goddess. (Orig.). 1994. pap. 5.95 (*1-55818-270-5*) Holmes Pub.

— Aceldama: Aleister Crowley's First Book. 1993. reprint ed. pap. 7.95 (*1-55818-249-7*) Holmes Pub.

— AHA! LC 83-82342. 96p. 1996. reprint ed. pap. 12.95 (*1-56184-035-1*) New Falcon Pubns.

— Ahab & Other Poems. 1973. lib. bdg. 250.00 (*0-87968-221-3*) Krishna Pr.

— Alexandra. Naylor, Anthony, ed. 1992. 60.00 (*1-872736-04-1*, Pub. by Mandrake Pr) Holmes Pub.

— Amphora. 1993. reprint ed. 35.00 (*1-55818-218-7*, First Impress) Holmes Pub.

— Appeal to the American Republic. 1993. reprint ed. pap. 9.95 (*1-55818-250-0*) Holmes Pub.

— The Argonauts. 1973. lib. bdg. 250.00 (*0-87968-222-1*) Krishna Pr.

— Book Four. 1973. lib. bdg. 250.00 (*0-87968-114-4*) Krishna Pr.

— Book Four. LC 70-146544. (Illus.). 128p. 1986. pap. 9.95 (*0-87728-513-6*) Weiser.

— The Book of Lies. 1973. lib. bdg. 250.00 (*0-87968-115-2*) Krishna Pr.

— Book of Lies. LC 79-16636. (Illus.). 198p. 1970. reprint ed. pap. 9.95 (*0-87728-516-0*) Weiser.

— Book of the Law. 128p. 1976. pap. 7.95 (*0-87728-334-6*) Weiser.

— The Book of Thoth. LC 79-16399. (Illus.). 287p. 1977. pap. 12.95 (*0-913866-12-1*, BK17) US Games Syst.

— The Book of Thoth Vol. III, No. 5: Being the Equinox. LC 79-16399. (Illus.). 308p. 1974. reprint ed. pap. 14.95 (*0-87728-268-4*) Weiser.

— Broadsheet Collection of Thirteen Rare Crowley Items. 1993. 19.95 (*1-55818-326-4*) Holmes Pub.

— Carmen Saeculare. 1993. reprint ed. pap. 9.95 (*1-55818-260-8*) Holmes Pub.

— City of God: A Rhapsody. 1993. reprint ed. pap. 6.95 (*1-55818-257-8*) Holmes Pub.

— Clouds Without Water. 1973. lib. bdg. 250.00 (*0-87968-111-X*) Krishna Pr.

C

An Asterisk (*) at the beginning of an entry indicates that the title is appearing for the first time.

— Clouds Without Water. Verey, C., ed. 140p. 1986. reprint ed. pap. 14.95 (0-934781-00-1) Bk Look.
— Clouds Without Water. 139p. 1973. reprint ed. pap. text 7.50 (0-911662-50-2) Yoga.
— Cocaine. 1992. lib. bdg. 79.95 (0-8490-9900-5) Gordon Pr.
— Cocaine: Impressions & Opinions. Arliss, Edward, ed. 1995. pap. 4.95 (1-55818-320-5) Holmes Pub.
— The Collected Works of Aleister Crowley, 3 vols., Set. 1974. lib. bdg. 900.00 (0-8490-3962-2) Krishna Pr.
— Collected Works of Aleister Crowley, Vol. 1. 269p. 1974. reprint ed. 18.00 (0-911662-51-0) Yoga.
— Collected Works of Aleister Crowley, Vol. 2. 282p. 1974. reprint ed. 18.00 (0-911662-52-9) Yoga.
— Collected Works of Aleister Crowley, Vol. 3. 248p. 1974. reprint ed. 18.00 (0-911662-53-7) Yoga.
— The Collected Writings of Aleister Crowley, 3 vols. 1973. 900.00 (0-685-01965-9) Gordon Pr.
— Commentaries on the Holy Books & Other Papers. 1998. pap. 29.95 (0-87728-905-0) Weiser.
— The Confessions of Aleister Crowley: An Autobiography. Symonds, John & Grant, Kenneth, eds. (Illus.). 960p. 1989. pap. 27.95 (0-14-019189-5, Penguin Bks) Viking Penguin.
— Creed of the Thelemites. 1973. lib. bdg. 250.00 (0-87968-500-X) Krishna Pr.
— Crowley Deck, Small. 1988. pap. 15.00 (0-88079-308-2, CR80) US Games Syst.
— Crowley on Drugs. rev. ed. Beta, Hymenaeons, ed. LC 97-75752. (Illus.). 192p. 2000. pap. 14.95 (1-56184-016-5) New Falcon Pubns.
— De Arte Magica. 1987. pap. 5.95 (0-916411-61-3, Sure Fire) Holmes Pub.
— Diary of a Drug Fiend. 1973. lib. bdg. 300.00 (0-87968-110-1) Krishna Pr.
— Diary of a Drug Fiend. LC 79-142495. 384p. 1970. pap. 12.50 (0-87728-146-7) Weiser.
— The Diary of a Drug Fiend. 384p. 1989. reprint ed. lib. bdg. 26.95 (0-89966-593-4) Buccaneer Bks.
— Dream of Scipio. 1973. lib. bdg. 250.00 (0-87968-501-8) Krishna Pr.
— Eight Lectures on Yoga. rev. ed. LC 85-70851. 128p. 1991. pap. 9.95 (1-56184-007-6) New Falcon Pubns.
— Eleusinian Rites & Why & How of Ecstasy. 1993. reprint ed. pap. 6.95 (1-55818-253-5) Holmes Pub.
— The Equinox, 2 vols., Vol. I, Nos. 1-10. unabridged ed. (Illus.). 4454p. 1999. reprint ed. boxed set 375.00 (0-87728-926-3) Weiser.
— The Equinox, Vol. 3, No. 1. unabridged ed. (Illus.). 464p. 1992. 55.00 (0-87728-210-2) Weiser.
— The Equinox: The Review of Scientific Illuminism, Vol. 3, No. 10. 288p. 1990. pap. 15.95 (0-87728-719-8) Weiser.
— The Equinox of the Gods. 1973. lib. bdg. 250.00 (0-87968-157-8) Krishna Pr.
— The Equinox of the Gods. Beta, Hymenaeus, ed. LC 91-60792. 208p. 1991. pap. 14.95 (1-56184-028-9) New Falcon Pubns.
— An Essay upon Number. 1988. reprint ed. pap. 6.95 (1-55818-106-7, Sure Fire) Holmes Pub.
— The Fish: An Unfinished Novel. Naylor, Anthony, ed. 128p. 1992. text 45.00 (1-872736-05-X, Pub. by Mandrake Pr) Holmes Pub.
— The Forbidden Lecture: Gilles de Rais. 1990. text 35.00 (1-872736-00-9, Pub. by Mandrake Pr) Holmes Pub.
— The Fun of the Fair. 1993. reprint ed. pap. 6.95 (1-55818-258-6) Holmes Pub.
— Gargoyles. 128p. 1992. reprint ed. pap. 24.95 (1-872736-16-5, Pub. by Mandrake Pr) Holmes Pub.
— Gems from the Equinox. rev. ed. LC 82-83309. 1184p. 1991. 49.95 (1-56184-019-X) New Falcon Pubns.
— The Giant's Thumb. 354p. (Orig.). 1992. pap. 45.00 (1-872736-14-9, Pub. by Mandrake Pr) Holmes Pub.
— Golden Twigs. Starr, Martin P., ed. LC 88-24810. (Illus.). 169p. 1988. 21.95 (0-933429-03-7) Teitan Pr.
— A Handbook of Geomancy. 1989. pap. 6.95 (1-55818-157-1) Holmes Pub.
— The Heart of the Master. rev. ed. LC 91-60793. (Illus.). 144p. 1992. pap. 12.95 (1-56184-027-0) New Falcon Pubns.
— The Holy Books of Thelema. LC 82-50829. (Illus.). 320p. 1989. pap. 19.95 (0-87728-686-8) Weiser.
— Improvement of Psycho-Analysis. (Orig.). 1993. reprint ed. pap. 5.95 (1-55818-265-9) Holmes Pub.
— In Residence: A Don's Guide to Cambridge. 1993. reprint ed. pap. 34.95 (1-872736-21-1, Pub. by Mandrake Pr) Holmes Pub.
— Jepthah & Other Mysteries. 1973. lib. bdg. 250.00 (0-87968-217-5) Krishna Pr.
— Konx Om Pax. 108p. 1973. reprint ed. pap. text 7.50 (0-911662-49-9) Yoga.
— Konx Om Pax: Essays in Light. LC 89-77963. (Illus.). 144p. 1990. 27.95 (0-933429-04-5) Teitan Pr.
— Last Ritual: The Thanatopsis of Aleister Crowley. (Illus.). 1993. reprint ed. pap. 9.95 (1-55818-254-3) Holmes Pub.
— The Law Is for All: The Authorized Popular Commentary to the Book of the Law. rev. ed. Wilkinson, Louis U., ed. LC 96-68645. (Illus.). 304p. 1996. pap. 16.95 (1-56184-090-4) New Falcon Pubns.
— Liber Aleph Vel CXI: The Book of Wisdom or Folly. LC 91-8023. 254p. 1991. pap. 19.95 (0-87728-729-5) Weiser.
— Little Essays Toward Truth. rev. ed. LC 91-60059. 96p. 1991. pap. 9.95 (1-56184-000-9) New Falcon Pubns.
— Magic in Theory & Practice. 1973. lib. bdg. 300.00 (0-87968-128-4) Krishna Pr.
— Magical Diaries of Aleister Crowley: Tunisia, 1923. Skinner, Stephen, ed. LC 95-50923. 272p. 1999. reprint ed. pap. 14.95 (0-87728-856-9) Weiser.
— Magick Bk. 4: Liber ABA. 2nd rev. ed. LC 97-37399. Vol. 4. (Illus.). 926p. 1997. 60.00 (0-87728-919-0) Weiser.
— Magick Without Tears. rev. ed. LC 82-83310. 560p. 1991. pap. 19.95 (1-56184-018-1) New Falcon Pubns.
— Moonchild. 1995. reprint ed. lib. bdg. 28.95 (1-56849-670-2) Buccaneer Bks.
— Moonchild. LC 72-142496. 336p. 1970. reprint ed. pap. 12.95 (0-87728-147-5) Weiser.
— Mortadello: or the Angel of Venice. 144p. 1993. reprint ed. pap. 37.50 (1-872736-17-3, Pub. by Mandrake Pr) Holmes Pub.
— The Mother's Tragedy & Other Poems. 1993. reprint ed. pap. 37.50 (1-872736-19-X, Pub. by Mandrake Pr) Holmes Pub.
— One Star in Sight. 1973. lib. bdg. 250.00 (0-87968-506-9) Krishna Pr.
— Orpheus. 1973. lib. bdg. 250.00 (0-87968-176-4) Krishna Pr.
— The Revival of Magick & Other Essays. Beta, Hymenaeus, ed. LC 97-75753. (Illus.). 240p. 1998. pap. 16.95 (1-56184-133-1) New Falcon Pubns.
— Rosa Decidua. 1993. pap. 7.95 (1-55818-251-9) Holmes Pub.
— Scented Garden of Abdullah the Satirist of Shiraz: A Facsimile Edition. fac. ed. LC 91-8493. 160p. 1991. 29.95 (0-933429-05-3) Teitan Pr.
— The Scrutinies of Simon Iff. Starr, Martin P., ed. LC 87-7122. (Illus.). 200p. 1987. 19.95 (0-933429-02-9) Teitan Pr.
— 777 & Other Qabalistic Writings. rev. ed. LC 83-160567. 311p. 1986. reprint ed. pap. 14.95 (0-87728-670-1) Weiser.
— Seven Seven Seven: A Study of the Kabbalah. 1973. lib. bdg. 250.00 (0-87968-105-5) Krishna Pr.
— Songs of Italy. 1993. reprint ed. pap. 6.95 (1-55818-252-7) Holmes Pub.
— Songs of the Spirit. 1973. lib. bdg. 250.00 (0-87968-220-5) Krishna Pr.
— Songs of the Spirit. 1992. reprint ed. pap. 27.50 (1-872736-18-1, Pub. by Mandrake Pr) Holmes Pub.
— The Soul of Osiris. 1973. lib. bdg. 250.00 (0-87968-177-2) Krishna Pr.
— The Soul of Osiris. 1992. reprint ed. pap. 37.50 (1-872736-20-3, Pub. by Mandrake Pr) Holmes Pub.
— The Star & the Garter. 1973. lib. bdg. 250.00 (0-87968-175-6) Krishna Pr.
— The Stategem & Other Stories. 1993. reprint ed. lib. bdg. 18.95 (0-89968-422-X, Lghtyr Pr) Buccaneer Bks.
— The Stratagem & Other Stories. 1973. lib. bdg. 250.00 (0-87968-117-9) Krishna Pr.
— The Stratagem & Other Stories. LC 74-167446. (Short Story Index Reprint Ser.). 1977. reprint ed. 13.95 (0-8369-3972-7) Ayer.
— Summa Spes. (Orig.). 1993. pap. 7.95 (1-55818-248-9) Holmes Pub.
— Tale of Archais. 1973. lib. bdg. 250.00 (0-87968-218-3) Krishna Pr.
— Tannhauser: A Story of All Time. 1973. lib. bdg. 250.00 (0-87968-215-9) Krishna Pr.
— Tao Te Ching, Liber CLXVII. rev. ed. LC 95-22270. (Illus.). 128p. 1995. pap. 12.95 (0-87728-846-1) Weiser.
— Tarot Divination. 72p. 1977. reprint ed. pap. 5.95 (0-87728-347-8) Weiser.
— Temperance: A Tract for the Times. 1993. reprint ed. pap. 9.95 (1-55818-256-X) Holmes Pub.
— Temple of Solomon the King. LC 92-64419. (Illus.). 704p. (Orig.). 2000. pap. 24.95 (1-56184-049-1) New Falcon Pubns.
— Thumbs Up: A Pentagram - A Pantacle to Win the War. 1993. reprint ed. pap. 6.95 (1-55818-255-1) Holmes Pub.
— The Vision & the Voice with Commentary & Other Papers Vol. IV, No. II: The Equinox. (Equinox Reprints Ser.). (Illus.). 448p. 1999. pap. 25.95 (0-87728-906-9) Weiser.
— The Whirlpool. 1973. lib. bdg. 250.00 (0-87968-507-7) Krishna Pr.
— The Winged Beetle. LC 92-21980. 256p. 1992. 29.95 (0-933429-06-1) Teitan Pr.
— Works of Aleister Crowley, 4 vols., Set. 1986. lib. bdg. 1500.00 (0-87968-130-6) Gordon Pr.
— World's Tragedy. rev. ed. LC 85-80865. 160p. 1991. pap. 12.95 (1-56184-014-9) New Falcon Pubns.

Crowley, Aleister, ed. The Goetia: The Lesser Key of Solomon the King. rev. ed. Mathers, S. L. MacGregor, tr. LC 95-37057. (Illus.). 160p. 1995. pap. 16.00 (0-87728-847-X) Weiser.

***Crowley, Aleister & Adams, Evangeline.** The General Practice of Astrology. (Illus.). 320p. 2000. (1-57863-908-5) Weiser.
— The General Principles of Astrology, Liber DXXXVI. Beta, Hymenaeus, ed. (Illus.). 608p. 2000. 49.95 (0-87728-908-5) Weiser.

***Crowley, Aleister & Adams, Evangeline Smith.** The General Principles of Astrology. LC 00-36517. 2000. pap. write for info. (0-87728-909-3) Weiser.

Crowley, Aleister, et al. Aleister Crowley's Illustrated Goetia: Sexual Evocation. LC 91-68244. (Illus.). 224p. 1991. pap. 14.95 (1-56184-048-3) New Falcon Pubns.
— The Enochian World of Aleister Crowley: Enochian Sex Magick. 2nd ed. LC 91-60791. (Illus.). 192p. 1991. pap. 14.95 (1-56184-029-7) New Falcon Pubns.
— The Equinox, Vol. 7, No. 1. Borland, Vance, ed. (Illus.). 272p. 1992. 34.50 (0-9626703-0-8) Silver Star Pubns.

Crowley, Aleister, jt. auth. see Fuller, J. F.

Crowley, Aleister, jt. auth. see Spare, Austin O.

Crowley, Aleister, tr. & illus. see Baudelaire, Charles.

Crowley, Alice L. Stanislavski & the Actor: The Method of Physical Action. LC 98-35563. 150p. 1959. pap. 5.00 (0-87830-090-2, D5987, Thtre Arts Bks) Routledge.

Crowley, Anna, tr. see Neumann, Richard K.

Crowley, Bill, jt. auth. see Wallace, Brian P.

Crowley, Brian, jt. auth. see Austin, Anthony.

Crowley, Brian L. The Self, the Individual, & the Community: Liberalism in the Political Thought F. A. Hayek & Sidney & Beatrice Webb. 304p. 1987. text 69.00 (0-19-827497-1) OUP.

Crowley, C. J. Persisting Latinisms in 'El Poema de Mio Cid' & Other Selected Old Spanish Literary Works. (LD Ser.: No. 48). 1952. pap. 25.00 (0-527-00794-3) Periodicals Srv.

Crowley, Carleen. All about Clothes. (Gregg-McGraw-Hill Series for Independent Living). 1978. text 10.41 (0-07-014765-5) McGraw.

Crowley, Charles. Operating Systems: A Design-Oriented Approach. 768p. (C). 1996. text 54.95 (0-256-15151-2, Irwn McGrw-H) McGrw-H Hghr Educ.

Crowley, Charles B. Aristotelian-Thomistic Philosophy of Measure & the International System of Units (SI) Correlation of International System of Units with the Philosophy of Aristotle & St. Thomas. Redpath, Peter A., ed. LC 96-20379. 318p. 1996. lib. bdg. 48.00 (0-7618-0401-3) U Pr of Amer.

Crowley, Charles L., jt. ed. see Feinschreiber, Robert.

Crowley, Chris, jt. auth. see Crowley, Vivianne.

Crowley, Christine B. Robinson, see Robinson Crowley, Christine B.

Crowley, D. A., ed. A History of the County of Wiltshire Vol. XV: Amesbury Hundred & Part of Branch & Dale Hundred, Vol. 15. (Victoria History of the Counties of England Ser.). (Illus.). 380p. 1995. 120.00 (0-19-722785-6) OUP.

Crowley, D. A., ed. A History of Wiltshire: Downton Hundred, Elstub & Everleigh Hundred, Vol. 11. (Victoria History of the Counties of England Ser.). (Illus.). 270p. 1980. 145.00 (0-19-722751-1) OUP.

Crowley, D. A., ed. A History of Wiltshire: Malmesbury Hundred, Vol. 14. (Victoria History of the Counties of England Ser.). (Illus.). 308p. 1991. 140.00 (0-19-722779-1, 6613) OUP.
— A History of Wiltshire: Ramsbury Hundred, Selkley Hundred, The Borough of Marlborough, Vol. 12. (Victoria History of the Counties of England Ser.). (Illus.). 1984. 150.00 (0-19-722759-7) OUP.

Crowley, D. A., ed. A History of Wiltshire: South-West Wiltshire: Chalk & Dunworth Hundreds, Vol. 13. (Victoria History of the Counties of England Ser.). (Illus.). 300p. 1987. 155.00 (0-19-722769-4) OUP.

Crowley, D. J. Understanding Communication: The Signifying Web, Vol. 2. (Communication & the Human Condition Ser.). xvi, 212p. 1982. text 106.00 (0-677-05920-5) Gordon & Breach.

Crowley, D. J. & Heyer, Paul. Communication in History: Technology, Culture, Society. 3rd ed. LC 98-28839. 368p. (C). 1998. pap. text 61.00 (0-8013-3133-1) Longman.

Crowley, Daniel J. I Could Talk Old-Story Good: Creativity in Bahamian Folklore. LC GR0040.C73. (University of California Publications, Folklore Studies: No. 17). 167p. reprint ed. pap. 51.80 (0-7837-4837-X, 204448400003) Bks Demand.

***Crowley, David.** Communication in History. 3rd ed. (C). 1999. pap. text 42.60 (0-8013-1791-6) Longman.

Crowley, David & Heyer, Paul, eds. Communication in History. 352p. (C). 1991. pap. text 32.95 (0-8013-0598-5, 78524) Longman.

Crowley, David & Mitchell, David, eds. Communication Theory Today. 340p. 1994. 47.50 (0-8047-2348-6); pap. 16.95 (0-8047-2347-8) Stanford U Pr.

Crowley, David, jt. ed. see Reid, Susan E.

Crowley, Dieter M. The Guardians of Truth: (The Awakening) 199p. (Orig.). 1994. pap. 19.95 (0-9644855-0-8) Sound Idea Prod.

Crowley, Donald, ed. Nathaniel Hawthorne. (Critical Heritage Ser.). 548p. (C). 1997. 160.00 (0-415-15930-X) Routledge.

Crowley, Donald & Heffron, Florence. The Idaho State Constitution: A Reference Guide, 19. LC 93-21486. (Reference Guides to the State Constitutions of the United States Ser.: No. 19). 328p. 1994. lib. bdg. 99.50 (0-313-27601-3, Greenwood Pr) Greenwood.

***Crowley, Douglas, et al, eds.** A History of the County of Wiltshire, Vol. XVI. (Victoria History of the Counties of England Ser.). (Illus.). 302p. 2000. text 120.00 (0-19-722793-7) OUP.

Crowley, Ed, tr. see Nodet, Etienne.

Crowley, Elaine. A Dublin Girl: Growing up in the 1930s. LC 97-18924. 172p. 1998. 21.00 (1-56947-112-6) Soho Press.
— A Dublin Girl: Growing up in the 1930s. LC 97-18924. 172p. 1999. pap. 10.00 (1-56947-137-1) Soho Press.
— A Family Cursed. 309p. 1996. 27.00 (1-85797-767-X, Pub. by Orion Pubng Grp) Trafalgar.

Crowley, F. K., ed. Modern Australia in Documents, 1901-1970. Incl. 1939-1970. 1973. 7.50 (0-85885-033-8); 1973. write for info. (0-318-51605-5) Trafalgar.

***Crowley, Frank.** Big John Forrest: A Founding Father of the Commonwealth of Australia. 536p. 2000. 45.00 (1-876268-44-1, Pub. by Univ of West Aust Pr) Intl Spec Bk.

Crowley, Haughy, Hanson, Toole & Dietrich Staff. Montana Environmental Law Handbook. 2nd ed. LC 96-217034. 391p. 1996. pap. text 89.00 (0-86587-531-6) Gov Insts.

Crowley, J. E. This Sheba, Self: The Conceptualization of Economic Life in Eighteenth-Century America. LC 73-19334. (Johns Hopkins University Studies in Historical & Political Science: Series 92, No. 2). 176p. reprint ed. pap. 54.60 (0-8357-6910-0, 203796800009) Bks Demand.

Crowley, J. Edward, tr. see Tournay, Raymond Jacques.

Crowley, J. L., ed. Vision As Process: Basic Research on Computer Vision Systems. (ESPRIT Basic Research Ser.). 464p. 1994. 93.95 (0-387-58143-X) Spr-Verlag.

Crowley, J. M., et al. Proceedings of the ESA-IEJ Joint Symposium on Electrostatics. 350p. 1994. pap. 9.95 (1-885540-00-0) Laplacian Pr.

Crowley, James C., jt. auth. see Hallmark, Bryan W.

Crowley, James F. Alliance for Change: A Plan for Community Action on Adolescent Drug Abuse. LC 84-71356. (Illus.). 226p. (Orig.). 1984. pap. 8.95 (0-9613416-0-2) Comm Intervention.

Crowley, James F., jt. auth. see Muldoon, Joseph A.

Crowley, Janice L. The Aegean & the East: An Investigation into the Transference of Artistic Motifs Between the Aegean, Egypt, & the Near East in the Bronze Age. (Studies in Mediterranean Archaeology & Literature: No. 51). (Illus.). 507p. (Orig.). 1989. pap. 95.00 (91-86098-55-1, Pub. by P Astroms) Coronet Bks.

Crowley, Jean Joy, jt. auth. see Wright, E. Deborah.

Crowley, Jimmy. Jimmy Crowley's Irish Song Book. 1986. pap. 9.95 (0-85342-773-9) Dufour.

Crowley, Joan F. & Vaillancourt, Dan. Lenin to Gorbachev: Three Generations of Soviet Communists Supplement. 216p. (C). 1989. pap. text, suppl. ed. 14.95 (0-88295-863-1) Harlan Davidson.

Crowley, John. Daemonomania. LC 99-44109. 640p. 2000. 24.95 (0-553-10004-1, Spectra) Bantam.

Crowley, John, et al, eds. Survival Analysis. LC 82-84316. (IMS Lecture Notes - Monographs: Vol. 2). x, 302p. 1983. pap. 25.00 (0-940600-02-1) Inst Math.

Crowley, John & Huitric, Ronan. Interenergy Competition in Natural Gas Price Formation: The Case of the United States since Deregulation. 24p. 1990. pap. 10.00 (0-918714-20-6) Intl Res Ctr Energy.

Crowley, John D. Developing a Vision: Strategic Planning & the Library Media Specialist. LC 94-2198. (Professional Guides in School Librarianship Ser.). 160p. 1994. 35.00 (0-313-28835-6, Greenwood Pr) Greenwood.

***Crowley, John E.** The Invention of Comfort: Sensibilities & Design in Early Modern Britain & Early America. LC 00-8958. (Illus.). 384p. 2000. 42.00 (0-8018-6437-2) Johns Hopkins Uni.

Crowley, John E. The Privileges of Independence: Neomercantilism & the American Revolution. LC 93-3563. (Early America: History, Context, Culture Ser.). 224p. (C). 1993. text 37.50 (0-8018-4667-6) Johns Hopkins.

Crowley, John Gordon, Jr. Primitive Baptists of the Wiregrass South: 1815 to the Present. LC 98-39624. (Illus.). 320p. 1999. 49.95 (0-8130-1640-1) U Press Fla.

Crowley, John W. The Black Heart's Truth: The Early Career of W. D. Howells. LC 84-20908. xv, 192p. 1985. 34.95 (0-8078-1632-9) U of NC Pr.
— The Dean of American Letters: The Late Career of William Dean Howells. LC 99-29050. 160p. 1999. 25.00 (1-55849-240-2) U of Mass Pr.
— Drunkard's Progress: Narratives of Addiction, Despair, & Recovery. LC 98-8732. 1999. 15.95 (0-8018-6007-5); 45.00 (0-8018-6008-3) Johns Hopkins.
— The Mask of Fiction: Essays on W. D. Howells. LC 88-39866. 288p. 1989. 32.50 (0-87023-674-1) U of Mass Pr.
— The White Logic: Alcoholism & Gender in American Modernist Fiction. LC 94-14809. 216p. (C). 1994. pap. 16.95 (0-87023-944-9) U of Mass Pr.

Crowley, John W., ed. New Essays on "Winesburg, Ohio" (American Novel Ser.). 141p. (C). 1990. pap. text 14.95 (0-521-38723-X) Cambridge U Pr.
— New Essays on "Winesburg, Ohio" (American Novel Ser.). 141p. (C). 1990. text 32.95 (0-521-38283-1) Cambridge U Pr.

Crowley, John W., ed. see Austen, Roger.

Crowley, Joseph Donald. Critical Essays on Walker Percy. (Critical Essays on American Literature Ser.). 264p. (C). 1989. 49.00 (0-8161-8880-7, G K Hall & Co) Mac Lib Ref.

Crowley, Joseph Donald, ed. Hawthorne: The Critical Heritage. 1978. 69.50 (0-7100-6886-7, Routledge Thoemms) Routledge.

Crowley, Joseph Donald, ed. see James, Henry.

Crowley, Joseph Donald, jt. ed. see Sattelmeyer, Robert.

Crowley, Joseph Donald, ed. & intro. see Defoe, Daniel.

Crowley, Joseph H., et al, eds. ESA 25th Annual Meeting Proceedings, 1997: Electrostatics Society of America Annual Meeting Proceedings. LC 97-72642. (Illus.). 172p. 1997. pap. text. write for info. (1-885540-05-1) Laplacian Pr.

***Crowley, Joseph M.** Fundamentals of Applied Electrostatics. LC 99-67687. (Illus.). 272p. 1999. pap. 45.00 (1-885540-11-6) Laplacian Pr.

Crowley, Joseph M. & Asano, Kazutoshi, eds. ESA-IEJ 1998 Proceedings of the Joint Symposium on Electrostatics. LC 98-66829. (Illus.). 493p. (C). 1998. pap. 30.00 (1-885540-08-6) Laplacian Pr.

Crowley, Joseph M. & Horenstein, Mark N., eds. Proceedings ESA Annual Meeting, 1999. LC 99-63141. (Illus.). 138p. (C). 1999. pap. 15.00 (1-885540-10-8) Laplacian Pr.

Crowley, Joseph M., et al. ESA 1995 Annual Meeting: Proceedings. 218p. 1995. pap. 25.00 (1-885540-01-9) Laplacian Pr.

Crowley, Joseph N. No Equal in the World: An Interpretation of the Academic Presidency. LC 93-37567. 320p. (C). 1994. 29.95 (0-87417-237-3) U of Nev Pr.

Crowley, Kate & Link, Mike. Boundary Waters Canoe Area Wilderness. (Voyageur Wilderness Ser.). (Illus.). 96p. (Orig.). 1996. pap. 14.95 (0-89658-071-7) Voyageur Pr.

***Crowley, Kate & Link, Mike.** Following the Pack: The World of Wolf Research. (Illus.). 199p. 1999. reprint ed. text 20.00 (0-7881-6684-0) DIANE Pub.

An Asterisk (*) at the beginning of an entry indicates that the title is appearing for the first time.

Crowley, Kate & Link, Mike. Lake Superior's North Shore & Isle Royale. LC 89-14782. (Voyageur Wilderness Ser.). (Illus.). 96p. (Orig.). 1996. pap. 14.95 (*0-89658-115-2*) Voyageur Pr.

Crowley, Kate, jt. auth. see Link, M.

Crowley, Kate, jt. auth. see Link, Mike.

Crowley, Kate, jt. ed. see Walker, Ken.

Crowley, Kathleen. The Day Room: A Memoir of Madness & Mending. LC 94-46756. 178p. 1995. 19.95 (*0-9643348-0-1*) Kennedy Carlisle.

Crowley, Kathleen, jt. auth. see Link, Mike.

Crowley, Kieran. Burned Alive. 352p. 1999. mass mkt. 6.50 (*0-312-97030-7*, St Martins Paperbacks) St Martin.

— Sleep My Little Dead: The True Story of the Zodiac Killer, Vol. 1. LC 97-210559. 1997. mass mkt. 5.99 (*0-312-96339-4*) St Martin.

Crowley, Kieran. True Crime. mass mkt. write for info. (*0-312-97641-0*) St Martin.

Crowley, Leonard. Introduction to Human Disease. 4th ed. (Health Science Ser.). 240p. 1996. pap., teacher ed. 10.00 (*0-7637-0330-3*) Jones & Bartlett.

Crowley, Leonard V. Introduction to Human Disease. 4th ed. (Health Science Ser.). 896p. (C). 1996. 58.75 (*0-86720-736-1*) Jones & Bartlett.

— Introductory Concepts in Anatomy & Physiology. LC 76-2249. (Illus.). 462p. reprint ed. 143.30 (*0-8357-9612-4*, 201507700092) Bks Demand.

Crowley, Leonard V., jt. auth. see Grindel, Cecelia G.

Crowley, Lillie R. Intermediate Algebra: An Introduction to Functions Through Applications. 240p. (C). 1997. pap. text 47.81 (*0-201-85361-2*) Addison-Wesley.

Crowley, Lisle. Creative Bluegrass Guitar. (Orig.). 1996. pap. 14.95 (*1-56922-101-4*, 07-4062) Creat Cncpts.

— Creative Gospel Guitar. (Illus.). 88p. 1996. pap. 12.95 (*1-56922-119-7*, 07-4071) Creat Cncpts.

***Crowley, Lisle.** Creative Sacred Guitar. (Illus.). 144p. 1998. pap. 14.95 (*1-56922-184-7*, 07-4086) Creat Cncpts.

***Crowley, M. Sue.** The Search for Autonomous Intimacy: Sexual Abuse & Young Women's Identity Development. LC 97-42851. (Adolescent Cultures, School & Society Ser.: Vol. 7). 256p. (C). 2000. pap. text 29.95 (*0-8204-3944-4*) P Lang Pubng.

***Crowley, Marilyn Bentz & Mackie, Joan.** The Best Soup Cookbook. (Illus.). 192p. 2000. pap. 17.95 (*0-7788-0017-2*, Pub. by R Rose Inc) Firefly Bks Ltd.

Crowley, Mart. 3 Plays by Mart Crowley. LC 96-13206. 368p. 1996. pap. text 13.95 (*1-55583-357-8*) Alyson Pubns.

Crowley, Mary V., jt. auth. see Trilling, Terry G.

Crowley-Meier, Cheri, ed. see Kearney, Patrick J.

Crowley-Milling, Michael C. John Adams, Engineer Extraordinary: A Tribute. LC 92-42697. (Classics in the History & Philosophy of Science Ser.). 194p. 1993. text 64.00 (*2-88124-875-6*); pap. text 38.00 (*2-88124-876-4*) Gordon & Breach.

Crowley, Miriam, jt. auth. see Nairn, Richard.

Crowley, Nancy. Help, She's Having a Baby. (Illus.). 64p. (Orig.). 1994. pap. write for info. (*0-9640358-0-4*) N Crowley.

— Help She's Having a Baby: Emergency Childbirth. rev. ed. LC 94-220147. (Illus.). 88p. 1994. pap. 8.95 (*0-9640358-1-2*) N Crowley.

Crowley, Patricia. Not My Child: A Mother Confronts Her Child's Sexual Abuse. 320p. 1991. mass mkt. 4.95 (*0-380-71276-8*, Avon Bks) Morrow Avon.

Crowley, Patty, ed. see Calvin, Larry.

Crowley, Paul G. In Ten Thousand Places: Dogma in a Pluralistic Church. LC 97-20777. 156p. 1997. pap. 19.95 (*0-8245-1698-2*) Crossroad NY.

Crowley, R. E., jt. auth. see Paquin, J. R.

Crowley, Rebecca Kaufmann. Hilton Head Guide. (Illus.). 144p. 1995. pap. 9.95 (*1-882943-04-X*) Coastal Villages.

Crowley, Richard. The Way to Wealth, Wherein Is Plainly Taught a Remedy for Sedicion. LC 74-28843. (English Experience Ser.: No. 724). 1975. reprint ed. 10.00 (*90-221-0724-8*) Walter J Johnson.

Crowley, Richard J., jt. auth. see Mills, Joyce C.

***Crowley, Robert.** Lectionary Scenes: 58 Vignettes. LC 96-46497. (Lectionary Ser.). 314p. 1999. pap. 25.85 (*0-7880-1373-4*) CSS OH.

Crowley, Robert. The Select Works of Robert Crowley, Printer, Archdeacon of Hereford, Vicar of St. Lawrence, Jewry. Cowper, J. M., ed. (EETS, ES Ser.: No. 15). 1974. reprint ed. 55.00 (*0-527-00230-5*) Periodicals Srv.

Crowley, Robert F. Lectionary Scenes: 52 Vignettes in Cycle C. LC 96-46497. 312p. (Orig.). 1997. pap. 34.50 (*0-7880-1060-3*) CSS OH.

— Lectionary Scenes: 57 Vignettes. (Lectionary Ser.). 1998. pap. 25.95 incl. disk (*0-7880-1276-2*) CSS OH.

— Lectionary Scenes: 57 Vignettes. LC 96-46497. (Lectionary Ser.). 340p. 1998. pap. 25.95 (*0-7880-1273-8*) CSS OH.

Crowley, Robert T. EDI: Charting a Course to the Future: A Guide to Understanding & Using Electronic Data Interchange. 2nd ed. Wainwright, John, ed. LC 93-2615. 201p. 1993. reprint ed. 42.50 (*1-883872-00-6*) Res Triangle.

Crowley, Ruth, tr. see Bohrer, Karl H.

Crowley, Ruth, tr. see Scharpf, Fritz W.

Crowley, Ruth A., tr. see Ingarden, Roman.

Crowley, Sarah. Reading for Ourselves. 24p. (C). 1993. pap. 5.00 (*0-85598-201-2*, Pub. by Oxfam Pub) Stylus Pub VA.

Crowley, Sharon. Composition in the University: Historical & Polemical Essays. LC 97-45367. (Pittsburgh Series in Composition, Literacy, & Culture). 240p. 1998. pap. 19.95 (*0-8229-5660-8*); text 40.00 (*0-8229-4056-6*) U of Pittsburgh Pr.

— The Methodical Memory: Invention in Current-Traditional Rhetoric. LC 89-37101. 360p. (C). 1990. 26.95 (*0-8093-1615-3*) S Ill U Pr.

Crowley, Sharon & Hawhee, Debra. Ancient Rhetorics for Contemporary Students. 2nd ed. LC 98-5535. 395p. 1998. 48.00 (*0-205-26903-6*) Allyn.

Crowley, Sharon, jt. auth. see Selzer, Jack.

Crowley, Sharon, jt. ed. see Selzer, Jack.

Crowley, Sharon R. Sexual Assault: The Medical-Legal Examination. LC 98-37949. (Illus.). 240p. (C). 1999. 59.95 (*0-8385-8533-7*, Apple Lange Med) McGraw.

Crowley, Shauna. The Screen Test Handbook. 282p. (C). 1990. pap. 19.95 (*0-86819-227-9*, Pub. by Currency Pr) Accents Pubns.

Crowley, Stephen. Hot Coal, Cold Steel: Russian & Ukrainian Workers from the End of the Soviet Union to the Post-Communist Transformation. LC 96-45812. 288p. (C). 1997. text 44.50 (*0-472-10783-6*, 10783) U of Mich Pr.

Crowley, Stewart. Mechanical Genuis. 1997. pap. 6.95 (*0-8167-2787-2*) Troll Communs.

Crowley, Suzanne C. Paisley. Irwin, Miriam D., ed. (Illus.). 48p. 1990. 28.00 (*0-88014-082-8*) Mosaic Pr OH.

Crowley, T. Clio's Craft. 1930. text. write for info. (*0-7730-4746-8*) Addison-Wesley.

Crowley, T. E. Beam Engines. (Album Ser.: No. 15). (Illus.). 32p. (C). 1989. pap. 4.75 (*0-85263-802-7*, Pub. by Shire Pubns) Parkwest Pubns.

Crowley, Terry. Beach-la-Mar to Bislama: The Emergence of a Natural Language in Vanuatu. (Oxford Studies in Language Contact). (Illus.). 444p. 1990. text 125.00 (*0-19-824893-8*) OUP.

— Erromangan (Sye) Grammar. LC 97-40792. (Oceanic Linguistics Special Publication Ser.: Vol. 26). 308p. 1998. pap. text 38.00 (*0-8248-1935-7*) UH Pr.

— An Introduction to Historical Linguistics. 3rd ed. (Illus.). 342p. 1998. pap. text 19.95 (*0-19-558378-7*) OUP.

Crowley, Terry, et al. A Concise History of Christianity in Canada. Murphy, Terrence & Perin, Roberto, eds. (Illus.). 352p. 1996. pap. text 29.95 (*0-19-540758-X*) OUP.

Crowley, Thomas J. & Burke, Kevin C., eds. Tectonic Boundary Conditions for Climate Reconstructions. LC 97-23987. (Oxford Monographs on Geology & Geophysics). (Illus.). 304p. 1998. text 75.00 (*0-19-511245-8*) OUP.

Crowley, Thomas J. & North, Gerald R. Paleoclimatology. (Illus.). 360p. (C). 1995. pap. 35.00 (*0-19-515338-3*) OUP.

Crowley, Tony. Language & History: Theories & Texts. LC 95-1855. (Politics of Language Ser.). 224p. (C). 1995. pap. 25.99 (*0-415-07245-X*) Routledge.

***Crowley, Tony.** Politics of Language in Ireland, 1366-1922: Sourcebook. LC 99-32500. (Politics of Language Ser.). 2000. pap. 25.99 (*0-415-15718-8*) Routledge.

Crowley, Tony. Standard English & the Politics of Language. LC 88-27887. 312p. 1989. pap. 15.95 (*0-252-06082-2*) U of Ill Pr.

***Crowley, Tony, ed.** Politics of Language in Ireland, 1366-1922: Sourcebook. LC 99-32500. 248p. (C). 2000. text. write for info. (*0-415-15717-X*) Routledge.

Crowley, Vivianne. Celtic Wisdom: Seasonal Rituals & Festivals. LC 98-50824. (Illus.). 128p. 1998. 19.95 (*0-8069-7056-1*) Sterling.

***Crowley, Vivianne.** Jung: A Journey of Transformation. LC 99-31192. 1999. 29.95 (*0-8356-0782-8*, Pub. by Theos Pub Hse) Natl Bk Netwk.

— Principles of Jungian Spirituality: The Only Introduction You'll Ever Need. LC 99-204414. (Illus.). 160p. 1998. pap. 11.00 (*0-7225-3578-3*, Pub. by Thorsons MD) Natl Bk Netwk.

Crowley, Vivianne. Principles of Wicca. 1998. pap. 11.00 (*0-7225-3451-5*) Thorsons PA.

***Crowley, Vivianne.** Woman's Kabbalah: Kabbalah for the 21st Century. 2000. 17.95 (*0-7225-3879-0*) Thorsons PA.

***Crowley, Vivianne & Crowley, Chris.** Myths, Magic & Mysticism: The Rituals, Rites & Superstitions of the World's Unorthodox Religions. (Illus.). 224p. 2000. 35.00 (*1-85868-987-2*, Pub. by Carlton Bks Ltd) Natl Bk Netwk.

Crowley, W. F., Jr. & Conn, P. Michael, eds. Modes of Action of GnRH & GnRH Analogs. (Serono Symposia Ser.). (Illus.). 416p. 1992. 180.00 (*0-387-97802-X*) Spr-Verlag.

Crowley, Walt. National Trust Guide/Seattle: America's Guide for Architecture & History Travelers. LC 97-34627. (Illus.). 288p. 1998. pap. 19.95 (*0-471-18044-0*) Wiley.

— Rites of Passage: A Memoir of the Sixties in Seattle. (Illus.). 352p. 1997. pap. 16.95 (*0-295-97493-1*) U of Wash Pr.

— Seattle University, a Century of Jesuit Education. (Illus.). 128p. 1991. 19.91 (*0-9630691-0-1*) Seattle Univ.

— Woodland Park Zoo Guide. (Illus.). 112p. (Orig.). 1995. pap. 11.95 (*0-945973-25-X*) Woodland Pk Zoo Soc.

Crowley, Walt & Crowley, William. Rites of Passage: A Memoir of the Sixties in Seattle. LC 95-38660. (Illus.). 352p. (C). 1995. 30.00 (*0-295-97492-3*) U of Wash Pr.

Crowley, Walt & Group Health Cooperative of Puget Sound Staff. To Serve the Greatest Number: A History of Group Health Cooperative of Puget Sound. LC 96-38972. (Illus.). 312p. 1997. 19.95 (*0-295-97587-3*) U of Wash Pr.

Crowley, Walt, ed. see Taial, Sidney.

Crowley, William, ed. Chemicals on the Internet Vol. 2: Inorganics & Minerals. 200p. 1997. pap. 69.00 incl. disk (*0-88415-140-9*, 5140) Gulf Pub.

— Rushtons Rowboats & Canoes: The 1903 Catalog in Perspective. 80p. 1993. reprint ed. pap. 9.95 (*0-910020-42-6*) Adirondack Mus.

Crowley, William, jt. auth. see Crowley, Walt.

Crowley,M.D., Leonard V. Introduction to Human Disease. 4th ed. (Health Science Ser.). 848p. (C). 1992. 50.00 (*0-86720-333-1*) Jones & Bartlett.

Crowling, Anthony. My Life with the Samurai: A POW in Indonesia. LC 96-176259. 1996. pap. text 16.95 (*0-86417-812-3*, Pub. by Kangaroo Pr) Seven Hills Bk.

Crown. Conversational Ingles. 1998. pap. 7.00 (*0-609-80297-6*) Liv Lang.

— Living Language French on a Rainy Day. LC 99-13172. (ANG, APA & FRE.). 1999. 14.95 (*0-609-60209-8*) Liv Lang.

— Living Language Italian on a Rainy Day. LC 99-13163. (ITA.). 1999. 14.95 (*0-609-60211-X*) Liv Lang.

— Living Language Spanish on a Rainy Day. LC 99-19112. (SPA.). 1999. 14.95 (*0-609-60210-1*) Liv Lang.

Crown, Alan D. A Bibliography of the Samaritans. 2nd ed. LC 92-42799. (American Theological Library Association Monograph: No. 32). (Illus.). 338p. 1993. 50.00 (*0-8108-2646-1*) Scarecrow.

Crown, Alan D., ed. The Samaritans: Their Religion, Literature, Society & Culture. 990p. 1988. 242.00 (*3-16-145237-2*, Pub. by JCB Mohr) Coronet Bks.

Crown, Alan D., et al, eds. Companion to Samaritan Studies. 500p. 1993. 137.50 (*3-16-145666-1*, Pub. by JCB Mohr) Coronet Bks.

Crown, Alan D., jt. auth. see Kessler, David.

Crown, Alan D., ed. see Kessler, David.

Crown, Bonnie & Atlas, Susan. D-I-V-O-R-C-E-S Spell Discover: A Kit to Help Children Express Their Feelings about Divorce. (Illus.). 52p. (Orig.). (J). (gr. 1-8). 1992. pap., spiral bd. 15.95 (*0-9633626-0-7*) Courageous Kids.

***Crown, Carol, ed.** Wonders to Behold: The Visionary Art of Myrtice West. LC 99-37638. (Illus.). 144p. 1999. 50.00 (*0-914457-99-3*, Pub. by Mustang Pub) Natl Bk Netwk.

***Crown, Cate & Rogers, Carol.** Trenton. LC 99-69060. (Images of America Ser.). (Illus.). 128p. 2000. pap. 18.99 (*0-7524-0961-1*) Arcadia Publng.

Crown, Conrad J. Finite Mathematics Student Manual. 3rd ed. (C). 1989. pap. text, student ed. 24.00 (*0-201-10816-X*) Addison-Wesley.

Crown Equipment Corporation Staff, jt. auth. see McNees, Pat.

Crown, Faith W. Mail Order Treasure in Your Library: How to Find It. (Illus.). x, 39p. 1993. reprint ed. pap. 6.00 (*0-9632462-0-8*) Juniper H Pubns.

Crown, Francis J., Jr. Surveys of the Confederate Postmasters' Provisionals. LC 81-52857. 1984. lib. bdg. 50.00 (*0-88000-124-0*) Quarterman.

Crown, J. Conrad & Bittinger, Marvin L. Finite Mathematics: A Modeling Approach. 2nd ed. LC 80-19472. (Mathematics Ser.). (Illus.). 480p. (C). 1981. text. write for info. (*0-201-03145-0*) Addison-Wesley.

Crown, J. Conrad, jt. auth. see Bittinger, Marvin L.

Crown, John, jt. auth. see Heinl, Robert D.

Crown, John, jt. auth. see Hough, Frank.

Crown, Judith & Coleman, Glenn. No Hands: The Rise & Fall of the Schwinn Bicycle Company, An American Institution. (Illus.). 384p. 1995. 25.00 (*0-8050-3553-2*) H Holt & Co.

Crown, Judston. The Search for Sebastian. LC 90-84909. (Orig.). 1991. pap. 9.95 (*0-9623497-6-3*) Los Hombres.

***Crown, Lawrence.** Penny Marshall: An Unauthorized Biography of the Director & Comedienne. 256p. 2000. pap. 15.95 (*1-58063-161-4*) Renaissance.

Crown Living Language Staff. Living Language Fast & Easy Arabic: The 60-Minute Survival Guide. (ARA.). 1992. 10.00 incl. audio (*0-517-58875-7*) Liv Lang.

— Living Language Fast & Easy Ingles para Hispanohablantes: 60 Minutos de Ingles Basico. (SPA & ENG.). 1992. 10.00 incl. audio (*0-517-58792-0*) Liv Lang.

— Living Language Fast & Easy Mandarin: The 60-Minute Survival Guide. 1992. 10.00 incl. audio (*0-517-58754-8*) Liv Lang.

— Living Language Fast & Easy Polish: The 60-Minute Survival Guide. (POL.). 1992. 10.00 incl. audio (*0-517-58794-7*) Liv Lang.

Crown, Patricia. Drawings by E. F. Burney: In the Huntington Collection. LC 82-21300. (Illus.). 88p. 1982. pap. 4.50 (*0-87328-124-1*) Huntington Lib.

Crown, Patricia L. & Judge, W. James, eds. Chaco & Hohokam: Prehistoric Regional Systems in the American Southwest. LC 90-26559. (Advanced Seminar Ser.). (Illus.). 384p. 1991. text 45.00 (*0-933452-75-6*); pap. text 24.95 (*0-933452-76-4*) Schol Am Res.

Crown, Patricia L., jt. ed. see Mills, Barbara J.

Crown, Patricia L., jt. ed. see Teague, Lynn S.

Crown, Patrick M., ed. From Globalism to Regionalism: New Perspectives on U. S. Foreign & Defense Policies. (Illus.). 259p. (Orig.). (C). 1994. pap. text 35.00 (*0-7881-0278-8*) DIANE Pub.

Crown-Pineiro, Carol. English for New America. 1999. pap. 39.95 incl. audio, VHS (*0-609-60470-8*) Liv Lang.

— English For New America. 1999. pap. 39.95 incl. audio, VHS (*0-609-60471-6*) Liv Lang.

— Lang English for New America. 1999. 39.95 (*0-609-60469-4*) Liv Lang.

Crown Pub Staff. All the Way. LC 97-45790. (Living Language Ser.). (SPA.). 1998. pap. 18.00 (*0-517-88502-6*) Liv Lang.

— All the Way Japanese. LC 97-43503. (Living Language Ser.). (JPN.). 1998. pap. 18.00 (*0-517-88504-2*) Liv Lang.

— All the Way Russian. 2nd ed. LC 98-24423. (Living Language Ser.). (RUS.). 1998. pap. 18.00 (*0-517-88505-0*) Liv Lang.

— Ultimate Italian Two. 2nd ed. LC 97-45802. (ITA.). 1998. pap. 18.00 (*0-517-88503-4*) Liv Lang.

Crown Publihing Group Staff. Living Language Ultimate Russian: Basic. LC 97-726. 1998. pap. 18.00 (*0-517-88284-1*) Liv Lang.

Crown Publishing Group. French Dictionary. (FRE.). 1998. mass mkt. 5.00 (*0-609-80299-2*) Liv Lang.

Crown Publishing Group Staff. German Dictionary. (GER.). 1998. pap. 5.00 (*0-609-80301-8*) Liv Lang.

— Ingles Dictionary. 1998. mass mkt. 5.00 (*0-609-80296-8*) Liv Lang.

— Italian Dictionary. (ITA.). 1998. pap. 5.00 (*0-609-80295-X*) Liv Lang.

— Living Language Russian Dictionary. (Living Language Ser.). (ENG & RUS.). 1998. pap. 5.00 (*0-609-80290-9*) Liv Lang.

— Living Language Spanish Dictionary. 1998. pap. 5.00 (*0-609-80289-5*) Liv Lang.

— Portuguese Dictionary. (POR.). 1998. pap. 5.00 (*0-609-80292-5*) Liv Lang.

— Ultimate German Manual: Basic-Intermediate. LC 98-143943. 1998. pap. 18.00 (*0-609-80250-X*) Liv Lang.

— Ultimate Spanish Manual: Basic Intermediate. LC 97-44325. (Living Language). 1998. pap. 18.00 (*0-609-80247-X*) Liv Lang.

Crown Publishing Staff. Basic Conversation, English to Chinese. (Living Language Ser.). 1999. write for info. (*0-609-60402-3*) Liv Lang.

— Living Language: Conversational German. rev. ed. (Living Language Ser.). (GER.). 1998. pap. 7.00 (*0-609-80300-X*) Crown Pub Group.

— Living Language: Conversational Italian. rev. ed. (Living Language Ser.). 1998. pap. 7.00 (*0-609-80294-1*) Crown Pub Group.

— Living Language: Conversational Portuguese. rev. ed. (Living Language Ser.). 1998. pap. 7.00 (*0-609-80293-3*) Crown Pub Group.

— Living Language: Conversational Russian. rev. ed. 1998. pap. 7.00 (*0-609-80291-7*) Crown Pub Group.

— Living Language: Conversational Spanish. rev. ed. (Living Language Ser.). 1998. pap. 7.00 (*0-609-80288-7*) Crown Pub Group.

— Living Language Complete Course: Portuguese (Brazillian) (Living Language Ser.). 1998. 22.50 incl. audio (*0-609-60269-1*, 903610) Crown Pub Group.

— Living Language Complete Course: Portuguese (Continental) (Living Language Ser.). 1998. 22.50 incl. audio (*0-609-60270-5*, 903611) Crown Pub Group.

— Living Language Conversational Japanese. rev. ed. 1998. pap. 7.00 (*0-609-80302-6*) Crown Pub Group.

Crown Publising Group Staff. Conversational French. rev. ed. (FRE.). 1998. pap. 7.00 (*0-609-80298-4*) Liv Lang.

Crown, Sidney & Freeman, Hugh, eds. The Book of Psychiatric Books. LC 92-49165. 440p. 1994. 50.00 (*0-87668-510-6*) Aronson.

Crown Staff. All the Way Russian. (Living Language Ser.). (RUS.). 1997. write for info. (*0-517-70238-X*) Liv Lang.

— All the Way Russian. (Living Language Ser.). 1996. write for info. (*0-517-70273-8*) Liv Lang.

— Living Language All the Way Japanese. (Living Language Ser.). (JPN.). 1998. write for info. (*0-517-70236-3*) Liv Lang.

— Living Language Ultimate French Advantage. LC 97-45798. 1998. pap. 18.00 (*0-609-80251-8*) Crown Pub Group.

— Living Language Ultimate German Advantage. LC 97-45801. 1998. pap. 18.00 (*0-609-80252-6*) Liv Lang.

— Living Language Ultimate Spanish Advantage. LC 97-43608. 1998. pap. 18.00 (*0-609-80253-4*) Crown Pub Group.

***Crown-Tamir, Hela.** How to Walk in the Footsteps of Jesus & the Prophets: A Scripture Reference Guide for Biblical Sites in Israel & Jordan. LC 99-45133. 2000. pap. text 14.95 (*965-229-229-X*) Gefen Pub Hse.

Crown, William H. Statistical Models for the Social & Behavioral Sciences: Multiple Regression & Limited-Dependent Variable Models. LC 97-5583. 200p. 1998. 65.00 (*0-275-95316-5*, Praeger Pubs) Greenwood.

Crown, William H., ed. Handbook on Employment & the Elderly. LC 95-42916. 464p. 1996. lib. bdg. 99.50 (*0-313-28598-5*, Greenwood Pr) Greenwood.

Crown, William H., jt. auth. see Wheat, Leonard F.

Crowne, Douglas P. & Marlowe, David. The Approval Motive: Studies in Evaluative Dependence. LC 80-475. (Illus.). 233p. 1980. reprint ed. lib. bdg. 59.50 (*0-313-22365-3*, CRAM, Greenwood Pr) Greenwood.

Crowne, Frances. Dangerous Symptoms. large type ed. 272p. 1993. 27.99 (*0-7505-0472-2*) Ulverscroft.

— Doctor in Demand. large type ed. 295p. 1993. 27.99 (*0-7505-0556-7*) Ulverscroft.

— Dreams Are for Tomorrow. large type ed. 249p. 1994. 27.99 (*0-7505-0603-2*, Pub. by Mgna Lrg Print) Ulverscroft.

— Instant Care. large type ed. (Magna Large Print Ser.). 1994. 27.99 (*0-7505-0670-9*, Pub. by Mgna Lrg Print) Ulverscroft.

— Nurse on the Move. large type ed. 269p. 1993. 27.99 (*0-7505-0470-6*, Pub. by Mgna Lrg Print) Ulverscroft.

— The Perfect Remedy. large type ed. 306p. 1994. 27.99 (*0-7505-0630-X*, Pub. by Mgna Lrg Print) Ulverscroft.

— The Road to Recovery. large type ed. 268p. 1992. 11.50 (*0-7505-0389-0*) Ulverscroft.

Crowne, Henry R. & Mitchell, Theodore D. Drowne Genealogy: Partial List of the Descendants of Leonard & Elizabeth (Abbott) Crowne of Sturgeon's Creek, Me., & Boston, Mass., 1646-1941. (Illus.). 141p. 1997. reprint ed. pap. 23.00 (*0-8328-8356-5*); reprint ed. lib. bdg. 33.00 (*0-8328-8355-7*) Higginson Bk Co.

Crowne, James D. Patent, Trademark, & Copyright Regulations, March 1999 Supplement. 561p. 1999. ring bd., suppl. ed. 75.00 (*1-57018-199-3*, 1199-PR9) BNA Books.

***Crowne, James D., ed.** Patent, Trademark, & Copyright Regulations: Includes I.P. Regulatory Developments Through October 1, 1999. 582p. 1999. ring bd. 75.00 (*1-57018-209-4*, 1209-PR9) BNA Books.

C

Crowne, James D., ed. Patent, Trademark & Copyright Regulations: 1998 Supplement. 780p. 1999. ring bd., suppl. ed. 75.00 (*1-57018-161-6*, 1161) BNA Books.

Crowne, John. City Politiques. Wilson, John H., ed. LC 67-12641. (Regents Restoration Drama Ser.). 179p. 1967. reprint ed. pap. 55.50 (*0-608-01850-3*, 206250000003) Bks Demand.

— The Dramatic Works of John Crowne, 4 vols., 1. Maidment, James & Logan, W. H., eds. LC 67-18423. 1972. reprint ed. 30.95 (*0-405-08408-0*, Pub. by Blom Pubns) Ayer.

— The Dramatic Works of John Crowne, 4 vols., 2. Maidment, James & Logan, W. H., eds. LC 67-18423. 1972. reprint ed. 30.95 (*0-405-08409-9*, Pub. by Blom Pubns) Ayer.

— The Dramatic Works of John Crowne, 4 vols., 3. Maidment, James & Logan, W. H., eds. LC 67-18423. 1972. reprint ed. 30.95 (*0-405-08410-2*, Pub. by Blom Pubns) Ayer.

— The Dramatic Works of John Crowne, 4 vols., 4. Maidment, James & Logan, W. H., eds. LC 67-18423. 1972. reprint ed. 30.95 (*0-405-08411-0*, Pub. by Blom Pubns) Ayer.

— The Dramatic Works of John Crowne, 4 vols., Set. Maidment, James & Logan, W. H., eds. LC 67-18423. 1972. reprint ed. 121.95 (*0-405-08407-2*, Pub. by Blom Pubns) Ayer.

Crowne, William. A True Relation of All the Remarkable Places Observed in the Travels of Thomas Lord Howard. LC 77-171742. (English Experience Ser.: No. 357). 1971. reprint ed. 30.00 (*90-221-0357-9*) Walter J Johnson.

Crowner. Impulse. LC 94-76497. (C). 1994. pap. text 40.36 (*0-395-66962-6*) HM.

— Impulse. (C). 1995. pap., teacher ed. 123.96 (*0-395-67325-9*) HM.

— Impulse. 2nd ed. LC 98-72014. 1998. pap. text 36.27 (*0-395-90934-1*) HM.

Crowner, Ann, ed. see Council for National Cooperation in Aquatics Staff.

Crowner, David & Lill, Klaus. Impulse: Kommunikatives Deutsch fur die Mittelstufe. (GER.). (C). 1995. text, teacher ed. 11.96 (*0-395-66964-2*) HM.

— Impulse: Kommunikatives Deutsch fur die Mittelstufe. (GER.). (C). 1998. pap. text, wbk. ed. 23.56 (*0-395-66963-4*) HM.

C

***Crowner, Martha L.** Understanding & Treating Violent Psychiatric Patients. LC 99-49869. (Progress in Psychiatry Ser.). 240p. 2000. 34.50 (*0-88048-752-6*) Am Psychiatric.

Crowner, Robert P. Developing a Strategic Business Plan with Cases: An Entrepreneur's Advantage. 6th ed. 256p. (C). 1990. text 16.25 (*0-256-08636-2*, 31-1128-96, Irwn McGrw-H) McGrw-H Hghr Educ.

Crownfield, Frederic R. White Plains Friends Meeting, 1850-1982. 1983. pap. 6.00 (*0-614-04686-6*) NC Frnds Hist Soc.

Crownhart, Maurice, ed. see Kanne, Eunice.

Crownhart-Vaughan, E. A., tr. see Golovin, Pavel N.

Crownhart-Vaughan, E. A., tr. see Kushnarev, Evgenii G.

Crownhart-Vaughan, E. A. P., tr. see Krasheninnikov, Stepan P.

Crowninshield, Benjamin W. A History of the First Regiment of Massachusetts Cavalry Volunteers. 2nd ed. (Army of the Potomac Ser.). (Illus.). 490p. (C). 1995. reprint ed. 65.00 (*0-935523-51-0*) Butternut & Blue.

Crowninshield, Francis W. Manners for the Metropolis: An Entrance Key to the Fantastic Life of the 400. LC 75-1838. (Leisure Class in America Ser.). (Illus.). 1975. reprint ed. 17.95 (*0-405-06907-3*) Ayer.

Crownover, Jerry. Life Is Simple - First Cutting. 180p. 1998. pap. text 14.95 (*1-890622-43-5*) Leathers Pub.

Crownover, Mary. Cheesecake Extraordinaire. LC 90-34639. 128p. 1990. 24.95 (*0-87833-721-0*) Taylor Pub.

— Cheesecake Extraordinaire: More than 100 Sumptuous Recipes for the Ultimate Dessert. (Illus.). 128p. 1994. pap. 15.95 (*0-8092-3544-7*, 354470, Contemporary Bks) NTC Contemp Pub Co.

Crownover, Richard M. Introduction to Fractals & Chaos. LC 94-34458. (Math Ser.). 320p. 1995. 58.75 (*0-86720-464-8*) Jones & Bartlett.

***Crowood Press Staff.** The Poultry Farmer's & Manager's Veterinary Handbook. 1999. 35.00 (*1-86126-261-2*, Pub. by Crolwood) Trafalgar.

Crowood Press Staff, ed. 100 Walks in Buchinghamshire & Hertfordshire. (Illus.). 192p. 1998. pap. 19.95 (*1-86126-102-0*, Pub. by Crolwood) Trafalgar.

— 100 Walks in Cambridgeshire & Bedfordshire. (Illus.). 192p. 1998. pap. 19.95 (*1-86126-103-9*, Pub. by Crolwood) Trafalgar.

***Crowsey, Linda.** Madame Alexande: Collector's Dolls Price Guide. 25th ed. (Illus.). 96p. 2000. pap. 9.95 (*1-57432-172-2*) Collector Bks.

— Madame Alexander Store Exclusives & Limited Editions: Identification & Values. (Illus.). 144p. 2000. pap. 24.95 (*1-57432-173-0*) Collector Bks.

Crowson, Andrew & Chen, Edward S., eds. Tungsten & Tungsten Alloys: Recent Advances: Proceedings of a Symposium by the Refractory Metals Committee, Held at the 120th Annual Meeting of the Minerals, Metals & Materials Society in New Orleans, LA, February 17-22, 1991. LC 91-62467. 314p. 1991. reprint ed. pap. 97.40 (*0-608-03826-1*, 206278800004) Bks Demand.

Crowson, Andrew & Metals & Materials Society. Molybdenum & Molybdenum Alloys: Proceedings of the Symposium Held at the 127th Annual Meeting & Exhibition of the Minerals, Metals & Materials Society in San Antonio, Texas, 16-19 February 1998 / LC 98-67688. x, 245p. 1998. 94.00 (*0-87339-411-9*) Minerals Metals.

Crowson, Lydia. The Esthetic of Jean Cousteau. LC 77-95326. 206p. reprint ed. pap. 63.90 (*0-608-14822-9*, 202563500045) Bks Demand.

***Crowson, N. J., ed.** Fleet Street, Press Barons & Politics: The Journals of Collin Brooks, 1932-1940. (Camden Fifth Ser.: No. 11). 322p. (C). 1999. 64.95 (*0-521-66239-7*) Cambridge U Pr.

Crowson, Noel & Brogden, John V., eds. Bloody Banners & Barefoot Boys: The 27th Alabama Infantry C. S. A. LC 96-40234. (Illus.). 156p. 1997. 19.95 (*1-57249-018-7*, Burd St Pr) White Mane Pub.

Crowson, Richard. Prairie Mirth: Crowson Cartoons from Wichita, Kansas. (Illus.). 160p. (Orig.). 1992. pap. 9.95 (*1-880652-10-2*) Wichita Eagle.

Crowson, Robert L. School-Community Relations, under Reform. 2nd ed. LC 97-76281. 317p. 1998. 38.00 (*0-8211-0233-8*) McCutchan.

Crowson, Robert L., et al, eds. Politics of Education & the New Institutionalism: Reinventing the American School: PEA Yearbook 1995. 208p. 1996. text 69.95 (*0-7507-0532-9*, Falmer Pr); pap. text 27.95 (*0-7507-0533-7*, Falmer Pr) Taylor & Francis.

Crowther-Alwyn, John. Business Roles. LC 97-180120. 112p. 1997. spiral bd. 31.95 (*0-521-46953-8*) Cambridge U Pr.

Crowther, Anne. Social Policy in Britain, 1914-1939. 2nd ed. (New Studies in Economic & Social History: No. 5). (Illus.). 96p. (C). 1997. text 27.95 (*0-521-55264-8*); pap. text 9.95 (*0-521-55789-5*) Cambridge U Pr.

Crowther, Betty, jt. auth. see Bates, William.

Crowther, Bill, jt. auth. see Crowther, Jean.

Crowther, Bill, jt. auth. see Crowther, Jean D.

Crowther, Bruce. Black Wednesday. large type ed. (Dales Mystery Ser.). 299p. 1992. pap. 18.99 (*1-85389-323-4*, Dales) Ulverscroft.

Crowther, Bruce & Pinfold, Mike. Singing Jazz: The Singers & Their Styles. (Illus.). 256p. 1998. pap. 17.95 (*0-87930-519-3*) Miller Freeman.

Crowther, C. Edward & Stone, Gayle. Intimacy: Strategies for Successful Relationships. LC 86-20694. 220p. (Orig.). 1987. 16.95 (*0-685-35403-2*) Curtis Pubns.

Crowther, Christopher D., jt. auth. see Durning, Alan T.

Crowther, Christy. Primary Orthopedic Care. LC 99-36528. (Illus.). 450p. (C). (gr. 13). 1999. pap. text 54.95 (*0-8151-1376-5*, 29560) Mosby Inc.

***Crowther, Christy & Campling, Jo.** Policing Urban Poverty. LC 99-40401. 2000. text 65.00 (*0-312-22846-5*) St Martin.

Crowther, Colin & Crowther, Mary. Hospital Visiting Made Easy. 160p. 1996. pap. 39.95 (*0-85439-456-7*, Pub. by St Paul Pubns) St Mut.

Crowther, D. & Veronesi, U., eds. Interferons: Mechanisms of Action & Role in Cancer Therapy. (ESO Monographs). (Illus.). 72p. 1991. 49.00 (*0-387-54302-3*) Spr-Verlag.

Crowther, Daphne, jt. ed. see Lafferranderie, Gabriel.

Crowther, David. Managment Accounting for Business. 320p. 1999. pap. 52.50 (*0-7487-2246-7*, Pub. by S Thornes Pubs) Trans-Atl Phila.

Crowther, Duane R. A Comprehensive Harmony of the Gospels. 48p. 1995. pap. 5.98 (*0-88290-518-X*, 1053) Horizon Utah.

Crowther, Duane S. America: God's Chosen Land of Liberty. LC 87-82115. 112p. 1987. 11.98 (*0-88290-320-9*) Horizon Utah.

Crowther, Duane S. Choral Concepts: Student Learning Guide, Unit 1. 32p. 1990. pap., student ed. 1.98 (*0-88290-411-6*, 2950) Horizon Utah.

— Choral Concepts: Student Learning Guide, Unit 2. 32p. 1990. pap., student ed. 1.98 (*0-88290-412-4*, 2951) Horizon Utah.

— Choral Concepts: Student Learning Guide, Unit 3. 32p. 1990. pap., student ed. 1.98 (*0-88290-413-2*, 2952) Horizon Utah.

— Choral Concepts: Student Learning Guide, Unit 4. 32p. 1990. pap., student ed. 1.98 (*0-88290-414-0*, 2953) Horizon Utah.

— Choral Concepts: Student Learning Guide, Teacher's Edition, Unit 1. 32p. 1992. pap., teacher ed. 4.98 (*0-88290-442-6*, 2946) Horizon Utah.

— Choral Concepts: Student Learning Guide, Teacher's Edition, Unit 2. 32p. 1992. pap., teacher ed. 4.98 (*0-88290-443-4*, 2947) Horizon Utah.

— Choral Concepts: Student Learning Guide, Teacher's Edition, Unit 3. 32p. 1992. pap., teacher ed. 4.98 (*0-88290-444-2*, 2948) Horizon Utah.

— Choral Concepts: Student Learning Guide, Teacher's Edition, Unit 4. 32p. 1992. pap., teacher ed. 4.98 (*0-88290-445-0*, 2949) Horizon Utah.

Crowther, Duane S. Come unto Christ. LC 70-173393. (Scripture Guide Ser.). 240p. 1971. pap. 9.98 (*0-88290-007-2*) Horizon Utah.

— Doctrinal Dimensions: Major Missionary Messages of the Restored Gospel. LC 86-81779. 303p. 1986. 18.98 (*0-88290-286-5*) Horizon Utah.

— Gifts of the Spirit. LC 65-29176. 352p. 1983. 19.98 (*0-88290-210-5*) Horizon Utah.

— God & His Church. LC 76-173392. (Scripture Guide Ser.). 244p. 1971. pap. 13.98 (*0-88290-006-4*) Horizon Utah.

— How to Understand the Book of Daniel. 176p. 1998. pap. 15.98 (*0-88290-637-2*, 1508) Horizon Utah.

— How to Understand the Book of Ezekiel. 176p. 1998. pap. 15.98 (*0-88290-638-0*, 1509) Horizon Utah.

— How to Understand the Book of Isaiah. 192p. 1998. pap. 17.98 (*0-88290-635-6*, 1506) Horizon Utah.

— How to Understand the Book of Jeremiah. 192p. 1998. pap. 16.98 (*0-88290-636-4*, 1507) Horizon Utah.

— How to Understand the Book of Mormon. rev. ed. LC 75-5322. 169p. 1975. pap. 14.98 (*0-88290-045-5*) Horizon Utah.

— How to Write with Power & Confidence: Writing Techniques & Book Industry Practices Every Author Should Know. 1998. pap. 17.98 (*0-88290-621-6*, 1212) Horizon Utah.

— How to Write Your Personal History. 96p. 1994. pap. 11.98 (*0-88290-503-1*, 1051) Horizon Utah.

— Inspired Prophetic Warnings. LC 87-82118. 320p. 1987. 19.98 (*0-88290-317-9*) Horizon Utah.

— Jesus of Nazareth, Savior & King. 304p. 1999. pap. 17.98 (*0-88290-656-9*) Horizon Utah.

— Life Everlasting: A Definitive Study of Life after Death. rev. ed. LC 98-71163. 528p. 1997. 23.98 (*0-88290-615-1*, 528) Horizon Utah.

— The Life of Joseph Smith: An Atlas, Chronological Outline & Documentation Harmony. 32p. 1989. pap. 4.98 (*0-88290-350-0*) Horizon Utah.

— My Family Heritage: Adult Personal History Starter Kit. LC 78-52120. 52p. 1981. pap. 9.98 (*0-88290-087-0*) Horizon Utah.

— A Personal History Journal for LDS Youth: From Birth Through High School. 1993. pap. 9.98 (*0-88290-089-7*, 1504) Horizon Utah.

— The Plan of Salvation & the Future in Prophecy. LC 72-173391. (Scripture Guide Ser.). 228p. 1971. pap. 12.98 (*0-88290-005-6*) Horizon Utah.

— La Profecia: Llave al Futuro. 1995. pap. 18.98 (*0-88290-532-5*) Horizon Utah.

— The Prophecies of Joseph Smith: Over Four Hundred Prophecies by & about Joseph Smith, & Their Fulfillment. LC 83-80664. 413p. 1873. 19.98 (*0-88290-221-0*) Horizon Utah.

Crowther, Duane S. Prophecy: Key to the Future. rev. ed. 368p. 1996. 19.98 (*0-88290-583-X*) Horizon Utah.

Crowther, Duane S. Prophets & Prophecies of the Old Testament. 2nd ed. LC 66-25508. (Illus.). 656p. 1993. reprint ed. 25.98 (*0-88290-022-6*) Horizon Utah.

— Tasks for Today: A Daily Job Planner. 100p. 1995. pap. 3.98 (*0-88290-528-7*, 1057) Horizon Utah.

***Crowther, Duane S.** Teaching Choral Concepts: Instructor's Kit. 600p. 1999. pap., teacher ed. 79.98 (*0-88290-675-5*, 2904) Horizon Utah.

Crowther, Duane S. Teaching Choral Concepts: Simple Lesson Plans & Teaching Aids for In-Rehearsal Choir Instruction. LC 79-89356. (Illus.). 447p. 1979. 39.98 (*0-88290-119-2*) Horizon Utah.

— This Is My Life: A Youth Genealogy Starter Kit. 76p. 1995. pap. 9.98 (*0-88290-582-1*, 1505) Horizon Utah.

— La Vida Sempiterna. LC 81-80953. Orig. Title: Life Everlasting. (SPA.). 353p. 1982. pap. 18.98 (*0-88290-185-0*) Horizon Utah.

***Crowther, Duane S.** You Can Read Music: A Quick Guide to Music Literacy. (Illus.). 64p. 2000. pap. 7.98 (*0-88290-680-1*) Horizon Utah.

Crowther, Duane S. & Crowther, Jean D., eds. The Joy of Being a Woman: Guidance for Meaningful Living by Outstanding LDS Women. LC 72-88910. 236p. 1988. reprint ed. 18.98 (*0-88290-015-3*) Horizon Utah.

Crowther, Duane S., ed. see Crowther, Jean D.

Crowther, Geoff, jt. auth. see Finlay, Hugh.

***Crowther, Hal.** Cathedrals of Kudzu: A Personal Landscape of the South. (Illus.). 192p. 2000. 24.95 (*0-8071-2594-6*) La State U Pr.

Crowther, Hal. Unarmed but Dangerous: Withering Attacks on All Things Phony, Foolish, & Fundamentally Wrong with America Today. 240p. 1995. 19.95 (*1-56352-193-8*) Longstreet.

Crowther, Ian. Chesterton. 101p. 1993. 19.95 (*1-870626-81-8*, Pub. by Claridge Pr); pap. 12.95 (*1-870626-86-9*, Pub. by Claridge Pr) Paul & Co Pubs.

Crowther, J. R., jt. auth. see Wardley, R. C.

Crowther, James G. Famous American Men of Science. LC 69-18925. (Essay Index Reprint Ser.). 1977. 30.95 (*0-8369-0040-5*) Ayer.

— Founders of British Science. LC 82-2954. (Illus.). 296p. 1982. reprint ed. lib. bdg. 75.00 (*0-313-23540-6*, CRFO, Greenwood Pr) Greenwood.

Crowther, Janice E., ed. see Sharp, Robert.

Crowther, Janis H., et al, eds. The Etiology of Bulimia Nervosa: The Individual & Family Context. 252p. 1992. 57.95 (*1-56032-206-3*) Hemisp Pub.

Crowther, Jean & Crowther, Bill. Fourteen New Mormon Temples: Counted Cross-Stitch Patterns of Temples of the Church of Jesus Christ of Latter-day Saints. 1988. 8.98 (*0-88290-335-7*) Horizon Utah.

Crowther, Jean D. Book of Mormon Puzzles & Pictures for Young Latter-Day Saints. LC 77-74495. (Books for LDS Children). (Illus.). 56p. (J). (gr. 3 up). 1977. pap. 6.98 (*0-88290-080-3*) Horizon Utah.

— The Bountiful Temple: Cross-Stitch Leaflet. 8p. 1994. pap. 3.98 (*0-88290-496-5*, 2838) Horizon Utah.

— Darling Dinosaurs: Charted for Counted Thread, Embroidery & Applique. 1988. pap. 5.98 (*0-88290-324-1*) Horizon Utah.

— Especially for Primary: Class Symbols & the Primary Theme in Counted Cross Stitch. 1990. 7.98 (*0-88290-391-8*) Horizon Utah.

— Especially for Women: Symbols, Seals & Scriptures in Counted Cross-Stitch. 1992. 7.98 (*0-88290-452-3*) Horizon Utah.

— Especially for Young Women: The Theme, Logo, Values & Class Symbols of the Young Women Program. 1990. pap. 7.98 (*0-88290-360-8*) Horizon Utah.

— Growing up a Mormon. rev. ed. (J). 1993. reprint ed. 10.98 (*0-88290-485-X*, 1300) Horizon Utah.

— Growing up in the Church: Gospel Principles & Practices for Children. rev. ed. LC 67-25433. (Illus.). 84p. (J). (gr. 2-6). 1973. reprint ed. 9.98 (*0-88290-024-2*) Horizon Utah.

— How to Get Married & Survive It: A Guide to Wedding, Reception & Honeymoon Planning. rev. ed. 96p. 1998. pap. 8.98 (*0-88290-650-X*, 2038) Horizon Utah.

— Jesus & the Children: Three Beautiful Adaptations of Artwork by Francis Hook (Cross-Stitch) 1984. 6.98 (*0-88290-241-5*) Horizon Utah.

— Jesus of Nazareth: Three Beautiful Adaptations of Artwork by Francis & Richard Hook (Cross-Stitch) 1985. 6.98 (*0-88290-271-7*) Horizon Utah.

— The Last Supper: Leonardo da Vinci's Masterpiece: A Counted Thread Design. 12p. 1987. 6.98 (*0-88290-293-8*, 2780) Horizon Utah.

— A Mother's Prayer. 14p. 1978. pap. 1.98 (*0-88290-099-4*) Horizon Utah.

— Murphy Strikes Again! More Murphy's Laws in Cross-Stitch. Crowther, Duane S., ed. 12p. 1987. 5.98 (*0-88290-292-X*, 2799) Horizon Utah.

Crowther, Jean D. The New Small Temples of the Church of Jesus Christ of Latter-day Saints: Counted Cross-stitch Patterns for Current & Future Small Temples. (Illus.). 24p. pap. 8.98 (*0-88290-682-8*) Horizon Utah.

Crowther, Jean D. Pedigree Patterns: 21 Original Counted Cross-Stitch Embroidery Charts of Family Relationships. 24p. (Orig.). 1981. pap. 6.98 (*0-88290-195-8*, 2880) Horizon Utah.

— Prayer: Three Beautiful Adaptations of Artwork by Francis Hook (Cross-Stitch) 1984. 6.98 (*0-88290-268-7*) Horizon Utah.

— Prophets of the Restoration: Portraits of Latter-Day Saint Presidents in Counted Cross Stitch. 24p. (Orig.). 1988. pap. 8.98 (*0-88290-321-7*) Horizon Utah.

— Puppies 'n Pooches: Charted for Counted Thread, Embroidery & Applique. 1988. 5.98 (*0-88290-325-X*) Horizon Utah.

— A Savior Is Born: Three Beautiful Adaptations of Artwork by Francis Hook (Counted Cross-Stitch) 1984. 6.98 (*0-88290-257-1*) Horizon Utah.

— Ten New Mormon Temples: Counted Cross-Stitch Patterns of Temples of the Church of Jesus Christ of Latter-Day Saints. (Illus.). 32p. 1997. pap. 8.98 (*0-88290-606-2*, 2810) Horizon Utah.

— The Very First Christmas: A Child's Story of the Savior's Birth. 48p. 1991. pap. 5.98 (*0-88290-432-9*) Horizon Utah.

— What Do I Do Now, Mom? Growing-up Guidance for Young Teen-age Girls. LC 80-82257. (Illus.). 86p. (J). (gr. 9-12). 1980. 10.98 (*0-88290-134-6*) Horizon Utah.

Crowther, Jean D. & Crowther, Bill. Thirteen New Mormon Temples: Counted Cross-Stitch Patterns of Temples of the Church of Jesus Christ of Latter-Day Saints. 1992. 8.98 (*0-88290-429-9*, 2809) Horizon Utah.

Crowther, Jean D., jt. auth. see Carboni, Polly.

Crowther, Jean D., jt. ed. see Crowther, Duane S.

Crowther, Joan, ed. see Youngblood, Charles E.

Crowther, John R. ELISA: Theory & Practice. LC 95-7859. (Methods in Molecular Biology Ser.: Vol. 42). (Illus.). 256p. 1995. pap. 79.50 (*0-89603-279-5*) Humana.

Crowther, John R. The ELISA Guidebook. LC 99-87692. (Methods in Molecular Biology Ser.: Vol. 149). 436p. 2000. boxed set 79.50 (*0-89603-728-2*) Humana.

***Crowther, John R.** The ELISA Guidebook. (Methods in Molecular Biology Ser.: Vol. 149). 436p. 2000. 99.50 (*0-89603-950-1*) Humana.

Crowther, Jonathan, et al, eds. Oxford Advanced Learner's Encyclopedic Dictionary. (Illus.). 1,120p. 1995. pap. text 23.95 (*0-19-431310-7*) OUP.

Crowther, Jonathan, jt. auth. see Miller, James M.

Crowther, Jonathan, ed. see Hornby, A. S.

Crowther, Karmen N. Researching Your Way to a Good Job. LC 92-9394. 240p. 1993. pap. 14.95 (*0-471-54827-8*) Wiley.

***Crowther, Kitty.** Jack & Jim. LC 00-39724. (Illus.). (J). 2000. lib. bdg. write for info. (*0-7868-1439-X*) Hyprn Child.

— Jack & Jim. (Illus.). 32p. (J). (ps-3). 2000. 15.99 (*0-7868-0614-1*, Pub. by Hyprn Child) Time Warner.

— Jack & Jim (Picturebook) (Illus.). 32p. (J). 2000. lib. bdg. 16.49 (*0-7868-2527-8*, Pub. by Disney Pr) Time Warner.

Crowther, Lane. Fresh & Light. LC 98-9459. (Williams-Sonoma Lifestyles Ser.). (Illus.). 112p. (gr. 11). 1999. 14.95 (*0-7835-4617-3*) Time-Life.

Crowther, M. A. & White, B. On Soul & Conscience: Forensic Medicine in Glasgow, 1839-1989. (Illus.). 248p. 1988. text 29.95 (*0-08-036406-3*, Pub. by Aberdeen U Pr); pap. text 16.00 (*0-08-036407-1*, Pub. by Aberdeen U Pr) Macmillan.

Crowther, Margaret, jt. auth. see Squire, David.

Crowther, Mary, jt. auth. see Crowther, Colin.

Crowther, Nicky. London Cycle Guide. (Illus.). 144p. 1998. pap. 14.95 (*1-85960-320-3*, Pub. by J H Haynes & Co) Motorbooks Intl.

***Crowther, Patricia.** High Priestess: The Life & Times of Patricia Crowther. (Illus.). 208p. 1999. pap. 16.50 (*0-919345-87-5*) Phoenix WA.

Crowther, Patricia. Lid off the Cauldron: A Handbook for Witches. LC 81-141202. 1985. pap. 7.95 (*0-08-772869-9*, Pergamon Pr) Elsevier.

— Lid off the Cauldron: A Wicca Handbook. (Illus.). 1998. pap. 22.95 (*1-86163-032-8*, Pub. by Capall Bann Pubng) Holmes Pub.

***Crowther, Patricia.** So Life Goes On. 163p. 2000. 21.95 (*0-7541-1168-7*, Pub. by Minerva Pr) Unity Dist.

Crowther, Patricia. Witches Were for Hanging. rev. ed. 266p. 1998. pap. 15.95 (*1-892137-07-0*) Mercury NC.

Crowther, Patricia P., et al. The Grand Kentucky Junction: Memoirs. Watson, Richard A. & Brucker, Roger W., eds. LC 83-26170. (Illus.). 96p. (Orig.). 1984. pap. 12.50 (*0-939748-08-8*) Cave Bks MO.

Crowther, Paul. Art & Embodiment. LC 92-44433. 218p. 1993. text 45.00 (*0-19-823996-3*, Clarendon Pr) OUP.

— Critical Aesthetics & Postmodernism. (Illus.). 230p. 1996. pap. text 24.00 (*0-19-823623-9*) OUP.

An Asterisk (*) at the beginning of an entry indicates that the title is appearing for the first time.

Crowther, Paul. The Kantian Sublime: From Morality to Art. (Oxford Philosophical Monographs). 182p. 1991. reprint ed. pap. text 28.00 (*0-19-823931-9*, 11074) OUP.

Crowther, Paul. The Language of Twentieth-Century Art: A Conceptual History. LC 97-5248. 240p. 1997. 40.00 (*0-300-07241-4*) Yale U Pr.

***Crowther, Peter.** Lonesome Roads. 145p. 1999. pap. 13.99 (*0-9531468-1-2*, Pub. by RazorBlade Pr) Firebird Dist.

— Longest Single Note. 1999. write for info. (*1-881475-56-5*) Cemetery Dance.

Crowther, Peter. Single-Handed Sailing in Galway Blazer. 1998. 29.95 (*1-85310-995-9*) Waterline.

— Tales in Space. (White Wolf Ser.). 1998. reprint ed. pap. 12.99 (*1-56504-867-9*, 11047, Borealis) White Wolf.

Crowther, Peter, ed. Dante's Disciples. 1998. pap. 5.99 (*1-56504-878-4*, Borealis) White Wolf.

— Heaven Sent. 1995. pap. 5.50 (*0-88677-656-2*, Pub. by DAW Bks) Penguin Putnam.

— Heaven Sent. 336p. 1999. pap. write for info. (*0-451-18445-9*, Sig) NAL.

— Moon Shots. 320p. 1999. mass mkt. 6.99 (*0-88677-848-4*, Pub. by DAW Bks) Penguin Putnam.

Crowther, Peter & Kramer, Edward E., eds. Dantes Disciples. 300p. (Orig.). 1996. pap. 14.99 (*1-56504-907-1*, 13007, Borealis) White Wolf.

Crowther, Peter & Lovegrove, James. Escardy Gap. 1998. pap. 6.99 (*0-8125-5539-2*, Pub. by Tor Bks) St Martin.

Crowther, Peter, ed. see De Lint, Charles, et al.

Crowther, Peter, ed. see Smith, Michael M., et al.

Crowther, Peter R., jt. auth. see Briggs, D. E. G.

Crowther, Peter R., jt. ed. see Briggs, Derek E.

Crowther, Richard L. Affordable Passive Solar Homes. 188p. 1983. pap. 20.00 (*0-89553-129-1*) Am Solar Energy.

Crowther, Richard L., ed. Ecologic Architecture: The Ecologic Perspective for Design. (Illus.). 320p. 1992. text 52.95 (*0-7506-9171-9*, Butterwrth Archit) Buttrwrth-Heinemann.

Crowther, Robert. Dump Trucks & Diggers. LC 95-71700. (Illus.). 12p. (J). (ps). 1996. 7.99 (*0-7636-0008-3*) Candlewick Pr.

— My Pop-Up Surprise A B C. LC 96-72255. (Illus.). 14p. (J). (ps-1). 1997. 16.95 (*0-531-30038-2*) Orchard Bks Watts.

— My Pop-Up Surprise 1 2 3. LC 96-72254. (Illus.). 12p. (J). (ps-1). 1997. 16.95 (*0-531-30039-0*) Orchard Bks Watts.

***Crowther, Robert.** Robert Crowther's Amazing Pop-up House of Inventions. LC 99-58306. 12p. (J). (gr. 1-4). 2000. 14.99 (*0-7636-0810-6*) Candlewick Pr.

Crowther, Robert. Robert Crowther's Deep Down Underground. LC 97-75072. (Illus.). 20p. (J). (gr. 1-4). 1998. 14.99 (*0-7636-0321-X*) Candlewick Pr.

— Robert Crowther's Incredible Animal Alphabet. LC 94-10566. (Illus.). (J). (gr. k-3). 1995. 14.95 (*1-56402-427-X*) Candlewick Pr.

— Robert Crowther's Most Amazing Hide-&-Seek Alphabet Book. LC 98-73307. (Illus.). 12p. (J). (ps-2). 1999. text 14.99 (*0-7636-0732-0*) Candlewick Pr.

***Crowther, Robert.** Robert Crowther's Most Amazing Hide-&-Seek 1-2-3 Numbers Book. LC 98-88043. (Illus.). 12p. (J). 1999. text 14.99 (*0-7636-0809-2*) Candlewick Pr.

Crowther, Robert. Robert Crowther's Pop-Up Olympics: Amazing Facts & Record Breakers. LC 95-69591. (Illus.). 12p. (J). (gr. 3-8). 1996. 19.99 (*1-56402-801-1*) Candlewick Pr.

— Tractors & Trucks. LC 95-71701. (Illus.). 12p. (J). (ps-2). 1996. 7.99 (*0-7636-0009-1*) Candlewick Pr.

— Who Lives in the Country? LC 91-58766. (Illus.). 10p. (J). (ps). 1992. 6.95 (*1-56402-090-8*) Candlewick Pr.

— Who Lives in the Garden? LC 91-58767. (Illus.). 10p. (J). (ps). 1992. 6.95 (*1-56402-091-6*) Candlewick Pr.

Crowther, Rodney G. Surname Index to Sixty-Five Volumes of Colonial & Revolutionary Pedigrees. 143p. 1964. lib. bdg. 19.00 (*0-915156-27-X*) Natl Genealogical.

Crowther, Samuel. Journal of an Expedition up the Niger & Tshadda Rivers Undertaken by MacGregor Laird in 1854. 248p. 1970. reprint ed. 59.50 (*0-7146-1866-7*, Pub. by F Cass Pubs) Intl Spec Bk.

— The Romance & Rise of the American Tropics. Bruchey, Stuart & Bruchey, Eleanor, eds. LC 76-4999. (American Business Abroad Ser.). (Illus.). 1976. reprint ed. lib. bdg. 47.95 (*0-405-09268-7*) Ayer.

Crowther, Samuel, jt. auth. see Ford, Henry J.

Crowther, Samuel, jt. auth. see Schon, James F.

Crowther, Terence G. Jimmy's Lucky Day, Level 2. LC 96-29782. (Illus.). 32p. 1997. pap. text 3.95 (*0-19-434962-4*) OUP.

— The Naughty Monkey, Level 1. (Illus.). 32p. 1997. pap. text 3.95 (*0-19-434955-1*) OUP.

— Sunny's Lucky Day, Level 2. LC 96-29787. (Illus.). 32p. 1997. pap. text 3.95 (*0-19-434963-2*) OUP.

Crowther, Terence G. Up & Away in English. LC 96-29781. (Illus.). 1997. write for info. (*0-19-434957-8*) OUP.

— Up & Away in English. LC 97-25400. (Illus.). 1998. write for info. (*0-19-434969-1*); write for info. (*0-19-434970-5*); write for info. (*0-19-434964-0*); write for info. (*0-19-434977-2*); write for info. (*0-19-434976-4*) OUP.

— Up & Away in English. LC 98-5338. (Illus.). 1999. write for info. (*0-19-434983-7*); write for info. (*0-19-434984-5*); write for info. (*0-19-434978-0*); write for info. (*0-19-434990-X*) OUP.

Crowther, Terence G. Up & Away in Phonics, Bk. 1. (Illus.). 48p. 1997. pap. text 6.95 (*0-19-434954-3*) OUP.

— Up & Away in Phonics, Bk. 2. 48p. 1997. pap. text 6.95 (*0-19-434961-6*) OUP.

— The Very Dangerous Driver, Level 1. (Illus.). 30p. 1997. pap. text 3.95 (*0-19-434956-X*) OUP.

***Crowther, Terence G. & Baxter, Brandon.** Up & Away in English. LC 98-37905. (Illus.). 1999. write for info. (*0-19-434985-3*) OUP.

***Crowther, Terence G. & Morris, Kelly Scott.** Up & Away in English. LC 98-10484. (Illus.). 1999. write for info. (*0-19-434971-3*) OUP.

***Crowther, Victor.** The Oratorio in Bologna 1650-1730. LC 98-33456. (Oxford Monographs on Music). (Illus.). 208p. 2000. text 74.00 (*0-19-816635-4*) OUP.

Crowther, William E. The Political Economy of Romanian Socialism. LC 87-29244. 212p. 1988. 65.00 (*0-275-92840-3*, C2840, Praeger Pubs) Greenwood.

Croxall, J., et al. The Distribution of Penguins on the Antarctic Peninsula & Islands of the Scotia Sea. 1800p. 1979. 25.00 (*0-85665-071-4*, Pub. by Brit Antarctic Surv) Balogh.

Croxall, J. P., ed. Seabird Status & Conservation: A Supplement. 320p. 1991. pap., suppl. ed. 37.95 (*1-56098-435-X*) Smithsonian.

Croxen, Caren. The Female Journey. 1987. pap. 9.95 (*0-944955-03-7*) Wissmann Pub.

— The Power of Self-Love. 1981. audio 6.95 (*0-944955-01-0*) Wissmann Pub.

— The Power of Self-Love. 1987. pap. 6.95 (*0-944955-00-2*) Wissmann Pub.

Croxford, Leslie. Solomon's Folly. LC 83-9199. (Phoenix Fiction Ser.). 208p. 1996. pap. 8.50 (*0-226-12149-6*) U Ch Pr.

Croxier, Ross H. & Pamilo, Pekka. Evolution of Social Insect Colonies: Sex Allocation & Kin Selection. LC 95-32182. (Illus.). 314p. (C). 1996. pap. text 35.00 (*0-19-854942-3*) OUP.

Croxton, C. A. Introductory Eigenphysics: An Approach to the Theory of Fields. LC 74-175. (Illus.). 285p. reprint ed. pap. 88.40 (*0-608-18841-7*, 203049700069) Bks Demand.

Croxton, Clive A. Introduction to Liquid State Physics. LC 74-13153. 295p. reprint ed. pap. 91.50 (*0-608-14672-2*, 205206300033) Bks Demand.

— Russian for the Scientist & Mathematician. LC 83-10209. 226p. reprint ed. pap. 70.10 (*0-608-15933-6*, 203092600072) Bks Demand.

— Statistical Mechanics of the Liquid Surface. LC 79-40819. (Illus.). 367p. reprint ed. pap. 113.80 (*0-608-17662-1*, 203037600069) Bks Demand.

Croxton, Clive A., ed. Fluid Interfacial Phenomena. LC 85-6437. 787p. reprint ed. pap. 200.00 (*0-7837-4016-6*, 204384600011) Bks Demand.

— Progress in Liquid Physics. LC 76-40166. 602p. 1978. reprint ed. pap. 186.70 (*0-608-08311-9*, 203054100069) Bks Demand.

Croxton Collaborative, Architects Staff, jt. auth. see National Audubon Society Staff.

Croxton, Derek. Peacemaking in Early Modern Europe: Cardinal Mazarin & the Congress of Westphalia, 1643-1648. LC 98-35304. (Illus.). 400p. 1999. 52.50 (*1-57591-017-9*) Susquehanna U Pr.

Croxton, Frederick E., jt. auth. see Williams, Pierce.

Croxton, P. C., et al. Structures & Materials: A Programmed Approach. (Illus.). 300p. 1974. 27.95 (*0-8464-0890-2*) Beekman Pubs.

Croxton, Ryan, jt. auth. see Neely, Paula K.

Croxton, Ryan, ed. see Poffenbarger, Amy & Poffenbarger, Mark.

Croxton, William L. Amazing Card Tricks Made Easy to Do. rev. ed. (Illus.). 61p. (J). (gr. 4 up). 1990. pap. 4.95 (*0-9623230-0-4*) WLC Enterprises.

Croy, Anne, ed. Uterine Natural Killer Cells. (Journal Ser.: Vol. 15, No. 1, 1996-97). (Illus.). 70p. 1997. pap. 26.25 (*3-8055-6395-7*) S Karger.

Croy, Dick. Dowsing for Love. LC 94-621798. 320p. (Orig.). 1995. pap. 14.95 (*0-9645252-1-6*) Watrshed Bks.

Croy, Greg, ed. see Christophersen, Susan & Farr, J. Michael.

Croy, Greg, ed. see Farr, J. Michael & Christophersen, Susan.

Croy, Greg, ed. see Farr, J. Michael & Pavlicko, Marie.

Croy, Homer. Cole Younger: Last of the Great Outlaws. LC 99-16421. 246p. 1999. pap. 12.00 (*0-8032-6400-3*, Bison Books) U of Nebr Pr.

— How Motion Pictures Are Made. Jowett, Garth S., ed. LC 77-11373. (Aspects of Film Ser.). (Illus.). 1978. reprint ed. lib. bdg. 25.95 (*0-405-11129-0*) Ayer.

— Jesse James Was My Neighbor. LC 97-163. 315p. 1997. pap. 14.00 (*0-8032-6380-5*, Bison Books) U of Nebr Pr.

Croy, N. Clayton. Endurance in Suffering: Hebrews 12:1-13 in Its Rhetorical, Religious, & Philosophical Context. LC 97-6079. (Society for New Testament Studies Monograph Ser.: No. 98). 260p. (C). 1998. text 59.95 (*0-521-59305-0*) Cambridge U Pr.

Croy, Norvin, et al. Using Information Technology to Support Knowledge Management. Elliott, Susan, ed. (Illus.). 163p. 1997. spiral bd. 595.00 (*1-928593-10-0*) Am Prodtv Qual.

Croy, R. R., ed. Plant Molecular Biology Labfax. (Labfax Ser.). (Illus.). 382p. 1994. text 63.00 (*0-12-198370-6*) Acad Pr.

Croy-Roeulx, R. De, see De Croy-Roeulx, R.

Croydon, Elizabeth, et al. Personal Values: Writings by Uncommon Women. LC 94-67994. 56p. (Orig.). 1994. pap. 11.95 (*0-9637704-0-3*) Red Dragon VA.

Croydon, Michael. Ivan Albright. (Illus.). 308p. 1995. 95.00 (*0-89659-002-X*) Abbeville Pr.

Croydon, Michael & Wesly, Ed, eds. Fourth International Exhibition of Holography. (Illus.). 33p. 1991. pap. 14.00 (*0-910535-09-4*) Lake Forest.

Croye, Marcia. Our Mc Connell Family of Ohio & West Virginia. (Illus.). 352p. 1993. 60.00 (*0-910973-05-9*) Arrowhead AZ.

Croyle, David J. Hear Ye . . . A Message to This Generation. LC 87-83660. 100p. 1988. 12.95 (*0-945371-00-4*); pap. 9.95 (*0-945371-01-2*) ICM Pubns.

Croyle, John. Bringing Out the Winner in Your Child. 256p. 1996. 19.99 (*0-345-40076-3*, Moorings) Ballantine Pub Grp.

— Bringing Out the Winner in Your Child. Abraham, Ken, ed. LC 96-52227. 250p. 1997. 19.95 (*1-888952-25-3*) Cumberland Hse.

— Bringing Out the Winner in Your Child. Abraham, Ken, ed. 272p. 1998. reprint ed. pap. 10.95 (*1-888952-90-3*) Cumberland Hse.

***Croyle, John & Abraham, Ken.** Bringing Out the Winner in Your Child. 252p. 2000. reprint ed. 20.00 (*0-7881-9326-0*) DIANE Pub.

Croyle, Robert T. Psychosocial Effects of Screening for Disease Prevention & Detection. (Illus.). 232p. 1995. text 45.00 (*0-19-507556-0*) OUP.

Croyston, Sean. Take One. 112p. 1995. pap. 19.95 (*0-86819-438-7*, Pub. by Currency Pr) Accents Pubns.

Crozat, Fran C. I Am a Little Kangaroo. LC 96-42522. (Illus.). 24p. (J). 1997. 3.50 (*0-8120-6435-6*); bds. 9.95 (*0-8120-6434-8*) Barron.

Crozat, Francois. I Am a Big Dinosaur. (I am Ser.). (Illus.). 24p. 1989. 9.95 (*0-8120-6097-0*) Barron.

— I Am a Big Dinosaur-Mini. (I am Ser.). (Illus.). 24p. (J). (ps). 1990. 3.50 (*0-8120-6193-4*) Barron.

— I Am a Little Alligator. (I am Ser.). (Illus.). 24p. (J). (ps-k). 1993. 8.95 (*0-8120-6342-2*); 3.50 (*0-8120-6343-0*) Barron.

— I Am a Little Bear. (I am Ser.). (Illus.). 24p. (J) (ps-k). 1989. 8.95 (*0-8120-5903-4*) Barron.

— I Am a Little Bear. (I am Ser.). (Illus.). 24p. (J) (ps-k). 1990. 3.50 (*0-8120-6191-8*) Barron.

— I Am a Little Cat. (I am Ser.). (Illus.). 24p. (J). (ps-k). 1992. 8.95 (*0-8120-6277-9*) Barron.

— I Am a Little Cat. 2nd ed. (Mini Version Ser.). (Illus.). 28p. (J). (ps). 1990. 3.50 (*0-8120-6287-6*) Barron.

— I Am a Little Caterpillar. LC 95-11744. (Illus.). 24p. (J). 1995. 3.50 (*0-8120-6484-4*) Barron.

— I Am a Little Deer: Large Size. (I Am a Little Ser.). (Illus.). 24p. (J). (ps-k). 1994. 8.95 (*0-8120-6418-6*) Barron.

— I Am a Little Deer: Miniature Size. (I Am a Little Ser.). (Illus.). 24p. (J). (ps-k). 1994. 3.50 (*0-8120-6419-4*) Barron.

— I Am a Little Dog. (Little Animal Stories Ser.). (Illus.). 24p. (J). (ps-k). 1992. 8.95 (*0-8120-6276-0*) Barron.

— I Am a Little Duck. (Little Animal Bks.). (Illus.). 24p. (J). (ps-k). 1989. 3.50 (*0-8120-6192-6*) Barron.

— I Am a Little Duck. (Little Animal Bks.). (Illus.). 24p. (J). (ps-k). 1989. 9.95 (*0-8120-5904-2*) Barron.

— I Am a Little Elephant. (Little Animal Stories Ser.). (Illus.). 24p. (J). (ps-k). 1993. 8.95 (*0-8120-6351-1*) Barron.

— I Am a Little Elephant: Mini Book. (Little Animal Stories Ser.). (Illus.). 24p. (J). (ps-k). 1993. 3.95 (*0-8120-6353-8*) Barron.

— I Am a Little Giraffe. (Illus.). 24p. (J). (ps-k). 1995. 3.50 (*0-8120-6421-6*) Barron.

— I Am a Little Giraffe. (Illus.). 24p. (J). (ps). 1995. 8.95 (*0-8120-6420-8*) Barron.

— I Am a Little Hedgehog: Miniature Edition. (Illus.). 24p. (J). 1996. 3.50 (*0-8120-6476-3*) Barron.

— I Am a Little Koala. (Little Animals Ser). (Illus.). 24p. (J). (ps up). 1995. 3.50 (*0-8120-6482-8*) Barron.

— I Am a Little Koala Bear. (Illus.). 24p. (J). 1995. 8.95 (*0-8120-6483-6*) Barron.

— I Am a Little Monkey: Large. (Little Animal Stories Ser.). (Illus.). 24p. (J). (ps-k). 1991. 9.95 (*0-8120-6149-7*) Barron.

— I Am a Little Monkey: Miniature. (Little Animal Stories Ser.). (Illus.). 24p. (J). (ps-k). 1991. 3.50 (*0-8120-6221-3*) Barron.

— I Am a Little Panda. LC 92-30962. (Little Animal Stories Ser.). (Illus.). 24p. (J). (ps-k). 1993. 3.50 (*0-8120-6312-0*) Barron.

— I Am a Little Panda. LC 92-30962. (Little Animal Stories Ser.). (Illus.). 24p. (J). (ps-k). 1993. 9.95 (*0-8120-6311-2*) Barron.

— I Am a Little Pig: Large. (Little Animal Stories Ser.). (Illus.). 24p. (J). (ps-k). 1991. 9.95 (*0-8120-6201-9*) Barron.

— I Am a Little Pig: Miniature. (Little Animal Stories Ser.). (Illus.). 24p. (J). (ps-k). 1991. 3.50 (*0-8120-6222-1*) Barron.

— I Am a Little Polar Bear. LC 96-84413. (Illus.). 24p. (J). 1996. 9.95 (*0-8120-6466-6*) Barron.

— I Am a Little Polar Bear: Mini Edition. (Illus.). 24p. (J). 1996. 3.50 (*0-8120-6467-4*) Barron.

— I Am a Little Rabbit. (Little Animal Bks.). (Illus.). 24p. (J). (ps-k). 1989. 9.95 (*0-8120-5905-0*) Barron.

— I Am a Little Rabbit. (Little Animal Bks.). (Illus.). 24p. (J). (ps-k). 1990. 3.50 (*0-8120-6194-2*) Barron.

— I am a Little Tiger: Little Animal Stories, Large. LC 92-21972. (Illus.). 24p. (J). (ps-k). 1992. 8.95 (*0-8120-6316-3*) Barron.

— I am a Little Tiger: Little Animal Stories, Min.. LC 92-21972. (Illus.). 24p. (J). (ps-k). 1992. 3.50 (*0-8120-6315-5*) Barron.

— I Am a Little Whale: Large. LC 94-32468. (Little Animal Stories Ser.). (Illus.). 24p. (J). 1995. 8.95 (*0-8120-6469-0*) Barron.

— I Am a Little Whale: Mini. LC 94-32468. (Little Animal Stories Ser.). (Illus.). 24p. (J). 1995. 3.50 (*0-8120-6470-4*) Barron.

Crozat, Marie-Louise, ed. see Freidman, Janet T.

Crozat, Marie-Louise, ed. see Yeiter, George M.

Crozatti, Carlo. A Divine Treason: The Trial of Judas Iscariot. LC 94-71913. 154p. (Orig.). 1994. pap. 14.95 (*1-885455-00-3*) DEC Unicorn.

***Croze, Harvey.** Pyramids of Life: Patterns of Life & Death in the Ecosystem. rev. ed. (Illus.). 2000. pap. 32.00 (*1-86046-613-3*) Harvill Press.

Crozel, H. Bibliographie Critique d'Origene: Supplement, No. I. 1982. pap. text 225.00 (*90-247-2704-9*) Kluwer Academic.

Crozer-Chester Medical Center Clinical Nutrition S. Manual of Medical Nutrition Therapy. 4th ed. 376p. 1998. ring bd. 100.00 (*0-9662274-0-9*) Crozer-Keystone.

***Crozes, Gil F. & Cushing, Robert S.** Evaluating Biological Regrowth in Distribution Systems. LC 00-40168. 2000. write for info. (*1-58321-025-3*) Am Water Wks Assn.

Crozes, Gil F., et al. Improving Clearwell Design for CT Compliance. LC 98-26501. 1998. write for info. (*0-89867-963-X*) Am Water Wks Assn.

Crozet, Felix. Revue de la Musique Dramatique en France. LC 80-2270. reprint ed. 48.50 (*0-404-18833-8*) AMS Pr.

Crozet, Yves. Dictionnaire de Banque et Bourse. (FRE.). 336p. 1993. pap. 32.95 (*0-7859-5612-3*, 2200213077) Fr & Eur.

Crozier. Electronic Instruments & Measurements. (Electronics Technology Ser.). 1985. text 52.95 (*0-8273-3874-0*) Delmar.

Crozier. International Handbook of Sociology. text. write for info. (*0-471-49129-2*) Wiley.

Crozier. Introduction to Electronics. 2nd ed. (Electronics Technology Ser.). 1987. text 57.95 (*0-8273-3896-1*) Delmar.

Crozier, Alan. Biochemistry & Physiology of Gibberellins, 2 vols., 1. LC 83-13862. 576p. 1983. 110.00 (*0-275-90963-8*, C09631, Praeger Pubs) Greenwood.

— Biochemistry & Physiology of Gibberellins, 2 vols., Vol. 2. LC 83-13862. 576p. 1983. 105.00 (*0-275-90964-6*, C09642, Praeger Pubs) Greenwood.

Crozier, Alan, jt. ed. see Rivier, Laurent.

Crozier, Alan, tr. see Frykman, Jonas & Lofgren, Orvar.

***Crozier, Amy, et al, eds.** Recovered: Absolute Victory over Alcoholism. LC 99-75781. 272p. 2000. pap. 15.95 (*1-893808-00-9*) Ursa Pub Co Inc.

Crozier, Andrew. All Where Each Is. (Agneau 2 Paperbook Ser.: 2). 320p. (Orig.). 1985. 26.00 (*0-907954-02-2*, Pub. by Allardyce Barnett); pap. 15.00 (*0-907954-03-0*, Pub. by Allardyce Barnett) SPD-Small Pr Dist.

Crozier, Andrew & Longville, Tim. A Various Art. 377p. 1995. pap. 12.95 (*1-85754-103-0*, Pub. by Carcanet Pr) Paul & Co Pubs.

Crozier, Andrew, ed. see Rakosi, Carl.

Crozier, Andrew J. The Causes of the Second World War. (History of the Contemporary World Ser.). (C). 1997. text 68.95 (*0-631-17128-2*); pap. text 28.95 (*0-631-18601-8*) Blackwell Pubs.

Crozier, Brian. Communism: Why Prolong Its Death-Throes? (C). 1990. 45.00 (*0-907967-17-5*, Pub. by Inst Euro Def & Strat) St Mut.

— The KGB Lawsuits. LC 95-220416. 280p. (Orig.). 1996. pap. text 19.95 (*1-870626-02-8*, Pub. by Claridge Pr) Paul & Co Pubs.

***Crozier, Brian.** The Rise & Fall of the Soviet Empire. 5th ed. 2000. reprint ed. pap. 18.95 (*0-7615-2555-6*) Prima Pub.

Crozier, Brian. Struggle for the Third World. LC 66-18563. 1966. 18.95 (*0-8023-1035-4*) Dufour.

Crozier, Brian, ed. The Granada Documents. 182p. (Orig.). 1987. reprint ed. pap. text 27.95 (*0-907671-27-6*, Pub. by Shepheard-Walwyn Pubs) Paul & Co Pubs.

Crozier, D. H. & Blench, R. M., eds. An Index of Nigerian Languages. 2nd ed. 142p. 1992. pap. 20.75 (*0-88312-611-7*) S I L Intl.

Crozier, Emmet. American Reporters on the Western Front, 1914 to 1918. LC 80-19400. (Illus.). xii, 299p. 1980. reprint ed. lib. bdg. 69.50 (*0-313-22655-5*, CRAR, Greenwood Pr) Greenwood.

Crozier, F. P. A Brasshat in No Man's Land. 254p. 1988. 60.00 (*0-947893-14-8*, Pub. by Gliddon Bks) St Mut.

Crozier-Hogle, Lois, et al. Surviving in Two Worlds: Contemporary Native American Voices. Leibold, Jay, ed. LC 96-25378. (Illus.). 287p. 1997. 35.00 (*0-292-74694-6*); pap. 14.95 (*0-292-74695-4*) U of Tex Pr.

***Crozier, Ida B.** Butterflies in the Wind. LC 99-95040. 2000. pap. 7.95 (*0-533-13270-3*) Vantage.

Crozier, Lorna. Angels of Flesh, Angels of Silence. 1997. pap. text 12.99 (*0-7710-2476-2*) McCland & Stewart.

— Everything Arrives at the Light. LC 95-156116. 152p. 1997. pap. text 14.99 (*0-7710-2479-7*) McCland & Stewart.

— Inventing the Hawk. LC 92-219952. 140p. 1997. pap. 12.99 (*0-7710-2477-0*) McCland & Stewart.

— Saving Grace: The Collected Poems of Mrs. Bentley. LC 97-196800. 96p. 1997. 19.99 (*0-7710-2480-0*) McCland & Stewart.

— What the Living Won't Let Go. 112p. 2000. pap. 12.95 (*0-7710-2481-9*) McCland & Stewart.

Crozier, Lorna & Hyland, Gary, eds. A Sudden Radiance: Saskatchewan Poetry. 296p. 1987. pap. 12.95 (*0-919926-66-5*, Pub. by Coteau) Genl Dist Srvs.

Crozier, Lorna & Hyland, Gary, eds. A Sudden Radiance: Saskatchewan Poetry. 296p. 1987. text 19.95 (*0-919926-67-3*, Pub. by Coteau) Genl Dist Srvs.

Crozier, Lorna, jt. ed. see Lane, Patrick.

Crozier, Maura & Froggart, Richard, eds. Cultural Traditions in Northern Ireland: Cultural Diversity in Contemporary Europe. LC 99-193949. (Illus.). 168p. 1998. pap. 15.95 (*0-85389-720-4*, Pub. by Inst Irish Studies) Irish Bks Media.

***Crozier, Michael.** After the Garden? 1999. pap. text 12.00 (*0-8223-6465-4*) Duke.

Crozier, Michael & Murphy, Peter, eds. The Left in Search of a Center. LC 95-16648. 224p. 1996. text 39.95 (*0-252-02199-1*); pap. text 16.95 (*0-252-06497-6*) U of Ill Pr.

C

Crozier, Michael J. Landslides: Causes, Consequences & Environment. 272p. 1986. 57.50 (*0-7099-0790-7*, Pub. by C Helm) Routldge.

Crozier, Michel. Bureaucratic Phenomenon. LC 63-20916. 1995. pap. text 12.95 (*0-226-12166-6*, P280) U Ch Pr.

— The Bureaucratic Phenomenon. LC 63-20916. (Phoenix Books in Sociology). (Illus.). 330p. reprint ed. pap. 102.30 (*0-608-09293-2*, 205416700004) Bks Demand.

— A Strategies for Change: The Future of French Society. Beer, William, tr. from FRE. (Organization Studies). 244p. 1982. 30.00 (*0-262-03082-9*) MIT Pr.

— World of the Office Worker. Landau, David, tr. from FRE. LC 76-141150. (Studies of Urban Society). (C). 1993. 22.00 (*0-226-12167-4*) U Ch Pr.

Crozier, Michel & Friedberg, Erhard. Actors & Systems: The Politics of Collective Action. Goldhammer, Arthur, tr. LC 80-13803. 272p. 1994. 30.00 (*0-226-12183-6*) U Ch Pr.

— Actors & Systems: The Politics of Collective Action. Goldhammer, Arthur, tr. LC 80-13803. 341p. reprint ed. pap. 105.80 (*0-608-09292-4*, 205416600004) Bks Demand.

Crozier, Ouida. Shadows after Dark. 224p. 1993. pap. 9.95 (*1-883061-50-4*) Rising AZ.

Crozier, Robin & Bennett, John M. Fake Fried Eggs. 6p. (Orig.). 1993. pap. 2.00 (*0-935350-44-6*) Luna Bisonte.

— Meat Click. 1980. pap. 2.00 (*0-935350-02-0*) Luna Bisonte.

Crozier, Robin, jt. auth. see Bennett, John M.

Crozier, Ronald D. Flotation. (Theory, Reagents & Ore Testing Ser.). (Illus.). 362p. 1992. 151.00 (*0-08-041864-3*, Pergamon Pr) Elsevier.

Crozier, Ross H. & Pamilo, Pekka. Evolution of Social Insect Colonies: Sex Allocation & Kin Selection. LC 95-32182. (Oxford Series in Ecology & Evolution). (Illus.). 320p. (C). 1996. text 79.00 (*0-19-854943-1*) OUP.

Crozier, W. A. Spotsylvania County Records. (Virginia County Records Ser.: Vol. I). (Illus.). 576p. 1996. reprint ed. lib. bdg. 49.00 (*0-8328-5134-5*) Higginson Bk Co.

Crozier, W. Ray. Individaul Learners: Personality Differences in Education. LC 96-43377. (Illus.). 256p. (C). 1997. 80.00 (*0-415-13329-7*); pap. 25.99 (*0-415-13330-0*) Routledge.

Crozier, W. Ray, ed. Shyness & Embarrassment: Perspectives from Social Psychology. (Illus.). 375p. (C). 1990. text 69.95 (*0-521-35529-X*) Cambridge U Pr.

Crozier, William A. Virginia County Records, 11 vols. Incl. Virginia County Records Vol. VI: Miscellaneous County Records. LC 67-29835. 326p. 1998. reprint ed. pap. 27.50 (*0-8063-0469-3*); Vol. 1. Spotsylvania County, 1721-1800. LC 67-29835. 576p. 1990. reprint ed. 35.00 (*0-8063-0468-5*); LC 67-29835. write for info. (*0-318-52677-8*) Genealog Pub.

— Virginia County Records: Miscellaneous County Records, Vol. IX. 151p. 1997. reprint ed. pap. 18.50 (*0-8063-0472-3*, 1249) Clearfield Co.

— Virginia County Records: Miscellaneous County Records, Vol. X. 95p. 1993. reprint ed. pap. 12.00 (*0-8063-0473-1*, 1250) Clearfield Co.

— Virginia County Records Vol. I: Westmoreland County. (New Ser.). 110p. 1997. reprint ed. pap. 13.50 (*0-8063-0474-X*, 1251) Clearfield Co.

— Williamsburg Wills: Virginia County Records, Vol. III. 77p. 1995. reprint ed. pap. 12.00 (*0-8063-0567-3*) Clearfield Co.

Crozier, William A., ed. Virginia County Records, Vol. 3. 77p. 1994. reprint ed. pap. 10.00 (*0-8328-4017-3*) Higginson Bk Co.

Crozier, William A., ed. see Virginia County Records Staff.

Crozon, Alain. I Can Fly! LC 98-48932. (Lift-the-Flap bks.). (Illus.). (J). 1999. 7.95 (*0-8118-2407-1*) Chronicle Bks.

— I Can Roll! LC 98-48931. (Lift-the-Flap bks.). (Illus.). (J). 1999. 7.95 (*0-8118-2408-X*) Chronicle Bks.

***Crozon, Alain & Lanchais, A.** Christmas! (What Am I? Ser.). (Illus.). 7p. (J). (ps). 1999. 7.95 (*0-8118-2613-9*) Chronicle Bks.

— Halloween! (What Am I? Ser.). (Illus.). 7p. (ps). 1999. 7.95 (*0-8118-2612-0*) Chronicle Bks.

Crozon, Alain & Lanchais, Aurelie. What Am I? (Illus.). (J). (ps). 1998. 7.95 (*0-8118-2102-1*) Chronicle Bks.

— Who Am I? Lift-the-Flap Book. (Illus.). (J). (ps). 1998. 7.95 (*0-8118-2103-X*) Chronicle Bks.

Crsboy, M. R. A Dictionary of Mosses. (C). 1988. text 60.00 (*81-85046-65-4*, Pub. by Scientific Pubs) St Mut.

CRSN Staff, jt. auth. see Wang, Ke-wen.

Cru, Jean N. War Books. 210p. 1988. pap. 12.50 (*0-916304-22-1*) SDSU Press.

***Crubaugh, Anthony.** Balancing the Scales of Justice: Local Courts & Rural Society in Southwest France, 1750-1800. LC 00-35684. (C). 2000. write for info. (*0-271-02078-4*) Pa St U Pr.

Crucefix, Martyn. Beneath Tremendous Rain. 99p. (Orig.). 1990. pap. 14.95 (*1-870612-26-4*, Pub. by Enitha Pr) Dufour.

— A Madder Ghost. LC 97-208586. 80p. 1997. pap. 17.95 (*1-900564-10-6*, Pub. by Enitha Pr) Dufour.

Crucq, A., ed. Catalysis & Automotive Pollution Control II: Proc. of the 2nd Internat. Symp., Brussels, 10-13 Sept., 1990. (Studies in Surface Science & Catalysis: Vol. 71). xiv,686p. 1991. 290.00 (*0-444-88787-3*) Elsevier.

***Cruddas, Colin.** Cobham: The Flying Years. (Transport Ser.). 1999. pap. 18.99 (*0-7524-0781-3*) Arcadia Publng.

***Cruddas, Rhonda.** Caffeine Free "Chocolate" Treats. LC TXu 730-666. 36p. 2000. write for info. (*0-9677251-0-0*) R Cruddas.

Crudele, John & Erickson, Richard. Making Sense of Adolescence: How to Parent from the Heart. 2nd ed. 271p. 1999. reprint ed. 22.95 (*0-9669924-0-7*); reprint ed. pap. 13.95 (*0-9669924-1-5*) J Crudele.

Cruden. Cruden's Complete Concordance. 1986. 29.95 (*0-932453-68-6*) Dugan Pubs Inc.

Cruden, Alexander. Cruden's Compact Concordance. abr. ed. 1988. 10.95 (*0-310-22919-7*) Zondervan.

— Cruden's Complete Concordance. 803p. 1967. 24.99 (*0-310-22920-0*, 9441) Zondervan.

— Cruden's Complete Concordance: To the Old & New Testaments. 784p. 1988. 15.95 (*0-917006-31-3*) Hendrickson MA.

— Cruden's Complete Concordance to the Old & New Testaments. 800p. 1991. pap. 9.95 (*0-943575-82-6*) Hendrickson MA.

— Cruden's Condensed Concordance. 1990. pap. text 7.95 (*1-55674-143-X*) Dugan Pubs Inc.

Cruden, Alexander, ed. Cruden's Complete Concordance to the Old & New Testaments. (Reference Library Edition). 24.99 (*0-529-06675-0*, CRU1) World Publng.

Cruden, David & Fell, Robin, eds. Landslide Risk Assessment: Proceedings of the Workshop on Landslide Risk Assessment, Honolulu, Hawaii, U. S. A., 19-21.02. 1997. (Illus.). 384p. (C). 1997. text 104.00 (*90-5410-914-9*, Pub. by A A Balkema) Ashgate Pub Co.

Cruden, Gordon N. Land Compensation & Valuation Law in Hong Kong. 508p. 1986. 151.00 (*0-409-99525-8*, MICHIE) LEXIS Pub.

Cruden, Loren. Compass of the Heart: Embodying Medicine Wheel Teachings. LC 95-48807. 192p. 1996. pap. 14.95 (*0-89281-600-7*, Destiny Bks) Inner Tradit.

— Coyote's Council Fire: Contemporary Shamans on Race, Gender & Community. LC 95-32363. 176p. 1995. pap. 14.95 (*0-89281-566-3*, Destiny Bks) Inner Tradit.

— Medicine Grove: A Shamanic Herbal. LC 97-18606. (Illus.). 176p. 1997. pap. 14.95 (*0-89281-647-3*) Inner Tradit.

— The Spirit of Place: A Workbook for Sacred Alignment. (Illus.). 232p. 1995. pap. 16.95 (*0-89281-511-6*, Destiny Bks) Inner Tradit.

— Walking the Maze: The Enduring Presence of Celtic Spirit. LC 98-39936. 256p. 1998. pap. 14.95 (*0-89281-623-6*) Inner Tradit.

Cruden, Robert. James Ford Rhodes: The Man, the Historian & His Work. LC 79-28196. 290p. 1980. reprint ed. lib. bdg. 59.75 (*0-313-22255-X*, CRJF, Greenwood Pr) Greenwood.

Cruden, Stewart. History of Bruntsfield Links Golfing Society. 110p. (C). 1989. text 45.00 (*0-85976-358-7*, Pub. by J Donald) St Mut.

Crudi & Larkin, Patricia. Core Curriculum for Intravenous Nursing. 368p. 1984. text 26.00 (*0-397-54516-9*, Lippnctt) Lppncott W & W.

Crues, John. Firestorm in Paradise. LC 97-50543. 224p. 1998. pap. 14.95 (*1-56474-260-1*) Fithian Pr.

Crues, John V., III, ed. MRI of the Musculoskeletal System. (MRI Teaching File Ser.). 242p. 1991. text 76.00 (*0-88167-705-1*) Lppncott W & W.

Cruess, Richard L. & Mitchell, Nelson S., eds. Surgical Management of Degenerative Arthritis of the Lower Limb. LC 75-20440. (Illus.). 248p. reprint ed. 76.90 (*0-8357-9421-0*, 201453900093) Bks Demand.

Cruess, Richard L. & Rennie, William R., eds. Adult Orthopaedics, 2 vols. (Illus.). 1566p. 1992. text 127.00 (*0-443-08107-7*) Church.

Cruetz, E. & Moriarty, J. Analysis of Several Percussion-Formed Artifacts. (Illus.). 16p. (C). 1962. reprint ed. pap. text 2.19 (*1-55567-408-9*) Coyote Press.

Cruft, Charles. Charles Cruft's Dog Book: Popular Breeds & Their Care. (Illus.). 96p. (Orig.). 1983. pap. 13.95 (*0-572-01208-X*) Trans-Atl Phila.

Cruft, Kitty & Fraser, Andrew. James Craig: Ingenious Architect of the New Town. 144p. 1989. pap. 40.00 (*1-873644-40-X*, Pub. by Mercat Pr Bks) St Mut.

Cruger, George, ed. see Danto, Arthur, et al.

Cruger, George A., ed. see Rewald, John & Near, Pinkney L.

Cruger, Laura. Return to Center, That Address Now Known: A Little Guide Towards Evolution in the Light. 72p. 1994. pap. 8.00 (*0-9643566-0-0*) Creat VA.

Crugier, Bice, jt. ed. see Neri, Louise.

Crugnola, Aldo M., jt. ed. see Deanin, Rudolph D.

Cruice, Gary, Jr., jt. auth. see Clanton, Candace.

Cruickshank, A. B., ed. Where Town Meets Country: Problems of Peri-Urban Areas of Scotland, Royal Scottish Geographical Society Symposium May 1981. (Illus.). 140p. 1982. 23.00 (*0-08-028442-6*, R130, Pergamon Pr); pap. 16.00 (*0-08-028443-4*, R145, Pergamon Pr) Elsevier.

Cruickshank, A. H. Pathology of the Pancreas. (Illus.). 290p. 1986. 173.00 (*0-387-16216-X*) Spr-Verlag.

Cruickshank, A. H. & Benbow, E. W. Pathology of the Pancreas. 2nd ed. LC 95-33. 358p. 1995. 145.00 (*3-540-19923-3*) Spr-Verlag.

Cruickshank, Allan D. Cruickshank's Photographs of Birds of America. LC 77-70078. (Illus.). 1977. pap. 10.95 (*0-486-23497-5*) Dover.

Cruickshank, Allan D. & Cruickshank, Helen. One Thousand & One Questions Answered about Birds. LC 75-41881. (One Thousand & One Questions Ser.). (Illus.). 320p. 1976. reprint ed. pap. 7.95 (*0-486-23315-4*) Dover.

Cruickshank, Bruce. Birds of the World in Philately, Vol. 2. (Illus.). 130p. (Orig.). 1990. pap. text 10.00 (*0-935991-08-5*) Am Topical Assn.

— Eighteen Years on the Gold Coast of Africa, 2 vols., Set. 1966. reprint ed. 95.00 (*0-7146-1802-0*, BHA-01802, Pub. by F Cass Pubs) Intl Spec Bk.

Cruickshank, Charles. Greece, 1940-1941. Frankland, Noble & Dowling, Christopher, eds. LC 79-52239. (Politics & Strategy of the Second World War Ser.). 206p. 1979. 21.50 (*0-87413-159-6*) U Delaware Pr.

Cruickshank, D. W., et al, eds. P. P. Ewald & His Dynamical Theory of X-Ray Diffraction. LC 92-9876. (International Union of Crystallography Monographs on Crystallography: No. 2). (Illus.). 172p. (C). 1992. text 69.00 (*0-19-855379-X*) OUP.

Cruickshank, D. W., jt. ed. see Gallagher, P.

Cruickshank, D. W., ed. see Wison, Edward M.

***Cruickshank, Dan, ed.** Architecture: The Critics' Choice. (Illus.). 352p. 2000. 50.00 (*0-8230-0289-6*) Watsn-Guptill.

Cruickshank, Dan, ed. see Fletcher, Banister.

***Cruickshank, Don W., ed.** A Lifetime's Reading: Hispanic Essays for Patrick Gallagher. 240p. 1999. 59.95 (*1-900621-21-5*, Pub. by Univ Coll Dublin Pr) Dufour.

Cruickshank, Don W., jt. auth. see Wilson, Edward M.

Cruickshank, Don W., ed. see Calderon de la Barca, Pedro.

Cruickshank, Donald R. Research That Informs Teachers & Teacher Educators. 160p. 1990. pap. 9.00 (*0-87367-446-4*) Phi Delta Kappa.

Cruickshank, Donald R., ed. Preparing America's Teachers. LC 96-68562. 150p. 1996. pap. 11.50 (*0-87367-486-3*) Phi Delta Kappa.

Cruickshank, Donald R., et al. The Act of Teaching. LC 94-25044. (C). 1994. text 49.00 (*0-07-014819-8*) McGraw.

— The Act of Teaching. 2nd ed. LC 98-6768. 496p. 1998. pap. 58.13 (*0-07-000789-6*) McGraw.

Cruickshank, Gordon & Austin, Alan. Cars & How They Work. LC 92-7623. (See & Explore Library). (Illus.). 64p. (J). (gr. 3 up). 1992. 11.95 (*1-56458-142-X*) DK Pub Inc.

Cruickshank, Graeme. Scottish Pottery. 1989. pap. 25.00 (*0-85263-849-3*, Pub. by Shire Pubns) St Mut.

Cruickshank, Helen, jt. auth. see Cruickshank, Allan D.

Cruickshank, Helen G., ed. John & William Bartram's America. (American Naturalists Ser.). (Illus.). 1990. 18.95 (*0-8159-5101-9*) Devin.

Cruickshank, Helen G., ed. see Bartram, J. & Bartram, W.

Cruickshank, Ian. Django's Gypsies - the Mystique of Django Reinhardt & His People. 138p. 23.95 (*0-614-20104-7*, 00183209, Pub. by Ashley Mark Pub) H Leonard.

— The Guitar Style of Django Reinhardt & the Gypsies. (Illus.). 48p. 1989. pap. 17.95 (*0-7119-1853-8*, AM73925) Music Sales.

Cruickshank, J. M. Beta Blockers in Clinical Practice. 2nd ed. 1994. text 205.00 (*0-443-04522-4*) Church.

Cruickshank, John. Albert Camus & the Literature of Revolt. LC 78-16380. 248p. 1978. reprint ed. lib. bdg. 45.50 (*0-313-20580-9*, CRAC, Greenwood Pr) Greenwood.

— Aspects of the Modern European Mind. LC 75-422041. (Problems & Perspectives in History Ser.). 212p. reprint ed. pap. 65.80 (*0-8357-5800-1*, 200638100058) Bks Demand.

— Benjamin Constant. LC 73-21952. (Twayne's World Authors Ser.). 170p. (C). 1974. lib. bdg. 20.95 (*0-8057-2242-4*) Irvington.

— Variations on Catastrophe: Some French Responses to the Great War. 1982. 34.95 (*0-19-212599-0*) OUP.

Cruickshank, John, ed. The Novelist As Philosopher: Studies in French Fiction, 1935-1960. LC 77-28882. 257p. 1978. reprint ed. lib. bdg. 35.00 (*0-313-20271-0*, CRNP, Greenwood Pr) Greenwood.

***Cruickshank, M. K.** Don't Dawdle Dorothy. (Illus.). (J). 1999. 18.99 (*0-7112-1215-5*) F Lincoln.

Cruickshank, Margrit. Circling the Triangle. 1991. pap. 7.95 (*1-85371-137-3*, Pub. by Poolbeg Pr) Dufour.

— S. K. U. N. K. & the Ozone Conspiracy. 235p. (YA). 1990. pap. 8.95 (*1-85371-067-9*, Pub. by Poolbeg Pr) Dufour.

Cruickshank, Ros. Body-Shaping for the Over-Thirties. 160p. 1995. pap. 7.95 (*0-572-01532-1*, Pub. by Foulsham UK) Assoc Pubs Grp.

Cruickshank, Steven. Mathematics & Statistics in Anaesthesia. (Illus.). 268p. 1998. text (*0-19-262313-3*) OUP.

— Mathematics & Statistics in Anaesthesia. LC 97-53170. (Illus.). 268p. 1998. pap. text 49.50 (*0-19-262312-5*) OUP.

Cruickshank, William. A Teaching Method for Brain-Injured & Hyperactive Children: A Demonstration-Pilot Study, 6. LC 81-6255. (Syracuse University Special Education & Rehabilitation Monograph Ser.: No. 6). (Illus.). 576p. 1981. reprint ed. lib. bdg. 95.00 (*0-313-23071-4*, CRTC) Greenwood.

Cruickshank, William M. Concepts in Learning Disabilities: Selected Writings, Vol. 2. LC 80-29024. 296p. 1981. text 45.00 (*0-8156-2239-2*) Syracuse U Pr.

— Concepts in Special Education Vol. 1: Selected Writings. LC 80-29024. 392p. 1981. text 45.00 (*0-8156-2238-4*) Syracuse U Pr.

Cruickshank, William M., ed. Cerebral Palsy: A Developmental Disability. 3rd rev. ed. LC 75-34275. 644p. reprint ed. pap. 199.70 (*0-608-17475-0*, 202996700067) Bks Demand.

— Teacher of Brain Injured Children: A Discussion of the Bases for Competency. LC 66-20050. (Special Education & Rehabilitation Monograph Ser.: No. 7). (C). 1966. 17.95 (*0-8156-2096-9*) Syracuse U Pr.

Cruickshank, William M. & Kliebhan, Joanne M., eds. Early Adolescence to Early Adulthood: The Best of ALCD, Vol. 5. LC 83-17968. (Best of ACLD Ser.). (Illus.). 208p. 1984. pap. text 19.95 (*0-8156-2301-1*) Syracuse U Pr.

Cruickshank, William M. & Lerner, Janet W., eds. Coming of Age: Selected Papers from the 18th International Conference of the Association for Children & Adults with Learning Disabilities. LC 81-21404. (Best of ACLD Ser.: No. 3). (Illus.). 251p. reprint ed. pap. 77.90 (*0-8357-3986-4*, 203668400003) Bks Demand.

Cruickshank, William M. & Silver, Archie A., eds. Bridges to Tomorrow: The Best of ACLD, Vol. 2. 1981. pap. 22.50 (*0-8156-2237-6*) Syracuse U Pr.

Cruickshank, William M. & Tash, Eli, eds. Academics & Beyond. (Best of ACLD Ser.: Vol. 4). 256p. 1983. pap. text 22.50 (*0-8156-2272-4*) Syracuse U Pr.

Cruickshank, William M., et al. Learning Disabilities: The Struggle from Adolescence Toward Adulthood. (Illus.). 304p. (C). 1980. pap. 19.95 (*0-8156-2221-X*) Syracuse U Pr.

— Misfits in the Public Schools. LC 69-13137. 230p. reprint ed. pap. 71.30 (*0-8357-3989-9*, 203668700005) Bks Demand.

— The Preparation of Teachers of Brain-Injured Children. LC 68-31430. (Syracuse University: Special Education & Rehabilitation Monograph Ser.: No. 8). (Illus.). 223p. reprint ed. pap. 69.20 (*0-8357-3988-0*, 203668600005) Bks Demand.

***Cruickshanks, Eveline.** The Glorious Revolution. LC 99-48546. (British History in Perspective Ser.). 2000. pap. 17.95 (*0-312-23009-5*); text 45.00 (*0-312-23008-7*) St Martin.

Cruickshanks, Eveline & Edward Corp. Staff, eds. The Stuart Court in Exile & the Jacobites. LC 95-49130. 1995. 55.00 (*1-85285-119-8*) Hambledon Press.

Cruijsen, Harry, jt. auth. see Keilman, Nico W.

Cruikshank, Barbara. Will to Empower: Democratic Citizens & other Subjects. 1999. write for info. (*0-8014-3480-7*) Cornell U Pr.

— The Will to Empower: Democratic Citizens & Other Subjects. LC 98-46489. 149p. 1999. pap. 16.95 (*0-8014-8599-1*) Cornell U Pr.

Cruikshank, Dale P., ed. Neptune & Triton. LC 95-32468. (Space Science Ser.). (Illus.). 1249p. 1996. 110.00 (*0-8165-1525-5*) U of Ariz Pr.

Cruikshank, Douglas E., jt. auth. see Sheffield, Linda Jensen.

Cruikshank, Ernest A., ed. Documentary History of the Campaign Upon the Niagara Frontier, 1812-1814, 4 vols. LC 74-146387. (First American Frontier Ser.). (Illus.). 1971. reprint ed. 209.95 (*0-405-02838-5*) Ayer.

— Documents Relating to the Invasion of Canada & the Surrender of Detroit, 1812. LC 70-146386. (First American Frontier Ser.). (Illus.). 1979. reprint ed. 35.95 (*0-405-02837-7*) Ayer.

Cruikshank, George. Graphic Works of George Cruikshank. Vogler, Richard A., ed. (Pictorial Archive Ser.). (Illus.). 200p. 1980. pap. 12.95 (*0-486-23438-X*) Dover.

Cruikshank, George. Punch & Judy. LC 70-174866. 1972. reprint ed. 26.95 (*0-405-09123-0*, Pub. by Blom Pubns) Ayer.

Cruikshank, George & Streatfeild, Thomas. Henry George: Printer, Bookseller, Publisher & Stationer in Westerham, Kent 1830-1846. 72p. (C). 1989. 59.00 (*0-7855-6529-9*, Pub. by Hurtwood Pr Ltd) St Mut.

Cruikshank, George, jt. auth. see Beckett, Gilbert Abbott.

***Cruikshank, Ginger.** Springfield, Vol. 1. (Images of America Ser.). 128p. 1999. pap. 18.99 (*0-7385-0229-4*) Arcadia Publng.

— Springfield Vol. II: Massachusetts. LC 99-69551. (Images of America Ser.). (Illus.). 128p. 2000. pap. 18.99 (*0-7385-0435-1*) Arcadia Publng.

Cruikshank, Ian. Django's Gypsies: The Mystique of Django Reinhart & His People. (Illus.). 138p. 1997. pap. 23.95 (*1-872639-06-2*, Pub. by Ashley Mark Pub) H Leonard.

Cruikshank, Jeffrey, jt. auth. see Campbell, Robert.

Cruikshank, Jeffrey L. & Korza, Pam. Going Public: A Field Guide to Developments in Art in Public Places. LC 87-73466. (Illus.). (Orig.). 1990. pap. 30.00 (*0-945464-00-2*) Univ MA Arts.

Cruikshank, Jeffrey L. & Sicilia, David B. The Engine That Could: Values-Driven Change at Cummins Engine Company, 1919-1994. LC 97-2746. 640p. 1998. 45.00 (*0-87584-613-0*) Harvard Busn.

Cruikshank, Jeffrey L., jt. auth. see Pagonis, William G.

Cruikshank, Jeffrey L., jt. auth. see Poorvu, William J.

Cruikshank, Jeffrey L., jt. auth. see Reiss, Bob.

Cruikshank, Jeffrey L., jt. auth. see Susskind, Lawrence.

Cruikshank, Jeffrey L., jt. ed. see McCraw, Thomas K.

Cruikshank, Julie. Life Lived Like a Story: Life Stories of Three Yukon Native Elders. LC 89-49361. (American Indian Lives Ser.). (Illus.). xvi, 404p. 1991. text 60.00 (*0-8032-1447-2*) U of Nebr Pr.

— Life Lived Like a Story: Life Stories of Three Yukon Native Elders. LC 89-49361. (American Indian Lives Ser.). (Illus.). xvi, 404p. 1991. reprint ed. pap. 16.00 (*0-8032-6352-X*, Bison Books) U of Nebr Pr.

— Reading Voices, Dan Dha Ts'edenintth'e: Oral & Written Interpretations of the Yukon's Past. (Illus.). 158p. 1997. 24.95 (*0-88894-728-3*) DGL.

Cruikshank, Julie. The Social Life of Stories: Narrative & Knowledge in the Yukon Territory. LC 97-22768. (Illus.). xxviii, 221p. 1998. text 50.00 (*0-8032-1490-1*) U of Nebr Pr.

***Cruikshank, Julie.** The Social Life of Stories: Narrative & Knowledge in the Yukon Territory. LC 97-22768. (Illus.). 221p. 2000. pap. text 19.95 (*0-8032-6409-7*) U of Nebr Pr.

Cruikshank, Ken. Close Ties: Railways, Government & the Board of Railway Commissioners, 1851-1933. 304p. 1991. text 65.00 (*0-7735-0854-6*, Pub. by McG-Queens Univ Pr) CUP Services.

Cruikshank, Margaret. The Gay & Lesbian Liberation Movement. LC 92-8622. (Revolutionary Thought & Radical Movements Ser.). 256p. (C). (gr. 13). 1992. pap. 19.99 (*0-415-90648-2*, A8173) Routledge.

C

An Asterisk (*) at the beginning of an entry indicates that the title is appearing for the first time.

— New Lesbian Writing. LC 83-22603. 220p. 1984. pap. 7.95 (*0-912516-81-X*) Grey Fox.

***Cruikshank, Margaret & Saunders, Dave.** Down by the Pond: A Surprise Farmyard Book. (Illus.). 32p. (J). (ps). 1999. pap. text 7.99 (*0-7112-0978-2*) F Lincoln.

Cruikshank, Margaret L., ed. The Lesbian Path. enl. rev. ed. LC 85-12519. 232p. 1985. reprint ed. pap. 10.95 (*0-912516-96-8*) Grey Fox.

Cruikshank, Moses. The Life I've Been Living. LC 86-51263. (Oral Biography Ser.: No. 1). (Illus.). 132p. 1986. pap. 9.95 (*0-912006-23-4*) U of Alaska Pr.

Cruim, Beverly & Daley, Jon. Shoshoni Texts. (Illus.). 283p. (C). 1997. pap. text 18.95 (*0-9639749-2-0*) Boise St U Dept Anthrop.

Cruise. New Class No. 11: Saved by the Bell. 1996. 3.95 (*0-689-80712-0*) S&S Childrens.

Cruise. Trust at Work. text. write for info. (*0-471-49130-6*) Wiley.

Cruise, A. M., et al. Principles of Space Instrument Design. LC 97-16356. (Aerospace Ser.: Vol. 9). (Illus.). 418p. (C). 1998. 110.00 (*0-521-45164-7*) Cambridge U Pr.

Cruise, Beth. Standing Room Only. (Saved by the Bell Ser.: No. 24). (J). 1996. pap. text 3.50 (*0-689-80625-6*) Aladdin.

Cruise, Boyd. Boyd Cruise. LC 76-24712. (Illus.). vi, 74p. 1976. 20.00 (*0-917860-01-2*) Historic New Orleans.

Cruise, Boyd & Harton, Merle. Signor Faranta's Iron Theatre. LC 82-83592. (Illus.). xii, 148p. 1982. 14.95 (*0-917860-13-6*) Historic New Orleans.

***Cruise, David.** Koskimo. 2000. 27.50 (*0-06-019787-0*); mass mkt. 7.99 (*0-06-103092-9*) HarpC.

Cruise, David & Griffiths, Allison. The Great Adventure: How the Mounties Conquered the West. LC 97-5813. 1997. text 26.95 (*0-312-15538-7*) St Martin.

Cruise, Edwina. English Grammar for Students of Russian. 2nd ed. Morton, Jacqueline, ed. 184p. 1993. pap. 12.95 (*0-934034-21-4*) Olivia & Hill.

***Cruise, James.** Governing Consumption: Needs & Wants, Suspended Characters & the "Origins" of Eighteenth-Century English Novels. LC 99-23974. 248p. 1999. 42.50 (*0-8387-5428-7*) Bucknell U Pr.

Cruise O'Brien, Donal, et al, eds. Contemporary West African States. 235p. (C). 1990. pap. text 19.95 (*0-521-36893-6*) Cambridge U Pr.

Cruise O'Brien, Donal B. Saints & Politicians: Essays in the Organisation of a Senegalese Peasant Society. LC 74-82221. (African Studies: No. 15). 221p. reprint ed. pap. 63.00 (*0-608-17522-6*, 2030612) Bks Demand.

Cruise-O'Brien, Kate, jt. ed. see Maher, Mary.

Cruise, Robert J., jt. auth. see Blitchington, Peter.

***Cruise, Robin.** Fiona's Private Pages. 176p. (J). (gr. 3-7). 2000. 15.00 (*0-15-202210-4*, Harcourt Child Bks) Harcourt.

Cruise, Robin. Match Point. Parker, Liz, ed. (Take Ten Bks.). (Illus.). 52p. (YA). (gr. 6-12). 1993. pap. text 3.95 (*1-56254-093-9*) Saddleback Pubns.

***Cruise, Robin.** Match Point. rev. ed. (Take Ten Ser.). (Illus.). 52p. (YA). (gr. 4-12). 1999. pap. 3.95 (*1-58659-035-9*) Artesian.

Cruise, Robin. The Nuclear Disaster at Chernobyl. Parker, Liz, ed. (Take Ten Bks.). 46p. (YA). (gr. 6-12). 1993. pap. text 3.95 (*1-56254-099-8*) Saddleback Pubns.

***Cruise, Robin.** The Nuclear Disaster at Chernobyl. rev. ed. (Take Ten Ser.). (Illus.). 46p. (YA). (gr. 4-12). 1999. pap. 3.95 (*1-58659-022-7*) Artesian.

— The Top-Secret Journal of Fiona Claire Jardin. 160p. (J). (gr. 3-7). 2000. pap. 6.00 (*0-15-202394-1*, Harcourt Child Bks) Harcourt.

Cruise, Robin. The Top-Secret Journal of Fiona Claire Jardin. LC 97-40363. 158p. (J). (gr. 4-6). 1998. 13.00 (*0-15-201383-0*) Harcourt Coll Pubs.

Cruise, T. E. Wings of Gold IV: Top Gun. 1990. mass mkt. 4.95 (*0-445-20975-5*, Pub. by Warner Bks) Little.

— Wings of Gold I: The Aces, Vol. 1. 384p. 1988. mass mkt. 3.95 (*0-445-20628-4*, Pub. by Warner Bks) Little.

— Wings of Gold II: The Flyboys. 352p. 1989. mass mkt. 4.95 (*0-445-20576-8*, Pub. by Warner Bks) Little.

Cruise, Valerie. When Do I Clap: A Guide to Classical Music. LC 97-223138. (Illus.). 172p. 1997. pap. 18.95 (*1-881907-13-9*) Two Bytes Pub.

Cruise, William. A Digest of the Laws of England Respecting Real Property, 7 vols. 4th enl. rev. ed. reprint ed. 695.00 (*1-56169-313-8*) Gaunt.

Cruisenaire. Learn Spanish with Books. 1993. pap. 16.95 (*0-201-48268-1*) Addison-Wesley.

Cruising Club of America Technical Committee, et al. Desirable & Undesirable Characteristics of Offshore Yachts. Rousmaniere, John, ed. 1987. 39.95 (*0-393-03311-2*) Norton.

***Cruising Guide Publications Staff.** Virgin Anchorages. (Illus.). 2000. pap. 24.95 (*0-944428-50-9*) Cruising Guide.

Cruit, Michael, jt. auth. see Lauderdale, Pat.

Crul, J. F., ed. Legal Aspects of Anaesthesia. (Developments in Critical Care, Medicine, & Anesthesiology Ser.). 146p. (C). 1989. lib. bdg. 80.00 (*0-7923-0393-8*) Kluwer Academic.

Crul, R. C. & Roest, F. C. Current Status of Fisheries & Fish Stocks of the Four Largest African Reservoirs. LC 96-121970. (CIFA Technical Papers: Vol.30). 140p. 1995. pap. 17.00 (*92-5-103683-7*) Food & Agri Org UN.

Crull. The 1995 Guide to the U. S. Membrane Industry. 175p. 1995. 1650.00 (*1-56965-319-4*, DMD95) BCC.

Crull & Park. Cancer Treatment & Diagnostic Products. LC 96-143455. 185p. 1995. 2650.00 (*1-56965-043-8*, C-047N) BCC.

Crull, Anna. High Tech Separations Industry Review. 284p. 1998. 1500.00 (*1-56965-500-6*, DST96) BCC.

— Membrane & Separations Technology Industry Review. 306p. 1998. 1500.00 (*1-56965-510-3*, DMS97) BCC.

Crull, Anna & Grant, Sandi, eds. Membrane & Separations Technology Industry Reviews. 316p. 1995. 1500.00 (*1-56965-331-3*) BCC.

Crull, Anna & Hilton, Richard. Synthetic Gems & Minerals. LC 98-143163. 133p. 1998. 2950.00 (*1-56965-463-8*, GB-215) BCC.

Crull, Anna & Jones, Michelle. Antioxidants: A Market Overview. 128p. 1998. 3150.00 (*1-56965-391-7*, C-020BN) BCC.

Crull, Anna, jt. auth. see Campbell, Craig.

Crull, Anna, jt. auth. see Clark, Nancy.

Crull, Anna, jt. auth. see Parrish, Alton.

Crull, Anna, jt. auth. see Santon, June.

Crull, Anna, jt. auth. see Wier, Patrick.

Crull, Anna, jt. contrib. by see Campbell, Craig.

Crull, Anna, jt. contrib. by see Hilton, Richard.

Crull, Anna, jt. contrib. by see Watson, David.

Crum. International Banking. (C). 1996. text. write for info. (*0-03-014539-2*); pap. text, teacher ed. write for info. (*0-03-014542-2*) Harcourt Coll Pubs.

— International Financial Management. (C). 1996. text. write for info. (*0-03-014537-6*) Harcourt Coll Pubs.

***Crum.** The Magic Of Conflict. 1998. per. 14.00 (*0-684-85448-1*) S&S Trade.

Crum, Alison & Jackson, Sonia. Play the Viol: The Complete Guide to Playing the Treble, Tenor, & Bass Viol. (Early Music Ser.: No. 10). (Illus.). 200p. 1992. pap. text 29.95 (*0-19-816311-8*) OUP.

Crum, Bartley. Behind the Silken Curtain. 300p. 1996. 24.95 (*0-9646886-1-1*) Milah.

Crum, Beverly, jt. auth. see Dayley, Jon.

Crum, Christopher P. & Nuovo, Gerard J. Genital Papillomaviruses & Related Neoplasms. LC 90-9232. (Illus.). 240p. 1991. reprint ed. pap. 74.40 (*0-608-05845-9*, 205981100007) Bks Demand.

Crum, Christopher P., et al. Pathology of Early Cervical Neoplasia. LC 96-29476. (Contemporary Issues in Surgical Pathology Ser.). 1996. text 95.00 (*0-443-07590-5*) Church.

Crum, Denny & Schaller, Bob. The State of the Game: Coach Denny Crums Perspective on College Basketball. 192p. 1999. pap. text 19.95 (*1-887002-94-4*) Cross Trng.

***Crum, Dorothy, ed.** Finnish Short Stories. Vaananen-Jensen, Inkeri & Vahanaki, K. Borje, trs. from FIN. (Illus.). 244p. 2000. pap. 17.95 (*1-57216-043-8*) Penfield.

Crum, Dorothy, jt. compiled by see Van Klompenburg, Carol.

Crum, Dorothy, ed. see Bourret, Joan Liffring-Zug.

Crum, Dorothy, ed. see Bradnan, Melinda.

Crum, Dorothy, ed. see Hughes, Helga.

Crum, Dorothy, ed. see Lagerlof, Selma.

Crum, Dorothy, ed. see Liffring-Zug, Joan.

Crum, Dorothy, ed. see Martin, Pat.

Crum, Dorothy, ed. see Stevens, Dianna.

Crum, Gary & McCormack, Thelma. Abortion: Pro-Choice or Pro-Life? 200p. (C). 1991. pap. 19.50 (*1-879383-04-7*) Am Univ Pr.

— Abortion: Pro-Choice or Pro-Life? 200p. (C). 1992. 50.00 (*1-879383-05-5*) Am Univ Pr.

Crum, H. A. Sphagnopsida - Sphagnaceae. LC 84-4705. (North American Flora Ser.: No. 2, Pt. 11). (Illus.). 180p. 1984. pap. 18.75 (*0-89327-252-3*) NY Botanical.

Crum, Howard & Planisek, Sandra. A Focus on Peatlands & Peat Mosses. Wagner, Warren H., Jr., ed. (Great Lakes Environment Ser.). 320p. (Orig.). (C). 1992. pap. text 22.95 (*0-472-06378-2*, 06378) U of Mich Pr.

Crum, Howard A. & Anderson, Lewis E. Mosses of Eastern North America, 2 vols. LC 79-24789. (Illus.). 576p. 1981. text 274.00 (*0-231-04516-6*) Col U Pr.

Crum, Howard A., jt. auth. see Steere, William C.

Crum, James, jt. ed. see Margalit, Yair.

Crum, Jessie K. The Art of Inner Listening: Pathway to Creativity. LC 74-21643. 1989. pap. 4.95 (*0-8356-0303-2*, Quest) Theos Pub Hse.

Crum, Jimmy & Gerber, Carole. How about That! 181p. 1993. pap. 12.00 (*0-9638284-0-1*) Gerber Crum.

Crum, John W. AP Exam in American History. 2nd ed. (AP Exam Guides Ser.). 320p. (YA). (gr. 9-12). 1990. pap. 10.95 (*0-685-31171-6*, Arco) Macmillan Gen Ref.

— AP United States History: Advanced Placement Examination. 6th ed. LC 97-81134. (Illus.). 352p. 1998. pap. text 14.95 (*0-02-862474-2*, Arc) IDG Bks.

Crum, Katherine B., jt. auth. see Castle, Frederick.

Crum, Kimball R. Brian's Lunch, Vol. 1. (Illus.). 24p. (Orig.). (J). (gr. 1-4). 1997. pap. 3.00 (*0-9645022-1-6*) Read Me Publ.

— My Sister Is Missing!! (Illus.). 24p. (Orig.). (J). (gr. k-2). 1995. pap. 3.00 (*0-9645022-0-8*) Read Me Publ.

Crum, Laura. Cutter. LC 94-1118. 1995. mass mkt. 4.99 (*0-312-95674-6*) St Martin.

— Roped. LC 98-21149. 256p. 1998. 22.95 (*0-312-19325-4*, Thomas Dunne) St Martin.

Crum, Lawrence A. Sonochemistry & Sonoluminescence. LC 98-51579. (NATO ASI Series, Series C, Mathematical & Physical Sciences). 16p. 1999. write for info. (*0-7923-5549-0*) Kluwer Academic.

Crum, Margaret, ed. First-Line Index of English Poetry, 1500-1800, in Manuscripts of the Bodleian Library, Oxford, 2 vols., Set. xi, 1257p. 1969. lib. bdg. 125.00 (*0-87352-018-1*, Z0060) Modern Lang.

***Crum, Mason.** The Story of Lake Junaluska. (Illus.). 168p. 1999. pap. text 10.00 (*0-9667928-2-3*) Intentional Growth Ctr.

***Crum, Paul.** Future Is Now: Breaking the Status Quo: God's Strategy for His Church of the 21st Century. 88p. 1999. pap. 8.00 (*1-929595-00-X*) Hrvst Pubns.

— Pressing on with Joy: Fulfilling Your Destiny Through Transformation. 173p. 1999. pap. 10.00 (*1-929595-03-4*) Hrvst Pubns.

— Spiritual Principles of Money: Practicing the Promises & Provisions. 63p. 1999. pap. 5.00 (*1-929595-0[illegible]-8*) Hrvst Pubns.

— Turning Regrets into Remembrances. 61p. 1999. pap. 5.00 (*1-929595-02-6*) Hrvst Pubns.

Crum, Ralph B. Scientific Thought in Poetry. LC 31-29142. reprint ed. 20.00 (*0-404-01868-8*) AMS Pr.

Crum, Richard, ed. see Spearman, C. H., Jr.

Crum, Robert. Eagle Drum: On the Powwow Trail with a Young Grass Dancer. LC 94-6034. (Illus.). 48p. (J). (gr. 1-6). 1994. mass mkt. 16.95 (*0-02-725515-8*) S&S Bks Yung.

— Let's Rodeo! Young Buckaroos & the World's Wildest Sport. LC 95-43540. (Illus.). 48p. (J). (gr. 2-9). 1996. mass mkt. 17.00 (*0-689-80075-4*) S&S Bks Yung.

Crum, Roy L. & Goldberg, Itzhak. Restructuring & Managing the Enterprise in Transition. LC 96-22711. (EDI Learning Resources Ser.). 424p. 1998. pap. 35.00 (*0-8213-3658-4*, 13658) World Bank.

Crum, Roy L., et al. Managing the Enterprise in Transition While Coping with Inflation. LC 93-40299. (EDI Seminar Ser.: No. 47). 44p. 1994. pap. 22.00 (*0-8213-2725-9*, 12725) World Bank.

Crum, Roy L., jt. auth. see Derkinderen, Frans G.

Crum, Sally. People of the Red Earth: Americans Indians of Colorado. LC 95-32115. (Illus.). 272p. 1986. 33.95 (*0-941270-88-2*) Ancient City Pr.

— People of the Red Earth: Americans Indians of Colorado. LC 95-32115. (Illus.). 272p. 1996. pap. 17.95 (*0-941270-89-0*) Ancient City Pr.

— Race to the Moonrise: An Ancient Journey. LC 98-60899. (Illus.). 99p. (J). 1998. pap. 12.95 (*1-890437-21-2*) Western Reflections.

Crum, Steven J. The Road on Which We Came - Po'i Pentun Tammen Kimmappeh: A History of the Western Shoshone. LC 93-39441. (Illus.). 248p. 1994. 29.95 (*0-87480-434-5*) U of Utah Pr.

— The Road on Which We Came - Po'i Pentun Tammen Kimmappeh: A History of the Western Shoshone. 248p. (C). 1996. reprint ed. pap. 19.95 (*0-87480-509-0*) U of Utah Pr.

Crum, Thomas. Magic of Conflict Video Seminar. Warner, Judith, ed. pap. 124.95 incl. audio, VHS (*1-877803-07-3*) Aiki Works.

Crum, Thomas & Warner, Judith. Your Conflict Cookbook: A Teacher's Handbook for Helping Students Deal with Anger & Violence. 80p. 1994. pap. text 15.00 (*1-877803-08-1*) Aiki Works.

Crum, Thomas, et al. The New Conflict Cookbook: A Parent/Teacher Guide for Helping Young People Deal with Anger & Conflict. Date not set. 15.00 (*1-877803-11-1*) Aiki Works.

Crum, Thomas F. Journey to Center: Lessons in Unifying Body, Mind & Spirit. LC 97-25840. 224p. 1997. pap. 12.00 (*0-684-83922-9*, Fireside) S&S Trade Pap.

— The Magic of Conflict: Personal Guidance System, Set. 1989. pap. text, student ed. 74.95 incl. audio (*1-877803-03-0*) Aiki Works.

— The Magic of Conflict: Turning a Life of Work into a Work of Art. (Illus.). 256p. 1988. pap. 14.00 (*0-671-66836-6*, Touchstone) S&S Trade Pap.

— The Magic of Conflict Workbook: Your Personal Guidance System. rev. ed. Warner, Judith, ed. (Illus.). 92p. 1997. pap. text 10.00 (*1-877803-02-2*) Aiki Works.

***Crum, Tom.** Know the Age of Your Deer. (Illus.). 48p. 2000. spiral bd. 12.95 (*1-890676-52-7*, Pub. by Beavers Pond) Bookman Bks.

Crum, Walter E. & Steindorff, Georg. Koptische Rechtsurkunden des Achten Jahrhunderts Aus Djeme (Theben) Herausgegeben und Ubersetzt. (GER.). iv, 470p. 1972. reprint ed. write for info. (*3-487-04115-4*) G Olms Pubs.

Crum, William L. Fiscal-Year Reporting for Corporate Income Tax. (Technical Papers: No. 11). 72p. 1956. reprint ed. 20.00 (*0-87014-417-0*) Natl Bur Econ Res.

Crum, William L., et al. Fiscal Planning for Total War. (Fiscal Studies Ser.: No. 1). 385p. 1942. reprint ed. 110.10 (*0-87014-117-1*) Natl Bur Econ Res.

Crumb, Dana. Still Eatin' It: A Dana Crumb Cookbook. Williams, Roger, ed. LC 96-32862. (Illus.). 120p. (YA). 1996. pap. 18.00 (*0-943389-18-6*) Snow Lion-SLG Bks.

Crumb, Dana & Cohen, Sherry. Eat It: A Cookbook. (Illus.). 1976. pap. 5.95 (*0-88388-019-9*) Bellerophon Bks.

Crumb, Dewitt & Goerlich, Shirley B., compiled by. Historical Addresses, Reminiscences & Roster of Survivors of the Civil War: 22nd NYV Cav., 2d Brig., 3rd Div., Cavalry Corps. (Illus.). 69p. 1996. reprint ed. pap. 12.00 (*1-887530-09-6*) RSG Pub.

Crumb, Herb S., ed. see Osborn, Thomas W.

Crumb, Lawrence N. Historic Preservation in the Pacific Northwest: A Bibliography of Sources, 1947-1978. (CPL Bibliographies Ser.: No. 11). 63p. 1979. pap. 7.00 (*0-86602-011-X*, Sage Prdcls Pr) Sage.

— The Oxford Movement & Its Leaders: A Bibliography of Secondary & Lesser Primary Sources. LC 88-10217. (American Theological Library Association Monograph: No. 24). 736p. 1988. 70.00 (*0-8108-2141-9*) Scarecrow.

— The Oxford Movement & Its Leaders: A Bibliography of Secondary & Lesser Primary Sources. LC 93-16025. (American Theological Library Association Monograph: No. 24). 320p. 1993. suppl. ed. 47.50 (*0-8108-2700-X*) Scarecrow.

Crumb, R. Big Yum Yum Book: The Story of Oggie & the Beanstalk. 2nd ed. LC 95-24604. (Illus.). 144p. 1995. reprint ed. pap. 20.00 (*0-943389-19-4*) Snow Lion-SLG Bks.

— Book of Mr. Natural. 1995. pap. text 12.95 (*1-56097-194-0*, Pub. by Fantagraph Bks) Seven Hills Bk.

— Carload O' Comics. (Illus.). 176p. 1996. reprint ed. 39.95 (*0-87816-439-1*) Kitchen Sink.

— Carload O'Comics. (Illus.). 176p. 1998. reprint ed. pap. 18.95 (*0-87816-403-0*) Kitchen Sink.

— Complete Crumb Vol. 14: Uncle Bob's Mid Life Crisis. (Illus.). 128p. 2000. 39.95 (*1-56097-365-X*, Pub. by Fantagraph Bks); pap. 18.95 (*1-56097-364-1*, Pub. by Fantagraph Bks) Seven Hills Bk.

***Crumb, R.** Complete Crumb Comics: Season of the Snoid, No. 13. (Illus.). 128p. 1998. 39.95 (*1-56097-313-7*) Fantagraph Bks.

Crumb, R. Complete Crumb Comics: Season of The Snoid, Vol. 13. (Illus.). 1998. pap. 18.95 (*1-56097-296-3*) Fantagraph Bks.

— The Complete Crumb Comics Vol. 1: The Early Years of Bitter Struggle. Groth, Gary & Fiore, Robert, eds. (Illus.). 144p. 1987. pap. 19.95 (*0-930193-42-3*, Pub. by Fantagraph Bks) Seven Hills Bk.

— The Complete Crumb Comics Vol. 2: Some More Early Years of Bitter Struggle. Groth, Gary & Fiore, Robert, eds. (Illus.). 144p. 1988. pap. 19.95 (*0-930193-62-8*) Fantagraph Bks.

— The Complete Crumb Comics Vol. 3: Starring Fritz the Cat. Groth, Gary & Fiore, Robert, eds. (Illus.). 144p. 1989. pap. 18.95 (*0-930193-75-X*) Fantagraph Bks.

— The Complete Crumb Comics Vol. 4: "Mr. Sixties!" Groth, Gary & Fiore, Robert, eds. (Illus.). 144p. 1988. pap. 18.95 (*0-930193-79-2*) Fantagraph Bks.

— The Complete Crumb Comics Vol. 5: Happy Hippy Comix. Groth, Gary & Boyd, Robert, eds. (Illus.). 144p. 1990. 39.95 (*0-930193-91-1*); pap. 18.95 (*0-930193-92-X*) Fantagraph Bks.

— The Complete Crumb Comics Vol. 6: On the Crest of a Wave. Groth, Gary & Boyd, Robert, eds. (Illus.). 144p. 1991. 39.95 (*1-56097-057-X*) Fantagraph Bks.

— The Complete Crumb Comics Vol. 7: "Hot 'n' Heavy" Groth, Gary & Boyd, Robert, eds. (Illus.). 144p. 1991. 39.95 (*1-56097-062-6*, Pub. by Fantagraph Bks); pap. 16.95 (*1-56097-061-8*) Fantagraph Bks.

— The Complete Crumb Comics Vol. 8: The Death of Fritz the Cat. 148p. 1992. 39.95 (*1-56097-077-4*); pap. 18.95 (*1-56097-076-6*) Fantagraph Bks.

— The Complete Crumb Comics Vol. 9: "R. Crumb vs. the Sisterhood" Groth, Gary & Boyd, Robert, eds. (Illus.). 144p. 1992. 39.95 (*1-56097-108-8*) Fantagraph Bks.

— The Complete Crumb Comics Vol. 10: Crumb Advocates Violent Overthrow. Thompson, Mark & Groth, Gary, eds. (Illus.). 118p. 1994. 39.95 (*1-56097-138-X*); pap. 18.95 (*1-56097-137-1*) Fantagraph Bks.

— The Complete Crumb Comics Vol. 11: Mr. Natural Commited to a Mental Institution. Thompson, Mark & Groth, Gary, eds. (Illus.). 126p. 1995. 39.95 (*1-56097-173-8*); pap. 18.95 (*1-56097-172-X*) Fantagraph Bks.

— The Complete Crumb Comics Vol. 12: We're Livin' in the Lap O' Luxury. 126p. 1997. 39.95 (*1-56097-265-3*); pap. 18.95 (*1-56097-264-5*) Fantagraph Bks.

— Complete Dirty Laundry Comics. (Illus.). 126p. 1993. pap. 16.95 (*0-86719-379-4*) Last Gasp.

— Crumb Family Comics. (Illus.). 170p. 1998. 19.95 (*0-86719-427-8*) Last Gasp.

— Crumb-Ology: The Works of R. Crumb 1981-1994. (Illus.). 120p. (C). 1995. 39.95 (*0-934953-24-4*) Water Row Pr.

— Crumb-Ology Supplement: The Works of R. Crumb, 1994-1998. Richter, Carl, ed. (Illus.). 45p. 1998. pap., suppl. ed. 5.95 (*0-934953-60-0*) Water Row Pr.

Crumb, R. Crumb Sketchbook, Vol. 4. 39.95 (*1-56097-139-8*, Pub. by Fantagraph Bks); pap. 19.95 (*1-56097-140-1*, Pub. by Fantagraph Bks) Seven Hills Bk.

— Crumb Sketchbook, Vol. 5. 39.95 (*1-56097-164-9*, Pub. by Fantagraph Bks); pap. 19.95 (*1-56097-163-0*, Pub. by Fantagraph Bks) Seven Hills Bk.

— Crumb Sketchbook, Vol. 6. 39.95 (*1-56097-270-X*, Pub. by Fantagraph Bks); pap. 19.95 (*1-56097-269-6*, Pub. by Fantagraph Bks) Seven Hills Bk.

Crumb, R. The Life & Death of Fritz the Cat. 96p. 1993. per. 9.95 (*1-56097-117-7*) Fantagraph Bks.

— My Troubles with Women. 80p. 1991. pap. 16.95 (*0-86719-374-3*) Last Gasp.

— The R. Crumb Coffee Table Art Book. LC 97-16339. (Illus.). 256p. (gr. 8). 1997. 40.00 (*0-316-16306-6*) Little.

— The R. Crumb Coffee Table Art Book: Crumb's Whole Career, from Shack to Chateau! (Illus.). 256p. 1998. pap. 25.00 (*0-316-16333-3*) Little.

— R. Crumb Comics. limited aut. ed. (Illus.). 28p. 1998. 125.00 (*3-927258-10-5*) Gingko Press.

— R. Crumb Draws the Blues. 16.95 (*0-86166-101-X*) Last Gasp.

— R. Crumb Draws the Blues. (Illus.). 64p. 1993. pap. 16.95 (*0-86719-401-4*) Last Gasp.

— R. Crumb Sketchbook, Vol. 3. Groth, Gary, ed. (Illus.). 144p. (Orig.). 1993. 39.95 (*1-56097-128-2*); pap. 19.95 (*1-56097-127-4*) Fantagraph Bks.

— R. Crumb Sketchbook, 1964-1965, Vol. 1. 176p. 1992. 39.95 (*1-56097-083-9*); pap. 19.95 (*1-56097-082-0*) Fantagraph Bks.

— R. Crumb Sketchbook, 1965-1966, Vol. 2. 176p. 1992. 39.95 (*1-56097-105-3*); pap. 19.95 (*1-56097-104-5*) Fantagraph Bks.

— R. Crumb's America. (Illus.). 90p. 1995. pap. text 16.95 (*0-86719-433-2*) Last Gasp.

— Robert Crumb Sketchbook, Vol. 7. (Illus.). 160p. 1999. 39.95 (*1-56097-328-5*); pap. 19.95 (*1-56097-327-7*) Fantagraph Bks.

— Waiting for Food: Restaurant Placemat Drawings. (Illus.). 96p. 1996. 29.95 (*0-87816-465-0*) Kitchen Sink.

— Weirdo Art of Robert Crumb: His Early Period, 1981-1985. 1999. pap. 19.95 (*0-86719-339-5*) Last Gasp.

C

— Your Vigor for Life Appalls Me: Robert Crumb Letters 1956-1972. 1998. pap. 14.95 (*1-56097-310-2*) Fantagraph Bks.

*Crumb, R. Your Vigor for Life Appalls Me: Robert Crumb Letters, 1956-1972. 250p. 1998. 29.95 (*1-56097-343-9*) Fantagraph Bks.

Crumb, R., et al. Flock of Dreamers: An Anthology of Dream Inspired Comics. (Illus.). 96p. 1998. pap. write for info. (*0-87816-549-5*) Kitchen Sink.

***Crumb, Robert.** The Complete Crumb Comics, Vol. 15. (Illus.). 2000. 39.95 (*1-56097-414-1*, Pub. by Fantagraph Bks); pap. 18.95 (*1-56097-413-3*, Pub. by Fantagraph Bks) Seven Hills Bk.

Crumbaugh, James C. Everything to Gain: A Guide to Self-Fulfillment Through Logoanalysis. LC 72-80164. 254p. 1988. pap. 9.95 (*0-917867-07-6*) V Frankl Inst.

Crumbaugh, James C., ed. A Primer of Projective Techniques of Psychological Assessment. LC 87-92178. 1989. 20.00 (*0-87212-215-8*) Libra.

Crumbaugh, James C., et al. Logotherapy: New Help for Problem Drinkers. LC 79-18635. 176p. 1981. text 27.95 (*0-88229-421-0*) Burnham Inc.

***Crumbie, Alison, et al.** Chronic Disease Management Quality Patient Care & Professional Issues. (Illus.). 256p. 2001. pap. 40.50 (*0-7506-4808-2*, Digital DEC) Buttrwrth-Heinemann.

Crumbley & Kratchman. Deadly Art Puzzle: Accounting for Murder. 1996. pap. 22.95 (*0-87393-606-X*) Dame Pubns.

Crumbley & Reps. Simon the Incredible. LC 97-77451. 1998. pap. 22.95 (*0-87393-729-5*) Dame Pubns.

Crumbley & Smith. Computer Encryption. LC 97-77454. (SWC-General Business). 1997. pap. 22.95 (*0-87393-739-2*) Dame Pubns.

Crumbley, et al. Chemistry in Whispering Caves. 1997. pap. 22.95 (*0-87393-654-X*) Dame Pubns.

— Nonprofit Sleuths: Follow the Money. 1997. pap. 22.95 (*0-87393-628-0*) Dame Pubns.

Crumbley, D. L. & Milam, Edward E. Keys to Estate Planning & Trusts. 2nd ed. LC 93-22031. (Barron's Business Keys Ser.). 160p. 1993. pap. 4.95 (*0-8120-1710-2*) Barron.

Crumbley, D. Larry. Barron's Guide to Tax Terms. 1995. pap. 14.95 (*0-8120-9373-9*) Barron.

— The Handbook of Accounting for Natural Resources. 432p. 1986. text 85.00 (*0-07-014809-0*) McGraw.

Crumbley, D. Larry & Milam, Edward E. Estate Planning in the 80s. rev. ed. LC 82-16314. 240p. reprint ed. pap. 74.40 (*0-608-14710-9*, 202357300033) Bks Demand.

***Crumbley, D. Larry & Milan, Edward E.** Keys to Estate Planning & Trusts. 3rd ed. (Barron's Business Keys Ser.). 208p. 1999. pap. 7.95 (*0-7641-0958-8*) Barron.

Crumbley, D. Larry & Nichols, Linda M., eds. Oil, Gas & Energy Quarterly, Vol. 46, No. 1. (Illus.). 1997. ring bd. 185.00 (*0-8205-1520-5*) Bender.

Crumbley, D. Larry & Smith, L. Murphy. Keys to Personal Financial Planning. 2nd ed. (Barron's Business Keys Ser.). 160p. 1994. pap. 4.95 (*0-8120-1919-9*) Barron.

Crumbley, D. Larry, et al. Dictionary of Tax Terms. LC 93-23218. 1994. pap. 9.95 (*0-8120-1780-3*) Barron.

Crumbley, D. Larry, jt. auth. see Apostolou, Nicholas G.

Crumbley, D. Larry, jt. auth. see Dickens, Thomas L.

Crumbley, D. Larry, jt. auth. see Milam, Edward E.

Crumbley, D. Lawrence. Keys to Surviving a Tax Audit. 160p. 1991. pap. 4.95 (*0-8120-4513-0*) Barron.

Crumbley, Joseph. Transracial Adoption & Foster Care: Practice Issues for Professionals. LC 99-26148. 1999. 18.95 (*0-87868-717-3*) Child Welfare.

Crumbley, Joseph & Little, Robert L., eds. Relatives Raising Children: An Overview of Kinship Care. LC 97-25669. 144p. 1997. pap. 16.95 (*0-87868-684-3*, CWLA Pr) Child Welfare.

Crumbley, Paul. Inflections of the Pen: Dash & Voice in Emily Dickinson. (Illus.). 224p. (C). 1997. text 29.95 (*0-8131-1988-X*) U Pr of Ky.

Crumbo, Kim. A River Runner's Guide to the History of the Grand Canyon. LC 81-84310. (Illus.). 96p. (Orig.). 1981. pap. 9.95 (*0-933472-61-7*) Johnson Bks.

***Crumbo, Wendy.** Briarwood Cove: Coming Together. LC 00-190659. 2000. 25.00 (*0-7388-1914-X*); pap. 18.00 (*0-7388-1915-8*) Xlibris Corp.

***Crume, Gene, ed.** Western Wisdom: Advice for Life. 144p. 1999. pap. 6.95 (*0-913383-65-1*) McClanahan Pub.

***Crume, Jeff.** Inside Internet Security: What Hackers Don't Want You to Know. 256p. 2000. pap. text (*0-201-67516-1*) Addison-Wesley.

Crume, Marion, ed. see Crume, Paul.

Crume, Marion W. Do You See Mouse? LC 94-30494. (Illus.). (J). 1995. 13.95 (*0-382-24684-5*); pap. 5.95 (*0-382-24685-3*); lib. bdg. 18.95 (*0-382-24683-7*) Silver Burdett Pr.

Crume, Paul. The World of Paul Crume. Crume, Marion, ed. LC 80-14072. 312p. 1999. reprint ed. 15.00 (*0-87074-176-4*) SMU Press.

Crume, Vic. The Ghost That Came Alive. 128p. (J). (gr. 4-7). 1992. pap. 2.95 (*0-590-46147-8*, Apple Paperbacks) Scholastic Inc.

Crumey, Andre N., ed. see Yatromanolakis, Yoryis.

Crumey, Andrew. D'Alembert's Principle. 208p. 1999. pap. 12.00 (*0-312-20401-9*, Picador USA) St Martin.

— D'Alembert's Principle: Memory, Reason & Imagination. LC 98-8725. 208p. (Orig.). 1998. text 21.00 (*0-312-19568-0*) St Martin.

— Music, in a Foreign Language. Date not set. 22.00 (*0-614-25847-2*, Picador USA) St Martin.

— Pfitz. LC 97-15517. 176p. 1997. text 20.00 (*0-312-16964-7*) St Martin.

— Pfitz. 192p. 1998. pap. 12.00 (*0-312-19550-8*, Picador USA) St Martin.

***Crumey, S. L.** The Tao of Dishwashing: Preparing Your Soul for the New Millennium. Thornton, Katherine, ed. LC 99-96349. 208p. 1999. pap. 17.95 (*1-929526-00-8*) I Am Unlimited.

Crumeyrolle, Albert. Orthogonal & Symplectic Clifford Algebras: Spinor Structures. (C). 1990. text 248.50 (*0-7923-0541-8*) Kluwer Academic.

***Crumeyrolle, Albert.** The 10-Step Method of Stress Relief: Decoding the Meaning & Significance of Stress. LC 00-9774. 2000. write for info. (*0-8493-0063-0*) CRC Pr.

***Crumley, Jack S., II.** Problems in Mind: Readings in Contemporary Philosophy of Mind. LC 99-33203. ix, 614p. 1999. pap. text 49.95 (*0-7674-0750-4*) Mayfield Pub.

***Crumley, Jack S., II, et al.** Readings in Epistemology. LC 98-50660. 652p. 1998. pap. text 46.95 (*0-7674-0009-7*, 0009-7) Mayfield Pub.

Crumley, Carole L., ed. Historical Ecology: Cultural Knowledge & Changing Landscapes. (Illus.). 304p. (C). 1994. pap. 24.95 (*0-933452-85-3*) Schol Am Res.

Crumley, Jack S. An Introduction to Epistemology. LC 98-3556. 384p. 1998. pap. text 29.95 (*0-7674-0008-9*, 0008-9) Mayfield Pub.

Crumley, James. Bordersnakes. 288p. 1997. mass mkt. 6.50 (*0-446-60448-8*, Pub. by Warner Bks) Little.

— The Last Good Kiss. (Contemporaries Ser.). 244p. 1988. pap. 11.00 (*0-394-75989-3*) Vin Bks.

— The Mexican Pig Bandit. (Illus.). 48p. 1998. 125.00 (*1-892011-01-8*); pap. 45.00 (*1-892011-00-X*) ASAP Pub.

— The Mexican Tree Duck. 256p. 1993. 19.95 (*0-89296-391-3*) Mysterious Pr.

— The Mexican Tree Duck. 272p. 1994. mass mkt. 5.99 (*0-446-40407-1*, Pub. by Warner Bks) Little.

— The Muddy Fork & Other Things: Short Fiction & Nonfiction. LC 91-61900. 224p. (Orig.). 1991. pap. 12.95 (*0-944439-39-X*) Clark City Pr.

— One to Count Cadence. LC 86-40468. (Vintage Contemporaries Ser.). 352p. 1987. pap. 13.00 (*0-394-73559-5*) Vin Bks.

— The Wrong Case. 272p. 1985. pap. 11.00 (*0-394-73558-7*) Random.

Crumley, James, jt. auth. see Crumley, Karen.

Crumley, Jim. The Company of Swans. (Illus.). 48p. 1998. 12.00 (*1-86046-558-7*) Harvill Press.

— Discovering the Pentland Hills. (Discovering Ser.). 200p. (C). 1996. pap. 22.50 (*0-85976-331-5*, Pub. by J Donald) St Mut.

— Gulfs of Blue Air: A Highland Journey. (Illus.). 192p. 1997. 35.00 (*1-85158-889-2*, Pub. by Mainstream Pubng) Trafalgar.

— The Road & the Miles: A Homage to Dundee. (Illus.). 192p. 1996. 29.95 (*1-85158-787-X*, Pub. by Mainstream Pubng) Trafalgar.

— The Royal Mile: Scotland's Most Romantic Way. (Illus.). 96p. (C). 1989. 70.00 (*0-948473-14-2*) St Mut.

— Shetland: Land of the Ocean. (Illus.). 120p. 1996. pap. 19.95 (*0-948661-65-8*, Pub. by Colin Baxter Ltd) Voyageur Pr.

Crumley, Jim. Waters of the Wild Swan. 1992. 34.95 (*0-224-03282-8*, Pub. by Random) Trafalgar.

***Crumley, Karen & Crumley, James.** Weapon of Jihad. 312p. 2000. 24.95 (*0-9674639-0-4*) Purple Sage Pubng.

Crumley, Malinda R., ed. see Hoover, William J.

Crumley, Marguerite. Church Hill: The St. John's Church Historic District. (Illus.). 132p. 1991. 19.95 (*1-889569-01-1*) Historic Richmond.

Crumlin, Rosemary & Knight, Anthony, eds. Aboriginal Art & Spirituality. (Illus.). 152p. 1991. 29.95 (*0-85924-998-0*) Harper SF.

Crumlish, Christian. Frontpage 2000 for Busy People. (Busy People Ser.). 305p. 1999. pap. 19.99 (*0-07-211981-0*) McGraw.

— The Internet - No Experience Required. 2nd ed. LC 98-88331. (No Experience Required Ser.). (Illus.). 496p. 1998. pap. text 19.99 (*0-7821-2385-6*) Sybex.

— Internet for Busy People. 2nd ed. 1997. pap. 24.99 (*0-07-882325-0*) McGraw.

— Internet for Busy People. 3rd ed. (Illus.). 352p. 1998. pap. text 24.99 (*0-07-882526-1*) Osborne-McGraw.

— Internet for Busy People. 4th ed. 264p. 1999. pap. 19.99 (*0-07-212116-5*) McGraw.

— Internet for Busy People, No. 4. (Busy People Bks.). (Illus.). 304p. 1995. pap. text 22.95 (*0-07-882108-8*) Osborne-McGraw.

— Word for Windows 95 for Busy People, No. 2. (Busy People Bks.). (Illus.). 304p. 1995. pap. text 22.95 (*0-07-882109-6*) McGraw.

— Word 97 for Busy People. LC 97-163007. 1997. pap. text 24.99 (*0-07-882282-3*) Osborne-McGraw.

***Crumlish, Christian.** Word 2000 for Busy People. 303p. 1999. pap. 19.99 (*0-07-211982-9*) McGraw.

Crumlish, Christian. WordPerfect X for Windows 95 Quick & Easy. 2nd ed. 224p. 1996. pap. 22.99 (*0-7821-1777-5*) Sybex.

Crumlish, Christian & Hadfield, Jeff. Netscape Communicator for Busy People. 320p. 1997. pap. text 24.99 (*0-07-882441-9*) McGraw.

Crumlish, Christian & Humes, Malcolm. Web Publishing with Netscape for Busy People, No. 6. (Busy People Bks.). 304p. 1996. pap. text 22.95 (*0-07-882144-4*) Osborne-McGraw.

Crumlish, Christian, jt. auth. see Asher, Levi.

Crummel, Alex. Africa & America. LC 72-79009. (Black Heritage Library Collection). 1977. 36.95 (*0-8369-8550-8*) Ayer.

***Crummel, Susan S.** Tumbleweed Stew. LC 99-50803. (Illus.). 24p. (ps-3). 2000. 10.95 (*0-15-202673-8*, Harcourt Child Bks); pap. 3.95 (*0-15-202628-2*, Harcourt Child Bks) Harcourt.

Crummel, Susan S., jt. auth. see Stevens, Janet.

Crummel, Susan Stevens, jt. auth. see Stevens, Janet.

Crummell, Alex. Africa & America: Addresses & Discourses. 468p. 1998. reprint ed. pap. 45.00 (*1-58073-000-0*) BCP Bks.

— Africa & America: Addresses & Discourses. 468p. 1998. reprint ed. pap. 45.00 (*0-933121-74-1*) Black Classic.

Crummell, Alexander. Africa & America: Addresses & Discourses. 1977. reprint ed. 18.00 (*0-403-07784-2*) Scholarly.

— Destiny & Race: Selected Writings, 1840-1898. Moses, Wilson J., ed. LC 91-44849. 320p. (C). 1992. lib. bdg. 35.00 (*0-87023-788-8*) U of Mass Pr.

— Future of Africa. LC 79-92424. 1862. 19.00 (*0-403-00156-0*) Scholarly.

Crummer, Roy E., jt. auth. see Plane, Donald R.

Crummett & Western. University Physics. 1994. teacher ed. 18.75 (*0-697-11201-2*) McGraw.

— University Physics. 1994. pap. text, teacher ed. 14.06 (*0-697-16425-X*) McGraw.

Crummett, William P. & Western, Arthur B. University Physics: Models & Applications. (Illus.). 1248p. (C). 1994. text. write for info. (*0-697-11199-7*, WCB McGr Hill) McGrw-H Hghr Educ.

— University Physics: Models & Applications. (Illus.). 1248p. (C). 1994. text, student ed. 30.00 (*0-697-11204-7*, WCB McGr Hill) McGrw-H Hghr Educ.

— University Physics: Models & Applications. 100p. 1994. student ed. write for info. (*0-697-27240-0*, WCB McGr Hill) McGrw-H Hghr Educ.

— University Physics: Models & Applications. (Illus.). 1248p. (C). 1995. text, student ed. 23.12 (*0-697-16426-8*, WCB McGr Hill) McGrw-H Hghr Educ.

Crummey, Donald. Land & Society in the Christian Kingdom of Ethiopia: From the Thirteenth to the Twentieth Century. LC 99-6218. 416p. 1999. 60.00 (*0-252-02482-6*) U of Ill Pr.

Crummey, Donald, ed. Banditry, Rebellion & Social Protest in Africa. LC 85-27352. 404p. (Orig.). (C). 1986. pap. text 27.50 (*0-435-08011-3*, 08011) Heinemann.

Crummey, Donald & Stewart, C. C., eds. Modes of Production in Africa: The Precolonial Era. LC 81-1433. (Sage Series on African Modernization & Development: No. 5). 256p. reprint ed. pap. 79.40 (*0-8357-8452-5*, 203471600091) Bks Demand.

Crummey, Donald E., jt. ed. see Bassett, Thomas J.

Crummey, Michael. Arguments with Gravity. 112p. 1996. pap. 14.95 (*1-55082-171-7*, Pub. by Quarry Pr) LPC InBook.

Crummey, Robert O. The Old Believers & the World of Antichrist: The Vyg Community & the Russian State, 1694-1855. LC 79-98121. (Illus.). 286p. reprint ed. pap. 88.70 (*0-8357-4743-3*, 203766400009) Bks Demand.

Crummey, Robert O., ed. Reform in Russia & the U. S. S. R. Past & Prospects. LC 88-39451. 328p. 1990. pap. text 16.95 (*0-252-06176-4*) U of Ill Pr.

Crummey, Robert O., jt. ed. see Berry, Lloyd E.

Crummy, Helen, ed. Let the People Sing! A Story of Craigmillar. 240p. (C). 1992. pap. 40.00 (*0-9518593-0-7*, Pub. by Argyll Pubng) St Mut.

Crump. Cases & Materials on Civil Procedure. 3rd ed. (Analysis & Skills Ser.). 1996. text 50.36 (*0-256-22157-X*) McGraw.

— Durango to Silverton: By Narrow Gauge Rails. LC 95-60598. 112p. 1996. pap. 5.95 (*0-918376-10-6*) Zeta Pubs Co.

— Evaluation of Clinical Evidence. 1993. text. write for info. (*0-582-21798-9*, Pub. by Addison-Wesley) Longman.

Crump, et al. Cases & Materials on Constitutional Law. 1989. write for info. (*0-8205-0261-8*, 479); teacher ed. write for info. (*0-8205-0262-6*) Bender.

— Cases & Materials on Constitutional Law. 1990. suppl. ed. write for info. (*0-8205-0264-2*) Bender.

— Cases & Materials on Constitutional Law. 1991. suppl. ed. write for info. (*0-8205-0265-0*) Bender.

Crump, jt. auth. see Dorsaneo.

***Crump, Andre, photos by.** Green Eyes: The Greenest Fields. (Illus.). 80p. 2000. pap. 24.95 (*0-9674898-0-6*) TCB Cafe.

Crump, Andy. Dictionary of Environment & Development: People, Places, Ideas, & Organizations. LC 92-36484. (Illus.). 272p. (C). 1993. 45.00 (*0-262-03207-4*); pap. text 22.50 (*0-262-53117-8*) MIT Pr.

***Crump, Andy & Ellwood, Wayne.** The A to Z of World Development. (Illus.). 304p. 1999. pap. 34.95 (*1-869847-46-6*, Pub. by New Intl Pubns) Stylus Pub VA.

Crump, Arthur. The Theory of Stock Speculation. LC 83-80982. 1983. reprint ed. pap. 12.00 (*0-87034-068-9*) Fraser Pub Co.

Crump, Beverly J. The Mother's Handbook Bk. 1: An Easy-to-Read Guide for Mothers. (Illus.). 192p. (Orig.). 1991. pap. 13.95 (*1-879520-09-5*) Cntry Ln Bks.

Crump, C. G. & Jacob, Ernest F., eds. Legacy of the Middle Ages. (Legacy Ser.). (Illus.). 1938. 48.00 (*0-19-821907-5*) OUP.

Crump, Charles G., ed. see Landor, Walter Savage.

Crump, Claudia, jt. auth. see Hoge, John D.

Crump, D. W. Contracts of Employment. 7th ed. 1994. pap. 165.00 (*0-406-01146-X*, MICHIE) LEXIS Pub.

Crump, David. Cases & Materials on Civil Procedure. 3rd ed. LC 98-11221. (Analysis & Skills Ser.). 1998. 43.00 (*0-8205-3099-9*) Bender.

— Cases & Materials on Civil Procedure: 1994 Supplement. 2nd ed. 512p. (C). 1994. per. 7.95 (*0-256-21262-7*, Irwn McGrw-H) McGrw-H Hghr Educ.

— Conflict of Interest: A Novel about Trial Lawyers, Greed, Passion, Power, Revenge...& Justice. LC 97-13272. 288p. (Orig.). 1997. pap. 14.95 (*0-89407-122-X*, 122X) Strawberry Hill.

***Crump, David.** The Holding Company: A Novel about Courtrooms, Lawyers, Money, Murder... And Justice. LC 99-55254. 282p. 2000. pap. 15.95 (*0-89407-131-9*) Strawberry Hill.

— Jesus: The Intercessor; Prayer & Christology in Luke-Acts. LC 99-30089. (Biblical Studies Libary). 295p. 1999. pap. 26.99 (*0-8010-2221-5*) Baker Bks.

Crump, David. Jesus the Intercessor. xiv, 295p. 1992. pap. 95.00 (*3-16-145821-4*, Pub. by JCB Mohr) Coronet Bks.

Crump, David & Berman, Jeffrey B. The Story of a Civil Suit: Dominguez vs. Scott's Food Stores. 2nd ed. 129p. 1985. pap. text 18.00 (*0-916081-03-6*) J Marshall Pub Co.

Crump, David & Curtis, J. Jerome, Jr. The Anatomy of a Real Property Transaction. 104p. (Orig.). 1984. pap. text 18.00 (*0-916081-02-8*) J Marshall Pub Co.

***Crump, David & Jacobs, George.** A Capital Case in America: How Today's Justice System Handles Death Penalty Cases, from Crime Scene to Ultimate Execution of Sentence. LC 99-69661. 288p. 2000. pap. 25.00 (*0-89089-729-8*) Carolina Acad Pr.

Crump, David & Mertens, William J. The Story of a Criminal Case: The State vs. Albert Delman Greene. 154p. (Orig.). 1984. pap. text 15.00 (*0-916081-00-1*) J Marshall Pub Co.

Crump, David, et al. Cases & Materials on Constitutional Law. 3rd ed. LC 98-10237. (Casebook Ser.). 1998. 59.00 (*0-8205-3113-8*) Bender.

Crump, Derrick. The Complete Guide to Wood Finishes. LC 92-20299. (Illus.). 176p. 1993. pap. 18.00 (*0-671-79669-0*, Fireside) S&S Trade Pap.

Crump, Donald J., ed. Adventures in Your National Parks. LC 88-31473. (Books for World Explorers Series 10: No. 2). (J). (gr. 3-8). 1989. 8.95 (*0-87044-702-5*) Natl Geog.

— Alaska's Magnificent Parklands. (Special Publications Series 18). 200p. 1984. 12.95 (*0-87044-442-5*); lib. bdg. 12.95 (*0-87044-447-6*) Natl Geog.

— Amazing Things Animals Do. (Books for World Explorers Series 10: No. 4). (J). (gr. 3-8). 1989. 8.95 (*0-87044-709-2*); lib. bdg. 12.50 (*0-87044-704-1*) Natl Geog.

— America's Hidden Wilderness: Lands of Seclusion. LC 88-9977. (Special Publications Series 23: No. 1). (Illus.). 200p. 1988. 12.95 (*0-87044-666-5*); lib. bdg. 16.00 (*0-87044-671-1*) Natl Geog.

— America's Majestic Canyons. LC 78-61263. (Special Publications Series 14: No. 1). (Illus.). 1979. 12.95 (*0-87044-271-6*) Natl Geog.

— America's Outdoor Wonders: State Parks & Sanctuaries. LC 87-11001. (Special Publications Series 22: No. 1). (Illus.). 200p. 1987. 12.95 (*0-87044-624-X*) Natl Geog.

— America's Seashore Wonderlands. LC 85-25848. (Special Publications Series 20: No. 2). (Illus.). 1985. 12.95 (*0-87044-543-X*) Natl Geog.

— America's Wild & Scenic Rivers. LC 83-47843. (Special Publications Series 18: No. 2). 200p. 1983. 12.95 (*0-87044-440-9*) Natl Geog.

— Animal Architects. LC 87-12198. (Books for World Explorers Series 8: No. 4). (Illus.). 104p. (J). (gr. 3-8). 1987. lib. bdg. 12.50 (*0-87044-617-7*) Natl Geog.

— Animals at Play, Set. (Books for Young Explorers: Set 15, No. 2). (Illus.). (J). (gr. k-4). 1988. lib. bdg. 16.95 (*0-87044-744-0*) Natl Geog.

— As We Live & Breathe: The Challenge of Our Environment. LC 74-151945. (Special Publications Series 6: No. 2). (Illus.). 1971. 12.95 (*0-87044-097-7*) Natl Geog.

— Blue Horizons: Paradise Isles of the Pacific. (Special Publications Series 20: No. 3). (Illus.). 1985. 12.95 (*0-87044-544-8*) Natl Geog.

— Books for Young Explorers, 4 vols., Set. (J). 1986. 13.95 (*0-87044-638-X*); lib. bdg. 16.95 (*0-87044-643-6*) Natl Geog.

— Books for Young Explorers: Along a Rocky Shore; Animal Families; Lions & Tigers & Leopards: The Big Cats; Our Amazing Animal Friends, 4 bks., Set 17. (J). (gr. k-4). 1994. 8.00 (*0-87044-821-8*) Natl Geog.

— Builders of the Ancient World: Marvels of Engineering. LC 86-5278. (Special Publications Series 21: No. 1). (Illus.). (YA). (gr. 8 up). 1986. 12.95 (*0-87044-585-5*) Natl Geog.

— Canada's Wilderness Lands. LC 81-48074. (Special Publications Series 17: No. 2). 200p. 1982. 12.95 (*0-87044-413-1*); lib. bdg. 12.95 (*0-87044-418-2*) Natl Geog.

— Computers: Those Amazing Machines. (Books for World Explorers Series 7: No. 2). (Illus.). 104p. 1986. 8.95 (*0-87044-574-X*); lib. bdg. 12.50 (*0-87044-579-0*) Natl Geog.

— Dolphins: Our Friends in the Sea. LC 86-18126. (Books for World Explorers Series 8: No. 1). (Illus.). 104p. (J). (gr. 4-5). 1986. 8.95 (*0-87044-609-6*) Natl Geog.

— Excursion to Enchantment. (Special Publications Series 23: No. 2). (Illus.). (YA). 1988. lib. bdg. 12.95 (*0-87044-672-X*) Natl Geog.

— Exploring America's Backcountry. LC 78-61265. (Special Publications Series 14: No. 3). (Illus.). 1979. 12.95 (*0-87044-273-2*); lib. bdg. 12.95 (*0-87044-278-3*) Natl Geog.

— The Far-Out Fact Book. LC 79-1793. (Books for World Explorers Series 1: No. 4). (Illus.). 104p. (J). (gr. 3-8). 1980. 8.95 (*0-87044-319-4*); lib. bdg. 12.50 (*0-87044-324-0*) Natl Geog.

— Fun with Physics. LC 86-8501. (Books for World Explorers Series 7: No. 4). (Illus.). 104p. (J). (gr. 5 up). 1986. 8.95 (*0-87044-576-6*); lib. bdg. 12.50 (*0-87044-581-2*) Natl Geog.

— Geo-Whiz! (Books for World Explorers Series 9: No. 2). 104p. (J). (gr. 3-8). 1988. 8.95 (*0-87044-657-6*); lib. bdg. 12.50 (*0-87044-662-2*) Natl Geog.

An Asterisk (*) at the beginning of an entry indicates that the title is appearing for the first time.

— Giants from the Past. LC 81-47893. (Books for World Explorers Series 4: No. 2). 104p. (J). (gr. 3-8). 1983. lib. bdg. 12.50 (*0-87044-429-8*) Natl Geog.

— Great American Journeys. LC 88-37216. (Special Publications Series 23: No. 4). (Illus.). (YA). 1989. 12.95 (*0-87044-669-X*); lib. bdg. 16.00 (*0-87044-674-6*) Natl Geog.

— Hidden Treasures of the Sea. (Books for World Explorers Series 9: Set 3). 104p. (J). (gr. 3-8). 1988. lib. bdg. 12.50 (*0-87044-663-0*) Natl Geog.

— Hidden Worlds. LC 79-3244. (Books for World Explorers Series 2: No. 4). (Illus.). 104p. (J). (gr. 3-8). 1981. 8.95 (*0-87044-336-4*); lib. bdg. 12.50 (*0-87044-341-0*) Natl Geog.

— How Animals Behave. LC 84-989. (Books for World Explorers Series 5: No. 4). (Illus.). 104p. (J). (gr. 3-8). 1984. 8.95 (*0-87044-500-6*); lib. bdg. 12.50 (*0-87044-505-7*) Natl Geog.

— How Things Are Made. LC 79-3242. (Books for World Explorers Series 2: No. 2). (Illus.). 104p. (J). (gr. 3-8). 1981. 8.95 (*0-87044-334-8*); lib. bdg. 12.50 (*0-87044-339-9*) Natl Geog.

— How Things Work. LC 81-47894. (Books for World Explorers Series 4: No. 3). (Illus.). 104p. (J). (gr. 7 up). 1983. lib. bdg. 12.50 (*0-87044-430-1*) Natl Geog.

— National Geographic Action Books, Set. Incl. Amazing Monkeys. Rinard, Judith E. 1985. Hide & Seek. Eugene, Toni. 1985. (Illus.). 1985. 21.95 (*0-87044-597-9*) Natl Geog.

— Nature's World of Wonders. LC 82-47842. (Special Publications Series 18: No. 1). 200p. 1983. 12.95 (*0-87044-439-5*) Natl Geog.

— New England: Land of Scenic Splendor. (Special Publications Series 24: No. 2). (Illus.). (YA). 1989. lib. bdg. 12.95 (*0-87044-720-3*) Natl Geog.

— On the Brink of Tomorrow: Frontiers of Science. LC 81-48075. (Special Publications Series 17: No. 3). 200p. (YA). (gr. 7 up). 1982. 12.95 (*0-87044-414-X*) Natl Geog.

— Pathways to Discovery: Exploring America's National Trails. LC 90-20750. (Special Publications Series 25: No. 4). (Illus.). (YA). 1990. 12.95 (*0-87044-792-0*) Natl Geog.

— Preserving America's Past. LC 81-48076. (Special Publications Series 17: No. 4). 200p. 1983. 12.95 (*0-87044-415-8*); lib. bdg. 12.95 (*0-87044-420-4*) Natl Geog.

— Secret Corners of the World. LC 81-48073. (Special Publications Series 17: No. 1). 200p. 1982. 12.95 (*0-87044-412-3*) Natl Geog.

— Secret World of Animals. (Books for World Explorers Series 7: No. 3). (Illus.). 104p. 1986. lib. bdg. 12.50 (*0-87044-580-4*) Natl Geog.

— Secrets of Animal Survival. LC 81-47895. (Books for World Explorers Series 4: No. 4). (Illus.). 104p. (J). (gr. 3 up). 1983. lib. bdg. 12.50 (*0-87044-431-X*) Natl Geog.

— Small Inventions That Make a Big Difference. LC 83-23770. (Books for World Explorers Series 5: No. 2). 104p. (J). (gr. 3-8). 1984. 8.95 (*0-87044-498-0*); lib. bdg. 12.50 (*0-87044-503-0*) Natl Geog.

— Surprising Lands Down Under. LC 89-14499. (Special Publications Series 24: No. 3). (Illus.). (YA). 1989. 12.95 (*0-87044-714-9*); lib. bdg. 12.95 (*0-87044-719-X*) Natl Geog.

— Why in the World. LC 85-18862. (Books for World Explorers Series 7: No. 1). (Illus.). 104p. 1985. lib. bdg. 12.50 (*0-87044-578-2*) Natl Geog.

— Wildlife: Making a Comeback. (Books for World Explorers Series 9: No. 1). 104p. (J). (gr. 3-8). 1987. 8.95 (*0-87044-656-8*); lib. bdg. 12.50 (*0-87044-661-4*) Natl Geog.

— The World's Wild Shores. LC 89-13952. (Special Publications Series 24: No. 4). (Illus.). (YA). 1990. 12.95 (*0-87044-716-5*); lib. bdg. 12.95 (*0-87044-721-1*) Natl Geog.

— Yosemite: An American Treasure. LC 90-5655. (Special Publications Series 25: No. 1). (Illus.). (YA). 1990. 12.95 (*0-87044-789-0*) Natl Geog.

Crump, Donald J., ed. see Amos, William H.

Crump, Donald J., ed. see Barry, S. L., et al.

Crump, Donald J., ed. see Fishbein, Seymour L.

Crump, Donald J., ed. see Fisher, Ron.

Crump, Donald J., ed. see Friedman, Herbert.

Crump, Donald J., ed. see Gibson, Barbara & Pinkney, Jerry.

Crump, Donald J., ed. see Gray, William R.

Crump, Donald J., ed. see Grove, Noel.

Crump, Donald J., ed. see Howarth, William L.

Crump, Donald J., ed. see Howarth, W., et al.

Crump, Donald J., ed. see Martin, Paul D.

Crump, Donald J., ed. see McGrath, Susan.

Crump, Donald J., ed. see McKelway, Margaret.

Crump, Donald J., ed. see National Geographic Society Staff.

Crump, Donald J., ed. see O'Neill, Catherine.

Crump, Donald J., ed. see O'Neill, Thomas.

Crump, Donald J., ed. see Rinard, Judy.

Crump, Donald J., ed. see Stuart, Gene S.

Crump, Donald J., ed. see Venino, S., et al.

Crump, Donald J., tr. see Pfister, Marcus.

Crump, Eric & Carbone, Nick. English Online: A Student's Guide to the Internet & World Wide Web. LC 96-76886. 200p. (C). 1996. pap. text 10.76 (*0-395-76749-0*) HM.

Crump, Freida M. The Coonridge Digest. Crowe, Robert L., ed. LC 94-74835. 96p. (Orig.). 1994. pap. 9.95 (*0-9644681-0-7*) Consortium IL.

Crump, Gail B. The Novels of Wright Morris: A Critical Interpretation. LC 77-15796. 266p. 1978. reprint ed. pap. 82.50 (*0-608-01851-1*, 206250100003) Bks Demand.

Crump, Galbraith M. The Mystical Design of "Paradise Lost" 194p. 1975. 29.50 (*0-8387-1519-2*) Bucknell U Pr.

Crump, Galbraith M., ed. Approaches to Teaching Milton's Paradise Lost. LC 85-21390. (Approaches to Teaching World Literature Ser.: No. 10). x, 201p. 1986. pap. 18.00 (*0-87352-494-2*, AP10P); lib. bdg. 37.50 (*0-87352-493-4*, AP10C) Modern Lang.

— Poems on Affairs of State Vol. 4: Augustan Satirical Verse, 1660-1714. LC 63-7938. (Illus.). 1968. 67.50 (*0-300-00389-7*) Yale U Pr.

Crump, I., ed. see Commonwealth Scientific & Industrial Research Orga.

***Crump, J. I.** Legends of the Warring States: Persuasions, Romances, & Stories from "Chan-kuo Ts'e" LC 98-36393. (Michigan Monographs in Chinese Studies: Vol. 83). (Illus.). xiv, 189p. 1999. text 45.00 (*0-89264-127-4*) Ctr Chinese Studies.

Crump, J. I. Legends of the Warring States: Persuasions, Romances & Stories from "Chan-Kuo Ts'e" LC 98-36393. (Michigan Monographs in Chinese Studies: Vol. 83). (Illus.). xiv, 189p. 1999. pap. 20.00 (*0-89264-129-0*) Ctr Chinese Studies.

Crump, J. I., tr. Chan-kuo Tse. rev. ed. LC 96-16933. (Michigan Monographs in Chinese Studies: Vol. 77). 1996. 75.00 (*0-89264-122-3*) Ctr Chinese Studies.

Crump, James. F. Holland Day: Suffering the Ideal. 144p. 1995. 75.00 (*0-944092-33-0*) Twin Palms Pub.

Crump, James I. Chinese Theater in the Days of Kublai Khan. LC 79-20046. (Illus.). 439p. reprint ed. pap. 136.10 (*0-7837-1905-1*, 204210900001) Bks Demand.

— Chinese Theater in the Days of Kublai Khan. 2nd ed. LC 90-20588. (Michigan Monographs in Chinese Studies: No. 62). 224p. (C). 1991. reprint ed. pap. text 25.00 (*0-89264-093-6*) Ctr Chinese Studies.

— Intrigues: Studies of the Chan-kuo Tse. LC 64-17440. 224p. reprint ed. pap. 69.50 (*0-608-30674-6*, 205082800060) Bks Demand.

— Song-Poems from Xanadu. LC 92-39788. (Michigan Monographs in Chinese Studies: No. 64). 1993. pap. text 15.00 (*0-89264-095-2*) Ctr Chinese Studies.

— Songs from Xanadu: Studies in Mongol Dynasty Song - Poetry. LC 83-7809. (Michigan Monographs in Chinese Studies: No. 47). (Illus.). xi, 232p. (C). 1983. pap. text 15.00 (*0-89264-047-2*) Ctr Chinese Studies.

Crump, James I., Jr., ed. Selections from Shui-hu Chuan. 1947. audio 7.95 (*0-88710-086-4*) Yale Far Eastern Pubns.

Crump, James I., Jr., jt. tr. see DeWoskin, Kenneth J.

Crump, John. Hatta Shuzo & Pure Anarchism in Interwar Japan. LC 93-26328. 1993. text 65.00 (*0-312-10631-9*) St Martin.

Crump, Karen C., jt. auth. see Roever, Dave.

Crump, M. Marjorie. The Epyllion from Theocritus to Ovid. viii, 284p. 3.5 hd. write for info. (*0-318-70733-0*) G Olms Pubs.

***Crump, Martha L.** In Search of the Golden Frog. LC 99-48238. (Illus.). 312p. 2000. 27.00 (*0-226-12198-4*) U Ch Pr.

Crump, Nancy C. Hearthside Cooking: An Introduction to Virginia Plantation Cuisine Including Bills of Fare, Tools & Techniques, & Original Recipes with Adaptions for Modern Fireplaces & Kitchens. LC 86-19808. (Illus.). 352p. 1986. spiral bd. 19.95 (*0-914440-94-2*, EPM) Howell Pr VA.

Crump, Owen. Southern Exposure: Manuscript Edition. 1957. pap. 13.00 (*0-8222-1310-9*) Dramatists Play.

Crump, R. W. Charlotte & Emily Bronte, 1846-1915: A Reference Guide. xvii, 194p. (C). 1982. 50.00 (*0-8161-7953-0*, Hall Reference) Macmillan.

— Charlotte & Emily Bronte, 1955-1983: A Reference Guide. (Reference Guides to Literature Ser.). 350p. 1986. 45.00 (*0-8161-8797-5*, Hall Reference) Macmillan.

Crump, R. W., ed. Order in Variety: Essays & Poems in Honor of Donald E. Stanford. LC 90-50934. 224p. 1991. 38.50 (*0-87413-420-X*) U Delaware Pr.

Crump, R. W., ed. see Rossetti, Christina Georgina.

Crump, Ray. Beneath the Grandstands. (Illus.). 326p. (Orig.). 1993. 11.95 (*0-685-68166-1*) Crump Pubng.

Crump, Rita. The Strange Illness: A Commedia Dell 'Arte. 12p. 1995. pap. 6.00 (*0-88734-346-5*) Players Pr.

***Crump, Robert.** Zap Art of R. Crumb. 2000. pap. 19.95 (*0-86719-347-6*) Last Gasp.

Crump, Robert & Nelson, Jon. The Prints of Lyman Byxbe. (Great Plains Art Ser.: No. 2). (Illus.). 32p. 1991. pap. text 10.00 (*0-938932-05-5*) U Nebr CFGPS.

Crump, Rusty, ed. see Gowen, Kenneth K.

Crump, Spencer. Route 66: America's First Main Street. LC 96-60658. 1997. pap. text 11.95 (*0-918376-18-1*) Zeta Pubs Co.

Crump, Steve & Haxhold, Suzanne. Animal Husbandry & Other Social Graces: Comments on Life in the Magic Valley. 150p. (Orig.). 1997. pap. 12.95 (*0-9659279-0-3*) Times-News.

Crump, Stuart, Jr. Yo-Yo Tricks & Tips, 1 vol. 1999. mass mkt. 5.99 (*0-451-19881-6*) NAL.

Crump, Susan, et al. Texas Objections at Trial. LC 92-20557. 192p. (Orig.). 1992. pap. 39.50 (*0-88063-827-3*, MICHIE) LEXIS Pub.

***Crumpacker, Bunny.** Old-Time Brand-Name Desserts. (Illus.). 96p. 2000. 12.98 (*0-7651-1653-7*) Smithmark.

— Old-Time Brand-Name Recipe Cookbook. LC 97-62144. (Illus.). 160p. 1998. 12.98 (*0-7651-9077-X*) Smithmark.

Crumpacker, Bunny & Crumpacker, Chick. Jazz Legends. (Illus.). 96p. 1995. 19.95 incl. audio compact disk (*0-87905-683-5*) Gibbs Smith Pub.

Crumpacker, Chick, jt. auth. see Crumpacker, Bunny.

Crumpacker, Harry L., jt. auth. see Orrick, Bentley.

Crumpacker, Laurie, ed. see Karlsen, Carol F. & Burr, Esther E.

Crumpacker, Mary M., tr. see Kreitmann, J.

Crumpe, Samuel. An Essay on the Best Means of Providing Employment for the People. 2nd ed. LC 67-29499. (Reprints of Economic Classics Ser.). xxviii, 339p. 1968. reprint ed. 49.50 (*0-678-00410-2*) Kelley.

Crumpecker, Christina, jt. auth. see Downing, Steve.

Crumplen, Rena M., ed. Laboratory Methods for Craft Brewers. LC 97-77521. (Illus.). 168p. 1997. pap. 65.00 (*1-881696-02-2*) Am Brewing Chems.

Crumpler, Anne B., jt. auth. see Wang, Joseph.

***Crumpler, Wendy.** Designer's Guide to Photoshop, Illustrator & Painter, Vol. 1. 304p. 2000. pap. 49.99 (*0-7821-2626-X*) Sybex.

Crumpler, Yvonne Shelton, ed. see Barefield, Marilyn Davis.

Crumplin, G., ed. The Four-Quinolones. (Applied Biology Ser.). (Illus.). 330p. 1990. 107.95 (*0-387-19597-1*) Spr-Verlag.

Crumpton, C. Management of Spent Radiation Sources in the European Union: Quantities Storage, EUR 16960. 130p. 1996. pap. 25.00 (*92-827-8289-1*, CRNA-16960-ENC, Pub. by Comm Europ Commun) Bernan Associates.

Crumpton, Landon S. Baja California Norte Almanac: Topographic Maps. 68p. 1997. pap. 12.50 (*0-9658663-0-0*, 0001) Baja Almanac.

— Baja California Sur Almanac: Topographic Maps. 68p. 1997. pap. 12.50 (*0-9658663-1-9*, 0002) Baja Almanac.

Crumpton, Laurie, et al. Hospital Care for Schizophrenia in California in 1984. (Working Paper Ser.: No. 54). 18p. 1989. pap. 5.00 (*0-89940-535-5*) LBJ Sch Pub Aff.

Crumpton, Nancy, jt. auth. see Plummer, David E.

Crumpton, Philip, ed. see Lawrence, D. H.

Crumrine, Boyd. History of Washington County PA, with Biographical Sketches. (Illus.). 1142p. 1994. text 90.00 (*0-7884-0044-4*) Heritage Bk.

— Virginia Court Records in Southwestern Pennsylvania: Records of the District of West Augusta & Ohio & Yohogania Counties, Virginia, 1775-1780. LC 74-7238. (Illus.). 542p. 1997. reprint ed. pap. 39.95 (*0-8063-0624-6*) Clearfield Co.

Crumrine, N. Ross. Ejidos & Regions of Refuge in Northwestern Mexico. Weigand, Phil C., ed. LC 86-24978. (Anthropological Papers: No. 46) (Illus.). 113p. 1987. pap. 24.95 (*0-8165-1002-4*) U of Ariz Pr.

Crumrine, N. Ross, ed. Pilgrimage in Latin America, 4. LC 89-11845. (Contributions to the Study of Anthropology Ser.: No. 4). 464p. 1991. 67.95 (*0-313-26110-5*, CPG/, Greenwood Pr) Greenwood.

Crumrine, N. Ross, jt. ed. see Spicer, Rosamond B.

Crumrine, Paul. Navigating the Yellow Stream: A Voyage into the Cesspool of Urine Collection for Drug Testing. LC 91-66421. 192p. 1991. pap. 9.95 (*0-9631221-0-X*) Nest Egg Pr.

Crumroy, Otto, Jr., et al. A Pastors Survival Guide. LC 97-41731. 48p. 1997. pap. 9.95 (*0-8192-1719-0*) Morehouse Pub.

Crunch. Beginner's Luck. LC 99-34884. (Crunch Fitness Ser.). (Illus.). 112p. 1999. pap. 14.95 (*1-57826-027-2*, Pub. by Hatherleigh) Norton.

— Get Fit in a Crunch. LC 99-34885. (Crunch Fitness Ser.). (Illus.). 144p. 1999. pap. 14.95 (*1-57826-026-4*, Pub. by Hatherleigh) Norton.

Crunden, Robert, ed. Traffic of Ideas Between India & America. 1985. 37.50 (*0-8364-1317-2*, Pub. by Chanakya) S Asia.

Crunden, Robert M. Body & Soul: The Making of American Modernism: Art, Music & Letter of the Jazz Age, 1919-1926. LC 99-48435. 464p. 2000 35.00 (*0-465-01484-4*, Pub. by Basic) HarpC.

— A Brief History of American Culture. LC 96-3536. 384p. (C). (gr. 13). 1996. pap. 24.95 (*1-56324-863-4*, N Castle) M E Sharpe.

— Ministers of Reform: The Progressives' Achievement in American Civilization, 1889-1920. 320p. 1985. pap. text 14.95 (*0-252-01167-8*) U of Ill Pr.

Crunden, Robert M., ed. The Superfluous Men: Conservative Critics of Modern Culture, 1900-1945. 1999. 24.95 (*1-882926-30-7*) ISI Books.

Crunk, T. Living in the Resurrection. LC 95-12681. (Series of Younger Poets: Vol. 90). 1995. 16.00 (*0-300-06525-6*); pap. 10.00 (*0-300-06526-4*) Yale U Pr.

***Crunk, Tony & Apple, Margot.** Big Mama. LC 99-34557. 32p. (J). 2000. 16.00 (*0-374-30688-5*) FS&G.

***Crunk, Tony & Nash, Scott.** Grandpa's Overalls. LC 00-39942. (Illus.). (J). 2001. lib. bdg. write for info. (*0-531-33321-3*) Orchard Bks Watts.

Crunkilton, John R., jt. auth. see Finch, Curtis R.

Crupa, Zutora. Leksikon Prava Medjunarodnih Privrednih Odnosa. (ENG, FRE, GER, RUS & SER.). 560p. 1982. 39.95 (*0-8288-0581-4*, F78530) Fr & Eur.

Crupi, Connie. The Pagoda-Skyline Drive: An Illustrated History of Reading's Mountaintop Landmarks. Adams, Charles J., ed. Date not set. pap. 5.95 (*1-887762-05-1*) His Soc Brks Cnty.

***Crupi, Susan R.** Vintage Chintz Year 2000 Calendar. deluxe ed. Barron, David M., tr. (Illus.). 28p. 1999. 13.95 (*0-9674589-0-0*) Vintage Chintz.

Cruptill, Paul. The Many Worlds of Larry Niven: A Checklist of Works by Larry Niven. (Booklet Ser.: No. 33). 63p. (Orig.). 1989. pap. text 4.50 (*0-936055-44-8*) C Drumm Bks.

Crurius, Timothy W., jt. auth. see Channell, Carolyn E.

Cruscial, William S. My Life As a Dragonfly: Swimmer to Flyer! LC 96-92629. (Illus.). 28p. (Orig.). (J). (ps-3). 1996. pap. 4.50 (*0-9654099-0-2*) Sawtooth Pr.

Cruse. Illustrated Dictionary of Immunology. 352p. 1994. boxed set 83.95 (*0-8493-4557-X*) CRC Pr.

Cruse. Stuck Rubber Baby. Taggart, B., ed. (Illus.). 216p. 1996. pap. 14.00 (*1-56389-255-3*, Pub. by DC Comics) Time Warner.

Cruse & Cunni. Money Puzzle. 3rd ed. (C). 1989. pap., student ed. 29.33 (*0-06-041454-5*) HarpC.

Cruse, Allan & Granberg, Millianne. Lectures on Freshman Calculus. 1971. pap. 25.95 (*0-201-01301-0*) Addison-Wesley.

Cruse, Amy. After the Victorians. 1988. reprint ed. lib. bdg. 49.00 (*0-685-55954-8*) Rprt Serv.

— After the Victorians. 256p. 1998. reprint ed. lib. bdg. 59.00 (*0-7812-7714-0*) Rprt Serv.

— After the Victorians. LC 76-158495. 1971. reprint ed. 39.00 (*0-403-01315-1*) Scholarly.

— Elizabethan Lyrists & Their Poetry. LC 76-120974. (Poetry & Life Ser.). reprint ed. 26.50 (*0-404-52507-5*) AMS Pr.

— Englishman & His Books in the Early Nineteenth Century. LC 68-20218. (Illus.). 300p. 1972. reprint ed. 23.95 (*0-405-08412-9*, Pub. by Blom Pubns) Ayer.

— The Englishman & His Books in the Early Nineteenth Century. (BCL1-PR English Literature Ser.). 300p. 1992. reprint ed. lib. bdg. 79.00 (*0-7812-7048-0*) Rprt Serv.

Cruse, D. A. Lexical Semantics. (Cambridge Textbooks in Linguistics Ser.). (Illus.). 310p. 1986. pap. text 24.95 (*0-521-27643-8*) Cambridge U Pr.

Cruse, D. Alan. Meaning in Language: An Introduction to Semantics & Pragmatics. LC 99-34409. (Oxford Textbooks in Linguistics Ser.). (Illus.). 416p. 2000. pap. text 24.95 (*0-19-870010-5*) OUP.

***Cruse, Eleonore.** Rosas. 1998. 25.99 (*3-8228-8037-X*) Benedikt Taschen.

Cruse, Eleonore. Roses. 1998. 19.99 (*3-8228-7761-1*) Taschen Amer.

Cruse, Harold. The Crisis of the Negro Intellectual: A Historical Analysis of the Failure of Black Leadership. LC 84-60452. 696p. 1984. pap. 15.95 (*0-688-03886-7*, Quil) HarperTrade.

Cruse, Holk. Neural Networks As Cybernetic Systems. LC 96-8521. 1996. 105.00 (*0-86577-672-5*) Thieme Med Pubs.

Cruse, Howard. Early Barefootz. (Illus.). 120p. 1990. pap. 11.95 (*1-56097-052-9*) Fantagraph Bks.

— Stuck Rubber Baby. (Illus.). 224p. 1995. 24.95 (*1-56389-216-2*, Pub. by DC Comics) Time Warner.

Cruse, J. M., ed. Highlights in Immunology. (Journal: Immunologic Research: Vol. 10, No. 1, 1991). (Illus.). 88p. 1991. pap. 33.25 (*3-8055-5394-3*) S Karger.

— Immunomodulation of Neoplasia. (Progress in Experimental Tumor Research Ser.: Vol. 32). (Illus.). vi, 246p. 1988. 207.00 (*3-8055-4595-9*) S Karger.

— The Year in Complement. (Journal: Immunologic Research: Vol. 12, No. 3, 1993). (Illus.). 108p. 1993. pap. 35.00 (*3-8055-5880-5*) S Karger.

Cruse, J. M. & Lewis, R. E., eds. Antigenic Variation: Molecular & Genetic Mechanisms of Relapsing Disease. (Contributions to Microbiology & Immunology Ser.: Vol. 8). (Illus.). vi, 246p. 1987. 169.75 (*3-8055-4343-3*) S Karger.

— Autoimmunity: Basic Concepts & Systemic & Selected Organ-Specific Diseases. (Concepts in Immunopathology Ser.: Vol. 1). (Illus.). viii, 362p. 1985. 172.25 (*3-8055-3908-8*) S Karger.

— Autoimmunoregulation & Autoimmune Disease. (Concepts in Immunopathology Ser.: Vol. 4). (Illus.). viii, 304p. 1987. 241.75 (*3-8055-4406-5*) S Karger.

Cruse, J. M. & Lewis, R. E., Jr., eds. Cellular Aspects of Autoimmunity. (Concepts in Immunopathology Ser.: Vol. 6). (Illus.). vi, 202p. 1988. 148.00 (*3-8055-4728-5*) S Karger.

— Clinical & Molecular Aspects of Autoimmune Diseases. (Concepts in Immunopathology Ser.: Vol. 8). (Illus.). x, 258p. 1991. 215.75 (*3-8055-5402-8*) S Karger.

— Complement Today. (Complement Profiles Ser.: Vol. 1). (Illus.). x, 156p. 1993. 106.25 (*3-8055-5673-X*) S Karger.

Cruse, J. M. & Lewis, R. E., eds. Immunoregulation & Autoimmunity. (Concepts in Immunopathology Ser.: Vol. 3). (Illus.). vii, 340p. 1986. 161.75 (*3-8055-4076-0*) S Karger.

— Organ Based Autoimmune Diseases. (Concepts in Immunopathology Ser.: Vol. 2). (Illus.). x, 278p. 1985. 129.75 (*3-8055-3929-0*) S Karger.

Cruse, J. M. & Lewis, R. E., Jr., eds. Therapy of Autoimmune Diseases. (Concepts in Immunopathology Ser.: Vol. 7). (Illus.). viii, 216p. 1989. 167.00 (*3-8055-4931-8*) S Karger.

— The Year in Immunology, Vol. 2, 1985-1986. (Illus.). vi, 386p. 1986. 256.75 (*3-8055-4342-5*) S Karger.

— The Year in Immunology, 1988, Vol. 4 & 5. (Illus.). xvi, 536p. 1989. 346.25 (*3-8055-5044-8*) S Karger.

— The Year in Immunology, 1988: Cellular, Molecular & Clinical Aspects. (Year in Immunology Ser.: Vol. 4). (Illus.). vii, 312p. 1989. 221.75 (*3-8055-4808-7*) S Karger.

— The Year in Immunology, 1988: Immunoregulatory Cytokines & Cell Growth. (Year in Immunology Ser.: Vol. 5). (Illus.). viii, 224p. 1989. 172.25 (*3-8055-4895-8*) S Karger.

— The Year in Immunology, 1984-1985. (Illus.). vi, 234p. 1985. 137.50 (*3-8055-4025-6*) S Karger.

— The Year in Immunology, 1989-1990: Molecules & Cells of Immunity. (Illus.). vi, 284p. 1990. 258.50 (*3-8055-5084-7*) S Karger.

— The Year in Immunology, 1986-1987. (Year in Immunology Ser.: Vol. 3). (Illus.). 350p. 1988. 224.50 (*3-8055-4616-5*) S Karger.

Cruse, J. M. & Lewis, R. E., eds. The Year in Immunopathology. (Journal: Pathology & Immunopathology Research: Vol. 5, No. 3-5, 1986). (Illus.). 248p. 1987. pap. 76.75 (*3-8055-4576-2*) S Karger.

C

Cruse, J. M. & Lewis, R. F., Jr., eds. Conjugate Vaccines. (Contributions to Microbiology & Immunology Ser.: Vol. 10). (Illus.). vi, 198p. 1989. 143.50 (*3-8055-4932-6*) S Karger.

Cruse, J. M. & Schwartz, L. M., eds. The Year in Immunology, 1983. (Journal: Survey of Immunologic Research: Vol. 3, No. 2-3). (Illus.). 156p. 1984. pap. 69.75 (*3-8055-3881-2*) S Karger.

Cruse, J. M., jt. ed. see Del Guercio, P.

Cruse, Joseph R., jt. auth. see Wegscheider-Cruse, Sharon.

Cruse, Julius M. Atlas of Immunology. LC 98-25823. 646p. 1998. boxed set 89.95 (*0-8493-9489-9*) CRC Pr.

Cruse, Julius M. & Lewis, R. E., eds. Genetic Basis of Autoimmune Disease: Cellular & Genetic Basis. (Concepts in Immunopathology Ser.: Vol. 5). (Illus.). vi, 202p. 1988. 148.00 (*3-8055-4635-1*) S Karger.

Cruse, Seymourina. Knopf City Guide: London. 1998. pap. 14.95 (*0-375-70255-5*) Knopf.

Cruse, Seymourina, jt. auth. see Goncalves, Madeleine.

Cruse, T. A. Boundary Element Analysis in Computational Fracture Mechanics. (C). 1988. text 137.50 (*90-247-3614-5*) Kluwer Academic.

Cruse, T. A., ed. Advanced Boundary Element Methods. (Illus.). 510p. 1988. 107.95 (*0-387-17454-0*) Spr-Verlag.

— Reliability Technology, 1992. (AD Ser.: Vol. 28). 276p. 1992. 62.50 (*0-7918-1095-X*, G00739) ASME.

Cruse, T. A., ed. see American Society of Mechanical Engineers Staff.

Cruse, Thomas A., ed. Fracture Mechanics: Nineteenth Symposium. LC 88-3320. (Special Technical Publication Ser.: No. 969). (Illus.). 923p. 1988. text 120.00 (*0-8031-0972-5*, STP969) ASTM.

— Reliability-Based Mechanical Design. LC 96-48240. (Mechanical Engineering Series of Reference Books & Textbooks: Vol. 108). (Illus.). 352p. 1997. text 125.00 (*0-8247-9793-0*) Dekker.

Cruse, Thomas A. & Griffin, Donald S., eds. Three-Dimensional Continuum Computer Programs for Structural Analysis: Presented at the Winter Annual Meeting of the American Society of Mechanical Engineers, New York, NY, November 26-30, 1972. LC 72-92593. 54p. reprint ed. pap. 30.00 (*0-608-11387-5*, 202206100024) Bks Demand.

Crusemann, Frank. The Torah: Theology & Social History of Old Testament Law. 480p. 1996. 47.00 (*0-8006-2856-X*, Fortress Pr) Augsburg Fortress.

Cruser, Patricia. Life is a Poem to God. vii, 70p. 1998. pap. 12.50 (*0-9667465-0-3*) ArtWord.

***Crush, Charles W.** The Montgomery County Story 1776 - 1957. (Illus.). 216p. 2000. 15.00 (*0-9701648-0-7*) Mont Mus.

Crush, Jonathan. The Struggle for Swazi Labour, 1890-1920. 320p. 1987. 65.00 (*0-7735-0569-5*, Pub. by McG-Queens Univ Pr) CUP Services.

Crush, Jonathan, ed. Power of Development. LC 94-40708. 304p. (C). 1995. pap. 27.99 (*0-415-11177-3*, C0062) Routledge.

— Power of Development. LC 94-40708. 304p. (C). (gr. 13). 1995. 85.00 (*0-415-11176-5*, C0061) Routledge.

Crush, Jonathan & Ambler, Charles, eds. Liquor & Labor in Southern Africa. LC 92-27473. 448p. (C). 1992. text 39.95 (*0-8214-1027-X*) Ohio U Pr.

Crush, Jonathan, jt. auth. see Jeeves, Alan.

Crush, Margaret. Take Care of Your Dog with the Home Vet Handbook. (Illus.). 63p. 1998. pap. text 15.00 (*0-7881-5897-X*) DIANE Pub.

***Crushshon, Mabel G.** Index to Hinds County, Mississippi Freedman's Bureau Labor Contracts. 90p. 1999. pap. 12.00 (*1-885480-34-2*) Pioneer Pubng.

Crusie, Jennifer. Anyone but You. (Love & Laughter Ser.). 1996. per. 3.50 (*0-373-44004-9*, 1-44004-9) Harlequin Bks.

— Crazy for You. LC 98-37169. 336p. 1999. text 24.95 (*0-312-19849-3*) St Martin.

***Crusie, Jennifer.** Crazy for You. 336p. 2000. mass mkt. 6.99 (*0-312-97112-5*) St Martin.

— Crazy for You. large type ed. LC 00-22868. 2000. 25.95 (*1-56895-853-6*) Wheeler Pub.

— Getting Rid of Bradley. 2000. mass mkt. 4.50 (*0-373-82233-2*, 1-82233-7) Harlequin Bks.

Crusie, Jennifer. Manhunting. (Temptation Ser.). 1993. per. 2.99 (*0-373-25563-2*, 1-25563-7) Harlequin Bks.

***Crusie, Jennifer.** Manhunting. 2000. mass mkt. 4.50 (*0-373-82215-4*, 1-82215-4) Harlequin Bks.

— Manhunting. 2000. mass mkt. 5.99 (*1-55166-618-9*, 1-66618-9, Mira Bks) Harlequin Bks.

Crusie, Jennifer. Sizzle. (Great Escapes Ser.). 1994. pap. 1.99 (*0-373-83271-0*, 1-83271-6) Harlequin Bks.

— Strange Bedpersons. (Temptation Ser.). 1994. per. 2.99 (*0-373-25598-5*, 1-25598-3) Harlequin Bks.

— Strange Bedpersons. (Temptation Ser.). 1994. per. 2.99 (*0-373-25620-5*, 1-25620-5) Harlequin Bks.

— Tell Me Lies. LC 97-36523. 322p. 1998. text 24.95 (*0-312-17940-5*) St Martin.

— Tell Me Lies. LC 98-24004. 1998. 25.95 (*1-56895-568-5*) Wheeler Pub.

***Crusie, Jennifer.** Tell Me Lies. 1. 368p. 1999. mass mkt. 6.50 (*0-312-96680-6*) St Martin.

— Welcome o Temptation. mass mkt. write for info. (*0-312-97425-6*) St Martin.

— Welcome to Temptation. LC 99-55739. 352p. 2000. text 24.95 (*0-312-25294-3*) St Martin.

— Welcome to Temptation. large type ed. LC 00-32502. 2000. write for info. (*1-56895-906-0*) Wheeler Pub.

Crusie, Jennifer. What the Lady Wants. LC 95-13946. (Temptation Ser.). 218p. 1995. per. 3.25 (*0-373-25644-2*, 1-25644-5) Harlequin Bks.

***Crusio, W. E. & Gerlai, R. T.** Handbook of Molecular-Genetic Techniques for Brain & Behavior Research. LC 99-38172. (Techniques in the Behavioral & Neural Sciences Ser.). 994p. 1999. 177.50 (*0-444-50239-4*) Elsevier.

Crusius, Christian A., et al. Die Philosophischen Hauptwerke. (GER.). xxxvi, 695p. 1987. 198.00 (*3-487-07883-X*) G Olms Pubs.

Crusius, Friedrich. Romissche Metrik. (GER.). vi, 148p. 1989. reprint ed. 20.00 (*3-487-07532-6*) G Olms Pubs.

Crusius, Otto. Die Mimiamben des Herondas. xvi, 206p. 1967. reprint ed. 50.00 (*0-318-70904-X*) G Olms Pubs.

Crusius, Timothy W. Kenneth Burke & the Conversation after Philosophy. LC 98-21997. (Rhetorical Philosophy & Theory Ser.). 1999. 44.95 (*0-8093-2206-4*); pap. 19.95 (*0-8093-2207-2*) S Ill U Pr.

— A Teacher's Introduction to Philosophical Hermeneutics. 105p. 1992. pap. 10.95 (*0-8141-5016-0*) NCTE.

Crusius, Timothy W., ed. Discourse: A Critique & Synthesis of Major Theories. LC 89-14571. vi, 167p. 1989. pap. 19.75 (*0-87352-190-0*, J307P); lib. bdg. 37.50 (*0-87352-189-7*, J307C) Modern Lang.

***Crusius, Timothy W. & Channell, Carolyn E.** The Aims of Argument: A Brief Rhetoric. 3rd ed. LC 99-28760. xxii, 312p. 1999. pap. text 22.95 (*0-7674-1132-3*) Mayfield Pub.

— The Aims of Argument: A Rhetoric & Reader. 3rd ed. LC 99-27621. xxii, 783p. 1999. pap. text 35.95 (*0-7674-1131-5*, 1131-6) Mayfield Pub.

Cruso, Thalassa. The Gardening Year. 260p. 1990. pap. 14.95 (*1-55821-082-2*) Lyons Pr.

Crusoe, Robinson & Miller, Madge. Robinson Crusoe. (J). (gr. 1-9). 1954. 6.00 (*0-87602-193-3*) Anchorage.

Cruson, Daniel. Newtown. (Images of America Ser.). (Illus.). 128p. 1998. pap. 16.99 (*0-7524-0948-4*) Arcadia Publng.

— Newtown's Slaves: A Case Study in Early Connecticut Rural Black History. (Illus.). 92p. 1995. pap. 10.00 (*1-888006-01-3*) Newtown Hist Soc.

***Cruson, Daniel.** Redding & Easton. LC 00-101910. (Images of America Ser.). (Illus.). 128p. 2000. pap. 18.99 (*0-7385-0421-1*) Arcadia Publng.

Crussard, Claude. Un Musicien Francais Oublie, Marc-Antoine Charpentier, 1634-1704. LC 76-43912. (Music & Theatre in France in the 17th & 18th Centuries Ser.). reprint ed. 32.50 (*0-404-60155-3*) AMS Pr.

***Crusz, Rienzi.** Lord of the Mountain: The Sardiel Poems. 160p. 1999. pap. 13.95 (*0-920661-82-3*) TSAR Pubns.

Crutcher & Sawrie. Sketches of the Master's Heart. 88p. 1996. pap. 8.99 (*0-8341-1586-7*) Nazarene.

Crutcher, Chris. Athletic Shorts. LC 91-4418. 160p. (YA). (gr. 7 up). 1991. 15.95 (*0-688-10816-4*, Grenwillow Bks) HarpC Child Bks.

Crutcher, Chris. Athletic Shorts: Six Short Stories. 176p. (YA). (gr. 7 up). 1992. mass mkt. 4.99 (*0-440-21390-8*, LLL BDD) BDD Bks Young Read.

Crutcher, Chris. Athletic Shorts: Six Short Stories. (Laurel-Leaf Contemporary Fiction Ser.). 1991. 9.60 (*0-606-00803-9*, Pub. by Turtleback) Demco.

Crutcher, Chris. Athletic Shorts: Six Short Stories. large type ed. LC 93-12. 202p. 1993. 16.95 (*1-56054-687-5*) Thorndike Pr.

— Chinese Handcuffs. 224p. (YA). 1991. mass mkt. 4.50 (*0-440-20837-8*, LLL BDD) BDD Bks Young Read.

— Chinese Handcuffs. LC 88-45809. 192p. (J). (gr. 7 up). 1989. 14.00 (*0-688-08345-5*, Grenwillow Bks) HarpC Child Bks.

Crutcher, Chris. Chinese Handcuffs. 1991. 9.60 (*0-606-04892-8*, Pub. by Turtleback) Demco.

Crutcher, Chris. The Crazy Horse Electric Game. LC 86-14592. 224p. (J). (gr. 7 up). 1987. 14.00 (*0-688-06683-6*, Grenwillow Bks) HarpC Child Bks.

Crutcher, Chris. Crazy Horse Electric Game. (Laurel-Leaf Contemporary Fiction Ser.). (J). 1987. 9.60 (*0-606-03763-2*, Pub. by Turtleback) Demco.

Crutcher, Chris. The Crazy Horse Electric Game. 224p. (YA). (gr. k-12). 1988. reprint ed. mass mkt. 4.50 (*0-440-20094-6*) Dell.

— The Deep End. 320p. 1994. mass mkt. 4.99 (*0-8217-4425-9*, Zebra Kensgtn) Kensgtn Pub Corp.

— Ironman. 240p. (YA). (gr. 7 up). 1996. mass mkt. 4.99 (*0-440-21971-X*, LLL BDD) BDD Bks Young Read.

— Ironman. LC 94-1657. (Illus.). 192p. (YA). (gr. 7 up). 1995. 15.00 (*0-688-13503-X*, Grenwillow Bks) HarpC Child Bks.

— Ironman: A Novel. LC 94-1657. (YA). 1996. 9.60 (*0-606-09477-6*, Pub. by Turtleback) Demco.

— Running Loose. 192p. (YA). (gr. 7 up). 1986. mass mkt. 4.99 (*0-440-97570-0*, LLL BDD) BDD Bks Young Read.

— Running Loose. LC 82-20935. 192p. (YA). (gr. 7-12). 1983. 17.95 (*0-688-02002-X*, Wm Morrow) Morrow Avon.

— Running Loose. 1986. 9.60 (*0-606-00387-8*, Pub. by Turtleback) Demco.

— Staying Fat for Sarah Byrnes. 216p. (YA). (gr. 7-12). 1995. mass mkt. 4.99 (*0-440-21906-X*) Dell.

Crutcher, Chris. Staying Fat for Sarah Byrnes. LC 91-40097. 224p. (YA). (gr. 7 up). 1993. 15.95 (*0-688-11552-7*, Grenwillow Bks) HarpC Child Bks.

Crutcher, Chris. Staying Fat for Sarah Byrnes. (J). 1993. 9.60 (*0-606-07156-3*, Pub. by Turtleback) Demco.

— Staying Fat for Sarah Byrnes. large type ed. (Teen Scene Ser.). (YA). (gr. 9-12). 1993. pap. 15.95 (*0-7862-0062-6*) Thorndike Pr.

— Stotan! 192p. (YA). (gr. k-12). 1988. mass mkt. 4.99 (*0-440-20080-6*, LLL BDD) BDD Bks Young Read.

Crutcher, Chris. Stotan! (Laurel-Leaf Contemporary Fiction Ser.). (J). 1986. 9.60 (*0-606-03931-7*, Pub. by Turtleback) Demco.

— Whale Talk. (J). Date not set. lib. bdg. 15.89 (*0-06-029369-1*, Grenwillow Bks) HarpC Child Bks.

— Whale Talk. (J). 2001. 15.95 (*0-688-18019-1*, Grenwillow Bks) HarpC Child Bks.

Crutcher, Ernest R., jt. auth. see Beeson, Richard D.

Crutcher, Jim. Windows on the Kingdom: Mission Illustrations for Pastors. 64p. 1996. pap. 6.99 (*0-8341-1587-5*) Nazarene.

Crutcher, Mark. Lime 5: Exploited by Choice. 320p. (Orig.). 1996. pap. 19.95 (*0-9648886-0-2*) Life Dynamics.

Crutchfield, Carolyn & Barnes, Marylou R. Motor Control & Motor Learning in Rehabilitation. (Illus.). 520p. (C). 1993. text 50.00 (*0-936030-06-2*) Stokesville Pub.

Crutchfield, Carolyn A. & Barnes, Marylou R. The Neurophysiological Basis of Patient Treatment: Peripheral Components of Motor Control, Vol. III. (Illus.). 1984. pap. 35.00 (*0-936030-03-8*) Stokesville Pub.

***Crutchfield, Donald E.** Confessions of a Hollywood P. I. 2000. pap. 16.95 (*1-889261-03-3*) SOS Beverly Hills.

Crutchfield, Donald E. Confessions of a Hollywood P. I. LC 97-6527. 250p. 1997. 24.95 (*0-935016-06-6*, Dunhill Pub Co) Zinn Pub Grp.

***Crutchfield, Elaine B.** Developing Human Capital in American Manufacturing: A Case Study of Barriers to Training & Development. LC 99-44757. (Studies on Industrial Productivity). 1999. write for info. (*0-8153-3584-9*) Garland.

Crutchfield, James, ed. see Canaday, Bob & Canaday, Jackie.

Crutchfield, James A. America's Yesteryears: Historic Vignettes from America's Past, 1492-1860. (Illus.). 198p. 1996. pap. 14.95 (*1-888608-15-3*) Cool Springs Pr.

— Eyewitness to American History. LC 97-164262. (Illus.). 224p. (Orig.). 1996. pap. 16.95 (*1-886609-04-7*) Tamarack Bks.

— The Harpeth River: A Biography. (Illus.). 148p. 1994. 19.95 (*1-57072-016-9*) Overmountain Pr.

— It Happened in Arizona. LC 94-27314. (Guide Ser.). (Illus.). 128p. 1994. pap. 9.95 (*1-56044-264-6*) Falcon Pub Inc.

— It Happened in Colorado. LC 92-55079. (Illus.). 137p. 1993. pap. 9.95 (*1-56044-364-2*) Falcon Pub Inc.

— It Happened in Montana. LC 92-53160. (Illus.). 109p. 1992. pap. 9.95 (*1-56044-073-2*) Falcon Pub Inc.

— It Happened in New Mexico. LC 95-61667. (Illus.). 118p. 1995. pap. 8.95 (*1-56044-319-7*) Falcon Pub Inc.

— It Happened in Oregon. LC 90-55078. (It Happened in... Ser.). (Illus.). 111p. 1994. pap. 9.95 (*1-56044-290-5*) Falcon Pub Inc.

— It Happened in Texas. LC 96-32818. (Illus.). 136p. 1996. pap. 8.95 (*1-56044-320-0*) Falcon Pub Inc.

— It Happened in Washington. LC 95-13094. (It Happened in... Ser.). (Illus.). 122p. (Orig.). 1994. pap. 8.95 (*1-56044-289-1*) Falcon Pub Inc.

Crutchfield, James A. Lewis & Clark Expedition: 1804-1806. 39.00 (*1-56696-098-3*) Jackdaw.

— Mountain Men & the Fur Trade. 39.00 (*1-56696-148-3*) Jackdaw.

Crutchfield, James A. Mountain Men of the American West. (Illus.). 200p. (Orig.). 1997. pap. 17.95 (*1-886609-07-1*) Tamarack Bks.

— The Natchez Trace: A Pictorial History. LC 85-11774. (Illus.). 160p. 1985. pap. 9.95 (*0-934395-03-9*) Rutledge Hill Pr.

— On This Day: A Brief History of Nashville & Middle Tennessee. (Illus.). 152p. 1995. pap. 9.95 (*0-9640392-1-4*) Cool Springs Pr.

— Primer of the North American Fur Trade. 1986. 9.50 (*0-913150-52-5*) Pioneer Pr.

— Santa Fe Trail. 208p. 1995. pap. 12.95 (*1-55622-462-1*, Rep of TX Pr) Wordware Pub.

— Timeless Tennesseans. (Illus.). 200p. 1983. 19.95 (*0-87397-186-8*, Strode Pubs) Circle Bk Service.

— Tragedy at Taos: The Revolt of 1847. LC 94-49513. 208p. 1995. pap. 12.95 (*1-55622-385-4*, Rep of TX Pr) Wordware Pub.

***Crutchfield, James A. & Holladay, Robert.** Franklin, Tennessee's Handsomest Town. LC 99-64290. (Tennessee Heritage Library Bicentennial Collection). (Illus.). 552p. 1999. 39.95 (*1-57736-147-4*, Hillsboro Pr) Providence Hse.

Crutchfield, James A. & LaPaglia, Peter S. The Tennessee Grassroots Writer. 96p. 1996. pap. 9.95 (*1-881576-51-5*) Providence Hse.

Crutchfield, James A. & Lawson, Rowena. West African Marine Fisheries: Alternatives for Management. LC 73-10843. (Program of International Studies of Fishery Arrangements. Papers: Paper No. 3). 78p. reprint ed. pap. 30.00 (*0-608-13832-0*, 202096000020) Bks Demand.

Crutchfield, James A. & Pontecorvo, Giulio. The Pacific Salmon Fisheries: A Study of Irrational Conservation. LC 72-75180. (Resources for the Future Ser.). (Illus.). 220p. 1969. 19.95 (*0-8018-1025-6*) Johns Hopkins.

Crutchfield, James A. & Sparkman, Winette. Miss Daisy Celebrates Tennessee. LC 95-79050. (Illus.). 266p. 1997. 19.95 (*0-9656547-0-2*) Side Dish.

Crutchfield, James Andrew. It Happened in Georgia. LC 99-23585. 1999. pap. 9.95 (*1-56044-845-8*, Two Dot) Falcon Pub Inc.

Crutchfield, James P. Computational Mechanics of Cellular Processes. 302p. 1998. text 49.50 (*0-691-01618-6*, Pub. by Princeton U Pr) Cal Prin Full Svc.

Crutchfield, Jean. Presumed Innocence. LC 99-224701. (Illus.). 80p. 1998. pap. 25.00 (*0-295-97718-3*) U of Wash Pr.

Crutchfield, Larry. The Origins of Dispensationalism: The Darby Factor. 254p. (Orig.). (C). 1991. lib. bdg. 52.50 (*0-8191-8467-5*) U Pr of Amer.

— The Origins of Dispensationalism: The Darby Factor. 254p. (Orig.). (C). 1992. pap. text 28.50 (*0-8191-8468-3*) U Pr of Amer.

Crutchfield, Malinda, ed. see Lovingood, Paul & Reiman, Robert.

Crutchfield, Philip. Annotated Corporate Voluntary Administration Law. 280p. 1994. pap. 70.00 (*0-455-21262-7*, Pub. by LawBk Co) Gaunt.

***Crutchfield, Robert D.** Crime. 2nd ed. LC 00-8037. 2000. pap. write for info. (*0-7619-8679-0*) Pine Forge.

Crutchfield, Robert D., et al, eds. Readings: Crime. LC 95-43519. (Crime & Society Ser.: No. 1). 1996. pap. 31.95 (*0-8039-9078-2*) Pine Forge.

Crutchfield, Roger S. English Vocabulary Quick Reference: A Comprehensive Dictionary Arranged by Word Roots. LC 97-94069. 382p. (Orig.). 1998. 39.95 (*0-9659138-0-5*) LexaDyne.

Crutchfield, Susan & Epstein, Marcy, eds. Points of Contact: Disability, Art & Culture. LC 99-86129. 312p. 2000. pap. 17.95 (*0-472-06711-7*, 06711); text 47.50 (*0-472-09711-3*, 09711) U of Mich Pr.

Crutchley, Anna. The Tassels Book: An Inspirational Guide to Tassels & Tassel-Making, with over 40 Practical Projects. (Illus.). 160p. 1996. 27.50 (*1-85967-222-1*, Lorenz Bks) Anness Pub.

Crutchley, Brooke, ed. see Morison, Stanley.

Crutchley, Zoe & Parnell, Veronica. My Bedtime Prayer Bear. (Illus.). 12p. (J). (ps-k). 1999. bds. 8.99 (*0-8054-1796-6*) Broadman.

Crute, I. R., et al, eds. The Gene-for-Gene Relationship in Plant-Parasite Interactions. LC 97-8473. (A CAB International Publication). 448p. 1997. text 120.00 (*0-85199-164-5*) OUP.

Crute, Joseph, Jr. Units of the Confederate States Army. 504p. 1988. 45.00 (*0-942211-53-7*) Olde Soldier Bks.

Crute, Joseph E., Jr. Emblems of Southern Valor: Battle Flags of the Confederacy. (Illus.). 112p. 1990. 35.00 (*1-56013-001-6*) Olde Soldier Bks.

Crute, Joseph H., Jr. Confederate Staff Officers, 1861-1865. 267p. 1984. 25.00 (*0-942211-33-2*) Olde Soldier Bks.

Crute, Sheree. Health & Healing for African-Americans: Straight Talk & Tips from More Than 150 Black Doctors on Our Top Health Concerns. (Illus.). 512p. 1999. pap. 15.95 (*1-57954-044-9*) Rodale Pr Inc.

Crute, Sheree, ed. Healthy & Healing for African Americans: Straight Talk from More Than 150 Black Doctors on Our Top Health Concerns. LC 97-5716. 512p. 1997. 29.95 (*0-87596-365-X*) Rodale Pr Inc.

***Cruts, Randy.** Controlled Insanity. Inbody, Mary, ed. 422p. 2000. pap. 14.95 (*1-58275-013-0*) Black Forest Pr.

Cruts, Randy. Dive into Terror. Knox, W. B. & Pearson, Anita, eds. (Illus.). 350p. 1996. pap. 12.95 (*1-881116-73-5*, Pub. by Black Forest Pr) Epic Bk Promo.

Crutsinger, Carla. Thinking Smarter: Skills for Academic Success, Set. 2nd ed. (YA). (gr. 4 up). 1992. reprint ed. pap. 39.95 (*0-944662-01-3*) Brainworks Inc.

Crutsinger, Carla & Hohner, Robin. Creative Memory: An Alternative to Rote Learning. (J). (gr. 4 up). 1994. pap. 39.95 (*0-944662-03-X*) Brainworks Inc.

Crutsinger, Carla & McDaniel, Katy. The Land of Sir Spell-a-Lot: A New Approach to Spelling, Writing, & Thinking. (Illus.). 220p. (Orig.). (J). (gr. 2). 1997. pap., wbk. ed. 39.95 (*0-944662-06-4*) Brainworks Inc.

— Sir Spell A-Lot: A Unique Procedure Emphasizing Spelling Accountability & Written Expression. (Illus.). 228p. (J). (gr. 5-6). 1997. pap. text 39.95 (*0-944662-09-9*) Brainworks Inc.

— Sir Spell A-Lot: A Unique Procedure Emphasizing Spelling Accountability & Written Expression. (Illus.). 240p. (J). (gr. 4-5). 1997. pap. text 39.95 (*0-944662-08-0*) Brainworks Inc.

— Sir Spell A-Lot: A Unique Procedure Emphasizing Spelling Accountability & Written Expression. (Illus.). 217p. (J). (gr. 3-4). 1997. pap. text 39.95 (*0-944662-07-2*) Brainworks Inc.

Crutsinger, Carla & Moore, Debra. ADD Quicktips: Practical Ways to Handle ADD Successfully. LC 97-229467. (Illus.). 250p. (Orig.). 1997. pap. 24.95 (*0-944662-05-6*) Brainworks Inc.

— The Most Wanted Words: A New Approach to Spelling, Writing & Thinking. (Illus.). 156p. (Orig.). (J). (gr. 2-6). 1995. pap. text 29.95 (*0-944662-04-8*) Brainworks Inc.

Cruttenden, Alan. Intonation. 2nd ed. 218p. 22.50 (*0-521-62902-0*) Cambridge U Pr.

Cruttenden, Alan. Intonation. 2nd ed. (Textbooks in Linguistics Ser.). 218p. (C). 1997. text 59.95 (*0-521-59182-1*); pap. text 23.95 (*0-521-59825-7*) Cambridge U Pr.

Cruttenden, Joseph. Atlantic Merchant-Apothecary: Letters of Joseph Cruttenden 1710-1717. Steele, I. K., ed. LC 77-2832. 161p. reprint ed. pap. 50.00 (*0-8357-5834-6*, 202644300049) Bks Demand.

Cruttenden, Pete & Rowthorn, Chris. Asia. (Read This First Ser.). (Illus.). 328p. 1999. pap. 14.95 (*1-86450-049-2*) Lonely Planet.

Cruttwell, C. R. History of the Great War, 1914-1918. 2nd ed. (Illus.). 671p. 1999. pap. 20.00 (*0-89733-315-2*) Academy Chi Pubs.

Cruttwell, Charles T. Literary History of Early Christianity, 2 vols. LC 76-129369. reprint ed. 95.00 (*0-404-01877-7*) AMS Pr.

Cruttwell, Maud. Donatello. LC 71-37334. (Select Bibliographies Reprint Ser.). (Illus.). 1977. reprint ed. 39.95 (*0-8369-6681-3*) Ayer.

— Luca Signorelli. LC 75-131677. (Illus.). xi, 144p. 1972. reprint ed. 59.00 (*0-403-00912-X*) Scholarly.

C

An Asterisk (*) at the beginning of an entry indicates that the title is appearing for the first time.

Cruttwell, Peter. History Out of Control: Confronting Global Anarchy. (Illus.). 240p. 1996. pap. 16.95 (*1-870098-61-7*, Pub. by Green Bks) Chelsea Green Pub.

Cruttwell, Robert W. Virgil's Mind at Work: An Analysis of the Symbolism of the Aeneid. LC 78-114505. 182p. 1971. reprint ed. lib. bdg. 35.00 (*0-8371-4733-6*, CRVM, Greenwood Pr) Greenwood.

Crutwell, Maud. Luca & Andrea Della Robbia. LC 79-155625. (Illus.). reprint ed. 39.50 (*0-404-01869-6*) AMS Pr.

Crutwell, Patrick, ed. & intro. see Johnson, Samuel.

Crutzen, P. & Ramanathan, V., eds. Clouds, Chemistry & Climate. (NATO ASI Ser.: Global Environmental Change: Series 1, Vol. 35). 260p. 1997. 129.00 (*3-540-60433-2*) Spr-Verlag.

Crutzen, Paul J., jt. auth. see Graedel, T. E.

Crutzen, Paul J., jt. auth. see Graedel, Thomas E.

Crutzen, Yves R., et al, eds. Industrial Application of Electromagnetic Computer Codes. (C). 1990. text 155.00 (*0-7923-0998-7*) Kluwer Academic.

Cruver, Donald R. Complying with the Foreign Corrupt Practices Act: A Guide for U. S. Firms Doing Business in the International Marketplace. 2nd ed. LC 99-14801. 1999. write for info. (*1-57073-702-9*) Amer Bar Assn.

Crux, Jason A. Calcareous Nannofossils & Their Applications. 424p. 1989. text 131.00 (*0-470-21203-9*) P-H.

Cruxton, Brad. Discovering Castle Days. (Illus.). 64p. 1997. pap. 12.95 (*0-19-541323-7*) OUP.

Cruxton, J. Bradley. Discovering the Amazon Rain Forest. (Illus.). 64p. 1998. pap. 12.95 (*0-19-541327-X*) OUP.

— Discovering the Amazon Rainforest: Teacher's Resource. (Illus.). 40p. 1998. pap. 12.95 (*0-19-541328-8*) OUP.

Cruysberg, J. R., jt. ed. see Deutman, A. F.

Cruysse, Inge Van der, see Shetter, William Z. & Van der Cruysse, Inge, eds.

Cruz, jt. auth. see Rodriguez.

***Cruz, Adriana.** 10 Proyectos con MS-Word Explicados en Espanol: Aplicaciones Practicas Listas para Usar. (PC Users Express Ser.). (SPA., Illus.). 263p. 1999. pap. 13.90 (*987-9131-94-0*, Pub. by MP Ediciones) Am Wholesale.

Cruz, Alberto. Como Triunfar Vendiendo Por Correo. (SPA., Illus.). 172p. (C). 1990. 29.95 (*0-9624747-0-3*) A Cruz.

Cruz, Alejandro. The Woman who Outshone the Sun: The Legend of Lucia Zenteno. LC 91-16646. Orig. Title: La Mujer que Brillaba Mas aun que el Sol: La Historia de Lucia Zenteno. 1991. 12.40 (*0-606-06891-0*) Turtleback.

Cruz, Amada, et al. Cindy Sherman. LC 97-26281. (Illus.). 256p. (Orig.). 1997. pap. 35.00 (*0-933856-49-0*) Mus Art Chicago.

— Cindy Sherman Retrospective. 2nd ed. LC 97-60467. (Illus.). 220p. 2000. reprint ed. pap. 34.95 (*0-500-27987-X*, Pub. by Thames Hudson) Norton.

***Cruz, Amada, et al.** Isaac Julien. (Illus.). 112p. 2000. pap. 24.95 (*0-941276-90-2*, Ctr Curatorial Studies) Bard Coll Pubns.

Cruz, Amada, et al. Jana Sterbak. LC 98-38138. (Illus.). 80p. 1998. 23.00 (*0-933856-55-5*) Mus Art Chicago.

Cruz, Amanda. Performance Anxiety: With CD. LC 97-8116. (Illus.). 112p. 1997. pap. text 29.95 (*0-933856-46-6*) Mus Art Chicago.

***Cruz, Amanda, et al, contrib. by.** Takashi Murakami: The Meaning of the Nonsense of the Meaning. (Illus.). 96p. 2000. 22.50 (*0-8109-6702-2*, Pub. by Abrams) Time Warner.

Cruz, Anne J. Imitacion y Transformacion: El Petrarquismo en la Poesia de Boscan y Garcilaso de la Vega. LC 87-36777. (Purdue University Monographs in Romance Languages: Vol. 26). x, 158p. (C). 1988. 47.00 (*1-55619-005-0*) J Benjamins Pubng Co.

Cruz, Anne J. & Johnson, Carroll B., eds. Cervantes & His Postmodern Constituencies. LC 98-35217. (Hispanic Issues Ser.: Vol. 17). 304p. 1998. 65.00 (*0-8153-3206-8*, H2114) Garland.

Cruz, Anne J. & Perry, Mary E., eds. Culture & Control in Counter-Reformation Spain. (Hispanic Issues Ser.: Vol. 7). 288p. (C). 1991. pap. 18.95 (*0-8166-2026-1*); text 47.95 (*0-8166-2025-3*) U of Minn Pr.

Cruz, Anne J., jt. ed. see Perry, Mary E.

Cruz, Arturo J. Nicaragua's Continuing Struggle: In Search of Democracy. Finn, James, ed. LC 87-28072. (Focus on Issues Ser.: No. 4). 1988. 12.95 (*0-932088-20-1*); pap. 5.95 (*0-932088-19-8*) Freedom Hse.

Cruz, Barbara. Americas. (Illus.). 200p. (C). 1993. pap. text, student ed. 23.95 (*0-19-507793-8*) OUP.

— Ruben Blades: Salsa Singer & Social Activist. LC 97-13031. (Hispanic Biographies Ser.). (Illus.). 128p. (YA). (gr. 6 up). 1997. lib. bdg. 20.95 (*0-89490-893-6*) Enslow Pubs.

***Cruz, Barbara.** School Dress Codes: A Pro/Con Issue. LC 00-21972. (Hot Pro/Con Issues Ser.). (Illus.). 2001. lib. bdg. 19.95 (*0-7660-1465-7*) Enslow Pubs.

— Separate Sexes, Separate Schools: A Pro/Con Issue. LC 99-37356. (Hot Pro/Con Issues Ser.). (Illus.). 64p. (gr. 6 up). 2000. lib. bdg. 19.95 (*0-7660-1366-9*) Enslow Pubs.

Cruz, Barbara C. Frida Kahlo: Portrait of a Mexican Painter. LC 96-851. (Hispanic Biographies Ser.). (Illus.). 112p. (YA). (gr. 6 up). 1996. lib. bdg. 20.95 (*0-89490-765-4*) Enslow Pubs.

— Jose Clemente Orozco: Mexican Artist. LC 98-26414. (Hispanic Biographies Ser.). (Illus.). 128p. (YA). (gr. 6 up). 1998. lib. bdg. 20.95 (*0-7660-1041-4*) Enslow Pubs.

— Raul Julia: Actor & Humanitarian. LC 97-37827. (Hispanic Biographies Ser.). (Illus.). 128p. (YA). (gr. 6 up). 1998. lib. bdg. 20.95 (*0-7660-1040-6*) Enslow Pubs.

Cruz, Barbara C., jt. auth. see Bermudez, Pedro R.

Cruz, Bartolomei De La, see De La Cruz, Bartolomei.

Cruz, Ben De la, see Kopp, Linda & De la Cruz, Ben.

Cruz, Ben De la, see De la Cruz, Ben.

Cruz-Bernal, Mairim. Cuando El es Adios. (Aqui y Ahora Ser.). 108p. 1997. pap. 6.95 (*0-8477-0306-1*) U of PR Pr.

Cruz-Bernal, Mairym. On Her Face the Light of la Luna. LC 96-71163. 1997. pap. 10.00 (*0-944854-22-2*) Provincetown Arts.

— On Her Face the Light of la Luna. LC 96-71163. 1998. 35.00 (*0-944854-23-0*) Provincetown Arts.

Cruz, Bill. The Official Generation 'n Pocket Guide to Bill Cruz's CubanAmericanisms. Teck, Bill, ed. (ENG & SPA.). 22p. 1997. pap. 4.95 (*0-9661173-0-1*) O A Prodns.

Cruz, Bill, jt. auth. see Teck, Bill.

Cruz, Bobby. Cuando Era Nino. (SPA.). 1997. pap. 9.99 (*0-88113-237-3*) Caribe Betania.

Cruz, C. Understanding Neural Networks. 156p. 1991. 157.50 (*0-943779-69-3*, Pub. by Elsvr Adv Tech) Elsevier.

Cruz, C. R. Dela, see Dela Cruz, C. R.

Cruz, Carlos, ed. see Cruz, Felix.

Cruz, Carlos, ed. see Cruz, Felix E.

Cruz, Christine M. Dela, see Dela Cruz, Christine M.

***Cruz, Contarini.** Ajilimojili. 1998. 7.95 (*84-241-3371-4*) Everest SP.

Cruz, Cynthia L., jt. auth. see Cruz, Isagani A.

Cruz, Eduardo R. A Theological Study Informed by the Theory of Paul Tillich & the Latin American Experience: The Ambivalence of Science. LC 96-50188. 354p. 1997. text 99.95 (*0-7734-2280-3*) E Mellen.

Cruz Emeric, Rafael. Principios del Diseno Escenografico. (SPA.). 262p. 1979. pap. 8.00 (*0-8477-3190-1*) U of PR Pr.

Cruz, Emmanuel M., ed. see Hopkins, Kevin D.

Cruz, Enrique B. De la, see De la Cruz, Enrique B.

Cruz, Felix. The Way: To Increase Your Will Power & to Better Understand Reality. Cruz, Carlos, ed. pap. 10.00 (*0-9665857-0-4*) EscritoPrime.

Cruz, Felix De La, see Lubs, Herbert A. & De La Cruz, Felix, eds.

***Cruz, Felix E.** The Way: To Increase Your Will Power & to Better Understand Reality. 2nd ed. Cruz, Carlos, ed. (Illus.). 110p. 1999. pap. 10.00 (*0-9665857-1-2*) EscritoPrime.

Cruz, Feodor F. John Dewey's Theory of Community. (American University Studies: Philosophy: Ser. V, Vol. 40). X, 213p. (C). 1987. text 33.50 (*0-8204-0488-8*) P Lang Pubng.

Cruz Fernandez Castro, Maria, jt. auth. see Cunliffe, Barry.

Cruz, Gilbert R. Let There Be Towns: Spanish Municipal Origins in the American Southwest, 1610-1810. LC 87-33553. (Illus.). 256p. (C). 1997. pap. 16.95 (*0-89096-677-X*) Tex A&M Univ Pr.

Cruz, Gladys, et al. Beyond the Culture Tours: Studies in Teaching & Learning with Culturally Diverse Texts. LC 97-955. 144p. 1997. 29.95 (*0-8058-2612-2*); pap. 16.00 (*0-8058-2613-0*) L Erlbaum Assocs.

Cruz Gonzalez, Jose. Calabasas Street. 34p. 1998. pap. 3.50 (*0-87129-829-5*, CA3) Dramatic Pub.

Cruz-Horta, Manuel, Jr., tr. see Schwartz, Robert M.

Cruz, Irving De la, see De la Cruz, Irving.

Cruz, Isagani A. & Cruz, Cynthia L. The Decisions & Dissents of Justice Isagani A. Cruz: Selected & Annotated. LC 96-946757. xviii, 518p. 1997. write for info. (*971-16-0359-4*) Cent Lawbk Sup.

Cruz, Isagani R. Beyond Futility: The Filipino as Critic. LC 84-169203. vii, 96p. (Orig.). (C). 1984. pap. 7.50 (*971-10-0160-8*, Pub. by New Day Pub) Cellar.

Cruz, Jesus. Gentlemen, Bourgeois & Revolutionaries: Political Change & Cultural Persistence among the Spanish Dominant Groups, 1750-1850. (Illus.). 362p. (C). 1996. text 80.00 (*0-521-48198-8*) Cambridge U Pr.

***Cruz, Joan C.** Angels & Devils. LC 98-61407. (Illus.). 301p. 1999. pap. 15.00 (*0-89555-638-3*, 1586) TAN Bks Pubs.

Cruz, Joan C. Eucharistic Miracles & Eucharistic Phenomena in the Lives of the Saints. LC 86-50850. 305p. 1994. pap. 15.00 (*0-89555-303-1*) TAN Bks Pubs.

— The Incorruptibles. LC 77-93992. (Illus.). 1994. pap. 13.50 (*0-89555-066-0*) TAN Bks Pubs.

— Miraculous Images of Our Lady: 100 Famous Catholic Portraits & Statues. LC 92-62149. (Illus.). 441p. (Orig.). 1993. pap. 20.00 (*0-89555-484-4*) TAN Bks Pubs.

— Miraculous Images of Our Lord. (Illus.). 235p. 1995. pap. 13.50 (*0-89555-496-8*) TAN Bks Pubs.

— Mysteries, Marvels, Miracles: In the Lives of the Saints. LC 96-60581. (Illus.). 581p. 1997. pap. 24.00 (*0-89555-541-7*, 1383) TAN Bks Pubs.

— Relics. LC 84-60744. (Illus.). 352p. 1984. pap. 12.95 (*0-87973-701-8*, 701) Our Sunday Visitor.

Cruz, Joan C., compiled by. Prayers & Heavenly Promises. LC 90-70225. (Illus.). 130p. (Orig.). 1990. pap. 5.00 (*0-89555-397-X*) TAN Bks Pubs.

***Cruz, Joan Carroll.** Secular Saints: 250 Canonized & Beatified Lay Men, Women & Children. (Illus.). 800p. 1999. pap. 35.00 (*0-89555-658-8*, 1738) TAN Bks Pubs.

Cruz, Jon. Culture on the Margins: The Black Spiritual & the Rise of American Cultural Interpretation. LC 98-43567. 280p. 1999. 18.95 (*0-691-00474-9*, Pub. by Princeton U Pr) Cal Prin Full Svc.

***Cruz, Jon.** Culture on the Margins: The Black Spiritual & the Rise of American Cultural Interpretation. LC 98-43567. 280p. 1999. 55.00 (*0-691-00473-0*, Pub. by Princeton U Pr) Cal Prin Full Svc.

Cruz, Jose E. Identity & Power: Puerto Rican Politics & the Challenge of Ethnicity. LC 97-45555. (Illus.). 376p. (C). 1998. text 59.95 (*1-56639-604-2*); pap. text 22.95 (*1-56639-605-0*) Temple U Pr.

Cruz, Joseph, jt. auth. see Pollock, John L.

Cruz, Juana I. de la, see De la Cruz, Juana I.

Cruz, Juana Inez De la, see De la Cruz, Juana Inez.

Cruz, Julia, tr. see Hinojosa, Rolando.

Cruz, Julio. Neurologic & Neurosurgical Emergencies. Zorab, Richard, ed. LC 98-7038. (Illus.). 624p. (C). 1998. text 145.00 (*0-7216-6105-X*, W B Saunders Co) Harcrt Hlth Sci Grp.

Cruz, Lopez. La Musica Folklorica de Puerto Rico. 1967. 19.95 (*0-87751-008-3*) E Torres & Sons.

Cruz, Loubel, et al. Identity: Who We Are. (Target Ser.). 160p. (Orig.). (J). (gr. 1-3). 1997. pap. text 11.95 (*0-8167-4276-6*) Troll Communs.

Cruz, M. Amal. 200p. (Orig.). 1987. pap. 9.95 (*0-915597-45-4*) Amana Bks.

— Exiles. LC 86-60588. 294p. 1986. 22.00 (*0-932966-71-3*) Permanent Pr.

— October in Cairo. LC 86-2807. 253p. 1988. 22.00 (*0-932966-84-5*) Permanent Pr.

Cruz, M. & Ignashev, S. P. Tagalog-Russian Dictionary. deluxe ed. (RUS & TAG.). 388p. 1959. 14.95 (*0-8288-6846-8*, M-9052) Fr & Eur.

Cruz, M. V. De la, see De la Cruz, M. V.

Cruz, Manny & Symington, Nikki. Alice Barnes: American Activist. Kern, Ann T., ed. LC 82-74177. (Illus.). 52p. (Orig.). 1982. pap. 7.50 (*0-911719-00-8*) Connections CA.

Cruz, Manuel & Cruz, Ruth. A Chicano Christmas Story. LC 80-69444. (SPA., Illus.). 48p. (Orig.). (J). (ps-5). 1981. pap. text 3.95 (*0-86624-000-4*, RM7) Bilingual Ed Serv.

Cruz, Martin De la, see De la Cruz, Martin.

Cruz-Melendez, Josefina, tr. Mexican Autobiography (La Autobiografia Mexicana) An Annotated Bibliography (Una Bibliografia Razonada), 13. LC 88-3129. 245p. 1988. lib. bdg. 75.00 (*0-313-25945-3*, WDX/) Greenwood.

Cruz Mendizabal, Juan, jt. auth. see Guerra Garrido, Raul.

Cruz, Michael M. Field of Screams: How to Promote Halloween & Haunted Attractions. Kennedy, John W., ed. (Illus.). 112p. (C). 1995. pap. text 19.95 (*1-887737-00-6*) Eureka Publng.

Cruz, Migdalia. Las Flores de Miriam. Presbyter's Peartree Staff, tr. from ENG. (SPA.). 53p. 1994. pap. text 3.95 (*1-885901-13-5*) Presbyters Peartree.

Cruz Monclava, Lidio. Historia de Puerto Rico: Siglo XIX, 6 vols., Set. (C). pap. 55.00 (*0-8477-0801-2*) U of PR Pr.

Cruz Monclava, Lidio, jt. auth. see Bothwell, Reece B.

Cruz, Nicky. Cegados por la Noche.Tr. of Blinded by the Night. (SPA.). 100. 8.99 (*1-56063-897-4*, 550137) Editorial Unilit.

Cruz, Nicky. Ciego por la Noche.Tr. of Blinded by the Night. (SPA.). 290p. 1995. pap. write for info. (*0-614-27001-4*) Editorial Unilit.

— Ciego Por la Noche - Blinded by the Night. (SPA.). 290p. 1995. write for info. (*0-614-24352-1*) Editorial Unilit.

— Code Blue: Respuesta a la Emergencia de la Crisis Juvenil.Tr. of Code Blue: Urgent Care for American Youth. (SPA.). 1996. 8.99 (*0-7899-0170-6*, 550138) Editorial Unilit.

— Como Contraatacar.Tr. of How to Fight Back. (SPA.). 211p. 1995. 7.99 (*1-56063-779-X*, 550133) Editorial Unilit.

— Corre! Nicky, Corre!Tr. of Run Baby Run. (SPA.). 304p. (J). 1972. pap. 6.99 (*0-8297-0434-5*) Vida Pubs.

— David Wilkerson: A Final Warning. LC 91-60215. 208p. 1991. reprint ed. pap. 9.95 (*0-89221-194-6*) New Leaf.

— David Wilkerson: La Ultima Advertencia.Tr. of David Wilkerson: A Final Warning. (SPA.). 183p. 1994. pap. 6.99 (*1-56063-508-8*, 550132) Editorial Unilit.

— David Wilkerson: The Final Warning. 207p. (C). 1990. pap. text 8.95 (*0-926557-21-1*) Omega Pubns OR.

— Despiertate, Iglesia - La Victoria Es Nuestra.Tr. of Brothers & Sisters, We Have a Problem. (SPA.). 160p. (Orig.). 1988. pap. 6.99 (*0-926557-07-6*, 490244) Editorial Unilit.

— Devuelveme Mi Dignidad.Tr. of Give Me Back My Dignity. (SPA.). 280p. write for info. (*1-56063-898-2*) Editorial Unilit.

Cruz, Nicky. Devuelveme Mi Dignidad.Tr. of Give Me Back My Dignity. (SPA.). 100. 10.99 (*1-56063-829-X*, 550135) Editorial Unilit.

Cruz, Nicky. Donde Estabas Tu Cuando Yo Estaba Herido?Tr. of Where Were You When I Was Hurting?. (SPA.). 166p. 1987. pap. 5.99 (*0-8423-6526-6*, 490243) Editorial Unilit.

— La Manana del Armagedon.Tr. of Armageddon by Morning. (SPA.). 275p. 1994. 7.99 (*1-56063-415-4*, 550131) Editorial Unilit.

— Rompiendo la Maldicion.Tr. of Devil on the Run. (SPA.). 259p. 6.99 (*1-56063-404-9*, 550130) Editorial Unilit.

Cruz, Nicky & Buckingham, Jamie. Run Baby Run: The Explosive True Story of a Savage Street Fighter. LC 68-23446. 360p. 1988. pap. 10.99 (*0-88270-630-6*) Bridge-Logos.

Cruz, Pedro Da, see Da Cruz, Pedro.

Cruz, Peter De, see De Cruz, Peter.

Cruz, Philip S. Aquaculture Feed & Fertilizer Resource Atlas of the Philippines. (FAO Fisheries Technical Paper Ser.: Series 09005681, No. 366). 274p. 1998. 29.00 (*92-5-104044-3*, F40443, Pub. by FAO) Bernan Associates.

Cruz, Rafael. Analisis Arqueologico del Yacimiento de Obsidiana de Sierra de las Navajas, Hidalgo. 122p. 1994. pap. 6.00 (*968-29-5130-5*, IN056) UCLAAP.

***Cruz, Rene.** Ricky Martin: Story Of. (Illus.). 48p. 1999. pap. 9.95 (*0-8256-1759-6*) Music Sales.

Cruz, Ricardo C. Five Days of Bleeding. 150p. (Orig.). 1995. pap. 7.95 (*1-57366-003-5*) Fiction Coll.

— Straight Outta Compton. 121p. 1992. 18.95 (*0-932511-60-0*); pap. 8.95 (*0-932511-61-9*) Fiction Coll.

Cruz, Rodolfo A. Instrucciones Practicas para Nuevos Creyentes. LC 77-71308. (SPA.). 78p. (Orig.). 1990. pap. text 3.99 (*0-89922-002-9*) Caribe Betania.

Cruz, Rosa Ana Dominguez, tr. see Amberlain, Robert.

Cruz, Rosa M., jt. ed. see Sanchez, Rosaura.

Cruz, Ruth, jt. auth. see Cruz, Manuel.

Cruz-Saenz, Michele S. De, see De Cruz-Saenz, Michele S.

Cruz, San Juan de la, see San Juan de la Cruz.

Cruz-Sanchez, F. F. Neuropathological Diagnostic Criteria for Brain Banking. LC 94-73422. (Biomedical & Health Research Ser.: Vol. 10). 166p. (gr. 12). 1995. 77.00 (*90-5199-208-4*) IOS Press.

Cruz-Sanchez, F. F. & Tolosa, E., eds. How to Run a Brain Bank. (Journal of Neural Transmission: Suppl. 39). (Illus.). 240p. 1993. 93.00 (*0-387-82426-X*) Spr-Verlag.

Cruz, Sor J. De La, see De La Cruz, Sor J.

Cruz, Stephen De, see Lyon, C. M. & De Cruz, Stephen.

***Cruz, Tomas.** Ultimate Health Secrets: Feel Great, Look Younger, Keep Fit! LC 99-93964. 100p. 2000. pap. 14.75 (*0-9672376-0-2*) TransGlobal Pubng.

Cruz-Trinidad, A., ed. Valuation of Tropical Coastal Resources: Theory & Application of Linear Programming. (ICLARM Studies & Reviews: No. 25). (Illus.). 108p. 1995. pap. 49.95 (*971-8709-72-X*, Pub. by ICLARM) Intl Spec Bk.

Cruz-Trinidad, A., et al. Bioeconomics of the Philippine Small Pelagics Fishery. (ICLARM Technical Reports: No. 38). 74p. 1993. write for info. (*971-8709-38-X*, Pub. by ICLARM) Intl Spec Bk.

Cruz-Uribe, Eugene. Hibis Temple Project, Vol. 1: Translations, Commentary, Discussions & Sign List. (Illus.). xvii, 276p. 1988. pap. 55,00 (*0-933175-14-0*) Van Siclen Bks.

Cruz-Uribe, Kathryn, jt. auth. see Klein, Richard G.

Cruz, Valdir. Catedral Basilica de Nossa Senhora da Luz dos Pinhais. (SPA., Illus.). 120p. (Orig.). 1996. 50.00 (*0-9652311-0-0*); pap. 35.00 (*0-9652311-1-9*) Brave Wolf.

Cruz, Victor H. Red Beans. LC 91-25377. 160p. (Orig.). 1991. pap. 11.95 (*0-918273-91-9*) Coffee Hse.

Cruz, Victor H., et al, eds. Paper Dance: 55 Latino Poets. 256p. (Orig.). 1995. pap. 13.95 (*0-89255-201-8*) Persea Bks.

Cruz, Virgil, jt. ed. see Coalter, Milton J.

Cruz, Wilfrido, et al. Urban & Industrial Management in Developing Countries: Lessons from Japanese Experience. LC 98-15951. (EDI Learning Resources Ser.). 65p. 1998. pap. 22.00 (*0-8213-4201-0*, 14201) World Bank.

Cruz, Wilfrido, jt. auth. see Repetto, Robert C.

Cruz, Yolanda P. Laboratory Exercises in Developmental Biology. (Illus.). 241p. 1993. pap. 19.95 (*0-12-198390-0*) Acad Pr.

Cruzan, Patricia. Sketches of Life: A Book of Poems. (Illus.). viii, 42p. (Orig.). 1996. pap. 7.95 (*0-9653543-0-X*) Clear Creek Pubs.

— Tall Tales of the United States. LC 96-92802. (Illus.). 38p. (Orig.). (J). (gr. 3-5). 1996. pap. 7.95 (*0-9653543-1-8*) Clear Creek Pubs.

— Tall Tales of the United States. LC 96-92802. (Illus.). 38p. (Orig.). (J). (gr. 3-5). 1997. lib. bdg. 13.95 (*0-9653543-2-6*) Clear Creek Pubs.

Cruzan, Ray. Applegate. LC 88-84113. 582p. 1989. 19.95 (*0-925774-00-6*) Ashton Woods.

Cruzeiro, A. B. & Zambrini, J. C., eds. Stochastic Analysis & Applications: Proceedings of the 1989 Lisbon Conference. (Progress in Probability Ser.: Vol. 26). vii, 197p. 1991. 69.00 (*0-8176-3567-X*) Birkhauser.

Crvenkovski, et al. Standard English - Macedonian, Macedonian - English Dictionary. (ENG & MAC.). 1000p. 1990. 95.00 (*0-8288-8225-8*, F131370) Fr & Eur.

Crwys-Williams, Jennifer. In the Words of Nelson Mandela: A Little Pocketbook LC 98-163097. xiii, 98 p. 1997. write for info. (*0-14-027049-3*, Penguin Bks) Viking Penguin.

— Thoughts of Nelson Mandela. LC 98-28561. (Illus.). 1998. pap. 12.95 (*1-55972-492-7*, Birch Ln Pr) Carol Pub Group.

Cryan-Hicks, Kathryn. W. E. B. Du Bois: Crusader for Peace. LC 91-70820. (Picture-Book Biography). (Illus.). 48p. (J). (gr. 4-8). 1991. 14.95 (*1-878668-05-6*); pap. 7.95 (*1-878668-09-9*) Disc Enter Ltd.

Cryan-Hicks, Kathryn, intro. Pride & Promise: The Harlem Renaissance. LC 93-72240. (Perspectives on History Ser.). (Illus.). 52p. (YA). (gr. 5-12). 1994. pap. 6.95 (*1-878668-30-7*) Disc Enter Ltd.

Cryan, Robert A. & Senior, John M., eds. All-Optical Communication Systems Vol. 2919: Architecture, Control & Network Issues II. 316p. 1996. 56.00 (*0-8194-2321-1*) SPIE.

Cryderman, Lynn. Glory Land: A Memoir of a Lifetime in Church. LC 99-10104. 176p. 2000. 14.99 (*0-310-22454-3*) Zondervan.

Cryer. Statistics F/business: Data Analys & Modeling. 3rd ed. (Business Statistics Ser.). 2001. pap. 53.75 (*0-534-52506-7*) PWS Pubs.

— Statistics for Business. 2nd ed. (Business Statistics Ser.). 1994. pap., student ed. 19.95 (*0-534-20391-4*) Wadsworth Pub.

— Swimming. 116p. 1997. pap. text 22.00 (*0-13-777871-6*) P-H.

Cryer & Lovelace. Statistics for Business. 2nd ed. (Business Statistics Ser.). 1994. pap., suppl. ed. 18.95 (*0-534-20393-0*) Wadsworth Pub.

Cryer, jt. auth. see Childre, Doc Lew.

Cryer, A., jt. auth. see Liddell, J. Eryl.

Cryer, Bruce, jt. auth. see Childre, Doc Lew.

Cryer, Bruce, ed. see Childre, Doc Lew.

Cryer, D., et al. Nutrition Activities for Preschoolers. (Illus.). 288p. (Orig.). (J). (ps). 1996. pap. 31.20 (*0-201-49452-3*) Addison-Wesley.

C

An Asterisk (*) at the beginning of an entry indicates that the title is appearing for the first time.

Cryer, Debby. Active Learning for Infants. 1987. text 20.95 (*0-201-21334-6*) Addison-Wesley.
— Active Learning for Threes. 1988. text 20.95 (*0-201-21337-0*) Addison-Wesley.
— Active Learning for Twos. 1988. text 20.95 (*0-201-21336-2*) Addison-Wesley.
***Cryer, Debby & Harms, Thelma.** Infants & Toddlers in Out-of-Home Care. LC 00-26375. 2000. write for info. (*1-55766-457-9*) P H Brookes.
Cryer, Debby, et al. Active Learning for Fives. (Active Learning Ser.). (Illus.). 450p. (Orig.). (J). (ps). 1995. pap. text 23.25 (*0-201-49401-9*) Addison-Wesley.
— Active Learning for Fours. (Active Learning Ser.). (Illus.). 402p. 1995. pap. text 23.25 (*0-201-49400-0*) Addison-Wesley.
Cryer, Debby, jt. auth. see Harms, Thelma.
Cryer, Frederick H. Divination in Ancient Israel & Its Near Eastern Environment: A Socio-Historical Investigation. LC 94-212235. (Journal for the Study of the Old Testament Supplement Ser.: No. 142). 367p. (C). 1994. 85.00 (*1-85075-353-9*, Pub. by Sheffield Acad) CUP Services.
Cryer, Frederick H. & Thompson, Thomas L., eds. Qumran Between the Old & New Testaments. (JSOTS Ser.: Vol. 290). 398p. 1998. 85.00 (*1-85075-905-7*, Pub. by Sheffield Acad) CUP Services.
Cryer, Jon & Cobb, George. Electronic Companion to Business Statistics. Venable, Alan, ed. (Electronic Companion Ser.). (Illus.). 300p. (Orig.). (C). 1997. pap. text, wbk. ed. 29.95 (*1-888902-24-8*); pap. text, wbk. ed. 29.95 incl. cd-rom (*1-888902-44-2*) Cogito Lrning.
Cryer, Jon, jt. auth. see Cobb, George.
Cryer, Jonathan D. & Miller, Robert B. Statistics for Business: Data Analysis & Modeling. 2nd ed. 883p. 1994. pap. 75.95 (*0-534-20388-4*) Wadsworth Pub.
— Statistics For Business:analy & Modeling. (Business Statistics). 848p. (C). 1990. pap. 51.25 (*0-534-92239-2*) Wadsworth Pub.
Cryer, Leona. Deaths & Burials in St. Mary's County, Maryland. 447p. (Orig.). 1995. pap. text 33.00 (*0-7884-0173-4*) Heritage Bk.
Cryer, Neil. Graphics on the BBC Microcomputer. 1983. 24.95 (*0-13-363283-0*) P-H.
Cryer, Neil & Cryer, Pat. BASIC Programming on the BBC Microcomputer. xii, 195p. 1982. pap. 11.95 (*0-685-07036-0*) P-H.
Cryer, Pat. The Research Student's Guide to Success. 192p. 1996. 87.95 (*0-335-19612-8*); pap. 27.95 (*0-335-19611-X*) OpUniv Pr.
***Cryer, Pat.** The Research Student's Guide to Success. 2nd ed. LC 00-37514. 2000. pap. write for info. (*0-335-20686-7*) Taylor & Francis.
Cryer, Pat, jt. auth. see Cryer, Neil.
Cryer, Philip E. Hypoglycemia: Pathophysiology, Diagnosis, & Treatment. LC 96-54723. (Illus.). 198p. (C). 1997. text 49.95 (*0-19-511325-X*) OUP.
Cryer, Sara. Reflections on Living. LC 99-159507. (Illus.). 304p. 1998. pap. 16.95 (*1-56589-098-1*) Crystal Clarity.
Cryer, Tom. Visual Testament & the Israelite Indian. (Illus.). 432p. 1999. pap. text 24.95 (*1-890558-48-6*, 58486) Granite UT.
Cryer, W. R. The Glory of God Revealed No. 1: The Divine Nature. LC 94-96167. 90p. (Orig.). 1995. pap. 7.95 (*0-9642412-0-X*) Glory Pubns.
Cryle, Denis. The Press in Colonial Queensland: A Social & Political History, 1845-1875. (Illus.). 350p. (Orig.). 1989. pap. text 29.95 (*0-7022-2181-3*, Pub. by Univ Queensland Pr) Intl Spec Bk.
Cryle, Denis, ed. Disreputable Profession: Journalism & Journalists in the 19th Century Australia. LC 97-179322. 178p. 1997. pap. 19.95 (*1-875998-18-7*, Pub. by Central Queensland) Accents Pubns.
Cryle, Denis, jt. auth. see Dornan, Dimity.
Cryle, Peter. Geometry in the Boudoir: Configurations of French Erotic Narrative. 328p. 1994. text 47.50 (*0-8014-2913-7*); pap. text 18.95 (*0-8014-8185-6*) Cornell U Pr.
Cryle, Peter M. The Thematics of Commitment: The Tower & the Plain. LC 84-42590. 470p. 1985. reprint ed. pap. 145.70 (*0-608-02890-8*, 206395400007) Bks Demand.
Crymes, Ruth. Some Systems of Substitution Correlations in Modern American English: With Implications for the Teaching of English As a Second Language. (Janua Linguarum, Ser. Major: No. 23). 1968. text 64.65 (*90-279-0614-9*) Mouton.
Crymes, Ruth H., jt. auth. see Shen, Yao.
Cryne. Criminal Law Review. (C). 2000. mass mkt., lab manual ed. 24.50 (*0-314-12594-9*) Delmar.
Crynes, Billy L., jt. ed. see Albright, Lyle F.
Cryogenic Engineering Conference Staff. International Advances in Cryogenic Engineering: Proceedings of the 1964 Cryogenic Engineering Conference. Timmerhaus, K. D., ed. LC 57-35598. 439p. 1965. reprint ed. pap. 136.10 (*0-608-05560-3*, 206602800006) Bks Demand.
Cryogenic Processes & Equipment Conference Staff. Cryogenic Processes & Equipment in Energy Systems: Presented at the Cryogenic Processes & Equipment Conference, Century 2-Emerging Technology Conference, San Francisco, CA, August 19-21, 1980. Toscano, W. M. et al, eds. LC 80-66045. 201p. reprint ed. pap. 62.40 (*0-608-17871-3*, 203270300080) Bks Demand.
Cryogenic Society of America, LNG Terminals & Safe. Applications of Cryogenic Technology: Proceedings, Vol. 9. Petsinger, Robert E. & Vance, Robert W., eds. LC 68-57815. 1979. 45.00 (*0-87936-014-3*) Scholium Intl.
Crysdale, Cynthia. Embracing Travail: Retrieving a Theology of the Cross for Today. LC 98-55485. 216p. 1999. 24.95 (*0-8264-1160-6*) Continuum.
Crysdale, Cynthia S., ed. Lonergan & Feminism. (Lonergan Studies). 228p. 1994. text 55.00 (*0-8020-5024-7*); pap. text 18.95 (*0-8020-7432-4*) U of Toronto Pr.
Crysdale, Stewart, et al. On Their Own: Making the Transition from School to Work in the Information Age. 222p. 55.00 (*0-7735-1785-5*); pap. 19.95 (*0-7735-1805-3*) McG-Queens Univ Pr.
Crysler, Julie. Get Stuffed Toronto: Eating Out in Toronto for under $15. 124p. 1998. mass mkt. write for info. (*1-895837-43-X*) Insomniac.
Crystal. Language A to Z, Bk. 2. 1991. pap. text. write for info. (*0-582-07564-5*, Pub. by Addison-Wesley) Longman.
Crystal, David. The Cambridge Encyclopedia of Language. 2nd ed. (Illus.). 488p. (C). 1997. text 69.95 (*0-521-55050-5*) Cambridge U Pr.
— The Cambridge Encyclopedia of Language. 2nd ed. (Illus.). 488p. (C). 1997. pap. 29.95 (*0-521-55967-7*) Cambridge U Pr.
— The Cambridge Encyclopedia of the English Language. (Illus.). 500p. 1995. text 64.95 (*0-521-40179-8*) Cambridge U Pr.
— The Cambridge Encyclopedia of the English Language. (Illus.). 500p. 1997. pap. 29.95 (*0-521-59655-6*) Cambridge U Pr.
— The Cambridge Factfinder. 3rd rev. ed. LC 97-35278. (Illus.). 912p. (C). 1998. pap. 16.95 (*0-521-63770-8*) Cambridge U Pr.
— Clinical Linguistics. 240p. 1981. 39.95 (*1-56593-521-7*, 0021) Singular Publishing.
— A Dictionary of Linguistics & Phonetics. 4th ed. LC 96-7651. (Language Library Ser.). 416p. 1996. pap. 28.95 (*0-631-20097-5*) Blackwell Pubs.
— English As a Global Language. LC 97-5003. (Illus.). 160p. (C). 1997. 19.95 (*0-521-59247-X*) Cambridge U Pr.
— English As a Global Language. (Canto Book Ser.). (Illus.). 160p. (C). 1998. pap. 12.95 (*0-521-62994-2*) Cambridge U Pr.
***Crystal, David.** Language Death. 208p. 2000. 19.95 (*0-521-65321-5*) Cambridge U Pr.
— Language Play. 272p. 1998. pap. 14.95 (*0-14-027385-9*, Pub. by Pnguin Bks Ltd) Trafalgar.
— Linguistics. 1990. pap. 15.95 (*0-14-013531-6*, Pub. by Pnguin Bks Ltd) Trafalgar.
— Listen to Your Child: A Parent's Guide. pap. 15.95 (*0-14-011015-1*, Pub. by Pnguin Bks Ltd) Trafalgar.
Crystal, David. Rediscover Grammar. (J). 1987. pap. text 15.08 (*0-582-00258-3*, 78071) Longman.
Crystal, David, ed. The Cambridge Biographical Dictionary. 505p. (C). 1996. pap. 17.95 (*0-521-56780-7*) Cambridge U Pr.
— The Cambridge Biographical Encyclopedia. 2nd rev. ed. LC 97-34577. (Illus.). 1264p. (C). 1998. 54.95 (*0-521-63099-1*) Cambridge U Pr.
***Crystal, David, ed.** The Cambridge Encyclopedia. (Illus.). 1341p. (C). 2000. 59.95 (*0-521-79099-9*) Cambridge U Pr.
Crystal, David, ed. The Cambridge Encyclopedia. 3rd ed. (Illus.). 1344p. (C). 1997. 54.95 (*0-521-58459-0*) Cambridge U Pr.
***Crystal, David, ed.** The Cambridge Factfinder. (Illus.). 912p. 2000. pap. 16.95 (*0-521-79435-8*) Cambridge U Pr.
— The Cambridge Paperback Encyclopedia. 3rd ed. LC 98-56011. (Illus.). 1088p. 1999. pap. 19.95 (*0-521-66800-X*) Cambridge U Pr.
***Crystal, David & Crystal, Hilary.** Words on Words: Quotations about Language & Languages. LC 00-39221. 2000. pap. write for info. (*0-226-12201-8*) U Ch Pr.
Crystal, David & Quirk, Randolph. Systems of Prosodic & Paralinguistic Features in English. (Janua Linguarum, Ser. Minor: No. 39). (Orig.). 1964. pap. text 26.15 (*90-279-0574-6*) Mouton.
Crystal, David & Varley, Rosemary. Introduction to Language Pathology. 3rd ed. (Illus.). 260p. (C). 1993. pap. text 45.00 (*1-56593-242-0*, 0564) Thomson Learn.
— Introduction to Language Pathology, 1. 4th ed. LC 99-166943. 267p. 1998. pap. text 34.95 (*1-86156-071-0*) Whurr Pub.
Crystal, David, et al. Grammatical Analysis of Language Disability. 2nd ed. (Illus.). 200p. (C). 1990. pap. text 39.95 (*1-879105-00-4*, A018) Singular Publishing.
Crystal, Graef S. In Search of Excess: The Overcompensation of American Executives. 272p. 1999. reprint ed. text 20.00 (*0-7881-6150-4*) DIANE Pub.
— Questions & Answers on Executive Compensation: How to Get What You're Worth. LC 84-11630. 196p. 1984. 27.50 (*0-13-748476-3*, Busn); pap. 9.95 (*0-13-748468-2*, Busn) P-H.
Crystal, Hilary, jt. auth. see Crystal, David.
Crystal, Michael R. Peterson's SAT Math Flash: The Quick & Easy Way to Learn & Apply Math Skills. 2nd rev. ed. Moscowitz, Mark, ed. LC 97-9127. 208p. (YA). 1997. pap. 8.95 (*1-56079-849-1*) Petersons.
— SAT Math Flash: The Quick Way to Build Math Power for the New SAT - & Beyond. LC 93-23413. 144p. (Orig.). 1993. pap. 7.95 (*1-56079-321-X*) Petersons.
***Crystal, Michael R.** SAT Math Flash 2001. 3rd ed. 222p. 2000. pap. 9.95 (*0-7689-0507-9*) Petersons.
Crystal, Michael R., jt. auth. see Carris, Joan.
Crystal, Nancy, jt. auth. see Tytla, Milan.
Crystal, Nathan. Professional Responsibility: Problems of Practice & the Profession. LC 95-80363. 736p. 1996. teacher ed. write for info. (*0-316-16379-1*, 63791) Aspen Law.
***Crystal, Nathan M.** Professional Responsibility: Problems of Practice & the Profession. 2nd ed. LC 00-20258. 2000. text 58.00 (*0-7355-1207-8*) Panel Pubs.
Crystal, Nathan M., jt. auth. see Knapp, Charles L.
Crystal Productions Staff. Cave Art Prints. (Illus.). (Orig.). 1996. pap., teacher ed. 29.95 (*1-56290-165-6*, 6063) Crystal.
Crystal, Ronald G., ed. Alpha 1-Antitrypsin Deficiency. (Lung Biology in Health & Disease Ser.: Vol. 88). (Illus.). 472p. 1995. text 190.00 (*0-8247-8848-6*) Dekker.
— The Biochemical Basis of Pulmonary Function. LC 75-25165. (Lung Biology in Health & Disease Ser.: Vol. 2). 556p. reprint ed. pap. 172.40 (*0-8357-7215-2*, 202707300054) Bks Demand.
Crystal, Ronald G., et al, eds. The Lung: Scientific Foundations, 2 vols. 2nd ed. LC 96-14140. 2,710p. 1996. text 352.00 (*0-397-51632-0*) Lppncott W & W.
Crystal, Ronald G. & West, John B., eds. Lung Injury. LC 91-32568. (Illus.). 416p. 1992. reprint ed. pap. 129.00 (*0-608-07188-9*, 206741300009) Bks Demand.
Crystal, Ruth C. Angel Talk. rev. ed. LC 95-61345. (Illus.). 192p. 1996. 19.95 (*1-887010-01-7*) Edin Bks.
Crystal, Ruth C. Think About Angels. (Illus.). 188p. 1997. write for info. (*1-882194-42-X*) TN Valley Pub.
Crystal, Stephen, et al. The Management of Home Care Services. 192p. 1987. 24.95 (*0-8261-5660-6*) Springer Pub.
Crystall, Ellen. Silent Invasion. 1996. mass mkt. 6.50 (*0-312-95935-4*) St Martin.
Crystian, Carol P. Payne & Pleasure of a Black Woman. (Orig.). 1997. pap. write for info. (*1-57553-433-9*) Watermrk Pr.
Cryz, S. J. Vaccines & Immunotherapy. (Illus.). 448p. 1991. 94.50 (*0-08-036083-1*, Pub. by PPI) McGraw.
Cryz, S. J., ed. Vaccines & Immunotherapy. 496p. 1991. text 94.50 (*0-07-105380-8*) McGraw-Hill HPD.
Cryz, Stanley. Immunotherapy & Vaccines. LC 90-13146. 150p. 1990. 90.00 (*0-89573-969-0*, Wiley-VCH) Wiley.
C.S. Mott Childrens Hospital Staff. Michigan Cooks: Favorite Recipes from Friends of C. S. Mott Childrens' Hospital University of Michigan. (Illus.). 1997. 16.95 (*0-9652189-0-2*) UMI Hlth System.
Csaba, G. The Ontogeny & Phylogeny of Hormone Receptors. (Monographs in Developmental Biology: Vol. 15). (Illus.). xii, 172p. 1981. 125.25 (*3-8055-2174-X*) S Karger.
Csaba, Gyorgy. Development of Hormone Receptors. (BioSeries-EXS: No. 53). 200p. 1987. 113.50 (*0-8176-1858-9*) Birkhauser.
Csaba, L., et al, eds. Computer Networking: Proceedings of the IFIP TC6 Conference (COMNET '90), Budapest, Hungary, 8-10 May, 1990. xii,508p. 1990. 160.00 (*0-444-88872-1*, North Holland) Elsevier.
Csaba, Laszlo. The Capitalist Revolution in Eastern Europe: A Contribution to the Economic Theory of Systemic Change. (Studies of Communism in Transition). 352p. 1995. 95.00 (*1-85278-672-8*) E Elgar.
— Eastern Europe in the World Economy. (Cambridge Russian, Soviet & Post-Soviet Studies: No. 68). 403p. (C). 1991. text 69.95 (*0-521-33426-8*) Cambridge U Pr.
— Privatization, Liberalization & Destruction: Recreating the Market in Central & Eastern Europe. 320p. 1994. 77.95 (*1-85521-398-2*, Pub. by Dartmth Pub) Ashgate Pub Co.
— Systemic Change & Stabilization in Eastern Europe. 152p. 1991. 72.95 (*1-85521-204-8*, Pub. by Dartmth Pub) Ashgate Pub Co.
Csaba, Varga. Codification As a Socio Historical Phenomenon. 391p. (C). 1991. pap. 95.00 (*963-05-6012-7*, Pub. by Akade Kiado) St Mut.
Csaki, C. Simulation & Systems Analysis in Agriculture. (Developments in Agricultural Engineering Ser.: Vol. 2). 262p. 1985. 142.00 (*0-444-99622-2*) Elsevier.
Csaki, Csaba & Lerman, Zvi. Land Reform in Ukraine: The First Five Years. LC 97-28277. (Discussion Paper Ser.: No. 371R). 126p. 1997. pap. 22.00 (*0-8213-4008-5*, 14008) World Bank.
— Land Reform in Ukraine: The First Five Years. (Discussion Paper Ser.: No. 371R). (RUS.). 139p. 1998. pap. 22.00 (*0-8213-4302-5*, 14302) World Bank.
Csaki, Csaba & Nash, John. Regional & International Trade Policy: Lessons for the EU Association in the Rural Sector World Bank/FAO Workshop June 20-23, 1998, Budapest, Hungary. LC 99-30860. (Technical Paper Ser.: No. 434). 112p. 1999. pap. 22.00 (*0-8213-4487-0*, 14487) World Bank.
Csaki, Csaba & Nash, John D. The Agrarian Economies of Central & Eastern Europe & the Commonwealth of Independent States: Situation & Perspective, 1997. LC 98-24255. (Discussion Paper Ser.: No. 387). 160p. 1998. pap. 22.00 (*0-8213-4238-X*, 14238) World Bank.
Csaki, Csaba, et al. Food & Agriculture in the Czech Republic: From a "Velvet" Transition to the Challenges of EU Accession. LC 99-29001. (Technical Paper Ser.: No. 437). 112p. 1999. pap. 22.00 (*0-8213-4502-8*, 14502) World Bank.
Csaki, F., et al, eds. Power Electronics, Problems Manual. 474p. (C). 1979. 114.00 (*963-05-1671-3*, Pub. by Akade Kiado) St Mut.
Csaki, F., et al. Power Electronics. 708p. (C). 1983. 168.00 (*963-05-3530-0*, Pub. by Akade Kiado) St Mut.
Csaki, N. Land Supply & International Specialisation in Agriculture. (Geography of World Agriculture Ser.: No. 3). 102p. (C). 1974. 25.00 (*963-05-0172-4*, Pub. by Akade Kiado) St Mut.
***Csala, Gottfried P.** Vienna, 1850-1950: History Through the Eyes of One Family. 268p. 1999. pap. 17.95 (*0-7392-0340-1*, PO3513) Morris Pubng.
Csampai, Attila. Callas: Images of a Legend. LC 96-67554. (Illus.). 264p. 1996. 75.00 (*1-55670-483-6*) Stewart Tabori & Chang.
Csanadi, Maria. Party-States & Their Legacies in Post-Communist Transformation. LC 97-25009. (Studies of Communism in Transition). 448p. 1997. 100.00 (*1-85898-645-1*) E Elgar.
Csanady, G. T. Circulation in the Coastal Ocean. 1982. text 176.50 (*90-277-1400-2*) Kluwer Academic.
— Turbulent Diffusion in the Environment. LC 72-92527. (Geophysics & Astrophysics Monographs: No. 3). (Illus.). 248p. 1973. pap. text 71.50 (*90-277-0261-6*) Kluwer Academic.
Csanyi, V. General Theory of Evolution. (Studia Biologica Hungarica Ser.: No. 18). 122p. (C). 1982. pap. 21.00 (*963-05-2823-1*, Pub. by Akade Kiado) St Mut.
Csanyi, Vilmos. Evolutionary Systems & Society: A General Theory. LC 88-7149. 304p. (C). 1988. text 59.95 (*0-8223-0836-3*) Duke.
Csapo, Georg, jt. ed. see Roskamm, Helmut.
***Csapo, Gizella M.** Nostalgia. LC 98-91051. 1999. pap. 5.95 (*0-533-13027-1*) Vantage.
Csapodi, Csaba. A Paris Book of Hours, Vol. 1. (Illus.). 1999. pap. 14.00 (*963-13-2397-8*, Pub. by Corvina Bks) St Mut.
— A Paris Book of Hours, Vol. 2. (Illus.). 1999. pap. 14.00 (*963-13-2398-6*, Pub. by Corvina Bks) St Mut.
Csapody, V. & Javorka, S. Iconographia Florae Partis Austro-Orientalis, Europae Centralis: Austro-Orientalis Europae Centralis. Priszter, J., ed. (ENG & LAT., Illus.). 576p. (C). 1991. 360.00 (*963-05-5896-3*, Pub. by Akade Kiado) St Mut.
Csapody, V. & Toth, I. A Colour Atlas of Flowering Trees & Shrubs. (Illus.). 310p. (C). 1982. 132.00 (*963-05-2783-9*, Pub. by Akade Kiado) St Mut.
— A Colour Atlas of Flowering Trees & Shrubs. 312p. 1982. 275.00 (*0-569-08743-0*) St Mut.
Csaszar, Sonia, tr. see Garbarino, James.
Csato, Eva Agnes, jt. ed. see Johanson, Lars.
Csatorday, Hajnal, tr. see Kun, Miklos.
CSB Staff. Clinician's Choice. 1994. 29.50 (*0-7616-3170-4*) Commun Skill.
Csboti, Mbarianna. People Skills for Young Adults. LC 98-45887. 1999. pap. 29.95 (*1-85302-716-2*) Taylor & Francis.
Csce121 Staff. Biology 121. 1998. pap. 6.25 (*0-07-234102-5*) McGraw.
***Csech, Werner V.** Die Raumlehre Johann Gottlieb Fichtes: Mit Berucksichtigung Philosophiegeschichtlicher Konstellationen. (Illus.). 463p. 1999. 67.95 (*3-631-34536-4*) P Lang Pubng.
Csecsei, G., et al. Primary & Secondary Brain Stem Lesions. (Illus.). 150p. 1987. 131.00 (*0-387-82025-6*) Spr-Verlag.
Csefalvay, Pal. The Christian Museum of Esztergom. (Illus.). 260p. 1999. 65.00 (*963-13-3896-7*, Pub. by Corvina Bks) St Mut.
Csellak, Bill, ed. see Simpson, Drake & Simpson, Debi.
***Csendes, Peter.** Historical Dictionary of Vienna. LC 98-35171. (Historical Dictionaries of Cities of the World Ser.: No. 8). (Illus.). 312p. 1998. 49.50 (*0-8108-3562-2*) Scarecrow.
***Csendes, Tibor.** Developments in Reliable Computing. LC 99-51736. 1999. write for info. (*0-7923-6057-5*) Kluwer Academic.
Csengeri, Karen, ed. The Collected Writings of T. E. Hulme. LC 93-43811. 526p. 1994. text 89.00 (*0-19-811234-3*, Clarendon Pr) OUP.
Csenki, Attila. Dependability for Systems with a Partitioned State Space: Markov & Semi-Markov Theory & Computational Implementation. LC 94-25788. (Lecture Notes in Statistics Ser.: Vol. 90). 1994. 48.95 (*0-387-94333-1*) Spr-Verlag.
Csepe, Valeria & Naatanen, Risto, eds. Evoked & Event-Related Potentials in Hearing Research & Clinical Application. (Audiology & Neuro-Otology Ser.: Vol. 2, No. 5, 1997). (Illus.). 138p. 1997. pap. 36.50 (*3-8055-6605-0*) S Karger.
Csepeli, Gyorgy & Orkeny, Elte A. Ideology & Political Beliefs in Hungary: The Twilight of Socialism. 200p. 1992. text 49.00 (*1-85567-000-3*, Pub. by P P Pubs) Cassell & Continuum.
Csepinszky, A. Input-Output Techniques: Proceedings of the Second Hungarian Conference on Input-Output Techniques. (Illus.). 408p. (C). 1976. 75.00 (*963-05-0891-5*, Pub. by Akade Kiado) St Mut.
Csere, Thomas. Psychic Horoscopes: The Birth Charts & Biographies of Famous Psychics & Sensitives. LC 85-80043. (Illus.). 456p. (Orig.). 1986. 29.95 (*0-935283-01-3*); pap. 19.95 (*0-935283-00-5*) Empyreal Press.
Cseres, Tibor. Titoist Artrocities in Vojvodina, 1944: Serbian Vendetta in Balska. Venerdy, Jozsef, ed. & tr. by. from HUN. 160p. (C). 1993. 25.00 (*1-882785-01-0*, HTA) Matthias Corvinus.
Cserhati, Tibor & Forgacs, Esther. Chromatography in Food Science & Technology. LC 99-62434. 568p. 1999. text 189.95 (*1-56676-749-0*) Technomic.
Cserhati, Tibor & Valko, Klara. Chromatographic Determination of Molecular Interactions: Applications in Biochemistry, Chemistry, & Biophysics. 352p. 1993. boxed set 147.95 (*0-8493-4437-9*, QP519) CRC Pr.
Cserhati, Tibor, jt. auth. see Forgacs, Esther.
Csermely, Peter, ed. Stress of Life: From Molecules to Man. LC 98-6826. (Annals of the New York Academy of Sciences Ser.: Vol. 851). 547p. 1998. 140.00 (*1-57331-116-2*); pap. 140.00 (*1-57331-117-0*) NY Acad Sci.
Csernai, L. P. Introduction to Relativistic Heavy Ion Collisions. 322p. 1994. 165.00 (*0-471-93420-8*) Wiley.
Csernai, L. P. & Strottman, D. D., eds. Relativistic Heavy Ion Physics, 2 vols. 748p. (C). 1991. pap. 52.00 (*981-02-0672-0*); text 150.00 (*981-02-0550-3*) World Scientific Pub.
Csernansky, J. G., ed. Antipsychotics, No. 120. (Handbook of Experimental Pharmacology Ser.: Vol. 120). (Illus.). 504p. 1996. 398.00 (*3-540-60118-X*) Spr-Verlag.
Csernansky, John, jt. ed. see Holister, Leo E.
Csernok, Elene, jt. ed. see Gross, Wolfgang L.

An Asterisk (*) at the beginning of an entry indicates that the title is appearing for the first time.

Csete, Marie, jt. auth. see Rippe, James M.

Csettkey, Laszlo. Az 1944 Oktoberi Esemenyek Es Az Osszeomlas Eloestejen. LC 81-50628.Tr. of Events of October, 1944, & on the Eve of the Downfall. (HUN.). 125p. (Orig.). 1981. pap. write for info. (*0-935484-08-6*) Universe Pub Co.

CSG National Committee on Suggested State Legislat. Suggested State Legislation, 1990, Vol. 49. 176p. 1989. pap. 30.00 (*0-87292-094-1*, SSL 090) Coun State Govts.

— Suggested State Legislation, 1991, Vol. 50. 152p. 1990. 30.00 (*0-87292-957-4*) Coun State Govts.

— Suggested State Legislation, 1992, Vol. 51. 192p. 1992. pap. 30.00 (*0-87292-965-5*, C-010-91) Coun State Govts.

— Suggested State Legislation, 1993, Vol. 52. 192p. 1992. pap. 30.00 (*0-87292-971-X*, C-040-92) Coun State Govts.

Csicsery-Ronay, Elizabeth, ed. & tr. see Berlioz, Hector.

Csicsery-Ronay, I., ed. Koltok Forradalma: Antologia, 1953-1956.Tr. of Poets Revolution. (HUN.). 103p. 1996. 8.00 (*0-911050-61-2*) Occidental.

Csicsery-Ronay, Istvan. Salata Kalman: Dokumentumdrama. LC 84-60250. (HUN.). 91p. 1984. 8.00 (*0-911050-55-8*); pap. 6.00 (*0-911050-54-X*) Occidental.

Csicsery-Ronay, Istvan, ed. Nagy Ferenc Miniszterelnok. (HUN., Illus.). 161p. 1995. 15.00 (*963-7871-05-5*) Occidental.

Csida, Joseph, ed. see Grove, Dick.

Csikai, Gyula J., ed. Handbook of Fast Neutron Generators, 3 vols., Set. 1987. 339.90 (*0-8493-2967-1*, QC793) CRC Pr.

— Handbook of Fast Neutron Generators, 3 vols., Vol. I. 256p. 1987. boxed set 239.00 (*0-8493-2968-X*) CRC Pr.

— Handbook of Fast Neutron Generators, 3 vols., Vol. 2. 240p. 1987. boxed set 239.00 (*0-8493-2969-8*) CRC Pr.

Csikor, F. & Pocsik, G. Electroweak Symmetry Breaking: Proceedings of the Budapest Workshop. 252p. 1995. text 81.00 (*981-02-2088-X*) World Scientific Pub.

Csikor, F. & Pocsik, G., eds. Standard Model at the Energy of Present. 165p. 1992. 165.00 (*1-56072-021-2*) Nova Sci Pubs.

Csikor, Ferena & Fodor, Zoltan, eds. Strong & Electroweak Matter '97: Proceedings of the Conference Eger, Hungary 21-25 May, 1997. LC 98-163810. 500p. 1998. 98.00 (*981-02-3257-8*) World Scientific Pub.

Csikos-Nagy, B. Socialist Price Theory & Price Policy. 372p. (C). 1975. 60.00 (*963-05-0357-3*, Pub. by Akade Kiado) St Mut.

— Towards a New Price Revolution. 190p. (C). 1979. 50.00 (*963-05-1851-1*, Pub. by Akade Kiado) St Mut.

Csikos-Nagy, B. & Bela-Elek, P. S. Price & Power: A Twentieth-Century Reinterpretation of Interconnected Phenomena. 166p. 1995. pap. 69.00 (*963-05-6802-0*, Pub. by Akade Kiado) St Mut.

Csikszenrmihalyi, Mark & Ivanhoe, Philip J., eds. Religious & Philosophical Aspects of the Laozi. LC 98-46708. (SUNY Series in Chinese Philosophy & Culture). (Illus.). 320p. (C). 1999. text 71.50 (*0-7914-4111-3*); pap. text 23.95 (*0-7914-4112-1*) State U NY Pr.

Csikszentmih, Mihaly. Creativity: Flow & the Psychology of Discovery & Invention. 464p. 1997. pap. 15.00 (*0-06-092820-4*, Perennial) HarperTrade.

Csikszentmihalyi, Isabella S., jt. ed. see Csikszentmihalyi, Mihaly.

Csikszentmihalyi, M., jt. ed. see Kubey, Robert.

***Csikszentmihalyi, Mihaly.** Beyond Boredom & Anxiety: Experiencing Flow in Work & Play. LC 99-56457. 2000. 34.95 (*0-7879-5140-4*) Jossey-Bass.

Csikszentmihalyi, Mihaly. The Evolving Self. LC 92-56220. 384p. 1994. pap. 15.00 (*0-06-092192-7*, Perennial) HarperTrade.

— Finding Flow: The Psychology of Engagement with Everyday Life. (MasterMinds Ser.). 144p. 1998. pap. 12.00 (*0-465-02411-4*, Pub. by Basic) HarpC.

— Flow: The Psychology of Optimal Experience. LC 89-45645. 320p. 1993. reprint ed. pap. 14.00 (*0-06-092043-2*, Perennial) HarperTrade.

Csikszentmihalyi, Mihaly & Csikszentmihalyi, Isabella S., eds. Optimal Experience: Psychological Studies of Flow in Consciousness. (Illus.). 430p. (C). 1992. pap. text 22.95 (*0-521-43809-8*) Cambridge U Pr.

Csikszentmihalyi, Mihaly & Larson, Reed. Being Adolescent: Conflict & Growth in the Teenage Years. LC 83-45253. (Illus.). 352p. 1986. pap. 21.00 (*0-465-00645-0*, Pub. by Basic) HarpC.

Csikszentmihalyi, Mihaly & Robinson, Rick E. The Art of Seeing: An Interpretation of the Aesthetic Experience. LC 90-41602. (Illus.). 222p. 1990. pap. 22.50 (*0-89236-156-5*, Pub. by J P Getty Trust) OUP.

Csikszentmihalyi, Mihaly & Rochberg-Halton, Eugene. The Meaning of Things: Symbols in the Development of the Self. LC 81-1443. 330p. 1981. pap. text 27.95 (*0-521-28774-X*) Cambridge U Pr.

***Csikszentmihalyi, Mihaly & Schneider, Barbara.** Becoming Adult: How Teenagers Prepare for the World of Work. 2000. 27.50 (*0-465-01540-9*, Pub. by Basic) HarpC.

Csikszentmihalyi, Mihaly, et al. Photography's Multiple Roles: Art, Document, Market, Science. Neff, Terry A., ed. LC 98-26380. (Illus.). 272p. 1998. write for info. (*0-9658887-1-1*) Mus Contemp Photo.

Csikszentmihalyi, Mihaly, jt. auth. see Jackson, Susan A.

Csikszentminalyi, Mihaly, et al. Talented Teenagers: The Roots of Success & Failure. LC 97-106421. 320p. 1996. pap. text 18.95 (*0-521-57463-3*) Cambridge U Pr.

CSIL (Centro Studi Industria Leggeia) Staff. The Furniture Industry in Argentina, Brazil & Chile. LC 99-33819. (Illus.). 150p. 1999. spiral bd. 1000.00 (*0-921577-94-X*) AKTRIN.

***Csil Staff.** The Furniture Industry in Australia & New Zealand. Wille, Stefan, ed. LC 98-932119. (Illus.). 92p. 1998. spiral bd. 1000.00 (*0-921577-88-5*) AKTRIN.

Csilla, Bertha, jt. ed. see Morse, Donald E.

***Csillag, Andrea.** Backstreet Boys Official Book. (Illus.). 128p. (YA). 2000. 14.95 (*0-385-32800-1*, Delacorte Pr Bks) BDD Bks Young Read.

Csillag, P. The Augustan Laws on Family Relations. 275p. (C). 1976. 48.00 (*963-05-0376-X*, Pub. by Akade Kiado) St Mut.

Csillik, B. & Csillik-Knyihar, E. The Protean Gate Structure & Plasticity of the Primary Nociceptive Analyzer: Structure & Plasticity of the Primary Nociceptive Analyzer. 294p. (C). 1986. 120.00 (*963-05-3928-4*, Pub. by Akade Kiado) St Mut.

Csillik-Knyihar, E., jt. auth. see Csillik, B.

Csilszent, Mihalyi, Mihaly. The Soul of Business. 2002. write for info. (*0-316-77527-4*) Little.

Csink, T., jt. ed. see Veghelyi, P.

Csirik, J., et al, eds. Fundamentals of Computation Theory. (Lecture Notes in Computer Science Ser.: Vol. 380). 1989. 56.00 (*0-387-51498-8*) Spr-Verlag.

Csirmaz, Laszlo, et al, eds. Logic Colloquium 1992: SiLLI & CSLI Co-Publications. (Studies in Logic, Language & Information: No. 1). 334p. 1995. 64.95 (*1-881526-97-6*) CSLI.

— Logic Colloquium 1992: SiLLI & CSLI Co-Publications. (Studies in Logic, Language & Information). (Illus.). 334p. 1995. pap. 22.95 (*1-881526-98-4*) CSLI.

CSIRO - Department of Industry, Science & Technolo, ed. Environmental Management: The Role of Eucalypts & Other Fast Growing Species. (Illus.). 218p. 1996. pap. 40.00 (*0-643-05993-8*, Pub. by CSIRO) Accents Pubns.

CSIRO Australia Staff. Conservation Tillage & Ley Farming Systems for the Semi-Arid Tropics. (Illus.). 170p. (Orig.). 1996. pap. 50.00 (*0-643-05841-9*, Pub. by CSIRO) Accents Pubns.

— Delta System: A General System for Processing Taxonomic Descriptions. 136p. 1995. pap. 460.00 incl. cd-rom (*0-643-05618-1*, Pub. by CSIRO) Accents Pubns.

— Gentianales. (Flora of Australia Ser.: Vol. 28). (Illus.). 356p. 1996. 79.95 (*0-643-05884-2*, Pub. by CSIRO); pap. 64.95 (*0-643-05885-0*, Pub. by CSIRO) Accents Pubns.

CSIRO Australia Staff, ed. Australia: State of the Environment 1996. (Illus.). 550p. 1996. 49.95 (*0-643-05830-3*, Pub. by CSIRO) Accents Pubns.

— Fungi of Australia, Vol. 1A. (Illus.). 434p. 1996. 69.95 (*0-643-05802-8*, Pub. by CSIRO); pap. 54.95 (*0-643-05889-3*, Pub. by CSIRO) Accents Pubns.

CSIRO Pub. Staff. Flora of Australia: Introduction, Vol. 1. 2nd ed. LC 98-176241. (Illus.). 350p. 1997. pap. write for info. (*0-643-05966-0*, Pub. by CSIRO) Accents Pubns.

— Introduciton. 2nd ed. (Flora of Australia Ser.: Vol. 1). (Illus.). 350p. 1999. 79.95 (*0-643-05965-2*, Pub. by CSIRO) Accents Pubns.

CSIRO Staff. The Insects of Australia, 2 vols., Set. 1991. 230.00 (*0-522-84454-5*, Pub. by Melbourne Univ Pr) Paul & Co Pubs.

— The Insects of Australia, Vol. 1. 1991. 115.00 (*0-522-84637-8*, Pub. by Melbourne Univ Pr) Paul & Co Pubs.

— The Insects of Australia, Vol. 2. 1991. 115.00 (*0-522-84638-6*, Pub. by Melbourne Univ Pr) Paul & Co Pubs.

CSIRO Staff, et al, eds. Greenhouse: Coping with Climate Change. LC 97-118500. (Illus.). 700p. 1995. 89.95 (*0-643-05688-2*, Pub. by CSIRO) Accents Pubns.

CSIS Energy & Strategic Resources Program Staff. Natural Gas Vehicles: A National Security Perspective: a Report. LC 84-23293. (Significant Issues Ser.: Vol. 6, No. 16). (Illus.). 79p. reprint ed. pap. 30.00 (*0-8357-6639-X*, 203530600094) Bks Demand.

CSIS Science & Technology Committee, Panel on Cris. America's Hidden Vulnerabilities: Crisis Management in a Society of Networks: a Report. Wilcox, Richard H. & Garrity, Patrick J., eds. LC 84-21414. 51p. reprint ed. pap. 30.00 (*0-8357-6638-1*, 203530500094) Bks Demand.

Csiszar, I. & Korner, J. Information Theory. 2nd ed. 452p. 1997. 237.00 (*963-05-7440-3*, Pub. by Akade Kiado) St Mut.

Csiszar, I., ed. see CISM (International Center for Mechanical Sciences.

Csiszar, Imre & Michaletzky, Gyorgy. Stochastic Differential & Difference Equations. LC 97-20913. (Progress in Systems & Control Theory Ser.). 1997. write for info. (*0-8176-3971-3*); write for info. (*3-7643-3971-3*) Birkhauser.

Csizmadia, E. & Szekely, Maria, eds. Food Economy in Hungary. 217p. (C). 1986. 75.00 (*963-05-3804-0*, Pub. by Akade Kiado) St Mut.

Csizmadia, I. G., jt. auth. see Ruff, Ferenc.

Csizmadia, Imre G., jt. ed. see Bertran, J.

Csizmadia, Imre G., jt. ed. see Ogretir, Cemil.

Csobadi, Peter, jt. auth. see Ludwig, Christa.

CSOF (Grime) Staff. Process Skills Development in Ambulatory Family Practice. 246p. 1999. ring bd. 47.96 (*0-7872-5591-2*, 41559101) Kendall-Hunt.

Csoka, Louis S. & Conference Board Staff. Rethinking Human Resources: A Research Report. LC 98-191565. (Report Ser.). 40 p. 1995. write for info. (*0-8237-0571-4*) Conference Bd.

Csokor, Franz T. A Critical Edition & Translation of Franz Theodor Czokor's European Trilogy, Vol. 1. Lichliter, Katherine M., tr. (Austrian Culture Ser.). (GER.). 252p. (C). 1995. text 49.95 (*0-8204-1512-X*) P Lang Pubng.

Csoma De Koros. Grammar of the Tibetan Language. (ENG & TIB.). 244p. 1983. pap. 38.00 (*0-7859-7482-2*) Fr & Eur.

Csoma, Sandor K. Tibetan Studies: Being a Reprint of the Articles Contributed to the Journal of the Asiatic Society of Bengal. Denilson, E., ed. LC 78-72400. reprint ed. 47.50 (*0-404-17259-8*) AMS Pr.

Csomos, G. & Feher, Janos, eds. Free Radicals & the Liver. (Illus.). 192p. 1992. 84.00 (*0-387-54445-3*) Spr-Verlag.

***Csomoss, Zoltan.** One Way Vol. I & II: The Quest for the Truth - Basics & Beyond Recovery, 8 vols. large type ed. 60p. 1998. pap. 10.00 (*0-9702409-1-0*) Zoltan.

Csonka, jt. ed. see Bocatius, Ionnes.

Csoori, Sandor. Barbarian Prayer: Selected Poems. 92p. 1999. pap. 21.00 (*963-13-3030-3*, Pub. by Corvina Bks) St Mut.

— Memory of Snow. Kolumban, Nicholas, tr. from HUN. (Translation Ser.). (Illus.). 72p. 1983. 22.50 (*0-915778-53-X*); 125.00 (*0-915778-54-8*); pap. 8.50 (*0-915778-52-1*) Penmaen Pr.

— Selected Poems of Sandor Csoori. Roberts, Len, tr. from HUN. & intro. by. LC 92-6972. 128p. (Orig.). 1992. pap. 11.00 (*1-55659-047-4*) Copper Canyon.

Csorba, I. P., ed. Selected Papers on Image Tubes. 736p. 1990. pap. 35.00 (*0-8194-0476-4*, VOL. MS20) SPIE.

Csordas, George, jt. auth. see Bleecker, David.

Csordas, George, jt. ed. see Bleecker, David.

Csordas, Thomas J. Language, Charisma, & Creativity: The Ritual Life of a Religious Movement. LC 95-50992. (Illus.). 251p. 1997. 45.00 (*0-520-20469-7*, Pub. by U CA Pr) Cal Prin Full Svc.

— The Sacred Self: A Cultural Phenomenology of Charismatic Healing. LC 93-34279. (Illus.). 1997. pap. 16.95 (*0-520-20884-6*, Pub. by U CA Pr) Cal Prin Full Svc.

Csordas, Thomas J., ed. Embodiment & Experience: The Existential Ground of Culture & Self. LC 93-45993. (Cambridge Studies in Medical Anthropology: Vol. 2). (Illus.). 306p. (C). 1995. pap. text 19.95 (*0-521-45890-0*) Cambridge U Pr.

***Csordos, Mark D.** Business Lessons for Young Entrepreneurs: 30 Things I Learned Before the Age of Thirty. 176p. (C). 2000. pap. 15.95 (*0-9679142-0-5*) Customer Ser.

Csorgo, M. & Szyszkowicz, Barbara. Asymptotic Methods in Probability & Statistics: A Volume in Honor of Miklos Csorgo. LC 98-37202. 889p. 1998. write for info. (*0-444-50083-9*) Elsevier.

Csorgo, Miklos. Quantile Processes with Statistical Applications. LC 83-60222. (CBMS-NSF Regional Conference Series in Applied Mathematics: No. 42). xiii, 156p. 1983. pap. text 33.00 (*0-89871-185-1*) Soc Indus-Appl Math.

Csorgo, Miklos & Horvath, L. Limit Theorems in Change-Point Analysis. LC 98-110380. (Probability & Mathematical Ser.). 438p. 1997. 165.00 (*0-471-95522-1*) Wiley.

— Weighted Approximations in Probability & Statistics. LC 92-27167. 464p. 1993. 210.00 (*0-471-93635-9*) Wiley.

Csorgo, Miklos, et al. An Asymptotic Theory for Empirical Reliability & Concentration Processes. (Lecture Notes in Statistics Ser.: Vol. 33). v, 171p. 1986. 47.95 (*0-387-96359-6*) Spr-Verlag.

***Csorgo, T.** Correlations & Fluctuations: From Qcd to Particle Interferometry Proceedings of the 8th Intern. 580p. 1999. 94.00 (*981-02-3823-1*) World Scientific Pub.

Csorna, S. E., jt. ed. see Panvini, R. S.

Csovanyos, Margaret F. A Varied Bouquet of Poems. 96p. 1991. 14.99 (*0-925037-14-1*) Great Lks Poetry.

CSS Publishing Company Staff. Advent/Christmas Resources for Young & Old: A Christmas Anthology. 1997. cd-rom 10.50 (*0-7880-0841-2*); mac bd 10.50 (*0-7880-0842-0*) CSS OH.

— First Lesson Sermon, 5 vols. (First Lessons Ser.). 1999. 42.95 (*0-7880-1528-1*) CSS OH.

CSS Publishing Company Staff. First Lesson Sermon, Set. (First Lessons Ser.). 1998. pap. 34.95 (*0-7880-1300-9*) CSS OH.

***CSS Publishing Company Staff.** Gospel Sermon, 5 vols. (Gospel Ser.). 1999. 44.95 (*0-7880-1534-6*) CSS OH.

— Second Lesson Sermon, 2 vols. 1999. pap. 22.95 (*0-7880-1531-1*) CSS OH.

— 2nd Lesson Sermon Series: For Use with the Revised Common Lectionary. 1998. cd-rom 16.95 (*0-7880-1298-3*) CSS OH.

CSS Publishing Company Staff, ed. Common Lectionary. (Gospel Ser.). 1998. pap. 36.50 (*0-7880-1304-1*) CSS OH.

— Common Lectionary Cycle A: Second Lesson Sermon Series. rev. ed. 1998. pap. 16.95 (*0-7880-1297-5*) CSS OH.

— First Lesson Sermon. (First Lessons Ser.). 1998. disk 34.95 (*0-7880-1303-3*) CSS OH.

CSS's Dept. of Public Policy Unit Staff. Separate, Unequal & Inequate: Educational Opportunities & Outcomes in New York City Public Schools. 30p. 1995. 5.00 (*0-88156-167-3*) Comm Serv Soc NY.

Csuhaj-Varju, Erzsebet, et al, eds. Grammar Systems: A Grammatical Approach to Distribution & Cooperation. (Topics in Computer Mathematics Ser.). 230p. 1994. text 109.00 (*2-88124-957-4*) Gordon & Breach.

Csuros, Maria. The Environmental Laboratory Handbook. Date not set. 99.50 (*1-56670-311-5*) Lewis Pubs.

— Environmental Sampling & Analysis for Technicians. 336p. 1994. lib. bdg. 75.00 (*0-87371-835-6*, L835) Lewis Pubs.

— Microbiological Examination of Water & Wastewater. LC 98-48684. 11p. 1999. 55.00 (*1-56670-179-1*) Lewis Pubs.

Csus. Intro to Windows 95 & Netscape Navigator. 112p. 1998. pap. text 19.80 (*0-536-01528-7*) Pearson Custom.

Csuti, Blair, et al. Atlas of Oregon Wildlife. LC 97-8467. (Illus.). 496p. 1997. 39.95 (*0-87071-395-7*) Oreg St U Pr.

Csuti, Blair A. Type Specimens of Recent Mammals in the Museum of Vertebrate Zoology, University of California, Berkeley. LC 80-13264. (University of California Publications in Social Welfare: No. 114). 83p. reprint ed. pap. 30.00 (*0-8357-6860-0*, 203555800095) Bks Demand.

CSZ Membership. Let Us Begin: The Sha'ar Zahav Haggadah. (ENG & HEB., Illus.). 64p. (Orig.). 1996. pap. 10.00 (*0-9619242-1-7*) Cong Shaar Zahav.

CTB Biotechnology News Staff, ed. Bioindustry Directory. 163p. (Orig.). 1995. pap., spiral bd. 157.00 (*0-9623391-7-2*, DBN-95) CTB Intl.

CTB Diagnostic Intelligence Group Staff, ed. Profiting from Gene-Based Diagnostics. 82p. 1996. spiral bd. 637.00 (*1-887566-04-X*, RPG-01) CTB Intl.

CTB Diagnostics Intelligence Staff, ed. Emerging Infectious Disease Test Markets. 170p. (Orig.). 1995. pap., spiral bd. 867.00 (*1-887566-01-5*, REI-01) CTB Intl.

— Guide to FDA Approved in Vitro Diagnostics. 438p. 1995. spiral bd. 464.00 (*1-887566-03-1*, GDI-01) CTB Intl.

CTB Directories Group Staff, ed. In Vitro Diagnostics Industry Directory, 1997-98. 318p. 1997. spiral bd. 267.00 (*1-887566-07-4*, DD1-97) CTB Intl.

— Pharma Industry Directory, 1999-2000. 1999. spiral bd. 188.00 (*1-887566-13-9*) CTB Intl.

CTB Emerging Pharmaceutical Group Staff, ed. Commercial Opportunites in Angiogenesis. 175p. 1996. spiral bd. 884.00 (*1-887566-06-6*, RAN-01) CTB Intl.

— Commercial Opportunities in Acute Stroke Treatment. 184p. 1997. spiral bd. 891.00 (*1-887566-08-2*, RAC-01) CTB Intl.

— Commercial Opportunities in Adhesion Molecules. 111p. 1997. spiral bd. 917.00 (*1-887566-10-4*, RAM-01) CTB Intl.

— Commercial Opportunities in Cardiovascular Diagnostics. 83p. 1998. spiral bd. 727.00 (*1-887566-12-0*, RCD-01) CTB Intl.

— Commercial Opportunities in Obesity Drug. 108p. 1996. spiral bd. 849.00 (*1-887566-05-8*, ROB-01) CTB Intl.

— Commercial Opportunities in Pharmacogenomics. 1998. spiral bd. 857.00 (*1-887566-11-2*, RPC-01) CTB Intl.

CTB Emerging Technologies Group, ed. Commercial Opportunities in Apoptosis. 213p. (Orig.). 1994. pap., spiral bd. 795.00 (*0-9623391-6-4*, RAP-01) CTB Intl.

— Cutting-Edge Technologies for Preventing Restenosis. 161p. (Orig.). 1995. pap. 877.00 (*1-887566-00-7*) CTB Intl.

CTBA Staff. Trilingual Dictionary of Round & Sawn Timber: French/English/German. (ENG, FRE & GER.). 223p. 1995. 79.95 (*0-320-00643-3*) Fr & Eur.

CTDNews Staff, ed. Cumulative Trauma Disorder: A Legal Guide to CTD Prevention, Regulation & Liability. LC 93-25971. 1993. 125.00 (*0-9636246-2-8*) Andrews Pubns.

***Ctein.** Post Exposure. 2nd ed. 208p. 2000. pap. text 32.95 (*0-240-80437-6*, Focal) Buttrwrth-Heinemann.

Ctein. Post-Exposure: Advanced Techniques for the Photographic Printer. LC 97-24532. (Illus.). 208p. 1997. pap. 29.95 (*0-240-80299-3*, Focal) Buttrwrth-Heinemann.

CTFA Staff. CTFA International Color Handbook. 2nd ed. 325p. 1992. 200.00 (*1-882621-03-4*) Cosmetic T&FA.

— International Regulatory/Resource Manual. Rempe, Jennifer M. & Santucci, Louis G., eds. LC 95-67181. 595p. 1995. text 325.00 (*1-882621-11-5*) Cosmetic T&FA.

CTI Center for Geography Geology & Meteorology, University of Leicester, U. K. Staff, ed. Geography Interactive: Learning & Teaching, 2 vols. Incl. Geography Interactive: Learning & Teaching: Geographical Methods & Techniques. 50p. 1998. 69.00 incl. cd-rom (*3-540-14694-6*); Geography Interactive: Learning & Teaching: Human Geography. 50p. 1998. 69.95 incl. cd-rom (*3-540-14692-X*); 169.00 (*3-540-14688-1*) Spr-Verlag.

— Geography Interactive: Learning & Teaching: Physical Geography. 50p. 1997. 69.95 incl. cd-rom (*3-540-14693-8*) Spr-Verlag.

CTIR Staff, jt. auth. see Arkansas International Center Staff.

Ctold, Donna, jt. auth. see Des Lauriers Cieri, Carol.

CTTS - Safety Products Staff. Finding 'em, Hiring 'em. 128p. 1995. pap. text 39.95 (*0-7872-1060-9*) Kendall-Hunt.

CTTS-Safety Prod. Staff. The CTTS CDL Study Manual. 400p. 1995. pap. text, per. 27.95 (*0-8403-9440-3*) Kendall-Hunt.

CTTS, Safety Prod. Staff. The CTTS CDL Study Manual. (SPA.). 386p. 1997. per. 29.95 (*0-7872-3758-2*) Kendall-Hunt.

CTTS Safety Products Staff. Controlled Substance Abuse & Alcohol Misuse Training. 3rd ed. LC 98-142093. 112p. 1997. per. 24.95 (*0-7872-3913-5*) Kendall-Hunt.

— CTTS Safety Products CDL Study Guide: Air Brakes. 32p. 1998. pap. 11.95 (*0-7872-5256-5*) Kendall-Hunt.

— CTTS Safety Products CDL Study Guide: Combination Vehicles. 32p. 1998. pap. 11.95 (*0-7872-5257-3*) Kendall-Hunt.

— CTTS Safety Products CDL Study Guide: General Knowledge. 94p. 1998. per. 11.95 (*0-7872-5254-9*) Kendall-Hunt.

— CTTS Safety Products CDL Study Guide: Hazardous Material. 50p. 1998. pap. 11.95 (*0-7872-5255-7*) Kendall-Hunt.

— CTTS Safety Products CDL Study Guide: Skill Test. 40p. 1998. pap. 11.95 (*0-7872-5253-0*) Kendall-Hunt.

C

— CTTS Safety Products CDL Study Guide: Transporting Passenger. 20p. 1998. pap. 11.95 (*0-7872-5258-1*) Kendall-Hunt.

CTTS Staff & Safety Products Staff. CTTS Cdl Study Manual. 3rd ed. LC 97-210496. 400p. 1997. per. 29.95 (*0-7872-3925-9*) Kendall-Hunt.

— Drug Abuse & Alcohol Misuse Training Guide for CDL Drivers. 3rd ed. 48p. 1998. per. 2.95 (*0-7872-1962-2*) Kendall-Hunt.

Cua, A. S. Moral Vision & Tradition: Essays in Chinese Ethics. LC 96-53933. (Studies in Philosophy & the History of Philosophy). 357p. 1998. text 66.95 (*0-8132-0890-4*) Cath U Pr.

Cua, Florence T. Element Concentrations in Teeth. 267p. 1992. 40.00 (*0-9645418-1-5*) F T Cua.

— Po, Pb, Ra, Pu, Cur, U, Th, Am, CF, Mo, & Tc Radionuclides in Teeth & Bones. 363p. 1994. 50.00 (*0-9645418-2-3*) F T Cua.

— SR 90 from Worldwide Fallout in Teeth & Bones. 175p. 1992. 40.00 (*0-9645418-0-7*) F T Cua.

***Cuadra, Angel.** Diez Sonetos Ocultos. (Coleccion Espejo de Paciencia). (SPA.). 55p. 2000. pap. 3.95 (*0-89729-917-5*) Ediciones.

Cuadra, Angel. La Voz Inevitable. LC 94-70870. (Coleccion Espejo de Paciencia). (SPA.). 93p. (Orig.). 1994. pap. 9.95 (*0-89729-732-6*) Ediciones.

Cuadra, Carlos, et al, eds. The Annual Review of Information Science & Technology, Vol. 10. LC 66-25096. 1975. 27.50 (*0-87715-210-1*) Am Soc Info Sci.

Cuadra, Pablo A. The Birth of the Sun: Selected Poems 1935-1985. White, Steven F., tr. from SPA. (Illus.). 171p. 1988. pap. 14.95 (*0-87775-205-2*) Unicorn Pr.

Cuadrado-Roura, Juan R., et al, eds. Moving Frontiers: Economic Restructuring, Regional Development & Emerging Networks. 368p. 1994. 96.95 (*1-85628-905-2*, Pub. by Avebry) Ashgate Pub Co.

Cuadras, C. M. & Rao, C. R., eds. Multivariate Analysis: Future Directions 2. (North-Holland Series in Statistics & Probability: 7). 504p. 1993. 200.00 (*0-444-81531-7*, North Holland) Elsevier.

Cuadriello, Jaime, et al. La Reina de las Americas: Works of Art from the Museum of the Basilica de Guadalupe. (ENG & SPA., Illus.). 136p. (Orig.). 1996. pap. 24.95 (*1-889410-01-2*) Mexican Fine Arts.

Cuadros, F., jt. ed. see Velarde, M. G.

Cuadros, Gil. City of God. 160p. (Orig.). 1994. pap. 9.95 (*0-87286-295-X*) City Lights.

Cuartas, A., jt. auth. see Chavarria, Andres S.

Cuartero Sancho, Maria P., ed. see Timoneda, Joan.

Cuatrecasas, Jose. Brunelliaceae. LC 85-13613. (Flora Neotropica Monographs: No. 2S). (Illus.). 104p. 1985. pap. text 21.00 (*0-89327-265-5*) NY Botanical.

— Brunelliaceae. LC 72-91637. (Flora Neotropica Monographs: No. 2). (Illus.). 190p. 1984. reprint ed. 15.00 (*0-89327-263-9*) NY Botanical.

Cuatrecasas, P. & Roth, T. Receptor Mediated Endocytosis. (Receptors & Recognition Series B: Vol. 15). (Illus.). 1984. 77.00 (*0-412-24820-4*, NO. 6827) Chapman & Hall.

Cuba, Lee J. American Government. 3rd ed. LC 96-34858. 192p. (C). 1999. pap. 24.20 (*0-673-52494-9*) Longman.

Cuba, Prince. Before Adam: The Original Man. (Orig.). 1992. pap. 6.95 (*1-56411-026-5*) Untd Bros & Sis.

— To the Woman: Three Essays. (Illus.). 17p. (Orig.). 1984. pap. 2.95 (*1-56411-112-1*) Untd Bros & Sis.

Cuba, Prince, ed. see Benyon, E. D.

Cuba, Prince A. Lynch Law Through Due Process. (Illus.). 12p. (Orig.). reprint ed. pap. 3.00 (*1-56411-145-8*) Untd Bros & Sis.

— Musa & the All-Seeing-Eye: A History of Moses. (Illus.). 74p. (Orig.). 1991. pap. 6.95 (*1-56411-009-5*) Untd Bros & Sis.

Cuba, Roland De, see Howe, Kate & De Cuba, Roland.

Cuba, Stanley L. Olive Rush: A Hoosier Artist in New Mexico. (Illus.). vii, 91p. (Orig.). 1992. pap. write for info. (*0-9623291-4-2*) Minnetrista.

Cuban American National Foundation Staff. The Cuban Revolution at Thirty: A Conference by the Cuban American National Foundation. 1989. 4.00 (*0-685-37919-1*) Cuban Amer Natl Fndtn.

Cuban, Larry. How Scholars Trumped Teachers: Constancy & Change in University Curriculum, Teaching, & Research, 1890-1990. LC 98-56523. 288p. 1999. text 63.00 (*0-8077-3865-4*) Tchrs Coll.

— How Teachers Taught: Constancy & Change in American Classrooms, 1890-1990. 2nd ed. LC 92-31867. (Research on Teaching Ser.). 384p. (C). 1993. 53.00 (*0-8077-3227-3*); pap. 26.95 (*0-8077-3226-5*) Tchrs Coll.

— The Managerial Imperative & the Practice of Leadership in Schools. LC 87-6512. (SUNY Series, Educational Leadership). 293p. (C). 1988. text 24.50 (*0-88706-593-7*) State U NY Pr.

— Teachers & Machines: The Classroom Use of Technology Since 1920. 144p. (C). 1985. pap. text 14.95 (*0-8077-2792-X*) Tchrs Coll.

***Cuban, Larry & Shipps, Dorothy.** Reconstructing the Common Good in Education: Coping with Intractable American Dilemmas. LC 00-27258. 2000. pap. write for info. (*0-8047-3863-7*) Stanford U Pr.

Cuban, Larry & Tyack, David B. Tinkering Toward Utopia: A Century of Public School Reform. LC 94-47545. (Illus.). 192p. (C). 1995. 23.50 (*0-674-89282-8*) HUP.

***Cuban, Larry & Woodward, John, eds.** Technology, Curriculum & Professional Development: Adapting Schools to Meet the Needs of Students with Disabilities. 256p. 2000. pap. 32.95 (*0-7619-7743-0*); lib. bdg. 69.95 (*0-7619-7742-2*) Corwin Pr.

Cuban Museum of Arts & Culture Staff. The Miami Generation: Nine Cuban Americans. (Illus.). 1985. 3.00 (*0-614-32311-8*) Balch IES Pr.

Cuban National Heritage Staff, ed. see De la Costa, Fernando, et al.

Cuban National Planning Council, et al. The Cuban Minority in the U. S. The Preliminary & Final Reports on Need Identification & Program Evaluation, 2 vols., Set. 1981. 82.95 (*0-405-13199-2*) Ayer.

Cuban Research Institute Staff & Florida International University Staff. Transition in Cuba: New Challenges for U. S. Policy. 674p. 1993. pap. 35.00 (*1-879862-05-0*) FL Intl U Latin.

Cuban Studies Conferences Staff. Problems of Succession in Cuba. Suchlicki, Jaime, ed. 105p. (Orig.). (C). 1985. pap. text 16.95 (*1-56000-661-7*) Transaction Pubs.

Cubano-Iguina, Astrid. Hilo en el Laberinto: Claves de la Lucha Politica en Puerto Rico, Siglo XIX. LC 90-80513. 166p. 1990. pap. 10.50 (*0-929157-04-4*) Ediciones Huracan.

Cubas, Zalmir, jt. ed. see Fowler, Murray E.

Cubbage, jt. auth. see Steves.

Cubbage, Brenda T., jt. auth. see Steves, Sterling W.

Cubbage, Frederick W. & O'Laughlin, Jay. Forest Resource Policy. Bullock, Charles S., III, ed. LC 00-565. 592p. 1993. text 90.95 (*0-471-62245-1*) Wiley.

Cubbage, Sue A. & Williams, Marcia. National Job Hotline Directory: The Job Finder's Hot List, 1999-2001. LC 98-65912. (Illus.). 376p. 1999. pap. text 16.95 (*1-884587-12-7*) Planning Comns.

Cubberley, Carol W. Tenure & Promotion for Academic Librarians: A Guidebook with Advice & Vignettes. LC 96-23959. 135p. 1996. lib. bdg. 32.50 (*0-7864-0238-5*) McFarland & Co.

Cubberley, Carol W., jt. auth. see Lundin, Anne H.

Cubberley, Ellwood P. School Funds & Their Apportionment, a Consideration of the Subject with Reference to a More General Equalization of Both the Burdens & the Advantages of Education. LC 72-176681. (Columbia University. Teachers College. Contributions to Education Ser.: No. 2). reprint ed. 37.50 (*0-404-55002-9*) AMS Pr.

Cubberley, Paul. Handbook of Russian Affixes. 144p. (Orig.). (C). 1994. pap. text 14.95 (*0-89357-254-3*) Slavica.

Cubberly, W., ed. see SME Staff.

Cubberly, William H., ed. ISA Handbook of Measurement Equations & Tables. LC 93-27096. 200p. 1993. pap. 50.00 (*1-55617-486-1*) ISA.

Cubbin, G. P., ed. Anglo-Saxon Chronicle 6 MS D. (Illus.). 286p. (C). 1996. 75.00 (*0-85991-467-4*) Boydell & Brewer.

Cubbin, J. S. Market Structure & Performance: The Empirical Research, Vol. 28. viii, 80p. 1988. pap. text 44.00 (*3-7186-4842-3*) Gordon & Breach.

Cubbin, J. S., jt. auth. see Ganley, J. A.

Cubbison, Shirley, jt. auth. see Stouffer, Cindy.

Cubbler, jt. auth. see Olivo, C. Thomas.

Cubbon, A. M. Crosses of the Isle of Man. 1972. pap. 7.50 (*0-89979-068-2*) British Am Bks.

Cubbon, A. M. Health & Safety in Ceramics 3rd Edition. 41p. 1991. pap. 12.00 (*0-901092-42-8*) Institute of Management Consultants.

Cubbs, Joanne. Religious Visionaries. (Illus.). 40p. 1991. pap. 19.95 (*0-932718-31-0*) Kohler Arts.

Cubbs, Joanne, contrib. by. Eccentric Machines. (Illus.). 48p. 1987. pap. 15.95 (*0-932718-22-1*) Kohler Arts.

— Second Hand: An Exhibition of Contemporary Found Object Art. (Illus.). 16p. 1989. pap. 5.00 (*0-932718-27-2*) Kohler Arts.

— Visual Paradox: Truth & Fiction in the Photographic Image. (Illus.). 80p. 1988. pap. 21.95 (*0-932718-24-8*) Kohler Arts.

Cubbs, Joanne & Von Bruenchenhein, Eugene, contrib. by. Eugene Von Bruenchenhein: Obsessive Visionary. (Illus.). 160p. 1988. pap. 35.00 (*0-932718-25-6*) Kohler Arts.

Cube, Felix-Eberhard Von, see Von Cube, Felix-Eberhard.

Cubeddu, Raimondo. The Philosophy of the Austrian School. LC 92-46097. 288p. (C). (gr. 13). 1993. 85.00 (*0-415-08647-7*, B2386) Routledge.

Cubeddu, Rinaldo, ed. Medical & Biological Applications, Vol. 6. 1996. pap. 55.00 (*1-55752-464-5*) Optical Soc.

***Cubells, Jose Maria.** Por Que Lloras? 1999. pap. 14.95 (*84-270-2450-9*) Planeta.

Cubena. Los Nietos de Felicidad Dolores. LC 89-83579. (Coleccion Ebano y Canela). (SPA.). 233p. (Orig.). 1991. pap. 18.00 (*0-89729-528-5*) Ediciones.

Cubenas, Jose A. Spanish & Hispanic Presence in Florida from the Discovery to the Bicentennial. 1979. pap. 4.00 (*84-499-2888-5*) Edit Mensaje.

Cubert, Harold M. The PLFP's Changing Role in the Middle East. LC 96-42486. 256p. 1997. 52.50 (*0-7146-4772-1*, Pub. by F Cass Pubs); pap. 24.50 (*0-7146-4329-7*, Pub. by F Cass Pubs) Intl Spec Bk.

Cubias, Daniel, jt. auth. see Raisglid, Ron.

Cubic Media, Staff. Multimedia Parallels. (C). 1995. 73.33 (*0-13-186347-9*) P-H.

Cubicciotti, D. D., ed. see Symposium on High Temperature Metal Halide Chemist.

Cubicciotti, Daniel, ed. see Symposium on High Temperature Materials Chemistry.

Cubillo De Aragon, Alvaro. El Enano De las Musas. (Textos y Estudios Clasicos De las Literaturas Hispanicas Ser.). xiv, 478p. 1973. reprint ed. 120.00 (*3-487-04081-6*) G Olms Pubs.

Cubillos. Sempre Adelante. (College Spanish Ser.). (SPA.). (C). 1996. text, wbk. ed. 30.95 (*0-8384-6489-0*) Heinle & Heinle.

— Sempre Adelante. annot. ed. (College Spanish Ser.). (SPA.). (C). 1995. text, teacher ed. 36.95 (*0-8384-6488-2*) Heinle & Heinle.

— Temas. LC 99-47130. (C). 1999. pap. 40.00 (*0-8384-8217-1*); pap. text, wbk. ed. 28.00 (*0-8384-8154-X*) Heinle & Heinle.

***Cubillos.** Temas. 2002. mass mkt. 1.00 (*0-8384-5039-3*) Heinle & Heinle.

Cubillos. Temas-student Text. LC 99-47130. (C). 2000. pap. 56.95 (*0-8384-8226-0*) Heinle & Heinle.

— Temas-testing Program. (C). 2000. pap. 1.00 (*0-8384-8235-X*) Heinle & Heinle.

Cubillos, jt. auth. see Mccone.

Cubillos, Julio C., jt. auth. see Duque, Luis.

Cubitt, Catherine, jt. auth. see Brooks, Nicholas.

Cubitt, Catherine R. Anglo-Saxon Church Councils, 650-850. (Studies in the Early History of Britain). 280p. (C). 1995. text 59.00 (*0-7185-1436-X*) St Martin.

Cubitt, Geoffrey. The Jesuit Myth: Conspiracy Theory & Politics in Nineteenth-Century France. LC 93-18391. 360p. (C). 1993. text 69.00 (*0-19-822868-6*, Clarendon Pr) OUP.

Cubitt, Geoffrey, ed. Imagining Nations. 256p. 1998. pap. 24.95 (*0-7190-5460-5*, Pub. by Manchester Univ Pr) St Martin.

— Imagining Nations. LC 97-47408. 256p. 2000. 89.95 (*0-7190-5115-0*, Pub. by Manchester Univ Pr) St Martin.

Cubitt, Gerald. Journey Through South Africa. (Illus.). 208p. 1992. 29.95 (*1-56757-014-3*) Appleton Comms.

— Zimbabwe: The Beautiful Land. (Illus.). 80p. 1992. 18.95 (*1-56757-008-9*) Appleton Comms.

Cubitt, Gerald, jt. auth. see Cochrane, Janet.

Cubitt, Gerald S. & Joyce, Peter. This Is Namibia. LC 93-215905. 158p. 1992. write for info. (*1-86825-186-1*) Struik Pubs.

— This Is Zimbabwe LC 93-159472. 160p. 1992. write for info. (*1-86825-234-5*) Struik Pubs.

Cubitt, J. M., ed. Mathematical Models in the Earth Sciences: Proceedings of the 7th Geochautauqua, Syracuse University, Oct. 1978. 90p. 1980. pap. 50.00 (*0-08-025305-9*, Pergamon Pr) Elsevier.

Cubitt, J. M. & England, W. A., eds. The Geochemistry of Reservoirs. (Geological Society Special Publication Ser.: No. 86). (Illus.). 328p. 1995. 108.00 (*1-897799-26-8*, 256, Pub. by Geol Soc Pub Hse) AAPG.

Cubitt, J. M. & Reyment, Richard A., eds. Quantitative Stratigraphic Correlation. LC 81-21926. (International Geological Correlation Programme Ser.: No. 148). 321p. reprint ed. pap. 99.60 (*0-7837-3228-7*, 204324600007) Bks Demand.

Cubitt, Sean. Digital Aesthetics. LC 98-61161. (Theory, Culture & Society Ser.). 172 p. 1998. pap. 22.95 (*0-7619-5900-9*) Sage.

— Timeshift: On Video Culture. (Illus.). 200p. 1991. 49.95 (*0-685-50225-2*, A5097) Routledge.

— Videography: Video Media As Art & Culture. LC 93-25196. 1993. pap. 18.95 (*0-312-10296-8*); text 45.00 (*0-312-10295-X*) St Martin.

Cubley, Kahtleen, ed. see Warren, Jean.

Cubley, Kathleen. On the Farm. (Illus.). 32p. (J). (ps-k). 1999. pap. 3.95 (*1-57029-257-4*, 01109) Totline Pubns.

— Things That Go. (Rhyme & Reason Workbook Ser.). (Illus.). 32p. (J). (ps-k). 1999. pap. 3.95 (*1-57029-258-2*, 01110) Totline Pubns.

Cubley, Kathleen, ed. Cobbler, Cobbler. (Cut & Tell Cutout Ser.). (Illus.). 8p. (J). (ps). 1995. 2.95 (*1-57029-029-6*, MPH 2219) Totline Pubns.

— Four Seasons - Math. LC 96-60131. (Four Seasons Ser.). (Illus.). 64p. (Orig.). (J). (ps). 1996. pap. 7.95 (*1-57029-089-X*) Totline Pubns.

Cubley, Kathleen, ed. see Backer, Barbara F.

Cubley, Kathleen, ed. see Bittinger, Gayle.

Cubley, Kathleen, jt. ed. see Bittinger, Gayle.

Cubley, Kathleen, ed. see Clark, Silvana.

Cubley, Kathleen, ed. see Claycomb, Patty & Bittinger, Gayle.

Cubley, Kathleen, ed. see Hodge, Mary A., et al.

Cubley, Kathleen, ed. see Hodges, Susan.

Cubley, Kathleen, ed. see Kranwinkel, Sonya.

Cubley, Kathleen, ed. see McKinnon, Elizabeth.

Cubley, Kathleen, ed. see McKinnon, Elizabeth S.

Cubley, Kathleen, ed. see Petersen, Evelyn.

Cubley, Kathleen, ed. see Spewock, Theodosia.

Cubley, Kathleen, ed. see Spewock, Theodosia & Warren, Jean.

Cubley, Kathleen, ed. see Totline Staff.

Cubley, Kathleen, ed. see Warren, Jean.

Cubley, Stewart, jt. auth. see Cassou, Michelle.

Cuc. Jumpstart: Spanish. 1997. 24.00 incl. cd-rom (*1-56997-304-0*) Knowldge Adv.

Cuc, Le T., et al, eds. Red Books, Green Hills: The Impact of Economic Reform on Restoration Ecology in the Midlands of Northern Vietnam. 1995. write for info. (*0-86638-179-1*) EW Ctr HI.

Cuca, Roberto & Pierce, Catherine S. Experiments in Family Planning: Lessons from the Developing World. LC 77-4602. 278p. reprint ed. pap. 86.20 (*0-7837-4233-9*, 204392200012) Bks Demand.

Cucari, Attilio, jt. auth. see Angelucci, Enzo.

Cucarro, Elio. Alliance Academic Review 1996. (Orig.). pap. 9.99 (*0-87509-690-5*) Chr Pubns.

Cucarro, Elio, ed. Alliance Academic Review 1997. pap. 9.99 (*0-87509-741-3*) Chr Pubns.

— Alliance Pulpit Review. LC 97-191815. 9.99 (*0-87509-740-5*) Chr Pubns.

Cuccarese, James, jt. auth. see Redmon, Ronald.

Cuccaro-Alamin, Stephanie. Postsecondary Persistence & Attainment. 34p. 1997. pap. 4.25 (*0-16-049222-X*) USGPO.

***Cuccaro-Alamin, Stephen.** Postsecondary Financing Strategies: How Undergraduates Combine Work, Borrowing & Attendance. 77p. 1998. pap. 6.00 (*0-16-063650-7*) USGPO.

Cuccaro-Alamin, Stephen & Choy, Susan P. Postsecondary Financing Strategies: How Undergraduates Combine Work, Borrowing & Attendance. Carroll, C. Dennis, ed. (Illus.). 67p. (C). 1999. pap. text 20.00 (*0-7881-7763-X*) DIANE Pub.

Cuccaro, Elio, ed. Alliance Academic Review 1995. 130p. (Orig.). 1995. pap. 9.99 (*0-87509-623-9*, 0016239) Chr Pubns.

Cucchi, Enzo. The Ceremony of Things. limited ed. Martinelli, Franco, tr. from ITA.Tr. of La/Ceremonia Delle Cose. (ENG & ITA., Illus.). 88p. 1985. pap. 35.00 (*0-935875-02-6*) P Blum Edit.

— Enzo Cucchi: Italia. (Illus.). 50p. 1987. 45.00 (*0-947564-40-3*, Pub. by A D'Offay Gallery) Dist Art Pubs.

— Rome. Eccher, Danilo & Bonito Oliva, Achile, eds. (Special Editions for Bibliofiles Ser.). (Illus.). 160p. 1993. 175.00 (*84-343-0660-3*) Elliots Bks.

— Sparire, 2 vols., Set. Shore, Meg & Schelbert, Catherine, trs. (ENG, GER & ITA., Illus.). 45p. (Orig.). 1987. bds. 22.50 (*0-935875-05-0*) P Blum Edit.

Cucchi, Enzo, creator. Mario Botta/Enzo Cucchi: The Chapel of Monte Tamaro. (ENG & ITA., Illus.). 132p. 1998. pap. 59.95 (*88-422-0531-1*) Gingko Press.

Cucchi, Enzo & Botta, Mario. Chapel of Monte Tamaro. 1998. 75.00 (*88-422-0712-8*) Dist Art Pubs.

Cucchiara, Roy F., et al. Clinical Neuroanesthesia. 2nd ed. LC 97-41358. (Illus.). 704p. 1997. text 125.00 (*0-443-07928-5*, C9409) Church.

Cucci, Frank. The Ofay Watcher: Manuscript Edition. 1970. pap. 13.00 (*0-8222-0836-9*) Dramatists Play.

Cuccio, Joan F. The Geometry of Love. LC 96-19009. 1997. 22.00 (*1-877946-82-6*) Permanent Pr.

***Cuccione, Michael & MacSporran, Jane.** There Are Survivors: The Michael Cuccione Story. 1998. pap. 19.95 (*0-9683188-0-0*) Mak a Diff Pub.

Cucco, Ulisse, jt. auth. see Joseph, Lou.

Cuchi, Jose A. Heraldica's Armorial General: A Collection of over 11,000 Drawings of Coats of Arms for Family Names of European Origin. LC 96-95242. 512p. (Orig.). 1997. pap. 145.00 (*0-9656408-0-9*) Heraldica Imports.

Cuchi, Jose C. Un Problema en America: The American Problem, Spanish Text. LC 74-14227. (Puerto Rican Experience Ser.). (Illus.). 246p. 1975. reprint ed. 20.95 (*0-405-06217-6*) Ayer.

Cuchi, Paloma, jt. auth. see Duran, Carmen.

Cuciti, Peggy, jt. ed. see Kaplan, Marshall.

***Cucker, F. & Wong, R., eds.** The Collected Papers of Stephen Smale, 3 vols. 1800p. 2000. 260.00 (*981-02-4307-3*) World Scientific Pub.

Cucker, Felipe & Shub, Michael. Foundations of Computational Mathematics: Selected Papers of a Conference Held at Rio De Janeiro, January 1997. LC 96-37588. 500p. 1997. pap. 102.00 (*3-540-61647-0*) Spr-Verlag.

Cucuel, G. La Poupliniere et la Musique de Chambre Au XVIII Siecle. LC 70-158961. (Music Ser.). (FRE.). 1971. reprint ed. lib. bdg. 55.00 (*0-306-70186-3*) Da Capo.

Cuculescu, I. & Oprea, A. G. Noncommutative Probability. LC 94-32310. (Mathematics & Its Applications Ser.: Vol. 305). 368p. (C). 1994. text 217.50 (*0-7923-3133-8*) Kluwer Academic.

Cucumber Group Staff. Why Cucumbers Are Better Than Men. LC 82-24194. (Illus.). 32p. 1983. pap. 3.95 (*0-87131-483-5*) M Evans.

Cuda, Heide Siegmund, jt. auth. see Alexander, Frank.

Cuda, Margaret C. Milk & Honey: A Collection of Poems. (Illus.). 48p. (Orig.). 1994. pap. 6.95 (*1-881692-07-8*) Trillium WV.

Cudahy, Brian J. Around Manhattan Island & Other Maritime Tales of New York. LC 96-50263. (Illus.). xii, 269p. 1997. 35.00 (*0-8232-1760-4*); pap. 16.00 (*0-8232-1761-2*) Fordham.

— Cash, Tokens, & Transfers: A History of Urban Mass Transit in North America. LC 90-82348. (Illus.). x, 266p. 1990. pap. 19.95 (*0-8232-1278-5*) Fordham.

— The Malbone Street Wreck. LC 99-25764. 144p. 1999. 32.50 (*0-8232-1931-3*, Pub. by Fordham); pap. 19.95 (*0-8232-1932-1*, Pub. by Fordham) BookMasters.

— Over & Back: The History of Ferryboats in New York Harbor. LC 89-84357. (Illus.). 472p. 1990. 39.95 (*0-8232-1245-9*) Fordham.

— Twilight on the Bay: The Excursion Boat Empire of B. B. Wills. LC 98-16065. 240p. 1998. 29.95 (*0-87033-509-X*) Cornell Maritime.

— Under the Sidewalks of New York: The Story of the Greatest Subway System in the World. 2nd rev. ed. LC 95-18861. xxiii, 194p. 1995. pap. 19.95 (*0-8232-1618-7*) Fordham.

Cudahy, Sheila. The Bristle Cone Pine & Other Poems. 61p. 1976. 5.95 (*0-15-114185-1*) Harcourt.

— Crow Time. (New American Fiction Ser.: No. 32). 250p. (Orig.). 1995. pap. 11.95 (*1-55713-202-X*) Sun & Moon CA.

— Nectar at Noon. 1989. 16.95 (*0-15-152170-0*) Harcourt.

Cudakov, N. G., et al. Number Theory & Analysis. LC 88-19373. (Translations Ser.: Series 1, Vol. 2). 532p. 1962. reprint ed. 44.00 (*0-8218-1602-0*, TRANS1/2) Am Math.

Cudanes, Christine, jt. auth. see Lefevre, Holly.

Cudco, Lorin, ed. see Drucker, Johanna, et al.

Cuddeback, William L. Caudebec in America: Descendants of Jacques Caudebec, 1700-1920. 276p. 1997. reprint ed. pap. 41.50 (*0-8328-7896-0*); reprint ed. lib. bdg. 51.50 (*0-8328-7895-2*) Higginson Bk Co.

An Asterisk (*) at the beginning of an entry indicates that the title is appearing for the first time.

Cuddeford, Derek. Equine Nutrition. (Illus.). 160p. 1997. 35.00 (*1-85223-852-6*, Pub. by Crolwood) Trafalgar.

Cuddeke, Christof. Marine Claims. 295p. 1993. 105.00 (*1-85044-540-0*) LLP.

Cuddigan, Maureen & Hanson, Mary B. Growing Pains: Helping Children Deal with Everyday Problems. LC 88-3451. 180p. reprint ed. pap. 55.80 (*0-7837-5920-7*, 204571900007) Bks Demand.

Cuddington, David B. Echoes of Frank Lloyd Wright. LC 98-91060. (Illus.). 64p. 1999. pap. 19.95 (*0-9669053-0-X*) Tiffany Dragon.

Cuddington, John T. Capital Flight: Estimates, Issues, & Explanations. LC 86-21386. (Studies in International Finance: No. 58). 44p. 1986. pap. text 13.50 (*0-88165-230-X*) Princeton U Int Finan Econ.

***Cuddon, J. A.** Dictionary of Literary Terms & Literary Theory. 1024p. 2000. pap. 16.95 (*0-14-051363-9*, Penguin Bks) Viking Penguin.

Cuddon, J. A. A Dictionary of Literary Terms & Literary Theory. 4th ed. LC 98-9226. (Language Library). 1163p. 1998. 89.95 (*0-631-20271-4*) Blackwell Pubs.

Cuddon, J. A., ed. The Penguin Book of Ghost Stories. (Fiction Ser.). 512p. 1985. pap. 13.95 (*0-14-006800-7*, Penguin Bks) Viking Penguin.

— The Penguin Book of Horror Stories. (Fiction Ser.). 608p. 1985. pap. 14.95 (*0-14-006799-X*, Penguin Bks) Viking Penguin.

Cuddon, J. A., ed. see Hogg, James.

Cuddy. Contemporary American Immigration Interpretive Essays Non European. 1982. 21.50 (*0-8057-8420-9*, Twyne) Mac Lib Ref.

Cuddy, Beverley. Cavalier King Charles Spaniels. (Illus.). 1996. pap. 9.95 (*0-7938-2392-7*, KW-193S) TFH Pubns.

Cuddy, Beverley & Bell, Chris. Instant Guide to Dogs. LC 99-50247. 2000. 4.99 (*0-517-12356-8*) Random Hse Value.

Cuddy, Dennis L. An American Commentary. 130p. (Orig.). 1993. pap. 6.95 (*1-879366-40-1*) Hearthstone OK.

***Cuddy, Dennis L.** Grab for Power. 2000. pap. text 7.95 (*1-57558-052-7*) Hearthstone OK.

— New World Order: Now if the Dawning of the New Age. 2000. pap. 12.95 (*1-57558-059-4*) Hearthstone OK.

Cuddy, Dennis L. President Clinton Will Continue the New World Order. 70p. (Orig.). 1994. pap. 2.95 (*1-879366-87-8*) Hearthstone OK.

— Secret Records Revealed. 1999. 11.95 (*1-57558-031-4*) Hearthstone OK.

Cuddy, Jeffrey A. The Ultimate Breakthrough in Market Turning Point Detection: Catching Every Major Pivot in Stocks. 1998. 50.00 (*0-930233-61-1*) Windsor.

Cuddy, John D. & Cuddy, Teresa. Growing Blueberries: A Guide for the Small Commercial Grower. 127p. (Orig.). 1996. pap. 23.45 (*1-888863-00-5*) Rush River Pubns.

***Cuddy, John D. & Cuddy, Teresa M.** Growing Blueberries: A Guide for the Serious Gardener & Commercial Grower. 2nd ed. 2000. pap. 25.00 (*1-888863-02-1*) Rush River Pubns.

Cuddy, Joseph E. Irish-America & National Isolationism, 1914-1920. LC 76-6332. (Irish Americans Ser.). 1976. 24.95 (*0-405-09328-4*) Ayer.

***Cuddy, Lois A.** T. S. Eliot & the Poetics of Evolution: Sub-Versions of Classicism, Culture & Progress. LC 99-27226. 288p. 2000. 46.50 (*0-8387-5422-8*) Bucknell U Pr.

Cuddy, Robbin. Anastasia, No. 1. 12p. (J). (gr. k-4). 1997. 12.95 (*0-694-01087-1*, HarpFestival) HarpC Child Bks.

— Cinderella. LC 94-70524. (Illustrated Classics Ser.). 96p. (J). 1995. 14.95 (*0-7868-3014-X*, Pub. by Disney Pr) Little.

— Cinderella: The Fairy Godmother's Magic. LC 93-73820. (Surprise Lift-the-Flap Bk.). (J). 1994. 9.95 (*1-56282-624-7*, Pub. by Disney Pr) Little.

— The Hunchback of Notre Dame Illustrated Classic. LC 95-83652. 96p. (J). 1996. 14.95 (*0-7868-3089-1*, Pub. by Disney Pr) Time Warner.

Cuddy, Teresa, jt. auth. see Cuddy, John D.

Cuddy, Teresa M., jt. auth. see Cuddy, John D.

Cudell, J. R., et al. What Next? Exploring the Future of High-Energy Physics: Proceedings of the 16th Annual Montreal. 332p. 1994. text 106.00 (*981-02-2073-1*) World Scientific Pub.

Cudich, Sylvia, tr. see Annacondia, Carlos & Sawin, Gisela.

Cudilleire, Manuel B., et al. En Pos la Democracia Economica. LC 87-81417. (Coleccion Cuba y sus Jueces). (SPA.). 138p. (Orig.). 1987. pap. 15.00 (*0-89729-443-2*) Ediciones.

Cudimano, Patricia. Works of Heart. 64p. 1993. 6.50 (*1-56245-038-7*) Great Quotations.

Cudinach, Salvidor, ed. & tr. see Piarist Fathers Staff.

Cudjoe, Selwyn R. Movement of the People. 224p. (Orig.). 1983. text 18.95 (*0-686-39680-4*); pap. text 8.95 (*0-911565-22-1*) Calaloux Pubns.

***Cudjoe, Selwyn R.** Tacarigua: A Village in Trinidad. LC 98-16086. xx, 78p. 1998. write for info. (*0-911565-24-8*) Calaloux Pubns.

Cudjoe, Selwyn R. V. S. Naipaul: A Materialist Reading. LC 87-35768. 304p. (Orig.). (C). 1988. 35.00 (*0-87023-619-9*); pap. text 18.95 (*0-87023-620-2*) U of Mass Pr.

Cudjoe, Selwyn R., ed. Caribbean Women Writers: Essays from the First International Conference. LC 90-80896. 400p. (C). 1990. pap. 20.95 (*0-87023-732-2*); lib. bdg. 40.00 (*0-87023-731-4*) U of Mass Pr.

— Eric E. Williams Speaks. 200p. (Orig.). 1991. 35.00 (*0-911565-12-4*); pap. 14.95 (*0-911565-13-2*) Calaloux Pubns.

Cudjoe, Selwyn R. & Cain, William E., eds. C. L. R. James: His Intellectual Legacies. LC 94-4518. 488p. (C). 1995. pap. 20.95 (*0-87023-907-4*); lib. bdg. 55.00 (*0-87023-906-6*) U of Mass Pr.

Cudjoe, Selwyn R., ed. see Philip, Maxwell, et al.

Cudkowicz, Merit E. & Irizarry, Michael C., eds. Neurologic Disorders in Women. LC 96-50469. 184p. 1997. text 59.95 (*0-7506-9745-8*) Buttrwrth-Heinemann.

Cudkowicz, Merit E., jt. auth. see Batchelor, Tracy.

Cudlip, William B. University of Michigan: Its Legal Profile. (University of Michigan Legal Publications). xv, 367p. 1994. 42.50 (*1-57588-377-5*, 300190) W S Hein.

***Cudmore, Bob.** You Can't Go Wrong: Stories from Nero, New York & Other Tales. (Illus.). 125p. 2000. 16.95 (*1-929529-02-3*); pap. 11.95 (*1-929529-03-1*) Nero Pubg Co.

Cudmore, Dana. The Remarkable Howe Caverns Story. (Illus.). 192p. 1990. 14.95 (*0-87951-387-X*, Pub. by Overlook Pr) Penguin Putnam.

Cudney, Milton R. & Hardy, Robert E. Self-Defeating Behaviors: Free Yourself from the Habits, Compulsions, Feelings, & Attitudes That Hold You Back. LC 90-84903. 256p. 1993. reprint ed. pap. 14.00 (*0-06-250197-6*, Pub. by Harper SF) HarpC.

Cudsi, Alexander S. & Dessouki, Ali E., eds. Islam & Power. LC 81-47608. 208p. reprint ed. pap. 64.50 (*0-608-15868-2*, 203074400070) Bks Demand.

Cudworth, Arthur G., Jr., ed. Flood Hydrology Manual. (C). 1990. 180.00 (*0-7855-6698-8*, Pub. by Scientific) St Mut.

Cudworth, Marsha. Self-Guided Architectural Tours of Cape May, NJ. LC 84-81044. (Illus.). 1985. pap. 6.95 (*0-9608554-2-4*) Lady Raspbrry.

— Self Guided Architectural Tours of Cape May, N.J. An Illustrated Guide to Cape Mays Rich Architectural Heritage - 2 Walking Tours & 1 Auto Tour Featuring over 100 Historical Sights. LC 84-81044. 82p. 1987. pap. 8.95 (*0-317-01463-3*) Bric-A-Brac.

Cudworth, Ralph. Ralph Cudworth: A Treatise Concerning Eternal & Immutable Morality: With A Treatise of Freewill. Hutton, Sarah, ed. LC 96-10996. (Cambridge Texts in the History of Philosophy Ser.). 254p. (C). 1996. text 59.95 (*0-521-47362-4*); pap. text 19.95 (*0-521-47918-5*) Cambridge U Pr.

— A Treatise Concerning Eternal & Immutable Morality & a Treatise of Freewill. (Collected Works: Vol. II). viii, 95p. 1979. reprint ed. 110.00 (*3-487-06010-8*) G Olms Pubs.

— The True Intellectual System of the Universe: The First Part; Wherein All the Reason & Philosophy of Atheism Is Confuted, & Its Impossibility Demonstrated. (Collected Works: Vol. I). 899p. 1977. reprint ed. 305.00 (*3-487-06009-4*) G Olms Pubs.

— The True Intellectual System of the Universe: 1845 Edition, 3 vols., Set. LC 95-232456. (Cambridge Platonists Ser.). 2060p. 1996. reprint ed. 395.00 (*1-85506-357-3*) Bks Intl VA.

Cue Canovas, Agustin. Los Estados Unidos y el Mexico Olvidado. Cortes, Carlos E., ed. LC 76-5224. (Chicano Heritage Ser.). (SPA.). 1977. reprint ed. 17.95 (*0-405-09498-1*) Ayer.

***Cuellar, Carlos J., et al.** Extending Access to Health Care Through Public-Private Partnerships: The Prosalud Experience. (Stubbs Monograph Ser.: No. 2). 108p. 2000. pap. 15.00 (*0-913723-63-0*) Mgmt Sci Health.

Cuellar, Carol. The Best in Popular Sheet Music. 96p. 1997. pap. text 12.95 (*0-7692-0031-1*) Wrner Bros.

— Biggest Country Hits of 95-96. 152p. (Orig.). 1996. pap. text 14.95 (*1-57623-451-7*, MF9628) Wrner Bros.

— Fantastic TV & Movie Songs. 72p. (YA). 1995. pap. text 9.95 (*0-89724-715-9*, AF9525) Wrner Bros.

— Great Original Solos for Piano. 144p. (YA). 1995. pap. text 14.95 (*0-89724-723-X*, MF9533) Wrner Bros.

— Prince - Sign o' the Times. 112p. (Orig.). (C). 1987. pap. text 16.95 (*0-7692-0538-0*, VF1393) Wrner Bros.

Cuellar, Carol, ed. Abba/Live. 60p. (Orig.). (C). 1986. pap. text 12.95 (*0-7692-0211-X*, VF1344) Wrner Bros.

— The Absolutely Very Best of Peter Combe...(So Far!) 68p. (Orig.). (C). 1991. pap. text 16.95 (*0-7692-0283-7*, VF1761) Wrner Bros.

— Academy Award Winning Music from "Dr. Zhivago" 40p. 1967. pap. text 12.95 (*0-7692-1507-6*, TSF0024) Wrner Bros.

— Again & 24 Top Movie & TV Hits. 124p. (Orig.). (C). 1994. pap. text 12.95 (*0-89724-214-9*, VF2114) Wrner Bros.

— Alabama: Greatest Hits, Vol. III. 56p. (C). 1995. pap. text 16.95 (*0-614-31159-4*, PF9505) Wrner Bros.

— Alabama: Live. 72p. (Orig.). (C). 1988. pap. text 12.95 (*0-7692-0216-0*, VF1485) Wrner Bros.

— Alabama: Pass It on Down. 56p. (Orig.). (C). 1990. pap. text 14.95 (*0-7692-0206-3*, VF1661) Wrner Bros.

— The Alan & Marilyn Bergman Songbook. 184p. (Orig.). (C). 1991. pap. text 22.95 (*0-7692-0209-8*, VF1706) Wrner Bros.

— Alan Jackson: A lot about Livin' & a Little 'Bout Love. 52p. (Orig.). (C). 1993. pap. text 16.95 (*0-7692-0762-6*, VF1902) Wrner Bros.

— Alan Jackson: Don't Rock the Jukebox. 72p. (Orig.). (C). 1991. pap. text 16.95 (*0-7692-0755-3*, VF1750) Wrner Bros.

— Alan Jackson: Who I am. 72p. (Orig.). (C). 1994. pap. text 16.95 (*0-7692-0763-4*, VF2168) Wrner Bros.

— Alice Cooper/Welcome to My Nightmare. 52p. (Orig.). (C). 1975. pap. text 6.95 (*0-7692-0284-5*, VF0328) Wrner Bros.

— All-American Songbook. 148p. (Orig.). (C). 1984. pap. text 9.95 (*0-7692-0830-4*, TMF0113) Wrner Bros.

— All My Love: 56 Beautiful Love Songs. 132p. (Orig.). (C). 1984. pap. text 8.95 (*0-7692-0868-1*, SF0066) Wrner Bros.

— All the Best Adult Contemporary Hits. 196p. (Orig.). (C). 1984. pap. text 12.95 (*0-7692-0864-9*, VF1474) Wrner Bros.

— All the Best Big Band Sounds. 132p. (Orig.). (C). 1996. pap. text 9.95 (*0-7692-0840-1*, SF0162) Wrner Bros.

— All the Best Country Superstars. rev. ed. 260p. (Orig.). (C). 1985. pap. text 14.95 (*0-7692-0842-8*, VF1608) Wrner Bros.

— All the Best Easy Listening. rev. ed. 256p. (Orig.). (C). 1994. pap. text 16.95 (*0-89724-412-5*, VF2163) Wrner Bros.

— All the Best Heavy Metal Ballads. rev. ed. 244p. (Orig.). (C). 1990. pap. text 16.95 (*0-7692-0867-3*, VF1970) Wrner Bros.

— Alto Sax Showstoppers. rev. ed. 112p. 1997. pap. 12.95 (*0-7692-1696-X*, F2947ASE) Wrner Bros.

— America/Deluxe Anthology. 148p. (Orig.). (C). 1977. pap. text 17.95 (*0-89724-163-0*, VF1365) Wrner Bros.

— America/History: Greatest Hits. 64p. (Orig.). (C). 1995. pap. text 16.95 (*0-7692-0212-8*, VF0523) Wrner Bros.

— Anita Baker: Rhythm of Love. 72p. (Orig.). (C). 1995. pap. text 17.95 (*0-7604-0075-X*, P1087SMX) Wrner Bros.

— Annie: Vocal Selections. 68p. (Orig.). (C). 1979. pap. text 13.95 (*0-89898-629-X*, TSF0006) Wrner Bros.

— Annie Warbucks: Vocal Selections. 88p. (Orig.). (C). 1994. pap. text 16.95 (*0-7692-0202-0*, TSF0073) Wrner Bros.

— Anything Goes Revival Edition: Vocal Selections. 68p. (Orig.). (C). 1983. pap. text 16.95 (*0-7692-0213-6*, VF1450) Wrner Bros.

— The Artistry of Bill Evans. 96p. (Orig.). (C). 1989. pap. text 14.95 (*0-89898-551-X*, TPF0148) Wrner Bros.

— Assassins: Revised Vocal Selections. 84p. (Orig.). (C). 1993. pap. text 21.95 (*0-7692-0204-7*, VF1978) Wrner Bros.

— Assassins: Vocal Score. 152p. (Orig.). (C). 1992. pap. text 75.00 (*0-7692-0208-X*, VF1765) Wrner Bros.

— Babes in Toyland: Vocal Score. 144p. (Orig.). (C). 1954. pap. text 40.00 (*0-7692-0205-5*, OP0001) Wrner Bros.

— Babes in Toyland: Vocal Selections. 52p. (Orig.). (C). 1985. pap. text 9.95 (*0-89724-351-X*, SF0144) Wrner Bros.

— Baby: Vocal Selections. 80p. (Orig.). (C). 1995. pap. text 12.95 (*0-7692-0214-4*, VAL2012A) Wrner Bros.

— Bach, Beethoven & Brahms Vol. 10: Piano/Vocal Folio. 148p. (Orig.). 1993. pap. 12.95 (*0-89898-724-5*, WFM00010) Wrner Bros.

— Bacharach Hall of Fame. 100p. (Orig.). (C). 1991. pap. text 14.95 (*0-7692-0210-1*, VF1733) Wrner Bros.

— The Baker's Wife: Vocal Selections. 36p. (Orig.). (C). 1990. pap. text 12.95 (*0-7692-0207-1*, VF1668) Wrner Bros.

— Balancing Act: Vocal Selections. 68p. (Orig.). (C). 1992. pap. text 14.95 (*0-7692-0215-2*, VF1904) Wrner Bros.

— The Band Wagon: Movie Selections. 52p. (Orig.). (C). 1995. pap. text 10.95 (*0-89724-515-6*, VF2177) Wrner Bros.

— Barnum: Vocal Score. 212p. (Orig.). (C). 1989. pap. text 50.00 (*0-7692-0203-9*, TSF0065) Wrner Bros.

— Because You Loved Me & Other Hot Pop Singles. 60p. (Orig.). (YA). 1996. pap. text 8.95 (*1-57623-533-5*, AF9674) Wrner Bros.

— Because You Loved Me & 14 Pop Chart Toppers. 92p. (Orig.). (YA). 1996. pap. text 9.95 (*1-57623-511-4*, MF9633) Wrner Bros.

— The Best in Christmas Sheet (Easy Piano) 64p. (YA). 1997. pap. 9.95 (*0-7692-0229-2*, AF9755) Wrner Bros.

— The Best in Christmas Sheet Music Piano/Vocal. 68p. (YA). 1997. pap. 9.95 (*0-7692-0085-0*, MF9728) Wrner Bros.

— The Best in Country Love Songs. 184p. (Orig.). (J). 1997. pap. text 16.95 (*1-57623-885-7*) Wrner Bros.

— The Best in Country Sheet Music. 104p. (Orig.). (YA). 1996. pap. text 12.95 (*1-57623-584-X*, MF9642) Wrner Bros.

— The Best in Popular Sheet Music. 120p. (YA). 1996. pap. text 14.95 (*1-57623-338-3*, MF9541A) Wrner Bros.

— The Best of Al Green. 76p. (Orig.). 1995. pap. text 14.95 (*0-89724-517-2*, P1093SMX) Wrner Bros.

— The Best of Chicago. 52p. (Orig.). (C). 1986. pap. text 10.95 (*0-7692-0240-3*, P0694SMX) Wrner Bros.

— The Best of Creedence Clearwater Revival. 68p. (Orig.). (C). 1986. pap. text 14.95 (*0-89898-454-8*, P0700SMX) Wrner Bros.

— The Best of Dwight Yoakam. 52p. (Orig.). (C). 1990. pap. text 10.95 (*0-7692-0845-2*, VF1699) Wrner Bros.

— The Best of Garth Brooks: Easy Piano. 60p. (Orig.). (C). 1992. pap. text 12.95 (*0-7692-0449-X*, P0942P2X) Wrner Bros.

— The Best of Genesis. 68p. (Orig.). (C). 1983. pap. text 10.95 (*0-7692-0460-0*, VF1053) Wrner Bros.

— The Best of Herb Alpert. 104p. (Orig.). (C). 1983. pap. text 18.95 (*0-7692-0733-2*, P0448SMX) Wrner Bros.

— The Best of Howard Jones. 52p. (Orig.). (C). 1987. pap. text 10.95 (*0-7692-0703-0*, VF1408) Wrner Bros.

— The Best of Marty Robbins. (Legendary Performers Ser.). 84p. (Orig.). (YA). 1995. pap. text 13.95 (*0-89724-523-7*, TPF0168) Wrner Bros.

— The Best of Popular Wedding Music. 180p. 1992. pap. 14.95 (*0-89898-996-5*) Wrner Bros.

— The Best of Randy Travis. 52p. (Orig.). (C). 1990. pap. text 10.95 (*0-7692-0841-X*, VF1650) Wrner Bros.

— The Best of Rush. 68p. (Orig.). (C). 1985. pap. text 10.95 (*0-7692-0913-0*, VF1201) Wrner Bros.

— The Best of Stevie Nicks - Timespace. 108p. (Orig.). (C). 1991. pap. text 16.95 (*0-7692-0773-1*, VF1785) Wrner Bros.

— The Best of the Temptations. 52p. (Orig.). (C). 1987. pap. text 10.95 (*0-89898-511-0*, P0772SMX) Wrner Bros.

— The Best of Vince Gill. 68p. (Orig.). (C). 1995. pap. text 16.95 (*0-89724-665-9*, PF9521) Wrner Bros.

— Beth Nielsen Chapman/You Hold the Key. (Personality Folio Ser.). 70p. (Orig.). (C). 1994. pap. text 19.95 (*0-89724-099-5*, VF2081) Wrner Bros.

— Beverly Hills, 90210 Soundtrack. 72p. (Orig.). (C). 1993. pap. text 18.95 (*0-7692-0227-6*, VF1938) Wrner Bros.

— Biggest Country Hits of 1996-1997. 148p. 1997. pap. 14.95 (*0-7692-1472-X*, MF9733) Wrner Bros.

— The Biggest Country Hits/1995. 256p. (Orig.). 1995. pap. 16.95 (*0-89724-781-7*, MF9548) Wrner Bros.

— Biggest Hits of 1995. 96p. (Orig.). (YA). 1995. pap. text 12.95 (*0-89724-914-3*, AF9550) Wrner Bros.

— Biggest Hits of 1995-1996: Easy Piano Arrangements by Dan Coates. 136p. (Orig.). 1996. pap. text 12.95 (*1-57623-463-0*, AF9662) Wrner Bros.

— Biggest Pop Hits of 1996-1997. 188p. 1997. pap. 14.95 (*0-7692-1426-6*, MF9732) Wrner Bros.

— Biggest Pop Hits of 1996-1997: Easy Piano. 112p. 1997. pap. 12.95 (*0-7692-1568-8*, AF9759) Wrner Bros.

— Bitter Sweet: Vocal Selections. 44p. (Orig.). (C). 1985. pap. text 9.95 (*0-7692-0220-9*, SF0141) Wrner Bros.

— BMI Top 50 Motion Picture Songs: Alto Sax. 60p. (Orig.). 1994. pap. 10.95 (*0-89898-763-6*, F3406ASX) Wrner Bros.

— BMI Top 50 Motion Picture Songs: Flute. 60p. (Orig.). 1994. pap. 10.95 (*0-89898-760-1*, F3406FLX) Wrner Bros.

— BMI Top 50 Motion Picture Songs: Trumpet. 60p. (Orig.). 1994. pap. 10.95 (*0-89898-762-8*, F3406TRX) Wrner Bros.

— Bob Seger & the Silver Bullet Band - It's a Mystery. 68p. (Orig.). (C). 1997. pap. text 19.95 (*1-57623-873-3*, PF9557) Wrner Bros.

— Bob Seger & the Silver Bullet Band Anthology. 144p. (Orig.). 1994. pap. 18.95 (*0-89724-237-8*, VF1507) Wrner Bros.

— Bob Seger & the Silver Bullet Bank - The Distance. 56p. (Orig.). (C). 1983. pap. text 12.95 (*0-7692-0920-3*, VF1028) Wrner Bros.

— Book of Golden Country Music: Piano/Vocal/Chords. rev. ed. 132p. 1992. pap. 14.95 (*0-89898-605-2*, F2926SMA) Wrner Bros.

— Book of Golden Hawaiian Songs: Piano/Vocal/Chords. 96p. (Orig.). 1995. pap. 12.95 (*0-89724-704-3*, F3113SMA) Wrner Bros.

— The Book of Great Love Songs. 204p. (Orig.). 1997. pap. 14.95 (*0-7692-0069-9*, MF9725) Wrner Bros.

— The Book of Great Rock & Roll Classics. 132p. 1997. pap. 14.95 (*0-7692-0081-8*) Warner Bros.

— The Book of Great TV Hits. 136p. (Orig.). 1997. pap. 14.95 (*0-7692-0070-2*, MF9723) Wrner Bros.

— Boston/the First Two Albums. 84p. (Orig.). (C). 1987. pap. text 14.95 (*0-7692-0226-8*, VF1375) Wrner Bros.

— Box Office Blockbusters: Fifty-Five Movie Songs & Themes. 164p. (Orig.). (YA). 1994. pap. text 12.95 (*0-89898-779-2*, F3407P2X); pap. text 14.95 (*0-89898-778-4*, F3407SMX) Wrner Bros.

— The Broadway Music Collection. 224p. (Orig.). (YA). 1994. pap. 16.95 (*0-7692-0130-X*, F3468SMX) Wrner Bros.

— Broadway Showstoppers. 386p. (Orig.). 1994. pap. 18.95 (*0-89898-824-1*, F2878SMC) Wrner Bros.

— Bruce Hornsby - Harbor Lights. (Illus.). 96p. (Orig.). (C). 1994. pap. text 19.95 (*0-89724-059-6*, VF1967) Wrner Bros.

— Bruce Hornsby Anthology. 256p. (Orig.). 1994. pap. 24.95 (*0-89724-425-7*, VF1947) Wrner Bros.

— Bruce Springsteen - Born in the U. S. A. 84p. (Orig.). (C). 1984. pap. text 18.95 (*0-89898-294-4*, P0579SMX) Wrner Bros.

— Bryan Adams/Reckless. 56p. (Orig.). (C). 1985. pap. text 14.95 (*0-89898-354-1*, P0608SMX) Wrner Bros.

— Bryan Adams/So Far So Good. 68p. (Orig.). (C). 1994. pap. text 14.95 (*0-7692-0241-1*, P1049SMX) Wrner Bros.

— Bryan White: Between Now & Forever. (Illus.). 68p. (Orig.). 1996. pap. text 16.95 (*1-57623-464-9*, PF9618) Wrner Bros.

— Butterfly Kisses & Other Great Hits. 72p. 1997. pap. text 9.95 (*0-7692-0977-7*, MF9731) Wrner Bros.

— Butterfly Kisses & Other Hot Pop Singles for Alto Sax. 28p. 1997. pap. 6.95 (*0-7692-1582-3*, IF9715) Wrner Bros.

— Butterfly Kisses & Other Hot Pop Singles for Clarinet. 28p. 1997. pap. 6.95 (*0-7692-1581-5*, IF9714) Wrner Bros.

— Butterfly Kisses & Other Hot Pop Singles for Tenor Sax. 28p. 1997. pap. 6.95 (*0-7692-1583-1*, IF9716) Wrner Bros.

— Butterfly Kisses & Other Hot Pop Singles for Trombone. 28p. 1997. pap. 6.95 (*0-7692-1585-8*, IF9718) Wrner Bros.

— Butterfly Kisses & Other Hot Pop Singles for Trumpet. 28p. 1997. pap. 6.95 (*0-7692-1584-X*, IF9717) Wrner Bros.

— Bye Bye Birdie. 72p. (Orig.). (YA). 1996. pap. text 14.95 (*1-57623-470-3*, PF9604) Wrner Bros.

— Bye Bye Birdie: Vocal Score. 164p. (Orig.). (C). 1988. pap. text 38.50 (*0-7692-0243-8*, TSF0064) Wrner Bros.

— Candlebox/Candlebox. 92p. (Orig.). (C). 1994. pap. text 19.95 (*0-89724-219-X*, VF2118) Wrner Bros.

— Carnival: Vocal Selections. 36p. (Orig.). (C). 1979. pap. text 10.95 (*0-7692-0244-6*, TSF0014) Wrner Bros.

— Carole Bayer Sager Anthology. 164p. (Orig.). (C). 1990. pap. text 19.95 (*0-7692-0921-1*, VF1601) Wrner Bros.

— Carpenters/Greatest Hits. 80p. (Orig.). (C). 1984. pap. text 16.95 (*0-7692-0239-X*, P0593SMX) Wrner Bros.

— The Cars: Complete. 292p. (Orig.). (C). 1988. pap. text 19.95 (*0-7692-0254-3*, VF1473) Wrner Bros.

— The Cars: Greatest Hits. 68p. (Orig.). (C). 1985. pap. text 12.95 (*0-7692-0251-9*, VF1265) Wrner Bros.

— Catch the Christmas Spirit. 96p. (Orig.). 1994. pap. 10.95 (*0-89724-379-X*, VF1957) Wrner Bros.

— Celine Dion: Falling for You. (Illus.). 88p. (Orig.). 1997. pap. text 18.95 (*1-57623-895-4*, 4813A) Wrner Bros.

C

— The Celine Dion Songbook. 76p. (Orig.). (YA). 1995. pap. text 16.95 (*0-89724-669-1*, PF9520) Wrner Bros.
— The Charlie Daniels Band/a Decade of Hits. 72p. (Orig.). (C). 1992. pap. text 16.95 (*0-7692-0253-5*, VF1860) Wrner Bros.
— The Chieftains: The Long Black Veil. 60p. (Orig.). 1995. pap. text 16.95 (*0-89724-870-8*, PF9530) Wrner Bros.
— Children's Song Vol. 1: Piano/Vocal. 160p. (Orig.). (YA). 1993. pap. 12.95 (*0-89898-709-1*, WFM00001) Wrner Bros.
— Chipmunk Christmas: Five Finger Coloring. (Illus.). 32p. (Orig.). (YA). 1993. pap. text 9.95 (*0-7692-0032-X*) Wrner Bros.
— Chitty Chitty Bang Bang: Vocal Selections. 36p. (Orig.). (C). 1992. pap. text 9.95 (*0-7692-0242-X*, TSF0070) Wrner Bros.
— Chris Isaak - Forever Blue. 56p. (Orig.). (C). 1995. pap. text 17.95 (*0-89724-746-9*, PF9522) Wrner Bros.
— Chris Isaak - Heart-Shaped World. 62p. (Orig.). (C). 1991. pap. text 16.95 (*0-7692-0756-1*, VF1745) Wrner Bros.
— Chris Isaak - San Francisco Days. 76p. (Orig.). (C). 1993. pap. text 19.95 (*0-7692-0760-X*, VF1937) Wrner Bros.
— The Christmas Fake Book: C Edition. 116p. (Orig.). (YA). 1995. pap. text 10.95 (*0-89724-860-0*) Wrner Bros.
— Christmas Favorites. (Warner Brothers Presents Ser.). 196p. (Orig.). 1995. pap. text 18.95 (*0-89724-853-8*, MF9556) Wrner Bros.
— Christmas Greatest Hits. 132p. (Orig.). 1995. reprint ed. pap. text 10.95 (*0-89724-852-X*, F3357P2A) Wrner Bros.
— Christmas Greatest Hits: Big Note Piano. 140p. (Orig.). (YA). 1993. pap. text 10.95 (*0-7692-0142-3*, F335793X) Wrner Bros.
— Christmas Music: Made Easy for Piano. 68p. (Orig.). 1995. pap. text 8.95 (*0-89724-866-X*, AF9540) Wrner Bros.
— Christmas Popular & Traditional Favorites - Schultz: Early Grade Piano. 116p. (Orig.). (YA). 1992. pap. text 12.95 (*0-7692-0143-1*, F302793X) Wrner Bros.
— Christmas Showstoppers: Piano - Vocal. rev. ed. 216p. 1997. pap. 17.95 (*0-89724-763-9*, F2868SMC) Wrner Bros.
— City of Angels: Vocal Score. 252p. (Orig.). (C). 1994. pap. text 75.00 (*0-89724-142-8*, VF2099) Wrner Bros.
— Clarinet Showstoppers. 112p. (Orig.). 1997. pap. text 12.95 (*0-7692-0025-7*) Wrner Bros.
— Clarinet Showstoppers. rev. ed. (Showstoppers Ser.). 112p. (Orig.). (YA). 1995. pap. text 12.95 (*0-89724-550-4*, F2947CLE) Wrner Bros.
— Classic Rhythm & Blues: The Greatest R & B Hits of the Sixties & Seventies. 188p. 1995. pap. text 16.95 (*0-89724-823-6*, MF9542) Wrner Bros.
— Clint Black: Looking for Christmas. 40p. (Orig.). (YA). 1995. pap. text 14.95 (*0-89724-994-1*, PF9550) Wrner Bros.
— Clint Black: One Emotion. (Illus.). 48p. (Orig.). 1995. pap. text 16.95 (*0-89724-503-2*, PF9501) Wrner Bros.
— Clint Black: The Greatest Hit. (Illus.). 80p. (Orig.). 1997. pap. text 16.95 (*1-57623-620-X*, PF9654) Wrner Bros.
— Closer Than Ever: Vocal Score. 272p. (Orig.). (C). 1996. pap. text 50.00 (*0-7692-0278-0*, VAL2002) Wrner Bros.
— Closer Than Ever: Vocal Selections. 48p. (Orig.). (C). 1996. pap. text 8.95 (*0-7692-0286-1*, VAL2001) Wrner Bros.
— Cole Porter - Cole Porter Years. 100p. (Orig.). (C). 1996. pap. text 10.95 (*0-7692-0511-9*, SF0005) Wrner Bros.
— Collin Raye/in This Life. 48p. (Orig.). (C). 1993. pap. text 13.95 (*0-7692-0266-7*, P0975SMX) Wrner Bros.
— The Comden & Green Songbook. 96p. (Orig.). (C). 1996. pap. text 17.95 (*1-57623-336-7*, PF9607) Wrner Bros.
— The Commitments. 56p. (Orig.). (C). 1991. pap. text 14.95 (*0-7692-0265-9*, P0935SMX) Wrner Bros.
— The Commitments, Vol. 2. 40p. (Orig.). (C). 1992. pap. text 10.95 (*0-7692-0270-5*, P0956SMX) Wrner Bros.
— Common Thread: The Songs of the Eagles. (Personality - Piano-Vocal Ser.). 80p. (Orig.). (C). 1994. pap. text 16.95 (*0-89724-136-3*, VF2097) Wrner Bros.
— The Complete Movie Music Collection. 330p. (Orig.). (YA). 1993. pap. text 16.95 (*0-89898-585-4*, F3325SMX) Wrner Bros.
— Complete Rock 'n' Roll Collection. 256p. (Orig.). (YA). (gr. 9-12). 1996. pap. 16.95 (*0-89898-966-3*, F3429SMA) Wrner Bros.
— A Connecticut Yankee: Vocal Selections. 44p. (Orig.). (C). 1984. pap. text 9.95 (*0-7692-0272-1*, SF0107) Wrner Bros.
— Country Favorites. (Warner Brothers Presents Ser.). 304p. (Orig.). 1995. pap. text 18.95 (*0-89724-521-0*, MF9503) Wrner Bros.
— Country Showstoppers, Vol. 2. 292p. (Orig.). 1994. pap. text 18.95 (*0-89898-850-0*) Wrner Bros.
— Cracker/Kerosene Hat. 56p. (Orig.). (C). 1994. pap. text 18.95 (*0-89724-286-6*, VF2128) Wrner Bros.
— Cristy Lane: One Day at a Time. 48p. (Orig.). (YA). 1994. pap. text 12.95 (*0-7604-0010-5*, P1076SMX) Wrner Bros.
— Crosby, Stills, Nash & Young. 108p. (Orig.). (C). 1994. pap. text 18.95 (*0-7692-0275-6*, VF0035) Wrner Bros.
— Crosby, Stills, Nash & Young/American Dream. 80p. (Orig.). (C). 1989. pap. text 14.95 (*0-7692-0281-0*, VF1542) Wrner Bros.
— Crosby, Stills, Nash & Young/Live It Up. 64p. (Orig.). (C). 1990. pap. text 14.95 (*0-7692-0276-4*, VF1673) Wrner Bros.
— Cryer & Ford. 48p. (Orig.). (C). 1996. pap. text 9.95 (*0-7692-0285-3*, VAL2003) Wrner Bros.
— Damn Yankees: Vocal Score. 152p. (Orig.). (C). 1988. pap. text 38.50 (*0-7692-0269-1*, TSF0058A) Wrner Bros.
— Dan Coates: Movie Music Made Easy for Piano. 56p. (Orig.). 1995. pap. text 8.95 (*0-89724-617-9*, AF9514) Wrner Bros.
— Dan Coates Country Music: Made Easy for Piano. 52p. (Orig.). Date not set. pap. text 8.95 (*0-7692-0096-6*, AF9511) Wrner Bros.
— Dan Coates Golden Collection of Movie Themes. 200p. (Orig.). 1994. pap. 17.95 (*0-89724-305-6*, PF0915) Wrner Bros.
— Dan Coates Popular Music: Made Easy for Piano. 60p. (Orig.). (YA). 1995. pap. text 8.95 (*0-89724-616-0*, AF9513) Wrner Bros.
— Dan Coates' Popular Music Collection: For the Advanced Player. (Professional Touch Ser.). 56p. (Orig.). 1996. pap. text 14.95 (*0-89724-938-0*, AF9555) Wrner Bros.
— Dave Brubeck/Points on Jazz: Jazz Ballet. (Dave Brubeck Classics Ser.). 52p. (Orig.). (C). 1993. pap. text 10.95 (*0-7692-0289-6*, TPF0165) Wrner Bros.
— Davekoz: Off the Beaten Path. 132p. (Orig.). (YA). 1997. pap. text 19.95 (*1-57623-805-9*, PF9706) Wrner Bros.
— Desert Song: Vocal Score. 212p. (Orig.). (C). 1985. pap. text 50.00 (*0-7692-0303-5*, VP0004) Wrner Bros.
— Desert Song: Vocal Selections. 36p. (Orig.). (C). 1985. pap. text 9.95 (*0-89724-158-4*, SF0140) Wrner Bros.
— Dire Straits/Money for Nothing. 92p. (Orig.). (C). 1988. pap. text 21.95 (*0-7692-0305-1*, P0817SMX) Wrner Bros.
— A Doll's Life: Vocal Selections. 40p. (Orig.). (C). 1996. pap. text 8.95 (*0-7692-0292-6*, VAL2004) Wrner Bros.
— Dolly Parton: I Will Always Love You & Other Greatest Hits. 48p. (Orig.). 1996. pap. text 14.95 (*1-57623-552-1*, PF9629) Wrner Bros.
— Don Henley - Greatest Hits (Actual Miles) 92p. (Orig.). (C). 1996. pap. text 19.95 (*1-57623-333-2*, PF9610) Wrner Bros.
— Don Henley - The End of Innocence. 64p. (Orig.). 1994. pap. 19.95 (*0-89724-199-1*, VF1604) Wrner Bros.
— Donald Fagan/Kamakiriad: Kamakiriad. (Illus.). 68p. (Orig.). (C). 1993. pap. text 19.95 (*0-89724-022-7*, VF1992) Wrner Bros.
— Don't Bother Me, I Can't Cope: Vocal Selections. 24p. (Orig.). (C). 1996. pap. text 9.95 (*0-7692-0293-4*, VAL2005) Wrner Bros.
— The Doors Greatest Hits. 60p. (C). 1983. pap. text 13.95 (*0-89898-200-6*, P0442SMX) Wrner Bros.
— Dreamgirls: Vocal Selections. 104p. (Orig.). (C). 1994. pap. text 18.95 (*0-7692-0301-9*, VF0961) Wrner Bros.
— Dwight Yoakam - Buenos Noches. 52p. (Orig.). (C). 1988. pap. text 12.95 (*0-7692-0874-6*, VF1504) Wrner Bros.
— Dwight Yoakam - If There Was a Way. 60p. (Orig.). (C). 1991. pap. text 14.95 (*0-7692-0857-6*, VF1698) Wrner Bros.
— Dwight Yoakam - Just Lookin' for a Hit. 56p. (Orig.). (C). 1990. pap. text 14.95 (*0-7692-0843-6*, VF1617) Wrner Bros.
— Dwight Yoakam - This Time. 52p. (Orig.). (C). 1993. pap. text 18.95 (*0-89724-422-2*, VF1961) Wrner Bros.
— Eagles - Their Greatest Hits. 56p. (Orig.). 1994. pap. 16.95 (*0-89724-434-6*, VF0425) Wrner Bros.
— Eagles/Hell Freezes Over. 92p. (Orig.). (C). 1995. pap. text 19.95 (*0-89724-559-8*, PF9512) Wrner Bros.
— Elvis Costello: A Singing Dictionary. 328p. 1980. pap. text 29.95 (*0-7692-1505-X*, VF0813) Wrner Bros.
— Elvis Presley - Hollywood Years. 92p. (Orig.). (C). 1992. pap. text 16.95 (*0-89724-445-1*, VF1865) Wrner Bros.
— Encyclopedia of Pop Music. 208p. (Orig.). 1997. pap. text 14.95 (*0-7692-0050-8*, 0054B) Wrner Bros.
— Enjoy Big Note Christmas. 64p. (Orig.). (YA). 1993. pap. text 8.95 (*0-7692-0033-8*) Wrner Bros.
— Enlarged Notes American Favorites. 72p. (Orig.). 1993. pap. 9.95 (*0-89898-608-7*, F3281SMX) Wrner Bros.
— Eric Clapton Signature Licks: Guitar Personality. 36p. (Orig.). (C). 1997. pap. 31.95 (*0-7692-0515-1*, 00695038) Wrner Bros.
— The Fabulous Christmas Fakebook. 108p. (Orig.). 1994. pap. 16.95 (*0-89724-383-8*, VF1816) Wrner Bros.
— Faith Hill: Take Me As I Am & It Matters to Me. 96p. (Orig.). (YA). 1996. pap. text 18.95 (*1-57623-454-1*, PF9616) Wrner Bros.
— Fame: Vocal Selections. 52p. (Orig.). (C). 1983. pap. text 13.95 (*0-7692-0452-X*, TSF0048) Wrner Bros.
— The Family Christmas Songbook. 160p. (Orig.). 1995. pap. text 16.95 (*0-89724-770-1*, VF1570A) Wrner Bros.
— Fantastic TV & Movie Songs. rev. ed. (Dan Coates Professional Touch Ser.). 96p. 1994. pap. 12.95 (*0-89724-358-7*, PF0825) Wrner Bros.
— Fantastic TV & Movie Songs: Big Note Arrangements by Dan Coates. 80p. (Orig.). 1995. pap. text 9.95 (*0-89724-709-4*, AF9532) Wrner Bros.
— Favorite Country Ballads: For Alto Saxophone. 56p. (Orig.). (J). 1996. pap. text 8.95 (*0-89724-882-1*, IF9557) Wrner Bros.
— Favorite Country Ballads: For Clarinet. 56p. (Orig.). (J). 1996. pap. text 8.95 (*0-89724-880-5*, IF9555) Wrner Bros.

Cuellar, Carol, ed. Favorite Country Ballads: For Flute. 56p. (Orig.). (J). 1996. pap. text 8.95 (*0-89724-879-1*, IF9554) Wrner Bros.

Cuellar, Carol, ed. Favorite Country Ballads: For Piano Accompaniment. 60p. (Orig.). 1996. pap. text 8.95 (*0-89724-878-3*, MF9563) Wrner Bros.
— Favorite Country Ballads: For Trumpet. 56p. (Orig.). (J). 1996. pap. text, wbk. ed. 8.95 (*0-89724-881-3*, IF9556) Wrner Bros.
— 50's & 60's Showstoppers. rev. ed. 260p. 1997. pap. 18.95 (*0-89724-450-8*, F2864SMD) Wrner Bros.
— Fifty Years of Popular Music. rev. ed. 224p. 1993. pap. text 14.95 (*0-89898-630-3*, F3145SMA) Wrner Bros.
— Fiorello: Vocal Selections. 28p. (Orig.). (C). 1991. pap. text 9.95 (*0-7692-0454-6*, VF1796) Wrner Bros.
— Fleetwood Mac/Greatest Hits. 72p. (Orig.). (C). 1989. pap. text 14.95 (*0-7692-0468-6*, VF1547) Wrner Bros.
— Floyd Cramer/Great Piano Hits. 48p. (Orig.). (C). 1988. pap. text 11.95 (*0-7692-0451-1*, P0756P9X) Wrner Bros.
— Foreigner: Double Vision. 56p. 1978. pap. text 12.95 (*0-7692-1509-2*, VF0617) Wrner Bros.
— Forever Plaid: Vocal Selections. 36p. (Orig.). (C). 1993. pap. text 12.95 (*0-7692-0462-7*, VF1931) Wrner Bros.
— 40 Years of Country Hits: 1955-1995. 264p. (Orig.). (YA). 1996. pap. text 19.95 (*1-57623-351-0*, MF9607) Wrner Bros.
— Four Decades of Great Popular Music. 336p. (Orig.). (J). 1997. pap. text 18.95 (*1-57623-920-9*) Wrner Bros.
— Free Willy: Soundtrack Selections. 36p. (Orig.). (C). 1993. pap. text 9.95 (*0-89724-078-2*, VF2075) Wrner Bros.
— Friends/TV Soundtrack. 64p. (Orig.). (C). 1996. pap. text 18.95 (*0-7692-0445-7*, PF9551) Wrner Bros.
— Garth Brooks: Beyond the Season. 36p. (Orig.). (C). 1992. pap. text 12.95 (*0-89898-927-2*, P0957SMX) Wrner Bros.
— Garth Brooks: Fresh Horses. 60p. (Orig.). (C). 1996. pap. text 18.95 (*0-7692-0446-5*, PF9558) Wrner Bros.
— Garth Brooks: Garth Brooks. 52p. (Orig.). (C). 1990. pap. text 13.95 (*0-7692-0447-3*, P0895SMX) Wrner Bros.
— Garth Brooks: No Fences. 52p. (Orig.). (C). 1991. pap. text 13.95 (*0-7692-0450-3*, P0909SMX) Wrner Bros.
— Gay Divorce: Vocal Selections. 32p. (Orig.). (C). 1988. pap. text 9.95 (*0-7692-0464-3*, VF1528) Wrner Bros.
— The Gay Life/Jennie: Vocal Selections. 36p. (Orig.). (C). 1988. pap. text 9.95 (*0-7692-0466-X*, VF1480) Wrner Bros.
— Genesis Anthology. 140p. (Orig.). (C). 1984. pap. text 16.95 (*0-7692-0461-9*, VF1113) Wrner Bros.
— Genesis/Abacab. 72p. (Orig.). (C). 1982. pap. text 12.95 (*0-7692-0465-1*, VF0923) Wrner Bros.
— Genesis/Deluxe Anthology. 276p. (Orig.). (C). 1993. pap. text 19.95 (*0-614-31157-8*, VF1903); pap. text 19.95 (*0-7692-0458-9*) Wrner Bros.
— Genesis/Deluxe Anthology. 44p. (Orig.). (C). 1995. pap. text 12.95 (*0-7692-0457-0*, VF0070) Wrner Bros.
— Genesis/Invisible Touch. 68p. (Orig.). (C). 1986. pap. text 12.95 (*0-7692-0467-8*, VF1326) Wrner Bros.
— The Genius of Art Pepper. 96p. (Orig.). (C). 1996. pap. text 19.95 (*0-7692-0448-1*, IF0481) Wrner Bros.
— The Genius of Art Tatum. 52p. (Orig.). (C). 1979. pap. text 10.95 (*0-7692-0200-4*, TPF0077) Wrner Bros.
— The Genius of Dave Brubeck, Bk. 1. 84p. (Orig.). (C). 1984. pap. text 11.95 (*0-7692-0267-5*, TPF0130) Wrner Bros.
— The Genius of Duke Ellington. 52p. (Orig.). (C). 1979. pap. text 10.95 (*0-7692-0290-X*, TPF0024) Wrner Bros.
— The Genius of Fats Waller. 56p. (Orig.). (C). 1983. pap. text 10.95 (*0-7692-0834-7*, TPF0120) Wrner Bros.
— The Genius of George Shearing. 48p. (Orig.). (C). 1985. pap. text 10.95 (*0-7692-0481-3*, TPF0052B) Wrner Bros.
— The George David Weiss Songbook: What a Wonderful World. 76p. (Orig.). (C). 1992. pap. text 14.95 (*0-7692-0878-9*, VF1848) Wrner Bros.
— Gin Blossoms - New Miserable Experience. 72p. (Orig.). (C). 1994. pap. text 19.95 (*0-89724-151-7*, VF2105) Wrner Bros.
— Giovanni: A Collection of Original Piano Solos. (Illus.). 88p. (YA). 1997. pap. text 18.95 (*1-57623-981-0*, 0046B) Wrner Bros.
— Girl Crazy: Vocal Selections. 32p. (Orig.). (C). 1984. pap. text 9.95 (*0-89724-258-0*, SF0094) Wrner Bros.
— Glenn Frey/Strange Weather. 84p. (Orig.). (C). 1992. pap. text 18.95 (*0-7692-0463-5*, VF1874) Wrner Bros.
— Golden Standards: Enlarged Notes. 100p. (Orig.). 1992. pap. 9.95 (*0-89898-609-5*, F3205SMX) Wrner Bros.
— The Goodbye Girl: Vocal Selections. 78p. (Orig.). (C). 1993. pap. text 18.95 (*0-7692-0725-1*, VF1954) Wrner Bros.
— Gordon Lightfoot - Deluxe Anthology. 196p. (Orig.). (C). 1989. pap. text 19.95 (*0-89724-760-4*, VF1597) Wrner Bros.
— Gospel & Inspirational Showstoppers. 312p. (Orig.). 1997. pap. 18.95 (*1-57623-490-8*, F3283SMB) Wrner Bros.
— Grateful Dead, Vol. 2. 108p. (Orig.). (C). 1976. pap. text 18.95 (*0-7692-0739-1*, VF0434) Wrner Bros.
— Grateful Dead - Built to Last. 60p. (Orig.). (C). 1990. pap. text 14.95 (*0-7692-0734-0*, VF1612) Wrner Bros.
— Grateful Dead - In the Dark. 64p. (Orig.). (C). 1988. pap. text 12.95 (*0-7692-0740-5*, VF1435) Wrner Bros.
— Grateful Dead - Without a Net. 80p. (Orig.). (C). 1991. pap. text 19.95 (*0-7692-0737-5*, VF1699) Wrner Bros.
— Great Ladies of Pop. 200p. (Orig.). (YA). 1996. pap. text 14.95 (*1-57623-469-X*, MF9629) Wrner Bros.
— Great Piano Christmas Hits. 52p. (Orig.). 1996. pap. text 9.95 (*1-57623-548-3*, AF9681) Wrner Bros.
— Great Popular Movie Hits. 124p. (Orig.). (YA). 1996. pap. text 12.95 (*1-57623-534-3*, MF9635) Wrner Bros.
— Great Popular Music: Simplified Piano Arrangements by Dan Coates. 80p. (Orig.). 1995. pap. text 9.95 (*0-89724-538-5*, AF9506) Wrner Bros.
— Great Popular Songs from the 80s & 90s. 392p. (Orig.). (YA). 1996. pap. text 19.95 (*1-57623-521-1*, MF9619) Wrner Bros.
— The Great Songs of Cole Porter. 260p. (Orig.). (C). 1986. pap. text 21.95 (*0-89724-424-9*, SF0155) Wrner Bros.
— The Great Songs of Gershwin. 228p. (Orig.). (C). 1985. pap. text 19.95 (*0-7692-0726-X*, SF0147) Wrner Bros.
— The Great Songs of Harry Warren. 212p. (Orig.). (C). 1989. pap. text 19.95 (*0-7692-0846-0*, VF1602) Wrner Bros.
— The Greatest Country Hits of the 90s. 2nd ed. 192p. (Orig.). (YA). 1996. pap. text 16.95 (*0-89724-834-1*, MF9580) Wrner Bros.
— The Greatest Country Hits of 1996-1997: Piano/Vocal/Chords. 184p. (Orig.). 1997. pap. text 16.95 (*1-57623-869-5*, MF9708) Wrner Bros.
— The Greatest Hits of 1996-1997. 136p. (Orig.). (J). 1997. pap. text 14.95 (*1-57623-889-X*) Wrner Bros.
— The Greatest Hits of 1996-1997: Alto Sax. 60p. (Orig.). (J). 1997. pap. text 9.95 (*1-57623-898-9*) Wrner Bros.
— The Greatest Hits of 1996-1997: Clarinet. 60p. (Orig.). (J). 1997. pap. text 9.95 (*1-57623-897-0*) Wrner Bros.
— The Greatest Hits of 1996-1997: Easy Piano. 148p. (Orig.). 1997. pap. text 14.95 (*1-57623-891-1*, AF9728) Wrner Bros.
— The Greatest Hits of 1996-1997: Flute. 60p. (Orig.). (J). 1997. pap. text 9.95 (*1-57623-896-2*) Wrner Bros.
— The Greatest Hits of 1996-1997: Tenor Sax. 60p. (Orig.). (YA). 1997. pap. text 9.95 (*1-57623-899-7*) Wrner Bros.
— The Greatest Hits of 1996-1997: Trombone. 60p. (Orig.). (J). 1997. pap. text 9.95 (*1-57623-901-2*) Wrner Bros.
— The Greatest Hits of 1996-1997: Trumpet. 60p. (Orig.). (YA). 1997. pap. text 9.95 (*1-57623-900-4*) Wrner Bros.
— The Greatest Pop Hits of the 90s: Easy Piano. 5th ed. 228p. (Orig.). (YA). 1995. pap. 14.95 (*0-89724-526-1*, AF9501) Wrner Bros.
— The Greatest Pop Hits of 1996-1997: Piano/Vocal/Chords. 208p. (Orig.). 1997. pap. text 16.95 (*1-57623-892-X*, MF9707) Wrner Bros.
— The Greatest Songs of 1960-1975. rev. ed. 112p. (YA). 1997. pap. text 12.95 (*0-89724-693-4*, THL1004E) Wrner Bros.
— Green Day - Dookie. 76p. (Orig.). (C). 1994. pap. text 16.95 (*0-7692-0736-7*, VF2167) Wrner Bros.
— Happy Anniversary, Charlie Brown! Featuring Songs from the T. V. Special. 36p. 1990. pap. text 12.95 (*0-7692-1508-4*, P0868SMX) Wrner Bros.
— Have Yourself a Merry Christmas. 84p. (YA). 1996. pap. 9.95 (*0-89898-995-7*, TXF0072A) Wrner Bros.
— Heart - Brigade. 100p. (Orig.). (C). 1990. pap. text 14.95 (*0-7692-0741-3*, VF1663) Wrner Bros.
— The Heart of Country. 132p. (Orig.). (C). 1995. pap. text 9.95 (*0-7692-0738-3*, VF1395) Wrner Bros.
— High Button Shoes: Vocal Selections. 24p. (Orig.). (C). 1989. pap. text 9.95 (*0-7692-0764-2*, VF1582) Wrner Bros.
— Hot Rock Ballads. 136p. (Orig.). (YA). (gr. 9-12). 1994. pap. text 14.95 (*0-89898-969-8*, F3430SMX) Wrner Bros.
— I Love My Wife: Vocal Selections. 76p. (Orig.). (C). 1992. pap. text 12.95 (*0-7692-0761-8*, VF1883) Wrner Bros.
— Ian Anderson: Flute Solos. 52p. (Orig.). (C). 1994. pap. text 9.95 (*0-89898-893-4*, P1073FLX) Wrner Bros.
— I'm Not Supposed to Love You Anymore & 14 Country Chart Toppers. 68p. (Orig.). (YA). 1996. pap. text 9.95 (*1-57623-512-2*, MF9634) Wrner Bros.
— The Inspirational Songs of Marijohn Wilkin. 96p. (Orig.). (YA). 1995. pap. text 12.95 (*0-7604-0072-5*, P1075SMX) Wrner Bros.
— Ira Gershwin Songbook. 212p. (Orig.). (C). 1984. pap. text 18.95 (*0-7692-0759-6*, SF0079) Wrner Bros.
— Jackson Browne/I'm Alive. 80p. (Orig.). (C). 1994. pap. text 19.95 (*0-89724-128-2*, VF2093) Wrner Bros.
— Jackson Browne/21 Songs for Piano & Guitar. 132p. (Orig.). (C). 1976. pap. text 12.95 (*0-7692-0252-7*, VF0398) Wrner Bros.
— James Taylor - Never Die Young. 80p. (Orig.). (C). 1988. pap. text 12.95 (*0-7692-0847-9*, VF1470) Wrner Bros.
— Janet Jackson - Design of a Decade. 104p. (Orig.). (C). 1996. pap. text 19.95 (*0-7692-0752-9*, PF9553) Wrner Bros.
— Jazz Classics - Trombone. 32p. (Orig.). 1994. pap. 9.95 (*0-89724-277-7*, IF0451) Wrner Bros.
— Jazz Classics - Violin. 32p. (Orig.). 1994. pap. 9.95 (*0-89724-276-9*, IF0446) Wrner Bros.
— Jim Croce Complete. 212p. (Orig.). (C). 1984. pap. text 19.95 (*0-7692-0277-2*, VF1131) Wrner Bros.
— Joe Henderson - Improvised Sax Solos. 44p. (Orig.). (C). 1987. pap. text 9.95 (*0-7692-0746-4*, SB284) Wrner Bros.
— John Cougar - American Fool. 56p. (Orig.). (C). 1982. pap. text 12.95 (*0-7692-0722-7*, VF0988) Wrner Bros.
— John Cougar Mellencamp - Scarecrow. 68p. (Orig.). (C). 1985. pap. text 12.95 (*0-7692-0718-9*, VF1256) Wrner Bros.
— John Cougar Mellencamp - The Lonesome Jubilee. 76p. (Orig.). (C). 1987. pap. text 12.95 (*0-7692-0720-0*, VF1426) Wrner Bros.
— John Mellencamp - Dance Naked. 80p. (Orig.). (C). 1995. pap. text 18.95 (*0-89724-502-4*, VF2165) Wrner Bros.
— John Michael Montgomery. 48p. (Orig.). 1995. pap. text 16.95 (*0-89724-762-0*) Wrner Bros.
— John Michael Montgomery: Kickin' It Up. 48p. (Orig.). (YA). 1994. pap. text 14.95 (*0-89898-849-7*, P1063SMX) Wrner Bros.
— John Prine - John Prine. 100p. (Orig.). (C). 1972. pap. text 16.95 (*0-7692-0523-2*, VF0157) Wrner Bros.
— John Williams - Fanfares & Themes. 132p. (Orig.). (C). 1989. pap. text 19.95 (*0-89724-350-1*, VF1588) Wrner Bros.
— John Williams Anthology. rev. ed. 180p. (Orig.). (C). 1987. pap. text 18.95 (*0-7692-0851-7*, VF1774) Wrner Bros.
— Joni Mitchell: Misses. 112p. 1997. pap. 21.95 (*1-57623-754-0*, PG9667) Wrner Bros.
— Joni Mitchell: Turbulent Indigo. 54p. (Orig.). (YA). 1995. pap. text 19.95 (*0-89724-656-X*, PF9506) Wrner Bros.
— Joni Mitchell Anthology. 148p. (Orig.). (C). 1983. pap. text 18.95 (*0-7692-0714-6*, VF1052) Wrner Bros.
— Journey - Escape - Frontiers. 108p. (Orig.). (C). 1984. pap. text 14.95 (*0-7692-0713-8*, VF1169) Wrner Bros.
— Journey - Greatest Hits. 64p. (Orig.). (C). 1984. pap. text 16.95 (*0-7692-0710-3*, VF1175) Wrner Bros.

An Asterisk (*) at the beginning of an entry indicates that the title is appearing for the first time.

— Kenny Loggins - Leap of Faith. 84p. (Orig.). (C). 1992. pap. text 19.95 (*0-7692-0697-2*, VF1782) Wrner Bros.

— Kids Korner: Color Me Chanukah. 32p. (Orig.). (YA). 1992. pap. text 6.50 (*0-7692-0034-6*) Wrner Bros.

— The Kid's Music Collection. 184p. 1997. pap. 16.95 (*0-7692-0023-0*, 0159B) Wrner Bros.

— Kiss - Crazy Nights. 56p. (Orig.). (C). 1988. pap. text 12.95 (*0-7692-0707-3*, VF1448) Wrner Bros.

— Lady, Be Good! Vocal Selections. 36p. (Orig.). (C). 1988. pap. text 9.95 (*0-7692-0706-5*, SF0212) Wrner Bros.

— Late Night Grande Hotel & Other Nanci Griffith Classics. 80p. (Orig.). (C). 1992. pap. text 14.95 (*0-7692-0768-5*, P0940SMX) Wrner Bros.

— Late Nite Comic: Broadway Selections. 36p. (Orig.). (C). 1991. pap. text 10.95 (*0-7692-0711-1*, VF1737) Wrner Bros.

— Laurindo Almeida: Contemporary Moods for Classica Guitar. 68p. (C). 1979. pap. text 14.95 (*0-7692-0201-2*, TPF0085) Wrner Bros.

— Led Zeppelin - Complete II. 260p. (Orig.). (C). 1993. pap. text 29.95 (*0-7692-0708-1*, VF1940) Wrner Bros.

— Led Zeppelin Complete. 232p. (Orig.). (C). 1973. pap. text 19.95 (*0-7692-0705-7*, VF0266) Wrner Bros.

— Legends of Liverpool: 25 Classics Recorded by the Beatles. 84p. (Orig.). 1996. pap. text 12.95 (*1-57623-433-9*, MF9630) Wrner Bros.

— Leonard Bernstein/I Hate Music! 20p. (Orig.). (C). 1995. pap. text 7.95 (*0-7692-0225-X*, VF0513) Wrner Bros.

— Linda Ronstadt - 'Round Midnight: With Nelson Riddle & His Orchestra. 292p. (Orig.). (C). 1986. pap. text 22.95 (*0-7692-0489-9*, VF1284) Wrner Bros.

— Little Me: Vocal Selections. 48p. (Orig.). (C). 1993. pap. text 10.95 (*0-7692-0701-4*, VF1941) Wrner Bros.

— Little Texas - Greatest Hits. 64p. (Orig.). (C). 1995. pap. text 16.95 (*0-7692-0693-X*, PF9549) Wrner Bros.

— Lullahits. 36p. (Orig.). (YA). 1996. pap. text 9.95 (*1-57623-538-6*, MF9631) Wrner Bros.

— Macarena & Party Time Favorites. (Illus.). 144p. (Orig.). (YA). 1996. pap. text 14.95 (*1-57623-640-4*, MF9646) Wrner Bros.

— Madonna - Erotica. 116p. (Orig.). (C). 1992. pap. text 18.95 (*0-7692-0702-2*, VF1911) Wrner Bros.

— Madonna - Like a Prayer. 76p. (Orig.). (C). 1989. pap. text 14.95 (*0-7692-0698-0*, VF1571) Wrner Bros.

— Madonna - Something to Remember. 76p. (Orig.). (C). 1996. pap. text 18.95 (*0-7692-0694-8*, PF9555) Wrner Bros.

— Madonna/The Immaculate Collection. 112p. 1990. pap. text 17.95 (*0-7692-1502-5*, VF1697) Wrner Bros.

— The Magic of Christmas: Big Note Piano Edition. 32p. (Orig.). (YA). (gr. 9-12). 1994. pap. text 4.50 (*0-89898-982-5*, F3439P3X) Wrner Bros.

— The Magic of Christmas: Easy Piano Duets Edition. 32p. (Orig.). (YA). (gr. 9-12). 1994. pap. text 4.50 (*0-89898-985-X*, F3442P8X) Wrner Bros.

— The Magic of Christmas: Easy Piano Edition. 32p. (Orig.). (YA). (gr. 9-12). 1994. pap. text 4.50 (*0-89898-981-7*, F3438P2X) Wrner Bros.

— The Magic of Christmas: Intermediate - Advanced Piano Edition. 32p. (Orig.). (YA). (gr. 9-12). 1994. pap. text 4.50 (*0-89898-983-3*, F3440P1X) Wrner Bros.

— The Magic of Christmas - Alto Sax Edition: Popular Songs & Traditional Carols. rev. ed. 32p. (Orig.). (YA). (gr. 9-12). 1994. pap. text 4.50 (*0-89724-738-8*, F3445ASA) Wrner Bros.

— The Magic of Christmas - Easy Organ Edition: Popular Songs & Traditional Carols. 32p. (Orig.). (YA). (gr. 9-12). 1994. pap. text 4.50 (*0-910957-45-2*, F3451EOX) Wrner Bros.

— The Magic of Christmas - Five Finger Piano Edition: Popular Songs & Traditional Carols. 32p. (Orig.). (YA). (gr. 9-12). 1994. pap. text 4.50 (*0-89898-984-1*, F3441PFX) Wrner Bros.

— The Magic of Christmas - French Horn Edition: Popular Songs & Traditional Carols. 32p. (Orig.). (YA). (gr. 9-12). 1994. pap. text 4.50 (*0-910957-48-7*, F3454FHX) Wrner Bros.

— The Magic of Christmas - Guitar Edition: Popular Songs & Traditional Carols. 32p. (Orig.). (YA). (gr. 9-12). 1994. pap. text 4.50 (*0-910957-42-8*, F3448GTX) Wrner Bros.

— The Magic of Christmas - Harmonica Edition: Popular Songs & Traditional Carols. 32p. (Orig.). (YA). (gr. 9-12). 1994. pap. text 4.50 (*0-910957-47-9*, F3453HAX) Wrner Bros.

— The Magic of Christmas - Piano-Vocal-Chords: Popular Favorites. 32p. (Orig.). (YA). (gr. 9-12). 1994. pap. 4.50 (*0-89898-977-9*, F3436SMX) Wrner Bros.

— The Magic of Christmas - Piano-Vocal-Chords: Traditional Favorites. 32p. (Orig.). (YA). (gr. 9-12). 1994. pap. text 4.50 (*0-89898-978-7*, F3437SMX) Wrner Bros.

— The Magic of Christmas - Recorder Edition: Popular Songs & Traditional Carols. 32p. (Orig.). (YA). (gr. 9-12). 1994. pap. text 4.50 (*0-910957-43-6*, F3449REX) Wrner Bros.

— The Magic of Christmas - Violin Edition: Popular Songs & Traditional Carols. 32p. (Orig.). (YA). (gr. 9-12). 1994. pap. text 4.50 (*0-910957-46-0*, F3452V1X) Wrner Bros.

— Marty Stuart - Honky Tonkin's What I Do Best. 64p. (Orig.). (C). 1996. pap. text 16.95 (*1-57623-659-5*, PF9641) Wrner Bros.

— Melissa Etheridge. 56p. (Orig.). (C). 1989. pap. text 14.95 (*0-7692-0716-2*, P0839SMX) Wrner Bros.

— Melissa Etheridge - Brave & Crazy. 80p. (Orig.). (C). 1990. pap. text 14.95 (*0-7692-0715-4*, P0866SMG) Wrner Bros.

— Michael Bolton - Soul Provider. 68p. (Orig.). (C). 1990. pap. text 16.95 (*0-7692-0223-3*, VF1635) Wrner Bros.

— Michael Bolton - Time, Love, & Tenderness. 60p. (Orig.). (C). 1991. pap. text 16.95 (*0-7692-0224-1*, VF1739) Wrner Bros.

— Michael Bolton - Timeless. 52p. (Orig.). (C). 1992. pap. text 16.95 (*0-7692-0228-4*, VF1908) Wrner Bros.

— The Michael Franks Songbook. 132p. (Orig.). (C). 1986. pap. text 16.95 (*0-7692-0456-2*, VF1301) Wrner Bros.

— Michael Jackson - Bad. 104p. (Orig.). (C). 1987. pap. text 16.95 (*0-7692-0758-8*, VF1423) Wrner Bros.

— Michael Jackson - Dangerous. 112p. (Orig.). (C). 1994. pap. text 19.95 (*0-7692-0754-5*, VF1799) Wrner Bros.

— Mighty Morphin Power Rangers: The Movie. 84p. (Orig.). (C). 1995. pap. text 16.95 (*0-89724-741-8*, PF9527) Wrner Bros.

— Mike & the Mechanics: Anthology. 124p. (Orig.). (C). 1993. pap. text 18.95 (*0-7692-0721-9*, VF1920) Wrner Bros.

— Mr. Wonderful: Vocal Selections. 28p. (Orig.). (C). 1989. pap. text 9.95 (*0-7692-0767-7*, VF1603) Wrner Bros.

— Motley Crue - Selections from Two Albums. 60p. (Orig.). (C). 1984. pap. text 12.95 (*0-7692-0766-9*, VF1114) Wrner Bros.

— Movie. rev. ed. (Showstoppers Ser.). 280p. (Orig.). 1995. pap. text 18.95 (*0-89724-551-2*, F2866SMD) Wrner Bros.

— Movie Classics. (World's Greatest Music Ser.). 240p. (YA). 1996. pap. text 16.95 (*1-57623-680-3*, MF9645) Wrner Bros.

— Movie Songs of the 90's. 148p. (YA). 1993. pap. 12.95 (*0-89898-687-7*, F3165SMX) Wrner Bros.

— Movies Songs & Themes. (Warner Brothers Presents Ser.). 328p. 1995. pap. text 18.95 (*0-89724-593-8*, MF9508A) Wrner Bros.

— Music from Star Wars Trilogy: Arranged by Dan Coates. (Illus.). 36p. (Orig.). (J). 1997. pap. text 12.95 (*1-57623-938-1*, 0020B) Wrner Bros.

— The Music of Sigmund Romberg. 104p. 1977. pap. text 12.95 (*0-7692-1504-1*, SF0018) Wrner Bros.

— The Music of Victor Herbert. 116p. 1976. pap. text 14.95 (*0-7692-1506-8*, SF0011) Wrner Bros.

— My Favorite Year: Vocal Selections. 96p. (Orig.). (C). 1993. pap. text 22.95 (*0-7692-0771-5*, VF1945) Wrner Bros.

— The Mystery of Edwin Drood: Vocal Selections. 88p. (Orig.). (C). 1986. pap. text 16.95 (*0-7692-0772-3*, VF1299) Wrner Bros.

— Neal Hefti - Anthology. 84p. (Orig.). (C). 1988. pap. text 12.95 (*0-7692-0735-9*, SF0196) Wrner Bros.

— Neal McCoy - You Gotta Love That! 44p. (Orig.). (YA). 1995. pap. text 14.95 (*0-89724-747-7*, PF9525) Wrner Bros.

— Neil Young - Complete Music, 1966-1969. 192p. (Orig.). (C). 1994. pap. text 22.95 (*0-7692-0879-7*, VF0263) Wrner Bros.

— Neil Young - Freedom. 60p. (Orig.). (C). 1990. pap. text 14.95 (*0-7692-0844-4*, VF1611) Wrner Bros.

— Neil Young - Harvest. 64p. (Orig.). (C). 1972. pap. text 16.95 (*0-7692-0852-5*, VF0219) Wrner Bros.

— Neil Young - Harvest Moon. 72p. (Orig.). (C). 1994. pap. text 19.95 (*0-7692-0872-X*, VF1907) Wrner Bros.

— Neil Young - Mirror Ball. 56p. (Orig.). (C). 1995. pap. text 18.95 (*0-89724-899-6*, PF9535) Wrner Bros.

— Neil Young - Sleeps with Angels. 68p. (Orig.). (C). 1995. pap. text 18.95 (*0-7692-0869-X*, VF2172) Wrner Bros.

— Neil Young & Crazy Horse - Life. 72p. (Orig.). (C). 1987. pap. text 12.95 (*0-7692-0859-2*, VF1418) Wrner Bros.

— Neil Young & Crazy Horse - Ragged Glory. 64p. (Orig.). (C). 1990. pap. text 16.95 (*0-7692-0866-5*, VF1688) Wrner Bros.

— Neil Young & Crazy Horse - Weld. 84p. (Orig.). (C). 1992. pap. text 16.95 (*0-7692-0849-5*, VF1800) Wrner Bros.

— Neil Young & the Blue Notes - This Note's for You. 52p. (Orig.). (C). 1988. pap. text 12.95 (*0-7692-0828-2*, VF1481) Wrner Bros.

— The New Best of Cole Porter. 68p. (Orig.). (C). 1995. pap. text 12.95 (*0-7692-0916-5*, VF1885) Wrner Bros.

— The New Best of David Gates. 44p. (Orig.). 1994. pap. 12.95 (*0-89724-210-6*, VF1754) Wrner Bros.

— The New Best of David Lee Roth. 64p. (Orig.). (C). 1994. pap. text 12.95 (*0-89724-339-0*, VF2149) Wrner Bros.

— The New Best of George Gershwin. 68p. (Orig.). (C). 1992. pap. text 12.95 (*0-89724-335-8*, VF1839) Wrner Bros.

— The New Best of Gordon Lightfoot. 48p. (Orig.). 1994. pap. 12.95 (*0-89724-430-3*, VF2166) Wrner Bros.

— The New Best of Jackson Browne. 68p. (Orig.). (C). 1994. pap. text 12.95 (*0-89724-293-9*, VF2136) Wrner Bros.

— The New Best of James Taylor. 68p. (Orig.). (C). 1991. pap. text 12.95 (*0-7692-0856-8*, VF1716) Wrner Bros.

— The New Best of Jim Croce. 68p. (Orig.). (C). 1996. pap. text 12.95 (*0-7692-0279-9*, VF1913) Wrner Bros.

— The New Best of Joni Mitchell. 52p. (Orig.). (C). 1993. pap. text 12.95 (*0-7692-0717-0*, VF1951) Wrner Bros.

— The New Best of Journey. 76p. (Orig.). (C). 1993. pap. text 12.95 (*0-7692-0709-X*, VF1968) Wrner Bros.

— The New Best of Led Zeppelin. 58p. (Orig.). (C). 1982. pap. text 12.95 (*0-7692-0704-9*, VF1798) Wrner Bros.

— The New Best of Michael Franks. 76p. (Orig.). (C). 1992. pap. text 12.95 (*0-7692-0459-7*, VF1871) Wrner Bros.

— The New Best of Moody Blues. 52p. (Orig.). (C). 1989. pap. text 12.95 (*0-7692-0719-7*, VF1973) Wrner Bros.

— The New Best of Neil Young. 52p. (Orig.). (C). 1992. pap. text 12.95 (*0-7692-0860-6*, VF1877) Wrner Bros.

— The New Best of Peter, Paul & Mary. 60p. (Orig.). (C). 1991. pap. text 12.95 (*0-7692-0503-8*, VF1778) Wrner Bros.

— The New Best of Phil Collins. 92p. (Orig.). (C). 1994. pap. text 12.95 (*0-89724-302-1*, VF2138) Wrner Bros.

— The New Best of Roy Orbison. 36p. (Orig.). (C). 1993. pap. text 12.95 (*0-7692-0495-3*, VF1944) Wrner Bros.

— The New Best of the Doobie Brothers. (New Best of Ser.). 52p. (Orig.). (C). 1993. pap. text 12.95 (*0-89724-241-6*, PG9663) Wrner Bros.

— The New Best of Toto. 52p. (Orig.). (C). 1985. pap. text 12.95 (*0-7692-0848-7*, VF1760) Wrner Bros.

— The New Best of Van Morrison. 60p. (Orig.). (C). 1984. pap. text 12.95 (*0-7692-0770-7*, VF1780) Wrner Bros.

— The New Best of Yes. 68p. (Orig.). (C). 1993. pap. text 12.95 (*0-7692-0839-8*, VF1950) Wrner Bros.

— The New Book of Golden Wedding Songs. 152p. (YA). 1994. pap. 14.95 (*0-89898-843-8*) Wrner Bros.

— The New Dan Coates Easy Piano Encyclopedia. 216p. (Orig.). 1995. pap. text 19.95 (*0-89724-942-9*, PF0792A) Wrner Bros.

— The New Dan Coates Professional Touch Encyclopedia. 192p. (Orig.). (J). 1997. pap. text 19.95 (*1-57623-801-6*) Wrner Bros.

— The New Dan Coates Professional Touch Encyclopedia. rev. ed. 192p. (Orig.). 1997. pap. text 19.95 (*0-89724-631-4*, PF0562B) Wrner Bros.

— New Giant Book of Rock. 448p. (Orig.). (YA). 1997. pap. text 19.95 (*1-57623-277-8*, VF1942B) Wrner Bros.

— The New Moon: Vocal Selections. 36p. (Orig.) (C). 1984. pap. text 10.95 (*0-7692-0769-3*, SF0118) Wrner Bros.

— The New of Grateful Dead. 76p. (Orig.). (C). 1994. pap. text 12.95 (*0-7692-0727-8*, VF1735) Wrner Bros.

— The New Phil Collins Deluxe Anthology. 240p. (Orig.). (C). 1993. pap. text 19.95 (*0-7692-0280-2*, VF1909) Wrner Bros.

— The New Television Showstoppers. rev. ed. 256p. (Orig.). (YA). 1996. pap. text 18.95 (*1-57623-519-X*, MF9637) Wrner Bros.

— Nymph Errant: Vocal Selections. 36p. (Orig.). (C). 1991. pap. text 9.95 (*0-7692-0776-6*, VF1712) Wrner Bros.

— Of Thee I Sing: Vocal Score. 202p. (Orig.). (C). 1932. pap. text 50.00 (*0-7692-0775-8*, VP0012) Wrner Bros.

— Of Thee I Sing: Vocal Selections. 36p. (Orig.). (C). 1984. pap. text 9.95 (*0-7692-0765-0*, SF0139) Wrner Bros.

— Oh, Kay! Vocal Selections. 56p. (Orig.). (C). 1984. pap. text 9.95 (*0-7692-0774-X*, SF0106) Wrner Bros.

— On a Clear Day You Can See Forever: Vocal Selections. 40p. (Orig.). (C). 1994. pap. text 10.95 (*0-85724-287-4*, VF2132) Wrner Bros.

— On Bended Knee & Other Hot Pop Singles. 72p. (Orig.). (YA). 1995. pap. text 9.95 (*0-89724-610-1*, MF9519) Wrner Bros.

— On the Town: Vocal Selections. 24p. (Orig.). (C). 1989. pap. text 9.95 (*0-89724-397-8*, VF1568) Wrner Bros.

— On the Twentieth Century: Vocal Selections. 100p. (Orig.). (C). 1992. pap. text 12.95 (*0-7692-0540-2*, VF1841) Wrner Bros.

— 100 Easy Listening. 228p. (Orig.). 1995. pap. text 17.95 (*0-89724-801-5*, PF0540A) Wrner Bros.

— 100 Great Christmas Songs. 212p. (Orig.). 1995. pap. text 19.95 (*0-89724-873-2*, MF9549) Wrner Bros.

— 100 Great Country Songs. 392p. (Orig.). 1995. pap. text 19.95 (*0-89724-871-6*, MF9550) Wrner Bros.

— 101 Greatest Rock 'n' Roll Classics Vol. 1: Piano/Vocal Mixed Folio. 3rd rev. ed. 272p. (Orig.). 1994. pap. 18.95 (*0-89898-816-0*, TMF0219C) Wrner Bros.

— 101 Most Popular Songs of the Rock Era. 392p. (Orig.). 1995. pap. text 22.95 (*0-89724-795-7*, VF1559A) Wrner Bros.

— Pachelbel's Canon in D & 19 Movie Themes. 80p. (Orig.). 1995. pap. 12.95 (*0-89724-251-3*, VF1753A) Wrner Bros.

— Passion: Vocal Score. 208p. (Orig.). (C). 1996. pap. text 85.00 (*1-57623-294-8*, PF9608) Wrner Bros.

— The Paul Davis Songbook. 100p. (Orig.). (C). 1996. pap. text 18.95 (*1-57623-432-0*, PF9613) Wrner Bros.

— Performance Plus Children Favorites, Bk. 3. 24p. 1997. pap. 6.95 (*0-7692-0021-4*) Warner Bros.

— Performance Plus Family Favorites, Bk. 4. 32p. 1997. pap. 6.95 (*0-7692-0020-6*) Warner Bros.

— Peter, Paul & Mary - Late Again. 36p. (Orig.). (C). 1968. pap. text 10.95 (*0-7692-0918-1*, VF0146) Wrner Bros.

— The Peter, Paul & Mary Songbook. 148p. (Orig.). (C). 1965. pap. text 16.95 (*0-943351-94-4*, VF0138) Wrner Bros.

— Phil Collins Anthology. 152p. (Orig.). (C). 1986. pap. text 18.95 (*0-7692-0273-X*, VF1273) Wrner Bros.

— Phil Collins/Both Sides. (Personality - Piano-Vocal Ser.). 76p. (Orig.). (C). 1993. pap. text 19.95 (*0-89724-148-7*, VF2095) Wrner Bros.

— Phil Collins/Serious Hits . . . Live! 88p. (Orig.). (C). 1991. pap. text 16.95 (*0-7692-0274-8*, VF1705) Wrner Bros.

— Phil Spector: Back to Mono. (Illus.). 308p. 1994. 39.95 (*0-89898-718-0*, P0966SMH) Wrner Bros.

— Placido Domingo - Bajo el Cielo Espanol. 84p. (Orig.). (C). 1997. pap. text 16.95 (*0-7692-0024-9*) Wrner Bros.

— Popular Favorites. (Grand Duets for Piano Ser.). 112p. (Orig.). (YA). 1997. pap. text 12.95 (*0-7692-0108-3*) Wrner Bros.

— Popular Music Collection for the Advanced Player. 52p. (Orig.). 1997. pap. 14.95 (*0-7692-0127-X*, AF9754) Wrner Bros.

— Porter on Broadway. 260p. (Orig.). (C). 1995. pap. text 24.95 (*0-7692-0508-9*, SF0202) Wrner Bros.

— Prince - Come. 60p. (Orig.). (C). 1995. pap. text 16.95 (*0-89724-470-2*, VF2173) Wrner Bros.

— Prince - The Gold Experience. 92p. (Orig.). (C). 1996. pap. text 19.95 (*0-7692-0478-3*, PF9552) Wrner Bros.

— Prince & the New Power Generation. 92p. (Orig.). (C). 1993. pap. text 18.95 (*0-7692-0922-X*, VF1905) Wrner Bros.

— Prince & the New Power Generation - Diamonds & Pearls. 84p. (Orig.). (C). 1991. pap. text 17.95 (*0-7692-0510-0*, VF1748) Wrner Bros.

— Prince & the Revolution - Parade. 64p. (Orig.). (C). 1986. pap. text 12.95 (*0-7692-0505-4*, VF1308) Wrner Bros.

— Prince & the Revolution - Purple Rain. 72p. (Orig.). (C). 1984. pap. text 16.95 (*0-7692-0552-6*, VF1179) Wrner Bros.

— Prince of Tides: Movie Selections. 32p. (Orig.). (C). 1992. pap. text 14.95 (*0-7692-0488-0*, P0941SMX) Wrner Bros.

— Promises, Promises: Vocal Selections. 52p. (Orig.). (C). 1989. pap. text 9.95 (*0-7692-0915-7*, VF1536) Wrner Bros.

— Quincy Jones - Q's Jook Joint. 132p. (Orig.). (C). 1996. pap. text 24.95 (*1-57623-288-3*, PF9545) Wrner Bros.

— Rags: Broadway Selections. 76p. (Orig.). (C). 1992. pap. text 14.95 (*0-7692-0483-X*, TSF0071) Wrner Bros.

— Randy Travis - An Old Time Christmas. 44p. (Orig.). (C). 1990. pap. text 14.95 (*0-7692-0858-4*, VF1659) Wrner Bros.

— Randy Travis - Anthology. 212p. (Orig.). (C). 1994. pap. text 19.95 (*0-89724-308-0*, VF2140) Wrner Bros.

— Randy Travis - Greatest Hits. 56p. (Orig.). (C). 1992. pap. text 16.95 (*0-7692-0881-9*, VF1893) Wrner Bros.

— Randy Travis - Greatest Hits, Vol. 2. 60p. (Orig.). (C). 1992. pap. text 16.95 (*0-7692-0871-1*, VF1894) Wrner Bros.

— Randy Travis - Heroes & Friends. 62p. (Orig.). (C). 1991. pap. text 14.95 (*0-7692-0876-2*, VF1689) Wrner Bros.

— Randy Travis - This Is Me. 52p. (Orig.). (C). 1994. pap. text 16.95 (*0-89724-331-5*, VF2148) Wrner Bros.

— Restless Heart - Wheels & Highlights from Their First Album. 84p. (Orig.). (C). 1987. pap. text 12.95 (*0-7692-0543-7*, VF1400) Wrner Bros.

— Restless Hearts - Big Dreams in a Small Town. 40p. (Orig.). (C). 1989. pap. text 12.95 (*0-7692-0914-9*, VF1521) Wrner Bros.

— Richard Marx - Paid Vacation. 64p. (Orig.). (C). 1994. pap. text 14.95 (*0-7692-0480-5*, P1066SMX) Wrner Bros.

— The Roches. 100p. (Orig.). (C). 1981. pap. text 9.95 (*0-7692-0923-8*, VF0900) Wrner Bros.

— Rock Music Collection. 352p. (Orig.). (YA). 1996. pap. text 18.95 (*1-57623-621-8*) Wrner Bros.

— Rock 'n Roll Classics. (World's Greatest Music Ser.). 180p. (Orig.). (YA). 1996. pap. text 16.95 (*1-57623-337-5*, MF9582) Wrner Bros.

— Rock 'n' Roll Showstoppers. 264p. (Orig.). 1994. pap. 18.95 (*0-89898-830-6*, F3366SMA) Wrner Bros.

— A Rockin' Christmas Sing-a-Long. 64p. (Orig.). (YA). 1996. pap. text 18.95 (*1-57623-587-4*, MF9640G); pap. text 9.95 (*1-57623-586-6*, MF9640) Wrner Bros.

— Rockin' Country. 156p. (Orig.). (YA). 1996. pap. text 14.95 (*0-7692-0097-4*, MF9609) Wrner Bros.

— Rod Stewart - Blondes Have More Fun. 68p. (Orig.). (C). 1979. pap. text 12.95 (*0-7692-0880-0*, VF0662) Wrner Bros.

— Roger Williams - Contemporary Piano Solos. 76p. (Orig.). (C). 1984. pap. text 11.95 (*0-7692-0484-8*, TPF0133) Wrner Bros.

— The Rolling Stones - Singles Collection: The London Years for Guitar. 336p. (Orig.). 1991. reprint ed. pap. text 29.95 (*0-89898-739-3*, P08708GTX) Wrner Bros.

— Romance, Romance: Vocal Selections. 60p. (Orig.). (C). 1988. pap. text 14.95 (*0-7692-0542-9*, VF1496) Wrner Bros.

— The Rose & 49 Top Professional Touch Hits. 2nd ed. 196p. (Orig.). 1997. reprint ed. pap. text 16.95 (*1-57623-980-2*, PF0826A) Wrner Bros.

— Rush - A Show of Hands. 120p. (Orig.). (C). 1989. pap. text 16.95 (*0-7692-0925-4*, VF1522) Wrner Bros.

— Rush - Chronicles. 196p. (Orig.). 1994. pap. 22.95 (*0-89724-349-8*, VF1682) Wrner Bros.

— Rush - Complete. 436p. (Orig.). (C). 1983. pap. text 29.95 (*0-7692-0551-8*, VF1060) Wrner Bros.

— Rush - Complete, Vol. 2. 276p. (Orig.). (C). 1995. pap. text 22.95 (*0-7692-0506-2*, VF1285) Wrner Bros.

— Rush - Deluxe Anthology. 210p. (Orig.). (C). 1981. pap. text 17.95 (*0-7692-0550-X*, VF0901) Wrner Bros.

— Rush - Hold Your Fire. 96p. (Orig.). (C). 1987. pap. text 12.95 (*0-7692-0479-1*, VF1424) Wrner Bros.

— Rush - Moving Pictures. 60p. (Orig.). (C). 1981. pap. text 12.95 (*0-7692-0477-5*, VF0872) Wrner Bros.

— Rush - Permanent Waves. 60p. (Orig.). (C). 1980. pap. text 12.95 (*0-7692-0924-6*, VF0766) Wrner Bros.

— Rush - Presto. 100p. (Orig.). (C). 1990. pap. text 16.95 (*0-7692-0475-9*, VF1622) Wrner Bros.

— Rush - Retrospective. 260p. (Orig.). (C). 1988. pap. text 16.95 (*0-7692-0544-5*, VF1475) Wrner Bros.

— Sam Cooke's Night Beat. 80p. (Orig.). 1995. pap. 18.95 (*0-89724-748-5*, PF9528) Wrner Bros.

— Sam Cooke's Sar Records Story. 292p. (Orig.). (C). 1994. pap. text 32.95 (*0-910957-80-0*, P1081SMX) Wrner Bros.

— Scorpions - World Wide Live. 96p. (Orig.). (C). 1985. pap. text 12.95 (*0-7692-0496-1*, VF1258) Wrner Bros.

— Secret Garden: Vocal Score. (Illus.). 356p. (Orig.). (C). 1993. pap. text 100.00 (*0-89724-112-6*, VF2084) Wrner Bros.

— Seesaw: Vocal Selections. 60p. (Orig.). (C). 1992. pap. text 12.95 (*0-7692-0917-3*, VF1896) Wrner Bros.

— Selections from "Home Alone" 20p. (Orig.). (C). 1990. pap. text 10.95 (*0-7692-0757-X*, VF1695) Wrner Bros.

— Selections from the Fiddler on the Roof: Alto Sax. 20p. (Orig.). (J). 1995. pap. text 4.95 (*0-89724-677-2*, IF9523) Wrner Bros.

— Selections from the Fiddler on the Roof: Clarinet. 20p. (Orig.). (J). 1995. pap. text 4.95 (*0-89724-675-6*, IF9521) Wrner Bros.

C

— Selections from the Fiddler on the Roof: Piano Accompaniment. 40p. (Orig.). 1995. pap. text 6.95 (*0-89724-673-X*, MF9535) Wrner Bros.

— Selections from the Fiddler on the Roof: Trombone. 20p. (Orig.). (J). 1995. pap. text 4.95 (*0-89724-679-9*, IF9525) Wrner Bros.

— Selections from the Wizard of Oz: Alto Sax. (Illus.). 16p. (Orig.). 1995. pap. text 4.95 (*0-89724-684-5*, IF9529) Wrner Bros.

— Selections from the Wizard of Oz: Clarinet. (Illus.). 16p. (Orig.). 1995. pap. text 4.95 (*0-89724-682-9*, IF9527) Wrner Bros.

— Selections from the Wizard of Oz: Flute. (Illus.). 16p. (Orig.). 1995. pap. text 4.95 (*0-89724-681-0*, IF9526) Wrner Bros.

— Selections from the Wizard of Oz: Piano Accompaniment. (Illus.). 28p. (Orig.). 1995. pap. text 6.95 (*0-89724-680-2*, MF9536) Wrner Bros.

— Selections from the Wizard of Oz: Tenor Sax. (Illus.). 16p. (Orig.). 1995. pap. text 4.95 (*0-89724-685-3*, IF9530) Wrner Bros.

— Selections from the Wizard of Oz: Trombone. (Illus.). 16p. (Orig.). 1995. pap. text 4.95 (*0-89724-686-1*, IF9531) Wrner Bros.

— Selections from the Wizard of Oz: Trumpet. (Illus.). 16p. (Orig.). 1995. pap. text 4.95 (*0-89724-683-7*, IF9528) Wrner Bros.

— Seven Brides for Seven Brothers: Vocal Selections. 32p. (Orig.). (C). 1992. pap. text 9.95 (*0-7692-0482-1*, TSF0069) Wrner Bros.

— 70's & 80's Pop Music. (Warner Brothers Presents Ser.). 372p. (Orig.). 1995. pap. text 18.95 (*0-7692-0057-5*, MF9502) Wrner Bros.

— 70's & 80's Showstoppers. 368p. 1997. pap. 18.95 (*1-57623-541-6*, F2863SMJ) Wrner Bros.

— The Sheldon Harnick Songbook. 136p. (Orig.). (C). 1996. pap. text 19.95 (*1-57623-347-2*, PF9539) Wrner Bros.

— Sheryl Crow - Tuesday Night Music Club. 60p. (Orig.). (C). 1995. pap. text 16.95 (*0-89724-459-1*, VF2174) Wrner Bros.

— Showstoppers - Trumpet. rev. ed. 112p. 1997. pap. 12.95 (*0-89724-650-0*, F2947TRE) Wrner Bros.

— Showstoppers - Xmas Big Note: Big Note. rev. ed. 180p. (YA). 1994. pap. 15.95 (*0-89898-847-0*, F2925P3A) Wrner Bros.

— Sigmund Spaeth - Song Session. 200p. (Orig.). (C). 1995. pap. text 9.95 (*0-7692-0536-4*, VF0247) Wrner Bros.

— Sing - Bein' Green & Other Joe Raposo Classics. 52p. (Orig.). (C). 1996. pap. text 11.95 (*1-57623-293-X*, AF9559) Wrner Bros.

— Sleepless in Seattle: Soundtrack. 48p. (Orig.). (C). 1993. pap. text 14.95 (*0-89898-690-7*, P1019SMX) Wrner Bros.

— Song Session Community Songbook. 128p. (Orig.). 1994. pap. 8.95 (*0-89724-419-2*, VF0248) Wrner Bros.

— Songs of the Gay 90s Vol. 3: Piano/Vocal Mixed Folio. 132p. (Orig.). 1993. pap. 12.95 (*0-89898-711-3*, WFM00003) Wrner Bros.

— Soul Asylum - Grave Dancers Union. (Illus.). 72p. (Orig.). (C). 1993. pap. text 19.95 (*0-89724-092-8*, VF1985) Wrner Bros.

— The Sounds of Christmas. 128p. (Orig.). (YA). 1996. pap. text 9.95 (*1-57623-589-0*, AF9680) Wrner Bros.

— Soundtrack Selections from "The Mambo Kings" 28p. (Orig.). (C). 1992. pap. text 10.95 (*0-7692-0699-9*, VF1834) Wrner Bros.

— Standing Outside the Fire & Other Hot Country Singles. 44p. (Orig.). (YA). 1994. pap. text 7.95 (*0-89898-886-1*, F3421SMX) Wrner Bros.

— A Star Is Born: Vocal Selections. 36p. (Orig.). (C). 1995. pap. text 9.95 (*0-7692-0853-3*, SF0064) Wrner Bros.

— Star 69. 68p. 1997. pap. 21.95 (*0-7692-0145-8*, PG9715) Wrner Bros.

— The Stingiest Man in Town: Vocal Selections. 148p. (Orig.). (C). 1957. pap. text 25.00 (*0-7692-0875-4*, OP0009) Wrner Bros.

— Student Prince: Vocal Score. 170p. (Orig.). (C). 1995. pap. text 45.00 (*0-7692-0870-3*, VP0016) Wrner Bros.

— Student Prince: Vocal Selections. 32p. (Orig.). (C). 1984. pap. text 9.95 (*0-7692-0850-9*, SF0126) Wrner Bros.

— Suzanne Vega - 99.9. 72p. (Orig.). (C). 1992. pap. text 18.95 (*0-7692-0861-4*, VF1867) Wrner Bros.

— A Tale of Cinderella: Vocal Selections. 48p. (Orig.). (C). 1995. pap. text 14.95 (*0-89724-952-6*, PF9515) Wrner Bros.

— Talking Heads - Anthology. 112p. (Orig.). (C). 1986. pap. text 16.95 (*0-7692-0854-1*, VF1294) Wrner Bros.

— Tenor Sax Showstoppers. 116p. 1995. pap. text 12.95 (*0-7692-1557-2*, F2947TSD) Wrner Bros.

— Themes of 007 - Bond's Greatest Hits. 72p. (Orig.). (C). 1996. pap. text 12.95 (*0-7692-0831-2*, TSF0053A) Wrner Bros.

— 30 Family Christmas Favorites: Arranged for Easy Piano by Dan Coates. 80p. (Orig.). 1995. pap. text 10.95 (*0-89724-884-8*, AF9539) Wrner Bros.

— Three Decades of Rhythm & Blues Classics. 152p. (Orig.). 1997. pap. text 14.95 (*1-57623-888-1*, 5202A) Wrner Bros.

— Tim McGraw - Not a Moment Too Soon. 52p. (Orig.). (C). 1994. pap. text 14.95 (*0-910957-66-5*, P1077SMX) Wrner Bros.

— Timeless Wedding, Bk. 2. 140p. (Orig.). (YA). 1997. pap. 10.95 (*0-89724-544-X*, MF9515A) Wrner Bros.

— Timeless Wedding Standards, Bk. 1. 132p. (Orig.). (YA). 1996. pap. 10.95 (*0-89724-543-1*, MF9514A) Wrner Bros.

— Timeless Wedding Standards, Bk. 3. rev. ed. 144p. (Orig.). 1997. pap. 10.95 (*0-89724-545-8*, MF9516A) Wrner Bros.

— Tish Hinojosa - Culture Swing - Destiny's Gate. 100p. (Orig.). (C). 1994. pap. text 19.95 (*0-7692-0753-7*, VF2125) Wrner Bros.

— Tito Rodriguez - Inolvidable. 52p. (Orig.). (C). 1995. pap. text 10.95 (*0-7692-0835-5*, A0062OPX) Wrner Bros.

— Today's Kings of Country Music, Vol. 2. 172p. (Orig.). (YA). 1994. pap. text 12.95 (*0-89898-780-6*, F3306SMA) Wrner Bros.

— Todays' Ladies of Country Music. 148p. (Orig.). (YA). 1991. pap. 12.95 (*0-89898-591-9*, F3191SMX) Wrner Bros.

— Tom T. Hall's Country Songs for Children. 68p. (Orig.). (C). 1996. pap. text 12.95 (*1-57623-460-6*, PF9620) Wrner Bros.

— Tony Bennett: Here's to the Ladies. 64p. (Orig.). (C). 1995. pap. text 19.95 (*1-57623-274-3*, PF9548) Wrner Bros.

— Tony Bennett: Steppin' Out. (Illus.). 88p. (Orig.). (C). 1993. pap. text 19.95 (*0-89724-095-2*, VF2078) Wrner Bros.

— The Tony Bennett Songbook. 156p. (Orig.). (C). 1996. pap. text 22.95 (*1-57623-468-1*, PF9619) Wrner Bros.

— Tony Bennett Unplugged. 80p. (Orig.). (C). 1994. pap. text 19.95 (*0-89724-393-5*, VF2155) Wrner Bros.

— The Top Country Hits of 1996. 308p. (Orig.). (YA). 1996. pap. text 18.95 (*1-57623-700-1*, MF9650) Wrner Bros.

— The Top Pop Hits of 1996. 328p. (Orig.). (YA). 1996. pap. text 18.95 (*1-57623-697-8*) Wrner Bros.

— The Top Pop Hits of 1996: Easy Piano Edition. 160p. (Orig.). (YA). 1996. pap. text 16.95 (*1-57623-701-X*, AF9694) Wrner Bros.

— The Top Pop Hits of the 90's. 5th ed. 176p. (Orig.). (YA). 1995. pap. text 12.95 (*0-89724-539-3*, F3471P2X) Wrner Bros.

— The Top Pop Hits of the 90's. 6th ed. 390p. (Orig.). 1995. pap. text 19.95 (*0-89724-828-7*, MF9568) Wrner Bros.

— The Top Pop Hits of the 90's. 6th ed. 188p. (Orig.). (YA). 1996. pap. text 14.95 (*1-57623-268-9*, AF9563) Wrner Bros.

— Toto - Fahrenheit. 52p. (Orig.). (C). 1987. pap. text 12.95 (*0-7692-0855-X*, VF1350) Wrner Bros.

— Toto - Past to Present. 72p. (Orig.). 1994. pap. 16.95 (*0-89724-439-7*, VF1692) Wrner Bros.

— Toto - The Seventh One. 68p. (Orig.). (C). 1988. pap. text 12.95 (*0-7692-0862-2*, VF1463) Wrner Bros.

— The Tractors. 44p. (Orig.). (C). 1995. pap. text 14.95 (*0-89724-571-7*, VF2176) Wrner Bros.

— Traditional & Popular Wedding Music. (Orig.). (C). 1997. pap. text 16.95 (*1-57623-971-3*, MF9720) Wrner Bros.

— Tripping Daisy. 104p. (Orig.). (YA). 1996. pap. text 22.95 (*1-57623-282-4*, PG9548) Wrner Bros.

— Universal Showstoppers. (Showstoppers Ser.). 276p. (Orig.). (YA). 1994. pap. text 18.95 (*0-89898-832-2*, F3409SMX) Wrner Bros.

— Vern Gosdin - Anthology. 96p. (Orig.). (C). 1992. pap. text 18.95 (*0-7692-0732-4*, VF1836) Wrner Bros.

— Vince Gill: When Love Finds You. 48p. (Orig.). 1994. pap. 16.95 (*0-89724-340-4*, VF2150) Wrner Bros.

— Vince Gill - I Still Believe in You. 56p. (Orig.). (C). 1992. pap. text 16.95 (*0-7692-0729-4*, VF1873) Wrner Bros.

— Vince Gill - Selections from Pocket Full of Gold & When I Call Your Name Plus Other Hits. 72p. (Orig.). (C). 1994. pap. text 16.95 (*0-7692-0728-6*, VF1742) Wrner Bros.

— Warner Bros. Presents Children's Favorite Songs. 180p. (Orig.). (YA). 1995. pap. text 18.95 (*0-89724-619-5*, MF9521) Wrner Bros.

— Warner Bros. Presents Christmas Favorites. 200p. (Orig.). 1995. pap. text 16.95 (*0-89724-885-6*, AF9547) Wrner Bros.

— Warner Bros. Presents Mellow Rock Classics. 392p. (Orig.). (YA). 1995. pap. text 18.95 (*0-89724-606-3*, MF9509) Wrner Bros.

— Warner Bros. Presents Television Favorites. (Warner Bros. Presents Ser.). 252p. (YA). 1995. pap. text 18.95 (*0-89724-944-5*, MF9561) Wrner Bros.

— Warner Bros. Presents Wedding Favorites. 320p. (Orig.). (YA). 1995. pap. text 18.95 (*0-89724-712-4*, MF9534) Wrner Bros.

— The Wedding Fake Book: C Edition, More Than 150 Traditional & Popular Songs for Piano - Vocal - Guitar. 164p. (Orig.). (YA). 1991. pap. text 12.95 (*0-7692-0140-7*, F3101FBX) Wrner Bros.

— The White Cliffs of Dover Songbook. 228p. (Orig.). (C). pap. 19.95 (*0-943748-57-7*, VF1832) Ekay Music.

— Wizard of Oz Easy Piano Coates. 32p. (YA). 1995. pap. 9.95 (*0-7692-0095-8*, AF9502) Wrner Bros.

— The Wonder of Stevie - Stevie Wonder Fakebook. (Orig.). (C). 1989. pap. text 9.95 (*0-7692-0833-9*, P0846FBX) Wrner Bros.

— Wonderful Music of Christmas. 196p. 1997. pap. 18.95 (*0-7692-0198-9*, MF9729) Wrner Bros.

— World Famous Music Vol. 2: Nostalgia's Golden Greats. 144p. 1993. pap. text 12.95 (*0-89898-710-5*) Wrner Bros.

— World Famous Music Vol. 4: Irish Melodies. 128p. (Orig.). 1993. pap. text 12.95 (*0-89898-712-1*) Wrner Bros.

— World Famous Music Vol. 6: Piano Classics. 160p. (Orig.). 1993. pap. text 12.95 (*0-89898-721-0*) Wrner Bros.

— World Famous Music Vol. 7: Light Classics. 160p. (Orig.). (YA). 1993. pap. text 12.95 (*0-89898-722-9*) Wrner Bros.

— World Famous Music Vol. 11: Classic Piano Solos. 148p. (Orig.). 1993. pap. 12.95 (*0-89898-725-3*, WIM00011) Wrner Bros.

— World Famous Music Enchanting Songs Vol. 8: Piano/Vocal Mixed Folio. 164p. (Orig.). 1993. pap. 12.95 (*0-89898-708-3*, WFM00008) Wrner Bros.

— World Famous Music Piano Selections, Vol. 9. 160p. (YA). 1993. pap. 12.95 (*0-614-31160-8*) Wrner Bros.

— Yentl: Movie Selections. 100p. (Orig.). (C). 1983. pap. text 16.95 (*0-7692-0829-0*, TSF0049) Wrner Bros.

— Yes - Complete Deluxe Edition. 484p. (Orig.). (C). 1981. pap. text 29.95 (*0-7692-0865-7*, VF0896) Wrner Bros.

— Yes - Talk. 80p. (Orig.). (C). 1994. pap. text 19.95 (*0-7692-0873-8*, VF2156) Wrner Bros.

— Yes - The Big Generator. 92p. (Orig.). (C). 1988. pap. text 12.95 (*0-7692-0863-0*, VF1444) Wrner Bros.

— Your Arms Are Too Short to Box with God: Vocal Selections. 20p. (C). 1996. pap. text 8.95 (*0-614-31162-4*, VAL2011) Wrner Bros.

— ZZ Top - Recycler. 56p. (Orig.). (C). 1995. pap. text 16.95 (*0-7692-0877-0*, VF1684) Wrner Bros.

— ZZ Top - Rhythmeen (Guitar) Rhythmeen. (Illus.). 92p. (Orig.). (C). 1997. pap. text 21.95 (*1-57623-514-9*, 0056B) Wrner Bros.

— ZZ Top Complete. 180p. (Orig.). (C). 1990. pap. text 24.95 (*0-7692-0827-4*, VF1642) Wrner Bros.

— ZZ Top Greatest Hits. 84p. (Orig.). (C). 1992. pap. text 18.95 (*0-89724-014-6*, VF1826) Wrner Bros.

Cuellar, Carol & Olson, David C., eds. Top 50 Country Classics: BMI 50th Anniversary Songbook. 160p. (Orig.). (YA). 1997. pap. text 16.95 (*1-57623-930-6*) Wrner Bros.

Cuellar, Carol & Quinones, Manny, eds. Country Wedding Favorites. rev. ed. 96p. (Orig.). (YA). 1995. pap. text 12.95 (*0-89724-467-2*, F3417SMA) Wrner Bros.

Cuellar, Carol & Stang, Aaron. Garth Brooks: No Fences. 84p. (Orig.). (YA). 1994. pap. text 17.95 (*0-89898-781-4*, P0909GTX) Wrner Bros.

Cuellar, Carol & Stang, Aaron, eds. The Best of ZZ Top for Bass Guitar. (Orig.). (YA). 1994. pap. text 18.95 (*0-89898-769-5*, P0986BGX) Wrner Bros.

— Cry of Love: Brother. 84p. (Orig.). (YA). 1994. pap. text 17.95 (*0-89898-837-3*, P1051GTX) Wrner Bros.

— Joni Mitchell: Hits. Perez, Zobeida, tr. 124p. (Orig.). 1997. pap. text 21.95 (*1-57623-753-2*) Wrner Bros.

— The Willie Nelson Guitar Songbook. rev. ed. 56p. (YA). 1995. pap. text 16.95 (*0-89724-533-4*, P0896GTA) Wrner Bros.

— ZZ Top Greatest Hits for Guitar. 220p. (Orig.). (YA). 1993. pap. text 24.95 (*0-89898-638-9*, P078GTX) Wrner Bros.

Cuellar, Carol, ed. see Belwin, C.

Cuellar, Carol, ed. see Schultz, Robert.

Cuellar, Carol, ed. see Shearing, George.

Cuellar, Carole, ed. Neil Young - Decade. 142p. (Orig.). (C). 1994. pap. text 18.95 (*0-7692-0825-8*, VF0476) Wrner Bros.

Cuellar, Fred. Diamonds for Profit. (Illus.). 245p. 1998. pap. 23.95 (*0-9668131-1-1*) City Desktop Prods.

— Fredisms. vi, 506p. 1998. pap. write for info. (*0-9668131-0-3*) City Desktop Prods.

— How to Buy a Diamond: Insider Secrets for Getting Your Money's Worth. 2nd rev. ed. LC 98-15723. 232p. 1998. pap. 14.95 (*1-57071-392-8*) Sourcebks.

***Cuellar, Fred.** The World's Greatest Proposals. 2000. pap. 9.95 (*1-57071-579-3*, Casablanca) Sourcebks.

Cuellar, Gabriel. Graphics Made Easy for the IBM PC & PC XT. (Illus.). 442p. 18.95 (*0-317-12839-6*) P-H.

***Cuellar, Israel.** Handbook of Multi-Cultural Mental Health: Assessment & Treatment of Diverse Populations. LC 99-66278. (Illus.). 512p. 1999. 79.95 (*0-12-199370-1*) Acad Pr.

Cuellar, Jose Tomas de, see de Cuellar, Jose Tomas.

Cueller, Carol, ed. see Warner Brothers Staff.

Cuello, A. C. & Collier, B., eds. Pharmacological Sciences: Perspectives for Research & Therapy in the Late 1990s. xxi, 519p. 1995. 159.00 (*3-7643-5072-5*) Birkhauser.

Cuello, A. Claudio, ed. Cholinergic Function & Dysfunction. LC 93-2319. (Progress in Brain Research Ser.: Vol. 98). 484p. 1993. 273.50 (*0-444-89717-8*) Elsevier.

Cuello, A. Claudio & Collier, Brian, eds. Pharmacological Sciences: Perspectives for Research & Theraphy in the Late 1990s. LC 95-17107. 1995. 159.00 (*0-8176-5072-5*) Birkhauser.

Cuello, H. Jose Israel. Contratacion de Mano de Obra Haitiana Destinada a la Industria Azucarera Dominicana, 1952-1986: Detalles y comparaciones de los Documentos Que Regularon. (Biblioteca Taller 310 Ser.). (SPA.). 458p. 1997. pap. 30.00 (*84-8400-241-1*) Editora Taller.

Cuena, J., ed. Knowledge Engineering & Agent Technology. (Frontiers In Artificial Intelligence Applications Ser.: Vol. 52). 1999. 76.00 (*0-9673355-8-2*) IOS Press.

Cuena, J., jt. ed. see Campbell, J. A.

Cuenca, Alejandro M. Sandinista Economics in Practice: An Insider's Critical Reflections. 178p. (Orig.). 1992. 30.00 (*0-89608-432-9*); pap. 12.00 (*0-89608-431-0*) South End Pr.

Cuenca, M. Spanish-English, English-Spanish Dictionary of False Friends. (ENG & SPA.). 215p. 1989. pap. 34.95 (*0-7859-7483-0*, 8420515485) Fr & Eur.

Cuenca, Miguel. Diccionario de Terminos Equivicos Ingles - Espanol, Ingles - Espanol. (ENG & SPA.). 224p. 1989. pap. 39.95 (*0-7859-5713-8*, 8420515485) Fr & Eur.

Cuenca, Mike. ACE Photoshop, Vol. 5. LC 98-40659. (Exam Cram Ser.: Vol. 5). (Illus.). 435p. 1998. pap. text 29.99 (*1-57610-374-9*) Coriolis Grp.

***Cuenca, Mike.** The Adobe Photoshop 5.5 Workshop. (Illus.). 375p. 2000. pap. 34.99 (*0-7897-2282-8*, Waite Grp Pr) Sams.

Cuenca, Mike. Mastering Adobe InDesign. 3rd ed. (Mastering Ser.). 864p. 1999. 39.99 (*0-7821-2552-2*) Sybex.

Cuenca, Pilar De, see De Cuenca, Pilar.

Cuenco, M. L. Aquaculture Systems Modeling. 46p. 1989. pap. 5.25 (*971-10-2277-X*, Pub. by ICLARM) Intl Spec Bk.

***Cueni, R. Robert.** Dinosaur Heart Transplants: Renewing Mainline Congregations. LC 99-47608. 2000. pap. 15.00 (*0-687-08466-0*) Abingdon.

Cueni, R. Robert. What Ministers Can't Learn in Seminary: A Survival Manual for the Parish Ministry. LC 88-6325. 160p. 1988. pap. 4.78 (*0-687-44652-X*) Abingdon.

Cueni, Robert. The Vital Church Leader. Miller, Herb, ed. (Effective Church Ser.). 128p. 1991. pap. 7.77 (*0-687-43793-8*) Abingdon.

Cuenod, M. A., ed. see IFAC Symposium, Zurich, Switzerland, 29-31 Aug. 19.

Cuenther, Bruce. 1997 Biennial. Neff, Terry A., ed. (Illus.). 40p. 1997. pap. 14.95 (*0-917493-25-7*) Orange Cnty Mus.

Cuervo, Rufino J. Diccionario de Construccion y Regimen de la Lengua Castellana, 8 vols. (SPA.). 8366p. Date not set. write for info. (*0-7859-9576-5*) Fr & Eur.

Cuesta, Benedicto. El Paisano: Nuevo Mexico: Vida y Dilema. 1976. pap. 4.95 (*0-913270-59-8*) Sunstone Pr.

Cuesta-Camacho, David E. Environmental Injustices, Political Struggles: Race, Class, & the Environment. LC 98-16749. 1998. 49.95 (*0-8223-2225-0*); pap. 17.95 (*0-8223-2242-0*) Duke.

Cuesta, Esther, tr. see Schlessman, Amy & Saunders, T. Frank.

Cuesta, Esther B., tr. see Saunders, I. Frank & Schlessman, Amy.

Cuesta, Felipe Arroyo De La, see Arroyo De La Cuesta, Felipe.

***Cuesta, Jorge.** Antologia de la Poesia Mexicana Moderna. LC 99-508395. 276p. 1998. pap. 13.99 (*968-16-5498-6*) Fondo CA.

Cuesta, Laureano Fueyo, see Fueyo Cuesta, Laureano.

Cuesta Mendoza, Antonio. Historia de la Educacion en Puerto Rico (1512-1826) LC 73-3581. (Catholic University of America. Studies in Romance Languages & Literatures: No. 27). reprint ed. 39.50 (*0-404-57777-6*) AMS Pr.

Cuesta, Miguel A. & Nagy, Alexander G., eds. Minimally Invasive Surgery in Gastrointestinal Cancer. LC 93-29876. (Illus.). 1993. text 120.00 (*0-443-04987-4*) Church.

Cuesta, Raf. Urban Design: Method & Techniques. LC 99-24321. 195p. 1999. text 59.95 (*0-7506-4102-9*) Buttrwrth-Heinemann.

Cuetara, Mittie. The Crazy Crawler Crane & Other Very Short Truck Stories. LC 98-3724. 31p. (J). (ps-2). 1998. 14.99 (*0-525-45951-0*, Dutton Child) Peng Put Young Read.

Cueter, Barbara. Money! Money! Money! Where It Comes from & Where It Goes. LC 94-66532. 102p. 1994. pap. 16.95 (*1-882792-03-3*) Proctor Pubns.

Cueto, Marcos, ed. Missionaries of Science: The Rockefeller Foundation & Latin America. LC 93-24416. (Philanthropic Studies). 196p. (C). 1994. 24.95 (*0-253-31583-2*) Ind U Pr.

Cueto-Rua, Julio C. Judicial Methods of Interpretation of the Law. 508p. 1981. 33.00 (*0-940448-08-4*) LSU Law Pubns.

Cueva, Agustin. The Process of Political Domination in Ecuador. Salti, Danielle, tr. LC 79-809. 109p. 1981. 34.95 (*0-87855-338-X*) Transaction Pubs.

Cueva, Juan De La, see De la Cueva, Juan.

Cueva, R., jt. auth. see Jordan, J.

Cuevas, Antonio & Lee, Jennifer, eds. Martial Arts Are Not Just for Kicking Butt: An Anthology of Writings on Martial Arts. LC 97-50055. (Illus.). 200p. 1998. pap. 15.95 (*1-55643-266-6*) North Atlantic.

— 2 Sex E: Urban Tales on Love, Liberty & the Pursuit of Gettin' It On. LC 98-52309. (Illus.). 200p. 1999. pap. 12.95 (*1-883319-94-3*) Frog Ltd CA.

Cuevas-Cancino, Francisco. FDR's Good Neighbor Policy Revisited: Third Morgenthau Memorial Lecture on Morality & Foreign Policy. 28p. 1983. pap. 4.00 (*0-87641-224-X*) Carnegie Ethics & Intl Affairs.

Cuevas, David S. Painting Landscapes in Watercolors. LC 95-37534. (Easy Painting & Drawing Ser.). 64p. 1996. 12.95 (*0-8120-9399-2*) Barron.

— Painting the Figure in Pastels. (Easy Painting & Drawing Ser.). (Illus.). 64p. 1996. 12.95 (*0-8120-9398-4*) Barron.

Cuevas, David S. & Parramon Studios Staff. The Human Figure in Watercolor. (Easy Painting & Drawing Ser.). (Illus.). 64p. 1996. pap. 13.95 (*0-8120-9747-5*) Barron.

Cuevas, Eugenio. El Ultimo de la Brigada. (SPA.). 1994. pap. 16.00 (*0-89729-568-4*) Ediciones.

Cuevas, Gilbert J. & Driscoll, Mark, eds. Reaching All Students with Mathematics. LC 92-44679. (Illus.). 244p. 1993. pap. 10.95 (*0-87353-357-7*) NCTM.

Cuevas, Gilbert J., jt. auth. see Coffland, Jack A.

Cuevas, Guillermo & Hoague, Eleanor C. Butterworth's Spanish & English Legal Dictionary, 2. pap. 105.00 (*0-327-12215-3*) LEXIS Pub.

Cuevas, Jose L. Gato Macho (Tom Cat) (SPA.). 728p. 1994. 39.99 (*968-16-4297-X*, Pub. by Fondo) Continental Bk.

Cuevas, Judy. Bliss. 384p. (Orig.). 1995. mass mkt. 5.99 (*0-515-11587-8*, Jove) Berkley Pub.

— Dance. 384p. (Orig.). 1996. mass mkt. 5.99 (*0-515-11763-3*, Jove) Berkley Pub.

Cuevas, Lou. Anasazi Legends, Songs of the Wind Dancer. LC 99-87981. 176p. 2000. pap. 9.95 (*0-87961-256-8*) Naturegraph.

— Apache Legends: Songs of the Wind Dancer. Brown, Keven, ed. LC 91-31366. (Illus.). 128p. (Orig.). (YA). 1991. pap. text 8.95 (*0-87961-219-3*) Naturegraph.

— In the Valley of the Ancients: A Book of Native American Legends. LC 97-3439. (Illus.). 64p. 1997. pap. 5.95 (*1-877856-82-7*) SW Pks Mnmts.

An Asterisk (*) at the beginning of an entry indicates that the title is appearing for the first time.

Cuevas, Tomasa. Prison of Women: Testimonies of War & Resistance in Spain, 1939-1975. Giles, Mary E., ed. & tr. by. from SPA. LC 97-33352. (Illus.). 256p. (C). 1998. text 65.50 (*0-7914-3857-0*); pap. text 21.95 (*0-7914-3858-9*) State U NY Pr.

Cuezva, J. M., et al, eds. Endocrine & Biochemical Development of the Fetus & Neonate. LC 90-7827. (Reproductive Biology Ser.). (Illus.). 330p. 1990. 95.00 (*0-306-43675-2*, Plenum Trade) Perseus Pubng.

Cuff. Super Spelling, Bk. 1. Date not set. pap. text. write for info. (*0-582-39104-0*, Pub. by Addison-Wesley) Longman.

— Super Spelling, Bk. 2. Date not set. pap. text. write for info. (*0-582-39105-9*, Pub. by Addison-Wesley) Longman.

— Super Spelling, Bk. 3. Date not set. pap. text. write for info. (*0-582-39106-7*, Pub. by Addison-Wesley) Longman.

— Super Spelling, Bk. 4. Date not set. pap. text. write for info. (*0-582-39107-5*, Pub. by Addison-Wesley) Longman.

— Super Spelling, Bk. 5. Date not set. pap. text. write for info. (*0-582-39108-3*, Pub. by Addison-Wesley) Longman.

— Super Spelling, Bk. 6. Date not set. pap. text. write for info. (*0-582-39109-1*, Pub. by Addison-Wesley) Longman.

Cuff, Carolyn K. Reasoning with a Computer in Pascal. 44p. 1986. teacher ed. write for info. (*0-318-60949-5*) Addison-Wesley.

Cuff, Courtney & Erskine, Lynn, eds. Green Scissors, 1998: Cutting Wasteful & Environmentally Harmful Spending. (Illus.). 85p. 1998. pap. 20.00 (*0-913890-79-0*) Friends of Earth.

Cuff, Courtney, et al. The Green Scissors Report: Cutting Wasteful & Environmentally Harmful Spending & Subsidies. 48p. (Orig.). 1995. pap. 10.00 (*0-913890-99-5*) Friends of Earth.

Cuff, Dana. Architecture: The Story of Practice. (Illus.). 320p. 1992. reprint ed. pap. text 21.00 (*0-262-53112-7*) MIT Pr.

***Cuff, Dana.** The Provisional City: Los Angeles Stories of Architecture & Urbanism. (Illus.). 400p. 2000. 40.00 (*0-262-03276-7*) MIT Pr.

Cuff, David J. & Mattson, Mark T. Thematic Maps. (Illus.). 176p. 1983. 15.95 (*0-415-90158-8*, NO. 2893); teacher ed. 4.95 (*0-416-34320-1*, NO. 3731) Routledge.

Cuff, E. C. Problems of Versions in Everyday Situations. LC 93-27025. (Studies in Ethnomethodology & Conversation Analysis: No. 2). 148p. (Orig.). (C). 1993. pap. text 26.00 (*0-8191-9292-9*); lib. bdg. 48.00 (*0-8191-9149-3*) U Pr of Amer.

Cuff, E. C. & Payne, G. C., eds. Perspectives in Sociology. 2nd ed. 1983. pap. text 15.95 (*0-04-301157-8*) Routledge.

Cuff, E. C. & Sharrock, W. W. Perspectives in Sociology. 4th ed. LC 97-30113. 368p. (C). 1998. 85.00 (*0-415-17371-X*) Routledge.

Cuff, E. C., et al. Perspectives in Sociology. 3rd ed. 257p. (C). 1990. pap. text 16.95 (*0-04-445684-0*) Routledge.

— Perspectives in Sociology. 4th ed. LC 97-30113. 368p. (C). 1998. pap. 24.99 (*0-415-15979-2*) Routledge.

Cuff, Kevin, et al. Stories in Stone. rev. ed. Fairwell, Kay et al, eds. (Great Explorations in Math & Science Ser.). (Illus.). 164p. (J). (gr. 4-8). 1999. pap. 16.00 (*0-924886-20-X*, GEMS) Lawrence Science.

Cuff, Penelope, jt. auth. see Page, Clint.

Cuff, Robert D. The War Industries Board: Business-Government Relations During World War I. LC 72-4022. 316p. 1973. reprint ed. pap. 98.00 (*0-608-05942-0*, 206627900008) Bks Demand.

Cuff, W. R. & Tomczak, M., Jr., eds. Synthesis & Modeling of Intermittent Estuaries. (Lecture Notes on Coastal & Estuarine Studies: Vol. 3). 302p. 1983. pap. 42.00 (*0-387-12681-3*) Spr-Verlag.

Cuff, Yvonne H. Ceramic Technology for Potters & Sculptors. (Illus.). 440p. (Orig.). (C). 1996. pap. 24.95 (*0-8122-1377-7*); text 45.00 (*0-8122-3071-X*) U of Pa Pr.

Cuffaro, Harriet. Experimenting with the World: John Dewey & Early Education. (Early Childhood Education Ser.). 144p. (C). 1994. text 32.00 (*0-8077-3372-5*); pap. text 16.95 (*0-8077-3371-7*) Tchrs Coll.

Cuffe, Mary. The Woman of Too Many Days. LC 99-31447. 96p. 1999. 25.95 (*0-934971-69-2*, Pub. by Calyx Bks); pap. 12.95 (*0-934971-68-4*, Pub. by Calyx Bks) Consort Bk Sales.

Cuffee, Clarence V. Holding Serve in Black America. (Illus.). 62p. 1996. pap. 8.00 (*0-9654022-0-7*) Ivory Publns.

Cuffel, Victoria, ed. see Chatterjee, Choitali.

Cuffel, Victoria, ed. see Cohen, Jeffrey H.

Cuffel, Victoria, jt. ed. see Conway, Dennis.

Cuffel, Victoria, ed. see Goss, Benjamin M.

Cuffel, Victoria, ed. see Gray, Christopher.

Cuffel, Victoria, ed. see Schonfeld, Martin.

Cuffel, Victoria, ed. see Seel, Peter B.

Cuffel, Victoria, ed. see Sisken, Daniel S.

Cuffel, Victoria, ed. see Wagoner, Paula A.

Cuffel, Victoria, ed. see Walker, Juliet E.

Cuffel, Victoria, ed. see Willnat, Lars.

Cuffel, Victoria J., ed. see Light, Nathan.

Cuffel, Victoria J., ed. see Peach, Lucinda J.

Cuffel, Victoria J., ed. see Schanker, David R.

Cuffey, Robyn, jt. auth. see Donovan-Wright, Mary A.

***Cuffie, Terrasita A.** Maya Angelou. LC 99-20045. (Importance of Ser.). (Illus.). 80p. (YA). (gr. 4-9). 1999. lib. bdg. 23.70 (*1-56006-532-X*) Lucent Bks.

***Cuganesan, Suresh, et al.** Controls in Strategic Supplier Relationships. 64p. 1999. pap. 19.95 (*0-86840-721-6*, Pub. by New South Wales Univ Pr) Intl Spec Bk.

Cugat, Xavier. Rumba Is My Life. (Ballroom Dance Ser.). 1985. lib. bdg. 250.00 (*0-87700-848-5*) Revisionist Pr.

— Rumba Is My Life: American Autobiography. 210p. 1995. lib. bdg. 79.00 (*0-7812-8493-7*) Rprt Serv.

Cugini, John V. General Purpose Programming Languages: A Source Book. (Illus.). 240p. pap. 19.95 (*0-89433-296-1*, 8229) Petrocelli.

Cugoano, Ottobah & Carretta, Vincent. Thoughts & Sentiments on the Evil of Slavery & Other Writings. LC 98-41172. (Penguin Classics Ser.). 1999. pap. 11.95 (*0-14-044750-4*) Viking Penguin.

Cuhaj, George. Standard Price Guide to U. S. Scouting Collectibles: ID & Price Guide for Cub, Scout & Explorer Programs. LC 97-80596. (Illus.). 328p. 1998. pap. 24.95 (*0-87341-520-5*, SCOUT) Krause Pubns.

Cuhaj, George, jt. ed. see Baumann, Fred.

***Cuhaj, Joe.** Hike America: Alabama. (Illus.). 2000. pap. 17.95 (*0-7627-0843-3*) Globe Pequot.

Cuhls, K. & Kuwahara, Takeo. Outlook for Japanese & German Future Technology: Comparing Technology Forecast Survey. (Technology, Innovation, & Policy Ser: Vol. 1). 238p. 1994. 68.95 (*3-7908-0800-8*) Spr-Verlag.

***Cuhulain, Kerr.** Wiccan Warrior: Walking a Spiritual Path in a Sometimes Hostile World. LC 99-89966. 216p. 2000. pap. 12.95 (*1-56718-252-6*) Llewellyn Pubns.

Cui. Debris Flow & Disaster Mitigation. text 121.00 (*0-471-98567-8*) Wiley.

Cui, Dan. The Cultural Contribution of British Protestant Missionaries & British-American Cooperation to China's National Development During the 1920's. LC 97-52587. 432p. (C). 1998. 59.00 (*0-7618-1029-3*) U Pr of Amer.

***Cui, Geng & Choudhury, Pravat K.** Marketing to Ethnic Consumers: An Annotated Bibliography. LC 00-44760. (Bibliography Ser.). 2000. pap. write for info. (*0-87757-285-2*) Am Mktg.

Cui, Gurangi J., jt. ed. see Gan, Z. Z.

Cui Jinzhong, jt. auth. see Li Chengsen.

Cui-Lan, Yan. Treatment of External Diseases with Acupuncture Moxibustion. Flaws, Bob, ed. Shou-Zhong, Yang, tr. from CHI. LC 96-80188.Tr. of Zhong Yi Wai Ke Zhen Jin Zhi Liao. viii, 253 p. (Orig.). 1997. pap. 29.95 (*0-936185-80-5*) Blue Poppy Pr.

Cuilleanain, Ni, jt. ed. see Pheifer, J.

Cuimmin. On the Saints of Ireland. Stokes, Whitley, ed. & tr. by. from IRI. 1996. pap. 3.00 (*0-89979-081-X*) British Am Bks.

Cuisenaire. Exploring with Power Polygons. 1995. pap. 9.95 (*0-201-44785-1*) Addison-Wesley.

— Learning with Cuisenaire Rods Booklet. 1995. 9.95 (*0-201-48270-3*) Addison-Wesley.

Cuisenaire. One-Digit Addition & Subtraction with Cuisenaire Rods. 1995. pap. write for info. (*0-201-48223-1*) Addison-Wesley.

Cuisenaire Company of America Staff. Super Source Geometry. 1998. pap. 15.95 (*1-57452-171-3*) Cuisenaire.

— Super Source Measurement. 1998. pap. 15.95 (*1-57452-172-1*) Cuisenaire.

— Super Source Number. 1998. pap. 15.95 (*1-57452-174-8*) Cuisenaire.

— Super Source Patterns & Functions. 1998. pap. 15.95 (*1-57452-173-X*) Cuisenaire.

— Super Source Probability & Statistics. 1998. pap. 15.95 (*1-57452-175-6*) Cuisenaire.

Cuisenaire Staff. Super Source: Cuisenaire Rods. (J). (gr. k-2). 1996. pap. text 15.95 (*1-57452-003-2*) Cuisenaire.

— Super Source: Cuisenaire Rods. (J). (gr. 3-4). 1996. pap. text 15.95 (*1-57452-004-0*) Cuisenaire.

— Super Source: Cuisenaire Rods. (J). (gr. 5-6). 1996. pap. text 15.95 (*1-57452-005-9*) Cuisenaire.

— Super Source: Geoboards. (J). (gr. k-2). 1996. pap. text 15.95 (*1-57452-006-7*) Cuisenaire.

— Super Source: Geoboards. (J). (gr. 3-4). 1996. pap. text 15.95 (*1-57452-007-5*) Cuisenaire.

— Super Source: Geoboards. (J). (gr. 5-6). 1996. pap. text 15.95 (*1-57452-008-3*) Cuisenaire.

— Super Source: Index. 45p. 1996. pap. text. write for info. (*0-938587-99-4*) Cuisenaire.

— Super Source: Pattern Blocks. (Illus.). 96p. (J). (gr. k-2). 1996. pap. text 15.95 (*1-57452-009-1*) Cuisenaire.

— Super Source: Pattern Blocks. (Illus.). 96p. (J). (gr. 3-4). 1996. pap. text 15.95 (*1-57452-010-5*) Cuisenaire.

— Super Source: Pattern Blocks. (Illus.). 96p. (J). (gr. 5-6). 1996. pap. text 15.95 (*1-57452-011-3*) Cuisenaire.

— Super Source: Snap Cubes. (Illus.). 96p. (J). (gr. k-2). 1996. pap. text 15.95 (*1-57452-012-1*) Cuisenaire.

— Super Source: Snap Cubes. (Illus.). 96p. (J). (gr. 3-4). 1996. pap. text 15.95 (*1-57452-013-X*) Cuisenaire.

— Super Source: Snap Cubes. (Illus.). 96p. (J). (gr. 5-6). 1996. pap. text 15.95 (*1-57452-014-8*) Cuisenaire.

— Super Source: Tangrams. (J). (gr. k-2). 1996. pap. text 15.95 (*1-57452-015-6*) Cuisenaire.

— Super Source: Tangrams. (J). (gr. 3-4). 1996. pap. text 15.95 (*1-57452-016-4*) Cuisenaire.

— Super Source: Tangrams. (J). (gr. 5-6). 1996. pap. text 15.95 (*1-57452-017-2*) Cuisenaire.

Cuisenier. Jules Romain, l'unanimisme et les Hommes de Bonne Volonte. 8.50 (*0-685-37080-1*, F122350) Fr & Eur.

Cuisenier, Jean, ed. Europe as a Cultural Area. (World Anthropology Ser.). 281p. 1979. text 44.65 (*90-279-7790-9*) Mouton.

Cuisinier, Jeanne. Danses magiques de Kelantan. LC 77-87024. 1977. reprint ed. 27.00 (*0-404-16809-4*) AMS Pr.

***Cuitino, Luis Martinez.** Garcia Lorca for Beginners. (Illus.). 192p. 1999. pap. 11.95 (*0-86316-290-8*) Writers & Readers.

***Cuito, Aurora.** Mountain Houses. (Illus.). 2000. pap. 35.00 (*0-8230-7392-0*) Watsn-Guptill.

— Stunning Houses. (Illus.). 160p. 2000. pap. write for info. (*0-8230-7463-3*) Watsn-Guptill.

— Working & Living Spaces: Working at Home. (Illus.). 176p. 2000. pap. 35.00 (*0-8230-5870-0*) Watsn-Guptill.

Cukier, Daniel & McCullough, Virginia E. Coping with Radiation Therapy: A Ray of Hope. 240p. 1994. pap. 14.95 (*1-56565-147-2*) Lowell Hse.

***Cukier, Daniel & McCullough, Virginia E.** Coping with Radiation Therapy: A Ray of Hope. 208p. 2000. reprint ed. 24.00 (*0-7881-9273-6*) DIANE Pub.

Cukier, Daniel & McCullough, Virginia E. Coping with Radiation Therapy: A Ray of Hope. 2nd ed. 240p. 1996. pap. 16.00 (*1-56565-436-6*, 04366W, Pub. by Lowell Hse) NTC Contemp Pub Co.

Cukierman, Alex. Central Bank Strategy, Credibility & Independence: Theory & Evidence. (Illus.). 450p. 1992. 65.00 (*0-262-03198-1*) MIT Pr.

Cukierman, Alex, et al, eds. Political Economy, Growth, & Business Cycles. (Illus.). 400p. 1992. 55.00 (*0-262-03194-9*) MIT Pr.

***Cuklanz, Lisa M.** Rape on Prime Time: Television, Masculinity & Sexual Violence. LC 99-38729. 1999. pap. 17.50 (*0-8122-1710-1*) U of Pa Pr.

Cuklanz, Lisa M. Rape on Trial: How the Mass Media Construct Legal Reform & Social Change. 160p. 1995. text 35.00 (*0-8122-3321-2*); pap. text 12.95 (*0-8122-1559-1*) U of Pa Pr.

Cukor, P., jt. auth. see Sandman, D.

Culanovski, I. V., et al. Twenty-Five Papers on Statistics & Probability. LC 61-9803. (Selected Translations in Mathematical Statistics & Probability Ser.: Vol. 1). 306p. 1961. 51.00 (*0-8218-1451-6*, STAPRO/1) Am Math.

Cular, James A. Weapons Women Use: A Guide to the Man Going Through Divorce. 36p. (Orig.). 1995. 6.95 (*0-9647707-0-9*) QQs Inc.

Culatta, Barbara, jt. auth. see Merritt, Donna D.

Culatta, Richard & Goldberg, Stanley. Stuttering Therapy: An Integrated Approach to Theory & Practice. (Illus.). 442p. 1994. 77.00 (*0-02-326311-3*, Macmillan Coll) P-H.

Culatta, Richard, jt. auth. see Dworkin, James P.

Culatta, Richard A. & Tompkins, James R. Fundamentals of Special Education: What Every Teacher Needs to Know. LC 98-17010. 472p. 1998. pap. text 47.00 (*0-13-256991-4*, Scribners Ref) Mac Lib Ref.

Culberson, Chicita F. Chemical & Botanical Guide to Lichen Products. (Illus.). 672p. 1979. reprint ed. pap. 99.00 (*3-87429-165-0*, 002099, Pub. by Koeltz Sci Bks) Lubrecht & Cramer.

Culberson, Ed. Obsessions Die Hard: Motorcycling the Pan-American Highway's Jungle Gap. 2nd ed. LC 97-180134. (Incredible Journeys Ser.). (Illus.). 272p. (Orig.). 1996. reprint ed. pap. 19.95 (*1-884313-06-X*, CULB) Whitehorse NH.

Culberson, Linda C. Arrowheads & Spear Points in the Prehistoric Southeast: A Guide to Understanding Cultural Artifacts. LC 93-8455. (Illus.). 160p. 1993. pap. 13.95 (*0-87805-638-6*); text 29.95 (*0-87805-643-2*) U Pr of Miss.

Culberson, Nancy, jt. ed. see Lawrence, Harold A.

Culberson, Nancy B. More Writing Wizardry. 64p. 1992. 10.95 (*0-8403-8143-3*) Kendall-Hunt.

— Writing Wizardry: The Basics, Vol. I. 144p. 1992. per. 18.95 (*0-8403-8125-5*) Kendall-Hunt.

— Writing Wizardry: The Basics, Vol. II. 144p. (C). 1993. per. 18.95 (*0-8403-8597-8*) Kendall-Hunt.

Culberson, W. L., ed. see Tuckerman, E.

Culberson, William C. Vigilantism: Political History of Private Power in America. LC 89-26555. (Contributions in Criminology & Penology Ser.: No. 28). (Illus.). 184p. 1990. pap. 19.95 (*0-275-93548-5*, B3548) Greenwood.

— Vigilantism: Political History of Private Power in America, 28. LC 89-26555. (Contributions in Criminology & Penology Ser.: No. 28). (Illus.). 184p. 1990. 55.00 (*0-313-27238-7*, CUV/) Greenwood.

Culbert, David, ed. Mission to Moscow. (Warner Bros. Screenplay Ser.). (Illus.). 280p. 1980. 14.95 (*0-299-08380-2*); pap. 9.95 (*0-299-08384-5*) U of Wis Pr.

Culbert, David & Wood, Richard. Film & Propaganda in America: A Documentary History, 5 vols., Set. LC 88-38490. 1991. lib. bdg. 795.00 (*0-313-20857-3*, Greenwood Pr) Greenwood.

Culbert, David, jt. auth. see Chambers, John W., 2nd.

Culbert, David H. News for Everyman: Radio & Foreign Affairs in Thirties America. LC 75-23862. 238p. 1976. 62.95 (*0-8371-8260-3*, CRC/, Greenwood Pr) Greenwood.

Culbert, David H., ed. Film & Propaganda in America: A Documentary History, World War II, Pt. 1, Vol. 2. LC 88-38490. 544p. 1990. lib. bdg. 105.00 (*0-313-20859-X*, CFP02, Greenwood Pr) Greenwood.

— Film & Propaganda in America: A Documentary History, World War II, Pt. 2, Vol. 3. LC 88-38490. 544p. 1990. lib. bdg. 105.00 (*0-313-20860-3*, CFP03, Greenwood Pr) Greenwood.

Culbert, David H., jt. ed. see Suid, Lawrence H.

Culbert, Michael, jt. auth. see Brodie, Douglas S.

Culbert, Michael L. Medical Armageddon, 4 vols. in 2 bks. Incl. Bk. 1, Vols. I & II. (Illus.). 1997. pap. (*0-9636487-1-3*); Bk. 2, Vols. III & IV. (Illus.). 1997. pap. (*0-9636487-2-1*); write for info. (*0-9636487-3-X*) C&C Communs.

— Medical Armageddon. rev. ed. LC 97-69817. (Illus.). 830p. 1997. pap. 29.95 (*0-9636487-5-6*) C&C Communs.

Culbert, Patrick T. Tikal Report No. 25A: Ceramics of Tikal. LC 93-14674. (University Museum Monographs: Vol. 81). (Illus.). xi, 345p. (C). 1993. text 65.00 (*0-924171-20-0*) U Museum Pubns.

Culbert, S. J. Your Lucky Number: Understand Its Vibration & Impact on Your Personality & Relationships. 96p. 1995. pap. 6.95 (*0-572-01398-1*, Pub. by Foulsham UK) Assoc Pubs Grp.

Culbert, Samuel A. Mind-Set Management: The Psychology of Effective Management. (Illus.). 368p. 1996. 30.00 (*0-19-509746-7*) OUP.

Culbert, Samuel A. & McDonough, John J. Radical Management: Power-Politics & the Pursuit of Trust. 240p. (C). 1985. 35.00 (*0-02-905940-2*) Free Pr.

Culbert, Steven. Reveal the Secrets of the Sacred Rose Tarot. 125p. 1990. pap. 9.95 (*0-88079-370-8*, BK81) US Games Syst.

Culbert, Steven T. Lovesong for the Giant Contessa. LC 96-51156. xiii, 278 p. 1997. 20.00 (*1-56858-082-7*) FWEW.

Culbert, Steven T. Sacred Rose Tarot Deck & Book Set. (Illus.). 1992. pap. 26.00 (*0-88079-417-8*) US Games Syst.

Culbert, T. Patrick, jt. auth. see Schusky, Ernest L.

Culbert, Tom & Dawson, Andy. Pan Africa: Across the Sahara in 1941 with Pan Am. Davies, R. E., ed. (Illus.). 184p. 1998. lib. bdg. 30.00 (*1-888962-12-7*) Paladwr Pr.

Culbertson, A. B. Culbertson. John Culbertson, Ransom Thacker, John Cummings & Related Families. (Illus.). 28p. 1997. reprint ed. pap. 5.50 (*0-8328-8162-7*); reprint ed. lib. bdg. 15.50 (*0-8328-8161-9*) Higginson Bk Co.

Culbertson, B. M., ed. Contemporary Topics in Polymer Science, Vol. 6: Multiphase Macromolecular Systems. (Illus.). 708p. 1989. 155.00 (*0-306-43374-5*, Plenum Trade) Perseus Pubng.

Culbertson, B. M., jt. auth. see Trivedi, B. C.

Culbertson, Barry & Vaughn, Penny. Everyday Prayers for Nurses. 96p. 1996. pap. 5.00 (*0-687-18423-1*) Dimen for Liv.

Culbertson, Barry, jt. auth. see Culbertson, LeNoir.

Culbertson, Barry L. Everyday Prayers for Teens. LC 94-164695. 96p. (gr. 7 up). 1994. pap. 5.00 (*0-687-31694-4*) Dimen for Liv.

Culbertson, Cathleen & Schmidt, Karen, eds. St. Anthony's DRG Guidebook (DRG) 620p. 1997. pap. 79.95 (*1-56329-470-2*) St Anthony Pub.

— 1999 Drg Guidebook. rev. ed. 620p. (C). 1999. pap. 79.95 (*1-56329-571-7*) Thomson Learn.

Culbertson, Charles V. Managing Your Safety Manager. 46p. 1981. 4.95 (*0-937802-01-8*) RMSP.

Culbertson, Diana. The Poetics of Revelation: Recognition in the Narrative Tradition. LC 88-37662. 120p. (C). 1988. 24.95 (*0-86554-310-0*, MUP/H251); pap. 16.95 (*0-86554-351-8*, MUP/P081) Mercer Univ Pr.

***Culbertson, Diana, ed.** Invisible Light: Poems about God. LC 00-35850. 2000. 19.95 (*0-231-12062-1*) Col U Pr.

Culbertson, Evelyn D. He Heard America Singing: Arthur Farwell, Composer, & Crusading Music Educator. LC 92-11172. (Composers of North America Ser.: No. 9). (Illus.). 885p. 1992. 94.00 (*0-8108-2580-5*) Scarecrow.

Culbertson, Hugh M. & Chen, Ni, eds. International Public Relations: A Comparative Analysis. (LEA's Communication Ser.). 424p. 1996. 79.95 (*0-8058-1684-4*) L Erlbaum Assocs.

Culbertson, Hugh M., et al. Social, Political, & Economic Concepts & Contexts in Public Relations: Theory & Cases. (Communication Textbook (Public Relations) Ser.). 328p. 1993. pap. 34.50 (*0-8058-1288-1*); text 69.95 (*0-8058-1013-7*) L Erlbaum Assocs.

Culbertson, Jack & Cunningham, Luvern L., eds. Microcomputers & Education: 85th Yearbook of the National Society for the Study of Education. LC 85-62667. xii, 308p. 1986. lib. bdg. 22.00 (*0-226-60141-2*) U Ch Pr.

Culbertson, Jack A. Building Bridges: UCEA'S First Two Decades. LC 98-209967. x, 365 p. 1995. write for info. (*1-55996-159-7*) Univ Council Educ Admin.

Culbertson, Jack A., et al. Performance Objectives for School Principals. LC 74-75367. 235p. 1974. 31.00 (*0-8211-0223-0*) McCutchan.

Culbertson, Jack A., jt. ed. see Willower, Donald J.

Culbertson, James T. Consciousness: Natural & Artificial. LC 81-81617. 1983. 13.95 (*0-87212-152-6*) Libra.

— The Minds of Robots: Sense Data, Memory Images & Behavior in Conscious Automata. LC 63-7256. (Illus.). 480p. reprint ed. 148.80 (*0-8357-9690-6*, 201173400079) Bks Demand.

— Sensations, Memories & the Flow of Time: A Theory of Subjective States - Reductive Materialism Using a Spacetime Analysis. LC 75-30170. (Illus.). 1976. 12.00 (*0-916298-01-9*) Cromwell.

Culbertson, Jan L., et al, eds. Sudden Infant Death Syndrome: Medical Aspects & Psychological Management. LC 88-45399. (Johns Hopkins Series in Contemporary Medicine & Public Health). (Illus.). 286p. 1988. reprint ed. pap. 88.70 (*0-608-05943-9*, 206628000008) Bks Demand.

Culbertson, Jan L. & Willis, Diane J., eds. Testing Young Children: A Reference Guide for Developmental, Psychoeducational, & Psychosocial Assessments. LC 92-11515. 496p. 1993. text 41.00 (*0-89079-550-9*, 1924) PRO-ED.

Culbertson, John J. Operation Tuscaloosa: 2nd Battalion, 5th Marines, at An Hoa. (Orig.). 1997. mass mkt. 5.99 (*0-8041-1565-6*) Ivy Books.

— A Sniper in the Arizona: 2nd Battalion, 5th Marines, in the Arizona Territory, 1967. LC 98-93522. 1999. mass mkt. 6.99 (*0-8041-1870-1*) Ivy Books.

Culbertson, Joseph. Indian Scout: Memoirs Eighteen Seventy-Six to Eighteen Ninety-Five. rev. ed. Trout, M. D., ed. LC 84-50262. Orig. Title: Joseph Culbertson-Boy Scout. (Illus.). 181p. 1985. pap. 16.95 (*0-917071-00-X*) Ocean Allen Pub.

Culbertson, Judi & Randall, Tom. Permanent Italians: An Illustrated Guide to the Cemeteries of Italy. LC 95-41353. (Permanent Ser.). (Illus.). 230p. (Orig.). 1996. pap. 16.95 (*0-8027-7431-8*) Walker & Co.

— Permanent Londoners: An Illustrated Guide to the Cemeteries of London. (Permanent Ser.). (Illus.). 230p. (Orig.). 1996. pap. 16.95 (*0-8027-7471-7*) Walker & Co.

— Permanent Parisians: An Illustrated Guide to the Cemeteries of Paris. (Permanent Ser.). (Illus.). 230p. 1996. pap. 16.95 (*0-8027-7470-9*) Walker & Co.

*Culbertson, Judi & Randall, Tom.** Permanent Parisians: An Illustrated Guide to the Cemeteries of Paris. (Illus.). 230p. 1999. reprint ed. pap. text 16.00 (*0-7881-6841-X*) DIANE Pub.

Culbertson, LeNoir & Culbertson, Barry. New Devotions for Any Occasion! 64p. 1997. pap. 6.95 (*0-687-05288-2*) Abingdon.

Culbertson, Manie. Louisiana: The Land & Its People. 4th ed. (Illus.). 128p. (C). 1986. teacher ed. 9.95 (*0-88289-894-9*) Pelican.

— Louisiana: The Land & Its People Student Skillbuilder. 2nd ed. (Illus.). 128p. (J). (gr. 4-7). 1999. pap. 9.95 (*1-56554-625-3*) Pelican.

Culbertson, Manie, jt. auth. see Eakin, Sue.

Culbertson, Margaret. American House Designs: An Index to Popular & Trade Periodicals 1850-1915, 19. LC 94-30280. (Art Reference Collection Ser.). 360p. 1994. lib. bdg. 85.00 (*0-313-29202-7*, Greenwood Pr) Greenwood.

— Texas Houses Built by the Book: The Use of Published Designs, 1850-1925. (Sara & John Lindsey Series in the Arts & Humanities: Vol. 3). (Illus.). 160p. 1999. 39.95 (*0-89096-863-2*) Tex A&M Univ Pr.

Culbertson, Nancy. Late Harvest. (Illus.). 35p. (Orig.). 1996. pap. 9.95 (*0-9655880-0-9*) N Culbertson.

Culbertson, Paul T. & Wiley, H. Orton. Introduction to Christian Theology. 472p. 1946. 32.99 (*0-8341-0217-X*) Beacon Hill.

Culbertson, Philip. Caring for God's People: Counseling & Christian Wholeness. LC 99-45725. 1999. pap. 29.00 (*0-8006-3187-0*, Fortress Pr) Augsburg Fortress.

Culbertson, Philip L. Counseling Men. LC 94-2825. (Creative Pastoral Care & Counseling Ser.). 96p. 1994. pap. 15.00 (*0-8006-2786-5*, 1-2786, Fortress Pr) Augsburg Fortress.

— A Word Fitly Spoken: Context, Transmission, & Adoption of the Parables of Jesus. LC 94-9989. (SUNY Series in Religious Studies). 390p. (C). 1995. text 74.50 (*0-7914-2311-5*); pap. text 24.95 (*0-7914-2312-3*) State U NY Pr.

Culbertson, Ralph. Air Logic. 1988. 37.50 (*0-932905-03-X*) Penton Pub.

Culbertson, Robert G. & Weisheit, Ralph A., eds. Order under Law: Readings in Criminal Justice. 5th rev. ed. LC 97-204852. (Illus.). 352p. (C). 1996. pap. text 18.95 (*0-88133-926-1*) Waveland Pr.

Culbertson, Robert G., jt. ed. see Weisheit, Ralph A.

Culbertson, S. M., jt. auth. see Smith, R. H.

Culbertson, Sidney M. Hunter Family of Virginia & Connections, Embracing Portions of Families of Alexander, Pearson, Chapman, Travers, Tyler, West, et al. (Illus.). 299p. 1997. reprint ed. pap. 45.00 (*0-8328-9271-8*); reprint ed. lib. bdg. 55.00 (*0-8328-9270-X*) Higginson Bk Co.

Culbertson, Thaddeus A. Journal of an Expedition to the Mauvaises Terres & the Upper Missouri in 1850. 1986. pap. 14.95 (*0-87770-387-6*) Ye Galleon.

Culbertson, Thaddeus A., ed. Journal of an Expedition to the Mauvaises Terres & the Upper Missouri in 1850. (Bureau of American Ethnology Bulletins Ser.). 164p. 1995. lib. bdg. 79.00 (*0-7812-4147-2*) Rprt Serv.

Culbertson, Todd, jt. ed. see MacKenzie, Ross.

Culbertson, William P., Jr., jt. ed. see Breit, William.

Culbertson, William R. & Tanner, Dennis C. Introductory Anatomy & Physiology Workbook. (Illus.). 224p. 1996. pap., wbk. ed. 35.00 (*0-205-26317-8*) Allyn.

***Culbreath, Alice N. & Neal, Saundra K.** Testing the Waters: A Teen's Guide to Career Exploration. LC 99-95344. 250p. (YA). 1999. pap. 24.95 (*0-9672502-0-X*) JRC Consultng.

Culbreath, Myrna, jt. auth. see Marshak, Sondra.

Culbreath, Susan E. How to Avoid Legal Traps in Workforce Reduction. LC 98-37864. 54p. 1998. spiral bd. 47.00 (*0-925773-46-8*) M Lee Smith.

— New Employment Issues in the Electronic Workplace. LC 98-11391. 52p. 1998. spiral bd. 47.00 (*0-925773-42-5*) M Lee Smith.

Culbreth, Cecil. Pray the Promises. 168p. 1999. ring bd. 10.00 (*0-9671852-1-1*) Book of Hope.

Culbreth, Cecil, ed. see Wilson, John.

Culbreth, David M. A Manual of Materia Medica & Pharmacology. 7th ed. 667p. 1996. reprint ed. pap. 35.00 (*0-7873-0229-5*) Hlth Research.

Culbreth, Linda. Christian "Wo-Mentoring" A Study from Titus Z. 107p. 1999. spiral bd. 14.95 (*1-893784-02-9*) Aunt Matilda.

— Laying Aside the Weight of Guilt. 23p. (Orig.). 1999. pap. 4.95 (*1-893784-01-0*) Aunt Matilda.

— Practical Strategies When Johnny Can't Learn or Behave. 54p. 1999. spiral bd. 9.95 (*1-893784-00-2*) Aunt Matilda.

Culbreth, Luann & Kaut, Carolyn. Principles & Clinical Applications of MRI Technology. Allen, Andrew & Biello, Lisa, eds. LC 97-134. (Illus.). 480p. 1998. text 65.00 (*0-7216-6632-9*, W B Saunders Co) Harcrt Hlth Sci Grp.

***Culclasure, Scott P.** The Past as Liberation from History. LC 98-30526. (Counterpoints Studies in the Postmodern Theory of Education: Vol. 63). 184p. (C). 1999. pap. text 29.95 (*0-8204-3840-5*) P Lang Pubng.

Culclasure, Scott P., jt. ed. see Bolton, Charles C.

Cule, John. A Doctor for the People: Two Thousand Years of General Practice in Britain. (Illus.). 1980. text 88.00 (*0-906141-29-X*) Kluwer Academic.

***Cule, John.** The Timetables of Medicine: An Illustrated Chronological Chart of the History of Medicine. (Illus.). 128p. 2000. 19.98 (*1-57912-156-X*) Blck Dog & Leventhal.

Cule, John. Wreath on the Crown. 140p. (C). 1967. pap. 20.00 (*0-85088-077-7*, Pub. by Gomer Pr) St Mut.

Cule, John, ed. Wales & Medicine. 249p. (C). 1975. pap. 20.00 (*0-85088-260-5*, Pub. by Gomer Pr) St Mut.

***Culea, John.** In the Air - On the Air: One TV News Anchor Will Report the Greatest News Story Ever. LC 99-66071. 389p. 1999. pap. 14.95 (*1-57921-251-4*) WinePress Pub.

Culea, John. Light the Night. 3rd ed. 389p. 1997. reprint ed. pap. 10.00 (*0-9671167-0-8*) J & P Pubg.

— Promised Land. LC 98-17112. 350p. 1998. 11.99 (*1-56476-722-1*) SP Pubns.

***Culebras, A.** Sleep Disorders & Neurological Disease. LC 99-40800. (Neurological Disease & Therapy Ser.). (Illus.). 421p. 1999. text 185.00 (*0-8247-7605-4*) Dekker.

Culebras, Antonio. Clinical Handbook of Sleep Disorders: Diagnosis & Management. 524p. 1996. pap. text 52.50 (*0-7506-9644-3*) Buttrwrth-Heinemann.

Culeen, Aufoy B. In Cage: Welat. (C). 1988. 13.50 (*0-945028-02-4*) Studio Nineteen Seventy-Six.

— John F. Kennedy. 80p. 1992. pap. 5.00 (*0-945028-03-2*) Studio Nineteen Seventy-Six.

Culham, Phyllis, et al, eds. Classics: A Discipline & Profession in Crisis? LC 89-34188. (Illus.). 410p. (Orig.). (C). 1989. pap. text 42.00 (*0-8191-7450-5*) U Pr of Amer.

Culhane, Alys, jt. auth. see Praetorius, Pete.

Culhane, Claire. No Longer Barred from Prison: Social Injustice in Canada. rev. ed. 216p. (C). 1991. write for info. (*0-921689-95-0*) Black Rose.

Culhane, Dara. An Error in Judgement: Politics of Medical Care in an Indian - White Community. (NFS Canada Ser.). 280p. 1993. pap. 16.95 (*0-88922-246-0*, Pub. by Talonbks) Genl Dist Srvs.

— The Pleasure of the Crown: Anthropology, Law & First Nations. LC 98-150773. 416p. 1998. pap. 21.95 (*0-88922-315-7*, Pub. by Talonbks) Genl Dist Srvs.

Culhane, Hind R. East - West an Ambiguous State of Being Vol. 4: The Construction & Representation of Egyptian Cultural Identity in Egyptian Film. LC 94-31805. (Intercultural Studies: Vol. 4). XIII, 226p. (C). 1996. 48.95 (*0-8204-2639-3*) P Lang Pubng.

Culhane, J. L. & Hiei, E. Solar Flare, Coronal & Heliospheric Dynamics. (Advances in Space Research (RJ) Ser.: Vol. 17/4-5). 392p. 1995. 207.50 (*0-08-042644-1*, Pergamon Pr) Elsevier.

Culhane, John. The American Circus: An Illustrated History. (Illus.). 512p. 1995. pap. 19.95 (*0-8050-1647-3*, Owl) H Holt & Co.

Culhane, John. Disney's Aladdin: The Making of an Animated Film. LC 92-28187. (Illus.). 128p. (J). 1992. 24.45 (*1-56282-892-4*, Pub. by Hyperion) Time Warner.

— Disney's Aladdin: The Making of an Animated Film. (Illus.). 128p. (J). 1993. pap. 14.45 (*1-56282-757-X*, Pub. by Hyperion) Time Warner.

Culhane, John. Fantasia 2000: A Vison of Hope. LC 99-39168. (Illus.). 19p. 1999. text 75.00 (*0-7868-6198-3*, Pub. by Hyperion) Time Warner.

Culhane, Jolane, ed. see Gardner, A. Dudley & Brinkerhoff, Val.

Culhane, Kevin R. Model Interrogatories. 2nd ed. 1997. ring bd. 119.00 incl. disk (*0-938065-33-5*) James Pub Santa Ana.

Culhane, P. T. & Bivon, R. Russian Language & People. LC 97-45922. 1997. write for info. (*0-8442-4205-5*) NTC Contemp Pub Co.

Culhane, Paul J. Public Lands Politics: Interest Group Influence on the Forest Service & the Bureau of Land Management. LC 80-8776. 416p. reprint ed. pap. 129.00 (*0-8357-4680-1*, 203762700008) Bks Demand.

Culhane, Shamus. Animation from Script to Screen. 6th ed. 1990. text 14.95 (*0-312-05052-6*) St Martin.

— Talking Animals & Other People: The Autobiography of a Legendary Animator. LC 97-43027. (Illus.). 477p. 1998. reprint ed. pap. 17.95 (*0-306-80830-7*) Da Capo.

***Culhane, Terry.** I Beheld a Maiden... The Bahai Faith & the Life of the Spirit. (Illus.). 150p. 2000. pap. 19.95 (*1-890688-10-X*, 10-X) Kalimat.

Culhane, Terry & Bivon, Roy. Russian Language & People: A Course for Beginners Learning Russian. LC 97-51167. (ENG & RUS.). 192p. 1997. pap. 39.95 incl. audio (*0-8442-4208-X*, 4208X, Natl Textbk Co) NTC Contemp Pub Co.

Culi, Yaacov. Torah Anthology Book of Esther. Kaplan, Aryeh, tr. (Torah Anthology - Meam Loez Ser.). 252p. 1978. 18.00 (*0-940118-13-0*) Moznaim.

— Torah Anthology Spanish Edition Genesis 2. Jabif, Israel, tr. from HEB. (Torah Anthology - Meam Loez Ser.: No. 2). (SPA.). 479p. 1993. 22.00 (*1-885220-09-X*) Moznaim.

— Torah Anthology Spanish Edition Genesis 3. Jabif, Israel, tr. from HEB. (Torah Anthology - Meam Loez Ser.: No. 3). (SPA.). 483p. 1994. 22.00 (*1-885220-10-3*) Moznaim.

Culi, Yaakov. Torah Anthology Spanish Edition Genesis 1. Jabif, Israel, tr. from HEB. (Torah Anthology - Meam Loez Ser.: No. 1). (SPA.). 362p. 1992. 22.00 (*1-885220-08-1*) Moznaim.

Culianu, I. P., ed. Libra: Etudes Roumanies Offertes a Willem Noomen a L'Occasion de Son Soixantieme Anniversaire. (FRE.). 204p. (Orig.). (C). 1983. pap. text 46.15 (*3-11-013319-9*) Mouton.

Culican, William. Opera Selecta: From Tyre to Tartessos. (Studies in Mediterranean Archaeology & Literature: No. 40). (Illus.). 685p. (Orig.). 1986. pap. 97.50 (*91-86098-41-1*, Pub. by P Astroms) Coronet Bks.

Culick, F., et al, eds. Unsteady Combustion: Proceedings of the NATO Advanced Study Institute, Praia da Granja, Portugal, September 6-17, 1993. (NATO ASI Series E: Applied Sciences: Vol. 306). 568p. (C). 1996. text 291.00 (*0-7923-3888-X*) Kluwer Academic.

Culick, F. E., ed. Guggenheim Aeronautical Laboratory at the California Institute of Technology: The First Fifty Years. LC 82-50314. (Illus.). 1983. 20.00 (*0-911302-46-8*) San Francisco Pr.

Culicover, Peter & Mc Nally, Louise, eds. Syntax & Semantics Vol. 29: The Limits of Syntax. (Illus.). 401p. 1997. text 99.00 (*0-12-613529-0*) Morgan Kaufmann.

Culicover, Peter W. Principles & Parameters: An Introduction to Syntactic Theory. LC 96-22237. (Oxford Textbooks in Linguistics). (Illus.). 460p. (C). 1997. pap. text 31.95 (*0-19-870014-8*) OUP.

— Syntactic Nuts: Hard Cases, Syntactic Theory & Language Acquisition. LC 99-16105. (Foundations of Grammar Ser.: Vol. 1). (Illus.). 256p. 1999. text 78.00 (*0-19-870024-5*); pap. text 24.95 (*0-19-870023-7*) OUP.

***Culicover, Peter W. & Postal, Paul M., eds.** Parasitic Gaps. (Current Studies in Linguistics: No. 35). (Illus.). 496p. (C). 2001. 55.00 (*0-262-03284-8*) MIT Pr.

Culin, Robert S. Games of the North American Indians. LC 73-8094. (Illus.). reprint ed. 85.00 (*0-404-11201-3*) AMS Pr.

Culin, Stewart. Chess & Playing-Cards. LC 75-35065. (Studies in Play & Games). (Illus.). 1976. reprint ed. 34.95 (*0-405-07916-8*) Ayer.

— Games of the North American Indians. LC 74-12653. (Illus.). 864p. 1975. reprint ed. 19.95 (*0-486-23125-9*) Dover.

— Games of the North American Indians, 2 vols., Vol. 1: Games of Chance. LC 92-15261. (Illus.). 402p. (C). 1992. pap. 15.95 (*0-8032-6355-4*, Bison Books) U of Nebr Pr.

— Games of the North American Indians, 2 vols., Vol. 2: Games of Skill. LC 92-15261. (Illus.). xvii, 490p. (C). 1992. pap. 15.95 (*0-8032-6356-2*, Bison Books) U of Nebr Pr.

— Korean Games: With Notes on the Corresponding Games of China & Japan. (Puzzles Ser.). (Illus.). 256p. 1991. reprint ed. pap. 9.95 (*0-486-26593-5*) Dover.

Culinary Arts Institute Staff & Berolzheimer, Ruth, eds. Culinary Arts Institute Encyclopedic Cookbook. rev. ed. (Illus.). 1040p. 1988. pap. 18.00 (*0-399-51388-4*, Perigee Bks) Berkley Pub.

Culinary Institute of America, Inc., Staff. The New Professional Chef. 6th ed. LC 95-35590. (Culinary Arts Ser.). (Illus.). 1216p. 1996. text 59.95 (*0-442-01961-0*, VNR) Wiley.

***Culinary Institute of America Ser.** Garde Manger: The Art & Craft of the Cold Kitchen. LC 98-29510. 488p. 1999. 54.95 (*0-471-32367-5*) Wiley.

***Culinary Institute of America Staff.** Cooking at the C. I. A. The Culinary Institute of America. 2000. pap. 19.95 (*0-9651095-6-9*, Pub. by M Poore Prods) Bristol Pub Ent CA.

Culinary Institute of America, Staff. Cooking Essentials for the New Professional Chef. 6th ed. LC 96-21066. (Sax/Lewis Program Ser.). (Illus.). 800p. 1996. text 49.95 (*0-442-02109-7*, VNR) Wiley.

Culinary Institute of America Staff. Cooking Secrets of the C. I. A. Favorite Recipes from the Culinary Institute - America's Most Celebrated Cooking School. LC 95-22251. (Companion to the PBS Series). (Illus.). 144p. 1995. pap. 14.95 (*0-8118-1163-8*) Chronicle Bks.

— Exploring Wine. (Hospitality, Travel & Tourism Ser.). 1996. pap. 19.95 (*0-442-02479-7*, VNR) Wiley.

Culinary Institute of America Staff. Exploring Wine. (Hospitality, Travel & Tourism Ser.). 1997. pap., wbk. ed. 19.95 (*0-442-02512-2*, VNR) Wiley.

Culinary Institute of America Staff. From Our Kitchens. (Illus.). 256p. 1993. text 20.95 (*0-442-01766-9*, VNR) Wiley.

— From Our Kitchens. Donovan, Mary D., ed. (Illus.). 304p. 1993. 20.95 (*0-471-28609-5*, VNR) Wiley.

— The New Professional Chef. 5th ed. (Illus.). 848p. 1991. pap., teacher ed. 23.95 (*0-442-00831-7*, VNR) Wiley.

— New Professional Chef. 5th ed. 869p. 1991. 49.95 (*0-471-29372-5*, VNR) Wiley.

Culinary Institute of America Staff. The New Professional Chef. 5th ed. 1992. 49.95 (*0-471-29367-9*, VNR) Wiley.

— New Professional Chef. 6th ed. (Illus.). 1190p. 1997. 64.95 (*0-471-28679-6*, VNR) Wiley.

Culinary Institute of America Staff. The Professional Chef's Knife. LC 77-26689. (Illus.). 64p. 1978. pap. 33.95 (*0-8436-2125-7*, VNR) Wiley.

— The Professional Chef's Knife. (Professional Chef's Photo-Text Ser.). (Illus.). 64p. 1983. pap. 34.95 (*0-471-28986-8*, VNR) Wiley.

— The Professional Chef's Techniques of Healthy Cooking. 2nd ed. LC 98-52145. 656p. 2000. 59.95 (*0-471-33269-0*) Wiley.

***Culinary Institute of America Staff.** Remarkable Service. 324p. 2000. text. write for info. (*0-471-38022-9*) Wiley.

Culinary Institute of America Staff & Donovan, Mary D. Cooking Essentials for the New Professional Chef. 816p. 1996. 54.95 (*0-471-28717-2*, VNR) Wiley.

Culinary Institute of America Staff & Donovan, Mary D. The Professional Chef's Techniques of Healthy Cooking. 640p. 1992. 49.95 (*0-471-28483-1*, VNR) Wiley.

— The Professional Chef's Techniques of Healthy Cooking. LC 92-19495. (Illus.). 614p. 1992. 49.95 (*0-442-01126-1*, VNR); pap. 34.95 (*0-442-02555-6*, VNR) Wiley.

Culinary Institute of America Staff & Donovan, Mary D. The Professional Chef's Techniques of Healthy Cooking. 640p. 1997. pap. 34.95 (*0-471-28836-5*, VNR) Wiley.

Culioli, Antoine. Cognition & Representation in Linguistic Theory. Liddle, Michel & Stonham, John T., eds. & trs. by. from FRE. LC 95-2051. (Current Issues in Linguistic Theory Ser.: No. 112). x, 161p. 1995. lib. bdg. 45.00 (*1-55619-566-4*) J Benjamins Pubng Co.

Culioli, Gabriel-Xavier. Dictionary French to Corsican. (FRE.). 1998. 69.95 (*0-320-00406-6*) Fr & Eur.

Culjak, Michael K. The Expert, the Prince & a Naked Witch. LC 96-86727. 272p. (Orig.). 1997. pap. 12.00 (*0-9654771-2-6*) Eau Gallie Pub.

Culkin. Fundamentals of Psychology. (General Business & Business Education Ser.). 1995. student ed. 14.95 (*0-8273-6802-X*) Delmar.

— Fundamentals of Psychology: Applications for Life & Work. (CA - Career Development Ser.). 1995. mass mkt. 44.95 (*0-538-65048-6*); mass mkt., wbk. ed. 11.00 (*0-538-65049-4*) S-W Pub.

Culkin, John M. Film Study in the High School: An Analysis & Rationale. 90p. (C). 1995. write for info. (*0-9649723-0-1*) Ctr Understanding.

Culkin, Mary L., et al. Building Blocks: A Legislator's Guide to Child Care Policy. LC 98-210023. x, 97 p. 1997. 30.00 (*1-55516-757-8*) Natl Conf State Legis.

***Cull, Brian.** Spitfires over Sicily. 2000. 29.95 (*1-902304-32-2*, Pub. by Grub St) Seven Hills Bk.

Cull, Brian. 249 at War: The Authorized History of the RAF's Top Claiming Squadron of WWII. (Illus.). 384p. 1997. 44.95 (*1-898697-49-3*, Pub. by Grub St) Seven Hills Bk.

— Wings over Suez: The First Authoritative Account of the Anglo-French Involvement in the Sinai. 1997. 49.95 (*1-898697-48-5*, Pub. by Grub St) Seven Hills Bk.

Cull, Brian & Lander, Bruce. Twelve Days in May: The Air Battle for France & the Low Countries, 10-21 May 1940, As Told by the Allied & German Pilots Themselves. (Illus.). 256p. 1995. 29.95 (*1-898697-20-5*, Pub. by Grub St) Seven Hills Bk.

Cull, Brian & Minterne, Don. Hurricanes over Tobruk: The Pivotal Role of the Hurricane in the Battle for Tobruk, Western Desert, January-June 1941. (Illus.). 224p. 1999. 29.95 (*1-902304-11-X*, Pub. by Grub St) Seven Hills Bk.

***Cull, Brian & Newton, Dennis.** With the Yanks in Korea Vol. 1: The First Definitive Account of British & Commonwealth Particiapation in the Air War, June 1950-December 1951. 2000. 45.00 (*1-902304-49-7*, Pub. by Grub St) Seven Hills Bk.

Cull, Brian, et al. Spitfires over Israel: The First Authoritative Account of Air Conflict During the Israeli War of Independence, 1948-49. (Illus.). 400p. 1994. 39.95 (*0-948817-74-7*, Pub. by Grub St) Seven Hills Bk.

Cull, Brian, jt. auth. see Nomis, Leo.

Cull, Christine & Goldstein, Laura H. The Clinical Psychologist's Handbook of Epilepsy: Assessment & Management. LC 96-52980. (Illus.). 248p. (C). 1997. 80.00 (*0-415-13050-6*); pap. 25.99 (*0-415-13051-4*) Routledge.

Cull, Helen A. & Allen, David W. Human Rights Advocacy in the Philippines: Report on Mission to the Philippines, August, 1985. LC 89-103582. 72p. reprint ed. pap. 30.00 (*0-7837-5638-0*, 205249000005) Bks Demand.

Cull, John, ed. see Gordonio, Bernardo.

Cull, John G., jt. auth. see Hardy, Richard E.

Cull, Julie M. Magic Herbs: More Than 200 Delicious & Healthy Recipes That Are Naturally Low-Fat & Fat-Free. 240p. 1996. pap. 12.95 (*1-56561-087-3*) Wiley.

Cull, Julie Metcalf. Magic Herbs: More Than 200 Delicious & Healthy Recipes That Are Naturally Low-Fat & Fat-Free. 240p. 1996. pap. 12.95 (*0-471-34748-5*) Wiley.

***Cull, Mark E. & Gale, Kate, eds.** Blue Cathedral. 376p. 2000. pap. 19.95 (*1-888996-21-8*, Red Hen Press) Valentine CA.

Cull, Mark E., jt. ed. see Gale, Kate.

Cull, Nicholas J. Selling War: The British Propaganda Campaign Against American "Neutrality" in World War II. (Illus.). 304p. 1996. reprint ed. pap. 22.00 (*0-19-511150-8*) OUP.

Cull, P., ed. The Sourcebook of Medical Illustration. (Illus.). 481p. 1989. 85.00 (*1-85070-255-1*) Prthnon Pub.

Cull, Robert J. & Davis, Lance E. International Capital Markets & American Economic Growth, 1820-1914. LC 93-43815. (Illus.). 176p. (C). 1994. text 47.95 (*0-521-46054-9*) Cambridge U Pr.

Cullamar, Evelyn T. Babaylanism in Negros: 1896-1907. (Illus.). 133p. (Orig.). 1986. pap. 12.50 (*971-10-0293-0*, Pub. by New Day Pub) Cellar.

Cullari, Salvatore. Foundations of Clinical Psychology: Instructor's Manual & Test Bank. 160p. (C). 1997. text, teacher ed. write for info. (*0-205-28008-0*, T8008-9) Allyn.

— Treatment Resistance: A Guide for Practitioners. 288p. (C). 1996. 53.00 (*0-205-15572-3*) Allyn.

***Cullari, Salvatore, ed.** Foundations of Clinical Psychology. LC 97-38141. 448p. (C). 1998. 83.00 (*0-205-26202-3*) Allyn.

Cullather, Nick. Illusions of Influence: The Political Economy of United States-Philippines Relations, 1942-1960. LC 93-36104. xiv, 264p. (C). 1994. 32.50 (*0-8047-2280-3*) Stanford U Pr.

— Secret History: The CIA's Classified Account of Its Operations in Guatemala, 1952-1954. 160p. 1999. 39.50 (*0-8047-3310-4*); pap. 14.95 (*0-8047-3311-2*) Stanford U Pr.

Cullather, Nick, ed. Managing Nationalism: United States National Security Council Documents on the Philipines, 1953-1960. 198p. (Orig.). 1993. pap. 12.50 (*971-10-0471-2*, Pub. by New Day Pub) Cellar.

Cullen. Breakdown in Adaptation. 1983. text 530.50 (*0-89838-608-X*) Kluwer Academic.

— Corrections. (C). 1997. text 38.00 (*0-15-500328-3*) Harcourt Coll Pubs.

***Cullen.** Criminology. 2001. pap. 45.00 (*0-534-56457-7*) Thomson Learn.

— Economics for Hospitality & Toursim. 1997. pap. 22.99 (*1-86152-179-0*) Thomson Learn.

Cullen. Food & Beverage Management. 2001. text. write for info. (*0-13-147340-9*) P-H.

Cullen & Molina. Communications System Using Matlab, Vol. 1. (ITCP-UK Computer Science Ser.). 1997. mass mkt. 35.95 (*1-85032-120-5*) ITCP.

An Asterisk (*) at the beginning of an entry indicates that the title is appearing for the first time.

Cullen, et al. Fundamentals of Math (FM) Vol. 1: Answer Key. 1983. pap. 20.95 (*0-8120-2692-6*) Barron.
Cullen, jt. auth. see Benson.
Cullen, jt. auth. see Zill, Dennis G.
Cullen, A. & Wait, James R. Electromagnetic Waves in Stratified Media. LC 68-22065. (International Series of Monographs on Electronics & Instrumentation: Vol. 3). 1962. reprint ed. 170.00 (*0-08-009734-0*, Pub. by Pergamon Repr) Franklin.
Cullen, A., jt. auth. see Banos, A.
Cullen, A., jt. auth. see Brown, J.
Cullen, A., jt. auth. see Clemmow, P.
Cullen, A., jt. auth. see Jordan, E.
Cullen, A., jt. auth. see Watt, A.
Cullen, A. C. & Frey, C. Probabilistic Techniques in Exposure Assessment: A Handbook for Addressing Variability & Uncertainty in Models & Inputs. LC 98-44311. (Illus.). 333p. (C). 1998. 99.50 (*0-306-45956-6*, Plenum Trade); pap. 49.00 (*0-306-45957-4*, Plenum Trade) Perseus Pubng.
Cullen, Alan. The Beeple. (J). 1968. 6.00 (*0-87602-108-9*) Anchorage.
— The Golden Fleece. 74p. (J). 1971. 6.00 (*0-87602-130-5*) Anchorage.
— The Man in the Moon. (J). 1964. 6.00 (*0-87602-153-4*) Anchorage.
— Trudi & the Minstrel. (J). (gr. 1-9). 1957. 6.50 (*0-87602-214-X*) Anchorage.
Cullen, Alexander. Adventures in Socialism: New Lanark Establishment & Orbiston Community. LC 70-134404. reprint ed. 27.50 (*0-404-08448-6*) AMS Pr.
— Adventures in Socialism: New Lanark Establishment & Orbiston Community. LC 68-55519. (Illus.). 329p. 1972. reprint ed. 25.00 (*0-678-00804-3*) Kelley.
Cullen, Allan. Niccolo & Nicolette. (J). (gr. 1-9). 1957. 6.00 (*0-87602-162-3*) Anchorage.
***Cullen, Angela.** Frankfurt Condensed. 2000. pap. 11.99 (*1-86450-223-1*) Lonely Planet.
***Cullen, Ann.** Emma Parchen: Twelve Years of Her American Dream. 203p. 2000. pap. 9.95 (*0-9670759-1-2*, Pub. by Bk Montana) Partners-West.
Cullen, Ann. Lilly Cullen: Helena, Montana 1894. 267p. 1999. pap. 9.95 (*0-9670759-0-4*) Bk Montana.
Cullen, Barbara, jt. auth. see Burke, Theresa K.
Cullen, Barbara N., ed. see Chernecky, Cynthia C. & Berger, Barbara J.
Cullen, Barbara N., ed. see Czerwinski, Sandra & Moloney-Harmon, Patricia A.
Cullen, Barbara N., ed. see Fenstermacher, Karen & Hudson, Barbara T.
Cullen, Barbara N., ed. see Hansen, Margie.
Cullen, Barbara N., ed. see Hartshorn, Jeanette & Sole, Mary L.
Cullen, Barbara N., ed. see Jarvis, Carolyn.
Cullen, Barbara N., ed. see Kingdon, Ruth T., et al.
Cullen, Barbara N., ed. see Leasia, Shelly.
Cullen, Barbara N., ed. see Melander, Sheila D.
Cullen, Barbara N., ed. see Miaskowski, Christine.
Cullen, Barbara N., ed. see Monahan, Frances D. & Neighbors, Marianne.
Cullen, Barbara N., ed. see Paul, Sara & Hebra, Jennifer D.
Cullen, Barbara N., ed. see Selfridge-Thomas, Judy.
Cullen, Barbara N., ed. see Tipsord-Klinkhammer, Beverley & Andreoni, Coleen P.
Cullen, Barbara N., ed. see Ulrich, Susan P., et al.
Cullen, Barnara N., ed. see Dow, Karen H., et al.
Cullen, Bernard, ed. Hegel Today. 133p. 1988. text 72.95 (*0-566-05353-5*, Pub. by Avebry) Ashgate Pub Co.
Cullen, Bill, et al, eds. Corrective Services in New South Wales. xxii, 347p. 1988. pap. 43.00 (*0-455-20781-X*, Pub. by LawBk Co) Gaunt.
***Cullen, Bob.** Why Golf? The Mystery of the Game Revisited. LC 00-20260. 256p. 2000. 20.00 (*0-684-86722-2*) S&S Trade.
Cullen, Bob, jt. auth. see Rotella, Robert J.
Cullen, Bryan R., ed. Human Retroviruses: Fionbicis in Molecular Biology. LC 92-48274. (Fionbicis in Molecular Biology Ser.). 240p. 1993. 69.00 (*0-19-963383-5*) OUP.
— Human Retroviruses: Fionbicis in Molecular Biology. LC 92-48274. (Fionbicis in Molecular Biology Ser.). (Illus.). 236p. 1993. pap. text 43.00 (*0-19-963382-7*) OUP.
Cullen, C. & Hollingum, H. Implementing Total Quality. 181p. (C). 1987. 290.00 (*0-7855-5715-6*, Pub. by Inst Pur & Supply) St Mut.
Cullen, Catherine. Collecting Civil Judgments: With Forms on Disk. LC 95-78126. 1996. pap. text 145.00 (*0-944490-92-1*) Mass CLE.
Cullen, Catherine Ann. The Magical, Mystical, Marvelous Coat. 2001. write for info. (*0-316-16334-1*) Little.
Cullen, Cecilia. Fundamentals of Mathematics (FM), Vol. 1. 1982. pap. 19.95 (*0-8120-2501-6*) Barron.
Cullen, Charles G. Linear Algebra & Differential Equations. 1979. mass mkt. 45.00 (*0-87150-262-3*, PWS 2131) PWS Pubs.
— Linear Algebra with Applications. (C). 1997. text 59.33 (*0-673-18570-2*) Addson-Wesley Educ.
— Linear Algebra with Applications: Solutions Manual. 2nd ed. 192p. (C). 1997. pap. text, student ed. 25.00 (*0-673-98317-X*) Addison-Wesley.
— Matrices & Linear Transformations. 336p. 1990. pap. 9.95 (*0-486-66328-0*) Dover.
Cullen, Charles T. The Papers of Thomas Jefferson Vol. 22: 6 August-31 December 1791, Vol. 22. LC 50-7486. (Illus.). 556p. 1986. text 85.00 (*0-691-04728-6*, Pub. by Princeton U Pr) Cal Prin Full Svc.
Cullen, Charles T., ed. see Jefferson, Thomas.
Cullen, Charles T., ed. see Marshall, John.
Cullen, Cheryl, et al. Global Graphics: Symbols: Designing with Symbols for an International Market. (Illus.). 192p. 2000. pap. 40.00 (*1-56496-512-0*) Rockport Pubs.
Cullen, Cheryl, jt. auth. see Peterson, L. K.
***Cullen, Cheryl Dangel.** Best of Annual Report Design, 1vol. 2000. 45.00 (*1-56496-633-X*) Rockport Pubs.
— Direct Response Graphics: The Best Print & Electronic Dirst Marketing Design, 2000. 45.00 (*1-56496-629-1*) Rockport Pubs.
Cullen, Cheryl Dangel. Graphic Idea Resource, Photography: Creating Effective Graphic Design with Photography. Rockport Publishers Staff, ed. (Graphic Idea Resource Ser.). (Illus.). 96p. 1999. pap. 17.99 (*1-56496-597-X*) Rockport Pubs.
***Cullen, Cheryl Dangel.** Large Graphics: Design Innovations for Oversized Spaces. (Illus.). 2000. 45.00 (*1-56496-692-5*) Rockport Pubs.
— Small Graphics: Design Innovation for Limited Spaces. 2000. 45.00 (*1-56496-693-3*) Rockport Pubs.
Cullen, Chris. Human Operant Conditioning & Behavior Modification. fac. ed. Davey, Graham, ed. LC 87-13321. 280p. 1988. reprint ed. pap. 86.80 (*0-7837-8281-0*, 204906200009) Bks Demand.
Cullen, Christopher. Astronomy & Mathematics in Ancient China: The Zhou Bi Suan Jing. (Needham Research Institute Studies: Vol. 1). (Illus.). 255p. (C). 1996. text 74.95 (*0-521-55089-0*) Cambridge U Pr.
Cullen, Countee. Color. 1975. 17.95 (*0-88143-155-9*) Ayer.
— Color. LC 70-101515. (American Negro: His History & Literature. Series 3). 1970. reprint ed. 14.00 (*0-405-01919-X*) Ayer.
Cullen, Countee, jt. auth. see Cat, Christopher.
Cullen, D., jt. auth. see Rawstron, D. D.
Cullen, D. E., et al, eds. Applications in Nuclear Data & Reactor Physics: ICTP, February 17-March 21, 1986, Trieste, Italy. 1008p. 1986. text 181.00 (*9971-5-0132-5*) World Scientific Pub.
Cullen, D. E., et al. Reactor Physics Calculations for Applications in Nuclear Technology, Workshop on. 756p. 1991. text 147.00 (*981-02-0517-1*) World Scientific Pub.
Cullen, Daniel. Freedom in Rousseau's Political Philosophy. LC 93-16549. 256p. (C). 1993. lib. bdg. 32.00 (*0-87580-180-3*) N Ill U Pr.
Cullen, David J. Historical Northern California. LC 84-62823. (Mother Lode Ser.: No. 2). 85p. 19.00 (*0-934827-00-1*) Heritage Map Co.
— Historical Northern California: Mother Lode-1. 2nd ed. LC 84-62823. (Mapsearch Ser.: Vol. 1, No. 1). (Illus.). 85p. 1986. pap. 19.00 (*0-934827-03-6*) Heritage Map Co.
— Historical Northern California: Mother Lode-3. LC 84-62823. (Mapsearch Ser.: Vol. 1, No. 3). (Illus.). 87p. 1986. pap. text 19.00 (*0-934827-02-8*) Heritage Map Co.
— Historical Northern Nevada. LC 84-62823. (North-West Ser.: Vol. 3, No. 1). 85p. 1986. pap. 19.00 (*0-934827-12-5*) Heritage Map Co.
— Historical Southern Arizona. LC 84-62823. (South-East Ser.: Vol. 3, No. 1). 85p. 1986. pap. 19.00 (*0-934827-10-9*) Heritage Map Co.
— Historical Southern Arizona. LC 84-62823. (South-East Ser.: Vol. 3, No. 2). 85p. (C). 1987. pap. 19.00 (*0-934827-19-2*) Heritage Map Co.
— Historical Southern California. LC 84-62823. (South-East Ser.: Vol. 1, No. 5). 85p. 1986. pap. 19.00 (*0-934827-06-0*) Heritage Map Co.
— Historical Southern California. LC 84-62823. (South-East Ser.: Vol. 1, No. 6). 85p. 1986. pap. 19.00 (*0-934827-08-7*); pap. text 14.95 (*0-934827-09-5*) Heritage Map Co.
— Historical Southern California. LC 84-62823. (South-East Ser.: Vol. 1, No. 7). 85p. 1986. pap. 19.00 (*0-934827-14-1*) Heritage Map Co.
— Historical Southern California. LC 84-62823. (South-West Ser.: Vol. 1, No. 8). 1986. pap. 19.00 (*0-934827-17-6*) Heritage Map Co.
— Historical Southern California: Central East-1. LC 84-62823. (Mapsearch Ser.: Vol. 1, No. 4). (Illus.). 87p. 1986. pap. 19.00 (*0-934827-04-4*) Heritage Map Co.
— Historical Southern California: South-West-1. LC 84-62823. (Mapsearch Ser.: Vol. 1, No. 9). (Illus.). 87p. 1986. pap. 19.00 (*0-934827-05-2*) Heritage Map Co.
— Historical Southern Nevada. LC 84-62823. (Mapsearch Ser., South East 3: Vol. 3, No. 2). 85p. 1987. pap. 19.00 (*0-934827-21-4*) Heritage Map Co.
— Historical Southern Nevada. LC 84-62823. (Mapsearch Ser., South East 4: Vol. 3, No. 3). 85p. 1987. pap. 19.00 (*0-934827-23-0*) Heritage Map Co.
Cullen, Deborah. Bataille's Eye & ICI Field Notes 4. Institute of Cultural Inquiry Staff, ed. (ICI Field Notes Ser.: Vol. 4). (Illus.). 128p. 1997. pap. 16.95 (*1-889917-00-1*) Inst of Cult Inquiry.
— Child Care Law: England & Wales. 1992. pap. 22.00 (*1-873868-06-5*) BAAF.
Cullen, Deborah, compiled by. BAAF Response to the Draft Adoption Bill: Adoption - A Service for Children. 1996. pap. 22.00 (*1-873868-33-2*) BAAF.
Cullen, Deborah & Ponce de Leon, Carolina. The S-Files: The Selected Files. (ENG & SPA., Illus.). 40p. 1999. pap. write for info. (*1-882454-08-1*) El Museo Barrio.
***Cullen, Deborah & Ramirez, Yasmin.** The S-Files: The Selected Files. (ENG & SPA., Illus.). 36p. 2000. pap. write for info. (*1-882454-10-3*) El Museo Barrio.
Cullen, Deborah L., jt. auth. see Luna, Gaye.
Cullen, Dolores. Pilgrim Chaucer: Center Stage. LC 99-11191. (Illus.). 208p. 1999. pap. 14.95 (*1-56474-306-3*) Fithian Pr.
Cullen, Dolores L. Chaucer's Host: Up-So-Doun. LC 97-44211. 192p. 1998. pap. 14.95 (*1-56474-254-7*) Fithian Pr.
***Cullen, Dolores L.** Chaucer's Pilgrims: The Allegory. LC 99-50529. 480p. 2000. pap. 16.95 (*1-56474-334-9*) Fithian Pr.
***Cullen, Don, et al.** Risk Management for Public Entities. Head, George L. & Wong, Kwok-Sze R., eds. LC 98-75367. 546p. 1999. pap. text 90.00 (*0-89462-127-0*, 35202) IIA.
Cullen-Dupont, Kathryn. Elizabeth Cady Stanton & Women's Liberty. Scott, John A., ed. (Makers of America Ser.). (Illus.). 144p. (YA). (gr. 6-12). 1992. lib. bdg. 19.95 (*0-8160-2413-8*) Facts on File.
Cullen-DuPont, Kathryn. The Encyclopedia of Women's History in America. LC 95-4308. 352p. 1996. 45.00 (*0-8160-2625-4*) Facts on File.
— The Encyclopedia of Women's History in America. LC 98-19338. (Illus.). 368p. 1998. reprint ed. pap. 22.50 (*0-306-80868-4*) Da Capo.
***Cullen-DuPont, Kathryn.** The Encyclopedia of Women's History in America. 2nd ed. LC 99-87498. (Illus.). 400p. 2000. lib. bdg. 50.00 (*0-8160-4100-8*) Facts on File.
***Cullen-DuPont, Kathryn, intro.** Margaret Sanger: An Autobiography. (Illus.). 516p. 1999. pap. 17.95 (*0-8154-1015-8*) Cooper Sq.
Cullen-DuPont, Kathryn, jt. auth. see Frost-Knappman, Elizabeth.
Cullen, Emily A., ed. see Bybee, Sandra.
Cullen, Emily A., ed. see Cohen, Leslie & Falco, Antoinette.
Cullen, Emily A., ed. see Collins, Melvin, Jr.
Cullen, Emily A., ed. see Georgantonis-Keah, Anna.
Cullen, Emily A., ed. see George, Bonnie S.
Cullen, Emily A., ed. see Kenner, Donald.
Cullen, Emily A., ed. see Salazar, Yolanda L.
Cullen, Emily A., ed. see Sternfeld, Norman I.
Cullen, Emily A., ed. see Stevens, Bill.
Cullen, Eric, et al. Therapeutic Communities for Offenders. LC 96-30405. (Wiley Series on Offender Rehabilitation). 296p. 1997. pap. 59.95 (*0-471-96980-X*) Wiley.
***Cullen, Fintan.** Sources on Irish Art: A Reader. 320p. 1999. 65.00 (*1-85918-154-6*); pap. 45.00 (*1-85918-155-4*) Intl Spec Bk.
Cullen, Fintan & Murphy, William M. The Drawings of John Butler Yeats. LC 86-73179. (Illus.). 100p. (Orig.). 1987. pap. 10.50 (*0-939072-07-6*) Albany Hist & Art.
Cullen, Francis T. Rethinking Crime & Deviance Theory: The Emergence of a Structuring Tradition. LC 83-17796. 200p. 1987. pap. 22.50 (*0-8476-7551-3*); text 50.00 (*0-86598-073-X*) Rowman.
Cullen, Francis T. & Agnew, Robert S., eds. Criminological Theory: Past to Present (Essential Readings). LC 97-33460. (Illus.). 375p. (C). 1998. pap. text. write for info. (*0-935732-91-8*) Roxbury Pub Co.
Cullen, Francis T. & Applegate, Brandon K., eds. Offender Rehabilitation: Effective Correctional Intervention. LC 97-7873. (International Library of Criminology, Criminal Justice & Penology). 490p. 1997. text 179.95 (*1-85521-798-8*, Pub. by Ashgate Pub) Ashgate Pub Co.
Cullen, Francis T. & Burton, Velmer S., Jr., eds. Contemporary Criminological Theory. LC 93-25713. (International Library of Essays in Law & Legal Theory: Vol. 11). (C). 1994. lib. bdg. 150.00 (*0-8147-1501-X*) NYU Pr.
Cullen, Francis T., jt. auth. see Benson, Michael L.
Cullen, G. W., jt. ed. see Jensen, K. F.
Cullen, George M. By George! A Farmer Remembers. Goodrich, Donna et al, eds. LC 89-80011. (Illus.). 284p. (Orig.). 1989. 19.95 (*0-9622258-1-9*); pap. 9.95 (*0-9622258-0-0*) GMC Pr.
Cullen, Gordon. Concise Townscape. LC 95-194548. (Illus.). 200p. 1995. pap. text 34.95 (*0-7506-2018-8*, Architectural Pr) Buttrwrth-Heinemann.
Cullen, Greg. Mary Morgan - Tarzanne - Frida & Diego: Three Plays. 180p. 1998. pap. 21.95 (*1-85411-223-6*) Seren Bks.
Cullen, J. The Identification of Flowering Plant Families. 4th ed. (Illus.). 227p. (C). 1997. pap. text 21.95 (*0-521-58550-3*) Cambridge U Pr.
— The Identification of Flowering Plant Families: Including a Key to Those Native & Cultivated in North Temperate Regions. 4th ed. LC 96-41206. (Illus.). 227p. (C). 1997. text 59.95 (*0-521-58485-X*) Cambridge U Pr.
— Subgenus Rhododendron Sections Rhododendron & Pogonanthum, Vol. 39, No. 1. (Revision of Rhododendron Ser.). (Illus.). 1980. 7.50 (*0-11-491649-7*, Pub. by Royal Botanic Edinburgh) Balogh.
Cullen, J., et al, eds. Breakdown in Human Adaptation to 'Stress' Towards a Multidisciplinary Approach, 2 vols. 1983. lib. bdg. 144.00 (*0-89838-607-1*) Kluwer Academic.
— The European Garden Flora: A Manual for the Identification of Plants in Europe, Both Out-of-Doors & under Glass. (European Garden Flora Ser.). (Illus.). 666p. (C). 1997. text 160.00 (*0-521-42096-2*) Cambridge U Pr.
— The European Garden Flora Vol. 4, Pt. 2: Dicotyledons, Dilleniaceae to Polygalaceae, a Manual for the Identification of Plants Cultivated in Europe, both Out-of-Doors & under Glass. (Illus.). 620p. (C). 1995. text 160.00 (*0-521-42095-4*) Cambridge U Pr.
Cullen, Jack & D'Innocenzo, Len. The Agile Manager's Guide to Customer-Focused Selling. LC 98-87070. (Agile Manager Ser.). (Illus.). 112p. 1998. pap. 10.95 (*1-58099-012-6*) Velocity Busn.
Cullen, Jack, jt. auth. see D'Innocenzo, Len.
Cullen, James, ed. The Orchid Book: A Guide to the Identification of Cultivated Orchid Species. (Illus.). 555p. (C). 1992. text 57.95 (*0-521-41856-9*) Cambridge U Pr.
Cullen, James, jt. ed. see The European Garden Flora Editorial Committee.
Cullen, Jim. The Art of Democracy: A Concise History of Popular Culture in the United States. (Illus.). 352p. 1995. 36.00 (*0-85345-919-3*, CL9193, Pub. by Monthly Rev); pap. 18.00 (*0-85345-920-7*, PB9207, Pub. by Monthly Rev) NYU Pr.
***Cullen, Jim.** Born in the U. S. A. Bruce Springsteen & the American Tradition. (Illus.). 254p. 2000. 23.00 (*0-7881-9344-9*) DIANE Pub.
Cullen, Jim. Born in the USA: Bruce Springsteen & the American Tradition. 272p. 1998. pap. 13.00 (*0-06-092911-1*, Perennial) HarperTrade.
— The Civil War in Popular Culture: A Reusable Past. LC 94-25072. (Illus.). 264p. 1995. 29.95 (*1-56098-459-7*) Smithsonian.
— The Civil War in Popular Culture: A Reusable Past. 254p. 1996. pap. 13.95 (*1-56098-687-5*) Smithsonian.
— The Civil War in Popular Culture: A Reusable Past. (Illus.). 253p. 1997. reprint ed. text 20.00 (*0-7881-5038-3*) DIANE Pub.
***Cullen, Jim.** Popular Culture in American History. 2000. 64.95 (*0-631-21957-9*); pap. 29.95 (*0-631-21958-7*) Blackwell Pubs.
Cullen, Joe & Hollingum, Jack. Implementing Total Quality. 181p. (C). 1988. 145.00 (*0-7855-3768-6*, Pub. by Inst Pur & Supply) St Mut.
Cullen, John & Broadbent, Mick. Managing Resources Project Planning & Financial Control: Activity Pack. 300p. 1999. pap. text 175.00 (*0-7506-3504-5*) Buttrwrth-Heinemann.
Cullen, John, jt. auth. see Broadbent, Michael.
Cullen, John, tr. see Holl, Adolf.
Cullen, John, tr. see Tamaro, Susanna.
Cullen, John B. Multinational Management: A Strategic Approach. LC 98-13178. 1998. 87.95 (*0-538-89034-7*) Thomson Learn.
Cullen, John B., jt. auth. see Carter, Nancy M.
Cullen, Joseph, jt. auth. see Luvaas, Jay.
Cullen, Joseph P. Richmond National Battlefield Park, Virginia. 46p. 1961. pap. 5.00 (*0-16-003410-8*) USGPO.
Cullen, Kathryn S., ed. The Obituaries of University of Washington Presidents, 1861-1958. (Illus.). 150p. 1989. 22.50 (*0-685-27005-X*) NW Ctr Study Ed.
Cullen, Kathy, ed. see Singh, Ravi.
Cullen, L. M. The Brandy Trade under the Ancient Regime: Regional Specialisation in the Charente. LC 97-27258. 302p. (C). 1998. text 69.95 (*0-521-59248-8*) Cambridge U Pr.
— The Emergence of Modern Ireland 1600-1900. LC 81-6548. 292p. 1981. 45.00 (*0-8419-0727-7*) Holmes & Meier.
Cullen, Leo. Clocking Ninety on the Rd. to Cloughjordan & other: Stories. 240p. 1995. pap. 14.95 (*0-85640-537-X*, Pub. by Blackstaff Pr) Dufour.
Cullen, Lesley, jt. auth. see Young, Michael.
Cullen, Linda, jt. auth. see Cullen, Noel.
Cullen, Louis. The Hidden Ireland: Reassessment of a Concept. 1996. pap. 10.95 (*0-946640-31-9*, Pub. by Lilliput Pr) Irish Bks Media.
Cullen, Luke. Insurgent Wicklow, 1798: The Story As Written by Luke Cullen O. D. C. 3rd rev. ed. O'Donnell, Ruan, ed. LC 98-145944. 191p. 1998. pap. 19.95 (*1-900505-55-X*, Pub. by Kestrel Bks) Irish Bks Media.
Cullen, Lynn. The Backyard Ghost. 160p. (J). 1995. reprint ed. pap. 3.50 (*0-380-72370-0*, Avon Bks) Morrow Avon.
Cullen, Lynn. Diary of Nelly Vandorn. 128p. (gr. 3 up). 14.95 (*0-06-029133-8*); 14.89 (*0-06-029134-6*) HarpC.
— Diary Of Nelly Vandorn. 128p. (gr. 3 up). mass mkt. 4.95 (*0-06-440926-0*) HarpC.
Cullen, Lynn. Meeting the Make-Out King. LC 93-38850. 144p. (J). 1995. pap. 3.99 (*0-380-72576-2*, Avon Bks) Morrow Avon.
— Meeting the Make-Out King. 1995. 9.09 (*0-606-09606-X*, Pub. by Turtleback) Demco.
— Ready, Set - Regina! 96p. (J). 1996. pap. 3.99 (*0-380-78427-0*, Avon Bks) Morrow Avon.
— Ready, Set - Regina! LC 95-95105. (J). 1996. 9.09 (*0-606-10111-X*, Pub. by Turtleback) Demco.
— Regina Calhoun Eats Dog Food. 1997. 9.09 (*0-606-10909-9*, Pub. by Turtleback) Demco.
— Stink Bomb. LC 97-16741. 128p. (J). (gr. 3-7). 1998. 14.00 (*0-380-97647-1*, Avon Bks) Morrow Avon.
— Stink Bomb. LC 97-16741. 128p. (J). (gr. 3-7). 1999. mass mkt. 3.99 (*0-380-78507-2*, Avon Bks) Morrow Avon.
— The Three Lives of Harris Harper. 160p. (J). (gr. 5-7). 1996. 14.95 (*0-395-73680-3*, Clarion Bks) HM.
— The Three Lives of Harris Harper. 160p. 1998. mass mkt. 3.99 (*0-380-72901-6*, Avon Bks) Morrow Avon.
Cullen, M. Girls Don't Do Honours. 1993. 56.00 (*0-7855-7043-8*) St Mut.
Cullen, Mark R., ed. Workers with Multiple Chemical Sensitivities. LC 86-642306. (Occupational Medicine Ser.: Vol. 2, No. 4). 160p. 1987. reprint ed. pap. 49.60 (*0-608-01985-2*, 206264000003) Bks Demand.
Cullen, Mark R., jt. auth. see Rosenstock, Linda.
Cullen, Mary & Luddy, Maria. Notable Women, 2 vols., 2. 1992. 47.00 (*1-85594-079-5*) St Mut.
Cullen, Mary & Luddy, Maria, eds. Women Power & Consciousness in 19th Century Ireland: Eight Biographical Studies. LC 96-121473. 304p. 1996. pap. 32.99 (*1-85594-078-7*, Pub. by Attic Press) Intl Spec Bk.
Cullen, Marygael & Green, Michelle. Illinois: An Economic Celebration. LC 98-37133. (Illus.). 200p. 1998. 39.00 (*1-885352-92-1*) Community Comm.
Cullen, Matthew, ed. see World Congress on Land Policy Staff.
Cullen, Michael R. Essential Precalculus with Applications. (C). 1997. text. write for info. (*0-201-84779-5*) Addison-Wesley.
— Mathematics for the Biosciences. (Illus.). 783p. (C). 1992. reprint ed. text 89.00 (*1-878907-57-3*) TechBooks.

Cullen, Michael R., jt. auth. see Zill, Dennis G.
***Cullen, Mike.** Anna Weiss. 66p. 1999. pap. 5.60 (*0-87129-950-X*, A79) Dramatic Pub.
Cullen, Mike. Anna Weiss. (Nick Hern Bks.). 96p. 1998. pap. 14.95 (*1-85459-388-9*) Theatre Comm.
Cullen, Murray. Cage Your Rage: An Inmate's Guide to Anger Control. (Illus.). 94p. 1992. pap. 12.50 (*0-929310-76-4*) Am Correctional.
— Enjaula Tu Furia: Manual del Prisionero para Controlar la Ira. Bravo-Guzman, Pedro, tr. from ENG. (SPA., Illus.). 101p. (Orig.). 1993. pap. text 12.50 (*0-929310-88-8*) Am Correctional.
Cullen, Murray & Wright, Joan. Cage Your Rage for Teens: A Guide to Anger Control. (Illus.). 100p. (YA). (gr. 7-12). 1996. pap., wbk. ed. 10.50 (*1-56991-036-7*, 555) Am Correctional.
Cullen, Murray C. & Cullen, Ronald B. Cage Your Rage Leader's Guide. 102p. (Orig.). 1997. pap. 50.00 (*1-56991-058-8*) Am Correctional.
Cullen, Murray C. & Cullen, Ronald R. Setting the Stage: How to Deliver an Anger Management Program: The Cage Your Rage for Teens Facilitator's Manual. Fins, Alice, ed. LC 96-218134. 95p. 1996. pap. 50.00 (*1-56991-037-5*, 555) Am Correctional.
Cullen, Noel & Cullen, Linda. Quantity Food Production. 516p. (C). 2001. 65.33 (*0-13-242165-8*, Macmillan Coll) P-H.
***Cullen, Noel C.** The World of Culinary Supervision, Training & Management. 2nd ed. LC 99-30939. (Illus.). 366p. 1999. 71.00 (*0-13-022543-6*) P-H.
Cullen, Noreen P. One Spirit Wrapped in Flesh: A Personal Transformation. La Fond, Elizabeth B., ed. (Illus.). 146p. (Orig.). 1996. pap. 8.95 (*0-9654368-0-2*) N Cullen.
Cullen, Nuala. Savoring Ireland: Cooking Through the Seasons. 1998. 12.99 (*1-85833-395-4*) Quadrillion Pubng.
Cullen, P. Economics for Hospitality Management. (Illus.). 224p. 1996. pap. 23.95 (*0-412-60540-6*) Chapman & Hall.
Cullen, Patrick. Spenser, Marvell, & Renaissance Pastoral. LC 76-123566. 224p. reprint ed. pap. 69.50 (*0-608-16213-2*, 201465300093) Bks Demand.
Cullen, Patrick, et al, eds. The Early Modern Englishwoman Vol. 2, Pt. 1: A Facsimile Library of Essential Works: Printings Writings, 1500-1640: Elizabeth Cary. 345p. 1996. 61.95 (*1-85928-093-5*, Pub. by Scolar Pr) Ashgate Pub Co.
— The Early Modern Englishwoman Vol. 3, Pt. 1: A Facsimile Library of Essential Works: Printings Writings, 1500-1640: Katherine Parr. 1996. 51.95 (*1-85928-094-3*, Pub. by Scolar Pr) Ashgate Pub Co.
— The Early Modern Englishwoman Vol. 4, Pt. 1: A Facsimile Library of Essential Works: Printings Writings, 1500-1640: Jane Anger, Rachel Speght, Ester Sowernam & Constantia Munda. 175p. 1996. 51.95 (*1-85928-095-1*, Pub. by Scolar Pr) Ashgate Pub Co.
— The Early Modern Englishwoman Vol. 5, Pt. 1: A Facsimile Library of Essential Works: Printed Writings, 1500-1640: Susan DuVerger. 400p. 1996. 99.95 (*1-85928-096-X*, Pub. by Scolar Pr) Ashgate Pub Co.
— The Early Modern Englishwoman Vol. 6, Pt. 1: A Facsimile Library of Essential Works: Printings Writings, 1500-1640: Mary Sidney Herbert. 200p. 1996. 51.95 (*1-85928-097-8*, Pub. by Scolar Pr) Ashgate Pub Co.
— The Early Modern Englishwoman Vol. 8, Pt. 1: A Facsimile Library of Essential Works: Printings Writings, 1500-1640: Margaret Tyler. 370p. 1996. 69.95 (*1-85928-099-4*, Pub. by Scolar Pr) Ashgate Pub Co.
Cullen, Patrick & Roche, Thomas P., Jr., eds. Spenser Studies: A Renaissance Poetry Annual, 1980-1993, 11 vols. 1980. write for info. (*0-404-19200-9*) AMS Pr.
Cullen, Patrick & Travistsky, Betty S., eds. The Early Modern Englishwoman: A Facsimile Library of Essential Works, 10 vols., Set. 1996. 516.95 (*1-85928-226-1*, Pub. by Scolar Pr) Ashgate Pub Co.
Cullen, Patrick & Travitsky, Betty S., eds. The Early Modern Englishwoman Vol. 1, Pt. 1: A Facsimile Library of Essential Works: Printed Writings, 1500-1640: Anne Askew. 1996. 51.95 (*1-85928-092-7*, Pub. by Scolar Pr) Ashgate Pub Co.
— The Early Modern Englishwoman Vol. 7, Pt. 1: A Facsimile Library of Essential Works: Printings Writings, 1500-1640: Alice Sutcliffe. 260p. 1996. 51.95 (*1-85928-098-6*, Pub. by Scolar Pr) Ashgate Pub Co.
— The Early Modern Englishwoman Vol. 9, Pt. 1: A Facsimile Library of Essential Works: Printings Writings, 1500-1640: Anne Wheathill. 312p. 1996. 52.95 (*1-85928-100-1*, Pub. by Scolar Pr) Ashgate Pub Co.
Cullen, Patrick, jt. ed. see Travitsky, Betty S.
Cullen, Patrick, ed. see Weamys, Anne.
***Cullen, Paul.** Refugees & Asylum-Seekers in Ireland. (Undercurrents Ser.). 72p. 2000. pap. 8.95 (*1-85918-242-9*, Pub. by Cork Univ) Stylus Pub VA.
Cullen, Paul & Boyle, Ken. Dublin. (Direct from Ireland Ser.). 218p. 1995. pap. 12.95 (*0-614-95631-5*, Passprt Bks) NTC Contemp Pub Co.
Cullen, Paula B. Journey of Storms. LC 93-79885. 152p. 1994. 16.00 (*0-9637906-6-8*); pap. 12.00 (*0-9637906-4-1*) Millstone Riv.
Cullen, Peggy. Cookie Magic. 1998. write for info. (*0-609-60220-9*) C Potter.
***Cullen, Peggy.** Got Milk? The Cookie Book. LC 00-26903. (Illus.). 2000. pap. 16.95 (*0-8118-2646-5*) Chronicle Bks.
Cullen, Peter J., jt. ed. see Goetz, Klaus H.
Cullen, Richard. Federalism in Action, the Australian & Canadian Offshore Disputes. 249p. 1990. pap. 43.00 (*1-86287-032-2*, Pub. by Federation Pr) Gaunt.
Cullen, Robert. Cover Story. LC 93-40751. 312p. 1994. 20.00 (*0-689-12198-9*) Atheneum Yung Read.
Cullen, Robert. Heirs of the Fire. LC 97-15070. 368p. 1997. 23.00 (*0-449-00025-7*) Fawcett.
Cullen, Robert. Rhetoric for a Multicultural America. LC 99-23610. 301p. (C). 1999. pap. text 32.00 (*0-205-28219-9*, Macmillan Coll) P-H.
— Thomas L. Synnott: The Career of a Dublin Catholic, 1830-1870. (Maynooth Studies in Local History). 64p. 1997. pap. 9.95 (*0-7165-2630-1*, Pub. by Irish Acad Pr) Intl Spec Bk.
***Cullen, Ron & Cushman, Donald P.** Transitions to Competitive Government: Speed, Consensus & Performance. LC 99-54267. (C). 2000. text 73.50 (*0-7914-4657-3*) State U NY Pr.
— Transitions to Competitive Government: Speed, Consensus, & Performance. LC 99-54267. 2000. pap. 24.95 (*0-7914-4658-1*) State U NY Pr.
Cullen, Ronald R., jt. auth. see Cullen, Murray C.
***Cullen, Shelley, et al.** Margaret River Style. (Illus.). 200p. 1999. pap. 24.95 (*1-86368-285-6*, Pub. by Fremantle Arts) Intl Spec Bk.
Cullen, Simon. Soldier Talk: A Squaddie's Handbook. 240p. (Orig.). 1995. pap. 11.95 (*0-85052-459-8*, Pub. by Leo Cooper) Trans-Atl Phila.
Cullen, Stephen. Children in Society: A Libertarian Critique. (Anarchist Discussion Ser.). 43p. (Orig.). 1991. pap. 3.00 (*0-900384-62-X*) Left Bank.
Cullen, Stuart C. & Larson, C. Philip, Jr. Essentials of Anesthetic Practice. LC 73-86838. 358p. reprint ed. pap. 111.00 (*0-608-16239-6*, 202650400049) Bks Demand.
Cullen, Sue, jt. ed. see Adams, Ruth.
Cullen, T., jt. ed. see Foss, C.
Cullen, Timothy, tr. see Averoff-Tossizza, Evangelos.
Cullen, Timothy, tr. see Christophilopoulou, Aikaterina.
Cullen, V. Alexander. Pawnbroker's Handbook: How to Get Rich Buying & Selling Guns, Gold & Other Good Stuff. (Illus.). 208p. 1995. pap. 20.00 (*0-87364-857-9*) Paladin Pr.
Cullen, Vicky, ed. see Stommel, Henry M.
Cullen, W. H., et al, eds. Automated Test Methods for Fracture & Fatigue Crack Growth-STP 877. LC 85-15710. (Illus.). 311p. 1985. text 47.00 (*0-8031-0421-9*, STP877) ASTM.
Cullen, W. H., jt. ed. see Strauss, B. M.
Cullenberg, Paula. Gillnet Hanging. 3rd rev. ed. (Marine Advisory Bulletin Ser.: No. 29). (Illus.). 20p. 1997. pap. text 4.00 (*1-56612-045-4*) AK Sea Grant CP.
Cullenberg, Stephen. The Falling Rate of Profit: Recasting the Marxian Debate. (New Directions - Rethinking Marxism Ser.). 154p. (C). 1994. 49.95 (*0-7453-0878-3*, Pub. by Pluto GBR); pap. 15.95 (*0-7453-0877-5*, Pub. by Pluto GBR) Stylus Pub VA.
Cullenberg, Stephen, jt. ed. see Magnus, Bernd.
Cullens, Carol, jt. ed. see McDonald, Linda.
Cullens, Chane & Blackwell, Ken. Cross-Platform Development Using Visual C++ 550p. 1995. pap. 39.95 incl. disk (*1-55851-428-7*, M&T Bks) IDG Bks.
Cullens, Chris, tr. see Kittler, Friedrich A.
Culler. Skiffs & Schooners. 1990. 26.87 (*0-07-014934-8*) McGraw.
Culler, Arthur D. Imaginative Reason: The Poetry of Matthew Arnold. LC 76-42264. (Illus.). 1976. reprint ed. lib. bdg. 65.00 (*0-8371-8979-9*, CUIR, Greenwood Pr) Greenwood.
— The Imperial Intellect. LC 55-8700. 327p. 1973. reprint ed. lib. bdg. 65.00 (*0-8371-7683-2*, CUII, Greenwood Pr) Greenwood.
Culler, Arthur D., ed. see Newman, John Henry.
Culler, Daniel L. Black Hole of Wauwilermoos: An Airman's Story. (Illus.). 400p. (Orig.). 1995. pap. 16.50 (*1-887776-01-X*) D L Culler.
— The Circle of Thorns: Birth & the Learning Years. (Illus.). 296p. (Orig.). 1992. pap. 14.95 (*1-887776-00-1*) D L Culler.
Culler, John & Wechsler, Chuck, eds. River Gods & Spotted Devils. 2nd ed. (Illus.). 284p. 1991. 12.95 (*0-929822-00-5*) LiveOak Pr.
Culler, John M. Purple Heaven. 200p. 1997. 21.95 (*1-887269-01-0*) J Culler & Sons.
— Purple Heaven. 1997. pap. text 21.95 (*1-887269-30-4*) J Culler & Sons.
Culler, Jonathan. Ferdinand de Saussure. rev. ed. LC 86-6302. 160p. 1986. text 35.00 (*0-8014-1917-4*); pap. text 10.95 (*0-8014-9389-7*) Cornell U Pr.
— Framing the Sign: Criticism & Its Institutions. LC 87-40552. (Project for Discourse & Theory Ser.: Vol. 3). 224p. 1989. 32.95 (*0-8061-2127-0*); pap. 16.95 (*0-8061-2184-X*) U of Okla Pr.
— Literary Theory. LC 97-17713. (Very Short Introductions Ser.). (Illus.). 152p. 1998. pap. 8.95 (*0-19-285318-X*) OUP.
— On Deconstruction: Theory & Criticism after Structuralism. LC 82-7414. 312p. 1982. text 42.50 (*0-8014-1322-2*); pap. text 14.95 (*0-8014-9201-7*) Cornell U Pr.
— The Pursuit of Signs: Semiotics, Literature, Deconstruction. LC 80-70539. 256p. (C). 1981. pap. text 14.95 (*0-8014-9224-6*) Cornell U Pr.
— Structuralist Poetics: Structuralism, Linguistics & the Study of Literature. LC 74-11608. 316p. 1976. pap. text 14.95 (*0-8014-9155-X*) Cornell U Pr.
Culler, Jonathan, jt. auth. see Empson, William.
Culler, Jonathan D., ed. The Harvard Advocate Centennial Anthology. 512p. 1966. 29.95 (*0-87073-120-3*) Schenkman Bks Inc.
Cullerton, Brenda, text. Geoffrey Beene. LC 95-7848. (Illus.). 144p. 1995. 55.00 (*0-8109-3141-9*, Pub. by Abrams) Time Warner.
Cullet, Philippe, jt. auth. see Dommen, Caroline.
Culleton, Beatrice. In Search of April Raintree. 196p. (C). 1992. pap. 7.00 (*1-895411-46-7*) Peguis Pubs Ltd.
— Spirit of the White Bison. LC 89-32047. (Illus.). 64p. (J). (gr. 5 up). 1989. reprint ed. pap. 5.95 (*0-913990-64-7*) Book Pub Co.
— Spirit of the White Bison. (Illus.). 64p. (J). (gr. 5-9). 1993. reprint ed. pap. 8.00 (*1-895411-43-2*) Peguis Pubs Ltd.
Culleton, Claire A. Names & Naming in Joyce. LC 94-15380. 160p. 1994. pap. 15.95 (*0-299-14384-8*) U of Wis Pr.
— Names & Naming in Joyce. LC 94-15380. 160p. 1994. 40.00 (*0-299-14380-5*) U of Wis Pr.
***Culleton, Claire A.** Working Class Women in First World War Britain. LC 99-27686. 2000. text 45.00 (*0-312-22541-5*) St Martin.
***Culleton, Edward.** Celtic & Early Christian Wexford, Ad 400-1166. 240p. 1999. 29.95 (*1-85182-515-0*, Pub. by Four Cts Pr) Intl Spec Bk.
Culleton, R. Gerald. The Prophets & Our Times. 1994. reprint ed. pap. 13.50 (*0-89555-050-4*) TAN Bks Pubs.
— The Reign of AntiChrist. 1974. reprint ed. pap. 13.50 (*0-89555-047-4*) TAN Bks Pubs.
Culley, John H. Cattle, Horses & Men of the Western Range. LC 84-2769. (Illus.). 337p. 1984. reprint ed. pap. 18.95 (*0-8165-0865-8*) U of Ariz Pr.
Culley, Lou A. Themes Through Time: Readings in Art History. 192p. (C). 1992. pap. text 29.95 (*0-8403-8048-8*) Kendall-Hunt.
— Transformations: Art & Society in the Modern Era. 256p. (C). 1992. pap. text, per. 35.95 (*0-8403-8367-3*) Kendall-Hunt.
Culley, LouAnn. Themes Through Time: Readings in Art History. 2nd ed. 208p. (C). 1997. per. 56.95 (*0-7872-3866-X*) Kendall-Hunt.
Culley, LouAnn. Transformations: Art & Society in the Modern Era. 2nd ed. 284p. (C). 1997. per. 54.95 (*0-7872-4554-2*, 41455401) Kendall-Hunt.
Culley, Margo, ed. A Day at a Time: The Diary Literature of American Women Writers from 1764 to the Present. LC 85-13140. 368p. 1985. pap. 16.95 (*0-935312-51-X*) Feminist Pr.
Culley, Margo, ed. American Women's Autobiography: Fea(s) ts of Memory. LC 91-46700. (Studies in American Autobiography). 352p. (Orig.). (C). 1992. pap. 17.95 (*0-299-13294-3*) U of Wis Pr.
Culley, Margo, jt. ed. see Hoffman, Leonore.
Culley, Peter. The Climax Forest. 112p. 1995. pap. 8.00 (*1-895679-00-1*, Pub. by Leech Pr) Genl Dist Srvs.
Culley, Sue. Integrative Counselling Skills in Action. (Counselling in Action Ser.: Vol. 12). 160p. 1991. 49.95 (*0-8039-8276-3*); pap. 21.50 (*0-8039-8277-1*) Sage.
Culley, Thomas D. Jesuits & Music. 401p. 1970. 29.00 (*88-7041-582-1*) Jesuit Hist.
Culley, Tom. Beating the Odds in Small Business. LC 97-36427. 320p. 1998. per. 20.00 (*0-684-84183-5*) Free Pr.
Culley, W. T. & Furnivall, F. J., eds. Caxton Eneydos. (EETS Extra Ser.: Vol. 57). 1963. reprint ed. 30.00 (*0-19-722564-0*, Pub. by EETS) Boydell & Brewer.
Culley, William C. Environmental & Quality Systems Integration. LC 98-12651. 328p. 1998. boxed set 64.95 (*1-56670-288-7*) CRC Pr.
Cullhed, Mats. Conservator Urbis Suae: Studies in the Politics & Propaganda of the Emperor Maxentius. LC 96-130748. (Acta Instituti Romani Regni Sueciae, Series in 4 Degrees: Vol. XX). (Illus.). 108p. 1994. pap. 43.50 (*91-7042-149-8*, Pub. by P Astroms) Coronet Bks.
***Cullick, Jonathan S.** Making History: The Biographical Narratives of Robert Penn Warren. LC 99-57982. (Southern Literary Studies). 192p. 2000. 45.00 (*0-8071-2558-X*); pap. 18.95 (*0-8071-2603-9*) La State U Pr.
Cullicott, John F. Terri's Winter. (Orig.). (J). (gr. 1-3). 1995. pap. 3.00 (*0-89824-219-3*) Royal Fireworks.
Culligan, Emmett J. The Last World War & the End of Time. (Illus.). 210p. 1981. reprint ed. pap. 13.50 (*0-89555-034-2*) TAN Bks Pubs.
Culligan, Joe. Joe Culligan's Back-to-Basics Management for the 21st Century. (C). 1993. pap. text 14.95 (*0-13-512112-4*) P-H.
Culligan, Joseph J. Adoption Searches Made Easier. LC 95-61932. (Illus.). 584p. 1995. pap. 34.95 (*1-57296-100-7*) FJA.
— Requirements to Become a P. I. in the Fifty States & Elsewhere. rev. ed. LC 92-64222. (Illus.). 576p. 1999. reprint ed. pap. 19.95 (*0-9630621-1-5*) Research Invest.
— When in Doubt, Check Him Out. rev. ed. LC 93-83775. (Illus.). 344p. 1999. reprint ed. pap. 19.95 (*0-9630621-2-3*) Research Invest.
— You Too Can Find Anybody. rev. ed. LC 91-91166. (Illus.). 370p. 1999. reprint ed. pap. 19.95 (*0-9630621-0-7*) Research Invest.
Culligan, Judy. Heroes & Pioneers. LC 98-38909. (Macmillan Profiles Ser.). 414p. 1998. 75.00 (*0-02-865059-X*) Macmillan.
— Macmillan Profiles: Myths & Legends. LC 99-51558. (Profiles Ser.). 400p. 1999. 75.00 (*0-02-865376-9*) Macmillan.
Culligan, Kevin, et al. Purifying the Heart: Buddhist Meditation for Christians. 176p. (Orig.). 1994. pap. 14.95 (*0-8245-1420-3*) Crossroad NY.
***Culligan, Kevin G. & Jordan, Regis.** Carmel & Contemplation: Transforming Human Consciousness. LC 99-56939. 384p. (C). 2000. pap. 14.95 (*0-935216-63-4*) ICS Pubns.
Culligan, Matthew J. Ronald Reagan & the Isle of Destiny: A Fascinating Journey into a Proud Irish History. (Illus.). 175p. 25.00 (*0-8063-4868-2*) Clearfield Co.
Culligan, Matthew J. & Cherici, Peter. The Wandering Irish in Europe: Their Influence from the Dark Ages to Modern Times. 256p. pap. 19.95 (*0-8063-4835-6*) Clearfield Co.
Culligan, Matthew J. & Cherici, Peter. The Wandering Irish in Europe: Their Influence from the Dark Ages to Modern Times. (Illus.). 350p. 1996. 22.95 (*0-9651244-0-1*) Derrynane Pr.
Culligan, Michael & Morehouse, Cynthia T., eds. International Directory of Youth Internships: With the United Nations, Its Specialized Agencies & Non-Governmental Organizations. 5th ed. 58p. 1993. pap. 7.50 (*0-945257-47-3*) Apex Pr.
Culligan, Pat, jt. auth. see Brown, Vera.
***Cullimore, D. Roy.** Practical Handbook for Bacterial Identification. (Illus.). 232p. (C). 2000. boxed set 79.95 (*1-56670-392-1*) Lewis Pubs.
Cullimore, D. Roy, ed. see International Symposium on Biofouled Aquifers Staf.
***Cullimore, Roy.** Microbiology of Well Biofouling. LC 99-35336. (Sustainable Well Ser.). 435p. 1999. 79.95 (*1-56670-400-6*) Lewis Pubs.
Cullimore, Roy, jt. auth. see Alford, George.
***Cullin, Mitch.** Branches. LC 99-34827. (Illus.). 182p. 2000. 22.00 (*1-57962-061-2*) Permanent Pr.
— Tideland: A Novel. LC 00-27918. 2000. 22.00 (*0-8023-1335-3*) Dufour.
Cullin, Mitch. Whompyjawed. LC 98-34205. 160p. 1999. 22.00 (*1-57962-023-X*) Permanent Pr.
***Cullina, William.** New England Wild Flower Society Guide to Growing & Propagating Wildflowers of the United States & Canada. LC 00-20513. 2000. 40.00 (*0-395-96609-4*) HM.
Cullinan. Angry River. 1994. text 13.90 (*0-15-302376-7*) Harcourt.
— Angry River. (J). 1994. text 17.80 (*0-15-302196-9*, Harcourt Child Bks) Harcourt.
— Astronaut. 1994. text 13.90 (*0-15-302295-7*) Harcourt.
— Authur Sails. 1994. text 13.90 (*0-15-302313-9*) Harcourt.
— Ballon Race. 1994. text 13.90 (*0-15-302328-7*) Harcourt.
— Big Book Collection Passports. 1994. text 233.50 (*0-15-303263-4*); text 203.50 (*0-15-303264-2*) H Holt & Co.
— Blast Off. 1994. text 13.90 (*0-15-302351-1*) Harcourt.
— Business Communication. (C). 1989. pap. text, teacher ed., suppl. ed. 40.50 (*0-03-029898-9*, Pub. by Harcourt Coll Pubs) Harcourt.
— Collin Powell. 1994. text 13.90 (*0-15-302443-7*) Harcourt.
— Earthquake. 1994. text 23.00 (*0-15-302262-0*) Harcourt.
— Ellis Island. 1994. text 13.90 (*0-15-302371-6*) Harcourt.
— Family Farm. (J). 1994. text 25.80 (*0-15-302222-1*, Harcourt Child Bks) Harcourt.
— Frog & Toad. (J). 1994. text 13.90 (*0-15-302321-X*) Harcourt.
— Gallant Pig. (J). 1994. text 13.90 (*0-15-302408-9*) Harcourt.
— Good Morning. (J). 1994. text 13.90 (*0-15-302284-1*) Harcourt.
— Gorilla. (J). 1994. text 13.90 (*0-15-302311-2*) Harcourt.
— Green Song. (J). 1994. 18.00 (*0-15-302197-7*, Harcourt Child Bks) Harcourt.
— Hail to Mail. 1994. text 13.90 (*0-15-302344-9*) Harcourt.
— Hermit Crab. 1994. text 13.90 (*0-15-302324-4*); text 57.80 (*0-15-302468-2*) Harcourt.
— King's Equal. 1994. text 13.90 (*0-15-302375-9*) Harcourt.
— Last Summer. 1994. text 13.90 (*0-15-302431-3*) Harcourt.
— Literature & Child. 4th ed. (C). 1997. pap. text, teacher ed. write for info. (*0-15-508173-X*) Harcourt Coll Pubs.
— Literature & the Child. 3rd ed. (C). 1993. pap. text, teacher ed. 5.50 (*0-15-501740-3*) Harcourt Coll Pubs.
— Little Bird. 1994. text 13.90 (*0-15-302283-3*) Harcourt.
— Little Pig. 1994. text 13.90 (*0-15-302314-7*) Harcourt.
— Man from the Sky. 94th ed. (J). 1994. text 17.40 (*0-15-302201-9*, Harcourt Child Bks) Harcourt.
— Mr. Blueberry. 1994. text 13.90 (*0-15-302316-3*) Harcourt.
— Mr. Henshaw. (J). 1994. text 20.20 (*0-15-302223-X*, Harcourt Child Bks) Harcourt.
— Pancakes. 1994. text 13.90 (*0-15-302280-9*) Harcourt.
— Principles of Business Communication. 5th ed. (C). 1993. pap. text, teacher ed. 5.50 (*0-03-096875-5*) Harcourt Coll Pubs.
— Red Hen. 1994. text 13.90 (*0-15-302302-3*) Harcourt.
— Sleepover. 1994. text 13.90 (*0-15-302438-0*) Harcourt.
— Smell of the Rain. 1994. text 13.90 (*0-15-302384-8*) Harcourt.
— Smell the Rain. LC 95-105683. (J). 1994. 18.00 (*0-15-302204-3*, Harcourt Child Bks) Harcourt.
— Two of a Kind. 1994. text 13.90 (*0-15-302382-1*) Harcourt.
— Volcano. (J). 1994. text 27.10 (*0-15-302224-8*, Harcourt Child Bks); text 13.90 (*0-15-302404-6*, Harcourt Child Bks) Harcourt.
Cullinan, Alice R. Sorting It Out: Discerning God's Call to Ministry. LC 98-49515. 1999. pap. 13.00 (*0-8170-1302-4*) Judson.
— Time for a Checkup. 30p. (Orig.). 1995. teacher ed., wbk. ed. 2.95 (*0-87508-717-5*, 717) Chr Lit.
— Time for a Checkup. 128p. (Orig.). 1994. pap. 5.95 (*0-87508-739-6*) Chr Lit.
— Time for a Checkup. (Illus.). 15p. (Orig.). 1995. pap., student ed., wbk. ed. 2.95 (*0-87508-718-3*, 718) Chr Lit.
Cullinan, Angeline. Producing Quality Radiographs. (Illus.). 289p. 1987. text 41.50 (*0-397-50778-X*, Lppnctt) Lppncott W & W.
— Producing Quality Radiographs. 2nd ed. 352p. 1993. text 51.00 (*0-397-55031-6*) Lppncott W & W.
***Cullinan, Bernice.** Easy Poetry Lessons That Dazzle & Delight: Reproducible Poems & Activities That Inspire Children. 112p. 1999. pap. 14.95 (*0-590-12050-6*) Scholastic Inc.
Cullinan, Bernice, ed. A Jar of Tiny Stars: Poems by NCTE Award-Winning Poets. LC 93-60466. (Illus.). 104p. (J). (gr. k-7). 1995. 16.95 (*1-56397-087-2*, Wordsong) Boyds Mills Pr.

An Asterisk (*) at the beginning of an entry indicates that the title is appearing for the first time.

Cullinan, Bernice & Bagert, Brad. Helping Your Child Learn to Read: With Activities for Childern from Infancy Through Age 10. Perkinson, Kathryn, ed. (Illus.). 64p. (Orig.). (C). 1993. pap. text 15.00 (*0-7881-0007-6*) DIANE Pub.

Cullinan, Bernice, et al. Three Voices: An Invitation to Poetry Across the Curriculum. (Illus.). 152p. (C). 1995. pap. text 19.50 (*1-57110-015-6*) Stenhse Pubs.

Cullinan, Bernice E. Read to Me: Raising Kids Who Love to Read. (Illus.). 160p. 1992. pap. 4.50 (*0-590-45206-1*) Scholastic Inc.

***Cullinan, Bernice E.** Read to Me: Raising Kids Who Love to Read. rev. ed. LC 00-27178. (Illus.). 160p. (J). 2000. pap. 6.95 (*0-439-08721-X*) Scholastic Inc.

Cullinan, Bernice E., ed. Children's Literature in the Reading Program. LC 86-27786. (Illus.). 181p. reprint ed. pap. 56.20 (*0-7837-4585-0*, 204430400002) Bks Demand.

— Children's Voices: Talk in the Classroom. LC 93-13319. (Illus.). 103p. reprint ed. pap. 32.00 (*0-608-05988-9*, 206631600008) Bks Demand.

— Pen in Hand: Children Become Writers. LC 93-25880. (Illus.). 95p. reprint ed. pap. 30.00 (*0-608-05989-7*, 206631700008) Bks Demand.

Cullinan, Bernice E. & Galda, Lee. Literature & the Child. 4th ed. LC 97-73555. 608p. (C). 1997. text 69.00 (*0-15-503956-3*, Pub. by Harcourt Coll Pubs) Harcourt.

***Cullinan, Bernice E. & Person, Diane G., eds.** The Continuum Encyclopedia of Children's Literature. 864p. 2001. 150.00 (*0-8264-1271-8*) Continuum.

Cullinan, Bernice E., jt. ed. see Hickman, Janet.

Cullinan, Mary. Business English for Industry & the Professions. 464p. (C). 1987. pap. text, teacher ed. 36.50 (*0-03-008152-1*) Dryden Pr.

Cullinan, Mary, jt. auth. see Barrett, Eileen.

Cullinan, Mary, jt. ed. see Barrett, Eileen.

Cullinan, Mary P. Business Communication: Principles & Processes. 2nd ed. 320p. (C). 1993. text 49.00 (*0-03-079098-0*, Pub. by Harcourt Coll Pubs) Harcourt.

Cullinan, Thomas. Mrs. Lincoln. 1969. pap. 5.25 (*0-8222-0786-9*) Dramatists Play.

Cullinane, S. & Stokes, G. Rural Transport Policy. LC 99-162981. 352p. 1998. 106.00 (*0-08-043070-8*) Elsevier.

Cullinane, John J. Understanding Architectural Drawings: A Guide for Non-Architects. (Illus.). 140p. 1995. pap. 24.95 (*0-471-14429-0*) Wiley.

Cullinane, M. John, et al. Contaminated Dredged Material: Control, Treatment & Disposal Practices. LC 89-70988. (Pollution Technology Review Ser.: No. 179). (Illus.). 772p. 1990. 85.00 (*0-8155-1229-5*) Noyes.

Culliney, John L. & Crockett, Edward S. Bike Touring: The Sierra Club Guide to Scuba & Snorkling. LC 79-21944. (Sierra Club Guides). (Illus.). 352p. 1982. pap. 15.00 (*0-87156-270-7*, Pub. by Sierra) Random.

Culliney, John L. & Koeble, Bruce P. A Native Hawaiian Garden: How to Grow & Care for Island Plants. LC 99-15190. (Illus.). 176p. 1999. pap. 24.95 (*0-8248-2176-9*) UH Pr.

Culling, Louis T. The Pristine Yi King: Pure Wisdom of Ancient China. LC 84-48090. (Inner Guide Ser.). 224p. (Orig.). 1999. pap. 7.95 (*0-87542-107-5*) Llewellyn Pubns.

***Cullingford, Benita.** British Chimney Sweeps: A Definitive Social History. (Illus.). 256p. 2000. 34.50 (*1-85776-452-8*, Pub. by Book Guild Ltd) Trans-Atl Phila.

Cullingford, Cedric. Assessment Versus Evaluation. 1997. pap. text 35.00 (*0-304-33620-3*) Continuum.

***Cullingford, Cedric.** The Causes of Exclusion: Home, School & the Development of Young Criminals. 224p. 1999. pap. 29.95 (*0-7494-3039-7*, Kogan Pg Educ) Stylus Pub VA.

Cullingford, Cedric. The Effective Teacher. (Cassell Education Ser.). (Illus.). 1995. pap. 33.95 (*0-304-33180-5*) Continuum.

— The Formative Years: Children's Tastes in Reading. LC 97-11790. (Children, Teachers, & Learning Ser.). 218p. 1997. 75.00 (*0-304-70092-4*); pap. 24.95 (*0-304-70093-2*) Cassell.

***Cullingford, Cedric.** The Human Experience: The Early Years. LC 99-76357. 298p. 1999. text 69.95 (*0-7546-1156-6*, Pub. by Ashgate Pub) Ashgate Pub Co.

— An Inspector Calls: OFSTED & Its Effect on School Standards. 192p. 1999. pap. 29.95 (*0-7494-3053-2*, Kogan Pg Educ) Stylus Pub VA.

Cullingford, Cedric. The Politics of Primary Education. LC 96-52126. 1997. 108.00 (*0-335-19579-2*); pap. 30.95 (*0-335-19578-4*) OpUniv Pr.

Cullingford, Cedric, ed. Assessment vs. Evaluation. LC 97-179503. (Children, Teachers, & Learning Ser.). 282p. 1997. 99.50 (*0-304-33621-1*, LB3056, Pub. by Cassell) LPC InBook.

— Children & Society: Children's Attitudes to Politics & Power. (Children, Teachers & Learning Ser.). 172p. 1992. pap. text 33.95 (*0-304-32437-X*) Continuum.

— Parents, Education & the State. LC 96-85136. (Monitoring Change in Education Ser.). 196p. 1996. text 55.95 (*1-85742-338-0*, Pub. by Arena) Ashgate Pub Co.

Cullingford, Cedric & Husemann, Harald. Anglo-German Attitudes. 221p. 1995. 72.95 (*1-85972-137-0*, Pub. by Avebry) Ashgate Pub Co.

Cullingford, Cedric, ed. see Emerson, Adrian.

Cullingford, Cedric, ed. see Gentle, Keith.

Cullingford, Cedric, ed. see Hartley, David.

Cullingford, Cedric, ed. see Stevenson, Rosemary J.

Cullingford, Cedric, ed. see Wiegand, Patrick.

Cullingford, Cedric, ed. see Winkley, Linda.

Cullingford, Elizabeth B. Gender & History in Yeats's Love Poetry. LC 95-40268. (Irish Studies). 356p. (C). 1996. pap. 19.95 (*0-8156-0331-2*, CUGHP) Syracuse U Pr.

***Cullingford, Guy.** Post Mortem. 222p. 1999. 21.95 (*0-7540-8525-2*, Black Dagger) Chivers N Amer.

Cullingford, R. A., et al, eds. Timescales in Geomorphology. LC 79-40517. (Illus.). 370p. reprint ed. pap. 114.70 (*0-8357-3075-1*, 203933200012) Bks Demand.

***Cullingworth, Barry, ed.** British Planning. LC 99-22497. 392p. 1999. 95.00 (*0-485-00404-6*); pap. 33.95 (*0-485-00604-9*) Athlone Pr.

Cullingworth, J. B. Planning in the U. S. A. Policies, Issues & Processes. LC 96-33158. (Illus.). 304p. (C). 1997. pap. 32.99 (*0-415-15012-4*) Routledge.

— Planning in the U. S. A. Policies, Issues & Processes. LC 96-33158. (Illus.). 304p. (C). 1997. 100.00 (*0-415-15011-6*) Routledge.

Cullingworth, J. B. & Nadin, Vincent. Town & Country Planning in Britain. 12th ed. LC 96-52768. (Illus.). 416p. (C). 1997. 85.00 (*0-415-13912-0*); pap. 35.00 (*0-415-13913-9*) Routledge.

Cullingworth, J. Barry. Urban & Regional Planning in Canada. 460p. 1987. 49.95 (*0-88738-135-9*) Transaction Pubs.

Cullingworth, J. Barry, ed. Energy, Land, & Public Policy Vol. 5: Energy Policy Studies. 250p. 1989. 29.95 (*0-88738-770-5*) Transaction Pubs.

Cullingworth, Nick, et al. BTEC Public Services Assignments: Core Units. 128p. 1998. pap. 210.00 (*0-7487-3967-X*) St Mut.

— BTEC Public Services Assignments: Option Units. 128p. 1998. pap. 210.00 (*0-7487-3960-2*) St Mut.

Cullins, Judy, ed. see Caveglia, Rico.

Cullins, Warren, et al. Zeballos, Its Gold Its People Yesterday & Today: An Historical Documentation. (Orig.). (YA). (gr. 6-8). 1982. pap. 7.75 (*0-9608386-0-0*) Cullins.

***Cullis, A. G.** Microscopy of Semiconducting Materials 1999: Proceedings of the Institute of Physics Conference, Vol. 164. LC 99-58027. (Institute of Physics Conference Ser.). 1999. 275.00 (*0-7503-0650-5*) IOP Pub.

Cullis, A. G. & Staton-Bevan, A. E., eds. Microscopy & Semiconducting Materials, 1995: Proceedings of the Institute of Physics Conference Held at Oxford University, 20-23 March 1995. (Institute of Physics Conference Ser.: Vol. 146). (Illus.). 795p. 1996. 353.00 (*0-7503-0347-6*) IOP Pub.

Cullis, A. G., ed. see Oxford Conference on Microscopy of Semiconducting.

Cullis, Adrian & Pacey, Arnold. A Development Dialogue: Rainwater Harvesting in Turkana. 182p. 1991. 50.00 (*1-85339-116-6*, Pub. by Intermed Tech); pap. 23.00 (*1-85339-104-2*, Pub. by Intermed Tech) Stylus Pub VA.

Cullis, John & Jones, Philip. Public Finance & Public Choice. 2nd ed. (Illus.). 448p. 1998. text 78.00 (*0-19-877580-6*); pap. text 39.95 (*0-19-877579-2*) OUP.

Cullis, John G. & West, Peter A. The Economics of Health: An Introduction. (Modern Revivals in Economics Ser.). 336p. 1992. 63.95 (*0-7512-0026-3*, Pub. by Gregg Revivals) Ashgate Pub Co.

Cullis, Midge. Volunteers Plus Votes Equal Victory: A Resource Manual for Volunteer Program Management of Election Campaigns. 150p. 1989. pap. 10.00 (*0-9624539-0-0*) Diakonos Pubns.

Cullis, Ray. Healing Hands, Healing Words: Positive Suggestion & Loving Touch for Family & Friends. LC 97-28383. (Illus.). 177p. 1998. pap. 12.95 (*0-87604-394-5*, 490) ARE Pr.

Cullison & Lowery. Feeds & Feeding. 5th ed. LC 98-408885. 676p. 1998. 100.00 (*0-13-319294-6*) P-H.

Cullison, Alan. The South Americans. (Peoples of North America Ser.). (Illus.). 120p. (J). (gr. 5 up). 1991. lib. bdg. 19.95 (*0-87754-863-3*) Chelsea Hse.

Culliton, Joseph T. Non-Violence Central to Christian Spirituality: Perspectives from Scripture to the Present. LC 82-7964. (Toronto Studies in Theology: Vol. 8). 312p. (C). 1982. lib. bdg. 99.95 (*0-88946-964-4*) E Mellen.

Cullity, B. D. Elements of X-Ray Diffraction 3rd ed. (C). 2000. text. write for info. (*0-201-61091-4*) Addison-Wesley.

Cullity, Berrard D. Elements of X-Ray Diffraction. 2nd ed. LC 77-73950. (Illus.). 575p. (C). 1978. 100.00 (*0-201-01174-3*) Addison-Wesley.

Cullity, Garrett & Gaut, Berys, eds. Ethics & Practical Reason. LC 97-15977. 430p. 1998. pap. text 22.00 (*0-19-823669-7*) OUP.

— Ethics & Practical Reason. LC 97-15977. 430p. (C). 1998. text 77.00 (*0-19-823646-8*) OUP.

Cullity, Maurice. A History of Dairying in Western Australia. 488p. 1983. 29.95 (*0-85564-177-0*, Pub. by Univ of West Aust Pr) Intl Spec Bk.

Culliver, Concetta C., ed. Female Criminality: The State of the Art. LC 92-27490. (Library of Sociology: Vol. 22). 568p. 1993. text 30.00 (*0-8153-0484-6*, SS796) Garland.

Cullman, Heather. For All Eternity. (Historical Romance Ser.). 352p. 1998. mass mkt. 5.99 (*0-451-40814-4*, Topaz) NAL.

Cullman, Joseph F. I'm a Lucky Guy. LC 98-13468. 1998. write for info. (*0-934037-48-5*) P Morris.

Cullman, Oscar. Prayer in the New Testament. Bowden, John, tr. (Overtures to Biblical Theology Ser.). 244p. 1995. pap. 20.00 (*0-8006-2944-2*) Augsburg Fortress.

Cullmann, Oscar. Early Christian Worship. LC 87-51009. 126p. (C). 1987. pap. 16.00 (*1-55605-018-6*) Wyndham Hall.

Cullom, Shelby. Fifty Years of Public Service: Personal Recollections of Shelby M. Cullom. LC 75-87504. (American Public Figures Ser.). 1969. reprint ed. lib. bdg. 55.00 (*0-306-71410-8*) Da Capo.

Cullop, Floyd G. Constitution of the United States: An Introduction. 160p. 1969. mass mkt. 5.99 (*0-451-62724-5*, Ment) NAL.

***Cullum, Albert.** Geranium on the Windowsill Just Died, but Teacher You Went Right On. 2000. 15.95 (*0-8252-0500-X*, Pub. by Quist) Allnce Hse.

Cullum, Albert. Geranium on Windowsill Died. 1978. pap. 3.95 (*0-8252-3105-1*) Quist.

— Greek & Roman Plays for the Intermediate Grades. (J). (gr. 4-8). 1993. pap. 18.99 (*0-86653-941-7*) Fearon Teacher Aids.

— Shakespeare in the Classroom. 272p. (J). (gr. 4-8). 18.99 (*0-86653-903-4*, FE0903) Fearon Teacher Aids.

Cullum, Albert & Aesop. Aesop's Fables: Plays for Young Children. (J). (gr. k-3). 1993. pap. 14.99 (*0-86653-940-9*) Fearon Teacher Aids.

***Cullum, Carolyn N.** The Storytime Sourcebook: A Compendium of Ideas & Resources for Storytellers. 2nd ed. LC 99-46420. 325p. 1999. pap. 45.00 (*1-55570-360-7*) Neal-Schuman.

***Cullum, Lee.** Genius Came Early: Creativity in the Twentieth Century. LC 99-72792. 383p. 1999. 25.95 (*1-881636-90-9*, Pub. by Windsor Hse Pub Grp) Baker & Taylor.

Cullum, Linda, jt. auth. see Alvine, Lynne.

Cullum-Swan, Betsy & Manning, Peter K. Imaginative Ethnography: Social Theory & Fieldwork at the End of Time. 1997. pap. 49.95 (*0-8133-2288-X*) Westview.

Cully, Barbara. New Intimacy. LC 96-49453. 80p. 1997. pap. 14.95 (*0-14-026480-9*) Viking Penguin.

— Shoreline Series. deluxe ed. 28p. 1996. pap. 10.00 (*1-888553-05-7*) Kore Pr.

Cully, Iris V. The Bible in Christian Education. LC 95-3486. 144p. 1995. pap. 15.00 (*0-8006-2806-3*, 1-2806, Fortress Pr) Augsburg Fortress.

— We Give Thanks: Preparation for Early Communion, Parents Edition. (Illus.). 24p. 1989. pap., teacher ed. 3.95 (*0-8192-4071-0*) Morehouse Pub.

— We Give Thanks: Preparation for Early Communion, Pupils Edition. (Illus.). 32p. 1989. pap., student ed. 4.95 (*0-8192-4070-2*) Morehouse Pub.

— We Give Thanks: Preparation for Early Communion, Teachers Manual. (Illus.). 48p. 1989. pap., teacher ed. 6.50 (*0-8192-4069-9*) Morehouse Pub.

***Cully, Mark.** Britain at Work: 1998 Workplace Relations Survey. LC 99-34133. 1999. pap. write for info. (*0-415-20637-5*) Routledge.

***Cully, Mark, et al.** Britain at Work: 1998 Workplace Relations Survey. LC 99-34133. 502p. (C). 1999. text. write for info. (*0-415-20636-7*) Routledge.

Culman, L. Cultural Revolution in the Provinces. LC 77-162858. (East Asian Monographs: No. 42). 224p. 1971. pap. 20.00 (*0-674-17985-4*) HUP.

Culme, John. The Directory of Gold & Silversmiths, Jewellers & Allied Traders 1838-1914, 2 vols., Set. (Illus.). 1988. 350.00 (*0-907462-46-4*) Antique Collect.

Culme-Seymour, Angela, tr. see Al-Jili, Abd A.

Culme-Seymour, Angela, tr. see Ibn al-Arabi.

***Culmination Mennonite Writ. Proj. Staff, prod.** Mennonite Experience in America, 4 vols. 1999. 79.99 (*0-8361-3120-7*) Herald Pr.

***Culos, Karen.** Christmas Memories: Preserving Family Histories. 116p. 1998. 29.95 (*0-9684364-0-4*) Quail Pubng.

Culot, Maurice & Lejeune, Jean-Francois, eds. Miami: Architecture of the Tropics. (Illus.). 192p. (Orig.). 1993. pap. 39.95 (*1-878271-75-X*) Princeton Arch.

Culotta-Andonian, Cathleen. Samuel Beckett: A Reference Guide. 1988. 65.00 (*0-8161-8570-0*, Hall Reference) Macmillan.

***Culotta, Felicia.** Britney: Every Step of the Way. 2000. pap. 12.00 (*0-451-40970-1*, Onyx) NAL.

Culotta, Wendy A. & Pickwell, George V. The Venomous Sea Snakes: A Comprehensive Bibliography. 526p. (C). 1993. lib. bdg. 79.50 (*0-89464-469-6*) Krieger.

Culp. Principles of Energy Conversion. 2nd ed. 1991. student ed. 27.50 (*0-07-014929-1*) McGraw.

Culp, Archie W. Principles of Energy Conversion. 2nd ed. (Mechanical Engineering Ser.). 576p. (C). 1990. 92.50 (*0-07-014902-X*) McGraw.

***Culp, Bruce & Culp, Melody.** The Value of the Gift: A Spiritual Guide to Love & Intimacy, for Young Adults. large type ed. 96p. (YA). (gr. 7 up). 2000. pap. 8.95 (*0-9672616-1-9*) Oak Hammock.

Culp, Christine P., jt. auth. see Collins, J. Wesley.

Culp, Clif. We've Been Screwed: The Attorneys "Done" It. LC 94-237616. 166p. (Orig.). 1994. pap. 19.94 (*0-9640840-0-7*) Clif Culp.

Culp, Daniel W., ed. Twentieth Century Negro Literature. LC 73-89416. (Black Heritage Library Collection). 1977. 26.95 (*0-8369-8551-6*) Ayer.

— Twentieth Century Negro Literature. LC 69-18586. (American Negro: His History & Literature. Series 2). 1969. reprint ed. 25.95 (*0-405-01856-8*) Ayer.

Culp, David A. & Loening, Stefan A., eds. Genitourinary Oncology. LC 83-19583. 644p. reprint ed. pap. 199.70 (*0-7837-2697-X*, 204307500006) Bks Demand.

Culp, Edwin D. Early Oregon Days. LC 86-23294. (Illus.). 170p. (Orig.). 1988. pap. 22.95 (*0-87004-314-5*) Caxton.

— Oregon, the Way It Was. LC 81-1266. (Illus.). 235p. 1981. pap. 15.95 (*0-87004-285-8*) Caxton.

Culp, George H. Educator's Guide to Hypercard & Hypertalk: Revised Edition for Hypercard 2.2 & Color. 2nd rev. ed. LC 95-127147. 256p. (C). 1994. pap. text 56.00 (*0-205-16652-0*) Allyn.

Culp, Gordon, ed. Trihalomethane Reduction in Drinking Water: Technologies, Costs, Effectiveness, Monitoring, Compliance. LC 84-14906. (Pollution Technology Review Ser.: No. 114). (Illus.). 251p. 1985. 42.00 (*0-8155-1002-0*) Noyes.

Culp, Gordon & Smith, Anne. Managing People (Including Yourself) for Project Success. 320p. 1992. 69.95 (*0-471-29018-1*, VNR) Wiley.

Culp, Gordon L. & Smith, R. Anne. Managing People, (Including Yourself) for Project Success. (Project Management Ser.). (Illus.). 307p. 1992. text 58.95 (*0-442-00952-6*, VNR) Wiley.

Culp, Gordon L., ed. see Culp/Wesner/Culp Staff.

Culp, Jesse. The Good Ole Days: Collected Columns by Jesse Culp. LC 88-92503. (Illus.). 200p. (Orig.). 1988. pap. 8.95 (*0-929835-00-X*) Mountntop Pr.

Culp, Melody, jt. auth. see Culp, Bruce.

Culp, Mildred L. Be WorkWise: Retooling Your Work for the 21st Century. 2nd ed. LC 94-94116. (Illus.). 85p. (Orig.). 1994. reprint ed. pap. 8.95 (*0-9640712-5-8*) Exec Direct.

Culp, Robert D., ed. Guidance & Control 1979, Feb. 24-28, 1979, Keyston, CO. LC 57-43769. (Advances in the Astronautical Sciences Ser.: Vol. 39). (Illus.). 492p. 1979. 45.00 (*0-87703-100-2*, Am Astronaut Soc) Univelt Inc.

Culp, Robert D., et al, eds. Guidance & Control 1982, Jan. 30-Feb. 3, 1982, Keystone, CO: 1982. LC 97-43769. (Advances in the Astronautical Sciences Ser.: Vol. 48). (Illus.). 558p. 1982. 65.00 (*0-87703-170-3*, Am Astronaut Soc); pap. 50.00 (*0-87703-171-1*, Am Astronaut Soc) Univelt Inc.

— Guidance & Control 1995, Feb. 1-5, 1995, Keystone, CO. LC 57-43769. (Advances in the Astronautical Sciences Ser.: Vol. 88). (Illus.). 600p. 1995. 120.00 (*0-87703-399-4*, Am Astronaut Soc) Univelt Inc.

— Guidance & Control 1985, Feb. 2-6, 1985, Keystone, CO: Feb. 2-6, 1985, Keystone, CO. LC 57-43769. (Advances in the Astronautical Sciences Ser.: Vol. 57). (Illus.). 618p. 1985. 65.00 (*0-87703-211-4*, Am Astronaut Soc); pap. 50.00 (*0-87703-212-2*, Am Astronaut Soc) Univelt Inc.

Culp, Robert D. & Bickley, George, eds. Guidance & Control 1993, Feb. 6-10, 1993, Keystone, CO. LC 57-43769. (Advances in the Astronautical Sciences Ser.: Vol. 81). (Illus.). 648p. 1993. 120.00 (*0-87703-365-X*, Am Astronaut Soc); pap. 90.00 (*0-87703-366-8*, Am Astronaut Soc) Univelt Inc.

Culp, Robert D. & Durrett, John C., eds. Guidance & Control 1986, Feb. 1-5, 1986, Keystone, CO. LC 57-43769. (Advances in the Astronautical Sciences Ser.: Vol. 61). (Illus.). 460p. 1986. 60.00 (*0-87703-257-2*, Am Astronaut Soc); pap. 50.00 (*0-87703-258-0*, Am Astronaut Soc) Univelt Inc.

Culp, Robert D. & Gravseth, Ario D., eds. Guidance & Control 1990, Feb. 3-7, 1990, Keystone, CO. LC 57-43769. (Advances in the Astronautical Sciences Ser.: Vol. 72). (Illus.). 676p. 1990. 95.00 (*0-87703-320-X*, Am Astronaut Soc); pap. 80.00 (*0-87703-321-8*, Am Astronaut Soc) Univelt Inc.

Culp, Robert D. & Igli, David A., eds. Guidance & Control, February 4-8 1998, Breckenridge, Colorado. (Advances in the Astronautical Science Ser.: Vol. 98). 706p. 1998. 120.00 (*0-87703-448-6*, Am Astronaut Soc); pap. 90.00 (*0-87703-449-4*, Am Astronaut Soc) Univelt Inc.

Culp, Robert D. & Kelly, Terry J., eds. Guidance & Control 1987, Jan. 31-Feb. 4, 1987, Keystone, CO. LC 57-43769. (Advances in the Astronautical Sciences Ser.: Vol. 63). (Illus.). 638p. 1987. 75.00 (*0-87703-268-8*, Am Astronaut Soc); pap. 60.00 (*0-87703-269-6*, Am Astronaut Soc) Univelt Inc.

Culp, Robert D. & Lewis, Robert A., eds. Guidance & Control 1989, Feb. 4-8, 1989, Keystone, CO. LC 57-43769. (Advances in the Astronautical Sciences Ser.: Vol. 68). (Illus.). 708p. 1989. 85.00 (*0-87703-299-8*, Am Astronaut Soc); pap. 70.00 (*0-87703-300-5*, Am Astronaut Soc) Univelt Inc.

Culp, Robert D. & McQuerry, James P., eds. Guidance & Control 1991, Feb. 2-6, 1991, Keystone, CO. LC 57-43769. (Advances in the Astronautical Sciences Ser.: Vol. 74). (Illus.). 730p. 1991. 120.00 (*0-87703-334-X*, Am Astronaut Soc); pap. 90.00 (*0-87703-335-8*, Am Astronaut Soc) Univelt Inc.

Culp, Robert D. & Medbery, James D., eds. Guidance & Control 1995, Feb. 1-5, 1995, Keystone, CO. LC 57-43769. (Advances in the Astronautical Sciences Ser.: Vol. 88). 600p. 1995. pap. 90.00 (*0-87703-400-1*, Am Astronaut Soc) Univelt Inc.

Culp, Robert D. & Odefey, Marvin L., eds. Guidance & Control 1996, Feb. 7-11, 1996, Breckenridge, CO. LC 57-43769. (Advances in the Astronautical Sciences Ser.: Vol. 92). (Illus.). 744p. 1996. 120.00 (*0-87703-412-5*, Am Astronaut Soc); pap. 90.00 (*0-87703-413-3*, Am Astronaut Soc) Univelt Inc.

Culp, Robert D. & Rausch, Ronald D., eds. Guidance & Control 1994, Feb. 2-6, 1994, Keystone, CO. LC 57-43769. (Advances in the Astronautical Sciences Ser.: Vol. 86). (Illus.). 700p. 1994. 120.00 (*0-87703-384-6*, Am Astronaut Soc); pap. 90.00 (*0-87703-385-4*, Am Astronaut Soc) Univelt Inc.

Culp, Robert D. & Shattuck, Paul L., eds. Guidance & Control 1988, Jan. 30-Feb. 3, 1988, Keystone, CO. LC 57-43769. (Advances in the Astronautical Sciences Ser.: Vol. 66). 576p. 1988. 75.00 (*0-87703-288-2*, Am Astronaut Soc) Univelt Inc.

— Guidance & Control 1988, Jan. 30-Feb. 3, 1988, Keystone, CO. LC 57-43769. (Advances in the Astronautical Sciences Ser.: Vol. 66). (Illus.). 576p. 1988. pap. 60.00 (*0-87703-289-0*, Am Astronaut Soc) Univelt Inc.

Culp, Robert D. & Stafford, Parker S., eds. Guidance & Control 1984, Feb. 4-8, Keystone, CO. LC 57-43769. (Advances in the Astronautical Sciences Ser.: Vol. 55). 500p. 1984. 60.00 (*0-87703-199-1*, Am Astronaut Soc); pap. 50.00 (*0-87703-200-9*, Am Astronaut Soc) Univelt Inc.

***Culp, Robert D. & Wiemer, Douglas, eds.** Guidance & Control 1999. (Advances in the Astronautical Sciences Ser.: Vol. 101). (Illus.). 528p. 1999. pap. 90.00 (*0-87703-457-5*, Am Astronaut Soc); lib. bdg. 120.00 (*0-87703-456-7*, Am Astronaut Soc) Univelt Inc.

C

Culp, Robert D. & Wiens, Stuart B., eds. Guidance & Control 1997, Feb. 5-9, 1997, Breckenridge, CO. LC 57-43769. (Advances in the Astronautical Sciences Ser.: Vol. 94). (Illus.). 458p. 1997. 120.00 (*0-87703-430-3*, Am Astronaut Soc); pap. 90.00 (*0-87703-431-1*, Am Astronaut Soc) Univelt Inc.

Culp, Robert D. & Zietz, Richard P., eds. Guidance & Control 1992, Feb. 2-6, 1992, Keystone, CO. LC 57-43769. (Advances in the Astronautical Sciences Ser.: Vol. 78). (Illus.). 754p. 1992. 120.00 (*0-87703-353-6*, Am Astronaut Soc); pap. 90.00 (*0-87703-354-4*, Am Astronaut Soc) Univelt Inc.

Culp, Stephanie. How to Conquer Clutter. 184p. 1989. pap. 12.99 (*0-89879-362-9*, Wrtrs Digest Bks) F & W Pubns Inc.

— How to Get Organized When You Don't Have the Time. (Illus.). 216p. 1986. pap. 14.99 (*0-89879-230-4*, Wrtrs Digest Bks) F & W Pubns Inc.

— 611 Ways to Do More in a Day. LC 98-10401. 128p. 1998. pap. 12.99 (*1-55870-475-2*, Betrwy Bks) F & W Pubns Inc.

— Stephanie Culp's 12 Month Organizer & Project Planner. 192p. 1995. pap. 12.99 (*1-55870-360-8*, Betrwy Bks) F & W Pubns Inc.

— Streamlining Your Life. 142p. 1991. pap. 11.99 (*0-89879-462-5*, Wrtrs Digest Bks) F & W Pubns Inc.

— You Can Find More Time for Yourself Every Day. LC 94-18456. 208p. 1994. pap. 12.99 (*1-55870-358-6*, Betrwy Bks) F & W Pubns Inc.

Culp, Wesner, Clup, Inc. & Owen, William P. Energy in Wastewater Treatment. (Illus.). 368p. (C). 1982. 56.00 (*0-13-277665-0*) P-H.

Culp/Wesner/Culp Staff. Handbook of Public Water Systems. Williams, Robert B. & Culp, Gordon L., eds. 1113p. 1986. 175.00 (*0-471-28871-3*, VNR) Wiley.

Culpan, Refik, ed. Multinational Strategic Alliances. LC 92-20709. (Illus.). 374p. 1993. pap. 24.95 (*1-56024-323-6*) Haworth Pr.

— Multinational Strategic Alliances. LC 92-20709. (Illus.). 374p. 1993. lib. bdg. 79.95 (*1-56024-322-8*) Haworth Pr.

Culpan, Refik Nino & Kumar, Brij, eds. Transformation Management in Postcommunist Countries: Organizational Requirements for a Market Economy. LC 94-31461. 272p. 1995. 69.50 (*0-89930-840-6*, Quorum Bks) Greenwood.

Culpeper, Jonathan. History of English. LC 97-215389. (Language Workbooks Ser.). 120p. (C). 1997. pap. 14.99 (*0-415-14591-0*) Routledge.

Culpeper, Jonathan, et al. Exploring the Language of Drama: From Text to Context. LC 97-42989. 192p. (C). 1998. 65.00 (*0-415-13794-2*); pap. 20.99 (*0-415-13795-0*) Routledge.

Culpeper, Nicholas. Complete Herbal. (Illus.). 1960. 29.95 (*0-685-21926-7*) Wehman.

— Culpeper's Complete Herbal & English Physician. enl. ed. (Illus.). 440p. 1987. reprint ed. pap. 12.50 (*0-916638-20-0*); reprint ed. text 35.00 (*0-916638-38-3*) Meyerbooks.

— Culpeper's Herbal Remedies. 1980. pap. 5.00 (*0-87980-025-9*) Wilshire.

Culpeper, Roy. The Multilateral Development Banks Vol. 5: Titans or Behemoths? 196p. 1997. 38.00 (*1-55587-470-3*); pap. 19.95 (*1-55587-496-7*) L Rienner.

Culpeper, Thomas. A Tract Against Usurie. LC 74-80170. (English Experience Ser.: No. 649). 22p. 1974. reprint ed. 15.00 (*90-221-0649-7*) Walter J Johnson.

Culpepper & Associates Inc. Staff. Employee Benefits in the Software Industry: A Survey of Current Practices. LC 98-178906. 168p. 1998. ring bd. 795.00 (*1-58128-020-3*) Culpepper.

Culpepper & Associates Inc. Staff & Coopers & Lybrand L. L. P. Staff. Financial Operating Ratios for Software Companies: A Benchmark for Financial Performance. 302p. 1998. ring bd. 995.00 (*1-58128-021-1*) Culpepper.

Culpepper & Associates Staff. Electronic Marketing Practices: The Internet, E-Mail & More. (Illus.). 220p. 1996. 695.00 (*1-58128-003-3*, QZ) Culpepper.

— Executive Pay: The Facts You Need to Establish Motivational Pay Plans for Software. (Illus.). 134p. 1997. ring bd. 695.00 (*1-58128-015-7*, XR) Culpepper.

— Marketing/Administrative Pay: The Facts You Need to Establish Motivational Pay Plans for Software Marketing & Administrative Professionals. (Illus.). 252p. 1997. ring bd. 695.00 (*1-58128-014-9*, DR) Culpepper.

— Phone Power: An Executive's Guide to Telesales & Telemarketing. (Illus.). 198p. 1996. pap. 295.00 (*1-58128-004-1*, LM) Culpepper.

— Re-Engineering the Software Company. 216p. 1995. pap. 295.00 (*1-58128-001-7*, HY) Culpepper.

— Sales Pay: The Facts You Need to Establish Motivational Pay Plans for Software Sales Professionals. (Illus.). 231p. 1997. ring bd. 795.00 (*1-58128-012-2*, CR) Culpepper.

— Small Company Pay: The Facts You Need to Establish an Affordable & Motivational Plan. (Illus.). 1997. ring bd. 495.00 (*1-58128-016-5*, UG) Culpepper.

— Software Industry Pay Library: The Software Industry's Definitive Source. (Illus.). 941p. 1997. ring bd. 2384.00 (*1-58128-017-3*, PL) Culpepper.

— Structures, Staffing, Turnover & Performance Management: Everything You Need to Structure Your Company, Plan Its Staffing Resources, Monitor Turnovers, & Develop Performance Plans. (Illus.). 160p. 1997. 650.00 (*1-58128-009-2*, JN/JT) Culpepper.

— Technical Pay: The Facts You Need to Attract & Retain Software Technical Professionals. (Illus.). 324p. 1997. ring bd. 795.00 (*1-58128-013-0*, TR) Culpepper.

— Workplace Issues in the Software Industry: A Comprehensive Look at the Relationship Between Human Resource Programs & Organization Performance. (Illus.). 200p. 1997. 495.00 (*1-58128-011-4*, IR) Culpepper.

Culpepper & Associates Staff & Vertana Consulting Staff. Software Pricing Trends: A Benchmark Guide to Boosting Revenue & Marketshare. (Illus.). 284p. 1997. ring bd. 795.00 (*1-58128-018-1*) Culpepper.

Culpepper & Associates Staff, jt. auth. see Bridges & Dunn-Raskin, LPP Staff.

Culpepper & Associates Staff, jt. auth. see Brinks, Jim.

Culpepper & Associates Staff, jt. auth. see Kormos, Joseph G.

Culpepper & Associates Staff, jt. auth. see Lewis, Ken.

Culpepper, Brandt. Establishing & Implementing Universal Newborn Hearing Screening Programs. 250p. 2000. pap. 49.95 (*1-56593-895-X*, 1750) Thomson Learn.

Culpepper, John. Laomi Is Not Home. 200p. (Orig.). (C). 1989. pap. 4.95 (*0-685-29152-9*) Warm Days Retirement.

Culpepper, John, jt. auth. see Amaro, Juan.

Culpepper, John, ed. & illus. see Amaro, Juan & Elder, Cindy.

Culpepper, Karen G. My Favorite Recipes. 150p. 1998. pap. 12.95 (*1-57502-928-6*, PO2558) Morris Pubng.

***Culpepper, Larry.** Softwood Drying. 350p. 2000. 54.00 (*0-87930-581-9*) Miller Freeman.

Culpepper, Marilyn M. Trials & Triumphs: Women of the American Civil War. 1994. pap. 18.95 (*0-87013-368-3*) Mich St U Pr.

Culpepper, Pat & Heard, Robert. Goal Line. LC 84-82423. (Illus.). 187p. 1984. 16.95 (*0-937642-02-9*) Honey Hill.

***Culpepper, Pepper D. & Finegold, David, eds.** The German Skills Machine: Sustaining Comparative Advantage in a Global Economy. LC 99-23020. (Policy & Institutions Ser.: Vol. 3). (Illus.). 496p. 1999. 85.00 (*1-57181-144-3*) Berghahn Bks.

***Culpepper, R. A., ed.** The Johannine Literature: An Introduction. 360p. 2000. pap. 25.00 (*1-84127-081-4*, Pub. by Sheffield Acad) CUP Services.

Culpepper, R. Alan. Anatomy of the Fourth Gospel: A Study in Literary Design. LC 82-16302. 256p. 1987. text 20.00 (*0-8006-2068-2*, 1-2068, Fortress Pr) Augsburg Fortress.

— Critical Readings of John 6. LC 98-112695. (Biblical Interpretation Ser.: No. 22). xiii, 289p. 1997. 97.00 (*90-04-10579-4*) Brill Academic Pubs.

— The Gospel & Letters of John. LC 98-18486. (Interpreting Biblical Texts Ser.). 1998. pap. write for info. (*0-687-01239-2*) Abingdon.

— The Gospel & Letters of John. Matthews, Rex, ed. LC 98-18486. (Interpreting Biblical Texts Ser.). 224p. 1998. pap. 19.95 (*0-687-00851-4*) Abingdon.

— The Johannine School: An Evaluation of the Johannine-School Hypothesis Based on an Investigation of the Nature of Ancient Schools. LC 75-34235. (Society of Biblical Literature. Dissertation Ser.: No. 26). 328p. reprint ed. pap. 101.70 (*0-8357-9576-4*, 201752500007) Bks Demand.

— John, the Son of Zebedee: The Life of a Legend. (Personalities of the New Testament Ser.). 2000. pap. 24.00 (*0-8006-3167-6*, Fortress Pr) Augsburg Fortress.

Culpepper, R. Alan. John, the Son of Zebedee: The Life of a Legend. LC 93-27796. 400p. 1994. text 39.95 (*0-87249-962-6*) U of SC Pr.

Culpepper, R. Alan & Black, C. Clifton, eds. Exploring the Gospel of John. 488p. 1996. 42.00 (*0-664-22083-5*) Westminster John Knox.

Culpepper, R. Brian, jt. auth. see Hanna, Karen C.

Culpepper, Raymond F. Powerliving: Practical Principles for Living in the Spirit. 143p. 1997. pap. 9.99 (*0-87148-974-0*) Pathway Pr.

Culpepper, Robert H. Evaluating the Charismatic Movement: A Theological & Biblical Approach. 192p. 1987. reprint ed. pap. 6.95 (*0-913029-17-3*) Stevens Bk Pr.

— Interpreting the Atonement. 170p. 1986. reprint ed. pap. 9.95 (*0-913029-13-0*) Stevens Bk Pr.

Culpepper, Rodney E. Breaking the Cycle of Date: A Cutting-Edge Approach to Church Stewardship. 160p. (Orig.). 1995. pap. 11.95 (*0-9647937-0-9*) Pepperfield Pubng.

Culpepper, Roy & Pestieau, Caroline, eds. Development & Global Governance: Conference Proceedings, May 2, 1995, Ottawa, Canada. LC 96-900352. 147p. 1996. pap. 12.00 (*0-88936-805-8*, Pub. by IDRC Bks) Stylus Pub VA.

Culpepper, William V. Crack. 86p. 1997. 29.95 (*1-892024-01-2*); pap. 29.95 (*1-892024-00-4*) Vicker Staff.

— Expressions. (Illus.). 72p. 1998. 29.95 (*1-892024-03-9*); pap. 25.00 (*1-892024-02-0*) Vicker Staff.

Culpin, D. J. Marivaux & Reason: A Study in Early Enlightenment Thought. LC 92-34832. (American University Studies: Romance Languages & Literature: Ser. II, Vol. 200). IX, 152p. (C). 1993. text 37.95 (*0-8204-2024-7*) P Lang Pubng.

Culpitt, Ian. Welfare & Citizenship: Beyond the Crisis of the Welfare State? (Theory, Culture & Society Ser.). 224p. (C). 1992. 65.00 (*0-8039-8617-3*); pap. 24.95 (*0-8039-8618-1*) Sage.

Culshaw, B. Optical Fibre Sensing & Signal Processing. Flood, J. E. & Hughes, C. J., eds. 256p. 1984. boxed set 99.00 (*0-906048-99-0*, TE904) INSPEC Inc.

Culshaw, B., et al. First European Conference on Smart Structures & Materials: Proceedings of the International Conference Held in Glasgow, 12-14 May 1992. (Smart Materials & Structures Ser.). (Illus.). 436p. 1992. 200.00 (*0-7503-0222-4*) IOP Pub.

Culshaw, Brian. Smart Structures & Materials. LC 95-48914. 280p. 1995. 79.00 (*0-89006-681-7*) Artech Hse.

Culshaw, Brian & Dakin, John, eds. Optical Fiber Sensors, Vol. III. (Optoelectronics Engineering Ser.). 237p. 1996. 89.00 (*0-89006-932-8*) Artech Hse.

— Optical Fiber Sensors Vol. IV: Applications, Analysis, & Future Trends. (Optoelectronics Engineering Ser.). 540p. 1997. 109.00 (*0-89006-940-9*) Artech Hse.

Culshaw, Brian & Jones, Julian D., eds. European Workshop on Optical Fibre Sensors, Vol. 3483. LC 98-233171. 324p. 1998. 80.00 (*0-8194-2938-4*) SPIE.

Culshaw, Brian, jt. ed. see Marcus, Michael A.

Culshaw, David. The Complete Catalog of British Cars, 1895-1975. (Illus.). 496p. 1997. 39.95 (*1-874105-93-6*, Pub. by Vloce Pub) Motorbooks Intl.

Culshaw, John. The Concerto. LC 78-60138. (World of Music Ser.). (Illus.). 71p. 1979. reprint ed. lib. bdg. 35.00 (*0-313-20547-7*, CUCO, Greenwood Pr) Greenwood.

— The Concerto: Music Book Index. 71p. 1993. reprint ed. lib. bdg. 69.00 (*0-7812-9643-9*) Rprt Serv.

Culshaw, Murray, jt. auth. see Norton, Michael.

Culter, Horace & Cutler, Stephen J. Biologically Active Products. LC 99-13027. 296p. 1999. boxed set 99.95 (*0-8493-1887-4*) CRC Pr.

Culter, Suzanne. Managing Decline: Japan's Coal Industry Restructuring & Community Response. LC 98-48397. (Illus.). 256p. (C). 1999. pap. 29.95 (*0-8248-2145-9*) UH Pr.

— Managing Decline: Japan's Coal Industry Restructuring & Community Response. LC 98-48397. (Illus.). 256p. (C). 1999. text 53.00 (*0-8248-2060-6*) UH Pr.

Cultice, Wendell W. Youth's Battle for the Ballot: A History of Voting Age in America, 291. LC 91-26373. (Contributions in Political Science Ser.: No. 291). 288p. 1992. 59.95 (*0-313-27962-4*, CYB/, Greenwood Pr) Greenwood.

Culton, Martha. Promises Kept. (Illus.). 264p. 1995. text 18.99 (*0-9645306-0-0*) United Gospel.

Culton, Sarah A. Psychology of Stress. 207p. (Orig.). 1991. pap. text 18.95 (*0-89420-281-2*, 345000) Natl Book.

Culton, Wilma. Down at the Billabong. LC 92-31951. (Voyages Ser.). (Illus.). (J). 1993. 3.75 (*0-383-03565-1*) SRA McGraw.

Cultru, P. Premier Voyage du Sieur de la Courbe Fait a la Coste d'Afrique en 1685. (B. E. Ser.: No. 164). (FRE.). 1913. 45.00 (*0-8115-3079-5*) Periodicals Srv.

Cultural Alliance of Greater Hampton Roads Staff. Sketches: Cultural Resource Directory. (Illus.). 81p. (Orig.). 1993. pap. 10.00 (*0-943133-05-X*) Cultural Alliance.

— Sketches: Cultural Resource Directory, 1989-90. (Illus.). 190p. 1989. pap. 10.00 (*0-943133-02-5*) Cultural Alliance.

— Sketches: Cultural Resource Directory, 1992-93. 8th ed. (Illus.). 75p. (Orig.). 1992. pap. 10.00 (*0-943133-04-1*) Cultural Alliance.

— Sketches Plus: Cultural Resource Directory Addendum. (Illus.). 52p. (Orig.). 1990. pap. 10.00 (*0-943133-03-3*) Cultural Alliance.

Cultural Environment Movement, jt. auth. see Duncan, Kate.

Cultural Heritage of the Plains Symposium Staff. The Great Plains: Environment & Culture. Blouet, Brian W. & Luebke, Frederick C., eds. LC 79-1152. (Illus.). 274p. reprint ed. pap. 85.00 (*0-608-08691-6*, 206921400004) Bks Demand.

Cultural Ministers Council (Australia) Staff. National Conservation & Preservation Policy for Movable Cultural Heritage. LC 97-162210. iv, 8 p. 1995. write for info. (*0-642-23354-3*, Pub. by Aust Inst Criminology) Advent Bks Div.

Cultural Relics Exchange Center of the PRC Staff, ed. Treasures: 300 Best Excavated Antiques from China. (Illus.). 331p. 1992. 69.95 (*0-934643-01-6*) Cypress Co.

Culver. Facets of Physics. Date not set. text, teacher ed. write for info. (*0-314-01720-8*) West Pub.

Culver Alumni Staff. American Traditions: Art from the Collections of the Culver Alumni. LC 93-61168. (Illus.). 356p. 1996. 50.00 (*0-8061-9942-3*) U of Okla Pr.

Culver-Aversa, Amy, ed. see Orchard, Paul.

Culver, Bruce. Afrika Korps in Action. (Combat Troops in Action Ser.: Vol. 4). (Illus.). 50p. 2000. reprint ed. pap. 9.95 (*0-89747-079-6*, 3004) Squad Sig Pubns.

— Panzer Colors: Markings of the German Army Panzer Forces 1939-45, Vol. 2. (Illus.). 96p. 1996. reprint ed. pap. 14.95 (*0-89747-069-9*, 6253) Squad Sig Pubns.

— The SdKfz 251 Half Track. (New Vanguard Ser.: Vol. 25). (Illus.). 48p. 1999. pap. 12.95 (*1-85532-846-1*, Pub. by Ospry) Stackpole.

— Tiger in Action. (Armor in Action Ser.). (Illus.). 50p. 1989. pap. 9.95 (*0-89747-230-6*, 2027) Squad Sig Pubns.

Culver, Bruce & Feist, Uwe. "Schwere Panzer" Konigstiger - Jagdtiger - Elefant. (Illus.). 176p. 1998. 45.00 (*0-9633824-9-7*) Ryton Pubns.

— Tiger I & Stormtiger in Detail. (Illus.). (YA). 40.00 (*0-9633824-0-3*) Ryton Pubns.

Culver, Bruce, jt. auth. see Feist, Uwe.

Culver, Carolyn S., et al. Identification & Management of the Exotic Sabellid Pest in California Cultured Abalone. (Illus.). 30p. 1997. pap. text 6.00 (*1-888691-05-0*, T-041) U CA Calif Sea.

Culver, Chuck. The Carousel Shoppe & Other Stories. 201p. 1996. 22.95 (*0-9654951-0-8*); pap. 11.95 (*0-9654951-1-6*) Thumbprint CA.

***Culver, Chuck.** We Happy Few: A Novel. 1999. pap. 12.50 (*0-9654951-3-2*) Thumbprint CA.

***Culver, Dan.** My Little Everest: A Story about Dealing with Fear. (Illus.). 48p. 2000. 11.95 (*1-55039-105-4*) Sono Nis Pr.

Culver, David C., et al. Adaptation & Natural Selection in Caves: The Evolution of Gammarus Minus. LC 94-5362. (Illus.). 240p. (C). 1995. text 44.00 (*0-674-00425-6*, CULADA) HUP.

Culver, Dennis J. Albion & Ariel Vol. 166: British Puritanism & the Birth of Political Zionism. LC 94-16473. (American University Studies: No. VII). IX, 238p. (C). 1995. text 48.95 (*0-8204-2303-3*) P Lang Pubng.

Culver, Diann. Dinosaurs: A Thematic Unit. (Thematic Units Ser.). (Illus.). 80p. (J). (gr. 3-5). 1993. student ed. 9.95 (*1-55734-238-5*) Tchr Create Mat.

***Culver, Diann.** Thematic Unit Earthquakes & Volcanoes. (Illus.). 80p. 2000. pap., teacher ed. 9.95 (*1-57690-591-8*, TCM 2591) Tchr Create Mat.

Culver, Dorothy C. Bibliography of Crime & Criminal Justice: Nineteen Twenty-Seven to Nineteen Thirty-One. LC 69-16228. (Criminology, Law Enforcement, & Social Problems Ser.: No. 99). 1969. reprint ed. 30.00 (*0-87585-099-5*) Patterson Smith.

Culver, Dorothy C., ed. Bibliography of Crime & Criminal Justice: Nineteen Thirty-Two to Nineteen Thirty-Seven. LC 69-16227. (Criminology, Law Enforcement, & Social Problems Ser.: No. 100). 1969. reprint ed. 30.00 (*0-87585-100-2*) Patterson Smith.

Culver, Edith D. Talespins: A Story of Early Aviation Days. LC 85-17359. (Illus.). 148p. (Orig.). 1986. pap. 10.95 (*0-86534-073-0*) Sunstone Pr.

Culver, Francis B., ed. Society of Colonial Wars in the State of Maryland Vol. II: Genealogies of the Members & Record of Services of Ancestors. 399p. 1997. reprint ed. pap. 35.00 (*0-8063-4687-6*) Clearfield Co.

Culver, Gregory L. E-Z Abegeez: Arterial Blood Gases. LC 98-90061. 1998. pap. 10.95 (*0-533-12697-5*) Vantage.

Culver, Henry B. The Book of Old Ships: From Egyptian Galleys to Clipper Ships. unabridged ed. LC 92-21987. (Pictorial Archive Ser.). (Illus.). 256p. 1992. reprint ed. pap. text 7.95 (*0-486-27332-6*) Dover.

Culver, Joann, tr. see Joy, Janet.

Culver, John C., jt. auth. see Hyde, John.

Culver, John H. Politics & Public Policies in California. 1995. pap. text. write for info. (*0-07-015095-8*) McGraw.

— Politics & Public Policies in California. LC 96-18017. 304p. (C). 1996. pap. 34.06 (*0-07-015094-X*) McGraw.

Culver, John H., jt. auth. see Brudney, Kent M.

Culver, John H., jt. auth. see Stumpf, Harry P.

Culver, Keith, ed. Readings in the Philosophy of Law. 600p. 1999. pap. 34.95 (*1-55111-179-9*) Broadview Pr.

Culver, Kenneth W. Gene Therapy: A Handbook for Physicians. (Illus.). 128p. 1994. lib. bdg. 44.95 (*0-913113-63-8*) M Liebert.

Culver Meadows, Iris & Meadows, Carolyn Jean. Jenny of the Ozarks, Grown Up. (Illus.). 128p. Date not set. pap. 5.95 (*0-9624710-3-8*) Culver-Meadows.

Culver, R. B. & Ianna, Philip A. The Gemini Syndrome: A Scientific Evaluation of Astrology. LC 84-42791. (Science & the Paranormal Ser.). (Illus.). 234p. 1984. reprint ed. pap. 18.95 (*0-87975-264-5*) Prometheus Bks.

Culver, Raymond B. Horace Mann & Religion in the Massachusetts Public Schools. LC 72-89168. (American Education: Its Men, Institutions, & Ideas. Series 1). 1974. reprint ed. 19.95 (*0-405-01406-6*) Ayer.

Culver, Robert. A Wakeup Call. 1993. pap. 6.95 (*1-883858-22-4*) Witness CA.

Culver, Robert D. The Histories & Prophecies of Daniel. 192p. (Orig.). 1980. pap. 9.99 (*0-88469-131-4*) BMH Bks.

Culver, Roger B. & Ianna, Philip A. Astrology: True or False? rev. ed. LC 88-43054.Tr. of Gemini Syndrome. 228p. 1988. pap. 19.95 (*0-87975-483-4*) Prometheus Bks.

Culver, Ruth. How to Hold a Quilt Show: A Practical Guide. (Illus.). 176p. (Orig.). 1995. pap. 20.00 (*0-9615155-0-3*) Culver Pubns.

Culver, Shannon M., ed. see Fisher, Dale.

Culver, Stephen, jt. auth. see Buzas, Martin A.

Culver, Stephen J. Distribution of Recent Benthic Foraminifera off the North American Pacific Coast from California to Baja. LC 86-600087. (Smithsonian Contributions to the Marine Sciences Ser.: No. 28). 638p. reprint ed. pap. 197.80 (*0-608-15494-6*, 202968300063) Bks Demand.

***Culver, Stephen J. & Rawson, Peter F., eds.** Biotic Responses to Global Change: The Last 145 Million Years. LC 99-16232. (Illus.). 400p. 2000. write for info. (*0-521-66304-0*) Cambridge U Pr.

Culver, Todd A. Discover Birds. (Discover Ser.). (Illus.). 48p. (J). (gr. 3-6). 1992. lib. bdg. 15.95 (*1-878363-66-2*, HTS Bks) Forest Hse.

Culver, Tom & Iland, Nancy G., eds. The Murder, She Wrote Cookbook: Recipes from the Cast & Crew. LC 97-5961. 288p. 1997. pap. 16.95 (*1-55652-316-5*) Chicago Review.

Culver, Will, tr. see Crepin, Joseph.

Culverhouse, Cecil. To Not be Afraid. 130p. 1998. pap. 8.00 (*1-57502-148-X*, PO2415) Morris Pubng.

Culverhouse, Mark, et al. Special Edition Using Visual J Plus Plus. LC 96-69952. 704p. 1996. pap. text 49.99 incl. cd-rom (*0-7897-0884-1*) Que.

Culverson, Donald. Contesting Apartheid: U. S. Activism, 1960-1987. LC 99-22528. 175p. 1999. 75.00 (*0-8133-6669-0*, Pub. by Westview) HarpC.

Culverwel, Nathanael. An Elegant & Learned Discourse on the Light of Nature, 1652: Nathanael Culverwel (1618-1651) Wellek, Rene, ed. LC 75-11215. (British Philosophers & Theologians of the 17th & 18th Centuries Ser.). 456p. 1978. lib. bdg. 10.00 (*0-8240-1769-2*) Garland.

Culverwell, Geoffrey, tr. see Stang, Ragna.

Culwick, Arthur T. & Culwick, G. M. Ubena of the Rivers. LC 76-44707. reprint ed. 69.50 (*0-404-15883-8*) AMS Pr.

Culwick, G. M., jt. auth. see Culwick, Arthur T.

C

An Asterisk (*) at the beginning of an entry indicates that the title is appearing for the first time.

Cumming, Robert B., Jr. Archaeological Investigations at the Tuttle Creek Dam, Kansas, Paper No. 10. fac. ed. (Smithsonian Institution, Bureau of American Ethnology Ser.: Bulletin 169). 52p. (C). 1958. reprint ed. pap. text 6.56 (*1-55567-691-X*) Coyote Press.

Cumming, Robert D. Human Nature & History: A Study of the Development of Liberal Political Thought, 2 vols. LC 68-54081. 1003p. 1969. lib. bdg. 54.00 (*0-226-12364-2*) U Ch Pr.

— Phenomenology & Deconstruction: Method & Imagination, Vol. 2. 404p. 1992. pap. text 28.00 (*0-226-12369-3*) U Ch Pr.

— Phenomenology & Deconstruction: Method & Imagination, Vol. 2. 404p. 1992. lib. bdg. 61.00 (*0-226-12368-5*) U Ch Pr.

— Phenomenology & Deconstruction Vol. 1: The Dream Is Over. LC 91-12696. 268p. 1991. lib. bdg. 60.00 (*0-226-12366-9*) U Ch Pr.

— Phenomenology & Deconstruction Vol. 1: The Dream Is Over. LC 91-12696. 268p. 1991. pap. text 21.00 (*0-226-12367-7*) U Ch Pr.

— The Philosophy of Sartre. 1972. pap. 11.00 (*0-394-71808-9*, V808) Vin Bks.

— Starting Point: An Introduction to the Dialectic of Existence. LC 78-16317. 596p. 1996. lib. bdg. 48.00 (*0-226-12347-2*) U Ch Pr.

— Starting Point: An Introduction to the Dialectic of Existence. LC 78-16317. 596p. reprint ed. pap. 184.80 (*0-608-08813-7*, 206945200004) Bks Demand.

Cumming, Susanna. Functional Change: The Case of Malay Constituent Order. (Discourse Perspectives on Grammar Ser.: No. 2). (Illus.). xiii, 253p. (C). 1991. lib. bdg. 113.85 (*0-89925-524-8*) Mouton.

Cumming, Valerie. Royal Dress: The Image & the Reality, 1580 to the Present. 225p. 1989. 49.95 (*0-8419-1267-X*) Holmes & Meier.

— The Visual History of Costume Accessories: From Hats to Shoes - 400 Years of Costume Accessories. (Illus.). 192p. 1998. pap. 29.95 (*0-89676-233-5*, Costume & Fashion Pr) QSMG Ltd.

Cumming, Valerie, et al. Museum of London: A Souvenir Guide to the Collection. (Illus.). 128p. 1997. 35.00 (*1-85759-126-7*, Pub. by P Wilson) Scala Books.

Cumming, Valerie, jt. auth. see Ribeiro, Aileen.

Cumming, Valerie, ed. see Baker, Patricia.

Cumming, Valerie, ed. see Carnegy, Vicky.

Cumming, Valerie, ed. see Connikie, Yvonne.

Cumming, Valerie, ed. see Costantino, Maria.

Cumming, Valerie, ed. see Feldman, Elane.

Cumming, Valerie, ed. see Herald, Jacqueline.

Cumming, W. J. A Color Atlas of Muscle Pathology. LC 94-42133. (Illus.). 1994. 130.00 (*0-7234-2016-5*) Wolfe Pub.

Cumming, W. P., ed. The Revelations of Saint Birgitta. (EETS, OS Ser.: No. 178). 1974. reprint ed. 40.00 (*0-527-00175-9*) Periodicals Srv.

Cumming, William K. Follow ME. 6.95 (*0-917920-01-5*); pap. 1.95 (*0-917920-00-7*) Mustardseed.

Cumming, William P. British Maps of Colonial America. LC 73-84190. 126p. reprint ed. pap. 39.10 (*0-8357-7425-2*, 202408900035) Bks Demand.

— Mapping the North Carolina Coast: Sixteenth-Century Cartography & the Roanoke Voyages. (America's 400th Anniversary Ser.). (Illus.). xii, 144p. (Orig.). 1988. pap. 12.00 (*0-86526-232-2*) NC Archives.

— North Carolina in Maps. viii, 36p. 1992. pap. 30.00 (*0-86526-137-7*) NC Archives.

— The Southeast in Early Maps. LC 97-45978. (Fred W. Morrison Series in Southern Studies). (Illus.). 504p. 1998. 90.00 (*0-8078-2371-6*) U of NC Pr.

Cummingham, Edward P. Digital Filtering: An Introduction. 560p. 1994. text 96.95 (*0-471-12475-3*) Wiley.

Cumminghan, William A., jt. auth. see Davis, Grant M.

Cummings. Current Perspectives Biology, 1998. LC 97-223395. (Biology Ser.). 1997. 17.95 (*0-314-20638-8*) Wadsworth Pub.

— Current Perspectives in Genetics. 2nd ed. LC 99-462691. (Environmental Science Ser.). 1999. 18.95 (*0-534-25280-X*) Wadsworth Pub.

— Current Prespectives Genetics: 1997 Edition. 1997. 12.00 (*0-314-20639-6*) Wadsworth Pub.

Cummings. Human Heredity. 4th ed. LC 97-999. 550p. 1997. 52.50 (*0-314-09578-0*) West Pub.

Cummings. Human Heredity: Principles & Issues. 5th ed. (Environmental Science Ser.). 1999. pap. text 50.50 (*0-534-37376-3*) Brooks-Cole.

— Human Heredity: Principles & Issues. 5th ed. LC 99-37549. (Environmental Science Ser.). 1999. 50.50 (*0-534-52372-2*) Wadsworth Pub.

— Human Heredity: Prinipies & Issues. 4th ed. (Environmental Science Ser.). 1997. 13.50 (*0-314-22461-0*) Wadsworth Pub.

— Human Heredity with Infotrac. 4th ed. (Environmental Science Ser.). 1997. 52.50 (*0-534-54093-7*) Wadsworth Pub.

***Cummings.** A L'aventure: A Four Skills Approach to Beginning French Student Text 487p. 1998. text 75.95 incl. audio (*0-471-17723-7*) Wiley.

— A L'aventure A Four Skills Approach to Beginning French Student Text. 487p. 1997. 75.95 incl. audio (*0-471-17720-2*) Wiley.

Cummings. Organizational Development. 5th ed. Date not set. pap. text, teacher ed. write for info. (*0-314-01983-9*) West Pub.

— PH Training Handbook. 1994. text 69.95 (*0-13-030578-2*) S&S Trade.

— Science & Life. Date not set. write for info. (*0-314-09586-1*) West Pub.

— Student Notetaking Guide to Biology. 1996. pap. 12.25 (*0-314-21310-4*) Wadsworth Pub.

— U. S. & Texas - Government: Telecourse Study Guide. (C). 1998. pap. text, student ed. 21.00 (*0-15-507190-4*, Pub. by Harcourt Coll Pubs) Harcourt.

— U. S. & Texas - Politics: Telecourse Study Guide. (C). 1998. pap. text, student ed. 26.50 (*0-15-507191-2*) Harcourt.

Cummings, jt. auth. see Klug.

Cummings, A. J. & Devine, T. M., eds. Industry, Business & Society in Scotland since 1700: Essays in Honour of John Butt. 200p. (Orig.). 1997. text 60.00 (*0-85976-401-X*, Pub. by J Donald) St Mut.

Cummings, A. L., et al. The Crowninshield-Bentley House. LC 76-16905. (Historic House Booklet Ser.: No. 2). 1976. 3.00 (*0-88389-060-7*, PEMP201, Essx Institute) Peabody Essex Mus.

Cummings, Abbott L. The Framed Houses of Massachusetts Bay, 1625-1725. LC 78-8390. (Illus.). 275p. 1982. pap. 29.95 (*0-674-31681-9*) Belknap Pr.

Cummings, Abbott L. & Little, Nina F. Bed Hangings: A Treatise on Fabrics & Styles in the Curtaining of Beds, 1650-1850. LC 94-28239. (Illus.). 74p. 1994. reprint ed. pap. 15.95 (*0-87451-972-1*) U Pr of New Eng.

Cummings, Alan, jt. auth. see Bailey-Cummings, Joanne.

Cummings, Alyece. Painless Fractions. LC 98-23068. (Illus.). 224p. (J). 1998. pap. 8.95 (*0-7641-0445-4*) Barron.

Cummings, Anne C. & Charvier-Berman, Evelyne. A l'Aventure: An Introduction to French Language & Francophone Cultures. LC 96-44828. 576p. 1996. text. write for info. (*0-471-30943-5*) Wiley.

Cummings, Anne C., jt. auth. see Charvier-Berman, Evelyne.

Cummings, Anthony, ed. see Owens, Jessie A.

Cummings, Anthony M. The Politicized Muse: Medici Festivals, 1512-1537. (Essays on the Arts Ser.). (Illus.). 250p. 1992. text 49.50 (*0-691-09142-0*, Pub. by Princeton U Pr) Cal Prin Full Svc.

Cummings, Anthony M. University Libraries & Scholarly Communication: A Study Prepared for the Andrew W. Mellon Foundation. LC 92-44941. 205p. 1992. pap. 8.00 (*0-918006-22-8*) Assn Res Lib.

Cummings, Barbara & Power, Jo-Ann. Prime Time. 384p. 1992. mass mkt. 4.99 (*1-55817-667-5*, Pinncle Kensgtn) Kensgtn Pub Corp.

— Risks. 480p. 1993. mass mkt. 4.99 (*1-55817-747-7*, Pinncle Kensgtn) Kensgtn Pub Corp.

Cummings, Barton. Binh Minh for Solo Piano. (Contemporary Keyboard Ser.: No. 1). 2p. 1989. pap. text 3.00 (*1-56571-004-5*) PRB Prods.

— Brief Moments for Solo Tuba. (Contemporary Instrumental Ser.: No. 3). i, 5p. 1989. pap. text 5.00 (*1-56571-020-7*) PRB Prods.

— Fantasia Breve for Tuba & Piano. (Contemporary Instrumental Ser.: No. 1). i, 16p. 1989. pap. text 12.00 (*1-56571-002-9*) PRB Prods.

— From the Psalms, for a Cappella SATB Chorus. (University Choral Ser.: No. 2). 12p. 1992. pap. text 2.00 (*1-56571-074-6*, UC002) PRB Prods.

— Miniatures for Tuba & Piano. (Contemporary Instrumental Ser.: No. 5). 9p. 1991. pap. text 7.00 (*1-56571-000-2*) PRB Prods.

Cummings, Barton, ed. see Edwards, Clara.

Cummings, Bernice & Schuck, Victoria. Women Organizing: An Anthology. LC 79-18956. 422p. 1979. 37.00 (*0-8108-1245-2*) Scarecrow.

Cummings, Bill. A Master's Guide to Atlantic Salmon Fishing. LC 95-10516. (Illus.). 288p. 1995. pap. 34.95 (*0-07-015059-1*, Ragged Mntain) McGraw-Hill Prof.

Cummings, Calvin K. Confessing Christ. 3rd rev. ed. (Orig.). 1977. pap. 1.45 (*0-934688-04-4*) Great Comm Pubns.

Cummings, Carol. Copy the Cat. (Learn with Me Ser.). (Illus.). 24p. (Orig.). (J). (ps-3). 1994. pap. 4.99 (*1-881660-01-X*) Teaching WA.

— Finding Feelings. (Learn with Me Ser.). (Illus.). 24p. (Orig.). 1992. pap. 4.99 (*1-881660-00-1*) Teaching WA.

— The Get-Alongs. (Illus.). 68p. 1993. pap. 5.99 (*1-881660-02-8*) Teaching WA.

— I'm Always in Trouble. (Learn with Me Ser.). (Illus.). 24p. (Orig.). (J). (ps-3). 1991. pap. 4.99 (*0-9614574-5-7*) Teaching WA.

— Managing a Cooperative Classroom. rev. ed. (Illus.). 108p. (C). 1997. reprint ed. pap. 5.00 (*1-881660-04-4*) Teaching WA.

— Managing a Diverse Classroom. (Illus.). 132p. 1995. pap. 14.95 (*1-881660-03-6*) Teaching WA.

— Managing to Teach. 2nd ed. (Illus.). 168p. (Orig.). (C). 1996. pap. text 14.95 (*0-9614574-0-6*) Teaching WA.

— Peering in on Peers: Coaching Teachers. (Illus.). 167p. (C). 1985. pap. 8.95 (*0-9614574-2-2*) Teaching WA.

— Plan to Teach: Page a Day. (Illus.). 224p. (J). (gr. k-12). 1987. pap. 5.95 (*0-685-40556-7*) Teaching WA.

— Plan to Teach: 2 Pages per Week. (Illus.). 176p. (C). 1988. pap. 5.95 (*1-881660-05-2*) Teaching WA.

— Sharing Is Caring. (Learn with Me Ser.). (Illus.). 24p. (Orig.). (J). (ps-3). 1992. pap. 4.99 (*0-9614574-9-X*) Teaching WA.

— Sticks & Stones. (Illus.). 24p. (Orig.). (J). (ps-3). 1992. pap. 4.99 (*0-9614574-8-1*) Teaching WA.

— Tattlin' Madeline. (Learn with Me Ser.). (Illus.). 24p. (Orig.). (J). (ps-3). 1991. pap. 4.99 (*0-9614574-4-9*) Teaching WA.

— Teaching Makes a Difference. 2nd ed. (Illus.). 224p. (C). 1990. reprint ed. pap. text 8.95 (*0-9614574-1-4*) Teaching WA.

— Win-Win Day. (Learn with Me Ser.). (Illus.). 24p. (Orig.). (J). (ps-3). 1991. pap. 4.99 (*0-9614574-6-5*) Teaching WA.

— Won't You Ever Listen? (Illus.). 24p. (Orig.). (J). (ps-3). 1992. pap. 4.99 (*0-9614574-7-3*) Teaching WA.

Cummings, Carolyn. Creating Good Schools for Young Children: Right from the Start. 2nd ed. 48p. 1995. pap. 12.00 (*1-58434-002-9*) NASBE.

Cummings, Charles. Eco-Spirituality: Toward a Reverent Life. 1991. pap. 9.95 (*0-8091-3251-6*) Paulist Pr.

— Monastic Practices. pap. 8.95 (*0-87907-975-4*); pap. 8.95 (*0-87907-875-8*) Cistercian Pubns.

Cummings, Charles, tr. see Hausherr, Irenee.

Cummings, Charles F., jt. auth. see Cunningham, John T.

Cummings, Charles L. The Great War Relic. (Illus.). 48p. 1995. reprint ed. pap. 7.50 (*0-914905-51-1*) Detroit Bk Pr.

Cummings, Charles M. Yankee Quaker Confederate General: The Curious Career of Bushrod Rust Johnson. (Illus.). 420p. 1993. reprint ed. 28.95 (*0-9626034-3-0*) Generals Bks.

Cummings, Charles W. Otolaryngology: Head & Neck Surgery. 1996. text 495.00 incl. cd-rom (*0-8151-2071-0*); text 895.00 incl. cd-rom (*0-8151-2076-1*) Mosby Inc.

Cummings, Charles W., et al. Otolaryngology: Head & Neck Surgery. 3rd ed. (Illus.). 3000p. (C). (gr. 13). 1998. text 495.00 (*0-8151-2067-2*, 29857) Mosby Inc.

***Cummings, Charles W., Jr., et al.** Otolaryngology: Head & Neck Surgery Review. 320p. (C). 1998. text. write for info. (*0-323-00688-4*) Mosby Inc.

Cummings, Cherilyn, jt. ed. see Ragan, Andrew.

Cummings, Connie. Cracker Still Lives Here: A Story of Living, Loving & Healing. Arden, Dan, ed. (Illus.). 128p. (Orig.). 1995. pap. 7.95 (*0-9641683-0-8*) Rivers Edge.

Cummings, Cynthia, jt. auth. see Broome, Betsy.

Cummings, Cynthia H. Christmas Bells. (Illus.). 84p. (J). (ps up). 1995. 10.95 (*1-881811-10-7*) H Peterson Pr.

— Christmas Dreams. (Illus.). 112p. 1992. 39.95 (*1-881811-09-3*) H Peterson Pr.

— Christmas Friends. (Illus.). 84p. (J). (ps up). 1996. 10.95 (*1-881811-11-5*) H Peterson Pr.

— Christmas Joy. (Illus.). 84p. (J). (ps up). 1986. 10.95 (*1-881811-05-0*) H Peterson Pr.

— Christmas Love. 5th ed. (Illus.). 84p. 1984. reprint ed. 10.95 (*1-881811-03-4*) H Peterson Pr.

— Christmas Memories. 4th ed. (Illus.). 84p. 1982. reprint ed. 10.95 (*1-881811-02-6*) H Peterson Pr.

— Christmas Ribbons. 8th ed. (Illus.). 84p. 1980. reprint ed. 10.95 (*1-881811-01-8*) H Peterson Pr.

— Christmas Spirit. (Illus.). 84p. (J). (ps up). 1989. 10.95 (*1-881811-08-5*) H Peterson Pr.

— Christmas Surprise. 2nd ed. (Illus.). 84p. (J). (ps up). 1985. reprint ed. 10.95 (*1-881811-04-2*) H Peterson Pr.

— Christmas Treasures. (Illus.). 84p. 1988. 10.95 (*1-881811-07-7*) H Peterson Pr.

— Christmas Wishes. (Illus.). 84p. 1987. 10.95 (*1-881811-06-9*) H Peterson Pr.

Cummings, D., tr. see Makrakis, Apostolos.

Cummings, D., tr. see Philaretos, Sotirios D.

Cummings, D. W. American English Spelling: An Informal Description. LC 86-30537. 608p. 1988. text 65.00 (*0-8018-3443-0*) Johns Hopkins.

Cummings, Darc. Singing a Mass for the Dead. 24p. (Orig.). 1995. 5.00 (*0-936908-07-6*) Broncho Pr.

Cummings, Darold B. & Johnson, Gary. What Not to Name Your Baby. (Illus.). 64p. (Orig.). 1982. pap. 2.95 (*0-914743-01-5*) Matrix Design Pubns.

***Cummings, Dave.** Just Looking. 1999. pap. write for info. (*1-58235-138-4*) Watermrk Pr.

Cummings, David. India. (Economically Developing Countries Ser.). (Illus.). 48p. (J). (gr. 6-8). 1995. lib. bdg. 24.26 (*1-56847-384-2*) Raintree Steck-V.

Cummings, David & McIntire, Dennis, eds. International Who's Who in Music & Musicians Directory, 1994-95. 14th ed. 1358p. 1994. 175.00 (*0-948875-71-2*) Intl Pubns Serv.

— The International Who's Who in Music & Musician's Directory, 1996-97. 15th ed. 1357p. 1996. 175.00 (*0-948875-22-4*, Pub. by Melrose) Taylor & Francis.

Cummings, David, jt. auth. see Pipkin, Bernard.

Cummings, Deborah H. Lad in a Kilt. (Illus.). 32p. (Orig.). (J). (gr. k-2). 1994. pap. 7.95 (*0-9641224-0-5*) Tartan Pr.

Cummings, Delano. Moon Dash Warrior: The Story of an American Indian in Vietnam, a Marine from the Land of the Lumbee. unabridged ed. Novak, Marian & Novak, David, eds. (Illus.). 266p. 1998. 22.00 (*0-9651858-3-4*) Signal Tree.

Cummings, Dennis J. The Men Behind the Trident: SEAL Team One in Vietnam. LC 96-52042. (Special Warfare Ser.). (Illus.). 288p. 1997. 29.95 (*1-55750-139-4*) Naval Inst Pr.

— The Men Behind the Trident: Seal Team One in Vietnam. 272p. 1998. reprint ed. mass mkt. 6.50 (*0-553-57928-2*) Bantam.

Cummings, Denver, ed. see Makrakis, Apostolos.

Cummings, Denver, tr. see Agapius, et al.

Cummings, Denver, tr. see Livadeas, Themistocles & Charitos, Minas.

Cummings, Denver, tr. see Makrakis, Apostolos.

Cummings, E. E. Another E. E. Cummings. Kostelanetz, Richard & Rocco, John, eds. LC 95-45471. (Illus.). 288p. 1998. 25.00 (*0-87140-157-6*, Pub. by Liveright) Norton.

— Another E. E. Cummings. Kostelanetz, Richard, ed. LC 95-45471. 336p. 1999. pap. 14.00 (*0-87140-174-6*, Pub. by Liveright) Norton.

Cummings, E. E. The Complete Poems, 1904-1962. Firmage, George J., ed. 1100p. (C). 1994. 50.00 (*0-87140-152-5*, Pub. by Liveright) Norton.

Cummings, E. E. A Concordance to the Complete Poems of e. e. Cummings. McBride, Katharine, ed. LC 88-47749. 984p. 1989. text 85.00 (*0-8014-2239-6*) Cornell U Pr.

— Democracy under Pressure. 8th ed. (C). 1997. pap. text, teacher ed. 29.75 (*0-15-503196-1*) Harcourt Coll Pubs.

— Democracy under Pressure. 8th ed. (C). 1997. pap. text 35.00 (*0-15-503198-8*, Pub. by Harcourt Coll Pubs) Harcourt.

Cummings, E. E. E.E. Cummings Reads: Cummings,&E.E. abr. ed. 1993. audio 12.00 (*1-55994-831-0*, DCN 1017) HarperAudio.

— E.E. Cummings Nonlect 3 CAS. abr. ed. 1977. audio 14.00 (*0-694-50139-5*, SWC 1188, Caedmon) HarperAudio.

— E.E. Cummings Nonlect 6 CAS. abr. ed. 1977. audio 14.00 (*0-694-50142-5*, SWC 1191, Caedmon) HarperAudio.

Cummings, E. E. Eimi. (American Biography Ser.). 432p. 1991. reprint ed. lib. bdg. 89.00 (*0-7812-8095-8*) Rprt Serv.

— The Enormous Room. 1994. lib. bdg. 29.95 (*1-56849-513-7*) Buccaneer Bks.

— The Enormous Room. 252p. 1999. mass mkt. 4.95 (*0-451-52669-4*, Penguin Classics) Viking Penguin.

— The Enormous Room. Hynes, Samuel L., ed. LC 98-11675. (Penguin Twentieth-Century Classics Ser.). 1999. pap. 11.95 (*0-14-118124-9*) Viking Penguin.

— The Enormous Room. 2nd ed. Firmage, George J., ed. (Illus.). 304p. (C). 1994. pap. 13.95 (*0-87140-150-9*, Pub. by Liveright) Norton.

— Etcetera: The Unpublished Poems of e. e. cummings. Firmage, George J. & Kennedy, Richard S., eds. (Liveright Bk.). 1983. 16.95 (*0-87140-644-6*); pap. 17.95 (*0-87140-128-2*) Norton.

***Cummings, E. E.** Etcetera: The Unpublished Poems of E. E. Cummings. 192p. 2000. pap. 13.00 (*0-87140-176-2*) Norton.

Cummings, E. E. Fairy Tales. 1965. 6.95 (*0-15-227080-9*, Harcourt Child Bks) Harcourt.

— Fairy Tales. LC 65-18727. (Illus.). 39p. (J). (gr. k up). 1975. pap. 7.00 (*0-15-629895-3*, Voyager Bks) Harcourt.

— Him. (Orig.). pap. 4.95 (*0-87140-038-3*) Liveright.

— Is Five... Poems. 2nd rev. ed. LC 85-5164. 116p. 1996. pap. 12.00 (*0-87140-164-9*, Pub. by Liveright) Norton.

— May I Feel Said He: Poem. (Illus.). 32p. 1995. 17.95 (*1-55670-422-4*) Stewart Tabori & Chang.

— May I Feel Said He: Poem. Sunshine, Linda, ed. LC 95-30234. (Illus.). 32p. 1995. reprint ed. 17.95 (*0-941807-00-2*) Welcome Enterprises.

— No Thanks. LC 78-3827. 96p. 1998. pap. 12.00 (*0-87140-172-X*) Norton.

— One Hundred Selected Poems. LC 59-15193. 128p. (Orig.). 1988. pap. 10.00 (*0-8021-3072-0*, Grove) Grove-Atltic.

— Selected Poems. LC 94-29263. 224p. 1994. pap. 10.95 (*0-87140-154-1*, Pub. by Liveright) Norton.

Cummings, E. E. Six Non-Lectures. LC 53-10472. (Charles Eliot Norton Lectures: 1952-1953). 118p. 1953. pap. text 9.95 (*0-674-44010-2*) HUP.

Cummings, E. E. Tulips & Chimneys: Poems. rev. ed. LC 76-10204. 188p. 1996. pap. 13.00 (*0-87140-165-7*, Pub. by Liveright) Norton.

***Cummings, E. E.** 22 & 50 Poems. 96p. 2000. pap. 12.00 (*0-87140-177-0*) Norton.

Cummings, E. E. ViVa. 2nd ed. Firmage, George J., ed. LC 79-4212. 80p. 1997. pap. 12.00 (*0-87140-169-X*, Pub. by Liveright) Norton.

— W. 2nd rev. ed. Firmage, George J., ed. & afterword by. (Transcript Edition Ser.). 1979. 9.95 (*0-87140-636-5*, Pub. by Liveright) Norton.

— Xaipe. Firmage, George J., ed. 71p. 1979. 9.95 (*0-87140-633-0*, Pub. by Liveright) Norton.

— Xaipe. Firmage, George J., ed. 80p. (C). 1997. pap. 12.00 (*0-87140-168-1*, Pub. by Liveright) Norton.

Cummings, E. Mark & Davies, Patrick. Children & Marital Conflict: The Impact of Family Dispute & Resolution. LC 93-43572. (Series on Social & Emotional Development). 216p. 1994. pap. text 22.00 (*0-89862-303-0*); lib. bdg. 45.00 (*0-89862-304-9*) Guilford Pubns.

Cummings, Earl E. What Manner of Man Is This? 1992. pap. 10.00 (*1-56186-515-X*) Pilgrim Pubns.

Cummings, Edward M. What's Happening: A Manifesto for the Future: a Human Affairs Manifesto of Individual & Social Behaviors with Two Hundred Questions & Answers to Help People Adapt to Changes in the Twenty-First Century. LC 93-3722. 1993. 34.95 (*0-9636276-0-0*) Cummings Assocs.

Cummings, Eileen, ed. & illus. see Elliott, Jayne.

Cummings, Eileen B. Ojo de Dios: Eye of God. (ENG & SPA., Illus.). 14p. 1993. pap. 29.00 (*0-926272-02-0*) E C Pr.

Cummings, F. Jay. The Future of Commercial Banking: Proceedings of the 1982 Political Economy Research Institute Conference on Banking & Financial Institutions. Jones, Deborah G., ed. (Illus.). 146p. (Orig.). (C). 1983. pap. text 22.00 (*0-8191-3294-2*) U Pr of Amer.

Cummings, Frank. Capitol Hill Manual. 2nd ed. LC 83-21048. (Illus.). 338p. reprint ed. pap. 104.80 (*0-7837-4598-2*, 204431700002) Bks Demand.

Cummings, George. A Common Journey: Black Theology (U. S. A.) & Latin American Liberation Theology. LC 93-16995. (Bishop Henry McNeal Turner Studies: Vol. 6). 225p. 1992. 25.00 (*0-88344-825-4*) Orbis Bks.

Cummings, Gerald R. & Meixner, Elizabeth. Corectec's Comprehensive Set of Review Questions for Radiography. 2nd ed. 300p. (C). 1991. pap. text 18.50 (*1-880890-00-3*) Corectec.

— Corectec's Comprehensive Set of Review Questions for Radiography. 3rd ed. (Illus.). 284p. (C). 1993. pap. text 22.00 (*1-880890-03-8*) Corectec.

— Corectec's Comprehensive Set of Review Questions for Radiography. 4th ed. (Illus.). 292p. 1998. pap. text 28.00 (*1-880890-08-9*) Corectec.

Cummings, Gordon, et al. Soft Tissue Changes in Contractures, Vol. 1. (Orthopedic Physical Therapy Ser.). (Illus.). 1983. pap. 30.00 (*0-936030-02-X*) Stokesville Pub.

***Cummings, Helen A.** Spirit Imagining. LC 99-75270. 64p. 2001. 12.95 (*0-8158-0542-X*) Chris Mass.

Cummings, Helen B. Amanda's Secret Journal. 250p. (Orig.). 1997. pap. write for info. (*0-9657417-0-2*) H B Cummings.

Cummings, Hildegard. Faces of Change: The Art of Ivan Olinsky, 1878-1962. LC 96-621130. (Illus.). 32p. (Orig.). 1995. pap. 14.00 (*1-880897-05-9*) Lyme Hist.

Cummings, Hildegard & Anderson, Jeffrey W. Faces of Change: The Art of Ivan Olinsky, 1878-1962. (Illus.). 32p. (Orig.). 1995. 14.00 (*0-614-10436-X*) W Benton Mus.

Cummings, Hildegard, et al. Harvey Sadow: Toward a Vessel Aesthetic: Ceramics Works 1968-1988. (Illus.). 72p. 18.50 (*0-918386-39-X*) W Benton Mus.

— J. Alden Weir: A Place of His Own. (Illus.). 99p. 14.50 (*0-918386-43-8*) W Benton Mus.

Cummings, Homer & McFarland, Carl. Federal Justice. LC 76-109552. (American Constitutional & Legal History Ser). 1970. reprint ed. lib. bdg. 59.50 (*0-306-71906-1*) Da Capo.

Cummings, Hubertis. Indebtedness of Chaucer's Works to the Italian Works of Boccacio. LC 65-21098. (Studies in Comparative Literature: No. 35). 1969. reprint ed. lib. bdg. 75.00 (*0-8383-0534-2*) M S G Haskell Hse.

Cummings, Hubertis M. Indebtedness of Chaucer's Works to the Italian Works of Boccaccio. (BCL1-PR English Literature Ser.). 202p. 1992. reprint ed. lib. bdg. 79.00 (*0-7812-7172-X*) Rprt Serv.

***Cummings, J. A.** Nightchild: A Clans Novel. (Vampire Clans Ser.). 328p. 1999. pap. 15.95 (*0-9670668-0-8*) Kresnak Pr.

Cummings, J. H., et al, eds. Physiological & Clinical Aspects of Short Chain Fatty Acids. (Illus.). 595p. (C). 1995. text 150.00 (*0-521-44048-3*) Cambridge U Pr.

Cummings, J. S. Jesuit & Friar in the Spanish Expansion to the East. (Collected Studies: No. CS237). 334p. (C). 1986. reprint ed. lib. bdg. 109.95 (*0-86078-185-2*, Pub. by Variorum) Ashgate Pub Co.

Cummings, Jack. Business Traveller's Survival Guide. (C). 1989. 24.95 (*0-13-107848-8*, Macmillan Coll) P-H.

— Dead Man's Medal. 256p. 1992. reprint ed. mass mkt. 3.50 (*1-55817-664-0*, Pinncle Kensgtn) Kensgtn Pub Corp.

Cummings, Jack. The Deserter Troop. 192p. 1991. 18.95 (*0-8027-4121-5*) Walker & Co.

Cummings, Jack. Escape from Yuma. 224p. 1993. mass mkt. 3.50 (*1-55817-697-7*, Pinncle Kensgtn) Kensgtn Pub Corp.

Cummings, Jack. Escape from Yuma. 187p. 1990. 18.95 (*0-8027-4111-8*) Walker & Co.

Cummings, Jack. Escape from Yuma. large type ed. LC 90-46133. 285p. 1990. reprint ed. lib. bdg. 15.95 (*1-56054-074-5*) Thorndike Pr.

— The Indian Fighter's Return. LC 92-42326. 182p. 1993. 19.95 (*0-8027-1268-1*) Walker & Co.

— The Indian Fighter's Return. large type ed. LC 94-9341. 268p. 1994. lib. bdg. 16.95 (*0-8161-5991-2*, G K Hall Lrg Type) Mac Lib Ref.

— The Last Lawmen. LC 94-8811. 177p. 1994. 19.95 (*0-8027-4143-6*) Walker & Co.

— Lynch's Revenge. 256p. 1993. mass mkt. 3.50 (*1-55817-752-3*, Pinncle Kensgtn) Kensgtn Pub Corp.

— Lynch's Revenge. large type ed. LC 94-9244. 290p. 1994. lib. bdg. 18.95 (*0-7862-0219-X*) Thorndike Pr.

— The McGraw-Hill Thirty-Six Hour Real Estate Investing Course. 358p. 1992. pap. 19.95 (*0-07-015048-6*) McGraw.

Cummings, Jack. Once a Legend. 1988. 16.95 (*0-8027-4075-8*) Walker & Co.

Cummings, Jack. Once a Legend. large type ed. LC 92-25936. 275p. 1992. reprint ed. lib. bdg. 15.95 (*1-56054-436-8*) Thorndike Pr.

— Once a Legend. 224p. 1992. reprint ed. mass mkt. 3.50 (*1-55817-650-0*, Pinncle Kensgtn) Kensgtn Pub Corp.

— One Thousand Dollars down Can Make You Rich: Tactics for Real Estate Investors. 320p. 1985. 24.95 (*0-317-18450-4*) P-H.

— Real Estate Finance & Investment Manual. 2nd ed. LC 96-29527. 480p. 1997. pap. text 34.95 (*0-13-493388-5*) P-H.

— The Real Estate Investor's Answer Book. 303p. 1993. pap. 19.95 (*0-07-015052-4*) McGraw.

— The Real Estate Investor's Answer Book. 1994. pap. text 17.95 (*0-07-015152-0*) McGraw.

— Rebels West. 1991. mass mkt. 3.50 (*1-55817-525-3*, Pinncle Kensgtn) Kensgtn Pub Corp.

— The Reit Revolution: Profiting from Real Estate Investment Trusts. 288p. 1999. 40.00 (*0-7352-0090-4*) PH Pr.

— The Rough Rider. 1991. mass mkt. 3.50 (*1-55817-481-8*, Pinncle Kensgtn) Kensgtn Pub Corp.

Cummings, Jack. The Rough Rider. 192p. 1988. 17.95 (*0-8027-4089-8*) Walker & Co.

Cummings, Jack. The Rough Rider. large type ed. LC 93-21818. 1993. pap. 15.95 (*1-56054-437-6*) Thorndike Pr.

— Sergeant Gringo. 1993. mass mkt. 3.50 (*1-55817-744-2*, Pinncle Kensgtn) Kensgtn Pub Corp.

— Sergeant Gringo. large type ed. LC 93-7856. 275p. 1993. lib. bdg. 16.95 (*1-56054-438-4*) Thorndike Pr.

— The Surrogate Gun. 224p. 1992. mass mkt. 3.50 (*1-55817-607-1*, Pinncle Kensgtn) Kensgtn Pub Corp.

— The Surrogate Gun. large type ed. 339p. 1990. lib. bdg. 14.95 (*1-56054-007-9*) Thorndike Pr.

— Tiger Butte. 1992. mass mkt. 3.50 (*1-55817-583-0*, Pinncle Kensgtn) Kensgtn Pub Corp.

— Tiger Butte. LC 85-20288. 178p. 1986. 14.95 (*0-8027-4055-3*) Walker & Co.

— Tiger Butte. large type ed. LC 92-36426. (Western Ser.). 269p. 1993. reprint ed. 17.95 (*1-56054-439-2*) Thorndike Pr.

— The Trick Shot. LC 95-46723. 180p. 1996. 19.95 (*0-8027-4153-3*) Walker & Co.

— The Trick Shot. large type ed. LC 96-36487. 284p. 1997. write for info. (*0-7862-0907-0*) Thorndike Pr.

Cummings, James, ed. see Connelly, Mary J., et al.

Cummings, Jean. Alias the Buffalo Doctor. LC 80-81714. (Illus.). 272p. 1980. 11.95 (*0-8187-0039-4*) Harlo Press.

***Cummings, Jean. Buffalo in Our Backyard. unabridged ed. LC 00-91377. 270p. 2000. pap. 12.50 (*0-9679959-0-6*) Rx Ranch.**

This is a true story of a family who learned how to care for a buffalo herd. The author, Jean Cummings, her husband--a newly trained surgeon--& their children settled in Stanwood, a village tucked into the wild forests of central Michigan. It was not the life Mrs. Cummings had expected. When her husband announced he was going to raise buffalo she didn't take him seriously, but in the spring of 1964 the arrival of thirteen buffalo changed their lives. Her husband was known as The Buffalo Doctor. You'll find out all about it in this charming account--Kahtanka crowned herd bull; the donkey who thought he was a buffalo; an exotic dancer in a buffalo-fur bikini for a buffalo-fur fashion show. There are herds of facts & information about buffalo history, the killing off of the great herds & anything else you could possibly want to know about this monstrous but lovable animal *Publisher Paid Annotation.*

–Shinglebolt. unabridged ed. LC 00-190939. (Illus.). 129p. 2000. pap. 8.50 (*0-9679959-2-2*) Rx Ranch.

Shinglebolt is a tale about a boy named Corky who sets out to find his father's lumbering camp on the Muskegon River. A St. Bernard dives out of the woods to save Corky from being hit by a widowmaker, a fall branch. They name the dog "Shinglebolt." Corky meets all sorts of interesting characters at his Pa's lumber camp, including a pair of murderers & log rustlers. Throughout, runs the theme, "Don't be afraid of something or somebody just because they are different." When Jean Cummings moved into a log home on the Muskegon River, she grew interested in river's history. The home had been built in the 1920s with "deadheads," stray logs which sank during the lumbering times of the 19th century. The builder of the home pulled these logs from the river bottom & milled the lumber. When the author researched lumbering & Muskegon River history she came upon an old news item about a St. Bernard dog found wandering in the woods. This ignited her imagination & sparked this engaging yarn about the glory days of lumbering. *Publisher Paid Annotation.*

–Stardancer. LC 00-190937. 313p. (Orig.). 2000. pap. 12.50 (*0-9679959-1-4*) Rx Ranch.

Stardancer is a tale about two adventurous women who, during their youth, turn westward to escape impossible situations. The novel begins in the Michigan lumbering era, where great fortunes were being made in timber. Both women, Cath & Gitty--aunt & niece--settle in Stardancer, a frontier town in the Black Hills of South Dakota, where cattlemen are making fortunes. Gitty marries a wealthy English cattleman & she becomes instrumental in helping save the American buffalo from extinction. She is unable to put aside her love for an unacceptable man & this passion brings her much grief. The author, Jean Cummings & her husband raised buffalo in Michigan for 20 years. Because her husband was born & raised on an Indian reservation, native lore is a great part of their lives. Research into buffalo & the western United States brought to life the colorful places & people of this story. Mrs. Cummings weaves an exciting tale of romance & adventure set in the nineteenth century. *Publisher Paid Annotation.*

Cummings, Jean. They Call Him the Buffalo Doctor. LC 73-147172. 320p. 1980. reprint ed. 7.00 (*0-8187-0035-1*) Harlo Press.

Cummings, Jeffrey L. & Benson, D. Frank. Dementia: A Clinical Approach. 2nd ed. 548p. 1992. pap. text 99.50 (*0-7506-9065-8*) Buttrwrth-Heinemann.

Cummings, Jeffrey L. & Trimble, Michael R. Behavioral Neurology. 544p. 1996. text 95.00 (*0-7506-2360-8*) Buttrwrth-Heinemann.

— Concise Guide to Neuropsychiatry & Behavioral Neurology. (Concise Guides Ser.). 368p. 1995. pap. text 22.00 (*0-88048-493-4*, 8493) Am Psychiatric.

Cummings, Jeffrey L., jt. auth. see Coffey, C. Edward.

Cummings, Jeffrey L., jt. auth. see Huber, Steven J.

Cummings, Jeffrey L., jt. auth. see Trimble, Michael R.

Cummings, Jeffrey L., jt. ed. see Bogousslavsky, Julien.

Cummings, Jeffrey L., jt. ed. see Miller, Bruce L.

Cummings, Jim. A Friend in the Water: Tales of Sea & Sky. LC 88-80396. 112p. (Orig.). 1988. pap. 7.95 (*0-945401-23-X*) EarthEar.

Cummings, Joe. Lao Phrasebook: A Language Survival Kit. (LAO., Illus.). 176p. 1994. pap. 5.95 (*0-86442-276-8*) Lonely Planet.

— Lonely Planet Bangkok. 4th ed. 240p. 1999. pap. 14.95 (*0-86442-666-6*) Lonely Planet.

— Lonely Planet Laos. 2nd ed. (Illus.). 272p. 1996. pap. 15.95 (*0-86442-381-0*) Lonely Planet.

— Lonely Planet Laos: Travel Survival Kit. 3rd ed. (Lonely Planet Travel Guides Ser.). (Illus.). 272p. 1998. pap. text 15.95 (*0-86442-617-8*) Lonely Planet.

— Lonely Planet Thailand. 8th ed. 976p. 1999. pap. 21.95 (*0-86442-636-4*) Lonely Planet.

— Lonely Planet Thailand Travel Atlas. (Illus.). 44p. 1995. pap. 8.95 (*0-86442-269-5*) Lonely Planet.

***Cummings, Joe.** Lonely Planet Thailand's Islands & Beaches. 2nd ed. (Illus.). 496p. 2000. pap. 15.95 (*0-86442-728-X*) Lonely Planet.

Cummings, Joe. The Meditation Temples of Thailand: A Guide. (Illus.). 100p. (Orig.). 1990. pap. 10.95 (*1-879220-15-6*) Wayfarer Bks.

— Moon Handbooks: Baja: Tijuana to Cabo San Lucas. 3rd rev. ed. LC 98-657868. (Illus.). 540p. 1998. pap. 16.95 (*1-56691-120-6*, Moon Handbks) Avalon Travel.

— Moon Handbooks: Cabo: La Paz to Cabo San Lucas. 2nd rev. ed. (Illus.). 270p. 1998. pap. 14.95 (*1-56691-119-2*, Moon Handbks) Avalon Travel.

— Moon Handbooks: Northern Mexico: Including the Copper Canyon. 2nd rev. ed. Vol. 2. (Illus.). 610p. 1998. pap. 17.95 (*1-56691-118-4*, Moon Handbks) Avalon Travel.

— Moon Handbooks: Texas. 4th rev. ed. (Illus.). 690p. 1998. pap. 18.95 (*1-56691-112-5*, Moon Handbks) Avalon Travel.

***Cummings, Joe.** Moon Handbooks - Baja: Tijuana to Cabo San Lucas. 4th rev. ed. (Moon Handbks.). (Illus.). 540p. 2000. pap. 17.95 (*1-56691-208-3*, Pub. by Avalon Travel) Publishers Group.

— Moon Handbooks - Cabo: La Paz to Cabo San Lucas. 3rd rev. ed. (Moon Handbks.). (Illus.). 270p. 2000. pap. 14.95 (*1-56691-207-5*, Pub. by Avalon Travel) Publishers Group.

Cummings, Joe. Thai Phrasebook: A Language Survival Kit. 3rd ed. (THA., Illus.). 208p. 1995. pap. 5.95 (*0-86442-275-X*) Lonely Planet.

— Thai Phrasebook: With Two-Way Dictionary. 4th ed. 250p. 1999. pap. 6.95 (*0-86442-658-5*) Lonely Planet.

***Cummings, Joe.** World Food Thailand. (World Food Ser.). (Illus.). 208p. 2000. pap. 12.95 (*1-86450-026-3*) Lonely Planet.

Cummings, Joe, contrib. by. Lonely Planet Laos Travel Atlas. (Illus.). 48p. 1997. pap. 12.95 (*0-86442-375-6*) Lonely Planet.

***Cummings, Joe & Clark, Michael.** Myanmar (Burma) 7th ed. (Illus.). 432p. 1999. pap. 16.95 (*0-86442-703-4*) Lonely Planet.

Cummings, Joe & Goncharoff, Nicko. Thailand's Islands & Beaches. 2nd ed. (Illus.). 496p. 1998. pap. 15.95 (*0-86442-540-6*) Lonely Planet.

***Cummings, Joe & Humphrey, Chris.** Moon Handbooks: Mexico City. (Illus.). 250p. 2000. pap. 14.95 (*1-56691-186-9*, Moon Handbks) Avalon Travel.

Cummings, Joe & Mallan, Chicki. Moon Handbooks: Mexico. 2nd rev. ed. LC 97-649746. (Illus.). 1220p. 1999. pap. 21.95 (*1-56691-123-0*, Moon Handbks) Avalon Travel.

Cummings, Joe & Wheeler, Tony. Lonely Planet Myanmar (Burma) Travel Survival Kit. 6th ed. (Illus.). 400p. 1996. pap. 13.95 (*0-86442-324-1*) Lonely Planet.

Cummings, Joe, jt. ed. see Lofaro, Michael A.

Cummings, John. Negro Population in the United States, 1790-1915. LC 68-28992. (American Negro: His History & Literature. Series 1). 1969. reprint ed. 31.95 (*0-405-01811-8*) Ayer.

— Poor Laws of Massachusetts & New York. 135p. 1993. reprint ed. lib. bdg. 69.00 (*0-7812-5246-6*) Rprt Serv.

Cummings, John, et al, eds. Short Chain Fatty Acids. LC 93-48419. 304p. (C). 1994. text 123.00 (*0-7923-8849-6*) Kluwer Academic.

Cummings, John & Volkman, Ernest. Goombata: The Improbable Rise & Fall of John Gotti & His Gang. 336p. 1992. reprint ed. mass mkt. 6.99 (*0-380-71487-6*, Avon Bks) Morrow Avon.

Cummings, John, jt. auth. see Reed, Terry.

Cummings, John T., jt. auth. see Askari, Hossein.

Cummings, Jonathan W. You & Your Handicap: The Arithmetic of Golf. 56p. 1997. pap. 8.00 (*0-8059-4062-6*) Dorrance.

Cummings, Judith A. Plan A: An Optimist Prepares for Y2K. 160p. 1998. pap. 21.95 (*0-9668348-0-5*) Rehoboth Publ.

Cummings, Karen. Guide to Owning a Birman Cat. LC 99-36717. (Illus.). 64p. 1999. 19.95 (*0-7910-5460-8*) Chelsea Hse.

— Guide to Owning an American Shorthair Cat. LC 99-36715. (Illus.). 64p. 1999. 19.95 (*0-7910-5458-6*) Chelsea Hse.

— Guide to Owning an Exotic Shorthair Cat. LC 99-36714. (Illus.). 64p. 1999. 19.95 (*0-7910-5462-4*) Chelsea Hse.

***Cummings, Karen, et al.** Fundamentals of Physics Pt. 1: Alternate Edition. 368p. 2000. pap. write for info. (*0-471-38864-5*) Wiley.

Cummings, Katherine. Telling Tales: The Hysteric's Seducton in Fiction & Theory. LC 90-41802. 320p. 1991. 39.50 (*0-8047-1825-3*) Stanford U Pr.

Cummings, Keith. The Techniques of Kiln-Formed Glass. (Illus.). 192p. 1997. 49.95 (*0-8122-3402-2*) U of Pa Pr.

Cummings, Keith. Techniques of Kiln Formed Glass. (Illus.). 176p. 1997. text. write for info. (*90-5703-561-8*, Harwood Acad Pubs) Gordon & Breach.

Cummings, Kevin S. & Mayer, Christine A. Field Guide to Freshwater Mussels of the Midwest. LC 92-83870. (Manual Ser.: No. 5). (Illus.). xii, 192p. 1992. text 15.00 (*1-882932-00-5*) Ill Nat Hist.

Cummings, L. L. & Frost, Peter J. Publishing in the Organizational Sciences. 2nd ed. (Foundations for Organizational Ser.: 1). 320p. 1995. text 58.00 (*0-8039-7144-3*) Sage.

Cummings, L. L., jt. auth. see Harnett, D. L.

Cummings, L. L., jt. ed. see Staw, Barry M.

Cummings, L. L., jt. ed. see Staw, Barry M.

Cummings, Larry L. & Staw, Barry M., eds. Evaluation & Employment in Organizations. LC 90-4533. (Research in Organizational Behavior Ser.). 256p. 1990. pap. 25.75 (*1-55938-219-8*) Jai Pr.

— Information & Cognition in Organizations. LC 90-4523. (Research in Organizational Behavior Ser.). 320p. 1990. pap. 25.75 (*1-55938-218-X*) Jai Pr.

— Leadership, Participation, & Group Behavior. LC 90-4529. 386p. 1990. pap. 25.75 (*1-55938-220-1*) Jai Pr.

Cummings, Larry L., jt. ed. see Staw, Barry M.

Cummings, Leslie. Nutrition Management for Food Services. (Food & Hospitality Ser.). 1989. text 44.25 (*0-8273-3522-9*) Delmar.

— Nutrition Management for Food Services. (Food & Hospitality Ser.). 1990. pap., teacher ed. 11.95 (*0-8273-3523-7*) Delmar.

Cummings, Leslie, et al. AIX Command Summary. (Orig.). 1991. spiral bd. 99.95 incl. disk (*0-9628940-0-1*) Secutron.

Cummings, Linda, tr. Old Time Gospel Piano. 96p. 1996. 15.98 incl. audio compact disk (*0-7866-2502-3*, 96320) Mel Bay.

Cummings, Linda C., jt. compiled by see Cummings, Pat.

Cummings, Louise. Eyes Wide Open. 128p. Date not set. pap. 15.95 (*1-55145-038-0*, Pub. by Wood Lake Bks) Logos Prods.

Cummings, M. E. & Greene, Karraker, eds. Life-Span Developmental Psychology: Perspectives on Stress & Coping. 352p. (C). 1991. text 69.95 (*0-8058-0371-8*) L Erlbaum Assocs.

Cummings, M. F. & Miller, C. C. Designs for Street Fronts, Suburban Houses & Cottages. LC 97-25653. (Illus.). 112p. 1999. pap. 9.95 (*0-486-29878-7*) Dover.

Cummings, Margaret A. Touched by AIDS. Butler, Cathy, ed. (Illus.). 22p. (Orig.). (YA). (gr. 7-12). 1992. pap. text 1.95 (*1-56309-024-4*, C926105, Wrld Changers Res) Womans Mission Union.

Cummings, Marion S. Hamilton Family Records: Descendants of John & Jane Hamilton, of Cayuga County, New York. (Illus.). 65p. 1997. reprint ed. pap. 13.00 (*0-8328-8924-5*); reprint ed. lib. bdg. 23.00 (*0-8328-8923-7*) Higginson Bk Co.

Cummings, Mark. A Disimprisoned Epic: Form & Vision in Carlyle's French Revolution. LC 88-18844. 204p. (C). 1988. text 37.50 (*0-8122-8117-9*) U of Pa Pr.

Cummings, Marlene A. Individual Differences: A Program for Elementary School Age Children. 588p. (gr. 1-6). 17.95 (*0-686-74870-0*) ADL.

Cummings, Martha, jt. auth. see Genzel, Rhona B.

Cummings, Martha C. Mono Lake: Stories. LC 95-68710. 172p. 1995. pap. 8.95 (*0-9646201-2-X*) Rowbarge Pr.

Cummings, Martha G., jt. auth. see Genzel, Rhona B.

Cummings, Martha Graves. Listen, Speak, Present. (J). 1991. mass mkt. 26.95 (*0-8384-3012-0*) Heinle & Heinle.

— Listen, Speak, Present. (J). 1992. mass mkt., teacher ed. 8.95 (*0-8384-3013-9*) Heinle & Heinle.

Cummings, Martha T. Straddling the Borders: The Year I Grew up in Italy. Caso, Adolph, ed. LC 99-18280. 226p. 1999. pap. 14.95 (*0-8283-2036-5*) Branden Bks.

Cummings, Mary. Lives of the Buddha in the Art & Literature of Asia. LC 80-67341. (Michigan Papers on South & Southeast Asia: No. 20). (Illus.). xiii, 225p. (C). 1982. pap. 16.95 (*0-89148-023-4*) Ctr S&SE Asian.

— Southampton. LC 96-227595. (Images of America Ser.). 1996. pap. 16.99 (*0-7524-0459-8*) Arcadia Publng.

Cummings, Merilyn. The Diet to Lose & Win. enl. rev. ed. 52p. 1987. teacher ed. 30.00 (*0-9617195-2-4*); audio 19.95 (*0-9617195-9-1*); audio 24.95 (*0-9617195-1-6*) Abrahamson Pub.

— The Diet to Lose & Win. 3rd enl. rev. ed. 52p. 1987. pap. 19.95 (*0-9617195-8-3*) Abrahamson Pub.

— The Good Food Game. 112p. (Orig.). 1989. pap. 19.95 (*0-9617195-0-8*); write for info. (*0-318-64738-9*) Abrahamson Pub.

Cummings, Michael, jt. auth. see Dolbeare, Kenneth.

Cummings, Michael J. Country Doctor's Book of Medical Wisdom & Cures. LC 97-150941. (Illus.). 160p. 1997. write for info. (*0-7853-2307-4*) Pubns Intl Ltd.

Cummings, Michael R. Biology: Science & Life. LC 95-45983. 650p. (C). 1996. 92.95 (*0-314-06400-1*) West Pub.

— Human Heredity: Principles & Issues. 3rd ed. Westby, ed. LC 93-26154. 500p. (C). 1993. text 60.25 (*0-314-02747-5*) West Pub.

C

An Asterisk (*) at the beginning of an entry indicates that the title is appearing for the first time.

Cummings, Michael R. Human Heredity: Principles & Issues. 4th ed. (Illus.). 560p. 1997. write for info. (*0-314-12981-2*) Brooks-Cole.

Cummings, Michael R. Perspectives in Biology. 225p. 1996. pap. 12.25 (*0-314-07562-3*) West Pub.

***Cummings, Michael S.** Beyond Political Correctness: Social Transformation in the United States. (Transformations in Politics & Society Ser.). 350p. 2000. lib. bdg. 52.00 (*1-55587-863-6*) L Rienner.

Cummings, Michael S. & Smith, Nicholas D., eds. Utopian Studies, 2 bks., Set, Nos. III & IV. 242p. (C). 1990. lib. bdg. 49.50 (*0-8191-7841-1*) U Pr of Amer.

Cummings, Michael S., jt. ed. see Tillman, Ray M.

***Cummings, Milton C.** Democracy under Pressure. 8th ed. 1999. 76.50 (*0-15-512834-5*) Harcourt Coll Pubs.

— Democracy under Pressure & Century Update; An Introduction to the American Politcal System. 8th ed. 1999. pap. text 59.00 (*0-15-512907-4*) Harcourt Coll Pubs.

Cummings, Milton C., Jr. & Wise, David. Democracy under Pressure. 8th ed. 248p. (C). 1997. pap. text, student ed. 25.00 (*0-15-503197-X*) Harcourt Coll Pubs.

— Democracy under Pressure: An Introduction to the American Political System. 6th ed. 797p. (C). 1989. VHS. write for info. (*0-318-65138-6*) Harcourt Coll Pubs.

— Democracy under Pressure: An Introduction to the American Political System. 7th ed. 797p. (C). 1993. 5.25 hd 16.50 (*0-15-500711-4*) Harcourt Coll Pubs.

— Democracy under Pressure: An Introduction to the American Political System. 7th ed. 797p. (C). 1994. write for info. (*0-15-500710-6*) Harcourt Coll Pubs.

— Democracy under Pressure: An Introduction to the American Political System. 8th ed. LC 96-75316. 898p. (C). 1996. text 69.50 (*0-15-503195-3*, Pub. by Harcourt Coll Pubs) Harcourt.

— Democracy under Pressure Brief Edition: An Introduction to the American Political System. 8th ed. 720p. (C). 1996. pap. text 53.00 (*0-15-505423-6*, Pub. by Harcourt Coll Pubs) Harcourt.

***Cummings, Missy.** Hornet's Nest: The Experiences of One of the Navy's First Female Fighter Pilots. 416p. 2000. pap. 19.95 (*0-595-00190-4*) iUniversecom.

Cummings, Monette. Crossed Hearts. 256p. 1993. mass mkt. 3.99 (*0-8217-4338-4*, Zebra Kensgtn) Kensgtn Pub Corp.

Cummings, N. A., et al. Medicaid, Managed Behavioral Health, & Implications for Public Policy: Report of the Hawaii Medicaid Project & Other Readings. (Readings in Behavioral Health Ser.: No. 2). 60p. 1993. pap. text. write for info. (*0-9637577-0-9*) Fnd Behav Hlth.

***Cummings, Neil & Lewandowska, Marysia.** The Value of Things. (Illus.). 240p. 2000. pap. 42.00 (*3-7643-6316-9*, Pub. by Birkhauser) Princeton Arch.

***Cummings, Nicholas A.** Essence of Psychotherapy: Reinventing the Art for the New Era of Data. (Illus.). 296p. 2000. pap. text 49.95 (*0-12-198760-4*) Acad Pr.

— First Session with Substance Abusers: A Step-by-Step Guide. LC 00-8844. 224p. 2000. write for info. (*0-7879-4933-7*) Jossey-Bass.

Cummings, Nicholas A., et al, eds. Surviving the Demise of Solo Practice: Mental Health Practitioners Prospering in the Era of Managed Care. LC 96-14756. 1996. 52.50 (*1-887841-03-2*, Psychosocial) Intl Univs Pr.

Cummings, Nicholas A., et al. The Value of Psychological Treatment: Collected Papers of Nicholas A. Cummings. LC 98-50582. 2000. 48.95 (*1-891944-12-6*) Zeig Tucker.

Cummings, Nicholas A., ed. see Baker, Neil J.

Cummings, Nick & Sayama, Mike. Focused Psychotherapy: A Casebook of Brief, Intermittent Psychotherapy Throughout the Lifecycle. 272p. 1995. text 32.95 (*0-87630-789-6*) Brunner-Mazel.

***Cummings, O. R.** Manchester Streetcars. LC 00-100094. (Images of America Ser.). (Illus.). 128p. 2000. pap. 18.99 (*0-7385-0412-2*) Arcadia Publng.

Cummings, O. R. The Shore Line Electric Railway. LC 98-8025. 1998. pap. write for info. (*0-933449-33-X*) Transport Trails.

— Trolleys to Augusta, Maine. (Transportation Bulletin Ser.: No. 76). (Illus.). 1969. 7.50 (*0-910506-03-5*) De Vito.

— Trolleys to Beaver Lake: A History of the Chester & Derry Railroad Association, 1891-1928. (Illus.). 34p. (Orig.). 1990. pap. 6.00 (*0-911940-48-0*) Cox.

***Cummings, O. R.** York's Trolleys. (Images of America Ser.). 1999. pap. 18.99 (*0-7385-0137-9*) Arcadia Publng.

Cummings, O. R. & Leavitt, Edward D. Street Cars to Old Orchard Beach: The Biddeford & Saco Railroad & Connecting Lines. (Illus.). 64p. (Orig.). 1989. pap. 9.00 (*0-911940-46-4*) Cox.

Cummings, O. R., jt. auth. see Clarke, Bradley H.

Cummings, Ora, tr. see Halamish, Aviva.

Cummings, Ora, tr. see Kaspit, Ben & Kfir, Ilan.

Cummings, Ora, tr. see Yehoshua, Abraham B.

***Cummings, Owen F.** The Basics of Christian Faith: Introducing Theology through the Sacraments. 192p. 2000. pap. 25.95 (*0-8245-1870-5*, Pub. by Crossroad NY) Natl Bk Netwk.

Cummings, Owen F. Coming to Christ: A Study in Christian Eschatology. LC 98-34836. 320p. 1998. 42.00 (*0-7618-1223-7*) U Pr of Amer.

***Cummings, Owen F.** Mystical Women, Mystical Body. LC 00-33963. 2000. pap. write for info. (*1-56929-036-9*, Pastoral Press) OR Catholic.

Cummings, P. Howard. Drugs Protocols Prehospital Emergency Care. (Nursing-Health Science Ser.). 459p. (C). 1993. pap. text 35.00 (*0-86720-214-9*) Jones & Bartlett.

Cummings, Pamela R., et al, eds. The Role of the Hospitality Industry in the Lives of Individuals & Families. LC 98-8597. 290p. 1998. 49.95 (*0-7890-0524-7*); pap. 24.95 (*0-7890-0526-3*) Haworth Pr.

Cummings, Pat. Angel Baby. LC 99-11502. (Illus.). 24p. (YA). (ps-3). 2000. lib. bdg. 15.89 (*0-688-14822-0*) Morrow Avon.

***Cummings, Pat.** Angel Baby. LC 99-11502. (Illus.). 24p. (YA). (ps-3). 2000. 15.95 (*0-688-14821-2*) Morrow Avon.

Cummings, Pat. The Blue Lake. LC 92-24354. (Illus.). 64p. (J). (gr. 1-5). 2001. 14.95 (*0-06-021535-6*); lib. bdg. 14.89 (*0-06-021536-4*) HarpC Child Bks.

— Carousel. LC 93-8708. (Illus.). 32p. (J). (ps-3). 1994. text, lib. bdg. 14.95 (*0-02-725512-3*, Bradbury S&S) S&S Childrens.

— Clean Your Room, Harvey Moon! (J). 1998. pap. 4.95 (*0-87628-335-0*) Ctr Appl Res.

— Clean Your Room, Harvey Moon! LC 89-23863. 32p. (J). (ps-2). 1991. lib. bdg. 16.00 (*0-02-725511-5*, Bradbury S&S) S&S Childrens.

— Clean Your Room, Harvey Moon! (J). 1994. 10.15 (*0-606-05789-7*, Pub. by Turtleback) Demco.

— Clean Your Room, Harvey Moon! LC 93-20571. (Illus.). 32p. (J). (gr. k-2). 1994. reprint ed. mass mkt. 4.95 (*0-689-71798-9*) Aladdin.

— My Aunt Came Back. LC 96-49374. (Illus.). 14p. (J). (ps up). 1998. write for info. (*0-694-01059-6*) HarpC.

— Purrrrr. (Chapter Book Charmers Ser.). (Illus.). 14p. (J). (ps up). 1999. 5.95 (*0-694-01056-1*) HarpC.

— Talking with Artists. LC 91-9982. (Illus.). 96p. (J). (gr. 4 up). 1992. lib. bdg. 22.00 (*0-02-724245-5*, Bradbury S&S) S&S Childrens.

— Talking with Artists. 1997. 11.95 (*0-689-81298-1*) S&S Childrens.

— Talking with Artists, Vol. III. (Illus.). 96p. (YA). (gr. 4 up). 1999. teacher ed. 20.00 (*0-395-89132-9*) HM.

***Cummings, Pat.** Why the Lizard Stretches His Neck. 2001. text 16.95 (*0-8050-6476-1*) H Holt & Co.

Cummings, Pat, ed. Talking with Artists, Vol. 2. LC 91-9982. Vol. 2. (Illus.). 96p. (J). (gr. 4-7). 1995. 19.95 (*0-689-80310-9*) Macmillan.

Cummings, Pat, ed. Talking with Artists. large type ed. 1995. 25.50 (*0-614-09611-1*, L-81885-00) Am Printing Hse.

Cummings, Pat. Pickin' Peas. LC 95-26133. 32p. (J). (ps-3). 1998. 15.95 (*0-06-027235-X*) HarpC.

Cummings, Pat & Cummings, Linda C., compiled by. Talking with Adventurers: Conversations with Christina M. Allen, Robert Ballard, Michael L. Blakey, Ann Bowles, David Doubilet, Jane Goodall, Dereck & Beverly Joubert, Michael Novacek, Johan Reinhard, Rick C. West & Juris Zarins. LC 98-11457. (Illus.). 96p. (J). (gr. 4-6). 1998. per. 19.95 (*0-7922-7068-1*, Pub. by Natl Geog) S&S Trade.

Cummings, Patricia. The Haunted Willow. LC 97-93451. 202p. (Orig.). (YA). (gr. 6-12). 1997. pap. 4.95 (*0-9657962-1-3*) Blue Line.

— The Secret in the Walnut Banister. LC 98-92912. 190p. (YA). (gr. 5-12). 1998. pap. 5.95 (*0-9657962-2-1*) Blue Line.

Cummings, Paul. Dictionary of Contemporary American Artists. 1999. text 85.00 (*0-312-17524-8*) St Martin.

— Irving Petlin: Pastels, 1961-1987. (Illus.). 84p. 1988. 30.00 (*1-878607-01-4*) Kent Gallery.

— Sculpture in Stone. (Illus.). 76p. (Orig.). (C). 1989. pap. 9.00 (*0-9624620-0-4*) Tree Gallery.

Cummings, Paul, ed. Dictionary of Contemporary American Artists. 6th ed. (Illus.). 800p. 1994. text 85.00 (*0-312-08440-4*) St Martin.

Cummings, Paul & Jenkins, Paul. Mark Tobey: Paintings (1920-1960) Iglesia, Ivy S., ed. (Illus.). 80p. (Orig.). 1994. pap. 25.00 (*0-9626731-9-6*) Yoshii Gallery.

Cummings, Paul, jt. auth. see Bame, E. Allen.

Cummings, Paul D. Lessons at the Fence Post. (Orig.). 1999. pap. 7.95 (*0-345-43287-8*, Ballantine) Ballantine Pub Grp.

— Lessons at the Fence Post. 208p. (Orig.). 1996. pap. 7.95 (*0-9655098-0-X*) Trning Strategies.

Cummings, Peggy. Connected Riding, an Introduction: Synchronizing Movements of Horse & Rider for Ease. (Illus.). 108p. 1999. pap. 14.95 (*0-9611314-9-7*) Primedia Enthusiast.

Cummings, Priscilla. Chadwick & the Garplegrungen. LC 87-71087. (Illus.). 30p. (J). (gr. k-4). 1987. 8.95 (*0-87033-377-1*, Tidewtr Pubs) Cornell Maritime.

— The Chadwick Coloring Book. (Illus.). 32p. (J). (gr. k-4). 1988. pap. 3.95 (*0-87033-389-5*, Tidewtr Pubs) Cornell Maritime.

— Chadwick Forever. (Illus.). 30p. (J). (gr. k-4). 1993. 8.95 (*0-87033-450-6*, Tidewtr Pubs) Cornell Maritime.

— Chadwick the Crab. LC 85-41005. (Illus.). 30p. (J). (gr. k-4). 1986. 8.95 (*0-87033-347-X*, Tidewtr Pubs) Cornell Maritime.

— Chadwick's Wedding. LC 88-51677. (Illus.). 30p. (J). (gr. k-4). 1989. 8.95 (*0-87033-390-9*, Tidewtr Pubs) Cornell Maritime.

***Cummings, Priscilla.** Chesapeake ABC. (Illus.). 30p. (J). (ps-k). 2000. 11.95 (*0-87033-525-1*, Tidewtr Pubs) Cornell Maritime.

— Meet Chadwick & His Chesapeake Bay Friends. (Illus.). 30p. (J). (ps). 1999. 11.95 (*0-87033-516-2*, Tidewtr Pubs) Cornell Maritime.

— Sid & Sal's Famous Channel Marker Diner. LC 91-65255. (Illus.). 30p. (J). (gr. k-5). 1991. 8.95 (*0-87033-423-9*, Tidewtr Pubs) Cornell Maritime.

Cummings, Priscilla. Toulouse: The Story of a Canada Goose. (Illus.). 30p. (J). (gr. 1-3). 1996. 9.95 (*0-87033-460-3*, Tidewtr Pubs) Cornell Maritime.

Cummings, R. D., tr. see Plato.

Cummings, R. M. Edmund Spencer. 363p. (C). 1996. 125.00 (*0-415-13402-1*) Routledge.

Cummings, Ralph W., Jr., jt. auth. see Wortman, Sterling.

Cummings, Ray. Girl in the Golden Atom. 1976. lib. bdg. 12.95 (*0-89968-175-1*, Lghtyr Pr) Buccaneer Bks.

— The Man Who Mastered Time. LC 74-15960. (Science Fiction Ser.). 362p. 1975. reprint ed. 29.95 (*0-405-06284-2*) Ayer.

Cummings, Renee. Fundamental Phonics. Ideal Instructional Fair, INSTRUCTIONAL FAIR, ed. 128p. 1999. pap. text 10.95 (*1-56822-855-4*) Instruct Fair.

Cummings, Rhoda Woods. Adolescence. (C). 1994. pap. text, student ed. 26.50 (*0-15-500393-3*, Pub. by Harcourt Coll Pubs) Harcourt.

— Adolescence. (C). 1994. pap. text, teacher ed. 33.75 (*0-15-502971-1*) Harcourt Coll Pubs.

— The Survival Guide for Teenagers with LD (Learning Differences) (YA). 1993. 17.05 (*0-606-05632-7*, Pub. by Turtleback) Demco.

Cummings, Rhoda Woods & Fisher, Gary L. The School Survival Guide for Kids with LD (Learning Differences) Ways to Make Learning Easier & More Fun. Espeland, Pamela, ed. LC 91-14489. (Illus.). 176p. (J). (gr. 2 up). 1991. pap. 12.95 (*0-915793-32-6*) Free Spirit Pub.

— The Survival Guide for Teenagers with LD: (Learning Differences) unabridged ed. Espeland, Pamela, ed. (YA). (gr. 7 up). audio 19.95 (*0-915793-56-3*, FS173) Free Spirit Pub.

— The Survival Guide for Teenagers with LD (Learning Differences) Espeland, Pamela, ed. LC 93-6798. (Illus.). 200p. (YA). (gr. 7 up). 1993. pap. 11.95 (*0-915793-51-2*) Free Spirit Pub.

Cummings, Rhoda Woods, jt. auth. see Fisher, Gary L.

Cummings, Richard, Jr. One Hundred One Costumes for All Ages, All Occasions. rev. ed. LC 87-20298. (Illus.). 200p. 1987. pap. 12.95 (*0-8238-0286-8*) Kalmbach.

— Simple Makeup for Young Actors. LC 89-23118. 1990. pap. 14.95 (*0-8238-0290-6*) Kalmbach.

Cummings, Richard, Jr., ed. see Lerner, Max.

Cummings, Richard O. American & His Food: A History of Food Habits in the United States. LC 74-112536. (Rise of Urban America Ser.). (Illus.). 1979. reprint ed. 22.95 (*0-405-02445-2*) Ayer.

***Cummings, Richard W.** Cummings' Vocabulary of Delaware. LC 99-51923. (American Language Reprints Ser.: Vol. 15). 47p. 1999. 16.00 (*1-889758-13-2*) Evol Pubng & Manuf.

Cummings, Robert. Basketmath: Elementary. (J). (gr. 4-6). mass mkt. 19.95 (*0-9623926-6-9*, BME) Sci Academy Soft.

— Basketmath: JHS-HS. (Illus.). (Orig.). (YA). (gr. 6-12). 1993. pap. text 19.95 (*0-9623926-5-0*) Sci Academy Soft.

— Basketmath en Espanol. (SPA., Illus.). 12p. (J). (gr. 4-6). 1997. pap. text 19.95 incl. disk (*0-9623926-7-7*) Sci Academy Soft.

***Cummings, Robert, ed.** Seventeenth-Century Poetry: An Annotated Anthology. LC 99-33568. (Annotated Anthologies Ser.). 576p. 1999. pap. 39.95 (*0-631-21066-0*) Blackwell Pubs.

— Seventeenth-Century Poetry: An Annotated Anthology. LC 99-33568. (Annotated Anthologies Ser.). 576p. 2000. 74.95 (*0-631-21065-2*) Blackwell Pubs.

Cummings, Robert & Gillespie, Stuart, eds. Translation & Literature, Vol. 1. 224p. 1993. pap. 30.00 (*0-7486-0310-7*, Pub. by Edinburgh U Pr) Col U Pr.

— Translation & Literature, Vol. 2. 224p. 1994. pap. 40.00 (*0-7486-0366-2*, Pub. by Edinburgh U Pr) Col U Pr.

Cummings, Robert D., jt. auth. see Church, F. J.

Cummings, Ronald, et al. New Evaluation Procedures for a New Generation of Water-Related Projects. LC 96-39266. (Technical Papers: No. 349). 64p. 1996. pap. 22.00 (*0-8213-3829-3*, 13829) World Bank.

Cummings, Ronald G. Water Resource Management in Northern Mexico. LC 72-3612. 80p. reprint ed. pap. 30.00 (*0-608-12532-6*, 202379400034) Bks Demand.

Cummings, S. J. R., et al. Gender Training: The Source Book. LC 99-204423. 160p. 1998. pap. 23.95 (*0-85598-404-X*, Pub. by Oxfam Pub) Stylus Pub VA.

***Cummings, Sally.** Centre-Periphery Relations in Kazakhstan. 2000. pap. 14.95 (*1-86203-100-2*) Royal Inst Intl Affairs.

***Cummings, Sarah.** Women's Information Services & Networks. 1999. pap. text 23.95 (*0-85598-425-2*) Oxfam Pubns.

Cummings, Scott. Left Behind in Rosedale: Race Relations & the Collapse of Community Institutions. LC 97-32511. (C). 1998. pap. 24.00 (*0-8133-3421-7*, Pub. by Westview) HarpC.

Cummings, Scott, ed. Business Elites & Urban Development: Case Studies & Critical Perspectives. LC 87-6456. (SUNY Series in Urban Public Policy). 395p. (C). 1988. pap. text 24.95 (*0-88706-578-3*) State U NY Pr.

Cummings, Scott & Monti, Daniel J., eds. Gangs: The Origins & Impact of Contemporary Youth Gangs in the United States. LC 92-2533. (SUNY Series in Urban Public Policy). 355p. (C). 1993. pap. text 24.95 (*0-7914-1326-8*) State U NY Pr.

Cummings, Shelly. Current Perspectives in Genetics: Insights & Applications in Molecular, Classical, & Human Genetics. 225p. 1996. pap. text 13.75 (*0-314-07563-1*) West Pub.

Cummings, Stephen & Ullman, Dana. Everybody's Guide to Homeopathic Medicines: Safe & Effective Remedies for You & Your Family. 3rd rev. ed. LC 96-31021. 304p. (Orig.). 1997. pap. 16.95 (*0-87477-843-3*, Tarcher Putnam) Putnam Pub Group.

Cummings, Stephen D. The Dixification of America: The American Odyssey into the Conservative Economic Trap. LC 97-49279. 240p. 1998. 39.95 (*0-275-96208-3*, Praeger Pubs) Greenwood.

Cummings, Steve. Home Banking with Quicken for Windows 95. 89p. 1996. pap. 16.95 (*1-55828-477-X*, MIS Pr) IDG Bks.

Cummings, Steve. Office 2000 Secrets. 1296p. 1999. 49.99 (*0-7645-3262-6*) IDG Bks.

— VBA for Dummies. 2nd ed. 432p. 1999. pap. 24.99 incl. cd-rom (*0-7645-0567-X*) IDG Bks.

Cummings, Steve & Cowart, Robert. Office 97 Secrets. LC 96-79757. 900p. 1997. pap. 49.99 (*0-7645-3015-1*) IDG Bks.

Cummings, Steve & Dummies Technical Press Staff. VBA for Dummies. LC 97-80869. 416p. 1998. pap. 29.99 incl. cd-rom (*0-7645-0258-1*) IDG Bks.

Cummings, Steve, jt. auth. see Williams, Robin.

Cummings, Stuart & Cummings, Susanne. Lonely Planet Diving & Snorkeling Guide to Turks & Caicos Islands. LC 92-34115. (Pisces Diving & Snorkeling Guides Ser.). 1993. pap. 14.95 (*1-55992-067-X*, Pisces Books) Lonely Planet.

Cummings, Stuart, jt. auth. see Cummings, Susanne.

Cummings, Susan H., jt. auth. see Loveridge, Catherine E.

Cummings, Susanne & Cummings, Stuart. Lonely Planet Diving & Snorkeling Guide to the Best Caribbean Diving. LC 95-12828. (Diving & Snorkeling Guides Ser.). (Illus.). 96p. 1995. pap. 14.95 (*1-55992-082-3*, 2082, Pisces Books) Lonely Planet.

— Lonely Planet Diving & Snorkeling Guide to U. S. Virgin Islands: St. Croix, St. Thomas & St. John. 2nd ed. (Pisces Diving & Snorkeling Guides Ser.). 96p. 1992. pap. 14.95 (*1-55992-053-X*, Pisces Books) Lonely Planet.

— Miami. (Florida Sights & Scenes Ser.). 64p. 1995. pap. 7.95 (*0-88415-644-3*, 5644) Gulf Pub.

Cummings, Susanne, jt. auth. see Cummings, Stuart.

Cummings, T., jt. auth. see Bailey, T. Grahame.

Cummings, Thomas & Worley, Christopher G. Organization Development & Change. 5th ed. Fenton, ed. LC 92-41858. (SWC-Management). 600p. (C). 1993. mass mkt. 64.25 (*0-314-01253-2*) West Pub.

Cummings, Thomas F. Polky Dot's Gift. LC 97-91104. (Illus.). 28p. (J). (ps-6). 1998. pap. 5.95 (*0-9660798-0-9*, PD1) ToLo Pub CT.

— Urdu Manual of the Phonetic Inductive or Direct Method: With a Progressive Introduction to the Constructions of the Urdu Language. (C). 1993. 20.00 (*81-206-0856-9*, Pub. by Asian Educ Servs) S Asia.

Cummings, Thomas G., ed. Systems Theory for Organization Development. LC 79-42906. (Wiley Series on Individuals, Groups & Organizations). 380p. reprint ed. pap. 117.80 (*0-608-16354-6*, 202669100051) Bks Demand.

Cummings, Thomas G. & Worley, Christopher G. Organization Development & Change. 6th ed. LC 96-50329. 725p. 1997. mass mkt. 87.95 (*0-314-20149-1*) S-W Pub.

***Cummings, Thomas G. & Worley, Christopher G.** Organization Development & Change. 7th ed. LC 00-41276. 2001. write for info. (*0-324-01987-4*) Sth-Wstrn College.

Cummings, Thomas S. Historic Annals of the National Academy of Design. LC 71-87503. (Library of American Art). 1969. reprint ed. lib. bdg. 47.50 (*0-306-71411-6*) Da Capo.

***Cummings, Tim.** Apocalypso. 74p. 1999. pap. 12.95 (*1-900152-38-X*, Pub. by Stride Pubns) SPD-Small Pr Dist.

***Cummings, Urban K.** Ronson the World's Greatest Lighter: Wick Lighters 1913-2000. 432p. 2000. pap. 24.95 (*0-9632796-1-0*) Bird Dog Bks.

Cummings, Val R. & Porter, David W. Chez Gators' Backyard Guide to Alligator Farming. LC 98-88588. (Illus.). 360p. 1999. pap. 24.95 (*1-891490-00-1*, 04-9902) StarSide Pr.

Cummings, W. K., ed. see Gopinathan, S.

Cummings, W. M., jt. ed. see Harwood, N.

Cummings, William & McGinn, Noel F., eds. International Handbook of Education & Development: Preparing Schools, Students & Nations for the Twenty First Century. LC 97-26288. 600p. 1997. 130.00 (*0-08-043067-8*, Pergamon Pr) Elsevier.

Cummings, William, jt. auth. see Scaglione, Robert.

Cummings, William H. Purcell. LC 68-25285. (Studies in Drama: No. 39). 1969. reprint ed. lib. bdg. 75.00 (*0-8383-0285-8*) M S G Haskell Hse.

— Purcell. 124p. 1990. reprint ed. lib. bdg. 59.00 (*0-7812-9080-5*) Rprt Serv.

Cummings, William John, compiled by. All Aboard! Along the Tracks in Dickinson County, Michigan. LC 94-13987. (Illus.). 154p. 1994. 26.00 (*0-933249-12-8*) Mid-Peninsula Lib.

Cummings, William K. & Altbach, Philip G., eds. The Challenge of Eastern Asian Education: Implications for America. LC 96-34722. (SUNY Series, Frontiers in Education). 340p. (C). 1997. text 65.50 (*0-7914-3283-1*); pap. text 21.95 (*0-7914-3284-X*) State U NY Pr.

Cummings, William K., et al. Changes in the Japanese University: A Comparative Perspective. LC 78-19787. 261p. 1979. 42.95 (*0-275-90344-3*, C0344, Praeger Pubs) Greenwood.

Cummings, William K., jt. auth. see Nielsen, H. Dean.

Cummings, William K., jt. ed. see Hawkins, John N.

Cummins. Basics of Legal Document Preparation. (General Business & Business Education Ser.). 1996. teacher ed. 17.95 (*0-8273-6800-3*, VNR) Wiley.

***Cummins.** Sucesos de las Islas Filipinas by Antonio De Marga. 1998. 52.95 (*0-521-01035-7*) Ashgate Pub Co.

Cummins, jt. auth. see Steckley.

Cummins, Thomas B. Toasts with the Incas: Andean Abstraction & Colonial Images on Kero Vessels. (History, Languages & Cultures of the Spanish & Portuguese Worlds Ser.). (Illus.). 380p. Date not set. text 59.50 (*0-472-11051-9*, 11051) U of Mich Pr.

Cummins, A. O. Isaac Cummings, 1601-1677, of Ipswich in 1638, & Some of His Descendants. (Illus.). 661p. 1989. reprint ed. pap. 99.00 (*0-8328-0445-2*); reprint ed. lib. bdg. 107.00 (*0-8328-0444-4*) Higginson Bk Co.

Cummins, Alex G., jt. auth. see Wade, Rex A.

Cummins, Ann F. Cattle Annie. LC 87-62832. (Illus.). 182p. (Orig.). 1988. pap. 9.95 (*0-943149-04-5*) Alpha Bks OR.

Cummins, Blair, jt. ed. see Cummins, Julie.

Cummins, Bryan. The Working Airedale. LC 94-14298. (Illus.). 192p. 1994. 24.95 (*0-940269-07-4*) OTR Pubns.

Cummins, C. Lyle, Jr. The Diesel Odyssey of Clessie Cummins. LC 98-73433. (Illus.). xiii, 399p. 1998. 37.00 (*0-917308-04-2*, B-777) Carnot Pr.

— Diesel's Engine Vol. 1: From Conception to 1918. Cummins, Jeanne, ed. LC 93-74475. (Illus.). xiv, 746p. 1993. 55.00 (*0-917308-03-4*) Carnot Pr.

Cummins, Carrice, jt. auth. see Benson, Vicki.

Cummins, Cedric C. Indiana Public Opinion & the World War, 1914-1917. 292p. 1945. 5.00 (*1-885323-10-7*) IN Hist Bureau.

Cummins, Cindy. Serge It in an Hour or Less. LC 96-8945. (Illus.). 112p. 1996. pap. 14.95 (*0-8019-8773-3*) Krause Pubns.

— Serge Something Super for Your Kids. LC 94-26848. (Illus.). 160p. 1995. pap. 19.95 (*0-8019-8607-9*) Krause Pubns.

Cummins, D. Duane. A Handbook for Today's Disciples: In the Christian Church (Disciples of Christ) rev. ed. 72p. (Orig.). 1991. pap. 3.25 (*0-8272-1425-1*) Chalice Pr.

— Un Manual para los Discipulos de Hoy. rev. ed. Delgado, Conchita, tr. from ENG. LC 83-15489.Tr. of Handbook for Today's Disciples. (SPA.). 80p. (Orig.). 1999. pap. 3.75 (*0-8272-2326-9*) Chalice Pr.

***Cummins, David L. & Thompson, E. Wayne.** This Day in Baptist History II: 366 Daily Devotions. LC 00-36057. 2000. write for info. (*1-57924-363-0*) Bob Jones Univ.

Cummins, David L., jt. auth. see Thompson, E. Wayne.

***Cummins, Denise D.** The Other Side of Psychology: How Experimental Psychologists Find Out about the Way We Think & Act. 240p. 2000. reprint ed. text 23.00 (*0-7881-6968-8*) DIANE Pub.

Cummins, Denise D. & Allen, Colin. The Evolution of Mind. (Illus.). 272p. 1998. 35.00 (*0-19-511053-6*) OUP.

Cummins, Denise D., jt. ed. see Cummins, Robert.

Cummins, Elizabeth. Understanding Ursula K. Le Guin. rev. ed. Bruccoli, Matthew J., ed. LC 89-70435. (Understanding Contemporary American Literature Ser.). 269p. 1993. pap. 12.95 (*0-87249-869-7*) U of SC Pr.

Cummins, Eric. The Rise & Fall of California's Radical Prison Movement. LC 93-17831. (Illus.). 352p. (C). 1993. 47.50 (*0-8047-2231-5*); pap. 17.95 (*0-8047-2232-3*) Stanford U Pr.

Cummins, Fred A., jt. auth. see Sadiq, Wagar.

Cummins, G. B. & Hiratsuka, Y. Illustrated Genera of Rust Fungi. rev. ed. LC 83-72397. 152p. 1983. spiral bd. 31.00 (*0-89054-058-6*) Am Phytopathol Soc.

Cummins, Genevieve. Chatelaines: Utility to Glorious Extravagance. LC 97-156249. (Illus.). 312p. 1994. 69.50 (*1-85149-206-2*) Antique Collect.

Cummins, George B. Rust Fungi on Legumes & Composites in North America. LC 78-60541. (Illus.). 436p. 1978. pap. 135.20 (*0-608-05632-4*, 206608800006) Bks Demand.

Cummins, George W. History of Warren County. (Illus.). 431p. 1997. reprint ed. lib. bdg. 46.00 (*0-8328-6080-8*) Higginson Bk Co.

Cummins, Geraldine. The Fate of Colonel Fawcett. 148p. 1985. spiral bd. 15.50 (*0-7873-0230-9*) Hlth Research.

Cummins, Harold. Dermatoglyphics in Indians of Southern Mexico & Central America: Santa Eulalia, Tzeltal, Lacondon & Maya Tribes. LC QL0941.C85. (Middle American Research Series Publication: No. 4). 27p. reprint ed. pap. 30.00 (*0-608-13719-7*, 205161600004) Bks Demand.

Cummins, Harold, et al. Measures of Men. (Publications: No. 7). 331p. 1936. 25.00 (*0-939238-08-X*) Tulane MARI.

Cummins, Herman Z., jt. auth. see Williamson, Samuel J.

Cummins, J., ed. see Kong, Shiu L. & Samuda, Ronald J.

Cummins, J. C. Licensing Law in Scotland. 400p. 1993. boxed set 121.00 (*0-406-11547-8*, UK, MICHIE) LEXIS Pub.

Cummins, J. David. Development of Life Insurance Surrender Values in the United States. LC 73-87483. (S. S. Huebner Foundation Monographs: No. 2). 81p. (C). 1973. pap. 12.00 (*0-918930-02-2*) Huebner Foun Insur.

— Investment Activities of Life Insurance Companies. (C). 1977. 23.95 (*0-256-01974-6*, Irwn McGrw-H) McGrw-H Hghr Educ.

— Strategic Planning & Modeling in Property-Liability Insurance. (S. S. Huebner International Ser.). 1985. lib. bdg. 82.00 (*0-89838-159-2*) Huebner Foun Insur.

Cummins, J. David & Derrig, R. A. Classical Insurance Solvency Theory. (C). 1988. 290.00 (*0-7855-4254-X*, Pub. by Witherby & Co) St Mut.

Cummins, J. David & Derrig, Richard A., eds. Classical Insurance Solvency Theory. (C). 1988. lib. bdg. 63.00 (*0-89838-272-6*) Huebner Foun Insur.

— Financial Models of Insurance Solvency. (C). 1989. lib. bdg. 115.50 (*0-7923-9018-0*) Huebner Foun Insur.

— Managing the Insolvency Risk of Insurance Companies. (S. S. Huebner International Ser.). 1991. lib. bdg. 110.00 (*0-7923-9152-7*) Huebner Foun Insur.

***Cummins, J. David & Santomero, Anthony M.** Changes in the Life Insurance Industry. LC 99-30333. (Innovations in Financial Markets & Institutions Ser.). 1999. write for info. (*0-7923-8535-7*) Kluwer Academic.

Cummins, J. David & Tennant, Joan L. Financial Management of Life Insurance Companies. LC 93-19221. (International Ser.). 1993. lib. bdg. 63.50 (*0-7923-9354-6*) Huebner Foun Insur.

Cummins, J. David, et al. Risk Based Capital: An Economic Overview. 1992. pap. text 7.50 (*1-887271-08-2*) Alliance Am Insurers.

— Risk Classification in Life Insurance. (S. S. Huebner International Ser.). 1983. lib. bdg. 78.00 (*0-89838-114-2*) Huebner Foun Insur.

Cummins, J. David, jt. auth. see Schwartz, Eduardo S.

Cummins, J. David, jt. intro. see Bachman, James E.

Cummins, J. S. A Question of Rites: Friar Domingo Navarrete & the Jesuits in China. 320p. 1992. 91.95 (*0-85967-880-6*, Pub. by Scolar Pr) Ashgate Pub Co.

Cummins, J. S., ed. Christianity & Missions, 1450-1800. LC 96-40399. (Expanding World Ser.: Vol. 28). 350p. Date not set. text 138.95 (*0-86078-519-X*, Pub. by Variorum) Ashgate Pub Co.

Cummins, J. S., ed. see de Vega, Lope.

Cummins, Jackie. Legislative Requirement under the Clear Air Act Amendments of 1990. (State Legislative Reports: Vol. 18, No. 2). 7p. 1993. 15.00 (*1-55516-299-1*, 7302-1802) Natl Conf State Legis.

Cummins, Jackie & Skiiema, Eric. Transportation, Clear Air, & Energy Efficiency: A Look at Overlapping Federal Legislation. (State Legislative Reports: Vol. 18, No. 11). 3p. 1993. 15.00 (*1-55516-337-8*, 7302-1811) Natl Conf State Legis.

Cummins, Jackie, et al. Alternative Fuels: A Case Study Report. LC 97-170652. 40p. 1995. pap. 20.00 (*1-55516-368-8*, 4116) Natl Conf State Legis.

Cummins, Jacqueline. End of Innocence. 1961. 11.95 (*0-8392-1028-0*) Astor-Honor.

Cummins, James. Portrait in a Spoon: Poems by James Cummins. LC 97-4723. 90p. 1997. pap. 9.95 (*1-57003-192-4*); text 15.95 (*1-57003-191-6*) U of SC Pr.

Cummins, James & Ferrer, Martin L. Proceedings-Memoria Conference on Books in Spanish for Young Readers: First Annual. Schon, Isabel, ed. (ENG & SPA.). 28p. (Orig.). (C). 1991. pap. 5.00 (*0-9639354-0-2*) Ctr Bks Spanish.

***Cummins, Jean Seitter.** The Doomsday Group. 264p. 1999. (*1-885663-04-8*) Franklin Mills.

Cummins, Jeanne, ed. see Cummins, C. Lyle, Jr.

Cummins, Jeff. Cars, Boats, Trains & Planes: A Pop-Up Book. LC 97-65901. 10p. (J). (ps-1). 1998. pap. 12.95 (*0-531-30058-7*) Orchard Bks Watts.

Cummins, Jim. Bilingualism & Special Education: Issues in Assessment & Pedagogy. 306p. 1984. write for info. (*0-905028-14-7*, MM6, Pub. by Multilingual Matters); pap. write for info. (*0-905028-13-9*, Pub. by Multilingual Matters) Taylor & Francis.

— Bilingualism & Special Education: Issues in Assessment & Pedagogy. LC 90-22601. 306p. (C). 1984. pap. text 31.00 (*0-89079-363-8*, 1639) PRO-ED.

— Bilingualism Education. LC 85-23149. 1989. pap. text 34.24 (*0-582-55380-6*, Pub. by Addison-Wesley) Longman.

Cummins, Jim & Corson, David. Bilingual Education. LC 97-43143. (Encyclopedia of Language & Education Ser.). 1997. lib. bdg. write for info. (*0-7923-4806-0*) Kluwer Academic.

Cummins, Jim & Sayers, Dennis. Brave New Schools: Challenging Cultural Illiteracy Through Global Learning Networks. 362p. 1997. pap. 17.95 (*0-312-16358-4*) St Martin.

Cummins, Jim & Skutnabb-Kangas, Tove, eds. Minority Education: From Shame to Struggle. 1988. 99.00 (*1-85359-004-5*, Pub. by Multilingual Matters); pap. 34.90 (*1-85359-003-7*, Pub. by Multilingual Matters) Taylor & Francis.

Cummins, John. Francis Drake. 348p. 1997. pap. 16.95 (*0-312-16365-7*) St Martin.

— Resources for Teachers of Adults. 64p. (C). 1987. pap. 80.00 (*0-900559-60-8*) St Mut.

Cummins, John, jt. auth. see Nichols, Kevin.

Cummins, John G. El Habla de Coria y Sus Cercanias. (Monagrafias A Ser.: Vol. XXXVIII). (SPA., Illus.). 256p. (Orig.). (C). 1969. pap. 69.00 (*0-900411-81-3*, Pub. by Tamesis Bks Ltd) Boydell & Brewer.

Cummins, John G., ed. see De Ayala, Pero L.

Cummins, Joseph E. Not One Dollar More! How to Save 3000 to 30000 Dollars Buying Your Next Home. LC 93-79861. 260p. (Orig.). 1995. pap. 19.95 (*0-9638215-9-8*) Kells Media.

***Cummins, Jospeh E.** Not One Dollar More! How To Save $3,000 to $30,000 Buying Your Next Home. 2nd ed. LC 99-23040. 286p. 1999. pap. 16.95 (*0-471-35726-X*) Wiley.

Cummins, Julian. Sales Promotion: How to Create & Implement Campaigns That Really Work. 2nd ed. 224p. 1998. pap. 35.00 (*0-7494-2447-8*) Kogan Page Ltd.

Cummins, Julie. Children's Book Illustration & Design, Vol. 2. (Illus.). 192p. 1998. 55.00 (*0-86636-393-9*) PBC Intl Inc.

***Cummins, Julie.** City Kid, Country Kid. 2001. text 15.95 (*0-8050-6467-2*) H Holt & Co.

— Tomboy of the Air. (J). 16.95 (*0-06-029138-9*, Wm Morrow); lib. bdg. 16.89 (*0-06-029243-1*, Wm Morrow) Morrow Avon.

***Cummins, Julie, intro.** Wings of an Artist: Children's Book Illustrators Talk about Their Art. LC 99-25906. (Illus.). 31p. (YA). (gr. 4 up). 1999. 17.95 (*0-8109-4552-5*, Pub. by Abrams) Time Warner.

Cummins, Julie & Cummins, Blair, eds. Choices Vol. 2: A Core Collection for Young Reluctant Readers. 544p. 1990. 45.00 (*0-934272-22-0*) J G Burke Pub.

Cummins, Kenneth, jt. auth. see Merritt, Richard.

Cummins, Kenneth W. & Wuycheck, John C. Caloric Equivalents for Investigations in Ecological Energetics. (International Association of Theoretical & Applied Limnology, Communications Ser.: No. 18). (Illus.). 158p. (Orig.). 1971. pap. 19.00 (*3-510-52018-1*, Pub. by E Schweizerbartsche) Balogh.

Cummins, Kent, jt. auth. see Britton, Tom.

Cummins, Lauren. Healthy Choices, Healthy Lives. (J). (ps-k). 1993. pap. 9.99 (*0-86653-935-2*) Fearon Teacher Aids.

***Cummins, Light T.** Austin College: A Sesquicentennial History, 1849-1999. LC 99-16895. 1999. 39.95 (*1-57168-317-8*, Eakin Pr) Sunbelt Media.

Cummins, Light T. Spanish Observers & the American Revolution, 1775- 1783. LC 91-13795. 280p. 1991. text 40.00 (*0-8071-1690-4*) La State U Pr.

Cummins, Light T. & Bailey, Alvin R., Jr., eds. A Guide to the History of Texas. LC 87-15021. (Reference Guides to State History & Research Ser.). 308p. 1988. lib. bdg. 69.50 (*0-313-24563-0*, CGT/, Greenwood Pr) Greenwood.

Cummins, Light T. & Jeansonne, Glen, eds. A Guide to the History of Louisiana. LC 82-6108. (Reference Guides to State History & Research Ser.). 298p. 1982. lib. bdg. 59.95 (*0-313-22959-7*, JLO/, Greenwood Pr) Greenwood.

Cummins, Louise. The Decennial Dilemma: Redistricting. (Illus.). 1984. pap. text 1.25 (*0-915757-02-8*) League Women Voters TX.

Cummins, Louise, ed. see Gamso, Jeffrey M.

Cummins, Maria. The Lamplighter. 1981. reprint ed. lib. bdg. 79.00 (*0-686-71927-1*) Scholarly.

Cummins, Mary. Carriage for Two. large type ed. (Linford Romance Library). 288p. 1998. pap. 17.99 (*0-7089-5238-0*) Ulverscroft.

***Cummins, Mary.** Fingala, Maid of Rathay. large type ed. 288p. 1999. pap. 18.99 (*0-7089-5467-7*, Linford) Ulverscroft.

— The Monkey Puzzle. large type ed. 304p. 2000. 20.99 (*1-84137-015-0*, Pub. by Mgna Lrg Print) Ulverscroft.

— Sea Tangle. 320p. 2000. 18.99 (*0-7089-5660-2*) Ulverscroft.

Cummins, Mary. Shadow over Flodden. large type ed. LC 97-18508. 211p. 1997. pap. 17.95 (*0-7838-8217-3*, G K Hall Lrg Type) Mac Lib Ref.

Cummins, MaryAnne D., ed. St. Peter's Episcopal Church, Delaware, Ohio - The First 100 Years, 1817-1918: A Collection of Documents & Genealogical Data. 389p. (Orig.). 1994. pap. text 28.50 (*1-55613-926-8*) Heritage Bk.

Cummins, Maureen, contrib. by. Crazy Quilt. limited ed. (Illus.). 18p. 1999. 6.00 (*1-893125-03-3*) Womens Studio Wrkshop.

***Cummins, Michael & Miller, Philip.** LAN Technologies Explained. (Illus.). 776p. 2000. pap. 49.95 (*1-55558-234-6*, Digital DEC) Buttrwrth-Heinemann.

Cummins, P. D. Medicine Marriage & the Marketplace. 2nd ed. LC 87-81723. 1988. reprint ed. write for info. (*0-9618819-2-5*) Foghrn Pr.

Cummins, P. D. & Zoeller, G., eds. Minds, Ideas, & Objects: Essays on the Theory of Representation in Modern Philosophy. (North American Kant Society Studies in Philosophy: Vol. 2). vi, 378p. (Orig.). 1992. pap. text 27.00 (*0-924922-13-3*); lib. bdg. 49.00 (*0-924922-63-X*) Ridgeview.

Cummins, P. D., ed. see Dyke, Peter C.

Cummins, Patricia W., ed. Literary & Historical Perspectives of the Middle Ages: Proceedings of the 1981 SEMA Conference. 232p. 1982. pap. 12.00 (*0-937058-15-7*) West Va U Pr.

Cummins, Patrick, tr. see Garrigou-Lagrange, Reginald.

Cummins, Paul F. Dachau Song. LC 91-28480. 308p. (C). 1992. text 29.95 (*0-8204-1729-7*) P Lang Pubng.

— For Mortal Stakes: Solutions for Schools & Society. 1998. pap. text 16.95 (*1-883647-08-8*) Bramble Co.

— For Mortal Stakes: Solutions for Schools & Society. LC 97-19044. (Counterpoints: Vol. 61). XVI, 213p. (C). 1998. pap. text 24.95 (*0-8204-3811-1*) P Lang Pubng.

Cummins, Peter, ed. Growth Factors & the Cardiovascular System. LC 93-11507. (Developments in Cardiovascular Medicine Ser.: Vol. 147). 400p. (C). 1993. text 191.00 (*0-7923-2401-3*) Kluwer Academic.

***Cummins, Richard.** Ireland. LC 99-29916. (Let's Investigate Ser.). 2000. lib. bdg. 21.30 (*1-58341-032-5*, Creat Educ) Creative Co.

Cummins, Richard, jt. auth. see Bjork, Patrick B.

Cummins, Richard O. ACLS Scenarios: Core Concepts for Case-Based Learning. 2nd ed. (Illus.). 320p. (C). (gr. 13). 1995. pap. text 25.00 (*0-8151-1517-2*, 25095) Mosby Inc.

Cummins, Richard O., ed. see American Heart Association Staff.

***Cummins, Rick & Scoullar, John.** The Little Prince - Str., Large Cast. 89p. 2000. pap. 5.60 (*1-58342-005-3*, LA3) Dramatic Pub.

Cummins, Robert. Meaning & Mental Representation. 173p. 1989. 25.00 (*0-262-03139-6*, Bradford Bks) MIT Pr.

— Meaning & Mental Representation. 173p. 1991. reprint ed. pap. text 15.00 (*0-262-53096-1*, Bradford Bks) MIT Pr.

— Representations, Targets, & Attitudes. LC 95-22502. (Representation & Mind Ser.). (Illus.). 168p. 1996. 25.00 (*0-262-03235-X*, Bradford Bks) MIT Pr.

Cummins, Robert & Cummins, Denise D., eds. Minds, Brains & Computers - The Foundations of Cognitive Science: An Anthology. LC 99-30789. (Philosophy Anthologies Ser.). (Illus.). 576p. (C). 1999. text 74.95 (*1-55786-876-X*) Blackwell Pubs.

***Cummins, Robert & Cummins, Denise D., eds.** Minds, Brains & Computers - The Foundations of Cognitive Science: An Anthology. LC 99-30789. (Philosophy Anthologies Ser.). (Illus.). 576p. (C). 1999. pap. text 39.95 (*1-55786-877-8*) Blackwell Pubs.

Cummins, Robert & Owen, David. Central Readings in the History of Modern Philosophy: Descartes to Kant. 483p. (C). 1991. pap. 33.50 (*0-534-16272-X*) Wadsworth Pub.

Cummins, Robert & Pollack, John, eds. Philosophy & AI: Essays at the Interface. (Illus.). 320p. 1991. 40.00 (*0-262-03180-9*, Bradford Bks) MIT Pr.

Cummins, Robert & Pollock, John, eds. Philosophy & AI: Essays at the Interface. (Bradford Bk.). 1995. pap. text 17.50 (*0-262-53135-6*, Bradford Bks) MIT Pr.

Cummins, Robert A. Improvement & Distribution of Practice. LC 76-176682. (Columbia University. Teachers College. Contributions to Education Ser.: No. 97). reprint ed. 37.50 (*0-404-55097-5*) AMS Pr.

— The Neurologically-Impaired Child: Doman-Delacato Techniques Reappraised. 272p. 1988. lib. bdg. 55.00 (*0-7099-4859-X*, Pub. by C Helm) Routldge.

Cummins, Robert C. & Christiano, Thomas D. Modern Moral & Political Philosophy. LC 98-8247. 568p. 1998. pap. text 45.95 (*0-7674-0283-9*, 0283-9) Mayfield Pub.

Cummins, Robert R. Basics of Legal Document Preparation. LC 96-17180. (General Business & Business Education Ser.). 352p. (C). 1996. pap. 69.95 (*0-8273-6799-6*) Delmar.

— Tort Law. LC 98-16766. 294p. 1998. pap. text 61.00 (*0-13-660994-5*) P-H.

Cummins, Roger & Whelan, Robert. Making a Lottery of Good Causes: The National Lottery & the Politicisation of Charity. LC 96-164286. (Choice in Welfare Ser.: No. 25). 28p. 1995. pap. 7.95 (*0-255-36362-1*, Pub. by Inst Economic Affairs) Coronet Bks.

***Cummins, Ronnie & Lilliston, Ben.** Genetically Engineered Food: A Self-Defense Guide for Consumers. 2000. pap. 12.95 (*1-56924-635-1*, Pub. by Marlowe & Co) Publishers Group.

Cummins, Sarah, jt. auth. see LeBlanc, Louise.

Cummins, Sarah, tr. see Crotean, Marie-Danielle.

Cummins, Sarah, tr. see Gauthier, Bertrand.

Cummins, Sarah, tr. see Gauthier, Gilles.

Cummins, Sarah, tr. see Leblanc, Louise.

Cummins, Sarah J. Autobiography & Reminiscences. 1997. reprint ed. pap. 12.95 (*0-87770-042-7*) Ye Galleon.

***Cummins, Susan, et al.** Beyond the Obvious: Rethinking Jewelry. (Illus.). 64p. 1999. pap. write for info. (*1-877742-06-6*) SF Craft & Folk.

Cummins, Suzanne, jt. auth. see Marlowe, Joelyn D.

Cummins, Thomas, et al. Arte Prehispanico del Ecuador: Huellas del Pasado: Los Sellos de Jama-Coaque. (ENG & SPA., Illus.). 255p. 1996. pap. 22.00 (*1-877812-50-1*, UC013) UPLAAP.

Cummins, Thomas J., jt. compiled by see Dunphy, Thomas.

Cummins, Tom, jt. ed. see Boone, Elizabeth H.

Cummins, Virginia R. Rookwood Pottery Potpourri. (Illus.). 136p. (Orig.). 1991. reprint ed. pap. 26.00 (*0-943633-03-6*) Cinc Art Gal.

Cummins, W. A. The Age of the Picts. LC 96-162451. (Illus.). 176p. 1996. 33.95 (*0-7509-0924-2*, Pub. by Sutton Pub Ltd) Intl Pubs Mktg.

— The Age of the Picts. (Illus.). 176p. 1998. pap. 21.95 (*0-7509-1608-7*, Pub. by Sutton Pub Ltd) Intl Pubs Mktg.

— The Picts & Their Symbols. 1999. 34.95 (*0-7509-2207-9*, Pub. by Sutton Publng) Intl Pubs Mktg.

Cummins, Walter. Where We Live. LC 82-22922. (Short Stories Ser.: Vol. 2). 94p. (Orig.). 1983. pap. text 7.50 (*0-89924-037-2*) Lynx Hse.

Cummins, Walter, ed. Shifting Borders: East European Poetry of the '80s. LC 91-58885. 488p. 1993. 59.50 (*0-8386-3497-4*) Fairleigh Dickinson.

Cummins, William & Scaglione, Robert. Shorin-Ryu: Okinawan Karate Question & Answer Book. (Illus.). 86p. 1985. pap. 11.95 (*0-8048-1426-0*) Tuttle Pubng.

Cummins, William, ed. & illus. see Scaglione, Robert.

Cummins/Owen & Owen. Central Readings in the History of Modern Philosophy. 2nd ed. (Philosophy Ser.). 1998. pap. 52.95 (*0-534-52347-1*) Wadsworth Pub.

Cummiskey, David. Kantian Consequentialism. 208p. 1996. text 45.00 (*0-19-509453-0*) OUP.

Cummiskey, Gary R. The Changing Face of Horror in the Nineteenth Century French Fantastic Short Story. LC 91-40091. (Age of Revolution & Romanticism: Interdisciplinary Studies: Vol. 3). 170p. (C). 1992. text 39.95 (*0-8204-1775-0*) P Lang Pubng.

Cummis, Worley. Essentials of Organizational Development & Change. 2001. 3300.00 (*0-324-02399-5*) Thomson Learn.

Cummuta, John M. The Debt-Free & Prosperous Living Basic Course. LC 94-240066. (Illus.). 248p. 1992. pap. 59.00 incl. audio (*1-883113-03-2*) Debt-FREE.

— The Debt-Free & Prosperous Living Basic Course. 6th ed. 1994. pap. 79.00 incl. audio (*1-883113-07-5*) Debt-FREE.

— The Debt-Free & Prosperous Living Basic Course. 7th rev. ed. 1997. pap. 79.00 (*1-883113-10-5*) Debt-FREE.

— Increase Your Profits Through Customer-Focused Direct Marketing: How to Get More Customers, How to Keep More Customers, How to Make More Money from the Customers You Have. 336p. 1989. pap. 79.00 (*1-883113-05-9*) Debt-FREE.

— The Personal Financial Success: Basic Course. 130p. 1991. pap. 49.00 (*1-883113-04-0*) Debt-FREE.

— Sales Machine Database Direct Marketing Course, 2 bks. 2nd ed. (Illus.). 240p. 1998. pap. 59.00 (*1-883113-12-1*) Debt-FREE.

— Sales Machine Database Direct Marketing Course Pt. 1: Database Direct Marketing. 2nd ed. (Illus.). 80p. 1998. pap. write for info. (*1-883113-13-X*) Debt-FREE.

— Sales Machine Database Direct Marketing Course Pt. 2: The Sales Machine System - Front-End Through Back-End Marketing. 2nd ed. (Illus.). 160p. 1998. pap. write for info. (*1-883113-14-8*) Debt-FREE.

— Sales Machine Direct Marketing Course, Pt. 1. rev. ed. (Illus.). 123p. 1993. write for info. (*1-883113-01-6*) Debt-FREE.

— Sales Machine Direct Marketing Course, Pt. 2. rev. ed. (Illus.). 62p. 1993. write for info. (*1-883113-02-4*) Debt-FREE.

— Sales Machine Direct Marketing Course, 2 pts., Set. rev. ed. (Illus.). 1993. pap. 98.00 (*1-883113-00-8*) Debt-FREE.

Cummuta, John M. & Wild, Mel. A Biblical Perspective on Debt-Free & Prosperous Living. 56p. 1998. pap. 7.95 (*1-883113-11-3*) Debt-FREE.

Cumnock, Frances, ed. Catalog of the Salem Congregation Music. (Illus.). 682p. 1980. 31.50 (*0-8078-1398-2*) Moravian Music.

Cumo. Thermal Hydraulic Design of Components for Steam Generation Plant. 408p. 1990. lib. bdg. 295.00 (*0-8493-6792-1*, TJ290) CRC Pr.

Cumo, Christopher. A History of the Ohio Agricultural Experiment Station, 1882-1997. unabridged ed. LC 97-72923. (Illus.). vi, 169p. (Orig.). 1997. per. 24.95 (*0-9646524-2-0*) Midwest Pr.

Cumo, Maurizio & Naviglio, Antonio. Thermal Hydraulics: Physical Properties & Characteristic Dimensions, Vol. 1. LC 87-15524. 176p. 1988. 96.00 (*0-8493-6789-1*, TJ260, CRC Reprint) Franklin.

— Thermal Hydraulics: Physical Properties & Characteristic Dimensions, 2 vols., Vol. II, Nucleate Boiling Heat Transfer. 160p. 1988. 90.00 (*0-8493-6790-5*, 6790, CRC Reprint) Franklin.

Cumo, Maurizio & Naviglio, Antonio, eds. Safety Design Criteria for Industrial Plants, 2 Vols., Vol. I. 288p. 1989. lib. bdg. 219.00 (*0-8493-6383-7*, T55) CRC Pr.

— Safety Design Criteria for Industrial Plants, 2 Vols., Vol. II. 304p. 1989. lib. bdg. 219.00 (*0-8493-6384-5*, T55) CRC Pr.

Cumont, Franz. Astrology & Religion among the Greeks & Romans. 208p. 1994. reprint ed. pap. 16.95 (*1-56459-459-9*) Kessinger Pub.

— The Mysteries of Mithra. 256p. 1996. reprint ed. pap. 14.95 (*1-56459-690-7*) Kessinger Pub.

— The Mysteries of Mithra. 2nd ed. McCormack, Thomas J., tr. (Illus.). 239p. 1956. pap. 8.95 (*0-486-20323-9*) Dover.

— The Mysteries of Mithra. 2nd ed. 239p. 1996. reprint ed. spiral bd. 15.50 (*0-7873-0231-7*) Hlth Research.

— The Oriental Religions in Roman Paganism, 1911. 325p. 1996. reprint ed. pap. 24.95 (*1-56459-537-4*) Kessinger Pub.

— Recherches Sur le Symbolisme Funeraire des Romains. LC 75-10632. (Ancient Religion & Mythology Ser.). (FRE., Illus.). 1976. reprint ed. 63.95 (*0-405-07007-1*) Ayer.

Cumont, Franz, jt. auth. see Bidez, Joseph.

Cumoulin, Heinrich. Zen Buddhism in the Twentieth Century. O'Leary, Joseph S., tr. from GER. 192p. (Orig.). (C). 1992. pap. 14.95 (*0-8348-0247-3*) Weatherhill.

***Cumper, Patricia.** One Bright Child. large type ed. 288p. 1999. 31.99 (*0-7089-4086-2*) Ulverscroft.

Cumper, Peter & Wheatley, Steven C. Minority Rights in the 'New' Europe. LC 98-47104. 1999. 135.00 (*90-411-1124-7*) Kluwer Law Intl.

Cumper, Peter, jt. auth. see McVea, Harry.

Cumpian, Carlos. Armadillo Charm. 80p. (Orig.). 1996. pap. 10.95 (*1-882688-09-0*) Tia Chucha Pr.

— Coyote Sun. (Illus.). 64p. (Orig.). 1990. pap. 6.50 (*1-877636-08-8*) March Abrazo.

Cumpian, Carlos, ed. Mas Sal Que Dulce Saltier Than Sweet: Bilingual English-Spanish Poetry. LC 94-72876. 82p. (Orig.). 1995. pap. 7.95 (*1-877636-13-4*) March Abrazo.

Cumpian, Carlos, et al. Emergency Tacos: Seven Poets con Picante. fac. ed. (Illus.). 40p. (Orig.). 1989. pap. 20.00 (*1-877636-07-X*) March Abrazo.

Cumpian, Carlos, ed. see Turcotte, Mark.

Cumpiano, Ina. Buen Tiempo, Mal Tiempo, Que Tiempo Hace? Big Book. (Que Maravilla! Ser.). (SPA., Illus.). 24p. (Orig.). (J). (gr. 1-3). 1992. pap. text 29.95 (*1-56334-026-7*) Hampton-Brown.

— Buen Tiempo, Mal Tiempo, Que Tiempo Hace? Small Book. (Que Maravilla! Ser.). (SPA.). 24p. (Orig.). 1992. pap. 6.00 (*1-56334-215-4*) Hampton-Brown.

— Homes Are for Living: Big Book. (Illus.). 24p. (Orig.). (J). (gr. 1-3). 1991. pap. text 29.95 (*1-56334-047-X*) Hampton-Brown.

— Homes Are for Living: Small Book. (Wonders! Ser.). (Illus.). 24p. (Orig.). (J). (gr. 1-3). 1991. pap. text 6.00 (*1-56334-053-4*) Hampton-Brown.

— Hugo Hogget: Big Book. (Wonders! Ser.). (Illus.). 24p. (Orig.). (J). (gr. 1-3). 1992. pap. text 29.95 (*1-56334-064-X*) Hampton-Brown.

— Hugo Hogget: Small Book. (Wonders! Ser.). (Illus.). 24p. (Orig.). (J). (gr. 1-3). 1992. pap. text 6.00 (*1-56334-070-4*) Hampton-Brown.

— Pan, Pan, Gran Pan: Big Book. (Rimas y Risas Red Ser.). (SPA., Illus.). 16p. (Orig.). (J). (gr. k-3). 1990. pap. text 29.95 (*0-917837-52-5*) Hampton-Brown.

— Pan, Pan, Gran Pan: Small Book. (Rimas y Risas Red Ser.). (SPA., Illus.). 16p. (Orig.). (J). (gr. k-3). 1992. pap. text 6.00 (*1-56334-085-2*) Hampton-Brown.

— Que Semana, Luchito! Big Book. (Que Maravilla! Ser.). (SPA., Illus.). 24p. (Orig.). (J). (gr. 1-3). 1991. pap. text 29.95 (*1-56334-023-2*) Hampton-Brown.

— Que Semana, Luchito! Small Book. (Que Maravilla! Ser.). (SPA., Illus.). 24p. (Orig.). (J). (gr. 1-3). 1991. pap. text 6.00 (*1-56334-037-2*) Hampton-Brown.

— Rosario y el Dinosaurio: Big Book. (Que Maravilla! Ser.: Level 1). (SPA., Illus.). 24p. (Orig.). (J). (gr. 1-3). 1992. pap. text 29.95 (*1-56334-168-9*) Hampton-Brown.

— Rosario y el Dinosaurio: Small Book. (Que Maravilla! Ser.: Level 1). (SPA., Illus.). 24p. (Orig.). (J). (gr. 1-3). 1992. pap. text 6.00 (*1-56334-170-0*) Hampton-Brown.

— Ton-Ton el Giganton: Big Book. (Que Maravilla! Ser.). (SPA., Illus.). 24p. (Orig.). (J). (gr. 1-3). 1992. pap. text 29.95 (*1-56334-025-9*) Hampton-Brown.

— Ton-Ton el Giganton: Small Book. (Que Maravilla! Ser.). (SPA., Illus.). 24p. (Orig.). (J). (gr. 1-3). 1992. pap. text 6.00 (*1-56334-039-9*) Hampton-Brown.

— Weather Watch: Big Book. (Wonders! Ser.). (Illus.). 24p. (Orig.). (J). (gr. 1-3). 1992. pap. text 29.95 (*1-56334-065-8*) Hampton-Brown.

— Weather Watch: Small Book. (Wonders! Ser.). (Illus.). 24p. (Orig.). (J). (gr. 1-3). 1992. pap. text 6.00 (*1-56334-071-2*) Hampton-Brown.

— Y Tu, Donde Vives? Big Book. (SPA., Illus.). 24p. (Orig.). (J). (gr. 1-3). 1992. pap. text 29.95 (*1-56334-019-4*) Hampton-Brown.

— Y Tu, Donde Vives? Small Book. (Que Maravilla! Ser.). (SPA., Illus.). 24p. (Orig.). (J). (gr. 1-3). 1992. pap. text 6.00 (*1-56334-045-3*) Hampton-Brown.

Cumpiano, William R. & Natelson, Jonathan D. Guitarmaking, Tradition & Technology: A Complete Reference for the Design & Construction of the Steel-String Folk Guitar & the Classical Guitar. LC 93-6160. (Illus.). 392p. 1994. reprint ed. 40.00 (*0-8118-0615-4*); reprint ed. pap. 29.95 (*0-8118-0640-5*) Chronicle Bks.

Cumpston, I. M. Indians Overseas in British Territories: 1839-1854. 198p. 1969. reprint ed. 27.00 (*0-8464-0506-7*) Beekman Pubs.

Cumpsty, John S. Religion As Belonging: A General Theory of Religion. 528p. (Orig.). (C). 1991. pap. text 39.50 (*0-8191-8359-8*); lib. bdg. 69.50 (*0-8191-8358-X*) U Pr of Amer.

Cumpsty, N. A. Compressor Aerodynamics. 32p. (C). 1997. 107.95 (*0-582-01364-X*) Addison-Wesley.

Cumpsty, Nicholas. Jet Propulsion: A Simple Guide to the Aerodynamic & Thermodynamic Design & Performance of Jet Engines. LC 97-7323. (Engine Technology Ser.: Vol. 2). (Illus.). 298p. (C). 1998. text 74.95 (*0-521-59330-1*); pap. text 29.95 (*0-521-59674-2*) Cambridge U Pr.

***Cumpton, Lonnie, et al.** Architectural Desktop 2 - Fundamentals: Instructor Version. 2nd ed. Aarhus, Jeanne & Ross, Jim, eds. (Illus.). 500p. 1999. pap. text, teacher ed. 125.00 (*1-891502-63-8*, ADT20FUNI) Tech Learn Co.

— Architectural Desktop 2 - Fundamentals: Student Version. 2nd ed. Aarhus, Jeanne & Ross, Jim, eds. (Illus.). 500p. 1999. pap. text, student ed. 112.50 (*1-891502-64-6*, ADT20FUNS) Tech Learn Co.

***Cumucio, Juan Carlos.** Hierarchy, Utility & Metaphor in Mapuche Botany. (Studies in Cultural Anthropology Twenty-Seven). 210p. 1999. pap. 32.50 (*91-554-4560-8*, Pub. by Uppsala Universitet) Coronet Bks.

Cumyn, Alan. Between Families & the Sky. LC 96-138757. 236p. 1995. pap. 16.95 (*0-86492-169-1*, Pub. by Goose Ln Edits) Genl Dist Srvs.

— Waiting for Li Ming. 274p. 1993. pap. write for info. (*0-86492-146-2*) Goose Ln Eds.

Cumyn, Richard. The Limit of Delta Y over Delta X. LC 94-218162. 190p. 1994. pap. 12.95 (*0-86492-176-4*, Pub. by Goose Ln Edits) Genl Dist Srvs.

Cuna. M31 Budgeting & Accounting for Nonaccounting Managers. 176p. per. 33.26 (*0-7872-6273-0*) Kendall-Hunt.

— V102 Planning. 4th ed. 64p. pap. text 18.74 (*0-7872-6692-2*) Kendall-Hunt.

Cunaccia. Hidden Tuscany: Unusual Destinations & Secret Places. (Illus.). 92p. 2000. 60.00 (*0-8478-2223-0*, Pub. by Rizzoli Intl) St Martin.

Cunaccia, Cesare M. Venice: Hidden Splendors. (Illus.). 128p. 1996. 35.00 (*2-08-013573-2*, Pub. by Flammarion) Abbeville Pr.

Cunaccia, Cesare M. & Listri, Massimo. Italian Parks & Gardens. LC 95-72946. (Illus.). 252p. 1996. 55.00 (*0-8478-1952-3*, Pub. by Rizzoli Intl) St Martin.

Cunan, Michael. Qualified Retirement & Other Employee Benefit Plans, 1995: Practitioner Edition - Text Table. (West's Employment Law Ser.). 1250p. (C). 1995. pap. text. write for info. (*0-314-06034-0*) West Pub.

Cunard, Nancy. Negro: An Anthology. LC 81-70126. (Illus.). 496p. 1996. pap. 39.50 (*0-8264-0862-1*) Continuum.

Cundall, A. E. Genesis & Exodus. (Bible Study Commentaries Ser.). 126p. 1981. pap. 4.95 (*0-87508-150-9*) Chr Lit.

Cundall, Arthur E. & Morris, Leon. Judges & Ruth. LC 68-31426. (Tyndale Old Testament Commentary Ser.). 318p. 1968. pap. 12.99 (*0-87784-257-4*, 257) InterVarsity.

Cundall, Frank. Bibliography of the West Indies. 197p. 1998. reprint ed. 45.00 (*1-57898-116-6*) Martino Pubng.

Cundall, Joseph. Joseph Cundall on Bookbinding History, Vol. 7. (History of Bookbinding & Design Ser.). 350p. 1990. text 40.00 (*0-8240-4020-1*) Garland.

Cundall, P. A., et al, eds. Key Questions in Rock Mechanics: Proceedings of the U. S. Symposium, 29th, Minneapolis, 13-15 April 1988. 791p. (C). 1988. text 168.00 (*90-6191-835-9*, Pub. by A A Balkema) Ashgate Pub Co.

Cundall, R., jt. auth. see Jennings, K. R.

Cundall, R. B., jt. ed. see Jennings, K. R.

Cundell, John. Radio Control in Model Boats. 3rd ed. (Illus.). 178p. (Orig.). 1996. pap. 24.50 (*1-85486-142-5*) Nexus Special Interests.

Cundick, Robert, ed. A First Album for Church Organists. (Illus.). 64p. 1967. pap. 11.95 (*0-8258-0227-X*, 0-4655) Fischer Inc NY.

Cundiff, Bette M. The Children's Material: A Complete "Miracles" Course for Children. rev. ed. (Illus.). 112p. (J). (gr. 1-6). 1998. pap. 10.95 (*0-9618309-1-3*) Miracle Dist.

Cundiff, Brad. The Hike Ontario Guide to Walks in Carolman Ontario. (Illus.). 176p. 1998. pap. 13.50 (*1-55046-270-9*, Pub. by Boston Mills) Genl Dist Srvs.

— Hike Ontario's Guide to Walks Around Toronto. LC 96-135807. (Illus.). 176p. 1994. pap. 11.95 (*1-55046-100-1*, Pub. by Boston Mills) Genl Dist Srvs.

Cundiff, David. Euthanasia Is Not the Answer: A Hospice Physician's View. LC 92-17245. 190p. 1992. 22.95 (*0-89603-237-X*) Humana.

Cundiff, David & McCarthy, Mary Ellen. The Right Medicine: How to Make Health Care Reform Work Today. LC 94-27992. 220p. 1994. 29.50 (*0-89603-284-1*) Humana.

Cundiff, Julian. Successful Carp Fishing. (Illus.). 208p. 1996. 45.00 (*1-85223-902-6*, Pub. by Crolwood) Trafalgar.

Cundiff, Lou G. Steps of Time. (Orig.). 1997. pap. write for info. (*1-57553-438-X*) Watermrk Pr.

***Cundiff, Margaret.** Called to Be Me. 1999. pap. text 10.95 (*0-281-05168-2*) Abingdon.

Cundiff, Michael J. Ten Knights in a Bar Room: Missing in Action in the Southwest Pacific, 1943. LC 89-48526. (Illus.). 132p. 1990. reprint ed. pap. 41.00 (*0-608-00020-5*, 206078600006) Bks Demand.

Cundill, Gordon. A Hunter's Africa. limited ed. LC 98-60928. (Illus.). 309p. 1998. 125.00 (*1-882458-20-6*) Trophy Rm Bks.

Cundy, Catherine. Salman Rushdie. LC 96-9826. (Contemporary World Writers Ser.). 320p. 1997. text 69.95 (*0-7190-4408-1*); text 19.95 (*0-7190-4409-X*, Pub. by Manchester Univ Pr) St Martin.

Cundy, Dale R. & Brown, Rick. Introduction to Avionics. LC 96-2321. 214p. (C). 1996. lab manual ed. 90.00 (*0-13-227489-2*) P-H.

Cundy, Dennis R. Gifts from the Seventh Heaven: Verses & Rhymes to Share. (Illus.). 77p. (Orig.). 1995. pap. 10.95 (*0-9645811-2-4*) Heaven Sent.

Cundy, H. M. & Rollett, A. P. Mathematical Models. 1996. pap., teacher ed. 18.95 (*0-906212-20-0*, Pub. by Tarquin Pubns) Parkwest Pubns.

Cundy, Ian. Ephesians-Thessalonians. (Bible Study Commentaries Ser.). 1981. pap. 4.95 (*0-87508-173-8*) Chr Lit.

Cundy, K. R., et al, eds. Infection Control: Dilemmas & Practical Solutions. LC 89-26613. (Illus.). 224p. (C). 1990. text 102.00 (*0-306-43397-4*, Kluwer Plenum) Kluwer Academic.

Cundy, Percival, tr. see Ukrainka, Lesja.

Cuneen, Joseph, tr. see Sulivan, Jean.

Cunegine, Hattie. Choices for Teenagers. LC 96-70471. 150p. (Orig.). (YA). (gr. 7 up). 1996. pap. 14.95 (*1-882792-34-3*) Proctor Pubns.

Cuneo, Carl J. Pay Equity: The Labour-Feminist Challenge. 240p. 1990. pap. 17.95 (*0-19-540782-2*) OUP.

Cuneo, Diane. Gifted & Talented Story Starters: My First Stories. (Gifted & Talented Ser.). (Illus.). 80p. (J). (gr. 1-3). 1995. pap. 5.95 (*1-56565-240-1*, 02401W, Pub. by Lowell Hse Juvenile) NTC Contemp Pub Co.

— Gifted & Talented Story Starters: Stories About Me. (Gifted & Talented Ser.). (Illus.). 80p. (J). (gr. 1-3). 1995. pap. 5.95 (*1-56565-242-8*, 02428W, Pub. by Lowell Hse Juvenile) NTC Contemp Pub Co.

***Cuneo, Diane.** Mary Louise Loses Her Manners. (Illus.). (J). 2000. pap. 6.99 (*0-440-41445-8*) Dell.

Cuneo, Diane. Mary Louise Loses Her Manners. LC 97-27875. (Illus.). 32p. (J). 1999. 15.95 (*0-385-32538-X*) Doubleday.

— Scary Story Starters. 64p. (J). 1995. pap. 5.95 (*1-56565-313-0*, 03130W, Pub. by Lowell Hse) NTC Contemp Pub Co.

***Cuneo, Louis.** Open Mike: Handbook for Creation & Operation of a Poetry Reading. 56p. 2000. pap. 9.95 (*0-9647373-1-0*) Marimbo Commun.

Cuneo, Louis, ed. see Angilly, Natica.

Cuneo, Marilyn M., jt. ed. see Richmond, Naima.

Cuneo, Mary L. Anne Is Elegant. LC 92-42417. 176p. (J). (gr. 4 up). 1993. 15.00 (*0-06-022992-6*); lib. bdg. 14.89 (*0-06-022993-4*) HarpC Child Bks.

— How to Grow a Picket Fence. LC 91-36444. (Illus.). 32p. (J). (ps-3). 1993. 15.00 (*0-06-020863-5*) HarpC Child Bks.

— Mail for Husher Town. 2000. lib. bdg. write for info. (*0-688-16526-5*, Grenwillow Bks) HarpC Child Bks.

Cuneo, Mary Louise. Mail for Husher Town. LC 98-52877. (Illus.). 24p. (J). (ps-3). 2000. 15.95 (*0-688-16525-7*, Grenwillow Bks) HarpC Child Bks.

Cuneo, Michael W. Catholics Against the Church: Anti-Abortion Protest in Toronto, 1969-1985. 1989. pap. 18.95 (*0-8020-6758-1*); text 40.00 (*0-8020-2726-1*) U of Toronto Pr.

— The Smoke of Satan: Conservative & Traditionalist Dissent in Contemporary American Catholicism. LC 99-24075. 226p. 1999. pap. 16.95 (*0-8018-6265-5*) Johns Hopkins.

— The Smoke of Satan: Conservative & Traditionalist Dissent in Contemporary American Catholicism. LC 96-34719. 224p. (C). 1997. 27.50 (*0-19-511350-0*) OUP.

Cuneo, Michael W., jt. auth. see Blasi, Anthony J.

Cuneo, Pablo. Bronka Stooler Boo Boo Boo: Stories & Art of a Child Author. 3rd ed. (Mucho Somos Ser.: No. 5). (Illus.). 9p. (gr. 1-5). 1986. 1.25 (*0-914370-50-2*) Mothers Hen.

Cuneo, Pia F. Art & Politics in Early Modern Germany: Jorg Breu the Elder & the Fashioning of Political Identity. LC 98-25296. (Studies in Medieval & Reformation Thought: Vol. 67). (Illus.). 240p. 1998. 94.00 (*90-04-11184-0*) Brill Academic Pubs.

***Cunerty, Bill & Lansdell, Lyle.** The Complete Quarterback. 70p. 2000. pap. 24.95 (*0-941873-15-3*) Sports Publishing.

Cuney & Hare, Maud C. Norris Wright Cuney: A Tribune of the Black People, Vol. 6. LC 94-19856. (African American Women Writers, 1910-1940 Ser.). 1995. reprint ed. 25.00 (*0-8161-1631-8*, G K Hall & Co) Mac Lib Ref.

Cuney-Hare, Maud. Negro Musicians & Their Music. LC 74-4108. (Music Reprint Ser.). 1974. reprint ed. 49.50 (*0-306-70652-0*) Da Capo.

Cunha. Clinical Infectious Disease: Diagnosis-Management. 1998. text. write for info. (*0-7216-4672-7*, W B Saunders Co) Harcrt Hlth Sci Grp.

***Cunha, A. M. & Fakirov, Stofiko.** Structure Development During Polymer Processing. LC 00-42664. (NATO ASI Ser.). 2000. write for info. (*0-7923-6449-X*) Kluwer Academic.

Cunha, A. Pinto Da, see Da Cunha, A. Pinto, ed.

Cunha, Burke, ed. Infectious Disease Pearls. (Pearls Ser.). (Illus.). 220p. (Orig.). 1998. pap. text 39.00 (*1-56053-203-3*) Hanley & Belfus.

Cunha, Burke A., ed. Infectious Diseases in Critical Care Medicine. LC 98-7036. (Infectious Disease & Therapy Ser.: 0). (Illus.). 872p. 1998. text 235.00 (*0-8247-0114-3*) Dekker.

Cunha, Burke A., jt. ed. see Ristuccia, Angela M.

Cunha, Carlos A. The Portuguese Communist Party's Strategy for Power, 1921-1986. rev. ed. LC 91-41523. (Modern European History Ser.: No. 2). 432p. 1992. text 25.00 (*0-8153-0676-8*) Garland.

Cunha, Derek Da, see Da Cunha, Derek, ed.

Cunha, Dorothy G., jt. auth. see Cunha, George M.

Cunha, Euclydes Da. Rebellion in the Backlands. Putnam, Samuel, tr. (Illus.). xxx, 562p. 1957. reprint ed. pap. text 19.95 (*0-226-12444-4*, P22) U Ch Pr.

Cunha, Frank Da, see Da Cunha, Frank.

Cunha, George M. & Cunha, Dorothy G. Conservation of Library Materials: A Manual & Bibliography on the Care, Repair, & Restoration of Library Materials, 2 vols. 2nd ed. LC 77-163871. 1972. 62.50 (*0-8108-2015-3*) Scarecrow.

— Conservation of Library Materials: A Manual & Bibliography on the Care, Repair, & Restoration of Library Materials, Vol. 1. 2nd ed. LC 77-163871. 1972. 47.50 (*0-8108-0427-1*) Scarecrow.

— Conservation of Library Materials: A Manual & Bibliography on the Care, Repair, & Restoration of Library Materials, Vol. 2. 2nd ed. LC 77-163871. 1972. 50.00 (*0-8108-0525-1*) Scarecrow.

— Library & Archives Conservation: 1980's & Beyond, Vol. I. LC 82-10806. 220p. 1983. 29.00 (*0-8108-1587-7*) Scarecrow.

Cunha, J. Gerson Da, see Gerson Da Cunha, J.

Cunha, L. V. Da, see Da Cunha, L. V.

Cunha, Luis V., et al. Management & Law for Water Resources. LC 77-76111. 1977. 40.00 (*0-918334-20-9*) WRP.

Cunha, M. Rachel, et al. The Portuguese in Rhode Island: A History. Conley, Patrick T., ed. (Rhode Island Ethnic Heritage Pamphlet Ser.). (Illus.). 33p. (Orig.). 1985. pap. 6.75 (*0-917012-72-0*) RI Pubns Soc.

Cunha-Ribeiro, L. M., jt. ed. see Campos, M.

Cunha, Rivara D. Archivo Portuguese Oriental in Six Fasciculo Em 10 Parties, 6 vols., Set. (C). 1992. reprint ed. 700.00 (*81-206-0777-5*, Pub. by Asian Educ Servs) S Asia.

Cunha Rivara, J. H. Da, see Da Cunha Rivara, J. H.

Cunha, Tony J. Horse Feeding & Nutrition. 2nd ed. (Animal Feeding & Nutrition Ser.). 445p. 1990. text 58.00 (*0-12-196561-9*) Acad Pr.

Cunha, Tony J., ed. see McDowell, Lee R.

Cunha-Vaz, J. G. & Leite, E. B., eds. Ocular Fluorophotometry & the Future. LC 89-19845. (Illus.). 167p. 1989. pap. text 57.50 (*90-6299-054-1*, Pub. by Kugler) Kugler Pubns.

Cuniberti, John M. The Birth of a Nation: A Formal Shot-by-Shot Analysis Together with Microfiche. (Illus.). 232p. 1979. 175.00 (*0-89235-016-4*) Primary Srce Media.

Cunico, Robert L., et al. Basic HPLC & CE of Biomolecules. unabridged ed. LC 98-70600. (Illus.). 400p. 1998. pap. 39.95 (*0-9663229-0-8*) Bay Bioanalytical.

Cuninggim, Merrimon. Uneasy Partners: The College & the Church. 200p. (Orig.). 1994. pap. 14.95 (*0-687-01151-5*) Abingdon.

Cuningham, Charles E. Timothy Dwight, 1752-1817: A Biography. LC 75-41069. reprint ed. 34.50 (*0-404-14746-1*) AMS Pr.

Cuningham, Eugene. Buckaroo. 1998. 17.50 (*0-7540-8031-5*) Chivers N Amer.

Cunkle, Carol, jt. auth. see Cunkle, James R.

Cunkle, James R. Treasures of Time: A Fully Illustrated Guide to Prehistoric Ceramics of the Southwest. LC 94-16275. 1994. pap. 14.95 (*0-914846-92-2*) Golden West Pub.

Cunkle, James R. & Cunkle, Carol. Kokopelli's Cookbook: Authentic Recipes of the Southwest. LC 97-40447. 112p. 1997. ring bd. 9.95 (*1-885590-24-5*) Golden West Pub.

An Asterisk (*) at the beginning of an entry indicates that the title is appearing for the first time.

Cunliffe. Gunter Grass. 1974. 13.50 (*0-8057-2400-1*, Twyne) Mac Lib Ref.
— Gunter Grass. reprint ed. pap. 13.50 (*0-608-30783-1*) Bks Demand.
Cunliffe & Trotte. 1st Read Alone: Ice. (Illus.). (J). pap. text 7.95 (*0-340-71666-5*, Pub. by Hodder & Stought Ltd) Trafalgar.
— 1st Read Home Alone: Firework. (Illus.). (J). mass mkt. 7.95 (*0-340-71665-7*, Pub. by Hodder & Stought Ltd) Trafalgar.
Cunliffe, B. W. Excavations at Portchester Castle Vol. II: Saxon. (Illus.). 352p. 1976. 20.00 (*0-85431-229-3*, Pub. by Soc Antiquaries) David Brown.
— Excavations at Portchester Castle Vol. III: Medieval, the Outer Bailey & Its Defences. (Illus.). 300p. 1977. 20.00 (*0-85431-222-6*, Pub. by Soc Antiquaries) David Brown.
Cunliffe, B. W., ed. Excavations at Richborough, No. 5. (Illus.). 414p. 1968. 20.00 (*0-85431-194-7*, Pub. by Soc Antiquaries) David Brown.
Cunliffe, B. W. & Fulford, M. G. Bath & the Rest of Wessex, Fascicule 2. (Corpus Signorum Imperii Romani, Great Britain: Vol. I). (Illus.). 1982. 98.00 (*0-19-726004-7*) OUP.
Cunliffe, B. W. & Munby, J. Excavations at Portchester Castle Vol. IV: Medieval, the Inner Bailey. (Illus.). 370p. 1985. 39.98 (*0-500-99039-5*, Pub. by Soc Antiquaries) David Brown.
***Cunliffe, Barry.** The Ancient Celts. (Illus.). 360p. 2000. pap. 21.95 (*0-14-025422-6*, Penguin Bks) Viking Penguin.
Cunliffe, Barry. English Heritage Book of Iron Age Britain. (Illus.). 128p. 1995. pap. 32.00 (*0-7134-7299-5*, Pub. by B T B) Balogh.
— Excavations at Fishbourne, 1961-1969 Vol. 1: The Site. LC 74-872142. (Reports of the Research Committee of the Society of Antiquaries of London: No. 26-27). (Illus.). 440p. reprint ed. pap. 136.40 (*0-7837-6403-0*, 204611900001) Bks Demand.
— Excavations at Fishbourne, 1961-1969 Vol. 2: The Finds. LC 74-872142. (Reports of the Research Committee of the Society of Antiquaries of London: No. 26-27). (Illus.). 448p. reprint ed. pap. 138.90 (*0-7837-6404-9*, 204611900002) Bks Demand.
— Fishbourne: A Roman Palace & Its Garden. LC 79-139850. (Illus.). 228p. reprint ed. pap. 70.70 (*0-608-17951-5*, 202789700057) Bks Demand.
— Fishbourne Roman Palace. (Illus.). 176p. 1998. pap. 24.99 (*0-7524-1408-9*, Pub. by Tempus Pubng) Arcadia Publng.
— Greeks, Romans & Barbarians: Spheres of Interaction. 256p. 1988. text 29.95 (*0-416-01991-9*) Routledge.
— Hengistbury Head Vol. I: The Prehistoric & Roman Settlement 3500 BC - AD 500. (Illus.). 363p. 1987. 39.98 incl. fiche (*0-947816-13-5*, Pub. by Oxford Univ Comm Arch) David Brown.
— Mount Batten, Plymouth: A Prehistoric & Roman Port. (Illus.). 108p. 1988. pap. 32.50 (*0-947816-26-7*, Pub. by Oxford Univ Comm Arch) David Brown.
— WESSEX AD 1000. (C). 1993. pap. text 39.95 (*0-582-49280-7*) Addison-Wesley.
Cunliffe, Barry, ed. The Ancient Celts. LC 96-53308. (Illus.). 336p. 1997. 49.95 (*0-19-815010-5*) OUP.
***Cunliffe, Barry, ed.** The Danebury Programme: The Prehistory of a Wessex Landscape, Vol. I. (Archaeology Monograph Ser.: Vol. 48). (Illus.). 233p. (C). 2000. 89.95 (*0-947816-48-8*, Pub. by Oxbow Bks) David Brown.
— The Danebury Programme: The Prehistory of a Wessex Landscape, Vol. II. (Archaeology Monograph Ser.: Vol. 49). (Illus.). 842p. (C). 2000. 125.00 (*0-947816-49-6*, Pub. by Oxbow Bks) David Brown.
Cunliffe, Barry, ed. The Oxford Illustrated Prehistory of Europe. (Illus.). 544p. 1994. 49.95 (*0-19-814385-0*) OUP.
— Prehistoric Europe: An Illustrated History. (Illus.). 544p. 1998. reprint ed. pap. 24.95 (*0-19-288063-2*) OUP.
Cunliffe, Barry & Cruz Fernandez Castro, Maria. The Guadajoz Project Vol. 1: Andalucia in the First Millennium BC: Torreparedones & Its Hinterland. (Monograph Ser.: Vol. 47). (Illus.). 469p. 1999. 150.00 (*0-947816-47-X*, Pub. by Oxford Univ Comm Arch) David Brown.
Cunliffe, Barry & Garratt, Beverley. Excavations at Portchester Castle Vol. V: Post Medieval 1609-1819. (Research Reports of the Society of Antiquaries of London: No. 52). (Illus.). 177p. 1995. 90.00 (*0-85431-264-1*, Pub. by Soc Antiquaries) David Brown.
Cunliffe, Barry & Keay, Simon, eds. Social Complexity & the Development of Towns in Iberia: From the Copper Age to the Second Century A. D. LC 96-112937. (Proceedings of the British Academy Ser.: No. 86). (Illus.). 480p. 1995. text 65.00 (*0-19-726157-4*) OUP.
Cunliffe, Barry & Miles, David. Aspects of the Iron Age in Central Southern Britain. (Illus.). 315p. 1984. pap. 19.95 (*0-947816-02-X*, Pub. by Oxford Univ Comm Arch) David Brown.
Cunliffe, Barry & Remfrew, Colin, eds. Science & Stonehenge. (Proceedings of British Academy Ser.: Vol. 92). (Illus.). 376p. 1998. text 65.00 (*0-19-726174-4*) OUP.
Cunliffe, Barry, jt. ed. see Bahn, Paul G.
Cunliffe, Barry, ed. see Todd, Malcolm.
Cunliffe, Barry, ed. see Wilkes, John.
Cunliffe, Barry W. Roman Bath. LC 72-856399. (Society of Antiquaries of London, Research Committee Reports: No. 24). 364p. reprint ed. pap. 112.90 (*0-608-13815-0*, 202078500018) Bks Demand.
Cunliffe-Beamer, Terrie L. The Laboratory Mouse. (Laboratory Animal Pocket Reference Ser.). 1998. 39.95 (*0-8493-2563-3*) CRC Pr.
Cunliffe, Christopher, ed. Joseph Butler's Moral & Religious Thought: Tercentenary Essays. (Illus.). 334p. 1992. text 78.00 (*0-19-826740-1*) OUP.
Cunliffe, J. Beast of Greendale, Bk. 12. (Illus.). (J). mass mkt. 8.95 (*0-340-71332-1*, Pub. by Hodder & Stought Ltd) Trafalgar.
— The Big Surprise. (Illus.). (J). mass mkt. 8.95 (*0-340-70409-8*, Pub. by Hodder & Stought Ltd) Trafalgar.
— The Mystery Tour. (Illus.). (J). mass mkt. 8.95 (*0-340-71333-X*, Pub. by Hodder & Stought Ltd) Trafalgar.
— Postman Pat: Follows a Trail. (Illus.). (J). 1996. text 17.95 (*0-340-67809-7*, Pub. by Hodder & Stought Ltd) Trafalgar.
— Postman Pat: Has the Best Village. (Illus.). (J). 1996. text 17.95 (*0-340-67810-0*, Pub. by Hodder & Stought Ltd) Trafalgar.
— Postman Pat: Hole in the Road. (Illus.). (J). 1996. text 17.95 (*0-340-67294-3*, Pub. by Hodder & Stought Ltd) Trafalgar.
— Postman Pat: In a Muddle. (Illus.). (J). 1996. text 17.95 (*0-340-67807-0*, Pub. by Hodder & Stought Ltd) Trafalgar.
— Postman Pat: Misses the Show. (Illus.). (J). 1996. text 7.99 (*0-340-67808-9*, Pub. by Hodder & Stought Ltd) Trafalgar.
— Postman Pat: Suit of Armour. (Illus.). (J). 1996. text 17.95 (*0-340-67806-2*, Pub. by Hodder & Stought Ltd) Trafalgar.
— Postman Pat & Christmas Baby. (Illus.). (J). 1998. text 17.95 (*0-340-69811-X*, Pub. by Hodder & Stought Ltd) Trafalgar.
— Postman Pat & Frog Pie Dinner. (Illus.). (J). 1998. mass mkt. 7.95 (*0-340-71436-0*, Pub. by Hodder & Stought Ltd) Trafalgar.
— Postman Pat & Goat Supper. (Illus.). (J). 1998. mass mkt. 7.95 (*0-340-71438-7*, Pub. by Hodder & Stought Ltd) Trafalgar.
— Postman Pat & Mushroom Tea. (Illus.). (J). 1998. mass mkt. 7.95 (*0-340-71440-9*, Pub. by Hodder & Stought Ltd) Trafalgar.
— Postman Pat & Surpise Breakfast. (Illus.). (J). 1998. mass mkt. 7.95 (*0-340-71434-4*, Pub. by Hodder & Stought Ltd) Trafalgar.
— Postman Pat & the Beast of Greendale, Bk. 12. (Illus.). (J). text 17.95 (*0-340-67816-X*, Pub. by Hodder & Stought Ltd) Trafalgar.
— Postman Pat & the Big Surprise. (Illus.). (J). text 17.95 (*0-340-67813-5*, Pub. by Hodder & Stought Ltd) Trafalgar.
— Postman Pat & the Cure for Hiccups. (Illus.). (J). mass mkt. 8.95 (*0-340-71626-6*, Pub. by Hodder & Stought Ltd) Trafalgar.
— Postman Pat & the Mystery Tour. (Illus.). (J). text 17.95 (*0-340-67817-8*, Pub. by Hodder & Stought Ltd) Trafalgar.
— Postman Pat & the Robot. (Illus.). (J). text 17.95 (*0-340-67814-3*, Pub. by Hodder & Stought Ltd); mass mkt. 8.95 (*0-340-70915-4*, Pub. by Hodder & Stought Ltd) Trafalgar.
— Postman Pat Follows a Trail. (J). mass mkt. 8.95 (*0-340-70387-3*, Pub. by Hodder & Stought Ltd) Trafalgar.
— Postman Pat Has Many Parcels. (Illus.). (J). mass mkt. 8.95 (*0-340-70408-X*, Pub. by Hodder & Stought Ltd) Trafalgar.
— Postman Pat Has Too Many Parcels. (Illus.). (J). text 17.95 (*0-340-67812-7*, Pub. by Hodder & Stought Ltd) Trafalgar.
— Postman Pat in a Muddle, No. 3. (Illus.). (J). mass mkt. 8.95 (*0-340-70385-7*, Pub. by Hodder & Stought Ltd) Trafalgar.
— Postman Pat Misses the Show. (Illus.). (J). mass mkt. 8.95 (*0-340-70386-5*, Pub. by Hodder & Stought Ltd) Trafalgar.
— Postman Pat 1: Hole in the Road. (Illus.). (J). mass mkt. 8.95 (*0-340-70384-9*, Pub. by Hodder & Stought Ltd) Trafalgar.
— Postman Pat Paints a Ceiling. (Illus.). (J). mass mkt. 8.95 (*0-340-70407-1*, Pub. by Hodder & Stought Ltd) Trafalgar.
— Postman Pat Paints the Ceiling. (Illus.). (J). text 17.95 (*0-340-67811-9*, Pub. by Hodder & Stought Ltd) Trafalgar.
— Postman Pat Takes Flight. (Illus.). (J). mass mkt. 8.95 (*0-340-71331-3*, Pub. by Hodder & Stought Ltd) Trafalgar.
— Postman Pat Takes Flight 11. (Illus.). (J). text 17.95 (*0-340-67815-1*, Pub. by Hodder & Stought Ltd) Trafalgar.
— Postmas Pat Has the Best Village. (Illus.). (J). mass mkt. 8.95 (*0-340-70388-1*, Pub. by Hodder & Stought Ltd) Trafalgar.
Cunliffe, John W. Early English Classical Tragedies. 1988. reprint ed. lib. bdg. 79.00 (*0-7812-0128-4*) Rprt Serv.
— English Literature During the Last Half-Century. 2nd enl. rev. ed. LC 70-156636. (Essay Index Reprint Ser.). 1977. reprint ed. 23.95 (*0-8369-2276-X*) Ayer.
— English Literature in the Twentieth Century. LC 67-23199. (Essay Index Reprint Ser.). 1977. 21.95 (*0-8369-0355-2*) Ayer.
— The Great Victorians, Vol. 14. Date not set. 30.95 (*0-8369-4830-0*) Ayer.
— Influence of Seneca on Elizabethan Tragedy. 1973. 250.00 (*0-87968-079-2*) Gordon Pr.
— The Influence of Seneca on Elizabethan Tragedy: An Essay. (BCL1-PR English Literature Ser.). 155p. 1992. reprint ed. lib. bdg. 69.00 (*0-7812-7103-7*) Rprt Serv.
— Modern English Playwrights: Short History of English Drama from 1825. (BCL1-PR English Literature Ser.). 260p. 1992. reprint ed. lib. bdg. 79.00 (*0-7812-7111-8*) Rprt Serv.
— Romantic Revival in England, Vol. 13. Date not set. 30.95 (*0-8369-4804-1*) Ayer.
— Shakespeare to Dryden, Vol. 11. Date not set. 30.95 (*0-8369-4802-5*) Ayer.
Cunliffe, John W., ed. Early English Classical Tragedies. 1971. reprint ed. 69.00 (*0-403-00913-8*) Scholarly.
— Poems of the Great War. LC 72-160904. (Granger Index Reprint Ser.). 1977. reprint ed. 21.95 (*0-8369-6267-2*) Ayer.
Cunliffe, John W., intro. Pope to Burns, Vol. 12. Date not set. 30.95 (*0-8369-4803-3*) Ayer.
Cunliffe, John W., ed. see Gascoigne, George.
Cunliffe-Jones, Hubert & Drewery, Benjamin, eds. A History of Christian Doctrine. 618p. 1997. pap. 39.95 (*0-567-08580-5*, Pub. by T & T Clark) Bks Intl VA.
Cunliffe-Jones, Hubert & Drewery, Benjamin, eds. A History of Christian Doctrine. 618p. 1979. 42.50 (*0-567-02352-4*) T & T Clark.
Cunliffe, Juliette. Complete Shih Tzu. (Illus.). 160p. 1993. 24.95 (*0-948955-47-3*, Pub. by Ringpr Bks) Seven Hills Bk.
Cunliffe, Julliette. The Chinese Shar-Pei Today. (Illus.). 160p. 1995. 25.95 (*0-87605-095-X*) Howell Bks.
Cunliffe, Marcus. In Search of America: Transatlantic Essays, 1951-1990, 98. LC 90-47538. (Contributions in American Studies: No. 98). 470p. 1991. 75.00 (*0-313-27712-5*, CSQ/, Greenwood Pr) Greenwood.
— Nation Takes Shape, 1789-1837. LC 59-5770. (Chicago History of American Civilization Ser.). 231p. 1960. pap. text 16.00 (*0-226-12667-6*, CHAC3) U Ch Pr.
— Soldiers & Civilians: The Martial Spirit in America, 1775-1865. (Modern Revivals in Military History Ser.). 512p. 1993. 87.95 (*0-7512-0126-X*, Pub. by Gregg Revivals) Ashgate Pub Co.
Cunliffe, Marcus, ed. see Weems, Mason L.
Cunliffe, R., jt. auth. see Raymond, S.
Cunliffe, Richard J. A Lexicon of the Homeric Dialect. LC 63-17165. 456p. 1977. pap. 24.95 (*0-8061-1430-4*) U of Okla Pr.
— A New Shakespearean Dictionary. 1977. lib. bdg. 69.95 (*0-8490-2340-8*) Gordon Pr.
— A New Shakespearean Dictionary. LC 76-39872. reprint ed. 52.50 (*0-404-01377-5*) AMS Pr.
Cunliffe, Roger, jt. auth. see Raymond, Santa.
Cunliffe, Tom. Celestial Navigation. (Illus.). 63p. (C). 1998. pap. 12.95 (*0-906754-39-9*, 128339AE, Pub. by Fernhurst Bks) St Mut.
— Coastal & Offshore Navigation. 64p. (C). 1990. text 59.00 (*0-906754-55-0*, Pub. by Fernhurst Bks) St Mut.
— Coastal & Offshore Navigation. 2nd ed. (Illus.). 96p. 1998. pap. (*0-906754-92-5*) Fernhurst Bks.
— Coastal Navigation. (U. S. Sailing Certification Ser.). 1996. pap. 19.95 (*1-882502-34-5*) US Sail Assn.
— Coastal Navigation. 1999. pap. 20.95 (*1-882502-72-8*) US Sail Assn.
— The Complete Yachtmaster. 1996. text 39.00 (*0-07-015106-7*) McGraw.
— Cunliffe on Cruising. (Illus.). 128p. (Orig.). 1992. pap. 17.95 (*0-924486-25-2*) Sheridan.
— Hand, Reef & Steer. LC 92-14844. (Illus.). 192p. 1992. 39.50 (*0-924486-40-6*) Sheridan.
— Heavy Weather Cruising. 64p. (C). 1990. text 65.00 (*0-906754-36-4*, Pub. by Fernhurst Bks) St Mut.
— Heavy Weather Cruising. 2nd ed. (Illus.). 93p. 1998. pap. 16.95 (*1-898660-27-1*) Motorbooks Intl.
— Inshore Navigation. 64p. (C). 1990. text 59.00 (*0-906754-31-3*, Pub. by Fernhurst Bks) St Mut.
***Cunliffe, Tom.** Ocean Sailing: Celestial Navigation, Weather, Passage Planning. (Illus.). 96p. 1999. pap. text 18.95 (*1-898660-61-1*, 129045AE) Fernhurst Bks.
— Passage Making. (Keelboat Certification Ser.: Vol. 5). (Illus.). 2000. pap. 24.95 (*1-882502-86-8*, Pub. by US Sail Assn) Partners Pubs Grp.
Cunliffe, Tom. The Shell Channel Pilot: The South Coast of England & the North Coast of France. 320p. 1997. 125.00 (*0-85288-386-2*, Pub. by Laurie Norie & Wilson Ltd) St Mut.
***Cunliffe, Tom.** The Shell Channel Pilot: The South Coast of England & the North Coast of France. 340p. 2000. 125.00 (*0-85288-421-4*, Pub. by Laurie Norie & Wilson Ltd) St Mut.
Cunliffe, Tom. Shell Pilot to the English Channel. (Illus.). 350p. (C). 1995. text 57.95 (*0-85288-278-5*, Pub. by Laurie Norie & Wilson Ltd) Bluewater Bks.
— Topsail & Battleaxe: A Voyage in the Wake of the Vikings. (Illus.). 182p. 1998. pap. 17.95 (*1-57409-045-3*) Sheridan.
Cunliffe, Tom, jt. auth. see Anderson, Bill.
Cunliffe, W. J. & Miller, Arthur, eds. Retinoid Therapy: A Review of Clinical & Laboratory Research. 376p. 1983. text 49.00 (*0-85200-740-X*) Kluwer Academic.
Cunliffe, W. J., jt. ed. see Marks, Ronald.
Cunnally, John. Images of the Illustrious: The Numismatic Presence in the Renaissance. LC 98-24951. 1998. 45.00 (*0-691-01668-2*, Pub. by Princeton U Pr) Cal Prin Full Svc.
Cunnane, S. & Thompson, L., eds. Flaxseed in Human Nutrition. 1995. 90.00 (*0-935315-60-8*) Am Oil Chemists.
Cunnane, Stephen C. Zinc: Clinical & Biochemical Significance. 224p. 1988. 126.00 (*0-8493-6733-2*, QP535, CRC Reprint) Franklin.
Cunnane, Tony & Bennett, Chris. A Year in the Life of the Red Arrows. (Illus.). 160p. 1998. 35.00 (*0-233-99119-0*, Pub. by Andre Deutsch) Trafalgar.
Cunneen, C., et al. Dynamics of Collective Conflict: Riots at the Bathurst 'Bike Races. (Illus.). xxviii, 207p. 1989. 57.00 (*0-455-20816-6*, Pub. by LawBk Co); pap. 30.50 (*0-455-20817-4*, Pub. by LawBk Co) Gaunt.
Cunneen, Chris, et al, eds. Faces of Hate: Hate Crime in Australia. LC 98-134396. 250p. 1997. pap. 29.00 (*1-876067-05-5*, Pub. by Federation Pr) Gaunt.
Cunneen, Chris & White, Robert. Juvenile Justice: An Australian Perspective. (Illus.). 304p. 1996. pap. text 49.95 (*0-19-553613-4*) OUP.
Cunneen, Sally. In Search of Mary: The Woman & the Symbol. LC 96-96361. 368p. (Orig.). 1996. pap. 14.00 (*0-345-38246-3*) Ballantine Pub Grp.
— Mother Church: What the Experience of Women Is Teaching Her. 1991. pap. 11.95 (*0-8091-3265-6*) Paulist Pr.
Cunneff, Tom. Hollywood on the Links. LC 97-43787. (Illus.). 224p. 1998. pap. 14.95 (*0-8092-2945-5*, 294550, Contemporary Bks) NTC Contemp Pub Co.
Cunni, jt. auth. see Cruse.
Cunnick, Elizabeth, ed. see Ottmann, Klaus & Bleckner, Ross.
Cunnick, Elizabeth, ed. see Yau, John.
***Cunniff, Patrick F., et al.** Product Engineering & Manufacturing. LC 99-210799. (Illus.). 344p. 1998. pap. text 42.60 (*0-9655911-3-1*) College Hse.
Cunniff, Patrick F., jt. auth. see Anand, Davinder K.
***Cunningham Devoto, Pat.** Out of the Night That Covers Me. 368p. 2001. 23.95 (*0-446-52751-3*) Warner Bks.
Cunnigham, Peter. The Story of Nell Gwyn & the Sayings of Charles the Second. Drinkwater, John, ed. (Illus.). 176p. 1972. 19.95 (*0-405-18145-0*) Ayer.
***Cunnigham, Sharon.** Colt Automatic Pistols. rev. ed. 354p. 1999. reprint ed. pap. 9.95 (*1-877704-39-3*) Pioneer Press.
Cunning, Robert. The Encyclopedia of Picture Framing Techniques. (Encyclopedia of Art Ser.). (Illus.). 176p. 1998. pap. 17.95 (*0-7624-0257-1*) Running Pr.
***Cunningham.** Accounting Information for Business. (C). 1999. pap. text, student ed. 25.00 (*0-03-022432-2*) Harcourt.
Cunningham. Accounting Information for Business Decisions, Vol. 2. (C). 1998. pap. text 33.50 (*0-03-022439-X*) Harcourt.
— Adirondack Regiment, One Hundred Eighteenth NY Volunteers. 1976. 25.00 (*0-8488-0244-6*) Amereon Ltd.
Cunningham. Architectural Drawings pap. text. write for info. (*0-471-48949-2*) Wiley.
Cunningham. Basic Circuit Analysis. 2nd ed. 959p. 1995. text 68.00 (*0-471-12733-7*) Wiley.
Cunningham. Basic Circuit Analysis: Student Problem Supplement to Accompany. 311p. 1994. pap., suppl. ed. 33.95 (*0-471-12480-X*) Wiley.
Cunningham. Charity Philanthropy & Reform: From the 1690s to 1850. LC 98-10081. 276p. 1998. text 69.95 (*0-312-21435-9*) St Martin.
— Chemical Aspects of the Atomic Nucleus. 1989. 10.00 (*0-85186-779-0*) CRC Pr.
— Culture Values. 2nd ed. (C). 1990. pap. text, teacher ed. 34.25 (*0-03-026767-6*) Harcourt Coll Pubs.
— Culture Values, Vol. 1. 2nd ed. (C). 1990. pap. text 63.00 (*0-03-026589-4*, Pub. by Harcourt Coll Pubs) Harcourt.
— Culture Values, Vol. 2. 2nd ed. (C). 1990. pap. text 63.00 (*0-03-026592-4*, Pub. by Harcourt Coll Pubs) Harcourt.
— Educational Administration: A Problem-Based Approach. LC 99-14377. 446p. (C). 1999. 70.00 (*0-205-18459-6*, Macmillan Coll) P-H.
— Educational Technology. (C). 1998. pap. text 16.36 (*0-395-90260-6*) HM.
Cunningham. Environmental Optics. text. write for info. (*0-471-48911-5*); pap. text. write for info. (*0-471-48910-7*) Wiley.
Cunningham. Environmental Science. 3rd ed. 1994. 113.43 (*0-697-15897-7*) McGraw.
— Environmental Science. 3rd ed. 1994. pap. 15.31 (*0-697-24310-9*, WCB McGr Hill); pap. text 61.74 (*0-697-31560-6*, WCB McGr Hill) McGrw-H Hghr Educ.
— Environmental Science. 3rd ed. 1994. boxed set 54.25 (*0-697-28760-2*, WCB McGr Hill) McGrw-H Hghr Educ.
— Environmental Science. 3rd ed. 1995. 59.25 (*0-697-28383-6*, WCB McGr Hill) McGrw-H Hghr Educ.
— Environmental Science. 3rd ed. 1995. text 84.25 (*0-697-31245-3*, WCB McGr Hill) McGrw-H Hghr Educ.
— Environmental Science. 4th ed. 1997. pap. 61.50 (*0-07-561249-6*) McGraw.
— Environmental Science. 4th ed. 1996. 55.74 (*0-697-41492-2*, WCB McGr Hill) McGrw-H Hghr Educ.
— Environmental Science: Taking Sides. 3rd ed. 1995. pap. 62.74 (*0-697-31563-0*, WCB McGr Hill) McGrw-H Hghr Educ.
— How to Play Trumpet. 1990. 6.95 (*0-685-32186-X*, H023) Hansen Ed Mus.
— Introduction to Asteroids. 1988. pap. 19.95 (*0-943396-16-6*) Willmann-Bell.
— Jefferson vs. Hamilton, Vol. 1. 2000. pap. 11.95 (*0-312-08585-0*) St Martin.
— Phonics They Use. 170p. (C). 1997. pap. text 30.60 (*0-673-46433-4*) Addson-Wesley Educ.
— Phonics They Use: Words for Reading & Writing. 3rd ed. LC 99-15343. 196p. (C). 1999. pap. text 26.00 (*0-321-02055-3*) Addson-Wesley Educ.
***Cunningham.** Reading & Writing in Elementary Classrooms: Strategies & Observations. 4th ed. LC 98-56205. 536p. 1999. 74.00 (*0-8013-3063-7*) Addison-Wesley.

C

— Strategies & Observations: Reading & Writing In Elementary Classrooms. 4th ed. 1999. 24.00 (*0-8013-1908-0*) Longman.

Cunningham. Tall Ships & Master Mariners. 1985. 9.95 (*0-919519-58-X*, Pub. by Breakwater Bks) BookWorld.

— Textbook of Veterinary Physiology. 2nd ed. (C). 1998. text. write for info. (*0-8089-2140-1*, Grune & Strat) Harcrt Hlth Sci Grp.

Cunningham, ed. Who's Telling the Story? 1995. pap. 12.95 (*0-614-11373-3*, Pub. by Oxfam Pub) Stylus Pub VA.

***Cunningham & Dawes.** Exercises for Developing Coaching Capability 1998 (uk Edition) 2000. boxed set 495.00 (*0-8464-5053-4*) Beekman Pubs.

Cunningham & Saig. Environmental Science. 2nd ed. 1992. teacher ed. 13.75 (*0-697-14295-7*, WCB McGr Hill) McGrw-H Hghr Educ.

Cunningham & Saigo. Understanding the Environment. 1994. pap. text, teacher ed. 14.06 (*0-697-20479-0*, WCB McGr Hill) McGrw-H Hghr Educ.

Cunningham & Stuller, John R. Basic Circuit Analysis. 2nd ed. 768p. 1994. text 96.95 (*0-471-12484-2*) Wiley.

Cunningham, jt. auth. see Mandelker.

Cunningham, ed. see Shakespeare, William.

Cunningham, A. Essential Chemistry. (Essential Guides Ser.). (Illus.). 64p. (YA). (gr. 7-11). 1992. pap. 6.95 (*0-7460-0727-2*, Usborne) EDC.

— Essential Chemistry. (Essential Guides Ser.). (Illus.). 64p. (YA). (gr. 7-11). 1999. lib. bdg. 14.95 (*0-88110-508-2*, Usborne) EDC.

Cunningham, A., jt. auth. see Claybourne, A.

Cunningham, A. B. Early Correspondence of Richard Wood, 1831-41. (Camden Fourth Ser.). 63.00 (*0-901050-70-9*) David Brown.

Cunningham, A. W. Shadows on the Grass. (C). 1989. 35.00 (*0-7223-2160-0*, Pub. by A H S Ltd) St Mut.

Cunningham, Agnes & Friesen, Gordon. Red Dust & Broadsides: A Joint Autobiography. Cohen, Ronald D., ed. LC 98-53049. (Illus.). 416p. 1999. 60.00 (*1-55849-209-7*); pap. 24.95 (*1-55849-210-0*) U of Mass Pr.

Cunningham, Alain. Canadian Indian Policy & Development Planning Theory. LC 99-33786. 1998. 50.00 (*0-8153-3224-6*) Garland.

***Cunningham, Alastair J.** The Healing Journey: Overcoming the Crisis of Cancer. rev. ed. (Illus.). 176p. 2000. pap. 14.95 (*1-55263-107-9*, Pub. by Key Porter) Firefly Bks Ltd.

Cunningham, Alexander. The Ancient Geography of India. 1990. reprint ed. 16.50 (*81-85395-47-0*) S Asia.

— Bhilsa Topes of Buddhist Monuments of Central India: Comprising a Brief Historical Sketch of the Rise Progress & Decline of Buddhism, with an Account of the Opening & Examination of the Various Groups of Topes Around Bhilsa. (C). 1997. 49.00 (*81-215-0759-6*, Pub. by M Manoharial) Coronet Bks.

— The Bhilsa Topes: or Buddhist Monuments of Central India. LC 78-72401. reprint ed. 47.50 (*0-404-17263-6*) AMS Pr.

— Ladbak, Physical, Statistical & Historical, with Notices of the Surrounding Countries. LC 98-905008. xii, 485 p. 1998. write for info. (*81-206-1296-5*) Asian Educ Servs.

— Mahabohdi: or The Great Buddhist Temple under the Bohdl Tree at Buddha-Gaya. LC 78-72402. reprint ed. 28.00 (*0-404-17264-4*) AMS Pr.

— Stupa of Bharhut: Buddhist Monument Ornamented with Numerous Sculpture. 1998. reprint ed. 56.00 (*81-215-0793-6*, Pub. by M Manoharial) Coronet Bks.

Cunningham, Alice. Introduction to Bioanalytical Sensors. LC 97-38100. (Techniques in Analytical Chemistry Ser.). 418p. 1998. 69.95 (*0-471-11861-3*, Wiley-Interscience) Wiley.

Cunningham, Allan. The Eastern Questions in the Nineteenth Century Vol. 2: Collected Essays. Ingram, Edward, ed. LC 92-17166. 304p. 1992. 52.50 (*0-7146-3453-0*, Pub. by F Cass Pubs) Intl Spec Bk.

— Life & Land of Burns. LC 76-144554. reprint ed. 47.50 (*0-404-08512-1*) AMS Pr.

— The Songs of Scotland, Ancient & Modern, 4 vols. LC 75-144551. reprint ed. 295.00 (*0-404-08640-3*) AMS Pr.

Cunningham, Allen, ed. Modern Movement Heritage: A Challenge to Manage. LC 98-8314. (Illus.). 224p. (C). (gr. 13). 1998. pap. 39.99 (*0-419-23230-3*, D6229, E & FN Spon) Routledge.

Cunningham, Amy. Grand Old Hotels of Northern California. (Umbrella Guides Ser.). (Illus.). 160p. (Orig.). 1996. pap. 12.95 (*0-945397-48-8*, Umbrella Bks) Epicenter Pr.

***Cunningham-Andersson, Una.** Growing Up with Two Languages: A Practical Guide. LC 99-14500. 1999. pap. 14.99 (*0-415-21257-X*) Routledge.

— Teachers, Pupils & the Internet. 1999. pap. (*0-7487-4307-3*) S Thornes Pubs.

***Cunningham-Andersson, Una & Andersson, Staffan.** Growing up with Two Languages: Practical Guide. 200p. (C). 1999. text 50.00 (*0-415-21256-1*) Routledge.

Cunningham, Andrew. Anatomical Renaissance. LC 96-47303. (Illus.). 304p. 1997. text 83.95 (*1-85928-338-1*, Pub. by Scolar Pr) Ashgate Pub Co.

Cunningham, Andrew, jt. auth. see French, Roger.

Cunningham, Andrew, jt. ed. see Grell, Ole P.

Cunningham, Andrew, jt. ed. see Grell, Peter.

Cunningham, Ann M. & Wicks, Wendy. Guide to Careers in Abstracting & Indexing. 126p. (Orig.). (C). 1992. pap. 29.00 (*0-942308-38-7*) NFAIS.

Cunningham, Ann M. & Wicks, Wendy, eds. Changing Roles in Information Distribution. (Report Series, 1994: No. 1). 160p. (Orig.). (C). 1993. pap. 75.00 (*0-942308-43-3*) NFAIS.

— Flexible Workstyles in the Information Industry. (Report Series, 1993: No. 2). 124p. (Orig.). 1993. pap. text 75.00 (*0-942308-41-7*) NFAIS.

— Three Views of the Internet. (Report Series, 1993: No. 3). 128p. (Orig.). (C). 1993. pap. 75.00 (*0-942308-42-5*) NFAIS.

Cunningham, Ann M., jt. auth. see White, Ryan.

Cunningham, Ann M., ed. see DiRenzo, Thomas G.

Cunningham, Ann M., ed. see Hodge, Gail M.

Cunningham, Annalisa. Yoga Vacations: A Guide to International Yoga Retreats. LC 99-24841. (Illus.). 240p. 1999. pap. 16.95 (*1-56261-474-6*) Avalon Travel.

Cunningham, Anne R., ed. see Rowe, John.

***Cunningham, Anne S.** Crystal Palaces: Garden Conservatories of the United States. (Illus.). 176p. 2000. 45.00 (*1-56898-242-9*) Princeton Arch.

Cunningham, Annette S. Aunts. LC 97-20728. 176p. 1997. pap. 11.95 (*0-8092-3057-7*, 305770, Contemporary Bks) NTC Contemp Pub Co.

Cunningham, Anthony, jt. auth. see Brull, Sorin.

Cunningham, Antonia. Rainforest Wildlife. (World Wildlife Ser.). (Illus.). 32p. (J). (gr. 3-7). 1993. pap. text 6.95 (*0-7460-0940-2*, Usborne); lib. bdg. 14.95 (*0-88110-640-2*, Usborne) EDC.

Cunningham, Antonia, jt. auth. see Claybourne, A.

Cunningham, B., jt. auth. see Cunningham Grahame, R. B.

Cunningham, Barry. Highway to Heaven. 1987. pap. 4.95 (*0-89137-817-0*) Quality Pubns.

— Superiority of the Son. 1990. pap. 3.85 (*0-89137-113-3*) Quality Pubns.

***Cunningham, Bernadette.** The World of Geoffrey Keating: History, Myth & Religion in Seventeenth-Century Ireland. 264p. 2000. 55.00 (*1-85182-533-9*, Pub. by Four Cts Pr) Intl Spec Bk.

Cunningham, Beryl M. & Holtrop, Wm. Woodshop Tool Maintenance. rev. ed. (Illus.). 296p. (C). 1974. pap. text 23.96 (*0-02-666280-9*) Glencoe.

Cunningham, Bess V. The Prognostic Value of a Primary Group Test: A Study of Intelligence & Relative Achievement in the First Grade. LC 70-176683. (Columbia University. Teachers College. Contributions to Education Ser.: No. 139). reprint ed. 37.50 (*0-404-55139-4*) AMS Pr.

Cunningham, Beverly. Quick Thinking, Grades K-6: Critical & Creative Thinking Challenges. 80p. 1992. pap. text 11.95 (*0-944459-47-1*) ECS Lrn Systs.

— Quick Thinking, Grades 7-12: Critical & Creative Thinking Challenges. 80p. 1992. pap. text 11.95 (*0-944459-48-X*) ECS Lrn Systs.

Cunningham, Beverly, et al. TAAS Master Math, Grade 2-3: Teacher's Handbook for Texas Assessment of Academic Skills. (Illus.). 144p. 1990. pap. text, teacher ed. 17.95 (*0-944459-14-5*) ECS Lrn Systs.

— TAAS Master Reading, Grade 4-5: Teacher's Handbook for Texas Assessment of Academic Skills. (Illus.). 112p. 1990. pap. text, teacher ed. 14.95 (*0-944459-20-X*) ECS Lrn Systs.

— TAAS Master Reading, Grade 2-3: Teacher's Handbook for Texas Assessment of Academic Skills. (Illus.). 112p. 1990. pap. text, teacher ed. 14.95 (*0-944459-19-6*) ECS Lrn Systs.

Cunningham, Beverly, jt. auth. see Klar, Elizabeth.

Cunningham, Bill. Castle: The Story of a Kentucky Prison. LC 94-79333. (Illus.). 256p. 1994. 18.95 (*0-913383-32-5*) McClanahan Pub.

— Children of Promise: The Story of a Kentucky Boy with a Future Growing up in a Town Without a Future. LC 97-74253. 376p. 1997. 23.95 (*0-913383-47-3*) McClanahan Pub.

— Flames in the Wind: An Inspiring Collection of Stories about Courageous West Kentuckians. LC 97-72210. (Illus.). 184p. 1997. 18.95 (*0-913383-52-X*) McClanahan Pub.

***Cunningham, Bill.** Hiking New Mexico's Gila Wilderness. 1999. pap. 19.95 (*1-56044-738-9*) Falcon Pub Inc.

— Lighting Grandma's Fire: Mountain Skills & Valley Pastimes. LC 99-64981. (Illus.). 180p. 1999. pap. 9.95 (*1-890437-33-6*) Western Reflections.

Cunningham, Bill. On Bended Knees: The Night Rider Story. 224p. 1996. 18.95 (*0-913383-43-0*) McClanahan Pub.

— Rendezvous: Back to a Simpler Time. (Illus.). 96p. 1995. pap. 19.95 (*0-87905-722-X*) Gibbs Smith Pub.

— Rocky Mountain Brave. LC 94-67350. (Illus.). 240p. (Orig.). 1994. pap. 12.95 (*0-9640890-1-7*) Parchment CO.

— Rocky Mountain Proud. Arnold, Karen S., ed. (Illus.). 274p. (Orig.). 1997. pap. 12.95 (*0-9640890-2-5*, RM3) Parchment CO.

— Rocky Mountain Tough. (Illus.). 220p. (Orig.). 1993. pap. 12.95 (*0-9640890-0-9*) Parchment CO.

— Wild Montana: A Recreation Guide to 55 Roadless Areas. LC 95-52631. (Illus.). 326p. (Orig.). 1995. pap. 14.95 (*1-56044-393-6*) Falcon Pub Inc.

Cunningham, Bill & Burke, Polly. Hiking California's Desert Parks. LC 96-46375. (Illus.). 384p. (Orig.). 1997. pap. 16.95 (*1-56044-508-4*) Falcon Pub Inc.

— Wild Utah: A Guide to 45 Roadless Recreation Areas. LC 97-38573. (Illus.). 352p. 1998. pap. 19.95 (*1-56044-616-1*) Falcon Pub Inc.

Cunningham, Billie M. Accounting Information for Business. (C). 1999. text 103.00 (*0-03-022429-2*) Harcourt.

— Accounting Information for Business Decisions, 2 vols., Vol. 1. (C). 1999. pap. text 34.00 (*0-03-022444-6*) Harcourt Coll Pubs.

***Cunningham, Billie M.** Accounting Information for Business Decisions, Vol. 1. (C). 1999. pap. text 66.00 (*0-03-031509-3*, Pub. by Harcourt Coll Pubs) Harcourt.

— Accounting Information for Business Decisions, 2 vols., Vol. 2. (C). 1999. pap. text 34.00 (*0-03-022447-0*) Harcourt Coll Pubs.

***Cunningham, Billie M.** Accounting Information for Business Decisions, Vol. 2. (C). 1999. pap. text 66.00 (*0-03-031511-5*, Pub. by Harcourt Coll Pubs) Harcourt.

Cunningham, Billie M. & Nikolai, Loren A. Account Information for Business Decisions, 1. 540p. (C). 1998. pap. text 33.50 (*0-03-022438-1*) Harcourt Coll Pubs.

Cunningham, Bradley S. Tucket Teddy's Day at Work. 7.95 (*0-9653674-0-1*) Nantucket Cblestns.

***Cunningham, Brian J.** Lessons for the Trail of Life Conversations Starters for Parents & Children. 80p. 1999. pap. 13.00 (*1-55833-223-5*) Natl Cath Educ.

Cunningham-Brow. Girls of Lechdale College. (J). mass mkt. 6.95 (*0-7472-5408-7*, Pub. by Headline Bk Pub) Trafalgar.

Cunningham, Bruce. Naval Fighters Vol. 45, Pt. 1: Douglas A3D Skywarrior: Design/Structures/Testing. (Illus.). 136p. 1998. pap. 22.95 (*0-942612-45-0*, NF45) Naval Fighters.

Cunningham, Bruce L., jt. auth. see McKinney, Peter.

Cunningham, C. Michael. The Nominal Christian Handbook. 1991. pap. 5.95 (*1-55673-306-2*, 9130) CSS OH.

Cunningham, Carl L., jt. auth. see Fox, Richard H.

Cunningham, Carmela & Coombs, Norman. Information Access & Adaptive Technology. LC 97-11048. 216p. 1997. boxed set 34.95 (*0-89774-992-8*) Oryx Pr.

Cunningham, Carol & Berger, Joel. Horn of Darkness: Rhinos on the Edge. LC 96-22323. (Illus.). 256p. 1997. 25.00 (*0-19-511113-0*) OUP.

***Cunningham, Carol & Berger, Joel.** Horn of Darkness: Rhinos on the Edge. (Illus.). 272p. 2000. pap. 14.95 (*0-19-513880-5*) OUP.

Cunningham, Carol & Berger, Joel. Horns of Darkness: Rhinos on the Edge. 1997. 25.00 (*0-614-28264-0*) OUP.

Cunningham, Carol, jt. auth. see Berger, Joel.

Cunningham, Carole. Carole Cunningham's Directory of Networking Organizations in the Greater Los Angeles Area - 1994 Edition: A Guidebook to Networking in Los Angeles. 150p. (Orig.). 1994. pap., spiral bd. 25.00 (*0-9638287-1-1*) Grande Vista.

— Carole Cunningham's Directory of Networking Organizations in the Inland Empire - 1994 Edition: A Guidebook to Networking in the Inland Empire & Los Angeles. 150p. (Orig.). 1994. pap., spiral bd. 25.00 (*0-9638287-9-7*) Grande Vista.

— Carole Cunningham's Directory of Networking Organizations in the San Fernando Valley - 1994 Edition: A Guidebook to Networking in the San Fernando Valley & Los Angeles. 150p. (Orig.). 1994. pap., spiral bd. 25.00 (*0-9638287-4-6*) Grande Vista.

— Carole Cunningham's Directory of Networking Organizations in the San Gabriel Valley, 1993: A Guidebook to Networking in the San Gabriel Valley & Los Angeles. 150p. (Orig.). 1993. pap., spiral bd. 25.00 (*0-9638287-7-0*) Grande Vista.

— Expanding Your Network Through Seminars, Workshops & Public Speaking. 408p. (Orig.). 1994. pap. 20.00 (*0-9638287-8-9*) Grande Vista.

Cunningham, Carole, et al. L. A. Connects: Westside/Downtown. (Illus.). 112p. (Orig.). 1995. pap. 9.95 (*0-9653445-0-9*) L A Connects.

Cunningham, Carole, ed. see Hargrove, Liz.

Cunningham, Carolyn. All Kinds of Separation. (Illus.). 24p. (J). (gr. k-6). 1988. student ed. 3.95 (*0-685-20040-X*, 0494) Kidsrights.

Cunningham, Carolyn & MacFarlane, Kee. When Children Abuse: Group Treatment Strategies for Children with Impulse Control Problems. rev. ed. Bear, Euan, ed. (Illus.). 272p. 1996. pap. text 28.00 (*1-884444-23-7*) Safer Soc.

Cunningham, Carolyn, jt. auth. see MacFarlane, Kee.

Cunningham, Cecil W. Feminine Attitudes in the Nineteenth Century. LC 72-2089. (English Literature Ser.: No. 33). 1972. reprint ed. lib. bdg. 75.00 (*0-8383-1483-X*) M S G Haskell Hse.

Cunningham, Charles. Germany Today & Tomorrow. LC 70-180396. reprint ed. 38.00 (*0-404-56117-9*) AMS Pr.

— Tennis for Everyone: Uncommon Solutions to Common Problems. 2nd ed. 146p. (C). 1997. per. 24.95 (*0-7872-4620-4*, 41462001) Kendall-Hunt.

Cunningham, Charles & Porter, Andrew J. R., eds. Recombinant Protein from Plants: Production & Isolation of Clinically Useful Compounds. LC 97-35760. (Methods in Biotechnology Ser.: Vol. 3). (Illus.). 308p. 1997. 89.50 (*0-89603-390-2*) Humana.

Cunningham, Charles H. Audiencia in the Spanish Colonies As Illustrated by the Audiencia in Manila, 1583-1800. LC 72-131250. 479p. 1971. reprint ed. 75.00 (*0-87752-130-1*) Gordian.

Cunningham, Chet. The Avenger No. 2: Houston Hellground. 192p. (Orig.). 1988. mass mkt. 2.95 (*0-446-34738-8*, Pub. by Warner Bks) Little.

— Comanche Massacre. large type ed. LC 97-39745. (Western Ser.). 279p. 1997. lib. bdg. 19.95 (*0-7862-1249-7*) Thorndike Pr.

***Cunningham, Chet.** Crazy Horse: War Chief of the Oglalas. LC 99-37845. (A&E Biography Ser.). (Illus.). 128p. (YA). (gr. 4-7). 2000. 25.26 (*0-8225-4978-6*, Lerner Publctns) Lerner Pub.

Cunningham, Chet. Cripple Creek Bonanza. LC 95-20831. 208p. 1995. pap. 12.95 (*1-55622-399-4*, Rep of TX Pr) Wordware Pub.

***Cunningham, Chet.** Cripple Creek Bonanza. rev. ed. 220p. 2000. 12.95 (*0-943727-22-7*) Wayfinder Pr.

Cunningham, Chet. Die of Gold. large type ed. 218p. 1992. pap. 14.95 (*0-8161-5486-4*, G K Hall Lrg Type) Mac Lib Ref.

***Cunningham, Chet.** The Fibromyalgia Relief Handbook. LC 00-131420. 224p. 2000. pap. 14.95 (*1-887053-13-1*) United Res CA.

Cunningham, Chet. Fifty Secrets: How to Meet People & Make Friends. LC 91-68345. 224p. (Orig.). 1993. pap. 12.95 (*0-9614924-7-3*) United Res CA.

— The Irritable Bowel Syndrome (IBS) & Gastrointestinal Solutions Handbook. LC 95-60171. 240p. 1997. pap. 14.95 (*0-9614924-9-X*) United Res CA.

— Jim Steel No. 5: Gold Train. large type ed. (Linford Western Library). 320p. 1993. pap. 16.99 (*0-7089-7445-7*) Ulverscroft.

— Line Rider's Revenge. 256p. 1994. mass mkt. 3.50 (*1-55817-787-6*, Pinncle Kensgtn) Kensgtn Pub Corp.

— The Macular Degeneration Handbook: Natural Ways to Prevent & Reverse It. LC 98-61570. (Illus.). 278p. 1998. pap. 14.95 (*1-887053-11-5*) United Res CA.

***Cunningham, Chet.** Nuke Down. 2000. mass mkt. 5.99 (*0-553-58077-9*) Bantam.

Cunningham, Chet. The Prostate Problem. 1995. pap. 8.95 (*0-8217-4892-0*) NAL.

***Cunningham, Chet.** The Sciatica Relief Handbook. LC 97-60209. (Illus.). 261p. 1998. pap. 14.95 (*1-887053-09-3*) United Res CA.

Cunningham, Chet. Sioux Slaughter: Pony Soldiers. large type ed. LC 98-30795. 1998. pap. 18.95 (*0-7862-1643-3*) Mac Lib Ref.

***Cunningham, Chet.** The Specialists: Plunder. 320p. 1999. mass mkt. 5.99 (*0-553-58071-X*) Bantam.

Cunningham, Chet. Three Simple Steps to Flatten Your Belly. LC 94-60412. (Illus.). 176p. (Orig.). 1995. pap. 12.95 (*0-9614924-8-1*) United Res CA.

— Your Prostate: What Every Man over Forty Needs to Know, Now! LC 90-71251. (Illus.). 192p. (Orig.). 1994. pap. 12.95 (*0-9614924-6-5*) United Res CA.

Cunningham, Chris, ed. see Gronseth, George & Broze, Matt.

Cunningham, Christine, ed. see McFarlane, Marilyn.

Cunningham, Clark E., jt. ed. see Russell, Susan D.

Cunningham, Cliff. Understanding Down Syndrome: An Introduction for Parents. LC 95-25997. 244p. 1998. pap. 14.95 (*1-57129-009-5*) Brookline Bks.

Cunningham, Colin. Stones of Witness Introduction to Church Architecture. 1999. 44.95 (*0-7509-1225-1*) Bks Intl VA.

Cunningham, Colin & Waterhouse, Prudence. Alfred Waterhouse, 1830-1905: Biography of a Practice. (Clarendon Studies in the History of Art). (Illus.). 436p. 1992. 210.00 (*0-19-817511-6*) OUP.

Cunningham, Colin, jt. ed. see Perry, Gill.

***Cunningham, Cyril.** Beaulieu: Finishing School for Secret Agents. 1998. 34.95 (*0-85052-598-5*, Pub. by Leo Cooper) Trans-Atl Phila.

— The Secret Underground City: Central Ammunition Depot of Corsham. 1998. 39.95 (*0-85052-585-3*, Pub. by Leo Cooper) Trans-Atl Phila.

Cunningham, D. R. Basic Circuit Analysis. 940p. 1995. pap. 6.76 (*0-471-14247-6*) Wiley.

Cunningham, Daniel P. Advanced Swaps & Derivative Financial Products. 266p. 1991. pap. text 17.50 (*0-685-49924-3*, B4-6973) PLI.

Cunningham, David. Gigabit Ethernet Networking. LC 98-84223. 1999. 50.00 (*1-57870-062-0*) Macmillan Tech.

— Nightfall, Country Lake. LC 94-26352. (Illus.). (J). (gr. 1-4). 1995. lib. bdg. 15.95 (*0-8075-5624-6*) A Whitman.

Cunningham, David, jt. auth. see Rand McNally Staff.

Cunningham, David R. & Stuller, John A. Circuit Analysis. 192p. 1994. pap. 6.95 (*0-471-12489-3*) Wiley.

Cunningham, David R. & Stuller, John R. Basic Circuit Analysis. (C). 1991. pap. text. write for info. (*0-395-51203-4*) HM Soft Schl Col Div.

Cunningham, David S. Faithful Persuasion: In Aid of a Rhetoric of Christian Theology. LC 91-50565. (C). 1991. text 34.50 (*0-268-00984-8*) U of Notre Dame Pr.

— Faithful Persuasion: In Aid of a Rhetoric of Christian Theology. LC 91-50565. (C). 1993. pap. text 19.50 (*0-268-00985-6*) U of Notre Dame Pr.

— These Three Are One: The Practice of Trinitarian Theology. LC 97-40904. (Challenges in Contemporary Theology Ser.: Vol. 2). 340p. 1997. text 57.95 (*1-55786-962-6*); pap. text 29.95 (*1-55786-963-4*) Blackwell Pubs.

Cunningham, David S., et al. Ecumenical Theology in Worship, Doctrine & Life: Essays Presented to Geoffrey Wainwright on His Sixtieth Birthday. LC 99-10430. 336p. 2000. text 49.95 (*0-19-513136-3*) OUP.

***Cunningham-Davis, Beatrice.** I Cry No More. 122p. 1999. pap. text 12.00 (*1-881524-64-7*, Prof Busn) Milligan Bks.

Cunningham, Denise. Clinical Ocular Photography. LC 98-13365. (Basic Bookshelf for Eyecare Professionals Ser.). (Illus.). 160p. 1998. pap. text 30.00 (*1-55642-377-2*, 63772) SLACK Inc.

***Cunningham, Diane.** Abstract & Index Collection in the National Institute of Standards & Technology Research Library. 32p. 1999. pap. 3.00 (*0-16-056914-1*) USGPO.

Cunningham, Diane K., compiled by. Easter Program Builder, No. 20. 39p. 1988. 4.99 (*0-8341-9588-7*, ME-120) Lillenas.

— Mother's Day & Father's Day Program Builder, No. 8. 37p. 1988. 4.50 (*0-8341-9061-3*, MP-308) Lillenas.

— Thanksgiving Program Builder, No. 3. 1989. 4.50 (*0-685-68755-4*, MP-405) Lillenas.

***Cunningham, Don & Bleiel, Jeff.** Add Some Music to Your Day: Analyzing & Enjoying the Music of the Beach Boys. LC 99-68551. (Illus.). 208p. 2000. pap. 19.95 (*0-9675973-0-7*) Tiny Ripple Bks.

Cunningham, Donald H. & Harris, Jeanette. The Simon & Schuster Guide to Writing. 2nd abr. ed. LC 96-31246. 1996. pap. text 38.00 (*0-13-456583-5*) P-H.

Cunningham, Donald H., jt. auth. see Pearsall, Thomas E.

Cunningham, Donald H., ed. see Stuart, Jesse H.

C

Cunningham, Donna. An Astrological Guide to Self-Awareness. 2nd rev. ed. 204p. 1994. pap. 12.00 (*0-916360-57-1*) CRCS Pubns CA.
— Astrology & Spiritual Development. (Illus.). 144p. (Orig.). 1989. pap. 9.95 (*0-945946-03-1*) Cassandra Pr.
— Astrology & Vibrational Healing. (Illus.). 168p. (Orig.). 1988. pap. 9.95 (*0-9615875-8-X*) Cassandra Pr.
— The Consulting Astrologer's Guidebook. LC 93-42845. (Illus.). 256p. (Orig.). 1994. pap. 14.95 (*0-87728-790-2*) Weiser.
— Flower Remedies Handbook: Emotional Healing & Growth with Bach & Other Flower Essences. LC 91-16851. (Illus.). 160p. 1991. pap. 14.95 (*0-8069-8204-7*) Sterling.
— Healing Pluto Problems. LC 85-52190. 320p. (Orig.). 1986. pap. 10.95 (*0-87728-398-2*) Weiser.
— How to Read Your Astrological Chart: Aspects of the Cosmic Puzzle. LC 99-37880. (Illus.). 224p. 1999. pap. 12.95 (*1-57863-114-9*, Pub. by Weiser) ACCESS Pubs Network.
— The Moon in Your Life: Being a Lunar Type in a Solar World. LC 95-52002. Orig. Title: Being a Lunar Type in a Solar World. (Illus.). 384p. 1996. reprint ed. pap. 15.95 (*0-87728-837-2*) Weiser.
— Moon Signs: The Key to Your Inner Life. 1989. mass mkt. 0.05 (*0-345-34724-2*) Ballantine Pub Grp.
Cunningham, Donna & Ramer, Andrew. Further Dimensions of Healing Addictions. (Illus.). 168p. (Orig.). 1988. pap. 9.95 (*0-945946-00-7*) Cassandra Pr.
— The Spiritual Dimensions of Healing Addictions. 172p. 1988. 9.95 (*0-9615875-5-5*) Cassandra Pr.
***Cunningham, Douette.** More Life Vol. 1: Principles & Practices for Purposeful Living. Gordon, Africa & Nichols, Derek, eds. 128p. 1999. pap. 16.99 (*0-9674320-0-6*) DOC Commns.
Cunningham, E. T., jt. auth. see Haller, G. F.
Cunningham, Edward. The Port Hudson Campaign, 1862-1863. LC 63-16655. (Illus.). 200p. 1994. pap. 14.95 (*0-8071-1925-3*) La State U Pr.
Cunningham, Elaine. Daughter of the Drow. 1996. pap. 5.99 (*0-7869-0514-X*, Pub. by TSR Inc) Random.
***Cunningham, Elaine.** Elfshadow. (Forgotten Realms Ser.). 320p. 2000. mass mkt. 5.99 (*0-7869-1660-5*) TSR Inc.
Cunningham, Elaine. Elfsong. (Forgotten Realms Harpers Ser.: No. 8). 320p. (Orig.). 1994. pap. 4.95 (*1-56076-679-4*, Pub. by TSR Inc) Random.
— Evermeet: Island of the Elves. 1999. pap. 6.99 (*0-7869-1354-1*) TSR Inc.
— Forgotten Realms: Elfshadow. LC 90-71501. (Harpers Ser.: Bk. 2). 320p. 1991. pap. 5.99 (*1-56076-117-2*, Pub. by TSR Inc) Random.
— Haldor Lillenas: The Marvelous Music Maker. (Illus.). 72p. (Orig.). (J). (gr. 5-6). 1992. pap. 5.99 (*0-8341-1443-7*) Beacon Hill.
***Cunningham, Elaine.** The Magehound. (Forgotten Realms Ser.: Bk. 1). (Illus.). 320p. 2000. mass mkt. 5.99 (*0-7869-1561-7*) TSR Inc.
Cunningham, Elaine. Silver Shadows. (Forgotten Realms Ser.). 1996. pap. 5.99 (*0-7869-0498-4*, Pub. by TSR Inc) Random.
***Cunningham, Elaine.** Songs & Swords Bk. 2: Elfsong. (DragonLance Ser.). 320p. 2000. mass mkt. 5.99 (*0-7869-1661-3*) TSR Inc.
Cunningham, Elaine. Thornhold. 1998. pap. 5.99 (*0-7869-1177-8*, Pub. by TSR Inc) Random.
Cunningham, Eldon C., ed. Printmaking: A Primary Form of Expression. (Illus.). 264p. 1992. 39.95 (*0-87081-247-5*) Univ Pr Colo.
***Cunningham, Elizabeth.** Daughter of the Shining Isles. LC 00-36072. (Magdalen Trilogy Ser.: Vol. 1). 416p. 2000. 24.95 (*1-58177-060-X*) Barrytown Ltd.
Cunningham, Elizabeth. How to Spin Gold: A Woman's Tale. LC 96-51167. 240p. 1997. 19.95 (*1-886449-12-0*) Barrytown Ltd.
— Return of the Goddess. 388p. 1993. pap. 12.95 (*0-88268-157-5*) Station Hill Pr.
— The Return of the Goddess: A Divine Comedy. LC 92-10395. 1992. 22.50 (*0-88268-115-X*) Station Hill Pr.
— Small Bird: Poems & Prayers. LC 99-54908. 80p. 1999. pap. text 12.95 (*1-58177-058-8*, Pub. by Barrytown Ltd) Consort Bk Sales.
— West, West, West. LC 91-71392. (Illus.). 132p. 1991. pap. text 27.50 (*0-9629111-0-0*, Bison Books) U of Nebr Pr.
— The Wild Mother. LC 93-2998. 1993. 20.95 (*0-88268-147-8*) Station Hill Pr.
— The Wild Mother. 208p. 1995. pap. 12.95 (*0-88268-197-4*) Station Hill Pr.
Cunningham, Elmo E. Prince Elmo. LC 99-70101. 112p. 1999. pap. 11.95 (*1-57197-163-7*) Pentland Pr.
Cunningham, Ernest G. & Rongstad, Richard H. Peacekeeping & U. N. Operational Control: A Study of Their Effect on Unit Cohesion. 222p. 1995. pap. text 19.95 (*1-887897-02-X*) Vikng-Phoenix.
Cunningham, Ernest W. The Ultimate Barbra. (Illus.). 256p. 1998. pap. 16.95 (*1-58063-041-3*) Renaissance.
***Cunningham, Ernest W.** Ultimate Bogie. LC 99-36166. 288p. 1999. pap. 16.95 (*1-58063-093-6*) Renaissance.
Cunningham, Ernest W. The Ultimate Marilyn: All the Facts, Fantasies, & Scandals about the World's Best-Known Sex Symbol. LC 97-53167. (Illus.). 256p. 1998. pap. 16.95 (*1-58063-003-0*) Renaissance.
Cunningham Et Al. Environmental Science. 3rd ed. 1995. 70.50 (*0-697-33069-9*, WCB McGr Hill) McGrw-H Hghr Educ.
— Environmental Science. 4th ed. 1996. (*0-697-36540-9*, WCB McGr Hill) McGrw-H Hghr Educ.
***Cunningham, Eugene.** Border Guns. large type ed. LC 99-30710. 1999. 18.95 (*1-57490-184-2*, Sagebrush LP West) T T Beeler.
— The Bravo Trail. 2000. 20.95 (*1-57490-268-7*, Sagebrush LP West) T T Beeler.
Cunningham, Eugene. Pistol Passport. large type ed. LC 94-2967. 321p. 1994. pap. 17.95 (*0-8161-7418-0*, G K Hall Lrg Type) Mac Lib Ref.
***Cunningham, Eugene.** Ranger Way. large type ed. LC 98-21231. (Large Print Western (Bath, England) Ser.). 227 p. 1998. write for info. (*0-7540-3433-X*) Chivers N Amer.
Cunningham, Eugene. Ranger Way. large type ed. LC 98-21231. (Nightingale Western Ser.). 241p. 1998. pap. 18.95 (*0-7838-0243-9*, G K Hall Lrg Type) Mac Lib Ref.
— Texas Sheriff. large type ed. LC 93-26430. 370p. 1993. lib. bdg. 16.95 (*1-56054-777-4*) Thorndike Pr.
— Texas Triggers: A Western Novel. large type ed. LC 97-13094. (Nightingale Ser.). 317p. 1997. pap. 17.95 (*0-7838-8204-1*, G K Hall Lrg Type) Mac Lib Ref.
— Triggernometry: A Gallery of Gunfighters. LC 95-38776. (Illus.). 504p. 1996. pap. 18.95 (*0-8061-2837-2*) U of Okla Pr.
— Triggernometry: A Gallery of Gunfighters. 1993. reprint ed. lib. bdg. 75.00 (*0-7812-5923-1*) Rprt Serv.
Cunningham, Everett W., jt. auth. see Jewell, Malcolm E.
Cunningham, F. Gary, et al. Williams Obstetrics. 20th ed. LC 96-78941. (C). 1996. pap. text 125.00 (*0-8385-9638-X*, A9638-6, Apple Lange Med) McGraw.
Cunningham, F. Gary, jt. auth. see Gant, Norman.
Cunningham, Frank. General Stand Watie's Confederate Indians. LC 98-17396. (Illus.). 272p. 1998. pap. 14.95 (*0-8061-3035-0*) U of Okla Pr.
— The Real World of Democracy Revisited: And Other Essays on Democracy & Socialism. LC 93-14234. 176p. (C). 1994. text 45.00 (*0-391-03837-0*) Humanities.
— The Real World of Democracy Revisited: And Other Essays on Democracy & Socialism. LC 93-14234. 176p. (C). 1994. pap. 15.00 (*0-391-03838-9*) Humanities.
— The Sculler at Ease: What Makes Boats Go. (Illus.). 168p. 1993. write for info. (*0-937321-02-8*) Avery Pr CO.
***Cunningham, Frank & Strom, Leslie S.** The Sculler at Ease. (Illus.). 167p. 1999. pap. 17.95 (*0-9674651-0-9*) Granview St Pr.
Cunningham, Frank R. Sidney Lumet: Film & Literary Vision. LC 91-10230. (Illus.). 304p. 1991. text 36.00 (*0-8131-1745-3*) U Pr of Ky.
Cunningham, G. A. History of Neenah: Being a Complete Historical Sketch from the "Early Days" to (1878), with Interesting Incidents & Personal Reminiscences. (Illus.). 307p. 1995. reprint ed. lib. bdg. 39.00 (*0-8328-5149-3*) Higginson Bk Co.
Cunningham, G. R., et al, eds. Regulation of Male Fertility. (Clinics in Andrology Ser.: No. 5). (Illus.). 245p. 1980. text 206.50 (*90-247-2373-6*) Kluwer Academic.
Cunningham, Gail. The New Woman & the Victorian Novel. LC 78-6179. 172p. 1978. text 44.00 (*0-06-491347-3*, N6417) B&N Imports.
Cunningham, Gail. The New Woman & the Victorian Novel LC 79-301111. viii, 172 p. 1978. write for info. (*0-333-21617-2*) Trans-Atl Phila.
Cunningham, Gary M. American Military Bayonets of the 20th Century: A Guide for Collectors, Including Notes on Makers, Markings, Finishes, Variations, Scabbards & Production Data LC 98-140317. iv, 115 p. 1996. write for info. (*1-888722-08-8*) S A Duff.
Cunningham, George. Assessment in the Classroom: Constructing & Interpreting Texts. LC 98-106194. 230p. 1997. 85.00 (*0-7507-0733-X*, Falmer Pr); pap. 27.95 (*0-7507-0732-1*, Falmer Pr) Taylor & Francis.
— Burren. (Illus.). 48p. 1998. pap. text 8.95 (*1-86059-079-9*, Pub. by Town Hse) Roberts Rinehart.
Cunningham, George, ed. Central & Eastern Eurobarometer: Public Opinion & the European Union (18 Countries Survey) (Illus.). 91p. 1998. pap. text 20.00 (*0-7881-7174-7*) DIANE Pub.
Cunningham, George P., jt. auth. see Blount, Marcellus.
***Cunningham, Geraldine & King, Kathleen.** Leadership in Nursing. (Illus.). 256p. 2000. pap. text 35.00 (*0-7506-3837-0*) Buttrwrth-Heinemann.
Cunningham, Gerry. Cruising Guide to the Lower Gulf. LC 98-70664. 1998. pap. text. write for info. (*0-9642450-7-8*) Cruising Charts.
Cunningham, Ginny. The Spirituality of Work: Military Personnel. 64p. 1996. pap. 2.95 (*0-87946-149-7*, 138) ACTA Pubns.
Cunningham, Glen. Stage Lighting Revealed: A Design & Execution Handbook. (Illus.). 176p. (Orig.). 1993. pap. 18.99 (*1-55870-290-3*, Betrwy Bks) F & W Pubns Inc.
Cunningham, Gloria. Effective Employee Assistance Programs: A Guide for EAP Counsellors & Managers. LC 93-41408. (Sourcebooks for the Human Services Ser.: Vol. 28). 1994. 56.00 (*0-8039-5205-8*); pap. 26.00 (*0-8039-5206-6*) Sage.
— Touched by the African Soul. LC 98-65154. (Illus.). 288p. 1998. pap. 10.95 (*1-889902-10-1*) Prtnrshp Bk Servs.
Cunningham, Graham. Religion & Magic: Approaches & Theories. 160p. 1999. text 45.00 (*0-8147-1587-7*); pap. text 16.50 (*0-8147-1588-5*) NYU Pr.
Cunningham Graham, R. B. & Carpenter, Edward. With the Northwest Wind. 1972. 59.95 (*0-8490-1312-7*) Gordon Pr.
Cunningham Grahame, R. B. & Cunningham, B. Vanished Arcadia. 1973. 59.95 (*0-8490-1254-6*) Gordon Pr.
Cunningham, Gregg L. & Independence Editorial Staff. Globalism in the Schools: Education or Indoctrination? The Cunningham Report. (Issue Papers: No. 9-86). 24p. 1986. pap. text 8.00 (*1-57655-000-1*) Independ Inst.
Cunningham, Gustavus W. Five Lectures on the Problem of the Mind. LC 75-3007. (Philosophy in America Ser.). reprint ed. 36.50 (*0-404-59123-X*) AMS Pr.
— Idealistic Argument in Recent British & American Philosophy. LC 67-23200. (Essay Index Reprint Ser.). 1977. 30.95 (*0-8369-0356-0*) Ayer.
Cunningham, H. H. Doctors in Gray: The Confederate Medical Service. LC 57-11544. (Illus.). 339p. (C). 1993. pap. 16.95 (*0-8071-1856-7*) La State U Pr.
Cunningham, H. H. Doctors in Gray: The Confederate Medical Service. (Illus.). 1990. 17.50 (*0-8446-0566-2*) Peter Smith.
Cunningham, Harry A. Material Facilities Needed in the Training of Intermediate Grade Teachers in Science. LC 73-176684. (Columbia University. Teachers College. Contributions to Education Ser.: No. 812). reprint ed. 37.50 (*0-404-55812-7*) AMS Pr.
Cunningham, Hazel. The Tamoxifen Papers. (Orig.). 1995. pap. 9.95 (*0-9643829-2-X*) Blue-Green Delta.
Cunningham, Helen. Majolica Figures. LC 96-71097. (Illus.). 176p. 1997. 34.95 (*0-7643-0214-0*) Schiffer.
Cunningham, Helen C. Clarice Cliff & Her Contemporaries: Susie Cooper, Keith Murray, Charlotte Rhead & the Carlton Ware Designers. LC 98-43306. (Illus.). 192p. 1999. 49.95 (*0-7643-0706-1*) Schiffer.
Cunningham, Hilary. God & Caesar at the Rio Grande: Sanctuary & the Politicization of Religion in the United States. LC 94-31786. 1995. pap. 19.95 (*0-8166-2457-7*) U of Minn Pr.
Cunningham, Homer F. The Presidents' Last Years: George Washington to Lyndon B. Johnson. LC 88-35089. 349p. 1989. lib. bdg. 37.50 (*0-89950-408-6*) McFarland & Co.
Cunningham, Hugh. Children & Childhood in Western Society since 1500. Morrill, John & Cannadine, David, eds. LC 94-49402. (Studies in Modern History). 224p. (C). 1995. pap. 24.60 (*0-582-23854-4*) Longman.
— Children & Childhood Western Society. Morrill, John & Cannadine, David, eds. LC 94-49402. (Studies in Modern History). 216p. (C). 1995. text 43.95 (*0-582-23853-6*, Pub. by Addison-Wesley) Longman.
Cunningham, I. C., tr. see Rusten, Jeffrey, et al, eds.
Cunningham, Ian. Strategic Learning. 272p. 1994. pap. 24.95 (*0-07-707894-2*) McGraw.
— The Wisdom of Strategic Learning: The Self Managed Learning Solution. 2nd ed. LC 98-27582. 270p. 1998. 76.95 (*0-566-08079-6*, Pub. by Gower) Ashgate Pub Co.
Cunningham, Ian & Dawes, Graham. Exercises for Developing Coaching Capability. 1988. pap. 585.00 (*0-85292-703-7*, Pub. by IPM Hse) St Mut.
***Cunningham, Ian, et al.** Self Managed Learning in Action: Putting SML into Practice. 264p. 2000. 96.95 (*0-566-08214-4*, Pub. by Gower) Ashgate Pub Co.
Cunningham, Ian C. & Simpson-Wells, Hugh. OCT Superbase Advanced Workbook. 672p. (Orig.). 1993. pap. 49.95 (*1-873664-07-9*, Pub. by Oxford Comp Trning) Cromland.
— OCT Superbase Developer's Workbook. 672p. (Orig.). 1993. pap. 49.95 (*1-873664-08-7*, Pub. by Oxford Comp Trning) Cromland.
— OCT Superbase Intermediate Workbook. (Illus.). 672p. (Orig.). 1993. pap. 49.95 (*1-873664-06-0*, Pub. by Oxford Comp Trning) Cromland.
— The OCT Superbase Version 2: Introductory Workbook. Alexander, Eric, ed. (Illus.). 640p. (Orig.). 1992. pap. 49.95 incl. disk (*1-873664-05-2*, Pub. by Oxford Comp Trning) Cromland.
Cunningham, Imogen. Imogen Cunningham: The Poetry of Form. (Illus.). 96p. 1995. 45.00 (*3-905514-07-9*) Dist Art Pubs.
Cunningham, Imogen, photos by. Imogen Cunningham: The Modernist Years. (Master Photo Ser.). (JPN., Illus.). 72p. 1993. 19.95 (*4-8457-0835-3*) RAM Publications.
— Imogen Cunningham Portraiture: Portraiture. (Illus.). 200p. 1998. 50.00 (*0-8212-2437-9*, Pub. by Bulfinch Pr) Little.
Cunningham, Imogen, jt. auth. see Adams, Ansel.
Cunningham, Ineke. Modernity & Academic Performance: A Study of Students in a Puerto Rican High School. 193p. 1972. 3.50 (*0-8477-2705-X*); pap. 2.50 (*0-8477-2706-8*) U of PR Pr.
Cunningham, Irma A. A Syntactic Analysis of Sea Island Creole. LC 90-26133. (Publications of the American Dialect Society: No. 75). 160p. 1992. pap. text 17.00 (*0-8173-0537-8*) U of Ala Pr.
Cunningham, Isabel S. Frank N. Meyer, Plant Hunter in Asia. LC 83-12920. (Illus.). 335p. 1984. reprint ed. pap. 103.90 (*0-608-00188-0*, 206097000006) Bks Demand.
Cunningham, J., jt. auth. see Sasse, M. A.
Cunningham, J., jt. auth. see Williams, D. F.
Cunningham, J. Barton. Action Research & Organizational Development. LC 92-1744. 288p. 1993. 65.00 (*0-275-94265-1*, C4265, Praeger Pubs) Greenwood.
***Cunningham, J. Barton.** Stress Management Sourcebook. 2nd ed. 2000. pap. 16.95 (*0-7373-0508-8*) Lowell Hse.
Cunningham, J. Barton. The Stress Management Sourcebook: Everything You Need to Know. LC 97-37447. 336p. 1998. pap. 16.00 (*0-7373-0012-4*, 00124W) NTC Contemp Pub Co.
— The Stress Management Sourcebook: Everything You Need to Know. LC 97-37447. 336p. 1998. reprint ed. 27.00 (*1-56565-792-6*, 07926W, Pub. by Lowell Hse) NTC Contemp Pub Co.
Cunningham, J. Brendonly. A Quarter's Worth of Blessings. 160p. (Orig.). 1994. pap. write for info. (*0-9623295-3-6*) Blue Hse NY.
Cunningham, J. O. The History of Champaign County. Schlipf, Frederick A., ed. LC 84-72777. (Champaign County Historical Archives Historical Publications Ser.: No. 7). (Illus.). 538p. 1984. reprint ed. 34.00 (*0-9609646-2-2*) Urbana Free Lib.
Cunningham, J. R. & Jones, D. K., eds. Experimental Results for Phase Equilibria & Pure Components Properties. (DIPPR Data Ser.: Vol. 1). 144p. 1991. pap. text 35.00 (*0-8169-0563-0*, R-1) Am Inst Chem Eng.
Cunningham, J. S., ed. see Marlowe, Christopher.
Cunningham, J. V. Let Thy Words Be Few. 17p. (Orig.). 1986. 45.00 (*0-936576-11-1*) Symposium Pr.
— The Poems of J. V. Cunningham. Steele, Timothy, ed. LC 97-355. 253p. 1997. pap. 16.95 (*0-8040-0998-8*); text 28.95 (*0-8040-0997-X*) Swallow.
Cunningham, James. Shakespeare's Tragedies & Modern Critical Theory. LC 96-38007. 240p. 1997. 37.50 (*0-8386-3711-6*) Fairleigh Dickinson.
Cunningham, James, ed. All Is Well: Poems & Readings in Rememberance. (Illus.). 192p. 1998. 11.95 (*0-00-255797-5*, Pub. by HarpC) Trafalgar.
Cunningham, James & Herr, Norman. Hands-on Physics Activities with Real-Life Applications. 672p. 1994. pap. text 29.95 (*0-87628-845-X*) Ctr Appl Res.
Cunningham, James B., jt. auth. see Herr, Norman.
Cunningham, James G. Textbook of Veterinary Physiology. 2nd ed. Kersey, Ray, ed. LC 96-29043. 688p. 1997. text 82.50 (*0-7216-6424-5*, W B Saunders Co) Harcrt Hlth Sci Grp.
Cunningham, James J., et al. Structuring Secured Commercial Loan Documents. 1991. ring bd. 135.00 (*0-685-69629-4*, SSL) Warren Gorham & Lamont.
Cunningham, James K. & Thielemeir, Margaret A. Trends & Regional Variations in Amphetamine-Related Emergency Admissions Vol. 1: California, 1984-1993. (Illus.). 98p. (Orig.). 1995. reprint ed. pap. 16.00 (*0-9651259-3-9*) Public Statistics.
Cunningham, James V. & Kotler, Milton. Building Neighborhood Organizations. LC 83-1182. 224p. 1983. pap. text 11.50 (*0-268-00669-5*) U of Notre Dame Pr.
Cunningham, James W. A Vanquished Hope: The Movement for Church Renewal in Russia, 1905-1906. LC 81-9077. 384p. 1981. pap. text 12.95 (*0-913836-70-2*) St Vladimirs.
Cunningham, Janet. Inner Selves: The Feminine (for Men & Women Who Value Their Intuitive Nature) Path to Weight Loss. (Illus.). 140p. (Orig.). 1994. pap. 9.95 (*0-919848-17-6*) Two Suns Pr.
— A Tribe Returned. Lucas, Winafred B., ed. LC 94-72318. (Illus.). 200p. 1994. 18.85 (*1-882530-09-8*) Deep Forest Pr.
Cunningham, Janet & Ranucci, Michael. Caution: Soul Mate Ahead! Spiritual Love in the Physical Dimension. LC 94-90007. (Illus.). 115p. (Orig.). 1994. pap. 9.95 (*0-9640026-9-8*) Two Suns Pr.
Cunningham, Jere. Love Object. 198p. 1985. lib. bdg. 12.50 (*0-910489-03-3*) Scream Pr.
Cunningham, Jill, pseud. Just One Women's Journey. (Illus.). 35p. (Orig.). 1989. pap. text 4.95 (*0-317-93239-X*) G Cozzo.
Cunningham, Jim C. Vermont Unveiled: A Photographic Guide to Nudism in the Green Mountain State. 2nd ed. Cunningham, Maggie, ed. (Illus.). 96p. (Orig.). 1996. pap. 19.50 (*0-9655540-0-7*) Naturist LIFE.
Cunningham, Jo. The Best of Collectible Dinnerware. 2nd rev. ed. LC 98-54684. (Illus.). 192p. 1999. 29.95 (*0-7643-0817-3*) Schiffer.
— The Best of Collectible Dinnerware: With Values. LC 95-8474. (Books for Collectors Ser.). (Illus.). 192p. 1995. 29.95 (*0-88740-833-8*) Schiffer.
— Collector's Encyclopedia of American Dinnerware. (Illus.). 320p. 1995. 24.95 (*0-89145-199-4*, 1373) Collector Bks.
— Homer Laughlin China: "A Giant among Dishes," 1873-1937. 192p. 1998. 29.95 (*0-7643-0417-8*) Schiffer.
***Cunningham, Jo.** Homer Laughlin China: Nineteen Forties to Nineteen Fifties. (Illus.). 176p. 2000. 29.95 (*0-7643-1164-6*) Schiffer.
Cunningham, Joe. Interborough Fleet: History of the IRT Subway Fleet. LC 96-61449. (Illus.). 156p. (Orig.). 1997. pap. 36.95 (*0-9645765-3-8*) Xplorer Pr.
— St. John's Home: From Brooklyn to Rockaway Park. 128p. 1993. pap. write for info. (*0-9636989-0-7*) SJH Pr.
***Cunningham, Joe & Granick, Eve Wheatcroft.** Amish Quilts 1880 to 1940 from the Collection of Faith & Stephen Brown. (Illus.). 80p. 2000. pap. 19.95 (*1-930561-01-6*) Michigan Mus.
Cunningham, Joe, jt. auth. see Marston, Gwen.
Cunningham, John. Adam Smith: Critical Assessments, 7 vols., Set. (Critical Assessments of Leading Economists Ser.). (Illus.). 3280p. (C). (gr. 13 up). 1994. text, boxed set 1275.00 (*0-415-11247-8*) Routledge.
***Cunningham, John.** Florham Park. (Images of America Ser.). 128p. 1999. pap. 18.99 (*0-7385-0003-8*) Arcadia Publng.
Cunningham, John. Madison. (Images of America Ser.). 1998. pap. 16.99 (*0-7524-0837-2*) Arcadia Publng.
— The Rainbow Runner. 288p. 1993. mass mkt. 4.99 (*0-8125-1359-2*, Pub. by Tor Bks) St Martin.
— Starfall. 352p. 1993. mass mkt. 4.99 (*0-8125-1361-4*) Tor Bks.
— Warhorse. 1992. mass mkt. 3.99 (*0-8125-1360-6*) Tor Bks.
Cunningham, John & Woods, Ronald N. Sir John Hicks: Critical Assessments, 4 vols., Set. (Critical Assessments Ser.). (Illus.). 1136p. (C). 1989. text, boxed set 700.00 (*0-415-01272-4*) Routledge.
Cunningham, John Christopher. Literary Intersections of Masculinity & Race: Contemporary Writing by U.S. Men. (Studies in American Popular History & Culture). 200p. 1999. 50.00 (*0-8153-3139-8*) Garland.
Cunningham, John G. The Past Will Happen Again: A Survey of Biblical Prophecy. LC 94-93860. 250p. (Orig.). 1995. pap. text 11.95 (*0-9643287-6-3*, Shekinah Hse) Cunningham Copywrt.
Cunningham, John J. Introduction to Nutritional Physiology. LC 83-61164. (Illus.). 228p. 1983. text 16.00 (*0-686-38084-3*) Lppncott W & W.
***Cunningham, John M.** Drafting Limited Liability Company Operating Agreement: Law, Tax, Forms. LC 98-44977. 1998. write for info. (*0-7355-0286-2*) Aspen Law.

C

An Asterisk (*) at the beginning of an entry indicates that the title is appearing for the first time.

Cunningham, John M. High Noon: A Screen Adaptation, Directed by Fred Zinneman. Garrett, George P. et al, eds. LC 71-135273. (Film Scripts Ser.). 1989. pap. text 19.95 (0-89197-788-0) Irvington.

Cunningham, John R. & Jones, Dennis K., eds. Experimental Results for DIPPR 1990-91 Projects on Phase Equilibria & Pure Component Properties. LC 94-35055. (DIPPR Data Ser.: Vol. 2). 226p. 1994. 125.00 (0-8169-0657-2, R-2) Am Inst Chem Eng.

— Results from the Design Institute for Physical Property Data: Experimental Results & Data Compilation Procedures. LC 91-21323. (Symposium Ser.: Vol. 86, No. 279). 155p. (Orig.). 1990. pap. 35.00 (0-8169-0496-0) Am Inst Chem Eng.

Cunningham, John R., jt. auth. see Johns, Harold E.

***Cunningham, John T.** Atlantic City. LC 00-102557. (Images of America Ser.). (Illus.). 128p. 2000. pap. 18.99 (0-7385-0426-2) Arcadia Publng.

Cunningham, John T. Chatham. (Images of America Ser.). 1999. pap. 16.99 (0-7524-0830-5) Arcadia Publng.

***Cunningham, John T.** Drew University: New Jersey. LC 00-104048. (College History Ser.). (Illus.). 128p. 2000. pap. 19.99 (0-7385-0453-X) Arcadia Publng.

Cunningham, John T. The East of Jersey: A History of the General Board of Proprietors of the Eastern Division of New Jersey. LC 92-24645. 1992. 24.95 (0-911020-24-1) NJ Hist Soc.

— New Jersey: A Mirror on America. 1996. student ed. write for info. (0-89359-012-6) Afton Pub.

— New Jersey, America's Main Road, 1976. 1976. reprint ed. pap. 18.95 (0-89359-007-X) Afton Pub.

— The New Jersey Sampler. (Historic Tales of Old New Jersey Ser.). 1977. write for info. (0-89359-014-2) Afton Pub.

— The New Jersey Shore: Maps by William N. Canfield. LC 58-6287. 272p. reprint ed. pap. 84.40 (0-7837-5682-8, 20591000005) Bks Demand.

— On the Go in New Jersey. 1996. pap., teacher ed. write for info. (0-89359-116-5) Afton Pub.

— On the Go in New Jersey. 1998. pap. 5.50 (0-89359-115-7) Afton Pub.

— Railroads in New Jersey: The Formative Years. (Illus.). 328p. 1997. 49.95 (0-89359-015-0) Afton Pub.

— This Is New Jersey. rev. ed. (Illus.). 285p. (C). 1994. reprint ed. pap. 15.95 (0-8135-2141-6) Rutgers U Pr.

— This Is New Jersey. 3rd ed. LC 78-5884. (Illus.). 301p. 1978. reprint ed. pap. 93.40 (0-7837-9214-X, 204996400004) Bks Demand.

— This Is New Jersey. 4th rev. ed. (Illus.). 285p. (C). 1994. reprint ed. text 35.00 (0-8135-2140-8) Rutgers U Pr.

— University in the Forest. La Clair, Ruth, ed. (Illus.). 384p. 1990. write for info. (0-89359-017-7) Afton Pub.

***Cunningham, John T.** Ustedes, New Jersey y el Mundo. Cunningham, Patricia, ed. Zanzo, Eliana, tr.Tr. of You, New Jersey & the World. (SPA., Illus.). 256p. (J). (gr. 4). 2000. text 43.95 (0-89359-125-4) Afton Pub.

Cunningham, John T. You New Jersey & the World. 256p. 1999. write for info. (0-89359-106-8) Afton Pub.

Cunningham, John T. & Cummings, Charles F. Remembering Essex: A Pictorial History of Essex County, New Jersey. LC 95-35729. 1995. write for info. (0-89865-949-3) Donning Co.

Cunningham, John T. & Sinclair, Donald A. Murder Did Pay: Nineteenth Century New Jersey Murders. (Classics Ser.). (Illus.). 193p. 1981. text 10.95 (0-911020-04-7) NJ Hist Soc.

Cunningham, Joseph. The Jets - New Haven EP-5 Electrics. (Classic Power Ser.: No. 9). 1991. pap. 29.95 (0-934088-26-8) NJ Intl Inc.

Cunningham, Joseph D. History of the Sikhs from the Origin of the Nation to the Battles of the Sutlej. (C). 1994. reprint ed. text 27.00 (81-206-0950-6, Pub. by Asian Educ Servs) S Asia.

Cunningham, Joseph W., jt. auth. see Soper, Katharine B.

Cunningham, J.S., ed. see Marlowe, Christopher.

Cunningham, Juann. Unbridled: Horse Thoughts & Tales. LC 99-94386. (Illus.). 80p. 1999. pap. 11.95 (0-9671551-0-X) Bravado Pubg.

Cunningham, Julia. Burnish Me Bright. 1990. 18.75 (0-8446-6252-6) Peter Smith.

— The Shadow Heart: Poems. LC 99-27139. 72p. 1999. pap. 10.00 (1-56474-314-4) Fithian Pr.

***Cunningham, Julia.** The Stable Rat & Other Poems. (J). 2001. 15.95 (0-688-17799-9, Grenwillow Bks); lib. bdg. 15.89 (0-688-17800-6, Grenwillow Bks) HarpC Child Bks.

Cunningham, Julie, ed. see Vander Vlist, Abraham.

Cunningham, K., jt. ed. see Soukop, M.

***Cunningham, Kathy.** Frumpy's Grumpy Day. (Illus.). 32p. (J). 2000. pap. 14.95 (1-57532-290-0) Press-Tige Pub.

Cunningham, Keith. American Indians' Kitchen-Table Stories: Contemporary Conversations with Cherokee, Sioux, Hopi, Osage, Navajo, Zuni, & Members of Other Nations. 296p. 1992. 25.95 (0-87483-203-9); pap. 16.95 (0-87483-202-0) August Hse.

***Cunningham, Keith.** Community Development: Weak Management Controls Compromise Integrity of Four Hud Grant Programs. (Illus.). 81p. 1999. pap. text 20.00 (0-7881-8429-6) DIANE Pub.

Cunningham, Keith. Two Zuni Artists: A Tale of Art & Mystery. LC 98-5212. (Folk Art & Artists Ser.). (Illus.). 96p. 1998. 25.00 (1-57806-062-1) U Pr of Miss.

Cunningham, Keith & Snider, Leslie. Human Biology Laboratory Manual. 3rd ed. 336p. (C). 1996. spiral bd. 35.00 (0-7872-2752-8) Kendall-Hunt.

***Cunningham, Keith & Snider, Leslie.** Human Biology Laboratory Manual. 3rd ed. 336p. (C). 1999. pap. text, lab manual ed. 36.95 (0-7872-6422-9) Kendall-Hunt.

***Cunningham, Kelly.** Out of Sight--Out of Mind? A Report on Anti-Homeless Laws, Litigation & Alternatives in 50 U. S. Cities. 90p. 1999. pap. text 25.00 (0-7881-8276-5) DIANE Pub.

Cunningham, Kevin, ed. see Sargeson, Frank.

Cunningham, L. Sleeping Arrangements. 14.00 (0-06-097773-6) HarpC.

Cunningham, Laura. A Place in the Country. 2000. 24.00 (0-06-019398-0) HarpC.

***Cunningham, Laura.** A Place in the Country. LC 99-59914. 304p. 2000. 24.95 (1-57322-157-0, Riverhead Books) Putnam Pub Group.

Cunningham, Laura, jt. auth. see Cunningham, Noel.

***Cunningham, Laura Shaine.** Sleeping Arrangements. 2000. pap. 12.00 (1-57322-823-0, Riverhd Trade) Berkley Pub.

Cunningham, Lawrence. Culture & Values. 4th ed. LC 97-70872. (C). 1997. pap. text 62.50 (0-15-505458-9, Pub. by Harcourt Coll Pubs) Harcourt.

— Culture & Values, Vol. I. 3rd ed. (C). 1994. pap. text, teacher ed., suppl. ed. 50.25 (0-15-500838-2) Harcourt Coll Pubs.

— Culture & Values, Vol. 1. 4th ed. (C). 1997. pap. text 57.50 (0-15-505459-7, Pub. by Harcourt Coll Pubs) Harcourt.

— Culture & Values, Vol. 2. 4th ed. (C). 1997. pap. text 61.00 (0-15-505461-9, Pub. by Harcourt Coll Pubs) Harcourt.

***Cunningham, Lawrence.** Culture & Values, Vol. 2. 4th ed. 1998. pap. 69.50 (0-15-567776-4) Harcourt.

— Culture & Values: A Survey of the Western Humanities. 4th ed. 1999. pap. 63.00 (0-15-567711-X) Harcourt.

— Culture & Values: A Survey of the Western Humanities. 4th ed. 1997. pap. text 76.00 (0-15-567643-1) Harcourt Coll Pubs.

Cunningham, Lawrence. Introductory Accounting & Finance for Lawyers. (American Casebook Ser.). 75p. 1997. pap. text, teacher ed., suppl. ed. write for info. (0-314-22785-7) West Pub.

Cunningham, Lawrence & Kelsay, John. The Sacred Quest: An Invitation to the Study of Religion. 2nd ed. 192p. (C). 1994. pap. text 30.60 (0-02-326336-9, Macmillan Coll) P-H.

Cunningham, Lawrence, ed. see Tantur Ecumenical Center (Jerusalem) Staff.

Cunningham, Lawrence A. & Buffett, Warren E. The Essays of Warren Buffett: Lessons for Corporate America. 224p. 1998. pap. 17.45 (0-9664461-0-0) Cunningham Grp.

Cunningham, Lawrence A. & Jacobson, Arthur J. Corbin on Contracts, 1999 Supplement. 1500p. 1998. pap. 135.00 (0-327-00764-8, 6333012) LEXIS Pub.

— Corbin on Contracts: 1999 Spring Cumulative Supplement, 14 vols. Incl. Corbin on Contracts Vol. 3: 1999 Spring Cumulative Supplement. 1999. pap., suppl. ed. (0-327-01177-7, 63334-13); Corbin on Contracts Vol. 3: 1999 Spring Cumulative Supplement. rev. ed. 1999. pap., suppl. ed. (0-327-01174-2, 63335-13); Corbin on Contracts Vol. 3A: 1999 Spring Cumulative Supplement. 1999. pap., suppl. ed. (0-327-01178-5, 63336-13); Corbin on Contracts Vol. 4: 1999 Spring Cumulative Supplement. rev. ed. 1999. pap., suppl. ed. (0-327-01175-0, 63344-13); Corbin on Contracts Vol. 5: 1999 Spring Cumulative Supplement. rev. ed. 1999. pap., suppl. ed. (0-327-01176-9, 63345-13); Vol. 1. Corbin on Contracts: 1999 Spring Cumulative Supplement. 1999. suppl. ed. (0-327-01172-6, 63331-13); Vol. 2. Corbin on Contracts: 1999 Spring Cumulative Supplement. 1999. suppl. ed. (0-327-01173-4, 63333-13); Vol. 4. Corbin on Contracts: 1999 Spring Cumulative Supplement. 1999. suppl. ed. (0-327-01179-3, 63337-13); Vol. 5. Corbin on Contracts: 1999 Spring Cumulative Supplement. 1999. suppl. ed. (0-327-01180-7, 63338-13); Vol. 5A. Corbin on Contracts: 1999 Spring Cumulative Supplement. 1999. suppl. ed. (0-327-01181-5, 63339-13); Vol. 6. Corbin on Contracts: 1999 Spring Cumulative Supplement. 1999. suppl. ed. (0-327-01182-3, 63340-13); Vol. 6A. Corbin on Contracts: 1999 Spring Cumulative Supplement. 1999. suppl. ed. (0-327-01183-1, 63341-13); Vol. 7. Corbin on Contracts: 1999 Spring Cumulative Supplement. 1999. suppl. ed. (0-327-01184-X, 63342-13); Vol. 8. Corbin on Contracts: 1999 Spring Cumulative Supplement. 1999. suppl. ed. (0-327-01185-8, 63343-13); 1283p. 1999. suppl. ed. write for info. (0-327-01171-8, 63329-10) LEXIS Pub.

Cunningham, Lawrence J. Ancient Chamorro Society. LC 91-78031. (Illus.). 240p. 1992. text 44.95 (1-880188-05-8) Bess Pr.

— Ancient Chamorro Society Activity Book. (Illus.). 160p. (Orig.). 1992. pap., student ed. 10.95 (1-880188-07-4) Bess Pr.

Cunningham, Lawrence J. & Beaty, Janice J. Guam: A Natural History. (Illus.). 208p. (J). (gr. 3-4). 2000. text. write for info. (1-57306-067-4); pap. text. write for info. (1-57306-069-0) Bess Pr.

Cunningham, Lawrence J., et al. A History of Guam. (Illus.). 336p. (J). (gr. 4-5). 2000. text. write for info. (1-57306-068-2) Bess Pr.

— A History of Guam: Skills Books. (Illus.). 80p. (J). (gr. 4-5). 2000. pap. text. write for info. (1-57306-070-4) Bess Pr.

Cunningham, Lawrence S. The Catholic Faith: An Introduction. LC 86-25450. 192p. (Orig.). 1987. pap. 8.95 (0-8091-2859-4) Paulist Pr.

— Cultures & Values Alt, Vol. 3E. 3rd ed. (C). 1993. pap. text 65.00 (0-15-500195-7) Harcourt.

— Faith Rediscovered: Coming Home to Catholicism. 1988. pap. 5.95 (0-8091-2923-X) Paulist Pr.

— Thomas Merton & the Monastic Vision. LC 99-34656. (Library of Religious Biography). 233p. 1999. pap. 16.00 (0-8028-0222-2) Eerdmans.

Cunningham, Lawrence S., intro. Thomas Merton: Spiritual Master: The Essential Writings. LC 92-9072. 464p. 1992. pap. 14.95 (0-8091-3314-8) Paulist Pr.

Cunningham, Lawrence S. & Egan, Keith J. Christian Spirituality: Themes from the Tradition. LC 96-24740. 224p. (Orig.). 1996. pap. 14.95 (0-8091-3660-0) Paulist Pr.

Cunningham, Lawrence S., ed. see Merton, Thomas.

Cunningham, Leon W., ed. Structural & Contractile Proteins Pt. D: Extracellular Matrix. (Methods in Enzymology Ser.: Vol. 144). 521p. 1987. text 157.00 (0-12-182044-0) Acad Pr.

— Structural & Contractile Proteins Pt. E: Extracellular Matrix. (Methods in Enzymology Ser.: Vol. 145). 396p. 1987. text 157.00 (0-12-182045-9) Acad Pr.

Cunningham, Leon W., jt. ed. see Colowick, Sidney P.

Cunningham, Linda. The Copper Angel of Piper's Mill & How She Saved Her Town. LC 89-83406. (Illus.). 48p. (J). (gr. 3-5). 1989. 12.95 (0-89272-274-6) Down East.

Cunningham, Linda, ed. Thorndike-Barnhart Children's Dictionary. (Illus.). 832p. (J). (gr. 4-7). 1996. 15.95 (0-06-270162-2, Harper Ref) HarpC.

Cunningham, Linda G., et al. The Changing Face of the Newsroom. Stinnett, Lee, ed. (Illus.). 120p. (Orig.). 1989. pap. 9.50 (0-943086-05-1) Nwspaper Assn Amer.

Cunningham, Lisa, ed. see Seewald, Jacqueline.

Cunningham, Liz. Talking Politics: Choosing the President in the Television Age. LC 94-21694. 192p. 1995. 19.95 (0-275-94187-6, Praeger Pubs) Greenwood.

Cunningham, Lois, ed. Full Circle: A Celebration of Billings Past & Present in Photographs. (Illus.). 80p. (Orig.). 1995. pap. 12.95 (0-9648728-0-3) Schaer Pubng.

Cunningham, Loren. Daring to Live on the Edge: The Adventure of Faith & Finances. 200p. 1991. pap. 8.99 (0-927545-06-3) YWAM Pub.

— Is That Really You, God? Hearing the Voice of God. 157p. 1984. pap. 8.99 (0-927545-22-5) YWAM Pub.

— Making Jesus Lord: The Dynamic Power of Laying down Your Rights. Orig. Title: Winning God's Way. 160p. 1997. pap. 8.99 (1-57658-012-1) YWAM Pub.

Cunningham, Loren & Rogers, Janice. Eres Tu, Senor? Araujo, Juan S., tr. from ENG.Tr. of Is That Really You, God?. (SPA.). 176p. 1986. pap. 8.99 (0-88113-061-3) Caribe Betania.

Cunningham, Louisa. The Spirit of Place: Japanese Paintings of the Sixteenth through Nineteenth Centuries. Neill, Peter, ed. (Illus.). 80p. (Orig.). 1984. pap. 7.00 (0-89467-030-1) Yale Art Gallery.

Cunningham, Lucia, tr. see Bombal, Maria L.

Cunningham, Lucia G. Texto e Ideologia en la Narrativa Chilena. LC 87-20006. (Towards a Social History of Hispanic & Luso-Brazilian Literature Ser.). (SPA.). 256p. (Orig.). 1988. pap. 9.95 (0-910235-28-7) Prisma Bks.

Cunningham, Luvern L., jt. ed. see Culbertson, Jack.

Cunningham, Luvern L., jt. ed. see Mitchell, Brad.

***Cunningham, Madeleine W. & Fujinami, Robert J., eds.** Molecular Mimicry, Microbes, & Autoimmunity. 400p. 2000. 99.95 (1-55581-194-9) ASM Pr.

Cunningham, Maggie, ed. see Cunningham, Jim C.

Cunningham, Margaret, ed. The Story of Little Woodcote & Woodcote Hall. (C). 1985. pap. 35.00 (0-907335-20-9, Pub. by Sutton Libs & Arts) St Mut.

Cunningham, Marian L., ed. see George, King.

Cunningham, Marilyn. On the Edge. (Intimate Moments Ser.). 1993. per. 3.50 (0-373-07527-8, 5-07527-0) Silhouette.

— Place of Power. Kratoville, Betty Lou, ed. (Meridian Bks.). (Illus.). 64p. (J). (gr. 3-9). 1989. lib. bdg. 4.95 (0-87879-651-7) High Noon Bks.

— Under the Midnight Sun. 1998. per. 3.99 (0-373-22492-3, 1-22492-2) Harlequin Bks.

Cunningham, Marilyn & Scariano, Margaret M. Nine to Five Series, Set. (Illus.). (J). (gr. 3-9). 1985. pap. 17.00 (0-87879-502-2) High Noon Bks.

Cunningham, Marion. The Breakfast Book. LC 96-47642. (Illus.). 336p. 1997. write for info. (0-517-18694-2) Wings Bks.

— Cooking with Children: 15 Lessons for Children, Ages 7 & Up, Who Really Want to Learn to Cook. LC 95-13580. (Illus.). 184p. (J). (gr. 2 up). 1995. 21.00 (0-679-42297-8) Knopf.

— Fannie Farmer Cookbook. 1994. mass mkt. 7.95 (0-553-85046-6) Bantam.

— Fannie Farmer Cookbook. LC 97-162330. 1996. 30.00 (0-679-45081-5) Knopf.

— Fanny Farmer Cookbook. 13th rev. ed. 1248p. 1994. mass mkt. 7.99 (0-553-56881-7) Bantam.

— Marion Cunningham's Good Eating: The Breakfast Book & the Supper Book. LC 98-28799. (Illus.). 576p. 1999. 9.99 (0-517-20402-9) Random Hse Value.

— The Supper Book. (Illus.). 1992. 22.00 (0-679-40144-X) Knopf.

— Fannie Farmer Cook Book. 1994. mass mkt. 9.99 (0-553-85029-6) Bantam.

Cunningham, Marion & Hirsheimer, Christopher. Learning to Cook with Marion Cunningham. LC 98-31102. (Illus.). 303p. 1999. 29.95 (0-375-40118-0) Knopf.

Cunningham, Mark E. Good Vibrations: A History of Record Production. 2nd ed. (Illus.). 438p. 1999. pap. text 19.95 (1-86074-242-4, SG00661) Sanctuary Pub.

***Cunningham, Mark E.** Live & Kicking: The Rock Concert Industry in the Nineties. 1999. pap. text 19.95 (1-86074-217-3) Sanctuary Pr.

Cunningham, Martin, ed. see El Sabio, Alfonso X.

Cunningham, Mary, jt. ed. see Bryer, Anthony.

Cunningham, Mary B., et al. The Preacher & His Audience: Studies in the Early Christian & Byzantine Homiletics. LC 98-17575. 275p. 1998. 103.00 (90-04-10681-2) Brill Academic Pubs.

Cunningham, Mary K. What Is Theological Exegesis? Interpretation & Use of Scripture in Barth's Doctrine of Election. LC 95-6389. 96p. (Orig.). (C). 1995. pap. 10.00 (1-56338-115-X) TPI PA.

Cunningham, Mary M. Heinz Warneke, 1895-1983: A Sculptor First & Last. LC 92-50685. (American Art Ser.). 1994. 85.00 (0-87413-470-6) U Delaware Pr.

Cunningham, Matthew. Finding Work Overseas: How & Where to Contact International Recruitment Agencies, Consultants & Employers. (Living & Working Abroad Ser.). 205p. 1996. pap. 19.95 (1-85703-409-0, Pub. by How To Bks) Trans-Atl Phila.

***Cunningham, Maurice T.** Race, Redistricting, & the Department of Justice in the Nineties. LC 00-35969. 232p. 2000. 59.00 (0-275-96649-6, Praeger Pubs) Greenwood.

Cunningham, Merce. The Dancer & the Dance: Merce Cunningham in Conversation with Jacqueline Lesschaeve. (Illus.). 256p. 1991. reprint ed. pap. 18.00 (0-7145-2931-1) M Boyars Pubs.

Cunningham, Merce & Lesschaeve, Jacqueline. The Dancer & the Dance: Merce Cunningham in Conversation with Jacqueline Lesschaeve. Nathan, Henry, ed. (Illus.). 224p. 1985. 27.50 (0-7145-2809-9) M Boyars Pubs.

Cunningham, Merce & Vaughan, David. Merce Cunningham: Fifty Years. LC 97-70518. (Illus.). 320p. 1997. 114.00 (0-89381-624-8) Aperture.

***Cunningham, Merle & Acker, Duane.** Animal Science & Industry. 6th ed. LC 99-89044. (Illus.). 768p. 2000. 98.00 (0-13-082653-7) P-H.

Cunningham, Merle, jt. auth. see Acker, Duane.

Cunningham, Michael. Flesh & Blood. LC 94-24628. 400p. 1995. text 22.00 (0-374-18113-6) FS&G.

— Flesh & Blood. 480p. 1996. per. 13.00 (0-684-87431-8) S&S Trade.

— Flesh & Blood, 5 pks. (Reading Group Guides Ser.). 1997. pap. write for info. (0-684-00284-1, Touchstone) S&S Trade Pap.

Cunningham, Michael, Jr. The History of Computation, Vol. 1. 4th ed. LC 00-. (Illus.). Date not set. 9.95 (0-9657152-1-3) AtlantiSoft.

Cunningham, Michael. A Home at the End of the World: A Novel. 320p. 1998. pap. 13.00 (0-374-52578-1) FS&G.

— A Home at the End of the World: A Novel. LC 98-42825. 342p. 1998. pap. 14.00 (0-312-20231-8) St Martin.

***Cunningham, Michael.** The Hours: A Novel. 1998. pap. write for info. (0-374-93947-0) FS&G.

Cunningham, Michael. The Hours: A Novel. LC 98-34188. 230p. 1998. text 22.00 (0-374-17289-7) FS&G.

***Cunningham, Michael.** The Hours: A Novel. LC 99-41903. 230p. 2000. pap. 13.00 (0-312-24302-2, Picador USA) St Martin.

— The Hours: A Novel. large type ed. LC 99-35098. 1999. 29.95 (0-7838-8715-9, G K Hall Lrg Type) Mac Lib Ref.

***Cunningham, Michael.** The Hours: A Novel. large type ed. LC 99-35098. 2000. pap. 30.00 (0-7838-8714-0) Mac Lib Ref.

***Cunningham, Michael & Marberrry, Craig.** Crowns: Portraits of Black Women in Church Hats. (Illus.). 240p. 2000. 27.50 (0-385-50086-6) Doubleday.

Cunningham, Michael, jt. auth. see Denson, Wil.

Cunningham, Michael, tr. see Kester, Gerard & Sidibe, Ousmane O.

Cunningham, Michael G. The Inner World of Traditional Theory. LC 89-22500. (Illus.). 70p. (Orig.). (C). 1990. pap. text 26.50 (0-8191-7572-2) U Pr of Amer.

***Cunningham, Michael J.** B2B: How to Build a Profitable E-Commerce Strategy. 2000. 27.00 (0-7382-0334-3) Perseus Pubng.

Cunningham, Michael R. Attracting & Loving People: The Psychology of Romantic Relationships. (Social Psychology Ser.). 1998. pap. 55.00 (0-8133-3107-2); pap. 21.00 (0-8133-3108-0) Westview.

— The Triumph of Japanese Style: 16th-Century Art in Japan. (Illus.). 168p. 1991. text 50.00 (0-940717-12-3); pap. text 30.00 (0-940717-13-1) Cleveland Mus Art.

Cunningham, Michael R., et al. Buddhist Treasures from Nara. LC 98-27230. (Illus.). 270p. 1998. 65.00 (0-940717-48-4) Cleveland Mus Art.

— Buddhist Treasures from Nara. LC 98-27230. (Illus.). 270p. 1999. pap. 40.00 (0-940717-49-2) Cleveland Mus Art.

***Cunningham, Michael R., et al.** Japanese & Korean Painting, Calligraphy & Ceramics from the George Gund Collection. Cleveland Museum of Art Staff, ed. LC 00-20245. (Illus.). 2000. write for info. (0-940717-58-1) Cleveland Mus Art.

Cunningham, Michael R., et al. Masterworks of Asian Art. LC 97-62327. (Illus.). 256p. 1998. 75.00 (0-500-97466-7, Pub. by Thames Hudson) Norton.

Cunningham, Michael R., jt. auth. see Cleveland Museum of Art Staff.

Cunningham, Mike. Smart Things to Know about E-Commerce. (Smart Things to Know about... Ser.). 1999. pap. text 16.99 (1-84112-040-5) Capstone Pub NH.

— Walking Point: An Infantryman's Untold Story. (Illus.). 252p. 1997. pap. 15.00 (0-9668627-0-8) Mike Cunningham.

Cunningham, Nancy B. Feeding the Spirit: How to Create Your Own Ceremonial Rites, Festivals, & Celebrations. LC 88-15051. 128p. (C). 1988. pap. 9.95 (0-89390-117-2) Resource Pubns.

— I Am Woman by Rite: A Book of Women's Rituals. LC 95-2847. (Illus.). 192p. (Orig.). 1995. pap. text 12.95 (0-87728-843-7) Weiser.

Cunningham, Nancy B., jt. auth. see Amaral, Geraldine.

C

An Asterisk (*) at the beginning of an entry indicates that the title is appearing for the first time.

Cunningham, Noble E., Jr. The Image of Thomas Jefferson in the Public Eye: Portraits for the People, 1800-1809. LC 80-22757. (Illus.). 185p. 1981. text 19.50 (*0-8139-0821-3*) U Pr of Va.

— In Pursuit of Reason: The Life of Thomas Jefferson. 1988. pap. 14.00 (*0-345-35380-3*) Ballantine Pub Grp.

— In Pursuit of Reason: The Life of Thomas Jefferson. LC 86-27626. (Southern Biography Ser.). (Illus.). 488p. 1987. 29.95 (*0-8071-1375-1*) La State U Pr.

Cunningham, Noble E. The Jeffersonian Republicans: The Formation of Party Organization, 1789-1801. LC 58-1263. 294p. reprint ed. pap. 91.20 (*0-8357-3909-0*, 203664300004) Bks Demand.

Cunningham, Noble E., Jr. Popular Images of the Presidency: From Washington to Lincoln. (Illus.). 328p. (C). 1991. 39.95 (*0-8262-0782-0*) U of Mo Pr.

— The Presidency of James Monroe. LC 95-34157. (American Presidency Ser.). 256p. (C). 1996. 29.95 (*0-7006-0728-5*) U Pr of KS.

Cunningham, Noble E. The Process of Government under Jefferson. LC 77-85535. 371p. 1978. reprint ed. pap. 115.10 (*0-608-04569-1*, 206534100003) Bks Demand.

— The United States in 1800: Henry Adams Revisited. LC 88-5514. (Douglas Southall Freeman Lectures: No. 1986). 83p. reprint ed. pap. 30.00 (*0-7837-4348-3*, 204405800012) Bks Demand.

Cunningham, Noel & Cunningham, Laura. The Logic of Subchapter K: A Conceptual Approach to the Taxation of Partnership. LC 96-23920. 236p. (C). 1996. 21.00 (*0-314-20017-7*) West Pub.

Cunningham, Oswald Joffre. Tombstone. LC 98-194506. 91p. 1993. write for info. (*976-625-061-8*) Kingston Pub.

Cunningham, P., ed. Soccer Mom Cookbook. LC 98-84810. (Illus.). 128p. 1998. pap. 10.95 (*0-913383-59-7*, Commwlth Bk Co) McClanahan Pub.

***Cunningham, P., et al, eds.** Derby Entertaining: Traditional Kentucky Recipes. 192p. 2000. 19.95 (*0-913383-69-4*) McClanahan Pub.

***Cunningham, P. & Froeschl, F.** Electronic Business Revolution: Opportunities & Challenges in the 21st Century. LC 99-49726. 250p. 1999. 48.00 (*3-540-66211-1*) Spr-Verlag.

Cunningham, P. Adradg, jt. auth. see Smyth, Barry.

***Cunningham, Patricia.** Teachers in Action: K-5 Chapters from Reading & Writing. LC 99-22406. 231p. (C). 1999. pap. text 28.00 (*0-8013-3424-1*) Longman.

Cunningham, Patricia & Goetz, Paul. Pisces Guide to Venomous & Toxic Marine Life of the World. LC 95-34470. 152p. 1996. pap. 18.95 (*1-55992-088-2*, 2088, Pisces Books) Lonely Planet.

***Cunningham, Patricia & Hall, Dorothy.** Month-by-Month Phonics for Upper Grades. Ruppard, Lynn & Vaughn, Louise, eds. (Professional Resources Ser.). (Illus.). 158p. 1998. pap. text 19.99 (*0-88724-473-4*, CD-2405) Carson-Dellos.

Cunningham, Patricia & Lab, Susan V., eds. Dress & Popular Culture. LC 90-86155. 165p. 1991. 39.95 (*0-87972-507-9*); pap. 15.95 (*0-87972-508-7*) Bowling Green Univ Popular Press.

Cunningham, Patricia, ed. see Cunningham, John T.

Cunningham, Patricia, ed. see Seewald, Jacqueline.

Cunningham, Patricia A. & Lab, Susan V., eds. Dress in American Culture. LC 93-70441. 221p. 1993. 29.95 (*0-87972-578-8*); pap. 15.95 (*0-87972-579-6*) Bowling Green Univ Popular Press.

Cunningham, Patricia M. Classrooms That Work: They Can All Read & Write. 2nd ed. LC 97-52381. (Illus.). 284p. (C). 1998. pap. text 25.00 (*0-321-01339-5*) Addson-Wesley Educ.

***Cunningham, Patricia M.** Making More Words: Multilevel, Hands-On Phonics & Spelling Activities. (Illus.). (J). 2000. pap. 17.99 (*1-56417-900-1*) Good Apple.

Cunningham, Patricia M. Phonics They Use: Words for Reading & Writing. 2nd ed. LC 94-34943. (C). 1995. pap. 22.50 (*0-673-99087-7*) Addson-Wesley Educ.

Cunningham, Patricia M. & Hall, Dorothy P. Making Big Words: Multilevel, Hands-On Spelling & Phonics Activities. (Illus.). 160p. 1994. 14.99 (*0-86653-807-0*) Good Apple.

— Making Words: Multilevel, Hands-On, Developmentally Appropriate Spelling & Phonics Activities. (Illus.). 192p. (J). (gr. 1-3). 1994. 15.99 (*0-86653-806-2*, GA1498) Good Apple.

Cunningham, Patricia M. & Hall, Dorothy P. Month-by-Month Phonics for First Grade. McIntyre, Chris, ed. (Professional Resources Ser.). (Illus.). 128p. 1997. pap. text 17.99 (*0-88724-397-5*, CD-2402) Carson-Dellos.

— Month-by-Month Phonics for Third Grade. (Professional Resources Ser.). (Illus.). 174p. 1997. pap. 17.99 (*0-88724-493-9*, CD-2404) Carson-Dellos.

Cunningham, Patricia M., et al. Reading & Writing Elementary Classrooms. 3rd rev. ed. LC 94-29678. 560p. (C). 1994. text 65.63 (*0-8013-1264-7*) Longman.

Cunningham, Patricia M., jt. auth. see Allington, Richard L.

Cunningham, Patricia M., jt. auth. see Hall, Dorothy P.

Cunningham, Patrick M. Welfare Reform: A Response to Unemployed Two-Parent Families. LC 92-32112. (Children of Poverty Ser.). 184p. 1993. text 15.00 (*0-8153-1114-1*) Garland.

Cunningham, Paul. Military Tokens of the U. S., 2 vols. (Illus.). 461p. 1998. 49.95 (*0-945008-01-5*) MI Exonumia Pubs.

Cunningham, Paul A. Michigan Trade Tokens. LC 87-91297. (Illus.). 752p. 1988. 32.50 (*0-945008-00-7*) MI Exonumia Pubs.

***Cunningham, Paul R.** Guide to Purchasing Electricity & Gas. 180p. 1999. 82.00 (*0-13-012652-7*) P-H.

Cunningham, Paul R. & Burrell, David. Guide to Purchasing Electricity & Gas. LC 98-38594. (Illus.). 163p. 1998. 79.00 (*0-88173-293-1*, 0422) Fairmont Pr.

Cunningham, Peter. All Risks Mortality. 1988. 17.95 (*0-316-16460-7*) Little.

— Birds of the Outer Hebrides. 243p. (C). 1989. pap. 24.00 (*0-906664-19-5*, Pub. by Mercat Pr Bks) St Mut.

***Cunningham, Peter.** Consequences of the Heart. 2000. 25.00 (*1-86046-498-X*) Harvill Press.

Cunningham, Peter. Extracts from the Accounts of the Revels at Court, in the Reigns of Queen Elizabeth & King James One. LC 74-127902. reprint ed. 47.50 (*0-404-01885-8*) AMS Pr.

— A Hebridean Naturalist. 1985. 35.00 (*0-86152-025-4*, Pub. by Acair Ltd) St Mut.

***Cunningham, Peter & Gardner, Philip.** Elementary School Teachers. 288p. 1999. 49.50 (*0-7130-0213-1*); pap. 27.50 (*0-7130-4032-7*) Intl Spec Bk.

Cunningham, Peter S. & Mickey, Robert S. Peter "Sugarfoot" Cunningham's Civilized Warring: Fundamental Kickboxing Techniques. (Illus.). 192p. (Orig.). 1996. pap. 19.95 (*0-9649331-0-1*, Ragnars Bks) Galt Pubng.

Cunningham, Phil, jt. auth. see Hines, Stephen E.

Cunningham, Philip. Proclaiming Shalom: Lectionary Introductions to Foster the Catholic & Jewish Relationship. 152p. (Orig.). 1995. pap. text 16.95 (*0-8146-6142-4*, Pueblo Bks) Liturgical Pr.

Cunningham, Philip, ed. see Vander Vlist, Abraham.

Cunningham, Philip A. Education for Shalom: Religion Textbooks & the Enhancement of the Catholic-Jewish Relationship. LC 94-10630. 192p. 1995. pap. 11.95 (*0-8146-2248-8*) Liturgical Pr.

Cunningham, Philip A. & Starr, Arthur F., eds. Sharing Shalom: A Process for Local Interfaith Dialogue Between Christians & Jews. LC 98-38566. 128p. 1998. pap. 7.95 (*0-8091-3835-2*) Paulist Pr.

Cunningham, Philip J. A Believer's Search for the Jesus of History. LC 98-38565. 154p. 1999. pap. 14.95 (*0-8091-3814-X*) Paulist Pr.

— Mark: The Good News Preached to the Romans. LC 94-41670. 192p. (Orig.). 1995. pap. 10.95 (*0-8091-3554-X*) Paulist Pr.

— Zakennayo: The Real Japanese You Were Never Taught in School. (Illus.). 96p. 1995. pap. 9.95 (*0-452-27506-7*, Plume) Dutton Plume.

Cunningham, Phyllis M., jt. ed. see Merriam, Sharan B.

Cunningham, Randy & Ethell, Jeffrey L. Fox Two. 176p. 1989. mass mkt. 3.95 (*0-446-35458-9*, Pub. by Warner Bks) Little.

Cunningham, Ray. Bad Case of the Sillies. 57p. (Orig.). 1992. pap. 4.95 (*0-9631251-2-5*) R Cunningham.

— How to Read Florida Legal Descriptions & Locate Property on Maps. 37p. 1991. pap. 6.95 (*0-9631251-0-9*) R Cunningham.

— Off the Interstates & Away from Tourist Traps: Wonderful Things to See & Do for Little or Nothing. LC 96-96291. 110p. (Orig.). 1996. pap. 7.95 (*0-9631251-4-1*) R Cunningham.

— Simpler Times. 215p. 1991. pap. 9.95 (*0-9631251-1-7*) R Cunningham.

— Southern Talk: A Disappearing Language. enl. ed. LC 93-30379. 192p. 1994. pap. 8.95 (*0-914875-22-1*) Bright Mtn Bks.

— The Way We Were in Marion County. LC 95-92146. 77p. (Orig.). 1995. pap. 5.95 (*0-9631251-3-3*) R Cunningham.

Cunningham, Ray E. Old Timey Southern Talk. 1986. 6.95 (*0-8187-0069-6*) Harlo Press.

Cunningham, Reba. How Do You Do It Ask Kids. 1991. pap. 8.95 (*0-939644-71-1*) Media Pub.

Cunningham, Rebecca. Costume Design: From Conception to Curtain. (Illus.). 288p. 1986. 29.95 (*0-671-61266-2*) P-H.

— The Magic Garment: Principles of Costume Design. (Illus.). 395p. (C). 1994. reprint ed. pap. text 32.95 (*0-88133-762-5*) Waveland Pr.

Cunningham, Richard, tr. see Bombal, Maria L.

***Cunningham, Richard B.** Archaeology, Relics & the Law. LC 99-38191. 726p. 1999. boxed set 80.00 (*0-89089-721-2*) Carolina Acad Pr.

Cunningham, Richard G. Annotated Bibliography of the Work of the Canon Law Society of America 1965-1980. 121p. (Orig.). 1982. pap. 3.00 (*0-943616-06-9*) Canon Law Soc.

Cunningham, Richard G., ed. Reflections on the Occasion of the Fiftieth Anniversary. 66p. (Orig.). 1988. pap. 4.00 (*0-943616-41-7*) Canon Law Soc.

Cunningham, Richard L. Fifty Common Birds of the Southwest. Priehs, T. J., ed. LC 89-61676. (Illus.). 64p. (Orig.). 1990. pap. 7.95 (*0-911408-83-5*) SW Pks Mnmts.

Cunningham, Richard W. California Indian Watercraft. LC 88-24426. (Illus.). (Orig.). 1990. pap. 12.95 (*0-945092-01-6*) EZ Nature.

Cunningham, Rob. La Guerre du Tabac: L'Experience Canadienne. LC 96-980414. (FRE.). 440p. 1997. pap. 17.50 (*0-88936-813-9*, Pub. by IDRC Bks) Stylus Pub VA.

Cunningham, Robert, 3rd & Cunningham, Robert M., Jr. The Blues: A History of the Blue Cross & Blue Shield System. LC 96-54810. 328p. 1997. 36.00 (*0-87580-224-9*) N Ill U Pr.

Cunningham, Robert, tr. see Boros, Ladislaus.

Cunningham, Robert, tr. see Schneider, Reinhold.

Cunningham, Robert B. The Bank & the Bureau: Organizational Development in the Middle East. LC 88-312. 164p. 1988. 47.95 (*0-275-92978-7*, C2978, Praeger Pubs) Greenwood.

Cunningham, Robert B. & Sarayrah, Yasin A. The Hidden Force in Middle Eastern Society. LC 92-36274. 224p. 1993. 55.00 (*0-275-94402-6*, C4402, Praeger Pubs) Greenwood.

Cunningham, Robert C. Filled with the Spirit. LC 73-190446. 46p. 1972. pap. 1.50 (*0-88243-712-7*, 02-0712) Gospel Pub.

Cunningham, Robert C., ed. see Burke, Bob.

***Cunningham, Robert E., Jr.** Sergei Rachmaninoff: A Bio-bibliography. Vol. 81. 2000. lib. bdg. write for info. (*0-313-30907-8*) Greenwood.

Cunningham, Robert E. Stillwater Through the Years. LC 79-89768. (Illus.). 1980. reprint ed. text 14.95 (*0-934188-05-X*) Evans Pubns.

Cunningham, Robert E., intro. Stillwater Where Oklahoma Began. LC 79-89767. (Illus.). 1979. reprint ed. text 14.95 (*0-934188-04-1*) Evans Pubns.

Cunningham, Robert M. Asking & Giving: A Report on Hospital Philanthropy. LC 79-28315. x, 139p. 1980. write for info. (*0-87258-300-7*) Am Hospital.

Cunningham, Robert M., Jr., jt. auth. see Cunningham, Robert, 3rd.

Cunningham, Rodger. Apples on the Flood: Minority Discourse & Appalachia. LC 90-22053. 248p. 1987. pap. 18.95 (*0-87049-629-8*) U of Tenn Pr.

Cunningham, Roger A., et al. Hornbook on the Law of Property. 2nd ed. (Hornbook Ser.). 987p. 1993. 46.00 (*0-314-01389-X*) West Pub.

Cunningham, Roger K., ed. see Van Oss, Carel J., et al.

Cunningham, Ronald, ed. see Peterson, Christina & Love, Bertha.

Cunningham, Ronald M. Discipleship 2000: Reclaiming the Vision. Coleman, George et al, eds. LC 96-76062. (Reader Resource Ser.). 165p. 1996. pap. text 5.00 (*1-883667-17-8*) Christian Meth.

Cunningham, Ronald M., et al. Diligent in Study, Growing in Faith, Active in Witness. LC 96-78092. (Reader Resource Ser.). 120p. (Orig.). 1996. pap. text 6.00 (*1-883667-18-6*) Christian Meth.

Cunningham-Rundle, Susanna, ed. Nutrient Modulation of the Immune Response. LC 92-49727. (Illus.). 576p. 1992. text 215.00 (*0-8247-8448-0*) Dekker.

Cunningham, Ruth A. Pinewoods Country Scroll Patterns, Vol. 1. (Illus.). 36p. 1997. pap. 11.95 (*0-9659393-0-8*) Pinewoods Cntry Crafts.

Cunningham, S. Electrostatics 1995: Proceedings of the 9th International Conference, York, U. K., 2-5 April 1995. (Institute of Physics Conference Ser.: Vol. 143). 1995. 186.00 (*0-7503-0337-9*) IOP Pub.

Cunningham, S. Language & the Phenomenological Reductions of E. Husserl. (Phaenomenologica Ser.: No. 70). 112p. 1976. pap. text 66.50 (*90-247-1823-6*, Pub. by M Nijhoff) Kluwer Academic.

Cunningham, S. A., ed. Confederate Veteran, 40 vols. (Illus.). 20000p. 1990. reprint ed. 1500.00 (*0-916107-14-0*) Broadfoot.

— The Confederate Veteran, 43 vols., Set. (Illus.). 20000p. 1988. reprint ed. 1500.00 (*1-56837-051-2*) Broadfoot.

Cunningham, Saig. Environmental Science: A Global Concern. 7th ed. 2002. 56.74 (*0-07-029426-7*) McGraw.

Cunningham, Sally Jean. Great Garden Companions: A Companion Planting System for a Beautiful, Chemical-Free Vegetable Garden. LC 97-33933. 288p. 1998. text 27.95 (*0-87596-781-7*) Rodale Pr Inc.

***Cunningham, Sally Jean.** Great Garden Companions: A Companion Planting System for a Beautiful, Chemical-Free Vegetable Garden. (Illus.). 2000. pap. 16.95 (*0-87596-847-3*) Rodale Pr Inc.

Cunningham, Sandra, jt. auth. see Reed, Kathlyn L.

Cunningham, Sarah, ed. We Belong Together: The Churches in Solidarity with Women. (Orig.). 1992. pap. 7.95 (*0-377-00242-9*) Friendship Pr.

Cunningham, Scott. The Complete Book of Incense, Oils & Brews. expanded rev. ed. LC 89-35510. (Llewellyn's Practical Magick Ser.). (Illus.). 269p. 1989. pap. 12.95 (*0-87542-128-8*) Llewellyn Pubns.

— Cunningham's Encyclopedia of Crystal, Gem & Metal Magic. LC 87-46256. (Illus.). 240p. 1987. pap. 14.95 (*0-87542-126-1*) Llewellyn Pubns.

— Cunningham's Encyclopedia of Magical Herbs. 2nd ed. LC 84-48091. (Illus.). 336p. (Orig.). 1985. pap. 14.95 (*0-87542-122-9*) Llewellyn Pubns.

***Cunningham, Scott.** Dreaming the Divine: Techniques for Sacred Sleep. 2nd ed. LC 99-39673. 360p. 1999. pap. 9.95 (*1-56718-192-9*) Llewellyn Pubns.

Cunningham, Scott. Earth, Air, Fire & Water: More Techniques of Natural Magic. LC 91-31198. (Practical Magick Ser.). (Illus.). 240p. (Orig.). 1991. pap. 9.95 (*0-87542-131-8*) Llewellyn Pubns.

— Earth Power: Techniques of Natural Magic. LC 83-81244. (Practical Magick Ser.). (Illus.). 176p. 1983. pap. 9.95 (*0-87542-121-0*) Llewellyn Pubns.

— Enciclopedia de Cristales, Gemas y Metales Magicos. LC 98-43646. (SPA., Illus.). 240p. 1999. 14.95 (*1-56718-189-9*, Llewellyn Esp) Llewellyn Pubns.

— Enciclopedia de las Hierbas Magicas. (SPA., Illus.). 336p. 1999. 12.95 (*1-56718-883-4*) Llewellyn Pubns.

***Cunningham, Scott.** Hawaiian Magic & Spirituality. 2nd ed. (Illus.). 256p. 2000. pap. 12.95 (*1-56718-188-0*) Llewellyn Pubns.

Cunningham, Scott. Hawaiian Religion & Magic. LC 94-32923. (World Religion & Magic Ser.). (Illus.). 256p. 1999. pap. 12.95 (*1-56718-199-6*) Llewellyn Pubns.

— Inciensos, Aceites e Infusiones: Recetario Magico. LC 96-53045. Orig. Title: spa. (SPA.). 304p. 1999. pap. 9.95 (*1-56718-930-X*) Llewellyn Pubns.

— Living Wicca: A Further Guide for the Solitary Practitioner. LC 93-24673. (Illus.). 208p. 1999. reprint ed. pap. 12.95 (*0-87542-184-9*) Llewellyn Pubns.

— Magical Aromatherapy: The Power of Scent. LC 89-38755. (New Age Ser.). (Illus.). 224p. (Orig.). 1989. mass mkt. 3.95 (*0-87542-129-6*) Llewellyn Pubns.

— Magical Herbalism: The Secret Craft of the Wise. 2nd ed. LC 83-80172. (Practical Magick Ser.). (Illus.). 2604p. 1983. pap. 9.95 (*0-87542-120-2*) Llewellyn Pubns.

— Pocket Guide to Fortunetelling. LC 97-26024. (Crossing Press Pocket Ser.). (Illus.). 140p. (Orig.). 1997. pap. 6.95 (*0-89594-875-3*) Crossing Pr.

***Cunningham, Scott.** Poderes Terrenales: Tecnicas Para la Magia Natural. 2000. pap. text 8.95 (*1-56718-187-2*) Llewellyn Pubns.

Cunningham, Scott. Sea Kayaking in Nova Scotia: A Guide to Paddling Routes along the Coast of Nova Scotia. (Illus.). 204p. 1996. pap. 16.95 (*1-55109-156-9*) Nimbus Publ.

***Cunningham, Scott.** Sea Kayaking in Nova Scotia: A Guide to Paddling Routes along the Coast of Nova Scotia. rev. ed. (Illus.). 276p. 2000. pap. 18.95 (*1-55109-317-0*) Nimbus Publ.

Cunningham, Scott. Through Many Tribulations: The Theology of Persecution in Luke-Acts. LC 98-103769. (JSNT Supplement Ser.: Vol. 142). 376p. 1997. 85.00 (*1-85075-661-9*, Pub. by Sheffield Acad) CUP Services.

— The Truth about Herb Magic. (Truth About Ser.). 64p. 1993. mass mkt. 1.99 (*0-87542-132-6*) Llewellyn Pubns.

— The Truth about Witchcraft. (Truth about Ser.). 64p. 1991. mass mkt. 1.99 (*0-87542-357-4*) Llewellyn Pubns.

— The Truth about Witchcraft Today. LC 88-45197. (New Age Ser.). 208p. (Orig.). 1999. mass mkt. 4.99 (*0-87542-127-X*) Llewellyn Pubns.

— La Verdad Sobre la Brujeria Americana (The Truth about Witchcraft) Rojas, Edgar, ed. (Verdad Sobre Ser.). (SPA.). 64p. 1999. mass mkt. 1.99 (*1-56718-878-8*) Llewellyn Pubns.

— La Verdad Sobre la Magia de las Hierbas. Rojas, Edgar, ed. (Verdad Sobre Ser.).Tr. of Truth about Herb Magic. (SPA.). 64p. 1999. mass mkt. 1.99 (*1-56718-875-3*) Llewellyn Pubns.

— Wicca: A Guide for the Solitary Practitioner. LC 88-45279. (Llewellyn's Practical Magick Ser.). (Illus.). 218p. 1999. pap. 9.95 (*0-87542-118-0*) Llewellyn Pubns.

— La Wicca: Magie Blanche et Art de Vivre. (FRE.). 1998. 22.95 (*2-89466-019-7*) Edns Roseau.

Cunningham, Scott, et al, eds. World War III Illustrated: Confrontational Comics. LC 95-32930. (Illus.). 256p. 1995. pap. 19.95 (*1-56858-039-8*) FWEW.

Cunningham, Scott & Harrington, David. La Casa Magica: Fortalezca su Hogar con Amor Salud y Felicidad.Tr. of Magical Household. (SPA., Illus.). 224p. (Orig.). 1999. pap. 7.95 (*1-56718-931-8*) Llewellyn Pubns.

— The Magical Household: Empower Your Home with Love Protection, Health & Happiness. LC 87-45740. (Practical Magick Ser.). (Illus.). 208p. (Orig.). 1987. pap. 9.95 (*0-87542-124-5*) Llewellyn Pubns.

— Spell Crafts; Creating Magical Objects. LC 93-24190. (Practical Magick Ser.). (Illus.). 224p. 1993. pap. 10.00 (*0-87542-185-7*) Llewellyn Pubns.

Cunningham, Scott, et al. Alternative Healing Gift Set. (Illus.). (Orig.). 1996. pap. 12.89 (*1-56718-894-X*) Llewellyn Pubns.

Cunningham, Scott, jt. auth. see Vangronsveld, Jaco.

Cunningham, Scott, jt. ed. see Vangronsveld, Jaco.

Cunningham, Sharon, ed. Longhunter Society Big Game Record Book. (Illus.). 175p. 1992. 35.00 (*0-9606428-2-X*) Natl Muzzle Load.

Cunningham, Sharon, ed. see Dresslar, Jim.

Cunningham, Sharon A. Manitou, Saratoga of the West. 2nd ed. LC 99-173079. 75 p. 1998. write for info. (*0-9663939-0-2*) S A Cunningham.

Cunningham, Shawn. The B & O Railroad Museum: A Visitor's Guide. (Illus.). 112p. (Orig.). 1994. pap. 12.95 (*1-886248-00-1*) B&O Railrd.

Cunningham, Simon. The Copper Industry in Zambia: Foreign Mining Companies in a Developing Country. LC 81-11869. 342p. 1981. 80.00 (*0-275-90602-7*, C0602, Praeger Pubs) Greenwood.

Cunningham, Stephen K. The Bartender's Black Book: Ten Best Guesses about the Meaning of God & of Life. 4th rev. ed. (Illus.). 176p. 1998. reprint ed. pap. 9.95 (*0-9657746-0-0*) Diversfd Intl.

— Learn Microsoft Assembler in a Day. (Popular Applications Ser.). 144p. (Orig.). 1993. pap. 15.95 incl. disk (*1-55622-331-5*) Wordware Pub.

— Learn Turbo Assembler in a Day: Version 3.0. LC 92-24952. (Popular Applications Ser.). (Illus.). 144p. 1992. pap. 15.95 incl. disk (*1-55622-300-5*) Wordware Pub.

Cunningham, Steve & White, Beth A. Their Deeds Are Their Monuments: Celebrating the Centennial Anniversary of the Dedication of the West Virginia Monuments at Gettysburg, 1898-1998. (Illus.). 48p. 1998. pap. 6.95 (*0-9664534-0-9*) WV Book Co.

Cunningham, Steven L., compiled by. Confirmation Workbook: A Workbook Based on the Book of Common Prayer 1979. 24p. 1989. pap. 4.25 (*0-8192-4106-7*) Morehouse Pub.

Cunningham, Stuart. Framing Culture: Criticism & Policy in Australia. 224p. (Orig.). 1992. pap. text 19.95 (*1-86373-172-5*, Pub. by Allen & Unwin Pty) Paul & Co Pubs.

Cunningham, Stuart & Jacka, Elizabeth. Australian Television & International Mediascapes. (Illus.). 288p. (C). 1996. text 59.95 (*0-521-47003-X*); pap. text 19.95 (*0-521-46974-0*) Cambridge U Pr.

***Cunningham, Stuart & Sinclair, John, eds.** Floating Lives: The Media & Asian Diasporas: Negotiating Cultural Identity Through Media. 244p. 2000. pap. 29.95 (*0-7022-3122-3*, Pub. by Univ Queensland Pr) Intl Spec Bk.

C

Cunningham, Stuart & Turner, Graeme. The Media in Australia: Industries, Texts, Audiences. LC 97-189485. 512p. 1997. pap. 35.00 (*1-86448-273-7*, Pub. by Allen & Unwin Pty) Paul & Co Pubs.

Cunningham, Stuart, et al. Contemporary Australian Television. 240p. 1994. pap. 24.95 (*0-86840-397-0*, Pub. by New South Wales Univ Pr) Intl Spec Bk.

Cunningham, Sue & Cates, Jean. Chuck Wagon Recipes & Others. (Illus.). 115p. 1994. write for info. (*0-9645414-0-8*) Chuck Wagon.

***Cunningham, Sue & Cates, Jean.** More Chuck Wagon Recipes & Others, Vol. 2. (Illus.). 1999. pap. 15.00 (*0-9645414-1-6*) Chuck Wagon.

***Cunningham, Sunny Anne.** BooBook: Guide to Guardian Angel Communication. 108p. 2000. pap. 16.00 (*1-892323-99-0*, Mystic Oracle Bks) Vivisphere.

Cunningham, Suzanne. Philosophy & the Darwinian Legacy. 272p. (C). 1996. 55.00 (*1-878822-61-6*) Univ Rochester Pr.

***Cunningham, Suzanne.** What Is a Mind? An Integrative Introduction to the Philosophy of Mind. LC 00-31905. 2000. pap. write for info. (*0-87220-518-5*) Hackett Pub.

Cunningham, T. Laine, ed. see Marchel, John.

Cunningham, Teresa, jt. ed. see DeCarlo, Montez.

Cunningham, Thomas J., Jr., jt. auth. see Ellis, William D.

Cunningham, Tim & Smith, Thomas. Who Do You Think You Are? (Illus.). 156p. 1998. pap. 12.95 (*1-57901-032-6*) Intl Promotions.

Cunningham, Timothy W. & Mansfield, Clay B. Pay Yourself First: A Commonsense Guide to Life Cycle Retirement Investing. LC 96-29256. (Illus.). 272p. 1996. pap. 16.95 (*0-471-16248-5*) Wiley.

Cunningham, Timothy W., jt. auth. see Mansfield, Clay B.

Cunningham, Tom. The Browning Collection at the University of Texas. LC 66-63479. (Tower Bibliographical Ser.: No. 4). 1966. 15.00 (*0-87959-036-X*) U of Tex H Ransom Ctr.

***Cunningham, Twyla R., ed.** National Conference on Juvenile Justice Records: Appropriate Criminal & Noncriminal Justice Uses. 97p. 1999. pap. text 25.00 (*0-7881-7993-4*) DIANE Pub.

Cunningham, Valentine. British Writers of the Thirties. LC 93-26236. 544p. 1990. reprint ed. pap. text 29.95 (*0-19-282655-7*) OUP.

— In the Reading Gaol: Postmodernity, Texts, & History. 304p. 1994. pap. text 29.95 (*0-631-15198-2*) Blackwell Pubs.

Cunningham, Valentine, ed. The Victorians: An Anthology of Poetry & Poetics. LC 99-34412. (Anthologies Ser.). 1100p. (C). 1999. text 74.95 (*0-631-19915-2*) Blackwell Pubs.

***Cunningham, Valentine, ed.** The Victorians: An Anthology of Poetry & Poetics. LC 99-34412. (Anthologies Ser.). 1100p. (C). 1999. pap. 39.95 (*0-631-19916-0*) Blackwell Pubs.

Cunningham, Vance & O'Brien, Tom. Vance Cunningham's New Mexico Real Estate Digest. (Illus.). 214p. 1993. pap. text 24.95 (*0-9636213-0-0*) Manzano Mtn.

Cunningham, Vickie, jt. ed. see Vickers, Betty.

Cunningham, Vickie C., jt. auth. see Vickers, Betty B.

Cunningham, Vickie C., jt. ed. see Vickers, Betty B.

Cunningham, W. J. Agony at Galloway: One Church's Struggle with Social Change. LC 79-56698. 181p. reprint ed. pap. 56.20 (*0-7837-1400-9*, 204158100021) Bks Demand.

Cunningham, W. Jack. Engineering at Yale: School, Department, Council, 1932-1982. (Transactions Ser.: Vol. 51). (Illus.). 224p. 1992. pap. 24.50 (*1-878508-06-7*) CT Acad Arts & Sciences.

Cunningham, W. Patrick, jt. auth. see McMurtrey, Martin.

Cunningham, Walker, ed. see Bull, John.

Cunningham, Walker, ed. see Merulo, Claudio.

Cunningham, Walker E. The Keyboard Music of John Bull. Buelow, George J., ed. LC 84-59. (Studies in Musicology: No. 71). 292p. reprint ed. 90.60 (*0-8357-1466-7*, 207033100078) Bks Demand.

Cunningham, Walter. All-American Boys. LC 77-22721. 1977. 9.95 (*0-02-529240-4*) Macmillan.

Cunningham, Walter F. Notes on Epistemology. LC 59-33496. (Fordham Philosophy Ser.). 204p. reprint ed. pap. 63.30 (*0-7837-5574-0*, 204535600005) Bks Demand.

Cunningham, Will. Sins of the Father: A Novel. LC 97-17334. 288p. 1997. pap. 12.99 (*0-7852-8129-0*) Nelson.

Cunningham, William. Alien Immigrants to England. 2nd ed. (Illus.). 286p. 1969. reprint ed. 35.00 (*0-7146-1295-2*, Pub. by F Cass Pubs) Intl Spec Bk.

— The Growth of English Industry & Commerce, 3 vols. in 2. Set. LC 66-21667. (Reprints of Economic Classics Ser.). (Illus.). 1968. reprint ed. 90.00 (*0-678-00288-6*) Kelley.

— Growth of the English Industry & Commerce, 2 vols., Set. 5th ed. 1968. reprint ed. 95.00 (*0-7146-1296-0*, BHA-01296, Pub. by F Cass Pubs) Intl Spec Bk.

— Historical Theology, 2 vols., Set. 1994. reprint ed. 67.99 (*0-85151-360-3*) Banner of Truth.

— An Introduction to Theological Studies: From "Theological Lectures" by William Cunningham. 98p. (C). 1994. reprint ed. pap. text 8.95 (*1-884416-02-0*) A Press.

— Reformers & the Theology of Reformation. 1979. 31.99 (*0-85151-013-2*) Banner of Truth.

Cunningham, William A., jt. auth. see Rase, Howard F.

Cunningham, William B., ed. Canada, the Commonwealth & the Common Market: A Report of the 1962 Summer Institute, Mount Allison University. LC 63-25277. 150p. reprint ed. pap. 46.50 (*0-8357-7991-2*, 202382500034) Bks Demand.

Cunningham, William C., et al. Private Security Trends, 1970-2000: The Hallcrest Report II. 384p. 1990. 59.95 (*0-7506-9179-4*) Buttrwrth-Heinemann.

Cunningham, William G. Empowerment: Vitalizing Personal Energy & Spirit. LC 90-48613. 176p. 1991. lib. bdg. 24.95 (*0-89334-203-3*) Humanics Ltd.

— Systematic Planning for Educational Change: An Activities Approach for Classroom Teachers. LC 81-84692. 323p. 1982. text 48.95 (*0-87484-551-3*, 551) Mayfield Pub.

Cunningham, William G. & Gresso, Donn W. Cultural Leadership: The Culture of Excellence in Education. LC 93-542. 304p. (C). 1993. 69.00 (*0-205-14709-7*, Longwood Div) Allyn.

Cunningham, William G., jt. auth. see Carter, Gene R.

Cunningham, William H., et al. Business in a Changing World. 3rd ed. LC 92-16799. (C). 1992. mass mkt. 65.75 (*0-538-81391-1*) S-W Pub.

— Integer Programming & Combinatorial Optimization: 5Th International IPCO Conference, Vancouver, Canada, June 1996, Proceedings, Vol. 108. LC 96-25589. (Lecture Notes in Computer Science Ser.). 505p. 1996. pap. 81.00 (*3-540-61310-2*) Spr-Verlag.

Cunningham, William P. Environmental Science. 6th ed. 672p. 2000. 75.31 (*0-07-290932-3*) McGraw.

— Environmental Science. 6th ed. 2000. pap., student ed. 16.50 (*0-07-290937-4*) McGraw.

Cunningham, William P., ed. Environmental Encyclopedia. 1998. 2nd ed. LC 98-153941. 1200p. 1997. 220.00 (*0-8103-9314-X*, 101457) Gale.

Cunningham, William P. & Saigo, Barbara. Environmental Science: A Global Concern. 4th ed. 656p. (C). 1997. per. write for info. (*0-07-114299-1*, WCB McGr Hill) McGrw-H Hghr Educ.

Cunningham, William P. & Saigo, Barbara W. Environmental Science: A Global Concern. 2nd ed. 640p. (C). 1991. text. write for info. (*0-697-14478-X*, WCB McGr Hill) McGrw-H Hghr Educ.

— Environmental Science: A Global Concern. 3rd ed. 640p. (C). 1994. text. write for info. (*0-697-15894-2*, WCB McGr Hill) McGrw-H Hghr Educ.

— Environmental Science: A Global Concern. 3rd ed. 612p. (C). 1994. text 57.50 (*0-697-15893-4*, WCB McGr Hill) McGrw-H Hghr Educ.

— Environmental Science: A Global Concern. 3rd ed. 320p. (C). 1995. text, student ed. 23.12 (*0-697-23631-5*, WCB McGr Hill) McGrw-H Hghr Educ.

— Environmental Science: A Global Concern. 4th ed. LC 96-83891. 640p. (C). 1996. text 62.35 (*0-697-28671-1*, WCB McGr Hill) McGrw-H Hghr Educ.

— Environmental Science: A Global Concern. 5th ed. LC 97-48876. 1998. 61.88 (*0-697-36023-7*, WCB McGr Hill) McGrw-H Hghr Educ.

— Understanding Our Environment: An Introduction. (Illus.). 408p. (C). 1993. text. write for info. (*0-697-20456-1*, WCB McGr Hill) McGrw-H Hghr Educ.

— Understanding Our Environment: An Introduction. (Illus.). 408p. (C). 1994. text, student ed. 20.00 (*0-697-20480-4*, WCB McGr Hill) McGrw-H Hghr Educ.

Cunningham, William P., et al. Environmental Science. 4th ed. 280p. (C). 1996. text, student ed. 19.37 (*0-697-28673-8*, WCB McGr Hill) McGrw-H Hghr Educ.

— Environmental Science: A Global Concern. 2nd ed. 124p. (C). 1991. text, wbk. ed. 24.37 (*0-697-10273-4*, WCB McGr Hill) McGrw-H Hghr Educ.

Cunninghame-Graham, Robert B. Brazilian Mystic. LC 70-146856. (Select Bibliographies Reprint Ser.). 1977. 21.95 (*0-8369-5623-0*) Ayer.

— Jose Antonio Paez. LC 73-146857. (Select Bibliographies Reprint Ser.). 1977. reprint ed. 28.95 (*0-8369-5624-9*) Ayer.

— Writ in Sand. LC 69-17571. (Essay Index Reprint Ser.). 1977. 19.95 (*0-8369-0068-5*) Ayer.

Cunninghame-Green, R. A. Minimax Algebra. LC 79-1314. (Lecture Notes in Economics & Mathematical Systems Ser.: Vol. 166). 1979. 28.00 (*0-387-09113-0*) Spr-Verlag.

Cunninghan, K., jt. ed. see Smyth, J.

Cunninghis, Richelle N. Reality Activities: A How to Manual for Increasing Orientation. 2nd rev. ed. (Illus.). 50p. 1995. pap. 10.00 (*1-882883-21-7*, 189) Idyll Arbor.

— A Survival Guide for Activity Professionals. 2nd rev. ed. DeBolt, Nancy, ed. LC 97-16966. 92p. 1997. pap. 12.00 (*1-882883-16-0*, 313) Idyll Arbor.

Cunninghis, Richelle N. & Best-Martini, Elizabeth. Quality Assurance for Activity Programs. 2nd rev. ed. Burlingame, Joan, ed. (Illus.). 110p. 1996. pap. 12.00 (*1-882883-23-3*, 185) Idyll Arbor.

Cunnington, Bert, jt. auth. see Limerick, David.

Cunnington, C. W. The History of Underclothes. 1976. lib. bdg. 250.00 (*0-8490-2011-5*) Gordon Pr.

— Why Women Wear Clothes. 1979. lib. bdg. 250.00 (*0-8490-2821-3*) Gordon Pr.

Cunnington, C. Willett. English Women's Clothing in the Nineteenth Century. (Illus.). 460p. 1990. pap. 24.95 (*0-486-26323-1*) Dover.

Cunnington, C. Willett & Cunnington, Phyllis. The History of Underclothes. (Illus.). 272p. 1992. reprint ed. pap. 9.95 (*0-486-27124-2*) Dover.

Cunnington, Phyllis, jt. auth. see Cunnington, C. Willett.

Cunnison, J., jt. auth. see Scott, William R.

Cunnison, Sheila & Stageman, Jane. Feminizing the Unions. 304p. 1995. pap. 35.95 (*1-85972-100-1*, Pub. by Avebry) Ashgate Pub Co.

Cunnius, Edward L., jt. ed. see Schnase, John L.

Cunnyngham, Blair. Edmond in the Twilight: An Angel Trilogy. LC 90-90457. 350p. (Orig.). 1992. pap. 12.95 (*0-9628603-0-1*) Still Meadow Pubs.

— Southeast, Forgotten Memories: An Angel Trilogy. LC 94-67745. 489p. (Orig.). (YA). (gr. 11-12). 1995. pap. 13.95 (*0-9628603-2-8*) Still Meadow Pubs.

Cunnyngham, Jerry. Kamache & the Medicine Bead: An Apache Story. Gilliland, Hap, ed. (Illus.). 48p. (J). (gr. 4-8). 1991. pap. 5.95 (*0-89992-123-X*) Coun India Ed.

Cuno, James, ed. French Caricature & the French Revolution, 1789-1799. (Illus.). 280p. 1988. 60.00 (*0-943739-06-3*); pap. 29.95 (*0-943739-05-5*) F S Wight Art.

Cunqueiro, Alvaro. Merlin & Company. Smith, Colin, tr. 224p. 1996. pap. 6.95 (*0-460-87731-3*, Everyman's Classic Lib) Tuttle Pubng.

Cunsolo. Applied Calculus. 171p. (C). 1997. pap. text, lab manual ed. 20.00 (*0-201-33825-4*) Addison-Wesley.

Cunsolo, Ronald S. Italian Nationalism: From Its Origins to World War II. (Anvil Ser.). 280p. 1990. reprint ed. pap. 14.50 (*0-89874-938-7*) Krieger.

Cuntz, Joachim J. & Khalkhali, Masoud, eds. Cyclic Cohomology & Noncommutative Geometry. LC 97-22462. (Fields Institute Communications Ser.: Vol. 17). 189p. 1997. text 65.00 (*0-8218-0823-0*) Am Math.

Cuntz, Otto. Die Geographie Des Ptolemaeus: Galliae, Germania, Raetia, Noricum, Pannoniae, Illyricum, Italia. LC 75-7310. (Roman History Ser.). 1975. reprint ed. 21.95 (*0-405-07192-2*) Ayer.

***Cuny, Christopher & Lubochinsky, Catherine.** Managing Interest Rate Risk. 256p. 2000. text 95.00 (*1-85573-513-X*, Pub. by Woodhead Pubng) Am Educ Systs.

CUNY Conference on History & Politics Staff & Weiner, Joel H., eds. Innovators & Preachers: The Role of the Editor in Victorian England, 5. LC 85-17658. (Contributions to the Study of Mass Media & Communications Ser.: No. 5). 335p. 1985. 75.00 (*0-313-24164-3*, WIN/) Greenwood.

Cuny, Frederick C. Famine, Conflict & Response: A Basic Guide. LC 98-49090. 192p. 1999. pap. 23.95 (*1-56549-090-8*) Kumarian Pr.

Cuny, Hubert, jt. auth. see Sirjean, Gaston.

Cuny, Jean, jt. auth. see Beauchamp, Gerald.

Cuny, Jean-Marie. Dictionnaire de la Cuisine Lorraine. (FRE.). 159p. 1992. 39.95 (*0-7859-8119-5*, 2862531367) Fr & Eur.

Cuny, Lynn Marie. Through Animals' Eyes: True Stories from a Wildlife Sanctuary. LC 98-32109. (Illus.). 149p. 1999. 19.95 (*1-57441-062-8*) UNTX Pr.

CUNY Staff, jt. auth. see Pre-Precalculus Grou SUNY Staff.

Cunyus, John. Handmade Christians in a Cookie-Cutter World. LC 97-6718. 144p. (Orig.). 1997. pap. 12.99 (*0-8272-1426-X*) Chalice Pr.

— Is It True? Examining the Core of Christian Faith. 136p. (Orig.). 1993. pap. 10.00 (*0-89896-163-7*) Larksdale.

— Soulmapping: A Spiritual Exercise. (Illus.). 48p. 1997. pap. 10.00 (*0-9644609-3-9*, 2) Srchlight Pr.

Cunyus, John G. Handmade Christians in a Cookie-Cutter World. 180p. (Orig.). 1995. pap. text 12.00 (*0-9644609-1-2*) Srchlight Pr.

— Is It True? Examining the Core of Christian Faith. 112p. (Orig.). 1994. pap. text 10.00 (*0-9644609-0-4*) Srchlight Pr.

Cunyus, Lucy. History of Bartow County Georgia (Formerly Cass Country. (Illus.). 404p. 1983. reprint ed. 40.00 (*0-89308-005-5*) Southern Hist Pr.

Cuoco, Albert A. Investigations in Algebra: An Approach to Using Logo. (Explorations in Logo Ser.). 350p. (Orig.). 1990. 70.00 (*0-262-03144-2*); pap. text 35.00 (*0-262-53071-6*) MIT Pr.

Cuoco, Daniel A. & American Society of Civil Engineers Staff. Guidelines for the Design of Double-Layer Grids. LC 97-19514. 87p. 1997. 14.00 (*0-7844-0253-1*) Am Soc Civil Eng.

Cuoco, Lorin, ed. The Dual Muse: The Writer as Artist, the Artist as Writer: Papers from the International Writers Center Symposium, 7-9 November 1997. LC 99-15505. (Illus.). 128p. 1999. lib. bdg. 35.00 (*1-55619-523-0*) J Benjamins Pubng Co.

Cuoco, Lorin, jt. auth. see Gass, William H.

Cuoco, Lorin, jt. ed. see Gass, William H.

Cuomo, Andrew. Guidebook on Military Base Reuse & Homeless Assistance. (Illus.). 44p. 1997. pap. text 25.00 (*0-7881-4686-6*) DIANE Pub.

***Cuomo, Andrew.** The State of the Cities (1998) (Illus.). 46p. (C). 2000. reprint ed. pap. text 20.00 (*0-7881-8594-2*) DIANE Pub.

***Cuomo, Andrew, frwd.** Colleges & Communities: Partners in Urban Revitalization. (Illus.). 49p. 1999. pap. text 15.00 (*0-7881-8079-7*) DIANE Pub.

— Mapping Your Community: Using Geographic Information to Strengthen Community Initiatives. (Illus.). 145p. (C). 2000. reprint ed. pap. text 25.00 (*0-7881-8589-6*) DIANE Pub.

Cuomo, Celia. In All Probability: Investigations in Probability & Statistics. rev. ed. Bergman, Lincoln et al, eds. (Great Explorations in Math & Science (GEMS) Ser.). (Illus.). 108p. 1998. reprint ed. pap., teacher ed. 13.50 (*0-924886-03-X*, GEMS) Lawrence Science.

Cuomo, Chris J. Feminism & Ecological Communities: An Ethic of Flourishing. LC 97-11037. 192p. (C). 1998. 65.00 (*0-415-15805-2*); pap. 20.99 (*0-415-15806-0*) Routledge.

Cuomo, Chris J. & Hall, Kim, eds. Whiteness: Feminist Philosophical Narratives. LC 99-15041. 141p. 1999. 58.00 (*0-8476-9294-9*); pap. 18.00 (*0-8476-9295-7*) Rowman.

Cuomo Commission on Competitiveness. America's Agenda: Rebuilding Economic Strength. Kaden, Lewis B. & Smith, Lee Orr, eds. LC 92-26858. 378p. (C). (gr. 13). 1992. pap. 34.95 (*1-56324-094-7*) M E Sharpe.

Cuomo Commission on Competitiveness, et al, eds. America's Agenda: Rebuilding Economic Strength. LC 92-26858. 378p. (C). (gr. 13). 1992. 65.95 (*1-56324-086-6*) M E Sharpe.

Cuomo, Gaetano, jt. auth. see Jossa, Bruno.

Cuomo, George. Geronimo & the Girl Next Door. LC 81-670248. 1973. pap. 1.00 (*0-933532-16-4*) BkMk.

Cuomo, Glenn R., ed. National Socialist Cultural Policy. 320p. 1995. text 55.00 (*0-312-09094-3*) St Martin.

Cuomo, Jerome J., et al, eds. Handbook of Ion Beam Processing Technology: Principles, Deposition, Film Modification & Synthesis. LC 88-38244. (Illus.). 438p. 1989. 129.00 (*0-8155-1199-X*) Noyes.

Cuomo, Kerry K., ed. see Greenberg, Marcia & Merkling, Helet.

Cuomo, Kerry Kennedy & Adams, Eddie. Truth to Power: Human Rights Defenders Who Are Changing Our World. (Illus.). 200p. 2000. 50.00 (*0-8129-3062-2*, Times Bks) Crown Pub Group.

Cuomo, Luisa F. Anatomia Di Un'Immagine: Inferno 2.127-132: Saggio d'Lessicologia E Di Semantica Strutturale. LC 93-17010. (Studies in Italian Culture: Literature in History: Vol. 14). IX, 200p. (C). 1994. text 44.95 (*0-8204-2204-5*) P Lang Pubng.

Cuomo, Mario. The Blue Spruce. LC 99-33431. (Illus.). 48p. (J). (gr. k-4). 1999. 17.95 (*1-886947-76-7*) Sleepng Bear.

— Common Sense. 1995. 21.00 (*0-614-15454-5*) S&S Trade.

— More Than Words. LC 94-18982. 1994. pap. 13.95 (*0-312-11385-4*) St Martin.

— More Than Words: The Speeches of Mario Cuomo. limited ed. 320p. 1993. text 150.00 (*0-312-10005-1*) St Martin.

— Reason to Believe. LC 95-39865. 182p. 1995. 21.00 (*0-684-81517-6*) S&S Trade.

— Reason to Believe. 208p. 1996. per. 11.00 (*0-684-82533-3*) S&S Trade.

***Cuomo, Matilda Raffa, ed.** The Person Who Changed My Life: Prominent Americans Recall Their Mentors. LC 98-56541. (Illus.). 240p. 1999. 21.95 (*1-55972-508-7*, Birch Ln Pr) Carol Pub Group.

Cuomo, Paul & Minnick, Roy. Advanced Land Descriptions: Manual of Instruction for Preparing Land Descriptions. (Illus.). 181p. 1993. 55.00 (*0-910845-53-0*) Landmark Ent.

Cuomo, Paul A. Surveying Principles for Civil Engineers: Review for the Engineering Surveying Section of the California Special Civil Engineer Exam. LC 97-12592. 139p. (Orig.). 1997. pap. 34.95 (*1-888577-08-8*, SPCE) Prof Pubns CA.

***Cuomo, Serafina.** Pappus of Alexandria & the Mathematics of Late Antiquity. (Cambridge Classical Studies). (Illus.). 244p. (C). 2000. text 59.95 (*0-521-64211-6*) Cambridge U Pr.

Cup Choy, Robert K. Life's Road: The Legacy of David Ah Fong Cup Choy. (Illus.). 74p. Date not set. pap. text. write for info. (*0-9670036-0-1*) R K H Cup Choy.

Cupach, W. R., jt. auth. see Spitzberg, Brian H.

Cupach, William R. & Canary, Daniel J. Competence in Interpersonal Conflict. LC 96-19841. 279p. (C). 1996. pap. 40.63 (*0-07-015056-7*) McGraw.

Cupach, William R. & Metts, Sandra. Facework. (Series on Close Relationships: Vol. 7). 88p. (C). 1994. text 42.00 (*0-8039-4711-9*) Sage.

Cupach, William R. & Spitzberg, Brian H., eds. The Dark Side of Interpersonal Communication. (Communication Ser.). 344p. 1994. text 69.95 (*0-8058-1167-2*) L Erlbaum Assocs.

Cupach, William R., jt. ed. see Spitzberg, Brian H.

Cupchik, Gerald C. & Laszlo, Janos, eds. Emerging Visions of the Aesthetic Process: In Psychology, Semiology, & Philosophy. (Illus.). 343p. (C). 1992. text 59.95 (*0-521-40051-1*) Cambridge U Pr.

Cupchik, Will. Why Honest People Shoplift or Commit Other Acts of Theft: Assessment & Treatment of 'Atypical Theft Offenders' LC 96-932325. 375p. 1997. write for info. (*1-896342-07-8*); pap. write for info. (*1-896342-02-7*) Tagami Communs.

Cuperez, Edwin. La Beatificacion del Santo. (SPA.). 88p. 1996. pap. 7.95 (*1-56328-117-1*) Edit Plaza Mayor.

Cupido, Joe. Chino: Warbirds Past & Present. (Illus.). 180p. 44.95 (*0-9701815-0-7*) Fox Two Prod.

Cupido, Joe. Light Strike: Skyhawks, Hornets & Corsair IIs. (Osprey Colour Library). (Illus.). 128p. 1993. 15.95 (*1-85532-309-5*, Pub. by Ospry) Motorbooks Intl.

Cupit, Geoffrey. Justice as Fittingness. 196p. 1999. pap. text 19.95 (*0-19-823862-2*) OUP.

— Justice As Fittingness. LC 96-26274. 196p. (C). 1997. text 49.95 (*0-19-823901-7*) OUP.

Cupit, Jerry. Nashville Songwriting. (Illus.). 203p. 1995. pap. 19.95 (*0-9649904-0-7*) Cupit Bks.

Cupit, John T. Brief History of Vernon Parish, Louisiana. 1963. 15.00 (*1-57980-021-1*) Claitors.

— Cupit. History of the Cupit Family. (Illus.). 204p. 1997. reprint ed. pap. 32.00 (*0-8328-8166-X*); reprint ed. lib. bdg. 42.00 (*0-8328-8165-1*) Higginson Bk Co.

Cupito, Mary Carmen, jt. auth. see Feiertag, Joe.

Cupitt, Don. After All: Religion Without Alienation. 1994. pap. 16.00 (*0-334-00036-X*) TPI PA.

Cupitt, Don. After God: The Future of Religion. LC 96-45050. 1997. 20.00 (*0-465-04514-6*, Pub. by Basic) HarpC.

— Creation Out of Nothing. LC 90-38813. 240p. (Orig.). (C). 1990. pap. 15.00 (*0-334-02463-3*) TPI PA.

Cupitt, Don. Last Philosophy. 1995. pap. 18.00 (*0-334-02586-9*) TPI PA.

— Meaning of It All in Everyday Speech. 1998. pap. 16.00 (*0-334-02786-1*) TPI PA.

— New Religion of Life in Every Speech. 1998. pap. 16.00 (*0-334-02763-2*) TPI PA.

— Religion of Being. 1998. pap. 17.00 (*0-334-02731-4*) S C M Pr Ltd.

Cupitt, Don. The Sea of Faith. (Illus.). 288p. 1988. text 54.95 (*0-521-34420-4*) Cambridge U Pr.

Cupitt, Don. Time Being. 1992. pap. 18.50 (*0-334-02522-2*) TPI PA.

Cupitt, Don, ed. Mysticism after Modernity. LC 97-11925. 200p. (C). 1997. text 57.95 (*0-631-20763-5*); pap. text 23.95 (*0-631-20764-3*) Blackwell Pubs.

***Cupitt, Richard T.** Reluctant Champions: U. S. Presidential Policy & Strategic Export Controls Truman Eisenhower Bush & Clinton. LC 99-35015. 304p. (C). 2000. text. write for info. (*0-415-92439-1*) Routledge.

— Reluctant Champions: U.S. Presidential Policy & Strategic Export Controls, Truman, Eisenhower, Bush & Clinton. LC 99-35015. 2000. pap. 25.99 (*0-415-92440-5*) Routledge.

Cupo, Hortense. No Way Out but Through. LC 93-29519. 150p. (J). 1994. pap. 4.95 (*0-8198-5130-2*) Pauline Bks.

Cupp, Easter E. Marine Plankton Diatoms of the West Coast of North America. (Bulletin of the Scripps Institute of Oceanography, Techn. Ser.: Vol. 5, Pt. 1). (Illus.). 237p. 1977. reprint ed. 95.00 (*3-87429-125-1*, 002145, Pub. by Koeltz Sci Bks) Lubrecht & Cramer.

Cupp, G. Wayne. Condensed Version of Revelation News: Bible of the End Time. (Illus.). 116p. 1996. pap. 7.95 (*1-889360-01-5*) Revel News.

— Revelation News: Bible Prophecy of the End-Time. 2nd ed. (Illus.). 176p. 1992. reprint ed. pap. 9.95 (*1-889360-00-7*) Revel News.

***Cupp, Melanie Johns.** Toxicology & Clinical Pharmacology of Herbal Products. (Forensic Science & Medicine Ser.). 344p. 2000. 89.50 (*0-89603-791-6*) Humana.

Cupp, Peggy & Mueller, Virginia. Make-a-Bible-Verse Acrostics. Fittro, Pat, ed. 48p. 1996. pap. 1.49 (*0-7847-0496-1*, 02596) Standard Pub.

Cuppage, Francis E. James Cook & the Conquest of Scurvy, 40. LC 94-3050. (Contributions in Medical Studies: No. 40). 192p. 1994. 59.95 (*0-313-29181-0*, Greenwood Pr) Greenwood.

Cuppens, Harry. Genetic Studies of the Cystic Fibrosis Transmembrane Conductance Regulator Gene in Belgian CF Patients. (Acta Biomedica Lovaniensia Ser.: Vol. 110). (Illus.). 138p. (Orig.). 1995. pap. 36.50 (*90-6186-682-0*, Pub. by Leuven Univ) Coronet Bks.

Cupper, Dan. Our Priceless Heritage: Pennsylvania State Parks, 1893-1993. (Illus.). 90p. 1993. pap. 12.95 (*0-89271-056-X*, 0916) Pa Hist & Mus.

— Pennsylvania Turnpike. (Pennsylvania History Ser.). (Illus.). 1990. pap. 5.50 (*0-911410-91-0*) Applied Arts.

— Seventy-Fifth Farm Show: A History of Pennsylvania's Annual Agricultural Exposition. (Illus.). 89p. (Orig.). 1991. pap. 7.95 (*0-89271-048-9*) Pa Hist & Mus.

Cuppett, Susan L. & Aruona, Okezie I., eds. Antioxidant Methodology: In-Vivo & In-Vitro Concepts. LC 97-3214. 1997. 85.00 (*0-935315-79-9*) Am Oil Chemists.

Cuppleditch, D. Hong Kong. (Best of Britain in Old Photographs Ser.). (Illus.). 128p. 1998. pap. 17.95 (*0-7509-1542-0*, Pub. by Sutton Pub Ltd) Intl Pubs Mktg.

Cupples, Carole. Welcome Speeches & More. 64p. (Orig.). 1993. pap. 6.95 (*0-687-27192-4*) Abingdon.

Cupples, Joseph E. Cupples Family, a Record & Family Memorial. 69p. 1997. reprint ed. pap. 14.00 (*0-8328-8168-6*); reprint ed. lib. bdg. 24.00 (*0-8328-8167-8*) Higginson Bk Co.

Cupples, Pat, jt. auth. see Wyatt, Valerie.

Cupples, Patricia, jt. auth. see Wyatt, Valerie.

Cupples, Terry. From Market to Millions. LC 90-92960. (Illus.). 175p. 1990. write for info. (*0-9625726-1-6*) Why Didnt I.

— How to Protect Your Idea-Invention for under 30 Dollars. 2nd ed. 80p. 1993. write for info. (*0-318-72240-2*) Why Didnt I.

— Protect Your Idea-Invention for under Thirty Dollars! LC 90-92959. 204p. 1990. write for info. (*0-9625726-0-8*) Why Didnt I.

Cupples, Vince, jt. auth. see Mohar, Ronald E.

Cupps, Perry T. Reproduction in Domestic Animals. 4th ed. 670p. (C). 1990. text 83.00 (*0-12-196575-9*) Acad Pr.

Cuppy, Will. The Decline & Fall of Practically Everybody. LC 83-48892. (Illus.). 256p. 1984. pap. 14.95 (*0-87923-514-4*) Godine.

***Cuppy, Will.** How to Attract the Wombat. (Illus.). 2000. pap. 15.95 (*1-56792-156-6*) Godine.

Cuppy, Will. How to Attract the Wombat. LC 82-20072. (Illus.). 192p. 1994. pap. 7.95 (*0-226-12828-8*) U Ch Pr.

— How to Be a Hermit, Or, a Bachelor Keeps House. 320p. 1987. reprint ed. pap. 7.95 (*0-87140-144-4*, Pub. by Liveright) Norton.

— How to Become Extinct. LC 82-17649. (Illus.). x, 114p. 1983. pap. 5.95 (*0-226-12826-1*) U Ch Pr.

— How to Tell Your Friends from the Apes. large type ed. LC 97-30816. 160p. 1997. text 19.95 (*1-56000-531-9*) Transaction Pubs.

Cura, Saraya, ed. & illus. see Duskis, Ronald A.

Curami, Andrea. Fifty Years of Ferrari. LC 97-39811. 112p. 1997. 14.98 (*0-7603-0454-8*) MBI Pubg.

Curammeng, Jose, Jr., jt. auth. see Petersen, Robert A.

Curammeng, Jose, Jr., ed. see Peterson, Robert.

Curan, Michael, ed. Professional Practice Guide to Risk. (Illus.). 1100p. 1998. ring bd. 245.00 (*1-885517-10-6*) AACE Intl.

Curan, Robert E., ed. American Jesuit Spirituality: The Maryland Tradition, 1634-1900. (Sources of American Spirituality Ser.). 384p. 1988. 19.95 (*0-8091-0381-8*) Paulist Pr.

Curant Road Elementary & Middle School Students. The Poacher's Payback. LC 95-83048. (Illus.). 27p. (J). (gr. k-6). 1995. write for info. (*0-9649125-0-3*) Durant Rd Elem.

Curato, Guy, pseud. Batting One Thousand - Baseball's Leading Hitters: A Tribute to Lou Gehrig. LC 88-82916. 124p. (Orig.). (YA). (gr. 9). 1989. pap. write for info. (*0-9621591-0-7*) T Assicurato.

Curatola, Heather, et al. Hengeyokai: Shapeshifters of the East. (Vampire Ser.). (Illus.). 1998. pap. 20.00 (*1-56504-338-3*, 3063) White Wolf.

Curatolo, Marisa. Appetizers: Easy & Delicious. (Illus.). 256p. 1999. pap. 14.95 (*1-55110-859-3*) Whitecap Bks.

***Curatolo, Ornella.** Made from Scratch: A Recipe for Success. 1999. pap. 17.95 (*0-9660092-3-1*) Puget Sound.

Curatorial Staff, jt. ed. see De Montebello, Philippe.

Curators of University of Missouri Staff. Gender, Equity & Schooling: Policy & Practice. Bank, Barbara J. & Hall, Peter M., eds. LC 96-40988. (Missouri Symposium on Research & Educational Policy Ser.: Vol. 2). 264p. 1997. text 43.00 (*0-8153-2534-7*); pap. text 21.95 (*0-8153-2535-5*) Garland.

— Race, Ethnicity, & Multiculturalism. Hall, Peter, ed. LC 96-40991. (Missouri Symposium on Research & Educational Policy Ser.: Vol. 1). (Illus.). 248p. 1997. pap. text 20.95 (*0-8153-2442-1*) Garland.

Curaudeau, Veroniques & Fargetton, Brigitte. Joyeux Noel. (Illus.). 79p. 1996. pap. 22.95 (*1-889825-00-X*) R C W Publng.

Curb, Rosemary & Manahan, Nancy. Lesbian Nuns. 400p. 1986. mass mkt. 5.95 (*0-446-32659-3*, Pub. by Warner Bks) Little.

Curb, Rosemary K., ed. Amazon All Stars: Thirteen Lesbian Plays. 426p. 1996. pap. 18.95 (*1-55783-220-X*) Applause Theatre Bk Pubs.

Curbeam, Nicole, et al. A Profile of North Carolina's African American & Native American Populations. (Illus.). 74p. 1994. write for info. (*0-9633115-2-2*) NC Inst Min Econ Devel.

Curbelo, Silvia. The Secret History of Water. (Florida Poetry Ser.: No. 1). 96p. (Orig.). 1997. 18.95 (*0-938078-53-4*); pap. 10.95 (*0-938078-52-6*) Anhinga Pr.

Curbow, John & Hurley, Evelyn, eds. Red Mountain Rendezvous. (Rendezvous Ser.: Vol. 1). (Orig.). 1993. pap. 5.00 (*0-9632842-3-1*) Curbow Pubns.

Curbow, John C. The Ninth Statue. (Illus.). 80p. (Orig.). 1992. pap. 10.00 (*0-9632842-0-7*) Curbow Pubns.

Curby, William A., jt. auth. see Gall, Lorraine S.

Curchak, Norma, et al. Legal Typewriting. 2nd ed. (Illus.). 1981. text 34.29 (*0-07-014940-2*) McGraw.

Curchin, Leonard A. The Local Magistrates of Roman Spain. (Phoenix Supplementary Volumes Ser.). 276p. 1990. text 65.00 (*0-8020-5841-8*) U of Toronto Pr.

— Roman Spain: Conquest & Assimilation. (Illus.). 240p. 1991. 49.95 (*0-415-06451-1*, A6147) Routledge.

Curchy, Christopher & Kyker, Keith. Educator's Survival Guide to TV Production Equipment & Setup. LC 97-24477. (Illus.). 150p. 1997. pap. 22.50 (*1-56308-582-8*) Libs Unl.

Curchy, Christopher, jt. auth. see Kyker, Keith.

Curci-Gonzalez, Lucy & French, Sharon K. Managing the Private Law Library: Management Challenges, New Technology & Planning for the 1990's. 531p. 1991. pap. text 17.50 (*0-685-49932-4*, G4-3862) PLI.

Curci, Lois. Shock Masters of the Cinema. Winick, Margot, ed. (Illus.). 151p. (Orig.). 1996. pap. 19.95 (*1-888214-00-7*) Fantasma Bks.

Curci, Paula. Letters Never Sent: One Woman's Cathartic Release in Poetry. (Illus.). 24p. (Orig.). 1996. pap. 9.00 (*0-9654831-0-X*) P Curci.

Curcic, Slobodan, ed. Hilandar Monastery: An Archive of Architectural Drawings, Sketches, & Photographs. LC 87-61105. (Princeton University Department of Art & Archaeology Collections: Vol. 1). (Illus.). 57p. 1987. reprint ed. pap. 30.00 (*0-608-04523-3*, 206526800001) Bks Demand.

Curcic, Slobodan. Gracanica: King Milutin's Church & Its Place in Late Byzantine Architecture. LC 79-11984. (Illus.). 1980. 40.00 (*0-271-00218-2*) Pa St U Pr.

Curcio, Anthony. The Psychology of Motocross. Walls, Barbara, ed. (Illus.). xiv, 240p. 1999. pap. 49.00 (*0-9669578-0-6*) Two Thous Twelve.

Curcio, Frances, ed. see Reys, Barbara J., et al.

Curcio, Frances R. & Bezuk, Nadine S. Understanding Rational Numbers & Proportions. LC 94-15966. (Curriculum & Evaluation Standards for School Mathematics Addenda Series, Gr. 5-8). (Illus.). 95p. 1994. pap. 17.95 (*0-87353-325-9*) NCTM.

Curcio, Frances R., jt. auth. see Sorrentino, Frank M.

Curcio, Frances R., ed. see Geddes, Dorothy, et al.

Curcio, Frances R., ed. see Phillips, Elizabeth, et al.

Curcio, Frances R., jt. ed. see Stiff, Lee V.

Curcio, Frances R., ed. see Zawojewski, Judith S., et al.

Curcio, Joan L. & First, Patricia F. Violence in the Schools: How to Proactively Prevent & Diffuse It. Herman, Jerry L. & Herman, Janice L., eds. LC 93-22348. (Road Maps to Success Ser.). 64p. 1993. pap. 14.95 (*0-8039-6058-1*) Corwin Pr.

Curcio, Joan L., et al. Sexuality & the Schools: Handling the Critical Issues. LC 95-37402. (Road Maps to Success Ser.). 72p. 1995. pap. 14.95 (*0-8039-6265-7*) Corwin Pr.

Curcio, Joan L., jt. auth. see First, Patricia F.

Curcio, Linda. How to Meet & Marry Mr. Right: (... & Live Happily Ever After) (Illus.). 72p. 1998. pap. 13.95 (*0-9666250-0-5*) Linda Curcio.

Curcio, Michele. Dictionnaire ee l'Astrologie: Dictionary of Astrology. (ENG & FRE.). 1980. pap. 19.95 (*0-8288-1189-X*, M6607) Fr & Eur.

Curcio-Nagy, Linda, jt. auth. see Beezley, William H.

Curcio, Rana C., jt. auth. see Augustine, Timothy J.

***Curcio, Vincent.** Chrysler: The Life & Times of an Automotive Genius. (Illus.). 688p. 2000. 35.00 (*0-19-507896-9*) OUP.

Curcione, Nick. Baja on the Fly. (Illus.). 72p. 1997. 29.95 (*1-57188-102-6*); pap. 19.95 (*1-57188-101-8*) F Amato Pubns.

— The Orvis Guide to Saltwater Fly Fishing. LC 93-44243. (Illus.). 256p. 1993. 24.95 (*1-55821-252-3*) Lyons Pr.

— The Orvis Guide to Saltwater Fly Fishing. 1996. pap. text 18.95 (*1-55821-491-7*) Lyons Pr.

Curd, Bruce R. Marry Only in the Lord. 72p. (Orig.). 1987. pap. 1.95 (*0-940999-12-9*, C-2062) Star Bible.

Curd, Martin & Cover, Jan A. Philosophy of Science: The Central Issues. LC 97-39387. 1000p. (C). 1998. pap. text 50.00 (*0-393-97175-9*) Norton.

Curd, Martin, jt. auth. see Russow, Lilly-Marlene.

***Curd, Patricia.** The Legacy of Parmenides: Eleatic Monism & Later Presocratic Thought. LC 97-8636. 280p. 1998. text 45.00 (*0-691-01182-6*, Pub. by Princeton U Pr) Cal Prin Full Svc.

Curd, Patricia, ed. A Presocratics Reader: Selected Fragments & Testimonia. McKirahan, Richard D., Jr., tr. LC 95-39291. 144p. 1996. pap. text 8.95 (*0-87220-326-3*); lib. bdg. 32.95 (*0-87220-327-1*) Hackett Pub.

Curd, Rollin C. A History of the Boundaries of Nebraska & Indian-Surveyor Stories. Ray, Kathleen C., ed. LC 99-63397. (Illus.). 344p. 1999. pap. 19.95 (*0-9672214-1-2*) Boundaries Pubg.

— A History of the Boundaries of Nebraska & Indian-Surveyor Stories. Ray, Kathleen C., ed. LC 99-63397. (Illus.). 344p. 1999. 34.95 (*0-9672214-0-4*) Boundaries Pubg.

Curd, William B. & Truog, Lucy P. Curd & Allied Families. 96p. 1997. reprint ed. pap. 18.00 (*0-8328-8170-8*); reprint ed. lib. bdg. 28.00 (*0-8328-8169-4*) Higginson Bk Co.

Curds, C. R. & Hawkes, H. A., eds. Ecological Aspects of Used Water Treatment: Biological Activities & Treatment Processes, Vol. 2. 308p. 1983. text 157.00 (*0-12-199502-X*) Acad Pr.

Cure, Adib, ed. see Plater-Zyberk, Elizabeth, et al.

Curemmeng, Jose, Jr., ed. see Petersen, Robert A.

Curemmeng, Jose, Jr., ed. see Peterson, Robert A.

Curen, Barbara Van, see Van Curen, Barbara.

Curen, Cathi. The Secret Journey. LC 98-93531. (Illus.). 80p. (J). (gr. 1-6). 1998. pap. 5.95 (*0-9667442-0-9*) Curen Enterp.

***Curenton, Ginevar.** Poetry of the Past & Present. 2000. 8.95 (*0-533-11835-2*) Vantage.

Curet, jt. auth. see Go, Angelka.

Curet, Bernard. Our Pride: Pointe Coupee. Woolfolk, Doug, ed. (Illus.). 112p. 1981. 20.00 (*0-86518-020-2*) Moran Pub Corp.

Curet De Anda, Miriam. La Poesia de Jose Gautier Benitez. LC 80-17629. (Coleccion Mente y Palabra). (Illus.). 158p. 1980. 5.00 (*0-8477-0570-6*); pap. 4.00 (*0-8477-0571-4*) U of PR Pr.

— El Sistema Expresivo de Ricardo Guiraldes. LC 76-8166. (Coleccion Mente y Palabra). (SPA.). 383p. (Orig.). 1976. 5.00 (*0-8477-0532-3*); pap. 4.00 (*0-8477-0533-1*) U of PR Pr.

Curet, Jose. Crimen en la Calle Tetuan. (Aqui y Ahora Ser.). 1996. pap. 6.95 (*0-8477-0274-X*) U of PR Pr.

Cureton, Ben. Rival Schools: United by Fate; Official Fighting Guide. LC 98-74211. 1998. pap. text 11.99 (*1-56686-851-3*) Brady Pub.

Cureton, Bill. Factor Analysis. 1993. pap. 55.00 (*0-8058-1546-5*) L Erlbaum Assocs.

— Software Engineering on the Sun Workstation. 396p. 1993. 64.95 (*0-387-97480-6*) Spr-Verlag.

Cureton, Charles H. The United States Marine Corps. LC 97-19007. (G. I. Series). 1997. pap. 13.95 (*1-85367-289-0*) Greenhill Bks.

— The United States Marine Corps: From 1775 to Modern Day. LC 99-21376. (G.I. Ser.). (Illus.). 84p. 1999. 19.95 (*0-7910-5373-3*) Chelsea Hse.

— United States Marine Corps in the Persian Gulf, 1990-1991: With the 1st Marine Division in Desert Shield & Desert Storm. 162p. 1993. per. 17.00 (*0-16-041826-7*) USGPO.

Cureton, Glenda B. Face Facts: A Guide to Facial Skin Care. (Illus.). 46p. (Orig.). 1992. pap. 7.95 (*0-9622568-6-2*) Earthtide Pubns.

Cureton, Richard. Rhythmic Phrasing in English Verse. (English Language Ser.). 432p. (C). 1995. pap. text 47.20 (*0-582-55267-2*) Longman.

Cureton, Thomas K. Encyclopedia of Physical Education, Fitness & Sports. 49.95 (*0-88314-293-7*) Natl Assn Sport.

Cureton, W. & Rieu, Charles, eds. Catalogus Codicum Manuscriptorum Orientalium Qui in Murso Britannico Asservantur, Pt. 2: Codices Arabicos Complectens. xiv, 882p. reprint ed. write for info. (*0-318-71496-5*) G Olms Pubs.

Curez, William B. & Jablow, Martha M. Understanding Your Child's Temperament. 1997. write for info. (*0-614-30158-0*) Childrens Hospital of Philadelphia.

Curfman, F. L. Automotive Radiator Construction & Restoration for Antique & Classic. LC 76-6299. Orig. Title: Manual of Automotive Radiator Construction & Repair. (Illus.). 1976. reprint ed. 6.95 (*0-911160-00-0*) Post Group.

Curfman-Falvey, Melissa, jt. auth. see Hampton, Cecil M.

Curhan, Leona & Garfinkle, Irwin. New England GolfGuide: The Directory for Public Play, 2000 Edition. 11th ed. 512p. (Orig.). 1999. pap. 17.95 (*0-9624717-6-3*) New Engl Golf.

Curhan, Leona, et al. New England Golf Guide: The Directory for Public Play, 1999 Edition. 488p. (Orig.). 1998. 17.95 (*0-9624717-5-5*) New Engl Golf.

Curi, U., jt. ed. see Bertola, F.

Curie, Eva. Madame Curie. (FRE.). 1985. pap. 12.95 (*0-7859-2194-X*, 207031068X) Fr & Eur.

Curie, Eve. Madame Curie. Sheean, Vincent, tr. (Illus.). 394p. 1986. pap. 14.95 (*0-306-80281-3*) Da Capo.

Curie, Marie Sklodowska, jt. ed. see David, J.

Curiel, D., et al. Trends in the Study of Morbidity & Mortality. (Public Health Papers: No. 27). (ENG, FRE, RUS & SPA.). 196p. 1965. pap. text 8.00 (*92-4-130027-2*, 1110027) World Health.

Curiel, Frances. Take Charge of Your Job Search! A Handbook to Empower Unemployed People to Find Their Own Jobs. LC 96-30051. 101p. (Orig.). 1997. pap. 20.00 (*1-883302-11-0*) Trning Res.

Curiel, Herman, jt. ed. see Sotomayor, Marta.

Curiel, Jonathan. The College Student's Guide to Credit. LC 86-50629. 230p. (Orig.). (C). 1987. pap. 4.95 (*0-9616978-0-6*) Univ Pr San Francisco.

Curien, Pierre-Louis. Categorical Combinators, Sequential Algorithms, & Functional Programming. 2nd ed. LC 93-281. (Progress in Theoretical Computer Science Ser.). xx, 403p. 1993. 76.50 (*0-8176-3654-4*) Birkhauser.

Curien, Pierre-Louis, jt. auth. see Amadio, Roberto M.

Curiger, Bice. Birth of the Cool: American Painting from Georgia O'Keeffe to Christopher Wool. 1997. 45.00 (*3-89322-884-5*, Pub. by Edition Cantz); 45.00 (*3-89322-902-7*, Pub. by Edition Cantz) Dist Art Pubs.

— Meret Oppenheim. Schelbert, Catherine, tr. (Illus.). 54p. 1988. pap. 20.00 (*0-685-50295-3*) Kent Gallery.

— Meret Oppenheim: A Different Retrospective. (Illus.). 236p. 1998. 45.00 (*3-908161-08-8*) Abbeville Pr.

— Meret Oppenheim: Defiance in the Face of Freedom. (Illus.). 290p. 1989. 62.50 (*0-262-03165-5*) MIT Pr.

Curiger, Bice, jt. auth. see Burckhardt, Jacqueline.

***Curio, Antonio.** Guitar Collection of Antonio Curio. 64p. 1999. pap. 19.95 incl. audio compact disk (*0-7866-3192-9*, 96800BCD) Mel Bay.

Curio, Augustine. A Notable History of the Saracens. Newton, Thomas, ed. LC 77-6870. (English Experience Ser.: No. 863). 1977. reprint ed. lib. bdg. 35.00 (*90-221-0863-5*) Walter J Johnson.

Curione, Maryann & Frantz, Lurene, eds. State College, Pennsylvania: A Photographic Celebration. (Illus.). 124p. 1995. 34.95 (*0-9647274-1-2*); pap. 24.95 (*0-9647274-6-3*) State Col Cent.

Curiotto, Aldo, ed. see Gelmini, Don P.

Curjel, Caspar R. Exercises in Multivariable & Vector Calculus. 840p. (C). 1990. pap. 28.13 (*0-07-014949-6*) McGraw.

Curl, jt. auth. see Hooper.

Curl, Alan & Lopez, Raul A. Vincent Price: Actor & Art Collector. (Illus.). 48p. 1982. pap. 10.00 (*0-935661-08-5*) Riverside Mus Pr.

***Curl, B. Jaime.** North Fork. Jones, Kara L. C., ed. (Illus.). 30p. 2000. pap. 10.00 (*1-929359-04-7*) Kota Pr.

Curl, Caroline, ed. see Edgemont Centennial Committee Staff, et al.

***Curl, Cathleen M., et al.** California Mechanics' Liens & Related Construction Remedies - 12/99 Update. 3rd ed. Maly, Bonnie C., ed. LC 98-72412. 470p. 1999. ring bd. 60.00 (*0-7626-0382-8*, RE-32682) Cont Ed Bar-CA.

Curl, Darryl. Chiropractic Approach to Head Pain. LC 93-44372. (Illus.). 384p. 1994. 70.00 (*0-683-02250-4*) Lppncott W & W.

Curl, David H. Photo/Imaging: How to Communicate with Camera & Computer. 4th rev. ed. LC 97-4064. Orig. Title: Photocommunication. (Illus.). 288p. (Orig.). (C). 1997. pap. text 30.00 (*0-88196-009-8*) Oak Woods Media.

Curl, David H., ed. see Driscoll, Cynthia B.

Curl, Donald, et al. Palm Beach County: In a Class by Itself. (Illus.). 208p. 1997. 39.95 (*0-9647106-2-5*) Copperfld Pubns.

***Curl, Donald W.** Florida Atlantic University. (College History Ser.). (Illus.). 128p. 2000. pap. 19.99 (*0-7385-0614-1*) Arcadia Publng.

Curl, Donald W. Mizner's Florida: American Resort Architecture. LC 83-22205. (American Monograph Newhouse Ser.). (Illus.). 264p. 1987. pap. text 17.50 (*0-262-53068-6*) MIT Pr.

— Murat Halstead & the Cincinnati Commercial. LC 80-12046. (Illus.). 196p. reprint ed. pap. 60.80 (*0-7837-4943-0*, 204460900004) Bks Demand.

Curl, Donald W., ed. see Pierce, Charles W.

Curl, E. A. & Truelove, B. The Rhizosphere. (Advanced Series in Agricultural Sciences: Vol. 15). (Illus.). 328p. 1985. 232.95 (*0-387-15803-0*) Spr-Verlag.

Curl, James Stevens. The Art & Architecture of Freemasonry. LC 92-35041. (Illus.). 272p. 1993. 60.00 (*0-87951-494-9*, Pub. by Overlook Pr) Penguin Putnam.

Curl, James Stevens. Classical Architecture: An Introduction to Its Vocabulary & Essentials, with a Select Glossary of Terms. 231p. 1992. pap. text 54.95 (*0-471-28965-5*, VNR) Wiley.

Curl, James Stevens. Classical Architecture: An Introduction to Its Vocabulary & Essentials, with a Select Glossary of Terms. LC 92-29975. 1993. pap. 46.95 (*0-442-30896-5*, VNR) Wiley.

— A Dictionary of Architecture. LC 98-20544. (Illus.). 848p. 1999. 45.00 (*0-19-210006-8*) OUP.

***Curl, James Stevens.** Dictionary of Architecture. (Illus.). 848p. 2000. pap. 16.95 (*0-19-280017-5*) OUP.

Curl, James Stevens. The Egyptian Revival: An Introductory Study of a Recurring Theme in the History of Taste. LC 93-44615. 1994. text 35.00 (*0-7190-4127-9*, Pub. by Manchester Univ Pr) St Martin.

Curl, James Stevens. The Londonderry Plantation, 1609-1914: The History, Architecture & Planning of the Estates of the City of London & Its Livery Companies in Ulster. LC 89-205110. xxiii, 503 p. 1986. write for info. (*0-85033-577-9*) Phillimore & Co.

Curl, John. Columbus in the Bay of Pigs. 2nd rev. ed. 80p. 1991. pap. 6.00 (*0-938392-10-7*) Homeward Pr.

— History of Work Cooperation in America: Cooperatives,

C

Cooperative Movements, Collectivity & Communalism from Early America to the Present. LC 80-84234. (Illus.). 64p. 1980. pap. 8.00 (*0-938392-00-X*) Homeward Pr.

— Tidal News. 108p. (Orig.). 1982. pap. 5.00 (*0-938392-02-6*) Homeward Pr.

Curl, John, et al. History of Collectivity in the San Francisco Bay Area. (Illus.). 64p. 1982. pap. 8.00 (*0-938392-01-8*) Homeward Pr.

Curl, M. Wade. Arterial Blood Withdrawal: Direct & from Arterial-Lines. LC 91-67113. (Illus.). 82p. (Orig.). (C). 1991. pap. 25.99 (*1-880610-13-2*) PRO-ACT Pub.

— How to Turn Your Healthcare Experience Into Cash. LC 91-92499. (Illus.). 108p. (C). 1992. pap. text 35.99 (*1-880610-00-0*) PRO-ACT Pub.

Curl, Michael. Dictionary of Anagrams. (Reference Library). 1998. pap. 6.95 (*1-85326-350-8*, 3508WW, Pub. by Wrdsworth Edits) NTC Contemp Pub Co.

Curl, Robert S. Analyzing Field Measurements: Air Conditioning & Heating. LC 96-54291. 242p. 1997. 64.00 (*0-88173-254-0*) Fairmont Pr.

— Building Owner's & Manager's Guide: Optimizing Facility Performance. LC 98-38503. (Illus.). 164p. 1998. 69.00 (*0-88173-290-7*, 0419) Fairmont Pr.

***Curl, Robert S.** Building Owner's & Manager's Guide: Optimizing Facility Performance. LC 98-38503. 180p. 1999. 69.00 (*0-13-083831-4*) P-H.

Curl, Robert S. Successful Industrial Energy Reduction Programs. LC 97-16391. xi, 157p. 1997. 65.00 (*0-88173-280-X*) Fairmont Pr.

— Successful Industrial Energy Reduction Programs. 169p. (C). 1997. 75.00 (*0-13-675059-1*) P-H.

Curl, Traci S., jt. ed. see Frajzyngier, Zygmunt.

Curl, Wade, jt. auth. see Dolson, Marianne.

Curland, David. Beauty & the Beast. (Language-Film Study Guide Ser.). 52p. (Orig.). (gr. 9-12). 1984. pap. text 4.95 (*0-913349-02-X*) Public Media Inc.

Curland, David, ed. The Green Wall. (Language-Film Study Guide Ser.). (Illus.). 42p. 1983. pap. text 4.95 (*0-913349-01-1*) Public Media Inc.

Curland, David J. Zarabanda: Beginning Spanish. 5th ed. 512p. 1991. per. 34.59 (*0-8403-6814-3*) Kendall-Hunt.

Curland, David J. & Fondo de Cultura Economica, South America. The Buried Mirror. 160p. (C). 1993. wbk. ed. 28.13 (*0-07-015049-4*) McGraw.

***Curland, Matthew J. & Storage, Bill.** Advanced Visual Basic Six: Power Techniques for Everyday Programs. 400p. 2000. pap. 39.95 incl. cd-rom (*0-201-70712-8*) Addison-Wesley.

Curlander, John C. & McDonough, Robert N. Synthetic Aperture Radar: Systems & Signal Processing. LC 90-29175. (Remote Sensing & Image Processing Ser.). 672p. 1991. 175.00 (*0-471-85770-X*) Wiley.

Curle, Adam. Another Way: Positive Response to Contemporary Violence. LC 96-165821. 1996. pap. text 15.95 (*1-897766-22-X*, Pub. by Jon Carpenter) Paul & Co Pubs.

— Planning for Education in Pakistan: A Personal Case Study. LC 66-14440. (Illus.). 230p. 1966. 24.00 (*0-674-67100-7*) HUP.

***Curle, Adam.** Planning for Education in Pakistan: A Personal Case Study. 232p. 1999. 25.95 (*0-7351-0178-7*) Replica Bks.

Curle, Adam. Recognition of Reality: Reflections & Prose Poems. (Conflict & Peacemaking Ser.). 105p. 1987. pap. 14.95 (*1-869890-12-4*, 1292, Pub. by Hawthorn Press) Anthroposophic.

Curle, C. Pictish & Norse Finds from the Brough of Birsay. (Illus.). 141p. 1982. pap. 19.98 (*0-903903-01-6*) David Brown.

— Life Is a Dream. LC 78-106284. (Short Story Index Reprint Ser.). 1977. 21.95 (*0-8369-3321-4*) Ayer.

Curle, Richard H. Aspects of George Meredith. LC 71-176496. (English Biography Ser.: No. 31). ix, 309p. 1972. reprint ed. lib. bdg. 75.00 (*0-8383-1363-9*) M S G Haskell Hse.

— Caravansary & Conversation. LC 73-134070. (Essay Index Reprint Ser.). 1977. 21.95 (*0-8369-2151-8*) Ayer.

Curlee. Stuttering & Related Disorders of Fluency. 2nd rev. ed. (Illus.). 320p. 1998. 45.00 (*0-86577-764-0*) Thieme Med Pubs.

Curlee, Carole. A Casually Catered Affair, or, Who Forgot the Chocolate Cake? (Illus.). 196p. 1980. spiral bd. 17.99 (*0-9645657-0-6*) Casually Catered.

— The Mexican Collection. (Illus.). 196p. 1993. spiral bd. 18.99 (*0-9645657-1-4*) Casually Catered.

Curlee, Lynn. Brooklyn Bridge. LC 99-43771. (J). 2001. 18.00 (*0-689-83183-8*) S&S Trade.

***Curlee, Lynn.** Liberty. LC 98-44732. (Illus.). 2000. 18.00 (*0-689-82823-3*) Atheneum Yung Read.

— Rushmore. (J). (gr. 3-5). write for info. (*0-439-06013-3*) Scholastic Inc.

Curlee, Lynn. Rushmore. LC 98-16891. (Illus.). 48p. (J). (gr. 2-5). 1999. 17.95 (*0-590-22573-1*) Scholastic Inc.

— Rushmore: Monument for the Ages. LC 98-16891. (J). 1998. pap. 16.95 (*0-590-22201-5*) Scholastic Inc.

— Ships of the Air. LC 94-10746. (Illus.). 32p. (J). (gr. 3-7). 1996. 14.95 (*0-395-69338-1*) HM.

Curlee, Lynn. Into the Ice. LC 96-24125. 40p. (J). 1998. 16.00 (*0-395-83013-3*) HM.

Curlee, Richard F., ed. Stuttering & Related Disorders of Fluency. LC 92-49795. (Current Therapy of Communication Disorders Ser.). 1992. 47.00 (*0-86577-442-0*) Thieme Med Pubs.

Curlee, Richard F. & Siegel, Gerald M. The Nature & Treatment of Stuttering. 2nd ed. 452p. 1996. 69.00 (*0-205-16336-X*) Allyn.

Curlee, T. Randall. The Economic Feasibility of Recycling: A Case Study of Plastic Wastes. LC 86-22675. 219p. 1986. 57.95 (*0-275-92376-2*, C2376, Praeger Pubs) Greenwood.

Curlee, T. Randall, et al. Waste-to-Energy in the United States: A Social & Economic Assessment. LC 93-26467. 280p. 1994. 72.95 (*0-89930-844-9*, Quorum Bks) Greenwood.

Curlee, Thomas N. & Moell, Joseph D. Transmitter Hunting: Radio Direction Finding Simplified. 336p. 1987. pap. 24.95 (*0-07-156006-8*) McGraw.

Curless, Maura. Tx/td,kids,careers W/o Collegeseries. LC 93-7078. (Tech Prep). 120p. (YA). 1993. pap. 7.95 (*1-56079-251-5*) Petersons.

Curless, Maura R. Tx/td,fitness:careers W/o Collseries. LC 92-31182. (Tech Prep). 112p. 1992. pap. 7.95 (*1-56079-223-X*) Petersons.

Curless, Maura Rhodes. Fitness. (Careers Without College Ser.). 1992. 13.15 (*0-606-05187-2*, Pub. by Turtleback) Demco.

— Kids. (Careers Without College Ser.). 1993. 13.15 (*0-606-05191-0*, Pub. by Turtleback) Demco.

Curley. Water & Wastewater Project Financing. 256p. 1993. lib. bdg. 75.00 (*0-87371-486-5*, L486) Lewis Pubs.

Curley & Pynn Public Relations Management, Inc. St, ed. see Magruder, G. Brock & Gilbert, Walter R., Jr.

Curley, Arthur & Broderick, Dorothy M. Building Library Collections. 6th ed. LC 84-23665. 350p. 1985. 31.00 (*0-8108-1776-4*) Scarecrow.

Curley, Arthur, et al. Akers' Simple Library Cataloging. 7th rev. ed. LC 83-14423. 1985. 34.50 (*0-8108-1649-0*) Scarecrow.

Curley, Arthur, jt. ed. see Sellen, Betty-Carol.

Curley, Augustine J. Augustine's Critique of Skepticism: A Study of Contra Academicos. 2nd ed. (Studies in the Humanities: Vol. 14). XX, 167p. (C). 1997. reprint ed. pap. text 32.95 (*0-8204-3936-3*) P Lang Pubng.

***Curley, Carlo.** In the Pipeline. 1998. 29.95 (*0-00-627990-2*, Pub. by HarpC) Trafalgar.

Curley, Charles. From Ashes on to Life. 1991. pap. 9.25 (*1-55673-386-0*, 9204) CSS OH.

Curley, Charles J. The Way of the King: Sermons for Pentecost, First Lesson, Cycle B. LC 93-2756. 1993. pap. 6.95 (*1-55673-613-4*, 9338) CSS OH.

Curley, Daniel. The Curandero. LC 90-38357. 136p. 1991. 12.95 (*0-933532-76-8*) BkMk.

— Living with Snakes. LC 84-22773. (Flannery O'Connor Award for Short Fiction Ser.). 144p. 1985. 19.95 (*0-8203-0767-X*) U of Ga Pr.

— Love in the Winter: Stories. fac. ed. LC 76-7541. (Illinois Short Fiction Ser.). 124p. 1994. pap. 38.50 (*0-7837-7618-7*, 204737000007) Bks Demand.

Curley, Daniel, et al, eds. Accent: An Anthology, 1940-60. LC 73-76274. 519p. 1973. text 39.95 (*0-252-00349-7*) U of Ill Pr.

Curley, Daniel, jt. auth. see Ebert, Roger.

Curley, Dorothy. Community Service: Innovations in Outreach at the Brooklyn Public Library. LC 77-137361. (Public Library Reporter: No. 16). 64p. reprint ed. pap. 30.00 (*0-608-12605-5*, 202419300035) Bks Demand.

Curley, E. M. Descartes Against the Skeptics. LC 77-14366. 288p. 1978. 34.50 (*0-674-19826-3*) HUP.

Curley, Edwin & Moreau, Pierre-Francois, eds. Spinoza: Issues & Directions, the Proceedings of the Chicago Spinoza Conference. LC 90-49020. (Brill's Studies in Intellectual History: Vol. 14). (ENG & FRE.). xiv, 404p. 1990. 142.00 (*90-04-09334-6*) Brill Academic Pubs.

Curley, Edwin, ed. see Spinoza, Baruch.

Curley, Edwin, ed. & tr. see De Spinoza, Benedict.

Curley, Edwin, tr. & intro. see Hobbes, Thomas.

Curley, Edwin M. Spinoza's Metaphysics: An Essay in Interpretation. LC 70-85073. 190p. 1969. reprint ed. pap. 58.90 (*0-7837-4102-2*, 205792500011) Bks Demand.

Curley, Frederick J., jt. ed. see Rippe, James M.

***Curley, Helen.** Local Ireland Almanac & Yearbook of Facts, 2000. 494p. 2000. pap. 14.95 (*0-9536537-0-6*, Pub. by Local Ireland) Dufour.

Curley, James M. I'd Do It Again: A Record of All My Uproarious Years. LC 76-6333. (Irish Americans Ser.). (Illus.). 1976. reprint ed. 68.95 (*0-405-09329-2*) Ayer.

Curley, Kathleen F. Word Processing: First Step to the Office of the Future. LC 82-18948. 164p. 1983. 45.00 (*0-275-91717-7*, C1717, Praeger Pubs) Greenwood.

Curley, Lois, jt. ed. see Hestenes, Roberta.

Curley, Marie T. The Buckram Syndrome: A Critical Essay on Paperbacks in Public Libraries of the United States. LC 68-31033. (Public Library Reporter: NO. 13). 79p. reprint ed. pap. 30.00 (*0-8357-7454-6*, 202425800036) Bks Demand.

Curley, Mark & Curley, Sandra. The Natural Guide to Good Health: Nutritional Balance for a Life Time. LC 90-70943. 185p. (Orig.). 1990. pap. 14.95 (*0-9626875-9-6*) Supreme Pub.

Curley, Martha A., et al. Critical Care Nursing of Infants & Children. Rader, Ilze, ed. LC 95-45034. (Illus.). 1126p. 1996. text 102.00 (*0-7216-3120-7*, W B Saunders Co) Harcrt Hlth Sci Grp.

Curley, Melissa, jt. auth. see Pettiford, Lloyd.

Curley, Michael, tr. Saint Patrick's Purgatory: A Poem by Marie de France. (Medieval & Renaissance Texts & Studies: Vol. 94). 192p. 1997. reprint ed. 20.00 (*0-86698-108-X*, MR94) MRTS.

Curley, Michael J. Church & State in the Spanish Floridas, (1783-1822) LC 73-3584. (Catholic University of America. Studies in Romance Languages & Literatures: No. 30). reprint ed. 49.50 (*0-404-57780-6*) AMS Pr.

— Geoffrey of Monmouth. LC 94-14513. (Twayne's English Authors Ser.: No. 509). 200p. 1994. 32.00 (*0-8057-7055-0*, Twyne) Mac Lib Ref.

Curley, Michael T. & Walker, Joseph A. How to Prepare for the Stockbroker Exam: Series 7. 2nd ed. LC 99-11533. 384p. 2000. 16.95 (*0-7641-0766-6*) Barron.

— How to Prepare for the Stockbroker's Exam: Series 7. LC 96-16033. 1996. pap. 14.95 (*0-8120-9709-2*) Barron.

Curley, Richard T. Elders, Shades & Women: Ceremonial Change in Lango, Uganda. LC 70-634788. 233p. reprint ed. pap. 72.30 (*0-608-15838-0*, 203142900074) Bks Demand.

Curley, Robert. Rhode Island: Off the Beaten Path: A Guide to Unique Places. 2nd ed. LC 98-7145. (Off the Beaten Path Ser.). (Illus.). 256p. 1998. pap. 12.95 (*0-7627-0201-X*) Globe Pequot.

***Curley, Robert Patrick.** Rhode Island: Off the Beaten Path. 3rd ed. LC 00-29391. (Off the Beaten Path Ser.). (Illus.). 224p. 2000. pap. 12.95 (*0-7627-0645-7*) Globe Pequot.

Curley, Sandra, jt. auth. see Curley, Mark.

Curley, Stephen J., jt. auth. see Wetta, Frank J.

Curley, Steven A. M. D. Anderson Solid. Pollock, Raphael E., ed. LC 97-41042. (Tumor Oncology Ser.). (Illus.). 264p. 1998. 89.95 (*0-387-98370-8*) Spr-Verlag.

Curley, T. F. Camp Meeting. unabridged ed. vii, 87p. 1991. pap. 15.00 (*1-890715-00-X*) T Curley.

***Curley, T. F.** Tristan: A Sixties Romance. LC 99-90695. 428p. 1999. 25.00 (*0-7388-0468-1*); pap. 18.00 (*0-7388-0469-X*) Xlibris Corp.

Curley, Terence P. Console One Another: A Guide to Christian Funerals. LC 93-3540. 104p. (Orig.). 1993. pap. 8.95 (*1-55612-600-X*) Sheed & Ward WI.

— Healing the Brokenhearted. LC 94-49216. 80p. (Orig.). 1995. pap. 3.95 (*0-8189-0709-6*) Alba.

— The Ministry of Consolation: A Parish Guide for Comforting the Bereaved. LC 93-10315. 80p. (Orig.). 1993. pap. 3.95 (*0-8189-0651-0*) Alba.

— Six Steps for Managing Loss: A Catholic Guide Through Grief. LC 97-18065. 1997. pap. 3.95 (*0-8189-0801-7*) Alba.

— A Way of the Cross for the Bereaved. LC 95-48356. (Illus.). 64p. (Orig.). 1996. pap. 3.95 (*0-8189-0752-5*) Alba.

Curley, Thomas M. Sir Robert Chambers: Law, Literature & Empire in the Age of Johnson. LC 96-33813. (Illus.). xxii, 698p. 1998. 87.50 (*0-299-15150-6*) U of Wis Pr.

Curley, Thomas M., ed. see Chambers, Robert.

Curley, Timothy, et al. Health Professions Education Linkages: Community-Based Primary Care Training. Glass, Karen, ed. 68p. (Orig.). 1994. pap. text 15.00 (*1-55877-179-4*) Natl Governor.

— State Progress in Health Care Reform, 1992: Strategic Investments: Tough Choices for America's Future. Glass, Karen, ed. 70p. (Orig.). 1993. pap. text 15.00 (*1-55877-202-2*) Natl Governor.

Curley, Timothy E. Predicting Love, Marriage, Sex & Money: Predictive Astrology. 182p. 1995. pap. text 12.95 (*0-937533-18-1*) TEC Pubns.

Curley, Timothy Edward. How to Read Your Own Horoscope: Predictive Astrology. (Illus.). 175p. 1998. pap. 13.95 (*0-937533-89-0*) TEC Pubns.

***Curlin, Vashti.** How to Prepare for the NCLEX-PN with CAT. 4th ed. (Illus.). 480p. 2000. pap. 29.95 incl. cd-rom (*0-7641-7237-9*) Barron.

Curling, Audrey. The Running Tide. large type ed. 384p. 1987. 27.99 (*0-7089-1582-5*) Ulverscroft.

— Sparrow's Yard. large type ed. 320p. 1987. 27.99 (*0-7089-1683-X*) Ulverscroft.

Curlow, Barbara & Somerfield, Mark R., eds. Psychosocial Resource Variables in Cancer Studies: Conceptual & Measurement Issues. LC 95-23013. (Journal of Psychosocial Oncology: Vol. 13, No. 1-2). 216p. 1995. pap. 39.95 (*1-56024-758-4*, Hawrth Medical) Haworth Pr.

Curme, George O. A Grammar of the English Language, 2 vols., Set. 1983. 60.00 (*0-930454-03-0*) Verbatim Bks.

— A Grammar of the English Language Vol. I: Parts of Speech. LC 77-87423. xxiii, 382p. 1983. 29.95 (*0-930454-02-2*) Verbatim Bks.

— A Grammar of the English Language Vol. II: Syntax. LC 77-87422. xvi, 624p. 1983. 32.95 (*0-930454-01-4*) Verbatim Bks.

— A Grammar of the German Language, 2 vols, Set. 1974. 600.00 (*0-87968-213-2*) Gordon Pr.

Curme, Lynn M., jt. auth. see Polunin, Nicholas.

Curnan, Cynthia. The Care & Feeding of Perfectionists. 240p. 1998. text 14.95 (*1-880823-21-7*) N Star Pubns.

***Curnen, Mary G. McCrea.** Doctors Afield. LC 99-26479. (Illus.). 264p. 1999. 27.50 (*0-300-08020-4*) Yale U Pr.

Curnes, Michael. Val. LC 95-83611. 410p. 1996. pap. 15.95 (*1-885487-19-3*) Brownell & Carroll.

Curnette, jt. auth. see Solnit, Albert J.

Curnier, Alain. Computational Methods in Solid Mechanics. LC 94-4245. (Solid Mechanics & Its Applications Ser.: Vol. 29). 1994. text 251.00 (*0-7923-2761-6*) Kluwer Academic.

Curnock, Audrey. Quantitative Methods in Business. 448p. 1999. pap. 49.50 (*0-7487-2083-9*, Pub. by S Thornes Pubs) Trans-Atl Phila.

Curnoe, Greg. Deeds/Abstracts. LC 96-120514. (Illus.). 200p. 1995. pap. 16.95 (*0-919626-78-5*, Pub. by Brick Bks) Genl Dist Srvs.

Curnow, Allen. Early Days Yet: New & Collected Peoms 1941-1997. 320p. 1997. pap. 27.95 (*1-85754-297-5*, Pub. by Carcanet Pr) Paul & Co Pubs.

— The Loop in the Lone Kauri Road. 1987. pap. 8.95 (*0-19-648053-1*) OUP.

Curnow, Barry & Fox, Jonh M. Third Age Careers: Meeting the Corporate Challenge. 200p. 1994. 74.95 (*0-566-07493-1*, Pub. by Gower) Ashgate Pub Co.

Curnow, Celia. Italian Maiolica in the National Museums of Scotland. (Illus.). 128p. 1995. pap. 35.00 (*0-948636-31-9*, 6319, Pub. by Natl Mus Scotland) A Schwartz & Co.

Curnow, Ena. Manana "Detras del Generalisimo" (Biografia de Bernarda Gomez de Toro) LC 93-74825. (Coleccion Cuba y sus Jueces). (SPA., Illus.). 445p. (Orig.). 1995. pap. 29.00 (*0-89729-719-9*) Ediciones.

Curnow, Ray, jt. auth. see Barron, Iann.

Curnow, Richard D., jt. ed. see Fagerstone, Kathleen A.

Curnow, Trevor. Wisdom, Intuition & Ethics. LC 98-74446. (Series in Philosophy). 1p. 1999. text 78.95 (*1-84014-840-3*) Ashgate Pub Co.

***Curnow, Vera.** The Best of Colored Pencil 5. (Illus.). 144p. 1999. 24.99 (*1-56496-582-1*) Rockport Pubs.

Curnow, Vera. Creative Colored Pencil: Landscapes. (Creative Colored Pencil Ser.). (Illus.). 84p. 1996. 16.99 (*1-56496-266-0*, Quarry Bks) Rockport Pubs.

— Creative Colored Pencil: Portraits. (Creative Colored Pencil Ser.). (Illus.). 84p. 1996. 16.99 (*1-56496-265-2*, Quarry Bks) Rockport Pubs.

— Creative Colored Pencil: The Step-by-Step Guide & Showcase. (Illus.). 160p. 1995. 29.99 (*1-56496-141-9*) Rockport Pubs.

Curnow, Wystan. Imants Tillers & the Book of Power. (Illus.). 172p. 1997. text 80.00 (*90-5703-271-6*) Gordon & Breach.

Curns, Eileen. Negatives to Positives. (Illus.). 39p. 1982. pap. 10.00 (*0-942968-02-6*) ACCORD IL.

Curns, Eileen & Lowstuter, Clyde. Pathways to People. 2nd rev. ed. (Illus.). 73p. 1978. pap. 12.00 (*0-942968-00-X*) ACCORD IL.

Curns, Eileen B. From Stress to Balance. Orig. Title: Stress. (Illus.). 88p. 1989. teacher ed. 45.00 (*0-942968-03-4*) ACCORD IL.

— From Stress to Balance. enl. rev. ed. Orig. Title: Stress. (Illus.). 88p. 1989. pap. 18.95 (*0-942968-01-8*) ACCORD IL.

Curns, Eileen B. & McGarey, Gladys T. The Stages of Stress Leading to Disease: Predict It, Prevent It, What to Do. (Illus.). 32p. (Orig.). 1997. pap. 10.00 (*0-942968-04-2*) ACCORD IL.

Curnutt, Barbara, ed. see Trotter, Martha Pope.

***Curnutt, Jordan.** Animals & the Law: A Dictionary. 2000. lib. bdg. 55.00 (*1-57607-147-2*) ABC-CLIO.

Curnutt, Jordan, jt. auth. see Dienhart, John W.

***Curnutt, Kirk.** Ernest Hemingway & the Expatriate Modernist Movement. (Literary Topics Ser.: Vol. 2). (Illus.). 240p. 2000. 49.95 (*0-7876-3963-X*) Gale.

Curnutt, Kirk. Wise Economies: Brevity & Storytelling in American Short Stories. LC 96-50297. 312p. 1997. text 35.00 (*0-89301-202-5*) U of Idaho Pr.

***Curnutt, Kirk, ed.** The Critical Response to Gertrude Stein, 36. LC 00-20765. (Critical Responses in Arts & Letters Ser.: Vol. 36). 400p. 2000. lib. bdg. 79.50 (*0-313-30475-0*, GR0475, Greenwood Pr) Greenwood.

Curoe, Philip R. Educational Attitudes & Policies of Organized Labor in the United States. LC 76-176702. (Columbia University. Teachers College. Contributions to Education Ser.: No. 201). reprint ed. 37.50 (*0-404-55201-3*) AMS Pr.

— Educational Attitudes & Policies of Organized Labor in the United States. LC 76-89169. (American Education: Its Men, Institutions, & Ideas. Series 1). 1975. reprint ed. 18.95 (*0-405-01407-4*) Ayer.

Curott, Phyllis. Book of Shadows: A Modern Woman's Journey into the Wisdom & Magic of Witchcraft. 320p. 1999. pap. 13.00 (*0-7679-0055-3*) Broadway BDD.

Curotto, Alberto, tr. from FRE. Brancusi. LC 97-70935. (Great Modern Masters Ser.). (Illus.). 64p. 1997. 11.98 (*0-8109-4693-9*, Pub. by Abrams) Time Warner.

— Modigliani. LC 97-70937. (Great Modern Masters Ser.). (Illus.). 64p. 1997. 11.98 (*0-8109-4651-3*, Pub. by Abrams) Time Warner.

Curotto, Alberto, tr. see Faerna, Jose M., ed.

Curpisin, Jim & Lefenseld, Mark. Fee-Based Services: Using Fees to Increase Revenues & Retain Accounts. 78p. 1997. pap. text 30.00 (*1-878204-56-4*) APIS Inc.

Curr, John. Coal Viewer & Engine Builder's Practical Companion. 2nd ed. 96p. 1970. reprint ed. 28.50 (*0-7146-2429-2*, Pub. by F Cass Pubs) Intl Spec Bk.

Curr, Matthew, tr. see William of Conches.

***Curra, John.** The Relativity of Deviance. LC 99-6305. 197p. 2000. 54.95 (*0-7619-0777-7*) Sage.

Currah, L. & Proctor, F. J. Onions in Tropical Regions. 1990. pap. 75.00 (*0-85954-283-1*, Pub. by Nat Res Inst) St Mut.

Currall, Julian. Sex Discrimination in European Community Law. (European Community Law Ser.). (C). 1994. text 85.00 (*0-485-70005-0*, Pub. by Athlone Pr) Humanities.

***Curran.** Sap R/3 3.0 in a Box. 1998. pap. text 132.00 (*0-13-011934-2*, Prentice Hall) P-H.

Curran. Taking the Fear Out of Economics E1. (ITBP Textbooks Ser.). 1999. pap. text 19.99 (*1-86152-474-9*) Thomson Learn.

Curran, ed. Pleistocene & Holocene Carbonate Environments on San Salvador Island, Bahamas, No. T175. (IGC Field Trip Guidebooks Ser.). 56p. 1989. 21.00 (*0-87590-610-9*) Am Geophysical.

Curran & Renzetti. Social Problems. 5th ed. 1999. pap., student ed. 20.00 (*0-205-29375-1*, Longwood Div) Allyn.

Curran, jt. auth. see Renzetti.

Curran, jt. auth. see Williams.

***Curran, Thomas A.** Integrating With SAP R/3. 375p. 2000. pap. 54.99 (*0-13-014458-4*) P-H.

Curran, Alfred A. German Immigration to Pennsylvania: 1683-1933. 97p. 5.75 (*1-55630-004-2*) Brentwood Comm.

— Soviet-German Nationalism. LC 86-71860. 135p. (Orig.). 1986. pap. 8.50 (*0-9617186-0-9*) A A Curran.

Curran, Allan, jt. auth. see Curran, Richard.

Curran, Barbara A. & Carson, Clara N. The Lawyer Statistical Report: The U. S. Legal Profession in the 1990s. LC 85-72656. 247p. (Orig.). 1994. pap. 30.00 (*0-910059-13-6*) Am Bar Foun.

Curran, Barbara A. & Rosich, Katherine J. Data Manual for the Survey of the Legal Needs of the Public. LC 80-66657. xvii, 381p. 1980. 100.00 (*0-910058-83-0*, 305270) W S Hein.

C

Curran, Barbara A., et al. The Lawyer Statistical Report. LC 85-72656. 1985. 98.00 (*0-910059-07-1*, 306010); pap., suppl. ed. 30.00 (*0-910059-09-8*, 306010) W S Hein.

Curran, Barbara A., jt. auth. see American Bar Foundation Staff.

Curran, Bob. Banshees, Beasts & Brides from the Sea: Irish Tales of the Supernatural. 160p. (Orig.). 1996. pap. 13.95 (*0-86281-553-3*, Pub. by Appletree Pr) Irish Bks Media.

***Curran, Bob.** Creatures of Celtic Myth. (Illus.). 2000. 27.95 (*0-7137-2766-7*) Blandford Pr.

— An Encyclopedia of Celtic Mythology. (Illus.). 240p. 2000. 29.95 (*0-8092-2330-9*, 233090, Contemporary Bks) NTC Contemp Pub Co.

Curran, Bob. A Field Guide to Irish Fairies. (Illus.). 72p. 1998. 12.95 (*0-8118-2276-1*) Chronicle Bks.

Curran, Charles. Moral Theology: A Continuing Journey. LC 81-23160. 238p. 1982. text 26.50 (*0-268-01350-0*) U of Notre Dame Pr.

Curran, Charles A. & McCormick, Richard A., eds. John Paul II & Moral Theology. LC 98-16737. (Readings in Moral Theology Ser.: No. 10). 400p. 1998. pap. 29.95 (*0-8091-3797-6*) Paulist Pr.

Curran, Charles C., ed. Library Research Round Table: 1977 Research Forums Proceedings: Meetings Held at the 96th Annual Conference of the American Library Association, 1977. LC 79-15300. (Monograph Publishing). 299p. 1979. reprint ed. pap. 92.70 (*0-8357-0424-6*, 201985900015) Bks Demand.

Curran, Charles C., et al, eds. Library Performance, Accountability & Responsiveness: Essays in Honor of Ernest R. DeProspo. LC 89-78242. (Information Management, Policies & Services Ser.: Vol. 11). 192p. (C). 1990. text 73.25 (*0-89391-597-1*) Ablx Pub.

Curran, Charles E. The Catholic Moral Tradition Today: A Synthesis. LC 98-44646. (Moral Traditions & Moral Arguments Ser.). 255p. 1999. pap. 19.95 (*0-87840-717-0*); text 60.00 (*0-87840-716-2*) Georgetown U Pr.

— The Church & Morality: An Ecumenical & Catholic Approach. LC 92-47448. (Hein/Fry Lectureship Ser.). 128p. 1993. pap. 14.00 (*0-8006-2756-3*, 1-2756, Fortress Pr) Augsburg Fortress.

— Critical Concerns in Moral Theology. LC 83-40593. 280p. reprint ed. pap. 86.80 (*0-608-15652-3*, 203190900077) Bks Demand.

— Directions in Catholic Social Ethics. LC 84-28079. 304p. (Orig.). (C). 1985. pap. text 14.00 (*0-268-00853-1*) U of Notre Dame Pr.

— Directions in Fundamental Moral Theology. LC 85-2543. 304p. 1985. pap. text 14.00 (*0-268-00854-X*) U of Notre Dame Pr.

— History & Contemporary Issues: Studies in Moral Theology. LC 96-26514. 226p. 1996. 29.95 (*0-8264-0944-X*) Continuum.

— Issues in Sexual & Medical Ethics. LC 77-89767. 1979. pap. 14.00 (*0-268-01142-7*) U of Notre Dame Pr.

— The Origins of Moral Theology in the United States: Three Different Approaches. Keenan, James F., ed. LC 96-46601. (Moral Traditions & Moral Agruments Ser.). 224p. 1997. 55.00 (*0-87840-634-4*); pap. 24.95 (*0-87840-635-2*) Georgetown U Pr.

— Transition & Tradition in Moral Theology. LC 78-20877. 272p. 1979. text 15.00 (*0-268-01837-5*) U of Notre Dame Pr.

Curran, Charles E., ed. Absolutes in Moral Theology? LC 75-3988. 320p. 1976. reprint ed. lib. bdg. 65.00 (*0-8371-7450-3*, CUMT, Greenwood Pr) Greenwood.

Curran, Charles E., et al, eds. Feminist Ethics & the Catholic Moral Tradition. (Readings in Moral Theology Ser.: No. 9). 272p. (Orig.). 1996. pap. 29.95 (*0-8091-3669-4*) Paulist Pr.

Curran, Charles E. & McCormick, Richard A. The Historical Development of Fundamental Moral Theology in the United States No. 11: Readings in Moral Theology. LC 99-32353. (Readings in Moral Theology Ser.: No. 11). 368p. 1999. pap. 29.95 (*0-8091-3879-4*) Paulist Pr.

Curran, Charles E. & McCormick, Richard A., eds. Dialogue about Catholic Sexual Teaching. LC 93-4370. (Readings in Moral Theology Ser.: No. 8). 624p. 1993. pap. 24.95 (*0-8091-3414-4*) Paulist Pr.

Curran, Charles E. & McCormick, Richard S., eds. Readings in Moral Theology No. 7: Natural Law & Theology. 1991. pap. 14.95 (*0-8091-3179-X*) Paulist Pr.

Curran, Charles E., jt. auth. see McCormick, Richard A.

Curran, Chris, ed. Scale, Cost & Effectiveness in University Distance Teaching. (Illus.). 226p. 1999. text 69.95 (*1-85972-468-X*, Pub. by Ashgate Pub) Ashgate Pub Co.

Curran, Christine P. Sexually Transmitted Diseases. LC 97-44140. (Diseases & People Ser.). 128p. (YA). (gr. 6 up). 1998. lib. bdg. 20.95 (*0-7660-1050-3*) Enslow Pubs.

***Curran, Colleen.** Cake Walk. 96p. 2000. pap. 14.95 (*0-88754-586-6*) Theatre Comm.

Curran, Colleen. Sacred Hearts. LC 90-175668. 122p. (Orig.). 1997. pap. 9.95 (*0-88754-484-3*) Theatre Comm.

— Something Drastic. LC 96-138754. 216p. 1995. pap. 14.95 (*0-86492-171-3*, Pub. by Goose Ln Edits) Genl Dist Srvs.

Curran, Connie R. Shaping an Integrated Delivery Network: Home Care's Role in Improving Service, Outcomes & Profitability. LC 98-19918. 162p. 1998. 46.00 (*1-56793-085-9*) Health Admin Pr.

***Curran, Cynthia.** When I Thus Began the World Anew: Middleclass Widows in 19th Century Britain. 275p. 2000. pap. text 32.00 (*1-55605-307-X*) Wyndham Hall.

***Curran, Daniel.** Guide to American Cinema, 1965-1995. LC 96-53269. 528p. 1998. lib. bdg. 79.50 (*0-313-29666-9*) Greenwood.

Curran, Daniel. Social Problems: Society in Crisis. 5th ed. LC 99-49528. 576p. (C). 1999. 63.00 (*0-205-28260-1*, Macmillan Coll) P-H.

Curran, Daniel J. Living Sociology Interactive Edition. abr. ed. 1998. 66.75 (*0-205-28785-9*) PH Diversified.

Curran, Daniel J. & Renzetti, Claire M. Criminology. (C). 1995. 37.33 (*0-205-15974-5*, Macmillan Coll) P-H.

— Social Problems: Society in Crisis. 2nd ed. 600p. 1990. pap. text 43.00 (*0-205-12252-3*, H22528) Allyn.

— Theories of Crime. LC 93-25394. 324p. 1993. pap. text 36.00 (*0-205-14193-5*) Allyn.

Curran, Daniel J., jt. auth. see Renzetti, Claire M.

Curran, David. Brautigan, Richard: A Pilgrimage, August 1982. Curran, Patricia, ed. (Illus.). 48p. (Orig.). 1989. reprint ed. spiral bd. 29.95 (*1-881417-06-9*) D F Curran Prods.

— Ghosts: True Hauntings in Montana. Curran, Patricia, ed. (Illus.). 40p. (Orig.). 1989. reprint ed. pap. 4.00 (*1-881417-05-0*) D F Curran Prods.

Curran, David F. The Complete Ginseng Grower's Manual. rev. ed. Curran, Patricia A., ed. LC 83-70439. (Illus.). 185p. (Orig.). 1993. reprint ed. ring bd. 84.95 (*1-881417-02-6*) D F Curran Prods.

— The Ginseng Disease & Pest Reference Guide. Curran, Patricia A., ed. (Illus.). 134p. (Orig.). 1989. reprint ed. spiral bd. 84.95 (*1-881417-04-2*) D F Curran Prods.

Curran, David K. Adolescent Suicidal Behavior. LC 87-8650. 208p. (C). 1987. pap. text 28.95 (*0-89116-781-1*) Hemisp Pub.

— Tyranny of the Spirit: Domination & Submission in Adolescent Relationships. LC 96-11820. 1996. 50.00 (*1-56821-833-8*) Aronson.

Curran, Dennis P., ed. Advances in Cycloaddition, Vol. 1. 208p. 1987. 109.50 (*0-89232-861-4*) Jai Pr.

— Advances in Cycloaddition, Vol. 2. 220p. 1990. 109.50 (*0-89232-951-3*) Jai Pr.

— Advances in Cycloaddition, Vol. 3. 210p. 1993. 109.50 (*1-55938-319-4*) Jai Pr.

— Advances in Cycloaddition, Vol. 4. 1997. 109.50 (*1-55938-695-9*) Jai Pr.

— Advances in Cycloaddition, Vol. 6. 1999. 109.50 (*0-7623-0531-2*) Jai Pr.

Curran, Dennis P., et al. Stereochemistry of Radical Reactions: Concepts, Guidelines, & Synthetic Applications. (Illus.). 281p. 1996. pap. 84.95 (*3-527-29409-0*, Wiley-VCH) Wiley.

Curran, Dolores. Dolores Curran on Family Prayer. LC 96-60656. 152p. (Orig.). 1997. pap. 9.95 (*0-89622-703-0*) Twenty-Third.

— Family: A Church Challenge for the 80's. (Orig.). 1981. 3.50 (*0-86683-640-3*) Harper SF.

— Stress & the Healthy Family. 192p. 1985. 13.95 (*0-86683-863-5*) Harper SF.

— Tired of Arguing with Your Kids? Wisdom from Parents Who Have Been There. LC 99-61901. 125p. 1999. pap. 12.95 (*1-893732-06-1*) SORIN BKS.

— Traits of a Healthy Family. 336p. 1984. mass mkt. 5.99 (*0-345-31750-5*, Ballantine) Ballantine Pub Grp.

— Traits of a Healthy Family: Fifteen Traits Commonly Found in Healthy Families by Those Who Work With Them. LC 82-70489. 300p. 1984. 14.95 (*0-86683-643-8*) Harper SF.

— Who, Me Teach My Child Religion? rev. ed. 156p. 1985. 6.95 (*0-86683-619-5*) Harper SF.

— Working with Parents. 1989. teacher ed. 15.95 (*0-88671-271-8*, 6240) Am Guidance.

Curran, Donald J. Metropolitan Financing: The Milwaukee Experience, 1920-1970. LC 72-7984. (Illus.). 181p. reprint ed. pap. 56.20 (*0-8357-6788-4*, 203546500095) Bks Demand.

Curran, Doreen. Magic of Free Machine Embroidery. 112p. 1994. pap. 24.00 (*0-916896-58-7*) Lacis Pubns.

Curran, E. T., jt. ed. see Murthy, S. N.

Curran, Edward L. Judge "For Four Days" Rutherford. 32p. 1988. reprint ed. pap. 1.95 (*1-883858-48-8*) Witness CA.

***Curran, Edward Lodge.** Great Moments in Catholic History. (Illus.). 114p. 1998. reprint ed. 18.00 (*0-911845-71-2*) Neumann Pr.

Curran, Eileen. Birds Nests. LC 84-8658. (Illus.). 32p. (J). (gr. k-2). 1997. pap. 3.50 (*0-8167-0342-6*) Troll Communs.

— Hello, Farm Animals. LC 84-8657. (Illus.). 32p. (J). (gr. k-2). 1997. pap. 3.50 (*0-8167-0346-9*) Troll Communs.

— Home for a Dinosaur. LC 84-8627. (Giant First Start Reader Ser.). (Illus.). 32p. (J). (gr. k-2). 1997. pap. 3.95 (*0-8167-0431-7*) Troll Communs.

— Life in the Forest. LC 84-16455. (Illus.). 32p. (J). (gr. k-2). 1985. pap. 3.50 (*0-8167-0447-3*) Troll Communs.

— Life in the Meadow. LC 84-12384. (Illus.). 32p. (J). (gr. k-2). 1997. pap. 3.50 (*0-8167-0344-2*) Troll Communs.

— Life in the Pond. LC 84-16285. (Illus.). 32p. (J). (gr. k-2). 1985. pap. 3.50 (*0-8167-0453-8*) Troll Communs.

— Life in the Sea. LC 84-16190. (Illus.). 32p. (J). (gr. k-2). 1997. pap. 3.50 (*0-8167-0449-X*) Troll Communs.

— Little Christmas Elf. LC 84-8628. (Giant First Start Reader Ser.). (Illus.). 32p. (J). (gr. k-2). 1985. lib. bdg. 17.25 (*0-8167-0352-3*) Troll Communs.

— Little Christmas Elf. LC 84-8628. (Giant First Start Reader Ser.). (Illus.). 32p. (J). (gr. k-2). 1997. pap. 3.95 (*0-8167-0432-5*) Troll Communs.

— Look at a Tree. LC 84-8843. (Illus.). 32p. (J). (gr. k-2). 1985. pap. 3.50 (*0-8167-0350-7*) Troll Communs.

— Mountains & Volcanoes. LC 84-8638. (Illus.). 32p. (J). (gr. k-2). 1996. pap. 3.50 (*0-8167-0348-5*) Troll Communs.

***Curran, Ellen.** Guided Imagery for Healing Children. 2000. pap. 14.95 (*1-58270-041-9*) Beyond Words Pub.

Curran, Emily, jt. auth. see Willow, Diane.

Curran, Francis X. Catholics in Colonial Law. LC 63-24861. 139p. reprint ed. pap. 43.10 (*0-8357-8567-X*, 203493300091) Bks Demand.

Curran, George, jt. auth. see Duvall Curran, Pamela.

Curran, Gerald J. A Comprehensive Guide to Understanding Your Homeowners Insurance Policy. LC 95-33209. 236p. 1996. pap. 29.95 (*0-7734-4232-4*) E Mellen.

Curran, Gerald J., Jr. The History, Development, Purpose, & Function of the Certified Public Adjuster & Certified Public Insurance Consultant. LC 97-29962. (Illus.). 364p. 1997. text 99.95 (*0-7734-8540-6*) E Mellen.

Curran, H. Allen, ed. Biogenic Structures: Their Use in Interpreting Depositional Environments. LC 87-163435. (Society of Economic Paleontologists & Mineralogists Ser.: No. 35). (Illus.). 353p. 1985. reprint ed. pap. 109.50 (*0-608-02973-4*, 206344100006) Bks Demand.

— Guide to Bahamian Ichnology: Pleistocene, Holocene & Modern Environments. (Illus.). 61p. 1997. pap. text 10.00 (*0-935909-61-3*) Bahamian.

— Proceedings of the 3rd Symposium on the Geology of the Bahamas. 250p. 1987. pap. text 18.00 (*0-935909-24-9*) Bahamian.

Curran, H. Allen & White, Brian, eds. Terrestrial & Shallow Marine Geology of the Bahamas & Bermuda. (Special Papers: No. 300). (Illus.). 1995. pap. 53.00 (*0-8137-2300-0*) Geol Soc.

Curran, Harold. Fearful Crossing: The Central Overland Trail Through Nevada. 2nd rev. ed. Paher, Stanley W., ed. (Illus.). 212p. 1987. reprint ed. pap. 15.95 (*0-913814-85-7*) Nevada Pubns.

Curran, Helen M. Apricot Power: How Laetrile Cured My Cancer. 111p. (Orig.). 1994. pap. 12.00 (*0-9642185-0-X*) H M Curran.

Curran, J. B., jt. auth. see Cain, Gordon.

Curran, J. P., ed. see Kers, A. J., et al.

***Curran, James.** De-Westernizing Media Studies. (Communication & Society Ser.). 2000. pap. 27.99 (*0-415-19395-8*) Routledge.

***Curran, James, ed.** Media Organisations in Society. (An Arnold Publication). 256p. 2000. text 75.00 (*0-340-72014-X*); pap. text 19.95 (*0-340-72015-8*) OUP.

Curran, James, et al, eds. Cultural Studies & Communications. LC 95-36959. 1996. text 59.95 (*0-340-65268-3*, Pub. by E A); pap. text 21.00 (*0-340-61417-X*, Pub. by E A) OUP.

— Mass Communication & Society. LC 78-68700. 488p. 1979. reprint ed. pap. 151.30 (*0-608-02791-X*, 206385800007) Bks Demand.

Curran, James & Gurevitch, Michael, eds. Mass Media & Society. LC 91-23441. 352p. 1995. pap. text 18.95 (*0-340-51759-X*, A6112, Pub. by E A) St Martin.

— Mass Media & Society. 2nd ed. 384p. 1996. pap. text 19.95 (*0-340-61418-8*, Pub. by E A) OUP.

***Curran, James & Gurevitch, Michael, eds.** Mass Media & Society. 3rd ed. (An Arnold Publication). (Illus.). 432p. 2000. pap. 24.95 (*0-340-73201-6*, Pub. by E A) OUP.

Curran, James & Park, Myung-Jin, eds. De-Westernizing Media Studies. 352p. pap. 85.00 (*0-415-19394-X*) Routledge.

Curran, James & Seaton, Jean. Power Without Responsibility: The Press & Broadcasting in Britain. 5th ed. LC 97-7921. 432p. (C). 1997. 80.00 (*0-415-16810-4*); pap. 21.99 (*0-415-11407-1*) Routledge.

Curran, James & Storey, David J., eds. Small Firms in Urban & Rural Locations. LC 93-18756. (Small Business Ser.). 176p. (C). (gr. 13). 1993. pap. 59.95 (*0-415-10037-2*) Thomson Learn.

Curran, James, jt. auth. see Liebes, Tamar.

***Curran, James Michael, et al.** Forensic Interpretation of Glass Evidence. LC 00-30354. 2000. write for info. (*0-8493-0069-X*) CRC Pr.

Curran, James P. & Monti, Peter M., eds. Social Skills Training: A Practical Handbook for Assessment & Treatment. LC 81-6374. 459p. reprint ed. pap. 142.30 (*0-7837-3882-X*, 204373000010) Bks Demand.

Curran, James T., et al, eds. Police & Law Enforcement, 1973-1993, 6 vols. LC 73-7210. 1973. lib. bdg. write for info. (*0-404-19542-3*) AMS Pr.

Curran, Jan D. The Appalachian Trail: How to Prepare for & Hike It. (Illus.). 204p. (Orig.). 1995. 19.95 (*1-56825-050-9*); pap. 14.95 (*1-56825-051-7*) Rainbow Books.

— The Appalachian Trail: Journey of Discovery. LC 91-21920. 330p. (Orig.). 1991. pap. 12.95 (*0-935834-66-4*) Rainbow Books.

— The Appalachian Trail: Onward to Katahdin. LC 99-18373. 288p. 1999. pap. 14.95 (*1-56825-072-X*) Rainbow Books.

Curran, Jane V. Goethe's Wilhelm Meister's Apprenticeship: A Reader's Commentary. (GERM Ser.). 2001. 55.00 (*1-57113-118-3*) Camden Hse.

Curran, Jeanne, jt. auth. see Takata, Susan R.

***Curran, Jim.** High Achiever: The Life & Climbs of Chris Bonington. (Illus.). 256p. 2000. 24.95 (*0-89886-713-4*) Mountaineers.

Curran, Jim. K-2: Triumph & Tragedy. 224p. 1989. pap. 14.00 (*0-395-48590-8*) HM.

— K-2, Triumph & Tragedy. large type ed. 1989. 27.99 (*0-7089-2069-1*) Ulverscroft.

— K2: The Story of the Savage Mountain. (Illus.). 192p. 1995. 24.95 (*0-89886-455-0*) Mountaineers.

***Curran, Jim.** K2: The Story of the Savage Mountain. (Illus.). 272p. 2000. pap. 14.95 (*0-89886-683-9*) Mountaineers.

Curran, Jim. Trends in Advanced Avionics. LC 92-5963. (Illus.). 200p. 1992. text 35.95 (*0-8138-0749-2*) Iowa St U Pr.

***Curran, Joan F., et al.** Numbering Your Genealogy: Basic Systems, Complex Families & International Kin. LC 00-25929. (Special Publications). 2000. pap. write for info. (*0-915156-64-4*) Natl Genealogical.

***Curran, John.** Pagan City & Christian Capital: Rome in the Fourth Century. LC 99-36418. (Oxford Classical Monographs). (Illus.). 300p. 2000. text 80.00 (*0-19-815278-7*) OUP.

***Curran, John E.** How Will You Paint Your Life Today? LC 99-64483. (Illus.). 94p. 1999. pap. 12.95 (*0-9664126-3-X*) AMC Pubns.

— How Will You Paint Your Life Today? large type ed. LC 99-64483. (Illus.). 78p. 1999. pap. 12.95 (*0-9664126-2-1*) AMC Pubns.

Curran, Joseph M. Hibernian Green on the Silver Screen: The Irish & American Movies, 23. LC 88-24749. (Contributions to the Study of Popular Culture Ser.: No. 23). 172p. 1989. 49.95 (*0-313-26491-0*, CNH/, Greenwood Pr) Greenwood.

Curran, June. Drafting House Plans: A Whole House System. LC 90-81254. (Illus.). 200p. 1995. pap. 29.95 (*0-932370-04-7*) Brooks Pub Co.

— Drawing Home Plans: A Simplified Drafting System for Planning & Design. LC 78-72188. (Illus.). (C). 1979. pap. 22.95 (*0-932370-02-0*) Brooks Pub Co.

— Profile Your Lifestyle: Questions to Ask Yourself Before Building, Buying or Remodeling a Home. LC 78-72187. (C). 1979. pap. 7.95 (*0-932370-00-4*) Brooks Pub Co.

Curran, K. T. The First Time Club: An AIDS Awareness Play. (Illus.). iii, 25p. (Orig.). 1993. pap. 3.50 (*0-88680-392-6*) I E Clark.

— Freshman Year: A One-Act Play. (Illus.). 30p. (YA). 1997. pap. 4.00 (*0-88680-444-2*) I E Clark.

Curran, Kathleen, ed. Thomas Alexander Tefft: American Architecture in Transition, 1845-1860. LC 87-72847. (Illus.). 288p. (Orig.). 1988. pap. 20.00 (*0-933519-12-5*) D W Bell Gallery.

Curran, Keith. Dalton's Back. 1990. pap. 5.25 (*0-8222-0266-2*) Dramatists Play.

— Walking the Dead. 1992. pap. 5.25 (*0-8222-1218-8*) Dramatists Play.

***Curran, Kelly & Stenerson, Jon.** Computer Numerical Control: Operation & Programming. LC 00-36763. 450p. (C). 2000. 72.00 (*0-13-011980-6*) P-H.

Curran, Kelly, jt. auth. see Stenerson, Jon.

Curran, Kevin & Williams, Geoff. Manual of Remote Working. LC 96-32170. 352p. 1997. 113,95 (*0-566-07839-2*, Pub. by Gower) Ashgate Pub Co.

Curran, Leigh. Going Nowhere Sideways. LC 98-34547. 224p. 1999. pap. 14.95 (*1-56474-289-X*) Fithian Pr.

Curran, Linda, et al, eds. Research Needs in Non-Conventional Bioprocesses. LC 85-11065. 148p. 1985. 32.50 (*0-935470-21-2*) Battelle.

Curran, Lorna. Lessons for Little Ones: Language Arts & Cooperative Learning. rev. ed. (Illus.). 248p. 1994. pap. 25.00 (*1-879097-09-5*) Kagan Cooperative.

— Lessons for Little Ones: Mathematics & Cooperative Learning. (Illus.). 285p. 1994. pap. text 25.00 (*1-879097-19-2*) Kagan Cooperative.

Curran, Lyle. How to Be a Lawyer Without Attending Law School. (Orig.). 1995. pap. 9.95 (*0-9640433-1-9*) M Hardberger.

Curran, M. G. & White, G. K. InfoServices: A Typing Practice Set. 144p. 1987. pap. text 13.08 (*0-07-014943-7*) McGraw.

Curran, Mary A. Environmental Life-Cycle Assessment. 432p. 1996. 79.95 (*0-07-015063-X*) McGraw.

Curran, Mary B. Thinkers Through Time: Reading Ethics with Literature. LC 93-23843. 196p. 1993. pap. write for info. (*0-916078-31-0*) Iris Pr.

Curran, Mary D. The Parish & the Hill. LC 86-14247. 272p. 1986. reprint ed. pap. 12.95 (*0-935312-58-7*) Feminist Pr.

Curran, Michael. Uncle Sam's Misguided Children. (Illus.). 85p. 1998. pap. 15.95 (*1-892509-49-0*) Chambers Pubg Grp.

Curran, Michael G., Jr., jt. ed. see Villee, Pat A. G.

***Curran, Michael J.** Uncle Sam's Misguided Children. (Illus.). 81p. 1998. pap. 8.95 (*0-9672811-0-5*) Stonehvn Pubng.

Curran, Michael W., jt. auth. see Mackenzie, David.

Curran, Michael W., jt. auth. see MacKenzie, David.

Curran, Michael W., jt. auth. see Mackenzie, David.

Curran, Michael W., jt. auth. see MacKenzie, David.

Curran, Noel. The Logical Universe: The Real Universe. (Avebury Series in Philosophy). 176p. 1994. 66.95 (*1-85628-863-3*, Pub. by Avebry) Ashgate Pub Co.

— The Philosophy of Mathematics & Natural Laws: Another Copernican Revolution. LC 97-73212. (Avebury Series in Philosophy). 224p. 1997. text 69.95 (*1-85972-654-2*, Pub. by Ashgate Pub) Ashgate Pub Co.

Curran, Pam. Shawnee Pottery: The Full Encyclopedia. LC 95-20256. (Illus.). 304p. 1995. 59.95 (*0-88740-845-1*) Schiffer.

Curran, Patricia. Grace Before Meals: Food Ritual & Body Discipline in Convent Culture. 192p. 1989. text 22.95 (*0-252-01585-1*) U of Ill Pr.

Curran, Patricia, ed. see Curran, David.

Curran, Patricia A., ed. see Curran, David F.

Curran, Patrick J. The Town of Islip: A History of Its Communities & Schools. (Orig.). pap. text. write for info. (*0-9615532-0-0*) Town Islip.

Curran, Paul, jt. ed. see Foody, Giles.

Curran, Paul J., jt. ed. see Foody, Giles M.

Curran, Peggy, et al. Montreal: La Joie de Vivre. (Urban Tapestry Ser.). (Illus.). 1998. write for info. (*1-881096-47-5*) Towery Pub.

Curran, Peter A., jt. auth. see Long, Ron.

Curran, Peter F., jt. auth. see Katzir-Katchalsky, Aharon.

Curran, R. C. Atlas de Histopatologia. (SPA.). 96p. 1979. 95.00 (*0-8288-4720-7*, S37588) Fr & Eur.

***Curran, R. C. & Crocker, J.** Curran's Atlas of Histopathology. (A Harvey Miller Publication). 304p. 2000. 45.00 (*0-19-263220-5*) OUP.

C

Curran, R. C. & Jones, E. L. Atlas de Patologia Macroscopica. (SPA.). 148p. 1978. 85.00 (*0-8288-4862-9*, S37589) Fr & Eur.

— Tumors: Structure & Diagnosis. (A Harvey Miller Publication). (Illus.). 812p. 1991. text 275.00 (*0-19-261840-7*) OUP.

Curran, R. M., ed. Creep-Fatigue Interaction, 1976 ASME-EPC Symposium: Presented at the Winter Meeting of the ASME, New York, N. Y., December 5-10, 1976. LC 76-28849. 438p. reprint ed. pap. 135.80 (*0-608-30567-7*, 201681600005) Bks Demand.

Curran, Richard & Curran, Allan. All about Harvard Square - A Guide: Historic Walking Tours, Museums, Restaurants, Shopping & Entertainment. LC 89-50283. (Illus.). 112p. (Orig.). 1989. pap. 4.95 (*0-9622433-0-2*) Basement Graphics.

Curran, Robert. Haunted. 1991. mass mkt. 4.99 (*0-312-92800-9*, Pub. by Tor Bks) St Martin.

Curran, Robert E. The Bicentennial History of Georgetown University, Vol. 1: From Academy to University 1789-1889. LC 92-47499. (Illus.). 463p. 1993. 25.00 (*0-87840-485-6*) Georgetown U Pr.

— Michael Augustine Corrigan & the Shaping of Conservative Catholism in America, 1878-1902. 1978. 51.95 (*0-405-10814-1*) Ayer.

Curran, Ron. Little Gray Cloud. (Oracle of Delphi Chronicles). 1997. 20.00 (*0-9656372-0-4*) Venture Bks CA.

Curran, S. New Technology & Insurance. (C). 1980. 85.00 (*0-7855-4069-5*, Pub. by Witherby & Co) St Mut.

***Curran, Stephen, et al.** Treating Depression in the Elderly. 256p. 2000. pap. text 38.00 (*0-7506-4379-X*) Buttrwrth-Heinemann.

***Curran, Steven.** Motion Graphics: Graphic Design for Broadcast & Film. 2000. 45.00 (*1-56496-646-1*) Rockport Pubs.

Curran, Stuart. Poetic Form & British Romanticism. 288p. 1990. pap. text 22.00 (*0-19-506072-5*) OUP.

— Shelley's Annus Mirabilis: The Maturing of an Epic Vision. LC 75-318514. (Illus.). 277p. 1975. reprint ed. pap. 85.90 (*0-608-03173-9*, 206362600007) Bks Demand.

Curran, Stuart, ed. Le Bossu & Voltaire on the Epic: Rene le Bossu, Treatise of the Epic Poem, 1695 & Voltaire, Essay on Epic Poetry, 1727. LC 73-133363. 374p. 1970. 50.00 (*0-8201-1086-8*) Schol Facsimiles.

Curran, Stuart, jt. ed. see Bennett, Betty T.

Curran, Stuart, ed. see Shelley, Mary Wollstonecraft.

Curran, Stuart, ed. see Smith, Charlotte.

Curran, Stuart M., ed. The Cambridge Companion to British Romanticism. (Cambridge Companions to Literature Ser.). 325p. (C). 1993. pap. text 18.95 (*0-521-42193-4*) Cambridge U Pr.

Curran, Sue. I Saw Satan Fall Like Lightning. LC 98-13826. 1998. pap. 12.99 (*0-88419-546-5*) Creation House.

— The Joshua Generation. LC 95-139563. 154p. (Orig.). 1994. pap. 9.99 (*1-56043-827-4*, Treasure Hse) Destiny Image.

— The Praying Church. 160p. 1991. 10.99 (*1-56043-442-2*, Treasure Hse) Destiny Image.

***Curran, Susan.** Incorporating State of the Art Information on the Environment: Environment Handbook. 238p. 1998. 55.00 (*0-11-310155-4*, Pub. by Statnry Office) Balogh.

Curran, Susan. New Technology & Insurance. 1981. 60.00 (*0-7855-7333-X*, Pub. by Fourmat Pub) St Mut.

Curran, Taia K., ed. The Directory of Human Services for Warren County. 2nd ed. 112p. 1999. pap. 17.95 (*0-925133-54-X*) Volt Directory.

***Curran, Taia K., ed.** Georgia Substance Abuse Treatment Resource Guide. 128p. 1999. 54.90 (*0-925133-62-0*) Volt Directory.

***Curran, Taia K.** Florida Directory of Disability Services. 288p. 1999. 54.90 (*0-925133-61-2*) Volt Directory.

Curran, Terrie. All Booked Up. 224p. 1989. reprint ed. mass mkt. 3.50 (*0-373-26028-8*) Harlequin Bks.

Curran, Theresa I., ed. see Coleman, Mary Sullivan & Krueger, Laura.

***Curran, Thomas.** SAP R/3 Business Blueprint. (Illus.). 1999. pap. 149.99 incl. VHS (*0-13-026075-4*) P-H.

Curran, Thomas. SAP R/3 Business Blueprint: Understanding the Business Process Reference Model. LC 97-13166. 320p. (C). 1997. pap. 49.99 (*0-13-521147-6*) P-H.

***Curran, Thomas.** SAP R/3 Business Blueprint: Understanding the Business Process Reference Model. 2nd ed. LC 99-15767. 512p. (C). 1999. pap. 54.99 (*0-13-085340-2*) P-H.

— Sap R/3 Desk Reference. 400p. 2001. pap. write for info. (*0-13-017574-9*) P-H.

***Curran, Thomas & Ladd, Andrew.** SAP R/3 Business Blueprint: The Complete Video Course. 372p. 1999. VHS 95.00 (*0-13-026076-2*) P-H.

***Curran, Thomas, et al.** Sap R/3 Reporting & E-Business Intelligence. LC 00-29829. 460p. 2000. pap. 54.99 incl. audio compact disk (*0-13-022615-7*) P-H.

Curran, Thomas, jt. ed. see Morse, Edgar.

Curran, Thomas H. Doctrine & Speculation in Scheiermacher's Glaubenslehre. LC 94-17866. xx, 390p. (C). 1994. 152.35 (*3-11-013832-8*) De Gruyter.

***Curran, Timothy L.** Joys & Tears of a Doctor: How Irish Humor, Dedicated Care & Strong Faith Help to Solve Patients' Pains. 1998. pap. 15.95 (*0-9640096-5-X*) Woodstock Books.

Curran, Timothy L. Joys & Tears of a Doctor: How Irish Humor, Dedicated Care & Strong Faith Help to Solve Patients' Pains, Vol. 1. 261p. 1998. pap. 15.95 (*0-9671812-0-8*) T L Curran.

Curran, Trisha. Financing Your Film: A Guide for Independent Filmmakers & Producers. LC 85-16792. 169p. 1985. 45.00 (*0-275-90042-8*, C0042, Praeger Pubs); pap. 19.95 (*0-275-91762-2*, B1762, Praeger Pubs) Greenwood.

— A New Note on the Film. Jowett, Garth S., ed. LC 79-6671. (Dissertations on Film, 1980 Ser.). 1980. lib. bdg. 12.95 (*0-405-12905-X*) Ayer.

Curran, Virginia. The Key to Making Your Home Beautiful with Beginner's Interior Design. 52p. 1998. pap. 6.00 (*0-8059-4370-6*) Dorrance.

Curran, Vivian G. Learning French Through the Law. 300p. 1995. text 60.00 (*0-9650295-0-6*) Juris Pubng.

Curran, W. & Harding, T. The Law & Mental Health: Harmonizing Objectives: A Comparative Survey of Existing Legislation Together with Guidelines for Its Assessment & Alternative Approaches to Improvement. (International Digest of Health Legislation Offprints: Vol. 28, No. 4). 159p. 1977. 25.00 (*92-4-169284-7*) World Health.

Curran, Wanda L. Raising a Healthy Guinea Pig. LC 97-10460. 1997. pap. 2.95 (*0-88266-999-0*, Storey Pub) Storey Bks.

— Your Guinea Pig: A Kid's Guide to Raising & Showing. LC 94-42164. (Illus.). 160p. (J). 1995. pap. 14.95 (*0-88266-889-7*, Garden Way Pub) Storey Bks.

Curran, William. The Beauty of Los Angeles. LC 91-25683. 80p. 1991. 19.95 (*1-55988-075-9*); pap. 9.95 (*1-55988-074-0*) Am Prods.

Curran, William J. Health Care Law. 4th ed. 1344p. 1990. 56.00 (*0-316-16532-8*, Aspen Law & Bus) Aspen Pub.

— Health Care Law & Ethics. 5th ed. LC 97-42574. 1512p. 1998. boxed set 62.00 (*1-56706-809-X*) Panel Pubs.

— Law Medicine Notes: Progress in Medicolegal Relations. Relman, Arnold S., ed. 450p. 1989. 38.50 (*0-910133-26-3*) Mass Med Pub Div.

Curran, William J. & Gostin, Lawrence O. Acquired Immunodeficiency Syndrome: Legal & Regulatory Policy. (Special Studies on AIDS). 400p. 1988. text 45.00 (*1-55572-008-0*) Univ Pub Group.

Curran, William J. & Shapiro, E. Donald. Law, Medicine & Forensic Science. 3rd ed. LC 81-81207. 1181p. (C). 1982. 41.00 (*0-316-16510-7*, Aspen Law & Bus) Aspen Pub.

Curran, William J., et al. Electrical Safety & Hazards in Hospitals. 205p. (C). 1974. text 19.50 (*0-8422-7135-X*) Irvington.

***Curran, William J., et al.** Health Care Law & Ethics: With Teacher's Manual. 5th rev. ed. (Casebook Ser.). 1400p. 1998. 62.00 (*1-56706-691-7*, 66917) Panel Pubs.

Curran, William J., et al. Health Care Law, Forensic Science, & Public Policy. 4th ed. 1344p. 1991. teacher ed. write for info. (*0-316-16533-6*, 65336) Aspen Law.

***Currance, Phillip L. & Bronstein, Alvin C.** Hazardous Materials: Emergency Medical Response Practices & Procedures. 1999. teacher ed. write for info. (*0-8151-1985-2*) Mosby Inc.

Currance, Phillip L. & Bronstein, Alvin C. Hazardous Materials: Medical Response, Practices & Procedures. LC 98-56388. (Illus.). 231p. (C). (gr. 13). 1999. pap. text 34.95 (*0-8151-1984-4*, 28068) Mosby Inc.

Currance, Phillip L., jt. auth. see Bronstein, Alvin C.

Currant, Nanda. Cat Dreams. (Illus.). 12p. 1989. 35.00 (*0-934714-09-6*) Swamp Pr.

Currao, Tim & Sessions, Ron. Camaro Restoration. (Illus.). 208p. 1990. pap. 17.95 (*0-89586-375-8*, HP Books) Berkley Pub.

Currao, Tom. Chevrolet Big Block V-8 Interchange Manual. LC 96-35796. (Illus.). 192p. 1996. pap. 19.95 (*0-7603-0117-4*) MBI Pubg.

— How to Build & Modify Chevrolet Big Block V-8 Engines. LC 97-22612. (Power Pro Ser.). (Illus.). 160p. 1997. pap. 16.95 (*0-7603-0203-0*) MBI Pubg.

Curray, Joseph R., et al. Geology of Continental Margins: A 1977 Short Course. LC QE0039.G45. (Education Course Note Ser.: Vol. 5). 143p. reprint ed. pap. 44.40 (*0-608-08723-8*, 206936200004) Bks Demand.

Currell, D. Introduction to Puppets & Puppet Making. 80p. 1996. 12.98 (*0-7858-0630-X*) Bk Sales Inc.

***Currell, David.** Puppets & Puppet Theatre. (Illus.). 176p. 1999. 40.00 (*1-86126-135-7*, Pub. by Crolwood) Trafalgar.

Currell, Donald. Residential Construction & Estimating: An Addition to the Complete Arizona Contractors' Study Guide. (Illus.). 97p. (Orig.). 1991. text 75.00 (*1-879020-04-1*) ACS Assocs Pub.

Currelly, C. T. I Brought the Ages Home. (Illus.). 336p. 1994. pap. write for info. (*0-88854-186-4*) Royal Ontario.

Curren, Anna M. & Munday, Laurie D. Dimensional Analysis for Meds. LC 98-177565. (Illus.). (Orig.). (C). 1998. pap. text 36.95 (*0-918082-08-0*) WI Pubns Inc.

— Math for Meds - Dosages & Solutions. 7th rev. ed. (Illus.). 336p. (C). 1995. pap. text 28.95 (*0-918082-07-2*) WI Pubns Inc.

Curren-Aquino, Deborah T., compiled by. King John: An Annotated Bibliography. LC 93-47107. (Shakespeare Bibliographies Ser.: Vol. 23). 936p. 1994. text 40.00 (*0-8240-6626-X*, H770) Garland.

Curren-Aquino, Deborah T., ed. King John: New Perspectives. LC 87-40529. 205p. 1989. 33.50 (*0-87413-337-8*) U Delaware Pr.

Curren, Art. Kitbashing HO Model Railroad Structures. 2nd ed. LC 95-112972. (Illus.). 88p. (Orig.). 1994. per. 11.95 (*0-89024-245-3*) Kalmbach.

— Realistic Plastic Structures for Toy Train Layouts. LC 97-218850. (Illus.). 80p. (Orig.). 1997. pap. 14.95 (*0-89778-410-3*, 10-8050, Kalmbach Books) Kalmbach.

Curren, Mary T., et al, eds. An Index to Advances in Consumer Research Vols. 7-11: Proceedings of the 1980-84 Conferences. 89p. 1985. pap. 18.00 (*0-915552-12-4*) Assn Consumer Res.

Currence, Mary G., ed. Tennessee Statistical Abstract, 1969. (Illus.). 707p. (C). 1968. pap. text 5.95 (*0-940191-00-8*) Univ TN Ctr Bus Econ.

— Tennessee Statistical Abstract, 1971. (Illus.). 712p. (C). 1971. pap. text 5.75 (*0-940191-01-6*) Univ TN Ctr Bus Econ.

— Tennessee Statistical Abstract, 1974. (Illus.). 705p. (C). 1974. pap. text 7.50 (*0-940191-02-4*) Univ TN Ctr Bus Econ.

Current & Climaco, eds. Decision Support Systems for Multiobjective Transportation Problems. 250p. 1996. text. write for info. (*0-08-042583-6*, Pergamon Pr) Elsevier.

Current, Annie E. Current. Genealogy of the Current & Hobson Families, in Two Parts. (Illus.). 350p. 1997. reprint ed. pap. 53.50 (*0-8328-8174-0*); reprint ed. lib. bdg. 63.50 (*0-8328-8173-2*) Higginson Bk Co.

Current Architecture Catalogue Staff. Joao Luis Carrilho Da Graca. (Illus.). 96p. 1996. pap. text 29.95 (*84-252-1495-5*) Watsn-Guptill.

Current, Dean, et al, eds. Costs, Benefits, & Farmer Adoption of Agroforestry: Project Experience in Central America & the Caribbean. (World Bank Environment Paper: Vol. 14). 228p. 1996. pap. 22.00 (*0-8213-3428-X*) World Bank.

Current Digest of the Soviet Press Staff. Current Soviet Policies Vol. X: The Proceedings of the 19th CPSU Conference. (Current Soviet Policies Ser.). (Orig.). 1988. pap. 25.00 (*0-913601-10-1*) Current Digest.

Current Digest of the Soviet Press Staff, tr. see Bigelow, Ann C., ed.

Current Digest of the Soviet Press Staff, tr. see Ehlers, Robert & Bessel, Richard, eds.

Current Digest of the Soviet Press Staff, tr. see Ehlers, Robert & Goodrich, Malinda, eds.

Current Digest of the Soviet Press Staff, tr. see Livermore, Gordon.

Current Dist Staff, ed. Notes on Pathology, Part II. 260p. 1976. 80.00 (*0-7855-0799-X*, Pub. by Current Dist) St Mut.

Current European Anaesthesiology Staff. Current European Aesthesiology: The Yearbook of the European Academy of Anaesthesiology, Vol. 3, 1987. LC 85-7409. (Illus.). 266p. 1987. reprint ed. pap. 82.50 (*0-8357-5566-5*, 203519300003) Bks Demand.

— Current European Anesthesiology: The Yearbook of the European Academy of Anaesthesiology, Vol. 1, 1985. LC 85-7409. (Illus.). 319p. 1985. reprint ed. pap. 98.90 (*0-8357-5564-9*, 203519300001) Bks Demand.

— Current European Anesthesiology: The Yearbook of the European Academy of Anaesthesiology, Vol. 2, 1986. LC 85-7409. (Illus.). 336p. 1986. reprint ed. pap. 104.20 (*0-8357-5565-7*, 203519300002) Bks Demand.

Current-Garcia, Eugene. O. Henry. LC 93-776. (Studies in Short Fiction: No. 49). 170p. 1993. 29.00 (*0-8057-0859-6*, Twyne) Mac Lib Ref.

Current-Garcia, Eugene, ed. O. Henry. (United States Authors Ser.: No. 77). 192p. (C). 1965. 32.00 (*0-8057-0368-3*, Twyne) Mac Lib Ref.

Current-Garcia, Eugene & Hitchcock, Bert, eds. American Short Stories. 6th ed. LC 96-1024. 800p. (C). 1997. pap. text 44.00 (*0-673-46901-8*) Addson-Wesley Educ.

Current-Garcia, Eugene, ed. see Tuggle, William O.

Current Hematology & Oncology Staff. Current Hematology & Oncology, 1987, Vol. 5. Fairbanks, Virgil F., ed. LC 81-210176. (Illus.). 320p. reprint ed. pap. 99.20 (*0-8357-5559-2*, 203518800005) Bks Demand.

Current, Ira. Photographic Color Printing: Theory & Technique. (Illus.). 296p. 1987. text 52.95 (*0-240-51787-3*, Focal) Buttrwrth-Heinemann.

Current Kitchens Staff. Potatoes Vol. 34: Recipes for America's Favorite Vegetable. 64p. 1994. pap., per. 3.95 (*0-942320-46-8*) Am Cooking.

Current, Marcia E., jt. auth. see Current, Richard N.

Current, Marion E. Looking at Each Other: Korean Western Cultures in Contrast. (Illus.). 96p. 1983. pap. 4.95 (*0-8048-1415-5*, Pub. by Seoul Intl Tourist) Tuttle Pubng.

Current Mathematical Publications Staff. Current Mathematical Publications, 17 vols., Nos. 1-17. LC 75-648439. 140p. 1991. reprint ed. pap. 43.40 (*0-608-05681-2*, 206619700001) Bks Demand.

Current Nephrology Staff. Current Nephrology, Vol. 18, 1995. Gonick, Harvey C., ed. LC 77-643123. 483p. 1995. reprint ed. pap. 149.80 (*0-608-02409-0*, 206305100018) Bks Demand.

Current, Richard N. Arguing with Historians: Essays on the Historical & the Unhistorical. LC 87-13682. 217p. reprint ed. pap. 67.30 (*0-608-09076-X*, 206971000005) Bks Demand.

— Daniel Webster & the Rise of National Conservatism. (Illus.). 215p. (C). 1992. reprint ed. pap. text 11.95 (*0-88133-653-X*) Waveland Pr.

— Encyclopedia of the Confederacy, Vol. 1. 1995. 95.00 (*0-13-276015-0*) P-H.

— Encyclopedia of the Confederacy, Vol. 2. 1995. 95.00 (*0-13-276023-1*) P-H.

— Encyclopedia of the Confederacy, Vol. 3. 1995. 95.00 (*0-13-276031-2*) P-H.

— Encyclopedia of the Confederacy, Vol. 4. 1995. 95.00 (*0-13-276049-5*) Prntice Hall Bks.

— The History of Wisconsin Vol. II: The Civil War Era, 1848-1873. Hass, Paul & Holzhueter, Jack, eds. LC 72-12941. (Illus.). 676p. 30.00 (*0-87020-243-X*, CIWA2) State Hist Soc Wis.

— Lincoln & the First Shot. 230p. (C). 1990. reprint ed. pap. text 11.95 (*0-88133-498-7*) Waveland Pr.

— The Lincoln Nobody Knows. (American Century Ser.). 314p. 1963. pap. 9.95 (*0-8090-0059-8*) Hill & Wang.

— The Lincoln Nobody Knows. LC 80-16138. 314p. 1980. reprint ed. lib. bdg. 69.50 (*0-313-22450-1*, CULN, Greenwood Pr) Greenwood.

— Lincoln's Loyalists: Union Soldiers from the Confederacy. 224p. 1992. text 30.00 (*1-55553-124-5*) NE U Pr.

— The Typewriter & the Men Who Made It. (Illus.). 176p. 1988. 17.95 (*0-911160-88-4*) Post Group.

— What Is an American? Abraham Lincoln & "Multiculturalism" (Clement Lectures: No. 2). 25p. (C). 1993. pap. 5.00 (*0-87462-326-X*) Marquette.

Current, Richard N., ed. Sections & Politics: Selected Essays by William B. Hesseltine. LC 68-65095. 180p. 1968. 12.95 (*0-87020-027-5*) State Hist Soc Wis.

Current, Richard N., et al, eds. Encyclopedia of the Confederacy, 4 vols. LC 93-4133. 1993. 375.00 (*0-13-275991-8*) S&S Trade.

— Words That Made American History: From Colonial Times to the 1870's, Vol. I. 3rd ed. (C). 1978. pap. text 32.00 (*0-673-39332-1*) Addson-Wesley Educ.

— Words That Made American History since the Civil War, Vol. 2. 3rd ed. (C). 1997. pap. 32.66 (*0-673-39333-X*) Addson-Wesley Educ.

Current, Richard N. & Current, Marcia E. Loie Fuller: Goddess of Light. LC 96-52659. (Illus.). 400p. 1997. text 29.95 (*1-55553-309-4*) NE U Pr.

Current, Richard N. & Randall, James G. Lincoln the President: Last Full Measure. 440p. 1991. text 39.95 (*0-252-01785-4*) U of Ill Pr.

Current, Richard N., et al. Current History of the United States. 2nd ed. 1048p. (C). 1984. text 56.25 (*0-07-554632-9*) McGraw.

— Current History of the United States, 1. 2nd ed. 1048p. (C). 1984. pap. text 36.74 (*0-07-554630-2*) McGraw.

— Current History of the United States, Vol. 2. 2nd ed. 1048p. (C). 1984. pap. text 36.74 (*0-07-554631-0*) McGraw.

— The Essentials of American History, 2 vols. 1986. teacher ed. write for info. (*0-318-54008-8*) McGraw.

Current, Richard N., jt. auth. see Randall, J. G.

Current Scene Staff. Reports on Communist China (October 1956-April 1961), Set, Vols. 1-37. (China Classic & Contemporary Works in Reprint Ser.). 1995. reprint ed. 65.00 (*0-404-19568-7*) AMS Pr.

Current, Sharon S. McQuillken Finds His Purpose. large type ed. (Illus.). 24p. (J). (gr. k-2). 1998. pap. 9.95 (*0-9668072-0-0*) Sunshine Pr CO.

Currer-Briggs, Noel. The Carters of Virginia: Their English Ancestry. (C). 1979. 50.00 (*0-85033-307-5*) St Mut.

***Currer-Briggs, Noel.** Debrett'S Guide to Tracing Your Family Tree. 2000. pap. 17.95 (*0-7472-5908-9*, Pub. by Headline Bk Pub) Trafalgar.

Currer-Briggs, Noel. Shroud Mafia: The Creation of a Relic? (Illus.). 264p. 1995. pap. 20.00 (*1-85776-041-7*, Pub. by Book Guild Ltd) Trans-Atl Phila.

— Worldwide Family History. 200p. 1982. 32.50 (*0-7100-0934-8*, Routledge Thoemms) Routledge.

— Young Men at War. 240p. 1996. pap. 14.95 (*0-85449-236-4*, Pub. by Gay Mens Pr) LPC InBook.

Currer, Caroline & Stacey, Meg, eds. Concepts of Health, Illness & Disease: A Comparative Perspective. LC 85-20759. 324p. 1987. 49.50 (*0-907582-18-4*); pap. 19.50 (*0-907582-19-2*) Berg Pubs.

Curreri-Alibrandi, Gaetano & Markowitz, Yvonne. Beyond Visual Perspective. LC 95-45234. 226p. (C). 1996. pap. text 29.50 (*0-7618-0219-3*); lib. bdg. 52.50 (*0-7618-0218-5*) U Pr of Amer.

Curreri, Joseph. Virginia's Natural Bridge. (Illus.). 32p. 1984. 20.00 (*0-88014-054-2*) Mosaic Pr OH.

Currey, jt. auth. see French.

Currey, A. Albertine. (J). pap. text 11.95 (*0-340-68325-2*, Pub. by Hodder & Stought Ltd) Trafalgar.

Currey, Anna. Tickling Tigers. (Barron's Educational Ser.). (Illus.). 32p. (J). 1996. pap. 5.95 (*0-8120-9594-4*) Barron.

— Tickling Tigers. (Illus.). 32p. (J). (ps-3). 1996. 12.95 (*0-8120-6594-8*) Barron.

***Currey, Anna.** Truffle's Christmas. (Illus.). 32p. (J). (gr. k-1). 2000. 15.95 (*0-531-30266-0*) Orchard Bks Watts.

Currey, Bruce & Hugo, Graeme, eds. Famine As a Geographical Phenomenon. 1984. lib. bdg. 144.50 (*90-277-1762-1*) Kluwer Academic.

Currey, Cecil B. Edward Lansdale: The Unquiet American. LC 98-15768. (Association of the U. S. Army Book Ser.: Vol. 2). (Illus.). 464p. 1998. pap. 24.95 (*1-57488-176-0*) Brasseys.

— Long Binh Jail: An Oral History of Vietnam's Notorious U. S. Military Prison. LC 99-23634. (Illus.). 288p. 1999. 25.95 (*1-57488-186-8*) Brasseys.

— Road to Revolution: Benjamin Franklin in England, 1765-1775. (Illus.). 1990. 16.50 (*0-8446-1931-0*) Peter Smith.

— Victory at Any Cost: The Genius of Viet Nam's Gen. Vo Nguyen Giap. (Association of the U. S. Army Book Ser.). (Illus.). 432p. 1996. 26.95 (*1-57488-056-X*) Brasseys.

— Victory at Any Cost: The Genius of Viet Nam's Gen. Vo Nguyen Giap. LC 98-19497. (Illus.). 4014p. 1999. pap. 21.95 (*1-57488-194-9*) Brasseys.

Currey, H. L. Essentials of Rheumatology. 2nd ed. (Illus.). 200p. 1988. pap. text 23.00 (*0-443-03913-5*) Church.

Currey, Janie. Play 101. 108p. (Orig.). 1996. pap. 5.95 (*0-9652587-0-X*) Vegas Publng.

Currey, L. W. Science Fiction & Fantasy Authors: A Bibliography of First Printings of Their Fiction & Selected Fiction. 579p. 1979. pap. 78.50 (*0-89366-285-2*) Ultramarine Pub.

Currey, Muriel, tr. see Badoglio, Pietro.

Currey, Norman S. Aircraft Landing Gear Design: Principles & Practices. (Educ Ser.). (Illus.). 373p. 1988. 67.95 (*0-930403-41-X*, 41-X) AIAA.

An Asterisk (*) at the beginning of an entry indicates that the title is appearing for the first time.

Currey, R. N., tr. Formal Spring. LC 76-80372. (Granger Index Reprint Ser.). 1977. 18.95 (*0-8369-6054-8*) Ayer.
Currey, Richard. Crossing Over: The Vietnam Stories. LC 92-32124. (Illus.). 104p. 1993. pap. 11.00 (*0-944439-21-7*) Clark City Pr.
— Fatal Light. LC 97-10834. 208p. 1997. pap. 12.00 (*0-395-85995-6*, Mariner Bks) HM.
— The Lost Highway. 272p. 1998. pap. 12.00 (*0-395-92479-0*) HM.
— Rio Grande. 1999. text 23.95 (*0-670-84966-9*) Viking Penguin.
Curricula & Certification Council (American Production & Inventory Control Society) Staff. Inventory Management Reprints: Articles Selected by the Inventory Management Committee of the APICS Curricula & Certification Council. LC 98-232128. 1998. write for info. (*1-55822-136-0*) Am Prod & Inventory.
— Just-In-Time Reprints: Articles Selected by the Just-In-Time Committee of the APICS Curricula & Certification Council. LC 98-232122. 307 p. 1998. write for info. (*1-55822-137-9*) Am Prod & Inventory.
Curricula and Certification Council (American Production and Inventory Control Society). Staff. Delivering Products & Services Reprints. LC 99-165637. 163 p. 1998. write for info. (*1-55822-163-8*) Am Prod & Inventory.
Curriculum Concepts Staff, ed. Descubrimientos Nivel Elemental. (Descubrimientos Ser.). (SPA., Illus.). (J). (ps-1). 1998. pap. 118.80 (*1-58273-010-5*) Newbridge Educ.
— Descubrimientos Nivel Elemental, 16 vols., Set A. (Descubrimientos Ser.). (SPA., Illus.). (J). (ps-1). 1998. pap. 59.00 (*1-58273-012-1*) Newbridge Educ.
— Descubrimientos Nivel Elemental, 16 vols., Set B. (Descubrimientos Ser.). (Illus.). (J). (ps-1). 1998. pap. 59.00 (*1-58273-014-8*) Newbridge Educ.
— Descubrimientos Nivel Elemental Complete Set, 34 vols. (Descubrimientos Ser.).Tr. of Discovery Links. (SPA., Illus.). (J). (ps-1). 1998. pap. 648.00 (*1-58273-008-3*) Newbridge Educ.
***Curriculum Concepts Staff, ed.** Descubrimientos Nivel Elemental Vinculos Entre la Escuela y el Hogar. (Descubrimientos Ser.).Tr. of Discovery Links Home-School Connections. (SPA., Illus.). 112p. (J). (ps-1). 1998. pap. write for info. (*1-56784-083-3*) Newbridge Educ.
— Discovery Links Early Level Add to Pack, 16 vols., Set A. (Discovery Links Ser.). (Illus.). (J). (ps-1). 1998. pap. 59.00 (*1-58273-011-3*) Newbridge Educ.
Curriculum Concepts Staff, ed. Discovery Links Early Level Add to Pack English. (Discovery Links Ser.). (Illus.). (J). (ps-1). 1998. pap. 118.80 (*1-58273-009-1*) Newbridge Educ.
— Discovery Links Early Level Add to Pack Set B, 16 vols. (Discovery Links Ser.). (Illus.). 1998. pap., teacher ed. 59.00 (*1-58273-013-X*) Newbridge Educ.
— Discovery Links Early Level Complete Set English, 34 vols. (Discovery Links Ser.). (Illus.). (J). (ps-1). 1998. pap. 648.00 (*1-58273-007-5*) Newbridge Educ.
— Discovery Links Early Level Home-School Connections. (Discovery Links Ser.). (Illus.). 112p. (J). (ps-1). 1998. pap. write for info. (*1-56784-081-7*) Newbridge Educ.
Curriculum Concepts Staff, ed. see Anton, William.
Curriculum Concepts Staff, ed. see Economos, Christine.
Curriculum Concepts Staff, ed. see Parkes, Brenda.
Curriculum Corporation Staff. English: A Curriculum Profile for Australian Schools. LC 95-116358. 160p. 1994. pap. text 27.50 (*1-86366-207-3*, 00763) Heinemann.
— Science: A Curriculum Profile for Australian Schools. 121p. 1994. pap. text 27.50 (*1-86366-208-1*, 00775) Heinemann.
Currid & Co. Staff. Computing Strategies for Reengineering Your Organization. (Illus.). 304p. 1993. 29.95 (*1-55958-481-5*) Prima Pub.
Currid, Cheryl. Cheryl Currid's Guide to Business Techniques. LC 95-40376. (Communications Ser.). 282p. 1995. pap. 26.95 (*0-442-02119-4*, VNR) Wiley.
— Computing Strategies for Reengineering Your Organization. 304p. 1995. pap. 15.95 (*0-7615-0117-7*) Prima Pub.
— Reengineering Tool Kit: 15 Tools & Technologies for Reengineering Your Organization. (Illus.). 320p. 1996. per. 18.00 (*0-7615-0438-9*) Prima Pub.
Currid, Cheryl, et al. Reengineering Tool Kit: 15 Tools & Technologies for Reengineering. LC 93-48147. (Illus.). 320p. 1994. 24.95 (*1-55958-504-8*) Prima Pub.
Currid, Cheryl, & Company Staff. Make Your Point! LC 93-34367. 304p. 1995. boxed set 24.95 (*1-55958-414-9*) Prima Pub.
Currid, Cheryl C. Novells Introduction to Networking. LC 96-79758. 350p. 1997. pap. 19.99 (*0-7645-4525-6*) IDG Bks.
***Currid, Cheryl C.** Novell's Introduction to Networking. 2nd ed. (Illus.). 360p. 2000. pap. 24.99 (*0-7645-4700-3*) IDG Bks.
Currid, Cheryl C., & Company, Staff. Novell's Guide to NetWare 3.12 Networks. LC 93-60632. 842p. 1993. 34.99 (*0-7821-1093-2*) Sybex.
Currid, John D. Ancient Egypt & the Old Testament. LC 97-23829. (Illus.). 272p. (gr. 12 up). 1997. pap. 21.99 (*0-8010-2137-5*) Baker Bks.
— Doing Archaeology in the Land of the Bible: A Basic Guide. LC 99-30489. (Illus.). 176p. 1999. pap. 14.99 (*0-8010-2213-4*) Baker Bks.
***Currid, John D.** Exodus Vol. 1: Chapters 1-18. 2000. 24.99 (*0-85234-437-6*) Evangelical Pr.
Curriden, Mark & Phillips, Leroy. Contempt of Court: The Turn-of-the-Century Lynching That Launched 100 Years of Federalism. LC 99-19327. 400p. 1999. 25.00 (*0-571-19952-6*) Faber & Faber.
Currie. Basically Academic. (J). 1991. mass mkt., teacher ed. 12.95 (*0-8384-2912-2*) Heinle & Heinle.
— Constitution in Congress. 1999. pap. text 18.00 (*0-226-13115-7*) U Ch Pr.
— Postmodern Narrative Theory. LC 97-51294. 184p. 1998. text 55.00 (*0-312-21390-5*) St Martin.
— Postmodern Narrative Theroy. LC 97-51294. 184p. 1998. pap. 19.95 (*0-312-21391-3*) St Martin.
***Currie.** 2000 Years. 1999. 17.95 (*0-7459-3884-1*, Pub. by Lion Pubng) Trafalgar.
Currie, B. & Sharp, R. Structural Design. (Illus.). 208p. (Orig.). (C). 1990. 39.50 (*0-7487-0417-5*, Pub. by S Thornes Pubs) Trans-Atl Phila.
Currie, Barbara. Fabulous Shape Forever: Yoga - The Ultimate Shape System. (Illus.). 160p. 1997. 22.95 (*0-233-99294-4*, Pub. by Andre Deutsch) Trafalgar.
Currie, Barbara. Fodor's Fun in Barbados LC 88-118337. 118p. 1987. write for info. (*0-340-41961-X*) Church.
***Currie, Bob.** The Politics of Hunger in India: A Study of Democracy, Governance & Kalahandi's Poverty. LC 99-53055. 2000. text 65.00 (*0-312-22954-2*) St Martin.
Currie, Brainerd. Selected Essays on the Conflict of Laws. LC 63-17326. 771p. reprint ed. pap. 200.00 (*0-608-13825-8*, 201789600010) Bks Demand.
Currie, Brainerd, ed. Selected Essays on the Conflict of Laws. LC 63-17326. 774p. 1990. reprint ed. lib. bdg. 60.00 (*0-89941-700-0*, 305980) W S Hein.
Currie, Bruce L., et al. Medicinal Chemistry Case Study Workbook. 377p. 1996. pap. 34.00 (*0-683-02260-1*) Lppncott W & W.
Currie, Bruce W. Structure & Function of Domestic Animals. 464p. 1992. boxed set 73.95 (*0-8493-8766-3*) CRC Pr.
Currie, C. R. & Lewis, C. P., eds. A Guide to English County Histories. (History Handbooks Ser.). (Illus.). 496p. (Orig.). 1997. pap. 26.95 (*0-7509-1505-6*, Pub. by Sutton Pub Ltd) Intl Pubs Mktg.
Currie, Caroline, et al. Corporate Finance Companion, 1998/99. 328p. 1998. pap. 56.00 (*1-85431-864-0*) Gaunt.
Currie, Christa. Gingerbread Houses. LC 93-41695. (Illus.). 128p. 1994. pap. 12.95 (*0-385-47267-6*, Main St Bks) Doubleday.
Currie, Christine, ed. see Clark, Tracy, et al.
Currie, Claudia, jt. ed. see Adelberg, Ellen.
Currie, David. Amazing Discoveries in Bible Lands. 80p. 1996. pap. 12.99 (*1-873796-52-8*) Review & Herald.
— Born Fundamentalist Born Again Catholic. LC 95-79976. 216p. (Orig.). 1996. pap. 11.95 (*0-89870-569-X*) Ignatius Pr.
Currie, David & Levine, Paul. Rules, Reputation & Macroeconomic Policy Coordination. LC 92-30613. (Illus.). 440p. (C). 1993. text 69.95 (*0-521-44196-X*) Cambridge U Pr.
Currie, David & Vines, David, eds. Macroeconomic Interactions Between North & South. 304p. 1988. text 69.95 (*0-521-36121-4*) Cambridge U Pr.
Currie, David, jt. auth. see Golding, David.
Currie, David, jt. ed. see Vines, David.
Currie, David G. The Management of Head Injuries. LC 93-3454. (Oxford Handbooks in Emergency Medicine Ser.). (Illus.). 200p. (C). 1993. text 65.00 (*0-19-262385-0*, 7565) OUP.
***Currie, David G., et al.** The Management of Head Injuries: A Practical Guide for the Emergency Room. 2nd ed. LC 99-36446. (Illus.). 176p. 2000. pap. text 57.50 (*0-19-263078-4*) OUP.
Currie, David P. Cases & Materials on Federal Courts. 4th ed. (American Casebook Ser.). 783p. (C). 1990. 57.50 (*0-314-74485-1*) West Pub.
— The Constitution in Congress: The Federalist Period 1789-1801. LC 96-51493. 328p. 1997. 32.50 (*0-226-13114-9*) U Ch Pr.
— The Constitution in the Supreme Court: The First Hundred Years, 1789-1888. xiv, 520p. 1992. pap. text 32.00 (*0-226-13109-2*) U Ch Pr.
— The Constitution in the Supreme Court: The First Hundred Years, 1789-1888. LC 85-1205. xiv, 506p. 1995. 66.00 (*0-226-13108-4*) U Ch Pr.
— The Constitution in the Supreme Court: The Second Century, 1888-1986. 682p. (C). 1993. pap. text 29.95 (*0-226-13112-2*) U Ch Pr.
— The Constitution in the Supreme Court: The Second Century, 1888-1986. LC 90-34143. (Illus.). 640p. 1994. 70.00 (*0-226-13111-4*) U Ch Pr.
— The Constitution of the Federal Republic of Germany. 444p. 1994. 35.00 (*0-226-13113-0*) U Ch Pr.
***Currie, David P.** The Constitution of the United States. 2nd ed. LC 99-55538. 160p. 2000. pap. text 12.00 (*0-226-13104-1*) U Ch Pr.
Currie, David P. The Constitution of the United States: A Primer for the People. x, 160p. 1988. pap. text 9.00 (*0-226-13107-6*) U Ch Pr.
— The Constitution of the United States: A Primer for the People. x, 160p. 1997. lib. bdg. 30.00 (*0-226-13106-8*) U Ch Pr.
— Federal Jurisdiction in a Nutshell. 3rd ed. (Nutshell Ser.). 242p. (C). 1990. pap. 21.00 (*0-314-75121-1*) West Pub.
Currie, David P., ed. Federalism & the New Nations of Africa. LC 64-23421. 448p. reprint ed. pap. 138.90 (*0-608-30695-9*, 202005000016) Bks Demand.
Currie, David P. & Stevos, Joyce L. The Constitution: Student Text. (Government Resources Ser.). (gr. 7-12). pap. 12.09 (*0-673-35186-6*) Addson-Wesley Educ.
Currie, David P. & Stevos, Joyce L. The Constitution: Teacher's Handbook. (gr. 7-12). 6.24 (*0-673-35187-4*) Addson-Wesley Educ.
***Currie, David R.** Songs in the Desert. LC 99-29453. 112p. 1999. 11.00 (*1-57312-258-0*) Smyth & Helwys.
Currie, Dawn H. Girl Talk: Adolescent Magazines & Their Readers. (Illus.). 416p. 1999. text 60.00 (*0-8020-4415-8*); pap. text 24.95 (*0-8020-8217-3*) U of Toronto Pr.
Currie, Donald. Personnel in Practice. (Illus.). 256p. (Orig.). 1997. pap. 38.95 (*0-631-20089-4*) Blackwell Pubs.
***Currie, Dwight.** How We Behave at the Feast: Reflections on an Age of Plenty. LC 99-38737. 240p. 2000. 21.00 (*0-06-019531-2*) HarpC.
***Currie, Edwina.** The Ambassador. large type ed. 488p. 1999. 31.99 (*0-7089-9122-X*) Ulverscroft.
Currie, Ellen. Available Light. 304p. 1995. pap. 11.00 (*0-684-80414-X*, Scribner Pap Fic) S&S Trade Pap.
— Available Light. 1987. reprint ed. pap. 6.95 (*0-317-56210-X*, WSP) PB.
— Moses Supposes. 1994. 20.00 (*0-671-65673-2*) S&S Trade.
— Moses Supposes: Stories. 224p. 1995. pap. 10.00 (*0-684-80421-2*) S&S Trade.
— Moses Supposes: 5-Copy Reader's Guide. (Reading Group Guides Ser.). 1995. pap. text. write for info. (*0-684-00048-2*, Touchstone) S&S Trade Pap.
Currie, Elliot. Crime & Punishment in America. LC 97-30703. 230p. 1998. 23.00 (*0-8050-4835-9*) H Holt & Co.
Currie, Elliot, jt. auth. see Skolnick, Arlene S.
Currie, Elliott. Crime & Punishment in America. 208p. 1998. pap. 12.95 (*0-8050-6016-2*, Owl) H Holt & Co.
— Reckoning: Drugs, the Cities, & the American Future. 405p. 1994. pap. 12.00 (*0-8090-1571-4*) Hill & Wang.
Currie, Elliott & Skolnick, Jerome H. America's Problems. 2nd ed. (C). 1997. 85.00 (*0-673-39714-9*) Addson-Wesley Educ.
Currie, Gregory. Image & Mind: Film, Philosophy & Cognitive Science. 329p. (C). 1995. text 69.95 (*0-521-45356-9*) Cambridge U Pr.
Currie, Gregory & Musgrave, Alan E., eds. Popper & the Human Sciences. 225p. 1985. pap. text 34.00 (*90-247-3141-0*, Pub. by M Nijhoff) Kluwer Academic.
Currie, Gregory, ed. see Lakatos, Imre.
Currie, H. M. Silver Latin Epic. (Orig.). 1985. pap. 13.00 (*0-86516-129-1*) Bolchazy-Carducci.
Currie, Harold W. Eugene V. Debs. Bowman, Sylvia E., ed. LC 76-3780. (Twayne's United States Authors Ser.). 155p. (C). 1976. lib. bdg. 20.95 (*0-8057-7167-0*) Irvington.
Currie, I. G. Fundamental Mechanics of Fluids. 2nd ed. LC 92-40110. 454p. (C). 1993. 105.31 (*0-07-015000-1*) McGraw.
Currie, Ian. Visions of Immortality: The Incredible Findings of a Century of Research on Death. LC 97-37750. 1997. pap. 15.95 (*1-86204-345-0*, Pub. by Element MA) Penguin Putnam.
Currie, Ian. You Cannot Die: The Incredible Findings of a Century of Research on Death. 368p. pap. 19.95 (*0-921051-90-5*) Somerville Hse.
— You Cannot Die: Collector's Edition: The Incredible Findings of a Century of Research on Death. 368p. 35.00 (*0-921051-98-0*) Somerville Hse.
Currie, J. C. & Pepper, A. T., eds. Water & the Environment. LC 92-30401. (Ellis Horwood Series in Environmental Management, Science & Technology). 380p. 1993. text 95.00 (*0-13-950692-6*, Pub. by Tavistock-E Horwood) Routldge.
Currie, J. M. The Economic Theory of Agricultural Land Tenure. LC 80-41114. (Illus.). 208p. 1981. text 59.95 (*0-521-23634-7*) Cambridge U Pr.
Currie, Jack. Echoes in the Air: A Chronicle of Aeronautical Ghost Stories. 1998. 29.95 (*0-947554-74-2*) Crecy Publishing.
Currie, Jack, jt. auth. see Kaplan, Philip.
Currie, James S., tr. see Berger, Klaus.
Currie, James S., tr. see Schnackenburg, Rudolf.
Currie, James T. Twice the Citizen 1908-1995: A History of the United States Army Reserve. 704p. 1997. boxed set 37.00 (*0-16-048401-4*) USGPO.
— The United States House of Representatives. LC 87-16898. (Anvil Ser.). 248p. 1988. pap. 16.00 (*0-89874-882-8*) Krieger.
Currie, James T., jt. auth. see Crossland, Richard B.
Currie, Jan & Newson, Janice A. Universities & Globalization: Critical Perspectives. LC 98-9059. 339p. 1998. write for info. (*0-7619-1065-4*); pap. 26.95 (*0-7619-1066-2*) Sage.
Currie, Janet. Welfare & the Well-Being of Children, Vol. 59. (Fundamentals of Pure & Applied Economics Ser.). 176p. 1995. pap. text 25.00 (*3-7186-5624-8*, Harwood Acad Pubs) Gordon & Breach.
Currie, Jennie & Brun, Laura. Blood Dreams. LC 96-43889. 36p. 1996. pap. 8.00 (*1-886214-03-4*) Detour Pr.
***Currie, Jim.** The Mindful Traveler: A Guide to Journaling & Transformative Travel. (Illus.). 160p. 2000. pap. 16.95 (*0-8126-9421-X*) Open Court.
Currie, Lauchlin. The Role of Economic Advisors in Developing Countries, 44. LC 81-6623. (Contributions in Economics & Economic History Ser.: No. 44). (Illus.). 261p. 1981. 59.95 (*0-313-23064-1*, CUE/, Greenwood Pr) Greenwood.
Currie, Lloyd A., ed. Nuclear & Chemical Dating Techniques. LC 81-20649. (ACS Symposium Ser.: No. 176). 1982. 54.95 (*0-8412-0669-4*) Am Chemical.
— Nuclear & Chemical Dating Techniques: Interpreting the Environmental Record. LC 81-20649. (ACS Symposium Ser.: No. 176). (Illus.). 528p. 1982. reprint ed. pap. 163.70 (*0-608-03242-5*, 206376100007) Bks Demand.
Currie, Mark. Rough Framing Carpentry. (Illus.). 256p. (Orig.). 1993. pap. 26.50 (*0-934041-86-5*) Craftsman.
Currie, Mark, ed. Metafiction. LC 95-13071. (Critical Readers Ser.). 240p. (C). 1995. pap. 38.00 (*0-582-21292-8*) Addison-Wesley.
— Metafiction. LC 95-13071. (Critical Readers Ser.). 240p. (C). 1995. text 61.25 (*0-582-21291-X*) Longman.
Currie, Martin & Steedman, Ian. Wrestling with Time: Problems in Economic Theory. LC 89-35138. 272p. 1990. reprint ed. text 57.50 (*0-472-10152-8*, 10152) U of Mich Pr.
Currie, Mary. The Singing Sack. 80p. (J). (gr. 2 up). 1990. write for info. (*0-7136-3115-5*, Pub. by A & C Blk) Midpt Trade.
Currie-McDaniel, Ruth. Carpetbagger of Conscience: A Biography of Emory Bryant. LC 99-18335. (Reconstructing America Ser.: Vol. 3). 254p. 1999. pap. 19.95 (*0-8232-1938-0*, Pub. by Fordham) BookMasters.
***Currie-McDaniel, Ruth.** Carpetbagger of Conscience: A Biography of Emory Bryant. LC 99-18335. (Reconstructing America Ser.: Vol. 3). (Illus.). 254p. 1999. 35.00 (*0-8232-1937-2*, Pub. by Fordham) BookMasters.
Currie, N. Pierre et Gilles. (Illus.). 1994. pap. 12.99 (*3-8228-9377-3*) Taschen Amer.
Currie, Nicholas C., ed. Radar Reflectivity Measurement: Techniques & Applications. (Radar Library). (Illus.). 753p. 1989. text. write for info. (*0-89006-324-9*) Artech Hse.
— Techniques of Radar Reflectivity Measurement. LC 83-72777. (Illus.). 540p. reprint ed. pap. 167.40 (*0-8357-7924-6*, 203635000002) Bks Demand.
Currie, Nicholas C. & Brown, Charles E. Principles & Applications of Millimeter-Wave Radar. 874p. 1987. text. write for info. (*0-89006-202-1*) Artech Hse.
Currie, Nicholas C., et al. Millimeter-Wave Radar Clutter. LC 92-12921. (Radar Library). 240p. 1992. text 58.00 (*0-89006-345-1*) Artech Hse.
Currie, Nicola. Being Anglican in the Third Millenium: The Official Report of the 10th Meeting of the Anglican Consultative Council. Rosenthal, James, ed. LC 97-35832. 448p. 1997. pap. 19.95 (*0-8192-1729-8*) Morehouse Pub.
Currie, P. M. The Shrine & Cult of Mu'in Al-Din Chishti of Ajmer. (Oxford University South Asian Studies Ser.). (Illus.). 246p. 1989. 24.95 (*0-19-562202-2*) OUP.
Currie, Pamela. Literature As Social Action: Modernist & Traditionalist Narratives in Germany in the 17th & 18th Centuries. (GERM Ser.). x, 258p. 1995. 65.00 (*1-57113-022-5*) Camden Hse.
Currie, Patricia M. Basically Academic. (J). 1991. mass mkt. 26.95 (*0-8384-2911-4*) Heinle & Heinle.
Currie, Paula S., et al. One Hundred Twenty-Five Ways to Be a Better Student: A Program for Study Skills Success. 136p. (YA). 1987. spiral bd. 34.95 (*1-55999-063-5*) LinguiSystems.
Currie, Philip & Padian, Kevin, eds. Encyclopedia of Dinosaurs. LC 97-23430. (Illus.). 869p. 1997. text 99.95 (*0-12-226810-5*) Morgan Kaufmann.
Currie, Philip J. The Flying Dinosaurs: The Illustrated Guide to the Evolution of Flight. (Discovery Books). (Illus.). 164p. 1991. pap. 19.95 (*0-88995-078-4*, Pub. by Red Deer) Genl Dist Srvs.
Currie, Philip J. & Koppelhus, Eva B. 101 Questions Answered about Dinosaurs. (Illus.). 64p. (Orig.). 1996. pap. text 2.00 (*0-486-29172-3*) Dover.
Currie, Philip J., jt. ed. see Carpenter, Kenneth.
Currie, Phillip J. & Martin, Colleayan. The Newest & Coolest Dinosaurs. LC 96-910710. (Illus.). 32p. (J). (gr. 4-8). 1998. text 18.95 (*1-895910-41-2*) Grasshopper Bks.
Currie, Quinn. Beautiful Joe. abr. rev. ed. (Illus.). 72p. (J). (gr. k-8). 1990. reprint ed. pap. 10.95 (*0-9623072-1-1*) S Ink WA.
— Black Beauty. rev. ed. (Illus.). 128p. (J). (gr. k-8). 1990. reprint ed. pap. 11.95 (*0-9623072-2-X*) S Ink WA.
Currie, Quinn, ed. see Johnson, John H.
Currie, Robert. Industrial Politics. LC 78-40480. 1979. 49.95 (*0-19-827419-X*) OUP.
Currie, Robert. Klondike Fever. (Illus.). 112p. 1992. pap. 6.95 (*1-55050-033-3*, Pub. by Coteau) Genl Dist Srvs.
Currie Robert. Klondike Fever. (Illus.). 112p. 1992. text 19.95 (*1-55050-034-1*, Pub. by Coteau) Genl Dist Srvs.
Currie, Robert. Night Games. 120p. 1983. pap. 5.95 (*0-919926-19-3*) Coteau.
— Things You Don't Forget. 240p. 1999. pap. 14.95 (*1-55050-153-4*, Pub. by Coteau) Genl Dist Srvs.
Currie, Robin. Baby Bible: Stories about Jesus. LC 96-83456. (Illus.). 36p. (J). (gr. k up). 1996. 11.99 (*0-7814-0252-2*) Chariot Victor.
— Lord's Prayer. LC 98-192069. 1998. 7.99 (*0-7814-3035-6*) Chariot Victor.
Currie, Robin. Mini Easter Activity Book. (Illus.). 48p. (J). (gr. 1-5). 1993. pap. 2.99 (*0-7459-2149-3*) Lion USA.
Currie, Robin. My Bible Friends: Read-&-Do Book. LC 97-14056. (Illus.). 175p. (J). (ps-3). 1998. 19.95 (*0-8198-4795-X*) Pauline Bks.
— Noah & the Big Boat. LC 94-73989. (Bible Buddies Ser.). (Illus.). 12p. (J). 1995. bds. 4.29 (*0-7814-0198-4*) Chariot Victor.
— Peanut Butter Promises: Nap 'n Snack Devotions. LC 99-19055. 96p. 1999. 10.00 (*0-570-05557-1*) Concordia.
— Second Helpings: Books & Activities about Food. Irving, Jan, ed. (Peddler's Pack Ser.). (Illus.). 145p. 1994. pap. text 18.50 (*1-56308-073-7*) Teacher Ideas Pr.
— The Story of Christmas: Eyewitness Animals. (Eyewitness Animals Ser.). (Illus.). 64p. (J). (ps). 1997. 12.99 (*0-7847-0714-6*, 03814) Standard Pub.
— Toddlers' Action Bible. LC 97-24651. (Illus.). 96p. (J). (ps-k). 1998. bds. 9.99 (*0-570-05030-8*, 56-1854) Concordia.
— Zacchaeus, the Little Man. LC 94-73988. (Bible Buddies Ser.). (Illus.). 12p. (J). (ps-k). 1995. bds. 4.99 (*0-7814-0199-2*) Chariot Victor.
Currie, Robin, jt. auth. see Irving, Jan.
Currie, Ruth H., tr. see MacAdam, Henry I.

C

***Currie, Sheldon, selected by.** The Journey Prize Anthology 11: The Best of Canada's New Writers. 192p. 2000. pap. 18.99 (*0-7710-4424-0*) McCland & Stewart.

***Currie, Stephan.** The Liberator: Voice of the Abolitionist Movement. LC 99-41296. (Words That Changed History Ser.). (Illus.). 144p. (YA). (gr. 6-9). 2000. lib. bdg. 23.70 (*1-56006-672-5*) Lucent Bks.

— Life of a Slave on a Southern Plantation. LC 99-25966. (Way People Live Ser.). (Illus.). 96p. (YA). (gr. 6-9). 2000. lib. bdg. 18.96 (*1-56006-539-7*) Lucent Bks.

***Currie, Stephen.** Abortion. LC 99-42785. (Opposing Viewpoints Digests Ser.). (Illus.). 144p. (YA). (gr. 6-10). 2000. pap. 14.95 (*0-7377-0228-1*); lib. bdg. 18.96 (*0-7377-0229-X*) Greenhaven.

Currie, Stephen. Adoption. LC 96-34145. (Overview Ser.). (Illus.). (YA). (gr. 4-12). 1997. lib. bdg. 22.45 (*1-56006-183-9*) Lucent Bks.

— Birthday a Day. (J). (gr. 3 up). 1996. pap. 14.95 (*0-673-36171-3*, GoodYrBooks) Addson-Wesley Educ.

***Currie, Stephen.** Issues in Immigration. LC 99-88268. (Contemporary Issues Ser.). (Illus.). 128p. (J). (gr. 4-12). 2000. lib. bdg. 18.96 (*1-56006-377-7*) Lucent Bks.

Currie, Stephen. Issues in Sports. LC 97-27451. (Other America Ser.). (Illus.). (YA). (gr. 4-12). 1997. lib. bdg. 22.45 (*1-56006-477-3*) Harcrt Hlth Sci Grp.

— Life in a Wild West Show. LC 98-27233. (Way People Live Ser.). (Illus.). (YA). (gr. 4-12). 1998. lib. bdg. 23.70 (*1-56006-352-1*) Lucent Bks.

— The Olympic Games. LC 98-50360. (Overview Ser.). (Illus.). 128p. (YA). (gr. 4-12). 1999. lib. bdg. 23.70 (*1-56006-395-5*) Lucent Bks.

— Polynesians. LC 98-39780. (Endangered Cultures Ser.). (Illus.). 32p. (YA). (gr. 4 up). 1999. lib. bdg. 21.30 (*1-887068-94-5*) Smart Apple.

***Currie, Stephen.** Slavery. LC 98-36198. (Opposing Viewpoints Digests Ser.). (J). (gr. 4-7). 1998. lib. bdg. 23.70 (*1-56510-881-7*) Greenhaven.

Currie, Stephen. Slavery. LC 98-36198. (Opposing Viewpoints Digests Ser.). 144p. (J). (gr. 4-12). 1998. pap. 14.95 (*1-56510-880-9*) Greenhaven.

— We Have Marched Together: The Working Children's Crusade. LC 95-47686. (J). 1997. lib. bdg. 19.95 (*0-8225-1733-7*, Lerner Publctns) Lerner Pub.

Currie, Stuart, ed. Drawing 1400-1600: Invention & Innovation. LC 97-33668. (Illus.). 224p. 1997. text 78.95 (*1-85928-364-0*, Pub. by Ashgate Pub) Ashgate Pub Co.

Currie, Stuart & Motture, Peta, eds. The Sculpted Object, 1400-1700. LC 96-33443. (Illus.). 274p. 1997. text 87.95 (*1-85928-270-9*, Pub. by Scolar Pr) Ashgate Pub Co.

***Currie, Thomas W.** Prayers for the Road: Psalm Meditations for College Students. LC 00-35370. 115p. 2000. pap. write for info. (*0-664-50129-X*, Pub. by Geneva Press) Presbyterian Pub.

Currie, Violet, jt. auth. see Spicer, Kay.

Currie, Wendy. Management Strategy for Information Technology. 352p. 1995. pap. 64.50 (*0-273-60700-6*, Pub. by Pitman Pub) Trans-Atl Phila.

Currie, Wendy L. Management Information Systems: Perspectives on Management, Organization & Change. (Illus.). 528p. 1999. text 105.00 (*0-19-877533-4*); pap. text 45.00 (*0-19-877532-6*) OUP.

Currie, William. An Historical Account of the Climates & Diseases of the U. S. A. & of the Remedies & Methods of Treatment. LC 70-180570. (Medicine & Society in America Ser.). 428p. 1972. reprint ed. 25.95 (*0-405-03945-X*) Ayer.

Currie, William, jt. auth. see Webster, Noah.

Currie, William J. New Drug Approval in Japan. (Worldwide Pharmaceutical Regulation Ser.). 64p. (Orig.). 1995. pap. 125.00 (*1-882615-14-X*) Parexel Intl.

Currie, William J. & Lofgren, Monica. A Practical to the EMEA. 203p. (Orig.). 1996. pap. 175.00 (*1-882615-27-1*) Parexel Intl.

Currie, William S. LANs Explained: A Guide to Local Area Networks. 1989. pap. text 34.95 (*0-470-21427-9*) P-H.

Currier & Ives. Currier & Ives Prints. (Illus.). 1991. pap. 3.95 (*0-486-26657-5*) Dover.

Currier, Alvi. Miraculous Child. 1997. 14.95 (*3-9500271-2-2*, Pub. by Basic Luka) Conciliar Pr.

Currier, Alvin A. Alyosha's Apple: A Classic Tale of Old Russia. LC 97-37431. (Illus.). 1997. 14.95 (*1-888212-08-X*) Conciliar Pr.

Currier, Betty, jt. ed. see Gillette, Beverly.

Currier, Bob, jt. auth. see Jackman, Joan.

Currier, Charles W. Carmel in America: A Centennial History of the Discalced Carmelites in the U. S. LC 89-85818. (Carmelite Sources Ser.). (Illus.). 480p. (C). 1989. reprint ed. pap. text 19.95 (*0-9624104-0-3*) Carmelite Communities.

Currier, Dean. Elements of Research in Physical Therapy. 3rd ed. (Illus.). 352p. 1990. 35.00 (*0-683-02248-2*) Lppncott W & W.

Currier, Dean P. & Nelson, Roger M. Dynamics of Human Biologic Tissues. (Contemporary Perspectives in Rehabilitation Ser.: Vol. 8). 276p. (C). 1992. text 35.00 (*0-8036-2298-8*) Davis Co.

Currier, Dean P., jt. auth. see Nelson, Roger M.

Currier, Donald. Hot Slots: How to Find the Hottest Slots in Town & Leave with More $$$ in Your Pocket. 32p. (Orig.). 1996. pap. 10.00 (*1-890030-01-5*) Las Vegas Insider.

— How to Make a Killing at Keno Vol. 1: Keno Strategies the Pros Use to Beat the Casinos. (Illus.). 32p. 1997. mass mkt. 10.00 (*1-890030-08-2*) Las Vegas Insider.

— How to Play Successful Blackjack: Become an Expert Blackjack Player with Basic Strategy. 32p. (Orig.). 1996. pap. 10.00 (*1-890030-03-1*) Las Vegas Insider.

— How to Prepare for & How to Pass a Race Horse Trainers Test: How to Buy Your First Race Horse (And Do It Right) & How to Claim Your First Race Horse (And Not Be Sorry You Did) (Illus.). 75p. 1998. mass mkt. 20.00 (*1-890030-11-2*) Las Vegas Insider.

— Insider's Secrets for Winning at Roulette: Tips, Techniques & Strategies for Beating the Casinos at Their Own Game! 1997. pap. 10.00 (*1-890030-07-4*) Las Vegas Insider.

— The Lucky System Slot Book: Las Vegas Pro Reveals "Insider Slot Tricks" That Score Big Jackpot Wins. 32p. (Orig.). 1996. pap. 10.00 (*1-890030-02-3*) Las Vegas Insider.

— Slot Machine Magic: How to Be a Slot Wizard & Beat the One-Armed Bandits with Insider Slot Secrets. 32p. (Orig.). 1996. pap. 10.00 (*1-890030-04-X*) Las Vegas Insider.

— Super Successful Slot Systems. 32p. (Orig.). 1996. pap. 10.00 (*1-890030-00-7*) Las Vegas Insider.

— The Ultimate Dice Book: A Players Guide to Craps. 2nd ed. (Illus.). 80p. 1999. mass mkt. 12.00 (*1-890030-09-0*) Las Vegas Insider.

Currier, Donald, ed. How to Cash in on Video Poker Slot Machines: Beat the Casinos with Winning Strategy & Expert Know-How. 32p. 1996. pap. 10.00 (*1-890030-05-8*) Las Vegas Insider.

Currier, Donald, ed. see Marks, Nancy.

Currier, Donald R. 50 Mission Crush. LC 92-8964. (Illus.). 176p. 1992. 24.95 (*0-942597-43-5*, Burd St Pr) White Mane Pub.

— Fifty Mission Crush. 192p. 1993. mass mkt. 5.99 (*0-671-79575-9*) PB.

Currier, Glenn & Penney, Jane. Telecourse Stury Guide for the Social Imagination: Introduction to Sociology. 3rd ed. 368p. (C). 1996. pap. text 25.00 (*0-15-504004-9*, Pub. by Harcourt Coll Pubs) Harcourt.

Currier, H. L. & Currier, J. M. Genealogy of Richard Currier of Salisbury & Amesbury, Massachusettes & Many of His Descendants. Also, the Genealogy of Ezra Currier of Bath, N. H. & His Descendants. (Illus.). 271p. 1993. reprint ed. pap. 41.00 (*0-8328-1389-3*); reprint ed. lib. bdg. 51.00 (*0-8328-1388-5*) Higginson Bk Co.

Currier, Horace R. Getty. Genealogical Notes of the Getty & Lytle Families of Salem, New York, Preceded by a History of the Scotch-Irish of New Hampshire, Massachusetts & New York, & Facts Concerning the Settlement of Washington County & Salem New York. 87p. 1997. reprint ed. pap. 16.50 (*0-8328-8722-6*); reprint ed. lib. bdg. 26.50 (*0-8328-8721-8*) Higginson Bk Co.

Currier, Horace T., jt. auth. see Allerton, W. S.

Currier, J. M., jt. auth. see Currier, H. L.

Currier, Jameson. Where the Rainbow Ends. LC 98-16591. (Illus.). 432p. 1998. 24.95 (*0-87951-892-8*, Pub. by Overlook Pr) Penguin Putnam.

***Currier, Jameson.** Where the Rainbow Ends. 2000. pap. 14.95 (*1-58567-084-7*, Pub. by Overlook Pr) Penguin Putnam.

Currier, Jeff. Currier's Quick & Easy Guide to Saltwater Fly Fishing. LC 97-42075. (Illus.). 136p. 1998. per. 22.95 (*0-9626663-9-4*) Greycliff Pub.

Currier, John J. History of Newburyport, MA 1764-1909, 2 vols. (Illus.). 1445p. 1997. reprint ed. lib. bdg. 149.00 (*0-8328-5956-7*) Higginson Bk Co.

Currier, John K. Clovis, King of the Franks. LC 97-21233. 1997. pap. write for info. (*0-87462-052-X*) Marquette.

Currier, John M., ed. Annis. Genealogy of David Annis of Hopkinton & Bath, N. H., His Ancestors & Descendants. (Illus.). 73p. 1997. reprint ed. pap. 14.00 (*0-8328-7287-3*); reprint ed. lib. bdg. 24.00 (*0-8328-7286-5*) Higginson Bk Co.

Currier, Joseph. Gono & the Magic Hat. (WellinWorld Ser.). 36p. (J). (ps-4). 1985. 8.95 incl. audio (*0-88684-179-8*, TC:114591) Listen USA.

— Let's Play a Game Everyone Wins. (WellinWorld Ser.: 2-9). 36p. (J). (ps-4). 1985. 8.95 incl. audio (*0-88684-178-X*, TC:114604) Listen USA.

— Samit & the Dragon. (WellinWorld Ser.: 2-9). 36p. (J). (ps-4). 1985. 8.95 incl. audio (*0-88684-177-1*, TC:114578) Listen USA.

— Sweetie, a Sugar-Coated Nightmare. (WellinWorld Ser.: 2-9). 36p. (J). (ps-4). 1985. 8.95 incl. audio (*0-88684-175-5*, TC:114552) Listen USA.

— Wellin Magic. (WellinWorld Ser.: 2-9). 36p. (J). (ps-4). 1985. 8.95 incl. audio (*0-88684-180-1*, TC:114617) Listen USA.

Currier, Katherine A. & Eimermann, Thomas E. Introduction to Law for Paralegals: A Critical Thinking Approach. LC 97-49325. 1998. boxed set 56.00 (*1-56706-632-1*) Aspen Law.

— Introduction to Paralegal Studies: A Critical Thinking Approach. LC 98-33342. xxxiv, 494p. 1998. pap. text 48.95 (*0-7355-0276-5*) Panel Pubs.

Currier, Mary. Bible Memory Activity Book. (Illus.). 96p. 1993. pap. 10.99 (*0-8010-2578-8*) Baker Bks.

***Currier, Mary.** Easy Paper Crafts, Bk. 1. (Illus.). 119p. (J). 1998. pap. text 6.95 (*0-87813-570-7*) Christian Light.

— Easy Paper Crafts, Bk. 2. (Illus.). (J). 1999. pap. text 6.95 (*0-87813-586-3*) Christian Light.

Currier, Mary. The Gospels Activity Book. (Repro Bks.). 128p. 1997. pap. 11.99 (*0-8010-5771-X*) Baker Bks.

Currier, Mary, jt. auth. see De Vries, Nellie.

Currier, Paul J., et al. Migratory Bird Habitat on the Platte & North Platte Rivers in Nebraska. Lewis, James, ed. LC 86-61270. (Illus.). 177p. (Orig.). 1986. pap. text 11.00 (*0-938441-00-0*); lib. bdg. 21.00 (*0-938441-01-9*) PRWCT.

Currier, Philip J. Currier Family Records of U. S. A. & Canada, 3 Vols., Set. LC 84-71210. 1300p. 1984. lib. bdg. 90.00 (*0-9613636-0-6*) P J Currier.

— Currier Family Records of U. S. A. & Canada, Vol. II. LC 84-71210. 419p. 1984. lib. bdg. 35.00 (*0-9613636-2-2*) P J Currier.

— Currier Family Records of U. S. A. & Canada, Vol. III. LC 84-71210. 212p. 1984. lib. bdg. 20.00 (*0-9613636-3-0*) P J Currier.

— Currier Family Records of U. S. A. & Canada, Vol. IV. 492p. 1990. lib. bdg. 45.00 (*0-9613636-4-9*) P J Currier.

— Currier Family Records of U. S. A. & Canada Vol. I: Descendants of Richard Currier (1616-1686-7) of Salisbury & Amesbury Mass., Set. 685p. 1984. lib. bdg. 45.00 (*0-9613636-1-4*) P J Currier.

Currier, R. Organizational Behavior: Course Study Guide. 208p. 1994. spiral bd. Price not set. (*0-933195-08-7*) CA College Health Sci.

Currier, R. S. Genealogical History of the Dickey Family: Descendants of Adam & Elizabeth Dickey. (Illus.). 340p. reprint ed. pap. 54.00 (*0-8328-1665-5*); reprint ed. lib. bdg. 64.00 (*0-8328-1664-7*) Higginson Bk Co.

Currier, Richard S. Currier. Genealogical History of the Currier Family. (Illus.). 341p. 1997. reprint ed. pap. 52.00 (*0-8328-8176-7*); reprint ed. lib. bdg. 62.00 (*0-8328-8175-9*) Higginson Bk Co.

Currier, Robin. The Story of Easter. LC 96-38394. (Eyewitness Animals Ser.). (Illus.). 64p. (J). (ps-2). 1997. 12.99 (*0-7847-0593-3*, 03813) Standard Pub.

Currier, Thomas F. A Bibliography of Oliver Wendell Holmes. Tilton, Eleanor M., ed. LC 53-11420. 708p. reprint ed. pap. 200.00 (*0-8357-7198-9*, 205025700058) Bks Demand.

Currimbhoy, Nayana. Designing Entrances for Retail & Restaurant Spaces. (Illus.). 192p. 1999. 40.00 (*1-56496-482-5*) Rockport Pubs.

***Currin.** Introduction to Traffic Engineering: Manual F/data Collect. 2001. pap. 20.00 (*0-534-37867-6*) Thomson Learn.

Currin, Beverly M. The Search for the Lost Rectors: Reflections on the History of Old Christ Church & Pensacola. LC 98-61612. (Pioneer Ser.). (Illus.). 125p. 1999. 12.00 (*0-9659142-2-4*) U of West Fla.

Currin, Debbie. Currnaments: Easy Christmas Ornaments. (Illus.). 1995. pap. 6.95 (*1-883675-06-5*, 106) J Shaw Studio.

Currin, P. J. Principle Remote Sensing. (Illus.). 296p. (C). 1996. pap. 78.00 (*0-582-30097-5*) Longman.

Curris & Virgadamo. Florida Representing the Elderly, Issue 2. 600p. 1998. ring bd. write for info. (*0-327-00914-4*, 6111812) LEXIS Pub.

Curris, Constantine. Continuity & Change: President Curris' Annual Address to the Faculty, 1983-1993. Hovet, Grace A. & Davis, Darrel, eds. LC 95-128556. (Northern Iowa Texts Ser.: No. 2). (Illus.). 79p. (C). 1994. pap. 5.95 (*0-964151I-1-1*) Assn Text Study.

Curris, Jo H. & Virgadamo, Michael J. Representing the Elderly in Florida. LC 95-37164. (D & S Florida Practice Ser.). 1995. spiral bd. 95.00 (*1-55834-275-3*, 61115, MICHIE) LEXIS Pub.

Curris, Jo Hern, jt. auth. see Virgadamo, Michael J.

Curristine, Eileen. GED Writing Skills, No. I. 1989. pap. text, student ed. 14.95 (*1-56030-013-2*) Comex Systs.

Curristine, Eileen, jt. auth. see Garvin, Ann.

Curro, Ellen. No Need to Be Afraid... First Pelvic Exam: A Handbook for Young Women & Their Mothers. (Illus.). 80p. (YA). (gr. 9-12). 1991. pap. text 4.95 (*0-9629417-1-9*) Linking Ed Med.

Curro, Michael J. National Park Service: Efforts to Link Resources to Results Suggest Insights for Other Agencies. (Illus.). 54p. (C). 1999. pap. text 20.00 (*0-7881-7830-X*) DIANE Pub.

Curro, Michael J. & Baker, Linda F. Managing for Results: Using the Results Act to Address Mission Fragmentation & Program Overlap. (Illus.). 44p. 1998. pap. text 20.00 (*0-7881-7076-7*) DIANE Pub.

Curro, Michael J., et al. Budget Function Classification: Relating Agency Spending & Personnel Levels to Budget Functions. (Illus.). 125p. (Orig.). (C). 1995. pap. text 30.00 (*0-7881-2460-9*) DIANE Pub.

Currriculum Concepts Staff, ed. see Parkes, Brenda.

Curry. Dimensions of State & Local Politics. (Political Science Ser.). 1919. pap. 30.00 (*0-534-54900-4*) Wadsworth Pub.

— Entre Otras Cosas. (SPA.). (C). 1993. pap. text 16.50 (*0-07-015058-3*) McGraw.

— Entre Otras Cosas. 2nd ed. (SPA.). (C). 1996. pap. text 20.00 (*0-07-015114-8*) McGraw.

***Curry.** Plazas-Activities File. (C). 2000. pap. 15.00 (*0-8384-1187-8*) Heinle & Heinle.

Curry. Prenatal Diagnosis. text. write for info. (*0-7216-6813-5*, W B Saunders Co) Harcrt Hlth Sci Grp.

— Sociology. 1995. text. write for info. (*0-205-13981-7*) Allyn.

Curry. Sociology of the 21st Century. 1996. pap. text, teacher ed. write for info. (*0-13-476672-5*) Allyn.

— Sociology of the 21st Century. 1996. pap. text, teacher ed. write for info. (*0-13-476680-6*) Allyn.

Curry. Sociology 21st Century. 2nd ed. 168p. 1998. pap. text, student ed. 14.00 (*0-13-095655-4*) P-H.

Curry & Hammond. Introduction to Biology Laboratory Manual. (C). 1989. pap. text 30.40 (*0-536-57420-0*) Pearson Custom.

Curry & Jioubu. Sociology 21st Century. 2nd ed. LC 98-8125. 1998. pap. text 37.33 (*0-13-955394-0*) S&S Trade.

Curry, et al. Constitutional Government. 4th ed. 560p. 1999. per. 48.95 (*0-7872-5671-4*, 41567101) Kendall-Hunt.

Curry, jt. auth. see Durham.

Curry, jt. auth. see Schwartz, M. Wiliam.

Curry, Adam & Curry, Jay. Customer Marketing Method: How to Implement & Profit from Customer Relationship Management. LC 99-89747. 272p. 2000. 25.00 (*0-684-83943-1*) Free Pr.

Curry, Alan S. Poison Detection in Human Organs. 4th ed. (Illus.). 358p. 1988. 78.95 (*0-398-05425-8*); pap. 51.95 (*0-398-06082-7*) C C Thomas.

Curry, Alexander. Classified: Computer Hacker's Guide. Wilde, David, ed. (Illus.). 116p. 1993. pap. 25.00 (*1-882204-09-3*) Wilde Pub.

Curry, Allen D. Leader's Guide for John W. Sanderson's "The Fruit of the Spirit" A Teaching Manual for Use in Adult Study Groups. (Orig.). 1978. pap. 3.95 (*0-934688-07-9*) Great Comm Pubns.

***Curry, Alphonse, Sr.** Spiritual Food for the Soul: God's Message in Rhythm (Southern Style) 176p. 1998. pap. 11.95 (*1-893444-01-5*) Pub & Prof Ghost Writers.

***Curry, Andrea, et al.** Population Profile of the United States, 1997. (Illus.). 60p. (C). 2000. reprint ed. pap. text 20.00 (*0-7881-8727-9*) DIANE Pub.

***Curry, Anne.** The Battle of Agincourt: Sources & Interpretations. LC 00-42919. (Warfare in History Ser.). 2000. write for info. (*0-85115-802-1*, Boydell Pr) Boydell & Brewer.

***Curry, Anne, ed.** The Battle of Agincourt, 1415. (Illus.). 176p. 2000. 29.99 (*0-7524-1780-0*, Pub. by Tempus Pubng) Arcadia Publng.

Curry, Anne & Hughes, Michael, eds. Arms, Armies & Fortifications in the Hundred Years War. (Illus.). 264p. 1999. pap. 29.95 (*0-85115-755-6*, Suffolk Records Soc) Boydell & Brewer.

Curry, Anne, jt. ed. see Bates, David.

Curry, Anny. The Limits of Tolerance: Censorship & Intellectual Freedom in Public Libraries. LC 96-31670. 272p. 1997. 39.50 (*0-8108-3224-0*) Scarecrow.

Curry, Barbara K. Instituting Enduring Innovations: Achieving Continuity of Change in Higher Education. Fife, Jonathan D., ed. LC 93-83927. (ASHE-ERIC Higher Education Reports: No. 92-7). 111p. (Orig.). 1993. pap. text 24.00 (*1-878380-20-6*) GWU Grad Schl E&HD.

***Curry, Barbara K.** Women in Power: Pathways to Leadership in Education. LC 99-49364. (Athene Series in Women's Studies). 128p. 2000. write for info. (*0-8077-3911-1*); pap. text. write for info. (*0-8077-3910-3*) Tchrs Coll.

Curry, Barbara K. & Brodie, James M. Sweet Words So Brave: The Story of African American Literature. LC 96-18995. (Illus.). 64p. (J). (gr. 3 up). 1996. 24.95 (*1-55933-179-8*) Zino Pr.

Curry, Betty L., ed. see Van der Marck, Jan.

Curry, Bob, jt. auth. see Armstrong, K. M.

Curry, Boykin, ed. Essays That Worked for Law Schools. 112p. 1991. pap. 10.00 (*0-449-90515-2*, Columbine) Fawcett.

Curry, Boykin & Kasbar, Brian, eds. Essays That Worked: Fifty Essays from Successful Applications to the Nation's Top Colleges. 144p. 1990. pap. 10.00 (*0-449-90517-9*, Columbine) Fawcett.

— Essays That Worked for Business Schools. 128p. 1991. pap. 11.00 (*0-449-90516-0*, Columbine) Fawcett.

Curry, Cathleen. An Evening Walk: Steps Toward Wisdom & Grace. LC 99-23218. 160p. 1999. pap. 9.95 (*0-87793-678-1*) Ave Maria.

Curry, Cathleen L. When Your Spouse Dies: A Concise & Practical Source of Help & Advice. LC 89-81539. 128p. 1990. pap. 8.95 (*0-87793-416-9*) Ave Maria.

Curry, Chris. Panic. 1994. mass mkt. 4.99 (*0-671-74947-1*) PB.

***Curry, Chris.** Taste of Blood: The Films of Herschell Gordon Lewis. 1999. pap. text 22.95 (*1-871592-91-7*) Creation Books.

Curry, Chris. Thunder Road: Chris Curry's Terrifying & Hilarious Vision of the Apocalypse. 1995. mass mkt. 5.99 (*0-671-89737-3*) PB.

Curry, Christopher. Coyote North Level 13. 1998. mass mkt. 6.99 (*0-671-00210-4*) PB.

— Icehouse Level 13. 1998. mass mkt. 6.99 (*0-671-00209-0*) PB.

Curry, Constance. Silver Rights. LC 95-21731. 288p. 1999. 21.95 (*1-56512-095-7*, 72095) Algonquin Bks.

— Silver Rights. 1996. pap. 13.00 (*0-15-600485-2*) Harcourt.

— Silver Rights. (Illus.). 288p. 1996. pap. 13.00 (*0-15-600479-8*) Harcourt.

***Curry, Constance, et al.** Deep in Our Hearts: Nine White Women in the Freedom Movement. 400p. 2000. 29.95 (*0-8203-2266-0*) U of Ga Pr.

Curry, Constance, jt. auth. see Henry, Aaron.

Curry, Corrada B. Description & Meaning in Three Novels by Gustave Flaubert. LC 95-53005. (Currents in Comparative Romance Languages & Literatures Ser.: Vol. 43). XI, 197p. (C). 1997. 44.95 (*0-8204-3116-8*) P Lang Pubng.

Curry, Corrada B., tr. see Muir, Edward & Ruggiero, Guido, eds.

Curry, Dave. UNIX Systems Programming for SVR4. LC 96-221849. (Illus.). 620p. (Orig.). 1996. pap. 34.95 (*1-56592-163-1*) Thomson Learn.

— Using C on the UNIX System. (Computer Science). 250p. (Orig.). 1989. pap. 24.95 (*0-937175-23-4*) Thomson Learn.

Curry, David A. UNIX System Security: A Guide for Users & System Administrators. (Illus.). 296p. (C). 1992. text 37.95 (*0-201-56327-4*) Addison-Wesley.

Curry, David J. The New Marketing Research Systems: How to Use Strategic Database Information for Better Marketing Decisions. LC 92-9811. 432p. 1992. 147.50 (*0-471-53058-1*) Wiley.

Curry, David P. Faberge: Virginia Museum of Fine Arts. LC 95-20926. (Illus.). 132p. (Orig.). 1997. pap. 19.95 (*0-917046-40-4*) Va Mus Arts.

— James McNeill Whistler at the Freer Gallery of Art. (Illus.). 320p. (Orig.). 1984. pap. 30.00 (*0-934686-53-X*) Freer.

— The Western Spirit: Exploring New Territory in American Art. Chambers, Marlene, ed. LC 89-50092. (Illus.). 116p. (Orig.). 1989. pap. 14.95 (*0-914738-38-0*) Denver Art Mus.

— Winslow Homer: The Croquet Game. LC 84-50421. (Illus.). 40p. (Orig.). 1984. pap. 4.00 (*0-89467-031-X*) Yale Art Gallery.

Curry, David P. & Rogers, Pattiann. A Covenant of Seasons. LC 98-20354. (Illus.). 144p. 1998. 50.00 (*1-55595-155-4*, Pub. by Hudson Hills); 35.00 (*1-55595-156-2*, Pub. by Hudson Hills) Natl Bk Netwk.

Curry, David P., et al. American Dreams: Paintings & Decorative Arts from the Warner Collection. LC 97-30069. (Illus.). 88p. 1997. pap. 24.95 (*0-917046-48-X*) Va Mus Arts.

Curry, Dean. Experiencing English: A Reading & Speaking Practice Book for Beginning Students of EFL. (Illus.). 60p. 1999. reprint ed. pap. text 20.00 (*0-7881-7706-0*) DIANE Pub.

— A World Without Tyranny: Christian Faith & International Politics. LC 89-81259. (Turning Point Christian Worldview Ser.). 192p. 1990. pap. 14.99 (*0-89107-509-7*) Crossway Bks.

Curry, Dean C. Global Transformation & Foreign Economic Policy: The Case of U. S.-European Community Agricultural Relations. LC 90-43292. (Foreign Economic Policy of the United States Ser.: Vol. 11). 206p. 1990. reprint ed. text 10.00 (*0-8240-7433-5*) Garland.

Curry, Deborah A., et al, eds. Racial & Ethnic Diversity in Academic Libraries: Multicultural Issues. LC 94-5445. (Reference Librarian Ser.: Nos. 45 & 46). (Illus.). 374p. 1994. lib. bdg. 49.95 (*1-56024-656-1*) Haworth Pr.

Curry, Dennis. Feast of the Dead: Aboriginal Ossuaries in Maryland. xi, 108p. 1999. pap. 15.00 (*1-878399-72-1*, MD Hist Trust) Div Hist Cult Progs.

Curry, Don, ed. Descubrimentos Home/School Connection Book. Torres, Leyla, tr. (Descubrimientos Ser.). (SPA.). 80p. (J). (gr. k). 1997. pap. text 49.95 (*1-56784-933-4*) Newbridge Educ.

— Sound: Big Book. (Ranger Rick Science Spectacular Ser.). 16p. (J). (gr. 2-5). 1997. pap. 16.95 (*1-56784-453-7*) Newbridge Educ.

— Sound: Mini Book. (Ranger Rick Science Spectacular Ser.). 16p. (J). (gr. 2-5). 1997. pap. text 19.95 (*1-56784-478-2*) Newbridge Educ.

— Sound Theme Pack. (Early Science Ser.). (Illus.). (J). (ps-2). 1997. pap. text 49.95 (*1-56784-392-1*) Newbridge Educ.

— Spanish A & B Add-to-Pack. Torres, Leyla, tr. (Descubrimientos Ser.). (SPA.). 128p. (J). (ps-1). 1997. pap. text 44.00 (*1-56784-942-3*) Newbridge Educ.

— Spanish Add-to-Pack. Torres, Leyla, tr. (Descurimientos Ser.). (SPA.). 256p. (J). (ps-1). 1997. pap. text 88.00 (*1-56784-941-5*) Newbridge Educ.

— Spanish C & D Add-to-Pack. Torres, Leyla, tr. (Descubrimientos Ser.). (SPA.). 128p. (J). (ps-1). 1997. pap. text 44.00 (*1-56784-943-1*) Newbridge Educ.

— Spanish Complete Program: Emergent Level. Torres, Leyla, tr. (Descubrimientos Ser.). (SPA.). (J). (ps-1). 1997. pap. text 485.00 (*1-56784-940-7*) Newbridge Educ.

— A World of Sound: Theme Pack. (Ranger Rick Ser.). (Illus.). (J). (gr. 2-5). 1997. pap. text 36.90 (*1-56784-458-8*) Newbridge Educ.

Curry, Don & Evento, Susan, eds. Descubrimientos: Teacher's Guide, PreK-1. (ENG & SPA.). 88p. (Orig.). 1997. pap., teacher ed. write for info. (*1-56784-935-0*) Newbridge Educ.

Curry, Don, ed. see Cory, Chris.

Curry, Don, ed. see Cory, Christopher.

Curry, Don, ed. see Nayer, Judy.

Curry, Don, ed. see Parke, Brenda.

Curry, Don, ed. see Parkes, Brenda.

Curry, Don, ed. see Shook-Hazen, Barbara.

Curry, Don, ed. see Trumbauer, Lisa.

Curry, Don L. Counting ABCs. (Counting Bks.). (Illus.). 32p. (J). 21.00 (*0-7368-7041-5*) Capstone Pr.

— Counting Birds. LC 99-52182. (Counting Bks.). (Illus.). 32p. (J). 1999. 21.00 (*0-7368-7039-3*) Capstone Pr.

— Counting Bugs. LC 99-52181. (Counting Bks.). (Illus.). 32p. (J). 1999. 21.00 (*0-7368-7037-7*) Capstone Pr.

— Counting My ABCs. LC 99-49696. (Illus.). (J). 1999. pap. write for info. (*0-7368-7051-2*) Capstone Pr.

— How Things Move. LC 00-36473. (Illus.). 2000. write for info. (*0-7368-0724-1*) Capstone Pr.

— My ABC's. LC 99-50152. (Illus.). 1999. pap. write for info. (*0-7368-7048-2*) Capstone Pr.

— The Water Cycle. LC 00-38157. (Illus.). 2000. write for info. (*0-7368-0727-6*) Capstone Pr.

— What Hatches? LC 00-36518. (Illus.). (J). 2000. write for info. (*0-7368-0721-7*) Capstone Pr.

***Curry, Don L. & Kaufman, Johanna.** Bugs, More or Less? LC 99-52181. (Illus.). (J). 1999. write for info. (*0-7368-7053-9*) Capstone Pr.

— Counting with Birds. LC 99-52182. (Illus.). (J). 1999. write for info. (*0-7368-7052-0*) Capstone Pr.

Curry, Edward D. Change, Growth & Profit in the Nineties. (Illus.). 125p. (Orig.). 1992. pap. 59.95 (*0-9633590-0-2*) Target Mktg-Mgmt.

— The Little Jewel: The Key to Successful Telemarketing. Curry, Letha S., ed. (Orig.). (C). 1994. text 39.95 (*0-9633590-1-0*) Target Mktg-Mgmt.

— The Survival Guide for the Evolving Insurance Crisis. Curry, Letha S., ed. (Illus.). 174p. (Orig.). 1995. pap. 39.95 (*0-9633590-2-9*) Target Mktg-Mgmt.

Curry, Edward D. & Shelton Curry, Letha. The Survival Guide for the Evolving Insurance Crisis. expanded rev. ed. 193p. (Orig.). 1998. pap. 39.95 (*0-9633590-3-7*) Target Mktg-Mgmt.

Curry, Elizabeth A., jt. ed. see Baughman, Steven A.

***Curry, Erastus S.** The Pre-Historic Races of America & Other Lands As Disclosed Thru Indian Traditions, Comprehending Also the Origin of Matter & the Formation of the World, the Periodic Changes of the Earth, the Glacial Periods, & Astronomy Solving the Chronological Problems, Etc., Etc. (LC History-America-E). 373p. 1999. reprint ed. lib. bdg. 89.00 (*0-7812-4320-3*) Rprt Serv.

***Curry, Francis X.** Molly's Grandson. 99p. 1999. pap. 10.95 (*0-7414-0139-8*) Buy Books.

Curry, Frick W., ed. Protecting Human Rights. (WVSS in Public Policy & Public Systems Ser.). (C). 1996. pap. text 18.50 (*0-8133-7156-2*) Westview.

Curry, G. David & Decker, Scott H. Confronting Gangs: Crime & Community. LC 97-28935. (Illus.). 200p. (C). 1998. pap. text. write for info. (*0-935732-92-6*) Roxbury Pub Co.

***Curry, G. David & Decker, Scott H.** Confronting Gangs: Crime & Community. 2nd ed. (Illus.). 210p. 2001. pap. text. write for info. (*1-891487-52-3*) Roxbury Pub Co.

Curry, Gene. Hot as a Pistol - Wild, Wild Wild Women, 2 vols. in 1. (Saddler Double Ser.). 352p. 1994. mass mkt. 4.99 (*0-8439-3647-9*) Dorchester Pub Co.

Curry, George. Charles Dickens & Annie Fields. LC PR4583.C98. (Illus.). 80p. reprint ed. pap. 30.00 (*0-7837-6674-2*, 204629000011) Bks Demand.

Curry, George E., ed. The Affirmative Action Debate. 384p. 1996. pap. 16.00 (*0-201-47963-X*) Addison-Wesley.

Curry, Guy L., et al. Discrete Simulation: Fundamentals & Microcomputer Support. 312p. (C). 1989. 49.95 (*0-8162-2060-3*) Holden-Day.

Curry, Haskell B. Foundations of Mathematical Logic. 2nd ed. 416p. (C). 1977. pap. 12.95 (*0-486-63462-0*) Dover.

Curry, Hayden. A Legal Guide for Lesbian & Gay Couples. 10th ed. LC 98-28122. 344p. 1999. 25.95 (*0-87337-495-9*) Nolo com.

Curry, Hayden, et al. A Legal Guide for Lesbian & Gay Couples. 10th ed. LC 96-15945. 344p. 1999. pap. 24.95 (*0-87337-336-7*) Nolo com.

***Curry, Helen.** The Way of the Labyrinth: A Powerful Meditation for Everyday Life. (Illus.). 224p. 2000. pap. 15.00 (*0-14-019617-X*) Penguin Putnam.

Curry-Hyde, H. E. & Howe, R. F., eds. Natural Gas Conversion II: Proceedings of the Third Natural Gas Conversion Symposium, Sydney, July 4-9, 1993. LC 94-10953. (Studies in Surface Science & Catalysis: Vol. 81). 594p. 1994. 272.50 (*0-444-89535-3*) Elsevier.

Curry, J. Counting the Ways. 1997. mass mkt. 13.95 (*0-340-68019-9*, Pub. by Hodder & Stought Ltd) Trafalgar.

— Peacock's Acre. mass mkt. 13.95 (*0-340-68021-0*, Pub. by Hodder & Stought Ltd) Trafalgar.

Curry, J. W. Re: Views: Re: Sponses. 42p. (Orig.). 1991. pap. 10.00 (*0-926935-49-6*) Runaway Spoon.

Curry, J. W. & Smith, Steven. Between. (Illus.). 30p. (Orig.). 1989. pap. 3.00 (*0-926935-12-7*) Runaway Spoon.

***Curry, James, et al.** The American Constitutional Experience: Selected Readings & Supreme Court Opinions. 184p. (C). 1999. per. 19.95 (*0-7872-5760-5*) Kendall-Hunt.

Curry, James H. Iterative Methods: Historic & Modern Perspectives. (C). 1999. write for info. (*0-201-50062-0*) Addison-Wesley.

Curry, Jane. Marietta Holley. (Twayne's United States Authors Ser.: vol. 658). 114p. 1995. 32.00 (*0-8057-4020-1*) Macmillan.

— The River's in My Blood: Riverboat Pilots Tell Their Stories. LC 82-11068. 318p. 1983. reprint ed. pap. 98.60 (*0-608-01845-7*, 206249500003) Bks Demand.

— Robin Hood & His Merry Men. (Illus.). 48p. (J). (gr. 2-6). 1994. mass mkt. 13.95 (*0-689-50609-0*) McElderry Bks.

Curry, Jane, ed. see Holley, Marietta.

Curry, Jane, ed. see Holley, Marietta.

Curry, Jane Kathleen. Nineteenth-Century American Woman Theatre Managers, 143. LC 93-44133. (Contributions in Women's Studies). 168p. 1994. 55.00 (*0-313-29141-1*, Greenwood Pr) Greenwood.

Curry, Jane L. Back in the Beforetime: Tales of the California Indians. LC 86-21339. (Illus.). 144p. (J). (gr. 4-7). 1987. 15.00 (*0-689-50410-1*) McElderry Bks.

— The Big Smith Snatch. LC 89-8036. 224p. (J). (gr. 4-7). 1989. lib. bdg. 16.00 (*0-689-50478-0*) McElderry Bks.

— The Christmas Knight. LC 92-2277. (Illus.). 32p. (J). (gr. k-4). 1993. 14.95 (*0-689-50572-8*) McElderry Bks.

— Dark Shade. LC 97-30238. 168p. (YA). (gr. 7-12). 1998. per. 16.00 (*0-689-81812-2*, 870382) McElderry Bks.

— The Daybreakers. (Illus.). (J). (gr. 3-7). 1991. 21.00 (*0-8446-6474-X*) Peter Smith.

— The Great Smith House Hustle. LC 92-33073. 192p. (J). (gr. 4-7). 1993. 14.95 (*0-689-50580-9*) McElderry Bks.

— Little, Little Sister. LC 88-13079. (Illus.). 32p. (J). (ps-3). 1989. text 12.95 (*0-689-50459-4*) McElderry Bks.

— Mindy's Mysterious Miniature. (J). (gr. 4-7). 1990. 20.25 (*0-8446-6433-2*) Peter Smith.

— Moon Window. LC 95-52558. 170p. (J). (gr. 4-7). 1996. 16.00 (*0-689-80945-X*) S&S Bks Yung.

— Poland's Journalists: Professionalism & Politics. (Cambridge Russian, Soviet & Post-Soviet Studies: No. 66). 312p. (C). 1990. text 69.95 (*0-521-36201-6*) Cambridge U Pr.

— Press Control Around the World. LC 82-9837. 283p. 1982. 39.95 (*0-275-90775-9*, C0775, Praeger Pubs) Greenwood.

— Robin Hood in the Greenwood. (Illus.). 48p. (J). (gr. 2-6). 1995. mass mkt. 15.00 (*0-689-80147-5*) McElderry Bks.

***Curry, Jane L.** A Stolen Life. LC 98-51103. (Illus.). 208p. (YA). (gr. 5-9). 1999. per. 16.00 (*0-689-82932-9*) McElderry Bks.

Curry, Jane L. What the Dickens! LC 90-26864. 160p. (J). (gr. 4-7). 1991. lib. bdg. 13.95 (*0-689-50524-8*) McElderry Bks.

Curry, Jane L., ed. Dissent in Eastern Europe. LC 83-2168. 227p. 1983. 38.50 (*0-275-90965-4*, C0965, Praeger Pubs) Greenwood.

Curry, Jane L. & Fajfer, Luba, eds. Poland's Permanent Revolution: People vs. Elites, 1956-1990. 300p. (C). 1995. pap. text 30.50 (*1-879383-46-2*); lib. bdg. 71.50 (*1-879383-45-4*) Am Univ Pr.

Curry, Jay, jt. auth. see Curry, Adam.

Curry, Jeffrey. Passport Taiwan: Your Pocket Guide to Taiwanese Business, Culture, & Etiquette. Szerlip, Barbara, ed. LC 97-8028. (Passport to the World Ser.). (Illus.). 96p. (Orig.). 1997. pap. 6.95 (*1-885073-27-5*) Wrld Trade Pr.

— A Short Course in International Economics. LC 99-16123. (Short Course in International Trade Ser.). (Illus.). 184p. 1999. pap. 19.95 (*1-885073-53-4*) Wrld Trade Pr.

Curry, Jeffrey & Nguyen, Jim C. Passport Vietnam: Your Pocket Guide to Vietnamese Business, Customs & Etiquette. Szerlip, Barbara, ed. LC 96-14867. (Passport to the World Ser.). (Illus.). 96p. (Orig.). 1997. pap. 6.95 (*1-885073-25-9*) Wrld Trade Pr.

Curry, Jeffrey E. A Short Course in International Negotiating. LC 98-17850. (Short Course in International Trade Ser.). (Illus.). 184p. 1997. pap. 19.95 (*1-885073-51-8*) Wrld Trade Pr.

Curry, Jennifer. Counting the Ways. large type ed. (Ulverscroft Large Print Ser.). 464p. 1997. 27.99 (*0-7089-3821-3*) Ulverscroft.

Curry, Jerri. I Believe in Angels: You Have to Be Willing to Risk to Fly with the Angels. Miles, Claudia, ed. LC 95-90358. (Illus.). 192p. (Orig.). 1996. pap. 14.00 (*0-944586-09-0*, TXU 162) WIN Pub.

— The Swan: A Storybook for Adults & Other Children. unabridged ed. (Illus.). 21p. (YA). (gr. 7 up). 1988. 13.95 incl. audio (*0-944586-00-7*) WIN Pub.

Curry, Joel B. Public Relations for the Local Church: A Practical Guide for Ministry Leaders. Spear, Cindy G., ed. 130p. (C). 1991. student ed., ring bd. 89.95 incl. audio (*0-941005-36-4*) Chrch Grwth VA.

Curry, John Court, jt. auth. see Andrew, Christopher.

Curry, Judith A & Webster, Peter J. Thermodynamics of Atmospheres & Oceans. LC 99-212902. (International Geophysics Ser.: Vol. 65). 471p. 1999. 65.00 (*0-12-199570-4*) Acad Pr.

Curry, Katharine & Jaffe, Amy. Nutrition Counseling & Comunication Skills. Connor, Maura, ed. LC 97-34828. (Illus.). 384p. 1997. pap. text 32.95 (*0-7216-7298-1*, W B Saunders Co) Harcrt Hlth Sci Grp.

***Curry, Kathy Lee.** Tabula Rasa: An Easy Energy Balancing Technique for You & Your Family. 2nd ed. (Illus.). 120p. 2000. pap. 23.95 (*0-9701919-0-1*) Indepndt Writer.

Curry, Kenneth. Sir Walter Scott's Edinburgh Annual Register. LC 77-8136. 227p. reprint ed. 70.40 (*0-608-16854-8*, 202756300055) Bks Demand.

Curry, Kenneth, ed. see Southey, Robert.

Curry, Kenny & Curry, Lisa. Get Up & Go. 1999. 19.95 (*0-7322-5877-4*, Pub. by HarpC) Consort Bk Sales.

Curry, Landon. The Politics of Fiscal Stress: Organizational Management of Budget Cutbacks. LC 90-42937. 110p. (Orig.). 1990. pap. 9.95 (*0-87772-326-5*) UCB IGS.

Curry, Laurie. Romania: Country Commercial Guide: Fiscal Year, 1998. 76p. (C). 1999. pap. text 30.00 (*0-7881-7410-X*) DIANE Pub.

Curry, Lee S., ed. see Clark, Fred A.

Curry, Leonard P. Blueprint for Modern America Non-Military Legislation of the First Civil War Congress. LC 68-10827. 312p. reprint ed. pap. 96.80 (*0-8357-3252-5*, 203947300013) Bks Demand.

— The Corporate City: The American City As a Political Entity, 1800-1850, 172. LC 96-29278. (Emergence of American Urbanism Ser.). 392p. 1997. 75.00 (*0-313-30277-4*) Greenwood.

— The Free Black in Urban America, 1800-1850: The Shadow of the Dream. LC 80-27811. (Illus.). xx, 366p. (C). 1997. pap. 17.95 (*0-226-13125-4*) U Ch Pr.

Curry, Leslie. The Random Spatial Economy & Its Evolution. LC 98-71403. 6p. 1998. text 84.95 (*1-84014-391-6*, Pub. by Ashgate Pub) Ashgate Pub Co.

Curry, Letha S., ed. see Curry, Edward D.

Curry, Letha Shelton, see Curry, Edward D. & Shelton Curry, Letha.

Curry, Linda & Cox, Debra. Eyewitness History: A Personal, Literary & Creative Approach to Teaching Social Studies. 150p. (C). 1995. pap. text 15.95 (*0-89641-240-7*) American Pr.

Curry, Lindy S. A Tiger by the Tail & Other Stories from the Heart of Korea. Park, Chan-eung, ed. LC 99-10669. (World Folklore Ser.). (Illus.). 150p. 1999. 22.50 (*1-56308-586-0*) Teacher Ideas Pr.

Curry, Lisa, jt. auth. see Curry, Kenny.

Curry, Lynn & Wergin, Jon F. Educating Professionals: Responding to New Expectations for Competence & Accountability. LC 92-41686. (Higher & Adult Education Ser.). 403p. 1993. text 38.95 (*1-55542-523-2*) Jossey-Bass.

***Curry, Lynne.** Modern Mothers in the Heartland: Gender, Health, & Progress in Illinois, 1900-1930. LC 99-27611. (Women & Health Ser.). (Illus.). 224p. 1999. text 40.00 (*0-8142-0830-4*); pap. text 18.50 (*0-8142-5052-7*) Ohio St U Pr.

Curry, Marilyn, jt. auth. see Warner, Carolyn.

Curry, Mary C. Making the Gods in New York: The Yoruba Religion in the African American Community. rev. ed. LC 97-8411. (Studies in African American History & Culture). (Illus.). 216p. 1997. text 53.00 (*0-8153-2919-9*) Garland.

Curry, Mary J., ed. see Ecklund, Lois E.

Curry, Mary J., ed. see Fields, Ann, et al.

Curry, Michael, jt. auth. see Bragg, David F.

Curry, Michael R. Digital Places: Living with Geographic Information Technologies. LC 98-14913. 208p. (C). 1998. pap. 29.99 (*0-415-13015-8*) Routledge.

— Digital Places: Living with Geographic Information Technologies. LC 98-14913. (Illus.). 208p. (C). 1998. 90.00 (*0-415-13014-X*) Routledge.

— The Work in the World: Geographical Practice & the Written Word. LC 96-16478. 256p. (C). 1996. pap. 19.95 (*0-8166-2665-0*); text 49.95 (*0-8166-2664-2*) U of Minn Pr.

Curry, Morris A., Sr. A Pocket Book of Short Sermon Starters: A Help for All Ministers: Young & Experienced. 92p. (Orig.). 1995. pap. text 5.00 (*1-882581-09-1*) Campbell Rd Pr.

Curry, Nancy E., ed. The Feeling Child: Affective Development Reconsidered. LC 86-3068. (Journal of Children in Contemporary Society: Vol. 17, No. 4). 156p. 1986. text 39.95 (*0-86656-555-8*) Haworth Pr.

Curry, Nancy E. & Johnson, Carl N. Beyond Self-Esteem: Developing a Genuine Sense of Human Value. LC 90-62662. (Research Monograph Ser.: No. 4). (Illus.). 177p. (Orig.). 1990. pap. text 8.00 (*0-935989-39-0*, NAEYC #143) Natl Assn Child Ed.

Curry, Neil. The Bending of the Bow: A Version of the Closing Books of Homer's Odyssey. (Illus.). 84p. 1994. pap. 16.95 (*1-870612-04-3*, Pub. by Enitha Pr) Dufour.

— Ships in Bottles. 96p. 1988. reprint ed. pap. 12.95 (*1-870612-30-2*, Pub. by Enitha Pr) Dufour.

— Walking to Santiago. 66p. 1993. pap. 17.95 (*1-870612-13-2*, Pub. by Enitha Pr) Dufour.

Curry, Nigel. Countryside Recreation, Access & Land Use Planning: Participation, Preferences, Policies &... (Illus.). 276p. (C). 1994. 60.00 (*0-419-15550-3*, E & FN Spon) Routledge.

Curry, Nigel, jt. auth. see Blunden, John.

Curry, Nigel, jt. ed. see Blunden, John.

Curry, Patricia B., et al, eds. Methods of Pesticide Exposure Assessment: Proceedings of a Workshop Held in Ottawa, Canada, October 5-8, 1993. (NATO - Challenges of Modern Society Ser.: Vol. 19). (Illus.). 236p. 1995. 89.50 (*0-306-45130-1*, Kluwer Plenum) Kluwer Academic.

Curry, Patrick. Defending Middle-Earth: Tolkien: Myth & Modernity. LC 97-19564. 176p. 1997. text 35.00 (*0-312-17671-6*) St Martin.

— Introducing Machiavelli. (Illus.). 176p. 1996. pap. 9.95 (*1-874166-28-5*, Pub. by Totem Bks) Natl Bk Netwk.

Curry, Peggy S. LandMarked: Stories of Peggy Simson Curry. 320p. (Orig.). 1992. pap. 12.95 (*0-931271-17-7*) Hi Plains Pr.

— So Far from Spring: A Novel of the American West. LC 83-21179. 344p. 1993. pap. 16.95 (*0-87108-840-1*) Pruett.

Curry, Peggy S., et al. Wyoming Promises: Poetry about Frontier Women. Curtis, Nancy, ed. (Illus.). 24p. 1984. 3.95 (*0-931271-04-5*) Hi Plains Pr.

Curry, R. Bruce, jt. auth. see Peart, R. M.

Curry, R. W., ed. Modern Chlor-Alkali Technology, Vol. 6. 306p. 1995. 125.00 (*0-85404-735-2*) CRC Pr.

Curry, Ramona. Too Much of a Good Thing: Mae West As Cultural Icon. LC 95-25838. 288p. 1996. pap. 19.95 (*0-8166-2791-6*); text 49.95 (*0-8166-2790-8*) U of Minn Pr.

Curry, Renee. Perspectives on Woody Allen. 1996. 50.00 (*0-8161-1615-6*) Macmillan.

Curry, Renee R. White Women Writing White: H.D., Elizabeth Bishop, Sylvia Plath & Whiteness, 175. LC 99-21706. (Contributions in Women's Studies: Vol. 175). 200p. 2000. 59.95 (*0-313-31019-X*) Greenwood.

Curry, Renee R. & Allison, Terry L., eds. States of Rage: Emotional Eruption, Violence, & Social Change. (Illus.). 233p. (C). 1996. text 55.00 (*0-8147-1525-7*); pap. text 19.50 (*0-8147-1530-3*) NYU Pr.

Curry, Reva A. & Tempkin, Betty B., eds. Ultrasonography: An Introduction to Normal Structure & Functional Anatomy. (Illus.). 492p. 1995. teacher ed. write for info. (*0-7216-4748-0*, W B Saunders Co) Harcrt Hlth Sci Grp.

— Ultrasonography: An Introduction to Normal Structure & Functional Anatomy. LC 93-26475. (Illus.). 800p. 1995. text 71.00 (*0-7216-4585-2*, W B Saunders Co) Harcrt Hlth Sci Grp.

Curry, Reva Arnez. Exercises in Sonography. (C). 1995. pap. text 42.00 (*0-7216-4962-9*) Harcourt.

Curry, Richard A. Ramon de Mesonero Romanos. LC 76-25. (Twayne's World Authors Ser.). (C). 1976. lib. bdg. 20.95 (*0-8057-6226-4*) Irvington.

Curry, Richard A., jt. auth. see Rojas, Jorge N.

Curry, Richard O. An Uncertain Future: Thought Control & Repression During the Reagan-Bush Era. LC 92-82816. (Illus.). 100p. 1992. 12.00 (*0-9627705-1-5*) Frst Amendment.

Curry, Richard O., ed. Freedom at Risk: Secrecy, Censorship, & Repression in the 1980s. 448p. 1989. pap. 18.95 (*0-87722-660-1*) Temple U Pr.

— Radicalism, Racism, & Party Realignment: The Border States During Reconstruction. LC 72-90743. 360p. reprint ed. pap. 111.60 (*0-608-15147-5*, 202581100046) Bks Demand.

Curry, Richard O. & Goodheart, Lawrence B., eds. American Chameleon: Individualism in Trans-National Context. LC 91-7150. 288p. 1991. 35.00 (*0-87338-443-1*); pap. 17.50 (*0-87338-448-2*) Kent St U Pr.

Curry, Rick. The Secrets of Jesuit Breadmaking: Recipes & Traditions from Jesuit Bakers Around the World. 256p. 1995. pap. 17.00 (*0-06-095118-4*, Perennial) HarperTrade.

Curry, Robert. Bahamian Lore. 1976. lib. bdg. 250.00 (*0-8490-1378-X*) Gordon Pr.

Curry, Robert L., Jr., jt. auth. see Rothchild, Donald.

Curry, Robert M. & Durham, James G. Ohio Real Property Law & Practice: 1998 Cumulative Supplement, Vol. 1. 5th ed. 1998. write for info. (*0-327-00804-0*) LEXIS Pub.

C

— Ohio Real Property Law & Practice: 1998 Cumulative Supplement, Vol. 2. 1998. write for info. (0-327-00805-9) LEXIS Pub.

— Ohio Real Property Law & Practice: 1998 Cumulative Supplement, Vol. 3. 1998. write for info. (0-327-00806-7) LEXIS Pub.

Curry, Ronald H. Win at Chess: A Comprehensive Guide to Winning Chess for the Intermediate Player. Long, Robert B., ed. (Illus.). 270p. (Orig.). 1995. pap. 18.95 (0-938650-64-5) Thinkers Pr.

Curry, Rosalynn, ed. see Hamdon, Marshall.

Curry, Rosalynn A., ed. see Prothro, Crystaline J.

Curry, Rosalynn A., ed. see Prothro, James S.

Curry, S. H., jt. auth. see McCallum, W. C.

Curry, Samuel. Browning & the Dramatic Monologue. LC 65-26455. (Studies in Browning: No. 4). 1969. reprint ed. lib. bdg. 75.00 (0-8383-0535-0) M S G Haskell Hse.

Curry, Saundra. Anesthesiology: Pretest Self Assessment & Review. 2nd ed. LC 97-25675. (Illus.). 264p. 1997. pap. text 45.00 (0-07-015102-4) McGraw-Hill HPD.

***Curry, Sharon & Ahrendt, Delilah.** Canine Caper: The True Story of a Female Pet Vigilante. 2001. 24.95 (0-88282-197-0, Pub. by New Horizon NJ) Natl Bk Netwk.

Curry, Sheila M., jt. auth. see Farley, Kara Leverte.

Curry, Stephen H. Clinical Pharmacokinetics: The MCQ Approach. (Illus.). 180p. (C). 1988. lib. bdg. 59.95 (0-936923-03-2); lib. bdg. 39.95 (0-936923-02-4) Telford Pr.

Curry, Steven. Dancing the Waves. (Illus.). 68p. 1998. pap. 10.95 (0-9653971-5-7) Anoai Pr.

— Waxing the Lunar Mountain Apple. (Poetry Ser.: Vol. 1). 100p. 1997. pap. 9.95 (0-9653971-3-0) Anoai Pr.

Curry, Susan & Rich, Susan, eds. Kline Guide to the Chemical Industry. 4th ed. (Illus.). 590p. 1980. pap. 147.00 (0-917148-13-4) Kline.

Curry-Swan, Lynne. Won by One. 1997. pap. text 19.95 (0-9645892-0-6) Growth Co.

Curry, Thomas J. The First Freedoms: Church & State in America to the Passage of the First Amendment. 288p. 1987. pap. text 24.95 (0-19-505181-5) OUP.

Curry, Thomas S., III, et al. Christensen's Physics of Diagnostic Radiology. 4th ed. LC 90-5586. (Illus.). 522p. 1990. text 54.00 (0-8121-1310-1) Lppncott W & W.

Curry, Tim, et al. Sociology for the 21st Century. 482p. (C). 1996. pap. 43.00 (0-13-184045-2) P-H.

Curry, Vicki. Music in Culture. 96p. (C). 1995. student ed., spiral bd., suppl. ed. 8.95 (0-7872-1896-0) Kendall-Hunt.

Curry, W. H. Sun Rising on the West: The Saga of Henry Clay & Elizabeth Smith. 1979. 20.00 (0-9606940-2-1) Crosby County.

Curry, W. L. History of Jerome Township, Union County. (Illus.). 205p. 1997. reprint ed. lib. bdg. 29.00 (0-8328-6331-9) Higginson Bk Co.

***Curry, W. L.** History of Jerome Township, Union County, Ohio. (Illus.). 243p. 1999. 30.50 (0-7884-1210-8, C868) Heritage Bk.

Curry, Walter C. Demonic Metaphysics of Macbeth. (Studies in Shakespeare: No. 24). 1970. reprint ed. pap. 12.95 (0-8383-0020-0) M S G Haskell Hse.

— Essays in Honor of Walter Clyde Curry. LC PR0014.F55. (Vanderbilt Studies in the Humanities: No. 2). 300p. reprint ed. pap. 93.00 (0-8357-3266-5, 203948700013) Bks Demand.

— Middle English Ideal of Personal Beauty. LC 70-180443. reprint ed. 32.50 (0-404-01886-6) AMS Pr.

— Shakespeare's Philosophical Patterns. 1990. 16.50 (0-8446-0567-0) Peter Smith.

Curry, Wesley, ed. A Dictionary of Medical Management Terms & Initialisms. LC 97-78155. 178p. 1998. pap. 48.00 (0-924674-62-8) Am Coll Phys Execs.

— New Leadership in Health Care Management: The Physician Executive. 2nd ed. LC 94-72291. 329p. 1994. 45.00 (0-924674-30-X) Am Coll Phys Execs.

Curry, Wesley, jt. auth. see Letourneau, Barbara.

Curry, Wesley, ed. see Kennedy, Marilyn M.

Curry, William L. Raid of the Confederate Cavalry Through Central Tennessee in October, 1863, Commanded by General Joseph Wheeler: A Paper Read Before the Ohio Commandery of the Loyal Legion. Stewart, George R., ed. LC 87-37511. (Eyewitness Accounts of the Civil War Ser.). (Illus.). 24p. (C). 1987. reprint ed. pap. 10.00 (0-942301-03-X) Birm Pub Lib.

***Curryer, Betty Nelson.** Anchors: The Illustrated History. LC 99-491016. 1999. pap. 23.95 (1-55750-041-X) Naval Inst Pr.

Cursio, Joan, et al. Case Citations No. 15: School Governance. Russo, Charles J., ed. (Fifteenth Series - School Governance). 1993. pap. 30.00 (1-56534-054-X) Ed Law Assn.

Curson, Jon, et al. Warblers of the Americas: An Indentification Guide. LC 94-7470. (Illus.). 268p. 1994. 42.00 (0-395-70998-9) HM.

Curson, Julie P. A Guide's Guide to Philadelphia. 6th ed. LC 91-71426. (Illus.). 528p. (Orig.). 1991. pap. 11.95 (0-913694-06-1) Curson Hse.

Curson, Marjorie. Jonas Salk. Gallin, Richard, ed. (Pioneers in Change Ser.). (Illus.). 144p. (J). (gr. 5-9). 1990. pap. 6.95 (0-382-09971-0) Silver Burdett Pr.

Curson, Peter & McCracken, Kevin. Plague in Sydney - The Anatomy of an Epidemic. 220p. 1990. pap. 24.95 (0-86840-219-2, Pub. by New South Wales Univ Pr) Intl Spec Bk.

Curstedt, Tore, et al, eds. New Perspectives of Surfactant Research: Proceedings of the 12th International Workshop, Stockholm, May 1997. (Journal: Biology of the Neonate: Vol. 71, Suppl. 1, 1997). (Illus.). iv, 70p. 1997. pap. 22.75 (3-8055-6528-3) S Karger.

Curt, Beryl. Textuality & Tectonics: Troubling Social & Psychological Science. 192p. 1994. 114.95 (0-335-19064-2); pap. 33.95 (0-335-19063-4) OpUniv Pr.

Curtain, Helena & Pesola, Carol A. Languages & Children: Making the Match. (MFL Second Language Library). (Illus.). 368p. 1988. pap. text 31.44 (0-201-12290-1) Addison-Wesley.

— Languages & Children, Making the Match: Foreign Language Instruction for an Early Start Grades K-8. 2nd ed. LC 93-11014. 1994. pap. text 27.84 (0-8013-1140-3) Longman.

***Curtain-Phillips, Marilyn.** Math Attack: How to Reduce Math Anxiety in the Classroom, at Work & in... 120p. 1999. 15.00 (0-9673997-1-8) Curtain-Phillips.

Curtain, R. F., ed. Modelling, Robustness & Sensitivity Reduction in Control Systems. (NATO Asi Series F: Vol. 34). x, 492p. 1987. 119.95 (0-387-17845-7) Spr-Verlag.

Curtain, R. F., et al, eds. Analysis & Optimization of Systems: State & Frequency Domain Approaches for Infinite-Dimensional Systems: Proceedings of the 10th International Conference, Sophia-Antipolis, France, June 9-12, 1992. LC 92-37327. (Lecture Notes in Control & Information Sciences: Vol. 185). 1993. 193.95 (0-387-56155-2) Spr-Verlag.

Curtain, Ruth F. & Zwart, Hans. An Introduction to Infinite Dimensional Linear Systems Theory. LC 95-5549. (Texts in Applied Mathematics Ser.: Vol. 21). (Illus.). xx, 697p. 1995. 59.95 (0-387-94475-3) Spr-Verlag.

Curtain, Sara, ed. Jump for Joy: More Raps & Rhymes. (Illus.). 64p. (Orig.). 1993. teacher ed. 14.00 (1-875327-17-7, Pub. by E Curtain) Peguis Pubs Ltd.

Curtay & Lyon. Encyclopedie Pratique Vitamines, Sels Mineraux Olgoelements. (FRE.). 284p. 1996. 59.95 (0-320-00668-9) Fr & Eur.

Curtayne, Alice. Francis Ledwidge, a Life of the Poet LC 99-158598. 215p. 1998. write for info. (1-874597-80-4) New Island Books.

— St. Catherine of Siena. LC 80-53745. 1980. reprint ed. pap. 13.50 (0-89555-162-4) TAN Bks Pubs.

Curth, Michael A. & Edelmann, Helmut. APL: A Problem-Oriented Introduction. 1989. text 49.95 (0-470-21395-7) P-H.

Curthoys, Ann, ed. For & Against Feminism. 1989. pap. text 18.95 (0-04-310021-X, Pub. by Allen & Unwin Pty) Paul & Co Pubs.

Curthoys, Ann & Merritt, John, eds. Better Dead Than Red: Australia's First Cold War, Vol. 2. 226p. (C). 1987. text 49.95 (0-04-909022-4) Routledge.

***Curthoys, Ann & Schultz, Julianne.** Journalism: Print, Politics & Popular Culture. (Australian Studies). 1999. pap. 29.95 (0-7022-3137-1, Pub. by Univ Queensland Pr) Intl Spec Bk.

Curthoys, J. S., jt. ed. see Atrens, D. M.

Curthoys, Jean. Feminist Amnesia. LC 96-20529. 216p. (C). 1997. 70.00 (0-415-14806-5); pap. 20.99 (0-415-14807-3) Routledge.

Curthoys, M. C., jt. ed. see Brock, M. G.

***Curti, Anna.** Christmas Tree. (Portable Holidays Ser.). (Illus.). 10p. (J). 1999. 7.95 (0-8109-5634-9, Pub. by Abrams) Time Warner.

***Curti, Anna.** The Christmas Star. (Portable Holidays Ser.). 10p. (J). (ps-k). 1999. 7.95 (0-8109-5638-1, Pub. by Abrams) Time Warner.

— Christmas Star Boxed: Portables. (Portable Holidays Ser.). (J). 1999. 7.95 (0-8109-5647-0) Abrams.

— Christmas Tree Boxed Set: Portables. (Portable Holidays Ser.). (J). 1999. 7.95 (0-8109-5635-7) Abrams.

— Fun to Make Paper Craft. 40p. (J). (gr. k-3). 1999. pap. 13.95 (1-85479-381-0, Pub. by M OMara) Trafalgar.

Curti, Anna. My First Prayers & Psalms. (ps-3). 1999. 7.99 (0-375-80235-5, Pub. by Random Bks Yng Read) Random.

Curti, B., et al, eds. Flavins & Flavoproteins, 1990: Proceedings of the Tenth International Symposium, Como, Italy, July 15-20, 1990. (Illus.). xxiv, 920p. 1991. lib. bdg. 300.00 (3-11-012373-8) De Gruyter.

Curti, G. Philip. Seven Bridges of Paul of Tarsus: With Embers from St. Paul's Fire. (Illus.). 104p. 1997. pap. 15.00 (0-8059-4324-2) Dorrance.

Curti, Lidia. Female Stories, Female Bodies: Narrative, Identity & Representation. LC 97-34293. 256p. 1998. text 55.00 (0-8147-1572-9); pap. text 18.50 (0-8147-1573-7) NYU Pr.

Curti, Lidia, jt. ed. see Chambers, Iain.

Curti, Merle E. American Philanthropy Abroad. 656p. 1988. 54.95 (0-88738-711-X) Transaction Pubs.

— Growth of American Thought. 3rd ed. LC 81-3433. 949p. (C). 1991. reprint ed. pap. text 34.95 (0-87855-879-9) Transaction Pubs.

— Human Nature in American Thought: A History. LC 79-3965. 472p. reprint ed. pap. 146.40 (0-608-20421-8, 207167400002) Bks Demand.

— The Learned Blacksmith: The Letters & Journals of Elihu Burritt. LC 70-137536. (Peace Movement in America Ser.). ix, 241p. 1972. reprint ed. lib. bdg. 32.95 (0-89198-063-6) Ozer.

— The Making of an American Community: A Case Study of Democracy in a Frontier County. vii, 483p. 1959. 57.50 (0-8047-0534-8) Stanford U Pr.

— Peace or War: The American Struggle, 1636-1936. LC 70-143428. (Peace Movement in America Ser.). 374p. 1972. reprint ed. lib. bdg. 45.95 (0-89198-064-4) Ozer.

— The University of Wisconsin Vol. 2: A History, 1848-1925. 678p. 1949. 40.00 (0-299-80572-7) U of Wis Pr.

Curti, Merle E. & Birr, Kendall. Prelude to Point Four: American Technical Missions Overseas 1838 to 1938. LC 78-4874. 284p. 1978. reprint ed. lib. bdg. 65.00 (0-313-20397-0, CUPP, Greenwood Pr) Greenwood.

Curti, Merle E. & Carstensen, Vernon. The University of Wisconsin: A History, 1848-1925, Vol. 1. LC 48-47638. 759p. 1974. reprint ed. pap. 200.00 (0-608-01862-7, 206251300001) Bks Demand.

Curti, Merle E., et al. History of American Civilization. LC 68-29199. (Essay Index Reprint Ser.). 1977. 42.95 (0-8369-1031-1) Ayer.

— The Making of an American Community: A Case Study of Democracy in a Frontier County. LC 59-5051. 495p. 1959. reprint ed. pap. 30.00 (0-7837-5129-X, 204485700004) Bks Demand.

Curti, Merle E., jt. auth. see Burritt, Elihu.

Curtice, David & Patton James, Systems Control, Inc. Staff. Handbook of the Operation of Small Wind Turbines on a Utility Distribution System. (Illus.). 192p. 1984. pap. text 39.95 (0-88016-009-8) WindBks.

Curtice, Randolph. The Age of Curiosity: Especially for Grandmothers. (Illus.). 1978. 7.50 (0-9601722-0-3) North Lake Prod.

Curtice, Robert M. Access Mechanisms & Data Structure Support in Data Base Management Systems. LC 76-372283. (QED Monograph Series. Data Base Management: No. 1). 66p. reprint ed. pap. 30.00 (0-8357-5035-3, 203200500077) Bks Demand.

— Planning for Data Base Systems. LC 76-374222. (QED Monograph Series. Data Base Management: No. 2). 49p. reprint ed. pap. 30.00 (0-608-15621-3, 203175000076) Bks Demand.

Curtice, Robert W., jt. auth. see Jones, Paul E.

Curties, T. J. The Monk of Udolpho: A Romance. Varma, Devendra P., ed. LC 77-2037. (Gothic Novels III Ser.). 1977. lib. bdg. 101.95 (0-405-10136-8) Ayer.

Curtin. Information Technology. 2nd ed. 2001. 37.50 (0-07-229740-9) McGraw.

Curtin. Microsoft Excel 95 Pal. 1997. pap. write for info. (0-13-237546-X) P-H.

— Microsoft Word 95 Windows Pal. 1997. pap. write for info. (0-13-237553-2) P-H.

Curtin. Postnational Democracy. LC 97-189159. 1997. pap. text 28.00 (90-411-0447-X) Kluwer Academic.

Curtin, Bonnie R. Managing Micrographic Records. (Illus.). 75p. 1998. pap. text 25.00 (0-7881-4787-0) DIANE Pub.

Curtin, Cait. The Grand Lady of Fourth Avenue: Portland's Historic Multnomah Hotel. (Illus.). 96p. 1997. 26.95 (0-8323-0521-9) Binford Mort.

***Curtin, Dan.** Invincible Lady. 1999. pap. write for info. (1-58235-215-1) Watermrk Pr.

Curtin, Daniel J., Jr. Curtin's California Land Use & Planning Law. 20th rev. ed. 2000. pap., wbk. ed. 48.00 (0-923956-63-8) Solano Pr.

***Curtin, Daniel J., Jr.** Subdivision Map Act Manual. 2000. pap. 40.00 (0-923956-64-6) Solano Pr.

Curtin, Daniel J., Jr. & Merritt, Robert E. Subdivision Map Act Manual. 9th ed. 1998. wbk. ed. 25.00 (0-923956-53-0) Solano Pr.

Curtin, Dave & Lynde, Rob. Colorado Springs: Rocky Mountain Majesty. LC 94-48824. (Urban Tapestry Ser.). (Illus.). 192p. 1995. 39.50 (1-881096-15-7) Towery Pub.

***Curtin, Deane & Litke, Robert, eds.** Institutional Violence. (Value Inquiry Book Ser.: Vol. 88). xvii, 413p. 1999. 110.00 (90-420-0508-4); pap. 36.00 (90-420-0498-3) Editions Rodopi.

Curtin, Deane W. Chinagounder's Challenge: The Question of Ecological Citizenship LC 99-25161. 1999. write for info. (0-253-21330-4) Ind U Pr.

Curtin, Deane W. & Heldke, Lisa M., eds. Cooking, Eating, Thinking: Transformative Philosophies of Food. LC 91-23622. (Illus.). 412p. 1992. text 45.00 (0-253-31599-9); pap. text 19.95 (0-253-20704-5, MB-704) Ind U Pr.

***Curtin, Deanne.** Chinnagounder's Challenge: The Question of Ecological Citizenship. LC 99-25161. 1999. 29.95 (0-253-33576-0) Ind U Pr.

Curtin, Deirdre, ed. see Schermers, Henry G.

Curtin, Dennis. Into Your Darkroom Step-by-Step. rev. ed. (Illus.). 90p. 1991. pap. 17.95 (0-936262-06-0) Amherst Media.

— Microsoft Access 7.0 by Pictorial. LC 96-22054. 235p. 1996. spiral bd. 37.33 (0-13-238361-6) P-H.

Curtin, Dennis P. Application Software: Version A. 3rd ed. LC 92-14812. (Computer Application Software Ser.). 816p. 1993. pap. text 73.33 (0-13-041971-0) P-H.

— dBASE III Plus Procedures Manual. 128p. 1989. pap. 21.33 (0-685-26608-7) P-H.

— DOS 5: S.A.V.E Edition, SAVE ed. 144p. (C). 1993. pap. text 14.00 (0-13-045592-X) P-H.

— Information Technology: The Breaking Wave. LC 97-43356. 1998. 33.00 (0-256-21847-1, Irwn Prfssnl) McGraw-Hill Prof.

— Manager's Guide to Symphony: An Illustrated Short Course. 160p. 1985. pap. 18.95 (0-13-550047-8) P-H.

— Microcomputer Resource Manual: Software & Applications - IBM Edition. (Illus.). 432p. (C). 1986. 11.95 (0-317-45978-3) P-H.

— Microsoft Access 2.0 by PicTorial. LC 95-13810. (Pictorial Ser.). 240p. (C). 1995. pap. text 37.33 (0-13-376849-X) P-H.

— Microsoft Excel for Windows 95 (Version 7.0) by PicTorial. LC 96-4038. (Pictorial Ser.). 320p. (C). 1996. spiral bd. 37.33 (0-13-238379-9) P-H.

— Microsoft Word 5.5 Procedures Manual. 287p. 1991. pap. text 19.00 (0-13-581364-6, 220302) P-H.

— Microsoft Word for Windows 95 (Version 7.0) by PicTorial. (Pictorial Ser.). 352p. (C). 1996. spiral bd. 37.33 (0-13-238387-X) P-H.

— Microsoft Word 4 Procedures Manual. LC 88-12106. 1988. pap. 18.00 (0-13-964305-2) P-H.

— Windows 95 by Pictorial. 192p. 1995. spiral bd. 37.33 (0-13-456674-2) P-H.

Curtin, Dennis P. & Osgood, William R. Preparing Your Business Budget with SYMPHONY. (Illus.). 160p. 1985. pap. 34.95 (0-13-698804-0) P-H.

Curtin, Dennis P., jt. auth. see Osgood, William R.

Curtin, Dennis P., jt. auth. see Swabey, Daphne E.

Curtin, Hugh D., jt. ed. see Som, Peter M.

Curtin, Jack. Justice Demands: Criminal Justice Literature on Political Economy as a Paradigm (Pak) 278p. (C). 1997. 37.44 (0-7872-1860-X) Kendall-Hunt.

— Pak: Class Justice Essays. 272p. (C). 1995. 31.19 (0-7872-1302-0) Kendall-Hunt.

Curtin, James J. Elvis: Unknown Stories Behind the Legend. LC 98-24509. (Illus.). 288p. 1998. pap. 19.95 (1-58029-102-3, Celebrity Bks) Hambleton-Hill.

Curtin, Jennifer. Women & Trade Unions: A Comparative Perspective. LC 99-72328. 200p. 1999. 61.95 (1-84014-513-7, Pub. by Ashgate Pub) Ashgate Pub Co.

Curtin, Jeremiah. Creation Myths of Primitive America. 1980. 34.95 (0-405-13697-8, 1710) Ayer.

— Creation Myths of Primitive America. (Works of Jeremiah Curtin). 1990. reprint ed. lib. bdg. 79.00 (0-7812-2501-9) Rprt Serv.

— Fairy Tales of Eastern Europe. (Works of Jeremiah Curtin). 1990. reprint ed. lib. bdg. 79.00 (0-7812-2506-X) Rprt Serv.

— Hero Tales of Ireland. LC 99-45379. 610p. 1999. pap. text 14.95 (0-486-40909-0) Dover.

— Hero Tales of Ireland. (Works of Jeremiah Curtin). 1990. reprint ed. lib. bdg. 79.00 (0-7812-2499-3) Rprt Serv.

— Introduction to Seneca Fiction, Legends & Myths. (Works of Jeremiah Curtin). 1990. reprint ed. lib. bdg. 79.00 (0-7812-2507-8) Rprt Serv.

***Curtin, Jeremiah.** Irish Tales of Fairies & the Ghost World. 128p. 2000. pap. 6.95 (0-486-41139-7) Dover.

Curtin, Jeremiah. A Journey in Southern Siberia. (Works of Jeremiah Curtin). 1990. reprint ed. lib. bdg. 79.00 (0-7812-2502-7) Rprt Serv.

— A Journey in Southern Siberia: The Mongols, Their Religion & Their Myths. LC 77-115526. (Russia Observed Ser.). (Illus.). 1971. reprint ed. 26.95 (0-405-03079-7) Ayer.

— The Mongols: A History. (Works of Jeremiah Curtin). 1990. reprint ed. lib. bdg. 79.00 (0-685-44782-0) Rprt Serv.

— The Mongols in Russia. (Works of Jeremiah Curtin). 1990. reprint ed. lib. bdg. 79.00 (0-685-44781-2) Rprt Serv.

— Myths & Folk: Tales of the Russians, Western Slavs & Magyars. LC 99-45507. 584p. 2000. pap. 16.95 (0-486-40905-8) Dover.

— Myths & Folk-Tales of Ireland. LC 69-18206. 245p. 1975. reprint ed. pap. 6.95 (0-486-22430-9) Dover.

— Myths & Folk-Tales of the Russians, Western Slavs & Magyars. LC 74-160611. 1972. reprint ed. 34.95 (0-405-08414-5, Pub. by Blom Pubns) Ayer.

— Myths & Folk-Tales of the Russians, Western Slavs & Magyars. (Works of Jeremiah Curtin). 1990. reprint ed. lib. bdg. 79.00 (0-685-44766-9) Rprt Serv.

— Myths & Folklore of Ireland. 352p. 1995. 9.99 (0-517-18570-9) Wings Bks.

— Myths & Folklore of Ireland. (Works of Jeremiah Curtin). 1990. reprint ed. lib. bdg. 79.00 (0-685-44780-4) Rprt Serv.

— Myths of the Modocs. (Works of Jeremiah Curtin). 1990. reprint ed. lib. bdg. 79.00 (0-685-44783-9) Rprt Serv.

— Myths of the Modocs: Indian Legends from the Northwest. LC 74-170711. 1972. reprint ed. 23.95 (0-405-08415-3, Pub. by Blom Pubns) Ayer.

— Seneca Indian Myths. (Works of Jeremiah Curtin). 1990. reprint ed. lib. bdg. 79.00 (0-685-44787-1) Rprt Serv.

— Tales of the Fairies & of the Ghost-World. LC 75-152760. 1972. reprint ed. 23.95 (0-405-08416-1, Pub. by Blom Pubns) Ayer.

— Tales of the Fairies & of the Ghost-World. (Works of Jeremiah Curtin). 1990. reprint ed. lib. bdg. 79.00 (0-7812-2500-0) Rprt Serv.

— Wonder Tales from Russia. (Works of Jeremiah Curtin). 1990. reprint ed. lib. bdg. 90.00 (0-7812-2508-6) Rprt Serv.

— The Works of Jeremiah Curtin. 1990. reprint ed. lib. bdg. 63.00 (0-685-27759-3) Rprt Serv.

Curtin, Jeremiah, jt. ed. see Sapir, Edward.

Curtin, Jeremiah, tr. see Sienkiewicz, Henryk.

Curtin, Jim. Christmas with Elvis. LC 98-27720. 1999. 29.95 (1-58029-104-X, Celebrity Bks) Hambleton-Hill.

— Elvis, the Early Years: A 2001 Fact Odyssey. LC 99-33781. 1999. pap. 19.95 (1-58029-106-6, Celebrity Bks) Hambleton-Hill.

***Curtin, Jim.** Ultimate Elvis: The Fifties. (Illus.). 192p. 2000. 24.95 (0-7894-5849-7) DK Pub Inc.

Curtin, Jim. Unseen Elvis Easles. 1992. write for info. (0-8212-1990-1) Little.

Curtin, John. Pak: Equity & the Underclass in Criminal Justice. 226p. (C). 1997. pap. text 39.95 (0-7872-3404-4, 41340401) Kendall-Hunt.

Curtin, John, selected by. Bob Dylan: Greatest Hits for Easy Guitar. (Illus.). 56p. pap. 14.95 (0-8256-1416-3, AM86112) Music Sales.

Curtin, John P., jt. auth. see Morrow, C. Paul.

Curtin, Katie. Women in China. LC 74-14166. 95p. 1975. pap. 9.95 (0-87348-405-3); lib. bdg. 30.00 (0-87348-404-5) Pathfinder NY.

Curtin, L. S. By the Prophet of the Earth: Ethnobotany of the Pima. LC 83-24334. (Illus.). 156p. 1984. reprint ed. pap. 10.95 (0-8165-0854-2) U of Ariz Pr.

— Healing Herbs of the Upper Rio Grand: Traditional Medicine of the Southwest. rev. ed. Moore, Michael, ed. & intro. by. (Illus.). 248p. 1997. pap. text 14.95 (1-889921-01-7) Western Edge Pr.

C

An Asterisk (*) at the beginning of an entry indicates that the title is appearing for the first time.

Curtin, Lawrence & Bernardo, Karen. The History of Sweepstakes. 182p. (Orig.). Date not set. pap. 9.95 (*0-9658401-4-X*, 777) Sweepstakes News.

***Curtin, Leah.** Sunflowers in the Sand: Stories from Children of War. LC 99-32170. 2000. 39.95 (*1-56833-141-X*) Madison Bks UPA.

Curtin, Leonora S. Healing Herbs of the Upper Curtin. (Illus.). 281p. 1976. 25.95 (*0-405-09499-X*) Arno Press.

Curtin, Mark J., jt. auth. see Chang, Richard Y.

***Curtin, Mary Ellen.** Black Prisoners & Their World, Alabama, 1865-1900. LC 00-28214. 352p. 2000. 59.50 (*0-8139-1981-9*); pap. 19.50 (*0-8139-1984-3*) U Pr of Va.

Curtin, Mary L., jt. auth. see Grossman, Andrea.

Curtin, Michael. Redeeming the Wasteland: Television Documentary & Cold War Politics. LC 95-12436. (Communications, Media & Culture Ser.). (Illus.). 350p. (C). 1995. text 52.00 (*0-8135-2221-8*); pap. text 18.95 (*0-8135-2222-6*) Rutgers U Pr.

— Revolution Wasn't Televised. 320p. (C). 1997. 75.00 (*0-415-91121-4*) Routledge.

Curtin, Michael F. & Bell, Julia B. The Ohio Politics Almanac. LC 95-37710. (Illus.). 216p. (C). 1996. pap. 16.00 (*0-87338-540-3*) Kent St U Pr.

Curtin, Michael J. & Curtin, Ralph D. The False Hope. 405p. (Orig.). 1999. pap. 12.50 (*1-892614-17-0*, BWP-FH) Briarwood VA.

Curtin, Nancy J. The United Irishmen: Popular Politics in Ulster & Dublin 1791-1798. 328p. 1994. 59.00 (*0-19-820322-5*) OUP.

— The United Irishmen: Popular Politics in Ulster & Dublin, 1791-1798. (Illus.). 328p. 1998. reprint ed. pap. text 35.00 (*0-19-820736-0*) OUP.

Curtin, P. D. African History Edition. 2nd ed. LC 93-47290. 546p. (C). 1995. pap. 51.00 (*0-582-05070-7*) Addison-Wesley.

Curtin, Paul J. Tumbleweeds: A Therapist's Guide to Treatment of ACOAs. 90p. (Orig.). 1985. pap. 6.95 (*0-934391-03-3*) Quotidian.

***Curtin, Philip D.** The World & the West: The European Challenge & the Overseas Response in the Age of Empire. (Illus.). 304p. 2000. 27.95 (*0-521-77135-8*) Cambridge U Pr.

***Curtin, Philip D., et al.** Discovering the Chesapeake: The History of an Ecosystem. LC 00-42405. 2001. pap. write for info. (*0-8018-6468-2*) Johns Hopkins.

Curtin, Philip De Armond. Atlantic Slave Trade: A Census. 358p. 1972. pap. 19.95 (*0-299-05404-7*) U of Wis Pr.

— Cross-Cultural Trade in World History. LC 83-23202. (Cambridge Studies in Comparative World History). 316p. 1984. pap. text 19.95 (*0-521-26931-8*) Cambridge U Pr.

— Death by Migration: Europe's Encounter with the Tropical World in the Nineteenth Century. (Illus.). 271p. (C). 1990. pap. text 18.95 (*0-521-38922-4*) Cambridge U Pr.

— Disease & Empire: Military Medicine in the Conquest of Africa. LC 98-22027. (Illus.). 272p. (C). 1998. text 64.95 (*0-521-59169-4*); pap. text 19.95 (*0-521-59835-4*) Cambridge U Pr.

— Economic Change in Precolonial Africa: Senegambia in the Era of the Slave Trade. LC 74-5899. (Illus.). 424p. reprint ed. pap. 131.50 (*0-7837-1655-9*, 204195300001) Bks Demand.

— Economic Change in Precolonial Africa: Supplementary Evidence. LC 74-5899. 163p. reprint ed. pap. 50.60 (*0-7837-1656-7*, 204195300002) Bks Demand.

— The Image of Africa: British Ideas & Action, 1780-1850. LC 64-10922. 558p. reprint ed. pap. 173.00 (*0-8357-6772-8*, 203544700095) Bks Demand.

— The Rise & Fall of the Plantation Complex: Essays in Atlantic History. 2nd ed. LC 97-22511. (Studies in Comparative World History). (Illus.). 236p. (C). 1998. text 54.95 (*0-521-62076-7*); pap. text 17.95 (*0-521-62943-8*) Cambridge U Pr.

— The Tropical Atlantic in the Age of the Slave Trade. Adas, Michael, ed. LC 91-72611. (Essays on Global & Comparative History Ser.). 47p. 1991. pap. 6.00 (*0-87229-048-4*) Am Hist Assn.

— Two Jamaicas: The Role of Ideas in a Tropical Colony, 1830-1865. LC 69-10082. (Illus.). 270p. 1968. reprint ed. lib. bdg. 55.00 (*0-8371-0055-0*, CUTJ, Greenwood Pr) Greenwood.

— Why People Move: Migration in African History. unabridged ed. LC 95-77712. (Charles Edmondson Historical Lectures). 50p. (Orig.). 1995. pap. 5.95 (*0-918954-61-4*) Baylor Univ Pr.

Curtin, Philip De Armond, ed. Africa & the West: Intellectual Responses to European Culture. LC 77-176409. 272p. 1974. pap. 17.95 (*0-299-06124-8*) U of Wis Pr.

— Africa Remembered: Narratives by West Africans from the Era of the Slave Trade. (Illus.). 361p. (C). 1997. reprint ed. pap. text 17.95 (*0-88133-948-2*) Waveland Pr.

Curtin, Philip De Armond, et al, eds. African History. 612p. (C). 1989. pap. text 29.66 (*0-582-64663-4*, 74644) Longman.

Curtin, Philip De Armond & Knight, Franklin. The Two Jamaicas: The Role of Ideas in a Tropical Colony, 1830-1865. LC 98-15428. 296p. Date not set. reprint ed. pap. text 22.95 (*1-55876-190-X*) Wiener Pubs Inc.

Curtin, Philip De Armond, et al. African History. 2nd ed. LC 93-47290. (C). 1995. text 99.75 (*0-582-05071-5*, 74644, Pub. by Addison-Wesley) Longman.

Curtin, Philip De Armond, jt. auth. see Bohannan, Paul.

Curtin, Ralph D., jt. auth. see Curtin, Michael J.

Curtin, Robert E., ed. Settlin In: The Relocation Magazine for Massachusetts. 1995. per. 19.98 (*0-916247-15-5*) Suburban MA.

Curtin, Sharon. Mustang. LC 96-83438. (Illus.). 192p. 1996. 40.00 (*0-9649915-1-9*) Rufus Pubns Inc.

Curtin, Sharon, jt. auth. see Gordon, James.

Curtin, Thomas E., jt. auth. see Vossen, Ruediger.

***Curtin, Tom.** Managing Green Issues. LC 00-42078. 2000. write for info. (*0-312-23716-2*) St Martin.

Curtin, W. G., et al. Design of Reinforced & Prestressed Masonry. 256p. 1988. 95.00 (*0-7277-1314-0*, Pub. by T Telford) RCH.

— Structural Foundation Designer's Manual. LC 93-12682. 377p. 1997. pap. 79.95 (*0-632-04215-X*, TA775) Blackwell Sci.

Curtin, William M., ed. see Cather, Willa.

Curtis. Chimney & Stove Cleaning. 1983. pap. 2.95 (*0-88266-188-4*, Storey Pub) Storey Bks.

— Michael Graves. pap. text 47.00 (*0-471-98592-9*) Wiley.

Curtis. Prostaglandins & Eicosanoids. text. write for info. (*0-471-48984-0*) Wiley.

Curtis. Sensible Sex. 9.95 (*1-56684-236-0*) Evans Bk Dist.

***Curtis.** Tell Me a Boy Story. 2000. 16.95 (*0-06-029020-X*); pap. 6.95 (*0-06-443698-5*); lib. bdg. 16.89 (*0-06-029021-8*) HarpC.

— Tell Me a Girl Story. 2000. 16.95 (*0-06-029018-8*); pap. 6.95 (*0-06-443697-7*); lib. bdg. 16.89 (*0-06-029019-6*) HarpC.

Curtis. Tool Design for Manufacturing. 2nd ed. 500p. (C). 2001. 64.00 (*0-13-674623-3*, Macmillan Coll) P-H.

— When I Was Little. (Illus.). 32p. (J). (ps-3). 2000. 15.95 incl. audio (*0-06-028258-4*) HarpC.

Curtis & Barnes. Invitation to Biology. 5th ed. 862p. 1994. text 57.00 (*0-87901-679-5*) Worth.

— Invitation to Biology. 5th ed. 496p. 1994. pap. text, student ed. 13.60 (*0-87901-685-X*) Worth.

— Invitation to Biology, Pt. 1, Secs 1-4, 8. 5th ed. 584p. 1994. pap. text 40.80 (*0-87901-734-1*) Worth.

— Invitation to Biology, Pt. 2, Secs. 5-7. 5th ed. 474p. 1994. pap. text 39.60 (*0-87901-735-X*) Worth.

Curtis & Fox. Biology. 5th ed. 1991. student ed. 68.80 (*0-87901-542-X*) Worth.

Curtis, et al. Christmas One Hundred Years Ago. (Historical Ser.). (Illus.). 1976. pap. 3.50 (*0-89540-036-7*, SB-036) Sun Pub.

Curtis, jt. auth. see Wilkins.

Curtis & Barnes Staff. Curtis & Barnes Pt. 1: Invitation to Biology. 5th ed. 288p. 1994. pap. text, student ed. 9.00 (*0-87901-743-0*) Worth.

Curtis, A. Cecil, tr. see Mann, Thomas.

Curtis, A. Kenneth & Snyder, Ann T. Candle in the Dark Leader's Guide. (Illus.). 64p. Date not set. pap. text, teacher ed. 9.99 (*1-56364-314-6*) Christian Hist.

Curtis, A. Kenneth & Thiede, Carsten P. From Christ to Constantine: The Trial & Testimony of the Early Church. (Illus.). 96p. (C). 1991. pap. 14.99 (*1-56364-200-X*) Christian Hist.

Curtis, A. Kenneth, et al. The 100 Most Important Events in Christian History. LC 97-35333. 208p. 1998. pap. 11.99 (*0-8007-5644-4*, Dates With Dest) Revell.

Curtis, Adrian. Joshua. (Old Testament Guides Ser.: Vol. 7). 89p. 1994. pap. 12.50 (*1-85075-706-2*, Pub. by Sheffield Acad) CUP Services.

— Ugarit (Ras Shamra) LC 86-102759. (Cities of the Biblical World Ser.). (Illus.). 125p. reprint ed. pap. 38.80 (*0-7837-5555-4*, 204533000005) Bks Demand.

Curtis, Alan R. Practical Math for Business, 4 vols. 4th ed. (C). 1987. trans. 101.56 (*0-395-42401-1*) HM.

Curtis, Alice P. Every Cat Should Have a Home. (Illus.). 60p. (Orig.). (J). 1992. pap. write for info. (*0-9612126-0-8*) A P Walmsley.

Curtis, Alice T. A Little Maid of Maryland. LC 95-49353. (Little Maid Ser.). (Illus.). 192p. (J). (gr. 3-8). 1996. reprint ed. pap. 9.95 (*1-55709-327-X*) Applewood.

— A Little Maid of Massachusetts Bay Colony. LC 96-28380. (Little Maid Ser.). (Illus.). 192p. (J). (gr. 3-8). 1996. reprint ed. pap. 9.95 (*1-55709-329-6*) Applewood.

— A Little Maid of Narragansett Bay. LC 97-53230. (Little Maid Ser.). (Illus.). 210p. (J). (gr. 3-8). 1998. reprint ed. pap. 9.95 (*1-55709-334-2*) Applewood.

— A Little Maid of Old Connecticut. LC 96-28381. (Little Maid Ser.). (Illus.). 192p. (J). (gr. 3-8). 1998. reprint ed. pap. 9.95 (*1-55709-328-8*) Applewood.

— A Little Maid of Old New York. (Little Maid Ser.). (Illus.). 192p. (J). (gr. 3-8). 1996. reprint ed. pap. 9.95 (*1-55709-326-1*) Applewood.

— A Little Maid of Old Philadelphia. (Little Maid Ser.). (Illus.). 192p. (J). (gr. 3-8). 1998. reprint ed. pap. 9.95 (*1-55709-325-3*) Applewood.

— A Little Maid of Provincetown. LC 97-3987. (Little Maid Ser.). (Illus.). 224p. (J). (gr. 3-8). 1997. reprint ed. pap. 9.95 (*1-55709-331-8*) Applewood.

— A Little Maid of Ticonderoga. LC 96-28379. (Little Maid Ser.). (Illus.). 192p. (J). (gr. 3-8). 1996. reprint ed. pap. 9.95 (*1-55709-330-X*) Applewood.

— A Little Maid of Virginia. LC 97-53240. (Little Maid Ser.). (Illus.). 192p. (J). (gr. 3-8). 1998. reprint ed. pap. 9.95 (*1-55709-333-4*) Applewood.

***Curtis, Alice Turner.** Little Maid of Old Maine. LC 99-42220. 228p. (gr. 4-7). 1999. pap. 9.95 (*1-55709-336-9*, Pub. by Applewood) Consort Bk Sales.

— Yankee Girl at Fort Sumter. LC 98-55145. (Yankee Girl Ser.). 1999. pap. text 9.95 (*1-55709-525-6*) Applewood.

Curtis, Alice Turner. A Yankee Girl at Gettysburg. LC 98-56022. 204p. (J). (gr. 4-7). 1999. 9.95 (*1-55709-526-4*, Pub. by Applewood) Consort Bk Sales.

***Curtis, Alice Turner.** Yankee Girl at Shiloh. (Yankee Girl Ser.). (Illus.). 192p. (J). (gr. 4-7). 2000. pap. 9.95 (*1-55709-527-2*) Applewood.

Curtis, Alva. A Synopsis of Lectures on Medical Science. 27p. 1996. reprint ed. spiral bd. 8.00 (*0-7873-0232-5*) Hlth Research.

Curtis, Anita. Animal Wisdom: Communications with Animals. (Illus.). 169p. (Orig.). 1996. pap. 11.95 (*0-9653654-0-9*) Animal Communs.

— How to Hear the Animals. 88p. 1998. pap. 18.00 (*0-9653654-1-7*) Animal Communs.

***Curtis, Annabelle.** Butterflies on Display: To Cut Out & Glue Together. (Illus.). 1999. pap. 8.95 (*1-899618-27-9*, Pub. by Tarquin Pubns) Parkwest Pubns.

Curtis, Annabelle. Paper Animals. (Illus.). 36p. (Orig.). 1994. pap. 6.95 (*0-906212-94-4*, Pub. by Tarquin Pubns) Parkwest Pubns.

— Paper Fish. 1997. pap. 8.95 (*1-899618-20-1*, Pub by Tarquin Pubns) Parkwest Pubns.

— Paper People. (Illus.). 32p. (Orig.). (J). (gr. 3-4). 1991. pap. 6.95 (*0-906212-61-8*, Pub. by Tarquin Pubns) Parkwest Pubns.

Curtis, Anthony. Lit Ed. LC 99-218128. 356p. 1998. 45.00 (*1-85754-149-9*, Pub. by Carcanet Pr) Paul & Co Pubs.

— Lyle: What's It Worth? (Illus.). 1995. pap. 15.95 (*0-399-51937-8*, Perigee Bks) Berkley Pub.

***Curtis, Anthony.** Lyle: 1001 More Antiques Worth a Fortune. LC 99-12453. 512p. 1999. pap. 15.95 (*0-399-52507-6*, Perigee Bks) Berkley Pub.

Curtis, Anthony. Lyle Cashing in on Collecting Americana. (Illus.). 512p. (Orig.). 1993. pap. 15.95 (*0-399-51809-6*, Perigee Bks) Berkley Pub.

— Lyle Film & Rock n' Roll Collectibles. (Illus.). 512p. (Orig.). 1996. pap. 14.95 (*0-399-52205-0*, Perigee Bks) Berkley Pub.

— The Lyle Official Antiques Review, 1995. 672p. (Orig.). 1994. pap. 13.95 (*0-399-52146-1*, Perigee Bks) Berkley Pub.

— The Lyle Official Antiques Review, 1996. (Illus.). 672p. (Orig.). 1995. pap. 13.95 (*0-399-52164-X*, Perigee Bks) Berkley Pub.

— The Lyle Official Antiques Review, 1997. (Illus.). 672p. (Orig.). 1996. pap. 13.95 (*0-399-52246-8*, Perigee Bks) Berkley Pub.

***Curtis, Anthony.** Lyle Official Antiques Review 2000. 1999. pap. 16.95 (*0-399-52545-9*, Perigee Bks) Berkley Pub.

Curtis, Anthony. Lyle Official Antiques Review 1999. (Illus.). 672p. 1998. pap. 15.95 (*0-399-52450-9*, Perigee Bks) Berkley Pub.

— Lyle Price Guide to American Furniture. LC 98-9793. 512p. 1998. pap. 15.95 (*0-399-52410-X*, Perigee Bks) Berkley Pub.

— Lyle Price Guide to China. LC 97-12649. 512p. 1997. pap. 15.95 (*0-399-52310-3*, Perigee Bks) Berkley Pub.

***Curtis, Anthony.** Lyle Price Guide to Uncommon Antiques & Oddities. LC 00-27104. 512p. 2000. pap. 16.95 (*0-399-52606-4*, Perigee Bks) Berkley Pub.

Curtis, Anthony. Lyle's Official Antiques Review, 1998. rev. ed. (Illus.). 672p. 1997. pap. 14.95 (*0-399-52352-9*, Perigee Bks) Berkley Pub.

— Somerset Maugham. LC 77-6618. 216p. 1977. write for info. (*0-02-529280-3*) Glencoe.

— Somerset Maugham. LC 78-307701. 216 p. 1977. 6.50 (*0-297-77367-4*) Weidenfeld & Nicolson.

Curtis, Anthony, compiled by. Lyle: There's a Fortune in Your Attic. (Illus.). 512p. (Orig.). 1991. pap. 14.95 (*0-399-51677-8*, Perigee Bks) Berkley Pub.

— Lyle Antique Dealers Pocket Guide. (Illus.). 256p. (Orig.). 1994. pap. 10.95 (*0-399-51852-5*, Perigee Bks) Berkley Pub.

— The Lyle Price Guide to Collectibles & Memorabilia. (Illus.). 512p. 1988. pap. 13.00 (*0-399-51445-7*, Perigee Bks) Berkley Pub.

— The Lyle Price Guide to Collectibles & Memorabilia, No. 2. (Illus.). 512p. 1990. pap. 13.00 (*0-399-51515-1*, Perigee Bks) Berkley Pub.

— The Lyle Price Guide to Collectibles & Memorabilia, No. 3. (Illus.). 512p. 1994. pap. 15.95 (*0-399-51855-X*, Perigee Bks) Berkley Pub.

— Lyle's One Thousand One Antiques Worth a Fortune: Which Not a Lot of People Know About. (Illus.). 512p. (Orig.). 1992. pap. 14.95 (*0-399-51757-X*, Perigee Bks) Berkley Pub.

Curtis, Anthony & Whitehead, John, eds. W. Somerset Maugham. 480p. 1987. 69.50 (*0-7100-9640-2*, 96402, Routledge Thoemms) Routledge.

— W. Somerset Maugham. (Critical Heritage Ser.). 488p. (C). 1997. 140.00 (*0-415-15925-3*) Routledge.

Curtis, Anthony, ed. & intro. see James, Henry.

***Curtis, Anthony J.** Health Psychology. LC 99-32420. (Modular Psychology Ser.). 1999. pap. write for info. (*0-415-19273-0*) Routledge.

Curtis, Anthony R. Monitoring NASA Communications. 100p. 1992. 14.95 (*0-936653-30-2*) Tiare Pubns.

— The Outer Space Frequency Directory. 80p. 1994. pap. 17.95 (*0-936653-49-3*) Tiare Pubns.

— Space Satellite Handbook. 3rd ed. LC 93-37563. 346p. 1994. 39.00 (*0-88415-192-1*, 5642) Gulf Pub.

Curtis, Anthony R., ed. Space Almanac. 2nd ed. 746p. 1992. 36.95 (*0-88415-039-9*, 5039) Gulf Pub.

— Space Almanac. 2nd ed. (Illus.). 746p. 1992. pap. 24.95 (*0-88415-030-5*, 5030) Gulf Pub.

Curtis, Arthur F. Treatise on the Law of Arson. lxviii, 689p. 1936. 55.00 (*0-89941-371-4*, 500290) W S Hein.

***Curtis, Arthur-Walter J., Sr.** The Master Amateurs: The Story of Golf's Only Amateurs Who Have Won Both the United States Open & United States Amateur. (Illus.). 160p. 2000. 24.95 (*0-9659419-1-4*) Curtis Pub.

Curtis, Audrey. A Curriculum for the Pre-School Child: Learning to Learn. 2nd ed. LC 97-14150. 224p. (C). 1997. pap. 17.99 (*0-415-13976-7*) Routledge.

Curtis, Barbara. Ready, Set Read: A Start-to-Finish Reading Program Any Parent Can Use. LC 98-12865. 178p. 1998. pap. 9.99 (*0-8054-0167-9*) Broadman.

Curtis, Barry, jt. auth. see Curtis, Susan.

Curtis, Benjamin R. Jurisdictions, Practice & Peculiar Jurisprudence of the Courts of the United States. Curtis, George T., ed. & notes by. xviii, 298p. 1989. reprint ed. 42.50 (*0-8377-2015-X*, Rothman) W S Hein.

— A Memoir of Benjamin Robbins Curtis, 2 vols. LC 77-75298. (American Scene Ser.). 1970. reprint ed. 115.00 (*0-306-71267-9*) Da Capo.

Curtis, Bette K. Life with Labradors. (Illus.). 152p. 1995. 30.00 (*0-614-04545-2*) Donald R Hoflin.

Curtis, Bill. Blackpool Tower. 144p. 1994. 30.00 (*0-86138-064-9*, Pub. by T Dalton); pap. 21.00 (*0-86138-068-1*, Pub. by T Dalton) St Mut.

— Fleetwood: A Town Is Born. 128p. 1994. 30.00 (*0-86138-043-6*, Pub. by T Dalton); pap. 30.00 (*0-86138-052-5*, Pub. by T Dalton) St Mut.

Curtis, Brent. Guilt. (Institute of Biblical Counseling Discussion Guides Ser.). 72p. (Orig.). 1992. pap. 5.00 (*0-89109-692-2*) NavPress.

Curtis, Brent & Eldredge, John. The Sacred Romance: Drawing Closer to the Heart of God. 228p. 1997. pap. 9.97 (*0-7852-7342-5*, J Thoma Bks) Nelson.

Curtis, Brian. Life Story of the Fish. 2nd ed. 1961. pap. 6.95 (*0-486-20929-6*) Dover.

Curtis, Brian A. Neurosciences: The Basics. LC 90-5577. 172p. 1990. text 26.00 (*0-8121-1309-8*) Lppncott W & W.

***Curtis, Bruce.** Beginning Golf. (Illus.). 2000. 19.95 (*0-8069-4970-8*) Sterling.

Curtis, Bruce. True Government by Choice Men? Inspection, Education, & State Formation in Canada West. (State & Economic Life Ser.: No. 17). 320p. (Orig.). 1992. text 60.00 (*0-8020-5967-8*); pap. text 19.95 (*0-8020-6894-4*) U of Toronto Pr.

Curtis Bullard, Laura J. Now-a-Days. LC 76-48580. 309p. 1980. reprint ed. pap. 8.95 (*0-89101-042-4*) U Maine Pr.

Curtis, C. F., et al, contrib. by. Statistical Mechanics: Deformation, Ultrasonic & Spectroscopy. LC 96-159643. (Advances in Polymer Science Ser.: Vol. 125). (Illus.). viii, 206p. 1996. 133.00 (*3-540-60483-9*) Spr-Verlag.

Curtis, C. F., ed. Appropriate Technology in Vector Control. 256p. 1989. lib. bdg. 189.95 (*0-8493-4755-6*, RA639) CRC Pr.

Curtis, C. H. The Missouri U. S. 66 Tour Book. LC 94-94615. 274p. 1994. pap. 19.95 (*0-9633863-4-4*) Curtis Ent.

— Why'd They Name It That? A Look at Some Peculiar Missouri Towns. LC 92-90469. 1992. pap. 14.95 (*0-9633863-3-6*) Curtis Ent.

Curtis, C. Michael. God: Stories. LC 98-42585. 416p. 1998. 30.00 (*0-395-92677-7*) HM.

Curtis, C. Michael, ed. God: Stories. LC 98-42585. 416p. 1998. pap. 14.00 (*0-395-92971-7*) HM.

Curtis, C. S. Corbett, see Corbett Curtis, C. S.

Curtis, C. W. Linear Algebra: An Introductory Approach. (Undergraduate Texts in Mathematics Ser.). (Illus.). 340p. 1997. 39.95 (*0-387-90992-3*) Spr-Verlag.

Curtis, Caroline. Stories of Life in Old Hawai'i. LC 98-207935. Orig. Title: Life in Old Hawaii. (Illus.). 304p. (YA). (gr. 7-12). 1997. pap. 16.95 (*0-87336-046-X*) Kamehameha Schools.

Curtis, Caroline, jt. auth. see Puku'i, Mary K.

Curtis, Caroline, jt. auth. see Pukui, Mary K.

Curtis, Carolyn. A Man for All Nations: The Story of Clyde & Ruth Taylor. 30p. 1998. pap. 3.99 (*0-87509-776-6*) Chr Pubns.

— A Man for All Nations: The Story of Clyde & Ruth Taylor. Vol. 20. (Illus.). 195p. (gr. 4-7). 1998. pap. 9.99 (*0-87509-768-5*) Chr Pubns.

***Curtis, Carolyn A.** Synthesis: Computer Parented...with Rights & Equality for All. LC 99-96093. (C). 2000. 14.99 (*0-9674461-0-4*) Reality Pubng.

Curtis, Catherine B., jt. auth. see Curtis, Donald B.

Curtis, Chara M. All I See Is Part of Me. rev. ed. (Illus.). 48p. (J). (ps up). 1994. 15.95 (*0-935699-07-4*) Illum Arts.

All I See is Part of Me is a beautifully illustrated adventure of self-discovery. On his enchanting inner journey, a child finds that he is not just a small body in a huge unfriendly world. Sister Star tells him, "You have a body that is true. But look at what's inside of you! Your body is just a little part of the light that shines within your heart." Although classified as a children's book, this international best seller speaks directly to people of all ages. We are all one. Winner of a 1996 Body Mind Spirit Magazine Award of Excellence. "This warm, gentle, tender, trusting book is just what the world needs." Gerald G. Jampolsky, M.D. Author. *Publisher Paid Annotation.*

–Fun Is a Feeling. (Illus.). 32p. (J). (ps up). 1992. 15.95 (*0-935699-04-X*) Illum Arts.

Fun Is a Feeling teaches children that "Fun isn't something or somewhere or who: it's a feeling of joy that lives inside of you!" This brilliantly illustrated rhyming book encourages readers to discover the fun hidden in all of life's experiences. "Feel the kiss of a raindrop. See the wink of a star - Magic reminders of how loved you are." "The artwork is fantastic. The message of treasuring our feelings is outstanding & uplifting. This book is a must for children."-Gerald G. Jampolsky, M.D., author. "This vibrant text delights in the challenge of making fun the 'path' in life rather than the destination."-NAPRA Trade Journal. "here's a book about new ways to have fun.

Fun likes to hide, so look for it everywhere."-The Seattle Times. The child's imagination is challenged to view everyday events (including chores) in a creative, magical way. In the end, each reader is left with a secret smile -- knowing "fun can be found wherever you go." "The artwork is fantastic. The message of treasuring our feelings is outstanding & uplifting. This book is a 'must' for children."-- Gerald G. Jampolosky, M.D., author. "This vibrant text delights in the challenge of making fun the 'path' in life rather than the destination."--NAPRA Trade Journal. "here's book about new ways to have fun. Fun likes to hide, so look for it everywhere."-- The Seattle Times. *Publisher Paid Annotation.*

— Fun Is a Feeling. LC 91-41875. (Illus.). 32p. (J). (ps up). 1998. 15.95 (*0-935699-13-9*) Illum Arts.

–How Far to Heaven? LC 93-1918. (Illus.). 28p. (J). (ps up). 1993. 15.95 (*0-935699-06-6*) Illum Arts. How Far to Heaven is the tender story of Nanna & her granddaughter. The child discovers her grandmother "...having a nice chat with your grandpa." She protests, "You said he's in heaven." When the little girl asks, "Is heaven very far?" Nanna leads her out the back gate, "Let's find out just how far it is." They discover that heaven can be seen, heard, smelled & felt in the glories of nature. Heaven is wherever you find it. Alfred Currier's exquisite oil paintings help to make this a lovely healing book for those who have lost a loved one. *Publisher Paid Annotation.*

— No One Walks on My Father's Moon. LC 95-62447. (Illus.). 32p. (J). (gr. 2 up). 1996. lib. bdg. 16.95 (*0-9649454-1-X*) Voyage Pubng.

Curtis, Charles, et al. Perspectives on God: Sociological, Theological & Philosophical. LC 78-62943. 1978. pap. text 24.00 (*0-8191-0605-4*) U Pr of Amer.

Curtis, Charles H. & Gibson, W. The Book of Topiary. LC 84-50509. (Illus.). 80p. 1986. reprint ed. pap. 8.95 (*0-8048-1491-0*) Tuttle Pubng.

Curtis, Charles W. Pioneers of Representation Theory: Frobenius, Burnside, Schur & Brauer. LC 99-14983. (History of Mathematics Ser.). 287p. 1999. 49.00 (*0-8218-9002-6*) Am Math.

Curtis, Charles W. & Reiner, Irving. Methods of Representation Theory: With Applications to Finite Groups & Orders, Vol. 1. 848p. 1990. pap. 104.95 (*0-471-52367-4*) Wiley.

— Methods of Representation Theory Vol. 2: With Applications to Finite Groups & Orders, Vol. 2. LC 81-7416. (Pure & Applied Mathematics: A Wiley-Interscience Series of Texts, Monographs & Tracts). 951p. 1994. pap. 99.95 (*0-471-06004-6*) Wiley.

Curtis, Chris C. & Smith, Gene P. Systeme Lefaucheux: Continuing the Study of Pinfire Cartrige Arms. 2nd rev. ed. Orig. Title: The Pinfire System. (Illus.). 224p. 2000. 39.95 (*1-882824-19-9*) Graphic Pubs.

Curtis, Christine W., et al. Fundamental Properties of Asphalt-Aggregate Interaction Including Adhesion & Absorption. 603p. (Orig.). (C). 1993. pap. text 20.00 (*0-309-05614-4*, SHRP-A-341) SHRP.

Curtis, Christopher. Ki-Aikido on Maui: A Training Manual. (Illus.). 187p. (Orig.). 1995. pap. 20.00 (*0-9655021-0-4*) MAKS Pub.

Curtis, Christopher Paul. Bud, Not Buddy. LC 99-10614. (Illus.). 245p. (YA). (gr. 4-7). 1999. 15.95 (*0-385-32306-9*) Delacorte.

***Curtis, Christopher Paul.** Bud, Not Buddy. large type ed. LC 00-29913. 276p. (J). (gr. 8-12). 2000. 22.95 (*0-7862-2574-2*) Thorndike Pr.

Curtis, Christopher Paul. The Watsons Go to Birmingham - 1963. LC 95-7091. 224p. (YA). (gr. 4-7). 1995. 15.95 (*0-385-32175-9*, Delacorte Pr Bks) BDD Bks Young Read.

— The Watsons Go to Birmingham - 1963. LC 95-7091. 224p. (J). (gr. 4-10). 1997. pap. 5.50 (*0-440-41412-1*) BDD Bks Young Read.

Curtis, Christopher Paul. The Watsons Go to Birmingham - 1963. 210p. (YA). (gr. 5 up). pap. 5.50 (*0-8072-8336-3*) Listening Lib.

Curtis, Christopher Paul. The Watsons Go to Birmingham - 1963. 15p. (YA). 1998. pap. 15.95 (*1-58303-068-9*) Pthways Pubng.

— The Watsons Go to Birmingham - 1963. (YA). 1997. 10.09 (*0-606-10993-5*, Pub. by Turtleback) Demco.

***Curtis, Christopher Paul.** Watsons Go to Birmingham-1963. 2000. mass mkt. 5.99 (*0-440-22800-X*, LE) Dell.

— The Watsons Go to Birmingham, 1963. LC 00-34400. (Illus.). (J). 2000. write for info. (*0-7862-2741-9*) Thorndike Pr.

***Curtis, Christy, ed.** Destrega: Prima's Official Strategy Guide. LC 98-68558. 96p. 1999. pap. 12.99 (*0-7615-2016-3*, Prima Games) Prima Pub.

Curtis, Clive & Metcalf, Jane. Becoming a Care Supervisor. LC 92-34226. (Skills for Caring Ser.). 1992. pap. text 9.95 (*0-443-04621-2*) Church.

***Curtis, Craig.** Fabulous Hell: A Novel. unabridged ed. LC 99-89537. 256p. 2000. pap. 12.95 (*1-55583-479-5*, Pub. by Alyson Pubns) Consort Bk Sales.

Curtis, D., ed. Air Emission Monitoring & Control Handbook. 500p. 1996. text 204.00 (*1-85617-279-1*) Elsevier.

Curtis, D. Khayman. Gallows Dancing. DeBarr, Toby & DeBarr, Sally, eds. 32p. 1998. pap. write for info. (*1-893409-02-3*) LY Prods.

Curtis, Dan, et al. Business & Professional Communication. 486p. (C). 1996. pap. text, per. 38.95 (*0-7872-2327-1*) Kendall-Hunt.

Curtis, Darwin O. Return & Remembrance. 1995. pap. 6.95 (*0-9646390-7-6*) Wind Word Pr.

Curtis, David. The French Popular Front & the Catholic Discovery of Marx. 250p. 1998. pap. 25.00 (*0-85958-665-0*, Pub. by Univ of Hull Pr) Paul & Co Pubs.

— Learn While You Sleep. 2nd ed. LC 60-15692. 1964. 10.00 (*0-87212-007-4*); pap. 5.95 (*0-87212-008-2*) Libra.

— A Light Touch: Successful Painting in Oils. (Illus.). 128p. 1997. pap. 19.95 (*0-7153-0623-5*, Pub. by D & C Pub) Sterling.

— Teaching Secondary English. LC 92-8564. 1992. 31.95 (*0-335-15758-0*) OpUniv Pr.

Curtis, David, et al. German Study-Aid. (J). 1977. pap. 2.75 (*0-87738-034-1*) Youth Ed.

Curtis, David A., ed. see Castoriadis, Cornelius.

Curtis, David A., ed. & tr. see Castoriadis, Cornelius.

Curtis, David A., ed. & tr. see Vidal-Naquet, Pierre.

Curtis, David A., ed. & tr. see Vidal-Naquet, Pierre & Leveque, Pierre.

Curtis, David A., ed. & tr. see Vidal-Naquet, Pierre, et al.

Curtis, David A., tr. see Castoriadis, Cornelius.

Curtis, David Ames, ed. The Castoriadis Reader. LC 96-12037. (Blackwell Readers Ser.). 400p. 1997. text 75.95 (*1-55786-703-8*); pap. text 29.95 (*1-55786-704-6*) Blackwell Pubs.

Curtis, Deb & Carter, Margie. Reflecting Children's Lives: A Handbook for Planning Child-Centered Curriculum. LC 96-41080. (Illus.). 192p. (Orig.). 1996. pap. 21.95 (*1-884834-27-2*, 3043) Redleaf Pr.

— The Visionary Director: A Handbook for Dreaming, Organizing, & Improvising in Your Center. LC 98-30881. 1998. 25.95 (*1-884834-55-8*) Redleaf Pr.

Curtis, Deb, jt. auth. see Carter, Margie.

***Curtis, Debbie & Carter, Margie.** The Art of Awareness: How Observation Can Transform Your Teaching. LC 00-40290. 224p. 2000. pap. 29.95 (*1-884834-84-1*, 533901, Pub. by Redleaf Pr) Gryphon Hse.

Curtis, Deborah. Touching from a Distance: Tom Curtis & Jay Division. (Illus.). 212p. 1996. pap. 15.95 (*0-571-17445-0*) Faber & Faber.

Curtis, Delbert. Christ in North American. 280p. write for info. (*1-883266-24-6*) Srv Consolidate.

Curtis, Donald. Daily Power for Joyful Living. 1975. pap. 7.00 (*0-87980-300-2*) Wilshire.

— Enchanted Journey: Adventures in Inner Space. LC 95-2916. 224p. (Orig.). 1999. mass mkt. 10.99 (*0-446-67195-9*) Warner Bks.

— Happiness & Success Through Personal Power. LC 90-84239. 184p. (Orig.). 1991. pap. 9.95 (*0-87516-629-6*) DeVorss.

— Helping Heaven Happen. LC 92-1760. 252p. (Orig.). 1992. pap. 12.95 (*0-87728-759-7*) Weiser.

— New Age Understanding. LC 72-92276. 144p. (YA). 1990. reprint ed. pap. 7.95 (*0-941992-23-3*) Los Arboles Pub.

— The Twenty-Third Psalm. 64p. 1992. pap. 7.95 (*0-87516-644-X*) DeVorss.

— Understanding & Standing under the Bhagavad Gita. LC 96-70495. 111p. 1996. text. write for info. (*0-917849-24-8*) Sci of Mind.

Curtis, Donald, et al. Preventing Famine: Policies & Prospects for Africa. 250p. 1988. text 59.95 (*0-415-00711-9*) Routledge.

Curtis, Donald A. Fantasy on Sunset Mountain. LC 82-74122. 44p. (Orig.). (YA). (gr. 3-12). 1982. pap. write for info. (*0-9610284-0-8*) D A Curtis.

***Curtis, Donald B. & Curtis, Catherine B.** The Fine Art of Marriage: When Two Become One. 125p. 2000. pap. 20.00 (*0-9701715-0-1*) Marriage Workshop.

Curtis, Doris M. Sedimentary Processes: Diagenesis. LC QE0472.. (Society of Economic Paleontologists & Mineralogists, Special Publication Ser.: No. 1). 222p. reprint ed. pap. 68.90 (*0-608-12947-X*, 202474700038) Bks Demand.

Curtis, Dorothe B. The Hawaiian Carved Stone Image Bowl. (Bulletin in Anthropology Ser.: Vol. 6). (Illus.). 32p. (C). 1995. pap. 12.00 (*0-930897-86-2*) Bishop Mus.

***Curtis, Duncan.** North American F-86 Sabre. (Illus.). 200p. 2000. 54.95 (*1-86126-358-9*, 130700AE, Pub. by Crolwood) Motorbooks Intl.

Curtis, Eastman. Dare to Destinize. 80p. 1996. mass mkt. 4.99 (*0-89274-990-3*, HH-990) Harrison Hse.

— Every Day, I Pray for My Teenager: A Handbook of Scriptural Prayers for the Parents of Teenagers. LC 96-85028. 300p. 1996. pap. 11.99 (*0-88419-435-3*) Creation House.

— Kickin Devil Hiney. LC 98-114909. 1997. mass mkt. 4.99 (*0-89274-994-6*) Harrison Hse.

***Curtis, Eastman.** Raising Heaven Bound Kids in a Hell Bent World: Sound Advice & Spiritual Guidance to Train up Your Teenagers & Prepare Them for Daily Battle. 192p. 2000. pap. 9.99 (*0-7852-6872-3*) Nelson.

Curtis, Eastman. Straight Talk. 160p. 1998. pap. 8.99 (*1-57794-019-9*, HH2-019) Harrison Hse.

— Turn Loose of Your 'But' & Go with God. 80p. 1996. mass mkt. 4.99 (*0-89274-989-X*, HH989) Harrison Hse.

Curtis, Ed. Song of Songs. (Bible Study Commentary Ser.). 128p. (Orig.). 1988. pap. 6.99 (*0-310-36871-5*, 18288P) Zondervan.

Curtis, Edmund. History of Ireland. 1985. pap. 23.95 (*0-416-67730-4*) Routledge.

— History of Ireland. 6th ed. 448p. (C). 1961. reprint ed. pap. 24.99 (*0-415-02786-1*, NO. 2158) Routledge.

— Roger of Sicily & the Normans in Lower Italy, 1016-1154. LC 70-180443. (Heroes of the Nations Ser.). xii, 483 p. 1973. reprint ed. 30.00 (*0-404-56536-0*) AMS Pr.

***Curtis, Edward B. & Morrow, James A.** Inverse Problems for Electrical Networks. LC 99-53875. 200p. 2000. 55.00 (*981-02-4174-7*) World Scientific Pub.

Curtis, Edward E. The British Army in the American Revolution. 2nd unabridged ed. 235p. 1998. reprint ed. pap. 16.95 (*0-87928-122-7*) Corner Hse.

— The Organization of the British Army in the American Revolution. (BCL1 - U. S. History Ser.). 223p. 1991. reprint ed. lib. bdg. 79.00 (*0-7812-6118-X*) Rprt Serv.

— The Organization of the British Army in the American Revolution. LC 72-131679. 223p. 1972. reprint ed. 39.00 (*0-403-00566-3*) Scholarly.

Curtis, Edward L. & Madsen, Albert A. Chronicles I & II: Critical & Exegetical Commentary. Driver, Samuel R. et al, eds. LC 10-14958. (International Critical Commentary Ser.). 560p. 1994. 39.95 (*0-567-05007-6*, Pub. by T & T Clark) Bks Intl VA.

***Curtis, Edward M.** Song of Songs. 120p. 2000. pap. 16.00 (*1-57910-342-1*) Wipf & Stock.

Curtis, Edward P., jt. auth. see Rosenberg-Naparsteck, Ruth.

Curtis, Edward S. The North American Indian: The Complete Portfolios. (Klotz Ser.). (Illus.). 768p. 1997. pap. 29.99 (*3-8228-8183-X*) Taschen Amer.

— The North American Indian Vol. 12: Hopi. Hodge, Frederick W., ed. LC 94-71420. (Illus.). 448p. 1996. pap. 19.95 (*1-884865-00-3*) Curtis & Forrest.

— Portraits from North American Indian Life. 1989. 14.98 (*0-88394-004-3*) Promntory Pr.

— Portraits from North American Indian Life: Original Portfolio Edition. 1990. 39.98 (*0-88394-077-9*) Promntory Pr.

***Curtis, Edward S.** Sacred Legacy. (Illus.). 192p. 2000. 60.00 (*0-7432-0374-7*) S&S Trade.

Curtis, Edward S. Selected Writings of Edward S. Curtis. 3rd ed. Gifford, Barry, ed. LC 76-7891. (Illus.). 192p. 1976. pap. 6.95 (*0-916870-00-6*) Creat Arts Bk.

***Curtis, Edward S., photos by.** The Plains Indian Photographs of Edward S. Curtis. (Illus.). 219p. 2001. 50.00 (*0-8032-1512-6*) U of Nebr Pr.

Curtis, Edward S. & Brown, Joseph E. North American Indians. (Illus.). 96p. 1992. pap. 29.95 (*0-89381-492-X*) Aperture.

***Curtis, Edward S. & Lowinsky, Simon.** Sites & Structures: The Architectural Photographs of Edward Curtis. Solomon, Dan & Solomon, Mary, eds. LC 00-22730. (Illus.). 2000. 65.00 (*0-8118-2938-3*) Chronicle Bks.

Curtis, Elizabeth, jt. auth. see Curtis, Neil.

Curtis, Elyse. Act Five: The Perils of Paul. LC 97-94167. 60p. (Orig.). 1997. pap. 6.95 (*1-891058-06-1*, 116) Astral Projections.

— Ballad of the Revelation. LC 97-93966. 74p. 1997. pap. 7.95 (*0-9657282-2-6*, 102) Astral Projections.

— Behind the Veil: The Birth Caul As an Indicator of Innate Intuitive Abilities. 2nd rev. ed. LC 97-93964. 104p. 1997. pap. 8.95 (*0-9657282-4-2*, 104) Astral Projections.

— Body, Mind, Spirit Connections. LC 97-93965. 74p. 1997. pap. 7.95 (*0-9657282-3-4*, 103) Astral Projections.

— The Bright & Morning Star: (We Are Light) LC 97-94747. 52p. 1997. pap. 6.95 (*1-891058-13-4*, 123) Astral Projections.

***Curtis, Elyse.** Camelot Within: Symbology of the Arthurian Legend. LC 98-93125. 50p. 1998. pap. 3.95 (*1-891058-15-0*, 126) Astral Projections.

Curtis, Elyse. Celestial Influences. LC 97-93970. 52p. 1997. pap. 6.95 (*0-9657282-5-0*, 105) Astral Projections.

— Eugenie Grandet. 76p. 1997. pap. 7.95 (*1-891058-10-X*, 120) Astral Projections.

— Good Intentions. LC 97-94171. 60p. 1997. pap. 6.95 (*1-891058-08-8*, 118) Astral Projections.

— I Cried Before I Was Born: Tales My Mother Told Me. LC 97-94099. 56p. 1997. pap. 6.95 (*1-891058-01-0*, 111) Astral Projections.

— Jesus: A Journey to Ascension. LC 99-94786. 84p. 1999. pap. 8.95 (*1-891058-21-5*, 132) Astral Projections.

***Curtis, Elyse.** Jesus: What Jesus Said about That. LC 99-94786. 86p. 1999. pap. 7.95 (*1-891058-17-7*) Astral Projections.

Curtis, Elyse. Jesus Vol. II: The Miracles. LC 99-94786. 52p. 1999. pap. 7.95 (*1-891058-18-5*, 129) Astral Projections.

— Jesus Vol. III: Parables, Prayers & Promises. LC 99-94786. 68p. 1999. pap. 6.95 (*1-891058-20-7*, 131) Astral Projections.

— Let There Be Light: Creation & Evolution in the Bible. LC 97-93213. (Illus.). 145p. (Orig.). 1997. pap. 14.95 (*0-9657282-0-X*, 100) Astral Projections.

— Mad Blake. LC 97-94169. 76p. 1997. pap. 7.95 (*1-891058-07-X*, 117) Astral Projections.

***Curtis, Elyse.** Past Lives Vol. 1: The Edgar Cayce Soul Group. LC 00-90543. 50p. 2000. pap. 9.95 (*1-891058-23-1*, 134) Astral Projections.

Curtis, Elyse. Reflections on World Religions I: Hinduism, Buddhism, Jainism, Toroastrianism, Toaism. LC 97-93963. 68p. 1997. pap. 7.95 (*0-9657282-9-3*, 109) Astral Projections.

— Reflections on World Religions II: Judaism, Christianity, Islam. LC 97-93963. (Illus.). 102p. 1997. pap. 8.95 (*1-891058-00-2*, 110) Astral Projections.

— The Seven Stars: The Revelation. LC 97-94173. 54p. (Orig.). 1997. pap. 6.95 (*1-891058-05-3*, 115) Astral Projections.

— Son of God - Son of Man: Search for the Incarnation of Jesus. LC 97-93967. 56p. 1997. pap. 6.95 (*0-9657282-6-9*, 106) Astral Projections.

— Song of Songs: (Expressions of Love) LC 97-94745. 52p. 1997. pap. 6.95 (*1-891058-14-2*, 124) Astral Projections.

— Soul Quest: The Legacy. LC 97-94746. 52p. 1997. pap. 6.95 (*1-891058-12-6*, 122) Astral Projections.

— Transpersonal Perspectives. LC 97-93968. 1997. pap. 6.95 (*0-9657282-8-5*, 108) Astral Projections.

— Vision, Dreams & the Revelation. LC 97-94100. 78p. 1997. pap. 7.95 (*1-891058-02-9*, 112) Astral Projections.

— Viva Aida! LC 97-94168. 52p. (Orig.). 1997. pap. 6.95 (*1-891058-09-6*, 119) Astral Projections.

— Where Is Soul Mate? LC 97-94172. 52p. 1997. pap. 6.95 (*1-891058-11-8*, 121) Astral Projections.

— Who Was Who: A Past Life Directory Based on the Edgar Cayce Discourses. LC 97-93372. xiv, 454p. (Orig.). 1997. pap. 49.95 (*0-9657282-1-8*, 101) Astral Projections.

Curtis, Emily, et al, eds. The Proceedings of the Sixteenth West Coast Conference on Formal Linguistics. (Proceedings of the West Coast Conference on Formal Linguistics Ser.). 624p. (C). 1998. text 75.00 (*1-57586-143-7*); pap. text 27.95 (*1-57586-142-9*) CSLI.

Curtis, F. W. High-Frequency Induction Hardened Gears. (Technical Papers: Vol. P232). (Illus.). 8p. 1943. pap. text 30.00 (*1-55589-343-0*) AGMA.

Curtis, Francis. The Republican Party: A History of Its Fifty Years Existence, 2 vols. (BCL Ser. II). LC 75-41070. reprint ed. 95.00 (*0-404-14870-0*) AMS Pr.

Curtis, Francis D. A Digest of Investigations in the Teaching of Science in the Elementary & Secondary Schools. LC 74-153694. 369p. reprint ed. pap. 114.40 (*0-608-16184-5*, 202600000048) Bks Demand.

— Second Digest of Investigations in the Teaching of Science. LC 74-153694. 446p. reprint ed. pap. 138.30 (*0-608-14955-1*, 202600100048) Bks Demand.

— Some Values Derived from Extensive Reading of General Science. LC 75-177601. (Columbia University. Teachers College. Contributions to Education Ser.: No. 163). reprint ed. 37.50 (*0-404-55163-7*) AMS Pr.

— Third Digest of Investigations in the Teaching of Science. LC 74-153694. 439p. reprint ed. pap. 136.10 (*0-608-14951-9*, 202600200048) Bks Demand.

Curtis, Freddie, ed. Symposium on Central California Archaeology: Problems, Programs, & Interdisciplinary Approaches. fac. ed. (Sacramento Anthropological Society, Sacramento State College Ser.: No. 3). (Illus.). 128p. 1965. reprint ed. pap. text 14.38 (*1-55567-558-1*) Coyote Press.

Curtis, G. H., et al. Effect of Ethane & Propane Extraction on Supply of Natural Gas. 51p. 1973. pap. 5.00 (*0-318-12603-6*, F40102) Am Gas Assn.

Curtis, G. H., jt. auth. see Williams, Howell.

Curtis, Gail. Beautiful America's Oregon. rev. ed. LC 87-19565. (Illus.). 80p. 1995. reprint ed. 19.95 (*0-89802-432-3*); reprint ed. pap. 12.95 (*0-89802-428-5*) Beautiful Am.

Curtis, Galvin. The Bat Boy. (J). 1998. 15.00 (*0-689-80365-6*) S&S Bks Yung.

Curtis, Gavin. The Bat Boy & His Violin. LC 97-25417. (Illus.). 32p. (J). (ps-4). 1998. per. 16.00 (*0-689-80099-1*) S&S Childrens.

Curtis, George T. Life of James Buchanan, 2 vols., Set. 1993. reprint ed. lib. bdg. 150.00 (*0-7812-5444-2*) Rprt Serv.

— Life of James Buchanan, Fifteenth President of the United States, 2 Vols., Set. LC 69-16849. (Select Bibliographies Reprint Ser.). 1977. 48.95 (*0-8369-5004-6*) Ayer.

— Life of James Buchanan, Fifteenth President of the United States, 2 Vols., Vol. 2. LC 69-16849. (Select Bibliographies Reprint Ser.). 1977. 24.95 (*0-8369-9648-8*); 24.95 (*0-8369-9649-6*) Ayer.

Curtis, George T., ed. & notes see Curtis, Benjamin R.

Curtis, George W. Ars Reck Vivendi: Being Essays Contributed to "the Easy Chair" LC 72-4608. (Essay Index Reprint Ser.). 1977. reprint ed. 18.95 (*0-8369-2941-1*) Ayer.

— Early Letters to John S. Dwight: Brook Farm & Concord. (American Biography Ser.). 293p. 1991. reprint ed. lib. bdg. 69.00 (*0-7812-8096-6*) Rprt Serv.

— Potiphar Papers. LC 04-13872. 1995. 8.00 (*0-403-00098-X*) Scholarly.

— Potiphar Papers. LC 72-121280. (BCL Ser. I). reprint ed. 32.50 (*0-404-01888-2*) AMS Pr.

Curtis, George W., ed. see Downing, Andrew J.

Curtis, George W., ed. see Motley, John L.

Curtis, Gerald G., ed. Diccionario Espanol-Ingles - Ingles-Espanol Universidad de Miami. rev. ed.Tr. of English-Spanish - Spanish-English Dictionary, University of Miami. (ENG & SPA.). 584p. 1993. pap. 4.50 (*1-56259-028-6*) Editorial Amer.

Curtis, Gerald L. Election Campaigning: Japanese Style. LC 70-154343. (Studies of the East Asian Institute). 275p. 1971. text 57.50 (*0-231-03512-8*) Col U Pr.

— Japanese Way of Politics. (Studies of the East Asian Institute). 264p. 1989. pap. text 20.00 (*0-231-06681-3*) Col U Pr.

— The Logic of Japanese Politics: Leaders, Institutions, & the Limits of Change. LC 99-19910. 336p. 1999. 27.95 (*0-231-10842-7*) Col U Pr.

***Curtis, Gerald L.** The Logic of Japanese Politics: Leaders, Institutions & the Limits of Change. LC 99-19910. 2000. pap. 17.50 (*0-231-10843-5*) Col U Pr.

Curtis, Gerald L. United States, Japan, & Asia: Challenges in the Policy. 1994. 28.00 (*0-393-03633-2*) Norton.

— United States, Japan, & Asia: Challenges in the Policy. LC 94-15868. 288p. (C). 1994. pap. text 14.00 (*0-393-96583-X*) Norton.

Curtis, Gerald L., ed. Japanese-American Relations in the 1970's. LC 70-106895. 1970. pap. 3.00 (*0-910416-11-7*) Am Assembly.

— Japan's Foreign Policy after the Cold War: Coping with

Change. LC 93-9483. (Studies of the East Asian Institute, Columbia University). 416p. (gr. 13). 1993. pap. text 31.95 (*1-56324-217-6*, East Gate Bk) M E Sharpe.

— Japan's Foreign Policy after the Cold War: Coping with Change. LC 93-9483. 416p. (C). (gr. 13). 1993. text 88.95 (*1-56324-216-8*, East Gate Bk) M E Sharpe.

***Curtis, Gerard.** The Visual Word: Art & the Material Book in Victorian England. LC 99-36701. (Illus.). 352p. 1999. text 78.95 (*1-84014-657-5*, Pub. by Ashgate Pub) Ashgate Pub Co.

***Curtis, Glade & Schuler, Judith.** Baby's First Year Week by Week. (Illus.). 300p. 2000. 19.95 (*1-55561-257-1*); pap. 14.95 (*1-55561-232-6*) Fisher Bks.

— Week by Week Gift Set. (Illus.). 2000. pap. 27.00 (*1-55561-294-6*) Fisher Bks.

— Your Pregnancy Week by Week. 4th rev. ed. (Illus.). 384p. 2000. 19.95 (*1-55561-256-3*); pap. 14.95 (*1-55561-260-1*) Fisher Bks.

Curtis, Glade B. Su Embarazo: Semana a Semana. LC 94-29990. (SPA., Illus.). 436p. 1994. pap. 12.95 (*1-55561-061-7*) Fisher Bks.

— Your Pregnancy: Every Woman's Guide. LC 99-12270. Orig. Title: Your Pregnancy Questions & Answers. (Illus.). 320p. 1999. pap. 10.95 (*1-55561-154-0*) Fisher Bks.

— Your Pregnancy after 30. LC 96-22165. (Your Pregnancy Ser.). (Illus.). 384p. 1996. pap. 12.95 (*1-55561-088-9*) Fisher Bks.

— Your Pregnancy Questions & Answers. LC 95-24480. (Your Pregnancy Ser.). (Illus.). 432p. 1995. pap. 12.95 (*1-55561-150-8*) Fisher Bks.

— Your Pregnancy Week by Week. 3rd ed. LC 97-22933. (Your Pregnancy Ser.). (Illus.). 384p. 1997. pap. 12.95 (*1-55561-143-5*) Fisher Bks.

***Curtis, Glade B. & Schuler, Judith.** Your Pregnancy Recovery Guide. 1999. 64.75 (*1-86204-523-2*, Pub. by Element MA) Penguin Putnam.

Curtis, Glade B. & Schuler, Judith. Your Pregnancy Recovery Guide. (Illus.). 124p. 1999. pap. 12.95 (*1-86204-395-7*, Pub. by Element MA) Penguin Putnam.

Curtis, Glen E., ed. see Suny, Ronald G., et al.

Curtis, Glenn E. Armenia, Azerbaijan & Georgia: Country Studies. 354p. 1995. boxed set 35.00 (*0-16-061177-6*) USGPO.

— Bulgaria: A Country Study. 374p. 1993. boxed set 31.00 (*0-16-061158-X*) USGPO.

Curtis, Glenn E. Greece: A Country Study. 4th ed. LC 95-32388. (Illus.). 443p. 1995. boxed set 22.00 (*0-8444-0856-5*) USGPO.

Curtis, Glenn E. Kazakstan, Kyrgyzstan, Tajikistan, Turkmenistan & Uzbekistan: Country Studies. 632p. 1997. boxed set 38.00 (*0-16-061207-1*) USGPO.

— Poland: A Country Study. 405p. 1994. boxed set 30.00 (*0-16-061164-4*) USGPO.

— Russia: A Country Study. 835p. 1998. boxed set 44.00 (*0-16-061212-8*) USGPO.

— Yugoslavia: A Country Study. 391p. 1992. boxed set 29.00 (*0-16-061147-4*) USGPO.

Curtis, Glenn E., ed. Bulgaria: A Country Study. 2nd ed. LC 93-10955. (Area Handbook Ser.). 1993. 27.00 (*0-8444-0751-8*) Lib Congress.

— Kazakstan, Kyrgyzstan, Tajikistan, Turkmenistan, & Uzbekistan: A Country Study. (Illus.). 565p. (C). 1998. text 50.00 (*0-7881-7133-X*) DIANE Pub.

— Poland Country Studies: Area Handbook. 3rd ed. LC 93-46235. (Area Handbook Ser.). 1994. 21.00 (*0-8444-0827-1*) Lib Congress.

— Russia: A Country Study. (Illus.). 725p. (C). 1999. text 60.00 (*0-7881-7603-X*) DIANE Pub.

— Russia: A Country Study. LC 97-97563. 728p. 1997. 44.00 (*0-8444-0866-2*, Pub. by Lib Congress) Bernan Associates.

Curtis, Glenn E. & Library of Congress. Federal Research Division. Kazakstan, Kyrgyzstan, Tajikistan, Turkmenistan, & Uzbekistan: Country Studies. LC 97-5110. (Illus.). 1997. (*0-8444-0938-3*) Lib Congress.

Curtis, Glenn E., ed. see Federal Research Division Staff.

Curtis, Grahame. Business Information Systems. 3rd ed. (C). 1998. pap. text 61.00 (*0-201-33136-5*) Addison-Wesley.

Curtis, Grant. Cambodia Reborn? The Transition to Democracy & Development. LC 98-25364. 200p. 1998. 39.95 (*0-8157-1646-X*); pap. 16.95 (*0-8157-1645-1*) Brookings.

Curtis, Harriot. An Address. (Works of Harriot Curtis). 1990. reprint ed. lib. bdg. 79.00 (*0-685-27800-X*) Rprt Serv.

— Charles Sumner. (Works of Harriot Curtis). 1990. reprint ed. lib. bdg. 90.00 (*0-7812-2467-5*) Rprt Serv.

— Essays from the Easy Chair. (Works of Harriot Curtis). 1990. reprint ed. lib. bdg. 90.00 (*0-7812-2472-1*) Rprt Serv.

— The Howadji in Syria. (Works of Harriot Curtis). 1990. reprint ed. lib. bdg. 79.00 (*0-685-44775-8*) Rprt Serv.

— Lotus Eater. (Works of Harriot Curtis). 1990. reprint ed. lib. bdg. 79.00 (*0-685-44774-X*) Rprt Serv.

— Nile Notes of a Howadji. (Works of Harriot Curtis). 1990. reprint ed. lib. bdg. 79.00 (*0-685-44776-6*) Rprt Serv.

— Orations & Addresses. (Works of Harriot Curtis). 1990. reprint ed. lib. bdg. 79.00 (*0-685-44764-2*) Rprt Serv.

— Potiphar Papers. (Works of Harriot Curtis). 1990. reprint ed. lib. bdg. 79.00 (*0-7812-2464-0*) Rprt Serv.

— Prue & I. (Works of Harriot Curtis). 1990. reprint ed. lib. bdg. 79.00 (*0-7812-2465-9*) Rprt Serv.

— Robert Burns. (Works of Harriot Curtis). 1990. reprint ed. lib. bdg. 79.00 (*0-7812-2469-1*) Rprt Serv.

— Trumps. (Works of Harriot Curtis). 1990. reprint ed. lib. bdg. 79.00 (*0-7812-2466-7*) Rprt Serv.

— Washington Irving. (Works of Harriot Curtis). 1990. reprint ed. lib. bdg. 90.00 (*0-7812-2470-5*) Rprt Serv.

— William Cullen Bryant. (Works of Harriot Curtis). 1990. reprint ed. lib. bdg. 90.00 (*0-7812-2468-3*) Rprt Serv.

— The Works of Harriot Curtis. 1990. reprint ed. lib. bdg. 79.00 (*0-685-44777-4*) Rprt Serv.

Curtis, Helen, ed. see Winters, Manque.

Curtis, Helena. Biology. 4th ed. LC 82-83895. (Illus.). 1983. text 43.95 (*0-87901-186-6*) Worth.

— Biology. 4th ed. LC 82-83895. (Illus.). 1983. 9.95 (*0-87901-187-4*) Worth.

Curtis, Helena & Barnes, N. Sue. Biology of Cells, Pt. 1. 5th ed. 496p. 1989. pap. text 29.95 (*0-87901-435-0*) Worth.

— Biology of Cells, Pt. I. 5th ed. 225p. 1990. pap. text, student ed. 9.95 (*0-87901-475-X*) Worth.

— Biology of Organisms, Pt. 2. 5th ed. 668p. 1989. pap. text 25.95 (*0-87901-436-9*) Worth.

— Biology of Populations, Pt. 3. 5th ed. 308p. 1989. pap. text 25.95 (*0-87901-437-7*) Worth.

Curtis, Helena & Barnes, Sue N. Invitation to Biology. 4th ed. 730p. (C). 1985. text 62.95 (*0-87901-255-2*) Worth.

— Invitation to Biology. 4th ed. 403p. (C). 1985. student ed. 14.95 (*0-87901-256-0*) Worth.

Curtis, Helena, et al. Biology. 5th ed. 1192p. 1989. text 67.95 (*0-87901-394-X*) Worth.

— Biology. 5th ed. 694p. 1989. pap. text, student ed. 14.95 (*0-87901-395-8*) Worth.

Curtis, Henry. Beauties of the Rose. (Illus.). 120p. 1981. 65.00 (*0-936736-00-3*) Sweetbrier.

— The Play Movement & Its Significance. 1982. 26.95 (*0-8434-0431-0*) McGrath NH.

Curtis, Henry S. The Practical Conduct of Play. 1982. 26.95 (*0-8434-0429-9*, Pub. by McGrath NH) Ayer.

Curtis, Herb. The Americans Are Coming. 263p. 1989. pap. 12.95 (*0-86492-108-X*, Pub. by Goose Ln Edits) Genl Dist Srvs.

— The Brennen Siding Trilogy: The Americans Are Coming - The Last Tasmanian - The Lone Angler. 848p. 1997. pap. 24.95 (*0-86492-193-4*, Pub. by Goose Ln Edits) Genl Dist Srvs.

— The Lone Angler. 292p. 1993. pap. 12.95 (*0-86492-162-4*, Pub. by Goose Ln Edits) Genl Dist Srvs.

***Curtis, Herb.** Luther Corherns' Salmon Camp Chronicles. 196p. 2000. pap. text 14.95 (*0-86492-268-X*) Goose Ln Eds.

Curtis, Herb. The Silent Partner. 266p. 1996. pap. 14.95 (*0-86492-214-0*, Pub. by Goose Ln Edits) Genl Dist Srvs.

Curtis, Hilary, ed. Sexual Health Promotion in General Practice. 1995. write for info. (*1-85775-131-0*, Radcliffe Med Pr) Scovill Paterson.

***Curtis, Hillman.** Flash Web Design. 250p. 1999. pap. 45.00 (*0-7357-0896-7*) New Riders Pub.

Curtis, Howard, ed. Public Access Microcomputers in Academic Libraries: The Mann Library Model at Cornell University. fac. ed. LC 86-22315. 231p. 1987. pap. 71.70 (*0-7837-7319-6*, 204724600007) Bks Demand.

Curtis, Howard, tr. see Hellens, Franz.

Curtis, Howard, tr. see Lamarche, Caroline.

Curtis, Howard, tr. see Simenon, Georges.

Curtis, Howard D. A First Cause in Aircraft Structural Analysis. LC 95-47845. 800p. (C). 1996. text 74.95 (*0-256-19260-X*, Irwn McGrw-H) McGrw-H Hghr Educ.

Curtis, Howard W., ed. Haverhill Whittier Club, 1886-1986: A History & Record of Meetings; Constitution & By-Laws; Officers & Members. (Illus.). 32p. 1986. pap. 7.50 (*1-878651-06-4*) HPL Pr.

Curtis, J. Rolemaster Annual 1996. (Rolemaster Standard System Ser.). (Illus.). 96p. 1997. pap. 10.00 (*1-55806-299-8*, 5505) Iron Crown Ent Inc.

Curtis, J., ed. Bulgakov: Flight (Beg) (Russian Texts Ser.). (RUS.). 1997. pap. 18.95 (*1-85399-435-9*, Pub. by Brist Class Pr) Focus Pub-R Pullins.

Curtis, J. & Scott, W. Social Stratification: Canada. 2nd ed. 1979. pap. 16.00 (*0-13-818633-2*) P-H.

Curtis, J., jt. auth. see Bernhardt, M.

Curtis, J., jt. auth. see Danielson, S.

Curtis, J. E. & Reade, J. E., eds. Art & Empire: Treasures from Assyria in the British Museum. LC 94-47101. 1995. pap. 19.95 (*0-87099-738-6*, 0-8109-6491-0) Metro Mus Art.

Curtis, J. Jerome, Jr., jt. auth. see Crump, David.

***Curtis, J. Randall & Rubenfeld, Gordon D., eds.** Managing Death in the ICU: The Transition from Cure to Comfort. (Illus.). 384p. 2000. text 59.95 (*0-19-512881-8*) OUP.

Curtis, J. W. The Coinage of Pharaonic Egypt. 1979. pap. 5.00 (*0-89005-283-2*) Ares.

Curtis, Jack. Christmas in Calico: An American Fable. 220p. 1996. pap. text 8.95 (*0-9640537-1-3*) Monterey Pubng.

— Christmas in Calico: An American Fable. LC 97-40683. 192p. 1998. text 14.95 (*0-87596-543-1*) Rodale Pr Inc.

— Cut & Branded. Grad, Doug, ed. 228p. (Orig.). 1993. mass mkt. 3.99 (*0-671-79321-7*) PB.

— Dawn Waters: New & Selected Short Stories. (Illus.). 222p. 1998. 25.00 (*0-9653336-3-9*) Sprng Creek Pub.

***Curtis, Jack.** Easter in Calico: A Tale of Miracles. LC 99-65031. 192p. 2000. pap. 9.95 (*0-9640537-2-1*) Monterey Pubng.

Curtis, Jack. The Fight for San Bernardo. Grad, Doug, ed. 192p. (Orig.). 1993. pap. 3.50 (*0-671-79319-5*) PB.

— Hide-Out Canyon. Grad, Doug, ed. 192p. (Orig.). 1995. mass mkt. 4.99 (*0-671-79318-7*) PB.

— The Jury on Smoky Hill. Grad, Doug, ed. 192p. (Orig.). 1992. pap. 3.50 (*0-671-73189-0*) PB.

— Mirrors Kill. large type ed. LC 95-13855. 550p. 1995. lib. bdg. 25.95 (*0-7838-1298-1*, G K Hall Lrg Type) Mac Lib Ref.

— My Calling: Poems by Jack Curtis. LC 98-84881. (Illus.). 152p. 1998. pap. 8.95 (*0-9640537-8-0*) Monterey Pubng.

— No Mercy. 160p. 1995. 19.95 (*0-8027-4151-7*) Walker & Co.

— Pepper Tree Rider. 144p. 1994. 19.95 (*0-8027-4137-1*) Walker & Co.

— Pepper Tree Rider. large type ed. LC 94-33228. 224p. 1994. lib. bdg. 19.95 (*0-7838-1130-6*, G K Hall Lrg Type) Mac Lib Ref.

— The Quiet Cowboy. Grad, Doug, ed. 192p. 1994. mass mkt. 4.99 (*0-671-79317-9*) PB.

— Wild River Massacre. Grad, Doug, ed. 224p. (Orig.). 1993. mass mkt. 3.99 (*0-671-79320-9*) PB.

Curtis, Jack, jt. auth. see Abbey, Edward.

Curtis, Jack, jt. auth. see Hannon, Michael.

Curtis, James. James Whale: A New World of Gods & Monsters. 456p. 1998. pap. 22.95 (*0-571-19285-8*) Faber & Faber.

— Mind's Eye, Mind's Truth: FSA Photography Reconsidered. (American Civilization Ser.). 1991. pap. 24.95 (*0-87722-823-X*) Temple U Pr.

— Tetradrachms of Roman Egypt. 2nd ed. Durst, S., ed. LC 88-72315. (Illus.). 420p. 1994. text 65.00 (*0-942666-61-5*) S J Durst.

***Curtis, James.** W C Fields. 1999. write for info. (*0-375-40217-9*) Knopf.

Curtis, James, ed. Featured Player: An Oral Autobiography of Mae Clarke. LC 95-45660. (Filmmakers Ser.: No. 49). 334p. 1996. 42.00 (*0-8108-3044-2*) Scarecrow.

Curtis, James, ed. see Lewis, David.

Curtis, James C. Andrew Jackson & the Search for Vindication. (Library of American Biography). 194p. (C). 1997. pap. 20.20 (*0-673-39334-8*) Addison-Wesley Educ.

Curtis, James C. & Gould, Lewis L., eds. The Black Experience in America: Selected Essays. LC 73-111392. 209p. 1970. reprint ed. pap. 64.80 (*0-608-03572-6*, 206439500009) Bks Demand.

Curtis, James E. & Russell, Storm J., eds. Physical Activity in Human Experience: Interdisciplinary Perspectives. LC 96-8065. (Illus.). 304p. 1996. text 35.00 (*0-87322-765-4*, BCUR0765) Human Kinetics.

Curtis, James M. Culture As Polyphony: An Essay on the Nature of Paradigms. LC 77-25242. 208p. reprint ed. pap. 64.50 (*0-7837-2360-1*, AU0042500006) Bks Demand.

Curtis, James R. Shango. LC 95-37664. 197p. (Orig.). 1996. pap. 11.95 (*1-55885-096-1*) Arte Publico.

Curtis, James R., jt. auth. see Arreola, Daniel D.

Curtis, James R., jt. auth. see Boswell, Thomas D.

Curtis, James T. Lewis Is Dead & I Don't Feel So Good Myself! 208p. 1997. pap. 11.00 (*0-8059-4148-7*) Dorrance.

Curtis, James T., jt. auth. see Noonan, David C.

Curtis, James T., jt. auth. see Pedersen, Tom A.

Curtis, Jamie, ed. see Hoff, Robert M.

Curtis, Jamie Lee. Boy/Girl Book. (Illus.). 32p. (ps-3). 15.95 (*0-06-028761-6*); 5.95 (*0-06-443639-X*) HarpC.

— Cuentame Otra Vez la Noche Que Naci. (SPA., Illus.). (J). 1999. 14.95 (*1-880507-63-3*) Lectorum Pubns.

— My Mommy Hung the Moon. 32p. (ps-1). pap. 6.95 (*0-06-443696-9*) HarpC.

— My Mommy Hung the Moon. 32p. (ps-3). 16.95 (*0-06-029016-1*); lib. bdg. 16.89 (*0-06-029017-X*) HarpC.

Curtis, Jamie Lee. Tell Me Again About the Night I Was Born. LC 95-5412. (Illus.). 40p. (J). (ps-3). 1998. 15.95 incl. audio (*0-06-027954-0*) HarpC.

— Tell Me Again About the Night I Was Born. LC 95-5412. (Illus.). 40p. (J). (ps-3). 1996. 15.95 (*0-06-024528-X*); lib. bdg. 15.89 (*0-06-024529-8*, J Cotler) HarpC Child Bks.

— Tell Me Again About the Night I Was Born. LC 95-5412. (Illus.). 40p. (J). (ps-3). 2000. pap. 5.95 (*0-06-443581-4*, HarpTrophy) HarpC Child Bks.

— Today I Feel Silly Activity Book. (Illus.). (J). 1998. pap. write for info. (*0-06-028099-9*) HarpC Child Bks.

— Today I Feel Silly & Other Moods That Make My Day. LC 97-31416. (Illus.). 40p. (J). (ps-3). 1998. 15.95 (*0-06-024560-3*) HarpC.

— Today I Feel Silly & Other Moods That Make My Day. (Illus.). 32p. (J). (ps-3). 2000. 15.95 incl. audio (*0-06-028257-6*) HarpC.

***Curtis, Jamie Lee.** Today I Feel Silly & Other Moods That Make My Day. (J). 2000. 19.95 (*0-00-225523-6*) HarpC.

Curtis, Jamie Lee. Today I Feel Silly & Other Moods That Make My Day. 32p. (J). (ps). 2001. bds. 6.95 (*0-694-01343-9*) HarpC Child Bks.

***Curtis, Jamie Lee.** Today I Feely Silly / Canadian Edition. (Illus.). (ps-3). 1999. write for info. (*0-06-028842-6*) HarpC.

Curtis, Jamie Lee. When I Was Little: A Four-Year-Old's Memoir of Her Youth. LC 91-46188. (Trophy Picture Bk.). (Illus.). 32p. (J). (ps-3). 1995. pap. 5.95 (*0-06-443423-0*, HarpTrophy) HarpC Child Bks.

— When I Was Little: A Four-Year-Old's Memoir of Her Youth. 440th ed. LC 91-46188. (Illus.). 32p. (J). (ps-3). 1993. 15.95 (*0-06-021078-8*) HarpC Child Bks.

— When I Was Little a Four-Year-Old's Memoir of Her Youth. 1993. 11.15 (*0-606-08430-4*, Pub. by Turtleback) Demco.

— When I Was Little Board Book: A Four-Year-Old's Memoir of Her Youth. (Illus.). 32p. (J). (ps-1). 1999. bds. 6.95 (*0-694-01216-5*, HarpFestival) HarpC Child Bks.

***Curtis, Jamie Lee.** Where Do Balloons Go: An Uplifting Mystery. LC 00-23188. 32p. (J). (ps-3). 2000. 16.95 (*0-06-027980-X*); lib. bdg. 16.89 (*0-06-027981-8*) HarpC Child Bks.

— Where Do Balloons Go? Kit. (J). 2000. write for info. (*0-06-029313-6*) HarpC Child Bks.

Curtis, Jamie Lee & Cornell, Laura. Tell Me Again About the Night I Was Born Board Book. (Illus.). 32p. (J). (ps-k). 1999. bds. 6.95 (*0-694-01215-7*) HarpC Child Bks.

Curtis, Jamie Lee, et al. Baby Love Library: Runaway Bunny, Tell Me Again & You're Just What I Need, Set. (Illus.). (J). (ps). 1999. 19.95 (*0-694-01303-X*, HarpFestival) HarpC Child Bks.

Curtis, Jane, et al. Frederick Billings, Vermonter. (Illus.). 136p. 1986. 24.95 (*0-930985-05-2*); pap. 14.95 (*0-930985-04-4*) Curtis Lieberman.

— Green Mountain Adventure, Vermonts Long Trail. LC 85-80828. (Illus.). 96p. (Orig.). 1985. pap. 9.95 (*0-318-23115-8*) Green Mtn Club.

— Green Mountain Adventures: Vermont's Long Trail. LC 85-80828. (Illus.). 96p. 1985. 14.95 (*0-930985-03-6*); pap. 9.95 (*0-930985-02-8*) Curtis Lieberman.

— Monhegan, the Artists' Island. LC 94-48603. (Illus.). 192p. 1995. 50.00 (*0-89272-347-5*) Down East.

— Return to Theses Hills, The Vermont Years of Calvin Coolidge. LC 84-73356. (Illus.). 96p. 1985. 17.50 (*0-930985-00-1*); pap. 9.95 (*0-930985-01-X*) Curtis Lieberman.

Curtis, Jane, jt. auth. see Curtis, Will.

Curtis, Jared, ed. see Wordsworth, William.

Curtis, Jean. Out of the Past. (Rainbow Romances Ser.: No. 884). 160p. 1994. 14.95 (*0-7090-4936-6*) Parkwest Pubns.

— Out of the Past. large type ed. (Linford Romance Library). 272p. 1995. pap. 16.99 (*0-7089-7717-0*, Linford) Ulverscroft.

Curtis, Jean-Louis. Baccarat. LC 92-10479. (Illus.). 304p. 1992. 95.00 (*0-8109-3122-2*, Pub. by Abrams) Time Warner.

Curtis, Jennifer. Cary Grant: A Life in Pictures. LC 97-24188. 1997. write for info. (*1-56799-565-9*, MetroBooks) M Friedman Pub Grp Inc.

— Fields of Change: A New Crop of American Farmers Find Alternatives to Pesticides. (Illus.). 230p. 1998. pap. 14.00 (*1-893340-08-2*) Natl Resources Defense Coun.

Curtis, Jennifer, jt. auth. see Cohen, Ronnie A.

Curtis, Jenny. Bob Hope: A Life Remembered. LC 99-17310. 1999. text 19.98 (*1-56799-854-2*) M Friedman Pub Grp Inc.

— Grace Kelly: A Life in Pictures. LC 99-18047. 1998. 13.98 (*1-56799-646-9*, MetroBooks) M Friedman Pub Grp Inc.

Curtis, Jerome J., Jr. & Blake, D. Steven. California Real Estate Finance & Construction Law, 2 vols., Set. 1600p. Date not set. 180.00 (*1-56257-358-6*, 61100-10, MICHIE) LEXIS Pub.

Curtis, Jerry L. The Imprisoned Hero in Camus, Beckett, & Desvignes. Brady, Patrick, ed. 400p. (Orig.). 1994. pap. text 36.50 (*1-886935-08-4*) New Prdigm Pr.

***Curtis, Jerry L., ed.** Essays on the Work of 20th Century French Author Lucette Desuignes. LC 99-57088. (Studies in French Literature: Vol. 38). 288p. 2000. 89.95 (*0-7734-7843-4*) E Mellen.

Curtis, Jill. Making & Breaking Families. 200p. 1998. 55.00 (*1-85343-411-6*, Pub. by Free Assoc Bks); pap. 23.50 (*1-85343-412-4*) Free Assoc Bks.

Curtis, Jim. Rock Eras: Interpretations of Music & Society, 1954-1984. LC 87-72615. 363p. 1987. 34.95 (*0-87972-368-8*); pap. 17.95 (*0-87972-369-6*) Bowling Green Univ Popular Press.

***Curtis, Joan C.** Strategic Interviewing: Skills & Tactics for Savvy Executives. LC 99-462241. 250p. 2000. 67.00 (*1-56720-358-2*, Q358, Quorum Bks) Greenwood.

Curtis, Joe M. Building Small, Living Large. (Illus.). xxv, 188p. (Orig.). 1996. spiral bd. 22.50 (*0-9655094-0-0*) Jace Pub.

— Building Small, Living Large: Simple, Green, Homebuilding Solutions. 2nd rev. ed. (Illus.). 228p. 1998. 22.50 (*0-9655094-1-9*) Jace Pub.

Curtis, John. Ancient Persia. (British Museum Paperbacks Ser.). (Illus.). 72p. 1990. pap. 14.50 (*0-674-03415-5*) HUP.

***Curtis, John.** The Bluffer's Guide to Accountancy: Bluff Your Way in Accountancy. (Bluffer's Guides Ser.). 64p. 2000. pap. 5.95 (*1-902825-87-X*) Oval Bks.

Curtis, John, ed. Bronze-Working Centres of Western Asia 1000-539 B.C. (Studies in Egyptian Archaeology). (Illus.). 342p. 1988. text 59.95 (*0-7103-0274-6*) Routledge.

— Fifty Years of Mesopotamian Discovery. (Illus.). 122p. 1982. pap. 18.00 (*0-903472-05-8*, Pub. by Brit Sch Archaeol Iraq) David Brown.

Curtis, John & Green, Anthony. Excavations at Khirbet Khatuniyeh LC 98-135431. (Saddam Dam Reports.). xii, 120p. 1997. write for info. (*0-7141-1144-9*) British Mus Pr.

Curtis, John & Whitehouse, Graham. Radiology for the MRCP. (Arnold Publications). (Illus.). 400p. 1998. pap. text 42.50 (*0-340-71886-2*) OUP.

Curtis, John, jt. auth. see Esset, Matt.

Curtis, John B., et al. Natural Science Laboratory Manual. (Illus.). 87p. (C). 1996. pap. text, lab manual ed. 9.80 (*1-889766-01-1*) Columbus State Bks.

— Natural Science 1. (Illus.). 270p. (C). 1996. pap. text 15.72 (*1-889766-00-3*) Columbus State Bks.

Curtis, John D. Learn to Relax: A Fourteen Day Program. (Illus.). 112p. (Orig.). 1991. pap. 7.95 (*0-9611456-1-7*, Coulee Press) Adastra Pub.

— The Mindset for Winning: A 4-Step Mental Training Program for Athletes. (Illus.). 120p. 1989. student ed. 9.95 (*0-9611456-5-X*, Coulee Press); pap. 9.95 (*0-9611456-3-3*, Coulee Press) Adastra Pub.

— The Mindset for Winning: Coaching Manual. 130p. 1989. 39.95 (*0-9611456-7-6*, Coulee Press) Adastra Pub.

— The Mindset for Winning Athlete's Log. 50p. 1989. pap. 7.95 (*0-9611456-6-8*, Coulee Press) Adastra Pub.

C

Curtis, John D., et al. Teaching Stress Management & Relaxation Skills: An Instructor's Guide. (Illus.). 280p. 1985. text 26.50 (*0-9611456-2-5*, Coulee Press) Adastra Pub.

Curtis, John L. Cattle Embryo Transfer Procedure. (Illus.). 131p. (Orig.). (C). 1991. spiral bd. 37.00 (*0-12-200240-7*) Acad Pr.

— Cattle Embryo Transfer Procedure. (Orig.). (C). 1990. pap. text 39.50 (*0-9627130-0-7*) J Curtis KS.

Curtis, John M. Dodging the Bullet: Survival Strategies for Life in the Fast Lane. 245p. 1999. pap. 14.95 (*0-9670327-1-7*) Discobolos Pr.

— Operation Charisma: How to Get Charisma & Wind up at the Top. 250p. 1999. pap. 14.95 (*0-9670327-0-9*, 0071) Discobolos Pr.

Curtis, John M. & Hamer, Marc R. Marketing Yourself As a Psychotherapist. LC 96-96841. (Illus.). 103p. (C). 1997. per. 29.95 (*0-9653956-0-X*) Discobolos.

Curtis, John T. Vegetation of Wisconsin: An Ordination of Plant Communities. (Illus.). 672p. 1959. 44.95 (*0-299-01940-3*) U of Wis Pr.

Curtis, Joseph E., jt. auth. see Kraus, Richard G.

Curtis, Joy, jt. auth. see Benjamin, Martin.

Curtis, Juan. Bocados I: Commentarios Chistosos de Unas Gotitas y Pastillas. (SPA., Illus.). 1997. lib. bdg. 15.99 (*1-878382-33-0*) Book Gallery.

Curtis, Judith A. The Renal Patient's Guide to Good Eating. (Illus.). 214p. 1989. pap. 27.95 (*0-398-06083-5*) C C Thomas.

— The Renal Patient's Guide to Good Eating. (Illus.). 214p. (C). 1989. text 40.95 (*0-398-05611-0*) C C Thomas.

Curtis, Judith A., et al, eds. Michigan Family Law, 2 vols. 4th ed. LC 93-77007. 1300p. 1993. ring bd. 165.00 (*0-685-65990-9*, 93-011) U MI Law CLE.

Curtis, Judith A., et al. Gilmore on Michigan Civil Procedure Before Trial, 2 Vols. 3rd rev. ed. LC 91-78183. 1186p. 1992. ring bd. 155.00 (*0-685-22713-8*, 92-008) U MI Law CLE.

— Gilmore on Michigan Civil Procedure Before Trial, Suppl. only 1991. rev. ed. LC 91-78183. 1186p. 1992. write for info. (*0-685-44336-1*) U MI Law CLE.

Curtis, Judith G., ed. Favorite Recipes from America's Fifty States. 48p. 1986. 6.00 (*0-86668-059-4*) ARCsoft.

Curtis, Karen, jt. auth. see Tajgman, David.

Curtis, Kathleen. The Physical Therapist's Guide to Health Care. LC 98-46544. (Illus.). 320p. 1999. pap. 28.00 (*1-55642-378-0*, 43780) SLACK Inc.

***Curtis, Kathleen.** The Physical Therapist's Guide to Health Care, Instructor's Manual. 80p. (C). 1999. pap. text, teacher ed. write for info. (*1-55642-458-2*) SLACK Inc.

— PT Primer. 300p. 2000. pap. text 35.00 (*1-55642-411-6*) SLACK Inc.

— PTA Primer. 300p. (C). 2000. pap. text 35.00 (*1-55642-413-2*) SLACK Inc.

Curtis, Kathleen, jt. auth. see Fulkerson, Mary L.

Curtis, Katie K. Tulukaruunkuk Teq-llu. large type ed. (ESK., Illus.). 24p. (Orig.). (J). (gr. k-3). 1997. pap. text 6.00 (*1-58084-000-0*) Lower Kuskokwim.

Curtis, Keith. From Management Goal-Setting to Organization Results: Transforming Strategies into Action. LC 93-49031. 224p. 1994. 55.00 (*0-89930-902-X*, Quorum Bks) Greenwood.

Curtis, Ken, jt. auth. see Curtis, Nancy.

Curtis, Kent, jt. auth. see Manning, George.

***Curtis, Kimberly.** Our Sense of The Real: Aesthetic Experience & Arendtian Politics. LC 99-31256. 1999. pap. text 16.95 (*0-8014-8640-8*) Cornell U Pr.

Curtis-Klause, Annette. Blood & Chocolate, Class Set. unabridged ed. (J). 1997. boxed set 228.80 incl. audio (*0-7887-2758-3*, 46113) Recorded Bks.

— Blood & Chocolate, Homework Set. unabridged ed. (J). (gr. 5). 1997. boxed set 74.95 incl. audio (*0-7887-1717-0*, 12/1997) Recorded Bks.

Curtis, L. Perry, Jr. Apes & Angels: The Irishman in Victorian Caricature. 2nd rev. ed. LC 96-16744. (Illus.). 208p. 1997. text 55.00 (*1-56098-647-6*); pap. text 19.95 (*1-56098-733-2*) Smithsonian.

Curtis, Larry G. & Kuehn, David L. A Guide to Successful Instrumental Conducting. 224p. (C). 1992. text. write for info. (*0-697-12694-3*) Brown & Benchmark.

Curtis, Lee K. Open the Door to Global Communication. (Illus.). 32p. (Orig.). 1996. pap. 3.50 (*0-9646390-0-9*) Wind Word Pr.

Curtis, Leonard F., jt. auth. see Barrett, Eric C.

Curtis, Lewis P. Chichester Towers. LC 66-21514. (Illus.). 130p. 1966. reprint ed. 40.30 (*0-608-08215-5*, 201319900086) Bks Demand.

Curtis, Linda. Aquatic Plants of Northeastern Illinois. 80p. 1998. pap. 15.00 (*1-57502-797-6*, PO2201) Morris Pubng.

— Messages. 1998. pap. write for info. (*1-58235-019-1*) Watermrk Pr.

***Curtis, Linda.** Slivered Leaves. 2000. 12.95 (*0-533-13458-7*) Vantage.

Curtis, Lindsay R. Feminine & Fit. (Illus.). 128p. (Orig.). 1975. pap. 3.95 (*0-89036-049-9*) Liahona Pub Trust.

Curtis, Lisa. Gardens-by-the-Bay Cookbook. (Illus.). 148p. (Orig.). 1993. pap. 9.95 (*0-944627-37-4*) Sand River Pr.

Curtis, Liz. The Cause of Ireland: From the United Irishmen to Partition. (Illus.). 437p. 1995. pap. 26.95 (*0-9514229-6-0*, Pub. by Beyond the Pale) Irish Bks Media.

— Ireland - The Propaganda War: The British Media & the "Battle for Hearts & Minds" 2nd ed. 336p. (C). reprint ed. pap. 22.00 (*0-86104-757-5*, Pub. by Pluto GBR) Stylus Pub VA.

— Making Advances: What You Can Do about Sexual Harassment at Work. (Illus.). 122p. 1995. pap. 9.95 (*0-563-36960-4*, Pub. by BBC) Parkwest Pubns.

Curtis, Lucy D. Lucy's List: A Comprehensive Sourcebook for Making Larger Living Easier. LC 96-15769. 272p. 1996. mass mkt. 14.99 (*0-446-67283-1*, Pub. by Warner Bks) Little.

Curtis, Lynn. Picturing Change: An Illustrated Guide to Worldwide Literacy Programs. (Illus.). (Orig.). 1995. pap. 4.00 (*0-9623561-6-6*) Laubach Literacy.

Curtis, Lynn A. The State of Families 4: Family, Employment & Reconstruction - Policy Based on What Works. LC 87-24374. 158p. 1995. pap. 16.95 (*0-87304-270-0*) Manticore Pubs.

Curtis, Lynn A., ed. Policies to Prevent Crime: Neighborhood, Family & Employment Strategies, Vol. 494. 1987. 26.00 (*0-8039-3008-9*); pap. 17.00 (*0-8039-3009-7*) Sage.

Curtis, Lynn A., ed. see Milton S. Eisenhower Foundation Staff.

Curtis, M. Introduction to Comparative Politics: Instructor's Manual. 4th ed. 18.00 (*0-673-97574-6*) Addson-Wesley Educ.

Curtis, M. J., ed. Immunopharmacology of the Heart. (Handbook of Immunopharmacology Ser.). (Illus.). 162p. 1993. text 79.00 (*0-12-200245-8*) Acad Pr.

Curtis, M. L. Matrix Groups. 2nd ed. (Universitext Ser.). (Illus.). xiii, 210p. 1987. 42.95 (*0-387-96074-0*) Spr-Verlag.

Curtis, M. L. & Hempel, J. Abstract Linear Algebra. (Universitext Ser.). 184p. 1990. 37.95 (*0-387-97263-3*) Spr-Verlag.

***Curtis, Marcia.** Big Sister, Little Sister. LC 99-24796. (Illus.). 40p. (J). 2000. 12.99 (*0-8037-2482-9*, Dial Yng Read) Peng Put Young Read.

— The Composition of Our Selves. 2nd ed. 240p. (C). 2000. per. 50.95 (*0-7872-7152-7*) Kendall-Hunt.

Curtis, Marcia, jt. auth. see Herrington, Anne J.

Curtis, Margarita O. Guia de Lectura: Notas, Vocabulario y Ejercicios. 160p. (C). 1994. spiral bd. 16.95 (*0-8403-8062-3*) Kendall-Hunt.

— Guia de Lectura: Notas, Vocabulario y Ejercicios para Las Bicicletas Son Para El Verano. 184p. (C). 1996. pap. text, per. 25.95 (*0-7872-2069-8*, 41206901) Kendall-Hunt.

Curtis, Marjorie. Desert Surgeon. large type ed. (Linford Romance Library). 288p. 1996. pap. 16.99 (*0-7089-7959-9*, Linford) Ulverscroft.

— Doctor's Request. large type ed. (Linford Romance Library). 256p. 1996. pap. 16.99 (*0-7089-7902-5*) Ulverscroft.

— Hospital Encounter. large type ed. (Dales Large Print Ser.). 204p. 1998. pap. 19.99 (*1-85389-796-5*, Dales) Ulverscroft.

— Sister Harriet. large type ed. (Dales Large Print Ser.). 212p. 1997. pap. 18.99 (*1-85389-749-3*, Dales) Ulverscroft.

***Curtis, Marjorie.** Staff Nurse in Fiji. large type ed. 224p. 2000. 18.99 (*1-85389-995-X*) Dales Lrg Prnt.

Curtis, Mark. The Great Deception: Anglo-American Power & World Order. LC 98-16747. 272p. 1998. 59.95 (*0-7453-1239-X*, Pub. by Pluto GBR) Stylus Pub VA.

***Curtis, Mark.** The Great Deception: Anglo-American Power & World Order. LC 98-16747. 272p. 1998. pap. 24.95 (*0-7453-1234-9*, Pub. by Pluto GBR) Stylus Pub VA.

Curtis, Mark, jt. auth. see Farago, Francis T.

Curtis, Mark A. Process Planning Technology. LC 87-34605. 253p. 1988. text 27.95 (*0-471-83254-5*) P-H.

— Tool Design for Manufacturing. LC 85-22775. 451p. 1986. text 39.95 (*0-471-88106-6*) P-H.

Curtis, Mary. Loving Arms of the Law. (Special Edition Ser.: No. 730). 1992. per. 3.39 (*0-373-09730-1*, 5-09730-8) Harlequin Bks.

Curtis, Mary E., jt. ed. see McKeown, Margaret G.

Curtis, Matt. Elliot Drives Away. LC 95-43898. (Rookie Readers Ser.). (Illus.). 32p. (J). (ps-2). 1996. lib. bdg. 17.00 (*0-516-02058-7*) Childrens.

— Six Empty Pockets. LC 96-49441. (Rookie Readers Ser.). (Illus.). 32p. (J). (gr. k-2). 1997. 17.00 (*0-516-20399-1*) Childrens.

— Six Empty Pockets. (Rookie Readers Ser.). (Illus.). (J). 1998. pap. text 4.95 (*0-516-26253-X*) Childrens.

Curtis, Mavis, jt. auth. see Bishop, Julia C.

Curtis, Michael. Marxism: The Inner Dialogue. 2nd ed. LC 96-52289. 406p. 1997. pap. text 22.95 (*1-56000-945-4*) Transaction Pubs.

— Three Against the Third Republic: Sorel, Barres & Maurras. LC 76-26140. 313p. 1976. reprint ed. lib. bdg. 59.75 (*0-8371-9048-7*, CUTR, Greenwood Pr) Greenwood.

Curtis, Michael, ed. Great Pol Theories, Vol. I. 1981. mass mkt. 6.99 (*0-380-00785-1*, Avon Bks) Morrow Avon.

— Great Pol Theories, Vol. II. 1976. mass mkt. 7.99 (*0-380-01235-9*, Avon Bks) Morrow Avon.

Curtis, Michael, ed. People & Politics in the Middle East. LC 72-140617. 335p. 1971. 39.95 (*0-87855-000-3*); pap. 24.95 (*0-87855-500-5*) Transaction Pubs.

— Totalitarianism. LC 78-66238. (Issues in Contemporary Civilization Ser.). 128p. 1979. 29.95 (*0-87855-288-X*) Transaction Pubs.

Curtis, Michael & Blondel, Jean. Western European Government & Politics. LC 96-33112. 442p. (C). 1997. pap. text 58.00 (*0-673-98257-2*) Longman.

Curtis, Michael & Chertoff, Mordecai S., eds. Israel: Social Structure & Change. LC 73-78696. (Third World Ser.). 460p. 1973. pap. 24.95 (*0-87855-575-7*) Transaction Pubs.

Curtis, Michael & Gitelson, Susan A., eds. Israel in the Third World. LC 75-44817. 520p. (Orig.). 1976. 44.95 (*0-87855-130-1*); pap. text 24.95 (*0-87855-603-6*) Transaction Pubs.

Curtis, Michael, Jr., et al. Introduction to Comparative Government. 2nd ed. (C). 1990. pap. 50.33 (*0-06-041466-9*) Addson-Wesley Educ.

Curtis, Michael, jt. auth. see Brooke, Nicholas.

Curtis, Michael J., jt. auth. see Keller, Martha R.

Curtis, Michael K. No State Shall Abridge: The Fourteenth Amendment & the Bill of Rights. LC 86-6309. xii, 276p. 1990. text 49.95 (*0-8223-0599-2*) Duke.

— No State Shall Abridge: The Fourteenth Amendment & the Bill of Rights. LC 86-6309. xii, 276p. (C). 1990. reprint ed. pap. text 19.95 (*0-8223-1035-X*) Duke.

Curtis, Michael K., ed. The Constitution & the Flag, Vols. 1 & 2. LC 92-39286. (Controversies in Constitutional Law Ser.). 424p. 1993. text 30.00 (*0-8153-1267-9*); text 30.00 (*0-8153-1268-7*) Garland.

***Curtis, Michael Kent.** Free Speech, "The People's Darling Privilege" Struggles for Freedom of Expression in American History. LC 00-29394. 480p. 2000. 32.95 (*0-8223-2529-2*) Duke.

Curtis, Michele G., et al. Glass's Office Gynecology. 5th ed. LC 98-3829. (Illus.). 570p. 1998. 79.00 (*0-683-30201-9*) Lppncott W & W.

Curtis, Mike. C. Q. B. 1997. 32.95 (*0-593-04032-5*) Bantam.

Curtis, Mike & Mowat, Keith, eds. Shipboard Handling of Unitised Cargo. (C). 1979. 45.00 (*0-906297-02-8*, Pub. by ICHCA) St Mut.

Curtis, Munzee. When the Big Dog Barks. LC 96-10412. (Illus.). 24p. (J). 1997. lib. bdg. 14.93 (*0-688-09540-2*, Grenwillow Bks) HarpC Child Bks.

— When the Big Dog Barks. LC 96-10412. (Illus.). 24p. (J). (ps up). 1997. 15.00 (*0-688-09539-9*, Grenwillow Bks) HarpC Child Bks.

Curtis, Nancy. Behind the Crisis: An Unseen War. (Illus.). 60p. 1993. pap. 5.00 (*0-9615445-1-1*) MDI Inc.

— Beyond Survival: What to Do When the Past Is a Little Hard to Swallow. (Illus.). 250p. 1990. 10.95 (*1-877717-01-0*) MDI Inc.

Curtis, Nancy & Curtis, Ken. Tormented? God's Keys to Life. rev. ed. (Illus.). 1985. pap. 4.95 (*0-9615445-0-3*) MDI Inc.

Curtis, Nancy & Nylander, Richard C. Beauport: The Sleeper-McCann House. LC 90-41093. (Illus.). 112p. 1990. pap. 29.95 (*0-87923-876-3*) U Pr of New Eng.

Curtis, Nancy, ed. see Burke, Tina, et al.

Curtis, Nancy, ed. see Curry, Peggy S., et al.

Curtis, Nancy C. Black Heritage Sites Vol. I: The North, Vol. 1. (Illus.). 336p. 1998. pap. 19.95 (*1-56584-432-7*, Pub. by New Press NY) Norton.

— Black Heritage Sites Vol. II: The South, Vol. 2. (Illus.). 336p. 1998. pap. 19.95 (*1-56584-433-5*, Pub. by New Press NY) Norton.

— Finder's Guide to Black Heritage Sites: An African-American Odyssey. (Illus.). 677p. 1995. 75.00 (*0-8389-0643-5*, 0643-5-2045) ALA.

Curtis, Natalie. Indians' Book. rev. ed. (Illus.). 1968. pap. 14.95 (*0-486-21939-9*) Dover.

Curtis, Natalie, tr. see Joy, Janet L.

Curtis, Neil. How Do We Know the Earth Is Round? LC 94-16253. (How Do We Know? Ser.). (Illus.). 48p. (J). (gr. 4-8). 1995. lib. bdg. 24.26 (*0-8114-3879-1*) Raintree Steck-V.

— The Ridgeway. (National Trail Guides Ser.). 1994. pap. text 19.95 (*1-85410-268-0*, Pub. by Aurum Pr) London Brdge.

— The Ridgeway. (National Trail Guides Ser.). (Illus.). 168p. 1996. pap. 19.95 (*1-85410-019-X*, Pub. by Aurum Pr) London Brdge.

— Rocks & Minerals. (Spotlights Ser.). (Illus.). 46p. (J). 1998. 11.95 (*0-19-521392-0*) OUP.

Curtis, Neil & Curtis, Elizabeth. Touching the Past: Archaeology 5-14. 64p. 1990. pap. 21.00 (*1-899827-63-3*) St Mut.

Curtis, Neil, et al. Planet Earth. LC 93-20103. (Visual Factfinders Ser.). (Illus.). 96p. (J). (gr. 5 up). 1993. pap. 12.95 (*1-85697-847-8*, Kingfisher) LKC.

Curtis, O. M. History of the Twenty-Fourth Michigan of the Iron Brigade. 495p. 1989. reprint ed. 35.00 (*0-942211-46-4*) Olde Soldier Bks.

Curtis, Olivia. Chemical Dependency: A Family Affair. LC 98-21058. 1998. 22.95 (*0-534-35583-8*) Brooks-Cole.

Curtis, Oswald, jt. auth. see Norris, Herbert.

Curtis, Patricia. Animals You Never Even Heard Of. LC 96-54480. (Illus.). 32p. (J). (gr. k-3). 1996. 16.95 (*0-87156-594-3*, Pub. by Sierra Club Childrens) Little.

— The Indoor Cat: How to Understand, Enjoy & Care for House Cats. (Illus.). 192p. 1982. pap. 9.95 (*0-399-50596-2*, Perigee Bks) Berkley Pub.

— The Indoor Cat: How to Understand, Enjoy, & Care for House Cats. rev. ed. LC 97-11870. 208p. 1997. pap. 12.00 (*0-399-52350-2*, Perigee Bks) Berkley Pub.

***Curtis, Patrick & Laitin, Anna.** 1999 Salary Study. 1999. pap. 26.95 (*0-87868-782-3*) Child Welfare.

Curtis, Patrick A., et al, eds. The Foster Care Crisis: Translating Research into Policy & Practice. LC 99-13225. (Child, Youth, & Family Services Ser.). 1999. text 50.00 (*0-8032-1483-9*); pap. text 19.95 (*0-8032-6399-6*) U of Nebr Pr.

Curtis, Paul, tr. see Voronkov, M. G., et al.

Curtis, Paul D., jt. auth. see Jensen, Paul G.

Curtis, Penelope. Barbara Hepworth. (St. Ives Artists Ser.). (Illus.). 80p. 1998. pap. 19.95 (*1-85437-225-4*, Pub. by Tate Gallery) U of Wash Pr.

***Curtis, Penelope.** Sculpture, 1900-1945. (Oxford History of Art Ser.). (Illus.). 304p. 1999. 39.95 (*0-19-210045-9*); pap. 17.95 (*0-19-284228-5*) OUP.

Curtis, Penelope & Wilkinson, Alan G. Barbara Hepworth: A Retrospective. LC 94-240160. (Illus.). 168p. 1997. pap. 40.00 (*1-85437-141-X*, Pub. by Tate Gallery) U of Wash Pr.

Curtis, Peter S., et al, eds. Belowground Responses to Rising Atmospheric CO2 - Implications for Plants, Soil Biota & Ecosystem Processes: Proceedings of a Workshop Held May 29-June 2, 1993, University of Michigan Biological Station, Pellston, Michigan. LC 94-46911. (Developments in Plant & Soil Sciences Ser.: Vol. 60). 1995. text 115.00 (*0-7923-2901-5*) Kluwer Academic.

Curtis, Philip J. The Fall of the U. S. Consumer Electronics Industry: An American Trade Tragedy. LC 94-8538. 360p. 1994. 59.95 (*0-89930-880-5*, Quorum Bks) Greenwood.

Curtis, P.J. Notes from the Heart: A Celebration of Traditional Irish Music. (Illus.). 180p. 1995. pap. 13.95 (*1-898142-07-6*, Pub. by Torc) Dufour.

Curtis-Prior, P. B., ed. Prostaglandins: Biology & Chemistry of Prostaglandins & Related Eicosanoids. (Illus.). 720p. 1988. text 250.00 (*0-443-02519-3*) Church.

Curtis, R., tr. see Madelin, Louis.

Curtis, R. C. Self-Defeating Behaviors: Experimental Research, Clinical Impressions, & Practical Implications. (Social - Clinical Psychology Ser.). (Illus.). 398p. (C). 1989. 65.00 (*0-306-43129-7*, Plenum Trade) Perseus Pubng.

Curtis, R. C. & Stricker, G. How People Change: Inside & Outside Therapy. (Social-Clinical Psychology Ser.). (Illus.). 234p. (C). 1991. 49.50 (*0-306-43784-8*, Plenum Trade) Perseus Pubng.

Curtis, R. T. & Wilson, R. A., eds. The Atlas of Finite Groups Ten Years On, Vol. 249. LC 98-21344. (London Mathematical Society Lecture Note Ser.: No. 249). (Illus.). 320p. (Orig.). (C). 1998. pap. 44.95 (*0-521-57587-7*) Cambridge U Pr.

Curtis, Randall. The Heart of a Man Is a Woman: How to Find the One You've Always Wanted. LC 95-158288. 240p. 1995. pap. 14.95 (*0-9644459-6-4*) Amrita Pubns.

— No One Is a Mystery: How to Use the Planets to Understand Anybody. LC 99-172726. (Illus.). 242p. 1998. mass mkt. 15.95 (*0-9644459-5-6*) Amrita Pubns.

Curtis, Ray C. Israel & the Gathering Storm. LC 90-92294. (Illus.). 258p. (Orig.). 1991. pap. 9.95 (*0-9629351-0-7*) SouthCross Bks.

Curtis, Rebecca C., ed. The Relational Self: Theoretical Convergences in Psychoanalysis & Social Psychology. LC 90-15734. 319p. 1991. lib. bdg. 41.95 (*0-89862-558-0*) Guilford Pubns.

Curtis, Rebecca S. Charlotte Avery on Isle Royale. 192p. 1996. pap. 6.95 (*1-883953-13-8*) Midwest Trad.

***Curtis, Regina.** The Little Hands Playtime! Book: 50 Activities to Encourage Cooperation & Sharing. LC 99-88073. (Illus.). 144p. (J). (ps-1). 2000. pap. 12.95 (*1-885593-42-2*) Williamson Pub Co.

Curtis, Renee L. Le Roman de Tristan en Prose, Vol. II. LC 84-24337. (Arthurian Studies: No. XIII). 320p. 1985. text 75.00 (*0-85991-182-9*) Boydell & Brewer.

Curtis, Richard. Four Weddings & a Funeral. LC 96-134. (Illus.). 128p. 1996. pap. 9.95 (*0-312-14340-0*) St Martin.

— How to Be Your Own Literary Agent: The Business of Getting a Book Published. expanded rev. ed. LC 95-40556. 320p. 1996. pap. 13.95 (*0-395-71819-8*) HM.

— Mastering the Business of Writing: A Leading Literary Agent Reveals the Secrets of Success. LC 96-84618. 256p. (Orig.). 1996. pap. 18.95 (*1-880559-55-2*) Allworth Pr.

— Notting Hill. 1999. pap. 15.00 (*0-340-73844-8*, Pub. by Hodder & Stought Ltd) Trafalgar.

— This Business of Publishing: An Insider's View of Current Trends & Tactics. LC 98-70413. 224p. 1998. pap. 18.95 (*1-880559-98-6*) Allworth Pr.

Curtis, Richard & Kurtz, Trisha. Creating Consumer Choice in Healthcare: Measuring & Communicating Health Plan Performance Information. LC 98-10363. 244p. 1998. 42.00 (*1-56793-080-8*) Health Admin Pr.

***Curtis, Richard, et al.** Blackadder: The Whole Damn Dynasty, 1485-1917. (Illus.). 480p. 2000. pap. 16.00 (*0-14-029608-5*) Penguin Putnam.

Curtis, Richard A. The USA Today Design & Layout Manual. Blais, Jacqueline & Perri, Lynne, eds. (Illus.). 52p. 1995. pap. text 10.00 (*0-944347-03-7*) USA Today Bks.

Curtis, Richard J. One Percent Solution: How to Save Money Without Really Trying. LC 88-11845. (Illus.). 53p. (Orig.). 1988. pap. 8.95 (*0-945298-04-8*) Curtis Pubns.

— Retirement Planning Alert: Will Your Plans Meet Your Life Style Needs? LC 87-36488. (Illus.). 62p. (Orig.). 1988. pap. 8.95 (*0-945298-03-X*) Curtis Pubns.

Curtis, Rick. The Backpacker's Field Manual. LC 97-38922. (Illus.). 384p. 1998. pap. 14.95 (*0-517-88783-5*, Crown) Crown Pub Group.

Curtis, Robert H. Great Lives: Medicine. LC 92-5387. (Illus.). 336p. (J). (gr. 4-6). 1993. 24.00 (*0-684-19321-3*) Scribner.

Curtis, Robert I. Garum & Salsamenta: Production & Commerce in Materia Medica. LC 91-16000. (Studies in Ancient Medicine: No. 3). (Illus.). xv, 226p. 1991. 82.00 (*90-04-09423-7*) Brill Academic Pubs.

Curtis, Robert I., ed. Studia Pompeiana et Classica in Honor of Wilhelmina F. Jashemski: Vol. I: Pompeiana; Vol. II: Classica, 2 vols., Set. (Illus.). 1989. 160.00 (*0-89241-425-1*) Caratzas.

— Studia Pompeiana et Classica in Honor of Wilhelmina F. Jashemski, Vol. I: Pompeiana. (Illus.). xxii, 330p. 1988. lib. bdg. 90.00 (*0-89241-423-5*) Caratzas.

— Studia Pompeiana et Classica in Honor of Wilhelmina F. Jashemski, Vol. II: Classica. (Illus.). xxii, 271p. 1989. lib. bdg. 80.00 (*0-89241-424-3*) Caratzas.

***Curtis, Robert O.** Silviculture for Multiple Objectives in the Douglas-fir Region. (Illus.). 123p. (C). 2000. reprint ed. pap. text 30.00 (*0-7881-8660-4*) DIANE Pub.

C

An Asterisk (*) at the beginning of an entry indicates that the title is appearing for the first time.

Curtis, Rosme. Winged Tenacity: The Polish Air Force, 1918-1944. 4th rev. ed. (World War II Monograph: 305). (Illus.). 36p. 1997. reprint ed. 16.95 (*1-57638-063-7*, M305H); reprint ed. pap. 6.95 (*1-57638-020-3*, M305S) Merriam Pr.

Curtis, Ross & Webb, Farren. Shall This Nation Long Endure? Taming the Capitalist Beast. LC 92-12410. 224p. (Orig.). 1992. pap. 10.95 (*1-56474-027-7*) Fithian Pr.

Curtis, S., ed. From Asthma to Thalassaemia: Medical Conditions in Childhood. (C). 1989. 50.00 (*0-903534-69-X*, Pub. by Brit Ag for Adopt & Fost) St Mut.

Curtis, S. R. Bandidos Fantasmas. (Zorro Ser.). (SPA.). 1998. pap. text 9.95 (*1-58105-164-6*) Santillana.

— Los Muertos no Hablan. (Zorro Ser.). (SPA.). 1998. pap. text 9.95 (*1-58105-165-4*) Santillana.

— El Origen de la Leyenda. (Zorro Ser.). (SPA.). 1998. pap. text 9.95 (*1-58105-166-2*) Santillana.

Curtis, Samual R. Mexico under Fire: Being the Diary of Samuel Ryan Curtis, 3rd Ohio Volunteer Regiment, During... Chance, Joseph E., ed. 308p. (C). 1994. 29.95 (*0-87565-127-5*) Tex Christian.

Curtis, Sandra. The Joy of Movement in Early Childhood. LC 81-16520. (Early Childhood Education Ser.). (Illus.). 141p. 1982. pap. text 14.95 (*0-8077-2691-5*) Tchrs Coll.

***Curtis, Sandra.** Zorro Unmasked: The Official History. LC 97-36453. (Illus.). 320p. 1998. pap. 14.45 (*0-7868-8285-9*, Pub. by Hyperion) Time Warner.

Curtis, Sandra R. Alice & Eleanor: A Contrast in Style & Purpose. LC 93-72172. (Women Studies). (Illus.). 225p. (C). 1994. 35.95 (*0-87972-625-3*) Bowling Green Univ Popular Press.

— Gabriel's Ark. LC 98-22135. (Illus.). 64p. (J). (gr. 3-6). 1998. pap. 7.95 (*1-881283-23-2*) Alef Design.

***Curtis, Sarah.** Children Who Break the Law: Or Everybody Does It. 237p. 1999. pap. 39.00 (*1-872870-76-7*, Pub. by Waterside Pr) Gaunt.

Curtis, Sarah. The Geography of Welfare Provision. LC 88-28714. (Geography, Environment & Planning Ser.). 1989. write for info. (*0-415-03472-8*) Routledge.

Curtis, Sarah & Taket, Ann. Health & Societies: Changing Perspectives. (Arnold Publications). (Illus.). 384p. 1995. pap. text 35.00 (*0-340-62513-9*) OUP.

***Curtis, Sarah A.** Educating the Faithful: Religion, Schooling & Society in Nineteenth-Century France. LC 99-89652. 220p. 2000. 38.00 (*0-87580-262-1*) N Ill U Pr.

Curtis, Scott, et al, eds. Deaf Blind Children: Evaluating Their Multiple Handicaps. LC HV1597.C87. 180p. reprint ed. pap. 55.80 (*0-608-17504-8*, 203001500067) Bks Demand.

Curtis, Simon. The Law of Shipbuilding Contracts. (Lloyd's Shipping Law Library). 330p. 1991. 160.00 (*1-85044-334-3*) LLP.

Curtis, Stanley E. Environmental Management in Animal Agriculture. LC 83-8443. 418p. reprint ed. pap. 129.60 (*0-7837-2173-0*, 204251100004) Bks Demand.

Curtis, Stephanie, ed. see Verge, Roger.

Curtis, Stephanie, tr. see Bocuse, Paul.

Curtis, Susan. A Consuming Faith: The Social Gospel & Modern American Culture. LC 90-28696. (New Studies in American Intellectual & Cultural History). (Illus.). 320p. 1991. text 49.95 (*0-8018-4167-4*) Johns Hopkins.

— Dancing to a Black Man's Tune: A Life of Scott Joplin. LC 93-46116. (Missouri Biography Ser.). (Illus.). 288p. (C). 1994. text 29.95 (*0-8262-0949-1*) U of Mo Pr.

— The First Black Actors on the Great White Way. LC 98-27203. (Illus.). 304p. 1998. 29.95 (*0-8262-1195-X*) U of Mo Pr.

— Neal's Yard Remedies: Essentail Oils. (Illus.). 144p. 1996. pap. 14.95 (*1-85410-413-6*, Pub. by Aurum Pr) London Brdge.

— The Santa Fe School of Cooking Cookbook: Spirited Southwestern Recipes. 2nd ed. (Illus.). 176p. 1998. pap. 19.95 (*0-87905-873-0*) Gibbs Smith Pub.

Curtis, Susan & Curtis, Barry. Managing People & Activities. (Illus.). 325p. (Orig.). 1997. pap. 49.50 (*0-273-62066-5*, Pub. by Pitman Pub) Trans-Atl Phila.

Curtis, Susan & Fraser, Romy. Natural Healing for Women: Caring for Yourself with Herbs, Homeopathy, & Essential Oils. 304p. 1995. pap. 15.00 (*0-614-10599-4*) Harper SF.

— Natural Healing for Women: Caring for Yourself with Herbs, Homeopathy & Essential Oils. 422p. 1992. pap. 16.00 (*0-04-440645-2*, Pub. by Pandora) Routldge.

***Curtis, Susan & Long, Kathi.** Salsas. LC 00-24824. (Santa Fe School of Cooking Ser.). 48p. 2000. 12.95 (*0-87905-948-6*) Gibbs Smith Pub.

Curtis, Susan, et al. Neal's Yard Natural Remedies. (Illus.). 208p. 1990. pap. 12.95 (*0-14-019000-7*, Arkana) Viking Penguin.

***Curtis, Susan, et al.** Tacos. (Santa Fe School of Cooking Ser.). (Illus.). 48p. 2000. 12.95 (*0-87905-947-8*) Gibbs Smith Pub.

Curtis, Susan, jt. auth. see Neal's Yard Remedies Staff.

Curtis, Susan P. Take-Along Crafts. (Illus.). 72p. (Orig.). 1982. pap. 2.50 (*0-918178-28-2*) Simplicity.

Curtis, Suzanne, jt. auth. see DeVincenzi, Patti.

Curtis, T. Adrian, ed. American Cardinal Readers, Bk. 7. 452p. (YA). (gr. 7-8). 1996. reprint ed. text 25.00 (*0-911845-42-9*) Neumann Pr.

— American Cardinal Readers, Bk. 8. 556p. (YA). (gr. 8-9). 1996. reprint ed. text 27.00 (*0-911845-43-7*) Neumann Pr.

Curtis, T. Adrian, jt. ed. see McLaughlin, Edith M.

Curtis, Terry & Schement, Jorge R. Tendencies & Tensions of the Information Age: The Production & Distribution of Information in the United States. 285p. 1997. pap. text 21.95 (*1-56000-928-4*) Transaction Pubs.

Curtis, Terry, jt. auth. see Schement, Jorge R.

Curtis, Thomas B. & Westerfield, Donald L. Congressional Intent. LC 92-9567. 192p. 1992. 52.95 (*0-275-94197-3*, Praeger Pubs) Greenwood.

***Curtis, Thomas L.** From the Grassroots: A History of the United Methodist Volunteers in Mission Movement. LC 00-26737. 2000. write for info. (*0-687-07520-3*) Abingdon.

Curtis, Thomas S. High Frequency Apparatus. 248p. reprint ed. pap. 11.95 (*1-55918-003-X*) Lindsay Pubns.

***Curtis, Todd.** Understanding Aviation Safety Data: Using the Internet & Other Sources to Analyze Air Travel Risk. LC 00-26398. 2000. write for info. (*0-7680-0602-3*) Soc Auto Engineers.

Curtis, Tony. Arches, 1. LC 99-212498. 1999. 28.95 (*1-85411-236-8*); pap. text 15.95 (*1-85411-237-6*); pap. text 29.95 (*1-85411-245-7*) Seren Bks.

— Business & Marketing for Engineering & Scientists. LC 93-49026. 1994. 16.95 (*0-07-707868-3*) McGraw.

— Poems: Selected & New. LC 86-60368. (Poetry Ser.). 86p. (Orig.). 1986. 15.00 (*0-934257-07-8*); pap. 8.00 (*0-934257-06-X*) Story Line.

— Taken for Pearls: New Poems. 64p. 1994. pap. 14.95 (*1-85411-087-X*, Pub. by Seren Bks) Dufour.

— This Far North. 74p. 1994. pap. 11.95 (*1-873790-62-7*) Dufour.

Curtis, Tony, ed. The Art of Seamus Heaney. LC 85-4488. 180p. 1985. 30.00 (*0-8023-1279-9*) Dufour.

— How Poets Work. LC 96-181360. 180p. 1997. pap. 16.95 (*1-85411-131-0*, Pub. by Seren Bks) Dufour.

Curtis, Tony, et al, eds. The Art of Seamus Heaney. 3rd ed. LC 93-2209. 240p. 1994. pap. 16.95 (*0-8023-1302-7*) Dufour.

Curtis, Tony & Alston, David. Welsh Painters Talking. LC 98-112706. 224p. 1998. 37.95 (*1-85411-200-7*, Pub. by Seren Bks) Dufour.

Curtis, Tony, jt. ed. see James, Sian.

Curtis, Verna P. American Prints 1960-1980. LC 81-85990. (Illus.). 28p. (Orig.). 1982. pap. 3.00 (*0-944110-20-7*) Milwauk Art Mus.

— Photographs from the Collection of Floyd & Josephine Segel. LC 82-80088. (Illus.). 36p. (Orig.). 1982. pap. 4.00 (*0-944110-22-3*) Milwauk Art Mus.

Curtis, Verna P., et al, eds. F. Holland Day: Selected Texts & Bibliography. (World Photographers References Ser.: Vol. 8). 161p. 1996. 105.00 (*0-8161-0618-5*, G K Hall & Co) Mac Lib Ref.

Curtis, Verna P. & Mallach, Stanley. Photography & Reform: Lewis Hine & the National Child Labor Committee. Goldstein, Rosalie, ed. LC 81-85989. (Illus.). 87p. (Orig.). 1981. pap. 10.00 (*0-944110-45-2*) Milwauk Art Mus.

Curtis, Vesta S. Persian Myths. (Legendary Past Ser.). (Illus.). 80p. (Orig.). (C). 1994. pap. 12.95 (*0-292-71158-1*) U of Tex Pr.

Curtis, W. First Steps to Ear Training (B-8) Consignment. 80p. 1986. pap. 6.95 (*0-7935-5541-8*, 50449980) H Leonard.

Curtis, W. D. & Miller, F. R. Differential Manifold & Theoretical Physics. 416p. 1986. pap. text 77.00 (*0-12-200231-8*) Acad Pr.

Curtis, W. S. & Donlon, E. T. Observational Evaluation of Severely Multi-Handicapped Children. (Modern Approaches to the Diagnosis & Instruction of Multi-Handicapped Children Ser.: Vol. 18). viii, 204p. 1985. 36.25 (*90-265-0595-7*) Swets.

Curtis, Walt. Mala Noche: And Other "Illegal" Adventures.Tr. of Bad Night. (Illus.). 224p. 1997. pap. 14.95 (*0-9623683-4-2*) BridgeCity Bks.

— Peckerneck Country. 1978. 10.00 (*0-932191-05-3*) Mr Cogito Pr.

— Rhymes for Alice Bluelight. LC 83-23846. 66p. 1984. pap. 7.00 (*0-89924-040-2*) Lynx Hse.

Curtis, Walt, tr. see Garcia Lorca, Federico, et al.

Curtis, Walter G. Reminiscences of Wilmington & Smithville--Southport, 1848-1900. 2nd ed. (Illus.). vi, 85p. 1999. 12.95 (*1-892444-11-9*) Southport Hist.

Curtis, Walter J. Johnny Goodman - The Last Amateur Golfer to Win the U. S. Open. LC 96-96292. (Illus.). 222p. 1997. reprint ed. lib. bdg. 24.95 (*0-9659419-0-6*) Curtis Pub.

Curtis, Wayne. Currents in the Stream. 214p. 1988. pap. 9.95 (*0-86492-092-X*, Pub. by Goose Ln Edits) Genl Dist Srvs.

— Fishing in the Miramichi. rev. ed. (Illus.). 134p. 1997. pap. 12.95 (*0-86492-181-0*, Pub. by Goose Ln Edits) Genl Dist Srvs.

— Frommer's Northern New England. (Illus.). 1996. 15.95 (*0-02-861141-1*) Macmillan.

— Frommer's Vermont, New Hampshire & Maine. 408p. 1998. pap. 15.95 (*0-02-862227-8*, Pub. by Macmillan) S&S Trade.

***Curtis, Wayne.** Maine: Off the Beaten Path. 4th ed. (Off the Beaten Path Ser.). (Illus.). 208p. (Orig.). 2000. pap. 12.95 (*0-7627-0644-9*) Globe Pequot.

Curtis, Wayne. Maine: Off the Beaten Path: A Guide to Unique Places. 3rd ed. LC 98-17469. (Off the Beaten Path Ser.). (Illus.). 256p. (Orig.). 1998. pap. 12.95 (*0-7627-0190-0*) Globe Pequot.

— One Indian Summer. 200p. 1994. pap. 12.95 (*0-86492-151-9*, Pub. by Goose Ln Edits) Genl Dist Srvs.

— River Guides of the Miramichi. (Illus.). 120p. 1997. pap. 12.95 (*0-86492-224-8*, Pub. by Goose Ln Edits) Genl Dist Srvs.

Curtis, Wayne C. Microeconomic Concepts for Attorneys: A Reference Guide. LC 83-23051. 153p. 1984. 45.00 (*0-89930-060-X*, CMC/, Quorum Bks) Greenwood.

— Statistical Concepts for Attorneys: A Reference Guide. LC 82-24068. 230p. 1983. 55.00 (*0-89930-033-2*, CSA/, Quorum Bks) Greenwood.

Curtis, Will & Curtis, Jane. Antique Woodstoves: Artistry in Iron. (Illus.). 64p. 1975. pap. 15.00 (*0-89156-000-3*) Cobblesmith.

Curtis, William. A Short History of the Browntai Moth. 1969. 45.00 (*0-7855-0674-8*) St Mut.

Curtis, William, jt. auth. see Sekler, Eduard F.

Curtis, William D. Periculum Latinum. 87p. (J). 1998. spiral bd. 13.50 (*0-939507-53-6*, L8) Amer Classical.

Curtis, William E. The Capitals of Spanish America. 1976. lib. bdg. 59.95 (*0-8490-1570-7*) Gordon Pr.

— Children of the Sun. LC 74-7946. reprint ed. 39.50 (*0-404-11833-X*) AMS Pr.

Curtis, William J. Denys Lasdun: Architecture, City, Landscape. LC 95-128886. (Illus.). 240p. (C). 1994. text 75.00 (*0-7148-2871-8*, Pub. by Phaidon Press) Phaidon Pr.

— Le Corbusier: Ideas & Forms. rev. ed. (Illus.). 240p. (C). 1995. pap. 29.95 (*0-7148-2790-8*, Pub. by Phaidon Press) Phaidon Pr.

— Modern Architecture since 1900. 3rd ed. LC 97-112837. (Illus.). 736p. 1996. 49.95 (*0-7148-3524-2*, Pub. by Phaidon Press) Phaidon Pr.

— Modern Architecture since 1900. 3rd ed. LC 97-112837. (Illus.). 736p. 1996. pap. text 29.95 (*0-7148-3356-8*, Pub. by Phaidon Press) Phaidon Pr.

***Curtis, William J. R.** Denys Lasdun: Architecture, City & Landscape. 240p. 1999. pap. 29.95 (*0-7148-3902-7*) Phaidon Pr.

Curtis, William J. R. Modern Architecture since 1900. 3rd ed. LC 97-120714. 736p. (C). 1996. pap. text 70.67 (*0-13-232273-0*, Pub. by P-H) S&S Trade.

Curtis, William R. Lambeth Conferences: The Solution for Pan-Anglican Organization. LC 68-58565. (Columbia University. Studies in the Social Sciences: No. 488). reprint ed. 32.50 (*0-404-51488-X*) AMS Pr.

Curtis, Wynn J., jt. auth. see Graham, Sheila Y.

***Curtis, Zelda.** Life After Work: Stories of Freedom, Opportunity & Change. 1999. pap. 17.95 (*0-7043-4597-8*, Pub. by Womens Press) Trafalgar.

Curtiss, A. B. The Children of the Gods. LC 94-74030. (Illus.). 140p. (YA). 1995. 18.95 (*0-932529-57-7*) Oldcastle.

— Hallelujah a Cat Comes Back. LC 95-74768. (Illus.). 48p. (J). (ps up). 1996. 18.95 (*0-932529-52-6*) Oldcastle.

— In the Company of Bears. LC 93-86130. (Illus.). 157p. (J). (ps up). 1994. lib. bdg. 18.95 (*0-932529-72-0*) Oldcastle.

— Legend of the Giant Panda. LC 97-65548. (Illus.). 40p. (J). (gr. k-4). 1997. 18.95 (*0-932529-59-3*) Oldcastle.

— Time of the Wild. (Illus.). 40p. (J). (gr. 4-8). 1998. lib. bdg. 18.95 (*0-932529-55-0*) Oldcastle.

— A Train You Never Saw. LC 98-66044. (Illus.). 40p. (J). (gr. k-3). 1998. lib. bdg. 18.95 (*0-932529-74-7*) Oldcastle.

Curtiss Aeroplane & Motor Corp. Curtiss Standard JN-4D Military Tractor (Aircraft) Handbook. Rice, M. S., ed. (Illus.). 72p. 1974. reprint ed. pap. 8.25 (*0-87994-013-1*) Aviat Pub.

***Curtiss, Allen, Jr.** 1,001 Tips for Better Mail Management. Riggiero, Timothy J., ed. 300p. 2000. pap. 59.00 (*0-615-11384-2*) Excelsior Bks PA.

***Curtiss, Arline.** Depression Is a Choice: Winning the Fight Through Directed Thinking Without Drugs. 320p. 2001. 24.95 (*0-7868-6629-2*, Pub. by Hyperion) Time Warner.

Curtiss, Carol, ed. see Durham, Ron.

Curtiss, Carol P., jt. auth. see Haylock, Pamela J.

Curtiss, Dave. Developing Capable Youth: How to Help Your Kids Become... 1994. pap. 14.99 (*0-310-57561-3*) Zondervan.

Curtiss, Eleanor. For Young Souls. 1941. pap. 5.95 (*0-87516-303-3*) DeVorss.

Curtiss, F. H. A Genealogy of the Curtiss Family, Being a Record of the Descendants of Widow Elizabeth Curtis, Who Settled in Stratford, Conn. 1639-40. (Illus.). 283p. 1993. reprint ed. pap. 42.00 (*0-8328-1391-5*); reprint ed. lib. bdg. 52.00 (*0-8328-1390-7*) Higginson Bk Co.

Curtiss, F. Homer. Coming World Changes. 136p. 1981. pap. 12.50 (*0-89540-090-1*, SB-090) Sun Pub.

***Curtiss, F. Homer.** Inner Radiance (1935) 378p. 1998. reprint ed. pap. 24.95 (*0-7661-0351-X*) Kessinger Pub.

Curtiss, F. Homer. Reincarnation. 62p. 1993. pap. 6.00 (*0-89540-260-2*, SB-260) Sun Pub.

Curtiss, F. Homer, jt. auth. see Curtiss, Harriette A.

Curtiss, H. C., Jr., jt. auth. see Dowell, E. H.

Curtiss, Harriette A. The Key to the Universe. 392p. 1996. reprint ed. spiral bd. 25.00 (*0-7873-1233-9*) Hlth Research.

— The Truth about Evolution & the Bible (1928) 248p. 1998. reprint ed. pap. 19.95 (*0-7661-0185-1*) Kessinger Pub.

Curtiss, Harriette A. & Curtiss, F. Homer. Gems of Mysticism. 88p. 1991. pap. 10.00 (*0-89540-143-6*, SB-143) Sun Pub.

— The Inner Radiance. 369p. 1993. pap. 32.00 (*0-89540-149-5*, SB-149) Sun Pub.

— The Key of Destiny. 372p. 1981. pap. 32.00 (*0-89540-070-7*, SB-070) Sun Pub.

— The Key of Destiny. 328p. 1996. reprint ed. spiral bd. 21.50 (*0-7873-0234-1*) Hlth Research.

— The Key of Destiny (1919) 333p. 1996. reprint ed. pap. 24.95 (*1-56459-700-8*) Kessinger Pub.

— The Key to the Universe. 1991. lib. bdg. 88.95 (*0-8490-4962-8*) Gordon Pr.

— The Key to the Universe. 391p. 1981. pap. 34.00 (*0-89540-069-3*, SB-069) Sun Pub.

— The Key to the Universe: or A Spiritual Interpretation of Numbers & Symbols (1917) 392p. 1996. reprint ed. pap. 24.95 (*1-56459-707-5*) Kessinger Pub.

— The Message of Aquaria. 487p. 1981. pap. 38.00 (*0-89540-065-0*, SB-065) Sun Pub.

— The Voice of Isis. 472p. 1992. pap. 35.00 (*0-89540-130-4*, SB-130) Sun Pub.

— The Voice of Isis. 9th rev. ed. 440p. 1996. reprint ed. spiral bd. 26.50 (*0-7873-0233-3*) Hlth Research.

— The Voice of Isis (1913) 442p. 1996. reprint ed. pap. 24.95 (*1-56459-699-0*) Kessinger Pub.

Curtiss, J. H. Introduction to the Theory of Functions of a Complex Variable. (Pure & Applied Mathematics Ser.: Vol. 44). (Illus.). 416p. 1978. text 175.00 (*0-8247-6501-X*) Dekker.

Curtiss, J. H., ed. see Applied Mathematics Symposium Staff.

Curtiss, John S. The Russian Church & the Soviet State, 1917-1950. 1953. 16.50 (*0-8446-1141-7*) Peter Smith.

— The Russian Revolutions of 1917. LC 82-15180. (Anvil Ser.). 192p. 1982. reprint ed. pap. 11.50 (*0-89874-499-7*) Krieger.

— Russia's Crimean War. LC 76-28915. (Illus.). 617p. reprint ed. pap. 191.30 (*0-608-17317-7*, 205223500068) Bks Demand.

Curtiss, Mina. Bizet & His World. LC 76-55412. 477p. 1977. reprint ed. lib. bdg. 75.00 (*0-8371-9427-X*, CUBI, Greenwood Pr) Greenwood.

Curtiss, Mina, ed. see Degas, Hilaire G.

Curtiss, Richard H. A Changing Image: American Perceptions of the Arab-Israeli Dilemma. 2nd ed. 1986. 14.95 (*0-937165-00-X*) Am Educ Trust.

— Stealth PACs: How Israel's American Lobby Took Control of U. S. Middle East Policy. (Illus.). 170p. (Orig.). (C). 1990. pap. 9.95 (*0-937165-03-4*) Am Educ Trust.

— Stealth PACs: Lobbying Congress for Control of U. S. Middle East Policy. 4th ed. 1996. pap. 14.95 (*0-937165-05-0*) Am Educ Trust.

— Stealth PACs: Lobbying Congress for Control of U.S. Middle East Policy. 3rd ed. 1991. 14.95 (*0-937165-04-2*) Am Educ Trust.

Curtiss, Richard H. & McMahon, Janet, eds. Seeing the Light: Personal Encounters with the Middle East & Islam. LC 97-6644. (Illus.). 280p. (Orig.). 1997. pap. 18.95 (*0-937165-06-9*) Am Educ Trust.

Curtiss, Thomas Q. The Smart Set: George Jean Nathan & H. L. Mencken. LC 97-28457. (Illus.). 320p. 1998. 20.95 (*1-55783-312-5*) Applause Theatre Bk Pubs.

Curtiss, Ursula. Hours to Kill. 168p. 1995. 19.50 (*0-7451-8668-8*, Black Dagger) Chivers N Amer.

Curtiss, Ursula. In Cold Pursuit. large type ed. (Linford Mystery Library). 1988. pap. 16.99 (*0-7089-6510-5*) Ulverscroft.

***Curtiss, Ursula.** The Iron Cobweb. large type ed. LC 99-43304. (Thorndike Mystery Ser.). 1999. 25.95 (*0-7862-2152-6*) Thorndike Pr.

Curtiss, Ursula. The Second Sickle. large type ed. (Linford Mystery Library). 352p. 1989. pap. 16.99 (*0-7089-6732-9*, Linford) Ulverscroft.

— The Wasp. 160p. 1998. 19.50 (*0-7540-8517-1*, Black Dagger) Chivers N Amer.

— The Wasp. large type ed. (Linford Mystery Library). 329p. 1989. pap. 16.99 (*0-7089-6642-X*, Linford) Ulverscroft.

Curtiss, Vienna I. Cappy: Rollicking Rancher Atop Arizona's Mighty Rim. LC 79-84471. (Illus.). 1979. 12.00 (*0-9602742-0-0*) Collectors Choice.

— I Should Be Glad to Help You, Madame: Europe Minus One's Wardrobe. LC 79-58850. (Illus.). 1979. 6.00 (*0-9602742-1-9*) Collectors Choice.

— Pageant of Art. LC 77-280. (Illus.). 1979. 27.50 (*0-9602742-2-7*) Collectors Choice.

Curtiss, W. M. The Tariff Idea. LC 96-85396. 81p. 1996. reprint ed. pap. 2.95 (*0-910614-46-6*) Foun Econ Ed.

Curtiss-Wedge, Franklyn. History of Buffalo & Pepin Counties, 2 vols. (Illus.). 1047p. 1998. reprint ed. lib. bdg. 114.00 (*0-8328-9732-9*) Higginson Bk Co.

— History of Freeborn County, Minnesota. (Illus.). 883p. 1994. reprint ed. lib. bdg. 89.50 (*0-8328-3848-9*) Higginson Bk Co.

— History of Goodhue County, Minnesota. (Illus.). 1074p. 1994. reprint ed. lib. bdg. 110.00 (*0-8328-3853-5*) Higginson Bk Co.

— The History of Renville County, Minnesota, 2 vols. (Illus.). 1376p. 1994. reprint ed. lib. bdg. 139.00 (*0-8328-3837-3*) Higginson Bk Co.

— History of Wabasha County, Minnesota. (Illus.). 781p. 1994. reprint ed. lib. bdg. 79.50 (*0-8328-3845-4*) Higginson Bk Co.

— History of Wright County, Minnesota, 2 vols. (Illus.). 1111p. 1994. reprint ed. lib. bdg. 115.00 (*0-8328-3854-3*) Higginson Bk Co.

Curtiss-Wedge, Franklyn, et al, compiled by. History of Dunn County: With Biographical Sketches. (Illus.). 966p. 1995. reprint ed. lib. bdg. 95.00 (*0-8328-5142-6*) Higginson Bk Co.

— History of Rice & Steele Counties, 2 vols. (Illus.). 1560p. 1997. reprint ed. lib. bdg. 164.00 (*0-8328-6812-4*) Higginson Bk Co.

Curtiss-Wedge, Franklyn, ed. History of Dakota Co., Minnesota. (Illus.). 662p. 1993. reprint ed. lib. bdg. 69.00 (*0-8328-3175-1*) Higginson Bk Co.

Curtiss-Wegde, Franklyn, et al, eds. History of McLeod County. (Illus.). 862p. 1997. reprint ed. lib. bdg. 88.50 (*0-8328-6806-X*) Higginson Bk Co.

Curtius, Ernst R. Civilization of France: An Introduction. Wyon, Olive, tr. LC 70-148877. (Select Bibliographies Reprint Ser.). 1977. reprint ed. 18.95 (*0-8369-5648-6*) Ayer.

— Essays on European Literature. Kowal, Michael, tr. from GER. LC 72-9943. 538p. reprint ed. pap. 166.80 (*0-8357-4041-2*, 203673200005) Bks Demand.

— European Literature & the Latin Middle Ages. Trask, Willard R. & Godman, Peter, trs. (Bollingen Ser.: No. XXXVI). 707p. (C). 1973. text 105.00 (*0-691-09969-3*, Pub. by Princeton U Pr); pap. text 24.95 (*0-691-01899-5*, Pub. by Princeton U Pr) Cal Prin Full Svc.

C

Curtius, Georg, et al, eds. Leipziger Studien zur Classischen Philologie, 20 vols. in 10, Set. lxxx, 7348p. 1972. reprint ed. 1360.00 (*3-487-04335-1*) G Olms Pubs.

Curtius, Georg & Brugmann, Karl, eds. Studien Zur Griechischen und Lateinischen Grammatik, 10 vols. in 5, Set. xvi, 4667p. 1972. reprint ed. 1185.00 (*3-487-04284-3*) G Olms Pubs.

Curtius, H. C., et al, eds. Biochemical & Clinical Aspects of Pteridines Vol. 4: Cancer - Immunology - Metabolic Diseases. Proceedings, Fourth Winter Workshop on Pteridines, February 23-March 2, 1985, St. Christoph, Arlberg, Austria. (Illus.). xxi, 686p. 1985. 315.40 (*3-11-010182-3*) De Gruyter.

— Chemistry & Biology of Pteridines, 1989: Pteridines & Folic Acid Derivatives Proceedings of the Ninth Int'l Symposium on Pteridines & Folic Acid Derivatives. Chemical, Biological & Clinical Aspects. Zurich, Switzerland, Sept. 3-8, 1989. (Illus.). xxxvi, 1340p. (C). 1990. lib. bdg. 346.15 (*3-11-012199-9*) De Gruyter.

— Unconjugated Pterins & Related Biogenic Amines. 398p. (C). 1987. lib. bdg. 161.55 (*3-11-011341-4*) De Gruyter.

Curtius, Ludwig. Die Antike Kunst Bd. II: Die Klassische Kunst Griechenlands. 466p. 1959. 160.00 (*0-318-70734-9*) G Olms Pubs.

Curtius Rufus, Quintus. Curtius Rufus, Quintus: Quintus Curtius Rufus, Index Verborum - Releves Lexicaux et Grammaticaux. Therasse, Jean, ed. (Alpha-Omega, Reihe A Ser.: Bd. XXIX). 628p. 1976. 130.00 incl. 3.5 hd (*3-487-05977-0*) G Olms Pubs.

— De Rebus Gestis Alexandri Magni. Mutzell, Julius, ed. xc, 972p. 1976. reprint ed. 225.00 incl. 3.5 hd (*3-487-06003-5*) G Olms Pubs.

— A History of Quintus Curcius, Conteyning the Actes of the Greate Alexander. Brende, J., tr. LC 77-25709. (English Experience Ser.: No. 303). 452p. 1971. reprint ed. 55.00 (*90-221-0303-X*) Walter J Johnson.

Curtler, Hugh. A Theory of Art, Tragedy & Culture: The Philosophy of Eliseo Vivas. (World of Art Ser.). 224p. 1983. pap. text 11.00 (*0-930586-15-8*) Haven Pubns.

— What Is Art? (World of Art Ser.). (Illus.). 220p. (Orig.). 1983. pap. text 25.00 (*0-930586-17-4*) Haven Pubns.

Curtler, Hugh M. Ethical Argument: Critical Thinking in Ethics. 160p. 1992. pap. 12.95 (*1-55778-513-9*) Paragon Hse.

— Rediscovering Values: Coming to Terms with Postmodernism. LC 97-9281. 192p. (C). (gr. 13). 1997. text 61.95 (*0-7656-0059-5*) M E Sharpe.

— Rediscovering Values: Coming to Terms with Postmodernism. LC 97-9281. 192p. (gr. 13). 1997. pap. text 24.95 (*0-7656-0060-9*) M E Sharpe.

Curtler, Hugh Mercier, ed. Vivas As Critic: Essays in Poetics & Criticism by Eliseo Vivas. LC 82-50419. viii, 257p. (C). 1982. 45.00 (*0-87875-224-2*) Whitston Pub.

Curtner-Smith, Mary. Infants & Children. 3rd ed. 172p. 1999. pap. text 18.70 (*0-536-02388-3*) Pearson Custom.

Curtner-Smith, Mary & Fitch, Stanley. Insights into Middle Childhood Development. 120p. (C). 1995. pap. text 16.00 (*1-56226-231-9*) CAT Pub.

Curto, Raul E., et al, eds. Algebraic Methods in Operator Theory. LC 94-5179. 1994. 98.00 (*0-8176-3745-1*) Birkhauser.

— Multivariable Operator Theory: Proceedings: A Joint Summer Research Conference on Multivariable Operator Theory (1993: University of Washington, Seattle) LC 95-2345. (Contemporary Mathematics Ser.: Vol. 185). 380p. 1995. pap. 63.00 (*0-8218-0298-4*, CONM/185) Am Math.

Curto, Raul E. & Fialkow, Lawrence A. Flat Extensions of Positive Moment Matrices: Recursively Generated Relations. LC 98-35277. (Memoirs of the American Mathematical Society Ser.: Vol. 136, No. 648). 56p. 1998. pap. 36.00 (*0-8218-0869-9*) Am Math.

— Solution of the Truncated Complex Moment Problem for Flat Data. LC 95-39135. (Memoirs of the American Mathematical Society Ser.: Vol. 568). 52p. 1996. pap. 32.00 (*0-8218-0485-5*, MEMO/119/568) Am Math.

Curton, Josephine J. Hard Times Notes. (Cliffs Notes Ser.). 48p. 1964. pap. 4.95 (*0-8220-0578-6*, Cliff) IDG Bks.

Curtright, Carolee, jt. auth. see Kozak, Dorothy.

Curtright, Thomas, ed. Quantum Groups: Spring Workshop on Quantum Groups, Argonne Laboratory, April 16 to May 11, 1990. 344p. 1991. text 81.00 (*981-02-0381-0*) World Scientific Pub.

Curtright, Thomas, et al, eds. Quantum Field Theory, Statistical Mechanics, Quantum Groups & Topology: Proceedings of the NATO Advanced Research Workshop, University of Miami, 7-12 January 1991. LC 92-30893. 364p. 1992. pap. write for info. (*981-02-0960-6*) World Scientific Pub.

Curts, Paul. Luther's Variations in Sentence Arrangement from the Modern Literary Usage with Primary Reference to the Position of the Verb. 1910. pap. 49.50 (*0-686-83611-1*) Elliots Bks.

Curts, Paul H., tr. see Hebbel, Friedrich.

Curtsinger, E. C. Segoviana. 248p. 1992. per. 15.00 (*0-941179-40-0*) Latitudes Pr.

Curtsinger, E. G. Swimming to the Moon. 236p. 1996. per. 15.00 (*0-941179-42-7*) Latitudes Pr.

Curtsinger, George, jt. auth. see Coleman, Thomas J.

Curtus. Development: New Paradigms & Principles for the Twenty-First Century. LC 95-38685. (Rethinking Bretton Woods Ser.: No. 2). 1995. 45.00 (*0-7453-1048-6*) Westview.

— Poison in the Pot: The Legacy of Lead. LC 84-2296. 287p. 1984. 31.95 (*0-8093-1156-9*) S Ill U Pr.

Curtus & Barthelemy. Algorithmic Complexity. LC 97-141792. 256p. 1995. 49.95 (*1-85728-451-8*, Pub. by UCL Pr Ltd) Taylor & Francis.

Curtus & Gisolfi, Diana. The Rule, Bible & Council: The Library of the Benedictine Abbey at Praglia. LC 97-34406. (Illus.). 200p. 1997. 55.00 (*0-295-97661-6*) U of Wash Pr.

Curtus, et al. Mexic Cinema/Mexic Woman. LC 96-10110. (Illus.). 1996. pap. 16.95 (*0-8165-1637-5*) U of Ariz Pr.

— White Man's Medicine: Government Doctors & the Navajo, 1863-1955. LC 97-36481. 290p. 1998. 39.95 (*0-8263-1839-8*) Univ of New Mexico Schl.

Curtus, jt. ed. see Sheehan, Helen E.

Curty, Angelo D. I Danced Around the World: As a Gentleman Host Aboard Cruise Ships. Curty, Kay, ed. LC 97-72396. (Illus.). 112p. 1997. pap. write for info. (*0-9652491-2-3*) Ken Cook.

Curty, Kay, ed. see Curty, Angelo D.

***Curuso, Andy.** Soccer Coaching Development & Tatics. (Illus.). 195p. 1998. pap. 14.95 (*0-9651020-1-7*) Reedswain.

Curutchet, Mirina. A Self-Help Housing Project in Rural Tunisia in Retrospect. 138p. 1987. write for info. (*91-7106-261-0*, Pub. by Nordic Africa) Transaction Pubs.

Curvers, Hans & Hemelrijk, Jaap, eds. Turkey in Focus. (Illus.). 158p. 1992. 29.95 (*0-7103-0441-2*, A7657) Routledge.

Curvin, Robert & Porter, Bruce. Blackout Looting: New York City, July 13, 1977. LC 78-20817. 240p. 1979. pap. text 21.95 (*0-89876-059-3*) Gardner Pr.

***Curwell, Steve & March, Chris.** Hazardous Building Materials: Guide to Selection of Alternatives. 2nd ed. (Illus.). 304p. (C). 1999. pap. 49.99 (*0-419-23450-0*, E & FN Spon) Routledge.

Curwen, Charles A. Taiping Rebel: The Deposition of Li Hsiu-Ch'eng. LC 76-8292. (Cambridge Studies in Chinese History, Literature & Institutions). 365p. reprint ed. pap. 104.10 (*0-608-17506-4*, 2030588) Bks Demand.

Curwen, H., tr. see Poe, Edgar Allan.

Curwen, Henry Darcy, ed. see Johnson, Samuel.

Curwen, Peter & Else, Peter K. Principles of Microeconomics. 480p. (C). 1990. text 90.00 (*0-04-338151-0*) Routledge.

Curwen, Samuel. Journal & Letters of Samuel Curwen, an American in England, from 1775-1783. Ward, George A., ed. LC 70-14720. (Era of the American Revolution Ser.). 1970. reprint ed. lib. bdg. 85.00 (*0-306-71923-1*) Da Capo.

— Journal & Letters of the Late Samuel Curwen. Ward, G. A., ed. LC 72-1002. reprint ed. 64.50 (*0-404-01889-0*) AMS Pr.

— Journal & Letters of the Late Samuel Curwen. (American Biography Ser.). 578p. 1991. reprint ed. lib. bdg. 99.00 (*0-7812-8097-4*) Rprt Serv.

— The Journal of Samuel Curwen, Loyalist, 2 vols., Set. Oliver, Andrew, ed. LC 72-180150. (Illus.). 1133p. 1972. 55.00 (*0-674-48380-4*) HUP.

***Curwin & Slater.** Improve Your Mathematics. 1999. pap. 9.99 (*1-86152-551-6*) Thomson Learn.

— Quantative Methods for Business Decisions. 5th ed. 2001. pap. 39.95 (*1-86152-531-1*) Thomson Learn.

Curwin, J. & Slater, Roger. Quantitative Methods for Business Decisions. 3rd ed. 300p. 1991. mass mkt. 62.95 (*0-412-40240-8*, A6301) Chapman & Hall.

Curwin, Jon & Slater, Roger. Quantitative Methods for Business Decisions. 4th ed. 480p. 1996. mass mkt. 31.95 (*0-412-74940-8*) Chapman & Hall.

— Quantitative Methods for Business Decisions. 4th rev. ed. (Illus.). 480p. 1996. pap. 24.99 (*1-86152-027-1*) Thomson Learn.

— Quantitative Methods for Business Decisions, Lecturers' Resource Manual. 4th ed. 150p. 1997. pap., student ed. 34.95 (*1-86152-028-X*, Pub. by ITBP) Thomson Learn.

Curwin, Richard & Fuhrmann, Barbara. Discovering Your Teaching Self: Humanistic Approaches to Effective Teaching. LC 74-11371. (Curriculum & Teaching Ser.). (Illus.). 256p. 1975. pap. text 18.95 (*0-685-03837-8*) P-H.

Curwin, Richard & Timmerman, Tim. Making Evaluation Meaningful. (Series in Education). 1988. pap. 12.95 (*0-8290-1078-5*); text 22.50 (*0-8290-0555-2*) Irvington.

Curwin, Richard L. Rediscovering Hope: Our Greatest Teaching Strategy. LC 98-177438. 182p. (Orig.). 1992. pap. 21.95 (*1-879639-24-6*) Natl Educ Serv.

Curwin, Richard L. & Mendler, Allen N. As Tough As Necessary: Countering Violence, Aggression, & Hostility in Our Schools. LC 97-18652. 150p. (Orig.). 1997. pap. 15.95 (*0-87120-280-8*, 197017) ASCD.

***Curwin, Richard L. & Mendler, Allen N.** Discipline with Dignity. rev. ed. LC 99-6600. 276p. 1999. pap. 15.95 (*0-87120-357-X*, 199235) ASCD.

Curwood, James. Glory of Living. 1998. lib. bdg. 52.95 (*1-56723-119-5*) Yestermorrow.

Curwood, James O. Baree: The Story of a Wolf-Dog. LC 90-37875. (Medallion Edition Ser.). 256p. (J). (gr. 3-11). 1992. pap. 4.95 (*1-55704-132-6*, Pub. by Newmarket) Norton.

— Baree, Son of Kazan. reprint ed. lib. bdg. 22.95 (*0-88411-858-4*) Amereon Ltd.

— Baree, Son of Kazan. 1990. reprint ed. lib. bdg. 18.95 (*0-89968-500-5*) Buccaneer Bks.

— Bear. LC 89-13247. (Medallion Edition Ser.). 208p. (J). (gr. 3-11). 1992. pap. 4.95 (*1-55704-131-8*, Pub. by Newmarket) Norton.

— Bear: A Novel. Date not set. lib. bdg. 21.95 (*0-8488-1703-6*) Amereon Ltd.

— Falkner of the Inland Seas. 1976. reprint ed. lib. bdg. 19.95 (*0-88411-851-7*) Amereon Ltd.

— The Flaming Forest. 1976. reprint ed. lib. bdg. 23.95 (*0-88411-852-5*) Amereon Ltd.

— God's Country: The Trail of Happiness. 1976. reprint ed. lib. bdg. 18.95 (*0-88411-853-3*) Amereon Ltd.

— The Gold Hunters. 1976. reprint ed. lib. bdg. 25.95 (*0-88411-854-1*) Amereon Ltd.

— Great Lakes. 1976. 78.00 (*0-8488-0961-0*) Amereon Ltd.

— Kazan. 1976. reprint ed. lib. bdg. 25.95 (*0-88411-855-X*) Amereon Ltd.

— Kazan. 1990. reprint ed. lib. bdg. 21.95 (*0-89968-501-3*) Buccaneer Bks.

— Kazan: Father of Baree. LC 95-969. 240p. (YA). 1995. pap. 4.95 (*1-55704-225-X*, Pub. by Newmarket) Norton.

— Nomads of the North. 1919. 69.00 (*0-403-00802-6*) Scholarly.

— Nomads of the North. LC 98-85545. 260p. 1998. reprint ed. pap. 12.00 (*1-892323-08-7*) Vivisphere.

— Nomads of the North: A Story of Romance & Adventure under the Open Stars. LC 78-127911. (BCL Ser. I). (Illus.). reprint ed. 37.50 (*0-404-01896-3*) AMS Pr.

— The River's End. 1976. reprint ed. lib. bdg. 23.95 (*0-88411-856-8*) Amereon Ltd.

Curwood, S. Uncommon Hero. 1999. 19.45 (*0-446-51448-9*, Pub. by Warner Bks) Little.

Cury, Ivan. Directing & Producing for Television: A Format Approach. LC 97-48424. 336p. 1998. pap. 36.95 (*0-240-80281-0*, Focal) Buttrwrth-Heinemann.

***Curzan, Anne L. & Damour, Lisa K.** First Day to Final Grade. LC 00-8010. (Illus.). 150p. (C). 2000. text, student ed. 32.50 (*0-472-09732-6*, 09732) U of Mich Pr.

— First Day to Final Grade: A Graduate Student's Guide to Teaching. LC 00-8010. (Illus.). 150p. (C). 2000. pap. text 15.95 (*0-472-06732-X*, 06732) U of Mich Pr.

Curzer. Ethical Theory & Moral Problems. LC 98-39126. (Philosophy Ser.). 1998. mass mkt. 43.95 (*0-534-52974-7*) Wadsworth Pub.

Curzi, Valler. I Ching. 1999. pap. text 6.95 (*84-270-2255-7*) Planeta.

***Curzio, Alberto Q. & Pellizzari, Fausta.** Rent, Resources, Technologies. LC 99-16713. (Illus.). xii, 259p. 1999. 94.00 (*3-540-66007-0*) Spr-Verlag.

Curzio, Alberto Quadrio, see Quadrio Curzio, Alberto.

Curzio, Anna G. Reflections Through a Glass. 80p. 1987. 55.00 (*0-7212-0777-4*, Pub. by Regency Pr GBR) St Mut.

Curzon. The Gospels in Our Image. 1997. pap. 13.00 (*0-15-600542-5*) Harcourt.

— Modern Poems on the Bible. 1997. pap. 13.00 (*0-15-600541-7*) Harcourt.

Curzon, Clare. All Unwary. LC 97-33068. (Thames Valley Mystery Ser.). 256p. 1998. text 21.95 (*0-312-18037-3*) St Martin.

— All Unwary. large type ed. LC 98-8442. 340p. 1999. pap. write for info. (*0-7540-3468-2*) Chivers N Amer.

— All Unwary. large type ed. LC 98-8442. 342p. 1999. 30.00 (*0-7862-1544-5*) Thorndike Pr.

— The Blue-Eyed Boy. large type ed. 416p. 1992. 27.99 (*0-7089-2585-5*) Ulverscroft.

— Cat's Cradle. (Worldwide Library Mysteries). 1994. per. 3.99 (*0-373-26151-9*, 1-26151-0) Harlequin Bks.

— Close Quarters. large type ed. 256p. 1998. per. 4.99 (*0-373-26292-2*, 1-26292-2, Wrldwide Lib) Harlequin Bks.

— Close Quarters. large type ed. LC 97-15222. 357p. 1997. lib. bdg. 21.95 (*0-7838-8214-9*, G K Hall Lrg Type) Mac Lib Ref.

— Close Quarters: A Thames Valley Mystery. large type ed. LC 96-43318. 192p. 1996. 20.95 (*0-312-15079-2*, Thomas Dunne) St Martin.

— Cold Hands. 2000. text 22.95 (*0-312-20464-7*) St Martin.

— Death Prone. LC 95-2373. (Mystery Ser.). 251p. 1996. per. 3.99 (*0-373-26189-6*, 1-26189-0, Wrldwide Lib) Harlequin Bks.

— First Wife, Twice Removed. LC 93-3478. (WWL Mystery Ser.). 1995. per. 3.99 (*0-373-26168-3*, 1-26168-4) Harlequin Bks.

***Curzon, Clare.** Guilty Knowledge. 288p. 2000. text 23.95 (*0-312-26169-1*) St Martin.

Curzon, Clare. Nice People. LC 95-1717. 1995. 20.95 (*0-312-13132-1*) St Martin.

— Nice People. large type ed. 336p. 1995. pap. 20.95 (*0-7862-0361-7*) Thorndike Pr.

— Past Mischief. 1997. per. 4.99 (*0-373-26256-6*, 1-26256-7, Wrldwide Lib) Harlequin Bks.

— Past Mischief. 1997. pap. text 20.95 (*0-7862-0923-2*) Thorndike Pr.

Curzon, Daniel. Among the Carnivores. Ashton, Sylvia, ed. LC 77-94071. 1979. 22.95 (*0-87949-124-8*) Ashley Bks.

— From Violent Men. 248p. (Orig.). 1983. pap. 4.95 (*0-930650-04-2*) IGNA Books.

— Human Warmth & Other Stories. LC 80-23270. 140p. 1981. pap. 4.95 (*0-912516-54-2*) Grey Fox.

— The Misadventures of Tim McPick: A Gay Comedy. LC 75-32707. 1980. reprint ed. pap. 4.95 (*0-930650-02-6*) IGNA Books.

— Not Necessarily Nice: Stories. LC 98-89872. 365p. 1999. 25.00 (*0-7388-0301-4*); pap. 15.00 (*0-7388-0302-2*) Xlibris Corp.

— Only the Good Parts: A Novel. LC 98-85381. 325p. 1998. 25.00 (*0-9663501-1-1*); pap. 15.00 (*0-7388-0020-1*) Xlibris Corp.

— The Revolt of the Perverts (Gay Short Stories) LC 77-83394. (Orig.). 1978. pap. 6.95 (*0-930650-01-8*) IGNA Books.

— Something You Do in the Dark. LC 77-150260. 1979. pap. 14.95 (*0-87949-138-8*) Ashley Bks.

— Superfag. 218p. (Orig.). 1996. pap. 9.95 (*0-930650-05-0*) IGNA Books.

Curzon, David. Confession of Faith. (Fine Editions Ser.). (Illus.). 1991. 50.00 (*0-89304-305-2*) Cross-Cultrl NY.

— Midrashim. (Review Jewish Writers Chapbook Ser.: No. 5). 1991. 15.00 (*0-89304-347-8*); pap. 5.00 (*0-89304-348-6*); audio 10.00 (*0-685-49056-4*); VHS 50.00 (*0-685-49057-2*) Cross-Cultrl NY.

— Midrashim. limited ed. (Review Jewish Writers Chapbook Ser.: No. 5). 1991. 35.00 (*0-685-49055-6*) Cross-Cultrl NY.

— Midrashim: Mini Book. (Review Jewish Writers Chapbook Ser.: No. 5). 1991. 15.00 (*0-685-49053-X*); pap. 5.00 (*0-685-49054-8*) Cross-Cultrl NY.

— Modern Poems on the Bible. 1997. pap. text 14.00 (*0-15-600526-3*, Harvest Bks) Harcourt.

— A View for Jacob's Ladder: One Hundred Midrashim. 200p. 1996. 11.00 (*0-8276-0568-4*) JPS Phila.

Curzon, David, ed. The Gospels in Our Image: An Anthology of Twentieth-Century Poetry Based on Biblical Texts. LC 95-11011. 320p. 1995. 30.00 (*0-15-100161-8*) Harcourt.

Curzon, David, intro. Modern Poems on the Bible: An Anthology. 416p. 1994. 17.50 (*0-8276-0449-1*) JPS Phila.

Curzon, David, jt. ed. see Barkan, Stanley H.

Curzon, F., jt. auth. see Blokhin, M.

Curzon, George N. Persia & the Persian Question, 2 vols., Set. 1966. 145.00 (*0-7146-1969-8*, Pub. by F Cass Pubs) Intl Spec Bk.

— Russia in Central Asia in Eighteen Eighty-Nine & the Anglo-Russian Question. (Illus.). 477p. 1967. 57.50 (*0-7146-1465-3*, Pub. by F Cass Pubs) Intl Spec Bk.

Curzon, Gerald, ed. The Biochemistry of Psychiatric Disturbances. fac. ed. LC 80-40498. (Illus.). 156p. pap. 48.40 (*0-7837-7361-7*, 204717000005) Bks Demand.

Curzon, Gerald, jt. ed. see Takada, Akikazu.

Curzon, Jean. Yesterday Once More. large type ed. (Linford Romance Library). 288p. 1994. pap. 16.99 (*0-7089-7506-2*, Linford) Ulverscroft.

Curzon, Julian. The Great Cyclone at St. Louis & East St. Louis, May 27, 1896: Being a Full History of the Most Terrifying & Destructive Tornado in the History of the World. LC 96-29716. (Illus.). 422p. 1997. pap. 12.95 (*0-8093-2124-6*) S Ill U Pr.

Curzon, L. B. Briefcase on Family Law. (Cavendish Briefcase Ser.). 209p. 1997. pap. 20.00 (*1-85941-246-7*, Pub. by Cavendish Pubng) Gaunt.

— Dictionary of Law. 5th rev. ed. 428p. 1998. pap. 42.50 (*0-273-63735-5*, Pub. by Pitman Pbg) Trans-Atl Phila.

— Equity & Trusts. (Lecture Notes Ser.). 312p. 1994. pap. write for info. (*1-874241-62-7*, Pub. by Cavendish Pubng) Gaunt.

— Equity & Trusts. 2nd ed. (Lecture Notes Ser.). 301p. 1996. pap. 30.00 (*1-85941-169-X*, Pub. by Cavendish Pubng) Gaunt.

— Family Law. (Lecture Notes Ser.). 386p. 1995. pap. 25.00 (*1-874241-70-8*, Pub. by Cavendish Pubng) Gaunt.

— Jurisprudence. (Lecture Notes Ser.). 266p. 1994. pap. write for info. (*1-874241-63-5*, Pub. by Cavendish Pubng) Gaunt.

— Jurisprudence. 2nd ed. (Questions & Answers Ser.). 332p. 1995. 18.00 (*1-85941-268-8*, Pub. by Cavendish Pubng) Gaunt.

— Jurisprudence. 2nd ed. (Lecture Notes Ser.). 350p. 1996. pap. write for info. (*1-85941-161-4*, Pub. by Cavendish Pubng) Gaunt.

— Teaching in Further Education: An Outline of Principles & Practice. 400p. 1990. pap. text 39.95 (*0-304-31961-9*) Continuum.

Curzon, M. E. & Ten Cate, J. M., eds. Diet, Nutrition & Dental Research. (Journal: Caries Research: Vol. 24, Suppl. 1, 1990). (Illus.). iv, 80p. 1990. pap. 36.75 (*3-8055-5305-6*) S Karger.

— Efficacy of Caries Preventive Strategies. (Journal: Caries Research: Vol. 27, Suppl. 1, 1993). (Illus.). iv, 96p. 1993. pap. 26.25 (*3-8055-5816-3*) S Karger.

Curzon Price, Victoria, et al. The Enlargement of the European Union: Issues & Strategies. LC 98-38316. (Studies in the European Economy Ser.). 1999. write for info. (*0-415-20292-2*) Routledge.

Curzon, Robert. Visits to Monasteries in the Levant. Hogg, James, ed. LC 96-129588. 496p. 1996. reprint ed. text 109.95 (*0-7734-4198-0*) E Mellen.

— Visits to the Monasteries in the Levant. (Curzon Travellers Ser.). (Illus.). 288p. (C). 1996. reprint ed. 70.00 (*0-7007-0346-2*, Pub. by Curzon Pr Ltd) Paul & Co Pubs.

Curzon, Susan C. Managing Change: A How to Do It Manual for Planning, Implementing & Evaluating Change in Libraries. Katz, Bill, ed. (How-to-Do-It Ser.). 128p. (Orig.). 1989. pap. text 45.00 (*1-55570-032-2*) Neal-Schuman.

— Managing the Interview: A-How-to-Do-It Manual. LC 94-47336. (How-to-Do-It-Ser.: Vol. 47). (Illus.). 160p. (Orig.). 1995. pap. 45.00 (*1-55570-160-4*) Neal-Schuman.

Cusa, Nicholas De, see De Cusa, Nicholas.

Cusack. HIV & AIDS Care: Practical Approaches. 160p. 1994. pap. 41.50 (*1-56593-144-0*, 0456) Singular Publishing.

Cusack, Barbara A. & Sullivan, Therese G., eds. Pastoral Care in Parishes Without a Pastor: Applications of Canon 517, Section 2. 88p. 1995. pap. 8.00 (*0-943616-68-9*) Canon Law Soc.

Cusack, Bridget, ed. Everyday English, 1500-1700: A Reader. LC 99-191110. (Illus.). 368p. 1998. text 49.50 (*0-472-09686-9*, 09686); pap. text 19.95 (*0-472-06686-2*, 06686) U of Mich Pr.

Cusack, Carole M. Conversion among the Germanic Peoples. LC 97-45096. 1998. 75.00 (*0-304-70155-6*) Continuum.

***Cusack, Carole M.** Rise of Christianity in Northern Europe, 300-1000. 2000. pap. 26.95 (*0-304-70735-X*) Continuum.

Cusack, Cyril. Between the Acts & Other Poems. 80p. 1990. pap. 11.95 (*0-86140-332-0*) Dufour.

Cusack, Dymphna. Jungfrau. 1997. pap. 14.95 (*0-86819-511-1*, Pub. by Currency Pr) Accents Pubns.

Cusack, Dymphna & Adelaide, Debra. A Window in the Dark LC 94-220998. v, 175p. 1991. write for info. (*0-642-10514-6*) Aust Inst Criminology.

Cusack, Dymphna, jt. auth. see Freehill, Norman.

C

An Asterisk (*) at the beginning of an entry indicates that the title is appearing for the first time.

Cusack, James S. Always Aware. Colby, J., ed. & pref. by. Ewing, Jeanne B., pref. LC 95-75583. (Self-Help Ser.). 200p. 1995. pap. text 9.95 (*1-883283-07-8*, 1-800-68-BRICK) Brick Tower.

Cusack, Lynette, jt. auth. see Navin, Sheryl.

Cusack, Michael. Online Customer Care: Applying Today's Technology to Achieve World-Class Customer Interaction. LC 97-46441. (Illus.). 265p. 1998. 39.50 (*0-87389-383-2*, H0972) ASQ Qual Pr.

Cusack, N. E. The Physics of Structurally Disordered Matter: An Introduction. (Graduate Student Series in Physics). (Illus.). 424p. 1987. 210.00 (*0-85274-591-5*); pap. 62.00 (*0-85274-829-9*) IOP Pub.

Cusack, Odean, intro. Pets & Mental Health. LC 88-9671. 241p. 1988. text 39.95 (*0-86656-652-X*); pap. text 14.95 (*0-86656-801-8*) Haworth Pr.

Cusack, Odean & Smith, Elaine, eds. Pets & the Elderly: The Therapeutic Bond. LC 83-26409. (Activities, Adaptation & Aging Ser.: Vol. 4, Nos. 2 & 3). (Illus.). 257p. 1984. text 49.95 (*0-86656-259-1*, B259) Haworth Pr.

Cusack, Pearse. An Interpretation of the Second Dialogue of Gregory the Great: Hagiography & St. Benedict. LC 93-21951. (Studies in the Bible & Early Christianity: Vol. 31). (Illus.). 204p. 1993. text 89.95 (*0-7734-9272-0*) E Mellen.

Cusack, Ralph. Cadenza. LC 84-21372. 228p. 1984. reprint ed. 20.00 (*0-916583-04-X*); reprint ed. pap. 7.95 (*0-916583-05-8*) Dalkey Arch.

Cusack, Sandra, jt. auth. see Seymour, Sylvia.

***Cusack, Sandra A. & Thompson, Wendy J.** Leadership for Older Adults: Aging with Purpose & Passion. LC 98-28100. 207p. 1998. pap. 29.95 (*0-87630-931-7*) Brunner-Mazel.

Cusack, Stephen, et al, eds. Biological Macromolecular Dynamics: Proceedings of a Workshop on Inelastic & Quasielastic Neutron Scattering in Biology, Institut Laue-Langevin, Grenoble, France, 14-15 October 1996. LC 97-21521. 1997. write for info. (*0-940030-49-7*) Adenine Pr.

Cusack, Suzanne B. Women & Relapse. 36p. (Orig.). 1984. pap. 3.00 (*0-89486-237-5*, 1379B) Hazelden.

Cusack, Thomas, jt. ed. see Bremer, Stuart.

Cusack, Victor. Bamboo Rediscovered: Growing & Using Non-Invasive, Clumping Bamboo Species Selection. 1998. pap. 19.95 (*0-9595889-8-1*) Chelsea Green Pub.

***Cusack, Victor.** Bamboo World: The Growing & Use of Clumping Bamboos. (Illus.). 2000. 45.00 (*0-7432-0066-7*) Simon & Schuster.

Cusak, Victor. Bamboo World: Clumping Bamboos & How to Use Them. 160p. 1999. 29.95 (*0-86417-934-0*, Pub. by Kangaroo Pr) Seven Hills Bk.

Cusano, John. Investing in Dreams: Connecticut's Commitment to Imagination, 1995. LC 63-62002. (Illus.). 79p. 1995. 19.95 (*0-614-10434-3*) W Benton Mus.

Cusatelli, G. Dizionario Garzanti Della Lingua Italiana: Garzanti Dictionary of the Italian Language. (ITA.). 1008p. 1979. 45.00 (*0-8288-4729-0*, M9189) Fr & Eur.

— Garzanti Dictionary of the Italian Language: Dizionario Garzanti della Lingua Italiana. 19th ed. (ITA.). 2272p. 1980. 150.00 (*0-8288-1988-2*, M9190) Fr & Eur.

Cusatelli, G. & Brunacci, G. Garzanti French-Italian, Italian-French Dictionary: Dizionario Garzanti Francese-Italiano, Italiano-Francese. Salati, U. et al, eds. (FRE & ITA.). 2048p. 1980. 150.00 (*0-8288-3371-0*, M6143) Fr & Eur.

Cusatis, Casimer De, see Das, Pankaj K. & De Cusatis, Casimer.

Cusato, Michael, ed. That Others Might Know & Love: Essays in Honor of Zachary Hayes, OFM. (Theology Ser.). 342p. 1997. pap. text 24.00 (*1-57659-130-1*) Franciscan Inst.

Cuschieki, A., jt. auth. see Buess, G. F.

Cuschieri, A. Disorders of the Spleen. (Illus.). 256p. 1994. 135.00 (*0-632-03314-2*) Blackwell Sci.

***Cuschieri, A.** Essential Surgical Practice. 4th ed. 1700p. 2000. 210.00 (*0-7506-3729-3*); 210.00 (*0-7506-4780-9*) Buttrwrth-Heinemann.

Cuschieri, A., et al. Essential Surgical Practice. 3rd ed. Moossa, A. R., ed. LC 94-24687. (Illus.). 1656p. 1995. text 165.00 (*0-7506-1850-7*) Buttrwrth-Heinemann.

Cuschieri, A., jt. auth. see Forbes, C. D.

Cuschieri, Alfred, et al. Clinical Surgery. (Illus.). 450p. (Orig.). 1996. pap. text 64.95 (*0-632-03146-8*) Blackwell Sci.

— Operative Manual of Endoscopic Surgery. LC 92-2421. (Illus.). 380p. 1992. 175.00 (*0-387-53486-5*) Spr-Verlag.

Cuschieri, Alfred, jt. auth. see Berci, George.

Cuschieri, Alfred, ed. see Perissat, J.

Cuschieri, Andrew. The Sacrament of Reconciliation: A Theological & Canonical Treatise. 366p. (Orig.). (C). 1992. lib. bdg. 65.00 (*0-8191-8655-4*) U Pr of Amer.

— The Sacrament of Reconciliation: A Theological & Canonical Treatise. 366p. (Orig.). (C). 1992. pap. text 37.50 (*0-8191-8656-2*) U Pr of Amer.

Cuschieri, Joseph M., et al, eds. Noise Control for Industry: NOISE-CON '94. (NOISE-CON Ser.). xxvii, 1060p. pap. 95.00 (*0-614-25012-9*) Noise Control.

***Cuscuna, Michael, et al.** Blue Note: The Jazz Photography of Francis Wolff. (Illus.). 176p. 2000. pap. 29.95 (*0-7893-0493-7*) Universe.

Cuscuna, Michael, et al. The Blue Note Years: The Jazz Photography of Francis Wolff. LC 95-7383. (Illus.). 204p. 1995. 65.00 (*0-8478-1912-4*, Pub. by Rizzoli Intl) St Martin.

Cuse, Arthur. Financial Guideline: Divorce. 160p. (Orig.). 1971. pap. 9.95 (*0-917474-03-1*) Guideline Pub.

— How to Make it in Gold & Not Get @#$[! (Orig.). 1974. pap. 9.95 (*0-917474-02-3*) Guideline Pub.

Cusens, Anthony R. & Pama, R. P. Bridge Deck Analysis. LC 74-3726. (Illus.). 294p. reprint ed. pap. 91.20 (*0-8357-6707-8*, 203533800095) Bks Demand.

Cuseo, Allan A. Homosexual Characters in YA Novels: A Literary Analysis, 1969-1982. LC 91-48008. 538p. 1992. 58.00 (*0-8108-2537-6*) Scarecrow.

Cuseo, Joseph B. Cooperative Learning: A Pedagogy. 48p. (C). 1996. pap. 6.95 (*0-913507-80-6*) New Forums.

— The Freshman Orientation Seminar: A Research-Based Rationale for Its Value, Delivery, & Content. (Freshman Year Experience Monograph: No. 4). 28p. (Orig.). 1991. pap. 20.00 (*1-889271-03-9*) Nat Res Ctr.

Cush, Cathie. Artists Who Created Great Works. (Twenty Events Ser.). (Illus.). 48p. (J). (gr. 5-6). 1994. lib. bdg. 24.26 (*0-8114-4933-5*) Raintree Steck-V.

— Depression. LC 93-14252. (Teen Hotline Ser.). (Illus.). 80p. (J). (gr. 6-7). 1993. lib. bdg. 25.68 (*0-8114-3529-6*) Raintree Steck-V.

— Disasters That Shook the World. LC 93-10299. (Twenty Events Ser.). (Illus.). 48p. (J). (gr. 5-6). 1993. lib. bdg. 24.26 (*0-8114-4929-7*) Raintree Steck-V.

— Pregnancy. LC 93-25155. (Teen Hotline Ser.). (Illus.). 80p. (J). (gr. 6-7). 1993. lib. bdg. 25.68 (*0-8114-3530-X*) Raintree Steck-V.

— Shipwrecks. LC 97-141. (Illus.). 120p. 1997. 16.98 (*1-56799-475-X*, Friedman-Fairfax) M Friedman Pub Grp Inc.

— Women Who Achieved Greatness. (Twenty Events Ser.). (Illus.). 48p. (J). (gr. 5-6). 1994. lib. bdg. 24.26 (*0-8114-4938-6*) Raintree Steck-V.

***Cush, Indus Khamit.** Enoch, the Ethiopian: Lost Prophet of the Bible : Greater Than Abraham, Holier Than Moses. LC 00-33135. 2000. pap. write for info. (*1-886433-03-8*) A&B Bks.

***Cushenbery, D. & Meyer.** Critical Reading. 2000. pap. 4.95 (*0-13-030397-6*) P-H.

— Drawing Conclusions. 2000. pap. 4.95 (*0-13-030380-1*) P-H.

— Following Directions. 2000. pap. 4.95 (*0-13-030392-5*) P-H.

— Locating Hidden Meaning. 2000. pap. 4.95 (*0-13-030394-1*) P-H.

— Recognizing Main Ideas. 2000. pap. 4.95 (*0-13-030387-9*) P-H.

— Understanding Details. 2000. pap. 4.95 (*0-13-030385-2*) P-H.

Cushenbery, Donald C. & Cushenbery, Rita C. Coping with Life after Your Mate Dies. 2nd rev. ed. LC 97-8996. 112p. (Orig.). 1997. pap. 7.99 (*0-8010-5765-5*) Baker Bks.

Cushenbery, Rita C., jt. auth. see Cushenbery, Donald C.

Cushieri. An Atlas of Minimal Access Surgical Anatomy. LC 99-53181. 1997. text. write for info. (*0-397-51459-X*) Lppncott W & W.

Cushieri, A. Common Bile Duct Exploration. (Developments in Surgery Ser.). 1984. lib. bdg. 212.50 (*0-89838-639-X*) Kluwer Academic.

Cushieri, Andrew. Introductory Reading in Canon Law. LC 87-29820. 532p. 1988. lib. bdg. 119.95 (*0-88946-210-0*) E Mellen.

Cushing, Angela. A Contextual Perspective to Female Nursing in Victoria, 1850-1914 - (DINROO) (Research Monographs: No. 7). 1993. pap. 35.00 (*0-7300-2028-2*, Pub. by Deakin Univ) St Mut.

Cushing, Barry. Accounting Information Systems. 5th ed. 1990. text 62.50 (*0-201-50158-9*) Addison-Wesley.

— Comparison of Audit Methodologies of Large Accounting Firms. (Studies in Accounting Research: vol. 26). 97p. 1986. 12.00 (*0-86539-060-6*) Am Accounting.

Cushing, Barry E. & Romney, Marshall B. Accounting Imformation Systems & Business Organizations. 4th ed. LC 86-17301. (Illus.). 775p. (C). 1987. text. write for info. (*0-201-10317-6*) Addison-Wesley.

Cushing, Barry E. & Romney, Marshall D. Accounting Information Systems: A Comprehensive Survey of Accounting Systems in Organizations. 5th ed. (Illus.). 900p. (C). 1989. text. write for info. (*0-318-64908-X*) Addison-Wesley.

Cushing, Barry E., jt. auth. see Davis, James R.

Cushing, C. E. Freshwater Ecosystems & Climate Change in North America: A Regional Assessment. LC 97-30261. (Advances in Environmental Science & Technology Ser.). 270p. 1998. pap. 80.00 (*0-471-97822-1*) Wiley.

***Cushing, Caleb.** Beyond the Rocky Mountains: Report on the Territory of Oregon. LC 99-27090. (Illus.). 212p. 2000. reprint ed. pap. 14.95 (*0-87770-694-8*) Ye Galleon.

Cushing, Caleb. Beyond the Rocky Mountains, Report on the Territory of Oregon. 210p. 2000. 19.95 (*0-87770-442-2*) Ye Galleon.

— Treaty of Washington: Its Negotiation, Execution & the Discussions Relating Thereto. LC 72-114872. (Select Bibliographies Reprint Ser.). 1977. 21.95 (*0-8369-5277-4*) Ayer.

Cushing, Carol C. Longstreet Highroad Guide to the New Hampshire Mountains. LC 98-89177. (Illus.). 320p. 1999. pap. 18.95 (*1-56352-503-8*) Longstreet.

***Cushing, Christine.** Dish It Out: Simple Recipes that Inspire. (Illus.). 208p. 2000. pap. 24.95 (*0-13-026815-1*) P-H.

Cushing, D. H. Detection of Fish. 220p. (C). 1973. 99.00 (*0-08-017123-0*, Pub. by Pergamon Repr) Franklin.

— Fisheries Biology: A Study in Population Dynamics. 2nd ed. LC 79-5405. (Illus.). 320p. 1981. 24.95 (*0-299-08110-9*) U of Wis Pr.

— The Provident Sea. (Illus.). 336p. 1988. text 85.00 (*0-521-25727-1*) Cambridge U Pr.

Cushing, David. Population Production & Regulation in the Sea: A Fisheries Perspective. (Illus.). 366p. (C). 1995. text 80.00 (*0-521-38457-5*) Cambridge U Pr.

Cushing, Edward J., jt. ed. see Shane, Linda C.

Cushing, Elizabeth H. No Race of Imitators: Lynn & Her People, an Anthology. LC 92-73334. 225p. 1992. pap. 18.50 (*1-882162-01-3*) Lynn Hist Soc.

Cushing, Elizabeth Hope. The Lynn Album: A Pictoral History. (Illus.). 192p. 1990. 38.10 (*0-89865-807-1*) Lynn Hist Soc.

Cushing, Frank H. Cushing at Zuni: The Correspondence & Journals of Frank Hamilton Cushing, 1879-1884. Green, Jesse, ed. LC 89-70751. (Illus.). 451p. 1990. reprint ed. pap. 139.90 (*0-608-04118-1*, 206485100011) Bks Demand.

***Cushing, Frank H.** Exploration of Ancient Key Dwellers' Remains on the Gulf Coast of Florida. LC 99-39305. (Southeastern Classics in Archaeology, Anthropology & History). (Illus.). 160p. 2000. reprint ed. pap. 29.95 (*0-8130-1791-2*) U Press Fla.

Cushing, Frank H. Explorations of Key Dwellers' Remains on the Gulf Coast of Florida. LC 72-5007. (Antiquities of the New World Ser.: Vol. 13). (Illus.). reprint ed. 37.50 (*0-404-57313-4*) AMS Pr.

— My Adventures in Zuni: American Autobiography. 125p. 1995. lib. bdg. 69.00 (*0-7812-8494-5*) Rprt Serv.

— Outlines of Zuni Creation Myths. LC 74-7947. reprint ed. 42.50 (*0-404-11834-8*) AMS Pr.

— Zuni: Selected Writings of Frank Hamilton Cushing. Green, Jesse, ed. & intro. by. LC 78-14295. (Illus.). xiv, 449p. 1979. pap. 15.95 (*0-8032-7007-0*, Bisor Books) U of Nebr Pr.

— Zuni Breadstuff. LC 74-7948. reprint ed. 62.50 (*0-404-11835-6*) AMS Pr.

— Zuni Fetishes. LC 66-23329. (Illus.). 52p. 1966 pap. 3.00 (*0-916122-03-4*) KC Pubns.

***Cushing, Frank H.** Zuni Fetishes. LC 99-60068. (Illus.). 48p. 1999. pap. 7.95 (*0-88714-144-7*) KC Pubns.

Cushing, Frank H. Zuni Folk Tales. 1977. lib. bdg. 59.95 (*0-8490-2858-2*) Gordon Pr.

— Zuni Folk Tales. LC 74-7949. reprint ed. 62.50 (*0-404-11836-4*) AMS Pr.

Cushing, Frank H., compiled by. Zuni Coyote Tales. LC 97-51899. 104p. 1998. pap. 7.95 (*0-8165-1892-0*) U of Ariz Pr.

Cushing, Frank H. & Baxter, Sylvester. My Adventurers in Zuni: Including Father of the Pueblos & an Aboriginal Pilgrimage. (American Historical Reprints Ser.). (Illus.). 79p. 1999. pap. 8.95 (*0-86541-045-3*) Filter.

***Cushing, G. F.** Chapters from the History of Hungarian Literature. Czigany, Lorant, ed. 416p. 1999. text 32.00 (*963-13-4818-0*, Pub. by Corvina Bks) St Mut.

Cushing, G. F., tr. see Warriner, Doreen, ed.

Cushing, George M. Great Buildings & Sights of Boston: A Photographic Guide. Urquhart, Ross, Jr., ed. (Illus.). 160p. 1982. pap. 11.95 (*0-486-24219-6*) Dover.

Cushing, Harry A. History of the Transition from Provincial to Commonwealth Government in Massachusetts. LC 78-120212. (Columbia University. Studies in the Social Sciences: No. 17). reprint ed. 30.00 (*0-404-51017-5*) AMS Pr.

Cushing, Harvey, jt. auth. see Bailey, Percival.

Cushing, Harvey W. Consecratio Medici & Other Papers. LC 70-99688. (Essay Index Reprint Ser.). 1977. 23.95 (*0-8369-1565-8*) Ayer.

Cushing, Helen G. Children's Song Index: An Index to More Than Twenty-Two Thousand Songs. 1988. reprint ed. lib. bdg. 159.00 (*0-7812-9714-1*) Rprt Serv.

— Children's Song Index: An Index to More Than Twenty-Two Thousand Songs. 798p. 1936. reprint ed. 195.00 (*0-403-01530-8*) Scholarly.

Cushing, J. M. An Introduction to Structured Population Dynamics. LC 98-19033. (CBMS-NSF Regional Conference Series in Applied Mathematics: No. CB71). (Illus.). xiii, 93p. 1998. pap. 36.00 (*0-89871-417-6*, BKCB0071) Soc Indus-Appl Math.

Cushing, J. S. The Genealogy of the Cushing Family: Ancestors & Descendants of Matthew Cushing Who Came to America in 1638. (Illus.). 668p. 1989. reprint ed. pap. 99.00 (*0-8328-0447-9*); reprint ed. lib. bdg. 107.00 (*0-8328-0446-0*) Higginson Bk Co.

Cushing, James. The Length of an Afternoon. 100p. 1999. pap. 12.00 (*0-9649240-6-4*) Cahuenga Pr.

— You & the Night & the Music. 86p. 1991. pap 10.00 (*0-9649240-2-1*) Cahuenga Pr.

Cushing, James S. The Genealogy of the Cushing Family: An Account of the Ancestors & Descendants of Matthew Cushing, Who Came to America in 1638. LC 79-55650. (Illus.). 668p. 1979. reprint ed. 25.00 (*0-9603588-0-3*) H G Cushing.

Cushing, James T. Philosophical Concepts in Physics: The Historical Relation Between Philosophy & Scientific Theories. (Illus.). 500p. (C). 1998. text 74.95 (*0-521-57071-9*); pap. text 30.95 (*0-521-57823-X*) Cambridge U Pr.

— Quantum Mechanics: Historical Contingency & the Copenhagen Hegemony. LC 94-8427. (Science & Its Conceptual Foundations Ser.). 328p. 1994. pap. text 27.00 (*0-226-13204-8*) U Ch Pr.

— Quantum Mechanics: Historical Contingency & the Copenhagen Hegemony. LC 94-8427. (Science & Its Conceptual Foundations Ser.). 328p. 1994. lib. bdg. 65.00 (*0-226-13202-1*) U Ch Pr.

— Theory Construction & Selection in Modern Physics. (Illus.). 427p. (C). 1990. text 105.00 (*0-521-38181-9*) Cambridge U Pr.

Cushing, James T., et al, eds. Bohmian Mechanics & Quantum Theory: An Appraisal. LC 96-11973. (Boston Studies in the Philosophy of Science: Vol. 184). 408p. (C). 1996. text 164.00 (*0-7923-4028-0*) Kluwer Academic.

Cushing, James T. & McMullin, Ernan, eds. Philosophical Consequences of Quantum Theory: Reflections on Bell's Theorem. LC 89-40014. (Studies in Science & the Humanities from the Reilly Center for Science, Technology, & Values: Vol. II). 336p. (C). 1989. pap. text 23.00 (*0-268-01579-1*) U of Notre Dame Pr.

Cushing, Jean, tr. see Cole, Bernedette K.

Cushing, John D., compiled by. A Bibliography of the Laws & Resolves of the Massachusetts Bay: 1642-1780. LC 83-82991. 372p. 1984. 60.00 (*0-89453-383-5*, 33835G) Scholarly Res Inc.

Cushing, John D., et al, compiled by. Catalogue of Books in the Massachusetts Historical Library: An Annotated Edition of the 1796 Library Catalogue of the Massachusetts Historical Society. LC 96-51572. (Illus.). 638p. 1997. 85.00 (*0-934909-69-5*, Pub. by Mass Hist Soc) NE U Pr.

Cushing, John D., compiled by. The First Laws of the Commonwealth of Massachusetts, 1788. LC 81-80445. 60.00 (*0-89453-212-X*, 32120G) Scholarly Res Inc.

— The First Laws of the State of Connecticut, 1784. LC 81-80466. (Earliest Laws of the Original Thirteen States Ser.). 307p. 1982. 60.00 (*0-89453-219-7*, 32197G) Scholarly Res Inc.

— The First Laws of the State of Delaware, 4797, 4 vols., Set. LC 81-80446. (Earliest Laws of the Original Thirteen States Ser.). 1981. 240.00 (*0-89453-216-2*, 32162G) Scholarly Res Inc.

— The First Laws of the State of Georgia, 1800, 2 vols., Set. LC 81-80447. (Earliest Laws of the Original Thirteen States Ser.). 1981. 120.00 (*0-89453-218-9*, 32189G) Scholarly Res Inc.

— The First Laws of the State of Maryland, 1787. LC 81-80448. (Earliest Laws of the Original Thirteen States Ser.). 1981. 60.00 (*0-89453-213-8*, 32138G) Scholarly Res Inc.

— The First Laws of the State of New Hampshire, 1790. LC 81-80443. (Law Ser.). 235p. 1981. 60.00 (*0-89453-215-4*, 32154G) Scholarly Res Inc.

— The First Laws of the State of New Jersey, 1783. LC 81-80467. (Earliest Laws of the Original Thirteen States Ser.). 455p. 1981. 60.00 (*0-89453-217-0*, 32170G) Scholarly Res Inc.

— The First Laws of the State of New York, 1782. LC 83-81642. (Earliest Laws of the Original Thirteen States Ser.). 255p. 1984. 60.00 (*0-89453-223-5*, 32235G) Scholarly Res Inc.

— The First Laws of the State of North Carolina, 1791, 2 vols., Set. LC 83-83022. (Earliest Laws of the Original Thirteen States Ser.). 1984. 120.00 (*0-89453-222-7*, 32227G) Scholarly Res Inc.

— The First Laws of the State of Rhode Island, 1798, 2 vols., Set. LC 82-84404. (Earliest Laws of the Original Thirteen States Ser.). 1983. 120.00 (*0-89453-224-3*, 32243G) Scholarly Res Inc.

— The First Laws of the State of South Carolina, 1790, 2 vols., Set. LC 81-80444. (Earliest Laws of the Original Thirteen States Ser.). 1984. 120.00 (*0-89453-214-6*, 32146G) Scholarly Res Inc.

— The First Laws of the State of Virginia, 1795. LC 82-81270. (Earliest Laws of the Original Thirteen States Ser.). 235p. 1982. 60.00 (*0-89453-221-9*, 32219G) Scholarly Res Inc.

Cushing, John D., intro. The Laws & Liberties of Massachusetts, 1641-1691, 3 vol., Set. LC 75-24575. 1976. 125.00 (*0-8420-2074-8*) Scholarly Res Inc.

Cushing, Kathleen. Papacy & Law in the Gregorian Revolution: The Canaonistic Work of Anselm of Lucca. (Oxford Historical Monographs). 264p. 1998. text 74.00 (*0-19-820724-7*) OUP.

Cushing, L. Genealogy of the Cushing Family. 117p. 1993. reprint ed. pap. 23.50 (*0-8328-1393-1*); reprint ed. lib. bdg. 33.50 (*0-8328-1392-3*) Higginson Bk Co.

Cushing, L. S., tr. see Pothier, Robert Joseph.

Cushing, Leo J., et al. Preparing Estate Tax Returns. LC 96-80039. 780p. 1997. ring bd. 95.00 (*1-57589-053-4*, 97-08.06-BK) Mass CLE.

Cushing, Luther S. An Introduction to the Study of the Roman Law. LC 89-83502. xi, 243p. 1989. reprint ed. 40.00 (*0-89941-686-1*, 305850) W S Hein.

— Lex Parliamentaria Americana: Elements of Law & Practice of Legislative Assemblies in the United States of America. (Lex Parliamentaria Americana Ser.). xxxvi, 1063p. 1989. reprint ed. 95.00 (*0-8377-2014-1*, Rothman) W S Hein.

***Cushing, Luther Stearns.** Elements of the Law & Practice of Legislative Assemblies in the United States of America: Lex Parliamentaria Americana. LC 99-73240. 1063p. 1999. 220.00 (*1-56169-543-2*) Gaunt.

Cushing, Mary. Nursing Jurisprudence. 534p. (C). 1988. pap. text 48.95 (*0-8385-7039-9*, A7039-9) Appleton & Lange.

Cushing, Mary W. The Rainbow Bridge. Farkas, Andrew, ed. LC 76-29932. (Opera Biographies Ser.). (Illus.). (J). (gr. k-5). 1977. reprint ed. lib. bdg. 33.95 (*0-405-09674-7*) Ayer.

Cushing, Michael A., jt. auth. see O'Neill, James L.

Cushing, Peter. Peter Cushing: An Autobiography. (Illus.). 320p. 1999. 55.00 (*1-887664-29-7*); pap. 20.00 (*1-887664-26-2*) Midnght Marquee Pr.

Cushing, Raymond & Moreau, Jeffrey. America's First Transcontinental Railway: A Pictorial History of the Pacific Railroad. LC 95-115873. (Illus.). 1994. pap. 9.95 (*1-56342-002-3*) Pentrex Media.

Cushing, Robert S., jt. auth. see Crozes, Gil F.

Cushing, Steven. Fatal Words: Communication Clashes & Aircraft Crashes. 1997. pap. text 11.95 (*0-226-13201-3*) U Ch Pr.

— Fatal Words: Communication Clashes & Airplane Crashes. LC 93-24615. 176p. 1994. 23.50 (*0-226-13200-5*) U Ch Pr.

Cushing, Thomas. History of Allegheny County, Pennsylvania. 1993. reprint ed. lib. bdg. 89.00 (*0-7812-5445-0*) Rprt Serv.

C

An Asterisk (*) at the beginning of an entry indicates that the title is appearing for the first time.

Cushing, Thomas, ed. A Genealogical & Biographical History of Allegheny County, Pennsylvania. LC 75-21638. 577p. 2000. reprint ed. 25.00 (*0-8063-0686-6*) Genealog Pub.

Cushing, Thomas & Sheppard, Charles E. History of the Counties of Gloucester, Salem & Cumberland, New Jersey, with Biographical Sketches of Their Prominent Citizens. (Illus.). 720p. 1992. reprint ed. lib. bdg. 73.50 (*0-8328-2449-6*) Higginson Bk Co.

— History of the Counties of Gloucester, Salem, & Cumberland New Jersey with Biographical Sketches of Their Prominent Citizens, 2 vols., Set. (Illus.). 1995. reprint ed. pap. text 74.00 (*0-7884-0227-7*) Heritage Bk.

Cushing, Thomas, tr. see Cossery, Albert.

Cushing, Tom, jt. auth. see Bowman, Martin.

Cushing, Val M. The Ceramic Design Book: A Gallery of Contemporary Work. Rich, Chris, ed. LC 98-7319. (Illus.). 192p. 1998. 34.95 (*1-57990-058-5*, Pub. by Lark Books) Random.

Cushing, William. Anonyms: A Dictionary of Revealed Authorship. iv, 829p. 1969. reprint ed. 210.00 (*0-685-67778-8*, 05102516) G Olms Pubs.

— Initials & Pseudonyms: A Dictionary of Literary Disguises, 2 vols., Set. 1969. reprint ed. 225.00 (*0-685-66457-0*, 05102714) G Olms Pubs.

Cushion, John & Cushion, Margaret. A Collector's History of British Porcelain. (Illus.). 448p. 1992. 89.50 (*1-85149-155-4*) Antique Collect.

Cushion, Margaret, jt. auth. see Cushion, John.

***Cushman.** Environmental Fluid Mechanics. 480p. 2000. text. write for info. (*0-471-34437-0*) Wiley.

Cushman & Koukoutchos & Koukoutchos. Cases in Constitutional Law. 9th ed. LC 99-19734. 615p. 1999. 70.00 (*0-13-083279-0*) P-H.

Cushman, Anne & Jones, Jerry. From Here to Nirvana: The Yoga Journal Guide to Spiritual India. 416p. 1999. pap. 15.95 (*1-57322-715-3*, Riverhd Trade) Berkley Pub.

Cushman, Barry. Rethinking the New Deal Court: The Structure of a Constitutional Revolution. LC 97-8904. 336p. 1998. pap. 24.95 (*0-19-512043-4*); text 60.00 (*0-19-511532-5*) OUP.

Cushman, Carolyn. Witch & Wombat. 320p. (Orig.). 1994. mass mkt. 5.50 (*0-446-60086-5*, Pub. by Warner Bks) Little.

C

Cushman, Charlotte. Charlotte Cushman: Her Letters & Memories of Her Life. Stebbins, Emma, ed. LC 76-82823. (Illus.). 316p. 1972. reprint ed. lib. bdg. 20.95 (*0-405-08417-X*, Pub. by Blom Pubns) Ayer.

Cushman, Chris, compiled by. Flip-Sort. 24p. 1998. 29.95 (*1-878383-40-X*) C Lee Pubns.

Cushman, Christopher L. First Aid Flipper. 49p. (YA). (gr. 7 up). 1995. 7.95 (*1-878383-33-7*) C Lee Pubns.

Cushman, Clare, ed. The Supreme Court Justices: Illustrated Biographies, 1789-1995. 2nd ed. LC 93-1446. (Illus.). 588p. (YA). (gr. 11). 1996. text 59.95 (*1-56802-127-5*) Congr Quarterly.

— The Supreme Court Justices: Illustrated Biographies, 1789-1995. 2nd ed. LC 93-1446. (Illus.). 588p. 1997. pap. 36.95 (*1-56802-126-7*) Congr Quarterly.

***Cushman, Dan.** Badlands Justice. 2000. 19.00 (*0-7540-8075-7*, Gunsmoke) Chivers N Amer.

Cushman, Dan. Blood on the Saddle: A Western Story. LC 99-11207. 1999. 20.95 (*0-7862-1032-X*) Mac Lib Ref.

— Blood on the Saddle: A Western Story. LC 98-2608. 1998. 18.95 (*0-7862-0993-3*) Thorndike Pr.

— Cow Country Cookbook. LC 91-58826. (Illus.). 176p. 1992. pap., per. 8.95 (*0-940666-18-9*) Clear Light.

— Dan Cushman's Cow-Country Cook Book. LC 67-21434. (Illus.). 1967. 12.95 (*0-911436-02-2*) Stay Away.

— The Fastest Gun. large type ed. LC 94-42796. 272p. 1995. pap. 16.95 (*0-7838-1152-7*, G K Hall Lrg Type) Mac Lib Ref.

— In Alaska with Shipwreck Kelly. large type ed. LC 95-35741. 1997. 20.00 (*0-7838-1474-7*, G K Hall Lrg Type) Mac Lib Ref.

— In Alaska with Shipwreck Kelly: A North-Western Story. large type ed. LC 95-23524. (Five-Star Western Ser.). 220p. 1996. 16.95 (*0-7862-0534-2*) Thorndike Pr.

***Cushman, Dan.** Jewell of the Java Sea. LC 98-48260. 1999. 22.95 (*0-7838-8494-X*) Macmillan Gen Ref.

Cushman, Dan. The Long Riders. large type ed. (Linford Western Library). 304p. 1995. pap. 16.99 (*0-7089-7697-2*, Linford) Ulverscroft.

— Montana - The Gold Frontier. LC 73-83492. 1973. 21.95 (*0-911436-03-0*) Stay Away.

— Montana, Here I Be! large type ed. (Sagebrush Large Print Westerns Ser.). 196p. 1995. lib. bdg. 17.95 (*1-57490-008-0*) T T Beeler.

— The Muskrat Farm. LC 59-6988. 1977. 12.95 (*0-911436-05-7*) Stay Away.

— The Old Copper Collar. 17.50 (*0-7540-8017-X*, Gunsmoke) Chivers N Amer.

— The Pecos Kid. LC 99-35656. (Westerns Ser.). (Orig.). 1999. 19.95 (*0-7862-1895-9*, Five Star MI) Mac Lib Ref.

***Cushman, Dan.** The Pecos Kid: A Western Duo. LC 00-42576. (YA). 2000. write for info. (*0-7862-2779-6*) Thorndike Pr.

Cushman, Dan. Plenty of Room & Air. LC 75-20626. 1975. 16.95 (*0-911436-04-9*) Stay Away.

— The Silver Mountain. 448p. 1995. pap. text 4.99 (*0-8439-3846-3*) Dorchester Pub Co.

— Stay Away, Joe. LC 52-12887. 249p. 1981. reprint ed. 21.95 (*0-911436-01-4*); reprint ed. pap. 10.95 (*0-911436-06-5*) Stay Away.

— Tall Wyoming. large type ed. LC 93-32758. 285p. 1994. lib. bdg. 16.95 (*0-8161-5856-8*, G K Hall Lrg Type) Mac Lib Ref.

— Valley of a Thousand Smokes. large type ed. 1999. 20.00 (*0-7838-1674-X*, G K Hall Lrg Type) Mac Lib Ref.

— Valley of a Thousand Smokes: A North-Western Story. LC 96-5873. 1996. 16.95 (*0-7862-0663-2*) Five Star.

— Valley of the Thousand Smokes: A North-Western Story. large type ed. LC 97-28190. (Western Ser.). 324p. 1997. lib. bdg. 19.95 (*0-7862-1194-6*) Thorndike Pr.

— Voyageurs of the Midnight Sun. large type ed. LC 96-43604. (Orig.). 1996. lib. bdg. 18.95 (*1-57490-049-8*, Sagebrush LP West) T T Beeler.

Cushman-de Vries, C. H., tr. see Souriau, J. M.

Cushman, Donald P. & Cahn, Dudley D., eds. Communication in Interpersonal Relationships. LC 83-24228. (SUNY Series, Human Communication Processes). 170p. (C). 1985. pap. text 16.95 (*0-87395-910-8*) State U NY Pr.

Cushman, Donald P. & King, Sarah S. Communication & High-Speed Management. LC 94-41034. (SUNY Series, Human Communication Processes). 277p. (C). 1995. text 59.50 (*0-7914-2535-5*); pap. text 19.95 (*0-7914-2536-3*) State U NY Pr.

— Continuously Improving an Organization's Performance: High-Speed Management. LC 96-22754. (SUNY Series in Management-Communication). 158p. (C). 1997. text 49.50 (*0-7914-3311-0*); pap. text 16.95 (*0-7914-3312-9*) State U NY Pr.

Cushman, Donald P. & King, Sarah S., eds. Communicating Organizational Change: A Management Perspective. LC 94-27492. (SUNY Series in International Management). 334p. (C). 1995. text 59.50 (*0-7914-2495-2*); pap. text 19.95 (*0-7914-2496-0*) State U NY Pr.

Cushman, Donald P. & Kovacic, Branislav, eds. Watershed Research Traditions in Human Communication Theory. LC 94-37655. (SUNY Series, Human Communication Processes). 312p. (C). 1995. text 64.50 (*0-7914-2597-5*); pap. text 21.95 (*0-7914-2598-3*) State U NY Pr.

Cushman, Donald P., jt. auth. see Cullen, Ron.

Cushman, Donald P., jt. auth. see Ju, Yanan.

Cushman, Donald P., jt. ed. see King, Sarah S.

Cushman, Donald P., jt. ed. see Kozminski, Andrzej K.

Cushman, Doug. ABC Mystery. LC 92-9621. (Trophy Picture Bk.). (Illus.). 32p. (J). (ps-2). 1996. pap. 5.95 (*0-06-443459-1*, HarpTrophy) HarpC Child Bks.

Cushman, Doug. ABC Mystery. LC 92-9621. 1993. 10.15 (*0-606-08961-6*, Pub. by Turtleback) Demco.

Cushman, Doug. Aunt Eater Loves a Mystery. (I Can Read Bks.). (Illus.). 64p. (J). (gr. 1-3). 1987. 13.00 (*0-06-021326-4*); lib. bdg. 15.89 (*0-06-021327-2*) HarpC Child Bks.

— Aunt Eater Loves a Mystery. LC 87-73. (I Can Read Bks.). (Illus.). 64p. (J). (ps-3). 1989. pap. 3.95 (*0-06-444126-1*, HarpTrophy) HarpC Child Bks.

— Aunt Eater Loves a Mystery. (I Can Read Bks.). (J). (gr. 1-3). 1987. 8.95 (*0-606-04162-1*, Pub. by Turtleback) Demco.

Cushman, Doug. Aunt Eater Loves a Mystery. unabridged ed. (I Can Read Bks.). (Illus.). (J). (gr. 1-3). 1991. audio 8.95 (*1-55994-435-8*) HarperAudio.

Cushman, Doug. Aunt Eater's Mystery Christmas. (I Can Read Bks.). (Illus.). 64p. (J). (gr. 1-3). 1996. pap. 3.75 (*0-06-444221-7*, HarpTrophy) HarpC Child Bks.

— Aunt Eater's Mystery Christmas. (I Can Read Bks.). (J). (gr. 1-3). 1996. 9.20 (*0-606-10130-6*) Turtleback.

— Aunt Eater's Mystery Halloween. LC 97-38606. (I Can Read Bks.). (Illus.). 64p. (J). (gr. 1-3). 1999. pap. 3.95 (*0-06-444266-7*) HarpC Child Bks.

— Aunt Eater's Mystery Halloween. LC 97-38606. (Illus.). 64p. (J). (gr. k-3). 1998. 14.95 (*0-06-027803-X*, Perennial) HarperTrade.

— Aunt Eater's Mystery Halloween. LC 97-38606. (Illus.). 64p. (J). (ps-3). 1998. lib. bdg. 14.89 (*0-06-027804-8*, Perennial) HarperTrade.

— Aunt Eater's Mystery Vacation. LC 91-25059. (I Can Read Bks.). (Illus.). 64p. (J). (ps-3). 1992. lib. bdg. 15.89 (*0-06-020514-8*) HarpC Child Bks.

Cushman, Doug. Aunt Eater's Mystery Vacation. LC 91-25059. (I Can Read Bks.). (Illus.). 64p. (J). (ps-3). 1993. pap. 3.95 (*0-06-444169-5*, HarpTrophy) HarpC Child Bks.

— Aunt Eater's Mystery Vacation. (I Can Read Bks.). (J). (gr. 1-3). 1993. 8.70 (*0-606-05732-3*, Pub. by Turtleback) Demco.

Cushman, Doug. Camp Big Paw. LC 89-26867. (I Can Read Bks.). (Illus.). 64p. (J). (ps-3). 1993. pap. 3.95 (*0-06-444166-0*, HarpTrophy) HarpC Child Bks.

Cushman, Doug. Camp Big Paw. (I Can Read Bks.). (J). (gr. 1-3). 1993. 8.95 (*0-606-05182-1*, Pub. by Turtleback) Demco.

Cushman, Doug. Inspector Hopper. LC PZ7.C959In 2000. (I Can Read Bks.). (Illus.). 64p. (J). (gr. 1-3). 2000. 14.95 (*0-06-028382-3*) HarpC Child Bks.

***Cushman, Doug.** Inspector Hopper. LC 99-30878. (I Can Read Bks.). (Illus.). 64p. (J). (ps-3). 2000. lib. bdg. 14.89 (*0-06-028383-1*) HarpC Child Bks.

— Inspector Hopper. (I Can Read Bks.). 64p. (J). (gr. 1-3). 2001. pap. 3.95 (*0-06-444260-8*) HarpC Child Bks.

Cushman, Doug. The Mystery of King Karfu. LC 95-31064. (Illus.). 32p. (J). (ps-3). 1996. 14.95 (*0-06-024796-7*) HarpC Child Bks.

— The Mystery of King Karfu. LC 95-31064. (Illus.). 32p. (J). (ps-3). 1998. pap. 5.95 (*0-06-443503-2*) HarpC Child Bks.

— The Mystery of King Karfu. 1998. 11.15 (*0-606-13638-X*, Pub. by Turtleback) Demco.

— The Mystery of the Monkey's Maze. LC 98-39424. (Illus.). 32p. (J). (ps-3). 1999. 15.95 (*0-06-027719-X*); lib. bdg. 15.89 (*0-06-027720-3*) HarpC Child Bks.

— Uncle Foster's Hat Tree. (Easy-to-Read Bks.). (Illus.). 48p. (J). (gr. k-3). 1996. pap. 3.99 (*0-14-037995-9*, PuffinBks) Peng Put Young Read.

Cushman, Doug. Uncle Foster's Hat Tree. (Puffin Easy-to-Read Ser.). (J). 1996. 8.70 (*0-606-08653-6*, Pub. by Turtleback) Demco.

Cushman, Ellen. The Struggle & the Tools: Oral & Literate Strategies in an Inner City Community. LC 98-13321. (Illus.). 352p. (C). 1998. text 65.50 (*0-7914-3981-X*); pap. text 21.95 (*0-7914-3982-8*) State U NY Pr.

Cushman, Glenn, jt. auth. see Cushman, Ruth C.

Cushman, H. B. The History of the Choctaw, Chickasaw, & Natchez Indians. LC 98-44030. 1999. pap. text 15.95 (*0-8061-3127-6*) U of Okla Pr.

Cushman, H. W. A Historical & Biographical Genealogy of the Cushmans: The Descendants of Robert Cushman, Puritan, 1617 -1855. (Illus.). 666p. 1989. reprint ed. pap. 99.00 (*0-8328-0449-5*); reprint ed. lib. bdg. 107.00 (*0-8328-0448-7*) Higginson Bk Co.

Cushman, Helen B. The Mill on the Third River: A History of the Davey Company Makers of Binders Board since 1842. Burnett, Robert & Bagger, Donald, eds. (Illus.). 147p. (C). 1992. write for info. (*0-9628551-0-3*) Davey NJ.

Cushman, J. A. The American Species of Orthophragmina & Lepidocyclina. 1971. reprint ed. 16.00 (*0-934454-06-X*) Lubrecht & Cramer.

— A Lower Miocene Foraminifera of Florida. 1972. reprint ed. 10.00 (*0-934454-58-2*) Lubrecht & Cramer.

— Upper Cretaceous Foraminifera of the Gulf Coastal Region. 1965. reprint ed. 21.80 (*0-934454-79-5*) Lubrecht & Cramer.

— Upper Eocene Foraminifera of the Southeastern U. S. 1971. reprint ed. 15.20 (*0-934454-80-9*) Lubrecht & Cramer.

Cushman, J. A. & Cahill, E. D. Miocene Foraminifera of the Coastal Plain of the Eastern U. S. 1971. reprint ed. 15.00 (*0-934454-64-7*) Lubrecht & Cramer.

Cushman, J. A. & Cooke, C. W. The Foraminifera of the Bryam Calcareous Marl at Byram, Mississippi & the Byram Calcareous Marl at Mississippi. 1971. 15.00 (*0-934454-36-1*) Lubrecht & Cramer.

— The Foraminifera of the Vicksburg Group. 1972. reprint ed. 12.50 (*0-934454-38-8*) Lubrecht & Cramer.

Cushman, J. A., jt. auth. see Cooke, C. W.

Cushman, Jack L. Math Flipper: A Guide to Basic Mathematics. (Illus.). 49p. (J). (gr. 6 up). 1989. reprint ed. 6.95 (*1-878383-02-7*) C Lee Pubns.

— Punctuation & Capitalization Flipper. (Illus.). 49p. (J). (gr. 5 up). 1989. reprint ed. 6.95 (*1-878383-00-0*) C Lee Pubns.

Cushman, Jean. Do You Wanna Bet? Your Chance to Find Out about Probability. (Illus.). 112p. (J). (gr. 3-7). 1991. 16.00 (*0-395-56516-2*, Clarion Bks) HM.

Cushman, Jennifer. Family & State: The Formation of a Sino-Thai Tin-Mining Dynasty 1797-1932. Reynolds, Craig J., ed. (South-East Asian Historical Monographs). (Illus.). 216p. 1992. 45.00 (*0-19-588966-5*) OUP.

— Fields from the Sea: Chinese Junk Trade with Siam During the Late Eighteenth & Early Nineteenth Centuries. (Studies on Southeast Asia: No. 12). 216p. (Orig.). 1993. pap. 16.00 (*0-87727-711-7*) Cornell SE Asia.

Cushman, Jennifer & Gungwu, Wang, eds. Changing Identities of the Southeast Asian Chinese since World War II. 354p. (Orig.). 1988. pap. 43.50 (*962-209-207-1*, Pub. by HK Univ Pr) Coronet Bks.

Cushman, Jerome. Affenpinscher: A Complete & Reliable Handbook. (Illus.). 96p. Date not set. 19.95 (*0-7938-0766-2*, RX-116) TFH Pubns.

Cushman, John H. Command & Control of Theatre Forces: The Future of Force Projection Operations. unabridged ed. LC 95-197738. 111p. (Orig.). 1995. pap. text 480.00 (*1-879716-24-0*, P-95-1) Ctr Info Policy.

— The Physics of Fluids in Hierarchical Porous Media: Angstroms to Miles. LC 97-13423. (Theory & Applications of Transport in Porous Media Ser.: No. 10). 467p. 1997. text 220.50 (*0-7923-4742-0*) Kluwer Academic.

— Thoughts for Joint Commanders. 64p. (C). 1993. pap. text. write for info. (*0-9637932-0-9*) J H Cushman.

Cushman, John H., ed. Dynamics of Fluids in Hierarchical Porous Media. 505p. 1990. text 154.00 (*0-12-200260-1*) Acad Pr.

Cushman, Joseph A. Foraminifera: Their Classification & Economic Use. 4th rev. ed. LC 48-9473. (Illus.). 613p. 1948. 62.00 (*0-674-30801-8*) HUP.

Cushman, Joseph D., Jr. The Sound of Bells: The Episcopal Church in South Florida, 1892-1969. LC 75-30946. (Illus.). 1976. 24.95 (*0-8130-0518-3*) U Press Fla.

Cushman, Joseph D. The Sound of Bells: The Episcopal Church in South Florida, 1892-1969. LC 75-30946. (Illus.). 412p. 1976. reprint ed. pap. 127.80 (*0-608-04474-1*, 206521900001) Bks Demand.

Cushman, Karen. The Ballad of Lucy Whipple. LC 95-45257. 195p. (J). (gr. 3-7). 1996. 15.00 (*0-395-72806-1*, Clarion Bks) HM.

— The Ballad of Lucy Whipple. LC 95-45257. 224p. (J). (gr. 3-7). 1998. pap. 4.95 (*0-06-440684-9*, HarpTrophy) HarpC Child Bks.

— The Ballad of Lucy Whipple. (J). 1998. 10.30 (*0-606-13177-9*) Turtleback.

— Catherine, Called Birdy. 224p. (YA). (gr. 6 up). 1994. 14.95 (*0-395-68186-3*, Clarion Bks) HM.

— Catherine, Called Birdy. (Trophy Bk.). 224p. (YA). (gr. 12 up). 1995. pap. 5.95 (*0-06-440584-2*, HarpTrophy) HarpC Child Bks.

***Cushman, Karen.** Catherine, Called Birdy. (Illus.). 16p. 1999. pap. text 3.95 (*0-590-38940-8*) Scholastic Inc.

Cushman, Karen. Catherine, Called Birdy. (YA). (gr. 6 up). 1995. 10.05 (*0-606-07355-8*, Pub. by Turtleback) Demco.

***Cushman, Karen.** Matilda Bone. (Illus.). 176p. (J). (gr. 4-7). 2000. 15.00 (*0-395-88156-0*, Clarion Bks) HM.

Cushman, Karen. The Midwife's Apprentice. LC 94-13792. 122p. (J). (gr. 6-9). 1995. 10.95 (*0-395-69229-6*, Clarion Bks) HM.

— The Midwife's Apprentice. (Trophy Bk.). (Illus.). 128p. (J). (gr. 12 up). 1996. pap. 5.95 (*0-06-440630-X*, HarpTrophy) HarpC Child Bks.

— The Midwife's Apprentice. 1996. 10.05 (*0-606-09612-4*, Pub. by Turtleback) Demco.

Cushman, Karen, jt. auth. see Lenski, Lois.

Cushman, Kathleen. Circus Dreams: The Making of a Circus Artist. (J). (gr. 4-7). 1990. 15.95 (*0-316-16561-1*, Joy St Bks) Little.

***Cushman, Kathleen & Steinberg, Adria.** Schooling for the Real World: A Guide to Providing Enriching Classroom Learning Experiences. LC 99-6487. 128p. 1999. pap. 19.95 (*0-7879-5041-6*) Jossey-Bass.

Cushman, Keith. D. H. Lawrence at Work: The Emergence of the Prussian Officer Stories. LC 77-22149. 255p. reprint ed. pap. 79.10 (*0-8357-6995-X*, 203904800010) Bks Demand.

Cushman, Keith & Jackson, Dennis, eds. D. H. Lawrence's Literary Inheritors. LC 90-44895. 270p. 1991. text 45.00 (*0-312-05577-3*) St Martin.

Cushman, Keith, ed. see Lawrence, D. H.

Cushman, Keith, jt. ed. see Squires, Michael.

Cushman, Kenneth M., et al, eds. Construction Litigation. 2nd ed. 750p. 1992. 125.00 (*0-685-69400-3*) PLI.

Cushman, Kenneth M. & Practising Law Institute. Handling Construction Risks: Allocate Now or Litigate Later LC 98-169654. (Real Estate Law & Practice Course Handbook Ser.). 328p. 1998. 129.00 (*0-87224-442-3*) PLI.

Cushman, Laura A. & Scherer, Marcia J., eds. Psychological Assessment in Medical Rehabilitation. LC 95-11109. (Measurement & Instrumentation in Psychology Ser.). 471p. 1995. text 29.95 (*1-55798-299-6*) Am Psychol.

Cushman, Michael J. Ships & Sailing: Poetry, Folklore, Sayings, Comics. 40p. 1995. pap. 3.00 (*0-9648667-0-6*) Cushmn Pubng.

Cushman, Philip. Constructing the Self, Constructing America: A Cultural History of Psychotherapy. 448p. 1996. pap. 14.00 (*0-201-44192-6*) Addison-Wesley.

Cushman, Priscilla. Introduction to Algebra with Business Technology Emphasis. 304p. (C). 1998. spiral bd. 29.95 (*0-7872-5364-2*) Kendall-Hunt.

Cushman, R. H. & Bates, L. M. Global Aspects of Classical Integrable Systems. LC 96-52345. 448p. 1997. 54.95 (*3-7643-5485-2*) Birkhauser.

Cushman, R. H., ed. see Souriau, J. M.

Cushman, Ralph B. Jesse Chisholm: Texas Trail Blazer & Sam Houston's Troubleshooter. (Illus.). 288p. 1997. pap. 16.95 (*1-57168-032-2*, Eakin Pr) Sunbelt Media.

— Young Bussey, Young Stud: An All-American Legend. 248p. 1993. 22.95 (*0-9637761-0-X*) Bigco Pr.

Cushman, Richard H. & Bates, Larry M. Global Aspects of Classic Integrable Systems. LC 96-52345. (Illus.). xvi, 435p. 1997. 54.95 (*0-8176-5485-2*) Birkhauser.

Cushman, Robert & Behlmer, Stacey Endress. Hollywood at Your Feet: The Story of the World Famous Chinese Theatre. (Illus.). 352p. 1992. pap. 19.95 (*0-938817-08-6*) Pomegranate Pr.

Cushman, Robert, jt. auth. see Brownlow, Kevin.

Cushman, Robert, jt. auth. see Endres, Stacey.

Cushman, Robert E. Therapeia: Plato's Conception of Philosophy. LC 76-6518. 322p. 1976. reprint ed. lib. bdg. 67.50 (*0-8371-8879-2*, CUTP, Greenwood Pr) Greenwood.

Cushman, Robert F. Cases in Civil Liberties. 3rd ed. 1979. 18.95 (*0-685-03776-2*) P-H.

— Cases in Constitutional Law. 5th ed. 1979. 29.95 (*0-685-03777-0*) P-H.

— Construction Change Order Claims. 1. 384p. 1994. boxed set 150.00 (*0-471-30369-0*) Wiley.

— Proving & Pricing Construction Claims, 1. 2nd ed. LC 96-585. 624p. 1997. boxed set 150.00 (*0-471-11424-3*) Wiley.

Cushman, Robert F., ed. Fifty State Construction Lien & Bond Law, 3 vols., Vol. 3. (Construction Law Library). 1490p. 1992. boxed set 370.00 (*0-471-12731-0*) Wiley.

Cushman, Robert F., et al, eds. Construction Litigation: Representing the Owner, 1. 2nd ed. LC 00-89. (Construction Law Library). 576p. 1989. boxed set 150.00 (*0-471-61914-0*) Wiley.

Cushman, Robert F. & Doyle, William J., eds. Construction Bidding Law, 1. LC 89-37695. (Construction Law Library). 352p. 1989. boxed set 150.00 (*0-471-50118-2*) Wiley.

Cushman, Robert F. & Hedemann, G. Christian. Architect & Engineer Liability: Claims Against Design Professionals, 1. 2nd ed. LC 95-21485. (Construction Law Library). 664p. 1995. boxed set 150.00 (*0-471-11221-6*) Wiley.

Cushman, Robert F. & Koniak, Susan P. Cases in Civil Liberties. 6th ed. LC 93-1893. 416p. (C). 1993. pap. text 45.00 (*0-13-146622-4*) P-H.

***Cushman, Robert F. & Myers, James J.** Construction Law Handbook LC 99-22241. 1999. write for info. (*0-7355-0670-1*) Panel Pubs.

Cushman, Robert F. & Taub, Kathy S. Design-Build Contracting Formbook. LC 97-7142. xxxii, 486 p. 1997. write for info. (*0-471-19076-4*) Halsted Pr.

Cushman, Robert F. & Taub, Kathy S., eds. Design-Build Contracting Formbook, 1. LC 97-7142. (Construction Law Library). 520p. 1997. boxed set 155.00 (*0-471-15478-4*) Wiley.

***Cushman, Robert Frank & Butler, Stephen D.** Fifty State Construction Lien & Bond Law. 2nd ed. LC 99-55748. 1999. boxed set 265.00 (*0-7355-1063-6*) Panel Pubs.

Cushman, Roger, jt. auth. see Bloodworth, Bryan.

An Asterisk (*) at the beginning of an entry indicates that the title is appearing for the first time.

Cushman-Roisin, Benoit. Introduction to Geophysical Fluid Dynamics. LC 93-44584. 320p. 1994. 93.33 (*0-13-353301-8*) P-H.

***Cushman, Ruth C. & Cushman, Glenn.** Hiking Trails of Boulder: The Best of the Plains, Foothills & Mountains. 2nd rev. ed. LC 99-51546. (Illus.). 225p. 1999. pap. 18.50 (*0-87108-907-6*) Pruett.

Cushman, Ruth C., et al. Boulder County Nature Almanac: What to See Where & When. LC 93-6251. (Illus.). 340p. 1993. pap. 19.95 (*0-87108-819-3*) Pruett.

Cushman, Ruth C., jt. auth. see Jones, Stephen.

Cushman, Stephen. Bloody Promenade: Reflections on a Civil War Battle. LC 99-11730. (American South Ser.). 1999. 29.95 (*0-8139-1874-X*) U Pr of Va.

— Blue Pajamas. LC 98-18936. 64p. 1998. pap. 11.95 (*0-8071-2303-X*); text 19.95 (*0-8071-2302-1*) La State U Pr.

— Fictions of Form in American Poetry. LC 92-39503. 236p. 1993. text 29.50 (*0-691-06963-8*, Pub. by Princeton U Pr) Cal Prin Full Svc.

Cushman, Stephen & Newlin, Paul, eds. Nation of Letters Vol. I: A Concise Anthology of American Literature. (Illus.). 408p. (C). 1998. pap. text 23.97 (*1-881089-89-4*) Brandywine Press.

— Nation of Letters Vol. II: A Concise History of American Literature. (Illus.). 420p. (C). 1998. pap. text 23.97 (*1-881089-90-8*) Brandywine Press.

Cushman, Thomas. Notes from Underground: Rock Music Counterculture in Russia. LC 95-1541. (SUNY Series in the Sociology of Culture). 403p. (C). 1995. text 59.50 (*0-7914-2543-6*); pap. text 19.95 (*0-7914-2544-4*) State U NY Pr.

Cushman, Thomas & Mestrovic, Stjepan G., eds. This Time We Knew: Western Responses to Genocide in Bosnia. 320p. (C). 1996. pap. text 19.50 (*0-8147-1535-4*) NYU Pr.

— This Time We Knew: Western Responses to Genocide in Bosnia. 320p. (C). 1996. text 50.00 (*0-8147-1534-6*) NYU Pr.

Cushman, W. H. & Rosenberg, D. J. Human Factors in Product Design. (Advances in Human Factors-Ergonomics Ser.: No. 14). xx,340p. 1991. 189.00 (*0-444-87434-8*); pap. 60.00 (*0-685-48201-4*) Elsevier.

Cushner. Human Diversity Education. 3rd ed. LC 99-27510. 384p. 1999. pap. 52.80 (*0-07-228724-1*) McGraw.

— Human Diversity in Action. 216p. 1998. pap., wbk. ed. 28.13 (*0-07-289371-0*) McGraw.

Cushner, Kenneth, ed. International Perspectives on Intercultural Education. LC 98-17268. 288p. 1998. write for info. (*0-8058-2745-5*); pap. write for info. (*0-8058-2746-3*) L Erlbaum Assocs.

Cushner, Kenneth & Brislin, Richard, eds. Improving Intercultural Interactions: Modules for Cross-Cultural Training Programs, Vol. 2. (Multicultural Aspects of Counseling Ser.: Vol. 8). 256p. (C). 1997. 49.95 (*0-7619-0536-7*, 05367); pap. 22.95 (*0-7619-0537-5*, 05375) Sage.

Cushner, Kenneth & Brislin, Richard W. Intercultural Interactions: A Practical Guide. 2nd ed. LC 95-35480. (Cross-Cultural Research & Methodology Ser.: Vol. 9). 384p. 1995. 37.00 (*0-8039-5990-7*); pap. 16.99 (*0-8039-5991-5*) Sage.

Cushner, N. P. Documents Illustrating the British Conquest of Manila 1762-63. (Camden Fourth Ser.). 27.00 (*0-901050-66-0*) David Brown.

Cushner, Nicholas P. Escape: The Honeymoon Travel Book. (Illus.). 104p. (Orig.). 1989. pap. 6.95 (*0-317-93054-0*) Travel Lite Assocs.

— Farm & Factory: The Jesuits & the Development of Agrarian Capitalism in Colonial Quito. LC 81-13537. 231p. (C). 1983. text 74.50 (*0-87395-570-6*); pap. text 24.95 (*0-87395-571-4*) State U NY Pr.

— Jesuit Ranches & the Agrarian Development of Colonial Argentina, 1650-1767. LC 82-19503. 206p. (C). 1984. pap. text 24.95 (*0-87395-706-7*) State U NY Pr.

— Landed Estates in the Colonial Philippines. LC 75-27615. (Monographs: No. 20). 146p. 1976. 11.50 (*0-938692-10-0*) Yale U SE Asia.

Cushner, Susie & Hamilton, David, photos by. Deruta: A Tradition of Italian Ceramics. LC 97-44652. (Illus.). 168p. 1998. 35.00 (*0-8118-1794-6*) Chronicle Bks.

***Cushnie, John.** Ground Cover: A Thousand Beautiful Plants for Difficult Places. (Illus.). 2000. 29.95 (*1-85626-326-6*, Pub. by Cathie Kyle) Trafalgar.

***Cushnir, Howard Raphael.** Unconditional Bliss: Finding Happiness in the Face of Hardship. 184p. 2000. pap. 15.95 (*0-8356-0792-5*, Pub. by Theos Pub Hse) Natl Bk Netwk.

Cushway, Delia & Sewell, Robyn. Counselling with Dreams & Nightmares. (Counselling in Practice Ser.: Vol. 6). (Illus.). 160p. (C). 1993. text 49.95 (*0-8039-8599-1*); pap. text 21.50 (*0-8039-8600-9*) Sage.

Cusic, David, jt. auth. see Mettling, Stephan R.

Cusic, Don. Cowboys & the Wild West: An A-Z Guide from the Chisholm Trail to the Silver Screen. LC 93-45584. (Illus.). 310p. 1995. pap. 19.95 (*0-8160-3030-8*) Facts on File.

— Eddy Arnold: I'll Hold You in My Heart. LC 97-7218. (Illus.). 256p. 1997. 19.95 (*1-55853-492-X*) Rutledge Hill Pr.

— Music in the Market. LC 95-47158. 189p. 1996. pap. 22.95 (*0-87972-694-6*) Bowling Green Univ Popular Press.

— The Poet As Performer. 136p. (Orig.). (C). 1991. pap. text 18.00 (*0-8191-8397-0*); lib. bdg. 44.00 (*0-8191-8396-2*) U Pr of Amer.

— The Sound of Light: A History of Gospel Music. LC 90-82744. 256p. (C). 1990. 19.95 (*0-87972-497-8*); pap. 40.95 (*0-87972-498-6*) Bowling Green Univ Popular Press.

Cusic, Don, ed. see Williams, Hank, Sr.

Cusich. Music & Feminism. 1995. 26.95 (*0-8057-9758-0*, Twyne) Mac Lib Ref.

Cusick. Progressive Casting & Splinting. 1998. 58.00 (*0-12-784576-3*) Acad Pr.

— Serial Casts. (C). 1998. pap. 29.95 (*0-12-784575-5*) Acad Pr.

Cusick, Allison W. & Silberhorn, Gene M. The Vascular Plants of Unglaciated Ohio. (Bulletin New Ser.: Vol. 5, No. 4). 1977. pap. text 10.00 (*0-86727-081-0*) Ohio Bio Survey.

Cusick, Beverly D. Progressive Casting & Splinting: For Lower Extremity Deformities in Children with Neuromotor Dysfunction. (Illus.). 410p. (C). 1990. pap. text 59.00 (*0-7616-4182-3*) Commun Skill.

Cusick, Dawn. The Button Craft Book. (Illus.). 128p. (Orig.). 1996. pap. 14.95 (*0-8069-3198-1*) Sterling.

— Cat Crafts. LC 96-35792. (Illus.). 128p. 1997. 14.95 (*0-8069-9553-X*) Sterling.

— Dried Flower Crafts: Capturing the Best of Your Garden to Decorate Your Home. LC 95-44155. (Illus.). 96p. 1996. 19.95 (*0-8069-6120-1*) Sterling.

— Dried Flower Crafts: Capturing the Best of Your Garden to Decorate Your Home. (Illus.). 96p. 1997. pap. 9.95 (*0-8069-6121-X*) Sterling.

***Cusick, Dawn.** Dried Flower Crafts: Capturing the Best of Your Garden to Decorate Your Home. (Illus.). 96p. 2000. reprint ed. text 20.00 (*0-7881-9111-X*) DIANE Pub.

Cusick, Dawn. Fabric Lovers' Christmas Scrapcrafts. LC 93-10659. (Illus.). 128p. (YA). (gr. 10-12). 1993. 27.95 (*0-8069-0437-2*) Sterling.

— Fabric Lovers' Christmas Scrapcrafts. (Illus.). 128p. 1994. pap. 14.95 (*0-8069-0438-0*) Sterling.

— The Lamp Shade Book: 80 Traditional & Innovative Projects to Create Exciting Lighting Effects. (Illus.). 128p. pap. 14.95 (*0-8069-8700-6*) Sterling.

***Cusick, Dawn.** Making Bead & Wire Jewelry: Simple Techniques, Stunning Designs. LC 99-55035. (Illus.). 128p. 2000. 27.95 (*1-57990-148-4*, Pub. by Lark Books) Sterling.

Cusick, Dawn. Nature Crafts with a Microwave: Over 80 Projects. (Illus.). 128p. 1995. pap. 14.95 (*0-8069-0667-7*) Sterling.

— Paper & Fabric Mache: 100 Imaginative & Ingenious Projects to Make. (Illus.). 128p. 1995. pap. 14.95 (*0-8069-0609-X*) Sterling.

— A Scented Christmas. (Illus.). 112p. 1990. pap. 9.95 (*0-8069-7470-2*) Sterling.

***Cusick, Dawn.** Tabletop Fountains. 2000. pap. 17.95 (*1-57990-189-1*, Pub. by Lark Books) Sterling.

Cusick, Dawn. Tabletop Fountains: 40 Easy & Great-Looking Projects to Make. LC 99-30747. (Illus.). 128p. 1999. 24.95 (*1-57990-105-0*) Lark Books.

— Wreath Making Basics: More Than Eighty Wreath Ideas. LC 92-41411. (Illus.). 96p. 1993. pap. 9.95 (*0-8069-0279-5*) Sterling.

Cusick, Dawn & Taylor, Carol. Nature Crafts for Christmas: A Step-by-Step Guide to Making Wreaths, Ornaments & Decorations. LC 94-15975. 256p. 1994. 27.95 (*0-87596-622-5*) Rodale Pr Inc.

Cusick, Dawn, jt. auth. see LaRose-Weaver, Diane.

Cusick, Dawn, ed. see Blose, Nora & Lovejoy, Sharon.

Cusick, Dawn, ed. see Dairy Barn Southeastern Ohio Cultural Arts Center.

Cusick, Dawn, ed. see Dairy Barn Staff.

Cusick, Dawn, ed. see Ham, Cathy.

Cusick, Dawn, ed. see Parker, Mary.

Cusick, Dawn, ed. see Sandberg, Gosta.

Cusick, Heidi. Sonoma: The Ultimate Winery Guide. LC 94-34732. (Illus.). 120p. 1995. pap. 18.95 (*0-8118-0773-8*) Chronicle Bks.

Cusick, Heidi, ed. Scones, Muffins, & Tea Cakes: Breakfast Breads & Teatime Spreads. LC 95-24699. (Illus.). 96p. 1996. 14.00 (*0-00-225201-5*) Collins SF.

Cusick, Heidi H. Chicken for Dinner. LC 97-27309. (Williams-Sonoma Lifestyles Ser.). (Illus.). 112p. (gr. 11). 1998. 14.95 (*0-7835-4611-4*) Time-Life.

— Mendocino: The Ultimate Wine & Food Lover's Guide. LC 96-30618. 1997. pap. 19.95 (*0-8118-1391-6*) Chronicle Bks.

— Soul & Spice: African Cooking in the Americas. (Illus.). 320p. 1995. pap. 16.95 (*0-8118-0419-4*) Chronicle Bks.

Cusick, Heidi H., et al, eds. Picnics: Country Garden Cookbook. LC 94-21598. (Illus.). 96p. 1995. 9.95 (*0-00-255484-4*, Pub. by Harper SF) HarpC.

Cusick, Heidy H. The International Pantry: Quick Home Cooking with Today's Best Seasonings, Prepared Sauces, & Spices. LC 97-10549. 1997. pap. 18.95 (*0-8118-1670-2*) Chronicle Bks.

Cusick High School, Class of 'Ninety-Two Staff. From 'Ninety-Two to You: A Collection of Stories & Poems. Agan, Melissa, ed. (Illus.). 44p. (Orig.). 1988. pap. text 3.50 (*0-317-90580-5*) Cusick Pub Co.

Cusick, James G., ed. Studies in Culture Contact: Interaction, Culture Change, & Archaeology. LC 96-83282. (Center for Archaeological Investigations Occasional Paper Ser.: Vol. 25). x, 502p. (C). 1998. pap. 40.00 (*0-88104-082-7*) Center Archaeol.

Cusick, Joyce E. Crafting with Lace: More than 40 Enchanting Projects to Make. LC 93-24784. (Illus.). 160p. 1993. 27.95 (*0-8069-0443-7*) Sterling.

— Crafting with Lace: More Than 40 Enchanting Projects to Make. (Illus.). 160p. 1995. pap. 14.95 (*0-8069-0444-5*) Sterling.

Cusick, Lois. Waldorf Parenting Handbook: Useful Information on Child Development & Education from Anthroposophical Sources. 2nd rev. ed. 1988. pap. 17.95 (*0-916786-75-7*, Saint George Pubns) R Steiner Col.

Cusick, Philip. The Educational Systems: Its Nature & Logic. 288p. (C). 1991. 40.00 (*0-07-014972-0*) McGraw.

Cusick, Philip A. The Egalitarian Ideal & the American High School: Studies of Three Schools. LC 83-1159. 159p. reprint ed. pap. 49.30 (*0-7837-3884-6*, 204373200010) Bks Demand.

Cusick, Richie T. Blood Roots. Zion, Claire, ed. 352p. (Orig.). 1992. mass mkt. 4.99 (*0-671-73497-0*) PB.

Cusick, Richie T. Buffy the Vampire Slayer. (J). (gr. 8-12). 1997. per. 3.99 (*0-671-01700-4*) PB.

Cusick, Richie T. Help Wanted. 224p. (YA). (gr. 7 up). 1993. mass mkt. 3.99 (*0-671-79403-5*, Archway) PB.

— The Mall. MacDonald, Patricia, ed. 224p. (Orig.). (YA). (gr. 7 up). 1992. mass mkt. 3.99 (*0-671-70955-5*, Archway) PB.

— Scarecrow. Zion, Claire, ed. 288p. (Orig.). 1990. mass mkt. 4.99 (*0-671-69020-5*) PB.

— Silent Stalker. MacDonald, Patricia, ed. 224p. (YA). (gr. 7 up). 1993. mass mkt. 3.99 (*0-671-79402-7*, Archway) PB.

— Silent Stalker. 1993. 9.09 (*0-606-05601-7*, Pub. by Turtleback) Demco.

— Someone at the Door. Clancy, Lisa, ed. 240p. (Orig.). (YA). (gr. 7 up). 1994. per. 3.99 (*0-671-88742-4*, Archway) PB.

— Starstruck. (YA). (gr. 7 up). 1996. per. 3.99 (*0-671-55104-3*) PB.

— Summer Secrets. 224p. (YA). (gr. 7 up). 1996. per. 3.99 (*0-671-54927-8*) PB.

— Teacher's Pet. 224p. (Orig.). (YA). (gr. 7-9). 1990. pap. 3.50 (*0-590-43114-5*) Scholastic Inc.

— Trick or Treat. 224p. (YA). (gr. 7-9). 1989. pap. 3.50 (*0-590-44235-X*) Scholastic Inc.

— Vampire. MacDonald, Patricia, ed. 224p. (Orig.). (YA). (gr. 7 up). 1991. mass mkt. 3.99 (*0-671-70956-9*, Archway) PB.

Cusick, Richie Tankersley. Drifter. 1994. 9.09 (*0-606-06338-2*, Pub. by Turtleback) Demco

— The Harvest. (Buffy the Vampire Slayer Ser.: No. 1). (YA). (gr. 7 up). 1997. pap. 4.50 (*0-671-01712-8*) PB.

Cusick, Richie Tankersley. Overdue. (J). 1995. 9.09 (*0-606-07986-6*, Pub. by Turtleback) Demco

Cusick, Suzanne G. Romanesca Ones Own. 1997. pap. text 25.00 (*0-226-13213-7*); lib. bdg. 75.00 (*0-226-13212-9*) U Ch Pr.

Cusick, Suzanne G. Valerio Dorico: Music Printer in Sixteenth-Century Rome. Buelow, George, ed. LC 81-4745. (Studies in Musicology: No. 43). (Illus.). 329p. 1981. reprint ed. pap. 102.00 (*0-8357-1173-0*, 207026200065) Bks Demand.

Cusick, T. & Flahive, E. The Markhoff & Lagrange Spectra. LC 89-14867. (Mathematical Surveys & Monographs: Vol. 30). 97p. 1989. text 49.00 (*0-8218-1531-8*, SURV/30) Am Math.

Cusick, Thomas W., et al. Stream Ciphers & Number Theory. LC 98-10345. (North-Holland Mathematical Library: 55). 446p. 1998. 143.50 (*0-444-82873-7*) Elsevier.

Cusick, Tim, jt. auth. see Kranz, Rachel.

Cusick, William D. Canine Nutrition: Choosing the Best Food for Your Breed of Dog. rev. ed. Luther, Luana, ed. LC 97-65218. (Illus.). 205p. 1997. pap. 14.95 (*0-944875-50-5*, Pub. by Doral Pub) Natl Bk Netwk.

— Canine Nutrition & Choosing the Best Food for Your Breed of Dog. LC 90-85146. (Illus.). (Orig.). 1990. pap. 21.95 (*1-879229-00-5*) Adele Pub.

Cusimano. Beyond Sovereignty. Date not set. 23.50 (*1-57259-751-8*) Worth.

— Beyond Sovereignty: Issues for a Global Agenda. LC 98-85002. 331p. 1999. text 35.00 (*0-312-21351-2*) St Martin.

Cusimano, jt. auth. see Roberts.

Cusimano, Gregory S. & Roberts, Michael L. Alabama Tort Law, 1998 Cumulative Supplement. 2nd ed. 470p. 1998. pap., suppl. ed. write for info. (*0-327-00561-0*, 6664715) LEXIS Pub.

Cusimano, Gregory S., jt. auth. see Roberts, Michael L.

Cusimano, Maryann K. Operation Restore Hope: The Bush Administration's Decision to Intervene in Somalia. (Pew Case Studies in International Affairs). 50p. (C). 1995. pap. text 3.50 (*1-56927-463-0*, GU Schl Foreign) Geo U Inst Dplmcy.

Cusimano, Richard C., tr. see Suger, Abbot of St. Denis.

Cusimano, Vincent J. & Halpern, Stephen C. Contemporary Issues in Science: Course Manual. 139p. (Orig.). 1982. pap. text 15.95 (*0-914639-25-0*) SI Cont Ed Inc.

— Contemporary Issues in Science: Implementation Manual. 98p. (Orig.). 1982. pap. text 15.95 (*0-914639-26-9*) SI Cont Ed Inc.

Cusine, D., jt. ed. see Templeton, A.

Cusine, D. J., jt. auth. see Maher, G.

Cusine, Douglas J. Cusine: Standard Securities. 1991. pap. 52.00 (*0-406-10587-1*, MICHIE) LEXIS Pub.

— New Reproductive Techniques: A Legal Perspective. (Medico-Legal Issues Ser.). 280p. 1988. text 87.95 (*0-566-05410-8*, Pub. by Dartmth Pub) Ashgate Pub Co.

— New Reproductive Techniques: A Legal Perspective. (Medico-Legal Issues Ser.). 1990. pap. 39.95 (*1-85521-007-X*, Pub. by Dartmth Pub) Ashgate Pub Co.

Cusine, Douglas J. & Rennie, Robert. Missives. 230p. 1993. boxed set 60.00 (*0-406-00593-1*, UK MICHIE) LEXIS Pub.

Cusine, Douglas J., jt. auth. see Rennie, Robert.

Cusizk, Richie T. Overdue. Clancey, Lisa, ed. 256p. (YA). (gr. 7 up). 1995. mass mkt. 3.99 (*0-671-88743-2*, Archway) PB.

Cusk, Rachel. The Country Life. LC 98-31292. 341p. 1998. text 24.00 (*0-312-19848-5*, Picador USA) St Martin.

***Cusk, Rachel.** The Country Life. LC 98-31292. 341p. 2000. pap. 14.00 (*0-312-25280-3*, Picador USA) St Martin.

— Saving Agnes: Novel. LC 99-53450. 224p. 2000. text 23.00 (*0-312-25256-0*, Picador USA) St Martin.

Cusmano, Anne M. Thoughts & Visions: Poems of the Heart & the Imagination. 50p. (Orig.). 1995. pap. 7.50 (*0-9645160-0-4*) Dutchess Angel.

Cusmano, Domenic, tr. see Salvatore, Filippo.

Cuspidi, Cesare, jt. ed. see Leonetti, Gastone.

Cuss, Camerer. The Camerer Cuss Book of Antique Watches. 336p. 1976. 79.50 (*1-85149-204-6*) Antique Collect.

Cussen, Antonio. Bello & Bolivar: Poetry & Politics in the Spanish American Revolution. (Cambridge Studies in Latin American & Iberian Literature: No. 6). 222p. (C). 1992. text 59.95 (*0-521-41248-X*) Cambridge U Pr.

Cussen, Debra T., ed. see Doughty, Charles W.

Cussen, Joseph A., jt. auth. see Dominicis, Maria C.

Cussen, Margaret. A Useful Guide to Irish Crochet Lacemaking. 87p. (C). 1989. pap. 40.00 (*0-7223-2096-5*, Pub. by A H S Ltd) St Mut.

Cusset, Catherine. No Tomorrow: The Ethics of Pleasure in the French Enlightenment. LC 98-55780. 224p. 1999. 35.00 (*0-8139-1860-X*) U Pr of Va.

Cusset, Catherine, ed. Yale French Studies, 94: Libertinage & Modernity. 224p. 1998. pap. 18.00 (*0-300-07738-6*) Yale U Pr.

Cusset, F. Technical Dictionary: French-English, English-French. 7th rev. ed. (ENG & FRE.). 434p. 1967. 175.00 (*0-7859-7146-7*) Fr & Eur.

Cusset, Francis. English-French & French-English Technical Dictionary. rev. ed. (ENG & FRE.). 1967. 65.00 (*0-8206-0043-1*) Chem Pub.

— Vocabulaire Technique Allemand-Francais, Francais-Allemand. 8th ed. (FRE & GER.). 474p. 1977. 49.95 (*0-8288-5532-3*, M6097) Fr & Eur.

— Vocabulaire Technique Anglais-Francais, Francais-Anglais. 9th ed. (FRE & GER.). 434p. 1977. 69.95 (*0-8288-5533-1*, M6098) Fr & Eur.

Cussianovich, Alejandro. Religious Life & the Poor: Liberation Theology Perspectives. Drury, John, tr. LC 78-16740. Orig. Title: Desde los Pobres de la Tiera. 176p. (Orig.). reprint ed. pap. 54.60 (*0-8357-7008-7*, 203357300086) Bks Demand.

Cussini, Eleonora, jt. auth. see Hillers, Delbert R.

***Cussler, Clive.** Atlantis Found. LC 99-55055. (Basic Ser.). 534p. 2000. 31.95 (*0-7862-2283-2*) Thorndike Pr.

— Atlantis Found. abr. ed. LC 99-39883. 534p. 1999. 26.95 (*0-399-14588-5*) Putnam Pub Group.

— Atlantis Found. large type ed. LC 99-55055. (Basic Ser.). 1950. 29.95 (*0-7862-2284-0*) Thorndike Pr.

Cussler, Clive. Clive Cussler & Dirk Pitt Revealed. (Dirk Pitt Novel Ser.). (Illus.). 516p. 1998. mass mkt. 7.99 (*0-671-02622-4*) PB.

— Cyclops. McCarthy, Paul, ed. 480p. 1989. per. 7.99 (*0-671-70464-8*) PB.

— Cyclops: A Dirk Pitt Adventure. 1997. mass mkt. 3.99 (*0-671-01130-8*) PB.

— Deep Six. McCarthy, Paul, ed. 480p. 1990. mass mkt. 7.99 (*0-671-70945-3*) PB.

— Dragon. 1990. 263.40 (*0-671-94486-X*) S&S Trade.

— Dragon. abr. ed. 1990. pap. 17.00 incl. audio (*0-671-70302-1*) S&S Trade.

— Dragon. large type ed. (General Ser.). 654p. 1991. 24.95 (*0-8161-5096-6*, G K Hall Lrg Type) Mac Lib Ref.

— Dragon. McCarthy, Paul, ed. 544p. 1991. reprint ed. per. 7.99 (*0-671-74276-0*) PB.

— Flood Tide. 548p. 1998. per. 7.99 (*0-671-00031-4*) PB.

— Flood Tide: A Novel. LC 97-26660. 511p. 1997. 26.00 (*0-684-80298-8*) Simon & Schuster.

— Flood Tide: A Novel. large type ed. LC 97-38617. 914p. 1998. 29.95 (*0-7862-1269-1*) Mac Lib Ref.

— Flood Tide: A Novel. large type ed. LC 97-38617. 914p. 2001. pap. 27.95 (*0-7862-1270-5*) Thorndike Pr.

***Cussler, Clive.** Flood Tide & Cyclops. 2001. 14.99 (*0-517-16277-6*) Crown Pub Group.

Cussler, Clive. Iceberg. 1984. mass mkt. 3.95 (*0-553-14641-6*) Bantam.

— Iceberg. McCarthy, Paul, ed. 1991. per. 7.99 (*0-671-73777-5*) PB.

— Iceberg. 224p. 1996. 24.00 (*0-684-82689-5*) Simon & Schuster.

***Cussler, Clive.** Iceberg. abr. ed. (YA). 2000. mass mkt. 4.99 (*0-671-78626-1*, Archway) PB.

Cussler, Clive. Iceberg. 1994. reprint ed. lib. bdg. 32.95 (*1-56849-270-7*) Buccaneer Bks.

— Inca Gold: A Novel. 1994. 24.00 (*0-671-68156-7*) S&S Trade.

— Inca Gold: A Novel. McCarthy, Paul, ed. LC 94-14545. 592p. 1995. mass mkt. 7.99 (*0-671-51981-6*) S&S Trade.

— Inca Gold: A Novel. abr. ed. (YA). (gr. 5 up). 1998. mass mkt. 4.99 (*0-671-02056-0*, Archway) PB.

— The Mediterranean Caper. 1984. mass mkt. 3.95 (*0-553-23328-9*) Bantam.

— The Mediterranean Caper. 256p. 1996. 24.00 (*0-684-82690-9*) Simon & Schuster.

***Cussler, Clive.** The Mediterranean Caper. large type ed. LC 99-52923. 328p. 2000. lib. bdg. 27.95 (*1-58547-014-7*) Ctr Point Pubg.

Cussler, Clive. The Mediterranean Caper. 1994. reprint ed. lib. bdg. 32.95 (*1-56849-271-5*) Buccaneer Bks.

— The Mediterranean Caper. rev. ed. McCarthy, Paul, ed. 256p. 2000. mass mkt. 7.99 (*0-671-73778-3*) PB.

— Night Probe! 352p. 1984. mass mkt. 7.99 (*0-553-27740-5*) Bantam.

— Pacific Vortex. 288p. 1984. mass mkt. 7.99 (*0-553-27632-8*) Bantam.

— Raise the Titanic! McCarthy, Paul, ed. 352p. 1990. per. 7.99 (*0-671-72519-X*) PB.

***Cussler, Clive.** Raise the Titanic! large type ed. 489p. 2000. lib. bdg. 28.95 (*1-58547-003-1*) Ctr Point Pubg.

Cussler, Clive. Raise the Titanic! 1994. reprint ed. lib. bdg. 32.95 (*1-56849-269-3*) Buccaneer Bks.

C

— Sahara. (Dirk Pitt Adventure Ser.). 576p. 1995. per. 7.99 (*0-671-52110-1*) S&S Trade.

***Cussler, Clive.** Serpent: From the NUMA Files. 474p. 1999. pap. 16.00 (*0-671-02670-4*, Pocket Books) PB.

Cussler, Clive. Shock Wave. 592p. 1996. per. 7.99 (*0-671-00030-6*, Pocket Star Bks) PB.

— Shock Wave. 1999. pap. 9.98 (*0-671-04413-3*) PB.

— Shock Wave. 448p. 1996. 25.00 (*0-684-80297-X*) S&S Trade.

— Shock Wave. large type ed. 1997. pap. 25.95 (*0-7838-1578-6*, G K Hall Lrg Type) Mac Lib Ref.

— Shock Wave. large type ed. 860p. 1999. lib. bdg. 27.95 (*0-7838-1579-4*) Mac Lib Ref.

— Shock Wave: Archway. 1998. mass mkt. 4.99 (*0-671-02055-2*) PB.

— Treasure. McCarthy, Paul, ed. 560p. 1989. per. 7.99 (*0-671-70465-6*) PB.

— Vixen 03. 1976. 23.95 (*0-8488-0470-8*) Amereon Ltd.

Cussler, Clive. Vixen 03. 384p. 1984. mass mkt. 7.99 (*0-553-27390-6*) Bantam.

— Vixen 03. large type ed. LC 00-23382. (Famous Authors Ser.). 615p. 2000. 28.95 (*0-7862-2492-4*, MML06400-171841) Thorndike Pr.

Cussler, Clive. Vixen 03. 1994. reprint ed. lib. bdg. 32.95 (*1-56849-272-3*) Buccaneer Bks.

Cussler, Clive & Dirgo, Craig. The Sea Hunters: True Adventures with Famous Shipwrecks. 1997. per. 7.99 (*0-671-00180-9*) PB.

— The Sea Hunters: True Adventures with Famous Shipwrecks. LC 96-28656. 368p. 1996. 24.00 (*0-684-83027-2*) S&S Trade.

— The Sea Hunters: True Adventures with Famous Shipwrecks. large type ed. LC 96-49136. (Wheeler Large Print Book Ser.). 1997. 26.95 (*1-56895-407-7*) Wheeler Pub.

***Cussler, Clive & Kemprecos, Paul.** Blue Gold. Vol. 2. 2000. audio 25.00 (*0-7435-0030-X*) S&S Audio.

— Blue Gold: A Novel from the NUMA Files. 480p. 2000. pap. 16.00 (*0-671-78546-X*, PB Trade Paper) PB.

— Serpent: From the NUMA Files. large type ed. LC 99-52169. 1999. pap. 24.95 (*1-56895-796-3*, Wheeler) Wheeler Pub.

Cussler, Clive & Kemprecos, Paul. Serpent: From the NUMA Files. 480p. 2000. reprint ed. mass mkt. 7.99 (*0-671-02668-2*, Pocket Books) PB.

Cussler, E. L. Diffusion: Mass Transfer in Fluid Systems. 2nd ed. (Illus.). 600p. (C). 1997. pap. text 44.95 (*0-521-56477-8*) Cambridge U Pr.

— Diffusion: Mass Transfer in Fluid Systems. 2nd ed. (Illus.). 598p. (C). 1997. text 100.00 (*0-521-45078-0*) Cambridge U Pr.

Cusson, Gilles. Biblical Theology & the Spiritual Exercises: A Method Toward a Personal Experience of God as Accomplishing within Us His Plan of Salvation. Ganss, George E. & Roduit, Mary A., trs. LC 87-81796. (Modern Scholarly Studies about the Jesuits, in English Translations Series II: No. 7).Tr. of Pedagogie de l'experience spirituelle personelle: Bible et Exercices. xvi, 385p. 1988. pap. 19.95 (*0-912422-00-9*) Inst Jesuit.

— Spiritual Exercises Made in Everyday Life: A Method & a Biblical Interpretation. Ganss, G. E., ed. Roduit, Mary A., tr. LC 88-83844. (Modern Scholarly Studies about the Jesuits, in English Translations Series II: No. 8). xii, 161p. 1989. 15.95 (*0-912422-90-4*) Inst Jesuit.

Cusson, Maurice. Why Delinquency? LC 84-167472.Tr. of Delinquents pourquoi?. 203p. (Orig.). reprint ed. pap. 63.00 (*0-8357-3636-9*, 203636400003) Bks Demand.

Cussons, Eileen. Elaine. (C). 1989. text 35.00 (*0-948929-12-X*) St Mut.

Cust, Anna M. The Ivory Workers of the Middle Ages. LC 70-178523. reprint ed. 34.50 (*0-404-56537-9*) AMS Pr.

Cust, Edward. Lives of the Warriors of the Civil Wars of France & England: Warriors of the Seventeenth Century, 2 vols. LC 76-38737. (Essay Index Reprint Ser.). 1977. reprint ed. 44.95 (*0-8369-2642-0*) Ayer.

— Lives of the Warriors of the Thirty Years' War: Warriors of the Seventeenth Century, 2 vols. LC 75-38742. (Essay Index Reprint Ser.). 1977. reprint ed. 39.95 (*0-8369-2643-9*) Ayer.

Cust, Elizabeth. Stuart: Some Account of the Stuarts of Aubigny, in France, 1422-1672. (Illus.). 130p. 1992. reprint ed. pap. 24.00 (*0-8328-2593-X*); reprint ed. lib. bdg. 34.00 (*0-8328-2592-1*) Higginson Bk Co.

Cust, Katherine I., ed. see De Deguilleville, Guillaume.

Cust, Kenneth F. A Just Minimum of Health Care: Selected Texts, Parallel Analysis & Comparative Approach. LC 97-12077. 168p. 1997. pap. 24.50 (*0-7618-0754-3*) U Pr of Amer.

— A Just Minimum of Health Care: Selected Texts, Parallel Analysis & Comparative Approach. LC 97-12077. 168p. 1997. 46.50 (*0-7618-0753-5*) U Pubns Amer.

Cust, R. N. A Sketch of the Modern Languages of the East Indies. (Illus.). 198p. 1986. reprint ed. 24.00 (*0-8364-1689-9*, Pub. by Abhinav) S Asia.

Cust, Richard. The Forced Loan & English Politics 1626-1628. (Illus.). 368p. 1987. 90.00 (*0-19-822951-8*) OUP.

Cust, Richard & Hughes, Ann, eds. The English Civil War. LC 97-152036. (Arnold Readers in History Ser.). 384p. 1997. text 65.00 (*0-340-66199-2*, Pub. by E A) OUP.

Custance, Arthur C. Doorway Papers, Vol. 8. 1986. pap. 9.95 (*0-310-23031-4*) Zondervan.

— Doorway Papers, vol. 10. 1985. pap. 9.95 (*0-310-38651-9*) Zondervan.

— The Doorway Papers: The Virgin Birth & the Incarnation, Vol. 5. 400p. (C). 1985. pap. text 10.45 (*0-310-22991-X*, 10663P) Zondervan.

— Evolution or Creation, vol. 4. 1981. pap. 8.95 (*0-310-22981-2*) Zondervan.

Custance, Arthur C. The Flood. 1979. 9.95 (*0-310-23040-3*) Zondervan.

Custance, Arthur C. Journey Out of Time: A Study of the Interval Between Death & the Resurrection of the Body. 303p. 1981. reprint ed. pap. 13.95 (*0-919857-01-9*, Pub. by Doorway USA) Doorway USA.

— The Seed of the Woman. 604p. 1980. 34.95 (*0-919857-00-0*, Pub. by Doorway USA) Doorway USA.

— The Sovereignty of Grace. 398p. 1989. reprint ed. 24.95 (*0-919857-03-5*, Pub. by Doorway USA) Doorway USA.

— Two Men Called Adam: A Fresh Look at the Creation-Evolution Controversy. 273p. 1983. pap. 14.95 (*0-919857-02-7*, Pub. by Doorway USA) Doorway USA.

— Without Form & Void: A Study of the Meaning of Genesis 1.2. 211p. 1970. reprint ed. pap. 9.95 (*0-919857-65-5*, Pub. by Doorway USA) Doorway USA.

Custance, David R., jt. auth. see King, Gillian M.

Custance, Olive. Opals: With, Rainbows. (Decadents, Symbolists, Anti-Decadents Ser.). 1996. 49.50 (*1-85477-137-X*) Continuum.

Custance, Roger. Winchester College: Sixth-Centenary Essays. (Illus.). 1982. 55.00 (*0-19-920103-X*) OUP.

***Custard, Edward T.** The Best 331 Colleges: 2000 Edition. LC 97-664258. Vol. 331. (Illus.). 746p. 1999. pap. 20.00 (*0-375-75411-3*) Random.

Custen, George F. Bio-Pics: How Hollywood Constructed Public History. LC 91-26427. (Illus.). 300p. 1992. pap. 15.95 (*0-8135-1755-9*); text 40.00 (*0-8135-1754-0*) Rutgers U Pr.

— Twentieth Century's Fox: Darryl F. Zanuck & the Culture of Hollywood. LC 97-23961. (Illus.). 384p. 1997. pap. 27.50 (*0-465-07619-X*, Pub. by Basic) HarpC.

— Twentieth Century's Fox: Darryl F. Zanuck & the Culture of Hollywood. 384p. 1998. pap. text 17.50 (*0-465-07620-3*, Pub. by Basic) HarpC.

Custer. Driving Down Health Care Costs. 420p. 1992. 89.00 (*1-56706-002-1*, 60021) Panel Pubs.

Custer, Richard L. P. & Meacham, Brian J. Introduction to Performance-based Fire Safety. LC 97-67356. xii, 260 p. 1997. 78.00 (*0-87765-422-0*) Natl Fire Prot.

Custer, Bobbie G. I Choose to Continue. 106p. 1991. pap. 9.95 (*0-685-39479-4*) BGC Pub Co.

— Two Choose to Continue. 2nd rev. ed. 106p. 1991. reprint ed. pap. text 9.95 (*0-9620061-0-6*) BGC Pub Co.

***Custer, Brice C.** Sacrificial Lion George Armstrong Custer. LC 99-61574. (Montana & the West Ser.: Vol. XIII). (Illus.). 293p. 1999. 42.50 (*0-912783-32-X*) Upton & Sons.

Custer, Carol E. Tomtit Poems Vol. 1: Poems of Nature & Life. 55p. 1991. pap. 10.00 (*0-9631565-0-0*, 3-141-875) Tomtit Ent.

Custer, Chester E. Lay Speakers Interpret to Others Our United Methodist Heritage: Advanced Course for the 1997-2000 Quadrennium. 16p. 1997. pap. 5.95 (*0-88177-199-6*, DR199) Discipleship Res.

— United Methodist Primer. 3rd ed. LC 85-73470. 112p. (Orig.). 1986. pap. 7.95 (*0-88177-024-8*, DR024) Discipleship Res.

Custer, Cliff. Love Is an Inside Job. 196p. 1993. pap. text. write for info. (*0-9637419-1-8*) Cyber Pub.

Custer, Dan. The Miracle of Mind Power. 263p. (C). 1985. reprint ed. pap. 9.95 (*0-930298-20-9*) Westwood Pub Co.

Custer, Elizabeth. Following the Guidon: Into the Indian Wars with General Custer & the Seventh Cavalry. LC 66-23766. (Western Frontier Library: Vol. 33). (Illus.). 342p. 1994. reprint ed. pap. 12.95 (*0-8061-1354-5*) U of Okla Pr.

Custer, Elizabeth B. Boots & Saddles: Or Life in Dakota with General Custer. 1976. 23.95 (*0-8488-0471-6*, J M C & Co) Amereon Ltd.

— Boots & Saddles: Or Life in Dakota with General Custer. LC 61-8999. (Western Frontier Library: No. 17). (Illus.). 276p. 1961. pap. 12.95 (*0-8061-1192-5*) U of Okla Pr.

— Boots & Saddles: Or Life in Dakota with General Custer. 307p. 1969. reprint ed. 27.95 (*0-87928-006-9*) Corner Hse.

— Boots & Saddles: Or Life in Dakota with General Custer. 307p. 1974. reprint ed. pap. 14.95 (*0-87928-125-1*) Corner Hse.

— Boots & Saddles: Or Life in Dakota with General Custer. unabridged ed. LC 96-44045. xi, 307p. 1996. reprint ed. 27.95 (*1-889881-05-8*) Old Bks Pub.

— Following the Guidon. (Illus.). xiii, 344p. (YA). (gr. 10). 1999. pap. 19.95 (*1-58218-116-0*) Digital Scanning.

— Following the Guidon. LC 94-14464. (Illus.). xxxii, 370p. 1994. reprint ed. pap. 12.95 (*0-8032-6362-7*, Bison Books) U of Nebr Pr.

— Tenting on the Plains: Or, General Custer in Kansas & Texas. abr. ed. LC 94-11743. (Illus.). 403p. 1994. pap. write for info. (*0-8061-2668-X*) U of Okla Pr.

Custer, Frederick, ed. Guide to Departments of Anthropology, 1998-1999. 29th ed. 1998. 55.00 (*0-913167-89-4*) Am Anthro Assn.

Custer, George. Buffalo Bill. (Buckaroos Ser.). (Illus.). 32p. (Orig.). (J). (gr. 2 up). 1996. pap. 1.50 (*1-55709-370-9*) Applewood.

— Indian Sign Language. (Buckaroos Ser.). (Illus.). 32p. (J). (gr. 2 up). 1996. pap. 1.50 (*1-55709-366-0*) Applewood.

— Sitting Bull. (Buckaroos Ser.). (Illus.). 32p. (Orig.). (J). (gr. 2 up). 1996. pap. 1.50 (*1-55709-365-2*) Applewood.

Custer, George A. My Life on the Plains. 1995. 9.98 (*0-88394-091-4*) Promntory Pr.

— My Life on the Plains. Quaife, Milo M., ed. & intro. by. LC 67-2618. (Illus.). xlii, 632p. 1966. pap. 15.00 (*0-8032-5042-8*, Bison Books) U of Nebr Pr.

— My Life on the Plains: Or Personal Experiences with Indians. (Western Frontier Library: No. 52). 1977. pap. 12.95 (*0-8061-1357-X*) U of Okla Pr.

— Wild Life on the Plains & Horrors of Indian Warfare. LC 79-90403. (Mass Violence in America Ser.). (Illus.). 1978. reprint ed. 54.95 (*0-405-01300-0*) Ayer.

Custer, Helen. Inside Windows NT. 2nd ed. LC 97-31952. 600p. 1997. pap. text 49.99 incl. cd-rom (*1-57231-677-2*) Microsoft.

Custer, Jay. Prehistoric Cultures of Eastern Pennsylvania. (Illus.). 425p. 1995. 29.95 (*0-89271-062-4*) Pa Hist & Mus.

Custer, Jay F. Delaware Prehistoric Archaeology: An Ecological Approach. (Illus.). 224p. 1984. 35.00 (*0-87413-233-9*) U Delaware Pr.

— Late Woodland Cultures of the Middle Atlantic Region. LC 84-40807. (Illus.). 216p. 1986. 36.50 (*0-87413-285-1*) U Delaware Pr.

— Prehistoric Cultures of the Delmarva Peninsula: An Archaeological Study. LC 86-40619. (Illus.). 448p. 1989. 57.50 (*0-87413-320-3*) U Delaware Pr.

Custer, Jim & Hoose, Bob. Another Helping of Dramastuff. LC 97-173647. 1997. 15.99 (*0-8341-9629-8*, MP-697) Lillenas.

— The Best of the Jeremiah People: Humorous Sketches & Performance Tips by America's Leading Christian Repertory Group. Wray, Rhonda, ed. LC 91-34195. 192p. (Orig.). (YA). (gr. 9 up). 1991. pap. 14.95 (*0-916260-81-X*, B117) Meriwether Pub.

— Dramastuff. 67p. 1993. 15.99 (*0-8341-9721-9*, MP-687) Lillenas.

— Little Book of Theatre Games Vol. 1. 1998. pap. 14.99 (*0-8341-9773-1*) Nazarene.

— The Worship Drama Library: 13 Sketches for Enhancing Worship, Vol. 7. 61p. 1994. 19.99 (*0-8341-9102-4*, MP-707) Lillenas.

Custer, John. The Old Testament: A Byzantine Perspective. 247p. (Orig.). 1995. pap. 10.00 (*1-887158-08-1*) God With Us.

Custer, Joseph A., et al. Kansas Legal Research & Reference Guide. 2nd ed. LC 97-70906. 1997. write for info. (*1-890452-01-7*) KS Bar.

Custer, Lisa, et al. Ssri Anaylsis Variance. LC 92-33531. (Six Sigma Research Institute Ser.). 1993. pap. text 25.95 (*0-201-63402-3*) Addison-Wesley.

Custer, M. James. The Unspeakable Gift. 290p. 1998. pap. 14.95 (*1-890828-14-9*, 14-9, Pub. by Camden Ct) Origin Bk Sales.

Custer, Milo. Custer Genealogies. (Illus.). 148p. 1997. reprint ed. pap. 23.00 (*0-8328-8188-0*); reprint ed. lib. bdg. 33.00 (*0-8328-8187-2*) Higginson Bk Co.

Custer, Robert L. & Milt, Harry. When Luck Runs Out: Help for Compulsive Gamblers & Their Families. LC 84-26055. 247p. reprint ed. pap. 76.60 (*0-8357-3445-5*, 203970500013) Bks Demand.

Custer, Rodney, ed. see Council on Technology Teacher Education Staff.

Custer, Stewart. The Stars Speak: Astronomy in the Bible. (Illus.). 205p. 1977. pap. 9.95 (*0-89084-059-8*, 001255) Bob Jones Univ.

— Tools for Preaching & Teaching the Bible. 2nd ed. LC 97-36578. 1998. pap. 11.95 (*0-89084-764-9*) Bob Jones Univ.

— A Treasury of New Testament Synonyms. 161p. 1975. 11.95 (*0-89084-025-3*, 002345) Bob Jones Univ.

***Custer, Stewart.** Witness to Christ: A Commentary on Acts. LC 00-23507. (Illus.). 496p. 2000. 31.95 (*1-57924-355-X*, 124560) Bob Jones Univ.

Custer, Susan H., et al. SMARTS (Studying, Memorizing, Active Listening, Reviewing, Test-Taking, & Survival SKills) A Study Skills Resource Guide. 2nd ed. (Illus.). 116p. 1995. pap. text, teacher ed. 19.50 (*1-57035-045-0*, 10SMARTS) Sopris.

Custers. Capital Accumulate Womens Labour, Vol. 1. 401p. 1998. pap. text 65.00 (*1-85649-575-2*, Pub. by Zed Books); pap. text 25.00 (*1-85649-576-0*) Zed Books.

Custers, Peter. Women in the Tebhaga Uprising: Rural Poor Women & Revolutionary Leadership 1946-47. 247p. (C). 1987. 18.00 (*0-8364-2174-4*, Pub. by Naya Prokash) S Asia.

Custine, Astolphe M. De, see De Custine, Astolphe M.

Custis, Peter, jt. auth. see Freeman, Thomas.

Custodio, Brenda. The Pocket Guide to Columbus. (Illus.). 120p. (Orig.). 1992. pap. 6.95 (*0-9632245-0-6*) Pocket Guide.

— The Pocket Guide to Columbus: 1992 Update. rev. ed. (Illus.). 1992. pap. 2.95 (*0-9632245-1-4*) Pocket Guide.

— Study Guide for "The Return" by Sonia Levitin. (Ethnic Explorations Ser.). 32p. (YA). 1994. teacher ed., wbk. ed. 11.95 (*1-882628-11-X*) Lotus Hse.

Custodio, E., et al, eds. Groundwater Flow & Quality Modelling. (C). 1988. text 365.50 (*90-277-2655-8*) Kluwer Academic.

Custodio, Isabel, tr. see Caudill-Slosberg, Margaret.

Custom Editorial Productions Staff. Claris Filemaker Pro 3.0 for Macintosh-Windows Quicktorial. (DF - Computer Applications Ser.). (C). 1996. pap. text, mass mkt. 21.95 incl. disk (*0-538-71567-7*) S-W Pub.

Customs Creations Staff. Wedding Treasures. (Illus.). 28p. (Orig.). 1986. pap. 5.95 (*0-933491-15-8*) Hot off Pr.

Custred, Glynn, jt. ed. see Orlove, Benjamin S.

Custudio, Jose. National Palace, Sintra. (Illus.). 128p. 1998. 35.00 (*1-85759-181-X*) Scala Books.

Custy, Mary C., jt. auth. see Dowling, Shelley L.

Custy, Mary C., jt. auth. see Van Wyk, J. J.

Cusulos, Anastasia. Case Study: The Case of Janis. LC 98-34166. (Walkin' in Your Shoes Ser.: Vol. 2). 54p. 1999. pap. text 12.00 (*1-877864-67-6*) Intercult Pr.

— Case Study: The Case of Vanessa. LC 98-11634. (Walkin' in Your Shoes Ser.: Vol. 4). 62p. 1999. pap. text 12.00 (*1-877864-69-2*) Intercult Pr.

— Facilitator's Guide: The Case of Vanessa. LC 98-11634. (Walkin' in Your Shoes Ser.: Vol. 3). 87p. 1999. spiral bd. 40.00 (*1-877864-68-4*) Intercult Pr.

— Facilitator's Manual: The Case of Janis. LC 98-34166. (Walkin' in Your Shoes Ser.: Vol. 1). 83p. 1999. spiral bd. write for info. (*1-877864-66-8*) Intercult Pr.

***Cusumano, Camille.** The Last Cannoli: A Novel: A Sicilian American Family Comes of Age Through the Ancient Power of Storytelling. 240p. 1999. per. 19.00 (*1-881901-20-3*) LEGAS.

Cusumano, J. P., et al, eds. Aerospace Structures: Nonlinear Dynamics & System Response. LC 93-73263. 105p. 1993. pap. 40.00 (*0-7918-1027-5*) ASME.

***Cusumano, Joseph D.** If You Build It: Creating Your Own Spiritual Field of Dreams. LC 99-91066. (Illus.). 96p. 1999. pap. 10.95 (*0-9674605-0-6*) Psychospirit.

Cusumano, Joseph D. Transforming Scrooge: Dickens' Blueprint for a Spiritual Awakening. LC 96-22000. (Illus.). 312p. (Orig.). 1999. pap. 17.95 (*1-56718-198-8*) Llewellyn Pubns.

Cusumano, Michael. Microsoft Secrets. 1997. pap. 14.00 (*0-684-82552-X*) S&S Trade.

Cusumano, Michael & Nobeoka, Ketaro. Thinking Beyond Lean: How Multi-Project Management Is Transforming Product Development at Toyota & Other Companies. LC 98-3545. (Illus.). 272p. 1998. 27.00 (*0-684-84918-6*) S&S Trade.

Cusumano, Michael A. The Japanese Automobile Industry: Technology & Management at Nissan & Toyota. LC 85-14033. (East Asian Monographs: No. 122). 400p. 1985. pap. 15.00 (*0-674-47256-X*) HUP.

— The Japanese Automobile Industry: Technology & Management at Nissan & Toyota. LC 85-14033. (East Asian Monographs: No. 122). 400p. 1995. 25.00 (*0-674-47255-1*) HUP.

— Japan's Software Factories: A Challenge to U. S. Management. (Illus.). 528p. 1991. text 60.00 (*0-19-506216-7*) OUP.

Cusumano, Michael A. & Selby, Richard W. Microsoft Secrets: How the World's Most Powerful Software Company Creates Technology, Shapes Markets, & Manages People. (Illus.). 416p. 1995. 29.50 (*0-02-874048-3*) Free Pr.

— Microsoft Secrets: How the World's Most Powerful Software Company Creates Technology, Shapes Markets, & Manages People. 544p. 1998. pap. 16.00 (*0-684-85531-3*, Touchstone) S&S Trade Pap.

***Cusumano, Michael A. & Yoffie, David B.** Competing on Internet Time: Lessons from Netscape & Its Battle with Microsoft. 288p. 1998. 26.00 (*0-684-85319-1*) Free Pr.

— Competing on Internet Time: Lessons from Netscape & Its Battle with Microsoft. 384p. 2000. per. 15.00 (*0-684-86345-6*) S&S Trade Pap.

Cusumano, S., et al. Contracts. (Butterworths Tutorial Ser.). 256p. 1996. pap. write for info. (*0-409-30399-2*, MICHIE) LEXIS Pub.

Cutaiar, M. Beth, jt. auth. see Hoekstra, Elizabeth M.

Cutburth, Ronald. Intuitive Science for Organizations. 60p. (Orig.). 1997. pap., spiral bd. 9.00 (*1-878291-18-1*) Love From Sea.

— Operations Analysis of Engineering Sciences: The Case of Lawrence Livermore National Laboratory. (Illus.). 300p. 1998. spiral bd. 76.00 (*1-878291-27-0*) Love From Sea.

— Science Research Programs: Showing Intractable Decision Conflict. (Illus.). 65p. 1997. spiral bd. 9.00 (*1-878291-35-1*) Love From Sea.

Cutburth, Ronald W. Complex Science Research Organizations. 115p. 1998. ring bd. 4.50 (*1-878291-38-6*) Love From Sea.

Cutburth, Ronald W. Concept Fusion. (Illus.). 100p. (C). 1997. pap. 48.00 (*1-878291-36-X*) Love From Sea.

Cutburth, Ronald W. Kantian Relativity for Research Measure. 102p. 1997. spiral bd. 15.00 (*1-878291-32-7*) Love From Sea.

— Love from the Sea. Naumann, Cynthia E., ed. Witt, Hannelore, tr. (GER., Illus.). 27p. (J). (gr. 5-8). 1989. pap. write for info. (*1-878291-03-3*) Love From Sea.

— Love from the Sea. Naumann, Cynthia E., ed. Witt, Hannelore, tr. (FRE., Illus.). 27p. (J). (gr. 5-8). 1989. pap. write for info. (*1-878291-07-6*) Love From Sea.

— Love from the Sea. Naumann, Cynthia E., ed. Lander, Kerstin, tr. (SWE., Illus.). 27p. (J). (gr. 5-8). 1989. pap. write for info. (*1-878291-06-8*) Love From Sea.

— Love from the Sea. Naumann, Cynthia E., ed. (Illus.). 27p. (J). (gr. 4-7). 1990. pap. 3.50 (*1-878291-01-7*) Love From Sea.

— Love from the Sea. Naumann, Cynthia E., ed. Tostado, Rocio G., tr. (SPA., Illus.). 27p. (J). (gr. 5-8). 1990. pap. write for info. (*1-878291-09-2*) Love From Sea.

— Love from the Sea. Naumann, Cynthia E., ed. West, Bobbie, tr. (CHI., Illus.). 27p. (J). (gr. 5-8). 1990. pap. write for info. (*1-878291-11-4*) Love From Sea.

— Social Structure Theory & Elements of Knowledge. unabridged ed. 220p. 1996. spiral bd. 26.00 (*1-878291-24-6*) Love From Sea.

— System Structure Theory. unabridged ed. 105p. 1996. spiral bd. 12.00 (*1-878291-30-0*) Love From Sea.

— Systems Analysis: How to Establish Quality of a New Product from Inception to Design Planning. Rodolff, Rebecca, ed. (Illus.). 100p. 1994. ring bd. 12.00 (*1-878291-25-4*) Love From Sea.

Cutcher-Gershenfeld, Joel, et al. Knowledge Driven Work: The Cross-Cultural Diffusion of Japanese & U. S. Work Practices. LC 98-20116. (Japan Business & Economics Ser.). (Illus.). 208p. 1998. 35.00 (*0-19-511454-X*) OUP.

Cutcher-Gershenfeld, Joel E., et al. Pathways to Change: Strategic Choices in Labor Negotiations. LC 95-39190. 265p. (C). 1995. 37.00 (*0-88099-156-9*); pap. 19.00 (*0-88099-155-0*) W E Upjohn.

Cutcher, J., ed. see Grotstein, J. S., et al.

Cutchin, Diane G., jt. auth. see Bromley, David G.

Cutchin, Kay L., et al. Landscapes & Language: English for American Academic Disourse. 256p. (C). 1998. pap. text 19.95 (*0-521-65766-0*) Cambridge U Pr.

An Asterisk (*) at the beginning of an entry indicates that the title is appearing for the first time.

— Landscapes & Language: English for American Academic Disourse: Instructor's Manual. 256p. (C). 1998. pap., teacher ed. 6.00 (*0-521-65765-2*) Cambridge U Pr.

***Cutchins, Judy.** Ice Age Giants of the South Vol. 1: Southern Fossil Discoveries. LC 99-87670. Vol. 1. (Illus.). 48p. (J). (gr. 3-7). 2000. 14.95 (*1-56164-195-2*) Pineapple Pr.

Cutchins, Margaret. Ladders We Climb to Who We Are. 116p. 1996. pap. 9.00 (*0-9655119-0-1*) Holly Creek Pr.

***Cutcliffe, Stephen H.** Ideas, Machines, & Values: An Introductory Overview of Science, Technology, & Society Studies. LC 99-57149. 224p. 2000. pap. text 22.95 (*0-7425-0067-5*) Rowman.

— Ideas, Machines, & Values: An Introductory Overview of Science, Technology, & Society Studies. LC 99-57149. 224p. 2000. 62.00 (*0-7425-0066-7*) Rowman.

Cutcliffe, Stephen H., et al, eds. New Worlds, New Technologies, New Issues. LC 91-58102. (Research in Technology Studies: Vol. 6). 240p. 1992. 36.50 (*0-934223-24-6*) Lehigh Univ Pr.

Cutcliffe, Stephen H. & Reynolds, Terry S. Technology & American History. LC 97-5925. 448p. 1997. pap. text 18.95 (*0-226-71028-9*); lib. bdg. 37.50 (*0-226-71027-0*) U Ch Pr.

Cutcliffe, Stephen H., jt. auth. see Reynolds, Terry S.

Cuteco. The Magic Apple House. (DA - Computer Education Ser.). (J). (gr. k-8). 1996. pap., suppl. ed. 7.95 (*0-538-66385-5*); pap., suppl. ed. 24.95 (*0-538-66386-3*) S-W Pub.

— The Magic Apple House. (DA - Computer Education Ser.). (J). (gr. k-8). 1996. pap. 7.95 (*0-538-66389-8*); pap., suppl. ed. 7.95 (*0-538-66387-1*); pap., suppl. ed. 24.95 (*0-538-66388-X*); pap., suppl. ed. 24.95 (*0-538-66390-1*) S-W Pub.

***Cuthand, Beth.** The Little Duck. (Illus.). 28p. (J). (gr. k-3). 1999. pap. 7.95 (*0-919441-74-2*, Pub. by Theytus Bks) Orca Bk Pubs.

Cuthbert. And Down Will Come Baby. Date not set. write for info. (*0-671-01515-X*) PB.

Cuthbert, A. R. Architecture, Society & Space - The High-Density Question Re-Examined. (Illus.). 90p. 1985. pap. 22.00 (*0-08-033227-7*, Pub. by PPL) Elsevier.

Cuthbert, Arthur A. The Life & World-Work of Thomas Lake Harris, Written from Direct Personal Knowledge. LC 72-2954. reprint ed. 42.50 (*0-404-10719-2*) AMS Pr.

***Cuthbert, Bob.** Friends & More. LC 98-94884. (Illus.). 36p. (J). (gr. k-3). 1999. 14.95 (*0-9670394-0-1*) Billy B.

Cuthbert Brandt, Gail, jt. auth. see Black, Naomi.

***Cuthbert, Chris.** Rink: Stories from Hockey's Hometowns. 320p. 1998. 32.00 (*0-670-87550-3*, PuffinBks) Peng Put Young Read.

Cuthbert, Clifton. Another Such Victory. LC 74-22777. (Labor Movement in Fiction & Non-Fiction Ser.). reprint ed. 45.00 (*0-404-58417-9*) AMS Pr.

Cuthbert, David. Figures. (Seeing Things Simply Ser.). 64p. 1994. 6.98 (*0-7858-0065-4*) Bk Sales Inc.

— The Pastel Painter's Solution Book. (Illus.). 144p. 1996. 27.99 (*0-89134-705-4*, North Lght Bks) F & W Pubns Inc.

Cuthbert, John A. West Virginia Folk Music. 185p. 1982. 7.95 (*0-937058-12-2*) West Va U Pr.

Cuthbert, John A. & Poesch, Jesse. David Hunter Strother: One of the Best Draughtsman the Country Posseses. LC 99-207041. (Illus.). 168p. 1997. 44.95 (*0-937058-39-4*); pap. 29.95 (*0-937058-43-2*) West Va U Pr.

Cuthbert, John A. & Ward, Barry J. Vernacular Architecture in America: A Selective Bibliography. 145p. 1984. 210.00 (*0-8161-0436-0*, Hall Reference) Macmillan.

Cuthbert, L. G. & Sapanel, J. C. ATM: The Broadband Telecommunications Solution. (Telecommunications Ser.: No. 29). 176p. 1993. boxed set 55.00 (*0-85296-815-9*, TE029) INSPEC Inc.

Cuthbert, Mabel J. & Verhoek, Susan. Spring Flowers. 2nd ed. (Pictured Key Nature Ser.). 256p. (C). 1982. text. write for info. (*0-697-04782-2*, WCB McGr Hill) McGrw-H Hghr Educ.

Cuthbert, Margaret. The Silent Cradle. 486p. 1999. mass mkt. 6.99 (*0-671-01514-1*) S&S Trade.

— The Silent Cradle. abr. ed. LC 97-52677. 352p. 1998. 23.00 (*0-671-01513-3*, PB Hardcover) PB.

Cuthbert, Marjorie, et al, eds. Management in Nursing. (Illus.). 327p. 1992. text 45.00 (*0-7295-0380-1*) Bailliere Tindall.

Cuthbert, Melbourne E. & Lockerbie, Jeannie, eds. Missions in the Local Church. rev. ed. 237p. (Orig.). 1998. pap. text 8.95 (*1-888796-06-5*) ABWE Pubng.

Cuthbert, Mike. European Community Law. 2nd ed. (Questions & Answers Ser.). 265p. 1995. 18.00 (*1-85941-264-5*, Pub. by Cavendish Pubng) Gaunt.

Cuthbert, Robert E. Working in Higher Education. LC 96-25915. 208p. 1996. 118.00 (*0-335-19722-1*); pap. 38.95 (*0-335-19721-3*) OpUniv Pr.

Cuthbert, Ros. Portraits. (Seeing Things Simply Ser.). 64p. 1994. 6.98 (*0-7858-0064-6*) Bk Sales Inc.

Cuthbert, Rosalind. Introduction to Painting Portraits. (Illus.). 1998. 14.99 (*0-7858-0932-5*) Bk Sales Inc.

— Oil Painter's Pocket Palette. (Pocket Palette Ser.). (Illus.). 64p. 1993. 16.99 (*0-89134-543-4*, 30521, North Lght Bks) F & W Pubns Inc.

Cuthbert, Sheila L. The Irish Harp Book. 254p. 1997. 29.95 (*0-8256-9383-7*, MP 10000) Omnibus NY.

Cuthbert, Thomas R., Jr. Broadband Direct-Coupled & Matching RF Network. 224p. 69.95 (*0-9669220-0-X*) TRCPEP.

Cuthbertson, Brian. John Cabot & the Voyage of the Matthew. (Illus.). 72p. 1997. pap. 16.95 (*0-88780-416-0*, Pub. by Formac Publ Co) Formac Dist Ltd.

Cuthbertson, Brian. Johnny Bluenose at the Polls. 344p. 1994. 29.95 (*0-88780-295-8*, Pub. by Formac Publ Co); pap. 19.95 (*0-88780-294-X*, Pub. by Formac Publ Co) Formac Dist Ltd.

— Lunenburg: An Illustrated History. (Illus.). 66p. 1997. pap. 16.95 (*0-88780-358-X*, Pub. by Formac Publ Co) Formac Dist Ltd.

— Wolfville & Grand Pre: Past & Present. (Illus.). 72p. 1997. pap. 16.95 (*0-88780-360-1*, Pub. by Formac Publ Co) Seven Hills Bk.

Cuthbertson, D. & Sinclair, H. Assessment of Factors Affecting Requirements of Farm Livestock. LC 69-14229. (International Encyclopedia of Food & Nutrition Ser.: Vol. 17, Pt. 2). 1969. 367.00 (*0-08-012710-X*, Pub. by Pergamon Repr) Franklin.

— Nutrition of Animals of Agricultural Importance, 2 vols., Set. LC 69-14229. 1969. 629.00 (*0-08-006943-6*, Pub. by Pergamon Repr) Franklin.

— Science of Nutrition of Farm Livestock. LC 69-14229. (International Encyclopedia of Food & Nutrition Ser.: Vol. 17, Pt. 1). 1969. 263.00 (*0-08-012709-6*, Pub. by Pergamon Repr) Franklin.

Cuthbertson, David. A Tragedy of the Reformation: Being the Authentic Narrative of the History & Burning of the "Christianismi Restitution", 1553, with a Succinct Account of the Theological Controversy Between Michael Servetus, Its Author, & the Reformer, John Calvin. LC 83-45608. reprint ed. 37.50 (*0-404-19826-0*) AMS Pr.

Cuthbertson, Duane. Raising Your Child, Not Your Voice. 168p. 1986. pap. 9.99 (*0-89693-342-3*, 6-2342, Victor Bks) Chariot Victor.

Cuthbertson, Ian M., ed. Redefining the CSCE: Challenges & Opportunities in the New Europe. LC 92-18018. 1992. 12.85 (*0-913449-33-4*) Inst EW Stud.

Cuthbertson, Joanne & Schevill, Susanna. Helping Your Child Sleep Through the Night. LC 84-18807. (Illus.). 256p. 1985. pap. 11.95 (*0-385-19250-9*) Doubleday.

Cuthbertson, Joanne, jt. auth. see Cornell, Gary.

Cuthbertson, Joanne, ed. see Cohn, David S.

Cuthbertson, Joanne, ed. see Matthews, Martin S.

Cuthbertson, Joanne, ed. see Rose, Lance.

Cuthbertson, John. Register of Marriages & Baptisms Performed by Rev. John Cuthbertson, Covenantor Minister, 1751-1791. Fields, S. Helen, ed. LC 83-81655. (Illus.). 301p. 1998. reprint ed. pap. 28.50 (*0-8063-1047-2*, Pub. by Clearfield Co) ACCESS Pubs Network.

Cuthbertson, K., jt. auth. see Barr, D. G.

Cuthbertson, Keith. Quantitative Financial Economics: Stocks, Bonds & Foreign Exchange. LC 95-48355. (Financial Economics & Quantitative Analysis Ser.). 492p. 1996. pap. 85.00 (*0-471-95360-1*) Wiley.

Cuthbertson, Keith & Gasparro, David. Inventories, Technological Change, Financial Effects & Risk. LC HB3720.5.C87. (Bank of England, Discussion Papers: Vol. 40). 26p. 1991. reprint ed. pap. 30.00 (*0-608-01650-0*, 206230200002) Bks Demand.

Cuthbertson, Keith & Gripaios, Peter. The Macroeconomy: A Business Perspective. 3rd ed. LC 97-3292. 1997. pap. 17.99 (*1-86152-088-3*) Thomson Learn.

— The Macroeconomy: A Guide for Business. 2nd ed. LC 92-11036. 160p. 1992. pap. 24.95 (*0-415-08673-6*) Thomson Learn.

— The Macroeconomy: A Guide for Business. 2nd ed. LC 92-11036. 160p. (C). (gr. 13). 1992. pap. 60.95 (*0-415-08672-8*, A9715) Thomson Learn.

Cuthbertson, Ken. Nobody Said Not to Go: The Life, Loves & Adventures of Emily Hahn. (Illus.). 400p. 1999. pap. 16.00 (*0-571-19965-8*) Faber & Faber.

— Nobody Said Not to Go: The Remarkable Life of Emily Hahn. LC 97-43687. (Illus.). 386p. 1998. 29.95 (*0-571-19950-X*) Faber & Faber.

Cuthbertson, Lydia. Guide to the Maldives. (Illus.). 128p. (C). 1994. pap. 24.00 (*0-907151-80-9*, Pub. by IMMEL Pubng) St Mut.

Cuthbertson, Michael. Playing in the Digital Funhouse. LC 94-37487. 250p. 1994. pap. 21.95 (*1-55828-368-4*, MIS Pr) IDG Bks.

Cuthbertson, Milbre. Broward County: Gateway to the World. LC 99-25327. (American Enterprise Ser.). (Illus.). 144p. 1999. 39.00 (*1-885352-99-9*) Community Comm.

Cuthbertson, Paul. Electronic Constructor's Guide. (Illus.). 288p. 1995. pap. text 54.95 (*0-7506-2211-3*) Buttrwrth-Heinemann.

— Troubleshooting Digital Electronics & Microprocessor Systems. (Illus.). 208p. 1999. pap. text 28.95 (*0-7506-3098-1*) Buttrwrth-Heinemann.

Cuthbertson, R. Andrew, tr. see De Boulogne, Duchenne.

***Cuthbertson, Tom.** Anybody's Bike Book. rev. ed. (Illus.). 256p. 1998. pap. 11.95 (*0-89815-996-2*) Ten Speed Pr.

Cuthbertson, Yvonne. Women Gardeners: A History. LC 98-25082. (Illus.). 244p. 1999. 36.00 (*0-912869-21-6*) Arden Pr.

Cuthill, J. R., ed. see Metallurgical Society of AIME Staff.

Cuthill, J. R., ed. see Symposium on Surface Analysis Techniques for Metal.

Cuthill, Mary-Catherine, jt. ed. see White, Kris.

Cuthrell, Jack. Letters of the Soul: From the Silence of the Mind. (Illus.). 208p. (Orig.). 1997. per. 11.95 (*0-9650525-6-7*) Spiritual Quest.

Cuticchia, A. J., et al, eds. Chromosome Coordinating Meeting, 1992 (CCM92) Baltimore Conference (1992), Update to the 10th International Workshop on Human Gene Mapping. (Genome Priority Reports: No. 1). (Illus.). vi, 892p. 1993. pap. 431.50 (*3-8055-5763-9*) S Karger.

Cuticchia, A. Jamie, ed. Human Gene Mapping, 1995: A Compendium. 1355p. (Orig.). (C). 1996. pap. text 150.00 (*0-8018-5343-5*) Johns Hopkins.

Cuticchia, A. Jamie, ed. Human Gene Mapping 1994: A Compendium. 1218p. (Orig.). 1995. pap. 95.00 (*0-8018-5180-7*) Johns Hopkins.

Cuticchia, A. Jamie & Pearson, Peter L., eds. Human Gene Mapping 1993: A Compendium. LC 94-648558. (Illus.). 1053p. 1994. reprint ed. pap. 200.00 (*0-608-05944-7*, 206628100008) Bks Demand.

***Cutietta, Robert A. & Lindeman, Carolynn A.** Strategies for Teaching Specialized Ensembles. (Strategies for Teaching Ser.). 99p. (Orig.). 1999. pap. 20.00 (*1-56545-090-6*, 1653) MENC.

Cutietta, Robert A. & Mead, Virginia H. Encountering the Fundamentals of Music: An Activities Approach for Classroom Teachers. LC 88-13856. xii, 233p. (C). 1989. 39.95 (*0-87484-886-5*, 886) Mayfield Pub.

— Encountering the Fundamentals of Music, Instructor's Manual: An Activities Approach for Classroom Teachers. (C). 1989. pap. text, teacher ed. write for info. (*0-87484-912-8*, 912) Mayfield Pub.

Cutilli, Bruce J., jt. auth. see Braun, Robert J.

Cutillo, Antonio G., ed. Application of Magnetic Resonance to the Study of Lung. (Illus.). 624p. 1996. 98.00 (*0-87993-611-8*) Futura Pub.

Cutillo, Brian, tr. see Milarepa.

***Cutillo, Susan B.** Journey Through Mind's Eye. 80p. 1999. per. 6.95 (*1-56002-834-3*) S B Cutillo.

Cutino, Peter & Bledsoe, Dennis, eds. Polo: The Manual for Coach & Player. LC 75-20710. (Illus.). 225p. 1975. pap. 13.45 (*0-685-56491-6*) Swimming.

Cutino, Peter J. Monterey: A View from Garlic Hill. LC 95-44754. (Illus.). 213p. (Orig.). 1995. pap. 14.95 (*0-940168-37-5*) Boxwood.

Cutis, jt. auth. see Robinson.

Cutkomp, Laurence K., jt. auth. see Chu, H. F.

Cutkomp, Laurence K., jt. auth. see Eesa, Naeem M.

Cutland, N. J. Computability: An Introduction to Recursive Function Theory. LC 79-51823. 264p. 1980. pap. text 32.95 (*0-521-29465-7*) Cambridge U Pr.

Cutland, N. J., ed. An Introduction to Non-Standard Analysis & Its Applications. No. 10. 350p. 1988. write for info. (*0-318-62526-1*) Cambridge U Pr.

Cutland, N. J., jt. auth. see Capinski, M.

***Cutler.** Highland High Diaries. 224p. 2000. pap. 19.95 (*1-57500-142-X*, Pub. by TV Bks) HarpC.

Cutler. Im T/a Stud.gen Chem:a Lab-based Apprch. (C). 1999. pap. text 44.50 (*0-03-025036-6*) Harcourt Coll Pubs.

— Psychiatry Review. 1999. pap. text. write for info. (*0-7216-6053-3*, W B Saunders Co) Harcrt Hlth Sci Grp.

— Tree Roots & Buildings. 1989. pap. text. write for info. (*0-582-03410-8*, Pub. by Addison-Wesley) Longman.

Cutler, A. Claire, et al, eds. Private Authority & International Affairs. LC 98-20843. (SUNY Series in Global Politics). 416p. (C). 1999. text 73.50 (*0-7914-4119-9*); pap. text 24.95 (*0-7914-4120-2*) State U NY Pr.

Cutler, A. J., jt. ed. see Hart, A. B.

Cutler, Alan. Studio General Chemistry: A Lab-Based Approach. 1999. pap. text 33.00 (*0-03-020652-9*) Harcourt Coll Pubs.

***Cutler, Andrew Hall.** Amalgam Illness: Diagnosis & Treatment: What You Can Do to Get Better, How Your Doctor Can Help You. (Illus.). vi, 226p. 1999. pap. 35.00 (*0-9676168-0-8*, Andrew Hall Cutler) Minerva Labs.

Cutler, Andrew J., ed. Equity & Trusts. 456p. 1996. pap. 95.00 (*0-7510-0690-4*, Pub. by HLT Pubns) St Mut.

— Equity & Trusts Cases. 376p. 1996. pap. 120.00 (*0-7510-0657-2*, Pub. by HLT Pubns) St Mut.

Cutler, Ann & McShane, Rudolph, trs. The Trachtenberg Speed System of Basic Mathematics. LC 81-13439. 270p. 1982. reprint ed. lib. bdg. 55.00 (*0-313-23200-8*, CUTS, Greenwood Pr) Greenwood.

Cutler, Anne, ed. Slips of the Tongue & Language Production. 293p. 1982. pap. 30.80 (*90-279-3120-8*) Mouton.

Cutler, Anne, jt. ed. see Otake, Takashi.

Cutler, Anthony. The Craft of Ivory: Sources, Techniques, & Uses in the Mediterranean World, A.D. 200-1400. (Byzantine Collection Publications: No. 8). (Illus.). 64p. (Orig.). 1985. pap. 8.00 (*0-88402-147-5*) Dumbarton Oaks.

— The Hand of the Master: Craftsmanship, Ivory, & Society in Byzantium (9th-11th Centuries) LC 93-14332. 320p. 1994. text 75.00 (*0-691-03366-8*, Pub. by Princeton U Pr) Cal Prin Full Svc.

— Imagery & Ideology in Byzantine Art. (Collected Studies: No. CS358). 336p. 1992. text 144.95 (*0-86078-313-8*, Pub. by Variorum) Ashgate Pub Co.

— Late Antique & Byzantine Ivory Carving. LC 98-74057. (Variorum Collected Studies Ser.: No. 617). (Illus.). 350p. 1998. text 161.95 (*0-86078-683-8*, Pub. by Ashgate Pub) Ashgate Pub Co.

— Transfigurations: Studies in the Dynamics of Byzantine Iconography. LC 75-1482. (Illus.). 226p. 1976. 35.00 (*0-271-01194-7*) Pa St U Pr.

Cutler, Anthony & Franklin, Simon, eds. Homo Byzantinus: Papers in Honor of Alexander Kazhdan. LC 92-8248. (Dumbarton Oaks Papers: No. 46). (Illus.). 338p. 1992. 65.00 (*0-88402-198-X*, Dumbarton Rsch Lib) Dumbarton Oaks.

Cutler, Antony, et al. Marx's Capital & Capitalism Today, Vol. 1. 1977. pap. 13.95 (*0-7100-8746-2*, Routledge Thoemms) Routledge.

Cutler, Art. Career Delivery Units: Student Reproducible Worksheets, Vol. 2. 72p. (Orig.). (YA). (gr. 6-12). 1994. pap. 54.99 (*0-934783-77-2*, CDUWK) CFKR Career.

— Career Delivery Units: Teaching Guide, Vol. 1. (Orig.). 1994. pap., teacher ed. 24.00 (*0-934783-76-4*, CDUTG) CFKR Career.

— College Paths. (Illus.). 16p. (YA). (gr. 7 up). 1998. pap. text 3.00 (*0-934783-94-2*, GLGP) CFKR Career.

***Cutler, Art, et al.** Job-o 2000. (Illus.). 16p. (YA). (gr. 7 up). 1999. pap. 4.20 (*1-887481-08-7*) CFKR Career.

Cutler, Art, ed. see CFKR Career Materials Staff.

Cutler, Barbara C. You, Your Child, & Special Education: A Guide to Making the System Work. LC 92-18844. 272p. (C). 1993. pap. text 24.00 (*1-55766-115-4*, 1154) P H Brookes.

Cutler, Brian L. & Penrod, Steven D. Mistaken Identification: The Eyewitness, Psychology & the Law. (Illus.). 300p. (C). 1995. pap. text 19.95 (*0-521-44572-8*) Cambridge U Pr.

Cutler, Bruce. Afterlife, Vol. 63. (Juniper Books Ser.). 79p. 1997. pap. 7.00 (*1-55780-175-4*) Juniper Pr ME.

— Dark Fire. LC 84-73435. 1985. pap. 6.25 (*0-933532-47-4*) BkMk.

— The Doctrine of Selective Depravity. 2nd ed. (Inland Seas Ser.: No. 1). 1988. pap. 8.00 (*1-55780-081-2*) Juniper Pr ME.

— The Massacre at Sand Creek: Narrative Voices. LC 94-31306. (American Indian Literature & Critical Studies Ser.: Vol. 16). xi, 252p. 1997. pap. 11.95 (*0-8061-2990-5*) U of Okla Pr.

— Seeing the Darkness. LC 97-44942. 96p. 1998. pap. 11.95 (*1-886157-16-2*) BkMk.

***Cutler, Bruce.** A West Wind Rises: Massacre at Marais des Cygnes. Averill, Tom, ed. 88p. 1999. reprint ed. pap. 7.50 (*0-939391-26-0*) B Woodley Pr.

Cutler, Bruce, jt. auth. see Jerome, Judson.

Cutler, Carolyn. Strike Commander Playtesters' Guide. (Illus.). 96p. (Orig.). 1993. pap. 14.95 (*0-929373-14-6*) Origin Syst.

Cutler, Charles L. How We Made It to One Hundred: Wisdom from the Super Old. LC 77-87771. 1978. 9.95 (*0-9601502-1-8*) Rockfall Pr.

— O Brave New Words! Native American Loanwords in Current English. LC 94-15764. (Illus.). 304p. 1994. 19.95 (*0-8061-2655-8*) U of Okla Pr.

***Cutler, Charles L.** O Brave New Words! Native American Loanwords in Current English. 304p. 2000. pap. text 13.95 (*0-8061-3246-9*) U of Okla Pr.

Cutler, Chris. File under Popular. 184p. Date not set. 10.00 (*0-936756-34-9*) Autonomedia.

Cutler, Colleen D. & Kaplan, Daniel. Nonlinear Dynamics & Time Series: Building a Bridge Between the Natural & Statistical Sciences. LC 96-44411. (Fields Institute Communications Ser.: No. 11). 252p. 1996. text 79.00 (*0-8218-0521-5*) Am Math.

Cutler, D. F. & Gregory, Mary, eds. The Anatomy of the Dicotyledons: Saxifragales, Vol. IV. 2nd ed. (Illus.). 336p. 1998. text 175.00 (*0-19-854792-7*) OUP.

Cutler, Daniel S. One Hundred Monkeys. LC 90-22446. (Illus.). 40p. (J). 1991. pap. 13.95 (*0-671-73564-0*) Litle Simon.

Cutler, David. Literary Washington: A Complete Guide to the Literary Life in the Nation's Capital. 2nd ed. 356p. (Orig.). 1991. pap. 12.95 (*0-8191-8245-1*) Madison Bks UPA.

Cutler, David F., jt. auth. see Fahn, Abraham.

Cutler, Donald. Dear Parents Please: Your Kids Want to Talk with You about Alcohol & Other Drugs. LC 95-77904. 123p. (Orig.). 1995. pap. 14.95 (*0-9647081-1-6*) Broadhearth.

Cutler, Donald I. Introduction to Computer Programming. 2nd ed. LC 79-160256. x, 303p. 1972. write for info. (*0-13-479634-9*) Prntice Hall Bks.

Cutler, Ebbitt. I Once Knew an Indian Woman. (Illus.). 72p. (J). (gr. 5 up). 1985. pap. 7.95 (*0-88776-068-6*) Tundra Bks.

— If I Were a Cat I Would Sit in a Tree. (Illus.). 28p. (J). (gr. k-4). 1985. 12.95 (*0-88776-177-1*) Tundra Bks.

Cutler, Ebbitt, tr. see Nickl, Peter.

Cutler, Edward. A Manual of Musical Copyright Law for the Use of Music-Publishers & Artists & of the Legal Profession. xx, 132, lxiiip. 1996. reprint ed. 35.00 (*0-8377-2058-3*, Rothman) W S Hein.

Cutler, Edward B. The Sipuncula: Their Systematics, Biology, & Evolution. (Comstock Bk.). (Illus.). 480p. 1994. text 75.00 (*0-8014-2843-2*) Cornell U Pr.

Cutler, Ellen W. Winning the War Against Asthma & Allergies: A Drug Free Alternative Treatment Plan for Asthma Sufferers & Their Families. LC 97-9404. (Instructor Material TV). 450p. 1997. pap. 17.95 (*0-8273-8622-2*) Delmar.

— Winning the War Against Immune Disorders & Allergies. LC 98-23746. 608p. 1998. pap. text 21.95 (*0-7668-0059-8*) Delmar.

Cutler, Ellen W., et al. Winning War against Headaches & Allergies. 256p. pap. 16.95 (*0-7668-0058-X*, Pub. by Delmar) Thomson Learn.

Cutler, Ellie, jt. auth. see O'Reilly & Associates Staff.

***Cutler, Everett.** Why We Ski: Poems for Skiers. 2nd ed. 85p. 2000. pap. 10.95 (*0-9701750-0-0*) E Cutler.

Cutler, Gordon B., Jr., jt. ed. see Grave, Gilman D.

Cutler, H. G., jt. auth. see Chu, C. K.

Cutler, Henry. Cutler. History of the Holliston Branch of the Cutler Family, Pts. 1 & 2. (Illus.). 136p. 1997. reprint ed. pap. 22.00 (*0-8328-8190-2*); reprint ed. lib. bdg. 32.00 (*0-8328-8189-9*) Higginson Bk Co.

Cutler, Horace G., ed. Biologically Active Natural Products: Potential Use in Agriculture. LC 88-7859. (Symposium Ser.: No. 380). (Illus.). 496p. 1988. 94.95 (*0-8412-1556-1*, Pub. by Am Chemical) OUP.

— Biologically Active Natural Products: Potential Use in Agriculture. LC 88-7859. (ACS Symposium Ser.: Vol. 380). 496p. 1988. reprint ed. pap. 153.80 (*0-608-03288-3*, 206380600007) Bks Demand.

C

Cutler, Horace G., et al, eds. Brassinosteriods: Chemistry, Bioactivity, & Applications. LC 91-12345. (ACS Symposium Ser.: No. 474). (Illus.). 358p. 1991. text 89.00 (*0-8412-2126-X*, Pub. by Am Chemical) OUP.

Cutler, Horace G., jt. auth. see Cutler, Stephen J.

***Cutler, Howard C.** The Art of Happiness: A Handbook for Living. LC 99-38401. 1999. write for info. (*1-56895-767-X*, Compass) Wheeler Pub.

Cutler, Hugh C. Corn, Cucurbits & Cotton from Glen Canyon. (Glen Canyon Ser.: No. 30). reprint ed. 26.00 (*0-404-60680-6*) AMS Pr.

***Cutler, Irving.** Jewish Chicago: A Pictorial History. (Images of America Ser.). (Illus.). 128p. 2000. pap. 18.99 (*0-7385-0130-1*) Arcadia Publng.

Cutler, Irving. The Jews of Chicago: From Shtetl to Suburb. LC 94-47591. (Ethnic History of Chicago Ser.). (Illus.). 368p. 1995. 29.95 (*0-252-02185-1*) U of Ill Pr.

Cutler, James E. Lynch-Law: An Investigation into the History of Lynching in the United States. LC 69-14920. (Criminology, Law Enforcement, & Social Problems Ser.: No. 70). (Illus.). 1969. reprint ed. 18.00 (*0-87585-070-7*) Patterson Smith.

Cutler, Jane. The Cello of Mr. O. LC 98-42692. (Illus.). 32p. (J). (gr. 1-4). 1999. 15.99 (*0-525-46119-1*, Dutton Child) Peng Put Young Read.

— Darcy & Gran Don't Like Babies. LC 91-42214. (Illus.). 32p. (J). (ps-2). 1993. 14.95 (*0-590-44587-1*, Scholastic Hardcover) Scholastic Inc.

— Darcy & Gran Don't Like Babies. 32p. (J). (ps-2). 1995. pap. 4.95 (*0-590-44588-X*, Cartwheel); pap. 4.95 (*0-590-72126-7*, Cartwheel) Scholastic Inc.

— Darcy & Gran Don't Like Babies. 1993. 10.15 (*0-606-07414-7*, Pub. by Turtleback) Demco.

— Family Dinner. (Sunburst Ser.). 112p. (J). (gr. 3-6). 1995. pap. 4.95 (*0-374-42258-3*) FS&G.

— Family Dinner. (ANTA Series of Distinguished Plays). (J). 1995. 10.30 (*0-606-07496-1*) Turtleback.

***Cutler, Jane.** 'Gator Aid. LC 98-49033. (Illus.). 144p. (J). (gr. 2-5). 1999. 16.00 (*0-374-32502-2*) FS&G.

Cutler, Jane. Mr. Carey's Garden. LC 93-13720. (Illus.). 32p. (J). (ps-3). 1996. 14.95 (*0-395-68191-X*) HM.

— My Wartime Summers. LC 94-9845. 176p. (J). (gr. 5 up). 1994. 15.00 (*0-374-35111-2*) FS&G.

— My Wartime Summers. LC 94-9845. 160p. (YA). (gr. 5-9). 1997. pap. 4.95 (*0-374-45463-9*, Sunburst Bks) FS&G.

— My Wartime Summers. LC 94-9845. 1997. 10.05 (*0-606-11658-3*, Pub. by Turtleback) Demco.

— No Dogs Allowed. 112p. (J). (gr. 4-7). 1992. 14.00 (*0-374-35526-6*) FS&G.

— No Dogs Allowed. (Illus.). 112p. (J). (gr. 2-5). 1994. pap. 4.95 (*0-374-45508-2*, Sunburst Bks) FS&G.

— No Dogs Allowed. LC 92-7206. (J). 1994. 9.05 (*0-606-09687-6*, Pub. by Turtleback) Demco.

— Rats! (Illus.). 128p. (J). (gr. 2-5). 1998. pap. text 4.95 (*0-374-46203-8*, Sunburst Bks) FS&G.

— Rats! 1998. 10.05 (*0-606-13727-0*, Pub. by Turtleback) Demco.

— Rats! abr. ed. LC 95-22953. (Illus.). 114p. (J). (gr. 4-7). 1996. 14.00 (*0-374-36181-9*) FS&G.

— The Song of the Molimo. LC 98-3285. (Illus.). 192p. (YA). (gr. 4-7). 1998. 16.00 (*0-374-37141-5*) FS&G.

— Spaceman. LC 96-46224. 176p. (J). (gr. 4-8). 1997. 14.99 (*0-525-45636-8*) NAL.

— Spaceman. LC 96-46224. (Illus.). 138p. (J). (gr. 3-7). 1999. pap. 4.99 (*0-14-038150-3*) Viking Penguin.

Cutler, Jay & Field, David. The Ultimate Tiny Book. 1991. ring bd. 89.95 (*0-9629742-0-X*) Separacolor.

***Cutler, Jeff.** Greater Boston: An Atlas of Eastern Massachusetts' Greatest Off-Road Bicycle Rides. (Mountain Bike America Guidebks.). (Illus.). 192p. 2000. pap. 17.95 (*0-7627-0701-1*) Globe Pequot.

Cutler, Jeff. Mountain Bike Southern New England: An Atlas of Southern New Englands' Greatest Off-Road Bicycle Rides. (Mountain Bike America Ser.). 256p. 1998. pap. 15.95 (*1-882997-15-8*) Beachway Pr.

Cutler, Jervis. Topographical Description of the State of Ohio, Indiana Territory, & Louisiana. LC 78-146388. (First American Frontier Ser.). (Illus.). 1977. reprint ed. 27.95 (*0-405-02839-3*) Ayer.

Cutler, Jill, ed. see Urban, Erin.

Cutler, Jody. Glen Hansen - The Venice Series: Glen Hansen - Paintings of Venice. Dicarco, Lawrence, ed. (Illus.). 33p. 1999. pap. 10.00 (*1-891848-00-3*) Fischbach Gal.

Cutler, John. Understanding Aircraft Structures. 2nd ed. (Illus.). 192p. 1992. pap. 39.95 (*0-632-03241-3*) Blackwell Sci.

— Understanding Aircraft Structures. 3rd ed. LC 98-40842. 1999. pap. 42.95 (*0-632-05001-2*) Blackwell Corp.

Cutler, John L. & Thompson, Lawrence S., eds. American Notes & Queries Supplement, Vol. 1. LC 77-93778. (Studies in English & American Literature). xx, 339p. 1980. 18.50 (*0-87875-139-4*) Whitston Pub.

Cutler, Jonathan, jt. ed. see Aronowitz, Stanley.

Cutler, Judith. Dying Fall. large type ed. (Magna Large Print Ser.). 350p. 1998. 29.99 (*0-7505-1213-X*, Pub. by Mgna Lrg Print) Ulverscroft.

— Dying to Write. large type ed. (Magna Large Print Ser.). 432p. 1998. 29.99 (*0-7505-1214-8*, Pub. by Mgna Lrg Print) Ulverscroft.

Cutler, Judy G., jt. auth. see Cutler, Laurence S.

Cutler, Julia P. Life & Times of Ephraim Cutler Prepared from His Journals & Correspondence by His Daughter Julia Perkins Cutler with Biographical Sketches of Jervis Cutler & William Parker Cutler. LC 71-146389. (First American Frontier Ser.). (Illus.). 1971. reprint ed. 35.95 (*0-405-02840-7*) Ayer.

Cutler, Julia P., jt. auth. see Cutler, William P.

Cutler, Karan, ed. Tantalizing Tomatoes: Smart Tips & Tasty Picks for Gardeners Everywhere. (Illus.). 1997. pap. 9.95 (*1-889538-00-0*) Bklyn Botanic.

Cutler, Karan D., ed. Flowering Vines: Beautiful Climbers. (Twenty-First Century Gardening Ser.). (Illus.). 112p. 1999. pap. 9.95 (*1-889538-10-8*) Bklyn Botanic.

Cutler, Karan D. & Brooklyn Botanic Garden Botanists, eds. Salad Gardens: Gourmet Greens & Beyond. LC 96-124519. (21st-Century Gardening Ser.). (Illus.). 120p. 1995. pap. 9.95 (*0-945352-89-1*) Bklyn Botanic.

Cutler, Karan D. & Marinelli, Janet, eds. Starting from Seed: The Natural Gardener's Guide to Propagating Plants. (Twenty-First Century Gardening Ser.). (Illus.). 112p. 1998. pap. 9.95 (*1-889538-09-4*) Bklyn Botanic.

Cutler, Karan Davis. Burpee Complete Vegetable & Herb Gardener: A Guide to Growing Your Garden Organically. LC 97-14564. (Illus.). 438p. 1997. 29.95 (*0-02-862005-4*) Macmillan.

Cutler, Lance. Making Wine at Home the Professional Way. 50p. (Orig.). 1996. pap. 11.95 (*0-9637438-3-X*) Wine Patrol Pr.

— The Tequila Lover's Guide to Mexico. LC 97-91335. 256p. 1998. 16.95 (*0-9637438-5-6*) Wine Patrol Pr.

***Cutler, Lance.** The Tequila Lover's Guide to Mexico & Mezcal: Everything There Is to Know about Tequila & Mezcal Including How to Get There. 2nd ed. Orig. Title: The Tequila Lover's Guide to Mexico. (Illus.). 260p. 2000. pap. 17.95 (*0-9637438-1-3*) Wine Patrol Pr.

Cutler, Laurence & Skoloff, Gary N. New Jersey Family Law Practice, 3 vols., Set. 6th ed. (Illus.). 1302p. 1990. ring bd. 175.00 (*0-685-65973-9*) NJ Inst CLE.

Cutler, Laurence S. & Cutler, Judy G. Maxfield Parrish: A Retrospective. LC 95-71810. 176p. 1996. 45.00 (*0-87654-599-1*) Pomegranate Calif.

— Parrish & Poetry: A Gift of Words & Art. LC 95-30368. (Illus.). 96p. 1995. 19.95 (*0-87654-486-3*) Pomegranate Calif.

Cutler, Laurence S., jt. ed. see Dietz, Albert G.

Cutler, Lawrence J., jt. auth. see Skoloff, Gary N.

Cutler, Lloyd N., et al, eds. Regulating Campaign Finance. LC 85-72102. (Annals of the American Academy of Political & Social Science Ser.: Vol. 486). 200p. (Orig.). 1986. text 26.00 (*0-8039-2542-5*); pap. text 17.00 (*0-8039-2543-3*) Sage.

Cutler, Lloyd N. & Sundquist, James L. Divided Government. (C). 1999. text 39.95 (*0-8133-0950-6*); pap. text 12.95 (*0-8133-0951-4*) Westview.

Cutler, Lynn W. Baggage to London. (Annikins Ser.: Vol. 13). (Illus.). 24p. (Orig.). (J). (ps-1). 1994. pap. 0.99 (*1-55037-345-5*, Pub. by Annick) Firefly Bks Ltd.

Cutler, Marika Moore, jt. auth. see Timberlake, Elizabeth M.

Cutler, Marjory & Cutler, Maxwell. S. N. I. C. K. E. R. Same Names in Cities, Kingdoms, Empires & Regions. LC 94-96433. 296p. 1994. pap. 12.95 (*0-9643131-0-3*) M Lee Ent.

Cutler, Mark, jt. auth. see Freud, Sally.

Cutler, Maxine. Voltaire, the Enlightenment & the Comic Mode: Essays in Honor of Jean Sareil. 284p. (C). 1990. text 29.95 (*0-8204-1289-9*) P Lang Pubng.

Cutler, Maxwell & Robinson-Cutler, Marjory L. W. H. I. M. P. U. R. Map: Where Is My Public Radio. 1986. write for info. (*0-9643131-1-1*) Snicker Pub.

Cutler, Maxwell, jt. auth. see Cutler, Marjory.

Cutler, Michael, ed. International Cooperation in Space Operations & Exploration, 9th Goddard Memorial Symposium, Mar. 11, 1971, Washington, D.C. 9th Goddard Memorial Symposium, Washington, D. C., Mar. 11, 1971. (Science & Technology Ser.: Vol. 27). 194p. 1971. 20.00 (*0-87703-058-8*, Am Astronaut Soc) Univelt Inc.

Cutler, N. R. & Narang, P. K. Drug Studies in the Elderly: Methodological Concerns. LC 86-18738. (Illus.). 464p. (C). 1986. text 120.00 (*0-306-42311-1*, Kluwer Plenum) Kluwer Academic.

Cutler, N. S. A Cutler Memorial & Genealogical History. (Illus.). 665p. 1989. reprint ed. pap. 99.50 (*0-8328-0451-7*); reprint ed. lib. bdg. 109.50 (*0-8328-0450-9*) Higginson Bk Co.

Cutler, Neal, ed. Aging & Public Policy. (Orig.). 1984. pap. 15.00 (*0-918592-76-3*) Pol Studies.

Cutler, Neal R. Accelerating CNS Drug Development. LC 97-50438. 194p. 1998. 99.95 (*0-471-98128-1*) Wiley.

Cutler, Neal R., et al, eds. Alzheimer's Disease: Clinical & Treatment Perspectives. LC 94-22396. 198p. 1995. 225.95 (*0-471-95039-4*) Wiley.

Cutler, Neal R. & Sramek, John J. Understanding Alzheimer's Disease. LC 96-20284. (Understanding Health & Sickness Ser.). 1996. pap. 12.00 (*0-87805-911-3*); text 28.00 (*0-87805-910-5*) U Pr of Miss.

Cutler, Neal R. & Sramek, John J., eds. Pharmacodynamics: Perspectives in Clinical Pharmacology. LC 94-6103. 508p. 1994. 334.95 (*0-471-95052-1*) Wiley.

Cutler, Neal R., et al. Alzheimer's Disease: Optimizing Drug Development Strategies. LC 94-10062. 178p. 1994. 145.00 (*0-471-95145-5*) Wiley.

— Anxiolytic Compounds: Perspectives in Drug Development. LC 95-39622. 176p. 1996. 99.95 (*0-471-95713-5*) Wiley.

— Optimizing the Clinical Devlopment of Antipsychotic Drugs. LC 97-3041. 216p. 1998. 79.95 (*0-471-97011-5*) Wiley.

Cutler, Norman. Songs of Experience: The Poetics of Tamil Devotion. LC 86-45051. (Religion in Asia & Africa Ser.). (Illus.). 224p. 1987. 31.50 (*0-253-35334-3*) Ind U Pr.

Cutler, Paul. Problem Solving in Clinical Medicine: From Data to Diagnosis. 2nd ed. (Illus.). 550p. 1997. pap. text 35.00 (*0-683-02252-0*) Lppncott W & W.

— Problem Solving in Clinical Medicine: From Data to Diagnosis. 3rd ed. 531p. 1997. 49.95 (*0-683-30377-5*); pap. 35.00 (*0-683-30167-5*) Lppncott W & W.

Cutler, Phoebe. The Public Landscape of the New Deal. LC 85-2437. 200p. 1986. 35.00 (*0-300-03256-0*) Yale U Pr.

Cutler, R. G., ed. Cellular Ageing Pt. 1: Concepts & Mechanisms: General Concepts. Mechanisms I: Fidelity of Information Flow, 2 pts. (Interdisciplinary Topics in Gerontology Ser.: Vol. 9). (Illus.). 150p. 1976. pap. 99.25 (*3-8055-2283-5*) S Karger.

— Cellular Ageing Pt. 2: Concepts & Mechanisms: Mechanisms II: Translation, Transcription & Structural Properties, 2 pts. (Interdisciplinary Topics in Gerontology Ser.: Vol. 10). (Illus.). 150p. 1976. pap. 65.25 (*3-8055-2284-3*) S Karger.

Cutler, R. G., et al, eds. Oxidative Stress & Aging. LC 95-105254. (Molecular & Cell Biology Updates Ser.). 1995. write for info. (*3-7643-5039-3*, Pub. by Birkhauser) Princeton Arch.

Cutler, R. G., et al. Oxidative Stress & Aging. Packer, Lester, ed. LC 95-105254. (Molecular & Cell Biology Updates Ser.: Vol. 12). 396p. 1995. 149.00 (*0-8176-5039-3*, Pub. by Birkhauser) Princeton Arch.

Cutler, Robert M. Harmonizing EEC-CMEA Relations: Never the Twain Shall Meet? (CISA Working Papers: No. 57). 31p. (Orig.). 1987. pap. 15.00 (*0-86682-074-4*) Ctr Intl Relations.

Cutler, Robert M., ed. from RUS. The Basic Bakunin: Writings, 1869-1871. LC 92-5386. (Great Books in Philosophy). 248p. (Orig.). (C). 1992. pap. 11.95 (*0-87975-745-0*) Prometheus Bks.

***Cutler, Robert W. P.** The Tin Box. 325p. 1999. pap. write for info. (*0-7392-0473-4*, 3804) Morris Pubng.

Cutler, Sandra M. Dwarf & Unusual Conifers Coming of Age: A Guide to Mature Garden Conifers. LC 96-97053. (Illus.). 176p. (Orig.). 1997. pap. 40.00 (*0-9654717-0-5*) Barton-Bradley.

Cutler, Stephen J. & Cutler, Horace G. Biologically Active Natural Products: Agrochemicals. LC 99-20202. 320p. 1999. boxed set 99.95 (*0-8493-1885-8*) CRC Pr.

Cutler, Stephen J., jt. auth. see Culter, Horace.

Cutler, Susan K., jt. auth. see Stein, Franklin.

Cutler, Thomas J. The Battle of Leyte Gulf. 1996. mass mkt. 6.50 (*0-671-53670-2*) PB.

***Cutler, Thomas J.** The Bluejackets' Manual. 22nd ed. (Illus.). 800p. 1998. 29.95 (*1-55750-065-7*) Naval Inst Pr.

Cutler, Thomas J. Brown Water, Black Berets. 416p. 1989. per. 6.99 (*0-671-67280-0*) PB.

***Cutler, Thomas J.** Brown Water, Black Berets: Coastal & Riverine Warfare in Vietnam. (Bluejacket Bks.). (Illus.). 448p. 2000. pap. 18.95 (*1-55750-196-3*) Naval Inst Pr.

Cutler, Thomas R. Gays & Television. 192p. (Orig.). 1989. pap. 8.95 (*0-318-65966-2*) TRC Pub.

Cutler, Thomas R., jt. auth. see International Gay & Lesbian Franchise Association.

Cutler, Timothy G. An Old Morristown Postcard Album. (Illus.). 32p. 1995. pap. 7.99 (*1-58057-057-7*, PA001) Digital Antiq.

Cutler, Timothy G., ed. see Parker, Richard W.

Cutler, Tony & Waine, Barbara. Managing the Welfare State: Text & Sourcebook. LC 98-215871. 1998. pap. text 19.50 (*1-85973-932-6*) NYU Pr.

— Managing the Welfare State: The Politics of Public Sector Management. LC 93-23931. 192p. 1994. 47.00 (*0-85496-843-1*) Berg Pubs.

Cutler, Tony, et al. Keynes, Beveridge & Beyond LC 86-11851. xi, 162p. 1986. write for info. (*0-7102-0992-4*) R&K.

Cutler, W. G. & Davis, R. C., eds. Detergency: Theory & Test Methods, Pt. 3. LC 79-163921. (Surfactant Science Ser.: Vol. 5). 343p. 1981. reprint ed. pap. 106.40 (*0-608-03578-5*, 206440100009) Bks Demand.

— Detergency Pt. 2: Theory & Test Methods. fac. ed. LC 79-163921. (Surfactant Science Ser.: No. 5). (Illus.). 292p. 1972. pap. 90.60 (*0-7837-7306-4*, 204334000002) Bks Demand.

Cutler, W. Gale. Detergency Pt. 4: Theory & Test Methods. Kissa, Erik, ed. (Surfactant Science Ser.: Vol. 20). (Illus.). 568p. 1986. text 195.00 (*0-8247-7503-1*) Dekker.

Cutler, W. Gale & Davis, R. C., eds. Detergency: Theory & Test Methods, Part 1. LC 79-163921. (Surfactant Science Ser.: No. 5). (Illus.). 463p. 1972. reprint ed. pap. 143.60 (*0-7837-3382-8*, 204334000001) Bks Demand.

Cutler, Wade E. Triple Your Reading Speed: The Acceleread Method. 3rd ed. 224p. 1993. per. 12.95 (*0-671-84644-2*, Arc) IDG Bks.

Cutler, Wayne, et al, eds. Correspondence of James K. Polk Vol. 8: September-December 1844. LC 75-84005. 624p. (C). 1993. text 45.00 (*0-87049-777-4*) U of Tenn Pr.

Cutler, Wayne & Hall, Robert G., eds. Correspondence of James K. Polk: January-June 1845, Vol. 9. 648p. 1996. 55.00 (*0-87049-947-5*) U of Tenn Pr.

Cutler, William P. Life, Journals & Correspondence of Rev. Manasseh Cutler, 2 vols., Set. 1993. reprint ed. lib. bdg. 150.00 (*0-7812-5353-5*) Rprt Serv.

Cutler, William P. & Cutler, Julia P. The Life, Journals & Correspondence of Rev. Manasseh Cutler, L L.D., 2 vols., Set. LC 86-23894. (Illus.). 1032p. 1987. text 60.00 (*0-8214-0859-3*) Ohio U Pr.

***Cutler, William W., III.** Parents & Schools: The 150-Year Struggle for Control in American Education. LC 99-88447. 296p. 2000. 25.00 (*0-226-13216-1*) U Ch Pr.

Cutler, William W., 3rd & Gillette, Howard, Jr., eds. The Divided Metropolis: Social & Spatial Dimensions of Philadelphia, 1800-1975, 85. LC 79-7729. (Contributions in American History Ser.: No. 85). (Illus.). 308p. 1980. 65.00 (*0-313-21351-8*, GDM/) Greenwood.

Cutler, Winnifred B. Hysterectomy Before & After: A Comprehensive Guide to Preventing, Preparing for, & Maximizing Health after Hysterectomy. LC 87-46132. 464p. 1990. reprint ed. 16.00 (*0-06-091629-X*, Perennial) HarperTrade.

— Love Cycles: The Science of Intimacy. (Illus.). 330p. 1996. reprint ed. write for info. (*0-9651753-0-8*) Athena Inst.

— Searching for Courtship: The Smart Woman's Guide to Finding a Good Husband. (Illus.). 352p. 1996. write for info. (*0-9651753-1-6*) Athena Inst.

— Searching for Courtship: The Smart Woman's Guide to Finding a Good Husband. (Illus.). 352p. 1998. reprint ed. pap. 16.50 (*0-9651753-2-4*) Athena Inst.

Cutler, Winnifred B. & Garcia, Delso-Ramon. Menopause: A Medical Guide for Women. 2nd rev. ed. 432p. 1993. pap. 14.95 (*0-393-30995-9*) Norton.

Cutliff, Lewis D., jt. auth. see Wagoner, John J.

***Cutliffe, Stephen H. & Mitcham, Carl, eds.** Visions of STS: Counterpoints in Science, Technology, & Society Studies. LC 00-38772. (C). 2001. pap. text 17.95 (*0-7914-4846-0*) State U NY Pr.

— Visions of STS: Counterpoints in Science, Technology, & Society Studies. LC 00-38772. (C). 2001. text 54.50 (*0-7914-4845-2*) State U NY Pr.

Cutlip, Eldon R. Cooking Wild from Idaho: A Collection of Wild Game & Sausage Recipes. 236p. spiral bd. 14.95 (*0-9644922-0-2*) EKC-Eldon.

— Sausage & Jerky Handbook: Everything You Need to Know for Making Smoked Sausage & Jerky at Home. (Illus.). 114p. pap. 9.95 (*0-9644922-1-0*) EKC-Eldon.

***Cutlip, Glen.** Transonic Consciousness. LC 99-96813. 2000. pap. 8.95 (*0-533-13356-4*) Vantage.

***Cutlip, Glen C.** Cosmic Reconciliation. LC 99-91773. 2000. 25.00 (*0-7388-1258-7*); pap. 18.00 (*0-7388-1259-5*) Xlibris Corp.

— How to Overcome Death: The Final Victory. LC 99-91668. 2000. 25.00 (*0-7388-1182-3*); pap. 18.00 (*0-7388-1183-1*) Xlibris Corp.

— The Unveiling of God: The Revelation of the God Self Within. 50p. 1999. pap. 9.95 (*0-7414-0325-0*) Buy Books.

Cutlip, Harley V. Cutlip's Quotem Pole. 80p. 1992. pap. write for info. (*0-9632843-0-4*) H V Cutlip.

Cutlip, Kimbra L. Sailor's Night Before Christmas. LC 99-30579. (Illus.). 32p. (J). (gr. k-3). 1999. 14.95 (*1-56554-395-5*) Pelican.

Cutlip, Michael B., jt. auth. see Shacham, Mordechai.

Cutlip, Ralph V. Mountain Massacres & Other Stories of Appalachia. (Illus.). 167p. (Orig.). (J). (gr. 8 up). 1986. pap. 6.50 (*0-317-47675-0*) B Cutlip.

Cutlip, Scott M. Effective Public Relations. 8th ed. LC 99-21943. (Illus.). 588p. 1999. 93.33 (*0-13-541211-0*) P-H.

— Fund Raising in the United States. 575p. 1989. 49.95 (*0-88738-317-3*) Transaction Pubs.

— A Public Relations Bibliography. 2nd ed. LC 65-16360. 319p. 1965. pap. 98.90 (*0-608-01903-8*, 206255500003) Bks Demand.

— Public Relations History: From the 17th to the 20th Century. (LEA's Communication Ser.). 320p. 1995. pap. 32.50 (*0-8058-1780-8*); text 59.95 (*0-8058-1779-4*) L Erlbaum Assocs.

— The Unseen Power: Public Relations. A History. (Communication Ser.). 808p. 1994. pap. 45.00 (*0-8058-1465-5*); text 135.00 (*0-8058-1464-7*) L Erlbaum Assocs.

Cutlip, William W. Precious Memories: The Life of a Minister. Erickson, Beverly H., ed. LC 95-60695. (Illus.). 300p. 1996. write for info. (*1-885527-03-9*) Feather Fables.

***Cutman, Marie E.** As He Leads Is Joy: Dora M. Taylor, Missionary Nurse in Honduras. (Illus.). 1999. pap. write for info. (*0-9672285-4-9*) MecPublishing.

— A Little Bit of Love: Ada & Ida Stoltzfus in India, Three Years of Relief Work. (Illus.). xiii, 199p. 1994. 14.95 (*0-9672285-0-6*); pap. 9.95 (*0-9672285-1-4*) MecPublishing.

— We Sat Where They Sat: Ada & Ida Stoltzfus, Thirty-Seven & One-Half Years in the Ancient City of Hebron. (Illus.). xv, 312p. 1996. 19.99 (*0-9672285-2-2*); pap. 14.99 (*0-9672285-3-0*) MecPublishing.

Cutmore, Max. Collecting & Repairing Watches. 1999. 24.95 (*0-7153-0819-X*) D & C Pub.

Cutmore, William H. Shaw's Ready Reckoner for the Calculation of (Metric) Areas. (C). 1982. 30.00 (*0-7219-0390-8*, Pub. by Scientific) St Mut.

Cutnell. Physics 4th ed. 1997. text, student ed. 76.00 (*0-471-29147-1*) Wiley.

Cutnell. Physics, Vol. 1. 4th ed. 1999. pap. text, student ed. 48.00 (*0-471-37750-3*) Wiley.

— Physics, Vol. 2. 5th ed. 1999. pap. text, student ed. 46.00 (*0-471-37751-1*) Wiley.

***Cutnell.** Physics, Vol.1&2. 4th ed. 1998. text 78.00 (*0-471-31871-X*) Wiley.

Cutnell. Physics: Chapters 1-5. 4th ed. 1998. pap. text 15.00 (*0-471-32456-6*) Wiley.

— Physics MCAT Student Survey. 4th ed. 1999. text 93.00 (*0-471-37020-7*) Wiley.

— Physics: Selected Chapters. 4th ed. 1998. pap. text 21.75 (*0-471-32240-7*) Wiley.

Cutnell. Physics: Take Note, vol. 2. 4th ed. pap. text 46.00 (*0-471-38069-5*) Wiley.

— Physics: Take Notes Ideas. 4th ed. text 78.00 (*0-471-38068-7*) Wiley.

Cutnell. Physics Study Guide Set. 4th ed. 1997. text 76.00 (*0-471-28381-9*) Wiley.

Cutnell. Student Solutions Manual to Accompany Physics. 4th ed. 304p. 1997. pap. 37.95 (*0-471-16410-0*) Wiley.

Cutnell, John D. Physics. 4th ed. 640p. 1997. pap. 37.95 (*0-471-16411-9*) Wiley.

Cutnell, John D. & Johnson, Kenneth W. Physics. 4th ed. 1984p. 1997. text, student ed. 177.85 (*0-471-25254-9*) Wiley.

C

An Asterisk (*) at the beginning of an entry indicates that the title is appearing for the first time.

***Cutnell, John D. & Johnson, Kenneth W.** Physics, 2 vols., Set. 5th ed. (C). 2000. write for info. (*0-471-39377-0*) Wiley.

— Physics, Vol. 1. 4th ed. LC 97-21746. 584p. 1997. pap. 70.95 (*0-471-19112-4*) Wiley.

— Physics, Vol. 1. 5th ed. 584p. (C). write for info. (*0-471-38717-7*) Wiley.

— Physics, Vol. 2. 4th ed. LC 97-21746. 544p. 1997. pap. 67.95 (*0-471-19113-2*); pap. text 80.00 (*0-471-19768-8*) Wiley.

— Physics, Vol. 2. 5th ed. 544p. (C). 2000. write for info. (*0-471-38718-5*) Wiley.

Cutnell, John D. & Johnson, Kenneth W. Physics Vol. 1. 4th ed. LC 97-21746. 1064p. 1997. text 114.95 (*0-471-15519-5*) Wiley.

Cutner, Herbert. Jesus: God, Man or Myth. 298p. 1986. reprint ed. spiral bd. 17.50 (*0-7873-0235-X*) Hlth Research.

Cutney, Barbara. Challenges & Pleasures: Living Ethically in a Competitive World. LC 97-30567. 128p. (C). 1997. pap. 19.50 (*0-7618-0910-4*) U Pr of Amer.

Cutolo, Chuck. Notes from the Hidden Years: Reflections on Spirituality, Politics & Other Stuff. LC 99-93215. 230p. 1999. pap. 16.95 (*0-9672093-0-7*) Denise Pubns.

***Cutolo, M.** Neuroendocrine Immune Basis of the Rheumatic Diseases LC 99-26842. (Annals Ser.). 1999. pap. write for info. (*1-57331-216-9*) NY Acad Sci.

Cutrer, Clyde W., Sr. Frog Pond Millennial Tales & More. LC 98-67683. (Illus.). 128p. 1998. 12.95 (*1-57736-128-8*) Providence Hse.

— Son of Frog Pond: Tales of the Not-So-Hot Preacher from the Swamp. LC 96-71627. 160p. 1996. 12.95 (*1-57736-026-5*) Providence Hse.

Cutrer, Emily F. The Art of the Woman: The Life & Work of Elisabet Ney. LC 87-19077. 287p. reprint ed. pap. 89.00 (*0-608-05993-5*, 206632100008) Bks Demand.

Cutrer, Thomas W. Ben McCulloch & the Frontier Military Tradition. LC 92-50812. (Civil War America Ser.). (Illus.). xiv, 402p. 1993. 45.00 (*0-8078-2076-8*) U of NC Pr.

— The English Texans. (Illus.). 188p. 1986. 7.95 (*0-86701-012-6*) U of Tex Inst Tex Culture.

— Parnassus on the Mississippi: The Southern Review & the Baton Rouge Literary Community, 1935-1942. LC 83-24913. (Southern Literary Studies). (Illus.). 291p. 1984. text 35.00 (*0-8071-1143-0*) La State U Pr.

Cutrer, Thomas W., ed. Longstreet's Aide: The Civil War Letters of Major Thomas J. Goree. LC 94-37521. (Nation Divided Ser.). (Illus.). 304p. (C). 1995. 32.50 (*0-8139-1574-0*) U Pr of Va.

Cutrer, Thomas W. & Parrish, T. Michael, eds. Brothers in Gray: The Civil War Letters of the Pierson Family. LC 97-11123. (Illus.). 336p. 1997. 34.95 (*0-8071-2134-7*) La State U Pr.

***Cutrer, William & Glahn, Sandra.** La Intimidad Sexual en el Matrimonio. (SPA.). 224p. 1999. pap. 8.99 (*0-8254-1145-9*, Edit Portavoz) Kregel.

— Lethal Harvest. 400p. 2000. pap. 10.99 (*0-8254-2371-6*) Kregel.

Cutrer, William & Glahn, Sandra. Sexual Intimacy in Marriage. LC 97-34279. 208p. 1997. pap. 11.99 (*0-8254-2354-6*) Kregel.

Cutrer, William, jt. auth. see Glahn, Sandra.

Cutright, Paul R. Great Naturalists Explore South America. LC 68-8454. (Essay Index Reprint Ser.). 1977. 29.95 (*0-8369-0357-9*) Ayer.

— Lewis & Clark: Pioneering Naturalists. LC 88-38522. (Illus.). xvi, 522p. 1989. reprint ed. pap. 24.00 (*0-8032-6334-1*, Bison Books) U of Nebr Pr.

— Theodore Roosevelt: The Making of a Conservationist. LC 84-16205. (Illus.). 306p. 1985. text 29.95 (*0-252-01190-2*) U of Ill Pr.

Cutright, Paul R. & Brodhead, Michael J. Elliott Coues: Naturalist & Frontier Historian. LC 80-12424. (Illus.). 510p. 1981. text 39.95 (*0-252-00802-2*) U of Ill Pr.

***Cutright, Paul Russell.** Contributions of Philadelphia to Lewis & Clark History. 3rd ed. (We Proceeded on Supplementary Publication Ser.: Vol. 6). (Illus.). 52p. 2000. reprint ed. pap. 8.00 (*0-9678887-0-0*) L & C Trail.

— A History of the Lewis & Clark Journals. (Illus.). 311p. 2000. 75.00 (*1-57898-247-2*) Martino Pubng.

— A History of the Lewis & Clark Journals. (Illus.). 336p. 2000. pap. text 25.95 (*0-8061-3247-7*) U of Okla Pr.

Cutrofello, Andrew. Discipline & Critique: Kant, Poststructuralism, & the Problem of Resistance. LC 93-3843. (SUNY Series in Contemporary Continental Philosophy). 168p. (C). 1994. text 59.50 (*0-7914-1855-3*); pap. text 19.95 (*0-7914-1856-1*) State U NY Pr.

— Imagining Otherwise: Metapsychology & the Analytic a Posteriori. LC 97-6363. (Studies in Phenomenology & Existential Philosophy). 1997. 79.95 (*0-8101-1399-6*); pap. 22.95 (*0-8101-1400-3*) Northwestern U Pr.

— The Owl at Dawn: A Sequel to Hegel's Phenomenology of Spirit. LC 94-24303. (SUNY Series in Radical Social & Political Theory). 196p. (C). 1995. text 57.50 (*0-7914-2583-5*); pap. text 18.95 (*0-7914-2584-3*) State U NY Pr.

Cutrona, Carolyn E. Social Support in Couples: Marriage As a Resource in Times of Stress. (Series in Close Relationships: Vol. 13). 150p. (C). 1996. pap. 17.95 (*0-8039-4884-0*); 42.00 (*0-8039-4883-2*) Sage.

Cutrubus, C. Nina, jt. auth. see Hamilton, Charles M.

Cutrubus, C. Nina, jt. ed. see Hamilton, Charles M.

***Cutrufelli, Maria Rosa.** Forbidden. 1998. lib. bdg. 25.00 (*0-226-13223-4*) U Ch Pr.

***Cutrufelli, Maria Rosa & Bertolini, Vincent J.** In the Forbidden City: An Anthology of Erotic Fiction by Italian Women. LC 00-24265. 1999. pap. 11.00 (*0-226-13224-2*) U Ch Pr.

Cutshall, Bryan. Pilgrims Promise. LC 98-65572. 216p. 1998. pap. 9.99 (*0-87148-987-2*) Pathway Pr.

Cutshall, Euel R., ed. see Minerals, Metals & Materials Society Staff.

Cutshall, John. 155 Awesome Ideas to Energize Any VBS! LC 98-21731. 112p. 1998. per. 14.99 (*0-7644-2118-2*, Vital Ministry) Group Pub.

Cutshall, John, jt. auth. see Keefer, Mikal.

Cutshall, Mark, jt. auth. see Cheatham, Melvin L.

Cutshall, Mark, jt. auth. see Horlsey, James.

Cutshall, Mark, jt. auth. see Mulder, Dennis M.

Cutshall, Mark, ed. see Staub, Dick & Troutman, Jeff.

Cutshall, Mark, ed. see Troutman, Jeff.

Cutshall, Susan & Frederick, Ruth. Treat 'Em Right: Tasty Ideas for Encouraging Volunteers. 80p. 1999. 8.99 (*0-7847-0920-3*, 03525) Standard Pub.

Cutshaw, Charlie. The New World of Russian Small Arms & Ammo. LC 99-190375. (Illus.). 160p. 1998. 39.95 (*0-87364-993-1*) Paladin Pr.

***Cutshaw, Charlie & Shilin, Valery.** Legends & Reality of the AK: A Behind-the-Scenes Look at the History, Design & Impact of the Kalashnikov Family of Weapons. (Illus.). 192p. 2000. pap. 35.00 (*1-58160-069-0*, 10011351) Paladin Pr.

Cutshaw, Kenneth A. & Zhang, Jianyi. Corporate Counsel's Guide to Doing Business in China. LC 95-205235. 275p. 1995. ring bd. 115.00 (*1-56789-022-9*, 150) Busn Laws Inc.

Cutshell, Mark, jt. auth. see Cheatham, Melvin L.

Cutsinger, James S. Advice to the Serious Seeker: Meditations on the Teaching of Frithjof Schuon. LC 96-12876. (SUNY Series in Western Esoteric Traditions). 225p. (C). 1997. text 59.50 (*0-7914-3249-1*); pap. text 19.95 (*0-7914-3250-5*) State U NY Pr.

— The Form of Transformed Vision: Coleridge & the Knowledge of God. LC 87-15234. 160p. (C). 1987. text 24.95 (*0-86554-280-5*, MUP-H241) Mercer Univ Pr.

Cutsinger, James S., ed. Reclaiming the Great Tradition: Evangelicals, Catholics & Orthodox in Dialogue. LC 96-39119. 214p. (Orig.). 1997. pap. 18.99 (*0-8308-1889-8*, 1889) InterVarsity.

Cutsinger, John W., Jr., ed. Magazine Fundamentals. 3rd ed. (Illus.). 24p. 1984. pap. text 8.50 (*0-916084-15-9*) Columbia Scholastic.

Cutsumbis, Michael M. A Bibliographic Guide to Materials on Greeks in the United States: 1890-1968. LC 74-130283. 100p. 1970. 9.95 (*0-913256-02-1*) CMS.

Cutt, James. Comprehensive Auditing in Canada: Theory & Practice. LC 88-14105. 281p. 1988. 65.00 (*0-275-93006-8*, C3006, Praeger Pubs) Greenwood.

Cutt, James & Dobell, Rodney, eds. Public Purse, Public Purpose: Autonomy & Accountability in the Groves of Academe. 300p. 1992. pap. text 19.95 (*0-88645-129-9*, Pub. by Inst Res Pub) Ashgate Pub Co.

***Cutt, James & Murray, Victor V.** Accountability & Effectiveness Evaluation in Non-Profit Organizations. LC 99-87024. 2000. write for info. (*0-415-21339-8*) Routledge.

Cutt, Thomas, ed. see Arbiter, Petronius.

Cuttance, Peter & Ecob, Russell, eds. Structural Modelling by Example: Applications in Educational, Sociological & Behavioural Research. (Illus.). 336p. 1988. text 74.95 (*0-521-26195-3*) Cambridge U Pr.

Cutten, George B. The Psychology of Alcoholism. Grob, Gerald N., ed. LC 80-1223. (Addiction in America Ser.). 1981. reprint ed. lib. bdg. 35.95 (*0-405-13579-3*) Ayer.

— Silversmiths of Virginia. (Illus.). 1976. reprint ed. 17.50 (*0-87517-040-4*) Dietz.

— Speaking with Tongues: Historically & Psychologically Considered. 1927. 59.50 (*0-685-69805-X*) Elliots Bks.

— The Threat of Leisure. 1982. 18.95 (*0-8434-0435-3*) McGrath NH.

Cutten, George B., et al. The Silversmiths of Georgia: Early Silversmiths & Silver Trade in Georgia. LC 98-65952. (Illus.). 176p. 1998. reprint ed. 25.00 (*1-891495-07-0*) Oglethorpe Pr.

Cutten, George B., jt. auth. see Burton, E. Milby.

Cutten History Committee of the Fitzroy History So, ed. Fitzroy: Melbourne's First Suburb. (Illus.). 368p. 1991. 45.00 (*0-522-84476-6*, Pub. by Melbourne Univ Pr) Paul & Co Pubs.

Cutter, Benjamin. Cutter. History of the Cutter Family of New England. (Illus.). 363p. 1995. reprint ed. pap. 52.00 (*0-8328-4764-X*); reprint ed. lib. bdg. 62.00 (*0-8328-4763-1*) Higginson Bk Co.

Cutter, Benjamin & Cutter, William R. History of the Town of Arlington, Mass., 1635-1879, with a Genealogical Register. (Illus.). 368p. 1989. reprint ed. lib. bdg. 39.00 (*0-8328-0803-2*, MA0007) Higginson Bk Co.

Cutter, C. A. C. A. Cutter's Three-Figure Author Table: Swanson-Swift Revision. 29p. 1969. lib. bdg. 17.00 (*0-87287-209-2*) Libs Unl.

— C. A. Cutter's Two-Figure Author Table: Swanson-Swift Revision. 4p. 1969. lib. bdg. 11.00 (*0-87287-208-4*) Libs Unl.

Cutter, C. A. & Sanborn. Cutter-Sanborn Three-Figure Author Table: Swanson-Swift Revision. 34p. 1969. lib. bdg. 18.00 (*0-87287-210-6*) Libs Unl.

***Cutter, Charles H.** Africa 1999 Edition. 34th ed. (Africa Ser.). 1999. pap. 11.50 (*1-887985-17-4*) Stryker-Post.

Cutter, Charles H. Africa, 1998. 33rd ed. (World Today Ser.). 1998. pap. 11.50 (*1-887985-10-7*) Stryker-Post.

Cutter, Daniel B. History of the Town of Jaffrey, from the Date of the Masonian Charter to the Present Time, 1749-1880, with a Genealogical Register of the Jaffrey Families. 648p. 1997. reprint ed. lib. bdg. 68.50 (*0-8328-5998-2*) Higginson Bk Co.

Cutter, Donald & Engstrand, Iris H. Quest for Empire: Spanish Settlement in the Southwest. (Illus.). 360p. 1996. 27.95 (*1-55591-230-3*) Fulcrum Pub.

Cutter, Donald C. California in 1792: A Spanish Naval Visit. LC 90-50231. (American Exploration & Travel Ser.: Vol. 71). (Illus.). 192p. 1990. 26.95 (*0-8061-2306-0*) U of Okla Pr.

— California in 1792: A Spanish Naval Visit. LC 90-50231. (American Exploration & Travel Ser.: Vol. 71). (Illus.). 192p. 1995. pap. 12.95 (*0-8061-2731-7*) U of Okla Pr.

Cutter, Donald C., ed. The Diary of Ensign Gabriel Morega's Expedition of Discovery in the Sacramento Valley 1808. (Early California Travels Ser.: Vol. XLI). (Illus.). 41p. 1957. pap. text 4.69 (*1-55567-665-0*) Coyote Press.

Cutter, Donald C., ed. The Defenses of Northern New Spain: Hugo O'Conor's Report to Teodoro de Croix, July 22, 1777. LC 93-18212. (DeGolyer Library: No. 4). 184p. 1994. text 47.50 (*0-87074-347-3*) SMU Press.

Cutter, Donald C., tr. The Letters of Father Payeras: The Last Days of Spain in California. 380p. 1995. 29.95 (*0-88388-187-X*) Bellerophon Bks.

Cutter, Donald C., ed. & epil. see Whitehead, Richard S.

Cutter, Donald S., ed. see Whitehead, Richard S.

Cutter, Douglas, ed. see Engstrand, Iris H.

Cutter, Elizabeth G. PLANT ANAT:INTERPRTN PT1. 2nd ed. (Illus.). 1978. text 24.00 (*0-201-01236-7*) Addison-Wesley.

***Cutter, Fred.** Suicide Prevention Triangle: A Manual for Everyone. LC TX 1-170-95. (Illus.). xii, 233p. 1999. pap. 74.95 (*0-9675519-0-0*) Triangle Bks CA.

Cutter, John M. Cutter's Official Guide to Hot Springs, Arkansas. Jones, William R., ed. (Illus.). 55p. 1979. reprint ed. pap. 4.95 (*0-89646-057-6*) Vistabooks.

Cutter, Lawrence, jt. auth. see Winger, Douglas E.

Cutter, Lawrence, jt. auth. see Winter, Douglas E.

Cutter, M., ed. see Prusinkiewicz, P. & Lindenmayer, A.

Cutter, Martha. Unruly Tongue: Indentity & Voice in American Women's Writing, 1850-1930. LC 98-36109. (Illus.). 224p. 1999. text 40.00 (*1-57806-085-0*) U Pr of Miss.

Cutter, Mary A. & Shelp, Earl E., eds. Competency: A Study of Informal Competency Determinations in Primary Care. (Philosophy & Medicine Ser.). 308p. 1991. lib. bdg. 155.50 (*0-7923-1304-6*, Pub. by Kluwer Academic) Kluwer Academic.

Cutter, Mary A., jt. ed. see Delkeskamp-Hayes, Corinna.

Cutter, Michael. GMP "How to" Essentials: How to Apply Quality Assurance Principles. (GMP Training Ser.). (Illus.). 150p. 1995. teacher ed., ring bd. 175.00 (*0-935184-93-7*) Interpharm.

— GMP "How to" Essentials: How to Organize a Validation File. (GMP Training Ser.). (Illus.). 150p. 1995. teacher ed., ring bd. 175.00 (*0-935184-95-3*) Interpharm.

— GMP "How to" Essentials: How to Perform Retrospective Validation. (GMP Training Ser.). (Illus.). 150p. 1995. teacher ed., ring bd. 175.00 (*0-935184-97-X*) Interpharm.

— GMP "How to" Essentials: How to Prepare for an FDA Inspection. (GMP Training Ser.). (Illus.). 150p. 1995. teacher ed., ring bd. 175.00 (*0-935184-89-9*) Interpharm.

— GMP "How to" Essentials: How to Review & Redesign SOP Systems. (GMP Training Ser.). (Illus.). 150p. 1995. teacher ed., ring bd. 175.00 (*0-935184-99-6*) Interpharm.

— GMP "How to" Essentials: How to Write Policies & Procedures. (GMP Training Ser.). (Illus.). 150p. 1995. teacher ed., ring bd. 175.00 (*0-935184-91-0*) Interpharm.

Cutter, Nancy C., jt. auth. see Kevorkian, C. George.

Cutter, Paul F. Early Lubbock: A Cultural View. 120p. 1997. 15.00 (*0-89015-845-2*, Eakin Pr) Sunbelt Media.

Cutter, Ralph. Sierra Trout Guide. rev. ed. (Illus.). 112p. (Orig.). 1991. reprint ed. pap. 19.95 (*1-878175-02-5*) F Amato Pubns.

Cutter, Robert J. The Brush & the Spur: Chinese Culture & the Cockfight. (Illus.). 268p. 1989. 47.50 (*962-201-417-8*, Pub. by Chinese Univ) Coronet Bks.

Cutter, Robert Joe, et al. Empresses & Consorts: Selections from Chen Shou's Records of the Three States with Pei Songzhi's Commentary. LC 98-41899. 312p. (C). 1999. text 50.00 (*0-8248-1945-4*) UH Pr.

Cutter, Susan L. Environmental Risks & Hazards. LC 96-6925. 413p. (C). 1993. pap. text 55.60 (*0-13-753856-1*) P-H.

Cutter, Susan L. & Renwick, William. Exploitation, Conservation, Preservation: A Geographic Perspective on Natural Resource Use. 3rd ed. 391p. 1998. text 86.95 (*0-471-01810-4*) Wiley.

Cutter, Susan L., jt. auth. see Mitchell, Jerry T.

Cutter, William, ed. see Behrman House, Inc. Staff.

Cutter, William, ed. see Lamm, Maurice.

Cutter, William, ed. see Pasachoff, Naomi.

Cutter, William, ed. see Rossel, Seymour.

Cutter, William C. Families of Western New York: Excerpted from Genealogical & Family History of Western New York - A Record of the Achievements of Her People in the Making of a Commonwealth & the Building of a Nation. 511p. 1996. reprint ed. pap. 49.95 (*0-8063-4660-4*, 9186) Clearfield Co.

— Organizing Time: Understanding Rhythm - A Method For... Foss, Scott, ed. 47p. (C). 1999. pap. text 6.00 (*0-89328-152-2*, 30/1373R) Lorenz Corp.

Cutter, William R. New England Families, Genealogical & Memorial: A Record of the Achievements of Her People in the Making of Commonwealths & the Founding of a Nation, 4 vols, (Illus.). 2149p. 1997. reprint ed. pap. 200.00 (*0-8063-4537-3*, 9175, Pub. by Clearfield Co) ACCESS Pubs Network.

Cutter, William R., compiled by. Genealogical & Family History of Northern New York: A Record of the Achievements of Her People in the Making of the Commonwealth & the Building of a Nation, 3 vols. (Illus.). 1247p. 1997. reprint ed. lib. bdg. 122.50 (*0-8328-5465-4*) Higginson Bk Co.

Cutter, William R., ed. New England Families, Genealogical & Memorial: Record of the Achievements of Her People in the Making of Commonwealths & the Founding of a Nation. (Illus.). 1259p. 1997. reprint ed. lib. bdg. 126.00 (*0-8328-5706-8*) Higginson Bk Co.

Cutter, William R., et al. Genealogical & Family History of the State of Connecticut: A Record of the Achievements of Her People in the Making of a Commonwealth & the Building of a Nation, 4 vols. (Illus.). 2842p. 1997. pap. 200.00 (*0-8063-4521-7*, 9177) Clearfield Co.

— Genealogical & Family History of the State of Connecticut: Record of the Achievements of Her People in the Making of a Commonwealth & the Founding of a Nation, 4 vols. (Illus.). 2208p. 1997. reprint ed. lib. bdg. 230.00 (*0-8328-5622-3*) Higginson Bk Co.

Cutter, William R., jt. auth. see Cutter, Benjamin.

***Cutter, William Richard.** Genealogical & Family History of Central New York: A Record of the Achievements of Her People in the Making of a Commonwealth & the Building of a Nation, 3 vols., Set. 1612p. 2000. reprint ed. pap. 150.00 (*0-8063-4972-0*, Pub. by Clearfield Co) ACCESS Pubs Network.

— Genealogical & Personal Memoirs: Relating to the Families of Boston & Eastern Massachusetts, 4 vols., Set. (Illus.). 2201p. 2000. reprint ed. pap. 200.00 (*0-8063-4549-7*, Pub. by Clearfield Co) ACCESS Pubs Network.

Cutterbuck, Ivan. A Church in Miniature. 202p. 1996. pap. 14.95 (*0-85244-345-5*, 6321, Pub. by Gralcewing) Morehouse Pub.

Cutting-Gray, Joanne. Woman As 'Nobody' & the Novels of Fanny Burney. 176p. (C). 1992. 39.95 (*0-8130-1106-X*) U Press Fla.

Cutting, John C. Principles of Psychopathology: Two Worlds - Two Minds - Two Hemispheres. LC 96-29144. (Illus.). 604p. (C). 1997. text 120.00 (*0-19-262240-4*) OUP.

Cutting, Jorge. La Salvacion: Su Seguridad, Creteza y Gozo. 2nd ed. Daniel, Roger P., ed. Bautista, Sara, tr. from ENG. (Serie Diamante).Tr. of Safety, Certainity & Enjoyment. (SPA., Illus.). 48p. 1982. pap. 0.85 (*0-942504-05-4*) Overcomer Pr.

— La Venida del Senor. 2nd ed. Bennett, Gordon H., ed. Bautista, Sara, tr. from ENG. (Serie Diamante).Tr. of Lord's Coming. (SPA., Illus.). 48p. 1982. pap. 0.85 (*0-942504-10-0*) Overcomer Pr.

Cutting, Linda K. Memory Slips: A Memoir of Music & Healing. 256p. 1998. pap. 13.00 (*0-06-092879-4*, Perennial) HarperTrade.

Cutting, Lynda, jt. auth. see Wilson, Jeni.

Cutting, Mary S. Little Stories of Courtship. LC 79-98566. (Short Story Index Reprint Ser.). 1977. 19.95 (*0-8369-3140-8*) Ayer.

— Little Stories of Married Life. LC 70-152968. (Short Story Index Reprint Ser.). 1977. reprint ed. 19.95 (*0-8369-3796-1*) Ayer.

— More Stories of Married Life. LC 75-37264. (Short Story Index Reprint Ser.). 1977. reprint ed. 19.95 (*0-8369-4075-X*) Ayer.

— Refractory Husbands. LC 79-128729. (Short Story Index Reprint Ser.). 1977. 17.95 (*0-8369-3620-5*) Ayer.

Cutting, Michael. The Little Crooked Christmas Tree. (Illus.). 24p. (J). (ps-2). 1995. pap. 5.95 (*1-895565-76-6*) Firefly Bks Ltd.

Cutting, R. E., jt. ed. see Gibson, R. J.

Cutting, Simon M., jt. ed. see Harwood, Colin R.

Cutting, Starr W. Der Conjunctiv Bei Hartmann Von Aue. LC 76-173037. (Chicago. University. Germanic Studies: No. 1). reprint ed. 29.50 (*0-404-50271-7*) AMS Pr.

Cutting, T. A. Cutting Kin. (Illus.). 224p. 1997. reprint ed. pap. 34.00 (*0-8328-8192-9*); reprint ed. lib. bdg. 44.00 (*0-8328-8191-0*) Higginson Bk Co.

Cutting, Tom. Can You Stand Forgiveness? Jacks, Sherry, ed. LC 90-71174. 160p. 1990. write for info. (*0-9627096-0-3*) Whitehead TX.

Cutting, W., et al, eds. Annual Review of Pharmacology, Vol. 2. LC 61-5649. 1962. text 40.00 (*0-8243-0402-0*) Annual Reviews.

— Annual Review of Pharmacology, Vol. 3. LC 61-5649. 1963. text 40.00 (*0-8243-0403-9*) Annual Reviews.

— Annual Review of Pharmacology, Vol. 5. LC 61-5649. 1965. text 40.00 (*0-8243-0405-5*) Annual Reviews.

Cutting, Windsor C., ed. Annual Review of Medicine, Vol. 2. LC 51-1659. 1951. 40.00 (*0-8243-0502-7*) Annual Reviews.

— Annual Review of Medicine, Vol. 3. LC 51-1659. 1952. 40.00 (*0-8243-0503-5*) Annual Reviews.

Cuttino, G. P. Gascon Calendar of 1322. (Camden Third Ser.). 35.00 (*0-86193-070-3*) David Brown.

— Gascon Register A, 3 vols., Vols. 1 & 2. (Illus.). 1975. 69.00 (*0-19-725950-2*) OUP.

Cuttino, G. P., ed. Gascon Register A, Vol. 3. (British Academy Ser.). (C). 1976. 22.50 (*0-19-725966-9*) OUP.

Cuttino, George P. English Medieval Diplomacy. LC 84-48297. 172p. reprint ed. pap. 53.40 (*0-7837-3695-9*, 205787300009) Bks Demand.

Cuttitta, F., jt. ed. see Martinez, A.

Cuttler, Charles. Northern Painting: From Purcelle to Bruegel - 14th, 15th, & 16th Centuries. 500p. (C). 1973. pap. text 68.00 (*0-03-089476-X*, Pub. by Harcourt Coll Pubs) Harcourt.

Cuttler, Dona. The History of Hyattstown (MD) LC 98-226149. (Illus.). 129p. 1998. pap. 15.00 (*0-7884-0985-9*, CUTT) Heritage Bk.

Cuttler, Dona L. The History of Comus. (Illus.). 88p. 1999. pap. 16.50 (*0-7884-1115-2*, C877) Heritage Bk.

C

***Cuttler, Dona L.** The History of Dickerson, Mouth of Monacacy, Oakland Mills & Sugarloaf Mountain (MD) (Illus.). 174p. 1999. pap. 18.50 (*0-7884-1347-3*, C879) Heritage Bk.

***Cuttler, Dona L. & Elgin, Dorothy J.** The History of Poolesville. (Illus.). 202p. 2000. pap. 26.00 (*0-7884-1450-X*, 1450) Heritage Bk.

Cuttler, Dona Lou. The Cemeteries of Hyattstown. LC 99-183595. 88p. 1999. pap. 14.00 (*0-7884-1077-6*, CUTL) Heritage Bk.

***Cuttler, Dona Lou.** Montgomery Circuit Records, 1788-1988: Methodist Episcopal, Methodist Episcopal South & United Methodist. 278p. 2000. pap. 34.00 (*0-7884-1427-5*, 1427) Heritage Bk.

Cuttler, Dona Lou & Brown, Ida Lu. The History of Barnesville & Sellman. (Illus.). 147p. 1999. pap. 23.50 (*0-7884-1180-2*, C878) Heritage Bk.

Cutts, Dana S. & Cutts, Gretchen S., eds. Old Family Recipes: Now You Can Cook Like Grandma. (Illus.). 120p. 1996. spiral bd. 10.95 (*0-9658705-0-2*) Old Fmly Recipes.

Cutts, David. The Adventures of Tom Thumb. LC 87-10980. (Illus.). 32p. (J). (gr. k-3). 1997. pap. 3.95 (*0-8167-1072-4*) Troll Communs.

— Creatures of the Night. LC 97-224921. (I Can Read about Ser.). (Illus.). (J). (ps-3). 1997. pap. 29.95 incl. audio (*0-8167-4345-2*) Troll Communs.

— El Galleton de Jengibre. (J). 1995. pap. 3.95 (*0-8167-3345-7*) Troll Communs.

— I Can Read about Bees & Wasps. deluxe ed. LC 98-137731. (I Can Read about Ser.). (Illus.). 48p. (J). (ps-3). 1998. pap. 4.95 (*0-8167-4444-0*) Troll Communs.

— I Can Read About Creatures of the Night. LC 78-68468. (Illus.). (J). (gr. 2-5). 1997. pap. 2.95 (*0-89375-202-9*) Troll Communs.

— I Can Read About Thunder & Lightning. LC 78-66273. (Illus.). (J). (gr. 2-6). 1997. pap. 2.95 (*0-89375-217-7*) Troll Communs.

— I Can Read about Thunder & Lightning. deluxe ed. (I Can Read about Ser.). (Illus.). 48p. (J). (ps-3). 1998. pap. 4.95 (*0-8167-4445-9*) Troll Communs.

— Look - a Butterfly. LC 81-11369. (Now I Know Ser.). (Illus.). 32p. (J). (gr. k-2). 1997. pap. 3.50 (*0-89375-663-6*) Troll Communs.

— More about Dinosaurs. LC 81-11432. (Now I Know Ser.). (Illus.). 32p. (J). (gr. k-2). 1982. lib. bdg. 17.25 (*0-89375-668-7*) Troll Communs.

— More about Dinosaurs. LC 81-11432. (Now I Know Ser.). (Illus.). 32p. (J). (gr. k-2). 1997. pap. 3.50 (*0-89375-669-5*) Troll Communs.

— Reptiles. (I Can Read about Ser.). (Illus.). (J). (ps-3). 1997. pap. 29.95 incl. audio (*0-8167-4346-0*) Troll Communs.

Cutts, David, ed. see Grimm, Jacob W. & Grimm, Wilhelm K.

Cutts, David, ed. see Grimm, Wilhelm K. & Grimm, Jacob W.

Cutts, Edward L. Parish Priests & Their People in the Middle Ages in England. LC 74-107457. reprint ed. 42.50 (*0-404-01898-X*) AMS Pr.

— Scenes & Characters of the Middle Ages. 1977. lib. bdg. 59.95 (*0-8490-2569-9*) Gordon Pr.

Cutts, Felicity T. & Smith, Peter G., eds. Vaccination & World Health: The LSHTM Fourth Annual Public Health Forum. LC 94-37790. 308p. 1995. 157.95 (*0-471-95242-7*) Wiley.

Cutts, Grace. On Call. (Junior Jaffray Collection: Bk. 3). 30p. (J). (ps-2). 1991. pap. 3.99 (*0-87509-452-X*) Chr Pubns.

— To China & Back. (Junior Jaffray Collection: Bk. 4). 27p. (J). (ps-2). 1991. pap. 3.99 (*0-87509-453-8*) Chr Pubns.

Cutts, Gracie. Angel at the Bridge. LC 97-185273. 207p. (Orig.). 1997. pap. 11.00 (*1-885729-10-3*) Toccoa Falls.

— Weak Thing in Moni Land. (Junior Jaffray Collection: Bk. 2). 29p. (J). (ps-2). 1991. pap. 3.99 (*0-87509-451-1*) Chr Pubns.

Cutts, Gretchen S., jt. ed. see Cutts, Dana S.

Cutts, J. H., jt. auth. see Krause, W. J.

Cutts, Joe, jt. auth. see Walsh, Molly.

Cutts, John. World's Fastest Motorcycles. 1991. 12.98 (*1-55521-708-7*) Bk Sales Inc.

Cutts, John P. The Shattered Glass: A Dramatic Pattern in Shakespeare's Early Plays. LC 68-22253. 154p. reprint ed. 47.80 (*0-608-16994-3*, 202760300055) Bks Demand.

Cutts, John P., ed. Seventeenth Century Songs & Lyrics. LC 70-80373. (Granger Index Reprint Ser.). 1977. 23.95 (*0-8369-6055-6*) Ayer.

Cutts, John P., ed. & intro. see Sidney, Philip.

Cutts, Joseph W., jt. auth. see Walsh, Molly K.

Cutts, Karen. A Practical Guide to Purchasing Groups: A Comprehensive Reference Source on Formation, Operation & Regulation of Purchasing Groups Formed under the Liability Risk Retention Act. LC 96-112043. 245p. 1995. text 495.00 (*0-9625840-9-6*) Insure Commns.

— Risk Retention Group Directory & Guide, 1999. 160p. (C). 1999. pap. text 210.00 (*1-891025-02-3*) Insure Commns.

Cutts, Karen, ed. Purchasing Group Users' Handbook. 410p. (C). 1999. ring bd. 540.00 (*1-891025-03-1*) Insure Commns.

Cutts, Norma E., ed. see Thayer Conference on the Functions, Qualifications.

Cutts, Paddy. Cat Breeds of the World. (Illustrated Encyclopedias Ser.). (Illus.). 1999. pap. 9.95 (*0-7548-0030-X*, Lorenz Bks) Anness Pub.

— Cat Care. (Practical Handbook Ser.). 1999. pap. 9.95 (*0-7548-0027-X*, Lorenz Bks) Anness Pub.

— Cats: A Comprehensive Guide to the World's Breeds. LC 98-47972. 1999. 19.98 (*1-57145-170-6*) Advantage Pubs.

— Identifying Guide to Cat Breeds. 80p. 1995. 6.98 (*0-7858-0325-4*) Bk Sales Inc.

— State Tax Handbook, 1999. 386p. 1999. pap. 41.95 (*0-8080-0322-4*) CCH INC.

***Cutts, Paddy.** Your Kitten: Choice & Care. (Illus.). 144p. 1999. reprint ed. text 17.00 (*0-7881-6830-4*) DIANE Pub.

Cutts, Robert L. An Empire of Schools: Japan's Universities & the Molding of a National Power Elite. LC 96-49365. 286p. (C). (gr. 13). 1997. 35.95 (*1-56324-843-3*, East Gate Bk) M E Sharpe.

Cutts, Simon. Piano Stool: Footnotes. 1982. pap. 12.50 (*0-912330-55-4*) Jargon Soc.

— Seepages. 1990. 20.00 (*0-912330-68-6*) Jargon Soc.

Cutts, Simon, et al. The Coracle: Coracle Press Gallery, 1975-1987. (Illus.). 132p. (Orig.). 1989. pap. 12.95 (*0-685-38946-4*) Yale Ctr Brit Art.

Cutts, William A. Weak Thing in Moni Land: The Story of Bill & Gracie Cutts. LC 90-80454. (Jaffray Collection of Missionary Portraits: Bk. 2). (Illus.). 168p. (Orig.). (YA). 1990. pap. 8.99 (*0-87509-429-5*) Chr Pubns.

Cutz, Ernest. Cellular & Molecular Biology of Airway Chemoreceptors. LC 97-24582. (Medical Intelligence Unit Ser.). 132p. 1997. text 99.00 (*1-57059-473-2*) Landes Bioscience.

Cuvalay-Haak, Martin. The Verb in Literary & Colloquial Arabic. (Functional Grammar Ser.: Vol. 19). xx, 278p. 1997. lib. bdg. 109.00 (*3-11-015401-3*) Mouton.

Cuvalo, Ante. Historical Dictionary of Bosnia & Herzegovina. LC 97-14417. (European Historical Dictionaries: No. 25). 1997. 45.00 (*0-8108-3344-1*) Scarecrow.

Cuvelier, C., et al. Finite Element Methods & Navier-Strokes Equations. 1986. text 225.50 (*90-277-2148-3*) Kluwer Academic.

Cuvelier, Eugene. Eugene Cuvelier: The Legend of the Forest. LC 98-101798. 1997. 65.00 (*3-89322-857-8*, Pub. by Edition Cantz) Dist Art Pubs.

Cuviella, Patrick & Woosley, Hugh. Basic Medical Laboratory Subjects. LC 74-18675. (Allied Health Ser.). 1975. pap. write for info. (*0-672-61383-2*) Macmillan.

Cuviep, Remi. The Superdome Murders. unabridged ed. (New Orleans Murder Ser.: No. 1). 100p. 1998. pap. 6.95 (*1-892651-05-X*) Columbia Pubns.

Cuvier. Cuvier's Animals. (Illus.). 128p. pap. 11.95 (*0-486-29102-2*) Dover.

Cuvier, Georges. The Class Mammalia: The Animal Kingdom Arranged in Conformity with Its Organization by the Baron Cuvier, Set, Vols 1[00ad]5. Sterling, Keir B., ed. LC 77-81117. (Biologists & Their World Ser.). (Illus.). 1978. reprint ed. lib. bdg. 237.95 (*0-405-10746-3*) Ayer.

— The Class Mammalia: The Animal Kingdom Arranged in Conformity with Its Organization by the Baron Cuvier, Vol. 1[00ad]5. Sterling, Keir B., ed. LC 77-81117. (Biologists & Their World Ser.). (Illus.). 1978. reprint ed. lib. bdg. 47.95 (*0-405-10765-X*) Ayer.

— The Class Mammalia: The Animal Kingdom Arranged in Conformity with Its Organization by the Baron Cuvier, Vol. 2. Sterling, Keir B., ed. LC 77-81117. (Biologists & Their World Ser.). (Illus.). 1978. reprint ed. lib. bdg. 47.95 (*0-405-10766-8*) Ayer.

— The Class Mammalia: The Animal Kingdom Arranged in Conformity with Its Organization by the Baron Cuvier, Vol. 3. Sterling, Keir B., ed. LC 77-81117. (Biologists & Their World Ser.). (Illus.). 1978. reprint ed. lib. bdg. 47.95 (*0-405-10767-6*) Ayer.

— The Class Mammalia: The Animal Kingdom Arranged in Conformity with Its Organization by the Baron Cuvier, Vol. 4. Sterling, Keir B., ed. LC 77-81117. (Biologists & Their World Ser.). (Illus.). 1978. reprint ed. lib. bdg. 47.95 (*0-405-10768-4*) Ayer.

— The Class Mammalia: The Animal Kingdom Arranged in Conformity with Its Organization by the Baron Cuvier, Vol. 5. Sterling, Keir B., ed. LC 77-81117. (Biologists & Their World Ser.). (Illus.). 1978. reprint ed. lib. bdg. 47.95 (*0-405-10769-2*) Ayer.

***Cuvier, Georges.** Encyclopaedia of Life Sciences, 16 vols. 9000p. 1998. pap. 9000.00 (*81-7041-665-5*, Pub. by Print Hse) St Mut.

Cuvier, Georges. Essay on the Theory of the Earth: Mineralogical Notes, & an Account of Cuvier's Geological Discoveries. Albritton, Claude C., Jr., ed. Kerr, Robert, tr. LC 77-6517. (History of Geology Ser.). (Illus.). 1978. reprint ed. lib. bdg. 35.95 (*0-405-10439-1*) Ayer.

— Memoirs on Fossil Elephants & on Reconstruction of the Genera Palaeotherium & Anoplotherium. Gould, Stephen Jay, ed. LC 79-8327. (FRE., Illus.). 1980. reprint ed. lib. bdg. 88.95 (*0-405-12709-X*) Ayer.

Cuvier, Georges & Simpson, Abby J. Historical Portrait of the Progress of Ichthyology, from Its Origins to Our Own Time. Pietsch, Theodore W., ed. & tr. by. (Foundations of Natural History Ser.). (Illus.). 504p. 1995. text 65.00 (*0-8018-4914-4*) Johns Hopkins.

***Cuvier, Remi.** Murder in Congo Square. unabridged ed. Wegeng, Lana & Price, Julie, eds. (New Orleans Murders Ser.: Vol. 2). (Illus.). 1999. pap. 7.95 (*1-892651-20-3*) Columbia Pubns.

Cuvillier, Armand. Diccionario de Filosofia: Dictionary of Philosophy. (SPA.). 228p. 1961. 22.50 (*0-8288-6815-8*, S-33052) Fr & Eur.

Cuvillier, Rolande. The Reduction of Working Time: Scope & Implications in Industrialised Market Economies. vi, 150p. (C). 1984. pap. 22.50 (*92-2-102702-3*); text 31.50 (*92-2-103817-3*) Intl Labour Office.

Cuvo, Anthony J., jt. auth. see Thaw, Jack.

Cuyas. Diccionario Cuyas "Junior" de Bolstillo Espanol-Ingles-Espanol.Tr. of "Junior" Cuyas Spanish-English, English-Spanish. (ENG & SPA.). 339p. 1980. pap. 7.95 (*0-8288-2322-7*, S50350) Fr & Eur.

Cuyas Armengol, Arturo. Appleton-Cuyas Dictionary. rev. ed. (ENG & SPA.). 548p. 1981. per. 5.95 (*0-13-615559-6*) P-H.

— Diccionario de Bolsillo Frances-Espanol, Espanol-Francais: Pocket Spanish - French, French - Spanish Dictionary.Tr. of Pocket Spanish - French, French - Spanish. (FRE & SPA.). 670p. 1971. pap. 6.95 (*0-8288-6436-5*, S-50391) Fr & Eur.

— Diccionario Manual Frances-Espanol, Espagnol-Francais: French & Spanish. 36th ed. (FRE & SPA.). 830p. 1977. 14.95 (*0-8288-5353-3*, S50390) Fr & Eur.

— Diccionario Manual Ingles-Espanol, Spanish-English. 35th ed. (ENG & SPA.). 768p. 1978. pap. 9.95 (*0-8288-5144-1*, S12389) Fr & Eur.

Cuyas Armengol, Arturo, ed. New Appleton's Cuyas English-Spanish & Spanish-English Dictionary. 5th ed. (ENG & SPA.). 1974. 26.95 (*0-13-611749-X*) P-H.

***Cuyckens, Hubert & Zawada, Britta, eds.** Polysemy in Cognitive Linguistics: Selected Papers from the International Cognitive Linguistics Conference, Amsterdam, 1997. (Current Issues in Linguistic Theory Ser.: Vol. 177). 330p. 2000. write for info. (*1-55619-894-9*) J Benjamins Pubng.

***Cuyjet, Michael J.** Helping African American Men Succeed. 1998. pap. 23.00 (*0-7879-9883-4*) Jossey-Bass.

Cuyjet, Michael J., jt. ed. see Terrell, Melvin C.

Cuyle, Deborah. Kidding Around Portland: What to Do, Where to Go & How to Have Fun in Portland. LC 00-503372. (Kidding Around Ser.). (Illus.). 144p. (J). (gr. 1-5). 1998. pap. 7.95 (*1-56261-374-X*) Avalon Travel.

Cuyler. Invisible in the Third Grade. (J). 1995. 14.95 (*0-8050-4684-4*) H Holt & Co.

Cuyler, Lewis. Bike Rides in the Berkshire Hills. rev. ed. LC 94-41377. (Berkshire Outdoors Ser.). (Illus.). 200p. 1995. pap. 9.95 (*0-936399-68-6*) Berkshire Hse.

Cuyler, Louise E. The Symphony. 2nd ed. LC 95-13538. (Detroit Monographs in Musicology: Studies in Music: No. 16). 248p. 1995. 45.00 (*0-89990-072-0*) Harmonie Park Pr.

Cuyler, Margery. The Battlefield Ghost. LC 99-19146. (Illus.). 103p. (J). (gr. 2-4). 1999. 15.95 (*0-590-10848-4*, Pub. by Scholastic Inc) Penguin Putnam.

— The Biggest, Best Snowman. LC 97-36720. (Illus.). 32p. (J). (ps-2). 1998. 15.95 (*0-590-13922-3*, Pub. by Scholastic) Scholastic Inc.

***Cuyler, Margery.** The Biggest, Best Snowman. LC 97-36720. (Illus.). (J). (ps-2). 1998. pap. 15.95 (*0-590-13493-0*) Scholastic Inc.

Cuyler, Margery. The Christmas Snowman. (Illus.). 32p. (J). (ps-3). 1992. 14.45 (*1-55970-066-1*, Pub. by Arcade Pub Inc) Time Warner.

— Daisy's Crazy Thanksgiving. LC 90-4323. (Illus.). 32p. (J). (ps-2). 1995. 14.95 (*0-8050-0559-5*, Owlet BYR) H Holt & Co.

— Fat Santa. LC 86-31962. 32p. (J). (ps-2). 1995. 14.95 (*0-8050-0423-8*, Bks Young Read) H Holt & Co.

— Fat Santa. LC 86-31962. (Illus.). 32p. (J). (ps-2). 1995. pap. 4.95 (*0-8050-1167-6*, Bks Young Read) H Holt & Co.

— From Here to There. LC 98-19647. (Illus.). (J). (ps-2). 1999. 16.95 (*0-8050-3191-X*) H Holt & Co.

***Cuyler, Margery.** Invisible in the Third Grade. (Illus.). 82p. (J). (gr. 3-4). 1999. reprint ed. text 15.00 (*0-7881-6641-7*) DIANE Pub.

— 100th Day Worries. LC 98-562887. (Illus.). 32p. (J). (gr. k-2). 2000. per. 16.00 (*0-689-82979-5*) S&S Trade.

Cuyler, Margery. That's Good! That's Bad! LC 90-49353. (Illus.). 32p. (J). (ps-2). 1995. 15.95 (*0-8050-1535-3*, Bks Young Read); pap. 5.95 (*0-8050-2954-0*, Bks Young Read) H Holt & Co.

— That's Good That's Bad. 1993. 11.15 (*0-606-06054-5*, Pub. by Turtleback) Demco.

— That's Good, That's Bad. unabridged ed. (Illus.). (J). (ps-3). 1996. pap. 15.95 (*0-87499-376-8*) Live Oak Media.

— That's Good, That's Bad, 4 bks., Set. unabridged ed. (Illus.). (J). (ps-3). 1996. pap., teacher ed. 37.95 incl. audio (*0-87499-378-4*) Live Oak Media.

— Weird Wolf. LC 89-7541. (Illus.). 80p. (J). (gr. 2-4). 1995. 12.95 (*0-8050-0835-7*, Bks Young Read); pap. 4.95 (*0-8050-1643-0*, Owl) H Holt & Co.

— Weird Wolf. (J). 1991. 10.05 (*0-606-12142-0*, Pub. by Turtleback) Demco.

***Cuyler, Margery & LeVert, Mireille.** Goldilocks & the Three Bears. LC 99-43668. (J). 2000. 9.95 (*0-307-10235-1*, Goldn Books) Goldn Bks Pub Co.

Cuyler, Margery, ed. see Adkins, Jan.

Cuyler, Susanna. B. Rugged Books' Prime Material. (Illus.). 80p. (Orig.). 1993. pap. 10.00 (*0-9612018-6-X*) B RUGGED.

— A Companion to Japanese Literature, Culture, & Language. (Illus.). 93p. (Orig.). 1992. pap. 10.00 (*0-9612018-5-1*) B RUGGED.

— Jeanne Owens: Pictorial Biography. (Illus.). 125p. (Orig.). 1986. pap. 21.00 (*0-9612018-3-5*) B RUGGED.

— Modern Rugmaking & Tapestry Techniques: Speed Hook Tufting, Rya & Double-Time Latch. (Illus.). 120p. (Orig.). 1985. pap. 10.00 (*0-9612018-1-9*) B RUGGED.

— One Who Goes Everywhere: The Ubiquarian's Dictionary. (Illus.). 160p. (Orig.). 1988. pap. 10.00 (*0-9612018-4-3*) B RUGGED.

— Patriarchy's Demolition: A Year of Action. (Illus.). 178p. (Orig.). (C). 1993. pap. 20.00 (*0-9612018-8-6*) B RUGGED.

Cuypers, Stefaan E., jt. auth. see Bransen, Jan.

Cuyt, Annie. Pade Approximants for Operators: Theory & Applications. (Lecture Notes in Mathematics Ser.: Vol. 1065). ix, 138p. 1984. 29.95 (*0-387-13342-9*) Spr-Verlag.

Cuyt, Annie, ed. Nonlinear Numerical Methods & Rational Approximation. (C). 1988. text 206.50 (*90-277-2669-8*) Kluwer Academic.

— Nonlinear Numerical Methods & Rational Approximation II. LC 94-20809. (Mathematics & Its Applications Ser.: Vol. 296). 464p. (C). 1994. text 276.00 (*0-7923-2967-8*) Kluwer Academic.

Cuyt, Annie & Wuytack, L., eds. Nonlinear Methods in Numerical Analysis. (North-Holland Mathematics Studies: No. 136). x,278p. 1987. 114.00 (*0-444-70189-3*, North Holland) Elsevier.

Cuyugan, Ruben S., ed. see Lim King, Betty.

***Cuyuna Country Heritage Society Governing Board.** Cuyuna Country: A Peoples' History, Vol. I. LC 99-76697. (Illus.). 336p. 2000. 35.00 (*0-9677450-0-4*) Cuyuna Cntry Hert Pres.

Cuyvers, Luc. Into the Rising Sun: Vasco de Gama & the Search for the Sea Route to the East. (Illus.). 176p. 1999. 29.95 (*1-57500-064-4*, Pub. by TV Bks) HarpC.

— The Strait of Dover. 1986. lib. bdg. 96.00 (*90-247-3252-2*) Kluwer Academic.

***Cuyvers, Ludo & Kerremans, Bart, eds.** The International Social Issue: Social Dumping & Social Competition in the Global Economy. 125p. 1998. pap. 60.00 (*90-5095-065-5*, Pub. by Intersentia Uitgevers) Gaunt.

Cuza-Male, Belkis. Elvis - la Tumba Sin Sosiego: O la Verdadera Historia de Jon Burrows. (SPA., Illus.). 340p. (Orig.). (YA). 1994. pap. write for info. (*0-913827-09-6*) Linden Ln Pr.

— Elvis - the Unquiet Grave: Or the True Story of Jon Burrows. Padilla, Barbara, ed. Miller, David, tr. from SPA. (Illus.). 340p. (Orig.). (YA). 1994. pap. write for info. (*0-913827-10-X*) Linden Ln Pr.

Cuzan, Alfred G. & Behar, Joseph E. At the Crossroads of Development. viii, 174p. 1996. 66.00 (*90-04-10732-0*) Brill Academic Pubs.

Cuzin, Jean-Pierre. Fragonard: Life & Work. (Illus.). 384p. 1988. 85.00 (*0-8109-0949-9*, Pub. by Abrams) Time Warner.

Cuzin, Jean-Pierre, jt. auth. see Laclotte, Michel.

Cuzma, Kay, ed. The Ladder of Life Series: Activity & Song Book. 160p. (J). 1998. pap. 9.99 (*0-8280-1125-7*) Review & Herald.

— The Ladder of Life Series Nos. 1 & 2: Faith & Virtue Storybooks & Cassette. (J). 1998. 14.99 incl. audio (*0-8280-1302-0*) Review & Herald.

— The Ladder of Life Series Nos. 5 & 6: Patience & Godliness Storybooks & Cassette. (J). 1998. 14.99 incl. audio (*0-8280-1304-7*) Review & Herald.

— The Ladder of Life Series Nos. 7 & 8: Kindness & Love Storybooks & Cassette. (J). 1998. 14.99 incl. audio (*0-8280-1305-5*) Review & Herald.

Cuzner, Bernard. Silversmith's Manual. 2nd ed. (Illus.). 209p. 1979. 35.00 (*0-7198-0062-5*, Pub. by NAG Press) Antique Collect.

Cuzzort, Kindred E. Creation Therapy. 142p. 1997. pap. text 9.95 (*0-9662952-0-X*) Qatsiyr.

Cuzzort, R. P. Using Social Thought: The Nuclear Issue & Other Concerns. LC 88-34581. 342p. (C). 1989. pap. text 38.95 (*0-87484-800-8*, 800) Mayfield Pub.

Cuzzort, R. P. & King, Edith W. Twentieth-Century Social Thought. 5th ed. LC 94-78728. (Illus.). 512p. (C). 1994. pap. text 59.50 (*0-15-501750-0*, Pub. by Harcourt Coll Pubs) Harcourt.

Cvak, Ladislav, jt. ed. see Kren, Vladimik.

Cvancara, Alan M. Exploring Nature in Winter. LC 92-12560. (Naturalist's Bookshelf Ser.). (Illus.). 194p. 1992. pap. 17.95 (*0-8027-7385-0*) Walker & Co.

— A Field Manual for the Amateur Geologist: Tools & Activities for Exploring Our Planet. rev. ed. LC 94-18496. 352p. 1995. pap. 17.95 (*0-471-04430-X*) Wiley.

Cve, M. Donald, jt. auth. see Burns, E. Robert.

Cvelbar, R., jt. ed. see Emri, I.

Cvengros, Jerry, ed. Youth Football: A Complete Handbook. LC 88-43249. (Illus.). 296p. 1992. reprint ed. pap. 30.00 (*1-884125-45-X*) Cooper Pubng.

Cvernavaca language School Staff. Hablai Complete Spanish Video Course. (Illus.). 1200p. (YA). (gr. 6-12). 1998. pap. text 299.00 (*1-58214-049-9*) Mltilingl Bks.

Cvetan, Edward J. Hard Places: 15 Uncommon Short Stories. 175p. 1999. pap. 12.00 (*0-7392-0227-8*, PO3263) Morris Pubng.

Cvetanovska, Danica, et al, trs. The Moon in the Well: And Other Macedonian Folk Tales. (Illus.). 84p. 1990. 7.95 (*0-912678-74-7*) Greenfld Rev Lit.

Cvetic, Mirjam & Langacker, Paul, eds. Testing the Standard Model: TASI Workshop 1990. 936p. (C). 1991. text 124.00 (*981-02-0314-4*); pap. text 61.00 (*981-02-0315-2*) World Scientific Pub.

Cveticanin, L. Dynamics of Machines with Variable Mass. (Stability & Control Ser.: Vol. 7). 300p. 1998. text 120.00 (*90-5699-096-9*, ECU108) Gordon & Breach.

Cvetkov. Psychologie Sociale. (C). 1991. pap. write for info. (*0-03-998283-1*) Harcourt Coll Pubs.

Cvetkov, Alexander. Pawn Endings. Marfia, Jim, tr. from BUL. 69p. 1985. pap. 6.00 (*0-931462-47-9*) Chess Ent.

Cvetkov, Nikolai. Proletariat of the World Unite! . . . So We United! 1989, a Year to Remember. (Illus.). 38p. (Orig.). 1990. pap. 12.95 (*0-945490-01-1*) Carolina Pacific.

Cvetkovic, Dragos, et al. Eigenspaces of Graphs. LC 96-2860. (Encyclopedia of Mathematics & Its Applications Ser.: No. 66). 271p. (C). 1997. text 69.95 (*0-521-57352-1*) Cambridge U Pr.

Cvetkovic, Dragos M., et al. Spectra of Graphs: Theory & Applications. 1998. 125.00 (*3-527-29685-9*) Wiley.

Cvetkovich, Ann. Mixed Feelings: Feminism, Mass Culture & Victorian Sensationalism. LC 92-4457. x, 227p. (C). 1992. pap. text 19.00 (*0-8135-1857-1*) Rutgers U Pr.

An Asterisk (*) at the beginning of an entry indicates that the title is appearing for the first time.

Cvetkovich, Ann & Kellner, Douglas M., eds. Articulating the Global & the Local: Globalization & Cultural Studies. LC 96-9473. (Cultural Studies Ser.: No. 5). 1996. text 75.00 (0-8133-3219-2, Pub. by Westview) HarpC.
Cvetkovich, George, jt. ed. see Vlek, Charles.
Cvetkovich, George T., jt. auth. see Earle, Timothy C.
Cvetlovic, Dragos, et al, eds. Spectra of Graphs: Theory & Applications. LC 79-50490. (Pure & Applied Mathematics Ser.). 1980. text 142.00 (0-12-195150-2) Acad Pr.
Cviic, Christopher. Remaking the Balkans. (Chatham House Papers). 144p. 1991. pap. 14.95 (0-87609-114-1) Coun Foreign.
— Remaking the Balkans. 2nd ed. LC 98-130291. (Chatham House Papers). 128p. 1995. pap. 15.95 (1-85567-295-2) Bks Intl VA.
Cvijetic, Milorad. Coherent & Nonlinear Lightwave Communications. 315p. 1996. 109.00 (0-89006-590-X) Artech Hse.
Cvikota, Mark. Successful Hiring: A Practical Guide to Interviewing & Selecting Employees. LC 97-93288. 63p. (Orig.). 1997. pap. 9.95 (0-9656915-0-0) Inland Mgmt.
Cvikota, Tom, jt. ed. see Albers, Maura.
Cvitanovic, P., et al, eds. Quantum Chaos-Quantum Measurement. (C). 1992. text 202.50 (0-7923-1599-5) Kluwer Academic.
Cvitanovic, Predrag. Universality in Chaos. 2nd ed. (Illus.). 648p. 1989. pap. 62.00 (0-85274-260-6) IOP Pub.
***Cvitkovich, Eileen.** Bay County. (Images of America Ser.). (Illus.). 128p. 2000. pap. 18.99 (0-7385-0603-6) Arcadia Publng.
Cvjetanovic, B. & Grab, B. Dynamics of Acute Bacterial Diseases Epidemiological Models & Their Application in Public Health. (Bulletin Supplement Ser.: No. 56). 143p. 1978. text 12.00 (92-4-068561-8) World Health.
***Cvjetnicanin, George D., et al.** Film into Video: A Guide to Merging the Technologies. 2nd ed. LC 99-87344. (Illus.). 400p. 2000. pap. 49.95 (0-240-80411-2, Focal) Buttrwrth-Heinemann.
Cvjetnicanin, George D., jt. auth. see Kallenberger, Richard H.
C.W. Jamieson (formerly Chairman of the British Journal of Surgery, President of the Vascular S, ed. Concise Vascular Surgery. (Illus.). 352p. 1997. text 60.00 (0-412-82450-7, Pub. by E A) OUP.
Cwayna, Kevin. Knowing Where the Fountains Are: Stories & Stark Realities of Homeless Youth. 160p. 1993. 16.95 (0-925190-71-3) Fairview Press.
CWC Sports Inc., ed. see Atlanta Falcons Staff.
CWC Sports Inc., ed. see Buffalo Bills Staff.
CWC Sports Inc., ed. see Chicago Bears Staff.
CWC Sports Inc, ed. see Dallas Cowboys Staff.
CWC Sports Inc., ed. see Denver Broncos Staff.
CWC Sports Inc., ed. see Detroit Lions Staff.
CWC Sports Inc., ed. see Indianapolis Colts Staff.
CWC Sports Inc., ed. see Jacksonville Jaguars Staff.
CWC Sports Inc., ed. see Miami Dolphins.
CWC Sports Inc., ed. see Minnesota Vikings Staff.
CWC Sports Inc., ed. see New York Giants.
CWC Sports Inc., ed. see New York Jets.
CWC Sports Inc., ed. see Oakland Raiders Staff.
CWC Sports Inc., ed. see San Diego Chargers Staff.
CWC Sports Inc, ed. see Seattle Seahawks Staff.
CWC Sports Inc., ed. see Tampa Bay Buccaneers Staff.
CWC Sports Inc., ed. see Washington Redskins Staff.
Cwiakala, Martin, jt. auth. see Mayo, William E.
Cwieka, Raymond. Sources of the Polish Tradition, 3 vols., Set. pap. 25.00 (0-915277-01-8) R Cwieka.
Cwiekowski, Frederick J. The Beginnings of the Church. 1988. pap. 14.95 (0-8091-2926-4) Paulist Pr.
Cwikel, Michael, et al, eds. Interpolation Spaces & Related Topics. (Israel Mathematical Conference Proceedings Ser.: Vol. 5). 294p. 1992. pap. 40.00 (0-685-70694-X, IMCP/5C) Am Math.
Cwikel, Michael & Peetre, J. Interpolation Spaces & Allied Topics in Analysis: Proceedings of the Conference Held in Lund, Sweden, August 29 - September 1, 1983. (Lecture Notes in Mathematics Ser.: Vol. 1070). iii, 239p. 1984. 37.95 (0-387-13363-1) Spr-Verlag.
Cwikiel, Wilfred & Ford, Thomas W. Living with Michigan's Wetlands: A Landowner's Guide. LC 98-165323. viii, 132 p. 1997. write for info. (1-889313-00-9) Tip of Mitt.
Cwiklik, Robert. A. Philip Randolph & the Labor Movement. LC 92-32167. (Gateway Civil Rights Ser.). (Illus.). 32p. (J). (gr. 2-4). 1993. pap. 4.95 (1-56294-788-5); lib. bdg. 20.90 (1-56294-326-X) Millbrook Pr.
— Albert Einstein. (Barron's Solutions Ser.). (Illus.). 144p. (J). (gr. 3-6). 1987. pap. 6.95 (0-8120-3921-1) Barron.
— Bill Clinton: President of the 90's. LC 97-797. (Gateway Biographies Ser.). (Illus.). 48p. (J). (gr. 2-4). 1997. lib. bdg. 20.90 (0-7613-0129-1) Millbrook Pr.
— Bill Clinton: President of the 90's. rev. ed. (Gateway Biographies Ser.). (Illus.). 48p. (J). (gr. 2-4). 1997. pap. 8.95 (0-7613-0146-1) Millbrook Pr.
— King Philip. Furstinger, Nancy, ed. (Alvin Josephy's Biography of the American Indians Ser.). (Illus.). 144p. (J). (gr. 5-7). 1989. pap. 7.95 (0-382-09762-9); lib. bdg. 12.95 (0-382-09573-1, Silver Pr NJ) Silver Burdett Pr.
— Malcolm X & Black Pride. LC 92-23687. (Gateway Civil Rights Ser.). (Illus.). 32p. (J). (gr. 2-4). 1991. pap. 5.95 (1-878841-73-4); lib. bdg. 20.90 (1-56294-042-2) Millbrook Pr.
— Malcolm X & Black Pride. (Gateway Civil Rights Ser.). (J). 1991. 10.15 (0-606-01450-0, Pub. by Turtleback) Demco.
— Sequoyah. Furstinger, Nancy, ed. (Alvin Josephy's Biography of the American Indians Ser.). (Illus.). 142p. (J). (gr. 5-7). 1989. pap. 7.95 (0-382-09759-9); lib. bdg. 12.95 (0-382-09570-7, Silver Pr NJ) Silver Burdett Pr.
— Stokely Carmichael & Black Power. LC 92-11560. (Gateway Civil Rights Ser.). (Illus.). 32p. (J). (gr. 2-4). 1993. pap. 4.95 (1-56294-839-3); lib. bdg. 20.90 (1-56294-276-X) Millbrook Pr.
***CWIN Staff.** State of the Right of the Child 1998. 1998. pap. 23.00 (0-7855-7635-5) St Mut.
Cwinn, A. Adam & Grahovac, Steven. Emergency CT Scans of the Head: A Practical Atlas. LC 97-42384. (Illus.). 224p. 1998. text 69.95 (0-8151-2621-2, 31882) Mosby Inc.
CWL. Breaking the Law. (Security & Survival Ser.). 50p. 1985. pap. 18.00 (0-939856-55-7) Tech Group.
— Defensive Design & Construction in Retreat Buildings. LC 87-50170. (Urban & Rural Survival Ser.). (Illus.). 100p. (Orig.). (C). 1987. pap. 25.00 (0-939856-70-0) Tech Group.
— Document Preparation: Or Form-Filing for Fun & Profit. LC 87-51188. (Illus.). 80p. (Orig.). 1987. pap. 30.00 (0-939856-82-4) Tech Group.
— Financial & Personal Privacy. (Security & Survival Ser.). 75p. (Orig.). 1989. pap. 20.00 (0-939856-94-8) Tech Group.
— Force Major. 60p. (Orig.). 1987. pap. 20.00 (0-939856-83-2) Tech Group.
— How to Fix What Is Wrong with America. LC 88-51970. 55p. (Orig.). 1989. pap. 20.00 (0-939856-91-3) Tech Group.
— Individual Action: Sticking It to Someone or the System. 48p. (Orig.). 1987. pap. 15.00 (0-939856-78-6) Tech Group.
— Lifestyle Modifications: Urban & Rural Survival. (Security & Survival Ser.). (Illus.). 48p. 1987. pap. 20.00 (0-939856-73-5) Tech Group.
— Mail Drops. 2nd ed. (Security & Survival Ser.). 48p. (Orig.). 1987. pap. 18.00 (0-939856-76-X) Tech Group.
— Nasty Letter Writing for Revenge, Fun & Profit: (The Snitches' Handbook) LC 89-51054. (Illus.). 65p. 1989. 20.00 (0-939856-99-9) Tech Group.
— Rational Anarchy & What It Can Do for You. LC 88-50190. 54p. (Orig.). 1988. pap. 15.00 (0-939856-84-0) Tech Group.
— Retreat & Small Farm Management: Urban & Rural Survival. (Security & Survival Ser.). (Illus.). 48p. 1987. pap. 25.00 (0-939856-74-3) Tech Group.
— Surviving the Law. LC 86-61881. (Breaking the Law Ser.: Vol. 2). (Illus.). 55p. (Orig.). 1986. pap. 25.00 (0-939856-62-X) Tech Group.
CWLA North American Commission on Chemical Dependency & Child Welfare Staff. Children at the Front: A Different View of the War on Alcohol & Drugs. 1992. pap. 15.95 (0-87868-502-2) Child Welfare.
CWLA North American Kinship Care Policy & Practice. Kinship Care: A Natural Bridge. 1994. pap. 8.95 (0-87868-584-7) Child Welfare.
CWLA Staff. CWLA Agency Self-Improvement Checklist & Membership Requirements. rev. ed. 1996. pap. 8.95 (0-87868-529-4) Child Welfare.
— CWLA Cultural Competence Self-Assessment Instrument. 1993. pap. 25.95 (0-87868-506-5, CWLA Pr) Child Welfare.
Cworetzky, et al. Psychology, Human Relations & Organizations Communication. (Adaptable Courseware Ser.). pap. 22.25 (0-314-11357-6) Brooks-Cole.
CWRT Staff & Center for Waste Reduction & American Institute fo. Pollution Prevention: Homework & Design Problems for Engineering Curricula. 156p. 1992. pap. 40.00 (0-8169-0581-9, C-1) Am Inst Chem Eng.
Cy DeCosse Inc., Staff. Costura Con Acholchado Maguina. (Singer Sewing Reference Library). (SPA., Illus.). 128p. 1992. 17.95 (0-86573-280-9) Creat Pub Intl.
Cy DeCosse Inc. Staff. Costura Con Maquina de Overlock. (SPA., Illus.). 128p. 17.95 (0-86573-273-6) Creat Pub Intl.
— Costura Para el Hogar: Singer Biblioteca De Costura. (SPA., Illus.). 128p. 1987. 17.95 (0-86573-219-1) Creat Pub Intl.
Cy DeCosse Inc., Staff. Mas Costura para el Hogar. (Singer Sewing Reference Library). (SPA., Illus.). 128p. 1992. 17.95 (0-86573-271-X) Creat Pub Intl.
— Pantalones Con Ajuste Perfecto. (Singer Sewing Reference Library). (SPA., Illus.). 128p. 1992. 17.95 (0-86573-281-7) Creat Pub Intl.
— A Portfolio of Flooring Ideas. LC 94-49672. (Illus.). 96p. 1995. pap. 9.95 (0-86573-958-7) Creat Pub Intl.
— Quick & Easy Decorating Projects. LC 94-49671. (Singer Sewing Reference Library). (Illus.). 128p. 1995. 18.95 (0-86573-302-3); pap. 16.95 (0-86573-303-1) Creat Pub Intl.
Cy DeCosse Inc. Staff. Sewing for the Home. rev. ed. (Illus.). 128p. 1994. 18.95 (0-86573-305-8) Creat Pub Intl.
Cy DeCosse Incorporated Staff. Advanced Home Wiring. LC 91-37337. (Black & Decker Home Improvement Library). (Illus.). 128p. 1992. 16.95 (0-86573-718-5); pap. 14.95 (0-86573-719-3) Creat Pub Intl.
— America's Favorite Wild Game Recipes. LC 94-32784. (Hunting & Fishing Library). (Illus.). 128p. 1994. 19.95 (0-86573-044-X) Creat Pub Intl.
— Basic Wiring & Electrical Repairs, Vol. 7. LC 90-42688. (Black & Decker Home Improvement Library). (Illus.). 128p. 1990. 16.95 (0-86573-714-2); pap. 14.95 (0-86573-715-0) Creat Pub Intl.
— Bathroom Remodeling. LC 93-14916. (Black & Decker Home Improvement Library). 128p. 1993. 16.95 (0-86573-728-2) Creat Pub Intl.
— Bathroom Remodeling. LC 93-14916. (Black & Decker Home Improvement Library). (Illus.). 128p. 1993. pap. 14.95 (0-86573-729-0) Creat Pub Intl.
— Bedroom Decorating. LC 91-807. (Arts & Crafts for Home Decorating Ser.). (Illus.). 128p. 1991. 18.95 (0-86573-350-3); pap. 16.95 (0-86573-351-1) Creat Pub Intl.
— Building Decks, Vol. 5. LC 89-23708. (Black & Decker Home Improvement Library). (Illus.). 128p. 1990. 16.95 (0-86573-708-8); pap. 14.95 (0-86573-709-6) Creat Pub Intl.
— Building Porches & Patios. LC 95-46568. (Black & Decker Home Improvement Library). (Illus.). 128p. 1996. 16.95 (0-86573-697-9); pap. 14.95 (0-86573-698-7) Creat Pub Intl.
— Built-in Projects for the Home. LC 93-8783. (Black & Decker Home Improvement Library). (Illus.). 128p. 1993. 16.95 (0-86573-730-4); pap. 14.95 (0-86573-731-2) Creat Pub Intl.
— Carpentry: Remodeling. LC 92-16327. (Black & Decker Home Improvement Library). (Illus.). 128p. 1992. 16.95 (0-86573-720-7); pap. 14.95 (0-86573-721-5) Creat Pub Intl.
— Carpentry: Tools, Shelves, Walls, Doors. LC 88-23718. (Black & Decker Home Improvement Library). (Illus.). 128p. 1989. 16.95 (0-86573-704-5) Creat Pub Intl.
— Carpinteria - Carpentry: Herramientas Anaqueles-Paredes-Pyertas - Tools, Shelves, Walls, Doors.Tr. of Carpentry. (SPA., Illus.). 128p. 1993. 16.95 (0-86573-722-3) Creat Pub Intl.
— Como Ahorrar Tiempo en la Costura. (SPA., Illus.). 128p. 1991. 17.95 (0-86573-275-2) Creat Pub Intl.
— Construccion de Terrazas - Building Decks: Black & Decker. (SPA., Illus.). 128p. 1993. 16.95 (0-86573-725-8) Creat Pub Intl.
— Creative Accessories for the Home. LC 93-18665. (Arts & Crafts for Home Decorating Ser.). 128p. 1993. 18.95 (0-86573-359-7) Creat Pub Intl.
— Creative Accessories for the Home. LC 93-18665. (Arts & Crafts for Home Decorating Ser.). (Illus.). 128p. 1993. pap. 16.95 (0-86573-360-0) Creat Pub Intl.
— Creative Sewing Ideas. LC 90-42685. (Singer Sewing Reference Library). (Illus.). 128p. 1990. 18.95 (0-86573-258-2); pap. 16.95 (0-86573-259-0) Creat Pub Intl.
— Creative Window Treatments. LC 91-42084. (Arts & Crafts for Home Decorating Ser.). (Illus.). 128p. 1992. 18.95 (0-86573-352-X); pap. 16.95 (0-86573-355-4) Creat Pub Intl.
— Deck & Landscaping Ideas. LC 96-1752. (Black & Decker Home Improvement Library). (Illus.). 192p. 1996. 18.95 (0-86573-688-X) Creat Pub Intl.
— Decoracion de Alcobas: Bedroom Decorating. (Illus.). 128p. 1995. 18.95 (958-9345-13-1) Creat Pub Intl.
— Decorating for Christmas. LC 92-5358. (Arts & Crafts for Home Decorating Ser.). (Illus.). 128p. 1992. 18.95 (0-86573-353-8) Creat Pub Intl.
— Decorating with Paint & Wallcovering, Vol. 2. LC 88-9558. (Black & Decker Home Improvement Library). (Illus.). 128p. 1988. 16.95 (0-86573-702-9); pap. 14.95 (0-86573-703-7) Creat Pub Intl.
— Embellished Quilted Projects. LC 96-32855. (Singer Sewing Reference Library). (Illus.). 128p. 1996. 18.95 (0-86573-309-0); pap. 16.95 (0-86573-310-4) Creat Pub Intl.
— Everyday Home Repairs, Vol. 1. LC 87-30486. (Black & Decker Home Improvement Library). (Illus.). 1988. 16.95 (0-86573-700-2); pap. 14.95 (0-86573-701-0) Creat Pub Intl.
— Exterior Home Repairs & Improvements. LC 95-12393. (Black & Decker Home Improvement Library). (Illus.). 128p. 1995. 16.95 (0-86573-744-4); pap. 14.95 (0-86573-745-2) Creat Pub Intl.
— Flooring Projects & Techniques. LC 96-26990. (Black & Decker Home Improvement Library). (Illus.). 128p. 1996. 16.95 (0-86573-678-2); pap. 14.95 (0-86573-679-0) Creat Pub Intl.
— Home Accessories with Style: Step-by-Step Creative Decorating Ideas. LC 95-44654. (Illus.). 320p. 1996. 32.95 (0-86573-397-X) Creat Pub Intl.
— Home Masonry Projects & Repairs. LC 95-20877. (Black & Decker Home Improvement Library). (Illus.). 128p. 1995. 16.95 (0-86573-732-0); pap. 14.95 (0-86573-733-9) Creat Pub Intl.
— Home Plumbing Projects & Repairs, Vol. 6. LC 90-32979. (Black & Decker Home Improvement Library). (Illus.). 128p. 1990. 16.95 (0-86573-710-X); pap. 14.95 (0-86573-711-8) Creat Pub Intl.
— Installaciones Electricas Basicas. (Black & Decker Home Improvement Library). (Illus.). 128p. 1994. 16.95 (0-86573-734-7) Creat Pub Intl.
— Kitchen Remodeling, Vol. 4. LC 89-11833. (Black & Decker Home Improvement Library). (Illus.). 128p. 1989. 16.95 (0-86573-706-1) Creat Pub Intl.
— Landscape Design & Construction. LC 92-34457. (Black & Decker Home Improvement Library). (Illus.). 128p. 1993. 16.95 (0-86573-726-6); pap. 14.95 (0-86573-727-4) Creat Pub Intl.
— Metallic Finishes Etc. LC 96-28583. (Creative Touches Ser.). (Illus.). 64p. 1996. pap. 9.95 (0-86573-875-0) Creat Pub Intl.
— More Creative Sewing Ideas. LC 92-9272. (Singer Sewing Reference Library). (Illus.). 128p. 1992. 18.95 (0-86573-276-0); pap. 16.95 (0-86573-277-9) Creat Pub Intl.
— More Sewing for the Home, Vol. 9. LC 87-24556. (Singer Sewing Reference Library). (Illus.). 128p. 1987. 18.95 (0-86573-235-3); pap. 16.95 (0-86573-236-1) Creat Pub Intl.
— 101 Sewing Secrets, Vol. 12. LC 89-1416. (Singer Sewing Reference Library). (SPA.). 128p. 1989. 18.95 (0-86573-249-3) Creat Pub Intl.
— Painted Designs Etc. LC 96-26995. (Creative Touches Ser.). (Illus.). 64p. 1996. pap. 9.95 (0-86573-999-4) Creat Pub Intl.
— Papering Projects Etc. LC 96-28584. (Creative Touches Ser.). (Illus.). 64p. 1996. pap. 9.95 (0-86573-877-7) Creat Pub Intl.
— A Portfolio of Bathroom Ideas. LC 93-41245. (Illus.). 96p. 1994. pap. 9.95 (0-86573-926-9) Creat Pub Intl.
— A Portfolio of Bedroom Ideas. LC 95-21129. (Illus.). 96p. 1995. pap. 9.95 (0-86573-962-5) Creat Pub Intl.
— A Portfolio of Ceramic & Natural Tile Ideas. LC 96-15845. (Illus.). 96p. 1996. pap. 9.95 (0-86573-991-9) Creat Pub Intl.
— A Portfolio of Fence & Gate Ideas. LC 96-18889. (Illus.). 96p. (Orig.). 1996. pap. 9.95 (0-86573-992-7) Creat Pub Intl.
— A Portfolio of Fireplace Ideas. LC 96-7947. (Illus.). 96p. 1996. pap. 9.95 (0-86573-990-0) Creat Pub Intl.
— A Portfolio of Landscaping Ideas. LC 94-20074. (Illus.). 96p. 1994. pap. 9.95 (0-86573-940-4) Creat Pub Intl.
— A Portfolio of Lighting Ideas. LC 95-40811. (Illus.). 96p. 1996. pap. 9.95 (0-86573-963-3) Creat Pub Intl.
— A Portfolio of Outdoor Furnishing Ideas. LC 96-31463. (Illus.). 96p. (Orig.). 1996. pap. 9.95 (0-86573-885-8) Creat Pub Intl.
— A Portfolio of Storage Ideas. LC 96-1754. (Illus.). 96p. 1996. pap. 9.95 (0-86573-964-1) Creat Pub Intl.
— A Portfolio of Unique Deck Ideas. LC 95-20475. (Illus.). 96p. 1995. pap. 9.95 (0-86573-974-9) Creat Pub Intl.
— A Portfolio of Water Garden & Specialty Landscape Ideas. LC 95-44655. (Illus.). 96p. 1996. pap. 9.95 (0-86573-975-7) Creat Pub Intl.
— A Portfolio of Window & Window Treatment Ideas. LC 94-36571. (Illus.). 96p. 1995. pap. 9.95 (0-86573-956-0) Creat Pub Intl.
— Quick & Easy Sewing Projects. LC 93-25891. (Singer Sewing Reference Library). (Illus.). 128p. 1993. 18.95 (0-86573-288-4); pap. 16.95 (0-86573-289-2) Creat Pub Intl.
— Quilt Projects by Machine. LC 92-19930. (Singer Sewing Reference Library). (Illus.). 128p. 1992. 18.95 (0-86573-278-7); pap. 16.95 (0-86573-279-5) Creat Pub Intl.
— Quilted Projects & Garments. LC 95-12392. (Singer Sewing Reference Library). (Illus.). 128p. 1995. 18.95 (0-86573-300-7); pap. 16.95 (0-86573-301-5) Creat Pub Intl.
— Quilting by Machine, Vol. 14. LC 89-49031. (Singer Sewing Reference Library). (Illus.). 128p. 1990. 18.95 (0-86573-253-1); pap. 16.95 (0-86573-254-X) Creat Pub Intl.
— Refinishing & Finishing Wood. LC 94-30079. (Black & Decker Home Improvement Library). (Illus.). 128p. 1994. 16.95 (0-86573-739-8); pap. 14.95 (0-86573-740-1) Creat Pub Intl.
— Remodelaciones de Cocinas. (Black & Decker Home Improvement Library). (SPA., Illus.). 128p. 1994. 16.95 (0-86573-736-3) Creat Pub Intl.
— Reparaciones Frecuentes en el Hogar - Everyday Home Repairs: Black & Decker. (SPA., Illus.). 128p. 1993. 16.95 (0-86573-724-X) Creat Pub Intl.
— Reparaciones y Proyectos de Plomeria. (Black & Decker Home Improvement Library). (SPA., Illus.). 128p. 1994. 16.95 (0-86573-735-5) Creat Pub Intl.
— Ropa Fina Tecnicas de Alta Costura: Singer Biblioteca de Costura. (SPA., Illus.). 128p. 17.95 (0-86573-223-X) Creat Pub Intl.
— Ropa para Deportistas: Singer Biblioteca de Costura. (SPA., Illus.). 128p. 1994. 17.95 (0-86573-227-2) Creat Pub Intl.
— Ropa para Ninos - Sewing for Children. (Singer Biblioteca de Costura Ser.). (SPA., Illus.). 128p. 1992. 17.95 (0-86573-272-8) Creat Pub Intl.
— Sewing for Children, Vol. 10. LC 88-23701. (Singer Sewing Reference Library). (Illus.). 128p. 1988. 18.95 (0-86573-243-4); pap. 16.95 (0-86573-244-2) Creat Pub Intl.
— Sewing for Special Occasions. LC 93-17641. (Singer Sewing Reference Library). (Illus.). 128p. 1994. pap. 16.95 (0-86573-287-6) Creat Pub Intl.
— Sewing for Special Occasions, Vol. 4. LC 93-17641. (Singer Sewing Reference Library). (Illus.). 128p. 1994. 18.95 (0-86573-286-8) Creat Pub Intl.
— Sewing for the Home. rev. ed. (Illus.). 128p. 1994. pap. 16.95 (0-86573-299-X) Creat Pub Intl.
— Sewing Projects for the Home. LC 91-4680. (Singer Sewing Reference Library). (Illus.). 128p. 1991. 18.95 (0-86573-262-0); pap. 16.95 (0-86573-263-9) Creat Pub Intl.
— Sewing with an Overlock, Vol. 11. LC 88-31343. (Singer Sewing Reference Library). (Illus.). 128p. 1989. 18.95 (0-86573-247-7) Creat Pub Intl.
— Singer Children's Clothes, Toys & Gifts Step-by-Step. LC 95-30810. (Illus.). 320p. 1995. 29.95 (0-86573-304-X) Creat Pub Intl.
— Singer Creative Gifts & Projects Step-by-Step. LC 93-17642. (Illus.). 320p. 1993. 29.95 (0-86573-290-6) Creat Pub Intl.
— Sponging Etc. LC 96-15848. (Creative Touches Ser.). (Illus.). 64p. 1996. pap. 9.95 (0-86573-996-X) Creat Pub Intl.
— Stenciling Etc. LC 96-15849. (Creative Touches Ser.). (Illus.). 64p. 1996. pap. 9.95 (0-86573-995-1) Creat Pub Intl.
— Stone Finishes, Etc. LC 96-15846. (Creative Touches Ser.). (Illus.). 64p. 1996. pap. 9.95 (0-86573-997-8) Creat Pub Intl.
— Swags Etc. LC 96-26996. (Creative Touches Ser.). (Illus.). 64p. 1996. pap. 9.95 (0-86573-876-9) Creat Pub Intl.
— Tecicas e Ideas para Eiupar Su Taller. (Black & Decker Home Improvement Library). (SPA., Illus.). 128p. 1994. 16.95 (0-86573-737-1) Creat Pub Intl.

C

— Timesaving Sewing, Vol. 8. LC 87-649. (Singer Sewing Reference Library). (Illus.). 128p. 1987. 18.95 (*0-86573-215-9*) Creat Pub Intl.

— Valances Etc. LC 96-15847. (Creative Touches Ser.). (Illus.). 64p. 1996. pap. 9.95 (*0-86573-998-6*) Creat Pub Intl.

— Window Treatments. LC 96-41124. (Singer Sewing Reference Library). (Illus.). 128p. 1996. 18.95 (*0-86573-407-0*); pap. 16.95 (*0-86573-408-9*) Creat Pub Intl.

Cy DeCosse Incorporated Staff & Black & Decker Incorporated Staff. Maximizing Minimal Space. LC 96-18878. (Portable Workshop Ser.). (Illus.). 96p. 1996. spiral bd. 14.95 (*0-86573-670-7*) Creat Pub Intl.

Cy DeCosse Incorporated Staff, jt. auth. see Clancy, Gary.

Cy Decosse Staff. Accesorios Creativos Para el Hogar: 76 Proyectos e Ideas. (SPA., Illus.). 128p. 1995. 18.95 (*958-9345-14-X*, Pub. by Monteverde Ltd) Creat Pub Intl.

Cy DeCosse Staff. Arreglos Con Flores Secas y de Seda. (SPA., Illus.). 128p. 1996. 17.95 (*0-86573-400-3*) Creat Pub Intl.

Cy Decosse Staff. Arreglos con Flores Secas y de Seda. (SPA.). 1995. 18.95 (*958-9345-17-4*, Pub. by Monteverde Ltd) Creat Pub Intl.

Cy DeCosse Staff. Creating Fashion Accessories. LC 92-32804. (Singer Sewing Reference Library). (Illus.). 128p. 1993. 18.95 (*0-86573-284-1*); pap. 16.95 (*0-86573-285-X*) Creat Pub Intl.

— Decoracion De Cocinas. (SPA., Illus.). 128p. 1996. 17.95 (*0-86573-395-3*) Creat Pub Intl.

— Decoracion De Comedores. (SPA., Illus.). 128p. 1996. 17.95 (*0-86573-393-7*) Creat Pub Intl.

Cy Decosse Staff. Decoracion de Salas: 104 Proyectos e Ideas. (SPA., Illus.). 128p. 1995. 18.95 (*958-9345-15-8*, Pub. by Monteverde Ltd) Creat Pub Intl.

Cy DeCosse Staff. Decorando Su Hogar Para Navidad. (SPA., Illus.). 128p. 1996. 17.95 (*0-86573-394-5*) Creat Pub Intl.

— Pintura Decorativa. (SPA., Illus.). 128p. 1996. pap. text 17.95 (*0-86573-392-9*) Creat Pub Intl.

Cyba, Eva, jt. ed. see De Bruijn, Jeanne.

Cybenko, G., et al, eds. The Mathematics of Information Coding, Extraction & Distribution. LC 98-31464. (IMA Volumes in Mathematics & Its Applications Ser.: Vol. 107). (Illus.). 143p. 1999. 59.95 (*0-387-98665-0*) Spr-Verlag.

Cybenko, George, jt. ed. see Bojanczyk, Adam.

***Cybergeek Group Staff.** Bizarre Internet Sites. (Illus.). 64p. 2000. pap. 5.95 (*1-889647-53-5*) Boston Am.

***Cybergnostics Inc. Staff.** Cyberstats: An Introduction to Statistics. 2000. 38.00 (*0-534-37828-5*) Thomson Learn.

Cyberia Staff. Webwise: The Cyberia Guide to Smart Web Publishing. 1997. pap. text 39.95 incl. cd-rom (*0-07-709312-7*) McGraw.

Cyberkath@traveltales.com. Cybercafes: A Worldwide Guide for Travelers. 2nd ed. 1998. pap. text 9.95 (*1-890762-01-6*) Wandering Trav.

CyberMedia Staff. Official Tech Support Yellow Pages. 1996. pap. text 19.95 incl. cd-rom (*1-887556-21-4*) Cybermedia.

Cybernautice Staff. Net Results: Web Marketing that Works. LC 97-72165. 392p. 1998. 29.99 (*1-56830-414-5*) Hayden.

Cyberspace Consortium Staff. Perv's Guide to the Net. 316p. (Orig.). 1996. mass mkt. 6.95 (*1-56333-471-2*, Rhinoceros) Masquerade.

Cybriwsky, Roman. Historical Dictionary of Tokyo. LC 96-38164. (Historical Dictionaries of Cities Ser.: No. 1). 256p. 1996. 49.00 (*0-8108-3234-8*) Scarecrow.

— Toyko: The Shogun's City at the 21st Century. 2nd ed. LC 97-50189. 272p. 1998. pap. 49.95 (*0-471-97187-1*) Wiley.

Cybriwsky, Roman A. Japan: Nippon. LC 94-9227. (American Geographical Society Around the World Program Ser.). 64p. 1994. pap. 13.95 (*0-939923-41-6*) M & W Pub Co.

***Cybriwsky, Roman A.** Tokyo, the Shogun's City at the 21st Century. 2nd ed. LC 97-50189. (World Cities Ser.). 272p. 1998. 100.00 (*0-471-97869-8*) Wiley.

Cybulski, Andrzej & Moulijn, Jacob A. Structured Catalysts & Reactors. LC 97-33104. (Chemical Industries Ser.). (Illus.). 664p. 1997. text 215.00 (*0-8247-9921-6*) Dekker.

Cybulski, Jerome S. A Greenville Burial Ground: Human Remains & Mortuary Elements in British Columbia Coast Prehistory. (Mercury Ser.: ASC No. 146). (Illus.). 268p. 1994. pap. 19.95 (*0-660-14008-X*, Pub. by CN Mus Civilization) U of Wash Pr.

Cybulski, Jerome S., jt. ed. see Sigmon, Becky A.

Cychowski, Lucille, ed. see Everett, Joann M.

Cyclops Design Team Staff. Project Cyclops: A Design Study of a System for Detecting Extraterrestrial Intelligence. 2nd ed. Oliver, Bernard M. & Billingham, John, eds. (Illus.). 256p. 1996. pap. 20.00 (*0-9650707-0-0*) SETI League.

Cycon, H. L., et al, eds. Schrodinger Operators: With Application to Quantum Mechanics & Global Geometry. (Texts & Monographs in Physics). (Illus.). ix, 319p. 1987. 49.95 (*0-387-16758-7*) Spr-Verlag.

Cycon, Robert & Sitarz, Darrell. Go Karting! A Guide to the World's Most Popular Motorsport. 2nd rev. ed. (Illus.). 112p. 1997. pap. 4.95 (*0-9661467-1-9*) Kart Mktg Grp.

— 1998 Karting Industry Buyer's Guide. 4th rev. ed. (Illus.). 106p. 1998. pap. 5.95 (*0-9661467-0-0*) Kart Mktg Grp.

Cycon, Robert, jt. ed. see Sitarz, Darrell.

Cydulka, Rita K., jt. auth. see Herr, Robert D.

Cyert, Richard M. Behavioral Theory of the Firm. 2nd ed. 1992. 43.95 (*0-631-17451-6*) Blackwell Pubs.

Cyert, Richard M. & DeGroot, Morris H. Bayesian Analysis & Uncertainty in Economic Theory. (Probability & Statistics Ser.). (Illus.). 224p. 1986. 65.00 (*0-8476-7471-1*) Rowman.

Cyert, Richard M. & Mowery, David C., eds. The Impact of Technological Change on Employment & Economic Growth. 480p. 1988. text 39.95 (*0-88730-290-4*, HarpBusn) HarpInfo.

— Technology & Employment: Innovation & Growth in the U. S. Economy. LC 87-42807. (Illus.). 239p. 1987. reprint ed. pap. 74.10 (*0-608-04257-9*, 206501200012) Bks Demand.

Cyert, Richard M., jt. auth. see Cohen, Kalman J.

***Cyford, Janet.** The Ring of Chairs: A Medium's Story of Her Training by Spirit Guides. xviii, 214p. 2000. 21.95 (*0-9678296-0-7*) Thirteen.

Cygan, Adam Jan. The United Kingdom Parliament & European Union Legislation. LC 98-185196. (Studies in Law: Vol. 2). 248p. 1998. 73.00 (*90-411-9650-1*) Kluwer Law Intl.

***Cyganski, David, et al.** Information Technology: Inside & Outside. 500p. 2000. 80.00 (*0-13-011496-0*, Prentice Hall) P-H.

***Cygelman, Adele.** Palm Springs Modern: Houses in the California Desert. LC 98-48811. (Illus.). 192p. 1999. 50.00 (*0-8478-2091-2*, Pub. by Rizzoli Intl) St Martin.

Cygne, Patrice De, see De Cygne, Patrice.

Cygnus Solutions Staff, jt. auth. see Stallman, Richard M.

Cyliani. Hermes Unveiled. Smith, Patrick, ed. Smith, Patrick J., tr. from FRE. (Alchemical Studies Ser.: No. 2). (Orig.). 1997. pap. 8.95 (*1-55818-357-4*, Alchemical) Holmes Pub.

Cylinder, Paul D., et al. Wetlands Regulation: A Complete Guide to Federal & California Programs. (Illus.). 384p. 1995. pap. text 40.00 (*0-923956-20-4*) Solano Pr.

Cylke, F. Kurt, Jr. The Environment. LC 93-7472. 100p. (C). 1997. pap. text 14.00 (*0-06-501638-6*) Addson-Wesley Educ.

Cylke, F. Kurt, Jr., jt. auth. see Buechler, Steven M.

Cylke, F. Kurt, Jr., jt. ed. see Scarpitti, Frank R.

Cylkowski, G. J. Developing a Career in Sports & Athletics. (Illus.). 175p. 1988. pap. 24.95 (*0-317-59360-9*) Mouvement Pubns.

Cylkowski, Greg J. The Almanac of Sports Contacts: The Global Resource Guide for Addresses in the Sports Marketplace. 345p. (Orig.). (C). 1998. pap. text 18.95 (*0-9636449-1-2*) Athletic Achieve.

— Developing a Lifelong Contract in the Sports Marketplace. 2nd rev. ed. (Illus.). 400p. (C). 1998. pap. text, per. 20.95 (*0-9636449-0-4*) Athletic Achieve.

Cylkowski, Greg J. & Staiffer, Kathleen. The Womansport Directory: The Women's Sports Bible. (Illus.). 195p. (Orig.). (C). 1995. pap. write for info. (*0-9636449-3-9*) Athletic Achieve.

CYMA-McGraw Hill Staff. The CYMA Bookkeeper. 1987. student ed. 49.00 incl. disk (*0-07-830800-3*) McGraw.

***Cymbala, Jim.** Fe Viva. (SPA.). 1999. pap. text 8.99 (*0-8297-2176-2*) Vida Pubs.

Cymbala, Jim. Fresh Faith: What Happens When Real Faith Ignites God's People. LC 99-35508. 192p. 1999. 17.99 (*0-310-23007-1*) Zondervan.

— Fresh Wind, Fresh Fire: What Happens When God's Spirit Invades the Hearts of His People. LC 96-50966. 188p. 1997. 16.99 (*0-310-21188-3*) Zondervan.

— Fresh Wind, Fresh Fire ITPE: What Happens When God's Spirit Invades the Heart of His People. 224p. 1997. pap. 10.99 (*0-310-21416-5*) Zondervan.

— Fuego Vivo, Viento Fresco.Tr. of Fresh Wind, Fresh Fire. (SPA.). 2000. pap. 7.99 (*0-8297-0621-6*) HarpC.

Cymbala, Jim & Merrill, Dean. Fresh Faith: What Happens When Real Faith Ignites God's People. pap. 10.99 (*0-310-23189-2*) HarpC.

Cymbala, Michael A., jt. ed. see Batastini, Robert J.

Cymbala, Michael A., ed. see Haugen, Marty.

Cymbula, Michael A., jt. ed. see Batastini, Robert J.

Cymbula, Michael A., ed. see Haugen, Marty.

Cymerman, John E. Farm Animals Punch-Out Stencils. (Illus.). (J). (gr. k-3). 1993. pap. 3.95 (*0-486-27437-3*) Dover.

— Reptiles & Amphibians Punch-Out Stencils. (Illus.). (J). (gr. 4-7). 1993. pap. 3.95 (*0-486-27665-1*) Dover.

— Wild Animals Punch-Out Stencils. (Illus.). (J). (gr. k-3). 1994. pap. 3.95 (*0-486-27971-5*) Dover.

Cymet, David. From Ejido to Metropolis, Another Path: An Evaluation on Ejido Property Rights & Informal Land Development in Mexico City. LC 92-10122. (American University Studies: Regional Studies: Ser. XXI, Vol. 6). XIV, 275p. (C). 1993. text 51.95 (*0-8204-1908-7*) P Lang Pubng.

Cymri, Chrys. Dragon Reforged. LC 94-68161. 320p. (Orig.). 1995. pap. 5.99 (*0-7869-0177-2*, Pub. by TSR Inc) Random.

— Dragons Can Only Rust. 320p. (Orig.). 1995. pap. 0.05 (*0-7869-0157-8*, Pub. by TSR Inc) Random.

Cymrot, Allen. Critical Real Estate Issues in the Nineties. 200p. 1992. 18.95 (*0-9633472-0-9*) C R Pub.

— Street Smart Real Estate Investing: Allen Cymrot's Strategies for Increasing Your Net Worth. (Illus.). 288p. 1993. reprint ed. 21.95 (*0-9633472-2-5*); reprint ed. pap. 19.95 (*0-9633472-1-7*) C R Pub.

Cynar, ed. Conference on Simulation in Engineering Education, 1989. 128p. 1989. pap. 30.00 (*0-911801-46-4*, SEE89-1) Soc Computer Sim.

Cynaumon, Dana, jt. auth. see Cynaumon, Greg.

Cynaumon, Greg & Cynaumon, Dana. Empowering Single Parents: Ten Ways to Increase Your Effectiveness. pap. 10.99 (*0-8024-7942-1*, 132) Moody.

Cynewulf. The Christ of Cynewulf. (BCL1-PR English Literature Ser.). 294p. 1992. reprint ed. lib. bdg. 79.00 (*0-7812-7164-9*) Rprt Serv.

— The Christ of Cynewulf: A Poem in Three Parts; the Advent, the Ascension, & the Last Judgement. Cook, Albert S., ed. LC 74-114906. (Select Bibliographies Reprint Ser.). 1977. 28.95 (*0-8369-5310-X*) Ayer.

— The Christ of Cynewulf: A Poem in Three Parts; the Advent, the Ascension, & the Last Judgement. Cook, Albert S., ed. LC 73-178524. reprint ed. 46.50 (*0-404-56538-7*) AMS Pr.

— Elene. Gradon, P. O., ed. (Old English Ser.). 1966. pap. text 9.95 (*0-89197-573-X*) Irvington.

— Elene: An Old English Poem. Kent, Charles W., ed. LC 77-178525. reprint ed. 32.50 (*0-404-56539-5*) AMS Pr.

— Juliana. Woolf, Rosemary, ed. (Old English Ser.). 1966. pap. text 7.95 (*0-89197-574-8*) Irvington.

Cynk, Jerzy B. The Polish Air Force at War: The Official History, 1939-1943. 336p. 1998. 59.95 (*0-7643-0559-X*) Schiffer.

— The Polish Air Force at War The Official History: The Official History, 1943-1945. 336p. 1998. 59.95 (*0-7643-0560-3*) Schiffer.

Cynkin, Simme. Occupational Therapy. 1979. 17.00 (*0-316-16610-3*, Little Brwn Med Div) Lppncott W & W.

Cynkin, Simme & Robinson, Anne M. Occupational Therapy. 2nd ed. 384p. 1989. text 48.00 (*0-316-16611-1*) Lppncott W & W.

Cynober, L., et al. Pharmacological Nutrition Immune Nutrition. (Illus.). 147p. 1995. pap. text 45.00 (*3-88603-543-3*, Pub. by W Zuckschwerdt) Scholium Intl.

Cynober, Luc A., ed. Amino Acid Metabolism & Therapy in Health & Nutritional Disease. LC 94-37722. 480p. 1995. boxed set 244.95 (*0-8493-8962-3*) CRC Pr.

Cynthia. The Night There Was Thunder & Stuff. (Illus.). 32p. (J). Date not set. pap. 4.95 (*1-895562-67-8*, Pub. by Wood Lake Bks) Logos Prods.

Cynthia, Nicole. Sweet Foolishness. 36p. (Orig.). 1985. pap. 2.95 (*0-9609794-2-5*) A Foster.

Cyparski, Emisha A. Reflections. 1997. 8.95 (*0-533-12410-7*) Vantage.

Cypert, Chuck. Mountain Bike! Texas & Oklahoma. (Mountain Bike Ser.). 384p. 1998. pap. text 14.95 (*0-89732-258-4*) Menasha Ridge.

Cypert, Samuel. The Power of Self-Esteem. 80p. 1993. pap. 10.95 (*0-8144-7798-4*) AMACOM.

Cypert, Samuel A. Believe & Achieve: W. Clement Stone's 17 Principles of Success. 288p. 1991. mass mkt. 5.99 (*0-380-76377-X*, Avon Bks) Morrow Avon.

— The Success Breakthrough: Get What You Want from Your Career, Your Relationships, & Your Life. 256p. (Orig.). 1993. mass mkt. 4.99 (*0-380-77151-9*, Avon Bks) Morrow Avon.

Cypert, Samuel A., ed. see Hill, Napoleon.

Cypess, Sandra M., ed. Essays in Romance Languages & Literature Including Latin American. 196p. 1979. reprint ed. 12.50 (*0-87291-130-6*) Coronado Pr.

Cypess, Sandra M., et al. Women Authors of Modern Hispanic South America: A Bibliography of Literary Criticism & Interpretation. LC 89-10889. 168p. 1989. 26.00 (*0-8108-2263-6*) Scarecrow.

Cypher, Ellen, ed. Watch What I Do: Programming by Demonstration. LC 93-18319. 672p. 1993. 60.00 (*0-262-03213-9*) MIT Pr.

Cypher, James M. & Dietz, James L. The Process of Economic Development. LC 96-38305. 576p. (C). 1997. 110.00 (*0-415-11027-0*); pap. 32.99 (*0-415-11028-9*) Routledge.

Cypher, John. Bob Kleberg & the King Ranch: A World-Wide Sea of Grass. (Illus.). 251p. (Orig.). 1996. pap. 14.95 (*0-292-71187-5*) U of Tex Pr.

— Bob Kleberg & the King Ranch: A Worldwide Sea of Grass. LC 94-22454. (Illus.). 280p. 1995. 29.95 (*0-292-71171-9*) U of Tex Pr.

Cypher, Robert & Sanz, Jorge L. The SIMD Model of Parallel Computation. LC 93-27497. (Illus.). 149p. 1994. 49.95 (*0-387-94139-8*) Spr-Verlag.

Cyphers, Ann. Chalcatzingo, Morelos: Estudio de Ceramica y Sociedad. 366p. 1992. pap. 14.00 (*968-36-2185-6*, UN004) UPLAAP.

— Descifrando los Misterios de la Cultura Olmeca: Una Exposicion Museografica de los Resultados del Proyecto Arqueologico San Lorenzo Tenochtitlan. (SPA., Illus.). 32p. 1995. pap. 11.50 (*1-877812-69-2*, UN047) UPLAAP.

***Cyphert.** Communication at Work. 2002. pap. 44.00 (*0-324-07067-5*) Sth-Wstrn College.

Cypres, Linda. Let's Speak Business English, Set. 256p. pap. 18.95 incl. audio (*0-7641-7306-5*) Barron.

Cypress, Harold, jt. auth. see Gopal, Christopher.

Cypress, Sandra M. La Malinche in Mexican Literature: From History to Myth. LC 91-15702. (Texas Pan American Ser.). (Illus.). 255p. (C). 1991. pap. 15.95 (*0-292-75134-6*); text 27.50 (*0-292-75131-1*) U of Tex Pr.

Cypress, Sandra M., jt. ed. see Nigro, Kirsten F.

Cypress Semiconductor Staff. Learning VHDL with WARP2. 600p. (C). 1996. 80.00 (*0-201-89573-0*) Addison-Wesley.

Cypress Woodlands Junior Forum Staff. Wild about Texas: A Bouquet of Recipes, Wild Flowers & Wines. (Illus.). 244p. 1989. reprint ed. write for info. (*0-9622009-0-5*) Cypress-Woodlands.

Cyprian. The World Council of Churches & the Interfaith Movement. LC 97-69632. 1997. write for info. (*0-911165-28-2*) Ctr Trad Orthodox.

Cyprian, Judy. Teaching Human Sexuality: A Guide for Parents & Other Caregivers. LC 97-49122. 1998. pap. 18.95 (*0-87868-661-4*, 6614, CWLA Pr) Child Welfare.

Cyprian of Carthage, St. De Lapsis & de Ecclesiae Catholicae Unitate. Benevot, Maurice, ed. (Oxford Early Christian Texts Ser.). 1971. 36.00 (*0-19-826804-1*) OUP.

— The Lapsed & the Unity of the Church. 1982. pap. 3.95 (*0-89981-038-1*) Eastern Orthodox.

— Letters, 1-81. Donna, Rose B., tr. LC 65-12906. (Fathers of the Church Ser.: Vol. 51). 352p. 1964. 21.95 (*0-8132-0051-2*) Cath U Pr.

— Life & Works of St. Cyprian of Carthage, 10 vols., Set. pap. 15.00 (*0-89981-040-3*) Eastern Orthodox.

— On Mortality. 1986. pap. 1.50 (*0-89981-064-0*) Eastern Orthodox.

Cyprian, Saint. Exhortation to Martyrdom. 1993. pap. 1.95 (*0-89981-145-0*) Eastern Orthodox.

Cyprian, Saint. St. Cyprian, the Lapsed, the Unity of the Catholic Church. Burghardt, Walter J. et al, eds. LC 57-7364. (Ancient Christian Writers Ser.: No. 25). 132p. 1957. 12.95 (*0-8091-0260-9*) Paulist Pr.

Cyprian, St. Treatises. Deferrari, Roy J. et al, trs. LC 77-81349. (Fathers of the Church Ser.: Vol. 36). 372p. 1958. 21.95 (*0-8132-0036-9*) Cath U Pr.

Cyprys, Ruth A. A Jump for Life. large type unabridged ed. 368p. 1998. 25.95 (*0-7531-5086-7*, 150867) ISIS Pub.

— A Jump for Life: A Survivor's Journal from Nazi-Occupied Poland. Potter, Elaine, ed. (Illus.). 256p. 1999. reprint ed. pap. 17.95 (*0-8264-1097-9*) Continuum.

***Cyprys, Ruth Altbeker.** Jump for Life. large type unabridged ed. 1999. pap. 19.95 (*0-7531-5057-3*, 150573, Pub. by ISIS Lrg Prnt) ISIS Pub.

Cypser, Cora E. The Creation of Kindness. (Illus.). 328p. (C). 1994. 15.00 (*0-9625774-3-X*) Kim Pathways.

— Lion & Lamb. (Illus.). 95p. (Orig.). 1992. pap. 7.95 (*0-9625774-4-8*) Kim Pathways.

— The Rocks Are Shouting! LC 97-68489. (Illus.). 368p. 1997. pap. 15.00 (*0-9625774-2-1*) Kim Pathways.

— Seasonings. (Illus.). 86p. (Orig.). 1992. pap. 7.95 (*0-9625774-5-6*) Kim Pathways.

— Think on These Things. LC 98-68153. (Illus.). 104p. 1998. pap. 9.00 (*1-892063-01-8*) Kim Pathways.

— Versings & Conversings. 1992. pap. 7.95 (*0-9625774-7-2*) Kim Pathways.

— Wandering in the Wilderness. (Illus.). 160p. 1995. pap. 8.00 (*0-9625774-1-3*) Kim Pathways.

Cypser, Rudolph J. Communications Architecture for Distributed Systems. LC 76-52673. (Illus.). 1978. text 52.75 (*0-201-14458-1*) Addison-Wesley.

Cypser, Rudolph J., ed. Communications for Cooperating Systems: OSI, SNA, & TCP-IP. (Systems Programming Ser.). (Illus.). 736p. (C). 1991. 67.00 (*0-201-50775-7*) Addison-Wesley.

Cyr, Annette. Goodnews Bees & Tulip Trees. (J). (gr. k-2). 1995. pap. 8.95 incl. audio (*0-7608-0490-7*); pap. 4.95 (*1-56801-790-1*) Sundance Pub.

— Goodnews Bees & Tulip Trees, Big bk. (J). (gr. k-2). 1995. pap. 17.95 (*1-56801-789-8*) Sundance Pub.

Cyr, Arthur. British Defense: Policy & Process. (CISA Working Papers: No. 13). 35p. (Orig.). 1978. pap. 15.00 (*0-86682-012-4*) Ctr Intl Relations.

— Liberal Politics in Britain. rev. ed. 290p. 1988. 39.95 (*0-88738-209-6*) Transaction Pubs.

Cyr, Arthur I. After the Cold War: American Foreign Policy in Europe & Asia. LC 96-40848. 1997. text 40.00 (*0-8147-1559-1*) NYU Pr.

— After the Cold War: American Foreign Policy in Europe & Asia. LC 99-50151. 1999. pap. text 20.00 (*0-8147-1595-8*) NYU Pr.

Cyr, Casey. Metta Morpheus. (Illus.). 80p. (Orig.). 1995. pap. 7.00 (*1-885175-05-1*) Hozomeen Pr.

Cyr, Cheryl, jt. auth. see Shumate, Shelia.

Cyr, Dianne H. & Reich, Blaize H., eds. Scaling the Ivory Tower: Stories from Women in Business School Faculties. LC 95-45416. 224p. 1996. 57.95 (*0-275-95085-9*, Praeger Pubs); pap. 21.95 (*0-275-95673-3*, Praeger Pubs) Greenwood.

Cyr, Dianne J. The Human Resource Challenge of International Joint Ventures. LC 95-19465. 224p. 1995. 62.95 (*0-89930-919-4*, Quorum Bks) Greenwood.

Cyr, Donald G. Marketing Your Product. 3rd ed. 170p. 1998. pap. text 14.95 (*1-55180-145-0*) Self-Counsel Pr.

Cyr, Frank W. Responsibility for Rural-School Administration: Allocation of Responsibilities in the Administration of Schools in Rural Areas. LC 70-176703. (Columbia University. Teachers College. Contributions to Education Ser.: No. 579). reprint ed. 37.50 (*0-404-55579-9*) AMS Pr.

Cyr, Geneieve St., see St. Cyr, Geneieve.

Cyr, Helen W. A Filmography of the Third World, 1976-1983: An Annotated List of 16mm Films. LC 84-23564. 285p. 1985. 31.00 (*0-8108-1768-3*) Scarecrow.

— The Third World in Film & Video, 1984-1990. LC 90-25883. 256p. 1991. 31.00 (*0-8108-2380-2*) Scarecrow.

Cyr, Helene. Handmade Forests: The Treeplanter's Experience. LC 98-31181. (Illus.). 144p. 1999. pap. 19.95 (*0-86571-393-6*, Pub. by New Soc Pubs) Consort Bk Sales.

Cyr, John E., et al. Real Estate Brokerage. 4th ed. 470p. 1995. pap. 37.95 (*0-7931-1065-3*, 1965-0104, Real Estate Ed) Dearborn.

***Cyr, John E., et al.** Real Estate Brokerage a Management Guide. 5th ed. LC 99-10261. 1999. pap. 43.40 (*0-7931-3155-3*) Dearborn.

Cyr, Mary. Performing Baroque Music. 256p. (C). 1998. pap. 25.95 (*1-84014-659-1*, Pub. by Ashgate Pub) Ashgate Pub Co.

— Performing Baroque Music. (Illus.). 254p. 1998. pap. 19.95 (*1-57467-043-3*, Amadeus Pr) Timber.

Cyr, Mary, ed. see Martin, Francois.

Cyr, Ruth N. Ruth's Primer of Africa. 368p. 1996. 59.00 (*1-880836-07-6*) Pine Isl Pr.

An Asterisk (*) at the beginning of an entry indicates that the title is appearing for the first time.

— Ruth's Primer of Africa. rev. ed. Alward, Edgar C., ed. (Illus.). 388p. 1998. text 89.00 (*1-891016-27-X*) Esparto Pr.

CYRCE - Circle for Youth Research Cooperation in E, ed. The Puzzle of Integration. (European Yearbook on Youth Policy & Research Ser.: Vol. 1). xv, 339p. (C). 1995. lib. bdg. 101.55 (*3-11-014565-0*) De Gruyter.

Cyre, Walling, jt. ed. see Tepfenhart, William M.

Cyrelson, David. Great Tips: The Ultimate "How To" Manual for Waiters & Waitresses. 2nd rev. ed. 112p. 1996. pap. 14.95 (*0-9669681-0-7*) Great Tips.

Cyrene, Joseph. Brzemie Krzyza. LC 85-62388.Tr. of Burden of the Cross. (POL., Illus.). 80p. (Orig.). 1985. pap. text 8.00 (*0-930401-03-4*) Artex Pub.

Cyrgatis, Ray. Golf Directories - U. S. A. Vol. 1: Philadelphia Metro Edition. (Illus.). 1999. mass mkt. 11.95 (*1-928696-25-2*) Golf Direct USA.

— Golf Directories - U. S. A. Vol. 3: New York Metro Edition. (Illus.). 376p. 1999. mass mkt. 11.95 (*1-928696-00-7*) Golf Direct USA.

Cyriax, George, ed. World Index of Economic Forecasts. LC 78-56982. (Praeger Special Studies). 395p. 1978. 295.00 (*0-275-90288-9*, C0288, Praeger Pubs) Greenwood.

Cyriax, James. The Slipped Disc. 1986. 5.95 (*0-684-16646-1*) S&S Trade.

— Textbook of Orthopaedic Medicine. 8th ed. 1983. text 89.00 (*0-7216-0777-2*, W B Saunders Co) Harcrt Hlth Sci Grp.

— Textbook of Orthopaedic Medicine, Vol. 2. 11th ed. 1984. text 63.00 (*0-7216-0960-0*, W B Saunders Co) Harcrt Hlth Sci Grp.

— Textbook of Orthopaedic Medicine: Diagnosis of Soft Tissue Lesions, Vol. 1. 8th ed. (Illus.). 1982. text 89.00 (*0-7020-0935-0*) Bailliere Tindall.

Cyriax, James & Coldham, Margaret. Textbook of Orthopaedic Medicine: Treatment by Manipulation, Massage & Injection, Vol. 2. 11th ed. (Illus.). 288p. 1984. text 63.00 (*0-7020-1037-5*) Bailliere Tindall.

Cyriax, Oliver. Crime: An Encyclopedia. (Illus.). 468p. 1995. 35.00 (*0-233-98821-1*, Pub. by Andre Deutsch) Trafalgar.

Cyril. St. Cyril of Alexandria Vol. 1: Letters 1-50. McEnerney, John I., tr. LC 85-5692. (Fathers of the Church Ser.: Vol. 76-77). 253p. 1987. reprint ed. pap. 78.50 (*0-7837-9149-6*, 204994900004) Bks Demand.

***Cyril & Russell, Norman.** Cyril of Alexandria. LC 99-55830. (Early Church Fathers Ser.). 272p. (C). 2000. text. write for info. (*0-415-18250-6*) Routledge.

Cyril of Alexandria. Cyril of Alexandria: Select Letters. Wickham, Lionel R., ed. & tr. by. (Oxford Early Christian Texts Ser.). 284p. 1983. text 65.00 (*0-19-826810-6*) OUP.

Cyril of Alexandria, St. Letters, 51-110. McEnerney, John, tr. LC 85-5692. (Fathers of the Church Ser.: Vol. 77). 204p. 1987. 31.95 (*0-8132-0077-6*) Cath U Pr.

Cyril of Jerusalem. On the Christian Sacraments. Cross, F. L., ed. 83p. 1977. pap. 7.95 (*0-913836-39-7*) St Vladimirs.

— Works, Vol. I. McCauley, Leo P. & Stephenson, Anthony A., trs. LC 68-55980. (Fathers of the Church Ser.: Vol. 61). 287p. 1969. 17.95 (*0-8132-0061-X*) Cath U Pr.

— Works, Vol. II. McCauley, Leo P. & Stephenson, Anthony A., trs. LC 68-55980. (Fathers of the Church Ser.: Vol. 64). 273p. 1970. 16.95 (*0-8132-0064-4*) Cath U Pr.

Cyril of Scythopolis. Cyril of Scythopolis: The Lives of the Monks of Palestine. Price, R. M., tr. from GER. (Cistercian Studies: No. 114). 368p. 1991. 34.95 (*0-87907-714-X*); pap. 17.95 (*0-87907-914-2*) Cistercian Pubns.

Cyrillus, Salvator. Codices Graeci Manuscripti: Regiae Bibliothecae Borbonicae, 2 vols. in 1. viii, 802p. 1992. reprint ed. 200.00 incl. 3.5 hd (*3-487-09602-1*) G Olms Pubs.

Cyrino, Monica S. In Pandora's Jar: Lovesickness in Early Greek Poetry. 208p. (C). 1995. lib. bdg. 39.50 (*0-8191-9752-1*) U Pr of Amer.

***Cyrkozuch, Alonda.** The Lovell Legend. LC 99-93969. (Illus.). 28p. (J). (ps-12). 1999. pap. 5.95 (*1-929098-00-6*, 01) Stry Teller.

— Queenie's Pond: The Barker Brothers Arrive. LC 99-93968. 24p. (J). (ps-12). 1999. pap. 5.95 (*1-929098-01-4*, 02) Stry Teller.

Cyrot, Michel & Pavuna, Davor. Elemental & High-TC Superconductivity. LC 92-14874. 300p. (C). 1992. text 55.00 (*981-02-0143-5*); pap. text 30.00 (*981-02-0144-3*) World Scientific Pub.

Cyrpinski, Andy J. Audio-Visual Aids in Health Biology: Index of Modern Information. LC 88-47968. 150p. 1990. pap. 44.50 (*1-55914-211-1*) ABBE Pubs Assn.

— Audio-Visual Aids in Health Biology: Index of Modern Information. LC 88-47968. 150p. 1990. 47.50 (*1-55914-210-3*) ABBE Pubs Assn.

Cyrs, Thomas E. Essential Skills for College Teaching: An Instructional Systems Approach. 3rd ed. (Illus.). 300p. (Orig.). 1994. pap. text 45.00 (*0-9628477-1-2*) NM State U CED.

— Teaching at a Distance with the Merging Technologies: An Instructional Systems Approach. Conway, Eugenia D., ed. & des. by. (Illus.). 300p. (Orig.). 1997. pap. text 48.00 (*0-9628477-3-9*) NM State U CED.

Cyrs, Thomas E. & Smith, Frank A. Teleclass Teaching: A Resource Guide. 2nd ed. (Illus.). 368p. (C). 1990. pap. text 38.00 (*0-9628477-0-4*) NM State U CED.

Cyrus. Bug Garden C. LC 99-6799. 2001. Price not set. (*0-15-202205-8*) Harcourt Coll Pubs.

Cyrus, Cinda. Well Cementing. Paxson, Jeanette R., ed. (Oil & Gas Production Ser.). (Illus.). 82p. (Orig.). (C). 1983. pap. text 15.00 (*0-88698-112-3*, 3.30610) PETEX.

Cyrus, Cinda, ed. see Hosmanek, Max.

Cyrus, Digby & Robson, Nigel. Bird Atlas of Natal. (Illus.). 340p. 1980. 19.95 (*0-86980-215-1*, Pub. by Univ Natal Pr) Intl Spec Bk.

Cyrus, Duane, ed. Vital Grace: The Black Male Dancer. (Illus.). 208p. 1999. 60.00 (*3-908161-31-2*) Abbeville Pr.

Cyrus, Harry R., pseud. Righteousness Exalts a Nation. Klemm, Barbara A., ed. LC 94-70326. 232p. pap. 15.00 (*0-9639386-0-6*) Fortune Prnting.

Cyrus, Kurt. Slow Train to Oxmox. LC 98-10732. 32p. (J). (ps-k). 1998. 16.00 (*0-374-37047-8*) FS&G.

— Tangle Town. LC 96-24269. (Illus.). 32p. (J). (ps-3). 1997. 16.00 (*0-374-37384-1*) FS&G.

***Cyrus, Virginia.** Experiencing Race, Class & Gender in the United States. 1999. pap. text. write for info. (*0-7674-1179-X*, 1179-X) Mayfield Pub.

— Experiencing Race, Class & Gender in the United States. 3rd ed. LC 99-33824. 515p. 1999. pap. text 33.95 (*0-7674-1003-3*, 1003-3) Mayfield Pub.

Cyrus William Rice & Co. Copper in Feedwater to Supercritical Steam Generating Units. 55p. 1965. 8.25 (*0-317-34503-6*, 69) Intl Copper.

Cyrusa, Lee, jt. auth. see Mundt, Richard W.

Cyscon, Philip. The Collected Adventures of the Monkey Man. (Illus.). 96p. (Orig.). 1993. pap. 9.95 (*1-879260-18-2*) Evanston Pub.

Cytowic, Richard E. The Man Who Tasted Shapes. LC 97-38214. (Illus.). 252p. 1998. pap. text 16.00 (*0-262-53152-6*, Bradford Bks) MIT Pr.

— The Man Who Tasted Shapes: A Bizarre Medical Mystery Offers Revolutionary Insights into Emotions, Reasoning & Consciousness. 272p. 1995. mass mkt. 11.99 (*0-446-67068-5*, Pub. by Warner Bks) Little.

— Nerve Block for Common Pain. (Illus.). viii, 96p. 1991. 30.00 (*0-387-97147-5*) Spr-Verlag.

— Synesthesia. (Neuropsychology Ser.). (Illus.). 315p. 1989. 111.95 (*0-387-96807-5*) Spr-Verlag.

— The Neurological Side of Neuropsychology. LC 95-1528. (Illus.). 529p. 1996. 62.50 (*0-262-03231-7*, Bradford Bks) MIT Pr.

Cytron, Barry D. Fire! The Library Is Burning. (Illus.). 56p. (J). (gr. 4 up). 1988. lib. bdg. 15.93 (*0-8225-0525-8*, Lerner Publctns) Lerner Pub.

Cytron, Phyllis. Myriam Mendilow: The Mother of Jerusalem. LC 93-15119. (YA). (gr. 5 up). 1993. lib. bdg. 23.93 (*0-8225-4919-0*, Lerner Publctns) Lerner Pub.

Cytryn, Leon & McKnew, Donald H., Jr. Growing up Sad: Childhood Depression & Its Treatment. 216p. 1998. pap. 13.95 (*0-393-31788-9*) Norton.

— Growing Up Sad: Childhood Depression & Its Treatment. LC 95-41233. 240p. 1996. 25.00 (*0-393-03827-0*) Norton.

Cytrynbaum, Solomon & Lee, Susan A., eds. Transformations in Global & Organizational Systems: Changing Boundaries in the 90s (Proceedings of the 10th Scientific Meeting of the A. K. Rice Institute) LC 93-84339. 170p. 1993. 28.00 (*0-614-19469-5*) Rice Inst.

Cytter, N. & Hutchison, J. Dictionary of the Kanuri Language. (PALL Ser.: No. 13). (ENG & KAU.). 200p. 1990. pap. 75.40 (*90-6765-412-4*) Mouton.

Cyvin, S. J. & Gutman, I. Kekule Structures in Benzenoid Hydrocarbons. (Lecture Notes in Chemistry Ser.: Vol. 46). xv, 348p. 1988. 59.95 (*0-387-18801-0*) Spr-Verlag.

Cyvin, S. J., et al. Theory of Coronoid Hydrocarbons. (Lecture Notes in Chemistry Ser.: Vol. 54). (Illus.). 172p. 1991. 35.95 (*0-387-53577-2*) Spr-Verlag.

— Theory of Coronoid Hydrocarbons II. LC 94-19284. (Lecture Notes in Chemistry Ser.: Vol. 62). 1994. 80.95 (*0-387-58138-3*) Spr-Verlag.

Cywinski, Jozef. The Essentials in Pressure Monitoring: Blood & Other Body Fluids. (Tardieu Ser.: No. 3). (Illus.). 120p. 1980. pap. text 59.00 (*90-247-2385-X*) Kluwer Academic.

Cywinski, Steve, ed. 1994 National Directory of Fire Chiefs & Emergency Departments, Vol. 3. 950p. 1994. 41.00 (*1-880245-06-X*) SPAN Pub.

— 1992 National Directory of Fire Chiefs, Rescue & Emergency Departments, Vol. I. 1992. 30.00 (*1-880245-02-7*) SPAN Pub.

Cywinski, Steve, ed. see Span Publishing, Inc., Staff.

Cyzevs'kyj, Dmytro & Luckyj, George S. A History of Ukrainian Literature: From the 11th to the End of the 19th Century. 2nd ed. Ferguson, Dolly et al, trs. from UKR. LC 96-25814. 800p. 1997. lib. bdg. 75.00 (*1-56308-522-4*) Libs Unl.

Cyzyk, Janet L. Baltimore County Design: Administrator's Manual. Maryland State Dept. of Education, ed. (Correlates Test to Adult Literacy Ser.). (Illus.). 128p. 1988. pap. text, student ed. 3.20 (*0-8428-9500-0*) Cambridge Bk.

— Entering the Reader's World, 3 bks., Bk. 1. Mendyk, Dennis, ed. (Adult Literacy Training Ser.). (Illus.). 160p. 1988. pap. text 6.00 (*0-8428-9503-5*) Cambridge Bk.

— Entering the Reader's World, 3 bks., Bk. 2. Mendyk, Dennis, ed. (Adult Literacy Training Ser.). (Illus.). 160p. 1988. pap. text 6.00 (*0-8428-9504-3*) Cambridge Bk.

— Entering the Reader's World, 3 bks., Bk. 3. Mendyk, Dennis, ed. (Adult Literacy Training Ser.). (Illus.). 160p. 1988. pap. text 6.30 (*0-8428-9505-1*) Cambridge Bk.

Czada, R. M., et al, eds. Institutions & Political Choice: On the Limits of Rationality. 340p. 1997. pap. 47.50 (*90-5383-498-2*, Pub. by VUB Univ Pr) Paul & Co Pubs.

Czaikowski, John, jt. auth. see Kidd, Steven.

Czaja, Albert J. & Dickinson. Chronic Active Hepatitis: The Mayo Clinic Experience. (Gastroenterology Ser.: Vol. 2). 368p. 1986. 160.00 (*0-8247-7615-1*) Dekker.

Czaja, Ludwik, jt. ed. see Chlebus, Bogdan.

Czaja, Paul C. Writing with Light: A Simple Workshop in Basic Photography. LC 72-93261. 96p. (J). (gr. 6 up). 1973. 12.95 (*0-85699-068-X*) Chatham Pr.

Czaja, Ronald & Blair, Johnny. Designing Surveys: A Guide to Decisions & Procedures. LC 94-48280. (Research Methods & Statistics Ser.). 1995. pap. 19.95 (*0-8039-9056-1*) Pine Forge.

Czaja, W., ed. Synchrotron Radiation: Selected Experiments in Condensed Matter Physics. (Monte Verita Ser.). viii, 179p. 1991. 53.00 (*0-8176-2594-1*) Birkhauser.

Czajkowski, Alexandre C. Amazing Creatures. LC 98-7126. Orig. Title: The Animal World. (Illus.). 80p. (J). (gr. 4 up). 2000. lib. bdg. 25.30 (*0-88682-945-3*, Creat Educ) Creative Co.

Czajkowski, Chris. Diary of a Wilderness Dweller. (Illus.). 224p. (Orig.). 1997. pap. 13.95 (*1-55143-059-2*) Orca Bk Pubs.

— Nuk Tessli: The Life of a Wilderness Dweller. (Illus.). 224p. 1999. pap. 14.95 (*1-55143-133-5*) Orca Bk Pubs.

Czajkowski, John, jt. auth. see Kidd, J. Steven.

Czajkowski, S. M., jt. ed. see Shumaker, S. A.

Czajowski, Chris. To Stalk the Oomingmak . . . An Artist's Arctic Journal. LC 89-85389. (Illus.). 112p. 1989. 19.95 (*0-9616679-1-5*) Aquarelle Pr.

Czaki, F., et al. Power Electronics. 708p. 1980. 410.00 (*0-569-08185-8*, Pub. by Collets) St Mut.

— Power Electronics, Problems Manual. Karpati, A. & Magyar, P., eds. 476p. 1979. 435.00 (*0-569-08554-3*, Pub. by Collets) St Mut.

Czamanski, Daniel. Privatization & Restructuring of Electricity Provision. LC 98-41088. (Privatizing Government Ser.). 168p. 1999. 59.95 (*0-275-95687-3*, Praeger Pubs) Greenwood.

Czandema, A. W., ed. Methods of Surface Analysis. (Methods & Phenomena Ser.: Vol. 1). xiv, 482p. 1989. reprint ed. 198.50 (*0-444-41344-8*) Elsevier.

Czander, William M. The Psychodynamics of Work & Organizations: Theory & Application. LC 93-13405. 408p. 1993. lib. bdg. 48.00 (*0-89862-284-0*) Guilford Pubns.

***Czanderna, A. W., et al, eds.** Beam Effects, Surface Topography, & Depth Profiling in Surface Analysis. (Methods of Surface Characterization Ser.: Vol. 5). (Illus.). 450p. (C). 1998. 125.00 (*0-306-45896-9*, Plenum Trade) Perseus Pubng.

Czanderna, A. W., et al, eds. Specimen Handling, Preparation, & Treatments for Surface Characterization. LC 98-45737. (Methods of Surface Characterization Ser.: No. 4). (Illus.). 320p. (C). 1999. text 127.50 (*0-306-45887-X*, Kluwer Plenum) Kluwer Academic.

Czanderna, A. W. & Hercules, D. M. Ion Spectroscopies for Surface Analysis. (Methods of Surface Characterization Ser.: Vol. 2). (Illus.). 486p. (C). 1991. text 125.00 (*0-306-43792-9*, Kluwer Plenum) Kluwer Academic.

Czaplewski, Russ. Captive of the Cheyenne: The Story of Nancy Jane Morton & the Plum Creek Massacre. Wallace, Bob, ed. LC 93-72732. (Illus.). 230p. (Orig.). (C). 1993. 17.95 (*0-9637898-1-3*); pap. 12.95 (*0-9637898-0-5*) Daw Cnty Hist Mus.

Czaplewski, Russ, jt. auth. see German, Rex.

Czaplicka, John, et al, contrib. by. Emigrants & Exiles: A Lost Generation of Austrian Artists in America 1920-1950. LC 96-17716. 1996. write for info. (*0-941680-16-9*) M&L Block.

Czaplicki, Jon S., et al, contrib. by. Hohokam Archaeology along Phase B of the Tucson Aqueduct-Central Arizona Project, No. 1, Pt. 1. (Archaeological Ser.: Vol. 178). (Illus.). 252p. 1989. 14.95 (*1-889747-62-9*) Ariz St Mus.

— Hohokam Archaeology along Phase B of the Tucson Aqueduct-Central Arizona Project, No. 1, Pt. 2. (Archaeological Ser.: Vol. 178). (Illus.). 244p. 1989. 14.95 (*1-889747-63-7*) Ariz St Mus.

— Hohokam Archaeology along Phase B of the Tucson Aqueduct-Central Arizona Project: Excavations at Water World (AZ AA:16:94) A Rillito Phase Ballcourt Village in the Avra Valley, No. 1, Pt. 2. (Archaeological Ser.: Vol. 178). (Illus.). 327p. 1989. 14.95 (*1-889747-64-5*) Ariz St Mus.

Czaplicki, Jon S. & Mayberry, James D. An Archaeological Assessment of the Middle Santa Cruz River Basin, Rillito to Green Valley, Arizona, for the Proposed Tucson Aqueduct Phase B, Central Arizona Project. (Archaeological Ser.: No. 164). (Illus.). 134p. 1983. pap. 8.95 (*1-889747-35-1*) Ariz St Mus.

Czaplinski, Czeslaw. Styka Family Saga. (Illus.). 202p. 1990. pap. 25.00 (*0-912757-16-7*) Bicenten.

Czaplinski, Lane. Making the Basketball Team: Get off the Bench & into the Game. (Illus.). 144p. (YA). (gr. 7 up). 1996. pap. 12.00 (*1-885758-08-1*) Quality Sports.

Czaplinski, Suzanne M. Sexism in Award-Winning Picture Books. (Illus.). 1973. pap. 2.50 (*0-912786-21-3*) Know Inc.

Czapski, G., ed. Fifth Conference on Superoxide & Superoxide Dismutase. (Free Radical Research Communications Ser.). 460p. 1991. pap. text 1050.00 (*3-7186-5125-4*, Harwood Acad Pubs) Gordon & Breach.

Czar, Catherine C., jt. auth. see Hrones, Stephen.

***Czaran, Tamas.** Spatiotemporal Models of Population & Community Dynamics. LC 97-68492. 304p. 1998. write for info. (*0-412-57550-7*) Kluwer Academic.

Czarkowski, Dariusz, jt. auth. see Kazimierczuk, Marian K.

Czarnecka, Ewa & Fiut, Aleksander. Conversations with Czeslaw Milosz. Lourie, Richard, tr. 1987. 27.95 (*0-15-122591-5*) Harcourt.

Czarnecki, Charles A., jt. auth. see Selman, Belle F.

Czarnecki, D. B. & Blinn, D. W. Diatoms of Southwestern U. S. A. Diatoms of the Colorado River in Grand Canyon National Park & Vicinity, Vol. 2. (Illus.). 1978. pap. text 40.00 (*3-7682-1182-7*) Lubrecht & Cramer.

Czarnecki, George A., ed. see Killen-Courtney, Dawn.

Czarnecki, Gerald M. Our Way of Life: CVQ Customer Valued Quality. 46p. 1995. pap. write for info. (*0-9648538-3-3*) UNC Inc.

Czarnecki, Greg & Czarnecki, Karen. Highroad Guide to the Pennsylvania Mountains, 5 vols. LC 98-87786. (Highroad Guides Ser.). (Illus.). 352p. 1998. pap. 18.95 (*1-56352-474-0*) Longstreet.

Czarnecki, J., ed. Chemistry of Interfaces. (Materials Science Forum Ser.: Vols. 25 & 26). 600p. 1988. text 200.00 (*0-87849-567-3*, Pub. by Trans T Pub) Enfield Pubs NH.

Czarnecki, Jack. A Cook's Book of Mushrooms. LC 94-48906. (Illus.). 208p. 1995. 30.00 (*1-885183-07-0*) Artisan.

— Joe's Book of Mushroom Cookery. 352p. 1997. 17.95 (*0-02-862174-3*) Macmillan.

— Portobello Cookbook. LC 96-47967. (Illus.). 84p. 1997. 14.95 (*1-885183-75-5*) Artisan.

Czarnecki, Jan. The Goths in Ancient Poland. LC 74-20750. 1975. 12.95 (*0-87024-264-4*) U of Miami Pr.

Czarnecki, John, jt. auth. see Long, Howie.

Czarnecki, Karen, jt. auth. see Czarnecki, Greg.

***Czarnecki, Krysztof & Eisenecker, Ulrich.** Generative Programming: Methods, Tools, & Applications. 640p. 2000. pap. 44.95 (*0-201-30977-7*) Addison-Wesley.

Czarnecki, Lois R. The Six Wrinkled Woos. (Illus.). 32p. (J). (gr. k-3). 1992. 17.95 (*0-9627275-0-4*) Ohana Pr.

Czarnecki, Mark, tr. see Bourassa, Andre G.

Czarnecki, Mark T. Benchmarking Strategies for Health Care Management. LC 94-18369. 1994. 99.00 (*0-8342-0604-8*, S153) Aspen Pub.

— Managing by Measuring: How to Improve Your Organization's Performance Through Effective Benchmarking. LC 98-35080. xi, 271 p. 1999. 50.95 (*0-8144-0390-5*) AMACOM.

Czarnecki, Michael, jt. ed. see Franklin, Walt.

Czarnek, Robert, jt. ed. see Indebetouw, Guy.

***Czarniawska, Barbara.** A City Reframed: Managing Warsaw in the 1990s. (Cities & Regions Ser.: Vol. 4). 186p. 2000. text 42.00 (*90-5700-565-4*, Harwood Acad Pubs) Gordon & Breach.

Czarniawska, Barbara. Writing Management: Organization Theory as a Literary Genre. LC 99-31593. (Illus.). 144p. 1999. pap. 24.95 (*0-19-829614-2*); text 65.00 (*0-19-829613-4*) OUP.

Czarniawska, Barbara & Sevon, Guje, eds. Translating Organizational Change. (De Gruyter Studies in Organization: No. 56). xii, 284p. (C). 1996. pap. text 29.95 (*3-11-014868-4*) De Gruyter.

— Translating Organizational Change. (Studies in Organization: Vol. 56). xii, 284p. 1996. text 79.95 (*3-11-014869-2*) De Gruyter.

Czarniawska-Joerges, Barbara. Economic Decline & Organizational Control. LC 88-36483. 168p. 1989. 55.00 (*0-275-93277-X*, C3277, Praeger Pubs) Greenwood.

— Exploring Complex Organizations: A Cultural Perspective. LC 91-36605. 256p. 1992. pap. 79.40 (*0-608-04808-9*, 205258500004) Bks Demand.

— Exploring Complex Organizations: A Cultural Perspective. 264p. 1992. 48.00 (*0-8039-4454-3*); pap. 22.95 (*0-8039-4455-1*) Sage.

— Ideological Control in Non-Ideological Organizations. LC 87-32759. 153p. 1988. 57.95 (*0-275-92794-6*, C2794, Praeger Pubs) Greenwood.

— Narrating the Organization: Dramas of Institutional Identity. LC 96-20954. (New Practices of Inquiry Ser.). 1997. lib. bdg. 45.00 (*0-226-13228-5*) U Ch Pr.

— Narrative Approach in Organization Studies. LC 97-21225. (Qualitative Research Methods Ser.). 1998. 24.00 (*0-7619-0662-2*); pap. 10.50 (*0-7619-0663-0*) Sage.

Czarniawska-Joerges, Barbara, ed. Good Novels, Better Management: Reading Organisational Realities in Fiction. 335p. 1994. text 59.00 (*3-7186-5646-9*, Harwood Acad Pubs); pap. text 27.00 (*3-7186-5647-7*, Harwood Acad Pubs) Gordon & Breach.

Czarnik, Anthony W., ed. Fluorescent Chemosensors for Ion & Molecule Recognition. LC 93-21067. (ACS Symposium Ser.: Vol. 538). (Illus.). 238p. 1993. text 75.00 (*0-8412-2728-4*, Pub. by Am Chemical) OUP.

Czarnik, Anthony W. & DeWitt, Sheila H., eds. A Practical Guide to Combinatorial Chemistry. LC 97-36358. (ACS Professional Reference Bks.). 360p. 1997. text 89.95 (*0-8412-3485-X*, Pub. by Am Chemical) OUP.

Czarnik, Anthony W., jt. auth. see Wilson, Stephen R.

***Czarnopys, Theresa S. & Santa, Thomas M.** Marian Shrines of the United States Series 1: A Pilgrim's Travel Guide. LC 98-20164. (Illus.). 240p. 1998. pap. 13.95 (*0-7648-0227-5*) Liguori Pubns.

Czarnota, Adam W., jt. auth. see Krygier, Martin.

***Czarnota, Lorna MacDonald.** Medieval Tales: That Kids Can Read & Tell. 96p. 2000. 21.95 (*0-87483-589-5*) August Hse.

— Medieval Tales: That Kids Can Read & Tell. 96p. (gr. 4-7). 2000. pap. 12.95 (*0-87483-588-7*) August Hse.

Czarnowski, M. S. Productive Capacity of Locality As a Function of Soil & Climate with Particular Reference to Forest Land. LC 64-16087. (Louisiana State University Studies, Biological Science Ser.: No. 5). 192p. reprint ed. pap. 59.60 (*0-608-14376-6*, 205187800013) Bks Demand.

Czarnowski, Stefan. Le Culte Des Heros et Ses Conditions Sociales. LC 74-25745. (European Sociology Ser.). 472p. 1975. reprint ed. 39.95 (*0-405-06500-0*) Ayer.

Czarra, Fred. Germany & the World. (ENG & GER.). 68p. (C). 1992. teacher ed., ring bd. 30.00 (*0-614-02982-1*) Amer Forum.

Czarra, Fred, ed. Guide to Historical Reading: Non-Fiction. 11th ed. 1983. 20.00 (*0-916882-03-9*) Heldref Pubns.

Czarsty. Stdy Gde/wkprs Acctng-baud 232. 2nd ed. 1998. 32.00 (*0-07-233039-2*) McGraw.

C

Czasak, Asia A. Nebula: Poetry. (Illus.). 30p. 1997. pap. 6.00 (*0-9642344-2-4*) A A Czasak.

Czaszar, A. & Czaszar, K. Foundations of General Topology. LC 62-9189. (International Series of Monographs on Pure & Applied Mathematics: Vol. 35). 1963. 174.00 (*0-08-010041-4*, Pub. by Pergamon Repr) Franklin.

Czaszar, K., jt. auth. see Czaszar, A.

Czatt, Milton S. The International Bible Students: Jehovah's Witnesses. (Yale Studies in Religion: No. 4). 44p. 1988. reprint ed. pap. 2.95 (*1-883858-47-X*) Witness CA.

Czaykowski, Bogdan, tr. see Bialoszewski, Miron.

***Czech, Brian.** Shoveling Fuel for a Runaway Train: Errant Economists, Shameful Spenders, & a Plan to Stop Them All. LC 00-22311. (Illus.). 206p. 2000. 22.50 (*0-520-22508-2*) U CA Pr.

***Czech, Brian, et al.** The Endangered Species Act: History, Conservation Biology & Public Policy. LC 00-8847. 2000. write for info. (*0-8018-6504-2*) Johns Hopkins.

Czech, Danuta. Auschwitz Chronicle, Nineteen Thirty-Nine to Nineteen Forty-Five. LC 89-35351. (Illus.). 88p. 1995. 124.50 (*0-8050-0938-8*) H Holt & Co.

— Auschwitz Chronicle, 1939-1945. 1997. pap. text 45.00 (*0-8050-5238-0*, Owl) H Holt & Co.

Czech, Danuta, jt. ed. see Bezwinska, J.

***Czech Heritage Society of Texas Staff.** Texas Military Veterans of Czech Descent. LC 99-38310. 1999. 45.00 (*1-57168-344-5*) Sunbelt Media.

Czech, J., ed. see Sedlacek, H. H., et al.

Czech, Jan M. An American Face. LC 98-47305. (Illus.). (J). 2000. 8.95 (*0-87868-718-1*, Child-Family Pr) Child Welfare.

Czech, Michael P., ed. Molecular Basis of Insulin Action. LC 84-26423. 488p. 1985. 120.00 (*0-306-41843-6*, Plenum Trade) Perseus Pubng.

Czechowicz, A. S., jt. auth. see Talalaj, S.

Czechowicz, Dorynne, ed. Detoxification from Alcohol & Other Drugs: A Treatment Improvement Protocol. 95p. (C). 1999. pap. text 20.00 (*0-7881-7597-1*) DIANE Pub.

Czegel, Barbara. Help Desk Practitioner's Handbook. LC 98-31159. 432p. 1998. pap. 39.99 (*0-471-31992-9*) Wiley.

— Running an Effective Help Desk. 2nd ed. LC 97-46069. 464p. 1998. pap. 39.99 (*0-471-24816-9*) Wiley.

Czeipek, Philipp. Die Herrendistanzfahrt Berlin Totis 1899. (Illus.). 168p. 1997. reprint ed. 63.00 (*3-487-08386-8*) G Olms Pubs.

Czeisler, Charles A. & Guilleminault, Christian, eds. REM Sleep: Its Temporal Distribution. LC QP0425.. 156p. 1980. reprint ed. pap. 48.40 (*0-608-00419-7*, 206113400007) Bks Demand.

Czeisler, Charles A., jt. ed. see Moore-Ede, Martin C.

Czeizel, A., et al, eds. Genetics of the Hungarian Population: Ethnic Aspects, Genetic Markers, Ecogenetics & Disease Spectrum. Sankaranarayanan, K., tr. (Illus.). 350p. 1991. 71.95 (*0-387-53580-2*) Spr-Verlag.

Czeizel, Andrew, et al. Genetics of the Hungarian Population: Ethnic Aspects, Genetic Markers, Ecogenetics & Disease Spectrum. 358p. 1991. 150.00 (*963-05-5767-3*, Pub. by Akade Kiado) St Mut.

Czeizel, Balazs. Journey Without Title - Utazas Cim Nelkul. (Artists' Books Ser.). (Illus.). 80p. (Orig.). 1995. pap. 15.00 (*0-89822-114-5*) Visual Studies.

— This Is Not America, Either. (Illus.). 96p. (Orig.). 1993. pap. 25.00 (*0-89822-107-2*) Visual Studies.

Czeizel, E. & Tusnady, G. Aetiological Studies of Isolated Common Congenital Abnormalities in Hungary. 358p. (C). 1984. 90.00 (*963-05-3223-9*, Pub. by Akade Kiado) St Mut.

Czeizel, E., et al. Congenital Limb Deficiencies in Hungary: Genetic & Teratologic Epidemiological Studies. LC 95-177096. 420p. 1994. pap. 195.00 (*963-05-6631-1*, Pub. by Akade Kiado) St Mut.

Czekanowska, Anna. Polish Folk Music: Slavonic Heritage - Polish Tradition - Contemporary Trends. (Cambridge Studies in Ethnomusicology). (Illus.). 240p. (C). 1991. text 74.95 (*0-521-30090-8*) Cambridge U Pr.

Czekierda, K. Dictionary of Environmental Protection. (ENG & POL.). 679p. 1996. 52.50 (*83-85792-35-X*, Pub. by Ekonomia Srod) IBD Ltd.

— Dictionary of Environmental Protection, English-Polish/Polish-English. (ENG & POL.). 1996. 52.50 (*0-7859-9715-6*) Fr & Eur.

Czelnai, R. & Szepesi, D. Technical Explanatory Dictionary: Meteorology. (ENG, FRE, GER, HUN & RUS.). 456p. 1986. 75.00 (*0-8288-1475-9*, F10024) Fr & Eur.

Czempiel, Ernst O. Amerikanische Sicherheitssystem, 1945-1949: Studie zur Aussenpolitik der buergerlichen Gesellschaft. (Beitraege zur Auswaertigen und Internationalen Politik Ser.: Vol. 1). (C). 1966. 100.00 (*3-11-000527-1*) De Gruyter.

Czempiel, Ernst-Otto & Krell, Gert, eds. The Future of European Arms Control. (New Approaches to Peace & Security Ser.). 288p. (C). 1988. pap. text. write for info. (*0-8133-7607-6*) Westview.

Czempiel, Ernst-Otto, jt. ed. see Rosenau, James N.

Czepiel, John. Competitive Marketing Strategy. 510p. (C). 1995. pap. 56.00 (*0-536-58829-5*) Pearson Custom.

— Competitive Marketing Strategy. 510p. (C). 1995. text 61.00 (*0-536-58868-6*) Pearson Custom.

Czepiel, John & Backman, Jules. Changing Marketing Strategies in a New Economy. LC 77-11109. (Key Issues Lecture Ser.). 1977. pap. write for info. (*0-672-97199-2*) Macmillan.

Czepiel, John A., et al, eds. The Services Challenge: Integrating for Competitive Advantage. LC 87-12543. (American Marketing Association, Proceedings Ser.). (Illus.). 114p. 1987. reprint ed. pap. 35.40 (*0-7837-9763-X*, 206049100005) Bks Demand.

Czepiel, Tomas M. Music at the Royal Court & Chapel in Poland, c. 1543-1600. LC 95-51816. (Outstanding Dissertations in Music from British Universities Ser.). 1996. write for info. (*0-614-10485-8*) Garland.

Czepiel, Tomasz M. Music at the Royal Court & Chapel in Poland, c. 1543-1600. rev. ed. LC 95-51816. (Outstanding Dissertations in Music from British Universities Ser.). (Illus.). 432p. 1996. text 105.00 (*0-8153-2237-2*) Garland.

***Czepil & NYU staff, ed.** Business Strategic Analysis B01-1101. 238p. 1999. pap. text 29.20 (*0-536-02629-7*) P-H.

Czepko, Daniel. Saemtliche Werke: Erster Band, Erster Teil: Lyrik in Zyklen. Szyrocki, Marian & Roloff, Hans-Gert, eds. iv, 381p. (C). 1989. lib. bdg. 242.30 (*3-11-011316-3*) De Gruyter.

— Saemtliche Werke: Erster Band, Zweiter Teil: Lyrik in Zyklen. Szyrocki, Marion & Roloff, Hans-Gert, eds. (Ausgaben Deutscher Literatur des XV bis XVIII Jahrhunderts Ser.). (GER.). iv, 450p. (C). 1989. lib. bdg. 288.50 (*3-11-012251-0*) De Gruyter.

— Saemtliche Werke Bd. II: Vermischte Gedichte, Zweiter Teil: Deutsche Gedichte. Roloff, Hans-Gert, ed. (Ausgaben Deutscher Literatur des 15. Bis 18. Jahrhunderts Ser.). (GER.). 672p. (C). 1997. lib. bdg. 199.00 (*3-11-014163-9*) De Gruyter.

— Saemtliche Werke Vol. II: Vermischte Gedichte, Pt. 1: Lateinische Gedichte. Roloff, Hans-Gert & Szyrocki, Marian, eds. (Ausgaben Deutscher Literatur des XV. bis XVIII. Jahrhunderts Ser.). (GER.). iv, 821p. (C). 1996. lib. bdg. 462.85 (*3-11-014164-7*) De Gruyter.

— Saemtliche Werke, 7 Baende Sechster Band: Briefwechsel und Dokumente Zu Leben und Werke. Roloff, Hans-Gert & Szyrocki, Marian, eds. (GER.). vi, 474p. (C). 1995. lib. bdg. 326.15 (*3-11-013425-X*) De Gruyter.

Czepulkowski, B. H., jt. auth. see Rooney, D. E.

Czepulkowski, B. H., jt. ed. see Rooney, D. E.

Czerepanov, S. K. Vascular Plants of Russia & Adjacent States (The Former U. S. S. R.) (Illus.). 528p. (C). 1995. text 110.00 (*0-521-45006-3*) Cambridge U Pr.

Czerkas, Sylvia J. Dinosaurs Past Present, Vol. 1. LC 87-60944. Vol. I. (Illus.). 180p. (Orig.). 1988. pap. 29.95 (*0-295-96707-2*) U of Wash Pr.

— Dinosaurs Past Present, Vol. 2. Vol. II. (Illus.). 164p. (Orig.). 1988. pap. 29.95 (*0-295-96708-0*) U of Wash Pr.

Czerkas, Sylvia J. & Olson, Everett C., eds. Dinosaurs Past & Present, Vol. 1. LC 87-60944. (Illus.). 180p. (Orig.). 1987. pap. 29.95 (*0-938644-24-6*) Nat Hist Mus.

— Dinosaurs Past & Present, Vol. 2. LC 87-60944. (Illus.). 164p. (Orig.). 1988. pap. 29.95 (*0-938644-23-8*) Nat Hist Mus.

Czerkawski, C. J. Theoretical & Policy-Oriented Aspects of the External Debt Economics. Bos, Dieter et al, eds. (Studies in Contemporary Economics). viii, 150p. 1991. 42.95 (*0-387-54282-5*) Spr-Verlag.

Czerkawski, J. W. An Introduction to Rumen Studies. LC 85-9400. (Pergamon International Library Science Technology Engineering & Social Studies). (Illus.). 220p. 1986. 115.00 (*0-08-025487-X*, Pub. by Pergamon Repr) Franklin.

Czerlinski, George H. Chemical Relaxation: An Introduction to Theory & Application of Stepwise Perturbation. LC 66-16501. 328p. reprint ed. pap. 101.70 (*0-608-16763-0*, 202707700054) Bks Demand.

***Czerlinsky, Thomas & Chandler, Shirley K.** Tips for Using the Vocational Decision-Making Interview. Pines, Susan, ed. 4p. 1999. pap. write for info. (*1-56370-650-4*) Park Ave.

— Vocational Decision-Making Interview Administration Manual. 3rd ed. Pines, Susan, ed. 1999. spiral bd. 24.95 (*1-56370-613-X*, JA613X) JIST Works.

Czermak, Herberth. Kafka's Short Stories Notes. (Cliffs Notes Ser.). 104p. (C). 1973. pap. 4.95 (*0-8220-0700-2*, Cliff) IDG Bks.

— The Trial Notes. (Cliffs Notes Ser.). 56p. (Orig.). 1976. pap. text 4.95 (*0-8220-1304-5*, Cliff) IDG Bks.

***Czernecki, Stefan.** Beastly Boys & Ghastly Girls. 48p. (J). (gr. 2-5). 2000. 14.95 (*0-06-024952-8*) HarpC Child Bks.

Czernecki, Stefan. The Cricket's Cage. large type ed. (Illus.). 32p. (J). (gr. k-4). 1996. write for info. (*1-895340-14-4*) Hyperion Pr.

— The Cricket's Cage: A Chinese Folktale. LC 96-15407. (Illus.). 32p. (J). (ps-2). 1997. lib. bdg. 14.89 (*0-7868-2234-1*, Pub. by Hyprn Child) Little.

— The Cricket's Cage: A Chinese Folktale. LC 96-15407. (Illus.). 32p. (J). (ps-2). 1997. 14.95 (*0-7868-0296-0*, Pub. by Hyprn Child) Time Warner.

Czernecki, Stefan. Dear Shell, You Curve So Well. 14.95 (*0-06-027173-6*) HarpC Child Bks.

— Don't Forget Winona. LC 99-27255. 32p. (J). (ps-2). 2000. 14.95 (*0-06-027197-3*) HarpC Child Bks.

— Female Indiana Jones, 2. 15.00 (*0-06-026205-2*) HarpC Child Bks.

— Female Indiana Jones: Book #3. 15.00 (*0-06-026207-9*) HarpC Child Bks.

Czernecki, Stefan. Female Indiana Jones Book 1. (Illus.). 15.00 (*0-06-026203-6*) HarpC.

Czernecki, Stefan. Frances Omnibus. 1995. 4.50 (*0-06-026804-2*) HarpC.

— How a Baby Begins. 40p. 15.95 (*0-06-025412-2*) HarpC Child Bks.

— I Do Not Understand Arf. 40p. (J). (ps-3). 14.95 (*0-06-027081-0*) HarpC Child Bks.

— If You Give a Cat a Cupcake. 32p. (J). (ps-2). 15.95 (*0-06-026683-X*) HarpC Child Bks.

— Mildred & Sam. 40p. (J). (ps-2). 14.95 (*0-06-026681-3*) HarpC Child Bks.

Czernecki, Stefan. Mystery at Midnight Museum. 32p. (J). 14.95 (*0-06-026199-4*) HarpC Child Bks.

— Pancho's Pinata. LC 92-7325. 1994. 10.15 (*0-606-06655-1*, Pub. by Turtleback) Demco.

Czernecki, Stefan. Rainforests of the World. 48p. 15.95 (*0-06-025354-1*) HarpC Child Bks.

— Rose Wilder Lane Biography. 256p. (J). (gr. 3-7). 2001. 14.95 (*0-06-026420-9*) HarpC Child Bks.

Czernecki, Stefan. Scary Stories Omnibus. 1995. 5.00 (*0-06-026786-0*) HarpC.

— Singing Snake. (J). 1995. 10.15 (*0-606-08166-6*) Turtleback.

Czernecki, Stefan. Spinster Sprout & the Spider Plants. 32p. (J). (gr. k-4). Date not set. 14.95 (*0-06-026435-7*) HarpC Child Bks.

Czernecki, Stefan. Still More of the World's Best Dirty Jokes. (Illus.). 144p. 1981. pap. 3.95 (*0-8065-0834-5*, Citadel Pr) Carol Pub Group.

Czernecki, Stefan. What Is a Kiss. 32p. (J). (ps-2). 14.95 incl. audio (*0-06-026255-9*) HarpC Child Bks.

Czernecki, Stefan. Wild Queen. 80p. (J). (gr. 1-4). lib. bdg. 13.89 (*0-06-026264-8*) HarpC.

— Wild Queen. 80p. (J). (gr. 1-4). 13.95 (*0-06-026263-X*) HarpC Child Bks.

***Czernecki, Stefan.** You & Me. 64p. 2001. 14.95 (*0-06-026698-8*) HarpC Child Bks.

Czernecki, Stefan. Zorah's Magic Carpet. large type ed. (Illus.). 32p. (J). (gr. k-4). 1995. write for info. (*1-895340-06-3*) Hyperion Pr.

— Zorah's Magic Carpet. LC 94-24529. (Illus.). 32p. (J). (gr. k-4). 1996. 14.95 (*0-7868-0081-X*, Pub. by Hyprn Child); lib. bdg. 14.89 (*0-7868-2066-7*, Pub. by Hyprn Child) Little.

***Czernecki, Stefan & Haijtink, Michael.** The Most Incredible Cardboard Toys in the Whole Wide World. (Illus.). 112p. 1999. pap. 19.95 (*1-57990-161-1*) Lark Books.

Czernecki, Stefan & Haijtink, Michael. The Most Incredible Cardboard Toys in the Whole Wide World. Dover Doran, Laura, ed. LC 99-33603. (Illus.). 112p. 1999. pap. 19.95 (*1-57990-137-9*, Pub. by Lark Books) Random.

***Czernecki, Stefan & Rhodes, T.** Pancho's Pinata. (SPA.). (J). 1999. pap. 15.49 (*0-7868-2189-2*, Pub. by Hyprn Child) Little.

Czernecki, Stefan & Rhodes, Timothy. The Hummingbirds' Gift. LC 93-19369. (Illus.). 32p. (J). (gr. k-4). 1994. 14.95 (*1-56282-604-2*, Pub. by Hyprn Child) Little.

— The Hummingbirds' Gift. large type ed. (Illus.). 32p. (J). (gr. k-4). 1994. write for info. (*0-920534-99-6*) Hyperion Pr.

— Nina's Treasures. large type ed. (Illus.). 40p. (J). (gr. k-4). 1994. pap. write for info. (*1-895340-02-0*) Hyperion Pr.

— Pancho's Pinata. LC 92-7325. (Illus.). 40p. (J). (ps-4). 1992. 14.95 (*1-56282-277-2*, Pub. by Hyprn Child); lib. bdg. 14.89 (*1-56282-278-0*, Pub. by Hyprn Child) Little.

— Pancho's Pinata. LC 92-7235. (Illus.). 40p. (J). (ps-4). 1994. pap. 4.95 (*0-7868-1007-6*, Pub. by Hyprn Ppbks) Little.

— Pancho's Pinata. large type ed. (Illus.). 40p. (J). (gr. k-4). 1992. write for info. (*0-920534-98-8*) Hyperion Pr.

— The Singing Snake. LC 92-85515. (Illus.). 40p. (J). (ps-2). 1993. lib. bdg. 14.89 (*1-56282-400-7*, Pub. by Hyprn Child) Little.

— The Singing Snake. LC 92-85515. (Illus.). 40p. (J). (ps-2). 1995. pap. 4.95 (*0-7868-1036-X*, Pub. by Hyprn Ppbks) Little.

— The Singing Snake. large type ed. (Illus.). 40p. (J). (ps-2). 1993. write for info. (*0-920534-97-X*) Hyperion Pr.

— The Sleeping Bread. LC 91-75422. (Illus.). 40p. (J). (gr. k-4). 1992. 14.95 (*1-56282-183-0*, Pub. by Hyprn Child) Little.

— The Sleeping Bread. large type ed. (Illus.). 40p. (J). (gr. k-4). 1992. write for info. (*0-920534-84-8*) Hyperion Pr.

Czernecki, Stefan, jt. auth. see Fleischman.

Czernecki, Stefan, jt. auth. see Geringer.

Czernecki, Stefan, jt. auth. see Hunter.

***Czerneda, Julia E.** Changing Vision. 2000. 6.99 (*0-88677-904-9*, Pub. by DAW Bks) Penguin Putnam.

Czerneda, Julie. Great Careers for People Interested in Living Things, Vol. 3. LC 93-78080. (Career Connections Ser.: Series 1). (Illus.). 48p. (J). (gr. 6-9). 1993. text 23.00 (*0-8103-9387-5*, GML00597-102105, UXL) Gale.

Czerneda, Julie E. Beholder's Eye. 368p. 1998. mass mkt. 5.99 (*0-88677-818-2*, Pub. by DAW Bks) Penguin Putnam.

— No Limits: Developing Scientific Literacy Using Science Fiction. (Illus.). (YA). (gr. 7-10). 1999. pap., teacher ed. write for info. (*1-895579-94-5*) Trifolium Inc.

— A Thousand Words for Stranger. 320p. 1997. mass mkt. 5.99 (*0-88677-769-0*, Pub. by DAW Bks) Penguin Putnam.

— Ties of Power. (Trade Pact Universe Ser.: No. 2). 416p. 1999. mass mkt. 6.99 (*0-88677-850-6*, Pub. by DAW Bks) Penguin Putnam.

Czerneda, Julie E., ed. Packing Fraction: And other Tales of Science & Imagination. (Illus.). 128p. (YA). (gr. 7-10). 1998. pap. 4.95 (*1-895579-89-9*) Trifolium Inc.

***Czerner, Thomas B.** What Makes You Tick? The Brain in Plain English. LC 00-26289. (Illus.). 256p. 2000. 24.95 (*0-471-37100-9*) Wiley.

Czerni, Sergiusz. Slownik Lotniczo - Kosmonautyczny. (ENG, GER, POL & RUS.). 123p. 1984. 49.95 (*0-8288-0024-3*, M15567) Fr & Eur.

Czerni, Sergiusz & Skrzynska, Maria. English-Polish Dictionary of Science & Technology. 9th ed. (ENG & POL.). 1032p. 1990. 150.00 (*0-8288-0649-7*, M 8490) Fr & Eur.

— Polish-English Dictionary of Science & Technology. 846p. 1983. 49.75 (*83-204-1380-X*) IBD Ltd.

— Polish-English Dictionary of Science & Technology. 8th ed. (ENG & POL.). 881p. 1994. 150.00 (*0-8288-0650-0*, M15313) Fr & Eur.

Czerniak, jt. auth. see Dorfman.

Czerniak, Robert J., et al. Applications of GPS for Surveying & Other Positioning Needs in Departments of Transportation. LC 98-165431. 46 p. 1998. write for info. (*0-309-06116-4*) Natl Acad Pr.

Czerniakow, Adam. The Warsaw Diary of Adam Czerniakow: Prelude to Doom. Hilberg, Raul et al, eds. LC 98-42718. 444p. 1999. reprint ed. pap. 18.95 (*1-56663-230-7*, Elephant Paperbacks) I R Dee.

Czerniakow, Adam, et al. The Warsaw Diary of Adam Czerniakow: Prelude to Doom. Hilberg, Raul et al, eds. LC 78-9272. (Illus.). 448p. 1982. pap. 12.95 (*0-8128-6110-8*, Scrbrough Hse) Madison Bks UPA.

***Czerniawska, Fiona.** Management Consultancy in the 21st Century. LC 99-40915. 236p. 1999. 34.95 (*1-55753-178-1*, Ichor Busn Bks) Purdue U Pr.

***Czerniawska, Fiona & Potter, Gavin.** Business in a Virtual World: Exploiting Information for Competitive Advantage. LC 00-32670. 2000. pap. 24.95 (*1-55753-194-3*) Purdue U Pr.

Czerniawski, A., tr. see Staff, Leopold.

Czerniawski, A., tr. see Szymborska, Wislawa.

Czerniawski, Adam, ed. The Mature Laurel: Essays on Modern Polish Poetry. LC 90-24814. 320p. 1990. 35.00 (*0-8023-1292-6*) Dufour.

Czerniawski, Adam, ed. from POL. The Burning Forest. LC 87-73053. (Illus.). 192p. (Orig.). 1988. pap. 18.95 (*1-85224-009-1*, Pub. by Bloodaxe Bks) Dufour.

Czerniawski, Adam, jt. auth. see Rozewicz, Tadeusz.

Czerniawski, Adam, tr. see Kolakowski, Leszek.

Czerniawski, Adam, tr. see Michalski, Krzysztof.

Czerniawski, Adam, tr. see Rozewicz, Tadeusz.

Czerniawski, Richard D. & Maloney, Michael W. Creating Brand Loyalty: The Management of Power Positioning & Really Great Advertising. LC 99-26211. 240p. 1999. pap. 21.95 (*0-8144-0501-0*) AMACOM.

Czerniawski, Stefan, tr. see Kolakowski, Leszek.

Czernichow, P. & Robinson, A. D., eds. Diabetes Insipidus in Man. (Frontiers of Hormone Research Ser.: Vol. 13). (Illus.). x, 326p. 1985. 143.50 (*3-8055-3921-5*) S Karger.

Czernichow, P., jt. ed. see Levy-Marschal, Claire.

Czernielewski, J. M., ed. Immunological & Pharmacological Aspects of Atopic & Contact Eczema. (Pharmacology & the Skin Ser.: Vol. 4). (Illus.). x, 254p. 1992. 215.75 (*3-8055-5433-8*) S Karger.

***Czerniewicz-Umer, Teresy.** Cracow. LC 00-31832. (Travel Guides Ser.). (Illus.). 2000. write for info. (*0-7894-6644-9*) DK Pub Inc.

Czerniewska, Pam. Learning about Writing: The Early Years. (Language in Education Ser.). 160p. (C). 1994. pap. 31.95 (*0-631-16963-6*) Blackwell Pubs.

Czernik, Daniel E. Gasket Handbook. LC 95-36623. (Illus.). 335p. 1996. 49.95 (*0-07-015113-X*) McGraw.

Czernis, Loretta. Weaving a Canadian Allegory: Anonymous Writing, Personal Reading. 134p. (C). 1994. text 29.95 (*0-88920-232-X*) W Laurier U Pr.

***Czernis-Ryl, Eva, ed.** Australian Gold & Silver, 1851-1900. (Illus.). 88p. 2000. pap. 30.00 (*1-86317-052-9*) Museum Applied Arts.

Czerny. Czerny/160 Eight-Measure Exercises, Opus 821. Hinson, Maurice, ed. (Masterwork Edition Ser.). 80p. 1991. pap. 8.95 (*0-7390-0714-9*, 4832) Alfred Pub.

Czerny. Etudes III: Kunst Der Fingerfertigkeit I. 1998. pap. text 7.95 (*963-9059-93-5*) Konemann.

— Etudes IV: Kunst Der Fingerfertigkelt II. 1998. pap. text 7.95 (*963-9059-94-3*) Konemann.

Czerny, Carl. The Complete School of Velocity for the Piano Opus 299. 104p. 1986. per. 6.95 (*0-7935-5290-7*) H Leonard.

— Little Pianist Opus 823: Complete for the Piano. 64p. 1986. pap. 5.95 (*0-7935-2597-7*) H Leonard.

— One Hundred Practical Exercises for Piano, Op. 139. (Carl Fischer Music Library: No. 371). 76p. (J). 1905. pap. 9.95 (*0-8258-0134-6*) Fischer Inc NY.

— School of Practical Composition, 3 vols., Set. LC 79-21105. (Music Reprint Ser.). 1979. reprint ed. lib. bdg. 110.00 (*0-306-79595-7*) Da Capo.

— School of Velocity for Piano, Op. 299, Complete Edition. 101p. (J). 1903. pap. 7.50 (*0-8258-0108-7*, L 338) Fischer Inc NY.

— Thirty New Studies in Technics Opus 849 (Etudes de Mecanisme) 56p. 1986. pap. 7.95 (*0-7935-5293-1*) H Leonard.

— Thirty New Studies in Technique for Piano, Op. 849. (Carl Fischer Music Library: No. 487). 56p. (J). 1907. pap. 8.95 (*0-8258-0127-3*, L 487) Fischer Inc NY.

Czerny, Carl, ed. see Bach, Johann Sebastian.

Czerny, Charles C. Letters to a Young Lady on the Art of Playing the Pianoforte. Hamilton, J. A., tr. from GER. (Music Ser.). vii, 82p. 1982. reprint ed. lib. bdg. 24.50 (*0-306-76123-8*) Da Capo.

Czerny, Robert, tr. see Ricoeur, Paul.

Czerny, Zigmund, jt. auth. see Teder, pseud.

Czervinske, Michael P., jt. auth. see Barnhart, Sherry L.

Czervinske, Michael P., jt. ed. see Barnhart, Sherry L.

Czervionke, Leo F. & Haughton, Victor M. Pocket Atlas of Spinal MRI. 90p. 1989. pap. text 16.95 (*0-88167-546-6*) Lppncott W & W.

Czerwien, Anthony S. POW: Tears That Never Dry. LC 94-33329. (Illus.). 256p. 1994. 22.00 (*0-912526-69-6*) Lib Res.

Czerwinski, E. J. Contemporary Polish Theatre & Drama, 1957-1984, 26. LC 87-31787. (Contributions to the Study of World Literature Ser.: No. 26). 174p. 1988. 47.95 (*0-313-24402-2*, CZC/, Greenwood Pr) Greenwood.

An Asterisk (*) at the beginning of an entry indicates that the title is appearing for the first time.

Czerwinski, E. J. Dictionary of Polish Literature. LC 93-49540. 504p. 1994. lib. bdg. 89.50 (*0-313-26222-5*, Greenwood Pr) Greenwood.

Czerwinski, Edward J., tr. see Kott, Jan.

Czerwinski, Frank L., jt. auth. see Samaras, Thomas T.

Czerwinski, Sandra & Moloney-Harmon, Patricia A. Review of Pediatric Critical Care. Cullen, Barbara N., ed. (Illus.). 250p. 1996. pap. text 34.00 (*0-7216-6159-9*, W B Saunders Co) Harcrt Hlth Sci Grp.

Czerwinski, Stanley. Housing Finance: FHA's Risk-Sharing Programs Offer Alternatives for Financing Affordable Multifamily Housing. (Illus.). 100p. (C). 1999. pap. text 25.00 (*0-7881-7782-6*) DIANE Pub.

***Czerwinski, Stanley J. & Fishkin, Christine M. B., eds.** Multifamily Housing: HUD Missed Opportunities to Reduce Costs on Its Uninsured Section 8 Portfolio. (Illus.). 86p. (C). 1999. pap. text 20.00 (*0-7881-8459-8*) DIANE Pub.

Czerwinski, Thomas J. Coping with the Bounds: Speculations on Nonlinearity in Military Affairs. LC 98-14653. 1998. write for info. (*1-57906-009-9*) Natl Defense.

Czerwinski, Thomas J., jt. auth. see Alberts, David S.

Czerwionka, Frederick J. Illinois Tax Handbook. 1987th ed. 1986. pap. 17.00 (*0-13-450322-8*) P-H.

Czerwionka, Frederick J., et al. Illinois Tax Handbook. 368p. 1988. 17.50 (*0-13-450256-6*) P-H.

— Illinois Tax Handbook, 1984. 250p. 1983. 11.00 (*0-317-07500-4*) P-H.

— Illinois Tax Handbook, 1989. 350p. 1988. 18.95 (*0-13-450330-9*, Busn) P-H.

Czeschin, Robert W. The Last Wave. 5th ed. 216p. 1991. 14.95 (*0-945332-23-8*) Agora Inc MD.

Czestochowski, Joseph S. Arthur Davies: A Catalogue Raisonne of the Prints. LC 83-40542. (American Art Ser.). (Illus.). 256p. 1987. 85.00 (*0-87413-242-8*) U Delaware Pr.

— Works of Arthur B. Davies. LC 79-11546. (Illus.). 110p. 1980. lib. bdg. 90.00 (*0-226-68946-8*) U Ch Pr.

Czestochowski, Joseph S., ed. Contemporary Polish Posters in Full Color. LC 78-64945. (Illus.). 1979. pap. 7.95 (*0-486-23780-X*) Dover.

Czetli, Nancy & Czetli, Steve N. Silent Witness: The True Story of a Psychic Detective. 224p. 1993. 17.95 (*1-55972-200-2*, Birch Ln Pr) Carol Pub Group.

Czetli, Steve N., jt. auth. see Czetli, Nancy.

Czichas, Casey. The Candlelight Reader: Ten Stories of Horror & Humor. LC 98-90536. 1999. pap. 14.95 (*0-533-12835-8*) Vantage.

Czichos, Raymond L. Frederic Remington - Eighteen Sixty-One to Nineteen Nine: He Knew the Horse. (Illus.). 108p. 1987. 34.50 (*0-9618420-0-8*) Pioneer Mus Western Art.

— Frederic Remington - Eighteen Sixty-One to Nineteen Nine: He Knew the Horse. deluxe ed. (Illus.). 108p. 1987. lthr. 75.00 (*0-9618420-1-6*) Pioneer Mus Western Art.

Cziesla, Wolfgang. Aktaion Polypragmon: Variationen Eines Antiken Themas in der Europaischen Renaissance. (Literarische Studien: Bd. 2). (GER., Illus.). 175p. 1990. 40.80 (*3-631-42431-0*) P Lang Pubng.

Cziesla, Wolfgang, jt. auth. see Glaser, Rita.

Czigany, Lorant. The Oxford History of Hungarian Literature: From Earliest Times to the Present. LC 83-3997. 582p. 1984. 79.00 (*0-19-815781-9*) OUP.

Czigany, Lorant, ed. see Cushing, G. F.

Czikann-Zichy, Maurice. My Life-Politics & Diplomacy in Turbulent Times. LC 86-51433. (Program of the Hungarian Historical Research Society Ser.). 105p. (Orig.). 1986. pap. 9.00 (*0-935484-12-4*) Universe Pub Co.

***Cziko, Gary.** The Things We Do: Using the Lessons of Bernard & Darwin to Understand the What, Why & How of Our Behavior. LC 99-51843. (Illus.). 350p. 2000. 37.95 (*0-262-03277-5*, Bradford Bks) MIT Pr.

Cziko, Gary. Without Miracles: Universal Selection Theory & the Second Darwinian Revolution. (Illus.). 400p. 1997. reprint ed. pap. text 19.50 (*0-262-53147-X*, Bradford Bks) MIT Pr.

Czimbal, Bob & Zadikov, Maggie. A Guide to Healthy Touch: Vitamin T. Allen, Ruby, ed. (Illus.). 240p. (Orig.). 1991. pap. 18.00 (*1-878793-00-4*) Open Bk OR.

— Stress Survival Kit: Fifty Two Stress Management Tools. 2nd ed. Tobin, L., ed. (Illus.). 160p. 1993. pap. 18.00 (*1-878793-03-9*) Open Bk OR.

***Czinkota.** International Business. 5th ed. (C). 1999. text. write for info. (*0-03-031626-X*) Harcourt.

Czinkota. International Business. 5th ed. LC 98-28009. (C). 1998. text 90.00 (*0-03-022378-4*, Pub. by Harcourt Coll Pubs) Harcourt.

— Oht T/A International Business. 5th ed. (C). 1998. pap. text 515.00 (*0-03-021593-5*) Harcourt Coll Pubs.

— Oht-teaching - International Business 4e. 4th ed. (C). 1995. pap. text 246.00 (*0-03-016213-0*) Harcourt Coll Pubs.

— Readings in Global Marketing. 1998. pap. 21.99 (*1-86152-429-3*) Thomson Learn.

***Czinkota, et al.** Web Tutor On Webct to Accompany Marketing Management. 2nd ed. 2000. pap. 19.00 (*0-324-06455-1*) Sth-Wstrn College.

Czinkota, Michael R. Global Business. (C). 1994. pap. text, teacher ed., suppl. ed. 12.00 (*0-03-094882-7*) Harcourt Coll Pubs.

— Global Business. 2nd ed. (C). 1997. pap. text 74.50 (*0-03-027382-X*) Dryden Pr.

— Global Business. 2nd ed. (C). 1997. pap. text, teacher ed. 66.50 (*0-03-024932-5*) Harcourt Coll Pubs.

— Global Business. 2nd ed. LC 97-77736. (C). 1997. text 59.00 (*0-03-024888-4*, Pub. by Harcourt Coll Pubs) Harcourt.

— Global Marketing. (C). 1995. text 91.00 (*0-03-010649-4*, Pub. by Harcourt Coll Pubs); pap. text, teacher ed., suppl. ed. 74.25 (*0-03-017029-X*) Harcourt Coll Pubs.

— International Business. 4th ed. (C). 1995. pap. text, teacher ed. 70.00 (*0-03-016203-3*); pap. text, student ed. 26.75 (*0-03-016204-1*) Harcourt Coll Pubs.

— International Marketing. 5th ed. (C). 1997. pap. text, teacher ed. 70.00 (*0-03-024467-6*) Harcourt Coll Pubs.

— Marketing: Best Practices. (C). 1999. text 88.50 (*0-03-021109-3*, Pub. by Harcourt Coll Pubs) Harcourt.

Czinkota, Michael R., ed. Export Controls: Building Reasonable Commercial Ties with Political Adversaries. LC 84-4735. 208p. 1984. 55.00 (*0-275-91143-8*, C1143, Praeger Pubs) Greenwood.

— Export Promotion: The Public & Private Sector Interaction. (Illus.). 346p. 1983. 65.00 (*0-275-90967-0*, C0967, Praeger Pubs) Greenwood.

Czinkota, Michael R. & Kotabe, Masaaki, eds. The Japanese Distribution System: Opportunities & Obstacles - Structure & Practices. 450p. 1992. text 75.00 (*1-55738-424-X*, Irwn Prfssnl) McGraw-Hill Prof.

— Readings in International Business. LC 97-29587. 352p. (C). 1998. text 64.95 (*0-631-20799-6*) Blackwell Pubs.

***Czinkota, Michael R. & Kotabe, Masaaki, eds.** Readings in International Business. LC 97-29587. 352p. (C). 1998. pap. text 34.95 (*1-57718-127-1*) Blackwell Pubs.

Czinkota, Michael R. & Marciel, Scot, eds. U. S. - Arab Economic Relations: A Time of Transition. LC 85-3614. 368p. 1985. 46.95 (*0-275-90081-9*, C0081, Praeger Pubs) Greenwood.

Czinkota, Michael R. & Ronkainen, Ilkka A. International Marketing. 4th ed. 518p. (C). 1994. pap. text, teacher ed. 82.25 (*0-03-010439-4*) Harcourt Coll Pubs.

— International Marketing. 5th ed. LC 97-66269. 912p. (C). 1997. text 102.50 (*0-03-024401-3*) Dryden Pr.

— International Marketing Strategy. LC 93-72078. 353p. (C). 1993. pap. text 54.50 (*0-03-098373-8*) Dryden Pr.

Czinkota, Michael R. & Tesar, George, eds. Export Policy: A Global Assessment. LC 81-17874. 175p. 1982. 45.00 (*0-275-90778-3*, C0778, Praeger Pubs) Greenwood.

Czinkota, Michael R. & Woronoff, Jon. Unlocking Japan's Markets: Seizing Marketing & Distribution Opportunities in Today's Japan. 225p. 1991. text 29.95 (*1-55738-213-1*, Irwn Prfssnl) McGraw-Hill Prof.

— Unlocking Japan's Markets: Seizing Marketing & Distribution Opportunities in Today's Japan. 228p. 1993. pap. 12.95 (*0-8048-1899-1*) Tuttle Pubng.

Czinkota, Michael R., et al. International Business. 3rd ed. LC 93-2282. 748p. (C). 1994. disk 25.00 (*0-03-098022-4*) Dryden Pr.

— Marketing Management. (Illus.). 700p. 1996. 74.95 (*1-55786-694-5*) Blackwell Pubs.

Czinkota, Michael R., jt. ed. see Cavusgil, S. Tamer.

Czinkota, Michael R., ed. see Colaiacovo, Juan Luis, et al.

Czitrom, A. Veronica & Spagon, eds. Statistics in Industry Case Studies of Semiconductor Process-Equipment Characterization. (Interdisciplinary Statistics Ser.). 330p. 59.95 (*0-412-99701-0*, Chap & Hall NY) Chapman & Hall.

Czitrom, A. Veronica & Spagon, Patrick, eds. Statistical Case Studies for Industrial Process Improvement. LC 97-12582. (ASA-SIAM Series on Statistics & Applied Probability: Vol. 1). (Illus.). xxvii, 514p. 1997. pap. text 52.00 (*0-89871-394-3*) Soc Indus-Appl Math.

Czitrom, Andrei A. & Gross, Allan E. Allografts in Orthopaedic Practice. (Illus.). 240p. 1992. 75.00 (*0-683-02300-4*) Lppncott W & W.

Czitrom, Andrei A. & Winkler, Heinz. Orthopaedic Allograft Surgery. LC 96-15022. (Illus.). 300p. 1996. 215.00 (*3-211-82647-5*) Spr-Verlag.

Czitrom, Daniel. Mysteries of the City: Culture Politics & the Underworld in New York, 1870-1920. (C). (gr. 13). 1999. 25.00 (*0-415-90470-6*) Routledge.

Czitrom, Daniel J. Media & the American Mind: From Morse to McLuhan. LC 81-14810. xiv, 254p. 1982. pap. 17.95 (*0-8078-4107-2*) U of NC Pr.

Czmpofridano, Anna M., jt. ed. see Alisio, Giancarlo.

Czobor, Agnes. The Budapest Museum of Fine Arts. 116p. (C). 1988. 50.00 (*0-7855-4539-5*, Pub. by Collets) St Mut.

— The Budapest Museum of Fine Arts. (Illus.). 116p. (C). 1988. text 50.00 (*0-7855-5861-6*, Pub. by Collets) St Mut.

Czoch, R. & Francik, A. Instrumental Effects in Homodyne Electron Paramagnetic Resonance Spectrometers. 1989. text 69.95 (*0-470-20897-X*) P-H.

***Czogala, E. & Leski, J.** Fuzzy & Neuro-Fuzzy Intelligent Systems. (Studies in Fuzziness & Soft Computing: Vol. 47). (Illus.). xvi, 195p. 2000. text 72.00 (*3-7908-1289-7*, Pub. by Physica-Verlag) Spr-Verlag.

Czogalla, C. D. & Boberg, F. Sulfur Compounds in Fossil Fuels 1, Vol. 3. 50p. 1983. pap. text 85.00 (*3-7186-0260-1*) Gordon & Breach.

Czolczynski, Krzysztof. Rotordynamics of Gas-Lubricated Journal Bearing Systems. LC 99-24755. (Mechanical Engineering Ser.). (Illus.). 152p. 1999. 49.00 (*0-387-98677-4*) Spr-Verlag.

Czompo, Andor, jt. auth. see Czompo, Ann I.

Czompo, Andor, ed. see Czompo, Ann I.

Czompo, Ann I. Recreational Jazz Dance. 2nd ed. Czompo, Andor, ed. LC 79-26223. (Illus.). (C). 1979. pap. text 9.95 (*0-935496-00-9*) AC Pubns.

Czompo, Ann I. & Czompo, Andor. Dance Fundamentals. (Illus.). 54p. (Orig.). (C). 1982. pap. text 5.00 (*0-935496-02-5*) AC Pubns.

Czou Jui-Lin, et al. Four Papers on Partial Differential Equations. LC 51-5559. (Translations Ser.: Series 2, Vol. 41). 317p. 1964. text 37.00 (*0-8218-1741-8*, TRANS2/41) Am Math.

Czovek, Erna. Music & the Child. 84p. 1989. pap. 25.00 (*963-13-0700-X*, Pub. by Corvina Bks) St Mut.

Czubaroff, Jeanine, ed. see Bailey, Alison.

Czuchajowski, Leszek. Wiersze na dwu Strunach (Two String Poems) (POL.). 80p. (Orig.). 1989. pap. text 7.00 (*0-930401-23-9*) Artex Pub.

Czuchna-Curl, Ardyce. Mountains & Rainbows: Modern Pioneers--How Alaska Changed Their Lives. LC 89-3079. (Illus.). 220p. (Orig.). 1989. 16.95 (*0-88196-002-0*); pap. 9.95 (*0-88196-001-2*) Oak Woods Media.

Czuckrey, William N. Games for Fundraising. LC 95-20296. (Illus.). 130p. 1995. pap. 24.95 (*1-56164-074-3*) Pineapple Pr.

Czuczka, George T. Imprints of the Future: Politics & Individuation in Our Time. LC 97-17272. 112p. 1995. pap. 10.95 (*3-85630-513-0*) Continuum.

Czudner, Gad. Small Criminals among Us: How to Recognize & Change Children's Antisocial Behavior Before They Explode. LC 98-68327. 280p. 1999. pap. 14.95 (*0-88282-180-6*) New Horizon NJ.

Czudnowski, Moshe M., ed. Does Who Governs Matter? LC 82-22495. (International Yearbook for Studies of Leaders & Leadership Ser.). 292p. 1982. pap. 18.00 (*0-87580-529-9*) N Ill U Pr.

— Political Elites & Social Change: Studies of Elite Roles & Attitudes. LC 83-2461. (International Yearbook for Studies of Leaders & Leadership Ser.). 255p. 1983. 32.00 (*0-87580-093-9*); pap. 18.00 (*0-87580-530-2*) N Ill U Pr.

Czudnowski, Moshe M., jt. ed. see Clarke, Harold D.

Czukor, John C. Beginning Clerical Worker: Account Clerk - Audit Clerk - Statistical Clerk - File Clerk - Payroll Clerk - Receptionist. 11th ed. 304p. 1989. per. 13.95 (*0-13-068206-3*, Arc) IDG Bks.

— File Clerk - General Clerk: Federal - State - Municipal. 9th ed. LC 92-17676. 224p. 1993. per. 12.95 (*0-671-84714-7*, Arc) IDG Bks.

Czukor, John C., jt. auth. see Hammer, Hy.

Czulewicz, Gerald. The Foremost Guide to Uncle Sam Collectibles. 288p. 1995. 24.95 (*0-89145-650-3*, 3976) Collector Bks.

Czupryna, G. In Situ Immobilization of Heavy-Metal-Contaminated Soils. LC 89-22799. (Pollution Technology Review Ser.: No. 173). (Illus.). 155p. 1989. 39.00 (*0-8155-1219-8*, 900102) Noyes.

Czury, Craig. God's Shiny Glass Eye. 40p. 1987. pap. 5.00 (*0-9613465-5-8*) Great Elm.

Czyz, Janusz. Paradoxes of Measures & Dimensions Originating in Felix Hausdorff's Ideas. 300p. (C). 1994. text 109.00 (*981-02-0189-3*) World Scientific Pub.

Czyz, Joann. Don't Count Me Out: A Different Perception of Fear. 272p. 1995. 16.95 (*0-9645587-0-X*); pap. 12.95 (*0-9645587-1-8*) LAF Pub.

Czyz, Vincent. Adrift in a Vanishing City. LC 98-61077. xiv, 234p. 1998. pap. 10.00 (*0-9665998-0-2*) Voyant Pubg.

Czyzycka, Magdalena, tr. see Ali, Ansara.

C15.1 Committee on RFP Guidelines Staff. Electronic Imaging Request for Proposal (RFP) Guidelines: ANSI/AIIM TR27-1996. (Technical Reports). 53p. 1996. 52.00 (*0-89258-222-7*, TR27) Assn Inform & Image Mgmt.

C18 Public Records Committee Staff. The Expungement of Information Recorded on Optical Write-Once-Read-Many (WORM) Systems: ANSI/AIIM TR28-1991. (Technical Reports). 11p. 1991. 33.00 (*0-89258-223-5*, TR28) Assn Inform & Image Mgmt.

C18.2 Committee on Digital Imaging for Public Records Staff. The Use of Optical Disks for Public Records. (Technical Reports). (Illus.). 41p. 1995. 45.00 (*0-89258-214-6*, TR25) Assn Inform & Image Mgmt.

C3.1 Meeting of COSPAR Scientific Commission C Sta. The Atmospheres of Venus & Mars: Proceedings of the C3.1 Meeting of COSPAR Scientific Commission C Which Was Held During the 30th COSPAR Scientific Assembly, Hamburg, Germany, 11-21 July, 1994. Taylor, F. W., ed. (Advances in Space Research Ser.: Vol. 16). 118p. 1995. pap. 97.75 (*0-08-042626-3*, Pergamon Pr) Elsevier.

C808, 42B. St Joseph 1st Mass Set-blk Pad. 1993. 12.95 (*0-89942-765-0*) Catholic Bk Pub.

C808, 42W. St Joseph 1st Mass Set-wht Pad. (J). 1993. 12.95 (*0-89942-764-2*) Catholic Bk Pub.

D

D. A. P. Plubishing Staff. Poliester #27 Death. 1999. pap. text 10.00 (*1-56466-066-4*) Archer Fields.

— Poliester #28 Design. 1999. pap. text 10.00 (*1-56466-071-0*) ACOA.

D. A. P. Staff. Radical Images. (Illus.). 1997. pap. text 45.00 (*3-900508-17-8*) Dist Art Pubs.

D. A. R. P. A. Staff, ed. Speech & Natural Language: Proceedings ofthe Summer Workshop, 1990. (Illus.). 300p. (C). 1998. pap. text 40.00 (*1-55860-157-0*) Morgan Kaufmann.

— The Speech & Natural Language Workshop: October, 1989 Proceedings. (C). 1998. pap. text 40.00 (*1-55860-111-2*) Morgan Kaufmann.

D A R Systems International Staff, ed. see Seiden, Eric A.

D A R Systems International Staff, ed. see Seiden, Eric A., et al.

***D. A. R. Thronateeska Chapter.** History & Reminiscences of Dougherty County Georgia. (Illus.). 411p. 2000. reprint ed. 62.50 (*0-8328-3419-X*) Higginson Bk Co.

D. A. R. Thronateeska Chapter, compiled by. History & Reminiscences of Dougherty County Georgia. LC 78-12903. 1978. reprint ed. 30.00 (*0-87152-282-9*) Reprint.

D' Andrea, Salovey. Peer Counseling. 2nd ed. 422p. 1996. pap. 29.95 (*0-8314-0084-6*) Sci & Behavior.

D. B. & Associates Staff, jt. auth. see Sykes, Diane L.

D. C. Bureau of National Affairs Washington Staff. Zero Tolerance: An Employer's Guide to Preventing Sexual Harassment & Healing the Workplace. 2nd ed. Cornish, Tony, ed. LC 98-52101. 144p. 1999. 29.00 (*1-55871-391-3*) BNAC.

D C C, Incorporated Staff. A LifeCare Digest on Helping Children Adjust to New Caregivers. 4p. 1999. pap. 1.95 (*1-58559-003-7*) DCC Inc.

— A LifeCare Digest on Sunburn Protection. 3p. 1999. pap. 1.75 (*1-58559-001-0*) DCC Inc.

— A LifeCare Guide to Caregiving. 1999. pap. 14.95 (*1-58559-000-2*) DCC Inc.

— A LifeCare Guide to In-Home Care. 64p. 1999. pap. 12.95 (*1-58559-002-9*) DCC Inc.

D. C. Comics Staff. Batman Collector's Set: Batman #520, 521, 522 & Detective Comics #687, 687, 689 with Cards, 6 vols. (Illus.). 1996. pap. 11.70 (*1-56389-284-7*, Pub. by DC Comics) Time Warner.

D. C. Comics Staff. DC Superheroes, Vol. 1. 1995. 8.98 (*1-57042-141-2*) Warner Bks.

— Dream: Beyond the Shores of Night. LC 98-123590. (Illus.). 208p. 1998. pap. text 19.95 (*1-56389-393-2*, Pub. by DC Comics) Time Warner.

D. C. Comics Staff. Superman Collector's Set: Includes Superman, 6 vols. (Illus.). 1996. pap. 11.70 (*1-56389-283-9*, Pub. by DC Comics) Time Warner.

D. C. Comics Staff. Superman Lives. 1993. 17.00 (*1-57042-024-6*) Warner Bks.

D., Chuck & Jah, Yusaf. Fight the Power: Rap, Race & Reality. (Illus.). 288p. 1998. pap. 12.95 (*0-385-31873-1*) Dell.

D D C Publishing Staff. Access 97: Just the Basics. (One-Day Course Ser.). 1997. pap. text 22.00 incl. cd-rom (*1-56243-519-1*) DDC Pub.

— Excel 97: Just the Basics. (One-Day Course Ser.). 1997. pap. text 22.00 incl. cd-rom (*1-56243-521-3*, DC-4) DDC Pub.

— Learning Microsoft Powerpoint 97. (Learning Ser.). 1997. pap. text 27.00 (*1-56243-442-X*, Z22) DDC Pub.

— Learning Windows 98. (Learning Ser.). pap. text 29.00 (*1-56243-569-8*, Z26HC) DDC Pub.

— Learning Windows 98. LC 99-168123. (Learning Ser.). 1998. pap. text 27.00 (*1-56243-487-X*, Z26) DDC Pub.

— One Day Course for Create a Web Page with Word 97. (One-Day Course Ser.). 1997. pap. text 22.00 (*1-56243-568-X*, DC23) DDC Pub.

— One Day Course for Frontpage. (One-Day Course Ser.). 1997. pap. text 22.00 (*1-56243-448-9*, DC22) DDC Pub.

— One Day Course for Windows NT 4.0. (One-Day Course Ser.). 1997. pap. text 22.00 (*1-56243-297-4*, DC24) DDC Pub.

— Outlook, '97: Just the Basics. (One-Day Course Ser.). 1997. pap. text 22.00 incl. cd-rom (*1-56243-528-0*, DC-11) DDC Pub.

— PowerPoint 97: Just the Basics. (One-Day Course Ser.). 1997. pap. text 22.00 incl. cd-rom (*1-56243-531-0*, DC-14) DDC Pub.

— Quick Reference Guide for Corel Wordperfect Suite 8. (Quick Reference Guides Ser.). 1997. pap. text 12.00 (*1-56243-543-4*, G32) DDC Pub.

— Quick Reference Guide for Lotus Smart Suite. LC 98-127516. (Quick Reference Guides Ser.). 1997. pap. text 12.00 (*1-56243-542-6*, G34) DDC Pub.

— Quick Reference Guide for Powerpoint 97. LC 97-207321. (Quick Reference Guides Ser.). 1997. pap. text 12.00 (*1-56243-490-X*, G-31) DDC Pub.

— Short Course for Access 97 Introductory. LC 99-162342. (Short Course Ser.). 1997. pap. text 25.00 (*1-56243-500-0*, AB29) DDC Pub.

— Short Course for Excel 97 Advanced. LC 98-153004. (Short Course Ser.). 1997. pap. text 25.00 (*1-56243-513-2*, AB37) DDC Pub.

— Short Course for Excel 97 Intermediate. LC 98-226437. (Short Course Ser.). 1997. pap. text 25.00 (*1-56243-512-4*, AB36) DDC Pub.

— Short Course for Excel 97 Introductory. LC 99-162344. (Short Course Ser.). 1997. pap. text 25.00 (*1-56243-511-6*, AB35) DDC Pub.

— Short Course for Office 97 Introductory. LC 99-162350. (Short Course Ser.). 1997. pap. text 25.00 (*1-56243-505-1*, AB26) DDC Pub.

— Short Course for Outlook Introduction. LC 98-170778. (Short Course Ser.). 1997. pap. text 25.00 (*1-56243-517-5*, AB41) DDC Pub.

— Short Course for Paradox 7 for Windows 95 Introductory. (Short Course Ser.). 1997. pap. text 25.00 (*1-56243-558-2*, AB42) DDC Pub.

— Short Course for Powerpoint 97 Introductory. LC 99-162347. (Short Course Ser.). 1997. pap. text 25.00 (*1-56243-514-0*, AB38) DDC Pub.

— Short Course for Word 97 Advanced. (Short Course Ser.). 1997. pap. text 25.00 (*1-56243-510-8*, AB34) DDC Pub.

— Short Course for Word 97 Intermediate. LC 98-180410. (Short Course Ser.). 1997. pap. text 25.00 (*1-56243-509-4*, AB33) DDC Pub.

— Short Course for Word 97 Introductory. LC 98-193900. (Short Course Ser.). 1997. pap. text 25.00 (*1-56243-508-6*, AB32) DDC Pub.

— Word 97: Just the Basics. (One-Day Course Ser.). 1997. pap. text 22.00 incl. cd-rom (*1-56243-535-3*, DC-18) DDC Pub.

***D D C Publishing Staff, et al.** Investing & Personal Finance. (Internet-in-an-Hour Ser.). (Illus.). 213p. 1999. pap. 10.00 (*1-56243-758-5*) DDC Pub.

D

An Asterisk (*) at the beginning of an entry indicates that the title is appearing for the first time.

D. D. Prentice Staff & P.R.G. Holland Staff. Contemporary Issues in Corporate Governance. LC 93-443. (Illus.). 246p. 1993. text 70.00 (*0-19-825859-3*) OUP.

D. E. A. Staff. D. E. A. Undercover. 1999. text 17.95 (*0-312-00029-4*) St Martin.

D. Gupta, Sobhanlal, jt. auth. see Mukhopadhyay, Amal K.

D K Multi-Media Staff. Eyewitness Encyclopedia of Space & the Universe. (Eyewitness Books). (YA). (gr. 4 up). 1997. 29.95 incl. cd-rom (*0-7894-0886-4*) DK Pub Inc.

***D K Publishing Staff.** Amazing Animals Lego Modelers. (LEGO Modelers Ser.). 32p. (J). (gr. k-5). 1999. pap. text 4.95 (*0-7894-4775-4*) DK Pub Inc.

D K Publishing Staff. Baby's Bathtime. 1999. pap. text 4.95 (*0-7894-4323-6*) DK Pub Inc.

— Body Art Gift Box. 1999. 12.99 (*0-7894-4792-4*) DK Pub Inc.

— Budapest. LC 98-50720. (Eyewitness Travel Guides Ser.). 264p. 1999. pap. 19.95 (*0-7894-4180-2*) DK Pub Inc.

— Bunny. LC 99-209406. (Find Out-Fold Out Bks.). 1999. 3.95 (*0-7894-4310-4*) DK Pub Inc.

— Car. (Funpax Ser.). 1999. 4.95 (*0-7894-4318-X*) DK Pub Inc.

— Chick. LC 99-209413. (Find Out-Fold Out Bks.). 1999. 3.95 (*0-7894-4309-0*) DK Pub Inc.

***D K Publishing Staff.** Children's History of the 20th Century. (DK Millennium Ser.). 344p. (J). (gr. 4-8). 1999. 29.95 (*0-7894-4722-3*) DK Pub Inc.

— Dance. (Eyewitness Books). (Illus.). (J). (gr. 4-7). 2000. 19.99 (*0-7894-6625-2*) DK Pub Inc.

D K Publishing Staff. Dk Great Dinosaur Atlas. 1999. 19.95 (*0-7894-4728-2*) DK Pub Inc.

— Dublin: The Guides That Show You What Others Only Tell You. LC 98-32196. (Eyewitness Travel Guides Ser.). 176p. 1999. pap. 19.95 (*0-7894-4178-0*) DK Pub Inc.

— Essential World Atlas. LC 98-18243. (Illus.). 256p. 1998. pap. text 14.95 (*0-7894-3250-1*) DK Pub Inc.

***D K Publishing Staff.** Fabulous Figures Lego Modelers. (LEGO Modelers Ser.). 32p. (J). (gr. k-5). 1999. pap. text 4.95 (*0-7894-4777-0*) DK Pub Inc.

D K Publishing Staff. Flowering Shrubs: American Horticultural Society. LC 98-48212. (AHS Practical Guides Ser.). 1999. pap. 8.95 (*0-7894-4157-8*) DK Pub Inc.

***D K Publishing Staff.** Formula One Yearbook: 1999 Edition. 128p. 1999. 19.95 (*0-7894-4642-1*) DK Pub Inc.

— Friendship. (DK Sticker Gift Box Ser.). 1999. 9.99 (*0-7894-4327-9*) DK Pub Inc.

D K Publishing Staff. Friendship Stationery. 1999. 6.99 (*0-7894-4328-7*) DK Pub Inc.

***D K Publishing Staff.** Future. (Eyewitness Books). (Illus.). (J). (gr. 4-7). 2000. 19.99 (*0-7894-6626-0*) DK Pub Inc.

D K Publishing Staff. Gardening in Shade: American Horticultural Society, Expert Advice from a Trusted Name in Gardening. LC 98-48214. (AHS Practical Guides Ser.). 1999. pap. 8.95 (*0-7894-4154-3*) DK Pub Inc.

— Lamb. LC 99-202129. 1999. 3.95 (*0-7894-4312-0*) DK Pub Inc.

— Madrid. LC 98-32197. (Eyewitness Travel Guides Ser.). 224p. (Orig.). 1999. pap. 22.95 (*0-7894-4179-9*) DK Pub Inc.

— Magic. (Funpax Ser.). 1999. 4.95 (*0-7894-4315-5*) DK Pub Inc.

***D K Publishing Staff.** Millennium 20th Century Day by Day. (DK Millennium Ser.). 1542p. 1999. 49.95 (*0-7894-4640-5*) DK Pub Inc.

D K Publishing Staff. My Big Book. LC 99-191131. (J). 1999. 9.95 (*0-7894-4325-2*) DK Pub Inc.

— My Big Machine Book. LC 99-191139. (J). 1999. 9.95 (*0-7894-4326-0*) DK Pub Inc.

— My Millennium Record Book. (DK Millennium Ser.). 1999. 9.95 (*0-7894-4713-4*) DK Pub Inc.

***D K Publishing Staff.** Mythology. (Eyewitness Books). (Illus.). (J). (gr. 4-7). 2000. 19.99 (*0-7894-6627-9*) DK Pub Inc.

D K Publishing Staff. Pig. LC 99-209408. (Watch the Fun Unfold Ser.). 1999. 3.95 (*0-7894-4311-2*) DK Pub Inc.

— Planes. (FunFax Sticker Ser.). 1999. pap. text 3.95 (*0-7894-4319-8*) DK Pub Inc.

— Playtime. (Bath Bks.). 1999. pap. text 4.95 (*0-7894-4324-4*) DK Pub Inc.

***D K Publishing Staff.** Renaissance. (Eyewitness Books). (Illus.). (J). (gr. 4-7). 2000. 19.99 (*0-7894-6624-4*) DK Pub Inc.

D K Publishing Staff. Reward. (DK Sticker Gift Box Ser.). 1999. pap. 9.99 (*0-7894-4793-2*) DK Pub Inc.

***D K Publishing Staff.** Rock Raiders Lego Game Books. (Lego Puzzle Bks.). 32p. (J). (gr. k-5). 1999. pap. text 4.95 (*0-7894-4707-X*) DK Pub Inc.

D K Publishing Staff. Rocks & Minerals. LC 92-12643. (Eyewitness Explorers Ser.). (Illus.). 64p. (J). (gr. k-3). 1997. pap. 5.95 (*0-7894-1682-4*) DK Pub Inc.

— Roses in the Garden. LC 98-48213. (AHS Practical Guides Ser.). 80p. 1999. pap. 8.95 (*0-7894-4155-1*) DK Pub Inc.

— Seashore. LC 93-31075. (Eyewitness Explorers Ser.). (Illus.). 64p. (J). (gr. k-3). 1997. pap. 5.95 (*0-7894-1681-6*) DK Pub Inc.

— Spacecraft. (FunFax Sticker Ser.). 1999. pap. text 3.95 (*0-7894-4322-8*) DK Pub Inc.

— Timeline Sticker Book. (DK Millennium Ser.). 1999. pap. 6.95 (*0-7894-4717-7*) DK Pub Inc.

— Tractor. (J). (ps). 1999. pap. 4.95 (*0-7894-4307-4*); pap. 4.95 (*0-7894-4308-2*) DK Pub Inc.

— Tractors. (FunFax Sticker Ser.). 8p. 1999. pap. text 3.95 (*0-7894-4321-X*) DK Pub Inc.

— Trains. (FunFax Sticker Ser.). 8p. 1999. pap. text 3.95 (*0-7894-4320-1*) DK Pub Inc.

— Trees. LC 92-54310. (Eyewitness Explorers Ser.). (Illus.). 64p. (J). (gr. k-3). 1997. pap. 5.95 (*0-7894-1679-4*) DK Pub Inc.

***D K Publishing Staff.** Ultimate Lego Book: Discover the Lego Universe. 128p. (J). (gr. 3). 1999. 19.95 (*0-7894-4691-X*) DK Pub Inc.

D K Publishing Staff. Water-wise Gardening. LC 98-48211. (AHS Practical Guides Ser.). 1999. pap. 8.95 (*0-7894-4161-6*) DK Pub Inc.

— Weather. LC 91-58210. (Eyewitness Explorers Ser.). (Illus.). 64p. (J). (gr. 4-7). 1998. pap. 5.95 (*0-7894-2985-3*) DK Pub Inc.

***D K Publishing Staff, ed.** Story of Joseph. (Bible Sticker Activity Bks.). (Illus.). (J). 2000. pap. 5.95 (*0-7894-5330-4*, D K Ink) DK Pub Inc.

D K Publishing Staff, jt. auth. see Reynolds, David West.

D., Lisa, ed. Stepping Stones to Recovery for Young People. LC 91-8676. 240p. (Orig.). (YA). (gr. 9-12). pap. 10.95 (*0-934125-19-8*) Hazelden.

D., Michael. The Healing Rosary: For Those in Recovery from Alcoholism & Addiction. LC 97-75616. (Illus.). 80p. 1998. pap. 5.95 (*1-878718-40-1*, Resurrection Pr) Catholic Bk Pub.

D. R. Myers Distributing Co., Inc. Staff. I. D. Checking Guide, 1993. (Illus.). 96p. 1993. 17.45 (*0-938964-24-0*) Drivers License Guide.

— U. S. Identification Manual, 1993. (Illus.). 700p. 1993. 149.00 (*0-938964-25-9*) Drivers License Guide.

D., Tremayne. Ferrari - Formula 1 Racing Team. LC 98-72320. (Illus.). 160p. 1998. pap. 24.95 (*1-85960-422-6*, Pub. by J H Haynes & Co) Motorbooks Intl.

Da, Adi. Drifted in the Deeper Land: Talks on Relinquishing the Superficiality of Mortal Existence... LC 97-66305. 1997. pap. text 14.95 (*1-57097-037-8*) Dawn Horse Pr.

— The Heart's Shout: Perfect & Urgent Wisdom from the Living Heart of Reality, the Incarnate Divine Person, Adi Da - The Da Avatar. rev. ed. LC 96-83384. 388p. 1996. pap. 17.95 (*1-57097-019-X*) Dawn Horse Pr.

— Ishta: The Way of Devotional Surrender to the Divine Person Da Avabhasa. LC 94-71522. (Illus.). 342p. 1994. reprint ed. pap. 14.95 (*0-918801-98-2*) Dawn Horse Pr.

— The Knee of Listening: The Early Life Ordeal & Radical Spiritual Realization of the Divine World-Teacher. rev. ed. (Illus.). 624p. 1996. mass mkt. 4.95 (*1-57097-023-8*) Dawn Horse Pr.

— The Method of the Siddhas: Talks on the Spiritual Technique of the Saviors of Mankind. (Illus.). 528p. 1996. pap. 7.95 (*1-57097-015-7*) Dawn Horse Pr.

— The Order of My Free Names: The Self-Revelation of the Incarnate Divine Person, Adi Da, & How to Call Him by Name. LC 97-149387. 200p. 1996. pap. text 17.95 (*1-57097-024-6*) Dawn Horse Pr.

— See My Brightness Face to Face: A Celebration of The Ruchira Buddha, Avatar Adi Da Samraj & the First 25 Years of His Divine Revelation Work. 1997. pap. 19.95 (*1-57097-038-6*) Dawn Horse Pr.

Da Angelious, Therese. Gregory Hines - Performer. De Angelis, Gina, ed. LC 99-17790. (Illus.). 144p. (YA). (gr. 5-9). 1999. 19.95 (*0-7910-5197-8*) Chelsea Hse.

Da Avabhasa. Easy Death: Spiritual Discourses & Essays on the Inherent & Ultimate Transcendence of Death & Everything Else. rev. ed. Grisso, Connie et al, eds. LC 91-45959. (Illus.). 432p. (Orig.). 1991. pap. 14.95 (*0-918801-30-3*) Dawn Horse Pr.

— Twirling & Jet Lag: A Simple & Effective Method for Overcoming Jet Lag, Tension & Fatigue. Gottlieb, Bill, ed. 48p. 1994. pap. 2.95 (*0-918801-27-3*) Dawn Horse Pr.

Da Avabhasa, Adi. The Lion Sutra: On Perfect Transcendence of the Primal Act, Which Is the Ego-"I", the Self-Contraction, or Attention Itself & All the Illusions of Separateness, Otherness, Relatedness & Difference. 508p. 1995. pap. 24.95 (*1-57097-012-2*) Dawn Horse Pr.

Da Basticci, Vespasiano. The Vespasiano Memoirs: Lives of Illustrious Men of the XVth Century. 7th ed. Waters, Emily & George, William, trs. from ITA. LC 97-189468. 492p. 1997. pap. text 22.50 (*0-8020-7968-7*) U of Toronto Pr.

Da Brescia, Bonaventura. Brevis Collectio Artis Musicae. Seay, Albert, ed. (Critical Texts Ser.: No. 11). (Illus.). vi, 93p. 1981. pap. text 6.00 (*0-933894-01-5*) Colo Coll Music.

— Regula Musice Plane. fac. ed. (Monuments of Music & Music Literature in Facsimile Ser., Series II: Vol. 77). (ITA., Illus.). 46p. 1975. lib. bdg. 20.00 (*0-8450-2277-6*) Broude.

Da Col, Ivar. Hamamelis y el Secreto.Tr. of Hamamelis & the Secret. (SPA., Illus.). 24p. (J). (ps-1). 1993. pap. text 6.95 (*980-257-100-8*, Pub. by Ediciones Ekare) Kane-Miller Bk.

Da Coll, Ivar. Hamamelis, Miosotis y el Senor Sorpresa.Tr. of Hamamelis, Miosotis & Mr. Sorpresa. (SPA., Illus.). 24p. (J). (ps-1). 1993. pap. 6.95 (*980-257-113-X*) Ediciones Ekare.

— Hamamelis, Miosotis y el Senor Sorpresa.Tr. of Hamamelis, Miosotis & Mr. Sorpresa. (SPA., Illus.). 24p. (J). (gr. 2-3). 1994. pap. 12.95 (*980-257-049-4*, Pub. by Santillana) T R Bks.

D'A-Collyer, A. Despatches & Correspondence of John Second Earl of Buckinghamshire Vol. II: Ambassador to the Court of Catherine II of Russia. (Camden Third Ser.). 63.00 (*0-86193-003-7*) David Brown.

Da Conceicao, Maria, jt. auth. see Kitchen, K. A.

Da Cortona, Pietro. The Anatomical Plates of Pietro Da Cortona: 27 Baroque Masterpieces. 64p. (Orig.). 1986. pap. 7.95 (*0-486-25081-4*) Dover.

***Da Costa.** Itinerario of Jeronime Lobo. 1998. 52.95 (*0-904180-15-8*) Ashgate Pub Co.

Da Costa Carvalho, Olivio. Dicionario de Frances Portuges - French - Portuguese Dictionary. (POR & SPA.). 798p. 1991. 65.00 (*0-8288-8539-7*) Fr & Eur.

— Dicionario de Portugues Frances - Portuguese - French Dictionary. (FRE & POR.). 853p. 1991. 65.00 (*0-8288-8537-0*) Fr & Eur.

Da Costa, Emilia V. Crowns of Glory, Tears of Blood: The Demerara Slave Rebellion of 1823. LC 96-51478. (Illus.). 400p. (C). 1997. pap. 19.95 (*0-19-510656-3*) OUP.

Da Costa, Emilia Viotti. The Brazilian Empire: Myths & Histories. LC 85-16456. (Illus.). xxvi, 314p. 1996. 29.00 (*0-226-85667-4*) U Ch Pr.

***Da Costa, Emilia Viotti.** The Brazilian Empire: Myths & Histories. rev. ed. LC 99-42037. 320p. 2000. pap. 16.95 (*0-8078-4840-9*) U of NC Pr.

Da Costa Fontes, Manuel. Folklore & Literature: Studies in the Portuguese, Brazilian, Cephardic & Hispanic Oral Traditions. LC 99-39443. (C). 2000. text 57.50 (*0-7914-4491-0*); pap. text 18.95 (*0-7914-4492-9*) State U NY Pr.

Da Costa Fontes, Manuel, et al. O Romanceiro Portugues e Brasileiro: Indice Tematico e Bibliografico, 2 vols.Tr. of Portuguese & Brazilian Balladry: A Thematic & Bibliographic Index. v, 695p. 1997. 60.00 (*1-56954-063-2*) Hispanic Seminary.

Da Costa, Francisco, jt. auth. see Mickle, M. M.

Da Costa, Hippolyto J. Dionysian Artificers. 47p. reprint ed. 11.50 (*0-89314-405-3*) Philos Res.

Da Costa, J. R., jt. ed. see Loucks, Daniel P.

Da Costa, Jaki. Menopausal Woman on the Run: A Wicked Woman's Guide to Growing Old. 1994. pap. 19.95 (*1-898307-19-9*) Holmes Pub.

Da Costa, Nicolaci & Renzini, Alvio, eds. Galaxy Scaling Relations: Origins, Evolution & Applications: Proceedings of the ESO Workshop, Held at Garching, Germany, 18-20 November, 1996. LC 97-38999. (ESO Astrophysics Symposia Ser.). xx, 404p. 1997. 32.95 (*3-540-63822-9*) Spr-Verlag.

Da Costa Nunez, Ralph. Hopes Dreams & Promises: The Future of Homeless Children in America. (Illus.). 252p. (Orig.). 1994. pap. 15.95 (*0-9641784-0-0*) Homes Homeless.

Da Costa Nunez, Ralph & Mandel, Jenna. Our Wish. (Illus.). 23p. (J). (ps-k). 1997. pap. 4.95 (*0-9641784-1-9*) Homes Homeless.

Da Costa, Patricia. The Devil Inside. (Black Lace Ser.). 1995. mass mkt. 5.95 (*0-352-32993-9*, Pub. by Virgin Bks) London Brdge.

Da Costa, Pedro, tr. see Dominguez, Walter.

Da Costa, Portia. Black Lace Shadowplay. 1999. mass mkt. 6.95 (*0-352-33313-8*) BLA4.

— Continuum. 256p. (Orig.). 1997. mass mkt. 5.95 (*0-352-33120-8*, Pub. by BLA4) London Brdge.

— Gemini Heat. (Black Lace Ser.). 1995. mass mkt. 5.95 (*0-352-32912-2*, Pub. by Virgin Bks) London Brdge.

— Gothic Blue. (Black Lace Ser.). 300p. 1996. mass mkt. 5.95 (*0-352-33075-9*, Pub. by Virgin Bks) London Brdge.

— The Stranger. (Black Lace Ser.). (Orig.). 1997. mass mkt. 5.95 (*0-352-33211-5*, Pub. by BLA4) London Brdge.

— The Tutor. (Black Lace Ser.). 1995. mass mkt. 5.95 (*0-352-32946-7*, Pub. by Virgin Bks) London Brdge.

Da Costa, Rafael S., tr. see Dror, Eli.

Da Costa, Suneeta Peres. Homework. 288p. 1999. 23.95 (*1-58234-060-9*) Bloomsbury Pubg.

Da Costa, Uriel. Examination of Pharisaic Traditions: Supplemented by Semuel da Silva's Treatise on the Immortality of the Soul. Salomon, H. P. & Sassoon, I. S., trs. LC 93-26266. (Studies in Intellectual History: Vol. 44). (Illus.). xxiii, 578p. 1993. 197.50 (*90-04-09923-9*) Brill Academic Pubs.

Da Cruz. American Government Reader. 1999. pap. 24.38 (*0-07-235489-5*) McGraw.

Da Cruz, Daniel. Boot. 1987. mass mkt. 6.99 (*0-312-90060-0*) St Martin.

***Da Cruz, Frank & Gianone, Christine.** Using C-Kermit. 3rd ed. 2001. pap. 49.95 (*1-55558-250-8*, Digital DEC) Buttrwrth-Heinemann.

Da Cruz, Frank & Gianone, Christine M. Using C-Kermit Communication Software. 2nd ed. LC 96-38354. (Illus.). 648p. 1996. pap. text 39.95 (*1-55558-164-1*, Digital DEC) Buttrwrth-Heinemann.

Da Cruz, Pedro. Vessel Management Positioning & Mooring Systems for Offshore Production Vessels. 1989. 125.00 (*90-6314-563-2*, Pub. by Lorne & MacLean Marine) St Mut.

Da Cunha. Southeast Asian Affairs 1998. 400p. 1998. text 55.00 (*0-312-21599-1*) St Martin.

Da Cunha, A. Correia. Dicionario Etimologico Nova Fronteira da Lingua Portuguesa.Tr. of Etymological Dictionary of the Portuguese Language. (POR.). 839p. 1982. 45.00 (*0-8288-1992-0*, M14426) Fr & Eur.

— Portuguese-English Banking Dictionary: Dicionario Bancario Portugues-Ingles. (ENG & POR.). 379p. 1984. pap. 39.95 (*0-8288-0322-6*, M8062) Fr & Eur.

Da Cunha, A. Pinto, ed. Scale Effects in Rock Masses, '93: Proceedings of the Second International Workshop on Scale Effects in Rock Masses, Lisbon, Portugal, June 1993. (Illus.). 350p. 1993. text 136.00 (*90-5410-322-1*, Pub. by A A Balkema) Ashgate Pub Co.

Da Cunha, Carneiro. Antropologica da Brasil. 1999. pap. text 14.95 (*0-226-09354-9*); lib. bdg. 34.95 (*0-226-09353-0*) U Ch Pr.

— Negros Estrangeiros. 1999. pap. text 14.95 (*0-226-09352-2*); lib. bdg. 34.95 (*0-226-09351-4*) U Ch Pr.

Da Cunha, Derek, ed. The Evolving Pacific Power Structure. (Illus.). 276p. (C). 1998. pap. 50.00 (*0-7881-3876-6*) DIANE Pub.

***Da Cunha, Frank.** Read? 1999. pap. write for info. (*1-58235-205-4*) Watermrk Pr.

Da Cunha, J. Gerson. Contributions to the Study of Indo-Portuguese Numismatics. (C). 1995. reprint ed. 26.00 (*81-206-0588-8*, Pub. by Asian Educ Servs) S Asia.

— Origin of Bombay. (C). 1993. reprint ed. text 48.00 (*81-206-0815-1*, Pub. by Asian Educ Servs) S Asia.

Da Cunha, J. Gerson, see Gerson Da Cunha, J.

Da Cunha, L. V., et al. Coping with Droughts. Yevjevich, Vujica, ed. LC 83-50242. 450p. 1984. 45.00 (*0-918334-52-7*) WRP.

Da Cunha Rivara, J. H. Goa & the Revolt of 1787. LC 97-901107. (C). 1996. 36.00 (*81-7022-646-5*, Pub. by Concept) S Asia.

Da Fonseca, Branquinho & Fernandez, Franciso C. The Baron. LC 96-71744. (Publication Ser.).Tr. of O Barao. 62p. 1996. pap. 10.00 (*0-942208-30-7*) Bandanna Bks.

Da Fonseca, Eduardo G. Beliefs in Action: Economic Philosophy & Social Change. 270p. (C). 1991. text 54.95 (*0-521-39306-X*) Cambridge U Pr.

Da Fonseca, Giannetti, jt. ed. see Willumsen, Maria J.

Da Fonseca, Gustavo A., et al. Lista Anotada dos Mamiferos do Brasil: Annotated List of Brazilian Mammals. (Occasional Papers in Conservation Biology). (ENG & POR., Illus.). 35p. (Orig.). (C). Date not set. pap. text 10.00 (*1-881173-17-8*) Conser Intl.

Da Free John. I Am Happiness: A Rendering for Children of the Spiritual Adventure of Master Da Free John. Bodha, Daji & Closser, Lynne, eds. (Illus.). 59p. (Orig.). (J). (gr. 2 up). 1982. pap. 8.95 (*0-913922-68-4*) Dawn Horse Pr.

***Da Free John.** What, Where, When, How, Why & Who to Remember to Be Happy. LC 00-8488. (Illus.). 2000. write for info. (*1-57097-074-2*) Dawn Horse Pr.

Da Graca Carvalho, Maria, et al, eds. Clean Combustion Technologies Pt. A: Proceedings of the Second International Conference. (Energy, Combustion & the Environment Ser.: Vol. 2). 620p. 1998. text 120.00 (*90-5699-608-8*, ECU154, Harwood Acad Pubs) Gordon & Breach.

***Da Graca Carvalho, Maria, et al, eds.** Clean Combustion Technologies Pts. A & B: Proceedings of the 2nd International Conference, 2 Pts. 1192p. 1998. text 295.00 (*90-5699-622-3*, Harwood Acad Pubs) Gordon & Breach.

Da Graca Carvalho, Maria, ed. see Papadopoulos, Christos.

Da Graca Hughes, Maria. Nascida De Novo. (POR.). 135p. Date not set. pap. 10.00 (*0-9668384-0-8*) M D Hughes.

***Da Graca, John.** Heads of State & Government. 2nd ed. 1056p. 2000. lib. bdg. 150.00 (*1-56159-269-2*) Groves Dictionaries.

Da, Heart-Master. Vegetable Surrender: or Happiness Is Not Blue. LC 87-72668. (Illus.). 46p. (J). 1987. 10.95 (*0-918801-02-8*) Dawn Horse Pr.

Da Knowledge Transfer Staff. Personal Money Management. LC 99-67835. pap. 9.95 (*1-885003-34-X*, Pub. by R D Reed Pubs) Midpt Trade.

Da Matta, Roberto. A Divided World: Apinaye Social Structure. (Harvard Studies in Cultural Anthropology: No. 6). (Illus.). 200p. 1982. 54.00 (*0-674-21288-6*) HUP.

Da Matta, Roberto, jt. ed. see Hess, David J.

Da Mosto, Alvise Ca, see Ca da Mosto, Alvise.

Da Mota, A. Teixeira. Some Aspects of Portuguese Colonization & Sea Trade in West Africa in the 15th & 16th Centuries. (Hans Wolff Memorial Lectures). 29p. (Orig.). 1978. pap. text 2.50 (*0-941934-22-5*) Indiana Africa.

Da Palestrina, Giovanni P. Masses & Motets. 240p. 1993. pap. 11.95 (*0-486-27631-7*) Dover.

***Da Paor, Louis.** An Illuminated Celtic Book of Days. LC 99-14269. 136p. 1999. 14.95 (*1-58008-102-9*) Ten Speed Pr.

Da Pian, R., jt. ed. see Pasqualin, A.

***Da Ponte, Lorenzo.** Memoirs. Abbott, Elisabeth, tr. from ITA. LC 99-46014. 512p. 2000. pap. 14.95 (*0-940322-35-8*) NY Rev Bks.

Da Ponte, Lorenzo. Memoirs of Lorenzo da Ponte. Abbott, Elizabeth, tr. from ITA. (Music Reprint Ser.). (Illus.). 512p. 1987. reprint ed. lib. bdg. 49.50 (*0-306-76290-0*) Da Capo.

Da Pra, Vic, jt. auth. see Scott, Jay.

Da Prato, G. & Zabczyk, J. W. Ergodicity for Infinite Dimensional Systems. (London Mathematical Society Lecture Note Ser.: No. 229). 350p. (C). 1996. pap. text 49.95 (*0-521-57900-7*) Cambridge U Pr.

Da Prato, Giuseppe & Tubaro, Luciano, eds. Control of Partial Differential Equations. (Lecture Notes in Pure & Applied Mathematics Ser.: Vol. 165). (Illus.). 296p. 1994. pap. text 145.00 (*0-8247-9240-8*) Dekker.

— Stochastic Partial Differential Equations & Applications II. (Lecture Notes in Mathematics Ser.: Vol. 1390). vi, 258p. 1989. 41.95 (*0-387-51510-0*) Spr-Verlag.

Da Prato, Giuseppe & Turvato, L., eds. Stochastic Partial Differential Equations & Applications. (Lecture Notes in Mathematics Ser.: Vol. 1236). v, 257p. 1987. 42.95 (*0-387-17211-4*) Spr-Verlag.

Da Prato, Giuseppe & Zabczyk, J. W. Stochastic Equations in Infinite Dimensions: Theory & Applications. (Encyclopedia of Mathematics & Its Applications Ser.: No. 45). 472p. (C). 1993. text 110.00 (*0-521-38529-6*) Cambridge U Pr.

Da Prato, Giuseppe & Zolesio, J. P. Partial Differential Equation Methods in Control & Shape Analysis. LC 96-29978. (Lecture Notes in Pure & Applied Mathematics Ser.: Vol. 188). (Illus.). 352p. 1997. pap. text 145.00 (*0-8247-9837-6*) Dekker.

— Shape & Stochastic Control in Partial Differential Equations. (Lecture Notes in Pure & Applied Mathematics Ser.). Date not set. write for info. (*0-8247-0027-9*) Dekker.

Da Prato, Giuseppe, ed. see Krylov, N. V., et al.

D

An Asterisk (*) at the beginning of an entry indicates that the title is appearing for the first time.

Da Providencia, Joao, jt. ed. see Dreizler, Reiner M.

Da Ravenna, Giovanni. Dragmalogia de Elgibili Vite Genere, by Giovanni di Conversino da Ravenna. Eaker, Helen L. & Kohl, Benjamin G., eds. LC 79-2342. (Bucknell Renaissance Texts in Translation Ser.). (ENG & LAT.). 296p. 1980. 38.50 (*0-8387-1897-3*) Bucknell U Pr.

da Ravenna, Giovanni Di Conversino, see Di Conversino da Ravenna, Giovanni.

Da Rocha, A. F. Neural Nets: A Theory for Brains & Machines, Vol. 638. LC 92-31542. (Lecture Notes in Computer Science Ser.). xv, 393p. 1992. 63.95 (*0-387-55949-3*) Spr-Verlag.

Da Rocha, Antonio F. Goncalves, see Harbert, John C. & Goncalves Da Rocha, Antonio F.

Da Rocha, Fernando J., jt. ed. see Callicott, J. Baird.

Da Rosa, Aldo V. Fundamentals of Electronics. LC 89-38295. (University Series in Modern Engineering). (Illus.). 376p. 1991. pap. text 52.00 (*0-911575-55-3*) Optimization Soft.

Da Ruan, ed. Intelligent Hybrid Systems: Fuzzy Logic, Neural Networks, & Genetic Algorithms. LC 97-34161. 376p. 1997. text 148.50 (*0-7923-9999-4*) Kluwer Academic.

Da Samara, Ruchira Avatar Adi, see Adi Da Samra, Ruchira Avatar.

Da-Samraj, Adi. The Master Dancer. 176p. 1993. pap. 12.95 (*0-918801-74-5*) Dawn Horse Pr.

Da Silva. New York City from a Cab Driver's View. 1994. 5.50 (*0-9644600-1-7*) NY Publ.

Da Silva, A. Martins, et al, eds. Biorhythms & Epilepsy. LC 85-11860. (Illus.). 254p. 1985. reprint ed. pap. 78.80 (*0-7837-9570-X*, 206031900005) Bks Demand.

— Neutrotraumatology: Progress & Perspectives - Proceedings of the International Conference on Recent Advances in Neurotraumatology Porto, Portugal, November 1990. (Acta Neurochirugica - Supplementum Ser.: No. 55). (Illus.). 90p. 1992. 96.95 (*0-387-82378-6*) Spr-Verlag.

Da Silva, C. E. Goncalves, see Goncalves da Silva, C. E.

Da Silva, Ed. RF & Microwave Engineering. (Illus.). 320p. 1998. pap. text 47.95 (*0-7506-3930-X*, Newnes) Buttrwrth-Heinemann.

da Silva, Esmeralda. Tarot. LC 98-207999. (Illus.). 72p. 1998. 9.95 (*1-85368-947-5*, Pub. by New5 Holland) Sterling.

da Silva, F. A. Pina, see Montalvao e Silva, J. M. & Pina da Silva, F. A., eds.

Da Silva, F. H. Lopes, see Pfurtscheller, G. & Lopes Da Silva, F. H., eds.

Da Silva, Fernando L., jt. ed. see Niedermeyer, Ernst.

da Silva, F.H., jt. ed. see Pfurtscheller, G.

da Silva Gracias, Fatima. Health & Hygiene in Colonial Goa, 1510-1961. (C). 1994. text 40.00 (*81-7022-506-X*, Pub. by Concept) S Asia.

Da Silva, J. J. Frausto, see Frausto da Silva, J. J.

da Silva, J. J. R. Frausto, jt. auth. see Williams, Robert Joseph Paton.

Da Silva, John. Golfing in New England: The Essential Guide for the New England Golfer. Vaughan, Valerie, ed. LC 97-67647. (Illus.). 200p. (Orig.). 1997. pap., per. 16.95 (*1-889787-00-0*) NE Cartographics.

Da Silva, Jose Lopes, see Lopes Da Silva, Jose, ed.

Da Silva, Luiz B., jt. ed. see Rocca, Jorge J.

Da Silva, M. & Minter, D. W. Fungi from Brazil Recorded by Batista & Co-Workers. (Mycological Paper Ser.: No. 168). 600p. 1995. pap. 115.00 (*0-85198-989-6*) C A B Intl.

Da Silva, M. Fernanda, jt. ed. see Kelly, Roger.

Da Silva, Manuel A., ed. Thermochemistry & Its Applications to Chemical & Biochemical. 1984. text 397.00 (*90-277-1698-6*) Kluwer Academic.

Da Silva, Maria B., ed. Families in the Expansion of Europe. LC 98-26155. (Expanding World Ser.: Vol. 29). 368p. 1998. text 107.95 (*0-86078-520-3*, Pub. by Variorum) Ashgate Pub Co.

Da Silva, Marlene F., jt. auth. see Prance, Ghillean T.

Da Silva, Nicholas. Dread & Alive: Night of the Animals, Vol. 2. Lin, Maria, ed. (Illus.). 32p. (Orig.). 1997. pap. 4.95 (*0-9656228-1-9*) Zoolook.

— Dread & Alive: Welcome to the Jungle, Vol. 3. Lin, Maria, ed. (Illus.). 50p. (Orig.). Date not set. pap. 4.95 (*0-9656228-2-7*) Zoolook.

Da Silva, Nicholas & Taylor, Benito. Dread & Alive: In the Beginning. Lin, Maria, ed. (Illus.). 32p. 1996. pap. 4.95 (*0-9656228-0-0*) Zoolook.

Da Silva, Owen F., tr. see Bienbar, Arthur, ed.

Da Silva, Rachel. Leading Out: Mountaineering Stories of Adventurous Women. 2nd ed. (Illus.). 450p. 1998. pap. 16.95 (*1-58005-010-7*) Seal Pr WA.

Da Silva, Zenia S. Usted y Yo: Primer Paso. (SPA.). 1975. write for info. (*0-02-270900-2*) Macmillan.

— Vuelo, Vol. 3. (SPA.). 1971. write for info. (*0-02-270770-0*) Macmillan.

***Da Silveira, Arnaldo V. K.** Can the Pope Go Bad? Vaillancourt, Kevin, ed. Spann, John, tr. from POR. 1998. reprint ed. pap. 8.50 (*1-929968-00-0*) Catholic Research Inst.

Da Veiga, H. Beirao, ed. Fluid Dynamics: Lectures Given at the 3rd 1982 Session of the Centro Internazionale Matematico Estivo (C. I. M. E.) Held at Varenna, Italy, August 22-September 1, 1982. (Lecture Notes in Mathematics Ser.: Vol. 1047). (ENG & FRE.). vii, 193p. 1984. 32.95 (*0-387-12893-X*) Spr-Verlag.

***Da Viadana, Lodovico G.** Lodovico Grossi Da Viadana: Salmi a Quattro Chori. Wielakker, Gerhard, ed. (Recent Researches in the Music of the Baroque Era Ser.: Vol. RRB86). (Illus.). xxiii, 179p. 1998. pap. 65.00 (*0-89579-398-9*) A-R Eds.

Da Vignola, Jiacomo B. LeDue Regole della Prospettiva Practica: Ed. I. Danti. (ITA., Illus.). 176p. 1998. reprint ed. pap. 495.00 (*1-85297-025-1*, Pub. by Archival Facs) St Mut.

***da Vinci, Leonardo.** Leonardo da Vinci. (Illus.). 96p. 2000. pap. 4.95 (*3-8290-4152-7*) Konemann.

da Vinci, Leonardo. The Notebooks of Leonardo da Vinci. Richter, Irma A., ed. & selected by by. LC 99-186641. (Illus.). 432p. 1999. pap. 9.95 (*0-19-283897-0*) OUP.

— The Notebooks of Leonardo da Vinci, Vols. 1 & 2. Richter, Jean-Paul, ed. (Illus.). 1970. 61.00 (*0-8446-4535-4*) Peter Smith.

Da Vinci Nichols, Nina & Bazzoni, Jana O. Pirandello & Film. LC 94-32071. (Illus.). xxviii, 248p. 1995. text 55.00 (*0-8032-3336-1*) U of Nebr Pr.

Da-wei, Kwo. Chinese Brushwork in Calligraphy & Painting: Its History Aesthetics & Techniques. 224p. 1990. pap. 13.95 (*0-486-26481-5*) Dover.

Da-Wei, Liu, tr. see Qing-Zhu, Fu.

Daab, Marcia J. Science Fair Workshop. (J). (gr. 4-8). 1990. pap. 7.99 (*0-8224-6374-1*) Fearon Teacher Aids.

Daae, E. English-Norwegian, Norwegian-English, Lommeordbok. (ENG & NOR.). 568p. 1980. pap. 15.95 (*0-7859-0859-5*, M9462) Fr & Eur.

— French-Norwegian, Norwegian-French Pocket Dictionary: Francais-Norvegien-Francais Lommerorbok. (FRE & NOR.). 455p. 1981. pap. 12.95 (*0-7859-0860-9*, M9461) Fr & Eur.

Daalder, Hans. Comparative European Politics: An Intellectual Autobiography. LC 96-22205. 384p. 1997. 85.00 (*1-85567-399-1*) Bks Intl VA.

Daalder, Hans, ed. Comparative European Politics: The Story of a Profession. LC 82-7278. 384p. 1999. pap. 24.95 (*1-85567-607-9*) Continuum.

Daalder, Hans & Irwin, Galen I., eds. Politics in the Netherlands: How Much Change. 1989. lib. bdg. 30.00 (*0-7146-3361-5*, F3361, Pub. by F Cass Pubs) Intl Spec Bk.

Daalder, Hans & Mair, Peter, eds. Western European Party Systems: Continuity & Change. 466p. 1983. pap. 16.95 (*0-8039-9702-7*) Sage.

Daalder, Ivo. Getting to Dayton: The Making of America's Bosnia Policy in 1995. LC 99-50468. 1999. 39.95 (*0-8157-1692-3*); pap. 16.95 (*0-8157-1691-5*) Brookings.

Daalder, Ivo H. Anthony Lake & the War in Bosnia. (Pew Case Studies in International Affairs). 50p. (C). 1995. pap. text 3.50 (*1-56927-467-3*, GU Schl Foreign) Geo U Inst Dplmcy.

***Daalder, Ivo H.** NATO in the 21st Century What Purpose? What Mission? 1999. pap. text 11.95 (*0-8157-1695-8*) Brookings.

Daalder, Ivo H. The SDI Challenge to Europe. LC 86-28781. 200p. 1987. text 26.00 (*0-88730-197-5*, HarpBusn) HarpInfo.

***Daalder, Ivo H. & O'Hanlon, Michael E.** Winning Ugly: NATO's War to Save Kosovo. 224p. 2000. pap. 24.95 (*0-8157-1696-6*) Brookings.

Daalder, Ivo H., jt. ed. see Burwell, Francis G.

Daalder, Ivoh & Terriff, Terry, eds. Rethinking the Unthinkable: New Directions for Nuclear Arms. 270p. 1993. text 39.50 (*0-7146-4518-4*, Pub. by F Cass Pubs) Intl Spec Bk.

Daalder, Yvo. The Clinton Administration & Multilateral Peace Operations. (Pew Case Studies in International Affairs). 50p. (C). 1995. pap. text 3.50 (*1-56927-462-2*, GU Schl Foreign) Geo U Inst Dplmcy.

Daams, B. J. Human Force Exertion in Used-Product Interaction: Background for Design. (Physical Ergonomics Ser.: No. 2). (Orig.). 1994. pap. 67.50 (*90-6275-995-5*, Pub. by Delft U Pr) Coronet Bks.

Daams, J. L., et al. Atlas of Crystal Structure Types for Intermetallic Phases, 4 vols. (Illus.). 7026p. (C). 1991. 1509.00 (*0-87170-421-8*, 57731G) ASM.

Daane, Dewey, jt. ed. see Colander, David C.

Daath, Heinrich. Medical Astrology. 108p. 1992. pap. 10.00 (*0-89540-195-9*, SB-195, Sun Bks) Sun Pub.

— Medical Astrology. 108p. 1996. reprint ed. spiral bd. 10.00 (*0-7873-0237-6*) Hlth Research.

— Medical Astrology. 115p. 1996. reprint ed. pap. 7.95 (*1-56459-758-X*) Kessinger Pub.

Dabac, Ulatko. Technisches Woerterbuch: Serbocroatian & German Technical Dictionary, 2 vols. (CRO, GER & SER.). 1969. 195.00 (*0-8288-6617-1*, M7653) Fr & Eur.

D'Abadal y Vinyals, Ramon & Taberner, Ferran V., eds. Ustages de Barcelona. LC 80-1999. reprint ed. 26.00 (*0-404-18552-5*) AMS Pr.

Dabagh, Thomas S. Legal Research Guide for California Practice. LC 85-60262. (Legal Bibliographic & Research Reprint Ser.: Vol. 5). 66p. 1985. reprint ed. lib. bdg. 35.00 (*0-89941-398-6*, 303650) W S Hein.

Dabagian, Marc. Don't Grow up Too Soon. (Illus.). 48p. (Orig.). (J). 1995. pap. 6.95 (*0-9646396-0-2*) Ogden Pr.

***Dabak, Prasad, et al.** UnDocumented Windows NT. LC 99-46008. (Out of Ser.). (Illus.). 350p. 1999. pap. 34.99 (*0-7645-4569-8*) IDG Bks.

Dabars, Zita. The Russian Way. (The...Way Ser.). (Illus.). 96p. 1995. pap. 12.95 (*0-8442-4296-9*, 42969, Passprt Bks) NTC Contemp Pub Co.

Dabars, Zita, et al. Russian Face to Face Level 2: Intermediate. annot. ed. (RUS.). Date not set. teacher ed. 49.50 (*0-8442-4312-4*, X4312-4) NTC Contemp Pub Co.

— Russian Face to Face Level 2: Intermediate, Level 2. (RUS.). 200p. pap., wbk. ed. 9.95 (*0-8442-4311-6*, x4311-6) NTC Contemp Pub Co.

— Russian Face to Face Level 2: Intermediate, Level 2. (RUS.). 528p. (C). student ed. 42.35 (*0-8442-4310-8*, X4310-8) NTC Contemp Pub Co.

— Russian Face to Face Level 2: Workbook Answer Key, Workbook Answer Key. (RUS.). pap. 13.95 (*0-8442-4316-7*, X4316-7) NTC Contemp Pub Co.

Dabas, M. S., tr. see Sabiq, As-Sayyed.

Dabashi, Hamid. Authority in Islam: From the Rise of Muhammad to the Establishment of the Umayyads. 256p. 1989. 44.95 (*0-88738-288-6*); pap. 24.95 (*1-56000-586-6*) Transaction Pubs.

— Ayn al-Qudat al-Hamadhani: An Intellectual Portrait. (Sufi Ser.: No. 6). 220p. (C). 1996. pap. 25.00 (*0-7007-0360-8*, Pub. by Curzon Pr Ltd) Paul & Co Pubs.

— Theology of Discontent: The Ideological Foundations of the Islamic Revolution in Iran. 600p. (C). 1992. text 75.00 (*0-8147-1839-6*); pap. text 25.00 (*0-8147-1840-X*) NYU Pr.

***Dabashi, Hamid.** Truth & Narrative: The Untimely Thoughts of Ayn al-Qudat. 752p. 1999. (*0-7007-1002-7*, Pub. by Curzon Pr Ltd) Paul & Co Pubs.

Dabashi, Hamid, jt. auth. see Chelkowski, Peter J.

Dabashi, Hamid, ed. see Sayyad, Parviz.

***Dabate, Lorraine.** Is It Hot in Here or Is It Me? Mastering the Maze of Menopause. 2000. pap. 9.95 (*1-890838-12-8*) Indus Pub.

D'Abate, Richard. To Keep the House from Falling In. 39p. 1973. 2.95 (*0-87886-028-2*, Greenfld Rev Pr) Greenfld Rev Lit.

D'Abate, Richard, ed. see Prosser, Albert L.

Dabbagh, Maureen. The Recovery of Internationally Abducted Children: A Comprehensive Guide. LC 97-14081. 236p. 1997. pap. 42.50 (*0-7864-0289-X*) McFarland & Co.

Dabbah, Mat. Sabe UD . . . Como? Cuando? Donde? Tecnicas de Investigacion. Zylberglait, Tobias, ed. (SPA., Illus.). 307p. (Orig.). 1996. pap. 29.95 (*0-945406-06-1*) Magnum Schl.

Dabbah, Max. Private Detective & Investigator Course. (ENG & SPA., Illus.). (Orig.). 1987. 450.00 (*0-945406-00-2*) Magnum Schl.

Dabbah, Maximo, jt. auth. see Zylberglait, Tobias.

Dabbah, Roger. Total Project Management: Strategies & Tactics for the Healthcare Industries. (Illus.). 340p. 1993. 98.00 (*0-935184-45-7*) Interpharm.

— Total R & D Management for Healthcare Manufacturers: Strategies & Tactics for the 21st Century. 2nd ed. (Total Management Ser.). 658p. 1998. 169.00 (*1-57491-071-X*) Interpharm.

Dabbert, Stephan, et al, eds. The Economics of Landscape & Wildlife Conservation. (A CAB International Publication). 296p. 1998. 90.00 (*0-85199-222-6*) OUP.

Dabbour, Mohammed M., tr. see Mansour, Awad & Rumman, Ali.

Dabbs. Heroes, Rogues & Lovers. 256p. 2000. 24.95 (*0-07-135739-4*) McGraw.

***Dabbs.** Immunopathology. 2000. text. write for info. (*0-443-06566-7*) Harcrt Hlth Sci Grp.

Dabbs, jt. auth. see Breitenkamp, Edward C.

Dabbs, Christine. Crazy Quilting. 1999. pap. 19.95 (*1-55853-694-9*) Rutledge Hill Pr.

Dabbs, Debbye. Beyond the Grill: A Cookbook for Men. (Illus.). 80p. 1997. pap. 12.00 (*0-9645899-3-1*) D Dabbs.

— Light Take Five, a Cookbook. 112p. 1994. pap. 12.00 (*0-9645899-1-5*) D Dabbs.

— Take Five, a Christmas Cookbook. (Illus.). 120p. 1995. pap. 12.00 (*0-9645899-2-3*) D Dabbs.

— Take Five, a Cookbook. 109p. 1993. pap. 12.00 (*0-9645899-0-7*) D Dabbs.

***Dabbs, Denton.** World War II: Shared Memories. 1999. 21.95 (*1-56311-518-2*) Turner Pub KY.

Dabbs, Henry. Black Brass: Black Generals & Admirals in the Armed Forces of the United States. (Illus.). 228p. 1998. pap. 12.95 (*1-57427-047-8*) Howell Pr VA.

Dabbs, Jack A. The French Army in Mexico, 1861-67: A Study in Military Government. (Studies in American History: No. 2). (Illus.). 1963. 60.00 (*90-279-0228-3*) Mouton.

Dabbs, Mark. The Sistrum. (Illus.). 96p. 1998. pap. 8.00 (*1-891948-04-0*, Pub. by Luxor Press) New Leaf Dist.

Dabbs, Thomas W. Reforming Marlowe: The Nineteenth-Century Canonization of a Renaissance Dramatist. LC 89-46399. 1991. 32.50 (*0-8387-5192-X*) Bucknell U Pr.

Dabcovich, Lydia. Busy Beavers. (J). (ps-2). 1989. 19.95 (*0-590-72455-X*) Scholastic Inc.

— Follow the River. (Illus.). (J). (gr. k-3). 1995. pap. 4.95 (*1-56801-802-9*) Sundance Pub.

— The Polar Bear Son: An Inuit Tale. (FRE., Illus.). 32p. (J). (ps-2). 1999. pap. 5.95 (*0-395-97567-0*) HM.

***Dabcovich, Lydia.** The Polar Bear Son: An Inuit Tale. LC 96-4780. (Illus.). 32p. (J). (ps-2). 1999. 16.00 (*0-395-72766-9*, Clarion Bks) HM.

Dabcovich, Lydia. Sleepy Bear. (Illus.). (J). 1993. pap. 5.99 (*0-14-054785-1*) NAL.

Dabcovich, Lydia. Sleepy Bear. (J). 1985. 11.19 (*0-606-01746-1*, Pub. by Turtleback) Demco.

***Dabczynski, Andrew & Phillips, Bob.** Fiddler's Philharmonic Encore, Cello & Bass. (Fiddler's Philharmonic Encore! Ser.). 48p. 1999. pap. 7.95 (*0-7390-0436-0*, 18082) Alfred Pub.

— Fiddlers Philharmonic Encore, Conductor's Score: Traditional Fiddling in the String Orchestra. 120p. 1999. pap. 21.95 (*0-7390-0546-4*, 18083) Alfred Pub.

— Fiddler's Philharmonic Encore, Viola. (Fiddler's Philharmonic Encore! Ser.). 48p. 1999. pap. 7.95 (*0-7390-0435-2*, 18081) Alfred Pub.

— Fiddler's Philharmonic Encore, Violin. (Fiddler's Philharmonic Encore! Ser.). 48p. 1999. pap. 7.95 (*0-7390-0434-4*, 18080) Alfred Pub.

— Fiddlers Philharmonic, Teacher's Score. 116p. 1996. pap., teacher ed. 19.95 (*0-7390-0889-7*, 11249) Alfred Pub.

Dabczynski, Andrew H. & Phillips, Bob. Fiddlers Philharmonic, Violin. 1996. pap. 6.95 (*0-88284-802-X*) Alfred Pub.

Dabel, Gregory J. Saving Money in Nonprofit Organizations: More Than 100 Money-Saving Ideas, Tips, & Strategies for Reducing Expenses Without Cutting Your Budget. LC 98-36782. (Nonprofit & Public Management Ser.). 1998. 22.95 (*0-7879-4515-3*) Jossey-Bass.

Dabelko, Geoffrey D., jt. ed. see Conca, Kenneth.

Dabezies. CLAO-Allergan. 1989. 130.00 (*0-316-17061-5*, Little Brwn Med Div) Lppncott W & W.

— CLAO LL Set. 2nd ed. 1989. 85.00 (*0-316-17060-7*, Little Brwn Med Div) Lppncott W & W.

— CLAO Set. 2nd ed. 1989. 295.00 (*0-316-17055-0*, Little Brwn Med Div) Lppncott W & W.

— CLAO Update LL, No. 4. 1989. 45.00 (*0-316-17054-2*, Little Brwn Med Div) Lppncott W & W.

— CLAO Update LL, No. 5. 1989. 45.00 (*0-316-17062-3*, Little Brwn Med Div) Lppncott W & W.

— CLAO Update LL, No. 6. 1990. 45.00 (*0-316-17063-1*, Little Brwn Med Div) Lppncott W & W.

— CLAO Update LL, No. 7. 1990. 45.00 (*0-316-17065-8*, Little Brwn Med Div) Lppncott W & W.

— CLAO Update LL, No. 8. 1991. 45.00 (*0-316-17066-6*, Little Brwn Med Div) Lppncott W & W.

Dabir-Alai, Parviz & Odekon, Mehmet, eds. Economic Liberalization & Labor Markets, 51. LC 97-37971. (Illus.). 296p. 1998. 65.00 (*0-313-30358-4*, GM0358, Greenwood Pr) Greenwood.

Dabit, Eugene. L' Hotel du Nord. (FRE.). 220p. 1990. pap. 10.95 (*0-7859-2139-7*, 2070382451) Fr & Eur.

Dabit, Raji. War & Peace: Between Israel & Its Neighbors. viii, 208p. 1997. pap. write for info. (*0-9657058-0-3*) R P Caudill.

Dabiwale, S. M. Emerging Entrepreneurship among Scheduled Castes of Contemporary India. (C). 1989. 24.00 (*81-7022-261-3*, Pub. by Concept) S Asia.

Dabla, Bashir A. Working Women in Kashmir. (C). 1991. 15.00 (*81-7033-132-3*, Pub. by Rawat Pubns) S Asia.

Dabney, Charles W. Universal Education in the South, 2 vols. LC 70-89170. (American Education: Its Men, Institutions, & Ideas. Series 1). 1970. reprint ed. 60.95 (*0-405-01408-2*) Ayer.

***Dabney, Colleen.** The Great Gilly Hopkins: A Guide for Using in the Classroom. Rosenfeld, Sara R., ed. (Illus.). 48p. 1999. pap., teacher ed. 7.95 (*1-57690-343-5*, TCM2343) Tchr Create Mat.

Dabney, Colleen. A View from Saturday. (Literature Unit Ser.). 48p. (J). (gr. 1-3). 1997. pap. 7.95 (*1-57690-348-6*) Tchr Create Mat.

Dabney, D. Lyle, jt. auth. see Moltmann, Jurgen.

Dabney, Eric, ed. see Burke, Bob & Franks, Kenny.

Dabney, Gene. Swimming: A Step-by-Step Guide. LC 89-27346. (Be the Best! Ser.). (Illus.). 64p. (J). (gr. 4-8). 1990. lib. bdg. 15.85 (*0-8167-1945-4*) Troll Communs.

— Swimming: A Step-by-Step Guide. LC 89-27346. (Be the Best! Ser.). (Illus.). 64p. (J). (gr. 4-8). 1997. pap. 3.95 (*0-8167-1946-2*) Troll Communs.

— Swimming: A Step-By-Step Guide. (Be the Best Ser.). 1990. 8.15 (*0-606-04821-9*, Pub. by Turtleback) Demco.

Dabney, James B. & Harman, Thomas L. Mastering Simulink, Vol. 2. LC 97-47332. Vol. 2. 345p. (C). 1997. pap. 56.00 (*0-13-243767-8*, Prentice Hall) P-H.

***Dabney, James B. & Harman, Thomas L.** Mastering Simulink 3. 400p. 2000. write for info. (*0-13-017085-2*) P-H.

Dabney, Joseph E. Herk: Hero of the Skies. LC 84-14330. (Illus.). 448p. 1984. 34.95 (*0-89783-039-3*); pap. 19.95 (*0-89783-028-8*) Cherokee.

— More Mountain Spirits: The Continuing Chronicle of Moonshine Life. LC 85-10932. (Illus.). 208p. 1985. reprint ed. pap. 8.95 (*0-914875-03-5*) Bright Mtn Bks.

— Mountain Spirits: A Chronicle of Corn Whiskey. LC 84-17442. (Illus.). 288p. 1984. reprint ed. pap. 10.95 (*0-914875-02-7*) Bright Mtn Bks.

— Smokehouse Ham, Spoon Bread & Scuppernong Wine: The Folklore & Art of Appalachian Cooking. LC 98-24662. (Illus.). 372p. 1998. 27.95 (*1-888952-93-8*); pap. 19.95 (*1-58182-004-6*) Cumberland Hse.

Dabney, Joy. A Book about Me. 32p. (J). (gr. k-3). 1987. student ed. 2.50 (*0-939985-00-4*) Creative Dimensions.

Dabney, Julia P. Musical Basis of Verse. LC 79-119650. (BCL Ser. I). reprint ed. 22.50 (*0-404-01916-1*) AMS Pr.

***Dabney, Lewis.** Biography of Edmund Wilson. 2000. text. write for info. (*0-374-11312-2*) FS&G.

Dabney, Lewis M. Edmund Wilson: Centennial Reflections. LC 97-12888. 352p. 1997. pap. 12.95 (*0-691-01671-2*, Pub. by Princeton U Pr) Cal Prin Full Svc.

Dabney, Lewis M., ed. see Wilson, Edmund.

Dabney, Melodye L. Incest Annotated Bibliography. (Illus.). 68p. (Orig.). 1984. pap. text 25.00 (*0-9614155-0-9*) Dabney.

Dabney, Norma & Lewis, Shirley, eds. Successful Black & Minority Schools. rev. ed. 96p. (C). 1990. reprint ed. pap. text. write for info. (*0-318-67015-1*) J Richardson.

Dabney, R. L. Christ Our Penal Substitute. 1992. 10.99 (*0-87377-983-5*) GAM Pubns.

— A Defense of Virginia & the South. 1992. 19.99 (*0-87377-929-0*) GAM Pubns.

***Dabney, R. L.** Evangelical Eloquence: A Course of Lectures of Preaching. 361p. 1999. reprint ed. pap. 8.99 (*0-85151-773-0*) Banner of Truth.

Dabney, R. L. The Life & Campaigns of Lt. Gen. T. J. "Stonewall" Jackson. 1992. 34.99 (*0-87377-982-7*); pap. 23.99 (*0-87377-981-9*) GAM Pubns.

— Practical Philosophy. 1992. 23.99 (*0-87377-980-0*) GAM Pubns.

— Systematic Theology. 903p. 1996. reprint ed. 37.99 (*0-85151-453-7*) Banner of Truth.

Dabney, R. L. & Dickinson, Curtis. Five Points of Calvinism. 1997. 19.99 (*0-87377-180-X*) GAM Pubns.

D

Dabney, Robert L. The Sensualistic Philosophy of the 19th Century. LC 75-3008. reprint ed. 32.50 (*0-404-59124-8*) AMS Pr.

Dabney, Viginius. Collected Works of Viginius Dabney: Gold That Did Not Glitter, 2 vols. 1990. reprint ed. lib. bdg. 75.00 (*0-318-67672-9*) Rprt Serv.

— Collected Works of Viginius Dabney: The Story of Don Miff, 2 vols. (Notable American Authors Ser.). 1990. reprint ed. lib. bdg. 75.00 (*0-7812-2600-7*) Rprt Serv.

— Gold That Did Not Glitter. (Notable American Authors Ser.). 1992. reprint ed. lib. bdg. 90.00 (*0-7812-2602-3*) Rprt Serv.

— The Story of Don Miff. (Notable American Authors Ser.). 1992. reprint ed. lib. bdg. 75.00 (*0-7812-2601-5*) Rprt Serv.

Dabney, Virginia B. Once There Was a Farm: A Country Childhood Remembered. LC 98-4241. (Virginia Bookshelf Ser.). 283p. 1998. reprint ed. pap. 14.95 (*0-8139-1847-2*) U Pr of Va.

Dabney, Virginia Bell. Once There Was a Farm . . . large type ed. 1990. lib. bdg. 18.95 (*1-56054-030-3*) Thorndike Pr.

Dabney, Virginius. The Jefferson Scandals: A Rebuttal. (Illus.). 172p. 1990. pap. 14.95 (*0-8191-7821-7*) Madison Bks UPA.

— Liberalism in the South. LC 77-128983. (BCL Ser. II). reprint ed. 49.50 (*0-404-00146-7*) AMS Pr.

— Mr. Jefferson's University: A History. LC 81-3392. (Illus.). 642p. 1981. pap. text 16.95 (*0-8139-1213-X*) U Pr of Va.

— Richmond: The Story of a City. expanded rev. ed. LC 89-38881. 504p. 1990. reprint ed. pap. 156.30 (*0-608-04567-5*, 206530600001) Bks Demand.

— Virginia: The New Dominion, a History from 1607 to the Present. LC 78-157580. (Illus.). 629p. 1983. pap. text 22.50 (*0-8139-1015-3*) U Pr of Va.

— Virginia Commonwealth University: A Sesquicentennial History. fac. ed. LC 87-1982. (Illus.). 451p. 1987. reprint ed. pap. 139.90 (*0-7837-8113-X*, 204792000008) Bks Demand.

Dabney, Virginius, et al, eds. New Virginia Review Anthology 3. (Illus.). 304p. (Orig.). 1984. 13.50 (*0-318-01379-7*) New VA.

Dabney, William H. Dabney. Sketch of the Dabneys of Virginia, with Some of Their Family Records. 107p. 1997. reprint ed. pap. 18.00 (*0-8328-8196-1*); reprint ed. lib. bdg. 28.00 (*0-8328-8195-3*) Higginson Bk Co.

***Dabney, William H.** Sketch of the Dabneys of Virginia: With Some of Their Family Records. 207p. 1999. reprint ed. pap. 19.50 (*0-7884-1242-6*, D005) Heritage Bk.

Daboni, L., et al. Recent Developments in the Foundations of Utility & Risk Theory. 1986. lib. bdg. 200.00 (*90-277-2201-3*) Kluwer Academic.

Daborn, Graham, jt. ed. see Conley, Marshall.

Dabourne, Wendy. Purpose & Cause in Pauline Exegesis: Romans 1.16-4.25 & a New Approach to the Letters. LC 98-20490. (Society for New Testament Studies Monograph Ser.: No. 104). 272p. (C). 1999. text 59.95 (*0-521-64003-2*) Cambridge U Pr.

Dabout, E., ed. Diccionario de Medicina. (SPA.). 24.95 (*0-7859-0587-1*, S-37586) Fr & Eur.

Dabovich, Sebastian. Holy Orthodox Church: Its Ritual, Services, & Sacraments. 1898. pap. 2.95 (*0-89981-030-6*) Eastern Orthodox.

— The Life of St. Nicholas. 1990. pap. 0.50 (*0-89981-085-3*) Eastern Orthodox.

— St. Panteleimon. 1978. pap. 0.25 (*0-89981-086-1*) Eastern Orthodox.

D

D'Aboville, Gerard. Alone: The Man Who Braved the Angry Pacific - & Won. Seaver, Richard, tr. from FRE. (Illus.). 176p. 1993. 21.45 (*1-55970-218-4*, Pub. by Arcade Pub Inc) Time Warner.

— Alone: The Man Who Braved the Vast Pacific - & Won. Seaver, Richard, tr. from FRE. (Illus.). 176p. 1994. pap. 13.45 (*1-55970-246-X*, Pub. by Arcade Pub Inc) Time Warner.

Dabral, Sanjay & Maloney, Timothy J. Basic ESD & IO Design. 328p. 1998. 84.95 (*0-471-25359-6*, Wiley-Interscience) Wiley.

D'Abramo, Louis R., et al, eds. Crustacean Nutrition. unabridged ed. LC 97-208952. (Advances in World Aquaculture Ser.: Vol. 6). (Illus.). xiii, 587p. (C). 1997. text 50.00 (*1-888807-00-8*) World Aquaculture.

Dabree, Bonamy, ed. see Stanhope, Phillip D.

Dabrio, Cristino J., jt. ed. see Friend, Peter F.

***Dabroski, Craig.** The Accounting Guide: A Comprehensive Resource for Community Banks. 150p. 1999. write for info. (*1-882097-71-8*) Amers Comm Bank.

Dabrowska-Bernstein, Barbara K., jt. auth. see Dabrowski, Marek P.

Dabrowska, Ewa. Cognitive Semantics & the Polish Dative. LC 97-23314. 240p. 1997. text 105.00 (*3-11-015218-5*) Mouton.

Dabrowski, A. Adsorption & Its Applications in Industry & Enviromntal Protection, Vol. 1. LC 98-48805. (Studies in Surface Science & Catalysis). 1090p. 1998. 431.00 (*0-444-50165-7*) Elsevier.

Dabrowski, A., ed. Adsorption & Its Application in Industry & Environmental Protection. LC 98-48805. (Studies in Surface Science & Catalysis). 1998. write for info. (*0-444-82828-1*) Elsevier.

— Adsorption & Its Applications in Industry & Enviromntal Protection, Vol. 2. LC 98-48805. (Studies in Surface Science & Catalysis). 1090p. 1998. pap. text 431.00 (*0-444-50166-5*) Elsevier.

Dabrowski, A. & Tertykh, V. A., eds. Adsorption on New & Modified Inorganic Sorbents. LC 95-50055. (Studies in Surface Science & Catalysis: Vol. 99). 944p. 1996. 377.00 (*0-444-82179-1*) Elsevier.

Dabrowski, H. P. Dornier DO 23. (Illus.). 48p. 1996. pap. 9.95 (*0-7643-0093-8*) Schiffer.

— Flying Wings of the Horten Brothers. Johnston, David, tr. from GER. LC 95-70704. (Illus.). 80p. 1995. pap. 14.95 (*0-88740-886-9*) Schiffer.

— The Horten Flying Wing in World War II: The History & Development of the HO229. Johnston, David, tr. from GER. LC 91-62748. (Illus.). 52p. 1991. pap. 9.95 (*0-88740-357-3*) Schiffer.

— Messerschmitt Me 321/323: Giants of the Luftwaffe. (Illus.). 48p. (YA). (gr. 10-13). 1994. pap. 9.95 (*0-88740-671-8*) Schiffer.

Dabrowski, Hans P. Heinkel HE 100: World Record & Propaganda Aircraft. Force, Edward, tr. from GER. LC 91-66339. (Illus.). 48p. 1991. pap. 9.95 (*0-88740-345-X*) Schiffer.

Dabrowski, Hans-Peter. Heinkel He 112. LC 98-131795.Tr. of JAGDEINSITZER HE 112. (Illus.). 48p. 1998. pap. 9.95 (*0-7643-0392-9*) Schiffer.

— Lippisch P 13A: The Experimental DM-1. Carle, James, tr. (Illus.). 48p. (Orig.). 1993. pap. 9.95 (*0-88740-479-0*) Schiffer.

— Mistel: The Piggy-Back Aircraft of the Luftwaffe. (Illus.). 52p. 1994. pap. 9.95 (*0-88740-668-8*) Schiffer.

Dabrowski, Hans-Peter & Koos, Volker. Arado Ar 196: Germany's Multi-Purpose Seaplane. Cox, Don, tr. (Illus.). 48p. (Orig.). 1993. pap. 9.95 (*0-88740-481-2*) Schiffer.

Dabrowski, J. & Mussig, H. J. Silicon Surfaces & Formation of Interfaces: Microscopic & Mesoscopic Structures. LC 99-89210. 350p. 1999. 52.00 (*981-02-3286-1*) World Scientific Pub.

Dabrowski, Konrad & Champigneulle, Alexis, eds. Advances in Fishery Biology - Biology, Exploitation, Rearing & Propagation of Coregonid Fishes: Proceedings of the Symposium on Coregonid Fishes Held October 2-4, 1984 at Thonon, France. (Advances in Limnology Ser.: Vol. 22). (GER., Illus.). viii, 386p. 1986. pap. 92.00 (*3-510-47020-6*, Pub. by E Schweizerbartsche) Balogh.

***Dabrowski, Konrad & Lutz, Peter L.** Ascorbic Acid in Aquatic Organisms: Status & Perspectives. 1999. 139.00 (*0-8493-9881-9*) CRC Pr.

Dabrowski, Magdalena. Contrasts of Form: Geometric Abstract Art 1910-1980. (Illus.). 302p. 1985. pap. 24.95 (*0-87070-289-0*) Mus of Modern Art.

— The Drawings of Philip Guston. (Illus.). 176p. (Orig.). 1988. pap. 24.95 (*0-87070-352-8*) Mus of Modern Art.

***Dabrowski, Magdalena.** French Landscape: The Modernist Vision 1880-1920. (Illus.). 144p. 1999. pap. 19.95 (*0-87070-027-8*) Mus of Modern Art.

Dabrowski, Magdalena. French Landscape & Paris: A Modernist Vision. 1999. pap. 24.95 (*0-8109-6204-7*, Pub. by Abrams) Time Warner.

— Kandinsky: Compositions. (Illus.). 128p. 1997. pap. 22.50 (*0-8109-6180-6*, Pub. by Abrams) Time Warner.

— Kandinsky: Compositions. (Illus.). 128p. 1995. 40.00 (*0-87070-405-2*, 0-8109-6142-3, Pub. by Mus of Modern Art); pap. 22.50 (*0-87070-406-0*, 0-8109-6180-6, Pub. by Mus of Modern Art) Abrams.

— Liubov Popova. (Illus.). 136p. 1991. 39.95 (*0-8109-6090-7*, Pub. by Abrams) Time Warner.

— Liubov Popova. (Illus.). 136p. 1991. 39.95 (*0-87070-567-9*, 0-8109-6090-7) Mus of Modern Art.

— Vasily Kandinsky Compositions. (Illus.). 128p. 1995. 45.00 (*0-8109-6142-3*, Pub. by Abrams) Time Warner.

Dabrowski, Magdalena, et al. Aleksandr Rodchenko: Russian Revolutionary Modernist. LC 98-65575. (Illus.). 336p. 1998. 65.00 (*0-8109-6187-3*, Pub. by Abrams) Time Warner.

— Alexander Rodchenko. (Illus.). 344p. 1998. 65.00 (*0-87070-063-4*, 0-8109-61873, Pub. by Mus of Modern Art) Abrams.

— Alexander Rodchenko. (Illus.). 344p. 1998. pap. 32.50 (*0-87070-064-2*) Mus of Modern Art.

Dabrowski, Marek P. & Dabrowska-Bernstein, Barbara K. Immunoregulatory Role of Thymus. 240p. 1989. lib. bdg. 190.00 (*0-8493-6178-8*, QR185) CRC Pr.

Dabscheck, Braham. Australian Industrial Relations in the 1980s. 192p. 1989. pap. text 19.95 (*0-19-554921-X*) OUP.

Dabscheck, Braham. The Struggle for Australian Industrial Relations. (oup). (Illus.). 208p. (C). 1996. pap. text 38.00 (*0-19-553486-7*) OUP.

Dabson, Brian, et al. Enterprising Youth in America: A Review of Youth Enterprise Programs. pap. 15.00 (*1-883187-19-2*) Corp Ent Dev.

Dabson, Brian, jt. auth. see Schweke, William.

Dabuisson, jt. auth. see IFAC Symposium Staff.

Dabundo, Laura, ed. Encyclopedia of Romanticism: Culture in Britain, 1780s-1830s. LC 92-2682. (Illus.). 688p. 1992. text 40.00 (*0-8240-6997-8*, H#1299) Garland.

***Dabundo, Laura, ed.** Jane Austen & Mary Shelley & Their Sisters. LC 99-87446. 192p. 2000. 49.00 (*0-7618-1611-9*); 27.50 (*0-7618-1612-7*) U Pr of Amer.

Dabydeen, Cyril. Black Jesus & Other Stories. LC 97-157742. 172p. 1997. pap. 12.95 (*0-920661-57-2*, Pub. by TSAR Pubns) LPC InBook.

— Coastline: New & Selected Poems. 120p. 1996. pap. 12.95 (*0-88962-419-4*) Mosaic.

— Discussing Columbus: Discussing Columbus. 96p. 1997. pap. 12.95 (*0-948833-57-2*, Pub. by Peepal Tree Pr) Paul & Co Pubs.

Dabydeen, Cyril, ed. Another Way to Dance: Contemporary Asian Poetry from Canada & the United States. LC 97-132442. 200p. 1997. pap. 19.95 (*0-920661-59-9*, Pub. by TSAR Pubns) LPC InBook.

— A Shapely Fire: Black Writers in Canada. 175p. 1987. 24.95 (*0-88962-345-7*); pap. 12.95 (*0-88962-344-9*) Mosaic.

Dabydeen, David. The Counting House. LC 97-107976. xi, 179 p. 1996. write for info. (*0-224-04343-9*, Pub. by Jonathan Cape) Trafalgar.

— Handbook for Teaching Caribbean Literature. 121p. (Orig.). (C). 1988. pap. text 17.50 (*0-435-91185-6*, 91185) Heinemann.

***Dabydeen, David.** Hogarths Blacks: Images of Blacks in Eighteenth Century. 2000. pap. 19.95 (*1-86064-587-9*) I B T.

Dabydeen, David, jt. ed. see Edwards, Paul.

Dacal-Moure, Ramon & Rivero-De-La-Calle, Manuel. Art & Archaeology of Pre-Columbian Cuba. LC 96-25207. (Latin American Ser.). (Illus.). 134p. 1997. text 35.00 (*0-8229-3955-X*) U of Pittsburgh Pr.

D'Acci, Julie. Defining Women: Television & the Case of Cagney & Lacey. LC 93-32536. (Illus.). xiv, 344p. (C). 1994. pap. text 19.95 (*0-8078-4441-1*); lib. bdg. 55.00 (*0-8078-2132-2*) U of NC Pr.

— Women Feminism & Television. (C). (gr. 13). 1999. 55.00 (*0-415-90252-5*) Routledge.

D'Accone, Frank A. The Civic Muse: Music & Musicians in Siena During the Middle Ages & Renaissance. LC 96-46888. 1997. 70.00 (*0-226-13366-4*) U Ch Pr.

D'Accone, Frank A., et al. Musica Franca: Essays in Honor of Frank A. D'Accone. LC 96-21129. (Festschrift Ser.). 1996. 54.00 (*0-945193-92-0*) Pendragon NY.

Daccord, Brian. Hockey Goaltending. LC 98-12412. (Illus.). 200p. 1998. pap. 16.95 (*0-88011-791-5*, PDAC0791) Human Kinetics.

Dace, Jacqueline K., compiled by. Gateway Heritage Index, Set, Vols. 1-15. LC 95-81188. 114p. (Orig.). 1995. pap. 14.95 (*1-883982-08-1*) MO Hist Soc.

Dace-Lombard, Joyce, jt. auth. see Wheeler, Eugenie G.

Dace, Peggy, jt. auth. see Whitaker, Julian M.

Dace Publishing Staff. The Basic Guide to the Akita. (Basic Guide Ser.). (Illus.). 128p. 1997. pap. text 9.95 (*0-932045-17-0*) Dace Pub.

— The Basic Guide to the Labrador Retriever. Zervas, Michael R., ed. (Basic Guide Breed Ser.). (Illus.). 128p. 1995. pap. 9.95 (*0-932045-01-4*) Dace Pub.

Dace, Rosalind, ed. see Dawson, Pam.

Dace, Rosalind, ed. see Purves, Pamela.

Dace, Wallace. Elements in Dramatic Structure. 1972. pap. 7.95 (*0-686-00365-9*) AG Pr.

— Elements of Dramatic Structure. LC 72-81889. 72p. 1972. pap. 2.95 (*0-686-05609-4*) AG Pr.

— Subsidies for the Theatre: A Study of the Central European System of Financing Drama, Opera & Ballet. LC 72-84841. 188p. 1973. pap. 7.95 (*0-686-05610-8*) AG Pr.

Dacey & Travers. Human Development. 3rd ed. 1995. teacher ed. 23.12 (*0-697-21005-7*, WCB McGr Hill) McGrw-H Hghr Educ.

Dacey, Florence, ed. The Dream of the Whale. (Illus.). 163p. 1994. pap. 9.00 (*0-927663-24-4*) COMPAS.

Dacey, Florence Chard, see Chard Dacey, Florence.

***Dacey, John S. & Fiore, Lisa.** Your Anxious Child: How Parents & Teachers Can Relieve Anxiety in Children. LC 99-50517. 240p. 2000. 24.00 (*0-7879-4997-3*, Pfffr & Co) Jossey-Bass.

Dacey, John S. & Kenny, Maureen E. Adolescent Development. 560p. (C). 1994. text, student ed. 21.87 (*0-697-20997-0*) Brown & Benchmark.

— Adolescent Development. 2nd ed. LC 95-83236. 592p. (C). 1996. text. write for info. (*0-697-21012-X*); per. write for info. (*0-07-114171-5*) Brown & Benchmark.

Dacey, John S. & Lennon, Kathleen H. Understanding Creativity: The Interplay of Biological, Psychological & Social Factors. LC 98-19770. (Health & Psychology Ser.). 320p. 1998. 37.95 (*0-7879-4032-1*) Jossey-Bass.

Dacey, John S. & Travers, John P. Human Development Across the Lifespan. 3rd ed. LC 95-75268. 612p. (C). 1995. text 44.87 (*0-697-21004-9*) Brown & Benchmark.

Dacey, John S. & Vestal, Lynne A. B. Human Development Across the Lifespan. 2nd ed. 256p. (C). 1994. text, student ed. 23.75 (*0-697-12734-6*) Brown & Benchmark.

Dacey, Karen H. In the Shadow of the Great Blue Hill. LC 95-3171. 188p. (C). 1995. lib. bdg. 38.50 (*0-8191-9879-X*) U Pr of Amer.

Dacey, Mark S. Principles & Practice of Insurance. 110p. (C). 1989. pap. 95.00 (*0-948691-83-2*, Pub. by Witherby & Co) St Mut.

— Property & Pecuniary Insurance. 115p. (C). 1987. pap. 60.00 (*0-948691-70-0*, Pub. by Witherby & Co) St Mut.

— Property & Pecuniary Insurance. 115p. (C). 1989. pap. 75.00 (*0-948691-85-9*, Pub. by Witherby & Co) St Mut.

Dacey, Michael F. Status of Pattern Analysis: Identification of Problems in the Statistical Analysis of Spatial Arrangement. (Discussion Papers: No. 3.). 1963. pap. 10.00 (*1-55869-122-7*) Regional Sci Res Inst.

Dacey, Michael F. & Karaska, Gerald J. Some Experimental Evidence of the Perception of Dot Patterns & Two-Dimensional Shapes. (Discussion Papers: No. 2). 1963. pap. 10.00 (*1-55869-115-4*) Regional Sci Res Inst.

Dacey, Norman F. Democracy in Israel. 74p. 1976. pap. 4.75 (*0-911038-68-X*, 0326, Inst Hist Rev) Legion Survival.

— What's Wrong with Your Life Insurance? 448p. 1989. 24.95 (*0-02-529350-8*) Macmillan.

Dacey, Philip. The Boy under the Bed. LC 80-8858. (Poetry & Fiction Ser.). 1981. text 16.50 (*0-8018-2601-2*) Johns Hopkins.

— Deathbed Playboy: Poems. LC 99-19706. 88p. 1999. 24.00 (*0-910055-48-3*); pap. text 14.00 (*0-910055-47-5*) East Wash Univ.

— Fives. 32p. (Orig.). 1984. pap. 3.00 (*0-933180-63-2*) Spoon Riv Poetry.

— What's Empty Weighs the Most. 32p. 1997. 5.00 (*0-9638516-1-6*, Black Dirt) Elgin Comm Coll.

Dacey, Philip & Jauss, David. Strong Measures: Contemporary American Poetry in Traditional Forms. 415p. (C). 1997. pap. 49.00 (*0-06-041471-5*) Addson-Wesley Educ.

Dacey, Philip, et al. Quarterly Preview of Literature Poetry Book Series: 50th Anniversary Anthology, Vols. XXXVII-XXXVIII. 1999. 40.00 (*1-888545-43-7*) Quarterly Rev.

Dacey, Ralph G., Jr., et al, eds. Trauma of the Central Nervous System. LC 85-10715. (Seminars in Neurological Surgery Ser.). (Illus.). 356p. 1985. reprint ed. pap. 110.40 (*0-608-05846-7*, 205981200007) Bks Demand.

Dach, Cindy. Fish Tales. (Illus.). 18p. 1998. mass mkt. 8.00 (*1-891070-00-2*) Eye of the Tiger.

Dach, Julie. African Greys: An Owner's Guide to a Happy Healthy Pet. LC 97-31329. 128p. 1998. pap. 12.95 (*0-87605-443-2*) Howell Bks.

Dacher, Elliott. Intentional Healing: A Guide to the Mind/Body Healing System. 2nd ed. 219p. 1996. pap. 14.95 (*1-56924-831-1*, Pub. by Marlowe & Co) Publishers Group.

Dacher, Elliott S. PNI: The New Mind - Body Healing Program. 224p. 1994. pap. 12.95 (*1-56924-928-8*) Marlowe & Co.

— Whole Healing: A Step-by-Step Program to Reclaim Your Power to Heal. (Illus.). 237p. 1998. text 24.00 (*0-7881-5960-7*) DIANE Pub.

D'Achilli, Kathy. Pharmacy Policy & Procedure Manual, 1992. 350p. 1992. ring bd. 93.00 incl. disk (*0-934322-12-0*) Am Soc Consult Phar.

Dachinger, Penny, jt. ed. see Ulman, Elinor.

Dachis, Chuck. Radios by Hallicrafters. LC 95-45247. (Illus.). 225p. (YA). (gr. 10-13). 1995. pap. 29.95 (*0-88740-929-6*) Schiffer.

— Radios by Hallicrafters. 2nd rev. ed. LC 99-17189. (Illus.). 225p. 1999. pap. 29.95 (*0-7643-0807-6*) Schiffer.

Dachman, Kenneth & Kinnan, Joen. The Self-Health Handbook: Low-Cost, Easy-to-Use Therapies from Around the World. LC 95-46516. 304p. 1996. 26.75 (*0-8160-3201-7*) Facts on File.

Dachman, Kenneth & Kinnan, Joen P. The Self-Health Handbook: Low-Cost, Easy-to-Use Therapies from Around the World. LC 95-46516. 304p. 1996. pap. 14.95 (*0-8160-3227-0*) Facts on File.

Dachman, Kenneth A., jt. auth. see Abdo, John.

Dachman, Kenneth A., jt. auth. see Leving, Jeffery M.

Dachner, Don. A Traveler's Guide to Caribbean History. (Illus.). 350p. (Orig.). 1997. per. 17.95 (*0-9657780-0-2*) Travelers Pr.

Dachowski, L., ed. Current Topics in Animal Learning: Brain, Emotion, & Cognition. 456p. (C). 1991. text 89.95 (*0-8058-0441-2*) L Erlbaum Assocs.

Dachs, H., ed. Neutron Diffraction. LC 78-2969. (Topics in Current Physics Ser.: Vol. 6). (Illus.). 1978. 48.95 (*0-387-08710-9*) Spr-Verlag.

Dachslager, Howard. Statistics & Probability Theory. 856p. 1997. pap. text 64.00 (*1-891037-01-3*) Copley Ridge Pr.

— Statistics & Probability Theory: A Tutorial Approach. unabridged ed. 800p. (C). 1998. pap. text 64.00 (*1-893260-00-3*) Harrison Pubg.

Dachtler, Doc. Drawknife. LC 83-19942. 1983. pap. 8.00 (*0-914134-07-8*) Konocti Bks.

Dacie. Haemolytic Anemias, Vol. 5. 3rd ed. (C). 1999. text 175.00 (*0-443-06269-2*) Church.

Dacie, John. The Haemolytic Anaemias Vol. 4: Secondary or Symptomatic Haemolytic Anaemias, Vol. 4. 3rd ed. 434p. 1995. text 110.00 (*0-443-03503-2*, 68660) Church.

Dacie, John V. The Haemolytic Anaemias - Three: The Haemolytic Anemicas of Immune Origin. 3rd ed. (Illus.). 528p. 1992. text 225.00 (*0-443-03502-4*) Church.

Dacie, John V. & Lewis, S. M. Practical Hematology. 8th ed. 1995. pap. text 83.00 (*0-443-04931-9*) Church.

Dacie, John V. & Lewis, S. M., eds. Practical Hematology. 7th ed. (Illus.). 556p. 1991. text 59.00 (*0-443-03952-6*) Church.

Dacier, Andre, tr. & comment see Aristotle.

Dacier, Anne. Des Causes De la Corruption Du Gout. 624p. reprint ed. write for info. (*0-318-71335-7*) G Olms Pubs.

Dacier, Liz, jt. auth. see Alpoge, Atila.

D'Acierno, Pellegrino, et al, eds. Modern Naples: A Documentary History: c.1799-1999. (Documentary History of Naples Ser.: Vol. 5). (Illus.). 300p. 2001. pap. 25.00 (*0-934977-53-4*) Italica Pr.

D'Acierno, Pellegrino, jt. ed. see Barnaby, Karin.

D'Acierno, Pellegrino, ed. see Leonard, George J.

D'Acierno, Pellegrino, tr. see Tafuri, Manfredo.

Dacin, Peter & Wadsworth, F. Marketing Credit Union Services: The Role of Perceived Value. 50p. 1995. pap. 100.00 (*1-880572-20-6*) Filene Res.

Dacin, Tina, jt. auth. see Amburgey, Terry.

Dacin, Tina, jt. auth. see Burger, Albert E.

Dacio, Juan. Diccionario de los Papas. (SPA.). 59.95 (*0-7859-0863-3*, S50110) Fr & Eur.

Dacke, C., et al. The Comparative Endocrinology of Calcium Regulations. 238p. 1996. text 85.00 (*1-898099-08-1*) Blackwell Sci.

Dacker, Bill. Te Mamae Me Te Aroha (The Pain & the Love) A History of the Kai Tahu Whanui in Otago, 1844-1994. LC 94-230496. 104p. 1994. pap. 29.95 (*0-908569-89-0*, Pub. by Univ Otago Pr) Intl Spec Bk.

Dackerman, Gerald, jt. auth. see Sohl, Marcia.

Dackombe, R., jt. auth. see Gardiner, Vince.

Daco, Pierre, ed. The Mammoth Book of Dreams. 544p. 1995. pap. 9.95 (*0-7867-0215-X*) Carroll & Graf.

Daconta. Java & JavaScript. 2nd rev. ed. 896p. 1999. pap. text 64.99 incl. cd-rom (*0-471-32719-0*) Wiley.

Daconta, Michael. Java for C/C++ Programmers. 1996. 39.95 incl. disk (*0-614-14509-0*) Wiley.

Daconta, Michael C. C Pointers & Dynamic Memory Management. 368p. 1993. pap. 44.95 incl. disk (*0-471-56152-5*) Wiley.

— C++ Pointers & Dynamic Memory Management. LC 94-48020. 496p. 1995. pap. 49.99 incl. disk (*0-471-04998-0*) Wiley.

An Asterisk (*) at the beginning of an entry indicates that the title is appearing for the first time.

***Daconta, Michael C., et al.** Java Pitfalls: Time-Saving Solutions & Workarounds to Improve Programs. LC 00-25724. (Illus.). 304p. 2000. pap. 39.99 (*0-471-36174-7*) Wiley.

Dacor Bacon House Foundation Staff. American Diplomacy in the Information Age. (Herbert Wilson Griffin Seminars in International Affairs Ser.). (Illus.). 162p. (C). 1991. lib. bdg. 38.50 (*0-8191-7987-6*) U Pr of Amer.

Dacorogna, B. Direct Methods in the Calculus of Variations. (Applied Mathematical Sciences Ser.: Vol. 79). (Illus.). ix, 308p. 1989. 74.95 (*0-387-50491-5*) Spr-Verlag.

***Dacorogna, Bernard & Marcellini, P.** Implicit Partial Differential Equations Vol. 37: Progress in Nonlinear Differential Equations & Their Applications. LC 99-38323. 288p. 1999. 59.95 (*0-8176-4121-1*, Pub. by Birkhauser) Spr-Verlag.

***Dacorogna, Bernard & Marcellini, Paolo.** Implicit Partial Differential Equations LC 99-38323. (Progress in Nonlinear Partial Differential Equations Ser.). 1999. write for info. (*3-7643-4121-1*) Birkhauser.

DaCosta, Cornel, jt. ed. see Gokulsing, K. Moti.

DaCosta, I. Noble Families among the Sephardic Jews. 1976. lib. bdg. 134.95 (*0-8490-2349-1*) Gordon Pr.

Dacque, Edgar. Vergleichende Biologische Formenkunde der Fossilen Niederen Tiere: Biological Comparative Morphology of Lower Fossil Animals. Gould, Stephen Jay, ed. LC 79-8329. (History of Paleontology Ser.). (GER., Illus.). 1980. reprint ed. lib. bdg. 81.95 (*0-405-12710-3*) Ayer.

***Dacquino, V. T.** Sybil Ludington: The Call to Arms. (Illus.). 104p. 2000. pap. 15.00 (*1-930098-09-X*) Purple Mnt Pr.

Dacquino, Vinny, jt. auth. see Messina, Kathlyn.

Dacre, Charlotte. Confessions of the Nun of St. Omer: A Tale, 2 vols., Set. LC 76-131314. (Gothic Novels Ser.). 1972. reprint ed. 46.95 (*0-405-00803-1*) Ayer.

— The Libertine, 4 vols., Set. LC 73-22761. 997p. 1979. reprint ed. 96.95 (*0-405-06012-2*) Ayer.

— The Passions, 4 vols. LC 73-22762. (Gothic Novels Ser.). 1979. reprint ed. 96.95 (*0-405-06013-0*) Ayer.

— Zafloya: or The Moor: A Romance of the Fifteenth Century, 3 vols., Set. LC 73-22763. (Gothic Novels Ser.). 802p. 1979. reprint ed. 94.95 (*0-405-06014-9*) Ayer.

— Zofloya. Craciun, Adriana, ed. 303p. (C). 1997. pap. text 12.95 (*1-55111-146-2*) Broadview Pr.

***Dacre, Charlotte.** Zofloya: Or the Moor. (Oxford World Classics Ser.). (Illus.). 306p. 2000. pap. 11.95 (*0-19-283934-9*) OUP.

Dacre, Charlotte. Zofloya: or The Moor. Michasiw, Kim I., ed. & intro. by. LC 96-32014. (The World's Classics Ser.). 316p. 1997. pap. 11.95 (*0-19-283239-5*) OUP.

D'Acre, Jacqueline. Between Extremities. unabridged ed. Neil, Winter C., ed. 352p. 1997. pap. 11.50 (*0-9653145-2-9*, 97-03, Autumn Bks) Pontalba Pr.

Dacre, Jane & Nicol, Maggie. The Clinical Skills Matrix. 1996. write for info. (*1-85775-195-7*, Radcliffe Med Pr) Scovill Paterson.

Dacre, Maxwell W., jt. auth. see Cook, Allison M.

Dacres, Edward, tr. see Machiavelli, Niccolo.

***D'Acres, Lilia & Luxton, Donald.** Lions' Gate. 160p. 2000. 26.95 (*0-88922-416-1*) Talonbks.

***Dacso, Clifford C.** Managed Care Answer Book. 1. 4th ed. 1128p. 1999. boxed set 136.00 (*0-7355-0464-4*) Panel Pubs.

Dacso, Clifford C., jt. auth. see Dacso, Sheryl T.

Dacso, Sherly T. Managed Care Answer Book. 2nd ed. LC 97-122155. 536p. 1996. 125.00 (*1-56706-357-8*) Panel Pubs.

Dacso, Sheryl T. Managed Care Answer Book. annuals 2nd ed. 536p. boxed set 125.00 (*1-56706-398-5*, S154) Panel Pubs.

Dacso, Sheryl T. & Dacso, Clifford C. Managed Care Answer Book. annuals 536p. 1994. 118.00 (*1-56706-127-3*, S154) Panel Pubs.

— Managed Care Answer Book: Forms & Checklists. annuals 400p. Date not set. pap. 96.00 incl. disk (*1-56706-407-8*, 64078) Panel Pubs.

— Risk Contracting & Capitation Answer Book: Strategies for Managed Care. LC 99-11154. 432p. 1999. 99.00 (*0-8342-0988-8*, 09888) Aspen Pub.

Dacunha-Castelle, D. & Duflo, M. Probability & Statistics I. McHale, D., tr. from FRE. (Illus.). vi, 362p. 1985. 72.95 (*0-387-96067-8*) Spr-Verlag.

— Probability & Statistics II. McHale, D., tr. from FRE. (Illus.). 400p. 1986. 71.95 (*0-387-96213-1*) Spr-Verlag.

Dacunha-Castelle, D., jt. auth. see Azencott, R.

Dacus Food Group, Inc. Staff. Mrs. Wages New Home Canning Guide. 1986. pap. text 5.95 (*0-9649067-1-6*) Precision Foods.

Dacus, Joseph A. Annals of the Great Strikes in the United States. LC 72-89728. (American Labor, from Conspiracy to Collective Bargaining Ser., No. 1). 480p. 1976. reprint ed. 28.95 (*0-405-02115-1*) Ayer.

Dacus, Rachel. Earth Lessons. 72p. 1998. pap. 11.00 (*0-944920-30-6*) Bellowing Ark Pr.

Dacy. What's Wrong with Your Life Insurance? 1994. pap. 5.00 (*0-02-009471-X*) Macmillan.

Dacy, Douglas C. Foreign Aid, War & Economic Development: South Vietnam, 1955-1975. (Illus.). 320p. 1986. text 89.95 (*0-521-30327-3*) Cambridge U Pr.

Dacyczyn, Amy. The Best of Tightwad Gazette. LC 98-39515. 912p. 1998. pap. 19.99 (*0-375-75225-0*) Villard Books.

— The Tightwad Gazette: Promoting Thrift As a Viable Alternative Lifestyle. 1992. pap. 12.99 (*0-679-74388-X*) Villard Books.

— The Tightwad Gazette: Promoting Thrift As a Viable Alternative Lifestyle. LC 92-22876. 1993. 9.95 (*0-679-74403-7*) Villard Books.

— The Tightwad Gazette III, Vol. 3. LC 96-27802. 1996. pap. 12.99 (*0-679-77766-0*) Villard Books.

— The Tightwad Gazette II. LC 94-12490. (Illus.). 1995. pap. 12.99 (*0-679-75078-9*) Villard Books.

Dada, Larry. Elderhosteling, U. S. A! An Elderhostel How-to Guide. LC 94-94145. 154p. 1994. pap. 12.95 (*0-9640140-0-9*) Eldertime Pubng.

Dada, Omar E. OKD's Cruise Ship Jobs Guide. 100p. (Orig.). text. write for info. (*0-9642899-0-3*) O K D Mgmt.

Dada, Rudolfo, tr. see Anglesey, Zoe, ed.

Dada, Tunde. Tasha What Time Is It? (Illus.). 32p. (J). (gr. k-3). 1994. pap. 6.95 (*1-882920-00-7*) Tunde Dada-Hse.

— Tasha What Time Is It? (Illus.). 17p. (J). (gr. k-3). 1995. write for info. (*1-882920-02-3*) Tunde Dada-Hse.

Dadaji. Look Within: Inspirations of Love. Mills, Ann, ed. LC 87-71489. (Illus.). 260p. (Orig.). 1995. pap. 11.95 (*0-942687-01-9*) Amida Pr.

D'Adam, ed. see Diderot, Denis.

D'Adamo, Amadeo F., ed. see Baruch, Elaine H.

Dadamo, Dick. The Laws of Management Physics: A Handbook for Hands-On Managers. 386p. 1994. pap. 19.95 (*0-929392-35-3*) Annabooks.

— Will the Real Inventory Please Stand up & Be Counted: Unscrambling the Methods & Madness of Manufacturing Inventories. (Illus.). 172p. 1998. pap. 24.95 (*0-929392-61-2*) Annabooks.

***D'Adamo, Peter.** Live Right 4 Your Type. 416p. 2001. 24.95 (*0-399-14673-3*) Putnam Pub Group.

***D'Adamo, Peter J. & Whitney, Catherine.** Cook Right 4 Your Type. 464p. 2000. reprint ed. pap. 13.95 (*0-425-17329-1*) Berkley Pub.

— Cook Right 4 Your Type: The Practical Kitchen Companion to "Eat Right 4 Your Type" LC 98-28749. (Illus.). 450p. 1998. 24.95 (*0-399-14437-4*, G P Putnam) Peng Put Young Read.

D'Adamo, Peter J. & Whitney, Catherine. Eat Right for Your Type: The Individualized Diet Solution to Staying Healthy, Living Longer & Achieving Your Ideal Weight. LC 96-35510. 392p. 1997. 23.95 (*0-399-14255-X*, G P Putnam) Peng Put Young Read.

***D'Adamo, Peter J. & Whitney, Catherine.** Eat Right for Your Type: The Individualized Diet Solution to Staying Healthy, Living Longer & Achieving Your Ideal Weight. Set. abr. ed. 1998. audio 18.00 (*0-694-52088-8*, 396087, Pub. by HarperAudio) Lndmrk Audiobks.

D'Adamo, Tony, jt. auth. see Ames, Lee J.

D'Adamo-Weinstein, Lisa, jt. auth. see Jensen, Jane.

Dadant & Sons, Incorporated Staff. The Honey Kitchen: The Best Honey Recipes in the World. LC 79-50568. (Illus.). 199p. 1997. pap. 8.95 (*0-915698-06-4*) Dadant & Sons.

Dadant & Sons, Incorporated Staff, ed. First Lessons in Beekeeping. LC 75-38347. (Illus.). 140p. 1997. pap. 4.00 (*0-915698-02-1*) Dadant & Sons.

Dadape, E. V. & Apte, D. G. Bhaminivilasa. (C). 1994. reprint ed. 17.00 (*81-208-1170-4*, Pub. by Motilal Bnarsidass) S Asia.

Dadarwal, K. R. Biotechnological Approaches in Soil Microorganisms for Sustainable Crop Production. LC 97-900713. 1997. pap. 150.00 (*81-7233-147-9*, Pub. by Scientific Pubs) St Mut.

Dadd, Bill. Great Trans-Continental Railroad Guide. LC 76-155931. (Illus.). 1971. reprint ed. pap. 8.00 (*0-912382-06-6*) Black Letter.

Dadd, Debra L. Home Safe Home: Protecting Yourself & Your Family from Everyday Toxics & Harmful Household Products. 384p. (Orig.). 1997. pap. 18.95 (*0-87477-859-X*, Tarcher Putnam) Putnam Pub Group.

Dadd, Debra L., jt. auth. see Good, Clint.

D'Addario, Francis J. The Manager's Violence Survival Guide. (Illus.). 74p. (Orig.). 1995. pap. 15.00 (*0-9648103-1-X*); pap., wbk. ed. 15.00 (*0-9648103-0-1*) Crime Prevent Assocs.

D'Addario, Francis J., jt. auth. see National Crime Prevention Institute Staff.

Daddario, Gina. Women's Sport & Spectacle: Gendered Television Coverage & the Olympic Games. LC 97-38544. 184p. 1998. 49.95 (*0-275-95856-6*, Praeger Pubs) Greenwood.

D'Addario, Joseph D. Build it: Out of Sight Sewing Center. 1972. pap. 5.95 (*0-686-01898-2*) Classic Furn Kits.

Daddazio, R. P., et al, eds. Acoustics, Vibrations, & Rotating Machines Vol. 3, Pt. B: Acoustics, Vibrations, & Rotating Machines, DE-Vol. 84-2. LC 95-81249. (Proceedings of the 1995 ASME Design Technical Engineering Conferences Ser.: Vol. 3, Pt. B). 1508p. 1995. 420.00 (*0-7918-1719-9*, H1000B) ASME.

D'Adderio, Mercedes, tr. & illus. see Kochane, Ariel, ed.

Daddesio, Thomas C. On Minds & Symbols: The Relevance of Cognitive Science for Semiotics, 117. (Approaches to Semiotics Ser.: No. 117). 271p. (C). 1994. lib. bdg. 118.70 (*3-11-013866-2*) Mouton.

D'Addetta, Joseph. American Folk Art Designs & Motifs for Artists & Craftspeople. LC 84-6136. 96p. 1984. pap. 6.95 (*0-486-24717-1*) Dover.

— Treasury of Chinese Design Motifs. (Illus.). 112p. 1981. pap. 7.95 (*0-486-24167-X*) Dover.

D'Addetta, Joseph. Traditional Japanese Design Motifs. (Pictorial Archive Ser.). 96p. 1984. pap. 7.95 (*0-486-24629-9*) Dover.

Daddieh, Cyril, jt. ed. see Mengisteab, Kidane.

***Daddio, Jim.** The Wind. 200p. 2000. pap. 12.99 (*1-57532-249-8*) Press-Tige Pub.

Daddio, Monica. Portrait of a Superstar: Humanizing the Jaguar. 235p. (Orig.). 1998. pap. 12.00 (*0-9667783-0-8*) Francella.

Daddio, Ralph, jt. ed. see Kennedy, Joan.

***Daddona, Cynthia.** Diary of a Modern-Day Goddess. 150p. 2000. pap. 10.95 (*1-55874-825-3*) Health Comm.

***Daddone, Peter.** Tug of War: A Triumph of Faith. LC 98-93745. 192p. 1999. pap. 12.95 (*0-9666754-0-1*) Aeron House.

Dadds, Marion. Passionate Enquiry & School Development: A Story about Teacher Action Research. LC 94-23561. 202p. 1995. pap. 27.95 (*0-7507-0433-0*, Falmer Pr) Taylor & Francis.

Dadds, Mark R. Families, Children, & the Development of Dysfunction: The Role of the Family. (Developmental Clinical Psychology & Psychiatry Ser.: Vol. 32). 120p. 1994. 42.00 (*0-8039-5191-4*) Sage.

Dadds, Mark R., jt. ed. see Vasey, Michael W.

Daddy Bob. The Only Reasons I Mention This: The Best of Daddy Bob. Fifield, Bob, ed. 120p. (Orig.). 1996. pap. 12.95 (*0-9652638-1-9*) Leather Jrnl.

Daddy, S. Kwaku. The Folklore of Ghana. 2nd rev. ed. Cogburn, Nan, ed. LC 94-73541. (Illus.). 70p. (C). 1997. pap. text 19.95 (*0-9644553-1-5*) Afr Heritage Recs.

Daddysman, James W. The Matamoros Trade: Confederate Commerce, Diplomacy, & Intrigue. LC 81-72031. (Illus.). 216p. 1984. 32.50 (*0-87413-215-0*) U Delaware Pr.

Dade, George C. Picture History of Aviation on Long Island, 1908-1938. 38th ed. (Illus.). 160p. 1998. pap. 13.95 (*0-486-26008-9*) Dover.

Dade, J. Animals in Education: A Resource List for Teachers. (C). 1988. 35.00 (*0-7855-3760-0*) St Mut.

Dade, Pat, jt. auth. see Evans, Karen L.

Dade, Tom. The Quest for Megalodon. Billac, Pete, ed. 385p. (Orig.). 1993. pap. 12.95 (*0-943629-06-3*) Swan Pub.

***Dadeppo.** Introduction to Structure & Mechanics. 1998. pap. text, student ed. write for info. (*0-13-921131-4*) P-H.

Dadeppo, Donald A. Introduction to Structural Mechanics. LC 98-10926. 480p. 1998. 105.00 (*0-13-859794-4*) P-H.

Dadesho, Sargon O. The Assyrian National Question at the United Nation: (A Historical Injustice Redressed) (Illus.). 308p. 1987. text 25.00 (*0-9618344-0-4*) Bet Nahrain.

D'Adesky, Anne-Christine. Under the Bone. LC 93-11962. 1994. 23.00 (*0-374-28066-5*) FS&G.

Dadey. Bailey Shelf Talker. (J). 1999. pap. write for info. (*0-590-06805-9*) Scholastic Inc.

Dadey, Debbie. Adventure of the Bailey School Kids. (J). 1995. pap. 14.00 (*0-590-62435-0*) Scholastic Inc.

— Angels Don't Know Karate. (Adventures of the Bailey School Kids Ser.: No. 23). (J). (gr. 2-4). 1996. 8.70 (*0-606-10124-1*, Pub. by Turtleback) Demco.

— Buffalo Bill & the Pony Express. LC 94-70798. (Disney's American Frontier Ser.: Bk. 13). (Illus.). 80p. (J). (gr. 1-4). 1994. pap. 3.50 (*0-7868-4005-6*, Pub. by Disney Pr); lib. bdg. 12.89 (*0-7868-5004-3*, Pub. by Disney Pr) Little.

***Dadey, Debbie.** Dracula Doesn't Rock & Roll. (Illus.). (J). 2000. 9.44 (*0-606-18537-2*) Turtleback.

— Happy Boo Day. (Illus.). (J). 2000. 9.34 (*0-606-18515-1*) Turtleback.

Dadey, Debbie. King of the Kooties. LC 99-13054. (Illus.). 84p. (J). (gr. 2-4). 1999. 15.95 (*0-8027-8709-6*) Walker & Co.

— Shooting Star: Annie Oakley, the Legend. LC 96-24821. (Illus.). 32p. (J). (gr. k-3). 1997. 15.95 (*0-8027-8484-4*); lib. bdg. 16.85 (*0-8027-8485-2*) Walker & Co.

— Shooting Star: Annie Oakley, the Legend. (Illus.). 32p. (J). (ps-2). 1999. pap. 6.95 (*0-8027-7559-4*) Walker & Co.

***Dadey, Debbie.** Snow Monster Mystery. (Illus.). (J). 1999. 9.34 (*0-606-18514-3*) Turtleback.

Dadey, Debbie. Will Rogers: Large Than Life. LC 98-35224. (Illus.). 32p. (J). (ps-2). 1999. 15.95 (*0-8027-8681-2*) Walker & Co.

— Will Rogers: Larger Than Life. LC 98-35224. (Illus.). 32p. (J). (gr. k-3). 1999. lib. bdg. 16.85 (*0-8027-8682-0*) Walker & Co.

Dadey, Debbie. Witches Don't Do Backflips. (Adventures of the Bailey School Kids Ser.: No. 10). (J). (gr. 2-4). 1994. 8.60 (*0-606-06888-0*, Pub. by Turtleback) Demco.

Dadey, Debbie. Wizards Don't Need Computers. LC 00-5674. (The Adventures of the Bailey School Kids Ser.: No. 20). (Illus.). 63p. (J). (gr. 2-5). 1996. pap. 3.50 (*0-590-50962-4*) Scholastic Inc.

— Wizards Don't Need Computers. (Adventures of the Bailey School Kids Ser.: No. 20). (J). (gr. 2-4). 1996. 8.70 (*0-606-10079-2*, Pub. by Turtleback) Demco.

Dadey, Debbie & Burr, Daniella. Bailey School Kids Joke Book. (J). (gr. 2-4). 1997. pap. 3.50 (*0-590-99552-9*) Scholastic Inc.

— Bailey School Kids Joke Book. (J). (gr. 2-4). 1997. 8.70 (*0-606-11026-7*, Pub. by Turtleback) Demco.

Dadey, Debbie & Jones, Marcia Thornton. Aliens Don't Wear Braces. (Adventures of the Bailey School Kids Ser.: No. 7). (J). (gr. 2-4). 1993. 8.70 (*0-606-05112-0*, Pub. by Turtleback) Demco.

Dadey, Debbie & Jones, Marcia Thornton. Angels Don't Know Karate. LC 49-117660. (Adventures of the Bailey School Kids Ser.: No. 23). (Illus.). 67p. (J). (gr. 2-5). 1996. pap. 3.99 (*0-590-84902-6*) Scholastic Inc.

— Bigfoot Doesn't Square Dance. (Adventures of the Bailey School Kids Ser.: No. 25). 80p. (J). (gr. 2-5). 1997. pap. 3.99 (*0-590-84905-0*, Little Apple) Scholastic Inc.

— Bigfoot Doesn't Square Dance. (Adventures of the Bailey School Kids Ser.: No. 25). (J). (gr. 2-4). 1997. 8.70 (*0-606-11128-X*, Pub. by Turtleback) Demco.

— Bogeymen Don't Play Football. (Adventures of the Bailey School Kids Ser.: No. 27). (Illus.). 80p. (J). (gr. 2-5). 1997. pap. 3.50 (*0-590-25701-3*) Scholastic Inc.

— Bogeymen Don't Play Football. (Adventures of the Bailey School Kids Ser.: No. 27). (Illus.). (J). (gr. 2-4). 1997. 8.70 (*0-606-11145-X*, Pub. by Turtleback) Demco.

— Cupid Doesn't Flip Hamburgers. (Adventures of the Bailey School Kids Ser.: No. 12). (Illus.). 96p. (J). (gr. 2-5). 1995. pap. 2.99 (*0-590-48114-2*) Scholastic Inc.

— Cupid Doesn't Flip Hamburgers. (Adventures of the Bailey School Kids Ser.: No. 12). (J). (gr. 2-4). 1995. 8.70 (*0-606-07405-8*, Pub. by Turtleback) Demco.

— Cyclops Doesn't Roller Skate. (Adventures of the Bailey School Kids Ser.: No. 22). (J). (gr. 2-5). 1996. pap. text 3.99 (*0-590-84886-0*) Scholastic Inc.

— Cyclops Doesn't Roller-Skate. (Adventures of the Bailey School Kids Ser.: No. 22). (J). (gr. 2-4). 1996. 8.70 (*0-606-09176-9*, Pub. by Turtleback) Demco.

— Dracula Doesn't Drink Lemonade. (Adventures of the Bailey School Kids Ser.: No. 16). 80p. (J). (gr. 4-7). 1995. pap. 3.99 (*0-590-22638-X*) Scholastic Inc.

Dadey, Debbie & Jones, Marcia Thornton. Dracula Doesn't Drink Lemonade. (Adventures of the Bailey School Kids Ser.: No. 16). (J). (gr. 2-4). 1995. 8.70 (*0-606-07444-9*, Pub. by Turtleback) Demco.

— Dracula Doesn't Rock & Roll. (Adventures of the Bailey School Kids Ser.: No. 39). (Illus.). 80p. (J). (gr. 2-5). 2000. pap. 4.99 (*0-439-04399-9*, Little Apple) Scholastic Inc.

Dadey, Debbie & Jones, Marcia Thornton. Dragons Don't Cook Pizza. LC 49-242810. (Adventures of the Bailey School Kids Ser.: No. 24). 80p. (J). (gr. 2-5). 1997. pap. 3.99 (*0-590-84904-2*) Scholastic Inc.

— Dragons Don't Cook Pizza. (Adventures of the Bailey School Kids Ser.: No. 24). (J). (gr. 2-4). 1997. 8.70 (*0-606-10790-8*, Pub. by Turtleback) Demco.

— Elves Don't Wear Hard Hats. (Adventures of the Bailey School Kids Ser.: No. 17). (J). (gr. 4-7). 1995. pap. 3.99 (*0-590-22637-1*) Scholastic Inc.

— Elves Don't Wear Hard Hats. (Adventures of the Bailey School Kids Ser.: No. 17). (J). (gr. 2-4). 1995. 8.70 (*0-606-08514-9*, Pub. by Turtleback) Demco.

— Frankenstein Doesn't Plant Petunias. LC 00-5619. (Adventures of the Bailey School Kids Ser.: No. 6). 80p. (J). (gr. 4-7). 1993. pap. 2.99 (*0-590-47071-X*) Scholastic Inc.

— Frankenstein Doesn't Plant Petunias. (Adventures of the Bailey School Kids Ser.: No. 6). (J). (gr. 2-4). 1993. 8.70 (*0-606-05298-4*, Pub. by Turtleback) Demco.

— Frankenstein Doesn't Slam Hockey Pucks. (Adventures of the Bailey School Kids Ser.: No. 34). (Illus.). 76p. (J). (gr. 2-4). 1999. pap. 3.99 (*0-590-18984-0*) Scholastic Inc.

— Gargoyles Don't Drive School Buses. (Adventures of the Bailey School Kids Ser.: No. 18). (Illus.). 80p. (J). (gr. 2-5). 1996. pap. 3.99 (*0-590-50961-6*) Scholastic Inc.

Dadey, Debbie & Jones, Marcia Thornton. Gargoyles Don't Drive School Buses. (Adventures of the Bailey School Kids Ser.: No. 19). (J). (gr. 2-4). 1996. 8.70 (*0-606-08750-8*, Pub. by Turtleback) Demco.

Dadey, Debbie & Jones, Marcia Thornton. Genies Don't Ride Bicycles. (Adventures of the Bailey School Kids Ser.: No. 8). (FRE., Illus.). (J). (gr. 2-4). pap. 5.99 (*0-590-24377-2*) Scholastic Inc.

— Genies Don't Ride Bicycles. LC 94-148224. (Adventures of the Bailey School Kids Ser.: No. 8). 80p. (J). (ps-3). 1994. pap. 2.99 (*0-590-47297-6*) Scholastic Inc.

Dadey, Debbie & Jones, Marcia Thornton. Genies Don't Ride Bicycles. (Adventures of the Bailey School Kids Ser.: No. 8). (J). (gr. 2-4). 1993. 8.70 (*0-606-06403-6*, Pub. by Turtleback) Demco.

Dadey, Debbie & Jones, Marcia Thornton. Ghosts Don't Eat Potato Chips. (Adventures of the Bailey School Kids Ser.: No. 5). (FRE.). (J). (gr. 2-4). pap. 5.99 (*0-590-74836-X*) Scholastic Inc.

— Ghosts Don't Eat Potato Chips. LC 93-163863. (Adventures of the Bailey School Kids Ser.: No. 5). (Illus.). 96p. (J). (gr. 2-5). 1992. pap. 3.99 (*0-590-45854-X*) Scholastic Inc.

Dadey, Debbie & Jones, Marcia Thornton. Ghosts Don't Eat Potato Chips. (Adventures of the Bailey School Kids Ser.: No. 5). (J). (gr. 2-4). 1992. 8.70 (*0-606-01843-3*, Pub. by Turtleback) Demco.

— Ghouls Don't Scoop Ice Cream. (Adventures of the Bailey School Kids Ser.: No. 31). (J). (gr. 2-4). 1998. 8.60 (*0-606-13426-3*, Pub. by Turtleback) Demco.

Dadey, Debbie & Jones, Marcia Thornton. Giants Don't Go Snowboarding. (Adventures of the Bailey School Kids Ser.: No. 33). (Illus.). (J). (gr. 2-4). 1998. pap. 3.50 (*0-590-18983-2*, Pub. by Scholastic Inc) Penguin Putnam.

***Dadey, Debbie & Jones, Marcia Thornton.** Goblins Don't Play Video Games. (Adventures of the Bailey School Kids Ser.: No. 37). (Illus.). 82p. (J). (gr. 2-5). 1999. pap. 3.99 (*0-439-04397-2*) Scholastic Inc.

Dadey, Debbie & Jones, Marcia Thornton. Gremlins Don't Chew Bubble Gum. (Adventures of the Bailey School Kids Ser.: No. 13). 96p. (J). (gr. 4-7). 1995. pap. 2.99 (*0-590-48115-0*) Scholastic Inc.

Dadey, Debbie & Jones, Marcia Thornton. Gremlins Don't Chew Bubble Gum. (Adventures of the Bailey School Kids Ser.: No. 13). (J). (gr. 2-4). 1995. 8.70 (*0-606-07602-6*, Pub. by Turtleback) Demco.

Dadey, Debbie & Jones, Marcia Thornton. Hercules Doesn't Pull Teeth. (Adventures of the Bailey School Kids Ser.: No. 30). (Illus.). 70p. (J). (gr. 2-5). 1998. pap. 3.50 (*0-590-25809-5*, Little Apple) Scholastic Inc.

***Dadey, Debbie & Jones, Marcia Thornton.** Hercules Doesn't Pull Teeth. (Adventures of the Bailey School Kids Ser.: No. 30). (J). (gr. 2-4). 1998. 8.70 (*0-606-13475-1*, Pub. by Turtleback) Demco.

— Knights Don't Teach Piano. (Adventures of the Bailey School Kids Ser.: No. 29). (Illus.). 66p. (J). (gr. 2-5). 1998. pap. 3.50 (*0-590-25804-4*, Little Apple) Scholastic Inc.

Dadey, Debbie & Jones, Marcia Thornton. Knights Don't Teach Piano. (Adventures of the Bailey School Kids Ser.: No. 29). (J). (gr. 2-4). 1998. 8.70 (*0-606-12975-8*, Pub. by Turtleback) Demco.

D

— Martians Don't Take Temperatures. LC 00-5333. (Adventures of the Bailey School Kids Ser.: No. 18). 67p. (J). (gr. 4-7). 1996. pap. 2.99 (*0-590-50960-8*) Scholastic Inc.

Dadey, Debbie & Jones, Marcia Thornton. Martians Don't Take Temperatures. (Adventures of the Bailey School Kids Ser.: No. 18). (J). (gr. 2-4). 1995. 8.70 (*0-606-08565-3*, Pub. by Turtleback) Demco.

Dadey, Debbie & Jones, Marcia Thornton. Mermaids Don't Run Track. (Adventures of the Bailey School Kids Ser.: No. 26). (Illus.). 72p. (J). (gr. 4-7). 1997. pap. 3.50 (*0-590-84906-9*, Little Apple) Scholastic Inc.

— Mermaids Don't Run Track. (Adventures of the Bailey School Kids Ser.: No. 26). (J). (gr. 2-4). 1997. 8.70 (*0-606-11620-6*, Pub. by Turtleback) Demco.

— Monsters Don't Scuba Dive. (Adventures of the Bailey School Kids Ser.: No. 14). (FRE., Illus.). 80p. (J). (gr. 2-4). pap. 5.99 (*0-590-24550-3*) Scholastic Inc.

— Monsters Don't Scuba Dive. LC 00-5206. (Adventures of the Bailey School Kids Ser.: No. 14). (Illus.). 96p. (J). (gr. 2-5). 1995. pap. 2.99 (*0-590-22635-5*) Scholastic Inc.

— Monsters Don't Scuba Dive. (Adventures of the Bailey School Kids Ser.: No. 14). (J). (gr. 2-4). 1995. 8.70 (*0-606-07884-3*, Pub. by Turtleback) Demco.

— Mrs. Jeepers' Batty Vacation. (Adventures of the Bailey School Kids Super Special Ser.: No. 2). (Illus.). (J). (gr. 2-4). 1997. 4.99 (*0-590-21243-5*) Scholastic Inc.

— Mrs. Jeepers in Outer Space. (Adventures of the Bailey School Kids Super Special Ser.: No. 4). (Illus.). 124p. (J). (gr. 2-5). 1999. pap. 3.99 (*0-439-04396-4*) Scholastic Inc.

— Mrs. Jeepers Is Missing. (Adventures of the Bailey School Kids Super Special Ser.: No. 1). (Illus.). (J). (gr. 2-4). 1996. pap. 4.99 (*0-590-88134-5*) Scholastic Inc.

— Mrs. Jeepers' Secret Cave. (Adventures of the Bailey School Kids Super Special Ser.: No. 3). (Illus.). 128p. (J). (gr. 2-4). 1998. pap. 4.99 (*0-590-11712-2*, Little Apple) Scholastic Inc.

— Mrs. Jeepers' Secret Cave. (Adventures of the Bailey School Kids Ser.: No. 3). (J). (gr. 2-4). 1998. 10.09 (*0-606-13626-6*, Pub. by Turtleback) Demco.

— Mummies Don't Coach Softball. (Adventures of the Bailey School Kids Ser.: No. 21). (J). (gr. 4-7). 1996. pap. 3.99 (*0-590-22639-8*) Scholastic Inc.

— Mummies Don't Coach Softball. (Adventures of the Bailey School Kids Ser.: No. 21). (J). (gr. 2-4). 1996. 8.70 (*0-606-09644-2*, Pub. by Turtleback) Demco.

— Ninjas Don't Bake Pumpkin Pies. (Adventures of the Bailey School Kids Ser.: No. 38). (Illus.). 70p. (J). (gr. 2-5). 1999. pap. 3.99 (*0-439-04398-0*) Scholastic Inc.

— Phantoms Don't Drive Sports Cars. (Adventures of the Bailey School Kids Ser.: No. 32). (Illus.). 76p. (J). (gr. 2-5). 1998. pap. 3.99 (*0-590-18982-4*, Pub. by Scholastic Inc) Penguin Putnam.

— Phantoms Don't Drive Sports Cars. (Adventures of the Bailey School Kids Ser.: No. 32). (J). (gr. 2-4). 1998. 8.60 (*0-606-13702-5*, Pub. by Turtleback) Demco.

— Pirates Don't Wear Pink Sunglasses. (Adventures of the Bailey School Kids Ser.: No. 9). 80p. (J). (gr. 4-7). 1994. pap. 3.50 (*0-590-47298-4*) Scholastic Inc.

Dadey, Debbie & Jones, Marcia Thornton. Pirates Don't Wear Pink Sunglasses. (Adventures of the Bailey School Kids Ser.: No. 9). (J). (gr. 2-4). 1994. 8.70 (*0-606-06671-3*, Pub. by Turtleback) Demco.

Dadey, Debbie & Jones, Marcia Thornton. Santa Claus Doesn't Mop Floors. LC 92-107363. (Adventures of the Bailey School Kids Ser.: No. 3). 80p. (J). (gr. 4-7). 1991. pap. 3.99 (*0-590-44477-8*) Scholastic Inc.

— Santa Claus Doesn't Mop Floors. (Adventures of the Bailey School Kids Ser.). (J). (gr. 2-6). 1991. 8.70 (*0-606-01936-7*, Pub. by Turtleback) Demco.

***Dadey, Debbie & Jones, Marcia Thornton.** Sea Monsters Don't Ride Motorcycles. (Adventures of the Bailey School Kids Ser.: No. 40). (Illus.). 80p. (J). (gr. 2-5). 2000. pap. 3.99 (*0-439-04401-4*, Little Apple) Scholastic Inc.

— Sea Monsters Don't Ride Motorcycles. (Adventures of the Bailey School Kids Ser.: No. 40). (J). (gr. 2-4). 2000. write for info. (*0-606-18601-8*, Pub. by Turtleback) Demco.

Dadey, Debbie & Jones, Marcia Thornton. Skeletons Don't Play Tubas. LC 00-5052. (Adventures of the Bailey School Kids Ser.: No. 11). 96p. (J). (gr. 4-7). 1994. pap. 2.99 (*0-590-48113-4*) Scholastic Inc.

— Sorciers/Ne Croient/Ordinateur. (Adventures of the Bailey School Kids Ser.). (FRE., Illus.). 88p. (J). mass mkt. 5.99 (*0-590-16024-9*) Scholastic Inc.

— Triplet Trouble & the Bicycle Race. (Triplet Trouble Ser.: No. 8). (Illus.). (J). (gr. 2-4). 1997. pap. 3.50 (*0-614-29027-9*, Little Apple) Scholastic Inc.

— Triplet Trouble & the Bicycle Race. (Triplet Trouble Ser.: No. 8). (J). (gr. 2-4). 1997. 8.70 (*0-606-12007-6*, Pub. by Turtleback) Demco.

— Triplet Trouble & the Class Trip. LC 49-254990. (Triplet Trouble Ser.: No. 7). 64p. (J). (gr. 1-4). 1997. pap. 3.50 (*0-590-90730-1*) Scholastic Inc.

— Triplet Trouble & the Class Trip. (Triplet Trouble Ser.: No. 7). (J). (gr. 2-4). 1997. 8.70 (*0-606-12008-4*, Pub. by Turtleback) Demco.

Dadey, Debbie & Jones, Marcia Thornton. Triplet Trouble & the Cookie Contest. (Triplet Trouble Ser.: No. 5). (J). (gr. 2-4). 1996. 8.70 (*0-606-12009-2*, Pub. by Turtleback) Demco.

Dadey, Debbie & Jones, Marcia Thornton. Triplet Trouble & the Field Day Disaster. (Triplet Trouble Ser.: No. 4). (J). (gr. 2-4). 1996. pap. 2.99 (*0-614-15776-5*, Little Apple) Scholastic Inc.

— Triplet Trouble & the Field Day Disaster. (Triplet Trouble Ser.: No. 4). (Illus.). 64p. (J). (gr. 1-4). 1996. pap. text 2.99 (*0-590-58107-4*) Scholastic Inc.

— Triplet Trouble & the Field Day Disaster. (Triplet Trouble Ser.: No. 4). (Illus.). (J). (gr. 2-4). 1996. 8.19 (*0-606-09992-1*, Pub. by Turtleback) Demco.

— Triplet Trouble & the Pizza Party. (Triplet Trouble Ser.: No. 6). (Illus.). (J). (gr. 2-4). 1996. pap. 2.99 (*0-590-90729-8*) Scholastic Inc.

Dadey, Debbie & Jones, Marcia Thornton. Triplet Trouble & the Pizza Party. (Triplet Trouble Ser.: No. 6). (J). (gr. 2-4). 1996. 8.70 (*0-606-12010-6*, Pub. by Turtleback) Demco.

Dadey, Debbie & Jones, Marcia Thornton. Triplet Trouble & the Red Heart Race. (Triplet Trouble Ser.: No. 3). (Illus.). (J). (gr. 2-4). 1996. pap. 2.99 (*0-590-58106-6*) Scholastic Inc.

— Triplet Trouble & the Red Heart Race. (Triplet Trouble Ser.: No. 3). (J). (gr. 2-4). 1996. 8.70 (*0-606-08650-1*, Pub. by Turtleback) Demco.

— Triplet Trouble & the Runaway Reindeer. (Triplet Trouble Ser.: No. 2). (J). (ps-3). 1995. pap. 2.99 (*0-590-25473-1*) Scholastic Inc.

— Triplet Trouble & the Runaway Reindeer. (Triplet Trouble Ser.: No. 2). (J). (gr. 2-4). 1995. 8.70 (*0-606-08651-X*, Pub. by Turtleback) Demco.

— Triplet Trouble & the Talent Show Mess. (Triplet Trouble Ser.: No. 1). 64p. (J). (gr. 2-4). 1995. pap. 3.50 (*0-590-25472-3*) Scholastic Inc.

— Triplet Trouble & the Talent Show Mess. (Triplet Trouble Ser.: No. 1). (J). (gr. 2-4). 1995. 8.70 (*0-606-08317-0*, Pub. by Turtleback) Demco.

— Trolls Don't Ride Roller Coasters. (Adventures of the Bailey School Kids Ser.: No. 35). (Illus.). 68p. (J). (gr. 2-5). 1999. pap. 3.99 (*0-590-18985-9*, Little Apple) Scholastic Inc.

— Unicorns Don't Give Sleigh Rides. (Adventures of the Bailey School Kids Ser.: No. 28). (Illus.). (J). (gr. 2-5). 1997. pap. 3.50 (*0-590-25783-8*) Scholastic Inc.

Dadey, Debbie & Jones, Marcia Thornton. Unicorns Don't Give Sleigh Rides. (Adventures of the Bailey School Kids Ser.: No. 28). (J). (gr. 2-4). 1997. 8.70 (*0-606-12837-9*, Pub. by Turtleback) Demco.

Dadey, Debbie & Jones, Marcia Thornton. Vampires Don't Wear Polka Dots. LC 00-5188. (Adventures of the Bailey School Kids Ser.: No. 1).Tr. of Vampires Ne Portent Pas de Robe a Pois. (Illus.). 78p. (J). (gr. 2-5). 1990. pap. 3.99 (*0-590-43411-X*) Scholastic Inc.

— Vampires Don't Wear Polka Dots. (Adventures of the Bailey School Kids Ser.: No. 1).Tr. of Vampires Ne Portent Pas de Robe a Pois. (J). (gr. 2-4). 1990. 8.70 (*0-606-04839-1*, Pub. by Turtleback) Demco.

— Wolfman Doesn't Hula Dance. (Adventures of the Bailey School Kids Ser.: No. 36). (Illus.). 71p. (J). (gr. 2-5). 1999. pap. 3.99 (*0-590-18986-7*) Scholastic Inc.

— Zombies Don't Play Soccer. LC 00-4964. (Adventures of the Bailey School Kids Ser.: No. 15). (Illus.). 70p. (J). (gr. 2-5). 1995. pap. 3.99 (*0-590-22636-3*, Little Apple) Scholastic Inc.

— Zombies Don't Play Soccer. (Adventures of the Bailey School Kids Ser.: No. 15). (J). (gr. 2-4). 1995. 8.70 (*0-606-08417-7*, Pub. by Turtleback) Demco.

Dadey, Debbie, et al. Aliens Don't Wear Braces. LC 94-146019. (Adventures of the Bailey School Kids Ser.: No. 7). (Illus.). 74p. (J). (gr. 2-5). 1993. pap. 2.99 (*0-590-47070-1*) Scholastic Inc.

— Ghouls Don't Scoop Ice Cream. (Adventures of the Bailey School Kids Ser.: No. 31). (Illus.). 66p. (J). (gr. 2-5). 1998. pap. 3.50 (*0-590-25819-2*, Little Apple) Scholastic Inc.

— Leprechauns Don't Play Basketball. (Adventures of the Bailey School Kids Ser.: No. 4). (Illus.). 71p. (J). (gr. 2-5). 1992. pap. 3.99 (*0-590-44822-6*) Scholastic Inc.

Dadey, Debbie, et al. Skeletons Don't Play Tubas. (Adventures of the Bailey School Kids Ser.: No. 11). (J). (gr. 2-4). 1994. 8.70 (*0-606-07086-9*, Pub. by Turtleback) Demco.

Dadey, Debbie, et al. Werewolves Don't Go to Summer Camp. LC 00-5266. (Adventures of the Bailey School Kids Ser.: No. 2). (Illus.). 93p. (J). (gr. 2-5). 1991. pap. 3.99 (*0-590-44061-6*) Scholastic Inc.

— Witches Don't Do Back Flips. LC 00-5589. (Adventures of the Bailey School Kids Ser.: No. 10). 96p. (J). (gr. 4-7). 1994. pap. 2.99 (*0-590-48112-6*) Scholastic Inc.

Dadey, Debbie, jt. auth. see Jones, Marcia Thornton.

Dadge, David, jt. ed. see Campbell, Dennis.

Dadhich, Naresh. Gandhi & Existentialism. (C). 1993. 18.00 (*81-7033-200-1*, Pub. by Rawat Pubns) S Asia.

***Dadhich, Naresh & Kembhavi, Ajit.** The Universe - Visions & Perspectives. 360p. 2000. 150.00 (*0-7923-6210-1*) Kluwer Academic.

Dadi, Marcel. CD a la Guitare Acoustique et Electroacoustique. Lefferts, Michael, ed. (FRE.). 44p. (Orig.). (C). 1997. pap. text 26.95 (*0-7692-1315-4*, 01010315) Wrner Bros.

— Marcel Dadi: Fingers Crossing. (Illus.). 80p. 1996. pap. 22.95 incl. audio compact disk (*0-7866-1461-7*, 95677BCD) Mel Bay.

Dadi, Marcel. Marcel Dadi/Fingerpicking Guitar Legend, Vol. 1. 128p. 1997. spiral bd. 22.95 incl. audio compact disk (*0-7866-3142-2*, 94851BCD) Mel Bay.

— Marcel Dadi/Fingerpicking Guitar Legend, Vol. 2. 84p. 1997. spiral bd. 22.95 incl. audio compact disk (*0-7866-3143-0*, 95115BCD) Mel Bay.

Dadi, Yang, jt. ed. see Boling, Guo.

Dadie, Bernard B. An African in Paris. Hatch, Karen C., tr. from FRE. LC 93-30915.Tr. of Negre a Paris. (ENG.). 184p. 1994. text 29.95 (*0-252-02040-5*); pap. text 14.95 (*0-252-06407-0*) U of Ill Pr.

— Beatrice du Congo. (FRE.). 148p. 1971. pap. 27.95 (*0-7859-4883-X*) Fr & Eur.

— The Black Cloth: A Collection of African Folk Tales. Hatch, Karen C., tr. from FRE. LC 86-25043.Tr. of Le Pagne Noir. 176p. 1987. pap. 15.95 (*0-87023-557-5*) U of Mass Pr.

— The City Where No One Dies. Mayes, Janis A., tr. from FRE. LC 86-50451. (FRE., Illus.). 139p. (Orig.). 1986. 10.00 (*0-89410-498-5*, Three Contnts) L Rienner.

— Hommes de Tous les Continents. pap. 8.95 (*0-685-35631-0*) Fr & Eur.

— Legendes Africaines. (FRE.). 1982. pap. 10.95 (*0-7859-3225-9*, 2266028545) Fr & Eur.

— Monsieur Thogo-gnini. pap. 8.95 (*0-685-33976-9*) Fr & Eur.

— Monsieur Thogo-Gnini. Brewster, Townsend T., tr. from FRE. 104p. (Orig.). 1986. pap. text 8.95 (*0-913745-16-2*) Ubu Repertory.

— One Way: Bernard Dadie Observes America. Patterson, Jo, tr. from FRE. LC 93-27875. 184p. 1994. pap. text 14.95 (*0-252-06408-9*) U of Ill Pr.

— One Way: Bernard Dadie Observes America. Patterson, Jo, tr. from FRE. LC 93-27875. 184p. 1994. text 29.95 (*0-252-02039-1*) U of Ill Pr.

— Le Pagne Noir. (FRE.). 160p. 1970. pap. 14.95 (*0-7859-3453-7*) Fr & Eur.

— Patron de New-York. pap. 6.50 (*0-685-35940-9*) Fr & Eur.

— Textes. Mercier, R. et al, eds. (Classiques du Monde, Litterature Africaine Ser.). pap. 8.95 (*0-685-35632-9*) Fr & Eur.

— La Ville ou Nul ne Meurt. pap. 8.95 (*0-685-35633-7*) Fr & Eur.

Dadisman, Kenny. Shooting the Bull. LC 96-96567. 117p. 1996. pap. 9.50 (*0-87012-563-X*) McClain. A collection of Barbour County, West Virginia folklore. *Publisher Paid Annotation.*

***Dadlez, Anna.** Journey from Innocence. 240p. 1998. text 21.00 (*0-88033-411-8*, 513, Pub. by East Eur Monographs) Col U Pr.

Dadlez, Anna R. Political & Social Issues in Poland, As Reflected in the Polish Novel. 289p. 1989. text 55.50 (*0-88033-166-6*, Pub. by East Eur Monographs) Col U Pr.

Dadlez, E. M. What's Hecuba To Him? Fictional Events & Actual Emotions. LC 96-42211. 1997. 35.00 (*0-271-01650-7*); pap. 16.95 (*0-271-01651-5*) Pa St U Pr.

Dadly, Bridget M., jt. auth. see Harris, Richard I.

Dadmun, Mark D., ed. see American Chemical Society, Division of Polymeric M.

Dadnguilan, Marilen J. & Philippine Center for Investigative Journalism Staff. Women in Bracket: A Chronicle of Vatican Power & Control. LC 97-946601. xv, 230 p. 1997. write for info. (*971-8686-14-2*) PCFIJ.

***Dadon, Jackie.** Showbiz Calendar 2000: Showbiz Calendar. (Illus.). 16p. 1999. pap. 12.95 (*0-9670789-0-3*) StoneQuest Ent.

Dadoo, Y. M. Facts about the Ghetto Act (1946) & a Historical Synopsis of the Indian Question in South Africa (1945) (Colin Webb Natal & Zululand Ser.: No. 5). 52p. 1993. pap. 16.50 (*0-86980-889-3*, Pub. by Univ Natal Pr) Intl Spec Bk.

Dadoyan, Seta B. The Fatimid Armenians: Cultural & Political Interaction in the Near East. LC 97-9135. (Islamic History & Civilization). 1997. 68.00 (*90-04-10816-5*) Brill Academic Pubs.

Dadras, Aly S. Electrical Systems for Architects. LC 94-47176. 416p. 1995. 49.00 (*0-07-015078-8*) McGraw.

Dadrian, Vahakn N. German Responsibility in the Armenian Genocide: A Review of the Historical Evidence of German Complicity. 2nd ed. LC 96-10409. (Illus.). 320p. 1997. 45.00 (*1-886434-01-8*); pap. 25.00 (*1-886434-02-6*) Blue Crane Bks.

— The History of the Armenian Genocide: Ethnic Conflict from the Balkans to Anatolia to the Caucasus. LC 95-1611. 480p. (C). 1995. 39.95 (*1-57181-016-1*) Berghahn Bks.

— Warrant for Genocide: Key Elements of Turko-Armenian Conflict. 219p. 1999. 32.95 (*1-56000-389-8*) Transaction Pubs.

Dadson, ed. Avisos a un Cortesano. (Exeter Hispanic Text Ser.: No. 41). (SPA.). 161p. Date not set. pap. text 17.95 (*0-85989-276-X*, Pub. by Univ Exeter Pr) Northwestern U Pr.

Dadson, Philip & McGlashan, Don. The From Scratch Rhythm Workbook. rev. ed. LC 95-10195. 102p. 1995. pap. text 21.50 (*0-435-08670-7*, 08670) Heinemann.

Dadson, Trevor, et al, eds. New Frontiers in Hispanic & Luso-Brazilian Scholarship: Como se Fue el Maestro. (Illus.). 584p. 1994. text 119.95 (*0-7734-9117-1*) E Mellen.

Dadswell, M. J., et al, eds. Common Strategies of Anadromous & Catadromous Fishes. LC 87-70241. (Symposium Ser.: No. 1). 561p. 1987. text 54.00 (*0-913235-42-3*, 540.01) Am Fisheries Soc.

Dadswell, Mary. Circles of Faces. 192p. (Orig.). 1987. pap. 11.95 (*0-7022-1969-X*, Pub. by Univ Queensland Pr) Intl Spec Bk.

Daduna, Joachim R., et al, eds. Computer-Aided Transit Scheduling: Proceedings, Lisbon, Portugal, July 1993, Vol. XIV. (Lecture Notes in Economics & Mathematical Systems Ser.: Vol. 430). (Illus.). 374p. 1995. 78.00 (*3-540-60193-7*) Spr-Verlag.

***Dadvison, Victor L. & Sittman, Donald B.** Biochemistry Chpts. 1-22. 4th ed. LC 98-52792. (National Medical Series for Independent Study). 16p. 1999. write for info. (*0-683-30503-4*) Lppncott W & W.

Dadyburjor, D. Eli Ruckenstein: A Special Issue in His Honor. 316p. 1987. pap. text 774.00 (*2-88124-257-X*) Gordon & Breach.

***Dadzie, Stells.** Tool-Kit for Tackling Racism in School. 80p. 1999. pap. text 17.95 (*1-85856-188-4*, Trentham Bks) Stylus Pub VA.

Dae, Edwina. Our Little Secret. 254p. mass mkt. 4.99 (*1-55197-183-6*) Picasso Publ.

Dae-Jung, Kim. Kim Dae-Jung's "Three-Stage" Approach to Korean Unification: Focusing on the South-North Confederal Stage. Tong-Chin, Rhee, tr. from KOR. 424p. Date not set. 39.95 (*1-884445-32-2*); pap. 19.95 (*1-884445-33-0*) C Schlacks Pub.

Dae, Michale W. Radionuclide Assessment of Congenital Heart Disease & Cardiac Positron Imaging. LC 98-27502. 127p. 1998. pap. text 50.00 (*0-932004-54-7*) Soc Nuclear Med.

***Daedalus.** Daedalus Online. 1999. pap. text 30.00 (*0-321-06126-8*) Addison-Wesley.

Daedalus. Little Brown Handbook with daedalus. 7th ed. (C). 1999. 39.00 (*0-321-06489-5*) Addison-Wesley.

***Daedalus.** The Longman Handbook for Writers & Readers. 2nd ed. 1999. 40.00 (*0-321-06490-9*) Longman.

Daedalus. Longman Writing Environment. (C). 1999. text. write for info. (*0-321-02405-2*) Addison-Wesley.

— The Writer's Workshop to Accompany Lannon: Technical Writing. 7th ed. (C). 1997. pap. text. write for info. (*0-321-01710-2*) Addison-Wesley.

— The Writer's Workshop to Accompany Lannon: Technical Writing, Windows Version. 7th ed. (C). 1997. pap. text 10.25 (*0-321-01711-0*) Addison-Wesley.

Daedalus, A. The Little, Brown Compact Handbook. 2nd ed. 1997. cd-rom 17.86 (*0-673-97260-7*) Addison-Wesley Educ.

Daeffler, Reidun & Petrosino, Barbara A. Manual of Oncology Nursing Practice: Nursing Diagnoses. 314p. 1990. 100.00 (*0-8342-0114-3*, 20114) Aspen Pub.

Daehlen, Morten, et al, eds. Mathematical Methods for Curves & Surfaces II: Lillehammer, 1997. LC 98-15040. (Innovations in Applied Mathematics Ser.). (Illus.). 576p. (C). 1998. text 55.00 (*0-8265-1315-8*) Vanderbilt U Pr.

Daehlen, Morten & Tveito, Aslak, eds. Numerical Methods & Software Tools in Industrial Mathematics. LC 97-185. (Illus.). 400p. 1997. 69.95 (*0-8176-3973-X*) Birkhauser.

Daehler, Marvin W. & Bukatko, Danuta. Cognitive Development. 432p. (C). 1985. text 48.74 (*0-07-554432-6*) McGraw.

Daehler, Marvin W., jt. auth. see Bukatko, Danuta.

Daehncke, Rose M. Twelve Hundred Pilze in Farbfotos. (GER., Illus.). 1179p. 1993. lib. bdg. 102.95 (*3-85502-503-7*) Lubrecht & Cramer.

— Two Hundred Pilze: One Hundred Eighty Pilze fuer die Kueche und ihre giftigen Doppelgaenger. (GER., Illus.). 246p. 1982. lib. bdg. 25.00 (*3-85502-145-7*) Lubrecht & Cramer.

Da'Ehu, B. D. With All My Heart, with All My Soul. 328p. 1993. 21.95 (*1-880880-01-6*) Israeli Trad.

Daele, Patrick Van, see Van Daele, Patrick.

Daellenbach, Hans G. Systems & Decision Making: A Management Science Approach. 560p. 1994. 118.95 (*0-471-95094-7*) Wiley.

Daellenbach, Hans G. & George, John A. Introduction to Operations Research Techniques. 2nd ed. 1983. teacher ed. write for info. (*0-205-07719-6*, H77191) Allyn.

Daemen, Jaak J. & Schultz, Richard A., eds. Rock Mechanics: Proceedings of the 35th U. S. Symposium, University of Nevada, Reno, 5-7 June 1995. (Illus.). 922p. (C). 1995. text 142.00 (*90-5410-552-6*, Pub. by A A Balkema) Ashgate Pub Co.

Daemion, Jai J. The Medicine Family Vision: Deep-Heart Sharing in the Wisdom & Guidance of the Earth. LC 96-76583. (Illus.). 400p. (Orig.). 1997. pap. 16.95 (*0-9651534-3-6*, 1010) Ajna Media.

Daemion, Jonathon. The Healing Power of Breath: An Introduction to Wholistic Breath Therapy. 256p. (Orig.). 1989. pap. write for info. (*1-85327-015-6*, Pub. by Prism Pr) Assoc Pubs Grp.

Daemmrich, Horst S. The Shattered Self: E. T. A. Hoffmann's Tragic Vision. LC 73-1490. 143p. reprint ed. pap. 44.40 (*0-608-17805-5*, 203228500079) Bks Demand.

Daemmrich, Horst S. & Daemmrich, Ingrid G. Spirals & Circles: A Key to Thematic Patterns in Classisism & Realism, 2 vols. LC 93-27275. (Studies on Themes & Motifs in Literature: Vols. 7 & 8). VII, 452p. 1994. 39.95 (*0-8204-2338-6*); text 39.95 (*0-8204-2337-8*) P Lang Pubng.

— Spirals & Circles: A Key to Thematic Patterns in Classisism & Realism, 2 vols., Set. LC 93-27275. (Studies on Themes & Motifs in Literature: Vols. 7 & 8). 1994. write for info. (*0-8204-2404-8*) P Lang Pubng.

Daemmrich, Horst S. & Haenicke, Diether H., eds. The Challenge of German Literature. LC 75-131425. 433p. reprint ed. pap. 134.30 (*0-608-10541-4*, 207116100009) Bks Demand.

Daemmrich, Ingrid. Enigmatic Bliss: The Paradise Motif in Literature. LC 96-13916. (Studies on Themes & Motifs in Literature: Vol. 25). (Illus.). VIII, 240p. (C). 1997. text 46.95 (*0-8204-3002-1*) P Lang Pubng.

Daemmrich, Ingrid G., jt. auth. see Daemmrich, Horst S.

Daemon, Laga. Tulo, the Cat Who Loved Zucchini. (Illus.). 52p. (Orig.). (J). (gr. 6-8). 1996. pap. 9.95 (*1-882427-15-7*, 315-7) Aspasia Inc.

Daems, Herman. The Holding Company & Corporate Control. 1978. lib. bdg. 111.00 (*90-207-0690-X*) Kluwer Academic.

Daems, Herman & Thomas, Howard. Strategic Groups, Strategic Moves & Performance. LC 94-3388. 364p. 1994. text 70.00 (*0-08-037768-8*, Pergamon Pr) Elsevier.

Daems, Herman, jt. ed. see Chandler, Alfred D., Jr.

Daems, Hugo. Kianza's Congo: A Portrait of Life in Unspoiled Africa. LC 98-86465. (Illus.). 275p. 1999. pap. 14.95 (*0-88739-189-3*) Creat Arts Bk.

Daems, W. T., et al, eds. Cell Biological Aspects of Disease: The Plasma Membrane & Lysosomes. (Boerhaave Series for Postgraduate Medical Education: No. 19). 330p. 1981. text 184.00 (*90-6021-466-8*) Kluwer Academic.

D

An Asterisk (*) at the beginning of an entry indicates that the title is appearing for the first time.

Daems, Willem F. Nomina Simplicium Medicinarum ex Synonymariis Medii Aevi Collecta: Semantische Untersuchungen zum Fachwortschatz Hoch- & Spaetmittelalterlicher Drogenkunde. LC 92-42058. (Studies in Ancient Medicine: Vol. 6). (GER.). 563p. 1993. 186.00 (*90-04-09672-8*) Brill Academic Pubs.

Daenell, E. Bluetezeit der Deutsche Hanse: Hansische Geschichte von der Zweiten Haelfte des XIV bis zum Cetzten Viertel des XV Jahrhunderts, 2 vols., Set. 1035p. (C). 1973. reprint ed. 280.75 (*3-11-004562-1*) De Gruyter.

Daeniker, Daniel. Swiss Securities Regulation: An Introduction to the Regulation of the Swiss Financial Market with a Translation of the Stock Exchange Act of 1995 (SESTA) & Implementing Ordinances. LC 99-159610. 354p. 1998. 122.00 (*90-411-0588-3*) Kluwer Law Intl.

Daeninckx, Didier. La Mart n'Oublie Personne. (FRE.). 192p. 1990. pap. 10.95 (*0-7859-2142-7*, 2070382567) Fr & Eur.

— Meurtres pour Memoire. (FRE.). 215p. 1988. pap. 10.95 (*0-7859-2094-3*, 2070380491) Fr & Eur.

— Murder in Memoriam. Heron, Liz, tr. from FRE. (Masks Ser.). 176p. (Orig.). 1992. pap. 13.95 (*1-85242-206-8*) Serpents Tail.

— A Very Profitable War. martin, Sarah, tr. from FRE. 192p. (Orig.). 1995. pap. 11.99 (*1-85242-247-5*) Serpents Tail.

Daennke, Kevin J., et al. Business Continuity Planning for Local Infrastructures: A Y2K Guide for Cities & Counties. 600p. 1999. pap. 55.00 (*0-9672565-0-X*) Ctr Year Two Thousand.

Daenzer, Dave. City Maps of Ohio. (Illus.). 1994. pap. 16.95 (*1-882062-01-9*) CITMAP.

— The Complete City Maps of Michigan. (Illus.). 574p. 1994. pap. 19.95 (*1-882062-02-7*) CITMAP.

***Daeron, M., et al, eds.** Immunoreceptor Tyrosine-Based Inhibition Motifs. (Current Topics in Microbiology & Immunology Ser.: Vol. 244). (Illus.). 200p. 1999. 129.00 (*3-540-65789-4*) Spr-Verlag.

Daes, Erica-Irene A. & United Nations High Commissioner for Human Rights Staff. Protection of the Heritage of Indigenous People LC 98-160628. (Human Rights Study Ser.). vi, 30p. 1997. pap. write for info. (*92-1-154126-3*) UN.

Daesch, Geraldine. Women Who Lived, Cities That Died. (International Poetry Chapbook Ser.). 21p. (Orig.). 1985. write for info. (*0-936600-05-5*) Riverstone Foothills.

Daeschler, Ted. The Dinosaur Hunter's Kit. (Discovery Kit Ser.). (Illus.). 64p. (Orig.). (J). (gr. 4-7). 1990. pap. 18.95 (*0-89471-804-5*) Running Pr.

Daeschner, C. William, Jr., ed. Pediatrics: An Approach to Independent Learning. LC 82-8438. 658p. reprint ed. pap. 200.00 (*0-8357-3060-3*, 203931600012) Bks Demand.

Daeschner, C. William, Jr. & Richardson, C. Joan, eds. Pediatrics: An Approach to Independent Learning. 3rd ed. LC 96-36967. (Illus.). 400p. 1997. text 65.00 (*0-8018-5603-5*); pap. text 34.95 (*0-8018-5604-3*) Johns Hopkins.

Daetz, Doug, et al. Customer Integration: The Quality Function Deployment (QFD) Leader's Guide for Decision Making. LC 95-36688. 300p. 1995. 45.00 (*0-471-13277-2*) Wiley.

Dafa, Xiulian, tr. & photos by see Hongzhi, Li.

Dafashy. Management Accounting. 364p. 2000. pap. text 20.50 (*0-536-01630-5*) Pearson Custom.

***Dafermos, C. M.** Hyperbolic Conservation Laws in Continuum Physics. LC 99-49545. (Grundlehren der Mathematischen Wissenschaften Ser.: Bd. 325). (Illus.). xviii, 350p. 1999. 99.00 (*3-540-64914-X*) Spr-Verlag.

Dafermos, C. M., et al, eds. The Breadth & Depth of Continuum Mechanics. (Illus.). 790p. 1986. reprint ed. 89.95 (*0-387-16219-4*) Spr-Verlag.

— Oscillation Theory, Computation, & Methods of Compensated Compactness. (IMA Volumes in Mathematics & Its Applications Ser.: Vol. 2). (Illus.). 415p. 1986. 65.95 (*0-387-96401-0*) Spr-Verlag.

Dafermos, C. M., et al. Amorphous Polymers & Non-Newtonian Fluids. (IMA Ser.: Vol. 6). (Illus.). 215p. 1987. 59.95 (*0-387-96556-4*) Spr-Verlag.

Dafermos, C. M., et al. Differential Equations: Proceedings of the 1987 EQUADIFF Conference. (Lecture Notes in Pure & Applied Mathematics Ser.: Vol. 118). (Illus.). 816p. 1989. pap. text 210.00 (*0-8247-8077-9*) Dekker.

Daffa, Ali A. & Stroyls, John J. Studies in the Exact Sciences in Medieval Islam. LC 83-21847. (Illus.). 253p. reprint ed. pap. 78.50 (*0-608-05290-6*, 206582800001) Bks Demand.

Daffe, Jerald. In the Face of Evil: You Can Find Faith. 153p. 1995. pap. 9.99 (*0-87148-343-2*) Pathway Pr.

— Life Challenges for Men. 195p. 1997. pap. 9.99 (*0-87148-039-5*) Pathway Pr.

Daffe, Jerald J. Revival: God's Plan for His People. LC 97-75573. 156p. 1997. pap. 9.99 (*0-87148-743-8*) Pathway Pr.

Daffern, Tony. Avalanche Safety for Skiers & Climbers. 2nd ed. 1999. pap. 16.95 (*0-89886-647-2*) Mountaineers.

— Avalanche Safety for Skiers & Climbers. 2nd enl. rev. ed. (Illus.). 192p. 1992. pap. 16.95 (*0-938567-33-0*) Mountaineers.

Dafflitto, Chiara. Michelangelo Pistoletto. (Illus.). 200p. 1996. pap. text 39.95 (*88-8158-050-0*, Pub. by Charta) Dist Art Pubs.

Daffner, Kirk R., jt. ed. see Scinto, Leonard F. M.

Daffner, Richard H. Clinical Radiology. LC 92-12314. (Illus.). 408p. 1993. 35.00 (*0-683-02330-6*) Lppncott W & W.

— Clinical Radiology: The Essentials. 2nd ed. LC 98-27066. 590p. 1998. pap. 38.00 (*0-683-30517-4*) Lppncott W & W.

— Imaging of Vertebral Trauma. 2nd ed. 304p. 1996. text 131.00 (*0-397-51680-0*) Lppncott W & W.

Dafforn, Erik, ed. see Farr, J Michael & Christophersen, Susan.

Dafforn, Erik, ed. see Farr, J. Michael & Christophersen, Susan.

Daffron, Susan C., jt. auth. see Sams Publishing Staff.

***Daffy, Chris.** Once a Customer, Always a Customer: How to Deliver Customer Service That Creates Customers for Life. 3rd ed. 320p. 2000. pap. 16.95 (*1-86076-164-X*, Pub. by Oak Tr) Midpt Trade.

Dafni, A. Pollution Ecology: A Practical Approach. LC 92-15944. (Practical Approach Ser.). 272p. 1993. 79.00 (*0-19-963299-5*) OUP.

***Dafni, Amots, et al.** Pollen & Pollination. LC 00-44575. 2000. write for info. (*3-211-83514-8*) Spr-Verlag.

Dafni, Jacob. Eilat: Routes & Trails in the Eilat Region - Hiker's Guide. LC 96-180911. (Illus.). 120p. 1995. 15.95 (*965-229-147-1*, Pub. by Gefen Pub Hse) Gefen Bks.

Dafoe, John W. Canada: An American Nation. LC 71-110739. reprint ed. 20.00 (*0-404-00616-7*) AMS Pr.

— Clifford Sifton in Relation to His Times. LC 79-157331. (Select Bibliographies Reprint Ser.). 1977. reprint ed. 35.95 (*0-8369-5791-1*) Ayer.

— Laurier, a Study in Canadian Politics. (BCL1 - History - Canada Ser.). 182p. 1991. reprint ed. lib. bdg. 69.00 (*0-7812-6363-8*) Rprt Serv.

DaFoe, William A., jt. ed. see Pashkow, Fredric J.

Daft. Essentials Of Organizational. LC 97-11016. 1997. pap. 48.95 (*0-538-87927-0*) S-W Pub.

— Essentials of Organizational Theory & Design. 2nd ed. 2000. 48.95 (*0-324-02097-X*) Thomson Learn.

— Leadership. LC 98-71914. (C). 1998. text 71.00 (*0-03-022417-9*) Harcourt Coll Pubs.

— Organization Theory & Design. 7th ed. (SWC-General Business). 2000. pap. text 85.95 (*0-324-02100-3*) Thomson Learn.

— Understanding Management. 2nd ed. (C). 1997. pap. text, teacher ed. 26.75 (*0-03-024734-9*) Harcourt Coll Pubs.

— Understanding Management. 2nd ed. (C). 1997. pap. text 31.50 (*0-03-024736-5*) Harcourt Coll Pubs.

— Understanding Management. 2nd ed. (C). 1997. 167.00 (*0-03-024739-X*) Harcourt Coll Pubs.

— Understanding Management. 2nd ed. 1997. 221.00 (*0-03-024738-1*) Harcourt Coll Pubs.

Daft, Richard L. Management. 4th ed. (C). 1996. text 89.00 (*0-03-017989-0*, Pub. by Harcourt Coll Pubs) Harcourt.

— Management. 4th ed. (C). 1996. pap. text, teacher ed. 49.50 (*0-03-017994-7*); pap. text, teacher ed. 82.00 (*0-03-017999-8*, Pub. by Harcourt Coll Pubs); audio compact disk 246.00 (*0-03-017992-0*, Pub. by Harcourt Coll Pubs) Harcourt.

— Management. 5th ed. (C). 1999. pap. text, student ed. Price not set. (*0-03-026511-8*) Harcourt Coll Pubs.

***Daft, Richard L.** Management. 5th ed. LC 99-72430. (Illus.). 2000. text. write for info. (*0-03-025967-3*) Harcourt Coll Pubs.

Daft, Richard L. Media BankT/A Management. 4th ed. (C). 1997. audio compact disk 246.00 (*0-03-018008-2*) Harcourt Coll Pubs.

— Media Instructor's Manual to Accompany Understanding Management. 176p. (C). 1995. pap. text, teacher ed. 32.00 (*0-03-098908-6*) Dryden Pr.

— Org Theory & Design 4e. 4th ed. Fenton & Craig, eds. (SWC-Management). 558p. (C). 1991. mass mkt. 62.50 (*0-314-93365-4*) West Pub.

— Org Theory & Design 5e. 5th ed. LC 94-34070. (SWC-Management). 750p. (C). 1994. pap. 65.75 (*0-314-04452-3*) West Pub.

— Organizational Theory & Design. 6th ed. LC 97-20922. (Miscellaneous/Catalogs Ser.). (C). 1997. mass mkt. 85.95 (*0-538-87902-5*) S-W Pub.

— Study Guide Management. 4th ed. (C). 1996. pap. text, student ed. 30.00 (*0-03-017993-9*, Pub. by Harcourt Coll Pubs) Harcourt.

— Understanding Management. (C). 1994. teacher ed. 144.50 (*0-03-098902-7*, Pub. by Harcourt Coll Pubs) Harcourt.

— Understanding Management: Test Bank. (C). 1995. pap. text, teacher ed., suppl. ed. 40.00 (*0-03-098899-3*, Pub. by Harcourt Coll Pubs) Harcourt.

Daft, Richard L. & Becker, Selwyn W. Innovations in Organizations: Innovation Adoption in School Organizations. LC 78-15711. Orig. Title: The Innovative Organization. 278p. 1981. lib. bdg. 42.50 (*0-444-00286-3*, DII/) Greenwood.

Daft, Richard L. & Lengel, Robert H. Fusion Leadership: Unlocking the Subtle Faces That Change People & Organizations. LC 97-52979. 282p. 1998. 27.95 (*1-57675-023-X*) Berrett-Koehler.

***Daft, Richard L. & Lengel, Robert H.** Fusion Leadership: Unlocking the Subtle Forces That Change People & Organizations. 302p. 2000. reprint ed. pap. 19.95 (*1-57675-080-9*, Pub. by Berrett-Koehler) Publishers Group.

Daft, Richard L. & Marcic, Dorothy. Understanding Management. 2nd ed. 368p. (C). 1997. pap. text, student ed. 28.50 (*0-03-024737-3*) Dryden Pr.

— UNDERSTANDING MANAGEMENT 2E. 2nd ed. LC 97-65945. 688p. (C). 1997. text 60.00 (*0-03-024593-1*) Dryden Pr.

Daft, Richard L. & Sharfman, Mark P. Organization Theory: Cases & Applications. 3rd ed. Fenton, ed. 379p. (C). 1990. pap. text 35.50 (*0-314-66769-5*) West Pub.

— Organizational Theory: Cases & Applications. 4th ed. LC 95-112704. 516p. (C). 1994. mass mkt. 50.95 (*0-314-04453-1*) West Pub.

Daft, Richard L., et al. Understanding Management. 344p. (C). 1995. pap. text, teacher ed. 61.00 (*0-03-098897-7*) Dryden Pr.

Daftari, Fereshteh. The Influence of Persian Art on Gauguin, Matisse, & Kandinsky. LC 91-24785. (Garland Publications in the Fine Arts). (Illus.). 560p. 1991. text 50.00 (*0-8153-0715-2*) Garland.

***Daftary, Farhad.** Intellectual Traditions in Islam. 2000. text 45.00 (*1-86064-435-X*) I B T.

Daftary, Farhad. The Isma'ilis: Their History & Doctrines. (Illus.). 822p. (C). 1990. text 125.00 (*0-521-37019-1*) Cambridge U Pr.

— The Isma'ilis: Their History & Doctrines. (Illus.). 821p. (C). 1992. pap. text 44.95 (*0-521-42974-9*) Cambridge U Pr.

— A Short History of the Ismailis: Traditions of a Muslim Community. LC 98-22131. 248p. 1998. text 59.95 (*1-55876-193-4*); pap. text 24.95 (*1-55876-194-2*) Wiener Pubs Inc.

Daftary, Farhad, ed. Medieval Isma'ili History & Thought. 349p. (C). 1996. text 69.95 (*0-521-45140-X*) Cambridge U Pr.

***Dafter, Helen.** Embroidered Treasures for Silk Ribbon. (Illus.). 2000. pap. 17.95 (*1-86351-240-3*) Sally Milner.

Dafter, Helen. Garden Landscapes in Silk Ribbon Embroidery. (Illus.). 112p. 1997. pap. 14.95 (*1-86351-195-4*, Pub. by Sally Milner) Sterling.

— Little Book of Silk Ribbon Flowers. 1999. 9.95 (*1-86351-229-2*) Sally Milner.

Dafydd ab Hugh. Arthur War Lord. 400p. (Orig.). 1994. mass mkt. 4.99 (*0-380-77028-8*, Avon Bks) Morrow Avon.

Dafydd, Ab Hugh. The Mountain. (Swept Away Ser.). 1996. 9.60 (*0-606-10338-4*, Pub. by Turtleback) Demco.

— The Pit. (Swept Away Ser.). 1996. 9.60 (*0-606-10339-2*, Pub. by Turtleback) Demco.

— Swept Away. (Swept Away Ser.). 1996. 9.60 (*0-606-09948-4*, Pub. by Turtleback) Demco.

Dag Hammarskjold Library Staff. Index to Proceedings of the Security Council: 48th Year. 326p. 30.00 (*92-1-100531-0*) UN.

Dagall, H. Creating a Good Impression: 300 Years of the Stamp Office & Stamp Duties. 130p. 1994. 40.00 (*0-11-641418-9*, Pub. by Statnry Office) Balogh.

Dagan, Avigdor. The Court Jesters. Harshav, Barbara, tr. 184p. 1990. 15.95 (*0-8276-0324-X*) JPS Phila.

— The Court Jesters. 1991. mass mkt. 4.95 (*0-446-36067-8*, Pub. by Warner Bks) Little.

Dagan, Gedeon. Theory of Flow & Transport in Porous Formations. (Illus.). 470p. 1989. 74.95 (*0-387-51098-2*) Spr-Verlag.

Dagan, Gedeon, et al, eds. Mathematical Modeling for Flow & Transport Through Porous Media. (C). 1992. text 186.00 (*0-7923-1616-9*) Kluwer Academic.

Dagan, Gedeon & Neuman, Shlomo P., eds. Subsurface Flow & Transport: A Stochastic Approach. LC 96-37796. (International Hydrology Ser.). (Illus.). 254p. (C). 1997. text 110.00 (*0-521-57257-6*) Cambridge U Pr.

Dagan, Gedeon & Russo, David A., eds. Water Flow & Solute Transport in Soils: Developments & Applications. LC 92-47096. (Advanced Series in Agricultural Sciences: Vol. 20). 1993. 145.00 (*0-387-56216-8*) Spr-Verlag.

Dagan, Hanoch. Unjust Enrichment: A Study of Private Law & Public Values. LC 96-49354. (Cambridge Studies in International & Comparative Law). (Illus.). 210p. (C). 1997. text 59.95 (*0-521-58468-X*) Cambridge U Pr.

Dagan, R. & Syrogiannopoulos, G., eds. Clinical Trial Methodology in Pediatric RTI. (Journal: Chemotherapy: Vol. 38, Suppl. 2, 1992). (Illus.). iv, 40p. 1992. pap. 12.25 (*3-8055-5651-9*) S Karger.

Daganzo, Carlos. Fundamentals of Transportation & Traffic Operations. LC 97-19182. 300p. 81.50 (*0-08-042785-5*, Pergamon Pr) Elsevier.

— Multinomial Probit: The Theory & Its Application to Demand Forecasting. LC 79-51674. (Economic Theory, Econometrics & Mathematical Economics Ser.). 1979. text 84.95 (*0-12-201150-3*) Acad Pr.

Daganzo, Carlos F. Logistics Systems Analysis. (Lecture Notes in Economics & Mathematical Systems Ser.: Vol. 361). (Illus.). x, 321p. 1991. pap. 40.00 (*0-387-54069-5*) Spr-Verlag.

— Logistics Systems Analysis. 2nd enl. rev. ed. LC 95-52401. (Illus.). 324p. 1996. 98.00 incl. 5.25 hd (*3-540-60639-4*) Spr-Verlag.

***Daganzo, Carlos F.** Logistics Systems Analysis. 3rd ed. LC 99-233285. (Illus.). xiv, 242p. 1999. 89.95 (*3-540-65533-6*) Spr-Verlag.

Daganzo, Carlos F., ed. Transportation & Traffic Theory: Proceedings of the 12th International Symposium on the Theory of Traffic Flow & Transportation, Berkeley, CA, U. S. A., 21-23 July--A Symposium in Honor of Gordon F. Newell. LC 93-1826. 614p. 1993. 279.50 (*0-444-89439-X*) Elsevier.

***D'Agata, John.** Halls of Fame. 256p. 2001. 24.95 (*1-55597-314-0*) Graywolf.

***Dagati, Mauro.** Softly Walking. 2000. 19.95 (*88-8158-234-1*) Charta.

D'Agati, Vivette D., et al. The Renal Biopsy. 3rd ed. Day, Lesley, ed. 336p. 1997. text 84.00 (*0-7216-6412-1*, W B Saunders Co) Harcrt Hlth Sci Grp.

Dagavarian, Debra A. A Century of Children's Baseball Stories. (J). (gr. 4-7). 1990. pap. 7.95 (*0-9625132-0-2*) Cyberbooks.

Dagavarian, Debra A., ed. A Century of Children's Baseball Stories. 200p. (J). 1992. lib. bdg. 16.95 (*0-88736-832-8*) Mecklermedia.

— A Century of Children's Baseball Stories, No. 2. 200p. (J). (gr. 5 up). 1993. 16.95 (*0-9625132-2-9*) Mecklermedia.

Dagcet, Dan. Beyond the Rangeland Conflict: Toward a West That Works. 2nd ed. (Illus.). vii, 104p. 1998. reprint ed. pap. 24.95 (*0-9666229-0-1*) Good Stewards Proj.

Dage, John H. La, see La Dage, John H.

Dageforde, Linda, ed. see Jauken, Arlene F.

Dageforde, Linda, ed. see Pati, Geeta.

Dageforde, Linda J., ed. see Bartels, Diane R.

Dageforde, Linda J., ed. see Bond, Garnett.

Dageforde, Linda J., ed. see Brase, Kristin.

Dageforde, Linda J., ed. see Burch, Hobart & Burch, Jan.

Dageforde, Linda J., ed. see Cavett, Dorcas.

Dageforde, Linda J., ed. see Cope, Thom K.

Dageforde, Linda J., ed. see Foreman, Tracie.

Dageforde, Linda J., ed. see Fox, John.

Dageforde, Linda J., ed. see Gilfert, Shirley K.

Dageforde, Linda J., ed. see Huffman, Karen.

Dageforde, Linda J., ed. see O'Donnell, Jeff.

Dageforde, Linda J., ed. see Orr, Clarice C.

Dageforde, Linda J., ed. see Owens-Navslar, JoAnne & Sime, Wes.

Dageforde, Linda J., ed. see Robb, Betty J.

Dageforde, Linda J., ed. see St. Peter, Sarah.

Dageforde, Linda J., ed. see Suttle, Courtney.

Dageforde, Linda J., ed. see Underwood, Larry.

Dageforde, Linda J., ed. see Underwood, Larry D.

Dageforde, Linda J., ed. see Walstrom, Veryl.

Dagel, Gena, jt. ed. see Oliphant, Dave.

Dagel, John F. Diesel Engine & Fuel System Repair. 2nd ed. 618p. 1988. student ed. write for info. (*0-318-63147-4*); pap. text, wbk. ed. 21.50 (*0-471-63833-1*) P-H.

Dagel, John F. & Brady, Robert N. Diesel Engine & Fuel System Repair. 4th ed. LC 97-8259. 777p. (C). 1997. 85.00 (*0-13-399692-1*) P-H.

Dagen, Margaret W., jt. auth. see Kimbrough, Mary.

Dagenais, Bernard, jt. auth. see Raboy, Marc.

Dagenais, Huguette & Piche, Denise, eds. Women, Feminism & Development. 456p. (C). 1994. 65.00 (*0-7735-1184-9*, Pub. by McG-Queens Univ Pr); pap. text 22.95 (*0-7735-1185-7*, Pub. by McG-Queens Univ Pr) CUP Services.

Dagenais, J. J. Models of Man: A Phenomenological Critique of Some Paradigms in the Human Sciences. 173p. 1972. pap. text 57.00 (*90-247-1290-4*, Pub. by M Nijhoff) Kluwer Academic.

Dagenais, John, ed. see De Valladolid, Alfonso.

Dagenais, M. G. & Muet, P. A. International Trade Modelling. 256p. (gr. 13). 1992. ring bd. 135.95 (*0-412-45000-3*, A6998, Chap & Hall CRC) CRC Pr.

Dagenais, Mario, et al, eds. Integrated Optoelectronics. (Quantum Electronics - Principles & Applications Ser.). (Illus.). 686p. 1994. text 90.00 (*0-12-200420-5*) Acad Pr.

***Dagenais, Michaele, et al.** Des Pouvoirs et des Hommes: L'Administration Municipales de Montrial, 1900-1950. (Canadian Public Administration Ser.). 240p. 1999. text 60.00 (*0-7735-1889-4*) McG-Queens Univ Pr.

***Dagenais, Michele.** Des Pouvoirs & des Hommes. (Canadian Public Administration Ser.). 1999. pap. 29.95 (*0-7735-1890-8*) McG-Queens Univ Pr.

Dagenbach, Dale & Carr, Thomas H., eds. Inhibitory Processes in Attention, Memory, & Language. LC 93-31495. (Illus.). 461p. 1994. text 69.95 (*0-12-200410-8*) Acad Pr.

Dagenias, Gerard. Dictionnaire des Difficultes de la Langue Francaise au Canada. 2nd ed. (FRE.). 538p. 1984. 39.95 (*0-7859-8023-7*, 2761810376) Fr & Eur.

Dagens, Bruno. Angkor: Heart of an Asian Empire. Sharman, Ruth, tr. LC 94-77943. (Discoveries Ser.). (Illus.). 192p. 1995. pap. 12.95 (*0-8109-2801-9*, Pub. by Abrams) Time Warner.

Dagens, Bruno, ed. Mayamatam: Treatise of Housing, Architecture & Iconography, 2 vols., Set. (C). 1995. 98.50 (*81-208-1026-0*, Pub. by Motilal Bnarsidass); 98.50 (*0-614-09993-5*, Pub. by Motilal Bnarsidass) S Asia.

Dager, Albert J. Vengeance Is Ours: The Church in Dominion. 288p. 1990. pap. 9.95 (*0-9626632-0-4*) Sword Pubs.

Dagg, A. J. Running, Walking & Jumping: The Science of Locomotion. 143p. 1977. pap. 18.00 (*0-85109-530-5*) Taylor & Francis.

Dagg, Anne I & Foster, J. Bristol. The Giraffe: Its Biology, Behavior & Ecology. LC 80-21839. 248p. (C). 1982. reprint ed. text 29.50 (*0-89874-275-7*) Krieger.

Dagg, Anne I., jt. auth. see Gauthier-Pilters, Hilde.

***Dagg, Jillian.** Family Affairs. LC 99-90980. 192p. 1999. 18.95 (*0-8034-9385-1*, Avalon Bks) Bouregy.

— Racing Hearts. LC 99-90720. 192p. 1999. 18.95 (*0-8034-9377-0*, Avalon Bks) Bouregy.

— Tropical Dreams. LC 98-96847. 192p. 1999. lib. bdg. 18.95 (*0-8034-9336-3*, Avalon Bks) Bouregy.

Dagg, John L. Manual of Church Order. 1992. 21.99 (*0-87377-976-2*) GAM Pubns.

— Manual of Theology, 3 vols. in 1. 1992. 23.99 (*0-87377-977-0*) GAM Pubns.

— Manual of Theology . . . Christian Doctrine . . . Church Order, 2 Vols. Gaustad, Edwin S., ed. LC 79-52592. (Baptist Tradition Ser.). 1980. reprint ed. lib. bdg. 63.95 (*0-405-12459-7*) Ayer.

Daggatt, W. Russell, jt. auth. see Griffin, Trenholme J.

Dagger, D., jt. auth. see Mukherjee, S.

Dagger, Richard. Civic Virtues: Rights, Citizenship, & Republican Liberalism. LC 96-28697. (Oxford Political Theory). 272p. 1997. pap. 19.95 (*0-19-510634-2*); text 60.00 (*0-19-510633-4*) OUP.

Daggett. Dynamics of Work. 2nd ed. (CA - Career Development Ser.). 1990. mass mkt. 43.95 (*0-538-80476-9*); mass mkt., wbk. ed. 15.95 (*0-538-80477-7*) S-W Pub.

— Dynamics of Work. 2nd ed. (CA - Career Development Ser.). (C). 1997. mass mkt. 43.95 (*0-538-68178-0*) S-W Pub.

— Dynamics of Work. 2nd ed. (CA - Career Development Ser.). (C). 1997. mass mkt., wbk. ed. 15.95 (*0-538-68179-9*) S-W Pub.

D

— Dynamics of Work, Tests. 2nd ed. (CA - Career Development Ser.). 1990. 2.95 (*0-538-80478-5*) S-W Pub.

— Solving Problems - Making Decisions. (CA - Career Development Ser.). 1982. pap. 16.95 (*0-538-07600-3*) S-W Pub.

— Your Future - Student Supplement: Plans & Choices. (CA - Career Development Ser.). 1984. mass mkt. 9.95 (*0-538-16351-8*) S-W Pub.

Daggett & Williams. Technology for Tomorrow: A Survey of Technology. (GB - Basic Business Ser.). 1985. text 35.95 (*0-538-16250-3*) S-W Pub.

Daggett, et al. The Brownfield, Denmark, Hiram & Porter Town Register, 1907 (Town Histories & Directories) 208p. 1997. reprint ed. pap. 28.00 (*0-8328-5818-8*) Higginson Bk Co.

Daggett, jt. auth. see Mitchell.

Daggett, jt. auth. see Vanhuss.

Daggett, jt. compiled by see Mitchell.

Daggett, Emerson. The Sentinel. 12p. (Orig.). 1981. pap. 2.00 (*0-932942-01-6*) Pacific NW Labor.

Daggett, Harriet S., jt. ed. see Charmatz, Jan P.

Daggett, James. Illustrator 8.0 Made Easy. LC 99-13252. 127p. 1999. 29.95 incl. cd-rom (*1-881795-15-2*) Bellwether-Cross.

Daggett, John. History of Attleborough, Massachusetts. (Illus.). 788p. 1993. reprint ed. lib. bdg. 79.00 (*0-8328-3088-7*) Higginson Bk Co.

— Sketch of the History of Attleborough, Massachusetts. 136p. 1993. reprint ed. lib. bdg. 23.00 (*0-8328-3137-9*) Higginson Bk Co.

Daggett, Karen, jt. auth. see Levy-Konesky, Nancy.

Daggett, Kendrick P. Fifty Years of Fortitude: The Maritime Career of Captain Jotham Blaisdell of Kennebunk, Maine, 1810-1860. (American Maritime Library: Vol. 12). (Illus.). 173p. 1988. 19.95 (*0-913372-43-9*) Mystic Seaport.

Daggett, Lyle. The Act of Resistance & Other Poems. (U. S. A. Poetry Chapbook Ser.: No. 3). 36p. 1983. pap. 3.00 (*0-937724-03-3*) Shadow Pr.

Daggett, Mala, ed. see Bloom, Louise, et al.

Daggett, R. M., ed. & illus. see Kalakaua, David.

***Daggett, Sharron.** A Guide to Basic & 12-Lead ECG Interpretation. (Illus.). ii, 93p. 2000. pap. 29.95 (*0-9701171-1-6*, 2702) Natl Inst Nurse.

— Handbook of Arterial Blood Gas Interpretation & Ventilator Management. iii, 69p. 1999. pap. 29.95 (*0-9701171-0-8*, 2701) Natl Inst Nurse.

Daggett, Stephen & English, Robert D. Breaking the Deadlock: A CNS Arms Control Proposal. 45p. (Orig.). 1987. pap. write for info. (*0-937115-05-3*) Comm Natl Security.

Daggett, Stuart. Chapters on the History of the Southern Pacific. LC 66-22621. (Library of Early American Business & Industry: No. 10). (Illus.). vi, 470p. 1966. reprint ed. 49.50 (*0-678-00181-2*) Kelley.

— Railroad Consolidation West of the Mississippi River. Bruchey, Stuart, ed. LC 80-1302. (Railroads Ser.). (Illus.). 1981. reprint ed. lib. bdg. 15.95 (*0-405-13771-0*) Ayer.

— Railroad Reorganization. LC 67-18576. (Library of Early American Business & Industry: No. 9). x, 404p. 1967. reprint ed. 49.50 (*0-678-00239-8*) Kelley.

Daggett, Wayne E. Capitol. 1997. pap. write for info. (*1-57553-704-4*) Watermrk Pr.

— Dad's Poetry. 1998. pap. write for info. (*1-57553-970-5*) Watermrk Pr.

Daggett, Willard R. Strategic Vision & Planning: Keys to Educational Improvement. 26p. 1984. 3.00 (*0-318-22203-5*, OC100); VHS 100.00 (*0-317-01419-6*, VS103VHS, VS103UM) Ctr Educ Trng Employ.

Daggett, Willard R. & Adams. Computers & Information Technology. (DC - Introduction to Computing Ser.). 1985. mass mkt. 43.95 (*0-538-04550-7*) S-W Pub.

Daggett, Willard R. & Kruse, Benedict. Education Is Not a Spectator Sport. unabridged ed. Kruse, Bettijune, ed. LC 96-95411. (Illus.). 352p. 1997. pap. 28.00 (*0-9656553-0-X*) Intl Ctr Ldrship.

Daggett, Willard R., jt. auth. see Kadamus, James A.

Daggett, Williard R. & Adams. Computer Information Technology. (DC - Introductino to Computing Ser.). 1985. 5.95 (*0-538-04553-1*) S-W Pub.

Daggy, Robert E., et al, eds. The Merton Annual: Studies in Thomas Merton, Religion, Culture, Literature, & Social Concerns, 1988-1993, 5 vols., Set. LC 87-47815. 1993. write for info. (*0-404-63800-7*) AMS Pr.

Daggy, Robert E., selected by. The Road to Joy: The Letters of Thomas Merton to New & Old Friends. LC 92-33540. 400p. 1993. pap. 15.95 (*0-15-677818-1*) Harcourt.

Daggy, Robert E., jt. auth. see Merton, Thomas.

Daggy, Robert E., ed. see Merton, Thomas.

***Dagher, Carole.** Bring down the Walls. LC 99-41936. 2000. text 39.95 (*0-312-22920-8*) St Martin.

Dagher, Joseph P. Think/Write: The Process of Translating Thought. rev. ed. 252p. 1998. pap. text. write for info. (*0-9671967-0-1*, Pub. by J Dagher) Amazon Com.

Dagher, Yusuf. Arabic Dictionary of Pseudonyms & the Writers Who Use Them. (ARA.). 1982. 19.95 (*0-86685-300-6*) Intl Bk Ctr.

Daghir, N. J. Poultry Production in Hot Climates. (CAB International Publication Ser.). (Illus.). 320p. 1995. text 100.00 (*0-85198-907-1*) OUP.

Daghistani, Shaykh A. Mercy Oceans I. 144p. (Orig.). 1995. pap. 9.95 (*0-934905-31-2*) Kazi Pubns.

— Mercy Oceans II. 144p. (Orig.). 1995. pap. 9.95 (*0-934905-32-0*) Kazi Pubns.

Daghlian, Philip B., ed. Essays in Eighteenth-Century Biography. LC 68-27341. 141p. reprint ed. pap. 43.80 (*0-608-13185-7*, 205603200044) Bks Demand.

Daghlian, Philip B., jt. ed. see Jenkinson, Edward B.

Daghlian, Philip B., ed. see Walpole, Horace.

Dagion, John W., ed. Hot Tricks. (True Revelations & Strange Happenings Ser.: Vol. 5). 192p. (Orig.). 1990. pap. 10.95 (*0-943595-17-7*) Leyland Pubns.

— Meat Rack. (True Revelations & Strange Happenings Ser.: Vol. 6). 160p. (Orig.). 1992. pap. 12.95 (*0-943595-34-7*) Leyland Pubns.

— Rough Trade. (True Revelations & Strange Happenings Ser.: Vol. 7). 160p. (Orig.). 1996. pap. 14.95 (*0-943595-58-4*) Leyland Pubns.

— Sex Stop. (True Revelations & Strange Happenings Ser.: Vol. 3). 192p. (Orig.). 1987. pap. 10.95 (*0-943595-03-7*) Leyland Pubns.

— Trucker. (True Revelations & Strange Happenings Ser.: Vol. 2). (Illus.). 192p. (Orig.). 1986. pap. 10.95 (*0-917342-22-4*) Leyland Pubns.

Dagit, Rosi. Grandmother Oak. (Illus.). 32p. (J). (gr. k-3). 1996. pap. 6.95 (*1-57098-114-0*) Roberts Rinehart.

Daglarca, Fazil Husnu. Beacon. Barkan, Stanley H. & Halman, Talat S., eds. (Review Turkish Writers Chapbook Ser.: No. 1).Tr. of Turkish & English. 48p. 1989. 15.00 (*0-89304-275-7*); 15.00 (*0-89304-277-3*); pap. 5.00 (*0-89304-276-5*); pap. 5.00 (*0-89304-278-1*) Cross-Cultrl NY.

— The Bird & I. Barkan, Stanley H., ed. Halman, Talat S., tr. (Cross-Cultural Review Chapbook Ser.: No. 4:). (ENG & TUR.). 16p. 1980. 15.00 (*0-89304-846-1*, CCC129) Cross-Cultrl NY.

— The Bird & I. Barkan, Stanley H., ed. Halman, Talat S., tr. (Cross-Cultural Review Chapbook Ser.: No. 4: Turkish Poetry 1). (ENG & TUR.). 16p. 1980. pap. 5.00 (*0-89304-803-8*); audio 10.00 (*0-89304-828-3*) Cross-Cultrl NY.

— Secme Siirler: Selected Poems. Halman, Talat S., tr. LC 69-12329. (Pitt Poetry Ser.: No. 46). 200p. 1969. pap. 62.00 (*0-608-05086-5*, 206564000005) Bks Demand.

Dagle, Gerald E., ed. see Benjamin, Stephen A.

Dagli, C. H. & Kusiak, Andrew, eds. Intelligent Systems in Design & Manufacturing. 380p. 1994. 95.00 (*0-7918-0034-2*, 800342) ASME Pr.

***Dagli, Cihan H., ed.** Intelligent Engineering Systems Through Artificial Neural Networks Vol. 9: Smart Engineering System Design, Neural Networks, Fuzzy Logic, Evolutionary Programming, Data Mining & Complex Systems. 1999. 185.00 (*0-7918-0098-9*) ASME Pr.

Dagli, Cihan H., ed. Intelligent Engineering through Artificial Neural Networks, Vol. 4. 1994. 185.00 (*0-7918-0045-8*, 800458) ASME Pr.

Dagli, Cihan H., et al, eds. ANNIE '95 - Intelligent Engineering Systems Through Artificial Neural Networks Vol. 5: Fuzzy Logic & Evolutionary Programming. 1056p. 1996. 185.00 (*0-7918-0048-2*, 800482) ASME.

— Intelligent Engineering Systems Through Artificial Neural Networks, Vol. 3. LC 93-30949. 1993. 185.00 (*0-7918-0038-5*) ASME Pr.

— Intelligent Engineering Systems Through Artificial Neural Networks: Proceedings of the Artificial Neural Networks in Engineering (ANNIE '92) Conference, Held November 15-18, 1992, in St. Louis, Missouri, U.S.A. LC 92-30949. (ASME Press Series on International Advances in Design Productivity). 1992. write for info. (*0-7918-0029-6*) ASME.

— Intelligent Engineering Systems Through Artificial Neural Networks: Proceedings of the 1998 Artificial Neural Networks in Engineering Conference, Vol. 8. LC 92-30949. (ASME Press Ser.). 910p. 1998. 185.00 (*0-7918-0082-2*) ASME Pr.

— Intelligent Engineering Systems Through Artificial Neural Networks: Smart Engineering Systems, Neural Networks, Fuzzy Logic, Data Mining & Evolutionary Programming, Proceedings, Vol. 7. LC 92-30949. (ASME Press Series on Intelligent Engineering Systems Through Artificial Neural Networks). 1078p. 1997. 185.00 (*0-7918-0064-4*) ASME.

Dagli, Vadilal, ed. Science & Technology in India. 345p. 1982. text 22.00 (*0-685-13747-3*) Coronet Bks.

Daglio, S. Daniel, tr. see Yates, Kyle M. & Owens, J. J.

Daglish, Neil D. Education Policy-Making in England & Wales: The Crucible Years, 1895-1911. LC 95-44531. (Woburn Education Ser.). (Illus.). 496p. (C). 1996. text 65.00 (*0-7130-0200-X*, Pub. by Woburn Pr) Intl Spec Bk.

Daglish, R. C., jt. ed. see Taube, A. M.

Daglish, Robert, tr. see Sholokhov, Mikhail Aleksandrovich.

Daglish, W. E., jt. auth. see Riley, Joe S.

Dagmar, tr. see Tichy, M. & Rakosnik, J.

Dagmar, Engels. Beyond Purdah: Women in Bengal 1890-1939. LC 96-902119. (Studies on South Asia). (Illus.). 294p. (C). 1996. text 26.00 (*0-19-563720-8*) OUP.

Dagmar, Engles. Beyond Purdah? Women in Bengal 1890-1930. (School of Oriental & African Studies). 296p. 1999. pap. text 14.95 (*0-19-564709-2*) OUP.

Dagnan, Cindy. Pay Day: Treasures for Stay-At-Home Moms. 105p. 1999. pap. text 6.99 (*0-89900-829-1*) College Pr Pub.

— Scribbles: Sketches for Stressed-Out Moms. 1997. pap. text 5.99 (*0-89900-721-X*) College Pr Pub.

Dag'Naud, Alain & Dazat, Olivier. Dictionnaire Inattendu des Citations. (FRE.). 1992. 95.00 (*0-7859-7612-4*, 2010177363) Fr & Eur.

Dagneau, Jacques. Les Agences Regionales du Credit Lyonnais: Annees 1870-1914. Bruchey, Stuart, ed. LC 77-81826. (Dissertations in European Economic History Ser.). (FRE., Illus.). 1978. lib. bdg. 65.95 (*0-405-10778-1*) Ayer.

Dagnello. Introduction to Real Analysis. LC 99-71719. 1999. text 64.17 (*0-395-95933-0*) HM.

D'Agnenica, Ellen, jt. auth. see Stevenson, N.

***D'agnese, Joseph.** Blockhead: The Story of Fibonnaci. 2000. text 15.95 (*0-8050-6305-6*) H Holt & Co.

Dagnini, G. Clinical Laparoscopy. 308p. 1980. text 112.00 (*1-57235-056-3*) Piccin Nuova.

— Laparoscopy & Imaging Techniques. Pearcey, S., tr. from ITA. (Illus.). 272p. 1990. 217.00 (*0-387-50999-2*) Spr-Verlag.

Dagognet, Francois. Etienne - Jules Marey: A Passion for the Trace. Galeta, Robert & Herman, Jeanine, trs. LC 92-22139. 204p. 1992. 31.00 (*0-942299-64-7*) Zone Bks.

— In Favor of Today's Art. (Illus.). 160p. (Orig.). 1992. pap. 24.95 (*2-906571-25-3*, Pub. by Editions Dis Voir) Dist Art Pubs.

— Trois Philosophies Revisitees: Saint-Simon, Fourier, Proudhon. (Europaea Memoria Ser.: Bd. 1). 171p. 1997. 45.00 (*3-487-10266-8*) G Olms Pubs.

Dagogo-Jack, S., jt. auth. see Johansen, K.

Dagort, Aida. Harps Are Not for Angels. LC 98-89481. 365p. 1999. 25.00 (*0-7388-0267-0*); pap. 15.00 (*0-7388-0268-9*) Xlibris Corp.

D'Agostino, Annette. Soap Stars to Superstars: Celebrities Who Started Out in Daytime Drama. LC 99-21726. (Illus.). 272p. 1958. pap. 16.95 (*1-58063-075-8*, Pub. by Renaissance) St Martin.

D'Agostino, Annette M. Harold Lloyd: A Bio-Bibliography, 54. LC 94-8273. (Bio-Bibliographies in the Performing Arts Ser.: No. 54). 320p. 1994. lib. bdg. 69.50 (*0-313-28986-7*, Greenwood Pr) Greenwood.

— The Index to Short & Feature Film Reviews in the Moving Picture World: The Early Years, 1907-1915, 20. LC 95-9907. (Bibliographies & Indexes in the Performing Arts Ser.: No. 20). 432p. 1995. lib. bdg. 85.00 (*0-313-29381-3*, Greenwood Pr) Greenwood.

D'Agostino, Annette M., ed. Filmmakers in the Moving Picture World: An Index of Articles, 1907-1927. LC 96-29894. 392p. 1997. lib. bdg. 75.00 (*0-7864-0290-3*) McFarland & Co.

D'Agostino, Anthony. Gorbachev's Revolution. LC 97-30236. 496p. 1998. text 50.00 (*0-8147-1898-1*) NYU Pr.

— Soviet Succession Struggles: Kremlinology & the Russian Question from Lenin to Gorbachev. 274p. 1989. pap. 19.95 (*0-685-28246-5*) Routledge.

D'Agostino, Carla T. & Byrd, Byron K. The Christmas Tree at Rockefeller Center. LC 97-22055. (Illus.). 112p. 1997. 27.50 (*0-9650308-7-3*) Lickle Pubng.

D'Agostino, Frank J. All about the Presidents Search-a-Word Puzzles. (Illus.). 64p. 1997. pap. 1.00 (*0-486-29910-4*) Dover.

— All about the States Search-a-Word Puzzles. (Illus.). pap. 1.00 (*0-486-29400-5*) Dover.

— Sports Search-a-Word Puzzles. (Illus.). (J). 1996. pap. 1.00 (*0-486-29348-3*) Dover.

Dagostino, Frank R. Estimating in Building Construction. 5th ed. LC 98-27457. 354p. 1998. 81.00 (*0-13-377938-6*) P-H.

— Light Frame Construction. (Construction & Building Trades Ser.). 1997. teacher ed. 13.95 (*0-8273-7122-5*); text 55.95 (*0-8273-7121-7*) Delmar.

— Materials of Construction. (Construction & Building Trades Ser.). 1997. teacher ed. 13.95 (*0-8273-7118-7*); text 55.95 (*0-8273-7117-9*) Delmar.

— Mechanical & Electrical Systems in Construction. 3rd ed. 450p. 1995. 91.00 (*0-13-181462-1*) P-H.

— Methods of Construction. (Construction & Building Trades Ser.). 1997. teacher ed. 13.95 (*0-8273-7120-9*); text 55.95 (*0-8273-7119-5*) Delmar.

Dagostino, Frank R. & Gallagher, Katy. California Real Estate Appraisal. 4th ed. Miller, George H., ed. 528p. (C). 1995. 22.80 (*0-13-378829-6*, Pub. by P-H) S&S Trade.

D'Agostino, Fred. Free Public Reason: Making It up As We Go. 216p. 1996. text 55.00 (*0-19-509761-0*) OUP.

D'Agostino, Fred & Gaus, Gerald F., eds. Public Reason. LC 97-37026. (International Research Library of Philosophy). 470p. 1998. text 153.95 (*1-85521-954-9*, Pub. by Ashgate Pub) Ashgate Pub Co.

D'Agostino, Fred & Jarvie, I. C., eds. Freedom & Rationality: Essays in Honor of John Watkins. (Boston Studies in the Philosophy of Science: No. 117). 392p. 1989. lib. bdg. 223.00 (*0-7923-0264-8*, Pub. by Kluwer Academic) Kluwer Academic.

D'Agostino, Giovanna. I'm Mama D. 1991. 3.98 (*0-931714-44-3*, Pub. by Nodin Pr) Bookmen Inc.

D'Agostino, Guido. Olives on the Apple Tree. LC 74-17924. (Italian American Experience Ser.). 1975. reprint ed. 21.95 (*0-405-06397-0*) Ayer.

D'Agostino, Guido & Nigro, A. Deep Inelastic Scattering & Related Phenomena: DIS 96. LC 96-49787. 1997. write for info. (*981-02-3008-7*) World Scientific Pub.

D'Agostino, Joseph D. Tarot: The Path to Wisdom. rev. ed. LC 94-36189. (Illus.). 128p. 1994. pap. 9.95 (*0-87728-819-4*) Weiser.

D'Agostino, L. V. Our Family. (Illus.). 1973. 6.95 (*0-9601076-1-4*) L V D'Agostino.

***D'Agostino, Marcello.** Handbook of Tableau Methods. LC 99-13568. 1999. write for info. (*0-7923-5627-6*) Kluwer Academic.

D'Agostino, Peppino. Contemporary Acoustic Guitar. Stang, Aaron, ed. (Acoustic Masters Ser.). 104p. (C). 1997. pap. text 24.95 (*1-57623-401-0*, EL96102CD) Wrner Bros.

D'Agostino, Peter & Tafler, David, eds. Transmission: Toward a Post-Television Culture. 2nd ed. (Communication & Human Values Ser.: Vol. 16). 258p. 1994. 52.00 (*0-8039-4268-0*); pap. 24.95 (*0-8039-4269-9*) Sage.

D'Agostino, Ralph B. & Stephens, Michael A. Goodness-of-Fit Techniques. (Statistics: Textbooks & Monographs: Vol. 68). (Illus.). 576p. 1986. text 137.50 (*0-8247-7487-6*) Dekker.

D'Agostino, Ralph B., et al. Mathematical Modeling: Applications in Emergency Health Services. LC 84-12917. (Emergency Health Services Review Ser.: Vol. 2, Nos. 2-3). 118p. 1984. 29.95 (*0-86656-373-3*) Haworth Pr.

D'Agostino, Ralph B., jt. auth. see Schiff, Daniel B.

D'Agostino, Riccardo, ed. Plasma Deposition, Treatment & Etching of Polymers, Plasma-Materials Interactions. 528p. 1990. text 136.00 (*0-12-200430-2*) Acad Pr.

D'Agostino, Riccardo, et al, eds. Plasma Processing of Polymers: Proceedings of the NATO Advanced Study Institute on Plasma Treatments & Deposition of Polymers, Acquafredda di Maratea, Italy, May 19-June 2, 1996. LC 97-45510. (NATO Advanced Science Institutes Ser.: No. 346). 544p. 1997. text 307.50 (*0-7923-4859-1*) Kluwer Academic.

D'Agostino, Robert J., jt. ed. see Krason, Stephen M.

D'Agostino, Rose, ed. see Trollope, Anthony.

D'Agostino, Thomas. Litigating Ada Claims: Forms, Pleadings, & Practical Guidance. LC 96-39407. 1996. write for info. (*1-57834-001-2*) LRP Pubns.

D'Agostino, Thomas J., jt. auth. see Hillman, Richard S.

Dagot, Edilberto P. What Time Does the Rally Start & Other Poems. (Illus.). 102p. (Orig.). (C). 1990. pap. 9.50 (*971-10-0409-7*, Pub. by New Day Pub) Cellar.

Dagpunar, John. Principles of Random Variate Generation. (Illus.). 248p. 1988. 75.00 (*0-19-852202-9*) OUP.

Dagtoglou, P. D., ed. Air Transport & the European Community: Recent Developments. (European Air Law Association Conference Papers: No. I). 120p. 1991. 60.00 (*90-6544-508-0*) Kluwer Law Intl.

Dagtoglou, P. D., et al, eds. Seventh Annual Conference in London: Euro Air Law Association Conference. 93p. 1998. text 68.50 (*90-411-0336-8*) Kluwer Law Intl.

Dagtoglou, P. D. & Ehlers, P. N., eds. Airline Liability: A Seminar on Liability & Claims Handling in the Airline & Aeropsace Industries. LC 98-168051. Date not set. text 68.00 (*90-411-0542-5*) Kluwer Academic.

Dagtoglou, P. D., jt. ed. see Slot, P. J.

Dague, Carrie M. Dague: The History & Genealogy of the Dague Family. (Illus.). 253p. 1992. reprint ed. pap. 39.00 (*0-8328-2401-1*); reprint ed. lib. bdg. 49.00 (*0-8328-2400-3*) Higginson Bk Co.

Daguer, D. & Mulcherjee, S. National Trends for Persons in Juvenile Corrective Institutions & Adult Prisons, 1981-1992. LC 96-145367. 25p. 1994. pap. 12.00 (*0-642-20067-X*, Pub. by Aust Inst Criminology) Advent Bks Div.

Daguerre, Mercedes & Hollenstein, Roman. Birkhauser Architectural Guide Switzerland: 20th Century. LC 97-38620. (Birkhauser Architectural Guides Ser.). (Illus.). 444p. 1997. 40.00 (*3-7643-5713-4*, Pub. by Birkhauser) Princeton Arch.

D'Aguiar, Fred. Bill of Rights. pap. 16.95 (*0-7011-6525-1*, Pub. by Random) Trafalgar.

D'Aguiar, Fred. British Subjects. 64p. 1994. pap. 12.95 (*1-85224-248-5*, Pub. by Bloodaxe Bks) Dufour.

— Dear Future. 224p. 1996. 22.00 (*0-679-44248-0*) McKay.

— Dear Future. 224p. 1998. pap. 12.00 (*0-380-72967-9*, Avon Bks) Morrow Avon.

— Feeding The Ghosts. LC 98-15708. 240p. 1999. 23.00 (*0-88001-623-X*) HarpC.

***D'Aguiar, Fred.** Feeding the Ghosts: A Novel. 240p. 2000. pap. 13.00 (*0-06-095593-7*, Ecco Press) HarperTrade.

D'aguilar & Dommanger. Dragonflies of Britian, Europe. 1987. 34.95 (*0-685-43767-1*) Viking Penguin.

D'Aguilar, George C., tr. see Bonaparte, Napoleon.

Daguin, Ariane & Faison, George. D'Artagnan's Glorious Game Cookbook. 336p. (gr. 8). 1999. 35.00 (*0-316-17075-5*) Little.

Dagum, C., et al, eds. Income & Wealth Distribution, Inequality & Poverty: Proceedings of the Second International Conference on Income Distribution by Size: Generation, Distribution, Measurement & Applications Held at the University of Pavia, Italy, September 28-30, 1989. (Studies in Contemporary Economics). (Illus.). xiii, 415p. 1990. 63.95 (*0-387-52863-6*) Spr-Verlag.

Dagut, M., tr. see Kaufman, Yehezkel.

Dagut, Menachem, tr. see Hacohen, David.

Dagwell, Carol V., jt. auth. see Koontz, Thomas.

Dagys, Andrew. Ontario Retirement Handbook: A Comprehensive Guide to Services & Programs for Retirees. 208p. 1996. pap. 15.00 (*1-55022-289-9*, Pub. by ECW) Genl Dist Srvs.

Dah Ming, Chiu & Sudama, Ram. Network Monitoring Explained. 207p. (C). 1992. 100.00 (*0-13-614710-0*) P-H.

Dahal & Mund. Social Economy & National Development: Lessons from Napalese Experience. 1996. pap. 40.00 (*0-7855-7495-6*, Pub. by Ratna Pustak Bhandar) St Mut.

Dahal, D. R. Decentralization & Development in Nepal. 1994. pap. 35.00 (*0-7855-0435-4*, Pub. by Ratna Pustak Bhandar) St Mut.

Dahal, D. R., jt. auth. see Dahal, M. K.

Dahal, D. R., jt. auth. see Verma, V.

Dahal, Fricke. Tamang Family Research Project. (C). 1991. text 30.00 (*0-7855-0161-4*, Pub. by Ratna Pustak Bhandar) St Mut.

Dahal, Kishor. Indo-Nepal Trade: Problems & Prospects. 1987. 40.00 (*0-7855-0242-4*, Pub. by Ratna Pustak Bhandar) St Mut.

— Indo-Nepal Trade: Problems & Prospects. 76p. (C). 1987. 190.00 (*0-89771-047-9*, Pub. by Ratna Pustak Bhandar) St Mut.

***Dahal, M. K.** Impact of Globalization in Nepal. 1998. pap. 34.00 (*0-7855-7601-0*) St Mut.

***Dahal, M. K. & Dahal, D. R.** Environment & Sustainable Development Issues in Nepalese Perspective. 1998. pap. 43.00 (*0-7855-7545-6*) St Mut.

An Asterisk (*) at the beginning of an entry indicates that the title is appearing for the first time.

Dahal, Raj, contrib. by. The Challenge of Good Governnance: Decentralization of Development in Nepal. 1996. pap. 22.00 (*0-7855-7369-0*, Pub. by Ratna Pustak Bhandar) St Mut.

Dahan, Albert & Van Beek, Johannes H. Physiology & Pharmacology of Cardio-Respiratory Control. Teppema, Luc, ed. LC 98-22537. 1998. 59.00 (*0-7923-5135-5*) Kluwer Academic.

Dahan, Bonnie T. Wise Concoctions: Natural Elixirs & Tonics for Health & Energy. LC 98-11973. (Illus.). 120p. 1998. pap. 16.95 (*0-8118-1744-X*) Chronicle Bks.

***Dahan, Fernand W.** Laboratories: A Guide to Planning, Programming & Design. (Illus.). 2000. 100.00 (*0-393-73058-1*) Norton.

Dahan, Gilbert. The Christian Polemic Against the Jews in the Middle Ages. Gladding, Jody, tr. from FRE. LC 98-16301. 130p. 1998. pap. 10.00 (*0-268-00830-2*) U of Notre Dame Pr.

Dahanayake, K., et al, eds. Direct Application of Phosphate Rock & Appropriate Technology Fertilizers in Asia: What Hinders Acceptance & Growth (Proceedings of International Workshop) unabridged ed. (Special Publications: No. SP-24). (Illus.). 278p. (Orig.). 1995. pap. 35.00 (*955-26-0030-8*) Intl Fertilizer.

Dahanayake, Mauilal, jt. auth. see Rosen, Milton J.

Dahanukar, S. & Thatte, U. Ayurveda Revisited. 1989. 21.50 (*0-86132-223-1*, Pub. by Popular Prakashan) S Asia.

DaHarb, Peggy, jt. auth. see Brunson, Dorothy.

Dahbany-Miraglia, Dina. Speaking American English Well. 240p. (C). 1998. per. 42.95 (*0-7872-5431-2*, 41543101) Kendall-Hunt.

Dahbour, Omar & Ishtay, Micheline, eds. The Nationalism Reader. LC 94-12537. 376p. (C). 1995. pap. 18.50 (*0-391-03867-2*) Humanities.

Dahbura, Tony, jt. see Weltman, Rob.

Dahdah, Antoine. Dictionary of Universal Arabic Grammar, in Charts & Tables. (ARA & ENG., Illus.). 1982. 35.00 (*0-86685-292-1*) Intl Bk Ctr.

Daheim, David C. We Regret to Inform You. 37p. Date not set. pap. 3.60 (*0-87129-995-X*, W86) Dramatic Pub.

***Daheim, Mary.** The Alpine Menace. 2000. mass mkt. 6.99 (*0-345-42124-8*) Ballantine Pub Grp.

— A Streetcar Named Expire. 2001. mass mkt. 6.50 (*0-380-80080-2*, Avon Bks) Morrow Avon.

Daheim, Mary R. The Alpine Advocate. 1992. mass mkt. 5.99 (*0-345-37672-2*) Ballantine Pub Grp.

— The Alpine Advocate. large type ed. LC 93-18807. 350p. 1993. lib. bdg. 17.95 (*1-56054-732-4*) Thorndike Pr.

— The Alpine Betrayal. 1993. mass mkt. 5.99 (*0-345-37937-3*) Ballantine Pub Grp.

— The Alpine Betrayal. large type ed. LC 93-22678. 378p. 1993. lib. bdg. 17.95 (*1-56054-874-6*) Thorndike Pr.

— The Alpine Christmas. (Holiday Mysteries Ser.). 1993. mass mkt. 5.99 (*0-345-38270-6*) Ballantine Pub Grp.

— The Alpine Christmas. large type ed. LC 93-38619. 378p. 1993. lib. bdg. 17.95 (*0-7862-0001-4*) Thorndike Pr.

— The Alpine Decoy. (Northwest Mysteries Ser.). 1994. mass mkt. 5.99 (*0-345-38841-0*) Ballantine Pub Grp.

— The Alpine Escape. (Orig.). 1995. mass mkt. 5.99 (*0-345-38842-9*) Ballantine Pub Grp.

— The Alpine Fury. 320p. (Orig.). 1995. mass mkt. 5.99 (*0-345-38843-7*) Ballantine Pub Grp.

— The Alpine Gamble. 1996. mass mkt. 5.99 (*0-345-39641-3*) Ballantine Pub Grp.

***Daheim, Mary R.** The Alpine Gamble. large type ed. LC 99-35485. (Beeler Large Print Mystery Ser.). 1999. write for info. (*1-57490-210-5*, Beeler LP Bks) T T Beeler.

Daheim, Mary R. The Alpine Hero. 1997. mass mkt. 5.99 (*0-345-39642-1*) Ballantine Pub Grp.

***Daheim, Mary R.** The Alpine Hero. large type ed. LC 98-50926. (Beeler Large Print Mystery Ser.). 1999. 31.19 (*1-57490-203-2*, Beeler LP Bks) T T Beeler.

Daheim, Mary R. The Alpine Icon. 1997. mass mkt. 5.99 (*0-345-39643-X*) Ballantine Pub Grp.

— The Alpine Icon. large type ed. LC 98-16228. 1998. 24.95 (*1-57490-138-9*, Beeler LP Bks) T T Beeler.

— The Alpine Journey: An Emma Lord Mystery. 1998. mass mkt. 5.99 (*0-345-39644-8*) Ballantine Pub Grp.

— The Alpine Kindred. 309p. 1999. mass mkt. 5.99 (*0-345-42122-1*) Ballantine Pub Grp.

***Daheim, Mary R.** The Alpine Legacy. 1999. mass mkt. 5.99 (*0-345-42123-X*, Ballantine) Ballantine Pub Grp.

Daheim, Mary R. Auntie Mayhem. 272p. 2000. mass mkt. 6.50 (*0-380-77878-5*) Morrow Avon.

***Daheim, Mary R.** Bantam of the Opera. 256p. (Orig.). 1999. mass mkt. 6.50 (*0-380-76934-4*, Avon Bks) Morrow Avon.

— Creeps Suzette. (Bed & Breakfast Mystery Ser.). 336p. 2000. mass mkt. 6.50 (*0-380-80079-9*, Avon Bks) Morrow Avon.

— Dune to Death. 240p. (Orig.). 1999. mass mkt. 6.50 (*0-380-76933-6*, Avon Bks) Morrow Avon.

Daheim, Mary R. A Fit of Tempera. 256p. 2000. reprint ed. mass mkt. 6.50 (*0-380-77490-9*, Avon Bks) Morrow Avon.

***Daheim, Mary R.** Fowl Prey. 272p. (Orig.). 1999. mass mkt. 6.50 (*0-380-76296-X*, Avon Bks) Morrow Avon.

— Holy Terrors. 256p. (Orig.). 1999. mass mkt. 6.50 (*0-380-76297-8*, Avon Bks) Morrow Avon.

— Just Desserts. (Bed & Breakfast Mystery Ser.). 252p. (Orig.). 1999. mass mkt. 6.50 (*0-380-76295-1*, Avon Bks) Morrow Avon.

Daheim, Mary R. Legs Benedict: A Bed-&-Breakfast Mystery. LC 98-93760. (Bed & Breakfast Mystery Ser.). 320p. 1999. mass mkt. 6.50 (*0-380-80078-0*, Avon Bks) Morrow Avon.

***Daheim, Mary R.** Major Vices. 256p. (Orig.). 2000. mass mkt. 6.50 (*0-380-77491-7*, Avon Bks) Morrow Avon.

— Murder, My Suite. 272p. (Orig.). 2000. mass mkt. 5.99 (*0-380-77877-7*, Avon Bks) Morrow Avon.

Daheim, Mary R. Nutty As a Fruitcake. LC 96-96422. 272p. 2000. mass mkt. 5.99 (*0-380-77879-3*) Morrow Avon.

— Passion's Triumph. 432p. 1988. pap. 3.95 (*0-380-89850-0*, Avon Bks) Morrow Avon.

— September Mourn: A Bed-&-Breakfast Mystery. LC 96-95484. (Bed & Breakfast Mystery Ser.). (Illus.). 320p. (Orig.). 2000. mass mkt. 5.99 (*0-380-78518-8*, Avon Bks) Morrow Avon.

— Snow Place to Die: Where There's Ice... There's Vice. (Bed & Breakfast Mystery Ser.: No. 13). 304p. 1998. mass mkt. 5.99 (*0-380-78521-8*, Avon Bks) Morrow Avon.

***Daheim, Mary R.** Wed & Buried. (Bed & Breakfast Mystery Ser.). 304p. 2000. mass mkt. 5.99 (*0-380-78520-X*, Avon Bks) Morrow Avon.

Dahesh. Al-Muhannad Al-Batir. (ARA & ENG., Illus.). 215p. 1991. 50.00 (*0-935359-22-2*) Daheshist.

— Al-Rahalat Al-Dahishiyyah Hawla Al-Kurah Al-Ardiyyah, Al-Rihlah Al-'Ashirah 'Am 1976, Vol. 10. (ARA & ENG., Illus.). 375p. 1992. 30.00 (*0-935359-26-5*) Daheshist.

— Al-Rahalat Al-Dahishiyyah Hawla Al-Kurah Al-Ardiyyah, Al-Rihlah Al-Hadiyah 'Asharah 'Am 1976, Vol. 11. (ARA & ENG., Illus.). 275p. 1993. 25.00 (*0-935359-27-3*) Daheshist.

— Al-Rahalat Al-Dahishiyyah Hawla Al-Kurah Al-Ardiyyah, Al-Rihlah Al-Kamisah 'Am 1971, Vol. 5. (ARA & ENG., Illus.). 230p. 1991. 22.00 (*0-935359-05-2*) Daheshist.

— Al-Rahalat Al-Dahishiyyah Hawla Al-Kurah Al-Ardiyyah, Al-Rihlah Al-Khamisah 'Asharah 'Am 1979-1980, Vol. 15. (ARA & ENG., Illus.). 286p. 1992. 25.00 (*0-935359-31-1*) Daheshist.

— Al-Rahalat Al-Dahishiyyah Hawla Al-Kurah Al-Ardiyyah, Al-Rihlah Al-Rabi'ah 'Asharah 'Am 1978, Vol. 14. (ARA & ENG., Illus.). 479p. 1992. 36.00 (*0-935359-30-3*) Daheshist.

— Al-Rahalat Al-Dahishiyyah Hawla Al-Kurah Al-Ardiyyah, Al-Rihlah Al-Sabi'ah 'Am 1972, Vol. 7. (ARA & ENG., Illus.). 214p. 1990. 22.00 (*0-935359-07-9*) Daheshist.

— Al-Rahalat Al-Dahishiyyah Hawla Al-Kurah Al-Ardiyyah, Al-Rihlah Al-Sabi'ah 'Ashrah 'Am 1972, Vol. 17. (ARA & ENG., Illus.). 523p. 1994. 40.00 (*0-935359-33-8*) Daheshist.

— Al-Rahalat Al-Dahishiyyah Hawla Al-Kurah Al-Ardiyyah, Al-Rihlah Al-Sadisah 'Am 1972, Vol. 6. (ARA & ENG., Illus.). 423p. 1990. 30.00 (*0-935359-06-0*) Daheshist.

— Al-Rahalat Al-Dahishiyyah Hawla Al-Kurah Al-Ardiyyah, Al-Rihlah Al-Sadisah 'Asharah 'Am 1980, Vol. 16. (ARA & ENG., Illus.). 158p. 1992. 20.00 (*0-935359-32-X*) Daheshist.

— Al-Rahalat Al-Dahishiyyah Hawla Al-Kurah Al-Ardiyyah, Al-Rihlah Al-Tasi'ah 'Am 1973-1974, Vol. 9. (ARA & ENG., Illus.). 431p. 1992. 30.00 (*0-935359-25-7*) Daheshist.

— Al-Rahalat Al-Dahishiyyah Hawla Al-Kurah Al-Ardiyyah, Al-Rihlah Al-Tasi'ah 'Asharah 'Am 1982, Vol. 19. (ARA & ENG., Illus.). 599p. 1994. 50.00 (*0-935359-35-4*) Daheshist.

— Al-Rahalat Al-Dahishiyyah Hawla Al-Kurah Al-Ardiyyah, Al-Rihlah Al-Thalithah 'Asharah 'Am 1978, Vol. 13. (ARA & ENG., Illus.). 182p. 1992. 24.00 (*0-935359-29-X*) Daheshist.

— Al-Rahalat Al-Dahishiyyah Hawla Al-Kurah Al-Ardiyyah, Al-Rihlah Al-Thaminah 'Asharah 'Am 1981-1982, Vol. 18. (ARA & ENG., Illus.). 603p. 1994. 48.00 (*0-935359-34-6*) Daheshist.

— Al-Rahalat Al-Dahishiyyah Hawla Al-Kurah Al-Ardiyyah, Al-Rihlah Al-Thaniyah 'Asharah 'Am 1977, Vol. 12. (Illus.). 275p. 1992. 25.00 (*0-935359-28-1*) Daheshist.

— Al-Rahalat Al-Dahishiyyah Hawla Al-Kurah Al-Aridiyyah, Al-Rihlah Al-Thaminah 'Am 1972, Vol. 8. (ARA & ENG., Illus.). 126p. 1990. 16.00 (*0-935359-08-7*) Daheshist.

— Anashid Hazinah. Mehdi, Majed, ed. (ARA & ENG., Illus.). 239p. 1991. 20.00 (*0-935359-10-9*) Daheshist.

— Awham Sarabiyyah Wa-Takhayyulat Turabiyyah. (ARA & ENG., Illus.). 131p. 1991. 18.00 (*0-935359-14-1*) Daheshist.

— Buruq Wa-Ru'ud Al-Nathry. 2nd ed. (ARA & ENG., Illus.). 136p. pap. write for info. (*0-935359-21-4*) Daheshist.

— Le Cantique des Cantiques. (ARA, ENG & FRE., Illus.). 147p. 1990. 45.00 (*0-935359-17-6*) Daheshist.

— Das Hohelied. (ARA, ENG & GER., Illus.). 147p. 1990. 45.00 (*0-935359-18-4*) Daheshist.

— Jahim Al-Duktur Dahesh, Vol. 1. 2nd ed. (ARA & ENG., Illus.). 346p. 1989. 200.00 (*0-935359-03-6*) Daheshist.

— Madhakkirat Yasu' Al-Nasiry, Vol. 1. (ARA & ENG., Illus.). 150p. 1991. 40.00 (*0-935359-11-7*) Daheshist.

— Memoiren eines Dinar. (ARA, ENG & GER., Illus.). 383p. 1990. 35.00 (*0-935359-20-6*) Daheshist.

— Memoires d'un Dinar. (ARA, ENG & FRE., Illus.). 399p. 1988. 35.00 (*0-935359-02-8*) Daheshist.

— Memoirs of Jesus of Nazareth, Vol. 1.Tr. of Mudhakkirat Yasu' Al-Nasiry Al-Juz' Al-Awwal. (ARA & ENG., Illus.). 159p. 1993. 40.00 (*0-935359-40-0*) Daheshist.

— Memorias de un Dinar. (ARA, ENG & SPA., Illus.). 382p. 1990. 35.00 (*0-935359-19-2*) Daheshist.

— Merkwurdige Erzahlungen und Wundersame Geschichten, Vol. 1. (ARA, ENG & GER., Illus.). 246p. 1988. 20.00 (*0-935359-04-4*) Daheshist.

— Mudhakkirat Dinar. 2nd ed. (ARA & ENG., Illus.). 462p. 1986. 30.00 (*0-935359-01-X*) Daheshist.

— Nashid Al-Anshad. (ARA & ENG., Illus.). 143p. 1985. 40.00 (*0-935359-24-9*) Daheshist.

— Le Reve Aile ou la Vie des Vivants sur la Lune & Longues Moustaches et Barbes Funestes. (ARA, ENG & FRE., Illus.). 79p. 1991. 25.00 (*0-935359-23-0*) Daheshist.

— The Song of Songs. (Illus.). 147p. 1990. 40.00 (*0-935359-16-8*) Daheshist.

Dahesh & Dammons, Halim. Buruq Wa-Ru'ud Al-Shi'ry. (ARA & ENG., Illus.). 136p. pap. write for info. (*0-935359-36-2*) Daheshist.

Dahesh & Hadad, Zeina. Al-Hamama Al-Dhabiha Aw Al-Shahida Al-Dahishiyyah Al-Ula Majda Hadad. (ARA & ENG., Illus.). 380p. 1991. 25.00 (*0-935359-09-5*) Daheshist.

Dahi, Lynda M. The Wizards of Consciousness: Making the Imponderable Practical. LC 96-49174. 208p. (Orig.). 1997. pap. 13.95 (*1-889964-03-4*, WBB008) Woodbridge Grp.

Dahir, Mubarak S. Take This Book to the Chiropractor with You. 1999. pap. text 14.95 (*1-882606-46-9*) Peoples Med Soc.

Dahiya. Keller Physics. 2nd ed. 1993. text, student ed. 17.19 (*0-07-033910-4*) McGraw.

Dahiya, L. N. Dynamics of Economic Life in Rural India: A Case Study. (C). 1991. 20.00 (*81-212-0391-0*, Pub. by Gian Publng Hse) S Asia.

Dahiya, R. P., ed. Progress in Hydrogen Energy. 1987. text 169.00 (*90-277-2440-7*) Kluwer Academic.

Dahiya, Yajan V. Panini As a Linguist: Ideas & Patterns. (C). 1995. 62.00 (*81-86339-09-4*, Pub. by Eastern Bk Linkers) S Asia.

Dahk Knox, W. B. The Jericho Syndrome: A God Centered Approach to Human Potential. LC 96-61351. 172p. 1999. pap. 11.99 (*1-56384-136-3*, Pub. by Huntington Hse) BookWorld.

Dahl. Russian Diction, Vol. 4. 1981. 40.00 (*0-08-023589-1*, Pergamon Pr) Elsevier.

— Structured Programming Applications. 1972. text 65.00 (*0-12-200550-3*) Acad Pr.

Dahl, et al, eds. Danish Law in a European Perspective. LC 96-184582. 543p. 1996. 96.00 (*87-607-0355-5*) Gaunt.

Dahl & Tate, Charles D., eds. The Lectures on Faith in Historical Perspective. (Monograph Ser.: Vol. 15). 1990. 11.95 (*0-88494-725-4*) Bookcraft Inc.

Dahl, A., jt. ed. see Retterstol, Nils.

Dahl, A. M. Directory of Directors in the City of New York & Tri-State Area. 727p. 1985. 150.00 (*0-936612-06-1*) DODC.

Dahl, A. M., ed. Directory of Directors in the City of New York & Tri State Area. 85th rev. ed. 700p. 1996. 225.00 (*0-936612-17-7*) DODC.

Dahl, Alf A. & Wilson, J. Douglas. Cabinetmaking & Millwork: Tools, Materials, Layout. LC 53-11586. (Books of the Building Trade). 359p. reprint ed. pap. 111.30 (*0-8357-7955-6*, 200611100060) Bks Demand.

Dahl, Andrew & Lesnick, Leslie. Internet Commerce. (Illus.). 382p. 1999. reprint ed. pap. text 25.00 (*0-7881-6521-6*) DIANE Pub.

Dahl, Andrew, jt. auth. see Lesnick, Leslie.

Dahl, Ann-Sofie, ed. Security in Our Time: Four Essays on the Future of Europe. 94p. 1996. reprint ed. pap. text 25.00 (*0-7881-3350-0*) DIANE Pub.

Dahl, Anne. German-English English-German Dictionary. (ENG & GER.). 1998. mass mkt. 5.99 (*0-345-91355-8*) Ballantine Pub Grp.

— Random House German-English, English-German Dictionary. LC 97-93536. 1997. mass mkt. 5.99 (*0-345-41439-X*) Ballantine Pub Grp.

— Random House German-English, English-German Dictionary. LC 98-21926. (ENG & GER.). 1998. pap. 12.95 (*0-375-70085-4*) Random Ref & Info.

Dahl, Anthony G. Literature of the Bahamas, 1724-1992: The March Towards National Identity. 236p. (C). 1995. lib. bdg. 42.50 (*0-7618-0092-1*) U Pr of Amer.

Dahl, Arlene. Arlene Dahl's Lovescopes. LC 83-6387. 224p. 1983. write for info. (*0-672-52770-7*) Macmillan.

Dahl, Arthur L. Ecological Foundations for a New Economics: The Theory of ECOs & Its Implications for New Paradigms. 192p. 1996. text 19.95 (*1-85649-434-9*, Pub. by Zed Books) St Martin.

— Unless & Until: A Baha'i Focus on the Environment. 96p. 1990. pap. 10.95 (*1-870989-09-0*) Bahai.

Dahl, Arthur L., et al. Mark Tobey: Art & Belief. (Illus.). 128p. (Orig.). 1984. 24.95 (*0-85398-179-5*); pap. 13.95 (*0-85398-180-9*) G Ronald Pub.

Dahl, Barding. Marching to Zaragoza: A Novel of Mexico. LC 97-44158. 228p. 1998. pap. 14.95 (*1-56474-256-3*) Fithian Pr.

Dahl, Basil. To the Toilers & Other Verses. 1972. 59.95 (*0-8490-1217-1*) Gordon Pr.

Dahl, Bonnie. The Users' Guide to GPS: The Global Positioning System. Ault, Steve et al, eds. (Illus.). 253p. 1993. pap. 24.95 (*0-932647-12-X*) Rchrdsns Pubng.

— User's Guide to the Loran-C. 2nd rev. ed. Haskins, Wally & Sherman, Hal, eds. (Illus.). 263p. (Orig.). 1991. reprint ed. pap. 19.95 (*0-932647-09-X*) Rchrdsns Pubng.

Dahl, Borghild. Finding My Way. large type ed. 1972. reprint ed. 27.99 (*0-85456-101-3*) Ulverscroft.

Dahl, Carolyn. Transforming Fabrics. LC 97-39715. (Illus.). 192p. 1997. 29.95 (*1-57432-700-3*, 4919, Am Quilters Soc) Collector Bks.

Dahl, Chris. Mrs. Dahl in the Season of Cub Scouts. Warren, Shirley, ed. 40p. 1991. pap. 5.00 (*1-877801-15-1*) Still Waters.

Dahl, Curtis. Robert Montgomery Bird. (Twayne's United States Authors Ser.). (C). 1963. lib. bdg. 20.95 (*0-317-38184-9*) Irvington.

***Dahl, Curtis, ed.** Around the World in 500 Days: Hattie Atwood Freeman. (Illus.). 225p. 1999. pap. 24.95 (*0-913372-90-0*) Mystic Seaport.

Dahl, Curtis, ed. see Bird, Robert M.

Dahl, Daniel, ed. & tr. see Skotte, Anders.

Dahl, David R. The Blue Deer: And Other Dreamtales. LC 98-8785. 158p. 1998. pap. 9.95 (*0-88496-433-7*, Pub. by Capra Pr) SPD-Small Pr Dist.

Dahl, Deanna, ed. see Stanley, Charles A.

Dahl, Del. The Complete Poodle. LC 93-38104. (Illus.). 288p. 1994. 25.95 (*0-87605-257-X*) Howell Bks.

Dahl, Dolores. Autumn Wine: And Other Seasonings. LC 89-92836. (Illus.). 133p. (Orig.). 1991. pap. 10.95 (*0-9608960-6-6*) Single Vision.

— Don't Stir the Stew: Inspirational Poetry, a Heart's Sharing I Must Stop Stewing, Mulling so- I need to Just Be Still, Let Go- (Illus.). 98p. 1998. pap. 10.95 (*1-892541-00-9*) Single Vision.

— Everything's a Mountain: A Revealing Look at the Empty Nest Syndrome. (Illus.). 88p. (Orig.). 1999. pap. 10.95 (*1-892541-01-7*) Single Vision.

— HeartStrings Thought Provoking Poetry: A Heart's Dictation. (Illus.). 171p. 1996. pap. 10.95 (*0-9608960-8-2*) Single Vision.

— Memories Ago Reminiscings of a Northern Minn. Childhood. (Illus.). 39p. (Orig.). 1985. pap. 9.95 (*0-9608960-4-X*) Single Vision.

— The Pearl Within the Shell: A Collection of Inspirational Poetry that Speaks tp You. LC 83-60744. (Illus.). 119p. (Orig.). 1983. pap. 10.95 (*0-9608960-1-5*) Single Vision.

— Suddenly Alone: A Progression of Emotions Embraced by a Widow on the Path of Healing. LC 87-90686. (Illus.). 144p. 1987. pap. 10.95 (*0-9608960-5-8*) Single Vision.

— Where Heavens Hide A Heart's Renewing: A 24-hr. Chronolgy of Ocean Viewing. LC 84-51375. (Illus.). 48p. (Orig.). 1984. pap. 9.95 (*0-9608960-2-3*) Single Vision.

Dahl, Donald. Progression Blackjack: Exposing the Cardcounting Myth. LC 92-38085. 1993. pap. 11.95 (*0-8065-1396-9*) Carol Pub Group.

Dahl, Doug. The Elephant Sits Amidst Words of Anger & Other Poems. 1992. 8.95 (*0-533-10025-9*) Vantage.

— Rock Moon Rock Harmonies & Other Poems. 1995. 8.95 (*0-533-11195-1*) Vantage.

— Units of Lovers. 1994. 8.95 (*0-533-10754-7*) Vantage.

Dahl, Eilif. The Phytogeography of Northern Europe: British Isles, Fennoscandia, & Adjacent Areas. LC 96-37970. (Illus.). 310p. (C). 1998. text 95.00 (*0-521-38358-7*) Cambridge U Pr.

Dahl, Enrique, jt. ed. see Levasseur, Alain A.

Dahl, Fred, jt. auth. see Sippl, Charles J.

Dahl, Gary. Jazz Accordion Solos: Intermediate Level. 40p. 1997. pap. 17.95 incl. audio compact disk (*0-7866-2480-9*, 96309BCD) Mel Bay.

***Dahl, Gary & Beuscher, Paul.** French Tangos for Accordian. 88p. 1998. pap. 19.95 incl. audio compact disk (*0-7866-0803-X*, 96927BCD) Mel Bay.

Dahl, Gary, tr. see Chenier, Clifton.

Dahl, George. The Material for the History of Dor. (Connecticut Academy of Arts & Sciences Ser., Trans.: Vol. 20). 1915. pap. 75.00 (*0-685-22848-7*) Elliots Bks.

Dahl, George K. Newspaper Records Management. rev. ed. 64p. 1988. pap. 49.95 (*1-877888-04-4*) Intl Newspaper.

Dahl, Gudrun, ed. Green Arguments & Local Subsistence. (Stockholm Studies in Social Anthropology: No. 31). 248p. (Orig.). 1993. pap. 49.50 (*91-7153-131-9*) Coronet Bks.

Dahl, Gudrun, jt. auth. see Ornas, Anders H.

***Dahl, Gunnar.** Trade, Trust, & Networks: Commercial Culture in Late Medieval Italy. 355p. 1998. 60.00 (*91-89116-05-4*, Pub. by Nordic Acad Pr) Intl Spec Bk.

Dahl, Hans F. Quisling: A Study in Treachery. Stanton-Ife, Anne-Marie, tr. from NOR. LC 98-35102. (Illus.). 350p. (C). 1999. text 54.95 (*0-521-49697-7*) Cambridge U Pr.

Dahl, Henry. Dahl's Law Dictionary: Spanish English / English Spanish. LC 92-25881. (ENG & SPA.). 600p. 1992. 55.00 (*0-89941-807-4*, 307520) W S Hein.

Dahl, Henry S. Dahl's Law Dictionary: Dictionnaire Juridique Dahl, Francais-Anglais, French-English. LC 94-45365.Tr. of Dictionnaire Juridique Dahl. (ENG & FRE.). 876p. 1995. pap. 49.95 (*0-89941-919-4*, 307720) W S Hein.

— Dahl's Law Dictionary Diccionario Juridico Dahl Spanish - English/Ingles - Espanol. 3rd ed. LC 98-42654. xli, 913p. 1999. 79.95 (*1-57588-496-8*, 311850) W S Hein.

— Dahl's Law Dictionary Diccionario Juridico Dahl Spanish - English/Ingles - Espanol: Spanish - English/Ingles - Espanol. 3rd ed. LC 98-42654. (ENG & SPA.). 974p. 1999. pap. 54.95 (*1-57588-452-6*, 311850) W S Hein.

— Dahl's Law Dictionary Diccionario Juridico Dahl Spanish-English - English-Spanish. 2nd ed. LC 96-17347.Tr. of Diccionario Juridico. (ENG & SPA.). (19) 801p. 1996. 79.95 (*1-57588-082-2*, 310750) W S Hein.

***Dahl, Hosten & Typology of Languages in Europe (Project) Staff.** Tense & Aspect in the Languages of Europe. LC 00-29180. (Empirical Approaches to Language Typology Ser.). 2000. write for info. (*3-11-015752-7*) Mouton.

Dahl, JoAnne C. Epilepsy: A Behavior Medicine Approach to Assessment & Treatment in Children: A Handbook for Professionals Working with Epilepsy. LC 92-49951. (Illus.). 187p. 1993. pap. 38.00 (*0-88937-106-7*) Hogrefe & Huber Pubs.

Dahl, Jonathan. Lost in America. 1992. write for info. (*0-679-74018-X*) McKay.

Dahl, June W. Footprints: A History of St. Paul Red Cross. (Illus.). 233p. 1981. 10.00 (*0-9605584-0-3*) Red Cross St Paul.

Dahl, Karin L. & Farnan, Nancy. Children's Writing: Perspectives from Research. LC 97-51433. (Literacy Studies Ser.). 166p. 1998. pap. 19.95 (*0-87207-189-8*, 189) Intl Reading.

Dahl, Karin L., jt. auth. see Smith, Carl B.

Dahl, Kevin. Wild Foods of the Sonoran Desert. LC 95-78196. (Illus.). 24p. (Orig.). 1995. pap. 4.95 (*1-886679-03-7*) Ariz-Sonora Des Mus.

Dahl, Larry E. & Cannon, Donald Q. The Teachings of Joseph Smith. 1997. 27.95 (*1-57008-311-8*) Bookcraft Inc.

D

Dahl, Larry E., jt. auth. see Holzapfel, Richard N.

***Dahl, Linda.** Morning Glory: A Biography of Mary Lou Williams. LC 99-34970. 480p. 2000. 30.00 (0-375-40899-1) Pantheon.

Dahl, Linda. Stormy Weather: The Music & Lives of a Century of Jazzwomen. LC 89-12352. (Illus.). 371p. 1989. reprint ed. pap. 18.95 (0-87910-128-8) Limelight Edns.

Dahl, Lucy. Disney's Flubber: Special Collector's Edition. LC 97-80129. (Illus.). 96p. (J). (gr. 3-7). 1997. 14.95 (0-7868-3149-9, Pub. by Disney Pr) Time Warner.

— Flubber. LC 97-80129. (Illus.). 96p. (J). 1997. lib. bdg. 14.89 (0-7868-5061-2, Pub. by Disney Pr) Little.

— 101 Dalmatians Movie Scrapbook: Behind the Scenes of the Live-Action Movie. LC 97-65446. (Illus.). 32p. (J). (gr. 2-5). 1997. pap. 7.95 (0-7868-4173-7, Pub. by Disney Pr) Time Warner.

Dahl, Lynda M. Beyond the Winning Streak: Using Conscious Creation to Consistently Win at Life. LC 92-39769. 208p. 1993. reprint ed. pap. 11.95 (0-9634629-0-3) Woodbridge Grp.

— Ten Thousand Whispers: A Guide to Conscious Creation. LC 96-39535. 208p. 1995. pap. 13.95 (1-889964-06-9) Woodbridge Grp.

— Wizards of Conscious Creations. 1997. pap. 13.95 (1-889964-05-0) Woodbridge Grp.

Dahl, Mark V. Clinical Immunodermatology. LC 80-19466. (Illus.). 292p. reprint ed. pap. 90.60 (0-8357-6311-0, 203558400096) Bks Demand.

— Clinical Immunodermatology. 3rd ed. LC 95-43751. (Illus.). 448p. (C). (gr. 13). 1995. text 96.00 (0-8151-2312-4, 25101) Mosby Inc.

— Current Opinion in Dermatology. 3rd ed. (Illus.). 268p. 1996. text 110.00 (1-85922-702-3) Rapid Science.

— Current Opinion in Dermatology, Vol. 4. Lord, Lynwood, ed. (Illus.). 312p. 1997. text 135.00 (1-85922-809-7) Rapid Science.

Dahl, Mark V. & Lynch, Peter J. Current Opinion in Dermatology. (Illus.). 328p. 1994. text 99.95 (1-870485-77-7) Rapid Science.

— Current Opinion in Dermatology. 2nd ed. (Illus.). 300p. 1995. text 99.95 (1-85922-686-8) Rapid Science.

Dahl, Mary K. Political Violence in Drama: Classical Models, Contemporary Variations. Brockett, Oscar G., ed. LC 86-19246. (Theater & Dramatic Studies: No. 36). 171p. reprint ed. pap. 53.10 (0-8357-1754-2, 207070700004) Bks Demand.

Dahl, Michael. Crawl Low under Smoke. 1999. 14.00 (0-516-21756-9) Capstone Pr.

— Home Fire Drills. 1999. 14.00 (0-516-21757-7) Capstone Pr.

— Horizontal Man, Vol. 1. (Finnegan Zwake Ser.: No. 1). 182p. (J). (gr. 4-8). 1999. mass mkt. 3.99 (0-671-03269-0) S&S Trade.

***Dahl, Michael.** Ruby Raven, Vol. 1. (Finnegan Zwake Ser.). 1999. per. 3.99 (0-671-03271-2) PB.

Dahl, Michael. Smoke Alarms. 1999. 14.00 (0-516-21758-5) Capstone Pr.

— Stop, Drop, & Roll. 1999. 14.00 (0-516-21759-3) Capstone Pr.

***Dahl, Michael.** Stop, Drop & Roll. LC 98-48482. (J). (gr. 3-4). 1999. 15.93 (0-7368-0197-9) Capstone PC.

Dahl, Michael. Worm Tunnel, 1, 2. (Finnegan Zwake Ser.). 1999. per. 3.99 (0-671-03270-4) PB.

***Dahl, Michael & Raatma, Lucia.** Crawl Low under Smoke. LC 98-46538. (Fire Safety Ser.). 24p. (J). (gr. 3-4). 1999. 15.93 (0-7368-0194-4, Bridgestone Bks) Capstone Pr.

Dahl, Michael & Raatma, Lucia. Home Fire Drills. LC 98-47053. (Fire Safety Ser.). 24p. (J). (gr. 3-4). 1999. 14.00 (0-7368-0195-2) Capstone Pr.

***Dahl, Michael & Raatma, Lucia.** Smoke Detectors. LC 98-44798. (Fire Safety Ser.). (J). (gr. 3-4). 1999. 15.93 (0-7368-0196-0, Bridgestone Bks) Capstone Pr.

Dahl, Michael J. The Pharaoh's Son. LC 98-73040. 262p. 1998. pap. 12.95 (0-9667244-0-2, 217) Astabora Publ.

Dahl, Michael S. Cuba. (Countries of the World Ser.). (J). 1998. 14.00 (0-516-21350-4) Childrens.

— France. LC 97-44466. (Countries of the World Ser.). 24p. (J). 1998. 13.75 (1-56065-737-5, Bridgestone Bks) Capstone Pr.

— Guatemala. LC 97-44465. (Countries of the World Ser.). (J). 1998. lib. bdg. 19.00 (1-56065-738-3, Bridgestone Bks) Capstone Pr.

— Simple Machines Series, 4 bks. Incl. Inclined Planes. LC 96-27768. 24p. (J). (gr. 1-2). 1996. lib. bdg. 13.75 (1-56065-447-3, Bridgestone Bks); Levers. LC 96-27770. 24p. (J). (gr. 1-2). 1996. lib. bdg. 13.75 (1-56065-444-9, Bridgestone Bks); Pulleys. LC 96-27769. 24p. (J). (gr. 1-2). 1996. lib. bdg. 13.75 (1-56065-445-7, Bridgestone Bks); Wheels & Axles. LC 96-27771. 24p. (J). (gr. 1-2). 1996. lib. bdg. 13.75 (1-56065-446-5, Bridgestone Bks); 55.00 (1-56065-634-4, Bridgestone Bks) Capstone Pr.

— South Africa. LC 97-44467. (Countries of the World Ser.). 24p. (J). 1998. 13.75 (1-56065-739-1, Bridgestone Bks) Capstone Pr.

— Vietnam. LC 97-41867. (Countries of the World Ser.). (J). 1998. lib. bdg. 14.00 (1-56065-740-5, Bridgestone Bks) Capstone Pr.

***Dahl, Ottar.** Syndicalism, Fascism & Post-Fascism in Italy, 1900-1950. 179p. 1999. 36.00 (82-560-1187-4, Pub. by Solum Verlag) Intl Spec Bk.

Dahl, Otto. Preparation of Nucleoside Phosphorothioates, Phosphorodithioates & Related Compounds, Vol. 11. (Sulfur Reports). 209p. 1991. pap. text 338.00 (3-7186-5236-6, Harwood Acad Pubs) Gordon & Breach.

Dahl, Oyvind. Meanings in Madagascar: Cases of Intercultural Communication. LC 98-41386. 216p. 1999. 59.95 (0-89789-642-4, Bergin & Garvey) Greenwood.

Dahl, Patricia, et al. Where to Go with Kids in the Capital District. (Illus.). 50p. (Orig.). 1982. pap. text 2.50 (0-9611292-0-4) With Kids.

Dahl, Patrick, jt. ed. see Pence, Richard A.

Dahl, Per F. Flash of the Cathode Rays: A History of J. J. Thomson's Electron. LC 97-13642. (Illus.). 472p. 1997. 49.50 (0-7503-0453-7) IOP Pub.

***Dahl, Per F.** Heavy Water & the Wartime Race for Nuclear Energy. LC 99-33672. 1999. 60.00 (0-7503-0633-5) IOP Pub.

Dahl, Per F. Superconductivity. 424p. 1992. 64.95 (0-88318-848-1) Spr-Verlag.

Dahl, Ragna & Gilliland, Mary E. Seasons in the Sun. LC 86-71400. 173p. 1986. 9.95 (0-9603624-4-4) Alpenrose Pr.

Dahl, Richard C. & Davis, Robert. Effective Speaking for Lawyers. LC 75-93751. 150p. 1969. lib. bdg. 38.50 (0-930342-11-9, 300200) W S Hein.

Dahl, Roald. Ah, Sweet Mystery of Life: The country stories of Roald Dahl. 176p. 1991. pap. 11.95 (0-14-011847-0) Viking Penguin.

— The Best of Roald Dahl. LC 89-40287. 1990. pap. 15.00 (0-679-72991-7) Vin Bks.

***Dahl, Roald.** The BFG. 1999. 16.95 (0-7540-6054-3) Chivers N Amer.

Dahl, Roald. The BFG. LC 93-22605. (Children's Classics Ser.). (J). 1993. 13.95 (0-679-42813-5) Everymns Lib.

— The BFG. LC 85-566. (Illus.). 221p. (YA). (gr. 1 up). 1982. 16.00 (0-374-30469-6) FS&G.

— The BFG. (Illus.). 208p. (J). (gr. 3-7). 1998. pap. 4.99 (0-14-130105-8, PuffinBks) Peng Put Young Read.

Dahl, Roald. The BFG. (J). 1984. 10.09 (0-606-00262-6, Pub. by Turtleback) Demco.

Dahl, Roald. The BFG. (Illus.). 1984. pap. 3.95 (0-14-031597-7) Viking Penguin.

— Bizarre! Bizarre! (FRE.). 1973. pap. 11.95 (0-7859-1747-0, 2070363953) Fr & Eur.

— Boy: Tales of Childhood. LC 85-117335. (Illus.). 176p. (J). (gr. 5-9). 1984. 16.00 (0-374-37374-4) FS&G.

— Boy: Tales of Childhood. (J). (gr. 4-6). 1986. pap. 5.99 (0-14-031890-9, PuffinBks) Peng Put Young Read.

— Boy: Tales of Childhood. (J). 1986. 11.09 (0-606-01511-6, Pub. by Turtleback) Demco.

— Boy: Tales of Childhood. 160p. 1992. pap. 9.95 (0-14-008917-9) Viking Penguin.

— Las Brujas. 1985. 14.05 (0-606-10447-X, Pub. by Turtleback) Demco.

— Las Brujas: Witches. Date not set. pap. text 8.95 (84-204-3655-0) Santillana.

— Charlie & the Chocolate Factory. 174p. (J). Date not set. 19.95 (0-8488-2241-2) Amereon Ltd.

— Charlie & the Chocolate Factory. (J). 1984. pap. 2.75 (0-553-15454-0) Bantam.

— Charlie & the Chocolate Factory. (J). 1976. pap. 5.95 (0-87129-220-3, C53) Dramatic Pub.

— Charlie & the Chocolate Factory. (Illus.). (J). (gr. 5 up). 1964. lib. bdg. 18.99 (0-394-91011-7, Pub. by Knopf Bks Yng Read) Random.

— Charlie & the Chocolate Factory. (Illus.). (J). (gr. 5 up). 1966. 17.00 (0-394-81011-2, Pub. by Knopf Bks Yng Read) Random.

— Charlie & the Chocolate Factory. LC 98-218806. (Illus.). 176p. (J). (gr. 3-7). 1998. pap. 5.99 (0-14-130115-5, PuffinBks) Peng Put Young Read.

Dahl, Roald. Charlie & the Chocolate Factory. (J). 1988. 10.09 (0-606-04032-3, Pub. by Turtleback) Demco.

Dahl, Roald. Charlie & the Chocolate Factory. (Illus.). 174p. (J). 1992. reprint ed. lib. bdg. 14.95 (0-89966-904-2) Buccaneer Bks.

— Charlie & the Great Glass Elevator. (J). 1984. pap. 2.75 (0-553-15455-9) Bantam.

Dahl, Roald. Charlie & the Great Glass Elevator. 73p. (J). (gr. 1 up). 1984. pap. 5.00 (0-87129-887-2, C64) Dramatic Pub.

Dahl, Roald. Charlie & the Great Glass Elevator. (Illus.). 176p. (J). (gr. 3-7). 1998. pap. 4.99 (0-14-130112-0, PuffinBks) Peng Put Young Read.

— Charlie & the Great Glass Elevator: The Further Adventures of Charlie Bucket & Willie Wonka, the Chocolate-Maker Extraordinaire. (Illus.). (J). (gr. k-7). 1972. 17.00 (0-394-82472-5, Pub. by Knopf Bks Yng Read); lib. bdg. 18.99 (0-394-92472-X, Pub. by Knopf Bks Yng Read) Random.

Dahl, Roald. Charlie & the Great Glass Elevator: The Further Adventures of Charlie Bucket & Willy Wonka. (J). 1988. 10.09 (0-606-04033-1, Pub. by Turtleback) Demco.

Dahl, Roald. Charlie et la Chocolaterie. (Folio - Junior Ser.: No. 446). (FRE., Illus.). 190p. (J). (gr. 5-10). 1987. pap. 9.95 (2-07-033446-5) Schoenhof.

Dahl, Roald. Charlie Et La Chocolaterie. 4th ed. 1997. pap. 13.95 (2-07-051333-5) Distribks Inc.

— Charlie Et La Grand Ascenseur. 3rd ed. 1998. pap. 14.95 (2-07-051517-6) Distribks Inc.

Dahl, Roald. Charlie et le Grand Ascenseur de Verre. (Folio - Junior Ser.: No. 65). (FRE., Illus.). 151p. (J). (gr. 5-10). 1978. pap. 7.95 (2-07-033065-6) Schoenhof.

— Charlie y El Gran Ascensor de Cristal. Orig. Title: Charlie & the Great Glass Elevator. (SPA.). (J). 8.95 (84-204-3214-8) Santillana.

— Charlie y El Gran Ascensor de Cristal. Orig. Title: Charlie & the Great Glass Elevator. 1981. 14.05 (0-606-10387-2, Pub. by Turtleback) Demco.

— Charlie y la Fabrica de Chocolate. Orig. Title: Charlie & the Chocolate Factory. (SPA.). (J). 8.95 (968-6026-71-1) Santillana.

Dahl, Roald. Charlie y la Fabrica de Chocolate. Orig. Title: Charlie & the Chocolate Factory. 1996. 14.05 (0-606-10388-0, Pub. by Turtleback) Demco.

Dahl, Roald. Charlie y la Fabrica de Chocolate: Charlie & the Chocolate Factory. (FRE.). (J). 1995. pap. 8.95 (84-204-4771-4) Santillana.

— El Cocodrilo Enorme. 1981. 11.70 (0-606-10404-6, Pub. by Turtleback) Demco.

Dahl, Roald. Danny, Campeon del Mundo, 2nd ed. 1982. 13.05 (0-606-10399-6, Pub. by Turtleback) Demco.

Dahl, Roald. Danny, Champion of the World. (J). (gr. 3 up). 1984. pap. 2.75 (0-553-15505-9) Bantam.

— Danny, Champion of the World. (Scholastic Literature Guide Ser.). 16p. (J). 1997. pap. text 3.95 (0-590-37361-7) Scholastic Inc.

— Danny, el Campeon del Mundo (Danny, the Champion of the World) (SPA.). 1996. pap. text 7.95 (84-279-3117-4) Lectorum Pubns.

***Dahl, Roald.** Danny, the Champion of the World. (Illus.). 205p. (YA). (gr. 5-9). 1998. pap. 5.99 (0-14-130114-7, PuffinBks) Peng Put Young Read.

— Danny, the Champion of the World. (J). (gr. 5-9). 1999. 19.50 (0-8446-7025-1) Peter Smith.

Dahl, Roald. Danny, the Champion of the World. (J). 1988. 9.84 (0-606-04034-X, Pub. by Turtleback) Demco.

— El Dedo Magico. (J). 1991. 15.40 (0-606-10407-0) Turtleback.

— El Dedo Magico: The Magic Finger. 1995. pap. text 5.95 (84-204-3656-9) Santillana.

— Dirty Beasts. LC 85-594. (Picture Puffin Ser.). (Illus.). 32p. (J). (gr. 1 up). 1986. pap. 5.99 (0-14-050435-4, PuffinBks) Peng Put Young Read.

— Dirty Beasts. (Picture Puffin Ser.). (Illus.). (J). 1986. 10.19 (0-606-01560-4, Pub. by Turtleback) Demco.

— Doigt Magique. (Folio - Cadet Bleu Ser.: No. 185). (FRE., Illus.). 63p. (J). (gr. 1-5). 1989. pap. 9.95 (2-07-031185-6) Schoenhof.

***Dahl, Roald.** The Enormous Crocodile. (Illus.). 64p. (J). (gr. 1-5). 2000. lib. bdg. 15.95 (0-375-81046-3, Pub. by Knopf Bks Yng Read); lib. bdg. 16.99 (0-375-91046-8, Pub. by Knopf Bks Yng Read) Random.

Dahl, Roald. The Enormous Crocodile. (Illus.). 32p. (J). (gr. 2-5). 1993. pap. 4.99 (0-14-036556-7, PuffinBks) Peng Put Young Read.

— The Enormous Crocodile. (J). 1993. 8.94 (0-606-05267-4, Pub. by Turtleback) Demco.

— The Enormous Crocodile. 1999. pap. 3.99 (0-14-050342-0) Viking Penguin.

Dahl, Roald. The Enormous Crocodile & the Magic Finger Audio. unabridged ed. LC 79-740794. (J). (gr. 4-7). 1988. audio 11.95 (0-89845-823-4, CPN 1633, Caedmon) HarperAudio.

Dahl, Roald. Esio Trot. LC 92-16931. (Illus.). 63p. (J). (gr. 2-6). 1999. pap. 4.99 (0-14-130464-2, PuffinBks) Peng Put Young Read.

— Esio Trot. (J). 1992. 10.19 (0-606-02634-7, Pub. by Turtleback) Demco.

***Dahl, Roald.** Esio Trot. (Illus.). (J). 1999. 10.44 (0-606-18402-3) Turtleback.

Dahl, Roald. Fantastic Mr. Fox. 43p. (J). 1985. pap. 5.50 (0-87129-670-5, F40) Dramatic Pub.

— Fantastic Mr. Fox. LC 74-118704. (Illus.). 72p. (J). (gr. 3-6). 1970. lib. bdg. 18.99 (0-394-90497-4, Pub. by Knopf Bks Yng Read) Random.

— Fantastic Mr. Fox. LC 74-118704. (Illus.). 72p. (J). (gr. 3-6). 1986. 17.00 (0-394-80497-X, Pub. by Knopf Bks Yng Read) Random.

— Fantastic Mr. Fox. (Illus.). 96p. (J). (gr. 2-6). 1998. pap. 4.99 (0-14-130113-9, PuffinBks) Peng Put Young Read.

— Fantastic Mr. Fox. (J). 1988. 10.09 (0-606-04221-0, Pub. by Turtleback) Demco.

— Fantastic Mr. Fox Audio. unabridged ed. LC 77-741116. (J). (gr. 4-6). 1989. audio 11.95 (0-89845-902-8, CPN 1576, Caedmon) HarperAudio.

— Fantastique Maitre Renard. (Folio - Cadet Rouge Ser.: No. 174). (FRE., Illus.). 119p. (J). (gr. 3-7). 1989. pap. 12.95 (2-07-031174-0) Schoenhof.

— George's Marvelous Medicine. (Illus.). 96p. (J). (gr. 2-6). 1998. pap. 4.99 (0-14-130111-2, PuffinBks) Peng Put Young Read.

— George's Marvelous Medicine. (J). 1991. 10.09 (0-606-05309-3, Pub. by Turtleback) Demco.

— The Giraffe & the Pelly & Me. LC 98-15787. 64p. (J). (gr. 2-6). 1998. 4.99 (0-14-130228-3, PuffinBks) Peng Put Young Read.

— The Giraffe & the Pelly & Me. 1994. 9.19 (0-606-06412-5, Pub. by Turtleback) Demco.

Dahl, Roald. Going Solo. (J). 1988. 10.09 (0-606-05320-4, Pub. by Turtleback) Demco.

Dahl, Roald. Going Solo. 224p. (J). 1988. pap. 9.95 (0-14-010306-6, Penguin Bks) Viking Penguin.

— Going Solo: The Thrilling Sequel to Boy. LC 98-8403. 224p. (J). (gr. 7 up). 1999. pap. 5.99 (0-14-130310-7, PuffinBks) Peng Put Young Read.

— El Gran Gigante Bonachon - The BFG. 1996. pap. text 7.95 (84-320-6178-6) Lectorum Pubns.

— La Grande Enterloupe.Tr. of James & the Giant Peach. (FRE.). 1984. pap. 10.95 (0-7859-2225-3, 207037520X) Fr & Eur.

***Dahl, Roald.** The Great Switcheroo. 2000. pap. 3.95 (1-86092-034-9, Pub. by Travelman Pub) IPG Chicago.

Dahl, Roald. James & El Melocoton Gigante. 1996. 14.05 (0-606-10428-3, Pub. by Turtleback) Demco.

— James & Giant Peach. limited ed. (Illus.). 48p. (J). 1996. 100.00 (0-7868-3112-X, Pub. by Disney Pr) Little.

— James & the Giant Peach. (J). 1984. pap. 2.95 (0-553-15317-X) Bantam.

— James & the Giant Peach. (J). 1982. pap. 5.95 (0-87129-321-8, J18) Dramatic Pub.

— James & the Giant Peach. LC 88-42879. (Illus.). 144p. (J). (gr. 4-7). 1996. pap. 4.99 (0-14-037424-8) Peng Put Young Read.

***Dahl, Roald.** James & the Giant Peach. (J). (gr. 3-7). 2000. 19.25 (0-8446-7142-8) Peter Smith.

Dahl, Roald. James & the Giant Peach. LC 95-81684. (Illus.). 144p. (J). (gr. 1-6). 1996. lib. bdg. 17.99 (0-679-98090-3) Random.

— James & the Giant Peach. 128p. (J). 1990. reprint ed. lib. bdg. 19.95 (0-89966-702-3) Buccaneer Bks.

— James & the Giant Peach: A Children's Story. LC 95-81684. (Illus.). 144p. (J). (gr. 1-7). 1996. 16.00 (0-679-88090-9) Random.

Dahl, Roald. James & the Giant Peach: A Children's Story. (J). 1988. 10.09 (0-606-04035-8, Pub. by Turtleback) Demco.

Dahl, Roald. James & the Giant Peach: The Book & Movie Scrapbook. (Illus.). 64p. (J). 1996. pap. 7.95 (0-7868-4085-4, Pub. by Disney Pr) Time Warner.

— James & the Giant Peach: The Book & Movie Scrapbook. (Illus.). 64p. (J). (gr. 3). 1996. 15.95 (0-7868-3106-5, Pub. by Disney Pr) Little.

Dahl, Roald. James & the Giant Peach Audio. abr. ed. LC 76-741306. (Illus.). (J). (gr. 4-7). 1989. audio 11.95 (0-89845-883-8, CPN 1543, Caedmon) HarperAudio.

Dahl, Roald. James et la Grosse Peche. (Folio - Junior Ser.: No. 517). (FRE., Illus.). 174p. (J). (gr. 5-10). 1988. pap. 9.95 (2-07-033517-8) Schoenhof.

— James y el Melocoton Gigante. Orig. Title: James & the Giant Peach. (SPA.). (J). 8.95 (84-204-3524-4) Santillana.

— Kiss, Kiss. (FRE.). 304p. 1978. pap. 11.95 (0-7859-1873-6, 2070370291) Fr & Eur.

— Kiss, Kiss. large type ed. 340p. 1989. reprint ed. 19.95 (1-85089-314-4, Pub. by ISIS Lrg Prnt) Transaction Pubs.

— The Magic Finger. LC 66-18657. (Illus.). 46p. (J). (gr. 3-6). 1966. 15.00 (0-06-021381-7) HarpC Child Bks.

— The Magic Finger. LC 66-18657. (Trophy Picture Bk.). (Illus.). 48p. (J). (gr. 3-6). 1983. pap. 3.95 (0-06-443045-6, HarpTrophy) HarpC Child Bks.

— The Magic Finger. (Illus.). 64p. (J). (ps-12). 1996. 16.99 (0-670-85252-X, Viking Child) Peng Put Young Read.

— The Magic Finger. LC 96-45417. (Illus.). 63p. (J). (gr. 2-6). 1998. pap. 4.99 (0-14-130229-1, PuffinBks) Peng Put Young Read.

— The Magic Finger. LC 96-45417. 1997. 9.19 (0-606-11588-9, Pub. by Turtleback) Demco.

— The Magic Finger of Dahl. 64p. 1997. pap. write for info. (0-14-037158-3) Viking Penguin.

— La Maravillosa Medician de Jorge: George's Marvelous Medicine. (J). 1995. pap. text 8.95 (84-204-3609-7) Santillana.

— La Maravillosa Medicina de Jorge. 1996. 14.05 (0-606-10442-9, Pub. by Turtleback) Demco.

— Matilda. (Illus.). 224p. (J). (gr. 3-7). 1988. 15.99 (0-670-82439-9, Viking Child) Peng Put Young Read.

— Matilda. LC 89-10604. (Illus.). 240p. (J). (gr. 3-7). 1998. pap. 4.99 (0-14-130106-6, PuffinBks) Peng Put Young Read.

— Matilda. (J). 1995. pap. text 12.95 (84-204-4638-6) Santillana.

— Matilda. (J). 1989. 18.05 (0-606-10484-4, Pub. by Turtleback) Demco.

— Matilda. (J). 1996. 10.09 (0-606-02745-9, Pub. by Turtleback) Demco.

***Dahl, Roald.** Matilda. 6th ed. (J). 1998. pap. 17.95 (2-07-051784-5) Distribks Inc.

— Mildenhall Treasure. LC 00-24683. (Illus.). 80p. (J). (ps up). 2000. 22.95 (0-375-81035-8, Pub. by Knopf Bks Yng Read) Random.

Dahl, Roald. The Minpins. (J). 1991. 17.00 (0-670-84168-4, Viking Child) Peng Put Young Read.

— The Minpins. (Illus.). 48p. (J). (ps-3). 1994. pap. 5.99 (0-14-054970-6, PuffinBks) Peng Put Young Read.

— The Minpins. 1993. 11.19 (0-606-07039-7, Pub. by Turtleback) Demco.

— Mon Oncle Oswald. (FRE.). 315p. 1986. pap. 11.95 (0-7859-2038-2, 2070377458) Fr & Eur.

— My Uncle Oswald. 208p. 1990. pap. 11.95 (0-14-005577-0, Penguin Bks) Viking Penguin.

— My Year. (J). 1999. pap. 3.99 (0-14-037680-1, Viking) Viking Penguin.

— A Novel Study Based on James & the Giant Peach. Brookes, Diane, ed. (J). 1998. pap. text, teacher ed. 7.95 (0-9683234-9-9) RRP.

— Over to You. LC 74-158082. 160p. 1990. pap. 10.95 (0-14-003574-5, Penguin Bks) Viking Penguin.

— Potion Magique de Georges Bouillon. (Folio - Junior Ser.: No. 463). (FRE., Illus.). 148p. (J). (gr. 5-10). 1990. pap. 8.95 (2-07-033463-5) Schoenhof.

— Revolting Recipes 10. 1997. 12.19 (0-606-13024-1, Pub. by Turtleback) Demco.

— Rhyme Stew. (J). 1999. pap. 3.99 (0-14-034365-2, Viking) Viking Penguin.

— Roald Dahl: Charlie & the Chocolate Factory, Charlie & the Great Glass Elevator & The BFG, 3 bks., Set. (J). 1989. pap. 11.95 (0-685-30573-2, Viking Child) Peng Put Young Read.

Dahl, Roald. The Roald Dahl Audio Collection. abr. ed. (gr. 4-6). 1991. audio 24.95 (1-55994-499-4) HarperAudio.

Dahl, Roald. The Roald Dahl Treasury. (Illus.). (J). 1997. 35.00 (0-614-29321-9) Viking Penguin.

— The Roald Dahl Treasury. LC 97-60691. (Illus.). 448p. (J). (gr. 4-7). 1997. 35.00 (0-670-87769-7) Viking Penguin.

— Roald Dahl's Book of Ghost Stories. 1984. 17.10 (0-606-10912-9, Pub. by Turtleback) Demco.

— Roald Dahl's Revolting Recipes. LC 94-76366. (Illus.). 64p. (J). (gr. 3 up). 1994. 15.99 (0-670-85836-6, Viking Child) Peng Put Young Read.

— Roald Dahl's Revolting Recipes. (Illus.). 64p. (J). (gr. 3 up). 1997. pap. 6.99 (0-14-037820-0, PuffinBks) Peng Put Young Read.

— Roald Dahl's Revolting Rhymes. LC 94-29459. (Illus.). 48p. (J). (gr. 1-8). 1995. pap. 5.99 (0-14-037533-3, PuffinBks) Peng Put Young Read.

An Asterisk (*) at the beginning of an entry indicates that the title is appearing for the first time.

— Roald Dahl's Tales of the Unexpected. 480p. 1990. pap. 15.00 (*0-679-72989-5*) Random.

— Roald Dahl's Tales of the Unexpected. 1979. pap. 7.95 (*0-394-74081-5*, V-81) Vin Bks.

***Dahl, Roald.** Skin & Other Stories. LC 99-58600. (Illus.). (J). 2000. 15.99 (*0-670-89184-3*, Viking Child) Peng Put Young Read.

Dahl, Roald. El Superzorro. 1977. 14.05 (*0-606-10417-8*, Pub. by Turtleback) Demco.

— El Superzorro: Fantastic Mr. Fox. (J). 1995. pap. text 8.95 (*84-204-3102-8*) Santillana.

— El Superzorro - Fantastic Mr. Fox. Buckley, Ramon, tr. (SPA., Illus.). 153p. (J). (gr. 2-4). 1992. pap. write for info. (*84-204-0013-0*) Santillana.

— Switch Bitch. 144p. 1989. pap. 11.95 (*0-14-004179-6*, Penguin Bks) Viking Penguin.

— The Twits. 96p. (J). 1985. pap. 2.75 (*0-553-15568-7*) Bantam.

— The Twits. LC 99-165477. (Illus.). 96p. (J). (gr. 2-6). 1998. pap. 4.99 (*0-14-130107-4*, PuffinBks) Peng Put Young Read.

— The Twits. (J). 1991. 10.09 (*0-606-05674-2*, Pub. by Turtleback) Demco.

— Two Fables. (Illus.). 63p. 1987. 12.95 (*0-374-28018-5*) FS&G.

— The Umbrella Man & Other Stories. LC 97-32549. 288p. (YA). (gr. 7-12). 1998. 16.99 (*0-670-87854-5*) Viking Penguin.

***Dahl, Roald.** Umbrella Man & Other Stories. (Illus.). 288p. (J). (gr. 7-12). 2000. pap. 6.99 (*0-14-130271-2*, PuffinBks) Peng Put Young Read.

Dahl, Roald. The Vicar of Nibbleswicke. (Illus.). 48p. (YA). (gr. 5 up). 1994. pap. 5.99 (*0-14-036837-X*, PuffinBks) Peng Put Young Read.

— The Vicar of Nibbleswicke. 1993. 10.19 (*0-606-06849-X*, Pub. by Turtleback) Demco.

— The Witches. LC 83-14195. (Illus.). 208p. (J). (gr. 3-7). 1983. 16.00 (*0-374-38457-6*) FS&G.

— The Witches. LC 99-165483. (Illus.). 208p. (J). (gr. 3-7). 1998. pap. 4.99 (*0-14-130110-4*, PuffinBks) Peng Put Young Read.

— The Witches. LC 85-519. (Illus.). 200p. (J). (gr. 3-7). 1999. pap. 3.95 (*0-14-031730-9*, Viking Child) Peng Put Young Read.

— The Witches. (J). 1985. 10.09 (*0-606-00540-4*, Pub. by Turtleback) Demco.

— The Wonderful Story of Henry Sugar & Six More. 224p. (J). 1988. pap. 4.99 (*0-14-032874-2*, PuffinBks) Peng Put Young Read.

***Dahl, Roald.** The Wonderful Story of Henry Sugar & Six More. (Illus.). 240p. (J). (gr. 7-12). 2000. pap. 5.99 (*0-14-130470-7*, PuffinBks) Peng Put Young Read.

Dahl, Roald. The Wonderful Story of Henry Sugar & Six More. (J). 1988. 10.09 (*0-606-04109-5*, Pub. by Turtleback) Demco.

— The Wonderful Story of Henry Sugar & Six More. large type rev. ed. 280p. (J). 1989. lib. bdg. 14.95 (*1-85089-984-3*) BDD LT Grp.

Dahl, Roald, ed. Roald Dahl's Book of Ghost Stories. 240p. (YA). (gr. 5 up). 1984. pap. 12.00 (*0-374-51868-8*) FS&G.

***Dahl, Roald & Blake, Quentin.** Matilda. 1999. 16.95 (*0-7540-6060-8*) Chivers N Amer.

Dahl, Roald, jt. auth. see Brookes, Diane.

Dahl, Robert. Controlling Nuclear Weapons. 1985. 39.95 (*0-8156-2334-8*) Syracuse U Pr.

— Controlling Nuclear Weapons: Democracy Versus Guardianship. 1985. pap. 16.95 (*0-8156-0196-4*) Syracuse U Pr.

Dahl, Robert, ed. see Davis Publishing Company Staff.

Dahl, Robert A. After the Revolution? Authority in a Good Society. rev. ed. 168p. (C). 1990. pap. 14.00 (*0-300-04964-1*) Yale U Pr.

— Congress & Foreign Policy. LC 82-25123. 305p. 1983. reprint ed. lib. bdg. 65.00 (*0-313-23788-3*, DACF, Greenwood Pr) Greenwood.

— Decision Making in a Democracy: The Supreme Court As a National Policy Maker. (Reprint Series in Social Sciences). (C). 1993. reprint ed. pap. text 1.00 (*0-8290-3570-2*, PS-53) Irvington.

— Democracy & Its Critics. 405p. (C). 1991. reprint ed. pap. 20.00 (*0-300-04938-2*) Yale U Pr.

— Democracy in the United States: Promise & Performance. 4th ed. LC 93-4898. 1993. reprint ed. 36.00 (*0-8191-9004-7*) U Pr of Amer.

— Democracy, Liberty, & Equality. (Norwegian University Press Publication Ser.). 288p. 1988. 29.95 (*0-318-36420-4*) OUP.

— Dilemmas of Pluralist Democracy: Autonomy vs. Control. LC 81-16111. (Studies in Political Science: No. 31). 1983. pap. 19.00 (*0-300-03076-2*) Yale U Pr.

— Modern Political Analysis. 5th ed. 176p. (C). 1990. pap. text 34.67 (*0-13-595406-1*, Pub. by P-H) S&S Trade.

***Dahl, Robert A.** On Democracy. LC 98-21375. 224p. 1998. 25.00 (*0-300-07627-4*) Yale U Pr.

— On Democracy. 224p. 2000. pap. 10.95 (*0-300-08455-2*) Yale U Pr.

Dahl, Robert A. Polyarchy: Participation & Opposition. LC 70-140534. 1971. pap. 17.00 (*0-300-01565-8*, Y254) Yale U Pr.

— Preface to Democratic Theory. LC 56-6642. (Walgreen Foundation Lectures). 160p. 1963. pap. text 7.95 (*0-226-13426-1*, P115) U Ch Pr.

— A Preface to Economic Democracy. LC 84-8483. (Quantum Bks.: No. 28). 1985. pap. 15.95 (*0-520-05877-1*, Pub. by U CA Pr) Cal Prin Full Svc.

Dahl, Robert A. Size & Democracy. pap. 5.95 (*0-8047-0889-4*) Stanford U Pr.

Dahl, Robert A. Toward Democracy: A Journey: Reflections: 1940-1997. LC 97-12132. 1160p. 1997. 95.00 (*0-87772-372-9*) UCB IGS.

— Who Governs? Democracy & Power in an American City. LC 61-16913. (Studies in Political Science: No. 4). (Illus.). 1963. pap. 19.00 (*0-300-00051-0*, Y73) Yale U Pr.

Dahl, Robert A., ed. Regimes & Oppositions. LC 79-151571. 415p. reprint ed. pap. 128.70 (*0-8357-8757-5*, 203370000087) Bks Demand.

Dahl, Robert A. & Flanigan, William. New Haven Community Study, 1959. 2nd ed. LC 75-38491. 1975. reprint ed. write for info. (*0-89138-024-8*) ICPSR.

Dahl, Robert A. & Lindblom, Charles E. Politics, Economics, & Welfare. 612p. (C). 1991. pap. text 29.95 (*1-56000-575-0*) Transaction Pubs.

Dahl, Robert A. & Tufte, Edward R. Size & Democracy. LC 72-97200. xii, 148p. 1973. 24.50 (*0-8047-0834-7*) Stanford U Pr.

Dahl, Robert A., et al. The New American Political Disorder: An Essay. LC 94-530. 102p. 1994. pap. 10.95 (*0-87772-355-9*) UCB IGS.

Dahl, Ruby W., et al. Lander: One-Shot Antelope Hunt. (Illus.). 129p. 1986. 19.95 (*0-9617178-0-7*) One-Shot Antelope Hunt.

— Lander: One-Shot Antelope Hunt. deluxe limited ed. (Illus.). 129p. 1986. 50.00 (*0-9617178-1-5*) One-Shot Antelope Hunt.

Dahl, S. G., et al, eds. Clinical Pharmacology in Psychiatry: Strategies in Psychotropic Drug Development. (Psychopharmacology Ser.: Vol. 10). (Illus.). 264p. 1993. 132.00 (*0-387-56329-6*) Spr-Verlag.

Dahl, S. G. & Gram, L. F., eds. Clinical Pharmacology in Psychiatry. (Psychopharmacology Ser.: Vol. 7). (Illus.). 330p. 1989. 66.00 (*0-387-50770-1*, 3077) Spr-Verlag.

***Dahl, Shawn.** Time Out New York's Eating & Drinking, 2000. 1999. pap. 9.95 (*0-9675240-0-8*) Time Out.

Dahl, Shawn & Bozza, Antony, eds. Rolling Stone Raves: What Your Rock & Roll Favorites Favor. LC 99-24546. 368p. 1999. pap. 15.00 (*0-688-16304-1*, Quil) HarperTrade.

Dahl, Solveig. Rape - A Hazard to Health. (Illus.). 154p. (C). 1993. 12.00 (*82-00-21809-0*, 14448) Scandnvan Univ Pr.

Dahl, Stephanie H. Modern Bride Just Married: Everything You Need to Know to Plan Your New Life Together. 239p. 1994. pap. write for info. (*0-471-59669-8*) Wiley.

Dahl, Stephanie H., jt. auth. see Lalli, Cele G.

Dahl, Svein Olaf, jt. auth. see Nesje, Atle.

Dahl, Sven-Erik, jt. auth. see Drazen, Jeffrey M.

Dahl, Taffy, jt. auth. see Kaufman, Donald.

Dahl, Tessa. Babies Babies Babies. 1999. pap. 3.99 (*0-14-054949-8*) NAL.

— Working for Love. large type ed. 190p. 1989. reprint ed. 19.95 (*1-85089-319-5*, Pub. by ISIS Lrg Prnt) Transaction Pubs.

Dahl, Tove S. The Muslim Family: A Study of Women's Rights in Islam. 211p. (C). 1997. text 31.00 (*82-00-22420-1*) Scandnvan Univ Pr.

Dahl, V., jt. auth. see Abramson, Harvey.

Dahl, Vladimir I. Dahl's Russian Dictionary. LC 79-40161. (Illus.). 1981. 290.00 (*0-317-67671-7*, Pergamon Pr) Elsevier.

— Dahl's Russian Dictionary, Vol. 3. LC 80-41732. 1980. 252.00 (*0-08-023592-1*) Franklin.

— Dahl's Russian Dictionary, Vol. 4. LC 80-41733. 1980. 302.00 (*0-08-023593-X*) Franklin.

Dahlan, H. M. Asian in the Global System. LC 98-944184. 348 p. 1997. write for info. (*967-942-383-2*) Penerbit U KB.

Dahlauser, Bonita. Faith, Family & Friends, Vol. 5. 229p. (Orig.). 1993. pap. 13.30 (*1-55833-088-7*) Natl Cath Educ.

Dahlback, Helena. My Sister Lotta & Me. Lesser, Rika, tr. from SWE. (Illus.). 32p. (J). (gr. k-3). 1995. 15.95 (*0-8050-2558-8*, Bks Young Read) H Holt & Co.

Dahlback, Nils. Representations of Discourse: Cognitive & Computational Aspects. 298p. (Orig.). 1991. pap. 84.00 (*91-7870-850-8*) Coronet Bks.

Dahlberg, Albert A. & Graber, Thomas M., eds. Orofacial Growth & Development. (World Anthropology Ser.). (Illus.). xiv, 354p. 1977. 52.35 (*90-279-7889-1*) Mouton.

Dahlberg, Albert E., jt. ed. see Zimmerman, Robert A.

Dahlberg, Annika. Contesting Views & Changing Paradigms: The Land Degradation Debate in Southern Africa. LC 96-128526. (Discussion Papers: Vol. 6). 59p. 1994. pap. text 12.95 (*91-7106-357-9*) Transaction Pubs.

Dahlberg, Arthur A. Jobs, Machines & Capitalism. LC 70-91296. (BCL Ser. I). reprint ed. 20.00 (*0-404-01917-X*) AMS Pr.

Dahlberg, Arthur O. How to Reduce Interest Rates & Poverty. LC 82-22029. (Illus.). 149p. 1984. 14.95 (*0-8159-5718-1*) Hope Pub Hse.

— How to Save Free Enterprise. LC 74-75390. (Illus.). 346p. 1974. 19.95 (*0-8159-5708-4*) Hope Pub Hse.

Dahlberg, B., et al, eds. Partial Differential Equations with Minimal Smoothness & Applications. (IMA Volumes in Mathematics & Its Applications Ser.: Vol. 42). 224p. 1992. 62.95 (*0-387-97774-0*) Spr-Verlag.

Dahlberg, Bruce T., pref. Tell El-Hesi Vol. 4-Phase One: The Site & the Expedition. (American Schools of Oriental Research Excavation Reports). (Illus.). 212p. (C). 1989. text. write for info. (*0-918401-01-1*) U Wake Forest.

Dahlberg, Bruce T. & O'Connell, Kevin G., eds. Tell El-Hesi: The Site & the Expedition. LC 80-21724. (Joint Archaeological Expedition to Tell el-Hesi Ser.: No. 4). xix, 214p. 1989. text 47.50 (*0-931464-57-9*) Eisenbrauns.

Dahlberg, Charles. The Literature of Unlikeness. LC 87-22730. 221p. reprint ed. pap. 68.60 (*0-7837-6203-8*, 204592400009) Bks Demand.

Dahlberg, Charles, tr. see De Lorris, Guillaume & De Meun, Jean.

Dahlberg, E. C. Applied Hydrodynamics in Petroleum Exploration. (Illus.). 161p. 1982. pap. 36.50 (*0-387-90677-0*) Spr-Verlag.

Dahlberg, E. H. Small-Scale Gold Mining: A Manual for Suriname. 54p. (Orig.). 1984. pap. 14.00 (*1-85339-049-6*, Pub. by Intermed Tech) Stylus Pub VA.

Dahlberg, Edward. ALMS for Oblivion, Essays. LC 64-13767. 176p. reprint ed. pap. 54.60 (*0-8357-5326-3*, 203321400084) Bks Demand.

— Because I Was Flesh. LC 64-10079. 1967. pap. 9.95 (*0-8112-0029-9*, NDP227, Pub. by New Directions) Norton.

— Bottom Dogs. 1994. lib. bdg. 24.95 (*1-56849-392-4*) Buccaneer Bks.

— Bottom Dogs. LC 74-22778. (Labor Movement in Fiction & Non-Fiction Ser.). reprint ed. 37.50 (*0-404-58418-7*) AMS Pr.

— The Flea of Sodom. LC 73-18392. (American Literature Ser.: No. 49). 1974. lib. bdg. 75.00 (*0-8383-1739-1*) M S G Haskell Hse.

— Leafless American. limited ed. (Illus.). 1967. 32.00 (*0-911796-02-9*) Beacham.

— The Leafless American & Other Writings. Billings, Harold, ed. & intro. by. LC 86-18185. (Recovered Classics Ser.). 128p. 1986. reprint ed. 20.00 (*0-914232-83-5*) McPherson & Co.

— The Leafless American & Other Writings. Billings, Harold, ed. & intro. by. Burns, Gerald, intro. LC 86-18185. (Recovered Classics Ser.). 128p. 1986. reprint ed. pap. 10.00 (*0-914232-80-0*) McPherson & Co.

— Samuel Beckett's Wake & Other Uncollected Prose. Moore, Steven, ed. LC 89-7856. 345p. 1989. 19.95 (*0-916583-42-2*) Dalkey Arch.

— Those Who Perish. LC 75-41070. reprint ed. 37.50 (*0-404-14528-0*) AMS Pr.

Dahlberg, Eric C. Applied Hydrodynamics in Petroleum Exploration. 2nd ed. LC 93-50624. (Illus.). 306p. 1994. 80.95 (*0-387-97880-1*) Spr-Verlag.

Dahlberg, Frances, ed. Woman the Gatherer. LC 80-25262. 1983. reprint ed. pap. 16.00 (*0-300-02989-6*, Y-476) Yale U Pr.

Dahlberg, Gunilla. Context & the Child's Orientation to Meaning: A Study of the Child's Way of Organizing the Surrounding World in Relation to Public, Institutionalized Socialization. 228p. (Orig.). 1985. pap. text 40.00 (*91-40-05120-X*) Coronet Bks.

Dahlberg, Gunilla, et al. Beyond Quality in Early Childhood & Care: Postmodern Perspectives. LC 99-208603. 268p. 1999. pap. 28.95 (*0-7507-0769-0*, Falmer Pr) Taylor & Francis.

— Beyond Quality in Early Childhood Education & Care: Postmodern Perspectives. LC 99-208603. 268p. 1999. 79.00 (*0-7507-0770-4*, Falmer Pr) Taylor & Francis.

— Children, Work & Ideology: A Cross-Cultural Comparison of Children's Understanding of Work & the Social Division of Labour. (Stockholm Studies in Education & Psychology: No. 24). 116p. (Orig.). 1987. pap. 35.00 (*91-22-01178-1*) Coronet Bks.

Dahlberg, James E., et al, eds. RNA Processing Pt. A: General Methods. (Methods in Enzymology Ser.: Vol. 180). 530p. 1989. text 136.00 (*0-12-182081-5*) Acad Pr.

Dahlberg, Keith. Edwin T. Dahlberg: Pastor, Pacemaker, Prophet. LC 97-49381. 162p. 1998. 22.00 (*0-8170-1277-X*) Judson.

Dahlberg, Kenneth A., ed. New Directions for Agriculture & Agricultural Research: Neglected Dimensions & Emerging Alternatives. LC 85-22046. 448p. (C). 1986. 79.50 (*0-8476-7417-7*, R7417); pap. 29.50 (*0-8476-7418-5*, R7418) Rowman.

Dahlberg, Kenneth A., et al. Environment in the Global Arena: Actors, Values, Policies, & Futures. Harf, James E. & Trout, B. Thomas, eds. LC 84-21251. (Global Issues Ser.). (Illus.). xix, 188p. (Orig.). 1985. pap. text 17.95 (*0-8223-0621-2*) Duke.

Dahlberg, Laurie, contrib. by. Duncan Hannah: Mythic Times. (Illus.). 56p. 1990. per. 18.00 (*0-945558-08-2*) ISU Univ Galls.

***Dahlberg, Laurie, ed.** On Site: Contemporary Photography of Place. (Illus.). 28p. 1999. pap. write for info. (*0-941276-81-3*) Bard Coll Pubns.

***Dahlberg, Linda L.** Measuring Violence Related Attitudes, Beliefs & Behaviors Among Youths: Assessment Tools. 272p. 1998. per. 21.00 (*0-16-061505-4*) USGPO.

Dahlbom, Bo, ed. Dennett & His Critics: Demystifying Mind. LC 92-43145. (Philosophers & Their Critics Ser.). 272p. 1993. 61.95 (*0-631-18549-6*) Blackwell Pubs.

— Dennett & His Critics: Demystifying Mind. (Philosophers & Their Critics Ser.). 248p. 1995. pap. 27.95 (*0-631-19678-1*) Blackwell Pubs.

Dahlbom, Bo & Mathiassen, Lars. Computers in Context: The Philosophy & Practice of Systems Design. LC 93-6779. (Illus.). 256p. 1993. pap. 26.95 (*1-55786-405-5*) Blackwell Pubs.

Dahlbom, Ulla. Estimation of Regression Functions with Certain Monotonicity & Concavity/Convexity Restrictions. (Illus.). 253p. (Orig.). 1995. pap. 48.50 (*91-22-01641-4*) Coronet Bks.

Dahlby, Mark, ed. see Tenzin Wangyal Rinpoche.

Dahle, Eric R., tr. see Wessels, Allison & Champion, George.

Dahle, John, ed. Library of Christian Hymns, 3 vols. in 2. LC 72-1649. reprint ed. 125.00 (*0-404-13202-2*) AMS Pr.

Dahleh, M. A., jt. auth. see Elia, N.

Dahleh, Marie D., jt. auth. see Thomson, William T.

Dahleh, Mohammed A., jt. auth. see Salapaka, Murti V.

Dahleh, Munther A. & Diaz-Bobillo, Ignacio J. Control of Uncertain Systems: A Linear Programming Approach. LC 94-10824. 432p. 1994. text 70.00 (*0-13-280645-2*) P-H.

Dahlem, Franz. Arnulf Rainer: Young Cross. 127p. 1992. pap. 19.95 (*0-939594-29-3*, Menil Collection) Menil Found.

Dahlem, James T. How to Make & Mend Cast Nets. 2nd rev. ed. 96p. 1996. pap. 6.95 (*0-8200-0612-2*) Great Outdoors.

Dahlem, Konferenzen & Goldammer, J. G., eds. Fire in the Environment: Its Ecological, Climatic & Atmospheric Chemical Importance. (Dahlem Workshop Reports - Physical, Chemical, Earth Sciences). 416p. 1993. 275.00 (*0-471-93604-9*) Wiley.

Dahlem, Konferenzen, et al. The Changing Atmosphere. LC 88-17138. (Dahlem Workshop Reports - Physical, Chemical, Earth Sciences). 296p. 1988. 315.00 (*0-471-92047-9*) Wiley.

Dahlem, Ted. How to Smoke Seafood. 44p. 1971. pap. 2.95 (*0-8200-0803-6*) Great Outdoors.

Dahlem Workshop on Humic Substances & Their Role i. Humic Substances & Their Role in the Environment: Report of the Dahlem Workshop on Humic Substances & Their Role in the Environment, Berlin 1987, March 29-April 3. Frimmel, F. H. & Christman, R. F., eds. LC 88-10625. (Life Sciences Research Report: No. 41). (Illus.). 285p. reprint ed. pap. 88.40 (*0-7837-4729-2*, 204451300004) Bks Demand.

Dahlen, Beverly. A Reading. 101p. (Orig.). (YA). (gr. 6-12). 1989. pap. 8.50 (*0-937013-33-1*) Potes Poets.

— Reading (8-10) 158p. (Orig.). 1992. pap. 12.00 (*0-925904-08-2*) Chax Pr.

Dahlen, F. A. & Tromp, Jeroen. Theoretical Global Seismology. LC 98-15199. 944p. 1998. text 80.00 (*0-691-00116-2*, Pub. by Princeton U Pr); pap. text 45.00 (*0-691-00124-3*, Pub. by Princeton U Pr) Cal Prin Full Svc.

***Dahlen, Lester A.** Pathways of Faith: A Story of Widening Opportunities in Mission. LC 99-43329. (Illus.). 228p. 1999. pap. 12.00 (*1-886513-04-X*) Kirk Hse Pubs.

Dahlen, Martha & Wong Kang Ying. Streetwise Guide to Chinese Herbal Medicine. (Illus.). 1996. pap. 11.95 (*962-7316-02-4*) China Bks.

Dahlen, Sven-Erik, jt. auth. see Holgate, Stephen T.

Dahlen, Sven-Erik, ed. see International Symposium on Trends in Eicosanoid Biology Staff.

Dahlen, Tommy. Among the Interculturalists: An Emergent Profession & Its Packaging of Knowledge. (Stockholm Studies in Social Anthropology: No. 38). 217p. 1997. pap. 49.50 (*91-7153-620-5*, Pub. by Almqvist Wiksell) Coronet Bks.

Dahlerup, Pil. Dekonstruktion: Die Literaturtheorie der 1990. 130p. 1998. pap. 12.00 (*3-11-015516-8*) De Gruyter.

Dahlgaard, H., ed. Nordic Radioecology: The Transfer of Radionuclides Through Nordic Ecosystems to Man. LC 95-188023. (Studies in Environmental Science: Vol. 62). 498p. 1994. 222.00 (*0-444-81617-8*) Elsevier.

Dahlgren, Anders. Wisconsin Library Building Project Handbook. rev. ed. 219p. 1991. pap. text 27.00 (*1-57337-058-4*) WI Dept Pub Instruct.

Dahlgren, Anders C. & Heyns, Erla P., compiled by. Planning Library Buildings: A Select Bibliography. 4th ed. LC 95-2767. 63p. 1995. pap. 15.00 (*0-8389-7800-2*) Library Admin.

Dahlgren, Anders C., jt. auth. see Library Administration & Management Association Pr.

Dahlgren, B. E., ed. see Standley, Paul C.

Dahlgren, Barbro. La Grana Cochinilla. 366p. 1990. pap. 9.20 (*968-36-1584-8*, UN028) UPLAAP.

— La Mixteca: Su Cultura e Historia Prehispanicas. 4th ed. 312p. 1990. pap. 9.20 (*968-36-0692-X*, UN037) UPLAAP.

Dahlgren, Barbro, et al, eds. Homenaje a Roman Pina Chan. 596p. 1987. pap. 11.43 (*968-837-966-2*, UN005) UPLAAP.

Dahlgren, Barbro & Soto de Arechavaleta, Ma. D., eds. Arqueologia del Norte y del Occidente de Mexico: Homenaje al Doctor J. Charles Kelley. (SPA.). 368p. 1995. pap. 23.00 (*968-36-4288-8*, UN042) UPLAAP.

Dahlgren, Bror E. & Noe, A. C. Index of American Palms, by B. E. Dahlgren. Fossil Palms, by A. C. Noe, Vol. 1. LC 36-23868. (Field Museaum of Natural History Botanical Ser.: No. 14). (Illus.). 456p. 1959. reprint ed. pap. 141.40 (*0-608-02693-X*, 206334700001) Bks Demand.

— Index of American Palms, by B. E. Dahlgren. Fossil Palms, by A. C. Noe, Vol. 2. LC 36-23868. (Field Museaum of Natural History Botanical Ser.: No. 14). (Illus.). 416p. 1959. reprint ed. pap. 129.00 (*0-608-02694-8*, 206334700002) Bks Demand.

Dahlgren, Colleen. Look for the Butterfly. Wightman, Christina C., ed. 100p. 1999. pap. 9.95 (*1-888911-11-5*) Benson Smythe.

Dahlgren, Dorothy & Kincaid, Simone C. In All the West No Place Like This: A Pictorial History of the Coeur d'Alene Region. 268p. 1995. 34.95 (*0-9643647-0-0*) Mus North Idaho.

— In All the West No Place Like This: A Pictorial History of the Coeur d'Alene Region. (Illus.). 268p. 1995. pap. 24.95 (*0-9643647-1-9*) Mus North Idaho.

Dahlgren, Emily & Maggio, Joseph A. Randolph Wardell Johnston: Feel Intensely, Imagine Vividly, Control Precisely. LC 93-93605. (Illus.). 100p. 1993. pap. 45.00 (*0-9638244-1-4*) Mag St Pr.

— Randolph Wardell Johnston: Feel Intensely, Imagine Vividly, Control Precisely. deluxe limited ed. LC 93-93605. (Illus.). 100p. 1993. 125.00 (*0-9638244-0-6*) Mag St Pr.

Dahlgren, Erik W. Were the Hawaiian Islands Visited by the Spaniards Before Their Discovery by Captain Cook in 1778? LC 75-35187. (Illus.). reprint ed. 67.50 (*0-404-14216-8*) AMS Pr.

Dahlgren, J. Elmer, tr. see Rosenius, Carl O.

D

Dahlgren, Kathleen. Naive Semantics for Natural Language Understanding. (C). 1988. text 104.50 (*0-89838-287-4*) Kluwer Academic.

Dahlgren, Marsiea & Young, Linda. Teams a Management Approach for Cities & Counties. 72p. 1994. pap. 29.95 (*1-882403-13-4*) The Innovation Grps.

Dahlgren, Martin, et al. "Portraits" - Music, Art & Poetry. (Illus.). 34p. 1998. spiral bd. 20.00 (*1-893365-00-X*) Barefooted Friar.

Dahlgren, Peter. Television & the Public Sphere: Citizenship, Democracy & the Media. (Media, Culture & Society Ser.: Vol. 10). 208p. 1995. 69.95 (*0-8039-8922-9*); pap. 26.95 (*0-8039-8923-7*) Sage.

Dahlgren, Peter & Sparks, Colin. Communication & Citizenship: Journalism & the Public Sphere. (Communication & Society Ser.). 256p. (C). 1993. pap. 23.99 (*0-415-10067-4*) Routledge.

Dahlgren, Peter & Sparks, Colin, eds. Journalism & Popular Culture. (Media, Culture & Society Ser.). (Illus.). 224p. (C). 1992. 55.00 (*0-8039-8670-X*); pap. 25.95 (*0-8039-8671-8*) Sage.

Dahlgren, R. Fabaceae, Pt. 3. (Flora of Southern Africa Ser.: Vol. 16). (Illus.). 430p. 1988. 38.00 (*0-621-11263-1*, Pub. by Natl Botanical Inst) Balogh.

Dahlgren, R. M. & Clifford, H. T. The Monocotyledon: A Comparative Study. LC 81-67906. (Botanical Systematics Ser.: No. 2). 1982. text 209.00 (*0-12-200680-1*) Acad Pr.

Dahlgren, R. M., et al. The Families of the Monocotyledons. 1985. 395.95 (*0-387-13655-X*) Spr-Verlag.

Dahlgren, Stellan & Norman, Hans. The Rise & Fall of New Sweden: Governor Johan Risingh's Journal in Its Historical Context, 1654-1655. (Acta Bibliothecae R. Universitatis Upsaliensis Ser.: Vol. XXVII). (Illus.). 303p. 1988. 81.00 (*91-554-2137-7*, Pub. by Uppsala Univ Acta Univ Uppsaliensis) Coronet Bks.

***Dahlgren, Sven-Olof.** Word Order in Arabic. LC 98-210486. (Orientalia Gothoburgensia Ser.: No. 12). 273p. 1998. pap. 62.50 (*91-7346-328-0*, Pub. by Almqvist Wiksell) Coronet Bks.

***Dahlgrun, Corinna & Darmstadt, Hans.** Neue Musik in der Kirche: Visionen Gegen die Zeit: Interdisziplinare Tage Fur Neue Musik und Theologie 11.-14. Juni 1998 - Dokumentation und Auswertung. 116p. 1999. 17.95 (*3-631-35232-8*) P Lang Pubng.

Dahlhaus, Barbara. Fertigkeit Horen. Neuner, Gerd, ed. (Fernstudienangebot Ser.). (GER.). 192p. 1996. 11.25 (*0-614-14080-3*) Langenscheidt.

— Fertigkeit Horverstehen, Set. (GER.). 200p. wbk. ed. 12.25 incl. audio (*3-468-49675-3*) Langenscheidt.

Dahlhaus-Beilner, Barbara. Wahnsinn: Symptom und Befreiung: Funktion und Narrative Vermittlung extremen Irrationalismus im Werk Doris Lessing. (Bochum Studies in English: Vol. 17). iv, 261p. (Orig.). (C). 1984. pap. 30.00 (*90-6032-259-2*, Pub. by B R Gruner) Humanities.

Dahlhaus, Carl. Analysis & Value Judgment. 2nd ed. Levarie, Siegmund, tr. from GER. LC 82-12251. (Monographs in Musicology & Aesthetics in Music). Orig. Title: Analyse und Werturteil. 95p. 1983. lib. bdg. 55.00 (*0-918728-20-7*) Pendragon NY.

— Between Romanticism & Modernism: Four Studies in the Music of the Later Nineteenth Century. Whittall, Mary, tr. from GER. LC 78-54793. (California Studies in 19th Century Music: No. 1). 129p. 1980. pap. 13.95 (*0-520-06748-7*, Pub. by U CA Pr) Cal Prin Full Svc.

— The Idea of Absolute Music. Lustig, Roger, tr. 186p. 1991. pap. text 14.00 (*0-226-13487-3*) U Ch Pr.

— The Idea of Absolute Music. Lustig, Roger, tr. LC 89-4829. 160p. 1993. 29.95 (*0-226-13486-5*) U Ch Pr.

— Ludwig Van Beethoven: Approaches to His Music. Whittall, Mary, tr. (Illus.). 304p. 1991. text 55.00 (*0-19-816148-4*) OUP.

— Ludwig Van Beethoven: Approaches to His Music. Whittall, Mary, tr. (Illus.). 282p. 1994. pap. text 24.95 (*0-19-816399-1*) OUP.

— Nineteenth-Century Music. Robinson, J. Bradford, tr. (Illus.). 427p. 1991. reprint ed. pap. 24.95 (*0-520-07644-3*, Pub. by U CA Pr) Cal Prin Full Svc.

— Studies on the Origin of Harmonic Tonality. Gjerdingen, Robert O., tr. LC 90-8696. 405p. reprint ed. pap. 125.60 (*0-608-20148-0*, 207142000011) Bks Demand.

Dahlhaus, Carl & Eggebrecht, Hans H. Brockhaus Riemann Musiklexikon, Vol. 1, A-K. (GER.). 1978. 175.00 (*3-7653-0303-8*) Eur-Am Music.

— Brockhaus Riemann Musiklexikon, Vol. 1, A-K. deluxe ed. (GER.). 1978. 195.00 (*0-685-73242-8*) Eur-Am Music.

Dahlhaus, Carl, jt. auth. see Katz, Ruth.

Dahlhaus, Carl, jt. ed. see Katz, Ruth.

Dahlhauser, Eric. Money & Freedom: The New American Game. 1993. pap. 9.95 (*0-9631782-1-0*) C Y W & D Accts.

Dahlhauser, Eric B. & Wolf, Stephen J. Money & Freedom: The New American Game. 127p. 1991. 24.95 (*0-9631782-0-2*) C Y W & D Accts.

***Dahlhauser, Margaret M.** Core Review for the NCLEX/CAT-RN. 512p. 2000. pap. 39.95 (*0-07-135339-9*) McGraw.

— Core Review Packaage for the: NCLEX RN CAT. 2nd ed. 256p. 2000. write for info. (*0-07-135335-6*) McGraw.

Dahlhauser, Margaret M. NCLEX/CAT-RN: PreTest Self-Assessment & Review. (Illus.). 800p. 1996. pap. text 29.00 incl. disk (*0-07-912082-2*) McGraw-Hill HPD.

Dahlheim, Marilyn E. A Photographic Catalog of Killer Whales, Orcinus Orca, from the Central Gulf of Alaska to the Southeastern Bering Sea. (Illus.). 64p. 1998. 13.00 (*0-89904-779-3*, Seascape Res Alliance); spiral bd. 8.00 (*0-89904-780-7*, Seascape Res Alliance) Crumb Elbow Pub.

Dahlheim, Werner. Gewalt & Herrschaft das Provinziale Herrschaftssystem der Roemischen Republik. (C). 1977. 157.70 (*3-11-006973-3*) De Gruyter.

***Dahlheimer, Charles M.** 20/20 Vision: A Focus on the Future of the Real Estate Industry. 232p. 2000. pap. 24.95 (*0-9623018-3-3*) NAC Group Inc.

Dahlheimer, Charles M., jt. auth. see Dooley, Thomas W.

Dahlheimer, John C. Mechanical Face Seal Handbook. LC 72-6443. 200p. reprint ed. pap. 62.00 (*0-608-13411-2*, 205574600035) Bks Demand.

Dahlia, Blag & Rude, Marc. Armed to the Teeth with Lipstick. (Illus.). 128p. (Orig.). 1998. pap. 12.00 (*0-9664432-0-9*) Greedy.

Dahlie, Hallvard. Isolation & Commitment: F. P. Grove's Settlers of the Marsh. (Canadian Fiction Studies: No. 16). 79p. (C). 1993. pap. text 14.95 (*1-55022-097-7*, Pub. by ECW) Genl Dist Srvs.

Dahlie, Jorgen. A Social History of Scandinavian Immigration, Washington State, 1895-1910. LC 80-849. (American Ethnic Groups Ser.). 1981. lib. bdg. 23.95 (*0-405-13412-6*) Ayer.

Dahlin, Amber, ed. see George, Marilyn J.

Dahlin, Amber, ed. see George, Marilyn Jordan.

***Dahlin, Bill.** The Pig & the Whale. (Illus.). 15p. (J). 1999. pap. 8.97 (*0-9678028-0-6*) B Dahlin.

***Dahlin, Dennis.** Earth Friendly Inns: Environmental Travel: Northeast Edition. (Illus.). 384p. 2000. pap. 18.95 (*0-9677076-0-9*, Pub. by WPM) Chelsea Green Pub.

Dahlin, Donald A. Chiropractic for Natural Health & Wellness Care. 136p. 1993. pap. 10.95 (*1-883243-00-9*) D A Dahlin.

Dahlin, Donald C. Impact of the Twenty-Sixth Amendment: The Residence Status of College Students. 1972. 1.00 (*1-55614-050-9*) U of SD Gov Res Bur.

— Law Enforcement Planning in South Dakota: A First Report. 1970. 1.00 (*1-55614-057-6*) U of SD Gov Res Bur.

— Rural Crime Prevention in South Dakota. LC 84-621635. (Special Project Ser.: No. 47). (Illus.). viii, 193p. 1982. write for info. (*1-55614-111-4*) U of SD Gov Res Bur.

— South Dakota Jails: Current Conditions & Proposed Directions. 1971. 5.00 (*1-55614-000-2*) U of SD Gov Res Bur.

Dahlin, Tom, ed. 1997 U. S. Market Forecasts: Economic & Demographic Profiles of 14,639 U. S. Markets. 500p. (Orig.). 1996. pap. write for info. (*0-9646364-4-1*) ASM Communs.

Dahlinger, Charles W. Drunk Driving Enforcement & Investigations: Learn the Four D's (Detection, Dexterity, Detention, Detailing) (Illus.). 87p. (Orig.). (C). 1995. pap. text 9.95 (*0-87563-622-5*) Stipes.

***Dahlinger, Fred, Jr.** Show Trains of the 20th Century. (Photo Archives Ser.). (Illus.). 128p. 2000. pap. 29.95 (*1-58388-030-5*, 130665AE, Pub. by Iconografix) Motorbooks Intl.

***Dahlinger, Fred, Jr., ed.** Trains of the Circus, 1876-1956. LC 99-76045. (Illus.). 128p. 2000. pap. 29.95 (*1-58388-024-0*, 130085AE, Pub. by Iconografix) Motorbooks Intl.

Dahlinger, Fred & Thayer, Stuart. Badger State Showmen: History of Wisconsin's Circus Heritage. LC 98-45989. (Illus.). 160p. 1998. 29.95 (*0-9663436-1-1*) Grote Publ.

Dahlitz, Julie. Avoidance & Settlement of Arms Control Disputes: Arms Control & Disarmament Law. LC 96-165690. 239p. 35.00 (*92-1-100680-5*) UN.

Dahlkamp, F. J. Uranium Ore Deposits. (Illus.). 512p. 1993. 262.95 (*3-540-53264-1*) Spr-Verlag.

Dahlke, Nanette C. Naturalistic Articulation Carryover Experiences. (Illus.). 1990. student ed. 13.95 (*0-9626939-2-8*) Janelle Pubns.

Dahlke, Paul. Buddhism & Its Place in the Mental Life of Mankind. LC 78-72403. reprint ed. 29.00 (*0-404-17265-2*) AMS Pr.

— Buddhist Essays. Silicara, Bhikkhu, tr. from GER. LC 78-72404. reprint ed. 37.50 (*0-404-17266-0*) AMS Pr.

— Buddhist Stories. Silacara, Bhikkhu, tr. LC 71-106285. (Short Story Index Reprint Ser.). 1977. 21.95 (*0-8369-3322-2*) Ayer.

Dahlke, Rudiger. Everyday Initiations: How to Survive Crises Using Rituals. LC 98-16528. 384p. 1999. pap. 16.95 (*1-885394-23-3*) Bluestar Communs.

— Heart-Aches: Heart Disease & the Psychology of the Broken Heart. (Illus.). 320p. (Orig.). 1996. pap. 14.50 (*1-885394-14-4*) Bluestar Communs.

Dahlke, Rudiger & Von Martius, Katharina. Mandalas of the World. LC 91-42009. (Illus.). 286p. 1992. pap. 21.95 (*0-8069-8526-7*) Sterling.

Dahllof, Urban & Selander, Staffan, eds. Expanding Colleges & New Universities: Selected Case Studies from Non-Metropolitan Areas in Australia, Scotland & Scandinavia. (Uppsala Studies in Education: No. 66). 339p. (Orig.). 1996. pap. 57.50 (*91-554-3697-8*, Pub. by Uppsala Univ Acta Univ Uppsaliensis) Coronet Bks.

— New Universities & Regional Context: Papers from an International Seminar. 291p. (Orig.). 1994. pap. 62.50 (*91-554-3337-5*) Coronet Bks.

Dahllof, Urban, et al. Dimensions of Evaluation in Higher Education: Report of the I.H.M.E. Study Group on Evaluation in Higher Education. (Higher Education Policy Ser.: No. 13). 160p. 1991. 49.95 (*1-85302-526-7*) Taylor & Francis.

***Dahlman, Carl J. & Thaler, David E.** Assessing Unit Readiness: Case Study of an Air Force Fighter Wing. 43p. (C). 2000. pap. 6.00 (*0-8330-2828-6*, DB-296) Rand Corp.

Dahlmann, Hellfried. Kleine Schriften. 271p. 1970. write for info. (*0-318-71105-2*) G Olms Pubs.

— Varro und die Hellenistische Sprachtheorie. 89p. 1964. write for info. (*3-296-12110-2*) G Olms Pubs.

Dahlmann, Hellfried, ed. see Varro.

Dahlquist, Alfred, ed. Every Name Index to Minnesota Genealogical Journal, Issues 1 & 2. 1985. pap. 12.00 (*0-915709-60-0*) Pk Geneal Bk.

Dahlquist, Alfred J. Your French-Canadian Connection Guide, No. 1. 32p. 1989. pap. 5.00 (*0-915709-00-7*) Pk Geneal Bk.

Dahlquist, Alfred J., et al. The Grave Markers of Hennepin County Minnesota, Vol. 1. 1983. pap. 6.00 (*0-915709-03-1*) Pk Geneal Bk.

— The Grave Markers of Hennepin County Minnesota, Vol. 2. LC 83-122629. (Illus.). 59p. 1993. pap. 10.00 (*0-915709-04-X*) Pk Geneal Bk.

Dahlquist, Allan. Megasthenes & Indian Religion. 1977. 11.50 (*0-89684-277-0*, Pub. by Motilal Bnarsidass) S Asia.

Dahlquist, Anna M. Burgess of Guatemala. 2nd ed. LC 95-94881. 172p. 1995. pap. 7.95 (*0-9641261-1-7*) Kings River.

— Daughter of the Covenants. LC 94-76457. 200p. (Orig.). 1994. pap. 7.95 (*0-9641261-0-9*) Kings River.

— Trailblazers for Translators: The Influence of the "Chichicastenago Twelve" LC 91-65732. 1995. pap. 10.95 (*0-87808-205-0*) William Carey Lib.

Dahlquist, Anna M. & Alen, Rupert. Royal Families of Medieval Scandinavia, Flanders, & Kiev. LC 96-80004. 248p. (Orig.). 1997. pap. 12.99 (*0-9641261-2-5*) Kings River.

Dahlquist, Julie R., jt. auth. see Bauer, Richard J.

***Dahlquist, Kathleen C.** "Hop-a-Long's Adventures" Erickson, Beverly H., ed. LC 99-72409. (Illus.). 81p. (J). (gr. 1-4). 2000. pap. 7.95 (*1-885527-18-7*) Feather Fables.

Dahlquist, Kathleen C. Jack: Venice's Beloved Donkey. Drake, Alice, ed. (Illus.). 28p. (Orig.). 1995. pap. 4.95 (*1-885527-08-X*) Feather Fables.

— The Little Brown Donkey. Drake, Alice, ed. LC 94-71676. (Illus.). 64p. (Orig.). (J). (gr. 3). 1994. pap. 7.95 (*0-9634122-8-0*) Feather Fables.

***Dahlquist, Kathleen C.** Tales of Erin: March 17th. large type ed. Erickson, Beverly H., ed. LC 99-75695. (Illus.). 80p. (J). (gr. 1-5). 2000. pap. 15.00 (*1-885527-20-9*) Feather Fables.

Dahlquist, L. M. Pediatric Pain Management. LC 98-43928. (Clinical Child Psychology Library). (Illus.). 172p. (C). 1999. pap. text 24.95 (*0-306-46085-8*, Kluwer Plenum) Kluwer Academic.

— Pediatric Pain Management. LC 98-43928. (Clinical Child Psychology Library). (Illus.). 172p. (C). 1999. 75.00 (*0-306-46084-X*, Plenum Trade) Perseus Pubng.

Dahlqvist, Gosta, jt. auth. see Speilman, Patrick.

Dahlqvist, Reine. The Keyed Trumpet & Its Greatest Virtuoso: Anton Weidinger. LC 75-16223. (Brass Research Ser.: No. 1). (Illus.). 25p. 1975. pap. 3.00 (*0-914282-13-1*) Brass Pr.

Dahlstedt, Marden A. The Terrible Wave: Memorial Edition. LC 72-76687. (Illus.). 125p. (YA). (gr. 7 up). 1988. reprint ed. pap. 5.00 (*0-9621827-0-2*) R R Dahlstedt.

Dahlsten, Donald L. Eradication of Exotic Pests: Analysis with Case Histories. LC 89-37234. 304p. (C). 1989. 45.00 (*0-300-04332-5*) Yale U Pr.

Dahlstrand, Frederick C. Amos Bronson Alcott: An Intellectual Biography. LC 80-65282. (Illus.). 500p. 1982. 48.50 (*0-8386-3016-2*) Fairleigh Dickinson.

Dahlstrom & Company. Don't Believe Everything You Read. (Illus.). 40p. 1984. pap. text 3.99 (*0-940712-29-6*) Dahlstrom & Co.

Dahlstrom, Ake & Brost, Leif. The Amber Book. Leijonhufvud, Jonas, tr. from SWE. LC 96-77632. Orig. Title: Stenen Som Flyter och Brinner. (Illus.). 144p. 1996. 27.00 (*0-945005-23-7*) Geoscience Pr.

Dahlstrom, Carl E. Strindberg's Dramatic Expressionism. LC 64-14697. 264p. 1972. reprint ed. 29.95 (*0-405-08426-9*, Pub. by Blom Pubns) Ayer.

Dahlstrom, Carol, ed. Mary Engelbreit Cross-Stitch for All Seasons. LC 97-71327. (Illus.). 192p. 1998. 29.95 (*0-696-20707-9*, Meredith Pr) Meredith Bks.

Dahlstrom, Carol F., ed. More Incredibly Awesome Crafts for Kids. LC 97-71328. (Illus.). 144p. 1997. pap. 16.95 (*0-696-20691-9*) Meredith Bks.

— 101 Full-Size Quilt Blocks & Borders. LC 97-75842. (Illus.). 216p. 1998. 34.95 (*0-696-20739-7*, Better Homes) Meredith Bks.

***Dahlstrom, Carol Field.** Simply Christmas: Renew the Spirit. 201 Easy Crafts, Food & Decorating Ideas. (Illus.). 192p. 2000. 29.95 (*0-9679764-0-5*, Brave Ink Pr) C F Dahlstrom.

Dahlstrom, Carol Field, ed. see Engelbreit, Mary.

Dahlstrom, Cecile. Pleasure Time Stories for Girls & Boys. (Illus.). 64p. (Orig.). pap. 9.95 (*1-886094-03-9*) Chicago Spectrum.

— Some Things Never Change. 96p. (Orig.). 1996. pap. 10.95 (*1-886094-53-5*) Chicago Spectrum.

***Dahlstrom, Daniel, ed.** Proceedings of the Twentieth World Congress of Philosophy Vol. VIII, Pt. II: Contemporary Philosophy: The Enlightenment & Its Critics. LC 99-66878. 250p. (C). 2000. 45.00 (*1-889680-12-5*) Philos Document.

***Dahlstrom, Daniel O.** Heidegger's Concept of Truth. (Modern European Philosophy Ser.). 388p. (C). 2001. text Price not set. (*0-521-64317-1*) Cambridge U Pr.

Dahlstrom, Daniel O., ed. Existential Personalism. LC 86-62500. (Proceedings of the American Catholic Philosophical Association Ser.: Vol. 60, 1986). 250p. (Orig.). (C). 1987. pap. 20.00 (*0-918090-20-2*) Am Cath Philo.

— Hermeneutics & the Tradition. LC 88-60862. (Proceedings of the American Catholic Philosophical Association Ser.: Vol. 62). 1988. 20.00 (*0-918090-22-9*) Am Cath Philo.

— Metaphysics of Substance: ACPA Proceedings, 1987, Vol. 61. 250p. (Orig.). 1987. pap. 20.00 (*0-918090-21-0*) Am Cath Philo.

— Nature & Scientific Method. LC 89-70817. (Studies in Philosophy & the History of Philosophy: Vol. 22). 328p. 1991. 48.95 (*0-8132-0723-1*) Cath U Pr.

— Philosophy & Art. LC 89-77750. (Studies in Philosophy & the History of Philosophy: Vol. 23). 266p. 1991. text 44.95 (*0-8132-0724-X*) Cath U Pr.

— Practical Reasoning: ACPA Proceedings, 1984, Vol. 58. 250p. 1985. pap. 20.00 (*0-918090-18-0*) Am Cath Philo.

— Realism. (Proceedings of the American Catholic Philosophical Association Ser.: Vol. 59). 250p. 1985. 20.00 (*0-918090-19-9*) Am Cath Philo.

Dahlstrom, Daniel O., tr. Moses Mendelssohn: Philosophical Writings. LC 97-16141. (Cambridge Texts in the History of Philosophy Ser.). 361p. 1997. text 64.95 (*0-521-57383-1*); pap. text 21.95 (*0-521-57477-3*) Cambridge U Pr.

Dahlstrom, Daniel O., jt. auth. see Baur, Michael.

Dahlstrom, Daniel O., ed. see Schiller, Friedrich.

Dahlstrom, Grant. Assessing Readability MMPI Instrument. Date not set. pap. 6.00 (*0-8166-2580-8*) U of Minn Pr.

Dahlstrom, Harry S. Don't Let People Rip You Off. (Illus.). 40p. (Orig.). 1984. pap. text 3.99 (*0-940712-26-1*) Dahlstrom & Co.

— Hey, That's Me: The American Teenager. (Illus.). 40p. (Orig.). 1984. pap. text 3.99 (*0-940712-30-X*) Dahlstrom & Co.

— Job Hunting Handbook. (Illus.). 50p. (Orig.). 1995. pap. text 3.99 (*0-940712-09-1*, Study Buddy) Dahlstrom & Co.

— Out of Hock. (Illus.). 50p. (Orig.). 1994. pap. 3.99 (*0-940712-54-7*) Dahlstrom & Co.

— Surviving a Layoff. LC 98-214993. (Illus.). 50p. (Orig.). 1994. pap. text 3.99 (*0-940712-76-8*) Dahlstrom & Co.

— Thinking Skills. (Illus.). 50p. (Orig.). 1987. pap. text 3.99 (*0-940712-55-5*) Dahlstrom & Co.

Dahlstrom, Kathryn. Captives in the Wilderness. (Good News Club Ser.). (J). (gr. 4-11). Date not set. pap. 4.99 (*1-55976-828-2*) CEF Press.

— Hate Fighters. (Good News Club Ser.). (J). (gr. 4-11). Date not set. pap. 4.99 (*1-55976-832-0*) CEF Press.

— Peppy's Rescue. (Good News Club Ser.). (J). (gr. 4-11). Date not set. pap. 4.99 (*1-55976-826-6*) CEF Press.

— Street Games. (Good News Club Ser.). Date not set. pap. 4.99 (*1-55976-830-4*) CEF Press.

— Street Games. (Good News Club Ser.). (J). Date not set. pap. 4.99 (*1-55976-829-0*) CEF Press.

— Trapped by an Earthquake. (Good News Club Ser.). (J). (gr. 4-11). Date not set. pap. 4.99 (*1-55976-827-4*) CEF Press.

Dahlstrom, Kathy. Sent into Hiding. (God News Club Ser.: Bk. 5). (J). (gr. 4 up). 1996. pap. 4.99 (*1-55976-831-2*) CEF Press.

Dahlstrom, Lars, jt. auth. see Zeichner, Kenneth.

Dahlstrom, Lorraine M. Doing the Days: A Year's Worth of Creative Journaling, Drawing, Listening, Reading, Thinking, Arts & Crafts Activities for Children Ages 8-12. LC 93-38119. (Free Spirited Classroom Ser.). (Illus.). 240p. (J). (gr. 3-6). 1994. pap., teacher ed. 21.95 (*0-915793-62-8*) Free Spirit Pub.

— Writing down the Days: 365 Creative Journaling Ideas for Young People. LC 88-29616. (Illus.). 176p. (YA). (gr. 6 up). 1990. pap. 12.95 (*0-915793-19-9*) Free Spirit Pub.

***Dahlstrom, Lorraine M.** Writing down the Days: 365 Creative Journaling Ideas for Young People. 2nd rev. ed. (Illus.). 176p. 2000. pap. 14.95 (*1-57542-086-4*) Free Spirit Pub.

Dahlstrom, Paul T. Love Has a Thousand Ways to Tell. 69p. (Orig.). 1993. pap. 8.00 (*0-9635690-3-1*) TA Pubns.

— Worshiping: Present & Future Hope: A Critique & Proposal. 1996. pap. 10.95 (*0-7880-0901-X*, Fairway Pr) CSS OH.

Dahlstrom, W. Grant, et al. An MMPI Handbook, Vol. 2. rev. ed. LC 74-172933. 600p. 1975. reprint ed. pap. 186.00 (*0-608-00835-4*, 206162600010) Bks Demand.

— An MMPI Handbook: Clinical Interpretation, Vol. 1. rev. ed. LC 74-172933. (Illus.). 1972. text 49.95 (*0-8166-0589-0*) U of Minn Pr.

— MMPI Patterns of American Minorities. 440p. 1986. text 44.95 (*0-8166-1530-6*) U of Minn Pr.

Dahlstrom, William S., jt. auth. see Anderson, Arthur J.

Dahm. Southpark the Tourist Guide to Southpark Shrink Wrap. 1998. 25.00 (*0-671-03540-1*) PB.

Dahm, Christof. Israel Im Markusevangelium. (Europaische Hochschulschriften Ser.: Reihe 23, Bd. 420). (GER., Illus.). V, 358p. 1991. 61.80 (*3-631-43657-2*) P Lang Pubng.

Dahm, Clifford N., jt. auth. see Markwiese, James T.

Dahm, Cynthia. Final Choice. LC 93-71327. 1995. 15.95 (*0-8158-0494-6*) Chris Mass.

Dahm, H. Vladimir Solovyev & Max Scheler: A Contribution to History of Phenomenology in Attempt to a Comparing Interpretation. Wright, Kathleen, tr. LC 74-83007. (Sovietica Ser.: No. 34). (Illus.). 406p. 1975. lib. bdg. 191.50 (*90-277-0507-0*) Kluwer Academic.

Dahm, Henrich. French & Japanese Economic Relations with Vietnam since 1975. 166p. 1998. text 36.00 (*0-7007-1084-1*, Pub. by Curzon Pr Ltd) UH Pr.

Dahm, Paul. Jean le Vingt-Troisieme: Pape du Concile. 1987. lib. bdg. 14.95 (*0-8288-2639-0*) Fr & Eur.

— Jean Vingt-Troisieme, le Pape du Concile. (FRE., Illus.). 152p. 1963. lib. bdg. 19.95 (*0-8288-3945-X*) Fr & Eur.

— The Rainbow Bridge. unabridged ed. 150p. 1998. pap. 14.95 (*0-9663022-0-6*) Running Tide Pr.

Dahm, Ralph & Brescoll, James. Opportunities in Sales Careers. (Illus.). 160p. 1993. 13.95 (*0-8442-6498-9*, VGM Career) NTC Contemp Pub Co.

— Opportunities in Sales Careers. (Illus.). 160p. 1994. pap. 10.95 (*0-8442-6499-7*, VGM Career) NTC Contemp Pub Co.

Dahm, Ralph M., jt. auth. see Brescoll, James.

D

An Asterisk (*) at the beginning of an entry indicates that the title is appearing for the first time.

Dahmane. Dahmane. (FO Ser.). 1998. pap. 14.99 (3-8228-9769-8) Taschen Amer.

Dahmani, M. The Fisheries Regime of the Exclusive Economic Zone No. 11: Publications on Ocean Development. 200p. 1987. lib. bdg. 115.00 (90-247-3374-X) Kluwer Academic.

Dahmann, Donald C. Locals & Cosmopolitans: Patterns of Spatial Mobility During the Transition from Youth to Early Adulthood. LC 82-2721. (University of Chicago, Department of Geography, Research Paper Ser.: No. 204). 163p. 1982. reprint ed. pap. 50.60 (0-608-02243-8, 206288400004) Bks Demand.

Dahmen, H. D., jt. auth. see Brandt, S.

Dahmen, Hans D., jt. auth. see Brandt, Siegmund.

Dahmen-Ray, Patricia, et al. Spokane's Celebrity Chefs: The MS Cookbook. (Illus.). 118p. (Orig.). 1990. pap. 15.95 (0-9615201-7-5) BCG Ltd.

Dahmen, U., et al, eds. High-Resolution Electron Microscopy of Defects in Materials Vol. 183: Symposium Proceedings Ser. 392p. 1991. text 17.50 (1-55899-072-0) Materials Res.

Dahmen, Wolfgang, et al, eds. Computation of Curves & Surfaces. (C). 1990. text 273.00 (0-7923-0724-0) Kluwer Academic.

— Multiscale Wavelet Methods for Partial Differential Equations. LC 97-12672. (Wavelet Analysis & Its Applications Ser.: Vol. 6). (Illus.). 570p. 1997. text 59.95 (0-12-200675-5) Morgan Kaufmann.

Dahmer, Fred. Caddo Was-- A Short History of Caddo Lake. LC 94-17945. 1995. pap. 9.95 (0-292-71576-5) U of Tex Pr.

Dahmer, Sondra. The Waiter & Waitress Training Manual. 4th ed. (Hospitality, Travel & Tourism Ser.). 162p. 1996. text 34.95 (0-442-02110-0, VNR) Wiley.

Dahmer, Sondra J. & Kahl, Kurt W. The Waiter & Waitress Training Manual. 4th ed. (Hospitality, Travel & Tourism Ser.). 162p. 1995. pap. 37.95 (0-471-28718-0, VNR) Wiley.

Dahmes, Sallie. The Breakthrough Bird Taxidermy Manual. Williamson, Bob & Edwards, Ken, eds. (Illus.). 156p. (C). 1988. pap. text 24.95 (0-925245-08-9) WASCO Manufact.

Dahmke, Mark. Using Concurrent PC DOS. 144p. 1986. pap. 26.95 (0-07-015073-7, BYTE Bks) McGraw.

Dahmke, Mark & Ciarcia, Steve. The Byte Guide to CP-M. 216p. 1983. pap. text 21.95 (0-07-015072-9, BYTE Bks) McGraw.

Dahms, Alan M. Emotional Intimacy: Overlooked Requirement for Survival. LC 72-78443. (Illus.). 154p. (C). 1972. 8.95 (0-87108-184-9) Publishers Consult.

Dahms, Alan M., jt. auth. see Clifton, Robert L.

Dahms, B. B. & Qualman, S., eds. Gastrointestinal Diseases. (Perspectives in Pediatric Pathology Ser.: Vol. 20). (Illus.). x, 176p. 1997. 189.75 (3-8055-6343-4) S Karger.

Dahms, Cathy W. & Geils, Brian W., eds. An Assessment of Forest Ecosystem Health in the Southwest. (Illus.). 97p. 1998. pap. text 25.00 (0-7881-7190-9) DIANE Pub.

Dahms, David. Rocky Mountain National Park: Jewel of the Rockies. (Illus.). 60p. (Orig.). 1997. pap. 12.95 (0-9646359-1-7) Paragon Pr.

— Rocky Mountain Wildflowers Pocket Guide. (Illus.). 112p. 1999. pap. 6.95 (0-9646359-2-5) Paragon Pr.

— Rocky Mountain Wildlife. 60p. (Orig.). 1995. pap. 11.95 (0-9646359-0-9) Paragon Pr.

Dahms, Edward & Gordh, Gordon. A Review of the Genera of Australian Encyrtidae (Hymenoptera - Chalcidoidea) Described from Australia by A. A. Girault with a Checklist of Included Species. Gupta, Virendra K., ed. LC 97-41194. (Memoirs on Entomology International Ser.: No. 9). (Illus.). 518p. (C). 1997. 75.00 (1-56665-065-8) Assoc Pubs FL.

Dahms, Erna M. Zeit und Zeiterlebnis in den Werken Max Frischs: Bedeutung und Technische Darstellung. (Quellen und Forschungen zur Sprach und Kulturgeschichte der Germanischen Voelker). (C). 1976. 80.80 (3-11-006679-3) De Gruyter.

Dahms, Hans-Uwe & Pottek, Mark. Microfauna Marina Band 7: Metahuntemannia Smirnov. (Illus.). 342p. 1964. pap. 59.00 (3-437-30698-7) Gustav Fischer.

***Dahms, Harry F., ed.** Transformations of Capitalism: Economy, Society, & the State in the Twentieth Century. LC 98-38573. (Main Trends of the Modern World Ser.). 440p. 1999. text 60.00 (0-8147-1902-3) NYU Pr.

Dahms, Harry F., ed. Transformations of Capitalism: Economy, Society & the State in the Twentieth Century. LC 98-38573. (Main Trends of the Modern World Ser.). 440p. 1999. pap. text 20.00 (0-8147-1903-1) NYU Pr.

Dahmus, Joseph. Seven Medieval Historians. LC 81-11332. 320p. (C). 1981. text 35.95 (0-88229-712-0) Burnham Inc.

Dahn, Felix. Die Konige der Germanen. (GER.). 1973. reprint ed. write for info. (3-487-04721-7) G Olms Pubs.

Dahne, Robert A. Keep Safe from Poisonous Animals, Insects, Plants, Trees in the United States of America. (Illus.). 80p. (Orig.). 1995. pap. 6.95 (0-9645585-0-5) Keep Safe Pubns.

D'Ahne, Siegfried, et al. Near-Infrared Dyes for High Technology Applications. LC 98-7675. (NATO ASI Series: Partnership Sub-Series 3). 458p. 1998. write for info. (0-7923-5101-0) Kluwer Academic.

Dahneke, Barton E., ed. Measurement of Suspended Particles by Quasi-Elastic Light Scattering. LC 82-17334. (Wiley-Interscience Publications). 584p. 1983. reprint ed. pap. 181.10 (0-7837-2393-8, 204007800006) Bks Demand.

Dahnert, Wolfgang. Radiology Review Manual. 3rd ed. LC 95-21072. (Illus.). 871p. 1996. 85.00 (0-683-02338-1) Lppncott W & W.

— Radiology Review Manual. 3rd ed. 1997. 139.00 incl. cd-rom (0-683-30083-0, D1128); 139.00 incl. cd-rom (0-683-30082-2, D0788); 139.00 incl. cd-rom (0-683-30081-4, D0789) Lppncott W & W.

— Radiology Review Manual. 4th ed. LC 98-27272. 1007p. 1998. pap. 89.00 (0-683-30623-5) Lppncott W & W.

Dahnert, Wolfgang F. Radiology Review Manual. 2nd ed. LC 92-49039. (Illus.). 742p. 1993. 76.00 (0-683-02340-3) Lppncott W & W.

Dahnert, Wolfgang F. Radiology Review Manual. 4th ed. 952p. 150.00 (0-7817-2169-5) Lppncott W & W.

***Dahnoun, Naim.** Digital Signal Processing Implementation. LC 99-49510. 234p. (C). 2000. 39.00 (0-201-61916-4) Addison-Wesley.

Dahon, Linda. The Vending Start-Up-Kit. 70p. 1996. ring bd. 108.95 (0-9667065-0-1) Vend Conn.

Dahood, Karen J., ed. see Ives, Ronald L.

Dahood, Mitchell, ed. Psalms I, 1-50. (Anchor Bible Ser.: Vol. 16). 384p. 1966. 29.00 (0-385-02765-6, Anchor NY) Doubleday.

— Psalms III, 101-150. LC 66-11766. (Anchor Bible Ser.: Vol. 17A). 544p. 1970. 35.00 (0-385-00607-1, Anchor NY) Doubleday.

— Psalms II, 51-100. LC 66-11766. (Anchor Bible Ser.: Vol. 17). 432p. 1968. 35.00 (0-385-03759-7, Anchor NY) Doubleday.

Dahood, Roger, ed. The Avowing of King Arthur. LC 83-48232. (Medieval Texts Ser.: Vol. 10). 160p. 1984. 15.00 (0-685-74483-3) Garland.

Dahood, Roger, jt. ed. see Ackerman, Robert W.

Dahorte, N., jt. auth. see Sudarshan, T. S.

Dahotre, N. B. & Hampikian, J. M., eds. Elevated Temperature Coatings: Science & Technology II. LC 96-76538. (Illus.). 310p. 1996. 20.00 (0-87339-313-9) Minerals Metals.

***Dahotre, Narendra B., ed.** Lasers in Surface Engineering. LC 98-73964. (Surface Engineering Ser.: Vol. 1). 599p. 1998. 118.00 (0-87170-665-2) ASM.

Dahotre, Narendra B., et al, eds. Elevated Temperature Coating: Science & Technology I. (Illus.). 440p. 1995. 20.00 (0-87339-289-2, 2892) Minerals Metals.

***Dahotre, Narendra B. & Hampikian, Janet M., eds.** Elevated Temperature Coatings: Science & Technology III. LC 98-68628. (Illus.). 20p. 1999. 136.00 (0-87339-421-6, 4216) Minerals Metals.

Dahr, Michael. Deductive Databases: Theory & Applications. LC 96-52954. (Illus.). 256p. 1997. mass mkt. 32.95 (1-85032-138-8) ITCP.

Dahrendorf, Ralf. After 1989: Morals, Revolution & Civil Society. LC 97-3225. (St. Antony's Ser.). 190p. 1997. text 35.00 (0-312-17613-9) St Martin.

— Class & Class Conflict in Industrial Society. xvi, 336p. 1959. pap. 16.95 (0-8047-0561-5) Stanford U Pr.

— Classes & Conflits de Classes Dans la Societe Industrielle. (Oeuvre Sociologique Ser.: No. 1). 1972. pap. 26.95 (90-279-7014-9) Mouton.

— Life Chances: Approaches to Social & Political Theory. LC 79-18685. x, 182p. (C). 1994. pap. text 8.95 (0-226-13443-1) U Ch Pr.

— Life Chances: Approaches to Social & Political Theory. LC 79-18685. 192p. reprint ed. pap. 59.60 (0-608-09440-4, 205424000005) Bks Demand.

— The Modern Social Conflict: An Essay on the Politics of Liberty. 1990. pap. 15.95 (0-520-06861-0, Pub. by U CA Pr) Cal Prin Full Svc.

— On Britain. LC 82-60102. 198p. 1996. pap. text 8.50 (0-226-13410-5) U Ch Pr.

— Out of Utopia: Toward a Reorientation of Sociological Analysis. (Reprint Series in Social Sciences). (C). 1993. reprint ed. pap. text 5.00 (0-8290-2719-X, S-58) Irvington.

— Society & Democracy in Germany. (Modern Revivals in Sociology Ser.). 496p. 1993. 72.95 (0-7512-0117-0, Pub. by Gregg Pub) Ashgate Pub Co.

— Society & Democracy in Germany. LC 79-15142. 457p. 1980. reprint ed. lib. bdg. 75.00 (0-313-22027-1, DASO, Greenwood Pr) Greenwood.

Dahrendorf, Ralf, ed. Europe's Economy in Crisis. 274p. 1982. 37.95 (0-8419-0806-0) Holmes & Meier.

Dahringer, jt. auth. see Mulbacher.

Dai, Bingham. Opium Addiction in Chicago. LC 72-124503. (Criminology, Law Enforcement, & Social Problems Ser.: No. 126). 1970. 26.00 (0-87585-126-6) Patterson Smith.

***Dai, Fan.** Butterfly Lovers: A Tale of the Chinese Romeo & Juliet. LC 99-68429. 250p. 2000. pap. 16.95 (0-9665421-4-2) Homa & Sekey.

Dai, Fan, et al, eds. Virtual Reality for Industrial Applications. LC 97-43400. (Computer Graphics - Systems & Applications Ser.). (Illus.). 500p. 1997. 59.95 (3-540-63348-0) Spr-Verlag.

Dai, H-H. & Sachdev, P. L., eds. Recent Advances in Differnetial Equations. 256p. 1998. ring bd. 64.95 (0-582-32219-7, LM2219, Chap & Hall CRC) CRC Pr.

Dai, H. L. & Field, R. W., eds. Molecular Dynamics & Spectroscopy by Stimulated Emission Pumping. (Advanced Series in Physical Chemistry). 1000p. 1995. text 177.00 (981-02-1749-8) World Scientific Pub.

— Molecular Dynamics & Spectroscopy by Stimulated Emission Pumping. (Advanced Series in Physical Chemistry: Vol. 4). 1000p. 1995. pap. 95.00 (981-02-2111-8) World Scientific Pub.

Dai, H. L. & Ho, W. Laser Spectroscopy & Photochemistry on Metal Surfaces. (Advanced Series in Physical Chemistry). 1995. text 158.00 (981-02-1748-X) World Scientific Pub.

— Laser Spectroscopy & Photochemistry on Metal Surfaces, 2 Pts. 1000p. 1995. text 112.00 (981-02-2998-4) World Scientific Pub.

— Laser Spectroscopy & Photochemistry on Metal Surfaces, 2 vol. set. LC 96-146533. (Advanced Series in Physical Chemistry: Vol. 5). 1000p. 1995. text 112.00 (981-02-2999-2) World Scientific Pub.

Dai, H. L. & Ho, W., eds. Laser Spectroscopy & Photochemistry on Metal Surfaces, Vol. 1. (Advanced Series in Physical Chemistry: Vol. 5). 1000p. 1995. pap. 61.00 (981-02-2996-8) World Scientific Pub.

— Laser Spectroscopy & Photochemistry on Metal Surfaces, Vol. 2. (Advanced Series in Physical Chemistry: Vol. 5). 600p. 1995. pap. 61.00 (981-02-2997-6) World Scientific Pub.

Dai, Hai-Lung & Freund, Hans-Joachim, eds. Laser Techniques for Surface Science III, Vol. 3272. LC 98-233175. 318p. 1998. 80.00 (0-8194-2711-X) SPIE.

Dai, L. Singular Control Systems. (Lecture Notes in Control & Information Sciences: Vol. 118). (Illus.). ix, 332p. 1989. 61.95 (0-387-50724-8) Spr-Verlag.

Dai, Phyllis C. & Miller, Paul E. Having the Mind of Christ: A Years Worth of Prayer, Scripture, Meditation, & Exercise for Spiritual Growth. 376p. (Orig.). 1996. pap. 14.95 (0-687-10941-8) Abingdon.

Dai, Q, et al, eds. Recent Advances of Chemistry & Molecular Biology in Cancer Research: Proceedings from the International Symposium on Recent Advances of Chemistry & Molecular Biology in Cancer Research. xiii, 404 p. 1994. 157.95 (0-387-57384-4) Spr-Verlag.

Dai, Wing-Fu. Ninety-Nine Basic Points for Learners of British English. (Orig.). 1995. pap. 9.95 (0-533-11345-8) Vantage.

Dai, Xingde & Larson, David R. Wandering Vectors for Unitary Systems & Orthogonal Wavelets. LC 98-4219. (Memoirs of the American Mathematical Society Ser.: Vol. 134, No. 640). (Illus.). 68p. 1998. pap. 36.00 (0-8218-0800-1, MEMO/134/640) Am Math.

Dai, Xiudian. Corporate Strategy, Public Policy & New Technologies: Philips & the European Consumer Electronics Industry. (Technology, Innovation, Entrepreneurship, & Competitive Strategy Ser.). 368p. 1996. text 65.50 (0-08-042581-X, Pergamon Pr) Elsevier.

Dai Zovi, Lonnie. Cantos, Rimos y Rimas. (SPA.). 67p. (Orig.). (YA). (gr. 7 up). 1990. pap. 28.50 incl. audio (0-935301-73-9); pap. 30.50 incl. audio compact disk (0-935301-79-8) Vibrante Pr.

— Mariachi... Y Mas. (SPA.). 71p. 1994. pap. 28.50 incl. audio (0-935301-67-4); pap. 31.50 incl. audio compact disk (0-935301-77-1) Vibrante Pr.

— Spanish Alive! Songbook - Cassette, Level I. (Spanish Alive! Spanish for Young Children Ser.). (SPA., Illus.). 33p. (J). (ps-3). 1990. reprint ed. pap. 13.95 incl. audio (0-935301-72-0) Vibrante Pr.

Daianu, Daniel. Transformation of Economy As a Real Process: An Insider's Perspective. LC 98-34300. 4p. 1998. text 68.95 (1-84014-475-0, Pub. by Ashgate Pub) Ashgate Pub Co.

***Daiber, Andreas.** Bekannte Helden in Neuen Gewandern? Intertextuelles Erzahlen im 'Biterolf und Dietleib' Sowie am Beispiel Keies und Gaweins im 'Lanzelet', 'Wigalois' und der 'Crone' (Mikrokosmos. Beitraege zur Literaturwissenschaft und Bedeutungsforschung Ser.). 288p. 1999. 45.95 (3-631-35479-7) P Lang Pubng.

***Daiber, Hans.** Bibliography of Islamic Philosophy, 2 vols. LC 99-31637. (Handbook of Oriental Studies). 1522p. 1999. 463.00 (90-04-11347-9) Brill Academic Pubs.

— Bibliography of Islamic Philosophy , 2 vols. LC 99-31637. (Handbook of Oriental Studies Ser.). 1999. write for info. (90-04-11348-7) Brill Academic Pubs.

Daiber, Hans. Ein Kompendium der Aristolischen Meteorologie der Fassung des Hunain Ibn Ishaq. 122p. pap. 28.25 (0-7204-8302-6) Elsevier.

— Naturwissenschaft bei den Arabern im 10. Jahrhundert n. Chr. Briefe des Abu l-Fadl Ibn al-'Amid, gest. 360-970, an Adudaddaula. LC 92-40571. (Islamic Philosophy, Theology & Science, Studies & Texts Ser.: Vol. 13). (ARA & GER.). vi, 244p. 1993. 60.50 (90-04-09755-4) Brill Academic Pubs.

— Neuplatonische Pythagorica in Arabischem Gewande. 148p. pap. 37.50 (0-444-85784-2) Elsevier.

— The Ruler As Philosopher. (Mededelingen der Koninklijke Nederlandse Akademie van Wetenschappen, Afd. Letterkunde Ser.: No. 49(4)). 1986. pap. text 13.75 (0-444-85657-9) Elsevier.

Daiber, Robert A. Manufacturing Technology Today & Tomorrow. 1990. 38.47 (0-02-675751-6) Glencoe.

Daiber, Robert A. & Erekson. Manufacturing Technology: Today & Tomorrow. 152p. 1999. teacher ed. 10.13 (0-02-675752-4) Glencoe.

— Manufacturing Technology: Today & Tomorrow. (Illus.). 192p. (YA). (gr. 6-12). 1999. student ed., wbk. ed. 8.87 (0-02-675753-2) Glencoe.

— Manufacturing Technology: Today & Tomorrow. annot. ed. 510p. 1999. teacher ed. 44.40 (0-02-675757-5) Glencoe.

Daiches, D., jt. auth. see Gaster, G.

Daiches, David. The King James Version of the English Bible. LC 68-16338. vii, 228p. (C). 1968. reprint ed. lib. bdg. 27.50 (0-208-00493-9, Archon Bks) Shoe String.

— Literature & Society. LC 74-95422. (Studies in Comparative Literature: No. 35). 1970. reprint ed. lib. bdg. 75.00 (0-8383-0970-4) M S G Haskell Hse.

— New Literary Values. LC 68-54342. (Essay Index Reprint Ser.). 1977. 18.95 (0-8369-0358-7) Ayer.

— The Novel & the Modern World. rev. ed. LC 60-11134. xii, 220p. 1984. reprint ed. pap. text 13.00 (0-226-13470-9, Midway Reprint) U Ch Pr.

— Robert Burns the Poet. (C). 1993. pap. 55.00 (0-85411-060-7, Pub. by Saltire Soc) St Mut.

— Scotch Whiskey: Its Past & Present. (Illus.). 192p. 1998. pap. 9.95 (1-874744-36-X, Pub. by Birlinn Ltd) Dufour.

— The Scottish Enlightenment. 48p. 1986. 22.00 (0-85411-032-1, Pub. by Saltire Soc) St Mut.

— A Study of Literature for Readers & Critics. LC 71-152593. 240p. 1972. reprint ed. lib. bdg. 35.00 (0-8371-6026-X, DARC, Greenwood Pr) Greenwood.

— Two Worlds. 224p. 1997. pap. 12.95 (0-86241-704-X, Pub. by Canongate Books) Interlink Pub.

— Virginia Woolf. LC 78-12655. 169p. 1979. reprint ed. lib. bdg. 35.00 (0-313-21187-6, DAVW, Greenwood Pr) Greenwood.

— Willa Cather: A Critical Introduction. LC 71-136061. 193p. 1971. reprint ed. lib. bdg. 35.00 (0-8371-5211-9, DAWC, Greenwood Pr) Greenwood.

Daiches, David, ed. The New Companion to Scottish Culture. 1993. pap. 12.95 (0-7486-6148-4, Pub. by Polygon) Subterranean Co.

Daiches, David & Flower, John. Literary Landscapes of the British Isles: A Narrative Atlas. LC 78-11446. 287p. reprint ed. pap. 89.00 (0-608-16427-5, 202721700054) Bks Demand.

Daiches, David & Jones Staff. The Scottish Enlightenment. 1993. pap. 60.00 (0-85411-069-0, Pub. by Saltire Soc) St Mut.

Daiches, Sol. People in Distress: A Geographical Perspective on Psychological Well-Being. LC 81-4308. (University of Chicago, Department of Geography, Research Paper Ser.: No. 197). 216p. 1981. reprint ed. pap. 67.00 (0-608-02241-1, 206288200004) Bks Demand.

Daichman, Graciela. Wayward Nuns in Medieval Literature. (Illus.). 240p. (Orig.). 1986. pap. text 17.95 (0-8156-2379-8) Syracuse U Pr.

Daichman, Graciela, tr. see Valdivieso, Mercedes.

***Daidoji, Yuzan.** The Code of the Samurai: The Bushido Shoshinshu of Taira Shigesuke. Cleary, Thomas F., tr. from JPN. LC 98-52721. 112p. 1999. 14.95 (0-8048-3190-4) Tuttle Pubng.

Daiei, Kaneko. The Essence of Shin. Steimetz, Calvin, ed. Yokoyama, W. S., tr. from JPN. 100p. (Orig.). (C). 1989. pap. 10.00 (1-877604-01-1) Pure Land.

Daiell, Saralyn, ed. see Dounuts, Kevin.

Daifuku, Alice. Small French & English Lexicon of Animal Physiology & Nutrition: Petit Lexique de Physiologie et de Nutrition Animales. (ENG & FRE.). 52p. 1986. pap. 27.95 (0-8288-0749-3, F25160) Fr & Eur.

Daifuku, H. Jeddito Two Sixty-Four: A Basket Maker Three, Pueblo One Site in Northeastern Arizona. LC 61-2973. (HU PMP Ser.). 1961. 25.00 (0-527-01285-8) Periodicals Srv.

Daigger, Glen T. & Buttz, John A. Upgrading Wastewater Treatment Plants. 2nd ed. (Water Quality Management Library: Vol. 2). 256p. 1998. 104.95 (1-56676-644-3) Technomic.

Daigle, A., jt. auth. see Maranda, D.

Daigle, Alan, jt. auth. see Zimmer, Gregory R.

Daigle, Barbara. HIV Homecare Handbook. LC 98-43154. (Jones & Bartlett Oncology Ser.). 382p. 1998. 33.75 (0-7637-0703-1) Jones & Bartlett.

***Daigle, France.** Just Fine. Majzels, Robert, tr. from FRE. 1999. pap. 14.95 (0-88784-639-4, Pub. by Hse1 of Anansi) Genl Dist Srvs.

Daigle, France. 1953: Chronicle of a Birth Foretold. Majzels, Robert, tr. from FRE. LC 98-104627. (ENG & FRE.). 176p. 1999. pap. 13.95 (0-88784-604-1) Genl Dist Srvs.

— Real Life. Ross, Sally, tr. LC 95-194223. 96p. 1995. pap. text 10.95 (0-88784-561-4, Pub. by Hse of Anansi Pr) Genl Dist Srvs.

Daigle, Gilles A. & Stinson, Michael R., eds. Proceedings of the International Conference on Noise Control Engineering Held July 20-22, 1992, in Toronto, Canada, Vols. 1 & 2. (Inter-Noise Ser.). lxiv, 1264p. 125.00 (0-931784-25-5) Noise Control.

Daigle, Jules O. Cajun Self-Taught: Learning to Speak the Cajun Language. 2nd ed. (FRE.). 540p. 1992. 31.95 (0-9614245-4-0) Swallow Pubns.

— A Dictionary of the Cajun Language. 6th ed. (FRE.). 632p. 1984. 30.00 (0-9614245-3-2) Swallow Pubns.

Daigle, Lesley. Child Welfare Services along the U. S.-Mexico Border. (Working Paper Ser.: No. 74). 74p. 1994. pap. 5.50 (0-89940-556-8) LBJ Sch Pub Aff.

Daigle, Leslie L., jt. auth. see Faltstrom, Patrik.

Daigle, Marsha, tr. see Fuchs, Eric.

Daigle, Paul H. Perkins Formerly of Hillmorton. (Illus.). 385p. 1997. pap. 68.50 (0-8328-9487-7); lib. bdg. 58.50 (0-8328-9486-9) Higginson Bk Co.

Daigle, Pierre V. Tears, Love & Laughter: The Story of the Cajuns & Their Music. 4th rev. ed. 160p. 1987. pap. 9.95 (0-9614245-1-6) Swallow Pubns.

Daigle, Rufus, ed. & illus. see Sufur.

Daigler, Robert T. Advanced Options Trading: The Analysis & Evaluation of Trading Strategies Hedging Tactics & Pricing Models. LC 94-138106. 325p. 1993. text 55.00 (1-55738-552-1, Irwn Prfssnl) McGraw-Hill Prof.

— Managing Risk with Financial Futures: Pricing, Hedging & Arbitrage. 375p. 1993. text 65.00 (1-55738-455-X, 455, Irwn Prfssnl) McGraw-Hill Prof.

Daignault, Daniel. Goalies: Guardians of the Net. (Illus.). 304p. 1996. 45.00 (1-55013-745-X) Firefly Bks Ltd.

Daignault, Frank. Striper Hot Spots. 2nd rev. ed. LC 96-23060. (Illus.). 256p. 1996. pap. 14.95 (1-56440-994-5) Globe Pequot.

— Striper Surf. LC 91-30129. (Illus.). 272p. 1996. pap. 16.95 (1-56440-278-9) Globe Pequot.

— The Trophy Striper. LC 99-32060. (Illus.). 192p. 1999. pap. 16.95 (1-58080-040-8) Burford Bks.

***Daignault, Taylor.** An Offer of Truth. (Another Great American First Novel Ser.: Vol. 9). 320p. 2000. 24.95 (0-947993-89-4, Pub. by Mlvrn Pubg Co) Brit Bk Co Inc.

Daigneault, Aubert, jt. auth. see Broer, A.

***Daigneault, Sylvie.** Bruno & the Bees. (J). 2000. pap. 6.99 (0-00-648145-0) HarpC Child Bks.

D

— Bruno Falls Asleep. (Bruno Bks.). (J). 2000. 16.00 (0-00-224557-4) HarpC Child Bks.

Daigon, Ruth. Between One Future & the Next. LC 94-38906. 128p. 1995. 12.00 (0-918949-67-X); pap. 8.00 (0-918949-66-1) Daigon.

***Daigon, Ruth.** The Moon Inside. (Contemporary Poetry Ser.: Vol. 1). 96p. 1999. pap. 11.95 (0-9667228-3-3) Newtons Baby.

Daihl, Richard E. Christian Faith in 3D: Why Today's Christians Are Disillusioned, Deceived & Divided. large type ed. LC 97-91284. 160p. 1998. pap. 10.95 (0-9661705-0-4) Words of Wisdom.

Daiken, Leslie. Children's Games Throughout the Year. LC 75-35067. (Studies in Play & Games). (Illus.). 1976. reprint ed. 25.95 (0-405-07918-4) Ayer.

Daiker, Donald, et al. New Directions in Portfolio Assessment: Reflective Practice, Critical Theory & Large-Scale Scoring. LC 93-43350. 367p. (Orig.). 1994. pap. text 27.50 (0-86709-338-2, 0338, Pub. by Boynton Cook Pubs) Heinemann.

Daiker, Donald A., et al, eds. Sentence Combining: A Rhetorical Perspective. LC 84-14026. 408p. 1985. 21.95 (0-8093-1191-7) S Ill U Pr.

Daiker, Donald A. & Morenberg, Max, eds. The Writing Teacher As Researcher: Essays in the Theory & Practice of Class-Based Research. LC 89-36957. 357p. (Orig.). (C). 1990. pap. text 27.50 (0-86709-255-6, 0255, Pub. by Boynton Cook Pubs) Heinemann.

Daiker, Donald A., et al. Literature: Options for Reading & Writing. 2nd ed. 1328p. (C). 1997. pap. text 59.00 (0-06-041483-9) Addson-Wesley Educ.

Dail. Pulmonary Pathology. 2nd ed. LC 92-2383. (Illus.). 1640p. 1993. 330.00 (0-387-97897-6) Spr-Verlag.

Dail, C. W. & Thomas, C. S. Simple Remedies for the Home. LC 91-61468. (Illus.). 158p. (Orig.). 1991. per. 11.95 (0-945383-30-4, 945-5820) Teach Servs.

Dail, Clarence & Thomas, Charles. Hydrotherapy: Simple Treatments for Common Ailments. rev. ed. LC 89-50071. (Illus.). 160p. (Orig.). 1996. per. 8.95 (0-945383-08-8, 945-5813) Teach Servs.

Dail, D. H. & Hammar, Samuel P., eds. Pulmonary Pathology. (Illus.). 1190p. 1987. 267.00 (0-387-96491-6) Spr-Verlag.

Dail, David H., et al. Pulmonary Pathology. 2nd ed. LC 94-17331. (Illus.). 1608p. 1995. 165.00 (0-387-94315-3) Spr-Verlag.

Dail, Laura, tr. see Taibo, Paco I., II.

Dail, Laura C., tr. see Taibo, Paco I., II.

Dail, Paula W. & Jewson, Ruth H., eds. In Praise of Fifty Years: The Groves Conference on the Conservation of Marriage & the Family. LC 85-91444. 156p. (Orig.). 1986. pap. 8.95 (0-89279-079-2) Graphic Pub.

Dail, Shirley M. Jesus Said "Leave Her Alone" (Illus.). 1979. pap. 2.95 (0-9602440-0-X) Jesus-First.

Daileader, Celia R. Eroticism on the Renaissance Stage: Transcendence, Desire, & the Limits of the Visible. LC 97-47555. (Cambridge Studies in Renaissance Literature & Culture: No. 30). (Illus.). 200p. (C). 1998. 49.95 (0-521-62379-0) Cambridge U Pr.

Dailer, Stephen, jt. contrib. by see Danziger, James.

***Dailey.** Electronic Devices & Circuitry. (Illus.). 2001. text. write for info. (0-13-081110-6) P-H.

Dailey. Scrooge Wore Spurs. 1997. per. 6.99 (1-55166-293-0, Mira Bks) Harlequin Bks.

***Dailey, Barbara Pfister & Pfister, Pamela.** Ruston, Louisiana. (Images of America Ser.). (Illus.). 128p. 2000. pap. 18.99 (0-7385-0584-6) Arcadia Publng.

***Dailey, D. C.** Guns Are Not for Fun. (Illus.). 34p. (J). (gr. 1-3). 1999. pap. 3.75 (1-929662-00-9) Brighter Horizons.

— Guns Are Not for Fun: Educators Edition. (Illus.). 38p. 1999. pap. 4.50 (1-929662-01-7) Brighter Horizons.

— Use Your Brains Stay Out of Gangs. (Illus.). 37p. (J). (gr. 1-3). 1999. pap. 3.75 (1-929662-02-5) Brighter Horizons.

— Use Your Brains Stay Out of Gangs: Educators Edition. Boudreau, Dawn, tr. (Illus.). 41p. 1999. pap. 4.50 (1-929662-03-3) Brighter Horizons.

Dailey, Daniel J., jt. auth. see Elliott, Scott D.

Dailey, Dennis M. The Sexually Unusual: Guide to Understanding & Helping. LC 88-24668. (Journal of Social Work & Human Sexuality: Vol. 7, No. 1). (Illus.). 169p. 1989. pap. text 14.95 (0-918393-63-9, Harrington Park) Haworth Pr.

Dailey, Dennis M., ed. The Sexually Unusual: Guide to Understanding & Helping. LC 88-15292. (Journal of Social Work & Human Sexuality: Vol. 7, No. 1). (Illus.). 169p. 1989. text 39.95 (0-86656-786-0) Haworth Pr.

Dailey, Denton J. Operational Amplifiers & Linear Integrated Circuits: Theory & Applications. (C). 1989. text 78.92 (0-07-039931-X) McGraw.

Dailey, Dianne K., ed. Environmental Damage Claims & Property Insurance Coverage: Issues under First-Party Policies. LC 96-79113. 360p. 1996. pap. 59.95 (1-57073-417-8, 519-0263, ABA Tort) Amer Bar Assn.

***Dailey, Donna.** Insight Pocket Guide Denver with Map. (Illus.). 2000. pap. 12.95 (1-58573-011-4, Insight Guides) Langenscheidt.

— Ireland. LC 99-89670. (Thomas Cook Signpost Guides Ser.). (Illus.). 1999. pap. 22.95 (0-7627-0682-1) Globe Pequot.

— Signpost Guide: Scotland. 2000. pap. 22.95 (0-7627-0679-1) Globe Pequot.

Dailey, Donna, text. Los Angeles: Pocket Guide. LC 99-222004. 1999. pap. text 8.95 (2-8315-6327-5) Berlitz.

Dailey, Dwight M. Concert Pieces for the Tenor Saxophone. 1983. pap. 13.00 (0-911586-07-5) Wahr.

Dailey, E. J. Practical Muskrat Raising. (Illus.). 136p. pap. 4.00 (0-936622-17-2) A R Harding Pub.

Dailey, Frank. The Complete Guide to Data Storage Technologies for Network-Centric Computing. (Illus.). 242p. 1997. pap. 275.00 (1-56607-995-0) Comput Tech Res.

***Dailey, Franklyn E., Jr.** Joining the War at Sea, 1939-1945. 2nd unabridged aut. ed. LC 99-188572. (Illus.). 460p. 1999. pap. 21.95 (0-9666251-0-2) Dailey Intl Pub.

— My Times with the Sisters: And Other Events. unabridged ed. (Illus.). vi, 134p. 2000. per. 9.50 (0-9666251-1-0) Dailey Intl Pub.

Dailey, Franklyn E., Jr. & Rosenthal, Morris. Electronic Imaging Applications & Markets: Desktop Publishing, Electronic Document Management, Multimedia Publishing. Lindgren, Brian J., ed. (Illus.). 124p. (Orig.). 1996. pap. 125.00 (0-9648176-1-6) Pink Hse.

Dailey, Fred. Polo Is a Four Letter Word. pap. 7.95 (0-914916-77-7) Ku Paa.

Dailey, G. Wayne. Next Door to Power. Date not set. 24.95 (0-8488-2088-6); pap. 14.95 (0-8488-2089-4) Amereon Ltd.

— Next Door to Power: Human Interest Stories about 45 Vice Presidents. (Illus.). 268p. (Orig.). 1997. pap. 11.95 (0-9653544-0-7) G W Dailey.

Dailey, Gene. Secrets of a Successful Entrepreneur: How to Start & Succeed at Running Your Own Business. LC 93-91403. 352p. 1993. pap. 24.95 (1-883635-01-2) K & A Pubns.

Dailey, J. R. The Yellow Ribbon Snake. LC 99-22460. 144p. 2000. pap. 12.00 (1-880284-37-5, Pub. by J Daniel) SCB Distributors.

***Dailey, Jane.** Before Jim Crow: The Politics of Race in Postemancipation Virginia. (Gender & American Culture Ser.). (Illus.). 288p. 2000. pap. 17.95 (0-8078-4901-4); lib. bdg. 39.95 (0-8078-2587-5) U of NC Pr.

***Dailey, Jane E.** Jumpin' Jim Crow: Southern Politics from Civil War to Civil Rights. LC 00-27861. (Illus.). 280p. 2000. 55.00 (0-691-00192-8) Princeton U Pr.

***Dailey, Jane Elizabeth, et al.** Jumpin' Jim Crow: Southern Politics from Civil War to Civil Rights. LC 00-27861. 280p. 2000. pap. 17.95 (0-691-00193-6) Princeton U Pr.

Dailey, Janet. Alabama - Dangerous Masquerade. (Janet Dailey Americana Ser.: No. 1). 1991. per. 3.50 (0-373-89851-7) Harlequin Bks.

— Alaska - Northern Magic. (Janet Dailey Americana Ser.: No. 2). 1991. per. 3.50 (0-373-89852-5) Harlequin Bks.

— Arizona - Sonora Sundown. (Janet Dailey Americana Ser.: No. 3). 1991. per. 3.50 (0-373-89853-3) Harlequin Bks.

— Arkansas Valley of the Vapours. (Janet Dailey Americana Ser.: No. 4). 1991. per. 3.50 (0-373-89854-1) Harlequin Bks.

— Aspen Gold. 416p. 1992. mass mkt. 5.99 (0-316-17153-0) Little.

***Dailey, Janet.** Bed of Grass. LC 00-34368. 2000. write for info. (0-7862-2692-7) Thorndike Pr.

Dailey, Janet. The Best Way to Lose. 1993. mass mkt. 5.99 (0-671-87499-3) PB.

— Beware of the Stranger. (Janet Dailey Americana Ser.: No. 882). 1992. per. 3.59 (0-373-89882-7, 1-89882-4) Harlequin Bks.

— Big Sky Country. (Janet Dailey Americana Ser.: No. 876). 1992. per. 3.59 (0-373-89876-2, 1-89876-6) Harlequin Bks.

Dailey, Janet. Bluegrass King. LC 77-368790. 187p. 1977. write for info. (0-263-09130-9, Pub. by Mills & Boon) Chivers N Amer.

Dailey, Janet. Boss Man from Ogallala. (Janet Dailey Americana Ser.: No. 877). 1992. per. 3.59 (0-373-89877-0, 1-89877-4) Harlequin Bks.

— Calder Born, Calder Bred. (Orig.). 1999. pap. 26.00 (0-7278-5469-0, Pub. by Severn Hse) Chivers N Amer.

— Calder Born, Calder Bred, 4. (Orig.). 1999. pap. 6.99 (0-671-04049-9) PB.

— Calder Pride. LC 97-23991. 368p. 1999. 23.95 (0-06-017699-7) HarpC.

***Dailey, Janet.** Calder Pride. 416p. 2000. mass mkt. 7.50 (0-06-109459-5, HarpTorch) Morrow Avon.

— Calder Pride. large type ed. 560p. 1999. pap. 23.95 (0-06-093302-X) HarpC.

Dailey, Janet. California - Fire & Ice. (Janet Dailey Americana Ser.: No. 5). 1991. per. 3.50 (0-373-89855-X) Harlequin Bks.

— Colorado - After the Storm. (Janet Dailey Americana Ser.: No. 6). 1991. per. 3.50 (0-373-89856-8) Harlequin Bks.

— Dakota Dreamin' (Janet Dailey Americana Ser.). 1992. per. 3.59 (0-373-89891-6, 1-89891-5) Harlequin Bks.

Dailey, Janet. Dangerous Masquerade. large type ed. LC 77-376625. 186p. 1976. write for info. (0-263-06059-4, Pub. by Mills & Boon) Chivers N Amer.

Dailey, Janet. Darling Jenny. (Americana Ser.). 1993. mass mkt. 3.59 (0-373-89900-9, 1-89900-4) Harlequin Bks.

— Difficult Decision. (Janet Dailey Americana Ser.: No. 7). 1991. per. 3.50 (0-373-89857-6) Harlequin Bks.

— Enemy in Camp. (Americana Ser.: No. 872). 1991. per. 3.59 (0-373-89872-X) Harlequin Bks.

***Dailey, Janet.** Enemy in Camp. large type ed. LC 99-16095. 1999. 27.95 (0-7862-2064-3, G K Hall Lrg Type) Mac Lib Ref.

Dailey, Janet. Father Christmas. (Superromance Ser.: No. 767). 1979. per. 1.25 (0-373-70767-3, 1-70767-8) Harlequin Bks.

— Fiesta San Antonio. 1991. mass mkt. 3.50 (0-373-83234-6) Harlequin Bks.

— Fire & Ice, Set. abr. ed. (Best of the Best Ser.). 1995. pap. 11.99 incl. audio (0-373-15295-7) Harlequin Bks.

— For Bitter or Worse. 1991. mass mkt. 3.50 (0-373-83235-4) Harlequin Bks.

— For Mike's Sake. 1993. per. 3.59 (0-373-89897-5, 1-89897-2) Harlequin Bks.

— For the Love of God. 1994. mass mkt. 6.50 (0-671-87501-9) PB.

— Foxfire Light. 1993. mass mkt. 5.99 (0-671-87502-7, PB Trade Paper) PB.

— The Glory Game. 1993. mass mkt. 6.99 (0-671-87503-5, PB Trade Paper) PB.

— The Great Alone. 1987. per. 6.99 (0-671-87504-3) PB.

— The Great Alone. 1997. pap. 14.00 (0-671-01932-5, PB Trade Paper) PB.

— Green Mountain Man. 1992. per. 3.59 (0-373-89895-9, 1-89895-6) Harlequin Bks.

— Green Mountain Man. large type ed. LC 99-34246. 2000. pap. 30.00 (0-7862-2072-4) Mac Lib Ref.

— The Healing Touch. LC 94-18397. (Janet Dailey's Love Scenes Ser.). 1994. 3.50 (1-56420-099-X) New Readers.

— Heart of Stone. (Janet Dailey Americana Ser.: No. 879). 1992. per. 3.59 (0-373-89879-7, 1-89879-0) Harlequin Bks.

— Heiress. 1988. mass mkt. 6.99 (0-449-13436-9, GM) Fawcett.

Dailey, Janet. Heiress. 470p. pap. write for info. (1-58754-102-5, Pub. by Olmstead Pr) LPC Group.

— The Homeplace. large type ed. LC 99-33011. (Core Ser.). 192p. 2000. 29.95 (0-7838-8686-1, G K Hall Lrg Type) Mac Lib Ref.

Dailey, Janet. Honourable Friends. large type ed. 1990. 27.99 (0-7089-2295-3) Ulverscroft.

— The Hostage Bride. 1984. mass mkt. 4.99 (0-671-87505-1) PB.

— Illusions. large type ed. LC 97-15892. (Wheeler Large Print Book Ser.). 1997. 26.95 (1-56895-455-7) Wheeler Pub.

— Illusions: A Novel. 464p. 1999. mass mkt. 6.99 (0-06-109460-9) HarpC.

— The Indy Man. (Americana Ser.: No. 864). 1991. per. 3.50 (0-373-89864-9) Harlequin Bks.

— Iowa the Homeplace. (Janet Dailey Americana Ser.: No. 15). 1991. per. 3.59 (0-373-89865-7) Harlequin Bks.

— Kansas the Mating Season. (Janet Dailey Americana Ser.: No. 16). 1991. per. 3.59 (0-373-89866-5) Harlequin Bks.

— Kona Winds. (Americana Ser.: No. 861). 1991. per. 3.50 (0-373-89861-4) Harlequin Bks.

— The Lancaster Men. 1994. mass mkt. 4.99 (0-671-87506-X) PB.

— A Land Called Deseret. 1992. per. 3.59 (0-373-89894-0, 1-89894-9) Harlequin Bks.

— Land of Enchantment. (Janet Dailey Americana Ser.: No. 881). 1992. per. 3.59 (0-373-89881-9, 1-89881-6) Harlequin Bks.

— Leftover Love. 1993. per. 6.99 (0-671-87507-8, PB Trade Paper) PB.

— Legacies. 1995. 22.95 (0-614-15482-0) Little.

— Legacies. 400p. 1996. mass mkt. 6.99 (0-446-60348-1, Pub. by Warner Bks) Little.

— Legacies. large type ed. (Wheeler Large Print Bks.). 1996. 26.95 (1-56895-295-3) Wheeler Pub.

— Lord of the High Lonesome. (Janet Dailey Americana Ser.: No. 884). 1992. per. 3.59 (0-373-89884-3, 1-89884-0) Harlequin Bks.

— Low Country Liar. 1992. per. 3.59 (0-373-89890-8, 1-89890-7) Harlequin Bks.

— A Lyon's Share. (Americana Ser.: No. 863). 1991. per. 3.50 (0-373-89863-0) Harlequin Bks.

— A Lyon's Share. LC 99-34773. 2000. pap. 30.00 (0-7862-2073-2) Thorndike Pr.

— Maine Summer Mahogany. (Janet Dailey Americana Ser.: No. 19). 1991. per. 3.59 (0-373-89869-X) Harlequin Bks.

— Maryland Bed of Grass. (Janet Dailey Americana Ser.: No. 20). 1991. per. 3.59 (0-373-89870-3) Harlequin Bks.

— Masquerade. 384p. 1991. mass mkt. 5.95 (0-316-17147-6) Little.

— The Master Fiddler. 1991. mass mkt. 3.50 (0-373-83230-3) Harlequin Bks.

***Dailey, Janet.** The Master Fiddler. large type ed. LC 99-31431. 1999. pap. 28.95 (0-7838-8678-0, G K Hall Lrg Type) Mac Lib Ref.

Dailey, Janet. Matchmakers. (Janet Dailey Americana Ser.: No. 8). 1991. per. 3.50 (0-373-89858-4) Harlequin Bks.

— Mistletoe & Holly. 1993. mass mkt. 4.99 (0-671-87508-6, Pocket Books) PB.

Dailey, Janet. The Night of the Cotillion. large type ed. LC 77-376591. 188p. (J). 1976. write for info. (0-263-09032-9, Pub. by Mills & Boon) Chivers N Amer.

Dailey, Janet. Nightway. 1993. per. 6.99 (0-671-87509-4) PB.

— No Quarter Asked. 1991. mass mkt. 3.50 (0-373-83233-8) Harlequin Bks.

— Notorious. 1995. 24.00 (0-614-96256-0) HarpC.

— Notorious. large type ed. LC 96-16390. 1996. lib. bdg. 26.95 (0-7862-0707-8) Thorndike Pr.

— Notorious. large type ed. LC 96-16390. 550p. 1997. pap. 24.95 (0-7862-0706-X) Thorndike Pr.

— One of the Boys. (Janet Dailey Americana Ser.: No. 880). 1992. per. 3.59 (0-373-89880-0, 1-89880-8) Harlequin Bks.

***Dailey, Janet.** One of the Boys. LC 00-33500. 2001. write for info. (0-7838-9119-9, G K Hall & Co) Mac Lib Ref.

Dailey, Janet. The Pride of Hannah Wade. 1994. mass mkt. 5.99 (0-671-87510-8) PB.

— The Prodigal Daughter. (Superromance Ser.). 1979. per. 1.25 (0-373-70775-4, 1-70775-1) Harlequin Bks.

— The Proud & the Free. large type ed. LC 94-42585. 647 p. 1995. 26.95 (1-56895-167-1) Wheeler Pub.

— Reilly's Woman. (Janet Dailey Americana Ser.: No. 878). 1992. per. 3.59 (0-373-89878-9, 1-89878-2) Harlequin Bks.

— Reilly's Woman. large type ed. (Nightingale Ser.). 200p. 1990. pap. 14.95 (0-8161-4964-X, G K Hall Lrg Type) Mac Lib Ref.

— Ride the Thunder. 1993. mass mkt. 5.99 (0-671-87511-6) PB.

— Riding High. LC 94-18547. (Janet Dailey's Love Scenes Ser.). 1994. pap. 3.50 (1-56420-098-1) New Readers.

— Rivals. 448p. 1990. mass mkt. 6.99 (0-449-14613-8, GM) Fawcett.

— The Rogue. 1993. mass mkt. 5.99 (0-671-87512-4) PB.

— Savage Land. 1992. per. 3.59 (0-373-89893-2, 1-89893-1) Harlequin Bks.

— Savage Land. large type ed. LC 99-34465. 1999. pap. 28.95 (0-7862-2074-0) Mac Lib Ref.

— The Second Time. 1994. mass mkt. 4.99 (0-671-87513-2) PB.

— Sentimental Journey. (Janet Dailey Americana Ser.). 1992. per. 3.59 (0-373-89892-4, 1-89892-3) Harlequin Bks.

— Separate Cabins. 1994. mass mkt. 4.99 (0-671-87514-0) PB.

— Show Me. (Janet Dailey Americana Ser.: No. 875). 1992. per. 3.59 (0-373-89875-4, 1-89875-8) Harlequin Bks.

***Dailey, Janet.** Show Me. LC 00-31959. 2000. 0.00 (0-7838-9111-3, G K Hall & Co) Mac Lib Ref.

— Show Me. large type ed. LC 77-355748. 188p. (J). 1976. write for info. (0-263-72273-2, Pub. by Mills & Boon) Chivers N Amer.

Dailey, Janet. Silver Wings Santiago Blue. 1994. pap. 6.50 (0-671-87515-9) PB.

Dailey, Janet. Six White Horses. large type ed. LC 77-378561. 188p. (J). 1977. write for info. (0-263-09116-3, Pub. by Mills & Boon) Chivers N Amer.

Dailey, Janet. Something Extra. 1991. mass mkt. 3.50 (0-373-83231-1) Harlequin Bks.

***Dailey, Janet.** Southern Nights. large type ed. LC 99-33016. 193p. 2000. pap. 30.00 (0-7838-8685-3) Mac Lib Ref.

— A Spring Bouquet. 2000. mass mkt. 6.99 (0-8217-6612-0, Zebra Kensgtn) Kensgtn Pub Corp.

Dailey, Janet. Stands a Calder Man. 1993. mass mkt. 6.99 (0-671-87516-7) PB.

— Stands a Calder Man. (Calder Saga Ser.: Vol. 2). 432p. 1998. 26.00 (0-7278-5383-X) Severn Hse.

— Stands a Calder Man, 2. 1999. per. 6.99 (0-671-04050-2) PB.

— Strange Bedfellow. 1992. per. 3.59 (0-373-89889-4, 1-89889-9) Harlequin Bks.

***Dailey, Janet.** Strange Bedfellow. LC 00-42566. 2000. write for info. (0-7862-2745-1) Thorndike Pr.

Dailey, Janet. Summer Mahogany. large type ed. 218p. 1995. 20.95 (0-7862-0349-8) Thorndike Pr.

— Sweet Promise. 1991. mass mkt. 3.50 (0-373-83232-X) Harlequin Bks.

— Sweet Promise. 1996. mass mkt. 5.99 (0-373-83329-6, 1-83329-2) Harlequin Bks.

— Tangled Vines. 448p. 1993. mass mkt. 5.99 (0-316-17163-8) Little.

— Terms of Surrender. 1993. mass mkt. 5.99 (0-671-87519-1) PB.

***Dailey, Janet.** That Boston Man. LC 00-33491. 2000. write for info. (0-7838-9122-9, G K Hall & Co) Mac Lib Ref.

Dailey, Janet. That Carolina Summer. (Janet Dailey Americana Ser.: No. 883). 1992. per. 3.59 (0-373-89883-5, 1-89883-2) Harlequin Bks.

***Dailey, Janet.** That Carolina Summer. LC 00-33489. 2001. write for info. (0-7838-9123-7, G K Hall & Co) Mac Lib Ref.

Dailey, Janet. The Thawing of Mara. (Americana Ser.: No. 888). 1992. per. 3.59 (0-373-89888-6) Harlequin Bks.

— This Calder Range. 1993. mass mkt. 6.99 (0-671-87517-5) PB.

— This Calder Range. 448p. 1998. pap. 25.00 (0-7278-5291-4) Severn Hse.

— This Calder Range, 1. Vol. 1. 1999. per. 6.99 (0-671-04048-0) PB.

— This Calder Sky. write for info. PB.

— This Calder Sky. 1993. mass mkt. 6.99 (0-671-87518-3) PB.

— This Calder Sky. 496p. 1999. 26.00 (0-7278-5401-1, Pub. by Severn Hse) Chivers N Amer.

***Dailey, Janet.** This Calder Sky. large type ed. 560p. 1999. 31.99 (0-7505-1327-6, Pub. by Mgna Lrg Print) Ulverscroft.

Dailey, Janet. This Calder Sky, 3. 1999. per. 6.99 (0-671-04051-0) PB.

— Tidewater Lover. 1992. per. 3.59 (0-373-89896-7, 1-89896-4) Harlequin Bks.

***Dailey, Janet.** Tidewater Lover. LC 00-33490. 2000. write for info. (0-7838-9124-5, G K Hall & Co) Mac Lib Ref.

Dailey, Janet. To Tell the Truth. (Americana Ser.: No. 887). 1992. per. 3.59 (0-373-89887-8) Harlequin Bks.

— Touch the Wind. 304p. 1994. reprint ed. per. 5.99 (0-671-87520-5) PB.

— A Tradition of Pride. (Americana Ser.: No. 874). 1992. mass mkt. 3.59 (0-373-89874-6) Harlequin Bks.

— The Travelling Kind. (Americana Ser.: No. 862). 1991. per. 3.50 (0-373-89862-2) Harlequin Bks.

***Dailey, Janet.** The Travelling Kind. large type ed. LC 99-33010. 2000. pap. 30.00 (0-7838-8684-5) Mac Lib Ref.

— Valley of the Vapours. large type ed. LC 77-357207. 187p. (J). 1976. write for info. (0-263-06097-7, Pub. by Mills & Boon) Chivers N Amer.

Dailey, Janet. Western Man. 1993. mass mkt. 5.99 (0-671-87521-3) PB.

— Western Man. 1988. pap. 3.50 (0-671-68178-8) S&S Trade.

— The Widow & the Wastrel. (Americana Ser.: No. 885). 1992. mass mkt. 3.59 (0-373-89885-1) Harlequin Bks.

— Wild Action. 1978. per. 1.25 (0-373-70748-7, 1-70748-8) Harlequin Bks.

— Wild & Wonderful. 1993. per. 3.59 (0-373-89898-3, 1-89898-0) Harlequin Bks.

An Asterisk (*) at the beginning of an entry indicates that the title is appearing for the first time.

— Wild & Wonderful. large type ed. LC 99-33138. 208p. 1999. 27.95 (*0-7862-2058-9*) Mac Lib Ref.

— With a Little Luck. (Americana Ser.). 1993. per. 3.59 (*0-373-89899-1*, 1-89899-8) Harlequin Bks.

***Dailey, Janet.** With a Little Luck. large type ed. LC 99-32483. 1999. 26.95 (*0-7838-8680-2*, G K Hall Lrg Type) Mac Lib Ref.

Dailey, Janet, et al. Flower Girls. 1996. mass mkt. 5.99 (*0-312-95940-0*) St Martin.

— Homecoming: Homecoming. 384p. 1997. mass mkt. 5.99 (*0-06-108508-1*) HarpC.

— Santa's Little Helpers. (Orig.). 1995. per. 4.99 (*0-373-48311-2*, 5-48311-0) Harlequin Bks.

— A Spring Bouquet. LaFarge, Ann, ed. 1996. pap. text 6.99 (*0-8217-5309-6*, Zebra Kensgtn) Kensgtn Pub Corp.

— Summer Lovers: Strange Bedfellows; First, Best & Only; Granite Man. (Harlequin Promotion Ser.). 1997. per. 9.99 (*0-373-83352-0*, 1-883352-4) Harlequin Bks.

Dailey, Janet, jt. auth. see Gage, Elizabeth.

Dailey, Joel. Lower 48. (Illus.). 96p. 1999. pap. 9.00 (*0-9663846-2-8*) Lavender Ink.

— Public Storage. unabridged ed. (Modern Poetry in English Ser.: No. 46). (Illus.). 28p. 1995. pap. 5.00 (*1-879457-49-0*) Norton Coker Pr.

Dailey, John F. Blood. Manley, Jane E., ed. LC 98-91736. (Illus.). 576p. 1998. per. 54.00 (*0-9631819-5-5*, BLD1) Med Cnslt Grp.

— Dailey's Notes on Blood. 2nd ed. (Illus.). 178p. (Orig.). (C). 1998. pap. text 18.00 (*0-7881-5232-7*) DIANE Pub.

— Dailey's Notes on Blood. 3rd ed. Manley, Jane E., ed. LC 93-214993. (Illus.). 173p. (Orig.). 1996. pap. text 24.00 (*0-9631819-4-7*, DNB3) Med Cnslt Grp.

Dailey, Jonathan D. The Journey Worth Taking. (Illus.). 288p. (C). 1993. 24.95 (*1-880047-12-8*); pap. text 12.95 (*1-880047-09-8*) Creative Des.

Dailey, Mary B. Getting Ready for Grade 1. (Home Workbooks Ser.). (Illus.). 64p. (Orig.). (J). (gr. 1). 1996. pap., wbk. ed. 2.49 (*0-88724-359-2*, CD-6856) Carson-Dellos.

— Grade 1 Activities. (Home Workbooks Ser.). (Illus.). 64p. (Orig.). (J). (gr. 1). 1996. pap., wbk. ed. 2.49 (*0-88724-360-6*, CD-6857) Carson-Dellos.

Dailey, Murray D., et al, eds. Ecology of the Southern California Bight: A Synthesis & Interpretation. LC 93-34699. 1993. 125.00 (*0-520-07578-1*, Pub. by U CA Pr) Cal Prin Full Svc.

Dailey, Nancy. When Baby Boom Women Retire. LC 97-27003. 168p. 1998. 55.00 (*0-275-96070-6*, Praeger Pubs) Greenwood.

***Dailey, Nancy.** When Baby Boom Women Retire. 160p. 2000. pap. 19.95 (*0-275-97097-3*, Praeger Trade) Greenwood.

Dailey, Nils L. Profiles in Management: Roles of the Value-Adding Manager. Cannarella, Deborah, ed. (Illus.). 100p. (Orig.). 1987. pap. text 14.95 (*0-941837-00-9*) N L Dailey Assocs.

Dailey, Pat. The New Pressure Cooker Cookbook. (Illus.). 160p. 1990. pap. 14.95 (*0-8092-4186-2*, 418620, Contemporary Bks) NTC Contemp Pub Co.

Dailey, Ralph. They Call Me Black Magic. 322p. 1998. pap. write for info. (*1-57502-946-4*, PO2306) Morris Pubng.

Dailey, Sheila. Putting the World in a Nutshell: The Art of the Formula Tale. LC 94-829. 126p. 1994. 35.00 (*0-8242-0860-9*) Wilson.

— Tales As Tools: The Power of Storytelling in the Classroom. 224p. 1994. pap. 19.95 (*1-879991-15-2*) Natl Storytlng Network.

Dailey, Stephanie, tr. see Seleskovitch, Danica.

Dailey, Thomas F. Bibliographies for Biblical Research Vol. XIII: The Book of Job. LC 97-45906. (Old Testament Ser.). 168p. 1997. text 59.95 (*0-7734-2437-7*) E Mellen.

— Parying with Francis de Sales. Koch, Carl, ed. LC 98-130091. (Companions for the Journey Ser.). (Illus.). 120p. 1997. pap. 8.95 (*0-88489-495-9*) St Marys.

— The Repentant Job: A Ricoeurian Icon for Biblical Theology. LC 94-21285. 256p. (Orig.). (C). 1994. reprint ed. pap. text 32.50 (*0-8191-9590-1*); reprint ed. lib. bdg. 59.50 (*0-8191-9589-8*) U Pr of Amer.

Dailey, Thomas V., jt. auth. see Church, Kevin E.

Dailey, Timothy J. Healing Through the Power of Prayer LC 97-67159. 256 p. 1997. write for info. (*0-7853-2434-8*) Pubns Intl Ltd.

— The Millennial Deception: Angels, Aliens & the Antichrist. LC 95-16266. 240p. (gr. 10). 1995. pap. 11.99 (*0-8007-9233-5*) Chosen Bks.

— Muhammad Ali: The Greatest of All Time. 224p. 1999. mass mkt. 5.99 (*0-451-19784-4*) NAL.

Dailey, Victoria. Frances H. Gearhart: California Block Prints. 20p. 1990. pap. 10.95 (*0-910524-15-7*) Eastern Wash.

Dailey, Victoria & Turner, Steve. Danish Posters, Nineteen Hundred Ten to Nineteen Forty. (Illus.). 40p. 1988. pap. 16.00 (*0-915148-17-X*) Wm Dailey.

Dailey, Victoria, jt. auth. see Turner, Steve.

Dailey, Victoria, ed. see Jaeger, Roland.

***Daillant, J., et al, eds.** X-Ray & Neutron Reflectivity: Principles & Applications. LC 99-42744. (Lecture Notes in Physics & Monographs: Vol. 58). xviii, 331p. 1999. 56.00 (*3-540-66195-6*) Spr-Verlag.

D'Ailly, Gisele. Parian Poems. (Illus.). 48p. 1995. 40.00 (*0-930126-48-3*) Typographeum.

***Daily.** The Brain Droppings 1999. 736p. 1998. pap. 9.95 (*0-7868-8342-1*) Hyperion.

— Day-by-Day Cholesterol. 1999. pap. 12.95 (*1-883205-72-7*) Intl Med Pub.

— Day-by-Day Hypertension. 1999. pap. 12.95 (*1-883205-62-X*) Intl Med Pub.

— Doctors. 2000. pap. 9.99 (*0-7407-0807-4*) Andrews & McMeel.

— Lawyers. 2000. pap. 9.99 (*0-7407-0809-0*) Andrews & McMeel.

— Murphy's Law, 1. 1998. text 9.99 (*0-8431-7432-3*) Pssblts Denver.

— Teacher's Calendar 2000 - 2001: The Day-by-Day Directory to Holidays, Historic Events, Birthdays & Special Occasions. (Illus.). 288p. 2000. pap. 19.95 (*0-8092-2521-2*, 252120, Contemporary Bks) NTC Contemp Pub Co.

— Technology in a Hemodynamic Monitor. 5th ed. (C). 1999. text. write for info. (*0-323-01151-9*) Mosby Inc.

— Three Hundred & Sixty-Five Sports Illustrated Pro & College Basketball. 1996. pap. 9.99 (*0-7819-1662-3*) Landmark General Corp.

Daily, Benjamin W. Ability of High School Pupils to Select Essential Data in Solving Problems. LC 73-176704. (Columbia University. Teachers College. Contributions to Education Ser.: No. 190). reprint ed. 37.50 (*0-404-55190-4*) AMS Pr.

Daily, Bev, jt. auth. see Thomas, Dayfydd.

Daily, Catherine M., jt. auth. see Dollinger, Marc J.

Daily, Dale N. Enlightenment Deism: The Foremost External Threat to Christianity & the Role It Has Played in American Protestantism. 152p. 1999. pap. 13.00 (*0-8059-4631-4*) Dorrance.

Daily, Dick & Cayce, Edgar. The Edgar Cayce Bible Companion: Biblical Treasures from the Edgar Cayce Readings. LC 97-33437. 219p. 1998. pap. 14.95 (*0-87604-398-8*, 506) ARE Pr.

***Daily, Don.** Classic Treasury of Aesop's Fables. 56p. 1999. 9.98 (*0-7624-0413-2*) Running Pr.

— Twelve Days of Christmas. (Illus.). 2000. 9.98 (*0-7624-0764-6*) Running Pr.

Daily, Edward. Custer to MacArthur: The 7th U.S. Cavalry (1866-1945) (Illus.). 204p. Date not set. 34.95 (*1-56311-233-7*) Turner Pub KY.

— Skirmish - Red, White & Blue: The History of the 7th U.S. Cavalry (1945-1953) (Illus.). 128p. Date not set. 29.95 (*1-56311-088-1*) Turner Pub KY.

Daily, Edward L. Legacy of Custer's 7th U. S. Cavalry in Korea. LC 90-70004. (Illus.). 128p. 1990. 39.95 (*0-938021-84-2*) Turner Pub KY.

Daily Express Staff. Crosswords New Daily Express, No. 1. 144p. 1996. pap. 9.95 (*0-14-025158-8*, Pub. by Pnguin Bks Ltd) Trafalgar.

— Crosswords New Daily Express, Vol. 2. 1996. pap. 7.95 (*0-14-025159-6*, Pub. by Pnguin Bks Ltd) Trafalgar.

Daily, Frederick W. Stand up to the IRS: How to Handle Audits, Tax Bills & Tax Court. 3rd ed. Leonard, Robin, ed. LC 96-16422. 368p. 1996. pap. 24.95 (*0-87337-337-5*) Nolo com.

— Surviving an IRS Audit. LC 99-29725. (Quick & Legal Ser.). 220p. 1999. pap. 24.95 (*0-87337-537-8*) Nolo com.

— Tax Savvy for Small Business. 2nd rev. ed. LC 96-39243. (Illus.). 352p. (Orig.). 1997. pap. 26.95 (*0-87337-372-3*) Nolo com.

— Tax Savvy for Small Business: Year-Round Tax Strategies to Save You Money, 4th ed. 4th ed. LC 99-20273. 1999. pap. text 29.95 (*0-87337-534-3*) Nolo com.

Daily, Fredrick W. Stand up to the IRS. 5th ed. 400p. 1999. pap. text 24.95 (*0-87337-500-9*) Nolo com.

Daily, Gretchen C., ed. Nature's Services: Societal Dependence on Natural Ecosystems. LC 96-40401. (Illus.). 416p. 1997. pap. text 24.95 (*1-55963-476-6*, Shearwater Bks) Island Pr.

Daily, Guangming, ed. The People's Republic of China. (Illus.). 608p. 1990. 130.00 (*1-86305-004-3*, Pub. by Lotus Pub) Intl Spec Bk.

***Daily Guideposts Staff.** Daily Guideposts 2001: Spirit-Lifting Thoughts for Every Day of the Year. 416p. 2000. 16.99 (*0-7852-6995-9*) Nelson.

Daily, J. W. & Harleman, D. R. Fluid Dynamics. 1966. 24.00 (*0-201-01421-1*) Addison-Wesley.

Daily, Jay E. The Anatomy of Censorship. LC 72-95841. (Books in Library & Information Science: No. 6). 423p. reprint ed. pap. 131.20 (*0-7837-3353-4*, 204331100008) Bks Demand.

— Cataloging Phonorecordings: Problems & Possibilities. LC 73-90723. (Practical Library & Information Science: No. 1). 192p. reprint ed. pap. 59.60 (*0-7837-0927-7*, 204123200019) Bks Demand.

— Organizing Nonprint Materials. 2nd ed. (Books in Library & Information Science: Vol. 48). (Illus.). 320p. 1986. text 115.00 (*0-8247-7504-X*) Dekker.

Daily, John. Fundamentals of Applied Physics for Traffic Accident Investigations LC 98-232533. (Traffic Accident Reconstruction Ser.). 441 p. 1997. write for info. (*1-884566-26-X*) Inst Police Tech.

— Fundamentals of Traffic Accident Reconstruction. 268p. (C). 1988. pap. text 34.95 (*1-884566-04-9*) Inst Police Tech.

Daily, Kathleen K. & Guenin, Gaylord T. Aspen: The Quiet Years. Borneman, Diane, ed. (Illus.). 320p. 1994. 50.00 (*0-9641399-0-1*) Red Ink.

Daily, Lois, ed. see New Hope Church Family & Friends Staff.

Daily, Marla. California's Channel Islands: 1001 Questions Answered. 3rd rev. ed. (Illus.). 284p. 1997. pap. 15.00 (*1-885375-01-8*, Shore Line Pr) Pacific Books.

Daily, Marla, ed. Santa Cruz Island Anthology. 2nd ed. 161p. pap. 10.95 (*1-886342-00-8*) Pacific Books.

Daily, Mike. Valley. Alexiadou, Artemis, ed. (Bend Ser.: No. 018). (Illus.). 222p. 1998. pap. 13.00 (*0-9643598-2-0*) Bend Pr CA.

Daily Nonpareil Office. Sketches of Springfield in 1856. fac. ed. (Annual Monograph). 96p. 1973. reprint ed. pap. 3.00 (*0-686-29090-9*) Clark County Hist Soc.

Daily Racing Form Staff. Graded Stakes 1998 Yearbook, Vol. 4. (Graded Stakes Yearbks.). (Illus.). 826p. 1999. text 39.95 (*0-9648493-2-1*) Daily Racing.

Daily, Robert. Earth. (Illus.). 64p. (J). (gr. 4-6). 1996. reprint ed. pap. 6.95 (*0-531-15767-9*) Watts.

— Elvis Presley: The King of Rock 'n' Roll. (Impact Biographies Ser.). 114p. 1996. lib. bdg. 24.00 (*0-531-11288-8*) Watts.

— Elvis Presley: The King of Rock 'n' Roll. (Impact Biographies Ser.). 144p. (YA). (gr. 7-12). 1997. pap. 9.95 (*0-531-15821-7*) Watts.

— Mercury. (First Bks.). (Illus.). 64p. (J). (gr. 4-6). 1996. reprint ed. pap. 5.95 (*0-531-15769-5*) Watts.

— Pluto. LC 94-58. (First Bks.). 64p. (J). (gr. 4-6). 1994. lib. bdg. 22.00 (*0-531-20166-X*) Watts.

— Pluto. (First Bks.). (Illus.). 64p. (J). (gr. 4-6). 1996. reprint ed. pap. 6.95 (*0-531-15770-9*) Watts.

— The Sun. (First Bks.). (Illus.). 64p. (J). (gr. 4-6). 1996. reprint ed. pap. 6.95 (*0-531-15776-8*) Watts.

Daily, Sean K. Migrating to Windows NT 4.0. LC 96-45904. 475p. (Orig.). 1997. pap. 39.95 (*1-882419-50-2*) News Four-Hund.

— Optimizing Windows NT. LC 97-74804. 1032p. 1998. pap. 49.99 (*0-7645-3110-7*) IDG Bks.

Daily Staff. Conservations with God. 1999. 9.95 (*0-7683-3559-0*) CEDCO Pub.

— Daily Bible. 1999. pap. 19.99 (*0-7369-0198-1*) Harvest Hse.

— Doodle-a-Day, 1. 1998. 9.95 (*1-56247-619-X*) Pleasant Co.

— Teachers: Jokes, Quotes & Anecdotes, 1. 1999. 9.99 (*0-8362-0883-8*) Andrews & McMeel.

***Daily Study for Women Staff.** Daily Study Bible for Women. 1999. 26.99 (*0-8423-3334-7*); pap. 19.99 (*0-8423-3335-5*) Tyndale Hse.

Daily, Susan. Graphics for Sunday. 1991. 29.95 (*0-85924-594-2*) Harper SF.

— More Graphics for Sundays & Feast Days. 1991. 29.95 (*0-85924-921-2*) Harper SF.

Daily Variety Staff. Variety Obituaries, 1991-1992, Vol. 14. LC 10-730184. 296p. 1994. text 180.00 (*0-8240-0848-0*) Garland.

Daimay Lin-Vien, et al. The Handbook of Infrared & Raman Characteristic Frequencies of Organic Molecules. (Illus.). 503p. (C). 1991. text 105.00 (*0-12-451160-0*) Acad Pr.

Daimon Verlag Staff. Talking with Angles. 1998. pap. 19.95 (*3-85630-564-5*) Continuum.

***Dain, Catherine.** Angel in the Dark. LC 99-46553. 222p. 1999. 19.95 (*0-7862-2251-4*) Five Star.

Dain, Catherine. Bet Against the House. 224p. (Orig.). 1995. mass mkt. 4.99 (*0-425-14580-8*, Prime Crime) Berkley Pub.

— Dead Man's Hand. 224p. 1997. mass mkt. 5.99 (*0-425-15760-1*, Prime Crime) Berkley Pub.

***Dain, Catherine.** Death of the Party: A Faith Cassidy Mystery. LC 00-24587. 222p. 2000. 21.95 (*0-7862-2538-6*) Five Star.

Dain, Catherine. Lament for a Dead Cowboy. 208p. (Orig.). 1994. pap. 4.50 (*0-425-14328-7*, Prime Crime) Berkley Pub.

— The Luck of the Draw. (Orig.). 1996. mass mkt. 5.99 (*0-425-15230-8*) Berkley Pub.

— Sing a Song of Death. 176p. (Orig.). 1993. mass mkt. 3.99 (*0-515-11057-4*, Jove) Berkley Pub.

— Walk a Crooked Mile. 208p. (Orig.). 1994. mass mkt. 3.99 (*0-515-11310-7*, Jove) Berkley Pub.

***Dain, Claudia.** Tell Me Lies. 368p. 2000. pap. 5.50 (*0-8439-4692-X*, Leisure Bks) Dorchester Pub Co.

Dain, Norman. Clifford W. Beers: Advocate for the Insane. LC 79-24290. (Contemporary Community Health Ser.). (Illus.). 424p. 1980. text 49.95 (*0-8229-3419-1*) U of Pittsburgh Pr.

Dain, Phyllis. The New York Public Library: A History of Its Founding & Early Years. LC 70-163359. (Illus.). 466p. (Orig.). 1972. 35.00 (*0-87104-131-6*) NY Pub Lib.

***Dain, Phyllis.** The New York Public Library: A Universe. (Illus.). 144p. 2000. pap. write for info. (*1-85759-234-4*, Pub. by Scala Books) Antique Collect.

Dain, Phyllis & Cole, John Y., eds. Libraries & Scholarly Communication in the United States: The Historical Dimension, 2. LC 89-23248. (Beta Phi Mu Monograph: No. 2). 164p. 1990. 55.00 (*0-313-26807-X*, DLS/, Greenwood Pr) Greenwood.

Dain, Phyllis, jt. auth. see Molz, Redmond K.

Dainard, J. A., ed. Editing Correspondence. LC 79-11603. (Conference on Editorial Problems Ser.: No. 14). 1987. 42.50 (*0-404-63664-0*) AMS Pr.

Daines & Graham. Adult Learning Adult Teaching. (C). 1992. 35.00 (*1-85041-065-8*, Pub. by Univ Nottingham) St Mut.

Daines, et al. Changes in Student Participation in Adult Education. (C). 1982. 35.00 (*0-902031-73-2*, Pub. by Univ Nottingham) St Mut.

***Daines, Brian & Perrett, Angelina.** Psychodynamic Approaches to Sexual Problems. LC 99-39401. 2000. pap. 25.95 (*0-335-20159-8*) OpUniv Pr.

Daines, Brian, et al. Medical & Psychiatric Issues for Counselors. (Professional Skills for Counselors Ser.). 160p. 1997. 39.95 (*0-8039-7506-6*); pap. 18.95 (*0-8039-7507-4*) Sage.

Daines-Gibeaut, Nicole & Daines-Gibeaut, Robert. Remember: A Story for the Child Within Us All. LC 95-94022. (Illus.). 156p. 1996. 14.95 (*0-9645055-6-8*) Heart-Heart Pub.

Daines-Gibeaut, Robert, jt. auth. see Daines-Gibeaut, Nicole.

Daines, J., et al, eds. Policy & Research in Adult Education. 150p. (C). 1982. text 65.00 (*0-7855-3193-9*, Pub. by Univ Nottingham) St Mut.

Daines, J., et al. Changes in Student Participation in Adult Education. 62p. (C). 1982. text 45.00 (*0-7855-3188-2*, Pub. by Univ Nottingham) St Mut.

Daines, John, et al. Adult Learning Adult Teaching. 3rd ed. 136p. 1994. 29.95 (*1-85041-071-2*, Pub. by U of Nottingham) Paul & Co Pubs.

— Adult Learning Adult Teaching. 3rd ed. 136p. 1998. reprint ed. pap. 12.95 (*1-85041-070-4*, Pub. by U of Nottingham) St Mut.

Dainiak, N., et al. Radiation Injury & the Chernobyl Catastrophe, Vol. 15, Supplement 2. LC 97-73747. 336p. 1997. pap. 49.00 (*1-880854-22-8*) AlphaMed Pr.

Dainian, Fan & Cohen, Robert S., eds. Chinese Studies in the History & Philosophy of Science & Technology. (Boston Studies in the Philosophy of Science: Vol. 179). 504p. (C). 1996. lib. bdg. 251.00 (*0-7923-3463-9*, Pub. by Kluwer Academic) Kluwer Academic.

Dainian, Fan, jt. auth. see Liang-Ying Hsu.

Daino, Peter. Mary, Mother or Sorrows, Mother of Defiance. LC 92-34370. (Illus.). 102p. reprint ed. pap. 31.70 (*0-608-20200-2*, 207145900012) Bks Demand.

Dainoff, Marilyn H., jt. auth. see Dainoff, Marvin J.

Dainoff, Marvin J. & Dainoff, Marilyn H. A Manager's Guide to Ergonomics in the Electronic Office. LC 86-32493. (Illus.). 242p. reprint ed. pap. 75.10 (*0-7837-6728-5*, 204635600011) Bks Demand.

Dainoff, Marvin J., jt. auth. see Rutter, Bryce G.

Dainora, Audra, et al, eds. Papers from the 31st Regional Meeting of CLS, Vol. 1. 535p. 1995. pap. 16.00 (*0-614-16723-X*) Chicago Ling.

— Parasession on Clitics, Vol. 2. 315p. 1995. pap. 16.00 (*0-914203-48-7*) Chicago Ling.

Dainora, J., et al. Materials of Construction for Use in an LNG Pipeline. 130p. 1968. 7.00 (*0-318-12652-4*, L40000) Am Gas Assn.

***Dainotto, Roberto M.** Place in Literature: Regions, Cultures, Communities. LC 99-38957. 2000. 35.00 (*0-8014-3683-4*) Cornell U Pr.

Dainow, Sheila. Working & Surviving in Organisations: A Trainer's Guide to Developing Organisational Skills. LC 97-44534. 252p. 1998. pap. 60.50 (*0-471-98151-6*) Wiley.

Dains, Joyce, et al. Advanced Assessment & Clinical Diagnosis. LC 98-14984. (Illus.). 464p. (C). (gr. 13). 1998. pap. text 49.95 (*0-8151-3627-7*, 30504) Mosby Inc.

Dains, Mary K., jt. ed. see Hurt, R. Douglas.

Daintith, J., et al, eds. Biographical Encyclopedia of Scientists, 2 vols., Set. 2nd ed. (Illus.). 1100p. 1994. 220.00 (*0-7503-0287-9*) IOP Pub.

Daintith, John, ed. A Dictionary of Chemistry. 3rd ed. LC 96-226025. (Oxford Paperback Reference). (Illus.). 538p. 1996. pap. 13.95 (*0-19-280031-0*) OUP.

***Daintith, John, ed.** A Dictionary of Chemistry. 4th ed. (Oxford Paperback Reference). (Illus.). 550p. 2000. pap. 15.95 (*0-19-280101-5*) OUP.

Daintith, John, ed. The Facts on File Dictionary of Chemistry. expanded rev. ed. (Illus.). 256p. 1990. pap. 12.95 (*0-8160-2367-0*) Facts on File.

Daintith, John, et al, eds. The Facts on File Dictionary of Physics. LC 88-45703. 240p. 1988. reprint ed. pap. 74.40 (*0-608-02863-0*, 206392700007) Bks Demand.

Daintith, John & Clark, John, eds. The Facts on File Dictionary of Chemistry. rev. ed. LC 99-17787. (Illus.). 272p. 1999. 27.95 (*0-8160-3909-7*, Checkmark) Facts on File.

— The Facts on File Dictionary of Mathematics. 3rd rev. ed. LC 99-17789. (Illus.). 256p. 1999. 27.95 (*0-8160-3913-5*, Checkmark) Facts on File.

— The Facts on File Dictionary of Physics. rev. ed. LC 99-17780. (Illus.). 256p. 1999. 40.00 (*0-8160-3911-9*, Checkmark) Facts on File.

Daintith, John & Clark, John O., eds. The Facts on File Dictionary of Physics. 3rd ed. LC 99-17780. 250p. 1999. pap. 17.95 (*0-8160-3912-7*) Facts on File.

***Daintith, John & Facts on File Publishers Staff.** The Facts on File Dictionary of Chemistry. 3rd ed. LC 99-17787. 266p. 1999. 17.95 (*0-8160-3910-0*) Facts on File.

Daintith, John & Stibbs, Anne. Quotations for Speeches. 198p. 1998. pap. text 14.00 (*0-7881-5406-0*) DIANE Pub.

Daintith, John, et al. The Facts on File Dictionary of Mathematics. 3rd ed. LC 99-17789. 241p. 1999. pap. 17.95 (*0-8160-3914-3*) Facts on File.

Daintith, John, jt. auth. see Illingworth, Valerie.

Daintith, John, jt. ed. see Illingworth, Valerie.

Daintith, T. C., ed. Journal of Energy, Vol. 8. (C). 1990. lib. bdg. 155.00 (*1-85333-479-0*, Pub. by Graham & Trotman) Kluwer Academic.

— Journal of Energy & Natural Resources Law, Vol. 9, Nos. 1-4. 380p. (C). 1992. lib. bdg. 170.00 (*1-85333-637-8*, Pub. by Graham & Trotman) Kluwer Academic.

Daintith, Terence & Hancher, Leigh. Energy Strategy in Europe: The Legal Framework. (European University Institute, Series A (Law): No. 4). x, 190p. 1986. 65.40 (*3-11-010646-9*) De Gruyter.

Daintith, Terence & Page, Alan. The Executive in the Constitution: Structure, Autonomy & Internal Control. LC 99-25366. 472p. 1999. text 45.00 (*0-19-826870-X*) OUP.

Daintith, Terence & Teubner, Gunther, eds. Contract & Organisation: Legal Analysis in the Light of Economic & Social Theory. (European University Institute, Series A (Law): No. 5). viii, 300p. 1986. 100.80 (*3-11-010705-8*) De Gruyter.

Daintith, Terence & University of London Staff. Implementing EC Law in the United Kingdom: Structures for Indirect Rule LC 95-171690. xxiii, 377 p. 1995. text 184.95 (*0-471-95225-7*) Wiley.

Daintith, Terrence, ed. Law As an Instrument of Economic Policy: Comparative & Critical Approaches. (European University Institute, Series A (Law): No. 7). 432p. (C). 1987. lib. bdg. 142.35 (*3-11-011430-5*) De Gruyter.

***Dainton, Barry.** Stream of Consciousness: Unity & Continuity in Conscious Experience. LC 99-59597. (International Library of Philosophy). 256p. 2000. 75.00 (*0-415-22382-2*) Routledge.

D

Dainton, Gary R., jt. auth. see Johnston, Christine A.

Dainty, Anton M., jt. ed. see Husebye, Eystein S.

Dainty, C., jt. auth. see Ageorges, N.

Dainty, Chris, ed. Current Trends in Optics. (Lasers & Optics Engineering Ser.). (Illus.). 352p. 1994. text 79.00 (*0-12-200720-4*) Acad Pr.

Dainty, Christopher & Bissonnette, Luc R., eds. Image Propagation Through the Atmosphere, Vol. 2828. 554p. 1996. 102.00 (*0-8194-2216-9*) SPIE.

Dainty, Christopher, jt. ed. see Bissonnette, Luc R.

Dainty, J. C. & Maystre, Daniel, eds. Modern Analysis of Scattering Phenomena. (Illus.). 208p. 1991. 137.00 (*0-7503-0156-2*) IOP Pub.

Dainty, Paul, jt. ed. see Smith, N. Craig.

Dainville, F. Langage des Geographes Termes, Signes, Couleurs des Cartes Anciennes, 1500-1800. (FRE.). 404p. 1964. pap. 75.00 (*0-8288-6777-1*, M-6100) Fr & Eur.

Dair, Carl. Design with Type. LC 66-23932. 1982. pap. text 19.95 (*0-8020-6519-8*) U of Toronto Pr.

Dair, Christina. Hesitant Hero. 1994. per. 3.50 (*0-373-09917-7*, 1-09917-5) Harlequin Bks.

Dairou, Yaya, jt. auth. see Tourneux, Henry.

Dairy Barn Cultural Arts Center Staff, jt. prod. see Beadwork Magazine Staff.

Dairy Barn Quilt National Staff. New Quilt Two, No. 2. Timmons, Christine, ed. (Illus.). 96p. 1993. pap. 21.95 (*1-56158-056-2*) Taunton.

Dairy Barn Southeastern Ohio Cultural Arts Center. Contemporary Quilts: Quilt National 1997. Cusick, Dawn, ed. LC 97-7736. 112p. 1997. 21.95 (*1-887374-35-3*) Lark Books.

Dairy Barn Staff. The Best in Contemporary Quilts: From Quilt National 1999. Cusick, Dawn, ed. LC 99-13374. (Illus.). 112p. 1999. 24.95 (*1-57990-110-7*, Pub. by Lark Books) Random.

Dairy Feeding Systems Management Components Staff & Natural Resource, Agriculture & Engineering Service Conference Staff. Dairy Feeding Systems: Management, Components & Nutrients, Vol. 116. LC 98-46912. 1998. pap. text 30.00 (*0-935817-36-0*) NRAES.

Dairy Practices Council Staff, ed. see Graves, Robert E.

Dairy Practices Council Staff, ed. see Weeks, Stanley.

Dairy Practices Council Staff, ed. see Wright, Peter E. & Graves, Robert E.

Dais, Eugene E., ed. Law & the Ecological Challenge: Amintaphil, Vol. 2. LC 78-61842. xxiv, 265p. 1979. lib. bdg. 42.00 (*0-930342-66-6*, 300220) W S Hein.

***Daise, Benjamin.** Kierkegaard's Socratic Art. LC 99-48303. 160p. 1999. pap. 18.00 (*0-86554-655-X*) Mercer Univ Pr.

Daise, Natalie. Gullah. LC 96-80320. (Gullah Island Ser.: No. 7). (Illus.). 24p. (J). (ps-1). 1997. 3.25 (*0-689-81242-6*) S&S Childrens.

Daise, Natalie E. & Ranger, Mike. Ranger Mike's Animal ABCs: A Sticker Book from A to (Almost) Z. LC 96-231937. 24p. (J). (ps-3). 1996. 4.99 (*0-689-80422-9*) Litle Simon.

Daise, Natalie E., jt. auth. see Daise, Ronald.

Daise, Ronald. Gullah Gullah Island Sticker Book: Charleston Market. 24p. (J). (ps-2). 1996. pap. 4.99 (*0-689-80831-3*) S&S Childrens.

***Daise, Ronald.** Reminiscences of Sea Island Heritage. (Illus.). 128p. 1998. pap. 12.95 (*0-87844-149-2*) Sandlapper Pub Co.

Daise, Ronald & Daise, Natalie E. Miss Natalie's Garden: A Gullah Gullah Island Sticker Book. (Illus.). 24p. (J). (ps-2). 1996. 4.99 (*0-689-80830-5*) S&S Childrens.

Daise, Ronald H. Little Muddy Waters: A Gullah Folk Tale. Tuynman, Carol E., ed. LC 97-80693. (Illus.). 32p. (J). (gr. 2-6). 1998. 14.95 (*1-891503-01-4*, CP101) G O G Enter.

Daisey, Rosalyn. Baby Bird & Chick Carving. (Illus.). 208p. 1994. 49.95 (*0-88740-590-8*) Schiffer.

Daisey, Rosalyn L. Shorebird Carving. LC 89-63675. (Illus.). 256p. 1990. text 49.95 (*0-88740-219-4*) Schiffer.

— Upland Game Bird Carving. LC 91-67015. (Illus.). 240p. 1991. text 49.95 (*0-88740-349-2*) Schiffer.

Daisey, Roslyn L. & Kurman, Sina P. Songbird Carving, Vol. I. LC 85-52376. (Illus.). 256p. 1986. 45.00 (*0-88740-057-4*) Schiffer.

— Songbird Carving, Vol. II. LC 85-52376. (Illus.). 1988. 45.00 (*0-88740-119-8*) Schiffer.

Daish, Elizabeth. Avenue of Poplars. 256p. 1998. 24.00 (*0-7278-5309-0*) Severn Hse.

***Daish, Elizabeth.** Avenue of Poplars. large type ed. 352p. 1999. 31.99 (*0-7505-1375-6*, Pub. by Mgna Lrg Print) Ulverscroft.

Daish, Elizabeth. Catrina. 224p. 1999. 26.00 (*0-7278-2224-1*, Pub. by Severn Hse) Chivers N Amer.

***Daish, Elizabeth.** Catrina LC 98-51860. 288 p. 1999. write for info. (*0-7540-3700-2*) Chivers N Amer.

Daish, Elizabeth. Catrina. large type ed. LC 98-51860. 1999. 24.95 (*0-7862-1775-8*) Thorndike Pr.

Daish, Elizabeth. The Clouded Mountain. 192p. 25.00 (*0-7278-5528-X*) Severn Hse.

— Emma's Christmas Rose. large type ed. 320p. 1997. 29.99 (*0-7505-1247-4*) Ulverscroft.

Daish, Elizabeth. Emma's Family. 256p. 1996. 24.00 (*0-7278-4904-2*) Severn Hse.

— Emma's Family. large type ed. (Magna Large Print Ser.). 368p. 1998. 29.99 (*0-7505-1162-1*, Pub. by Mgna Lrg Print) Ulverscroft.

— Emma's Haven. 256p. 1996. 20.00 (*0-7278-4831-3*) Severn Hse.

— Emma's Haven. large type ed. (Magna Large Print Ser.). 359p. 1997. 27.99 (*0-7505-1036-6*) Ulverscroft.

***Daish, Elizabeth.** Emma's Journey. 256p. 1999. 25.00 (*0-7278-2256-X*, Pub. by Severn Hse) Chivers N Amer.

— Emma's Journey. 336p. 2000. 31.99 (*0-7505-1473-6*) Ulverscroft.

Daish, Elizabeth. Emma's Peace. 256p. 1995. 20.00 (*0-7278-4745-7*) Severn Hse.

— Emma's Peace. large type ed. (Magna Large Print Ser.). (Illus.). 347p. 1996. 27.99 (*0-7505-0977-5*) Ulverscroft.

— Emma's War. 400p. 1998. reprint ed. 25.00 (*0-7278-5277-9*) Severn Hse.

— Ryan's Quadrangle. 256p. 1996. 22.00 (*0-7278-4891-7*) Severn Hse.

***Daish, Elizabeth.** Summer Romance. 1999. 25.00 (*0-7278-5449-6*, Pub. by Severn Hse) Chivers N Amer.

Daishonin, Nichiren. Selected Writings of Nichiren. Watson, Burton, tr. from JPN. (Translations from the Oriental Classics Ser.). 508p. 1990. text 57.50 (*0-231-07260-0*) Col U Pr.

Daisley, J., jt. auth. see Willis, L.

Daisley, R., jt. auth. see Fuchs, N.

Daiss, Timothy. In the Saddle: Exploits of the 5TH Georgia Cavalry During the Civil War. (Illus.). 200p. 1999. 29.95 (*0-7643-0972-2*) Schiffer.

***Daitch, Richard W.** Northwest Territories. (Hello Canada Ser.). 1999. pap. 7.95 (*1-55041-265-5*) Fitzhenry & W Ltd.

Daitch, Richard W. Northwest Territories. LC 95-4222. (Hello Canada Ser.). (Illus.). 76p. (J). (gr. 3-6). 1996. 18.95 (*0-8225-2761-8*) Lerner Pub.

Daitch, Susan. The Colorist. 40p. (Orig.). 1985. pap. 3.00 (*0-917061-22-5*) Top Stories.

— The Colorist. (Vintage Contemporaries Ser.). (Orig.). 1990. pap. 8.95 (*0-679-72492-3*) Vin Bks.

— The Shawl. 1990. pap. 6.95 (*0-679-72942-9*) Random.

— Storytown: Stories. LC 95-26578. (Illus.). 192p. (Orig.). 1996. pap. 12.95 (*1-56478-094-5*) Dalkey Arch.

Daitch, Susan, et al. A VLS Reader. Mark, M., ed. 320p. (Orig.). 1991. pap. 12.95 (*1-85242-245-9*) Serpents Tail.

Daiter, Stephen, jt. contrib. by see Danziger, James.

Daito, Eisuke, jt. ed. see Kawabe, Nobuo.

Daity, Peggy, et al. Christmas Joy. 305p. 1995. pap. 9.99 (*0-88070-780-1*, Palisades OR) Multnomah Pubs.

Daitz, ed. see Euripides.

Daitz, Stephen G. Euripides' Hekabe. unabridged ed. (Living Voice of Greek & Latin Ser.). (GRE.). 60p. pap. text 39.95 incl. audio (*0-88432-084-7*, S23650) Audio-Forum.

— Jerusalem Palimpsest of Euripides. (Illus.). (C). 1970. 106.95 (*3-11-001193-X*) De Gruyter.

— Plato's Portrait of Sokrates. (Living Voice of Greek & Latin Ser.). (GRE.). 68p. 1988. pap. text 39.95 incl. audio (*0-88432-254-8*, S23695) Audio-Forum.

— Pronunciation & Reading of Ancient Greek: A Practical Guide. 2nd rev. ed. LC 85-740005. (Living Voice of Greek & Latin Ser.). 20p. 1985. pap. 34.95 incl. audio (*0-88432-138-X*, S23660) Audio-Forum.

— The Pronunciation & Reading of Classical Latin: A Practical Guide. LC 85-740004. (Living Voice of Classical Latin Ser.). 1984. pap. 34.95 incl. audio (*0-88432-125-8*, S23675) Audio-Forum.

— A Recital of Ancient Greek Poetry. (Living Voice of Greek & Latin Ser.). 52p. 1978. pap. 59.50 incl. audio (*0-88432-029-4*, S23600) Audio-Forum.

Daitz, Stephen G., reader. The Iliad of Homer, Pt. I. unabridged ed. pap. text 59.50 incl. audio (*0-88432-288-2*, S23810) Audio-Forum.

— The Iliad of Homer, Pt. II. unabridged ed. (Living Voice of Greek & Latin Ser.). pap. text 59.50 incl. audio (*0-88432-373-0*, S23817) Audio-Forum.

— Iliad of Homer, Pt. III. unabridged ed. 1994. pap. text 59.50 incl. audio (*0-88432-435-4*, S23824) Audio-Forum.

— Iliad of Homer, Pt. IV. unabridged ed. 1994. pap. text 59.50 incl. audio (*0-88432-621-7*, S23830) Audio-Forum.

Daitz, Stephen G. & Sonkowsky, Robert P. Selections from Vergil. (Living Voice of Classical Latin Ser.). (LAT.). 44p. pap. text 39.95 incl. audio (*0-88432-139-8*, S23685) Audio-Forum.

Daitz, Stephen G., jt. auth. see Aristophanes.

Daitz, Stephen G., ed. see Homer.

Daiute, Colette. Computers & Writing. 200p. 1985. text 19.00 (*0-201-10368-0*) Addison-Wesley.

Daiute, Colette, ed. The Development of Literacy Through Social Interaction. LC 85-644581. (New Directions for Child Development Ser.: No. CD 61). 129p. (Orig.). 1993. pap. 25.00 (*1-55542-720-0*) Jossey-Bass.

Daiuto, B. J., et al. The Hyperbolic Map & Applications to the Linear Quadratic Regulator. (Lecture Notes in Control & Information Sciences: Vol. 110). (Illus.). v, 132p. 1989. 43.95 (*0-387-96741-9*) Spr-Verlag.

Daive, Jean. A Lesson in Music: Poems. Kalendek, Julie, tr. from FRE. (Serie d'Ecriture: No. 6). 64p. 1992. pap. 6.00 (*0-930901-80-0*) Burning Deck.

Daix, Pierre. Picasso. (Illus.). 160p. 1995. 35.00 (*0-8050-1792-5*) H Holt & Co.

Daix, Pierre & Boudaille, Georges. Picasso's Paintings, 1900-1906. (FRE., Illus.). 360p. 1989. 200.00 (*1-55660-048-8*) A Wofsy Fine Arts.

Daix, Pierre & Rosselet, Joan. Picasso's Cubist Paintings, 1907-16: Catalogue Raisonne. (FRE., Illus.). 378p. 1979. 225.00 (*1-55660-101-8*) A Wofsy Fine Arts.

Daiyun, Yue. Intellectuals in Chinese Fiction. LC 87-82667. (China Research Monographs: No. 33). 143p. (Orig.). (C). 1988. pap. 10.00 (*0-912966-97-1*) IEAS.

Daizovi, Lonnie. Cantiques, Rhythmes et Rimes: Chants, Rhythms & Rhymes for the French Classroom. Voges, Ginny, tr. from SPA. (FRE.). 60p. (YA). (gr. 7-12). 1991. pap. 28.50 (*0-935301-63-1*) Vibrante Pr.

— Cantos Calientes: Musically Accompanied Chants for the Spanish Student. (SPA.). 76p. (YA). (gr. 7-12). 1998. pap. 28.50 incl. audio (*0-935301-70-4*) Vibrante Pr.

— Francais Joyeux: Simple Songs That Teach French. (FRE., Illus.). 32p. (J). 1999. pap. 13.95 (*0-935301-78-X*) Vibrante Pr.

— Perfect Pics. (Illus.). 53p. 1991. 12.95 (*0-935301-62-3*) Vibrante Pr.

Daizovi, Lonnie G. Spanish Alive! Teacher's Manual, Level I. (Spanish Alive! Spanish for Young Children Ser.). (SPA., Illus.). 177p. (J). (ps-3). 1990. reprint ed. teacher ed. 18.95 (*0-935301-59-3*) Vibrante Pr.

Dajani, Laika. Black Bart, Elusive Highwayman-Poet. (Illus.). 184p. 1996. pap. 18.95 (*0-89745-195-3*) Sunflower U Pr.

Dajani-Shareel, Hadia & Messier, Ronald A., eds. The Jihad & Its Times. (Michigan Series on the Middle East: No. 4D). 135p. (Orig.). 1991. pap. 12.95 (*0-685-59625-7*) UM Ctr MENAS.

Dajani, Souad R. Eyes Without Country: Searching for a Palestinian Strategy of Liberation. LC 94-21706. 256p. (C). 1994. text 59.95 (*1-56639-240-3*); pap. text 24.95 (*1-56639-241-1*) Temple U Pr.

Dajani, Zahia R. Egypt & the Crisis of Islam. LC 89-13227. (American University Studies: History: Ser. IX, Vol. 56). X, 255p. 1990. text 45.95 (*0-8204-1060-8*) P Lang Pubng.

Dajcovic, Jovan. English-Serbian-English Dictionary of Synonyms & Antonyms. (ENG & SER.). 780p. 1986. 29.95 (*0-8288-0501-6*, F22680) Fr & Eur.

Dajkovic. English-Serbocroatian Technical Dictionary. (ENG & SER.). 452p. 1982. 14.95 (*0-8288-0655-1*, F14122) Fr & Eur.

Dajkovic, J. English-Serbocroatian & VV: Dictionary of Synonyms & Antonyms. 778p. (C). 1986. 110.00 (*0-89771-930-1*, Pub. by Collets) St Mut.

— English-Serbocroation & Serbocroatian-English Dictionary of Synonyms & Antonyms. 778p. (C). 1986. 270.00 (*0-7855-6455-1*, Pub. by Collets) St Mut.

Dajkovic, Jovan. An English-Serbo Croatian & Serbo Croatian-English Dictionary of Synonyms & Antonyms. 800p. 1981. 25.00 (*0-918660-30-0*) Ragusan Pr.

***Dajoz, R.** Insects & Forests: The Role & Diversity of Insects in the Forest Environment. 620p. 2000. (*1-898298-68-8*) Intercept UK.

***Dak, Martin.** Spellbound. x, 365p. 2000. 49.00 (*0-615-11606-X*) Skylight Bks.

Dak, T. M., ed. Rural Industrialization Challenges & Perspectives. 1989. 31.00 (*81-85119-46-5*, Pub. by Northern Bk Ctr) S Asia.

— Social Transformation in India. 1990. 29.50 (*81-202-0284-8*, Pub. by Ajanta) S Asia.

Dakan, Peggy, jt. auth. see Bruno, Janet.

***Dakan, Richard.** Dream Given Form: A Supplement for the Roleplaying Game Based on Babylon 5. 1999. pap. text 21.00 (*1-887990-18-6*) Chameleon Eclectic.

Dakan, Richard. League: A Supplement for the Roleplaying Game Based on Babylon 5. 1998. pap. text 25.00 (*1-887990-17-8*) Chameleon Eclectic.

— Murder in Drivespace. (Alternity Ser.). 1999. 13.95 (*0-7869-1407-6*, Pub. by TSR Inc) Random.

Dakan, Richard & Freidman, Markleford. Dark Kingdom of Jade. (Wruith Ser.). 1996. 15.00 (*1-56504-615-3*, 6010) White Wolf.

***Dake Annotation Reference Library Staff.** Dake Annotated Reference Bible. 1999. 117.99 (*1-55829-127-X*) Dake Publishing.

***Dake, Cindy Lewis.** The Best of Prayer Patterns. Turrentine, Jan, ed. (Illus.). 378p. 1999. pap. 12.99 (*1-56309-292-1*) Womans Mission Union.

Dake, Finis J., Sr. Another Time... Another Place... Another Man: A Biblical Alternative to the Traditional View of Creation. Allison, Mark & Patton, David, eds. (Doctrinal Ser.: Vol. 1). 170p. (Orig.). 1997. pap. 9.99 (*1-55829-110-5*) Dake Publishing.

— God's Plan for Man. 1018p. 1999. 34.99 (*1-55829-026-5*) Dake Publishing.

— Heavenly Hosts. LC 96-105645. 1995. pap. 9.99 (*1-55829-067-2*) Dake Publishing.

— Help for Today. 36p. 1988. pap. 3.00 (*1-55829-030-3*) Dake Publishing.

— The Rapture & the Second Coming of Christ. 119p. 1987. pap. 9.99 (*1-55829-028-1*) Dake Publishing.

— Revelation Expounded. 320p. 1999. pap. 12.99 (*1-55829-027-3*) Dake Publishing.

Dake, Henry C. Art of Gem Cutting. 7th ed. (Illus.). 96p. 1987. pap. 4.50 (*0-910652-07-4*) Gembooks.

Dake, L. The Practice of Reservoir Engineering. LC 93-35471. (Developments in Petroleum Science Ser.: No. 36). 556p. 1994. 242.00 (*0-444-88538-2*) Elsevier.

Dake, L. P. Fundamentals of Reservoir Engineering. (Developments in Petroleum Science Ser.: Vol. 8). xvi,444p. (gr. 7 up). 1979. pap. 70.00 (*0-444-41830-X*) Elsevier.

— The Practice of Reservoir Engineering. (Developments in Petroleum Science Ser.: Vol. 36). 556p. 1994. pap. 100.00 (*0-444-82094-9*) Elsevier.

Dake, Lorelei, jt. auth. see Freeman, Sabrina.

***Dake Publishing Staff.** Dake Annotated Reference Bible. large type ed. 1999. 59.99 (*1-55829-123-7*) Dake Publishing.

***Dake Publishing Staff, contrib. by.** The Interactive Dake Bible: Step Compatible. 1999. 89.99 (*1-55829-111-3*) Dake Publishing.

Dakenbing, William F. The Creation Book. LC 75-39840. (Illus.). 70p. (J). (gr. 3 up). 1976. 5.95 (*0-685-68397-4*); pap. 3.95 (*0-685-68398-2*) Triumph Pub.

Dakers, Andrew. Robert Burns: His Life & Genius. LC 72-3378. (English Literature Ser.: No. 33). 1972. reprint ed. lib. bdg. 75.00 (*0-8383-1507-0*) M S G Haskell Hse.

Dakers, Caroline. Clouds: Biography of a Country House. LC 93-13472. (Illus.). 224p. 1993. 50.00 (*0-300-05776-8*) Yale U Pr.

***Dakers, Caroline.** Holland Park Circle: Artists & Victorian Society. LC 99-16247. (Illus.). 303p. 2000. 39.95 (*0-300-08164-2*) Yale U Pr.

Dakers, Lionel. The Church Anthem Handbook. 76p. 1995. pap. 5.95 (*0-19-353108-9*) OUP.

— Places Where They Sing: Memoirs of a Church Musician. (Illus.). 244p. 1995. lib. bdg. 24.95 (*1-85311-122-8*, 853, Pub. by Canterbury Press Norwich) Morehouse Pub.

Dakers, Lionel, compiled by. The New Church Anthem Book: 100 Anthems. 592p. 1992. 43.95 (*0-19-353107-0*) OUP.

— The New Church Anthem Book: 100 Anthems. 592p. 1995. pap. 18.95 (*0-19-353109-7*) OUP.

Dakers, Lionel & Scott, John. Ash Wednesday to Easter for Choirs. 234p. 1999. pap. text 14.95 (*0-19-353111-9*) OUP.

Dakin, A., Jr. & Reed, Emily L. Dakin. Descendants of Thos. Dakin of Concord, Massachusetts & Reverand Simon Dakin of North East, New York, 1624-1920. (Illus.). 79p. 1997. reprint ed. pap. 16.00 (*0-8328-8198-8*); reprint ed. lib. bdg. 26.00 (*0-8328-8197-X*) Higginson Bk Co.

Dakin, A. H. Dakin: Descendants of Thomas Dakin of Concord, MA. (Illus.). 716p. 1991. reprint ed. pap. 99.00 (*0-8328-1737-6*); reprint ed. lib. bdg. 109.00 (*0-8328-1736-8*) Higginson Bk Co.

Dakin, Arthur H. Paul Elmer More. LC 59-11076. 434p. 1960. reprint ed. pap. 134.60 (*0-7837-9326-X*, 206006600004) Bks Demand.

Dakin, Douglas. British & Americans Philhellenes During the War of Greek Independence, 1821-1833. xii, 247p. 1987. reprint ed. pap. 60.00 (*90-256-0947-3*, Pub. by AM Hakkert) BookLink Distributors.

Dakin, Edwin F., jt. auth. see Dewey, Edward R.

Dakin, H. S. High-Voltage Photography. 1978. pap. 9.95 (*0-930420-00-4*) H S Dakin.

— High-Voltage Photography. 3rd ed. LC 74-77233. 1978. pap. 4.95 (*0-685-82476-4*) H S Dakin.

Dakin, John, jt. ed. see Culshaw, Brian.

***Dakin, John P., et al, eds.** Fiber Optic & Laser Sensors & Applications, Vol. #354. LC 99-208076. 1999. 89.00 (*0-8194-3003-X*) SPIE.

Dakin, John P., jt. ed. see Kersey, Alan D.

Dakin, Karen, jt. ed. see Miller, Wick R.

Dakin, Nick. Book of the Marine Aquarium. 1993. 49.95 (*1-56465-102-9*, 16049) Tetra Pr.

— The Marine Aquarium Problem Solver: Over 500 Questions Answered. (Illus.). 208p. 1996. 28.95 (*1-56465-187-8*) Tetra Pr.

Dakin, Shaun, jt. auth. see Deans, Candance.

Dakin, Susan, ed. Skills for Practical Writing: A Workbook for Training in Work-Related Writing. 2nd ed. (Illus.). 326p. 1994. student ed. 30.00 (*1-883314-01-1*) NC Writers Network.

Dakin, Susanna. The Perennial Adventure: A Tribute to Alice Eastwood, 1859-1943. 48p. 1954. 10.00 (*0-940228-09-2*) Calif Acad Sci.

Dakin, Theodora P. A History of Women's Contribution to World Health. LC 91-46383. (Studies in Health & Human Services: Vol. 21). 128p. 1992. lib. bdg. 59.95 (*0-7734-9624-6*) E Mellen.

Dakins, Wallace W. AIDS & Its Early, Late & Final Symptoms for Death: Index of New Information. 160p. 1997. pap. 44.50 (*0-7883-1659-1*) ABBE Pubs Assn.

— AIDS & Its Early, Late & Final Symptoms for Death: Index of New Information. 160p. 1997. 47.50 (*0-7883-1658-3*) ABBE Pubs Assn.

***Dakkand, et al.** Total Quality Management: Text & Cases. 2nd ed. LC 99-87382. 380p. 2000. pap. text 49.95 (*0-7506-3952-0*) Buttrwrth-Heinemann.

Daknewa, Tashi, jt. auth. see Leo, Veronica.

Dakolias, Maria. Court Performance Around the World: A Comparative Perspective LC 99-21219. (Technical Paper Ser.). 1999. pap. 22.00 (*0-8213-4436-6*) World Bank.

— The Judicial Sector in Latin America & the Caribbean: Elements of Reform. (Technical Papers: No. 319). 104p. 1996. pap. 22.00 (*0-8213-3612-6*, 13612) World Bank.

Dakos. Don't Read This Book Whatever You Do! More Poems about School. LC 92-23236. (Illus.). 64p. (J). (gr. 2-4). 1998. per. 3.99 (*0-689-82132-8*) S&S Childrens.

— Our Principal Kissed a Pig. (J). 2000. 17.00 (*0-689-81117-9*) S&S Childrens.

Dakos, Kalli. The Bug in Teacher's Coffee: And Other School Poems. LC 98-54209. (I Can Read Bks.). (Illus.). 48p. (J). (gr. k-3). 1999. lib. bdg. 14.89 (*0-06-027940-0*) HarpC.

— The Bug in Teacher's Coffee: And Other School Poems. LC 98-54209. (I Can Read Bks.). (Illus.). 48p. (J). (ps-3). 1999. 14.95 (*0-06-027939-7*) HarpC Child Bks.

— Don't Read This Book Whatever You Do! More Poems about School. LC 92-23236. (Illus.). 64p. (J). (gr. 2-6). 1993. lib. bdg. 15.00 (*0-02-725582-4*, Four Winds Pr) S&S Childrens.

— Get Out of the Alphabet, Number 2! Wacky Wednesday Puzzle Poems. LC 96-19965. (Illus.). 32p. (J). (ps-2). 1997. 15.00 (*0-689-81118-7*) S&S Trade.

— The Goof Who Invented Homework: And Other School Poems. LC 95-38294. (Illus.). 80p. (J). (gr. 2-6). 1996. 15.99 (*0-8037-1927-2*, Dial Yng Read) Peng Put Young Read.

— If You're Not Here, Please Raise Your Hand. LC 89-71530. (Illus.). 64p. (J). 1995. mass mkt. 3.95 (*0-689-80116-5*) Aladdin.

— If You're Not Here, Please Raise Your Hand. 1995. 9.40 (*0-606-07698-0*) Turtleback.

— If You're Not Here, Please Raise Your Hand: Poems about School. LC 89-71530. (Illus.). 64p. (J). (gr. 2-6). 1990. lib. bdg. 14.00 (*0-02-725581-6*, Four Winds Pr) S&S Childrens.

Dakos, Kalli. If You're Not Here, Please Raise Your Hand: Poems about School, Class Set. (J). 1997. boxed set 70.30 incl. audio (*0-7887-3151-3*, 46271) Recorded Bks.

An Asterisk (*) at the beginning of an entry indicates that the title is appearing for the first time.

— If You're Not Here, Please Raise Your Hand: Poems about School, Homework. (J). 1997. boxed set 22.20 incl. audio (*0-7887-1830-4*, 40610) Recorded Bks.

Dakos, Kalli. Mrs. Cole on an Onion Roll: And Other School Poems. LC 94-8018. (Illus.). 40p. (gr. k-3). 1999. pap. 5.99 (*0-689-82687-7*, 076714005990) Aladdin.

— Mrs. Cole on an Onion Roll: And Other School Poems. LC 94-8018. (Illus.). 40p. (J). 1995. mass mkt. 14.00 (*0-02-725583-2*) S&S Bks Yung.

Dakos, Kally D. What's There to Write? (J). 1993. mass mkt. 7.95 (*0-590-73354-0*) Scholastic Inc.

***Dakota, Heather.** Realistic Wildlife Painting for Decorative Artists. LC 99-50231. (Illus.). 128p. 2000. pap. 23.99 (*0-89134-939-1*, North Lght Bks) F & W Pubns Inc.

Dakota, Wes. Under Two Heavens. (Illus.). 240p. 1991. pap. 14.95 (*0-933025-22-X*) Blue Bird Pub.

Dakoulas, Panos, et al. Geotechnical Earthquake Engineering & Soil Dynamics III: University of Washington, Seattle, WA, August 3-6, 1998, 2. LC 98-25845. 1616p. 1998. 169.00 (*0-7844-0361-9*) Am Soc Civil Eng.

Dakoulas, Panos, ed. see American Society of Civil Engineers Geotechnical E.

Dakron, Ron. Given Nightingale Sleep. 25p. 1989. pap. 4.95 (*0-930773-09-8*) Black Heron Pr.

— Hammers. unabridged ed. LC 97-213716. 230p. 1997. 22.95 (*0-930773-48-9*) Black Heron Pr.

— Infra. 239p. (Orig.). 1987. pap. 10.95 (*0-930773-04-7*) Black Heron Pr.

— Newt. 205p. 1992. pap. 10.95 (*0-930773-19-5*) Black Heron Pr.

Dakshinamurti, Krishnamurti, ed. Vitamin Receptors: Vitamins As Ligands in Cell Communication-Metabolic Indicators. (Intercellular & Intracellular Communications Ser.: No. 6). (Illus.). 277p. (C). 1994. text 85.00 (*0-521-39280-2*) Cambridge U Pr.

Dakubu, Mary E. Korle Meets the Sea: A Sociolinguistic History of Accra. (Illus.). 240p. (C). 1997. text 70.00 (*0-19-506061-X*) OUP.

Dakyns, H. G., tr. see Xenophon.

Dakyns, Jannie R. The Middle Ages in French Literature, 1851-1900. (Oxford Modern Languages & Literature Monographs). 1973. 29.95 (*0-19-815522-0*) OUP.

Dal-Bianco, P., jt. auth. see Deecke, L.

Dal-Bianco, P., jt. ed. see Deecke, L.

Dal Bozzo, Jerry. The Stinking Cookbook: From the Stinking Rose, a Garlic Restaurant. LC 94-4157. (Illus.). 76p. 1995. pap. 9.95 (*0-89087-730-0*) Celestial Arts.

Dal Canton, Antonio, jt. ed. see Andreucci, Vittorio E.

Dal Co, Francesco & De Micelis, Marco, notes. O. M. Ungers: Works & Projects, 1990-1998. LC 99-23548. (Illus.). 368p. 1999. 85.00 (*1-58093-030-1*, Pub. by Monacelli Pr) Penguin Putnam.

Dal Co, Francesco & Forster, Kurt. Frank O. Gehry. LC 98-42480. (Illus.). 592p. 1997. 75.00 (*1-885254-63-6*, Pub. by Monacelli Pr) Penguin Putnam.

Dal, Hughes-Alain. Why I Am a Monster (Pourquoi Je Suis un Monstre) limited ed. Crowe, Thomas R., tr. from FRE. 44p. 1990. pap. 4.50 (*0-685-64798-6*) New Native Pr.

Dal Masetto, Antonio. El Ojo de la Perdiz. (SPA.). 214p. 1980. pap. 9.00 (*0-910061-01-7*, 1102) Ediciones Norte.

Dal Maso, Gianni. Introduction to (Gamma)-Convergence. LC 92-34990. (Progress in Nonlinear Differential Equations & Their Applications Ser.: Vol. 8). xiv, 340p. 1992. 84.00 (*0-8176-3679-X*) Birkhauser.

Dal Negro, R., jt. auth. see Allegra, L.

***Dal Porto, Richard, et al.** Syphon Filter: Prima's Official Strategy Guide. LC 99-70032. (Illus.). 111p. 1999. pap. 12.99 (*0-7615-2058-9*) Random.

Dal Porto, Richard, jt. auth. see Eberly, Eric.

Dal Pra, Roberto, jt. auth. see Gimenez, Juan.

Dal Santo, G. A Laboratory Basis for Anesthesiology. 764p. 1993. text 60.00 (*1-57235-009-1*, Pub. by Piccin Nuova) Gordon & Breach.

Dal Santo, G. A Laboratory Basis for Anesthesiology. (Illus.). 764p. 1993. text 66.00 (*88-299-1018-X*, Pub. by Piccin Nuova) Gordon & Breach.

Dal Santo, G. A Rational Basis for Anesthesiology. 934p. 1990. text 80.00 (*1-57235-010-5*) Piccin Nuova.

Dal Santo, G. A Rational Basis for Anesthesiology. (Illus.). 934p. 1990. text 88.00 (*88-299-0809-6*, Pub. by Piccin Nuova) Gordon & Breach.

Dal Sasso, Cristiano. Animals: Origin & Evolution. Serini, Rocco, tr. from ITA. LC 94-2541. (Beginnings Origins & Evolution Ser.). (Illus.). 48p. (J). (gr. 3-10). 1994. lib. bdg. 24.26 (*0-8114-3333-1*) Raintree Steck-V.

Dal Toso, Giampietro. La Nozione Di Proairesis in Gregorio Di Nissa: Analisi Semiotico-Linguistica E Prospettive Antropologiche. X, 348p. 1998. 51.95 (*3-631-33700-0*) P Lang Pubng.

Dal', V. Proverbs of the Russian People, 2 vols. (RUS.). 1984. 49.95 (*0-8288-2287-5*, M15187) Fr & Eur.

Dal Verme, Francesco. Seeing America & Its Great Men: The Journal & Letters of Count Francesco Dal Verme, 1783-1784. Cometti, Elizabeth, ed. LC 69-17333. (Illus.). 196p. reprint ed. 60.80 (*0-8357-9818-6*, 201116400074) Bks Demand.

Daladier, Edouard. In Defense of France. LC 74-156637. (Essay Index Reprint Ser.). 1977. reprint ed. 20.95 (*0-8369-2352-9*) Ayer.

Dalafi, H. & Hassan, M. H. Renaissance of Sciences in Islamic Countries - Muhammad Abdus Salam. 376p. 1994. pap. text 39.00 (*9971-5-0713-7*) World Scientific Pub.

Dalafi, H., et al. Renaissance of Sciences in Islamic Countries - Muhammad Abdus Salam. 420p. (C). 1994. text 78.00 (*9971-5-0946-6*) World Scientific Pub.

***Dalai, Anita.** Argentina. LC 00-27150. 2000. 31.40 (*0-7398-1279-3*) Raintree Steck-V.

Dalai Lama, VII. Meditations to Transform the Mind. Mullin, Glenn H., ed. & tr. by. LC 99-16633. 285p. 1999. pap. 16.95 (*1-55939-125-1*, Pub. by Snow Lion Pubns) Natl Bk Netwk.

Dalai Lama, VI. Stallion on a Frozen Lake: Love Poems of the Sixth Dalai Lama. Barks, Coleman, tr. from TIB. & intro. by. 95p. (C). 1993. pap. 8.00 (*0-9618916-5-3*) Maypop.

***Dalai Lama.** Buddha Heart, Buddha Mind: Living the Four Nobel Truths. Rinpoche, Jigme, tr. 240p. 2000. pap. 18.95 (*0-8245-1866-7*, Pub. by Crossroad NY) Natl Bk Netwk.

— Simple Path: Basic Buddhist Teachings. 2000. 19.95 (*0-00-710550-9*) Thorsons.

Dalai Lama XIV. Awakening the Mind, Lightening the Heart: Core Teachings of Tibetan Buddhism. Lopez, Donald S., Jr., ed. LC 95-11538. (Path to Enlightenment Ser.: Vol. 2). 256p. 1995. 21.00 (*0-06-061688-1*, Pub. by Harper SF) HarpC.

— Beyond Dogma: Dialogues & Discourses. Dresser, Marianne, ed. Anderson, Alison, tr. LC 95-51791. 230p. (Orig.). 1996. pap. 14.95 (*1-55643-218-6*) North Atlantic.

— The Bodhgaya Interviews. Cabezon, Jose Ignacio, ed. & intro. by. LC 88-6713. (Illus.). 97p. 1988. pap. 8.95 (*0-937938-62-9*) Snow Lion Pubns.

— The Buddha Nature: Death & Eternal Soul in Buddhism. LC 96-27536. 88p. (Orig.). 1997. pap. 9.95 (*1-885394-19-5*, 94195) Bluestar Communs.

— The Buddhism of Tibet. Hopkins, Jeffrey, ed. & tr. by. LC 87-13049. 81p. 1987. reprint ed. pap. 12.95 (*0-937938-48-3*) Snow Lion Pubns.

— Consciousness at the Crossroads: Conversations with Dalai Lama on Brain Science & Buddhism. Houshmand, Zara et al, eds. Wallace, B. Alan & Jinpa, Geshe Thupten, trs. LC 99-34728. 185p. 1999. pap. 15.95 (*1-55939-127-8*, Pub. by Snow Lion Pubns) Natl Bk Netwk.

***Dalai Lama XIV.** Dalai Lama's Book of Wisdom. 2000. pap. 8.95 (*0-7225-3955-X*) Thorsons PA.

Dalai Lama XIV. Dharma Gaia: A Harvest of Essays in Buddhism & Ecology. Hunt-Badiner, Allan, ed. LC 90-34216. (Illus.). 267p. (Orig.). 1990. pap. 15.00 (*0-938077-30-9*) Parallax Pr.

— Disarmament, Peace, & Compassion. 24p. (Orig.). 1995. pap. 3.50 (*1-884519-13-X*) Open Media.

— Essential Teachings: His Holiness the Dalia Lama. Dresser, Marianne, ed. Pollon, Zelie, tr. from FRE. LC 94-24038. 200p. (Orig.). (C). 1995. pap. 14.95 (*1-55643-192-9*) North Atlantic.

Dalai Lama XIV. A Flash of Lightning in the Dark of Night: A Guide to the Bodhisattva's Way of Life. Padmakara Translation Group Staff, tr. from TIB. LC 93-36511. (Dragon Editions Ser.). 141p. 1994. pap. 13.95 (*0-87773-971-4*, Pub. by Shambhala Pubns) Random.

— The Four Noble Truths. 1997. audio Price not set. (*1-56176-937-1*) Mystic Fire.

Dalai Lama XIV. The Four Noble Truths. Side, Dominique, ed. 166p. 1998. pap. 11.00 (*0-7225-3550-3*) Thorsons PA.

— Freedom in Exile. large type ed. 432p. 1991. 23.95 (*1-85089-531-7*, Pub. by ISIS Lrg Prnt) Transaction Pubs.

— Freedom in Exile: The Autobiography of the Dalai Lama. LC 89-46523. (Illus.). 304p. 2000. reprint ed. pap. 14.00 (*0-06-098701-4*, Perennial) HarperTrade.

— The Good Heart: A Buddhist Perspective on the Teachings of Jesus. Kiely, Robert, ed. Jinpa, Geshe Thupten, tr. & anno. by. LC 96-24684. (Illus.). 224p. 1996. 24.00 (*0-86171-114-9*) Wisdom MA.

— The Good Heart: A Buddhist Perspective on the Teachings of Jesus. Kiely, Robert, ed. Jinpa, Geshe Thupten, tr. & anno. by. 224p. 1998. pap. 14.95 (*0-86171-138-6*) Wisdom MA.

— Healing Anger: The Power of Patience from a Buddhist Perspective. Jinpa, Geshe Thupten, tr. from TIB. LC 96-53235. (Illus.). 160p. (Orig.). 1997. pap. 12.95 (*1-55939-073-5*) Snow Lion Pubns.

***Dalai Lama XIV.** The Heart of the Buddha's Path. 228p. 1999. 18.00 (*0-7225-3932-0*) Thorsons PA.

— The Joy of Living & Dying in Peace: Core Teachings of Tibetan Buddhism, Vol. 3. Lopez, Donald S., Jr., ed. LC 96-52543. 208p. 1997. 17.00 (*0-06-061725-X*, Pub. by Harper SF) HarpC.

Dalai Lama XIV. Kalachakra Tantra: Rite of Initiation. 2nd ed. Hopkins, Jeffrey, ed. & tr. by. LC 99-18615. (Illus.). 512p. 1999. reprint ed. pap. 22.95 (*0-86171-151-3*) Wisdom MA.

— Kindness, Clarity & Insight. Hopkins, Jeffrey, ed. & tr. by. Napper, Elizabeth, ed. LC 84-51198. (Illus.). 232p. (Orig.). 1984. pap. 12.95 (*0-937938-18-1*) Snow Lion Pubns.

— The Meaning of Life from a Buddhist Perspective. Hopkins, Jeffrey, ed. & tr. by. from TIB. LC 91-30315. (Illus.). 114p. 1993. pap. 12.50 (*0-86171-096-7*) Wisdom MA.

— My Land & My People. LC BL1489.N44A3. (Illus.). 271p. 1983. reprint ed. 6.95 (*0-9611474-0-7*) Potala.

Dalai Lama XIV. My Land & My People: The Original Autobiography of His Holiness the Dalai Lama of Tibet. LC 97-23849. xiv, 238p. 1997. mass mkt. 12.99 (*0-446-67421-4*, Pub. by Warner Bks) Little.

Dalai Lama XIV. Nyung Na: The Means of Achievement of the Eleven-Faced Great Compassionate One, Avalokiteshvara of the (Bhikshuni) Lakshmi Tradition. Miller, Constance & Thresher, Sarah, eds. Rinpoche, Lama Thubten Zopa & Churinoff, George, trs. from TIB. (Illus.). 208p. 1995. pap. 16.00 (*0-86171-250-1*) Wisdom MA.

— The Opening of the Wisdom Eye. LC 70-152732. (Illus.). 178p. 1991. reprint ed. pap. 12.95 (*0-8356-0549-3*, Quest) Theos Pub Hse.

— Path to Bliss: A Practical Guide to Stages of Meditation. Cox, Christine, ed. Huboam, G. T. & Jinpa, Geshe Thupten, trs. LC 90-2650. 240p. 1991. pap. 14.95 (*0-937938-92-0*) Snow Lion Pubns.

— The Path to Enlightenment. rev. ed. Mullin, Glenn H., ed. & tr. by. LC 94-39647. (Illus.). 237p. 1994. pap. 14.95 (*1-55939-032-8*) Snow Lion Pubns.

— Path to Enlightenment, Vol. 4. 16.00 (*0-06-061726-8*) HarpC.

— Path to Enlightenment, Vol. 5. 16.00 (*0-06-061727-6*) HarpC.

— Path to Enlightenment, Vol. 6. 16.00 (*0-06-061728-4*) HarpC.

— Path to Enlightenment, Vol. 7. 16.00 (*0-06-061729-2*) HarpC.

— Path to Enlightenment, Vol. 8. 16.00 (*0-06-061732-2*) HarpC.

— The Quintessence Tantras of Tibetan Medicine. Clark, Barry, tr. 260p. (Orig.). 1995. pap. 22.95 (*1-55939-009-3*) Snow Lion Pubns.

— Sleeping, Dreaming, & Dying: An Exploration of Consciousness with the Dalai Lama. Varela, Francisco J., ed. Wallace, B. Alan & Jinpa, Geshe Thupten, trs. LC 97-2448. (Illus.). 264p. (Orig.). 1997. pap. 16.95 (*0-86171-123-8*) Wisdom MA.

— Spiritual Advice for Buddhists & Christians. Mitchell, Donald, ed. LC 98-16984. 100p. 1998. pap. 9.95 (*0-8264-1076-6*) Continuum.

— Transcendent Wisdom: A Teaching on the Wisdom Section of Shantidera's Guide to the Bodhisattva Way of Life. 2nd ed. Wallace, B. Alan, ed. & tr. by. LC 94-7562. (Illus.). 142p. 1994. pap. 12.95 (*1-55939-030-1*) Snow Lion Pubns.

***Dalai Lama XIV.** Transforming the Mind: Teachings on Generating Compassion. 208p. 2000. 20.00 (*0-7225-4030-2*, Pub. by Thorsons PA) HarpC.

Dalai Lama XIV. Union of Bliss & Emptiness: A Commentary on Guru Yoga Practice. Cox, Christine, ed. Jinpa, Geshe Thupten, tr. & intro. by. LC 88-31948. (Illus.). 191p. 1988. pap. 14.95 (*0-937938-69-6*) Snow Lion Pubns.

Dalai Lama XIV. The Way to Freedom: Core Teachings of Tibetan Buddhism. Lopez, Donald S., Jr., ed. LC 94-31891. (Illus.). 192p. 1994. 19.00 (*0-06-061722-5*, Pub. by Harper SF) HarpC.

Dalai Lama XIV. The World of Tibetan Buddhism: An Overview of Its Philosophy & Practice. Jinpa, Geshe Thupten, ed. & tr. by. LC 94-30512. xii, 210p. 1995. 25.00 (*0-86171-100-9*); pap. 15.95 (*0-86171-097-5*, Pub. by Wisdom MA) Natl Bk Netwk.

Dalai Lama XIV, frwd. The Buddha's Art of Healing: Tibetan Paintings Rediscovered. LC 97-51770. (Illus.). 208p. 1998. 65.00 (*0-8478-2089-0*, Pub. by Rizzoli Intl) St Martin.

— The Buddha's Art of Healing: Tibetan Paintings Rediscovered. LC 97-51770. (Illus.). 208p. 1998. pap. 35.00 (*0-8478-2090-4*, Pub. by Rizzoli Intl) St Martin.

Dalai Lama XIV, pref. Tibet: The Sacred Realm, Photographs 1880-1950. (Illus.). 159p. 1997. pap. 41.95 (*0-89381-121-1*) Aperture.

Dalai Lama XIV & Hopkins, Jeffrey. The Dalai Lama at Harvard: Lectures on the Buddhist Path to Peace. LC 88-39486. 82p. 1989. pap. 14.95 (*0-937938-71-8*) Snow Lion Pubns.

***Dalai Lama XIV & Lopez, Donald S., Jr.** Opening the Eye of New Awareness. 2nd rev. ed. LC 99-28438. 160p. 1999. pap. 14.95 (*0-86171-155-6*) Wisdom MA.

Dalai Lama XIV & Norman, Alexander. Ethics for the New Millennium, Vol. 2. LC 99-15138. 237p. 1999. 24.95 (*1-57322-025-6*) Putnam Pub Group.

Dalai Lama XIV & Ouaki, Fabien. Imagine All the People: A Conversation with the Dalai Lama on Money, Politics & Life as It Could Be. LC 99-11860. 224p. 1999. pap. 14.95 (*0-86171-150-5*) Wisdom MA.

Dalai Lama XIV, et al. Art of Happiness: A Handbook for Living. LC 98-20431. 322p. 1998. 23.95 (*1-57322-111-2*, Riverhead Books) Putnam Pub Group.

— The Dalai Lama, A Policy of Kindness: An Anthology of Writings by & about the Dalai Lama. 2nd ed. Piburn, Sidney D., ed. & compiled by by. 144p. (Orig.). 1993. pap. 10.95 (*1-55939-022-0*) Snow Lion Pubns.

Dalai Lama XIV, et al. Deity Yoga: In Action & Performance Tantra. LC 87-16562. 274p. 1987. reprint ed. pap. 19.95 (*0-937938-50-5*) Snow Lion Pubns.

Dalai Lama XIV, et al. MindScience: An East-West Dialogue. Goleman, Daniel & Thurman, Robert, eds. LC 91-30288. (Illus.). 137p. 1993. pap. 13.95 (*0-86171-066-5*) Wisdom MA.

— Tantra in Tibet. Hopkins, Jeffrey et al, eds. LC 87-16561. 252p. (Orig.). 1987. reprint ed. pap. 14.95 (*0-937938-49-1*) Snow Lion Pubns.

— Worlds in Harmony: Dialogues on Compassionate Action. LC 92-16826. (Illus.). 139p. 1992. pap. 12.50 (*0-938077-77-5*) Parallax Pr.

Dalai Lama XIV, jt. auth. see Berzin, Alexander.

Dalaigh, Brian O., ed. Corporation Book of Ennis, 1660-1810. (Illus.). 472p. 1991. 39.50 (*0-7165-2469-4*, Pub. by Irish Acad Pr) Intl Spec Bk.

Dalal. Measurement of Free Radicals in Human Disease Process. 1992. write for info. (*0-8493-0173-4*, CRC Reprint) Franklin.

Dalal, A. S. Psychology, Mental Health & Yoga. LC 90-85067. 166p. (Orig.). 1991. pap. 9.95 (*0-941524-64-7*) Lotus Pr.

Dalal, A. S. Psychology, Mental Health & Yoga: Essays on Sri Aurobindo's Psycholigical Thought; Implications of Yoga for Mental Health. 2nd ed. 166p. 1996. pap. 9.95 (*81-7058-231-8*, Pub. by SAA) E-W Cultural Ctr.

Dalal, A. S., ed. see Aurobindo, Sri.

Dalal, A. S., ed. see Aurobindo, Sri & Mother.

Dalal, A. S., ed. see Aurobindo, Sri & Mother, The.

Dalal, C. B., ed. see Desai, Mahadev.

***Dalal-Clayton, Barry & Dent, David.** Knowledge of the Land: Land Resources Information & Its Use in Rural Developments. (Illus.). 300p. 2000. text 85.00 (*0-19-829601-0*) OUP.

Dalal-Clayton, Diksha. The Adventures of Young Krishna: The Blue God of India. LC 92-19072. (Illus.). 114p. (YA). (gr. 5-12). 1992. 15.00 (*0-19-508113-7*) OUP.

Dalal, D., et al. Guide to Notes on Company Accounts & Reports. 3rd ed. (C). 1989. 350.00 (*0-7855-6125-0*) St Mut.

Dalal, Farhad. Taking the Group Seriously: Towards a Post-Foulkesian Group Analytic Theory. LC 98-215220. (International Library of Group Analysis). 239p. 1998. write for info. (*1-85302-642-5*) Jessica Kingsley.

Dalal, Ghulam A. Ethics in Persian Poetry, with Special Reference to Thimurid Period. (C). 1995. 34.00 (*81-7017-314-0*, Pub. by Abhinav) S Asia.

Dalal, K. L., ed. Human Development: An Indian Perspective. 1991. 25.00 (*0-7069-5831-4*) Advent Bks Div.

Dalal, Suresh, ed. Prateechi: A Literary Digest of West Indian Languages 1987. (C). 1992. pap. text 10.00 (*81-7201-089-3*, Pub. by National Sahitya Akademi) S Asia.

Dalal, T. The Delights of Vegetarian Cooking. 182p. 1993. 14.95 (*0-318-36304-6*) Asia Bk Corp.

Dalalyan, S. G., et al. Eight Papers Translated from the Russian. LC 89-17983. (Translations Ser.: Series 2, Vol. 145). 117p. 1989. 64.00 (*0-8218-3129-1*, TRANS2/145) Am Math.

***Dalamatian Press Staff.** Printing. (J). (gr. k-1). 1999. pap. text 2.99 (*1-57759-136-4*) Dalmatian Pr.

Dalaney, Cornelius F. Rationality & Religious Belief. LC 79-63359. (University of Notre Dame Studies in the Philosophy of Religion: No. 1). 176p. 1979. reprint ed. pap. 54.60 (*0-608-00881-8*, 206167500010) Bks Demand.

Dalang, R., et al, eds. Seminar on Stochastic Analsis, Random Fields & Applications. LC 99-14457. (Progress in Probability Analysis Ser.: Vol. 45). 320p. 1999. 125.00 (*3-7643-6106-9*) Birkhauser.

Dalang, Robert C., jt. auth. see Cairoli, R.

D'Albas, Andrieu. Death of a Navy: Japanese Naval Action in World War II. 1957. 14.95 (*0-8159-5302-X*) Devin.

***Dalbeck, Ruth.** I'll Take the Sun - Conflict Solving & Image Building for Use in Families & Classrooms. 1999. 11.95 (*0-7541-0685-3*, Pub. by Minerva Pr) Communs Plus.

Dalberth, Paul, et al. Oracle 8 How-To: Intermediate - Advanced. LC 97-40533. 720p. 1998. pap. 39.99 (*1-57169-123-5*) Sams.

D'Alberti, Sarah, ed. see Tasso, Torquato.

D'Albertis, Deirdre. Dissembling Fictions: Elizabeth Gaskell & the Victorian Social Text. LC 97-4103. 246p. 1997. text 39.95 (*0-312-17304-0*) St Martin.

Dalbey, Alice F. The Visitor's Guide to Point Reyes National Seashore. LC 73-89770. (Orig.). 1974. pap. 5.95 (*0-85699-098-1*) Chatham Pr.

Dalbey, Gordon. Healing the Masculine Soul. 1991. pap. 10.99 (*0-8499-3257-2*) Word Pub.

Dalbey, Ross E. & Tartakoff, Alan M., eds. Advances in Cell & Molecular Biology of Membranes & Organelles Vol. 4: Protein Export & Membrane Biogenesis. 276p. 1995. 128.50 (*1-55938-924-9*) Jai Pr.

Dalbiez, Roland. Psychoanalytical Method & the Doctrine of Freud, 2 Vols. Lindsay, T. F., tr. from FRE. (Select Bibliographies Reprint Ser.). 1977. reprint ed. 52.95 (*0-8369-6715-1*) Ayer.

Dalbor. Spanish in Review. 2nd ed. Ep. 1992. cd-rom 50.95 (*0-471-54568-6*) Wiley.

Dalbor, J. B. Spanish in Review Workbook. 2nd ed. 184p. 1991. pap. 36.95 (*0-471-54569-4*) Wiley.

Dalbor, John B. SPANISH PRONOUNCIATION, 3E. 3rd ed. LC 96-77795. 418p. (C). 1996. pap. text 64.50 (*0-03-018077-5*) Holt R&W.

Dalbor, John B. & Sturcken, H. Tracy. Spanish in Review. 2nd ed. 352p. (C). 1992. pap. 65.95 (*0-471-60093-8*) Wiley.

Dalbor, John B., jt. auth. see Yates, Donald A.

Dalby & Rubenstone. The International Student's Guide to American Colleges. 1996. per. 11.95 (*0-671-52000-8*) S&S Trade.

***Dalby, Andrew.** Dangerous Tastes: The Story of Spices. (California Studies in Food & Culture). (Illus.). 196p. 2000. 27.50 (*0-520-22789-1*) U CA Pr.

— Dictionary of Languages: The Definitive Reference to More Than 400 Languages. 1999. pap. 35.00 (*0-7475-3118-8*, Pub. by Blmsbury Pub) Trafalgar.

Dalby, Andrew. Dictionary of Languages: The Definitive Reference to More Than 400 Languages. LC 98-87178. 734p. 1999. 50.00 (*0-231-11568-7*) Col U Pr.

***Dalby, Andrew.** Empire of Pleasures: Luxury & Indulgence in the Roman World. LC 00-35317. 2000. pap. write for info. (*0-415-18624-2*) Routledge.

Dalby, Andrew. Siren Feasts: A History of Food & Gastronomy in Greece. (Illus.). 336p. (C). 1997. pap. 24.99 (*0-415-15657-2*) Routledge.

Dalby, Andrew, ed. South-East Asia: A Guide to Reference Material. (Regional Reference Guides Ser.: No. 2). xiv, 302p. 1993. 100.00 (*1-873836-00-7*, Pub. by H Zell Pubs) Seven Hills Bk.

Dalby, Andrew & Grainger, Sally. The Classical Cookbook. LC 95-82386. (Illus.). 144p. 1996. 24.95 (*0-89236-394-0*, Pub. by J P Getty Trust) OUP.

Dalby, Arnold, ed. A Guide to World Language Dictionaries. 470p. 1998. lib. bdg. 95.00 (*1-57958-069-6*) Fitzroy Dearborn.

Dalby, Claus Z. Gift Boxes. (Illus.). 76p. 1996. 18.95 (*1-870586-18-2*, D Porteous-Parkwest) Parkwest Pubns.

***Dalby, Claus Z.** Gift Boxes. (Illus.). 76p. 1999. reprint ed. text 19.00 (*0-7881-6395-7*) DIANE Pub.

An Asterisk (*) at the beginning of an entry indicates that the title is appearing for the first time.

Dalby, David, et al, eds. Drought in Africa Two - Secheresse en Afrique. rev. ed. LC 78-310180. (African Environment: Special Reports: No. 6). 208p. reprint ed. pap. 64.50 (*0-8357-6950-X*, 203900900009) Bks Demand.

Dalby, J. T., jt. ed. see Williams, R.

Dalby, J. Thomas, ed. Mental Disease in History: A Selection of Translated Readings. LC 96-33891. (Reshaping of Psychoanalysis: No. 7). XIX, 264p. (C). 1997. text 51.95 (*0-8204-3056-0*) P Lang Pubng.

Dalby, John, compiled by. Rice County, Minnesota Cemetery Listing, Vol. 1. LC 97-3943. 1997. write for info. (*0-915709-30-9*) Pk Geneal Bk.

— Rice County, Minnesota Cemetery Listing, Vol 2. LC 97-3943. 1997. write for info. (*0-915709-31-7*) Pk Geneal Bk.

— Rice County, Minnesota Cemetery Listing, Vol. 3. LC 97-3943. 1997. write for info. (*0-915709-32-5*) Pk Geneal Bk.

— Rice County, Minnesota, Military Personnel Vol. 1: War of 1812, Mexican War, Civil War, Spanish American War & World War I. 1995. reprint ed. pap. 20.00 (*0-915709-29-5*) Pk Geneal Bk.

Dalby, Joseph. EU Law for the Construction Industry. LC 97-39127. 253p. 1998. pap. 99.95 (*0-632-04067-X*) Blackwell Sci.

Dalby, Judy N., jt. auth. see Hammond, Vicky L.

Dalby, L. J. Wilts & Berks Canal. 120p. (C). 1985. 39.00 (*0-85361-332-X*) St Mut.

Dalby, Liza. Geisha. LC 99-177015. (Illus.). 367p. 1998. pap. 17.95 (*0-520-20495-6*, Pub. by U CA Pr) Cal Prin Full Svc.

***Dalby, Liza Crihfield.** Little Songs of the Geisba. 2000. pap. 12.95 (*0-8048-3250-1*) Tuttle Pubng.

— The Tale of Murasaki. 448p. 2000. 24.95 (*0-385-49794-6*, N A Talese) Doubleday.

Dalby, Mark, ed. The Cocker Connection: Yorkshire, Van Diemen's Land Melbourne, British Columbia, Mexico, Tonga & Michigan. 160p. (C). 1989. 34.00 (*0-7212-0784-7*, Pub. by Regency Pr GBR) St Mut.

Dalby, Max F. Band Rehearsal Techniques. 1993. 16.00 (*0-614-01757-2*) Instrumental.

Dalby, Nina. Opus One Piano Tutor. 84p. Date not set. 9.95 (*0-946005-11-7*, OS 10125, Pub. by Ossian) Music Sales.

Dalby, Rex K., jt. auth. see Brooks, B. David.

Dalby, Richard. Ghosts & Scholars. 1987. pap. write for info. (*0-85030-614-0*) Aqrn Pr.

Dalby, Richard. Mistletoe & Mayhem. 1993. 8.98 (*1-55521-972-1*) Bk Sales Inc.

— Modern Ghost Stories: By Eminent Women Writers. 336p. 1994. pap. 10.95 (*0-7867-0089-0*) Carroll & Graf.

— Tales of Witchcraft. 1994. 8.98 (*0-7858-0137-5*) Bk Sales Inc.

Dalby, Richard, ed. The Mammoth Book of Ghost Stories. 600p. 1990. pap. 9.95 (*0-88184-590-6*) Carroll & Graf.

— The Mammoth Book of Victorian & Edwardian Ghost Stories. LC 96-154348. 544p. 1995. pap. 10.95 (*0-7867-0279-6*) Carroll & Graf.

— Shivers for Christmas. large type ed. (Large Print Ser.). 512p. 1996. 27.99 (*0-7089-3656-3*) Ulverscroft.

— Twelve Gothic Tales. LC 98-23332. (Oxford Twelves Ser.). 240p. 1999. pap. 9.95 (*0-19-288094-2*) OUP.

— Vampire Stories. 1993. 7.98 (*1-55521-900-4*) Bk Sales Inc.

Dalby, Richard, jt. auth. see Benson, E. F.

Dalby, Richard, ed. see Benson, E. F.

Dalby, Richard, ed. see Braddon, Mary Elizabeth.

Dalby, Richard, ed. see Edwards, Amelia B.

Dalby, Richard, ed. see Jackson, T. G.

Dalby, Richard, ed. see Lawrence, Margery.

Dalby, Richard, ed. see Wintle, W. J.

Dalby, Rob. God of the Door. LC 93-85368. 254p. (Orig.). 1993. pap. 14.95 (*1-883940-00-1*) Palmetto Lodge.

— God of the Door: A Novel. large type ed. LC 93-41535. 361p. 1994. lib. bdg. 17.95 (*0-7862-0117-7*) Thorndike Pr.

***Dalby, Rob.** O Bed! O Breakfast! 2000. pap. 14.95 (*1-58571-021-0*, 909-098, Pub. by Genesis Press) BookWorld.

Dalby, Sidonia, jt. auth. see Rubenstone, Sally.

Dalby, Sidonia M., et al. International Student's Guide to Going to College in America: How to Choose Colleges & Universities in the United States. 160p. 1996. 12.95 (*0-02-860581-0*) Macmillan.

Dalby, Simon & Tuathail, Gearoid. Rethinking Geopolitics. LC 97-50287. (Illus.). 352p. (C). 1998. 90.00 (*0-415-17250-0*) Routledge.

Dalby, Simon & Tuathail, Geroid. Rethinking Geopolitics. LC 97-50287. (Illus.). 336p. (C). 1998. pap. 29.99 (*0-415-17251-9*) Routledge.

Dalby, Terry L. & Rigby, William H. The PIC16C5X Microcontroller: A Practical Approach to Embedded Control. (Illus.). 100p. (C). 1997. text. write for info. (*0-9654740-0-3*) Tecksysts.

Dalby, Terry L., jt. auth. see Rigby, William H.

Dalby, Thomas. Historical Account of the Rise & Growth of the West-India Colonies, & of the Great Advantages They Are to England, in Respect to Trade, London, 1690. LC 75-141095. (Research Library of Colonial Americana). 1972. reprint ed. 20.95 (*0-405-03300-1*) Ayer.

Dalcanale, Enrico, jt. auth. see Ungaro, Rocco.

Dalche, Jean G. Economie et Societe dans les Pays de la Couronne de Castille. (Collected Studies: No. CS149). (FRE.). 352p. (C). 1982. reprint ed. lib. bdg. 128.95 (*0-86078-096-1*, Pub. by Variorum) Ashgate Pub Co.

Dalche, Patrick G. Geographie et Culture, de L'Antiquite Tardive au XIIe Siecle. (Variorum Collected Studies Ser.: No. 592). 352p. 1997. text 109.95 (*0-86078-655-2*, Pub. by Ashgate Pub) Ashgate Pub Co.

Dalcho, Frederick. An Historical Account of the Protestant Episcopal Church, in South Carolina, from the First Settlement of the Province, to the War of the Revolution. LC 71-38445. (Religion in America, Ser. 2). 180p. 1972. reprint ed. 46.95 (*0-405-04064-4*) Ayer.

Dalcin, Mario, et al. Dependable Computing for Critical Applications 6. LC 97-41366. (Dependable Computing & Fault-Tolerant Systems Ser.). 310p. 1997. 55.00 (*0-8186-8009-1*) IEEE Comp Soc.

Dalconzo, Joseph H. The Secret . . . Your Beliefs Create Your Reality: 15-Minutes That Could Change Your Life. unabridged ed. Gilbert, Lisa, ed. & des. by. iv, 76p. (Orig.). 1996. pap. 5.95 (*0-9656207-0-0*) Renaiss Ent.

Dalcourt, Gerard J. The Methods of Ethics. 254p. (C). 1984. pap. text 22.50 (*0-8191-3550-X*); lib. bdg. 50.00 (*0-8191-3549-6*) U Pr of Amer.

Dalcourt, Gerard J., ed. see Simon, Yves R.

Daldal, Fevzi, jt. ed. see Youvan, Douglas C.

Daldorph, Brian. The Holocaust & Hiroshima: Poems. LC 98-162161. 72p. 1997. pap. 10.00 (*0-910479-00-3*) Mid-America Pr.

— Luminous Details. 38p. (Orig.). 1992. pap. 3.00 (*1-880575-12-4*) Hot Pepper.

— Songs of Exile. Manaster, Robert A., ed. (Chapbook Ser.: No. 17). 56p. 1990. pap. 4.95 (*0-932884-17-2*) Red Herring.

Daldrup, Engelbert L., ed. see Flagge, Ingeborg & Hellmuth, Anette.

Daldrup, Roger J. & Gust, Dodie. Freedom from Anger. 3rd ed. LC 88-81097. 175p. 1996. reprint ed. pap. 7.95 (*0-9651209-0-2*) Resolution Press.

Daldrup, Roger J., et al. Focused Expressive Psychotherapy: Freeing the Overcontrolled Patient. LC 88-21183. 233p. 1988. lib. bdg. 33.00 (*0-89862-729-X*) Guilford Pubns.

Daldry, Graham. Charles Dickens & the Form of the Novel. LC 86-17315. 208p. 1987. 59.00 (*0-389-20675-X*, N8232) B&N Imports.

Daldry, Jeremy. The Teenage Guy's Survival Guide. LC HQ797.D35 1999. 136p. (YA). (gr. 5-12). 1999. pap. 8.95 (*0-316-17824-1*) Little.

Dale. Achieving Sustainable Development. LC 96-215201. (Sustainability & the Environment Ser.). 303p. 1996. text 75.00 (*0-7748-0556-0*) U of Wash Pr.

— Companion to Pharmacology. 2nd ed. 1996. pap. text 23.00 (*0-443-05385-5*, W B Saunders Co) Harcrt Hlth Sci Grp.

— Dictionary of Abbreviations & Acronyms. (Reference Library). 1998. pap. 6.95 (*1-85326-385-0*, 3850WW, Pub. by Wrdsworth Edits) NTC Contemp Pub Co.

Dale & Wolf. Speech Comment Made Simple. 2nd ed. LC 99-59705. 224p. 2000. pap. text 27.93 (*0-13-020797-7*) P-H.

Dale, Antony. Brighton Churches. LC 88-25459. (Illus.). 248p. reprint ed. pap. 76.90 (*0-608-20329-7*, 207158200002) Bks Demand.

Dale, A. I. A History of Inverse Probability from Thomas Bayes to Karl Pearson. (Studies in the History of Mathematics & Physical Sciences: Vol. 16). (Illus.). xx, 495p. 1995. 69.95 (*0-387-97620-5*) Spr-Verlag.

Dale, A. M., ed. Euripides: Helen. (Bristol Greek Texts Ser.). (GRE.). 216p. 1981. reprint ed. 29.95 (*0-906515-98-X*, Pub. by Brist Class Pr) Focus Pub-R Pullins.

Dale, Aimee, jt. auth. see Dale, Charles.

***Dale, Alan.** Comedy Is a Man in Trouble: Slapstick in American Movies. 2000. 25.95 (*0-8166-3657-5*) U of Minn Pr.

***Dale, Alan S.** Comedy Is a Man in Trouble: Slapstick in American Movies. LC 00-9080. (Illus.). 2000. pap. write for info. (*0-8166-3658-3*) U of Minn Pr.

Dale, Alfred G. Nuclear Power Development in the U. S. to 1960: A New Pattern in Innovation & Technological Change. Bruchey, Stuart, ed. LC 78-22670. (Energy in the American Economy Ser.). (Illus.). 1979. lib. bdg. 18.95 (*0-405-11974-7*) Ayer.

Dale, Alzina S. Maker & Craftsman: The Story of Dorothy L. Sayers. LC 92-23960. (Wheaton Literary Ser.). 172p. 1992. pap. 11.99 (*0-87788-523-0*, H Shaw Pubs) Waterbrook Pr.

— Mystery Reader's Walking Guide: Washington, D. C. LC 97-34072. (Mystery Reader's Walking Guide Ser.). (Illus.). 400p. 1998. pap. 16.95 (*0-8442-9480-2*, Passprt Bks) NTC Contemp Pub Co.

— The Outline of Sanity: A Biography of G. K. Chesterton. LC 82-11452. 376p. reprint ed. pap. 116.60 (*0-608-17707-5*, 203006300067) Bks Demand.

— T. S. Eliot: The Philosopher Poet. LC 88-4457. (Wheaton Literary Ser.). 209p. 1988. 17.99 (*0-87788-832-9*, H Shaw Pubs) Waterbrook Pr.

Dale, Alzina S., ed. Dorothy L. Sayers: The Centenary Celebration. LC 92-44894. 224p. 1993. 18.95 (*0-8027-3224-0*) Walker & Co.

Dale, Alzina S. & Hendershott, Barbara S. Mystery Reader's Walking Guide: Chicago. LC 94-33414. (Illus.). 400p. 1995. 16.95 (*0-8442-9607-4*, Passprt Bks) NTC Contemp Pub Co.

— Mystery Reader's Walking Guide: England. (Illus.). 416p. 1988. 16.95 (*0-8442-9551-5*, Passprt Bks) NTC Contemp Pub Co.

— Mystery Reader's Walking Guide: New York. (Illus.). 360p. 1995. 16.95 (*0-8442-9481-0*, Passprt Bks) NTC Contemp Pub Co.

Dale, Alzina S., jt. auth. see Hendershott, Barbara S.

Dale, Alzina Stone. Mystery Reader's Walking Guide: New York. (Illus.). 360p. 1997. pap. text 14.95 (*0-8442-9611-2*) NTC Contemp Pub Co.

Dale, Amy L. & Dale, Barry. Dinoflagellate Contributions to the Deep Sea. Honjo, Susumu, ed. (Ocean Biocoenosis Ser.: No. 5). (Illus.). 20p. (Orig.). 1992. pap. text 10.00 (*1-880224-04-6*) Woods Hole Ocean.

Dale, Andrew I. A History of Inverse Probability: From Thomas Bayes to Karl Pearson. 2nd ed. Buchwald, J. Z. et al, eds. LC 99-18596. (Sources & Studies in the History of Mathematics & Physical Sciences). (Illus.). 704p. 1999. 94.00 (*0-387-98807-6*) Spr-Verlag.

Dale, Andrew I., tr. see Laplace, Marquis Pierre Simon De.

Dale, Angela & Davies, Richard, eds. Analysing Social & Political Change: A Handbook of Research Methods. 256p. (C). 1994. text 69.95 (*0-8039-8298-4*); pap. text 24.95 (*0-8039-8299-2*) Sage.

***Dale, Angela, et al.** Analysing Census Microdata. (An Arnold Publication). 2000. 39.50 (*0-340-69228-6*, Pub. by E A) OUP.

Dale, Angela, et al. Housing Deprivation & Social Change. LC 98-211851. (Series LS). x, 127 p. 1996. 17.00 (*0-11-691666-4*) Sterling.

Dale, Angela, jt. auth. see Allen, Jeanne.

Dale, Ann & Robinson, John B., eds. Achieving Sustainable Development. LC 96-215201. 320p. 1996. pap. 25.95 (*0-7748-0540-4*) U of Wash Pr.

Dale, Anthony. Historic Preservation in Foreign Countries: France, England, Ireland, the Netherlands, & Denmark, Vol. 1. Stipe, Robert E., ed. (Illus.). 153p. (Orig.). 1984. 15.00 (*0-911697-00-4*); 15.00 (*0-685-08483-3*) US ICOMOS.

Dale, Anthony, tr. see Gochet, Paul.

Dale, B., ed. Mechanisms of Fertilization: Plants to Humans. (NATO ASI Series H: Cell Biology: Vol. 45). (Illus.). xvi, 708p. 1990. 225.00 (*0-387-51766-9*) Spr-Verlag.

Dale, B. & Aschheim, K. W. Esthetic Dentistry: A Clinical Approach to Techniques & Materials. (Illus.). 510p. 1992. text 135.00 (*0-8121-1467-1*) Lppncott W & W.

Dale, B., et al. Women with Guns: Six New American Plays. 299p. (Orig.). 1986. pap. 14.95 (*0-88145-035-9*) Broadway Play.

Dale, B., jt. auth. see Paige, J.

Dale, B. G. & Plunkett, J. J. Quality Costing. (Illus.). 192p. 1991. pap. 54.95 (*0-442-31369-1*) Chapman & Hall.

***Dale, B. G. & Plunkett, James J.** Quality Costing. 3rd ed. LC 99-34483. 1999. 87.95 (*0-566-08260-8*, Pub. by Gower) Ashgate Pub Co.

Dale, Barbara & Dale, Jim. Happy Birthday to Someone Who Isn't Very Old...in Dog Years. (Illus.). 80p. 1993. 4.95 (*0-8362-3050-7*) Andrews & McMeel.

— The Joys of Motherhood. (Illus.). 128p. 1987. pap. 7.95 (*0-8362-2097-8*) Andrews & McMeel.

— The Joys of Motherhood. (Illus.). 48p. 1993. 4.95 (*0-8362-3047-7*) Andrews & McMeel.

Dale, Barrie. Total Quality Management Blueprint. LC 99-25164. (Business Blueprints Ser.). 264p. 1999. pap. 34.95 (*0-631-19577-7*) Blackwell Pubs.

Dale, Barrie & Burnes, Bernard, eds. Working in Partnership: Best Practice in Customer - Supplier Relations. LC 97-42340. 167p. 1998. 74.95 (*0-566-07997-6*, Pub. by Gower) Ashgate Pub Co.

Dale, Barrie & McQuater, Ruth. Managing Business Improvement & Quality: Implementing Key Tools & Techniques. 200p. (C). 1998. text 68.95 (*0-631-20787-2*) Blackwell Pubs.

— Managing Business Improvement & Quality: Implementing Key Tools & Techniques. 200p. (C). 1998. pap. text 34.95 (*0-631-20788-0*) Blackwell Pubs.

Dale, Barrie & Oakland, John. Quality Improvement Through Standards. 2nd expanded rev. ed. LC 94-187536. 338p. (C). 1999. pap. 142.50 (*0-7487-1699-8*, Pub. by S Thornes Pubs) Trans-Atl Phila.

Dale, Barrie, et al. Managing Quality & Human Resources: A Guide to Continuous Improvement. 2nd ed. LC 97-39508. 256p. 1997. pap. text 43.95 (*0-631-20024-X*) Blackwell Pubs.

Dale, Barrie G., ed. Managing Quality. 3rd ed. LC 99-16395. 480p. 1999. text 69.95 (*0-631-21409-7*); pap. text 39.95 (*0-631-21410-0*) Blackwell Pubs.

Dale, Barry, jt. auth. see Dale, Amy L.

Dale, Bill. The History of Angels One Message, Many Faces. Hamrick, Gail, ed. (Illus.). 40p. 1993. 25.00 (*0-9624693-4-3*) Willitts Designs.

— Power Your Golf Swing with Centrifugal Force: Science of Circle Swing. Larson, Elsa, ed. (Illus.). 123p. (Orig.). 1996. pap. text 23.00 (*0-944972-07-1*) Dale Publishing Co.

Dale, Brian & Elder, Kay. In Vitro Fertilization. (Illus.). 201p. (C). 1997. pap. text 44.95 (*0-521-57567-2*) Cambridge U Pr.

Dale, Brian, jt. auth. see Elder, Kay.

***Dale, Bruce.** The Beauty of Life. LC 99-64396. 1999. 25.00 (*0-7388-0504-1*); pap. 18.00 (*0-7388-0505-X*) Xlibris Corp.

— On Missing Link Road. LC 99-90824. 1999. 25.00 (*0-7388-0528-9*); pap. 18.00 (*0-7388-0529-7*) Xlibris Corp.

Dale, Bruce, jt. auth. see Page, Jake.

Dale, Bruce E., ed. Liquid Fuels, Lubricants & Additives from Biomass. LC 94-71222. 200p. 1994. text 58.75 (*0-929355-49-0*) Am Soc Ag Eng.

***Dale, Catherine.** Schoenberg's Chamber Symphonies: The Crystallization & Rediscovery of a Style. LC 99-31936. (Illus.). 400p. 2000. text 70.95 (*1-85928-257-1*, Pub. by Ashgate Pub) Ashgate Pub Co.

Dale, Catherine & McQuattie, Shiela. Practical Musicianship: A Learning Package in Twenty Stages. 112p. (Orig.). 1992. pap. text 12.95 (*0-85958-499-2*, Pub. by Univ of Hull Pr) Paul & Co Pubs.

Dale, Celia. The Innocent Party. 1998. 19.50 (*0-7540-8509-0*, Black Dagger) Chivers N Amer.

Dale, Charles & Dale, Aimee. The Chefs' Guide to America's Best Restaurants. 2nd rev. ed. (Illus.). 336p. 1998. pap. 14.95 (*0-9657647-1-0*, Pub. by Chefs Guide) BookWorld.

Dale, Charles W. Basic Electricity & DC Circuits. rev. ed. (Illus.). 928p. (C). 1995. reprint ed. pap. 39.95 (*0-7906-1072-8*) Prompt Publns.

Dale, Chris, jt. ed. see Redmill, Felix.

Dale, Christine, jt. auth. see Redhead, Janet S.

***Dale, Clarence J.** Deep Rooted, & Can't Be Moved. 64p. 1999. pap. 12.00 (*0-7392-0397-5*, PO3617) Morris Pubng.

Dale, Corrine H. & Paine, J. H., eds. Women on the Edge: Ethnicity & Gender in Short Stories by American Women. LC 98-38847. (Wellesley Studies in Critical Theory, Literary History & Culture: Vol. 19). 192p. 1998. reprint ed. 45.00 (*0-8153-3247-5*, H2124) Garland.

Dale, Cyndi. New Chakra Healing: The Revolutionary 32-Center Energy System. LC 96-13288. (Illus.). 304p. 1999. pap. 19.95 (*1-56718-200-3*) Llewellyn Pubns.

Dale, D. & Federman, D., eds. Scientific American Medicine, 3 vols. LC 77-92625. (Illus.). 1996. ring bd. 328.00 (*0-89454-000-9*) Sci Am Medicine.

Dale, D. & Plunkett, P. Managing Quality. 357p. (C). 1990. 215.00 (*0-7855-5716-4*, Pub. by Inst Pur & Supply) St Mut.

Dale, D. D. & Baker, Thomas. Como Convertirse en Padre Eficaz De Su Adolescente: Guia Para Los Padres. Gonzalez, Gabriel et al, trs. (SPA.). 88p. 1994. pap. 12.00 (*1-885903-01-4*, TX 3882834) ParentingKids.

Dale, Daryl. Teaching Basics: Adult. (Illus.). 80p. (Orig.). 1985. pap. 3.50 (*0-87509-369-8*) Chr Pubns.

— Teaching Basics: Junior. (Illus.). 73p. (Orig.). 1985. pap. 3.50 (*0-87509-359-0*) Chr Pubns.

— Teaching Basics: Primary. (Illus.). 77p. (Orig.). 1985. pap. 3.50 (*0-87509-363-9*) Chr Pubns.

— Teaching Basics: Youth. (Illus.). 80p. (Orig.). 1985. pap. 3.50 (*0-87509-364-7*) Chr Pubns.

Dale, Daryl, ed. see Weidman, Mavis.

Dale, David. Montana Primer. (Illus.). 46p. (Orig.). 1996. pap. 8.95 (*0-9622429-5-0*) Big Mtn.

— The Way a Bear Is. 46p. (Orig.). 1993. pap. 8.95 (*0-9622429-4-2*) Big Mtn.

Dale, David, jt. auth. see Owen, Robert.

Dale, Doris. Bilingual Children's Literature in Spanish & English: An Annotated Bibliography. 50p. 1998. ring bd. 30.00 (*0-931510-62-7*) Hi Willow.

Dale, Duane & Mitiguy, Nancy. Planning for a Change: A Citizen's Guide to Creative Planning & Program Development. LC 79-624733. (Illus.). (Orig.). (C). 1978. pap. 10.00 (*0-934210-01-2*) Devlp Commy.

Dale, Duane, et al. Beyond Experts: A Guide for Citizen Group Training. LC 79-64419. (Orig.). (C). 1979. pap. 7.00 (*0-934210-07-1*) Devlp Commy.

Dale, Duane D. How to Make Citizen Involvement Work: Strategies for Developing Clout. LC 79-624734. (Illus.). (Orig.). (C). 1978. pap. 10.00 (*0-934210-04-7*) Devlp Commy.

Dale, E., jt. auth. see Alward, Edgar C.

Dale, Edgar. Children's Attendance at Motion Pictures. LC 75-125462. (Literature of Cinema Payne Fund Studies of Motion Pictures & Social Values). 1970. reprint ed. 18.95 (*0-405-01643-3*) Ayer.

— Content of Motion Pictures. LC 77-124026. (Literature of Cinema Ser.). 1970. reprint ed. 19.95 (*0-405-01644-1*) Ayer.

— How to Appreciate Motion Pictures. LC 70-124027. (Literature of Cinema Ser.). 1970. reprint ed. 15.95 (*0-405-01645-X*) Ayer.

Dale, Edgar, ed. The Educator's Quotebook. LC 83-63095. 108p. (Orig.). 1984. pap. 10.50 (*0-87367-429-4*) Phi Delta Kappa.

Dale, Edgar & O'Rourke, Joseph. Vocabulary Building: A Process Approach. Barbe, Walter B., ed. 1986. 14.95 (*0-88309-122-4*, 280199) Zaner-Bloser.

D

An Asterisk (*) at the beginning of an entry indicates that the title is appearing for the first time.

Dale, Edgar, et al. Motion Pictures in Education: A Summary of the Literature. LC 71-124003. (Literature of Cinema, Ser. 1). 1970. reprint ed. 31.95 (0-405-01609-3) Ayer.

Dale, Edgar, jt. auth. see Chall, Jeanne S.

Dale, Edward & Litton, Gaston. Cherokee Cavaliers: Forty Years of Cherokee History As Told in the Correspondence of the Ridge-Watie-Boudinot Family. LC 94-24337. (Civilization of the American Indian Ser.: Vol. 19). (Illus.). 319p. 1995. pap. 15.95 (0-8061-2721-X) U of Okla Pr.

Dale, Edward E. The Indians of the Southwest: A Century of Development Under the United States. (Civilization of the American Indian Ser.: No. 28). (Illus.). 1976. pap. 16.95 (0-8061-1314-6) U of Okla Pr.

— Tales of the Tepee. LC 97-53296. xv, 119p. 1998. pap. 8.00 (0-8032-6610-3, Bison Books) U of Nebr Pr.

Dale, Edward E., ed. see Canton, Frank M.

Dale, Edwin L., Jr. Conservatives in Power: A Study in Frustration. LC 60-5921. 214p. reprint ed. pap. 66.40 (0-608-14421-5, 205172300002) Bks Demand.

Dale, Edwin L., et al. The People's Budget: A Common Sense Plan for Shrinking the Government in Washington. LC 95-9253. (Illus.). 240p. (Orig.). 1995. pap. 14.95 (0-89526-722-5) Regnery Pub.

Dale, Elizabeth. How Long? LC 98-9317. (Illus.). 32p. (J). (ps-1). 1998. 14.95 (0-531-30101-X) Orchard Bks Watts.

— Scrumpy. (J). 1996. pap. text 7.50 (84-480-0150-8) Lectorum Pubns.

Dale, Eric S. Bringing Heaven Down to Earth: A Practical Spirituality of Work. LC 90-48098. (American University Studies: Theology & Religion: Ser. VII, Vol. 83). (Illus.). 158p. (C). 1991. text 31.95 (0-8204-1518-9) P Lang Pubng.

Dale, Frank. Delaware Diary: Episodes in the Life of a River. LC 95-39440. (Illus.). 200p. (C). 1996. pap. 17.95 (0-8135-2283-8); text 39.00 (0-8135-2282-X) Rutgers U Pr.

Dale, Godfrey. Peoples of Zanzibar: Their Customs & Religious Beliefs. LC 78-90112. 124p. 1969. reprint ed. lib. bdg. 45.00 (0-8371-2028-4, DAP&, Greenwood Pr) Greenwood.

Dale, Helen. Co-Authoring in the Classroom: Creating an Environment for Effective Collaboration. LC 96-44498. 104p. (Orig.). 1997. pap. 12.95 (0-8141-0695-1) NCTE.

Dale, Henry. Early Flying Machines. LC 92-21664. (Discoveries & Inventions Ser.). (Illus.). 64p. (YA). (gr. 7 up). 1993. text 20.00 (0-19-520966-4) OUP.

Dale, Henry H., frwd. A Catalogue of the Printed Books in the Wellcome Historical Medical Library Vol. 1: Books Printed Before 1641, 2 vols., Vol. 1. rev. ed. 422p. 1996. 100.00 (1-888262-02-8) Martino Pubng.

***Dale, Hilda.** The Coach & the Triumph of the Lamb: Two Poems by Marguerite de Navarre. 160p. 1999. pap. 29.95 (1-902454-04-9, Pub. by Elm Bank Pubns) Intl Spec Bk.

Dale, Holly, jt. auth. see Cole, Janis.

Dale, Iain. The Unofficial Book of Political Lists. 186p. 1999. pap. 17.95 (1-86105-145-X, Pub. by Robson Bks) Parkwest Pubns.

***Dale, Iain.** Wit & Wisdom of Tony Banks: A Tribute to a Parliamentary Character. 154p. 1999. pap. 10.95 (1-86105-200-6) Robson.

Dale, Iain, ed. As I Said to Dennis: The Margaret Thatcher Book of Quotations. LC 97-69432. (Illus.). 208p. 1997. 24.95 (1-86105-098-4, Robson-Parkwest) Parkwest Pubns.

— The Blair Necessities: The Tony Blair Book of Quotations. LC 98-70058. 184p. 1999. 22.95 (1-86105-139-5, Pub. by Robson Bks) Parkwest Pubns.

***Dale, Iain, ed.** British Political Party Manifestos, 1900-1997. LC 99-25226. 1312p. (C). 2000. text. write for info. (0-415-20588-3) Routledge.

Dale, Iain & Simmons, John, compiled by. The Bill Clinton Joke Book: Uncensored. 90p. 1998. pap. 6.95 (1-86105-194-8, Pub. by Robson Bks) Parkwest Pubns.

Dale, Ian. British Political Party Manifestos, 1900-1997. LC 99-25226. 1999. write for info. (0-415-20591-3) Routledge.

Dale, J. B. Indian Palmistry. 66p. 1996. pap. 6.00 (0-89540-221-1, SB-221) Sun Pub.

Dale, J. N., et al. Foundations for Reading & Writing, 2. Evans, A. R., ed. (Welcome to English Ser.). (Illus.). 1977. 3.45 (0-89285-034-5) ELS Educ Servs.

— Foundations for Reading & Writing, Bk. 1. Evans, A. R., ed. (Welcome to English Ser.). (Illus.). 1977. audio 12.00 (0-89285-044-2) ELS Educ Servs.

— Foundations for Reading & Writing, Bk. 2. Evans, A. R., ed. (Welcome to English Ser.). (Illus.). 1977. audio 12.00 (0-89285-045-0) ELS Educ Servs.

— Foundations for Reading & Writing, Bk. 3. Evans, A. R., ed. (Welcome to English Ser.). (Illus.). 1977. audio 12.00 (0-89285-046-9) ELS Educ Servs.

— Foundations for Reading & Writing, Bk. 4. Evans, A. R., ed. (Welcome to English Ser.). (Illus.). 1977. audio 12.00 (0-89285-047-7) ELS Educ Servs.

— Foundations for Reading & Writing, No. 1. Evans, A. R., ed. (Welcome to English Ser.). (Illus.). 1977. student ed. 3.45 (0-89285-033-7) ELS Educ Servs.

Dale, James W. Christic & Patristic Baptism: Baptizo: An Inquiry into the Meaning of the Word in the Holy Scriptures. LC 94-44997. 670p. 1995. pap. text 25.00 (0-86516-263-8) Bolchazy-Carducci.

Dale, James W. Christic Baptism & Patristic Baptism. LC 94-44997. 1995. pap. 19.99 (0-87552-234-3) P & R Pubng.

Dale, James W. Classic Baptism: An Inquiry into the Meaning of the Word Baptizo As Determined by the Usage of Classical Greek Writers. LC 88-92850. 376p. 1989. reprint ed. pap. 25.00 (0-86516-224-7) Bolchazy-Carducci.

— Classic Baptism: The Meaning of the Word in Classical Greek Writers. 1989. pap. 19.99 (0-87552-230-0) P & R Pubng.

— Johannic Baptism: An Inquiry into the Meaning of the Word As Determined by the Usage of the Holy Scriptures. 2nd ed. 428p. (C). 1993. reprint ed. pap. 19.99 (0-87552-232-7) P & R Pubng.

— Johannic Baptism Baptizo: An Inquiry into the Meaning of the Word As Determined by the Usage of the Holy Scriptures. 2nd ed. xvi, 428p. (C). 1993. reprint ed. pap. text 25.00 (0-86516-259-X) Bolchazy-Carducci.

— Judaic Baptism. 400p. 1991. reprint ed. pap. 25.00 (0-86516-247-6) Bolchazy-Carducci.

— Judaic Baptism: An Inquiry into the Meaning As Determined by the Usage of Jewish & Patristic Writers. 1991. pap. 19.99 (0-87552-231-9) P & R Pubng.

***Dale, Jean.** The Charlton Standard Catalogue of Royal Doulton Animals. 2nd rev. ed. (Illus.). 544p. 1998. pap. 24.95 (0-88968-198-8) Charlton Pr.

Dale, Jean. Honoring Jesus with My Life. 175p. 1992. pap. 3.25 (0-9634003-7-1) F Stellway.

Dale, Jean, ed. see Shaeffer, Ralph E.

Dale, Jennifer & Foster, Peggy. Feminists & State Welfare. 192p. (Orig.). (C). 1986. pap. text 11.95 (0-7102-0278-4, Routledge Thoemms) Routledge.

***Dale, Jenny.** Abandoned! (Puppy Patrol Ser.: Vol. 3). (Illus.). 112p. (J). (gr. 3-6). 2000. pap. 3.99 (0-439-11325-3) Scholastic Inc.

— Big Ben. (Puppy Patrol Ser.: Vol. 2). (Illus.). (J). 2000. pap. 3.99 (0-439-11324-5) Scholastic Inc.

— Double Trouble. (Puppy Patrol Ser.: Vol. 4). (Illus.). (J). 2000. pap. 3.99 (0-439-11326-1) Scholastic Inc.

— Gus the Greedy Puppy. (Illus.). 64p. (J). (gr. k-3). 2000. per. 3.99 (0-689-83423-3) Aladdin.

— Lenny the Lazy Puppy. (Puppy Friends Ser.: No. 4). (Illus.). 64p. (J). (gr. k-3). 2000. pap. 3.99 (0-689-83552-3) Aladdin.

— Lily the Lost Puppy. (Puppy Friends Ser.). 64p. (gr. k-3). 2000. per. 3.99 (0-689-83404-7) Aladdin.

— Max the Muddy Puppy. (Puppy Friends Ser.: No. 5). (Illus.). 64p. (J). (ps-3). 2000. pap. 3.99 (0-689-83553-1) Aladdin.

— Puppy Patrol: Teachers Pet. large type ed. (Illus.). (J). 1999. pap. write for info. (0-7540-6086-1) Chivers N Amer.

— Spot the Sporty Puppy. LC 99-87888. (Puppy Friends Ser.). (Illus.). (J). 2000. pap. 3.99 (0-689-83424-1) Aladdin.

— Star Paws. (Puppy Patrol Ser.: Vol. 5). (Illus.). (J). 2000. pap. 3.99 (0-439-11327-X) Scholastic Inc.

— Teacher's Pet, (Puppy Patrol Ser.). 128p. (J). (gr. 3-6). 2000. pap. 3.99 (0-439-11323-7) Scholastic Inc.

Dale, Jeremy. Molecular Genetics of Bacteria. 3rd ed. LC 97-32243. 324p. 1998. 115.00 (0-471-97782-9) Wiley.

***Dale, Jeremy.** Molecular Genetics of Bacteria. 3rd ed. LC 97-32243. 324p. 1998. pap. 45.00 (0-471-97783-7) Wiley.

Dale, Jeremy, jt. auth. see Ratledge, Colin.

Dale, Jeremy W. & Sanders, Peter G., eds. Methods in Gene Technology, Vol. 1. 300p. 1991. 128.50 (1-55938-263-5) Jai Pr.

— Methods in Gene Technology, Vol. 2. 354p. 1995. 128.50 (1-55938-264-3) Jai Pr.

***Dale, Jim.** The Too-Bad-It's-Your-Birthday Book: A Few Tender Thoughts to Put a Smile on Your Wrinkly Little Face. LC 00-31049. 2000. 7.95 (0-7407-1087-7) Andrews & McMeel.

Dale, Jim, jt. auth. see Crosby, Don.

Dale, Jim, jt. auth. see Dale, Barbara.

Dale, Jim, jt. auth. see Dunlop, Frank.

***Dale, Joan.** Create Greeting Cards with Glass Painting Techniques. (Illus.). 128p. 1999. pap. 22.99 (1-58180-007-X, 31502, North Lght Bks) F & W Pubns Inc.

Dale, John. Dark Angel. LC 95-68389. (Mask Noir Ser.). 304p. (Orig.). 1996. pap. 13.99 (1-85242-391-9) Serpents Tail.

— The Dogs Are Barking. LC 98-89859. (Illus.). 256p. 1999. pap. 12.99 (1-85242-609-8, Pub. by Serpents Tail) Consort Bk Sales.

Dale-Jones, Don. Raymond Garlick. 112p. 1996. pap. 9.95 (0-7083-1322-1, Pub. by Univ Wales Pr) Paul & Co Pubs.

Dale-Jones, Don & Jenkins, W. Randal. Wales Today. 144p. (C). 1976. pap. 45.00 (0-85088-377-6, Pub. by Gomer Pr) St Mut.

Dale-Jones, Don, jt. ed. see Croft, Julian.

Dale, Julie S. Art to Wear. LC 86-14041. (Illus.). 320p. 1986. 95.00 (0-89659-664-8) Abbeville Pr.

Dale, Kenneth G. Reading the Bible in One Year: A Complete Program: April 1st Version. 6p. 1997. pap. 2.50 (1-891481-04-5) TrueLife Creat.

— Reading the Bible in One Year: A Complete Program: August 1st Version. 6p. 1997. pap. 2.50 (1-891481-08-8) TrueLife Creat.

— Reading the Bible in One Year: A Complete Program: December 1st Version. 6p. 1997. pap. 2.50 (1-891481-12-6) TrueLife Creat.

— Reading the Bible in One Year: A Complete Program: February 1st Version. 1997. pap. 2.50 (1-891481-02-9) TrueLife Creat.

— Reading the Bible in One Year: A Complete Program: January 1st Version. 6p. 1997. pap. 2.50 (1-891481-01-0) TrueLife Creat.

— Reading the Bible in One Year: A Complete Program: July 1st Version. 6p. 1997. pap. 2.50 (1-891481-07-X) TrueLife Creat.

— Reading the Bible in One Year: A Complete Program: June 1st Version. 6p. 1997. pap. 2.50 (1-891481-06-1) TrueLife Creat.

— Reading the Bible in One Year: A Complete Program: March 1st Version. 6p. 1997. pap. 2.50 (1-891481-03-7) TrueLife Creat.

— Reading the Bible in One Year: A Complete Program: May 1st Version. 6p. 1997. pap. 2.50 (1-891481-05-3) TrueLife Creat.

— Reading the Bible in One Year: A Complete Program: November 1st Version. 6p. 1997. pap. 2.50 (1-891481-11-8) TrueLife Creat.

— Reading the Bible in One Year: A Complete Program: October 1st Version. 6p. 1997. pap. 2.50 (1-891481-10-X) TrueLife Creat.

— Reading the Bible in One Year: A Complete Program: September 1st Version. 6p. 1997. pap. 2.50 (1-891481-09-6) TrueLife Creat.

Dale, Larry & Gilbertie, James L. Economics for Classroom Teachers. rev. ed. 534p. 1997. pap. text 52.95 (1-56226-369-2) CAT Pub.

Dale, Larry L. & Dixon, Lloyd S. The Impact of Water Supply Reductions on San Joaquin Valley Agriculture During the 1986-1992 Drought. LC 98-20916. (Illus.). 94p. 1998. pap. 13.00 (0-8330-2620-8, MR-552-EPA) Rand Corp.

Dale, Laura A., jt. auth. see Murphy, Gardner.

Dale, Leigh & Ryan, Simon, eds. The Body in the Library. LC 99-171844. (Cross-Cultures Ser.: No. 33). 272p. 1998. pap. 22.00 (90-420-0753-2) Editions Rodopi.

Dale, Leon A. French Labor: A Bibliography with a Selection of Documents on the French Labor Movement. LC 72-95163. xxxvii, 317p. 1969. 57.50 (0-678-00543-5) Kelley.

Dale, Leslie. Dynamic Uses of Imagery. (Orig.). 1994. pap. 9.95 (0-913412-75-9) Brandon Hse.

Dale, M. B., jt. ed. see Mucina, L.

Dale, M. M. & Dickenson, A. H. Companion to Pharmacology: A Study Guide for Self Assessment & Revision. LC 92-19270. (Illus.). 206p. 1993. pap. text 19.95 (0-443-04178-4) Church.

Dale, M. M., jt. auth. see Rang, H. P.

Dale, M. Maureen, et al, eds. Textbook of Immunopharmacology. 3rd ed. LC 93-19411. (Illus.). 384p. 1994. pap. 79.95 (0-632-03025-9, Pub. by Blckwll Scitfc UK) Blackwell Sci.

Dale, Madeline M. Southern Cross. LC 98-16361. 256p. 1998. 24.95 (1-880090-61-9) Galde Pr.

Dale, Malcolm & Thomas, Klaude. Gurps Goblins. Punch, Sean & Pinsonneault, Susan, eds. (Illus.). 144p. 1996. pap. 21.95 (1-55634-317-5, 6078, Pub. by S Jackson Games) BookWorld.

Dale, Margaret. How to Be a Better Interviewer. (How to Be a Better...Ser.). 1997. pap. 15.95 (0-7494-1902-4) Kogan Page Ltd.

— Successful Recruitment Selection: A Practical Guide for Managers. 256p. 1995. 45.00 (0-7494-1422-7, Pub. by Kogan Pg) Cassell.

Dale, Marilyn. Moments Vol. 1: A Soul's Reflection. LC 97-66263. (Orig.). 1997. pap. 10.95 (0-9656685-3-3) Soul Message.

Dale, Mark R. Spatial Pattern Analysis in Plant Ecology. LC 98-15360. (Cambridge Studies in Ecology). (Illus.). 320p. (C). 1998. 69.95 (0-521-45227-9) Cambridge U Pr.

***Dale, Mark R.** Spatial Pattern Analysis in Plant Ecology. (Cambridge Studies in Ecology Ser.). (Illus.). 336p. 2000. pap. 35.95 (0-521-79437-4) Cambridge U Pr.

Dale, Martin. The Movie Game: The Film Business in Britain, Europe & America. (Film Studies). (Illus.). 416p. 1997. 70.00 (0-304-33386-7); pap. 19.95 (0-304-33387-5) Continuum.

***Dale, Monica.** Eurhythmics for Young Children: Six Lessons for Fall. LC 00-191235. (Illus.). xiv, 70p. 2000. 24.95 (0-9701416-0-2) Musikinesis.

Dale Nathanson, Martha. Home Care Fraud & Abuse: Critical Questions, Essential Answers. 448p. Date not set. boxed set 69.00 (0-8342-1188-2, 11882) Aspen Pub.

Dale, Nell. Ada Plus Data Structures: An Object-Based Approach. 840p. 1996. pap. text 52.50 (0-669-29265-6) Jones & Bartlett.

— Ada Plus Data Structures 3.5: An Object-Based Approach. 840p. 1996. pap. text 55.00 (0-669-41676-2) Jones & Bartlett.

***Dale, Nell.** Essentials of C++ As a Second Language: A Laboratory Course. (Illus.). 152p. (C). 1999. pap. text 21.25 (0-7637-0858-5) Jones & Bartlett.

Dale, Nell. Programming in Pascal. (Computer Science Ser.). 624p. 1997. pap. 51.25 (0-7637-0484-9) Jones & Bartlett.

***Dale, Nell & Headington, Mark.** C++ Plus Data Structures. (Illus.). (C). 1998. pap. text 10.00 (0-7637-0739-2) Jones & Bartlett.

Dale, Nell & Lilly, Susan C. Pascal + Data Structure: Test Item File. 4th ed. (Computer Science Ser.). 1995. pap. 10.00 (0-669-34722-1) Jones & Bartlett.

Dale, Nell & Orshalick, David. Introduction to Pascal & Structured Design. (Computer Science Ser.). 470p. (C). 1983. pap. 50.00 (0-669-06962-0) Jones & Bartlett.

Dale, Nell & Walker, Henry M. Abstract Data Types 3.5. 624p. 1996. 61.25 (0-669-40000-9) Jones & Bartlett.

Dale, Nell & Weems, Chip. Pascal. 4th ed. (Computer Science). Date not set. 58.75 (0-669-34218-1) Jones & Bartlett.

— Pascal. 4th ed. (Computer Science Ser.). 1996. pap. 50.00 (0-7637-0397-4) Jones & Bartlett.

— Pascal: Test Item File. 4th ed. (Computer Science Ser.). Date not set. pap. 10.00 (0-669-34221-1) Jones & Bartlett.

— Turbo Pascal. 4th ed. (Computer Science Ser.). 1997. pap. 55.00 (0-7637-0608-6) Jones & Bartlett.

— Turbo Pascal: Test Item File. 4th ed. (Computer Science Ser.). Date not set. pap. 10.00 (0-669-34955-0) Jones & Bartlett.

— Turbo Pascal: Transparencies Masters. 4th ed. (Computer Science Ser.). Date not set. pap. 50.00 (0-669-34956-9) Jones & Bartlett.

Dale, Nell, et al. Ada + Data Structures. (Computer Science Ser.). 1996. pap., teacher ed. 10.00 (0-669-29266-4) Jones & Bartlett.

— Data Types Data Structure & Algorithms in C++ LC 98-12284. (Computer Science Ser.). 773p. 1998. 61.25 (0-7637-0621-3) Jones & Bartlett.

***Dale, Nell, et al.** Instructor's Guide for C++ 2nd ed. (Illus.). 200p. (C). 1999. pap. text, teacher ed. 35.00 (0-7637-1144-6) JB Pubns.

Dale, Nell, et al. Program & Problem Solving C++ Test Item File. (Computer Science Ser.). 1996. pap., teacher ed. 10.00 (0-669-29775-5) Jones & Bartlett.

— Programming & Problem Solving Test Item File. (Computer Science Ser.). 1994. pap. 10.00 (0-669-29362-8) Jones & Bartlett.

— Programming & Problem Solving with ADA. LC 93-78374. 887p. 1996. pap. 56.25 (0-7637-0293-5) Jones & Bartlett.

***Dale, Nell, et al.** Programming & Problem Solving with ADA. 2nd ed. LC 99-49488. (Illus.). 896p. (C). 2000. pap. text 60.00 (0-7637-0792-9) Jones & Bartlett.

— Programming & Problem Solving with C++ (Illus.). 1312p. (C). 1998. text 63.75 (0-7637-0812-7) JB Pubns.

Dale, Nell, et al. Programming & Problem Solving with C++ LC 96-223831. 1155p. 1996. pap. 58.75 (0-7637-0292-7) Jones & Bartlett.

***Dale, Nell, et al.** Programming & Problem Solving with Java. (Illus.). 1184p. (C). 2000. pap. text 63.75 (0-7637-1064-4) Jones & Bartlett.

— Programming in C++ (Illus.). 320p. (C). 1996. pap. text 10.00 (0-7637-0711-2) Jones & Bartlett.

Dale, Nell, et al. Programming in C++ LC 98-3359. (Computer Science Ser.). 645p. 1998. pap. 50.00 (0-7637-0537-3) Jones & Bartlett.

Dale, Nell, et al. TM- Program & Problem Solve C++ Trans Masters. (Illus.). 408p. (C). 1996. pap. text 50.00 (0-7637-0320-6) Jones & Bartlett.

Dale, Nell, jt. auth. see Headington, Mark.

Dale, Nell B. Lab Course in Turbo Pascal 3.5. 2nd ed. LC 96-221851. 1997. 16.00 (0-7637-0333-8) Jones & Bartlett.

***Dale, Nell B.** A Laboratory Course in C++ LC 99-33648. 1999. write for info. (0-7637-1146-2) Jones & Bartlett.

Dale, Nell B. A Laboratory Course in Pascal: With a Tutorial on THINK. 176p. (C). 1991. disk. write for info. (0-318-70088-3) HM Trade Div.

— A Laboratory Course in Pascal: With a Tutorial on THINK. (Computer Science Ser.). 176p. (C). 1991. pap. 28.75 (0-669-26957-3) Jones & Bartlett.

— Programming in Pascal. 515p. (C). 1990. teacher ed. write for info. (0-318-70087-5) HM Trade Div.

— Programming in Pascal. (Computer Science Ser.). 515p. (C). 1990. pap. 51.25 (0-669-20042-5) Jones & Bartlett.

— Programming in Pascal with an Early Introduction to Procedures. (Computer Science Ser.). 523p. (C). 1990. pap. 50.00 (0-669-20249-5); pap. 10.00 (0-669-20246-0); pap., teacher ed. 10.00 (0-669-20244-4) Jones & Bartlett.

Dale, Nell B. & Lilly, Susan C. Pascal Plus Data Structures, Algorithms, & Advanced Programming. 4th ed. (Computer Science Ser.). 762p. (C). 1996. pap. 57.50 (0-669-39540-4) Jones & Bartlett.

— Pascal Plus Data Structures, Algorithms & Advanced Programming. 4th ed. (Computer Science Ser.). (C). 1995. pap., teacher ed. 10.00 (0-669-34721-3) Jones & Bartlett.

— Pascal Plus Data Structures, Algorithms, & Advanced Programming 4th ed. LC 94-76241. xxvii, 762p. 1995. write for info. (0-669-34720-5) Free Pr.

Dale, Nell B. & Orshalick, David W. A Laboratory Course in C++ 3.5. LC 96-32748. (Computer Science Ser.). 424p. 1996. pap. 27.50 (0-7637-0247-1) Jones & Bartlett.

Dale, Nell B. & Weems, Chip. Introduction to Pascal & Structured Design. 2nd ed. LC 86-80506. (Computer Science Ser.). 720p. (C). 1987. pap. 47.50 (0-669-09570-2) Jones & Bartlett.

— Introduction to Pascal 3.5 & Structured Design. 4th ed. 870p. (C). 1994. pap. 53.75 (0-669-34224-6); pap., teacher ed. 10.00 (0-669-34220-3) Jones & Bartlett.

— Introduction to Turbo Pascal & Software Design. 4th ed. (Computer Science Ser.). (C). Date not set. pap., teacher ed. 10.00 (0-669-34954-2) Jones & Bartlett.

— Introduction to Turbo Pascal 3.5 & Software Design. 4th ed. (Computer Science Ser.). 912p. (C). 1996. pap. 53.75 (0-669-39435-1) Jones & Bartlett.

— Introduction to Turbo Pascal 3.5 & Software Design: Casebook. 4th ed. (Computer Science Ser.). (C). 1995. pap. 10.00 (0-669-34957-7) Jones & Bartlett.

Dale, Nell B., et al. Programming & Problem Solving in C++ 2nd ed. LC 99-25436. 1999. write for info. (0-7637-1063-6) Jones & Bartlett.

— Programming & Problem Solving with ADA. (Computer Science Ser.). 887p. (C). 1994. pap., teacher ed. 10.00 (0-669-29361-X) Jones & Bartlett.

***Dale, Nell B., et al.** Programming in C++ 2nd ed. LC 00-44385. 2000. write for info. (0-7637-1424-0) Jones & Bartlett.

Dale-Nichols, Jan, ed. Competition in the Utility Industry: 31 Case Studies from the Pages of Chartwell's Industry Leading Publications. 2nd ed. 136p. 1996. pap., spiral bd. 98.00 (1-891790-04-8) Chartwell Inc.

Dale, Nora. The Best Trick of All. (Real Readers Ser.). (Illus.). 32p. (J). (gr. 1-4). 1989. pap. 4.95 (0-8114-6700-7) Raintree Steck-V.

Dale, Norman, jt. auth. see Corney, Bob.

Dale, Norman, tr. see Guillot, Rene.

D

Dale, Ole Johan. Urban Planning in Singapore: The Transformation of a City. (South-East Asian Social Science Monographs). (Illus.). 352p. 1999. text 47.50 (*967-65-3064-6*) OUP.

Dale, Owen, jt. auth. see Hill, Kim.

Dale, P., jt. auth. see Vein, R.

Dale, Paulette. "Did You Say Something, Susan?" How Women Can Gain Confidence with Assertive Communication. LC 98-25277. 208p. 1998. 19.95 (*1-55972-482-X*, Birch Ln Pr) Carol Pub Group.

— English Pronunciation for Japanese Speakers. 1994. pap. 49.00 incl. audio (*0-13-321407-9*) P-H.

Dale, Paulette & Poms, Lillian. English Pronunciation for International Students. LC 93-23687. 320p. (C). 1994. pap. text 31.53 (*0-13-279852-2*) P-H.

— English Pronunciation for Japanese Speakers. LC 93-41643. 320p. (C). 1994. pap. text 31.53 (*0-13-034372-2*) P-H.

— English Pronunciation for Japanese Students. 1994. write for info. (*0-318-72332-8*) P-H.

— English Pronunciation for Spanish Speakers: Consonants. (Illus.). 240p. (C). 1986. pap. text 28.20 (*0-13-281304-1*) P-H.

— English Pronunciation for Spanish Speakers: Vowels. (Illus.). 176p. (C). 1985. pap. text 28.20 (*0-13-281312-2*) P-H.

Dale, Paulette & Wolf, James C. Speech Communication for International Students. (Illus.). 160p. (C). 1988. pap. text 27.20 (*0-13-827312-X*) P-H.

Dale, Penny. All about Alice. LC 92-52991. (Illus.). 32p. (J). (ps-3). 1993. 13.95 (*1-56402-171-8*) Candlewick Pr.

— Bet You Can't. LC 87-3780. (Illus.). 32p. (J). (ps-1). 1988. 12.95 (*0-397-32235-6*); lib. bdg. 12.89 (*0-397-32256-9*) HarpC Child Bks.

— Big Brother, Little Brother. LC 96-30539. (Illus.). 32p. (J). (ps-2). 1997. 15.99 (*0-7636-0146-2*) Candlewick Pr.

— Daisy Rabbit's Tree House. LC 95-16171. (Illus.). 32p. (J). (ps-1). 1997. reprint ed. pap. 5.99 (*0-7636-0149-7*) Candlewick Pr.

— Ten in the Bed: Level One, Red. LC 98-88092. (Reading Together Ser.). (Illus.). 32p. (J). 1999. pap. write for info. (*0-7636-0868-8*) Candlewick Pr.

— Ten Out of Bed. LC 92-46116. (Illus.). 32p. (J). 1996. reprint ed. pap. 5.99 (*1-56402-834-8*) Candlewick Pr.

— Ten Play Hide-&-Seek. LC 97-32228. (Illus.). 40p. (J). (ps-k). 1998. 15.99 (*0-7636-0654-5*) Candlewick Pr.

— Wake up, Mr. B.! LC 91-58763. (Illus.). 32p. (J). (ps up). 1992. 14.95 (*1-56402-104-1*) Candlewick Pr.

— Wake up, Mr. B.! LC 91-58763. (Illus.). 32p. (J). (ps up). 1994. pap. 4.99 (*1-56402-382-6*) Candlewick Pr.

***Dale, Penny.** Big Brother, Little Brother. 32p. (J). 1999. pap. 5.99 (*0-7636-1249-9*) Candlewick Pr.

Dale, Penny, jt. auth. see Waddell, Martin.

Dale, Peter. Adults Abused as Children: Experiences of Counselling & Psychotherapy. LC 98-61270. 238 p. 1999. write for info. (*0-7619-5998-X*) Sage.

— Dangerous Families: Assessment & Treatment of Child Abuse. 280p. 1987. 47.50 (*0-422-60140-3*, 1129, Pub. by Tavistock); pap. 14.95 (*0-317-56157-X*, 1152, Pub. by Tavistock) Routldge.

— Directory of Library & Information Organizations in the United Kingdom. LC 94-143049. 192p. 1993. reprint ed. pap. 59.60 (*0-608-07777-1*, 206786500010) Bks Demand.

— The Divine Comedy: Hell Purgatory Heaven. LC 97-157812. (Poetica Ser.). 422p. 1997. pap. 19.95 (*0-85646-280-2*, Pub. by Anvil Press) Dufour.

— Edge to Edge. LC 97-178869. 172p. 1997. pap. 18.95 (*0-85646-272-1*, Pub. by Anvil Press) Dufour.

— Guide to Libraries & Information Sources in Medicine & Health Care. 2nd ed. LC 96-147051. (Key Resources Ser.). 192p. 1997. 69.95 (*0-7123-0839-3*, Pub. by SRIS) L Erlbaum Assocs.

— The Victorian Critic & the Idea of History: Carlyle, Arnold, Pater. 320p. 1977. 40.50 (*0-674-93581-0*) HUP.

Dale, Peter, compiled by. Guide to Libraries & Information Sources in Medicine & Health Care. (Key Resources Ser.). 162p. 1995. pap. 69.95 (*0-7123-0823-7*) L Erlbaum Assocs.

— Guide to Libraries in Key U.K. Companies. (Key Resources Ser.). 188p. 1993. pap. 39.95 (*0-7123-0796-6*, Pub. by SRIS) L Erlbaum Assocs.

Dale, Peter, ed. Guide to Libraries & Information Units: In Government Departments & Other Organisations. 32nd ed. (Key Resources Ser.). 208p. 1996. pap. 65.00 (*0-7123-0828-8*) L Erlbaum Assocs.

— Guide to Libraries & Information Units: In Government Departments & Other Organisations. 33rd ed. 200p. 1998. pap. 65.00 (*0-7123-0845-8*) L Erlbaum Assocs.

— Guide to Libraries in Western Europe: National, International & Government Libraries. 2nd ed. (Key Resources Ser.). 160p. 1994. pap. 65.00 (*0-7123-0810-5*) L Erlbaum Assocs.

Dale, Peter, tr. The Divine Comedy: Hell Purgatory Heaven. LC 97-157812. (Poetica Ser.). 422p. 1997. 45.00 (*0-85646-287-X*, Pub. by Anvil Press) Dufour.

Dale, Peter & British Library. Guide to Libraries in Western Europe: National, International & Government Libraries LC 98-105702. 122 P. ;p. 1991. write for info. (*0-7123-0785-0*) B23tish Library.

Dale, Peter, jt. auth. see Binns, Bernard.

Dale, Peter, jt. auth. see Laforgue, Jules.

Dale, Peter A. In Pursuit of a Scientific Culture: Science, Art, & Society in the Victorian Age. LC 89-40251. (Science & Literature Ser.). 348p. (Orig.). (C). 1989. pap. text 19.95 (*0-299-12264-6*) U of Wis Pr.

***Dale, Peter F. & McLaughlin, John D.** Land Administration. LC 99-36961. (Spatial Information Systems Ser.). 184p. 2000. write for info. (*0-19-823390-6*) OUP.

Dale, Peter F. & McLaughlin, John D. Land Information Management: An Introduction with Special Reference to Cadastral Problems in Third World Countries. (Illus.). 300p. 1988. 69.00 (*0-19-858404-0*) OUP.

Dale, R. English Pronunciation for Spanish Speakers, 2 vols. 1986. text 55.25 incl. audio (*0-13-281338-6*) P-H.

— World of Jazz. 192p. 1996. 15.98 (*0-7858-0599-0*) Bk Sales Inc.

Dale, R., ed. Education, Training & Employment: Towards a New Vocationalism? 138p. 1985. text 19.50 (*0-08-032673-0*, M110, M115, M125, Pub. by PPL); pap. text 9.00 (*0-08-032672-2*, Pub. by PPL) Elsevier.

Dale, R., et al, eds. Aspects of Automated Natural Language Generation: Sixth International Workshop, Trento, Italy, April 5-7, 1992: Proceedings. LC 92-9037. (Lecture Notes in Artificial Intelligence Ser.: Vol. 587). viii, 312p. 1992. 52.95 (*0-387-55399-1*) Spr-Verlag.

Dale, R. C. The Films of Rene Clair. LC 85-22235. (Illus.). 1986. 92.50 (*0-8108-1858-2*) Scarecrow.

Dale, Ralph A. Acupoint Exercises for the Six Senses: A Lay Person's Guide. 2nd rev. ed. (Illus.). 150p. 2001. pap. 29.00 (*1-877589-18-7*) Dialectic Pubng.

— Acupoint Exercises for the Six Senses: Professional Edition. (Illus.). 53p. 1996. spiral bd. 15.00 (*1-877589-10-1*) Dialectic Pubng.

— Acupuncture - The Five Element-Phases: The Theory, Command Points, Clinical Applications & Comprehensive Index. (Illus.). 400p. 2001. 95.00 (*1-877589-14-4*) Dialectic Pubng.

— Acupuncture - The One Thousand New Points: A Comprehensive Manual & Prescription Index. (Illus.). 500p. 2001. 125.00 (*1-877589-07-1*) Dialectic Pubng.

— Acupuncture - The Special Function Points. (Illus.). 205p. 1996. pap. 39.00 (*1-877589-12-8*) Dialectic Pubng.

— The Acupuncture Certification Examination Review Book of Questions & Answers. 87p. 1985. student ed., spiral bd. 25.00 (*1-877589-03-9*) Dialectic Pubng.

— The Acupuncture Comprehensive Prescription Index. (Illus.). 550p. 1997. 125.00 (*1-877589-16-0*) Dialectic Pubng.

— The Acupuncture Comprehensive Prescription Index. rev. ed. (Illus.). 550p. 1997. pap. 95.00 (*1-877589-15-2*) Dialectic Pubng.

— Acupuncture in Holistic Practice Vol. 5: Selected Journal Articles, 1976-2000. LC L11000xW08500. (Illus.). 600p. 2001. 125.00 (*1-877589-08-X*) Dialectic Pubng.

— The Acupuncture Manual Vol. 1: Points, Conduits, Functions & Indications. LC L11000xW08500. (Illus.). 600p. 2001. 125.00 (*1-877589-13-6*) Dialectic Pubng.

— Acupuncture with Your Fingers: An 18-Point Healing System. 6th rev. ed. (Illus.). 55p. 1988. 12.00 (*1-877589-00-4*) Dialectic Pubng.

— Acupuncture with Your Fingers: An 18-Point Healing System. 7th rev. ed. LC 99-161906. (Illus.). 55p. 1998. pap. 6.25 (*1-877589-01-2*) Dialectic Pubng.

— Acupuntura Con Sus Dedos: Sistema Curativo de Dieciocho Puntos. rev. ed. Lorenzana, Ronald, tr. (SPA., Illus.). 55p. (Orig.). 1987. pap. 6.25 (*1-877589-02-0*) Dialectic Pubng.

— Dictionary of Acupuncture Terms, Concepts & Points. LC 93-90608. (Illus.). 431p. 1993. pap. 69.00 (*1-877589-11-X*) Dialectic Pubng.

— The Micro-Acupuncture Comprehensive Manual & Prescription Index. LC L11000x08500. (Illus.). 400p. 2001. 125.00 (*1-877589-06-3*) Dialectic Pubng.

***Dale, Ralph Alan.** Acupuncture A-Z. 384p. 2002. pap. 50.00 (*0-7506-4827-9*) Buttrwrth-Heinemann.

— The Acupuncture Manual: Points, Conduits, Functions & Indications. LC L11000xW08500. (Illus.). 500p. 2000. pap. 95.00 (*1-877589-21-7*) Dialectic Pubng.

Dale, Richard. Bank Supervision Around the World. (Report Ser.). 76p. 1982. pap. 10.00 (*1-56708-056-1*) Grp of Thirty.

— Botswana's Search for Autonomy in Southern Africa, 358. LC 95-2087. (Contributions in Political Science Ser.: Vol. 358). 296p. 1995. 59.95 (*0-313-29571-9*, Greenwood Pr) Greenwood.

— Risk & Regulation in Global Se. LC 95-53020. 352p. 1996. 135.00 (*0-471-95781-X*) Wiley.

Dale, Richard S. & Mattione, Richard P. Managing Global Debt. LC 83-72567. 50p. 1983. pap. 8.95 (*0-8157-1717-2*) Brookings.

Dale, Robert. Generating Referring Expressions: Constructing Descriptions in a Domain of Objects & Processes. (Illus.). 288p. 1992. 39.95 (*0-262-04128-6*, Bradford Bks) MIT Pr.

Dale, Robert & Opyt, Barbara. Lotus Notes for Web Workgroups. LC 96-14280. 280p. (C). 1996. pap. 36.95 (*1-56690-110-3*) Thomson Learn.

Dale, Robert, jt. auth. see Reiter, Ehud.

Dale, Robert D. Good News from Great Leaders. LC 91-78150. 173p. (Orig.). 1992. pap., student ed. 15.95 (*1-56699-051-3*, AL130) Alban Inst.

— Leadership for a Changing Church: Charting the Shape of the River. LC 97-40921. 128p. 1998. pap. 14.95 (*0-687-01485-9*) Abingdon.

— Leading Edge: Leadership Strategies from the New Testament. LC 96-11267. 144p. 1996. pap. 12.95 (*0-687-01506-5*) Abingdon.

Dale, Robert E. Pastoral Leadership. 1986. 16.95 (*0-687-30349-4*) Abingdon.

Dale, Robin & Audio Preservation Task Force Staff. Audio Preservation: A Selective Annotated Bibliography & Brief Summary of Current Practices. LC 98-22579. 1998. 9.00 (*0-8389-7959-9*) ALA.

Dale, Rodney. Cats in Books. LC 97-71148. (Illus.). 112p. 1997. 16.95 (*0-8109-4045-0*, Pub. by Abrams) Time Warner.

— Jazz. LC 98-65248. (Teach Yourself Ser.). (Illus.). 192p. 1998. pap. 9.95 (*0-8442-0012-3*, 00123, Teach Yrslf) NTC Contemp Pub Co.

— Timekeeping. LC 92-21661. (Discoveries & Inventions Ser.). (Illus.). 64p. (YA). (gr. 7 up). 1993. 20.00 (*0-19-520968-0*) OUP.

Dale, Rodney, ed. Early Railways. (Discoveries & Inventions Ser.). (Illus.). 64p. (YA). (gr. 7 up). 1994. lib. bdg. 20.00 (*0-19-521003-4*) OUP.

Dale, Rodney & Weaver, Rebecca. Home Entertainment. (Discoveries & Inventions Ser.). (Illus.). 64p. (YA). (gr. 7 up). 1994. pap. 10.95 (*0-19-521005-0*); text 20.00 (*0-19-521001-8*) OUP.

— Machines in the Office. (Discoveries & Inventions Ser.). (Illus.). 64p. (YA). (gr. 7 up). 1994. lib. bdg. 20.00 (*0-19-521000-X*) OUP.

Dale, Rodney, jt. auth. see Sassoon, George.

Dale, Rodney, ed. see Sassoon, George.

Dale, Roger, et al. The TVEI Story: Policy, Practice & Preparation for the Workforce. 192p. 1990. 113.00 (*0-335-09563-1*); pap. 35.95 (*0-335-09562-3*) OpUniv Pr.

Dale, Ronald. The Price Guide to Black & White Pot Lids. 2nd ed. (Price Guide Ser.). (Illus.). 480p. 1987. pap. 19.50 (*1-85149-008-6*) Antique Collect.

Dale, Ruth J. Breakfast in Bed. (Romance Ser.: No. 3465). 1997. per. 3.25 (*0-373-03465-2*, 1-03465-1) Harlequin Bks.

— Breakfast in Bed. large type ed. (Mills & Boon Large Print Ser.). 288p. 1998. 24.99 (*0-263-15432-7*, Pub. by Mills & Boon) Ulverscroft.

— Breakfast in Bed (Simply the Best) 1997. per. 3.25 (*0-373-15711-8*) Harlequin Bks.

— Le Cow-Boy et L'Heritiere. (Horizon Ser.: No. 475). (FRE.). 1998. pap. 3.50 (*0-373-39475-6*, 1-39475-8) Harlequin Bks.

— The Cupid Chronicles (The Camerons of Colorado) (Superromance Ser.). 1996. per. 3.99 (*0-373-70687-1*, 1-70687-8) Harlequin Bks.

— The Cupid Conspiracy (Camerons of Colorado) (Temptation Ser.). 1996. per. 3.50 (*0-373-25679-5*, 1-25679-1) Harlequin Bks.

— Cupid's Revenge: Camerons of Colorado. (Superromance Ser.: No. 788). 1998. per. 4.25 (*0-373-70788-6*, 0-70788-5) Harlequin Bks.

— Ecos de Sociedad (Society News) (Deseo Ser.). (SPA.). 1998. per. 3.50 (*0-373-33450-8*, 1-33450-7) Harlequin Bks.

***Dale, Ruth J.** Une Famille Inseparable. (FRE.). 2000. mass mkt. 3.99 (*0-373-39542-6*) Harlequin Bks.

Dale, Ruth J. Kids, Critters & Cupid. LC 96-3671. (Superromance Ser.). 298p. 1996. per. 3.99 (*0-373-70678-2*, 1-70678-7) Harlequin Bks.

— Moonlighting. (Love & Laughter Ser.). 1997. per. 3.50 (*0-373-44015-4*, 1-44015-5) Harlequin Bks.

— Parents Wanted! (Romance Ser.: No. 3557). 1999. per. 3.50 (*0-373-03557-8*, 1-03557-5, Harlequin) Harlequin Bks.

— Parents Wanted! large type ed. (Larger Print Ser.: No. 403). 1999. per. 3.50 (*0-373-15803-3*, 1-15803-9, Harlequin) Harlequin Bks.

— La Petite Comedienne. (Horizon Ser.). (FRE.). 1997. pap. 3.50 (*0-373-39438-1*, 1-39438-6) Harlequin Bks.

— A Private Eyeful: (Hero for Hire) (Temptation Ser.: No. 709). 1998. per. 3.75 (*0-373-25809-7*, 0-25809-5) Harlequin Bks.

— Runaway Honeymoon. 1997. per. 3.25 (*0-373-03441-5*, 1-03441-2) Silhouette.

— Runaway Honeymoon. large type ed. 1997. per. 3.25 (*0-373-15687-1*) Harlequin Bks.

— Runaway Honeymoon. large type ed. 1997. 20.95 (*0-263-15167-0*) Mac Lib Ref.

— Runaway Wedding. large type ed. 1997. 20.95 (*0-263-14929-3*) Thorndike Pr.

— Runway Wedding. (Romance Ser.). 186p. 1996. per. 3.25 (*0-373-03413-X*, 1-03413-1) Harlequin Bks.

— The Seven-Year Itch. (Love & Laughter Ser.). 1996. per. 3.50 (*0-373-44006-5*, 1-44006-4) Harlequin Bks.

***Dale, Ruth J.** Shane's Last Stand. (Heart of the West Ser.: No. 8). 2000. per. 4.50 (*0-373-82592-7*, 1-82592-6, Harlequin) Harlequin Bks.

Dale, Ruth J. A Simple Texas Wedding. (Romance Ser.). 1996. per. 3.25 (*0-373-03424-5*, 1-03424-8) Harlequin Bks.

— Together Again. (Family Continuity Program Ser.: No. 37). 1999. mass mkt. 4.50 (*0-373-82185-9*, 1-82185-9) Harlequin Bks.

— Wild Horses. 1994. per. 2.99 (*0-373-03313-3*) Harlequin Bks.

Dale, Ruth J. & Raye, Kimberly. One in a Million. (Duets Ser.: No. 4). 1999. per. 5.99 (*0-373-44070-7*, 1-44070-0, Harlequin) Harlequin Bks.

Dale, Ruth Jean. Bachelor Available! (Romance Ser.: No. 3539). 1999. per. 3.50 (*0-373-03539-X*, 1-03539-3) Harlequin Bks.

— Bachelor Available: Texas Grooms Wanted. large type ed. 1999. 3.50 (*0-373-15785-1*, Harlequin) Harlequin Bks.

***Dale, Ruth Jean.** The Cowgirl's Man. Vol. 782. 2000. mass mkt. 3.99 (*0-373-25882-8*) Harlequin Bks.

Dale, Ruth Jean. Dash to the Altar. large type ed. (Whirlwind Weddings Ser.). 1998. per. 3.50 (*0-373-15737-1*, Harlequin) Harlequin Bks.

— Dash to the Altar: Whirlwind Weddings. (Romance Ser.: No. 3491). 1998. per. 3.50 (*0-373-03491-1*, 1-03491-7) Harlequin Bks.

— Family Secrets: The Lyon Legacy. 1999. per. 4.25 (*0-373-70853-X*, 1-70853-6) Harlequin Bks.

***Dale, Ruth Jean.** Fiance Wanted. 2000. per. 3.50 (*0-373-15839-4*) Harlequin Bks.

— Fiance Wanted! (Romance Ser.). 2000. mass mkt. 3.50 (*0-373-03593-4*) Harlequin Bks.

— Hitched! (Superromance Ser.). 2000. mass mkt. 4.50 (*0-373-70933-1*, 1-70933-6) Harlequin Bks.

— Wrangler's Woman. (Temptation Ser.: Vol. 774). 2000. per. 3.99 (*0-373-25874-7*) Harlequin Bks.

Dale, Samuel S., ed. see Oelsner, G. H.

Dale Seymour Staff. Mathematics: Problem Solving Activities. 1997. text 10.25 (*0-86651-255-1*) Seymour Pubns.

Dale, Sharon. Frederick Hurten Rhead: An English Potter in America. (Illus.). 150p. (Orig.). (C). 1986. pap. 29.95 (*0-9616623-0-1*) Erie Art Mus.

Dale, Sheila & Carty, Joan. Finding Out about Continuing Education: Sources of Information & Their Use. LC 84-18986. 112p. 1985. pap. 25.00 (*0-335-15024-1*) OpUniv Pr.

Dale, Shelley, jt. auth. see Burandt, Harriet.

Dale, Spencer. The Effect of Official Interest Rate Changes on Market Rates since 1987. LC HG1623.G7. (Bank of England, Economics Division: Vol. 10). (Illus.). 32p. 1993. reprint ed. pap. 30.00 (*0-608-05664-2*, 206618000006) Bks Demand.

Dale, Spencer & Haldane, Andrew G. Interest Rate Control in a Model of Monetary Policy. LC HG0230.3. (Working Papers: No. 17). 39p. 1993. pap. 30.00 (*0-7837-8446-5*, 204925100010) Bks Demand.

— Interest Rates & the Channels of Monetary Transmission: Some Sectoral Estimates. LC HG0949.. (Bank of England, Working Paper Ser.: Vol. 18). (Illus.). 48p. 1993. reprint ed. pap. 30.00 (*0-608-07953-7*, 206792600012) Bks Demand.

***Dale, Stephen.** Lost in the Suburbs: A Political Travelogue. 304p. 1999. 20.95 (*0-7737-3204-7*, Pub. by Stoddart Publ) Genl Dist Srvs.

Dale, Stephen F. Indian Merchants & Eurasian Trade, 1600-1750. LC 93-31404. (Studies in Islamic Civilization). (Illus.). 176p. (C). 1994. text 59.95 (*0-521-45460-3*) Cambridge U Pr.

Dale, Steve. Doggone Chicago. LC 98-10367. 368p. 1988. pap. 12.95 (*0-8092-2944-7*, 294470, Contemporary Bks) NTC Contemp Pub Co.

Dale, Stone & Hendershott, Barbara S. Mystery Reader's Walking Guide: London. 320p. 1993. 16.95 (*0-8442-9550-7*) NTC Contemp Pub Co.

— Mystery Reader's Walking Guide: London. (Illus.). 320p. 1994. pap. 12.95 (*0-8442-9552-3*) NTC Contemp Pub Co.

Dale, Theresa. Biotic Mac's Slow Foods Cookbook. (Illus.). 101p. 1995. pap. 10.00 (*0-9652947-1-4*) Wellness Ctr.

— Transform Your Emotional DNA: Understanding the Blueprint of Your Life. 2nd rev. ed. LC 96-90408. (Illus.). 103p. 1997. mass mkt. 19.95 (*0-9652947-6-5*) Wellness Ctr.

Dale, Theresa C., et al. ESL Through Content-Area Instruction: Mathematics, Science, Social Studies. Crandall, JoAnn, ed. LC 95-39034. (Language in Education Ser.: Vol. 69). 1995. pap. write for info. (*0-937354-72-4*) Delta Systems.

Dale, Thomas E. Relics, Prayer, & Politics in Medieval Venetia: Romanesque Painting in the Crypt of Aquileia Cathedral. LC 97-386. (Illus.). 282p. 1997. text 79.50 (*0-691-01175-3*, Pub. by Princeton U Pr) Cal Prin Full Svc.

***Dale, Tom & Cisco, Susan L.** Indexing Business Records - The Value Proposition. 213p. 1998. pap. 120.00 (*0-89258-374-6*) Assn Inform & Image Mgmt.

Dale, Virginia. Never Marry in Morocco: A Novel. 256p. (Orig.). 1996. pap. 12.95 (*1-56474-174-5*) Fithian Pr.

Dale, Virginia H., ed. Effects of Land Use Change on Atmospheric CO2 Concentrations: South & Southeast Asia As a Case Study. LC 93-5145. (Ecological Studies: Vol. 101). 1993. 105.00 (*0-387-94117-7*) Spr-Verlag.

Dale, Virginia H. & English, Mary R., eds. Tools to Aid Environmental Decision Making. LC 98-7730. (Illus.). 296p. 1998. 74.00 (*0-387-98555-7*); pap. 34.95 (*0-387-98556-5*) Spr-Verlag.

Dale, W. Andrew. Band of Brothers: Creators of Modern Vascular Surgery. Johnson, George, Jr. & DeWeese, James A., eds. (Illus.). 528p. 1996. 50.00 (*0-9649826-1-7*) G Johnson.

Dale, W. Andrew, et al, eds. Band of Brothers: Creators of Modern Vascular Surgery. (Illus.). 172p. 59.95 (*1-56757-000-3*) Appleton Comms.

Dale, William. Law of the Parish Church. 6th ed. 210p. 1989. reprint ed. pap. 38.00 (*0-406-11400-5*, UK, MICHIE) LEXIS Pub.

— The Modern Commonwealth. 1983. 105.00 (*0-406-17404-0*, U.K., MICHIE) LEXIS Pub.

Dale, Zila, jt. auth. see Hill, Marianne.

Dalebout. Intro the Legal Process: Business Law Text With Cases. 502p. (C). 1998. pap. text 24.25 (*0-536-01511-2*) Pearson Custom.

Dalebout, Lyn. Out of the Flames. 270p. (Orig.). 1996. pap. 15.00 (*0-9655247-0-1*) Blue Bison Pr.

DaleCarter, Glenn, jt. auth. see Cannon, Phil.

Daleckii, Ju. L. & Krein, M. G. Stability of Solutions of Differential Equations in Banach Space. LC 74-8403. (Translations of Mathematical Monographs: Vol. 43). 386p. 1974. 97.00 (*0-8218-1593-8*, MMONO/43) Am Math.

Dalecky, Yu. L. & Fomin, S. V. Measures & Differential Equations in Infinite-Dimensional Space. (C). 1991. text 215.00 (*0-7923-1517-0*) Kluwer Academic.

Dalecky, Yu L., jt. auth. see Belopolskaya, Y. I.

Daleiden, Jerome F., et al. Evaluations of the AASHTO Design Equations & Recommended Improvements. 214p. (C). 1994. pap. text 15.00 (*0-309-05803-1*, SHRP-P-394) SHRP.

Daleiden, Joseph L. The American Dream: Can It Survive the 21st Century? LC 98-55176. 550p. 1999. 35.95 (*1-57392-265-X*) Prometheus Bks.

— The Final Superstition: A Critical Evaluation of the Judeo-Christian Legacy. LC 94-15700. 490p. (C). 1994. 33.95 (*0-87975-896-1*) Prometheus Bks.

An Asterisk (*) at the beginning of an entry indicates that the title is appearing for the first time.

— Science of Morality: The Individual, Community & Future Generations. LC 98-7119. 460p. 1998. 35.95 (*1-57392-225-0*) Prometheus Bks.

D'Alelio, Ellen, jt. auth. see Dufau, Micheline.

D'Alelio, Gaetano F. & Parker, John A., eds. Ablative Plastics: Papers. LC 76-143687. (Illus.). 504p. reprint ed. pap. 156.30 (*0-8357-5005-1*, 205503200008) Bks Demand.

D'Alelio, Jane. I Know That Building! Discovering Architecture with Activities & Games. (Illus.). 88p. (J). (gr. 3 up). 1995. pap. 14.95 (*0-471-14396-0*) Wiley.

D'Alembert, Arthur. The Song of the Swan. LC 98-89520. 375p. 1998. text 25.00 (*0-7388-0209-3*); pap. text 15.00 (*0-7388-0210-7*) Xlibris Corp.

D'Alembert, Jean L. Essai sur les Elements de Philosophie. (FRE.). xxxviii, 518p. 1965. reprint ed. write for info. (*0-318-71312-8*) G Olms Pubs.

D'Alembert, Jean L., jt. ed. see Diderot, Denis.

D'Alembert, Jean-Le Rond. Elemens de Musique: Theorique et Pratique. fac. ed. (Monuments of Music & Music Literature in Facsimile Ser., Series II: Vol. 19). 1966. lib. bdg. 32.50 (*0-8450-2219-9*) Broude.

D'Alemberte, Talbot. The Florida State Constitution: A Reference Guide, 5. LC 90-43375. (Reference Guides to the State Constitutions of the United States Ser.: No. 5). 224p. 1991. lib. bdg. 65.00 (*0-313-26339-6*, DFD/, Greenwood Pr) Greenwood.

D'Alemberte, Talbot, et al. Florida Civil Trial Guide, 5 vols., Set. 1990. 510.00 (*0-8205-1320-2*, 320) Bender.

Dalen, D., et al. Computer Science Logic: 10th International Workshop, CSL 96, Annual Conference of the EACSL, Utrecht, the Netherlands, September 21-27, 1996 : Proceedings, Vol. 125. LC 97-23265. (Lecture Notes In Computer Science). viii, 473p. 1997. pap. write for info. (*3-540-63172-0*) Spr-Verlag.

Dalen, Dirk van. Logic & Structure. 3rd ed. 1997. 38.95 (*0-387-57839-0*) Spr-Verlag.

Dalen, H. P. Van, see Van Dalen, H. P.

***Dalen, James E., ed.** The Best of Archives of Internal Medicine. 250p. 1999. 50.00 (*1-57947-057-2*) AMA.

Dalen, James E. & Alpert, Joseph S. Valvular Heart Disease. 1986. 125.00 (*0-316-17171-9*, Little Brwn Med Div) Lppncott W & W.

***Dalenberg, Constance J.** Countertransference & the Treatment of Trauma. LC 00-24634. 320p. 2000. text 39.95 (*1-55798-687-8*, 431-748A) Am Psychol.

***Dalenberg, Dale D., et al.** Data Structures in Java. (Illus.). 800p. (C). 2000. pap. text 65.00 (*0-7637-1079-2*) JB Pubns.

Dalenoort, G. J. The Paradigm of Self-Organization II. (Studies in Cybernetics). 272p. 1994. pap. text 80.00 (*2-88124-976-0*) Gordon & Breach.

Dalenoort, G. J., ed. The Paradigm of Self-Organization: Current Trends in Self-Organization. (Studies in Cybernetics: Vol. 19). xii, 332p. 1989. pap. text 135.00 (*2-88124-709-1*) Gordon & Breach.

Dalenoort, G. J., jt. ed. see Atmanspacher, H.

Dalens, Bernard J. Local & Regional Anesthesia from Birth to Adulthood. LC 95-3775.Tr. of Anesthesie Locoregionale de la Naissance a L'age Adulte. (Illus.). 480p. 1995. 105.00 (*0-683-09653-2*) Lppncott W & W.

Dalens, Bernard J., ed. Pediatric Regional Anesthesia. 528p. 1989. lib. bdg. 159.00 (*0-8493-5629-6*, RD84) CRC Pr.

Dalens, Bernard J., jt. auth. see Bissonnette, Bruno.

D'Aleo, Michael & Edelglass, Stephen. Sensible Physics Teaching. LC 99-60170. (Illus.). 168p. 1999. pap., teacher ed. 16.75 (*1-888182-53-9*, Parker Courtney) Sci & Math Assn.

Daleo, Morgan S. The Book of Dreams & Visions: Creative Journaling with Night Dreams & Day Dreams for Understanding & Inspiration. (Illus.). 120p. 1996. wbk. ed. 15.00 (*0-9648799-6-4*) Grace Pubng.

— Curriculum of Love: Cultivating the Spiritual Nature of Children. (Illus.). 176p. 1996. pap. 17.95 (*0-9648799-4-8*) Grace Pubng.

— A Spirited Alphabet: An Alphabet Primer, Blending Lilting Rhyme with Tender Illustrations. (Illus.). 32p. 1996. write for info. (*0-9648799-5-6*) Grace Pubng.

***Daleo, Morgan S.** A Spirited Alphabet: From A to Z. 32p. 1999. 14.95 (*1-57174-148-8*) Hampton Roads Pub Co.

Daler, Edward N., et al, eds. Evolution of Refractory Metals & Alloys: Proceedings. (Illus.). 220p. 1994. 10.00 (*0-87339-234-5*, 2345) Minerals Metals.

Daler, T., et al. Security of Information & Data. 1989. text 47.95 (*0-470-21381-7*) P-H.

Dales, David N., jt. auth. see Thiessen, Frank J.

Dales, Davis N. & Thiessen, Frank J. Automotive Electronics & Engine Performance. 2nd ed. LC 94-26855. 375p. (C). 1994. pap. text 76.00 (*0-13-350547-2*) P-H.

— Automotive Principles. 4th ed. 1994. pap. text, student ed., wbk. ed. 20.80 (*0-13-370040-2*) P-H.

Dales, Davis N., jt. auth. see Thiessen, Frank J.

Dales, Douglas. Called to Be Angels: An Introduction to Anglo-Saxon Spirituality. 9.95 (*1-85311-229-1*, 6214, Pub. by Canterbury Press Norwich) Morehouse Pub.

Dales, Douglas. Dunstan: Saint & Statesman. 208p. 1998. 33.95 (*0-7188-2704-X*, Lutterworth-Parkwest) Parkwest Pubns.

— Light to the Isles: Missionary Theology in Celtic & Anglo Saxon Britain. 190p. 1998. pap. 25.95 (*0-7188-2965-4*, Lutterworth-Parkwest) Parkwest Pubns.

— Living Through Dying: The Spiritual Experience of Saint Paul. 100p. 1999. 28.95 (*0-7188-2898-4*, Lutterworth-Parkwest) Parkwest Pubns.

Dales, Gath. Truth in Mathematics. 392p. 1998. text 135.00 (*0-19-851476-X*) OUP.

Dales, George F. & Kenoyer, Jonathan M. Excavations at Mohenjo Daro Pakistan: The Pottery. (University Museum Monographs: No. 53). (Illus.). xxi, 586p. 1986. 149.00 (*0-934718-52-0*) U Museum Pubns.

Dales, George F. & Lipo, Carl P. Explorations on the Makran Coast, Pakistan: A Search for Paradise. LC 92-75530. (Contributions of the University of California Archaeological Research Facility Ser.). (Illus.). 274p. (Orig.). (C). 1992. pap. text 24.00 (*1-882744-00-4*) U CA Arch Res Fac.

Dales, H. G., tr. see Dieudonne, Jean A.

Dales, J., tr. see Dieudonne, Jean A.

Dales, Judy B. Curves in Motion: Quilt Design & Techniques. LC 98-15529. 160p. 1998. pap. 29.95 (*1-57120-052-5*, 10176) C & T Pub.

Dales, M. J. Controlling Insect Pest of Stored Products Using Insect Growth Regulators & Insecticides of Microbial Origin. 1994. pap. 30.00 (*0-85954-386-2*, Pub. by Nat Res Inst) St Mut.

Dales, R. C., ed. see Grosseteste, Robert.

Dales, R. P., jt. auth. see Pleijel, F.

Dales, Richard C. The Intellectual Life of Western Europe in the Middle Ages. 2nd rev. ed. LC 92-10587. 322p. 1992. pap. 50.00 (*90-04-09622-1*) Brill Academic Pubs.

— The Problem of the Rational Soul in the Thirteenth Century. LC 95-19416. (Studies in Intellectual History). vii, 214p. 1995. 72.00 (*90-04-10296-5*) Brill Academic Pubs.

— The Scientific Achievement of the Middle Ages. LC 73-77801. (Middle Ages Ser.). (Illus.). 184p. 1973. pap. text 16.95 (*0-8122-1057-3*) U of Pa Pr.

Dales, Richard C. & Argerami, Omar. Medieval Latin Texts on the Eternity of the World. LC 90-28369. (Studies in Intellectual History: No. 23). (ENG & LAT.). 229p. 1991. 87.00 (*90-04-09376-1*) Brill Academic Pubs.

Dales, Richard C., ed. see Grosseteste, Robert.

Dales, S. & Pogo, Beatriz G. Biology of Poxviruses. (Virology Monographs: Vol. 18). (Illus.). 140p. 1981. 55.00 (*0-387-81643-7*) Spr-Verlag.

Dalesandro, Gino. Gino's Kitchen: Nourishing the Soul. LC 97-24053. (Illus.). 248p. 24.95 (*1-56838-152-2*, 5665 A) Hazelden.

Daleski, H . M . The Divided Heroine: A Recurrent Pattern in Six English Novels. LC 83-12897. 164p. 1984. 39.50 (*0-8419-0885-0*) Holmes & Meier.

Daleski, H. M. Dickens & the Art of Analogy. LC 75-122330. 349p. 1970. write for info. (*0-8052-3373-3*) Schocken.

— Thomas Hardy & Paradoxes of Love. LC 97-15472. 240p. 1997. 34.95 (*0-8262-1125-9*) U of Mo Pr.

Daleski, Hillel M. The Forked Flame: A Study of D. H. Lawrence. LC 87-6005. 320p. reprint ed. pap. 99.20 (*0-608-09902-3*, 206924000003) Bks Demand.

Daleski, William, jt. ed. see Baumgarten, Murray.

D'Alessandro, Alex. The Clinician's Guide to Successful Treatment Planning for Managed Care. LC 95-21475. 1995. 79.00 (*0-935255-43-5*) Of Course Pubns.

— Patient Advocacy Strategies for Managed Care. LC 98-49709. 1998. pap. text 89.00 (*0-935255-62-1*) Of Course Pubns.

— Two Minute Management: Focusing on Two Special Minutes that You Spend with Yourself Before Approaching Your People. Edwards, Heidi, ed. LC 85-821901. (Illus.). 100p. (Orig.). 1985. pap. 8.95 (*0-935255-22-2*) Of Course Pubns.

D'Alessandro, Alex, ed. see American Board of Certified Managed Care Providers.

D'Alessandro, Frank M. The Verdict of History on Sacco & Vanzetti. 448p. (Orig.). 1997. pap. text 19.95 (*1-889534-07-2*) Jay St Pubs.

D'Alessandro, Giulietta. Child Across the River. 1958. 10.95 (*0-8392-1013-2*) Astor-Honor.

Dalessandro, Gloria. Blessed Is He Who Considers the Poor. MacKall, Phyllis, ed. 1989. text. write for info. (*0-318-64884-9*) G Dalessandro.

***D'Alessandro, Jacquie.** Kiss the Cook. (Zebra Bouquet Ser.: No. 47). 2000. mass mkt. 3.99 (*0-8217-6604-X*, Zebra Kensgtn) Kensgtn Pub Corp.

D'Alessandro, Jacquie. Red Roses Mean Love. 368p. 1999. mass mkt. 5.99 (*0-440-23553-7*) Dell.

***D'Alessandro, Jacquie.** Whirlwind Wedding. 384p. 2000. mass mkt. 5.99 (*0-440-23551-0*) Dell.

Dalessandro, James & Menhart, David. Citizen Jane: A True Story of Money, Murder, & One Woman's Mission to Put a Killer Behind Bars. (Onyx True Crime Ser.). 416p. 1999. mass mkt. 6.99 (*0-451-40904-3*, Onyx) NAL.

D'Alessandro, Joe, jt. auth. see Marino, Bob.

D'Alessandro, Natale, et al, eds. Cancer Therapy: Differentiation, Immunomodulation, & Angiogenesis. LC 93-10491. (NATO ASI Series H: Cell Biology: Vol. 75). 1993. 211.95 (*0-387-54603-0*) Spr-Verlag.

D'Alessandro, Nicolo. Casa Sulla Collina. (SPA., Illus.). 14p. 1988. pap. 75.00 (*0-89304-650-7*) Cross-Cultrl NY.

— Condottieri.Tr. of Soldiers. 1986. pap. 15.00 (*0-89304-651-5*) Cross-Cultrl NY.

— D'Alessandro. (Illus.). 54p. 1987. 50.00 (*0-685-49065-3*); pap. 25.00 (*0-685-49066-1*) Cross-Cultrl NY.

— Erotica: Italian Art. 48p. 1992. pap. 5.00 (*0-89304-693-0*) Cross-Cultrl NY.

— Erotica: Italian Art, Mini. 48p. 1992. 15.00 (*0-89304-694-9*); pap. 5.00 (*0-89304-695-7*) Cross-Cultrl NY.

— Nicolo d'Alessandro: Italian Art. 95p. 1985. 25.00 (*0-89304-570-5*, CCC181); pap. 10.00 (*0-89304-595-0*) Cross-Cultrl NY.

D'Alessandro, Nicolo, jt. auth. see Simpson, Louis.

D'Alessandro, P. The Conical Approach to Linear Programming. 300p. 1997. text 98.00 (*90-5699-031-4*) Gordon & Breach.

D'Alessandro, Patricia. Croce D'Oro. (Illus.). 32p. (Orig.). 1991. pap. 3.00 (*1-880575-10-8*) Hot Pepper.

— Famiglia e Amici Con Amore. Hildred, Debra C., ed. (Illus.). 78p. 1999. pap. 10.00 (*0-9670152-0-0*) P DAlessandro.

D'Alessandro, Stephanie & Gilman, Sander L. Weimar Bodies: Fantasies about the Body in Weimar Art, Science & Medicine. LC 99-194415. (Illus.). 16p. 1998. text. write for info. (*0-935573-23-2*) D & A Smart Museum.

D'Alessandro, Stephanie, ed. see Heller, Reinhold.

Dalessio, jt. auth. see Stolzenberg.

Dalessio, Donald J. & Silberstein, Stephen D., eds. Wolff's Headache & Other Head Pain. 6th ed. LC 92-48683. (Illus.). 552p. (C). 1993. text 69.50 (*0-19-508250-8*) OUP.

Dalessio, Donald J., jt. auth. see Diamond, Seymour.

***D'Alessio, Paolo.** Formula 1 2000 World Championship Yearbook. (Illus.). 144p. 2000. 34.95 (*0-89658-499-2*) Voyageur Pr.

D'Alessio, Paolo. Obrigado, Ayrton: Simply the Best. (Illus.). 160p. 1996. 34.95 (*88-7911-141-8*, Pub. by Giorgio Nada Editore) Howell Pr VA.

— Senna: The Best. (Illus.). 48p. (Orig.). 1996. pap. 39.95 (*88-7911-153-1*, Pub. by Giorgio Nada Editore) Howell Pr VA.

***D'Alessio, Paolo & Boccafogli, Roberto.** Formula 1: 1999 World Championship Yearbook. (MotorSport Library). (Illus.). 208p. 1999. 34.95 (*0-89658-485-2*) Voyageur Pr.

Dalet, R. Sante Naturelle - Encyclopedie Maladies, Traitements. (FRE.). 200p. 1996. 49.95 (*0-320-00647-6*) Fr & Eur.

***Dalewijk, Henk-Jan.** Master Clinicians Confront the Treatment of Borderline Personality Disorders. 2001. 45.00 (*0-7657-0294-0*) Aronson.

Daley. Organic Chemistry. 2nd ed. 1998. 14.50 (*0-697-24100-9*) McGraw.

— Organic Chemistry. 2nd ed. 2000. 28.25 (*0-697-24040-1*, WCB McGr Hill) McGrw-H Hghr Educ.

Daley, Ann S. Gustave Baumann: Woodblock Prints from the Holme Roberts & Owen Collection. Chambers, Marlene, ed. LC 91-71300. (Illus.). 32p. 1991. pap. 9.95 (*0-914738-41-0*) Denver Art Mus.

Daley, Anthony. Steel, State & Labor: Mobilization & Adjustment in France. LC 95-23147. 309p. (Orig.). (C). 1996. pap. 22.95 (*0-8229-5602-0*); text 49.95 (*0-8229-3918-5*) U of Pittsburgh Pr.

Daley, Anthony, ed. The Mitterrand Era: Policy Alternatives & Political Mobilization in France. 360p. (C). 1996. text 50.00 (*0-8147-1872-8*) NYU Pr.

Daley, Brian. The Adventures of Han Solo. 1994. pap. 10.00 (*0-345-39442-9*) Ballantine Pub Grp.

Daley, Brian. The Broken Country, Vol. 3. 1998. mass mkt. 6.99 (*0-345-42210-4*, Del Rey) Ballantine Pub Grp.

— Han Solo Adventures. 578p. 1992. mass mkt. 5.99 (*0-345-37980-2*) Ballantine Pub Grp.

— Han Solo Adventures. LC 94-96383. 566p. 1994. pap. 10.00 Ballantine Pub Grp.

— Han Solo & the Lost Legacy. (Star Wars: Bk. 3). 192p. (YA). (gr. 5 up). 1986. mass mkt. 5.99 (*0-345-34514-2*, Del Rey) Ballantine Pub Grp.

— Han Solo & the Lost Legacy. (Star Wars: Bk. 3). (YA). (gr. 5 up). 1998. mass mkt. 5.99 (*0-345-91210-1*, Del Rey Discovery) Ballantine Pub Grp.

— Han Solo at Stars' End. (Star Wars: Bk. 1). (YA). (gr. 5 up). 1980. mass mkt. 5.99 (*0-345-29664-8*, Del Rey) Ballantine Pub Grp.

— Han Solo at Stars' End. (Star Wars: Bk. 1). (YA). (gr. 5 up). 1997. mass mkt. 5.99 (*0-345-91208-X*, Del Rey) Ballantine Pub Grp.

— Han Solo at Stars' End. (Star Wars: No. 1). 80p. (YA). (gr. 5 up). 1997. pap. text 6.95 (*1-56971-254-9*) Dark Horse Comics.

— Han Solo's Revenge. (Star Wars: Bk. 2). (YA). (gr. 5 up). 1997. pap. 5.99 (*0-345-91209-8*, Del Rey) Ballantine Pub Grp.

— Millenium Jugdement or Jubilee. LC 97-14056. (Illus.). 42p. (J). 1997. pap. 2.95 (*0-8198-4796-8*) Pauline Bks.

— A Screaming Across the Sky. (GammaLAW Ser.: Bk. 2). 1998. mass mkt. 6.99 (*0-345-42209-0*, Del Rey) Ballantine Pub Grp.

— Smoke on the Water. (GammaLAW Ser.: Bk. 1). 1998. mass mkt. 5.99 (*0-345-35858-9*, Del Rey) Ballantine Pub Grp.

— To Waters' End, Vol. 4. (GammaLAW Ser.: Bk. 4). 356p. 1999. mass mkt. 6.99 (*0-345-42211-2*, Del Rey) Ballantine Pub Grp.

Daley, Brian J., tr. from GRE. On the Dormition: Early Patristic Homilies. LC 97-36467. 1997. pap. 9.95 (*0-88141-177-9*) St Vladimirs.

Daley, C. R. Daley Observations: The Best of C. R. Daley's Western Recorder Editorials. Colin, A. B. & Wingfield, Mark, eds. 192p. 1998. pap. text 14.95 (*1-57736-122-9*) Providence Hse.

***Daley, Caroline & Montgomerie, Deborah, eds.** The Gendered Kiwi. (Illus.). 300p. 2000. 29.95 (*1-86940-219-7*, Pub. by Auckland Univ) Paul & Co Pubs.

Daley, Caroline & Nolan, Melanie, eds. Suffrage & Beyond: International Feminist Perspectives. LC 94-33981. 1994. text 55.00 (*0-8147-1870-1*) NYU Pr.

***Daley, Catherine.** Spend the Day with Bear. (Bear in the Big Blue House Ser.). (Illus.). 12p. (J). (ps-k). 2000. bds. 8.99 (*1-57584-401-X*) Rdrs Digest.

Daley, Catherine. What's That Squeak? (Bear in the Big Blue House Ser.). (Illus.). 16p. (J). (ps-k). 2000. pap. 7.99 (*1-57584-399-4*, RD Childrens) Rdrs Digest.

Daley, Charlotte C., ed. see Gilmer, Chris & Milam, June M.

Daley, Charlotte C., ed. see Milam, June M.

Daley, Charlotte C., ed. see Milam, June M., et al.

Daley, Charlotte C., ed. see Milan, June M., et al.

Daley, D. & Vere-Jones, D. An Introduction to the Theory of Point Processes. (Series in Statistics). (Illus.). 700p. 1988. 116.95 (*0-387-96666-8*) Spr-Verlag.

Daley, D. J. & Gani, J. Modelling Epidemics: An Introduction. LC 98-44051. (Cambridge Studies in Mathematical Biology: No. 14). (Illus.). 200p. (C). 1999. text 44.95 (*0-521-64079-2*) Cambridge U Pr.

Daley, Dan. Nashville's Unwritten Rules: Inside the Business of Country Music. (Illus.). 352p. 1998. pap. 16.95 (*0-87951-889-8*, Pub. by Overlook Pr) Penguin Putnam.

— Nashville's Unwritten Rules: Inside the Business of Country Music. LC 96-45691. (Illus.). 288p. 1999. 27.95 (*0-87951-770-0*, Pub. by Overlook Pr) Penguin Putnam.

Daley, Daryl J., ed. see Stoyan, Dietrich.

Daley, Dennis. Group Drug Counseling: Participant Recovery Workbook. 32p. 1998. pap. 11.95 (*1-55691-136-X*) Learning Pubns.

— Group Drug Counseling Manual. 128p. 1998. pap. 19.95 (*1-55691-137-8*) Learning Pubns.

— Improving Communication & Relationships: An Adults-in Recovery Workbook. 81p. 1996. pap., wbk. ed. 12.95 (*1-55691-107-6*, 076) Learning Pubns.

Daley, Dennis. Managing Anger: An Adults-in-Recovery Workbook. 32p. pap. 11.95 (*1-55691-173-4*) Learning Pubns.

Daley, Dennis. Relapse Prevention Workbook: Spanish Edition. for Recovering Alcoholics & Drug Dependent Persons. 1993. pap. 11.50 (*1-55691-096-7*, 967) Learning Pubns.

Daley, Dennis, ed. The Politics & Administration of Privatization Vol. 24:4: Efforts among Local Governments. 51p. 1996. pap. 15.00 (*0-944285-48-1*) Pol Studies.

Daley, Dennis & Leslie, Bennett. Recovery from Psychiatric Illness: A Guide to Understanding the Psychiatric Hospital Experience. 1992. pap. 5.95 (*1-55691-091-6*, 916) Learning Pubns.

Daley, Dennis & Miller, Judy. Recovery & Relapse Prevention for Parents of Chemically Dependent Children. 1993. pap. 4.95 (*1-56246-027-7*, P183, HazeldenJohnson Inst) Hazelden.

— Taking Control: A Practical Family Guide to Dealing with Chemicl Dependency. 1993. pap. 12.95 (*1-55691-095-9*, 959) Learning Pubns.

Daley, Dennis & Roth, Loren. When Symptoms Return: A Guide to Relapse in Psychiatric Illness. 1992. pap. 5.95 (*1-55691-090-8*, 908) Learning Pubns.

***Daley, Dennis & Sproule, Charles.** Adolescent Relapse Prevention Workbook: A Guide to Staying off Drugs & Alcohol. rev. ed. 1999. pap. 11.95 (*1-55691-175-0*) Learning Pubns.

Daley, Dennis, jt. auth. see Montrose, Ken.

Daley, Dennis, jt. auth. see Sinberg, Janet.

Daley, Dennis C. Coping with Feelings Workbook: For Adults in Recovery from Chemical Dependency. rev. ed. 64p. 1998. pap., wbk. ed. 11.95 (*1-55691-154-8*, 084) Learning Pubns.

— Dual Diagnosis Workbook. 163p. 1994. pap. 15.95 (*0-8309-0666-5*, Indep Pr) Herald Pub Hse.

— Family Recovery Workbook: For Families Affected by Chemical Dependency, Set. 32p. (Orig.). 1987. 3.50 (*0-943519-03-9*, B1903) Sulzburger & Graham Pub.

— Kicking Addictive Habits Once & for All. LC 97-43205. 224p. 1998. pap. text 17.95 (*0-7879-4068-2*) Jossey-Bass.

— Living Sober Client Workbook. 27p. 1994. pap. text, wbk. ed. 3.95 (*1-56215-074-X*) GTR Inc.

— Living Sober Counseling Manual. 82p. 1994. pap. text, teacher ed. 8.95 (*1-56215-073-1*) GTR Inc.

— Living Sober II Client Workbook. 27p. 1996. pap. text, wbk. ed. 3.95 (*1-56215-078-2*) GTR Inc.

— Living Sober II Counselor Manual. 43p. 1996. pap. text, teacher ed. 8.95 (*1-56215-077-4*) GTR Inc.

— Managing Your Drug or Alcohol Problem Client Workbook. 1999. pap. text 26.00 (*0-12-785039-2*) Acad Pr.

— Managing Your Drug or Alcohol Problem Therapist Guide. 1999. pap. text 37.50 (*0-12-785038-4*) Acad Pr.

— Money & Recovery: An Adults-in-Recovery Workbook, 4 bks. 32p. 1997. pap. 11.50 (*1-55691-131-9*, 319) Learning Pubns.

— Relapse: A Guide to Successful Recovery. Joiner, Lee M., ed. LC 87-24385. 48p. (Orig.). 1987. pap. text 4.25 (*0-943519-02-0*, B1902) Sulzburger & Graham Pub.

— Relapse Prevention. 1989. pap. 14.95 (*0-8306-9004-2*) Sulzburger & Graham Pub.

— Relapse Prevention: Treatment Alternatives & Counseling Aids. Joiner, Lee M., ed. LC 88-873. 144p. (Orig.). 1988. pap. text 14.95 (*0-943519-06-3*, B1906) Sulzburger & Graham Pub.

— Relapse Prevention Workbook: For Recovering Alcoholics & Drug Dependent Persons, 4 bks. 2nd ed. 32p. (Orig.). 1997. pap., student ed. 11.50 (*1-55691-130-0*, 300) Learning Pubns.

Daley, Dennis C., pref. Relapse: Conceptual, Research & Clinical Perspectives. LC 89-15611. (Journal of Chemical Dependency Treatment: Vol. 2, No. 2). (Illus.). 257p. 1989. pap. text 19.95 (*0-86656-976-6*) Haworth Pr.

— Relapse: Conceptual, Research & Clinical Perspectives. LC 89-15611. (Journal of Chemical Dependency Treatment: Vol. 2, No. 2). (Illus.). 257p. 1994. text 49.95 (*0-86656-919-7*) Haworth Pr.

Daley, Dennis C. & Campbell, Frances. Coping with Dual Disorders: Counseling Clients with Chemical Dependency & Mental Illness. 23p. 1989. pap. 4.25 (*0-89486-586-2*, 5218B) Hazelden.

Daley, Dennis C. & Miller, Judy. Surviving Addiction Workbook: Practical Tips on Developing a Recovery Plan. rev. ed. 32p. 1997. pap. 11.50 (*1-55691-065-7*, 657) Learning Pubns.

D

— When Your Child Is Chemically Dependent. 16p. 1995. pap. 4.95 (1-56246-026-9, 3176, HazeldenJohnson Inst) Hazelden.

Daley, Dennis C. & Raskin, Miriam S., eds. Treating the Chemically Dependent & Their Families. (Sourcebooks for the Human Services Ser.: Vol. 16). (Illus.). 244p. (C). 1990. text 56.00 (0-8039-3297-9); pap. text 26.00 (0-8039-3298-7) Sage.

Daley, Dennis C. & Thase, Michael E. Dual Disorders Recovery Counseling. 170p. 1994. pap. 15.95 (0-8309-0694-0, Indep Pr) Herald Pub Hse.

Daley, Dennis C. & Zuckoff, Allan. Improving Treatment Compliance: Counseling & Systems Strategies for Substance Abuse & Dual Disorders. LC 98-47969. 254p. 1999. 19.95 (1-56838-281-2) Hazelden.

Daley, Dennis C., et al. Dual Disorders: Counseling Clients with Chemical Dependency & Mental Illness. 2nd ed. LC 92-48321. 141p. pap. 18.95 (0-89486-449-1, 5023A) Hazelden.

Daley, Dennis C., jt. auth. see Read, Edward M.

Daley, Dennis M. Performance Appraisal in the Public Sector: Techniques & Applications. LC 92-12121. 184p. 1992. 57.95 (0-89930-701-9, DPI/, Quorum Bks) Greenwood.

Daley, Henry W., jt. auth. see Hanson, Roger A.

Daley, Jacque. A String of Pearls: Poems about People, Places & Life. LC 98-92136. 1998. text 10.00 (0-9667429-0-7) Jacpak Bks.

— Verses for Kids: For Fun & Learning. large type ed. LC 98-92137. (Illus.). (J). (gr. k-6). 1998. 10.00 (0-9667429-1-5) Jacpak Bks.

Daley, James G., ed. Social Work Practice in the Military. LC 98-53340. 358p. (C). 1999. lib. bdg. 49.95 (0-7890-0625-1) Haworth Pr.

***Daley, James G., ed.** Social Work Practice in the Military. LC 98-53340. 358p. (C). 1999. pap. 24.95 (0-7890-0626-X) Haworth Pr.

***Daley, Janet, ed.** North Dakota History: Journal of the Northern Plains Cumulative Index, 1945-1998. 112p. 2000. pap. 16.95 (1-891419-19-6) State Hist ND.

Daley, Jon, jt. auth. see Cruim, Beverly.

Daley, Joseph C., et al. A Guide to Municipal Official Statements. 634p. 1990. ring bd. 116.00 (0-13-371543-4) Aspen Law.

Daley, Jr., Henry O. & O'Malley. Problems in Chemistry. 2nd ed. (Undergraduate Chemistry Ser.: Vol. 11). (Illus.). 504p. 1988. text 95.00 (0-8247-7826-X) Dekker.

Daley, Juanita. His Records Stand. write for info. (1-57074-306-1) Greyden Pr.

Daley, Ken. Basic Film Technique. (Media Manuals Ser.). 158p. 1980. pap. 32.95 (0-240-51016-X, Focal) Buttrwrth-Heinemann.

Daley, Kevin R. Socratic Selling: How to Ask the Questions That Get the Sale. 1997. 14.22 (0-7863-1232-7) McGraw.

Daley, Kevin R. & Wolfe, Emmett. Socratic Selling: How to Ask the Questions That Get the Sale. LC 95-20289. 228p. 1995. text 19.95 (0-7863-0455-3, Irwn Prfssnl) McGraw-Hill Prof.

Daley, Koos. The Triple Fool: A Critical Evaluation of Constantijn Huygens' Translations of John Donne. (Bibliotheca Humanistica & Reformatorica Ser.: No. XLVI). 238p. 1990. lib. bdg. 67.50 (90-6004-405-3, Pub. by B De Graaf) Coronet Bks.

Daley, Lane H. & Vigelaud, Robert L. Intermediate Accounting. (C). 1993. text. write for info. (0-538-02935-8) S-W Pub.

Daley, Leo C. Monarch Notes on Descartes' Philosophy. (Orig.). (C). 4.25 (0-671-00527-8, Arco) Macmillan Gen Ref.

Daley, Margaretmary. Women of Letters: A Study of Self & Genre in the Personal Correspondence of Caroline Schlegel-Schelling Rahel Levin Varnhagen, & Bettina von Arnim. LC 98-6066. (Studies in German Literature, Linguistics & Culture). 180p. 1999. 55.00 (1-57113-132-9) Camden Hse.

Daley, Mark, tr. see Rheaume, Manon & Gilbert, Chantal.

Daley, Mary D. Irish Laws. 1997. 7.95 (0-8118-1529-3) Chronicle Bks.

— Traditional Irish Laws. 1998. 10.95 (0-8118-1995-7) Chronicle Bks.

Daley, Maureen. Seventeenth Summer. (YA). (gr. 7-11). 1942. 10.95 (0-396-02322-3, G P Putnam) Peng Put Young Read.

Daley, Michael. Amazing Solar Science Activities. (Illus.). 112p. (J). (gr. 3-9). 1998. pap. 12.95 (0-07-015177-6) McGraw.

***Daley, Michael.** Original Sin. 36p. 2000. pap. 8.00 (0-9651413-6-5) Pleasure Boat.

Daley, Michael, jt. auth. see Beck, James.

Daley, Michael J. Nuclear Power: Promise or Peril? LC 96-19085. (Pro/Con Ser.). (J). 1996. lib. bdg. 21.27 (0-8225-2611-5, Lerner Publctns) Lerner Pub.

***Daley, Patrick.** Backstage Pass: Mandy Moore. (Illus.). (J). 2000. pap. 5.99 (0-439-22223-0) Scholastic Inc.

Daley, Patrick. Run, Gus, Run!, Level 1. LC 97-80105. (Disney First Reader Ser.: No. 10). (Illus.). 24p. (J). (gr. k-1). 1998. pap. 2.95 (0-7868-4169-9, Pub. by Disney Pr) Time Warner.

Daley, R. & Daley, S. Build Your Own. 1991. 24.95 (0-8306-6428-9) McGraw-Hill Prof.

***Daley, Rachel M. & Ganick, Peter.** Today It Starts into Light. 31p. 1998. 6.00 (0-937013-93-5, Pub. by Potes Poets) SPD-Small Pr Dist.

Daley, Rebecca S. Problem Solving Through Business & Technical Communication. 3rd ed. 228p. (C). 1994. spiral bd. 26.95 (0-8403-9151-X) Kendall-Hunt.

***Daley, Regan.** In the Sweet Kitchen. 2000. write for info. (0-679-30974-8) Random.

Daley, Richard, ed. Integration Technology for CASE. (UNICOM Applied Information Technology Ser.). 165p. 1993. 109.95 (0-291-39797-2, Pub. by Avebury Technical) Ashgate Pub Co.

Daley, Richard & Daley, Sally. Organic Chemistry: Preliminary Version. 1424p. (C). 1996. text. write for info. (0-697-35090-8, WCB McGr Hill) McGrw-H Hghr Educ.

Daley, Richard M., jt. auth. see Devine, Thomas E.

Daley, Robert. A Faint Cold Fear. 480p. 1992. mass mkt. 5.99 (0-446-36219-0, Pub. by Warner Bks) Little.

— The Innocents Within. LC 99-14155. 448p. 1999. 25.95 (0-375-50178-9) Villard Books.

— Nowhere to Run. 1997. mass mkt. 188.73 (0-446-16416-X) Warner Bks.

— Prince of the City: The True Story of a Cop Who Knew Too Much. 400p. 1994. mass mkt. 5.99 (0-446-36569-6, Pub. by Warner Bks) Little.

— Tainted Evidence. 1995. pap. 5.99 (0-446-36083-X) Warner Bks.

— To Kill a Cop. 400p. 1996. mass mkt. 6.50 (0-446-36571-8, Pub. by Warner Bks) Little.

— Wall of Brass. 1994. write for info. (0-318-72700-5) Little.

— Wall of Brass. 384p. 1995. mass mkt. 6.50 (0-446-36566-1, Pub. by Warner Bks) Little.

— Year of the Dragon. 528p. 1997. mass mkt. 6.99 (0-446-36572-6, Pub. by Warner Bks) Little.

Daley, Robert, et al. The Golden Age: Images from the Klemantaski Collection. Sachs, Peter G., ed. (Illus.). 32p. (YA). 1999. pap. 20.00 (0-9641689-2-8) Klemantaski.

Daley, Roger A. Hand Surgery. (Vademecum Ser.). 2000. spiral bd. 45.00 (1-57059-573-9) Landes Bioscience.

Daley, Rosie. In the Kitchen with Rosie: Oprah's Favorite Recipes. LC 94-9628. 112p. 1994. 18.95 (0-679-43404-6) Knopf.

Daley, S., jt. auth. see Daley, R.

Daley, Sally, jt. auth. see Daley, Richard.

Daley, Shannon, jt. auth. see Guy, Kathleen.

Daley, Sue & Gross, Steve. At Home with the Past: How the Love of Old Things Creates Beautiful Interiors. LC 97-20859. (Illus.). 208p. 1998. 40.00 (0-517-70371-8) Random Hse Value.

Daley, Susan, jt. photos by see Gross, Steve.

Daley, Todd. Apples & Oranges. 240p. (C). 1995. pap. text, per. 31.95 (0-7872-1581-3) Kendall-Hunt.

Daley, William. The Chinese Americans. LC 94-45788. (Immigrant Experience Ser.). 120p. 1995. pap. 9.95 (0-7910-3379-1) Chelsea Hse.

— The Chinese Americans. LC 94-45788. (Immigrant Experience Ser.). 120p. (YA). (gr. 5 up). 1995. lib. bdg. 19.95 (0-7910-3357-0) Chelsea Hse.

***Daley, William M., intro.** Export Programs Guide, 2000: A Business Guide to Federal Export Assistance. 64p. 2000. pap. text 20.00 (0-7881-8802-X) DIANE Pub.

***Daley, William M. & Scott, Daniel T., eds.** A Basic Guide to Exporting. 132p. 2000. pap. text 30.00 (0-7881-8782-1) DIANE Pub.

Dalfanso, Maureen. ISO 9000: Documentation, Training, & Checklist. 8p. 1996. pap. text 60.00 incl. disk (0-471-15572-1) Wiley.

Dalfen, ed. Marci Aurelii, Antonini, Libri XII. (GRE.). 1987. 39.50 (3-322-00355-8, T1046, Pub. by B G Teubner) U of Mich Pr.

Dalferth, Silfredo B. Die Zweireichelehre Martin Luthers Im Dialog Mit der Befreiungstheologie Leonardo Boffs: Ein Okumenischer Beitrag Zum Verhaltnis von Christlichem Glauben und Gesellschaftlicher Verantwortung. (Europaische Hochschulschriften Ser.: Reihe 23, Bd. 586). (GER.). 341p. 1996. 57.95 (3-631-30908-2) P Lang Pubng.

Dalfin, Chaim. Demystifying the Mystical: Understanding the Language & Concepts of Chasidism & Jewish Mysticism - A Primer for the Layman. LC 95-16069. 192p. 1995. 25.00 (1-56821-453-7) Aronson.

— A Model for Leadership - The Lubavitcher Rebbes. 224p. 1998. pap. 14.95 (1-880880-26-1) Israeli Trad.

— The Rebbe's Advice. 192p. (YA). 1997. pap. 12.95 (1-880880-24-5) Israeli Trad.

— The Rebbe's Advice, Bk. 2. 160p. (YA). Date not set. pap. 12.95 (1-880880-25-3) Israeli Trad.

— The Seven Chabad-Lubavitch Rebbes. Baron, Dov, ed. LC 97-41691. 1998. 30.00 (0-7657-6003-7) Aronson.

— To Be Chasidic: A Contemporary Guide. LC 96-13673. 280p. 1997. 30.00 (1-56821-905-9) Aronson.

Dalfin, Chaim X. Conversations with the Rabbi: Encouragement Wisdom & Advice. 256p. 1996. 21.95 (1-880880-16-4) Israeli Trad.

D'Alfonso, A., ed. Voix Off: Dix Poetes Anglophones du Quebec. (FRE.). 181p. 1985. pap. write for info. (2-89135-009-X) Guernica Editions.

D'Alfonso, A., jt. ed. see Caccia, F.

D'Alfonso, Antonio. Black Tongue, Vol. 1. 78p. 1983. pap. write for info. (0-919349-07-2) Guernica Editions.

— Duologue: On Culture & Identity. LC 97-74341. 96p. 1998. pap. 10.00 (1-55071-072-9) Guernica Editions.

— Fabrizio's Passion. LC 94-77152. (Prose Ser.: No. 34). 232p. 1995. pap. 15.00 (1-55071-023-0) Guernica Editions.

***D'Alfonso, Antonio.** Fabrizio's Passion. (Picas Ser.: No. 12). 214p. 2000. pap. 8.00 (1-55071-082-6, Pub. by Guernica Editions) Paul & Co Pubs.

D'Alfonso, Antonio. In Italics: In Defense of Ethnicity. LC 94-74387. (Essay Ser.: No. 21). (Illus.). 268p. 1996. pap. 18.00 (1-55071-016-8) Guernica Editions.

— The Other Shore. 164p. 1989. pap. 8.00 (0-920717-32-2) Guernica Editions.

— Panic Love, Vol. 1. 54p. 1993. pap. 8.00 (0-920717-63-2) Guernica Editions.

Dalfonso, Deborah, jt. auth. see Brooks, Jean O.

Dalfovo, A. T., et al. The Foundations of Social Life: Ugandan Philosophical Studies I. LC 91-58114. (Cultural Heritage & Contemporary Change Series II: Vol. 2). 1992. 45.00 (1-56518-007-0); pap. 17.50 (1-56518-006-2) Coun Res Values.

Dalgaard, Bruce R. South Africa's Impact on Britain's Return to Gold, 1925. Bruchey, Stuart, ed. LC 80-2801. (Dissertations in European Economic History Ser.). (Illus.). 1981. lib. bdg. 23.95 (0-405-13985-3) Ayer.

Dalgado, M. S. Diccionario Konkani-Portuguez. (SPA.). 602p. 1983. write for info. (0-8288-1774-X, F24950) Fr & Eur.

Dalgado, S. Dicionario Konkani to Portugues. (POR.). 602p. 1998. 175.00 (0-320-00678-6) Fr & Eur.

— Dicionario Portuguesto Konkani. (POR.). 940p. 1986. reprint ed. 195.00 (0-320-00679-4) Fr & Eur.

Dalgarno, A., et al, eds. Abstracts of the Sixteenth International Conference on the Physics of Electronic & Atomic Collisions: Abstracts of Contributed Papers from the XVI International ICPEAC held in New York, NY, July 26-August 1, 1989. (Illus.). 968p. 1989. pap. 70.00 (0-88318-631-4) Am Inst Physics.

— The Physics of Electronic & Atomic Collisions. LC 90-53183. (AIP Conference Proceedings Ser.: No. 205). 696p. 1990. lib. bdg. 99.00 (0-88318-390-0) Am Inst Physics.

Dalgarno, A. & Layzer, David, eds. Spectroscopy of Astrophysical Plasmas. (Illus.). 372p. 1987. pap. text 37.95 (0-521-26927-X) Cambridge U Pr.

Dalgarno, Alexander, jt. ed. see Bederson, Benjamin.

Dalgarno, George. Works of George Dalgarno of Aberdeen. Maitland, Thomas, ed. LC 74-165338. (Maitland Club, Glasgow. Publications: No. 29). reprint ed. 40.00 (0-404-52987-9) AMS Pr.

Dalgarno, Melvin & Matthews, Eric, eds. The Philosophy of Thomas Reid. 463p. (C). 1989. text 171.00 (0-7923-0190-0) Kluwer Academic.

Dalgish, Gerard M. A Dictionary of Africanisms: Contributions of Sub-Saharan Africa to the English Language. LC 82-9366. 203p. 1982. lib. bdg. 65.00 (0-313-23585-6, DDA/, Greenwood Pr) Greenwood.

Dalgleish. HIV & The New Viruses. 2nd ed. LC 98-83211. 576p. (C). 1999. 125.00 (0-12-200741-7) Acad Pr.

Dalgleish, A. G., et al, eds. The Impact of Biotechnology on Autoimmunity. LC 94-971. (Medical Science Symposia Ser.: Vol. 6). 148p. (C). 1994. text 89.00 (0-7923-2724-1) Kluwer Academic.

Dalgleish, A. G. & Browning, M. J., eds. Tumor Immunology. (Cancer: Clinical Science in Practice Ser.). (Illus.). 369p. (C). 1996. text 85.00 (0-521-47237-7) Cambridge U Pr.

Dalgleish, D. Douglas, et al. Trident. LC 83-16777. (Science & International Affairs Ser.). (Illus.). 384p. 1984. 36.95 (0-8093-1126-7) S Ill U Pr.

Dalgleish, D. I. An Introduction to Satellite Communications. (Telecommunications Ser.: No. 20). 1989. 99.00 (0-86341-132-0, TE020) INSPEC Inc.

Dalgleish, G. & Mechan, D. "I Am Come Home" Treasures of Prince Charles Edward Stuart. (Illus.). 24p. 1995. pap. 3.50 (0-948636-52-1, 6521, Pub. by Natl Mus Scotland) A Schwartz & Co.

Dalgleish, Julie G., jt. auth. see Morrison, Bradley G.

Dalgleish, Neil. World Survey. (Illus.). 128p. 1976. pap. 9.95 (0-7175-0750-5) Dufour.

Dalgleish, Tim. Risks & Decisions in Child Protection. pap. text 28.00 (0-471-98219-9) Wiley.

Dalgleish, Tim & Power, Michael J. Handbook of Cognition & Emotion. LC 98-27102. 866p. 1999. 108.95 (0-471-97836-1) Wiley.

Dalgleish, Tim, jt. auth. see Power, Michael J.

Dalgliesh, Alice. The Bears on Hemlock Mountain. 1981. 10.19 (0-606-01480-2, Pub. by Turtleback) Demco.

— The Bears on Hemlock Mountain. LC 89-27651. (Illus.). 64p. (J). (gr. 1-4). 1990. reprint ed. 15.00 (0-684-19169-5) Scribner.

— The Bears on Hemlock Mountain. 2nd ed. LC 91-40166. (Illus.). 64p. (J). (ps-3). 2000. reprint ed. mass mkt. 4.99 (0-689-71604-4) Aladdin.

— Coraje de Sarah Noble (The Courage of Sarah Noble) (SPA.). (YA). 1996. pap. 8.95 (84-279-3462-9) Lectorum Pubns.

— The Courage of Sarah Noble. LC 54-5922. (Illus.). 64p. (J). (gr. 1-5). 1987. reprint ed. 15.00 (0-684-18830-9) Scribner.

Dalgliesh, Alice. The Courage of Sarah Noble. unabridged ed. (J). 1954. 24.20 incl. audio (0-7887-2658-7, 40818) Recorded Bks.

— The Courage of Sarah Noble. 2nd ed. (J). 1991. 10.15 (0-606-02070-5, Pub. by Turtleback) Demco.

Dalgliesh, Alice. The Courage of Sarah Noble. 2nd ed. LC 91-15531. (Illus.). 64p. (J). (ps-3). 2000. reprint ed. mass mkt. 4.99 (0-689-71540-4) Aladdin.

— The Fourth of July Stories. 2nd ed. LC 94-29290. (Illus.). 32p. (J). (ps-3). 1995. mass mkt. 5.99 (0-689-71876-4) Macmillan.

— The Silver Pencil. (Illus.). 248p. (YA). (gr. 7 up). 1991. pap. 4.99 (0-14-034792-5, PuffinBks) Peng Put Young Read.

— The Silver Pencil. 1995. 19.00 (0-8446-6794-3) Peter Smith.

— The Thanksgiving Story. LC 87-11471. (Illus.). 32p. (J). (gr. k-3). 1985. mass mkt. 5.99 (0-689-71053-4) Aladdin.

Dalgliesh, Alice. The Thanksgiving Story. (J). 1954. 11.19 (0-606-00599-4, Pub. by Turtleback) Demco.

Dalgliesh, Alice. The Thanksgiving Story. LC 88-4448. (Illus.). 32p. (J). (gr. k-3). 1988. reprint ed. 15.00 (0-684-18999-2) Scribner.

— El Valor de Sarah Noble. 1992. 12.70 (0-606-10405-4, Pub. by Turtleback) Demco.

Dalgliesh, Malcom. The Sage of San Diego Said Choose Quality & Reason. (Illus.). 100p. (Orig.). 1996. pap. 6.95 (0-9646438-0-4) New Enlightenment.

Dalgliesh, Walter S. Shakespeare's Macbeth. 2nd ed. LC 74-163664. reprint ed. 24.50 (0-404-01918-8) AMS Pr.

Dalglish, Carol. Refugees from Vietnam. Campling, Jo, ed. LC 89-30607. 224p. 1989. text 49.95 (0-312-03165-3) St Martin.

***Dalglish, Cass.** Nin. 352p. 2000. pap. 12.00 (1-883523-39-7, Pub. by Spinsters Ink) Words Distrib.

Dalglish, Cass. Sweetgrass. Howe, Ray, ed. 134p. (Orig.). (C). 1992. pap. 10.95 (0-9627860-3-9) Lone Oak MN.

Dalglish, Doris N. People Called Quakers. LC 78-90628. (Essay Index Reprint Ser.). 1977. 18.95 (0-8369-1254-3) Ayer.

Dalglish, Kenny & Winter, Henry. Dalglish: My Autobiography. 320p. 1996. text 35.00 (0-340-66011-2, Pub. by Hodder & Stought Ltd) Trafalgar.

***Dalglish, Peter.** The Courage of Children: My Life with the World's Poorest Kids. LC 98-167611. 340p. 2000. pap. 18.00 (0-00-638567-2) HarpC.

Dalgran, Melinda. Start Smart: Answers to Questions Asked by First Year College Students. 94p. (YA). (gr. 11-12). 1994. pap. text 12.95 (0-07-015190-3) McGraw.

Dalheimer, Matthias K. Programming with Qt: Write Portable GUI Applications on UNIX & WIN32. (Illus.). 361p. 1999. pap. 32.95 (1-56592-588-2) OReilly & Assocs.

Dalhoff, Axel. Pharmacokinetics of Selected Antibacterial Agents. LC 97-33565. (Antibiotics & Chemotherapy Ser.: No. 49). (Illus.). vi, 148p. 1997. 148.00 (3-8055-6576-3) S Karger.

Dalhoff, Axel, ed. Bacterial Infections. (Chemotherapy Ser.: Vol. 45, No. 2 (1999)). (Illus.). 68p. 1999. pap. 25.25 (3-8055-6841-X) S Karger.

Dalhoff, Dietmar. Behaviorale Anpassung & Institutioneller Wandel in Mittel- & Osteuropa: Ein Ansatz zur Analyse Gesellschaftlicher Anpassung im Transformationsprozeb mit Besonderem Blick auf Polen. (GER., Illus.). XIII, 320p. 1996. 57.95 (3-631-30687-3) P Lang Pubng.

Dalhouse, Mark T. An Island in the Lake of Fire: Bob Jones University, Fundamentalism, & the Separatist Movement. LC 95-41978. 200p. (C). 1996. 24.95 (0-8203-1815-9) U of Ga Pr.

Dalhuisen, J. H. The New U. K. Securities Legislation & the E. C. 1992 Program. (Verhandelingen der Koninklijke Nederlandse Akademie van Wetenschappen, Afd. Letterkunde, Nieuwe Reeks Ser.: No. 142). viii, 158p. 1989. pap. text 47.00 (0-444-85709-5) Elsevier.

Dali, Salvador. Art Mini-Dali. (Illus.). 96p. 2000. pap. text 4.95 (3-8290-2934-9) Konemann.

***Dali, Salvador.** Dali. (Illus.). 2000. pap. 1.00 (0-486-41074-9) Dover.

Dali, Salvador. Dali on Modern Art: The Cuckolds of Antiquated Modern Art. Chevalier, Haakon M., tr. from FRE. LC 96-13351. (Illus.). 96p. 1996. reprint ed. pap. text 4.95 (0-486-29220-7) Dover.

Dali, Salvador. Dali Postcards Book: 24 Paintings from the Salvador Dali Museum. (Illus.). 1994. pap. 4.95 (0-486-28286-4) Dover.

Dali, Salvador. Diary of a Genius. 2nd rev. ed. (Illus.). 192p. 1998. reprint ed. pap. 19.95 (1-871592-76-3) Creation Books.

— Fifty Secrets of Magic Craftsmanship. (Illus.). 192p. 1992. reprint ed. pap. 11.95 (0-486-27132-3) Dover.

— Hidden Faces. Chevalier, Haakon, tr. from FRE. & frwd. by. LC 87-60972. (Illus.). 318p. 1996. reprint ed. pap. 22.00 (0-7206-0687-X, Pub. by P Owen Ltd) Dufour.

— Oui: The Paranoid-Critical Revolution, Writings, 1927-1933. Shafir, Yvonne, tr. 192p. 1998. pap. text 13.95 (1-878972-22-7) Exact Change.

— The Secret Life of Salvador Dali. Chevalier, Haakon M., tr. from FRE. LC 92-36763. (Illus.). 432p. 1993. reprint ed. pap. 9.95 (0-486-27454-3) Dover.

Dali, Salvador, jt. auth. see Bunuel, Luis.

Dali, Salvador, Foundation, Inc. Staff. Dali: The Salvador Dali Museum Collection. (Illus.). 176p. 1994. pap. 35.00 (0-8212-2086-1, Pub. by Bulfinch Pr) Little.

Dalibard, J., et al, eds. Fundamental Systems in Quantum Optics: Proceedings of the Les Houches Summer School, Course LIII, 25 June-27 July, 1990. (Houches Summer School Proceedings Ser.: Vol. 53). xxxviii, 1123p. 1992. 289.50 (0-444-89736-4) Elsevier.

Dalibard, J., jt. auth. see Basdevant, Jean-Louis.

Dalichow, Irene & Booth, Mike. Aura-Soma: Healing Through Color, Plant, & Crystal Energy. Burnham, Joan M., tr. from GER. LC 95-25375. 1996. pap. 13.95 (1-56170-291-9, 149T) Hay House.

— Aura-Soma: Healing Through Color, Plant, & Crystal Energy. 2nd ed. Burnham, Joan M., tr. from GER. LC 95-25375. (Illus.). 350p. 1996. reprint ed. 24.00 (1-56170-322-2, 149) Hay House.

Dalik, Richard. Manalapan & Englishtown. (Images of America Ser.). (Illus.). 128p. 1998. pap. 16.99 (0-7524-0910-7) Arcadia Pubng.

D'Alimonte, Roberto, ed. see Nelken, Davis.

Dalin, Anne. Creme de la Femme. Davis, Nancy, ed. LC 97-25306. 370p. 1997. pap. 16.95 (0-375-70056-0) Random Ref & Info.

Dalin, David G. American Jews & the Separationist Faith: The New Debate on Religion in Public Life. 182p. 1992. 19.95 (0-89633-176-8) Ethics & Public Policy.

Dalin, David G. & Rosenbaum, Jonathan. Making a Life, Building a Community: A History of the Jews of Hartford. LC 97-19875. (New Perspectives Ser.). (Illus.). 330p. 1997. 49.95 (0-8419-1374-9); pap. 24.95 (0-8419-1375-7) Holmes & Meier.

Dalin, David G. & Sarna, Jonathan D., eds. Religion & State in the American Jewish Experience: A Documentary History. LC 96-27119. 368p. 1997. text 40.00 (0-268-01654-2) U of Notre Dame Pr.

Dalin, David G., jt. auth. see Abrams, Elliott.

D

An Asterisk (*) at the beginning of an entry indicates that the title is appearing for the first time.

Dalin, David G., jt. auth. see Sarna, Jonathan D.

Dalin, David G., ed. & intro. see Herberg, Will.

Dalin, Per. Changing the School Culture. Hopkins, David & Reynolds, David, eds. (School Development Ser.). (Illus.). 208p. 1993. pap. text 33.95 (*0-304-32737-9*) Continuum.

— How Schools Improve: An International Report. Hopkins, David & Reynolds, David, eds. LC 95-197330. (School Development Ser.). (Illus.). 272p. 1994. pap. 37.95 (*0-304-32736-0*) Continuum.

— School Development: Theories & Strategies. LC 98-235189. (School Development Ser.). 1998. pap. text 28.95 (*0-304-33600-9*) Continuum.

Dalin, Per & Kitson, Katherine. School Development Theories & Strategies : An International Handbook. LC 98-235189. (School Development Ser.). xii, 273 p. 1998. pap. write for info. (*0-304-33599-1*) Continuum.

Dalin, Per & Rust, Val D. Toward Schooling for the Twenty-First Century. (School Development Ser.). (Illus.). 256p. 1996. pap. 35.95 (*0-304-33448-0*) Continuum.

Dalin, Per, jt. auth. see Rust, Val D.

Daling, Tjabel. Costa Rica in Focus: A Guide to the People, Politics & Culture. (In Focus Guides Ser.). (Illus.). 100p. 1998. pap. 12.95 (*1-56656-230-9*) Interlink Pub.

Dalis, Art & Jacobsen, John. Hurricane Smith & the Last Dutch Mine. LC 98-92033. 149p. 1998. pap. write for info. (*1-57502-923-5*, PO2467) Morris Pubng.

Dalis, Gus T., jt. auth. see Fodor, John T.

Dalisay, Jose Y., Jr. Sarcophagus & Other Stories. 144p. 1992. pap. text 18.00 (*971-10-5074-9*, Pub. by U of Philippines Pr) UH Pr.

Dalitz, R. & Stinchcombe, R., eds. A Breadth of Physics: Proceedings of the Peirels 80th Birthday Symposium, Oxford, United Kingdom. 252p. (C). 1988. pap. 29.00 (*9971-5-0520-7*); text 79.00 (*9971-5-0519-3*) World Scientific Pub.

Dalitz, R. H. & Nauenberg, M., eds. The Foundations of Newtonian Scholarship. LC 99-88303. 300p. 1999. 72.00 (*981-02-3920-3*) World Scientific Pub.

***Dalitz, R. H. & Nauenberg, Michael.** The Foundations of Newtonian Scholarship. LC 99-88303. 2000. pap. write for info. (*981-02-4044-9*) World Scientific Pub.

Dalitz, R. H., ed. see Dirac, P. A.

Dalka-Prysby, Sandra. Slow but Sure. LC 98-31097. 224p. 1999. 22.95 (*0-385-49217-0*) Doubleday.

Dalke, David. If Daddy Loved Me. 1994. 0.45 (*1-56123-120-7*) Centering Corp.

Dalkey, Kara. Bhagavati. LC 98-5548. 384p. 1998. text 24.95 (*0-312-86003-X*) St Martin.

— Bijapur. LC 96-41695. (Blood of the Goddess Ser.). 1997. 23.95 (*0-312-86001-3*, Pub. by Tor Bks) St Martin.

— Bijapur: Blood of the Goddess. 1998. mass mkt. 6.99 (*0-8125-4943-0*, Pub. by Tor Bks) St Martin.

— Blood of the Goddess: Goa, Vol. 1. 256p. 1996. 21.95 (*0-312-86000-5*) Tor Bks.

***Dalkey, Kara.** Genpei. 2000. text 25.95 (*0-312-89071-0*) St Martin.

Dalkey, Kara. The Heavenward Path. LC 97-28940. 230p. (J). 1998. 17.00 (*0-15-201652-X*, Harcourt Child Bks) Harcourt.

— Little Sister. LC 96-2556. (Jane Yolen Bks.). 208p. (J). 1996. 17.00 (*0-15-201392-X*) Harcourt.

— Little Sister. LC 97-28231. 208p. 1998. pap. 4.99 (*0-14-038631-9*) Viking Penguin.

Dalkey, Victoria & Davis, Randal. Gregory Kondos: Yosemite & Other California Landscapes. (Illus.). 36p. 1994. pap. 9.95 (*1-886091-08-0*) Hearst Art Gal.

Dalkibic, M. dBASE IV SmartStart. (SmartStart Ser.). (Illus.). 256p. 1993. 25.99 (*1-56529-251-0*) Que.

Dalkin, Monika & Hollis, Mignonne. The Other Rope Book. 30p. (J). (gr. 2-6). 10.95 (*0-9644524-0-5*) Jolly Geranium.

Dalkley, Kara. Crystal Sage. 352p. 1999. mass mkt. 5.99 (*0-451-45640-8*, ROC) NAL.

Dall, Caroline H. The College, the Market, & the Court: Woman's Relation to Education, Labor & Law. LC 72-2596. (American Women Ser.: Images & Realities). 540p. 1974. reprint ed. 30.95 (*0-405-04453-4*) Ayer.

— Margaret & Her Friends: or Ten Conversations with Margaret Fuller upon the Mythology of the Greeks & Its Expression in Art. LC 72-4961. (Romantic Tradition in American Literature Ser.). 166p. 1978. reprint ed. 20.95 (*0-405-04633-2*) Ayer.

Dall, Caroline W. Alongside. Baxter, Annette K., ed. LC 79-8785. (Signal Lives Ser.). 1980. reprint ed. lib. bdg. 18.95 (*0-405-12833-9*) APPA VA.

Dall, J. C., et al, eds. Prospects in Aging. (Sandoz Lectures in Gerontology). (Illus.). 314p. 1993. text 101.00 (*0-12-200745-X*) Acad Pr.

***Dall, Jeanette, et al.** My Time with God: 150 Ways to Start Your Own Quiet Time. LC 00-21068. (Heritage Builders Ser.). 208p. (J). (gr. 3-7). 2000. 9.99 (*1-56179-802-9*) Tyndale Hse.

Dall, Jeanette, jt. auth. see Washington, Linda.

Dall, Jeanette, ed. see Bible, Debbie.

***Dall, Mary Doerfler.** Children Discover the Mass: Lessons, Crafts, Cutouts & More! LC 00-8681. (Illus.). 128p. 2000. teacher ed., spiral bd. 16.95 (*0-87793-948-9*) Ave Maria.

Dall, W., et al, eds. Advances in Marine Biology: Biology of the Penaeidae, Vol. 27. (Illus.). 489p. (C). 1991. text 104.00 (*0-12-026127-8*) Acad Pr.

Dall, W. H., et al. A Manual of the Recent & Fossil, Marine Pelecypod Mollusks of the Hawaiian Islands. (BMB Ser.: No. 153). 1969. reprint ed. 40.00 (*0-527-02261-6*) Periodicals Srv.

Dall, William H. Alaska & Its Resources. LC 72-125736. (American Environmental Studies). (Illus.). 1974. reprint ed. 40.95 (*0-405-02661-7*) Ayer.

— A Critical Review of Bering's First Expedition, 1725-30: Together with a Translation of His Original Report upon It. LC 92-29918. write for info. (*0-87770-513-5*) Ye Galleon.

Dalla Bona, Luke, jt. ed. see Carlson, Roy.

Dalla Chiara, Maria L., ed. The Tenth International Congress of Logic, Methodology & Philosophy of Science, Florence, August 1995, 2 vols. Incl. Vol. 2. Structures & Norms in Science. LC 96-52731. 512p. (C). 1997. lib. bdg. 257.00 (*0-7923-4384-0*); Vol. 1. Logic & Scientific Methods. LC 96-52731. 552p. (C). 1997. lib. bdg. 275.00 (*0-7923-4383-2*); LC 96-52731. (Synthese Library). 1996. Set text 470.00 (*0-7923-4385-9*) Kluwer Academic.

***Dalla Chiara, Maria Luisa, et al, eds.** Language, Quantum, Music: Selected Contributed Papers of the 10th International Congress of Logic, Methodology & Philosophy of Science, Florence, August 1995. (Synthese Library). 368p. 1999. 252.00 (*0-7923-5867-8*, Kluwer Acad) Kluwer Academic.

Dalla Costa, Giovanna F., jt. ed. see Dalla Costa, Mariarosa.

Dalla Costa, John. The Ethical Imperative: Why Moral Leadership Is Good Business. 1998. write for info. (*0-201-38606-2*) Addison-Wesley.

Dalla Costa, Mariarosa & Dalla Costa, Giovanna F., eds. Women, Development & Labor Reproduction: Issues of Struggles & Movements. LC 99-25029. 223p. 1997. 59.95 (*0-86543-621-5*); pap. 18.95 (*0-86543-622-3*) Africa World.

Dalla-Costa, Raphael. Dictionnaire des Sports Aeriens Ultralegers: French-English, English-French. (ENG & FRE.). 88p. 1988. pap. 18.95 (*0-7859-8087-3*, 2854281829) Fr & Eur.

Dalla, Ismail. The Emerging Asian Bond Market. LC 95-48236. 168p. 1996. pap. 90.00 (*0-8213-3487-5*) World Bank.

Dalla, Ismail & Khatkhate, Deena. Regulated Deregulation of the Financial System in Korea. LC 95-30168. (Discussion Paper Ser.: Vol. 292). 42p. 1995. pap. 22.00 (*0-8213-3356-9*, 13356) World Bank.

Dalla Torre, K. W. Von, see Von Dalla Torre, K. W.

***Dalla Volta, Sergio, et al.** Cardiology. (Clinical Medicine Ser.). (Illus.). 891p. 1999. pap. text 67.50 (*0-07-709518-9*) McGraw-Hill HPD.

Dallagiacomo, Gene, ed. see Peck, Ennis.

Dall'Aglio, G., et al, eds. Advances in Probability Distributions with Given Marginals: Beyond the Copulas. (C). 1991. text 140.50 (*0-7923-1156-6*) Kluwer Academic.

Dallaglio, L. Dallaglio on Rugby. text 35.00 (*0-340-71839-0*, Pub. by Hodder & Stought Ltd) Trafalgar.

Dallago, Bruno. The Irregular Economy: The "Underground" Economy & the "Black" Labour Market. (Illus.). 224p. 1990. text 72.95 (*1-85521-013-4*, Pub. by Dartmth Pub) Ashgate Pub Co.

Dallago, Bruno, et al, eds. Convergence & System Change: The Convergence Hypothesis in the Light of Transition in Central & Eastern Europe. 247p. 1992. 66.95 (*1-85521-218-8*, Pub. by Dartmth Pub) Ashgate Pub Co.

Dallago, Bruno & Pegoretti, Giovanni, eds. Integration & Disintegration in European Economies. LC 95-5683. 310p. 1995. 77.95 (*1-85521-552-7*, Pub. by Dartmth Pub) Ashgate Pub Co.

Dallago, Bruno, jt. auth. see Kovacs, Janos.

D'Allaire, Micheline. Les Communautes Religieuses de Montreal. (FRE.). 1998. write for info. (*2-89415-201-9*) Edits Meridien.

***Dallaire, Natalie & Cole, Stephen.** Parallel 59. (Doctor Who Ser.). 288p. 2000. mass mkt. 6.95 (*0-563-55590-4*, Pub. by BBC Bks) Genl Dist Srvs.

Dallal, Ahmad S., ed. from ARA. An Islamic Response to Greek Astronomy. LC 95-12871. (Islamic Philosophy, Theology & Science, Studies & Texts Ser.: Vol. 23).Tr. of Kitab Tadil Hayat Al-Aflak of Sadr Al-Sharia. ix, 461p. 1995. 152.50 (*90-04-09968-9*) Brill Academic Pubs.

Dallal, Reading A., tr. see Ghanimah, Yusuf R.

Dallal, Shaw J. Scattered Like Seeds: A Novel. LC 98-8761. 1998. 26.95 (*0-8156-0553-6*) Syracuse U Pr.

Dallal, Sheila, ed. see Ghanimah, Yusuf R.

Dallal, Tamalyn. Diaries of a Feminist Belly Dancer: In Brazil. (Illus.). 176p. 1997. pap. 14.95 (*1-890916-20-X*) Talion Pub.

— Diaries of a Feminist Belly Dancer: In Cuba. (Illus.). 176p. 1997. pap. 14.95 (*1-890916-21-8*) Talion Pub.

— They Told Me I Couldn't: A Young Woman's Multicultural Adventures in Colombia. Harris, Bev, ed. (Travels of Tamalyn Dallal Ser.). (Illus.). 176p. 1997. pap. 14.95 (*1-890916-19-6*) Talion Pub.

Dallal, Tamalyn, jt. auth. see Long, Rod.

Dallal, Tamlyn. How to Play the Finger Cymbals: Dallal's Tutorial for Belly Dancers. 1996. pap. 11.95 incl. audio (*1-890916-64-1*) Talion Pub.

Dall'Alba, Gloria & Hasselgren, Biorn, eds. Reflections on Phenomenography: Toward a Methodology? LC 97-127733. (Goteborg Studies in Educational Sciences: No. 109). 202p. 1996. pap. 52.50 (*91-7346-299-3*, Pub. by Almqvist Wiksell) Coronet Bks.

Dallalis. Nursing the Whole Person. (LPN/LVN Nursing Ser.). 1995. text 59.95 (*0-8273-5459-2*) Delmar.

Dallapiccola, Anna L. Ramachandra Temple at Vijayanagara. (C). 1992. text 58.00 (*81-85425-27-2*, Pub. by Manohar) S Asia.

Dallard, Shyrlee. Ella Baker. (History of the Civil Rights Movement Ser.). (Illus.). 128p. (J). (gr. 5-8). 1990. pap. 7.95 (*0-382-24066-9*); lib. bdg. 12.95 (*0-382-09931-1*) Silver Burdett Pr.

DallaRiva, Lois, jt. auth. see Snow, Roslyn.

Dallas. Waterloo at Dawning, Vol. 1. 1950. pap. 15.95 (*0-8050-3185-5*) St Martin.

Dallas A & M University Mothers' Club Staff. Hullabaloo in the Kitchen. 384p. 1983. 12.95 (*0-9612446-0-7*) Dallas A & M Mothers.

— Hullabaloo in the Kitchen II. LC 98-86674. (Illus.). 320p. 1998. 19.95 (*0-9612446-1-5*) Dallas A & M Mothers.

Dallas Aids Planning Commission Staff. A Community Response to AIDS: Report of the Dallas Aids Planning Commission. Halcyon Press Staff, ed. (Illus.). 260p. (Orig.). 1988. pap. 7.00 (*0-9621114-0-6*) Halcyon TX.

Dallas, Alastair. Special Edition Using Collabra Share: Special Edition. (Illus.). 550p. (Orig.). 1995. 34.99 (*0-7897-0410-2*) Que.

Dallas County Community College District Staff. Out of Dallas: Fourteen Stories. Wood, Jane R. et al, eds. LC 88-38942. (Illus.). 208p. 1989. pap. 12.95 (*0-929398-03-3*) UNTX Pr.

Dallas County Community College Staff. Telecourse: Living with Health. (C). 1994. pap. text, student ed. 21.10 (*0-07-015187-3*) McGraw.

Dallas County Medical Society Staff, ed. Thyme to Remember: Generations of Recipes Handed down for Today. (Illus.). 1998. write for info. (*0-9664895-0-0*) Dallas Cty Med Soc.

Dallas Cowboys Staff. Dallas Cowboys. CWC Sports Inc, ed. (NFL Team Yearbooks Ser.). (J). (gr. 1-12). 1998. pap. 9.99 (*1-891613-06-5*) Everett Sports.

Dallas Cowboys' Wives Staff, compiled by. Cookin' with the Cowboys: Family Photo Album & Favorite Recipes. 1995. pap. 14.95 (*0-9634855-3-9*) Happy Hill Farm.

Dallas, Daniel B. Pressworking Aids for Designers & Diemakers. LC 77-90988. (Manufacturing Data Ser.). 275p. 1978. 42.00 (*0-87263-042-0*) SME.

Dallas, Eugenia. One Woman, Five Lives, Five Countries. Silici, Paula, ed. LC 98-67925. (Illus.). 257p. 1998. pap. 20.00 (*0-88100-107-4*) Natl Writ Pr.

Dallas, F. A. A., et al, eds. Recent Advances in Thin-Layer Chromatography. LC 88-17880. (Illus.). 262p. 1988. 85.00 (*0-306-42934-9*, Plenum Trade) Perseus Pubng.

Dallas, George. Waterloo at Dawning. LC 97-13625. 560p. 1995. 35.00 (*0-8050-3184-7*) H Holt & Co.

Dallas, Georgia. This Band of Gold. 224p. 1987. pap. 5.95 (*0-310-47321-7*, 15578P) Zondervan.

Dallas, Herb, Jr., ed. see Haversat, Trudy, et al.

Dallas I. S. D. Staff. The Bible Study Course of the New Treatment. 1993. reprint ed. pap. 4.95 (*0-925279-28-5*) Wallbuilders.

Dallas, Ian. The Book of Strangers: A Novel. LC 88-16114. 151p. (C). 1988. pap. text 17.95 (*0-88706-991-6*) State U NY Pr.

Dallas Independent School District Staff. Bible Study Course of the Old Testament. 96p. (Orig.). 1994. reprint ed. pap. 4.95 (*0-925279-44-7*) Wallbuilders.

Dallas, James. Dallas: The History of the Family of Dallas & Their Connections & Descendants from the Twelfth Century. (Illus.). 611p. 1992. reprint ed. pap. 89.50 (*0-8328-2479-8*); reprint ed. lib. bdg. 99.50 (*0-8328-2478-X*) Higginson Bk Co.

Dallas, James W., jt. auth. see Atkinson, David B.

Dallas, Joe. Desires in Conflict. 1991. pap. 10.99 (*0-89081-897-5*) Harvest Hse.

— A Strong Delusion: Confronting the Gay Christian Movement. 300p. (Orig.). 1996. pap. 10.99 (*1-56507-431-9*) Harvest Hse.

Dallas Junior Forum Staff. Deep in the Heart. LC 86-71410. (Illus.). 304p. 1986. spiral bd. 18.95 (*0-9617187-0-6*) Dallas Jr Forum.

Dallas, Kim. Fundamental Karate. LC 97-29623. (Fundamental Sports Ser.). (Illus.). (J). 1997. 19.93 (*0-8225-3462-2*) Lerner Pub.

Dallas, Mark, jt. auth. see Arthur, Linda.

Dallas, Melissa & Riegel, Carl. Hospitality & Tourism Careers: A Blueprint for Success. LC 97-21990. 252p. (C). 1997. pap. text 38.20 (*0-13-228545-2*) P-H.

Dallas, Michael. Men: Move to Paradise: Find Love, Sex & Money in Tropical Getaways. LC 95-95030. (Illus.). 265p. (Orig.). 1995. pap. 24.95 (*0-9649039-0-3*) Alex & Watson.

***Dallas Morning News Editors.** Dallas Stars: '99 NHL Champs. 96p. 1999. pap. 9.95 (*1-58261-193-9*, Pub. by Sprts Pubng) Partners-West.

Dallas Museum of Art League Staff. The Artful Table: Great Food from the Dallas Museum of Art League. (Illus.). 224p. 1995. 35.00 (*0-936227-14-1*) Dallas Mus.

Dallas Museum of Art Staff. The Quedlinburg Treasury. (Illus.). 30p. (Orig.). 1991. pap. 14.95 (*0-936227-10-9*) U of Wash Pr.

Dallas, Roland. King Hussein: A Life on the Edge. LC 99-37260. (Illus.). 336p. 1999. 28.00 (*0-88064-242-4*, Pub. by Fromm Intl Pub) FS&G.

***Dallas, Ruth.** The Black Horse & Other Stories. 112p. 2000. pap. 24.95 (*1-877133-85-X*, Pub. by Univ Otago Pr) Intl Spec Bk.

— Collected Poems. 208p. 2000. pap. 39.95 (*1-877133-86-8*, Pub. by Univ Otago Pr) Intl Spec Bk.

Dallas, Ruth. Curved Horizon. 192p. 1996. 19.95 (*0-908569-54-8*, Pub. by Univ Otago Pr) Intl Spec Bk.

***Dallas, Sandra.** Alice's Tulips. 240p. 2000. 22.95 (*0-312-20359-4*) St Martin.

Dallas, Sandra. Buster Midnight's Cafe. LC 97-50480. 224p. 1998. pap. 11.95 (*0-312-18062-4*) St Martin.

— Colorado Ghost Towns & Mining Camps. LC 84-17377. (Illus.). 254p. 1985. pap. 19.95 (*0-8061-2084-3*) U of Okla Pr.

— Colorado Ghost Towns & Mining Camps. LC 84-17377. (Illus.). 264p. 1988. 32.95 (*0-8061-1910-1*) U of Okla Pr.

— The Diary of Mattie Spenser. LC 96-53926. 229p. 1997. text 21.95 (*0-312-15515-8*) St Martin.

— The Diary of Mattie Spenser. 240p. 1998. pap. 11.95 (*0-312-18710-6*) St Martin.

— The Diary of Mattie Spenser. large type ed. LC 97-47196. (Large Print Bks.). 1998. pap. 23.95 (*1-56895-523-5*) Wheeler Pub.

— The Persian Pickle Club. LC 95-31032. 208p. 1995. text 20.95 (*0-312-13586-6*) St Martin.

— The Persian Pickle Club. large type ed. (Niagara Large Print Ser.). 270p. 1997. pap. 29.50 (*0-7089-5856-7*, Linford) Ulverscroft.

— The Persian Pickle Club. 8th ed. 208p. 1996. pap. 11.95 (*0-312-14701-5*) St Martin.

***Dallas, Sue.** Animal Biology & Care. LC 99-38885. (Illus.). 256p. 2000. pap. text 26.95 (*0-632-05054-3*, Pub. by Blckwell Science) Iowa St U Pr.

— Manual of Veterinary Care. (Illus.). 256p. 2000. pap. text 56.95 (*0-905214-49-8*, Pub. by BSAVA) Iowa St U Pr.

Dallas, Susan, ed. Diary of George Mifflin Dallas While United States Minister to Russia, 1837-1839. LC 70-115527. (Russia Observed, Series I). 1970. reprint ed. 17.95 (*0-405-03019-3*) Ayer.

Dallas, Wendy, jt. auth. see Pavarotti, Adua.

Dallas 1, Morning News Staff. November 22 - The Day Remembered. LC 89-71363. 160p. 1990. pap. 11.95 (*0-87833-711-3*) Taylor Pub.

Dallat, C. L., et al. Trio 7 Poetry. 57p. 1993. pap. 13.95 (*0-85640-486-1*, Pub. by Blackstaff Pr) Dufour.

Dallavo, William G. The Power Within Henry Washe. (Illus.). 51p. 1983. pap. 6.00 (*0-942494-74-1*) Coleman Pub.

Dalle & Thrush. Esl Guide Academic Writing. 1995. pap. 20.00 (*0-205-15175-2*) P-H.

Dalle Vacche, Angela. The Body in the Mirror: Shapes of History in Italian Cinema. LC 91-19142. (Illus.). 324p. reprint ed. pap. 100.50 (*0-608-20146-4*, 207141800011) Bks Demand.

— Cinema & Painting: How Art Is Used in Film. LC 95-32441. (Illus.). (C). 1996. pap. 19.95 (*0-292-71583-8*); text 45.00 (*0-292-71582-X*) U of Tex Pr.

Dallek, Geraldine. Medicare Managed Care: Securing Beneficiary Protections. (Illus.). 66p. 1998. pap. text 25.00 (*0-7881-7079-1*) DIANE Pub.

Dallek, Geraldine, ed. The Best from the States: The Text of Key State HMO Consumer Protection Provisions. 78p. (C). 1998. pap. text 25.00 (*0-7881-7078-3*) DIANE Pub.

***Dallek, Matthew.** The Right Moment: Ronald Reagan's First Victory & the Great Turning Point in American Politics. LC 00-37600. (Illus.). 320p. 2000. 24.50 (*0-684-84320-X*) Free Pr.

Dallek, Robert. Flawed Giant: Lyndon Johnson & His Times, 1961-1973. LC 97-39084. (Illus.). 784p. 1998. 35.00 (*0-19-505465-2*) OUP.

— Flawed Giant: Lyndon Johnson & His Times, 1961-1973. (Illus.). 784p. 1999. pap. 18.95 (*0-19-513238-6*) OUP.

— Franklin D. Roosevelt & American Foreign Policy, 1932-1945: With a New Afterword. LC 97-118779. (Illus.). 688p. 1995. pap. text 19.95 (*0-19-509732-7*) OUP.

— Hail to the Chief: The Making & Unmaking of American Presidents. LC 96-8033. 256p. (J). 1996. 22.95 (*0-7868-6205-X*, Pub. by Hyperion) Time Warner.

— Hail to the Chief: The Making & Unmaking of American Presidents. 256p. (J). 1997. reprint ed. pap. 15.45 (*0-7868-8265-4*, Pub. by Hyperion) Time Warner.

— Lone Star Rising: Lyndon Johnson & His Times, 1908-1960. (Illus.). 736p. 1991. text 35.00 (*0-19-505435-0*) OUP.

— Lone Star Rising: Lyndon Johnson & His Times, 1908-1960. (Illus.). 754p. 1992. pap. 16.95 (*0-19-507904-3*) OUP.

— Ronald Reagan: The Politics of Symbolism - With a New Preface. LC 98-50782. 1999. pap. 15.95 (*0-674-77941-X*) HUP.

Dallemagne-Cookson, Elise. The Bearded Lion Who Roars: Simba Mandefu Mabe. (Illus.). 288p. (Orig.). 1995. pap. 12.95 (*1-56474-115-X*) Fithian Pr.

— The Filmmaker. LC 99-25533. 264p. 2000. pap. 14.95 (*1-56474-313-6*, Pub. by Fithian Pr) SCB Distributors.

Dallemagne, Elise. The Ombu Tree. LC 98-6672. 288p. 1998. pap. 14.95 (*1-56474-261-X*) Fithian Pr.

D'Allemagne, Henry R. Decorative Antique Ironwork: A Pictorial Treasury. Ostoia, Vera K., tr. LC 67-20193. (Illus.). 420p. 1998. pap. 19.95 (*0-486-22082-6*) Dover.

***D'Allemand, Patricia.** Latin Americna Cultural Criticism: Re-Interpreting a Continent. LC 00-21154. (Studies in Latin American Literature & Culture : 7). 208p. 2000. pap. text 89.95 (*0-7734-7811-6*) E Mellen.

Dallen, James. The Dilemma of Priestless Sundays. LC 94-31579. 154p. (Orig.). 1994. pap. 11.00 (*1-56854-042-6*, DP/SUN) Liturgy Tr Pubns.

— The Reconciling Community: The Rite of Penance. 446p. 1992. pap. 19.95 (*0-8146-6076-2*, Pueblo Bks) Liturgical Pr.

Dallen, James & Favazza, Joseph A. Removing the Barriers: The Practice of Reconciliation. 76p. (Orig.). 1991. pap. 5.95 (*0-929650-37-9*, REMBAR) Liturgy Tr Pubns.

Dallen, Michael. The Seven Commandments: A Guide to Hebrew Revolutionary Morality & Universal Law (The Code of the Rainbow Covenant) LC 98-94941. (Illus.). xiv, 408p. 1999. pap. 31.95 (*0-9671330-0-9*) Emden Bks.

Dallenbach-Hellweg, G. & Poulsen, Hemming. Atlas of Endometrial Histopathology. 2nd expanded rev. ed. LC 96-16757. 240p. 1996. 195.00 (*3-540-60908-3*) Spr-Verlag.

Dallenbach-Hellweg, Gisela. Histopathology. (Illus.). 435p. 1987. 177.00 (*0-387-18156-3*) Spr-Verlag.

Dallenbach-Hellweg, Gisela & Poulsen, Hemming. Series of Slides for the Atlas of Histopathology of the Cervix Uteri. 1992. 224.00 incl. sl. (*0-387-92119-2*) Spr-Verlag.

D

Dallenbach-Hellweg, Gisela & Poulsen, Hemming, eds. Atlas of Histopathology of the Cervix Uteri. (Illus.). 200p. 1991. 182.00 (*0-387-52295-6*) Spr-Verlag.

Dallenbach-Hellweg, Gisela, jt. auth. see Stoll, Peter.

Dallenbach, K. M., jt. auth. see Dillenbeck, A. L.

Dallenbach, Lucien. The Mirror in the Text. Whiteley, Jeremy & Hughes, Emma, trs. LC 89-4898. 280p. 1989. 47.95 (*0-226-13491-1*) U Ch Pr.

***Daller, Helmut.** Migration und Mehrsprachigkeit: Der Sprachstand Turkischer Ruckkehrer Aus Deutschland. (GER., Illus.). VIII, 201p. 1999. 37.95 (*3-631-34559-3*) P Lang Pubng.

***Daller, Morton F.** Product Liability Desk Reference: 1999 Edition. 544p. 1999. pap. 122.00 (*0-7355-0508-X*) Panel Pubs.

Daller, Morton F., ed. Product Liability Desk Reference: A Fifty-State Compendium. annuals 496p. pap. 109.00 (*0-316-17241-3*, 72413) Aspen Law.

Dallery, Arleen B., et al, eds. Crises in Continental Philosophy. LC 90-34077. (Selected Studies in Phenomenology & Existential Philosophy). 283p. (C). 1990. pap. text 19.95 (*0-7914-0420-X*) State U NY Pr.

— Ethics & Danger: Essays on Heidegger & Continental Thought. LC 91-18875. (Selected Studies in Phenomenology & Existential Philosophy: No. 17). 358p. (C). 1992. text 59.50 (*0-7914-0983-X*); pap. text 19.95 (*0-7914-0984-8*) State U NY Pr.

— Transitions in Continental Philosophy. LC 93-1254. (Selected Studies in Phenomenology & Existential Philosophy). 353p. (C). 1994. text 59.50 (*0-7914-1849-9*); pap. text 19.95 (*0-7914-1850-2*) State U NY Pr.

Dallery, Arleen B. & Scott, Charles E., eds. The Question of the Other: Essays in Contemporary Continental Philosophy. LC 88-39152. (Selected Studies in Phenomenology & Existential Philosophy). 256p. 1989. text 19.50 (*0-7914-0032-8*) State U NY Pr.

Dalles, Heidi & Bras, Karin, eds. Tourism & Small Entrepreneurs. LC 99-22632. (Tourism Dynamics Ser.). 1999. 38.00 (*1-882345-24-X*); pap. 30.00 (*1-882345-27-4*) Cognizant Comm.

D'Allesandro, Sam, jt. auth. see Bellamy, Dodie.

D'Allessandro, M. & Bonne, A. Radioactive Waste Disposal into a Plastic Clay Formation: A Site-Specific Exercise of Probabilistic Assessment of Geological Containment. (Radioactive Waste Management Ser.). iv, 150p. 1981. text 123.00 (*3-7186-0084-6*) Gordon & Breach.

Dallet, J. Kabul-French Dictionary: Dictionnaire Kabyle-Francais. (ARA & FRE.). 1052p. 1983. 85.00 (*0-8288-1588-7*, F37550) Fr & Eur.

Dallett, Francis James, Jr. Dallett. Genealogy of the Dallett Family. (Illus.). 112p. 1997. reprint ed. pap. 17.50 (*0-8328-8200-3*); reprint ed. lib. bdg. 27.50 (*0-8328-8199-6*) Higginson Bk Co.

Dallett, Janet. When the Spirits Come Back. 160p. 1988. pap. 16.00 (*0-919123-32-5*, Pub. by Inner City Bks) BookWorld.

Dallett, Janet O. The Not-Yet-Transformed God: Depth Psychology & the Individual Religious Experience. LC 98-21648. 160p. 1998. pap. 16.95 (*0-89254-042-7*) Nicolas-Hays.

— Saturday's Child: Encounters with the Dark Gods. 128p. 1995. pap. 16.00 (*0-919123-52-X*, Pub. by Inner City Bks) BookWorld.

D'Alleva, Anne. Art & Artifacts of Polynesia. (Illus.). 64p. (Orig.). 1990. pap. 25.00 (*0-9628074-0-0*) Hurst Gal.

— Arts of the Pacific Islands. LC 97-22414. (Perspectives). (Illus.). 176p. 1998. pap. 18.95 (*0-8109-2722-5*, Pub. by Abrams) Time Warner.

— Native American Arts & Cultures. LC 93-73931. (Arts & Cultures Ser.). (Illus.). 136p. 1994. 25.95 (*0-87192-248-7*) Davis Mass.

Dalley, A. F., jt. auth. see Magee, D. F.

Dalley, Bernell K., jt. auth. see Pellev, John W.

Dalley, Bronwyn. Family Matters: Child Welfare in Twentieth-Century New Zealand. LC 98-198082. (Illus.). 280p. 1998. pap. 29.95 (*1-86940-190-5*, Pub. by Auckland Univ) Paul & Co Pubs.

***Dalley, Bronwyn & Labrum, Bronwyn, eds.** Fragments of Life. (Illus.). 300p. 2000. pap. 29.95 (*1-86940-185-9*, Pub. by Auckland Univ) Paul & Co Pubs.

***Dalley, Dave.** The Independent Hostel Guide 2000: Britain & Europe. 2000. pap. 7.95 (*0-9523381-9-X*, Pub. by Backpackers) Wilderness Pr.

Dalley, Gardiner F. Swallow Shelter & Associated Sites. (Anthropological Papers: No. 96). (Illus.). 1978. pap. 17.50 (*0-87480-143-5*) U of Utah Pr.

Dalley, Gardiner F., jt. auth. see Fry, Gary F.

Dalley, James & Dalley, Tamara. Pregnancy Journal. 136p. 1994. 18.95 (*0-9642259-0-5*) Castle Peak.

***Dalley, Jan.** Diana Mosley: A Life. LC 99-40737. (Illus.). 336p. 2000. 27.50 (*0-394-58736-7*) Knopf.

Dalley, Nicholas S., ed. see Dally, Jill.

Dalley, Robert J. Surfin' Guitars: Instrumental Surf Bands of the Sixties. 2nd ed. (Rock & Roll Remembrances Ser.: No. 13). (Illus.). 382p. 1996. lib. bdg. 55.00 (*1-56075-042-1*) Popular Culture.

Dalley, Stephanie. Myths from Mesopotamia: Creation, the Flood, Gilgamesh & Others. (Illus.). 360p. 1998. pap. 9.95 (*0-19-283589-0*) OUP.

Dalley, Stephanie & Yoffee, Norman, eds. Old Babylonian Texts in the Ashmolean Museum: Texts from Kish & Elsewhere. (Oxford Editions of Cuneiform Texts Ser.: Vol. XIII). (Illus.). 154p. 1991. pap. text 110.00 (*0-19-814479-2*) OUP.

Dalley, Stephanie, et al. The Legacy of Mesopotamia. LC 97-12948. (Illus.). 248p. (C). 1998. text 105.00 (*0-19-814946-8*) OUP.

— The Old Babylonian Tablets from Tell Al Rimah. (Illus.). 271p. 1976. 42.00 (*0-903472-03-1*, Pub. by Brit Sch Archaeol Iraq) David Brown.

Dalley, Tamara. Pregnancy Journal. 136p. 1994. 15.95 (*0-9642259-2-1*) Castle Peak.

Dalley, Tamara, jt. auth. see Dalley, James.

Dalley, Tessa, ed. Art As Therapy: An Introduction to the Use of Art As a Therapeutic Technique. 201p. 1984. pap. 16.95 (*0-422-78730-2*, NO. 9083) Routledge.

— Art as Therapy: Introduction to the Use of Art as a Therapeutic Technique. (Illus.). 224p. (C). 1984. pap. 25.99 (*0-415-04021-3*) Routledge.

Dalley, Tessa & Case, Caroline. Handbook of Art Therapy. LC 91-36908. (Illus.). 272p. (C). 1992. pap. 29.99 (*0-415-04381-6*, A7102) Routledge.

Dalley, Tessa, et al. Images of Art Therapy: New Developments in Theory & Practice. (Illus.). 264p. 1987. pap. 17.95 (*0-422-60400-3*) Routledge.

— Images of Art Therapy: New Developments in Theory & Practice. (Illus.). 264p. (C). 1987. lib. bdg. 69.95 (*0-422-60390-2*, Pub. by Tavistock) Routldge.

Dalley, Tessa, jt. ed. see Case, Caroline.

Dalley, Tessa, jt. ed. see Gilroy, Andrea.

D'Alleyrand, Marc R., ed. Networks & Imaging Systems in a Windowed Environment. LC 95-42036. 364p. 1995. 27.00 (*0-89006-654-X*, TA1637) Artech Hse.

Dallimore. Holly Yew & Box. LC 76-10174. (Illus.). 1976. reprint ed. 15.00 (*0-913728-12-8*) Theophrastus.

Dallimore, Arnold. Heart Set Free. 1988. pap. 13.99 (*0-85234-249-7*, Pub. by Evangelical Pr) P & R Pubng.

Dallimore, Arnold A. George Whitefield: God's Anointed Servant in the Great Revival of the Eighteenth Century. LC 89-81258. 224p. 1990. pap. 14.99 (*0-89107-553-4*) Crossway Bks.

— George Whitefield Vol. 1: The Life & Times of the Great Evangelist of the 18th Century Revival. 612p. (C). 1979. reprint ed. 49.99 (*0-85151-026-4*) Banner of Truth.

— George Whitefield Vol. 2: The Life & Times of the Great Evangelist of the 18th Century Revival. 620p. (C). 1980. 49.99 (*0-85151-300-X*) Banner of Truth.

— The Life of Edward Irving: The Fore-Runner of the Charismatic Movement. 179p. (C). 1983. pap. 13.99 (*0-85151-369-7*) Banner of Truth.

— Spurgeon: A New Biography. 272p. (C). 1985. reprint ed. pap. 14.99 (*0-85151-451-0*) Banner of Truth.

— Susanna Wesley. LC 92-41948. 176p. (YA). (gr. 10 up). 1993. pap. 9.99 (*0-8010-3018-8*) Baker Bks.

Dallin. Listener Guide to Music. 8th ed. 1993. teacher ed. 30.62 (*0-697-12510-6*) McGraw.

Dallin, A. Major Problems in Early Modern Russian History. Kollmann, Nancy S., ed. LC 91-46584. (Articles on Russian & Soviet History, 1500-1991 Ser.: Vol. 1). 472p. 1992. reprint ed. text 25.00 (*0-8153-0558-3*) Garland.

Dallin, Alexander. Imperial Russian History I, 1700-1861. Hamburg, Gary M., ed. LC 92-3226. (Articles on Russian & Soviet History, 1500-1991 Ser.: Vol. 2). 517p. 1992. text 25.00 (*0-8153-0559-1*) Garland.

— Imperial Russian History II, 1861-1917. Hamburg, Gary M., ed. LC 91-46583. (Articles on Russian & Soviet History, 1500-1991 Ser.: Vol. 3). 599p. 1992. text 30.00 (*0-8153-0560-5*) Garland.

— Odessa, 1941-1944: A Case Study of Soviet Territory under Foreign Rule. LC 98-208730. 296p. 1998. 48.00 (*973-98391-1-8*, Pub. by Ctr Romanian Studies) Intl Spec Bk.

— The Soviet Union at the United Nations: An Inquiry into Soviet Motives & Objectives. LC 75-27679. (Illus.). 244p. 1976. reprint ed. lib. bdg. 69.50 (*0-8371-8454-1*, DASU, Greenwood Pr) Greenwood.

Dallin, Alexander, compiled by. Soviet Conduct. LC 75-31359. 318p. 1975. reprint ed. lib. bdg. 65.00 (*0-8371-8511-4*, DASCW, Greenwood Pr) Greenwood.

Dallin, Alexander, ed. Between Totalitarianism & Pluralism. LC 91-48457. (Articles on Russian & Soviet History, 1500-1991 Ser.: Vol. 9). 456p. 1992. text 30.00 (*0-8153-0566-4*) Garland.

— Civil-Military Relations in the Soviet Union. LC 91-44950. (Articles on Russian & Soviet History, 1500-1991 Ser.: Vol. 12). 312p. 1992. text 20.00 (*0-8153-0569-9*) Garland.

— The Gorbachev Era. LC 92-1190. (Articles on Russian & Soviet History, 1500-1991 Ser.: Vol. 14). 376p. 1992. text 20.00 (*0-8153-0571-0*) Garland.

— The Kruschev & Brezhnev Years. LC 91-46853. (Articles on Russian & Soviet History, 1500-1991 Ser.: Vol. 10). 504p. 1992. text 25.00 (*0-8153-0567-2*) Garland.

— The Nature of the Soviet System. LC 91-46445. (Articles on Russian & Soviet History, 1500-1991 Ser.: Vol. 8). 552p. 1992. text 25.00 (*0-8153-0565-6*) Garland.

— Political Parties in Russia. LC 93-15341. (Research Ser.: No. 88): x, 102p. 1993. pap. text 10.95 (*0-87725-188-6*) U of Cal IAS.

— Soviet Foreign Policy, 1917-1990. LC 91-44951. (Articles on Russian & Soviet History, 1500-1991 Ser.: Vol. 13). 544p. 1992. text 30.00 (*0-8153-0570-2*) Garland.

Dallin, Alexander & Breslauer, George W. Political Terror in Communist Systems. xvi, 176p. 1970. pap. 11.95 (*0-8047-1085-6*) Stanford U Pr.

***Dallin, Alexander & Firsov, Fridrikh I., eds.** Dimitrov & Stalin, 1934-1943: Letters from the Soviet Archives. Staklo, Vadim A., tr. LC 99-39083. (Annals of Communism Ser.). 269p. 2000. 35.00 (*0-300-08021-2*) Yale U Pr.

Dallin, Alexander & Patenaude, Bertrand, eds. Soviet Scholarship under Gorbachev. 100p. (Orig.). 1988. pap. write for info. (*0-318-64415-0*) Stanford U CFREES.

Dallin, Alexander & Patenaude, Bertrand M., eds. Stalin & Stalinism. LC 91-44952. (Articles on Russian & Soviet History, 1500-1991 Ser.: Vol. 7). 408p. 1992. text 25.00 (*0-8153-0564-8*) Garland.

Dallin, David J. Soviet Foreign Policy after Stalin. LC 75-14596. (Illus.). 543p. 1975. reprint ed. lib. bdg. 85.00 (*0-8371-8223-9*, DASF, Greenwood Pr) Greenwood.

Dallin, Leon. Listeners Guide to Musical Understanding. 7th ed. 416p. (C). 1990. text. write for info. (*0-697-12883-0*) Brown & Benchmark.

— Listener's Guide to Musical Understanding. 8th ed. 376p. (C). 1993. text. write for info. (*0-697-12509-2*) Brown & Benchmark.

— Listener's Guide to Musical Understanding. 8th ed. 376p. (C). 1993. text. write for info. (*0-697-12513-0*); text, pap. text. write for info. incl. disk (*0-697-24597-7*); text, ring bd. write for info. incl. audio compact disk (*0-697-24598-5*); audio. write for info. (*0-697-12512-2*) Brown & Benchmark.

— Techniques of Twentieth-Century Composition: A Guide to the Materials of Modern Music. 3rd ed. 304p. (C). 1974. text. write for info. (*0-697-03614-6*) Brown & Benchmark.

Dallin, Leon & Dallin, Lynn. Heritage Songster. 2nd ed. 320p. (C). 1980. text. write for info. (*0-697-03481-X*) Brown & Benchmark.

Dallin, Leon, jt. auth. see Winslow, Robert W.

Dallin, Lynn. Cancer Causes & Natural Controls. LC 82-13765. 374p. 1984. 24.95 (*0-87949-224-4*) Ashley Bks.

Dallin, Lynn, jt. auth. see Dallin, Leon.

Dalling, M. Plant Proteolytic Enzymes, Vol. 1. LC 85-24319. 1986. 100.00 (*0-8493-5682-2*, CRC Reprint) Franklin.

— Plant Proteolytic Enzymes, Vol. 2. LC 85-24319. 176p. 1986. 103.00 (*0-8493-5683-0*, CRC Reprint) Franklin.

Dalling, Michael J., ed. Plant Proteolytic Enzymes, 2 vols. 1986. 239.90 (*0-8493-5684-9*, QK898) CRC Pr.

Dalling, Paula. Rivers of a Dream: A Compilation of Lifechanging & Inspirational Poetry. Sims, Wanda, ed. & illus. by. (Orig.). (YA). 1997. pap. text 3.99 (*0-9640854-1-0*) M J Beth.

Dallinger, Frederick W. Nominations for Elective Office in the United States. LC 73-19140. (Politics & People Ser.). 304p. 1974. reprint ed. 23.95 (*0-405-05865-9*) Ayer.

Dallinger, Jane. Grasshoppers. (Lerner Natural Science Ser.). (Illus.). 48p. (J). (gr. 4 up). 1981. reprint ed. pap. 5.95 (*0-8225-9568-0*, Lerner Publctns) Lerner Pub.

— Spiders. LC 80-27548. (Lerner Natural Science Bks.). (Illus.). 48p. (J). (gr. 4 up). 1981. lib. bdg. 22.60 (*0-8225-1456-7*, Lerner Publctns) Lerner Pub.

Dallinger, Jane & Kuribayashi, Satoshi. Spiders. LC 80-27548. (Natural Science Bks.). (Illus.). 48p. (J). (gr. 4 up). 1981. pap. 5.95 (*0-8225-9534-6*, First Ave Edns) Lerner Pub.

Dallinger, Reinhard. Ecotoxicology of Metals in Invertebrates. 480p. 1993. lib. bdg. 99.95 (*0-87371-734-1*, L734) Lewis Pubs.

Dallington, Robert. Aphorismes Civil & Militarie: A Briefe Inference upon Guicciardines Digression, 2 pts. LC 77-6869. (English Experience Ser.: No. 864). 1977. reprint ed. lib. bdg. 75.00 (*90-221-0864-3*) Walter J Johnson.

— A Survey of the Great Dukes State of Tuscany in 1596. LC 74-80171. (English Experience Ser.: No. 650). 74p. 1974. reprint ed. 20.00 (*90-221-0650-0*) Walter J Johnson.

Dallington, Robert, tr. see Colonna, Francesco.

Dallison, Dennis. Reflections of My Life: The Apology of John the Baptist. Norman, Ruth E., ed. (Illus.). 66p. (Orig.). 1982. pap. 5.00 (*0-932642-75-6*) Unarius Acad Sci.

— Yamamoto Returns: A True Story of Reincarnation. (Illus.). 132p. 1985. pap. 8.00 (*0-932642-98-5*) Unarius Acad Sci.

Dallman, Elaine, et al, eds. Woman Poet: The East. LC 81-69793. (Woman Poet Ser.). (Illus.). 123p. 1982. pap. 12.50 (*0-935634-02-9*); boxed set 19.95 (*0-935634-03-7*) Women-in-Lit.

— Woman Poet: The Midwest. LC 81-69793. (Woman Poet Ser.). (Illus.). 115p. 1985. pap. 12.50 (*0-935634-04-5*); boxed set 19.95 (*0-935634-05-3*) Women-in-Lit.

— Woman Poet: The West. LC 79-55988. (Woman Poet Ser.). (Illus.). 100p. (Orig.). 1980. boxed set 19.95 (*0-935634-01-0*) Women-in-Lit.

Dallman, Elaine, ed. see Clark, Patricia.

Dallman-Jones, Anthony S. & Black River Group Staff. The Handbook of Effective Teaching & Assessment Strategies. rev. ed. 230p. 1994. pap. 28.95 (*1-885435-01-0*) Twin Lights.

***Dallman, Margaret J. & Lamb, Jonathan R., eds.** Haematopoietic & Lymphoid Cell Culture. (Handbooks in Practical Animal Cell Biology Ser.). (Illus.). 198p. (C). 2000. 69.95 (*0-521-62043-0*); pap. 26.95 (*0-521-62969-1*) Cambridge U Pr.

Dallman, P., jt. auth. see DeMaeyer, E.

Dallman, Peter R. Plant Life in the World's Mediterranean Climates: California, Chile, South Africa, Australia, & the Mediterranean Basin. LC 97-52208. 255p. 1998. pap. 29.95 (*0-520-20809-9*, Pub. by U CA Pr) Cal Prin Full Svc.

Dallman, Peter R., et al. La Carence En Fer Chez le Nourrisson Et Che L'Enfant. Bothwell, Thomas H. et al, eds. (FRE., Illus.). 57p. (Orig.). 1985. pap. text 3.50 (*0-935368-45-0*) ILSI.

— Deficiencia De Hierro en la Infancia y la Ninez. Bothwell, Thomas H. et al, eds. Arroyave, Guillermo, tr. (SPA., Illus.). 83p. (Orig.). 1985. pap. text 3.50 (*0-318-35288-5*) ILSI.

— Iron Deficiency in Infancy & Childhood. Bothwell, Thomas H. et al, eds. (Illus.). 49p. (Orig.). 1979. pap. text 3.50 (*0-935368-08-6*) ILSI.

Dallman, R. J., jt. ed. see O'Brien, J. E.

Dallman, Robert E., jt. auth. see Weiss, Robert M.

Dallmann-Jones, Anthony. The Phoenix Flight Manual: Rising above the Ashes of Ordinary Existence. LC 95-196784. 209p. (Orig.). 1995. pap. 14.95 (*1-881952-49-5*) Three Blue Herons.

Dallmann-Jones, Anthony S. Busy Person's Guide to Dynamic Stress Management. 1998. pap. text 12.95 (*1-881952-10-X*) Three Blue Herons.

***Dallmann-Jones, Anthony S.** The Essential Guide to Living a Stress Free Life: Personal Rejuvenation for the New Millennium. (Primary Domino Thinking Ser.). (Illus.). 244p. 1998. pap. 14.95 (*1-881952-28-2*) Wolf Creek WI.

Dallmann-Jones, Anthony S. How to Set Yourself on Fire in the Workplace: The Fireball Business Manual. 1999. pap. text 12.95 (*1-881952-08-8*) Three Blue Herons.

— Primary Domino Thinking: Creating the Life You Want. (Source Book of the Primary Domino Thinking Ser.). 154p. (Orig.). 1997. pap. 12.95 (*1-881952-40-1*) Wolf Creek WI.

— Resolving Unfinished Business: Assessing the Effects of Being Raised in a Dysfunctional Environment. 160p. (Orig.). 1996. pap. 12.95 (*1-881952-26-6*) Three Blue Herons.

Dallmann-Jones, Anthony S., jt. auth. see Black River Group Staff.

Dallmann, William. The Midnight Lion - Gustav Adolf. 60p. 1997. reprint ed. pap. 3.50 (*1-891469-01-0*) Repristination.

— Robert Barnes - English Lutheran Martyr. 48p. 1997. reprint ed. pap. 3.00 (*1-891469-02-9*) Repristination.

Dallmayr, Fred. Alternative Visions: Paths in the Global Village. LC 97-29035. (Philosophy in the Global Context Ser.). 319p. 1997. 68.00 (*0-8476-8767-8*); pap. 24.95 (*0-8476-8768-6*) Rowman.

— Between Freiburg & Frankfurt: Toward a Critical Ontology. LC 91-15780. 256p. (C). 1991. text 35.00 (*0-87023-764-0*) U of Mass Pr.

— Beyond Orientalism: Essays on Cross-Cultural Encounter. LC 96-12033. 224p. (C). 1996. text 59.50 (*0-7914-3069-3*); pap. text 19.95 (*0-7914-3070-7*) State U NY Pr.

— Margins of Political Discourse. LC 88-30582. (SUNY Series in Contemporary Continental Philosophy). 271p. 1989. text 21.50 (*0-7914-0034-4*) State U NY Pr.

— The Other Heidegger. (Contestations Ser.). 248p. 1995. pap. text 15.95 (*0-8014-8140-6*) Cornell U Pr.

Dallmayr, Fred & Davy, G. N. Between Tradition & Modernity: India's Search for Identity. LC 97-51895. 375p. (C). 1998. 49.95 (*0-7619-9243-X*); pap. 24.95 (*0-7619-9244-8*) Sage.

Dallmayr, Fred R. Critical Encounters: Between Philosophy & Politics. LC 86-40240. 288p. (C). 1989. text 37.00 (*0-268-00760-8*); pap. text 15.00 (*0-268-00774-8*) U of Notre Dame Pr.

— G. W. F. Hegel: Modernity & Politics. (Modernity & Political Thought Ser.: Vol. 3). 264p. (C). 1993. text 48.00 (*0-8039-3615-X*); pap. text 22.95 (*0-8039-3616-8*) Sage.

— Polis & Praxis: Exercises in Contemporary Political Theory. 312p. 1987. pap. text 14.50 (*0-262-54048-7*) MIT Pr.

— Twilight of Subjectivity: Contributions to a Post-Individualist Theory of Politics. LC 80-23433. 376p. 1981. lib. bdg. 40.00 (*0-87023-314-9*) U of Mass Pr.

Dallmayr, Fred R., ed. Border Crossings: Toward a Comparative Political Theory. LC 99-33088. (Global Encounters Ser.). 416p. 1999. 75.00 (*0-7391-0042-4*); pap. 24.95 (*0-7391-0043-2*) Lxngtn Bks.

— From Contract to Community: Political Theory at the Crossroads. LC 78-884. (Publications in Political Science: No. 4). 190p. reprint ed. pap. 58.90 (*0-8357-6122-3*, 203452600090) Bks Demand.

Dallmayr, Fred R., jt. ed. see Benhabib, Seyla.

Dallmayr, Winfried R., jt. auth. see Rankin, Robert S.

Dallmeier, F. & Comiskey, J. A., eds. Forest Biodiversity in North Central, & South America, & the Caribbean: Research & Monitoring. LC 98-25187. (Man & the Biosphere Ser.: VOL. 21). (Illus.). 792p. 1998. 110.00 (*1-85070-964-5*) Prthnon Pub.

— Forest Biodiversity Research, Monitoring, & Modeling: Conceptual Background & Old World Case Studies. LC 98-10706. (Man & the Biosphere Ser.: Vol. 20). (Illus.). 696p. 1998. 95.00 (*1-85070-963-7*) Prthnon Pub.

***Dallmeyer, David, et al.** Home Back Program by Post Rehabilitation Fitness. (Illus.). 25p. 1998. 40.00 incl. vdisk (*1-930241-04-6*) F I Intl.

— Home Leg Program by Post Rehabilitation Fitness. (Illus.). 25p. 1998. 40.00 incl. VHS (*1-930241-05-4*) F I Intl.

— Home Shoulder Program by Post Rehabilitation Fitness. (Illus.). 28p. 1998. 40.00 incl. VHS (*1-930241-03-8*) F I Intl.

Dallmeyer, Dorinda G. Joining Together, Standing Apart: National Identities after NAFTA. LC 97-35852. (NAFTA Law & Policy Ser.: No. 4). 180p. 1997. 74.50 (*90-411-0483-6*) Kluwer Academic.

Dallmeyer, Dorinda G. & DeVorsey, Louis, Jr., eds. Rights to Oceanic Resources. (C). 1989. lib. bdg. 94.50 (*0-7923-0019-X*) Kluwer Academic.

Dallmeyer, Dorinda G. & Ike, Albert F., eds. Environmental Ethics & the Global Marketplace. LC 98-10309. 168p. (C). 1998. pap. 20.00 (*0-8203-2015-3*); text 45.00 (*0-8203-2003-X*) U of Ga Pr.

Dallmeyer, Dorothy S. Early Education of Toddlers. LC 84-73135. 65p. (Orig.). 1984. pap. 4.95 (*0-916109-01-1*) Summers Pub.

Dallmeyer, R. D., ed. Terranes in the Circum-Atlantic Paleozoic Orogens. LC 88-34622. (Geological Society of America Ser.: Vol. 230). (Illus.). 283p. 1989. reprint ed. pap. 87.80 (*0-608-07755-0*, 206784300010) Bks Demand.

Dallmeyer, R. D., et al, eds. Pre-Permian Geology of Central & Eastern Europe. (Illus.). 608p. 1995. 433.95 (*0-387-55472-6*) Spr-Verlag.

D

An Asterisk (*) at the beginning of an entry indicates that the title is appearing for the first time.

— Tectonostratigraphic Evolution of the Central & East European Orogens. 1995. write for info. (*3-540-55472-6*) Spr-Verlag.

Dallmeyer, R. D. & Lecorche, P. P., eds. The West African Orogens & Circum-Atlantic Correlatives: IGCP-Project 233. (Illus.). ix, 405p. 1991. 199.95 (*0-387-52412-6*) Spr-Verlag.

Dallmeyer, R. D. & Martinez-Garcia, E., eds. Pre-Mesozoic Geology of Iberia: IGCP-Project 233. (Illus.). 550p. 1991. 214.95 (*0-387-51792-8*) Spr-Verlag.

Dallmeyer, R. David. Earth Views: A Physical Geology Perspective on CD-ROM Text & Student Manual. 146p. (C). 1997. 14.95 incl. cd-rom (*0-7872-3390-0*) Kendall-Hunt.

***Dallmier, Kevin.** Fishing Georgia. LC 00-39384. (Illus.). 2000. pap. write for info. (*1-56044-777-X*) Falcon Pub Inc.

Dallos, Peter, et al, eds. The Cochlea. (Springer Handbook of Auditory Research Ser.: Vol. 8). (Illus.). 584p. 1996. 89.95 (*0-387-94449-4*) Spr-Verlag.

Dallos, Rudi. Interacting Stories: Narratives, Family Beliefs & Therapy. LC 98-150406. 256p. 1997. pap. 32.00 (*1-85575-095-3*, Pub. by H Karnac Bks Ltd) Other Pr LLC.

Dallos, Rudi & Draper, Rosalind. An Introduction to Family Therapy: Systemic Theory & Practice. LC 99-17598. 224p. 1999. pap. 29.95 (*0-335-20063-X*) OpUniv Pr.

Dallos, Rudi & McLaughlin, Eugene, eds. Social Problems & the Family. (Illus.). 320p. (C). 1993. text 69.95 (*0-8039-8836-2*); pap. text 25.95 (*0-8039-8837-0*) Sage.

Dallos, Rudi, jt. auth. see Foreman, Sally.

Dallos, Rudi, jt. ed. see Miell, Dorothy.

Dallow, Ellen, ed. A Whisper of Blood. 288p. 1995. mass mkt. 5.50 (*0-441-00266-8*) Ace Bks.

***Dallow, Theodore J.** How to Buy Foreclosed Real Estate for a Fraction of Its Value. 2nd ed. LC 00-35593. 176p. 2000. pap. 9.95 (*1-58062-258-5*) Adams Media.

Dalloway, Marie. Concentration: Focus Your Mind, Power Your Game. 62p. (Orig.). 1993. pap. text 14.95 (*0-9634933-1-0*) Optimal Perf.

— Drive & Determination: Developing Your Inner Motivation. 80p. 1993. pap. text 14.95 (*0-9634933-2-9*) Optimal Perf.

— Performing under Pressure: Mental Techniques for Handling Pressure in Tennis. LC 97-76203. 155p. 1997. pap. text 18.00 (*0-9634933-5-3*) Optimal Perf.

— Reflections on the Mental Side of Sports. LC 94-66323. 143p. 1994. pap. text 14.95 (*0-9634933-4-5*) Optimal Perf.

— Risk Taking: Performing Your Best During Critical Times. (Illus.). 62p. 1993. pap. 14.95 (*0-9634933-3-7*) Optimal Perf.

— Visualization: The Master Skill in Mental Training. 67p. 1992. pap. text 14.95 (*0-9634933-0-2*) Optimal Perf.

Dalloz, Jaques. The War in Indo-China, 1945-1954. 288p. (C). 1990. lib. bdg. 68.00 (*0-389-20897-3*) B&N Imports.

Dallum, Linda B. One Soul's Journey. (Illus.). (Orig.). 1986. pap. 6.95 (*0-9616937-0-3*) L B Dallum.

Dallwitz, M. J., jt. auth. see Watson, Leslie.

Dally, Ann. Understanding: Coming to Grips with Moments of Inadequacy, Neurosis, Isolation, Depression, Masochism, Frustration. LC 78-66254. 192p. (C). 1983. pap. 6.95 (*0-8128-6104-3*, Scrbrough Hse) Madison Bks UPA.

Dally, Emma. Tomorrow's Past. large type ed. (Ulverscroft Large Print Ser.). 528p. 1997. 27.99 (*0-7089-3822-1*) Ulverscroft.

Dally, J. W. Packaging of Electronic Systems: A Mechanical Engineering Approach. (C). 1989. text 73.00 (*0-07-015214-4*) McGraw.

Dally, James W. Experimental Stress Analysis. 3rd ed. 672p. (C). 1991. 95.94 (*0-07-015218-7*) McGraw.

— Introduction to Engineering Design Bk. 1: Solar Desalination. (Illus.). xvii, 231p. (Orig.). (C). 1997. pap. text 27.00 (*0-9655911-0-7*) College Hse.

— Introduction to Engineering Design Bk. 2: Weighing Machines. (Illus.). 341p. (Orig.). (C). 1997. pap. text 29.50 (*0-9655911-1-5*) College Hse.

***Dally, James W.** Introduction to Engineering Design Bk. 4: Human Powered Pumping Systems. (Illus.). 420p. (C). 1999. pap. text 32.00 (*0-9655911-7-4*) College Hse.

Dally, James W. & Riley, William F. Experimental Stress Analysis. 3rd ed. (C). 1991. pap. text, teacher ed. 37.50 (*0-07-015219-5*) McGraw.

***Dally, James W. & Rocheleau, David N.** Introduction to Engineering Design Vol. 3: Postal Scales. LC 99-182216. (Illus.). 434p. (C). 1998. pap. text 32.00 (*0-9655911-2-3*) College Hse.

Dally, James W., et al. Instrumentation for Engineering Measurements. 2nd ed. 608p. (C). 1993. text 96.95 (*0-471-55192-9*) Wiley.

Dally, Jill. The Meat & Potatoes of Breastfeeding: Easy Nutritional Guidelines for Breastfeeding Moms. Dalley, Nicholas S., ed. LC 97-141808. (Illus.). 220p. (Orig.). 1997. pap. 14.95 (*0-9652008-0-9*) Footprint Pr.

Dally, John, jt. ed. see Verdon, Timothy G.

Dally, Joseph W. Woodbridge & Vicinity: The Story of a New Jersey Township. 392p. 1989. reprint ed. lib. bdg. 27.50 (*0-912606-34-7*) Hunterdon Hse.

Dally, Kathleen L., jt. auth. see Folts, Harold C.

Dally, Peter. Marriage of Heaven & Hell. LC 99-52175. 352p. 1999. text 24.95 (*0-312-20559-7*) St Martin.

Dally, William J. A VLSI Architecture for Concurrent Data Structures. (C). 1987. text 92.50 (*0-89838-235-1*) Kluwer Academic.

Dally, William J. & Poulton, John. Digital Systems Engineering. LC 97-43730. (Illus.). 600p. (C). 1998. 54.95 (*0-521-59292-5*) Cambridge U Pr.

Dally, William R. & Zeidler, Ryszard B., eds. Coastal Dynamics, 1995: Proceedings of the International Conference on Coastal Research in Terms of Large Scale Experiments - Organized by the Polish Academy of Sciences, Institute of Hydro-Engineering, IBW PAN, Gdansk, Poland, September 4-8, 1995. LC 96-1377. 1080p. 1996. pap. 87.00 (*0-7844-0154-3*) Am Soc Civil Eng.

***Dalmage, Heather M.** Tripping on the Color Line: Black-White Multiracial Families in a Racially Divided World. LC 00-32350. 192p. (C). 2000. text 50.00 (*0-8135-2843-7*); pap. text 20.00 (*0-8135-2844-5*) Rutgers U Pr.

Dalmais, Ann Marie. The Beaver, Reading Level 3-4. (World Animal Library). (Illus.). 28p. (J). (gr. 2-5). 1983. lib. bdg. 21.27 (*0-86592-859-2*) Rourke Enter.

— The Duck, Reading Level 3-4. (World Animal Library). (Illus.). 28p. (J). (gr. 2-5). 1983. lib. bdg. 21.27 (*0-86592-862-2*) Rourke Enter.

— Kangaroo, Reading Level 3-4. (World Animal Library). (Illus.). 28p. (J). (gr. 2-5). 1983. lib. bdg. 14.60 (*0-685-58820-3*) Rourke Corp.

— Kangaroo, Reading Level 3-4. (World Animal Library). (Illus.). 28p. (J). (gr. 2-5). 1983. lib. bdg. 21.27 (*0-86592-864-9*) Rourke Enter.

— Penguin, Reading Level 3-4. (World Animal Library). (Illus.). 28p. (J). (gr. 2-5). 1983. 12.50 (*0-685-58823-8*) Rourke Corp.

— Penguin, Reading Level 3-4. (World Animal Library). (Illus.). 28p. (J). (gr. 2-5). 1983. lib. bdg. 21.27 (*0-86592-854-1*) Rourke Enter.

— Porcupine, Reading Level 3-4. (World Animal Library). (Illus.). 28p. (J). (gr. 2-5). 1983. 12.50 (*0-685-58824-6*) Rourke Corp.

— Porcupine, Reading Level 3-4. (World Animal Library). (Illus.). 28p. (J). (gr. 2-5). 1983. lib. bdg. 21.27 (*0-86592-852-5*) Rourke Enter.

— Squirrel, Reading Level 3-4. (World Animal Library). (Illus.). 28p. (J). (gr. 2-5). 1983. 12.50 (*0-685-58826-2*) Rourke Corp.

— Squirrel, Reading Level 3-4. (World Animal Library). (Illus.). 28p. (J). (gr. 2-5). 1983. lib. bdg. 21.27 (*0-86592-857-6*) Rourke Enter.

Dalmais, Anne M. Doctor Rabbits Vacation. (J). Date not set. pap. 4.50 (*0-448-14498-0*) Putnam Pub Group.

Dalmais, I. H. & Jounel, Pierre. The Church at Prayer Vol. IV: The Liturgy & Time. Martimort, Aime G., ed. 304p. 1989. pap. 15.95 (*0-8146-1366-7*) Liturgical Pr.

Dalmais, Paul. Seal, Reading Level 3-4. (World Animal Library). (Illus.). 28p. (J). (gr. 2-5). 1983. 12.50 (*0-685-58825-4*) Rourke Corp.

— Seal, Reading Level 3-4. (World Animal Library). (Illus.). 28p. (J). (gr. 2-5). 1983. lib. bdg. 21.27 (*0-86592-867-3*) Rourke Enter.

Dalman, G. Conrad, jt. auth. see Lee, Charles A.

Dalman, Gustaf. Aramaischesneuhebraisches Handworterbuch zu Targum, Talmud und Midrasch. (GER.). ix, 577p. 1997. reprint ed. write for info. (*3-487-01602-8*) G Olms Pubs.

— Arbeit und Sitte in Palastina, 8 vols. in 7, Set. lxxxix, 3033p. 1987. reprint ed. write for info. (*3-487-00480-1*) G Olms Pubs.

— Jerusalem und Sein Gelande. xi, 402p. 1972. reprint ed. write for info. (*3-487-04403-X*) G Olms Pubs.

— Jesus Christ in the Talmud, Midrash, Zohar, & the Liturgy of the Synagogue. LC 73-2190. (Jewish People; History, Religion, Literature Ser.). 1977. reprint ed. 17.95 (*0-405-05256-1*) Ayer.

— The Words of Jesus: Considered in the Light of Post-Biblical Jewish Writings & the Aramaic Language. 350p. 1997. pap. 25.00 (*1-57910-072-4*) Wipf & Stock.

Dalman, Gustav & Alt, Albrecht, eds. Palastina-Jahrbuch des Deutschen Evangelischen Instituts Fur Altertumswissenschaft des Heiligen Landes Zu Jerusalem. lvi, 4361p. 1975. reprint ed. write for info. (*3-487-05514-7*) G Olms Pubs.

Dalmas, John. The Bavarian Gate. 352p. 1997. per. 5.99 (*0-671-87764-X*) Baen Bks.

— The Lion of Farside. 448p. 1995. mass mkt. 5.99 (*0-671-87674-0*) Baen Bks.

— The Lion Returns. 1999. mass mkt. 6.99 (*0-671-57824-3*) S&S Trade.

— The Lizard War. 1989. mass mkt. 4.99 (*0-671-69851-6*) Baen Bks.

— The Regiment. 416p. 1991. reprint ed. mass mkt. 5.99 (*0-671-72065-1*) Baen Bks.

— Regiment's War. 368p. 1993. mass mkt. 4.99 (*0-671-72155-0*) Baen Bks.

— Three-Cornered War: The Regiment's Last Stand. 1999. mass mkt. 6.99 (*0-671-57783-2*) Baen Bks.

— The White Regiment. (Orig.). 1990. mass mkt. 4.99 (*0-671-69880-X*) Baen Bks.

Dalmases, Candido de. Ignatius of Loyola, Founder of the Jesuits: His Life & Work. Aixala, Jerome, tr. from SPA. LC 83-80349. (Modern Scholarly Studies about the Jesuits, in English Translations Series II: No. 6). xxii, 362p. 1985. 14.00 (*0-912422-58-0*) Inst Jesuit.

Dalmases, Candido De, see De Dalmases, Candido.

Dalmaso, G. & Dell'Antonio, G. Composite Media & Homogenization Theory. (Progress in Nonlinear Differential Equations & Their Applications Ser.). 1990. 86.50 (*0-8176-3511-4*) Birkhauser.

Dalmasso, A. P., ed. Complement in Laboratory Medicine. (Journal: Complement & Inflammation: Vol. 6, No. 1, 1989). (Illus.). 72p. 1988. pap. 51.50 (*3-8055-4914-8*) S Karger.

Dalmath, Gabe & Waxman, Jan L. The Image Is Rochester. LC 97-2082. (Urban Tapestry Ser.). (Illus.). 240p. 1997. 44.95 (*1-881096-40-8*) Towery Pub.

Dalmatian Press Staff. Alphabet. (Precious Moments Workbooks Ser.). (J). 1998. pap. 2.99 (*1-57759-113-5*) Dalmatian Pr.

***Dalmatian Press Staff.** Alphabet. (Tools Ser.). (J). (gr. k-1). 1999. pap. text 2.29 (*1-57759-141-0*) Dalmatian Pr.

— Alphabet. (Tools Ser.). (J). (ps). 1999. pap. text 2.29 (*1-57759-142-9*) Dalmatian Pr.

— Baby's Goodnight Blessings. (Illus.). (J). 2000. 2.99 (*1-57759-374-X*) Dalmatian Pr.

Dalmatian Press Staff. Beautiful Bible Stories for Children. (J). 1998. pap. 5.99 (*1-57759-120-8*) Dalmatian Pr.

***Dalmatian Press Staff.** Beginning Sounds. (Tools Ser.). (J). (ps). 1999. pap. text 2.29 (*1-57759-192-5*) Dalmatian Pr.

— Counting 1-10. (Tools Ser.). (Illus.). (J). 1999. pap. text 2.29 (*1-57759-144-5*) Dalmatian Pr.

— Daddy Loves Me. (Illus.). (J). 2000. 2.99 (*1-57759-372-3*) Dalmatian Pr.

— Daniel & the Lions Den. (Illus.). (J). 2000. pap. text 4.97 (*1-888567-34-1*) Dalmatian Pr.

— David & Goliath. (Illus.). (J). 2000. pap. text 4.97 (*1-888567-35-X*) Dalmatian Pr.

— Goodnight Baby. (Illus.). (J). 2000. 2.99 (*1-57759-370-7*) Dalmatian Pr.

— I'm a Baby. (Illus.). (J). 2000. 2.99 (*1-57759-371-5*) Dalmatian Pr.

— Lowercase Alphabet. (Tools Ser.). (Illus.). (J). (ps). 1999. pap. text 2.29 (*1-57759-143-7*) Dalmatian Pr.

— Math. (Tools Ser.). (J). (gr. 2). 1999. pap. text 2.29 (*1-57759-152-6*) Dalmatian Pr.

Dalmatian Press Staff. Math Skills. (Precious Moments Workbooks Ser.). (J). 1998. pap. 2.99 (*1-57759-116-X*) Dalmatian Pr.

***Dalmatian Press Staff.** Mommy Loves Me. (Illus.). (J). 2000. 2.99 (*1-57759-373-1*) Dalmatian Pr.

— Moses Baby in the Bulrushes. (Illus.). (J). 2000. pap. text 4.97 (*1-888567-36-8*) Dalmatian Pr.

— Multiplication. (J). (gr. 3-4). 1999. pap. text 2.99 (*1-57759-137-2*) Dalmatian Pr.

— Multiplication & Division. (J). (gr. 3-4). 1999. pap. text 2.29 (*1-57759-150-X*) Dalmatian Pr.

Dalmatian Press Staff. My Writing Tablet. (J). 1998. pap. 2.29 (*1-888567-10-4*) Dalmatian Pr.

***Dalmatian Press Staff.** NASCAR Racers Get on Track. (Illus.). (J). 2000. pap. 2.99 (*1-57759-298-0*) Dalmatian Pr.

— NASCAR Racers Maximum Performance. (Illus.). (J). 2000. pap. 2.99 (*1-57759-299-9*) Dalmatian Pr.

— NASCAR Racers Road Thunder. (Illus.). (J). 2000. pap. 2.50 (*1-57759-344-8*) Dalmatian Pr.

— Noah's Ark. (Illus.). (J). 2000. pap. text 4.97 (*1-888567-37-6*) Dalmatian Pr.

Dalmatian Press Staff. Phonics. (Precious Moments Workbooks Ser.). (J). 1998. pap. 2.99 (*1-57759-114-3*) Dalmatian Pr.

— Precious Moments Activity Art Tablet. (Precious Moments Ser.). (Illus.). (J). 1998. pap. 2.29 (*1-57759-057-0*) Dalmatian Pr.

— Precious Moments Activity Fun Tablet. (Precious Moments Ser.). (J). 1998. pap. 2.29 (*1-57759-058-9*) Dalmatian Pr.

***Dalmatian Press Staff.** Precious Moments Addition & Subtraction. (Precious Moments Workbooks Ser.). (Illus.). (J). 2000. pap. 2.99 (*1-57759-290-5*) Dalmatian Pr.

— Precious Moments Lowercase Alphabet. (Precious Moments Ser.). (Illus.). (J). (ps-3). 1999. pap., wbk. ed. 2.99 (*1-57759-208-5*) Dalmatian Pr.

— Precious Moments Lowercase Colors & Shapes. (Precious Moments Ser.). (Illus.). (J). (ps-3). 1999. pap., wbk. ed. 2.99 (*1-57759-207-7*) Dalmatian Pr.

— Precious Moments Reading Readiness. (Precious Moments Workbooks Ser.). (Illus.). (J). 2000. pap. 2.99 (*1-57759-288-3*) Dalmatian Pr.

— Precious Moments Transition Math. (Precious Moments Workbooks Ser.). (Illus.). (J). 2000. pap. 2.99 (*1-57759-289-1*) Dalmatian Pr.

— Reading Readiness. (Tools Ser.). (Illus.). (J). (gr. 1). 1999. pap. text 2.29 (*1-57759-146-1*) Dalmatian Pr.

— Saban's Power Rangers Lost Galaxy Cosmic Journey. (Illus.). (J). 1999. pap. 2.99 (*1-57759-251-4*) Dalmatian Pr.

— Saban's Power Rangers Lost Galaxy Mega Maze & Puzzle Book. (Illus.). (J). 1999. pap. 2.99 (*1-57759-252-2*) Dalmatian Pr.

Dalmatian Press Staff. Time, Money & Measurement. (Precious Moments Workbooks Ser.). (J). 1998. pap. 2.99 (*1-57759-115-1*) Dalmatian Pr.

— Ultimate Bible Fun Book: The Greatest Collection of Fun & Learning Ever Assembled. (Ultimate Fun Bks.). (J). 1998. pap. 5.99 (*1-57759-016-3*) Dalmatian Pr.

— Ultimate Fun Book: The Greatest Collection of Fun & Learning Ever Assembled. (Ultimate Fun Bks.). (J). 1998. pap. 5.99 (*1-57759-015-5*) Dalmatian Pr.

— Ultimate Holiday Fun Book: The Greatest Collection of Fun & Learning Ever Assembled. (Ultimate Fun Bks.). (J). 1998. pap. 5.99 (*1-888567-74-0*) Dalmatian Pr.

Dalmation Club of America Staff. The Official Book of the Dalmatian: AKC Rank #15. (Illus.). 352p. Date not set. 79.95 (*0-7938-2081-2*, TS-254) TFH Pubns.

Dalmatov, B. I. Soil Mechanics, Foundations & Footings: Selected Translations of Russian Geotechnical Literature. Zeidler, Ryszard B., ed. & tr. by. from RUS. (Geotechnika Ser.: No. 3). (Illus.). 408p. (C). 1991. text 168.00 (*90-6191-172-9*, Pub. by A A Balkema) Ashgate Pub Co.

Dalmau, Eduardo Martinez, see Martinez Dalmau, Eduardo.

Dalmau, Jose M. Pla, see Pla Dalmau, Jose M.

D'Almeida, G. A., et al. Atmospheric Aerosols: Global Climatology & Radiative Characteristics. LC 90-23500. 561p. 1991. text 110.00 (*0-937194-22-0*) A Deepak Pub.

D'Almeida, Irene A. Francophone African Women Writers: Destroying the Emptiness of Silence. (Illus.). 208p. 1994. lib. bdg. 44.95 (*0-8130-1302-X*) U Press Fla.

Dalmeny, Kath. Kath Dalmeny's World of Knitted Toys. LC 98-226145. (Illus.). 128p. 1998. 24.95 (*0-7153-0680-4*, Pub. by D & C Pub) Sterling.

Dalmeyer, Dorinda G. & Tsipis, Kosta. Heaven & Earth Vol. 16, USAS: Civilian Uses of Near-Earth Space. LC 96-21724. (Utrecht Studies in Air & Space Law). 1997. 120.00 (*90-411-0262-0*) Kluwer Law Intl.

Dalmia, Vasudha. The Nationalization of Hindu Traditions: Bharatendu Harishchandra & Nineteenth-Century Banaras. 502p. 1999. pap. text 16.50 (*0-19-564856-0*) OUP.

***Dalmia, Vasudha & Damsteegt, Th.** Narrative Strategies: Essays on South Asian Literature & Film. LC 99-937585. (Illus.). 1999. write for info. (*0-19-564975-3*) OUP.

Dalmia, Vasudha & Von Stietencron, Heinrich, eds. Representing Hinduism: The Construction of Religious Traditions & National Identity. LC 95-7978. 468p. 1995. pap. 22.95 (*0-8039-9195-9*) Sage.

— Representing Hinduism: The Construction of Religious Traditions & National Identity. LC 95-7978. 468p. 1995. 49.95 (*0-8039-9194-0*) Sage.

***Dalmolin, Eliane.** Cutting the Body. LC 99-50860. (Body, in Theory Ser.). (Illus.). 288p. (C). 2000. text 49.50 (*0-472-11073-X*, 11073) U of Mich Pr.

Dalmolin, Eliane, jt. ed. see Clestin, Roger.

Dalmonte, Rossana, ed. see Rossini, Gioachino.

Dalnoky, Christine, jt. auth. see Desvigne, Michel.

Dalokay, Vedat. Sister Shako & Kolo the Goat: Memories of My Childhood in Turkey. Ener, Guner, tr. (YA). (gr. 5 up). 1994. 14.00 (*0-688-13271-5*) Lothrop.

Dalon, George D. The Gathering. 58p. (Orig.). 1995. pap. 10.00 (*0-9635690-7-4*) TA Pubns.

D'Alonzo, G., jt. auth. see Criner, G.

***D'Alonzo, Mary Beth & Georgia Historical Society Staff.** Streetcars of Chatham County, GA. (Images of America Ser.). (Illus.). 128p. 1999. pap. 18.99 (*0-7385-0179-4*) Arcadia Publng.

D'Alonzo, Thomas L. Your Eyes! A Comprehensive Look at the Understanding & Treatment of Vision Problems. rev. ed. LC 91-71193. (Illus.). 251p. (C). 1991. pap. 14.95 (*0-9629063-5-2*) Avanti.

***Dalos, Gyorgy.** The Guest from the Future: Anna Akhmatova & Isaiah Berlin. Wood, Antony, tr. from GER. (Illus.). 256p. 2000. pap. 13.00 (*0-374-52720-2*) FS&G.

D'Alotto, Louis, et al. A Unified Signal Algebra Approach to Two-Dimensional Parallel Digital Signal Processing. LC 97-46946. (Illus.). 304p. 1998. text 135.00 (*0-8247-0025-2*) Dekker.

Dalotto, Todd. The Hemp Cookbook: From Seed to Shining Seed. LC 99-40750. (Illus.). 160p. 1999. pap. 14.95 (*0-89281-787-9*) Inner Tradit.

Daloz, Jean-Pascal, jt. auth. see Chabal, Patrick.

Daloz, Jean-Pascal, jt. ed. see Alden, Chris.

Daloz, Laurent A. Effective Teaching & Mentoring: Realizing the Transformational Power of Adult Learning Experiences. LC 86-10317. (Higher Education Ser.). 279p. 1986. text 35.45 (*1-55542-001-X*) Jossey-Bass.

***Daloz, Laurent A.** Mentor: Guiding the Journey of Adult Learners. 2nd ed. LC 99-6188. (Higher & Adult Education Ser.). 304p. 1999. pap. text 24.95 (*0-7879-4072-0*) Jossey-Bass.

Daloz, Laurent A., et al. Common Fire: Leading Lives of Commitment in a Complex World. LC 95-25499. 288p. 1997. pap. 15.00 (*0-8070-2005-2*) Beacon Pr.

Dalphin, John R. Persistence of Social Inequality in America. 2nd ed. 164p. 1987. pap. 14.95 (*0-87073-615-9*) Schenkman Bks Inc.

Dalphin, John R. Persistence of Social Inequality in America. 3rd ed. 192p. write for info. (*0-87047-119-8*) Schenkman Bks Inc.

— Persistence of Social Inequality in America. 3rd ed. 1999. pap. 18.95 (*0-87047-118-X*) Schenkman Bks Inc.

***Dalphond, Julie.** A Critical Review of the Main Variables in Offset Printing: Effects on Print Quality, Measurement & Control. 47p. 1999. 25.84 (*1-896742-42-4*) Pulp & Paper.

***Dalpiaz, Christina.** How to Depolarize Your Jerk Magnet: In Love, Life & Business. Holbrook, Yash, ed. 150p. 2000. pap. 19.95 (*0-9650669-2-4*) Chance.

— Parenting in the Aftermath of Family Violence: Changing the Dynamics Between Parent & Child. Holbrook, Yash, ed. 2000. pap. 14.95 (*0-9650669-1-6*) Chance.

Dalpiaz, P., jt. auth. see Cherubini, R.

Dalpino, Catharin E. Anchoring Third Wave Democracies: Prospects & Problems for U. S. Policy. (Institute for the Study of Diplomacy Monograph). 110p. 1998. pap. 7.00 (*0-934742-92-8*) Geo U Inst Dplmcy.

— Opening Windows: Promoting a Fourth Wave of Democracy. 100p. 1998. pap. 14.95 (*0-8157-1701-6*) Brookings.

D'Alpuget, Blanche. Turtle Beach. 256p. 1984. mass mkt. 3.50 (*0-345-31818-8*, Ballantine) Ballantine Pub Grp.

— White Eye. 1994. pap. 22.00 (*0-671-62005-3*) S&S Trade.

D'Alquen, Richard. Time, Mood & Aspect in German Tense. Kuxdorf, Manfred, ed. (German Studies in Canada: Vol. 8). (Illus.). xiv, 299p. 1997. pap. 57.95 (*3-631-30832-9*) P Lang Pubng.

— Time, Mood & Aspect in German Tense. Kuxdorf, Manfred, ed. (German Studies in Canada: Vol. 8). (Illus.). XIV, 299p. 1997. pap. 57.95 (*0-8204-3224-5*) P Lang Pubng.

Dalquest, Walter W. The Tehuantepec Jungle: A Memoir. LC 96-205979. 175p. 1996. 19.95 (*0-915323-10-9*) Midwestern St U Pr.

D

Dalquest, Walter W., et al, eds. Mammalian Zoogeography of a Rocky Mountain - Great Plains Interface in New Mexico, Oklahoma, & Texas. (Special Publications: No. 34). 1990. pap. 14.00 (*0-89672-230-9*) Tex Tech Univ Pr.

Dalquest, Walter W. & Horner, Norman V. Mammals of North-Central Texas. (Illus.). 261p. 1984. 15.00 (*0-915323-01-X*) Midwestern St U Pr.

Dalquest, Walter W. & Schultz, Gerald E. Ice Age Mammals of Northwestern Texas. (Illus.). 309p. 1992. text 29.95 (*0-915323-03-6*) Midwestern St U Pr.

Dalrymple. Marketing Management. 7th ed. 720p. (C). 1999. text 99.95 (*0-471-33238-0*) Wiley.

— Marketing Management 7th ed. pap. text. write for info. (*0-471-36201-8*) Wiley.

***Dalrymple, Alfred J. Meadowbrook under Thunder & Wind. 2nd ed. LC 99-93541. 104p. 1999. 6.50 (*0-9673338-2-2*) Dalrymple Bks.**

Part 1, is an essay containing thoughts about God, Fate, awareness, the soul...(metaphysics). Some of the section matter is: Sentience resides in all things; the body-mind & the soul; If the divine is in all things, should we embrace the bad as well as the good?; Is God personal?; We need to separate what a person is from what he does; Does God..as the "I" which is "Here"...occasionally intervene personally?; the signpost. (From "Sentience resides in all things:" Apparently, sentience resides in the area of harmonic movement at the center of things having nothing missing from it, or having everything present in it, in order for it to be as it has been. After the bang & the inflation & expansion, things harmonically maintain their existence, because they are the same as what they have been. This sentence is concerned with being what it is.) Part 2 is a three-act play. Two middleage American men in Shanghai. They're free to cross bridges. What they do is seriously silly. Dart, P.O. Box 744, Unalaska, AK 99685. 907-581-3701. Check or M.O. 3.00 postage. *Publisher Paid Annotation.*

–Murder in the Highest Places. 2nd unabridged ed. LC 99-93420. 206p. 1999. pap. 7.95 (*0-9673338-1-4*) Dalrymple Bks.

In Nepal...Oliver Faulkner is pursued by a murderer. In the company of 5 friends, including Molly, his soul mate, Oliver is on his way to Changri La (Pass)..pronounced Shangrila. So...also the murderer is on the way to Shangrila, or "the top" of the journey. Both will come to act, in Changri La, in a way relating to "love"...to the possession of it, or to a blinding loss of it. Oliver feels that even the soul of a murderer is innocent at birth. He thinks he ought to remember that a "sameness" has been altered..& so, try to hate only the acts of the other. Is any memorial due the murderer's entire life, after the end of it? If it ends in Shangrila..Oliver will depart from a shape in the snow. Then...aware of the murderer's victims..will he allot to the shape any part of the sad emptiness? Dec. 1999. Dart, P.O. Box 744, Unalaska, AK 99685. 907-581-3701/Fax: 907-581-5045. Check or money order. 3.00 postage *Publisher Paid Annotation.*

–A Wind under Heaven. 2nd unabridged ed. LC 99-93421. 240p. 1999. pap. 8.50 (*0-9673338-0-6*) Dalrymple Bks. In Nepal...the belief in reincarnation closes doors to separation of church & state. But democracy is magic there. They want it & don't want it. In each person is conflict between what seems to be God's will & what seems to be their own. So...for those born "lower than" by divine decree, heavy feelings of guilt occur while reaching out. They rarely do. But, when they do, the action is likely to be en masse & eruptive. Jim Bart has been to Nepal many times..is at a NYC lecture hall, for words about a scheduled climb of Everest. But..he speaks of case, saying that the concept of reincarnation ought to be redefined. In the audience is Hindu Fundamentalist Sadhev Raj Dahal, who will soon be Prime Minister of Nepal. In Nepal a parliamentary election is due & Jim is asked by a candidate to speak about democracy. He does. Eruptively...a sea of Nepalis follow him to the Palace & the National Secretariat. Some Nepalis die. Blamed for this by Dahal, Jim flees toward Everest, hoping to reach Tibet. *Publisher Paid Annotation.*

Dalrymple, Allison, jt. auth. see Clement, Ginny.

Dalrymple, Byron. Doves & Dove Shooting. 256p. 1991. 17.95 (*0-8329-0463-5*, Winchester Pr) New Win Pub.

— How to Call Wildlife. 1982. pap. 6.95 (*0-943822-07-6*) Times Mir Mag Bk Div.

Dalrymple, Byron & Precht, Dave. Modern Book of the Black Bass. 288p. 1995. 19.95 (*0-8329-0510-0*, Winchester Pr) New Win Pub.

Dalrymple, Byron W. Fresh Looks at Deer Hunting. 288p. 1992. 24.95 (*0-8329-0471-6*, Winchester Pr) New Win Pub.

— North American Big-Game Animals. 1985. 29.95 (*0-943822-56-4*) Times Mir Mag Bk Div.

— Outdoor Lifetime: Six Decades in a Writer's Life. 1994. 24.95 (*0-8329-0508-9*, Winchester Pr) New Win Pub.

Dalrymple-Champneys, Norma, ed. see Crabbe, George.

Dalrymple, D., ed. see Hales, John.

Dalrymple, David, ed. see Bannatyne, George.

Dalrymple, Douglas J. Basic Marketing Management. 6th ed. 670p. 1995. pap. text, teacher ed. 14.95 (*0-471-30643-6*) Wiley.

— The Web Site to Accompany Basic Market Management. 2nd ed. 2000. write for info. (*0-471-36202-6*) Wiley.

Dalrymple, Douglas J. & Cron, William L. Sales Management: Concept & Cases. 6th ed. LC 97-30041. 640p. 1997. text 95.95 (*0-471-19197-3*) Wiley.

— Sales Management: Concepts & Cases. 5th ed. 1995. pap. text 25.00 (*0-471-11495-2*) Wiley.

Dalrymple, Douglas J. & Cron, William L. Sales Management: Concepts & Cases. 5th ed. 1995. text 25.00 (*0-471-11477-4*) Wiley.

Dalrymple, Douglas J. & Cron, William L. Sales Management Simulation 4. 4th ed. 176p. 1995. pap. 34.95 (*0-471-08873-0*) Wiley.

Dalrymple, Douglas J. & Parsons, Leonard J. Basic Marketing Management. LC 94-26246. 480p. 1995. pap. 53.95 (*0-471-58603-X*) Wiley.

— Basic Marketing Management. 2nd ed. (Illus.). 336p. 2000. pap. write for info. (*0-471-35392-2*) Wiley.

— Marketing Management: Text & Cases. 6th ed. LC 94-26245. 1008p. 1994. text 92.95 (*0-471-55255-0*) Wiley.

Dalrymple, G. Brent. The Age of the Earth. (Illus.). xviii, 474p. 1991. 69.50 (*0-8047-1569-6*) Stanford U Pr.

— Age of the Earth. xviii, 474p. 1994. pap. 24.95 (*0-8047-2331-1*) Stanford U Pr.

Dalrymple-Hay, M. J., jt. auth. see Britto, J. A.

Dalrymple, Jane & Burke, Beverley. Anti-Oppressive Practice: Social Care & the Law. LC 94-26582. 208p. 1995. 31.95 (*0-335-19193-2*) OpUniv Pr.

Dalrymple, John. Essay Towards a General History of Feudal Property in Great Britain. vii, 332p. 1979. reprint ed. 45.00 (*0-8377-0508-8*, Rothman) W S Hein.

***Dalrymple, Larry.** Indian Basketmakers of California & the Great Basin: The Living Art & Fine Tradition. LC 99-39181. (Illus.). 76p. 2000. pap. 24.95 (*0-89013-337-9*, Pub. by Museum NM Pr) U of NM Pr.

— Indian Basketmakers of California & the Great Basin & Indian Basketmakers of the Southwest, 2 vols. (Illus.). 244p. 2000. pap., boxed set 60.00 (*0-89013-341-7*, Pub. by Museum NM Pr) U of NM Pr.

— Indian Basketmakers of the Southwest: The Living Art & Fine Tradition. LC 00-39182. (Illus.). 140p. 2000. pap. 29.95 (*0-89013-338-7*, Pub. by Museum NM Pr) U of NM Pr.

Dalrymple, Mary. Formal Issues in Lexical-Functional Grammar. LC 94-26186. (CSLI Lecture Notes Ser.: No. 47). 1995. 54.95 (*1-881526-37-2*) CSLI.

— The Syntax of Anaphoric Binding. LC 93-20413. (CSLI Lecture Notes Ser.: No. 36). 196p. 1993. 64.95 (*1-881526-07-0*); pap. 20.95 (*1-881526-06-2*) CSLI.

Dalrymple, Mary, ed. Semantics & Syntax in Lexical Functional Grammar: The Resource Logic Approach. LC 98-40622. (Language, Speech & Communication Ser.). (Illus.). 409p. 1999. 40.00 (*0-262-04171-5*) MIT Pr.

Dalrymple, Mary, et al. Formal Issues in Lexical-Functional Grammar. LC 94-26186. (CSLI Lecture Notes Ser.: No.47). 1995. pap. 24.95 (*1-881526-36-4*) CSLI.

Dalrymple, Priscilla H. American Victorian Costume in Early Photographs. (Illus.). 128p. 1991. pap. 12.95 (*0-486-26533-1*) Dover.

Dalrymple, Prudence W., jt. ed. see Smith, Linda C.

Dalrymple, R. A., ed. Physical Modelling in Coastal Engineering: Proceedings of an International Conference, Newark, Delaware, August 1981. 320p. (C). 1984. text 123.00 (*90-6191-516-3*, Pub. by A A Balkema) Ashgate Pub Co.

Dalrymple, R. A., jt. auth. see Dean, R. G.

Dalrymple, R. W., et al, eds. Incised-Valley Systems: Origin & Sedimentary Sequences. LC 95-141337. (Special Publications: No. 51). (Illus.). 380p. 1994. text 97.00 (*1-56576-015-8*) SEPM.

Dalrymple, Robert A., ed. Coastal Hydrodynamics. 812p. 1987. 10.00 (*0-87262-606-7*) Am Soc Civil Eng.

***Dalrymple, Roger.** Language & Piety in Middle English Romance. 282p. 2000. 75.00 (*0-85991-598-0*) Boydell & Brewer.

Dalrymple, Ron. Are You a Genius? 15p. 1978. pap. 1.00 (*0-935882-00-6*) Celestial Gifts.

— The Feeding: Corporate Cannibalism. LC 94-68049. (Orig.). 1996. pap. 12.95 (*0-935882-05-7*) Celestial Gifts.

— Increase Your Power of Creative Thinking in Eight Days. 122p. 1985. spiral bd. 14.95 (*0-912057-41-6*) Celestial Gifts.

— The Inner Manager: Mastering Business, Home & Self. LC 89-92088. 112p. (Orig.). 1989. pap. 8.95 (*0-935882-03-0*) Celestial Gifts.

— Mind Wars. 175p. 1981. text 12.95 (*0-935882-02-2*) Celestial Gifts.

— Richard the Liar-Hearted. 40p. (Orig.). 1979. pap. 2.95 (*0-935882-01-4*) Celestial Gifts.

Dalrymple, Theodore. If Symptoms Persist: Anecdotes from a Doctor. large type ed. 21.95 (*1-85695-058-1*, Pub. by ISIS Lrg Prnt) Transaction Pubs.

— Mass Listeria. 1998. 17.95 (*0-233-99137-9*, Pub. by Andre Deutsch) Trafalgar.

— So Little Done: The Testament of a Serial Killer. 144p. 1996. 17.95 (*0-233-98959-5*, Pub. by Andre Deutsch) Trafalgar.

***Dalrymple, William.** The Age of Kali: Indian Travels & Encounters. 375p. 2000. pap. 14.95 (*1-86450-172-3*) Lonely Planet.

Dalrymple, William. At the Court of the Fish-eyed Goddess: Travels in the Indian Subcontinent. LC 98-915501. xvi, 323p. 1998. 34.00 (*81-7223-332-9*) HarpC.

— From the Holy Mountain: A Journey among the Christians of the Middle East. (Illus.). 496p. 1999. pap. 16.95 (*0-8050-6177-0*, Pub. by H Holt & Co) VHPS.

— In Xanadu. 1990. 13.00 (*0-679-72853-8*) McKay.

— In Xanadu: A Quest. 318p. 2000. pap. 14.95 (*1-86450-173-1*) Lonely Planet.

Dalrymple, William. In Xanadu: A Quest. LC 89-40506. (Departures Ser.). 336p. 1990. pap. 9.95 (*0-685-29462-5*) Vin Bks.

Dalsass. New Good Cake Book. 1999. pap. 14.95 (*0-393-31882-6*) Norton.

***Dalsass, Diana.** New Chocolate Classics. LC 98-31268. (Illus.). 160p. 1999. 14.95 (*0-393-31881-8*) Norton.

Dalsass, Diana. The New Good Cake Book: Over 125 Delicious Recipes That Can Be Prepared in 30 Minutes or Less. large type ed. LC 96-48726. (Spec-Hall Ser.). 361p. 1997. lib. bdg. 26.95 (*0-7838-8050-2*, G K Hall Lrg Type) Mac Lib Ref.

Dalsgard, Ruby, ed. see Gregor, Jan T.

Dalsimer, Adele. Kate O'Brien. (English Authors Ser.: No. 471). 175p. (C). 1990. text 25.95 (*0-8057-6994-3*) Macmillan.

Dalsimer, Adele, ed. see Boston College Museum of Art Staff.

Dalsimer, John P. Como Comprender Os Demonstrativos Financeiros de Uma Organizacao Sem Fins Lucrativos: Uma Cartilha para Membros Do Conselho Diretoria.Tr. of Understanding Nonprofit Financial Statements. (POR.). 24p. (Orig.). 1996. pap. write for info. (*0-925299-62-6*) Natl Ctr Nonprofit.

— Self-Help Accounting: A Guide for the Volunteer Treasurer. Ellis, Susan J., ed. LC 88-83599. (Volunteer Energy Ser.). (Illus.). 104p. (Orig.). 1989. pap. 14.95 (*0-940576-08-2*) Energize.

Dalsimer, John P. Understanding Nonprofit Financial Statements: A Primer for Board Members. (Nonprofit Governance Ser.: No. 8). 24p. 1995. pap. 10.00 (*0-925299-43-X*) Natl Ctr Nonprofit.

Dalsimer, John P. Understanding Nonprofit Financial Statements: A Primer for Board Members. (Nonprofit Governance Ser.: No. 08). 24p. 1992. reprint ed. pap. text 12.00 (*0-925299-10-3*) Natl Ctr Nonprofit.

Dalsimer, Katherine. Female Adolescence. LC 85-26389. 160p. 1987. pap. 15.00 (*0-300-04031-8*) Yale U Pr.

Dalston, T., et al. Early Forged Stamps Detector. 1979. reprint ed. pap. 10.00 (*0-686-64444-1*); reprint ed. pap. 10.00 (*0-912574-39-8*) S J Durst.

Daltaban, T. S. & Wall, C. G. Fundamental & Applied Pressure Analysis. 500p. 1998. 98.00 (*1-86094-091-9*, Pub. by Imperial College) World Scientific Pub.

Daltabuit, Magali. Ecologia Humana en una Comunidad de Morelos. 144p. 1988. pap. 13.71 (*968-837-864-X*, UN035) UPLAAP.

Daltabuit, Magali, et al. Coba: Estrategias Adaptativas de Tres Familias Mayas. 114p. 1988. pap. 6.86 (*968-837-996-4*, UN034) UPLAAP.

Daltlin, Randy. Life with Love. 108p. 1998. pap. 9.95 (*1-57502-744-5*, PO2067) Morris Pubng.

Dalton. Cosmetologist. 4th ed. Date not set. pap. text, teacher ed. 24.50 (*0-314-00787-3*) West Pub.

— Cosmetologist Ace. 4th ed. Date not set. pap. text 69.95 (*0-314-00829-2*) West Pub.

— Dalton's Tables of Houses. 80p. 1975. 12.00 (*0-88053-750-7*, D2010-054) Am Fed Astrologers.

— Disorders of Fluency. 2nd ed. 1989. 61.50 (*1-56593-564-0*, 0022) Singular Publishing.

— The Gentlemen in Black. 2nd ed. Reginald, R. & Menville, Douglas A., eds. LC 75-46265. (Supernatural & Occult Fiction Ser.). (Illus.). 1976. reprint ed. lib. bdg. 26.95 (*0-405-08123-5*) Ayer.

— 1998 Tax Return Practice Problems for Corporation, S Corporations, & Partnerships. 1999. pap. 21.95 (*0-87393-883-6*) Dame Pubns.

— 1997 Tax Return Practice Problem for Corporations, S Corporations, & Partnerships. 1998. pap. 21.95 (*0-87393-789-9*) Dame Pubns.

— El Sid. LC 98-14762. 240p. 1998. pap. 11.95 (*0-312-18713-0*) St Martin.

— Two 1998 Individual Tax Returns Practice Problems. 1999. pap. 21.95 (*0-87393-882-8*) Dame Pubns.

— Two 1997 Individual Tax Returns Practice Problems. 1998. pap. 21.95 (*0-87393-788-0*) Dame Pubns.

Dalton, et al. Advance Medical Life Support. LC 98-21745. 480p. 1998. pap. 48.00 (*0-8359-5179-0*) P-H.

Dalton, A. A Manager's Guide to Safety Representatives. 1996. pap. 145.00 (*1-85953-080-X*, Pub. by Tech Comm) St Mut.

Dalton, A. J., jt. auth. see Janicki, Matthew P.

Dalton, Alan. Safety, Health & Environmental Hazards in the Workplace. LC 99-218020. 1998. 80.00 (*0-304-33289-5*); pap. 35.95 (*0-304-33291-7*) Continuum.

Dalton, Alice. Paramedic Refresher Course: A Case-Based Approach. (Illus.). 280p. (gr. 13). 1999. pap. text 19.95 (*0-8151-1729-9*, 30352) Mosby Inc.

Dalton, Alice T., et al. Pocket Guide to EMT Prehospital Care. LC 93-23587. (Illus.). 256p. 1994. pap. text 17.95 (*0-7216-3781-7*, W B Saunders Co) Harcrt Hlth Sci Grp.

***Dalton, Amanda.** How to Disappear. 64p. 2000. pap. 16.95 (*1-85224-500-X*, Pub. by Bloodaxe Bks) Dufour.

Dalton, Andrew. Making the Fast Track Pay. LC 99-488015. 112p. 1998. pap. 41.00 (*1-85811-193-5*, Pub. by CLT Prof) Gaunt.

***Dalton, Ann M.** Culture Shock! Ukraine. 1999. pap. 12.95 (*1-55868-420-4*) Gr Arts Ctr Pub.

Dalton, Anne, jt. auth. see Dalton, Mary.

Dalton, Annie. Out of the Ordinary. LC 89-39787. 256p. (YA). (gr. 7 up). 1990. 14.95 (*0-06-021424-4*) HarpC Child Bks.

— Out of the Ordinary. LC 89-39787. (Trophy Keypoint Bk.). 256p. (YA). (gr. 7 up). 1992. pap. 3.95 (*0-06-447081-4*, HarpTrophy) HarpC Child Bks.

***Dalton, Annie.** The Starlight Princess & Other Princess Stories. LC 99-13444. (Illus.). 109p. (J). (gr. 1-4). 1999. 19.95 (*0-7894-2632-3*) DK Pub Inc.

Dalton, Bill. Indonesia. 2nd ed. (Asia Guides Ser.). (Illus.). 368p. 1997. pap. 19.95 (*0-8442-4767-7*, Passprt Bks) NTC Contemp Pub Co.

***Dalton, Bill.** Indonesia. 3rd ed. LC 98-32319. 1999. pap. 19.95 (*962-217-615-1*) Norton.

— Indonesia. 4th rev. ed. (Illus.). 2000. pap. 19.95 (*962-217-676-3*) China Guides.

Dalton, Bill. Moon Handbooks: Bali. 2nd rev. ed. (Illus.). 750p. 1997. pap. 19.95 (*1-56691-073-0*, Moon Handbks) Avalon Travel.

— Moon Handbooks: Indonesia. 6th ed. LC 95-222255. (Illus.). 1380p. 1995. pap. 25.00 (*1-56691-062-5*, Moon Handbks) Avalon Travel.

Dalton, Bill, ed. see Williams, George J., III.

Dalton, Bill, ed. see Willliams, George, III.

Dalton, Billie J. Deterministic Explanation of Quantum Mechanics: Based on a New Trajectory-Wave Ordering Interaction. LC 94-29982. 1994. pap. 29.95 (*0-87839-091-X*) North Star.

Dalton-Brown, S., ed. Tolstaia: Three Stories (Tri Rasskasa) (Russian Texts Ser.). (RUS.). 88p. 1996. pap. 18.95 (*1-85399-475-8*, Pub. by Brist Class Pr) Focus Pub-R Pullins.

Dalton-Brown, Sally. Voices from the Void: The Genres of Liudmila Petrushevskaia. Date not set. write for info. (*1-57181-997-5*) Berghahn Bks.

Dalton, C. W. How to Raise a Winner. Herschler, Sara, ed. LC 86-71649. (Illus.). 126p. (Orig.). 1986. pap. 7.95 (*0-916969-01-0*) Big Blue Bks.

— Limericks & Rhymes for Critical Times. (Illus.). 204p. (Orig.). 1994. pap. 9.95 (*0-916969-03-7*) Big Blue Bks.

— The Right Brain & Religion: A Discussion of Religion in the Context of the Right-&-Left-Brain Theory. Garland, L. D., ed. LC 90-81587. (Illus.). 1990. pap. 11.95 (*0-916969-02-9*) Big Blue Bks.

— You're OK - The World's All Wrong. Herschler, Sara & Garland, L. D., eds. LC 84-70707. 542p. 1985. 17.95 (*0-916969-00-2*) Big Blue Bks.

Dalton, Charles, ed. see American Society of Mechanical Engineers Staff.

Dalton, Charlotte. Sparkle's Tidbits of Advice for Cats (And Their Owners) LC 95-68992. (Illus.). 68p. (Orig.). 1995. pap. 7.95 (*0-9646162-0-3*) C Dalton.

Dalton, Christiane & Seidhofer, Barbara. Pronunciation. Widdowson, H. G. & Candlin, C. N., eds. 206p. 1995. pap. text 14.95 (*0-19-437197-2*) OUP.

***Dalton, Cindy Devine.** Avoid Fatty Foods. LC 00-28020. (Why Should I... Ser.). 2000. write for info. (*1-55916-301-1*) Rourke Bk Co.

— Drink More Water. LC 00-28018. (Why Should I... Ser.). 2000. write for info. (*1-55916-302-X*) Rourke Bk Co.

— Eat Carbohydrates That Grow. LC 00-28021. (Why Should I... Ser.). 2000. write for info. (*1-55916-303-8*) Rourke Bk Co.

— Eat Power Proteins. LC 00-28019. (Why Should I... Ser.). 2000. write for info. (*1-55916-304-6*) Rourke Bk Co.

— Keep Cholesterol Low. LC 00-36929. (Why Should I... Ser.). (Illus.). 2000. pap. write for info. (*1-55916-305-4*) Rourke Bk Co.

— Love My Vitamins. LC 00-28017. (Why Should I... Ser.). 2000. write for info. (*1-55916-306-2*) Rourke Bk Co.

Dalton, Clive. Introduction to Practical Animal Breeding. 3rd ed. (Illus.). 174p. 1991. pap. 20.95 (*0-632-03126-3*) Blackwell Sci.

Dalton, Cornelius, et al. Leading the Way: A History of the General Court, 1629-1980. (Illus.). 528p. 1984. write for info. (*0-9613915-0-2*); pap. 4.50 (*0-9613915-1-0*) Mass Sec Commonw.

Dalton, Cyndi. The Blanket Brigade: The Soldiers Story of the 16th Maine, Vol. II. 300p. 1995. pap. 13.95 (*0-9642029-2-1*) Union Pubng.

Dalton, Cynthia, ed. see Small, Abne R.

Dalton, Cynthia S., jt. ed. see Wukasch, Ronald F.

Dalton, Dave. One Earth, Two Worlds: Environment. (Environment). 32p. (C). 1995. pap. 6.95 (*0-85598-276-4*, Pub. by Oxfam Pub) Stylus Pub VA.

***Dalton, David.** Been Here & Gone: A Memoir of the Blues. LC 00-25447. 432p. 2000. 25.00 (*0-380-97676-5*, Wm Morrow) Morrow Avon.

Dalton, David. A Buyer's Market: Global Trade, Southern Poverty & Northern Action; Trade, Aid & Debt. rev. ed. (Trade, Aid & Debt Ser.). (Illus.). 16p. (C). 1994. pap. 5.00 (*0-85598-280-2*, Pub. by Oxfam Pub) Stylus Pub VA.

— Mr. Mojo Risin' Jim Morrison: The Last Holy Fool. 1991. pap. 13.95 (*0-312-05899-3*) St Martin.

— Piece of My Heart: A Portrait of Janis Joplin. (Quality Paperbacks Ser.). (Illus.). 287p. 1991. reprint ed. pap. 14.95 (*0-306-80446-8*) Da Capo.

Dalton, David. Playing the Viola: Conversations with William Primrose. (Illus.). 256p. 1990. pap. text 32.00 (*0-19-816195-6*) OUP.

Dalton, David. El Sid: Saint Vicious. LC 97-2876. 1997. text 21.95 (*0-312-15520-4*) St Martin.

Dalton, David & Cayen, Ron. James Dean: American Icon. 256p. 1986. pap. 19.95 (*0-312-43962-8*) St Martin.

Dalton, David & Farren, Mick. Rolling Stones: In Their Own Words. rev. ed. (In Their Own Words Ser.). (Illus.). 144p. (Orig.). pap. 15.95 (*0-86001-541-6*, OP 40401, Pub. by Bobcat) Omnibus NY.

***Dalton, David & Hewlett-Packard Staff.** Dhcp: Implementation & Reference Guide. 350p. 2000. pap. text 44.99 (*0-13-084848-4*, Prentice Hall) P-H.

Dalton, David & Kaye, Lenny. Rock 100: The Greatest Stars of Rock's Golden Age. 2nd ed. LC 99-42119. (Illus.). 288p. 1999. pap. 19.95 (*0-8154-1017-4*) Cooper Sq.

Dalton, David, jt. auth. see Faithful, Marianne.

Dalton, David, jt. auth. see Scully, Rich.

Dalton, David R. The Alkaloids: The Fundamental Chemistry: A Biogenetic Approach. LC 79-4538. (Studies in Organic Chemistry: No. 7). (Illus.). 803p. reprint ed. pap. 200.00 (*0-7837-4423-4*, 205248300012) Bks Demand.

Dalton, Denise, et al, texts. Jesus Lives in Us. 144p. pap. 6.50 (*0-8198-3930-2*) Pauline Bks.

Dalton, Denise & Berger, Mary J. Jesus Lives in Us. 260p. teacher ed., spiral bd. 16.95 (*0-8198-3932-9*) Pauline Bks.

Dalton, Dennis. Mahatma Gandhi: Nonviolent Power in Action. 279p. 1995. pap. 18.50 (*0-231-08119-7*) Col U Pr.

***Dalton, Dennis.** Mahatma Gandhi: Nonviolent Power in Action. 2000. reprint ed. pap. 18.50 (*0-231-12237-3*) Col U Pr.

Dalton, Dennis. Security Management: Business Strategies for Success. 328p. 1994. 39.95 (*0-7506-9492-0*) Buttrwrth-Heinemann.

Dalton, Dennis, ed. see Gandhi, Mahatma.

Dalton, Dennis R. The Art of Successful Security Management. LC 97-5440. 240p. 1997. 42.95 (*0-7506-9729-6*) Buttrwrth-Heinemann.

Dalton, Dori. The Shamrock & the Feather: A Contemporary Spiritual Journey. 360p. 2000. pap. 16.95 (*0-9651576-3-6*) Heart Link.

Dalton, Douglas. West's California Criminal Law. LC 95-17931. 1995. text. write for info. (*0-314-06746-9*) West Pub.

Dalton Edition Staff. New Webster's Universal Dictionary. 1997. write for info. (*0-517-18554-7*) Random Hse Value.

Dalton, Elizabeth, jt. auth. see Hickey, Elizabeth.

Dalton, Emily. Dream Baby. (American Romance Ser.: Vol. 738). 1998. per. 3.99 (*0-373-16738-5*, 1-16738-6) Harlequin Bks.

— Elise & the Hotshot Lawyer. (American Romance Ser.). 1997. per. 3.75 (*0-373-16666-4*, 1-16666-9) Harlequin Bks.

— Heaven Can Wait. (American Romance Ser.). 1996. per. 3.75 (*0-373-16650-8*, 1-16650-3) Harlequin Bks.

— Instant Daddy. (Presents Ser.: Bk. 783). 1999. per. 3.99 (*0-373-16783-0*, 1-16783-2) Harlequin Bks.

— Make Room for Daddy. LC 95-13559. (American Romance Ser.). 249p. 1995. per. 3.50 (*0-373-16586-2*, 1-16586-9) Harlequin Bks.

— Marley & Her Scrooge. (American Romance Ser.: No. 706). 1997. per. 3.75 (*0-373-16706-7*, 1-16706-3) Harlequin Bks.

***Dalton, Emily.** A Precious Inheritance. 2000. per. 4.25 (*0-373-16823-3*) Harlequin Bks.

Dalton, Emily. Sign Me, Speechless in Seattle. (American Romance Ser.: Vol. 750). 1998. per. 3.99 (*0-373-16750-4*, 1-16750-1) Harlequin Bks.

— Wake Me with a Kiss. (American Romance Ser.: No. 685). 1997. per. 3.75 (*0-373-16685-0*, 1-16685-9) Harlequin Bks.

Dalton, George, jt. ed. see Isaac, Barry L.

Dalton, George, ed. see Murra, John V.

Dalton, H., jt. auth. see Murrell, J. C.

Dalton, H. R. & Reynolds, N. J. Final MB: A Guide to Success in Clinical Medicine. 2nd ed. LC 96-25827. 1997. pap. text 21.00 (*0-443-05332-4*) Church.

Dalton, Harlon L. Racial Healing: Confronting the Fear Between Blacks & Whites. 256p. 1996. pap. 12.95 (*0-385-47517-9*, Anchor NY) Doubleday.

Dalton, J. W. The Life Savers of Cape Cod. (Illus.). 176p. (YA). 1991. reprint ed. pap. 8.95 (*0-940160-49-8*) Parnassus Imprints.

— Lifesavers of Cape Cod. 1967. pap. 14.95 (*0-85699-002-7*) Chatham Pr.

***Dalton, Jack.** Gemini: A Novel. 231p. 1999. pap. 25.00 (*0-9679725-0-7*) Raven Feathers.

***Dalton, James.** City of Shadows. 2000. text 25.95 (*0-312-87643-2*) Forge NYC.

Dalton, James F. Mind over Markets: Power Trading with Market Generated Information. (Illus.). 345p. 1999. reprint ed. pap. 29.95 (*0-934380-53-8*) Traders Pr.

— Personal Financial Planning: Understanding Your Financial Calculator. LC 98-96599. 247p. (C). 1998. pap. text 35.00 (*1-890260-04-5*) Dalton Pub.

Dalton, James F., et al. Mind over Markets: Power Trading with Market Generated Information. 350p. 1993. reprint ed. per. 27.50 (*1-55738-489-4*, Irwn Prfssnl) McGraw-Hill Prof.

Dalton, James F., jt. auth. see Dalton, Michael A.

Dalton, Jerry O. The Tao Te Ching: A New Approach - Backward down the Path. 192p. 1996. mass mkt. 5.99 (*0-380-72560-6*, Avon Bks) Morrow Avon.

— The Tao Te Ching: Backward down the Path - A New Approach. LC 93-1946. (Illus.). 208p. 1995. lib. bdg. 26.95 (*0-89334-231-9*, 2319053) Humanics Ltd.

***Dalton, Jim L.** A Field Guide on the Hiring Process II: From Both Sides of the Desk. 2nd unabridged ed. 2000. pap. 14.95 (*0-9678640-0-3*) Uniquely.

Dalton, Joan. Adventures in Thinking: Creative Thinking & Co-Operative Talk in Small Groups. 189p. (Orig.). 1992. pap. text 21.50 (*0-17-006555-3*, 00723) Heinemann.

Dalton, Joan & Boyd, Julie. I Teach: A Guide to Inspiring Classroom Leadership. 138p. (C). 1992. pap. text 17.50 (*0-435-08782-7*, 08782) Heinemann.

Dalton, Joan & Watson, Marilyn. Among Friends: Classrooms Where Caring & Learning Prevail. (Illus.). 208p. 1997. pap. 16.95 (*1-57621-142-8*) Develop Studies.

Dalton, Joan, jt. auth. see Collis, Mark.

Dalton, Joe. The Omega Sanction. 320p. 1999. pap. 6.99 (*0-312-97188-5*, St Martins Paperbacks) St Martin.

Dalton, Joe, jt. auth. see McGuire.

Dalton, John. Fasciolosis. LC 98-38015. 562p. 1999. 160.00 (*0-85199-260-9*) OUP.

— How the Stock Market Works. 1988. 14.95 (*0-13-435082-0*) NY Inst Finance.

D'Alton, John. King James' Irish Army List, 1689 A. D. Illustrations, Historical & Genealogical (Of) (Illus.). 1000p. 1997. reprint ed. 125.00 (*0-940134-23-3*) Irish Genealog.

Dalton, John, tr. see Bellarmine, Robert.

Dalton, John C. John Call Dalton on Experimental Method: An Original Anthology. Cohen, I. Bernard, ed. LC 79-7957. (Three Centuries of Science in America Ser.). 1980. lib. bdg. 19.95 (*0-405-12538-0*) Ayer.

Dalton, John M. How the Stock Market Works: The New York Institute of Finance. 2nd ed. LC 93-36063. (C). 1993. pap. text 17.95 (*0-13-097866-3*) NY Inst Finance.

Dalton, John W. Fourth State Board Review. Date not set. pap. text 16.50 (*0-314-00786-5*) West Pub.

— The Professional Cosmetologist. (Illus.). 552p. (C). 1989. reprint ed. pap. text, teacher ed. 6.25 (*0-314-77883-7*); reprint ed. pap. text, teacher ed., student ed. 20.50 (*0-314-77879-9*) West Pub.

— The Professional Cosmetologist. 3rd ed. (Illus.). 552p. (C). 1989. reprint ed. text 35.50 (*0-314-77877-2*); reprint ed. pap. text 27.25 (*0-314-77878-0*) West Pub.

— The Professional Cosmetologist. 4th ed. 1992. text 42.50 (*0-314-73042-7*) West Pub.

— State Board Review Questions: The Professional Cosmetologist. 3rd ed. 361p. (C). 1991. reprint ed. pap. text 13.00 (*0-314-77882-9*) West Pub.

Dalton, Jon C., ed. Racism on Campus: Confronting Racial Bias Through Peer Interventions. LC 85-644751. (New Directions for Student Services Ser.: No. SS56). 1991. 22.00 (*1-55542-780-4*) Jossey-Bass.

Dalton, K. J. & Fawdry, R. D., eds. The Computer in Obstetrics & Gynecology. 244p. 1987. pap. 60.00 (*1-85221-010-9*) OUP.

Dalton, Karen C., jt. auth. see Wood, Peter H.

Dalton, Katharina. Once a Month: Understanding & Treating PMS. 6th ed. LC 99-10080. (Illus.). 320p. 1999. 25.95 (*0-89793-256-0*); pap. 15.95 (*0-89793-255-2*) Hunter Hse.

Dalton, Katharine & Holton, Wendy. Depression after Childbirth: How to Recognize, Treat, & Prevent Postnatal Depression. 3rd ed. (Illus.). 220p. 1997. pap. 19.95 (*0-19-286185-9*) OUP.

Dalton, Kit. Bawdy House. (Buckskin Giant Edition Ser.). 368p. (Orig.). 1994. pap. text, mass mkt. 4.99 (*0-8439-3657-6*) Dorchester Pub Co.

Dalton, Kit. Blazing Six-Guns, 2 vols. in 1. (Buckskin Double Edition Ser.). 352p. 1996. mass mkt. 5.99 (*0-8439-4115-4*) Dorchester Pub Co.

Dalton, Kit. 52 Caliber Shootout, Trick Shooter. (Buckskin Double Edition Ser.). 3852p. 1996. mass mkt. 5.99 (*0-8439-3940-0*) Dorchester Pub Co.

— Gold Town Gal/Morgan's Squaw, 2 vols. in 1. (Buckskin Double Edition Ser.). 352p. 1997. mass mkt. 5.99 (*0-8439-4159-6*) Dorchester Pub Co.

— Under the Black Flag. (Illus.). 236p. 1995. reprint ed. 24.95 (*0-9649732-6-X*) L J Tolbert.

***Dalton, Kyle.** Burned Orange: Tom Penders & 10 Years at the University of Texas. LC 99-88287. (Illus.). 224p. 2000. pap. 14.95 (*1-886110-92-1*) Addax Pubng.

Dalton, L. Venezuela. 1976. lib. bdg. 59.95 (*0-8490-2793-4*) Gordon Pr.

Dalton, L. C. The Civil Law of British Guiana Being the Civil Law of British Guiana Ordinance, 1916. With All Amendments & with Notes, Cases, Index & Appendix of Ordinances. xv, 157p. 1999. reprint ed. 60.00 (*1-56169-504-1*) Gaunt.

Dalton, L. R., et al, eds. Electrical, Optical, & Magnetic Properties of Organic Solid-State Materials III: Materials Research Society Symposium Proceedings, Vol. 413. 713p. 1996. 65.00 (*1-55899-316-9*) Materials Res.

Dalton, Larry R., et al, eds. EPR & Advanced EPR Studies of Biological Systems. 328p. 1985. 183.00 (*0-8493-6630-5*, QP519, CRC Reprint) Franklin.

Dalton, Lawrence. History of Randolph County: With Family Sketches. 359p. 1997. reprint ed. lib. bdg. 42.00 (*0-8328-6601-6*) Higginson Bk Co.

Dalton, Lee. The Feather of the Owl. LC 87-82114. (Illus.). 96p. 1987. pap. 6.98 (*0-88290-299-7*) Horizon Utah.

— When the Brave Ones Cried. LC 86-81778. 176p. 1986. 10.98 (*0-88290-282-2*) Horizon Utah.

Dalton, Leroy. Algebra in the Real World. 1997. text 19.95 (*0-86651-121-0*) Seymour Pubns.

Dalton, Margot. Angels in the Light. (Superromance Ser.). 1993. per. 3.50 (*0-373-70576-X*, 1-70576-3) Harlequin Bks.

— Another Woman. LC 95-6940. (Harlequin Promotion Ser.). 296p. 1994. per. 3.99 (*0-373-83306-7*, 1-83306-0) Harlequin Bks.

— Another Woman: Women Who Dare. (Superromance Ser.). 1993. mass mkt. 3.50 (*0-373-70558-1*, 1-70558-1) Harlequin Bks.

***Dalton, Margot.** Best Man in Wyoming. Vol. 12. 256p. 2000. per. 4.50 (*0-373-82596-X*) Harlequin Bks.

— Consequences: Crystal Creek, Vol. 928. (Superromance Ser.). 2000. mass mkt. 4.50 (*0-373-70928-5*, 1-70928-6) Harlequin Bks.

Dalton, Margot. Cottonwood Creek: Home on the Ranch. 1998. per. 4.25 (*0-373-70794-0*) Harlequin Bks.

— Cowboys & Cabernet. (Crystal Creek Ser.). 1993. per. 3.99 (*0-373-82514-5*, 1-82514-0) Harlequin Bks.

— Daniel & the Lion. 1993. per. 3.39 (*0-373-70533-6*, 1-70533-4) Harlequin Bks.

— Defis Pour un Tricheur. (OR Ser.). (FRE.). 1994. pap. 4.50 (*0-373-38161-1*, 1-38161-5) Harlequin Bks.

— Even the Nights Are Better. (Crystal Creek Ser.). 1993. per. 3.99 (*0-373-82517-X*, 1-82517-3) Harlequin Bks.

— A Family Likeness. 1996. per. 3.99 (*0-373-70714-2*, 1-70714-0) Harlequin Bks.

— La Femme Coupable. (Amours d'Aujourd'Hui Ser.). (FRE.). 1997. pap. 4.99 (*0-373-38274-X*, 1-38274-6) Harlequin Bks.

— First Impression. 384p. 1997. per. 5.99 (*1-55166-265-5*, 0-66265-0, Mira Bks) Harlequin Bks.

***Dalton, Margot.** Fourth Horseman. 378p. 1999. per. 5.99 (*1-55166-522-0*, Mira Bks) Harlequin Bks.

Dalton, Margot. French Twist. (Delta Justice Ser.). 1998. per. 4.50 (*0-373-82570-6*, 1-82570-2) Harlequin Bks.

— The Heart Won't Lie. (Crystal Creek Ser.: Vol. 23). 1994. per. 3.99 (*0-373-82535-8*, 1-82535-5) Harlequin Bks.

— The Hiding Place. (Superromance Ser.). 1996. per. 3.99 (*0-373-70693-6*, 1-70693-6) Harlequin Bks.

***Dalton, Margot.** In Plain Sight, Vol. 914. (Harlequin Super Romance Ser.). 2000. mass mkt. 4.50 (*0-373-70914-5*) Harlequin Bks.

Dalton, Margot. Les Jours de Tendresse. (Amours d'Aujourd'Hui Ser.: Vol. 296). 1998. mass mkt. 4.99 (*0-373-38296-0*, 1-38296-9) Harlequin Bks.

— Kim & the Cowboy: (Class of '78) (Superromance Ser.). 1994. per. 3.50 (*0-373-70622-7*, 1-70622-5) Harlequin Bks.

— Magic & Moonbeams. (Superromance Ser.: No. 431). 1990. per. 2.95 (*0-373-70431-3*) Harlequin Bks.

— Magic & Moonbeams. (Men at Work Ser.: Vol. 15). 1998. mass mkt. 4.50 (*0-373-81027-X*, 1-81027-4) Harlequin Bks.

— A Man I Used to Know: Love That Man. (Superromance Ser.: No. 831). 1999. per. 4.25 (*0-373-70831-9*, 1-70831-2, Harlequin) Harlequin Bks.

— Man of My Dreams. LC 96-336. 298p. 1995. per. 3.75 (*0-373-70664-2*, 1-70664-7) Harlequin Bks.

— Memories of You. (Superromance Ser.: No. 749). 1997. per. 3.99 (*0-373-70749-5*, 1-70749-6) Harlequin Bks.

— Mustang Heart. (Crystal Creek Ser.). 1994. per. 3.99 (*0-373-82525-0*, 1-82525-6) Harlequin Bks.

— Never Givin' Up on Love. (Crystal Creek Ser.). 1994. per. 3.99 (*0-373-82531-5*, 1-82531-4) Harlequin Bks.

***Dalton, Margot.** The Newcomer. (Superromance Ser.: Vol. 940). 2000. mass mkt. 4.50 (*0-373-70940-4*, 1-70940-1) Harlequin Bks.

Dalton, Margot. Sagebrush & Sunshine. (Superromance Ser.: No. 425). 1990. per. 2.95 (*0-373-70425-9*) Harlequin Bks.

— Sagebrush & Sunshine. LC 96-341. (Western Lovers Ser.). 249p. 1995. per. 3.99 (*0-373-88518-0*, 1-88518-5) Harlequin Bks.

— Second Thoughts. (Mira Bks.). 1998. per. 5.99 (*1-55166-421-6*, 1-66421-8, Mira Bks) Harlequin Bks.

— The Secret Years: (Showcase) LC 95-6884. (Superromance Ser.). 299p. 1995. per. 3.75 (*0-373-70638-3*, 1-70638-1) Harlequin Bks.

— Southern Nights. 1994. mass mkt. 3.99 (*0-373-82528-5*, 1-82528-0) Harlequin Bks.

— Sunflower. (Superromance Ser.: No. 502). 1992. per. 3.39 (*0-373-70502-6*, 1-70502-9) Harlequin Bks.

— Tangled Lives. 1996. pap. 5.50 (*0-614-07831-8*, 1-66047-1, Mira Bks); per. 5.50 (*1-55166-047-4*, Mira Bks) Harlequin Bks.

— Third Choice. 384p. 1998. per. 5.99 (*1-55166-441-0*, 1-66441-6) Harlequin Bks.

— Three Waifs & a Daddy. (Superromance Ser.: No. 480). 1991. per. 3.29 (*0-373-70480-1*) Harlequin Bks.

— Under Prairie Skies. (Superromance Ser.: No. 401). 1990. per. 2.95 (*0-373-70401-1*) Harlequin Bks.

***Dalton, Margot.** Under Prairie Skies. 2000. mass mkt. 5.99 (*1-55166-594-8*, 1-66594-2, Mira Bks) Harlequin Bks.

Dalton, Margot & Stuart, Anne. New Year's Resolution: Baby. 1997. per. 5.99 (*0-373-83320-2*, 1-83320-1) Silhouette.

Dalton, Margot, et al. My Valentine '94. (Promo Ser.). 1994. mass mkt. 4.99 (*0-373-83294-X*, 1-83294-8) Harlequin Bks.

Dalton, Mark M. Downeast Detectives: Six Tales of Mystery, Mayhem & Murder in Maine. 112p. (Orig.). 1993. pap. 9.95 (*1-880365-25-1*) Prof Pr NC.

***D'Alton, Mary.** Christmas Stocking Book: 50 Exquisite Designs That Celebrate the Season with Style. LC 97-44118. 1999. pap. 16.95 (*1-57990-141-7*, Pub. by Lark Books) Random.

D'Alton, Mary. The Christmas Stocking Book: 50 Exquisite Designs to Celebrate the Season with Style. LC 97-44118. (Illus.). 128p. 1998. 24.95 (*1-57990-050-X*, Pub. by Lark Books) Random.

Dalton, Mary & Dalton, Anne. It's Not in the Genes. 333p. 1996. pap. 15.00 (*0-9661360-0-4*) Boos Pub Co.

***Dalton, Mary M.** The Hollywood Curriculum: Teachers & Teaching in the Movies. LC 96-54029. (Counterpoints Ser.: Vol. 51). 117p. (C). 1999. pap. text 24.95 (*0-8204-3732-8*) P Lang Pubng.

***Dalton, Maxine A.** Becoming a More Versatile Learner. (Ideas into Action Guidebook Ser.). 25p. 1998. pap. text 6.95 (*1-882197-38-0*) Ctr Creat Leader.

Dalton, Maxine A. & Hollenbeck, George P. How to Design an Effective System for Developing Managers & Executives. LC 96-28862. 40p. 1996. pap. text 15.00 (*1-882197-24-0*) Ctr Creat Leader.

Dalton, Maxine A., jt. auth. see Wilson, Meena S.

Dalton, Melville. Conflicts Between Staff & Line Managerial Officers. (Reprint Series in Sociology). (C). 1993. reprint ed. pap. text 5.00 (*0-8290-3704-7*, S-59) Irvington.

Dalton, Michael. Blackjack: A Professional Reference: The Encyclopedia of Casino Twenty-One. 3rd rev. ed. (Illus.). 208p. (C). 1993. pap. text 19.95 (*1-879712-02-4*) Spur Moment.

— The Countrey Justice, Containing the Practise of the Justices of the Peace out of Their Sessions. LC 70-37969. (American Law: The Formative Years). 406p. 1972. reprint ed. 30.95 (*0-405-03996-4*) Ayer.

— Countrey Justice, Containing the Practise of the Justices of the Peace Out of Their Sessions. LC 74-28844. (English Experience Ser.: No. 725). 1975. reprint ed. 50.00 (*90-221-0725-6*) Walter J Johnson.

***Dalton, Michael A. & Dalton, James F.** Cases & Applications. 2nd ed. 308p. (C). 1999. pap. text, teacher ed. write for info. (*1-890260-12-6*) Dalton Pub.

Dalton, Michael A. & Dalton, James F. Dalton CFP Examination Review Vol. 2: Problems & Solutions. 3rd ed. 950p. (C). 1998. pap. text 125.00 (*1-890260-07-X*) Dalton Pub.

***Dalton, Michael A. & Dalton, James F.** Dalton CFP Examination Review Mock Exam & Solutions: Series A, Exam 1, 2000-2001 Edition. 3rd ed. 67p. (C). 1999. pap. text 25.00 (*1-890260-14-2*) Dalton Pub.

— Dalton CFP Examination Review Mock Exam & Solutions: Series A, Exam 2, 1999-2000. 2nd ed. 70p. (C). 1999. pap. text 25.00 (*1-890260-13-4*) Dalton Pub.

— Dalton CFP Examination Review Released Cases & Questions with Answers & Explanations. 2nd ed. 223p. (C). 1999. pap. text. write for info. (*1-890260-10-X*) Dalton Pub.

— Personal Financial Planning Cases & Applications. 2nd ed. (Personal Financial Planning Ser.). 433p. (C). 1999. pap. text 70.00 (*1-890260-11-8*) Dalton Pub.

Dalton, Michael A., et al. Dalton CFP Examination Review: Case Exam Book. 3rd rev. ed. 446p. (C). 1999. pap. text 70.00 (*1-890260-09-6*) Dalton Pub.

— Dalton CFP Examination Review Vol. 1: Outlines & Study Guides. 3rd ed. 950p. (C). 1998. pap. text 125.00 (*1-890260-06-1*) Dalton Pub.

Dalton, Mike. The New Jersey Joke Book. LC 95-19919. 160p. 1996. pap. 7.95 (*0-8065-1714-X*, Citadel Pr) Carol Pub Group.

— The North Dakota Joke Book. 160p. 1982. 8.95 (*0-8184-0336-5*) Carol Pub Group.

Dalton, Murphy L., Jr. Searching & the Delta Squared Magnetometer. (Illus.). 121p. 1993. pap. text 29.00 (*0-9613740-8-X*) M L Dalton Res.

Dalton, Ormonde M., jt. auth. see Read, Charles H.

Dalton, Pamela. And Baby Makes Six. (Romance Ser.: No. 1234). 1997. per. 3.25 (*0-373-19234-7*, 1-19234-3) Silhouette.

— Un Papa Comble. (Horizon Ser.: No. 484). (FRE.). 1998. 3.50 (*0-373-39484-5*, 1-39484-0) Harlequin Bks.

— The Prodigal Husband. (Romance Ser.). 1993. per. 2.75 (*0-373-08957-0*, 5-08957-8) Silhouette.

— Second Chance at Marriage. (Romance Ser.). 1995. per. 2.99 (*0-373-19100-6*, 1-19100-6) Silhouette.

***Dalton, Pamela.** Who's Been Sleeping in Her Bed? (Intimate Moments Ser.: Bk. 1020). 2000. mass mkt. 4.50 (*0-373-27090-9*, 1-27090-9) Silhouette.

Dalton, Pat. Twice in a Lifetime. large type ed. LC 96-5902. 1996. pap. 20.95 (*0-7838-1729-0*, G K Hall Lrg Type) Mac Lib Ref.

— Winds of Destiny. large type ed. 255p. 1995. pap. 17.95 (*0-7838-1455-0*, G K Hall Lrg Type) Mac Lib Ref.

Dalton, Patricia. Wildflowers of the Northeast: In the Audubon Fairchild Garden. LC 79-20296. (Illus.). 1979. pap. 6.95 (*0-914016-63-6*) Phoenix Pub.

Dalton, Patrick. Microsoft SQL Server Black Book. 1997. pap. 39.99 (*0-614-28448-1*) Coriolis Grp.

— Microsoft SQL Server Black Book. 10th ed. LC 98-123586. 500p. (C). 1997. pap. text 49.99 incl. cd-rom (*1-57610-149-5*) Coriolis Grp.

— New York Metro Directory, 1996-97. 1998. pap. 135.00 (*1-882893-17-4*) Dalton.

Dalton, Paul. Conquest, Anarchy & Lordship: Yorkshire, 1066-1154. (Cambridge Studies in Medieval Life & Thought: No. 27). (Illus.). 367p. (C). 1994. text 74.95 (*0-521-45098-5*) Cambridge U Pr.

Dalton, Peggy. Counseling People with Communication Problems. (Counselling in Action Ser.: Vol. 11). 192p. 1994. 49.95 (*0-8039-8894-X*); pap. 21.50 (*0-8039-8895-8*) Sage.

Dalton, Peggy, jt. auth. see Fransella, Fay.

Dalton, Peter. He Wants to Be Called Coach. 1999. pap. 12.95 (*0-533-12929-X*) Vantage.

Dalton, Peter, ed. see Small, Abne R.

Dalton-Puffer, Christiane. The French Influence on Middle English Morphology: A Corpus-Based Study of Derivation. LC 96-15692. (Topics in English Linguistics Ser.: Vol. 20). xiii, 284p. (C). 1996. lib. bdg. 117.05 (*3-11-014990-7*) Mouton.

Dalton, R. & Hamer, S. H. The Provincial Token Coinage of the 18th Century. (Illus.). 1990. write for info. (*0-9627694-0-1*) Davissons Ltd.

Dalton, Robb E. Lifeplanning. Messmer, Dale & Collins, Vicky, eds. (Illus.). 164p. (Orig.). 1987. pap. 14.95 (*0-9619467-0-9*) Lifeplanning.

Dalton, Robert E., jt. auth. see Wells, John E.

***Dalton, Roque.** Clandestine Poems. Paschke, Barbara & Weaver, Jack, eds. Hirschman, Jack, tr. from SPA. LC 83-51488. 183p. 1998. reprint ed. pap. 12.95 (*0-915306-91-3*) Curbstone.

Dalton, Roque. For the Record; Selected Poems. 1999. pap. text 14.95 (*1-885214-20-0*) Azul Edits.

— Miguel Marmol. Ross, Kathleen & Schaaf, Richard, trs. LC 87-71397. 503p. 1987. 19.95 (*0-915306-68-9*) Curbstone.

D

An Asterisk (*) at the beginning of an entry indicates that the title is appearing for the first time.

— Miguel Marmol. Ross, Kathleen & Schaaf, Richard, trs. LC 87-71397. 503p. 1988. pap. 12.95 (0-915306-67-0) Curbstone.

— Small Hours of the Night: Selected Poems of Roque Dalton. St. Martin, Hardie, ed. Cohen, Jonathan et al, trs. 204p. 1996. pap. 14.95 (1-880684-35-7) Curbstone.

Dalton, Roy C. The Jesuits' Estates Question, 1760-1888: A Study of the Background for the Agitation of 1889. LC 74-393033. (Canada Studies in History & Government: No. 11). 213p. reprint ed. pap. 66.10 (0-608-12842-2, 202360800033) Bks Demand.

Dalton, Russell J. Citizen Politics: Public Opinion & Political Parties in Advanced Industrial Democracies. 2nd ed. LC 96-4480. Orig. Title: Citizen Politics in Western Democracies. 352p. 1996. pap. text 32.95 (1-56643-026-7, Chatham House Pub) Seven Bridges.

— Citizen Politics: Public Opinion & Political Parties in Advanced Industrial Society. 3rd ed. (Illus.). 400p. (C). 2001. pap. text 27.95 (1-889119-32-6, Chatham House Pub) Seven Bridges.

— European Politics Today. LC 98-28448. 560p. (C). 1998. 71.00 (0-321-00281-4) Addson-Wesley Educ.

— The Green Rainbow: Environmental Groups in Western Europe. LC 94-4956. (Illus.). 328p. 1994. 40.00 (0-300-05962-0) Yale U Pr.

— Politics in West Germany. 376p. (C). 1989. pap. text 29.73 (0-673-39887-0) Addson-Wesley Educ.

Dalton, Russell J., ed. The New Germany Votes: Reunification & the Creation of a German Party System. (German Studies). 256p. 1993. text 39.50 (0-85496-314-6); pap. text 19.50 (0-85496-386-3) Berg Pubs.

Dalton, Russell J., et al, eds. Electoral Change in Advanced Industrial Democracies: Realignment or Dealignment? LC 84-42592. 532p. reprint ed. pap. 165.00 (0-8357-8867-9, 205227700085) Bks Demand.

Dalton, Russell J. & Kolinsky, Eva, eds. Germans Divided: The 1994 Bundestagswahl & the Evolution of the German Party System. (German Studies). 336p. 1996. 55.00 (1-85973-160-0, Pub. by Berg Pubs); pap. 19.50 (1-85973-165-1, Pub. by Berg Pubs) NYU Pr.

***Dalton, Russell J. & Wattenberg, Martin P., eds.** Parties Without Partisans: Political Change in Advanced Industrial Democracies. (Comparative Politics Ser.). 280p. 2000. text 45.00 (0-19-924082-5) OUP.

Dalton, Russell J., et al. Critical Masses: Citizens, Nuclear Weapon Production & Environmental Destruction in the United States & Russia. LC 99-28632. (American & Comparative Environmental Policy Ser.). (Illus.). 502p. 1999. 65.00 (0-262-04175-8); pap. text 27.50 (0-262-54103-3) MIT Pr.

Dalton, Sandra R. Christmas Gift from Vietnam. LC 96-85155. 220p. 1996. 15.95 (0-9652191-8-6) Four Sis Pr.

Dalton, Sean. Earth 2: Puzzle 2, Bk. 2. 240p. (Orig.). 1995. mass mkt. 4.99 (0-441-00148-3) Ace Bks.

— Termination. 224p. (Orig.). 1995. mass mkt. 4.99 (0-441-00201-3) Ace Bks.

— Turncoat. 192p. (Orig.). 1994. mass mkt. 4.99 (0-441-00117-3) Ace Bks.

Dalton, Sheila. Catalogue. LC 98-183125. (Illus.). 1998. text 32.95 (0-385-25703-1) Delacorte.

***Dalton, Sheila.** Trial by Fire. 216p. (YA). (gr. 9-12). 1998. pap. 7.95 (0-929141-63-6) Napoleon Publ.

Dalton, Sheila & Beeson, Bob. Bubblemania. (Illus.). 32p. (Orig.). (J). (gr. 1-4). 1992. pap. 5.95 (0-920501-75-3) Orca Bk Pubs.

Dalton, Sheila & Lafave, Wayne R. Doggerel. 32p. 1997. pap. 4.95 (0-385-25623-X) Doubleday.

Dalton, Stephan. Secret Worlds. (Illus.). 160p. 1999. text 35.00 (1-55209-384-0) Firefly Bks Ltd.

Dalton, Stephen. The Miracle of Flight. rev. ed. (Illus.). 184p. 1999. 40.00 (1-55209-378-6) Firefly Bks Ltd.

Dalton, Thomas & Bergenn, Victor, eds. Beyond Heredity & Environment: Myrtle McGraw & the Maturation Controversy. 328p. 1998. pap. text 23.00 (0-8133-9070-2, Pub. by Westview) HarpC.

Dalton, Thomas C. The State Politics of Judicial & Congressional Reform: Legitimizing Criminal Justice Policies, 135. LC 84-29763. (Contributions in Political Science Ser.: No. 135). (Illus.). 234p. 1985. 59.95 (0-313-24549-5, DSP/) Greenwood.

Dalton, Thomas F. The Effects of Heat & Stress on Cleanup Personnel Working with Hazardous Materials. 1984. 75.00 (0-318-01766-0) Spill Control Assn.

Dalton, Thomas M., jt. auth. see Pratt, James W.

Dalton, Tony, et al. Making Social Policy in Australia: An Introduction. LC 96-127321. 272p. 1996. pap. 29.95 (1-86448-023-8, Pub. by Allen & Unwin Pty) Paul & Co Pubs.

Dalton, Valerie. Book of Simple Truths. (Illus.). 92p. 1993. pap. text 4.95 (1-85398-061-7, Pub. by Ashgrove Pr) Words Distrib.

Dalton, Verona F. I've Been Lucky. LC 92-30751. 180p. 1992. 12.95 (0-944957-11-0) Rivercross Pub.

Dalton, Vicki. Australian Deaths in Custody & Custody-Related Police Operations, 1996. LC 98-201079. 65p. 1999. pap. 15.00 (0-642-24041-8, Pub. by Aust Inst Criminology) Advent Bks Div.

Dalton, Wayne, jt. auth. see Casad, Jose.

Dalton, William K. Technology of Metallurgy. LC 92-43577. 463p. (C). 1993. text 60.80 (0-02-326900-6, Macmillan Coll) P-H.

Daltow, Ellen & Windling, Terri, eds. The Year's Best Fantasy & Horror: Eighth Annual Collection. 1995. pap. 16.95 (0-312-13219-0) St Martin.

***D'Altroy, Terence N.** The Incas. 2001. 29.95 (0-631-17677-2) Blackwell Pubs.

Daluge, Agnes L. & Daluge, Willard. Rosa's Miracle Mouse: The True Story of a W. W. II Undercover Teenager. large type ed. Scott, Geoffrey L., ed. (Illus.). 227p. 1998. pap. 12.99 (0-9665887-0-3) Authors Direct.

Daluge, Willard, jt. auth. see Daluge, Agnes L.

D'Aluisio, Faith & Menzel, Peter. Women in the Material World. LC 96-15947. (Illus.). 256p. 1996. 35.00 (0-87156-398-3, Pub. by Sierra) Random.

D'Aluisio, Faith, jt. auth. see Menzel, Peter.

Daluiso, Ann. Life Management. 3rd ed. (Annual Ser.). (Illus.). 256p. 1995. pap. text 12.25 (1-56134-339-0, Dshkn McG-Hill) McGrw-H Hghr Educ.

DaLuz, P. L., jt. ed. see Weil, M. H.

Dalven, R. Introduction to Applied Solid State Physics: Topics in the Applications of Semiconductors, Superconductors, Ferromagnetism & the Nonlinear Optical Properties of Solids. 2nd ed. LC 89-72108. (Illus.). 426p. (C). 1990. text 55.00 (0-306-43434-2, Kluwer Plenum) Kluwer Academic.

Dalven, Rae. The Jews of Ioannina. (Illus.). 227p. 1990. 25.00 (0-930685-03-2, Pub. by Lycabettus Pr) Bosphorus Bks.

Dalven, Rae, ed. Daughters of Sappho. LC 91-58950. 1994. 39.50 (0-8386-3470-2) Fairleigh Dickinson.

Dalven, Rae, tr. see Cavafy, C. P.

DalVera, Rocco, jt. auth. see Barton, Robert.

D'Alverny, Marie T. Pensee Medievale en Occident: Theologie, Magique et Autres Textes du XIIe-XIIe Siecle. Burnett, Charles, ed. (Collected Studies: No. CS511). 352p. 1995. text 119.95 (0-86078-538-6, Pub. by Variorum) Ashgate Pub Co.

D'Alverny, Marie-Therese. Etudes Sur le Symbolisme de la Sagesse et l'Iconographie Medievale. Burnett, C. S., ed. (Collected Studies: No. CS 421). (Illus.). 352p. 1993. 122.95 (0-86078-390-1, Pub. by Variorum) Ashgate Pub Co.

— La Transmission des Textes Philosophiques et Ecientifiques au Moyen Age. Burnett, Charles, ed. (Collected Studies: CS 463). 368p. 1994. 119.95 (0-86078-448-7, Pub. by Variorum) Ashgate Pub Co.

D'Alverny, Marie-Therese & Burnett, Charles. La Connaissance de l'Islam dans l'Occident Medievale. (Collected Studies: No. CS 445). 342p. 1994. 119.95 (0-86078-440-1, Pub. by Variorum) Ashgate Pub Co.

Dalvi, Jayavant D. & Lad, P. A. Leaves of Life. LC 98-915451. 196p. 1998. write for info. (81-250-1591-4, Pub. by Orient Longman Ltd) S Asia.

D'Alviella, Eugene F. Goblet, see Goblet D'Alviella, Eugene F.

D'Alviella, Goblet. The Contemporary Evolution of Religious Thought in England, America & India (1886) 344p. 1998. reprint ed. pap. 24.95 (0-7661-0206-8) Kessinger Pub.

— Hibbert Lectures 1891: Lectures on the Origin & Growth of the Conception of God as Illustrated by Anthropology & History. 312p. 1998. reprint ed. pap. 24.95 (0-7661-0207-6) Kessinger Pub.

— The Migration of Symbols, 1894. 303p. 1994. reprint ed. pap. 19.95 (1-56459-442-4) Kessinger Pub.

***Dalvit, D. A. R.** Problems on Statistical Mechanics. LC 99-16504. 296p. 1999. 110.00 (0-7503-0520-7); pap. text 39.00 (0-7503-0521-5) IOP Pub.

Dalwood, C., jt. auth. see Biggs, P.

Dalwood, Mary, tr. see Bataille, Georges.

Daly. Characterizing Human Psycholocial Adaptations, Vol. 208. LC 97-24261. (CIBA Foundation Symposium Ser.). 304p. 1997. 128.00 (0-471-97767-5) Wiley.

Daly. Sex, Evolution & Behavior. (Biology Ser.). 1978. pap. 13.00 (0-87872-156-8) Wadsworth Pub.

Daly, et al. Pak: Interactive Reading Manual for College Students. 166p. (C). 1998. pap. text 36.95 (0-7872-4647-6, 41464701) Kendall-Hunt.

Daly, jt. auth. see Bland.

Daly, Adrian F., jt. auth. see Harris, Alan G.

Daly, Alfrieda, ed. Workplace Diversity: Issues & Perspectives. LC 98-12180. (Orig.). (C). 1998. pap. 27.95 (0-87101-281-2, NASW Pr) Natl Assn Soc Wkrs.

Daly, Ann. Oscar Romero: Martyr for the Poor. 1989. pap. 22.00 (1-85390-093-1, Pub. by Veritas Pubns) St Mut.

Daly, Audrey. Beauty & the Beast. (Favorite Tales Ser.). (Illus.). 28p. (J). 1994. 2.99 (0-7214-5453-4, Ladybrd) Penguin Putnam.

— The Emperor's New Clothes. (Favorite Tales Ser.). (Illus.). 28p. (J). 1994. 2.99 (0-7214-5450-X, Ladybrd) Penguin Putnam.

— Hansel & Gretel. (Favorite Tales Ser.). (Illus.). 28p. (J). 1994. 2.99 (0-7214-5452-6, Ladybrd) Penguin Putnam.

— Jack & the Beanstalk. (Favorite Tales Ser.). (Illus.). 28p. (J). 1994. 2.99 (0-7214-5448-8, Ladybrd) Penguin Putnam.

— The Little Mermaid. (Favorite Tales Ser.). (Illus.). 28p. (J). 1994. 2.99 (0-7214-5447-X, Ladybrd) Penguin Putnam.

— Tom Thumb. (Favorite Tales Ser.). (Illus.). 28p. (J). 1994. 2.99 (0-7214-5446-1, Ladybrd) Penguin Putnam.

Daly, Augustin. Under the Gaslight. Meserve, Walter J., ed. & intro. by. (On Stage, America! Ser.). 54p. 1996. spiral bd. 4.95 (0-937657-29-8) Feedbk Theabks & Prospero.

— Under the Gaslight. LC 76-108468. 1971. reprint ed. 19.00 (0-403-00428-4) Scholarly.

— Under the Gaslight: A Totally Original & Picturesque Drama of Life & Love in These Times, in Five Acts. (BCL1-PS American Literature Ser.). 47p. 1992. reprint ed. lib. bdg. 59.00 (0-7812-6699-8) Rprt Serv.

Daly, Barbara. Home Improvement. 1998. per. 3.50 (0-373-44060-X, 1-44060-1, Mira Bks) Harlequin Bks.

Daly, Barbara, ed. The Acute Care Nurse Practitioner. LC 96-46566. 192p. 1997. 34.95 (0-8261-9480-X) Springer Pub.

Daly, Barbara & Lacey, Meg. Great Genes!; Make Me Over, 2 bks. in 1. (Duets Ser.: No. 13). 1999. per. 5.99 (0-373-44079-0, 1-44079-1) Harlequin Bks.

Daly, Barbara, jt. auth. see Wainscott, Tina.

Daly-Bednarek, Janet R. The Changing Image of the City: Planning for Downtown Omaha, 1945-1973. LC 91-42758. (Illus.). xii, 304p. 1992. text 50.00 (0-8032-1692-0) U of Nebr Pr.

Daly, Brenda. Authoring a Life: A Woman's Survival in & Through Literary Studies. LC 97-45988. 268p. (C). 1998. text 59.50 (0-7914-3679-9); pap. text 19.95 (0-7914-3680-2) State U NY Pr.

— Lavish Self-Divisions: The Novels of Joyce Carol Oates. LC 96-11684. 232p. (C). 1996. 37.50 (0-87805-885-0) U Pr of Miss.

Daly, Brenda O. & Reddy, Maureen T., eds. Narrating Mothers: Theorizing Maternal Subjectivities. LC 90-27053. 310p. (C). 1991. pap. text 19.50 (0-87049-706-5) U of Tenn Pr.

Daly, Brian. Big & Hairy. Ashby, Ruth, ed. 144p. (Orig.). (J). (gr. 3-6). 1994. pap. 3.99 (0-671-87111-0, Minstrel Bks) PB.

Daly, Bridget & Skeels, Janet. 100th Boyfriend. LC 87-4714. (Illus.). 96p. (Orig.). 1987. pap. 5.95 (0-941104-05-2) Real Comet.

Daly, Cahal. Moral Philosophers in Britain: From Bradley to Wittgenstein. 220p. 1996. 45.00 (1-85182-227-5, Pub. by Four Cts Pr) Intl Spec Bk.

Daly, Cahal B. The Price of Peace. 251p. 1991. 24.00 (0-85640-471-3, Pub. by Blackstaff Pr) Dufour.

— The Price of Peace. 251p. 1991. pap. 12.95 (0-85640-472-1) Dufour.

— Tertullian the Puritan & His Influences. 240p. 1993. text 45.00 (1-85182-110-4, Pub. by Irish Acad Pr) Intl Spec Bk.

Daly, Carol H. Maine Coon Cats: Everything about Purchase, Care, Nutrition, Reproduction, Diseases & Behavior. LC 95-14958. (Complete Pet Owner's Manual Ser.). (Illus.). 1995. pap. 6.95 (0-8120-9038-1) Barron.

Daly, Carroll J. The Adventures of Race Williams. 352p. 1989. 9.95 (0-89296-959-8) Mysterious Pr.

— The Adventures of Satan Hall. 304p. 1988. 8.95 (0-89296-938-5) Mysterious Pr.

***Daly, Catherine.** Bugs, Bugs, Bugs. (Illus.). 32p. (J). (ps-3). 2000. pap. 3.49 (0-448-42189-5, Planet Dexter) Peng Put Young Read.

— Whiskers. LC 99-89175. (Road to Reading Mile 2 Ser.). (Illus.). (J). 2000. 10.99 (0-307-46214-5) Gldn Bks Pub Co.

***Daly, Catherine & Leonard, Thomas.** Whiskers. LC 99-89175. (Road to Reading Ser.). (J). 2000. pap. 3.99 (0-307-26214-6) Gldn Bks Pub Co.

***Daly, Charles J. & Rao, Navalgund Anant Hemant Kumar.** Scalar Diffraction from a Circular Aperture. LC 00-22042. (International Series in Engineering & Computer Science). 2000. write for info. (0-7923-7810-5) Kluwer Academic.

Daly, Charles P., et al. The Magazine Publishing Industry. LC 96-32138. 310p. 1996. pap. text 26.00 (0-205-16612-1) Allyn.

Daly, Chuck, intro. Allen Iverson. LC 97-33159. (Basketball Legends Ser.). (Illus.). 64p. (YA). (gr. 3 up). 1999. lib. bdg. 15.95 (0-7910-4852-7) Chelsea Hse.

— Alonzo Mourning. LC 97-46624. (Basketball Legends Ser.). (Illus.). 64p. (YA). (gr. 3 up). 1999. lib. bdg. 15.95 (0-7910-4577-3) Chelsea Hse.

— Antoine Walker. (Basketball Legends Ser.). (Illus.). 64p. (YA). (gr. 3 up). 1999. lib. bdg. 16.95 (0-7910-5008-4) Chelsea Hse.

— Basketball Legends, 18 bks., Set. (Illus.). (J). (gr. 3 up). 1995. lib. bdg. 269.10 (0-7910-2425-3) Chelsea Hse.

— Chris Webber. (Basketball Legends Ser.). (Illus.). 64p. (YA). (gr. 3 up). 1999. lib. bdg. 16.95 (0-7910-5010-6) Chelsea Hse.

— Gary Payton. LC 97-46623. (Basketball Legends Ser.). (Illus.). 64p. (YA). (gr. 3 up). 1999. lib. bdg. 15.95 (0-7910-4578-1) Chelsea Hse.

— The Head Coaches. LC 97-42865. (Basketball Legends Ser.). (Illus.). 64p. (YA). (gr. 3 up). 1999. lib. bdg. 15.95 (0-7910-4580-3) Chelsea Hse.

— John Stockton. LC 97-50120. (Basketball Legends Ser.). (Illus.). 64p. (YA). (gr. 3 up). 1999. lib. bdg. 15.95 (0-7910-4579-X) Chelsea Hse.

— Juwan Howard. LC 97-46645. (Basketball Legends Ser.). (Illus.). 64p. (YA). (gr. 3 up). 1999. lib. bdg. 15.95 (0-7910-4575-7) Chelsea Hse.

— Keith Van Horn. (Basketball Legends Ser.). (Illus.). 64p. (YA). (gr. 3 up). 1999. lib. bdg. 16.95 (0-7910-5009-2) Chelsea Hse.

— Kevin Garnett. (Basketball Legends Ser.). (Illus.). 64p. (YA). (gr. 3 up). 1999. lib. bdg. 16.95 (0-7910-5006-8) Chelsea Hse.

— Shawn Kemp. LC 97-43799. (Basketball Legends Ser.). (Illus.). 64p. (YA). (gr. 3 up). 1999. lib. bdg. 15.95 (0-7910-4576-5) Chelsea Hse.

Daly, Conor. Buried Lies. LC 96-75692. 320p. 1996. pap. 18.95 (1-57566-033-4) Kensgtn Pub Corp.

— Buried Lies. 304p. 1997. mass mkt. 5.50 (1-57566-168-3, Knsington) Kensgtn Pub Corp.

— Local Knowledge. 1996. pap. 4.99 (1-57566-036-9) Kensgtn Pub Corp.

— Local Knowledge. 1997. pap. 9.95 (1-57566-153-5) Kensgtn Pub Corp.

— Outside Agency. LC 96-79079. 320p. 1997. 18.95 (1-57566-162-4, Knsington) Kensgtn Pub Corp.

— Outside Agency. 288p. 1998. mass mkt. 5.99 (1-57566-319-8) Kensgtn Pub Corp.

Daly, D. J., ed. International Comparisons of Prices & Output. LC 76-171572. (Conference on Research in Income & Wealth. Studies in Income & Wealth Ser.: Vol. 37). 429p. reprint ed. pap. 133.00 (0-8357-2603-7, 201598500006) Bks Demand.

— International Comparisons of Prices & Output. (Studies in Income & Wealth: No. 37). 429p. 1972. reprint ed. text 111.60 (0-87014-244-5) Natl Bur Econ Res.

Daly, Dan & O'Donnell, Bob. The Pro Football Chronicle. (Illus.). 416p. (Orig.). 1990. pap. 16.95 (0-02-028300-8) Macmillan.

Daly, Daniel L. & Peter, Val J. National Performance Standards for Residential Care: A Policy Initiative from Father Flanagan's Boys' Home. 25p. 1996. pap. 4.99 (1-889322-10-5, 19-208) Boys Town Pr.

Daly, David A. A Comparison of Exhibition & Distribution Patterns in Three Recent Feature Motion Pictures. abr. ed. Jowett, Garth S., ed. LC 79-6672. (Dissertations on Film, 1980 Ser.). 1980. lib. bdg. 18.95 (0-405-12906-8) Ayer.

— The Source for Stuttering & Cluttering. LC 97-195128. 210p. 1996. spiral bd. 41.95 incl. audio (0-7606-0108-9) LinguiSystems.

Daly, David D. & Pedley, Timothy A. Current Practice of Clinical Electroencephalography. 2nd ed. 848p. 1990. text 120.00 (0-88167-635-7) Lppncott W & W.

Daly, David J. The Legend of Killer Noon. LC 99-94273. 223p. 2000. pap. 14.95 (0-9671411-0-9, Pub. by Green Boat Pr) ACCESS Pubs Network.

Daly, Donald. Managerial Macroeconomics: Canadian Edition. 480p. (C). 1987. text 49.95 (0-256-06000-2, Irwn McGrw-H) McGrw-H Hghr Educ.

— Managerial Macroeconomics: Canadian Edition. 104p. (C). 1987. teacher ed., per. write for info. (0-256-06653-1, Irwn McGrw-H) McGrw-H Hghr Educ.

Daly, Donald J. & Globerman, Steven. Tariff & Science Policies: Applications of a Model of Nationalism. LC 76-24911. (Ontario Economic Council Research Studies: No. 4). 135p. reprint ed. pap. 41.90 (0-8357-4021-8, 203671200005) Bks Demand.

Daly, E. Book of the Lion. 1995. 9.95 (0-8050-0806-3) H Holt & Co.

Daly, Edward & Devlin, Kieran. The Clergy of the Derry Diocese. 208p. 1997. boxed set 35.00 (1-85182-335-2, Pub. by Four Cts Pr) Intl Spec Bk.

Daly, Edward A. We've Got to Start Meeting Like This: A Primer on Visual Telephony. Hansen, Kathleen J., ed. (Illus.). Date not set. pap. text 49.50 (1-880145-04-9) KJH Comm.

Daly, Edward A. & Hansell, Kathleen J. Visual Telephony: Guide for Communications Managers. LC 99-10794. (Telecommunications Library). 257p. 1999. 65.00 (1-58053-023-0) Artech Hse.

Daly, Eleanor. The Amphibamidae: Amphibia: Temnospondyli, with a Description of a New Genus from the Upper Pennsylvanian of Kansas. Mengel, Robert M. et al, eds. LC 94-621020. (Miscellaneous Publications: No. 85). (Illus.). 61p. (Orig.). (C). pap. text. write for info. (0-89338-046-6) U KS Nat Hist Mus.

Daly, Elizabeth. Deadly Nightshade. large type ed. LC 92-46503. (Americana Series). 337p. 1993. reprint ed. lib. bdg. 20.95 (1-56054-321-3) Thorndike Pr.

— Murders in Volume Two: A Henry Gamadge Mystery. LC 93-38797. 320p. 1994. reprint ed. pap. 6.95 (1-883402-52-2) S&S Trade.

— Nothing Can Rescue Me. large type ed. 315p. 1991. reprint ed. lib. bdg. 20.95 (1-56054-217-9) Thorndike Pr.

— Unexpected Night. 1995. pap. 6.95 (1-883402-14-X) S&S Trade.

— Unexpected Night: A Henry Gamadge Mystery. LC 94-8930. 240p. 1994. reprint ed. per. 7.00 (1-883402-51-4) S&S Trade.

Daly, Elizabeth, ed. Monitoring Children's Language Development: Holistic Assessment in Classrooms. LC 90-5262. (Illus.). 169p. (C). 1991. pap. text 20.00 (0-435-08540-9, 08540) Heinemann.

Daly, Eugene J. Thy Will Be Done: A Guide to Wills, Taxation, & Estate Planning for Older Persons. 2nd ed. LC 94-4962. (Golden Age Books - Perspectives on Aging Ser.). 234p. (C). 1994. pap. 17.95 (0-87975-903-8) Prometheus Bks.

Daly, F., jt. auth. see Hand, D. J.

Daly, F. C. First Rebels: Strictly Confidential Notes on the Growth of the Revolutionary Movements in Bengal. 1983. reprint ed. 16.50 (0-8364-0939-6, Pub. by RDDHI) S Asia.

***Daly, Fergus.** Building & Testing Probability Models. (Arnold Texts in Statistics Ser.). 256p. 2001. pap. text 34.95 (0-340-73203-2) E A.

Daly, Gabriel. Transcendence & Imminence: A Study in Catholic Modernism & Integralism. 266p. 1980. text 59.00 (0-19-826652-9) OUP.

Daly-Gawenda, Debra. Manual of Medical-Surgical Nursing. LC 96-9848. (Nursing Fact Finder Ser.). 700p. 1996. spiral bd. 29.95 (0-316-21792-1) Lppncott W & W.

Daly-Gawenda, Debra, et al, eds. Occupational Health Nursing Care Guidelines. LC 96-8187. (Illus.). 336p. 1996. 49.95 (0-8261-9350-1) Springer Pub.

***Daly, Gayle H.** Scissors, Glue & Phonological Processes, Too! Interactive Activities for Remediating Phonological Processes. (Illus.). 174p. (J). (ps-4). 1999. spiral bd. 37.95 (0-7606-0303-0) LinguiSystems.

Daly, Gerald. Homeless. LC 95-26465. (Illus.). 312p. (C). 1996. pap. 24.99 (0-415-12029-2) Routledge.

— Homeless. LC 95-26465. (Illus.). 312p. (C). 1996. 85.00 (0-415-12028-4) Routledge.

Daly, Greg. Glazes & Glazing Techniques. 2nd ed. (Illus.). 143p. 1996. reprint ed. 29.95 (0-9650786-0-4) Gentle Br.

Daly, H. C. The U. S. S. Solace Was There: The History of a Hospital Ship During World War II. LC 90-84769. (Illus.). 735p. 1991. 39.95 (0-935902-17-1) Balboa Pub.

Daly, Helen, jt. auth. see Rosenberg, Ken.

Daly, Herman E. Beyond Growth: The Economics of Sustainable Development. LC 95-51311. 264p. 1997. pap. 17.00 (0-8070-4709-0) Beacon Pr.

D

An Asterisk (*) at the beginning of an entry indicates that the title is appearing for the first time.

Daly, Herman E. Ecological Economics & the Ecology of Economics: Essays in Criticism. LC 98-53414. 208p. 1999. 75.00 (*1-85898-968-X*) E Elgar.

***Daly, Herman E.** Ecological Economics & the Ecology of Economics: Essays in Criticism. LC 99-53414. 208p. 2000. pap. 25.00 (*1-84064-109-6*) E Elgar.

Daly, Herman E. & Cobb, John B., Jr. For the Common Good: Redirecting the Economy Toward Community, the Environment, & a Sustainable Future. 2nd ed. LC 93-24460. 544p. 1994. pap. 20.00 (*0-8070-4705-8*) Beacon Pr.

Daly, Herman E. & Townsend, Kenneth N. Valuing the Earth: Economics, Ecology, Ethics. (Illus.). 384p. 1992. 45.00 (*0-262-04133-2*) MIT Pr.

— Valuing the Earth: Economics, Ecology, Ethics. (Illus.). 384p. 1992. pap. text 23.50 (*0-262-54068-1*) MIT Pr.

Daly, Howell V. Bees of the New Genus Ctenoceratina in Africa South of the Sahara: Hymenoptera: Apoides. (Publications in Entomology: Vol. 108). 80p. 1988. pap. 16.95 (*0-520-09725-4*, Pub. by U CA Pr) Cal Prin Full Svc.

Daly, Howell V., et al. An Introduction to Insect Biology & Diversity. 2nd ed. LC 97-27059. (Illus.). 696p. (C). 1998. text 76.00 (*0-19-510033-6*) OUP.

Daly, J. A Concept for Using Controlled Shot Peening in Original Gear Design. (Nineteen Eighty-Seven Fall Technical Meeting Ser.: Vol. 87FTM13). (Illus.). 4p. 1987. pap. text 30.00 (*1-55589-489-5*) AGMA.

Daly, J. A., et al, eds. Teaching Communication: Theory, Research & Methods. 520p. (C). 1990. pap. 45.00 (*0-8058-0162-6*); text 125.00 (*0-8058-0645-8*) L Erlbaum Assocs.

Daly, Jack. Single Living. 100p. 1991. write for info. (*0-9631420-0-3*) Seacoast.

***Daly, Jackie & Carter, Tom.** Tammy Wynette: A Daughter Recalls Her Mother's Tragic Life & Death. LC 99-88604. (Illus.). 304p. 2000. 24.95 (*0-399-14598-2*) Putnam Pub Group.

Daly, James. Sir Robert Filmer & English Political Thought. LC 78-25913. 228p. reprint ed. pap. 70.70 (*0-8357-8323-5*, 203398200088) Bks Demand.

Daly, James & Bergman, Lee. A Hero's Welcome: The Conscience of Sergeant James Daly vs. the United States Army. LC 74-17652. (Illus.). 288p. 1975. 8.50 (*0-672-52030-3*, Bobbs) Macmillan.

***Daly, James A.** Black Prisoner of War: A Conscientious Objector's Vietnam Memoir. (Modern War Studies). 2000. 40.00 (*0-7006-1059-6*) U Pr of KS.

***Daly, James A. & Bergman, Lee.** Black Prisoner of War: A Conscientious Objector's Vietnam Memoir. 2000. reprint ed. pap. 17.95 (*0-7006-1060-X*) U Pr of KS.

Daly, James C. Fiber Optics. 1996. 84.95 (*0-614-18444-4*, B03035) Info Gatekeepers.

Daly, James C., ed. Fiber Optics. 256p. 1984. lib. bdg. 139.00 (*0-8493-5103-0*, TA1800) CRC Pr.

Daly, James C., jt. auth. see Galipeau, Denis P.

Daly, James J. Cheerful Ascetic, & Other Essays. LC 68-24847. (Essay Index Reprint Ser.). 1977. 17.95 (*0-8369-0359-5*) Ayer.

— Road to Peace. LC 78-107691. (Essay Index Reprint Ser.). 1977. 19.95 (*0-8369-1495-3*) Ayer.

***Daly, James W.** Recreation & Sport Planning & Design. 2nd ed. LC 99-42475. (Illus.). 240p. 2000. pap. 36.00 (*0-7360-0345-2*) Human Kinetics.

Daly, Janis J., jt. auth. see Karas, M. Ann.

Daly, Jay. Presenting S. E. Hinton. (Twayne's United States Authors Ser.: No. 528). 160p. (C). 1989. 28.00 (*0-8057-8211-7*, Twyne) Mac Lib Ref.

***Daly, Jeanette M.** Writer's Guide to Nursing Periodicals. LC 00-8048. 2000. pap. write for info. (*0-7619-1492-7*) Sage.

Daly, Jeanne, et al. The Public Health Researcher: A Methodological Guide. LC 98-148134. 232p. 1998. pap. text 34.50 (*0-19-554075-1*) OUP.

Daly, Jill, reader. Fanny Hill's Daughter. abr. ed. 1991. pap. 12.95 incl. audio (*1-882071-35-2*) B&B Audio.

Daly, John, jt. auth. see Holden, Benedict M.

Daly, John, ed. see O'Dugan, John.

Daly, John, jt. ed. see Romanini, Judith.

Daly, John, jt. ed. see Sommer, John.

Daly, John A. Peg Woffington: A Tribute to the Actress & the Woman. LC 70-91489. (Illus.). 182p. 1972. 20.95 (*0-405-08427-7*, Pub. by Blom Pubns) Ayer.

Daly, John A., et al, eds. Avoiding Communication: Shyness, Reticence & Communication Apprehension. 2nd ed. LC 97-9260. (Communication Ser.). (Illus.). 528p. (C). 1997. pap. text 35.00 (*1-57273-069-2*) Hampton Pr NJ.

— Avoiding Communication: Shyness, Reticence & Communication Apprehension. 2nd ed. LC 97-9260. (Communication Ser.). (Illus.). 528p. (C). 1997. text 89.50 (*1-57273-068-4*) Hampton Pr NJ.

Daly, John A. & McCroskey, James C., eds. Avoiding Communication: Shyness, Reticence, & Communication Apprehension. LC 83-27242. (Sage Focus Editions Ser.). (Illus.). 296p. reprint ed. pap. 91.80 (*0-7837-4563-X*, 204409200003) Bks Demand.

— Avoiding Communication: Shyness, Reticence, & Communication Apprehension. LC 83-27242. (Sage Focus Editions Ser.). 296p. 1984. reprint ed. pap. 84.40 (*0-608-02228-4*, 2044092) Bks Demand.

Daly, John A. & Miller, Robert R. Corporations' Use of the Internet in Developing Countries. LC 98-24487. (IFC Discussion Paper Ser.: No. 35). 32p. 1998. pap. 22.00 (*0-8213-4256-8*, 14256) World Bank.

Daly, John A. & Wiemann, John M., eds. Strategic Interpersonal Communication. LC 92-45190. (Interpersonal Communication Ser.). 320p. 1994. text 69.95 (*0-89859-957-1*) L Erlbaum Assocs.

Daly, John A., jt. ed. see McCroskey, James C.

Daly, John C. Russian Seapower & "The Eastern Question", 1827-41. LC 90-62893. (Illus.). 290p. 1991. 41.95 (*1-55750-726-0*) Naval Inst Pr.

Daly, John J., jt. auth. see Holden, Benedict M., Jr.

Daly, John J., jt. auth. see Holden, Benedict M.

Daly, John M. Current Opinion in General Surgery. 2nd ed. (Illus.). 288p. (Orig.). 1995. text 129.95 (*1-85922-671-X*) Rapid Science.

Daly, John M. & Cady, Blake, eds. Atlas of Surgical Oncology. LC 92-18763. 1992. text 129.00 (*0-8016-1272-1*) Mosby Inc.

Daly, John M., et al. Management of Upper Gastrointestinal Cancer. (Illus.). 304p. text. write for info. (*0-7020-2147-4*) W B Saunders.

Daly, Jonathan. Autocracy under Siege: Security Police & Opposition in Russia, 1866-1905. LC 98-25021. 290p. 1998. 38.00 (*0-87580-243-5*) N Ill U Pr.

Daly, Jonathan G. The Daly News - A Musical Memoir. 90p. 1996. pap. 5.95 (*0-87129-684-5*, D03) Dramatic Pub.

Daly, Joseph L., jt. auth. see Minnesota State Bar Association Staff.

***Daly, Jude.** Fair, Brown & Trembling: An Irish Cinderella Story. LC 99-34315. (Illus.). 32p. (J). (ps-2). 2000. 16.00 (*0-374-32247-3*) FS&G.

***Daly, K. S.** Ireland: An Encyclopedia for the Bewildered. (Illus.). 170p. 1999. reprint ed. text 20.00 (*0-7881-6647-6*) DIANE Pub.

Daly, K. S. Sex: An Encyclopedia for the Bewildered. LC 97-118632. (Illus.). 256p. 1996. 14.95 (*1-85410-359-8*, Pub. by Aurum Pr) London Brdge.

Daly, Karen A. Vietnamese Classifiers in Narrative Texts. LC 97-61945. (Publications in Linguistics: Vol. 125). 220p. 1998. pap. 29.00 (*1-55671-021-6*) S I L Intl.

Daly, Katherine & Watters, Ron. Kath & Ron's Guide to Idaho Paddling: Flatwater & Easy Whitewater Trips. LC 99-94741. (Illus.). 288p. 1999. pap. 18.95 (*1-877625-07-8*) Great Rift.

Daly, Kathleen. Gender, Crime & Punishment. LC 94-1582. 352p. 1994. 47.00 (*0-300-05955-8*) Yale U Pr.

— Gender, Crime & Punishment. 352p. 1996. pap. 17.00 (*0-300-06866-2*) Yale U Pr.

— Greek & Roman Mythology A to Z: A Young Reader's Companion. (Mythology A to Z Ser.). (Illus.). 144p. (YA). (gr. 7-12). 1992. lib. bdg. 19.95 (*0-8160-2151-1*) Facts on File.

Daly, Kathleen & Maher, Lisa, eds. Criminology at the Crossroads: Feminist Readings in Crime & Justice. LC 97-18731. (Readings in Crime & Punishment Ser.). 304p. (C). 1998. text 54.00 (*0-19-511343-8*); pap. text 22.95 (*0-19-511344-6*) OUP.

Daly, Kathleen N. A Book of Flowers. 2nd ed. Orig. Title: A Child's Book of Flowers. (Illus.). 44p. 1986. 10.00 (*0-937543-00-4*) Sacrum Pr.

Daly, Kerry J. Families & Time. (Understanding Families Ser.: Vol. 7). 200p. 1996. 44.00 (*0-8039-7340-3*); pap. 21.95 (*0-8039-7341-1*) Sage.

***Daly, Kevin J.** Financial Volatility & Real Economic Activity. LC 98-73755. 3p. 1998. text 65.95 (*1-84014-873-X*, Pub. by Ashgate Pub) Ashgate Pub Co.

Daly, Kieran. Catholic Church Music in Ireland: Lyra Ecclesiastica & the Cecilian Movement in Ireland. 240p. 1995. 45.00 (*1-85182-141-4*, Pub. by Four Cts Pr); pap. 30.00 (*1-85182-204-6*, Pub. by Four Cts Pr) Intl Spec Bk.

Daly, Laura, ed. Put It in Writing, Bk. 3. (Writing Ser.). 1988. student ed. 1.95 (*0-8428-9722-4*) Cambridge Bk.

Daly, Laura, jt. auth. see Schenk, Brian.

Daly, Lawrence W. Innocence, the Ragged Edge. Olson, David L., ed. (Illus.). 80p. (Orig.). (C). 1988. pap. text 19.95 (*0-9621127-0-4*) Daly Consulting.

Daly, Leila. Sensational Salads. 93p. 1994. write for info. (*1-57215-003-3*) World Pubns.

***Daly, Leslie E. & Bourke, Geoffrey J.** Interpretation & Uses of Medical Statistics. 5th ed. LC 99-45805. (Illus.). 576p. 2000. pap. 79.95 (*0-632-04763-1*) Blackwell Sci.

Daly, Lew. E. Dickinson on a Sleepwalk with the Alphabet Prowling Around Her. deluxe limited ed. (Burning Deck Poetry Pamphlets Ser.). 24p. 1990. pap. 15.00 (*0-930901-69-X*) Burning Deck.

— Nemesis. 224p. (Orig.). 1991. pap. 8.00 (*0-945926-28-6*) Paradigm RI.

— Nemesis. deluxe ed. 224p. (Orig.). 1991. pap. 20.00 (*0-945926-29-4*) Paradigm RI.

— Swallowing the Scroll: Late in a Prophetic Tradition with Poetry of Susan Howe & John Taggart. 1994. pap. 5.00 (*1-879645-08-4*) Garlic MA.

***Daly, Lewis C.** A Moment to Decide: The Crisis in Mainstream Presbyterianism. (Denominational Studies Ser.). 170p. 2000. pap. 25.00 (*0-9679106-0-9*) Inst for Democracy.

Daly, Lloyd W. Iohannis Philoponi: De Vocabulis Quae Diversum Significatum Exhibent Secundum Differentiam Accentus. LC 81-72156. (Memoirs Ser.: Vol. 151). 1983. 20.00 (*0-87169-151-5*, M151-DAL) Am Philos.

Daly, Lois K., ed. Feminist Theological Ethics: A Reader. LC 94-15935. (Library of Theological Ethics). 384p. 1994. pap. 26.00 (*0-664-25327-X*) Westminster John Knox.

Daly, Lorraine. Sherlock Holmes & the Lusitania. Wilks, Ian, ed. LC 98-40038. 192p. 1998. 30.00 (*0-86025-291-4*, Pub. by I Henry Pubns) Empire Pub Srvs.

Daly, Louise H. Alexander Cheves Haskell: The Portrait of a Man. (Illus.). 267p. 1989. reprint ed. 30.00 (*0-916107-13-2*) Broadfoot.

Daly, M. Wickerdary: A Dictionary. (C). 1990. 30.00 (*0-946211-52-3*) St Mut.

Daly, M., jt. auth. see Gilmore, Mike.

Daly, M. W., jt. auth. see Holt, P. M.

Daly, M. W., jt. ed. see Benavides, Gustavo.

Daly, Macdonald, ed. see Wells, H. G.

Daly, Macdonald, ed. & intro. see Gaskell, Elizabeth.

Daly, Margaret. Alleluia! Amen! Accompaniment Edition. 305p. 1989. 90.00 (*0-86217-146-6*, Pub. by Veritas Pubns) St Mut.

— Alleluia! Amen! People's Edition. 128p. 1989. pap. 30.00 (*0-905092-47-3*, Pub. by Veritas Pubns) St Mut.

— Cantate: Responsorial Psalms for Sundays of the Year B. 161p. 1993. 59.00 (*1-85390-280-2*, Pub. by Veritas Pubns) St Mut.

— Music for Weddings. 96p. 1989. pap. 55.00 (*1-85390-131-8*, Pub. by Veritas Pubns); pap. 22.00 (*1-85390-631-X*, Pub. by Veritas Pubns); audio 22.00 (*0-7855-6982-0*, Pub. by Veritas Pubns) St Mut.

— Nunc Dimittis: Night Prayer of the Church. 72p. 1991. pap. 7.95 (*1-85390-103-2*, Pub. by Veritas Pubns) St Mut.

— Responsorial Psalms for Sundays of the Year. 1989. pap. 30.00 (*1-85390-118-0*, Pub. by Veritas Pubns) St Mut.

Daly, Margo. The Mini Rough Guide to Sydney. (Illus.). 304p. 1999. 9.95 (*1-85828-453-8*, Pub. by Rough Guides) Penguin Putnam.

Daly, Margo, et al. The Rough Guide to Australia. 4th ed. (Illus.). 1999. 21.95 (*1-85828-461-9*, Pub. by Rough Guides) Penguin Putnam.

***Daly, Maria L.** Diary of a Union Lady, 1861-1865. Hammond, Harold E., ed. LC 99-89818. 448p. 2000. pap. 19.95 (*0-8032-6623-5*) U of Nebr Pr.

Daly, Mark. Air Defence Radar - Lane & Sea. (Military Systems - Related Special Reports). 1997. 695.00 (*0-7106-1427-6*) Janes Info Group.

— Radar for Combat Aircraft. (Air-Space - Related Special Reports). 1998. 695.00 (*0-7106-1428-4*) Janes Info Group.

Daly, Markate. Communitarianism: A New Public Ethics. 353p. (C). 1993. 26.75 (*0-534-20088-5*) Wadsworth Pub.

Daly, Marsha. Onto the Future. pap. 2.95 (*0-317-39728-1*) St Martin.

Daly, Martin, ed. Modernization in the Sudan. LC 85-19768. 177p. 1985. text 29.50 (*0-936508-11-6*) Barber Pr.

Daly, Martin & Wilson, Margo. Homicide. (Evolutionary Foundations of Human Behavior Ser.). 340p. 1988. pap. text 28.95 (*0-202-01178-X*); lib. bdg. 54.95 (*0-202-01177-1*) Aldine de Gruyter.

— Sex, Evolution, & Behavior. 2nd ed. 402p. (C). 1983. 29.75 (*0-87150-767-6*) Wadsworth Pub.

— The Truth about Cinderella: A Darwinian View of Parental Love. LC 99-28271. (Darwinism Today Ser.). 80p. 1999. pap. 9.95 (*0-300-08029-8*) Yale U Pr.

Daly, Martin W., Jr. The Sirdar: Sir Reginald Wingate & the British Empire in the Middle East. LC 96-79457. (Memoirs Ser.: Vol. 222). (Illus.). 345p. 1977. 30.00 (*0-87169-222-8*, M222-dam) Am Philos.

***Daly, Martin W.** Tonga. 224p. 1999. lib. bdg. 62.00 (*1-85109-293-5*) ABC-CLIO.

Daly, Martin W., ed. Modern Egypt, from 1517 to the End of the Twentieth Century: Modern Egypt, from 1517 to the End of the Twentieth Century, Vol. 2. (Illus.). 478p. (C). 1999. text 100.00 (*0-521-47211-3*) Cambridge U Pr.

Daly, Martin W. & Deng, Francis M. Bonds of Silk: The Human Factor in the British Administration of the Sudan. LC 89-43113. (African Studies: No. 1). (C). 1989. text 26.00 (*0-87013-279-2*) Mich St U Pr.

Daly, Martin W. & Sikainga, Ahmad A., eds. The Civil War in Sudan. 224p. 1993. text 69.50 (*1-85043-515-4*, Pub. by I B T) St Martin.

Daly, Martin W., jt. auth. see Forbes, Lesley.

Daly, Martin W., ed. see Lea, C. A.

Daly, Martin W., jt. ed. see Petry, Cary F.

Daly, Mary. Beyond God the Father: Toward a Philosophy of Women's Liberation. 2nd rev. ed. LC 84-45067. 257p. 1993. pap. 17.50 (*0-8070-1503-2*) Beacon Pr.

— The Church & the Second Sex. rev. ed. LC 85-47519. 240p. 1986. reprint ed. pap. 16.00 (*0-8070-1101-0*) Beacon Pr.

***Daly, Mary.** The Gender Division of Welfare: The Impact of the British & German Welfare States. LC 99-41039. (Illus.). 288p. (C). 2000. 64.95 (*0-521-62331-6*); pap. 22.95 (*0-521-62621-8*) Cambridge U Pr.

Daly, Mary. Gyn/Ecology: The Metaethics of Radical Feminism. LC 90-52596. 517p. 1990. pap. 19.00 (*0-8070-1413-3*) Beacon Pr.

— Outercourse: The Be-Dazzling Voyage. 478p. 1993. pap. 12.00 (*0-7043-4372-X*, Pub. by Womens Press) Trafalgar.

— Pure Lust: Elemental Feminist Philosophy. 470p. 1998. pap. 11.95 (*0-7043-3935-8*, Pub. by Womens Press) Trafalgar.

***Daly, Mary.** Quintessence... Realizing the Archaic Future: A Radical Elemental Feminist Manifesto. LC 98-15286. (Illus.). 304p. 1999. pap. 18.00 (*0-8070-6791-1*) Beacon Pr.

Daly, Mary. Quintessence... Realizing the Archaic Future: A Radical Elemental in the Feminist Manifesto. LC 98-15286. (Illus.). 304p. 1998. 24.00 (*0-8070-6790-3*) Beacon Pr.

Daly, Mary & Caputi, Jane. Websters' First Intergalactic Wickedary of the English Language. (Illus.). 310p. 1998. pap. 22.95 (*0-7043-4114-X*, Pub. by Womens Press) Trafalgar.

Daly, Mary, et al. The Sherry Fitzgerald Guide to Dublin's Victorian Houses. LC 98-234015. (Illus.). 208p. 1998. pap. 49.95 (*1-899047-42-5*, Pub. by A A Farmar) Irish Bks Media.

Daly, Mary C., ed. New York Code of Professional Responsibility: Opinions, Commentary & Caselaw, 2 vols. LC 97-37283. 1997. ring bd. 300.00 (*0-379-20677-3*) Oceana.

Daly, Mary C., et al, eds. Rights, Liability & Ethics in International Legal Practice: Ethics & Practice. LC 94-28869. 430p. 1994. 115.00 (*0-929179-98-6*) Juris Pubng.

Daly, Mary E. Industrial Development & Irish National Identity, 1922-1939. LC 91-42446. (Irish Studies). 216p. 1992. reprint ed. pap. 67.00 (*0-608-07604-X*, 205991900010) Bks Demand.

Daly, Maureen. First a Dream. 1990. pap. 12.95 (*0-590-40846-1*) Scholastic Inc.

— First a Dream. 224p. (YA). (gr. 7-9). 1991. 3.25 (*0-590-40847-X*, Point) Scholastic Inc.

— Seventeenth Summer. (YA). (gr. 7 up). 1985. mass mkt. 4.50 (*0-671-61931-4*, Archway) PB.

Daly, Maureen. Seventeenth Summer. 1968. 9.09 (*0-606-04805-7*, Pub. by Turtleback) Demco.

Daly, Maureen. Seventeenth Summer. 293p. (YA). (gr. 7 up). 1981. reprint ed. lib. bdg. 23.95 (*0-89966-355-9*); reprint ed. lib. bdg. 19.95 (*0-89967-029-6*, Harmony Rain) Buccaneer Bks.

Daly, Maurice. Daly's Billiard Book. (Illus.). 1988. pap. 8.95 (*0-486-25724-X*) Dover.

Daly, Meg, jt. auth. see Bondoc, Anna.

Daly, Muriel D. Ants' Nest. LC 79-37265. (Short Story Index Reprint Ser.). 1977. reprint ed. 20.95 (*0-8369-4076-8*) Ayer.

Daly, M.W., comment. Sudan. 2nd rev. ed. LC 94-131040. (World Bibliographical Ser.). 216p. 1992. lib. bdg. 81.00 (*1-85109-187-4*) ABC-CLIO.

***Daly, Nicholas.** Modernism, Romance & the "Fin de Siecle" Popular Fiction & British Culture. LC 98-55153. 232p. (C). 2000. 59.95 (*0-521-64103-9*) Cambridge U Pr.

Daly, Niki. The Boy on the Beach. LC 98-10786. (Illus.). 32p. (J). (ps-2). 1999. 16.00 (*0-689-82175-1*) S&S Childrens.

— Bravo, Zan Angelo! A Comedia Dell'Arte Tale with Story & Pictures. LC 97-39436. (J). (gr. k up). 1998. 16.00 (*0-374-30953-1*) FS&G.

***Daly, Niki.** Jamela's Dress. LC 98-42048. (Illus.). 32p. (YA). (ps-3). 1999. pap. text 16.00 (*0-374-33667-9*) FS&G.

Daly, Niki. Mama, Papa & Baby Joe. (Illus.). 32p. (J). 1999. pap. 4.99 (*0-14-054969-2*, PuffinBks) Peng Put Young Read.

— My Dad. LC 94-14455. (Illus.). 32p. (J). (ps-3). 1995. per. 16.00 (*0-689-50620-1*) McElderry Bks.

— Not So Fast, Songololo. LC 94-40984. (Illus.). (J). (gr. k-3). 1996. mass mkt. 4.95 (*0-689-80154-8*) Aladdin.

— Not So Fast, Songololo. (J). 1998. pap. 4.95 (*0-87628-975-8*) Ctr Appl Res.

— Not So Fast, Songololo. LC 85-70134. (Illus.). 32p. (J). (gr. k-3). 1986. 16.00 (*0-689-50367-9*) McElderry Bks.

— Not So Fast, Songololo. LC 94-40984. (J). 1996. 10.15 (*0-606-09700-7*, Pub. by Turtleback) Demco.

— Papa Lucky's Shadow. LC 91-24283. (Illus.). 32p. (J). (gr. k-3). 1999. per. 5.99 (*0-689-82430-0*) Aladdin.

— Papa Lucky's Shadow. LC 91-24283. (Illus.). 32p. (J). (ps-3). 1992. 16.00 (*0-689-50541-8*) McElderry Bks.

Daly, Niki. Why the Sun & Moon Live in the Sky. LC 93-47304. 32p. (J). (ps-3). 1995. 15.00 (*0-688-13331-2*) Lothrop.

Daly, Niki, jt. auth. see Hartmann, Wendy.

Daly, P., et al, contrib. by. Implementing Projects on the Information Highway. LC 96-5905. 1996. write for info. (*0-917599-17-9*) Natl Rural.

Daly, Padraig. The Voice of the Hare. LC 97-162576. 80p. 1997. 19.95 (*1-873790-97-X*, Pub. by Dedalus); pap. 12.95 (*1-873790-96-1*, Pub. by Dedalus) Dufour.

***Daly, Padraig J.** Last Dreamers: New & Selected Poems. 150p. 2000. 23.95 (*1-901233-46-4*, Pub. by Dedalus); pap. 15.95 (*1-901233-45-6*, Pub. by Dedalus) Dufour.

Daly, Patricia E., ed. Envisioning the New Adam: Empathic Portraits of Men by American Women Writers. LC 94-37879. 160p. 1997. pap. 17.95 (*0-275-95805-1*, Praeger Pubs) Greenwood.

— Envisioning the New Adam: Empathic Portraits of Men by American Women Writers, 149. LC 94-37879. (Contributions in Women's Studies: Vol. 149). 160p. 1995. 59.95 (*0-313-29095-4*, Greenwood Pr) Greenwood.

Daly, Patrick W., jt. auth. see Kopka, Helmut.

Daly, Paul V. The Supply of Illicit Drugs to the United States: The MMICC Report, 1995. (Illus.). 83p. 1998. pap. text 20.00 (*0-7881-3942-8*) DIANE Pub.

Daly, Peter. The Biotechnology Business: A Strategic Analysis. LC 85-10877. 150p. 1985. 42.00 (*0-8476-7460-6*) Rowman.

Daly, Peter M. Literature in the Light of the Emblem. 2nd ed. LC 99-180754. 312p. 1999. text 65.00 (*0-8020-0910-7*); pap. text 22.95 (*0-8020-7891-5*) U of Toronto Pr.

— Literature in the Light of the Emblem: Structural Parallels Between the Emblem & Literature in the Sixteenth & Seventeenth Centuries. LC 79-11863. 259p. reprint ed. pap. 80.30 (*0-608-15394-X*, 202932700060) Bks Demand.

Daly, Peter M., ed. Andrea Alciato & the Emblem Tradition. LC 88-39895. (AMS Studies in the Emblem: No. 4). 1989. 57.50 (*0-404-63704-3*) AMS Pr.

— Andreas Alciatus, 2 vols., Vol. I: The Latin Emblems. (Illus.). 368p. 1985. text 175.00 (*0-8020-2425-4*) U of Toronto Pr.

— Andreas Alciatus, 2 vols., Vol. II: Emblems in Translation. (Illus.). 464p. 1985. write for info. (*0-318-56150-6*) U of Toronto Pr.

— The English Emblem & the Continental Tradition. LC 87-45812. (Studies in the Emblem: No. 1). 1988. 58.50 (*0-404-63701-9*) AMS Pr.

— The English Emblem Tradition. (Index Emblematicus Ser.: Vol. 2). (Illus.). 576p. (C). 1994. text 110.00 (*0-8020-2922-1*) U of Toronto Pr.

— The Index of Emblem Art: Symposium. LC 89-45847. (Studies in the Emblem: No. 6). 1990. 57.50 (*0-404-63706-X*) AMS Pr.

D

An Asterisk (*) at the beginning of an entry indicates that the title is appearing for the first time.

Daly, Peter M., et al, eds. The English Emblem Tradition, Vol. 1. (Index Emblematicus Ser.). 483p. 1988. text 95.00 (*0-8020-5748-9*) U of Toronto Pr.

***Daly, Peter M., et al, eds.** Germany Reunified: A Five- & Fifty-Year Retrospective. 2nd ed. (McGill European Studies: Vol. 1). (Illus.). XVIII, 256p. 1999. pap. text 32.95 (*0-8204-4569-X*, 4569X) P Lang Pubng.

Daly, Peter M. & Dimler, G. Richard, eds. The Jesuit Series: Part 1, A-D. (Illus.). 296p. 1997. 100.00 (*0-7735-1551-8*, Pub. by McG-Queens Univ Pr) CUP Services.

Daly, Peter M. & Lappe, Claus O. Text und Variantenkonkordanz zu Schillers "Kabale und Liebe" (C). 1976. 484.65 (*3-11-002225-7*) De Gruyter.

Daly, Peter M. & Manning, John. Aspects of Renaissance & Baroque Symbol Theory, 1500-1700. LC 97-32551. (Studies in the Emblem). 283p. 1998. write for info. (*0-404-63714-0*) AMS Pr.

Daly, Peter M. & Russell, Daniel, eds. AMS Studies in the Emblem, 12 vols. (Numbered Monographic Ser.). 1993. write for info. (*0-404-63700-0*) AMS Pr.

— Emblematica: An Interdisciplinary Journal for Emblem Studies. 1994. write for info. (*0-404-99999-9*) AMS Pr.

Daly, Peter M. & Silcox, Mary V., eds. The English Emblem: Bibliography of Secondary Literature. (Illus.). 208p. 1996. 90.00 (*0-7735-1575-5*, Pub. by McG-Queens Univ Pr) CUP Services.

— The English Emblem Tradition, Vol. 4. (Index Emblematicus Ser.). 400p. 1999. text 110.00 (*0-8020-4367-4*) U of Toronto Pr.

— The Modern Critical Reception of the English Emblem. (Illus.). 353p. 1996. 90.00 (*0-7735-1576-3*, Pub. by McG-Queens Univ Pr) CUP Services.

Daly, Pierrette. Heroic Tropes: Gender & Intertext. LC 92-32623. 194p. (C). 1993. text 29.95 (*0-8143-2427-4*) Wayne St U Pr.

Daly, Pierrette, tr. see Konnyu, Leslie.

Daly, R., tr. see Stubhaug, A.

Daly, R. A. Law Teachers' Manual of the Analysis of Cases & the Use of Law Books. (Legal Bibliographic & Research Reprint Ser.: Vol. 11). vi, 226p. 1988. reprint ed. lib. bdg. 40.00 (*0-89941-651-9*, 305640) W S Hein.

— Legal Bibliographic & Research Reprint Series, 12 vols., Set. Surles, Richard H., ed. LC 94-76711. vi, 226p. 1980. reprint ed. write for info. (*0-89941-031-6*, 301600) W S Hein.

Daly, R. J. & Sand, E. A., eds. Psychological Treatment of Mental Illness. (Illus.). 170p. 1987. 79.95 (*0-387-17596-2*) Spr-Verlag.

Daly, R. J., jt. ed. see Helgason, Tomas.

***Daly, Richard.** God's Little Book of Calm: Words of Peace & Refreshment for Weary Souls. 160p. 1999. pap. 6.95 (*0-00-274049-4*, Pub. by HarpC) Trafalgar.

Daly, Richard H., jt. ed. see Lee, Richard B.

Daly, Richard T. Applications of the Mathematical Theory of Linguistics. (Janua Linguarum, Series Minor: No. 185). 1974. pap. text 71.55 (*90-279-2684-0*) Mouton.

Daly, Robert J. Christian Sacrifice: The Judaeo-Christian Background Before Origen. LC 78-12004. (Catholic University of American Studies in Christian Antiquity: No. 18). 605p. reprint ed. pap. 187.60 (*0-7837-1001-1*, 204130800020) Bks Demand.

— The Origins of the Christian Doctrine of Sacrifice. LC 77-78628. 160p. (Orig.). reprint ed. pap. 49.60 (*0-608-16321-X*, 202687500053) Bks Demand.

Daly, Robert J., ed. In All Things: Religious Faith & American Culture. LC 89-64479. 232p. (Orig.). (C). 1990. pap. 14.95 (*1-55612-315-9*) Sheed & Ward WI.

— Rising from History: U. S. Catholic Theology Looks to the Future. LC 87-2011. (College Theology Society Publications, 1988: Vol. 30). 234p. (Orig.). (C). 1987. lib. bdg. 44.00 (*0-8191-6155-1*) U Pr of Amer.

Daly, Robert J., ed. Origen: Treatise on the Passover & Dialogue with Heraclides. (Ancient Christian Writers Ser.: No. 54). 1992. 16.95 (*0-8091-0452-0*) Paulist Pr.

Daly, Robert J., ed. see Kilmartin, Edward J.

Daly, Robert J., tr. see Fries, Heinrich.

Daly, Robert J., tr. see Von Balthasar, Hans U., ed.

Daly, Robert W., ed. see Keeler, William F.

Daly, Russ T. Resistance: Rx to the Fountain of Youth. (Illus.). 52p. 1997. per. 9.95 (*0-9662688-0-6*) Challenger Pubns.

Daly, Saralyn. Katherine Mansfield. LC 93-29509. (New York Times Byline Bks.: No. 23). 168p. 1994. 32.00 (*0-8057-7056-9*) Macmillan.

Daly, Saralyn R., tr. & intro. see Ruiz, Juan.

Daly, Steve. Lotus Notes 4.5 Essentials. LC 96-68974. (Illus.). 240p. 1997. 22.99 (*1-57576-436-9*) Sams.

Daly, Steve, jt. auth. see Lasseter, John.

Daly, T. A., ed. Little Book of American Humorous Verse. LC 73-38597. (Granger Index Reprint Ser.). 1977. reprint ed. 18.95 (*0-8369-6329-6*) Ayer.

Daly, T. P. Sisyphus & Sycamore & Other Songs of Survival & Endurance. New York Society for General Semantics Staff, ed. 65p. (Orig.). 1988. pap. 12.50 (*0-9621550-0-4*) NY Genl Semantics.

Daly, Thomas A. The Art of Thomas Aquinas Day: The Painting Season. LC 98-92475. (Illus.). 152p. 1998. 60.00 (*0-9663104-0-3*) T A Daly.

— Canzoni. (Classics of Modern American Humor. Second Ser.). (Illus.). reprint ed. 26.00 (*0-404-19929-1*) AMS Pr.

***Daly, Tim.** Digital Photography Handbook: A User's Guide to Creating Digital Images. (Illus.). 160p. 2000. pap. 27.99 (*0-89879-945-7*, 10643, Wrtrs Digest Bks) F & W Pubns Inc.

Daly, Timothy. Kafka Dances. (Currency Plays Ser.). (Illus.). xvi, 78p. (Orig.). 1994. pap. 16.95 (*0-86819-388-7*, Pub. by Currency Pr) Accents Pubns.

Daly, Victor. Not Only War. Date not set. 21.95 (*0-8434-0002-1*) Ayer.

Daly, Wadman. Relocating Your Workplace: A User's Guide to Acquiring & Preparing Business Facilities. LC 92-54361. (Illus.). 365p. (Orig.). 1993. pap. 23.95 (*1-56052-186-4*) Crisp Pubns.

Daly, Wally, et al. Best Radio Plays of 1983: BBC Giles Cooper Award Winners. 200p. (C). 1984. write for info. (*0-413-55220-9*, A0028, Methuen Drama) Methn.

Daly-Weir, Catherine. All Aboard Cars. LC 95-22239. (All Aboard Bks.). (Illus.). 32p. (J). (ps-3). 1996. pap. 2.99 (*0-448-41102-4*, G & D) Peng Put Young Read.

Daly-Weir, Catherine. All Aboard Cars. LC 95-22239. (J). 1996. 8.15 (*0-606-08980-2*, Pub. by Turtleback) Demco.

Daly-Weir, Catherine. Are You Right for Him? Is He Right for You? Fun Quizzes All about You & Your Guy, 1 vol. 80p. (YA). (gr. 7-12). 1999. pap. 3.99 (*0-448-41985-8*, Grosset-Putnam) Putnam Pub Group.

***Daly-Weir, Catherine.** Coat of Arms. 32p. 2000. pap. 6.99 (*0-448-41975-0*, G & D) Peng Put Young Read.

— Daddy & Me, 1 vol. LC 99-10942. (ps-k). 1999. pap. text 2.99 (*0-448-41964-5*) Putnam Pub Group.

— Happily Never After: Tangled Tales. (Illus.). 48p. (ps-3). 2000. pap. 3.99 (*0-307-45408-8*) Gldn Bks Pub Co.

Daly-Weir, Catherine. Knights. LC 97-50347. (All Aboard Reading Ser.). (Illus.). 48p. (J). (gr. 1-3). 1998. lib. bdg. 13.89 (*0-448-41886-X*, G & D) Peng Put Young Read.

— Knights, Level 2. LC 97-50347. (All Aboard Reading Ser.). (Illus.). 48p. (J). (gr. 1-3). 1998. mass mkt. 3.99 (*0-448-41857-6*, G & D) Peng Put Young Read.

— A Simple Wish: Make a Simple Wish of Your Very Own. LC 97-72386. (Simple Wish Ser.). (Illus.). 24p. (Orig.). (J). (gr. 2-5). 1997. pap. 4.95 (*0-448-41635-2*, G & D) Peng Put Young Read.

— Treasure Hunt! (Jewel Sticker Stories Ser.). (Illus.). 24p. (J). (ps-2). 1998. mass mkt. 3.99 (*0-448-41848-7*, G & D) Peng Put Young Read.

Daly-Weir, Catherine & Greenburg, Dan. Who Is He Really? 25 Fun Quizzes about Guys & You, Vol. 10. (Illus.). 80p. (J). (gr. 3-8). 1997. mass mkt. 3.99 (*0-448-41648-4*, G & D) Peng Put Young Read.

Daly, Wendy. Bonnie Blair: Power on Ice. LC 95-23217. (Bullseye Biography Ser.). 1996. 9.09 (*0-606-09093-2*, Pub. by Turtleback) Demco.

— Tara & Michelle: The Road to Gold. LC 97-66957. (J). 1997. pap. 3.99 (*0-679-88930-2*, Pub. by Random Bks Yng Read) Random.

— Tara & Michelle: The Road to Gold. (J). 1997. lib. bdg. 11.99 (*0-679-98930-7*, Pub. by Random Bks Yng Read) Random.

Daly, Wendy. Tara & Michelle: The Road to Gold. 1997. 9.09 (*0-606-12821-2*, Pub. by Turtleback) Demco.

***Daly, Willaim P.** The Laborer Is Worthy of His Hire, Vol. 10. Stratman, Bernard F., ed. 71p. 1999. pap. 17.00 (*1-893060-04-7*) NFPC.

Daly, William. Jesus-Pivot of the Priesthood: A Gift for Seminarians & Aspirants. 120p. (Orig.). 1994. pap. 6.95 (*0-931888-57-3*) Christendom Pr.

Daly, William, tr. see Gershwin, George.

Daly, William T. Beyond Critical Thinking: Teaching the Thinking Skills Necessary to Academic & Professional Success. (Freshman Year Experience Monograph: No. 17). 30p. 1995. pap. 20.00 (*1-889271-14-4*) Nat Res Ctr.

Dalyell, Tam. A Science Policy for Britain. LC 83-190946. 141p. reprint ed. pap. 43.80 (*0-608-17087-9*, 202771400056) Bks Demand.

Dalzell, Alexander. The Criticism of Didactic Poetry: Essays on Lucretius, Virgil, & Ovid. (Robson Classical Lectures). 240p. 1996. text 50.00 (*0-8020-0822-4*) U of Toronto Pr.

Dalzell, Alexander, et al, eds. Acta Conventus Neo-Latini Torontonensis: Proceedings of Seventh International Congress, 1988, at Toronto. (Medieval & Renaissance Texts & Studies: Vol. 86). 896p. 1991. 60.00 (*0-86698-098-9*, MR86) MRTS.

Dalzell, Alexander, tr. The Correspondence of Erasmus: Letters 1535 to 1657 (1525) (Collected Works of Erasmus: No. 11). 544p. 1993. text 110.00 (*0-8020-0536-5*) U of Toronto Pr.

Dalzell, Frederick, jt. auth. see Smith, George David.

Dalzell, George W., jt. auth. see Canfield, George L.

Dalzell, James R. & Townsend, Gilbert. Masonry Simplified, Vol. 1. 3rd ed. LC 72-93804. 414p. reprint ed. pap. 128.40 (*0-608-15392-3*, 202941100060) Bks Demand.

Dalzell, Lee B., jt. auth. see Dalzell, Robert F., Jr.

Dalzell, Lee Baldwin, jt. auth. see Dalzell, Robert F., Jr.

Dalzell, Robert F., Jr. Enterprising Elite: The Boston Associates & the World They Made. LC 86-33649. (Studies in Business History: No. 40). (Illus.). 320p. 1987. 29.95 (*0-674-25765-0*) HUP.

— Enterprising Elite: The Boston Associates & the World They Made. 328p. 1993. pap. 12.95 (*0-393-31079-5*) Norton.

Dalzell, Robert F., Jr. & Dalzell, Lee B. George Washington's Mount Vernon: At Home in Revolutionary America. LC 98-23215. (Illus.). 322p. 1998. 30.00 (*0-19-512114-7*) OUP.

***Dalzell, Robert F., Jr. & Dalzell, Lee Baldwin.** George Washington's Mount Vernon: At Home in Revolutionary America. (Illus.). 320p. 2000. pap. 19.95 (*0-19-513628-4*) OUP.

Dalzell, Thomas G. The Dramatic Encounter of Divine & Human Freedom in the Theology of Hans Urs von Balthasar. Hollenweger, Walter J. et al, eds. LC 98-167111. (Studies in the Intercultural History of Christianity: Vol. 105). 316p. 1997. pap. 48.95 (*3-906759-05-9*, Pub. by P Lang) P Lang Pubng.

— The Dramatic Encounter of Divine & Human Freedom in the Theology of Hans Urs von Balthasar. LC 98-167111. (Studies in the Intercultural History of Christianity: Vol. 105). 316p. (C). 1997. pap. text 48.95 (*0-8204-3421-3*, Pub. by P Lang) P Lang Pubng.

***Dalzell, Thomas G.** The Dramatic Encounter of Divine & Human Freedom in the Theology of Hans Urs von Balthasar. 2nd ed. LC 99-50211. (Studies in the Intercultural History of Christianity: Vol. 105). 316p. (C). 1999. pap. 43.95 (*0-8204-4627-0*) P Lang Pubng.

***Dalzell, Thomas G., contrib. by.** The Dramatic Encounter of Divine & Human Freedom in the Theology of Hans Urs Von Balthasar. 2nd ed. LC 99-50211. (Studies in the Intercultural History of Christianity). 316p. 1999. pap. 43.95 (*3-906764-29-X*, Pub. by P Lang) P Lang Pubng.

Dalzell, Tom. Flappers 2 Rappers: American Youth Slang. LC 96-50258. (Illus.). 272p. 1996. pap. 14.95 (*0-87779-612-2*) Merriam-Webster Inc.

— The Slang of Sin. LC 98-26827. (Illus.). 1998. pap. 14.95 (*0-87779-627-0*) Merriam-Webster Inc.

Dalzell, William, ed. see MacDonald, Betty.

Dalziel, ed. Tectonics of the Scotia Arc, Antarctica, No. T180. (IGC Field Trip Guidebooks Ser.). 216p. 1989. 35.00 (*0-87590-550-1*) Am Geophysical.

Dalziel, Ian W. Tectonic Evolution of a Forearc Terrane, Southern Scotia Ridge, Antarctica. LC 84-21107. (Geological Society of America Ser.: Vol. 200). (Illus.). 38p. 1984. reprint ed. pap. 30.00 (*0-608-07729-1*, 206781700010) Bks Demand.

Dalziel, Pamela, ed. see Hardy, Thomas.

Dalziel, Pamela, ed. & intro. see Hardy, Thomas.

***Dalziel, Paul.** Money, Credit & Price Stability. LC 00-36894. (International Studies in Money & Banking). 2000. write for info. (*0-415-24056-5*) Routledge.

Dalziel, Paul. The New Zealand Macroeconomy: A Briefing on the Reforms. LC 96-225149. (Illus.). 142p. 1996. pap. text 28.00 (*0-19-558330-2*) OUP.

Dam, Andries Van, see Foley, James D. & Van Dam, Andries.

Dam, Bastiaan A. Van & Stoffel, Cornelis O. Chapters on English Printing, Prosody & Punctuation, 1550-1700. reprint ed. 27.50 (*0-404-06751-4*) AMS Pr.

Dam, C. P. Van, see Cheer, A. Y. & Van Dam, C. P., eds.

Dam, Hari N. The Intellectual Odyssey of Walter Lippmann. 1973. 69.95 (*0-87968-057-1*) Gordon Pr.

Dam, Herman Van, see Van Dam, Herman, ed.

Dam, Jacques Van, see Van Dam, Jacques.

Dam, James W. Van, see Van Dam, James W., ed.

Dam, James W. Van, see Breizman, Boris N. & Van Dam, James W., eds.

Dam, Jan D. Van, see Van Dam, Jan D.

Dam, Joop Van, see Van Dam, Joop.

Dam, Kenneth W. The GATT: Law & International Economic Organization. LC 75-93088. (Midway Reprint Ser.). 1994. pap. text 25.00 (*0-226-13496-2*) U Ch Pr.

— Oil Resources: Who Gets What How? LC 75-43239. 1993. pap. text 4.95 (*0-226-13498-9*, P 776) U Ch Pr.

— Oil Resources: Who Gets What How? LC 75-43239. 1995. lib. bdg. 24.00 (*0-226-13497-0*) U Ch Pr.

— The Role of Rules in the International Monetary System. LC 76-47303. 1976. pap. 1.50 (*0-916770-03-6*) Law & Econ U Miami.

— The Rules of the Game: Reform & Evolution in the International Monetary System. 408p. 1995. pap. text 16.95 (*0-226-13501-2*, Midway Reprint) U Ch Pr.

— The Rules of the Game: Reform & Evolution in the International Monetary System. LC HG3881.D326. 400p. reprint ed. pap. 124.00 (*0-608-09441-2*, 205424100005) Bks Demand.

Dam, Kenneth W., et al, eds. Cryptography's Role in Securing the Information Society. LC 96-68943. 720p. (Orig.). 1996. 44.95 (*0-309-05475-3*) Natl Acad Pr.

Dam, Kenneth W., jt. auth. see Shultz, George P.

Dam, Mogens, ed. A Practical Approach to Epilepsy. 300p. 1991. 49.50 (*0-08-041171-1*, Pub. by PPI) McGraw.

Dam, Mogens & Gram, Lennart, eds. Comprehensive Epileptology. LC 90-8076. 864p. 1991. reprint ed. pap. 200.00 (*0-608-03401-0*, 206409800008) Bks Demand.

Dam, Mogens, ed. see Epilepsy International Symposium Staff.

Dam, Raymond Van, see Van Dam, Raymond.

Damachi, Ukandi G. Nigerian Modernization. LC 75-183394. 160p. 1972. 24.95 (*0-89388-030-2*) Okpaku Communications.

Damachi, Ukandi G. & Diejomaoh, Victor P. Human Resources & African Development. LC 78-19133. (Praeger Special Studies). 378p. 1978. 80.00 (*0-275-90289-7*, C0289, Praeger Pubs) Greenwood.

***D'Amadeus.** The Boy in the Sailor Soup. unabridged ed. 1999. pap. 15.00 (*1-929326-26-2*) Hal Bar Pubg.

Damaj, Bassam B. Immunological Reagents & Solutions: A Laboratory Handbook. (Molecular Laboratory Methods Ser.). 150p. 2000. 34.95 (*1-881299-29-5*) Eaton Pub Co.

Damalas, Holly. Trustmate. LC 97-93760. 311p. 1997. 21.95 (*0-9657959-0-X*) Bandit Books.

Daman Singh, Sarva. Ancient Indian Warfare: With Special Reference to the Vedic Period. (C). 1997. reprint ed. 22.00 (*81-208-0486-4*, Pub. by Motilal Bnarsidass) S Asia.

***Damane, E. M.** Why Bother. 165p. 1998. 29.95 (*0-86543-688-6*) Africa World.

— Why Bother. 165p. 1999. pap. 12.95 (*0-86543-689-4*) Africa World.

Damani, L. A., ed. Sulphur-Containing Drugs & Related Organic Compounds: Chemistry, Biochemistry & Toxicology: Metabolism & Pharmacokinetics of Sulpher-Containing Drugs, Vol. 3, Pt. B. (Adolescent Medicine Ser.). 1989. text 74.95 (*0-470-21514-3*) P-H.

— Sulphur Containing Drugs & Related Organic Compounds: Chemistry, Biochemistry, & Toxicology; Metabolism of Sulphur Functional Groups, Vol. 1, Pt. B. 1989. text 89.95 (*0-470-21258-6*) P-H.

— Sulphur-Containing Drugs & Related Organic Compounds Vol. 1, Pt. A: Chemistry, Biochemistry & Toxicology: Metabolism of Sulphur Functional Groups. 1989. text 89.95 (*0-470-21257-8*) P-H.

— Sulphur-Containing Drugs & Related Organic Compounds Vol. 2, Pt. A: Chemistry, Biochemistry & Toxicology: Analytical, Biochemical & Toxicological Aspects of Sulphur Xenobiochemistry. (Adolescent Medicine Ser.). 1989. text 74.95 (*0-470-21500-3*) P-H.

— Sulphur-Containing Drugs & Related Organic Compounds Vol. 2, Pt. B: Chemistry, Biochemistry & Toxicology: Analytical, Biochemical & Toxicological Aspects of Sulphur Xenobiochemistry. (Adolescent Medicine Ser.). 1989. text 74.95 (*0-470-21501-1*) P-H.

— Sulphur-Containing Drugs & Related Organic Compounds Vol. 3, Pt. A: Chemistry, Biochemistry & Toxicology: Metabolism & Pharmacokinetics of Sulphur Containing Drugs. (Adolescent Medicine Ser.). 1989. text 74.95 (*0-470-21513-5*) P-H.

Damani, L. A., jt. ed. see Gorrod, J. W.

Damania, A. B., ed. Biodiversity & Wheat Improvement. 448p. 1994. 310.00 (*0-471-94137-9*) Wiley.

Damann, George, et al. Packard. 5th ed. LC 96-14073. (Illus.). 448p. 1996. 44.95 (*0-7603-0104-2*, Crestline Pub) MBI Pubg.

Damanpour, Faramarz. The Evolution of Foreign Banking Institutions in the United States. LC 89-10692. 265p. 1990. 67.95 (*0-89930-371-4*, DFB/, Greenwood Pr) Greenwood.

D'Amante, Elvo S. All about Chords: A Comprehensive Approach to Understanding Contemporary Chordal Structures & Progressions Through Solid Drills in Suggested Study Questions, Keyboard Drills, & Ear-Training Exercises. LC 88-24571. (Illus.). 120p. (Orig.). (C). 1988. pap. 14.95 (*0-9620941-0-2*) Encore Music Pub Co.

— Music Fundamentals: Pitch Structures & Rhythmic Design. (C). 1994. pap. text 35.95 (*1-880157-12-8*) Ardsley.

— Music Fundamentals: Through Pitch Structures & Rhythmic Design. 1994. pap. text, teacher ed. 10.95 (*1-880157-22-5*) Ardsley.

D'Amario, Patricia, jt. auth. see Bunting, Elaine.

Damas, David. Bountiful Island: A Study of Land Tenure on a Micronesian Atoll. (Illus.). xvi, 272p. (C). 1994. text 45.00 (*0-88920-239-7*) W Laurier U Pr.

Damas, David & Sturtevant, William C., eds. Arctic: Handbook of North American Indians, Vol. 5. LC 77-17162. (Illus.). 862p. 1985. 52.00 (*0-87474-185-8*, DAV5) Smithsonian.

Damas, David, jt. auth. see Sturtevant, William C.

Damas, Luis, jt. ed. see Filgueiras, Miguel.

Damascelli, D., et al, eds. Basic Concepts in Diagnostic Imaging. LC 90-9104. (Bracco R & D Monograph Ser.). (Illus.). 169p. 1991. reprint ed. pap. 52.40 (*0-608-05847-5*, 205981300007) Bks Demand.

Damascene. Christ the Eternal Tao. 1999. pap. text 19.00 (*0-938635-85-9*) St Herman Pr.

Damascene, John & Seventh Oecumenical Synod Staff. The Icon: It's Spiritual Basis & Purpose. Cavarnos, Constantine, tr. from GRE. (Illus.). 11p. 1999. pap. 2.00 (*0-914744-19-4*) Inst Byzantine.

Damasceno, Leslie. Cultural Space & Theatrical Conventions in the Works of Oduvaldo Vianna Filho. (Latin American Literature & Culture Ser.). (SPA., Illus.). 292p. 1996. 44.95 (*0-8143-2595-5*) Wayne St U Pr.

Damascenus, Nicolaus. On the Philosophy of Aristotle: Fragments of the First Five Books. 1969. pap. 34.00 (*90-04-01725-9*, PHA, 13) Brill Academic Pubs.

Damascus, John, et al. Sign of the Cross. 1987. pap. 1.00 (*0-89981-200-7*) Eastern Orthodox.

Damase, Jacques. Les Folies du Music Hall. (Univers Fableux Collection). (FRE., Illus.). 192p. 1960. lib. bdg. 24.95 (*0-8288-3934-4*) Fr & Eur.

— Sonia Delaunay: Fashion & Fabrics. LC 96-61494. (Illus.). 176p. 1997. pap. 34.95 (*0-500-27947-0*, Pub. by Thames Hudson) Norton.

Damashek, Barbara, jt. auth. see Newman, Molly.

Damashek, Marc, tr. see Lozinskaya, Tatjana A.

Damashek, Sandra. What Can You Do on Christmas Day? (Illus.). 12p. (J). 1998. 6.99 (*0-8054-1666-8*) Broadman.

Damashek, Sandra & Floyd-Jones, Salley. What Do Ducklings Do? (Illus.). 14p. (J). 1999. bds. 6.99 (*0-8054-1668-4*) Broadman.

Damasio, A. R., et al, eds. Neurobiology of Decision-Making. (Research & Perspectives in Neurosciences Ser.). 192p. 1995. 108.00 (*3-540-60143-0*) Spr-Verlag.

Damasio, Antonio. Descartes' Error: Emotion, Reason, & the Human Brain. (Illus.). 320p. 1994. 24.95 (*0-399-13894-3*, Grosset-Putnam) Putnam Pub Group.

— The Feeling of What Happens: Body & Emotion in the Making of Consciousness. LC 99-26357. 384p. (C). 1999. 28.00 (*0-15-100369-6*, Harvest Bks) Harcourt.

Damasio, Antonio R. Descartes' Error: Emotion, Reason & the Human Brain. 336p. 1995. pap. 13.50 (*0-380-72647-5*, Avon Bks) Morrow Avon.

***Damasio, Antonio R.** The Feeling of What Happens: Body & Emotion in the Making of Consciousness. (Illus.). 400p. 2000. pap. 15.00 (*0-15-601075-5*) Harcourt.

Damasio, Antonio R., jt. auth. see Damasio, Hanna.

Damasio, Antonio R., jt. ed. see Goodglass, H.

Damasio, Hanna. Human Brain Anatomy in Computerized Images. (Illus.). 304p. 1995. text 95.00 (*0-19-508204-4*) OUP.

Damasio, Hanna & Damasio, Antonio R. Lesion Analysis in Neuropsychology. (Illus.). 256p. 1989. text 59.50 (*0-19-503919-X*) OUP.

Damask, A., jt. auth. see Garcia, Nicholas.

Damask, Arthur C., et al. Injury Causation Analyses: Case Studies & Data Sources, 2. 150.00 (*0-327-12270-6*) LEXIS Pub.

An Asterisk (*) at the beginning of an entry indicates that the title is appearing for the first time.

Damask, Arthur C., et al. Injury Causation Analyses: Cases Studies & Data Sources, 2 vols., Set. 381p. 1990. 150.00 (*0-87473-660-9*, 61159-10, MICHIE) LEXIS Pub.

Damask, Arthur C., jt. ed. see Bohan, Thomas L.

Damaska, Mirjan R. Evidence Law Adrift. LC 96-39928. 224p. 1997. 30.00 (*0-300-06937-5*) Yale U Pr.

— The Faces of Justice & State Authority: A Comparative Approach to the Legal Process. 262p. (C). 1991. reprint ed. pap. 20.00 (*0-300-05119-0*) Yale U Pr.

— The Faces of Justice & State Authority: A Comparative Study of the Legal Process. LC 86-7729. 288p. 1986. 40.00 (*0-300-03567-5*) Yale U Pr.

Damaske, Charles H. Along the Right-of-Way to East Troy. (Illus.). 200p. (Orig.). 1989. pap. text. write for info. (*0-318-64881-4*) C H Damaske.

Damaskin, Boris B., et al. Absorption of Organic Compounds on Electrodes. Uvarov, E. Boris & Parsons, Roger, trs. from RUS. LC 69-17533. (Illus.). 515p. 1971. reprint ed. pap. 159.70 (*0-608-05487-9*, 206595600006) Bks Demand.

D'Amato, Al. Power, Pasta & Politics: The World According to Senator Al D'Amato. LC 95-9429. 384p. (J). 1996. reprint ed. pap. 12.45 (*0-7868-8182-8*, Pub. by Hyperion) Time Warner.

D'Amato, Alex, jt. auth. see D'Amato, Janet.

D'Amato, Alfonse, ed. The Homeowners Protection Act of 1997, S.318. (Illus.). 144p. 1999. reprint ed. pap. text 30.00 (*0-7881-8059-2*) DIANE Pub.

— Religious Intolerance in Europe Today: Hearing Before the Commission on Security & Cooperation in Europe. (Illus.). 164p. (C). 1999. reprint ed. pap. text 35.00 (*0-7881-7712-5*) DIANE Pub.

D'Amato, Alfonse M. Power, Pasta & Politics: The World According to Senator Al D'Amato. Orig. Title: Enough Is Enough. 384p. (J). 1995. 24.45 (*0-7868-6045-6*, Pub. by Hyperion) Time Warner.

***D'Amato, Alfonse M., ed.** Derivatives Disclosure & Accounting: Congressional Hearing. (Illus.). 436p. (C). 1999. reprint ed. pap. text 50.00 (*0-7881-8269-2*) DIANE Pub.

— The Federal Mass Transit Program & the Reauthorization of the Intermodal Surface Transportation Efficiency Act (ISTEA): Congressional Hearing. 123p. (C). 2000. pap. text 25.00 (*0-7881-8502-0*) DIANE Pub.

D'Amato, Alfonse M., ed. Swiss Banks & the Status of Assets of Holocaust Survivors or Heirs: Hearing Before the Committee on Banking, Housing, & Urban Affairs, U. S. Senate. 73p. (C). 1998. pap. text 25.00 (*0-7881-4954-7*) DIANE Pub.

Damato, Anthony. The Flounder Complex. 1968. pap. 3.25 (*0-8222-0410-X*) Dramatists Play.

D'Amato, Anthony. International Law: Process & Prospect. 2nd ed. 373p. (C). 1995. lib. bdg. 75.00 (*0-941320-84-7*) Transnatl Pubs.

— International Law & Political Reality: Collected Papers. LC 95-15796. 1995. 95.00 (*90-411-0036-9*) Kluwer Law Intl.

— International Law Coursebook. 400p. (C). 1994. 47.00 (*0-87084-420-2*) Anderson Pub Co.

— An Introduction to Law & Legal Thinking. Orig. Title: How to Understand the Law. 190p. (Orig.). 1996. pap. 30.00 (*1-57105-015-9*) Transnatl Pubs.

— Jurisprudence: A Descriptive & Normative Analysis of Law. LC 83-24964. 1984. lib. bdg. 136.50 (*90-247-2919-X*) Kluwer Academic.

D'Amato, Anthony, ed. Analytic Jurisprudence Anthology. LC 95-49866. 289p. 1995. pap. 29.95 (*0-87084-018-5*) Anderson Pub Co.

— International Law Anthology. LC 93-47686. 448p. 1994. pap. 19.90 (*0-87084-360-5*) Anderson Pub Co.

D'Amato, Anthony & Engel, Kirsten, eds. International Environmental Law Anthology. LC 96-124573. 702p. 1995. pap. 32.95 (*0-87084-375-3*) Anderson Pub Co.

D'Amato, Anthony & Long, Doris E., eds. International Intellectual Property Anthology. LC 96-7025. 604p. 1996. pap. 29.95 (*0-87084-373-7*) Anderson Pub Co.

— International Intellectual Property Law. LC 97-195573. 688p. 1997. 152.00 (*90-411-0694-4*) Kluwer Academic.

D'Amato, Anthony, jt. auth. see Steinhart, Ralph G.

D'Amato, Anthony, jt. ed. see Clark, David S.

D'Amato, Anthony, jt. ed. see Kole, Karen V.

D'Amato, Antionette. Cooking & Canning with Mamma D'Amato. LC 97-654. 160p. 1997. 15.95 (*0-06-039206-1*, ReganBks) HarperTrade.

***D'Amato, Barbara.** Authorized Personnel Only. 2000. text 24.95 (*0-312-86564-3*) St Martin.

D'Amato, Barbara. The Doctor, the Murder, the Mystery: The True Story of the Dr. John Branion Murder Case. 432p. 1997. mass mkt. 6.99 (*0-425-15624-9*, Prime Crime) Berkley Pub.

— The Doctor, the Murder, the Mystery: The True Story of the Dr. John Branion Murder Case. LC 91-51217. (Illus.). 319p. 1992. 20.95 (*1-879360-13-6*) Noble Pr.

— The Doctor, the Murder, the Mystery: The True Story of the Dr. John Branion Murder Case. LC 92-51081. (Illus.). 319p. 1993. reprint ed. pap. 11.95 (*1-879360-28-4*) Noble Pr.

— Good Cop, Bad Cop. 304p. 1999. mass mkt. 6.99 (*0-8125-9014-7*, Pub. by Forge NYC) St Martin.

— Hard Bargain: A Cat Marsala Mystery, 1 vol. 288p. 1999. mass mkt. 5.99 (*0-425-16898-0*) Berkley Pub.

— Hard Bargain: A Cat Marsala Mystery. LC 97-20622. 281 p. 1997. 20.50 (*0-684-83353-0*) S&S Trade.

— Hard Case. 240p. (Orig.). 1995. pap. 4.99 (*0-425-15009-7*, Prime Crime) Berkley Pub.

— Hard Christmas: A Cat Marsala Mystery. 288p. 1996. mass mkt. 5.99 (*0-425-15465-3*, Prime Crime) Berkley Pub.

— Hard Christmas: A Cat Marsala Mystery. 288p. 1995. 20.00 (*0-684-19687-5*) S&S Trade.

***D'Amato, Barbara.** Hard Evidence: A Cat Marsala Mystery. (Cat Marsala Mysteries Ser.). (Illus.). 255p. 2000. mass mkt. 6.50 (*0-425-17412-3*, Prime Crime) Berkley Pub.

D'Amato, Barbara. Hard Evidence: A Cat Marsala Mystery. LC 98-31785. 256p. 1999. 21.50 (*0-684-83354-9*) Scribner.

***D'Amato, Barbara.** Hard Evidence: A Cat Marsala Mystery. large type ed. LC 00-22866. (Wheeler Large Print Bks.). 2000. pap. 22.95 (*1-56895-861-7*) Wheeler Pub.

D'Amato, Barbara. Hard Luck: A Cat Marsala Mystery. (Mystery Ser.). 1993. per. 3.99 (*0-373-26124-1*, 1-26124-7) Harlequin Bks.

— Hard Luck: A Cat Marsala Mystery. 224p. 1992. text 20.00 (*0-684-19408-2*, Scribners Ref) Mac Lib Ref.

— Hard Tack: A Cat Marsala Mystery. (Worldwide Library Mysteries: No. 97). 1992. per. 3.99 (*0-373-26097-0*, 1-26097-5) Harlequin Bks.

— Hard Women: A Cat Marsala Mystery. 1994. per. 3.99 (*0-373-26150-0*, 1-26150-2) Harlequin Bks.

— Hardball. (Illus.). 1993. per. 3.99 (*0-373-83302-4*, 1-83302-9) Harlequin Bks.

***D'Amato, Barbara.** Help Me Please. 2nd ed. LC 99-22195. 336p. 1999. 23.95 (*0-312-86563-5*, Pub. by Forge NYC) St Martin.

D'Amato, Barbara. Killer.app. 1997. mass mkt. 5.99 (*0-8125-5391-8*, Pub. by Forge NYC) St Martin.

***D'Amato, Barbara.** Of Course you Know That Chocolate is a Vegetable & Other Stories. LC 00-24236. (Standard Print Mystery Ser.). 243p. 2000. 20.95 (*0-7862-2539-4*) Five Star.

***Damato, Bertil.** Ocular Tumours. (Illus.). 288p. 2000. 99.00 (*0-7506-2220-2*) Buttrwrth-Heinemann.

D'Amato, Donald. Block Island. (Images of America Ser.). (Illus.). 128p. 1998. pap. 16.99 (*0-7524-0486-5*) Arcadia Publng.

— Warwick. (Images of America Ser.). 128p. 1996. pap. 16.99 (*0-7524-0265-X*) Arcadia Publng.

D'Amato, Donald & Brown, Henry. Pawtuxet. (Images of America Ser.). 1997. pap. 16.99 (*0-7524-0588-8*) Arcadia Publng.

D'Amato, Donald A. Warwick's Three Hundred Fifty Year Heritage: A Pictorial History. LC 92-21790. 1992. write for info. (*0-89865-845-4*) Donning Co.

D'Amato, Donald A. & Tarantino, Richard A. Johnson & Wales: The Making of America's Career University. LC 98-23594. 1998. write for info. (*1-57864-038-5*) Donning Co.

D'Amato, Francesco. Nuclear Cytology in Relation to Development. LC 76-46045. (Developmental & Cell Biology Ser.: No. 6). 291p. reprint ed. pap. 83.00 (*0-608-15709-0*, 2031636) Bks Demand.

D'Amato, Gary & Christl, Cliff. Mudbaths & Bloodbaths: The Inside Story of the Bears-Packers Rivalry. LC 97-27098. (Illus.). 288p. 1997. 25.00 (*1-879483-41-6*); pap. 16.95 (*1-879483-44-0*) Prairie Oak Pr.

D'Amato, Gary, jt. auth. see Gentile, Domenic.

D'Amato, Guy A. Portraits of Ideas. (Illus.). 220p. 1977. 22.95 (*0-8369-8014-X*) Ayer.

D'Amato, James J. The Perpetuality of Marriage: A Matter of Faith. DeStefano, Josephine, ed. 33p. 1994. 14.95 (*0-9621266-3-2*) IPPD.

— Work & Stress: A Report on How Work Stress Can Affect the Quality of Life. De Stefano, Josephine & Buomaupina, Maryann, eds. 250p. 1988. 26.95 (*0-9621266-0-8*) IPPD.

D'Amato, Janet & D'Amato, Alex. Cardboard Carpentry. (Activity Bks.). (Illus.). (J). (gr. 2-5). 1966. lib. bdg. 13.95 (*0-87460-085-5*) Lion Bks.

— Handicrafts for Holidays. (Illus.). (J). (gr. 1-4). 1967. lib. bdg. 13.95 (*0-87460-086-3*) Lion Bks.

— Indian Crafts. (Illus.). (J). (gr. 2-5). 1968. lib. bdg. 13.95 (*0-87460-088-X*) Lion Bks.

— Native American Craft Inspirations. LC 92-35721. (Illus.). 224p. 1992. pap. 11.95 (*0-87131-707-9*) M Evans.

D'Amato, Peter. The Savage Garden: Cultivating Carnivorous Plants. (Illus.). 314p. 1998. pap. 19.95 (*0-89815-915-6*) Ten Speed Pr.

D'Amato, R., et al. Relevance of Animal Studies to the Evaluation of Human Cancer Risk. (Progress in Clinical & Biological Research Ser.). 482p. 1992. 350.00 (*0-471-56183-5*, Wiley-Interscience) Wiley.

D'Amato, R. C. & Dean, R. S., eds. The School Psychologist in Nontraditional Settings: Integrating Clients, Services, & Settings. 240p. 1989. 49.95 (*0-89859-996-2*) L Erlbaum Assocs.

D'Amato, Rik C. & Rothlisberg, Barbara A. Psychological Perspectives on Intervention: A Case Study Approach to Prescriptions for Change. (Illus.). 211p. (C). 1997. reprint ed. pap. text 15.95 (*0-88133-974-1*) Waveland Pr.

***D'Amato, Robert & Snyder, Joan.** Macular Degeneration: A Comprehensive Guide to Treatment, Breakthroughs & Coping Strategies. (Illus.). 192p. 2000. pap. 14.95 (*0-8027-1359-9*) Walker & Co.

DaMatta, Roberto. Carnivals, Rogues, & Heroes: An Interpretation of the Brazilian Dilemma. Drury, John, tr. LC 90-70861. (From the Helen Kellogg Institute for International Studies). (C). 1992. pap. text 19.50 (*0-268-00794-2*) U of Notre Dame Pr.

Damazio, Frank. Breaking the Bands of Barrenness. 197p. 1998. 16.99 (*0-8307-2337-4*, Regal Bks) Gospel Lght.

***Damazio, Frank.** Commentary on Colossians. 2000. pap. text 12.99 (*1-886849-72-2*) City Bible Pub.

— Crossing Rivers, Taking Cities: Lessons from Joshua on Reaching Cities for Christ. LC 99-23086. 303p. 1999. pap. 12.99 (*0-8307-2392-7*, Regal Bks) Gospel Lght.

Damazio, Frank. Developing the Prophetic Ministry. 76p. 1983. pap. 8.99 (*0-914936-85-9*) City Bible Pub.

— Effective Keys to Successful Leadership. 207p. 1993. pap. 10.50 (*0-914936-54-9*) City Bible Pub.

***Damazio, Frank.** Foundation Truth. (Foundation Truth Ser.). 2000. pap. text, teacher ed. 17.00 (*1-886849-33-1*) City Bible Pub.

— Foundation Truth: Students. (Foundation Truth Ser.). 2000. pap. text 13.00 (*1-886849-32-3*) City Bible Pub.

— From Barrenness to Fruitfulness: Restoration for the Heart & Soul of Leaders. LC 98-19263. 197p. 1998. pap. 10.99 (*0-8307-2369-2*, Regal Bks) Gospel Lght.

— Gate Church: Unlocking Heaven's Door for Your Community. 275p. 2000. 17.99 (*1-886849-75-7*) City Bible Pub.

— Harvesting Church Seminar: Syllabus. 2000. pap. text 13.00 (*1-886849-38-2*) City Bible Pub.

Damazio, Frank. The Lay Pastor Training Manual. 107p. 1997. pap., teacher ed. 21.99 (*1-886849-05-6*); pap., student ed. 14.99 (*1-886849-06-4*) City Bible Pub.

— The Making of a Leader. 332p. 1988. pap. 21.99 (*0-914936-84-0*) City Bible Pub.

— The Making of a Leader Study Guide. 50p. 1991. pap., student ed. 6.99 (*0-914936-57-3*) City Bible Pub.

***Damazio, Frank.** Maximizing Your Leadership Potential: Syllabus. 2000. pap. 13.00 (*1-886849-42-0*) City Bible Pub.

— Maximizing Your Vision Potential: Syllabus. 2000. pap. 13.00 (*1-886849-45-5*) City Bible Pub.

— Maximizing Your Warfare Potential: Syllabus. 2000. pap. 13.00 (*1-886849-47-1*) City Bible Pub.

— Prophetic Church Seminar. 2000. pap. text 13.00 (*1-886849-52-8*) City Bible Pub.

Damazio, Frank. Seasons of Intercession. 222p. 1998. pap. 12.99 (*1-886849-11-0*) City Bible Pub.

— Seasons of Revival: Understanding the Appointed Times of Spiritual Refreshing, Bk. 1. LC 97-201755. (Illus.). 409p. 1996. pap. 14.99 (*1-886849-04-8*) City Bible Pub.

— Timothy Training Program-Students. 57p. 1994. spiral bd. 10.99 (*0-914936-13-1*) City Bible Pub.

— Timothy Training Program-Teachers. 77p. 1994. spiral bd. 13.99 (*0-914936-12-3*) City Bible Pub.

— The Vanguard Leader. 320p. 1994. pap. 13.99 (*0-914936-53-0*) City Bible Pub.

Dambacher, M., jt. ed. see Broell, H.

Dambacher, M. A., jt. ed. see Broell, H.

Dambacher, P. Digital Terrestrial Television Broadcasting: Design & Operation. LC 98-6383. (Illus.). 290p. 1998. 89.95 (*3-540-63918-7*) Spr-Verlag.

Dambacher, Paul. Digital Broadcasting. (IEE Telecommunications Ser.: No. 34). 336p. 1996. boxed set 92.00 (*0-85296-873-6*) INSPEC Inc.

D'Amboise, Gerald. The Canadian Small & Medium-Sized Enterprise: Situation & Challenges. 230p. 1991. 23.00 (*0-88645-121-3*, Pub. by Inst Res Pub) Ashgate Pub Co.

D'Amboise, Jacqueline, tr. see Breton, Andre.

D'Amboise, Valery. Dictionnaire d'Amboise Pays de Savoie, 23 vols. (FRE.). 1988. pap. 2750.00 (*0-7859-8222-1*, 2903795134) Fr & Eur.

D'Ambra, Eve. Private Lives, Imperial Virtues: The Frieze of the Forum Transitorium in Rome. LC 92-11126. (Illus.). 250p. (C). 1993. text 39.50 (*0-691-04097-4*, Pub. by Princeton U Pr) Cal Prin Full Svc.

— Roman Art. LC 99-166514. (Illus.). 176p. 1999. pap. 18.95 (*0-521-64463-1*) Cambridge U Pr.

— Roman Art in Context: An Anthology. 256p. 1993. pap. text 21.80 (*0-13-781808-4*) P-H.

***Dambra, Gilles.** Measure Your EQ Factor: Discover & Develop Your Emotional Potential. 2000. pap. 11.95 (*0-572-02538-6*) W Foulsham.

D'Ambra, Michael & Alston, Theodore A. Hematology & Heart Surgery. 1999. 125.00 (*0-89603-723-1*) Humana.

Dambre, Marc. La Symphonie Pastorale et la Porte Etroite De Gide. (FRE.). 214p. 1991. pap. 12.95 (*0-7859-2181-8*, 2070384403) Fr & Eur.

***Dambriunas, Leonardus, et al.** Beginner's Lithuanian. (LIT.). 320p. 1998. reprint ed. pap. 19.95 (*0-7818-0678-X*) Hippocrene Bks.

Dambro, Amy L., et al. Community Mobilization: Strategies to Support Young Children & Their Families. 371p. (Orig.). 1996. pap. 22.00 (*1-888324-03-1*) Families & Work.

Dambro, M., jt. auth. see Griffith, H. Winter.

Dambro, Mark C. Griffith's 5-Minute Clinical Consultant, 1996. 1995. 54.95 (*0-683-02320-9*) Lppncott W & W.

Dambro, Mark R. The Five Minute Clinical Consult, 1995. Griffith, Jo, ed. 1252p. 1994. 52.95 (*0-683-03741-2*) Lppncott W & W.

— Griffith's 5 Minute Clinical Consult 1998. 1997. 54.95 (*0-683-30405-4*) Lppncott W & W.

— Griffith's 5 Minute Clinical Consult, 1998. 1997. write for info. (*0-683-23136-7*) Lppncott W & W.

Dambro, Mark R. Griffith's 5 Minute Clinical Consult 1999. 7th ed. 1,345p. 1999. 99.00 (*0-7817-2063-X*); text 54.95 (*0-7817-2011-7*) Lppncott W & W.

— Griffith's 5-Minute Clinical Consult, 2000. 1392p. 139.00 (*0-7817-2463-5*) Lppncott W & W.

— Griffith's 5 Minute Clinical Consult, 2001. 1400p. text 54.95 (*0-7817-2565-8*) Lppncott W & W.

***Dambro, Mark R., ed.** Griffith's 5 Minute Clinical Consult, 2000. 1344p. 2000. 54.95 (*0-7817-2436-8*) Lppncott W & W.

Dambro, Mark R. & Goldfarb, Bruce. The Five Minute Health Advisor. LC 97-24984. 527p. 1997. pap. 19.95 (*0-683-30435-6*) Lppncott W & W.

Dambro, Mark R., jt. ed. see Griffith, H. Winter.

D'Ambrogio, Kerry J. & Roth, George B. Positional Release Therapy: Assessment & Treatment of Musculoskeletol Dysfunction. (Illus.). 280p. (C). (gr. 13). 1997. text 79.95 (*0-8151-0096-5*, 26559) Mosby Inc.

D'Ambrosi, Sybil, et al. Quintessence. Bayes, Ron, ed. 114p. (Orig.). 1991. pap. 9.95 (*0-932662-57-9*) St Andrews NC.

D'Ambrosio, Anna T. The Distinction of Being Different: Joseph P. McHugh & the American Arts & Crafts Movement. (Illus.). 64p. 1993. 19.95 (*0-915895-15-3*) Munson Williams.

***D'Ambrosio, Anna Tobin, ed.** Masterpieces of American Furniture from the Munson-Williams-Proctor Institute. LC 98-45261. (Illus.). 171p. 1999. 50.00 (*0-8156-8127-5*) Syracuse U Pr.

d'Ambrosio, Antonio, jt. auth. see Guzzo, Piero Giovanni.

D'Ambrosio, Bobbe, et al. Spell Well. (Makemaster Bk.). (J). (gr. 1-6). 1980. pap. 12.99 (*0-8224-6455-1*) Fearon Teacher Aids.

D'Ambrosio, Carlo. In Passing: Poems. (Hummingbird Publications). 44p. 1998. pap. 5.00 (*1-886841-09-8*) Skylnds Writ & Artists.

D'Ambrosio, Charles. The Point. 256p. 1996. pap. 11.95 (*0-316-17125-5*) Little.

***D'Ambrosio, Charles.** The Point. 1998. pap. 11.95 (*0-316-19095-0*, Back Bay) Little.

D'Ambrosio, Margaret. Meggie's Journeys. LC 88-61446. 175p. (Orig.). 1988. pap. 10.95 (*0-685-31954-7*) Dufour.

D'Ambrosio, Paul S. & Emans, Charlotte S. Folk Art's Many Faces: Portraits in the New York State Historical Association. 1987. pap. 19.95 (*0-917334-15-9*) New York State College of.

Dambrosio, Richard A. No Language but a Cry. (Laurel-Leaf Library). (J). 1971. 11.09 (*0-606-04186-9*, Pub. by Turtleback) Demco.

D'Ambrumenil, Peter. Mediation & Arbitration. (Medico-Legal Practitioner Ser.). 154p. 1997. 72.00 (*1-85941-155-X*, 15671, Pub. by Cavendish Pubng) Gaunt.

***Dambska.** Normal & Pathologic Development of the Human Brain & Spinal Cord. 212p. 1999. pap. 79.00 (*0-86196-591-4*, Pub. by J Libbey Med) Bks Intl VA.

Dame, Enid. Anything You Don't See. 51p. (Orig.). 1992. pap. 6.95 (*0-931122-67-8*) West End.

— Confessions. Barkan, Stanley H., ed. (Cross-Cultural Review Chapbook Ser.: No. 12: American Poetry 6). 16p. 1980. 15.00 (*0-89304-730-9*, CCC139); pap. 5.00 (*0-89304-811-9*); audio 10.00 (*0-89304-836-4*) Cross-Cultrl NY.

— Lilith & Her Demons. Barkan, Stanley H., ed. (Review Woman Writers Chapbook Ser.: No. 2). 20p. 1989. reprint ed. 15.00 (*0-89304-405-9*, CCC161); reprint ed. 15.00 (*0-89304-407-5*); reprint ed. pap. 5.00 (*0-89304-406-7*); reprint ed. pap. 5.00 (*0-89304-408-3*) Cross-Cultrl NY.

— Monologhi: Fatti e Fantasie di Donne Detti Spudoratemente. Scammacca, Nina, tr. (Monologues Ser.: Women of Fact & Fancy Speak Their Minds). (ENG & ITA., Illus.). 95p. 1989. 25.00 (*0-89304-069-X*); pap. 10.00 (*0-89304-070-3*) Cross-Cultrl NY.

Dame, Enid, et al, eds. Which Lilith? Feminist Writers Re-Create the World's First Woman. LC 98-9252. 411p. 1998. 40.00 (*0-7657-6015-0*) Aronson.

Dame, Frederick W. Jean-Jacques Rousseau & Political Literature in Colonial America. LC 95-23504. 144p. 1996. write for info. (*0-7734-8919-3*) E Mellen.

— Jean-Jacques Rousseau in American Literature, Traces, Influence, Transformation, 1760-1860: A Paradigm of French-German Culture Emanation in America. LC 96-10172. (European University Papers, Series XIV: Vol. 310). 428p. 1996. pap. 69.95 (*0-8204-2970-8*, PS159) P Lang Pubng.

***Dame, Frederick W.** Jean-Jacques Rousseau on Adult Education & Revolution: Paradigma of Radical, Pedagogical Thought. 2nd rev. ed. 244p. 1999. pap. 39.95 (*3-631-34902-5*) P Lang Pubng.

Dame, Frederick W. Jean-Jacques Rousseau on Adult Education & Revolution: Paradigma of Radical, Pedagogical Thought. 2nd rev. ed. LC 99-28094. 244p. 1999. pap. 39.95 (*0-8204-4338-7*) P Lang Pubng.

Dame, Kevin T. Fenway in Your Pocket: The Red Sox Fan's Guide to Fenway Park. rev. ed. (Illus.). 126p. (Orig.). 1998. pap. 6.95 (*0-9640946-0-6*) Baseball Direct.

Dame, L. Yucatan. 1976. lib. bdg. 59.95 (*0-8490-2854-X*) Gordon Pr.

Dame, L. Thomas, jt. auth. see Stouffer, Donald C.

Dame, Lauren & Wolfe, Sidney M. The Failure of Private Hospital Regulation. 52p. (Orig.). 1996. pap. 15.00 (*0-937188-47-6*) Pub Citizen.

— Patient Dumping in Hospital Emergency Rooms. 18p. (Orig.). 1996. pap. 10.00 (*0-937188-06-9*) Pub Citizen.

Dame, Melvina A. Serving Linguistically & Culturally Diverse Students: Strategies for the School Library Media Specialist. 175p. 1993. 27.50 (*1-55570-116-7*) Neal-Schuman.

Dame of Sark. Dame of Sark: An Autobiography. Hathaway, ed. (Jersey Heritage Editions Ser.), 1991. write for info. (*0-86120-013-6*, Pub. by Aris & Phillips) David Brown.

Dame, Richard F. Ecology of Marine Bivalves: An Ecosystem Approach. LC 96-11641. (Marine Science Ser.). 272p. 1996. boxed set 104.95 (*0-8493-8045-6*) CRC Pr.

Dame, Richard F., ed. Bivalve Filter Feeders: In Estuarine & Coastal Ecosystem Processes. (NATO ASI Series G: Ecological Sciences: Vol. 33). (Illus.). vi, 580p. 1993. write for info. (*3-540-56952-9*) Spr-Verlag.

— Bivalve Filter Feeders in Estuarine & Coastal Ecosystem Processes. LC 93-28010. (NATO ASI Series G: Ecological Sciences: Series G, Vol. 33). 1993. 309.95 (*0-387-56952-9*) Spr-Verlag.

Damelio, Dan. Silvabamba. 1977. 16.60 (*0-606-02430-1*, Pub. by Turtleback) Demco.

D'Amelio, Dennis P. All Aboard the Alphabet Train. (Right Track Bks.: Vol. 3). (Illus.). (J). (ps). 1998. pap. write for info. (*1-891528-61-0*) Telescopic Pr.

— Colored Cars. (Right Track Bks.: Vol. 4). (Illus.). 24p. (J). (ps-3). 1998. pap. write for info. (*1-891528-66-1*) Telescopic Pr.

D

— Counting Cars. (Right Track Bks.: Vol. 1). (Illus.). (J). (ps). 1998. pap. write for info. (1-891528-50-5) Telescopic Pr.

— The Last Bear. (Illus.). 26p. (J). 1998. pap. write for info. (1-891528-71-8) Telescopic Pr.

— Shape Train Coming. (Right Track Bks.: Vol. 2). (Illus.). (J). (ps). 1998. pap. write for info. (1-891528-55-6) Telescopic Pr.

D'Amelio, Frank S., Sr. Botanical Phytocosmetic Desk Reference. LC 98-43782. 376p. 1998. boxed set 129.95 (0-8493-2118-2) CRC Pr.

D'Amelio, Joseph. Perspective Drawing Handbook. LC 83-12399. (Illus.). 96p. 1984. pap. 34.95 (0-442-21828-1, VNR) Wiley.

D'Amelio, Joseph. Perspective Drawing Handbook. (Illus.). 96p. 1984. pap. 34.95 (0-471-28873-X, VNR) Wiley.

Damelio, Robert. The Basics of Benchmarking. LC 96-119782. (Illus.). 74p. 1995. pap. 7.95 (0-527-76301-2, 763012) Productivity Inc.

— The Basics of Process Mapping. 77p. 1996. pap. 7.95 (0-527-76316-0) Productivity Inc.

Damelio, Robert & Englehaupt, William. An Action Guide to Making Quality Happen. LC 95-1340. 184p. 1995. pap. 26.00 (0-527-76291-1) Productivity Inc.

Damen, et al. Remote Sensing for Resources Development, Vol. 2. 1986. 168.00 (90-6191-676-3) Ashgate Pub Co.

Damen, M. C., et al, eds. Remote Sensing for Resources Development & Environmental Management: Proceedings of the 7th International Symposium, ISPRS Commission VII, Enschede, 25-29 August 1986, 3 vols., Set. 1300p. (C). 1986. text 459.00 (90-6191-674-7, Pub. by A A Balkema) Ashgate Pub Co.

Dameon. Damron Amsterdam: The Complete Guide to Amsterdam. 185p. 1997. pap. 9.95 (0-929435-28-1) Damron Co.

Damer. Attacking Faulty Reasoning. (Philosophy Ser.). 1980. pap. 9.50 (0-534-00750-3) Wadsworth Pub.

— Glasgow: Going for a Song. (C). 1990. pap. 17.50 (0-85315-727-8, Pub. by Lawrence & Wishart) NYU Pr.

Damer, Bruce. Avatars! Exploring & Building Virtual Worlds on the Internet. LC 98-119898. (Illus.). 592p. 1997. pap. 39.95 incl. cd-rom (0-201-68840-9) Peachpit Pr.

Damer, Eyre. When the Ku Klux Rode. LC 79-37588. (Black Heritage Library Collection). 1977. reprint ed. 23.95 (0-8369-8964-3) Ayer.

Damer, Mary, jt. auth. see McEwan, Elaine K.

Damer, Sean. From Moorepark to 'Wine Alley' The Rise & Fall of a Glasgow Housing Scheme. (Edinburgh Education & Society Ser.). 256p. 1989. 60.00 (0-85224-622-6, Pub. by Edinburgh U Pr) Col U Pr.

— From Moorepark to "Wine Alley" The Rise & Fall of a Glasgow Housing Scheme. 216p. 1991. pap. text 25.00 (0-85224-657-9, Pub. by Edinburgh U Pr) Col U Pr.

Damer, T. Edward. Attacking Faulty Reasoning. 2nd ed. 166p. (C). 1986. pap. 18.95 (0-534-07614-9) Wadsworth Pub.

— Attacking Faulty Reasoning: A Practical Guide to Fallacy-Free Arguments. 3rd ed. LC 94-15081. 200p. 1994. pap. 36.95 (0-534-21750-8) Wadsworth Pub.

*__Damer, T. Edward.__ Attacking Faulty Reasoning: A Practical Guide to Fallacy-Free Arguments. 4th ed. LC 00-36664. 2001. write for info. (0-534-55133-5) Wadsworth Pub.

Damerau, Burghard, jt. auth. see Brautigam, Bernd.

Damerau, Frederick J. Markov Models & Linguistic Theory: An Experimental Study of a Model for English. LC 78-135666. (Janua Linguarum, Ser. Minor: No. 95). (Orig.). 1971. pap. text 53.85 (90-279-1707-8) Mouton.

Damerell, Reginald G. Education's Smoking Gun: How Teachers Colleges Have Destroyed Education in America. LC 85-10113. 312p. 1985. 17.95 (0-88191-025-2) Freundlich.

Damerest, Nancy, ed. see McCann, Yvette B.

Dameron, jt. auth. see Salak.

Dameron, Dave. Benning's Brigade Vol. 1: A History & Roster of the Fifteenth Georgia. LC 96-6977. 1996. reprint ed. 24.00 (0-87152-498-8) Reprint.

Dameron, George W. Episcopal Power & Florentine Society, 1000-1320. LC 90-36715. (Historical Studies: No. 107). (Illus.). 296p. 1991. 45.00 (0-674-25891-6, DAMEPI) HUP.

Dameron, J. Lasley. Popular Literature: Poe's Not So Soon Forgotten Lore. Kadis, Averil J., ed. 1980. pap. 2.50 (0-910556-16-4) Enoch Pratt.

Dameron, J. Lasley & Mathews, James W., eds. No Fairer Land: Studies in Southern Literature Before 1900. LC 85-51200. x, 245p. 1986. 45.00 (0-87875-305-2) Whitston Pub.

Dameron, J. Lasley & Palmer, Pamela. An Index to the Critical Vocabulary of "Blackwood's Edinburgh Magazine," 1830-1840. LC 93-5478. 277p. (C). 1993. lib. bdg. 40.00 (0-933951-52-3) Locust Hill Pr.

Dameron, Joseph, jt. auth. see Engels, Dennis W.

Dameron, Ned, jt. auth. see Burroughs, Edgar Rice.

*__Dameron, R. A.__ Pretest Prediction Analysis & Posttest Correlation of the Sizewell-B 1: Ten Scale Prestressed Concrete Containment Model Test. 204p. 1998. per. 17.00 (0-16-062941-1) USGPO.

Dameron, Ronald F. Principally Speaking. LC 97-91405. (Illus.). 168p. 1998. pap. 10.95 (0-9662148-0-3) Walnut Vista.

Dameron, Steven. Star Quality. 90p. 1998. pap. 8.95 (1-57502-936-7, P02577) Morris Pubng.

*__Damerow, Diane, et al.__ Building Family Strengths: A Tool Kit for Families. Wolk, Phyllis E., ed. (Illus.). 51p. 1999. pap. 9.95 (1-888440-09-0) U MN Ext Serv.

Damerow, Gail. The Chicken Health Handbook. Haar, Amanda, ed. LC 93-33385. (Illus.). 352p. 1994. pap. 19.95 (0-88266-611-8, Garden Way Pub) Storey Bks.

— Fences for Pasture & Garden. Foster, Kim & Art, Pam, eds. LC 91-55486. (Illus.). 160p. 1992. pap. 16.95 (0-88266-753-X, Garden Way Pub) Storey Bks.

— A Guide to Raising Chickens: Care, Feeding, Facilities. Lappies, Pamela, ed. LC 95-18318. (Storey Animal Handbook Ser.). (Illus.). 352p. 1995. pap. 18.95 (0-88266-897-8, 897-8, Storey Pub) Storey Bks.

— Ice Cream! The Whole Scoop. LC 90-80207. (Illus.). 384p. 1991. 26.95 (0-944435-09-2) Glenbridge Pub.

— Ice Cream! The Whole Scoop. LC 90-80207. (Illus.). 384p. 1995. pap. 19.95 (0-944435-29-7) Glenbridge Pub.

— The Perfect Pumpkin. LC 97-12562. (Illus.). 224p. 1997. pap. 12.95 (0-88266-993-1, Storey Pub) Storey Bks.

*__Damerow, Gail.__ Storey's Guide to Raising Chickens. LC 00-30806. (Illus.). 2000. write for info. (1-58017-325-X) Storey Bks.

Damerow, Gail. Your Chickens: A Kid's Guide to Raising & Showing. Steege, Gwen & Driggs, Lorin, eds. LC 92-54655. (Illus.). 160p. (Orig.). 1993. pap. 14.95 (0-88266-823-4, Garden Way Pub) Storey Bks.

— Your Goats: A Kid's Guide to Raising & Showing. LC 92-54656. (Illus.). 160p. (Orig.). 1993. pap. 16.95 (0-88266-825-0, Garden Way Pub) Storey Bks.

Damerow, P., et al. Exploring the Limits of Preclassical Mechanics. (Illus.). xiii, 387p. 1991. 69.95 (0-387-97602-7) Spr-Verlag.

Damerow, Peter. Abstraction & Representation: Essays on Cultural Evolution of Thinking. (Boston Studies in the Philosophy of Science: Vol. 175). 428p. (C). 1996. lib. bdg. 170.00 (0-7923-3816-2) Kluwer Academic.

Dames & Moore Staff. Fundamentals of Environmental Science & Technology. Knowles, Porter C., ed. (Illus.). 138p. (Orig.). 1992. pap. text 32.00 (0-86587-302-X) Gov Insts.

Dames, Konstanze. Zeitliche Eigenschaften der Sprachproduktion Von Sprachentwicklungsgestorten Kindern: Entwicklungsverzogerung Oder Storung? (Illus.). 155p. 1998. 31.95 (3-631-33727-2) P Lang Pubng.

Dames, Michael. The Avebury Cycle. rev. ed. (Illus.). 240p. 1996. pap. 16.95 (0-500-27886-5, Pub. by Thames Hudson) Norton.

— A Journey Through Ancient Ireland. (Illus.). 256p. 1999. pap. 24.95 (1-86204-546-1, Pub. by Element MA) Penguin Putnam.

— A Journey Through Mythic Ireland LC 99-28817. 1999. write for info. (1-86204-446-5) Element MA.

— Mythic Ireland. LC 91-67303. (Illus.). 272p. 1996. pap. 16.95 (0-500-27872-5, Pub. by Thames Hudson) Norton.

Damesick, Peter & Wood, Peter H., eds. Regional Problems, Problem Regions & Public Policy in the U. K. (Illus.). 288p. 1987. 69.00 (0-19-823257-8) OUP.

Damewood, Glenn, et al. Noise Abatement at Gas Pipelines Installations: Blow-off Noise Suppression & Regulator Valve Noise Generation, Vol. III. 121p. 1961. pap. 5.50 (0-318-12661-3, L00280) Am Gas Assn.

Damewood, Graciela. The Soul of Healing: An Autobiography. (Orig.). 1996. pap. 14.00 (0-9650642-0-4) Openway.

Damewood, Marian D. The Johns Hopkins Handbook of in Vitro Fertilization & Assisted Reproductive Technologies. 1990. 42.95 (0-316-17194-8, Little Brwn Med Div) Lppncott W & W.

Damgaard, E., et al. The Politics of Economic Crisis: Lessons from Western Europe. 1989. text 77.95 (0-566-05517-1, Pub. by Dartmth Pub) Ashgate Pub Co.

Damgaard, Erik, et al, eds. Parliamentary Change in the Nordic Countries. (Illus.). 224p. 1993. 39.00 (82-00-21510-5) Scandnvan Univ Pr.

Damgaard, Erik, jt. ed. see Bergman, Torbjorn.

Damgaard, P. & Huffel, H. Stochastic Quantization. 508p. (C). 1988. text 99.00 (9971-5-0254-2); pap. text 40.00 (9971-5-0298-4) World Scientific Pub.

Damgaard, P. H., et al, eds. Probabilistic Methods in Quantum Field Theory & Quantum Gravity. (NATO ASI Ser.: Vol. 224). (Illus.). 384p. (C). 1990. text 150.00 (0-306-43602-7, Kluwer Plenum) Kluwer Academic.

Damgaard, Poul H. & Jurkiewicz, Jerzy, eds. New Developments in Quantum Field Theory: Proceedings of a NATO ARW Held in Zakopane, Poland, June 14-20, 1997. LC 97-48523. (NATO ASI Ser. Series B, Physics: Vol. 366). (Illus.). 374p. (C). 1998. text 125.00 (0-306-45816-0) Kluwer Academic.

Damgard, I. B. Lectures on Data Security: Modern Cryptology in Theory & Practice. LC 99-21384. (Lecture Notes in Computer Science Ser.: Vol. 1561). 250p. 1999. 39.00 (3-540-65757-6) Spr-Verlag.

Damgard, I. B., ed. Advances in Cryptology - EUROCRYPT '90: Proceedings of the Workshop on the Theory & Application of Cryptographic Techniques Aarhus, Denmark, May 21-24, 1990, Vol. 473. (Lecture Notes in Computer Science Ser.). viii, 500p. 1991. 53.95 (0-387-53587-X) Spr-Verlag.

Damhorst, Mary L., jt. auth. see Kaiser, Susan B.

Damia, Giorgio, ed. see Torri, Giorgio.

Damiamayan, Dikran. Analysis of Aperture Antennas in Inhomogeneous Media. LC 77-141023. 93p. 1969. 17.50 (0-403-04493-6) Scholarly.

Damian, Carol. The Virgin of the Andes. LC 94-73217. (Illus.). 112p. 1995. 48.00 (0-9628514-8-5) Grassfield Pr.

*__Damian, Carol, text.__ Isabel De Obaldia: Captive Spirits. (Illus.). 20p. 1999. pap. 15.00 (1-930191-10-3) M Martin Fine Art.

*__Damian, Carol & Bach, Caleb Ives, texts.__ Alfredo Castaneda: Nuestro Yo, y Mi Nosotros (Our Me, & My We) (Illus.). 24p. 1999. pap. 15.00 (1-930191-09-X) M Martin Fine Art.

*__Damian-Grint, Peter.__ The New Historians of the 12th-Century Renaissance: Authorising History in the Vernacular Revolution. LC 99-37949. 320p. 1999. 90.00 (0-85115-760-2, Suffolk Records Soc) Boydell & Brewer.

Damian, Jean-Michel. Dictionnaire des Disques et des Compacts Guide Critique de la Musique Classique Enregistree. 4th ed. (FRE.). 1367p. 1991. pap. 59.95 (0-7859-7807-0, 2221066820) Fr & Eur.

Damian, Kate, jt. auth. see Damian, Peter.

Damian, Peter. Letters, 91-120. Blum, Owen J., tr. from LAT. (Fathers of the Church Ser.: No. 5). 440p. 1998. text 42.95 (0-8132-0816-5) Cath U Pr.

— The Letters of Peter Damian, 61-90. Blum, Owen J., tr. from LAT. LC 88-25802. (Fathers of the Church: Mediaeval Continuation Ser.: Vol. 3). 397p. 1992. text 42.95 (0-8132-0750-9) Cath U Pr.

Damian, Peter & Damian, Kate. La Aromaterapia: El Olor y la Psique.Tr. of Aromatherapy. (SPA.). 272p. 1996. pap. 16.95 (0-89281-473-X) Inner Tradit.

— Aromatherapy - Scent & Psyche: Using Essential Oils for Physical & Emotional Well-Being. 256p. 1995. pap. 16.95 (0-89281-530-2) Inner Tradit.

*__Damian, Theodor, et al.__ Mai Am un Singur Dor: Simpozion Ocazional de Aniversarea a 145 Ani de la Nasterea Luceafarului: Poezie - Romanesti. 2nd ed. (RUM., Illus.). 52p. 1998. pap. write for info. (1-888067-05-5) Romanian Inst.

— Symposium: Rediscovering God: The Relation Between God & Man & It's Significance for Our Life Today. (Ecumenical Theological Symposium Ser.: No. 5). (Illus.). 62p. 1998. pap. 8.00 (1-888067-06-3) Romanian Inst.

— Symposium: The Theological Legacy of Father Dumitri Staniloae & Its Ecumenical Actuality. (Ecumenical Theological Symposium Ser.: No. 6). (Illus.). 72p. 1999. pap. 8.00 (1-888067-07-1) Romanian Inst.

Damian, Theodor, et al. Symposium Vol. I: Worship & Identity in Our Contemporary Society. The First Ecumenical Theological Symposium. 37p. (Orig.). 1994. pap. 8.00 (1-888067-00-4) Romanian Inst.

— Symposium Vol. II: Quo Vadis Homo? Salvation & the Modern World. The Second Ecumenical Theological Symposium. 60p. (Orig.). 1995. pap. 8.00 (1-888067-01-2) Romanian Inst.

— Symposium Vol. IV: Freedom & Responsibility in Contemporary Society. The Fourth Ecumenical Theological Symposium. (Illus.). 76p. (Orig.). 1997. pap. 8.00 (1-888067-04-7) Romanian Inst.

Damian, Theodor, ed. see Pentiuc, Eugen & Blackwell, John A.

Damiani, A. S. Creative Leadership: Mining the Gold in Your Workforce. LC 98-4451. 170p. 1998. 17.95 (1-57444-226-0, SL2260) St Lucie Pr.

Damiani, A. S. Migs. Moving up the Organization in Facilities Management: Proven Strategies for Improving the Productivity of Your Workforce. (Illus.). 134p. 1998. pap. 24.95 (1-891121-03-0) SciTech Pub.

Damiani, Anita. Enlightened Observers: British Travellers to the Near East, 1715-1850. LC 85-103370. (Illus.). 207p. 1979. reprint ed. pap. 64.20 (0-608-07603-1, 205991800010) Bks Demand.

Damiani, Anthony. Astronoesis: Philosophy's Empirical Context, Astrology's Transcendental Ground. (Illus.). 512p. 2000. 79.00 (0-943914-00-0) Larson Pubns.

— Living Wisdom: Revisioning the Philosophic Quest. LC 96-78529. (Illus.). 240p. (Orig.). 1996. pap. 15.95 (0-943914-69-8) Larson Pubns.

— Looking into Mind: How to Recognize Who You Are & How You Know. Widsom's Goldenrod Staff, ed. 298p. (Orig.). 1990. pap. 14.95 (0-943914-50-7) Larson Pubns.

— Standing in Your Own Way: Tales on the Nature of Ego. 270p. 1992. pap. 15.95 (0-943914-60-4) Larson Pubns.

Damiani, Bruno & Mulica, Barbara. ET in Arcadia Ego: Essays on Death in the Pastoral Novel. 186p. (Orig.). (C). 1990. pap. text 19.50 (0-8191-7773-3) U Pr of Amer.

Damiani, Bruno & Rodriguez, Benjamin. El Impacto del Humanismo en el Nuevo Mundo. (SPA.). vi, 307p. 75.00 (1-882528-10-7) Scripta.

Damiani, Bruno M. La Diana of Montemayor As Social & Religious Teaching. LC 83-3608. (Studies in Romance Languages: No. 28). 124p. reprint ed. pap. 38.50 (0-7837-5811-1, 204547800006) Bks Demand.

— Francisco Lopez de Ubeda. LC 76-409943. (Twayne's World Authors Ser.). 180p. (C). 1977. lib. bdg. 20.95 (0-8057-6271-X) Irvington.

— Montemayor's Diana, Music, & the Visual Arts. vi, 118p. 1983. 11.00 (0-942260-28-7) Hispanic Seminary.

Damiani, Bruno M., ed. Renaissance & Golden Age Essays in Honor of D. W. McPheeters. (SPA.). 1984. 25.00 (0-916379-10-8) Scripta.

Damiani, Bruno M., intro. La Celestina. 302p. 1990. 45.00 (0-916379-86-8) Scripta.

Damiani, Bruno M. & El Saffar, Ruth A., eds. Studies in Honor of Elias Rivers. 200p. 30.00 (0-916379-32-9) Scripta.

Damiani, Bruno M. & Imperiale, Louis. La Lozana Andaluza: A Traves de los Siglos. (SPA.). 244p. 1997. 74.95 (1-57309-250-9) Intl Scholars.

Damiani, Bruno M., tr. see Delicado, Francisco.

*__Damiani, Chad.__ WCW Fan Book. (Official Strategy Guides Ser.). (Illus.). 128p. (YA). 2000. pap. 14.99 (0-7615-2736-2, Prima Tech) Prima Pub.

Damiani, Giovanna. San Marco Florence: A Souvenir Guide to the Museum & Its Art. (Illus.). 96p. 1997. 30.00 (0-614-18272-7, Pub. by P Wilson) Scala Books.

— San Marco Florence: A Souvenir Guide to the Museum & Its Art. (Illus.). 96p. 1997. 30.00 (0-85667-474-5) Scala Books.

— San Marco, Florence: The Museum & Its Art. (Illus.). 96p. 1997. 30.00 (1-85759-138-0) Antique Collect.

Damiani, Roberto, et al, texts. James Rosenquist. 100p. 1996. pap. text 45.00 (88-8158-038-1, Pub. by Charta) Dist Art Pubs.

Damiano, Todd. Infrared Landscape Photography. LC 98-74044. (Illus.). 128p. 1999. pap. 29.95 (0-936262-82-6) Amherst Media.

Damiano, David B. Vector Calculus. (Mathematics Ser.). 1998. text 63.95 (0-534-95654-8) PWS Pubs.

Damiano, David B. & Little, John B. A Course in Linear Algebra. 384p. (C). 1988. text 86.00 (0-15-515134-7, Pub. by SCP) Harcourt.

— A Course in Linear Algebra. 384p. (C). 1988. text 24.50 (0-15-515135-5) SCP.

Damiano, Tony. Damiano's at the Tarrimore House. LC 93-73745. (Illus.). 1993. 16.95 (0-87197-393-6) Favorite Recipes.

D'Amico, jt. auth. see Barbarito.

D'Amico, jt. auth. see Zikmund.

Damico, Alfonso J. Democracy & the Case for Amnesty. LC 75-12502. (University of Florida Monographs: Social Sciences: No. 55). 86p. reprint ed. pap. 30.00 (0-7837-4950-3, 204461600004) Bks Demand.

Damico, Alfonso J., ed. Liberals on Liberalism. 240p. 1986. 39.50 (0-8476-7484-3); pap. 23.00 (0-8476-7485-1) Rowman.

Damico, Anthony, tr. see Aquinas, Thomas, Saint.

D'Amico, Anthony V. & Hanks, Gerald E. Radiotherapeutic Management of Prostate Adenocarcinoma. (An Arnold Publication). (Illus.). 224p. 1999. text 55.00 (0-340-74110-4, Pub. by E A) OUP.

D'Amico, Arnaldo & Sberveglieri, Giorgio. Sensors for Domestic Applications: Proceedings of the 1st European School of Sensors (ESS '94) 300p. 1995. text 86.00 (981-02-2246-7) World Scientific Pub.

D'Amico, Carol, jt. auth. see Judy, Richard W.

Damico, David. Influential Parent: How to Be the Person Your Teen Really Needs. LC 97-15025. 250p. 1997. pap. text 10.99 (0-87788-887-6, H Shaw Pubs) Waterbrook Pr.

D'Amico, Diane. Christina Rossetti: Faith, Gender & Time. 200p. 1999. pap. 18.95 (0-8071-2507-5); text 39.95 (0-8071-2375-7) La State U Pr.

D'Amico, Francesca, jt. auth. see Orr, James M.

D'Amico, Francine & Beckman, Peter R., eds. Women in World Politics: An Introduction. LC 94-21994. 248p. 1995. 59.95 (0-89789-410-3, Bergin & Garvey); pap. 21.95 (0-89789-411-1, Bergin & Garvey) Greenwood.

D'Amico, Francine & Weinstein, Laurie, eds. Gender Camouflage: Women & the U. S. Military. LC 98-40841. x, 279 p. 1999. pap. 19.95 (0-8147-1907-4) NYU Pr.

*__D'Amico, Francine & Weinstein, Laurie, eds.__ Gender Camouflage: Women & the U. S. Military. LC 98-40841. 230p. 1999. text 55.00 (0-8147-1906-6) NYU Pr.

D'Amico, Francine, jt. ed. see Beckman, Peter R.

D'Amico, G., et al, eds. IGA Mesangial Nephropathy. (Contributions to Nephrology Ser.: Vol. 40). (Illus.). x, 310p. 1984. 29.75 (3-8055-3877-4) S Karger.

D'Amico, G. & Colasanti, G., eds. Advances in Nephrology & Dialysis. (Contributions to Nephrology Ser.: Vol. 45). (Illus.). x, 214p. 1985. 113.25 (3-8055-3963-0) S Karger.

— Current Studies in Nephrology: Dialysis & Transplantation. (Contributions to Nephrology Ser.: Vol. 48). (Illus.). vi, 206p. 1986. 29.75 (3-8055-4141-4) S Karger.

— Nephrology & Dialysis Updated. (Contributions to Nephrology Ser.: Vol. 61). (Illus.). vi, 298p. 1988. 29.75 (3-8055-4673-4) S Karger.

D'Amico, G., jt. ed. see Colasanti, G.

Damico, Helen. Beowulf's Wealhtheow & the Valkyrie Tradition. LC 83-40262. 286p. 1984. text 30.00 (0-299-09500-2) U of Wis Pr.

— Medieval Scholarship Vol. 2: Biographical Studies of the Formation of a Discipline. LC 95-6189. 480p. 1998. text 95.00 (0-8153-2890-7, H2071) Garland.

*__Damico, Helen, ed.__ Medieval Scholarship Vol. 3: Biographical Studies on the Foundation of a Discipline: Philosophy & the Arts. (Reference Library of the Humanities). 368p. 1999. 90.00 (0-8153-3339-0, H2110) Garland.

Damico, Helen & Leyerle, John, eds. Heroic Poetry in the Anglo-Saxon Period: Studies in Honor of Jess B. Bessinger, Jr. LC 92-39522. (Studies in Medieval Culture: Vol. 32). 1993. boxed set 45.00 (1-879288-27-3) Medieval Inst.

Damico, Helen & Olsen, Alexandra Hennessey, eds. New Readings on Women in Old English Literature. LC 88-45459. (Illus.). 330p. 1990. 39.95 (0-253-33413-6); pap. 15.95 (0-253-20547-6) Ind U Pr.

— New Readings on Women in Old English Literature. LC 88-45459. 329p. Date not set. reprint ed. pap. 102.00 (0-608-20536-2, 205445000002) Bks Demand.

Damico, Helen & Zavadil, Joseph B., eds. Medieval Scholarship: Biographical Studies on the Formation of a Discipline. Incl. Medieval Scholarship Vol. I: History: Biographical Studies on the Formation of a Discipline: History. LC 95-6189. (Illus.). 347p. 1995. text 66.00 (0-8240-6894-7); LC 95-6189. write for info. (0-614-32276-6) Garland.

Damico, Helen, jt. ed. see Gallacher, Patrick J.

D'Amico, J. & Drummond, Karen E. The Science Chef: One Hundred Fun Food Experiments & Recipes for Kids. (Illus.). 180p. (J). 1994. pap. 12.95 (0-471-31045-X) Wiley.

D'Amico, Jack. The Moor in English Renaissance Drama. 288p. (C). 1991. lib. bdg. 49.95 (0-8130-1068-3) U Press Fla.

Damico, Jack S., jt. ed. see Hamayan, Else V.

Damico, Jack S., jt. ed. see Smith, Michael D.

D'Amico, Joan & Drummond, Karen E. The Healthy Body Cookbook: Fun Activities & Delicious Recipes for Kids. LC 98-2776. (Illus.). 184p. (J). (gr. 3-7). 1998. pap. 12.95 (*0-471-18888-3*) Wiley.
— The Math Chef: Over 60 Math Activities & Recipes for Kids. LC 96-22143. (Illus.). 180p. (J). (gr. 3-9). 1996. pap. 12.95 (*0-471-13813-4*) Wiley.
— The Science Chef Travels Around the World: Fun Food Experiments & Recipes for Kids. LC 95-32952. (Illus.). 192p. (J). (gr. 3-9). 1996. pap. 12.95 (*0-471-11779-X*) Wiley.
***D'Amico, Joan & Drummond, Karen E.** The United States Cookbook: Fabulous Foods & Fascinating Facts from All 50 States. LC 99-39548. (Illus.). 192p. (J). (gr. 3-7). 2000. pap. text 12.95 (*0-471-35839-8*) Wiley.
D'Amico, John. Renaissance Humanism in Papal Rome: Humanists & Churchmen on the Eve of the Reformation. (Studies in Historical & Political Science). 352p. 1991. reprint ed. pap. text 18.95 (*0-8018-4224-7*) Johns Hopkins.
D'Amico, John, jt. auth. see Weil-Garris, Kathleen.
D'Amico, John F. Roman & German Humanism, 1450-1550. Grendler, Paul F., ed. (Collected Studies: No. 413). 368p. 1993. 115.95 (*0-86078-388-X*, Pub. by Variorum) Ashgate Pub Co.
D'Amico, Joseph J. & Corbett, H. Dickson. How to Develop Your School's Readiness for Improvement: An Analysis Process & Recommendations. 51p. 1987. pap. 8.95 (*1-56602-015-8*) Research Better.
D'Amico, Joseph J., jt. auth. see Corbett, H. Dickson.
D'Amico, K. L., et al. Synchrotron Radiation Techniques in Industrial, Chemical, & Materials Science: Proceedings of the Combined Symposia on Applications of Synchrotron Research to Materials Science Held in Washington, D. C., August 1995, & Applications of Synchrotron Radiation in Chemistry & Related Fields Held in Chicago, Illinois, August 1995. LC 96-41921. (Illus.). 268p. (C). 1997. text 107.00 (*0-306-45389-4*, Kluwer Plenum) Kluwer Academic.
D'Amico, Klaudia M. Deckendekorationen Emilianischer Sakralbauten von 1530 bis 1630. (Schriften zur Buildenden Kunst Ser.: Bd. 6). (GER., Illus.). 435p. 1997. 76.95 (*3-631-31098-6*) P Lang Pubng.
D'Amico, M. & Santambrogio, G. C. Three Dimensional Analysis of Spinal Deformities. LC 94-77521. (Studies in Health Technology & Informatics: Vol. 15). 550p. (gr. 12). 1995. 130.00 (*90-5199-181-9*) IOS Press.
D'Amico, Martin. How to Predict Year End Cash & Energize Any Size Business. LC 97-20333. (Illus.). 292p. 1998. pap. 19.95 (*1-56825-063-0*, 063-0) Rainbow Books.
D'Amico, Michael, jt. auth. see Zikmund, William G.
D'Amico, Paolo, jt. ed. see Beletic, James W.
D'Amico, Pat. Reflections & Ironies: Packaged in Rhyme. LC 95-92830. (Illus.). 80p. (Orig.). 1996. pap. 8.95 (*0-9650543-0-6*) Pilot Pubns.
D'Amico, Paul M. Massive Myths with Simple Solutions: Revolutionary Breakthrough in Drug Dependencies Derived from Psychopharmacology. (Illus.). 290p. (YA). 1987. 10.00 (*0-89288-163-1*) Damico.
D'Amico, Raymond A. Werbel Life Insurance Primer. 256p. (C). 1999. pap. text 19.95 (*1-884803-03-2*) Werbel Pub.
D'Amico, Raymond A., et al. Health Insurance Primer: Werbel's Sickness & Accident. rev. ed. 172p. (C). 1998. pap. text 19.95 (*1-884803-02-4*) Werbel Pub.
D'Amico, Robert. Contemporary Continental Philosophy. LC 98-37834. (Dimensions of Philosophy Ser.). 280p. 1998. text 65.00 (*0-8133-3221-4*, Pub. by Westview); pap. text 25.00 (*0-8133-3222-2*, Pub. by Westview) HarpC.
— Historicism & Knowledge. 208p. 1988. text 35.00 (*0-415-90032-8*); pap. text 12.95 (*0-415-90033-6*) Routledge.
— Marx & Philosophy of Culture. LC 80-24405. (University of Florida Humanities Monographs: No. 50). viii, 108p. (Orig.). 1981. pap. 15.95 (*0-8130-0689-9*) U Press Fla.
— Marx & Philosophy of Culture. LC 80-24405. (University of Florida Monographs: Vol. 50). 118p. (Orig.). 1981. reprint ed. pap. 36.60 (*0-608-04465-2*, 206521000001) Bks Demand.
D'Amico, Serge, jt. auth. see Fortin, Francis.
D'Amico, Thomas A. Handbook of Surgical Intensive Care. 4th ed. Pruitt, Scott K., ed. (Illus.). 592p. (C). (gr. 13). 1995. pap. text 47.95 (*0-8151-2249-7*, 24275) Mosby Inc.
***D'Amico, V.** Smart Presentations - Everyone's Guide to Wooing Business Audiences. 81p. 1999. 11.95 (*0-7541-0632-2*, Pub. by Minerva Pr) Unity Dist.
D'Amico, Vic, jt. auth. see Palmer, Ted.
Damiecki, P. Time Trends in Cancer Incidence & Mortality. Coleman, M. et al, eds. (IARC Scientific Publications: No. 121). (Illus.). 814p. 1993. text 195.00 (*92-832-2121-4*) OUP.
Damien. Computer Knowledge Begin. 290p. 1998. pap. text 60.00 (*0-536-01298-9*) Pearson Custom.
Damien, Geradin, jt. ed. see Esty, Daniel.
Damien of Molokai & Milsome, John. No Greater Love. 112p. (C). 1989. 39.00 (*0-85439-308-0*, Pub. by St Paul Pubns) St Mut.
Damien, Paul. Death at C Minor. 368p. mass mkt. 5.99 (*1-55197-072-4*) Picasso Publ.
Damioli, Carol. Rogue Angel - A Novel of Fra Filippo Lippi. Caso, Adolfo, ed. (Illus.). 248p. 1994. reprint ed. text 21.95 (*0-937832-33-2*) Branden Bks.
Damisch, Hubert. The Judgment of Paris. Goodman, John, tr. (Analytic Iconology Ser.: Vol. 1). 1996. lib. bdg. 55.00 (*0-226-13510-1*) U Ch Pr.
— The Judgment of Paris. Goodman, John, tr. (Analytic Iconology Ser.: Vol. 1). (Illus.). 312p. 1996. pap. text 19.95 (*0-226-13512-8*) U Ch Pr.
— The Origin of Perspective. Goodman, John, tr. LC 93-21895. 504p. 1994. 55.00 (*0-262-04139-1*) MIT Pr.
— The Origin of Perspective. Goodman, John, tr. (Illus.). 504p. 1995. pap. text 26.50 (*0-262-54077-0*) MIT Pr.
Damitio, James W., jt. auth. see Schmidgall, Raymond S.
Damitz, Charlie. The Shot Not Heard Around the World. 86p. (J). (gr. 4-6). 1999. pap. 9.99 (*0-88092-440-3*, 4403) Royal Fireworks.
Damjan, Mischa. La Ardilla Gigante y el Pequeno Rinoceronte. (SPA., Illus.). 32p. (J). (gr. k-3). 1998. 15.95 (*1-55858-884-1*, Pub. by North-South Bks NYC); pap. 6.95 (*1-55858-883-3*, Pub. by North-South Bks NYC) Chronicle Bks.
— The Big Squirrel & the Little Rhinoceros. Hort, Lenny, tr. LC 91-17865. (Illus.). 32p. (J). (gr. k-3). 1998. pap. 6.95 (*1-55858-882-5*) North-South Bks NYC.
Damjan, Mischa. The False Flamingoes. LC 70-105399. (Illus.). 32p. (J). (ps-3). 13.95 (*0-87592-016-0*) Scroll Pr.
Damjano. Path. Health Related Profession. 1996. 365.00 (*0-7216-6850-X*) Harcourt.
Damjanov, Ivan. High-Yield Pathology. 150p. write for info. (*0-7817-2367-1*) Lppncott W & W.
Damjanov, Ivan. Histopathology: Color Atlas & Textbook. (Illus.). 560p. 1996. pap., spiral bd. 42.95 (*0-683-02334-9*) Lppncott W & W.
— Pathology for the Health-Related Professions. (Illus.). 570p. 1996. pap., teacher ed. write for info. (*0-7216-6473-3*, W B Saunders Co) Harcrt Hlth Sci Grp.
— Pathology for the Health-Related Professions. LC 99-27976. (Illus.). 555p. 2000. pap. text. write for info. (*0-7216-8118-2*, W B Saunders Co) Harcrt Hlth Sci Grp.
Damjanov, Ivan. Pathology for the Health Related Professions: Instructor's Manual. 2nd ed. 95p. Date not set. pap. text, teacher ed. write for info. (*0-7216-8119-0*, W B Saunders Co) Harcrt Hlth Sci Grp.
Damjanov, Ivan. Progress in Reproductive & Urinary Tract Pathology. 1989. 70.00 (*0-938607-13-8*) Field & Wood Inc Medical.
— Progress in Reproductive & Urinary Tract Pathology, Vol. 2. 1990. 89.00 (*0-938607-29-4*) Field & Wood Inc Medical.
Damjanov, Ivan, et al, eds. The Human Teratomas: Experimental & Clinical Biology. LC 82-48865. (Contemporary Biomedicine Ser.: Vol. 3). 374p. 1983. 99.50 (*0-89603-040-7*) Humana.
Damjanov, Ivan & Anderson. Color Atlas of Pathology. 544p. (C). (gr. 13). 1999. text 179.00 (*0-8151-2248-9*, 24114) Mosby Inc.
Damjanov, Ivan & Goldblatt. Pathology. LC 98-2713. (Rypins' Intensive Reviews Ser.). 432p. 1998. pap. text 21.95 (*0-397-51555-3*) Lppncott W & W.
Damjanov, Ivan & Linder, James. Anderson's Pathology. 10th ed. (Illus.). 3014p. (C). (gr. 13). 1995. text 295.00 (*0-8016-7236-8*, 07236) Mosby Inc.
Damjanov, Ivan & Rubin, Emanuel. Pocket Pathology. 550p. 1998. pap. text 23.95 (*0-397-58407-5*) Lppncott W & W.
— Pocket Pathology. 7th ed. LC 98-21735. 20p. 1999. text. write for info. (*0-7817-1636-5*) Lppncott W & W.
— Review of Pathology. 2nd ed. 225p. 1997. text 395.00 (*0-7817-1635-7*) Lppncott W & W.
— Review of Pathology. 2nd ed. LC 99-33310. 225p. 1998. pap. text 21.00 (*0-397-58408-3*) Lppncott W & W.
Damjanov, Ivan, jt. ed. see Rubin, Emanuel.
Damjanovic, Mijat & Voich, Dan, Jr., eds. The Impact of Culture-Based Value Systems on Management Policies & Practices: Yugoslav & United States Issues & Viewpoints. 1985th ed. LC 85-6580. 400p. 1985. 65.00 (*0-275-90199-8*, C0199, Praeger Pubs) Greenwood.
Damjanovich, S. Mobility & Proximity in Biomarkers. 352p. 1994. lib. bdg. 210.00 (*0-8493-4931-1*, QH601) CRC Pr.
Damjanovich, S., et al. New Trends in the Description of the General Mechanism & Regulation of Enzymes: Symposium on Enzyme Action, 9-12 July 1978, Debrecen, Hungary. (Symposia Biologica Hungarica Ser.: No. 21). 312p. (C). 1978. 75.00 (*963-05-1881-3*, Pub. by Akade Kiado) St Mut.
***Damjanovski, Vlado.** CCTV. LC 99-32637. 408p. 1999. 89.95 (*0-7506-7196-3*) Buttrwrth-Heinemann.
Damkani, Jacob. Why Me? LC 97-5104. 223p. 1997. pap. 12.99 (*0-88368-440-3*) Whitaker Hse.
Damke, Ciro. Sprachgebrauch und Sprachkontakt in der Deutschen Sprachinsel in Sudbrasilien. (Europaische Hochschulschriften Ser.: Reihe 21, Bd. 190). (Illus.). XVIII, 319p. 1997. 57.95 (*3-631-32453-7*) P Lang Pubng.
Damle, C. B. Land Reforms & Changing Agrarian Relations. (C). 1993. 29.00 (*81-7033-177-3*, Pub. by Rawat Pubns) S Asia.
Damm, Ellie. Treasure by the Bay: The Historic Architecture of Sandusky, Ohio. LC 87-47807. (Illus.). 192p. 1989. 45.00 (*0-8387-5133-4*) Bucknell U Pr.
***Damm, Gene & Damm, Mary.** Guide for Competitive Swimmers. (Illus.). 96p. 2000. pap. 9.95 (*0-9647782-2-X*) Sports Pubns.
Damm, Janet M. Germans from Russia: Index of Naturalization Records in Whitman County, Washington 1860-1942. 17p. 1986. pap. 6.00 (*0-943145-00-7*) Palouse Pubns.
Damm, Klaus-Werner & Pichowiak, Siegfried. Geodynamik und Magmengenese in der Kuestenkordillere Nordchiles Zwischen Taltal und Chanaral. (Geotektonische Forschungen Ser.: Vol. 61). (GER.). 166p. 1981. 88.00 (*3-510-50027-X*, Pub. by E Schweizerbartsche) Balogh.
Damm, Mary, jt. auth. see Damm, Gene.
Damm, Peter. The Water's Edge: Poems from a Five Month Journey in Bali, Indonesia & New Zealand. 112p. 1999. pap. 12.00 (*0-9668431-0-X*) O & W Pub.
***Damm, Robert J.** Repertoire, Authenticity & Instruction: The Presentation of American Indian Music in Oklahoma's Elementary Schools. LC 00-26419. (Native Americans Ser.). 2000. write for info. (*0-8153-3814-7*) Garland.
Damm, W., jt. ed. see Kloos, C. Delgado.
Dammaj, Zayd M. The Hostage. Jayyusi, May & Tingley, Christopher, trs. LC 94-2635. (Emerging Voices: New International Fiction Ser.). 168p. 1994. 24.95 (*1-56656-146-9*); pap. 10.95 (*1-56656-140-X*) Interlink Pub.
Damman, Gregory C. Collecting Child Support in the U. S. A. 12 Effective Strategies. 144p. (Orig.). 1997. pap. 11.95 (*1-55180-127-2*) Self-Counsel Pr.
Dammann, Arthur E. & Nellis, David W. Natural History Atlas to the Cays of the U. S. Virgin Islands. LC 92-23127. (Illus.). 160p. 1992. pap. 29.95 (*1-56164-022-0*) Pineapple Pr.
Dammann, Erik. The Future in Our Hands. (Illus.). 1979. 87.00 (*0-08-024284-7*, Pub. by Pergamon Repr) Franklin.
Dammann, George H. 90 Years of Ford. (Crestline Ser.). (Illus.). 608p. 1993. 44.95 (*0-87938-682-7*) MBI Pubg.
— 75 Years of Chevrolet. LC 86-72731. (Crestline Ser.). (Illus.). 536p. 1987. 44.95 (*0-87938-692-4*, Crestline Pub) MBI Pubg.
Dammann, Gordon. A Pictorial Encyclopedia of Civil War Medical Instruments & Equipment, 3 vols., Vol. 1. LC 83-80357. (Illus.). 104p. 1983. 8.95 (*0-933126-32-8*) Pictorial Hist.
— A Pictorial Encyclopedia of Civil War Medical Instruments & Equipment, Vol. II. LC 88-60472. (Illus.). 96p. 1988. pap. 8.95 (*0-933126-94-8*) Pictorial Hist.
— Pictorial Encyclopedia of Civil War Medical Instruments & Equipment, Vol. III. LC 83-80357. (Illus.). 132p. 1998. pap. text 9.95 (*1-57510-034-7*) Pictorial Hist.
Dammann, Nancy. We Tried: Government Service in India & Nepal. LC 95-71920. (Illus.). 196p. 1995. pap. 9.95 (*0-9609376-3-3*) Soc Change Pr.
Damme, Dirk Van, see Van Damme, Dirk.
Damme, E. J. Van, see Van Damme, E. J.
Damme, E. Van, see Van Damme, E.
Damme, J. P. Van, see Van Damme, J. P.
Damme, Lynn, ed. see Bailey, Bill.
Damme, Wilfried Van, see Van Damme, Wilfried.
Dammel, Judith, jt. auth. see Carlson, Laurie.
Dammel, Ralph. Diazonaphthoquinone-Based Resists. LC 92-25724. (Tutorial Texts in Optical Engineering Ser.: Vol. TT 11). 1992. pap. 42.00 (*0-8194-1019-5*) SPIE.
Dammer, Harry R., jt. auth. see Clear, Todd R.
Dammers, Horace. Sermons in Stone: Preaching in Cathedrals. 1997. pap. 14.95 (*0-264-67453-7*) G C Mowbray.
Dammeyer, Mark. Go the Extra Yard. (Illus.). 98p. (Orig.). 1995. pap. 25.00 (*0-935803-05-X*) Indus Fabrics.
Dammons, Halim, jt. auth. see Dahesh.
Damodar, Singhat. Pakistan: The Modern Nations in Historical Perspective. 214p. 1972. 9.95 (*0-13-648469-7*) Asia Bk Corp.
***Damodaran.** Applied Corporate Finance: Solutions Manual. 87p. 1998. pap. text 37.00 (*0-471-31416-1*) Wiley.
— Investment Philosophies. 288p. (C). 2000. 27.95 (*0-471-34503-2*) Wiley.
Damodaran & Paraf, A., eds. Food Proteins & Their Applications. LC 97-4028. (Food Science & Technology Ser.: Vol. 80). (Illus.). 704p. 1997. text 195.00 (*0-8247-9820-1*) Dekker.
Damodaran, Aditya. Vibrations - Poems. (C). 1992. text 10.00 (*81-220-0267-6*, Pub. by Konark Pubs Pvt Ltd) Advent Bks Div.
Damodaran, Ajit. Your Success Story: How to Rewrite Your Brain's Own Programs to Design a Perfect Life. LC 96-90759. (Illus.). 262p. (Orig.). 1997. pap. 14.95 (*0-9655084-4-7*) VSDN Pub.
Damodaran, Aswarth, jt. auth. see Bernstein, Peter L.
***Damodaran, Aswath.** Applied Corporate Finance. LC 98-5651. 592p. 1999. text 69.95 (*0-471-33042-6*) Wiley.
— Applied Corporate Finance: A User's Manual. LC 98-5651. (Illus.). 592p. 1998. pap. 77.95 (*0-471-23970-4*) Wiley.
Damodaran, Aswath. Corporate Finance: Theory & Practice. LC 96-21163. (Wiley Series in Finance). 912p. 1996. text 103.95 (*0-471-07680-5*) Wiley.
— Corporate Finance: Theory & Practice, Study Guide & Problems Manual. 384p. 1997. pap. 31.95 (*0-471-17388-6*) Wiley.
— Damodaran on Valuation: Security Analysis for Investment & Corporate Finance. 464p. 1994. 79.95 (*0-471-30465-4*); 169.95 incl. disk (*0-471-01450-8*); 69.95 (*0-471-12015-4*) Wiley.
— Damodaran on Valuation: Security Analysis for Investment & Corporate Finance. 232p. 1994. pap., student ed. 29.95 (*0-471-10897-9*) Wiley.
— Investment Valuation: Tools & Techniques for Determining the Value of Any Asset. LC 95-7418. (Frontiers in Finance Ser.). 544p. 1995. 69.95 (*0-471-13393-0*) Wiley.
— Investment Valuations: Tools 7 Techniques for Determining the Value of Any Asset. LC 95-7418. (Frontiers in Finance Ser.). 544p. 1995. pap. 69.95 (*0-471-11213-5*) Wiley.
Damodaran, Srinivasan, ed. Food Proteins & Lipids: Proceedings of the John E. Kinsella Memorial Symposium Held in Chicago, Illinois, August 22-23, 1995. LC 97-6056. (Advances in Experimental Medicine & Biology Ser.: No. 415). (Illus.). 220p. (C). 1997. text 79.50 (*0-306-45586-2*, Kluwer Plenum) Kluwer Academic.
Damodaran, Vinita. Broken Promises: Popular Protest, Indian Nationalism & the Congress Party in Bihar, 1935-1946. 412p. (C). 1993. 39.95 (*0-19-562979-5*) OUP.
Damoiseau, Louis. Hippoligische Wanderungen In Syrien und der Wuste, 2 vols. in 1. (Documenta Hippologica Ser.). xxi, 442p. 1979. reprint ed. write for info. (*3-487-08200-4*) G Olms Pubs.
***Damon.** Handbook of Child Psychology Vol. 1: Theoretical Models of Human Development. 5th ed. 1296p. 2000. pap. 55.00 (*0-471-34979-8*) Wiley.
Damon. Handbook of Child Psychology Vol. 2: Cognition, Perception & Language. 5th ed. 1056p. 2000. pap. 55.00 (*0-471-34980-1*) Wiley.
— Handbook of Child Psychology Vol. 3: Social, Emotional, & Personality Development. 5th ed. 1232p. 2000. pap. 55.00 (*0-471-34981-X*) Wiley.
— Handbook of Child Psychology Vol. 4: Child Psychology in Practice. 5th ed. 1216p. 2000. pap. 55.00 (*0-471-34982-8*) Wiley.
Damon, Albert. Human Biology & Ecology. LC 77-559. (Illus.). 367p. (C). 1977. pap. text 15.50 (*0-393-09103-1*) Norton.
Damon, Albert, et al. The Human Body in Equipment Design. LC 65-22067. 384p. reprint ed. pap. 119.10 (*0-7837-2243-5*, 205733100004) Bks Demand.
Damon, Barbara J. My Every Christmas Wish. (Illus.). (J). (gr. 3-6). 1997. 7.95 (*0-533-11102-1*) Vantage.
Damon, Bonnie, ed. see Association of Christian Schools International Staff.
Damon, Bonnie L., jt. auth. see Hobbs, Frank B.
Damon, Cynthia. The Mask of the Parasite: A Pathology of Roman Patronage. LC 97-33297. 320p. (C). 1997. text 44.50 (*0-472-10760-7*, 10760) U of Mich Pr.
— Nepos Life of Atticus. 40p. (Orig.). 1993. pap. text 5.00 (*0-929524-81-0*) Bryn Mawr Commentaries.
— Res Gestae Divi Augusti. (Greek Commentaries Ser.). 60p. (C). 1995. pap. text 5.00 (*0-929524-84-5*) Bryn Mawr Commentaries.
Damon, D. Bradford. Damon. Genealogy of Six Generations of Descendants of John Damon of Scituate, Massachusetts. 138p. 1997. reprint ed. pap. 21.00 (*0-8328-8204-6*); reprint ed. lib. bdg. 31.00 (*0-8328-8203-8*) Higginson Bk Co.
Damon, Dave, ed. see Damon, Valerie H.
Damon, Duane. When This Cruel War Is Over: The Civil War Home Front. LC 95-11740. (J). 1996. lib. bdg. 21.27 (*0-8225-1731-0*, Lerner Publctns) Lerner Pub.
Damon, Emma. A Kaleidoscope of Kids. LC 94-32157. (Illus.). (J). 1995. 10.99 (*0-8037-1845-4*, Dial Yng Read) Peng Put Young Read.
Damon, Frederick H. From Muyuw to the Trobriands: Transformations along the Northern Side of the Kula Ring. LC 90-35337. 285p. 1990. 48.50 (*0-8165-1191-8*) U of Ariz Pr.
Damon, J. Topological Triviality & Versality for Subgroups A&K. LC 88-15554. (Memoirs Ser.: No. 75/389). 106p. 1988. pap. text 18.00 (*0-8218-2452-X*, MEMO/75/389) Am Math.
Damon, James. Higher Multiplicities & Almost Free Divisors & Complete Intersections. LC 96-21896. (Memoirs of the American Mathematical Society Ser.: Vol. 123/589). 113p. 1996. pap. 36.00 (*0-8218-0481-2*, MEMO/123/589) Am Math.
— The Unfolding & Determinacy Theorems for Subgroups of A & K. LC 84-9333. (Memoirs of the American Mathematical Society Ser.: No. 50/306). 88p. 1984. pap. 17.00 (*0-8218-2306-X*, MEMO/50/306) Am Math.
Damon, Laura. Discovering Earthquakes & Volcanoes. LC 89-4974. (Illus.). 32p. (J). (gr. 2-4). 1990. lib. bdg. 17.25 (*0-8167-1757-5*) Troll Communs.
— Discovering Earthquakes & Volcanoes. LC 89-4974. (Illus.). 32p. (J). (gr. 2-4). 1996. pap. 3.50 (*0-8167-1758-3*) Troll Communs.
— Fun in the Snow. LC 87-10843. (Illus.). 32p. (J). (gr. k-2). 1988. lib. bdg. 17.25 (*0-8167-1081-3*) Troll Communs.
— Fun in the Snow. LC 87-10843. (Illus.). 32p. (J). (gr. k-2). 1997. pap. 3.95 (*0-8167-1082-1*) Troll Communs.
— Funny Fingers, Funny Toes. LC 87-10915. (Illus.). 32p. (J). (gr. k-2). 1988. lib. bdg. 17.25 (*0-8167-1089-9*) Troll Communs.
— Funny Fingers, Funny Toes. LC 87-10915. (Illus.). 32p. (J). (gr. k-2). 1996. pap. 3.95 (*0-8167-1090-2*) Troll Communs.
— Hide-&-Seek on the Farm. LC 87-13737. (First-Start Easy Readers Ser.). (Illus.). 32p. (J). (gr. k-2). 1988. lib. bdg. 13.05 (*0-8167-1231-X*) Troll Communs.
— Hide-&-Seek on the Farm. LC 87-13737. (First-Start Easy Readers Ser.). (Illus.). 32p. (J). (gr. k-2). 1997. pap. 2.50 (*0-8167-1232-8*) Troll Communs.
— Hide-And-Seek on the Farm. 1999. pap. text 1.95 (*0-8167-3191-8*) Troll Communs.
— Hide-And-Seek on the Farm. enl. ed. 1999. pap. text 16.95 (*0-8167-4083-6*) Troll Communs.
— Secret Valentine. LC 87-13736. (Giant First Start Reader Ser.). (Illus.). 32p. (J). (gr. k-2). 1988. lib. bdg. 17.25 (*0-8167-1101-1*) Troll Communs.
— Secret Valentine. LC 87-13736. (Giant First Start Reader Ser.). (Illus.). 32p. (J). (gr. k-2). 1996. pap. 3.95 (*0-8167-1102-X*) Troll Communs.
— Wonders of Plants & Flowers. LC 89-5003. (Illus.). 32p. (J). (gr. 2-4). 1997. pap. 3.50 (*0-8167-1762-1*) Troll Communs.
Damon, Linda, jt. auth. see Mandell, Joan G.
***Damon, Lisa M. & Cox, Marvel Kohlhof.** Ageless Women: A Collection of International Writings & Art. (Illus.). 54p. 1999. pap. 15.00 (*0-9675807-0-6*, AW1999) Damon Cox.
Damon, Maria. The Dark End of the Street: Margins in American Vanguard Poetry, Vol. 1. LC 92-21872. (American Culture Ser.: Vol. 7). (Illus.). 328p. (C). 1993. pap. 19.95 (*0-8166-1987-5*); text 49.95 (*0-8166-1986-7*) U of Minn Pr.
Damon, Matt, jt. auth. see Affleck, Ben.
Damon-Moore, Helen. Magazines for the Millions: Gender & Commerce in the Ladies' Home Journal & the Saturday Evening Post, 1880-1910. LC 93-33767. (Illus.). 263p. (C). 1994. text 59.50 (*0-7914-2057-4*); pap. text 19.95 (*0-7914-2058-2*) State U NY Pr.

D

An Asterisk (*) at the beginning of an entry indicates that the title is appearing for the first time.

Damon, Phillip. Modes of Analogy in Ancient & Medieval Verse. LC 72-95296. (California Library Reprint). 81p. reprint ed. pap. 30.00 (*0-608-18497-7*, 203150300075) Bks Demand.

Damon, Richard A. The Damon Family of Wayland, Massachusetts. LC 97-66204. vii, 439 p. 1997. write for info. (*0-89725-301-9*, Penobscot Pr) Picton Pr.

Damon, Roberta. Relationship Skills. Howard, Gina, ed. 66p. 1993. pap. text 5.95 (*1-56309-082-1*, N933105, New Hope) Womans Mission Union.

Damon, S. Foster. A Blake Dictionary: The Ideas & Symbols of William Blake. rev. ed. LC 87-40509. (Illus.). 560p. 1988. pap. 25.00 (*0-87451-436-3*) U Pr of New Eng.

Damon, S. Foster, ed. see Blake, William.

Damon, Sidney. Harold the Orange Juice Boy. 40p. (Orig.). (J). (gr. k-4). pap. write for info. (*0-937148-14-8*) Wild Horses.

Damon, Sue. Popcorn Clouds & Bubblegum Trees: Devotions for Young Children. LC 94-40241. (J). 1994. pap. 7.95 (*1-56212-076-X*) CRC Pubns.

Damon, Thomas D. Introduction to Astronautics. (Orbit Ser.). Date not set. write for info. (*0-89464-033-X*) Krieger.

— Introduction to Space: The Science of Spaceflight. 2nd ed. LC 94-34253. 278p. 1995. pap. 39.50 (*0-89464-053-4*) Krieger.

— Introduction to Space: The Science of Spaceflight. 2nd ed. LC 94-34253. 278p. (C). 1995. 49.50 (*0-89464-056-9*) Krieger.

Damon, Valerie H. Grindle Lamfoon & the Procurnious Fleekers. Damon, Dave, ed. LC 78-64526. (Illus.). (J). (gr. 1-12). 1979. 12.95 (*0-932356-05-2*); 14.95 (*0-932356-06-0*) Star Pubns MO.

— Tea with Adella Dine Crow. Damon, Dave, ed. LC 88-92261. (Illus.). 32p. (J). (ps-5). 1990. 9.95 (*0-932356-15-X*) Star Pubns MO.

— Willo Mancifoot (and the Mugga Killa Whomps) Damon, Dave, ed. LC 83-50739. (Illus.). (J). (gr. 2-6). 1985. 14.95 (*0-932356-07-9*) Star Pubns MO.

— Willo Mancifoot (and the Mugga Killa Whomps) limited ed. Damon, Dave, ed. LC 83-50739. (Illus.). (J). (gr. 2-6). 1985. 100.00 (*0-932356-08-7*) Star Pubns MO.

Damon, William. Greater Expectations: Overcoming the Culture of Indulgence in America's Homes & Schools. 285p. 1995. 23.00 (*0-02-906935-1*) Free Pr.

— Greater Expectations: Overcoming the Culture of Indulgence in America's Homes & Schools. 304p. 1996. per. 12.00 (*0-684-82505-8*) Free Pr.

***Damon, William.** Greater Expectations: Overcoming the Culture of Indulgence in America's Homes & Schools. 286p. 1999. reprint ed. text 23.00 (*0-7881-6611-5*) DIANE Pub.

Damon, William. The Moral Child: Nurturing Children's Natural Moral Growth. 224p. 1988. text 29.95 (*0-02-906932-7*) Free Pr.

— The Moral Child: Nurturing Children's Natural Moral Growth. 192p. 1990. per. 14.95 (*0-02-906933-5*) Free Pr.

— Social & Personality Development: Essays on the Growth of the Child. 504p. (C). 1983. pap. text 32.75 (*0-393-95307-6*) Norton.

— Social & Personality Development: From Infancy Through Adolescence. (Illus.). (C). 1983. pap. text 35.50 (*0-393-95248-7*) Norton.

— The Social World of the Child. LC 77-79480. (Jossey-Bass Behavioral Science Ser.). 377p. reprint ed. pap. 116.90 (*0-7837-0165-9*, 204046200017) Bks Demand.

— Youth Charter: How Communities Can Work Together to Raise the Standards for All Our Children. LC 97-23786. 256p. 1997. 23.50 (*0-684-82995-9*) Free Pr.

***Damon, William, ed.** Handbook of Child Psychology, 4 Vol.Set. 680p. 2000. pap. 220.00 (*0-471-37789-9*) Wiley.

Damon, William, ed. Handbook of Child Psychology, 4 vols. 5th ed. Incl. Child Psychology in Practice. 5th ed. Sigel, Irving E. & Renninger, K. Ann, eds. 1188p. 1997. 220.00 (*0-471-07663-5*); Cognition, Perception, & Language. 5th ed. Kuhn, Deanna & Siegler, Robert S., eds. 1030p. 1997. 220.00 (*0-471-05730-4*); Social, Emotional, & Personality Development. 5th ed. Eisenberg, Nancy, ed. 1232p. 1997. 220.00 (*0-471-07668-6*); Vol. 1, Theoretical Models of Human Development. Theoretical Models of Human Development. 5th ed. Lerner, Richard, ed. LC 96-49157. 1274p. 1997. 225.00 (*0-471-05527-1*); LC 96-49157. 3008p. 1997. 880.00 (*0-471-17893-4*) Wiley.

Damon, William, jt. auth. see Colby, Anne.

Damoose, John N., jt. auth. see Bright, Bill.

D'Amore, Gabriella, jt. auth. see Rothrock, Robert W.

D'Amore, Gerard V. The EsPolska Ploy. 256p. 1987. 16.95 (*0-933905-01-7*) Claycomb Pr.

Damore, Leo. The Cape Cod Years of John Fitzgerald Kennedy. LC 93-20153. (Illus.). 288p. 1993. pap. 12.95 (*1-888363-12-6*) Seven Stories.

— Senatorial Privilege: The Chappaquiddick Cover-Up. LC 88-11535. (Illus.). 496p. 1988. 21.95 (*0-89526-564-8*) Regnery Pub.

Damoreau, Laure-Cinthie. Classic Bel Canto Technique: The Method of the Paris Conservatoire (1834-1856) 112p. 1998. pap. 9.95 (*0-486-29984-8*) Dover.

Damos, Diane, ed. Multiple Task Performance. 350p. 1991. 110.00 (*0-85066-757-7*, Pub. by Tay Francis Ltd) Taylor & Francis.

DaMotta, Ronaldo S., jt. auth. see May, Peter H.

D'Amour, Cynthia. Networking - The Skill the Schools Forgot to Teach: What You Need to Know to Get Ahead in Business. viii, 120p. (Orig.). 1996. pap. 14.95 (*0-9654600-0-2*) Jump Start Bks.

D'Amour, Fred E., et al. Manual for Laboratory Work in Mammalian Physiology. 3rd ed. LC 65-17285. 1996. pap. text 23.00 (*0-226-13563-2*) U Ch Pr.

Damour, Lisa K., jt. auth. see Curzan, Anne L.

Damousi, Joy. Depraved & Disorderly: Female Convicts, Sexuality & Gender in Colonial Australia. LC 96-46423. 231p. (C). 1997. text 64.95 (*0-521-58323-3*); pap. text 19.95 (*0-521-58723-9*) Cambridge U Pr.

***Damousi, Joy.** The Labour of Loss: Mourning, Memory & Wartime Bereavement in Australia. LC 99-18523. (Studies in the Social & Cultural History of Modern Warfare: No. 7). 256p. (C). 1999. 64.95 (*0-521-66004-1*); pap. 22.95 (*0-521-66974-X*) Cambridge U Pr.

Damousi, Joy & Lake, Marilyn, eds. Gender & War: Australians at War in the Twentieth Century. (Studies in Australian History). (Illus.). 359p. (C). 1995. text 69.95 (*0-521-45100-0*) Cambridge U Pr.

Damp. Dahlias: The Complete Guide. (Illus.). 160p. 1995. pap. 22.95 (*1-85223-889-5*, Pub. by Crolwood) Trafalgar.

Damp, Dennis V. The Book of U. S. Government Jobs: Where They Are, What's Available, & How to Get One. 6th ed. Richards, Victor, ed. LC 95-7817. (Illus.). 288p. 1996. pap. 34.95 incl. disk (*0-943641-16-0*) Bookhaven Pr.

— The Book of U. S. Government Jobs: Where They Are, What's Available & How to Get One. 6th rev. ed. Macie, Michelle, ed. LC 95-7817. (Illus.). 288p. 1995. pap. 18.95 (*0-943641-12-8*) Bookhaven Pr.

— The Book of U. S. Government Jobs: Where They Are, What's Available & How to Get One. 7th ed. LC 99-35716. (Illus.). 256p. 2000. pap. 19.95 (*0-943641-18-7*) Bookhaven Pr.

— Health Care Job Explosion! High Growth Health Care Careers & Job Locator. 2nd rev. ed. Taylor, Erin M., ed. LC 98-18903. Orig. Title: Health Care Job Explosion! Careers in the 90's. (Illus.). 320p. 1998. pap. 17.95 (*0-943641-15-2*) Bookhaven Pr.

— Post Office Jobs: How to Get a Job with the U. S. Postal Service. LC 95-52578. (Illus.). 224p. 1996. pap. 17.95 (*0-943641-14-4*) Bookhaven Pr.

— Post Office Jobs: How to Get a Job with the U. S. Postal Service. 2nd rev. ed. LC 99-32727. (Illus.). 224p. 2000. pap. 17.95 (*0-943641-19-5*) Bookhaven Pr.

Damp, Dennis V., ed. see Preston, James F.

Dampfer, Meldeau. Something Fishy at the Panama Canal. (Illus.). 72p. (Orig.). 1986. pap. 16.00 (*0-937953-02-4*) Tiptoe Lit Serv.

Dampier, Louis. Your First Turtle. (Illus.). 32p. 1992. pap. 2.29 (*0-86622-108-5*, YF-117) TFH Pubns.

Dampier, William C. History of Science. 572p. (C). 1948. pap. text 39.95 (*0-521-09366-X*) Cambridge U Pr.

Damrell, Joseph. Billy Maki: A Novel. LC 97-16931. 256p. 1997. pap. 12.95 (*0-87839-118-5*) North Star.

— Gift: A Novel of the Upper Peninsula. LC 92-18789. 1992. pap. 9.95 (*0-87839-071-5*) North Star.

Damrell, Joseph, ed. Isaac Polvi: The Autobiography of a Finnish Immigrant. LC 91-35581. 208p. 1991. pap. 12.95 (*0-87839-066-9*) North Star.

Damrell, Joseph D. Seeking Spiritual Meaning: The World of Vedanta. LC 77-9145. (Sociological Observations Ser.: No. 2). 252p. reprint ed. pap. 78.20 (*0-608-30994-X*, 202188500026) Bks Demand.

***Damron.** Introductory Animal Science. LC 99-28115. (Illus.). 765p. 1999. 96.00 (*0-13-273392-7*) P-H.

Damron. Women's Traveler, 1995. 1995. pap. text 10.95 (*0-929435-16-8*) Damron Co.

— Women's Traveler, 1996. 1996. pap. text 11.95 (*0-929435-20-6*) Damron Co.

Damron Co. Staff. Damron Women's Traveller: 1999 Edition. 1998. pap. 12.95 (*0-929435-30-3*) Damron Co.

Damron Company Staff. Damron Accommodations. 3rd ed. 1998. pap. text 18.95 (*0-929435-27-3*) Damron Co.

— Damron Road Atlas. 7th ed. (Illus.). 400p. 1998. pap. text 17.95 (*0-929435-31-1*) Damron Co.

Damron, O. Rex & O'Neill, Daniel J. An Introduction to Interpersonal & Public Communication. 139p. 1981. pap. text 10.95 (*0-89641-021-8*) American Pr.

Damron Publishing Staff. Damron Accommodations. 4th ed. 2000. pap. 19.95 (*0-929435-35-4*, Pub. by Damron Co) Pubs Dist Ctr Inc.

— Damron Men's Travel Guide 2000. 36th ed. 1999. pap. 17.95 (*0-929435-32-X*, Pub. by Damron Co) Pubs Dist Ctr Inc.

— Damron Women's Traveller 2000. 11th ed. 600p. 1999. pap. 13.95 (*0-929435-33-8*, Pub. by Damron Co) Pubs Dist Ctr Inc.

— Women's Traveller: 1998. 1997. pap. text 12.95 (*0-929435-26-5*) Damron Co.

Damron, Stephen. Agricultural Animals. 140p. (C). 1998. per. 36.95 (*0-7872-4684-0*) Kendall-Hunt.

Damron, Troy. Moments of Memory. (Illus.). 20p. (Orig.). pap. 0.99 (*1-885729-01-4*) Toccoa Falls.

Damrosch. Adventure in Reading: Grade 9. 85th ed. 1985. text, student ed. 65.25 (*0-15-335042-3*) Holt R&W.

— Adventures in American Literature: Grade 11. 1985. text 66.50 (*0-15-335044-X*) Holt R&W.

— Adventures in English Literature: Grade 12. 1985. text 66.50 (*0-15-335045-8*) Holt R&W.

***Damrosch.** The Anthology of British Literature, Vol 1. 1999. (*0-201-58879-X*) Longman.

Damrosch. The Longman Anthology of British Literature. 18.00 (*0-321-02737-X*) Addson-Wesley Educ.

Damrosch, ed. The Harpercollins Introduction to British Literature, Vol. 1. LC 98-4325. 3008p. (C). 1998. pap. 53.00 (*0-321-01173-2*) Addson-Wesley Educ.

— The Harpercollins Introduction to British Literature, Vol. 2. LC 98-4325. 3008p. (C). 1998. pap. 53.00 (*0-321-01174-0*) Addson-Wesley Educ.

Damrosch, Barbara. The Garden Primer. LC 86-40545. (Illus.). 688p. 1995. pap. 16.95 (*0-89480-316-6*, 1316) Workman Pub.

— Theme Gardens. LC 82-60062. (Illus.). 224p. 1982. pap. 18.95 (*0-89480-217-8*, 487) Workman Pub.

***Damrosch, Barbara.** Theme Gardens. rev. ed. 224p. 2001. pap. 19.95 (*0-7611-2137-4*) Workman Pub.

Damrosch, David. Anthology of British Literature: Early Modern Period. LC 99-35637. 1453p. (C). 1999. pap. 30.13 (*0-321-06763-0*) Addison-Wesley.

— Anthology of British Literature: Middle Ages. LC 99-35638. 595p. (C). 1999. pap. 30.13 (*0-321-06762-2*) Addison-Wesley.

— Anthology of British Literature: Restoration & the 18th Century. LC 99-28424. 950p. (C). 1999. pap. 30.13 (*0-321-06764-9*) Addison-Wesley.

— Anthology of British Literature: The Romantics & Their Contemporaries. LC 99-35639. 1071p. (C). 1999. pap. 30.13 (*0-321-06765-7*) Addison-Wesley.

— Anthology of British Literature: The Victorian Age. LC 99-34561. 925p. (C). 1999. pap. 30.13 (*0-321-06766-5*) Addison-Wesley.

— Anthology of British Literature: The 20th Century. LC 99-35640. 959p. (C). 1999. pap. 30.13 (*0-321-06767-3*) Addison-Wesley.

***Damrosch, David.** Longman Anthology of British Literature: Compact Version. LC 99-56300. 2648p. 1999. pap. 51.00 (*0-321-07670-2*) Longman.

— The Longman Compact Anthology of British Literature. LC 99-56300. 1999. pap. text 35.00 (*0-321-07672-9*); pap. text 35.00 (*0-321-07673-7*) Longman.

— Meetings of the Mind. LC 99-87371. 224p. 2000. 19.95 (*0-691-05055-4*) Princeton U Pr.

— Meetings of the Mind: Life, Literature & the Pursuit of Agreement. LC 99-87371. 2000. pap. write for info. (*0-691-05056-2*) Princeton U Pr.

Damrosch, David. The Narrative Covenant: Transformations of Genre in the Growth of Biblical Literature. LC 86-43001. 368p. 1990. pap. text 17.95 (*0-8014-9934-8*) Cornell U Pr.

— We Scholars: Changing the Culture of the University. LC 94-32442. (Illus.). 240p. 1995. text 35.00 (*0-674-94842-4*, DAMWES); pap. text 17.50 (*0-674-94843-2*, DAMWEX) HUP.

Damrosch, Leo. Fictions of Reality in the Age of Hume & Johnson. LC 89-16619. 272p. 1989. pap. text 16.95 (*0-299-12384-7*) U of Wis Pr.

— The Sorrows of the Quaker Jesus: James Nayler & the Puritan Crackdown on the Free Spirit. (Illus.). 384p. 1996. 42.50 (*0-674-82143-2*) HUP.

Damrosch, Leopold, Jr. God's Plot & Man's Stories: Studies in the Fictional Imagination from Milton to Fielding. LC 84-8754. (Illus.). 352p. 1996. lib. bdg. 30.00 (*0-226-13579-9*) U Ch Pr.

Damrosch, Leopold. The Uses of Johnson's Criticism. LC 75-19431. 250p. reprint ed. pap. 77.50 (*0-608-15893-3*, 203078800074) Bks Demand.

Damrosch, Leopold, Jr., ed. Modern Essays on Eighteenth-Century Literature. 502p. 1988. pap. text 26.95 (*0-19-504924-1*) OUP.

Damrosch, Lori F., ed. The International Court of Justice at a Crossroads. 511p. 1987. pap. 75.00 (*0-941320-46-4*) Transnatl Pubs.

Damrosch, Walter J. My Musical Life. 376p. 1990. reprint ed. lib. bdg. 79.00 (*0-7812-9105-4*) Rprt Serv.

— My Musical Life. (American Biography Ser.). 376p. 1991. reprint ed. lib. bdg. 79.00 (*0-7812-8098-2*) Rprt Serv.

Dams, Bernd H. & Zega, Andrew. Pleasure Pavilions & Follies: In the Gardens of the Ancien Regime. LC 97-177521. (Illus.). 192p. 1995. 50.00 (*2-08-013561-9*, Pub. by Flammarion) Abbeville Pr.

Dams, Bernd H., jt. auth. see Zega, Andrew.

***Dams, D., et al, eds.** Practical Aspects of SPIN Model-Checking: 6th International Workshop, SPIN'99, Held As FM'99 User Group Meeting, Toulouse, France, September 21 & 24, 1999, Proceedings. LC 99-49725. (Lecture Notes in Computer Science Ser.: Vol. 1680). x, 277p. 1999. pap. 52.00 (*3-540-66499-8*) Spr-Verlag.

Dams, Jeanne M. The Body in the Transept: A Dorothy Martin Mystery. 224p. 1996. mass mkt. 5.99 (*0-06-101133-9*, Harp PBks) HarpC.

— The Body in the Transept: A Dorothy Martin Mystery. LC 95-19220. 216p. 1995. 19.95 (*0-8027-3275-5*) Walker & Co.

— The Body in the Transept: A Dorothy Martin Mystery. large type ed. LC 96-41688. 284p. 1996. pap. 21.95 (*0-7838-1992-7*) Thorndike Pr.

***Dams, Jeanne M.** Death in Lacquer Red: A Hilda Johansson Mystery. LC 99-48839. 1999. 24.95 (*1-57490-240-7*, Beeler LP Bks) T T Beeler.

Dams, Jeanne M. Death in Lacquer Red: A Hilda Johansson Mystery. LC 98-45223. 240p. 1999. 22.95 (*0-8027-3329-8*) Walker & Co.

— Holy Terror in the Hebrides: A Dorothy Martin Mystery. Vol. 3. 272p. 1999. mass mkt. 5.99 (*0-06-101346-3*, Harp PBks) HarpC.

— Holy Terror in the Hebrides: A Dorothy Martin Mystery. LC 97-22018. (Dorothy Martin Mystery Ser.). 224p. 1997. 21.95 (*0-8027-3311-5*) Walker & Co.

***Dams, Jeanne M.** Holy Terror in the Hebrides: A Dorothy Martin Mystery. large type ed. LC 99-89095. 2000. write for info. (*0-7862-2407-X*) Mac Lib Ref.

— Killing Cassidy. (Dorothy Martin Mystery Ser.). 2000. 23.95 (*0-8027-3347-6*) Walker & Co.

— Malice in Miniature: A Dorothy Martin Mystery. 272p. 2000. mass mkt. 5.99 (*0-06-101345-5*) HarpC.

Dams, Jeanne M. Malice in Miniature: A Dorothy Martin Mystery. LC 98-24415. (Dorothy Martin Mystery Ser.). (Illus.). 220p. (gr. 8). 1998. 22.95 (*0-8027-3322-0*) Walker & Co.

***Dams, Jeanne M.** Red, White & Blue Murders: A Hilda Johansson Mystery. LC 00-22216. 256p. 2000. 23.95 (*0-8027-3341-7*) Walker & Co.

Dams, Jeanne M. Trouble in the Town Hall: A Dorothy Martin Mystery. 256p. 1998. mass mkt. 5.99 (*0-06-101132-0*, Harp PBks) HarpC.

— Trouble in the Town Hall: A Dorothy Martin Mystery. LC 96-26485. (Dorothy Martin Mystery Ser.). 256p. 1996. 20.95 (*0-8027-3285-2*) Walker & Co.

***Dams, Jeanne M.** The Victim in Victoria Station. 2001. mass mkt. 5.99 (*0-373-26368-6*) Harlequin Bks.

— The Victim in Victoria Station: A Dorothy Martin Mystery. LC 99-89073. 2000. write for info. (*0-7862-2409-6*) Thorndike Pr.

Dams, Jeanne M. The Victim in Victoria Station: A Dorothy Martin Mystery. LC 99-26942. (Dorothy Martin Mystery Ser.). 256p. 1999. 23.95 (*0-8027-3337-9*) Walker & Co.

Dams, R., jt. auth. see Adams, F.

Damschrod. Listen & Sing. 1995. pap. write for info. (*0-02-870330-8*) Macmillan.

Damschrode, David A. Listen & Sing: Lessons in Ear-Training & Sight-Singing. LC 96-182413. 1995. pap., teacher ed. write for info. (*0-02-870667-6*, Schirmer Books) Mac Lib Ref.

Damschroder. Listen & Sing. 1997. 40.00 (*0-02-864933-8*) Mac Lib Ref.

Damschroder, David. Listen & Sing: Lessons in Ear-Training & Sight-Singing. (Illus.). 492p. (C). 1995. 40.00 (*0-02-870665-X*, Schirmer Books) Mac Lib Ref.

Damschroder, David & Williams, David R. Music Theory from Zarlino to Schenker: A Bibliography & Guide. LC 90-6952. (Harmonologia Ser.: No. 4). 550p. 1991. lib. bdg. 84.00 (*0-918728-99-1*) Pendragon NY.

Damschroder, David A. Foundations of Music & Musicianship. 480p. 1992. 35.00 (*0-02-870661-7*, Schirmer Books) Mac Lib Ref.

— Foundations of Music & Musicianship. 192p. 1992. pap. write for info. (*0-02-870663-3*, Schirmer Books) Mac Lib Ref.

***Damschroder, Natalie J.** Hunter's Song. 256p. 2000. mass mkt. 5.99 (*1-929613-30-X*, Kismet MI) Avid MI.

***Damsey, Joan.** Physician Office Letters 2000. 2000. pap. 60.00 (*1-57947-081-5*) AMA.

Damsgaard, J., jt. auth. see Vitek, J.

Damsgaard-Madsen, Aksel, et al, eds. Studies in Ancient History & Numismatics: Presented to Rudi Thomsen. (Illus.). 270p. (C). 1988. 48.00 (*87-7288-161-5*, Pub. by Aarhus Univ Pr) David Brown.

Damsker, Matt. Totally Tulips. (Totally Flowers Ser.). (Illus.). 96p. 1996. pap. 5.95 (*0-89087-780-7*) Celestial Arts.

Damskis, Horst & Moller, Barbel. Verwaltungskultur in den Neuen Bundeslandern: Werte und Einstellungen von Fuhrungskraften in den Ministerialverwaltungen von Brandenburg und Sachsen. (Berliner Schriften zur Demokratieforschung Ser.: Bd. 4). (GER.). 191p. 1997. pap. 42.95 (*3-631-49997-3*) P Lang Pubng.

Damsky, I., jt. auth. see Polugayevsky, Lyev.

Damsky, Iakov. The Heavy Pieces in Action. 160p. 1997. pap. text 19.95 (*1-85744-054-4*, Pub. by Cadgn Bks) Macmillan.

Damsky, Iakov, jt. auth. see Poolugayevsky, Lyev.

***Damsky, Lee, ed.** Sex & Single Girls: Women Write on Sexuality. 320p. 2000. pap. 16.95 (*1-58005-038-7*) Seal Pr WA.

Damsky, Sheldon W. & Coon, James A. All You Ever Wanted to Know about Zoning... Salkin, Patricia, ed. (Illus.). 195p. (Orig.). (C). 1989. pap. text 55.00 (*0-8113-0000-5*) NY Plan Fed.

Damsteegt, P. Gerard. Foundations of the Seventh-Day Adventist Message & Mission. 348p. 1977. pap. 19.99 (*0-943872-45-6*) Andrews Univ Pr.

Damsteegt, Th, jt. see Dalmia, Vasudha.

Damsteegt, Theo. Giriraj Kisor's "Yatraem" A Hindi Novel Analysed. LC 98-120667. (Gonda Indological Studies: No. VI). xiv, 354p. 1997. pap. 82.00 (*90-6980-112-4*, Pub. by Egbert Forsten) Hodler & Stoughton.

Damude, Noreen, et al. Texas Wildscapes: Gardening for Wildlife. (Illus.). 250p. 1999. pap. 24.95 (*1-885696-30-2*, Pub. by TX Prks & Wldlife) U of Tex Pr.

Damus, Karla, ed. see Biancuzzo, Marie & Freda, Margaret Comberford.

Damus, Karla, ed. see Freda, Margaret Comerford & Patterson, Ellen T.

Damus, Karla, ed. see Harvey, Mildred G.

Damus, Karla, ed. see McFarlane, Judith & Parker, Barbara J.

Damus, Karla, ed. see Moore, Mary L. & Givens, Susan R.

Damus, Karla, ed. see Moos, Merry K. & Freda, Margaret C.

Damus, Karla, ed. see Passero, Virginia A.

Damus, Karla, ed. see Wjite, Denise & Poole, Judith H.

Damuth, John D. & MacFadden, Bruce J., eds. Body Size in Mammalian Paleobiology: Estimation & Biological Implications. (Illus.). 409p. (C). 1990. text 69.95 (*0-521-36099-4*) Cambridge U Pr.

D'Amyot, tr. see Plutarque.

Dan. The Spy from Israel. 1969. pap. 12.50 (*0-85303-015-4*, Pub. by M Vallentine & Co) Intl Spec Bk.

Dan, Alice, ed. Reframing Women's Health: Multidisciplinary Research & Practice. LC 94-7456. 1994. 59.95 (*0-8039-5773-4*); pap. text 28.00 (*0-8039-5860-9*) Sage.

Dan, Alice J. & Lewis, Linda L., eds. Menstrual Health in Women's Lives. (Illus.). 312p. 1991. pap. text 16.95 (*0-252-06209-4*) U of Ill Pr.

— Menstrual Health in Women's Lives. (Illus.). 312p. 1992. text 37.50 (*0-252-01784-6*) U of Ill Pr.

Dan-an, Cheng. Acupuncture & Moxibustion Formulas & Treatments. Ming, Wu, ed. & tr. by. from CHI. LC 95-83248. (Great Masters Ser.). 225p. (Orig.). 1996. pap. 22.95 (*0-936185-68-6*) Blue Poppy Pr.

Dan, Asit, jt. auth. see Sitaram, Dinkar.

Dan, Barbara. Survival Strategies for the Holidays. 100p. (Orig.). 1995. 5.95 (*1-884898-08-4*) Eden Pubng OR.

An Asterisk (*) at the beginning of an entry indicates that the title is appearing for the first time.

— Vicky: God's Angel in Our Midst. Orig. Title: Vicky: The Death of Our Baby. 64p. (Orig.). 1996. reprint ed. pap., per. 4.95 (*1-884898-10-6*) Eden Pubng OR.

Dan, Barbara G., ed. see Macdougall, Alan Scott.

Dan, F., jt. auth. see Oprea, C.

Dan, John. Behold! the Lamb of God: An Easter Passover Seder Service for Christians. (Illus.). 64p. (Orig.). 1995. pap. 3.95 (*1-884898-05-X*) Eden Pubng OR.

— Power to Change. LC 94-70391. (Illus.). 288p. 1994. 12.00 (*1-884898-00-9*); pap. 8.00 (*1-884898-01-7*) Eden Pubng OR.

Dan, John, et al. Power to Choose: True Stories of Tragedy & Triumph. (Illus.). 256p. (Orig.). 1995. pap. 8.00 (*1-884898-07-6*) Eden Pubng OR.

Dan, Joseph. Gershom Scholem & the Mystical Dimension of Jewish History. (Modern Jewish Masters Ser.). 350p. (C). 1988. pap. text 18.50 (*0-8147-1812-4*) NYU Pr.

— Jewish Intellectual History in the Middle Ages, 3. LC 93-50086. (Studies in Jewish History, Culture, & Thought: Vol. 3). 224p. 1994. 69.50 (*0-275-94777-7*, Praeger Pubs) Greenwood.

— Jewish Mysticism Vol. 1: Late Antiquity. LC 98-42910. Vol. I. 321p. 1998. 50.00 (*0-7657-6007-X*) Aronson.

— Jewish Mysticism Vol. 2: The Middle Ages. 363p. 1998. 50.00 (*0-7657-6008-8*) Aronson.

— Jewish Mysticism Vol. 3: The Modern Period. 433p. 1998. 50.00 (*0-7657-6009-6*) Aronson.

— Jewish Mysticism Vol. 4: General Characteristics & Comparative Study. 301p. 1998. 50.00 (*0-7657-6010-X*) Aronson.

— The Teachings of Hasidism. (Orig.). 1983. pap. text 19.95 (*0-87441-223-4*) Behrman.

Dan, Joseph, ed. Binah: Studies in Jewish History, Vol. I. LC 88-5813. (Studies in Jewish History, Culture, & Thought). 205p. 1989. 69.50 (*0-275-93036-X*, C3036, Praeger Pubs) Greenwood.

Dan, Joseph, ed. Binah: Studies in Jewish History, Vol. I. LC 88-5813. (Studies in Jewish History, Culture, & Thought). 205p. 1989. pap. 59.95 (*0-275-93035-1*, B3035, Praeger Pubs) Greenwood.

Dan, Joseph, ed. Binah: Studies in Jewish Thought, Vol. 2. LC 88-5813. (Studies in Jewish History, Culture, & Thought). 262p. 1989. pap. 59.95 (*0-275-93037-8*, B3037, Praeger Pubs) Greenwood.

— Binah: Studies in Jewish Thought, Vol. II. LC 88-38727. (Studies in Jewish History, Culture, & Thought). 262p. 1989. 69.50 (*0-275-93038-6*, C3038, Praeger Pubs) Greenwood.

Dan, Joseph, ed. The Christian Kabbalah: Jewish Mystical Books & Their Christian Interpreters. 231p. 1998. pap. 35.00 (*0-914630-19-9*) HUP.

— Jewish Intellectual History in the Middle Ages. LC 93-50086. (Studies in Jewish History, Culture, & Thought). 216p. 1994. pap. 19.95 (*0-275-94778-5*, Praeger Pubs) Greenwood.

— Studies in Jewish Mysticism. 220p. 1981. 25.00 (*0-685-11699-9*) Assn for Jewish Studies.

***Dan, Joseph & Herrmann, Klaus, eds.** Studies in Jewish Manuscripts. (Texts & Studies in Medieval & Early Modern Judaism: Vol. 14). 276p. 1999. 157.50 (*3-16-147044-3*, Pub. by JCB Mohr) Coronet Bks.

Dan, Joseph & Kiener, Ronald C., eds. The Early Kabbalah. (Classics of Western Spirituality Ser.: Vol. 51). 224p. 1986. pap. 14.95 (*0-8091-2769-5*) Paulist Pr.

Dan, Joseph & Talmage, Frank, eds. Studies in Jewish Mysticism. 25.00 (*0-87068-803-0*) Ktav.

Dan, Joseph, jt. ed. see Schafer, Peter.

Dan, Lea. Lea Dan's Spiritual Reflections: Devotions/ Meditations. Davis, B. L., ed. (Value Ser.: Vol. 1). (Orig.). pap. 9.00 (*0-9640982-1-0*) B L Davis.

dan Pustaka, Dewan Bahasa. Istilah Diplomasi Dan Hubungan Antarabangsa: Bahasa Inggeris-bahasa Melayu, Bahasa Melayu-bahasa Inggeris. LC 98-944738. xxiii, 170p. 1998. write for info. (*983-62-6120-6*) Dewan Pustaka.

Dan, R. Accumulated Index of Jewish Bibliographical Periodicals. 276p. (C). 1979. 75.00 (*963-05-1047-2*, Pub. by Akade Kiado) St Mut.

Dan, Uri. Capture & Trial of Adolph Eichman. 1993. 19.95 (*0-671-68107-9*) S&S Trade.

Dan-xi, Zhu. Extra Treatises Based on Investigation & Inquiry: A Translation of Zhu Dan-Xi's Ge Zhi Ya Lun. Flaws, Bob, ed. Shou-zhong, Yang & Wu-jin, Duan, trs. from CHI. LC 93-74980. (Great Masters Ser.). (Illus.). 135p. (Orig.). 1994. pap. 16.95 (*0-936185-53-8*) Blue Poppy Pr.

— The Heart & Essence of Dan-xi's Methods of Treatment: A Translation of Zhu Dan-xi's Dan Xi Zhi Fa Xin Yao. Flaws, Bob, ed. Shou-zhong, Yang, tr. from CHI. & intro. by. LC 93-72799. 450p. 1993. pap. text 29.95 (*0-936185-50-3*) Blue Poppy Pr.

Dana, jt. auth. see Lewis.

***Dana, Amber.** The Butterfly Moon. LC 99-46300. 200p. 1999. 24.95 (*0-7862-2219-0*) Macmillan.

— The Kiss of Life. large type ed. LC 98-48526. 193 p. 1999. write for info. (*0-7540-3637-5*) Chivers N Amer.

Dana, Amber. The Kiss of Life. large type ed. LC 98-48526. Date not set. 30.00 (*0-7838-0444-X*) Mac Lib Ref.

***Dana, Amber.** Love Is Triumph. large type ed. 320p. 1999. pap. 18.99 (*0-7089-5545-2*, Linford) Ulverscroft.

— A Rich Girl's Love. large type ed. LC 99-54774. (G. K. Hall Nightingale Ser.). 2000. 20.95 (*0-7838-8845-7*, G K Hall & Co) Mac Lib Ref.

Dana, Amber. A Rose Without Love. large type ed. LC 97-30535. 230p. 1997. pap. 21.95 (*0-7838-8306-4*, G K Hall Lrg Type) Mac Lib Ref.

— A Scarlet Dawn. large type ed. LC 96-94426. (Nightingale Ser.). 1996. 17.95 (*0-7838-1888-2*, G K Hall Lrg Type) Mac Lib Ref.

Dana, Ann S., jt. auth. see Handler, Marianne G.

Dana, Anna M. Under the Texas Sun: Adventures of a Young Cowpuncher. LC 86-14401. (Wardlaw Book Ser.). 112p. 1986. 15.95 (*0-89096-284-7*) Tex A&M Univ Pr.

Dana, Barbara. Emily Dickinson: Fictionalized Biography. (gr. 3-7). 14.95 (*0-06-028704-7*); mass mkt. 4.95 (*0-06-440843-4*) HarpC.

— Emily Dickinson: Fictionalized Biography. (J). (gr. 3-7). 14.89 (*0-06-028705-5*) HarpC.

Dana, Barbara. Necessary Parties. LC 85-45267. (Charlotte Zolotow Bk.). 352p. (YA). (gr. 7 up). 1986. 14.95 (*0-06-021408-2*) HarpC Child Bks.

— Young Joan. LC 90-39494. (Charlotte Zolotow Bk.). 384p. (YA). (gr. 7 up). 1991. 17.95 (*0-06-021422-8*) HarpC Child Bks.

— Young Joan. LC 90-39494. 352p. (YA). (gr. 5-9). 1997. pap. 5.95 (*0-06-440661-X*, HarpTrophy) HarpC Child Bks.

— Young Joan. LC 90-39494. 1997. 10.05 (*0-606-12125-0*, Pub. by Turtleback) Demco.

Dana, Barbara. Zucchini. 160p. (J). 1984. pap. 3.99 (*0-440-41402-4*) BDD Bks Young Read.

Dana, Barbara. Zucchini. LC 80-8448. (Charlotte Zolotow Bk.). (Illus.). 128p. (J). (gr. 4-7). 1982. lib. bdg. 15.89 (*0-06-021395-7*) HarpC Child Bks.

— Zucchini. (Charlotte Zolotow Bks.). (J). 1988. 9.09 (*0-606-12588-4*, Pub. by Turtleback) Demco.

— Zucchini Out West. LC 96-28976. (Illus.). 160p. (J). (gr. 3-5). 1997. lib. bdg. 14.89 (*0-06-024898-X*) HarpC Child Bks.

Dana, Beth J. StableMotion: A Progressive Home Exercise Program. LC 96-90970. (Illus.). iv, 75p. 1996. spiral bd. 18.95 (*0-9655783-0-5*) TheraTool.

Dana, Bev, ed. see Haggerty, Brian A.

Dana, Bev, ed. see Unseld, Teresa S.

Dana, Bruce W., ed. Malignant Lymphomas, Including Hodgkin's Disease: Diagnosis, Management, & Special Problems, No. 66. LC 93-127. (Cancer Treatment & Research Ser.). 192p. (C). 1993. text 175.50 (*0-7923-2171-5*) Kluwer Academic.

Dana, C. A. Proudhon & His Bank of the People: How to Solve the Current U. S. Financial Mess. 1992. lib. bdg. 75.00 (*0-8490-5457-5*) Gordon Pr.

Dana, Carroll, ed. see Arrigoni, Patricia.

Dana, Catherine, tr. see Potter, Beatrix & Pomaska, Anna.

Dana, Charles A. Art of Newspaper Making. LC 71-125689. (American Journalists Ser.). 1974. reprint ed. 16.95 (*0-405-01666-2*) Ayer.

— Proudhon & His Bank of the People. 1974. 59.95 (*0-8490-0906-5*) Gordon Pr.

— Recollections of the Civil War. LC 95-50715. (Illus.). xxix, 296p. 1996. pap. 12.95 (*0-8032-6601-4*, Bison Books) U of Nebr Pr.

Dana, Charles A., ed. Household Book of Poetry. LC 77-12923. (Granger Index Reprint Ser.). 1977. 35.95 (*0-8369-6163-3*) Ayer.

Dana, Charles H. Two Years Before the Mast. (Regents Illustrated Classics Ser.). (gr. 7-12). 1987. pap. text 3.75 (*0-13-935123-X*, 20571) Prentice ESL.

Dana, Charles L. The Peaks of Medical History. 2nd ed. LC 75-23703. (Illus.). reprint ed. 55.00 (*0-404-13255-3*) AMS Pr.

Dana, Daniel. La Automediaciou (Managing Differences) Como Pasar del Conflicto al Acuerdo. 2nd rev. ed. (SPA.). 200p. 1998. pap. 19.95 (*0-9621534-4-3*) MTI Pubns.

***Dana, Daniel.** Conflict Resolution. (Briefcase Bks.). 2000. pap. 14.95 (*0-07-136431-5*) McGraw.

Dana, Daniel. Managing Differences: How to Build Better Relationships at Work & Home. 2nd rev. ed. 240p. (Orig.). 1998. pap. 19.95 (*0-9621534-3-5*) MTI Pubns.

***Dana, David D.** The Fireman: The Fire Departments of the United States with a Full Account of All Large Fires. LC 99-68873. (Illus.). 367p. 1999. reprint ed. pap. 30.00 (*1-930423-01-2*) Brohan Pr.

***Dana, David T., III.** A Generous Idea: St. Paul's School & Seikei Gakuen. (Illus.). 158p. 2000. pap. write for info. (*1-889274-13-5*) Posterity Press.

Dana, Edward S. Minerals & How to Study Them. 3rd rev. ed. LC 49-7833. 333p. 1949. reprint ed. pap. 103.30 (*0-7837-3437-9*, 205775900008) Bks Demand.

Dana, Edward S., et al, eds. A Century of Science in America. LC 72-94344. (American Scientific Community, 1790-1920 Ser.). 1973. reprint ed. lib. bdg. 37.00 (*0-8420-1654-6*) Scholarly Res Inc.

Dana, H. E. Manual de Eclesiologia: A Manual of Ecclesiology. Robleto, Adolfo, tr. 1987. 10.99 (*0-311-17018-8*) Casa Bautista.

— Manual of Grammar of Greek in the New Testament. 1957. 53.00 (*0-02-327070-5*, Macmillan Coll) P-H.

Dana, H. E. & Mantey, J. R. Gramatica Griega del Nuevo Testamento: A Manual: Grammar of the Greek N.T. Robleto, Adolfo et al, trs. 1977. reprint ed. pap. 16.50 (*0-311-42010-9*) Casa Bautista.

Dana, Henry S. History of Woodstock. (Illus.). 641p. 1997. reprint ed. lib. bdg. 67.50 (*0-8328-6510-9*) Higginson Bk Co.

Dana, Jacqueline. Tota Rosa. (FRE.). 256p. 1985. pap. 11.95 (*0-7859-2009-9*, 2070376370) Fr & Eur.

Dana, James. Sutter of California. lib. bdg. 69.00 (*0-403-08971-9*) Scholarly.

Dana, James D. Characteristacts of Volcanoes. (Notable American Authors Ser.). 1992. reprint ed. lib. bdg. 90.00 (*0-7812-2608-2*) Rprt Serv.

— Collected Works. 1990. reprint ed. lib. bdg. 75.00 (*0-7812-2603-1*); reprint ed. write for info. (*0-318-67673-7*); reprint ed. write for info. (*0-318-67674-5*); reprint ed. write for info. (*0-318-67675-3*); reprint ed. write for info. (*0-318-67676-1*) Rprt Serv.

— Corals & Coral Islands. (Notable American Authors Ser.). 1992. reprint ed. lib. bdg. 90.00 (*0-7812-2607-4*) Rprt Serv.

— Crustacea. (Notable American Authors Ser.). 1992. reprint ed. lib. bdg. 90.00 (*0-7812-2606-6*) Rprt Serv.

— Geology. (Notable American Authors Ser.). 1992. reprint ed. lib. bdg. 90.00 (*0-7812-2605-8*) Rprt Serv.

Dana, James D., et al, eds. Dana's New Mineralogy: The System of Mineralogy of James Dwight Dana & Edward Salisbury Dana. 8th ed. LC 96-46965. 1872p. 1997. 325.00 (*0-471-19310-0*) Wiley.

***Dana, Janice T., et al.** Standardized Quantity Recipe File for Quality & Cost Control. 2nd ed. 524p. 1999. pap. 79.95 (*0-8138-2379-X*) Iowa St U Pr.

Dana, John C. Libraries: Addresses & Essays. LC 67-22088. (Essay Index Reprint Ser.). 1977. 23.95 (*0-8369-1329-9*) Ayer.

— Libraries: Addresses & Essays. LC 67-22088. (Essay Index Reprint Ser.). 299p. 1982. reprint ed. lib. bdg. 20.00 (*0-8290-0476-9*) Irvington.

***Dana, John Cotton.** The New Museum: Selected Writings. Peniston, William A., ed. LC 99-44326. 262p. 1999. pap. 28.00 (*0-931201-64-0*) Am Assn Mus.

Dana, Julian. Rivers of America: The Sacramento River of Gold. Date not set. lib. bdg. 23.95 (*0-8488-1968-3*) Amereon Ltd.

— Sacramento, River of Gold. Skinner, Constance L., ed. LC 72-144963. (Illus.). 1971. reprint ed. 29.00 (*0-403-00932-4*) Scholarly.

— Sutter. 1992. reprint ed. lib. bdg. 75.00 (*0-7812-5022-6*) Rprt Serv.

— Sutter of California: A Biography. LC 74-11308. (Illus.). 423p. 1974. reprint ed. lib. bdg. 35.00 (*0-8371-7644-1*, DASC, Greenwood Pr) Greenwood.

Dana, Katherine F. Our Phil, & Other Stories. LC 74-113653. (Short Story Index Reprint Ser.). 1977. 17.95 (*0-8369-3382-6*) Ayer.

***Dana, Leo-Paul.** Entrepreneurship in Pacific Asia: Past, Present & Future. 1999. pap. text 26.00 (*981-02-3930-0*) WSC Inst MA Studies.

Dana, Malcolm M. Annals of Norwich. 395p. 1998. reprint ed. pap. 31.50 (*0-7884-0838-0*, D050) Heritage Bk.

— The Norwich Memorial: Annals of Norwich, New London County, in the Great Rebellion of 1861-65. (Illus.). 395p. 1997. reprint ed. lib. bdg. 45.00 (*0-8328-5678-9*) Higginson Bk Co.

Dana, Nancy B., jt. auth. see Price, Anne.

Dana, Nancy F. & Dana, Thomas N. Qualitative Research in Education: A Guide to Study Design & Proposal Preparation. Kincheloe, Joe & Steinberg, Shirley R., eds. (Critical Education Practice Ser.). 200p. 1997. text 30.00 (*0-8153-2198-8*) Garland.

Dana, Nancy F. & Vann, Allan S. Beginning to Teach: Breaking Down Walls of Teacher Isolation. (Beginning to Teach Booklet Ser.). 16p. (Orig.). 1995. pap. 1.50 (*0-912099-21-6*, 421) Kappa Delta Pi.

Dana, Napoleon J. Monterrey Is Ours: The Mexican War Letters of Lt. Dana, 1845-1847. Ferrell, Robert H., ed. LC 88-29351. (Illus.). 248p. 1990. text 29.95 (*0-8131-1703-8*) U Pr of Ky.

Dana, Richard. Multicultural Assessment Perspectives for Professional Psychology. LC 92-17630. 320p. (C). 1992. 74.00 (*0-205-14092-0*, Longwood Div) Allyn.

Dana, Richard. Multicultural Intervention Perspectives for Professional Psychology. (C). 2000. 45.95 (*0-205-15897-8*, Macmillan Coll) P-H.

***Dana, Richard.** Murderer's Moon. large type ed. 296p. 1999. pap. 18.99 (*0-7089-5600-9*, Linford) Ulverscroft.

Dana, Richard. The Seaman's Friend. LC 79-4623. 1979. reprint ed. lib. bdg. 50.00 (*0-8201-1330-1*) Schol Facsimiles.

— Two Years Before the Mast. 1981. reprint ed. lib. bdg. 27.95 (*0-89966-426-1*) Buccaneer Bks.

— Understanding Cultural Identity in Intervention & Assessment. LC 97-45247. (Multicultural Aspects of Counseling Ser.). 1997. pap. 26.95 (*0-7619-0364-X*) Sage.

Dana, Richard, ed. Handbook of Cross-Cultural & Multicultural Personality Assessment. LC 99-30954. (Personality & Clinical Psychology Ser.). 700p. 1999. write for info. (*0-8058-2789-7*) L Erlbaum Assocs.

***Dana, Richard & Paine, Lauran.** Death Was the Echo. large type ed. LC 99-57949. (Nightingale Ser.). 2000. pap. 20.95 (*0-7838-8846-5*) Mac Lib Ref.

Dana, Richard, jt. ed. see May, Theodore W.

Dana, Richard Henry. The Buccaneer & Other Poems. (Notable American Authors Ser.). 1992. reprint ed. lib. bdg. 75.00 (*0-7812-2610-4*) Rprt Serv.

— Collected Works. 1990. reprint ed. lib. bdg. 75.00 (*0-7812-2609-0*); reprint ed. lib. bdg. 75.00 (*0-7812-2612-0*); reprint ed. write for info. (*0-318-67677-X*); reprint ed. write for info. (*0-318-67678-8*); reprint ed. write for info. (*0-318-67679-6*) Rprt Serv.

— The Idle Man. 1972. 59.95 (*0-87968-271-X*) Gordon Pr.

Dana, Richard Henry. Poems & Prose Writings. (Notable American Authors Ser.). 1992. reprint ed. lib. bdg. 75.00 (*0-7812-2611-2*) Rprt Serv.

Dana, Richard Henry. The Seaman's Friend. (Notable American Authors Ser.). 1992. reprint ed. lib. bdg. 75.00 (*0-7812-2614-7*) Rprt Serv.

— The Seaman's Friend: A Treatise on Practical Seamanship. LC 97-24116. (Illus.). 234p. 1997. pap. 7.95 (*0-486-29918-X*) Dover.

— To Cuba & Back. (Notable American Authors Ser.). 1992. reprint ed. lib. bdg. 75.00 (*0-7812-2615-5*) Rprt Serv.

— Two Years Before the Mast. (Illustrated Classics Collection 3). 64p. 1994. pap. 4.95 (*0-7854-0727-8*, 40468) Am Guidance.

— Two Years Before the Mast. 219p. Date not set. 21.95 (*0-8488-2558-6*) Amereon Ltd.

— Two Years Before the Mast. 383p. 1964. mass mkt. 6.95 (*0-451-52369-5*, CE1764, Sig Classics) NAL.

***Dana, Richard Henry.** Two Years Before the Mast. (Classic Ser.). 2000. mass mkt. 6.95 (*0-451-52759-3*, Sig Classics) NAL.

Dana, Richard Henry. Two Years Before the Mast. Philbrick, Thomas, ed. (American Library). 576p. 1981. pap. 11.95 (*0-14-039008-1*, Penguin Classics) Viking Penguin.

— Two Years Before the Mast. abr. ed. Fago, John N., ed. (Now Age Illustrated III Ser.). (Illus.). (J). (gr. 4-12). 1977. pap. text 2.95 (*0-88301-270-7*) Pendulum Pr.

***Dana, Richard Henry.** Two Years Before the Mast. large type ed. LC 99-48426. 560p. 1999. 32.95 (*1-56000-464-9*) Transaction Pubs.

Dana, Richard Henry. Two Years Before the Mast. (Notable American Authors Ser.). 1992. reprint ed. lib. bdg. 75.00 (*0-7812-2613-9*) Rprt Serv.

— Two Years Before the Mast: A Personal Narrative. 1964. 12.05 (*0-606-01959-6*, Pub. by Turtleback) Demco.

— Two Years Before the Mast: A Personal Narrative of Life at Sea. large type ed. LC 98-5398. 227p. 1998. 24.95 (*0-7838-8453-2*, G K Hall Lrg Type) Mac Lib Ref.

— Two Years Before the Mast Readalong. (Illustrated Classics Collection 3). 64p. 1994. pap. 14.95 (*0-7854-0743-X*, 40470) Am Guidance.

— Understanding Cultural Identity in Intervention & Assessment. LC 97-45247. (Multicultural Aspects of Counseling Ser.). 1997. 58.00 (*0-7619-0363-1*) Sage.

Dana, Robert. Hello Stranger. 64p. (Orig.). 1996. 14.95 (*0-938078-46-1*); pap. 9.95 (*0-938078-43-7*) Anhinga Pr.

***Dana, Robert.** Summer. LC 99-67834. xiv, 82p. 2000. 21.00 (*0-938078-63-1*); pap. 12.00 (*0-938078-64-X*, Pub. by Anhinga Pr) SPD-Small Pr Dist.

Dana, Robert. What I Think I Know: New & Selected Poems. 174p. (Orig.). 1991. 18.95 (*1-893032-11-6*); pap. 10.95 (*1-893032-12-4*) Jensen Daniels.

Dana, Robert, ed. A Community of Writers: Paul Engle & the Iowa Writers' Workshop. LC 98-48369. (Illus.). 308p. 1999. pap. 17.95 (*0-87745-668-2*) U of Iowa Pr.

***Dana, Rocky & Harrington, Marie.** The Blond Ranchero: Memories of Juan Francisco Dana. LC 60-10572. (Illus.). 142p. 1999. reprint ed. pap. 9.95 (*0-9673464-0-1*) South County Historical.

Dana, Rose. Citadel of Love. large type ed. (Romance Ser.). 272p. 1995. pap. 16.99 (*0-7089-7660-3*, Linford) Ulverscroft.

Dana, Samuel T. & Fairfax, Sally K. Forest & Range Policy. 2nd ed. (Illus.). 480p. (C). 1980. 91.88 (*0-07-015288-8*) McGraw.

Dana, Samuel T. & Krueger, Myron. California Lands. Bruchey, Stuart, ed. LC 78-53561. (Development of Public Land Law in the U. S. Ser.). (Illus.). 1979. reprint ed. lib. bdg. 26.95 (*0-405-11374-9*) Ayer.

Dana, Suzanna E., jt. auth. see Di Maio, Vincent J.

Dana, Thomas N., jt. auth. see Dana, Nancy F.

Dana, Trudy K. Strangers Who Molest: Protecting Children from Sexual Predators. 49p. 1991. pap. 4.50 (*0-9632692-0-8*) Snohomish Cnty CC.

Dana, William F. The Optimism of Ralph Waldo Emerson. 1972. 59.95 (*0-8490-0771-2*) Gordon Pr.

Danaber, Annette D., ed. see Hess, Shelley.

Danae Staff. Diccionario Ilustrado Danae de la Lengua Espanola. deluxe ed. (SPA., Illus.). write for info. (*0-7859-0434-4*, S50207) Fr & Eur.

— Enciclopedia Universal Danae, 6 vols., Set. 4th ed. (SPA.). 2400p. 1976. 595.00 (*0-8288-5678-8*, S50522) Fr & Eur.

Danagelo. Workbook to Accompany Introductory Italian. 288p. 1997. pap. 36.95 (*0-471-30942-7*) Wiley.

Danahay, Martin A. A Community of One: Masculine Autobiography & Autonomy in Nineteenth-Century Britain. LC 92-38402. (SUNY Series, The Margins of Literature). 232p. (C). 1993. text 64.50 (*0-7914-1511-2*); pap. text 21.95 (*0-7914-1512-0*) State U NY Pr.

Danahay, Martin A., ed. see Stevenson, Robert Louis.

***Danaher, Geoff.** Visions of Mackay. 1998. pap. 24.95 (*1-875998-52-7*, Pub. by Central Queensland) Accents Pubns.

Danaher, Kevin. Beyond Safaris: A Guide to Building People-to-People Ties with Africa. LC 91-70803. 1991. 39.95 (*0-86543-204-X*); pap. 12.95 (*0-86543-205-8*) Africa World.

— Corporations Are Gonna Get Your Mama: Globalization & the Downsizing of the American Dream. LC 96-31851. 224p. 1997. pap. 15.95 (*1-56751-112-0*); lib. bdg. 29.95 (*1-56751-113-9*) Common Courage.

— Folktales from The Irish Countryside. 128p. 1998. reprint ed. pap. 8.95 (*0-85342-849-2*, Pub. by Mercier Pr) Irish Amer Bk.

— In Whose Interest? A Guide to U. S.-South Africa Relations. 280p. 1985. pap. 11.95 (*0-89758-038-9*) Inst Policy Stud.

— The Year in Ireland: Irish Calendar Customs. (Illus.). 276p. 1997. reprint ed. pap. 19.95 (*0-937702-13-7*) Irish Bks Media.

Danaher, Kevin, ed. Fifty Years Is Enough: The Case Against the World Bank & the International Monetary Fund. LC 94-15460. (Project of Global Exchange Ser.). 208p. 1994. 30.00 (*0-89608-496-5*); pap. 16.00 (*0-89608-495-7*) South End Pr.

***Danaher, Kevin & Burbach, Roger, eds.** Globalize This! The Battle Against the World Trade Organization & Corporate Rule. LC 00-29508. 211p. 2000. pap. 15.95 (*1-56751-196-1*, Pub. by Common Courage) LPC InBook.

— Globalize This! The Battle Against the World Trade Organization & Corporate Rule. LC 00-29508. 211p. 2000. lib. bdg. 29.95 (*1-56751-197-X*, Pub. by Common Courage) LPC InBook.

D

Danaher, Kevin & Shellenberger, Michael, eds. Fighting for the Soul of Brazil: A Project of Global Exchange. 288p. 1995. 30.00 (*0-85345-923-1*, CL9231, Pub. by Monthly Rev); pap. 18.00 (*0-85345-924-X*, PB924X, Pub. by Monthly Rev) NYU Pr.

***Danaher, Patrick.** Beyond the Ferris Wheel: Educating Queensland Show Children. 1998. pap. 24.95 (*1-875998-54-3*, Pub. by Central Queensland) Accents Pubns.

Danaher, Peter J., jt. auth. see Rossiter, John R.

Danaher, William J. Insight in Chemistry. LC 87-36001. 162p. (Orig.). (C). 1988. pap. text 19.50 (*0-8191-6865-3*) U Pr of Amer.

Danaher, William J., ed. Australian Lonergan Workshop. 318p. (C). 1993. lib. bdg. 49.50 (*0-8191-9066-7*) U Pr of Amer.

Danahy, Michael. The Feminization of the Novel. (University of Florida Monographs: No. 65). 248p. 1991. 49.95 (*0-8130-1038-1*) U Press Fla.

Danai, Kourosh, et al, eds. ASME Dynamic Systems & Control Divison: Proceedings, International Mechanical Engineering Congress & Exposition, Atlantic, GA, 1996. LC 94-78983. (DSC Ser.: Vol. 58). 937p. 1996. pap. 300.00 (*0-7918-1528-5*, TJ151) ASME.

Danakas, George T. Practical Guide to the Care of the Gynecologic-Obstetric Patient. (Illus.). 1072p. (C). (gr. 13). 1996. pap. text 39.95 (*0-8151-2316-7*, 25553) Mosby Inc.

Danakas, John. Curve Ball. 153p. (J). (gr. 3-8). 1995. 16.95 (*1-55028-423-1*); pap. 8.95 (*1-55028-433-9*) Formac Dist Ltd.

— Hockey Heroes. 95p. (J). (gr. 3-8). 1998. text 6.95 (*1-55028-596-3*, Pub. by J Lorimer) Formac Dist Ltd.

— Lizzie's Soccer Showdown. 124p. (J). (gr. 3-8). 1995. pap. 8.95 (*1-55028-464-9*); bds. 16.95 (*1-55028-465-7*) Formac Dist Ltd.

***Danaos, Kosta.** The Magus of Java: Teachings of an Authentic Taoist Immortal. (Illus.). 208p. 2000. pap. 14.95 (*0-89281-813-1*, Inner Trad) Inner Tradit.

Danara, Laurel. Riven: The Sequel to Myst Strategies & Secrets (Unofficial) LC 97-61773. 192p. 1997. pap. text 14.99 (*0-7821-2215-9*) Sybex.

Danas, Joseph, Jr. Two Years Before the Mast. (Military Library). pap. 3.95 (*1-85326-563-2*, 5632WW, Pub. by Wrdsworth Edits) NTC Contemp Pub Co.

Danaubauer, Edwin, jt. auth. see Ciesla, William.

Danbom, David B. Born in the Country: A History of Rural America. LC 94-42020. (Revisiting Rural America Ser.). (Illus.). 232p. 1995. text 45.00 (*0-8018-5039-8*); pap. text 15.95 (*0-8018-5040-1*) Johns Hopkins.

— Our Purpose Is to Serve: The First Century of the North Dakota Agricultural Experiment Station. LC 89-63044. (Illus.). 225p. 1990. 24.00 (*0-911042-38-5*) NDSU Inst Reg.

Danbom, S. & Domenico, S. N., eds. Shear-Wave Exploration. LC 87-60488. (Geophysical Developments Ser.: No. 1). 282p. 1987. text 61.00 (*0-931830-45-1*, 121A) Soc Expl Geophys.

Danbrot, Margaret. New Cabbage Soup Diet. LC 97-186861. 1997. mass mkt. 4.99 (*0-312-96228-2*) St Martin.

Danbury, Hazel. Bereavement Counseling Effectiveness: A Client-Opinion Study. LC 96-84593. 288p. 1996. pap. 68.95 (*1-85972-292-X*, Pub. by Avebry) Ashgate Pub Co.

— Teaching Practical Social Work. 3rd ed. 124p. 1994. 86.95 (*1-85742-160-4*, Pub. by Arena) Ashgate Pub Co.

Danbury, Hazel, jt. auth. see Sharp, Mavis.

Danbury, Richard, 3rd, ed. see Sevil.

Danbury, Richard J., III, ed. see Whealdon, Everett.

Danbury, Richard S., III, ed. Dan River Anthology, 1996. 128p. 1996. text 39.95 (*0-89754-124-3*) Dan River Pr.

— Dan River Anthology, 1985. 1985. 42.95 (*0-89754-040-9*) Dan River Pr.

— Dan River Anthology, 1985. 1985. pap. 13.95 (*0-89754-039-5*) Dan River Pr.

— Dan River Anthology, 1989. 140p. 1989. 42.95 (*0-89754-069-7*); pap. 13.95 (*0-89754-068-9*) Dan River Pr.

— Dan River Anthology, 1986. 180p. 1986. 42.95 (*0-89754-046-8*); pap. 13.95 (*0-89754-045-X*) Dan River Pr.

— Dan River Anthology, 1990. 136p. (YA). 1990. pap. 13.95 (*0-89754-072-7*) Dan River Pr.

— Dan River Anthology, 1988. 104p. 1988. 42.95 (*0-89754-067-0*); pap. 9.95 (*0-89754-066-2*) Dan River Pr.

— Dan River Anthology, 1999. LC 98-72675. 120p. 1999. 42.20 (*0-89754-166-9*) Dan River Pr.

— Dan River Anthology, 1991. 148p. 1991. 42.95 (*0-89754-079-4*); pap. 13.95 (*0-89754-078-6*) Dan River Pr.

Danbury, Richard S., 3rd, ed. Dan River Anthology, 1997. 148p. 1997. 42.95 (*0-89754-122-7*); pap. 13.95 (*0-89754-121-9*) Dan River Pr.

***Danbury, Richard S., III, ed.** Dan River Anthology, 2000. 180p. 2000. 42.95 (*0-89754-177-4*); pap. 13.95 (*0-89754-178-2*) Dan River Pr.

Danbury, Richard S., III, ed. Dan River Anthology, 1987. 200p. (Orig.). 1987. 19.95 (*0-89754-061-1*); pap. 9.95 (*0-89754-060-3*) Dan River Pr.

— Dan River Anthology, 1993. 160p. 1992. 19.95 (*0-89754-081-6*); pap. 9.95 (*0-89754-080-8*) Dan River Pr.

Danbury, Richard S., ed. Dan River Anthology, 1994. 104p. 1993. 29.95 (*0-89754-087-5*) Dan River Pr.

Danbury, Richard S., III, ed. Dan River Anthology, 1998. 148p. 1998. 39.95 (*0-89754-140-5*); pap. 12.95 (*0-89754-139-1*) Dan River Pr.

— Dan River Stories. 128p. (Orig.). 1996. 25.95 (*0-89754-123-5*) Dan River Pr.

— When the Mockingbird Sings. 100p. (Orig.). 1986. 19.95 (*0-89754-059-X*); pap. 9.95 (*0-89754-058-1*) Dan River Pr.

Danbury, Richard S., III, ed. see Laird, Thomas.

Danbury, Richard S., III, ed. see O'Sullivan, Kathleen F.

Danbury, Richard S., ed. see Reinbolt, William, III.

Danbury, Richard S., III, ed. see Seviul.

Danbury, Richard S., III, ed. see Webster, Sheldon.

Danby. Fundamentals of Celestial Mechanics. 2nd ed. 1988. 24.95 (*0-943396-20-4*) Willmann-Bell.

Danby, Hal. Make It Yourself. (Illus.). 127p. 1974. 19.00 (*0-8464-1187-3*) Beekman Pubs.

Danby, Herbert, tr. Mishnah. 876p. 1933. text 69.00 (*0-19-815402-X*) OUP.

Danby, J. M., et al. Astrophysics Simulations: The Consortium for Upper Level Physics Software. LC 94-38485. 224p. 1995. pap. 46.95 incl. disk (*0-471-54879-0*) Wiley.

Danby, Jack. Enjoying East Yorkshire. (C). 1989. text 45.00 (*0-948929-11-1*) St Mut.

— Enjoying More East Riding. (C). 1989. text 45.00 (*0-948929-37-5*) St Mut.

Danby, Miles. Moorish Style. 240p. 1999. pap. 29.95 (*0-7148-3861-6*) Phaidon Pr.

— Moorish Style. LC 96-147153. (Illus.). 240p. (C). 1995. 59.95 (*0-7148-2951-X*, Pub. by Phaidon Press) Phaidon Pr.

Danbym. Fires of Excellence. LC 97-173676. 1998. 75.00 (*1-85964-087-7*, 851491, Pub. by Garnet-Ithaca) LPC InBook.

Danca, Vince. A Man's Best Friend Is His Doggerel. 44p. 1992. pap. write for info. (*0-9602390-0-6*) V Danca.

— The 1998 Compleat Jazz Calendar. (Illus.). 28p. 1997. pap. 9.95 (*0-9602390-2-2*) V Danca.

Dance, Bill & Tucker, Tim. On Largemouth Bass. 1996. pap. text 12.95 (*0-937866-53-9*) Atlantic Pub Co.

Dance, Bill & Wirth, Don. Bill Dance's Fishing Tips: America's Favorite Fisherman. LC 98-66164. (Illus.). 128p. 1998. pap. 6.95 (*1-887654-46-1*) Premium Pr TN.

Dance, Bill, jt. auth. see Sosin, Marle.

Dance, Bill, jt. auth. see Tucker, Tim.

***Dance, Charles.** Izaak Walton: A Drama in Four Parts. limited ed. (Illus.). 67p. 2000. boxed set 50.00 (*1-886967-10-5*) Meadow Run Pr.

Dance, Cherilyn. Focus on Adoption: A Snapshot of Adoption Patterns in England, 1995. 1997. pap. 60.00 (*1-873868-48-0*) BAAF.

Dance Collection Staff, jt. auth. see New York Public Library Staff.

Dance, Daryl C. Folklore from Contemporary Jamaicans. LC 84-5061. (Illus.). 272p. 1985. pap. 17.00 (*0-87049-566-6*) U of Tenn Pr.

— Long Gone: The Mecklenberg Six & the Theme of Escape in Black Folklore. LC 86-7097. (Illus.). 208p. 1987. pap. 17.00 (*0-87049-581-X*) U of Tenn Pr.

— Shuckin' & Jivin': Folklore from Contemporary Black Americans. LC 77-23635. 416p. 1978. 35.00 (*0-253-35220-7*) Ind U Pr.

— Shuckin' & Jivin': Folklore from Contemporary Black Americans. LC 77-23635. 416p. 1981. pap. 15.95 (*0-253-20265-5*, MB-265) Ind U Pr.

Dance, Daryl C., ed. Fifty Caribbean Writers: A Bio-Bibliographical Critical Sourcebook. LC 85-10008. 542p. 1986. lib. bdg. 85.00 (*0-313-23939-8*, DWR/, Greenwood Pr) Greenwood.

— Honey, Hush! An Anthology of African American Women's Humor. LC 97-6772. 673p. 1997. 30.00 (*0-393-04557-9*) Norton.

— Honey, Hush! An Anthology of African American Women's Humor. 716p. 1998. pap. 17.95 (*0-393-31818-4*, Norton Paperbks) Norton.

Dance, Edward H. History the Betrayer. LC 73-16869. 162p. 1975. reprint ed. lib. bdg. 55.00 (*0-8371-7237-3*, DAHB, Greenwood Pr) Greenwood.

Dance Films Association Inc. Modern Dance & Ballet on Film & Video: A Catalog, Vol. 1. 1986. 19.95 (*0-317-41588-3*) Dance Films.

Dance, Frank E. X. & Zak-Dance, Carol C. Speaking Your Mind: Private Thinking & Public Speaking. LC 93-80571. 352p. (C). 1994. pap. text 28.95 (*0-8403-8691-5*) Kendall-Hunt.

Dance, J. B., jt. auth. see Turcu, I. C.

Dance, James. Get the Most Out of Sales Meetings. LC 97-30115. (Here's How Ser.). (Illus.). 160p. 1997. pap. 12.95 (*0-8442-2483-9*, NTC Learningworks) NTC Contemp Pub Co.

— How to Get the Most Out of Sales Meetings: 50 Proven Techniques to Improve Selling Skills. (Illus.). 160p. 1993. 34.95 (*0-8442-3467-2*, NTC Business Bks) NTC Contemp Pub Co.

Dance, James C. Public Relations for the Smaller Library. 1979. pap. 8.00 (*0-8389-5547-9*) ALA.

Dance Magazine Inc. Staff. Stern's Performing Arts Directory, 1999. rev. ed. Kaplan, Barbara, ed. (Illus.). 450p. 1998. pap. 65.00 (*0-930036-30-1*) Dance Mag Inc.

Dance, S. Peter. Art of Natural History. 1990. 85.00 (*0-685-33411-2*) Random Hse Value.

— Shells. LC 91-58223. (Eyewitness Handbooks Ser.). (Illus.). 256p. 1992. 29.95 (*1-56458-032-6*); pap. 18.95 (*1-56458-060-1*) DK Pub Inc.

Dance, S. Peter, ed. Seashells of Eastern Arabia. (Illus.). 300p. 1995. 75.00 (*1-873544-64-2*, Pub. by Motivate Pubg Ltd) Intl Bk Ctr.

Dance, Sadashiv A. Divine Hymns & Ancient Thought Vol. 2: Ritual & the Quest for Truth. (C). 1995. 48.00 (*81-7013-122-7*, Pub. by Navarang) S Asia.

Dance, Stanley. The World of Count Basie. (Quality Paperbacks Ser.). (Illus.). xxii, 399p. 1985. reprint ed. pap. 15.95 (*0-306-80245-7*) Da Capo.

— The World of Duke Ellington. LC 80-29358. (Quality Paperbacks Ser.). (Illus.). xii, 311p. 1980. reprint ed. pap. 12.95 (*0-306-80136-1*) Da Capo.

— The World of Swing. LC 79-15249. (Quality Paperbacks Ser.). (Illus.). 436p. 1979. pap. 14.95 (*0-306-80103-5*) Da Capo.

Dance, Stanley, ed. Jazz Era: The Forties. (Roots of Jazz Ser.). 253p. 1989. reprint ed. lib. bdg. 27.50 (*0-306-76191-2*) Da Capo.

Dance, Stanley, jt. auth. see Barnet, Charlie.

Dance Theater Workshop Staff. Poor Dancer's Almanac: A Survival Manual for Choreographers, Managers & Dancers. White, David R. & Levine, Mindy N., eds. LC 83-72080. 320p. (Orig.). 1984. pap. 15.00 (*0-9611382-0-3*) Dance Theater.

Dance, Tom. High Standard: A Collector's Guide to the Hamden & Hartford Target Pistols. LC 91-60415. (Illus.). 192p. 1991. pap. 24.00 (*0-917218-47-7*) A Mowbray.

Dancer, Catherine C. Living with Kids in Los Angeles & Orange County: A Comprehensive Family Resource Guide from Conception to College Planning. 288p. (Orig.). 1993. pap. 18.00 (*0-938737-29-5*) Denali Press.

Dancer, E. N. Realization of Vector Fields & Dynamics of Spatially Homogeneous Parabolic Equations. LC 99-14984. (Memoirs Ser.). 1999. write for info. (*0-8218-1182-7*) Am Math.

Dancer, Edward N. Weakly Nonlinear Dirichlet Problems on Long or Thin Domains. LC 93-2236. (Memoirs of the American Mathematical Society Ser.: No. 501). 66p. 1993. pap. 26.00 (*0-8218-2563-1*, MEMO/105/501) Am Math.

Dancer, J. B. The Hanged Man. large type ed. (Linford Western Library). 1989. pap. 16.99 (*0-7089-6769-8*) Ulverscroft.

— The Lawmen: Evil Breed. large type ed. (Linford Western Library). 240p. 1989. pap. 16.99 (*0-7089-6713-2*, Linford) Ulverscroft.

— The Lawmen: Kansas, Bloody Kansas. large type ed. (Linford Western Library). 256p. 1989. pap. 16.99 (*0-7089-6720-5*, Linford) Ulverscroft.

— One Way to Die. large type ed. 1990. pap. 16.99 (*0-7089-6854-6*, Linford) Ulverscroft.

— Vengeance Trail. large type ed. (Linford Western Library). 1989. pap. 16.99 (*0-7089-6761-2*) Ulverscroft.

Dancer, Lacey. Noelle. 1996. pap. 1.78 (*0-8217-5557-9*) Kensgtn Pub Corp.

Dancer, Rex. Bad Girl Blues. LC 93-47452. 1994. 20.00 (*0-671-88007-1*) S&S Trade.

— Postcard from Hell. LC 94-40420. 1995. 21.00 (*0-671-88009-8*) S&S Trade.

— Postcard from Hell: Andy Derain Novel. 320p. 1995. 22.00 (*0-684-80362-3*) S&S Trade.

Dancey, Elisabeth. The Cellulite Solution. LC 97-207670. 1997. mass mkt. 5.99 (*0-312-96252-5*) St Martin.

Dancey, Peter G., jt. auth. see Vajda, Ferenc A.

Dancey, William S. & Pacheco, Paul J., eds. Ohio Hopewell Community Organization. LC 96-27659. 1997. 45.00 (*0-87338-561-6*) Kent St U Pr.

Dancha, Kim. My Own Time: The Authorized Biography of John Wetton. LC 96-70725. (Illus.). 180p. (Orig.). 1997. pap. 19.95 (*0-9654847-1-8*) Northern Line.

***Dancheck, Michelle & Stephenson, David.** SwingS Instructional Manual. (Illus.). 50p. 1999. pap. 11.95 (*0-9672667-0-X*) Swing Systems.

Danchenko, Lesia. Folk Art from the Ukraine. 233p. 1982. 150.00 (*0-7855-1503-8*) St Mut.

Danchev. Fin de Siecle. 256p. 1995. text 65.00 (*1-85043-967-2*, Pub. by I B T) St Martin.

Danchev, Alex. Oliver Franks: Founding Father. LC 92-40948. (Illus.). 250p. (C). 1993. text 45.00 (*0-19-821577-0*, Clarendon Pr) OUP.

Danchev, Alex. On Specialness: Essays in Anglo-American Relations. LC 97-16439. 202p. 1998. text 59.95 (*0-312-17647-3*) St Martin.

Danchick, Gabrielle, ed. see Kapralov, Yuri.

Danchin, Sebastian. Blues Boy: The Life & Music of B. B. King. LC 97-9716. (American Made Music Ser.). Orig. Title: B. B. King. (Illus.). 224p. 1998. 28.00 (*1-57806-017-6*) U Pr of Miss.

***Danchin, Sebastian.** Earl Hooker, Blues Master. (American Made Music Ser.). (Illus.). 320p. 2001. pap. 22.00 (*1-57806-307-8*); lib. bdg. 48.00 (*1-57806-306-X*) U Pr of Miss.

Danchise & Hall. A College Journey. 214p. (C). 1997. per. 40.95 (*0-7872-4308-6*, 41430801) Kendall-Hunt.

Danciger, Elizabeth. Homeopathy: From Alchemy to Medicine. 128p. 1989. pap. 5.95 (*0-89281-290-7*, Heal Arts VT) Inner Tradit.

Dancik, Deborah B. & Shroder, Emelie J., eds. Building Blocks for Library Space: Functional Guidelines. (Illus.). 24p. (Orig.). 1995. pap. 15.00 (*0-8389-7746-4*) Library Admin.

***Dancing Bear Staff.** Prospero in Therapy. 40p. 1999. pap. 5.00 (*0-9659307-1-8*) Dream Horse Pr.

Dancing Bear Staff, ed. see McNeilley, Michael.

Dancing Jester Press Staff, jt. auth. see Daniel, Shiloh.

Dancis, J., jt. ed. see Schneider, H.

***Danckers, Ulrich, et al.** A Compendium of the Early History of Chicago to the Year 1835 When the Indians Left. unabridged ed. (Illus.). 340p. 2000. 60.00 (*0-9675823-0-X*) Early Chicago.

Danckert. The Fourth Wise Man. (J). 1999. mass mkt. 16.00 (*0-689-80253-6*) S&S Bks Yung.

Danckert, Ludwig. Directory of European Porcelain. (Illus.). 684p. 1990. 70.00 (*0-7198-0003-X*, Pub. by NAG Press) Antique Collect.

Danckert, Ruth Wells, see Wells Danckert, Ruth.

Danckwerts, P., jt. auth. see Bradley, D. A.

Danckwerts, P., jt. auth. see Hobler, T.

Dancla, Charles. Six Airs Varies for Violin & Piano, Opus 89. (Carl Fischer Music Library: No.125). 1911. pap. 8.50 (*0-8258-0027-7*, L125) Fischer Inc NY.

Dancla, L. School of Mechanism Opus 74: For the Violin. 20p. 1986. pap. 3.95 (*0-7935-5459-4*) H Leonard.

— Six Airs Varies for Violin & Piano, Opus 89: Violin & Piano. 36p. 1986. pap. 7.95 (*0-7935-5436-5*) H Leonard.

Danco, Katharine L. From the Other Side of the Bed: A Woman Looks at Life in the Family Business. LC 81-13032. 1997. reprint ed. 19.95 (*0-9603614-2-1*) Ctr Family Busn.

Danco, Leon A. Beyond Survival: A Guide for the Business Owner & His Family. LC 74-29583. (Illus.). 1998. reprint ed. 19.95 (*0-9603614-0-5*) Ctr Family Busn.

— L' Entreprise Familiale: Preparer l'Avenir... Le Secret d'Une Transmission Reussie. (FRE., Illus.). 247p. 1998. 33.95 (*0-9603614-6-4*) Ctr Family Busn.

— Inside the Family Business. LC 80-23512. 1995. reprint ed. 19.95 (*0-9603614-1-3*) Ctr Family Busn.

— Outside Directors in the Family Owned Business: Why, When, Who & How. LC 81-12931. 1995. reprint ed. 29.95 (*0-9603614-3-X*) Ctr Family Busn.

— Someday It'll All Be . . . Who's? The Lighter Side of the Family Business. LC 90-49915. 1990. 24.95 (*0-9603614-5-6*) Ctr Family Busn.

Dancocks, Daniel G. D-Day Dodgers: The Canadians in Italy, 1943-1945. 1996. pap. text 26.99 (*0-7710-2543-2*) McCland & Stewart.

— Welcome to Flanders Fields. 404p. 1996. mass mkt. 2.99 (*0-7710-2546-7*) McCland & Stewart.

D'Ancona, Jacob. The City of Light: An Authentic Traveler's Tale. Selbourne, David, tr. from ITA. LC 97-21859. 352p. 1999. 29.95 (*0-316-17353-3*) Little.

Dancona, Jacob. City of Light The Hidden Journal of the Man Who Entered China Four Years Before Marco Polo. Selbourne, David, tr. from ITA. LC 99-38715. 528p. 1999. 29.95 (*1-55972-523-0*) Carol Pub Group.

D'Ancona, Matthew & Thiede, Carsten P. Eye Witness to Jesus. 1996. 23.95 (*0-614-96931-X*) Doubleday.

— Eyewitness to Jesus: Amazing New Manuscript Evidence about the Origins of the Gospels. (Illus.). 224p. 1996. 23.95 (*0-385-48051-2*) Doubleday.

D'Ancona, Matthew & Thiede, Carsten Peter. The Jesus Papyrus: The Most Sensational Evidence on the Origin of the Gospel since the Discovery of the Dead Sea Scroll. 224p. 2000. pap. 12.95 (*0-385-48898-X*) Doubleday.

D'Ancona, P., ed. see Aeschlimann, E.

Dancu, David. Homeopathic Vibrations: A Guide for Natural Healing. LC 95-73146. 224p. (Orig.). 1996. pap. 19.95 (*1-888604-01-8*) SunShine CO.

Dancu, Dumitru, jt. auth. see Dancu, Juliana.

Dancu, Juliana & Dancu, Dumitru. Romanian Icons on Glass. Ciocaltea, Georgeta, tr. LC 82-10846. (Romanian Traditions & Customs Ser.). (Illus.). 179p. reprint ed. pap. 55.50 (*0-7837-3577-4*, 204343600009) Bks Demand.

Dancy, Britta, et al. Langenscheidt German-Swedish Dictionary: Langenscheidt Handwoerterbuch Deutsch-Schwedisch. (GER & SWE.). 736p. 1985. 95.00 (*0-8288-0526-1*, M15821) Fr & Eur.

— Langenscheidt Handwoerterbuch Schwedisch-Deutsch: Swedish & German. (GER & SWE.). 640p. 1980. 95.00 (*0-8288-0527-X*, F60990) Fr & Eur.

Dancy, Jonathan. An Introduction to Contemporary Epistemology. 288p. 1985. pap. 27.95 (*0-631-13622-3*) Blackwell Pubs.

— Moral Reasons. LC 92-21888. 256p. 1997. pap. 29.95 (*0-631-18792-8*) Blackwell Pubs.

***Dancy, Jonathan.** Normativity. (Ratio Special Issues Ser.). 160p. 2000. pap. 22.95 (*0-631-22041-0*) Blackwell Pubs.

— Practical Reality. 195p. 2000. 29.95 (*0-19-824115-1*) OUP.

Dancy, Jonathan, ed. Reading Parfit. LC 96-37737. (Illus.). 352p. 1997. pap. text 57.95 (*0-631-16871-0*) Blackwell Pubs.

— Reading Parfit. LC 96-37737. (Illus.). 352p. (C). 1997. pap. text 26.95 (*0-631-19726-5*) Blackwell Pubs.

Dancy, Jonathan, et al, eds. Human Agency: Language, Duty, & Value. LC 88-12306. 328p. 1988. 42.50 (*0-8047-1474-6*) Stanford U Pr.

Dancy, Jonathan & Sosa, Ernest, eds. A Companion to Epistemology. (Companions to Philosophy Ser.). 560p. 1994. pap. text 31.95 (*0-631-19258-1*) Blackwell Pubs.

Dancy, Jonathan, ed. see Berkeley, George.

Dancy-Jones, John. Performance Poems. (Illus.). 24p. 1988. pap. 5.00 (*0-929170-08-3*) Paper Plant.

Dancy, R. M. Sense & Contradiction: A Study in Aristotle. LC 75-2184. (Synthese Historical Library: No. 14). 196p. 1975. lib. bdg. 93.00 (*90-277-0565-8*, D Reidel) Kluwer Academic.

— Sense & Contradiction: A Study in Aristotle. (Synthese Historical Library). 196p. 1980. pap. text 48.00 (*90-277-1189-5*) Kluwer Academic.

— Two Studies in the Early Academy. LC 90-40610. (SUNY Series in Ancient Greek Philosophy). 231p. (C). 1991. pap. text 21.95 (*0-7914-0633-4*) State U NY Pr.

Dancy, R. M., ed. Kant & Critique: New Essays in Honor of W. H. Werkmeister. LC 93-3264. (Synthese Library). 204p. 1993. text 120.50 (*0-7923-2244-4*) Kluwer Academic.

Dancy, Rahima Baldwin. You Are Your Child's First Teacher. rev. ed. LC 88-3983. (Illus.). 380p. 2000. pap. 14.95 (*0-89087-519-7*) Celestial Arts.

***Dancy, Rahima Baldwin.** You Are Your Child's First Teacher: What Parents Can Do with & for Their Children from Birth. rev. ed. LC 00-24110. (Illus.). 396p. 2000. pap. 14.95 (*0-89087-967-2*) Celestial Arts.

Dancy, T. E. & Robinson, E. L., eds. Flat Rolled Products: Rolling & Treatment. LC 59-14888. (Metallurgical Society Conference Ser.: Vol. 1). 149p. reprint ed. pap. 46.20 (*0-608-11435-9*, 200066400038) Bks Demand.

D

An Asterisk (*) at the beginning of an entry indicates that the title is appearing for the first time.

Dancyger. Introduction to Filmmaking. (C). 1998. pap. text 40.50 (0-15-502861-8, Pub. by Harcourt Coll Pubs) Harcourt.

Dancyger, Ken. Broadcast Writing: Drama, Comedies, & Documentaries. (Electronic Media Guide Ser.). 112p. 1991. pap. 24.95 (0-240-80054-0, Focal) Buttrwrth-Heinemann.

***Dancyger, Ken.** Global Script Writing. 256p. 2001. pap. 22.95 (0-240-80428-7, Focal) Buttrwrth-Heinemann.

Dancyger, Ken. Technique of Film & Video Editing: Theory & Practice. 2nd ed. LC 96-30880. (Illus.). 380p. 1996. pap. 37.95 (0-240-80255-1, Focal) Buttrwrth-Heinemann.

***Dancyger, Ken.** Technique of Film & Video Editing: Theory & Practice. 3rd ed. (Illus.). 448p. 2001. pap. 35.95 (0-240-80420-1, Focal) Buttrwrth-Heinemann.

Dancyger, Ken & Rush, Jeff. Alternative Scriptwriting: Writing Beyond the Rules. 2nd ed. 300p. 1995. pap. 29.95 (0-240-80218-7, Focal) Buttrwrth-Heinemann.

Dancyger, Ken, jt. auth. see Cooper, Pat.

Dancyger, Ruth. The Temple - Tifereth Isreal, 1850-2000. Mcginty, Linda, ed. (Illus.). 1999. pap. write for info. (0-9621087-1-5) Temple-Tifereth.

Dancyger, Ruth & Glaubinger, Jane. The Art of Phyllis Seltzer. (Women's Ser.). 53p. 1995. pap. text 20.00 (1-893023-52-4) Ohio Artists.

Dancygier, Barbara. Conditionals & Prediction: Time, Knowledge & Causation in English. LC 98-13861. (Cambridge Studies in Linguistics: No. 87). 224p. (C). 1998. text 59.95 (0-521-59151-1) Cambridge U Pr.

— Gastroenterologic Endoscopic Sonography. LC 99-28831. (Illus.). 244p. 1999. 79.00 (0-86577-839-6) Thieme Med Pubs.

***Dancygier, Henryk, et al.** Gastroenterologic Endoscopic Ultrasonography. LC 99-28831. 1999. write for info. (3-13-116471-9) Thieme Med Pubs.

Dancz, Virginia H. Women & Party Politics in Peninsular Malaysia. (South-East Asian Social Science Monographs). (Illus.). 292p. 1987. text 35.00 (0-19-582689-2) OUP.

Dand, Robin. The International Cocoa Trade. (Wiley Trading Advantage Ser.). (Illus.). 375p. 1997. 95.00 (0-471-19055-1) Wiley.

Dand, Robin. International Cocoa Trade. 2nd ed. (Illus.). 304p. 1999. 159.95 (1-85573-434-6) Am Educ Systs.

***Dand, Robin.** International Cocoa Trade. 2nd ed. LC 99-32796. 1999. write for info. (0-8493-2266-9) CRC Pr.

Danda, Ajit K. Ethnicity in India. (C). 1991. 25.00 (81-210-0270-2, Pub. by Inter-India Pubns) S Asia.

— Research Methodology in Anthropology. (C). 1992. 17.00 (81-210-0295-8, Pub. by Inter-India Pubns) S Asia.

— Weaker Sections in Indian Villages, 2 vols., Set. (C). 1993. 64.00 (81-210-0303-2, Pub. by Inter-India Pubns) S Asia.

Dandamaev, M. A. A Political History of the Achaemenid Empire. Vogelsang, W. J., tr. from RUS. (Illus.). xv, 373p. 1990. 144.00 (90-04-09172-6) Brill Academic Pubs.

Dandamaev, Muhammad A. Slavery in Babylonia. Powell, Marvin A. & Weisberg, David B., eds. Powell, Victoria A., tr. from RUS. LC 84-10225.Tr. of Rabstov v Vavilonii. 836p. 1984. 55.00 (0-87580-104-8) N Ill U Pr.

Dandamell, Birgitta & Danielsson, Ulla. Twined Knitting. Hansen, Robin O., tr. from SWE. LC 89-83442. (Illus.). 120p. 1994. pap. 16.95 (1-883010-02-0) Interweave.

Dandamudi, Sivarama P. & Gries, D. Introduction to Assembly Language Programming: From 8086 to Pentium Processors. Schneider, F. B., ed. LC 98-17534. (Undergraduate Texts in Computer Science Ser.). (Illus.). 650p. 1998. 69.95 (0-387-98530-1) Spr-Verlag.

Dandaneau, Steven & Falcone, Maud. Social & Cultural Theory Vol. 1: A Wrong Life - Studies in Lifeworld-Grounded Critical Theory. 1998. 73.25 (0-7623-0466-9) Jai Pr.

Dandaneau, Steven P. A Town Abandoned: Flint, Michigan, Confronts Deindustrialization. LC 95-47289. (SUNY Series in Popular Culture & Political Change). 259p. (C). 1996. text 59.50 (0-7914-2877-X); pap. text 21.95 (0-7914-2878-8) State U NY Pr.

***Dandaneau, Steven P.** A Wrong Life: Studies in Lifeworld-Grounded Critical Theory. LC 98-28055. (Social & Cultural Theories Ser.: Vol. 1). 1998. 73.25 (0-7623-0478-2) Jai Pr.

Dandapani, Krishnan, jt. ed. see Haar, Jerry.

Dandavate, Madhu. As the Mind Unfolds: Issues & Personalities. Vivekanandan, B., ed. xxv, 322p. 1993. 30.00 (81-85402-19-1, Pub. by Shipra Pubns) Nataraj Bks.

— Yusuf Meherally: Quest for New Horizons. 1986. 19.00 (0-86132-139-1, Pub. by Popular Prakashan) S Asia.

Dandavate, Pramila, et al, eds. Widows & Destitute Women in India. 145p. 1989. text 15.95 (81-7027-139-8, Pub. by Radiant Pubs) S Asia.

Dandavati, Annie G. The Women's Movement & the Transition to Democracy in Chile. (American University Studies: Series 9, Vol. 172). XIV, 171p. (C). 1996. pap. text 24.95 (0-8204-2562-1) P Lang Pubng.

Dande, Leon. Blue Blood. LC 72-37589. (Black Heritage Library Collection). 1977. reprint ed. 40.95 (0-8369-8965-1) Ayer.

Dandekar, B. B. Bene Israel Tales. 143p. 1991. 11.95 (0-942387-08-2) AB Lit Hse.

— David Rahabi. Benjamin, B. S., ed. 177p. 1993. 14.95 (0-942387-10-4) AB Lit Hse.

— The Jewish Amendment. Benjamin, B. S., ed. 182p. 1992. 14.95 (0-942387-09-0) AB Lit Hse.

— A Nazi among Jews. Benjamin, B. S., ed. 272p. 1990. 14.95 (0-942387-06-6) AB Lit Hse.

— Rampaging Lovers. 312p. 1988. 14.95 (0-942387-04-X) AB Lit Hse.

Dandekar, Hemalata C. Beyond Curry: Quick & Easy Indian Cooking Featuring Cuisine from Maharashtra State. LC 82-74367. (Special Publications: No. 3). (Illus.). 162p. (Orig.). 1983. pap. 14.95 (0-89148-026-9) Ctr S&SE Asian.

— Men to Bombay, Women at Home: Urban Influence on Sugao Village, Deccan Maharashtra, India, 1942-1982. LC 85-48240. (Michigan Papers on South & Southeast Asia: No. 28). (Illus.). 325p. (C). 1986. 31.95 (0-89148-035-8); pap. 15.95 (0-89148-036-6) Ctr S&SE Asian.

— Shelter, Woman, & Development: First & Third World Perspectives. 1993. pap. 37.50 (0-911586-96-2) Wahr.

Dandekar, Hemalata C., ed. The Planner's Use of Information. LC 88-71130. (Illus.). 224p. 1988. reprint ed. pap. 33.95 (0-918286-56-5, Planners Press) Am Plan Assn.

Dandekar, Kumudini. The Elderly in India. LC 96-4407. 228p. 1996. 29.95 (0-8039-9301-3) Sage.

Dandekar, Surya, jt. auth. see Sinha, R. P.

Dandekar, Thomas & Sharma, Kishore. Regulatory RNA. LC 97-44012. (Biotechnology Intelligence Unit Ser.). 205p. 1998. 149.00 incl. 5.25 hd (1-57059-480-5) Landes Bioscience.

— Regulatory RNA. LC 97-44012. (Biotechnology Intelligence Unit Ser.). 205p. 1998. 149.00 incl. 5.25 hd (3-540-64343-5) Spr-Verlag.

Dandekar, V. M. The Indian Economy, 1947-92: Population, Poverty & Employment. (Indian Economy Ser.: Vol. 2). 444p. (C). 1996. 39.95 (0-8039-9270-X) Sage.

— Poverty in India. 159p. 1971. 8.95 (0-318-37213-4) Asia Bk Corp.

Dandekar, Vinayak M. The Indian Economy, 1947-92. LC 94-31777. (Indian Economy Ser.: Vol. 2). 1995. 29.95 (0-8039-9185-1) Sage.

Dandeker, Christopher, ed. Nationalism & Violence. LC 97-30500. 1997. text 34.95 (1-56000-339-1) Transaction Pubs.

Dandelion, Pink. A Sociological Analysis of the Theology of Quakers: The Silent Revolution. LC 96-23943. (Studies in Religion & Society: No. 34). 456p. 1997. text 109.95 (0-7734-8807-3) E Mellen.

Dandi. Christmas Buttons. (Illus.). 12p. (J). (ps-k). 1997. pap. 6.99 (1-57151-600-X, Nibble Me Bks) Picture Me Bks.

— Easter Buttons. (Illus.). 12p. (J). (ps-k). 1998. pap. 6.99 (1-57151-601-8, Nibble Me Bks) Picture Me Bks.

— Halloween Buttons. (Illus.). 12p. (J). (ps-k). 1998. pap. 6.99 (1-57151-602-6, Nibble Me Bks) Picture Me Bks.

— Picture Me As Goldilocks. LC 97-229323. (Fairy Tale Ser.). (Illus.). 8p. (Orig.). (J). (ps-1). 1997. bds. 6.99 (1-57151-529-1, 1-57151-529-1) Picture Me Bks.

— Picture Me As Jack & the Beanstalk. LC 97-229317. (Fairy Tale Ser.). (Illus.). 8p. (Orig.). (J). (ps-1). 1997. bds. 6.99 (1-57151-531-3, 1-57151-531-3) Picture Me Bks.

— Picture Me As Little Red Riding Hood. LC 97-229320. (Fairy Tale Ser.). (Illus.). 8p. (Orig.). (J). (ps-1). 1997. bds. 6.99 (1-57151-530-5, 1-57151-530-5) Picture Me Bks.

— Picture Me at the First Christmas. (Inspirational Picture Me Ser.). (Illus.). 8p. (J). (ps-k). 1997. bds. 6.99 (1-57151-534-8) Picture Me Bks.

— Picture Me on Halloween. (Picture Me Holiday Ser.). (Illus.). 8p. (J). (ps-3). 1997. bds. 6.99 (1-57151-536-4) Picture Me Bks.

— Picture Me on Noah's Ark. (Illus.). 8p. (J). (ps-k). 1997. bds. 6.99 (1-57151-532-1) Picture Me Bks.

— Picture Me on Santa's Knee. (Picture Me Holiday Ser.). (Illus.). 8p. (J). (ps-k). 1997. bds. 6.99 (1-57151-537-2) Picture Me Bks.

— Picture Me with Jonah & the Whale. (Inspirational Picture Me Ser.). (Illus.). 8p. (J). (ps-k). 1997. bds. 6.99 (1-57151-533-X) Picture Me Bks.

— Picture Me with My Friend Jesus: Boy Version. (Illus.). 8p. (Orig.). (J). (ps-2). 1998. bds. 6.99 (1-57151-541-0) Picture Me Bks.

— Picture Me with My Friend Jesus: Girl Version. (Illus.). 8p. (Orig.). (J). (ps-2). 1998. bds. 6.99 (1-57151-542-9) Picture Me Bks.

— Picture Me with the Easter Bunny. (Picture Me Holiday Ser.). (Illus.). 8p. (J). (ps-k). 1997. bds. 6.99 (1-57151-535-6) Picture Me Bks.

Dandin. Dandin's Dasha-Kumara-Charita: The Ten Princes. Ryder, Arthur W., tr. from SAN. LC PK3794.D4D3. 248p. reprint ed. pap. 76.90 (0-608-10849-9, 201203200079) Bks Demand.

Dandliker, R., et al, eds. Optical Sensors, Vol. 6. 658p. 1992. lib. bdg. 300.00 (0-89573-678-0, Wiley-VCH) Wiley.

Dandmayev, M., ed. Societies & Languages of the Ancient Near East: Studies in Honour of I. M. Diakonoff. 1982. pap. 69.95 (0-85668-205-5, Pub. by Aris & Phillips) David Brown.

Dando, Malcolm. Biological Warfare in the Twenty-First Century. 260p. 1994. 40.00 (1-85753-064-0, Pub. by Brasseys) Brasseys.

***Dando, Malcolm.** The New Biological Weapons: Threat, Proliferation & Control. 180p. 2000. 49.95 (1-55587-924-1) L Rienner.

Dando, Malcolm & Rogers, Paul. A Violent Peace: Global Security after the Cold War. 207p. 1992. 37.00 (0-08-036694-5, Pub. by Brasseys) Brasseys.

Dando, Malcolm R. A New Form of Warfare: The Rise of Non-Lethal Weapons. (Illus.). 200p. 1996. 39.95 (1-85753-127-2, Pub. by Brasseys) Brasseys.

Dando, Malcom, jt. ed. see Blunden, Margaret.

Dando, Marc & Burchett, Michael. SeaLife: A Guide to the Marine Environment. Waller, Geoffrey, ed. (Illus.). 432p. 1996. 49.95 (1-56098-633-6) Smithsonian.

Dando, Shigemitsu. Criminal Law of Japan: The General Part. George, B. J., tr. from JPN. LC 96-48547. (Wayne State University Law School Comparative Criminal Law Project Ser.: Vol. 19). xxiv, 523p. 1997. 85.00 (0-8377-0653-X, Rothman) W S Hein.

Dando, William A., et al. Russia & the Independent Nations of the Former U. S. S. R. Geofacts & Maps. 112p. (C). 1995. text. write for info. (0-697-27754-2, WCB McGr Hill) McGrw-H Hghr Educ.

Dandola, John. Dead at the Box Office. Orig. Title: West of Orange. 2000p. write for info. (1-878452-25-8, Compass Point Mysteries) Quincannon.

— Dead in Their Sights: An Edie Koslow-Tony del Plato Mystery. LC 00-27860. 2000. write for info. (1-878452-26-6, Compass Point Mysteries) Quincannon.

Dandola, John. Leif the Lucky. (Learning & Coloring Bks.). (Illus.). 24p. (J). (gr. k up). 1991. pap. 3.95 (1-878452-05-3, Tory Corner) Quincannon.

— Rogers' Rangers. (Learning & Coloring Bks.). (Illus.). 24p. (YA). (gr. k up). 1992. pap. 3.95 (1-878452-08-8, Tory Corner) Quincannon.

***Dandola, John.** Wicked Is the Wind: A Jeffrey Devereaux--Kirsten Eriksson Novel. LC 00-27859. 2000. write for info. (1-878452-28-2, Compass Point Mysteries) Quincannon.

— Wind of Time. write for info. (1-878452-27-4, Compass Point Mysteries) Quincannon.

Dandola, John, intro. The Prince Valiant Coloring Book: Authorized Edition. deluxe limited ed. (Illus.). 52p. 1990. reprint ed. pap. 6.95 (1-878452-00-2, Tory Corner) Quincannon.

D'Andrade, Diane, ed. see Bunting, Eve.

D'Andrade, Diane, ed. see Hall, Lynn.

D'Andrade, Diane, ed. see Hayes, Ann.

D'Andrade, Diane, ed. see Ingold, Jeanette.

D'Andrade, Diane, ed. see Johnson, Pamela.

D'Andrade, Diane, ed. see Lattimore, Eleanor F.

D'Andrade, Diane, ed. see McPhail, David.

D'Andrade, Diane, ed. see Most, Bernard.

D'Andrade, Diane, ed. see Walsh, Ellen S.

D'Andrade, Diane, ed. see Wilbur, Richard.

D'Andrade, Diane, ed. see Willard, Nancy.

D'Andrade, Ernesto, jt. auth. see Mateus, Maria Helena.

D'Andrade, Kendall, jt. ed. see Werhane, Patricia.

D'Andrade, Roy. The Development of Cognitive Anthropology. (Illus.). 286p. (C). 1995. text 59.95 (0-521-45370-4); pap. text 18.95 (0-521-45976-1) Cambridge U Pr.

D'Andrade, Roy G. & Strauss, Claudia, eds. Human Motives & Cultural Models. (Publications for the Society for Psychological Anthropology). (Illus.). 252p. (C). 1992. text 64.95 (0-521-41233-1) Cambridge U Pr.

D'Andraia, Frank, ed. The Academic Library Director: Reflections on a Position in Transition. LC 97-10967. 108p. 1997. 39.95 (0-7890-0320-1) Haworth Pr.

Dandre, Victor E. Anna Pavlova in Art & Life. LC 70-180025. (Illus.). 410p. 1979. reprint ed. 42.95 (0-405-08428-5, Pub. by Blom Pubns) Ayer.

D'Andrea, A., et al, eds. Materials for Photonic Devices - Italy, 27-31 May 1991. 300p. (C). 1991. text 93.00 (981-02-0648-8) World Scientific Pub.

— Optics of Excitons in Confined Systems: Proceedings of the International Meeting, Italy, 24-27 September 1991. (Institute of Physics Conference Ser.: No. 123). (Illus.). 376p. 1992. 170.00 (0-85498-413-5) IOP Pub.

D'Andrea, A. & Tomassini, N. Excitons & Polaritons in Semiconductor Confined Systems. 200p. 1998. text 44.00 (981-02-2264-5) World Scientific Pub.

D'Andrea, A. N., jt. auth. see Mengali, U.

***D'Andrea, Deborah.** Picture Me As a Ballerina. rev. ed. (Illus.). 10p. (J). (ps-1). 2000. bds. 5.99 (1-57151-575-5) Picture Me Bks.

— Picture Me As a Bunny. rev. ed. (Illus.). 10p. (J). (ps-1). 2000. bds. 5.99 (1-57151-577-1) Picture Me Bks.

— Picture Me As a Firefighter. rev. ed. (Illus.). 10p. (J). (ps-1). 2000. bds. 5.99 (1-57151-583-6) Picture Me Bks.

— Picture Me As a Pirate. rev. ed. (Illus.). 10p. (J). (ps-1). 2000. bds. 5.99 (1-57151-578-X) Picture Me Bks.

— Picture Me As a Reindeer. (Illus.). 10p. (J). (ps-1). 1999. bds. 5.99 (1-57151-580-1) Picture Me Bks.

— Picture Me Counting 1 - 2 - 3. rev. ed. (Illus.). 10p. (J). (ps-1). 2000. bds. 5.99 (1-57151-581-X) Picture Me Bks.

— Picture Me Learning Letters A, B, C. rev. ed. (Illus.). 10p. (J). (ps-1). 2000. bds. 5.99 (1-57151-582-8) Picture Me Bks.

D'Andrea, Deborah B. Count with Me 1, 2, 3. Guenther, Luisa, tr. (SPA., Illus.). 8p. (J). (ps). 1993. bds. 5.99 (1-878338-41-2) Picture Me Bks.

— Count With Me 1, 2, 3. Zavinski, Monique, tr. (FRE., Illus.). 8p. (J). (ps). 1993. bds. 5.99 (1-878338-35-8) Picture Me Bks.

— If I Were a Bunny, Or a Panda, Or a Monkey, Or... Zavinski, Monique, tr. (FRE., Illus.). 8p. (J). (ps). 1993. bds. 5.99 (1-878338-30-7) Picture Me Bks.

— If I Were a Bunny, Or a Panda, Or a Monkey, Or... Guenther, Luisa, tr. (SPA., Illus.). 8p. (J). (ps). 1993. bds. 5.99 (1-878338-36-6) Picture Me Bks.

— If I Were a Fairy, Or a Ballerina, Or a Witch, Or... Guenther, Luisa, tr. (SPA., Illus.). 8p. (J). (ps). 1993. bds. 5.99 (1-878338-38-2) Picture Me Bks.

— If I Were a Fairy, Or a Ballerina, Or a Witch, Or... Zavinski, Monique, tr. (FRE., Illus.). 8p. (J). (ps). 1993. bds. 5.99 (1-878338-32-3) Picture Me Bks.

— If I Were a Firefighter, Or a Doctor, Or an Astronaut, Or... Guenther, Luisa, tr. (SPA., Illus.). 8p. (J). (ps). 1993. bds. 5.99 (1-878338-39-0) Picture Me Bks.

— If I Were a Firefighter, Or a Doctor, Or an Astronaut, Or... Zavinski, Monique, tr. (FRE., Illus.). 8p. (J). (ps). 1993. bds. 5.99 (1-878338-33-1) Picture Me Bks.

— If I Were a Pirate, Or a Cowboy, Or a Knight, Or... Guenther, Luisa, tr. (SPA., Illus.). 12p. (J). (ps). 1993. bds. 5.99 (1-878338-37-4) Picture Me Bks.

— If I Were a Pirate, Or a Cowboy, Or a Knight, Or... Zavinski, Monique, tr. (FRE., Illus.). 8p. (J). (ps). 1993. bds. 5.99 (1-878338-31-5) Picture Me Bks.

D'Andrea, Domenick. Robin Hood. LC 90-23078. (Bullseye Step into Classics Ser.). 96p. (Orig.). (J). (gr. 2-6). 1991. pap. 3.99 (0-679-81045-5, Pub. by Random Bks Yng Read) Random.

D'Andrea, Frances M., jt. ed. see Wormsley, Diane P.

***D'Andrea, Frank.** LungMouth. 28p. 1999. pap. 2.79 (1-892061-01-5) Future Tense.

***D'Andrea, Guillermo & Quelch, John A.** Cases in Strategic Marketing Management: Latin America. 320p. 2000. pap. 60.00 (0-13-089490-7) P-H.

D'Andrea, Guy, ed. see Goddard, Thomas G.

***D'Andrea, Joseph.** Picture Me Playing Baseball. rev. ed. (Illus.). 10p. (J). (ps-1). 2000. bds. 5.99 (1-57151-584-4) Picture Me Bks.

D'Andrea, Joseph C. If I Played Baseball, Or Football, Or Soccer, Or... Guenther, Luisa, tr. (SPA., Illus.). 8p. (J). (ps). 1993. bds. 5.99 (1-878338-40-4) Picture Me Bks.

— If I Played Baseball, Or Football, Or Soccer, Or... Zavinski, Monique, tr. (FRE., Illus.). 8p. (J). (ps). 1993. bds. 5.99 (1-878338-34-X) Picture Me Bks.

— Picture Me with Grandma. (Illus.). 8p. (Orig.). (J). (ps-2). 1998. bds. 6.99 (1-57151-545-3) Picture Me Bks.

***D'Andrea, Michael J. & Daniels, Judy A.** Multicultural Counseling: Empowerment Strat F/diverse Soc. 2001. pap. 35.00 (0-534-57340-1) Thomson Learn.

D'Andrea, Tom. Color Works: A Practical Guide to Business Desktop Color. unabridged ed. (Illus.). viii, 88p. 1998. pap. 19.95 (0-9664824-0-9) Lexmark Intl.

D'Andria, Lou, jt. auth. see Gaylord, Richard J.

Dandridge, Danske. Historic Shepherdstown. (Illus.). 389p. 1997. reprint ed. lib. bdg. 44.00 (0-8328-6954-6) Higginson Bk Co.

***Dandridge, Derrick M.** The Maple Kids Go to the Zoo. large type ed. (Maple Kids Ser.). (Illus.). 32p. (ps-2). 1999. pap. 5.00 (1-928694-01-2, Pub. by Modern Star Bks) Allnce Hse.

— The Original Maple Kids. large type ed. (Maple Kids Ser.). (Illus.). 28p. (ps-2). 1999. pap. 5.00 (1-928694-00-4, Pub. by Modern Star Bks) Allnce Hse.

***Dandridge, Dorothy.** Everything & Nothing: The Dorothy Dandridge Tragedy. LC 99-462418. 240p. 2000. pap. 13.00 (0-06-095675-5, Perennial) HarperTrade.

Dandridge, Raymond G. The Poet & Other Poems. LC 73-18573. reprint ed. 21.50 (0-404-11384-2) AMS Pr.

Dandridge, Rita. Black Women's Blues: A Literary Anthology: 1934-Present. (G. K. Hall Reference Ser.). 300p. 1992. 45.00 (0-8161-9084-4, Hall Reference) Macmillan.

Dandridge, Rita B., compiled by. Ann Allen Shockley: An Annotated Primary & Secondary Bibliography, 18. LC 86-33471. (Bibliographies & Indexes in Afro-American & African Studies: No. 18). 136p. 1987. lib. bdg. 49.95 (0-313-25740-X, DGS/, Greenwood Pr) Greenwood.

Dandsberg, Randall H., jt. ed. see Novak, Giles.

Dandurand, Anne. The Cracks. pap. 11.95 (0-920544-93-2, Pub. by Mercury Bk) LPC InBook.

Dandurand, Anne, et al. Three by Three: Short Stories. Von Flotow, Luise, tr. from FRE. & selected by by. (Prose Ser.: No. 18). 122p. 1994. pap. 10.00 (0-920717-69-1) Guernica Editions.

Dandurand, Jeanette S., ed. Psalter: A Collection of Responsorial Psalms for Use at Mass. 1990. ring bd. 28.95 (0-915866-16-1) Am Cath Pr.

Dandy. Essential Orthopaedics. 4th ed. 1997. pap. text 37.95 (0-443-05724-9, W B Saunders Co) Harcrt Hlth Sci Grp.

Dandy, David J. Arthroscopic Management of the Knee. 2nd ed. (Illus.). 236p. 1987. text 82.00 (0-443-02958-X) Church.

— Essential Orthopaedics & Trauma. (Illus.). 456p. 1989. pap. text 34.95 (0-443-04003-6) Church.

Dandy, David S., jt. auth. see Liu, Huimin.

Dandy, Evelyn B. Black Communications: Breaking Down the Barriers. (Illus.). 186p. 1992. pap. 10.95 (0-913543-23-3) African Am Imag.

Dandy, J. M. A. Computer Modelling with CD. 1997. pap. text 29.95 (0-943396-52-2) Willmann-Bell.

Dandy, Walter E. Benign Tumors in the Third Ventricle of the Brain: Diagnosis & Treatment. (Illus.). 1970. reprint ed. 25.00 (0-87266-037-0) Argosy.

Dane, Barbara. Doing More with Less: Long-Term Skills in Short-Term Treatment. Date not set. 60.00 (0-7657-0296-7) Aronson.

Dane, Barbara O. & Levine, Carol. AIDS & the New Orphans: Coping with Death. LC 94-4755. 168p. 1994. pap. 18.95 (0-86569-249-1, Auburn Hse) Greenwood.

Dane, Barbara O. & Levine, Carol, eds. AIDS & the New Orphans: Coping with Death. LC 94-4755. 168p. 1994. 57.95 (0-86569-220-3, Auburn Hse) Greenwood.

Dane, Barbara O. & Miller, Samuel O. AIDS: Intervening with Hidden Grievers. LC 92-10959. 240p. 1992. 52.95 (0-86569-028-6, T028, Auburn Hse) Greenwood.

Dane, Bonnie J. Solitary Pussytoes: A Novel. LC 94-17138. 144p. 1995. pap. 9.50 (1-885187-00-9) Back Alley Pr.

Dane, Charles S. Life's Little Destruction Book. 1992. mass mkt. 6.99 (0-312-92927-7) St Martin.

Dane, Clemence. Women's Side. LC 70-99629. (Essay Index Reprint Ser.). 1977. 19.95 (0-8369-1566-6) Ayer.

Dane, Elizabeth. Painful Passages: Working with Children with Learning Disabilities. LC 90-6463. 221p. 1990. 24.95 (0-87101-175-1) Natl Assn Soc Wkrs.

Dane, Eva. A Lion by the Mane. large type ed. 336p. 1986. 27.99 (0-7089-1445-4) Ulverscroft.

— Shadows in the Fire. large type ed. 336p. 1986. 27.99 (0-7089-1416-0) Ulverscroft.

D

— The Vaaldorp Diamond. large type ed. 384p. 1985. 27.99 (0-7089-1279-6) Ulverscroft.

Dane, Francis C. The Common & Uncommon Sense of Social Behavior. LC 87-15833. 182p. (C). 1987. mass mkt. 17.00 (0-534-08406-0) Brooks-Cole.

***Dane, Frank.** Esteem, Awareness, Support, Empowerment (E. A. S. E.), Phase 1. (Illus.). 168p. 1998. pap., wbk. ed. 29.95 incl. audio (0-9672749-0-7) POUVANT.

— Esteem, Awareness, Support, Empowerment (E. A. S. E.), Phase 2. (Illus.). 110p. 1999. wbk. ed. 29.95 incl. audio (0-9672749-1-5) POUVANT.

Dane, Joseph A. Who Is Buried in Chaucer's Tomb? Studies in the Reception of Chaucer's Book. LC 98-2718. (Colleagues Bks.). (Illus.). 350p. 1998. text 45.95 (0-87013-432-9) Mich St U Pr.

Dane, Les. Surefire Sales Closing Techniques. 1978. pap. 8.95 (0-13-877894-9) P-H.

Dane, Nathan. General Abridgement & Digest of American Law with Occasional Notes & Comments, 9 vols., Set. LC 12-11277. 1979. reprint ed. 405.00 (1-57588-294-9, 200350) W S Hein.

Dane, Roslyn. The Assistance of Vice. 168p. (Orig.). 1989. pap. 8.95 (0-934411-19-0, Banned Bks) Edward-William Austin.

Dane, Sylvia, ed. see Moore, Jamie W. & Moore, Dorothy P.

Daneel, M. L. Old & New in Southern Shona, Independent Churches Vol. 1: Background & Rise of the Major Movements. (Change & Continuity in Africa Ser.). 1971. text 56.95 (90-279-6940-X) Mouton.

— Zionism & Faith-Healing in Rhodesia: Aspects of African Independent Churches. February, V. A., Communications Staff, tr. from DUT. (Illus.). 1970. pap. 29.25 (90-279-6278-2) Mouton.

***Daneel, Marthinus L.** African Earthkeepers: A Wholistic Interfaith Mission. 288p. 2000. pap. 30.00 (1-57075-329-6) Orbis Bks.

***Danegger, Anna E.** Juvenile Accountability Incentive Block Grants: Strategic Planning Guide - Summary. 51p. (C). 2000. pap. text 20.00 (0-7881-8591-8) DIANE Pub.

Danehy, James P., ed. see Conference on Enzyme Economics Staff.

***Danek, Jennifer.** Med School Survival Guide: How to Make the Challenges of Medical School Seem Like Small Stuff. 176p. 2000. pap. 12.00 (0-609-80595-9, STU014000, Three Riv Pr) Crown Pub Group.

Danek, Jennifer, jt. auth. see Danek, Marita.

Danek, Marita & Danek, Jennifer. Becoming a Physician: What You Need to Know to Make the Decision & Go for It. LC 96-25092. 217p. (Orig.). 1997. pap. 15.95 (0-471-12166-5) Wiley.

Daneke, Gregory, ed. Public & Private Enterprise & the Energy Future. 192p. (Orig.). 1985. pap. 15.00 (0-918592-78-X) Pol Studies.

Daneke, Gregory A. Systemic Choices: Nonlinear Dynamics, Institutional Ecology & Practical Management. LC 99-33759. (Illus.). 288p. 1999. text 42.50 (0-472-11049-7, 11049) U of Mich Pr.

Daneker, Gail, jt. ed. see Geisler, Charles C.

Danel, Adam D. A Case for Freedom: Machiavellian Humanism. LC 96-41721. 298p. 1996. 62.50 (0-7618-0557-5); pap. 29.50 (0-7618-0558-3) U Pr of Amer.

Danelius, Hans, jt. auth. see Burgers, Herman.

Danelski, David J. Rights, Liberties & Ideals: The Contributions of Milton R. Konvitz. viii, 182p. 1983. reprint ed. 29.50 (0-8377-0518-5, Rothman) W S Hein.

— A Supreme Court Justice Is Appointed. LC 80-21229. (Studies in Political Science). 242p. 1980. reprint ed. lib. bdg. 59.75 (0-313-22652-0, DASJ, Greenwood Pr) Greenwood.

Danelski, David J., jt. auth. see Cohen, William.

Danelski, David J., ed. see Hughes, Charles E.

Daneman, A. Pediatric Body CT. (Illus.). 390p. 1986. 377.00 (0-387-16217-8) Spr-Verlag.

Daneman, Denis, et al. When a Child Has Diabetes. (Your Personal Health Ser.). (Illus.). 218p. 1999. pap. 14.95 (1-55209-331-X) Firefly Bks Ltd.

Danenberg, Alvin H. More Than LIP Service: A Lifetime Investment Plan. LC 96-47762. (Illus.). 350p. 1996. 49.95 (0-87814-655-5) PennWell Bks.

Danermark, B. & Elander, I. Social Rented Housing in Europe: Policy Tenure & Design. 192p. (Orig.). 1994. pap. 47.50 (90-6275-942-4, Pub. by Delft U Pr) Coronet Bks.

Danes. Mark: A Gospel for Today. 1989. pap. 16.95 (0-7459-1504-3, Pub. by Lion Pubng) Trafalgar.

— Messiah. 1991. pap. 13.95 (0-7459-1943-X, Pub. by Lion Pubng) Trafalgar.

— Todays Issues & Christian Beliefs. 1994. pap. 15.95 (0-7459-2521-9, Pub. by Lion Pubng) Trafalgar.

Danes, B. Shannon, ed. In Vitro Epithelia & Birth Defects. (Alan R. Liss Ser.: Vol. 16, No. 2). 1980. 55.00 (0-685-03291-4) March of Dimes.

Danes, E. More Easy Piano Classics. (Learn to Play Ser.). (Illus.). 64p. (J). (gr. 1 up). 1994. text 9.95 (0-7460-1698-0, Usborne); lib. bdg. 17.95 (0-88110-703-4, Usborne) EDC.

Danes, E. & Buckton, R. Easy Guitar Tunes. (Tunebooks Ser.). (Illus.). 64p. (J). (gr. 1-4). 1995. pap. 10.95 (0-7460-1675-1, Usborne) EDC.

— Easy Guitar Tunes. (Tunebooks Ser.). (Illus.). 64p. (J). (gr. 1 up). 1995. lib. bdg. 18.95 (0-88110-715-8, Usborne) EDC.

Danes, E., jt. auth. see Elliot, K.

Danes, Emma. First Book of Music. (Illus.). 64p. (J). (gr. k up). 1994. lib. bdg. 16.95 (0-88110-658-5, Usborne) EDC.

— First Book of Music. (Illus.). 64p. (J). (gr. 1-4). 1994. pap. 8.95 (0-7460-1329-9, Usborne) EDC.

— Music Theory for Beginners. (Music Bks.). (Illus.). 48p. (J). (gr. 1 up). 1997. text 7.95 (0-7460-2416-9, Usborne); lib. bdg. 15.95 (0-88110-902-9, Usborne) EDC.

Danes, Emma, jt. auth. see Elliott, Kate.

Danes, Emma, ed. see Hooper, Caroline.

Danese, Andrea, ed. Sirens. (Illus.). 296p. 1997. 29.95 (0-446-91245-X, Pub. by Warner Bks) Little.

Danese, Andrea, ed. see Bender, Steve.

Danese, Andrea, jt. ed. see Kratovil, Laurie.

Danese, Andrea, ed. see Lelooska, Chief.

***Danese, Tracy E.** Claude Pepper & Ed Ball: Politics, Purpose & Power. LC 99-35314. (Florida History & Culture Ser.). (Illus.). 320p. 2000. 34.95 (0-8130-1744-0) U Press Fla.

Danesh, Abol H. Corridor of Hope: A Visual View of Informal Economy. (Illus.). 176p. 1999. 48.00 (0-7618-1403-5) U Pr of Amer.

***Danesh, Abol H.** Corridor of Hope: A Visual View of Informal Economy. LC 99-22100. (Illus.). 176p. 1999. pap. 27.50 (0-7618-1404-3) U Pr of Amer.

Danesh, Abol H. Rural Exodus & Squatter Settlements in the Third World: Case of Iran. LC 87-10627. (Illus.). 184p. (Orig.). (C). 1987. pap. text 22.50 (0-8191-6444-5); lib. bdg. 43.50 (0-8191-6443-7) U Pr of Amer.

Danesh, Ali. PVT & Phase Behaviour of Petroleum Reservoir Fluids. LC 98-18286. (Developments in Petroleum Science Ser.: 47). 1998. 158.00 (0-444-82196-1) Elsevier.

Danesh, Arman. JavaScript Interactive Course. LC 96-49086. 676p. 1997. pap. text 39.99 incl. cd-rom (1-57169-084-0) Sams.

***Danesh, Arman.** Mastering Cold Fusion 4. LC 99-61819. (Mastering Ser.). (Illus.). 880p. 1999. pap. 44.99 (0-7821-2452-6) Sybex.

— Mastering Coldfusion 4.5. (Illus.). 1008p. 2000. pap. 49.99 (0-7821-2773-8) Sybex.

Danesh, Arman. Mastering Linux. LC 98-86867. (Mastering Ser.). xxviii, 960p. 1998. pap. text 39.99 (0-7821-2341-4) Sybex.

— Mastering Linux: Premium Edition. (Mastering Ser.). 1248p. 1999. 49.99 (0-7821-2555-7) Sybex.

***Danesh, Arman.** Mastering Red Hat Linux 6. 3rd ed. (Mastering Ser.). (Illus.). 944p. 1999. pap. 39.99 (0-7821-2613-8) Sybex.

Danesh, Arman. Teach Yourself JavaScript in a Week. 1996. 39.99 (0-672-31213-1) Macmillan.

— Teach Yourself JavaScript in a Week. 576p. 1996. pap. text 39.99 incl. cd-rom (1-57521-073-8) Sams.

— Teach Yourself Javascript 1.1 in a Week. 2nd ed. LC 96-70388. 600p. 1996. pap. text 39.99 incl. cd-rom (1-57521-195-5) Sams.

— Sams Teach Yourself JavaScript 1.3 in 21 Days. 3rd ed. 600p. 1999. 29.99 (1-57521-304-4) Sams.

***Danesh, Arman.** Using Linux System Administration. 2nd ed. (Special Edition Using... Que Ser.). (Illus.). 900p. 2000. pap. 39.99 (0-7897-2352-2) Que.

***Danesh, Armand.** 1001 Linux Tips. (Illus.). 700p. 2000. pap. 54.95 incl. audio compact disk (1-884133-78-9, Jamsa Press) Gulf Pub.

***Danesh, John.** Bahai Faith in Words & Images. 2000. 28.95 (1-85168-216-3, Pub. by Onewrld Pubns); pap. 19.95 (1-85168-219-8, Pub. by Onewrld Pubns) Penguin Putnam.

Daneshagari, Perry. The Chase, 1. 1998. pap. text 14.95 (1-881116-95-6) Black Forest Pr.

Daneshvari, Abbas. Animal Symbolism in Warqa Wa Gulshah. (Oxford Studies in Islamic Art). (Illus.). 92p. 1987. text 45.00 (0-19-728003-X) OUP.

— Medieval Tomb Towers of Iran. (Islamic Art & Architecture Ser.: Vol. 2). (Illus.). 112p. (C). 1986. lib. bdg. 17.95 (0-939214-34-2) Mazda Pubs.

Daneshvari, Abbas, ed. Essays in Islamic Art & Architecture (In Honor of Katharina Otto-Dorn) LC 81-71740. (Islamic Art & Architecture Ser.: Vol. 1). (FRE., Illus.). x, 135p. 1981. pap. text 25.00 (0-89003-110-X) Undena Pubns.

Danesi. Adesso! (College Italian Ser.). (C). 1992. pap., student ed., wbk. ed. 36.95 (0-8384-1987-9) Heinle & Heinle.

— Adesso. (College Italian Ser.). (ITA.). (C). 1992. suppl. ed. 8.95 incl. audio (0-8384-3941-1) Heinle & Heinle.

— Adesso. 2nd ed. LC 96-32017. (College Italian Ser.). 1997. text 54.95 (0-8384-1991-7) Heinle & Heinle.

— Adesso. 2nd ed. (College Spanish Ser.). (C). 1997. pap., suppl. ed. 54.95 (0-8384-6707-5) Heinle & Heinle.

— Adesso! Workbook & Lab Manual. 2nd ed. (College Italian Ser.). (C). 1997. mass mkt., wbk. ed., lab manual ed. 32.95 (0-8384-6099-2) Heinle & Heinle.

— Adesso Tests. 2nd ed. (College Italian Ser.). (C). 1997. text 36.95 (0-8384-6706-7) Heinle & Heinle.

— Con Fantasia. (College Italian Ser.). (ITA.). (C). 1995. text, wbk. ed., lab manual ed. 34.95 (0-8384-5974-9) Heinle & Heinle.

— Con Fantasia. (College Italian Ser.). (ITA.). (C). 1995. text, suppl. ed. 69.95 (0-8384-5975-7) Heinle & Heinle.

— Con Fantasia. (College Italian Ser.). (ITA.). (C). 1995. text, teacher ed. 41.95 (0-8384-5973-0) Heinle & Heinle.

— Tapescript Adesso. (College Italian). (C). 1992. suppl. ed. 19.95 (0-8384-2067-2) Heinle & Heinle.

— Tests Adesso. (College Italian). (C). 1992. suppl. ed. 38.95 (0-8384-2046-X) Heinle & Heinle.

Danesi, jt. auth. see Danesi, Marcel.

Danesi, Marcal, et al, eds. Heritage Languages & Education: The Canadian Experience. 260p. 1996. pap. 18.95 (0-88962-480-1) Mosaic.

Danesi, Marcel. Adesso! Text & Audiocassette. 2nd ed. (College Italian Ser.). (C). 1997. pap. text, mass mkt. 75.95 incl. audio (0-8384-6117-4) Heinle & Heinle.

— Cool: The Signs & Meanings of Adolescence. (Toronto Studies in Semiotics). 168p. 1994. text 40.00 (0-8020-0467-9); pap. text 14.95 (0-8020-7483-9) U of Toronto Pr.

— Crossword Italian! Have Fund Learning Italian by Solving Crossword Puzzles. (ITA & ENG.). 200p. (Orig.). 1999. pap. text 17.95 (0-8020-4430-1) U of Toronto Pr.

— Giambattista Vico & the Cognitive Science Enterprise, Vol. 4. LC 94-10697. (Emory Vico Studies). XV, 184p. (C). 1995. pap. text 29.95 (0-8204-2402-1) P Lang Pubng.

— Increase Your Puzzle IQ: Tips & Tricks to Increase Your Logic Power. LC 96-34965. Orig. Title: Logic Puzzles Decoded. 201p. 1997. pap. 14.95 (0-471-15725-2) Wiley.

— Italian. 2nd ed. (Master the Basics Ser.). 290p. 1995. pap. 10.95 (0-8120-9002-0) Barron.

— Italian Grammar. (Grammar Ser.). (ITA & ENG.). 256p. 1990. pap. 6.95 (0-8120-4311-1) Barron.

— Italian the Easy Way. 2nd ed. (ITA.). 1996. pap. 12.95 (0-8120-9146-9) Barron.

— Italian Vocabulary. (ITA & ENG.). 256p. 1990. spiral bd. 6.95 (0-8120-4471-1) Barron.

— Language Games in Italian. 164p. 1985. pap. text 14.95 (0-8020-6596-1) U of Toronto Pr.

— Learn Italian the Fast & Fun Way Book. 2nd ed. Heywood, Wald, ed. LC 97-8788. (Barron's Fast & Fun Way Ser.). (ITA., Illus.). 260p. 1997. pap. 14.95 (0-7641-0210-9) Barron.

— Pronounce It Perfectly in Italian! (Pronounce It Perfectly Ser.). (ITA & ENG.). 140p. 1994. pap. 16.95 incl. audio (0-8120-8015-7) Barron.

— Robert A. Hall, Jr. & American Structuralism. (Edward Sapir Monographs in Language, Culture & Cognition: No. 15). viii, 92p. (Orig.). 1987. pap. 18.00 (0-933104-25-1) Jupiter Pr.

***Danesi, Marcel.** Semiotics in Language Education. LC 00-33862. (Approaches to Applied Semiotics Ser.). 2000. pap. write for info. (3-11-016915-0) De Gruyter.

Danesi, Marcel. Vico, Metaphor, & the Origin of Language. LC 92-30604. 212p. 1993. 35.00 (0-253-31607-3) Ind U Pr.

Danesi, Marcel, ed. Giambattista Vico & Anglo-American Science: Philosophy & Writing. (Approaches to Semiotics Ser.: No. 119). 283p. (C). 1994. lib. bdg. 136.95 (3-11-013665-1) Mouton.

— Issues in Language: Studies in Honor of Robert J. Di Pietro Presented to Him by His Students. LC 81-13647. (Edward Sapir Monographs in Language, Culture & Cognition: No. 9). viii, 165p. (Orig.). (C). 1981. pap. 24.00 (0-933104-13-8) Jupiter Pr.

Danesi, Marcel, et al, eds. Aboriginal Languages & Education: The Canadian Experience. 150p. 1996. pap. 18.95 (0-88962-479-8) Mosaic.

— Studies in Italian Applied Linguistics. (Biblioteca di Quaderni d'Italianistica Ser.: Vol. 1).Tr. of Studi di Linguistica Applicata Italiana. 236p. (Orig.). (C). 1984. pap. 15.00 (0-9691979-0-X, Pub. by Can Soc Ital Stu) Speedimpex.

Danesi, Marcel & Danesi. Italian on the Road, Level 2. (Languages on the Road Ser.). (ENG & ITA.). 1992. pap. 11.95 incl. audio (0-8120-7936-1) Barron.

Danesi, Marcel & McGroarty, Stephen. Spanish Verbs Skill Builder, Set. (SPA & ENG.). 1999. pap. 29.95 incl. audio (0-609-60444-9) Liv Lang.

— Spanish Verbs Skill Builder Manual. 1999. pap. 6.95 (0-609-80433-2) Liv Lang.

Danesi, Marcel & Wald, Heywood. Learn Italian the Fast & Fun Way. 2nd ed. LC 97-8788. (ENG & ITA.). 300p. 1997. 39.95 incl. audio (0-7641-7025-2) Barron.

Danesi, Marcel, et al. Con Fantasia: Reviewing & Expanding Functional Italian Skills. LC 95-15425. (SPA.). (C). 1995. mass mkt. 55.95 (0-8384-5972-2) Heinle & Heinle.

Danesi, Marcel, jt. auth. see Titone, Renzo.

***Danesi, Marcello.** Analyzing Cultures: An Introduction & Handbook. LC 99-28479. 1999. pap. text 19.95 (0-253-21298-7) Ind U Pr.

Danesi, Marcello. Of Cigarettes, High Heels & Other Interesting Things: An Introduction to Semiotics. LC 99-17390. (Semaphores & Signs Ser.). 192p. 1999. pap. 17.95 (0-312-21450-2) St Martin.

Daneski, Gavin. The Animal Man. large type ed. 1991. 27.99 (0-7089-2459-X) Ulverscroft.

Danesy, Frank C. Higher Education Credentials: A Guide to Educational Systems in Europe & North America. 186p. 1994. text 220.50 (0-471-94269-3) Wiley.

Danett, Thomas, tr. see Comines, Philippe de.

Danewalia, B. S. Police & Politics in 20th Century Punjab: A Saga of the Punjab. LC 99-931640. (C). 1997. 42.00 (81-202-0453-0, Pub. by Aditya Prakashan) S Asia.

Daney, Charles. Dictionnaire de la Lande Francaise. (FRE.). 347p. 1992. 115.00 (0-7859-8124-1, 2862661635) Fr & Eur.

— Programming in REXX. 299p. 1990. 49.00 (0-07-015305-1) McGraw.

Daney, Mike. Coaching Kids Lowhoop Basketball. (Illus.). 117p. (Orig.). 1989. pap. 8.50 (0-933715-01-3) Am Youth Sports Pub.

— Coaching Kids Teeball. (Illus.). 117p. (Orig.). 1985. pap. 7.50 (0-933715-00-5) Am Youth Sports Pub.

Danford, Andy. Japanese Management Techniques & British Workers. LC 97-52769. (Employment & Work Relations in Context Ser.). 256p. 1998. 82.50 (0-7201-2368-2) Continuum.

Danford, D. B., jt. auth. see Munro, H. N.

Danford, G. S., jt. ed. see Steinfeld, E.

Danford, Heath. You Might Be a Dallas If . . . (101 Ways to Tell If You've True Blue) Crowell, John, ed. (Illus.). 58p. 1997. pap. 6.95 (0-9662122-0-7) Fanatics Pub Gp.

Danford, John W. David Hume & the Problem of Reason: Recovering the Human Sciences. LC 89-29104. 240p. 1990. reprint ed. pap. 74.40 (0-608-07885-9, 205999200010) Bks Demand.

***Danford, John W.** Roots of Freedom. 2000. 24.95 (1-882926-47-1) ISI Books.

Danford, John W. Wittgenstein & Political Philosophy: A Re-Examination of the Foundations of Social Science. LC 78-6716. xiv, 166p. (C). 1981. reprint ed. pap. text 6.95 (0-226-13594-2) U Ch Pr.

— Wittgenstein & Political Philosophy: A Reexamination of the Foundations of Social Science. 280p. 1994. pap. text 17.95 (0-226-13595-0, Midway Reprint) U Ch Pr.

— Wittgenstein & Political Philosophy: A Reexamination of the Foundations of Social Science. LC 78-6716. 280p. reprint ed. pap. 86.80 (0-608-09442-0, 205424200005) Bks Demand.

Danford, Karen P. The Family in Adalbert Stifter's Moral & Aesthetic Universe: A Rarefied Vision. LC 90-46279. (North American Studies in Nineteenth-Century German Literature: Vol. 7). 190p. (C). 1991. text 37.95 (0-8204-0825-5) P Lang Pubng.

Danford, Natalie, jt. ed. see Kulka, John.

Danford, Robert E., ed. see Library Administration & Management Association Pr.

Danford, Scott, jt. ed. see Seidel, Andrew D.

Danforth, Art. Dashed Hopes, Broken Dreams. 60p. 1980. 5.50 (0-318-15067-0) NASCO.

— Living with Alzheimer's: Ruth's Story. LC 86-21052. Orig. Title: The Book of Ruth. 224p. (Orig.). 1986. 15.95 (0-939533-02-2); pap. 9.95 (0-939533-01-4) Howarth Pr.

***Danforth, Audrey & Kennedy, Jane.** Good Night Sky. (Illus.). 8p. (J). (gr. k-2). 1999. pap. 3.75 (1-58323-005-X) Seedling Pubns.

— Kite Dance. (Illus.). 8p. (J). (gr. k-2). 2000. pap. 3.75 (1-58323-003-3) Seedling Pubns.

Danforth, Audrey & Kennedy, Jane. Take a Bow Jody. (Illus.). 8p. (J). (gr. k-1). 1995. pap. 3.75 (1-880612-47-X) Seedling Pubns.

Danforth, Audrey, jt. auth. see Kennedy, Jane.

Danforth, Carol. Heard Through the Grapevine: Sayings, Expressions, Colloquialisms, & More! Brown, Virginia, ed. (Illus.). 168p. 1999. pap. write for info. (0-9667761-0-0) D Danforth.

Danforth, David N. & Scott, James R. Danforth's Obstetrics & Gynecology. 8th ed. LC 98-37809. 2000p. 1999. write for info. (0-7817-1206-8) Lppncott W & W.

Danforth, Doug, jt. auth. see Bailowitz, Richard A.

Danforth, Elizabeth & Stackpole, Michael A., eds. Citybook 2: Port 'O Call. (Illus.). 1984. 11.95 (0-940244-71-3) Flying Buffalo.

— Grimtooth's Traps Fore. (Illus.). 1986. 9.95 (0-940244-83-7) Flying Buffalo.

Danforth, Elizabeth, et al. Citybook 6: Uptown. Jaquays, Paul, ed. (Illus.). (Orig.). pap. 11.95 (0-940244-99-3) Flying Buffalo.

— Mage's Blood & Old Bones: A Tunnels & Trolls Anthology. (Illus.). 180p. (Orig.). 1992. pap. 7.95 (0-940244-66-7) Flying Buffalo.

Danforth, Elizabeth, ed. & illus. see St. Andre, Ken.

Danforth, Ellen Z. Nesting Weights, Einsatzgewichte, & Piles a Godets: A Catalog of Nested Cup Weights in the Edward Clark Streeter Collection of Weights & Measures. LC 87-33492. (Transactions Ser.: Vol. 50, Pt. 1). (Illus.). 117p. 1988. pap. 39.50 (0-208-02220-1) CT Acad Arts & Sciences.

Danforth Foundation Staff, jt. auth. see Twentieth Century Fund Staff.

Danforth, George E., jt. ed. see Schulze, Franz.

Danforth, Helen H. A Tale of Two Cabins. (Illus.). 36p. (Orig.). (J). (gr. 7 up). 1985. pap. 4.95 (0-9614899-0-1) Pioneer Farm.

Danforth, John C. Resurrection: The Confirmation of Clarence Thomas. 240p. 1994. text 22.95 (0-02-906936-X) Free Pr.

— Resurrection: The Confirmation of Clarence Thomas. LC 94-25005. 1994. 19.95 (0-453-03324-5, Viking) Viking Penguin.

Danforth, John C., jt. auth. see Kerrey, J. Robert.

Danforth, Kimberly, jt. auth. see Fassler, David.

***Danforth, Laurel.** Moments in Time. 1999. pap. write for info. (1-58235-369-7) Watermark Pr.

Danforth, Loring M. The Death Rituals of Rural Greece. LC 82-47589. (Illus.). 248p. 1982. pap. text 19.95 (0-691-00027-1, Pub. by Princeton U Pr) Cal Prin Full Svc.

— Firewalking & Religious Healing: The Anastenaria of Greece & the American Firewalking Movement. (Modern Greek Studies). (Illus.). 352p. (C). 1989. pap. text 18.95 (0-691-02853-2, Pub. by Princeton U Pr) Cal Prin Full Svc.

— The Macedonian Conflict: Ethnic Nationalism in a Transnational World. (Illus.). 290p. 1995. pap. text 15.95 (0-691-04356-6, Pub. by Princeton U Pr) Cal Prin Full Svc.

Danforth, Randi, jt. auth. see Chassman, Gary.

***Danforth, S. C., et al, eds.** Solid Freeform & Additive Fabrication -- 2000: Materials Research Society Symposium Proceedings, Vol. 625. 2000. text 73.00 (1-55899-533-1) Materials Res.

Danforth, Scot, jt. auth. see Shea, Thomas M.

Danforth, Scott, et al. Objects for OS/23. 500p. 1995. pap. 39.95 (0-471-13126-1) Wiley.

Danforth, Stephen C., jt. ed. see Sheldon, Brian W.

Danforth, Susan. Encountering the New World, 1493 to 1800. (Illus.). 108p. 1991. pap. 25.00 (0-916617-37-8, Pub. by J C Brown) Oak Knoll.

An Asterisk (*) at the beginning of an entry indicates that the title is appearing for the first time.

Danforth, Susan, compiled by. The Land of Norumbega: Maine in the Age of Exploration & Settlement. (Illus.). 80p. (Orig.). 1988. pap. 15.00 (*0-9621545-0-4*) ME Humanities.

Danforth, Wendy. Feelings You Always Had but Never Dared to Name. LC 98-93102. (Illus.). 168p. 1998. pap. 12.95 (*0-9664638-0-3*) Harold Pubns Inc.

Danforth, William H. I Dare You. 1931. 7.50 (*0-9602416-0-4*); pap. 5.50 (*0-685-02452-0*) I Dare You.

Dang, C. & Trockel, W. Triangulations & Simplicial Methods. Fandel, Gunter U., ed. (Lecture Notes in Economics & Mathematical Systems Ser.: Vol. 421). (Illus.). x, 196p. 1995. 59.00 (*3-540-58838-8*) Spr-Verlag.

Dang, Cassandra. Mrs. Greenthumbs Plows Ahead: The Five Secrets of a Gorgeous Home Garden. LC 97-30270. 1998. 25.00 (*0-517-70554-0*) Random.

Dang, Himraj. Human Conflict in Conservation: Protected Areas: The Indian Experience. (Development Alternatives Ser.). 1992. text 35.00 (*0-7069-5050-X*, Pub. by Vikas) S Asia.

Dang, Kim, jt. ed. see Toprac, Anthony J.

Dang, Nguyen D., et al, eds. Perspectives of Nuclear Physics in the Late Nineties: Proceedings of the International Conference on Nuclear Physics & Relation. 150p. 1995. text 150.00 (*981-02-2086-3*) World Scientific Pub.

***Dang, Rupin.** Flowers of the Western Himalayas. 1998. pap. 80.00 (*0-7855-7549-9*) St Mut.

Dang, Satyapal, ed. see Canandian, Darshan S.

Dang, Seong A. Ferraro: Programmer's Guide to the EGA & VGA Cards. 2nd ed. (C). 1993. pap. text. write for info. (*0-201-55694-4*) Addison-Wesley.

Dang Tran Con & Phan Huy Ich. The Song of a Soldier's Wife. Huynh Sanh Thong, tr. LC 85-73465. (Lac-Viet Ser.: No. 3). (Illus.). 118p. 1986. pap. 10.00 (*0-938692-24-0*) Yale U SE Asia.

Dang, Tri. Beginning Tai Chi. (Illus.). 64p. (Orig.). 1994. pap. 9.95 (*0-8048-2001-5*) Tuttle Pubng.

Dang, Tri T. Beyond the Known: The Real Meaning of the Martial Arts. (Illus.). 152p. 1993. pap. 12.95 (*0-8048-1891-6*) Tuttle Pubng.

Dang, Tri Thong. Toward the Unknown: Martial Artist, What Shall You Become? (Bruce Lee Library). 1997. pap. text 12.95 (*0-8048-2099-6*) Tuttle Pubng.

Dang, Yumei & Kauffman, Louis H. Hypercomplex Iterations, Distance Estimation & Higher Dimensional Fractals. (Series on Knots & Everything: Vol. 17). 150p. 1998. 26.00 (*981-02-3296-9*) World Scientific Pub.

Dangarembga, Tsitsi. Nervous Conditions. LC 89-4076. 210p. 1996. pap. 12.95 (*1-878067-77-X*) Seal Pr WA.

Dangberg, Grace. Guide to the Life & Works of F. J. Teggart. LC 81-96263. (Illus.). 568p. 1983. text 15.00 (*0-913205-00-1*) Grace Dangberg.

Dangberg, Grace M., ed. Letters to Jack Wilson, the Paiute Prophet, Written Between 1908 & 1911. fac. ed. (Smithsonian Institution, Bureau of American Ethnology, Bulletins Ser.: No. 164, Paper 55). 18p. (C). 1957. reprint ed. pap. text 2.19 (*1-55567-803-3*) Coyote Press.

Dange, Sadashiv Ambadas. Divine Hymns & Ancient Thought Vol. I: Rgveda Hymns & Ancient Thought. 1992. 36.00 (*0-8364-2862-5*, Pub. by Navarang) S Asia.

— Encyclopaedia of Puranic Beliefs & Practices, Vol. 1 (A-C) (C). 1986. 54.00 (*81-7013-006-9*, Pub. by Navarang) S Asia.

— Encyclopaedia of Puranic Beliefs & Practices, Vol. 3. (C). 1987. 48.50 (*0-685-35374-5*, Pub. by Navarang) S Asia.

— Encyclopaedia of Puranic Beliefs & Practices Vol. IV: O-S. (C). 1989. 54.00 (*81-7013-056-5*, Pub. by Navarang) S Asia.

— Encyclopedia of Puranic Beliefs & Practices, Vol. 2. 746p. (C). 1987. 54.50 (*0-685-19281-4*, Pub. by Navarang) S Asia.

— Myths from the Mahabharata. LC 97-905056. 1997. write for info. (*81-7305-116-X*) Aryan Bks Intl.

— Puranic Myth & Culture. (C). 1987. 21.00 (*81-202-0192-2*, Pub. by Ajanta) S Asia.

— Towards Understanding Hindu Myths. LC 96-900893. lxiv, 497p. (C). 1996. 60.00 (*81-7305-080-5*, Pub. by Aryan Bks Intl) Nataraj Bks.

Dange, Sadashiv Ambadas, ed. Encyclopedia of Puranic Beliefs, Vol. 5. 1989. 47.00 (*81-7013-069-7*, Pub. by Navarang) S Asia.

Dange, Sadashiv Ambadas & Dange, Sindhu S. Critiques on Sanskrit Dramas. (C). 1994. text 30.00 (*81-7305-033-3*, Pub. by Aryan Bks Intl) S Asia.

Dange, Sindhu S. Aspects of Speech in Vedic Ritual. xxi, 269p. (C). 1996. 32.00 (*81-7305-078-3*, Pub. by Aryan Bks Intl) Nataraj Bks.

Dange, Sindhu S., jt. auth. see Dange, Sadashiv Ambadas.

Dangeard, P. Le Vacuome de la Cellule Vegetale: Morphologie. (Protoplasmatologia Ser.: Vol. 3, Pt. D1, 2, 3a, 3b). (Illus.). iv, 41p. 1956. 57.90 (*0-387-80423-4*) Spr-Verlag.

Dangel, Leo. Hogs & Personals. 80p. (Orig.). 1992. pap. 5.95 (*0-944024-22-X*) Spoon Riv Poetry.

— Home from the Field. 233p. 1997. pap. 12.95 (*0-944024-31-9*) Spoon Riv Poetry.

— Old Man Brunner Country. 60p. 1987. pap. 4.95 (*0-933180-94-2*) Spoon Riv Poetry.

Dangelmayr, G., jt. ed. see Guttinger, W.

Dangelmayr, Gerhard. Dynamics of Nonlinear Waves in Dissipative Systems: Reduction, Bifurcation & Stability. (Pitman Research Notes in Mathematics Ser.). 1996. pap. 67.95 (*0-582-22929-4*, Pub. by Addison-Wesley) Longman.

D'Angelo. Composition in the Classical Tradition. LC 99-14267. 266p. (C). 1999. 44.00 (*0-02-327141-8*, Macmillan Coll) P-H.

D'Angelo, Al, Jr. Playing Smart: A Practical Guide to Slot Machine Play. D'Angelo, Barbara, ed. & intro. by. LC 95-83364. (Illus.). 73p. (Orig.). 1995. pap. 8.95 (*0-9644746-0-3*) A-Fortune.

Dangelo, Allen R. Fun, Creative, & Profitable Salon Marketing: 67 Ways to Grow Your Salon Business. 1998. pap. 19.95 (*1-57472-267-0*) Archer-Ellison.

D'Angelo, Anthony J. The College Blue Book: A Few Thoughts, Reflections & Reminders on How to Get the Most Out of College & Life. Lauterbach, Bernice et al, eds. LC 95-90377. 96p. (Orig.). (YA). (gr. 11 up). 1995. pap. 7.95 (*0-9646957-0-7*) Arkad Press.

D'Angelo, Barbara, ed. & intro. see D'Angelo, Al, Jr.

D'Angelo, Christine. A Child Is Waiting. (Intimate Moments Ser.). 1993. per. 3.50 (*0-373-07509-X*, 5-07509-8) Silhouette.

D'Angelo, Doreen. A Cookbook of Treasures: Recipes for Healthy Living. (Health & Fitness Series: Vol. 1). (Illus.). 150p. 1997. pap. 12.95 (*0-9658141-0-6*, 589-97) DAngelo Mktg.

***D'Angelo, Edward.** Blood Test: A Novel. 2000. 24.00 (*0-688-17493-0*, Wm Morrow) Morrow Avon.

D'Angelo, Edward, ed. Cuban & North American Marxism. iv, 214p. 1984. pap. 24.00 (*90-6032-265-7*, Pub. by B R Gruner) Humanities.

D'Angelo, Edward, et al. Contemporary East European Marxism, Vol. 1. (Praxis Ser.: Vol. 6). xii, 302p. 1980. pap. 35.00 (*90-6032-189-8*, Pub. by B R Gruner) Humanities.

— Contemporary East European Marxism, Vol. 2. (Praxis Ser.: Vol. 7). vi, 283p. 1982. pap. 35.00 (*90-6032-217-7*, Pub. by B R Gruner) Humanities.

D'Angelo, George V. Aerospace Agencies & Organizations: A Guide for Business & Government. LC 93-293. 192p. 1993. 55.00 (*0-89930-842-2*, Q842, Quorum Bks) Greenwood.

— Aerospace Business Law. LC 93-42764. 208p. 1994. 62.95 (*0-89930-892-9*, Quorum Bks) Greenwood.

D'Angelo, Jean. Ketone Enolates: Regiospecific Preparation & Synthetic Uses. 1977. pap. 14.00 (*0-08-021587-4*, Pergamon Pr) Elsevier.

D'Angelo, Jimmy, jt. auth. see Canter, W. Horace.

***D'Angelo, John P.** Mathematical Thinking: Problem-Solving & Proofs. 2nd ed. LC 99-50074. 412p. 1999. 81.33 (*0-13-014412-6*) P-H.

D'Angelo, John P. Several Complex Variables & the Geometry of Real Hypersurfaces. 288p. 1993. boxed set 99.95 (*0-8493-8272-6*, QA331) CRC Pr.

D'Angelo, Laura. FBI's Most Wanted. LC 97-611. 100p. (YA). (gr. 8 up). 1997. lib. bdg. 19.95 (*0-7910-4264-2*) Chelsea Hse.

— Hate Crimes. LC 97-39090. (Crime, Justice, & Punishment Ser.). (Illus.). 100p. (YA). (gr. 8 up). 1997. lib. bdg. 19.95 (*0-7910-4266-9*) Chelsea Hse.

***D'Angelo, Laura A. & Beck, Robert M., Jr.** Legal Aspects of Stallion Management & Syndication. 194p. 2000. pap. 50.00 (*1-58757-033-5*, HM038) Univ of KY.

D'Angelo, Louise. The Catholic Answer to the Jehovah's Witnesses: A Challenge Accepted. (SPA.). 177p. (Orig.). 1997. pap. 10.00 (*1-878886-11-8*) Maryheart Crusaders.

— Come Climb the Ladder & Rejoice Vol. I: A Spiritual Guide. 419p. (Orig.). 1993. pap. 9.50 (*1-878886-01-0*) Maryheart Crusaders.

— Come Climb the Ladder & Rejoice Vol. II: A Spiritual Guide. 430p. (Orig.). 1995. pap. 12.50 (*1-878886-02-9*) Maryheart Crusaders.

— Come Home...the Door Is Open: An Invitation to Reconciliation. 240p. (Orig.). 1977. reprint ed. pap. 7.00 (*1-878886-04-5*) Maryheart Crusaders.

— Mary's Light of Grace: Marian Lectures. (Illus.). 34p. (Orig.). 1973. pap. 3.00 (*1-878886-05-3*) Maryheart Crusaders.

— Too Busy for God? Think Again! LC 81-52423. 120p. 1992. reprint ed. pap. 5.00 (*0-89555-166-7*) TAN Bks Pubs.

— Too Busy for God? Think Again: A Spiritual Guide for Working Women & Housewives. 119p. 1975. reprint ed. pap. 5.00 (*1-878886-16-9*) Maryheart Crusaders.

D'Angelo, Mary R. Moses in the Letter to the Hebrews. LC 78-12917. (Society of Biblical Literature. Dissertation Ser.: No. 42). 280p. reprint ed. pap. 86.80 (*0-7837-5431-0*, 204519600005) Bks Demand.

D'Angelo, N., ed. see ESRIN-ESLAB Symposium Staff.

D'Angelo, N. E., jt. auth. see Zipfinger, F. P.

D'Angelo, Pascal. Son of Italy. LC 74-17925. (Italian American Experience Ser.). 200p. 1975. reprint ed. 17.95 (*0-405-06398-9*) Ayer.

D'Angelo, Rosetta & Blelloch, Paola. L' Arte di Comunicare. 352p. (C). 1993. per. 51.95 (*0-8403-8782-2*, 40878201) Kendall-Hunt.

D'Angelo, Rosetta, jt. auth. see Blelloch, Paola.

D'Angelo, Rudy A. Television's Cowboys, Gunfighters & Cap Pistols. LC 98-89185. (Illus.). 288p. 1999. pap. 31.95 (*0-930625-83-8*, AT5838, Antique Trader) Krause Pubns.

Danger, Eric Paxton. Selecting Color for Packaging. 1987. 86.95 (*0-291-39716-6*) Ashgate Pub Co.

— Selecting Color for Print. 1987. 86.95 (*0-291-39715-8*) Ashgate Pub Co.

Danger, Marilyn, ed. Simply Delicious. 3rd ed. (Illus.). 314p. (Orig.). 1983. reprint ed. pap. 9.95 (*0-9608666-0-4*) Miriam Hosp.

Dangerfield, Elizabeth, et al. Australian Secondary Science Book, Bk. 2. 248p. 1997. pap. text 26.95 (*0-521-45675-4*) Cambridge U Pr.

Dangerfield, George. The Awakening of American Nationalism 1815-1828. (Illus.). 331p. (C). 1994. reprint ed. pap. text 15.95 (*0-88133-823-0*) Waveland Pr.

— The Era of Good Feelings. 540p. 1989. reprint ed. pap. text 17.95 (*0-929587-14-6*, Elephant Paperbacks) I R Dee.

— The Strange Death of Liberal England. LC 96-70279. 384p. 1997. reprint ed. pap. 18.95 (*0-8047-2930-1*) Stanford U Pr.

Dangerfield, Michael L., ed. The Text & Concordances of Fernando del Pulgar - Claros Varones de Castilla & Letras, Seville, 1500. (Spanish Ser.: No. 29). 6p. 1986. 10.00 incl. fiche (*0-942260-71-6*) Hispanic Seminary.

Dangerfield, Royden, ed. see Gordon, David R.

Dangerfield, Royden J., jt. auth. see Ewing, Cortez A.

Dangerfield, Stanley & Howell, Elsworth. Encyclopedie Internationale des Chiens. (FRE.). 489p. 1984. 125.00 (*0-7859-4816-3*, M6099) Fr & Eur.

Dangerous Goods Panel of Air Navigation Commission. Instrucciones Tecnicas para el Transporte Sin Riesgos de Mercancias Peligrosas por Via Aerea, 1989-90. (SPA.). 535p. 1988. 42.00 (*0-940394-26-X*) Labelmaster.

— Instructions Techniques pour la Securite du Transport Aerien des Marchandises, 1989-90. (FRE.). 535p. 1988. 42.00 (*0-940394-27-8*) Labelmaster.

Dangerous Goods Panel of Air Navigations Commissio. Technical Instructions for the Safe Transport of Dangerous Goods by Air 1989-90. (Illus.). 535p. 1988. 42.00 (*0-940394-28-6*) Labelmaster.

Dangerous Goods Panel of Air Navigations Commissio & Commission of ICAO Staff. Technical Instructions for the Safe Transport of Dangerous Goods by Air, 1987-88. 535p. 1986. 40.00 (*0-940394-21-9*) Labelmaster.

Dangerous Goods Panel of Air Staff & Navigation Commission of ICAO Staff. Instrucciones Tecnicas para el Transporte Sin Riesgos de Mercancias Peligrosas Por Via Aerea 1987-88.Tr. of Technical Instructions for the Safe Transport of Dangerous Goods by Air. (SPA.). 535p. 1986. 40.00 (*0-940394-23-5*) Labelmaster.

— Instructions Techniques pour la Seucrite du Transport Aerien des Marchandises Dangereuses, 1987-88.Tr. of Technical Instructions for the Safe Transport of Dangerous Goods By Air. (FRE.). 535p. 1986. 40.00 (*0-940394-22-7*) Labelmaster.

D'Angers, J.-E. L' Humanisme Chretien au XVIlieme Siecle: St. Francois de Sales & Yves de Paris. (International Archives of the History of Ideas Ser.: No. 31). 216p. 1970. lib. bdg. 85.50 (*90-247-0210-0*) Kluwer Academic.

D'Angers, Julien E., pseud. Recherches sur le Stoicisme aux XVIe et XVIIe Siecles. (Studien und Materialien Zur Geschichte der Philosophie Ser.: Vol. XIX). xi, 532p. 1976. write for info. (*3-487-05580-5*) G Olms Pubs.

D'Anghiera, Pietro M. The History of Travayle in the West & East Indies. LC 92-16472. 984p. 1992. 100.00 (*0-8201-1473-1*) Schol Facsimiles.

D'Angieri, Alessandro. The Colored Atlas of Lovebirds. (Illus.). 192p. 1997. 29.95 (*0-7938-0473-6*, TS-282) TFH Pubns.

D'Angio, Giulio J., et al, eds. Practical Pediatric Oncology. 320p. 1992. 145.00 (*0-471-58835-0*) Wiley.

Dangl, J. L. Bacterial Pathogenesis of Plants & Animals. Capron, A. et al, eds. (Currents Topics in Microbiology & Immunology Ser.: Vol. 192). 330p. 1994. 158.95 (*0-387-57391-7*) Spr-Verlag.

Dangle, Lloyd. Next Stop: Troubletown. (Illus.). 120p. (Orig.). 1996. pap. 10.95 (*0-916397-44-0*) Manic D Pr.

D'Anglebert, Jean-Henry. Pieces de Clavecin, Livre Premier: Paris, 1689. fac. ed. (Monuments of Music & Music Literature in Facsimile Ser.: Vol. 4). 1964. lib. bdg. 60.00 (*0-8450-2004-8*) Broude.

Danglemayer, T. ESD Program Management: A Realistic Approach to Continuous, Measurable Improvement in Static Control. 288p. (C). (gr. 13). 1996. mass mkt. 62.95 (*0-412-09781-8*) Chapman & Hall.

Dangler, Charles. Pacific Rim Region: A World Marketplace Approach Through Trade & Investment. 178p. 1992. 21.95 (*0-8191-8629-5*) Madison Bks UPA.

Dangler, Charles A., ed. Nucleic Acid Analysis: Principles & Bioapplications. LC 95-47202. 284p. 1996. 119.95 (*0-471-10358-6*) Wiley.

Dangler, Jamie Faricellia. Hidden in the Home: The Role of Waged Homework in the Modern World Economy. LC 94-282. (SUNY Series on Women & Work). 225p. (C). 1994. text 49.50 (*0-7914-2129-5*); pap. text 16.95 (*0-7914-2130-9*) State U NY Pr.

***Dangler, Jean.** Mediating Fictions: Literature, Women Healers & the Go-Between in Medieval & Early Modern Iberia. LC 00-40383. 2001. write for info. (*0-8387-5452-X*) Bucknell U Pr.

D'Angleton, Cicely. A Cave of Overwhelming: A Collection of Poems by Cicely D'Angleton. LC 95-8111. 88p. (Orig.). 1996. pap. 10.95 (*1-882310-02-0*) Britain Bks.

Dangman & Miura, Dennis S. Electrophysiology & Pharmacology of the Heart: A Clinical Guide. (Illus.). 784p. 1991. text 250.00 (*0-8247-8449-9*) Dekker.

Dangoor, Daniella, tr. see Hocquenghem, Guy.

Dangor, Achmat. Kafka's Curse. 240p. 1999. 22.00 (*0-375-40510-0*) Pantheon.

***Dangor, Achmat.** Kafka's Curse. 2000. pap. 12.00 (*0-375-70462-0*) Vin Bks.

Dangor, Achmat. Waiting for Leila. (Writers Ser.). 140p. 1995. reprint ed. pap. text 12.95 (*0-86975-471-8*, Pub. by Ravan Pr) Ohio U Pr.

D'Angouleme, Marguerite. Chansons Spirituelles. Dottin, G., ed. (FRE.). 198p. 1971. 13.95 (*0-8288-9917-7*, F30250) Fr & Eur.

— La Coche: Poeme de Casuistique Amoureuse de Marguerite de Navarre dans la Tradition du Platonisme Repaissant. Marichal, Robert, ed. (FRE.). 265p. 1971. 24.95 (*0-8288-9918-5*, F30260) Fr & Eur.

— Les Marguerites de la Marguerite des Princesses, 4 vols. in 1. 1970. reprint ed. 90.00 (*0-8288-9919-3*, F30280) Fr & Eur.

D'Angouleme, Marguerite. The Prisons of Marguerite de Navarre. 152p. pap. 40.00 (*0-7049-0124-2*) Pegasus Pr.

D'Angouleme, Marguerite. Le Theatre Profane. Saulnier, V. L., ed. (FRE.). 357p. 1965. 17.95 (*0-8288-9920-7*, F30310) Fr & Eur.

D'Angour, Armand, jt. auth. see Shaw, Steven.

***Dangwal, Parmesh.** I Dare!" Kiran Bedi A Biography. 1999. reprint ed. pap. 18.50 (*81-7476-097-0*, Pub. by UBS Pubs) S Asia.

Danhauer, Jeffrey L., jt. auth. see Johnson, Carole E.

Danhauer, Jeffrey L., jt. auth. see Mendel, Lisa L.

Danhauser, A. Solfege des Solfeges Bk. 1: Vocal. 68p. 1986. pap. 5.95 (*0-7935-5326-1*, 50258490) H Leonard.

— Solfeo Do Los Solfeos Libro: 1 Vocal. (SPA.). 68p. 1986. pap. 5.95 (*0-7935-5354-7*) H Leonard.

Danhiez, Michel, jt. auth. see Goudaert, Michel.

Danhof, Clarence H. Change in Agriculture: The Northern United States, 1820-1870. LC 70-75430. (Illus.). 336p. 1969. 27.50 (*0-674-10770-5*) HUP.

— Government Contracting & Technological Change. LC 79-28531. (Illus.). 472p. 1980. reprint ed. lib. bdg. 65.00 (*0-313-22297-5*, DAGT, Greenwood Pr) Greenwood.

Danhof, Kenneth & Smith, Carol. Computing System Fundamentals: An Approach Based on Microcomputers. LC 79-14933. 1981. text. write for info. (*0-201-01298-7*) Addison-Wesley.

***Dani, A. H.** The Development of Sedentary & Nomadic Civilizations: 700 BC to AD 250, Vol. II. 573p. 1999. pap. 750.00 (*81-208-1408-8*, Pub. by Motilal Bnarsidass) St Mut.

— History of Civilizations of Central Asia, 4 vols. Masson, V. M. et al, eds. 2163p. 1999. pap. 3000.00 (*81-208-1409-6*, Pub. by Motilal Bnarsidass) St Mut.

***Dani, A. H., ed.** The Crossroads of Civilizations A. D. 250 to 750. 570p. 1999. pap. 750.00 (*81-208-1540-8*, Pub. by Motilal Bnarsidass) St Mut.

— The Dawn of Civilation Earliest Times to 700 B. C., Vol. I. 535p. 1999. pap. 750.00 (*81-208-1407-X*, Pub. by Motilal Bnarsidass) St Mut.

Dani, A. H. & Masson, V. M., eds. The Dawn of Civilization: Earliest Times to 700 BC. (History of the Civilizations of Central Asia Ser.: Vol. 1). (Illus.). 535p. 1999. text 35.00 (*1-85043-869-2*) St Martin.

Dani, Ah M., ed. see UNESCO Staff.

Dani, Ahmad H. Indian Palaeography. (C). 1986. 44.00 (*0-8364-2320-8*, Pub. by M Manoharial) S Asia.

Dani, S. U., et al, eds. Principles of Neural Aging. LC 97-218825. 490p. 1997. 120.00 (*0-444-82329-8*) Elsevier.

Danial, C. Ralph, 3rd. Diagnosis of Onychomycosis & Other Nail Disorders: A Pictorial Atlas. LC 95-46880. (Illus.). 96p. 1995. 40.00 (*0-387-94625-X*) Spr-Verlag.

Danial, M. Changing Landscape of Plant Science. LC 97-905511. 1997. pap. 375.00 (*81-7089-223-6*, Pub. by Intl Bk Distr) St Mut.

Danica, Elly. Don't: A Woman's Word. 96p. 1988. pap. 10.95 (*0-921881-05-3*, Pub. by Gynergy-Ragweed) U of Toronto Pr.

Danich, John, jt. auth. see Ball, Judy.

Danicola, Robert C., jt. auth. see Brown, Ralph S.

Daniec, Jadwiga I. The Message of Faith & Symbol in European Medieval Bronze Church Doors. (Illus.). 192p. 1998. pap. 17.95 (*1-887750-95-9*) Rutledge Bks.

Daniel. Advanced Coursebook. pap., teacher ed. 19.29 (*0-13-241266-7*) P-H.

— American Business English Program Higher Intermediate Course Book. 1995. pap. text, teacher ed. 19.29 (*0-13-241167-9*) P-H.

— American Business English Program Intermediate Level Course Book. 1995. pap. text 15.43 (*0-13-241068-0*) P-H.

— Analyzing Arguments. (C). 1996. pap. text 11.74 (*0-07-015303-5*) McGraw.

— Business Statistics. (C). 1994. pap., student ed. 19.96 (*0-395-71803-1*) HM.

— Business Statistics, 7 vols. (C). 1995. pap., teacher ed. 11.96 (*0-395-71930-5*) HM.

— Business Statistics, 6 vols. 6th ed. (C). 1991. pap. text, teacher ed. 6.36 (*0-395-59294-1*); pap. text, student ed. 9.16 (*0-395-59295-X*) HM.

— Business Statistics, 6 vols. 6th ed. (C). 1991. pap. text 76.76 (*0-395-62835-0*) HM.

— Business Statistics, 7 vols. 7th ed. LC 94-76499. (C). 1994. text 79.16 (*0-395-71231-9*) HM.

— Complete Dental Hygiene. 2001. text. write for info. (*0-323-00993-X*) Mosby Inc.

— Engineering Mechanics. 416p. 1994. 32.00 (*0-19-509738-6*) OUP.

***Daniel.** Hindu Response to Religious Pluralism. 2000. 40.00 (*81-86218-10-6*, Pub. by Kant Pubns) S Asia.

Daniel. Sphincters: Normal Function - Changes in Diseases. 464p. 1992. lib. bdg. 184.00 (*0-8493-6748-4*, QP322) CRC Pr.

Daniel. Story of Daniel & the Lion's Den. 1995. pap. text 9.98 (*1-886858-24-1*) Shepherds Tales.

Daniel. Teacher Solution Manual to Accompany Biostatistics. 196p. 1994. pap. text 28.95 (*0-471-12114-2*) Wiley.

***Daniel.** World of Risk. LC 99-55797. 328p. 2000. 29.95 (*0-471-84085-8*) Wiley.

Daniel & Barrier. Dictionary Perigourdin-Francais. (FRE.). 335p. 1988. 125.00 (*0-320-00897-5*) Fr & Eur.

Daniel, jt. auth. see Bodanis, David.

***Daniel, Brigid.** Child Development for Child Care & Protection Workers. LC 98-11672. 1999. pap. text 28.95 (*1-85302-633-6*) Taylor & Francis.

Daniel, Steve. Texas Whitewater. LC 98-41877. (Illus.). 224p. 1999. 25.95 (*0-89096-874-8*); pap. 14.95 (*0-89096-885-3*) Tex A&M Univ Pr.

Daniel, Abbot. Pilgrimage of the Abbot Daniel in the Holy Land, 1106-1107 AD. 1986. pap. 7.50 (*0-89981-070-5*) Eastern Orthodox.

D

Daniel, Abraham. Labor Enterprises in Israel: The Institutional Economy, Vol. 2. 232p. 1976. pap. text 24.95 (*0-87855-639-7*) Transaction Pubs.

Daniel, Adam R., jt. ed. see Conzen, Michael P.

Daniel, Alan. Good Families Don't. (Illus.). 32p. (J). (ps-3). 1991. pap. 4.99 (*0-440-40565-3*) Dell.

Daniel, Alan & Daniel, Lea. Sody Salleratus. unabridged ed. 32p. (J). (gr. k-2). 1998. 14.95 (*1-55074-281-7*, Pub. by Kids Can Pr) Genl Dist Srvs.

Daniel, Alan, jt. auth. see Rubin, Mark.

Daniel, Alfred H. The Home Inspection Manual: One Hundred & One Things to Know Before You Buy a House. Burns, Deborah, ed. LC 86-45973. 160p. 1987. 19.95 (*0-88266-457-3*, Garden Way Pub) Storey Bks.

Daniel, Alice. Asheville Cooks: Recipes & Profiles of Ashville, NC's Finest Restaurants. Rich, Dave et al, eds. (Illus.). 208p. (Orig.). 1997. pap. 15.95 (*0-9634607-9-X*) ThreeD Pr.

Daniel, Alma, et al. Ask Your Angels! 1992. pap. 12.00 (*0-345-36358-2*) Ballantine Pub Grp.

***Daniel, Andy.** Target Card Game. 2nd rev. ed. (Illus.). 1998. 9.95 (*1-929645-05-8*) Enginuity CA.

***Daniel, Andy & Daniel, Sara E.** Diangle! Board Game. 2nd rev. ed. (Illus.). 1999. 24.95 (*1-929645-06-6*) Enginuity CA.

— Doubles Wild Board Game. (Illus.). 1998. 19.95 (*1-929645-04-X*) Enginuity CA.

— Doubles Wild Board Game. 2nd ed. (Illus.). 1999. 19.95 (*1-929645-07-4*) Enginuity CA.

— Stack 21 Card Game. (Illus.). 1997. 9.95 (*1-929645-00-7*) Enginuity CA.

— Tilez! Board Game. (Illus.). 1998. 24.95 (*1-929645-03-1*) Enginuity CA.

Daniel, Ann, ed. Scapegoats for a Profession? Uncovering Procedural Injustice. 200p. 1998. text 28.00 (*90-5702-276-1*, Harwood Acad Pubs); pap. text 18.00 (*90-5702-277-X*, Harwood Acad Pubs) Gordon & Breach.

Daniel, Antoinette, jt. auth. see Viljoen, Andrbe.

Daniel, Arlie V., ed. Activities Integrating Oral Communication Skills for Students Grades K-8. 338p. (Orig.). (C). 1992. pap. text 32.00 (*0-944811-12-4*) Natl Comm Assn.

Daniel, Barbara, ed. see Berge, Jean-Michel, et al.

Daniel, Bartolomej. Geschichte der Roma in Bohmen, Mahren und der Slowakei. Hohmann, Joachim S., ed. (Studien Zur Tsiganologie und Folkloristik Ser.: Vol. 23). (Illus.). 221p. 1998. pap. 39.95 (*3-631-31987-8*) P Lang Pubng.

Daniel, Becky. Absolutely Autumntime. (Illus.). 192p. (Orig.). 1996. pap. text 12.95 (*1-56490-028-2*) G Grimm Assocs.

— Animals Love Their Alphabet. 32p. (J). (ps-k). 1991. 8.99 (*0-86653-579-9*, GA1307) Good Apple.

— Count. (Preschool Basic Skills Ser.). (Illus.). 64p. 1992. 7.99 (*0-86653-672-8*, GA1402) Good Apple.

— Following Directions Brain Boosters. (Illus.). 64p. (J). (gr. 1-4). 1992. 8.99 (*0-86653-654-X*, GA1349) Good Apple.

— Hooray for Addition Facts! (Illus.). 80p. (J). (gr. 1-3). 1990. 10.99 (*0-86653-517-9*, GA1133) Good Apple.

— Hooray for Division Facts! (Illus.). 80p. (J). (gr. 2-4). 1990. 10.99 (*0-86653-520-9*, GA1135) Good Apple.

— Hooray for Fraction Facts! 80p. (J). (gr. 2-5). 1990. 10.99 (*0-86653-568-3*, GA1165) Good Apple.

— Hooray for Multiplication Facts! (Illus.). 80p. (J). (gr. 2-4). 1990. 10.99 (*0-86653-519-5*, GA1136) Good Apple.

— Hooray for Subtraction Facts! (Illus.). 80p. (J). (gr. 1-3). 1990. 10.99 (*0-86653-518-7*, GA1134) Good Apple.

— Hooray for the Big Book of Math Facts! 288p. (J). (gr. 1-4). 1990. 24.95 (*0-86653-533-0*, GA1148) Good Apple.

— I Love You, Baby: Daily Affirmations for Newborns. (Illus.). 384p. (Orig.). 1996. pap. 10.00 (*1-885412-00-2*) R A Daniel.

***Daniel, Becky.** Illinois: The Prairie State: A Christian-Oriented History & Geography Teacher Guidebook. 80p. 1999. teacher ed. 20.95 (*0-88280-143-0*) ETC Pubns.

Daniel, Becky. Language Brain Boosters. (Illus.). 64p. (J). (gr. 1-4). 1992. 8.99 (*0-86653-653-1*, GA1348) Good Apple.

— Logic Brain Boosters. (Illus.). 64p. (J). (gr. 1-4). 1992. 8.99 (*0-86653-652-3*, GA1347) Good Apple.

— Logic Thinker Sheets. 64p. (J). (gr. 4-8). 1989. 8.99 (*0-86653-505-5*, GA1099) Good Apple.

— Math Brainstorms. 80p. (J). (gr. 1-4). 1990. 10.99 (*0-86653-565-9*, GA1170) Good Apple.

— Math Thinker Sheets. 64p. (J). (gr. 4-8). 1988. student ed. 8.99 (*0-86653-429-6*, GA1036) Good Apple.

— Mother Goose & Friends: A Number Activity Book. Mitchell, Judy, ed. (Illus.). 352p. (Orig.). (J). (ps-3). 1995. pap. 24.95 (*1-57310-011-0*) Teachng & Lrning Co.

— Mother Goose & Friends: An Alphabet Activity Book. Mitchell, Judy, ed. (Illus.). 352p. (J). (ps-3). 1994. pap., teacher ed. 24.95 (*1-57310-000-5*) Teachng & Lrning Co.

— Play, Baby, Play: Daily Affirmations for Toddlers. (Illus.). 388p. pap. 10.00 (*1-885412-01-0*) R A Daniel.

— Portraits in Black. (Illus.). 96p. (J). (gr. 4-7). 1990. 11.99 (*0-86653-531-4*, GA1147) Good Apple.

— Prince Poloka of Uli Loko. (Illus.). 48p. (J). (gr. 3-5). 1994. 9.95 (*0-9642050-0-9*) Great Creations.

— Read. (Preschool Basic Skills Ser.). (Illus.). 64p. 1992. 8.99 (*0-86653-671-X*, GA1401) Good Apple.

— Reading Brainstorms. 80p. (J). (gr. 1-4). 1990. 10.99 (*0-86653-560-8*, GA1171) Good Apple.

— Reading Thinker Sheets. 64p. (J). (gr. 4-8). 1989. 8.99 (*0-86653-501-2*, GA1097) Good Apple.

— Spell. (Preschool Basic Skills Ser.). (Illus.). 64p. 1992. 7.99 (*0-86653-673-6*, GA1403) Good Apple.

— Spelling Thinker Sheets. 64p. (J). (gr. 4-8). 1988. student ed. 8.99 (*0-86653-423-7*, GA1035) Good Apple.

— Star Spangled Summertime. (Illus.). 192p. (Orig.). 1996. pap. text 12.95 (*1-56490-027-4*) G Grimm Assocs.

— Surprise Studded Springtime. (Illus.). 192p. (Orig.). 1996. pap. text 12.95 (*1-56490-026-6*) G Grimm Assocs.

— Time-Out for January: An Activity for Every Day. (Illus.). 48p. (J). (gr. 1-4). 1994. 6.99 (*0-86653-828-3*, GA1520) Good Apple.

— Time-Out Trivia. annuals teacher ed. 49.99 (*1-56417-688-6*, GA1581) Good Apple.

— Time-Out Trivia for April: An Activity for Every Day. (Illus.). 48p. (J). (gr. 1-4). 1994. 6.99 (*0-86653-787-2*, GA1481) Good Apple.

— Time-Out Trivia for December: An Activity for Every Day. (Illus.). 48p. (J). (gr. 1-4). 1994. 6.99 (*0-86653-827-5*, GA1519) Good Apple.

— Time-Out Trivia for February: An Activity for Every Day. (Illus.). 48p. (J). (gr. 1-4). 1994. 6.99 (*0-86653-829-1*, GA1521) Good Apple.

— Time-Out Trivia for June/Summer. 48p. 1996. teacher ed. 6.99 (*1-56417-724-6*, GA1543) Good Apple.

— Time-Out Trivia for May: An Activity for Every Day. (Illus.). 48p. (J). (gr. 1-4). 1994. 6.99 (*0-86653-788-0*, GA1482) Good Apple.

— Time-Out Trivia for November. 48p. 1996. teacher ed. 6.99 (*1-56417-723-8*, GA1542) Good Apple.

— Time-Out Trivia for October. 48p. 1996. teacher ed. 6.99 (*1-56417-722-X*, GA1541) Good Apple.

— Time-Out Trivia for September. 48p. 1996. teacher ed. 6.99 (*1-56417-721-1*, GA1540) Good Apple.

— Warm & Wondrous Wintertime. (Illus.). 192p. (Orig.). 1996. pap. text 12.95 (*1-56490-023-1*) G Grimm Assocs.

— Word Thinker Sheets. 64p. (J). (gr. 4-8). 1988. student ed. 8.99 (*0-86653-394-X*, GA1034) Good Apple.

— Writing Brainstorms. 80p. (J). (gr. 1-4). 1990. 10.99 (*0-86653-569-1*, GA1172) Good Apple.

— Writing Thinker Sheets. 64p. (J). (gr. 4-8). 1989. 8.99 (*0-86653-490-3*, GA1098) Good Apple.

Daniel, Becky & Daniel, Charlie. Arithmetrix. 64p. (J). (gr. 5-8). 1980. 8.99 (*0-916456-75-7*, GA 188) Good Apple.

— The Division Book. 64p. (J). (gr. 3-6). 1980. 8.99 (*0-916456-77-3*, GA 190) Good Apple.

— Good Apple & Teacher Helpers. 144p. (gr. 3-7). 1981. 13.99 (*0-86653-047-9*, GA 282) Good Apple.

— The Multiplication Book. 64p. (J). (gr. 2-6). 1980. 8.99 (*0-916456-76-5*, GA 191) Good Apple.

— Strain Your Brain. (Enrichment & Gifted Ser.). (Illus.). 48p. (J). (gr. 4-6). 1980. pap. 6.95 (*0-88160-032-6*, LW 217) Learning Wks.

— Thinker Sheets. 64p. (J). (gr. 2-6). 1978. 8.99 (*0-916456-23-4*, GA78) Good Apple.

— What's Next? 64p. (J). (gr. k-6). 1979. 5.99 (*0-916456-41-2*, GA116) Good Apple.

Daniel, Becky & McClure, Nancee. Listen. 64p. teacher ed. 8.99 (*0-86653-728-7*, GA1450) Good Apple.

— Think. 64p. teacher ed. 8.99 (*0-86653-729-5*, GA1451) Good Apple.

Daniel, Becky, jt. auth. see Daniel, Charlie.

Daniel, Becky, jt. auth. see Mier, Naomi.

Daniel, Becky, jt. auth. see Schafer, Anna.

Daniel, Beverly, jt. auth. see Hernandez, Carolyn.

Daniel, Bonnie S., jt. auth. see Jenkins, John M.

Daniel, Bradford, ed. Black, White & Gray. LC 72-6796. (Essay Index Reprint Ser.). 1977. reprint ed. 30.95 (*0-8369-7271-6*) Ayer.

Daniel, C. W., jt. auth. see Neville, M. C.

Daniel, Carter A. MBA: The First Century. LC 97-25110. 336p. 1998. 48.50 (*0-8387-5362-0*) Bucknell U Pr.

Daniel, Carter A., ed. The Plays of John Lyly. LC 87-47849. 384p. 1988. 45.00 (*0-8387-5119-9*) Bucknell U Pr.

Daniel, Charles. The Autobiography of the Angel of Death. LC 94-71620. 242p. (Orig.). 1995. pap. 14.95 (*1-56883-053-X*) Colonial Pr AL.

— Kenjutsu: The Art of Japanese Swordsmanship. 150p. 1990. pap. 12.95 (*0-86568-148-1*, 323) Unique Pubns.

— Taijutsu: Ninja Art of Unarmed Combat. LC 86-51212. 200p. (Orig.). 1986. pap. 12.95 (*0-86568-085-X*, 125) Unique Pubns.

— Traditional Ninja Weapons & Ninjutsu Techniques. LC 85-52270. 147p. (Orig.). 1986. pap. 9.50 (*0-86568-075-2*, 108) Unique Pubns.

Daniel, Charles, jt. auth. see Smith, Page.

Daniel, Charles S. Ai: A Social Vision. LC 70-154438. (Utopian Literature Ser.). 1976. reprint ed. 26.95 (*0-405-03521-7*) Ayer.

Daniel, Charlie & Daniel, Becky. Super Spelling Fun. 64p. (J). (gr. 2-6). 1978. 8.99 (*0-916456-31-5*, GA82) Good Apple.

— Writing about My Feelings. 64p. (J). (gr. 1-4). 1978. 8.99 (*0-916456-18-8*, GA80) Good Apple.

Daniel, Charlie, jt. auth. see Daniel, Becky.

Daniel, Chloe. Butterfly in the Sky. (J). 1999. text 6.99 (*1-56799-889-5*) M Friedman Pub Grp Inc.

— Star Shapes. (J). 1999. text 6.99 (*1-56799-890-9*) M Friedman Pub Grp Inc.

— Teddy's Toy Box. (J). 1999. text 6.99 (*1-56799-892-5*) M Friedman Pub Grp Inc.

Daniel, Chock. Have You Heard the One About...?? 136p. 1996. pap. 9.95 (*0-9654803-0-5*) Jokes.

***Daniel, Christina H.** After the Flame. 190p. 2000. pap. 12.95 (*1-891929-45-3*) Four Seasons.

Daniel, Christopher S. Sundials. (Album Ser.: No. 176). (Illus.). 32p. 1989. pap. 5.25 (*0-85263-808-6*, Pub. by Shire Pubns) Parkwest Pubns.

Daniel, Claire. The Chick That Wouldn't Hatch. LC 98-55235. 20p. (J). (gr. 1-2). 1999. pap. 3.95 (*0-15-202269-4*) Harcourt.

— The Chick That Wouldn't Hatch. LC 98-55235. 20p. (J). (gr. 1-3). 1999. 10.95 (*0-15-202337-2*, Harcourt Child Bks) Harcourt.

***Daniel, Claire.** Chick That Wouldn't Hatch. (Green Light Reader Ser.). (Illus.). (J). 1999. 9.40 (*0-606-18170-9*) Turtleback.

Daniel, Claire, et al. Great Big Book of Fun Phonics Activities. 352p. 1999. pap. 23.95 (*0-439-08247-1*) Scholastic Inc.

Daniel, Clay. Death in Milton's Poetry. LC 92-56180. 1994. 34.50 (*0-8387-5248-9*) Bucknell U Pr.

Daniel, Clete. Chicano Workers & the Politics of Fairness: The FEPC in the Southwest, 1941-1945. 248p. 1991. text 30.00 (*0-292-76521-5*) U of Tex Pr.

Daniel, Clifton T. Growing up with My Grandfather: Memories of Harry Truman. (Illus.). 256p. 1995. 19.95 (*1-55972-286-X*, Birch Ln Pr) Carol Pub Group.

Daniel Coker Horton & Bell Staff, et al. Mississippi Environmental Law Handbook. 145p. 1994. pap. text 79.00 (*0-86587-309-7*) Gov Insts.

Daniel, Cuthbert. Applications of Statistics to Industrial Experimentation. (Probability & Mathematical Statistics Ser.). 320p. 1976. 174.95 (*0-471-19469-7*) Wiley.

Daniel, Cuthbert & Wood, Fred S. Fitting Equations to Data: Computer Analysis of Multifactor Data. 2nd ed. LC 79-11110. (Probability & Mathematical Statistics: Applied Probability & Statistics Section Ser.). 480p. 1980. 199.50 (*0-471-05370-8*) Wiley.

***Daniel, Cuthbert & Wood, Fred S.** Fitting Equations to Data: Computer Analysis of Multifactor Data. 2nd ed. (Wiley Classics Library). 458p. 1999. pap. 59.95 (*0-471-37684-1*) Wiley.

Daniel, D. F., jt. ed. see Reddy, M. S.

Daniel, D. M., jt. auth. see Pickell, Daniel.

Daniel, Dale M., ed. Knee Ligaments: Structure, Function, Injury, & Repair. 498p. 1990. text 140.00 (*0-88167-605-5*) Lppncott W & W.

Daniel, Darin, ed. see Garcia Lorca, Federico, et al.

Daniel, Darrin. Figo: Selected Poems, 1992-1996, Vol. 8. (Spike Ser.: No. 8). (Illus.). 28p. (Orig.). 1997. pap. 5.00 (*1-885089-01-5*) Cityful Pr.

Daniel, Darrin, ed. see Corman, Cid.

Daniel, Darrin, ed. see Hunter, Robert.

Daniel, Darrin, ed. see Jones, Jim.

Daniel, Darrin, ed. see Peters, Thomas R., Jr.

Daniel, David. The Orthodox Church of India: History. 1986. 14.95 (*0-318-36664-9*) Asia Bk Corp.

Daniel, David, jt. ed. see Lee, Don.

Daniel, David A. Poker: How to Win at the Great American Game. LC 96-21024. 384p. 1997. 20.00 (*1-56980-093-6*) Barricade Bks.

Daniel, David E. & Koerner, Robert M. Quality Assurance & Quality Control for Waste Containment Facilities. (Illus.). 305p. (Orig.). (C). 1995. pap. text 95.00 (*0-7881-1605-3*) DIANE Pub.

— Waste Containment Facilities: Guidance for Construction, Quality Assurance, & Quality Control of Liner & Cover Systems. LC 95-31293. 1995. 48.00 (*0-7844-0111-X*) Am Soc Civil Eng.

— Waste Containment Facilities: Guidance for Construction, Quality Assurance & Quality Control of Liner & Cover Systems. 354p. 1995. 48.00 (*0-7844-0003-2*) Am Soc Civil Eng.

Daniel, David E. & Trautwein, Stephen J., eds. Hydraulic Conductivity & Waste Contaminant Transport in Soil, STP 1142. LC 94-27568. (Special Technical Publication Ser.: Vol. 1142). 606p. 1994. text 75.00 (*0-8031-1442-7*, STP1142) ASTM.

Daniel, David E., jt. auth. see Koerner, Robert M.

Daniel, David E., ed. see ASCE Geotechnical Engineering Division Staff & ASCE Environmental Engineering Division Staff.

Daniel, Deborah & Fey, Samantha. The Insiders' Guide to North Carolina's Southern Coast & Wilmington. 6th ed. (Insiders' Guide Travel Ser.). 1999. pap. 15.95 (*1-57380-129-1*, The Insiders' Guide) Falcon Pub Inc.

Daniel, Dennis. Tales of the Tape: A Production Director's Odyssey. (Illus.). 200p. 1997. pap. 19.95 (*0-89324-269-1*, 3845) Natl Assn Broadcasters.

***Daniel, Dina.** Progressions. 300p. 2001. pap. 13.95 (*1-57532-275-7*, Pub. by Press-Tige Pub) Barnes & Noble Inc.

Daniel, Donald C. Anti-Submarine Warfare & Superpower Strategic Stability. LC 85-14158. 240p. 1986. text 32.50 (*0-252-01272-0*) U of Ill Pr.

Daniel, Donald C., et al. Coercive Inducement: And the Containment of International Crises. LC 98-49655. (Illus.). 288p. 1998. 35.00 (*1-878379-85-2*); pap. 14.95 (*1-878379-84-4*) US Inst Peace.

Daniel, Douglass K. Lou Grant: The Making of TV's Top Newspaper Drama. (Illus.). 380p. 1995. 45.00 (*0-8156-2675-4*); pap. 19.95 (*0-8156-0363-0*) Syracuse U Pr.

Daniel, E. E., jt. ed. see Grover, A. K.

Daniel, E. Randolph. The Franciscan Concept of Mission in the High Middle Ages. (Franciscan Pathways Ser.). 177p. 1992. pap. 15.00 (*1-57659-065-8*) Franciscan Inst.

Daniel, E. Valentine. Charred Lullabies: Chapters in an Anthropography of Violence. LC 96-20275. (Princeton Studies in Culture, Power & History). 272p. 1996. text 49.50 (*0-691-02774-9*, Pub. by Princeton U Pr); pap. text 15.95 (*0-691-02773-0*, Pub. by Princeton U Pr) Cal Prin Full Svc.

— Fluid Signs: Being a Person the Tamil Way. LC 84-163. 215p. (C). 1984. pap. 15.95 (*0-520-06167-5*, Pub. by U CA Pr) Cal Prin Full Svc.

Daniel, E. Valentine & Knudsen, John, eds. Mistrusting Refugees. LC 95-18975. 330p. 1996. 50.00 (*0-520-08898-0*, Pub. by U CA Pr); pap. 18.95 (*0-520-08899-9*, Pub. by U CA Pr) Cal Prin Full Svc.

Daniel, E. Valentine, ed. see Peck, Jeffrey M.

Daniel, Edwin E. Neuropeptide Function in the Gastrointestinal Tract. 520p. 1990. lib. bdg. 254.00 (*0-8493-6158-3*, QP572) CRC Pr.

Daniel, Eileen. Clashing Views on Controversial Issues in Health & Society. 2nd ed. (Taking Sides Ser.). (C). 1995. per. write for info. (*1-56134-444-3*, Dshkn McG-Hill) McGrw-H Hghr Educ.

Daniel, Eileen L. Clashing Views on Controversial Issues in Health & Society. 3rd ed. (Taking Sides Ser.). (Illus.). 400p. 1998. pap. text 13.00 (*0-697-39111-6*, Dshkn McG-Hill) McGrw-H Hghr Educ.

— Taking Sides: Clashing Views on Controversial Issues in Health & Society. 2nd ed. (C). 1997. text. write for info. (*0-697-39269-4*, WCB McGr Hill) McGrw-H Hghr Educ.

Daniel, Eleanor & Wade, John. Foundations of Christian Education. LC 99-32265. 430p. 1999. pap. 24.99 (*0-89900-855-0*) College Pr Pub.

***Daniel, Elton L.** The History of Iran. LC 00-33132. (Greenwood Histories of the Modern Nations Ser.). 296p. 2000. 35.00 (*0-313-30731-8*, GR0731, Greenwood Pr) Greenwood.

Daniel, Elton L. The Political & Social History of Khurasan under Abbasid Rule 747-820. LC 79-53302. 1979. 28.00 (*0-88297-025-9*) Bibliotheca.

Daniel, Elton L., ed. see Al-Ghazzali, Abu Hamid Muhammad.

Daniel, Elton L., tr. see Farahani, Mirza M.

Daniel, Eric D., et al, eds. Magnetic Recording: The First 100 Years. LC 98-8207. 360p. 1998. pap. 49.95 (*0-7803-4709-9*) Inst Electrical.

Daniel, Eric D., jt. auth. see Mee, C. Denis.

Daniel, Eugene L., Jr. In the Presence of Mine Enemies: An American Chaplain in WWII German Prison Camps. LC 85-70894. (Illus.). 112p. 1985. pap. 10.00 (*0-9617501-0-3*) E L Daniel.

Daniel, Eugene S., III & Burroughs, Jon, eds. New Hampshire's White Mountains: Presidential Range - Franconia-Pemigewasett. (Illus.). 1998. pap. 7.95 (*1-878239-61-9*) Applchn Pub.

Daniel-Falk, Lauren. Merchandising Strategies for the Competitive Nineties: How to Create the Total Shopping Experience. (Orig.). 1993. pap. 29.95 (*0-9638313-3-X*) RTW Review.

Daniel, Flake, jt. auth. see Coulanges, Claudine.

Daniel, Francois. Dictionnaire de Dermatologie. (FRE.). 760p. 1990. lib. bdg. 225.00 (*0-8288-2593-9*) Fr & Eur.

Daniel, Frank. Create Your Own Mad Scientist's Laboratory Sticker Picture: With 32 Reusable Stickers. (Illus.). (J). (gr. k-3). 1994. pap. 2.95 (*0-486-27919-7*) Dover.

— Creepy Crawly Stickers. (Illus.). (J). (gr. k-3). 1993. pap. 1.00 (*0-486-27455-1*) Dover.

— Funny Monster Stickers. (Illus.). (J). (gr. k-3). 1992. pap. 1.00 (*0-486-26988-4*) Dover.

Daniel, Frank. Little Monster. (Little Activity Bks.). (Illus.). (J). 1995. pap. 1.00 (*0-486-28416-6*) Dover.

— Scary Monster Sticker Book. (Little Activity Bks.). (Illus.). (J). 1994. pap. 1.00 (*0-486-27911-1*) Dover.

— Silly Clowns Punch-Out Masks. (Illus.). (J). 1995. pap. 3.95 (*0-486-28790-4*) Dover.

Daniel, Frank. Chanukah. (Fun Time Pop-Up Ser.). 20p. (J). (ps-k). 1993. mass mkt. 3.95 (*0-689-71733-4*) Aladdin.

— Christmas. (Fun Shapes Ser.). 20p. (J). (ps). 1993. mass mkt. 3.95 (*0-689-71734-2*) Aladdin.

— Halloween. (Fun Shapes Ser.). 20p. (J). (ps-k). 1993. mass mkt. 3.95 (*0-689-71736-9*) Aladdin.

Daniel, Frederick S. Richmond Howitzers in the War. 1976. 27.95 (*0-8488-0974-2*) Amereon Ltd.

Daniel, G. Enzyklopaedie der Archaologie. (GER.). 486p. 1997. 49.95 (*0-320-00448-1*) Fr & Eur.

Daniel, Glenda. Ancient Near Eastern Symbology: Traces from Antiquity. McCall, Yvonne, ed. (Art Traces Ser.: Vol. 2). (Illus.). 30p. (Orig.). 1997. spiral bd. 10.95 (*1-887003-95-9*) Dancng Jester.

— Dune Country: A Hiker's Guide to the Indiana Dunes. rev. ed. LC 84-10366. (Illus.). 186p. 1984. pap. 12.95 (*0-8040-0854-X*) Swallow.

Daniel, Glenda & Sullivan, Jerry. A Sierra Club Naturalist's Guide to Michigan, Wisconsin, Minnesota & Southern Ontario. LC 80-28742. (Naturalist's Guides Ser.). (Illus.). 384p. 1982. pap. 16.00 (*0-87156-277-4*, Pub. by Sierra) Random.

Daniel, Glyn E., jt. auth. see Piggott, Stuart.

Daniel, Gregory B., jt. ed. see Berry, Clifford R.

Daniel, Gwyn, jt. auth. see Burck, Charlotte.

Daniel, Hal J., III. Moksha. Hathaway, Michael, ed. Date not set. pap. 10.00 (*0-943795-34-6*) Chiron Rev.

Daniel, Hardie W. Magnificent Poet. LC 85-70859. (Illus.). 112p. 1986. 10.00 (*0-942172-01-9*) Endeavor Pub.

Daniel, Harry & Jorgensen, Mark C. Anza-Borrego Desert State Park. Houk, Rose, ed. LC 82-73296. (Illus.). 74p. 1982. 24.95 (*0-910805-00-8*); pap. 19.95 (*0-910805-01-6*) Anza-Borrego.

Daniel, Harry, ed. see Knaak, Manfred.

Daniel, Hawthorne. Islands of the East Indies. LC 77-86669. (Illus.). 1977. reprint ed. 37.50 (*0-404-16703-9*) AMS Pr.

Daniel, Helen & Dessaix, Robert. Picador New Writing LC 93-216482. xiii, 294 p. 1993. write for info. (*0-330-27397-3*) Trans-Atl Phila.

Daniel, Herbert. Physik: Band 4: Atome, Festkorper, Kerne, Teilchen. 350p. 1998. 80.00 (*3-11-016221-0*); pap. 61.00 (*3-11-014631-2*) De Gruyter.

Daniel, Herbert, jt. auth. see Parker, Richard.

Daniel, Hermann A. Thesaurus Hymnologicus. (GER.). lxii, 1843p. 1973. reprint ed. write for info. (*3-487-04912-0*) G Olms Pubs.

Daniel, Hilla. Big Bible Story Puzzle Book. (Illus.). (J). 1992. pap. 8.95 (*0-86653-737-6*) Good Apple.

***Daniel, Holdsworth.** Baby Love Comes to the Rescue. 32p. (J). (gr. k-2). 1999. 3.99 (*0-570-05499-0*) Concordia.

D

— Goodness the Paramedic & the Oily Rags, Vol. 1. 32p. (J). (gr. k-2). 1999. 3.99 (*0-570-05498-2*) Concordia.

— Joy the Clown Strengthens Heartland, Vol. 1. 32p. (J). (gr. k-2). 1999. 3.99 (*0-570-05497-4*) Concordia.

— Kiddie Kindness & the Good News, Vol. 1. 32p. (J). (gr. k-2). 1999. 3.99 (*0-570-05463-X*) Concordia.

Daniel, Howard A., 3rd. Democratic Republic of Viet Nam Coins & Currency, Vol. II, Part 3. LC 76-351167. (Catalog & Guidebook of Southeast Asian Coins & Currency Ser.: Vol. II, Pt. 3). (Illus.). 322p. (Orig.). 1992. text 34.95 (*1-879951-03-7*) Southeast Asian.

Daniel, Howard A., III. Republic of Viet Nam Coins & Currency. LC 76-351167. (Catalog & Guidebook of Southeast Asian Coins & Currency Ser.: Vol. II, Pt. 2). (Illus.). 160p. (Orig.). 1992. pap. 29.95 (*1-879951-02-9*) Southeast Asian.

Daniel Hughes, A. Bilingual Commercial, Accounting & Legal Dictionary: Diccionario Bilingue, Comercial Contable y Legal. (ENG & SPA.). 268p. 1982. 29.95 (*0-8288-0127-4*, S14503) Fr & Eur.

Daniel, I. M., ed. Composite Materials: Testing & Design (6th Conference) - STP 787. 587p. 1982. 55.00 (*0-8031-0695-5*, STP787) ASTM.

Daniel, I. Randolph, Jr. Hardaway Revisited: Early Archaic Settlement in the Southeast. LC 97-10131. 328p. 1998. pap. text 29.95 (*0-8173-0900-4*) U of Ala Pr.

Daniel Industries Staff & Upp, Loy. Fluid Flow Measurement. 192p. 1993. 45.00 (*0-88415-017-8*) Gulf Pub.

Daniel, Issac M. & Ishai, Ori. Engineering Mechanics of Composite Materials. (Illus.). 416p. 1994. text 68.00 (*0-19-507506-4*) OUP.

Daniel, J. Dictionary Francais-Perigourdin. (FRE.). 398p. 1978. 160.00 (*0-320-00917-3*) Fr & Eur.

Daniel, J. C., ed. A Century of Natural History, 1980-1989, Vol. 1. (Illus.). 958p. 1988. 38.00 (*0-19-562166-2*) OUP.

Daniel, J. C. & Datye, Hemant, eds. A Week with Elephants: Proceedings of the International Seminar on the Conservation of the Asian Elephants. LC 96-903474. (Illus.). 554p. 1999. text 24.95 (*0-19-563850-6*) OUP.

Daniel, J. C. & Serrao, J. S., eds. Conservation in Developing Countries: Problems & Prospects. (Illus.). 696p. 1991. text 45.00 (*0-19-562652-4*) OUP.

Daniel, J. Leland, jt. ed. see Edelson, Martin C.

Daniel, J. W., et al. Mercury Poisoning, No. 2. LC 72-13563. (Illus.). 220p. (C). 1972. text 32.50 (*0-8422-7073-6*) Irvington.

Daniel, Jack. My Recollection of Cherokee Alabama. (Illus.). 232p. 1998. pap. 20.00 (*1-884289-25-8*) Grandmother Erth.

— Southern Railway: From Stevenson to Memphis: A History of the Southern Railroad in Memphis. LC 96-76332. (Illus.). 384p. (Orig.). 1996. pap. 24.95 (*1-884289-17-7*) Grandmother Erth.

— Throughbreds of Railroading: Yesterday & Today: NS Norfolk Southern. (Illus.). 272p. 1998. pap. 29.95 (*1-884289-26-6*) Grandmother Erth.

Daniel, Jack L. Changing the Players & the Game: A Personal Account of the SCA Black Caucus Origins. 77p. 1995. pap. 10.00 (*0-944811-16-7*) Natl Comm Assn.

Daniel, Jacque. How to Network (& Prospect) Your Way to Prosperity. 159p. (Orig.). 1996. pap. 9.95 (*0-9651604-0-8*) J Daniel Ent.

Daniel, James & Bruchey, Stuart, eds. Private Investment: The Key to International Industrial Development: a Report of the San Francisco Conference. LC 80-606. (Multinational Corporations Ser.). 1981. reprint ed. lib. bdg. 33.95 (*0-405-13355-3*) Ayer.

Daniel, James W., jt. auth. see Noble, Ben.

Daniel, Jamie O. & Moylan, Tom, eds. Not Yet: Reconsidering Ernst Bloch. 240p. 1997. pap. 20.00 (*0-86091-683-9*, Pub. by Verso) Norton.

Daniel, Jamie O., tr. see Sloterdijk, Peter.

Daniel, Jean. Le Refuge at la Source. (FRE.). 1979. pap. 10.95 (*0-7859-1895-7*, 2070371212) Fr & Eur.

— Tomorrow Is Sunday. (C). 1988. 39.00 (*0-85439-141-X*, Pub. by St Paul Pubns) St Mut.

Daniel, Jean, ed. see Broach-Sowels, Holly.

Daniel, Jean E., ed. see Broach-Sowels, Holly.

Daniel, Jeffrey. Ellen DeGeneres up Close. 1994. mass mkt. 5.99 (*0-671-51734-1*) PB.

Daniel, Jennifer. Spin-a-Story, the Haunted Banana & Other Wacky Mysteries. (Spin-a-Story Ser.). (Illus.). 24p. (Orig.). (J). (gr. 4-7). 1990. pap. 2.95 (*1-878890-02-6*) Palisades Prodns.

— Spin-a-Story, Twenty Thousand French Fries under the Sea & Other Crazy Classics. (Spin-a-Story Ser.). (Illus.). 24p. (J). (gr. 4-7). 1990. pap. 2.95 (*1-878890-01-8*) Palisades Prodns.

Daniel, Jennifer, et al. My First Book of Questions. (Illus.). 128p. (J). (ps-2). 1992. 12.95 (*0-590-44942-7*, 032, Cartwheel) Scholastic Inc.

Daniel, Joan F., et al. Reflected Truth: Former Workers & Followers Unmask Life in a Large, Little-Known Sect. LC 96-67803. 450p. (Orig.). 1996. pap. 10.45 (*0-9639419-3-3*) Res Info Servs.

Daniel, John. All Things Touched by Wind. 65p. (Orig.). (C). 1994. pap. 9.95 (*0-9634000-5-3*) Salmon Run.

— Common Ground. LC 87-73557. 80p. 1988. pap. 7.95 (*0-917652-73-8*) Confluence Pr.

— The Druidic Idea of God. 1995. pap. 7.95 (*1-55818-319-1*, Sure Fire) Holmes Pub.

— Druidic Worship & Their Temples. 1998. reprint ed. pap. 7.95 (*1-55818-392-2*) Holmes Pub.

— Looking After: A Son's Memoir. 272p. 1997. pap. 14.00 (*1-887178-59-7*, Pub. by Counterpt DC) HarpC.

— Mega-Universities & Knowledge Media. (Illus.). 212p. 1998. pap. 24.95 (*0-7494-2634-9*, Kogan Pg Educ) Stylus Pub VA.

— Oregon Rivers. LC 97-8933. (Illus.). 166p. 1997. 45.00 (*1-56579-229-7*) Westcliffe Pubs.

— Scarlet & the Beast: A History of the War Between English & French, Vol. I. 2nd ed. (Illus.). 947p. (C). 1995. 43.00 (*0-9635079-8-2*) J Kregal Inc.

— Scarlet & the Beast: English Freemasonry, Banks, & the Illegal Drug Trade, Vol. 3. 175p. 1995. 12.00 (*0-9635079-4-X*) J Kregal Inc.

— Scarlet & the Beast: Mother of Modern Cults, Viv-a-Vis, Mystery Babylon, Mother of Harlots, Vol. 2. LC 95-139580. 200p. 1994. 12.00 (*0-9635079-2-3*) J Kregal Inc.

— Scarlet & the Beast: The War Between English & French Freemasonry. 2nd ed. (Illus.). 1000p. 1995. write for info. (*0-614-07570-X*) J Kregal Inc.

— Voting for Democracy: Watershed Elections in Contemporary Anglophone Africa. LC 98-37431. (Centre for Democratization Ser.). 292p. 1999. text 68.95 (*1-85521-996-4*, Pub. by Ashgate Pub) Ashgate Pub Co.

— The Woman by the Bridge: Stories. 144p. (Orig.). 1991. pap. 8.95 (*0-940475-62-6*) Dolphin-Moon.

Daniel, John, ed. Wild Song: Poems of the Natural World. LC 97-49514. (Illus.). 144p. 1998. pap. 14.95 (*0-8203-2011-0*) U of Ga Pr.

Daniel, John, et al, eds. Academic Freedom Three: Education & Human Rights. (World University Service Series on Academic Freedom). 256p. (C). 1995. text 25.00 (*1-85649-302-4*, Pub. by Zed Books) St Martin.

Daniel, John, jt. auth. see Robinson, Thomas.

Daniel, John, jt. ed. see Cohen, Dennis L.

Daniel, John, ed. see Finney, Charles G.

Daniel, John M. One for the Books: Confessions of a Small-Press Publisher. 128p. (Orig.). 1997. pap. 10.00 (*1-56474-224-5*) Fithian Pr.

— Richmond Examiner During the War. LC 76-125690. (American Journalists Ser.). 1977. reprint ed. 23.95 (*0-405-01667-0*) Ayer.

— Structure, Style, & Truth: Elements of the Short Story. LC 98-14825. (Illus.). 64p. 1998. pap. 8.95 (*1-56474-272-5*) Fithian Pr.

Daniel, John M., jt. ed. see Moss, Steve.

***Daniel, Joshua M.** Reflections: A Journey Through Revelation. LC 99-68553. 544p. 2000. pap. 30.00 (*1-57921-270-0*) WinePress Pub.

Daniel, Katinka S. Kodaly Approach: Method Book 1. 2nd ed. LC 79-53162. 204p. 1979. spiral bd. 29.95 (*0-916656-13-6*, MFBK 13); trans. 29.95 (*0-916656-14-4*, MFBK 14) Mark Foster Mus.

— Kodaly Approach: Method Book 2. (Illus.). 79p. 1985. trans. 21.50 (*0-916656-21-7*, MFBK 21) Mark Foster Mus.

— Kodaly Approach: Method Book 2. 197p. 1986. spiral bd. 29.95 (*0-916656-20-9*, MFBK 20) Mark Foster Mus.

— Kodaly Approach: Method Book 3. (Illus.). 56p. 1985. trans. 19.50 (*0-916656-23-3*, MFBK 23) Mark Foster Mus.

— Kodaly Approach: Method Book 3. (Illus.). 225p. 1987. spiral bd. 38.95 (*0-916656-22-5*, MFBK 22) Mark Foster Mus.

— Kodaly in Kindergarten: Fifty Lesson Plans, Curriculum, Song Collection. LC 81-68473. (Illus.). 190p. (Orig.). 1981. spiral bd. 27.95 (*0-916656-15-2*, MFBK 15) Mark Foster Mus.

Daniel, Kevin N. Reinventing the Truth: Historical Claims of One of the World's Largest Nameless Sects. 315p. (Orig.). 1993. pap. 9.45 (*0-9639419-0-9*) Res Info Servs.

Daniel, Kevin W. Thomas Daniel of Col. VA: And Eight Generations of His Descendants. (Illus.). 341p. (Orig.). 1995. pap. 25.00 (*0-7884-0235-8*) Heritage Bk.

Daniel, Kevin W. & Daniel, Mary C. Writing Naked: Principles of Writing for Realtime & Captioning. 105p. 1998. pap. 33.95 (*1-881859-50-9*) Natl Ct Report.

Daniel, LaNelle. American Drama Criticism: Supplement IV to the Second Edition. (Drama Explication Ser.). viii, 239p. (C). 1996. lib. bdg. 45.00 (*0-208-02393-3*) Shoe String.

Daniel, Larry, et al. Inside MapInfo Professional. 648p. (C). 1996. pap. 54.95 (*1-56690-088-3*, 2000) Thomson Learn.

Daniel, Larry, jt. auth. see Hutchinson, Scott.

Daniel, Larry J. Cannoneers in Gray: The Field Artillery of the Army of Tennessee, 1861-1865. LC 83-17989. (Illus.). 248p. 1989. pap. text 19.95 (*0-8173-0481-9*) U of Ala Pr.

— Shiloh: The Battle That Changed the Civil War. (Illus.). 432p. 1998. pap. 14.00 (*0-684-83857-5*, Touchstone) S&S Trade Pap.

— Soldiering in the Army of Tennessee: A Portrait of Life in a Confederate Army. LC 91-50250. (Illus.). xviii, 231p. (C). 1991. 32.50 (*0-8078-2004-0*) U of NC Pr.

Daniel, Larry J. & Bock, Lynn N. Island No. 10: Struggle for the Mississippi Valley. LC 95-31876. (Illus.). 216p. 1996. pap. text 24.95 (*0-8173-0816-4*) U of Ala Pr.

Daniel, Larry J. & Gunter, Riley W. Confederate Cannon Foundries. Pioneer Press, ed. LC 76-62878. 1977. pap. 17.50 (*0-913150-38-X*) Pioneer Pr.

Daniel, Lea, jt. auth. see Shapiro, Deborah.

Daniel, Lea, jt. illus. see Daniel, Alan.

Daniel, Linda. Kayak Cookery. (Illus.). 208p. (Orig.). 1997. pap. 12.95 (*0-89732-236-3*) Menasha Ridge.

Daniel, Lizzie C., ed. Confederate Scrapbook. (Illus.). 272p. 1996. reprint ed. pap. 14.95 (*1-888366-02-8*) Dixie Pr.

Daniel, Lois. How to Write Your Own Life Story: A Step-by-Step Guide for the Nonprofessional Writer. 4th ed. LC 96-52438. 248p. 1997. pap. 12.95 (*1-55652-318-1*) Chicago Review.

Daniel, Lusk. O, Rosie. LC 78-23579. (Illus.). (Orig.). 1979. pap. 12.50 (*0-914140-04-3*) Carpenter Pr.

Daniel, M. & Purkayastha, R. P., eds. Handbook of Phytoalexin Metabolism & Action. (Books in Soils, Plants & the Environment: Vol. 37). (Illus.). 632p. 1994. text 210.00 (*0-8247-9269-6*) Dekker.

Daniel, M., jt. ed. see Lakshmanan, M.

Daniel, Malcolm. Edgar Degas, Photographer. (Illus.). 144p. 1998. 49.50 (*0-8109-6524-0*, Pub. by Abrams) Time Warner.

— The Photographs of Edouard Baldus. LC 94-19297. (Illus.). 1994. 65.00 (*0-87099-714-9*); pap. write for info. (*0-87099-715-7*) Abrams.

Daniel, Malcolm R., et al. Edgar Degas, Photographer. LC 98-29432. 1998. 50.00 (*0-87099-883-8*) Metro Mus Art.

Daniel, Mano & Embree, Lester, eds. Phenomenology of the Cultural Disciplines. (Contributions to Phenomenology Ser.). 352p. (C). 1994. lib. bdg. 148.50 (*0-7923-2792-6*, Pub. by Kluwer Academic) Kluwer Academic.

Daniel, Marilyn S. & Strickland, Randy. Occupational Therapy Protocol Management in Adult Physical Dysfunction. 464p. 1992. ring bd. 93.00 (*0-8342-0314-6*, 20314) Aspen Pub.

Daniel, Mark. The Devil to Pay. 256p. 1995. mass mkt. 4.99 (*0-380-72328-X*, Avon Bks) Morrow Avon.

— Pity the Sinner. large type ed. 1995. 27.99 (*0-7505-0728-4*, Pub. by Mgna Lrg Print) Ulverscroft.

— Unbridled. 256p. 1992. mass mkt. 4.99 (*0-380-71443-4*, Avon Bks) Morrow Avon.

Daniel, Martha V., jt. auth. see Taylor, Barbara J.

Daniel, Mary C., jt. auth. see Daniel, Kevin W.

Daniel, Megan. A Time-Travel Christmas, 1 vol. 448p. (Orig.). 1998. mass mkt. 5.50 (*0-505-52319-1*) Dorchester Pub Co.

Daniel, Megan, et al. A Time-Travel Christmas. 448p. (Orig.). 1996. mass mkt. 5.99 (*0-505-52186-5*, Love Spell) Dorchester Pub Co.

— A Time-Travel Christmas. 448p. (Orig.). 1997. mass mkt. 5.50 (*0-505-52241-1*, Love Spell) Dorchester Pub Co.

Daniel, Michael. The Littledoobiddles & Doobetterdees. (Illus.). 40p. (J). 1995. pap. write for info. (*1-55673-998-2*, Fairway Pr) CSS OH.

Daniel, Michael & Hamm, Don. Mercury. (J). 1997. pap. 8.95 (*1-878406-15-9*, Paintbrsh) Parker Dstb.

Daniel, Mike & Weathered, Tom. Landlord-Tenant Relations. 49p. pap. 5.00 (*0-685-23166-6*, 41,575L) NCLS Inc.

Daniel, Norma, jt. auth. see Porrett, Theresa.

Daniel, Norman. Islam & the West: The Making of an Image. 467p. 1994. pap. 33.95 (*1-85168-043-8*, Pub. by Onewrld Pubns) Penguin Putnam.

— Islam & the West: The Making of an Image. 472p. 1997. pap. 25.95 (*1-85168-129-9*, Pub. by Onewrld Pubns) Penguin Putnam.

Daniel, Norman A. Heroes & Saracens: A Reinterpretation of the Chansons de Geste. 349p. 1984. 60.00 (*0-85224-430-4*, Pub. by Edinburgh U Pr) Col U Pr.

Daniel, Orville E. Harmony of the Four Gospels: The New International Version. 2nd ed. 224p. (gr. 10). 1996. pap. 16.99 (*0-8010-5642-X*) Baker Bks.

Daniel, P. A., ed. Romeo & Juliet: Parallel Texts of the First 2 Quartos; Quarto 1, 1597 & Quarto 2, 1599. Incl. Reprint of Q. 2, 1599. 1974. reprint ed. Reprint of Quarto 1, 1597. 1974. reprint ed. Revised Edition Quarto 2, 1599. 1974. reprint ed. (New Shakespeare Society, London, Ser. 2: Nos. 1-4). 1974. Set pap. 60.00 (*0-8115-0233-3*) Periodicals Srv.

Daniel, P. A., ed. see Brooke, Arthur.

Daniel, Patricia. In Heaven I Can Fly: A Poetic Journey of Faith. 60p. 1998. pap. 10.00 (*1-57502-865-4*, PO2357) Morris Pubng.

Daniel, Patricia A. One Father One Mother One Race. Mackey, Rosella, ed. (Illus.). 200p. (Orig.). pap. text 15.00 (*0-9628081-0-5*) Daw Enter.

Daniel, Pete. Breaking the Land: The Transformation of Cotton, Tobacco, & Rice Cultures since 1880. LC 84-197. (Illus.). 368p. 1987. pap. text 20.95 (*0-252-01391-3*) U of Ill Pr.

— Deep'n As It Come: The 1927 Mississippi River Flood. LC 95-35502. (Illus.). 224p. 1996. pap. text 22.00 (*1-55728-401-6*) U of Ark Pr.

***Daniel, Pete.** Lost Revolutions: The South in the 1950s. LC 99-48066. (Illus.). 488p. 2000. 45.00 (*0-8078-2537-9*); pap. 19.95 (*0-8078-4848-4*) U of NC Pr.

Daniel, Pete. The Shadow of Slavery: Peonage in the South, 1901-69. (Illus.). 240p. 1990. pap. text 14.95 (*0-252-06146-2*) U of Ill Pr.

— Standing at the Crossroads: Southern Life in the Twentieth Century. LC 96-34839. 259p. 1996. reprint ed. pap. text 14.95 (*0-8018-5495-4*) Johns Hopkins.

Daniel, Pete, et al. The Peonage Files of the U.S. Department of Justice, 1901-1945. LC 90-12380. (Black Studies Research Sources). 26 p. 1989. write for info. (*0-89093-991-8*) U Pubns Amer.

Daniel, Pete, ed. see Washington, Booker T.

Daniel, Peter, ed. Safecomp '97: The 16th International Conference on Computer Safety, Reliability & Security. York, U. K., September 7-10, 1997. LC 97-26958. xiii, 381p. 1997. pap. 119.00 (*3-540-76191-8*) Spr-Verlag.

Daniel, Peter A. Notes & Conjectural Emendations of Certain Doubtful Passages in Shakespeare's Plays. LC 78-163665. reprint ed. 22.50 (*0-404-01919-6*) AMS Pr.

Daniel, Phillippe A. & AWWA Research Foundation Staff. Balancing Multiple Water Quality Objectives. LC 97-31913. 1998. write for info. (*0-89867-940-0*) Am Water Wks Assn.

Daniel, R. K., jt. auth. see Ramirez, Oscar M.

Daniel, R. P. The Church: Its Beginning, Doctrine & Order. 76p. pap. 3.95 (*0-88172-161-1*) Believers Bkshelf.

— Dating, Marriage, Sex & Divorce. 75p. pap. 3.95 (*0-88172-147-6*) Believers Bkshelf.

— From Rapture to Reigning. 77p. 1993. pap. 3.95 (*0-88172-196-4*) Believers Bkshelf.

— Gospel & the Path of Separation. pap. 3.25 (*0-88172-016-X*) Believers Bkshelf.

— Let's Play Bible Detective. 36p. pap. 2.95 (*0-88172-017-8*) Believers Bkshelf.

— Outline of Booth's Chart of the Ages. pap. 3.25 (*0-88172-018-6*) Believers Bkshelf.

— The Tabernacle Talks Today. pap. 5.95 (*0-88172-020-8*) Believers Bkshelf.

Daniel, R. P., ed. see Dennett, E.

Daniel, R. P., ed. see Grant, F. W.

Daniel, R. P., ed. see Hole, F. B.

Daniel, R. R. & Sreekantan, B. V., eds. Essays on Particles & Fields: M. G. K. Menon Festschrift. (Illus.). 332p. 1990. 27.00 (*81-85324-09-3*) OUP.

Daniel, R. R., jt. ed. see Kasturirangan, K.

Daniel, Ralph, jt. auth. see Apel, Willi.

Daniel, Ralph T. The Anthem in New England before Eighteen Hundred. LC 78-31121. (Music Reprint Ser.). 1979. reprint ed. 39.50 (*0-306-79511-6*) Da Capo.

Daniel, Randy D. Soft Landing: Flights of Fantasy in Space & Time. LC 93-86888. 256p. (Orig.). 1993. pap. 15.00 (*1-884469-00-0*) Renegade Pr.

Daniel, Rebecca. I Love You, Baby: Daily Affirmations for Newborns. (Illus.). 376p. (Orig.). (J). (ps). 1996. mass mkt. 10.00 (*0-614-29349-9*) R A Daniel.

Daniel, Robert L. Athens, Ohio: The Village Years. LC 97-17328. (Illus.). 460p. 1997. text 36.95 (*0-8214-1195-0*); pap. text 17.95 (*0-8214-1196-9*) Ohio U Pr.

Daniel, Robert P. Psychological Study of Delinquent & Non-Delinquent Negro Boys. LC 75-176718. (Columbia University. Teachers College. Contributions to Education Ser.: No. 546). reprint ed. 37.50 (*0-404-55546-2*) AMS Pr.

Daniel, Robert R. The Poetry of Villon & Baudelaire: Two Worlds, One Human Condition. LC 96-24067. (Currents in Comparative Romance Languages & Literatures Ser.: Vol. 52). VI, 196p. (C). 1997. text 44.95 (*0-8204-3472-8*) P Lang Pubng.

Daniel, Roger P. God's Performance Review: Of the Seven Chuches of Asia. 139p. 1994. pap. 4.95 (*0-88172-212-X*) Believers Bkshelf.

— An Outline of Prophesy. 54p. (Orig.). 1990. pap. 3.95 (*0-88172-151-4*) Believers Bkshelf.

Daniel, Roger P., ed. see Cutting, Jorge.

Daniel, Roger P., ed. see Mackintosh, Carlos H.

Daniel, Rollin K. Rhinoplasty: An Atlas of Surgical Techniques. LC 98-27807. 1999. write for info. (*0-387-94458-3*) Spr-Verlag.

Daniel, Rollin K., ed. Aesthetic Plastic Surgery - Rhinoplasty. LC 92-48728. (Illus.). 1000p. 1993. text 425.00 (*0-316-17251-0*) Lppncott W & W.

Daniel, Rollin K., jt. auth. see Ramirez, Oscar M.

Daniel, Rollin K., jt. auth. see Regnault, Paule.

Daniel, Rollin K., jt. ed. see Ramirez, Oscar M.

Daniel, Ron W., jt. auth. see Fraser, Anthony R.

Daniel, Ronald S. Human Sexuality - Methods & Materials for the Education, Family Life & Health Professions, Volume 1: An Annotated Guide to the Audio-Visuals. LC 79-84564. (Illus.). 1979. pap. 35.00 (*0-934016-02-X*); lib. bdg. 45.00 (*0-934016-03-8*) Heuristicus.

Daniel-Rops. Combat pour Dieu 1870-1939. 963p. 1963. 29.95 (*0-8288-7478-6*) Fr & Eur.

— Eglise de la Cathedrale et de la Croisade. 830p. 1952. 9.95 (*0-8288-7490-5*) Fr & Eur.

Daniel-Rops, Henry. Two Men in Me. Meynier, Gil, tr. from FRE. LC 76-163024. (Short Story Index Reprint Ser.). 1977. reprint ed. 19.95 (*0-8369-3938-7*) Ayer.

Daniel, Rosy. Healing Foods. 1997. 9.95 (*0-7225-3280-6*) Thorsons PA.

Daniel, S. First Steps in Tamil. (ENG & TAM.). 122p. 1922. 10.95 (*0-7859-9813-6*) Fr & Eur.

Daniel, S. E., et al, eds. Dementia in Parkinsonism. (Illus.). 220p. 1997. text 119.00 (*3-211-82960-1*) Spr-Verlag.

Daniel, Sadie L. Women Builders. enl. rev. ed. (YA). 1990. 12.95 (*0-87498-084-4*); pap. 10.95 (*0-87498-085-2*) Assoc Pubs DC.

Daniel, Sally & Dirks, Laura M. Colorado's Kind of Cooking. (Illus.). 212p. 1997. 19.95 (*1-878681-02-8*) McCormick Pub.

Daniel, Sally, jt. auth. see Dirks, Lana.

Daniel, Sally H. & Dirks, Laura M. Marketing Without Mystery for NPOs: A Practical Guide to Marketing Fund Raisers. (Illus.). 196p. 1996. student ed. 34.95 (*1-878681-03-6*) McCormick Pub.

Daniel, Sami, et al, eds. Money & Macroeconomic Policy: Essays in Honour of Bernard Corry & Maurice Peston, Vol. 1. LC 98-22389. 256p. 1999. 95.00 (*1-85898-578-1*) E Elgar.

Daniel, Sami, ed. see Corry, Bernard & Peston, Maurice H.

Daniel, Samuel. Collection of the Historie of England. LC 86-10208. 252p. 1986. reprint ed. 60.00 (*0-8201-1413-8*) Schol Facsimiles.

— Hymen's Triumph by Samuel Daniel. Pitcher, John, ed. (Malone Society Reprints Ser.: No. 155). (Illus.). 114p. 1995. text 45.00 (*0-19-729032-9*) OUP.

— Selected Poetry & a Defense of Rhyme. Hiller, Geoffrey G. & Groves, Peter L., eds. LC 98-23254. 264p. 1998. pap. 14.95 (*1-889818-04-6*) Pegasus Pr.

Daniel, Samuel, tr. see Giovio, Paolo.

Daniel, Sara E., jt. auth. see Daniel, Andy.

Daniel, Scott, jt. auth. see Buscaino, Dale.

Daniel, Sergei. Claude Lorrain: Painter of Light. (Great Painters Ser.). (Illus.). 176p. 1996. 40.00 (*1-85995-193-7*) Parkstone Pr.

— French Painting. (Schools & Movements Ser.). (Illus.). 288p. 1996. 55.00 (*1-85995-215-1*) Parkstone Pr.

D

An Asterisk (*) at the beginning of an entry indicates that the title is appearing for the first time.

Daniel, Sergei, jt. auth. see Leek, Peter.

Daniel, Shiloh & Dancing Jester Press Staff. Canine Vegetarian: Dog-Eat-Veggies. Thomson, G. G., ed. LC 97-66526. (Illus.). 60p. 1997. pap. text 14.95 (*1-887003-42-8*) Dancng Jester.

Daniel, Sophia. Dream Healing: A Practical Guide to Unlocking the Healing Power of Your Dreams. LC 99-19415. 160p. 1999. pap. 12.95 (*1-86204-459-7*, Pub. by Element MA) Penguin Putnam.

Daniel, Stephen H. John Toland: His Methods, Manners & Mind. 1984. 65.00 (*0-7735-1007-9*, Pub. by McG-Queens Univ Pr) CUP Services.

— Myth & Modern Philosophy. 256p. (C). 1990. 37.95 (*0-87722-644-X*) Temple U Pr.

— The Philosophy of Jonathan Edwards: A Study in Divine Semiotics. LC 93-50171. (Indiana Series in the Philosophy of Religion). 224p. 1994. 22.95 (*0-253-31609-X*) Ind U Pr.

Daniel, Tabitha C. & Terry, Kay W. Multiage Classrooms by Design: Beyond the One-Room School. Herman, Jerry J. & Herman, Janice L., eds. LC 95-8842. (Practicing Administrator's Leadership Ser.). 88p. 1995. pap. 14.95 (*0-8039-6261-4*) Corwin Pr.

Daniel, Theodore W. & Helms, John. Baker's Principles of Silviculture. 2nd ed. (Illus.). 512p. (C). 1979. 91.88 (*0-07-015297-7*) McGraw.

***Daniel, Thesina C. How to Succeed Through Your Teenage Years: And Avoid Yielding to Drugs, Teen Pregnancy, Suicide & Serving Time in Jail. Bookmasters, Inc. Staff, ed. LC 00-90001. 130p. (YA). (gr. 8 up). 2000. per. 9.95 (*0-9678621-1-6*) Gardenia Pubng.**

Teenagers are a valuable part of our society. They are the ones who will continue & finish what we adults have started & find cures to many diseases. They need to focus throughout their teenage years in order to succeed. "How To Succeed Through Your Teenage Years & avoid yielding to Drugs, Teen Pregnancy, Suicide & Serving Time in Jail", will help encourage the teens to succeed. Why will it help? These four temptations are destroying the lives of many of our teenagers. Real life cases will show the reality & the effects to these four temptations & how it can affect their present & future lives. They will know how valuable they are. How they can accomplish their future dreams. How not to yield to dares & peer pressure, but instead can be preparing for their future career. Throughout their teen years they can be learning adult responsibility that will be helpful when they reach eighteen to journey on. They will know how valuable high school education is & how it will help them in their future endeavor. This book will show parents & others how to help & encourage the teenagers to succeed. *Publisher Paid Annotation.*

D

Daniel, Thomas F. Acanthaceae. Breedlove, Dennis E., ed. (Flora of Chiapas Ser.: Pt. 4). (Illus.). 158p. 1995. pap. 15.00 (*0-940228-35-1*) Calif Acad Sci.

— Carlowrightia (Acanthaceae) LC 82-24613. (Flora Neotropica Monographs: No. 34). (Illus.). 116p. (Orig.). 1983. pap. 20.50 (*0-89327-246-9*) NY Botanical.

— Systematics of Tetramerium (Acanthaceae) Anderson, Christiane, ed. LC 86-10852. (Systematic Botany Monographs: Vol. 12). (Illus.). 134p. 1986. pap. 16.50 (*0-912861-12-6*) Am Soc Plant.

Daniel, Thomas F., ed. see Anderson, Christiane.

Daniel, Thomas F., ed. see Strother, John L.

***Daniel, Thomas M.** Pioneers in Medicine & Their Impact on Tuberculosis. (Illus.). 270p. 2000. 59.00 (*1-58046-067-4*, Pub. by Univ Rochester Pr) Boydell & Brewer.

Daniel, Thomas M. & Robbins, Frederick C., eds. Polio. LC 97-18522. (Illus.). 216p. 1997. 29.95 (*1-878822-90-X*) Univ Rochester Pr.

***Daniel, Thomas M. & Robbins, Frederick C., eds.** Polio. (Illus.). 216p. 1999. pap. 19.95 (*1-58046-066-6*) Univ Rochester Pr.

Daniel, Thomas M., jt. ed. see Kaiser, Larry R.

Daniel, Tony. Earthling. LC 97-24800. 288p. 1997. text 22.95 (*0-312-85571-0*) St Martin.

— Earthling. 1998. pap. 14.95 (*0-312-86661-5*, Pub. by Tor Bks) St Martin.

***Daniel, Tony.** Metaplanetary. 2001. write for info. (*0-06-105142-X*) HarpC.

Daniel, Tony. The Robot's Twilight Companion. LC 99-21951. 336p. 1999. 24.95 (*0-9655901-5-1*) Golden Gryphon.

— Warpath. 320p. 1994. mass mkt. 4.99 (*0-8125-1966-3*, Pub. by Tor Bks) St Martin.

Daniel, Tony & Smith, Beau. The Tenth Vol. I: Collected Edition. (Illus.). 48p. 1998. pap. 4.95 (*1-58240-002-4*) Image Comics.

— The Tenth Miniseries: Abuse of Humanity. (Illus.). 112p. 1998. pap. 11.95 (*1-58240-036-9*) Image Comics.

Daniel, Ute. The War from Within: German Women in the First World War. Winter, Jay, ed. Ries, Margaret, tr. from GER. LC 98-115319. (Legacy of the Great War Ser.). 256p. 1997. 65.00 (*0-85496-892-X*, Pub. by Berg Pubs); pap. 18.50 (*1-85973-147-3*, Pub. by Berg Pubs) NYU Pr.

Daniel, W. Harrison. Jimmie Foxx: The Life & Times of a Baseball Hall of Famer, 1907-1967. LC 96-34665. (Illus.). 256p. 1996. lib. bdg. 28.50 (*0-7864-0196-6*) McFarland & Co.

Daniel, W. T. The History & Origin of Law Reports: England. LC 12-13803. 359p. 1961. reprint ed. lib. bdg. 47.50 (*0-89941-348-X*, 500300) W S Hein.

Daniel, W. W. Workplace Industrial Relations & Technical Change. 352p. 1987. 38.00 (*0-86187-917-1*) St Martin.

Daniel, W. W. & McIntosh, Neil. Right to Manage: A Study of Leadership & Reform in Employee Relations. 192p. 1972. pap. 19.95 (*0-8464-0798-1*) Beekman Pubs.

Daniel, Walter. The Life of Ailred of Rievaulx. Powicke, Maurice, ed. 272p. 1979. reprint ed. text 85.00 (*0-19-822256-4*) OUP.

Daniel, Walter C. Black Journals of the United States. LC 81-13440. (Historical Guides to the World's Periodicals & Newspapers Ser.). 432p. 1982. lib. bdg. 85.00 (*0-313-20704-6*, DBJ/, Greenwood Pr) Greenwood.

— De Lawd: Richard B. Harrison & The Green Pastures. 99. LC 86-7588. (Contributions in Afro-American & African Studies: No. 99). 188p. 1986. 45.00 (*0-313-25300-5*, DDL/, Greenwood Pr) Greenwood.

Daniel, Wayne & Minitab, Inc. Staff. Biostatistics: A Foundation for the Health Sciences. 6th ed. 968p. 1996. student ed. 115.95 incl. disk (*0-471-17445-9*) Wiley.

Daniel, Wayne W. Biostatistics: A Foundation for Analysis in the Health Sciences. 7th ed. LC 98-13102. 928p. 1998. text 99.95 (*0-471-16386-4*) Wiley.

— Essentials of Business Statistics, 2 vols. 2nd ed. 492p. (C). 1987. pap. text, teacher ed. 5.56 (*0-395-44699-6*) HM.

— Pickin' on Peachtree: A History of Country Music in Atlanta, Georgia. (Music in American Life Ser.). (Illus.). 328p. 1990. text 32.50 (*0-252-01687-4*) U of Ill Pr.

Daniel, Wayne W. & Terrell, James C. Business Statistics: Basic Concepts & Methodology. 4th ed. 800p. 1986. disk. write for info. (*0-318-60186-9*) HM.

— Business Statistics: Basic Concepts & Methodology. 5th ed. 1988. teacher ed. write for info. (*0-318-63306-X*); student ed. 16.76 (*0-318-36888-9*) HM.

— Business Statistics for Management & Economics. 7th ed. (C). 1995. pap. text, student ed. 23.96 (*0-395-71802-3*) HM.

Daniel, Werner G., et al, eds. Cardiogenic Embolism. LC 95-12357. (Illus.). 320p. 1996. 75.00 (*0-683-02359-4*) Lppncott W & W.

Daniel, William. Genetics & Human Variation. 4th ed. (Illus.). 585p. 1995. pap. 32.80 (*0-87563-556-3*) Stipes.

Daniel, Yvonne. Rumba: Dance & Social Change in Contemporary Cuba. LC 94-34363. (Blacks in the Diaspora Ser.). (Illus.). 224p. 1995. 35.00 (*0-253-31605-7*); pap. 14.95 (*0-253-20948-X*) Ind U Pr.

Daniele, Anthony, jt. auth. see Clair, Bernard E.

Daniele, Joseph. How to Build 35 Great Clocks. LC 83-24237. (Illus.). 192p. 1984. pap. 14.95 (*0-8117-2232-5*) Stackpole.

Daniele, Paul, jt. auth. see Stewart, Bruce.

***Daniele, R. Anthony.** Other People's Habits. 224p. 2000. pap. 21.95 (*0-07-135915-X*) McGraw.

Danielesson, Bengt, ed. Advances in Molecular & Cell Biology Vol. 15: Biochemical Technology, 2 pts. 688p. 1997. 257.00 (*0-7623-0114-7*) Jai Pr.

***Danielewski, M.** Diffusion & Reactions. (Solid State Phenomena Ser.: Vol. 72). (Illus.). 276p. (C). 2000. text 95.00 (*3-908450-51-9*, Pub. by Scitec Pubns) Enfield Pubs NH.

Danielewski, Mark Z. House of Leaves. LC 99-36024. 704p. 2000. pap. 19.95 (*0-375-70376-4*) Pantheon.

***Danielewski, Mark Z.** House of Leaves. 2000. 40.00 (*0-375-42052-5*) Pantheon.

Danielfour, R. Quintet for Piano & Strings: Study Score. 1994. pap. 14.95 (*0-7935-3040-7*) H Leonard.

Danieli, Fidel. Connie Zehr - Flash Back, 1970-1985: An Installation Using Mnemonic Fragments. LC 84-52883. (Illus.). 31p. (Orig.). 1985. pap. text 5.00 (*0-936429-03-8*, 84-052883) LA Municipal Art.

Danieli, Y. International Handbook of Multigenerational Legacies of Trauma. LC 98-26017. (The Plenum Series on Stress & Coping). (Illus.). 672p. 1998. 95.00 (*0-306-45738-5*, Kluwer Plenum) Kluwer Academic.

Danieli, Yael, et al, eds. International Responses to Traumatic Stress: Humanitarian, Human Rights, Justice, Peace, & Development Contributions, Collaborative Actions, & Future Initiatives. 484p. 1995. 46.00 (*0-89503-132-9*) Baywood Pub.

— The Universal Declaration of Human Rights: Fifty Years & Beyond. LC 98-39685. 480p. 1998. text 46.00 (*0-89503-192-2*) Baywood Pub.

Danielian, Noobar R. AT&T: The Story of Industrial Conquest. LC 74-7672. (Telecommunications Ser.). 486p. 1974. reprint ed. 33.95 (*0-405-06038-6*) Ayer.

Daniell, Andy. The Effects of Money, Inflation & Interest Rates on Residential Investment. LC 94-21347. (Financial Sector of the American Economy Ser.). (Illus.). 144p. 1994. text 15.00 (*0-8153-1762-X*) Garland.

Daniell, B. L., jt. auth. see Waldron, M. B.

Daniell, Christopher. Death & Burial in Medieval England. (Illus.). 272p. (C). 1998. pap. 24.99 (*0-415-18550-5*) Routledge.

— Death & Burial in Medieval England, 1066-1550. LC 96-7552. (Illus.). 268p. (C). 1996. 60.00 (*0-415-11629-5*) Routledge.

— Traveller's History of England. 4th ed. (Traveller's History Ser.). (Illus.). 304p. 1998. pap. 14.95 (*1-56656-244-9*, Interlink Bks) Interlink Pub.

Daniell, David. William Tyndale: A Biography. LC 94-17509. 429p. 1994. 35.00 (*0-300-06132-3*) Yale U Pr.

Daniell, David, ed. Tyndale's New Testament. Tyndale, William, tr. 1996. pap. 15.00 (*0-300-06580-9*) Yale U Pr.

Daniell, David, ed. see Tyndale, William.

Daniell, David, ed. & intro. see Buchan, John.

Daniell, Gene & Burroughs, Jon. Hiking Guide to Mount Washington & the Presidential Range. 6th ed. LC 98-29415. 1998. 14.95 (*1-878239-76-7*) AMC Books.

Daniell, Gene & Burroughs, Jon, eds. AMC White Mountain Guide. 26th rev. ed. LC 98-27283. 576p. 1998. pap. 21.95 (*1-878239-65-1*) AMC Books.

— Southern New Hampshire Trail Guide. LC 99-22411. 352p. 1999. pap. text 16.95 (*1-878239-73-2*) AMC Books.

Daniell, Gene S., jt. ed. see Burroughs, Jon.

Daniell, Jere R. Experiment in Republicanism: New Hampshire Politics & the American Revolution, 1741-1794. LC 75-122219. (Illus.). 277p. reprint ed. pap. 85.90 (*0-7837-1688-5*, 205721800024) Bks Demand.

***Daniell, Rosemary.** Fatal Flowers: On Sin, Sex & Suicide in the Deep South. (Illus.). 294p. 1999. pap. 15.95 (*1-892514-26-5*, Hill St Class) Hill St Pr.

Daniell, Rosemary. Sleeping with Soldiers. 320p. 1986. mass mkt. 3.95 (*0-446-30023-3*, Pub. by Warner Bks) Little.

— The Woman Who Spilled Words All over Herself: Writing & Living the Zona Rosa Way. 216p. 1998. pap. 13.95 (*0-571-19935-6*) Faber & Faber.

Daniell, S. Story of Cornwall. (C). 1989. pap. 40.00 (*0-85025-309-8*, Pub. by Tor Mark Pr) St Mut.

— Victorian Cornwall. (C). 1989. pap. text 24.95 (*0-85025-315-2*, Pub. by Tor Mark Pr) St Mut.

Daniell, S., ed. Churches of Cornwall. (C). 1988. pap. 24.95 (*0-85025-300-4*, Pub. by Tor Mark Pr) St Mut.

Daniell, Tina. The Companions. (DragonLance Meetings Sextet: Vol. 6). 320p. 1993. pap. 5.99 (*1-56076-340-X*, Pub. by TSR Inc) Random.

— Dark Heart. LC 90-71496. (DragonLance Meetings Sextet: Vol. 3). (Illus.). 320p. (Orig.). 1992. pap. 5.99 (*1-56076-116-4*, Pub. by TSR Inc) Random.

— Marquesta Kar-Thon. (DragonLance Warriors Ser.). 320p. (Orig.). 1995. pap. 5.99 (*0-7869-0134-9*, Pub. by TSR Inc) Random.

Danielli, James F., jt. auth. see Bourne, Geoffrey H.

Danielli, James F., jt. ed. see Bourne, Geoffrey H.

Danielli, Reuvik, tr. see Gazit, Shlomo.

D'Aniello, Charles, ed. Teaching Bibliographic Skills in History: A Sourcebook for Historians & Librarians. LC 92-8833. 392p. 1993. lib. bdg. 65.00 (*0-313-25266-1*, DTB, Greenwood Pr) Greenwood.

***D'Aniello, Joesh.** A Family Heirloom. LC 99-91971. 2000. 25.00 (*0-7388-1452-0*); pap. 18.00 (*0-7388-1453-9*) Xlibris Corp.

Daniells, Cory. Broken Vows. 336p. 1999. mass mkt. 5.99 (*0-553-58097-3*) Bantam.

Daniells, Greg. Let It Rip. (Illus.). 128p. 1997. 12.98 (*0-7858-0656-3*) Bk Sales Inc.

***Daniells, Greg & Kleh, Cindy.** Snowboarding: Experience the Thrill of the Ride. (Illus.). 144p. 2000. pap. 19.95 (*1-55209-544-4*) Firefly Bks Ltd.

Daniells, Jeff & Smith, Mike, eds. Post Flask Management of Tissue-Cultured Bananas. 1991. pap. 45.00 (*1-86320-042-8*, Pub. by ACIAR) St Mut.

Daniells, Lorna M. Business Information Sources. 3rd rev. ed. LC 92-41827. 1993. 42.50 (*0-520-08180-3*, Pub. by U CA Pr) Cal Prin Full Svc.

Daniells, Trenna & Sutphen, Trenna. Lifestyle Thin. 32p. 1986. pap. text 29.95 incl. digital audio (*0-918519-13-6*) Trenna Prods.

***Danielmeyer, H. G. & Takeda, Y., eds.** The Company of the Future: Markets, Tools & Strategies. LC 99-37748. 200p. 1999. 62.00 (*3-540-65861-0*) Spr-Verlag.

Danielopol, D., jt. ed. see Loffler, H.

Danielou, Alain. Gods of Love & Ecstasy: The Traditions of Shiva & Dionysus. LC 92-1042. 250p. 1992. pap. 14.95 (*0-89281-374-1*) Inner Tradit.

***Danielou, Alain.** The Hindu Temple: Deification of Eroticism. (Illus.). 128p. 2001. pap. 24.95 (*0-89281-854-9*) Inner Tradit.

Danielou, Alain. Introduction to the Study of Musical Scales. (C). 1979. 31.00 (*0-8364-2353-4*, Pub. by M Manoharial) S Asia.

***Danielou, Alain.** Introduction to the Study of Musical Scales. 292p. 1999. 28.50 (*81-215-0920-3*, Pub. by Munshiram) Coronet Bks.

Danielou, Alain. El Kama Sutra Completo: La Primera Traduccion Integra y Moderna Del Texto Clasico de la India.Tr. of Complete Kama Sutra. (SPA.). 576p. 1997. pap. 19.95 (*0-89281-584-1*, Inner Trad) Inner Tradit.

— The Myths & Gods of India. (Classic Work on Hindu Polytheism from the Princeton Bollingen Ser.). (Illus.). 480p. 1991. pap. 35.00 (*0-89281-354-7*) Inner Tradit.

— The Phallus: Sacred Symbol of Male Creative Power. LC 95-220292. (Illus.). 128p. 1995. pap. 19.95 (*0-89281-556-6*) Inner Tradit.

— Ragas of Northern Indian Music. 1981. 32.00 (*0-8364-0774-1*, Pub. by M Manoharial) S Asia.

— Virtue, Success, Pleasure, & Liberation: Four Aims of Life in the Tradition of Ancient India. 1993. pap. 14.95 (*0-89281-218-4*) Inner Tradit.

— The Way to the Labyrinth: Memories of East & West. Cournand, Marie-Claire, tr. from FRE. LC 86-28660.Tr. of Le/Chemin du Labyrinthe. 352p. 1987. 23.95 (*0-8112-1014-6*, Pub. by New Directions); pap. 13.95 (*0-8112-1015-4*, NDP634, Pub. by New Directions) Norton.

— While the Gods Play. 288p. (Orig.). 1987. pap. 12.95 (*0-89281-115-3*) Inner Tradit.

— Yoga: Mastering the Secrets of Matter & the Universe. 192p. (Orig.). 1990. pap. 14.95 (*0-89281-301-6*) Inner Tradit.

Danielou, Alain, tr. from SAN. The Complete Kama Sutra: The First Unabridged Modern Translation of the Classic Indian Text. 512p. 1993. 29.95 (*0-89281-492-6*) Inner Tradit.

— The Complete Kama Sutra: The First Unabridged Modern Translation of the Classic Indian Text. unabridged ed. 576p. 1995. pap. 19.95 (*0-89281-525-6*, Park St Pr) Inner Tradit.

Danielou, Alain, tr. see Adigal, Ilango.

Danielou, Alain, tr. see Shattan, Merchant-Prince.

Danielou, Jean. The Angels & Their Mission. LC 56-11414. 118p. (C). 1987. reprint ed. pap. 9.95 (*0-87061-056-2*, 6914) Chr Classics.

— The Bible & the Liturgy. LC 55-9516. 372p. 1955. text 18.50 (*0-268-00018-2*) U of Notre Dame Pr.

— The Dead Sea Scrolls & Primitive Christianity. Attanasio, Salvator, tr. from FRE. LC 78-21516. 128p. 1979. reprint ed. lib. bdg. 35.00 (*0-313-21144-2*, DADE, Greenwood Pr) Greenwood.

— God's Life in Us. 1969. pap. 9.95 (*0-87193-304-7*) Dimension Bks.

— Origen. Mitchell, Walter, tr. LC 82-48698. (Orthodoxies & Heresies in the Early Church Ser.). reprint ed. 36.00 (*0-404-62381-6*) AMS Pr.

— Prayer: The Mission of the Church. LC 96-9103. (Ressourcement Ser.). 140p. 1996. 15.00 (*0-8028-4105-8*) Eerdmans.

Danielou, Jean, ed. From Glory to Glory: Texts from Gregory of Nyssa's Mystical Writings. LC 79-38. 304p. 1979. pap. 13.95 (*0-913836-54-0*) St Vladimirs.

Danielpour, Debbie, ed. see Chapel, Hal J. & Clark, Richard G.

Danielpour, R. The Enchanted Garden Book 1: Piano Solo Preludes. 40p. 1993. pap. 12.95 (*0-7935-2533-0*) H Leonard.

— First Light Concerto for Chamber Orchestra in One Movement: Full Score. 92p. 1992. pap. 45.00 (*0-7935-0078-8*, 50481217) H Leonard.

— Quintet for Piano & Strings: Score & Parts. 100p. 1994. per. 100.00 (*0-7935-3037-7*) H Leonard.

— Sonnets to Orpheus: Score Book One for Soprano & Chamber Ensemble. 168p. 1995. per. 50.00 (*0-7935-4998-1*, 50482477) H Leonard.

— Urban Dances for Brass Quintet, Score & Parts. 72p. 1992. pap. 35.00 (*0-7935-1244-1*) H Leonard.

Daniels. Digital Design. 207p. 1996. pap., lab manual ed. 23.95 (*0-471-14686-2*) Wiley.

— Digital Design. 418p. 1997. pap. text, student ed. 25.00 (*0-471-14685-4*) Wiley.

— For Baby's Sake (Baby Boom) large type ed. 1997. per. 3.25 (*0-373-15707-X*, Harlequin) Harlequin Bks.

***Daniels.** International Business: Environments & Operations. 8th ed. 1998. (*0-201-53723-0*) P-H.

Daniels. International Money & Finance. LC 98-28157. (FV - International Finance Ser.). 1998. pap. 91.95 (*0-538-87533-X*) S-W Pub.

— Lost Fathers: Politics of Fatherlessness in America. 208p. 2000. pap. 16.95 (*0-312-22471-0*) St Martin.

— Over the Threshold. LC 98-47351. 272p. 1999. pap. 19.99 (*0-415-91805-7*) Routledge.

— Sweet Valentine. large type ed. 1997. per. 3.25 (*0-373-15692-8*, Harlequin) Harlequin Bks.

Daniels & Dewar. Programmed Proofreading. 3rd ed. (PS - Communication/English Ser.). (C). 1991. mass mkt. 19.00 (*0-538-70392-X*) S-W Pub.

Daniels, et al. Japanese Americans: From Relocation to Redress. rev. ed. LC 91-2892. (Illus.). 264p. 1992. pap. 22.95 (*0-295-97117-7*) U of Wash Pr.

***Daniels, et al.** Managing Telework. 2000. pap. 34.95 (*1-86152-572-9*) Thomson Learn.

— Windows 2000. LC 99-68975. (Illus.). 350p. 2000. pap. 34.99 (*0-7357-0973-4*) Macmillan Tech.

Daniels, jt. auth. see Allan.

Daniels, Kari & Schaper, Connie. Out & About. (Illus.). 166p. (J). (ps-12). 1998. spiral bd. 29.00 (*1-884135-37-4*) Mayer-Johnson.

***Daniels, Teri.** The Feet in the Gym. (Illus.). 32p. (J). (ps-3). 1999. 15.95 (*1-890817-12-0*, Pub. by Winslow Pr) Publishers Group.

— G-Rex. LC 99-30882. (Illus.). 32p. (J). (gr. k-4). 2000. lib. bdg. 17.99 (*0-531-33243-8*) Orchard Bks Watts.

— Just Enough. LC 00-8395. (Illus.). 32p. (J). (ps-k). 2000. 15.99 (*0-670-88873-7*, Viking Child) Peng Put Young Read.

Daniels, A. Pat. Bolivar! Gulf Coast Peninsula. LC 85-60991. (Illus.). 113p. (Orig.). 1985. pap. 8.95 (*0-9614885-0-6*) Peninsula Pr TX.

— Citizen First, Banker Second: History of a Texas Community Bank & Stories about Its Politically Liberal Leader. LC 95-69947. (Illus.). 241p. 1995. 25.00 (*0-9614885-3-0*) Peninsula Pr TX.

— A Fascinating Voyage on the Bolivar Ferry. LC 92-81012. (Illus.). 56p. 1992. pap. 4.95 (*0-9614885-1-4*) Peninsula Pr TX.

***Daniels, Abner P.** Tales from Iosco County. 1999. 24.95 (*0-9675028-0-2*) Beacon Light Bks.

Daniels, Alice G. After the Flowers: Life Beyond Widowhood. 112p. (Orig.). 1996. pap. 9.95 (*1-56474-173-7*) Fithian Pr.

Daniels, Alison. Feng Shui for You & Your Cat. (Illus.). 160p. 1999. pap. 19.95 (*0-8230-1655-2*) Watsn-Guptill.

Daniels, Allen, et al. Behavioral Healthcare Quality & Accountability Tool Kit, Version I. 1997. 745.00 (*1-887452-14-1*) Manisses Communs.

Daniels, Allen S., et al. Behavioral Group Practice Performance Characteristics: The Council of Behavioral Group Practices Benchmarking Study. (Managed Behavioral Healthcare Library). 1995. pap. 45.00 (*1-887452-00-1*) CentraLink.

Daniels, Annette. Timeless Moment. 416p. 1995. mass mkt. 4.99 (*0-7860-0114-3*) Kensgtn Pub Corp.

— Timeless Moment. 1996. mass mkt. 4.99 (*0-8217-5330-4*, Zebra Kensgtn) Kensgtn Pub Corp.

Daniels, Anthony. Coups & Cocaine: Journeys in South America. LC 86-18054. (Illus.). 240p. 1988. reprint ed. pap. 9.95 (*0-87951-311-X*, Pub. by Overlook Pr) Penguin Putnam.

Daniels, Anthony, jt. see Lawson, Denis.

Daniels, Arlene K. Invisible Careers: Women Civic Leaders from the Volunteer World. (Women in Culture & Society Ser.). xxxviii, 304p. 1995. 35.95 (*0-226-13610-8*) U Ch Pr.

Daniels, Arlene K., jt. ed. see Benet, James.

Daniels, Arthur, Jr. If God Heals Your Eyes, Don't Cut off Your Head: Thinking about God? xxx, 464p. 1998. 24.00 (*0-9666107-1-7*) Proaster Bks.

Daniels, Arthur M. A Journal of Sibley's Indian Expedition During the Summer of 1863 & Record of the Troops Employed. (Illus.). 154p. 1980. reprint ed. 30.00 (*0-911506-13-6*) Thueson.

***Daniels, Aubrey C.** Bringing Out the Best in People. 2nd ed. 245p. 1999. 21.95 (*0-07-135145-0*) McGraw.

Daniels, Aubrey C. Bringing Out the Best in People: How to Apply the Astonishing Power of Positive Reinforcement. 208p. 1994. 21.95 (*0-07-015358-2*) McGraw.

***Daniels, Aubrey C.** Gestion du Rendement (Performance Management) L'Amelioration de la Qualite de la Productivite par le Renforcement (Improving Quality Productivity Through Positive Reinforcement) 3rd ed. (FRE.). 247p. 1999. pap. 29.95 (*0-937100-06-4*) Perf Manage.

Daniels, Aubrey C. Performance Management: Improving Quality & Productivity Through Positive Reinforcement. 3rd rev. ed. LC 82-61868. (Illus.). 1989. 29.95 (*0-937100-01-3*) Perf Manage.

***Daniels, B. J.** The Agent's Secret Child. (Intrigue Ser.: Bk. 585). 2000. mass mkt. 4.25 (*0-373-22585-7*, 1-22585-3) Harlequin Bks.

Daniels, B. J. A Father for Her Baby: Lost & Found. (Intrigue Ser.: No. 493). 1998. per. 3.99 (*0-373-22493-1*, 1-22493-0) Harlequin Bks.

— Hotshot P. I. (Lawman Ser.). 1997. per. 3.75 (*0-373-22417-6*, 1-22417-9) Harlequin Bks.

***Daniels, B. J.** Love at First Sight. (Intrigue Ser.: Vol. 555). 2000. per. 4.25 (*0-373-22555-5*) Harlequin Bks.

Daniels, B. J. Outlawed! LC 96-3685. (Intrigue Ser.). 251p. 1996. per. 3.50 (*0-373-22353-6*, 1-22353-6) Harlequin Bks.

— Stand by Your Man. LC 95-6903. (Intrigue Ser.). 248p. 1995. per. 3.50 (*0-373-22312-9*, 1-22312-2) Harlequin Bks.

— Stolen Moments: Countdown 2000. (Intrigue Ser.: No. 533). 1999. per. 3.99 (*0-373-22533-4*, 1-22533-3) Harlequin Bks.

— Undercover Christmas. (Intrigue Ser.: No. 446). 1997. per. 3.75 (*0-373-22446-X*, 1-22446-8) Harlequin Bks.

***Daniels, B. J., et al, eds.** Magnetic Materials, Structures & Processing for Information Storage: Materials Research Society Symposium Proceedings, Vol. 614. 2000. text 73.00 (*1-55899-522-6*) Materials Res.

Daniels, B. K., ed. Safety of Computer Control Systems, 1990: Safety, Security & Reliability Related Computers for the 1990's. (IFAC Symposia Ser.: 9017). (Illus.). 196p. 1990. 100.00 (*0-08-040953-9*, Pergamon Pr) Elsevier.

Daniels, Barbara. The Woman Who Tries to Believe. 29p. (Orig.). 1996. pap. 6.95 (*0-9636545-6-X*) Wind Pubns.

Daniels, Barbara J., jt. auth. see Daniels, David I.

Daniels, Barbara L., ed. see Camilli, Eileen, et al.

Daniels, Barbara L., ed. see Kelley, Klara B.

Daniels, Barry, ed. Joseph Chaikin & Sam Shepard: Letters & Texts, 1972-1984. LC 94-29134. 251p. 1994. pap. 10.95 (*1-55936-095-X*) Theatre Comm.

Daniels, Barry V. Revolution in the Theatre: French Romantic Theories of Drama, 7. LC 83-1705. (Contributions in Drama & Theatre Studies: No. 7). 249p. 1983. 65.00 (*0-313-22476-5*, DRT/, Greenwood Pr) Greenwood.

Daniels, Belinda S., jt. compiled by see Davis, Lenwood G.

Daniels, Bill. Movie Money: Understanding Hollywood's (Creative) Accounting Practices. LC 98-18122. 300p. 1998. pap. 29.95 (*1-879505-33-9*) Silman James Pr.

Daniels, Bob. May It Please the Court: A Collection of Legal Episodes. LC 98-91750. 188p. 1998. write for info. (*0-9666068-0-9*) B Daniels Ink.

Daniels Brawley, Oletha. No Question about It God is Building Acmes: Associated Christian Ministries & Educational Serv, 1. 1998. pap. text 15.95 (*1-887918-15-9*) Brockton Pubng.

Daniels, Bruce B. Sunday on the Farm: Memoirs of a Horseshoer. LC 95-73230. xi, 164p. 1996. 30.00 (*0-9627965-1-4*) St Eloy.

Daniels, Bruce C. Dissent & Conformity on Narragansett Bay: The Colonial Rhode Island Town. LC 83-23265. 151p. 1984. reprint ed. pap. 46.90 (*0-608-03570-X*, 20596550009) Bks Demand.

— The Fragmentation of New England: Comparative Perspectives on Economic, Political, & Social Divisions in the Eighteenth Century, 131. LC 88-17775. (Contributions in American History Ser.: No. 131). (Illus.). 250p. 1988. 59.95 (*0-313-26358-2*, DNE/) Greenwood.

Daniels, Bruce C., ed. Power & Status: Officeholding in Colonial America. LC 84-21023. 333p. reprint ed. pap. 103.30 (*0-7837-0212-4*, 204052000017) Bks Demand.

Daniels, Bruce C., ed. see James, Sydney V.

Daniels, C. M. & Welsby, Derek A. Soba: Archaeological Research at a Medieval Capital on the Blue Nile. (Illus.). 363p. 1991. 72.00 (*1-872566-02-2*, Pub. by Brit Inst Estrn Africa) David Brown.

Daniels, Carl M. Museum Quality Orgasm. 2nd ed. 48p. 1997. pap. 5.00 (*0-9653194-4-X*) Future Tense.

***Daniels, Carl Miller.** Shy Boys at Home. Hathaway, Michael, ed. 80p. 1999. pap. 10.00 (*0-943795-35-4*) Chiron Rev.

Daniels, Carlos G., Jr. Life . . . with No Strings Attached! 155p. 1984. 7.95 (*0-89697-144-9*) Intl Univ Pr.

Daniels, Carole A. Polymers: Structure & Properties. LC 88-50948. 112p. 1989. 69.95 (*0-87762-552-2*) Technomic.

Daniels, Caroline, jt. auth. see Daniels, John L.

Daniels, Celia & Pederson, Cynthia. Fissures. 40p. (Orig.). 1993. pap. 6.00 (*1-880286-13-0*) Singular Speech Pr.

Daniels, Charles B. & Scully, Sam. What Really Goes on in Sophocles' Theban Plays. LC 96-6787. 160p. 1996. lib. bdg. 36.50 (*0-7618-0304-1*) U Pr of Amer.

Daniels, Charles B., et al. Toward an Ontology of Number Mind & Sign. (Scots Philosophical Monographs: No. 10). 176p. 1986. pap. 15.00 (*0-685-17182-5*, Pub. by Aberdeen U Pr); text 31.95 (*0-08-032462-2*, R132, K150, Pub. by Aberdeen U Pr) Macmillan.

Daniels, Charles I. Creative Imaging: A Student Study Guide. (Illus.). 158p. (Orig.). (C). 1986. pap. text 16.95 (*0-938465-00-7*) Zo Pub.

Daniels, Charles J. Dream House - Real House: The Adventure of Planning & Building a Custom Home. LC 87-90285. (Illus.). 168p. (Orig.). (C). 1988. pap. 11.95 (*0-9619422-0-7*) Daniels Pub.

Daniels, Chip. Conker's Pocket Tales: Official Strategy Guide. 1999. pap. text 12.99 (*0-7615-2281-6*) Prima Pub.

***Daniels, Chip.** Gauntlet Legends: Prima's Official Strategy Guide. 2000. pap. 14.99 (*0-7615-3101-7*) Prima Pub.

***Daniels, Chip & Joyce, P. D.** Breath of Fire 3: Prima's Official Strategy Guide. LC 97-69336. 176p. 1998. per. 14.99 (*0-7615-0924-0*) Prima Pub.

Daniels, Christian & Menzies, Nicholas K. Science & Civilization in China Vol. 6, Pt. 3: Biology & Biological Technology: Agro-Industries & Forestry. (Illus.). 767p. (C). 1996. text 155.00 (*0-521-41999-9*) Cambridge U Pr.

Daniels, Christian, jt. auth. see Grove, Linda.

Daniels, Christine & Kennedy, Michael V., eds. Over the Threshold: Intimate Violence in Early America. LC 98-47351. 272p. 1999. 75.00 (*0-415-91804-9*) Routledge.

***Daniels, Christine & Moch, Leslie Page, eds.** Negotiated Empires: Centers & Peripheries in the New World, 1500-1820. 320p. 2000. 80.00 (*0-415-92538-X*); pap. 19.99 (*0-415-92539-8*) Routledge.

Daniels, Clyde E. Man in the Universe. 73p. (Orig.). 1991. pap. 7.95 (*0-9634437-0-4*) Hall-Ware Pub.

Daniels, Coenraad, tr. see Roussel, A.

Daniels, Cynthia R. At Women's Expense: State Power & the Politics of Fetal Rights. LC 93-4102. 191p. 1993. text 19.95 (*0-674-05043-6*) HUP.

— At Women's Expense: State Power & the Politics of Fetal Rights. 192p. 1996. pap. 14.50 (*0-674-05044-4*) HUP.

— Lost Fathers: The Politics of Fatherlessness. LC 97-48633. 224p. 1998. text 24.95 (*0-312-21107-4*) St Martin.

Daniels, Cynthia R. & Brooks, Rachelle. Feminists Negotiate the State: The Politics of Domestic Violence. LC 97-30132. 136p. (C). 1997. 49.00 (*0-7618-0883-3*); pap. 29.50 (*0-7618-0884-1*) U Pr of Amer.

Daniels, Cynthia R., jt. ed. see Boris, Eileen.

Daniels, D. Surface-Penetrating Radar. (Radar, Sonar, Navigation & Avionics Ser.: No. 6). 320p. 1996. 139.00 (*0-85296-862-0*, RA006) INSPEC Inc.

***Daniels, D. & Price, V.** The Essential Enneagram: The Definitive Personality Test & Self-Discovery Guide. 128p. 2000. pap. 10.00 (*0-06-251676-0*, Pub. by Harper SF) HarpC.

Daniels, Dan. Paranoia & Dirty Feet. 6.00 (*0-921884-14-1*) Genl Dist Srvs.

Daniels D'Andrea, Lewis. Community Counseling. 3rd ed. 2002. pap. 43.75 (*0-534-50626-7*) Thomson Learn.

***Daniels, Daniel.** The Curse of Gutenberg: Storytelling with Dan Daniels. 152p. 2000. pap. 12.75 (*1-896647-23-5*) Genl Dist Srvs.

Daniels, Danny. Mortal Midnight. 224p. (Orig.). 1996. pap. 11.99 (*1-883893-64-X*) WinePress Pub.

Daniels, David. Orchestral Music: A Handbook. 3rd ed. LC 96-34819. 632p. 1996. 50.00 (*0-8108-3228-3*) Scarecrow.

Daniels, David, et al. A Basic Reader for College Writers. 358p. (C). 1989. pap. text 13.00 (*0-944210-75-9*) Townsend NJ.

— Sexually Transmitted Diseases & AIDS. LC 92-2331. (Brainscan MCQs Ser.). 1993. 40.95 (*0-387-19762-1*) Spr-Verlag.

Daniels, David I. & Daniels, Barbara J. HCO English Grammar. LC 90-56015. (College Outline Ser.). 288p. 1991. pap. 14.00 (*0-06-467109-7*, Harper Ref) HarpC.

Daniels, David L., et al, eds. Cranial & Spinal Magnetic Resonance Imaging: An Atlas & Guide. 332p. 1987. text 170.00 (*0-88167-185-1*) Lppncott W & W.

— Cranial & Spinal Magnetic Resonance Imaging: An Atlas & Guide. LC 87-9817. (Illus.). 331p. reprint ed. pap. 102.70 (*0-608-09748-9*, 206991800007) Bks Demand.

Daniels, David L., jt. auth. see Haughton, Victor M.

Daniels, David W., ed. see Daniels, Vann A.

***Daniels, Dawn M.** Souls of My Sisters: Black Women Break Their Silence, Tell Their Stories & Heal Their Spirits. (Illus.). 2000. pap. 15.00 (*1-57566-653-7*) Kensgtn Pub Corp.

Daniels, Denise. Love's Legacy. 384p. 1998. mass mkt. 4.99 (*0-8217-6060-2*, Zebra Kensgtn) Kensgtn Pub Corp.

***Daniels, Dianne.** Exercises for Osteoporosis. LC 00-37028. 2000. pap. 14.95 (*1-57826-076-0*, Pub. by Hatherleigh) Norton.

Daniels, Don, ed. see Fehl, Fred.

Daniels, Donald E., tr. see Barth, Karl.

Daniels, Doris G. Always a Sister: The Feminism of Lillian D. Wald. LC 89-1065. 224p. 1995. pap. 12.95 (*1-55861-113-4*) Feminist Pr.

Daniels, Doug & Nestel, Barry. Defining Critical Mass - The Case in Animal Research. 61p. 1993. pap. write for info. (*0-88936-649-7*) IDRC Bks.

Daniels, Douglas H. Pioneer Urbanites: A Social & Cultural History of Black San Francisco. (Illus.). 248p. 1991. pap. 15.95 (*0-520-07399-1*, Pub. by U CA Pr) Cal Prin Full Svc.

Daniels, Dwight R. Hosea & Salvation History: The Early Traditions of Israel in the Prophecy of Hosea. (Beiheft zur Zeitschrift fuer die Alttestamentliche Wissenschaft Ser.: Vol. 191). ix, 148p. (C). 1990. lib. bdg. 60.00 (*3-11-012143-3*) De Gruyter.

Daniels, Earl, ed. Art of Reading Poetry. LC 70-103087. (Granger Index Reprint Ser.). 1977. 26.95 (*0-8369-6102-1*) Ayer.

Daniels, Edmond F. The King That Never Was. LC 98-88287. 325p. 1998. 25.00 (*0-7388-0135-6*) Xlibris Corp.

Daniels, Edwin. Ghost Dancing: Sacred Medicine & the Art of J. D. Challenger. LC 97-53241. (Illus.). 156p. 1998. 75.00 (*1-55670-824-6*) Stewart Tabori & Chang.

Daniels, Edwin H., Jr. Eagle Seamanship: A Manual for Square-Rigger Sailing. 3rd rev. ed. LC 89-13739. (Illus.). 256p. 1990. pap. text 16.95 (*0-87021-251-6*) Naval Inst Pr.

Daniels, Elizabeth. Bridges to the World: Henry Noble MacCracken & Vassar College. LC 94-31965. (Illus.). 318p. (Orig.). 1994. pap. 18.50 (*1-883551-02-1*, College Ave Pr) Attic Studio Pub.

Daniels, Elizabeth, ed. see Allen, Barbara.

Daniels, Estelle. Astrologikal Magick. LC 95-3723. (Illus.). 352p. (Orig.). 1995. pap. 14.95 (*0-87728-826-7*) Weiser.

Daniels, Estelle, jt. auth. see Tuitean, Paul.

Daniels, Eugene. The Catholic Church in Mission. 52p. 1993. pap. 1.95 (*0-912552-80-8*) MARC.

Daniels, F. J. Basic English: Writer's Japanese-English Workbook. (ENG & JPN.). 720p. 1997. boxed set, wbk. ed. 49.95 (*4-590-00322-8*, Pub. by Hokuseido Pr) Book East.

Daniels, Farrington. Direct Use of the Sun's Energy. LC 64-20913. (Trends in Science Ser.: No. 5). (Illus.). 402p. reprint ed. pap. 124.70 (*0-7837-5309-8*, 208033200005) Bks Demand.

Daniels, Farrington & Duffie, John A., eds. Solar Energy Research. LC 55-6325. 306p. reprint ed. pap. 94.90 (*0-608-11601-7*, 200206900011) Bks Demand.

Daniels, Florence M. Why Art? LC 77-28084. (Illus.). 236p. 1978. text 33.95 (*0-88229-173-4*) Burnham Inc.

Daniels, Frank J. Petrified Wood: The World of Fossilized Wood, Cones, Ferns, & Cycads. (Illus.). vi, 170p. (YA). (gr. 9-12). 1998. 75.00 (*0-9662938-0-0*) W Colorado Publ.

Daniels, Fred. Endless Memories. Ehrlich, Benno, tr. from DUT. 168p. (Orig.). 1994. pap. text 8.95 (*965-229-094-7*, Pub. by Gefen Pub Hse) Gefen Bks.

— Shadows in Twilight: A 1940-1945 Testimony. 66p. 1992. pap. 8.95 (*965-229-076-9*, Pub. by Gefen Pub Hse) Gefen Bks.

Daniels, Fred J., et al, eds. Flechten Follmann: Contributions to Lichenology in Honour of Gerhard Follmann. (Illus.). viii, 580p. 1995. 144.50 (*3-87429-380-7*, 062484, Pub. by Koeltz Sci Bks) Lubrecht & Cramer.

Daniels, G. S., ed. Artists from the Royal Botanic Gardens, Kew. (Illus.). 73p. 1974. pap. 3.00 (*0-913196-17-7*) Hunt Inst Botanical.

— A Linnaean Keepsake. (ENG & LAT., Illus.). 70p. 1973. 13.00 (*0-913196-15-0*) Hunt Inst Botanical.

Daniels, Geoff. Genetics of the Human Blood Groups. LC 95-5792. 735p. 1995. 195.00 (*0-86542-914-6*) Blackwell Sci.

Daniels, George. Watchmaking. rev. ed. LC 99-495156. (Illus.). 472p. 1998. 80.00 (*0-85667-497-4*, Pub. by P Wilson) Antique Collect.

Daniels, George F. Daniels. Note on a Franklin, (Massachusetts) Branch of the Daniell of Daniels Family. 62p. 1997. reprint ed. pap. 12.00 (*0-8328-8206-2*); reprint ed. lib. bdg. 22.00 (*0-8328-8205-4*) Higginson Bk Co.

— Huguenots in the Nipmuck Country, or Oxford, Mass., Prior to 1713. (Illus.). 168p. 1996. reprint ed. pap. 22.50 (*0-8328-5207-4*); reprint ed. lib. bdg. 32.50 (*0-8328-5206-6*) Higginson Bk Co.

Daniels, George G. XIX Olympiad: Mexico City, 1968, Sapporo, 1972. LC 96-28503. (Olympic Century Ser.: Vol. 17). (Illus.). 184p. 1996. write for info. (*1-888383-17-8*) Wld Sport Resch.

Daniels, George H. American Science in the Age of Jackson. LC 94-31186. (History of American Science & Technology Ser.). 304p. reprint ed. pap. 94.30 (*0-608-09221-5*, 205272500005) Bks Demand.

Daniels, George H. & Rose, Mark H., eds. Energy & Transport: Historical Perspectives on Policy Issues. LC 82-5642. (Sage Focus Editions Ser.: No. 52). (Illus.). 287p. reprint ed. pap. 89.00 (*0-8357-8453-3*, 203471700091) Bks Demand.

Daniels, George M., ed. The Drums of War. LC 73-92611. 1974. 25.95 (*0-89388-126-0*) Okpaku Communications.

Daniels, Gilbert, ed. see Bonar, Ann.

Daniels, Gilbert S., jt. auth. see Fiala, John L.

Daniels, Gilbert S., ed. see Krussmann, Gerd.

Daniels, Gordon. Sir Harry Parkes: British Representative in Japan, 1865-1883. (Meiji Ser.: No. 2). 264p. (C). 1995. text 45.00 (*1-873410-36-0*, Pub. by Curzon Pr Ltd) UH Pr.

Daniels, Gordon & Drifte, Reinhard, eds. Europe & Japan: Changing Relationships since 1945. 124p. (C). 1996. pap. text 15.00 (*0-904404-44-7*, Pub. by Curzon Pr Ltd) UH Pr.

Daniels, Guy & Hedley, Leslie W., eds. Fiction. 1986. (Anthology of Innovative Fiction Ser.). 200p. (Orig.). 1986. pap. 8.95 (*0-933515-10-3*) Exile Pr.

Daniels, Guy, tr. see Casals, Felipe G.

Daniels, Guy, tr. see Mayakovsky, Vladimir.

Daniels, Guy, tr. see Turchin, Valentin F.

Daniels, H. MMF: The Practitioner's Guide. 1994. ring bd. write for info. (*0-409-02169-5*, MICHIE) LEXIS Pub.

Daniels, H. Caroline. Information Technology: The Management Challenge. LC 93-244581. 199p. (C). 1993. 32.81 (*0-201-63195-4*) Addison-Wesley.

Daniels, H. Frances, jt. auth. see Dewar, Thadys J.

Daniels, Harry. An Introduction to Vygotsky. LC 95-32749. (Illus.). 304p. (C). 1996. pap. 25.99 (*0-415-12865-X*) Routledge.

— Special Education Reformed: Inclusion: Beyond Rhetoric? LC 99-39366. (New Millennium Ser.). (Illus.). 304p. 1999. 90.00 (*0-7507-0893-X*, Pub. by Falmer Pr UK); pap. 27.95 (*0-7507-0892-1*, Pub. by Falmer Pr UK) Taylor & Francis.

Daniels, Harry, ed. Charting the Agenda: Educational Activity after Vygotsky. LC 94-9765. (Illus.). 256p. (C). 1994. pap. 25.99 (*0-415-11757-7*, B4716) Routledge.

— An Introduction to Vygotsky. LC 95-32749. (Illus.). 304p. (C). 1996. 85.00 (*0-415-12864-1*) Routledge.

Daniels, Harvey. Literature Circles: Voice & Choice in the Student-Centered Classroom. LC 94-17107. (Illus.). 216p. 1994. pap. text 20.00 (*1-57110-000-8*) Stenhse Pubs.

Daniels, Harvey & Bizar, Marilyn. Methods That Matter: Six Structures for Best Practice Classrooms. LC 97-47516. (Illus.). 272p. 1998. pap. text 19.50 (*1-57110-082-2*) Stenhse Pubs.

Daniels, Harvey, jt. auth. see Zemelman, Steven.

Daniels, J. Illustrated Guide to the Identification of Banana Varieties in the South Pacific. (Illus.). 1995. pap. 75.00 (*1-86320-138-6*, Pub. by ACIAR) St Mut.

Daniels, J. R. New Generation Engines, 1997. LC 99-185989. (Research Reports: No. R342). xviii, 268p. 1997. 945.00 (*0-85058-935-5*) Economist Intell.

Daniels, Jack. Daniels' Running Formula. LC 98-13356. (Illus.). 296p. 1998. pap. 17.95 (*0-88011-735-4*, PDAN0735) Human Kinetics.

Daniels, Jacquie, jt. auth. see Bingham, Rosie.

Daniels, James. Car Suspension. (Illus.). 176p. 1998. 39.95 (*1-899870-31-8*, Pub. by Motor Racing) Motorbooks Intl.

Daniels, James H., Jr. Daniels: The Daniels Family. (Illus.). 264p. 1991. reprint ed. pap. 41.50 (*0-8328-2218-3*); reprint ed. lib. bdg. 51.50 (*0-8328-2217-5*) Higginson Bk Co.

— Daniels Vol. II: The Daniels Family. (Illus.). 484p. 1991. reprint ed. pap. 73.00 (*0-8328-2220-5*); reprint ed. lib. bdg. 83.00 (*0-8328-2219-1*) Higginson Bk Co.

Daniels, Jane Z., et al. Realizing the Potential of Women & Minorities in Engineering: Four Perspectives from the Field. Glass, Karen, ed. 132p. (Orig.). 1990. pap. text 20.00 (*1-55877-118-2*) Natl Governor.

Daniels, Janie E. The Beanie Invasion. (Illus.). 176p. 1997. pap. text 14.95 (*0-9661302-0-0*) JED Universal.

Daniels, Janus, ed. see Taylor, Eldon.

***Daniels, Jaret C.** Your Florida Guide to Butterfly Gardening: A Guide for the Deep South. (Illus.). 104p. 2000. pap. 14.95 (*0-8130-1790-4*) U Press Fla.

Daniels, J.D. Digital Design from Zero to One. 11th ed. LC 95-50562. 640p. 1996. text 99.95 (*0-471-12447-8*) Wiley.

Daniels, Jeanne. Why the Stars Come Out at Night. (Illus.). (J). (ps up). 1995. 14.95 (*1-885108-05-2*) Armstrong CT.

Daniels, Jeff. The Anatomy of the Car. write for info. (*0-318-59660-1*) S&S Trade.

Daniels, Jeff. Apartment 3A. Date not set. pap. 5.95 (*0-8222-1759-7*) Dramatists Play.

— Boom Town. Date not set. pap. 5.95 (*0-8222-1760-0*) Dramatists Play.

Daniels, Jeff. Classic British Cars. 1999. 24.95 (*0-7522-1706-2*) Boxtree.

Daniels, Jeff. Escanaba in Da Moonlight. Date not set. pap. 5.95 (*0-8222-1761-9*) Dramatists Play.

— The Vast Difference. Date not set. pap. 5.95 (*0-8222-1762-7*) Dramatists Play.

Daniels, Jeffery. Michelangelo. 1990. 6.98 (*1-55521-600-5*) Bk Sales Inc.

Daniels, Jeremy. Anfernee Hardaway. LC 95-42478. (Basketball Legends Ser.). (Illus.). 64p. (J). (gr. 3 up). 1996. lib. bdg. 15.95 (*0-7910-2435-0*) Chelsea Hse.

Daniels, Jeremy L., ed. see Mignery, Herb.

***Daniels, Jerrod R.** Cunning Treatment. LC 99-80017. 160p. 2000. write for info. (*1-57197-212-9*, Pub. by Pentland Pr) Assoc Pubs Grp.

Daniels, Jerry. Hunting the Whitetail. (Illus.). 197p. 1991. 17.95 (*0-9625070-0-8*) Hunting Adventures.

Daniels, Jessie. White Lies: Race, Class, Gender & Sexuality in White Supremacist Discourse. 256p. (C). 1996. pap. 18.99 (*0-415-91290-3*) Routledge.

— White Lies: Race, Class, Gender, & Sexuality in White Supremacist Discourse. 256p. (C). (gr. 13 up). 1997. 70.00 (*0-415-91289-X*) Routledge.

Daniels, Jim. Blessing the House. LC 96-45917. (Poetry Ser.). 105p. 1997. pap. 12.95 (*0-8229-5636-5*); text 25.00 (*0-8229-3988-6*) U of Pittsburgh Pr.

***Daniels, Jim.** Blue Jesus. LC 99-74768. (Poetry Ser.). 80p. 2000. pap. 12.95 (*0-88748-332-1*, Pub. by Carnegie-Mellon) CUP Services.

Daniels, Jim. M-80. LC 92-62335. 100p. (C). 1993. pap. 10.95 (*0-8229-5497-4*); text 19.95 (*0-8229-3747-6*) U of Pittsburgh Pr.

— Niagara Falls. 39p. 1994. pap. 7.00 (*0-938566-63-6*) Adastra Pr.

D

An Asterisk (*) at the beginning of an entry indicates that the title is appearing for the first time.

— Places - Everyone. LC 85-40366. (Brittingham Prize in Poetry, 1985 Ser.). 96p. 1985. pap. 11.95 (*0-299-10354-4*) U of Wis Pr.

— Punching Out. LC 89-16662. 94p. (C). 1990. pap. 11.95 (*0-8143-2191-7*) Wayne St U Pr.

— Punching Out. LC 89-16662. 93p. reprint ed. pap. 30.00 (*0-608-10522-8*, 2054433) Bks Demand.

Daniels, Jim, ed. Letters to America: Contemporary American Poetry on Race. LC 95-19996. 230p. (Orig.). (C). 1995. pap. 21.95 (*0-8143-2542-4*) Wayne St U Pr.

Daniels, Jim, et al. Brooding the Heartlands: Poets of the Midwest. Liebler, M. L., ed. (Working Lives Ser.). 152p. 1998. 9.95 (*0-933087-50-0*) Bottom Dog Pr.

Daniels, Jim, jt. ed. see Costanzo, Gerald.

Daniels, Jim Ray. No Pets: Stories. (Working Lives Ser.). 133p. 1999. pap. 10.95 (*0-933087-54-3*, Pub. by Bottom Dog Pr) SPD-Small Pr Dist.

Daniels, Joan. The Folded Spiral in the Classroom: Circular Bookmaking Across the Curriculum. 2nd rev. ed. (Illus.). 32p. 1996. teacher ed. 12.95 (*0-9653835-0-4*) Folded Spiral.

Daniels, Joan E., jt. auth. see Udall, Anne J.

Daniels, Joanne & Smith, Loretta. Clinical Calculations: A Unified Approach. 4th ed. LC 98-15353. 368p. (C). 1998. text 45.95 (*0-7668-0167-5*) Delmar.

Daniels, Joanne M. & Smith, Loretta M. Clinical Calculations: A Unified Approach. LC 86-2131. 272p. (C). 1986. pap. 24.95 (*0-8273-2517-7*) Delmar.

— Clinical Calculations: A Unified Approach. LC 86-2131. 272p. (C). 1986. Apple II 49.95 (*0-8273-2516-9*) Delmar.

— Clinical Calculations: A Unified Approach - Instructor's Guide. 3rd ed. 132p. 1994. 14.95 (*0-8273-5946-2*) Delmar.

— Clinical Calculations 3e. 3rd ed. LC 93-19225. (Student Material TV). 375p. (C). 1993. mass mkt. 41.95 (*0-8273-5945-4*) Delmar.

Daniels, Jody J., jt. ed. see Aha, David.

Daniels, Joe. Oyster Cookery: Sixty Recipes. (Illus.). 64p. (Orig.). 1988. pap. 3.95 (*0-940828-18-9*) D Youra Studios.

Daniels, John. Abu Dhabi: A Portrait. LC 73-93277. (Illus.). 117p. reprint ed. pap. 36.30 (*0-8357-5026-4*, 203034800068) Bks Demand.

— In Freedom's Birthplace: A Study of Boston Negroes. LC 69-18575. (American Negro: His History & Literature. Series 2). 1969. reprint ed. 19.95 (*0-405-01857-6*) Ayer.

— International Business. 8th ed. (C). 1998. text. write for info. (*0-201-57154-4*) Addison-Wesley.

— International Business: Environments & Operations. 7th ed. Toland, Beth, ed. (C). 1996. text 51.00 (*0-201-84789-2*) Addison-Wesley.

— International Business: Environments & Operations. 8th ed. LC 97-20402. 909p. (C). 1997. 96.00 (*0-201-84618-7*, Prentice Hall) P-H.

— International Business & Globalization. 450p. (C). 2000. text. write for info. (*0-201-47148-5*) Addison-Wesley.

Daniels, John, jt. auth. see Stockman, Mike.

Daniels, John D. & Radebaugh, Lee H. Global Insights 1994. LC 93-25875. (C). 1994. pap. text 21.00 (*0-201-59658-X*) Addison-Wesley.

— International Business. 6th ed. LC 93-10135. (C). 1993. text 68.00 (*0-201-59090-5*) Addison-Wesley.

— International Business: Environments & Operations. 5th ed. (Illus.). (C). 1989. text 43.25 (*0-201-15747-0*) Addison-Wesley.

— International Business Environments & Operations. 4th ed. LC 35-11127. 816p. (C). 1986. text. write for info. (*0-201-10713-9*) Addison-Wesley.

Daniels, John D., et al. International Business Environments & Operations. 3rd ed. LC 81-170636. (Illus.). 531p. (C). 1982. text. write for info. (*0-201-10223-4*) Addison-Wesley.

Daniels, John D., jt. auth. see Cook, Steve.

Daniels, John H. Nothing Could Be Finer: Canden Polo 1898-1948. 200p. 1997. 49.95 (*1-887269-27-4*) J Culler & Sons.

Daniels, John L. & Daniels, Caroline. Global Vision: Building New Models for the Corporation of the Future. 224p. 1992. 27.95 (*0-07-015350-7*) McGraw.

***Daniels, John S.** The Nester. 1999. 19.00 (*0-7540-8074-9*, Gunsmoke) Chivers N Amer.

Daniels, John S. Smoke of the Gun. 1979. mass mkt. 1.95 (*0-451-08667-8*, J8667, Sig) NAL.

Daniels, Joleen. Inheritance. (Romance Ser.). 1993. per. 2.69 (*0-373-08939-2*, 5-08939-6) Silhouette.

— Jilted! (Romance Ser.). 1994. per. 2.75 (*0-373-08990-2*, 5-08990-9) Silhouette.

— Long Lost Husband. 1994. per. 2.75 (*0-373-19043-3*, 1-19043-8) Harlequin Bks.

Daniels, Jonathan. The End of Innocence. LC 73-37285. (FDR & the Era of the New Deal Ser.). 351p. 1972. reprint ed. 39.50 (*0-306-70423-4*) Da Capo.

— Frontier on the Potomac. LC 70-37284. (FDR & the Era of the New Deal Ser.). 262p. 1972. reprint ed. lib. bdg. 35.00 (*0-306-70425-0*) Da Capo.

— The Man of Independence. LC 98-22079. (Give 'Em Hell Harry Ser.). 384p. 1998. pap. 22.50 (*0-8262-1190-9*) U of Mo Pr.

Daniels, Jonathan, intro. A Southerner Discovers the South. LC 68-16228. (American Scene Ser.). 1970. reprint ed. lib. bdg. 42.50 (*0-306-71011-0*) Da Capo.

Daniels, Joseph P. The Meaning & Reliability of Economic Summit Undertakings, 1975-1989. LC 92-40358. (Foreign Economic Policy of the United States Ser.). 320p. 1993. text 10.00 (*0-8153-1253-9*) Garland.

Daniels, Joseph P., jt. auth. see Von Furstenberg, George M.

Daniels, Josephus. Editor in Politics. LC 74-2839. (Illus.). 644p. 1974. reprint ed. lib. bdg. 105.00 (*0-8371-7439-2*, DAEI, Greenwood Pr) Greenwood.

— Life of Woodrow Wilson, 1856-1924. LC 72-114509. (Illus.). 381p. 1971. reprint ed. lib. bdg. 69.50 (*0-8371-4729-8*, DAWW, Greenwood Pr) Greenwood.

— Life of Woodrow Wilson, 1856-1924. (History - United States Ser.). 381p. 1992. reprint ed. lib. bdg. 89.00 (*0-7812-6227-5*) Rprt Serv.

— Life of Woodrow Wilson, 1856-1924. LC 70-144965. (Illus.). 1971. reprint ed. 18.00 (*0-403-00934-0*) Scholarly.

— Shirt-Sleeve Diplomat. LC 73-11621. (Illus.). 547p. 1973. reprint ed. lib. bdg. 75.00 (*0-8371-7082-6*, DASD, Greenwood Pr) Greenwood.

— Tar Heel Editor. LC 74-2840. (Illus.). 544p. 1974. reprint ed. lib. bdg. 89.50 (*0-8371-7440-6*, DATH, Greenwood Pr) Greenwood.

— The Wilson Era: The Years of War & After, 1917-1923. (History - United States Ser.). 654p. 1993. reprint ed. lib. bdg. 109.00 (*0-7812-4924-4*) Rprt Serv.

Daniels, Judith. Beach Realities. (Voices Romance Ser.: No. 5). 224p. 1994. mass mkt. 3.50 (*0-8217-4765-7*, Zebra Kensgtn) Kensgtn Pub Corp.

Daniels, Judith M., jt. ed. see Marcus, Jacob R.

Daniels, Judy A., jt. auth. see D'Andrea, Michael J.

Daniels, Julie. Enjoying Dog Agility: From Back Yard to Competition. Luther, Luana, ed. LC 91-90231. (Illus.). 325p. 1991. 26.50 (*0-944875-16-5*) Doral Pub.

Daniels, Julie, jt. auth. see Zink, M. Christine.

Daniels, K. Air Technology in Covered Spaces. (C). 1983. 140.00 (*0-7855-4394-5*, Pub. by Build Servs Info Assn) St Mut.

***Daniels, Karen.** Dancing Suns. LC 00-101955. (ZaddackTrilogy Ser.: Bk. I). 342p. 2000. 24.00 (*1-892323-19-2*) Vivisphere.

— Mentor's Lair. (Zaddack Trilogy Ser.: Bk. II). 200p. 2000. pap. 16.00 (*1-892323-21-4*, Straw Hse Pr) Vivisphere.

Daniels, Karen, et al, eds. Courageous Journeys: A Literary Collection by Evolving Writers. annuals 140p. 1998. pap. 12.50 (*0-9656056-6-3*) Tenacity Pr.

Daniels, Karu F. Brandy: An Intimate Look. LC 99-30859. (Illus.). 96p. 1999. pap. 10.95 (*0-7407-0024-3*) Andrews & McMeel.

Daniels, Kate. Four Testimonies. LC 97-48849. (Southern Messenger Poets Ser.). 96p. 1998. pap. 16.95 (*0-8071-2260-2*); text 19.95 (*0-8071-2259-9*) La State U Pr.

— The Niobe Poems. LC 88-4754. (Pitt Poetry Ser.). 79p. (Orig.). 1988. reprint ed. pap. 30.00 (*0-608-07694-5*, 206778400010) Bks Demand.

— The White Wave. LC 83-40341. (Poetry Ser.). 64p. 1984. text 19.95 (*0-8229-3493-0*) U of Pittsburgh Pr.

Daniels, Kate, ed. see Rukeyser, Muriel.

Daniels, Kathleen. Minna's Story: The Secret Love of Dr. Sigmund Freud. (Illus.). 280p. 1992. 18.95 (*0-929173-08-2*) Health Press.

***Daniels, Kay.** Convict Women. (Illus.). 288p. 1999. pap. 24.95 (*1-86448-677-5*, Pub. by Allen & Unwin Pty) Paul & Co Pubs.

Daniels, Kay & Murnane, Mary. Australia's Women: A Documentary History. (Illus.). 335p. 1989. pap. text 29.95 (*0-7022-2235-6*, Pub. by Univ Queensland Pr) Intl Spec Bk.

***Daniels, Kayla.** Code Name - Santa: Families Are Forever. (Intimate Moments Ser.). 1999. mass mkt. 4.25 (*0-373-07969-9*) Silhouette.

Daniels, Kayla. The Daddy Trap: Families Are Forever. 1999. per. 4.25 (*0-373-07922-2*, 1-07922-7) Silhouette.

— Heiress Apparent. (Special Edition Ser.). 1993. mass mkt. 3.39 (*0-373-09814-6*, 5-09814-0) Silhouette.

— Her First Mother. 1998. per. 4.25 (*0-373-07844-7*, 1-07844-3) Silhouette.

— Marriage Minded. 1996. per. 3.99 (*0-373-24068-6*, 1-24068-8) Silhouette.

— Miracle Child. (Special Edition Ser.). 1994. per. 3.50 (*0-373-09911-8*, 1-09911-8) Harlequin Bks.

— Secondhand Dad: Families Are Forever. 1998. per. 4.25 (*0-373-07892-7*, 1-07892-2) Silhouette.

***Daniels, Kayla.** Sous Haute Protection. (FRE.). 2000. mass mkt. 5.50 (*0-373-38352-5*) Harlequin Bks.

Daniels, Kayla. Wanted: Mom & Me. 1997. per. 3.99 (*0-373-07760-2*, 1-07760-1) Silhouette.

Daniels, Keith A. Satan Is a Mathematician: Poems of the Weird, Surreal & Fantastic. 168p. 1998. pap. 12.95 (*0-9631203-6-0*) Anamnesis Pr.

— What Rough Book: Dark Poems & Light. LC 91-76733. 144p. (Orig.). 1992. pap. 10.95 (*0-9631203-2-8*) Anamnesis Pr.

Daniels, Keith A., et al. Hadrosaur Tales Vol. 6: Where Science Meets Fantasy. 5th ed. Summers, David L., ed. 135p. 1998. pap. 5.95 (*1-885093-12-8*) Hadrosaur Pr.

Daniels, Keith A., ed. see Blish, James.

Daniels, Keith A., ed. see Clarke, Arthur C.

***Daniels, Keith Allen.** Haiku by Unohu. 68p. 2000. pap. 9.95 (*1-892842-09-2*, Anamnesis) Anamnesis Pr.

— I Think, Therefore I Am: A Fascicle of Versicles. 56p. 2000. pap. 9.95 (*1-892842-12-2*, Anamnesis) Anamnesis Pr.

***Daniels, Keith Allen & Miller, Ryder, eds.** Arthur C. Clarke & C. S. Lewis: A Correspondence. 88p. 2000. pap. 14.95 (*1-892842-18-1*, Anamnesis) Anamnesis Pr.

***Daniels, Keith Allen, et al.** The Weird Sonneteers. 152p. 2000. pap. 12.95 (*1-892842-04-1*, Anamnesis) Anamnesis Pr.

Daniels, Ken. China Bombers: Chinese-American Composite Wing in WWII. LC 98-60160. 1999. pap. text 24.95 (*1-58007-006-X*) Specialty Pr.

***Daniels, Ken.** Contact Lenses. LC 99-23383. (Basic Bookshelf for Eyecare Professionals Ser.). (Illus.). 1999. pap. 30.00 (*1-55642-345-4*) SLACK Inc.

Daniels, Ken. Hear My Laughter...Feel My Pain: A Monolog Play for Young Adults. 12p. (Orig.). (J). (gr. 6-9). 1996. pap. 2.00 (*1-57514-253-8*, 3088) Encore Perform Pub.

***Daniels, Ken.** What Would Jesus Say. 110p. 2000. pap. 10.00 (*0-9679662-7-2*) Hardbound.

Daniels, Ken & Haimes, Erica, eds. Psychosocial Perspectives on Donor Insemination: International Social Science Perspectives. LC 97-40984. 192p. (C). 1998. text 59.95 (*0-521-49709-4*); pap. text 18.95 (*0-521-49783-3*) Cambridge U Pr.

***Daniels, Kenneth.** Caring Thoughts. 1999. pap. write for info. (*1-58235-228-3*) Watermrk Pr.

***Daniels, Kettlie J.** So I Have Knocked Knees: Yet Destined for More. (Illus.). 112p. 2000. pap. 10.95 (*1-57258-165-4*) Teach Servs.

Daniels, Kitty, et al. Getting Started with WordPerfect 6.0 for Windows. 192p. 1995. pap. 21.95 (*0-471-12068-5*) Wiley.

Daniels, Kitty, et al. Getting Started with WordPerfect 6.0 for Windows. (Getting Started Ser.). 192p. 1995. pap. text. write for info. (*0-471-12562-8*) Wiley.

Daniels, Klaus. Low-Tech, Light-Tech, High-Tech: Building in the Information Age. (Illus.). 240p. 1998. 60.00 (*3-7643-5861-0*) Birkhauser.

***Daniels, Klaus.** Low-Tech, Light-Tech, High-Tech: Special Edition. (Illus.). 240p. 2000. pap. 49.95 (*3-7643-6329-0*) Birkhauser.

Daniels, Klaus. The Technology of Ecological Building: Basic Principles & Measures, Examples & Ideas. Schwaiger, Elizabeth, tr. LC 97-13752. (Illus.). 304p. 1997. 70.00 (*3-7643-5461-5*, Pub. by Birkhauser) Princeton Arch.

Daniels, Leroy J. Tales of an Old Horsetrader: The First Hundred Years. LC 87-10932. (Bur Oak Original Ser.). 247p. 1987. pap. 14.95 (*0-87745-187-7*) U of Iowa Pr.

Daniels, Les. Batman: The Complete History: The Life & Times of the Dark Knight. LC 98-32409. (Illus.). 208p. 1999. 29.95 (*0-8118-2470-5*) Chronicle Bks.

***Daniels, Les.** Batman Masterpiece Edition. (Illus.). 96p. 2000. boxed set 65.00 (*0-8118-2782-8*) Chronicle Bks.

Daniels, Les. DC Comics: Sixty Years of the World's Favorite Super Heroes. LC 95-7243. (Illus.). 256p. 1995. 40.00 (*0-8212-2076-4*, Pub. by Bulfinch Pr) Little.

— Living in Fear: The History of Horror in the Mass Media. LC 82-25261. (Quality Paperbacks Ser.). (Illus.). 256p. 1983. reprint ed. pap. 12.95 (*0-306-80193-0*) Da Capo.

— Marvel: Five Fabulous Decades of the World's Greatest Comics. (Illus.). 288p. 1991. 49.50 (*0-8109-3821-9*) Abrams.

— Marvel: Five Fabulous Decades of the World's Greatest Comics. (Illus.). 288p. 1993. pap. 24.95 (*0-8109-2566-4*, Pub. by Abrams) Time Warner.

— No Blood Spilled. 1991. pap. 3.95 (*0-8125-0932-3*, Pub. by Tor Bks) St Martin.

— Superman: The Complete History: The Life & Times of the Man of Steel. (Illus.). 192p. 1998. 29.95 (*0-8118-2162-5*) Chronicle Bks.

— Superman Masterpiece Edition: The Golden Age of America's First Super Hero. LC 98-5836. (Illus.). 96p. 1999. boxed set 65.00 (*0-8118-2111-0*) Chronicle Bks.

***Daniels, Les.** Superman Masterpiece Edition: The Golden Age of America's First Super Hero. (Illus.). 96p. 1999. 9.95 (*0-8118-2269-9*) Chronicle Bks.

Daniels, Les. Yellow Fog. (Illus.). 1986. 30.00 (*0-937986-82-8*) D M Grant.

***Daniels, Les & Kidd, Chip.** Wonder Woman: The Complete History: The Life & Times of the Amazon Princess. LC 00-24215. (Illus.). (YA). 2000. 29.95 (*0-8118-2913-8*) Chronicle Bks.

Daniels, Linda. Decorative Birds Stained Glass Pattern Book. LC 92-14480. 64p. 1992. pap. 5.95 (*0-486-27267-2*) Dover.

Daniels, Lolee & Pollard, Rita. The Library Experience: Sharing the Responsibility. (Illus.). 121p. (YA). (gr. 6-8). 1987. teacher ed. 64.95 (*0-935637-08-7*); student ed. 11.99 (*0-935637-09-5*) Cambridge Strat.

— The Library Experience: Sharing the Responsibility, Set. (Illus.). 48p. (YA). (gr. 6-8). 1987. trans. 85.00 (*0-935637-10-9*) Cambridge Strat.

Daniels, Lucille & Worthingham, Catherine. Therapeutic Exercise for Body Alignment & Function. 2nd ed. LC 76-27058. (Illus.). 1977. pap. text 35.95 (*0-7216-2873-7*, W B Saunders Co) Harcrt Hlth Sci Grp.

***Daniels, Lucy.** Animal Ark: Goat in the Garden. large type ed. (Illus.). (J). 1999. pap. write for info. (*0-7540-6089-6*) Chivers N Amer.

Daniels, Lucy. Badger in the Basement. (Animal Ark Ser.: No. 7). (J). (gr. 3-5). 1996. 9.05 (*0-606-11090-9*, Pub. by Turtleback) Demco.

***Daniels, Lucy.** Cat Crazy. (Animal Ark Pets Ser.: No. 13). (Illus.). (J). (gr. 3-5). 2000. pap. 3.99 (*0-439-05170-3*) Scholastic Inc.

— Chick Challenge. (Animal Ark Pets Ser.: No. 6). (Illus.). 128p. (J). (gr. 3-5). 1999. pap. 3.99 (*0-439-05163-0*) Scholastic Inc.

Daniels, Lucy. Cub in the Cupboard. (Animal Ark Ser.: No. 8). (J). (gr. 3-5). 1996. 9.05 (*0-606-11226-X*, Pub. by Turtleback) Demco.

***Daniels, Lucy.** Doggy Dare. (Animal Ark Pets Ser.: No. 12). (Illus.). (J). (gr. 3-5). 2000. pap. 3.99 (*0-439-05169-X*) Scholastic Inc.

— Duckling Diary. (Animal Ark Pets Ser.: No. 10). (Illus.). (J). (gr. 3-5). 2000. pap. 3.99 (*0-439-05167-3*) Scholastic Inc.

— Gerbil Genius. (Animal Ark Pets Ser.: No. 9). (Illus.). 128p. (J). (gr. 3-5). 2000. pap. 3.99 (*0-439-05166-5*) Scholastic Inc.

— Guinea Pig Gang. (Animal Ark Pets Ser.: No. 8). (Illus.). (J). (gr. 3-5). 1999. pap. 3.99 (*0-439-05165-7*) Scholastic Inc.

Daniels, Lucy. Hamster Hotel. (Animal Ark Pets Ser.: No. 4). (J). (gr. 3-5). 1999. pap. text 3.99 (*0-439-05161-4*) Scholastic Inc.

Daniels, Lucy. Hedgehogs in the Hall. (Animal Ark Ser.: No. 5). (J). (gr. 3-5). 1996. 9.05 (*0-606-11452-1*, Pub. by Turtleback) Demco.

— Kitten Crowd. (Animal Ark Pets Ser.: No. 2). 128p. (J). (gr. 3-5). 1999. mass mkt. 3.50 (*0-439-05159-2*) Scholastic Inc.

— Kittens in the Kitchen. large type ed. (Animal Ark Ser.: No. 1). (J). (gr. 3-5). 1998. pap. 16.95 (*0-7540-6011-X*, Galaxy Child Lrg Print) Chivers N Amer.

— Lamb's Lessons. (Animal Ark Pets Ser.: No. 11). (Illus.). 128p. (J). (gr. 3-5). 2000. pap. 3.99 (*0-439-05168-1*) Scholastic Inc.

— Mouse Magic. (Animal Ark Pets Ser.: No. 5). (Illus.). 128p. (J). (gr. 3-5). 1999. pap. 3.99 (*0-439-05162-2*) Scholastic Inc.

Daniels, Lucy. Piglet in a Playpen. (Animal Ark Ser.: No. 9). (J). (gr. 3-5). 1996. 9.05 (*0-606-11748-2*, Pub. by Turtleback) Demco.

— Pony in the Porch. 1998. pap. text 16.95 (*0-7540-6038-1*) Chivers N Amer.

***Daniels, Lucy.** Pony Parade. (Animal Ark Pets Ser.: No. 7). (Illus.). 128p. (J). (gr. 2-5). 1999. pap. text 3.99 (*0-439-05164-9*) Scholastic Inc.

— Puppies in the Pantry. (Animal Ark Ser.: No. 3). (J). (gr. 3-5). 1999. 16.95 (*0-7540-6058-6*) Chivers N Amer.

Daniels, Lucy. Puppy Puzzle. (Animal Ark Pets Ser.: No. 1). (Illus.). 107p. (J). (gr. 1-4). 1999. mass mkt. 3.50 (*0-439-05158-4*) Scholastic Inc.

— Rabbit Race. (Animal Ark Pets Ser.: No. 3). (J). (gr. 3-5). 1999. pap. text 3.99 (*0-439-05160-6*) Scholastic Inc.

— Sheepdog in the Snow. (Animal Ark Ser.: No. 6). (J). (gr. 3-5). 1996. 9.05 (*0-606-11838-1*, Pub. by Turtleback) Demco.

Daniels, M. Harry, et al. Toward Excellence in Secondary Vocational Education: Developing Pretechnical Curricula. 48p. 1985. 5.50 (*0-318-22216-7*, IN295) Ctr Educ Trng Employ.

Daniels, M. S., jt. auth. see Haynes, J. H.

Daniels, Magdalen. Changing Woman's Workbook: Approaching Menopause As Journey of Spiritual Transformation. (Illus.). 152p. (Orig.). 1993. pap. 16.95 (*1-883230-08-X*) Purple Iris Pr.

Daniels, Marcus. Haynes BSA Unit Singles Owners Workshop Manual, No. 127: '58-'72. 1979. 23.95 (*0-85696-127-2*) Haynes Manuals.

Daniels, Marie C. The Function of Humor in the Spanish Romances of Chivalry. LC 91-43875. (Harvard Dissertations in the Romance Languages Ser.). 344p. (C). 1992. text 25.00 (*0-8240-0635-6*) Garland.

Daniels, Marilyn. Benedictine Roots in the Development of Deaf Education: Listening with the Heart. LC 96-23811. 160p. 1997. 55.00 (*0-89789-500-2*, Bergin & Garvey) Greenwood.

***Daniels, Marilyn.** Dancing with Words: Signing for Hearing Children's Literacy. LC 00-27239. 160p. 2000. 55.00 (*0-89789-723-4*, H723, Bergin & Garvey) Greenwood.

Daniels, Marjorie. Remember When . . .? (Illus.). 157p. (Orig.). 1988. pap. 4.95 (*0-940828-17-0*) D Youra Studios.

Daniels, Mark. Employment Law Guide to the Americans with Disabilities Act. 1216p. 1992. ring bd. 126.00 (*0-13-295015-4*) Aspen Law.

— Employment Law Guide to the Americans with Disabilities Act. LC 92-20237. 1992. 95.00 (*0-13-036260-3*) P-H.

Daniels, Mark R. Terminating Public Programs: An American Political Paradox. LC 97-10553. 124p. (C). (gr. 13). 1997. text 38.95 (*0-7656-0124-9*) M E Sharpe.

Daniels, Mark R. Terminating Public Programs: An American Political Paradox. LC 97-10553. 124p. (C). (gr. 13). 1997. pap. text 18.95 (*0-7656-0125-7*) M E Sharpe.

***Daniels, Mark R., ed.** Creating Sustainable Community Programs: Examples of Collaborative Public Administration. 2001. write for info. (*0-275-96774-3*) Greenwood.

Daniels, Mark R., ed. Medicaid Reform & the American States: Case Studies on the Politics of Managed Care. LC 97-23657. 320p. 1998. 59.95 (*0-86569-263-7*, Auburn Hse) Greenwood.

***Daniels, Marta.** Peace Is Everybody's Business: Half a Century of Peace Education with Elizabeth Evans Baker. (Illus.). 1999. pap. 7.95 (*0-9636610-0-0*) Juniata Coll.

Daniels, Martin. Cunning Stunts: The Best 500 Pub Tricks & Brain Teasers. 96p. 1995. pap. text 11.95 (*0-572-02051-1*, Pub. by W Foulsham) Trans-Atl Phila.

Daniels, Martin, jt. auth. see Pemberton, Steven.

Daniels, Mary, ed. A Patchwork of Blessings & Grace. LC 96-11332. 96p. 1996. pap. 5.00 (*1-57312-050-2*) Smyth & Helwys.

Daniels, May. The French Drama of the Unspoken, No. 3--3. LC 77-2374. (Edinburgh University Publications Language & Literature Ser.: No. 3). 263p. 1977. reprint ed. lib. bdg. 65.00 (*0-8371-9464-4*, DAFD, Greenwood Pr) Greenwood.

Daniels, Maygene F. & Walch, Timothy, eds. A Modern Archives Reader: Basic Readings on Archival Theory & Practice. (Illus.). 357p. 1984. 25.00 (*0-911333-11-8*, 100017); pap. 25.00 (*0-911333-12-6*, 200017) National Archives & Recs.

Daniels, Michael, ed. Going Where You Wheel. (Architecture of Independence Ser.). (Illus.). 128p. (Orig.). 1987. pap. 30.00 (*0-317-59705-1*) Center Independent.

— Going Where You Wheel: The Architecture of Independence, Pt. 2. (Illus.). 124p. 1986. pap. text 20.00 (*0-317-56075-1*) Center Independent.

Daniels, Michael Craig. Living, Loving, & Loathing: Modern Rhymes & Limericks for the Romantically Inclined & Humorously Correct. LC 97-94240. (Illus.). 96p. 1997. 12.95 (*0-9659946-2-7*) Good Knight Bks.

An Asterisk (*) at the beginning of an entry indicates that the title is appearing for the first time.

Daniels, Molly A. The Prophetic Novel. LC 91-17983. (American University Studies: English Language & Literature: Ser. IV, Vol. 166). XI, 158p. (C). 1991. text 34.95 (*0-8204-1266-X*) P Lang Pubng.

Daniels, Morna. Burundi. LC 93-202799. (World Bibliographical Ser.). 164p. 1992. lib. bdg. 63.50 (*1-85109-194-7*) ABC-CLIO.

— Victorian Book Illustration. 1988. pap. 14.75 (*0-7123-0157-7*, Pub. by B23tish Library) U of Toronto Pr.

Daniels, Mortimer B. Corporation Financial Statements. Brief, Richard P., ed. LC 80-1484. (Dimensions of Accounting Theory & Practice Ser.). 1980. reprint ed. lib. bdg. 18.95 (*0-405-13514-9*) Ayer.

Daniels-Moseley, Julia. "Come to My Sunland" Letters of Julia Daniels Moseley from the Florida Frontier, 1882-1886. Moseley, Julia W. & Crislip, Betty P., eds. LC 98-17500. (Florida History & Culture Ser.). (Illus.). 256p. 1998. 29.95 (*0-8130-1605-3*) U Press Fla.

Daniels, N. C., ed. see Mintz, S., et al.

Daniels, Natalie. Moonlight Shadows. large type ed. 203p. 1995. pap. 18.99 (*1-85389-564-4*, Dales) Ulverscroft.

Daniels, Neil, jt. auth. see Hudson, Anne.

Daniels, Neil M. The Morality Maze: An Introduction to Moral Ecology. LC 91-18489. 227p. 1991. 27.95 (*0-87975-697-7*) Prometheus Bks.

Daniels, Norman. Just Health Care. (Studies in Philosophy & Health Policy). 276p. 1985. pap. text 22.95 (*0-521-31794-0*) Cambridge U Pr.

Daniels, Norman. Justice & Justification: Reflective Equilibrium in Theory & Practice. (Cambridge Studies in Philosophy & Public Policy). 378p. (C). 1996. pap. text 20.95 (*0-521-46711-X*) Cambridge U Pr.

— Justice & Justification: Reflective Equilibrium in Theory & Practice. (Cambridge Studies in Philosophy & Public Policy). 378p. (C). 1996. text 59.95 (*0-521-46152-9*) Cambridge U Pr.

— Seeking Fair Treatment: From the AIDS Epidemic to National Health Care Reform. 216p. 1995. 25.00 (*0-19-505712-0*) OUP.

— Thomas Reid's 'Inquiry' The Geometry of Visibles & the Case for Realism. LC 88-60488. (Series in Philosophy). 196p. 1989. reprint ed. pap. 14.95 (*0-8047-1712-5*) Stanford U Pr.

Daniels, Norman, ed. Reading Rawls: Critical Studies on Rawls' "A Theory of Justice" LC 88-60487. (Series in Philosophy). 408p. 1989. reprint ed. pap. 17.95 (*0-8047-1503-3*) Stanford U Pr.

Daniels, Norman, et al. Benchmarks of Fairness for Health Care Reform. LC 95-47820. (Illus.). 208p. 1996. text 36.50 (*0-19-510237-1*) OUP.

***Daniels, Norman, et al.** Is Inequality Bad for Our Health? 112p. 2000. pap. 12.00 (*0-8070-0447-2*) Beacon Pr.

Daniels, Norman, ed. see Rosenberg, Alexander.

Daniels, P., jt. ed. see Greaves, P.

Daniels, P. A., Jr., jt. ed. see Catacosinos, Paul A.

Daniels, P. N., jt. ed. see McIntyre, J. E.

Daniels, P. W. Service Industries in the World Economy. LC 92-43005. (IBG Studies in Geography). (Illus.). 204p. 1993. pap. 24.95 (*0-631-18132-6*) Blackwell Pubs.

Daniels, P. W. & Lever, W. F. Global Economy in Transition. 256p. (C). 1996. pap. text 44.00 (*0-582-25328-4*) Longman.

Daniels, P. W. & Ronohardjo, Purnomo, eds. Malignant Catarrhal Fever in Asian Livestock. 127p. (Orig.). 1988. pap. 100.50 (*0-949511-71-4*) St Mut.

Daniels, P. W., jt. auth. see Bryson, J. R.

Daniels, Pamela K. Angelic Inspirations. LC 95-94618. 1995. pap. 9.95 (*0-9647670-0-7*) Angelic Inspir.

Daniels, Pat, ed. see Time-Life Books Editors.

Daniels, Patricia. Earth. LC 97-27748. (Nature Library). (J). 1998. write for info. (*0-7922-7046-0*) Natl Geog.

— The First Christmas. LC 95-36899. (Family Time Bible Stories Ser.). (Illus.). 28p. (J). (ps-2). 1999. 4.95 (*0-7835-4625-4*) Time-Life.

Daniels, Patricia. Imaginary Kingdoms. 1924. lib. bdg. write for info. (*0-688-17639-9*, Wm Morrow) Morrow Avon.

Daniels, Patricia. Noah's Ark. LC 95-36897. (Family Time Bible Stories Ser.). (Illus.). 28p. (J). (ps-2). 1999. 4.95 (*0-7835-4626-2*) Time-Life.

***Daniels, Patricia.** Oceans. LC 99-44330. (Nature Library). (Illus.). (J). 1999. write for info. (*0-7922-7545-4*) Natl Geog.

Daniels, Patricia, ed. New Approaches to Undergraduate Engineering Three. 380p. 1992. pap. text 50.00 (*0-939204-49-5*) Eng Found.

Daniels, Patricia, ed. see Gutelle, Andrew M.

Daniels, Patricia, ed. see Quattlebaum, Mary A.

Daniels, Patricia, ed. see Time-Life Books Editors.

Daniels, Patricia A. Asharel to Israel. Lawrence, Marie, ed. 196p. (Orig.). pap. text 15.00 (*0-9628081-3-X*) Daw Enter.

— Voices in the Solemn Wind. Mackey, Rosella, ed. (Illus.). 96p. (Orig.). (J). pap. text 10.00 (*0-9628081-1-3*) Daw Enter.

Daniels, Patricia S. The Ten Commandments. Crawford, Jean, ed. LC 96-15330. (Family Time Bible Stories Ser.). (Illus.). 28p. (J). 1999. 4.95 (*0-7835-4631-9*) Time-Life.

***Daniels, Paul.** Under No Illusion. (Illus.). 2000. 7.95 (*1-85782-314-1*) Blake Publng.

Daniels, Paul & Murray, Barry. You Don't Have to Be a Kid to Pull a Rabbit Out of a Hat: Magic for Adults. LC 97-17778. 160p. 1997. pap. 19.95 (*1-56980-119-3*) Barricade Bks.

Daniels, Paul A., jt. ed. see Catacosinos, Paul A.

Daniels, Peter. Success Is... Principles for Achieving Your Dreams. 1998. pap. 6.99 (*1-57757-036-7*) Trade Life.

Daniels, Peter, et al, eds. The Geography of the Services. LC 93-3012. 155p. 1993. text 42.50 (*0-7146-4520-6*, Pub. by F Cass Pubs) Intl Spec Bk.

Daniels, Peter T. Phonologies of Asia & Africa Vol. 1: Including the Caucasus. Kaye, Alan S., ed. LC 97-4964. xxi, 1041p. 1997. text 119.50 (*1-57506-017-5*) Eisenbrauns.

Daniels, Peter T. & Bright, William, eds. The World's Writing Systems. (Illus.). 968p. 1996. text 165.00 (*0-19-507993-0*) OUP.

Daniels, Peter T., jt. auth. see Bergstrasser, Gotthelf.

Daniels, Peter T., jt. auth. see Kaye, Alan S.

Daniels, Peter T., jt. ed. see Kaye, Alan S.

Daniels, Peter W. & Moulaert, Frank, eds. The Changing Geography of Advanced Producer Services: Theoretical & Empirical Perspectives. LC 91-19252. (Illus.). 224p. 1993. 215.00 (*0-471-94519-6*) Wiley.

Daniels, Philip. Alibi of Guilt. 1996. 19.50 (*0-7451-8693-9*, Black Dagger) Chivers N Amer.

— Cinderella Spy. large type ed. (Linford Mystery Library). 304p. 1989. pap. 16.99 (*0-7089-6729-9*, Linford) Ulverscroft.

— The Dracula Murders. large type ed. (Linford Mystery Library). 256p. 1988. pap. 16.99 (*0-7089-6565-2*) Ulverscroft.

— Enquiries Are Proceeding. large type ed. (Linford Mystery Library). 1989. pap. 16.99 (*0-7089-6753-1*) Ulverscroft.

— Foolproof. large type ed. (Linford Mystery Library). 259p. 1989. pap. 16.99 (*0-7089-6633-0*, Linford) Ulverscroft.

— A Genteel Little Murder. large type ed. (Linford Mystery Library). 244p. 1988. pap. 16.99 (*0-7089-6556-3*, Linford) Ulverscroft.

— Goldmine - London W. I. large type ed. (Linford Mystery Library). 256p. 1989. pap. 16.99 (*0-7089-6738-8*, Linford) Ulverscroft.

— The Inconvenient Corpse. large type ed. (Linford Mystery Library). 256p. 1988. pap. 16.99 (*0-7089-6618-7*, Linford) Ulverscroft.

— Nice Knight for Murder. large type ed. (Linford Mystery Library). 240p. 1988. pap. 16.99 (*0-7089-6625-X*, Linford) Ulverscroft.

— The Scarred Man. large type ed. (Linford Mystery Library). 273p. 1989. pap. 16.99 (*0-7089-6637-3*, Linford) Ulverscroft.

Daniels, Phillip. A Genteel Little Murder. LC 85-28691. 192p. 1986. reprint ed. pap. 5.95 (*0-89733-192-3*) Academy Chi Pubs.

Daniels, R. J. A Field Guide to the Birds of Southwestern India. (Illus.). 228p. 1997. text 39.95 (*0-19-563726-7*) OUP.

Daniels, R. P. Man Plus Woman: God's Design. 76p. pap. 4.95 (*0-88172-180-8*) Believers Bkshelf.

Daniels, R. W. Duralumin as Material for Worm & Other Gearing. (Technical Papers: Vol. P22A). (Illus.). 11p. 1921. pap. text 30.00 (*1-55589-317-1*) AGMA.

Daniels, Ray. Designing Great Beers: The Ultimate Guide to Brewing Classic Beer Styles. (Illus.). 404p. (Orig.). 1996. pap. 19.95 (*0-937381-50-0*) Brewers Pubns.

— Making Out in Chinese. (CHI & ENG.). 104p. 1998. pap. 6.95 (*4-900737-13-5*, Pub. by Yen Bks) Tuttle Pubng.

— 101 Ideas for Homebrew Fun. LC 97-47350. (Illus.). 144p. 1998. pap. 14.95 (*0-937381-57-8*) Brewers Pubns.

***Daniels, Ray & Larson, Geoff.** Smoked Beers: History, Brewing Techniques, Recipes. 2000. pap. 14.95 (*0-937381-76-4*) Brewers Pubns.

Daniels, Raymond B. & Hammer, Richard D. Soil Geomorphology. LC 92-3789. 256p. 1992. 120.00 (*0-471-51153-6*) Wiley.

Daniels, Rebecca. Family Addition. 1997. per. 3.25 (*0-373-19201-0*, 1-19021-2) Silhouette.

— Father Figure. (Intimate Moments Ser.). 1996. per. 3.99 (*0-373-07696-7*, 1-07696-7) Silhouette.

— Husband Wanted -- Fast! (Romance Ser.). 2000. per. 3.50 (*0-373-19419-6*, 1-19419-0) Silhouette.

— L. A. Midnight. (Intimate Moments Ser.: No. 431). 1992. per. 3.39 (*0-373-07431-X*, 5-07431-5) Harlequin Bks.

— Lawyers, Guns & Money. (Intimate Moments Ser.). 1994. per. 3.50 (*0-373-07563-4*, 5-07563-5) Silhouette.

— Loving the Enemy. (Romance Ser.). 1994. per. 2.75 (*0-373-08987-2*, 5-08987-5) Silhouette.

— Mind over Marriage. (Intimate Moments Ser.). 1997. per. 3.99 (*0-373-07765-3*, 1-07765-0) Silhouette.

— Tears of the Shaman. (Intimate Moments Ser.). 1995. per. 3.75 (*0-373-07654-1*, 1-07654-6) Silhouette.

— Way of the Wolf. (Montana Mavericks Ser.). 1995. per. 3.99 (*0-373-50171-4*, 1-50171-7) Harlequin Bks.

Daniels, Rebecca. Women Stage Directors Speak: Exploring the Influence of Gender on Their Work. LC 96-28188. 255p. 1996. lib. bdg. 29.50 (*0-7864-0235-0*) McFarland & Co.

Daniels, Rebecca. The Yuletide Bride. (Intimate Moments Ser.: No. 827). 1997. per. 3.99 (*0-373-07827-7*, 1-07827-8) Harlequin Bks.

Daniels, Rene. Rene Daniels. (Illus.). 188p. 1999. pap. 46.00 (*90-70149-66-4*, 915014) S V Abbemuseum.

Daniels, Rhonda L. Fair Housing Compliance Guide. 2nd rev. ed. O'Connor, Rosanne, ed. LC 94-44960. (Illus.). 121p. 1995. pap. 19.80 (*0-86718-404-3*) Home Builder.

Daniels, Richard. The Art of Playing Rock Guitar. (Illus.). 180p. 1995. pap. 18.95 (*0-89524-895-6*, 02509127, Pub. by Cherry Lane) H Leonard.

— Blues Guitar Inside & Out. (Illus.). (Orig.). 1982. pap. 19.95 (*0-89524-148-X*, Pub. by Cherry Lane) H Leonard.

***Daniels, Richard.** Fifty Blues Moves: By Richard Daniels. 1998. pap. 17.95 (*1-57560-087-0*, Pub. by Cherry Lane) H Leonard.

Daniels, Richard. The Heavy Guitar Bible. (Illus.). 104p. (YA). (gr. 8 up). 1979. reprint ed. pap. 18.95 (*0-89524-066-1*, Pub. by Cherry Lane) H Leonard.

— The Heavy Guitar Bible, Vol. 2. pap. 16.95 (*0-89524-598-1*) Cherry Lane.

Daniels, Robert. Arena Ball: The Building of Virginia's Soccer Dynasty - Collector's Edition. limited ed. (Illus.). 128p. 1994. 30.00 (*1-885758-01-4*) Quality Sports.

***Daniels, Robert.** Life's Trails. 1998. pap. write for info. (*1-57553-973-X*) Watermrk Pr.

Daniels, Robert. The War Within: Experiencing Victory in the Battle for Sexual Purity. LC 96-45359. 224p. 1997. pap. 12.99 (*0-89107-933-5*) Crossway Bks.

— Year of the Heroic Guerrilla: World Revolution & Counterrevolution in 1968. (Illus.). 288p. 1996. pap. 15.95 (*0-674-96451-9*) HUP.

Daniels, Robert A. & New York State Museum Staff. Guide to the Identification of Scales of Inland Fishes of Northeastern North America. LC 96-61274. (Bulletin Ser.). x, 97 p. 1996. write for info. (*1-55557-203-0*) NYS Museum.

Daniels, Robert E., et al. A Bibliography of the Kalenjin Peoples of East Africa. LC 87-31643. (Bibliographies in African Studies: No. 1). (Orig.). 1987. pap. 15.00 (*0-942615-03-4*) U Wis African Stud.

Daniels, Robert H., jt. auth. see Anderson, Frederick R.

Daniels, Robert V. Fourth Revolution. (C). (gr. 13). 1999. 55.00 (*0-415-91077-3*) Routledge.

— Gorbachev & the End of Communism. LC 92-22189. 240p. (C). (gr. 13). 1993. pap. 25.99 (*0-415-06150-4*, A6348) Routledge.

— Russia: The Roots of Confrontation. LC 85-27267. (American Foreign Policy Library). (Illus.). 432p. 1985. 42.00 (*0-674-77965-7*) HUP.

— Russia: The Roots of Confrontation. (American Foreign Policy Library). 432p. 1985. pap. 17.00 (*0-674-77966-5*) HUP.

— Russia's Transformation: Snapshots of a Crumbling System. LC 97-36039. 256p. (Orig.). 1997. 67.50 (*0-8476-8708-2*); pap. 24.95 (*0-8476-8709-0*) Rowman.

— Soviet Communism from Reform to Collapse. (Problems in European Civilization Ser.). 387p. (C). 1995. pap. text 19.96 (*0-669-33144-9*) HM Trade Div.

— The Stalin Revolution: Foundations of the Totalitarian Era. 4th ed. 288p. (C). 1996. pap. text 19.96 (*0-669-41693-2*) HM Trade Div.

Daniels, Robert V., ed. A Documentary History of Communism, 2 vols. rev. ed. Incl. Vol. II. Communism & the World. 480p. 1984. pap. 19.95 (*0-87451-300-6*); 1988. 45.00 (*0-87451-298-0*) U Pr of New Eng.

— The Stalin Revolution: Foundations of the Totalitarian Era. 3rd ed. LC 89-84257. (Problems in European Civilization Ser.). 269p. (C). 1990. pap. text 19.96 (*0-669-21165-6*) HM Trade Div.

Daniels, Robert V., ed. A Documentary History of Communism & the World: From Revolution to Collapse. 3rd ed. LC 93-46972. 418p. (C). 1994. reprint ed. pap. text 24.00 (*0-87451-678-1*) U Pr of New Eng.

— A Documentary History of Communism in Russia: From Lenin to Gorbachev. 4th ed. LC 92-56902. 428p. 1993. pap. text 24.00 (*0-87451-616-1*) U Pr of New Eng.

Daniels, Roger. Anti-Chinese Violence in North America: An Original Anthology. LC 78-54807. (Asian Experience in North America Ser.). 1979. lib. bdg. 19.95 (*0-405-11263-7*) Ayer.

— Archival Doc: Pre-Pearl Harbor July 1940-December 1941, Vol. 1. 150p. 1989. text 30.00 (*0-8240-2791-4*) Garland.

— Asian American: Chinese & Japanese in the United States since 1850. LC 88-5643. (Illus.). 402p. 1990. 18.95 (*0-295-97018-9*) U of Wash Pr.

— The Asian Experience in North America Series: Chinese & Japanese, 47 bks., Set. (Illus.). 1979. reprint ed. lib. bdg. 1345.50 (*0-405-18992-3*) Ayer.

— The Bonus March: An Episode of the Great Depression, 14. LC 75-133497. (Illus.). 370p. 1971. 35.00 (*0-8371-5174-0*, DBM/, Greenwood Pr) Greenwood.

— Coming to America: A History of Immigration & Ethnicity in American Life. LC 89-46524. (Illus.). 512p. 1991. reprint ed. pap. 17.00 (*0-06-092100-5*, Perennial) HarperTrade.

— Concentration Camps: North American Japanese in the United States & Canada During World War II. LC 80-19813. 262p. 1993. 23.50 (*0-89464-819-5*) Krieger.

Daniels, Roger. The Decision to Relocate the Japanese Americans. LC 85-12678. 150p. (C). 1985. reprint ed. pap. text 13.50 (*0-89874-879-8*) Krieger.

Daniels, Roger. Not Like Us: Immigrants & Minorities in America, 1890-1924. LC 97-16117. (American Ways Ser.). 192p. 1998. pap. text 12.95 (*1-56663-166-1*) I R Dee.

— Not Like Us: Immigrants & Minorities in Modern America, 1890-1924. LC 97-16117. (American Ways Ser.). 192p. 1997. 22.50 (*1-56663-165-3*, Pub. by I R Dee) Natl Bk Netwk.

— The Politics of Prejudice: The Anti-Japanese Movement in California & The Struggle for Japanese Exclusion. 1978. pap. 13.95 (*0-520-03411-2*) U CA Pr.

— The Politics of Prejudice: The Anti-Japanese Movement in California & The Struggle for Japanese Exclusion. 181p. 1999. pap. 14.95 (*0-520-21950-3*, Pub. by U CA Pr) Cal Prin Full Svc.

— Prisoners Without Trial: Japanese Americans in World War II. Foner, Eric, ed. LC 92-27144. (Critical Issue Ser.). 144p. 1993. pap. 9.00 (*0-8090-1553-6*) Hill & Wang.

Daniels, Roger, ed. American Concentration Camps: A Documentary History of the Relocation & Incarceration of Japanese Americans 1942-46, 9 vols. 2650p. 1989. 510.00 (*0-8153-0019-0*) Garland.

— Citizen 13660. LC 78-54830. (Asian Experience in North America Ser.). (Illus.). 1980. reprint ed. lib. bdg. 18.95 (*0-405-11287-4*) Ayer.

— Reports of the Royal Commission on Chinese Immigration. LC 78-54810. (Asian Experience in North America Ser.). 1979. reprint ed. lib. bdg. 52.95 (*0-405-11267-X*) Ayer.

— Three Short Works on Japanese Americans. LC 78-3223. (Asian Experience in North America Ser.). 1979. lib. bdg. 29.95 (*0-405-11291-2*) Ayer.

— Two Monographs on Japanese Canadians. LC 78-3222. (Asian Experience in North America Ser.). 1979. lib. bdg. 17.95 (*0-405-11304-8*) Ayer.

Daniels, Roger, et al, eds. Contented Among Strangers: Rural German-Speaking Women & Their Families in the Nineteenth-Century Midwest. LC 95-9849. (Statue of Liberty-Ellis Island Centennial Ser.). (Illus.). 336p. (C). 1995. pap. text 15.95 (*0-252-06472-0*) U of Ill Pr.

— Japanese Americans, from Relocation to Redress. LC 85-29583. (Illus.). 238p. reprint ed. pap. 73.80 (*0-8357-6844-9*, 203553900095) Bks Demand.

Daniels, Roger, jt. auth. see Kitano, Harry H.

Daniels, Roger, jt. auth. see O'Brien, Robert W.

Daniels, Roger, jt. auth. see Yoo, David K.

Daniels, Roger, ed. see Andracki, Stanislaw.

Daniels, Roger, ed. see Bell, Reginald.

Daniels, Roger, ed. see California, State Board of Control Staff.

Daniels, Roger, ed. see Canada Department of Labour Staff.

Daniels, Roger, ed. see Canada Royal Commission on Chinese & Japanese Immi.

Daniels, Roger, ed. see Coman, Katherine & Lind, Andrew W.

Daniels, Roger, ed. see Condit, Ira M.

Daniels, Roger, ed. see Conroy, Hilary.

Daniels, Roger, ed. see Dooner, W. Pierton.

Daniels, Roger, ed. see Flowers, Montaville.

Daniels, Roger, ed. see Gibson, Otis.

Daniels, Roger, ed. see Gulick, Sidney L.

Daniels, Roger, ed. see Hata, Donald T., Jr.

Daniels, Roger, ed. see Irwin, Wallace.

Daniels, Roger, ed. see Japanese General-Consulate Staff.

Daniels, Roger, ed. see Kachi, Teruko O.

Daniels, Roger, ed. see Kawakami, Kiyoshi K.

Daniels, Roger, ed. see Kil Young Zo.

Daniels, Roger, ed. see Kyne, Peter B.

Daniels, Roger, ed. see LaViolette, Forrest E.

Daniels, Roger, ed. see Lee, Rose H.

Daniels, Roger, ed. see Matsumoto, Toru.

Daniels, Roger, ed. see McClatchy, Valentine S.

Daniels, Roger, ed. see Mears, Eliot G.

Daniels, Roger, ed. see Millis, Harry A.

Daniels, Roger, ed. see Pickle, Linda S.

Daniels, Roger, jt. ed. see Saunders, Kay.

Daniels, Roger, ed. see Shapiro, Harry L.

Daniels, Roger, ed. see Steiner, Jesse F.

Daniels, Roger, ed. see Sugimoto, Howard H.

Daniels, Roger, ed. see Sung, Betty L.

Daniels, Roger, ed. see Thompson, Richard A.

Daniels, Roger, ed. see Tien-Lu Li.

Daniels, Roger, ed. see U. S. Department of State Staff & Morris, Roland.

Daniels, Roger, ed. see U. S. Department of War Staff.

Daniels, Roger, ed. see U. S. House of Representatives, Committee on the D.

Daniels, Roger, ed. see U. S. House of Representatives Select Committee on.

Daniels, Roger, ed. see U. S. Senate Joint Special Committee.

Daniels, Roger, ed. see Wong, Franklin E.

Daniels, Roger, ed. see Wynne, Robert E.

Daniels, Roger, ed. see Yatsushiro, Toshio.

Daniels, Roger, ed. see Young, Charles H., et al.

Daniels, Roger, jt. ed. see Yung, Wing.

Daniels, Ron, ed. New Cleaning Strategies: Environmental Issues & Technological Developments. LC 95-100492. (Illus.). 190p. (Orig.). 1994. pap. 49.00 (*0-87930-279-8*) Miller Freeman.

Daniels, Ronald J., ed. Ontario Hydro at the Millennium: Has Monopoly's Moment Passed? 409p. 1996. 22.95 (*0-7735-1430-9*, HD9685, Pub. by McG-Queens Univ Pr); 65.00 (*0-7735-1426-0*, Pub. by McG-Queens Univ Pr) CUP Services.

Daniels, Ruby & Johnson, Barbara. Ruby of Cochin: An Indian Jewish Woman Remembers. 1995. 29.95 (*0-8276-0539-0*) JPS Phila.

***Daniels, Rudolph.** Trains Across the Continent: North American Railroad History. (Illus.). 2000. 39.95 (*0-253-33762-3*); pap. 19.95 (*0-253-21411-4*) Ind U Pr.

Daniels, S., jt. ed. see Smith, E. B.

Daniels, Sarah. Beside Herself. (Women's Playhouse Plays Ser.). 73p. (Orig.). (C). 1990. pap. write for info. (*0-413-62400-5*, A0460, Methuen Drama) Methn.

— Beside Herself. 73p. (Orig.). 1995. pap. write for info. (*0-413-65910-0*, AO743, Methuen Drama) Methn.

— Daniels: Plays One. (Methuen World Dramatists Ser.). 420p. (Orig.). (C). 1991. pap. 14.95 (*0-413-64930-X*, A0537, Methuen Drama) Methn.

— Daniels Plays 2. 256p. 1995. pap. 15.95 (*0-413-69040-7*, A0733) Heinemann.

— Masterpieces. 2nd ed. (Methuen Modern Plays Ser.). 68p. (Orig.). (C). 1984. pap. write for info. (*0-413-41260-1*, A0432, Methuen Drama) Methn.

— Neaptide. (Royal Court Writers Ser.). 48p. (C). 1988. pap. write for info. (*0-413-57800-3*, A0182, Methuen Drama) Methn.

Daniels, Stephen. Fields of Vision: Landscape Imagery & National Identity in England & the United States. (Illus.). 266p. 1993. text 47.50 (*0-691-03273-4*, Pub. by Princeton U Pr) Cal Prin Full Svc.

— Humphry Repton: Landscape Gardening & the Geography of Georgian England LC 98-52787. 1999. write for info. (*0-300-07949-4*) Yale U Pr.

D

— Humphry Repton: Landscape Gardening & the Geography of Georgian England. LC 98-52787. (Illus.). 320p. 1999. 60.00 (*0-300-07964-8*) Yale U Pr.

— Joseph Wright: A Selection of Paintings from the Collection of Mr. & Mrs. Paul Mellon. (British Artists Ser.). (Illus.). 1999. pap. 13.95 (*0-691-02943-1*, Pub. by Princeton U Pr) Cal Prin Full Svc.

Daniels, Stephen. From A Delta's Heart. 2nd ed. 53p. 1995. reprint ed. mass mkt. 10.00 (*1-893719-00-6*) LEJ.

Daniels, Stephen, intro. Humphry Repton: The Red Books for Brandsbury & Glemham Hall. LC 94-19588. (Dumbarton Oaks Reprints & Facsimiles in Landscape Architecture Ser.: 3). (Illus.). 1994. 125.00 (*0-88402-227-7*, Dumbarton Rsch Lib) Dumbarton Oaks.

Daniels, Stephen & Lee, Roger, eds. Exploring Human Geography: A Reader. (Arnold Publications). (Illus.). 512p. 1995. pap. text 35.00 (*0-340-61429-3*) OUP.

Daniels, Stephen & Martin, Joanne. Civil Juries & the Politics of Reform. (American Bar Foundation Ser.). 320p. 1995. 35.00 (*0-8101-1121-7*) Northwestern U Pr.

Daniels, Stephen, jt. ed. see Cosgrove, Denis.

Daniels, Sterling N., 2nd. Yas. (Illus.). 36p. (J). (gr. k-3). pap. text 4.95 (*0-9628081-2-1*) Daw Enter.

Daniels, Steve. The Wild Lawn Handbook: Alternatives to the Traditional Front Lawn. LC 94-5369. 256p. 1995. 22.00 (*0-02-529445-8*) Macmillan.

— The Wild Lawn Handbook: Alternatives to the Traditional Front Lawn. (Illus.). 224p. 1997. pap. text 17.95 (*0-02-862004-6*) Macmillan.

Daniels, Steve & David, Nicholas. The Archaeology Workbook. LC 81-43519. (Illus.). 120p. (Orig.). (C). 1982. pap. 19.95 (*0-8122-1125-1*) U of Pa Pr.

***Daniels, Steve & MacLean, Jim.** GURPS Traveller:Far Trader: Profit & Pitfalls among the Stars. Punch, Sean, ed. (Illus.). 128p. 1999. pap. 20.95 (*1-55634-373-6*, Pub. by S Jackson Games) BookWorld.

***Daniels, Steven E. & Walker, Gregg B.** Working Through Environmental Conflicts: The Collaborative Learning Approach. LC 00-25460. 240p. 2000. 59.00 (*0-275-96473-6*, C6473) Greenwood.

Daniels, Stevie, ed. Easy Lawns: Low-Maintenance Native Grasses for Gardeners Everywhere. (21st-Century Gardening Ser.). 112p. 1999. pap. 9.95 (*1-889538-12-4*, Pub. by Bklyn Botanic) Storey Bks.

Daniels, Stevie O., ed. see Lawton, Barbara P. & Van Patten, George F.

Daniels, Stevie O., ed. see Solomon, Steve O.

Daniels, Stevie O., ed. see Van Patten, George F. & Solomon, Steve O.

Daniels, Stuart R. Inelastic Steel Structure. LC 65-25460. 205p. reprint ed. pap. 63.60 (*0-608-11383-2*, 202177400023) Bks Demand.

Daniels, Ted. A Doomsday Reader: Prophets, Predictors & Hucksters of Salvation. LC 99-6337. (Illus.). 256p. 1999. pap. 18.95 (*0-8147-1909-0*); text 55.00 (*0-8147-1908-2*) NYU Pr.

Daniels, Teresa. Blessing Talk: Teacher's Manual. (Training Ser.). 80p. 1998. text, teacher ed. 29.95 (*1-884061-27-3*) Womens Minist.

— Blessing Talk: The Art of Lifting with Words. (Training Ser.). 80p. 1998. text 29.95 (*1-884061-17-6*) Womens Minist.

Daniels, Teresa & Cox, Naomi I. Group Talk: The Art of Leadership in Groups. (Training Ser.). 80p. 1998. text 29.95 (*1-884061-21-4*) Womens Minist.

Daniels, Theodore T. Millennialism: An International Bibliography. LC 91-39298. 692p. 1992. text 35.00 (*0-8240-7102-6*, SS667) Garland.

Daniels, Thomas L. Land Gains Taxation: The Vermont Case. (Occasional Papers: No. 10). (Illus.). 58p. (Orig.). 1986. pap. text 5.00 (*0-944277-15-2*, D36) U VT Ctr Rsch VT.

Daniels, Thomas L., et al. The Small Town Planning Handbook. 2nd ed. LC 94-71489. (Illus.). 312p. (Orig.). 1995. pap. 35.95 (*1-884829-02-3*, Planners Press); lib. bdg. 50.00 (*1-884829-03-1*, Planners Press) Am Plan Assn.

Daniels, Tim. 1001 Secrets for Windows NT Registry. LC 97-33918. 500p. (Orig.). 1997. pap. 49.95 incl. cd-rom (*1-882419-68-5*) News Four-Hund.

Daniels, Tom. When City & Country Collide: Managing Growth in the Metropolitan Fringe. LC 98-42236. (Illus.). 420p. 1998. pap. text 32.50 (*1-55963-597-5*) Island Pr.

Daniels, Tom & Bowers, Deborah. Holding Our Ground: Protecting America's Farms. LC 96-52665. (Illus.). 350p. 1997. pap. text 34.95 (*1-55963-482-0*, Shearwater Bks) Island Pr.

Daniels, Tom D. & Spiker, Barry K. Perspectives on Organizational Communication. 3rd ed. 360p. (C). 1993. text. write for info. (*0-697-20134-1*) Brown & Benchmark.

— Perspectives on Organizational Communication. 4th ed. LC 96-83543. 384p. (C). 1996. text. write for info. (*0-697-28896-X*, WCB McGr Hill) McGrw-H Hghr Educ.

Daniels, V. G., jt. auth. see Huang, C. L.

Daniels, V. G., jt. ed. see Huang, C. L.

Daniels, Val. Between Dusk & Dawn. 1994. mass mkt. 3.50 (*0-373-27042-9*, 1-27042-0) Harlequin Bks.

— For Baby's Sake. (Romance Ser.: No. 3461). 1997. per. 3.25 (*0-373-03461-X*, 1-03461-0) Harlequin Bks.

— Forever Isn't Long Enough: Family Ties. (Harlequin Romance Ser.: No. 3377). 1995. per. 2.99 (*0-373-03377-X*) Harlequin Bks.

— Making Mr. Right. 1999. per. 3.50 (*0-373-15809-2*, 1-15809-6) Harlequin Bks.

— Making Mr. Right. 1999. per. 3.50 (*0-373-03563-2*, 1-03563-3) Harlequin Bks.

— Marriage on His Terms. (Romance Ser.). 1998. per. 3.50 (*0-373-03497-0*, 1-03497-4) Harlequin Bks.

— Marriage on His Terms. large type ed. (Bachelor Territory Ser.). 1998. per. 3.50 (*0-373-15743-6*, Harlequin) Harlequin Bks.

— A Ranch, a Ring & Everything. (Harlequin Romance Ser.: No. 3418). 1996. per. 3.25 (*0-373-03418-0*, 1-03418-0) Harlequin Bks.

— Santa's Special Delivery: (Baby Boom) (Romance Ser.: No. 3534). 1998. per. 3.50 (*0-373-03534-9*, 1-03534-4) Harlequin Bks.

— Santa's Special Delivery: (Baby Boom) large type ed. (Larger Print Ser.: No. 380). 1998. per. 3.50 (*0-373-15780-0*, 1-15780-9) Harlequin Bks.

— Sweet Valentine. (Romance Ser.). 1997. per. 3.25 (*0-373-03446-6*, 1-03446-1) Harlequin Bks.

— Their Marriage Contract. (Special Edition Ser.: No. 1248). 1999. per. 4.25 (*0-373-24248-4*, 1-24248-6) Silhouette.

Daniels, Vann A. Language of Love, Power & Health: Heal Your Life Through Language. Daniels, David W. et al, eds. (Orig.). 1992. pap. write for info. (*0-9633837-0-1*) Ctr Heal Lang.

Daniels, Velma S. Happy Anniversary. (Illus.). 1992. 8.50 (*0-8378-2531-8*) Gibson.

Daniels, Velma S. & King, Peggy E. Fountain of Love. (Serenade Serenata Ser.: No. 6). 192p. (Orig.). 1983. pap. 2.50 (*0-310-50012-5*, 17101P) Zondervan.

Daniels, Velma S., et al. Treasured Romance Vol. 1: On Wings of Love; Love's Late Spring; Fountain of Love, Vol. 1. 450p. 1996. 19.99 (*0-310-20952-8*) Zondervan.

Daniels, Vera, ed. & notes see Eluard, Paul.

Daniels, Victor. The Winds of Time. write for info. (*0-688-17110-9*, Wm Morrow) Morrow Avon.

Daniels, Victor & Horowitz, Laurence J. Being & Caring: A Psychology for Living. 2nd ed. 371p. (C). 1997. reprint ed. pap. text 30.95 (*0-88133-991-1*) Waveland Pr.

Daniels, W. H. Illustrated History of Methodism. 1977. lib. bdg. 75.00 (*0-8490-2036-0*) Gordon Pr.

Daniels, William R. The American Forty-Five & Seventy-Eight RPM Record Dating Guide, 1940-1959. 16. LC 84-22420. (Discographies Ser.: No. 16). 157p. 1985. lib. bdg. 49.95 (*0-313-24232-1*, DRP/, Greenwood Pr) Greenwood.

— Breakthrough Performance: Managing for Speed & Flexibility. PRC, Inc. Staff, ed. 1994. 39.95 (*1-882939-00-X*); pap. 24.95 (*1-882939-01-8*) ACT Pub.

— Change-ABLE Organization: Key Management Practices for Speed & Flexibility. LC 96-78804. 1997. 39.95 (*1-882939-03-4*) ACT Pub.

— Group Power One: A Manager's Guide to Using Task-Force Meetings. LC 86-24955. 94p. (Orig.). 1986. pap. 24.95 (*0-88390-204-4*, Pfffr & Co) Jossey-Bass.

— Group Power Two: A Manager's Guide to Conducting Regular Meetings. LC 89-20244. (Illus.). 172p. (Orig.). 1990. pap. text 24.95 (*0-88390-236-2*, Pfffr & Co) Jossey-Bass.

Daniels, William R. & Mathers, John G. Change-ABLE Organization: Key Management Practices for Speed & Flexibility. LC 96-78804. (Illus.). 304p. 1996. pap. 24.95 (*1-882939-02-6*) ACT Pub.

Daniels, Zeke. ZekeSpeak: Simple Truths in a Complex World. LC 93-60375. 160p. (Orig.). 1993. pap. 5.95 (*0-934239-70-3*, One Wrld CA) Timely Visions.

Daniels, Zoe. Year of the Cat: The Amulet. 240p. (Orig.). (YA). 1995. mass mkt. 3.99 (*0-425-14862-9*) Berkley Pub.

— Year of the Cat: The Dream. 240p. (Orig.). 1995. mass mkt. 3.99 (*0-425-14768-1*) Berkley Pub.

— Year of the Cat: The Hunt. 256p. (Orig.). (YA). 1995. mass mkt. 3.99 (*0-425-14778-9*) Berkley Pub.

Danielsen, Barbara J. & Ellison, Mary. Drug Policy in Minnesota: Charting the Course. (Illus.). 58p. (C). 1997. reprint ed. pap. text 25.00 (*0-7881-4213-5*) DIANE Pub.

Danielsen, Dan & Engle, Karen, eds. After Identity: A Reader in Law & Culture. 400p. (C). (gr. 13). 1994. pap. 26.99 (*0-415-90997-X*, B3881) Routledge.

***Danielsen, Margie.** Tainted Roses: A True Story of Murder, Mystery & a Dangerous Love. LC 99-70159. 310p. 2000. 24.95 (*0-88282-183-0*) New Horizon NJ.

— Tainted Roses: A True Story of Murder, Mystery & a Dangerous Love. 304p. 2000. pap. 6.50 (*0-312-97685-2*) St Martin.

Danielsen, Niels & Maher, Peter J. Papers in Theoretical Linguistics. Baerentzen, Per, ed. LC 91-39469. (Current Issues in Linguistic Theory Ser.: No. 23). xxii, 224p. 1992. 65.00 (*90-272-3509-0*) J Benjamins Pubng Co.

Danielsen, Rolf, et al. Norway: A History from the Vikings to Our Own Times. 486p. 1995. 41.00 (*82-00-21803-1*) Scandnvan Univ Pr.

Danielsen, Thore, ed. Scandinavian Conference on Artificial Intelligence, '88. (Frontiers in Artificial Intelligence & Applications Ser.). 382p. (gr. 12). 1988. pap. 68.00 (*90-5199-003-0*, Pub. by IOS Pr) IOS Press.

Danielson, et al. Meteorology. 272p. 1998. spiral bd., wbk. ed. 29.38 (*0-697-21715-9*) McGraw.

Danielson, Anders. The Economic Surplus: Theory, Measurement, Applications. LC 93-37880. 168p. 1994. 62.95 (*0-275-94765-3*, Praeger Pubs) Greenwood.

Danielson, Carol B. & Hamel-Bissec, Brenda. Families, Health & Illness. (Illus.). 427p. (C). (gr. 13). 1992. pap. text 35.00 (*0-8016-0360-9*, 00360) Mosby Inc.

Danielson, Charlotte. A Collection of Performance Tasks & Rubrics: Middle School Mathematics. LC 96-53629. (Illus.). 224p. 1997. pap. 27.95 (*1-883001-33-1*) Eye On Educ.

— A Collection of Performance Tasks & Rubrics: Upper Elementary School Mathematics. LC 97-10141. (Illus.). 224p. 1997. pap. 27.95 (*1-883001-39-0*) Eye On Educ.

— Enhancing Professional Practice: A Framework for Teaching. LC 96-25256. 140p. 1996. pap. 19.95 (*0-87120-269-7*, 196074) ASCD.

***Danielson, Charlotte.** Subverting the Family Romance: Women Writers, Kinship Structures & the Early French Novel. LC 99-33520. 192p. 2000. 36.00 (*0-8387-5410-4*) Bucknell U Pr.

Danielson, Charlotte & Abrutyn, Leslye. An Introduction to Using Portfolios in the Classroom. LC 97-21178. 1997. pap. 10.95 (*0-87120-290-5*) ASCD.

Danielson, Charlotte & Hansen, Pia. A Collection of Performance Tasks & Rubrics: Primary School Mathematics. LC 98-51694. (Illus.). 200p. 1999. pap. 24.95 (*1-883001-70-6*) Eye On Educ.

Danielson, Charlotte & Marquez, Elizabeth. A Collection of Performance Tasks & Rubrics: High School Mathematics. LC 97-38988. 225p. 1997. pap. 29.95 (*1-883001-49-8*) Eye On Educ.

***Danielson, Charlotte & McGreal, Thomas L.** Teacher Evaluation to Enhance Professional Practice. LC 00-9116. 2000. pap. write for info. (*0-87120-380-4*) ASCD.

Danielson, Dana, ed. & illus. see Van Laarhoven, Robert.

***Danielson, Dennis, ed.** The Book of the Cosmos: Imagining the Universe from Heraclitus to Hawking. 512p. 2000. text 35.00 (*0-7382-0247-9*, Pub. by Perseus Pubng) HarpC.

— The Cambridge Companion to Milton. 2nd ed. LC 99-10915. (Cambridge Companions to Literature Ser.). (Illus.). 304p. 1999. 59.95 (*0-521-65226-X*); pap. 18.95 (*0-521-65543-9*) Cambridge U Pr.

Danielson, Donald A. Vectors & Tensors in Engineering & Physics. 352p. (C). 1992. 49.95 (*0-201-52426-0*) Addison-Wesley.

— Vectors & Tensors in Engineering & Physics. 2nd ed. LC 96-44249. 290p. (C). 1997. 50.00 (*0-201-44210-8*) Addison-Wesley.

Danielson, Dorothy & Hayden, Rebecca W. Using English: Your Second Language. (Illus.). 228p. (C). 1973. pap. text 15.95 (*0-13-939678-0*) P-H.

Danielson, Dorothy & Porter. Using English. 2nd ed. 1990. pap. text 34.60 (*0-13-947367-X*) P-H.

Danielson, Eric W. & Levin, James. Meteorology. LC 97-27826. 544p. (C). 1997. per. write for info. (*0-697-21711-6*, WCB McGr Hill) McGrw-H Hghr Educ.

***Danielson, Eric W., et al.** Meteorology. 2nd ed. LC 00-25409. (Illus.). 2000. write for info. (*0-07-365963-0*) McGraw.

Danielson, J. David, tr. see Quiroga, Horacio.

Danielson, Karen, et al. Multifamily Development Handbook. LC 99-61429. 350p. Date not set. 89.95 (*0-87420-869-6*, M27) Urban Land.

Danielson, Kathy. On My Honor: A Study Guide. Friedland, Joyce & Kessler, Rikki, eds. (Novel-Ties Ser.). (J). (gr. 4-6). 1991. pap. text 15.95 (*0-88122-576-2*) Lrn Links.

Danielson, Kathy E. Counting on Literature: Primary Math with Picture Books. (Illus.). 48p. 1990. pap. 7.95 (*0-913839-82-5*, BL191) Pieces of Lrning.

Danielson, Kathy E. & LaBonty, Jan. Integrating Reading & Writing Through Children's Literature. LC 93-14086. 352p. (C). 1993. pap. text 61.00 (*0-205-15314-3*, Longwood Div) Allyn.

Danielson, Kathy Everts, jt. auth. see Rogers, Sheri Everts.

Danielson, Michael N. Home Team: Professional Sports & the American Metropolis. LC 96-35200. 397p. 1997. 29.95 (*0-691-03650-0*, Pub. by Princeton U Pr) Cal Prin Full Svc.

— Profits & Politics in Paradise: The Development of Hilton Head Island. LC 95-4364. 323p. 1995. pap. 19.95 (*1-57003-039-1*) U of SC Pr.

Danielson, Michael N. & Doig, Jameson W. New York: The Politics of Urban Regional Development. LC 81-7480. (Lane Studies in Regional Government: No. 4). 352p. 1982. 55.00 (*0-520-04371-5*, Pub. by U CA Pr); pap. 16.95 (*0-520-04551-3*, Pub. by U CA Pr) Cal Prin Full Svc.

Danielson, Michael N. & Keles, Rusen. The Politics of Rapid Urbanization: Government & Growth in Modern Turkey. (Illus.). 304p. 1985. 39.95 (*0-8419-0951-2*); pap. 19.50 (*0-8419-0952-0*) Holmes & Meier.

Danielson, Peter. Artificial Morality: Virtuous Robots for Virtual Games. LC 91-30432. 256p. (C). 1992. 75.00 (*0-415-03484-1*, A5029); pap. 25.99 (*0-415-07691-9*, A7338) Routledge.

— Modeling Rationality, Morality & Evolution. (Vancouver Studies in Cognitive Science: Vol. 7). 480p. 1998. pap. text 29.95 (*0-19-512550-9*) OUP.

Danielson, Peter A. Modeling Rationality, Morality & Evolution. (Vancouver Studies in Cognitive Science: Vol. 7). 480p. 1999. text 70.00 (*0-19-512549-5*) OUP.

***Danielson, Richard.** The Spirit of the Cove. LC 99-65730. 360p. 2000. pap. 17.25 (*0-88739-311-X*) Creat Arts Bk.

***Danielson, Rick.** Web Site Graphics: Flash Animation & DHTML: The Best Work from the Web. 2000. pap. 20.00 (*1-56496-722-0*) Rockport Pubs.

— Web Site Graphics: Home Page & Splash Page: The Best Work from the Web. 2000. pap. 20.00 (*1-56496-723-9*) Rockport Pubs.

— Web Site Graphics: Navigation 2: The Best Work from the Web. 2000. pap. 20.00 (*1-56496-721-2*) Rockport Pubs.

Danielson, Roswell S. Cuban Medicine. LC 76-1768. 247p. 1978. 39.95 (*0-87855-114-X*) Transaction Pubs.

Danielson, S. & Curtis, J. Martial Arts Companion. (Rolemaster Standard System Ser.). (Illus.). 128p. 1997. pap. 18.00 (*1-55806-313-7*, 5602) Iron Crown Ent Inc.

Danielson, Sarah P. The Miracle on 34th Street: A Hollywood Classic. (Illus.). 112p. 1993. 14.98 (*0-8317-4284-4*) Smithmark.

Danielson, Virginia. The Voice of Egypt: Umm Kulth Um, Arabic Song, & Egyptian Society in the Twentieth Century. LC 96-45394. (Studies in Ethnomusicology). 240p. 1997. pap. 17.95 (*0-226-13612-4*) U Ch Pr.

— The Voice of Egypt: Umm Kulthum, Arabic Song, & Egyptian Society in the Twentieth Century. LC 96-45394. (Studies in Ethnomusicology). 240p. 1997. lib. bdg. 45.00 (*0-226-13611-6*) U Ch Pr.

Danielson, Virginia, et al, eds. The Middle East. (Illus.). 900p. 1999. text 165.00 (*0-8240-6042-3*) Garland.

Danielsson, Anna, jt. auth. see Smith, Gudmund J.

Danielsson, B. Prisma Modern English-Swedish Dictionary. (ENG & SWE.). 394p. 1980. 49.95 (*0-7859-0912-5*, M9451) Fr & Eur.

Danielsson, Henry. Arthur Machen: A Bibliography. LC 74-130267. (Reference Ser.: No. 44). 1970. reprint ed. lib. bdg. 75.00 (*0-8383-1174-1*) M S G Haskell Hse.

Danielsson, Ulla, jt. auth. see Dandamell, Birgitta.

Danien, Elin C. & Sharer, Robert J., eds. New Theories on the Ancient Maya. (University Museum Monographs: University Museum Symposium Ser.: Nos. 77 & III). (Illus.). xvi, 224p. (C). 1992. text 50.00 (*0-924171-13-8*) U Museum Pubns.

D'Anier, Paul J. Economic Interdependence in Ukrainian-Russian Relations. LC 98-45360. (SUNY Series in Global Politics). 320p. (C). 1999. text 65.50 (*0-7914-4245-4*) State U NY Pr.

Danieri, Cheryl L. Credit Where Credit Is Due: The Mont-de-Piet of Paris 1771-1851. Besnick, Janet, ed. LC 91-13393. (Modern European History Ser.). 296p. 1991. text 20.00 (*0-8153-0415-3*) Garland.

***D'Anieri, Paul, et al.** Politics & Society in Ukraine. LC 99-30503. 352p. 1999. 60.00 (*0-8133-3537-X*); pap. 24.00 (*0-8133-3538-8*) Westview.

D'Anieri, Paul J. Economic Interdependence in Ukrainian-Russian Relations. LC 98-45360. (SUNY Series in Global Politics). 278p. (C). 1999. pap. text 21.95 (*0-7914-4246-2*) State U NY Pr.

Danieri, Silvia S., tr. see Berg-Sobre, Judith.

Daniggelis, Paul D. Rodant Pel Mon: Roaming about the World with Urbici Soler, Sculptor (1890-1953) 152p. 1995. 25.00 (*0-9648062-0-7*) Intl Assn Vis Arts.

Danila. Solution Chemistry of Macrocycles. text. write for info. (*0-471-48985-9*) Wiley.

Danil'chuk, A. P. Gnatyuk. see Gnatyuk Danil'chuk, A. P.

Danilenko, G. M. & Burnham, William. Law & Legal System of the Russian Federation. LC 98-18219. 1998. 105.00 (*1-57823-053-5*) Juris Pubng.

Danilenko, Gennady, jt. ed. see Carty, Anthony.

Danilenko, Gennady M. Law-Making in the International Community. LC 92-34503. (Developments in International Law Ser.: Vol. 15). 360p. 1993. lib. bdg. 123.50 (*0-7923-2039-5*) Kluwer Academic.

Danilewicz-Zielinska, Maria. Bibliografia-Kultura 1958-1994. (POL.). 1996. pap. 70.00 (*0-614-25055-2*) Szwede Slavic.

Danilian, Sergei, ed. see Gaevsky, Vadim.

Daniljuk, I. I., ed. On Integral Functionals with Variable Domain of Integration, Vol. 4. LC 76-12567. (Proceedings of the Steklov Institute of Mathematics Ser.: Vol. 118). 144p. 1976. pap. 55.00 (*0-8218-3018-X*, STEKLO/118) Am Math.

Daniloff, Nicholas. Two Lives, One Russia. 368p. 1990. mass mkt. 4.95 (*0-380-70841-8*, Avon Bks) Morrow Avon.

Daniloff, Raymond G., jt. ed. see Baken, Ronald J.

Danilov, Aleksei D. Chemistry of the Ionosphere. LC 68-31236. (Monographs in Geoscience). 312p. 1970. reprint ed. pap. 96.80 (*0-608-05455-0*, 206592400006) Bks Demand.

***Danilov, Oleg B., ed.** Gas, Liquid & Free-Electron Lasers. 158p. 1999. pap. text 62.00 (*0-8194-3160-5*) SPIE.

Danilov, V. G., et al. Mathematical Modelling of Heat & Mass Transfer Processes. (Mathematics & Its Applications Ser.: Vol. 348). 316p. (C). 1995. text 173.50 (*0-7923-3789-1*) Kluwer Academic.

Danilov, V. I. & Shokurov, V. V. Algebraic Curves, Algebraic Manifolds & Schemes. Shafarevich, I., ed. LC 98-153637. (Illus.). 307p. 1998. reprint ed. pap. 49.95 (*3-540-63705-2*) Spr-Verlag.

Danilov, V. I., et al. Algebraic Geometry II: Cohomologies of Algebraic Varieties, Algebraic Surfaces. Gamkrelidze, R. V., ed. Treger, R., tr. from RUS. (Encyclopedia of Mathematical Sciences Ser.: Vol. 35). (Illus.). 260p. 1996. 109.00 (*3-540-54680-4*) Spr-Verlag.

Danilov, Victor J. America's Science Museums. LC 90-33627. 496p. 1990. lib. bdg. 75.00 (*0-313-25865-1*, DVS, Greenwood Pr) Greenwood.

— Chicago's Museums: A Complete Guide to the City's Cultural Attractions. rev. ed. LC 90-27049. (Illus.). 304p. 1991. pap. 11.95 (*1-55652-135-9*) Chicago Review.

***Danilov, Victor J.** Colorado Museums & Historic Sites. (Illus.). 376p. 2000. 45.00 (*0-87081-572-5*, Pub. by Univ Pr Colo); pap. 21.95 (*0-87081-573-3*, Pub. by Univ Pr Colo) U of Okla Pr.

Danilov, Victor J. Corporate Museums, Galleries, & Visitor Centers: A Directory. LC 91-11324. 224p. 1991. lib. bdg. 57.95 (*0-313-27658-7*, DCI/, Greenwood Pr) Greenwood.

— Hall of Fame Museums: A Reference Guide. LC 97-16714. 288p. 1997. lib. bdg. 69.50 (*0-313-30000-3*, Greenwood Pr) Greenwood.

— Museum Careers & Training: A Professional Guide. LC 93-33518. 560p. 1994. lib. bdg. 89.50 (*0-313-28105-X*, Greenwood Pr) Greenwood.

— A Planning Guide for Corporate Museums, Galleries, & Visitor Centers. LC 91-28085. 224p. 1991. lib. bdg. 57.95 (*0-313-27657-9*, DPG/) Greenwood.

— University & College Museums, Galleries, & Related Facilities: A Descriptive Directory. LC 95-20544. 704p. 1996. lib. bdg. 110.00 (*0-313-28613-2*, Greenwood Pr) Greenwood.

Danilova, Alexandra. Choura: The Memoirs of Alexandra Danilova. LC 87-27496. (Illus.). 213p. 1987. reprint ed. pap. 11.95 (*0-88064-103-7*) Fromm Intl Pub.

D

An Asterisk (*) at the beginning of an entry indicates that the title is appearing for the first time.

Danilova, O. A., jt. auth. see Savchenko, O. N.

***Daniluh, David.** Private Cuisine: An Executive Chef's Secrets to Gourmet Cooking Made Easy. (Illus.). 1999. pap. 17.00 (*0-9673719-0-2*) D Daniluk.

Daniluk, Judith C. Women's Sexuality Across the Life Span: Challenging Myths, Creating Meanings. LC 98-22508. 416p. 1998. lib. bdg. 40.00 (*1-57230-350-6*) Guilford Pubns.

Danin, A. & Orshan, G. Vegetation of Israel: Desert & Coastal Vegetation. (Illus.). 357p. 1999. 149.00 (*90-73348-99-4*, Pub. by Backhuys Pubs) Balogh.

Danin, Avinoam. Plants of Desert Dunes. LC 95-37101. (Adaptations of Desert Organisms Ser.). (Illus.). 192p. 1996. 99.00 (*3-540-59260-1*) Spr-Verlag.

***Danin, Avionam, et al.** Flora of the Shroud of Turin. (Illus.). 52p. 1999. pap. write for info. (*0-915279-76-2*) Miss Botan.

Danin, Daniel. Probabilities in the Quantum World. 270p. (C). 1983. 50.00 (*0-7855-4976-5*, Pub. by Collets) St Mut.

Daninos, Pierre. Les Carnets du Bon Dieu. (FRE.). pap. 10.95 (*0-8288-9174-5*, F97920) Fr & Eur.

— Les Carnets du Major Thompson. (FRE.). 244p. 1968. 10.95 (*0-8288-9175-3*, F97931) Fr & Eur.

— Les Carnets du Major Thompson. (FRE.). (C). 1954. pap. 7.95 (*0-8442-1749-2*, VF1749-2) NTC Contemp Pub Co.

— Les Carnets Du Major W. Marmaduke Thompson, Decouverte de la France et des Francais. 1960. 11.95 (*0-685-11065-6*) Fr & Eur.

— Un Certain Monsieur Blot. (FRE.). 1964. pap. 10.95 (*0-8288-9181-8*, F97970) Fr & Eur.

— La France dans Tous Ses Etats. (FRE.). 1986. pap. 8.95 (*0-7859-3418-9*) Fr & Eur.

— La Galerie des Glaces. (FRE.). 1984. pap. 8.95 (*0-7859-3121-X*, 2253034347) Fr & Eur.

— Le Jacassin. 230p. 1967. pap. 19.95 (*0-7859-5238-1*) Fr & Eur.

— Ludovic Morateur Ou le Plus Que Parfait. (FRE.). 248p. 1970. 10.95 (*0-8288-9178-8*, M3357); pap. 8.95 (*0-686-55565-1*) Fr & Eur.

— Made in France: Recit. 247p. 14.95 (*0-686-55566-X*) Fr & Eur.

— Le Major Tricolore: Redecouverte de la France et des Francais par le Major W. Marmaduke Thompson. (FRE., Illus.). 192p. 1968. pap. 19.95 (*0-7859-5239-X*) Fr & Eur.

— Le Major Tricolore: Redecouverte de la France et des Francais par le Major W. Marmaduke Thompson. (FRE., Illus.). 160p. 1971. 10.95 (*0-8288-9172-9*, F97941) Fr & Eur.

— Le Major Tricolore, Comment Peut-On Etre Francais. 11.50 (*0-685-37286-3*) Fr & Eur.

— Meridiens. 8.95 (*0-686-55568-6*) Fr & Eur.

— Les Nouveaux Carnets du Major Thompson. (FRE.). 226p. 1973. 17.95 (*0-8288-9176-1*, M3358) Fr & Eur.

— Le Pouvoir aux Enfants. 8.95 (*0-686-55570-8*) Fr & Eur.

— La Premiere Planete a Droite en Sortant par la Voie Lactee. (FRE.). 1975. 15.95 (*0-8288-9170-2*, M3360) Fr & Eur.

— La Premiere Planete a Droite en Sortant par la Voie Lactee. (FRE.). 1975. pap. 3.95 (*0-686-55572-4*) Fr & Eur.

— Le Pyjama. (FRE.). 1972. 15.95 (*0-8288-9173-7*, FA880) Fr & Eur.

— Snobissimo. (FRE.). 256p. 1964. 11.95 (*0-8288-9179-6*, M3361); pap. 3.95 (*0-686-55575-9*) Fr & Eur.

— Le Thirty-SixE Dessous. (FRE.). 1990. pap. 10.95 (*0-7859-3054-X*, 2253000973) Fr & Eur.

— Les Touristocrates. (FRE.). 208p. 1974. 10.95 (*0-8288-9177-X*, M3363); pap. 8.95 (*0-686-55579-1*) Fr & Eur.

— Tout l'Humour du Monde. (FRE.). 224p. 1967. pap. 24.95 (*0-7859-5491-0*) Fr & Eur.

— Tout Sonia: Avec: Sonia les Autres et Moi, Comment Vivre avec ou sans Sonia. (FRE., Illus.). 435p. 1976. 10.95 (*0-8288-9180-X*, F66921) Fr & Eur.

— Les Trente - Sixieme Dessous. (FRE.). 1990. pap. 10.95 (*0-7859-5492-9*) Fr & Eur.

— Vacances a Tous Prix. (FRE.). 1972. 10.95 (*0-8288-9182-6*, F97980) Fr & Eur.

***Danis, Daniel.** That Woman. 1998. pap. text 10.95 (*0-88922-399-8*) Talonbks.

***Danis, Daniel & Gaboriau, Linda.** Song of the Say-Sayer.Tr. of Le Chant du Dire-Dire. 96p. 2000. pap. 10.95 (*0-88922-419-6*, Pub. by Talonbks) Genl Dist Srvs.

Danis, Edward J. The Professorenroman in America: A Study in Cultural Crossccurrents, Popular Acclaim, & Literary Survival. 184p. (C). 1993. lib. bdg. 44.00 (*0-8191-9104-3*) U Pr of Amer.

Danis, Helen. Fingerprints. LC 89-90799. (Illus.). 131p. (Orig.). 1989. reprint ed. pap. 11.95 (*0-9625117-0-6*) H Danis.

Danis, Naomi. Walk with Me. LC 94-16973. (Story Corner Ser.). (Illus.). 24p. (J). (ps). 1995. 6.95 (*0-590-45855-8*, Cartwheel) Scholastic Inc.

Danish, Barbara. The Dragon & the Doctor. 2nd rev. ed. LC 95-16733. (Illus.). 40p. (J). 1995. pap. 5.95 (*1-55861-117-7*) Feminist Pr.

Danish, Michele A., jt. auth. see Generali, Joyce.

Danish National Archives Staff, ed. Guide to the Sources for the History of Nations, 3rd Series, Vol. 3: Sources of the History of North Africa, Asia & Oceania in Scandinavia, Pt. 1: Sources of the History of North Africa, Asia & Oceania in Denmark. 842p. 1980. lib. bdg. 110.00 (*3-598-21474-X*) K G Saur Verlag.

Danish, Sherif & Gannon, Patrick. Building Database Driven Catalogs. LC 98-4245. 300p. 1998. pap. 39.95 (*0-07-015307-8*) McGraw.

Danish, Steven, et al. Helping Skills: A Basic Training Program. 2nd ed. 68p. 1980. teacher ed. 20.95 (*0-87705-483-5*, Kluwer Acad Hman Sci); pap., student ed. 20.95 (*0-87705-484-3*, Kluwer Acad Hman Sci) Kluwer Academic.

***Danish, Steven E.** One Soldier's Memories: World War II. (Illus.). 202p. 1999. pap. 20.00 (*0-913337-35-8*) Southfarm Pr.

Danish, Steven J., et al. Helping Skills II: Life Development Intervention. 160p. (C). 1983. student ed. 20.95 (*0-89885-146-7*, Kluwer Acad Hman Sci); 18.95 (*0-89885-145-9*, Kluwer Acad Hman Sci) Kluwer Academic.

Danishefsky, Isidore. Biochemistry for Medical Sciences. 1980. text 34.00 (*0-316-17198-0*) Little.

Danishvar, Simin. Daneshvar's Playhouse: A Collection of Stories. Mafi, Maryam, tr. from PER. & afterword by by. LC 89-2527. (Illus.). 184p. 1989. 22.00 (*0-934211-19-1*) Mage Pubs Inc.

— A Persian Requiem. Zand, Roxane, tr. from PER. LC 91-40933. 288p. 1992. 22.50 (*0-8076-1273-1*) Braziller.

— Revolution in Iran. LC 96-8633. 256p. 1996. text 59.95 (*0-312-16270-7*) St Martin.

— Savushun: A Novel about Modern Iran. Ghanoonparvar, M. R., tr. from PER. LC 90-5608. 320p. 1991. pap. 12.95 (*0-934211-31-0*) Mage Pubs Inc.

— Sutra & Other Stories. Javadi, Hassan & Neshati, Amin, trs. from PER. LC 94-17049. 192p. 1994. 24.95 (*0-934211-42-6*) Mage Pubs Inc.

Danjo, Yari. Astro-Metrics: Of Undiscovered Planets & Intelligent Life Forms. Perine, Roy, ed. (Illus.). 352p. (C). 1994. 29.95 (*0-9638989-0-6*) Privately Pub.

D'Anjou, Leo. Social Movements & Cultural Change: The First Abolition Campaign Revisited. (Sociological Imagination & Structural Change Ser.). 304p. 1996. pap. text 24.95 (*0-202-30522-8*); lib. bdg. 49.95 (*0-202-30521-X*) Aldine de Gruyter.

***Dank, Barry M. & Refinetti, Roberto, eds.** The Politics of Sexuality. (Sexuality & Culture Ser.: Vol. 3). 221p. 2000. pap. 24.95 (*0-7658-0651-7*) Transaction Pubs.

Dank, Barry M. & Refinetti, Roberto, eds. Sex Work & Sex Workers Vol. 2: Sexuality & Culture. 120p. 1998. pap. 24.95 (*0-7658-0491-3*) Transaction Pubs.

— Sexual Harassment & Sexual Consent. LC 99-163535. (Sexuality & Culture Ser.: Vol. 1). 170p. 1997. pap. text 21.95 (*1-56000-995-0*) Transaction Pubs.

Dank, Milton. Game's End. LC 78-12625. (YA). (gr. 7 up). 1979. 8.95 (*0-397-31821-9*) HarpC Child Bks.

***Dank, Milton.** The Glider Gang: An Eyewitness History of World War II Glider Combat. (World War II Monograph Ser.: Vol. 48). (Illus.). 158p. 1999. pap. 29.95 (*1-57638-172-2*, M48-S) Merriam Pr.

— The Glider Gang: An Eyewitness History of World War II Glider Combat. rev. ed. (World War II Monograph Ser.: Vol. 48). (Illus.). 158p. 1999. 39.95 (*1-57638-173-0*, M48-H) Merriam Pr.

Dankbaar, Ben, jt. ed. see Cannell, William.

***Dankberg, Tracy & Graham, Leland.** Math Bridge: 6th Grade. Willie, Kirsten et al, eds. (Illus.). 96p. (J). (gr. 6). 1999. pap., wbk. ed. 9.95 (*1-887923-18-7*, Pub. by Rainbow UT) Midpt Trade.

Dankberg, Tracy & Graham, Leland. Math Bridge: 8th Grade. Willie, Kirsten et al, eds. (Illus.). 96p. (YA). (gr. 8). 1999. pap., wbk. ed. 9.95 (*1-887923-20-9*, Pub. by Rainbow UT) Midpt Trade.

Dankberg, Tracy, jt. auth. see Graham, Leland.

Danke, William D., jt. auth. see Stanley, Thomas J.

Dankelman, Irene & Davidson, Joan. Women Environment - 3rd World: Alliance for the Future. (Illus.). 224p. (Orig.). 1987. 20.00 (*1-85383-003-8*, Pub. by Escan Pubns) Island Pr.

***Dankelmann, Otfried.** Entdeckung und Selbstentdeckung: Die Begegnung Europaischer Reisender Mit dem England und Irland der Neuzeit. 213p. 1999. 35.95 (*3-631-35074-0*) P Lang Pubng.

Dankenbring, Ray. The Mel Bay Story. LC 97-214629. (Illus.). 208p. 1997. pap. 9.95 (*0-7866-2608-9*, 96470) Mel Bay.

Dankenbring, William F. Beyond Star Wars. LC 78-60520. 1978. 10.95 (*0-917182-07-3*) Triumph Pub.

— The First Genesis: A New Case for Creation. LC 75-10841. (Illus.). 408p. 1975. 8.95 (*0-685-54180-0*) Triumph Pub.

— The First Genesis: The Saga of Creation Versus Evolution. LC 79-65131. (Illus.). 1979. 12.00 (*0-917182-14-6*) Triumph Pub.

— The Keys to Radiant Health. LC 74-19241. 281p. 1974. 7.50 (*0-685-61404-2*) Triumph Pub.

— The Last Days. LC 77-79265. 1977. 11.95 (*0-917182-05-7*) Triumph Pub.

Danker, Donald F., ed. see North, Luther H.

Danker, Frederick W. Augsburg Commentary on the New Testament: Second Corinthians. LC 89-51. 256p. 1989. kivar 23.00 (*0-8066-8868-8*, 10-9026, Augsburg) Augsburg Fortress.

— Greek-English Lexicon of the New Testament & Other Early Christian Literature. 3rd ed. 1998. lib. bdg. 65.00 (*0-226-03933-1*) U Ch Pr.

— Multipurpose Tools for Bible Study. LC 93-14303. 352p. 1994. pap. 24.00 (*0-8006-2598-6*, 1-2598) Augsburg Fortress.

— Shorter Lexicon of the Greek New Testament. 2nd rev. ed. LC 82-10933. 240p. 1983. pap. 30.00 (*0-226-13613-2*) U Ch Pr.

Dankers, N., et al, eds. Fishes & Fisheries of the Wadden Sea. 157p. 1979. pap. 60.00 (*90-6191-055-2*, Pub. by A A Balkema) Ashgate Pub Co.

— Invertebrates of the Wadden Sea: Final Report of the Section "Marine Zoology" of the Wadden Sea Working Group - Report 4. 221p. 1981. pap. 91.00 (*90-6191-054-4*, Pub. by A A Balkema) Ashgate Pub Co.

Dankert, P. & Kooyman, A., eds. Europe Without Frontiers. 118p. 1989. text 80.00 (*0-304-31842-6*) Continuum.

Dankleff, Richard. Westerns. LC 83-21979. 96p. 1984. pap. 9.95 (*0-87071-340-X*) Oreg St U Pr.

Dankmyer, Melissa & Scott, Jack. Effective Impressions: A Guide to Small Business Promotion. 62p. (Orig.). 1995. pap. text 12.95 (*0-9645440-0-8*) Phoenix Special.

Dankner, Harold, et al. Retiree Health Benefits: Field Test of the FASB Proposal. LC 89-84509. (Illus.). 215p. 1989. pap. 25.00 (*0-910586-74-8*, 079-89) Finan Exec.

Dankner, Harold, jt. auth. see Combe, Cynthia.

Dankner, Stuart R. Flight into Sight: Adventures in Ocular Space. LC 94-61877. (Illus.). 20p. (Orig.). (J). (gr. 1-6). 1996. pap. 6.95 (*0-9644017-0-3*) Eyecare Bear.

Danko. Live Nude Girls. LC 98-11780. 160p. 1998. pap. 14.95 (*0-312-18741-6*) St Martin.

***Danko-McGhee, Katherina.** The Aesthetic Preferences of Young Children. LC 00-23052. (Studies in Education: Vol. 49). 128p. 2000. text 59.95 (*0-7734-7756-X*) E Mellen.

Danko, Steven I. Black Holes: An Annotated Bibliography, 1975-1983. LC 85-14382. 1985. text 29.00 (*0-8108-1836-1*) Scarecrow.

Danko, W. D., jt. auth. see Stanley, T. J.

Danko, William D., jt. auth. see Stanley, Thomas J.

Dankoff, Robert. Evliya Celebi in Bitlis: The Relevant Section of the Seyahatname. (Evliya Celebi's Book of Travels: Vol. 2). (ENG & TUR., Illus.). xx, 435p. 1990. 159.00 (*90-04-09242-0*) Brill Academic Pubs.

Dankoff, Robert, tr. The Intimate Life of an Ottoman Statesman, Melek Ahmed Pasha (1588-1662) As Portrayed in Evliya Celebi's Book of Travels (Seyahat-name) LC 90-40379. (SUNY Series in Medieval Middle East History). (Illus.). 318p. (C). 1991. pap. text 24.95 (*0-7914-0641-5*) State U NY Pr.

***Dankoff, Robert & Elsie, Robert.** Evliya Celebi in Albania & Adjacent Regions (Kosovo, Montenegro, Ohrid) (Evliya Celebi's Book of Travels Ser.). (Illus.). 316p. 1999. text 94.50 (*90-04-11624-9*) Brill Academic Pubs.

Dankoff, Robert, et al. The Versified Armenian-Turkish Glossary by Kalayi, ca. 1800. LC 96-85914. (Orig.). (C). 1996. pap. 12.50 (*0-9652548-0-1*) CSU Armenian Pub.

Dankoff, Robert, tr. see Yusuf, Khass H.

Dankoff, Robert, tr. & intro. see Yusuf, Khass.

Dankovich, Dean D. Semiconductors: Index of New Information & Research Bible of Current Reviews. 150p. 1994. 47.50 (*0-7883-0028-8*); pap. 44.50 (*0-7883-0029-6*) ABBE Pubs Assn.

Dankowicz, H. Complex Dynamics in Hamiltonian Systems with Applications to Celestial Mechanics. LC 97-33097. (Series on Nonlinear Science: Vol. 25). 200p. 1997. text 38.00 (*981-02-3221-7*) World Scientific Pub.

***Danks, Brian & Sabol, Jon.** Active Server Pages: A4, Version 2.07. Oberman, David, ed. (CIW Application Developer Track A4 Ser.). (Illus.). 1999. pap. write for info. (*1-58143-078-7*) Prosoft I-net.

— Active Server Pages: Version 2.07. Oberman, David, ed. (CIW Application Developer Track Ser.). (Illus.). 1999. pap. write for info. (*1-58143-042-6*) Prosoft I-net.

Danks, Carol, et al, eds. Teaching for a Tolerant World: Essays & Resources. LC 98-47791. 413p. (gr. 9-12). 1999. pap. 26.95 (*0-8141-4296-6*) NCTE.

Danks, H. V., ed. Insect Life-Cycle Polymorphism: Theory, Evolution, & Ecological Consequences for Seasonality & Diapause Control. LC 94-13391. (Series Entomologica: Vol. 52). 376p. (C). 1994. text 276.00 (*0-7923-2828-0*) Kluwer Academic.

Danks, Harry. The Viola d'Amore. 2nd rev. ed. LC 79-313933. (Illus.). 128p. 1979. 48.00 (*0-900998-16-4*, Pub. by S Bonner) Theodore Front.

***Danks, Hugh.** The Bug Book & the Bug Bottle. (Hand in Hand with Nature Ser.). (Illus.). 64p. (Orig.). 1998. pap. 9.95 (*0-921051-10-7*) Somerville Hse.

Danks, Hugh. The Bug Book & the Bug Bottle. LC 86-40541. (Illus.). 64p. (Orig.). (J). (gr. k-5). 1987. pap. 9.95 (*0-89480-314-X*, 1314) Workman Pub.

Danks, Joseph H., et al, eds. Cognitive Processes in Translation & Interpreting. LC 96-45778. (Applied Psychology Ser.: Vol. 3). 276p. (C). 1997. 52.00 (*0-7619-0054-3*, 00543) Sage.

Danks, Joseph H. & Pezdek, Kathy. Reading & Understanding. Murray, Frank B., ed. LC 80-11688. (IRA Series on the Development of the Reading Process). 81p. (Orig.). reprint ed. pap. 30.00 (*0-8357-8659-5*, 203510600092) Bks Demand.

Danks, Joseph H., jt. auth. see Glucksberg, Sam.

Danks, Lia M. Building Your Ark: Your Personal Survival Guide to the Year 2000 Crisis. (Illus.). 277p. 1998. pap. 29.97 (*0-9671791-0-6*) DAL Ent.

Danks, Rabindra & Schneidre, P. Night Fell: Poems & Drawings. (Illus.). 48p. (Orig.). 1975. pap. 2.95 (*0-915242-06-0*) Pygmalion Pr.

Danks, S. Advanced Level Business Studies. 464p. 1995. pap. 59.95 (*1-85805-112-6*, Pub. by DP Publns) St Mut.

— A First Course in Business Studies. 350p. (C). 1991. 65.00 (*1-870941-73-X*) St Mut.

— GCSE Business Studies. 360p. (C). 1987. 60.00 (*0-905435-95-8*) St Mut.

— GNVQ Advanced Business. 566p. 1994. pap. 59.95 (*1-85805-083-9*, Pub. by DP Publns) St Mut.

— GNVQ Intermediate Business. 300p. 1993. pap. 59.95 (*1-85805-113-4*, Pub. by DP Publns) St Mut.

Danks, Sherryl, jt. auth. see Puckett, Ruby P.

Danksy, Rich. Guildbook: Masquers. (Wruith Ser.). (Illus.). 72p. (Orig.). 1996. pap. 12.00 (*1-56504-604-8*, 6011) White Wolf.

Danksy, Richard & White Wolf Publishing Staff, Wolf. Laws of Night: The Pocket Guide to Mind's Eye Theater. (Illus.). 144p. (Orig.). 1996. pap. 12.95 (*1-56504-506-8*, 5005) White Wolf.

Dankwa, Nano O., III. Christianity & African Traditional Beliefs. Branch, John W., ed. (Illus.). 70p. 1990. pap. text 7.00 (*0-9626487-0-1*) Power Word NY.

***Dankworth, J.** Jazz Revolution. 1999. 35.00 (*0-09-477570-2*) Arrow Bks.

***Dankworth, John.** Jazz in Revolution. (Illus.). 256p. 2000. reprint ed. pap. 22.95 (*0-09-479730-7*, Pub. by Constable & Co) Trafalgar.

Danky, James P., ed. Genealogical Research: An Introduction to the Resources of the State Historical Society of Wisconsin. LC 79-15148. 56p. 1979. pap. 5.95 (*0-87020-180-8*) State Hist Soc Wis.

— Native American Periodicals & Newspapers, 1828-1982: Bibliography, Publishing Record, & Holdings. LC 83-22579. (Illus.). 532p. 1984. lib. bdg. 85.00 (*0-313-23773-5*, DNP/, Greenwood Pr) Greenwood.

Danky, James P. & Hady, Maureen E., eds. African-American Newspapers & Periodicals: A National Bibliography. LC 98-26099. 740p. 1999. text 125.00 (*0-674-00788-3*) HUP.

Danky, James P. & Hady, Maureen E., intros. Newspapers in the State Historical Society of Wisconsin: A Bibliography with Holdings, 2 vols. Incl. Vol. I. Newspapers in the State Historical Society of Wisconsin: A Bibliography with Holdings. LC 92-60505. xiv, 256p. 1994. lib. bdg. (*0-88354-700-7*); Vol. II. Newspapers in the State Historical Society of Wisconsin: A Bibliography with Holdings. LC 92-60505. viii, 488p. 1994. lib. bdg. Not sold separately (*0-88354-701-5*); Set lib. bdg. 110.00 N Ross.

Danky, James P. & Wiegand, Wayne A. Print Culture in a Diverse America. LC 97-33935. (History of Communication Ser.). 336p. 1998. text 49.95 (*0-252-02398-6*); text 27.95 (*0-252-06699-5*) U of Ill Pr.

Danky, James P., jt. auth. see Berman, Sanford.

Danky, James P., jt. ed. see Berman, Sanford.

Danley, Jerry J. Useful Science. (Illus.). 92p. 1983. 1.25 (*0-88323-132-8*, 222); pap. 4.25 (*0-88323-181-6*, 216) Pendergrass Pub.

Danley, John R. The Role of the Modern Corporation in a Free Society. LC 93-2103. (Soundings: A Series in Ethics, Economics & Business). (C). 1994. text 46.00 (*0-268-01647-X*) U of Notre Dame Pr.

Danley, Karen, et al. Career Planning Curriculum: Instructor's Guide: For People with Psychiatric Disabilities. (Psychiatric Vocational Rehabilitation Ser.). 1998. teacher ed., spiral bd. 59.95 (*1-878512-07-2*) Boston Univ Ctr Psy Rehab.

— Career Planning Curriculum: Reference Handbook for People with Psychiatric Disabilities. (Psychiatric Vocational Rehabilitation Ser.). 104p. 1998. spiral bd. 39.95 (*1-878512-08-0*) Boston Univ Ctr Psy Rehab.

Danley, Susan. American Drawings & Watercolors from the Huntington Collection. LC 87-38073. 44p. (Orig.). 1988. pap. 10.00 (*0-87328-094-6*, 172, Pub. by Huntington Lib) A Schwartz & Co.

Danley, Susan, ed. Language As Object: Emily Dickinson & Contemporary Art. LC 96-21069. (Illus.). 104p. 1997. pap. 19.95 (*1-55849-066-3*) U of Mass Pr.

Danley, William, jt. auth. see Willis, Jerry.

Danly, D. E. Emerging Opportunities for Electroorganic Processes: A Critical Evaluation of Plant Design & Economics. LC 84-5882. (Series of Special Reports: No. 11). (Illus.). 279p. reprint ed. pap. 86.50 (*0-7837-3374-7*, 204333200008) Bks Demand.

Danly, Linda, ed. Hugo Friedhofer: The Best Years of His Life: A Hollywood Master of Music for the Movies. LC 98-50959. (Filmmakers Ser.: No. 66). (Illus.). 200p. 1999. 39.50 (*0-8108-3582-7*) Scarecrow.

Danly, Robert L. In the Shade of Spring Leaves: The Life of Higuchi Ichiyo, with Nine of Her Best Short Stories. 384p. 1992. pap. 10.95 (*0-393-30913-4*) Norton.

Danly, Susan. Facing the Past: Nineteenth-Century Portraits from the Collection of the Pennsylvania Academy of the Fine Arts. Mott, Jacolyn A., ed. (Illus.). 100p. (Orig.). 1992. pap. 24.95 (*0-943836-16-6*) Penn Acad Art.

— Light, Air, & Color: American Impressionist Paintings from the Collection of the Pennsylvania Academy of the Fine Arts. (Illus.). 91p. (Orig.). 1990. pap. 14.95 (*0-943836-13-1*) Penn Acad Art.

— Telling Tales: Nineteenth-Century Narrative Painting from the Collection of the Pennsylvania Academy of the Fine Arts. (Illus.). 100p. (Orig.). (C). 1991. pap. 22.50 (*0-943836-15-8*) Am Fed Arts.

Danly, Susan & Lafo, Rachel. Branching: The Art of Michael Mazur. LC 97-40175. (Illus.). (Orig.). 1997. pap. 9.95 (*0-914337-18-1*) Mead Art Mus.

Danly, Susan & Leibold, Cheryl. Eakins & the Photograph: Works by Thomas Eakins & His Circle in the Collection of the Pennsylvania Academy of the Fine Arts. LC 93-32940. (Illus.). 236p. 1994. 85.00 (*1-56098-352-3*) Smithsonian.

— Eakins & the Photograph: Works by Thomas Eakins & His Circle in the Collection of the Pennsylvania Academy of the Fine Arts. LC 93-32940. (Illus.). 236p. 1994. pap. 34.95 (*1-56098-353-1*) Smithsonian.

Danly, Susan & Weber, Bruce. For Beauty & for Truth: The William & Abigail Gerdts Collection of American Still Life. LC 98-9976. (Illus.). 1998. pap. 19.95 (*0-914337-19-X*) Mead Art Mus.

Danman, Gregory C. How to Form & Operate a Limited Liability Company: A Do-It-Yourself Guide. 2nd ed. LC 98-91028. (Self-Counsel Legal Ser.). (Illus.). 222p. (Orig.). 1998. write for info. (*1-55180-182-5*) Self-Counsel Pr.

Dann. Nebula Awards No. 32: SFWA's Choices for the Best Science Fiction & Fantasy of the Year. 352p. (J). 1998. pap. 13.00 (*0-15-600552-2*) Harcourt.

Dann, Allan & Underwood, John. How to Succeed in the Music Business. rev. ed. 133p. 1997. pap. text 19.95 (*0-7119-6195-6*, OP47873) Omnibus NY.

D

Dann, Bucky. More Children's Sermons. 96p. (Orig.). 1993. pap. 9.95 (0-664-25307-5) Westminster John Knox.

Dann, Colin, jt. auth. see Guthrie, Colin.

Dann, Geoff & Gravett, Chris. Knight. LC 92-1590. (Eyewitness Books). (Illus.). 64p. (J). (gr. 5 up). 1993. 19.00 (0-679-83882-1, Pub. by Knopf Bks Yng Read) Random.

Dann, Graham M. The Language of Tourism: A Sociolinguistic Perspective. LC 96-206040. (CAB International Publication Ser.). 310p. 1996. text 80.00 (0-85198-999-3) OUP.

Dann, Graham M., jt. auth. see Potter, Robert B.

Dann, Jack. Christs & Other Poems. 1978. pap. 6.00 (0-686-21111-1) Bellevue Pr.

— Clones. 1998. mass mkt. 5.99 (0-441-00522-5) Ace Bks.

— Future War. 1999. mass mkt. 5.99 (0-441-00639-6) Ace Bks.

— Hackers! 1996. mass mkt. 5.50 (0-441-00375-3) Ace Bks.

— Immortals. 1998. mass mkt. 5.99 (0-441-00539-X) Ace Bks.

— The Memory Cathedral: A Secret History of Leonardo da Vinci. LC 95-15109. 512p. 1996. reprint ed. pap. 10.95 (0-553-37857-0) Bantam.

— Nanotech. 1998. mass mkt. 5.99 (0-441-00585-3) Ace Bks.

— Nebula Awards No. 32: SFWA's Choices for the Best Science Fiction & Fantasy of the Year. 1998. 26.00 (0-15-100306-8) Harcourt.

***Dann, Jack.** The Silent: A Novel. 304p. 1999. reprint ed. pap. 12.95 (0-553-38038-9) Bantam.

Dann, Jack, ed. More Wandering Stars: An Anthology of Outstanding Stories of Jewish Fantasy & Science Fiction. LC 99-45347. 192p. 1999. pap. 16.95 (1-58023-063-6) Jewish Lights.

— Three in Space. (White Wolf Rediscovery Trio Ser.: No. 2). 1998. reprint ed. pap. 14.99 (1-56504-866-0, 11046, Borealis) White Wolf.

— Wandering Stars: An Anthology of Jewish Fantasy & Science Fiction. LC 98-10588. 272p. 1998. reprint ed. pap. 16.95 (1-58023-005-9) Jewish Lights.

Dann, Jack, et al, eds. Three in Time: White Wolf Rediscovery Trio, 3 bks. in 1. 1997. reprint ed. pap. 14.99 (1-56504-985-3, 10041, Borealis) White Wolf.

Dann, Jack & Dozois, Gardner. Angels! 240p. (Orig.). 1995. mass mkt. 4.99 (0-441-00220-X) Ace Bks.

— Timegates. 256p. 1997. mass mkt. 5.99 (0-441-04288-0) Ace Bks.

***Dann, Jack & Dozois, Gardner, eds.** Aliens among Us. 304p. 2000. mass mkt. 5.99 (0-441-00704-X) Ace Bks.

Dann, Jack & Dozois, Gardner, eds. Dinosaurs II. 272p. (Orig.). 1995. mass mkt. 4.99 (0-441-00285-4) Ace Bks.

— Hackers. (Orig.). mass mkt. 5.50 (0-614-13603-2) Ace Bks.

— Invaders! 256p. (Orig.). 1993. mass mkt. 4.50 (0-441-01519-0) Ace Bks.

— Timegates. 1997. pap. 5.99 (0-441-00428-8) Ace Bks.

Dann, Jack, jt. auth. see Haldeman, Jack C., II.

Dann, John C. The Revolution Remembered: Eyewitness Accounts of the War for Independence. LC 79-19254. 1980. 20.00 (0-226-13622-1) U Ch Pr.

— The Revolution Remembered: Eyewitness Accounts of the War for Independence. LC 79-19254. 1983. pap. 17.00 (0-226-13624-8) U Ch Pr.

Dann, John C. & Byrd, Cecil K. Liberty's Legacy: Our Celebration of the Northwest Ordinance & the United States Constitution. Peckham, Howard H., ed. 116p. 1987. pap. 5.00 (0-87758-020-0) Ohio Hist Soc.

Dann, John R. Axe Man & Spear Woman. text. write for info. (0-312-86984-3) St Martin.

Dann, Joshua. Timeshare: ATime for War. 280p. 1999. mass mkt. 5.99 (0-441-00638-8) Ace Bks.

— Timeshare: Do You Believe in Yesterday? 256p. 1997. mass mkt. 5.99 (0-441-00457-1) Ace Bks.

— Timeshare: Second Time Around. 256p. 1998. pap. 5.99 (0-441-00567-5) Ace Bks.

Dann, Kevin. Bright Colors Falsely Seen: Synaesthesia & the Search for Transcendental Knowledge. LC 98-15990. 240p. 1998. 30.00 (0-300-06619-8) Yale U Pr.

Dann, Kevin & Miller, Gordon. Thirty Walks in New Jersey. enl. rev. ed. LC 91-38199. (Illus.). 240p. (C). 1992. pap. 14.95 (0-8135-1812-1); text 25.00 (0-8135-1811-3) Rutgers U Pr.

***Dann, Kevin T.** Across the Great Border Fault: The Naturalist Myth in America. LC 99-53245. 328p. (C). 2000. text 50.00 (0-8135-2790-2) Rutgers U Pr.

Dann, Kevin T. Traces on the Appalachians: A Natural History of Serpentine in Eastern North America. (Illus.). 150p. (Orig.). (C). 1988. pap. 11.95 (0-8135-1324-3) Rutgers U Pr.

***Dann, Lucy & Riches, Francine.** Bardi Counting Book. (Illus.). 24p. (J). 2000. pap. 4.95 (1-875641-54-8, Pub. by Magabala Bks) Intl Spec Bk.

Dann, Mary H. Upstate Odyssey: The Lehigh Valley Railroad in Western New York. LC 96-71260. (Illus.). 144p. (Orig.). 1997. pap. 29.95 (1-884650-05-8) Railroad Res.

Dann, Max & Knight, Andrew. Spotswood. 82p. 1992. pap. 17.95 (0-86819-315-1, Pub. by Currency Pr) Accents Pubns.

Dann, O. & Dinwiddy, John R., eds. Nationalism in the Age of the French Revolution. 472p. 1988. 55.00 (0-907628-97-4) Hambledon Press.

Dann, Patty. The Baby Boat: A Memoir of Adoption. LC 97-41748. 256p. 1998. 22.45 (0-7868-6380-3, Pub. by Hyperion) Time Warner.

— The Baby Boat: A Memoir of Adoption. 272p. 1999. reprint ed. pap. 11.95 (0-7868-8411-8, Pub. by Hyperion) Time Warner.

— Mermaids. 1986. 13.95 (0-89919-471-0, Pub. by Ticknor & Fields) HM.

***Dann, Penny.** Book Buddy: A Child's First Book. (Illus.). (J). 2000. pap. text 16.95 (0-7624-0802-2) Running Pr.

Dann, Penny. Eensy Weensy Spider. (Little Barron's Toddler Bks.). (Illus.). 20p. (J). (ps). 1999. pap. 4.95 (0-7641-0857-3) Barron.

***Dann, Penny.** Five Little Ducks. (Toddler Bks.). 20p. (J). 1999. pap. text 4.95 (0-7641-0868-9) Barron.

Dann, Penny. A Little Book of Nature. LC 94-7881. (Quotations for Kids Ser.). 24p. 1998. lib. bdg. 18.50 (1-56766-152-1) Childs World.

— Old MacDonald Had a Farm. (Toddler Bks.). 20p. (J). 1999. pap. text 4.95 (0-7641-0869-7) Barron.

***Dann, Penny.** Secret Fairy Boutique. (Illus.). 16p. (J). 2000. 14.95 (0-531-30308-X) Orchard Bks Watts.

Dann, Penny. Secret Fairy Handbook: Or How to Be a Little Fairy. (Illus.). 20p. (J). (ps-3). 1997. per. 14.95 (0-689-81458-5) Litle Simon.

— The Secret Fairy Party Book: Or How to Have Your Own Secret Fairy Party. LC 98-68245. (Illus.). 16p. (J). (ps up). 1999. 14.95 (0-531-30183-4) Orchard Bks Watts.

— The Secret Mermaid Handbook: or How to Be a Little Mermaid. (Illus.). 20p. (J). (ps-3). 1998. per. 14.95 (0-689-82255-3) S&S Childrens.

***Dann, Penny.** The Wheels on the Bus. (Toddler Bks.). (Illus.). 20p. (J). 1999. pap. 4.95 (0-7641-0856-5) Barron.

***Dann, Penny.** Josh B'Gosh & the Doctor. 10p. (J). 1998. 5.99 (1-929174-09-8) Oshkosh BGosh.

— Learn How to Share with Josh B'Gosh. 10p. 1998. 5.99 (1-929174-06-3) Oshkosh BGosh.

Dann, Penny. A Little Book of Courage. LC 93-6640. (Quotations for Kids Ser.). 32p. (J). (gr. 1-8). 1994. lib. bdg. 18.50 (1-56766-094-0) Childs World.

— A Little Book of Friendship. LC 93-12918. (Quotations for Kids Ser.). 32p. (J). (gr. 1-8). 1994. lib. bdg. 18.50 (1-56766-095-9) Childs World.

Dann, Peter L., ed. Advances in Computer-Based Human Assessment. (C). 1991. lib. bdg. 201.00 (0-7923-1071-3) Kluwer Academic.

Dann, Richard. F4F Wildcat Walkaround. (Walk Around Ser.). (Illus.). 80p. 1995. pap. 14.95 (0-89747-347-7) Squad Sig Pubns.

— Grumman Biplanes in Action. LC 96-143636. (Aircraft in Action Ser.). (Illus.). 50p. 1996. pap. 9.95 (0-89747-353-1) Squad Sig Pubns.

***Dann, Richard S.** UH-60 Black Hawk Walk Around. (Walk Around Ser.: Vol. 19). (Illus.). 80p. 1999. pap. 14.85 (0-89747-405-8) Squad Sig Pubns.

Dann, Ruth, jt. ed. see Barber, Michael.

Dann, Sam, ed. The Twenty-Ninth Day of April 1945. LC 98-13755. (Illus.). 278p. 1998. 29.95 (0-89672-391-7) Tex Tech Univ Pr.

***Dann, Sarah & Crossingham, John.** Baseball in Action. LC 99-38037. (Sports in Action Ser.). (Illus.). 32p. (J). (gr. 1-4). 1999. pap. 5.95 (0-7787-0175-1); lib. bdg. 19.96 (0-7787-0163-8) Crabtree Pub Co.

Dann, Sarah, jt. auth. see Crossingham, John.

Dann, Sarah, jt. auth. see Walker, Niki.

Dann, Uriel. Hanover & Britain, 1740-1760. 288p. 1991. text 65.00 (0-7185-1352-5) St Martin.

— Hanover & Britain, 1740-1760. 184p. 1993. pap. 17.95 (0-7185-1489-0) St Martin.

— King Hussein & the Challenge of Arab Radicalism: Jordan, 1955-1967. (Studies in Middle Eastern History). 224p. 1991. reprint ed. pap. text 24.95 (0-19-507134-4) OUP.

— King Hussein's Strategy of Survival. LC 92-9685. (Policy Papers: No. 29). 1992. pap. 8.00 (0-944029-17-5) Wash Inst NEP.

Dann, Uriel, ed. The Great Powers in the Middle East, 1919-1939: Regional Politics in Their Global Context. LC 87-16103. 464p. 1988. 75.00 (0-8419-0875-3) Holmes & Meier.

Danna, A. R. & Kritz, Arnold H. Introduction to Problem Solving. (Illus.). 368p. (Orig.). 1986. pap. text 18.95 (0-938069-00-4) Lyn-Bar Pub.

Danna, Carl, ed. see Danna, Jo.

Danna, Jo. Starting Over: You in the New Workplace. rev. ed. LC 90-6119. (Illus.). 272p. (Orig.). 1990. pap. 12.95 (0-9610036-3-4) Palomino Pr.

— When Alzheimer's Hits Home. Danna, Carl, ed. LC 94-65719. (Illus.). 208p. (Orig.). 1995. pap. 14.95 (0-9610036-4-2) Palomino Pr.

— Winning the Job Interview Game: Tips for the High-Tech Era. LC 85-61451. (Illus.). 223p. (Orig.). 1986. pap. 10.95 (0-9610036-2-6) Palomino Pr.

***D'anna, Lynnette.** Fool's Bells. 176p. 2000. pap. 15.99 (1-895837-90-1) Insomniac.

D'anna, Lynnette. RagTimeBone. 186p. 1994. pap. 12.00 (0-921586-37-X, Pub. by New Star Bks) Genl Dist Srvs.

Danna, Mark. Great Word Search Puzzles for Kids. 1999. pap. text 4.95 (0-8069-2469-1) Sterling.

— Word Search Puzzles for Kids. 1999. pap. text 4.95 (0-8069-6557-6) Sterling.

Danna, Minta. Internal Medicine Words: Over 8000 Words, Terms, & Quick Definitions. Bowen, Pat, ed. 288p. (Orig.). 1997. pap. 29.95 (1-877810-68-1, IMW) Rayve Prodns.

Danna, Sammy R., ed. Advertising & Popular Culture: Studies in Variety & Versatility. LC 91-77257. (Illus.). 180p. (C). 1992. 29.95 (0-87972-527-3); pap. 14.95 (0-87972-528-1) Bowling Green Univ Popular Press.

Danna, Theresa M. Rollover, Mona Lisa! How Anyone Can Model for Artists. LC 91-77256. (Illus.). 64p. 1992. pap. 6.95 (0-9631074-0-2) T M Danna.

Dannatt, Adrian. United States Holocaust Memorial Museum: Washington DC, 1993. (Architecture in Detail Ser.). (Illus.). 60p. 1995. pap. 29.95 (0-7148-2939-0, Pub. by Phaidon Press) Phaidon Pr.

Danne, E. C. Some Aspects of Selecting & Applying Gears for Rolling Mill Equipment. (Technical Papers: Vol. P109.06). (Illus.). 14p. 1950. pap. text 30.00 (1-55589-388-0) AGMA.

Danne, Thomas & Weber, Bruno, eds. Quality Control of Diabetes Care & Chronic Compications in Young People after St. Vincent & Kos: 4th International Workshop "Diabetic Angiopathy in Children (DAC)", Berlin, September 4 - 6, 1997. (Hormone Research Ser.: Vol. 50, Suppl. 1). (Illus.). vi, 108p. 1998. pap. 48.75 (3-8055-6720-0) S Karger.

***Danneberg, Julie.** First Day Jitters. LC 99-50095. (Illus.). 32p. (J). (gr. k-4). 2000. 16.95 (1-58089-054-7, Whispering Coyote); pap. 6.95 (1-58089-061-X, Whispering Coyote) Charlesbridge Pub.

— First Day Jitters. (Illus.). (J). 2000. 12.40 (0-606-18748-0) Turtleback.

Danneberg, Julie. Margaret's Magnificent Colorado Adventure. LC 98-31232. (Illus.). 48p. (J). (gr. 4-7). 1999. pap. 14.95 (1-56579-329-3) Westcliffe Pubs.

Danneberger, T. Karl. Turfgrass Ecology & Management. Code, Cindy, ed. LC 93-78045. 201p. (C). 1993. 28.00 (1-883751-00-4) GIE Media.

Dannecker, Martin. Theories of Homosexuality. 1995. per. 3.95 (0-907040-05-5, Pub. by Gay Mens Pr) LPC InBook.

Danneels, Godfred. Christ or Aquinas? Exploring the New Age Movement. 53p. 1991. 3.95 (0-85390-109-0, Pub. by Veritas Pubns) St Mut.

Danneels, Godfried C. Words of Life. O'Connell, Matthew J., tr. from FRE. LC 91-62600. 224p. (Orig.). 1991. pap. 9.95 (1-55612-313-2) Sheed & Ward WI.

Dannehl, Adolf. Technical Dictionary of Railroads: Technik-Woerterbuch Eisenbahn. (ENG, FRE, GER & RUS.). 400p. 1983. 125.00 (0-8288-2373-1, M15065) Fr & Eur.

Dannehl, Charles. Politics, Trade & Development: Soviet Economic Aid to the Non-Communist Third World 1955-89. (Illus.). 150p. 1995. text 72.95 (1-85521-658-2, Pub. by Dartmth Pub) Ashgate Pub Co.

***Dannel, Kathy.** French Bulldog: An Owner's Guide to a Happy Healthy Pet. LC 00-35054. (Guide to a Happy Healthy Pet Ser.). (Illus.). 160p. 2000. write for info. (1-58245-163-X) Howell Bks.

Dannelley, Richard. Sedona - Beyond the Vortex: The Power of the Vortex, Sacred Geometry & the Merkba. (Sedona Ser.: Bk. 3). (Illus.). 128p. (Orig.). 1995. pap. 12.00 (0-9629453-7-4) Vortex Society.

— Sedona Power Spot, Vortex & Medicine Wheel Guide. (Illus.). 112p. 1991. pap. 11.00 (0-9629453-2-3) Vortex Society.

***Dannelley, Richard.** Sedona Vortex 2000. 2000. pap. text 12.00 (0-9629453-1-5) Vortex Society.

Dannells, Michael. From Discipline to Development: Rethinking Student Conduct in Higher Education. Fife, Jonathan D., ed. LC 96-79498. (ASHE-ERIC Higher Education Reports: No. 25-2). 114p. 1995. pap. 24.00 (1-878380-74-5, 95-8) GWU Grad Schl E&HD.

***Dannells, Michael & Stage, Frances K.** Linking Theory to Practice: Case Studies for Working with College Students. 2nd ed. LC 99-57551. (C). 2000. 29.95 (1-56032-865-7) Taylor & Francis.

Dannemann, Gerhard & Meyding, Thomas. An Introduction to German Civil & Commercial Law. 168p. 1993. pap. 75.00 (0-903067-35-8, Pub. by Brit Inst ICL) St Mut.

Dannemann, Silke, ed. JSD Conference Index in Economics & Finance Vol. 1, No. 1: Winter 1995. 140p. (Orig.). (C). pap. text 195.00 (1-886487-50-2) JSD Info Srvs.

Dannemeyer, William. Shadow in the Land: Homosexuality in America. LC 89-80470. 243p. 1989. pap. text 9.95 (0-89870-241-0) Ignatius Pr.

***Dannemiller Tyson Associates Staff.** Whole-Scale Change: Unleashing the Magic in Organizations. 280p. 2000. pap. 44.95 (1-57675-088-4, Pub. by Berrett-Koehler) Publishers Group.

— Whole-Scale Change Toolkit: Unleashing the Magic in Organizations. 280p. 2000. pap. 44.95 (1-57675-089-2, Pub. by Berrett-Koehler) Publishers Group.

Dannen, Donna, jt. auth. see Dannen, Kent.

***Dannen, Frederic & Long, Barry.** Hong Kong Babylon: An Insider's Guide to the Hollywood of the East. (Illus.). 416p. (J). 1998. pap. 12.45 (0-7868-8359-6, Pub. by Hyperion) Time Warner.

Dannen, Fredric. Hit Men: Power Brokers & Fast Money Inside the Music Business. LC 90-55680. (Illus.). 400p. 1991. pap. 16.00 (0-679-73061-3) Vin Bks.

Dannen, Kent & Dannen, Donna. Colorado Rocky Mountain Country. 18.50 (0-528-81121-5) Rand McNally.

Dannen, Kent & Dannen, Donna. Hiking Rocky Mountain National Park: Including Indian Peaks. 8th ed. LC 94-855. (Hiking & Nature Walks Guides Ser.). (Illus.). 288p. 1994. pap. 12.95 (1-56440-375-0) Globe Pequot.

— National Parks of the Rocky Mountains: Rocky Mountain, Grand Teton, Yellowstone, Glacier-Waterton Lakes. (Illus.). 120p. 1986. 14.95 (0-930487-20-6) Rocky Mtn Nature Assn.

— Rocky Mountain Wildflowers. LC 81-7439. (Illus.). 64p. (Orig.). 1981. pap. 5.95 (0-9606768-0-5) Tundra Pubns.

— Short Hikes in Rocky Mountain National Park. Orig. Title: Walks With Nature in Rocky Mountain National Park. (Illus.). 64p. (Orig.). 1986. reprint ed. pap. 5.95 (0-9606768-1-3) Tundra Pubns.

Dannen, Kent & Mills, Enos. The Story of Scotch with Supplementary Chapters by Kent Dannen. LC 98-9772. (Illus.). 144p. 1998. pap. 12.95 (1-57779-006-5) Alpine Pubns.

Dannenbauer, Heinrich, jt. auth. see Haller, Johannes.

Dannenbaum, Christine & Schill, Rainer. Die Entwicklung der Pollentetraden und Pollinien Bei Den Asclepiadaceae. (Bibliotheca Botanica: Vol. 141). (GER., Illus.). viii, 138p. 1991. 110.00 (3-510-48012-0, Pub. by E Schweizerbartsche) Balogh.

Dannenbaum, George. Boom to Bust: Remembrances of the Grants, New Mexico Uranium Boom. (Illus.). 224p. 1995. pap. 19.95 (1-880047-28-4) Creative Des.

Dannenbaum, Jed. Drink & Disorder: Temperance Reform in Cincinnati from the Washingtonian Revival to the WCTU. LC 83-3671. (Illus.). 260p. 1984. text 27.50 (0-252-01055-8) U of Ill Pr.

Dannenbaum, Julie. Fast & Fresh Cookbook. 1994. 12.98 (0-88365-847-X) Galahad Bks.

Dannenberg, Andrew J., jt. auth. see Zakim, David.

Dannenberg, H. D., ed. Schweinekrankheiten. (Illus.). 400p. 1987. 43.50 (3-8055-4547-9) S Karger.

Dannenberg, Konrad, ed. see Freeman, Marsha.

Dannenberg, Linda. French Tarts: 50 Savory & Sweet Recipes. LC 96-47965. (Illus.). 128p. 1997. 19.95 (1-885183-39-9) Artisan.

— Paris Bistro Cooking. (Illus.). 160p. 1991. 35.00 (0-517-57433-0) C Potter.

— Paris Boulangerie Cookbook. LC 93-36414. (Illus.). 160p. 1994. 35.00 (0-517-59221-5) Crown Pub Group.

***Dannenberg, Linda.** Perfect Vinaigrettes: Appetizer to Desserts. LC 99-16263. (Illus.). 112p. 1999. text 19.95 (1-55670-943-9) Stewart Tabori & Chang.

Dannenberg, Linda, jt. auth. see Ducasse, Alain.

Dannenfeldt, Karl H. Leonhard Rauwolf: Sixteenth-Century Physician, Botanist, & Traveler. LC 68-15634. (Monographs in the History of Science). (Illus.). 329p. 1968. 29.95 (0-674-52500-0) HUP.

Dannenfeldt, Karl H., ed. The Renaissance: Basic Interpretations. 2nd ed. (Problems in European Civilization Ser.). 220p. (C). 1974. pap. text 18.36 (0-669-90530-5) HM Trade Div.

Dannenmaier, Molly. A Child's Garden. LC 97-29057. 1998. 35.00 (0-684-83725-0) S&S Trade.

— Child's Garden. 1998. 35.00 (0-676-57282-0) Random Bks Yng Read.

Dannenmaier, William D. We Were Innocents: An Infantryman in Korea. LC 98-25403. 1999. 26.95 (0-252-02449-4) U of Ill Pr.

***Dannenmaier, William D.** We Were Innocents: An Infantryman in Korea. 248p. 2000. reprint ed. pap. 18.95 (0-252-06926-9) U of Ill Pr.

Danner. Modern Legal Research. 1996. text 26.36 (0-256-16485-1) McGraw.

Danner, Henry F. Roman Law Pleading: An Outline of Its Historical Growth & General Principles. 63p. 1983. reprint ed. 25.00 (0-8377-0519-3, Rothman) W S Hein.

Danner, Dan G. Pilgrimage to Puritanism: History & Theology of the Marian Exiles at Geneva, 1555-1560. LC 97-26602. (Studies in Church History: Vol. 9). 168p. (C). 1999. text 42.95 (0-8204-3884-7) P Lang Pubng.

Danner, Dauber. 1997 Core Release Supplement 8: 76 Chemicals. 440p. 1998. ring bd. 160.00 (1-56032-766-9) Hemisp Pub.

Danner, David L., jt. auth. see Mundel, Marvin E.

Danner, Dorothy S. What a Way to Spend a War: Navy Nurse POWs in the Philippines. LC 95-35862. (Illus.). 230p. 1995. 28.95 (1-55750-154-8) Naval Inst Pr.

— What a Way to Spend a War: Navy Nurse POWs in the Philippines. large type ed. LC 96-44456. 1997. pap. 21.95 (0-7838-2021-6, G K Hall Lrg Type) Mac Lib Ref.

Danner, Douglas. Medical Malpractice: Checklists & Discoveries. 3rd ed. LC 85-81408. 1994. ring bd. 350.00 (0-685-59893-4) West Group.

— Pattern Disc Product Liability. 3rd ed. LC 94-80029. 1995. ring bd. 270.00 (0-685-59895-0) West Group.

— Pattern Discovery Motor Vehicles, 2 vols. 3rd ed. LC 84-82253. 1994. ring bd. 245.00 (0-685-59892-6) West Group.

— Pattern Discovery Premises Liability. 2nd ed. LC 86-80670. 1986. 98.00 (0-685-59894-2) West Group.

— Pattern Discovery Tort Actions. 3rd ed. LC 86-82354. 1994. ring bd. 245.00 (0-685-59896-9) West Group.

Danner, Douglas & Toothman, John W. Trial Practice Checklists. LC 89-85093. 1990. 95.00 (0-317-01808-6) West Group.

— Trial Practice Checklists. LC 89-85093. 1993. suppl. ed. 45.00 (0-317-01809-4) West Group.

Danner, Douglas & Varn, Larry L. Expert Witness Checklists. 2nd ed. LC 93-77154. 1993. 160.00 (0-686-40192-1) West Group.

— Pattern Deposition Checklists. 3rd ed. LC 93-77906. 1993. 160.00 (0-318-02978-2) West Group.

Danner, Fred, jt. ed. see Worell, Judith.

Danner, Horace G. & Noel, Roger. Discover It! A Better Vocabulary, the Better Way. Date not set. pap. 29.95 (0-937600-01-6) Imprimis.

— A Thesaurus of Word Roots of the English Language. 788p. (Orig.). (C). 1992. lib. bdg. 75.00 (0-8191-8666-X) U Pr of Amer.

Danner, J. D. Danner. History of the Danner Family: Jacob Danner & His Four Sons, George, Samuel, Frederick & Jacob, Jr. (Illus.). 28p. 1997. reprint ed. pap. 6.00 (0-8328-8210-0); reprint ed. lib. bdg. 16.00 (0-8328-8209-7) Higginson Bk Co.

Danner, J. D. & Danner, Rose C. Carver - Danner: History of Christian Carver & Frederick Danner & Their Descentants. (Illus.). 47p. 1997. reprint ed. pap. 9.50 (0-8328-7878-2); reprint ed. lib. bdg. 19.50 (0-8328-7877-4) Higginson Bk Co.

Danner, John. Old Landmarks of Conton & Stark County, Ohio, 2 vols., Set. (Illus.). 1511p. 1994. reprint ed. lib. bdg. 150.00 (0-8328-4363-6) Higginson Bk Co.

D

An Asterisk (*) at the beginning of an entry indicates that the title is appearing for the first time.

Danner, Karen E. & Kurasaki, Karen S., eds. Prevention & School Transitions. LC 93-33337. (Prevention in Human Services Ser.). (Illus.). 222p. 1994. lib. bdg. 39.95 (*1-56024-576-X*) Haworth Pr.

***Danner-Kuhn, Cyndi.** Adobe Photoshop 5: Student Text. (Computer Applications Ser.). 2000. 36.95 (*0-538-69550-1*) S-W Pub.

Danner, Mark. The Massacre of El Mozote: A Parable of the Cold War. LC 94-2637. 1994. pap. 13.00 (*0-679-75525-X*) Vin Bks.

Danner, Mary A., tr. see Al-Iskandari, Ibn A.

Danner, Peter, ed. see Larsson, Jytte T.

Danner, Peter L. An Ethics for the Affluent. LC 80-5528. 424p. 1980. lib. bdg. 59.00 (*0-8191-1163-5*) U Pr of Amer.

— Getting & Spending: A Primer in Economic Morality. LC 93-40686. 264p. (Orig.). 1994. pap. 15.95 (*1-55612-552-6*) Sheed & Ward WI.

Danner, R. P., jt. auth. see Daubert, T. E.

Danner, R. P., jt. auth. see Myers, K. H.

Danner, Richard A. Strategic Planning: A Law Library Management Tool for the 90's & Beyond. 2nd ed. LC 96-29606. (Law Library Information Reports: Vol. 11). 67p. 1996. pap. 50.00 (*0-87802-110-8*) Glanville.

Danner, Richard A., ed. see American Association of Law Libraries Staff.

Danner, Ronald P. & High, Martin S. Handbook of Polymer Solution Thermodynamics. LC 92-38224. 1993. 125.00 (*0-8169-0579-7*) Am Inst Chem Eng.

Danner, Rose C., jt. auth. see Danner, J. D.

Danner, Victor & Thackston, Wheeler M. Ibn 'Ata Illah-Kwaja Abdullah Ansari: The Book of Wisdom-Intimate Conversations. LC 78-1022. (Classics of Western Spirituality Ser.). 256p. 1997. reprint ed. pap. 19.95 (*0-8091-2182-4*) Paulist Pr.

Danneskiold-Samsoe, Bente & Lund, Birger, eds. Musculoskeletal Pain, Myofascial Pain Syndrome, & the Fibromyalgia Syndrome: Proceedings from the Second World Congress on Myofascial Pain & Fibromyalgia. LC 93-30041. (Journal of Musculoskeletal Pain: Vol. 1, Nos. 3-4). (Illus.). 334p. 1993. pap. text 49.95 (*1-56024-508-5*); lib. bdg. 89.95 (*1-56024-485-2*) Haworth Pr.

Dannhaeuser, Norbert. Two Towns in Germany: Commerce & the Urban Transformation. LC 95-40690. (Contemporary Urban Studies). 328p. 1996. 69.50 (*0-89789-458-8*, Bergin & Garvey) Greenwood.

Dannhaus, Diane. My Mom, the Professional. (Illus.). 24p. (Orig.). (J). (gr. k-4). 1994. pap. 7.95 (*0-89896-104-1*) Larksdale.

Dannhauser, A. Teoria de la Musica Spanish: Nueva Edicion. (SPA.). 128p. 1986. per. 12.95 (*0-7935-5537-X*, 50326630) H Leonard.

***Dannhauser, Carol Leonetti.** AOL Official Guide to Personal Finance & Investing Online. LC 99-48362. (Illus.). 528p. 2000. 24.99 (*0-7645-3427-0*) IDG Bks.

Dannhauss, Dianne. Big Brother, Big Sister, Big Deal. Bowen, Debbie, ed. LC 98-37863. (Professional Mom Ser.). (Illus.). 14p. (J). (gr. 1-4). 1998. lib. bdg. 12.95 (*1-56763-151-7*) Ozark Pub.

— The Day My Mom Almost Enrolled in Preschool. Bowen, Debbie, ed. LC 98-37898. (Professional Mom Ser.). (Illus.). 15p. (J). (gr. 1-4). 1998. lib. bdg. 12.95 (*1-56763-149-5*) Ozark Pub.

— My Mom the Professional. Bowen, Debbie, ed. LC 98-37897. (Professional Mom Ser.). (Illus.). 23p. (J). (gr. 1-4). 1998. lib. bdg. 12.95 (*1-56763-147-9*) Ozark Pub.

Dannheisser, Ilana & Edwards, Penny. Homeopathy. LC 98-22373. (Illustrated Guide Ser.). (Illus.). 144p. 1998. pap. 19.95 (*1-86204-168-7*, Pub. by Element MA) Penguin Putnam.

Dannin, Ellen J. Working Free: New Zealand's Employment Contracts Act. LC 98-144023. 264p. 1997. pap. 27.95 (*1-86940-174-3*, Pub. by Auckland Univ) Paul & Co Pubs.

Danninger, Breant. Hedonic Damages: 1991 Supplement. 44p. 1991. pap. write for info. (*0-87473-786-9*, 65730-10, MICHIE) LEXIS Pub.

Danninger, Brent B. Hedonic Damages: Proving Damages for Lost Enjoyment of Living. 491p. 1990. 80.00 (*0-87473-647-1*, 65729-10, MICHIE) LEXIS Pub.

Dannis, Joe, jt. auth. see Bahan, Ben.

Dannon, Ann. I Am a Woman. Katz, Jonathan N., ed. LC 75-13750. (Homosexuality Ser.). 1975. reprint ed. 17.95 (*0-405-07406-9*) Ayer.

— Journey to a Woman. Katz, Jonathan N., ed. LC 75-13752. (Homosexuality Ser.). 1975. reprint ed. 15.95 (*0-405-07408-5*) Ayer.

— Odd Girl Out. Katz, Jonathan N., ed. LC 75-13735. (Homosexuality Ser.). 1975. reprint ed. 17.95 (*0-405-07405-0*) Ayer.

— Women in the Shadows. Katz, Jonathan N., ed. LC 75-13751. (Homosexuality Ser.). 1975. reprint ed. 11.95 (*0-405-07407-7*) Ayer.

Danns, George. Domination & the Power in Guyana: A Study of the Police in a Third World Context. LC 80-19179. 275p. 1982. 39.95 (*0-87855-418-1*) Transaction Pubs.

D'Annunzio, Gabriele. The Child of Pleasure. Harding, G., tr. from ITA. LC 89-26950. 311p. 1990. reprint ed. lib. bdg. 25.00 (*0-86527-396-0*) Fertig.

— The Child of Pleasure. 2nd ed. Harding, Georgina, tr. from ITA. (Decadence Ser.). 311p. 1999. reprint ed. pap. 11.95 (*0-946626-60-X*, Pub. by Dedalus) Hippocrene Bks.

— Daughter of Jorio: A Pastoral Tragedy. Porter, Charlotte et al, trs. LC 69-10064. 208p. 1968. reprint ed. lib. bdg. 59.50 (*0-8371-0005-4*, DADJ, Greenwood Pr) Greenwood.

***D'Annunzio, Gabriele.** Flame. 312p. 1999. pap. text 14.95 (*1-56886-062-5*, Pub. by Marsilio Pubs) Consort Bk Sales.

D'Annunzio, Gabriele. The Flame of Life. Vivarias, K., tr. from ITA. 403p. 1990. reprint ed. lib. bdg. 40.00 (*0-86527-250-6*) Fertig.

— Gabriele D'Annunzio: International Naval Disarmament Conference at Washington & Geneva, Nov. 1921-April 1922. 1930. 15.00 (*0-913298-58-1*) S F Vanni.

— Gioconda. Symons, Arthur, tr. from ITA. LC 87-38137. viii, 144p. 1989. reprint ed. lib. bdg. 29.50 (*0-86527-382-0*) Fertig.

— L' Innocente (The Victim) 2nd ed. Harding, Georgina, tr. from ITA. (Decadence Ser.). 333p. 1997. reprint ed. pap. 14.95 (*0-946626-64-2*, Pub. by Dedalus) Subterranean Co.

— Tales of My Native Town. Mantellini, Rafael, tr. LC 69-10065. 287p. 1968. reprint ed. lib. bdg. 65.00 (*0-8371-0056-9*, DANT, Greenwood Pr) Greenwood.

— The Triumph of Death. 2nd ed. Harding, Georgina, tr. (Decadence Ser.). 320p. 1999. reprint ed. pap. 11.95 (*0-946626-62-6*, Pub. by Dedalus) Hippocrene Bks.

Danny-Moebs. University Physics Vol. 1. 1995. (*0-697-36283-3*, WCB McGr Hill) McGrw-H Hghr Educ.

Dano, Helen M. The Little Makana. LC 94-77956. (Illus.). 32p. (J). (gr. k-3). 1994. 8.95 (*1-880188-93-7*) Bess Pr.

Dano, Linda & Kyle, Anne. Living Great: Style Expert & Television Star Linda Dano Shows You How to Bring Style Home with Her Easy, Affordable Decorating Ideas & Techniques. 224p. 1999. pap. 16.95 (*0-399-52484-3*, Perigee Bks) Berkley Pub.

— Looking Great... (Illus.). 208p. 1998. pap. 15.00 (*0-399-52387-1*, Perigee Bks) Berkley Pub.

Dano, S. Linear Programming in Industry, Theory & Applications: An Introduction. rev. ed. LC 73-13172. (Illus.). 180p. 1974. 39.95 (*0-387-81189-3*) Spr-Verlag.

Danoff, I. Michael. Art at Work. 20p. 1997. pap. 10.00 (*1-879003-18-X*) Edmundson.

Danoff, I. Michael. Contemplation: Five Installations. LC 96-85998. (Illus.). 39p. 1996. pap. 22.00 (*1-879003-16-3*) Edmundson.

— Richard Fleischner Critical Distance. (Illus.). 39p. 1992. pap. 16.00 (*1-879003-04-X*) Edmundson.

Danoff, I. Michael & Day, Holliday T. Iowa Artists, 1992. (Illus.). 59p. 1992. pap. 8.00 (*1-879003-05-8*) Edmundson.

Danoff, I. Michael & Farber, Janet L. Iowa Artists, 1996. (Illus.). 60p. 1996. pap. 15.00 (*1-879003-13-9*) Edmundson.

Danoff, I. Michael & Grachos, Louis. Iowa Artists 1997. 72p. 1997. pap. 12.00 (*1-879003-17-1*) Edmundson.

Danoff, I. Michael & Leveton, Deborah. Iowa Artists, 1995. (Illus.). 48p. 1995. pap. 10.00 (*1-879003-12-0*) Edmundson.

Danoff, I. Michael & Rowe, M. Jessica. Mary Miss Photo/Drawings. (Illus.). 31p. 1996. pap. 15.00 (*1-879003-15-5*) Edmundson.

Danoff, I. Michael, et al. Peter Halley: Paintings, 1989-92. LC 92-74506. (Illus.). 30p. (Orig.). 1992. pap. 20.00 (*1-879003-08-2*) Edmundson.

Danoff, I. Michael, jt. auth. see Leveton, Deborah.

Danoff, I. Michael, jt. auth. see Noun, Louise.

Danoff, I. Michael, jt. auth. see Torrence, Gaylord.

Danoff, Judith, et al. Open for Children: For Those Interested in Early Childhood Education. (Illus.). 225p. (C). 1991. pap. text 21.95 (*0-87411-482-9*) Copley Pub.

Danon, Jacques, et al. An Introduction to Mossbauer Spectroscopy. May, Leopold, ed. LC 76-137011. (Illus.). 213p. 1971. reprint ed. pap. 66.10 (*0-608-05459-3*, 206592800006) Bks Demand.

Danon, Ruth. Triangulation from a Known Point. 56p. 1990. 16.95 (*0-929654-97-8*); pap. 8.95 (*0-929654-93-5*) FoxRock.

Danon, Samuel, jt. auth. see Rosenberg, Samuel N.

Danon, Samuel, jt. tr. see Rosenberg, Samuel N.

Danon, Yehuda L. & Shemer, Joshua, eds. Chemical Warfare Medicine: Aspects & Perspectives from the Persian Gulf War. (Illus.). 228p. (C). 1994. text 95.00 (*965-229-103-X*, Pub. by Gefen Pub Hse) Gefen Bks.

Danopo, Constantine P., ed. see Magyar, Karl P.

Danopoulos, Constantine & Zirker, Daniel, eds. The Military & Society in the Former Eastern Bloc. LC 98-46210. 248p. 1998. 69.00 (*0-8133-3524-8*, Pub. by Westview) HarpC.

Danopoulos, Constantine P. & Watson, Cynthia, eds. The Political Role of the Military: An International Handbook. LC 95-46134. 536p. 1996. lib. bdg. 125.00 (*0-313-28837-2*, Greenwood Pr) Greenwood.

Danopoulos, Constantine P. & Zirker, Daniel G., eds. Civil-Military Relations in the Soviet & Yugoslav Successor States. 312p. (C). 1996. pap. 75.00 (*0-8133-8846-5*, Pub. by Westview) HarpC.

Danos, M. & Gillet, V. Angular Momentum Calculus in Quantum Physics. 176p. 1990. text 36.00 (*981-02-0412-4*) World Scientific Pub.

Danos, Paul. Introduction to Financial Accounting. 2nd ed. 1993. pap. text, teacher ed. 22.00 (*0-256-12442-6*) McGraw.

Danos, Paul & Imhoff, Eugene. Introduction to Financial Accounting. 2nd ed. (C). 1999. text, student ed. 75.95 (*0-256-17744-9*, Irwn McGrw-H) McGrw-H Hghr Educ.

Danov, Christo. Alttrakien. LC 73-75484. (C). 1976. 203.85 (*3-11-003434-4*) De Gruyter.

Danove, Paul L. The End of Mark's Story: A Methodological Study. LC 93-200. (Biblical Interpretation Ser.: Vol. 3). x, 293p. 1993. 92.00 (*90-04-09717-1*) Brill Academic Pubs.

Danovich, Mike, ed. see Singh, Swayam P.

Danovitch, Gabriel M. Handbook of Kidney Transplantation. 3rd ed. 400p. pap. text. write for info. (*0-7817-2066-4*) Lppncott W & W.

Danovitch, Gabriel M., ed. Handbook of Kidney Transplantation. 2nd ed. LC 96-16796. 512p. 1996. pap. text 43.00 (*0-316-17276-6*) Lppncott W & W.

Danovitz, Gloria, jt. auth. see Stern, Stacy.

Danow, David. Models of Narrative. LC 96-34402. 240p. 1996. text 39.95 (*0-312-16388-6*) St Martin.

Danow, David K. The Dialogic Sign: Essays on the Major Novels of Dostojefsky. LC 91-33847. (Studies in Russian Language & Literature). 219p. (C). 1992. text 42.95 (*0-8204-1628-2*) P Lang Pubng.

— The Spirit of Carnival: Magical Realism & the Grotesque. 192p. 1995. text 25.95 (*0-8131-1905-7*) U Pr of Ky.

— The Thought of Mikhail Bakhtin: From Word to Culture. LC 90-46988. 110p. 1991. pap. 16.95 (*0-312-05609-5*) St Martin.

***Danowski, Debbie & Lazaro, Pedro.** Why Can't I Stop Eating? Recognizing, Understanding & Overcoming Food Addiction. LC 99-86746. 350p. 2000. pap. 15.00 (*1-56838-365-7*) Hazelden.

Danowski, Michael P., jt. auth. see Chin, Wanda.

Danquah, Francis K. Cocoa Diseases & Politics in Ghana, 1909-1966, Vol. 143. LC 93-34296. (American University Studies: Series IX). XIII, 189p. (C). 1995. text 39.95 (*0-8204-2190-1*) P Lang Pubng.

Danquah, Meri N. Willow Weep for Me: A Black Woman's Journey Through Depression. LC 97-20515. 272p. 1998. 23.95 (*0-393-04567-6*) Norton.

Danquah, Meri N., ed. Becoming American: Personal Essays by First Generation Immigrant Women. LC 99-37345. 256p. 2000. text 22.95 (*0-7868-6589-X*, Pub. by Hyperion) Time Warner.

Danquah, Meri Nana-Ama. Willow Weep for Me: A Black Woman's Journey Through Depression. 1999. pap. 12.95 (*0-345-43213-4*) Ballantine Pub Grp.

Danriquez, Alan R., ed. see O'Leary, Kathlene J.

***Dans, Peter E.** Doctors in the Movies: Boil the Water & Just Say Aah. (Illus.). 408p. 2000. 34.95 (*0-936741-14-7*) Medi-Ed Pr.

Dansby & Kaliski. College Accounting. 2nd ed. (Swc-Accounting Ser.). Date not set. mass mkt., student ed. 31.25 (*0-538-82030-6*) S-W Pub.

Dansby & Kaliski, Burton S. College Accounting: Working Papers Chapter 1-11. 3rd ed. (AB - Accounting Principles Ser.). 1995. 33.95 (*0-538-85697-1*) S-W Pub.

— College Accounting: Working Papers Chapter 1-11. 3rd ed. (AB - Accounting Principles Ser.). 1996. text, student ed. 19.95 (*0-538-85698-X*) S-W Pub.

Dansby, Lee Ann. Forever, My Knight. 385p. 1996. mass mkt. 6.99 (*1-57343-007-2*) LionHearted.

Dansby, Robert. Paradigm College Accounting: Annotated Instructor's Edition 1, 11. 3rd rev. ed. 59.95 (*0-7638-0037-6*) EMC-Paradigm.

Dansby, Robert & Kaliski, Burton S. Paradigm Peachtree Accounting. 192p. 16.95 (*0-7638-0200-X*) EMC-Paradigm.

Dansby, Robert L. Basic Business Math. 256p. (C). 1991. pap. text 48.00 (*0-13-060971-4*) P-H.

— Business Math Essentials. LC 99-25814. (Illus.). 535p. 1999. pap. text 38.00 (*0-13-079978-5*, Prentice Hall) P-H.

Dansby, Robert L. & Kaliski, Burton S. Paradigm College Accounting. 4th ed. LC 98-27081. 1999. text. write for info. (*0-7638-0160-7*) Paradigm MN.

Dansby, Robert L. & Lawrence, Michael D. Paradigm Cost Accounting: Principles & Applications. LC 97-25595. 1997. text. write for info. (*0-7638-0075-9*) Paradigm MN.

Dansby, Robert L., et al. Paradigm College Accounting: Annotated Instructor's Edition 1,29. 3rd ed. 79.95 (*0-7638-0036-8*) EMC-Paradigm.

— Paradigm College Accounting: Annotated Instructor's Edition 1,29. 4th ed. 79.95 (*0-7638-0161-5*) EMC-Paradigm.

— Paradigm College Accounting: Complete Text, Chapters 1,27. 3rd rev. ed. 962p. 49.75 (*0-7638-0033-3*) EMC-Paradigm.

— Paradigm College Accounting: Solutions Manual 1,29. 953p. 49.95 (*0-7638-0165-8*) EMC-Paradigm.

— Paradigm College Accounting: Study Guide & Working Papers. 4th ed. 564p. 24.95 (*0-7638-0162-3*) EMC-Paradigm.

— Paradigm College Accounting: Study Guide & Working Papers 1, 18. 4th ed. 747p. 24.95 (*0-7638-0163-1*) EMC-Paradigm.

— Paradigm College Accounting: Study Guide & Working Papers, 19 ,29. 339p. 20.95 (*0-7638-0164-X*) EMC-Paradigm.

— Paradigm College Accounting: Text, Chapters 1,11. 421p. 33.95 (*0-7638-0034-1*) EMC-Paradigm.

— Paradigm College Accounting: Text, Chapters 1,12. 4th ed. 457p. 35.95 (*0-7638-0157-7*) EMC-Paradigm.

— Paradigm College Accounting: Text, Charters 1, 18. 677p. 39.95 (*0-7638-0159-3*) EMC-Paradigm.

— Paradigm College Accounting: Text 1, 12 & Study Guide. 4th ed. 54.95 (*0-7638-0274-3*) EMC-Paradigm.

— Paradigm College Accounting: Text 1, 29 & Study Guide 1, 18. 4th ed. 73.90 (*0-7638-0276-X*) EMC-Paradigm.

— Paradigm College Accounting: Text 1,18 & Study Guide 1, 18. 4th ed. 59.95 (*0-7638-0275-1*) EMC-Paradigm.

— Paradigm QuickBooks Accounting. 192p. 16.95 (*0-7638-0202-6*) EMC-Paradigm.

Danse, Ilene R. Common Sense Toxics in the Workplace. 272p. 1991. text 55.95 (*0-442-00154-1*, VNR) Wiley.

Dansel, Michael. Fifty Best Memory Methods & Tests. 224p. 1996. pap. 19.95 (*0-572-02282-4*, Pub. by W Foulsham) Trans-Atl Phila.

Danserau, Fred & Yammarino, F. Leadership: The Multiple Levels Approaches, 2 pts., Set. (Monographs in Organizational Behavior: Vol. 24). 1998. 157.00 (*0-7623-0469-3*) Jai Pr.

Dansereau, Diane M. Dansereau Savoir Dire & Casset. LC 89-82765. (FRE.). 240p. (C). 1990. pap. text 65.16 (*0-669-21830-8*) HM Trade Div.

— Savoir Dire: Cours de Phonetique et de Prononciation. LC 89-82765. (FRE.). 240p. (C). 1990. pap. text 55.96 (*0-669-20996-1*); teacher ed. 51.16 (*0-669-20997-X*); 2.66 (*0-669-20999-6*); audio 31.16 (*0-669-20998-8*) HM Trade Div.

Dansereau, Fred & Yammarino, Francis J. Leadership: The Multiple-Level Approaches. LC 98-11695. (Monographs in Organizational Behavior & Industrial Relations Ser.: Vol. 24A). 1998. 78.50 (*0-7623-0503-7*) Jai Pr.

— Leadership: The Multiple-Level Approaches. LC 98-11695. (Monographs in Organizational Behavior & Industrial Relations Ser.: Vol. 24B). 1998. 78.50 (*0-7623-0504-5*) Jai Pr.

Dansereau, Fred, et al. Data Enquiry That Tests Entity & Correlational-Causal Theories. LC 86-7426. 365p. (Orig.). 1986. pap. 40.00 (*0-937719-00-5*) Inst Theory Test.

Dansereau, Michel. La Recherche de l'Objet d'Amour Perdu. (FRE.). 1998. write for info. (*2-89415-167-5*) Edits Meridien.

Dansereau, Pierre M. Biogeography: An Ecological Perspective. LC 57-6819. 408p. reprint ed. pap. 126.50 (*0-8357-7224-1*, 205630500056) Bks Demand.

Dansereau, Raymond J. Tomorrow's Mission: World War II Diary of a Combat Aircrewman Aboard the U. S. S. Yorktown (CV-10), the Fighting Lady, During the Pacific War 1943-1945. LC 97-68498. (Illus.). 1997. pap. 20.00 (*0-923687-43-2*) Celo Valley Bks.

Dansereau, Serge. Food & Friends: A Chef's Gastronomic Journey Through France & Italy. 220p. 1999. 45.00 (*0-7322-5949-5*, Pub. by HarpC) Consort Bk Sales.

***Dansereau, Serge.** Food & Friends: A Chef's Journey Through France & Italy. (Illus.). 288p. 2000. pap. 14.95 (*0-7322-6446-4*) HarpC.

Dansker, Edward. Integrated Engineering - Construction Projects: Proposal to Completion. LC 91-48038. (Illus.). 192p. 1992. 79.00 (*0-8155-1303-8*) Noyes.

Danskin, David G. & Crow, Mark A. Biofeedback: An Introduction & Guide. LC 80-84020. 116p. (Orig.). (C). 1981. pap. text 20.95 (*0-87484-530-0*, 530) Mayfield Pub.

Danskin, Elizabeth. Women's Gymnastics. (Hancock House Physical Education Ser.). (Illus.). 120p. (Orig.). (J). (gr. 12). 1983. pap., teacher ed. 14.95 (*0-88839-045-9*) Hancock House.

Danskin, J., tr. see Krein, S. G.

Danskin, J. M., tr. see Aleksandrov, A. D. & Zalgaller, V. A.

Danskin, J. M., tr. see Nikol'skii, S. M.

Dansky, Miriam. As Heard from Rabbi Wagschal. 1997. 18.95 (*1-58330-002-3*) Feldheim.

— Rebbetzin Grunfeld. 20.99 (*0-89906-119-2*, GRUH); pap. 17.99 (*0-89906-120-6*, GOIP) Mesorah Pubns.

Dansky, Richard. Buried Secretes: Wraith 2nd Screen & Book. 2nd ed. (Wruith Ser.). (Illus.). 72p. 1996. pap. 15.00 (*1-56504-603-X*, 6601) White Wolf.

— Clan Novel Lasombra. 288p. 1999. pap. 5.99 (*1-56504-807-5*) White Wolf.

— Guildbook: Puppeteers & Pardoners. (Wruith Ser.). (Illus.) (Orig.). 1997. pap. 18.00 (*1-56504-665-X*, 6304) White Wolf.

— Wraith: The Oblivion. 2nd ed. (Illus.). 272p. 1996. 28.00 (*1-56504-600-5*, 6600) White Wolf.

Dansky, Richard & Ditchburn, Elizabeth. Clanbook: LaSombra. (Vampire Ser.). (Illus.). 72p. (Orig.). 1996. pap., suppl. ed. 12.00 (*1-56504-211-5*, 2062) White Wolf.

Dansky, Richard & Fischi, Beth. Guildbook: Sandmen. (Wruith Ser.). 72p. 1996. pap. 12.00 (*1-56504-662-5*, 6301) White Wolf.

Dansky, Richard & Huang, Ed. Shadow Players Guide. (Wruith Ser.). (Illus.). 144p. (Orig.). 1997. pap. 18.00 (*1-56504-602-1*, 6013) White Wolf.

Dansky, Richard & White Wolf Publishing Staff, Wolf. Guildbook: Artificers. (Wruith Ser.). (Illus.). 72p. 1996. pap. 12.00 (*1-56504-661-7*, 6300) White Wolf.

Dansky, Richard, et al. Charnel Houses of Europe: The Shoah. (Wruith Ser.). (Illus.). 144p. (Orig.). 1997. pap. 15.00 (*1-56504-651-X*, 6903, Black Dog Game) White Wolf.

— Dark Kingdom of Jade Adventures. (Wruith Ser.). (Illus.). 96p. (Orig.). (YA). 1996. pap. 15.00 (*1-56504-617-X*, 6012) White Wolf.

— Giovanni Chronicles No. II: Blood & Fire. (Vampire Ser.). (Illus.). 96p. (Orig.). 1996. pap. 18.00 (*1-56504-251-4*, 2091) White Wolf.

Dansky, Richard, jt. auth. see Baugh, Bruce.

Dansky, Richard, jt. auth. see Lemke, Ian.

Dansky, Richard, jt. auth. see Summers, Cynthia.

Dansky, Richard E. Corax: Changing Breeds Book. (Werewolf Ser.). 1998. pap. text 15.00 (*1-56504-337-5*) White Wolf.

— Guide to the Camarilla. (Vampire Ser.). (Illus.). 224p. 1999. 25.95 (*1-56504-261-1*, 2302) White Wolf.

***Dansky, Richard E.** Last Supper Blood & Rite. 2000. pap. 17.95 (*1-56504-253-0*) White Wolf.

— Walking Dead. (Hunter Ser.). 2000. pap. 15.95 (*1-56504-741-9*) White Wolf.

Dansky, Richard E., jt. auth. see Achilli, Justin.

Dansky, Steven. Nobody's Children: Orphans of the HIV Epidemic. LC 96-48940. 1995. 39.95 (*1-56024-881-5*) Haworth Pr.

— Now Dare Everything: Tales of HIV-Related Psychotherapy. LC 92-48376. 1994. pap. 17.95 (*1-56023-037-1*, Harrington Park) Haworth Pr.

D

Dansky, Steven F. Nobody's Children: Orphans of the HIV Epidemic. LC 96-48940. 178p. 1997. 54.95 (1-56023-855-0, Harrington Park); pap. 14.95 (1-56023-923-9, Harrington Park) Haworth Pr.

— Now Dare Everything: Tales of HIV-Related Psychotherapy. LC 92-48376. (Illus.). 332p. 1994. lib. bdg. 49.95 (1-56024-398-8) Haworth Pr.

Danson, Andrew. Unofficial Portraits. 1988. pap. 24.95 (0-385-25143-2) Doubleday.

***Danson, Edwin.** Drawing the Line: How Mason & Dixon Surveyed the Most Famous Border in America. 224p. 2001. 22.95 (0-471-38502-6) Wiley.

Danson, F. Mark & Plummer, Stephen E., eds. Advances in Environmental Remote Sensing. 198p. 1995. 140.00 (0-471-95464-0) Wiley.

***Danson, Gia E. & Danson, Julianna A.** Sun Sand & Surf: The Ultimate Guide to Orange County Beaches. Collins, Richard J., ed. (Illus.). xi, 101p. 2000. pap. write for info. (0-9679452-0-8) Vista Pacif.

Danson, Julianna A., jt. auth. see Danson, Gia E.

Danson, Lawrence. Max Beerbohm & the Act of Writing. (Illus.). 276p. 1991. reprint ed. pap. text 22.00 (0-19-811227-0) OUP.

— Max Beerbohm & the Mirror of the Past. (Illus.). 96p. 1982. 15.00 (0-87811-031-3) Princeton Lib.

— On King Lear. LC 81-47120. 194p. reprint ed. pap. 60.20 (0-8357-3700-4, 203642400003) Bks Demand.

***Danson, Lawrence.** Shakespeare's Dramatic Genres. LC 99-48533. 168p. 2000. 39.95 (0-19-871173-5); 18.95 (0-19-871172-7) OUP.

Danson, Lawrence. Tragic Alphabet: Shakespeare's Drama of Language. LC 74-79902. 212p. reprint ed. pap. 65.80 (0-8357-8768-0, 203370200087) Bks Demand.

— Wilde's Intentions: The Artist in His Criticism. 208p. (C). 1997. text 49.95 (0-19-818375-5) OUP.

— Wilde's Intentions: The Artist in His Criticism. 208p. 1999. reprint ed. pap. text 18.95 (0-19-818628-2) OUP.

Danson, M. J., et al, eds. The Archaebacteria: Biochemistry & Biotechnology. (Biochemical Society Symposium Ser.: Vol. 58). 212p. 1992. 110.50 (1-85578-010-0, Pub. by Portland Pr Ltd) Ashgate Pub Co.

Danson, Margaret. SmartMoves for the SmartKid in All of Us. (Illus.). 88p. (Orig.). 1996. pap. write for info. (0-9651529-0-1) SmartMoves.

Danson, Michael J., jt. ed. see Eisenthal, Robert.

Danson, Michael W., ed. Small Firm Formation & Regional Economic Development. LC 95-34494. (Small Business Ser.). (Illus.). 272p. (C). 1996. 90.00 (0-415-12970-2) Routledge.

Danson, Michael W., et al. The Role of Regional Development Agencies in Economic Regeneration. (Regional Policy & Development Ser.: Vol. 1). 160p. 1993. 55.00 (1-85302-067-2) Taylor & Francis.

***Danson, Mike & Cameron, Greta, eds.** Governance, Institutional Change & Regional Development. LC 99-75457. (Urban & Regional Planning & Development Ser.). 278p. 2000. text 74.95 (0-7546-1125-6, Pub. by Ashgate Pub) Ashgate Pub Co.

Danson, S. Liaison Blindfold. 1997. mass mkt. 6.95 (0-7472-5583-0, Pub. by Headline Bk Pub) Trafalgar.

Danson, Sheryl. The Ranger Man. (Temptation Ser.). 1994. per. 2.99 (0-373-25603-5, 1-25603-1) Harlequin Bks.

— The Spy Who Loved Her. (Temptation Ser.). 1994. per. 2.99 (0-373-25579-9, 1-25579-3) Harlequin Bks.

Danson, Sophie. Moon of Desire. (Black Lace Ser.). 1995. mass mkt. 5.95 (0-352-32911-4, Pub. by Virgin Bks) London Brdge.

— The Silken Cage. (Black Lace Ser.). 1995. mass mkt. 5.95 (0-352-32928-9, Pub. by Virgin Bks) London Brdge.

***Danspeckgruber, Wolfgang, ed.** The Self-Determination of Peoples: Community, Nation, & State in an Interdependent World. 350p. 2000. pap. 22.50 (1-55587-793-1) L Rienner.

— The Self-Determination of Peoples: Community, Nation, & State in an Interdependent World. 350p. 2000. lib. bdg. 59.95 (1-55587-768-0) L Rienner.

Danspeckgruber, Wolfgang & Watts, Arthur, eds. Self-Determination & Self-Administration: A Sourcebook. LC 97-32069. 516p. 1997. lib. bdg. 110.00 (1-55587-786-9) L Rienner.

Danspeckgruber, Wolfgang F. & Tripp, Charles R., eds. The Iraqi Aggression Against Kuwait: Strategic Lessons & Implications for Europe. 344p. (C). 1996. text 85.00 (0-8133-8623-3, Pub. by Westview) HarpC.

Dant, Doris R., jt. ed. see Walker, Ronald W.

Dant, Doris R., jt. ed. see Welch, John W.

Dant, Rajiv P., jt. ed. see Kaufmann, Patrick J.

***Dant, Tim.** Material Culture in the Social World: Values, Activities, Lifestyles. LC 99-14375. 1999. pap. 24.95 (0-335-19821-X) OpUniv Pr.

***Danta, Darrick.** Yearbook of the Associated of Pacific Coast Geographers, No. 60. (Illus.). 218p. 1999. pap. 20.00 (0-9668754-1-9) Assoc of Pacific Coast.

Danta, Darrick, ed. Yearbook of the Association of Pacific Coast Geographers, Vol. 59. (Illus.). 200p. (Orig.). 1998. pap. 20.00 (0-9668754-0-0) Assoc of Pacific Coast.

Danta, Darrick, jt. ed. see Hall, Derek.

Dante Alighieri. Cantos from Dante's Inferno. Schwerner, Armand, tr. from ITA. LC 99-47639. 72p. 1999. 33.95 (1-883689-98-8, Pub. by Talisman Hse) LPC Group.

— The Canzoniere of Dante Alighieri. xxxvi, 467p. 1985. reprint ed. lib. bdg. 79.00 (0-7812-0560-3) Rprt Serv.

— The Complete Lyric Poems of Dante Alighieri. Cirigliano, Marc, ed. & tr. by. from ITA. LC 96-50199. (Studies in Italian Literature: Vol. 3). 352p. 1997. text 99.95 (0-7734-8694-1) E Mellen.

— Dante: Monarchy. Shaw, Prue, ed. (Cambridge Texts in the History of Political Thought Ser.). 169p. (C). 1996. text 44.95 (0-521-56120-5) Cambridge U Pr.

— Dante Alighieri's Divine Comedy: Verse Translation & Commentary, 2 vols., Set, Vols. 1 & 2. Musa, Mark, tr. & comment by. Incl. Vol. 1. Dante Alighieri's Divine Comedy: Italian Text & Translation. LC 96-12746. 352p. 1997. text (0-253-32968-X); Vol. 2. Dante Alighieri's Divine Comedy: Commentary. LC 96-12746. 470p. 1997. text (0-253-32967-1); LC 96-12746. (Indiana Masterpiece Editions Ser.). 1997. 89.95 (0-253-33214-1) Ind U Pr.

— Dante & the Early Italian Love Poets, 1 vol. 1999. pap. 9.50 (0-460-87641-4) J M Dent & Sons.

— Dante's Comedy. Kilmer, Nicholas, tr. from ITA. (Illus.). (C). 1985. pap. 9.95 (0-8283-1884-0) Branden Bks.

— Dante's Inferno. Kilmer, Nicholas, tr. from ITA. (Illus.). 1985. 19.50 (0-937832-28-6) Dante U Am.

***Dante Alighieri.** Dante's Inferno. Halpern, Daniel, ed. LC 92-28061. 1998. 24.95 (0-88001-291-9) HarpC.

Dante Alighieri. Dante's Inferno: The Indiana Critical Edition. Musa, Mark, ed. & tr. by. from ITA. LC 94-20237. (Indiana Masterpiece Editions Ser.). 432p. 1995. pap. 12.95 (0-253-20930-7); text 39.95 (0-253-33943-X) Ind U Pr.

***Dante Alighieri.** Dante's Lyric Poems. DiScipio, Giuseppe C., ed. Tusiani, Joseph, tr. (Italian Poetry in Translation Ser.: No. III). (ITA & ENG.). 244p. 1999. per. 16.00 (1-881901-18-1) LEGAS.

Dante Alighieri. Dante's Paradise. Musa, Mark, tr. from ITA. & comment by. LC 83-48828. (Illus.). 416p. 1984. 45.00 (0-253-31619-7) Ind U Pr.

— Dante's Purgatory. Musa, Mark, tr. & notes by. LC 80-8098. (Illus.). 384p. 1981. 39.95 (0-253-17926-2) Ind U Pr.

— Dante's Vita Nuova: A Translation & an Essay. Musa, Mark, tr. from ITA. LC 72-79905. 224p. 1973. pap. 12.95 (0-253-20162-4, MB-162) Ind U Pr.

— De Vulgari Eloquentia. Botterill, Steven, ed. & tr. by. (Cambridge Medieval Classics Ser.: No. 5). 134p. (C). 1996. text 59.95 (0-521-40064-3) Cambridge U Pr.

— Divina Comedia. 1998. pap. 14.95 (84-320-4863-1) Planeta.

Dante Alighieri. La Divina Comedia. 441p. 1997. pap. text 9.98 (968-15-0680-4) Ed Mex.

Dante Alighieri. La Divina Comedia. 334p. 1959. 4.95 (0-8288-7452-2) Fr & Eur.

— La Divina Comedia. (SPA.). 512p. 1992. pap. 5.50 (0-8477-0729-6) U of PR Pr.

— La Divina Comedia. Grandgent, C. H., ed. LC 72-78429. 987p. 1972. reprint ed. pap. 200.00 (0-7837-1689-3, 205721900024) Bks Demand.

— La Divina Commedia, 3 vols. Ayres, Harry M., tr. (ITA & ENG.). (C). 1953. 50.00 (0-913298-29-8) S F Vanni.

Dante Alighieri. The Divine Comedy. Huse, H. R., ed. LC 54-7242. (Rinehart Editions Ser.). 492p. (C). 1954. pap. text 32.00 (0-03-008690-6, Pub. by Harcourt Coll Pubs) Harcourt.

Dante Alighieri. The Divine Comedy. Bergin, Thomas G., ed. & tr. by. from ITA. (Crofts Classics). 384p. 1955. pap. text 9.95 (0-88295-028-2) Harlan Davidson.

— The Divine Comedy. Ciardi, John, tr. from ITA. (Illus.). (C). 1977. 52.25 (0-393-04472-6) Norton.

— The Divine Comedy. Sisson, C. H., tr. (Oxford World's Classics Ser.). (Illus.). 742p. 1998. pap. 17.95 (0-19-283502-5) OUP.

— The Divine Comedy. 288p. 1994. 8.50 (0-460-87522-1, Everyman's Classic Lib) Tuttle Pubng.

— The Divine Comedy, 3 vols. Sayers, Dorothy L., tr. from ITA. (Classics Ser.). pap. write for info. (0-318-55027-X, Penguin Classics) Viking Penguin.

— Divine Comedy. Ciardi, John, tr. 1998. mass mkt. 5.99 (0-451-62804-7) Addson-Wesley Educ.

— Divine Comedy. 1955. pap. 12.00 (0-394-70126-7, V126) Vin Bks.

— The Divine Comedy. large type ed. 1997. pap. 19.95 (1-55701-211-3) BNI Pubns.

— The Divine Comedy: A New Translation & Introduction. Cotter, James F., tr. from ITA. (Illus.). 656p. 1993. pap. 14.95 (0-916349-18-7, Pub. by Element MA) Penguin Putnam.

— The Divine Comedy: Inferno. Mandelbaum, Allen, tr. from ITA. (Bantam Classics Ser.). (ENG & ITA., Illus.). 396p. 1982. mass mkt. 5.95 (0-553-21339-3, Bantam Classics) Bantam.

— The Divine Comedy: Inferno, Vol. 1. rev. ed. Sinclair, John D., tr. & comment by. 432p. 1961. pap. text 13.95 (0-19-500412-4) OUP.

— Divine Comedy: Paradise. Musa, Mark, ed. (Classics Ser.). 448p. 1986. pap. 10.95 (0-14-044443-2, Penguin Classics) Viking Penguin.

— The Divine Comedy: Paradiso. Mandelbaum, Allen, tr. from ITA. (Classics Ser.). 464p. (Orig.). 1986. mass mkt. 6.95 (0-553-21204-4) Bantam.

— The Divine Comedy: Paradiso, Vol. 3. Sinclair, John D., tr. & comment by. 432p. (Orig.). 1961. pap. 14.95 (0-19-500414-0) OUP.

— The Divine Comedy: Purgatorio. Mandelbaum, Allen, tr. from ITA. (Illus.). 448p. (Orig.). 1983. mass mkt. 6.95 (0-553-21344-X, Bantam Classics) Bantam.

— The Divine Comedy: Purgatorio, Vol. 2. Sinclair, John D., tr. & comment by. 432p. (Orig.). 1961. pap. 14.95 (0-19-500413-2) OUP.

— The Divine Comedy: Purgatory. Musa, Mark, tr. from ITA. & intro. by. 400p. 1985. pap. 10.95 (0-14-044442-4, Penguin Classics) Viking Penguin.

— The Divine Comedy: The Inferno, Vol. 1. (C). 1997. pap. text. write for info. (0-321-02597-0) Addson-Wesley Educ.

— The Divine Comedy, Inferno. Musa, Mark, tr. from ITA. & intro. by. (Classics Ser.). 432p. 1984. pap. 10.95 (0-14-044441-6) Viking Penguin.

— The Divine Comedy of Dante Alighieri: A Poetic Translation in Iambic Pentameter & Terza Rima. Arndt, Stephen W., tr. from ITA. LC 93-33759. 720p. 1993. text 139.95 (0-7734-9385-9) E Mellen.

— The Divine Comedy of Dante Alighieri: Inferno, Vol. 1. Durling, Robert M., ed. & tr. by. 672p. 1996. 39.95 (0-19-508740-2) OUP.

— The Divine Comedy of Dante Alighieri: Inferno, Vol. 1. Durling, Robert M., ed. & tr. by. (Illus.). 672p. 1997. reprint ed. pap. 14.95 (0-19-508744-5) OUP.

— The Divine Comedy of Dante Alighieri: Paradiso. Mandelbaum, Allen, tr. from ITA. & intro. by. LC 73-94441. (California Dante Ser.: Vol. III). (Illus.). 320p. 1984. 55.00 (0-520-04517-3, Pub. by U CA Pr) Cal Prin Full Svc.

— The Divine Comedy of Dante Alighieri: Purgatorio. Mandelbaum, Allen, tr. from ITA. (California Dante Ser.: Vol. II). (Illus.). 1982. 55.00 (0-520-04516-5, Pub. by U CA Pr) Cal Prin Full Svc.

— Episodios Famosos de la Divina Comedia: Primera Parte: Infierno. Cordaro, Philip & Ferracane, Gerardo, eds. Crespo, Angel, tr. from ITA. LC 76-8012. (UPREX, Humanidades Ser.: No. 49). (SPA.). (Orig.). 1976. pap. 1.50 (0-8477-0049-6) U of PR Pr.

— Hell. Ellis, Steve, tr. 224p. 1995. 25.95 (0-7011-6127-2, Pub. by Chatto & Windus) Trafalgar.

— The Inferno. Ciardi, John, tr. LC 96-17276. 1996. 15.50 (0-679-60209-7) Modern Lib NY.

— Inferno. 1999. pap. text 14.95 (88-17-15232-3) CE27.

***Dante Alighieri.** Inferno. Zappulla, Elio, tr. & notes by. LC 97-37482. 1998. 30.00 (0-679-44280-4) Pantheon.

Dante Alighieri. Inferno. (Mentor Bks.). 1982. 11.09 (0-606-03430-7, Pub. by Turtleback) Demco.

— Inferno. (Classics of World Literature Ser.). 432p. 1998. pap. 5.95 (1-85326-787-2, 7872WW, Pub. by Wrdsworth Edits) NTC Contemp Pub Co.

— Inferno: New Teaching. 1999. pap. 12.00 (0-679-75708-2) Vin Bks.

— Inferno of Dante. deluxe ed. Pinsky, Robert, tr. (ITA & ENG., Illus.). 464p. 1997. pap. 18.00 (0-374-52531-5) FS&G.

— The Inferno of Dante. LC 70-39797. 264p. reprint ed. pap. 81.90 (0-608-16193-4, 201464100096) Bks Demand.

— Literary Criticism of Dante Alighieri. Haller, Robert S., ed. LC 72-85402. (Regents Critics Ser.). 242p. reprint ed. pap. 75.10 (0-8357-2745-9, 203985400013) Bks Demand.

— The New Life.Tr. of La/Vita Nuova. 77p. reprint ed. 39.00 (0-932051-68-5) Rprt Serv.

Dante Alighieri. Oeuvres Completes. 1912p. 86.95 (0-686-56492-8) Fr & Eur.

— Oeuvres Completes. deluxe ed. (FRE.). 1920p. 1988. 125.00 (0-8288-3470-9, M5089) Fr & Eur.

Dante Alighieri. Offizin Schriftenreihe 20 Tex und Metafont - Offizin I. (GER.). (C). 1991. text. write for info. (0-201-57863-8) Addison-Wesley.

— Paradiso. Ciardi, John, tr. from ITA. 1970. mass mkt. 6.99 (0-451-62700-8, Ment) NAL.

— Paradiso. 1993. 75.00 (0-679-42821-6) Random.

— The Portable Dante. Musa, Mark, ed. 752p. 1995. pap. 15.95 (0-14-023114-5, Penguin Bks) Viking Penguin.

— Purgatorio. 1999. pap. text 14.95 (88-17-15233-1) CE27.

***Dante Alighieri.** Purgatorio. 2000. pap. write for info. (0-375-70839-1) Knopf.

Dante Alighieri. La Vita Nuova. Reynolds, Barbara, tr. from ITA. & intro. by. (Classics Ser.). 128p. 1969. pap. 9.95 (0-14-044216-2, Penguin Classics) Viking Penguin.

— Vita Nuova. Musa, Mark, ed. (Oxford World's Classics Ser.). 122p. 1999. pap. 8.95 (0-19-283935-7) OUP.

— Vita Nuova. Cervigni, Dino S. & Vasta, Edward, trs. LC 95-2300. (ENG & ITA.). 339p. (C). 1995. text 34.95 (0-268-01925-8) U of Notre Dame Pr.

— Vita Nuova. Cervigni, Dino S. & Vasta, Edward, trs. from ITA. LC 95-2300. 339p. 1996. pap. text 16.95 (0-268-01926-6) U of Notre Dame Pr.

— La Vita Nuova. Martin, Theodore, tr. from ITA. & intro. by. (Select Bibliographies Reprint Ser.). 1977. reprint ed. 18.95 (0-8369-6797-6, Penguin Classics) Viking Penguin.

Dante Alighieri & Sean. Echoes of Wolves. 30p. (J). 1992. pap. write for info. (0-9634867-3-X) Peyto Pub.

Dante Alighieri, jt. auth. see Lindskoog, Kathryn.

Dante Committee. Dante: Essays in Commemoration, 1321-1921. LC 74-132438. (Studies in Dante: No. 9). 1970. reprint ed. lib. bdg. 63.95 (0-8383-1194-6) M S G Haskell Hse.

Dante, Isabella & Edgren, Susanne Marie. This Season of Surety. 54p. 1998. pap. 17.00 (1-892922-37-1) Hunter & Co.

— When I Am Never Perfect. 64p. 1998. pap. 17.00 (1-892922-36-3) Hunter & Co.

Dante, Joe. Four Magic Moves to Winning Gold. 192p. 1995. pap. 13.95 (0-385-47776-7) Doubleday.

Dante, Joe & Elliot, Len. Four Magic Moves to Winning Golf. Date not set. lib. bdg. 21.95 (0-8488-1710-9) Amereon Ltd.

Dante, Mike. Shirtsleeve Philosophy. 1992. 10.95 (0-533-10019-4) Vantage.

— Telling It Like It Is. rev. ed. 1996. pap. 9.95 (0-533-11669-4) Vantage.

Dante, Nicholas, jt. auth. see Kirkwood, James.

Dante, Todd, et al. How? N. Y. S. Workers' Compensation Board & State Insurance Fund Maliciously Compromised our Mother's Health Mentally, Physically & Financially! 156p. (Orig.). 1994. pap. text 24.95 (1-885899-00-9) One Plus One.

***Dantec.** Dictionnaire du Marinier Illustre. (FRE.). 1998. 69.95 (0-320-00247-0) Fr & Eur.

Dantec, Denise Le, see Le Dantec, Denise.

Dantec, Jean-Pierre Le, see Le Dantec, Denise & Le Dantec, Jean-Pierre.

Dantes, Ligia. Your Fantasies May Be Hazardous to Your Health: How Your Thoughts Create Your World. 1995. pap. 10.95 (1-85230-687-4, Pub. by Element MA) Penguin Putnam.

Danthanarayana, W., ed. Insect Flight. (Proceedings in Life Sciences Ser.). (Illus.). 325p. 1986. 129.00 (0-387-16502-9) Spr-Verlag.

Danthine, A., ed. The OSI95 Transport Service with Multimedia Support. (Research Reports ESPRIT: Vol. 1). 1994. 75.95 (0-387-58316-5) Spr-Verlag.

Danthine, A. & Spaniol, Otto, eds. High Performance Networking, IV: Proceeding of the IFIP TC6-WG6.4 Fourth International Conference on High Performance Networking, Liege, Belgium, 14-18 December, 1992. LC 93-10968. (IFIP Transactions C: Communication Systems Ser.: 14). 468p. 1993. pap. 153.50 (0-444-81481-7, North Holland) Elsevier.

Danthine, A. L. High-Performance Networks for Multimedia Applications. LC 98-30759. 1998. 105.00 (0-7923-8274-9) Kluwer Academic.

Danthine, A. L., et al, eds. From Multimedia Services to Network Services: Proceedings, 4th International Cost 237 Workshop, Lisboa, Portugal, December 15-19, 1997. LC 97-51527. (Lecture Notes in Computer Science Ser.: Vol. 1356). xii, 180p. 1997. pap. 37.00 (3-540-63935-7) Spr-Verlag.

Danthine, Jean-Pierre, et al. The Impact of EMU on European Banking: Monitoring European Integration 9. 150p. 1998. pap. 14.95 (1-898128-38-3, Pub. by Ctr Econ Policy Res) Brookings.

***Danticat, Edwidge.** Beacon Best: Great Writing by Women & Men of All Colors & Cultures 2000. 2000. 28.50 (0-8070-6244-8); pap. 14.00 (0-8070-6245-6) Beacon Pr.

Danticat, Edwidge. Breath, Eyes, Memory. (Vintage Contemporaries Ser.). 1995. pap. 11.00 (0-679-75661-2) Vin Bks.

— Breath, Eyes, Memory. 1998. pap. 11.00 (0-375-70504-X) Vin Bks.

— Breath, Eyes, Memory. large type ed. LC 98-40405. 301p. 1998. 30.00 (0-7862-1654-9) Thorndike Pr.

— Breath, Eyes, Memory. large type ed. LC 98-40405. 1999. pap. 30.00 (0-7862-1655-7) Thorndike Pr.

— The Farming of Bones. LC 98-3655. 312p. 1998. 23.00 (1-56947-126-6) Soho Press.

***Danticat, Edwidge.** The Farming of Bones. 336p. 1999. pap. 12.95 (0-14-028049-9, Penguin Bks) Viking Penguin.

Danticat, Edwidge. Krik? Krak! LC 94-41999. 227p. 1995. 20.00 (1-56947-025-1) Soho Press.

— Krik? Krak! Stories. LC 95-43449. (Vintage Contemporaries Ser.). 224p. 1996. pap. 11.00 (0-679-76657-X) Vin Bks.

***Danticat, Edwidge, ed.** The Butterfly's Way: Voices from the Haitian Dyaspora in the United States. 2001. pap. 15.00 (1-56947-218-1) Soho Press.

Danticat, Edwidge, et al. Breath, Eyes, Memory. 2nd ed. LC 93-39256. Vol. 16. 230p. 1994. 20.00 (1-56947-142-8) Soho Press.

Dantico, John A. Paying for Time Not Worked: An Approach to Developing a Comprehensive Workplace Policy. (Building Blocks Ser.: Vol. 9). (Illus.). 19p. (Orig.). 1993. pap. 24.95 (1-57963-012-X, A0028) Am Compensation.

D'Antioche, Vettius V. Anthologies - Livre I. 1989. pap. 49.00 (90-04-08643-9, EPRO, 111) Brill Academic Pubs.

Danto, Arthur. Andy Warhol: $ (Illus.). 72p. 1997. pap. 20.00 (1-880154-13-7) Gagosian Gallery.

— Playing with the Edge: The Photographic Achievement of Robert Mapplethorpe. LC 94-38950. (Illus.). 208p. 1995. 29.95 (0-520-20051-9, Pub. by U CA Pr) Cal Prin Full Svc.

Danto, Arthur, et al. Art-Artifact: African Art in Anthropology Collections. LC 87-36845. (Illus.). 196p. 1988. pap. 30.00 (0-9614587-8-X) Museum African.

— Repicturing Abstraction. Cruger, George & Humphrey, Randee, eds. LC 94-72978. (Illus.). 108p. 1995. 15.00 (0-935519-20-3) Anderson Gal.

Danto, Arthur C. After the End of Art: Contemporary Art & the Pale of History. (A. W. Mellon Lectures in the Fine Arts). 262p. 1997. pap. text 12.95 (0-691-00299-1, Pub. by Princeton U Pr) Cal Prin Full Svc.

— After the End of Art: Contemporary Art & the Pale of History. LC 96-9027. (Bollingen Ser.). (Illus.). 239p. 1997. 26.95 (0-691-01173-7, Pub. by Princeton U Pr) Cal Prin Full Svc.

***Danto, Arthur C.** The Artistic Re-enchantment of the World. LC 99-86188. 320p. 2000. 30.00 (0-374-10613-4) FS&G.

Danto, Arthur C. Beyond the Brillo Box: The Visual Arts in Post-Historical Perspective. 264p. 1993. pap. 12.00 (0-374-52391-6) FS&G.

— Beyond the Brillo Box: The Visual Arts in Post-Historical Perspective. LC 98-15100. (Illus.). 275p. 1998. 16.95 (0-520-21674-1, Pub. by U CA Pr) Cal Prin Full Svc.

— The Body Body Problem: Selected Essays. LC 98-39125. 275p. 1999. 35.00 (0-520-21282-7, Pub. by U CA Pr) Cal Prin Full Svc.

— Connections to the World: The Basic Concepts of Philosophy. LC 96-37031. 306p. 1997. pap. 16.95 (0-520-20842-0, Pub. by U CA Pr) Cal Prin Full Svc.

— Embodied Meanings: Critical Essays & Aesthetic Meditations. (Illus.). 400p. 1995. pap. 14.00 (0-374-52458-0) FS&G.

— Encounters & Reflections: Art in the Historical Present. 355p. 1990. 22.95 (0-374-14819-8) FS&G.

— Encounters & Reflections: Art in the Historical Present. 356p. 1991. pap. 12.00 (0-374-52327-4) FS&G.

— Encounters & Reflections: Art in the Historical Present. LC 96-27590. 356p. 1997. pap. 17.95 (0-520-20846-3, Pub. by U CA Pr) Cal Prin Full Svc.

— Narration & Knowledge. LC 84-29362. 400p. 1985. pap. text 21.00 (0-231-06117-X) Col U Pr.

— Nietzsche As Philosopher. 250p. 1980. reprint ed. pap. text 19.50 (0-231-05053-4) Col U Pr.

An Asterisk (*) at the beginning of an entry indicates that the title is appearing for the first time.

— The Philosophical Disenfranchisement of Art. LC 86-2260. 1988. pap. text 20.00 (*0-231-06365-2*) Col U Pr.
— Philosophizing Art: Selected Essays. LC 98-38834. 285p. 1999. 35.00 (*0-520-21283-5*, Pub. by U CA Pr) Cal Prin Full Svc.
— The Transfiguration of the Commonplace: A Philosophy of Art. 222p. 1981. pap. 15.50 (*0-674-90346-3*) HUP.
— The Wake of Art: Criticism, Philosophy & the Ends of Taste. 150p. 1997. pap. 35.00 (*90-5701-221-9*) Dist Art Pubs.
Danto, Arthur C., contrib. by. The Wake of Art: Criticism, Philosophy & the Ends of Taste. 224p. 1998. pap. text 18.00 (*90-5701-301-0*) Gordon & Breach.
Danto, Arthur C., ed. Three Hundred Ninety-Seven Chairs. (Illus.). 96p. 1988. 34.95 (*0-8109-1698-3*, Pub. by Abrams) Time Warner.
***Danto, Arthur C. & Bailey, George W. S.** Theories of Art Today. Carroll, Noel, ed. LC 99-42502. 270p. 2000. 55.00 (*0-299-16350-4*); pap. 21.95 (*0-299-16354-7*) U of Wis Pr.
Danto, Arthur C. & Goodman, Susan T. From the Inside Out: Eight Contemporary Artists. LC 93-77955. (Illus.). 59p. (Orig.). 1993. pap. text 14.95 (*0-87334-067-1*) Jewish Mus NY.
Danto, Arthur C., et al. Howard Ben Tre. LC 99-36156. (Illus.). 164p. 2000. 50.00 (*1-55595-187-2*, Pub. by Hudson Hills) Natl Bk Netwk.
Danto, Arthur C., jt. auth. see Langer, Susanne K.
Danto, Arthur C., jt. auth. see Strassfield, Christina M.
Danto, Bruce L. Jail House Blues. LC 73-79482. 325p. 1973. 8.95 (*0-914244-01-9*) Epic Pubns.
— Prime Target: Security Measures for the Executive at Home & Abroad. LC 90-33084. 256p. 1990. pap. 20.95 (*0-914783-39-4*); text 34.95 (*0-914783-38-6*) Charles.
Danto, Bruce L., et al, eds. The Human Side of Homicide. LC 81-21617. 336p. 1982. text 57.50 (*0-231-04964-1*) Col U Pr.
— So You Want to See a Psychiatrist? LC 79-23225. 170p. 1980. lib. bdg. 18.95 (*0-405-12622-0*) Ayer.
Danto, Bruce L., et al. Suicide & Bereavement. 1980. 20.95 (*0-405-12505-4*) Ayer.
Danto, Bruce L., jt. auth. see Lester, David.
Danto, Eloise. Museums of New York. 3rd ed. (Illus.). 150p. (Orig.). 1998. pap. 12.95 (*0-9615128-9-X*) Eldan Pr.
— Museums of the San Francisco Bay Area. 2nd ed. (Illus.). 125p. (Orig.). 1998. pap. 12.95 (*0-9615128-8-1*) Eldan Pr.
Danton, George H. Germany Ten Years After. LC 79-150180. (Select Bibliographies Reprint Ser.). 1977. reprint ed. 23.95 (*0-8369-5693-1*) Ayer.
Danton, Graham. The Theory & Practice of Seamanship. 11th ed. LC 96-14277. 568p. (C). 1996. 125.00 (*0-415-14200-8*); pap. 39.99 (*0-415-15372-7*) Routledge.
D'Antoni, Francesca G. Dante's Burning Sands: Some New Perspectives. LC 91-34971. (Studies in Italian Culture: Vol. 4). 181p. (C). 1992. text 40.95 (*0-8204-1473-5*) P Lang Pubng.
Dantonio. Learning to Question. 224p. (C). 2000. pap. 33.27 (*0-205-28036-6*, Macmillan Coll) P-H.
D'Antonio, Bob. Garden of the Gods Pikes Peak. (Classic Rock Climbs Ser.: No. 4). (Illus.). 64p. (Orig.). 1996. pap. 9.95 (*1-57540-027-8*) Falcon Pub Inc.
— Mountain Biking Denver-Boulder. LC 97-13318. (Illus.). 136p. (Orig.). 1997. pap. 10.95 (*1-56044-532-7*) Falcon Pub Inc.
***D'Antonio, Bob,** Mountain Biking Grand Junction & Fruita. (Illus.). 128p. 2000. pap. 9.95 (*1-56044-945-4*) Falcon Pub Inc.
D'Antonio, Bob. Mueller State Park Elevenmile Canyon. (Classic Rock Climbs Ser.: No. 3). (Illus.). 60p. (Orig.). 1996. pap. 9.95 (*1-57540-031-6*) Falcon Pub Inc.
***D'Antonio, Bob.** Rock Climbing Colorado's San Luis Valley. 2nd ed. LC 99-29087. (Illus.). 150p. 1999. pap. 15.00 (*1-56044-914-4*) Falcon Pub Inc.
D'Antonio, Bob. San Luis Valley: Rock Climbing & Bouldering Guide. LC 97-134544. (Illus.). 88p. (Orig.). 1994. pap. 12.00 (*0-934641-79-X*) Falcon Pub Inc.
***D'Antonio, Dave.** The Giants Fan's Little Book of Wisdom. 2000. pap. 6.95 (*1-888698-34-9*) Diamond Communications.
Dantonio, Marylou. How Can We Create Thinkers? Questioning Strategies That Work for Teachers. 120p. (Orig.). 1990. pap. 22.95 (*1-879639-08-4*) Natl Educ Serv.
Dantonio, Marylou, jt. auth. see Beisenherz, Paul C.
D'Antonio, Michael. The Best Medicine. LC 99-15937. 1999. text 23.95 (*0-312-24184-4*) St Martin.
— Devouring the Young. 1996. 27.50 (*0-517-59957-0*) Random.
— Fall from Grace: The Failed Crusade of the Christian Right. LC 92-9453. 242p. (C). 1992. pap. 14.95 (*0-8135-1896-2*) Rutgers U Pr.
— Tin Cup Dreams: A Long Shot Makes It on the PGA Tour. LC 99-53824. 288p. 2000. 23.95 (*0-7868-6497-4*, Pub. by Hyperion) Time Warner.
D'Antonio, Nancy. Our Baby from China: An Adoption Story. LC 96-32327. 24p. (J). (ps-2). 1997. lib. bdg. 13.95 (*0-8075-6162-2*) A Whitman.
D'Antonio-Nocera, Anne, et al, eds. The Professional Activity Manager & Consultant. (Illus.). 452p. (Orig.). 1996. pap. 45.00 (*1-882883-24-1*, 297) Idyll Arbor.
D'Antonio, William V., et al, eds. Ecology, World Resources & the Quality of Social Life. LC 93-44900. 240p. (C). 1994. pap. text 24.95 (*1-56000-722-2*) Transaction Pubs.
D'Antonio, William V. & Aldous, Joan, eds. Families & Religions: Conflict & Change in Modern Society. LC 83-3310. 320p. reprint ed. pap. 99.20 (*0-7837-6577-0*, 204614200011) Bks Demand.
D'Antonio, William V., et al. Laity, American & Catholic: Transforming the Church. LC 95-48857. 192p. (Orig.). 1996. pap. 15.95 (*1-55612-823-1*, LL1823) Sheed & Ward WI.
D'Antonio, William V., jt. auth. see Lee, Bernard J.
D'Antonio, William V., ed. see Drucker, Peter F., et al.
Dantor, Mackinlay. Long Remember. 1993. reprint ed. lib. bdg. 89.00 (*0-7812-5475-2*) Rprt Serv.
Dantwala, M. L., ed. Indian Agricultural Development since Independence. (C). 1991. 30.00 (*81-204-0118-2*, Pub. by Oxford IBH) S Asia.
Dantwala, M. L., et al, eds. Dilemmas of Growth: The Indian Experience. LC 95-46608. 404p. (C). 1996. 38.00 (*0-8039-9266-1*) Sage.
Dantwala, M. L., et al. Social Change Through Voluntary Action. LC 98-30826. 1998. 45.00 (*0-7619-9297-9*); pap. write for info. (*0-7619-9298-7*) Sage.
Dantz, William R. Hunger. 352p. 1992. mass mkt. 4.99 (*0-8125-1957-4*, Pub. by Tor Bks) St Martin.
— Nine Levels Down. 320p. 1999. mass mkt. 6.99 (*0-8125-2416-0*, Pub. by Forge NYC) St Martin.
— Pulse. 288p. 1990. pap. 3.95 (*0-380-75714-1*, Avon Bks) Morrow Avon.
— The Seventh Sleeper. 368p. 1992. mass mkt. 4.99 (*0-380-71032-3*, Avon Bks) Morrow Avon.
Dantzer, David R. & Scharf, Steven M. Cardiopulmonary Critical Care. 3rd ed. Fletcher, Judy, ed. LC 96-36901. (Illus.). 800p. 1997. text 125.00 (*0-7216-6543-8*, W B Saunders Co) Harcrt Hlth Sci Grp.
Dantzer, R., jt. ed. see Zayan, R.
Dantzer, Robert. The Psychosomatic Delusion: Why the Mind Is Not the Source of All Our Ills. 247p. 1993. 24.95 (*0-02-906937-8*) Free Pr.
Dantzer, Robert, jt. ed. see Rothwell, Nancy.
***Dantzger.** Criminology & Criminal Justice. LC 97-33500. 208p. 1998. pap. 24.95 (*0-7506-9731-8*) Buttrwrth-Heinemann.
Dantzic. Drawing Dimensions. (Illus.). 344p. 1998. pap. text 53.33 (*0-13-220153-4*) P-H.
DANTZIG. Systems Development Hdbk. 1993. text 79.95 (*0-13-855339-4*) S&S Trade.
Dantzig, Albert Van, see Van Dantzig, Albert, ed.
Dantzig, G. & Veinott, A. F., Jr., eds. Mathematics of the Decision Sciences, Pt. 1. LC 62-21481. (Lectures in Applied Mathematics: Vol. 11). 429p. 1969. reprint ed. text 57.00 (*0-8218-1111-8*, LAM/11) Am Math.
Dantzig, G. B. & Veinott, A. F., Jr., eds. Mathematics of the Decision Sciences, Pt. 2. LC 62-21481. 443p. 1969. reprint ed. text 59.00 (*0-8218-1112-6*, LAM 12) Am Math.
Dantzig, G. B., et al. Linear Inequalities & Related Systems. Kuhn, Harold W. & Tucker, A. W., eds. LC 56-8385. (Annals of Mathematics Studies: No. 38). 346p. reprint ed. pap. 107.30 (*0-608-06437-8*, 206665000008) Bks Demand.
Dantzig, George B. Linear Programming & Extensions. (Rand Corporation Research Studies). 642p. 1963. text 95.00 (*0-691-08000-3*, Pub. by Princeton U Pr); pap. text 29.95 (*0-691-05913-6*, Pub. by Princeton U Pr) Cal Prin Full Svc.
Dantzig, George B. & Thapa, Mukund N. Linear Programming: Introduction. LC 96-36411. (Springer Series in Operations Research). (Illus.). 435p. 1997. 54.95 (*0-387-94833-3*) Spr-Verlag.
Dantzig, George B., et al. Essays in the History of Mathematics. Schlissel, Arthur, ed. LC 83-26642. (Memoirs of the American Mathematical Society Ser.: No. 298). 74p. 1987. reprint ed. pap. 16.00 (*0-8218-2298-5*, MEMO/48/298C) Am Math.
Dantzig, J. A., jt. ed. see Sekhar, J. A.
Dantzig, L. van, jt. ed. see Bakker, B. L. G.
Dantzig, Tobias. Number: The Language of Science. 4th rev. ed. (Illus.). 340p. 1967. pap. 18.95 (*0-02-906990-4*) Free Pr.
Dantzker, David R., et al. Comprehensive Respiratory Care. (Illus.). 1104p. 1995. text 66.00 (*0-7216-2844-3*, W B Saunders Co) Harcrt Hlth Sci Grp.
Dantzker, M. L., ed. Contemporary Policing: Personnel, Issues & Trends. LC 96-50435. 288p. 1997. pap. 36.95 (*0-7506-9736-9*) Buttrwrth-Heinemann.
***Dantzker, M. L. & Hunter, Ronald D.** Research Methods. LC 99-53865. 267p. 2000. 39.95 (*0-7506-9951-5*) Buttrwrth-Heinemann.
Dantzker, Mark L. Police Organization & Management: Yesterday, Today & Tomorrow. LC 98-18426. 298p. 1998. pap. 49.95 (*0-7506-7101-7*) Buttrwrth-Heinemann.
— Readings for Research Methods in Criminology & Criminal Justice. LC 98-22623. xi, 180 p. 1998. pap. 19.95 (*0-7506-7000-2*) Buttrwrth-Heinemann.
Dantzker, Mark L., et al. Practical Applications for Criminal Justice Statistics. LC 97-9588. 196p. 1997. 26.95 (*0-7506-9830-6*, BH Security) Buttrwrth-Heinemann.
Dantzker, Mark L., jt. auth. see Doerner, William G.
Dantzler, John, jt. auth. see Clark, John.
Dantzler, Lea, jt. ed. see Berliner, Nancy.
Dantzler, Mark. Let's Start Something! Riddles to Get You Going. (Illus.). 64p. (Orig.). (J). (gr. 2 up). 1994. pap. 3.95 (*0-9643953-0-4*) G T Bks.
— Riddles for Clever Kids! (Illus.). 26p. (J). 1994. pap. 9.50 (*0-930329-83-X*) Kabel Pubs.
Dantzler, W. H., ed. Comparative Renal Handling of Solutes & Water. (Journal: Renal Physiology & Biochemistry: Vol. 8, No. 4-5, 1985). (Illus.). 112p. 1985. pap. 54.00 (*3-8055-4147-3*) S Karger.
Dantzler, William H., ed. Comparative Psyiology Section 13, 2 vols., Set. LC 96-43735. (Handbook of Physiology Ser.). (Illus.). 1856p. 1997. text 325.00 (*0-19-507419-X*) OUP.
Danubio, Maria E., jt. ed. see Greene, Lawrence S.
Danuloff, Craig. Expert Advisor: Harvard Graphics. 400p. 1989. pap. text 22.95 (*0-201-52369-8*) Addison-Wesley.
Danuloff, Craig. MacWorld Pagemaker 5 Bible. LC 93-61312. (Bible Ser.). 650p. 1994. pap. 39.95 (*1-878058-84-3*) IDG Bks.
Danuloff, Craig & Sanders, William. Advanced Pagemaker 4.0 for Windows. (Illus.). 250p. (Orig.). 1991. pap. 27.95 (*1-55958-070-4*) Prima Pub.
Danuloff, Craig, jt. auth. see Harrel, William.
Danuloff, Craig, jt. auth. see McClelland, Deke.
Danusso, F., jt. auth. see Natta, G.
Danvers. Circuit of Heaven Reader's Guide. 1998. write for info. (*0-380-97256-5*, Eos) Morrow Avon.
Danvers, Dennis. Circuit of Heaven. LC 97-27462. 384p. 1998. mass mkt. 14.00 (*0-380-97447-9*, Eos) Morrow Avon.
— Circuit of Heaven. 384p. 1999. mass mkt. 5.99 (*0-380-79092-0*, Eos) Morrow Avon.
— End of Days. LC 99-20947. 384p. 1999. 16.00 (*0-380-97448-7*, Eos) Morrow Avon.
***Danvers, Dennis.** End of Days. LC 99-20947. 400p. 2000. mass mkt. 6.50 (*0-380-79093-9*, Avon Bks) Morrow Avon.
— The Fourth World. LC 99-52345.Tr. of Cuarto Mundo. 352p. 2000. 23.00 (*0-380-97761-3*, Eos) Morrow Avon.
Danvers, Dennis. Time & Time Again. 1995. mass mkt. 5.99 (*0-671-53448-3*, Pocket Books) PB.
— Time & Time Again. LC 94-11965. 304p. 1994. 22.00 (*0-671-78800-0*) S&S Trade.
***Danvers, Dennis.** Wilderness. Brehl, J. B., ed. 384p. 2000. mass mkt. 6.50 (*0-380-80646-0*, Avon Bks) Morrow Avon.
Danvers, Dennis. Wilderness. Rubenstein, Julie, ed. 320p. 1992. reprint ed. mass mkt. 5.99 (*0-671-72828-8*, Pocket Star Bks) PB.
Danvers, Frederick C. Portuguese in India, 2 vols. (Illus.). 1966. 95.00 (*0-7146-2005-X*, Pub. by F Cass Pubs) Intl Spec Bk.
— The Portuguese in India, 2 vols. (C). 1988. reprint ed. 64.00 (*81-206-0391-5*, Pub. by Asian Educ Servs) S Asia.
— The Portuguese in India, 2 vols. 1986. reprint ed. 84.00 (*0-685-14348-1*, Pub. by Usha) S Asia.
Danvy, Olivier, et al. Partial Evaluation International Seminar, Dagstuhl Castle, Germany, February 1996: Selected Papers. LC 96-2749. (Lecture Notes in Computer Science Ser.: Vol. 1110). 514p. 1996. 81.00 (*3-540-61580-6*) Spr-Verlag.
Dany, M. & Laloy, J. R. Le Francais de l'Hotellerie et du Tourisme (French for the Hotel & Tourism Industry) (FRE.). 186p. 1990. pap. 24.95 (*0-7859-4863-5*, M9311) Fr & Eur.
Danylchuk, Karen E. Managing Competitive Sport Programs in Schools. Zeigler, Earle F., ed. (Monograph Series on Sport & Physical Education Management). 56p. (C). 1993. pap. text 4.40 (*0-87563-450-8*) Stipes.
Danyluk, Andrea, ed. Predicting the Future: AI Approaches to Time-Series Problems: Papers from the AAAI Workshop. (Technical Reports: Vol. WS-98-07). (Illus.). 92p. 1998. spiral bd. 25.00 (*1-57735-060-X*) AAAI Pr.
Danysh, Romana, jt. auth. see Finnegan, John Patrick.
Danz, Cassandra. Mrs. Greenthumbs. LC 92-17969. 1993. pap. 12.00 (*0-517-58668-1*, Crown) Crown Pub Group.
— Mrs. Greenthumbs: How I Turned a Boring Yard into a Glorious Garden & How You Can Too. (Illus.). 256p. 1993. pap. 12.00 (*0-517-88010-5*) C Potter.
— Mrs. Greenthumbs Plows Ahead: Five Steps to Drop Dead Gorgeous Gardens of Your Dreams. 224p. (J). 1999. pap. 12.95 (*0-609-80265-8*) Crown Pub Group.
— Mrs. Greenthumbs Plows Ahead: Five Steps to Drop Dead Gorgeous Gardens of Your Dreams, 2. (J). 1999. pap. text 12.70 (*0-676-58495-0*) Random.
Danz, Harold P. Cougar! LC 98-43497. (Illus.). 310p. 1999. pap. 19.95 (*0-8040-1015-3*) Swallow.
***Danz, Harold P.** Cougar! LC 98-43497. (Illus.). 306p. 1999. 39.95 (*0-8040-1014-5*) Swallow.
Danz, Harold P. Of Bison & Man: From the Annals of a Bison Yesterday to a Refreshing Outcome from Human Involvement with America's Most Valiant of Beasts. LC 97-15918. (Illus.). 232p. 1997. 32.50 (*0-87081-454-0*) Univ Pr Colo.
Danz, Louis. Personal Revolution & Picasso. LC 74-3421. (Studies in Philosophy: No. 40). 1974. lib. bdg. 59.00 (*0-8383-2066-X*) M S G Haskell Hse.
***Danzberger, Jacqueline & Clark, Michele.** A Guide to Promising Practices in Educational Partnerships. 74p. 1999. pap. text 30.00 (*0-7881-4036-1*) DIANE Pub.
Danzberger, Jacqueline, jt. auth. see Friedman, Will.
Danzer. World History. (C). 1998. pap. text 24.00 (*0-13-095382-2*) P-H.
Danzer, Gerald A. America Its People: Mosaic Making, 1-31. (C). 1997. text 177.00 (*0-673-53766-8*) S&S Trade.
— The Americans: Reconstruction Through the 20th Century: Life, Liberty, Pursuit of Happiness LC 99-202522. 1020p. 1999. write for info. (*0-395-89081-0*) HM.
Danzer, Gerald A. Public Places: Exploring Their History. LC 97-541. (American Association for State & Local History Book Ser.). (Illus.). 152p. 1987. pap. 17.95 (*0-7619-8931-5*) AltaMira Pr.
Danzer, Hal, jt. auth. see Kass-Annese, Barbara.
Danzer, Klaus, jt. auth. see Eckschlager, Karel.
Danzer, Paul, ed. ARRL Operating Manual. LC 98-113805. 1997. pap. 25.00 (*0-87259-614-1*) Am Radio.
Danzi, Angela D. From Home to Hospital: Jewish & Italian American Women & Childbirth, 1920-1940. LC 97-33580. 244p. (C). 1997. 39.50 (*0-7618-0911-2*) U Pr of Amer.
Danzi, J. Thomas, ed. Positioning Your Practice for the Managed Care Market. LC 95-44935. (Illus.). 328p. 1996. pap. 29.00 (*0-683-02373-X*) Lppncott W & W.
Danzi, J. Thomas & Landman, Silviu. Case Atlas of Gastroenterology. (Illus.). 335p. 1995. 129.00 (*0-683-02366-7*) Lppncott W & W.
Danzi, Joseph & Scopelliti, Joseph. The Office Management of Digestive Diseases. (Illus.). 200p. 1992. text 45.00 (*0-8121-1436-1*) Lppncott W & W.
Danzig. The Capability Problem in Contract Law: Further Readings on Well-Known Cases. 1978. pap. text 13.50 (*0-88277-501-4*) Foundation Pr.
Danzig, Abraham ben Jehiel Michal & Cohen, Yehoshua. Chochmas Adam, the Laws of Niddah: Chochmas Adam, Hilkhot Nidah. LC 98-39790. 400p. 1999. 23.95 (*1-880582-40-6*) Judaica Pr.
— Chochmas Adam, the Laws of Tevilah: Chochmas Adam, Hilkhos Tevilah. LC 98-39184. 160p. 1999. 14.95 (*1-880582-41-4*) Judaica Pr.
Danzig, Allison & Brandwein, Peter, eds. Sport's Golden Age, a Closeup of the Fabulous Twenties. LC 68-58784. (Essay Index Reprint Ser.). 1977. 24.95 (*0-8369-0013-8*) Ayer.
Danzig, E. M. Coccids of the Far-Eastern U. S. S. R. (Homoptera Coccinea) Phylogenetic Analysis of Coccids in the World Fauna. (Illus.). 476p. 1990. 63.00 (*90-73348-03-X*, Pub. by Backhuys Pubs) Balogh.
Danzig, Jerry. Pushing the Envelope Vol. 1: New Trends in Direct Marketing. 1994. 45.00 (*0-86636-326-2*) PBC Intl Inc.
***Danzig, Marsha.** The Tiniest Acorn: A Story to Grow By. LC 98-37760. (J). 1999. 12.95 (*0-88391-001-2*) F Fell Pubs Inc.
***Danzig, Robert J.** Angel Threads: Weaving the Tapestry of Your Life. LC 99-50017. 196p. 2000. 14.95 (*0-88391-018-7*) F Fell Pubs Inc.
— The Leader Within You: Master 9 Powers to Be the Leader You Always Wanted to Be. 192p. 2000. pap. 14.95 (*0-88391-021-7*) F Fell Pubs Inc.
— Vitamins for the Spirit. LC 98-31626. 1999. 10.00 (*0-88391-000-4*) F Fell Pubs Inc.
Danzig, Sheila R. Power Publicity! A Simple, Comprehensive, Step-By-Step Program for Building Your Business Through Free Press Coverage. Danzig, William, ed. LC 89-92232. (How to Make People Buy Whatever You're Selling Whether They Know They Need It or Not Ser.). 107p. 1990. pap. 20.00 (*0-9624333-4-9*) Natl Success.
Danzig, William, ed. see Danzig, Sheila R.
Danziger. Supernovae Remnants. (International Astronomical Union Symposia Ser.). 1983. pap. text 112.00 (*90-277-1667-6*) Kluwer Academic.
Danziger, Charles. Japan for Starters: Almost Everything You Need to Know. Orig. Title: The American Who Couldn't Say Noh. (JPN., Illus.). 174p. 1996. reprint ed. 9.95 (*4-7700-2087-2*) Kodansha.
Danziger, Christopher. South African History, 1910-1970: Cartoons. (Illus.). 1978. 10.50 (*0-19-570117-8*) OUP.
***Danziger, Danny.** Year 1000. 2000. 25.00 (*0-06-019795-1*); pap. 13.00 (*0-06-095762-X*) HarpC.
Danziger, Danny, jt. auth. see Lacey, Robert.
Danziger, E. International Income Tax. 428p. 1991. pap. 102.00 (*0-409-10505-8*, SA, MICHIE) LEXIS Pub.
Danziger, E. & Stack, E. M. Tax Handbook 1992-93. 1992. pap. 48.00 (*0-614-05480-X*, SA, MICHIE) LEXIS Pub.
— Tax Handbook 1992-93. (Illus.). 711p. 1992. pap. 48.00 (*0-614-05468-0*, SA, MICHIE) LEXIS Pub.
Danziger, Edmund J., Jr. The Chippewas of Lake Superior. LC 78-58130. (Civilization of the American Indian Ser.: No. 148). (Illus.). 288p. 1990. pap. 16.95 (*0-8061-2246-3*) U of Okla Pr.
— Indians & Bureaucrats: Administering the Reservation Policy During the Civil War. LC 73-85486. 250p. 1974. text 24.95 (*0-252-00314-4*) U of Ill Pr.
Danziger, Edmund J. Indians & Bureaucrats: Administering the Reservation Policy During the Civil War. fac. ed. LC 73-85486. 258p. 1994. pap. 80.00 (*0-7837-7619-5*, 204737100007) Bks Demand.
Danziger, Edmund J. A People Living Apart: Indians of the Great Lakes, 1855-1900. (Illus.). (C). text. write for info. (*0-472-09690-7*); pap. text. write for info. (*0-472-06690-0*) U of Mich Pr.
Danziger, Edmund J., Jr. Survival & Regeneration: Detroit's American Indian Community. LC 90-29857. (Great Lakes Bks.). (Illus.). 262p. 1991. 34.95 (*0-8143-2348-0*, Great Lks Bks) Wayne St U Pr.
***Danziger, Eve.** Relatively Speaking: Language, Thought, & Kinship among the Mopan Maya. LC 99-86793. (Oxford Studies in Anthropological Linguistics). (Illus.). 272p. 2001. text 60.00 (*0-19-509910-9*) OUP.
Danziger, Gloria, jt. auth. see Simon, Rita J.
Danziger, Hillel. Mishnah-Nezikin Vol. 3B: Avodah Zarah-Horayos. Kempler, Naftali, ed. (ArtScroll Mishnah Ser.). 228p. 1988. 22.99 (*0-89906-299-7*) Mesorah Pubns.
Danziger, Hillel & Scherman, Nosson. The ArtScroll Tehillim: Psalms. (ArtScroll Mesorah Ser.). 326p. 1988. 18.99 (*0-89906-665-8*) Mesorah Pubns.
— The ArtScroll Tehillim: Psalms. (ArtScroll Mesorah Ser.). 326p. 1989. 13.99 (*0-89906-670-4*); pap. 9.99 (*0-89906-671-2*) Mesorah Pubns.
— The ArtScroll Tehillim: Psalms. deluxe ed. (ArtScroll Mesorah Ser.). 326p. 1988. 32.95 (*0-89906-672-0*) Mesorah Pubns.
— The ArtScroll Tehillim: Psalms. deluxe ed. (ArtScroll Mesorah Ser.). 326p. 1989. 24.95 (*0-89906-673-9*) Mesorah Pubns.
Danziger, Hillel, ed. see Sonnenfeld, Shlomo Z.
Danziger, Irene & Kennedy, Sandra. Adventures in SeeLogo Teacher Edition: Course Code 192-2. Schroeder, Bonnie, ed. (Illus.). 120p. (Orig.). 1989. 19.95 (*0-917531-69-8*) CES Compu-Tech.

D

Danziger, Irene & Weinberger, Paula. Computer Applications: Programming with SeeLogo Teacher Edition: Course Code S94-4, Grade 8. Doheny, Catherine & Schroeder, Bonnie, eds. (Illus.). 50p. 1989. reprint ed. 19.95 (0-917531-82-5) CES Compu-Tech.

— Computer Applications: Telecommunications: Course Code S94-4. Doheny, Catherine & Schroeder, Bonnie, eds. (Illus.). 42p. (J). (gr. 7). 1989. reprint ed. pap. text 5.95 (0-917531-57-4) CES Compu-Tech.

— Telecommunications: Lab Pack. Schroeder, Bonnie & Doheny, Catherine, eds. (Illus.). 99.95 (1-56177-097-3, L394-4) CES Compu-Tech.

— Telecommunications: Lab Pack. Doheny, Catherine & Schroeder, Bonnie, eds. (Illus.). teacher ed., student ed. 99.95 incl. disk (1-56177-049-3, L194-4) CES Compu-Tech.

— Telecommunications: Lab Pack. Schroeder, Bonnie & Doheny, Catherine, eds. (Illus.). disk 15.95 (1-56177-096-5, D394-4) CES Compu-Tech.

— Telecommunications: Lab Pack. Doheny, Catherine & Schroeder, Bonnie, eds. (Illus.). Apple II 15.95 (1-56177-048-5, D194-4) CES Compu-Tech.

Danziger, Irene, et al. Primary Program 2: Course Code 191-1. Doheny, Cathy & Schroeder, Bonnie, eds. (Illus.). 90p. 1989. teacher ed. 24.95 (0-917531-64-7) CES Compu-Tech.

— Primary Program 2: Course Code 191-1. Doheny, Cathy & Schroeder, Bonnie, eds. (Illus.). 54p. 1989. reprint ed. student ed. 5.95 (0-917531-39-6) CES Compu-Tech.

— Primary Program 2: Course Code 191-2. (Illus.). 120p. 1986. teacher ed. 24.95 (0-917531-65-5) CES Compu-Tech.

— Primary Program 2: Course Code 191-2. Doheny, Cathy & Schroeder, Bonnie, eds. (Illus.). 46p. 1989. student ed. 5.95 (0-917531-40-X) CES Compu-Tech.

— Primary Program 2 Pt. 2: Lab Pack. Doheny, Cathy & Schroeder, Bonnie, eds. (Illus.). teacher ed., student ed. 299.95 incl. disk (1-56177-017-5, L191-2) CES Compu-Tech.

— Primary Program 2, Pt. 1: Lab Pack. Schroeder, Bonnie, ed. (Illus.). teacher ed., student ed. 299.95 incl. disk (1-56177-016-7, L191-1); disk 15.95 (1-56177-012-4, D191-1A); disk 15.95 (1-56177-013-2, D191-1B) CES Compu-Tech.

Danziger, Irene, jt. auth. see Kennedy, Sandra.

Danziger, James. American Century. (Illus.). 464p. 90.00 (2-84323-155-8, Pub. by Assouline) Rizzoli Intl.

— Understanding the Political World. 3rd ed. (C). 1995. pap. text. write for info. (0-8013-1689-8) Addison-Wesley.

Danziger, James & Dailer, Stephen, contrib. by. The American Century Pt. 1: Photographs & Visions, 1900-1935. (Illus.). 1997. pap. 35.00 (0-9659835-0-1) J Danzier.

Danziger, James & Daiter, Stephen, contrib. by. The American Century Pt. II: Observations & Metaphors, 1936-1967. (Illus.). 232p. 1998. pap. write for info. (0-9659835-1-X) J Danzier.

***Danziger, James N.** American Century: Observations & Metaphors Pt. 2 1936-1967, 2. (American Century Ser.). 1999. pap. text 40.00 (0-9659835-2-8) J Danzier.

Danziger, James N. Understanding the Political World. 2nd ed. LC 93-2171. 450p. (C). 1993. pap. text 40.00 (0-8013-1179-9, 79703) Longman.

Danziger, James N. Understanding the Political World. 3rd ed. (C). 1995. pap. text 0.00 (0-8013-1777-0) HEPC Inc.

Danziger, James N. Understanding the Political World. 4th ed. (C). 1997. pap. text. write for info. (0-8013-1853-X) Addison-Wesley.

— Understanding the Political World: A Comparative Introduction to Political Science. 4th ed. LC 97-21717. 576p. (C). 1997. pap. text 57.00 (0-8013-1852-1) Addison-Wesley.

— Understanding the Political World: An Introduction to Political Science. 480p. (Orig.). (C). 1991. pap. text 35.95 (0-582-29025-2, 71724) Addison-Wesley.

— Understanding the Political World: An Introduction to Political Science. 2nd ed. LC 93-2171. 450p. (Orig.). (C). 1994. teacher ed. write for info. (0-8013-1180-2, 79704) Longman.

Danziger, Jeff. The Champlain Monster. (Illus.). 96p. (J). 1983. pap. 8.95 (0-933050-17-8) New Eng Pr VT.

— Teed Stories. LC 88-30789. (Illus.). 116p. (Orig.). 1988. pap. 7.95 (0-933050-60-7) New Eng Pr VT.

Danziger, John. Supernovae Remnants. (International Astronomical Union Symposia Ser.). 1983. lib. bdg. 211.50 (90-277-1666-8) Kluwer Academic.

Danziger, Kurt. Constructing the Subject: Historical Origins of Psychological Research. (Studies in the History of Psychology). (Illus.). 263p. (C). 1994. pap. text 18.95 (0-521-46785-3) Cambridge U Pr.

— Interpersonal Communication. 250p. 1976. 113.00 (0-08-018757-9, Pub. by Pergamon Repr) Franklin.

— Naming the Mind: How Psychology Found Its Language. 224p. 1997. 45.00 (0-8039-7762-X); pap. 14.99 (0-8039-7763-8) Sage.

Danziger, Marie F. Text - Countertext: Postmodern Paranoia in Samuel Beckett, Doris Lessing & Philip Roth. (Studies in Literary Criticism & Theory). 120p. (C). 1997. text 34.95 (0-8204-2871-X) P Lang Pubng.

Danziger, Nick. Danziger's Adventures: From Miami to Kabul. (Illus.). 290p. (Orig.). 1993. pap. 12.00 (0-586-09081-9, Pub. by HarpC) Trafalgar.

— Danziger's Britain: A Journey to the Edge. (Illus.). 368p. 1998. pap. 15.95 (0-00-638249-5, Pub. by HarpC) Trafalgar.

— Danziger's Travels: Beyond Forbidden Frontiers. (Vintage Departures Ser.). 1988. pap. 14.00 (0-679-73994-7) Vin Bks.

Danziger, Paula. Amber Brown Boxed Set: Amber Brown Is Not a Crayon; You Can't Eat Your Chicken Pox, Amber Brown; Amber Brown Goes Fourth; Amber Brown Wants Extra Credit. (Amber Brown Ser.: Nos. 1-4). (J). (gr. 4-7). 1997. pap., boxed set 14.00 (0-590-30018-0) Scholastic Inc.

***Danziger, Paula.** Amber Brown Goes Fourth. (Amber Brown Ser.: No. 3). (J). (gr. 3-6). 1999. write for info. (0-613-00276-8) Econo-Clad Bks.

Danziger, Paula. Amber Brown Goes Fourth. LC 94-41935. (Amber Brown Ser.: No. 3). 88p. (J). (ps-3). 1995. 13.99 (0-399-22849-7, G P Putnam) Peng Put Young Read.

— Amber Brown Goes Fourth. LC 94-41935. (Amber Brown Ser.: No. 3). (Illus.). 101p. (J). (gr. 2-5). 1996. pap. 3.50 (0-590-93425-2, Little Apple) Scholastic Inc.

— Amber Brown Goes Fourth. LC 94-41935. (Amber Brown Ser.: No. 3). (J). (gr. 3-6). 1996. 8.60 (0-606-10120-9, Pub. by Turtleback) Demco.

Danziger, Paula. Amber Brown Goes Fourth. (Amber Brown Ser.: No. 3). 112p. (J). (gr. 3-6). pap. 3.99 (0-8072-1291-1) Listening Lib.

Danziger, Paula. Amber Brown Is Feeling Blue. LC 98-11233. (Amber Brown Ser.: No. 7). (Illus.). (J). (gr. 3-6). 1998. 13.95 (0-399-23219-2) Putnam Pub Group.

— Amber Brown Is Feeling Blue. LC 98-11233. (Amber Brown Ser.: No. 7). (Illus.). 128p. (J). (gr. 3-6). 1998. 14.99 (0-399-23179-X) Putnam Pub Group.

***Danziger, Paula.** Amber Brown Is Feeling Blue. (Amber Brown Ser.: No. 7). (Illus.). 131p. (J). (gr. 2-5). 1999. pap. 3.99 (0-439-07168-2) Scholastic Inc.

— Amber Brown Is Not a Crayon. (Amber Brown Ser.: No. 1). (J). (gr. 3-6). write for info. (0-7857-7523-4) Econo-Clad Bks.

Danziger, Paula. Amber Brown Is Not a Crayon. (Amber Brown Ser.: No. 1). (Illus.). 80p. (J). (gr. 2-5). 1995. pap. 3.50 (0-590-45899-X) Little.

— Amber Brown Is Not a Crayon. LC 92-34678. (Amber Brown Ser.: No. 1). (Illus.). 80p. (J). (gr. 1-4). 1994. 13.99 (0-399-22509-9, G P Putnam) Peng Put Young Read.

— Amber Brown Is Not a Crayon. (Amber Brown Ser.: No. 1). (J). (gr. 3-6). 1995. 8.70 (0-606-07185-7, Pub. by Turtleback) Demco.

Danziger, Paula. Amber Brown Is Not a Crayon. (Amber Brown Ser.: No. 1). 80p. (J). (gr. 3-6). pap. 3.50 (0-8072-1289-X) Listening Lib.

— Amber Brown Sees Red. (Amber Brown Ser.: No. 6). (J). (gr. 3-6). write for info. (0-613-09442-5) Econo-Clad Bks.

— Amber Brown Sees Red. LC 96-41227. (Amber Brown Ser.: No. 6). (Illus.). 112p. (J). (gr. 3-7). 1997. 13.99 (0-399-22901-9, G P Putnam) Peng Put Young Read.

Danziger, Paula. Amber Brown Sees Red. (Illus.). 116p. (J). (gr. 2-5). 1998. pap. 3.50 (0-590-94728-1) Scholastic Inc.

***Danziger, Paula.** Amber Brown Sees Red. (Amber Brown Ser.: No. 6). (J). (gr. 3-6). 1998. 8.60 (0-606-12874-3, Pub. by Turtleback) Demco.

— Amber Brown Sees Red. (Amber Brown Ser.: No. 6). 116p. (J). (gr. 3-6). pap. 3.99 (0-8072-1294-6) Listening Lib.

— Amber Brown Wants Extra Credit. (Amber Brown Ser.: No. 4). (J). (gr. 3-6). write for info. (0-613-02015-4) Econo-Clad Bks.

Danziger, Paula. Amber Brown Wants Extra Credit. LC 95-586. (Amber Brown Ser.: No. 4). (Illus.). 120p. (J). (ps-3). 1996. 14.99 (0-399-22900-0, G P Putnam) Peng Put Young Read.

— Amber Brown Wants Extra Credit. LC 95-586. (Illus.). 120p. (J). (gr. 2-5). 1997. pap. 3.50 (0-590-94716-8, Little Apple) Scholastic Inc.

— Amber Brown Wants Extra Credit. (Amber Brown Ser.: No. 4). (J). (gr. 3-6). 1997. 8.60 (0-606-11035-6, Pub. by Turtleback) Demco.

Danziger, Paula. Amber Brown Wants Extra Credit. (Amber Brown Ser.: No. 3). 120p. (J). (gr. 3-6). pap. 3.99 (0-8072-1292-X) Listening Lib.

Danziger, Paula. Can You Sue Your Parents for Malpractice? 160p. (J). (gr. 5 up). 1998. pap. 3.99 (0-698-11688-7, PapStar) Peng Put Young Read.

Danziger, Paula. Can You Sue Your Parents for Malpractice? 144p. (J). (gr. 5-6). pap. 3.99 (0-8072-1375-6) Listening Lib.

— Can You Sue Your Parents for Malpractice? 152p. (YA). (gr. 5-8). pap. 3.99 (0-8072-1540-6) Listening Lib.

Danziger, Paula. The Cat Ate My Gymsuit. LC 74-8898. (Illus.). 147p. (J). (gr. 4-7). 1998. pap. 4.99 (0-698-11684-4, PapStar) Peng Put Young Read.

***Danziger, Paula.** The Cat Ate My Gymsuit. (J). 1998. 9.09 (0-606-13091-8, Pub. by Turtleback) Demco.

— The Cat Ate My Gymsuit. 128p. (J). (gr. 3-5). pap. 3.99 (0-8072-1368-3) Listening Lib.

Danziger, Paula. A Day No Pigs Would Fly. (J). 1979. mass mkt. 4.99 (0-440-80173-7) Dell.

— The Divorce Express. 160p. (J). (gr. 4 up). 1998. pap. 3.99 (0-698-11685-2, PapStar) Peng Put Young Read.

Danziger, Paula. The Divorce Express. 160p. pap. 3.99 (0-8072-1376-4) Listening Lib.

Danziger, Paula. Earth to Matthew: A Mathew Martin Book. 154p. (J). (gr. 3-7). 1998. pap. 4.99 (0-698-11692-5, PapStar) Peng Put Young Read.

— Everyone Else's Parents. (J). 1996. pap. 4.99 (0-440-91119-2) BDD Bks Young Read.

— Everyone Else's Parents Said Yes. 128p. (YA). (gr. k-6). 1990. pap. 3.99 (0-440-40333-2, YB BDD) BDD Bks Young Read.

— Everyone Else's Parents Said Yes. 126p. (J). (gr. 4-7). 1998. pap. 4.99 (0-698-11687-9, PapStar) Peng Put Young Read.

— Everyone Else's Parents Said Yes. (J). 1989. 9.09 (0-606-03267-3, Pub. by Turtleback) Demco.

***Danziger, Paula.** Forever Amber Brown. (Amber Brown Ser.: No. 5). (J). (gr. 3-6). 1999. write for info. (0-613-03623-9) Econo-Clad Bks.

Danziger, Paula. Forever Amber Brown. (Amber Brown Ser.: No. 5). (J). (gr. 3-6). 1998. pap. 15.98 incl. audio (0-8072-0366-1, FTR185SP) Listening Lib.

— Forever Amber Brown. LC PZ7.D2394Fo 1996. (Illus.). 112p. (J). (gr. 1-4). 1996. 13.95 (0-399-22932-9, G P Putnam) Peng Put Young Read.

— Forever Amber Brown. (Illus.). 96p. (J). (gr. 2-5). 1998. pap. 3.50 (0-590-94725-7) Scholastic Inc.

Danziger, Paula. Forever Amber Brown. 1997. 8.60 (0-606-11345-2, Pub. by Turtleback) Demco.

— Forever Amber Brown. (Amber Brown Ser.: No. 5). 101p. (J). (gr. 3-6). pap. 3.99 (0-8072-1293-8) Listening Lib.

— I, Amber Brown. LC 98-52884. (Amber Brown Ser.: No. 8). (Illus.). 140p. (J). (gr. 4-7). 1999. 14.99 (0-399-23180-3, Ace-Putnam) Putnam Pub Group.

— I, Amber Brown. (Amber Brown Ser.: No. 8). (J). (gr. 3-6). 2000. write for info. (0-399-23242-7) Putnam Pub Group.

— I, Amber Brown. (Illus.). (J). 2000. 9.34 (0-606-18877-0) Turtleback.

— I, Amber Brown. (Amber Brown Ser.: No. 8). (Illus.). 144p. (J). (gr. 2-5). 2000. pap. 3.99 (0-439-07169-0, Little Apple) Scholastic Inc.

Danziger, Paula. Ironman. (J). 1996. mass mkt. 5.99 (0-440-91150-8) BDD Bks Young Read.

— It's an Aardvark-Eat-Turtle World. 144p. (J). 1996. pap. 3.99 (0-440-41399-0) BDD Bks Young Read.

— It's an Aardvark-Eat-Turtle World. 1996. 9.09 (0-606-00305-3, Pub. by Turtleback) Demco.

***Danziger, Paula.** It's an Aardvark-Eat-Turtle World. (Illus.). (J). 2000. 10.34 (0-606-18469-4) Turtleback.

Danziger, Paula. Make Like a Tree & Leave. 126p. (J). (gr. 4-7). 1998. pap. 4.99 (0-698-11686-0, PapStar) Peng Put Young Read.

— Make Like a Tree & Leave. 1998. 10.09 (0-606-13593-6, Pub. by Turtleback) Demco.

— Not for a Billion Gazillion Dollars. (Illus.). 126p. (J). (gr. 3-7). 1998. pap. 4.99 (0-698-11693-3, PapStar) Peng Put Young Read.

— The Pistachio Prescription. LC 77-86330. 154p. (gr. 5-9). 1999. pap. 4.99 (0-698-11690-9) Putnam Pub Group.

Danziger, Paula. The Pistachio Prescription. 154p. (J). (gr. 4-6). pap. 3.99 (0-8072-1525-2); pap. 3.99 (0-8072-1374-8) Listening Lib.

— Remember Me to Harold Square. 1 vol. (YA). (gr. 5 up). 1999. pap. 3.99 (0-698-11694-1, PapStar) Peng Put Young Read.

— Remember Me to Harold Square. 139p. (YA). (gr. 6 up). pap. 3.99 (0-8072-1472-8) Listening Lib.

Danziger, Paula. Seguiremos Siendo Amigos (Amber Brown Is Not a Crayon) (SPA.). (J). 1995. pap. text 9.95 (84-204-4857-5) Santillana.

— Seguiremos Siendo Amigos (Amber Brown Is Not a Crayon) (J). 1994. 15.05 (0-606-10506-9, Pub. by Turtleback) Demco.

— Thames Doesn't Rhyme with James. 192p. (J). (gr. 5-9). 1995. pap. 3.99 (0-425-15015-1) Berkley Pub.

— Thames Doesn't Rhyme with James. 176p. (YA). 1994. 15.95 (0-399-22526-9, G P Putnam) Peng Put Young Read.

***Danziger, Paula.** Thames Doesn't Rhyme with James, 1 vol. (Illus.). 160p. (YA). (gr. 5-9). 1999. pap. 3.99 (0-698-11788-3, PapStar) Peng Put Young Read.

— Thames Doesn't Rhyme with James. 153p. pap. 3.99 (0-8072-1473-6) Listening Lib.

Danziger, Paula. There's a Bat in Bunk Five. LC 80-15581. 1980. 9.89 (0-440-08606-X) Dell.

— There's a Bat in Bunk Five. LC 80-15581. (Illus.). 154p. (J). (gr. 4-7). 1998. pap. 3.99 (0-698-11689-5, PapStar) Peng Put Young Read.

***Danziger, Paula.** There's a Bat in Bunk Five. 1998. 9.09 (0-606-13094-2, Pub. by Turtleback) Demco.

— There's A Bat in Bunk Five. 160p. pap. 160.00 (0-8072-1369-1) Listening Lib.

Danziger, Paula. This Place Has No Atmosphere. 160p. (J). (gr. k-6). 1989. pap. 3.99 (0-440-40205-0, YB BDD) BDD Bks Young Read.

— This Place Has No Atmosphere. LC 85-46070. 156p. (gr. 5-9). 1999. pap. 4.99 (0-698-11695-X) Putnam Pub Group.

Danziger, Paula. You Can't Eat Your Chicken Pox, Amber Brown. (Amber Brown Ser.: No. 2). (J). (gr. 3-6). write for info. (0-7857-7522-6) Econo-Clad Bks.

Danziger, Paula. You Can't Eat Your Chicken Pox, Amber Brown. LC 93-37761. (Amber Brown Ser.: No. 2). (Illus.). 80p. (J). (gr. 3-6). 1995. 13.95 (0-399-22702-4, G P Putnam) Peng Put Young Read.

— You Can't Eat Your Chicken Pox, Amber Brown. (Amber Brown Ser.: No. 2). (Illus.). 101p. (J). (gr. 2-5). 1996. pap. 3.50 (0-590-50207-7, Little Apple) Scholastic Inc.

Danziger, Paula. You Can't Eat Your Chicken Pox, Amber Brown. (Amber Brown Ser.: No. 2). (J). (gr. 3-6). 1996. 8.09 (0-606-08911-X, Pub. by Turtleback) Demco.

— You Can't Eat Your Chicken Pox, Amber Brown. (Amber Brown Ser.: No. 2). 101p. (J). (gr. 3-6). pap. 3.50 (0-8072-1290-3) Listening Lib.

Danziger, Paula & Martin, Ann M. P. S. Longer Letter Later. 234p. (J). (gr. 3-7). 1999. pap. 4.99 (0-590-21311-3) Scholastic Inc.

— P. S. Longer Letter Later: A Novel in Letters. LC 97-19120. 234p. (J). (gr. 5-8). 1998. 15.95 (0-590-21310-5) Scholastic Inc.

Danziger, Paula & Martin, Ann M. P. S. Longer Letter Later: A Novel in Letters. 240p. (J). (gr. 3-5). pap. 4.99 (0-8072-1537-6) Listening Lib.

— Snail Mail No More. LC 99-33593. (Illus.). 192p. (J). (gr. 4-7). 2000. 15.95 (0-439-06335-3, Scholastic Ref) Scholastic Inc.

— Snail Mail No More. LC 99-33593. (Illus.). (J). 2001. pap. 4.99 (0-439-06336-1) Scholastic Inc.

***Danziger, Paula & Ross, Tony.** It's Just in Time, Amber Brown. LC 99-89396. (A is for Amber Ser.). (J). 2001. write for info. (0-399-23470-5) Putnam Pub Group.

Danziger, Peter, ed. Representing People with Disabilities. LC 91-52548. 594p. 1991. ring bd. 95.00 (0-942954-38-6) NYS Bar.

Danziger, Raphael. Abd al-Qadir & the Algerians: Resistance to the French & Internal Consolidation. LC 76-18061. 1977. 49.50 (0-8419-0236-4, Africana) Holmes & Meier.

Danziger, Robert. The Musical Ascent of Herman Being: A How-To Novel. 3rd rev. ed. LC 95-75889. (Illus.). 112p. (C). 1995. pap. 11.95 (0-9613427-8-1) Jordan Pr.

— The Revelation of Music: Learning to Love the Classics. LC 91-90208. (Illus.). 253p. (Orig.). (C). 1991. pap. text 17.95 (0-9613427-6-5) Jordan Pr.

— The Revelation of Music: Learning to Love the Classics. 2nd enl. rev. ed. LC 95-75274. (Illus.). 312p. (Orig.). (C). 1995. pap. text 27.95 incl. audio compact disk (0-9613427-7-3) Jordan Pr.

Danziger, Sheldon. America Unequal. (Illus.). 240p. 1997. pap. text 17.00 (0-674-01811-7) HUP.

***Danziger, Sheldon, ed.** Economic Conditions & Welfare Reform. LC 99-49277. 350p. 1999. text 40.00 (0-88099-200-X); pap. text 22.00 (0-88099-199-2) W E Upjohn.

Danziger, Sheldon & Gottschalk, Peter. America Unequal. LC 95-11218. (Illus.). 240p. (C). 1996. text 31.00 (0-674-01810-9) HUP.

— Uneven Tides: Rising Inequality in America. LC 92-14233. (Illus.). 320p. 1992. 45.00 (0-87154-222-6) Russell Sage.

Danziger, Sheldon & Gottschalk, Peter, eds. Uneven Tides: Rising Inequality in America. (Illus.). 288p. 1994. reprint ed. pap. 16.95 (0-87154-227-7) Russell Sage.

***Danziger, Sheldon & Lin, Ann C., eds.** Coping with Poverty. (Illus.). 304p. (C). 2000. pap. text 27.95 (0-472-08697-9, 08697) U of Mich Pr.

— Coping with Poverty: The Social Contexts of Neighborhood, Work & Family in the African-American Community. LC 00-20956. (Illus.). 304p. (C). 2000. text 65.00 (0-472-11145-0, 11145) U of Mich Pr.

Danziger, Sheldon & Portney, Kent E. Distributional Impacts of Public Policies. (Orig.). 1984. pap. 15.00 (0-918592-68-2) Pol Studies.

Danziger, Sheldon & Witte, John F., eds. State Policy Choices: The Wisconsin Experience. LC 88-40232. (La Follette Public Policy Ser.). 312p. 1988. reprint ed. pap. 96.80 (0-608-01967-4, 206262200003) Bks Demand.

Danziger, Sheldon, jt. ed. see Cornia, Giovanni A.

Danziger, Sheldon, jt. ed. see Waldfogel, Jane.

Danziger, Sheldon H., et al, eds. Confronting Poverty: Prescriptions for Change. LC 93-50929. (Russell Sage Foundation Book). (Illus.). 576p. 1994. text 49.95 (0-674-16081-9); pap. text 22.95 (0-674-16082-7) HUP.

Danziger, Sheldon H. & Weinberg, Daniel H., eds. Fighting Poverty: What Works & What Doesn't. LC 85-24848. (Illus.). 448p. 1986. pap. 18.50 (0-674-30086-6) HUP.

— Fighting Poverty: What Works & What Doesn't. (Illus.). 448p. 1986. 43.00 (0-674-30085-8) HUP.

Danziger, Y., ed. Talmud Bavli - Tractate Shevuos: Schottenstein Edition. 1994. 46.99 (0-89906-746-8) Mesorah Pubns.

Danziger, Y., ed. see Eisemann, Moshe.

Danziger, Y., ed. see GoldWurm, Hersh.

Danziger, Y., ed. see Rabinnovitch, M. & Goldwurm, Hersh.

Danziger, Y., ed. see Rabinovitch, M. & Kalatsky, Y.

Danziger, Y., ed. see Rabinowitz, Y.

Danziger, Y., ed. see Roberts, M.

Danziger, Y., ed. see Rosenberg, A. J.

Danziger, Y., ed. see Rosenberg, A. Y.

Danziger, Y., tr. see Goldwurm, Hersh.

Danziger, Y. Eliezer, tr. see Schneersohn, Joseph I.

Danziger, Yehezkel, ed. see Roberts, Matis.

Danzigger, H., ed. see Rosenberg, Avrohom Y.

Danzinger, Eliezer Y., ed. Kuntres Ahavat Yisrael: Love of a Fellow Jew. 2nd rev. ed. Posner, Zalman I. & Mangel, Nissen, trs. from HEB. LC 98-6108. 80p. 1998. pap. 9.95 (0-8266-0458-7) Kehot Pubn Soc.

Danzinger, Lazer, tr. see Dov Ber Schneersohn, Shalom.

Danzinger, Y., ed. see Roberts, M.

Danzinger, Y. Elizer, jt. auth. see Schneersohn, Shalom Dov Baer.

Danzis, Steve. Behind the Lions: A Family Guide to the Art Institute of Chicago. LC 97-36122. (Illus.). 112p. (J). (gr. 2-8). 1998. pap. 15.95 (0-86559-156-3) Art Inst Chi.

Danzker, Jo-Anne B., et al, eds. Dreamings - Tjukurrpa: Aboriginal Art from the Western Desert. LC 95-225228. (Illus.). 152p. 1994. 55.00 (3-7913-1427-0, Pub. by Prestel) te Neues.

Danzker, Jo-Anne Birnie. Robert Wilson: Steel Velvet. (Illus.). 104p. 1998. pap. 35.00 (3-7913-1925-6) te Neues.

Danzo, Mark S. Marketing & Managing Your Refractive Surgery Venture. (Illus.). 158p. 1997. pap. write for info. (1-929196-07-5) Am Opthlmc Admin.

Danzon, Patricia M. Global Budgets vs. Competitive Cost-Control Strategies. (Studies in Health Reform). 200p. (Orig.). 1994. pap. 9.95 (0-8447-7023-X, AEI Pr) Am Enterprise.

— Medical Malpractice: Theory, Evidence, & Public Policy. (Illus.). 312p. 1985. 44.00 (0-674-56115-5) HUP.

Danzon, Patricia M. & Harrington, Scott. Rate Regulation of Workers' Compensation Insurance. LC 97-25288. 150p. 1997. 29.95 (0-8447-3932-4) Am Enterprise.

***Dao, Bei.** Blue House. 2000. pap. 13.95 (0-939010-58-5) Zephyr Pr.

An Asterisk (*) at the beginning of an entry indicates that the title is appearing for the first time.

— Unlock. Weinberger, Eliot & Man-Cheong, Iona, trs. from CHI. 2000. pap. 13.95 (*0-8112-1447-8*, Pub. by New Directions) Norton.

Dao, Ming, ed. see Lu, Zuyin.

Dao, N. Quy & Daudon, M., eds. Infrared & Raman Spectra of Calculi. 348p. 1997. pap. 200.00 incl. cd-rom (*2-84299-003-X*) Elsevier.

Dao, Nguyen Van, see Van Dao, Nguyen.

Dao Quang Chinh, Anthony. Dominican Laity & the Year 2000. 3rd rev. ed. LC 97-71122. viii, 133p. 1997. pap. 5.95 (*0-9657125-0-8*) Magnificat Inst.

Dao Thi Thanh Hieu, tr. see Albin, Francis M., ed.

Dao, Thomas L., ed. see International Symposium on Endogenous Factors Infl.

Dao, Thuy, et al, eds. 1999 4th International Symposium on Plasma Process-Induced Damage. (Illus.). 250p. 1999. pap. write for info. (*0-9651577-3-3*) Nrthrn CA Chapter.

Daoran, Li & Mingyuan, Wang. Company Law & Laws Relating to Foreign Investment of China. Date not set. ring bd. write for info. (*1-57823-062-4*) Juris Pubng.

Daoren, Huanchu. Back to Beginnings. 1998. pap. 10.00 (*1-57062-377-5*, Pub. by Shambhala Pubns) Random.

Daoshing Ni, jt. auth. see Maoshing Ni.

Daoud, Abu & Du Jonchay, Gilles. Paustine from Jerusalem to Munich, from Munich to Jerusalem: The Sole Survivor of Black September Tells His Story for the First Time. 400p. Date not set. 27.45 (*1-55970-429-2*, Pub. by Arcade Pub Inc) Time Warner.

Daoud, Hazim S. Flora of Kuwait: Dicotyledoneae, Vol. I. (Illus.). 288p. 1985. 95.00 (*0-7103-0075-1*) Routledge.

Daoud, M. & Williams, Claudine. Soft Matter Physics. LC 98-39229. 1998. 89.00 (*3-540-64665-5*) Spr-Verlag.

Daoudi, M. S. The Meaning of Kahlil Gibran. 160p. 1982. 9.95 (*0-8065-0804-3*, Citadel Pr) Carol Pub Group.

Daoust, Gene, jt. auth. see Daoust, Joyce.

Daoust, H., jt. auth. see Stepek, Jiri.

Daoust, Jean-Paul. Black Diva: (Selected Poems: 1982-1986) 48p. 1991. pap. 5.00 (*0-920717-54-3*) SPD-Small Pr Dist.

***Daoust, Jean-Paul.** Blue Ashes: Selected Poems, 1982-1998. Sloate, Daniel, tr. from FRE. (Essential Poets Ser.: No. 94). 144p. 1999. pap. 13.00 (*1-55071-093-1*, Pub. by Guernica Editions) SPD-Small Pr Dist.

Daoust, Joyce & Daoust, Gene. 40-30-30 Fat Burning Nutrition: The Dietary Hormonal Connection to Permanent Weight Loss & Better Health. LC 96-61472. 136p. 1996. pap. 16.95 (*1-56912-086-2*) Wharton Pub.

Daoutidis, Prodromos & Kumar, Aditya. Control of Nonlinear Differential Algebraic Equation Systems. LC 98-32277. (Pitman Research Notes in Mathematics Ser.). 1999. lib. bdg. 69.95 (*0-8493-0609-4*) CRC Pr.

Daoxian, Yuan & Zaihua, Liu, eds. Global Karst Correlation. (Illus.). 308p. 1998. 90.00 (*1-880132-32-X*) Sci Pr NY.

***Daoxian, Yuan & Zaihua, Liu, eds.** Global Karst Correlation: Final Report of UNESCO-IUGS Project 299. 328p. 1999. 127.50 (*90-6764-286-X*, Pub. by VSP) Coronet Bks.

Daoyi, Zhang. Art of Chinese Papercuts. 68p. 1989. pap. 14.95 (*0-8351-1577-1*) China Bks.

DaParma, Charles W., et al. Latin Study Aid. (J). 1987. pap. 2.75 (*0-87738-035-X*) Youth Ed.

Dapdap, Jerry A. Studies in Ear Training. (Illus.). 48p. (Orig.). (C). 1990. pap. 6.50 (*971-10-0417-8*, Pub. by New Day Pub) Cellar.

Daper, Peter, ed. see Pearce, Michael.

Daphinoff, Dimiter, jt. ed. see Klein, Holger.

Daphne, Clair & Robyn, Donald. Writing Romantic Fiction. unabridged ed. LC 99-488462. 160p. 1999. pap. 15.95 (*0-7136-4887-2*) A & C Blk.

DaPian, R., jt. ed. see Pasqualin, A.

D'Apice, Mary. The Pueblo. (Native American People Ser.). (Illus.). 32p. (J). (gr. 5-8). 1990. lib. bdg. 11.95 (*0-685-36390-2*) Rourke Corp.

— The Pueblo. (Native American People Ser.: Set II). (Illus.). 32p. (J). (gr. 4-8). 1990. lib. bdg. 22.60 (*0-86625-385-8*) Rourke Pubns.

D'Apice, Mary, jt. auth. see D'Apice, Rita.

D'Apice, Rita. Gamblers. (Wild West in American History Ser.). (Illus.). 32p. (J). (gr. 3-8). 1989. lib. bdg. 23.93 (*0-86625-371-8*) Rourke Pubns.

D'Apice, Rita & D'Apice, Mary. The Algonquian. (Native American People Ser.: Set II). (Illus.). 32p. (J). (gr. 4-8). 1990. lib. bdg. 22.60 (*0-86625-388-2*) Rourke Pubns.

— Los Pueblo. (Pueblos Americanos Nativos Ser.).Tr. of Pueblo. (SPA.). 32p. (J). (gr. 5-8). 1990. lib. bdg. 21.27 (*0-86625-453-6*) Rourke Pubns.

D'Apice, Rita, et al. Native American People, 6 bks., Set. (Illus.). 192p. (J). (gr. 5-8). 1990. lib. bdg. 71.70 (*0-685-36385-6*) Rourke Corp.

— Native American People, 6 bks., Set. (Illus.). 192p. (J). (gr. 5-8). 1990. lib. bdg. 95.64 (*0-86625-383-1*) Rourke Pubns.

Dapkus, Dave, jt. auth. see Mosby, Jack.

Daplyn, P., et al. The Uses of Geographical Information Systems in Socio-Economic Studies. 1994. pap. 49.00 (*0-85954-372-2*, Pub. by Nat Res Inst) St Mut.

Daplyn, P. F., jt. auth. see Poate, C. D.

D'Aponte, Mimi G., ed. Seventh Generation: An Anthology of Native American Plays. LC 98-4449. 300p. 1998. pap. 16.95 (*1-55936-147-6*) Theatre Comm.

***Dapor, Maurizio.** Electron Atom Scattering: An Introduction. LC 99-54396. 187p. 1999. text 59.00 (*1-56072-758-6*) Nova Sci Pubs.

Dapper, Michael & Klancher, Lee. Victory Motorcycle: The Making of a New American V-Twin. LC 98-14857. 96p. 1998. pap. 14.95 (*0-7603-0530-7*) MBI Pubg.

Dapper, Olfert & Jones, Adam. Olfert Dapper's Description of Benin. LC 98-29219. (DUT & ENG.). 1998. write for info. (*0-942615-34-4*) African Studies Assn.

Dapples, Edward C. & Hopkins, M. E., eds. Environments of Coal Deposition. LC 68-58108. (Geological Society of America, Special Paper: No. 114). 242p. reprint ed. pap. 75.10 (*0-608-11125-2*, 200796500067) Bks Demand.

D'Appolonia, B. L. & Kunerth, W. H., eds. The Farinograph Handbook. 3rd ed. 64p. 1984. 64.00 (*0-913250-37-6*) Am Assn Cereal Chem.

D'Appolonia, Elio. Leopold Hirschfeldt & James Robert Davis Memorial Lecture: Reflections on the Growth & Changes of the Private Practice of Geotechnical Engineering. 25.00 (*0-614-05239-4*, LHML04831.5M) ASFE.

DaPra, Vic. Sunburst Alley: A Pictorial Gallery of the Les Paul Sunburst, 1958-1960. (Illus.). 80p. (Orig.). pap. 24.95 (*1-57424-041-2*) Centerstream Pub.

D'Aprix, David. International Foreign Language Guide for Hotel & Restaurant Personnel. (Living Language Ser.). 1998. pap. 18.00 (*0-609-80283-6*) Crown Pub Group.

— The Non-Connoisseur's Menu Guide: For French, Italian, Latin American & Spanish Cuisines. LC 99-35433. 320p. 1999. pap. 10.95 (*0-609-80493-6*) Liv Lang.

D'Aprix, Roger. Communicating for Change: Connecting the Workplace with the Marketplace. LC 95-25894. (The Management Ser.). 176p. 1996. 29.95 (*0-7879-0199-7*) Jossey-Bass.

Dapson, Janet C. & Dapson, Richard W. Hazardous Materials in the Histopathology Laboratory: Regulations, Risks, Handling & Disposal. 3rd ed. (Illus.). (Orig.). 1995. pap. 75.00 (*0-9645197-0-4*) Anatech MI.

Dapson, Richard W., jt. auth. see Dapson, Janet C.

D'Aquila, Ignatus. Remembering Dixie. Pelton, Mimi, ed. (Illus.). 384p. 1997. 22.95 (*0-9659156-0-3*) Hot Aug Nights.

D'Aquili, Eugene & Newberg, Andrew B. The Mystical Mind: Probing the Biology of Religious Experience. LC 99-24098. (Theology & the Sciences Ser.). 240p. 1999. pap. 20.00 (*0-8006-3163-3*, 1-3163, Fortress Pr) Augsburg Fortress.

D'Aquili, Eugene G. The Regulation of Physical & Mental Systems: Systems Theory of the Philosophy of Science. LC 89-12984. (Studies in Sociology: Vol. 4). 200p. 1990. lib. bdg. 89.95 (*0-88946-633-5*) E Mellen.

D'Aquili, Eugene G., jt. auth. see Laughlin, Charles D., Jr.

Daquin, et al. French Noels for Organ. 1998. pap. 10.95 (*0-486-29696-2*) Dover.

DAR Alabama Society. Index to Alabama Wills, 1808-1870. 180p. 1999. reprint ed. pap. 20.00 (*0-8063-0765-X*, 70, Pub. by Clearfield Co) ACCESS Pubs Network.

Dar, Allen K. Dart Grammar Workbook No. 1, Vol. 1. 2nd ed. 384p. 1996. pap. text, wbk. ed. 31.53 (*0-13-518770-2*) P-H.

Dar, B. A. Quranic Ethics. 1994. pap. 5.50 (*0-933511-29-9*) Kazi Pubns.

Dar, G. Mn. Modern Book-Keeping & Accounting. 600p. 1992. 140.00 (*81-7041-644-2*, Pub. by Scientific Pubs) St Mut.

***Dar, R. K.** Governance & the IAS: In Search of Resilience. LC 99-940404. 1999. write for info. (*0-07-463093-8*) McGrw-H Hghr Educ.

Dar Rah Haqq. Teach Yourself Islamic Ideology. Bakhtiar, Laleh, tr. from PER. 1989. pap. text 6.70 (*1-871031-11-7*) Abjad Bk.

Dar Rah Haqq's Board of Writers Staff. A Glance at the Life of the Holy Prophet of Islam. Tawheedi, N., tr. from PER. LC 88-62666. 181p. (Orig.). 1989. reprint ed. pap. 7.95 (*0-922817-01-4*) Mostazafan Foun.

Dar, S. U. Impact of Integrated Rural Development Programme, 1992. 144p. 1992. 68.00 (*81-7041-601-9*, Pub. by Scientific Pubs) St Mut.

Dar Systems International Staff. LBASIC Reference Manual. 3rd ed. Partise, David A. & Seiden, Eric A., eds. 120p. 1986. pap. 24.95 (*0-916163-98-9*) DAR Syst.

Dar, Yehezkel & Resh, Nura. Classroom Composition & Pupil Achievement: A Study of the Effect of Ability-Based Classes. (Special Aspects of Education Ser.: Vol. 5). x, 200p. 1986. text 94.00 (*0-677-21450-2*) Gordon & Breach.

Dara, Evan. The Lost Scrapbook. 400p. 1995. 21.95 (*1-57366-006-X*) Fiction Coll.

— The Lost Scrapbook. 475p. 1998. pap. 14.95 (*1-57366-038-8*) Fiction Coll.

Darabi, Katherine F., et al, compiled by. Childbearing among Hispanics in the United States: An Annotated Bibliography, 4. LC 86-33716. (Bibliographies & Indexes in Women's Studies: No. 6). 179p. 1987. lib. bdg. 59.95 (*0-313-25617-9*, DCH/) Greenwood.

***Darabi, Parvin & Thomson, Romin P.** Rage Against the Veil: The Courageous Life & Death of an Islamic Dissident. LC 98-54854. (Illus.). 310p. 1999. 26.95 (*1-57392-682-5*) Prometheus Bks.

Darack, Arthur. Trade the OEX: Cut Risk Not Profit. 3rd ed. LC 95-6435. (Illus.). 247p. 1995. 29.95 (*1-56625-032-3*) Bonus Books.

Darack, Ed. 6194: Denali Solo. 168p. (Orig.). 1995. pap. 12.00 (*1-884980-80-5*) E Darack Photo.

— Wind - Water - Sun: A Solo Kayak Journey along Baja California's Desert Coastline. LC 98-65927. (Illus.). 320p. 1998. 29.95 (*1-881663-08-6*) Poudre Canyon Pr.

Daragahi. The Ultimate Flight Simulator Guidebook. 1997. 39.95 (*0-8052-8574-1*, M&T Bks) IDG Bks.

Daragan, Vladimir A., jt. auth. see Mayo, Kevin H.

D'Aragona, Tullia. Dialogue on Infinity of Love. Russell, Rinaldina & Merry, Bruce, trs. LC 96-28841. 1996. pap. 12.95 (*0-226-13639-6*) U Ch Pr.

— Dialogue on Infinity of Love. Russell, Rinaldina & Merry, Bruce, trs. LC 96-28841. 1997. lib. bdg. 26.00 (*0-226-13638-8*) U Ch Pr.

Darai, G., jt. ed. see Becker, Yechiel.

Darai, Gholamreza, ed. Virus Diseases in Laboratory & Captive Animals. (Developments in Veterinary Virology Ser.). (C). 1987. text 293.50 (*0-89838-988-7*) Kluwer Academic.

Darai, Gholamreza & Becker, Yechiel, eds. PCR: Protocols for Diagnosis of Human & Animal Virus Diseases. LC 95-9546. (Illus.). 448p. 1995. 139.95 (*3-540-58899-X*) Spr-Verlag.

Darai, Gyorgy. Langenscheidt Universal Hungarian-German, German-Hungarian Dictionary: Langenscheidt Universal Woerterbuch Ungarisch-Deutsch-Ungarisch. 6th ed. (GER & HUN.). 447p. 1981. 14.95 (*0-8288-1661-1*, M14527) Fr & Eur.

Daramy, Sheikh B. Constitutional Developments in the Post-Colonial State of Sierra-Leone 1961-1984. LC 93-14707. (African Studies: Vol. 30). (Illus.). 328p. 1993. text 99.95 (*0-7734-9290-9*) E Mellen.

Daras, Stephen. Things to Remember: A Handbook for Drivers. LC 98-96413. 72p. 1998. pap. text 7.95 (*1-56167-452-4*, Five Star Spec Ed) Am Literary Pr.

Daraul, Arkon. History of Secret Societies. (Illus.). 256p. 1983. pap. 12.00 (*0-8065-0857-4*, Citadel Pr) Carol Pub Group.

***Daraul, Arkon.** Secret Societies - a History. 256p. 1999. 7.98 (*1-56731-291-8*, MJF Bks) Fine Comms.

Darbandi, Afkham, tr. see Attar, Farid Al-Din.

Darbandi, Afkham, tr. see Modarres-Sadeqi, Jafar.

Darbel, Alain, jt. auth. see Bourdieu, Pierre.

Darbelne. Pensee et Structure Text. 2nd ed. 1985. 16.95 (*0-684-14882-X*) S&S Trade.

Darbelnet, Jean, jt. auth. see Vinay, Jean-Paul.

Darber, Daniel A., jt. auth. see Findley, Roger W.

Darbey, Barbara R., ed. see McMonagle, Gary R.

Darbishire, Helen. The Poet Wordsworth. LC 79-14336. 182p. 1980. reprint ed. lib. bdg. 35.00 (*0-313-21483-2*, DAWO, Greenwood Pr) Greenwood.

Darbishire, Helen, ed. Early Lives of Milton. LC 77-144967. (Illus.). 1971. reprint ed. 49.00 (*0-403-00935-9*) Scholarly.

Darbishire, Helen, ed. see Milton, John.

Darbishire, Helen, ed. see Wordsworth, William.

D'Arblay, Frances B. Dr. Johnson & Fanny Burney. (BCL1-PR English Literature Ser.). 252p. 1992. reprint ed. lib. bdg. 79.00 (*0-7812-7366-8*) Rprt Serv.

Darblay, Jerome, photos by. Living in Istanbul. (Illus.). 256p. 1994. 45.00 (*2-08-013563-5*, Pub. by Flammarion) Abbeville Pr.

Darblay, Jerome & D'Arnoux, Alexandra. Family Houses by the Sea. LC 92-16349. (Illus.). 240p. 1993. 50.00 (*0-517-59165-0*) C Potter.

Darbo, Peter, tr. see De Ley, Gerd, ed.

D'Arbois de Jubainville, Marie-Henri. Etudes Sur l'Etat Interieur des Abbayes Cistercinnes. xviii, 489p. 1976. reprint ed. write for info. (*3-487-05944-4*) G Olms Pubs.

Darbosa e Rosario, Pilar. Un Lustro Crucial, 1893-1898: El Concierto Conduce al Pacto, 1891-1896. LC 83-10612. 182p. 1986. 12.00 (*0-8477-0879-9*); pap. 8.00 (*0-8477-0880-2*) U of PR Pr.

Darboux, Gaston. Theorie Generale des Surfaces, 4 Vols. 2nd ed. LC 67-16997. 1968. 150.00 (*0-8284-0216-7*) Chelsea Pub.

Darbouze, Gilbert. Degenerecence & Regenereseence dans l'Oeuvre d'Emile Zola & Celle de Manuel Zeno Gandia: Etude Comparee. (Currents in Comparative Romance Languages & Literatures Ser.: Vol. 31). (FRE.). X, 183p. (C). 1997. text 43.95 (*0-8204-2540-0*) P Lang Pubng.

Darboven, Hanne. Hanne Darboven: 1971-1985. (Illus.). 232p. 1992. 55.00 (*3-89322-372-X*, Pub. by Edition Cantz) Dist Art Pubs.

Darbre, A. Practical Protein Chemistry: A Handbook. LC 84-26942. 640p. 1986. reprint ed. pap. 198.40 (*0-7837-8317-5*, 204910300010) Bks Demand.

Darbre, Philippa D. Basic Molecular Biology: Essential Techniques. LC 98-27199. 208p. 1998. pap. 44.95 (*0-471-97705-5*) Wiley.

Darbro, David, jt. auth. see Swope, Mary R.

***Darbro, Jon.** Chez Geek. 1999. boxed set 19.95 (*1-55634-411-2*, Pub. by S Jackson Games) BookWorld.

Darbshire, Owen, jt. auth. see Katz, Harry C.

***Darby.** Dental Hygiene Theory & Practice. 2nd ed. 2001. text. write for info. (*0-7216-9162-5*) Harcrt Hlth Sci Grp.

Darby. Japan & European Periphery. 288p. 1997. text 69.95 (*0-312-16161-1*) St Martin.

Darby, jt. auth. see Carr, Michael.

***Darby, Ann.** The Orphan Game. large type ed. LC 99-39089. 521p. 1999. 27.95 (*0-7838-8749-3*, G K Hall Lrg Type) Mac Lib Ref.

— The Orphan Game: A Novel. 336p. 2000. pap. 13.00 (*0-688-17782-4*, Quil) HarperTrade.

Darby, Ann. The Orphan Game: A Novel. LC 98-43778. 336p. 1999. 24.00 (*0-688-16778-0*, Wm Morrow) Morrow Avon.

Darby, Anthony. The Great American National Scholarships & Grants Guide. 130p. 1991. pap. 9.95 (*0-9630725-0-1*) DClaren Media.

— The Great American National Scholarships & Grants Guide. 2nd rev. ed. (Illus.). 150p. (C). 1993. pap. 19.95 (*0-9630725-1-X*) DClaren Media.

Darby, Barbara. Frances Burney, Dramatist: Gender, Performance, & the Late Eighteenth-Century Stage. LC 97-19459. (Illus.). 272p. (C). 1997. text 39.95 (*0-8131-2022-5*) U Pr of Ky.

Darby, Betty, jt. auth. see Wittish, Rich.

***Darby, Catherine.** Falcon to the Lure. large type ed. 336p. 1999. 31.99 (*0-7089-4097-8*, Linford) Ulverscroft.

— Falcon's Claw. large type ed. 360p. 1999. 31.99 (*0-7089-4131-1*) Ulverscroft.

— The Flaunting Moon. large type ed. 320p. pap. 18.99 (*0-7089-5437-5*) Ulverscroft.

Darby, Catherine. Frost on the Moon. large type ed. (Linford Mystery Library). 352p. 1998. pap. 17.99 (*0-7089-5209-7*, Linford) Ulverscroft.

— Moon in Pisces. large type ed. (Ulverscroft Large Print Ser.). 272p. 1998. 29.99 (*0-7089-3937-6*) Ulverscroft.

***Darby, Catherine.** Zabillet of the Snow. large type ed. 320p. 1999. pap. 18.99 (*0-7089-5468-5*, Linford) Ulverscroft.

***Darby, Chad.** Beginning Java Server Pages. 400p. 2000. pap. 39.99 (*1-86100-209-2*) Wrox Pr Inc.

Darby, D. J. Financing of Industry & Trade. 1970. 45.00 (*0-8464-0413-3*) Beekman Pubs.

— Financing of Industry & Trade. 251p. 1970. pap. 19.95 (*0-8464-0412-5*) Beekman Pubs.

Darby, David. Structures of Disintegration: Narrative Strategies in Elias Canetti's "Die Blendung" (Studies in Austrian Literature, Culture, & Thought). 240p. 1992. 33.00 (*0-929497-50-3*) Ariadne CA.

Darby, Douglas S., jt. auth. see Verma, Gajendra K.

Darby, Emma. A Conflict of Women. (Signet Double Romance Ser.). 1977. mass mkt. 1.50 (*0-451-07370-3*, W7370, Sig) NAL.

***Darby, Glenn.** How to Star in Your Own TV Show for $50 or Less: An Insider's Guide to Access Television. LC 99-94514. (Illus.). 248p. 2000. pap. 14.95 (*0-9669328-0-3*, Pub. by Big Red Barn) SCB Distributors.

Darby, Graham. Spain in the Seventeenth Century. LC 94-1990. (Seminar Studies in History). (C). 1995. pap. text 14.06 (*0-582-07234-4*, Pub. by Addison-Wesley) Longman.

Darby, H. C. & Terrett, I. B., eds. The Domesday Geography of Midland England. 2nd ed. LC 78-134626. 508p. reprint ed. pap. 144.80 (*0-608-13568-2*, 2022445) Bks Demand.

Darby, Henry C. Mediaeval Cambridgeshire. (Cambridge Town, Gown & County Ser.: Vol. 15). (Illus.). 1977. pap. 5.95 (*0-900891-11-4*) Oleander Pr.

Darby, Ian A., ed. In Situ Hybridization Protocols. 2nd ed. LC 98-48665. (Methods in Molecular Biology Ser.: Vol. 123). (Illus.). 368p. 1999. 79.50 (*0-89603-686-3*) Humana.

Darby, J. N. Letters of J. N. Darby, 3 vols., Set. 22.00 (*0-88172-060-7*) Believers Bkshelf.

— Notes & Comments on Scripture, 7 vols., Set. 37.00 (*0-88172-068-2*) Believers Bkshelf.

— Notes & Jottings on Scripture. 7.95 (*0-88172-069-0*) Believers Bkshelf.

Darby, Jaye T. & Geiogamah, Hanay, eds. Stories of Our Way: An Anthology of American Indian Plays. LC 98-74559. (Native American Theater Ser.: No. 1). 508p. (C). 1999. 60.00 (*0-935626-49-2*) U Cal AISC.

Darby, Jaye T., jt. ed. see Geiogamah, Hanay.

Darby, Jean. Alice: A Centennial History, 1888-1988. (Illus.). 104p. 1997. 14.95 (*0-89015-645-X*, Eakin Pr) Sunbelt Media.

— Douglas MacArthur. (Lerner Biography Ser.). (Illus.). 112p. (J). (gr. 5 up). 1989. lib. bdg. 23.93 (*0-8225-4901-8*, Lerner Publctns) Lerner Pub.

— Dwight D. Eisenhower: A Man Called Ike. LC 90-6452. (Lerner Biography Ser.). (Illus.). 100p. (YA). (gr. 5 up). 1990. lib. bdg. 23.93 (*0-8225-4900-X*, Lerner Publctns) Lerner Pub.

— Martin Luther King, Jr. (Lerner Biography Ser.). (Illus.). 112p. (YA). (gr. 6-9). 1990. lib. bdg. 23.96 (*0-8225-4902-6*, Lerner Publctns) Lerner Pub.

— Martin Luther King, Jr. (Illus.). 144p. (YA). (gr. 6-9). 1992. pap. 6.95 (*0-8225-9611-3*, Lerner Publctns) Lerner Pub.

— That's Me in Here. (Illus.). 42p. (Orig.). (J). (gr. 1-2). 1989. pap. 4.95 (*0-8198-7345-4*) Pauline Bks.

Darby, John. Intimidation & Control of Conflict in Northern Ireland. (Irish Studies). 199p. 1987. text 39.95 (*0-8156-2394-1*) Syracuse U Pr.

— Scorpions in a Bottle: Ethnic Conflict in Northern Ireland. 300p. 1997. 54.95 (*1-873194-11-0*, Pub. by Minority Rts Pubns); pap. 19.95 (*1-873194-16-1*, Pub. by Minority Rts Pubns) Paul & Co Pubs.

— Target Rabaul. (McLeane's Rangers Ser.: No. 2). 1983. mass mkt. 2.50 (*0-685-07874-4*, Zebra Kensgtn) Kensgtn Pub Corp.

Darby, John, ed. Northern Ireland: The Background to the Conflict. 176p. 1987. pap. 17.95 (*0-8156-2417-4*) Syracuse U Pr.

***Darby, John & MacGinty, Roger.** The Management of Peace Processes. LC 99-59427. 2000. 69.95 (*0-312-23198-9*) St Martin.

Darby, John F. Personal Recollections of Many Prominent People Whom I Have Known. LC 75-94. (Mid-American Frontier Ser.). 1975. reprint ed. 40.95 (*0-405-06860-3*) Ayer.

Darby, John T., jt. ed. see Davis, Lloyd S.

Darby, Joseph J., tr. from GER. Penal Code of the Federal Republic of Germany. LC 86-29731. (American Series of Foreign Penal Codes: Vol. 28). xxvi, 257p. 1987. 32.50 (*0-8377-0048-5*, Rothman) W S Hein.

Darby, Joseph J., tr. from GER. Alternative Draft of a Penal Code for the Federal Republic of Germany. (American Series of Foreign Penal Codes: Vol. 21). 157p. 1977. 22.50 (*0-8377-0041-8*, Rothman) W S Hein.

Darby, Judith M. Comfortably Fixed. LC 90-93015. (Illus.). 176p. 1990. 28.50 (*0-9626261-0-4*) J M Darby.

Darby, Ken. Hollywood Holyland: The Filming & Scoring of "The Greatest Story Ever Told" LC 91-47501. (Filmmakers Ser.: No. 30). (Illus.). 314p. 1992. 39.50 (*0-8108-2509-0*) Scarecrow.

Darby, Kit. Airline Pilot Career Decisions: A Personal Guide for Professional Pilots Entering the Airline Job Market. 4th ed. Waymire, Montina L. & Dean, Becky, eds. 44p. 1998. pap. 32.95 (*1-891726-03-X*) Aviation Info.

— Questions, Questions: A Comprehensive Listing of

D

Frequently Asked Technical & Human Resource Questions Used by Major, National & Regional Airlines. Dean, Becky & Waymire, Montina L., eds. 96p. 1998. pap. 28.95 (*1-891726-04-8*) Aviation Info.

Darby, Kit & Dean, Becky. Airline Pilot Application Handbook Vol. 1: A Comprehensive Guide to Getting & Completing Airline Employment Applications. 176p. 1997. pap. 34.95 (*1-891726-02-1*, AIR Inc) Aviation Info.

Darby, Kit & Gradwohl, Dan. 1999-2000 Airline Fleet & Sim Directory. Waymire, Montina L. & Dean, Becky, eds. 64p. 1999. pap. 29.95 (*1-891726-25-0*, AIR Inc) Aviation Info.

— 1999-2000 U. S. Airlines Salary Survey & Career Earnings Comparison. 3rd ed. Waymire, Montina L. & Dean, Becky, eds. 144p. 1999. pap. 40.00 (*1-891726-27-7*, AIR Inc) Aviation Info.

Darby, Kit, et al. Airline Pilot Test Kit Vol. 1: A Guide for Airline Pre-Employment Testing. 96p. 1997. pap. 39.00 (*1-891726-01-3*, AIR Inc) Aviation Info.

Darby, Kit, ed. see Komich, Norm.

Darby, M. I., jt. auth. see Taylor, K. N. R.

Darby, Maribeth. Land of Whistlepunks & Wild Things: Forests Yesterday & Today. LC 97-183210. (Illus.). 128p. (J). 1997. 14.95 (*1-57168-112-4*, Eakin Pr) Sunbelt Media.

Darby, Mark Stuart. Keeping Australia on the Left: A Catamatan Odyssey Around Australia. LC 99-37417. 225p. 1999. pap. text 13.95 (*1-55571-508-7*) PSI Resch.

Darby, Mary, jt. ed. see Namovicz-Peat, Susan.

Darby, Michael R. & Anderson, John E., eds. Reducing Poverty in America: Views & Approaches. LC 95-35748. 360p. 1995. 59.95 (*0-7619-0006-3*); pap. 28.00 (*0-7619-0007-1*) Sage.

Darby, Michael R., et al. The International Transmission of Inflation. LC 83-5785. (National Bureau of Economic Research Monographs). (Illus.). 742p. 1984. lib. bdg. 88.00 (*0-226-13641-8*) U Ch Pr.

— The International Transmission of Inflation. LC 83-5785. (National Bureau of Economic Research Monographs). (Illus.). 744p. 1985. pap. text 30.00 (*0-226-13642-6*) U Ch Pr.

Darby, Michele & Walsh, Margaret. Dental Hygiene Theory & Practice. (Illus.). 960p. 1994. text 62.95 (*0-7216-2966-0*, W B Saunders Co) Harcrt Hlth Sci Grp.

Darby, Michele L. Mosby's Comprehensive Review of Dental Hygiene. 4th ed. LC 97-34800. (Illus.). 912p. (C). (gr. 13). 1997. pap. text 45.95 (*0-8151-2267-5*, 29189) Mosby Inc.

Darby, N. J. & Creighton, T. E. Protein Structure. LC 92-27978. (In Focus Ser.). (Illus.). 112p. 1994. pap. text 19.95 (*0-19-963310-X*) OUP.

Darby, Philip. Three Faces of Imperialism. LC 86-24665. 256p. 1987. 40.00 (*0-300-03748-1*) Yale U Pr.

Darby, Phillip. At the Edge of International Relations: Postcolonialism, Gender & Dependency. LC 96-21544. 224p. (C). 1997. text 89.50 (*1-85567-438-6*) Bks Intl VA.

***Darby, Phillip.** At the Edge of International Relations: Postcolonialism, Gender & Dependency. 2000. pap. 24.95 (*1-85567-639-7*) Continuum.

Darby, Phillip, ed. The Fiction of Imperialism: Reading Between International Relations. LC 97-27690. (Writing Past Colonialism Ser.). 250p. 1998. 69.95 (*0-304-70158-0*); pap. 26.95 (*0-304-70159-9*) Continuum.

Darby, Robert, ed. But Not for Love: Stories of Majorie Barnard & M. Barnard Eldershaw. 240p. (Orig.). 1989. pap. text 12.95 (*0-04-351070-1*) Routledge.

Darby, Robert D. Outside My Window. 118p. (Orig.). 1996. pap. 5.95 (*1-57502-291-5*, PO1001) Morris Pubng.

Darby, Ron. Chemical Engineering & Fluid Mechanics. (Illus.). 512p. 1996. text 165.00 (*0-8247-9628-4*) Dekker.

Darby, Stephen E. & Simon, Andrew. Incised River Channels: Processes, Forms, Engineering & Management. LC 98-33225. 456p. 1999. 140.00 (*0-471-98446-9*) Wiley.

Darby, Stuart, et al, eds. Older People, Nursing & Mental Health. LC 98-29335. (Illus.). 192p. 1998. pap. text 32.50 (*0-7506-2440-X*) Buttrwrth-Heinemann.

Darby, Susan A., jt. auth. see Cramer, Gregory D.

Darby, W. J., et al, eds. Annual Review of Nutrition, Vol. 1. (Illus.). 1981. text 43.00 (*0-8243-2801-9*) Annual Reviews.

— Annual Review of Nutrition, Vol. 2. (Illus.). 1982. text 43.00 (*0-8243-2802-7*) Annual Reviews.

— Annual Review of Nutrition, Vol. 3. (Illus.). 1983. text 43.00 (*0-8243-2803-5*) Annual Reviews.

— Annual Review of Nutrition, Vol. 4. (Illus.). 1984. text 43.00 (*0-8243-2804-3*) Annual Reviews.

Darby, W. Thomas. The Feast: Meditations on Politics & Time. 256p. 1990. pap. 16.95 (*0-8020-6786-7*) U of Toronto Pr.

— The Feast, Meditations on Politics & Time. LC 82-216877. 250p. reprint ed. pap. 77.50 (*0-8357-3637-7*, 203636500003) Bks Demand.

***Darby, Wendy Joy.** Landscape & Identity: Geographies of Nation & Class in England. (Materializing Culture Ser.). 224p. 2000. 65.00 (*1-85973-425-1*, Pub. by Berg Pubs); pap. 22.50 (*1-85973-430-8*, Pub. by Berg Pubs) NYU Pr.

Darby, William. John Ford's Westerns: A Thematic Analysis, with a Filmography. LC 96-4041. (Illus.). 317p. 1996. lib. bdg. 39.95 (*0-7864-0080-3*) McFarland & Co.

— Masters of Lens & Light: A Checklist of Major Cinematographers & Their Feature Films. LC 91-20656. (Illus.). 1071p. 1991. 110.00 (*0-8108-2454-X*) Scarecrow.

— Necessary American Fictions: Popular Literature of the 1950s. LC 87-73250. 397p. 1987. 36.00 (*0-87972-389-0*); pap. 17.95 (*0-87972-390-4*) Bowling Green Univ Popular Press.

— A Tour from the City of New York to Detroit in the Michigan Territory. 1988. reprint ed. lib. bdg. 49.00 (*0-317-90011-0*) Rprt Serv.

— A Tour from the City of New York to Detroit in the Michigan Territory, Made Between the Second of May & the 22nd of September, 1818, Etc. 1977. reprint ed. 49.00 (*0-403-07894-6*) Scholarly.

Darby, William & Du Bois, Jack. American Film Music: Major Composers, Techniques, Trends, 1915-1990. LC 90-5973. (Illus.). 623p. 1990. lib. bdg. 62.50 (*0-89950-468-X*) McFarland & Co.

***Darby, William & Du Bois, Jack.** American Film Music: Major Composers, Techniques, Trends, 1915-1990. LC 90-5973. (Illus.). 623p. 1999. per. 30.00 (*0-7864-0753-0*, McFarland Cls) McFarland & Co.

Darby, William J. & Jukes, Thomas H., eds. Founders of Nutrition Science: Biographical Articles from the Journal of Nutrition. (Illus.). 1200p. 1992. 95.00 (*0-943029-02-3*) Am Soc Nutr Sci.

Darbyshire, Alan & Taylor, David Conrad. GNVQ Advanced Engineering: Systems, Process, Materials & Design. (GNVQ Ser.). (Illus.). 384p. (Orig.). (C). 1998. pap. 47.50 (*0-7487-2886-4*, Pub. by S Thornes Pubs) Trans-Atl Phila.

Darbyshire, Alan, et al. GNVQ Intermediate Engineering. (Illus.). 384p. (Orig.). (C). 1998. pap. 42.50 (*0-7487-2936-4*, Pub. by S Thornes Pubs) Trans-Atl Phila.

Darbyshire, Alfred. The Art of the Victorian Stage. LC 76-91898. 1972. 20.95 (*0-405-08429-3*, Pub. by Blom Pubns) Ayer.

Darbyshire, J. F. Soil Protozoa. (Illus.). 224p. 1994. text 90.00 (*0-85198-884-9*) OUP.

Darbyshire, J. F., jt. ed. see Tinsley, J.

Darbyshire, John. Badgers. (Illus.). 48p. 1998. pap. text 11.95 (*1-900455-58-7*, Pub. by Colin Baxter Ltd) Voyageur Pr.

Darbyshire, Lydia. Collector's Encyclopedia of Toys & Dolls. 1990. 19.98 (*1-55521-667-6*) Bk Sales Inc.

— Complete Identifier - Cats & Kittens. (Illus.). 224p. 1999. pap. 15.95 (*1-57715-066-X*) Knckerbocker.

— Identifying Guide to Antique Silver. 80p. 1994. 6.98 (*0-7858-0047-6*) Bk Sales Inc.

— Latin Cooking. 1999. 12.99 (*0-7858-1112-5*) Bk Sales Inc.

Darbyshire, Lydia, ed. Asian Cooking. (Illus.). 464p. 1997. 25.98 (*0-7858-0850-7*) Bk Sales Inc.

— The Magic Book. (Illus.). 224p. 1997. 19.98 (*0-7858-0791-8*) Bk Sales Inc.

Darbyshire, P. Living with a Sick Child in Hospital: The Experiences of Parents & Nurses. 240p. 1994. 54.25 (*1-56593-374-5*, 0721) Singular Publishing.

Darbyshire, Philip. Living with a Sick Child in Hospital. 225p. 1994. pap. 36.95 (*0-412-61050-7*) Chapman & Hall.

D'Arc, James V., ed. The Register of the Cecil B. De Mille Archives. LC 91-31992. (Illus.). xvi, 469p. 1991. 95.00 (*0-8425-2305-7*, Friends of the Library) Brigham.

D'Arc, Joan, ed. Paranoid Women Collect Their Thoughts: A Paranoia Annual Anthology. (Illus.). 155p. (Orig.). 1996. pap. 12.95 (*0-9653643-0-5*) Paranoia Pub.

D'Arc, Jon. Don't Drink the Eye Drops, Dream Rider. LC 96-83145. 168p. 1996. 21.00 (*0-915090-06-6*) Firefall.

D'Arcais, Francesca F. Giotto. LC 95-15262. (Illus.). 384p. 1995. 95.00 (*1-55859-774-3*) Abbeville Pr.

D'Arcais, G. B. Flores, see Levelt, Willem J. & Flores d'Arcais, G. B., eds.

D'Arcais, G. B. Flores, see Flores d'Arcais, G. B., ed.

D'Arcais, G. F. Diccionario de Ciencias de la Educacion. (SPA.). 1872p. 1990. 195.00 (*0-7859-3349-2*, 8428513317) Fr & Eur.

D'Arcangelo, Amelio M. A Guide to Sound Ship Structure. LC 64-18584. 314p. reprint ed. pap. 97.40 (*0-608-17202-2*, 202701600053) Bks Demand.

D'Arcangelo, Bartholomew, et al. Blueprint Reading for Plumbers: Residential & Commercial. 5th rev. ed. (Blueprint Reading Ser.). 1989. text 38.95 (*0-8273-3459-1*) Delmar.

— Blueprint Reading for Plumbers: Residential & Commercial. 5th rev. ed. (Blueprint Reading Ser.). 1989. pap., teacher ed. 13.50 (*0-8273-3460-5*) Delmar.

— Mathematics for Plumbers & Pipefitters. 5th ed. LC 95-34211. (Trade/Tech Math Ser.). 288p. 1995. mass mkt. 40.95 (*0-8273-7061-X*) Delmar.

— Mathematics for Plumbers & Pipefitters. 5th ed. (Trade/Tech Math Ser.). 64p. 1996. text, teacher ed. 16.95 (*0-8273-7062-8*) Delmar.

Darcangelo, David. Wealth Starts at Home: And 15 Other Financial Secrets That Could Make You a Fortune. LC 96-40001. 216p. 1997. text 22.95 (*0-7863-1128-2*, Irwn Prfssnl) McGraw-Hill Prof.

Darcey, John M., ed. The Language Teacher: Commitment & Collaboration. (Reports of the Northeast Conference on the Teaching of Foreign Languages). 138p. 1987. pap. 10.95 (*0-915432-87-0*) NE Conf Teach Foreign.

Darch, Colin, compiled by. Tanzania. (World Bibliographical Ser.: No. 54). 316p. 1985. lib. bdg. 65.00 (*0-903450-91-7*) ABC-CLIO.

Darch, Colin & Pacheleke, Calisto. Mozambique. LC 88-144644. (World Bibliographical Ser.: No. 78). 388p. 1988. lib. bdg. 70.00 (*1-85109-025-8*) ABC-CLIO.

D'Arch Smith, Timothy. Alembic. LC 92-12721. 226p. 1992. 19.95 (*1-56478-009-0*) Dalkey Arch.

Darchangelo. Math for Plumbers & Pipefitters. 4th ed. (Trade/Tech Math Ser.). 1989. pap., teacher ed. 16.00 (*0-8273-3954-2*) Delmar.

Darcovich, Nancy, et al. Literacy Skills for the Knowledge Society: Further Results from the International Adult Literacy Survey. LC 98-700475. (Illus.). 195p. 1997. 41.75 (*92-64-15624-0*) Org for Econ.

Darcovich, William & Yuzyk, Paul, eds. A Statistical Compendium on the Ukrainians in Canada, 1891-1976. LC 82-176005. 869p. 1980. reprint ed. pap. 200.00 (*0-608-01995-X*, 206265100003) Bks Demand.

Darcy. Cecilys of Young Lady of Quality. 1986. pap. 5.95 (*0-8027-7274-9*) Walker & Co.

Darcy, jt. auth. see Stewart.

***D'Arcy, Anne Marie.** The Fullness of Wisdom: The Image of the Vessel in the Queste Del Saint Graal & Malory's Tale of the Sankgreal. 400p. 2000. 65.00 (*1-85182-496-0*, Pub. by Four Cts Pr) Intl Spec Bk.

D'Arcy, Anne-Marie, et al, eds. Text & Gloss: Studies in Literature of Anglo-Saxon England. LC 99-229404. 224p. 1999. boxed set 55.00 (*1-85182-443-X*, Pub. by Four Cts Pr) Intl Spec Bk.

Darcy, Beruba. Religious Education at the Crossroads. 1998. pap. 9.95 (*0-8091-3829-8*) Paulist Pr.

***Darcy-Berube, Francoise & Berube, John Paul.** Growing up a Friend of Jesus: A Guide to Discipleship for Children. (Illus.). 128p. (J). (gr. 3-6). 2000. 17.95 (*0-86716-401-8*) St Anthony Mess Pr.

D'Arcy, C. J. & Burnett, P. A., eds. Barley Yellow Dwarf: Forty Years of Progress. 374p. 1995. 79.00 (*0-89054-167-1*) Am Phytopathol Soc.

Darcy, Catherine C. The Institute of the Sisters of Mercy of the Americas: The Canonical Development of the Proposed Governance Model. LC 92-45194. 1993. 59.50 (*0-8191-9044-6*); pap. 36.50 (*0-8191-9045-4*) U Pr of Amer.

Darcy, Clare. Cressida. 1991. mass mkt. 3.95 (*1-55817-512-1*, Pinncle Kensgtn) Kensgtn Pub Corp.

D'Arcy, Danya, ed. Literatia Macabre. (Illus.). 112p. (Orig.). 1996. pap. 11.95 (*0-9651215-0-X*) Strait-Jacket.

D'Arcy, E. Dangerous Passions. mass mkt. 11.95 (*0-340-68266-3*, Pub. by Hodder & Stought Ltd) Trafalgar.

— Interlover. mass mkt. 11.95 (*0-340-66645-5*, Pub. by Hodder & Stought Ltd) Trafalgar.

— Midnight Blue. 1997. mass mkt. 11.95 (*0-340-66644-7*, Pub. by Hodder & Stought Ltd) Trafalgar.

D'Arcy, Eithene. Irish Crochet Lace. 1990. pap. 12.95 (*0-85105-421-8*, Pub. by Smyth) Dufour.

***Darcy, Emma.** Amores Ocultos. (Bianca Ser.: Vol. 226). (SPA.). 2000. mass mkt. 3.50 (*0-373-33576-8*, Harlequin) Harlequin Bks.

Darcy, Emma. Breaking Point. (Presents Ser.: No. 433). 1992. per. 2.79 (*0-373-11433-8*, 1-11433-9) Harlequin Bks.

— Bride of Diamonds. (Presents Ser.: No. 1367). 1991. per. 2.75 (*0-373-11367-6*) Harlequin Bks.

***Darcy, Emma.** Bride of His Choice. (Presents Ser.: No. 2080). 2000. per. 3.99 (*0-373-12080-X*, 1-12080-7, Harlequin) Harlequin Bks.

— Bride of His Choice. large type ed. 288p. 2000. 22.95 (*0-263-16484-5*) Thorndike Pr.

Darcy, Emma. Burning with Passion: (Valentine) LC 95-4576. (Presents Ser.). 188p. 1995. per. 3.25 (*0-373-11721-3*, 1-11721-7) Harlequin Bks.

***Darcy, Emma.** The Cattle King's Mistress: Kings of the Outback. (Presents Ser.: Bk. 2110). 2000. per. 3.99 (*0-373-12110-5*, 1-12110-2) Harlequin Bks.

Darcy, Emma. Climax of Passion. LC 96-257. 187p. 1995. per. 3.25 (*0-373-11771-X*, 1-11771-2) Harlequin Bks.

— Climax of Passion. large type ed. 1996. 20.95 (*0-263-14590-5*) Mac Lib Ref.

— The Colour of Desire. (Presents Ser.: No. 385). 1991. per. 2.75 (*0-373-11385-4*) Harlequin Bks.

***Darcy, Emma.** Una Consulta Mas (One More Affair) The Marriage Decider. (Bianca Ser.: No. 186). 1999. per. 3.50 (*0-373-33536-9*, 1-33536-3) Harlequin Bks.

Darcy, Emma. Craving Jamie. (Top Author Ser.). 1997. per. 3.50 (*0-373-11881-3*, 1-11881-9) Harlequin Bks.

— Un Dangereux Refuge. (Azur Ser.: No. 785). (FRE.). 1999. mass mkt. 3.99 (*0-373-34785-5*, 1-34785-5) Harlequin Bks.

***Darcy, Emma.** Une Epouse a Reconquerir. (FRE.). 2000. mass mkt. 3.99 (*0-373-34814-2*) Harlequin Bks.

Darcy, Emma. Fantasy. (Sunsational - Brick Ser.: No. 236). 1991. per. 5.95 (*0-373-83236-2*) Harlequin Bks.

— The Father of Her Child. (Presents Ser.). 1996. per. 3.50 (*0-373-11833-3*) Harlequin Bks.

— The Father of Her Child. large type ed. (Harlequin Romance Ser.). 283p. 1997. 20.95 (*0-263-14918-8*) Mac Lib Ref.

— The Fatherhood Affair. LC 95-6878. (Presents Ser.). 186p. 1995. per. 3.25 (*0-373-11745-0*, 1-11745-6) Harlequin Bks.

— The Fatherhood Affair. (Promo Ser.). 1999. per. 4.50 (*0-373-21955-5*, 1-21995-9) Harlequin Bks.

— Fatherhood Fever! (Top Author/Man Talk) (Presents Ser.: Vol. 1984). 1998. per. 3.75 (*0-373-11984-4*, 1-11984-1) Harlequin Bks.

— Having Leo's Child. (Romance Ser.). 1999. per. 3.75 (*0-373-12050-8*, 1-12050-0) Harlequin Bks.

***Darcy, Emma.** Having Leo's Child. large type ed. (Harlequin Romance Ser.). 2000. 22.95 (*0-263-16307-5*) Mills & Boon.

Darcy, Emma. Heart of the Outback. 1993. per. 2.89 (*0-373-11519-9*, 1-11519-5) Harlequin Bks.

— High Risk. (Presents Ser.: No. 447). 1992. per. 2.89 (*0-373-11447-8*, 1-11447-9) Harlequin Bks.

— High Risk. large type ed. (Harlequin Ser.). 1993. lib. bdg. 19.95 (*0-263-13536-5*) Thorndike Pr.

— An Impossible Dream. (Presents Ser.). 1993. per. 2.89 (*0-373-11536-9*, 1-11536-9) Harlequin Bks.

— An Impossible Dream. large type ed. LC 94-2188. 217p. 1994. lib. bdg. 18.95 (*0-7862-0203-3*) Thorndike Pr.

— In Need of a Wife. (Promo Ser.). 1999. per. 4.50 (*0-373-21975-X*, 1-21975-7) Harlequin Bks.

— In Need of a Wife. large type ed. (Magna Large Print Ser.). 304p. 1998. 29.99 (*0-7505-1092-7*, Pub. by Mgna Lrg Print) Ulverscroft.

— Inherited One Nanny: Nanny Wanted! (Presents Ser.: Vol. 1972). 1998. per. 3.75 (*0-373-11972-0*, 1-11972-6) Harlequin Bks.

— Inherited One Nanny: Nanny Wanted! large type ed. 1998. 21.95 (*0-263-15748-2*, Pub. by Mills & Boon) Chivers N Amer.

***Darcy, Emma.** Innocente ou Intrigante? (Azur Ser.: No. 788). (FRE.). 1999. mass mkt. 3.99 (*0-373-34788-X*, 1-34788-9) Harlequin Bks.

Darcy, Emma. Jack's Baby. 1997. per. 3.50 (*0-373-11857-0*, 1-11857-9) Silhouette.

— Jack's Baby. large type ed. (Harlequin Romance Ser.). 1997. 20.95 (*0-263-15122-0*) Mac Lib Ref.

— The Last Grand Passion. (Presents Plus Ser.). 1993. mass mkt. 2.99 (*0-373-11592-X*, 1-11592-2) Harlequin Bks.

— The Last Grand Passion. large type ed. (Magna Large Print Ser.). 292p. 1998. 29.99 (*0-7505-1097-8*, Pub. by Mgna Lrg Print) Ulverscroft.

— Last Stop Marriage. LC 95-22378. (Presents Ser.). 188p. 1996. mass mkt. 3.25 (*0-373-11785-X*, 1-11785-2) Harlequin Bks.

***Darcy, Emma.** A Marriage Betrayed. (Harlequin Presents Ser.). 1999. mass mkt. 3.75 (*0-373-12069-9*, Harlequin) Harlequin Bks.

— A Marriage Betrayed. large type ed. (Harlequin Romance Ser.). 2000. 22.95 (*0-263-16406-3*) Mills & Boon.

— The Marriage Decider. 1999. per. 3.75 (*0-373-12020-6*, 1-12020-3, Harlequin) Harlequin Bks.

Darcy, Emma. The Marriage Decider. large type ed. (Harlequin Ser.). 1999. 21.95 (*0-263-16102-1*, Pub. by Mills & Boon) Ulverscroft.

— Marriage Meltdown. 1997. per. 3.50 (*0-373-11900-3*, 1-11900-7) Harlequin Bks.

— Marriage Meltdown. large type ed. (Harlequin Romance Ser.). 288p. 1998. 20.95 (*0-263-15398-3*) Thorndike Pr.

— Merry Christmas. (Presents Ser.: No. 1923). 1997. per. 3.50 (*0-373-11923-2*, 1-11923-9) Harlequin Bks.

— Mischief & Marriage. 1996. per. 3.50 (*0-373-11815-5*, 1-11815-7) Harlequin Bks.

— Necesito Esposa (In Need of a Wife) (Bianca Ser.).Tr. of I Need a Wife. (SPA.). 1997. per. 3.50 (*0-373-33431-1*, 1-33431-7) Harlequin Bks.

— No Risks, No Prizes. (Presents Ser.). 1993. per. 2.99 (*0-373-11570-9*, 1-11570-8) Harlequin Bks.

— Un Nuevo Comienzo (A New Beginning) (Deseo Ser.). (SPA.). 1998. per. 3.50 (*0-373-33449-4*, 1-33449-9) Harlequin Bks.

— Olvidar el Pasado. (Bianca Ser.: No. 33402).Tr. of Fatherhood Affair. (SPA.). 1997. per. 3.50 (*0-373-33402-8*, 1-33402-8) Harlequin Bks.

— Ombre sur un Mariage. (Azur Ser.: Bk. 741). 1999. mass mkt. 3.50 (*0-373-34741-3*, 1-34741-8) Harlequin Bks.

— One-Woman Crusade. (Presents Ser.: No. 1351). 1991. per. 2.75 (*0-373-11351-X*) Harlequin Bks.

— La Otra: Marriage Meltdown. (Bianca Ser.: Vol. 455).Tr. of Other. (SPA.). 1998. per. 3.50 (*0-373-33455-9*, 1-33455-6) Harlequin Bks.

— Otro en Tu Corazon. (Bianca Ser.: No. 171). (SPA.). 1999. per. 3.50 (*0-373-33521-0*) Harlequin Bks.

— Outback Heat. (Australians Ser.). 1998. per. 4.50 (*0-373-82573-0*) Harlequin Bks.

— Outback Heat. large type ed. 1999. 21.95 (*0-263-15845-4*, G K Hall & Co) Mac Lib Ref.

— Le Passe Ennemi. (Azur Ser.: Vol. 698). (FRE.). 1998. mass mkt. 3.50 (*0-373-34698-0*, 1-34698-0) Harlequin Bks.

— Passion Cruelle. (Azur Ser.: Vol. 707). 1998. mass mkt. 3.50 (*0-373-34707-3*, 1-34707-9) Harlequin Bks.

— Pattern of Deceit. (Romance Ser.: No. 3085). 1990. per. 2.50 (*0-373-03085-1*) Harlequin Bks.

— Pattern of Deceit. large type ed. 1990. reprint ed. lib. bdg. 18.95 (*0-263-12075-9*) Mac Lib Ref.

***Darcy, Emma.** The Playboy King's Wife: Kings of the Outback. (Harlequin Presents Ser.). 2000. mass mkt. 3.99 (*0-373-12116-4*, 1121169) Harlequin Bks.

— The Pleasure King's Bride. (Presents Ser.). 2000. mass mkt. 3.99 (*0-373-12122-9*, 1-12122-7) Harlequin Bks.

Darcy, Emma. Por Segunda Vez: A Wedding to Remember. (Born in the U. S. A. Ser.). (SPA.). 1996. per. 3.50 (*0-373-33390-0*, 1-33390-5) Harlequin Bks.

— The Power & the Passion. (Presents Ser.: No. 1272). 1990. per. 2.50 (*0-373-11272-6*) Harlequin Bks.

— Le Reve Trahi. (Azur Ser.: No. 723). (FRE.). 1998. mass mkt. 3.50 (*0-373-34723-5*, 1.34723-6) Harlequin Bks.

— Ride the Storm. (Presents Ser.: No. 1401). 1991. per. 2.79 (*0-373-11401-X*) Harlequin Bks.

— Ride the Storm. large type ed. 1993. 19.95 (*0-263-13315-X*) Thorndike Pr.

— The Secret Mistress: Presents Passion. (Presents Ser.: Bk. 2038). 1999. per. 3.75 (*0-373-12038-9*, 1-12038-5) Harlequin Bks.

***Darcy, Emma.** The Secret Mistress: Presents Passion. large type ed. 1999. 21.95 (*0-263-16205-2*, Pub. by Mills & Boon) Ulverscroft.

Darcy, Emma. Secrets Within. 1997. per. 5.99 (*1-55166-294-9*, Mira Bks) Harlequin Bks.

— Seducing the Enemy. 1997. per. 3.50 (*0-373-11906-2*, 1-11906-4) Harlequin Bks.

— Seducing the Enemy. large type ed. (Harlequin Ser.). 288p. 1997. 20.95 (*0-263-15318-5*) Thorndike Pr.

— The Seduction of Keira. (Presents Ser.: No. 1472). 1992. per. 2.89 (*0-373-11472-9*) Harlequin Bks.

— The Seduction of Keira. large type ed. 203p. 1995. 21.95 (*0-7838-1242-6*, G K Hall Lrg Type) Mac Lib Ref.

— The Sheikh's Revenge. (Presents Ser.). 1993. per. 2.99 (*0-373-11604-7*, 1-11604-5) Harlequin Bks.

An Asterisk (*) at the beginning of an entry indicates that the title is appearing for the first time.

— The Sheikh's Seduction. (Presents Ser.). 1998. per. 3.75 (*0-373-11953-4*, 0-11953-7) Harlequin Bks.
— The Shining of Love. (Presents Ser.). 1994. per. 2.99 (*0-373-11632-2*, 1-11632-6) Harlequin Bks.
— The Shining of Love. large type ed. (Magna Large Print Ser.). 258p. 1997. 27.99 (*0-7505-1093-5*, Pub. by Mgna Lrg Print) Ulverscroft.
— Les Silences du Coeur. (Azur Ser.: No. 714). (FRE.). 1998. pap. 3.50 (*0-373-34714-6*, 1-34714-5) Harlequin Bks.
— Their Wedding Day. 1996. per. 3.50 (*0-373-11848-1*, 1-11848-8) Harlequin Bks.
— Their Wedding Day. large type ed. (Harlequin Romance Ser.). 1997. 20.95 (*0-263-14992-7*) Mac Lib Ref.
— To Tame a Wild Heart. (Presents Ser.: No. 455). 1992. per. 2.89 (*0-373-11455-9*, 1-11455-2) Harlequin Bks.
— To Tame a Wild Heart. large type ed. 261p. 1992. reprint ed. lib. bdg. 16.95 (*1-56054-496-1*) Thorndike Pr.
— Too Strong to Deny. (Presents Ser.: No. 1335). 1991. per. 2.50 (*0-373-11335-8*) Harlequin Bks.
— Too Strong to Deny. large type ed. 1990. reprint ed. lib. bdg. 18.95 (*0-263-12267-0*) Mac Lib Ref.
— Ultima Parada: Matrimonio. (SPA.). 1997. per. 3.50 (*0-373-33403-6*, 1-33403-6) Harlequin Bks.
— The Upstairs Lover. (Presents Ser.). 1993. per. 2.89 (*0-373-11555-5*, 1-11555-9) Harlequin Bks.
— The Upstairs Lover. large type ed. LC 93-3644. 213p. 1993. lib. bdg. 18.95 (*1-56054-733-2*) Thorndike Pr.
— The Velvet Tiger. (Presents Ser.). 1992. per. 2.89 (*0-373-11496-6*, 1-11496-6) Harlequin Bks.
***Darcy, Emma.** The Velvet Tiger. large type ed. 304p. 1999. 31.99 (*0-7505-1465-5*, Pub. by Mgna Lrg Print) Ulverscroft.
Darcy, Emma. A Very Stylish Affair. (Presents Ser.). 1993. per. 2.99 (*0-373-11579-2*, 1-11579-9) Harlequin Bks.
— A Very Stylish Affair. large type ed. (Magna Large Print Ser.). 240p. 1997. 27.99 (*0-7505-1095-1*) Ulverscroft.
— The Wedding. (Presents Ser.: No. 463). 1992. per. 2.89 (*0-373-11463-X*, 1-11463-6) Harlequin Bks.
— The Wedding. large type ed. LC 95-53793. (Romance Collection). 217 p. 1996. write for info. (*0-7451-4883-2*, G K Hall Lrg Type) Mac Lib Ref.
— A Wedding to Remember. 1994. per. 2.99 (*0-373-11659-4*, 1-11659-9) Harlequin Bks.
— A Wedding to Remember. (And the Winner Is...Ser.). 1997. per. 3.99 (*0-373-48346-5*, 1-48346-0) Harlequin Bks.
— A Wedding to Remember. 1999. per. 4.50 (*0-373-65106-6*) Harlequin Bks.
— A Wedding to Remember. large type ed. (Magna Large Print Ser.). 263p. 1997. 27.99 (*0-7505-1096-X*) Ulverscroft.
— Whirlpool of Passion. large type ed. (Magna Large Print Ser.). (Illus.). 245p. 1996. 27.99 (*0-7505-0997-X*) Ulverscroft.
— Wrong Mirror. (Presents Ser.). 1991. per. 2.79 (*0-373-15154-3*) Harlequin Bks.
Darcy, G., jt. auth. see Thomas, Aug H.
D'Arcy, G. Minot. Investment Counsel. 1964. 10.95 (*0-8392-1052-3*) Astor-Honor.
D'Arcy, Gordon. Animals of Ireland. (Appletree Pocket Guides Ser.). (Illus.). 72p. (Orig.). 1988. pap. 7.95 (*0-86281-199-6*, Pub. by Appletree Pr) Irish Bks Media.
— Birds of Ireland. (Appletree Pocket Guides Ser.). (Illus.). 72p. (Orig.). 1986. pap. 7.95 (*0-86281-162-7*, Pub. by Appletree Pr) Irish Bks Media.
***D'Arcy, Gordon.** Ireland's Lost Birds. (Illus.). 176p. 2000. pap. 19.95 (*1-85182-529-0*, Pub. by Four Cts Pr) Intl Spec Bk.
— Ireland's Lost Birds. limited ed. (Illus.). 176p. 2000. 120.00 (*1-85182-526-6*, Pub. by Four Cts Pr) Intl Spec Bk.
D'Arcy, Gordon. The Natural History of the Burren. (Illus.). 168p. (C). 1990. 110.00 (*0-907151-64-7*, Pub. by IMMEL Pubng) St Mut.
D'Arcy, Gordon & Hayward, John. The Natural History of the Burren. 168p. 1995. 60.00 (*0-907151-23-X*, Pub. by IMMEL Pubng) St Mut.
Darcy, H. L. Russian-English Aerospace Dictionary. 407p. 1985. 110.00 (*0-8288-0016-2*, M15472) Fr & Eur.
D'Arcy, J. B. Sheep Management & Wool Technology. 3rd ed. 352p. 1990. reprint ed. pap. 34.95 (*0-86840-036-X*, Pub. by New South Wales Univ Pr) Intl Spec Bk.
D'Arcy, Jan. Dr. Jack's Adventure in Videoconferencing Land: A Guide to Communicating Effectively on Camera. (Illus.). 80p. 1990. 15.95 (*0-9627822-0-3*) J Darcy & Assocs.
— Technically Speaking: A Guide for Communicating Complex Information. 270p. 1998. pap. 29.95 (*1-57477-051-9*) Battelle.
— Technically Speaking: A Guide for Communicating Complex Information. 270p. 1999. pap. 29.95 (*0-7803-5367-6*) IEEE Standards.
***D'arcy, Julie.** Time of the Wolf. 1999. pap. 9.95 (*1-893896-08-0*) Ima Jinn.
D'Arcy, Leo, ed. European Community Law. 160p. (C). 1991. pap. 100.00 (*1-85352-387-9*, Pub. by HLT Pubns) St Mut.
— European Community Law & Human Rights. 160p. (C). 1991. 72.00 (*1-85352-876-5*, Pub. by HLT Pubns) St Mut.
— European Law & Practice. 160p. (C). 1991. pap. text 72.00 (*1-85352-839-0*, Pub. by HLT Pubns) St Mut.
Darcy, Lilian. The Baby Bond: Bundles of Joy. (Romance Ser.: No. 1390). 1999. per. 3.50 (*0-373-19390-4*, 1-19390-3) Silhouette.
***Darcy, Lilian.** Boda de Papel. Vol. 212.Tr. of Paper Wedding. (SPA.). 2000. per. 3.50 (*0-373-33562-8*, 1-33562-9) Harlequin Bks.
Darcy, Lilian. A Father's Love. large type ed. 288p. 1995. 23.99 (*0-263-14178-0*, Pub. by Mills & Boon) Ulverscroft.
— Full Recovery. large type ed. (Mills & Boon Large Print Ser.). 288p. 1997. 23.99 (*0-263-15142-5*, Pub. by Mills & Boon) Ulverscroft.
— A Gift for Healing. large type ed. (Mills & Boon Large Print Ser.). 288p. 1997. 22.50 (*0-263-15177-8*, Pub. by Mills & Boon) Ulverscroft.
***Darcy, Lilian.** Her Passion for Dr. Jones. (Readers Choice Ser.). 2000. mass mkt. 4.50 (*0-373-51125-6*, 1511252) Harlequin Bks.
— Her Passion for Dr. Jones. 288p. 2000. 26.99 (*0-263-16320-2*, Pub. by Mills & Boon) Ulverscroft.
Darcy, Lilian. Midwife's Dilemma. large type ed. 288p. 1996. 23.99 (*0-263-14519-0*, Pub. by Mills & Boon) Ulverscroft.
— Misleading Symptoms. large type ed. (Mills & Boon Large Print Ser.). 288p. 1997. 22.50 (*0-263-15229-4*, Pub. by Mills & Boon) Ulverscroft.
***Darcy, Lilian.** Raising Baby Jane. (Romance Ser.: Bk. 1478). 2000. mass mkt. 3.50 (*0-373-19478-1*, 1-19478-6) Silhouette.
Darcy, Lilian. Valentines for Nurse Cleo. large type ed. (Magna Large Print Ser.). (Illus.). 297p. 1996. 27.99 (*0-7505-1010-2*) Ulverscroft.
— Wanting Dr. Wilde. (Promo Ser.). 1999. per. 3.75 (*0-373-83381-4*, 1-83381-3) Harlequin Bks.
— Wanting Dr. Wilde. large type ed. 1999. 25.99 (*0-263-15727-X*) Mills & Boon.
D'Arcy, Margaretta, jt. auth. see Arden, John.
D'Arcy, Mark, jt. auth. see Gosling, Paul.
D'Arcy, Martin C. Communism & Christianity. 250p. 1957. 12.95 (*0-8159-5208-2*) Devin.
— The Nature of Belief. (Select Bibliographies Reprint Ser.). 1977. reprint ed. 23.95 (*0-8369-5930-2*) Ayer.
D'Arcy, Mary R. The Saints of Ireland. 241p. 1985. reprint ed. pap. 9.95 (*0-9614900-0-4*) Irish Am Cult.
Darcy, Michael D., jt. ed. see LaBerge, Jeanne M.
D'Arcy, P. F., et al, eds. Mechanisms of Drug Interactions. (Handbook of Experimental Pharmacology Ser.: Vol. 122). 400p. 1996. 349.00 (*3-540-60204-6*) Spr-Verlag.
D'Arcy, P. F. & Green, J. P., eds. Iatrogenic Diseases. 3rd ed. (Illus.). 950p. 1986. 195.00 (*0-19-261440-1*) OUP.
D'Arcy, P. F. & Griffin, J. P., eds. Iatrogenic Diseases: Annual Updates. 2nd ed. Incl. Update, 1981. (Illus.). 1981. 69.00 (*0-19-261263-8*); Update, 1983. 1984. 80.00 (*0-19-261399-5*); Update, 1982. 1983. 80.00 (*0-19-261356-1*); (C). write for info. (*0-318-54847-X*) OUP.
D'Arcy, P. F., jt. auth. see Griffin, J. P.
D'Arcy, Pat. Making Sense, Shaping Meaning: Writing in the Context of a Capacity-Based Approach to Learning. LC 89-31481. 163p. (Orig.). (YA). (gr. 11). 1989. pap. text 21.50 (*0-86709-245-9*, 0245, Pub. by Boynton Cook Pubs) Heinemann.
D'Arcy, Patrick F. Laboratory on the Nile: A History of the Wellcome Tropical Research Laboratories. LC 99-27047. 282p. 1999. 49.95 (*0-7890-0728-2*, Pharmctl Prods) Haworth Pr.
D'Arcy, Patrick F. & McElnay, James C., eds. The Pharmacy & Pharmacotherapy of Asthma. 1989. text 99.95 (*0-470-21522-4*) P-H.
D'Arcy, Paula. Gift of the Red Bird: A Spiritual Encounter. 168p. 1996. 14.95 (*0-8245-1590-0*) Crossroad NY.
— Song for Sarah: A Young Mother's Journey Through Grief & Beyond. LC 95-10816. 124p. 1995. 12.99 (*0-87788-762-4*, H Shaw Pubs) Waterbrook Pr.
— Song for Sarah: A Young Mother's Journey Through Grief & Beyond. 1999. pap. 12.99 (*0-87788-760-8*, H Shaw Pubs) Waterbrook Pr.
— When Your Friend Is Grieving: Building a Bridge of Love. 114p. (Orig.). 1990. pap. 7.99 (*0-87788-088-3*, H Shaw Pubs) Waterbrook Pr.
Darcy, R. & Rohrs, Richard C. A Guide to Quantitative History. LC 93-50069. 336p. 1995. 69.50 (*0-275-94897-8*, Praeger Pubs); pap. 24.95 (*0-275-95237-1*, Praeger Pubs) Greenwood.
Darcy, R., et al. Women, Elections, & Representation. 2nd rev. ed. LC 93-2301. (Women & Politics Ser.: Vol. 1). (Illus.). xiv, 276p. (Orig.). 1994. pap. text 20.00 (*0-8032-6597-2*, Bison Books) U of Nebr Pr.
— Women, Elections, & Representation. 2nd rev. ed. LC 93-2301. (Women & Politics Ser.: Vol. 1). (Illus.). xiv, 276p. (Orig.). 1994. text 45.00 (*0-8032-1696-3*) U of Nebr Pr.
D'Arcy, Stephen P. & Doherty, Neil A. Financial Theory of Pricing Property-Liability Insurance Contracts. LC 87-81433. (S. S. Huebner Foundation Monographs: No. 15). 1988. pap. 22.95 (*0-256-06124-6*) Huebner Foun Insur.
D'Arcy, W. G. Flora of Panama Pt. I: Checklist & Index: The Introduction & Checklist. 328p. 1987. 49.95 (*0-915279-08-8*, MSB-17) Miss Botan.
D'Arcy, W. G., ed. Solanaceae: Biology & Systematics. LC 85-17057. (Illus.). 608p. 1986. text 130.50 (*0-231-05780-6*) Col U Pr.
Darcy, Warren. Wagner's das Rheingold. (Studies in Musical Genesis & Structure). (Illus.). 274p. 1996. pap. text 26.00 (*0-19-816603-6*) OUP.
D'Arcy, William G. & Keating, Richard C., eds. The Anther: Form, Function & Phylogeny. (Illus.). 363p. (C). 1996. text 95.00 (*0-521-48063-9*) Cambridge U Pr.
Darda, R. S. From Feudalism to Democracy: A Study in the Growth of Representative Institutions in Rajasthan 1908-1948. 364p. 1971. text 24.00 (*0-685-13763-5*) Coronet Bks.
***Dardashti, Danielle.** Jewish Family Fun Book: Projects, Trips, Movies, Books & Games with Jewish Themes for the Whole Family, Vol. 1. LC 99-44914. 1999. pap. 12.00 (*0-8065-2152-X*) Carol Pub Group.
Darden, jt. auth. see McDaniel, Carl, Jr.
Darden, Anne S., jt. ed. see Bandy, Susan J.
Darden, Bessie. Hair Matters: African Ancestry. 122p. 1996. pap. text 37.95 (*0-7872-2122-8*) Kendall-Hunt.
***Darden, Bob.** On the 8th Day God Laughed. LC 00-8483. 2000. write for info. (*0-941037-84-3*, BIBAL Press) D & F Scott.
Darden, Carole, jt. auth. see Jean, Norma.
***Darden, Christopher A. & Lochte, Dick.** L. A. Justice. 448p. 2001. 25.95 (*0-446-52327-5*) Warner Bks.
— The Trials of Nikki Hill. LC 98-35768. 434p. 1999. 25.00 (*0-446-52326-7*, Pub. by Warner Bks) Little.
***Darden, Christopher A. & Lochte, Dick.** The Trials of Nikki Hill. 2000. mass mkt. write for info. (*0-446-60798-3*) Warner Bks.
Darden, Daniel Y., ed. see Lambee, Joshua B.
Darden, Ellington. Bigger Muscles in Forty-Two Days. (Illus.). 224p. (Orig.). 1992. pap. 16.95 (*0-399-51706-5*, Perigee Bks) Berkley Pub.
— Body Defining. (Illus.). 144p. 1996. pap. 14.95 (*0-8092-3232-4*, 32324, Contemporary Bks) NTC Contemp Pub Co.
— Especially for Women. LC 82-83949. 240p. reprint ed. pap. 74.40 (*0-608-15856-9*, 203147100074) Bks Demand.
— A Flat Stomach ASAP: The Breakthough Plan for the Look You Want in Just 6 Weeks. LC 97-31233. 1998. per. 16.00 (*0-671-01408-0*) PB.
— Grow. LC 93-19953. (Illus.). 192p. 1993. pap. 16.95 (*0-8092-3802-0*, 380200, Contemporary Bks) NTC Contemp Pub Co.
— Hot Hips & Fabulous Thighs. LC 90-20566. 204p. 1991. pap. 9.95 (*0-87833-733-4*) Taylor Pub.
— Living Longer & Stronger: The Six-Week Plan to Enhance & Extend Your Years Over Forty. LC 94-26838. 224p. (Orig.). 1995. pap. 13.95 (*0-399-51900-9*, Perigee Bks) Berkley Pub.
— The Nautilus Book. rev. ed. (Illus.). 344p. 1990. pap. 14.95 (*0-8092-4074-2*, 407420, Contemporary Bks) NTC Contemp Pub Co.
— The Six-Week Fat-to-Muscle Makeover. 176p. 1990. pap. 11.95 (*0-399-51562-3*, Perigee Bks) Berkley Pub.
— Soft Steps to a Hard Body. LC 92-37452. (Illus.). 184p. 1993. pap. 9.95 (*0-87833-795-4*) Taylor Pub.
— Thirty-Two Days to a Thirty-Two Inch Waist. LC 89-71364. 160p. 1990. pap. 8.95 (*0-87833-710-5*) Taylor Pub.
— Two Weeks to a Tighter Tummy. LC 91-46775. 128p. 1992. pap. 9.95 (*0-87833-790-3*) Taylor Pub.
Darden, Hunter D. The Everlasting Snowman. LC 96-92476. (Illus.). 37p. (J). (gr. k-5). 1996. 16.95 (*0-9653729-0-1*) Sunfleur.
— Pete's Angel - A Story of Self-Love. LC 98-90400. (Illus.). 40p. (J). (gr. k-7). 1998. 19.95 (*0-9653729-1-X*) Sunfleur.
Darden, Jim. Cowboy Craft. (Illus.). 48p. (Orig.). 1985. pap. 4.50 (*0-9614570-1-5*) Rodeo Studio.
— Great American Azaleas: A Guide to the Finest Azalea Varieties. (Illus.). 96p. 1986. pap. 9.95 (*0-9615912-0-X*) Greenhse Pr.
— Scrappy: A Rodeo Bull. (Illus.). iv, 169p. (Orig.). 1985. pap. 5.95 (*0-9614570-0-7*) Rodeo Studio.
Darden, Joseph. Toward a Healthier Sexuality: A Book of Readings. 168p. (C). 1996. pap. text, per. 31.95 (*0-7872-3236-X*) Kendall-Hunt.
— Toward a Healthier Sexuality: A Book of Readings. 142p. (C). 1998. per. 26.95 (*0-7872-5007-4*, 41500702) Kendall-Hunt.
Darden, Kathryn, ed. Anthology of Christian Poetry, 1997. 94p. 1997. pap. 11.95 (*1-888061-08-1*) Darden & Assocs.
— Creative Resource Directory: The Source for Middle Tennessee's Christian Music Industry. 64p. 1998. pap. 8.95 (*1-888061-09-X*) Darden & Assocs.
Darden, L. A. & Keirans, J. E., eds. Nymphs of the Genus Ixodes: (Acari: Ixodidae) of the United States: Taxonomy, Identification Key, Distribution, Hosts, & Medical/Veterinary Importance. (Thomas Say Publications in Entomology). 95p. 1996. pap. 35.00 (*0-938522-57-4*, ESATSP9) Entomol Soc.
Darden, Lindley. Theory Change in Science: Strategies from Mendelian Genetics. (Monographs in the History & Philosophy of Biology). (Illus.). 328p. 1991. text 55.00 (*0-19-506797-5*, 2394) OUP.
Darden, Mary M. & Proffitt, Margaret T. Food, Family & Friendships. (Illus.). vi, 244p. 1996. 15.95 (*0-9654643-1-8*) Darden & Proffitt.
Darden, Robert. I, Jesus: Stories from the Savior. 332p. 1997. 17.95 (*1-56530-185-4*) Summit TX.
Darden, Robert & Richardson, P. J. The Way of an Eagle: Professional Golfers Reveal Their Tips for Success On & Off the Course. LC 95-33301. (Illus.). 272p. 1996. 19.99 (*0-7852-7701-3*) Nelson.
Darden, Robert, jt. auth. see Richardson, P. J.
Darden, Robert F. Drawing Power: Knott, Ficklen, & McClanahan, Editorial Cartoonists of the Dallas Morning News. LC 81-86546. (Illus.). 120p. 1983. 19.95 (*0-918954-37-1*) Baylor Univ Pr.
Darden, William R. & Lucas, William H. The Decision Making Game: An Integrated Operations Management Simulation. LC 69-18739. iv, 165 p. 1969. write for info. (*0-390-25355-3*) McGraw.
Darden, William R., ed. see AMA Winter Educators' Conference Staff.
Darden, William R., jt. ed. see Lusch, Robert F.
D'Ardenne, A. J., jt. ed. see Stansfeld, Alfred G.
Dardenne, Robert, jt. auth. see Anderson, Rob M.
d'Ardenne, S. R., ed. Liflade Ant Te Passiun of Seinte Iuliene. (EETS Original Ser.: Vol. 248). 1963. reprint ed. 50.00 (*0-19-722248-X*, Pub. by EETS) Boydell & Brewer.
D'Ardenne, S. R. & Dobson, E. J., eds. Seinte Katerine: Re-Edited from Ms Bodley 34 & Other Manuscripts. (SS 7 Ser.). 1981. 47.50 (*0-19-722407-5*) OUP.
D'Ardennes, Patricia & Mahtani, Aruna. Transcultural Counselling in Action. (Counselling in Action Ser.: Vol. 6). 144p. (C). 1989. text 49.95 (*0-8039-8110-4*); pap. text 21.50 (*0-8039-8111-2*) Sage.
Darder. Living a Pedagogy of Love: Paulo Freire in Practice. (Cultural Studies Ser.). 128p. 1999. text 60.00 (*0-8133-9105-9*) Westview.
Darder, Andoria, ed. Latinos & Education. 485p. (C). 1997. 80.00 (*0-415-91181-8*) Routledge.
Darder, Antonia. Culture & Power in the Classroom: A Critical Foundation for Bicultural Education. LC 91-29793. (Critical Studies in Education & Culture). 192p. 1991. 55.00 (*0-89789-236-4*, H236, Bergin & Garvey); pap. 15.95 (*0-89789-239-9*, G239, Bergin & Garvey) Greenwood.
Darder, Antonia, ed. Bicultural Studies in Education: Transgressive Discourses of Resistance & Possibility. 2nd ed. (Bicultural Studies in Education). 260p. (C). 1995. pap. 20.00 (*0-941742-14-8*) Claremont Grad.
— Cultural Studies in Education: Schooling As a Contested Terrain. 250p. 1998. pap. 20.00 (*0-941742-19-9*) Claremont Grad.
— Culture & Difference: Critical Perspectives on the Bicultural Experience in the United States. LC 95-11211. (Critical Studies in Education & Culture). 288p. 1995. 69.50 (*0-89789-384-0*, Bergin & Garvey); pap. 24.95 (*0-89789-457-X*, Bergin & Garvey) Greenwood.
— Latinos & Education. 485p. (C). 1997. pap. 25.99 (*0-415-91182-6*) Routledge.
— The Struggle for Educational Justice: Bicultural Studies in Education. 208p. (Orig.). (C). 1993. pap. text 15.00 (*0-941742-12-1*) Claremont Grad.
Darder, Antonia & Torres, Rodolfo D., eds. The Latino Reader: Culture, Politics & Society. LC 97-14134. 448p. 1998. pap. text 31.95 (*1-55786-987-1*) Blackwell Pubs.
Darder, Antonio & Torres, Rodolfo D., eds. The Latino Reader: Culture, Politics & Society. LC 97-14134. 448p. 1997. text 73.95 (*1-55786-986-3*) Blackwell Pubs.
Dardes, Kathleen & Rothe, Andrea, eds. The Structural Conservation of Panel Paintings: Proceedings of a Symposium at the J. Paul Getty Museum, April 1995. LC 98-10541. (Symposium Proceedings Ser.). (Illus.). 600p. 1998. pap. 70.00 (*0-89236-384-3*, Pub. by J P Getty Trust) OUP.
Dardess, B. We Are One. 1.25 (*0-687-08192-0*) Abingdon.
Dardess, George, et al. Divine Inspiration: The Life of Jesus in World Poetry. LC 96-41983. 624p. 1997. 35.00 (*0-19-509351-8*) OUP.
Dardess, George, jt. auth. see Rosenthal, Peggy.
Dardess, John W. A Ming Society: T'ai-ho County, Kiangsi, Fourteenth to Seventeenth Centuries. LC 96-3631. (Illus.). 313p. 1997. 48.00 (*0-520-20425-5*, Pub. by U CA Pr) Cal Prin Full Svc.
Dardess, Margaret B., jt. ed. see Aoki, Michiko Y.
Dardia, Michael. Subsidizing Redevelopment in California. LC 97-53067. (Illus.). xxv, 110p. 1998. pap. 12.00 (*0-9653184-8-6*) Pub Policy Inst.
***Dardia, Michael & Luk, Sherman.** Rethinking the California Business Climate. LC 99-33965. (Illus.). xi, 49p. 1999. pap. 7.00 (*1-58213-011-6*) Pub Policy Inst.
Dardia, Michael, et al. Defense Cutbacks: Effects on California's Communities, Firms & Workers - Executive Summary. 14p. (Orig.). 1996. pap. text 7.50 (*0-8330-2361-6*, MR-689-OSD) Rand Corp.
— The Effects of Military Base Closures on Local Communities: A Short-Term Perspective. (MR-667-OSD Ser.). 64p. (Orig.). 1996. pap. text 15.00 (*0-8330-2354-3*) Rand Corp.
Dardick, Eileen & Ferrendelli, Sheila. Cooking the Lite Fantastic. 1994. 14.95 (*0-9641615-0-8*) Ideal Image.
— Lite-er & More Fantastic. 1994. 15.95 (*0-9641615-1-6*) Ideal Image.
Dardick, Geeta. Home Butchering & Meat Preservation. (Illus.). 288p. 1986. pap. 18.95 (*0-8306-2713-8*) McGraw-Hill Prof.
Dardick, Irving. Color Atlas/Text of Salivary Gland Tumor Pathology. LC 95-26461. (Illus.). 288p. 1996. 129.50 (*0-89640-308-4*) Igaku-Shoin.
Dardick, Irving, jt. auth. see Society for Ultrastructural Pathology Handbook Com.
Dardick, Irving, jt. auth. see Yazdi, Hossein.
Dardick, Simon & Marrelli, Nancy. Cheap Thrills: Great Montreal Meals for under 10 Dollars. 120p. (Orig.). 1995. pap. 8.95 (*1-55065-069-6*, Pub. by Vehicule Pr) Genl Dist Srvs.
Dardick, Simon, jt. auth. see Marrelli, Nancy.
Dardier. Early Stroke Patient. 1980. text 32.95 (*0-7216-0830-2*) Harcourt.
Dardis, G. F. & Moon, B. P., eds. Geomorphological Studies in Southern Africa: Proceedings of a Symposium, Transkei, 8-11 April, 1988. 519p. (C). 1988. text 129.00 (*90-6191-831-6*, Pub. by A A Balkema) Ashgate Pub Co.
***Dardis, Sharon & Rogers, Cindy.** As I Journey On: Meditations for Those Facing Death. LC 99-52772. 2000. pap. 10.99 (*0-8066-3889-3*, Augsburg) Augsburg Fortress.
Dardis, Tom. Some Time in the Sun: The Hollywood Years of F. Scott Fitzgerald, William Faulkner, Nathanael West, Aldous Huxley, & James Agee. LC 88-21562. (Illus.). 312p. 1989. reprint ed. pap. 12.95 (*0-87910-116-4*) Limelight Edns.
— The Thirsty Muse: Alcohol & the American Writer. 1989. 18.45 (*0-89919-376-5*, Pub. by Ticknor & Fields) HM.
Dardjowidjojo, Soenjono. Sentence Patterns of Indonesian. (PALI Language Text Ser.). 1994. audio 500.00 (*0-8248-1624-2*) Cooperative Natl Park Res Studies Unit.

D

— Sentence Patterns of Indonesian. LC 78-6687. (PALI Language Text Ser.). 448p. 1983. pap. text 27.00 (*0-8248-0418-X*) UH Pr.

— Vocabulary Building in Indonesian: An Advanced Reader. LC 84-5093. (Monographs in International Studies, Southeast Asia Ser.: No. 64). 664p. 1984. pap. text 30.00 (*0-89680-118-7*) Ohio U Pr.

Dardo, M. From Confrontation to Cooperation: Eighth International Seminar on Nuclear War. (Science & Culture Ser.). 316p. 1992. text 109.00 (*981-02-1191-0*) World Scientific Pub.

— Great Projects for Scientific Collaboration East-West-North-South: Seventh International Seminar on Nuclear War. (Science & Culture Ser.). 432p. 1992. text 121.00 (*981-02-1190-2*) World Scientific Pub.

Dardo, M. & Goebel, K. The New Emergencies: 9th International Seminar on Nuclear War. (Science & Culture Ser.). 352p. 1992. text 109.00 (*981-02-1192-9*) World Scientific Pub.

Dardour, J. C., jt. auth. see Bouhanna, F.

Dare. Amazing Las Vegas Trivia Book. 128p. 1996. pap. 9.95 (*0-9643183-2-6*) LV Trivia.

Dare, et al. Concepts of Leisure in Western Thought: Critical & Historical. 2nd ed. LC 98-161992. 316p. (C). 1997. per. 42.95 (*0-7872-2743-9*) Kendall-Hunt.

Dare, Alice. The Angel, the Spider & the Christmas Tree, Vol. 1. unabridged ed. Pillow, Martha, ed. LC 97-154818. (Illus.). 32p. (J). (gr. k-6). 1996. 14.95 (*1-57895-004-X*, Bridge Res) Curriculm Presbytrn KY.

Dare, Angela & O'Donovan, Margaret. Good Practice in Caring for Young Children with Special Needs. 224p. (Orig.). 1997. pap. 39.50 (*0-7487-2871-6*, Pub. by S Thornes Pubs) Trans-Atl Phila.

— A Practical Guide to Child Nutrition. 128p. 1996. pap. 22.50 (*0-7487-2375-7*, Pub. by S Thornes Pubs) Trans-Atl Phila.

— A Practical Guide to Working with Babies. 2nd ed. (Illus.). 192p. 1998. pap. 23.50 (*0-7487-3635-2*, Pub. by S Thornes Pubs) Trans-Atl Phila.

***Dare, Angela & O'Donovan, Margeret.** Good Practice in Child Safety. (Illus.). 224p. 2000. pap. 32.50 (*0-7487-4502-5*, Pub. by S Thornes Pubs) Trans-Atl Phila.

Dare, Angela, jt. auth. see O'Donovan, Margaret.

Dare, Chris, et al, eds. Handbook of Eating Disorders: Theory, Treatment & Research. 438p. 1996. pap. 89.95 (*0-471-96307-0*) Wiley.

Dare, Christopher, jt. ed. see Edwards, Griffith.

Dare, G. D. 1.3 Million Women Marched: Get a Glimpse of the Feeling of the Day. LC 99-94396. (Illus.). 54p. 1998. pap. text 16.95 (*0-9672481-0-8*) Buttrfly Press.

Dare, Gillian A. & Bakewell, K. G. The Manager's Guide to Getting the Answers. 2nd ed. LC 85-110400. (Illus.). 99p. reprint ed. pap. 30.70 (*0-7837-7012-X*, 204682600004) Bks Demand.

Dare, Justine. Dangerous Games, 1 vol. 326p. 1999. mass mkt. 5.99 (*0-451-40773-3*, Sig) NAL.

— Fire Hawk. 1997. mass mkt. 5.99 (*0-451-40762-8*, Onyx) NAL.

— Fire Hawk. 1999. mass mkt. 5.99 (*0-451-40633-8*, Onyx) NAL.

***Dare, Justine.** Night Fires. 2000. mass mkt. 6.50 (*0-451-40938-8*, Onyx) NAL.

***Dare, M. P.** The Shadow of the Rat: A Sherlock Holmes Adventure. 162p. 1999. pap. 19.50 (*1-899562-71-0*) Ash-Tree.

— Unholy Relics. xvi, 160p. 1997. 36.50 (*1-899562-23-0*) Ash-Tree.

Dare, Philip N. American Communes to Eighteen Sixty: A Bibliography. LC 89-16930. (Sects & Cults in America Ser.: Vol. 12). 212p. 1989. text 15.00 (*0-8240-8572-8*, SS348) Garland.

Dare-Plumpton, David, jt. ed. see Jones, Peter.

Dare, Robert, jt. auth. see Orchard, Lionel.

Dare, Sally A. Anna: Letters from the Attic. Groth, Shane & Erickson, Richard D., eds. LC 97-182522. Date not set. pap. 12.95 (*0-9649922-1-3*) Deforest Pr.

Dareau, Margaret, jt. auth. see Watson, Harry D.

***Dareini, Ali Akbar, tr.** The Rise & Fall of the Pahlavi Dynasty: Memoirs of Former General Hussein Fardust. 463p. 1999. pap. 400.00 (*81-208-1642-0*, Pub. by Motilal Bnarsidass) St Mut.

Daremberg, Charles. Histoire des Sciences Medicales. Comprenant l'Anatomie, la Physiologie, la Medicine, la Chirurgie et les Doctrines de Pathologie Generale. 2 vols. fac. ed. (FRE., Illus.). 1336p. 1974. reprint ed. 107.00 (*3-201-00907-5*, Pub. by Akademische Druck-und) Balogh.

— La Medecine: Histoire & Doctrines. 2nd ed. LC 75-13257. (History of Ideas in Ancient Greece Ser.). (FRE.). 1976. reprint ed. 35.95 (*0-405-07300-3*) Ayer.

Darenbourg, Marcetta Y., jt. ed. see Wayda, Andrea L.

Darensbourg, Joseph. Jazz Odyssey: The Autobiography of Joe Darensbourg, as Told to Peter Vacher. 231p. 1988. 19.95 (*0-8071-1442-1*) La State U Pr.

***Darensbourg, Marcetta Y.** Inorganic Syntheses, Vol. 32. 368p. 1998. 98.95 (*0-471-24921-1*, Wiley-Interscience) Wiley.

Darensbourg, Marcetta Y., jt. ed. see Wayda, Andrea L.

Daresh, John C. & Playko, Marsha A. Beginning the Principalship: A Practical Guide for New School Leaders. LC 96-51287. (Illus.). 120p. 1997. 55.95 (*0-8039-6566-4*); pap. 24.95 (*0-8039-6567-2*) Corwin Pr.

— Leaders Helping Leaders: A Practical Guide to Administrative Mentoring. LC 93-22401. 1995. 22.95 (*0-590-49219-5*, 17314D7 1993, Scholastic Ref) Scholastic Inc.

— Supervision As a Proactive Process: Concepts & Cases. 2nd ed. (Illus.). 397p. (C). 1995. pap. text 26.95 (*0-88133-814-1*) Waveland Pr.

Daresh, John C., jt. auth. see Capasso, Ronald L.

***D'Arezzo, Carol S. & Shannon-Nunn, Lauren.** Parrot-Toys & Play Areas: How to Put Some Fun into Your Parrot's Life. (Illus.). viii, 136p. 2000. pap. 16.95 (*0-9678820-0-1*) CrowFire Pubng.

D'Arezzo, Richard. Quick-Fix Home Repair. rev. ed. Alexander, Christie, ed. (Quick-Fix Ser.). (Illus.). 160p. 1987. pap. 6.95 (*0-939353-08-3*) Alexander & Alexander.

Darf Publ. Ltd. Staff & Horneman, F. Journal of Frederick Horneman's Travels from Cairo to Mourzouk. 226p. 1990. 125.00 (*1-85077-031-X*, Pub. by Darf Pubs Ltd) St Mut.

Darf Publishers Ltd. Staff. Travels in North Africa. (C). 1988. 135.00 (*1-85077-200-2*, Pub. by Darf Pubs Ltd) St Mut.

Darga, Kenneth. Sampling & the Census: A Case Against the Proposed Adjustments for Undercount. LC 99-11413. 140p. 1999. pap. 16.95 (*0-8447-4102-7*, Pub. by Am Enterprise) Pub Resources Inc.

Darga, Rita, jt. auth. see Nakane, Hisao.

Dargahi, Nick. Microsoft Flight Simulator: The Official Strategy Guide. LC 93-85785. (Secrets of the Games Ser.). (Illus.). 467p. 1994. pap. 19.95 (*1-55958-466-1*) Prima Pub.

— Microsoft Flight Simulator 5.1: The Official Strategy Guide. 1995. pap. text 19.95 (*0-7615-0155-X*) Prima Pub.

— SimCity 2000: Power, Politics, & Planning. LC 94-65409. (Illus.). 304p. 1994. pap. 19.95 (*1-55958-192-1*) Prima Pub.

— SimCity 2000: Power, Politics, & Planning. rev. ed. 1995. pap. 19.95 (*0-7615-0075-8*) Prima Pub.

— The Ultimate Flight Simulator Pilot's Guidebook. LC 97-38726. 704p. 1997. 39.95 (*1-55828-574-1*, MIS Pr) IDG Bks.

***Dargahi, Nick.** Ultimate Flight Simulator Pilot's Guidebook. 2nd ed. (Illus.). 870p. 2000. pap. 39.99 (*0-7645-3502-1*) IDG Bks.

***Dargahi-Noubary, G. R.** Time Series with Applications to Seismology. LC 98-44635. 240p. 1999. 85.00 (*1-56072-610-5*) Nova Sci Pubs.

Dargan, Amanda & Zeitlin, Steven. City Play. LC 90-30667. (Illus.). 220p. (C). 1990. 27.95 (*0-8135-1577-7*) Rutgers U Pr.

Dargan, E. Preston & Weinberg, Bernard. The Evolution of Balzac's "Comedie Humaine" LC 72-91802. 441p. 1973. reprint ed. lib. bdg. 52.00 (*0-8154-0452-2*) Cooper Sq.

Dargan, Elizabeth P., ed. The Civil War Diary of Martha Abernathy: Wife of Dr. C. C. Abernathy of Pulaski, Tennessee. (Illus.). 142p. (Orig.). 1994. pap. 11.95 (*0-9644094-0-2*, TX3 851 802) E P Dargan.

Dargan, James F. My Experiences in Service: or A Nine Months Man. Tanis, Norman E. & Matcha, Jack, eds. (American Classics Facsimile Ser.: Pt. I). 416p. 1974. pap. 10.00 (*0-937048-00-3*) Santa Susana.

Dargan, Joan. Balzac & the Drama of Perspective. LC 85-80419. (French Forum Monographs: No. 60). 172p. (Orig.). 1985. pap. 12.95 (*0-917058-61-5*) French Forum.

— Simone Weil: Thinking Poetically. LC 98-34052. (SUNY Series, Simone Weil Studies). 148p. (C). 1999. pap. text 17.95 (*0-7914-4224-1*) State U NY Pr.

— Simone Weil: Thinking Poetically. LC 98-34052. (SUNY Series, Simone Weil Studies). 176p. (C). 1999. text 54.50 (*0-7914-4223-3*) State U NY Pr.

Dargan, Joan, tr. see Escandell, Noemi.

Dargan, Joan, tr. see Veto, Miklos.

Dargan, Mary P. The Early English Kitchen Garden. 2nd ed. (Lost Art of Kitchen Gardening Ser.). (Illus.). 126p. (Orig.). 1982. pap. 12.00 (*0-9613313-0-5*) H Dargan Assocs.

Dargan, Olive T. From My Highest Hill: Carolina Mountain Folks. Elfenbein, Anna S., ed. LC 98-17522. Orig. Title: Highland Annals. (Illus.). 336p. 1998. reprint ed. pap. 22.50 (*1-57233-020-1*) U of Tenn Pr.

Dargan, Olive, pseud. Highland Animals. LC 72-6081. (Short Story Index Reprint Ser.). 1977. reprint ed. 21.95 (*0-8369-4207-8*) Ayer.

Dargan, Rosie. The Named Nurse in Practice. (Illus.). 110p. 1997. pap. 18.95 (*1-873853-37-8*) Bailliere Tindall.

***Dargan, William, et al.** Benjamin Lloyd's Hymn Book: A Primitive Baptist Song Tradition. 1999. pap. 18.00 (*0-9672672-1-8*) Alabama Folklife Assn.

Dargan, William, et al. Benjamin Lloyd's Hymn Book: A Primitive Baptist Song Tradition. LC 99-36078. (Illus.). 1999. 25.00 (*0-9672672-0-X*) Alabama Folklife Assn.

Dargatz, Jan. 52 Maneras de Ayudar a Tus Hijos a Vencer el Miedo. (52 Maneras de... Ser.). (SPA.). 150p. 1995. pap. 7.99 (*0-88113-354-X*) Caribe Betania.

— 52 Maneras Sencillas de Desarrollar la Autoestima y Confianza de Su Hijo. (Serie "52 Maneras"). (SPA.). 166p. 7.99 (*0-88113-228-4*, B001-2284) Caribe Betania.

— Fifty-Two Simple Ways to Tell Your Child "I Love You" 160p. (Orig.). 1991. pap. 7.99 (*0-8407-9591-2*) Nelson.

— Simple Truths. LC 94-43145. 1995. pap. text 10.99 (*0-8407-9139-9*) Nelson.

Dargavel, John. Fashioning Australia's Forests. LC 95-223958. (Illus.). 328p. (C). 1995. pap. text 35.00 (*0-19-553526-X*) OUP.

Dargavel, John & Tucker, Richard, eds. Changing Pacific Forests: Historical Perspectives on the Forest Economy of the Pacific Basin. LC 92-25130. 156p. (C). 1992. 39.95 (*0-8223-1262-X*); pap. 14.95 (*0-8223-1263-8*) Forest Hist Soc.

Dargay, Joyce. Factor Demand in Swedish Manufacturing: Econometric Analyses. (Studia Oeconomica Upsaliensia: No. 14). 138p. (Orig.). 1988. pap. 36.50 (*91-554-2258-6*, Pub. by Uppsala Univ Acta Univ Uppsaliensis) Coronet Bks.

D'Argenio, Constance. Implementing Nursing Diagnosis-Based Practice: Managing the Change. LC 90-14522. 192p. 1991. 55.00 (*0-8342-0215-8*, 20215) Aspen Pub.

D'Argenio, D. Z., ed. Advanced Methods of Pharmacokinetic & Pharmacodynamic Systems Analysis. (Illus.). 220p. (C). 1991. text 85.00 (*0-306-44028-8*, Kluwer Plenum) Kluwer Academic.

D'Argenio, David Z., ed. Advanced Methods of Pharmacokinetic & Pharmacodynamic Systems Analysis Vol. 2: Proceedings of a Meeting Held in Los Angeles, California, May 21-22, 1993, Vol. 2. (Illus.). 228p. (C). 1995. text 85.00 (*0-306-45018-6*, Kluwer Plenum) Kluwer Academic.

***Darger, Henry.** Henry Darger: Art & Selected Writings. (Illus.). 256p. 2000. 85.00 (*0-8478-2284-2*) Rizzoli Intl.

Dargie, Henry J., et al. Managing Heart Failure in Primary Care. (Illus.). 256p. 1996. pap. 49.95 (*0-86542-966-9*) Blackwell Sci.

***Dargie, Richard.** Castle under Seige. (Age of Castles Ser.). (Illus.). 48p. (J). (gr. 4-8), 1998. pap. 7.95 (*0-8172-8121-5*) Raintree Steck-V.

Dargie, Richard. Knights & Castles. LC 98-7003. (Age of Castles Ser.). 48 p. (J). (gr. 4-8). 1998. 25.69 (*0-8172-5122-7*) Raintree Steck-V.

***Dargie, Richard.** Knights & Castles. (Age of Castles Ser.). (Illus.). 48p. (J). (gr. 4-8). 1998. pap. 7.95 (*0-8172-8122-3*) Raintree Steck-V.

Dargo, George. Jefferson's Louisiana: Politics & the Clash of Legal Traditions. LC 74-25036. (Studies in Legal History). 272p. reprint ed. pap. 84.40 (*0-7837-2244-3*, 205733200004) Bks Demand.

Dargush, G. F., jt. auth. see Soong, T. T.

Dargys, Adolfas, jt. ed. see Asmontas, Steponas.

D'Ari, Paul, jt. ed. see Epler-Wood, Gregory.

Dari, Willie & Petit-Skinner, Solange. Fijian Protocol. 1985. pap. 8.00 (*0-9606272-1-9*) Macduff Pr.

Dari, Willie, et al. Adolescents in Fiji. LC 94-77219. 1994. pap. 15.00 (*0-9606272-2-7*) Macduff Pr.

Daria. A How to Book...Making Success Your Reality. LC 97-93298. 84p. (Orig.). 1997. pap. 9.95 (*0-9656846-0-1*) M Soderlind.

D'Aria, Daniel. You Shall Not Bear False Witness, Vol. 9. (Reflections on the Commandments Ser.). 63p. 1995. pap. 2.95 (*0-8198-8806-0*) Pauline Bks.

— You Shall Not Steal, Nor Covet Your Neighbor's Goods, Vol. 8. (Reflections on the Commandments Ser.). 63p. 1995. pap. 2.95 (*0-8198-8805-2*) Pauline Bks.

Daria, Gholamreza, ed. Molecular Biology of Iridoviruses. (Developments in Molecular Virology Ser.). 1989. text 210.50 (*0-7923-0506-X*) Kluwer Academic.

Daria, Irene, jt. auth. see Friedman, Lynn.

Darian, Shea. Grandpa's Garden. LC 96-164651. (Illus.). 36p. (J). (ps-5). 1996. 16.95 (*1-883220-42-4*); pap. 7.95 (*1-883220-41-6*) Dawn CA.

— Grandpa's Garden. 1996. 13.15 (*0-606-09350-8*, Pub. by Turtleback) Demco.

***Darian, Shea.** Seven Times the Sun: Guiding Your Child Through the Rhythms of the Day. 2nd ed. 224p. (Orig.). 1999. pap. 15.95 (*0-9675713-0-8*) Gilead Pr.

Darian-Smith, Eve. Bridging Divides: The Channel Tunnel & English Legal Identity in the New Europe. LC 98-46627. 280p. 1999. 50.00 (*0-520-21610-5*, Pub. by U CA Pr); 19.95 (*0-520-21611-3*, Pub. by U CA Pr) Cal Prin Full Svc.

Darian-Smith, Eve & Fitzpatrick, Peter, eds. Laws of the Postcolonial. LC 98-51222. (Law, Meaning & Violence Ser.). 320p. 1999. text 49.50 (*0-472-10956-1*, 10956) U of Mich Pr.

Darian-Smith, Ian, ed. Handbook of Physiology: Section 1, The Nervous System, 2 pts. (American Physiological Society Book). (Illus.). 1244p. 1988. text 275.00 (*0-19-520660-6*) OUP.

Darian-Smith, J., et al. The Anatomy of Manual Dexterity: The New Connectivity of the Primate Sensorimotor Thalamus & Cerebral Cortex. LC 96-17837. (Advances in Anatomy, Embryology & Cell Biology Ser.: Vol. 133). (Illus.). 140p. 1996. pap. 99.50 (*3-540-61111-8*) Spr-Verlag.

Darian-Smith, Kate. Australia & Oceania. LC 96-41314. (Continents Ser.). 48p. (J). 1997. lib. bdg. 25.69 (*0-8172-4778-5*) Raintree Steck-V.

— Exploration into Australia. LC 95-14456. (Exploration Into Ser.). (Illus.). 48p. (J). (gr. 4 up). 1996. pap. 7.95 (*0-382-39227-2*) Silver Burdett Pr.

Darian-Smith, Kate & Hamilton, Paula. Memory & History in Twentieth Century Australia. LC 94-217340. (Illus.). 264p. 1994. pap. text 35.00 (*0-19-553569-3*) OUP.

Darian-Smith, Kate & Lowe, David. The Australian Outback & Its People. (People & Places Ser.). (Illus.). 48p. (J). (gr. 5-8). 1995. lib. bdg. 24.26 (*1-56847-337-0*) Raintree Steck-V.

Darien, Georges. Gottlieb Krumm. (FRE.). 1991. pap. 14.95 (*0-7859-2172-9*, 2070384136) Fr & Eur.

Darien, Peter. Darien's World: Liveright Edition. (Illus.). 1964. 4.00 (*0-912156-02-3*) Masterwork Pr.

— Darien's World: Oriole Edition, 10 vols. 1961. boxed set 37.00 (*0-912156-01-5*) Masterwork Pr.

— Ecliptic: College Edition. (Illus.). 1969. pap. 2.00 (*0-912156-00-7*) Masterwork Pr.

D'Arienzo, Camille & Willis, Edgar E. Writing Scripts for Television, Radio & Film. 3rd ed. LC 92-53792. (Illus.). 352p. (C). 1993. pap. text 51.50 (*0-03-075011-3*, Pub. by Harcourt Coll Pubs) Harcourt.

D'Arienzo, Daria. Filing & Record-Keeping Manual for the University of Connecticut. 1984. pap. 3.00 (*0-317-61521-1*) Univ Conn Lib.

Darier, Eric. Theories of the Environment. LC 98-26079. 320p. 1999. 59.95 (*0-631-21122-5*); pap. 26.95 (*0-631-21123-3*) Blackwell Pubs.

Darilek, Richard E. A Crisis or Conflict Prevention Center for the Middle East. LC 95-12013. 52p. 1995. pap. text 7.50 (*0-8330-1636-9*, MR-499-USDP) Rand Corp.

— A Loyal Opposition in Time of War: The Republican Party & the Politics of Foreign Policy from Pearl Harbor to Yalta, 49. LC 75-44655. (Contributions in American History Ser.: No.49). 239p. (Orig.). 1976. 55.00 (*0-8371-8773-7*, DLO/) Greenwood.

***Darilek, Richard E.** Measures of Effectiveness for the Information-Age Army. LC 00-36615. 2000. write for info. (*0-8330-2847-2*) Rand Corp.

Darilek, Richard E. & Wendt, James C. Korean Arms Control: Political-Military Strategies, Studies & Games. LC 94-31163. 1994. pap. 13.00 (*0-8330-1589-3*, MR-489-A) Rand Corp.

Darin, Bobby & Murray, Jean. Splish Splash. (Sing-a-Song Storybooks Ser.). (Illus.). 24p. (J). 1993. 9.95 (*0-7935-1841-5*, 00183010) H Leonard.

Darin, Dodd. Dream Lovers: The Magnificent Shattered Lives of Bobby Darin & Sandra Dee by Their Son. 448p. 1995. mass mkt. 5.99 (*0-446-60246-9*, Pub. by Warner Bks) Little.

Darin, Dodd M., ed. see Mednis, Edmar.

Darin, Marcy, ed. Stories from the Circle: Women's Leadership in Community. LC 91-6754. 124p. 1991. pap. 8.95 (*0-8192-1536-8*) Morehouse Pub.

Darin, Marcy, ed. see Episcopal Church Women Staff.

Daringer, Helen F. & Eaton, Anne T., eds. Poet's Craft. LC 72-8284. (Granger Index Reprint Ser.). (Illus.). 1977. reprint ed. 23.95 (*0-8369-6385-7*) Ayer.

Dario, P., ed. Sensors & Sensory Systems for Advanced Robots. (NATO Asi Series F: Vol. 43). xi, 597p. 1988. 143.95 (*0-387-19089-9*) Spr-Verlag.

Dario, P., et al, eds. Robots & Biological Systems: Towards a New Bionics? (NATO ASI Series F: Computer & Systems Sciences, Special Programme AET: Vol. 102). xii, 796p. 1993. 215.95 (*0-387-56158-7*) Spr-Verlag.

Dario, R. Cantos de Vida y Esperanza. 148p. 1983. pap. 9.95 (*0-7859-5207-1*) Fr & Eur.

Dario, Ruben. Antologia. Ruiz Barrionuevo, Carmen, ed. (Nueva Austral Ser.: Vol. 269). (SPA.). 1991. pap. text 24.95 (*84-239-7269-0*) Elliots Bks.

— Azul, Cantos de Vida y de Esperanza. (SPA.). pap. 8.95 (*968-432-191-0*, Pub. by Porrua) Continental Bk.

— Carta Del Pais Azul. (Fondo 2000 Ser.). (SPA.). pap. 2.99 (*968-16-5048-4*, Pub. by Fondo) Continental Bk.

— Cuentos. (SPA.). pap. 10.95 (*84-239-0880-1*, Pub. by Espasa Calpe) Continental Bk.

— Cuentos Completos. 2nd ed. LC 87-672973. (Coleccion Popular Ser.). 1994. pap. 12.99 (*968-16-1441-0*) Fondo.

— Eleven Poems of Ruben Dario: Bilingual Edition. Walsh, Thomas & DeLa Selva, Salomon, trs. 1977. lib. bdg. 59.95 (*0-8490-1758-0*) Gordon Pr.

— Margarita. (Illus.). 48p. (J). 5.95 (*980-257-053-2*, Pub. by Ediciones Ekare) Kane-Miller Bk.

— El Mundo de los Suenos. (Coleccion Mente y Palabra). 233p. (C). 1973. 5.00 (*0-8477-0502-1*); pap. 4.00 (*0-8477-0503-X*) U of PR Pr.

***Dario, Ruben.** Poemas Escogidos. 1999. 13.00 (*84-481-0978-3*, McGrw-H College) McGrw-H Hghr Educ.

Dario, Ruben. Poesia. 8th ed. 144p. 1991. pap. 9.95 (*0-7859-5206-3*) Fr & Eur.

Dario, Ruben, et al. Beyond the Glitter: The Language of Gems in Modernista. LC 98-20794. 216p. 1999. 38.50 (*0-8387-5394-9*) Bucknell U Pr.

Darion, Joe & Wasserman, Dale. Man of La Mancha. 1966. pap. 9.95 (*0-394-40619-2*) Random.

Darion, Joe, jt. auth. see Leigh, Mitch.

Dariot, Claudius. Introduction to Astrology: A Brief & Most Easy Introduction to the Astrological Judgment of the Stars. large type ed. Wiggers, Carol A., ed. (Illus.). 102p. (C). 1992. text, wbk. ed. 20.00 (*1-878935-15-1*) JustUs & Assocs.

D'Arista, Jane W. The Evolution of U. S. Finance, Two-Vol. Set, Two-Vol. Set. Incl. Vol. I. Evolution of U. S. Finance Vol. I: Federal Reserve Monetary Policy 1915-1935. LC 93-36837. 272p. (C). (gr. 13). 1994. pap. text 42.95 (*1-56324-231-1*); Vol. II. Evolution of U. S. Finance Vol. II: Restructuring Institutions & Markets. LC 93-36837. 528p. (C). (gr. 13). 1994. pap. text 45.95 (*1-56324-233-8*); LC 93-36837. (Columbia University Seminars Ser.). 800p. (gr. 13). 1994. Set pap. text 74.95 (*1-56324-397-0*) M E Sharpe.

— The Evolution of U.S. Finance: Federal Reserve Monetary Policy, 1915-1935; & Volume II Restructuring Institutions, Two-Vol. Set, Two-Vol. Set. Incl. Vol. I. Evolution of U.S. Finance Vol. I: Federal Reserve Monetary Policy 1915-1935. LC 93-36837. 272p. (C). (gr. 13). 1994. text 85.95 (*1-56324-230-3*); Vol. II. Evolution of U.S. Finance Vol. II: Restructuring Institutions & Markets. LC 93-36837. 528p. (C). (gr. 13). 1994. text 100.95 (*1-56324-232-X*); LC 93-36837. (Columbia University Seminars Ser.). 800p. (gr. 13). 1994. Set text 166.95 (*1-56324-396-2*) M E Sharpe.

Darity, William, Jr., ed. Economics & Discrimination, 2 vols. LC 95-13443. (International Library of Critical Writings in Economics: Vol. 57). 1344p. 1995. 470.00 (*1-85278-790-2*) E Elgar.

— Labor Economics: Problems in Analyzing Labor Markets. LC 92-18985. (Recent Economic Thought Ser.). 320p. (C). 1992. lib. bdg. 152.00 (*0-7923-9260-4*) Kluwer Academic.

Darity, William A., Jr. & Horn, Bobbie L. The Loan Pushers: The Role of Commercial Banks in the International Debt Crisis. 224p. 1988. text 34.95 (*0-88730-067-7*, HarpBusn) HarpInfo.

Darity, William A., Jr. & Myers, Samuel L., Jr. Persistent Disparity: Race & Economic Inequality in the U. S. since 1945. LC 97-30626. 208p. 1998. 80.00 (*1-85898-658-3*) E Elgar.

An Asterisk (*) at the beginning of an entry indicates that the title is appearing for the first time.

Darity, William A. & Myers, Samuel L. Persistent Disparity: Race & Economic Inequality in the U. S. since 1945. LC 97-30626. 208p. 1999. pap. 25.00 (*1-85898-665-6*) E Elgar.

Darity, William A., ed. see Carson, Emmett.

Darius-Beautell, Eva. Contemporary Theories & Canadian Fiction: Shifting Sands. LC 99-11294. (Canadian Studies: Vol. 21). 267p. 1999. text 89.95 (*0-7734-8173-7*) E Mellen.

Darius, Robert G., et al, eds. Gulf Security into the Nineteen Eighties: Perceptual & Strategic Dimensions. (Publication Ser.: No. 291). xii, 134p. 1984. pap. 4.38 (*0-8179-7912-3*); lib. bdg. 8.78 (*0-8179-7911-5*) Hoover Inst Pr.

***Dariusz, Ko Odziejczyk.** Ottoman-Polish Diplomatic Relations (15th-18th Century) An Annotated Edition of Names & other Documents. annot. ed. LC 98-44347. (Ottoman Empire & Its Heritage Ser.). 1999. write for info. (*90-04-11280-4*) Brill Academic Pubs.

Darizcuren, Francis. Les Tablatures par l'Image: Special Basse. Lefferts, Michael, ed. 56p. (Orig.). (C). 1997. pap. text 19.95 (*0-7692-1329-4*, 01010323) Wrner Bros.

***Dark, Alice Elliot.** In the Gloaming: Stories. 2001. pap. 13.00 (*0-684-87005-3*, Scribner Pap Fic) S&S Trade Pap.

***Dark, Alice Elliott.** In the Gloaming: Stories. LC 99-27542. 288p. 2000. 22.50 (*0-684-86521-1*) S&S Trade.

Dark, Harris E. Auto Engines of Tomorrow: Power Alternatives for Cars to Come. LC 74-6518. 192p. reprint ed. pap. 59.60 (*0-8357-5903-2*, 205622300056) Bks Demand.

— The Wankel Rotary Engine: Introduction & Guide. LC 73-16676. 159p. reprint ed. pap. 49.30 (*0-608-17123-9*, 205622400056) Bks Demand.

Dark, Harris E., ed. see Leigh, Bob, et al.

Dark, Harry & Dark, Phyl. The Greatest Ozarks Guidebook. 2nd ed. LC 79-7733. 272p. (Orig.). 1980. pap. 7.95 (*0-936120-00-2*) Greatest Graphics.

Dark Horse Comics. Female War. (Aliens Ser.). (Illus.). 1997. pap. text 16.95 (*1-56971-190-9*) Dark Horse Comics.

Dark Horse Comics Staff. Dark Horse Short Story Collection. (Illus.). 1997. pap. text 12.95 (*1-56971-179-8*) Dark Horse Comics.

***Dark Horse Comics Staff.** Dominion. 3rd ed. 2000. pap. 16.95 (*1-56971-488-6*, Pub. by Dark Horse Comics) Penguin Putnam.

Dark Horse Comics Staff. Droid: Rebellion. (Star Wars Ser.). (Illus.). 1997. pap. text 14.95 (*1-56971-224-7*) Dark Horse Comics.

— The Early Adventures: Classic Star Wars. (Star Wars Ser.). (Illus.). 1997. pap. text 19.95 (*1-56971-178-X*) Dark Horse Comics.

— Mask: A Mask for All Seasons. (Illus.). 1997. pap. text 14.95 (*1-56971-177-1*) Dark Horse Comics.

— Nightmare Asylum. (Aliens Ser.). (Illus.). 1997. pap. text 16.95 (*1-56971-217-4*) Dark Horse Comics.

— Shadows of the Empire. (Star Wars Ser.). (Illus.). 1997. pap. text 17.95 (*1-56971-183-6*) Dark Horse Comics.

Dark Horse Comics Staff. Star Wars Empires End. (Star Wars Ser.). (Illus.). (J). 1997. pap. 5.95 (*1-56971-306-5*) Dark Horse Comics.

— Usagi Yojimbo: Daisho. 1998. pap. 14.95 (*1-56971-292-1*, Pub. by Dark Horse Comics) Penguin Putnam.

***Dark, Horton.** Terminator. (Illus.). (YA). 1999. pap. 9.95 (*1-56971-373-1*) Dark Horse Comics.

Dark, K. R. New Studies in Post-Cold War Security. LC 96-16535. 296p. 1996. text 82.95 (*1-85521-728-7*, Pub. by Dartmth Pub) Ashgate Pub Co.

***Dark, K. R.** Religion & International Relations. LC 99-53007. 2000. text 75.00 (*0-312-23067-2*) St Martin.

Dark, K. R. Theoretical Archaeology. LC 94-23209. 256p. 1995. text 49.95 (*0-8014-3125-5*); pap. text 19.95 (*0-8014-8252-6*) Cornell U Pr.

— The Waves of Time: Long-Term Change & International Relations. LC 97-10239. 224p. 1998. 85.00 (*1-85567-402-5*) Bks Intl VA.

***Dark, K. R.** Waves of Time: Long-Term Change & International Relations. 224p. 2000. pap. text 28.95 (*0-8264-4762-7*) Continuum.

Dark, K. R., ed. External Contacts & the Economy of Late-Roman & Post-Roman Britain. LC 96-38196. (Illus.). 192p. 1996. 75.00 (*0-85115-655-X*, Boydell Pr) Boydell & Brewer.

Dark, K. R. & Harris, A. L. The New World & the New World Order: Domestic Instability in the Americas & the End of the Cold War. (Illus.). 184p. 1996. text 59.95 (*0-312-16212-X*) St Martin.

***Dark, Ken.** Britain & the End of the Roman Empire. (Illus.). 176p. 2000. 32.50 (*0-7524-1451-8*, Pub. by Tempus Pubng) Arcadia Publng.

Dark, Ken. The Inscribed Stones of Dyfed. 1992. pap. 21.00 (*0-86383-818-9*, Pub. by Gomer Pr) St Mut.

Dark, Ken & Dark, Petra. The Landscape of Roman Britain. (Illus.). 192p. 1996. 33.95 (*0-7509-0964-1*, Pub. by Sutton Pub Ltd) Intl Pubs Mktg.

— The Landscape of Roman Britain. (Illus.). 192p. 1998. pap. 19.95 (*0-7509-1874-8*, Pub. by Sutton Pub Ltd) Intl Pubs Mktg.

Dark, Kenneth R. Civitas to Kingdom: British Political Continuity, 300-800. (Illus.). 322p. 1999. pap. 32.95 (*0-7185-0206-X*) Continuum.

— Civitas to Kingdom: British Political Continuity, 300-800. 224p. 1994. 59.00 (*0-7185-1465-3*, Pub. by Leicester U Pr) Cassell & Continuum.

Dark, Larry. A Literary Traveler. 1999. pap. 22.50 (*0-670-85333-X*) Viking Penguin.

— Prize Stories 1998: The O. Henry Awards. 464p. 1998. pap. 11.95 (*0-385-48958-7*) Doubleday.

Dark, Larry, ed. The Literary Ghost. LC 91-15052. 384p. 1992. pap. 13.00 (*0-87113-483-7*, Atlntc Mnthly) Grove-Atltic.

— The Literary Lover: Great Contemporary Stories of Passion & Romance. 384p. 1994. pap. 13.95 (*0-14-017164-9*, Penguin Bks) Viking Penguin.

***Dark, Larry, ed.** Prize Stories 1999: The O. Henry Awards. (Prize Stories: The O. Henry Awards Ser.). 464p. 1999. pap. 11.95 (*0-385-49358-4*, Anchor NY) Doubleday.

***Dark, Larry, ed.** Prize Stories 2000: The O Henry Awards. (Illus.). 464p. 2000. pap. 13.00 (*0-385-49877-2*, Anchor NY) Doubleday.

***Dark One.** Animal Mystic Water Wars, Vol. 1. (Illus.). 156p. 1999. pap. 19.95 (*1-57989-024-5*) Sirius Ent.

Dark One & Horan, Robb. Animal Mystic, Vol. 1. (Illus.). 156p. 1996. pap. 14.95 (*1-57989-004-0*) Sirius Ent.

Dark, Petra, jt. auth. see Dark, Ken.

Dark, Petra, jt. ed. see Mellars, Paul.

Dark, Philip J. An Illustrated Catalogue of Benin Art IV. 1982. 210.00 (*0-8161-0382-8*, G K Hall & Co) Mac Lib Ref.

Dark, Philip J. & Rose, Roger G., eds. Artistic Heritage in a Changing Pacific. LC 93-7844. (Illus.). 312p. (C). 1993. text 42.00 (*0-8248-1573-4*) UH Pr.

Dark, Phyl, jt. auth. see Dark, Harry.

Dark, Sandra. Old Flames. (Shadows Ser.). 1996. per. 3.50 (*0-373-27063-1*, 1-27063-6) Silhouette.

— Sleeping Tigers. 1994. per. 3.50 (*0-373-27044-5*, 1-27044-6) Harlequin Bks.

Dark Shadows Fan Club Staff, ed. Dark Shadows - The First Year. (Dark Shadows Television Show Ser.). (Illus.). 100p. (Orig.). 1997. pap. 30.00 (*0-317-05623-9*) L Wendruck.

— Dark Shadows - The Last Year. (Dark Shadows Television Show Ser.). (Illus.). 80p. (Orig.). 1997. pap. 30.00 (*0-317-05624-7*) L Wendruck.

— The Dark Shadows Announcement. (Dark Shadows Tel Show Ser.). (Illus.). 80p. (Orig.). 1997. pap. 30.00 (*0-614-04386-7*) L Wendruck.

— Dark Shadows Episode Guide. (Dark Shadows Television Show Ser.). (Illus.). 80p. (Orig.). 1997. pap. 30.00 (*0-317-05622-0*) L Wendruck.

Dark, Sidney. Charles Dickens. LC 75-38650. (Studies in Dickens: No. 52). 1976. lib. bdg. 75.00 (*0-8383-2113-5*) M S G Haskell Hse.

— Five Deans. LC 71-93332. (Essay Index Reprint Ser.). 1977. 20.95 (*0-8369-1285-3*) Ayer.

— Robert Louis Stevenson. LC 76-173849. (English Literature Ser.: No. 33). 1971. reprint ed. lib. bdg. 75.00 (*0-8383-1343-4*) M S G Haskell Hse.

— Twelve Bad Men. LC 68-54343. (Essay Index Reprint Ser.). 1977. 23.95 (*0-8369-0361-7*) Ayer.

— Twelve More Ladies. LC 70-86744. (Essay Index Reprint Ser.). 1977. 20.95 (*0-8369-1177-6*) Ayer.

— Twelve Royal Ladies. LC 73-99689. (Essay Index Reprint Ser.). 1977. 26.95 (*0-8369-1459-7*) Ayer.

Dark, Sidney & Grey, Rowland. Gilbert: His Life & Letters. LC 76-177509. (Illus.). 1972. reprint ed. 23.95 (*0-405-08430-7*, Pub. by Blom Pubns) Ayer.

Dark, Taylor E. The Unions & the Democrats: An Enduring Alliance. LC 98-30400. 304p. 1999. 37.50 (*0-8014-3576-5*, ILR Press) Cornell U Pr.

Dark, Tom. Practical Implementation of New Management Strategies: Managing Your Processes. (C). 1994. 97.50 (*0-7478-1839-8*, Pub. by S Thornes Pubs) Trans-Atl Phila.

Dark, Victoria. Marrying Mattie. 320p. 1999. mass mkt. 4.99 (*0-8217-6101-3*) Kensgtn Pub Corp.

Dark Videbeck, Sheila L., jt. auth. see Schultz, Judith M.

Darke. A Question of Courage. (Longman Literature Ser.). 1995. pap. text. write for info. (*0-582-25395-0*, Pub. by Addison-Wesley) Longman.

Darke, Alexander. Legacies. 1997. pap. 3.50 (*0-87129-714-0*, L86) Dramatic Pub.

Darke, David. Horrorshow. 352p. 1994. mass mkt. 4.50 (*0-8217-4783-5*, Zebra Kensgtn) Kensgtn Pub Corp.

Darke, Diana. Discovery Guide to Aegean & Mediterranean Turkey. 320p. (C). 1995. pap. 65.00 (*0-902743-70-8*, Pub. by IMMEL Pubng) St Mut.

— Discovery Guide to Eastern Turkey & the Black Sea Coast. 352p. (C). 1995. pap. 59.00 (*0-902743-74-0*, Pub. by IMMEL Pubng) St Mut.

— Discovery Guide to Jordan & the Holy Land. 232p. (C). 1995. pap. 59.00 (*0-907151-70-1*, Pub. by IMMEL Pubng) St Mut.

— Guide to North Cyprus. 2nd ed. LC 95-17759. (Bradt Country Guides Ser.). (Illus.). 240p. (Orig.). 1995. pap. 14.95 (*1-56440-819-1*, Pub. by Bradt Pubns) Globe Pequot.

***Darke, Diana.** North Cyprus: The Bradt Travel Guide. 3rd ed. LC 99-54343. (Illus.). 2000. pap. 14.95 (*1-84162-012-2*, Pub. by Bradt Pubns) Globe Pequot.

— Tunsia. 2nd ed. (Illustrated Travel Guides Ser.). (Illus.). 2000. pap. 14.95 (*0-658-00508-1*, Passprt Bks) NTC Contemp Pub Co.

Darke, Diane, et al. Turkey. LC 93-84399. (Illustrated Travel Guides from Thomas Cook Ser.). (Illus.). 192p. 1994. pap. 12.95 (*0-8442-9066-1*, Passprt Bks) NTC Contemp Pub Co.

***Darke, Dorothy Marie.** The Leaves Have Lost Their Trees. 115p. 1999. pap. 45.00 (*1-85072-226-9*, Pub. by W Sessions) St Mut.

Darke, Frederick & Griffiths, Mark. Manual of Grasses. (Illus.). 218p. 1995. 39.95 (*0-88192-300-1*) Timber.

***Darke, Hubert, tr.** The Book of Government of Rules for Kings: The Siyar al Muluk or Siyasatnama of Nizam Al-Mulk. 288p. 2000. 80.00 (*0-7007-1228-3*, Pub. by Curzon Pr Ltd) Paul & Co Pubs.

Darke, Jane, ed. see Labour Housing Group Staff.

***Darke, Nick.** Riot. 2000. pap. 10.95 (*0-413-73730-6*, Methuen Drama) Methn.

Darke, Nick. Ting Tang Mine & Other Plays. (Methuen Theatrescripts Ser.). 70p. (C). 1988. pap. write for info. (*0-413-17930-3*, A0296, Methuen Drama) Methn.

Darke, Peter G. G. & Bonogura. Color Atlas of Veterinary Cardiology. 1995. 71.00 (*0-7234-1907-8*) Mosby Inc.

Darke, Rick. The Color Encyclopedia of Ornamental Grasses: Sedges, Rushes, Restios, Cat-Tails & Selected Bamboos. LC 98-23440. (Illus.). 325p. 1999. 49.95 (*0-88192-464-4*) Timber.

***Darke, Rick.** In Harmony with Nature: Lessons from the Arts & Crafts Garden. LC 99-53510. (Illus.). 160p. 2000. 35.00 (*1-56799-904-2*, Friedman-Fairfax) M Friedman Pub Grp Inc.

Darke, Rick & Griffiths, Mark, eds. Manual of Grasses. (Illus.). 169p. 1994. 72.50 (*0-333-61535-2*, Pub. by Pan) Trans-Atl Phila.

***Darken, Kevin J.** Attorney's Guide to Preventing & Defending Health Care Fraud Investigations. LC 99-41031. 600p. 1999. 149.00 (*0-8342-1171-8*) Aspen Pub.

Darkenwald, Gordon G., jt. auth. see Beder, Harold W.

Darkhovsky, B. S., jt. auth. see Brodsky, B. E.

Darkin, Alida. The Jewel of Regeneration. LC 87-51373. (Humming Bird Bk.). (Illus.). 59p. (Orig.). 1987. pap. write for info. (*0-945126-01-8*) Undiscovd Worlds Pr.

***Darkins, Adam William & Cary, Margaret Ann.** Telemedicine & Telehealth: Principles, Policies, Performance & Pitfalls. (Illus.). 320p. 2000. text 42.95 (*0-8261-1302-8*) Springer Pub.

Darkins, Claudia M. A Name I Can't Read: The Rocky Road to Literacy, a Mother's Story. Butler, Marguerite L. & Willis, Brenda, eds. LC 97-92290. 200p. 1998. 14.95 (*0-9648154-0-0*, Cane Pub) Claudia Prodns.

Darklee, Dennis R., jt. auth. see Shoop, Robert J.

Darklight, Senya. Senya. Campbell, Marty, ed. LC 88-92537. (Illus.). 200p. 1989. pap. 9.00 (*0-929749-00-6*) Mar Crafs.

Darklight, Senya, et al. Companion to Senya. Campbell, Marty, ed. LC 88-92536. (Illus.). 160p. (Orig.). 1989. pap. 9.00 (*0-929749-01-4*) Mar Crafs.

Darknell, Frank A. Scholars Manque & Freeway Students: Repercussions of the Baby Boom at American State Colleges. LC 96-85164. (Illus.). 350p. (Orig.). 1999. pap. 19.95 (*0-9647412-7-X*) Capitola Hall Pr.

Darko, Amma. Beyond the Horizon. (African Writers Ser.). 140p. 1995. pap. 9.95 (*0-435-90990-8*, 90990) Heinemann.

Darko, Anna. The Housemaid. LC 99-210197. 107p. 1999. pap. 11.95 (*0-435-91008-6*) Heinemann.

Darko, S. Fordjour. Biblio-Catalog: A Guide to Eye-Opening Books on Africa. 87p. 1989. pap. 12.95 (*0-9624300-0-5*) Educ Servs Intl.

Darkow, Michael T. Real Characters. 155p. mass mkt. 4.99 (*1-55197-107-0*) Picasso Publ.

Darkwah, R. H. Shewa, Menilek, & the Ethiopian Empire. (Illus.). 233p. (C). 1976. 37.95 (*0-8419-5310-4*, Africana) Holmes & Meier.

Darkwhiaul, Jonathon A. The Creation. 377p. (Orig.). 1995. pap. 6.95 (*0-9638922-1-5*) Bristlecne Pr.

— Fearless. 256p. (Orig.). 1993. pap. 6.95 (*0-9638922-0-7*) Bristlecne Pr.

Darla Moore School of Business Staff. Transition into Business. LC 98-39132. 122p. (C). 1998. pap. text 13.80 (*0-13-081541-1*) P-H.

Darland, Carmen, jt. ed. see Whalen, Kim.

Darlen-De, jt. auth. see Master Teachers Staff.

Darley, Alex. Passionists of the Southwest: A Revelation of the Penitentes. LC 68-57290. (Beautiful Rio Grande Classics Ser.). 134p. 1968. lib. bdg. 17.50 (*0-87380-020-6*) Popular E Commerce.

***Darley, Andrew.** Visual Digital Culture. 2000. 75.00 (*0-415-16554-7*); pap. 32.99 (*0-415-16555-5*) Routledge.

Darley, Diana. Dictionnaire National des Communes de France. (FRE.). 1344p. 1992. 150.00 (*0-7859-9271-5*) Fr & Eur.

Darley, Frederic L., jt. ed. see Keith, Robert L.

Darley, Frederick L., et al. Motor Speech Disorders. LC 74-25475. (Illus.). 304p. 1975. text 68.00 (*0-7216-2878-8*, W B Saunders Co) Harcrt Hlth Sci Grp.

Darley, George. Complete Poetical Works. (BCL1-PR English Literature Ser.). 538p. 1992. reprint ed. lib. bdg. 99.00 (*0-7812-7506-7*) Rprt Serv.

***Darley, Gillian.** John Soane: An Accidental Romantic. LC 99-62198. (Illus.). 368p. 1999. 50.00 (*0-300-08165-0*); pap. 24.95 (*0-300-08695-4*) Yale U Pr.

Darley, H. C. & Gray, George R. Composition & Properties of Drilling & Completion Fluids. 5th ed. (Illus.). 644p. 1988. 125.00 (*0-87201-147-X*, 1147) Gulf Pub.

Darley-Hill, Susan, jt. ed. see Traina, Frank.

Darley, John M. & Cooper, Joel, eds. Attribution & Social Interaction: The Legacy of Edward E. Jones. LC 97-44346. (Illus.). 550p. 1998. text 49.95 (*1-55798-475-1*) Am Psychol.

Darley, John M., et al. Psychology. 5th ed. rev. ed. 752p. (C). 1990. text 66.00 (*0-13-734377-9*, 670106) P-H.

Darley, John M., jt. ed. see Zanna, Mark P.

Darley, Lois M. Caloriechex. 80p. (Orig.). 1988. student ed. 6.95 (*0-939909-02-2*) Scribe Write.

— Dietchex. 80p. (Orig.). 1988. student ed. 6.95 (*0-939909-01-4*) Scribe Write.

***Darley, Marshall.** Biology: Lecture Supplement. 112p. 2000. suppl. ed. 12.00 (*1-886855-44-7*, No. 1108) Tavenner Pub.

— Biology 1104-Lecture Supplements. 120p. 1999. 10.00 (*1-886855-32-3*) Tavenner Pub.

Darley, Marshall. Botany 1210 Lab Manual. 84p. 1998. pap., lab manual ed. 12.00 (*1-886855-99-4*) Tavenner Pub.

Darley-Ujmar, Victor, ed. see Balkwill, Fran.

Darley-Usmar, V. & Shapira, A. H., eds. Mitochondria: DNA, Proteins & Disease. LC 94-129580. (Portland Press Research Monographs: Vol. 5). (Illus.). xi, 286p. (C). 1994. text 102.00 (*1-85578-042-9*, Pub. by Portland Pr Ltd) Ashgate Pub Co.

***Darley, W. L.** An Easy Dictionary. (J). (gr. 2-4). 1999. pap. 35.00 (*0-7217-0035-7*, Pub. by Schofield) St Mut.

— An Easy Dictionary: Look It Up (Exercises) (J). (gr. 2-4). 1999. pap. 35.00 (*0-7217-0081-0*, Pub. by Schofield) St Mut.

— An Illustrated Dictionary. (Illus.). (J). (gr. 1-3). 1999. pap. 39.00 (*0-7217-0455-7*, Pub. by Schofield) St Mut.

— An Illustrated Dictionary: Exercises. (Illus.). (J). (gr. 1-3). 1999. pap. 39.00 (*0-7217-0676-2*, Pub. by Schofield) St Mut.

Darling. Molecular Visions Organic Mode. (C). 1998. 8.50 (*0-9648837-4-0*) Darling Models.

***Darling.** On the Eve of Contact. 2000. 27.00 (*0-465-01563-8*, Pub. by Basic); pap. 14.00 (*0-465-01564-6*, Pub. by Basic) HarpC.

***Darling & Benjamin.** Shakespeare on Love. 2000. write for info. (*0-684-01113-1*) S&S Trade.

Darling & Lynn. The Slut Museum. 2000. write for info. (*0-316-17327-4*) Little.

Darling, Aileen, tr. see Strobel, S.

Darling, Arthur B. The Central Intelligence Agency: An Instrument of Government, to 1950. 509p. (C). 1999. pap. text 25.00 (*0-7881-6319-1*) DIANE Pub.

— The Central Intelligence Agency: An Instrument of Government, to 1950. Berkowitz, Bruce D. & Goodman, Allan E., eds. 672p. 1990. 60.00 (*0-271-00715-X*); pap. 22.50 (*0-271-00717-6*) Pa St U Pr.

Darling, Benjamin. Be Still My Beating Heart: A Titillating Pictorial of Art Throughout the Ages. 1990. 15.95 (*0-942139-11-9*) Tale Weaver.

— Cakes Men Like: Fifty Fun-Filled Recipes. 60p. 1992. 9.95 (*0-8118-0007-5*) Chronicle Bks.

— Helpful Hints for Housewives: A Treasury of Tips for the Model Homemaker. (Illus.). 60p. 1992. 9.95 (*0-8118-0006-7*) Chronicle Bks.

— Robert & the Balloon Machine. (Illus.). 32p. (J). 1991. 11.95 (*0-88138-120-9*, Green Tiger S&S) S&S Childrens.

— Tips for Teens: Telephone Tactics, Petting Practices, & Other Milestones on the Road to Popularity. LC 93-35815. (Illus.). 60p. 1994. 9.95 (*0-8118-0520-4*) Chronicle Bks.

— Valerie & the Silver Pear. LC 90-24945. (Illus.). 32p. (J). (gr. k-3). 1992. mass mkt. 14.95 (*0-02-726100-X*, Four Winds Pr) S&S Childrens.

***Darling, Benjamin, ed.** Shakespeare on Love. (Illus.). 96p. 2000. 16.95 (*0-7352-0174-9*) PH Pr.

Darling, Benjamin, jt. compiled by see Edens, Cooper.

Darling, Candy. Candy Darling. (Illus.). 144p. (Orig.). 1992. pap. 5.95 (*0-937815-45-4*) Hanuman Bks.

Darling, Christina. Mirror. LC 96-84953. (Illus.). 32p. (J). (gr. k). 1997. 16.00 (*0-374-34720-4*) FS&G.

Darling, Curtis. Kern County Place Names. (Illus.). 135p. 1988. 12.00 (*0-943500-12-5*) Kern Historical.

Darling, D. C. & Morgan, S. J. Animal Cells - Culture & Media: Essential Data. LC 94-31441. (Bios Essential Data Ser.). 168p. 1995. pap. 39.95 (*0-471-94300-2*) Wiley.

Darling, Daniel, tr. see Schuller, Robert H.

Darling, David. Between Fire & Ice: The Science of Heat. LC 91-40966. (Experiment! Ser.). (Illus.). 60p. (YA). (gr. 5 up). 1992. lib. bdg. 13.95 (*0-87518-501-0*, Dillon Silver Burdett) Silver Burdett Pr.

— Computers of the Future: Intelligent Machines & Virtual Reality. LC 95-14212. (J). (gr. 5). 1995. pap. 7.95 (*0-382-39169-1*, Dillon Silver Burdett) Silver Burdett Pr.

— Computers of the Future: Intelligent Machines & Virtual Reality. LC 95-14212. (Beyond Two Thousand Ser.). (YA). (gr. 5 up). 1995. lib. bdg. 14.95 (*0-87518-617-3*) Silver Burdett Pr.

Darling, David. Equations of Eternity: Speculations on Consciousness, Meaning, & the Mathematical Rules That Orchestrate the Cosmos. LC 92-26440. 208p. (YA). 1993. 19.45 (*1-56282-875-4*, Pub. by Hyperion) Time Warner.

— The Extraterrestrial Encyclopedia: An Alphabetical Reference to All Life in the Universe. LC 99-38266. (Illus.). 544p. 2000. pap. 25.00 (*0-8129-3248-X*, Times Bks) Crown Pub Group.

Darling, David. The Health Revolution: Surgery & Medicine in the Twenty-First Century. LC 95-14223. (Beyond Two Thousand Ser.). (Illus.). (YA). (gr. 5 up). 1995. lib. bdg. 14.95 (*0-87518-616-5*, Dillon Silver Burdett) Silver Burdett Pr.

— The Health Revolution: Surgery & Medicine in the Twenty-First Century. LC 95-14223. (Beyond Two Thousand Ser.). (Illus.). (YA). (gr. 5 up). 1999. pap. 11.00 (*0-382-39170-5*, Dillon Silver Burdett) Silver Burdett Pr.

— Making Light Work: The Science of Optics. LC 91-3999. (Experiment! Ser.). (Illus.). 60p. (J). (gr. 4-6). 1991. lib. bdg. 13.95 (*0-87518-476-6*, Dillon Silver Burdett) Silver Burdett Pr.

— Micromachines & Nantechnology: The Amazing New World of the Ultrasmall. (Beyond Two Thousand Ser.). (Illus.). 64p. (J). (gr. 5-9). 1995. pap. 7.95 (*0-382-24953-4*, Dillon Silver Burdett) Silver Burdett Pr.

— Return to Child: Philosophy, Games & Techniques Developed by David Darling. 36p. 1993. 9.00 (*1-885617-00-3*) Music for People.

— Sounds Interesting: The Science of Acoustics. LC 91-4002. (Experiment! Ser.). (Illus.). 60p. (J). (gr. 4-6). 1991. lib. bdg. 13.95 (*0-87518-477-4*, Dillon Silver Burdett) Silver Burdett Pr.

D

— Spiderwebs to Skyscrapers: The Science of Structure. LC 91-4001. (Experiment! Ser.). (Illus.). 60p. (J). (gr. 4-6). 1991. lib. bdg. 13.95 (*0-87518-478-2*, Dillon Silver Burdett) Silver Burdett Pr.
— Up, up, & Away: The Science of Flight. LC 91-4000. (Experiment! Ser.). (Illus.). 60p. (J). (gr. 4-6). 1991. lib. bdg. 13.95 (*0-87518-479-0*) Silver Burdett Pr.
— Zen Physics: The Science of Death, the Logic of Reincarnation. LC 95-51829. 1996. write for info. (*0-614-95860-1*) HarpC.
Darling, David D., ed. Waterpower, '91: A New View of Hydro Resources, 3 vols., Set. LC 89-647159. 2328p. 1991. pap. 16.00 (*0-87262-814-0*) Am Soc Civil Eng.
Darling, Deborah Lynn. Blueberry Hill: The Power of Love. LC 98-92129. 64p. (Orig.). 1998. pap. 9.99 (*0-9667111-0-6*) Radiance Pubg.
— Upsize Woman in a Downsize World. Visser, Pieter Clark, ed. LC 98-92131. (Illus.). 176p. (Orig.). 1998. pap. 19.95 (*0-9667111-2-2*) Radiance Pubg.
Darling, Dennis C. Chameleon with Camera: A Unique Primer on Travel Photography & How to Survive the Trip. (Illus.). 96p. 1989. pap. 8.95 (*0-945618-02-6*) Dorsoduro Pr.
***Darling, Diana & Couteau, Jean.** Bali & Lombok. LC 00-31837. (Travel Guides Ser.). (Illus.). 2000. write for info. (*0-7894-6648-1*) DK Pub Inc.
Darling, Dorothy S. Nemesis. 218p. mass mkt. 4.99 (*1-55197-056-2*) Picasso Publ.
Darling, Frank C. Biblical Healing: Hebrew & Christian Roots. 274p. (Orig.). 1989. pap. 9.95 (*0-9622504-0-6*) Vista Publns.
— Christian Healing in the Middle Ages & Beyond. 1990. 11.95 (*0-9622504-1-4*) Vista Publns.
— The Restoration of Christian Healing: New Freedom in the Church since the Reformation. 1992. 15.95 (*0-9622504-2-2*) Vista Publns.
— The Westernization of Asia: A Comparative Political Analysis. 320p. 1980. pap. text 24.95 (*0-87073-971-9*) Transaction Pubs.
Darling, George K. & Chaston, James F., Jr. The Business of Banking for Bank Directors. Behr, Joan H., ed. (Illus.). 64p. (Orig.). 1995. pap. text 33.00 (*1-57070-010-9*, 31186) Robt Morris Assocs.
Darling, Gerald & Smith, Christopher. LOF Ninety & the New Salvage Convention. 256p. 1991. 110.00 (*1-85044-376-9*) LLP.
Darling, Gregory. An Evaluation of the Vedantic Critique of Buddhism. (C). 1987. 30.00 (*81-208-0363-9*, Pub. by Motilal Bnarsidass) S Asia.
Darling-Hammond, Linda. Authentic Assessment in Action: Studies of School & Students at Work. (Series on School Reform). 304p. (C). 1995. text 50.00 (*0-8077-3439-X*); pap. text 24.95 (*0-8077-3438-1*) Tchrs Coll.
— A License to Teach: Raising Standards for Teaching. LC 98-53975. (Illus.). 225p. 1999. pap. 23.00 (*0-7879-4680-X*) Jossey-Bass.
— The Right to Learn: A Blueprint for Creating Schools That Work. LC 97-4736. 394p. 1997. mass mkt. 27.00 (*0-7879-0261-6*, 455167) Jossey-Bass.
— Standards for Teachers. 1994. 12.00 (*0-89333-126-0*) AACTE.
Darling-Hammond, Linda, ed. Professional Development Schools: Schools for Developing a Professional. LC 93-31823. (Series on School Reform). 240p. (C). 1994. text 45.00 (*0-8077-3320-2*); pap. text 19.95 (*0-8077-3319-9*) Tchrs Coll.
Darling-Hammond, Linda & Grimmett, Peter P. Supervision in Transition. Glickman, Carl, ed. LC 44-6213. 222p. 1992. pap. 23.95 (*0-87120-188-7*, 610-92000) ASCD.
Darling-Hammond, Linda & Marks, Ellen L. The New Federalism in Education: State Responses to the 1981 Education Consolidation & Improvement Act. LC 83-136421. xvii, 86p. 1983. pap. 7.50 (*0-8330-0491-3*, R-3008-ED) Rand Corp.
Darling-Hammond, Linda & Sykes, Gary, eds. Teaching As the Learning Profession: Handbook of Policy & Practice. LC 99-19781. (Education Ser.). 320p. 1998. 39.95 (*0-7879-4341-X*) Jossey-Bass.
Darling-Hammond, Linda, et al. Excellence in Teacher Education. 54p. 1992. pap. 8.95 (*0-8106-1847-8*) NEA.
— Professional Development: International & National Perspectives. 60p. 1995. pap. 12.00 (*1-56377-041-5*, SC9501) Am Assn Higher Ed.
— Tuition Tax Deductions & Parent School Choice: A Case Study of Minnesota. LC 85-16965. 1985. pap. 10.00 (*0-8330-0670-3*, R-3294-NIE) Rand Corp.
Darling-Hammond, Linda, jt. auth. see Gonzalez, Josue M.
Darling-Hammond, Linda, jt. auth. see Millman, Jason.
Darling, Harold. Bon Voyage! Souvenirs from the Golden Age of Travel. (Illus.). 96p. 1990. 27.50 (*0-89659-898-5*) Abbeville Pr.
— From Mother Goose to Dr. Seuss: Children's Book Covers, 1880-1960. LC 98-48960. (Illus.). 176p. 1999. 22.95 (*0-8118-1898-5*) Chronicle Bks.
— Happy Book. (Illus.). 32p. (J). 1992. 8.95 (*0-9621131-5-8*) Laughing Elephant.
— I Love Old Things. (Illus.). 48p. 1996. 18.95 (*1-883211-09-3*) Laughing Elephant.
— Luggage Labels & the Golden Age of Travel. (Illus.). 56p. (Orig.). 1992. pap. 20.00 (*0-9621131-1-5*) Laughing Elephant.
Darling, Harold, et al. Invisible Art. (Illus.). 141p. 1999. pap. 25.00 (*1-883211-16-6*, Darling & Comp) Laughing Elephant.
Darling, Harold W. Man in His Right Mind. 158p. 1977. reprint ed. text 9.50 (*0-85364-097-1*) Attic Pr.
Darling, Harry. Essentials of Medical Astrology. LC 80-70672. 152p. 1981. 19.00 (*0-86690-004-7*, D1051-014) Am Fed Astrologers.
Darling, J. S. Little Keyboard Book: Eight Tunes of Colonial Virginia Set for Piano or Harpsichord. LC 71-165364. 16p. 1972. pap. 4.95 (*0-910412-93-6*) Colonial Williamsburg.
Darling, J. S., ed. Colonial Keyboard Tunes: Set for Piano or Harpsichord. LC 80-12691. 24p. 1980. pap. 4.95 (*0-87935-055-5*) Colonial Williamsburg.
Darling, James S., ed. see Bremner, Robert.
Darling, Janina. Margaret Rinkovsky: The "Odyssey Landscapes" Reconsidered. 1995. pap. 10.00 (*0-945952-01-5*) Mus Art Hist.
Darling, Jay N. As Ding Saw Herbert Hoover. Henry, John M., ed. LC 95-46890. (Iowa Heritage Collection). (Illus.). 144p. 1996. pap. 12.95 (*0-8138-2343-9*) Iowa St U Pr.
— As Ding Saw Hoover. Henry, John M., ed. LC 54-11723. 139p. reprint ed. pap. 43.10 (*0-8357-5780-3*, 200045400026) Bks Demand.
Darling, Jennifer, ed. Pasta Pronto! LC 97-75846. (Fresh & Simple Ser.). 96p. 1998. pap. 15.95 (*0-696-20784-2*, Better Homes) Meredith Bks.
— Quick-Toss Salad Meals. LC 97-75844. (Fresh & Simple Ser.). 96p. 1998. pap. 15.95 (*0-696-20790-7*, Better Homes) Meredith Bks.
— Vegetable Dinners, 12 vols. LC 98-68028. (Fresh & Simple Ser.). (Illus.). 96p. 1995. pap. 15.95 (*0-696-20789-3*, Better Homes) Meredith Bks.
Darling, Jennifer & Better Homes & Gardens. Better Homes & Gardens New Cook Book. 11th ed. 1168p. 1997. mass mkt. 7.99 (*0-553-57795-6*) Bantam.
Darling, Jennifer, ed. see Better Homes & Gardens.
***Darling, Jennifer D., ed.** Cookies for Christmas. LC 99-74181. (Illus.). 240p. 1999. 24.95 (*0-696-20963-2*) Meredith Bks.
Darling, Jennifer D., ed. New Cook Book. 11th ed. (Illus.). 544p. 1996. pap. 15.95 (*0-696-20614-5*, Better Homes); ring bd. 26.95 (*0-696-20188-7*, Better Homes) Meredith Bks.
Darling, Jim. Gray Whales. LC 99-20759. (WorldLife Library). (Illus.). 72p. 1999. pap. 16.95 (*0-89658-447-X*) Voyageur Pr.
Darling, Joan. Dream of Love. 1997. mass mkt. 1.78 (*0-8217-5778-4*) Kensgtn Pub Corp.
Darling, John. Bass Fishing on Shore & Sea. 168p. 1996. 45.00 (*1-85223-878-X*, Pub. by Crolwood) Trafalgar.
— Child Centered Education: And Its Critics. (One-Off Ser.). 128p. 1993. pap. (*1-85396-225-2*) Corwin Pr.
Darling, John & Glendinning, Anthony. Gender Matters in Schools: Pupils & Teachers. (Issues in Education Ser.). 128p. 1996. pap. 29.95 (*0-304-32805-7*) Continuum.
Darling, John R., jt. auth. see Nurmi, Raimo W.
***Darling, Julia.** Crocodile Soup: A Novel. LC 99-57063. 352p. 2000. 25.00 (*0-06-019602-5*) HarpC.
Darling, Justice. Scintillae Juris Meditations in the Tea Room: Meditations in the Tea Room. LC 88-80854. 225p. 1988. reprint ed. 55.00 (*0-912004-64-9*) Gaunt.
Darling, Kathy. ABC Cats. LC 97-44142. (Illus.). 32p. (J). (ps-3). 1998. 15.95 (*0-8027-8666-9*); lib. bdg. 16.85 (*0-8027-8667-7*) Walker & Co.
— ABC Dogs. LC 96-40225. (Illus.). 32p. (J). (ps-3). 1997. 15.95 (*0-8027-8634-0*); lib. bdg. 16.85 (*0-8027-8635-9*) Walker & Co.
— Amazon A B C. LC 95-23114. (Illus.). 32p. (J). (ps-2). 1996. 16.00 (*0-688-13778-4*); lib. bdg. 15.93 (*0-688-13779-2*) Lothrop.
— Arctic Babies. LC 95-37736. (Illus.). 32p. (J). (gr. 3-6). 1996. 15.95 (*0-8027-8413-5*) Walker & Co.
— Arctic Babies. LC 95-37736. (Illus.). 32p. (J). (ps-3). 1996. lib. bdg. 16.85 (*0-8027-8414-3*) Walker & Co.
— Arctic Babies. (Illus.). 32p. (J). (ps-3). 1997. pap. 5.95 (*0-8027-7504-7*) Walker & Co.
— Chameleons: On Location. LC 94-14584. (Illus.). 32p. (J). (gr. k up). 1997. lib. bdg. 15.93 (*0-688-12538-7*) Lothrop.
— Chameleons: On Location. LC 94-14584. (Illus.). 32p. (J). (gr. 1 up). 1997. 16.00 (*0-688-12537-9*) Lothrop.
— Desert Babies. LC 96-32912. (Illus.). 32p. (J). (ps-3). 1997. lib. bdg. 16.85 (*0-8027-8480-1*) Walker & Co.
— Desert Babies. LC 96-32912. (Illus.). 32p. (J). (ps-3). 1997. 15.95 (*0-8027-8479-8*) Walker & Co.
Darling, Kathy. Dinosaur Desert. 1924. write for info. (*0-688-17211-3*); lib. bdg. write for info. (*0-688-17212-1*) Lothrop.
Darling, Kathy. Holiday Hoopla: Multicultural Celebrations. LC 94-221315. (Illus.). 128p. 1994. pap. 12.95 (*1-878279-73-4*) Monday Morning Bks.
— Holiday Hoopla: Multicultural Folk Tales. LC 94-221320. (Illus.). 128p. 1994. pap. 12.95 (*1-878279-74-2*) Monday Morning Bks.
— How to Babysit an Orangutan. LC 96-5445. (Illus.). (J). 1996. 15.95 (*0-8027-8466-6*); lib. bdg. 16.85 (*0-8027-8467-4*) Walker & Co.
— In Praise of Dogs. LC 95-15999. (Illus.). 192p. 1995. 29.95 (*0-87605-650-8*) Howell Bks.
— Komodo Dragons: On Location. LC 93-3700. (On Location Ser.). (Illus.). 40p. (J). (gr. k up). 1997. 16.00 (*0-688-13776-8*); lib. bdg. 15.93 (*0-688-13777-6*) Lothrop.
— Lemurs: On Location. LC 97-36250. (Illus.). 40p. 1998. 16.00 (*0-688-12539-5*); lib. bdg. 15.93 (*0-688-12540-9*) Lothrop.
***Darling, Kathy.** Lions. LC 99-32632. (Nature Watch Ser.). (Illus.). 48p. (J). (gr. 2-5). 2000. 22.60 (*1-57505-404-3*, Carolrhoda) Lerner Pub.
Darling, Kathy. Manatee: On Location. (Illus.). (J). (gr. 4-7). 1991. 17.00 (*0-688-09030-3*) Lothrop.
— Math with Nursery Rhymes. (Math Is Everywhere Ser.). (Illus.). 48p. (J). (gr. k-1). 1994. pap. text, teacher ed. 6.45 (*1-55799-321-1*, EMC 093) Evan-Moor Edu Pubs.
— Rain Forest Babies. LC 95-37738. (Illus.). 32p. (J). (ps-3). 1996. 15.95 (*0-8027-8411-9*) Walker & Co.
— Rain Forest Babies. LC 95-37738. (Illus.). 32p. (J). (ps-3). 1996. lib. bdg. 16.85 (*0-8027-8412-7*) Walker & Co.
— Rain Forest Babies. (Illus.). 32p. (J). (ps-3). 1997. pap. 5.95 (*0-8027-7503-9*) Walker & Co.
— Seashore Babies. LC 96-26951. (Illus.). 32p. (J). (ps-3). 1997. lib. bdg. 16.85 (*0-8027-8477-1*) Walker & Co.
— Seashore Babies. LC 96-26951. (Illus.). 32p. (J). (ps-3). 1997. 15.95 (*0-8027-8476-3*) Walker & Co.
— Tasmanian Devil: On Location. LC 91-27561. (Illus.). 40p. (J). (gr. 2 up). 1992. 16.00 (*0-688-09726-X*) Lothrop.
***Darling, Kathy.** There's a Zoo on You! LC 99-47871. 48p. (J). (gr. 3-5). 2000. 24.90 (*0-7613-1357-5*) Millbrook Pr.
Darling, Kathy, jt. auth. see Cobb, Vicki.
***Darling, Kev.** English Electric Lightning. (WarbirdTech Ser.: Vol. 28). (Illus.). 100p. 2000. pap. 16.95 (*1-58007-028-0*, Pub. by Specialty Pr) Voyageur Pr.
— Royal Air Force Avro Vulcan. (WarbirdTech Ser.: Vol. 26). (Illus.). 100p. 2000. pap. 16.95 (*1-58007-023-X*, Pub. by Specialty Pr) Voyageur Pr.
Darling, Kjerstin & Giffin, James M. Veterinary Guide to Horse Breeding. LC 98-27929. (Illus.). 274p. 1999. 34.95 (*1-58245-003-X*) Howell Bks.
Darling, Laura & Archibaund, W. R., eds. Bears: Their Biology & Management. (Illus.). 448p. 1990. pap. text 46.00 (*0-944740-03-0*) Intl Assn Bear Res.
Darling, Linda T. Revenue-Raising & Legitimacy: Tax Collection & Finance Administration in the Ottoman Empire, 1560-1660. (Ottoman Empire & Its Heritage Ser.: Vol. 6). 1996. 123.00 (*90-04-10289-2*) Brill Academic Pubs.
Darling, Louise, ed. Handbook of Medical Library Practice, 3 vols. 4th ed. 368p. 1983. 73.50 (*0-8108-2446-9*) Scarecrow.
— Handbook of Medical Library Practice, Vol. 1. 4th ed. 344p. 1982. 20.50 (*0-8108-2424-8*) Scarecrow.
— Handbook of Medical Library Practice, Vol. II. 4th ed. 368p. 1983. 25.00 (*0-8108-2425-6*) Scarecrow.
Darling, Louise, et al, eds. Handbook of Medical Library Practice, Vol. III: Health Science Librarianship & Administration. 4th ed. 1988. 32.50 (*0-8108-2426-4*) Scarecrow.
Darling, Malcolm L. The Punjab Peasant in Prosperity & Debt. rev. ed. Dewey, Clive, ed. 1978. 14.00 (*0-8364-0070-4*) S Asia.
Darling, Mary, jt. auth. see Jones, Diane V.
Darling, Michael. A. J. M. Smith & His Works. (Illus.). 56p. (C). 1990. pap. text 9.95 (*1-55022-026-8*, Pub. by ECW) Genl Dist Srvs.
— Mordecai Richler: An Annotated Bibliography. 211p. (C). 1979. pap. 9.00 (*0-920763-62-6*, Pub. by ECW) Genl Dist Srvs.
Darling, Pamela W. New Wine: The Story of Women Transforming Leadership & Power in the Episcopal Church. LC 94-10734. 258p. 1994. pap. 16.95 (*1-56101-094-4*) Cowley Pubns.
Darling, Penny. Happy Holidays & Great Celebrations: A Culinary Treasure. 1994. 17.95 (*0-930440-34-X*) Royal Hse.
— Vegetarian Fast & Fancy: Great Garden of Eating. LC 94-66320. 1996. pap. 17.95 (*0-930440-35-8*) Royal Hse.
Darling, Peter. Identifing Crystals. 1998. 7.99 (*0-7858-0945-7*) Bk Sales Inc.
Darling, Philip. Training for Profit: A Guide to the Integration of Training in an Organization's Success. 2nd ed. LC 93-2921. (McGraw-Hill Training Ser.). 176p. 1993. pap. 24.95 (*0-07-707786-5*) McGraw.
Darling, R. R. Constructing Nonhomeomorphic Stochastic Flows. LC 87-19528. (MEMO Ser.: Vol. 70/376). 97p. 1987. pap. 18.00 (*0-8218-2439-2*, MEMO 70/376) Am Math.
Darling, R. W. Differential Forms & Connections. LC 93-46634. (Illus.). 268p. (C). 1994. text 64.95 (*0-521-46259-2*); pap. text 23.95 (*0-521-46800-0*) Cambridge U Pr.
Darling, Renny. Easiest & Best Coffee Cakes & Quick Breads. (Illus.). 1985. pap. 17.95 (*0-930440-19-6*) Royal Hse.
— Entertaining! Fast & Fancy: Cook Easy & Eat Grand. 344p. 1990. pap. 17.95 (*0-930440-22-6*) Royal Hse.
— Great Beginnings & Happy Endings: Hors D'Oeuvres & Desserts for Standing Ovations. (Illus.). 1979. pap. 16.95 (*0-930440-11-0*) Royal Hse.
— The Joy of Eating: A Simply Delicious Cookbook. LC 76-27499. (Illus.). 1976. pap. 14.95 (*0-930440-00-5*) Royal Hse.
— The Joy of Eating French Food: Great French Dishes Made Easy. 1980. pap. 16.95 (*0-930440-05-6*) Royal Hse.
— The Joy of Entertaining: Renny Darling's Party Planner. LC 78-53363. 1978. pap. 14.95 (*0-930440-10-2*) Royal Hse.
— The Love of Eating: Another Simple Delicious Cookbook. LC 77-85732. (Illus.). 1977. pap. 14.95 (*0-930440-01-3*) Royal Hse.
— The Moderation Diet: Cooking Great, Looking Great, Feeling Great. 1990. pap. 17.95 (*0-930440-30-7*) Royal Hse.
— The New Joy of Eating. 1991. 17.95 (*0-930440-32-3*) Royal Hse.
— With Love from Darling's Kitchen. 1982. pap. 16.95 (*0-930440-17-X*) Royal Hse.
Darling, Robert. A. D. Hope. LC 96-48186. 1997. 32.00 (*0-8057-7049-6*, Twyne) Mac Lib Ref.
— Mr. Fishrat. deluxe limited ed. (Alaska Christmas Ser.: No. II). (Illus.). 17p. 1992. 50.00 (*0-9630863-8-3*); pap. 20.00 (*0-9630863-7-5*) Limner Pr.
Darling, Roger. Custer's Seventh Cavalry Comes to Dakota: New Discoveries Reveal Custer's Tribulations Enroute to the Yellowstone Expedition. LC 88-62488. (Illus.). 240p. 1988. 28.50 (*0-9621488-0-6*) Potomac-Western Pr.
— Custer's Seventh Cavalry Comes to Dakota: New Discoveries Reveal Custer's Tribulations Enroute to the Yellowstone Expedition. LC 88-51070. (Custer Trails Ser.: Vol. 2). (Illus.). 230p. 1988. 75.00 (*0-912783-16-8*) Upton & Sons.
— General Custer's Final Hours: Correcting a Century of Misconceived History. LC 91-68408. (Illus.). 50p. (Orig.). 1992. pap. 8.00 (*0-9621488-2-2*) Potomac-Western Pr.
— A Sad & Terrible Blunder: Generals Terry & Custer at the Little Big Horn - New Discoveries. LC 90-60075. (Illus.). 310p. 1990. 28.50 (*0-9621488-1-4*) Potomac-Western Pr.
Darling, Roger, jt. auth. see Upton & Sons Publishers Staff.
Darling, Rosalyn B. & Baxter, Christine. Families in Focus: Sociological Methods in Early Intervention. 434p. (C). 1996. pap. text 38.00 (*0-89079-647-5*, 7806) PRO-ED.
Darling, Rosalyn B. & Peter, Margo I. Families, Physicians, & Children with Special Health Needs: Collaborative Medical Education Models. LC 93-40559. 224p. 1994. 57.95 (*0-86569-226-2*, Auburn Hse) Greenwood.
Darling, Rosalyn B., jt. auth. see Seligman, Milton.
***Darling, Rosalyn Benjamin.** The Partnership Model in Human Services: Sociological Foundations & Practices. LC 00-38632. (Clinical Sociology Ser.). 2000. write for info. (*0-306-46274-5*, Kluwer Plenum) Kluwer Academic.
Darling, Shari, jt. auth. see Bramble, Linda.
Darling, Sharon S. & Casterline, Gail F. Chicago Metalsmiths. LC 77-76503. (Illus.). 1977. 15.00 (*0-226-10412-5*) U Ch Pr.
Darling, Sharon S., jt. auth. see Chicago Historical Society Staff.
Darling-Smith, Barbara, ed. Can Virtue Be Taught? LC 93-4578. (Boston University Studies in Philosophy & Religion: Vol. 14). (C). 1993. text 37.00 (*0-268-00799-3*) U of Notre Dame Pr.
— Can Virtue Be Taught? LC 93-4578. (Boston University Studies in Philosophy & Religion: Vol. 14). (C). 1994. reprint ed. pap. text 13.00 (*0-268-00807-8*) U of Notre Dame Pr.
Darling-Smith, Barbara, jt. ed. see Rouner, Leroy S.
Darling, Stanton G., II, comment. Ohio Civil Justice Reform Act, 1987 House Bill. 302p. 1987. pap. 40.00 (*0-8322-0218-5*) Banks-Baldwin.
Darling, Stephen D. A Guide to Framework Molecular Modeling. (Illus.). 48p. (Orig.). 1996. pap. text 1.00 (*0-9648837-0-8*) Darling Models.
Darling, Tom. Antiquities: A Novel. 192p. (Orig.). 1996. pap. 10.00 (*1-889543-00-4*) Beachchair Pr.
Darling, Tom, ed. Manifesto Destiny: Radical Manifestos in American History. 224p. (Orig.). 1996. pap. 12.00 (*1-889543-01-2*) Beachchair Pr.
Darling, Tom, ed. see Melville, Herman.
Darling, Wayne. Fifth Dimensional Healing: Crystal Wizdom & the Five Elements of Multidimensional Healing. (Illus.). 108p. (Orig.). 1999. pap. 12.95 (*1-884695-11-6*) Wrds of Wizdom.
Darling, Wendy & Loeb, Evelyn. The 12 Cats of Christmas. LC 98-140867. (Pocket Gift Editions Ser.). (Illus.). 64p. 1997. 4.95 (*0-88088-063-5*) Peter Pauper.
Darlington, Anna, jt. auth. see Anderson, Robin.
Darlington, Beth, ed. see Wordsworth, William.
Darlington, C. D. Recent Advances in Cytology. 2nd ed. LC 88-21258. (Genes Cells & Organisms Ser.). (Illus.). 696p. 1988. text 10.00 (*0-8240-1376-X*) Garland.
Darlington, Cynthia L., jt. auth. see Smith, Paul.
Darlington, David. Area 51: The Dreamland Chronicles. LC 97-23507. (Illus.). 287p. 1997. 25.00 (*0-8050-4777-8*) H Holt & Co.
— Area 51: The Dreamland Chronicles. (Illus.). 320p. 1998. pap. 12.95 (*0-8050-6040-5*, Owl) H Holt & Co.
— The Mojave: A Portrait of the Definitive American Desert. 337p. 1995. 25.00 (*0-8050-1631-7*) H Holt & Co.
— The Mojave: A Portrait of the Definitive American Desert. 352p. 1997. pap. text 14.95 (*0-8050-5594-0*, Owl) H Holt & Co.
Darlington, G. Ronald, et al. Pennsylvania Appellate Practice, 2 vols. LC 86-82356. 1993. suppl. ed. 72.50 (*0-317-03797-8*) West Group.
— Pennsylvania Appellate Practice, 2 vols., Set. LC 86-82356. 1986. 285.00 (*0-317-04605-5*) West Group.
Darlington, Gail & Gamlin, Linda. Diet & Arthritis: A Comprehensive Guide to Controlling Arthritis Through Diet. 448p. 1998. pap. 17.95 (*0-09-178577-4*, Pub. by Vermilion) Trafalgar.
Darlington, Gail, jt. auth. see Stone, Trevor.
Darlington, George & Schaller, Bob. Football 101: Husker Style. (Illus.). 158p. 1998. pap. 10.95 (*1-887002-86-3*) Cross Trng.
Darlington, Hank. Complete Business Management Guide for Kitchen & Bathroom Professionals: Starting & Staying in Business. (Illus.). 233p. 1997. 30.00 (*1-887127-07-0*, 5308) Natl Kit Bath.
Darlington, J., et al, eds. Declarative Programming Sasbachwalden 1991: Phoenix Seminar & Workshop, Black Forest, Germany 18-22 November 1991. (Workshops in Computing Ser.). (Illus.). 336p. 1992. 64.95 (*0-387-19735-4*) Spr-Verlag.
— Functional Programming & Its Applications: An Advanced Course. LC 81-38503. 318p. reprint ed. pap. 90.70 (*0-608-16935-8*, 2056145) Bks Demand.
Darlington, Jean B. Why Milk Pasteurization? Plowing under the Truth. 18p. 1994. reprint ed. spiral bd. 5.00 (*0-7873-1030-1*) Hlth Research.
***Darlington, Jeff.** General Protection Fault: Mating Call of the North American Computer Geek. (Illus.). 152p. 2000. pap. 12.95 (*1-929462-04-2*) Plan Nine Publ.

D

An Asterisk (*) at the beginning of an entry indicates that the title is appearing for the first time.

Darlington, Joan R. Is It Poison Ivy? A Field Book on Poisonous Plants & Look-Alikes. (Illus.). 32p. (Orig.). (YA). 1993. pap. 9.00 (*1-882291-53-0*) Oyster River Pr.
— Is It Poison Ivy? Field Guide to Poison Ivy, Oak, Sumac & Their Lookalikes. 2nd rev. ed. (Illus.). 32p. 1999. pap. 10.00 (*1-882291-58-1*) Oyster River Pr.
Darlington, Joseph J. Treatise on the Law of Personal Property. LC 98-23664. viii, 469p. 1998. reprint ed. 65.00 (*0-8377-2044-3*, Rothman) W S Hein.
***Darlington, Keith.** The Essence of Expert Systems. LC 99-38354. (Essence of Computing Ser.). 1999. 55.01 (*0-13-022774-9*) P-H.
Darlington, L. Neil. Record of the Early Settlement of Lower Loup Creek: Fayette Co., 1798-1865. (Illus.). 68p. 1997. reprint ed. pap. 14.00 (*0-8328-6947-3*) Higginson Bk Co.
Darlington, Mansur. Haynes Moto-Guzzi 750, 850 & 1000 V-Twins Owners Workshop Manual, No. M339: '74-'78. 1979. 23.95 (*0-85696-339-9*) Haynes Manuals.
— Haynes Yamaha RD400 Twin Owners Workshop Manual, No. 333: '75-'79. 1977. 23.95 (*0-85696-548-0*) Haynes Manuals.
— Haynes Yamaha XS250, 360 & 400 Twins Owners Workshop Manual, No. 378: '75-'84. 23.95 (*1-85010-248-1*) Haynes Manuals.
— Haynes Yamaha XS750 (3-cyl) Models Owners Workshop Manual, No. 340: '76 On. 1978. 16.95 (*0-85696-547-2*) Haynes Manuals.
— Haynes Yamaha XT, TT, & SR 500 Singles Owners Workshop Manual, No. 342: '75-'83. pap. 23.95 (*1-85010-749-1*) Haynes Manuals.
Darlington, Mansur & Cox, Penny. Haynes Honda CX500 V-Twins Owners Workshop Manual, No. M442: '78-'86. pap. 16.95 (*1-85010-157-4*) Haynes Manuals.
Darlington, Mansur & Paul, Rik. Haynes Suzuki GS550 & GS750 Fours Owners Workshop Manual, No. M363: '76-'82. pap. 23.95 (*0-85696-946-X*) Haynes Manuals.
Darlington, Mansur & Rogers, Chris. Haynes Honda GL1000 Gold Wing Owners' Workshop Manual, No. M309: 1975-1990. 1981. 16.95 (*0-85696-710-6*) Haynes Manuals.
Darlington, Mary C., ed. Fort Pitt & Letters from the Frontier. LC 72-106087. (First American Frontier Ser.). (Illus.). 1979. reprint ed. 32.95 (*0-405-02842-3*) Ayer.
— History of Colonial Henry Bouquet & the Western Frontiers of Pennsylvania, 1747-1764. LC 75-106121. (First American Frontier Ser.). (Illus.). 1979. reprint ed. 30.95 (*0-405-02841-5*) Ayer.
Darlington, Philip J., Jr. Zoogeography. LC 79-26913. 690p. 1980. reprint ed. lib. bdg. 63.50 (*0-89874-109-2*) Krieger.
Darlington, R. R. & McGurk, Patrick, eds. The Chronicle of John of Worcester Vol. 2: The Annals for 450-1066. (Medieval Texts Ser.). (Illus.). 804p. 1995. text 145.00 (*0-19-822261-0*) OUP.
Darlington, Ralph. The Dynamics of Workplace Unionism: Shop Stewards' Organisation in Three Merseyside Plants. LC 93-46397. (Employment & Work Relations in Context Ser.). 320p. 1995. 95.00 (*0-7201-2168-X*) Continuum.
— The Political Trajectory of J. T. Murphy. LC 99-182477. 256p. 1998. 44.95 (*0-85323-733-6*, Pub. by Liverpool Univ Pr); pap. 19.95 (*0-85323-743-3*, Pub. by Liverpool Univ Pr) Intl Spec Bk.
Darlington, Richard B. Autotutorial: Workbook for Radicals & Squares. 1977. pap., student ed. 6.25 (*0-918610-02-8*) Logan Hill.
— Behavioral Statistics. 1987. wbk. ed. 9.95 (*0-02-907861-X*) S&S Trade.
— Radicals & Squares: Statistical Methods for the Behavioral Sciences. 1975. teacher ed. 30.00 (*0-918610-01-X*) Logan Hill.
— Regression & Linear Models. 480p. (C). 1990. 79.69 (*0-07-015372-8*) McGraw.
Darlington, Richard B. & Carlson, Patricia M. Behavioral Statistics: Logic & Methods. 640p. 1987. text 32.95 (*0-02-907860-1*) Free Pr.
***Darlington, Robert A.** Australia. (Nations of the World Ser.). (Illus.). 2000. 31.40 (*0-7398-1280-7*) Raintree Steck-V.
***Darlington, Tenaya.** Madame Deluxe. 96p. 2000. pap. 13.95 (*1-56689-105-1*, Pub. by Coffee Hse) Consort Bk Sales.
Darlington, W. A. J. M. Barrie. LC 73-20391. (English Literature Ser.: No. 33). 1974. lib. bdg. 75.00 (*0-8383-1768-5*) M S G Haskell Hse.
— Sheridan. LC 74-7188. (Studies in Drama: No. 39). 1974. lib. bdg. 75.00 (*0-8383-1926-2*) M S G Haskell Hse.
Darlington, William A. Literature in the Theatre, & Other Essays. LC 68-16924. (Essay Index Reprint Ser.). 1977. 19.95 (*0-8369-0362-5*) Ayer.
— Through the Fourth Wall. LC 68-16925. (Essay Index Reprint Ser.). 1977. 19.95 (*0-8369-0363-3*) Ayer.
— The World of Gilbert & Sullivan. 1977. 23.95 (*0-8369-5573-0*, 6637) Ayer.
Darlington, William A., ed. Christopher Gist's Journals. LC 65-27166. 296p. 1971. reprint ed. 31.95 (*0-405-03671-X*) Ayer.
Darlington, Yvonne. Moving On: Women's Experiences of Childhood Sexual Abuse & Beyond. LC 96-233040. 140p. 1996. pap. 29.00 (*1-86287-219-8*, Pub. by Federation Pr) Gaunt.
D'Arlon, Ben, jt. auth. see Cagno, Michael.
Darlow, Denys. Musical Instruments. (Junior Reference Ser.). (Illus.). (J). (gr. 6 up). 1983. 14.95 (*0-7136-2043-9*) Dufour.
Darlow, M. S. Balancing of High-Speed Machinery. (Mechanical Engineering Ser.). (Illus.). 185p. 1989. 79.95 (*0-387-96986-1*) Spr-Verlag.
Darlow, Michael & Hodson, Gillian. Terence Rattigan: The Man & His Work. 25.00 (*0-7043-2160-2*, Pub. by Quartet) Charles River Bks.
Darlow, Mike. The Fundamentals of Woodturning. LC 97-49054. (Illus.). 208p. 1998. pap. 24.95 (*1-55821-719-3*) Lyons Pr.
***Darlow, Mike.** Woodturning Methods. (Illus.). 187p. 1999. pap. 24.95 (*1-56523-125-2*, Pub. by Fox Chapel Pub) IPG Chicago.
***Darlow, Steve.** Lancaster Down: The Extraordinary Tale of Seven Young Bomber Crew at War. 2000. 29.95 (*1-902304-48-9*) Grub St.
Darlow, T. H. & Moule, H. E. Historical Catalogue of the Printed Editions of Holy Scripture in the Library of the British & Foreign Bible Society, 4 vols. 2278p. 1993. 250.00 (*1-57898-025-9*) Martino Pubng.
Darman, Peter. Insignia of World War II. 1999. 19.99 (*0-7858-1135-4*) Bk Sales Inc.
***Darman, Peter.** Insignia of World War II. (Illus.). 192p. 2000. 19.99 (*0-7858-1024-2*) Bk Sales Inc.
Darman, Peter. The Survival Handbook: Learn the Survival Skills of the World's Elite Forces. (Illus.). 256p. 1997. pap. 12.95 (*1-55046-194-X*, Pub. by Boston Mills) Genl Dist Srvs.
— Uniforms of World War II. 1998. 19.99 (*0-7858-0939-2*) Bk Sales Inc.
***Darman, Richard.** Who's in Control: Polar Politics & the Sensible Center. 384p. 1999. reprint ed. text 25.00 (*0-7881-6600-X*) DIANE Pub.
D'Armand, Roscoe C. DeArmond Families of America & Related Families (d'Armand, D'Armond, DeArman, Dearmont, Etc.) (Illus.). 699p. 1996. reprint ed. pap. 99.00 (*0-8328-5440-9*); reprint ed. lib. bdg. 109.00 (*0-8328-5439-5*) Higginson Bk Co.
Darmani, Lawrence. African Youth Speak. (Illus.). 32p. (Orig.). (YA). (gr. 9-12). 1994. pap. 4.95 (*0-377-00271-2*) Friendship Pr.
Darmaputera, Eka. Pancasila & the Search for Identity & Modernity in Indonesian Society: A Cultural & Ethical Analysis. x, 254p. (Orig.). 1988. pap. 72.00 (*90-04-08422-3*) Brill Academic Pubs.
***Darmer, Michael & Kuyper, Laurens.** Industry & the European Union: Analysing Policies for Business. LC 00-34796. 2000. write for info. (*1-84064-390-0*) E Elgar.
Darmesteter, Arsene, jt. auth. see Hatzfeld, Adophe.
Darmesteter, James. English Studies. Darmesteter, Mary, tr. LC 72-3420. (Essay Index Reprint Ser.). 1977. reprint ed. 23.95 (*0-8369-2896-2*) Ayer.
— Selected Essays. Jastrow, Morris, Jr., ed. LC 70-37149. (Essay Index Reprint Ser.). 1977. reprint ed. 23.95 (*0-8369-2492-4*) Ayer.
Darmesteter, James, tr. Zend-Avesta: Selections. 1984. pap. 7.95 (*0-916411-41-9*, Near Eastern) Holmes Pub.
Darmesteter, James & Mills, L. H. The Zend-Avesta, 3 vols, Set. 1974. lib. bdg. 900.00 (*0-87968-509-3*) Krishna Pr.
Darmesteter, Mary, tr. see Darmesteter, James.
Darmon, Michel & Blumenberg, M., eds. Molecular Biology of the Skin: The Keratinocyte. (Illus.). 291p. 1993. text 99.00 (*0-12-203455-4*) Acad Pr.
Darmon, Pierre. Damning the Innocent. 1999. pap. write for info. (*0-14-008529-7*, Penguin Bks) Viking Penguin.
Darmon, Rene Y. Effective Human Resource Management in the Sales Force. LC 92-3316. 336p. 1992. 65.00 (*0-89930-648-9*, DEU/, Quorum Bks) Greenwood.
Darms, Greg. Flora of Marin. (Wind Room Ser.: No. 6). 16p. (Orig.). 1996. pap. 4.00 (*1-887853-09-X*) Radiolarian.
— Walking Home Through Bear Valley. 32p. 1995. pap. 6.00 (*1-887853-02-2*) Radiolarian.
D'Arms, John H. Commerce & Social Standing in Ancient Rome. LC 80-25956. (Illus.). 224p. 1981. 35.00 (*0-674-14475-9*) HUP.
D'Arms, John H. & Eadie, John W., eds. Ancient & Modern: Essays in Honor of Gerald F. Else. LC 77-76612. 234p. (Orig.). 1977. pap. 10.00 (*0-89824-427-7*) Trillium Pr.
Darmstadt, Hans, jt. auth. see Dahlgrun, Corinna.
Darmstadter, Joel. Conserving Energy: Prospects & Opportunities in the New York Region. LC 75-15414. 120p. reprint ed. pap. 37.20 (*0-608-18338-5*, 203301500082) Bks Demand.
Darmstadter, Joel, ed. Global Development & the Environment: Perspectives on Sustainability. LC 91-68394. 92p. 1992. pap. 9.95 (*0-915707-63-2*) Resources Future.
Darmstadter, Joel & Toman, Michael A., eds. Assessing Surprises & Nonlinearities in Greenhouse Warming. 158p. 1993. pap. 25.00 (*0-915707-71-3*) Resources Future.
Darmstadter, Joel, et al. Energy in the World Economy: A Statistical Review of Trends in Output, Trade, & Consumption Since 1925. LC 70-155848. (Resources for the Future Ser.). (Illus.). 888p. 1972. 40.00 (*0-8018-1282-8*) Johns Hopkins.
— Energy in the World Economy: A Statistical Review of Trends in Output, Trade, & Consumption Since 1925. LC 70-155848. (Illus.). 888p. reprint ed. pap. 200.00 (*0-608-18085-8*, 203214700078) Bks Demand.
— How Industrial Societies Use Energy: A Comparative Analysis. LC 77-83780. (Resources for the Future Ser.). (Illus.). 300p. 1978. text 22.50 (*0-8018-2041-3*) Johns Hopkins.
— How Industrial Societies Use Energy: A Comparative Analysis. LC 77-83780. 300p. reprint ed. pap. 93.00 (*0-608-18086-6*, 203214800078) Bks Demand.
Darmstadter, Joel, jt. auth. see Lareau, Thomas J.
Darnall, Diane T. The Challengers: A Century of Ballooning. (Illus.). 224p. (Orig.). 1990. pap. 25.00 (*0-318-66930-7*) Hunter Ariz.
Darnall, Douglas. Divorce Casualties: Protecting Your Children from Parental Alienation. LC 98-25046. 288p. 1998. pap. 14.95 (*0-87833-208-1*) Taylor Pub.
Darnall, Jean. Heaven, Here I Come. LC 97-60809. 176p. 1998. pap. 9.99 (*1-57921-030-9*) WinePress Pub.
Darnall, Russell W. The World's Greatest Project: One Project Team on the Path to Quality. LC 96-36169. (Illus.). 173p. (Orig.). 1996. pap. 32.95 (*1-880410-46-X*) Proj Mgmt Inst.
Darnall, Steve. Uncle Sam. (Illus.). 112p. 1998. 17.95 (*1-56389-436-X*, Pub. by DC Comics) Time Warner.
Darnall, Steve, jt. auth. see Kayanan, Rafael.
D'Arnato. International Law Studies: Collected Papers, Vol. 2. LC 97-6095. 1997. 94.00 (*90-411-0380-5*) Kluwer Law Intl.
Darnay. American Cost of Living Survey. 2nd ed. 368p. 1995. 160.00 (*0-8103-4324-X*) Gale.
— Gale State Rankings Reporter. 2nd ed. 1580p. 1996. 110.00 (*0-8103-6412-3*) Gale.
— Statistical Abstract of the World. 2nd ed. 1120p. 1996. 70.00 (*0-8103-6433-6*) Gale.
— Statistical Record of Older Americans. 2nd ed. 1996. 109.00 (*0-8103-6431-X*) Gale.
Darnay, Arsen. Gale City & Metro Rankings Reporter, Rpt. 2. 2nd ed. 1492p. 1996. 134.00 (*0-7876-0061-X*) Gale.
— World Market Share Reporter, Vol. 2. 2nd ed. 1996. 315.00 (*0-7876-0062-8*) Gale.
Darnay, Arsen J. Market Share Reporter, 1997. 7th ed. 1996. 235.00 (*0-8103-0209-8*) Gale.
— Market Share Reporter, 1992. 2nd ed. 1992. 235.00 (*0-8103-7947-3*) Gale.
Darnay, Arsen J., ed. Market Share Reporter, 1991. 624p. 1990. 235.00 (*0-8103-7872-8*, 100913-M94801) Gale.
— Statistical Abstracts of the World 1. 3rd ed. 950p. 1994. 60.00 (*0-8103-9199-6*) Gale.
Darnay, Arsen J. & Lazich, Robert S., eds. Market Share Reporter, 1996: An Annual Compilation of Reported Market Share Data on Companies, Products, & Services, Set. 6th ed. (Market Share Reporter Ser.). 725p. 1995. 235.00 (*0-8103-0208-X*, 101968) Gale.
Darnay, Arsen J. & Reddy, Marlita A., eds. Market Share Reporter, 1995. 5th ed. 720p. 1994. 235.00 (*0-8103-8954-1*) Gale.
Darneille, Diane D. Season Mystery Kit: Animal Coat Change. (Season Science Ser.). (Illus.). 32p. (Orig.). (J). (gr. k-3). 1994. pap. text, boxed set 14.95 (*0-9634246-0-2*) Sci Passport.
— Season Science 1: Seasonal Mystery of Animal Coat Change. (Season Science Ser.). (Illus.). 32p. (Orig.). (J). (gr. k-3). 1992. pap. 13.95 (*0-9634246-1-0*) Sci Passport.
Darnel, Allen G. "Beginners-Only" Dance Book: Learn Social, Ballroom & Latin Dances. 4th ed. Wals, Robert & Wals, Pat, eds. LC 94-96842. (Illus.). 189p. 1999. reprint ed. 25.00 (*0-9644827-1-1*, 713-789-5959); reprint ed. pap. 25.00 (*0-9644827-0-3*, 713-789-5959) Beginners-Only.
Darnel, Michael R. Theory of Lattice-Ordered Groups. LC 94-35410. (Pure & Applied Mathematics Ser.: Vol. 187). (Illus.). 560p. 1994. text 195.00 (*0-8247-9326-9*) Dekker.
Darnell. Cell Biology. 2nd ed. (C). 1990. pap. text 56.00 (*0-7167-2078-7*) W H Freeman.
— Cell Biology & Composition. 2nd ed. (C). 1991. pap. text 56.80 (*0-7167-2311-5*) W H Freeman.
Darnell, A. C., ed. The Collected Economic Articles of Harold Hotelling. (Illus.). ix, 178p. 1989. 87.95 (*0-387-97011-8*, 2881) Spr-Verlag.
Darnell, Adrian & Baumol, William J., eds. Early Mathematical Economics, 6 vols. 1991. 650.00 (*1-85196-010-4*, Pub. by Pickering & Chatto) Ashgate Pub Co.
Darnell, Adrian C. A Dictionary of Econometrics. 480p. (Orig.). 1994. 150.00 (*1-85278-389-3*) E Elgar.
— A Dictionary of Econometrics. LC 93-39138. 480p. (Orig.). (C). 1996. pap. 45.00 (*1-85898-328-2*) E Elgar.
Darnell, Adrian C., ed. The History of Econometrics, 2 vols. (International Library of Critical Writings in Economics: Vol. 4). 880p. 1994. 320.00 (*1-85278-718-X*) E Elgar.
Darnell, Adrian C. & Evans, J. Lynne. The Limits of Econometrics. 192p. 1990. text 90.00 (*1-85278-048-7*) E Elgar.
— The Limits of Econometrics. 192p. 1991. pap. text 30.00 (*1-85278-517-9*) E Elgar.
Darnell, Bob & Golfen, Bob. How to Restore & Modify Your Vespa Motorscooter. LC 99-46372. (Authentic Restoration Guides Ser.). (Illus.). 160p. 1999. pap. text 19.95 (*0-7603-0623-0*, 128936AP, Pub. by MBI Pubg) Motorbooks Intl.
Darnell, Catherine M. Your Body Intuitive Series, 4 vols. Ghetie, Stella, ed. Incl. Understanding Your Body's Architecture. (Illus.). (Orig.). 1995. pap. 4.95 (*0-9650325-0-7*); Understanding Your Body's Inner Workings. (Illus.). (Orig.). 1995. pap. 6.95 (*0-9650325-3-1*); Understanding Your Body's Vascular Container. (Illus.). 1995. pap. 6.95 (*0-9650325-2-3*); Understanding Your Body's Wiring. (Illus.). (Orig.). 1995. pap. 6.95 (*0-9650325-1-5*); 28.95 (*0-9650325-7-4*) Cottage Wrks.
Darnell, Charles E. The Simple Index: An Index of Biblical Topic Sub-Headings. LC 97-220715. 160p. 1997. pap. 5.95 (*1-889949-06-X*) VisionQuest KY.
***Darnell, Daniel.** Java & the AS/400: Practical Examples Using VisualAge for Java. LC 99-6633. (Illus.). 238p. 1999. pap. 79.00 incl. cd-rom (*1-58304-033-1*) News Four-Hund.
***Darnell, Dave.** St. Francois County: Looking Back. LC 99-34160. 1999. write for info. (*1-57864-079-2*) Donning Co.
Darnell, Donald. James Fenimore Cooper: Novelist of Manners. LC 92-51015. 1994. 29.50 (*0-87413-487-0*) U Delaware Pr.
Darnell, Ermina J. Forks of Elkhorn Church: With Genealogies of Early Members. LC 79-92437. (Illus.). xvii, 322p. 2000. reprint ed. pap. 29.50 (*0-8063-0883-4*, Pub. by Clearfield Co) ACCESS Pubs Network.
Darnell, Frank & Hoem, Anton. Taken to Extremes: Education in the Far North. 320p. 1996. 36.00 (*82-00-22588-7*) Scandnvan Univ Pr.
Darnell, J. E. & Lodish, H. Molecular Cell Biology. 2nd ed. LC 89-70096. (Illus.). 1100p. (C). 1990. 160.00 (*0-7167-2164-3*) W H Freeman.
Darnell, J. E., jt. auth. see Lodish, H.
Darnell, Jane R. Rhyme Your Way to a Powerful Vocabulary. (Owl Bks.). 352p. 1995. pap. 6.95 (*0-8050-1258-3*) H Holt & Co.
Darnell, Jeanie & Piper, Buddy. How to Stop Overeating: Handbook to Stop Overeating, Using Tranquilizers, Diet Pills, Alcohol, Caffeine, Cigarettes & Being a Workaholic, People Pleaser, Hypochondriac, Anorexic or Having Bulimia. (Illus.). 128p. (Orig.). 1992. pap. 9.95 (*0-9633475-0-0*) Darnell & Piper.
Darnell, Jerome L. Interstate Banking: How Colorado Would Benefit. (Issue Papers: No. 16-87). 12p. 1987. pap. text 8.00 (*1-57655-013-3*) Independ Inst.
Darnell, M., et al, eds. Cryptography & Coding: 6th IMA International Conference, Cirencester, U. K., December 17-19, 1997. LC 97-48262. (Lecture Notes in Computer Science Ser.: Vol. 1355). ix, 337p. 1997. pap. text 55.00 (*3-540-63927-6*) Spr-Verlag.
Darnell, Michael, et al, eds. Functionalism & Formalism in Linguistics Vol. I: General Papers. LC 98-5867. (Studies in Language Companion Ser.: Vol. 41). (ENG & MUL.). vi, 484p. 1999. 98.00 (*1-55619-927-9*) J Benjamins Pubng Co.
— Functionalism & Formalism in Linguistics Vol. II: Case Studies. LC 98-5867. (Studies in Language Companion Ser.: Vol. 42). (ENG & MUL.). vi, 407p. 1999. 82.00 (*1-55619-928-7*) J Benjamins Pubng Co.
Darnell, Michael N. Left Behind: A Book of Comfort & Hope. Brown, Carol, ed. (Illus.). 102p. (Orig.). 1991. pap. 8.95 (*1-56325-005-5*, TB001) Davis Pub Law.
Darnell, P. A. & Margolis, Philip E. C: A Software Engineering Approach. 2nd ed. (Books on Professional Computing). (Illus.). 648p. 1995. 39.00 (*0-387-97389-3*) Spr-Verlag.
Darnell, P. A., jt. auth. see Margolis, Philip E.
Darnell, Pam, jt. auth. see Cocke, Earline.
***Darnell, Paul Jean.** Victorian to Vamp: Women's Clothing, 1900-1929. LC 99-72951. (Illus.). 112p. 2000. pap. 19.95 (*1-887402-15-2*) Fabric Fancies.
Darnell, Paula J. Victorian Bathing Costumes. LC 95-90477. 1995. pap. 19.95 (*1-887402-06-3*) Fabric Fancies.
— Victorian Millinery: Ladies' Hats 1850-1900. LC 95-61332. (Illus.). 105p. (Orig.). 1995. pap. 19.95 (*1-887402-08-X*) Fabric Fancies.
Darnell, Peter. System Modeling & Visual Simulation in Industry. 400p. 1997. text 59.99 (*1-85032-869-2*) ITCP.
Darnell, Peter A. & Margolis, Philip E. C, a Software Engineering Approach. 3rd ed. LC 96-808. 497p. 1996. pap. 44.95 (*0-387-94675-6*) Spr-Verlag.
***Darnell, Regna.** And along Came Boas: Continuity & Revolution in Americanist Anthropology. LC 98-28940. (Studies in the History of Language Sciences: Vol. 86). xviii, 333p. 1998. 89.00 (*1-55619-623-7*) J Benjamins Pubng Co.
Darnell, Regna. Edward Sapir: Linguist, Anthropologist, Humanist. 1990. 55.00 (*0-520-06678-2*, Pub. by U CA Pr) Cal Prin Full Svc.
***Darnell, Regna.** Invisible Genealogies: A History of Americanist Anthropology. (Critical Studies in the History of Anthropology Ser.). (Illus.). 2000. text 55.00 (*0-8032-1710-2*); pap. text 24.95 (*0-8032-6629-4*) U of Nebr Pr.
Darnell, Regna & Irvine, Judith T., eds. The Collected Works of Edward Sapir Vol. 4: Ethnology. LC 94-26271. (Collected Works of Edward Sapir: Vol. 4). 963p. (C). 1994. lib. bdg. 260.00 (*3-11-012858-6*) Mouton.
Darnell, Regna, jt. ed. see Valentine, Lisa P.
Darnell, Rick. HTML 4 Unleashed. 2nd ed. LC 98-85219. 1998. 39.99 (*0-672-31347-2*) Sams.
— StarOffice for Linux Bible. 720p. 2000. pap. 39.99 (*0-7645-3363-0*) IDG Bks.
***Darnell, Rick & Reisner, Trudi.** Microsoft Outlook 2000: One Step at a Time. LC 99-15721. 360p. 1999. pap. 29.99 (*0-7645-3293-6*) IDG Bks.
Darnell, Rick, et al. Dynamic Web Publishing Unleashed. 2nd ed. LC 97-68546. 844p. 1997. 39.99 (*1-57521-363-X*) Sams.
— HTML 4 Unleashed: Professional Reference Edition. 2nd ed. 1195p. 1997. pap. 59.99 (*1-57521-380-X*) Sams.
Darnell, Rick, jt. auth. see Phillips, Lee Ann.
***Darnell, Yolanda.** Almost There: A Series of Monologues. 75p. (YA). (gr. 8-13). 2000. pap. 11.99 (*1-884429-13-0*) First Choice Ent.
— Bellwood Village Vol. 1: The Remedial Room, 8 vols., Vol. 1. 125p. (YA). (gr. 8 up). 2000. pap. 11.99 (*1-884429-12-2*) First Choice Ent.
Darnell, Yolanda. Heresay. North Valley Press Staff, ed. & intro. by. 24p. (Orig.). (J). (gr. 6-9). 1996. pap. text 2.95 (*1-884429-01-7*) Frst Choice.
***Darnell, Yolanda.** Terror in the Darkness: The Story of a Stalked Fan. 150p. 2000. pap. 7.99 (*1-884429-11-4*) Frst Choice.
***Darner, Josephine.** The Dance Within. LC 99-90598. 96p. 1999. pap. 10.95 (*1-880016-31-1*, Ink Drop Pr) Road Pubs.
Darner, Kirt I. Hunting the Rockies - Home of the Giants. LaRocco, Rich, ed. LC 88-51289. (Illus.). 291p. 1988. 25.00 (*0-9614821-2-5*) Darner Bks.
Darney, Philip D., et al, eds. Protocols for Office Gynecologic Surgery. (Protocols in Obstetrics & Gynecology Ser.). 400p. 1996. pap. 49.95 (*0-86542-374-1*) Blackwell Sci.
Darney, Philip D., jt. auth. see Speroff, Leon.

D

An Asterisk (*) at the beginning of an entry indicates that the title is appearing for the first time.

D'Arnis, W. H. Lexicon Manuale Ad Scriptores Mediae et Infimae Latinitatis, Ex Glossariis Caroli Dufresne D. Ducangii, D. P. Carnentarii, Adelungii, Latingii, et Aliorum, in Compendium Accuratissimi Redactum. 1168p. 1977. reprint ed. write for info. (*3-487-06426-X*) G Olms Pubs.

Darnley, A. G., et al. A Global Geochemical Database for Environmental & Resource Management. 122p. 1995. pap. 26.00 (*92-3-103085-X*, UM3085, Pub. by UNESCO) Bernan Associates.

Darnley, Lyn, jt. auth. see Martin, Stephanie.

***Darnolf, Staffan.** Democratic Electioneering in Southern Africa: The Contrasting Cases of Botswana & Zimbabwe. LC 00-39629. (Ghoteborg Studies in Politics). (Illus.). 2000. pap. write for info. (*0-9679101-0-2*) Intl Academic Pubs.

D'Arnoux, Alexandra & De Chabaneix, Gilles. Family Houses in the Country. LC 99-36149. (Illus.). 256p. 2000. 50.00 (*0-517-70860-4*) C Potter.

D'Arnoux, Alexandra, jt. auth. see Darblay, Jerome.

Darnovsky, Marcy, et al, eds. Cultural Politics & Social Movements. 392p. (C). 1995. pap. text 22.95 (*1-56639-323-X*) Temple U Pr.

Darnton, A. Geoffrey & Darnton, Moksha. Business Process Analysis. 311p. 1997. pap. 32.50 (*1-86152-039-5*) Thomson Learn.

Darnton, G. & Darnton, M. Business Process Analysis. 300p. 1996. 39.00 (*0-614-20042-3*) Chapman & Hall.

Darnton, G., jt. auth. see Maddison, R.

Darnton, Geoffrey & Giacoletto, Sergio. Information in the Enterprise: Enterprise Information Systems, Practice & Theory. LC 92-11883. (Policy Ser.). (Illus.). 450p. 1992. text 34.95 (*1-55558-091-2*, EY-J821E-DP) DEC.

Darnton, John. The Experiment. LC 99-28860. 421p. 1999. 24.95 (*0-525-94517-2*) Dutton Plume.

***Darnton, John.** Experiment. 2000. mass mkt. 6.99 (*0-451-20010-1*) Signet.

Darnton, John. Neandertal. 1998. pap. text 11.95 (*84-08-02725-5*) Planeta.

— Neanderthal: A Novel. 416p. 1997. mass mkt. 7.99 (*0-312-96300-9*) St Martin.

— Neanderthal: A Novel. large type ed. 1996. 27.95 (*0-7862-0824-4*) Thorndike Pr.

— Neanderthal: A Novel. large type ed. LC PS3554.A727N43 1996b. 609p. 1997. pap. 25.95 (*0-7862-0834-1*) Thorndike Pr.

Darnton, M., jt. auth. see Darnton, G.

Darnton, Moksha, jt. auth. see Darnton, A. Geoffrey.

Darnton, Robert. Berlin Journal, 1989-1990. 335p. 1993. pap. 12.95 (*0-393-31018-3*) Norton.

Darnton, Robert. The Business of Enlightenment: A Publishing History of the Encyclopedie, 1775-1800. LC 78-23826. 636p. 1987. pap. text 14.95 (*0-674-08786-0*) Belknap Pr.

— The Business of Enlightenment: A Publishing History of the Encyclopedie, 1775-1800. LC 78-23826. (Illus.). 636p. 1979. 52.95 (*0-674-08785-2*) HUP.

— Corpus of Clandestine Literature in France, 1769-1789. 1995. 32.50 (*0-393-03745-2*) Norton.

— The Forbidden Bestsellers of Pre-Revolutionary France. (Illus.). 464p. 1996. pap. 14.95 (*0-393-31442-1*, Norton Paperbks) Norton.

— The Great Cat Massacre. 1985. pap. 14.00 (*0-394-72927-7*) Vin Bks.

— The Kiss of Lamourette: Reflections in Cultural History. 416p. 1991. pap. 12.95 (*0-393-30752-2*) Norton.

— The Literary Underground of the Old Regime. (Illus.). 272p. 1982. pap. text 10.50 (*0-674-53657-6*) HUP.

— Mesmerism & the End of the Enlightenment in France. (Illus.). 226p. 1968. pap. 15.95 (*0-674-56951-2*) HUP.

Darnton, Robert & Roche, Daniel, eds. Revolution in Print: The Press in France, 1775-1800. LC 88-20744. (Illus.). 367p. reprint ed. pap. 113.80 (*0-7837-4840-X*, 204448700003) Bks Demand.

D'Arnuk, Nanisi B. Outside In: A Cameron Andrews Mystery. LC 96-18719. 200p. (Orig.). 1996. pap. 10.95 (*0-934678-75-8*) New Victoria Pubs.

Daro, Deborah. Confronting Child Abuse: Research for Effective Program Design. 1988. 35.00 (*0-02-906931-9*) Free Pr.

Daro, Deborah, et al. The Role of Home Visiting in Preventing Child Abuse: An Evaluation of the Hawaii Healthy Start Program. LC 98-218177. 61p. 1998. write for info. (*0-937906-81-6*) Natl Comm Child Abuse.

Daroczy, J. & Racz, I. Diagnostic Electron Microscopy in Practical Dermatology. 213p. (C). 1987. 150.00 (*963-05-4152-1*, Pub. by Akade Kiado) St Mut.

Daroff, R. & Neetens, A., eds. Neurological Organization of Ocular Movement. LC 90-5225. (Illus.). 562p. 1989. lib. bdg. 146.00 (*90-6299-067-3*, Pub. by Kugler) Kugler Pubns.

Darold, Thomas. COBRA Handbook: Forms & Checklist. annuals 400p. Date not set. pap. 96.00 incl. disk (*1-56706-304-7*) Panel Pubs.

Darosky, Renee & Recker, Kristie. ACSA West Central Regional Conference Proceedings. Imai, Mika & Witzling, Lawerence, eds. (Publications in Architecture & Urban Planning Ser.: Vol. R94-10). (Illus.). 204p. 1994. pap. 10.00 (*1-886437-07-6*) U of Wis Ctr Arch-Urban.

Darouse, John N. The Purpose of Man: The Purpose of God. LC 98-92646. 190p. 1998. pap. 17.77 (*1-57502-771-2*, PO2126) Morris Pubng.

Darovic, Gloria O. Hemodynamic Monitoring: Invasive & Noninvasive Clinical Application. 2nd ed. LC 94-21276. (Illus.). 905p. 1995. pap. text 47.00 (*0-7216-4901-7*, W B Saunders Co) Harcrt Hlth Sci Grp.

Daroy, Esther V. The Hazards of Memory: TNT: Travails & Triumphs of a Pinoy Emigrant in the U. S. A. a Novel. 144p. (Orig.). 1993. pap. 10.75 (*971-10-0509-3*, Pub. by New Day Pub) Cellar.

Darpa. Image Understanding 1992. (C). 1998. pap. text 75.00 (*1-55860-244-5*) Morgan Kaufmann.

***DARPA Staff.** Broadcast News Transcription & Understanding Workshop Conference Proceedings. 334p. 1998. pap. 50.00 (*1-55860-564-9*) Morgan Kaufmann.

— Image Understanding: Proceedings of the 1987-98 DARPA Workshops. 1330p. 1998. pap. 95.00 (*1-55860-583-5*) Morgan Kaufmann.

DARPA Staff, ed. Image Understanding Workshop, 1989. 1150p. (Orig.). (C). 1998. pap. text 65.00 (*1-55860-070-1*) Morgan Kaufmann.

— Image Understanding Workshop 1990. (C). 1998. pap. text 75.00 (*1-55860-140-6*) Morgan Kaufmann.

— Innovative Approaches to Planning, Scheduling & Control: DARPA 1990 Proceedings. (Illus.). 400p. 1990. pap. text 40.00 (*1-55860-164-3*) Morgan Kaufmann.

— Radius: Image Understanding for Imagery Intelligence. 526p. 1997. pap. text 54.95 (*1-55860-450-2*) Morgan Kaufmann.

— RSTA: Reconnaissance, Surveillance, & Target Acquisition for the Unmanned Ground Vehicle. 456p. 1997. pap. text 54.95 (*1-55860-451-0*) Morgan Kaufmann.

— The Speech & Natural Language Workshop: Spring, 1989 Proceedings. 295p. (C). 1998. pap. text 19.95 (*1-55860-073-6*) Morgan Kaufmann.

DARPA Workshop Staff, ed. Image Understanding Workshop '97 Proceedings. (IUW Proceedings Ser.). 1531p. (C). 1998. pap. text 89.95 (*1-55860-490-1*) Morgan Kaufmann.

Darquea, Gustavo & Iglesias, Enrique V., intros. Grietas En el Crisol. LC 93-73843. (Coleccion Hispanica - Narrativa: No. 3). (SPA.). 123p. (Orig.). 1993. pap. 12.00 (*0-89729-709-1*) Ediciones.

Darr, A. Method for Zither. (GER.). 58p. 1950. pap. 13.95 (*0-8258-0237-7*, 0-630) Fischer Inc NY.

Darr, Alan P., et al. The Dodge Collection: Eighteenth-Century French & English Art in the Detroit Institute of Arts. LC 96-17761. (Illus.). 272p. 1996. 75.00 (*1-55595-135-X*) Hudson Hills.

Darr, Ann. Cleared for Landing. LC 78-6640. (Illus.). 1978. pap. 9.95 (*0-931848-01-6*) Dryad Pr.

— Confessions of a Skewed Romantic. 70p. (Orig.). 1993. pap. text 17.95 (*0-938572-04-0*) Bunny Crocodile.

— Do You Take This Woman? LC 85-52077. (Series Ten). 64p. (Orig.). 1986. pap. 7.00 (*0-931846-28-5*) Wash Writers Pub.

— Flying the Zuni Mountains: Poems by Ann Darr. Cavalieri, Grace et al, eds. LC 94-71525. 95p. (Orig.). 1994. pap. 10.00 (*0-938572-08-3*) Bunny Crocodile.

Darr, Ann, ed. Hungry As We Are: An Anthology of Washington Area Poets. 346p. (Orig.). 1995. pap. 17.95 (*0-931846-48-X*) Wash Writers Pub.

Darr, Clara. Nodes in Transit with Aspects. 44p. 1993. 6.00 (*0-86690-436-0*) Am Fed Astrologers.

Darr, David, jt. auth. see Boulter, David.

Darr, Jack & Horn, Delta T. Hot to Test Almost Everything Electronic. 3rd ed. 336p. 1993. pap. 19.95 (*0-07-030406-8*) McGraw.

Darr, Jack & Horn, Delton T. How to Test Almost Everything Electronic. 2nd ed. (Illus.). 180p. 1988. 16.95 (*0-8306-7925-1*, 2925); pap. 10.95 (*0-8306-2925-4*) McGraw-Hill Prof.

Darr, John A. Herod the Fox: Audience Criticism & Lukan Characterization. (Journal for the Study of the New Testament, Supplement Ser.: No. 163). 248p. 1998. 60.00 (*1-85075-883-2*, Pub. by Sheffield Acad) CUP Services.

Darr, Jurgen. Buro Komplett/Word Reihe Losungen. (GER.). (C). 1991. text. write for info. (*0-201-55979-X*) Addison-Wesley.

Darr, Katheryn P. Isaiah's Vision & the Family of God. (Literary Currents in Biblical Interpretation Ser.). 256p. (Orig.). 1994. pap. 28.95 (*0-664-25537-X*) Westminster John Knox.

Darr, Kurt. Ethics in Health Services Management. 3rd ed. LC 96-26874. 1997. pap. text 35.95 (*1-878812-36-X*) Hlth Prof Pr.

Darr, P., et al. The Demand for Urban Water. (Studies in Applied Regional Science: No. 6). 1976. pap. text 66.50 (*90-207-0647-0*) Kluwer Academic.

Darr, Richard K. A History of the Nashua & Lowell Railroad Corporation, 1835-1880. LC 75-41752. (Companies & Men: Business Enterprises in America Ser.). (Illus.). 1976. 34.95 (*0-405-08069-7*) Ayer.

Darr, S. C., ed. see Henderson, Shelia & George, Bonnie S.

Darraby, Jessica L. Art, Artifact & Architecture Law. LC 94-32104. (Entertainment & Communication Law Ser.). 1995. ring bd. 115.00 (*0-87632-221-6*) West Group.

Darrach, Tina. On the Corner to off the Corner. (Contemporary Literature Ser.: No. 10). 30p. 1981. pap. 5.95 (*0-940650-10-X*) Sun & Moon CA.

Darracott, Joseph, ed. All for Art: The Ricketts & Shannon Collection: Fitzwilliam Museum, Cambridge, 9 October-3 December 1979. LC 79-14089. 135p. reprint ed. pap. 38.50 (*0-8357-5311-5*, 2031650) Bks Demand.

Darracott, Joseph C., ed. The First World War in Posters. (Illus.). (Orig.). 1974. pap. 11.95 (*0-486-22979-3*) Dover.

***Darragh, Francis & Law, Louise Darragh.** Healing Your Child: An A-Z Guide to Using Natural Remedies. (Illus.). 224p. 2000. pap. 13.95 (*1-56924-614-9*) Marlowe & Co.

Darragh, James H., jt. ed. see Langsley, Donald G.

Darragh, John J. & Witten, Ian H. The Reactive Keyboard. (Cambridge Series in Human-Computer Interaction: No. 5). (Illus.). 198p. (C). 1992. text 54.95 (*0-521-40375-8*) Cambridge U Pr.

Darragh, Neil. When Christians Gather: Issues in the Celebration of the Eucharist. LC 96-32676. 176p. (Orig.). 1997. pap. 11.95 (*0-8091-3678-3*) Paulist Pr.

Darragh, P. J. & Stead, R. J., eds. International Ceramic Conference - AUSTCERAM, '90. 820p. 1991. text 300.00 (*0-87849-608-4*, Pub. by Trans T Pub) Enfield Pubs NH.

Darragh, Tina. Against the Odds. 72p. (Orig.). 1989. pap. 8.00 (*0-937013-28-5*) Potes Poets.

— Btpf/btyn. limited ed. 31p. (C). 1997. 26.00 (*0-937013-70-6*) Potes Poets.

— Striking Resemblance. (Burning Deck Poetry Ser.). 64p. (Orig.). 1989. pap. 7.00 (*0-930901-64-9*) Burning Deck.

— Striking Resemblance. deluxe ed. (Burning Deck Poetry Ser.). 64p. (Orig.). 1989. pap. 15.00 (*0-930901-65-7*) Burning Deck.

***Darragh, Tina, et al.** Etruscan Reader Vol. VIII: Tina Darragh/Douglas Oliver/Randolph Healy. 120p. 1998. pap. 13.95 (*1-901538-09-5*, Pub. by etruscan bks) SPD-Small Pr Dist.

Darrah, Charles N. Learning & Work: An Exploration in Industrial Ethnography. LC 95-42416. (Studies in Education & Culture: No. 8). 200p. 1996. text 44.00 (*0-8153-1455-8*, SS1069) Garland.

Darrah, D. D. History & Evolution of Freemasonry. 21.95 (*0-685-21969-0*) Wehman.

Darrah, Delmar D. The Evolution of Freemasonry: An Authentic Story of Freemasonry (1920) 420p. 1998. reprint ed. pap. 37.00 (*0-7661-0372-2*) Kessinger Pub.

— The Master's Assistant: A Complete Treatise on Freemasonry (1912) 150p. 1998. reprint ed. pap. 17.95 (*0-7661-0192-4*) Kessinger Pub.

Darrah, Delmore D. History & Evolution of Freemasonry. (Illus.). 1951. pap. 17.00 (*0-911164-13-8*) Powner.

Darrah, Johanna, jt. auth. see Piper, Martha C.

Darrah, John. Paganism in Arthurian Romance. LC 97-23497. 320p. 1997. pap. 35.00 (*0-85991-426-7*, DS Brewer) Boydell & Brewer.

Darrah, Lawrence B. Food Marketing. LC 74-175620. 397p. reprint ed. pap. 123.10 (*0-608-12416-8*, 205570900032) Bks Demand.

Darrah, Mary C. Sister Ignatia: Angel of Alcoholics Anonymous. 300p. 1992. pap. 12.95 (*0-8294-0712-X*) Loyola Pr.

Darrah-Morgan, D., jt. tr. see Linnard, William.

Darrah, Victoria W. My Father's Daughter: Continuing the Dream. (Illus.). 209p. (Orig.). 1994. pap. text 11.95 (*0-9644039-0-0*) Servant Warriors.

Darrah, William C. Cartes De Visite in Nineteenth Century Photography. (Illus.). 222p. 1981. 27.00 (*0-913116-05-X*) W C Darrah.

— A Critical Review of the Upper Pennsylvanian Floras of the Eastern United States. LC 74-113602. (Illus.). 224p. 1970. 36.00 (*0-913116-02-5*) W C Darrah.

— Pithole: The Vanished City. LC 72-78194. (Illus.). 260p. 1972. 8.50 (*0-913116-03-3*) W C Darrah.

— The World of Stereographs. LC 77-92123. 246p. 1977. 22.50 (*0-913116-04-1*) W C Darrah.

— The World of Stereographs. 2nd ed. (Illus.). 256p. 1997. reprint ed. pap. 21.95 (*0-9650513-1-5*) Land Yacht Pr.

Darrand, Tom C. & Shupe, Anson D. Metaphors of Social Control in a Pentecostal Sect. LC 83-9006. (Studies in Religion & Society: Vol. 6). 232p. 1984. lib. bdg. 89.95 (*0-88946-870-2*) E Mellen.

Darras, B. T., jt. ed. see Panteliadis, C. P.

D'Arras, Jean. Historia de la Linda Melosina. Corfis, Ivy A., ed. (Spanish Ser.: No. 32).Tr. of Melusine. (SPA., Illus.). xviii, 222p. 1986. text 20.00 (*0-942260-79-1*) Hispanic Seminary.

Darraugh, Barbara. A Building Service Contractor's Guide to Total Quality Management. (Illus.). vi, 214p. 1997. pap. 70.00 (*1-892725-10-X*, RP144) Building Serv.

— Letter Idea Book: Sample Business Letters That Communicate Clearly to Customers, Employees, & Vend. 1996. pap. 50.00 (*1-892725-09-6*, RP123) Building Serv.

— Marketing for Building Service Contractors. 1997. pap. 50.00 (*1-892725-11-8*, RP145) Building Serv.

— Model Proposals. vi, 110p. 1998. pap. 50.00 (*1-892725-30-4*) Building Serv.

— 1997-1998 Compensation & Benefits Survey. (Illus.). viii, 78p. 1998. pap. 49.00 (*1-892725-14-2*, RP150) Building Serv.

— 1996-1997 Financial & Operating Ratios Study. (Illus.). v, 60p. 1996. pap. 50.00 (*1-892725-07-X*, RP125) Building Serv.

— Selling for Building Service Success. (Illus.). vii, 142p. 1997. pap. 50.00 (*1-892725-13-4*, RP146) Building Serv.

Darraugh, Barbara, ed. Practical Guide for Technical & Skills Trainers Vols. 1 & 2, 2 vols., Set. LC 94-79054. 418p. 1994. pap. text 165.00 (*1-56286-014-3*) Am Soc Train & Devel.

Darraugh, Barbara & Tepper, Donald. Public Relations for Building Service Success. vi, 79p. 1997. pap. 50.00 (*1-892725-12-6*, RP147) Building Serv.

Darrell, jt. auth. see Abney, A. H.

Darrell, Elizabeth. The Gathering Wolves. large type ed. 656p. 1983. 27.99 (*0-7089-8156-9*) Ulverscroft.

— Victorious Passion. 1999. 26.00 (*0-7278-5495-X*) Severn Hse.

Darrell, Jesse, tr. see Koepke, Hermann.

Darrell, Jesse, tr. see Steiner, Rudolf.

Darrell, Kathryn, tr. see Stonov, Dmitry.

Darrell, Richard W., ed. Viral Diseases of the Eye. LC 84-7897. 342p. reprint ed. pap. 106.10 (*0-7837-1485-8*, 205718000023) Bks Demand.

Darren, Alison. Lesbian Film Guide: An Essential A-Z guide to the Celluloid Lesbian. LC 99-43640. (Sexual Politics Ser.). (Illus.). 224p. 1999. pap. 15.95 (*0-304-33376-X*) Continuum.

Darrid, Diana D. In the Wings: A Memoir. LC 99-27885. 1999. write for info. (*1-56980-151-7*) Barricade Bks.

Darrieussecq, Marie. My Phantom Husband. Allen, Esther, tr. from FRE. LC 98-55513. 160p. 1999. 19.95 (*1-56584-538-2*, Pub. by New Press NY) Norton.

— Pig Tales: A Novel of Lust & Transformation. 1997. 18.00 (*1-56584-361-4*, Pub. by New Press NY) Norton.

***Darrieussecq, Marie.** Truismes, Vol. 1. 2nd ed. (FRE.). 1998. pap. 13.95 (*2-07-040307-6*) CFR Pubns.

— Undercurrents. Coverdale, Linda, tr. from FRE. 2001. 21.95 (*1-56584-627-3*, Pub. by New Press NY) Norton.

***Darrigol, Olivier.** Electrodynamics from Ampere to Einstein. LC 99-49544. 544p. 2000. write for info. (*0-19-850594-9*) OUP.

Darrigol, Olivier. From c-Numbers to q-Numbers: The Classical Analogy in the History of Quantum Theory. LC 91-42469. 388p. 1992. 75.00 (*0-520-07822-5*, Pub. by U CA Pr) Cal Prin Full Svc.

Darring, Gerald. Blessed Are the Peacemakers: Meditations on the Church in the World. Easton, Laurine M., ed. 47p. (Orig.). 1989. pap. 2.95 (*1-55588-180-7*) St Michael Guild.

— Building Blocks of the Kingdom. (Orig.). 1994. pap. 16.95 (*1-55612-723-5*) Sheed & Ward WI.

— To Love & Serve: Lectionary-Based Meditations, Year C. 84p. (Orig.). 1994. pap. 6.95 (*1-55612-700-6*) Sheed & Ward WI.

— To Love & Serve: Lectionary-Based Meditations, Year A. 84p. (Orig.). 1994. pap. 6.95 (*1-55612-701-4*) Sheed & Ward WI.

— To Love & Serve: Lectionary-Based Meditations Year B. 88p. (Orig.). 1993. pap. 6.95 (*1-55612-672-7*) Sheed & Ward WI.

Darring, Walt, jt. auth. see Moore, N. M., Jr.

Darroch, Gordon & Soltow, Lee. Property & Inequality in Victorian Ontario: Structural Patterns & Cultural Communities in the 1871 Census. (Social History of Canada Ser.). (Illus.). 256p. (C). 1994. text 45.00 (*0-8020-0516-0*); pap. text 19.95 (*0-8020-6952-5*) U of Toronto Pr.

Darroch, James L. Canadian Banks & Global Competitiveness. pap. 24.95 (*0-7735-1868-1*) McG-Queens Univ Pr.

— Canadian Banks & Global Competitiveness. 352p. 1994. 55.00 (*0-7735-1138-5*, Pub. by McG-Queens Univ Pr) CUP Services.

Darroch-Lozowski, Vivian. Antarctica Body. (Illus.). 172p. 1990. pap. 14.95 (*0-921254-17-2*, Pub. by Penumbra Pr) U of Toronto Pr.

— Notebook of Stone. 71p. 1987. 9.95 (*0-920806-92-9*, Pub. by Penumbra Pr) U of Toronto Pr.

***Darroch-Lozowski, Vivian.** The Uncoded World: A Poetic Semiosis of the Wandered. LC 98-45615. (Semiotics & the Human Sciences Ser.: Vol. 18). X, 254p. (C). 1999. text 52.00 (*0-8204-4413-8*) P Lang Pubng.

Darrough, Masako N. & Blank, Robert H., eds. Biological Differences & Social Equality: Implications for Social Policy. LC 82-11914. (Illus.). 255p. 1983. 55.00 (*0-313-23022-6*, DAS/, Greenwood Pr) Greenwood.

Darrow, A. P. Pearson: Crispin Pearson of Bucks County, PA, 1748-1806. Armstrong, William C., ed. (Illus.). 166p. 1991. reprint ed. pap. 25.00 (*0-8328-1753-8*); reprint ed. lib. bdg. 35.00 (*0-8328-1752-X*) Higginson Bk Co.

Darrow, Clarence. Attorney for the Damned: Clarence Darrow in the Courtroom. Weinberg, Arthur, ed. LC 88-39520. xxiv, 576p. 1989. pap. 20.00 (*0-226-13649-3*) U Ch Pr.

— Clarence Darrow on Capital Punishment. 192p. 1991. pap. 11.95 (*0-685-53600-9*) CH Bookworks.

— Crime: Its Cause & Treatment. (C). 1990. 100.00 (*0-89771-161-0*) St Mut.

***Darrow, Clarence.** Crime & Criminal: Address to the Prisoners at Cook County Jail. 80p. 2000. pap. 10.00 (*0-88286-250-2*) C H Kerr.

Darrow, Clarence. Crime, Its Cause & Treatment. LC 70-172562. (Criminology, Law Enforcement, & Social Problems Ser.: No. 148). 320p. 1972. reprint ed. 31.50 (*0-87585-143-6*) Patterson Smith.

— Darrow on Capital Punishment: His Closing Argument in the Loeb-Leopold Trial & His Debate on Capital Punishment. (Illus.). 180p. 1991. reprint ed. pap. 11.95 (*0-685-49004-1*) CH Bookworks.

— Farmington. LC 98-20288. vi, 277p. 1998. reprint ed. 60.00 (*0-9631902-8-8*) Canonymous.

— Infidels & Heretics. 1975. 250.00 (*0-87968-240-X*) Gordon Pr.

— Insects & Men: Instinct & Reason-Reflections on the Observations & Discoveries of Henri Fabre, Naturalist. 1991. lib. bdg. 79.95 (*0-8490-4559-2*) Gordon Pr.

— A Persian Pearl: And Other Essays, 1899. LC 97-5174. 175p. 1997. reprint ed. lib. bdg. 50.00 (*1-886363-27-7*) Lawbk Exchange.

— A Persian Pearl & Other Essays. LC 74-1199. (American Literature Ser.: No. 49). 1974. lib. bdg. 75.00 (*0-8383-1770-7*) M S G Haskell Hse.

— Realism in Literature & Art. 1973. 59.95 (*0-8490-0932-4*) Gordon Pr.

— Resist Not Evil. 1998. pap. text 11.95 (*0-9666932-9-9*) Breakout Prods Inc.

— Resist Not Evil. 1994. lib. bdg. 250.95 (*0-8490-8839-9*) Gordon Pr.

— Resist Not Evil: With Intro. & Index Added. LC 78-172567. (Criminology, Law Enforcement, & Social Problems Ser.: No. 148). 200p. 1972. reprint ed. pap. 12.00 (*0-87585-903-8*); reprint ed. lib. bdg. 24.00 (*0-87585-148-7*) Patterson Smith.

— The Skeleton in the Closet. 5.95 (*0-8283-1438-1*) Branden Bks.

— The Story of My Life. 476p. 1992. reprint ed. lib. bdg. 47.95 (*0-89966-918-2*) Buccaneer Bks.

An Asterisk (*) at the beginning of an entry indicates that the title is appearing for the first time.

— Verdicts Out of Court. Weinberg, Arthur & Weinberg, Lila, eds. (New Reprints in Essay & General Literature Index Ser.). 1977. reprint ed. 34.95 (*0-518-10198-3*, 10198) Ayer.

— Why I Am An Agnostic & Other Essays. LC 94-22965. (Freethought Library). 107p. (C). 1995. pap. 14.95 (*0-87975-940-2*) Prometheus Bks.

Darrow, Clarence & LeSueur, Meridel, intros. Autobiography of Mother Jones: Pittston Strike Commemorative Edition. (Labor Classics Ser.). (Illus.). 320p. (Orig.). 1990. reprint ed. 25.95 (*0-88286-167-0*) C H Kerr.

Darrow, Clarence & Lewis, Arthur M. Darrow-Lewis Debate on the Theory of Non-Resistance to Evil. 37p. 1989. 5.00 (*0-911826-48-3*, 5076) Am Atheist.

Darrow, Clarence S. An Eye for an Eye. 1905. LC 99-47232. 213p. 1995. reprint ed. 40.00 (*1-886363-07-2*, 310530) Lawbk Exchange.

— The Story of My Life. LC 96-17195. 512p. 1996. pap. 18.00 (*0-306-80738-6*) Da Capo.

Darrow, Clarence S. & Lewis, Arthur M. Marx Versus Tolstoy: A Debate. LC 73-137537. (Peace Movement in America Ser.). 124p. 1972. reprint ed. lib. bdg. 22.95 (*0-89198-066-0*) Ozer.

Darrow, Diane & Maresca, Tom. The Seasons of the Italian Kitchen. 466p. 1998. text 25.00 (*0-7881-5423-0*) DIANE Pub.

— The Seasons of the Italian Kitchen. 480p. 1996. pap. 15.00 (*0-87113-657-0*, Atlntc Mnthly) Grove-Atltic.

Darrow, Geof, jt. auth. see Miller, Frank.

Darrow, Helen F. Independent Activities for Creative Learning. 2nd ed. LC 86-1763. (Illus.). 191p. 1986. reprint ed. pap. 59.30 (*0-608-00855-9*, 206164600010) Bks Demand.

— Social Studies for Understanding. LC 64-18225. (Practical Suggestions for Teaching Ser.). 103p. reprint ed. pap. 32.00 (*0-608-14947-0*, 202600300048) Bks Demand.

Darrow, Ken & Saxenian, Mike. Appropriate Technology Sourcebook: A Guide to Practical Books for Village & Small Community Technology. rev. ed. (Illus.). 800p. 1993. reprint ed. 29.95 (*0-917704-18-5*); reprint ed. pap. 23.95 (*0-917704-17-7*) Approp Tech Inst.

Darrow, Marc. The Santa Cruz Guru Murders. (Mystery in the Monterey Bay Area Ser.). 174p. (Orig.). 1995. pap. 9.95 (*0-9617681-8-5*) Otter B Bks.

— Shrinking the Truth. (Mystery in the Monterey Bay Area Ser.). 220p. (Orig.). 1997. pap. 9.95 (*0-9617681-9-3*) Otter B Bks.

Darrow, Margaret A., jt. ed. see Emener, William G.

***Darrow, Margaret H.** French Women & the First World War: War Stories from the Homefront. (Legacy of the Great War Ser.). (Illus.). 256p. 2000. 65.00 (*1-85973-361-1*, Pub. by Berg Pubs); pap. 19.50 (*1-85973-366-2*, Pub. by Berg Pubs) NYU Pr.

Darrow, Paul. Avon: A Terrible Aspect. 192p. 1991. pap. 4.50 (*0-8216-2503-9*, Carol Paperbacks) Carol Pub Group.

Darrow, R. Morton. The State of Families 2: Work & Family. LC 87-24374. 96p. (Orig.). 1987. pap. 10.00 (*0-87304-226-3*) Manticore Pubs.

Darrow, Robert L. Atlantic City Kitty. LC 97-91200. 1998. 18.95 (*0-533-12593-6*) Vantage.

***Darrow, Sharon.** Old Thunder & Miss Raney. LC 99-462361. (Illus.). 32p. (J). (ps-3). 2000. 15.95 (*0-7894-2619-6*, D K Ink) DK Pub Inc.

***Darsey, James.** Prophetic Tradition & Radical Rhetoric in America. 1999. pap. text 19.00 (*0-8147-1924-4*) NYU Pr.

Darsey, James F. The Prophetic Tradition & Radical Rhetoric in America. LC 97-4772. 1997. text 45.00 (*0-8147-1876-0*) NYU Pr.

***Darsey, Jerry A.** Neural Networks in Chemical & Physical Systems. 200p. 2000. 28.00 (*981-02-4070-8*) World Scientific Pub.

Darshana Shakti Ma, ed. see Svami Kripalvananda.

Darsinos, Spiros. Frozen Harps: Poetry from the Heart. Papadatos, Androa, tr. from GRE. Orig. Title: Petrines Arpes. 96p. (Orig.). 1997. mass mkt. 9.95 (*1-885778-12-0*) Seaburn.

Darsky, Joseph. Narodnyi Artist Ego Velichestva. . . Chaliapin. unabridged ed.Tr. of People's Artist of His Majesty. . . Chaliapin. (RUS., Illus.). 250p. 1999. mass mkt. 20.00 (*0-9655131-1-4*) J Stremlin.

Darsky, Joseph, ed. see Chaliapin, Lydia.

Darst. Lesson Plans for Dynamic Physical Education for Secondary Sc: Dynamic Physic Education. 3rd ed. 308p. 1997. pap. 26.00 (*0-205-26267-8*) Allyn.

Darst, David H. Converting Fiction: Counter Reformational Closure in the Secular Literature of Golden Age Spain, Vol. 259. LC 98-41810. (North Carolina Studies in the Romance Languages & Literatures). 179p. (C). 1999. pap. 22.50 (*0-8078-9263-7*) U of NC Pr.

Darst, David H., ed. International Albert Schweitzer Lecture Series at Yale University. (Illus.). 60p. (Orig.). pap. text 3.50 (*1-885007-06-X*) A Schweitzer.

Darst, David H., jt. auth. see Mullen, Edward J.

Darst, David H., ed. see Arias, Oscar.

Darst, David H., ed. see Goodall, Jane.

Darst, David H., ed. see Williams, Betty.

Darst, Paul & Armstrong, George. Outdoor Adventure Activities for School & Recreation Programs. (Illus.). 307p. (C). 1991. reprint ed. pap. text 23.95 (*0-88133-583-5*) Waveland Pr.

Darst, Paul W., jt. auth. see Pangrazi, Robert P.

Darst, Richard B., ed. Introduction to Linear Programming: Applications & Extension. (Pure & Applied Mathematics Ser.: Vol. 141). (Illus.). 376p. 1990. text 59.75 (*0-8247-8383-2*) Dekker.

***Darst, Robert G.** Smokestack Diplomacy: Cooperation & Conflict in East-West Environmental Politics. (Global Environmental Accord Ser.). (Illus.). 330p. (C). 2001. 55.00 (*0-262-04183-9*); pap. 22.00 (*0-262-54111-4*) MIT Pr.

Darst, Sheila S., ed. see Granader, Sherry L.

Darst, Sheila S., ed. see Kachelmeier, Glenda S.

Darst, Sheila S., ed. see Barrett, Anna P.

Darst, Shelia S., ed. see Evey, Ethel L.

Dart, Alan, jt. auth. see Dixson, Robert J.

***Dart, Allan, ed.** Starlog Celebrity Series Presents Vol. 31: TV Cartoons. 2001. pap. 4.99 (*0-88013-030-X*, Pub. by Starlog Grp Inc) Kable News Co Inc.

Dart, Allan K. ESL Grammar Exercise Book, No. 2. (Illus.). 250p. (C). 1985. pap. text 12.75 (*0-13-283904-0*) P-H.

Dart, Allan K. ESL Grammar Handbook for Intermediate to Advanced Students. 240p. (C). 1982. pap. text 25.80 (*0-13-283804-4*) P-H.

Dart, Allan K. Grammar Dialogues: An Interactive Approach. 336p. (C). 1991. pap. text 34.20 (*0-13-634460-7*) P-H.

Dart, Allen, et al. Ancient Hohokam Communities in Southern Arizona: The Coyote Mountains Archaeological District in the Altar Valley. (Technical Reports: No. 90-3). (Illus.). 134p. (Orig.). 1990. pap. 10.00 (*1-886398-05-4*) Desert Archaeol.

Dart, Allen, ed. see Davis, Carolyn O.

Dart, C. J. & Smith, D. A. Woodwork for Winemakers. (Illus.). 136p. 1993. reprint ed. pap. 10.95 (*0-9619072-4-X*) G W Kent.

Dart-Enander, Eva. The Matlab 5 Handbook. 2nd ed. 32p. (C). 1999. pap. text 51.95 (*0-201-39845-1*) Addison-Wesley.

Dart, Gregory. Rousseau, Robespierre & English Romanticism. LC 98-7920. (Studies in Romanticism: No. 32). (Illus.). 302p. (C). 1999. text 59.95 (*0-521-64100-4*) Cambridge U Pr.

Dart, Iris Rainer. I'll Be There. 384p. 1992. mass mkt. 6.50 (*0-446-36327-8*) Warner Bks.

— Show Business Kills. large type ed. 543p. 1995. reprint ed. 23.95 (*0-7862-0487-7*, G K Hall Lrg Type) Mac Lib Ref.

— When I Fall in Love. LC 98-45074. 272p. 1999. 25.00 (*0-688-16034-4*, Wm Morrow) Morrow Avon.

***Dart, Iris Rainer.** When I Fall in Love. 352p. 1999. mass mkt. 6.99 (*0-380-73198-3*, Avon Bks) Morrow Avon.

Dart, Iris Rainer. When I Fall in Love. large type ed. LC 99-22157. 1999. write for info. (*1-56895-734-3*) Wheeler Pub.

***Dart, John.** Gospel of Thomas. 2000. pap. 12.00 (*1-56975-231-1*) Ulysses Pr.

Dart, John & Riegert, Ray. Unearthing the Lost Words of Jesus: The Discovery & Text of the Gospel of Thomas. LC 98-4422. (Illus.). 112p. 1998. 17.00 (*1-56975-095-5*) Ulysses Pr.

Dart, M. C. & Jenkins, S. H. Disposal of Sludge to Sea, Vol. 14, No. 3. 1982. pap. 44.00 (*0-08-029093-0*, Pergamon Pr) Elsevier.

Dart, Martha. Marjorie Sykes - Quaker Grandhian. LC 99-936354. (Illus.). 1999. pap. 24.00 (*1-85072-125-4*, Pub. by W Sessions) St Mut.

— To Meet at the Source: Hindus & Quakers. LC 89-64310. (Orig.). 1990. pap. 4.00 (*0-87574-289-0*) Pendle Hill.

***Dart, Martha.** Transcending Tradition. 1999. pap. 24.00 (*1-85072-170-X*, Pub. by W Sessions) St Mut.

***Dart, Martha, ed.** In Quaker Friendship: Letters from Marjorie Sykes. 139p. 1999. pap. 45.00 (*1-85072-223-4*, Pub. by W Sessions) St Mut.

Dart, P. J., jt. ed. see Ayanabe, A.

Dart, Peter. Pudovkin's Films & Film Theory. LC 74-986. (Dissertations on Film Ser.). 1974. 18.95 (*0-405-04874-2*) Ayer.

Dart, Raymond A. Adventures with the Missing Link. 3rd ed. (Illus.). 255p. pap. 8.95 (*0-936676-29-9*) Inst Achieve Human Pot.

Dart, Richard C. 5 Minute Consult in Medical Toxicology. 1000p. 1998. 59.95 (*0-683-30202-7*) Lppncott W & W.

Dart, Ron & Packer, James I. In a Pluralist World. (Charting Our Course Ser.). 70p. (C). 1998. 5.95 (*1-57383-105-0*, Regent Coll Pub) Regent College.

Dart, S. Leonard & Tubbs F., Eldred. The Mini Module Manual. 1976. pap. text 3.00 (*0-915242-17-6*) Pygmalion Pr.

***Dart, Susan.** Configuration Management: The Missing Link in Web Engineering. 304p. 2000. 79.00 (*1-58053-098-2*) Artech Hse.

Dart, Susan. Edward Dart, Architect. LC 93-70276. 280p. 1993. 19.95 (*1-879260-09-3*) Evanston Pub.

— Old Home Place. (Illus.). 96p. 1997. pap. 12.00 (*1-886094-72-1*) Chicago Spectrum.

***Darte, Alain, et al.** Scheduling & Automatic Parallelization. LC 99-46585. 240p. 2000. 69.95 (*0-8176-4149-1*, Pub. by Birkhauser) Spr-Verlag.

Darte, Alain, jt. auth. see Perrin, Guy-Ren E.

Darter, Michael. Report on the 1992 U. S. Tour of European Concrete Highways. (Illus.). 147p. (C). 1996. reprint ed. pap. text 30.00 (*0-7881-3556-2*) DIANE Pub.

Darter, Michael I., jt. auth. see Rauhut, J. Brent.

Darter, Tom, ed. see Casabona, Helen, et al.

Dartez, C. Jenny Giraffe Discovers the French Quarter with Jenny Giraffe's Mardi Gras Ride. (Jenny Giraffe AudioCassette Ser.). (J). text 9.95 incl. audio (*1-56554-264-9*) Pelican.

Dartez, Cecilia C. Jenny Giraffe Discovers Papa Noel. LC 94-12719. (Illus.). 32p. (J). (ps-3). 1994. 14.95 (*1-56554-084-0*) Pelican.

— Jenny Giraffe Discovers the French Quarter. LC 90-48720. (Illus.). 32p. (J). (gr. 4-7). 1991. 14.95 (*0-88289-819-1*) Pelican.

— Jenny Giraffe's Mardi Gras Ride. LC 96-27300. (Illus.). 32p. (J). (gr. 1-4). 1997. 14.95 (*1-56554-182-0*) Pelican.

***Dartez, Cecilia Casrill.** Marmac Guide to New Orleans. 4th ed. LC 85-646121. (Illus.). 328p. 1999. pap. 14.95 (*1-56554-424-2*) Pelican.

Dartford, Gerald P. The French Revolution. (Illus.). 156p. (YA). (gr. 10-12). 1989. reprint ed. pap. text 8.67 (*1-877653-02-0*) Wayside Pub.

Dartford, James. Dining Spaces. (gr. 13). 1990. mass mkt. 36.95 (*0-442-30300-9*) Chapman & Hall.

Dartford, Mark, jt. ed. see Clarke, Donald.

Dartington Conference (1979) Staff. Aspects of Education: Selected Papers from the Dartington Conference. Braham, Mark, ed. LC 80-42315. (Illus.). 241p. reprint ed. pap. 74.80 (*0-8357-5796-X*, 203049400069) Bks Demand.

Dartmouth College Staff. Dictionary Catalog of the Stefansson Collection on the Polar Regions. 1982. 905.00 (*0-8161-1357-2*, G K Hall & Co) Mac Lib Ref.

Dartmouth Medical School, Center for the Evaluative. The Dartmouth Atlas of Health Care. LC 96-11510. (Illus.). 1996. 350.00 (*1-55648-155-1*, 044100) AHPI.

— The Dartmouth Atlas of Health Care. LC 96-11510. 230p. (C). 1996. pap. 75.00 (*1-55648-163-2*, 70369) AHPI.

Dartnall, Terry, ed. Artificial Intelligence & Creativity: An Interdisciplinary Approach. LC 94-26894. (Studies in Cognitive Systems: Vol. 17). 456p. 1994. lib. bdg. 178.50 (*0-7923-3061-7*, Pub. by Kluwer Academic) Kluwer Academic.

Dartnall, Terry & Kim, Steven, eds. Artificial Intelligence & Creativity: Papers from the 1993 Spring Symposium. (Technical Reports). (Illus.). 180p. (Orig.). (C). 1993. spiral bd. 25.00 (*0-929280-38-5*) AAAI Pr.

Dartnall, Terry, jt. auth. see Wiles, Janet.

Dartnell Corp Staff. The Extra Mile. LC 94-68815. (Customer Service Rep's Survival Guide Ser.). 237p. 1995. pap. 16.95 (*0-85013-211-8*) Dartnell Corp.

Dartnell Corp. Staff. Getting the Best of Stress. (Illus.). 88p. 1998. pap., wbk. ed. 16.95 (*0-85013-343-2*) Dartnell Corp.

— How to Develop Powerful Telephone Skills. LC 97-66683. (Illus.). 88p. 1997. pap., wbk. ed. 16.95 (*0-85013-293-2*) Dartnell Corp.

— How to Handle Objections. LC 97-66571. (Illus.). 88p. 1997. pap., wbk. ed. 16.95 (*0-85013-292-4*) Dartnell Corp.

— How to Handle Tough Customers. LC 97-66739. (Illus.). 96p. 1997. pap., wbk. ed. 16.95 (*0-85013-287-8*) Dartnell Corp.

— How to Make Teamwork WORK. LC 97-66737. (Illus.). 96p. 1997. pap., wbk. ed. 16.95 (*0-85013-290-8*) Dartnell Corp.

— Phone Me, Fax Me, Beep Me! Teleconnecting Your Way to Success in the New Cyberspaced Workplace. LC 97-68743. 225p. 1997. pap. 16.95 (*0-85013-311-4*) Dartnell Corp.

— Problem Solving Techniques for Teams. LC 97-66738. (Illus.). 88p. 1997. pap., wbk. ed. 16.95 (*0-85013-291-6*) Dartnell Corp.

— The 7 Classic Strategies in Selling, 7 vols. Incl. Vol. 5. Close it Right, Right Now! How to Close More Sales Fast. 64p. Date not set. pap. 7.95 (*0-85013-305-X*); Vol. 6. Closing Strong. 64p. Date not set. pap. 7.95 (*0-85013-306-8*); Set pap. 39.95 (*0-85013-300-9*) Dartnell Corp.

— Stand-Out Service. LC 94-68817. (Customer Service Rep's Survival Guide Ser.). 227p. 1995. pap. 16.95 (*0-85013-204-5*) Dartnell Corp.

Dartnell Corp Staff. Tough Customers. LC 94-68816. (Customer Service Rep's Survival Guide Ser.). 230p. 1995. pap. 16.95 (*0-85013-210-X*) Dartnell Corp.

Dartnell Corp. Staff. Winning New Accounts. LC 97-66740. (Illus.). 80p. 1997. pap., wbk. ed. 16.95 (*0-85013-288-6*) Dartnell Corp.

Dartnell Corp. Staff, ed. Quality Depends on You: 7 Simple Things You Can Do for Your Company & Your Career. LC 96-83847. (Illus.). 269p. 1996. pap. 18.95 (*0-85013-251-7*) Dartnell Corp.

Dartnell Corporation Editors, ed. The Communication Connection: How to Get Your Message Across Verbally & Nonverbally. 96p. Date not set. pap., wbk. ed. 16.95 (*0-85013-333-5*) Dartnell Corp.

— How to Be a Quality Performer. 88p. Date not set. pap., wbk. ed. 16.95 (*0-85013-340-8*) Dartnell Corp

— Make Your Team a Winner! Tips & Techniques for Success in Today's Work Teams. 184p. Date not set. pap. 14.95 (*0-85013-341-6*) Dartnell Corp.

— Quick Quizzes: 133 Ways to Measure Success. LC 98-72469. 168p. 1998. pap. 19.95 (*0-85013-339-4*) Dartnell Corp.

Dartnell Editors. Close It Right, Right Now! How to Close More Sales Fast. (Professional Selling Ser.: Vol. 2). 146p. 1995. pap. 13.95 (*0-85013-241-X*) Dartnell Corp.

— Do You Have Any Objections? Your Guide to Turning Buyer Resistance into Sales. (Professional Selling Ser.: Vol. 3). 132p. 1995. pap. 13.95 (*0-85013-240-1*) Dartnell Corp.

— First Team: Everthing You Need to Know to Start a Team...Lead a Team...& Be a Team, 1. (High Performance Teams Ser.). 176p. 1995. pap. 14.95 (*0-85013-234-7*) Dartnell Corp.

— More Than a Foot in the Door: The Sales Professional's Guide to Winning New Accounts. (Professional Selling Ser.: Vol. 1). 164p. 1995. pap. 13.95 (*0-85013-239-8*) Dartnell Corp.

— One-on-One: Where the Real Work in Teamwork Gets Done. (High Performance Teams Ser.). 171p. 1995. pap. 14.95 (*0-85013-235-5*) Dartnell Corp.

— The Professional Secretary's Survival Guide: Failsafe Tactics for the Corporate Jungle. 159p. 1992. pap. 12.95 (*0-85013-206-1*) Dartnell Corp.

— Telephone Terrific! 172p. 1994. pap. 14.95 (*0-85013-226-6*) Dartnell Corp.

— Ultra Teams. (High Performance Teams Ser.). 237p. 1995. pap. 14.95 (*0-85013-236-3*) Dartnell Corp.

Dartnell Editors, ed. Dazzle Me! How to Deliver Uncommonly Good Customer Service Every Time. LC 97-65283. (Illus.). 222p. 1997. pap. 16.95 (*0-85013-274-6*) Dartnell Corp.

Dartnell, G. E. & Goddard, E. H. A Glossary of Words Used in the County of Wiltshire. (English Dialect Society Publications: No. 69). 1969. reprint ed. pap. 30.00 (*0-8115-0488-3*) Periodicals Srv.

Dartnell, Michael Y. Action Directe: Ultra-Left Terrorism in France 1979-1987. LC 94-34936. 224p. 1995. 47.50 (*0-7146-4566-4*, Pub. by F Cass Pubs); pap. 19.50 (*0-7146-4212-6*, Pub. by F Cass Pubs) Intl Spec Bk.

***Darton.** Divided We Stand. 2000. pap. 15.00 (*0-465-01727-4*, Pub. by Basic) HarpC.

Darton, Eric. Divided We Stand: A Biography of New York City's World Trade Center. LC 99-32069. (Illus.). 260p. 2000. pap. 25.00 (*0-465-01701-0*, Pub. by Basic) HarpC.

Darton, F. J. Vincent Crummles: His Theatre & His Times. LC 79-173157. 1972. reprint ed. 26.95 (*0-405-08431-5*, Pub. by Blom Pubns) Ayer.

Darton, F. J. Harvey. Children's Books in England. 3rd rev. ed. LC 99-223278. 416p. 1999. 49.95 (*1-884718-88-4*, 53551) Oak Knoll.

Darton, Frederick. Arnold Bennett. LC 73-20384. (English Literature Ser.: No. 33). 1974. lib. bdg. 75.00 (*0-8383-1769-3*) M S G Haskell Hse.

— J. M. Barrie. LC 73-21740. (English Literature Ser.: No. 33). 1974. lib. bdg. 75.00 (*0-8383-1780-4*) M S G Haskell Hse.

Darton, Frederick J. Arnold Bennett. LC 70-131681. 1971. reprint ed. 19.00 (*0-403-00568-X*) Scholarly.

— J. M. Barrie. (BCL1-PR English Literature Ser.). 127p. 1992. reprint ed. lib. bdg. 69.00 (*0-7812-7432-X*) Rprt Serv.

— J. M. Barrie. LC 74-131682. 1970. reprint ed. 59.00 (*0-403-00569-8*) Scholarly.

Darton, Harvey. Plates Illustrative of the Vocabulary for the Deaf & Dumb. 1972. 69.95 (*0-8490-0841-7*) Gordon Pr.

Darton, J. M. Famous Girls Who Have Become Illustrious Women: Forming Models for Imitation for the Young Women of England. LC 79-38751. (Essay Index Reprint Ser.). 1977. reprint ed. 23.95 (*0-8369-2644-7*) Ayer.

Darton, Mike. Art Deco. (Illus.). 128p. 1996. write for info. (*1-57215-174-9*) World Pubns.

Darton, Nelson H. Catalogue & Index of Contributions to North American Geology: 1732-1891. Cohen, I. Bernard, ed. LC 79-7958. (Three Centuries of Science in America Ser.). 1980. reprint ed. lib. bdg. 94.95 (*0-405-12539-9*) Ayer.

Dartt, J., jt. auth. see Hubbard, C. H.

Dartt, Justus, jt. auth. see Hubbard, C. Horace.

Darty, Peggy. Angel Valley. 262p. 1995. pap. 9.99 (*0-88070-778-X*, Palisades OR) Multnomah Pubs.

— The Captured Bride of Aspenwood. 320p. 1992. mass mkt. 3.99 (*0-8217-3966-2*, Zebra Kensgtn) Kensgtn Pub Corp.

— Cimarron Sunset. (Serenade Saga Ser.: No. 29). 1986. pap. 1.49 (*0-310-47262-8*, 15572P) Zondervan.

— Kincaid of Cripple Creek. 192p. 1985. pap. 2.50 (*0-310-46982-1*, 15554P) Zondervan.

— Memories. LC 97-44218. 256p. 1998. pap. 9.99 (*1-57673-171-5*, Palisades OR) Multnomah Pubs.

— Moonglow. LC 97-12382. 286p. 1997. pap. 9.99 (*1-57673-112-X*, Palisades OR) Multnomah Pubs.

— A Mountain to Stand Strong, No. 8. (Serenade Serenata Ser.). 1984. pap. 1.49 (*0-310-46532-X*, 15513P) Zondervan.

— Promises. LC 97-26591. 280p. (Orig.). 1997. pap. 9.99 (*1-57673-149-9*, Palisades OR) Multnomah Pubs.

— Seascape. 262p. 1996. pap. 9.99 (*0-88070-927-8*, Palisades OR) Multnomah Pubs.

— Spirits. LC 98-29214. 250p. 1998. pap. 9.99 (*1-57673-460-9*) Multnomah Pubs.

— Sundance. LC 96-30681. 228p. 1996. pap. 9.99 (*0-88070-952-9*, Palisades OR) Multnomah Pubs.

— Wailing Winds of Juneau Abbey. (gr. k). 1990. mass mkt. 3.95 (*0-8217-3075-4*, Zebra Kensgtn) Kensgtn Pub Corp.

Darty, Peggy, et al. Fireside Christmas. 352p. 1999. pap. 4.97 (*1-57748-595-5*) Barbour Pub.

***Darty, Peggy, et al.** Getaways: Four Inspirational Love Stories to Sweep You Away to Other Lands. 352p. 2000. pap. 4.97 (*1-57748-711-7*) Barbour Pub.

Darty, Peter. The Pocketbook of Porcelain & Pottery Marks. 1974. 15.00 (*0-685-53252-6*) Ars Ceramica.

D'Arusmont, Frances W. Life, Letters & Lectures, 1834-1844. LC 72-2598. (American Women Ser.: Images & Realities). 1974. 23.95 (*0-405-04454-2*) Ayer.

— Views of Society & Manners in America. Baker, Paul R., ed. LC 63-10878. 317p. reprint ed. pap. 98.30 (*0-608-10980-0*, 200299600017) Bks Demand.

D'Arusmont, Francis. Views of Society & Manners in America. 1988. reprint ed. lib. bdg. 75.00 (*0-7812-0290-6*) Rprt Serv.

Darussalam, Brunei, jt. auth. see Begawan, Bandar S.

Daruty. Management: Leadership in Action. 5th ed. LC 95-8641. Orig. Title: Management: Concepts & Applications. (C). 1996. pap. text, student ed. 27.19 (*0-673-98020-0*) Addson-Wesley Educ.

Daruvala, J. C., ed. Tensions of Economic Development in Southeast Asia. LC 73-19306. (Illus.). 163p. (C). 1974. reprint ed. lib. bdg. 59.50 (*0-8371-7321-3*, DAED, Greenwood Pr) Greenwood.

***Daruvala, Susan.** Zhou Zuoren & an Alternative Chinese Response to Modernity. (Harvard East Asian Monographs: Vol. 189). 2000. text 39.50 (*0-674-00238-5*) HUP.

Daruvar, Ives De, see De Daruvar, Ives.

D

Darvall, Leanna. Medicine, Law & Social Change: How Bioethics, Feminism & Rights Movements Are Affecting Decision Making. (Medico-Legal Issues Ser.). 153p. 1993. 87.95 (*1-85521-077-0*, Pub. by Dartmth Pub) Ashgate Pub Co.

Darvas, Nicolas. How I Made Two Million Dollars in the Stock Market. 208p. 1986. reprint ed. pap. 9.95 (*0-8184-0396-9*) Carol Pub Group.

— Wall Street: The Other Las Vegas. 192p. 1986. reprint ed. pap. 7.95 (*0-8184-0398-5*) Carol Pub Group.

***Darvay, Amrit & Chu, Anthony.** Pocket Guide to Acne. LC 00-22607. (Illus.). 56p. 2000. pap. 29.95 (*0-632-05437-9*) Blackwell Sci.

Darve, F., ed. Geomaterials: Constitutive Equations & Modelling. 424p. 1990. mass mkt. 157.50 (*1-85166-384-3*) Elsevier.

Darve, F., et al. Proceedings of the Joint U. S.-France Workshop on Recent Advances in Geomechanical, Geotechnical & Geo Environmental Engineering. (Illus.). 190p. (C). 1993. 175.00 (*2-7108-0644-4*, Pub. by Edits Technip) Enfield Pubs NH.

Darveau, Mary, ed. see Winterflood, James.

Darvell, E. Drama & the Curriculum. 1992. pap. 40.00 (*0-7300-1477-0*, ECT465, Pub. by Deakin Univ) St Mut.

Darveniza, M. Lightning Protection for Power Systems. (High Voltage Power Transmission Ser.). 1999. 90.00 (*0-86380-241-9*) Research Studies Pr Ltd.

D'Arvieux. The Chevalier d'Arvieux's Travels in Arabia the Desert. xvi, 358p. reprint ed. write for info. incl. 3.5 hd (*0-318-71480-9*) G Olms Pubs.

Darvil, Giles & Smale, Gerald G., eds. Partners in Empowerment: Networks of Innovation in Social Work. (Pictures of Practice Ser.: Vol. 2). (C). 1990. 85.00 (*0-7855-0089-8*, Pub. by Natl Inst Soc Work) St Mut.

Darvill, Fred, Jr. Mountaineering Medicine. 14th rev. ed. LC 98-9968. (Illus.). 116p. 1998. pap. 7.95 (*0-89997-207-1*) Wilderness Pr.

Darvill, Fred T. Hiking the North Cascades. LC 98-13265. (Illus.). 396p. 1998. 19.95 (*0-8117-2791-2*) Stackpole.

Darvill, Fred T., Jr. North Cascades Highway Guide. Moore, Shirley T., ed. 63p. (Orig.). 1986. pap. text 3.95 (*0-914019-10-4*) NW Interpretive.

— Stehekin: A Guide to the Enchanted Valley. 2nd ed. (Illus.). 100p. 1996. pap. 9.95 (*0-915740-00-1*) Darvill Outdoor.

Darvill, Giles. Helping Your Staff to Learn: Improving Practice in the Social Services: An Update for Managers. 1997. pap. 23.00 (*1-899942-18-1*) Natl Inst Soc Work.

— Managing Contradiction & Avoidance: Discussion Paper & Self-Audit. 1997. pap. 23.00 (*1-899942-13-0*) Natl Inst Soc Work.

— Work-Based Learning: Examples of Practice. 1997. pap. 25.00 (*1-899942-14-9*) Natl Inst Soc Work.

Darvill, Giles & Smale, Gerald G., eds. Partners in Empowerment Networks of Innovation in Social Work Vol. 2: Pictures of Practice. (C). 1990. pap. 27.00 (*0-902789-71-6*, Pub. by Natl Inst Soc Work) St Mut.

Darvill, T. C. Billown Neolithic Landscape Project, Isle of Man, Third Report, 1997 LC 98-189546. (Bournemouth University School of Conservation Sciences Research Report.). 50p. 1998. write for info. (*1-85899-067-X*) Bournemouth Univ.

Darvill, Timothy. Prehistoric Britain. (Illus.). 223p. (C). 1997. pap. 29.99 (*0-415-15135-X*) Routledge.

— Prehistoric Britain from the Air: A Study of Space, Time & Society. (Air Surveys Ser.). (Illus.). 305p. (C). 1996. text 59.95 (*0-521-55132-3*) Cambridge U Pr.

***Darvill, Timothy, et al, eds.** The Cerne Giant: An Antiquity on Trial. (Bournemouth University School of Conversation Sciences Occasional Paper Ser.: Vol. 5). 172p. 1999. pap. 34.95 (*1-900188-94-5*, Pub. by Oxbow Bks) David Brown.

Darvill, Timothy & Thomas, Julian, eds. Neolithic Houses in North-West Europe & Beyond. (Monographs in Archaeology: Vol. 57). 213p. 1996. pap. 35.00 (*1-900188-08-2*, Pub. by Oxbow Bks) David Brown.

Darville, Ray, jt. auth. see Pavlidis, Stephen J.

***Darvis, Rick G., et al.** Guide to College Financial Aid, Vol. 1. 1999. ring bd. 79.00 (*0-7646-0735-9*) Prctnrs Pub Co.

— PPC'S College Financial Aid Seminar Package, Vol. 1. 1998. ring bd. write for info. (*0-7646-0546-1*) Prctnrs Pub Co.

***Darvonne, Gerogette R.** Human Obesity - Treatment & Therapy: Index of Authors & Subjects. rev. ed. LC 95-15284. 177p. 1999. 47.50 (*0-7883-2130-7*); pap. 44.50 (*0-7883-2131-5*) ABBE Pubs Assn.

Darwall, Stehpen. Philosophical Ethics: An Historical & Contemporary Introduction. LC 97-40578. (Dimensions of Philosophy Ser.). (C). 1997. pap. 27.00 (*0-8133-7860-5*, Pub. by Westview) HarpC.

Darwall, Stephen. The British Moralists & the Internal 'Ought' 1640-1740. 368p. (C). 1995. pap. text 21.95 (*0-521-45782-3*) Cambridge U Pr.

— The British Moralists & the Internal 'Ought' 1640-1740. 368p. (C). 1995. text 64.95 (*0-521-45167-1*) Cambridge U Pr.

Darwall, Stephen, et al, eds. Moral Discourse & Practice: Some Philosophic Approaches. 432p. (C). 1996. text 58.00 (*0-19-510749-7*); pap. text 36.95 (*0-19-509669-X*) OUP.

Darwall, Stephen, ed. see Butler, Joseph.

Darwall, Stephen L. Impartial Reason. LC 82-22046. 288p. (C). 1983. 39.95 (*0-8014-1560-8*) Cornell U Pr.

Darwall, Stephen L., ed. Equal Freedom. 408p. 1995. pap. text 22.95 (*0-472-08281-7*, 08281) U of Mich Pr.

Darweesh, Mahmud. Sand & Other Poems. Kagbbani, Rana, tr. 112p. 1986. 19.95 (*0-7103-0062-X*, 0062X) Routledge.

Darwen, Hugh, jt. auth. see Date, C. J.

Darwent, Brian, ed. see Saroyan, William.

Darwert, Melanie, et al. What to Do in a General Practice Emergency. (Illus.). 98p. 1997. 22.00 (*0-7279-1183-X*, Pub. by BMJ Pub) Login Brothers Bk Co.

Darwiche, Fawda A. The Gulf Stock Exchange Crash: The Rise & Fall of the Souq Al-Mankh. 224p. 1986. 42.50 (*0-7099-4534-5*, Pub. by C Helm) Routldge.

Darwin. Design of Steel & Composite Beams with Web Openings, 1990. 1990. 20.00 (*1-56424-031-2*, D802) Am Inst Steel Construct.

Darwin, Beatrice. If You Lived with the Sioux Indians. 80p. (J). (ps-3). 1992. pap. 4.95 (*0-590-45162-6*) Scholastic Inc.

Darwin, Bernard. Dickens. LC 73-8958. (Studies in Dickens: No. 52). 1973. reprint ed. lib. bdg. 75.00 (*0-8383-1710-3*) M S G Haskell Hse.

— Golf Between Two Wars. rev. ed. (Classics of Golf Ser.). (Illus.). 220p. 1984. reprint ed. 28.00 (*0-940889-04-8*) Classics Golf.

— The Golf Courses of the British Isles. LC 87-61796. (Illus.). 280p. 1988. 35.00 (*0-88266-485-9*, Garden Way Pub) Storey Bks.

— The Golf Courses of the British Isles (1910) rev. ed. (Classics of Golf Ser.). (Illus.). 1997. 24.95 (*0-940889-26-9*) Classics Golf.

Darwin, Bernard, et al. A History of Golf in Britain. rev. ed. (Illus.). 260p. 1991. reprint ed. 28.00 (*0-940889-30-7*) Classics Golf.

Darwin, Bernard A. Dickens Advertiser: A Collection of the Advertisements in the Original Parts of Novels by Charles Dickens. LC 72-152553. (Studies in Dickens: No. 52). 1971. reprint ed. lib. bdg. 75.00 (*0-8383-1234-9*) M S G Haskell Hse.

Darwin, Charles. Autobiography & Selected Letters. Darwin, Francis, ed. 365p. 1958. pap. 9.95 (*0-486-20479-0*) Dover.

— The Autobiography of Charles Darwin, 1809-1882: With Original Omissions Restored. Barlow, Nora, ed. & notes by. LC 93-17940. 253p. 1993. reprint ed. pap. 11.95 (*0-393-31069-8*) Norton.

— Charles Darwin's Letters: A Selection, 1825-1859. Burkhardt, Frederick, ed. (Illus.). 275p. (C). 1996. text 23.95 (*0-521-56212-0*) Cambridge U Pr.

— Charles Darwin's Letters: A Selection, 1825-1859. Burkhardt, Frederick, ed. (Canto Book Ser.). (Illus.). 272p. (C). 1998. pap. 14.95 (*0-521-56677-0*) Cambridge U Pr.

— Charles Darwin's Marginalia, Vol. 1. Di Gregorio, Mario A. & Gill, N. W., eds. LC 90-2970. 792p. 1990. text 35.00 (*0-8240-6639-1*, 783) Garland.

— Charles Darwin's Notebooks, 1836-1844: Geology, Transmutation of Species, Metaphysical Enquiries. Barrett, Paul H. et al, eds. LC 87-47953. 800p. (C). 1989. text 89.95 (*0-8014-1660-4*); pap. text 42.50 (*0-8014-9580-6*) Cornell U Pr.

— The Collected Papers of Charles Darwin, 2 vols. Barrett, Paul H., ed. LC 76-606. (Illus.). 1994. pap. 13.50 (*0-226-13658-2*, P886) U Ch Pr.

— The Collected Papers of Darwin. Barrett, Paul H., ed. 1977. lib. bdg. 40.00 (*0-226-13657-4*) U Ch Pr.

— Concordance to Darwin's Origin of Species. Barrett, Paul H. et al, eds. LC 80-66893. 864p. 1981. text 85.00 (*0-8014-1319-2*) Cornell U Pr.

— A Concordance to Darwin's "The Descent of Man, & Selection in Relation to Sex" Barrett, Paul H. et al, eds. LC 87-47699. 1168p. (C). 1988. text 95.00 (*0-8014-2085-7*) Cornell U Pr.

— A Concordance to Darwin's "The Expression of the Emotions in Man & Animals" Barrett, Paul H. et al, eds. LC 86-47707. 528p. 1986. text 80.00 (*0-8014-1990-5*) Cornell U Pr.

— Correspondence: 1837-1843, Vol. 2. Burkhardt, Frederick & Smith, Sydney, eds. 646p. 1987. text 69.95 (*0-521-25588-0*) Cambridge U Pr.

— Correspondence: 1843-1846, Vol. 3. Burkhardt, Frederick & Smith, Sydney, eds. 564p. 1988. text 69.95 (*0-521-25589-9*) Cambridge U Pr.

— Correspondence: 1847-1850, Vol. 4. Burkhardt, Frederick & Smith, Sydney, eds. (Illus.). 752p. 1989. text 69.95 (*0-521-25590-2*) Cambridge U Pr.

— Correspondence: 1851-1855, Vol. 5. Burkhardt, Frederick & Smith, Sydney, eds. (Illus.). 737p. (C). 1990. text 69.95 (*0-521-25591-0*) Cambridge U Pr.

— Correspondence: 1856-1857, Vol. 6. Burkhardt, Frederick & Smith, Sydney, eds. 708p. 1990. text 69.95 (*0-521-25586-4*) Cambridge U Pr.

— Correspondence: 1858-1859, Vol. 7. Burkhardt, Frederick & Smith, Sydney, eds. (Illus.). 709p. (C). 1992. text 69.95 (*0-521-38564-4*) Cambridge U Pr.

— Correspondence: 1861, Vol. 9. Burkhardt, Frederick et al, eds. (Illus.). 645p. (C). 1994. text 69.95 (*0-521-45156-6*) Cambridge U Pr.

— Correspondence: 1862, Vol. 8. Burkhardt, Frederick et al, eds. (Illus.). 862p. (C). 1993. text 69.95 (*0-521-44241-9*) Cambridge U Pr.

— The Correspondence of Charles Darwin, Vol. 1. Burkhardt, Frederick & Smith, Sydney, eds. 752p. 1985. text 69.95 (*0-521-25587-2*) Cambridge U Pr.

— The Correspondence of Charles Darwin Vol. 10: 1862. Burkhardt, Frederick et al, eds. (Illus.). 976p. (C). 1997. text 74.95 (*0-521-59032-9*) Cambridge U Pr.

***Darwin, Charles.** The Correspondence of Charles Darwin 1863, Vol. 11. Burkhardt, Frederick et al, eds. (Correspondence of Charles Darwin Ser.). (Illus.). 1086p. 2000. 85.00 (*0-521-59033-7*) Cambridge U Pr.

Darwin, Charles. Darwin. 3rd ed. Appleman, Philip, ed. (Critical Editions Ser.). (Illus.). (C). 1990. pap. write for info. (*0-393-95849-3*) Norton.

— Darwin on Earthworms: The Formation of Vegetable Mould Through the Action of Worms. (Illus.). 160p. 1976. reprint ed. 7.95 (*0-916302-10-5*); reprint ed. pap. 5.95 (*0-916302-06-7*) Bookworm Pub.

— The Darwin Reader. 2nd ed. Ridley, Mark, ed. LC 95-50297. (C). 1996. pap. text 17.50 (*0-393-96967-3*) Norton.

— The Descent of Man. 2nd ed. LC 97-36473. 728p. 1998. pap. text 18.95 (*1-57392-176-9*) Prometheus Bks.

— The Descent of Man & Selection in Relation to Sex. LC 80-8679. (Illus.). 935p. 1981. reprint ed. pap. text 27.95 (*0-691-02369-7*, Pub. by Princeton U Pr) Cal Prin Full Svc.

— The Different Forms of Flowers on Plants of the Same Species. (Illus.). (C). 1994. pap. 13.95 (*0-226-13664-7*) U Ch Pr.

— The Essential Darwin. Jastrow, Robert, ed. 348p. 1984. 19.95 (*0-316-45826-0*) Little.

— The Expression of the Emotions in Man & Animal. 3rd ed. (Series in Affective Science). (Illus.). 512p. 1998. 30.00 (*0-19-511271-7*) OUP.

— Expression of the Emotions in Man & Animals. LC 65-17286. (Illus.). 386p. 1965. pap. text 17.00 (*0-226-13656-6*, P526) U Ch Pr.

— Expression of the Emotions in Man & Animals. LC 73-90703. 372p. 1969. reprint ed. lib. bdg. 65.00 (*0-8371-2291-0*, DAEM, Greenwood Pr) Greenwood.

— Human Nature, Darwin's View. Alland, Alexander, Jr., ed. LC 85-4108. 232p. 1985. text 50.00 (*0-231-05898-5*) Col U Pr.

— Journal of Researches, 2 vols. unabridged ed. (Classic Reprint Ser.). 587p. 1997. reprint ed. 60.00 (*0-936128-56-9*) De Young Pr.

— Metaphysics, Materialism, & the Evolution of the Mind: Early Writings of Charles Darwin. LC 80-15763. 1994. pap. text 6.95 (*0-226-13659-0*, P906) U Ch Pr.

— The New Conceptions of Matter. (Select Bibliographies Reprint Ser.). 1977. reprint ed. 23.95 (*0-8369-6610-4*) Ayer.

— On Evolution: The Development of the Theory of Natural Selection. Glick, Thomas F. & Kohn, David, eds. LC 96-9388. (HPC Classics Ser.). 416p. 1996. pap. text 12.95 (*0-87220-285-2*) Hackett Pub.

— On Evolution: The Development of the Theory of Natural Selection. Glick, Thomas F. et al, eds. LC 96-9388. (HPC Classics Ser.). 416p. 1996. lib. bdg. 37.95 (*0-87220-286-0*) Hackett Pub.

— On the Formation of Vegetable Mould, Through the Action of Worms with Observation of Their Habits. (Illus.). xxx, 326p. 1985. pap. 12.95 (*0-226-13663-9*) U Ch Pr.

— On the Origin of Species: A Facsimile of the First Edition. LC 63-17196. 528p. 1964. pap. text 13.50 (*0-674-63752-6*) HUP.

— El Origen de las Especies. Jose, Jaume, ed. De Zulueta, Antonio, tr. (Nueva Austral Ser.: Vol. 16). (SPA.). 1991. pap. text 34.95 (*84-239-1816-5*) Elliots Bks.

— The Origin of Species. 1976. 31.95 (*0-8488-0975-0*) Amereon Ltd.

— The Origin of Species. 432p. 1999. mass mkt. 5.95 (*0-553-21463-2*) Bantam.

— The Origin of Species. 1986. mass mkt. 6.99 (*0-451-62776-8*) NAL.

Darwin, Charles. The Origin of Species. Appleman, ed. (Illus.). 0.00 (*0-393-05549-3*) Norton.

Darwin, Charles. The Origin of Species. Beer, Gillian, ed. & intro. by. (Oxford World's Classics Ser.). (Illus.). 472p. 1998. pap. 8.95 (*0-19-283438-X*) OUP.

— The Origin of Species. LC 90-63888. (Great Minds Ser.). 444p. (C). 1991. pap. 10.95 (*0-87975-675-6*) Prometheus Bks.

— The Origin of Species. Burrow, J. W., ed. (Classics Ser.). 480p. 1982. pap. 10.95 (*0-14-043205-1*, Penguin Classics) Viking Penguin.

— The Origin of Species. (Classics of World Literature Ser.). 480p. 1998. pap. 5.95 (*1-85326-780-5*, 7805WW, Pub. by Wrdsworth Edits) NTC Contemp Pub Co.

— The Origin of Species. abr. ed. (C). 1975. pap. text 11.25 (*0-393-09219-4*) Norton.

— The Origin of Species: Complete & Fully Illustrated. (Illus.). 544p. 1995. 9.99 (*0-517-12320-7*) Random Hse Value.

— The Origin of Species by Means of Natural Selection. LC 93-3598. 714p. 1993. 20.00 (*0-679-60070-1*) Modern Lib NY.

— The Origin of Species by Means of Natural Selection. LC 98-21225. 1998. pap. 8.95 (*0-375-75146-7*) Modern Lib NY.

— The Portable Darwin. Porter, Duncan M. & Graham, Peter W., eds. LC 93-17106. 640p. (Orig.). 1993. pap. 14.95 (*0-14-015109-5*, Penguin Bks) Viking Penguin.

***Darwin, Charles.** The Power of Movement in Plants. 592p. 2000. reprint ed. 79.95 (*1-930665-07-5*) Blackburn Pr.

Darwin, Charles. The Power of Movement in Plants. 2nd ed. LC 65-23402. 1966. reprint ed. lib. bdg. 55.00 (*0-306-70921-X*) Da Capo.

— Variation in Animals & Plants under Domestication, 2 vols. unabridged ed. (Classic Reprint Ser.). 700p. 1997. reprint ed. 100.00 (*0-936128-64-X*) De Young Pr.

— The Variation of Animals & Plants under Domestication, Vol. 1. LC 97-40164. (Foundations of Natural History Ser.). (Illus.). 496p. 1998. pap. text 18.95 (*0-8018-5866-6*) Johns Hopkins.

— The Variation of Animals & Plants under Domestication, Vol. 2. LC 97-40164. (Foundations of Natural History Ser.). 595p. 1998. pap. text 18.95 (*0-8018-5867-4*) Johns Hopkins.

— The Various Contrivances by Which Orchids Are Fertilised by Insects. LC 83-18186. (Illus.). 275p. (C). 1992. pap. 11.95 (*0-226-13662-0*) U Ch Pr.

— The Various Contrivances by Which Orchids Are Fertilised by Insects. LC 83-18186. (Illus.). 275p. (C). 1994. lib. bdg. 20.00 (*0-226-13661-2*) U Ch Pr.

— The Voyage of the Beagle. LC 99-26696. (Great Minds Ser.). 547p. 1999. pap. 15.95 (*1-57392-773-2*) Prometheus Bks.

— The Voyage of the Beagle. (Classics of World Literature Ser.). 1998. pap. 5.95 (*1-85326-476-8*, 4768WW, Pub. by Wrdsworth Edits) NTC Contemp Pub Co.

— The Voyage of the Beagle: Charles Darwin's Journal of Researches. Browne, Janet & Neue, Michael, eds. 448p. 1989. pap. 11.95 (*0-14-043268-X*, Penguin Classics) Viking Penguin.

— Works, 18 vols. LC 73-147085. reprint ed. 1485.00 (*0-404-08400-1*) AMS Pr.

— The Works of Charles Darwin, 29 vols., Set. Barrett, Paul H. & Freeman, R. B., eds. (Illus.). (C). 1990. lib. bdg. 2595.00 (*0-8147-1830-2*) NYU Pr.

— The Works of Charles Darwin: A Monograph of the Sub-Class Cirripedia, Vol. 11. Gautrey, Peter, ed. (Illus.). (C). 1989. lib. bdg. 95.00 (*0-8147-1800-0*) NYU Pr.

— The Works of Charles Darwin: Diary of the Voyage of H. M. S. Beagle, Vol. 1. Barrett, Paul H. & Freeman, R. B., eds. (Illus.). 464p. (C). 1987. lib. bdg. 95.00 (*0-8147-1796-9*) NYU Pr.

— The Works of Charles Darwin: Insectivorous Plants, Vol. 24. 2nd ed. Barrett, Paul H. & Freeman, R. B., eds. (C). 1990. lib. bdg. 95.00 (*0-8147-1822-1*) NYU Pr.

— The Works of Charles Darwin: Journal of Researches into the Geology & Natural History of the Various Countries Visitied by H. M. S. Beagle, Vol. II, Pt. I. Barrett, Paul H. & Freeman, R. B., eds. (Illus.). 256p. (C). 1987. lib. bdg. 95.00 (*0-8147-1787-X*) NYU Pr.

— The Works of Charles Darwin: Journal of Researches into the Geology & Natural History of the Various Countries Visited by H. M. S. Beagle, Vol. III, Pt. 2. Barrett, Paul H. & Freeman, R. B., eds. (Illus.). 264p. (C). 1987. lib. bdg. 95.00 (*0-8147-1788-8*) NYU Pr.

— The Works of Charles Darwin: Monographs of the Fossil Lepadidae & the Fossil Balanide, Vol. 14. Gautrey, Peter, ed. (Illus.). (C). 1989. lib. bdg. 95.00 (*0-8147-1803-5*) NYU Pr.

— The Works of Charles Darwin: On the Origin of Species, Vol. 15. Gautrey, Peter, ed. (Illus.). (C). 1989. lib. bdg. 95.00 (*0-8147-1804-3*) NYU Pr.

— The Works of Charles Darwin: Subset, 10 vols., Set. Barrett, Paul H. & Freeman, R. B., eds. (C). 1987. lib. bdg. 895.00 (*0-8147-1799-3*) NYU Pr.

— The Works of Charles Darwin: Subset, 10 vols., Set. Barrett, Paul H. & Freeman, R. B., eds. (C). 1989. lib. bdg. 895.00 (*0-8147-1810-8*) NYU Pr.

— The Works of Charles Darwin: Subset, 9 vols., Set. Barrett, Paul H. & Freeman, R. B., eds. (C). 1990. lib. bdg. 855.00 (*0-8147-1831-0*) NYU Pr.

— The Works of Charles Darwin: The Descent of Man, & Selection in Relation to Sex, Vol. 2. 2nd ed. Barrett, Paul H. & Freeman, R. B., eds. (C). 1989. lib. bdg. 95.00 (*0-8147-1820-5*) NYU Pr.

— The Works of Charles Darwin: The Descent of Man, & Selection in Relation to Sex, Vol. 2. 2nd ed. Barrett, Paul H. & Freeman, R. B., eds. (C). 1990. lib. bdg. 95.00 (*0-8147-1819-1*) NYU Pr.

— The Works of Charles Darwin: The Different Forms of Flowers on Plants of the Same Species, Vol. 26. 2nd ed. Barrett, Paul H. & Freeman, R. B., eds. (C). 1990. lib. bdg. 95.00 (*0-8147-1824-8*) NYU Pr.

— The Works of Charles Darwin: The Effects of Cross & Self Fertilization in the Vegetable Kingdom, Vol. 25. 2nd ed. Barrett, Paul H. & Freeman, R. B., eds. (C). 1990. lib. bdg. 95.00 (*0-8147-1823-X*) NYU Pr.

— The Works of Charles Darwin: The Expression of the Emotions in Man & Animals, Vol. 23. 2nd ed. Darwin, Francis et al, eds. (C). 1990. lib. bdg. 95.00 (*0-8147-1821-3*) NYU Pr.

— The Works of Charles Darwin: The Formation of Vegetable Mould Thhrough the Action of Worms, with Observations on Their Habits, Vol. 28. Barrett, Paul H. & Freeman, R. B., eds. (C). 1990. lib. bdg. 95.00 (*0-8147-1826-4*) NYU Pr.

— The Works of Charles Darwin: The Foundations of the Origin of the Species, Two Essays Written in 1842 & 1844, Vol. 10. Darwin, Frances et al, eds. 240p. (C). 1987. lib. bdg. 95.00 (*0-8147-1795-0*) NYU Pr.

— The Works of Charles Darwin: The Geology of the Voyage of H. M. S. Beagle, Vol. VII. 3rd ed. Barrett, Paul H. & Freeman, R. B., eds. (Illus.). 256p. (C). 1987. lib. bdg. 95.00 (*0-8147-1792-6*) NYU Pr.

— The Works of Charles Darwin: The Movements & Habits of Climbing Plants, Vol. 18. Gautrey, Peter, ed. (Illus.). (C). 1989. lib. bdg. 95.00 (*0-8147-1807-8*) NYU Pr.

— The Works of Charles Darwin: The Origin of Species, Vol. 16. Gautrey, Peter, ed. (Illus.). (C). 1989. lib. bdg. 95.00 (*0-8147-1805-1*) NYU Pr.

— The Works of Charles Darwin: The Power of Movement in Plants, Vol. 27. Barrett, Paul H. & Freeman, R. B., eds. (C). 1990. lib. bdg. 95.00 (*0-8147-1825-6*) NYU Pr.

— The Works of Charles Darwin: The Various Contrivances by Which Orchids are Fertilized by Insects, Vol. 17. Gautrey, Peter, ed. (Illus.). (C). 1989. lib. bdg. 95.00 (*0-8147-1806-X*) NYU Pr.

— The Works of Charles Darwin: The Zoology of the Voyage of H. M. S. Beagle, under the Command of Captain Fitzroy, During the Years 1832-1836, Vol. V, Pt. III. Barrett, Paul H. & Freeman, R. B., eds. (Illus.). 264p. (C). 1987. lib. bdg. 95.00 (*0-8147-1790-X*) NYU Pr.

— The Works of Charles Darwin: Variation of Animals & Plants under Domestication, Vol. 2. Cautrey, Peter, ed. (Illus.). (C). 1989. lib. bdg. 95.00 (*0-8147-1809-4*) NYU Pr.

— The Works of Charles Darwin: Variation of Animals & Plants under Domestication, Vol. 19. Gautrey, Peter, ed. (Illus.). (C). 1989. lib. bdg. 95.00 (*0-8147-1808-6*) NYU Pr.

Darwin, Charles & Nelson, Joseph L. Human Nature: Classical Selections on Human Nature. 2nd ed. LC 96-25024. (Lynchburg College Symposium Readings Ser.: Vol. 10). 305p. 1996. pap. text 26.50 (*0-7618-0451-X*) U Pr of Amer.

Darwin, Charles G. The Next Million Years. LC 73-5264. 210p. 1973. reprint ed. lib. bdg. 35.00 (*0-8371-6876-7*, DANM, Greenwood Pr) Greenwood.

Darwin, Cynthia E. Money, Power & the Sexes: Channeling Sexual Energy in the Workplace. LC 95-68814. 106p. (Orig.). 1995. pap. 9.57 (*0-9645975-4-3*) Cat Hill Prods.

Darwin, David, jt. auth. see Nilson, Arthur H.

Darwin, Erasmus. The Botanic Garden: A Poem in Two Parts. Reiman, Donald H., ed. LC 75-31194. (Romantic Context: Poetry 1789-1830 Ser.). 1978. reprint ed. lib. bdg. 103.00 (*0-8240-2145-2*) Garland.

— The Loves of the Plants. 214p. 1991. reprint ed. 85.00 (*1-85477-065-9*) Continuum.

— Zoonomia: or The Laws of Organic Life, 2 vols. LC 79-147964. reprint ed. write for info. (*0-404-08215-7*) AMS Pr.

Darwin, Frances, ed. see Darwin, Charles.

***Darwin, Francis.** Autobiography of Charles Darwin. (Great Minds Ser.). 365p. 2000. pap. 15.00 (*1-57392-834-8*) Prometheus Bks.

Darwin, Francis. Rustic Sounds & Other Studies in Literature & Natural History. LC 69-17572. (Essay Index Reprint Ser.). 1977. 19.95 (*0-8369-0069-3*) Ayer.

— Springtime, & Other Essays. LC 67-23201. (Essay Index Reprint Ser.). 1977. 19.95 (*0-8369-0364-1*) Ayer.

Darwin, Francis, ed. see Darwin, Charles.

Darwin, George E. & Buddery, J. H. Beryllium. LC TN0799.B4D3. (Metallurgy of the Rarer Metals Ser.: No. 7). 402p. reprint ed. pap. 124.70 (*0-8357-7145-8*, 202576100046) Bks Demand.

Darwin, Ian F. Checking C Programs with Lint. (Computer Science). 84p. (Orig.). 1988. pap. 12.95 (*0-937175-30-7*) Thomson Learn.

Darwin, John, jt. auth. see Madden, Frederick.

Darwin, John, jt. auth. see Merry, Barbara.

Darwin, John, jt. ed. see Madden, Frederick.

Darwin, Porter. Frommer's Portable London. 208p. 1997. 9.95 (*0-02-862232-4*) Macmillan.

Darwin, Robert. The History of the Union Pacific Railroad in Cheyenne: A Pictorial Odyssey to the Mecca of Steam. LC 87-80052. (Illus.). 400p. 1988. 175.00 (*0-941421-09-0*) Express Pr Ltd.

Darwin, Steven P. Systematics of Timonius Subgenus Abbottia (Rubiaceae-Guettardeae) Anderson, Christiane, ed. (Systematic Botany Monographs: Vol. 42). (Illus.). 86p. 1994. pap. 11.00 (*0-912861-42-8*) Am Soc Plant.

Darwin, Tess. The Scots Herbal. LC 98-177777. 208p. 1997. 52.00 (*1-873644-60-4*, Pub. by Mercat Pr Bks) St Mut.

Darwin, Tony. The Citebook. 8th ed. Fluharty, Barbara, ed. LC 90-71186. (Illus.). 270p. (C). 1990. pap. 16.95 (*0-9628328-0-4*, TX2-139-018) Starlite Inc.

— The Citebook. 12th ed. Fluharty, Barbara, ed. LC 90-71186. (Illus.). 300p. 1995. pap. 24.95 (*0-9628328-6-3*) Starlite Inc.

— The Citebook. 13th ed. Fluharty, Barbara, ed. LC 90-71186. 300p. 1996. pap. 18.70 (*0-9628328-7-1*) Starlite Inc.

— The Citebook. 14th ed. Fluharty, Barbara & Green, C., eds. LC 90-71186. 280p. 1997. pap. 24.95 (*0-9628328-8-X*) Starlite Inc.

Darwish, Adel & Alexander, Gregory. Unholy Babylon: The Secret History of Saddam's War. (Illus.). 335p. 1997. reprint ed. pap. text 14.00 (*0-7881-5108-8*) DIANE Pub.

Darwish, Mahmoud. From Beirut. Kessler, Stephen, tr. 20p. 1993. 3.00 (*0-944550-25-8*) Pygmy Forest Pr.

— Memory for Forgetfulness: August, Beirut, 1982. Muhawi, Ibrahim, tr. from ARA. LC 94-26351.Tr. of Dhairah lil-Nisyan. 1995. 40.00 (*0-520-08767-4*, Pub. by U CA Pr); pap. 14.95 (*0-520-08768-2*, Pub. by U CA Pr) Cal Prin Full Svc.

— Psalms. Bennani, Ben, tr. 70p. 1994. 15.00 (*0-89410-761-5*, Three Contnts); pap. 8.95 (*0-89410-762-3*, Three Contnts) L Rienner.

Darwish, Mustafa. Dream-Makers of the Nile: 75 Years of Egyptian Cinema. (Illus.). 72p. 1997. pap. 14.95 (*977-424-429-X*, Pub. by Am Univ Cairo Pr) Col U Pr.

Dary, David. The Buffalo Book: The Full Saga of the American Animal. LC 89-35104. (Illus.). 374p. 1989. pap. 18.95 (*0-8040-0931-7*) Swallow.

— Comanche. (Public Education Ser.: No. 5). 19p. 1976. pap. 2.00 (*0-89338-003-2*) U KS Nat Hist Mus.

— Cowboy Culture: A Saga of Five Centuries. LC 88-30449. (Illus.). xii, 388p. 1989. reprint ed. pap. 14.95 (*0-7006-0390-5*) U Pr of KS.

— Entrepreneurs of the Old West. LC 85-45590. (Illus.). 380p. 1997. reprint ed. 17.95 (*0-7006-0827-3*) U Pr of KS.

— More True Tales of Old-Time Kansas. LC 87-6152. (Illus.). x, 268p. 1987. 19.95 (*0-7006-0331-X*); pap. 9.95 (*0-7006-0329-8*) U Pr of KS.

— Red Blood & Black Ink: Journalism in the Old West. LC 97-34373. 1998. 30.00 (*0-679-44655-9*) Knopf.

— Red Blood & Black Ink: Journalism in the Old West. LC 98-53916. (Illus.). 360p. 1999. pap. 15.95 (*0-7006-0955-5*) U Pr of KS.

***Dary, David.** The Santa Fe Trail. 2000. 30.00 (*0-375-40361-2*, Pub. by Knopf) Random House.

Dary, David. Seeking Pleasure in the Old West. 364p. 1997. reprint ed. 14.95 (*0-7006-0828-1*) U Pr of KS.

— True Tales of Old-Time Kansas. LC 84-40065. Orig. Title: True Tales of the Old-Time Plains. (Illus.). x, 326p. (Orig.). 1984. pap. 9.95 (*0-7006-0250-X*) U Pr of KS.

Daryabadi, A. M. Holy Quran Arabic-English. 1986. 24.50 (*1-56744-039-8*) Kazi Pubns.

Daryanani, Gobind. Principles of Active Network Synthesis & Design. 512p. 1976. text 106.95 (*0-471-19545-6*) Wiley.

— Roth IRA Book: An Investor's Guide. (Illus.). 288p. 1998. pap. text 34.95 (*0-9665398-1-8*) DQI Inc.

***Daryani, Prem H.** The Art of Gear Fabrication. LC 00-31914. 2000. write for info. (*0-8311-3142-X*) Indus Pr.

Daryson, Diane & Francis, Leslie J. Learning with the Sunday Gospels Pt. 1: Advent to Pentecost. (Illus.). 1998. pap. 27.95 (*0-264-67445-6*, Pub. by A R Mowbray) Cassell & Continuum.

Darzano, Frank. Introduction to Technology Education. 28p. 1991. pap., wbk. ed. 7.00 (*0-943008-50-6*, T13) Bergwall.

— Introduction to Technology Education. (Technology Education Ser.). 26p. (YA). (gr. 10 up). 1991. student ed. 7.00 (*0-8064-0410-8*, T13) Bergwall.

Darzi. Atlas of Laparoscopic Surgery. 1997. text 110.00 (*0-7020-2011-7*, W B Saunders Co) Harcrt Hlth Sci Grp.

Darzi, A., et al. Techniques in the Management of Gallstone Disease. 272p. 1995. 150.00 (*0-632-03675-3*) Blackwell Sci.

Darzins, Egons. The Bacteriology of Tuberculosis. LC 57-8918. 500p. reprint ed. pap. 155.00 (*0-8357-5948-2*, 205585300039) Bks Demand.

D'Arzo, Silvio. The House of Others. Botsford, Keith, tr. from ITA. LC 95-23486. 200p. (C). 1995. pap. 14.95 (*0-8101-6001-3*, Marlboro); text 39.95 (*0-8101-6000-5*, Marlboro) Northwestern U Pr.

***Darzynkiewicz, Zbigniew, ed.** Flow Cytometry Pt. A. 3rd ed. 1999. 69.95 (*0-12-203053-2*) Acad Pr.

— Flow Cytometry Pt. B. 3rd ed. 1999. 69.95 (*0-12-203054-0*) Acad Pr.

— Methods in Cell Biology Vol. 63: Flow Cytometry, Pt. A. 500p. 1999. 110.00 (*0-12-544166-5*) Acad Pr.

— Methods in Cell Biology Vol. 64: Flow Cytometry, Pt. B. 500p. 1999. 110.00 (*0-12-544167-3*) Acad Pr.

Darzynkiewicz, Zbigniew, et al, eds. Methods in Cell Biology Vol. 42: Flow Cytometry, Pt. B. 2nd ed. (Illus.). 697p. 1994. pap. text 59.95 (*0-12-203052-4*) Acad Pr.

Darzynkiewicz, Zbigniew, jt. ed. see Gray, Joe W.

Das. Credit Derivatives. 2nd ed. (Illus.). 800p. 2000. 79.95 (*0-471-84031-9*) Wiley.

— Dynamics & Statistics in Engineering. 1994. 73.50 (*0-256-15439-2*) McGraw.

— Fundamentals of Geotechnical Engineering. LC 99-47729. 293p. 2000. pap. text 99.95 (*0-534-37114-0*) Brooks-Cole.

— Pedondontics. 1983. 60.00 (*0-7855-0746-9*, Pub. by Current Dist) St Mut.

— Pedondontics. 1985. 49.00 (*0-7855-0823-6*, Pub. by Current Dist) St Mut.

— Pesticides Analysis. (Illus.). 488p. 1981. text 185.00 (*0-8247-1087-8*) Dekker.

Das, A. Field Theory: A Path Integral Approach - Lecture Notes in Physics, Vol. 52. (Lecture Notes in Physics Ser.). 416p. 1993. pap. text 45.00 (*981-02-1397-2*) World Scientific Pub.

Das, A. & Koltun, Daniel S. From Statistical Processes to Chaos. 152p. 1995. text 48.00 (*981-02-2010-3*) World Scientific Pub.

Das, A. Andrew. Baptized into God's Family: The Doctrine of Infant Baptism for Today. LC 91-67125. 152p. (Orig.). 1992. pap. 8.99 (*0-8100-0409-7*, 15N0543) Northwest Pub.

Das, A. K. Dental Anatomy & Oral Histology Review. (C). 1991. 70.00 (*0-89771-344-3*, Pub. by Current Dist) St Mut.

— Metallurgy of Failure Analysis. LC 97-166769. (Illus.). 354p. 1997. 69.95 (*0-07-015804-5*) McGraw.

— Tribal Art & Craft. (C). 1993. 44.00 (*0-8364-2877-3*, Pub. by Agam) S Asia.

Das, A. R., jt. auth. see Thothathri, K.

Das, Amal, jt. auth. see Adderly, Brenda.

Das, Amita. India: Impact of the West. (C). 1995. 20.00 (*81-7154-790-7*, Pub. by Popular Prakashan) S Asia.

Das, Anadijiban. Field Theory: A Path Integral Approach. (Lecture Notes in Physics Ser.). 416p. 1993. text 86.00 (*981-02-1396-4*) World Scientific Pub.

— The Special Theory of Relativity: A Mathematical Approach. LC 93-10256. (Illus.). 214p. 1996. 39.95 (*0-387-94042-1*) Spr-Verlag.

— The Special Theory of Relativity: A Mathematical Exposition. (Illus.). 220p. 1993. write for info. (*3-540-94042-1*) Spr-Verlag.

Das, Anita K. The Oral OB GYN Board Exam: How to Prepare for the Exam, How to Take the Exam, How to Pass the Exam. LC 98-24808. 1998. 19.95 (*1-56053-303-X*) Hanley & Belfus.

Das, Arup K. Dental Anatomy & Oral Histology. 260p. 1972. 70.00 (*0-7855-2915-2*, Pub. by Current Dist) St Mut.

Das, Arup K. & Bom, H. B. Dental Anatomy & Oral History. 240p. 1972. pap. (*81-86793-05-4*) Current Bks Intl.

Das, Arvind. Agrarian Unrest & Socio-Economic Change, 1900-1980. 1983. 28.00 (*0-8364-0967-1*, Pub. by Manohar) S Asia.

— The State of Bihar: An Economic History Without Footnotes. 116p. 1993. pap. text 20.00 (*90-5383-135-5*, Pub. by VU Univ Pr) Paul & Co Pubs.

Das, ARvind N. India Invented: A Nation-in-the Making. (C). 1994. text 24.00 (*81-7304-019-2*, Pub. by Manohar) S Asia.

Das, Arvind N., ed. Agrarian Movements in India: Studies on 20th Century Bihar. (Library of Peasant Studies: No. 5). (Illus.). 200p. 1982. text 42.50 (*0-7146-3216-3*, Pub. by F Cass Pubs) Intl Spec Bk.

Das, Arvind N., jt. auth. see Breman, Jan.

Das, Ashok. Integrable Models. (Lecture Notes in Physics Ser.: Vol. 30). 356p. (C). 1989. text 68.00 (*9971-5-0910-5*); pap. text 36.00 (*9971-5-0911-3*) World Scientific Pub.

Das, Ashok, ed. From Symmetries to Strings: Forty Years of Rochester Conferences. 344p. (C). 1990. pap. 44.00 (*981-02-0333-0*); text 108.00 (*981-02-0332-2*) World Scientific Pub.

Das, Ashok & Ferbel, Thomas. Introduction to Nuclear & Particle Physics. LC 93-19307. 352p. 1993. text 87.95 (*0-471-57132-6*) Wiley.

***Das, Ashok & Ferbel, Thomas, eds.** Probing Luminous & Dark Matter. 250p. 2000. 76.00 (*981-02-4286-7*) World Scientific Pub.

Das, Ashok & Melissinos, Adrian C. Quantum Mechanics: A Modern Introduction. xviii, 640p. 1986. text 132.00 (*2-88124-053-4*); pap. text 59.00 (*2-88124-052-6*) Gordon & Breach.

Das, B. M. The Peoples of Assam. 98p. 1987. 16.95 (*0-685-21574-1*) Asia Bk Corp.

Das, B. S. Mission to Bhutan: Nation in Transition. (C). 1995. 21.00 (*0-7069-9470-1*, Pub. by Vikas) S Asia.

Das, Baul S. Crossing the River of Love: Music of the Bauls of Bengal. 1992. 11.95 incl. audio (*0-934252-38-6*) Hohm Pr.

Das, Bhagavan. The Essential Unity of All Religions. 740p. 1994. reprint ed. pap. 29.95 (*1-56459-456-4*) Kessinger Pub.

— It's Here Now (Are You?) A Spiritual Memoir. LC 97-17510. (Illus.). 320p. 1997. 22.22 (*0-7679-0008-1*) Broadway BDD.

— The Science of Peace: An Attempt at an Exposition of the First Principles of the Science of the Self (1904) 348p. 1998. reprint ed. pap. 27.95 (*0-7661-0337-4*) Kessinger Pub.

— The Science of Social Organization or the Laws of Manu in the Light of Theosophy. 358p. 1998. reprint ed. pap. 27.95 (*0-7661-0338-2*) Kessinger Pub.

***Das, Bhagirath L.** World Trade Organization: A Guide to New Frameworks for International Trade. 2000. text 69.95 (*1-85649-710-0*) St Martin.

Das, Bharat. Victims in the Criminal Justice System. LC 96-906699. (C). 1997. 30.00 (*81-7024-797-7*, Pub. by Ashish Pub Hse) S Asia.

Das, Bibekananda & Das, L. N. The Feminine Gender. (Illus.). vi, 163p. 1995. 20.00 (*81-85445-84-2*, Pub. by Manak Pubns Pvt Ltd) Nataraj Bks.

Das, Bina P. & Gupta, Virendra K. Social Wasps of India & the Adjacent Countries (Hymenoptera: Vespidae) (An Illustrated Account of the Vespid Fauna of the Indian Subregion) (Oriental Insects Monographs: No. 11). (Illus.). 300p. (C). 1989. 55.00 (*1-877711-22-5*) Assoc Pubs FL.

Das, Binod S. Studies in the Economic History of Orissa from Ancient Times to 1833. 1978. 11.50 (*0-8364-0200-6*) S Asia.

Das, Binod S., ed. Life & Culture in Orissa. 1985. 17.50 (*0-8364-1402-0*, Pub. by Minerva) S Asia.

Das, Bishnu Pada, see Pada Das, Bishnu.

***Das, Braja.** Shallow Foundations: Bearing Capacity & Settlement. LC 99-28608. 384p. 1999. boxed set 79.95 (*0-8493-1135-7*) CRC Pr.

Das, Braja. Soil Mechanics Laboratory Manual. 5th ed. (Illus.). 280p. (C). 1997. text 30.00 (*1-57645-010-4*, 104) Engineering.

Das, Braja, et al. Engineering Mechanics: Statics. 586p. (C). 1993. text 60.50 (*0-256-11452-8*, Irwn McGrw-H) McGrw-H Hghr Educ.

Das, Braja M. Civil Engineering Geotechnical Engineering: Review for the Professional Engineer's Exam. (Illus.). 58p. (Orig.). 1999. pap. 19.95 (*1-57645-046-5* 465) Engineering.

— Introduction to Soil Mechanics. LC 79-16729. 274p. reprint ed. pap. 85.00 (*0-608-12979-8*, 202386400034) Bks Demand.

— Principles of Foundation Engineering. 2nd ed. 624p. (C). 1990. text 69.95 (*0-534-92171-X*) PWS Pubs.

— Principles of Foundation Engineering. 3rd ed. LC 94-48565. (Engineering Ser.). 1995. 70.00 (*0-534-20646-8*) PWS Pubs.

— Principles of Foundation Engineering. 4th ed. LC 98-36450. 1998. 94.95 (*0-534-95403-0*) PWS Pubs.

— Principles of Geotechnical Engineering. 2nd ed. 606p. (C). 1990. text 69.95 (*0-534-92130-2*) PWS Pubs.

— Principles of Geotechnical Engineering. 3rd ed. LC 93-5738. 1993. mass mkt. 69.50 (*0-534-93375-0*) PWS Pubs.

— Principles of Geotechnical Engineering. 4th ed. LC 97-28512. (C). 1997. mass mkt. 102.95 (*0-534-95179-1*) PWS Pubs.

— Principles of Soil Dynamics. 1992. 70.50 (*0-534-93129-4*) PWS Pubs.

Das, Braja M., ed. Special Topics in Foundations. (Sessions Proceedings Ser.). 136p. 1988. 18.00 (*0-87262-645-8*) Am Soc Civil Eng.

Das, Braja M., et al. Engineering Mechanics: Dynamics. LC 92-36127. 526p. (C). 1994. text 60.50 (*0-256-11450-1*, Irwn McGrw-H) McGrw-H Hghr Educ.

Das, Chand N. Hours of Glory: Famous Battles of the Indian Army, 1801-1971. (Illus.). 600p. 1998. pap. text 60.00 (*0-7881-5467-2*) DIANE Pub.

Das, Chandra M. Philosophy of Rabindranath Tagore: His Social, Political, Religious, & Educational Views. (C). 1996. 30.00 (*81-7100-817-8*, Pub. by Deep & Deep Pubns) S Asia.

Das, Chandrahasa. The Wealth of Devotion. LC 97-65783. 128p. (Orig.). 1997. pap. 9.95 (*0-9657306-2-X*) Omegaman Prod.

Das, D. Clinical Surgery. 3rd ed. (C). 1989. 120.00 (*0-7855-4650-2*, Pub. by Current Dist) St Mut.

— MCQS in Surgery. (C). 1987. 60.00 (*0-8110-0134-2*, Pub. by Current Dist) St Mut.

— OP: Surgery. 3rd ed. (C). 1989. 105.00 (*0-7855-6115-3*, Pub. by Current Dist) St Mut.

Das, D., et al. College Botany Practical, Vol. I. (C). 1989. 50.00 (*0-89771-411-3*, Pub. by Current Dist) St Mut.

— College Botany Practical, Vol. II. (C). 1989. 75.00 (*0-89771-412-1*, Pub. by Current Dist) St Mut.

Das, D. K. & Essman, Walter B., eds. Oxygen Radicals: Systemic Events & Disease Processes. (Illus.). xii, 196p. 1990. 151.50 (*3-8055-5049-9*) S Karger.

Das, D. K. & Prabhudesai, R. K. Chemical Engineering License Problems & Solutions: For the Professional Engineer's Exam. (Illus.). 192p. 1998. reprint ed. pap. 31.50 (*1-57645-037-6*, 376) Engineering.

— Chemical Engineering License Review: For the Professional Engineer's Exam. 2nd ed. (Illus.). 565p. 1998. reprint ed. pap. 69.50 (*1-57645-036-8*, 368) Engineering.

Das, D. K. & Prabhudesai, R. K. Chemical Engineering License Review. (Illus.). 565p. 1996. student ed. 75.00 (*1-57645-000-7*) Engineering.

Das, Debendra K., ed. SAARC: Regional Cooperation & Development. (C). 1992. 26.00 (*0-8364-2808-0*, Pub. by Deep & Deep Pubns) S Asia.

Das, Deepa. Prostitutes & Prostitution in India. (C). 1993. 30.00 (*0-7069-5957-4*, Pub. by Vikas) S Asia.

Das, Deepak Kumar, jt. ed. see Swain, Mamata.

Das, Dilip & Prabhudesai, R. K. Chemical Engineering License Problems & Solutions. (Illus.). 192p. 1996. 35.00 (*1-57645-011-2*, 120) Engineering.

Das, Dilip K. Import Canalisation. (Illus.). 154p. (C). 1992. text 27.50 (*0-8039-9409-5*) Sage.

— The Yen Appreciation & the International Economy. 208p. (C). 1992. text 55.00 (*0-8147-1852-3*) NYU Pr.

***Das, Dilip K., ed.** Asian Exports: Past Trends & Future Prospects. LC 99-50351. 465p. 2000. pap. text 35.00 (*0-19-592100-3*) OUP.

— Asian Exports: Past Trends & Future Prospects. LC 99-50351. (The Practical Approach Ser.: No. 223). 465p. 2000. text 60.00 (*0-19-592128-3*) OUP.

Das, Dilip K., ed. Emerging Growth Pole: The Asia-Pacific Economy. LC 95-26812. 670p. (C). 1997. pap. 61.00 (*0-13-525841-3*) P-H.

— International Finance. LC 93-9646. (Illus.). 656p. (C). 1993. pap. 39.99 (*0-415-09281-7*, B0144) Routledge.

— Police Practices: An International Review. LC 94-18256. 475p. 1994. 58.00 (*0-8108-2908-8*) Scarecrow.

Das, Dilip K. & Prabhudesai, Raj K. EIT Chemical Review. 2nd ed. (Illus.). 208p. (C). 1998. pap. 29.95 (*1-57645-023-6*, 236) Engineering.

Das, Dipak K. Stress Adaptation, Prophylaxis & Treatment. LC 98-52740. (Developments in Molecular & Cellular BioChemistry Ser.). 185p. 1999. write for info. (*0-7923-8406-7*) Kluwer Academic.

Das, Dipak K., ed. Heart in Stress. LC 99-34749. 450p. 1999. text 140.00 (*1-57331-164-2*) NY Acad Sci.

***Das, Dipak K. & New York Academy of Sciences Staff.** Heart in Distress. LC 99-34749. (Annals of the New York Academy of Science Ser.). 1999. write for info. (*1-57331-165-0*) NY Acad Sci.

Das, Dipak K., et al. Myocardial Preservation, Preconditioning & Adaptation. LC 96-21067. (Annals of the New York Academy of Sciences: Vol. 793). 1996. 150.00 (*1-57331-024-7*) NY Acad Sci.

— Myocardial Preservation, Preconditioning, & Adaptation. LC 96-21067. (Annals of the New York Academy of Sciences). 1996. pap. 150.00 (*1-57331-025-5*) NY Acad Sci.

Das, Dipak K., jt. auth. see Bittar, E. Edward.

Das, Dipak K., jt. auth. see Mukhopadhyay, Satya N.

Das, Dipak Kumar. Revisiting Talwar: A Study in the Royal Indian Navy Uprising of February 1946. (C). 1994. 36.00 (*81-202-0349-6*, Pub. by Ajanta) S Asia.

Das, G. D., jt. ed. see Malhotra, Sudarshan.

Das, G. D., jt. ed. see Wallace, R. B.

Das, G. K., jt. ed. see Salgado, Gamini.

Das, G. N. Couplets from Kabir. (C). 1991. 17.50 (*81-208-0935-1*, Pub. by Motilal Bnarsidass) S Asia.

— Couplets from Thulasee Das. LC 97-904264. (C). 1997. 14.00 (*81-7017-352-3*, Pub. by Abhinav) S Asia.

— Love Songs of Kabir. (C). 1992. 17.50 (*81-7017-288-8*, Pub. by Abhinav) S Asia.

— Maxims of Vidur LC 97-905685. 148p. 1997. write for info. (*81-7017-353-1*) S Asia.

— Readings from Bhagabata. 1996. 14.00 (*81-7017-337-X*, Pub. by Abhinav) S Asia.

— Readings from Thirukkural. (C). 1997. 14.00 (*81-7017-342-6*, Pub. by Asian Educ Servs) S Asia.

Das, Gobind. Supreme Court in Quest of Identity. (C). 1989. 125.00 (*0-89771-760-0*, Pub. by Eastern Book) St Mut.

Das Goswami, Satsvarupa. Your Ever Well-Wisher. (Illus.). 363p. 1982. 10.95 (*0-89213-133-0*, YEWW) Bhaktivedanta.

Das, Gugudas. Tribes of Arunachal Pradesh in Transition. 1995. 25.00 (*0-7069-8648-2*, Pub. by Vikas) S Asia.

Das Gupta, A. K. A Theory of Wage Policy. (Illus.). 1976. pap. 3.95 (*0-19-560699-X*) OUP.

Das Gupta, Amitabha. The Second Linguistic Turn: Chomsky & the Philosophy of Language. xi, 220p. 1996. pap. 44.95 (*3-631-49866-7*) P Lang Pubng.

Das-Gupta, Arindam & Mookherjee, Dilip. Incentives & Institutional Reform in Tax Enforcement: An Analysis of Developing Country Experience. LC 98-905168. (Illus.). 494p. 1998. text 39.95 (*0-19-564286-4*) OUP.

Das Gupta, Ashin. Malabar in Asian Trade, 1740-1800. LC 66-44074. (Cambridge South Asian Studies). 216p. reprint ed. pap. 61.60 (*0-608-12224-6*, 2024446) Bks Demand.

D

Das Gupta, Ashin & Pearson, M. N. India & the Indian Ocean - 1500 to 1800. 374p. 1987. 49.95 (*0-318-36991-5*) Asia Bk Corp.

Das-Gupta, D. K. Ferroelectric Polymers & Ceramic-Polymer Composites. (Key Engineering Materials Ser.: Vols. 92-3). (Illus.). 352p. (C). 1994. text 166.00 (*0-87849-674-2*, Pub. by Trans T Pub) Enfield Pubs NH.

Das Gupta, D. K. & Lang, S. B. Proceedings of the 20th Century British Dielectrics Society Meeting on Ferroelectrics & Related Dielectric Phenomena in Ordered Material. 260p. 1987. pap. text 533.00 (*2-88124-276-6*) Gordon & Breach.

Das Gupta, Dipanker S. Molybdenum Nutrition in Rice. (International Bioscience Monographs: No. 4). 74p. 1978. 8.00 (*0-88065-046-X*) Scholarly Pubns.

Das Gupta, Dipanker S., ed. Principles & Practice of Acute Cardiac Care. LC 83-12340. (Illus.). 511p. 1984. reprint ed. pap. 158.50 (*0-8357-7671-9*, 205699900001) Bks Demand.

Das Gupta, Hemendra N. The Indian Theatre. 1988. 41.00 (*0-8364-2299-6*, Pub. by Gian Publng Hse) S Asia.

Das Gupta, Malabika, ed. Status of Tribal Women in Tripura. (C). 1993. 14.00 (*0-614-18156-9*, Pub. by Vikas) S Asia.

Das Gupta, Monica, et al, eds. Health, Poverty & Development in India. LC 96-902117. (Illus.). 380p. (C). 1996. text 27.50 (*0-19-563621-X*) OUP.

— Prospective Community Studies in Developing Countries. (International Studies in Demography). (Illus.). 358p. 1998. text 85.00 (*0-19-829209-0*) OUP.

Das Gupta, Pradeep, jt. auth. see Kalra, J. Inder.

Das Gupta, Prajna, jt. ed. see Lee, Victor.

Das Gupta, Ranajit. Economy, Society & Politics in Bengal: Jalpaiquri 1869-1947. 342p. (C). 1993. 28.00 (*0-19-562841-1*) OUP.

Das Gupta, Shashibhusan. Obscure Religious Cults. 1995. reprint ed. 28.00 (*81-7102-020-8*, Pub. by Firma KLM) S Asia.

Das, Gurudas. Tribes of Arunachal Pradesh in Transition. 1995. pap. 14.00 (*0-7069-9681-X*, Pub. by Vikas) S Asia.

Das, Gurudas & Purkayastha, R. K., eds. Liberalization & India's North East. LC 98-901510. 1998. 48.00 (*81-7169-498-5*, Commonwealth) S Asia.

Das, H. H. Federal & State Politics in India. (C). 1990. 150.00 (*0-89771-208-0*) St Mut.

Das, H. K., jt. auth. see Biswas, B. B.

Das, Hari H. & Mohapatra, S. Centre-State Relations in India: A Study of Subnational Aspirations. 271p. 1986. 32.00 (*81-7024-062-X*, Pub. by Ashish Pub Hse) S Asia.

Das, Hari H. & Rath, Rabindranath. Tribals of Andaman & Nicobar Islands. (C). 1991. text 22.50 (*81-7024-367-X*, Pub. by Ashish Pub Hse) S Asia.

Das, Indraneil. Biogeography of the Reptiles of South Asia. LC 94-48209. (Illus.). 112p. (C). 1996. 27.50 (*0-89464-935-3*) Krieger.

— Herpetological Bibliography of Indonesia. LC 97-50219. 96p. 1998. 22.50 (*1-57524-026-2*) Krieger.

Das, J. P. Prostitute & Other Stories. LC 95-905271. (C). 1995. 14.00 (*81-241-0262-7*, Pub. by Har-Anand Pubns) S Asia.

— Silences. 100p. 1989. text 10.95 (*0-317-93100-8*, Pub. by Vikas) S Asia.

— Spider's Web & Other Stories. 1990. text 15.95 (*0-7069-4958-7*, Pub. by Vikas) S Asia.

— The Working Mind: An Introduction to Psychology. LC 98-19164. 1998. 39.95 (*0-7619-9261-8*) Sage.

Das, J. P. & Gindis, Boris. Lev S. Vygotsky & Contemporary Educational Psychology Vol. 30, No. 2, 1995: A Special Issue of Educational Psychologist, Vol. 30, No. 2, 1995. 56p. 1995. pap. 20.00 (*0-8058-9938-3*) L Erlbaum Assocs.

Das, J. P. & Zide, A., eds. Under a Silent Sun: A Selection of Oriya Women's Poems. 80p. (C). 1992. text 12.95 (*0-7069-5968-X*, Pub. by Vikas) S Asia.

Das, J. P., et al. Cognitive Planning: The Psychological Basis of Intelligent Behavior. 202p. 1996. 29.95 (*0-8039-9287-4*) Sage.

Das, Jagannath. Krsna's Holy Land: Sri Vraja Mandula Parikrama. Roberts, John W., ed. (C). 1989. write for info. (*0-318-65393-1*) Gaudiya Vaisnava Pr.

Das, Jagannath P., et al. Assessment of Cognitive Processes: The PASS Theory of Intelligence. LC 93-13843. (Illus.). 256p. (C). 1993. 67.00 (*0-205-14164-1*, Longwood Div) Allyn.

Das, Jages. Folklore of Assam. 142p. 1980. 7.95 (*0-318-36317-8*) Asia Bk Corp.

***Das, Jibanananda & Chaudhuri, Sukanta.** A Certain Sense: Poems LC 99-932109. (ENG & BEN.). xix, 99 p. 1998. write for info. (*81-260-0541-6*) S Asia.

Das, K. B. & Mahapatra, L. K. Folklore of Orissa. 160p. 1979. 6.95 (*0-318-36319-4*) Asia Bk Corp.

Das, K. C. Modern Indian Short Stories, Vol. 4. 164p. 1983. 12.95 (*0-318-36918-4*) Asia Bk Corp.

Das, K. V. Main Group Elements & Their Compounds. 525p. 1997. 139.00 (*3-540-61425-7*) Spr-Verlag.

Das, Kamal. From the Reindeer to the Rhine: The Daring Adventures of an Indian Lady. 1990. 17.00 (*81-7099-210-9*, Pub. by Mittal Pubs Dist) S Asia.

Das, Kamala. My Story. (C). 1996. pap. write for info. (*81-207-1324-9*) Sterling Pubs.

Das, Kedarnath. Obstetric Forceps: Its History & Evolution. (Illus.). 903p. 1993. boxed set 125.00 (*1-897849-00-1*) Norman SF.

Das, Kumar B. Cement Industry of India. (Illus.). 465p. (C). 1987. 48.50 (*81-7024-083-2*, Pub. by Ashish Pub Hse) S Asia.

— Electrical Energy & Economic Development of Rural India. (C). 1990. 17.50 (*81-7024-370-X*, Pub. by Ashish Pub Hse) S Asia.

Das, L. D. V. Forage Crops. 315p. 1997. pap. 475.00 (*81-7089-170-1*, Pub. by Intl Bk Distr) St Mut.

Das, L. N., jt. auth. see Das, Bibekananda.

Das, Lama Surya. Awakening the Buddha Within: Eight Steps to Enlightenment: Tibetan Wisdom for the Western World. LC 97-8346. 432p. 1997. 26.00 (*0-553-06695-1*) Broadway BDD.

***Das, Lama Surya.** Awakening the Buddhist Heart: Integrating Love, Meaning, & Connection into Every Part of Your Life. 320p. 2000. 25.00 (*0-7679-0276-9*) Broadway BDD.

— Awakening to the Sacred. (Illus.). 400p. 2000. pap. 15.00 (*0-7679-0275-0*) Broadway BDD.

Das, Lama Surya. Awakening to the Sacred: Creating a Spiritual Life from Scratch. LC 99-10659. 400p. 1999. 26.00 (*0-7679-0274-2*) Broadway BDD.

Das, M. C. Biology of Enchytraeidae (Oligochaeta) 171p. 1983. pap. 225.00 (*81-7089-006-3*, Pub. by Intl Bk Distr) St Mut.

Das, M. P., ed. Topics in Condensed Matter Physics. (Illus.). 297p. (C). 1994. lib. bdg. 145.00 (*1-56072-180-4*) Nova Sci Pubs.

Das, M. P. & Mahanty, J. Modern Perspectives in Many-Body Physics: Proceeding of the Summer School. 456p. 1994. text 116.00 (*981-02-1560-6*) World Scientific Pub.

Das, M. P. & Neilson, D., eds. Strongly Correlated Election Systems. 255p. (C). 1992. text 175.00 (*1-56072-090-5*) Nova Sci Pubs.

Das, M. P., jt. auth. see Neilson, D.

Das, M. P., jt. ed. see Mahanty, J.

Das, M. S. & Bardis, P. D. Family in Asia. 451p. 1978. 24.95 (*0-7069-0606-3*) Asia Bk Corp.

Das, Man S. & Gupta, Vijay K., eds. Feminine Roles in Global Society. 182p. 1995. pap. 150.00 (*0-7855-2729-X*, Pub. by Print Hse) St Mut.

Das, Man Singh, see Kolaja, Jiri T. & Singh Das, Man, eds.

Das, Man Singh, see Singh Das, Man, ed.

Das, Manoj. Bulldozers & Fables & Fantasies for Adults. (New World Literature Ser.: No. 26). 1990. 19.50 (*81-7018-604-8*, Pub. by BR Pub) S Asia.

— India - A Tourist's Paradise. 490p. 1983. 19.95 (*0-318-36989-3*) Asia Bk Corp.

— Sri Aurobindo. 3rd ed. 1982. reprint ed. pap. 4.00 (*0-8364-1585-X*, Pub. by National Sahitya Akademi) S Asia.

— The Submerged Valley & Other Stories. 159p. (Orig.). 1986. pap. 6.95 (*0-941524-26-4*) Lotus Pr.

***Das, Manoranjan, et al.** The Ninth of August: A Play - August Na LC 98-908050. xi, 59 p. 1998. write for info. (*81-260-0484-3*, Pub. by Rabindra Bhawn) S Asia.

Das, Mitra & Kolack, Shirley. Technology, Values & Society: Social Forces in Technological Change. 2nd ed. Ser. XI, Vol. 27. (Illus.). 181p. (C). 1991. text 23.00 (*0-8204-0824-7*) P Lang Pubng.

Das, Mukunda P. Physics of Novel Materials. 1998. 48.00 (*981-02-3552-6*) World Scientific Pub.

Das, N. Disturbance of Homeostasis. (C). 1988. 60.00 (*0-7855-4651-0*, Pub. by Current Dist) St Mut.

— Handbook of Pedodontics. 2nd ed. (C). 1980. 65.00 (*0-7855-4652-9*, Pub. by Current Dist) St Mut.

Das, N., ed. Disturbance of Homeostasis. (C). 1987. 60.00 (*0-89771-342-7*, Pub. by Current Dist) St Mut.

— Handbook of Pedodontics. (C). 1985. 40.00 (*0-89771-345-1*, Pub. by Current Dist) St Mut.

Das, N. K. Ethinic Identity Ethnicity & Social Stratification in North-East India. (C). 1989. 45.00 (*81-210-0218-4*, Pub. by Inter-India Pubns) S Asia.

Das, N. K. & Bertoni, H. L. Directions for the Next Generation of MMIC Devices & Systems: Proceedings of the 1996 WRI International Symposium Held in New York City, September 11-13, 1996. LC 97-41794. (Language of Science Ser.). 427p. (C). 1997. 135.00 (*0-306-45769-5*, Kluwer Plenum) Kluwer Academic.

Das, Nagen C. Development of Handloom Industry: Organisation, Production, Marketing. 1986. 30.00 (*0-8364-1881-6*, Pub. by Deep & Deep Pubns) S Asia.

Das, Navayauvana. Lessons from the Ayurveda: Health for Devotees. Das, Nityananda, ed. 150p. 1989. pap. write for info. (*0-923519-04-1*) New Jaipur.

Das Neves, E. Maranha, ed. Advances in Rockfill Structures. (C). 1991. text 306.50 (*0-7923-1267-8*) Kluwer Academic.

Das, Nityananda. Someone Has Poisoned Me. 416p. 1999. pap. 10.00 (*0-923519-09-2*) New Jaipur.

Das, Nityananda, ed. see Das, Navayauvana.

Das, Nityananda, ed. see Das, Purnaprajna.

Das, P. & Jhingran, Arun G., eds. Fish Genetics in India: Proceedings of the Symposium on Conservation & Management of Fish Genetic Resources of India, 1986. (Current Trends in Life Sciences Ser.: Vol. 15). viii, 266p. 1989. 95.00 (*1-55528-177-X*) Scholarly Pubns.

Das, P. C. Textbook of Medicine. (C). 1989. 150.00 (*0-89771-343-5*, Pub. by Current Dist) St Mut.

Das, P. C., et al, eds. Hereditary Diseases & Blood Transfusion: Proceedings of the Nineteenth Annual International Symposium on Blood Transfusion, Groningen, 1994. (Developments in Hematology & Immunology Ser.: Vol. 30). 256p. (C). 1995. text 104.50 (*0-7923-3694-1*) Kluwer Academic.

— Supportive Therapy in Haematology. LC 85-4977. 1985. text 213.00 (*0-89838-700-0*) Kluwer Academic.

Das, P. C., jt. auth. see Sibinga, C. T.

Das, P. C., jt. ed. see Sibinga, C. T.

Das, P. K. Handbook of Human Physiology. 464p. 1995. pap. (*81-86793-26-7*) Current Bks Intl.

Das, P. K. Lasers & Optical Engineering. (Illus.). 480p. 1995. 69.95 (*0-387-97108-4*) Spr-Verlag.

— Optical Signal Processing: Fundamentals. (Illus.). 488p. 1991. 79.95 (*0-387-51476-7*) Spr-Verlag.

Das, P. K. & Srimani, S. L., eds. Handbook for the Design of Castellated Beams. 98p. (C). 1984. text 78.00 (*90-6191-428-0*, Pub. by A A Balkema) Ashgate Pub Co.

Das, P. K., jt. auth. see Chatterjee, B. N.

Das, Pankaj K. & De Cusatis, Casimer. Acousto-Optic Signal Processing: Fundamentals & Applications. (Acoustics Library). 425p. 1991. text 65.00 (*0-89006-464-4*) Artech Hse.

Das, Parag C., ed. Safety of Bridges. LC 99-178840. 249p. 1997. 74.00 (*0-7277-2591-2*, 2591, Pub. by T Telford) RCH.

Das, Paritosh. Sahajiya Cult of Bengal & Pancha Sakha Cult of Orissa. (C). 1988. 17.50 (*0-8364-2378-X*, Pub. by Firma KLM) S Asia.

Das, Pradip K. & Baruah, Hrishikesh. Petroleum & Coal. 139p. 1997. pap. 120.00 (*81-7533-042-2*, Pub. by Print Hse) St Mut.

Das, Prodeepta. I Is for India. LC 95-43424. (Illus.). 32p. (J). (ps-3). 1996. lib. bdg. 13.95 (*0-382-39278-7*) Silver Burdett Pr.

Das, Purna C. The Economic History of Orissa in the Nineteenth Century. 1989. 42.50 (*81-7169-009-2*, Pub. by Commonwealth) S Asia.

Das, Purnaprajna. Mahabharata: The Fifth Veda. Das, Nityananda, ed. 752p. 1998. pap. 17.95 (*0-923519-08-4*) New Jaipur.

Das, R. K. Temples of Vrindaban. 1990. 94.00 (*81-85067-47-3*, Pub. by Sundeep Prak) S Asia.

Das, R. L., ed. see Battery Conference on Applications & Advances Staf.

Das, Rahul P. Essays on Vaisnavism in Bengal. LC 97-902967. (C). 1997. 18.00 (*81-7102-082-8*, Pub. by Firma KLM) S Asia.

Das, Ram Narayan, see Narayan Das, Ram.

Das, Ranjan. Strategic Management of Services: Framework & Cases. LC 98-168211. (Illus.). 448p. (C). 1998. text 35.00 (*0-19-564170-1*) OUP.

Das, S. Exotic Options: Products, Applications & Pricing. 218p. 1996. pap. 95.00 (*0-455-21439-5*, Pub. by LawBk Co) Gaunt.

— Purdah: The Status of Indian Women. 287p. 1979. 19.95 (*0-318-37070-0*) Asia Bk Corp.

Das, S., ed. Aluminum Alloys for Packaging III. (Illus.). 230p. 1998. 94.00 (*0-87339-386-4*, 3864) Minerals Metals.

Das, S., et al, eds. International Colloquium on Modern Quantum Field Theory. 580p. (C). 1991. pap. 48.00 (*981-02-0200-8*); text 130.00 (*981-02-0199-0*) World Scientific Pub.

Das, S. K. Civil Service Reform & Structural Adjustment. LC 98-902977. (Illus.). 284p. (C). 1998. text 27.95 (*0-19-564305-4*) OUP.

***Das, S. K.** Civil Service Reform & Structural Adjustment. 284p. 1999. pap. 14.95 (*0-19-564851-X*) OUP.

Das, S. K. The Last Lambada LC 99-931543. 169 p. 1998. write for info. (*81-207-2117-9*) Sterling.

***Das, S. K.** Public Office, Private Interest: Bureaucracy & Corruption in India. (Illus.). 320p. 2000. text 24.95 (*0-19-565382-3*) OUP.

Das, S. K. & Kipouros, G. J., eds. Automotive Alloys. LC 96-80048. (Illus.), 214p. 1997. 60.00 (*0-87339-368-6*, 3686) Minerals Metals.

Das, S. K., ed. see Metallurgical Society of AIME Staff, et al.

Das, S. K., ed. see TMS Northeast Regional Symposium Staff.

Das, S. M. Handbook of Limnology & Water Pollution: With Practical Methodology. (C). 1988. 27.50 (*81-7003-097-8*, Pub. by S Asia Pubs) S Asia.

Das, S. N., jt. auth. see Thakur, R. S.

Das, S. R., et al, eds. Modern Quantum Field Theory II: Proceedings of the International Colloquium Tata Institute of Fundamental Research, Bombay, India 5 - 11 January 1994. 340p. 1995. text 86.00 (*981-02-2411-7*, PcahmMpPt-P2889) World Scientific Pub.

Das, Sakti & Crawford. Cancer of the Prostate. LC 92-48552. (Basic & Clinical Oncology Ser.: Vol. 3). (Illus.). 480p. 1993. text 185.00 (*0-8247-8863-X*) Dekker.

Das, Sakti & Crawford, E. David, eds. Laparoscopic Urology. LC 93-47167. 1994. text 105.00 (*0-7216-3766-3*, W B Saunders Co) Harcrt Hlth Sci Grp.

Das, Sakti, jt. auth. see Crawford, E. David.

Das, Sakti, jt. auth. see Hashmat, Azid.

Das, Santi, ed. Satyajit Ray, an Intimate Master. LC 98-903408. xvii, 238 p. 1998. write for info. (*81-7023-748-3*) Allied Pubs.

Das, Sarat C. Contributions on the Religion & History of Tibet. 1988. 35.00 (*0-7855-0309-9*, Pub. by Ratna Pustak Bhandar) St Mut.

— Indian Pandits in the Land of Snow. (C). 1992. reprint ed. 22.00 (*81-206-0776-7*, Pub. by Asian Educ Servs) S Asia.

— An Introduction to the Grammar of the Tibetan Language. 1983. 38.00 (*0-8364-2568-5*, Pub. by Motilal Bnarsidass) S Asia.

— An Introduction to the Grammar of the Tibetan Language. (ENG & TIB.). 1992. reprint ed. 75.00 (*0-8288-8432-3*, F66921) Fr & Eur.

— Journey to Lhasa & Central Tibet. 1988. 50.00 (*0-7855-0313-7*, Pub. by Ratna Pustak Bhandar) St Mut.

— Journey to Lhasa & Central Tibet. 285p. (C). 1988. 140.00 (*0-89771-097-5*, Pub. by Ratna Pustak Bhandar) St Mut.

— Tibetan-English Dictionary. 1987. 75.00 (*0-8288-1759-6*, F63570) Fr & Eur.

— Tibetan-English Dictionary. 1353p. (C). 1987. 220.00 (*0-89771-085-1*, Pub. by Ratna Pustak Bhandar) St Mut.

— A Tibetan-English Dictionary. (C). 1983. reprint ed. 54.00 (*0-8364-2194-9*, Pub. by Motilal Bnarsidass) S Asia.

— A Tibetan-English Dictionary: Compact Edition. 1987. 80.00 (*0-7855-0290-4*) St Mut.

— Tibetan Studies. Chattopadhyay, Alaka, ed. 1985. 24.00 (*0-8364-1501-9*, Pub. by KP Bagchi) S Asia.

Das, Sarat C., ed. Contributions on the Religion & History of Tibet. 210p. (C). 1988. 140.00 (*0-89771-118-1*, Pub. by Ratna Pustak Bhandar) St Mut.

Das, Satadal. Handbook of Microbiology. 185p. 1995. pap. (*81-86793-23-2*) Current Bks Intl.

Das, Satya. New Perspectives on Business Cycles: An Analysis of Inequality & Heterogeneity. 256p. 1993. 95.00 (*1-85278-800-3*) E Elgar.

Das, Satyait. Structured Notes & Derivative Embedded Securities. 557p. 1996. pap. 195.00 (*1-85564-566-1*, Pub. by Euromoney) Am Educ Systs.

***Das, Satyajit.** Credit Derivatives: Trading & Management of Credit & Default Risk. LC 97-53210. 350p. 1998. 79.95 (*0-471-24856-8*) Wiley.

Das, Satyajit. Global Swap Markets. 555p. 1991. 90.00 (*1-873446-10-1*, Pub. by IFR Pub) Am Educ Systs.

— Swap Financing. (Illus.). xxxv, 661p. 1989. pap. 148.50 (*0-455-20831-X*, Pub. by LawBk Co) Gaunt.

Das, Satyajit, ed. Risk Management & Financial Derivatives: A Guide to the Mathematics. LC 97-46822. (Irwin Library of Investment & Finance). 500p. 1998. 70.00 (*0-07-015378-7*) McGraw-Hill Prof.

Das, Saytyajit. Swap & Derivative Financing: The Global Reference to Products Pricing Applications & Markets Revised Edition. 2nd rev. ed. 1500p. 1993. text 95.00 (*1-55738-542-4*, Irwn Prfssnl) McGraw-Hill Prof.

Das, Shankar, pseud. God Alone Is: Essential Teachings from Talks by Shankar Das. 108p. (Orig.). 1989. pap. 4.95 (*0-9621660-0-6*) Sadhana Ashram.

Das Sharma, Amal. Musicians of India: Past & Present, Gharanas of Hindustani Music & Genealogies. (C). 1993. 22.00 (*81-85421-18-8*, Pub. by Naya Prokash) S Asia.

Das, Shiv. Highways of Higher Life: Principles & Practice of Bhaava Yoga & Spiritual Technology. LC 98-906996. 170 p. 1998. write for info. (*81-85402-99-X*) Shipra Pubns.

Das, Shukavak. The Life & Thought of Kedarnath Dutta Bhaktivinoda: A Hindu Encounter with Modernity. 400p. (C). 1996. pap. 40.00 (*1-889756-25-3*) Sanskrit Relgns Inst.

Das, Shukavak, jt. auth. see Dutta, Kedarnatha.

Das, Sisir K. A History of Indian Literature 1911-1956: Struggle for Freedom: Triumph & Tragedy. (C). 1995. 36.00 (*81-7901-798-2*, Pub. by Indian Pubs) S Asia.

Das, Sisir K., ed. English Writings of Rabindranath Tagore. LC 94-903179. (C). 1996. 44.00 (*81-7201-945-9*, Pub. by Indian Pubs) S Asia.

— English Writings of Rabindranath Tagore Vol. I: Poems. (C). 1994. 44.00 (*81-7201-547-X*, Pub. by Indian Pubs) S Asia.

***Das, Sitanshu.** Indian Nationalism: Study in Evolution. LC 99-938996. 232p. 1999. 20.00 (*81-241-0620-7*, Pub. by Har-Anand Pubns) Nataraj Bks.

Das, Sri K. Everybody's Guide to Palmistry. (C). 1993. write for info. (*81-207-0564-5*) Sterling Pubs.

DAS Staff. Pathophysiology of Reperfusion Injury. 528p. 1992. lib. bdg. 219.00 (*0-8493-4555-3*, RB144) CRC Pr.

Das, Subodh K. Automotive Alloys II: Proceedings, TMS Annual Meeting on Automotive Alloys, San Antonio, Texas, 1998. LC 96-80048. (Illus.). 207p. 1997. 88.00 (*0-87339-387-2*, TN775) Minerals Metals.

Das, Subrata, jt. auth. see Fox, John.

Das, Sudipta. Myths & Realities of French Imperialism in India, 1763-1783. LC 91-30733. (American University Studies: History: Ser. IX, Vols. 117). (Illus.). XVII, 459p. (C). 1993. text 54.95 (*0-8204-1676-2*) P Lang Pubng.

Das, Sukla. Socio-Economic Life of Northern India. 1980. 22.50 (*0-8364-0609-5*) S Asia.

***Das, Sumitra.** Handbook of Pedodontics. 162p. 1998. pap. (*0-7855-7518-9*) Current Bks Intl.

Das, Sunhit R., jt. auth. see Chopra, Kasturi L.

Das, Sur. Management Decisions. 1985. 69.00 (*0-7855-0742-6*, Pub. by Current Dist) St Mut.

Das, Suranjan. Communal Riots in Bengal, 1905-1947. (South Asian Studies). (Illus.). 328p. 1994. reprint ed. pap. text 8.95 (*0-19-563233-8*) OUP.

Das, Suranjan, ed. Caste & Communal Politics in South Asia. (University of Calcutta Monograph: No. 8). (C). 1993. 20.00 (*81-7074-137-8*, Pub. by KP Bagchi) S Asia.

Das, Surya. Awakening the Buddha: Tibetan Wisdom for the Western World. 432p. 1998. pap. 15.95 (*0-7679-0157-6*) Broadway BDD.

— The Snow Lion's Turquoise Mane: Wisdom Tales from Tibet. LC 90-55787. 288p. 1992. pap. 19.00 (*0-06-250849-0*, Pub. by Harper SF) HarpC.

Das, Surya, ed. see Rinpoche, Nyshul K.

Das, Sushanto. Dedication to Freedom: MN Roy - The Man & His Times. 1986. 14.00 (*81-202-0169-8*, Pub. by Ajanta) S Asia.

Das, Swaswati. Social Life in Ancient India: 800 B. C. - 183 B. C. (C). 1994. 20.00 (*81-7018-759-1*, Pub. by BR Pub) S Asia.

Das, T. K. The Subjective Side of Strategy Making: Future Orientations & Perceptions of Executives. LC 86-12344. (Illus.). 292p. 1986. 55.00 (*0-275-92340-1*, C2340, Praeger Pubs) Greenwood.

Das, T. K., compiled by. The Time Dimension: An Interdisciplinary Guide. LC 90-31137. 360p. 1990. 65.00 (*0-275-92681-8*, C2681, Praeger Pubs) Greenwood.

Das, T. K., jt. auth. see Flamholtz, Eric G.

Das, T. K., jt. ed. see Flamholtz, Eric G.

Das, V. Balamohan. Rural Banks & Rural Credit. (C). 1991. 46.00 (*81-7141-120-7*) S Asia.

Das, Varsha. Traditional Performing Arts. (C). 1992. 15.00 (*81-224-0407-3*) S Asia.

D

An Asterisk (*) at the beginning of an entry indicates that the title is appearing for the first time.

Das, Veena. Critical Events: An Anthropological Perspective on Contemporary India. 240p. 1997. pap. text 10.95 (*0-19-564052-7*) OUP.

***Das, Veena.** Violence & Subjectivity. LC 99-55800. (Illus.). 374p. 2000. 50.00 (*0-520-21607-5*, Pub. by U CA Pr); pap. 19.95 (*0-520-21608-3*, Pub. by U CA Pr) Cal Prin Full Svc.

***Das, Veena, et al.** Tradition, Pluralism & Identity: In Honour of T. N. Madan. LC 99-46675. (Contributions to Indian Sociology Ser.). 1999. write for info. (*0-7619-9381-9*) Sage.

Das, Victor. Jharkhand: Castle over the Graves. (Tribal Studies of India Series T: No. 155). (C). 1992. 27.50 (*81-210-0298-2*, Pub. by Inter-India Pubns) S Asia.

dasa, Adiraja. The Hare Krishna Book of Vegetarian Cooking. (Illus.). 318p. 1990. 19.95 (*0-902677-07-1*, HKVC) Bhaktivedanta.

Dasa, Amala-Bhakta. The Life of Tulasei Devei & Her Care & Worship. LC 98-175273. xvii, 100 p. 1997. write for info. (*0-89213-315-5*) BBT Sci Bks.

Dasa, Anadi K., jt. auth. see Arun.

Dasa, Banu, tr. see Thakur, Bhaktivinoda.

Dasa, Drutakarma & Goswami, Mukunda D. Divine Nature: A Spiritual Perspective on the Environmental Crisis. LC 95-5867. (Illus.). 108p. 1995. mass mkt. 4.95 (*0-89213-296-5*, DNM) Bhaktivedanta.

Dasa, Gaur K. Arcana-Paddhati: The Perfection of Deity Worship. 250p. 1993. pap. 14.95 (*1-889756-27-X*) Sanskrit Relgns Inst.

Dasa, Haridhama, jt. auth. see Goswami, Sripada D.

dasa, Kurma. Great Vegetarian Dishes: Over 240 Recipes from Around the World. (Illus.). 192p. 1990. 19.95 (*0-9593659-1-5*, VD, Pub. by Mandala Pub Grp) Words Distrib.

Dasa, Ravindra Svarupa, see Tamal Krishna Goswami & Svarupa Dasa, Ravindra.

Dasa, Shukavak. Hindu Encounter with Modernity: Kedarnath Datta Bhaktivinada, Vaisnava Theologian. rev. ed. LC 97-2565. (Illus.). 368p. 1999. 24.95 (*1-889756-30-X*) Sanskrit Relgns Inst.

Dasabodhisattappattikatha. Birth Stories of the Ten Bodhisattvas. Saddhatissa, Ven H., tr. from PLI. (C). 1975. 33.00 (*0-86013-089-4*, Pub. by Pali Text) Elsevier.

Dasan, Vima. His Word Lives: Sunday Homilies for Years A. B. C. 448p. 1996. pap. 39.95 (*0-85439-526-1*, Pub. by St Paul Pubns) St Mut.

Dasannacharya, B. A. & Wadnawan, V. K., eds. Y-Ba-Cu-O & Related Superconductors: Current Indian Work: A Special Issue of the Journal Phase Transitions, Section B. 146p. 1989. pap. 290.00 (*0-685-47166-7*) Gordon & Breach.

Dasarathy, Belur V., ed. Image Data Compression: Block Truncation Coding. LC 94-45993. 304p. 1995. pap. 50.00 (*0-8186-6847-4*, BP06847) IEEE Comp Soc.

— Sensor Fusion: Architecture, Algorithms & Applications. LC 98-119961. 27p. 1997. pap. 59.00 (*0-8194-2482-X*) SPIE.

***Dasarathy, Belur V., ed.** Sensor Fusion: Architectures, Algorithms & Applications 2. LC 98-184505. 250p. 1998. 59.00 (*0-8194-2825-6*) SPIE.

***Dasarathy, Belur V. & Society of Photo-optical Instrumentation Engineers.** Data Mining & Knowledge Discovery: Theory, Tools, & Technology: 5-6 April 1999, Orlando, Florida. LC 99-227065. (Illus.). 244p. 1999. 62.00 (*0-8194-3169-9*) SPIE.

Dasberg, S. & Or, Dani. Drip Irrigation. LC 98-55477. (Applied Agriculture Ser.). 190p. 1999. 139.00 (*3-540-65122-5*) Spr-Verlag.

Dascal, Marcelo. Cultural Relativism & Philosophy: North & Latin American Perspectives. LC 91-23928. (PHC Ser.: No. 7). xii, 316p. 1991. 114.50 (*90-04-09433-4*) Brill Academic Pubs.

— Leibniz, Language, Signs & Thought: A Collection of Essays. LC 86-15017. (Foundations of Semiotics Ser.: No. 10). xi, 203p. 1987. 59.00 (*90-272-3280-6*) J Benjamins Pubng Co.

— Pragmatics & the Philosophy of Mind Vol. 1: Thought in Language. (Pragmatics & Beyond Ser.: iv: 1). xii, 207p. 1983. pap. 59.00 (*90-272-2503-6*) J Benjamins Pubng Co.

Dascal, Marcelo, ed. Dialogue: An-Interdisciplinary Approach. LC 84-24202. (Pragmatics & Beyond Companion Ser.: No. 1). xiv, 473p. 1985. 130.00 (*0-915027-47-X*) J Benjamins Pubng Co.

Dascal, Marcelo, et al, eds. Sprachphilosophie - Philosophy of Language - La Philosophie Du Langage: An International Handbook of Contemporary Research. (Handbooks of Linguistics & Communication Science: No. 7.1). (ENG, FRE & GER.). xxxvi, 872p. (C). 1992. lib. bdg. 523.10 (*3-11-009583-1*) De Gruyter.

— Sprachpilosophie - Philosophy of Language - La Philosohie du Language Vol. 2: Ein Internationales Handbuch Zeitgenoessischer Forschung, an International Handbook of Contemporary Research Manuel International des Recherches Contemporaines. (Handbooks of Linguistics & Communication Science: Bd. 7.2). (ENG, FRE & GER.). xii, 1216p. (C). 1995. lib. bdg. 676.95 (*3-11-013991-X*) De Gruyter.

Dascal, Marcelo, jt. ed. see Cohen, Avner.

Dascalu, D. Transit Time Effects in Unipolar Solid-State Devices. (Abacus Bks.). xviii, 396p. 1974. text 112.00 (*0-85626-007-X*) Gordon & Breach.

Dasch, Clement E. Ichneumon-Flies of America North of Mexico, Pt. 10Subfamily Banchinae, Tribe Glyptini. (Memoir Ser.: No. 43). (Illus.). 644p. 1988. 75.00 (*1-56665-042-9*) Assoc Pubs FL.

— The Ichneumon-Flies of America North of Mexico, Pt. 12 Subfamilies Microleptinae, Helictinae, Cylloceriinae & Oxytorinae (Hymenoptera - Ichneumonidae) (Memoirs of the American Entomological Institute Ser.: No. 52). (Illus.). iv, 470p. 1992. 60.00 (*1-56665-052-6*) Assoc Pubs FL.

— Ichneumon-Flies of America North of Mexico, Pt. 5 Subfamily Diplazontinae. (Memoir Ser.: No. 3). (Illus.). 1964. 45.00 (*1-56665-002-X*) Assoc Pubs FL.

— Ichneumon-Flies of America North of Mexico, Pt. 8 Subfamily Cremastinae. (Memoir Ser.: No. 29). (Illus.). 702p. 1979. 75.00 (*1-56665-027-5*) Assoc Pubs FL.

— Ichneumon-Flies of America North of Mexico, Pt. 9 Subfamilies Theriinae & Anomaloninae. (Memoir Ser.: No. 36). 610p. 1984. 65.00 (*1-56665-034-8*) Assoc Pubs FL.

— Ichneumonidae of America North of Mexico, Pt. 6 Subfamily Mesochorinae. (Memoir Ser.: No. 16). (Illus.). 376p. 1971. 45.00 (*1-56665-014-3*) Assoc Pubs FL.

— Neotropic Mesochorinae (Hymenoptera - Icheumonidae) (Memoir Ser.: No. 22). (Illus.). 509p. 1974. 50.00 (*1-56665-020-8*) Assoc Pubs FL.

Dasch, Deborah. An Introduction to Court Reporter Technology. Wacht, Peter, ed. 339p. 1997. pap. 29.95 (*1-881859-21-5*) Natl Ct Report.

Dasch, Deborah, jt. auth. see Finney, Martha.

Dasch, Deborah A., jt. auth. see Finney, Martha I.

Dasch, E. Julius. Earth Science for Students, 4 Vols. LC 99-26905. 781p. 1999. write for info. (*0-02-865308-4*) Macmillan.

Daschbach, Edwin G., ed. Photo Essay: This Land Is Home to Me: A Pastoral Letter on Powerlessness in Appalachia by the Catholic Bishops of the Region. (Illus.). 160p. 1998. pap. 13.00 (*0-9664525-0-X*) Soc of Divine Word.

Dascher. Multiplan Managerial Accountng. (C). 1993. text 45.00 (*0-03-003708-5*) Harcourt Coll Pubs.

Dascher, jt. auth. see Brenner.

Daschner, Dominik. Die Gedruckten Mebbucher Suddeutschlands Bis zur Ubernahme des Missale Romanum Pius V. (1570) (Regensburger Studien Zur Theologie Ser.: Bd. 47). (GER., Illus.). LVII, 682p. 1994. 97.95 (*3-631-47990-5*) P Lang Pubng.

Dasef, John R., jt. auth. see Teller, Albert E.

Dasef, John W. History of Montcalm County: Its People, Industries & Institutions, 2 vols. (Illus.). 1185p. 1997. reprint ed. lib. bdg. 115.00 (*0-8328-6776-4*) Higginson Bk Co.

Daseler, Robert. Levering Avenue. LC 98-38948. x, 70p. 1998. 15.00 (*0-930982-50-9*); pap. 10.00 (*0-930982-51-7*) U of Evansville Pr.

Dasen, Veronique. Dwarfs in Ancient Egypt & Greece. LC 92-35446. (Oxford Monographs on Classical Archaeology). (Illus.). 384p. 1994. text 110.00 (*0-19-814699-X*) OUP.

Dasenbrock, Reed W. Imitating the Italians: Wyatt, Spenser, Synge, Pound, Joyce. LC 90-23519. 304p. 1991. text 38.50 (*0-8018-4147-X*) Johns Hopkins.

— The Literary Vorticism of Ezra Pound & Wyndham Lewis: Towards the Condition of Painting. LC 84-20179. 284p. 1985. reprint ed. pap. 88.10 (*0-608-03649-8*, 206447500009) Bks Demand.

Dasenbrock, Reed W., ed. Literary Theory after Davidson. LC 92-14885. 336p. (C). 1993. 50.00 (*0-271-00895-4*); pap. 19.95 (*0-271-00898-9*) Pa St U Pr.

Dasenbrock, Reed W., jt. ed. see Jussawalla, Feroza.

Dasenbrook, Norman C. & Mastroianni, Michael D. Harnessing the Power of Conflict: Business & Family. 2nd ed. 224p. (Orig.). 1997. pap. text 14.95 (*0-9643949-1-X*) Crysand Pr.

Dasenbrook, Norman C., jt. auth. see Mastroianni, Michael D.

Dasent, Arthur I. Nell Gwyn, 1650-1687. LC 70-82824. 1972. 24.95 (*0-405-08432-3*, Pub. by Blom Pubns) Ayer.

Dasent, G. W., tr. see Vigfusson, Gudbrand, ed.

Dasent, George W. East o' the Sun & West o' the Moon. LC 70-97214. (Illus.). 418p. (J). (gr. 1 up). 1970. reprint ed. pap. 8.95 (*0-486-22521-6*) Dover.

Dasent, George W., tr. see Asbjornsen, Peter C.

Dasent, George W., tr. see Lewis, Naomi, ed.

Dasent, W. E. Nonexistent Compounds: Compounds of Low Stability. LC 65-27436. 191p. reprint ed. pap. 59.30 (*0-608-30362-3*, 205503500008) Bks Demand.

Dasey, Diana. Beginner's Book of Breadmaking. 1996. pap. text 15.95 (*0-86417-767-4*, Pub. by Kangaroo Pr) Seven Hills Bk.

Dasgupta, A. K. Use & Misuse of People: The Indian Case. (C). 1989. 30.00 (*81-7018-550-5*, Pub. by BR Pub) S Asia.

Dasgupta, Abhijit. Growth with Equity: The New Technology & Agrarian Change in Bengal LC 98-909704. 180p. 1998. write for info. (*81-7304-245-4*) Manohar.

Dasgupta, Ajit K. Gandhi's Economic Thought. LC 96-10733. (Studies in the History of Economics). 224p. (C). 1996. 80.00 (*0-415-11430-6*) Routledge.

DasGupta, Amit, jt. ed. see Murty, K. Satchidananda.

DasGupta, Amit, ed. see Symposium on High Temp. Superconducting Oxides Pro.

Dasgupta, Atis K. Fakir & Sannyasi Uprisings. (C). 1992. 12.00 (*81-7074-109-2*) S Asia.

Dasgupta, Avijit, jt. auth. see Nemerow, Nelson L.

DasGupta, B. R. Botulinum & Tetanus Neurotoxins: Neurotransmission & Biomedical Aspects. LC 93-3845. (Illus.). 708p. (C). 1993. text 165.00 (*0-306-44412-7*, Kluwer Plenum) Kluwer Academic.

Dasgupta, Bidhu B. Trilingual Dictionary: Hindi - Bengali - English. 1991. 29.95 (*0-8288-8433-1*) Fr & Eur.

Dasgupta, Biplab. Oil Industry in India. 257p. 1971. 37.50 (*0-7146-2583-3*, Pub. by F Cass Pubs) Intl Spec Bk.

— Structural Adjustment, Global Trade & the New Political Economy of Development. 384p. 1999. text 69.95 (*1-85649-595-7*); text 25.00 (*1-85649-596-5*) Zed Books.

Dasgupta, Biplab, ed. Village Studies in the Third World. 400p. 1978. 39.95 (*0-87855-303-7*) Transaction Pubs.

Dasgupta, Biplab & Morris-Jones, W. H. Patterns & Themes in Indian Politics. 364p. 1975. 16.95 (*0-318-36596-0*) Asia Bk Corp.

Dasgupta, Biplab, et al. Village Society & Labour Use. (Illus.). 1977. text 6.95 (*0-19-560795-3*) OUP.

Dasgupta, D., ed. Artificial Immune Systems & Their Applications. LC 98-35558. 350p. 1998. 54.95 (*3-540-64390-7*) Spr-Verlag.

Dasgupta, D. & Michalewicz, Zbigniew. Evolutionary Algorithms in Engineering Applications. LC 97-7264. 552p. 1997. 69.95 (*3-540-62021-4*) Spr-Verlag.

Dasgupta, Dipankar. The Macroeconomy: A Textbook View. (Illus.). 234p. 1998. text 8.95 (*0-19-564306-2*) OUP.

Dasgupta, Gautam, jt. auth. see Marranca, Bonnie.

Dasgupta, Gautam, jt. ed. see Marranca, Bonnie.

Dasgupta, J. N. Bengal in the Sixteenth Century A. D. 1989. reprint ed. 26.00 (*81-85326-11-8*) S Asia.

Dasgupta, K. K., et al, eds. Studies in Ancient Indian History: (D. C. Sircar Commemoration Volume) (C). 1988. 110.00 (*81-85067-10-4*, Pub. by Sundeep Prak) S Asia.

Dasgupta, Kalyan K. Wood Carvings of Eastern India. (C). 1990. text 60.00 (*0-8364-2621-5*, Pub. by Firma KLM) S Asia.

***DasGupta, Minakshie.** Bangia Ranna: The Bengal Cookbook. 2nd rev. ed. 1998. 20.00 (*81-7476-205-1*, Pub. by UBS Pubs) S Asia.

Dasgupta, Nandini. Petty Trading in the Third World: The Case of Calcutta. 374p. 1992. 82.95 (*1-85628-270-8*, Pub. by Avebry) Ashgate Pub Co.

Dasgupta, Partha. The Control of Resources. (Illus.). 240p. 1983. 37.95 (*0-674-16980-8*) HUP.

— Environmental & Resource Economics in the World of the Poor. LC 97-50282. 40p. 1998. pap. text 9.95 (*0-915707-91-8*) Resources Future.

— An Inquiry into Well-Being & Destitution. (Illus.). 680p. 1995. pap. text 32.00 (*0-19-828835-2*) OUP.

Dasgupta, Partha, ed. Population, Economic Development, & the Environment. (Illus.). 312p. 1994. 35.00 (*0-19-828950-2*) OUP.

Dasgupta, Partha, et al, eds. Economic Analysis of Markets & Games: Essays in Honor of Frank Hahn. (Illus.). 656p. 1992. 76.50 (*0-262-04127-8*) MIT Pr.

— The Economics of Transnational Commons. LC 96-52403. (Illus.). 332p. 1998. text 87.00 (*0-19-829220-1*) OUP.

Dasgupta, Partha & Maler, Karl-Goran, eds. The Environment & Emerging Development Issues, Vol. 1. (WIDER Studies in Development Economics). (Illus.). 288p. 1997. text 55.00 (*0-19-828767-4*) OUP.

— The Environment & Emerging Development Issues, Vol. 2. (WIDER Studies in Development Economics). (Illus.). 358p. 1997. text 75.00 (*0-19-828768-2*) OUP.

Dasgupta, Partha S. & Heal, G. M. Economic Theory & Exhaustible Resources. LC 79-51749. (Cambridge Economic Handbook Ser.). 516p. 1980. pap. text 33.95 (*0-521-29761-3*) Cambridge U Pr.

Dasgupta, Rajaram. Nutritional Planning in India. (C). 1989. 27.50 (*81-7013-049-2*, Pub. by Navarang) S Asia.

Dasgupta, S. Yoga As Philosophy & Religion. 1974. lib. bdg. 300.00 (*0-87968-104-7*) Krishna Pr.

Dasgupta, S. N. Hindu Mysticism. 168p. 1987. reprint ed. pap. 6.95 (*81-208-0304-3*, Pub. by Motilal Bnarsidass) S Asia.

— Hindu Mysticism. 168p. 1987. reprint ed. 11.00 (*81-208-0303-5*) St Mut.

— Yoga Philosophy: In Relation to Other Systems of Indian Thought. (C). 1997. 30.00 (*81-208-0909-2*, Pub. by Motilal Bnarsidass) S Asia.

Dasgupta, Samira. Birjia: Society & Culture. (C). 1994. text 28.00 (*81-7102-018-6*, Pub. by Firma KLM) S Asia.

Dasgupta, Samira & Sarkar, Amitabha. Frontiers of Social Anthropology. (Illus.). 150p. 1996. 18.00 (*81-212-0528-X*, Pub. by Gyan Publishing Hse) Nataraj Bks.

Dasgupta, Satadal. The Community in Canada: Rural & Urban. LC 95-39579. 378p. (C). 1996. pap. text 39.50 (*0-7618-0209-6*); lib. bdg. 66.50 (*0-7618-0208-8*) U Pr of Amer.

— Rural Canada: Structure & Change. LC 87-21644. (Canadian Studies: Vol. 3). 232p. 1987. lib. bdg. 89.95 (*0-88946-196-1*) E Mellen.

Dasgupta, Sathi. On the Trail of an Uncertain Dream: Indian Immigrant Experience in America. LC 88-46198. (Immigrant Communities & Ethnic Minorities in the U. S. & Canada Ser.: No. 38). 1989. 47.00 (*0-404-19448-6*) AMS Pr.

DasGupta, Sayantani & Dasgupta, Shamita D. The Demon Slayers & Other Stories: Bengali Folk Tales. LC 94-1706. (International Folk Tale Ser.). 224p. 1994. 24.95 (*1-56656-164-7*); pap. 12.95 (*1-56656-156-6*) Interlink Pub.

Dasgupta, Sayantari. Her Own Medicine: A Woman's Journey from Student to Doctor. 1999. mass mkt. 5.99 (*0-449-00309-4*) Fawcett.

Dasgupta, Shahana. This India. (C). 1993. 14.00 (*81-7167-159-4*, Pub. by Rupa) S Asia.

DasGupta, Shamita D., ed. A Patchwork Shawl: Chronicles of South Asian Women in America. LC 97-49650. 256p. (C). 1998. text 49.00 (*0-8135-2517-9*); pap. text 19.00 (*0-8135-2518-7*) Rutgers U Pr.

Dasgupta, Shamita D., jt. auth. see DasGupta, Sayantani.

Dasgupta, Subrata. Creativity in Invention & Design: Computational & Cognitive Explorations of Technological Originality. LC 93-28650. (Illus.). 268p. (C). 1994. text 44.95 (*0-521-43068-2*) Cambridge U Pr.

— Design Theory & Computer Science. (Cambridge Tracts in Theoretical Computer Science Ser.: No. 15). 448p. (C). 1991. text 80.00 (*0-521-39021-4*) Cambridge U Pr.

— Jagadis Chandra Bose & the Indian Response to Western Science. (Illus.). 272p. 2000. text 29.95 (*0-19-564874-9*) OUP.

Dasgupta, Sugata. Towards a Philosophy of Social Work in India. 272p. 1967. 59.50 (*0-614-01823-4*) Elliots Bks.

Dasgupta, Surama. Development of Moral Philosophy in India. 256p. (C). 1994. reprint ed. 27.50 (*81-215-0627-1*, Pub. by M Manoharial) Coronet Bks.

Dasgupta, Surendranath. Mahabhasya of Patanjali. (C). 1991. 20.00 (*81-215-0530-5*, Pub. by M Manoharial) Coronet Bks.

— Natural Science of the Ancient Hindus. Chattopadhyaya, Debiprasad, ed. 99p. (C). 1987. 9.50 (*81-208-0329-9*, Pub. by Motilal Bnarsidass) S Asia.

— Philosophical Essays. 1990. reprint ed. 29.00 (*81-208-0750-2*, Pub. by Motilal Bnarsidass) S Asia.

— A Study of Patanjali. 2nd ed. (C). 1989. 18.00 (*81-208-0452-X*, Pub. by Motilal Bnarsidass) S Asia.

— Yoga As Philosophy & Religion. 200p. 1978. 15.95 (*0-318-37199-5*) Asia Bk Corp.

— Yoga As Philosophy & Religion. (C). 1995. reprint ed. 18.50 (*81-208-0217-9*, Pub. by Motilal Bnarsidass) S Asia.

Dasgupta, Tapati. Social Thought of Rabindranath Tagore: A Historical Analysis. (C). 1993. 24.00 (*81-7017-302-7*, Pub. by Abhinav) S Asia.

Dash, Baidya B. Fundamentals of Ayurvedic Medicine. (C). 1996. reprint ed. 14.00 (*81-220-0026-6*, Pub. by Konark Pubs) S Asia.

Dash, Barbara, ed. see Dunskaya, Irina.

Dash, Barbara, ed. see Goldberg, Mark.

Dash, Barbara, ed. see Yevsikov, Victor.

Dash, Barbara, ed. see Zamascikov, Sergei.

Dash, Barbara L. A Defector Reports: The Institute of the U. S. A. & Canada. 229p. (Orig.). 1982. pap. text 100.00 (*1-55831-061-4*) Delphic Associates.

Dash, Bhagavan D. Ayurvedic Cures for Common Diseases. 161p. (Orig.). 1986. pap. text 9.95 (*0-89744-055-2*) Auromere.

Dash, Bhagwan. Encyclopedia of Tibetan Medicine: Being the Tibetan Text of Rgyud Bzi & Sanskrit Restoration of Amrta Htrdaya Arsteagnga Guhyopadebsa Tantra & Expository Translation in English / LC 94-900815. (Indian Medical Science Ser.). (ENG & TIB.). 1994. 58.00 (*81-7030-397-4*) S Asia.

— Hand Book of Ayurveda: The Indian System of Medicine. 144p. 1987. 14.95 (*0-318-36356-9*) Asia Bk Corp.

Dash, Bhagwan & Kashyap, Lalitesh. Basic Principles of Ayurveda. (Illus.). 628p. 1980. 70.00 (*0-940500-34-5*) Asia Bk Corp.

— Materia Medica of Ayurveda. (C). 1988. 64.00 (*0-8364-2325-9*, Pub. by Concept) S Asia.

Dash, G. N. Hindus & Tribals: Quest for a Co-Existence, Social Dynamics in Medieval Orissa. LC 98-908467. xiv, 140p. 1998. 15.00 (*81-86921-01-X*, Pub. by Decent Bks) Nataraj Bks.

Dash, Helen. Brisbane - Our Town: A Century of Photographs. (Illus.). 218p. 1988. text 24.95 (*0-7022-2127-9*, Pub. by Univ Queensland Pr) Intl Spec Bk.

Dash, Irene G. Women's Worlds in Shakespeare's Plays. LC 96-2686. (Illus.). 304p. 1997. 45.00 (*0-87413-599-0*) U Delaware Pr.

Dash, J. G., et al, eds. Ice Physics & the Natural Environment. LC 98-48081. (Illus.). xvi, 355p. 1999. 198.00 (*3-540-65155-1*) Spr-Verlag.

***Dash, J. Michael.** Culture & Customs of Haiti. LC 00-33126. (Culture & Customs of Latin America & the Caribbean Ser.). 2000. write for info. (*0-313-30498-X*, Greenwood Pr) Greenwood.

Dash, J. Michael. Edouard Glissant. (Studies in African & Caribbean Literature: No. 3). 214p. (C). 1995. pap. text 19.95 (*0-521-47550-3*) Cambridge U Pr.

— The Other America: Caribbean Literature in a New World Context. LC 97-38884. (New World Studies Ser.). 224p. 1998. text 42.50 (*0-8139-1763-8*); pap. text 18.50 (*0-8139-1764-6*) U Pr of Va.

Dash, J. Michael, tr. & intro. see Glissant, Edouard.

Dash, Joan. The Longitude Prize: The Race Between the Moon & the Watch-Machine. LC 97-44257. (Illus.). 208p. 2000. 16.00 (*0-374-34636-4*) FS&G.

— The Triumph of Discovery: Women Scientists Who Won the Nobel Prize. 160p. (YA). (gr. 9 up). 1990. pap. 8.95 (*0-671-69333-6*, Julian Messner) Silver Burdett Pr.

— We Shall Not Be Moved: The Women's Factory Strike of 1909. LC 95-19404. (Illus.). 166p. (J). (gr. 3-7). 1996. 15.95 (*0-590-48409-5*) Scholastic Inc.

— We Shall Not Be Moved: The Women's Factory Strike of 1909. (J). 1998. pap. 5.99 (*0-590-48410-9*) Scholastic Inc.

— We Shall Not Be Moved: The Women's Factory Strike of 1909. 1998. 11.09 (*0-606-13892-7*, Pub. by Turtleback) Demco.

Dash, Judi & Schensul, Jill. Country Roads of New Jersey. (Country Roads Ser.). 192p. pap. 12.95 (*0-658-00179-5*, Cntry Rds Pr) NTC Contemp Pub Co.

Dash, Judi & Schensul, Jill. Country Roads of New Jersey. 2nd ed. LC 96-31091. (Country Roads Ser.). (Illus.). 140p. 1996. pap. 10.95 (*1-56626-173-2*, Cntry Rds Pr) NTC Contemp Pub Co.

Dash, Julie. Daughters of the Dust. 320p. 1999. pap. 13.95 (*0-452-27607-1*, Plume) Dutton Plume.

Dash, Julie, et al. Daughters of the Dust: The Making of an African American Woman's Film. LC 92-50333. (Illus.). 192p. 1992. 27.95 (*1-56584-029-1*, Pub. by New Press NY); pap. 18.95 (*1-56584-030-5*, Pub. by New Press NY) Norton.

Dash, Keshab C. Logic of Knowledge Base. (C). 1992. 12.00 (*81-7030-346-X*) S Asia.

Dash, Kimberly, et al. Discharge Planning for the Elderly: A Guide for Nurses. LC 95-25626. (Illus.). 280p. 1996. 35.95 (*0-8261-9230-0*) Springer Pub.

D

An Asterisk (*) at the beginning of an entry indicates that the title is appearing for the first time.

Dash, L. N. Women, Family Life, & Rural Welfare. (Illus.). 202p. 1993. 22.00 (81-85445-45-1, Pub. by Manak Pubns Pvt Ltd) Nataraj Bks.

Dash, Leon. Rosa Lee: A Mother & Her Family in Urban America. LC 96-19403. (Illus.). 224p. 1996. 23.00 (0-465-07092-2, Pub. by Basic) HarpC.

— Rosa Lee: A Mother & Her Family in Urban America. LC 97-11543. 288p. 1997. pap. 13.95 (0-452-27896-1) NAL.

Dash, M. C. & Kar, C. S., eds. The Turtle Paradise-Gahirmatha: (An Ecological Analysis & Conservation Strategy) 300p. (C). 1990. 500.00 (81-85017-48-4, Pub. by Interprint) St Mut.

Dash, Michael, jt. ed. see Arthur, Charles B.

Dash, Michael, tr. see Glissant, Edouard.

Dash, Michael, tr. see Pineau, Gisele.

Dash, Michael I., et al. Hidden Wholeness: An African American Spirituality for Individuals & Communities. LC 97-3691. 184p. (Orig.). 1997. pap. 14.95 (0-8298-1164-8) Pilgrim OH.

***Dash, Mike.** Borderlands. 2000. mass mkt. 6.99 (0-440-23656-8) Dell.

Dash, Mike. Borderlands: The Ultimate Exploration of the Unknown. LC 99-37203. 520p. 1999. 27.95 (0-87951-724-7, Pub. by Overlook Pr) Penguin Putnam.

***Dash, Mike.** Tulipomania: The Story of the World's Most Coveted Flower & the Extraordinary Passions It Aroused. LC 99-39186. 288p. 2000. 23.00 (0-609-60439-2, Crown) Crown Pub Group.

— Tulipomania: The Story of the World's Most Coveted Flower & the Extraordinary Passions It Aroused. 2001. reprint ed. pap. 12.00 (0-609-80765-X, Three Riv Pr) Crown Pub Group.

Dash, Narendra K. Purusottamadeva as Grammarian. (C). 1991. 22.00 (0-685-56362-6, Pub. by Agam) S Asia.

— Survey on Sanskrit Grammar in Tibetan Language. (C). 1993. 32.00 (81-7320-011-4, Pub. by Agam) S Asia.

Dash, Nilakanth, jt. auth. see All India Symposium on Veastu.

Dash, Paul. Traditions from the Caribbean. LC 98-23306. (Cultural Journeys Ser.). (J). 1999. 25.69 (0-8172-5384-X) Raintree Steck-V.

***Dash, Robert.** Notes from Madoo: Making a Garden in the Hamptons. LC 00-20062. 256p. 2000. 24.00 (0-618-01692-9) HM.

***Dash, S. K., et al.** Health Benefits of Probiotics. LC 99-45795. (Health Learning Handbook Ser.). 56p. 1999. pap. write for info. (1-890766-10-0, Pub. by B L Pubns) Nutri-Books Corp.

Dash, Samuel, et al. Eavesdroppers. LC 71-136498. (Civil Liberties in American History Ser.). (Illus.). 1971. reprint ed. lib. bdg. 35.00 (0-306-70074-3) Da Capo.

Dash, Subas C. Gangesa on Yogarudhi: Containing the Original Text of the Yogarudhivada of the Sabdakhanda of the Tattvacintamani with Its English Translation & a Detailed Introduction. (Sri Garib Dass Oriental Ser.: No. 163). xv, 205p. (C). 1992. 18.00 (81-7030-354-0) S Asia.

Dash, Tora. Chinese Fortunes - Straight from the Cookie. Dash, Turock, ed. 69p. 1996. pap. 5.95 (1-890081-32-9) T D Publng.

— Counting & Coloring Animals. Dash, Turock, ed. 44p. (J). (ps-k). 1996. pap. 3.95 (1-890081-39-6) T D Publng.

— 50 Thoughts That Will Help You Through Life!! Dash, Turock, ed. 53p. 1996. pap. 5.95 (1-890081-64-7) T D Publng.

Dash, Turock. The Milooka Chronicles, Bk. 1. 126p. (J). (gr. 3-8). 1996. pap. 3.95 (1-890081-57-4) T D Publng.

Dash, Turock, ed. see Dash, Tora.

Dash, Vaidya B. Formulary of Tibetan Medicine. (C). 1988. 72.00 (81-85132-04-6, Pub. by Classics India Pubns) S Asia.

— Fundamentals of Ayurvedic Medicine. 245p. 1984. text 20.00 (0-89744-052-8) Auromere.

— Fundamentals of Ayurvedic Medicine. 2nd ed. 246p. (C). 1987. text 21.95 (0-940500-05-1) Asia Bk Corp.

— Fundamentals of Ayurvedic Medicine. 7th rev. ed. 200p. 1990. text 27.50 (81-220-0117-3) Konark Pubs Pvt Ltd.

— Materia Medica of Indo-Tibetan Medicine. 647p. (C). 1987. 64.00 (81-85132-00-3, Pub. by Classics India Pubns) S Asia.

— Materia Medica of Tibetan Medicine. LC 93-908512. (C). 1994. 98.00 (81-7030-387-7, Pub. by Sri Satguru Pubns) S Asia.

— Pharmacopoeia of Tibetan Medicine. LC 93-908824. (C). 1994. 34.00 (81-7030-388-5, Pub. by Sri Satguru Pubns) S Asia.

— Tibetan Medicine: Theory & Practice. (C). 1997. 20.00 (81-7030-519-5, Pub. by Sri Satguru Pubns) S Asia.

Dash, Vaidya B. & Junius, Acarya M. Handbook of Ayurveda. 221p. (Orig.). 1983. text 10.95 (0-89744-053-6) Auromere.

Dash, Vaidya B. & Kashyap, Lalitesh. Diagnosis & Treatment of Diseases in Ayurveda, Pt. 4. 1987. 58.00 (81-7022-024-6, Pub. by Concept) S Asia.

Dash, Vaidya B. & Kashyap, Vaidya L. Iatro-Chemistry of Ayurveda (Rasa Sastra) LC 94-907330. (C). 1995. 44.00 (81-7022-527-2, Pub. by Concept) S Asia.

Dash, Vaidya B., tr. see Charaka.

Dash, Vaidya Bhagwan. Massage Therapy in Ayurveda. (Pancakarma Therapy of Ayurveda Ser.: No. 1). (C). 1992. 21.00 (81-7022-380-6, Pub. by Concept) S Asia.

Dashe, Alfred. The Men's Health Sourcebook: Everything You Need to Know. 288p. 1996. 25.00 (1-56565-465-X) Lowell Hse.

Dashe, Alfred M. Man's Health Sourcebook. 2nd ed. LC 99-43149. (Illus.). 288p. 1999. pap. 17.95 (0-7373-0109-0, 01090W) NTC Contemp Pub Co.

— The Man's Health Sourcebook. 2nd ed. (Illus.). 288p. 1997. reprint ed. pap. 15.00 (1-56565-813-2, Anodyne) Lowell Hse.

Dashefsky, A., et al. Americans Abroad: A Comparative Study of Emigrants from the United States. (Environment, Development, & Public Policy: Public Policy & Social Services Ser.). (Illus.). 184p. (C). 1991. 35.00 (0-306-43941-7, 589, Plenum Trade) Perseus Pubng.

Dashefsky, Arnold, ed. Contemporary Jewry, Vol. 7. 160p. 1986. 29.95 (0-87855-979-5) Transaction Pubs.

— Contemporary Jewry, Vol. 8. 160p. 1987. 29.95 (0-88738-097-2) Transaction Pubs.

Dashefsky, Arnold & Shapiro, Howard M. Ethnic Identification among American Jews: Socialization & Social Structure. 196p. (C). 1993. reprint ed. pap. text 26.50 (0-8191-8333-4) U Pr of Amer.

Dashefsky, H. Steve. Zoology: High School Science Fair Experiments. LC 94-29631. (Illus.). 160p. (YA). (gr. 9-12). 1994. pap. 12.95 (0-07-015687-5) McGraw-Hill Prof.

Dashefsky, H. Steven. Botany: High-School Science Fair Projects. LC 94-34890. (Illus.). 160p. (YA). (gr. 9-12). 1994. 21.95 (0-07-015684-0) McGraw-Hill Prof.

— Environmental Science: High School Science Fair Experiments. 177p. 1994. pap. 12.95 (0-07-015689-1) McGraw.

— Insect Biology: Forty-Nine Science Fair Projects. (Illus.). 208p. 1994. pap. 10.95 (0-8306-4032-0, 4178) McGraw-Hill Prof.

— Microbiology: High-School Science Fair Experiments. LC 94-23117. (Illus.). 160p. (YA). (gr. 9-12). 1994. 21.95 (0-07-015663-8) McGraw-Hill Prof.

— Zoology: Forty-Nine Science Fair Projects. 169p. (J). (gr. 4-7). 1995. pap. 11.95 (0-07-015683-2) McGraw.

— Zoology: High School Science Fair Experiments. LC 94-29631. (Illus.). 160p. (YA). (gr. 9-12). 1994. 21.95 (0-07-015686-7) McGraw-Hill Prof.

Dashefsky, H. Steven & Cooke, LeRoy. Environmental Science: High School Science Fair Experiments. LC 93-34615. (Illus.). 192p. 1993. pap. text 12.95 (0-8306-4586-1) TAB Bks.

Dashefsky, Helene, ed. see Andre, Joli.

Dasheiff, R. M. & Vincent, D. J., eds. Continuous Wave-Form Analysis. LC 97-101457. (Supplements to Electroencephalography & Clinical Neurophysiology Ser.: 45). 172p. 1996. 149.50 (0-444-82429-4) Elsevier.

Dashek, William V. Methods in Plant Biochemistry & Molecular Biology. LC 96-41196. 480p. 1997. spiral bd., lab manual ed. 99.95 (0-8493-9480-5) CRC Pr.

***Dashek, William V., ed.** Plant Electron Microscopy & Cytochemistry. 300p. 2000. spiral bd. 79.50 (0-89603-809-2) Humana.

Dashek, William V., jt. auth. see Zeidan, Henry.

Dasher, B., et al. Portal Design in Radiation Therapy. 168p. 1994. pap. text 45.00 (0-9642715-0-8) D W V.

Dasher, George R. On Station. (Illus.). 242p. 1994. 17.00 (1-879961-03-2, 07-0008) Natl Speleological.

Dashew, Linda, jt. auth. see Dashew, Steve.

Dashew, Steve & Dashew, Linda. Mariner's Weather Handbook: A Guide to Forecasting & Tactics. LC 98-93808. 594p. 1998. 69.95 (0-9658028-2-5) Beowulf.

Dashew, Steve & Dashew, Linda. Offshore Cruising Encyclopedia, Version II. rev. ed. (Illus.). 1232p. 1997. 109.90 incl. audio compact disk (0-9658028-6-8) Beowulf.

Dashew, Steve & Dashew, Linda. Offshore Cruising Encyclopedia, Version II. 2nd rev. ed. LC 97-72568. (Illus.). 1232p. 1997. 89.95 (0-9658028-1-7) Beowulf.

***Dashew, Steve & Dashew, Linda.** Surviving the Storm: Coastal & Offshore Tactics. LC 99-96375. 675p. 1999. 89.90 incl. audio compact disk (0-9658028-5-X) Beowulf.

— Surviving the Storm: Coastal & Offshore Tactics. LC 99-96376. (Illus.). 675p. 1999. 69.95 (0-9658028-9-2) Beowulf.

Dashiell, Alfred, ed. see Canby, Henry S.

Dashiell, Benjamin J. Dashiell Family Records Vol. III: Some Descendants of George Dashiell of Quantico. 214p. 1995. reprint ed. pap. 34.00 (0-8328-4766-6); reprint ed. lib. bdg. 44.00 (0-8328-4765-8) Higginson Bk Co.

— Dashiell Family Records, (Some Descendants of James Dashiell of Maryland), Vol. 1. (Illus.). 256p. 1997. reprint ed. pap. 39.00 (0-8328-8216-X); reprint ed. lib. bdg. 49.00 (0-8328-8215-1) Higginson Bk Co.

— Dashiell, Family Records, (Some Descendants of Thos. Dashiell of Maryland), Vol. 2. (Illus.). 330p. 1997. reprint ed. pap. 51.00 (0-8328-8218-6); reprint ed. lib. bdg. 61.00 (0-8328-8217-8) Higginson Bk Co.

Dashiell, David C. Invert, Oracle. (Illus.). 108p. (Orig.). 1989. pap. 30.00 (0-9623420-0-9) E J Wagner.

Dashiell, Jackie & Parrott, Wanda S. There's a Spirit in the Kitchen. LC 96-34493. 256p. (Orig.). 2000. pap. 16.95 (1-880090-25-2) Galde Pr.

Dashiell, Sallie, jt. auth. see Bolton, Susan Oakander.

Dashman, T. Laboratory Manual for Human Nutrition. xv, 237p. 1991. pap. text 46.00 (3-7186-0513-9, Harwood Acad Pubs) Gordon & Breach.

Dashman, Theodore & Blocker, Deborah E. Laboratory Manual for Human Nutrition. 2nd ed. 288p. 1996. pap. text 21.00 (3-7186-0608-9, Harwood Acad Pubs) Gordon & Breach.

Dashney, John. The Adventures of Mishka the Mousewere. LC 95-78871. (Illus.). 155p. (Orig.). (J). 1995. pap. 8.95 (0-9641357-2-8) Storm Peak.

— The Adventures of Walter the Weremouse. (Illus.). 164p. (Orig.). (J). (gr. 4-8). 1992. pap. 6.50 (0-9633236-0-1) J Dashney.

— The Adventures of Walter the Weremouse. (Illus.). 176p. (Orig.). (J). 1996. pap. 8.95 (0-9641357-4-4) Storm Peak.

— The Ballad of Big Ben's Boots & Other Tales for Telling. (Illus.). 157p. (Orig.). (J). 1996. pap. 8.95 (0-9641357-3-6) Storm Peak.

— King of Messy Potatoes. (J). 1997. pap. 8.95 (0-9641357-6-0) Storm Peak.

— The Orm. (J). 1998. 12.95 (0-9641357-8-7) Storm Peak.

Dashorst, Gilbert. Plants of the Adelaide Plains & Hills. (Illus.). 224p. 1990. 32.50 (0-86417-323-7, Pub. by Kangaroo Pr) Seven Hills Bk.

Dashow, Cookie & Templeton, Muffin. The Demented Divorcee Cookbook. LC 98-171251. (Illus.). 64p. 1997. pap., per. 6.95 (0-942320-57-3) Am Cooking.

Dashow, Ken. Da-Show Must Go On: Six Short Plays. LC 98-178306. Orig. Title: Six Plays by Ken Dashow. 1996. pap. 5.25 (0-8222-1535-7) Dramatists Play.

Dashti, Ali. Twenty Three Years: A Study of the Prophetic Career of Mohammad. Bagley, F. R., tr. from PER. 224p. (Orig.). 1985. 29.95 (0-04-297048-2) Routledge.

— Twenty Three Years: A Study of the Prophetic Career of Mohammad. Bagley, F. R., tr. from PER. (Bibliotheca Iranica Ser.: No. 2). 246p. (Orig.). (C). 1994. reprint ed. pap. 15.95 (1-56859-029-6) Mazda Pubs.

***Dashwood, Alan & Ward, Angela, eds.** The Cambridge Yearbook of European Legal Studies Vol. 1: 1998. 320p. 1999. 90.00 (1-84113-088-5, Pub. by Hart Pub) Intl Spec Bk.

Dashwood, Alan, et al. A Guide to the Civil Jurisdiction & Judgments Convention. 650p. 1987. 176.00 (90-6544-269-3) Kluwer Law Intl.

— Variable Geometry--A Recipe for Europe: A Monitoring European Integration Report. 190p. (C). 1996. pap. 14.95 (1-898128-22-7) Brookings.

Dashwood, Julie R., ed. Luigi Pirandello: The Theatre of Paradox. LC 97-29102. 300p. 1997. text 89.95 (0-7734-8746-8) E Mellen.

Dashwood, Julie R. & Everson, Jane E., eds. Writers & Performers in Italian Drama, from the Time of Dante to Pirandello: Essays in Honour of G.H. McWilliam. LC 91-26556. (Studies in Theatre Arts: Vol. 1). (Illus.). 204p. 1991. lib. bdg. 89.95 (0-7734-9717-X) E Mellen.

Dasi, Ananda Vrindavana-devi, jt. auth. see Dasi, Kalindi-devi.

***Dasi, Kalindi-devi & Dasi, Ananda Vrindavana-devi.** Sadhu Goes to Govardhana. (Illus.). 32p. (J). (gr. 1-6). 1998. pap. 4.50 (81-87216-10-7) Torchlght Pub.

— Sadhu Goes to the Yamuna. (Illus.). 32p. (J). (gr. 1-6). 1998. pap. 4.95 (81-87216-00-X) Torchlght Pub.

Dasi, Padmavati D. The Gift of Gopal. (Gopal Trilogy Ser.: No. 3). 48p. (J). (gr. k-4). 1999. 14.95 (1-886069-19-0, 1213, Pub. by Mandala Pub Grp) Words Distrib.

— Gopal the Infallible. (Gopal Trilogy Ser.: No. 1). 48p. (J). (gr. k-4). 1999. 14.95 (1-886069-17-4, 1212, Pub. by Mandala Pub Grp) Words Distrib.

— Miraculous Gopal. (Gopal Trilogy Ser.: No. 2). 48p. (J). (gr. k-4). 1999. 14.95 (1-886069-18-2, 1211, Pub. by Mandala Pub Grp) Words Distrib.

DaSilva. Experiencias. (College Spanish). (C). 1990. mass mkt. 41.95 (0-8384-3487-8); mass mkt. 36.95 (0-8384-3488-6); mass mkt., student ed., wbk. ed. 34.95 (0-8384-3490-8) Heinle & Heinle.

Dasilva. Experiencias. (College Spanish Ser.). (C). 1990. suppl. ed. 6.95 (0-8384-3492-4) Heinle & Heinle.

— Spanish: A Short Course. 4th ed. (College Spanish Ser.). (SPA.). (C). 1992. mass mkt., teacher ed. 6.95 (0-8384-5128-4) Heinle & Heinle.

— Spanish: Short Course. 4th ed. (College Spanish Ser.). (C). 1991. suppl. ed. 6.95 (0-8384-3517-3) Heinle & Heinle.

DaSilva, E. J., et al, eds. Biotechnology: Economic & Social Aspects: Issues for Developing Countries. (Illus.). 402p. (C). 1992. text 95.00 (0-521-38473-7) Cambridge U Pr.

— Microbial Technology in the Developing World: An Introduction. (Illus.). 456p. 1988. 65.00 (0-19-854719-6) OUP.

Dasilva, Fabio & Brunsma, David L., eds. All Music: Essays on the Hermeneutics of Music. (Avebury Series in Philosophy). 272p. 1996. text 72.95 (1-85972-360-8, Pub. by Avebry) Ashgate Pub Co.

Dasilva, Fabio B. & Kanjirathinkal, Mathew J. Politics & the End of History: Essays in Post-Modernist Thought. LC 92-32632. (Major Concepts in Politics & Political Theory Ser.). VII, 292p. (C). 1993. 49.95 (0-8204-2033-6) P Lang Pubng.

Dasilva, Fabio B. & Kanjirathinkal, Mathew J., eds. Her Voices: Hermeneutics of the Feminine. 194p. 1996. pap. text 28.50 (0-7618-0311-4); lib. bdg. 49.50 (0-7618-0310-6) U Pr of Amer.

Dasilva, Fabio B., jt. auth. see Pressler, Charles A.

DaSilva, Howard, et al. The Zulu & the Zayda: Manuscript Edition. 1966. pap. 13.00 (0-8222-1296-X) Dramatists Play.

DaSilva, Willard H. New York Domestic Relations Reporter. text 260.00 (0-8205-2083-7) Bender.

DaSilva, Willard H. New York Matrimonial Practice. LC 79-91156. (Practice Systems Library Manual). ring bd. 125.00 (0-317-00469-7) West Group.

— New York Matrimonial Practice. LC 79-91156. (Practice Systems Library Manual). 1993. suppl. ed. 60.00 (0-317-03180-5) West Group.

Daskal, Melvin H. The Sales Representatives' Business & Tax Handbook: How to Run Your Company & How to Sell It. LC 94-2844. 444p. 1994. text 85.00 (0-7863-0312-3, Irwn Prfssnl) McGraw-Hill Prof.

Daskalakis, C. N., ed. Using & Administering an Apollo Network. (Macmillan Computer Science Ser.). (Illus.). 285p. (C). 1989. pap. text 35.00 (0-333-46804-X) Scholium Intl.

Daskaloff, Alexander. Credit Card Debt: Reduce Your Financial Burden in Three Easy Steps. 224p. 1999. mass mkt. 5.99 (0-380-80700-9, Avon Bks) Morrow Avon.

***Daskalogiannakis, John.** Glossary of Orthodontic Terms. Van Der Linden, Frans P. G. M. et al, eds. (Dynamics of Orthodontics Ser.). (Illus.). 284p. 2000. pap. 98.00 incl. audio compact disk (3-87652-760-0, Pub. by Quintessenz Verlags) Quint Pub Co.

Daskarolis, George P. San Francisco's Greek Colony: An Evolution of an Ethnic Community. LC 95-81624. 208p. (Orig.). 1995. pap. 12.95 (1-880971-13-5) Light&Life Pub Co MN.

Daskin, Mark S. Network & Discrete Location: Models, Algorithms & Applications. LC 94-24488. 520p. 1995. 89.95 (0-471-01897-X) Wiley.

Dasmann, Raymond, jt. auth. see Yocom, Charles.

Dasmann, Raymond F. California's Changing Environment. Hundley, Norris, Jr. & Schutz, John A., eds. (Golden State Ser.). (Illus.). 100p. 1981. pap. 12.00 (0-929651-16-2) MTL.

Dasmann, Raymond F. California's Changing Environment. pap. write for info. (0-87835-116-7) Thomson Learn.

Dasmann, Raymond F. Environmental Conservation. 5th ed. LC 83-21767. 496p. (C). 1984. text 81.95 (0-471-89141-X) Wiley.

— Wildlife Biology. 2nd ed. LC 80-19006. 224p. (C). 1981. text 73.95 (0-471-08042-X) Wiley.

Dasmann, Raymond F., et al. Ecological Principles for Economic Development. LC 72-8597. (Illus.). 262p. reprint ed. pap. 81.30 (0-608-18842-5, 203049800069) Bks Demand.

Dasmann, Raymond F., ed. see Leopold, A. Starker, et al.

Dasnois, Alide, tr. see Meillassoux, Claude.

Daso, Dik. Architects of American Air Supremacy: General Hap Arnold & Dr. Theodore von Karman. LC 97-26768. (Illus.). 487p. 1997. pap. 28.00 (1-58566-042-6) Air Univ.

***Daso, Dik Alan.** Hap Arnold & the Evolution of American Airpower. (Illus.). 368p. 2000. 29.95 (1-56098-824-X) Smithsonian.

Daspin, Eileen, jt. auth. see Casella, Cesare.

Daspit, Toby & Weaver, John A., eds. Popular Culture & Critical Pedagogy: Reading, Constructing, Connecting. LC 98-8645. (Pedagogy & Popular Culture Ser.: Vol. 2). 280p. 1998. 60.00 (0-8153-2870-2, SS1163) Garland.

***Daspit, Toby & Weaver, John A., eds.** Popular Culture & Critical Pedagogy: Reading, Constructing, Connecting. (Pedagogy & Popular Culture Ser.: Vol. 2). 232p. (C). 2000. pap. 24.99 (0-8153-3864-3, Falmer Pr) Taylor & Francis.

Dass, Baba H. Guru Purnima Songs. 1988. pap. 2.00 (0-918100-11-9) Sri Rama.

— Jai Ma Kirtan: Songs to the Divine Mother. 1985. pap. 1.25 (0-918100-12-7) Sri Rama.

— Selfless Service: The Spirit of Karma Yoga. (Essays on the Search for Peace in Daily Life Ser.: No. 3). 24p. 1995. pap. 3.00 (0-918100-17-8) Sri Rama.

— Sri Ram Kirtan. 1984. pap. 2.50 (0-918100-13-5) Sri Rama.

***Dass, Baba Hari.** The Yoga Sutras of Patanjali: A Study Guide for Book I Samadhi Pada. Diffenbaugh, Dayanand, ed. (Illus.). 176p. 1999. pap. 16.95 (0-918100-20-8, YS20-B) Sri Rama.

Dass, Bhagwan. Diagnosis & Treatment of Diseases in Ayurveda, Pt. V. 1991. 74.00 (81-7022-348-2, Pub. by Concept) S Asia.

— Diagnosis & Treatment of Diseases in Ayurveda, Vols. 1-3. (C). 1988. 190.00 (0-7855-2281-6, Pub. by Scientific) St Mut.

— A Handbook of Ayurveda. (C). 1988. 55.00 (0-7855-2282-4, Pub. by Scientific) St Mut.

— Materia Medica of Ayurveda. (C). 1988. 75.00 (0-7855-2283-2, Pub. by Scientific) St Mut.

***Dass, Chhabil.** Principles & Practice of Biological Mass Spectrometry. 573p. (C). 2000. 94.95 (0-471-33053-1) Wiley.

Dass, F. A. The Andaman Islands. (C). 1988. reprint ed. 15.00 (81-206-0408-3, Pub. by Asian Educ Servs) S Asia.

Dass, Nirmal. The Avowing of King Arthur: A Modern Verse Translation. LC 86-26656. 126p. (Orig.). (C). 1987. pap. text 15.00 (0-8191-5770-8); lib. bdg. 34.00 (0-8191-5769-4) U Pr of Amer.

***Dass, Nirmal, tr. from HIN.** Songs of the Saints from the Adi Granth. LC 99-54419. (C). 2000. text 59.50 (0-7914-4683-2) State U NY Pr.

***Dass, Nirmal, tr. from HIN.** Songs of the Saints from the Adi Granth. LC 99-54419. 2000. pap. 19.95 (0-7914-4684-0) State U NY Pr.

Dass, Ram. Be Here Now. (Illus.). 380p. 1971. pap. 13.13 (0-517-54305-2) Harmony Bks.

— Journey of Awakening: A Mediator's Guidebook. 448p. 1990. mass mkt. 6.99 (0-553-28572-6) Bantam.

— Miracle of Love: Stories about Neem Karoli Baba. (Illus.). 432p. (Orig.). 1995. reprint ed. pap. 17.95 (1-887474-00-5) Hanuman Found.

— The Only Dance There Is. LC 73-14054. 192p. 1974. pap. 11.95 (0-385-08413-7, Anchor NY) Doubleday.

***Dass, Ram.** Still Here: Embracing Aging, Changing & Dying. LC 99-86015. 224p. 2000. 22.22 (1-57322-049-3, Riverhead Books) Putnam Pub Group.

Dass, Ram & Gorman, Paul. How Can I Help? Stories & Reflections on Service. Lippe, Toinette, ed. LC 84-48734. 1985. pap. 10.95 (0-394-72947-1) Knopf.

Dass, Ram & Levine, Stephen. Grist for the Mill. rev. ed. LC 76-40447. 176p. 1995. reprint ed. pap. 9.95 (0-89087-499-9) Celestial Arts.

Dass, Ram, et al. Timothy Leary: Outside Looking In: Appreciations, Castigations, & Reminiscences. LC 98-54344. (Illus.). 304p. 1999. pap. 16.95 (0-89281-786-0) Inner Tradit.

An Asterisk (*) at the beginning of an entry indicates that the title is appearing for the first time.

Dass, T. Symmetries Gauge Fields Strings & Fundamental Interact: Mathematical Techniques in Gauge & String Theories. 1993. write for info. (*81-224-0470-7*, Pub. by Wiley Estrn) Franklin.

***Dassanayake, Clayton.** The Flora of Ceylon, Vol. 12. rev. ed. 392p. 1999. 90.00 (*90-5410-270-5*, Pub. by A A Balkema) Ashgate Pub Co.

Dassanayake, D. Revised Handbook to the Flora of Ceylon, Vol. 5. (C). 1988. text 60.00 (*0-7855-3165-3*, Pub. by Scientific) St Mut.

— Revised Handbook to the Flora of Ceylon, Vols. 1-4. (C). 1988. text 40.00 (*0-7855-7056-X*, Pub. by Scientific) St Mut.

Dassanayake, M. D., ed. A Handbook to the Flora of Ceylon, Vol. IV. rev. ed. 545p. 1983. 43.50 (*90-6191-067-6*) Ashgate Pub Co.

— A Revised Handbook to the Flora of Ceylon, Vol. 9. (Illus.). 494p. (C). 1995. text 90.00 (*90-5410-267-5*, Pub. by A A Balkema) Ashgate Pub Co.

Dassanayake, M. D. & Clayton, W. D., eds. Flora of Ceylon. (Illus.). 436p. (C). 1996. 85.00 (*1-886106-79-7*) Science Pubs.

— A Revised Handbook to the Flora of Ceylon, Vol. 10. rev. ed. (Illus.). 434p. (C). 1996. text 85.00 (*90-5410-268-3*, Pub. by A A Balkema) Ashgate Pub Co.

— A Revised Handbook to the Flora of Ceylon, Vol. 11. 420p. 1997. 85.00 (*90-5410-269-1*, Pub. by A A Balkema) Ashgate Pub Co.

***Dassanayake, M. D. & Clayton, W. D., eds.** A Revised Handbook to the Flora of Ceylon, Vol. 13. (Illus.). 292p. (C). 1999. 90.00 (*90-5410-790-1*, Pub. by A A Balkema) Ashgate Pub Co.

— A Revised Handbook to the Flora of Ceylon, Vol. 14. (Illus.). 200p. (C). 2000. text 90.00 (*90-5410-791-X*, Pub. by A A Balkema) Ashgate Pub Co.

Dassanayake, M. D. & Fosberg, F. R., eds. Handbook of the Flora of Ceylon, Vol. 6. rev. ed. (Flora of Ceylon Ser.). (Illus.). 431p. (C). 1988. text 90.00 (*90-6191-069-2*, Pub. by A A Balkema) Ashgate Pub Co.

— Handbook to the Flora of Ceylon, 8 vols., Set. rev. ed. 4000p. (C). 1988. text 672.00 (*90-6191-063-3*, Pub. by A A Balkema) Ashgate Pub Co.

— A Revised Handbook of the Flora of Ceylon, Vol. 7. (Illus.). 446p. (C). 1991. text 90.00 (*90-6191-551-1*, Pub. by A A Balkema) Ashgate Pub Co.

— A Revised Handbook to the Flora of Ceylon, Vol. 1. 516p. 1980. 90.00 (*90-6191-064-1*, Pub. by A A Balkema) Ashgate Pub Co.

— A Revised Handbook to the Flora of Ceylon, Vol. 2. 518p. 1981. 90.00 (*90-6191-065-X*, Pub. by A A Balkema) Ashgate Pub Co.

— A Revised Handbook to the Flora of Ceylon, Vol. 3. 508p. 1981. 90.00 (*90-6191-066-8*, Pub. by A A Balkema) Ashgate Pub Co.

— A Revised Handbook to the Flora of Ceylon, Vol. 5. 484p. 1985. 90.00 (*90-6191-068-4*, Pub. by A A Balkema) Ashgate Pub Co.

Dassanayke, M. D., et al, eds. Handbook to the Flora of Ceylon Vol. 8. rev. ed. (Illus.). 464p. (C). 1994. text 98.00 (*90-6191-552-X*, Pub. by A A Balkema) Ashgate Pub Co.

Dassanowsky, Robert. Phantom Empires: The Novels of Alexander Lernet-Holenia & the Question of Postimperial Austrian Identity. (Studies in Austrian Literature, Culture, & Thought). 223p. 1996. 49.50 (*1-57241-030-2*) Ariadne CA.

***Dassanowsky, Robert & Lehman, Jeffrey.** Gale Encyclopedia of Multicultural America, 3 vols. 2nd ed. LC 99-44226. 1999. write for info. (*0-7876-3989-3*) Gale.

DasSarma, Shiladitya & Fleischmann, Esther M., eds. Archaea: A Laboratory Manual: Halophiles. (Illus.). 264p. (C). 1995. pap. 48.00 (*0-87969-438-6*) Cold Spring Harbor.

Dassbach, Carl H. Dynamics of the Internet. (Foundations in Library & Information Science: Vol. 42). Date not set. 78.50 (*0-7623-0409-X*) Jai Pr.

Dassbach, Elma. La Comedia Hagiografica del Siglo de Oro Espanol: Lope de Vega, Tirso de Molina y Calderon de la Barca. (Iberica Ser.: Vol. 22). (SPA.). IX, 200p. (C). 1997. text 44.95 (*0-8204-3317-9*) P Lang Pubng.

Dassel Area Historical Society Staff, compiled by. Stockholm Township (Wright County, Minnesota) Cemeteries. LC 94-48710. (Illus.). 32p. 1995. pap. 10.00 (*0-915709-18-X*) Pk Geneal Bk.

Dassesse, D., et al, eds. Retail Banking in the 1990's. (C). 1989. 85.00 (*0-85297-294-6*, Pub. by Chartered Bank) St Mut.

Dassesse, M., jt. auth. see Isaacs, S.

Dassesse, Marc, et al. EC Tax Law: VAT & Other Tax Provisions. boxed set. write for info. (*0-406-04366-3*, UK, MICHIE) LEXIS Pub.

D'Assier, Adolphe. Posthumous Humanity: A Study of Phantoms. Olcott, Henry S., ed. LC 81-50204. (Secret Doctrine Reference Ser.). 384p. 1981. reprint ed. 17.00 (*0-913510-36-X*) Wizards.

D'Assigny, Marius. The Art of Memory: A Treatise Useful for Such as Are to Speak in Public. LC 83-46046. (Scientific Awakening in the Restoration Ser.: No. 1). 128p. 1985. reprint ed. 45.00 (*0-404-63301-3*) AMS Pr.

D'Assigny, Marius, tr. see Gautruche, Pierre.

Dassin, Joan, ed. see Archdiocese of Sao Paulo Staff.

Dassios, G., et al, eds. Mathematical Methods in Scattering Theory & Biomedical Technology. (Pitman Research Notes in Mathematics Ser.: No. 390). 248p. 1998. pap. 51.00 (*0-582-36804-9*) Addison-Wesley.

***Dassios, George & Kleinman, Ralph E.** Low Frequency Scattering. LC 99-32310. (Oxford Mathematical Monographs). 320p. 2000. text 115.00 (*0-19-853678-X*) OUP.

Dassler, H. G. & Bortitz, S., eds. Air Pollution & Its Influence on Vegetation: Causes-Effects-Prophylaxis & Therapy. (Tasks for Vegetation Science Ser.). (C). 1987. text 168.00 (*90-6193-619-5*) Kluwer Academic.

Dasso. Real Estate. 13th ed. 592p. (C). 2001. 86.67 (*0-13-681693-2*, Macmillan Coll) P-H.

Dasso, jt. auth. see Guttery.

Dasso, Jerome, jt. auth. see Ring, Alfred A.

Dasso, Jerome, jt. auth. see Ringl.

Dasso, Margaret & Skelly, Maryan. Dirt Busters: The Best Little Cleaning Book Ever. 115p. (Orig.). 1990. pap. 7.95 (*0-9621757-0-6*) Peter & Thornton Pubs.

— Dirt Busters: The Best Little Cleaning Book Ever. rev. ed. 130p. (Orig.). (YA). (gr. 5 up). 1991. reprint ed. pap. 7.95 (*0-9621757-1-4*) Peter & Thornton Pubs.

Dassonville, G., ed. Water Supply: The Decade-Half Way: Part of the Proceedings of the Regional Conference of the IWSA Held in Conjunction with the 3rd Congress of the UADE in Libreville, Gabon, 10-15 June, 1985. 372p. 1986. pap. 66.00 (*0-08-034142-X*, Pub. by PPL) Elsevier.

Dassonville, Michel. Ronsard et Montaigne: Ecrivains Engages? LC 88-82136. (French Forum Monographs: No. 71). 128p. (Orig.). 1989. pap. 12.95 (*0-917058-72-0*) French Forum.

Dassow, Ethel, ed. see Fadich, Ray.

Dassow, J., ed. Developments in Theoretical Computer Science. (Topics in Computer Mathematics Ser.). 276p. 1994. text 134.00 (*2-88124-961-2*) Gordon & Breach.

Dassow, J., et al, eds. Aspects & Prospects of Theoretical Computer Science: Proceedings 6th International Meeting of Young Computer Scientists, Smolenice, Czechoslovakia, November 19-23, 1990. (Lecture Notes in Computer Science Ser.: Vol. 464). vi, 298p. 1990. 38.00 (*0-387-53414-8*) Spr-Verlag.

Dassow, J. & Keleman, J., eds. Machines, Languages & Complexity. (Lecture Notes in Computer Science Ser.: Vol. 381). vi, 244p. 1989. 34.00 (*0-387-51516-X*) Spr-Verlag.

Dassow, J. & Paun, G. Regulated Rewriting in Formal Language Theory. (EATCS Monographs on Theoretical Computer Science: Vol. 18). (Illus.). 308p. 1990. 93.95 (*0-387-51414-7*) Spr-Verlag.

Dassu, Marta & Saich, Anthony J., eds. The Reform Decade in China: From Hope to Despair. 220p. 1991. pap. 16.95 (*0-7103-0417-X*, A5505) Routledge.

Dasta, Joseph F., jt. auth. see Chernow, Bart.

Dastidar, Sachi G., ed. Bengal Studies 1994: Essays on Economics, Society & Culture. (Illus.). 264p. (Orig.). (C). 1996. pap. 12.95 (*0-9649957-0-0*) SUNY Coll Wstbry.

— Calcutta Three Hundred - Kolkata Memoirs of a Diverse City: Overseas Tribute to Calcutta on Her Tercentenary. (Illus.). 157p. (Orig.). 1993. pap. text 10.00 (*0-9634363-0-9*) S Asia Forum.

Dastidar, Sachi G., jt. auth. see Mukh, Firma K.

Dastjerdi, Hossein V., tr. see Sobhani, Jafar.

Dastmalchian, Ali, et al. The Climate of Workplace Relations. 240p. (C). (gr. 13). 1991. pap. 64.95 (*0-415-03738-7*, A5925) Thomson Learn.

Daston, George P., ed. Molecular & Cellular Methods in Developmental Toxicology. LC 96-14296. (Methods in Toxicology Ser.). 304p. 1996. spiral bd. 94.95 (*0-8493-3342-3*) CRC Pr.

Daston, George P., jt. auth. see Kavlock, Robert J.

Daston, Lorraine. Biographies of Scientific Objects. LC 99-43745. 288p. 1999. pap. text 19.00 (*0-226-13672-8*); lib. bdg. 55.00 (*0-226-13670-1*) U Ch Pr.

Daston, Lorraine & Park, Katharine. Wonders & the Order of Nature, 1150-1750. LC 96-49411. 1998. 34.00 (*0-942299-90-6*) Zone Bks.

Dastrup, Boyd L. Crusade in Nuremberg: Military Occupation, 1945-1949, 47. LC 85-927. (Contributions in Military Studies Ser.: No. 47). (Illus.). 159p. 1985. 47.95 (*0-313-24847-8*, DCN/, Greenwood Pr) Greenwood.

— The Field Artillery: History & Sourcebook. LC 93-1142. 240p. 1993. lib. bdg. 75.00 (*0-313-27264-6*, DFC/, Greenwood Pr) Greenwood.

— U. S. Army Command & General Staff College: A Centennial History. (Illus.). 157p. 1982. 40.00 (*0-89745-033-7*) Sunflower U Pr.

Dastrup, Linda. Creative Gift Ideas. (Illus.). 36p. (Orig.). 1992. student ed. 5.95 (*0-9621898-6-3*) Creative Changes.

— Creative Organizers System. (Illus.). 1990. student ed. 19.95 (*0-9621898-5-5*) Creative Changes.

— Holiday Fun. (Illus.). 46p. (Orig.). 1992. student ed. 5.95 (*0-9621898-7-1*) Creative Changes.

— Teaching Children Responsibility: Children & Jobs. rev. ed. (Illus.). 15p. 1986. student ed. 5.95 (*0-9621898-0-4*) Creative Changes.

Dastur, Francoise. Death: An Essay on Finitude. Llewelyn, John, tr. from FRE. 108p. 1996. 35.00 (*0-485-11487-9*, Pub. by Athlone Pr) Humanities.

— Heidegger & the Question of Time. Raffoul, Francois & Pettigrew, David E., trs. from FRE. LC 96-40852. (Contemporary Studies in Philosophy & the Human Sciences). 120p. (C). 1997. text 39.95 (*0-391-04032-4*) Humanities.

— Heidegger & the Question of Time. Raffoul, Francois & Pettigrew, David, trs. (Contemporary Studies in Philosophy & Human Sciences Ser.). 108p. 1999. 39.95 (*1-57392-395-8*, Humanity Bks) Prometheus Bks.

***Dastur, Franpcoise.** Telling Time: Sketch of a Phenomenological Chrono-Logy LC 99-36615. 2000. write for info. (*0-485-11520-4*) Humanities.

Dastur, J. F. Everybody's Guide to Ayurvedic Medicine. 212p. 1983. 14.95 (*0-318-36355-0*) Asia Bk Corp.

— Medicinal Plants of India & Pakistan. 212p. 1988. 11.95 (*0-318-36365-8*) Asia Bk Corp.

— Medicinal Plants of India & Pakistan. (C). 1988. 35.00 (*0-7855-2269-7*, Pub. by Scientific) St Mut.

— Useful Plants of India & Pakistan. (C). 1988. 40.00 (*0-7855-2268-9*, Pub. by Scientific) St Mut.

Dasu, Sriram, ed. Management of Design: Engineering & Management Perspectives. LC 94-34778. 304p. (C). 1994. lib. bdg. 124.50 (*0-7923-9509-3*) Kluwer Academic.

Dasun, Liu & Zhonjun, Lin. The I Ching: Text & Annotated Translation. annot. ed. Youde, Fu, tr. (CHI & ENG.). 141p. 1995. pap. 11.95 (*7-80551-696-0*) China Bks.

Dasupta, Gautam, jt. ed. see Marranda, Bonnie.

Dasypodius, Petrus. Dictionarium Latinogermanicum. (Documenta Linguistica, Reihe I: Worterbucher Des Vol. 15 & 16. Jahrhunderts Ser.). (LAT.). x, 982p. 1974. reprint ed. write for info. (*3-487-05325-X*) G Olms Pubs.

Data Communications Magazine Staff, ed. Interface Proceedings '84. 1984. pap. 40.00 (*0-07-606897-8*) McGraw.

Data Energy Research Institute Staff, et al. India & Thailand Social & Economic Effects of Petroleum Development. vii, 130p. (Orig.). 1987. pap. 15.75 (*92-2-105507-8*) Intl Labour Office.

Data Notes. Garlic Use Poetry Pages. 12p. (C). 1985. pap. text 5.95 (*0-911569-84-7*) Prosperity & Profits.

Data Notes Publishing. Recyclable Scrap Locating - A Workbook. 60p. 1983. ring bd. 29.95 (*0-317-00336-4*) Prosperity & Profits.

Data Notes Publishing Staff. Advertising Via Telemarketing Script Presentations Encyclopaedia. 150p. 1991. ring bd. 125.00 (*0-911569-73-1*) Prosperity & Profits.

— Colleges That Offer Credit for Life Experience. 300p. 1983. ring bd. 27.95 (*0-911569-07-3*) Prosperity & Profits.

— Envelope Addressing As a Small Business: A Business Workbook. (Illus.). 60p. 1992. ring bd., wbk. ed. 29.95 (*0-911569-87-1*) Prosperity & Profits.

— Flea Market Directories, Books, References, Etc. A How to Find or Locate Workbook. LC 83-90737. 200p. 1984. ring bd. 25.95 (*0-911569-57-X*) Prosperity & Profits.

— Furniture Recycling: Info Mapping Index. rev. ed. 30p. 1992. ring bd. 23.95 (*0-911569-45-6*) Prosperity & Profits.

— Gift Basket Greetings to Duplicate & Use Encyclopedia. Doyle, A. C., ed. 70p. 1991. ring bd. 49.95 (*0-911569-21-9*) Prosperity & Profits.

— How to Form a Corporation, Network, Cooperative, Barter Organization, Club, or Association: An At Your Own Pace Workbook. 50p. 1983. ring bd. 29.95 (*0-911569-56-1*) Prosperity & Profits.

— Resale Shop or Flea Market Business - A How to Find or Locate Merchandise Workbook. 62p. (Orig.). 1992. ring bd. 24.95 (*0-911569-83-9*) Prosperity & Profits.

— Telephone Repair & Operations - A Locating Services Workbook. rev. ed. LC 83-90725. 25p. 1996. ring bd. 29.95 (*0-911569-64-2*) Prosperity & Profits.

— Telesales Script Presentations Directory. 100p. (Orig.). (C). 1991. ring bd. 59.95 (*0-911569-91-X*) Prosperity & Profits.

— Vegetarian Associations, Organizations, Periodicals, Cooking Schools & More: A How to Find or Locate Reference. 60p. 1992. ring bd., wbk. ed. 24.95 (*0-911569-53-7*) Prosperity & Profits.

— Word Mapping for Educational Research Success: A Workbook. 14p. (YA). (gr. 11-12). 1988. student ed., ring bd. 25.95 (*0-911569-18-9*) Prosperity & Profits.

Data Notes Publishing Staff, compiled by. Creative Financing Data Notes Report. rev. ed. 65p. 1995. ring bd. 28.95 (*0-911569-00-6*) Prosperity & Profits.

— Word Mapping Reference Handbook. 250p. 1992. student ed., ring bd. 32.95 (*0-911569-01-4*) Prosperity & Profits.

Data Notes Research. Cooking School Alternatives, Southern Regional Guide: How to Find or Locate Workbook. rev. ed. 63p. 1998. student ed., ring bd. 24.95 (*0-911569-33-2*) Prosperity & Profits.

— Ginseng Use Poetry Pages. 18p. (C). 1985. pap. text 5.00 (*0-911569-82-0*) Prosperity & Profits.

Data Notes Research Project. Aloe Vera Use Poetry Pages. 6p. (C). 1985. pap. text 6.00 (*0-911569-81-2*) Prosperity & Profits.

— Ginger Use Poetry Pages. 11p. (C). 1985. pap. text 5.00 (*0-911569-80-4*) Prosperity & Profits.

Data Notes Research Staff. Direct Sales, Commission Sales, Etc. A Report. LC 83-90738. (Bibliography Ser.). 60p. 1984. ring bd. 35.95 (*0-911569-61-8*) Prosperity & Profits.

— Old Fashioned, Bygone, Yesteryear & Way Back When Products Catalogs: A Report. rev. ed. LC 83-90728. 100p. 1996. ring bd. 32.95 (*0-911569-62-6*) Prosperity & Profits.

— Pennystock Information: How to Find or Locate Information on Pennystock. rev. ed. LC 83-90739. 1997. ring bd. 29.95 (*0-911569-60-X*) Prosperity & Profits.

Data Notes Research Staff, ed. Debtors or Bill Payer's Reference: How to Find or Locate Information on Debt Repayment. 75p. 1992. ring bd. 27.95 (*0-911569-03-0*) Prosperity & Profits.

Data Notes Staff. Aluminum Recycling: A Self Paced Workbook. rev. ed. 93p. 1992. ring bd. 26.95 (*0-911569-40-5*) Prosperity & Profits.

— Aromatica Encyclopedia. 65p. 1992. ring bd. 32.95 (*0-911569-94-4*) Prosperity & Profits.

— Blessed Everyday with Miracles, Prosperity & Success: A Poetry Book. 22p. 1986. pap. text 5.00 (*0-911569-92-8*) Prosperity & Profits.

— Bread Pudding Encyclopedia. 150p. 1991. ring bd. 39.95 (*0-911569-75-8*) Prosperity & Profits.

— Business Idea Greetings: Letters for Gifts, Mailing, Faxing. (Illus.). 70p. 1992. student ed., ring bd. 49.95 (*0-911569-16-2*) Prosperity & Profits.

— Business Idea Publications, Bylaw Ideas, & More. 138p. 1993. ring bd. 79.95 (*0-911569-89-8*) Prosperity & Profits.

— Colds & Fever Cures Story Poem: Rye the Rhyming Detective in "Therm the Cold Germ" 18p. 1986. pap. text 5.00 (*0-911569-68-5*) Prosperity & Profits.

— Cooking School Alternatives: An International Directory. rev. ed. (Illus.). 63p. 1998. ring bd. 62.95 (*0-911569-55-3*) Prosperity & Profits.

— Cooking School Alternatives Located in the U. S. A Directory. (Illus.). 75p. 1998. pap. text 59.95 (*0-911569-54-5*) Prosperity & Profits.

— Cooking School Alternatives, Midwest Region: A How to Find or Locate Workbook. rev. ed. (Illus.). 63p. 1998. student ed., ring bd. 24.95 (*0-911569-34-0*) Prosperity & Profits.

— Cooking School Alternatives, Mountain States Region: A How to Find or Locate Workbook. rev. ed. (Illus.). 63p. 1998. student ed., ring bd. 24.95 (*0-911569-35-9*) Prosperity & Profits.

— Cooking School Alternatives, Northeast Region: A How to Find or Locate Workbook. rev. ed. (Illus.). 63p. 1998. student ed., ring bd. 24.95 (*0-911569-32-4*) Prosperity & Profits.

— Cooking School Alternatives, Pacific Coast, Alaska & Hawaii Regions: A How to Find or Locate Workbook. rev. ed. (Illus.). 63p. 1997. student ed., ring bd. 24.95 (*0-911569-38-3*) Prosperity & Profits.

— Cooking School Alternatives, Southwest Region: A How to Find or Locate Workbook. rev. ed. (Illus.). 63p. 1998. student ed., ring bd. 24.95 (*0-911569-36-7*) Prosperity & Profits.

— Family Businesses, Small Businesses, Home Businesses & General Business Possibilities, Encyclopedia. 150p. 1991. ring bd. 79.95 (*0-911569-99-5*) Prosperity & Profits.

— Food Businesses, Snack Shops, Specialty Food, Restaurants & Other Ideas: A Business Workbook. rev. ed. (Illus.). 75p. 1992. ring bd. 27.95 (*0-911569-69-3*) Prosperity & Profits.

— Frugal, Pennypinching, Money Saving Cookbook. (Illus.). 52p. ring bd. 23.95 (*0-911569-14-6*) Prosperity & Profits.

— Gift & Cookie Bag Greetings Encyclopedia. 60p. 1991. ring bd. 32.95 (*0-911569-17-0*) Prosperity & Profits.

— Information & Referral Services: A Business Possibility Workbook. rev. ed. (Illus.). 70p. 1992. ring bd. 25.95 (*0-911569-59-6*) Prosperity & Profits.

— Potpourri Simple & Easy Notebook. rev. ed. 83p. 1993. ring bd. 29.95 (*0-911569-22-7*) Prosperity & Profits.

— Refunding Periodicals, Books, Clubs, Associations: A How to Find or Locate Workbook. rev. ed. 63p. 1992. student ed., ring bd. 24.95 (*0-911569-06-5*) Prosperity & Profits.

— Salad Bar Recipe Pages: Restaurant, Catering & Food Business Edition. (Illus.). 60p. 1992. ring bd. 29.95 (*0-911569-26-X*) Prosperity & Profits.

Data, P. G., et al. Neurobiology & Cell Physiology of Chemoreception. (Advances in Experimental Medicine & Biology Ser.: Vol. 337). (Illus.). 466p. (C). 1993. text 135.00 (*0-306-44575-1*, Kluwer Plenum) Kluwer Academic.

***Data Research, Inc. (Rosemount, Minn.).** Federal Laws Prohibiting Employment Discrimination. 2nd ed. LC 99-461743. 1998. write for info. (*0-939675-74-9*) Data Res MN.

— Statutes, Regulations, & Case Law Protecting Individuals with Disabilities. 2nd ed. LC 98-120311. 1997. write for info. (*0-939675-61-7*) Data Res MN.

— Statutes, Regulations, & Case Law Protecting Individuals with Disabilities. 3rd ed. LC 99-461744. 1998. write for info. (*0-939675-77-3*) Data Res MN.

— U.S. Supreme Court Employment Cases. 3rd ed. LC 98-120317. 1997. write for info. (*0-939675-63-3*) Data Res MN.

Data Research, Inc. (Rosemount, Minn.), jt. auth. see United States. Supreme Court.

Data Resources Staff. Metro Insights. (Illus.). 1137p. 1988. 449.00 (*0-07-607001-8*) McGraw.

Database Consulting Group Staff. Using Informix Data Blades. 1997. 39.99 (*0-7897-1418-3*) Que.

DATADEScription Inc. Staff. Getting Started Datadesk Student Version 5.0. Guardino, Karen, ed. 32p. (C). 1997. lib. bdg. write for info. (*0-201-57122-6*) Addison-Wesley.

Datalized Slide Charts Staff. Duct Calculation Slide Rule. 1p. 1990. pap. 40.00 (*1-892765-14-4*) Air Conditioning Cont.

DataMyte Staff. DataMyte Handbook: A Practical Guide to Computerized Data Collection for Statistical Process Control. 3rd ed. Houston, Jerry, ed. 656p. 40.00 (*0-930345-02-9*) DataMyte Corp.

— DataMyte Handbook: A Practical Guide to Computerized Data Collection for Statistical Process Control. 4th ed. Houston, Jerry, ed. LC 84-71481. 640p. 1989. write for info. (*0-930345-03-7*) DataMyte Corp.

Datan, Nancy, et al, eds. Life-Span Developmental Psychology: Intergenenational Relations. 296p. (C). 1986. text 69.95 (*0-89859-536-3*) L Erlbaum Assocs.

Datan, Nancy, et al. A Time to Reap: The Middle Age of Women in Five Israeli Subcultures. LC 80-26776. 206p. 1981. reprint ed. pap. 63.90 (*0-608-05945-5*, 206628200008) Bks Demand.

Datapower A/S Staff. Microsoft Excel 7.0 for Windows 95: Advanced Coursebook. (Illus.). 1996. pap. text 32.95 (*1-888323-09-4*) DataPower Intl.

— Microsoft Word 7.0 for Windows 95: Advanced Coursebook. (Illus.). 1996. pap. text 32.95 (*1-888323-10-8*) DataPower Intl.

DataPower AS Staff. Microsoft Access 2.0: Introductory Coursebook. 141p. 1995. pap. text 29.95 (*1-888323-04-3*) DataPower Intl.

D

An Asterisk (*) at the beginning of an entry indicates that the title is appearing for the first time.

— Microsoft Excel 5.0 for Windows: Introductory Coursebook. 126p. 1995. pap. text 29.95 (*1-888323-02-7*) DataPower Intl.

— Microsoft Getting Started in Windows 95: Upgrader Coursebook. 46p. 1995. pap. text 14.95 (*1-888323-01-9*) DataPower Intl.

— Microsoft PowerPoint 4.0: Introductory Coursebook. 147p. 1995. pap. text 29.95 (*1-888323-03-5*) DataPower Intl.

— Microsoft Windows for Workgroups Version 3.11: Introductory Course Book. 116p. 1995. pap. text 29.95 (*1-888323-05-1*) DataPower Intl.

— Microsoft Windows 95: Introductory Coursebook. 151p. 1995. pap. text 29.95 (*1-888323-00-0*) DataPower Intl.

— Microsoft Word 6.0 for Windows: Introductory Course Book. 170p. 1995. pap. text 29.95 (*1-888323-06-X*) DataPower Intl.

Datapro-McGraw-Hill. Datapro-McGraw-Hill Guide to IBM PC Software. 2nd ed. 1985. pap. text 23.95 (*0-07-015407-4*) McGraw.

Datar, A. B. Civil Service: A Life-Time Experience. (C). 1994. 27.50 (*81-241-0144-2*, Pub. by Har-Anand Pubns) S Asia.

Datar, Arvind P. Guide to Central Excise Law & Practice. (C). 1990. 400.00 (*0-89771-234-X*) St Mut.

Datcher, Michael. Tough Love: Cultural Criticism & Familial Observations on the Life & Death of Tupac Shakur. Alexander, Kwame, ed. (Black Words Ser.). 132p. 1997. pap. 12.95 (*1-888018-05-4*, BlckWrds) Alexndr Pub.

Datcher, Michael, ed. see Toney, A. K., et al.

Date, A. R. & Gray, A. L. Applications of Inductively Coupled Plasma Mass Spectrometry. (Illus.). 272p. 1989. text 139.95 (*0-7514-0132-3*, Pub. by B Acad & Prof) Routldge.

Date, A. R. & Gray, A. L., eds. The Applications of Inductively Coupled Plasma Mass Spectrometry. (Illus.). 224p. 1988. text 105.00 (*0-412-01721-0*, Chap & Hall NY) Chapman & Hall.

Date-Bah, Eugenia, ed. Promoting Gender Equality at Work: Turning Vision into Reality. 241p. (C). 1997. pap. 25.00 (*1-85649-454-3*, Pub. by Zed Books); text 65.00 (*1-85649-453-5*, Pub. by Zed Books) St Martin.

***Date, C. J.** The Database Relational Model: A Retrospective Review & Analysis. 128p. 2000. pap. text 10.00 (*0-201-61294-1*) Addison-Wesley.

Date, C. J. A Guide to DB2. 1984. 37.75 (*0-201-11317-1*) Addison-Wesley.

— A Guide to DB2: A User's Guide to the IBM Product IBM DATABASE 2. (Illus.). (C). 1990. text 46.25 (*0-201-50113-9*) Addison-Wesley.

— A Guide to Ingres. LC 86-25566. (C). 1987. text 40.95 (*0-201-06006-X*) Addison-Wesley.

— A Guide to SQL Standard. LC 86-26511. (C). 1987. pap. text 27.95 (*0-201-05777-8*) Addison-Wesley.

— A Guide to the SQL Standard: A User's Guide to the Standard Relational Language (SQL) 2nd ed. (Illus.). 240p. (C). 1989. pap. text 32.25 (*0-201-50209-7*) Addison-Wesley.

— Introducion a los Sistemas de Bases de Datos. 5th ed. (SPA.). 896p. (C). 1992. pap. text 42.00 (*0-201-51859-7*) Addison-Wesley.

***Date, C. J.** An Introduction to Database Systems. 7th ed. LC 99-30439. 938p. (C). 1999. 69.00 (*0-201-38590-2*) Addison-Wesley.

Date, C. J. An Introduction to Database Systems, Vol. I. 3rd ed. LC 80-17603. (IBM Systems Programming Ser.). (Illus.). 704p. (C). 1981. text 21.95 (*0-201-14471-9*) Addison-Wesley.

— An Introduction to Database Systems, Vol. I. 4th ed. (Systems Programming Ser.). 1986. text 34.36 (*0-201-14201-5*) Addison-Wesley.

— Introduction to Database Systems, Vol. 3. (C). 1991. pap. text. write for info. (*0-201-55651-0*) Addison-Wesley.

Date, C. J. Relational Database Writings, 1985-1989. (Illus.). 528p. (C). 1990. 49.69 (*0-201-50881-8*) Addison-Wesley.

— What Not How: Business Rules Approach to Application Development. LC 00-131706. 128p. 2000. pap. 24.95 (*0-201-70850-7*) Addison-Wesley.

***Date, C. J. & Darwen, Hugh.** Foundation for Future Database Systems: The Third Manifesto. 2nd ed. 576p. 2000. 39.95 (*0-201-70928-7*) Addison-Wesley.

— Foundation for Object Relational Databases: The Third Manifesto. LC 98-10364. 528p. (C). 1998. 44.95 (*0-201-30978-5*) Addison-Wesley.

Date, C. J. & Darwen, Hugh. A Guide to the SQL Standard: A Users Guide to the Standard Database Language SQL. 4th ed. LC 96-35776. 522p. (Orig.). (C). 1996. pap. 44.95 (*0-201-96426-0*) Addison-Wesley.

Date, C. J. & McGoveran, David. A Guide to Sybase & SQL Server. (Illus.). 576p. (C). 1992. 55.95 (*0-201-55710-X*) Addison-Wesley.

— A Guide to Sybase & SQL Server. 2nd ed. (C). 1997. text 40.00 (*0-201-91434-4*) Addison-Wesley.

Date, C. J. & White, Colin J. A Guide to DB2. 2nd ed. (Illus.). 496p. (C). 1988. text 38.75 (*0-201-09428-2*) Addison-Wesley.

— A Guide to SQL-DS. 505p. (C). 1989. 45.94 (*0-201-14688-6*) Addison-Wesley.

Date General Corporation Staff & Burstein, Harvey. Hotel Security Management. 2nd ed. LC 84-17717. 188p. 1985. 49.95 (*0-275-90069-X*, C0069, Praeger Pubs) Greenwood.

Date, N. P., tr. see Bohnecke, Gunther.

Date, N. P., tr. see Wattenberg, Hermann.

Date, N. P., tr. see Wust, Georg & Defant, Albert.

Date, R. A., et al, eds. Plant-Soil Interactions at Low pH, Principles & Management: Proceedings of the 3rd International Symposium on Plant-Soil Interactions at Low pH Held 1993, Brisbane, Queensland, Australia. LC 95-34329. (Developments in Plant & Soil Sciences Ser.: Vol. 64). 822p. 1995. text 481.00 (*0-7923-3198-2*) Kluwer Academic.

Date, S. V. Final Orbit. 352p. 1997. mass mkt. 5.99 (*0-380-79625-2*, Avon Bks) Morrow Avon.

***Date, S. V.** Smokeout. 240p. 2000. 23.95 (*0-399-14649-0*) Putnam Pub Group.

Date, S. V. Speed Week. LC 98-50629. 224p. 1999. 22.95 (*0-399-14513-3*, G P Putnam) Peng Put Young Read.

Date, Shin, jt. ed. see Toki, Hiroshi.

Date, V. H. Upanisads Retold. 1999. reprint ed. 29.00 (*81-215-0873-8*, Pub. by M Manoharial) Coronet Bks.

Daten. Can You Do This? (J). 15.95 (*0-8126-0148-3*) Open Court.

Dates, Jannette L. & Barlow, William, eds. Split Image: African Americans in the Mass Media. 2nd ed. LC 92-47367. (C). 1993. 17.95 (*0-88258-179-1*) Howard U Pr.

Datesman, Kyle. Classical Banjo: 40 Classical Works Arranged for the 5 String Banjo. (Illus.). 86p. 1996. pap. text 12.95 (*1-57424-017-X*) Centerstream Pub.

Datesman, Maryanne K., et al. The American Ways: An Introduction to American Culture. 2nd ed. LC 96-44476. 240p. 1996. pap. text 29.67 (*0-13-342015-9*) P-H.

Datesman, Susan K., jt. ed. see Scarpitti, Frank R.

Dathe, jt. auth. see Montgomery.

Dathe, David. Astronomy, '99/'00. 2nd ed. (Annual Ser.). (Illus.). 240p. 1998. pap. text 12.25 (*0-07-039386-9*, Dshkn McG-Hill) McGrw-H Hghr Educ.

— Astronomy 98/99. (Annual Ser.). (Illus.). 256p. 1998. pap. text 12.25 (*0-697-39298-8*, Dshkn McG-Hill) McGrw-H Hghr Educ.

Dathe, David, jt. auth. see Kalmbach Publishing Co. Staff.

Dathe, David, jt. auth. see Montgomery, Carla W.

Dathenus, Petrus. The Pearl of Christian Comfort (Paarl of Christelijke Vertroosting) Blok, Arie W. & Beeke, Joel R., trs. from DUT. 87p. 1997. 7.50 (*1-892777-10-X*) Reform Heritage Bks.

Dathorne, O. R. Asian Voyages: Two Thousand Years of Constructing the Other. LC 95-39749. 328p. 1996. 65.00 (*0-89789-469-3*, Bergin & Garvey) Greenwood.

— The Black Mind: A History of African Literature. LC 74-76744. 539p. reprint ed. pap. 167.10 (*0-8357-7293-4*, 205585400039) Bks Demand.

— Dele's Child. LC 84-51445. 158p. (Orig.). 1986. 15.00 (*0-89410-421-7*, Three Contnts) L Rienner.

— In Europe's Image: The Need for American Multiculturalism. LC 94-4754. 232p. 1994. 59.95 (*0-89789-397-2*, Bergin & Garvey) Greenwood.

— Songs for a New World. 1988. 15.00 (*0-916057-01-1*) Assn Carib Stud.

***Dathorne, O. R.** Worlds Apart: Race in the Modern Period. 2000. write for info. (*0-89789-722-6*) Greenwood.

Dathorne, O. R., ed. Journal of Caribbean Studies, Vols. 1-9. 1993. write for info. (*0-318-69327-5*) Assn Carib Stud.

Dathrorne, O. R. Imagining the World: Mythical Belief Versus Reality in Global Encounters. LC 93-9016. 256p. 1994. 55.00 (*0-89789-364-6*, Bergin & Garvey) Greenwood.

Datig, Fred A. Cartridges for Collectors, Vol. II. 1956. 19.95 (*0-87505-097-2*) Pioneer Pr.

— Cartridges for Collectors: Centerfire, Vol. I. (Illus.). 176p. 1956. pap. 15.95 (*0-87505-096-4*) Pioneer Pr.

— Cartridges for Collectors: Centerfire-Rimfire-Plastic, Vol. III. (Illus.). 176p. 1956. 19.95 (*0-87505-098-0*) Pioneer Pr.

— Soviet Russian Tokarev "TT" Pistols & Cartridges 1929-1953. LC 90-71931. 168p. 1991. 29.95 (*1-882824-15-6*) Graphic Pubs.

Datig, William E. The Age of Androids: Expanding the Human Universe, an Introduction to a Unified Theory of Knowledge. LC 97-71648. (Illus.). xxi, 281p. 1997. 24.95 (*0-9657651-0-5*, HSA-01) Mill Pond Pub.

Datin, Richard C. Elegance on C Street: Virginia City's International Hotel. (Illus.). 48p. 1986. 4.95 (*0-913814-76-8*) Nevada Pubns.

— Reno: A View of the Past. LC 92-97115. (Comstock Papers: No. 2). (Illus.). 36p. (Orig.). 1993. pap. 9.75 (*0-9634452-0-0*) R C Datin.

— Tall Tales & Tarnished Truths (Of Nevada) (Comstock Papers: Vol. 3). (Illus.). 50p. (Orig.). 1999. pap. 10.00 (*0-9634452-1-9*) R C Datin.

***Datki, John, ed.** Krudy's Chronicles: Early Twentieth Century in Gyula Krudy's Non Fiction Works. 300p. (C). 2000. 44.95 (*963-9116-78-5*); pap. 21.95 (*963-9116-79-3*) Ctrl Europ Univ.

Datla, Raju U., ed. Optical Diagnostic Methods for Inorganic Transmissive Materials, Vol. 3425. LC 99-170354. 1998. 59.00 (*0-8194-2880-9*) SPIE.

Datlof, Natalie, et al. The World of George Sand, 122. LC 90-46700. (Contributions in Women's Studies: No. 122). 352p. 1991. 57.95 (*0-313-27584-X*, DGE/, Greenwood Pr) Greenwood.

***Datlow.** Ruby Slippers, Golden Tears. 2000. 22.00 (*0-380-97262-X*) Morrow Avon.

***Datlow & Windling.** Black Thorn White Rose. 2000. 22.00 (*0-380-97241-7*) Morrow Avon.

Datlow, Ellen. A Wolf at the Door: And Other Retold Fairytales. LC 99-38616. (Illus.). 192p. (J). (gr. 4-6). 2000. per. 16.00 (*0-689-82138-7*) S&S Bks Yung.

— The Year's Best Fantasy & Horror. 9th ed. 624p. 1996. 27.95 (*0-312-14449-0*) St Martin.

— The Year's Best Fantasy & Horror. 10th ed. Windling, Terri, ed. 624p. 1997. text 29.95 (*0-312-15700-2*) St Martin.

***Datlow, Ellen.** The Year's Best Fantasy & Horror. 13th ed. 640p. 2000. pap. 17.95 (*0-312-26416-X*) St Martin.

— Years Best Fantasy & Horror. 13th ed. 640p. 2000. text 29.95 (*0-312-26274-4*) St Martin.

Datlow, Ellen. The Year's Best Fantasy & Horror: Eleventh Annual Collection. 624p. 1998. text 29.95 (*0-312-18778-5*) St Martin.

— The Year's Best Fantasy & Horror: Tenth Annual Collection. 624p. 1997. pap. 17.95 (*0-312-15701-0*, St Martin Griffin) St Martin.

Datlow, Ellen, ed. The Fifth Omni Book of Science Fiction. 352p. 1987. mass mkt. 3.95 (*0-8217-2050-3*, Zebra Kensgtn) Kensgtn Pub Corp.

— Off Limits: Tales of Alien Sex. 304p. 1997. reprint ed. mass mkt. 5.99 (*0-441-00436-9*) Ace Bks.

— Omni Best Science Fiction One. 1992. 8.95 (*0-87455-277-X*) Omni Bks.

— Omni Best Science Fiction Three. 256p. 1993. pap. 10.00 (*0-87455-284-2*) Omni Bks.

— Omni Best Science Fiction Two. 1992. 8.95 (*0-87455-278-8*) Omni Bks.

— The Seventh Omni Book of Science Fiction. 384p. 1989. mass mkt. 4.50 (*0-8217-2688-9*, Zebra Kensgtn) Kensgtn Pub Corp.

***Datlow, Ellen, ed.** Vanishing Acts. 384p. 2000. 24.95 (*0-312-86962-2*, Pub. by Tor Bks) St Martin.

Datlow, Ellen, ed. The Year's Best Fantasy & Horror. 3rd ed. 1990. pap. 14.95 (*0-312-04450-X*) St Martin.

Datlow, Ellen & Windling, eds. Sirens & Other Demon Lovers. mass mkt. 5.99 (*0-06-105782-7*, HarperPrism) HarpC.

***Datlow, Ellen & Windling, Terri.** Black Heart, Ivory Bones. LC 99-50293. 384p. 2000. pap. 13.50 (*0-380-78623-0*, Avon Bks) Morrow Avon.

— Black Swan, White Raven. LC 96-33224. 384p. 1997. pap. 23.00 (*0-380-97523-8*, Avon Bks) Morrow Avon.

Datlow, Ellen & Windling, Terri. Black Swan, White Raven. 384p. 1998. pap. 13.00 (*0-380-78621-4*, Avon Bks) Morrow Avon.

Datlow, Ellen & Windling, Terri, eds. Black Thorn, White Rose. 1994. 22.00 (*0-688-13713-X*, Avon Bks) Morrow Avon.

— Black Thorn, White Rose. 400p. 1995. mass mkt. 5.99 (*0-380-77129-2*, Avon Bks) Morrow Avon.

— Ruby Slippers Golden Tears. 432p. 1996. mass mkt. 6.99 (*0-380-77872-6*, Avon Bks) Morrow Avon.

***Datlow, Ellen & Windling, Terri, eds.** Silver Birch, Blood Moon. LC 98-54639. 384p. 1999. pap. 13.50 (*0-380-78622-2*, Avon Bks) Morrow Avon.

Datlow, Ellen & Windling, Terri, eds. Snow White, Blood Red. 432p. 1993. mass mkt. 6.50 (*0-380-71875-8*, Avon Bks) Morrow Avon.

— The Year's Best Fantasy & Horror: Eleventh Annual Collection. 624p. 1998. pap. 17.95 (*0-312-19034-4*) St Martin.

— The Year's Best Fantasy & Horror: Fifth Annual Collection. 624p. 1992. pap. 15.95 (*0-312-07888-9*) St Martin.

— The Year's Best Fantasy & Horror: Twelfth Annual Collection. 2nd ed. 496p. 1999. pap. 17.95 (*0-312-20686-0*); text 29.95 (*0-312-20962-2*) St Martin.

Datnow, Amanda & Yonezawa, Susan, eds. The Integrated Reform Projects of Crede: A Special Issue of the Journal of Education for Students Placed at Risk. 128p. pap. 27.50 (*0-8058-9815-8*) L Erlbaum Assocs.

Datnow, Claire. Edwin Hubble: Discoverer of Galaxies. LC 96-37095. (Great Minds of Science Ser.). 128p. (J). (gr. 4-10). 1997. lib. bdg. 20.95 (*0-89490-934-7*) Enslow Pubs.

Datnow, Claire L. American Science Fiction & Fantasy Writers. LC 98-8846. (Collective Biographies Ser.). 128p. (YA). (gr. 6 up). 1999. lib. bdg. 20.95 (*0-7660-1090-2*) Enslow Pubs.

Dato, Daniel P. Grammatical Aspects of Foreign Accents: Spoken English Patterns for Practice & Reference. LC 93-70711. (Illus.). 400p. (C). 1993. pap. text, teacher ed. 39.95 (*1-881336-01-8*); pap. text, student ed. 34.95 (*1-881336-02-6*) Bilingual CI.

— Marketing & Selling Your Accent Reduction Programs: How to Find, & Contact Accented Speakers & Sell Your Program. LC 92-71984. 121p. 1992. pap. text 19.95 (*1-881336-00-X*) Bilingual CI.

— Psycholinguistic Aspects of Foreign Accents (PAFAS) A Complete Personalized Program for Achieving Clear, Pleasant-Sounding Speech. 312p. 1988. pap. text, student ed. 39.95 (*1-881336-04-2*) Bilingual CI.

— Psycholinguistic Aspects of Foreign Accents (PAFAT) A Complete Approach to Effective Accent Reduction. 318p. 1987. pap. text, teacher ed. 59.95 (*1-881336-03-4*) Bilingual CI.

Dato, Daniel P., ed. see Georgetown University Round Table on Languages & L.

Dato, Judith G. Parent Involvement Resource Manual. (Illus.). 211p. 1995. write for info. (*1-55997-177-0*) Websters Intl.

Dator, James, jt. auth. see Kim, Tae-Chang.

Dator, James, jt. ed. see Kim, Tae-Chang.

D'Atri, J. E. & Ziller, W. Naturally Reductive Metrics & Einstein Metrics on Compact Lie Groups. LC 79-7. (Memoirs Ser.: No. 18/215). 72p. 1982. reprint ed. pap. 21.00 (*0-8218-2215-2*, MEMO/18/215) Am Math.

Datsko, Joseph. Materials Selection for Design & Manufacturing: Theory & Practice. LC 96-50430. (Illus.). 392p. 1997. text 145.00 (*0-8247-9844-9*) Dekker.

Datt, Gaurav. Bargaining Power, Wages & Employment: An Analysis of Agricultural Labor Markets in India. LC 96-25152. 220p. (C). 1997. 32.00 (*0-8039-9338-2*, 93382) Sage.

Datt, Gaurav & Ravallion, Martin. Income Gains for the Poor from Public Works Employment: Evidence for Two Indian Villages. LC 93-43861. (Living Standards Measurement Study Working Papers: No. 100). 62p. 1994. pap. 22.00 (*0-8213-2724-0*, 12724) World Bank.

Datt, Ruddar, ed. Organising the Unorganised Workers. LC 98-906101. (C). 1997. 39.00 (*81-259-0342-9*, Pub. by Vikas) S Asia.

Datta. Anesthetic & Obstetric Management of High-Risk Pregnancy. 2nd ed. (Illus.). 656p. (C). (gr. 13). 1996. text 99.00 (*0-8151-2280-2*, 27531) Mosby Inc.

— Numerical Methods for Linear Control Systems & Analysis. 450p. 1997. write for info. (*0-12-203590-9*) Acad Pr.

Datta, A., et al, eds. Particle Phenomenology in the Nineties: Workshop on High Energy Phenomenology II, 2-15 January 1991, Calcutta, India. LC 92-11874. 700p. (C). 1998. text 130.00 (*981-02-0699-2*) World Scientific Pub.

Datta, A. K. Essential of Human Anatomy, Vol. 2: Head, Neck & Brain. (C). 1989. 150.00 (*0-7855-6116-1*, Pub. by Current Dist) St Mut.

— Essentials of Human Anatomy, Vol. I: Thorax-Abdomen. (C). 1991. 100.00 (*0-89771-347-8*, Pub. by Current Dist) St Mut.

— Essentials of Human Embryology. (C). 1991. 130.00 (*0-89771-346-X*, Pub. by Current Dist) St Mut.

Datta, A. K., ed. Essential of Human Anatomy, Vol. 1: Thorax & Abdomen. (C). 1986. 110.00 (*0-7855-6117-X*, Pub. by Current Dist) St Mut.

— Essentials of Human Anatomy, Vol. II: Head, Neck & Brain. (C). 1990. 140.00 (*0-89771-348-6*, Pub. by Current Dist) St Mut.

Datta, Amal. Sikkim since Independence. (C). 1991. 21.50 (*81-7099-267-2*, Pub. by Mittal Pubs Dist) S Asia.

Datta, Amaresh, ed. Encyclopaedia of Indian Literature, Ea., Vols. 1-6. 1014p. 1987. 59.95 (*0-318-36947-8*) Asia Bk Corp.

Datta, Amlan. An Introduction to India's Economic Development since the Nineteenth Century. (C). 1989. 17.00 (*0-86132-219-3*, Pub. by Popular Prakashan) S Asia.

— A New Radicalism & Other Essays. (C). 1989. 11.00 (*81-85195-22-6*, Pub. by Minerva) S Asia.

Datta, Amres, ed. Encyclopedia of Indian Literature Vol. III: K to Navalram. (C). 1989. 62.00 (*0-8364-2487-5*, Pub. by National Sahitya Akademi) S Asia.

Datta, Aniruddha. Adaptive Internal Model Control. LC 98-2771. (Advances in Industrial Control Ser.). 1998. 79.95 (*3-540-76252-3*) Spr-Verlag.

Datta, Anjan K. & Institute of Social Studies (Netherlands) Staff. Land & Labour Relations in South-West Bangladesh: Resources, Power & Conflict. LC 98-14874. 304p. 1998. text 69.95 (*0-312-21543-6*) St Martin.

***Datta, Ann & Gould, John.** John Gould in Australia: Letters & Drawings: With a Catalogue of Manuscripts, Correspondence & Drawings Relating to the Birds & Mammals of Australia Held in the Natural History Museum, London. LC 97-226485. (Miegunyah Press Ser.: Vol. 2.14). (Illus.). 350p. 2000. 85.00 (*0-522-84780-3*, Pub. by Melbourne Univ Pr) Paul & Co Pubs.

Datta, Asim K. & Roy, B. C. Essentials of Abdomen & Thorax. 1983. 60.00 (*0-7855-7514-6*, Pub. by Current Dist) St Mut.

— Essentials of Head, Neck & Brain. 1983. 65.00 (*0-7855-0788-4*, Pub. by Current Dist) St Mut.

— Essentials of Human Embryology. 458p. 1978. 85.00 (*0-7855-0815-5*, Pub. by Current Dist) St Mut.

Datta, Asim K. Essentials of Human Anatomy Pt. IV: Neuroanatomy. 289p. 1995. pap. (*81-86793-03-8*) Current Bks Intl.

— Essentials of Human Anatomy Pt. 11: Head & Neck. 372p. 1999. pap. (*81-86793-37-2*) Current Bks Intl.

— Essentials of Human Anatomy Pt. 111: Superior & Inferior Extremities. 290p. 1995. pap. (*81-86793-02-X*) Current Bks Intl.

— Essentials of Human Embryology. 299p. 1999. pap. (*81-86793-04-6*) Current Bks Intl.

***Datta, Asim Kumar.** Essentials of Human Anatomy: Thorax & Abdomen. 433p. 1998. pap. (*81-86793-32-1*) Current Bks Intl.

— Essentials of Human Osteology. 262p. 1997. pap. (*81-86793-29-1*) Current Bks Intl.

Datta, Asok, ed. Studies in Archaeology. (C). 1991. 100.00 (*81-85016-29-1*, Pub. by Bks & Bks) S Asia.

Datta, B. Applied & Computational Control, Signals & Circuits, Vol. 1. 385p. 1997. 59.95 (*0-8176-3954-3*) Birkhauser.

Datta-Barua, Lohit. Natural Gas Measurement & Control: A Guide for Operators & Engineers. 205p. 1991. 75.00 (*0-07-015608-5*) McGraw.

Datta, Bhabatosh. Indian Planning at Crossroads. (Illus.). 260p. 1992. text 28.00 (*0-19-562958-2*) OUP.

Datta, Birendranath, jt. ed. see Singh, K. S.

Datta, Biswa N. Numerical Linear Algebra & Applications. LC 94-30071. 750p. 1995. pap. 110.95 (*0-534-17466-3*) Brooks-Cole.

Datta, Biswa N., et al, eds. Applied & Computational Control, Signals & Circuits. annuals 1997. write for info. (*0-614-30185-8*) Spr-Verlag.

— Linear Algebra in Signals, Systems, & Control. LC 88-60026. (Proceedings in Applied Mathematics Ser.: No. 32). xiv, 667p. 1988. 65.75 (*0-89871-223-8*) Soc Indus-Appl Math.

Datta, D. Essentials of Human Embryology. 2nd ed. (C). 1990. 200.00 (*0-7855-4654-5*, Pub. by Current Dist) St Mut.

— General Anatomy. 3rd ed. (C). 1987. 100.00 (*0-7855-4655-3*, Pub. by Current Dist) St Mut.

— Textbook of Gynecology. (C). 1989. 160.00 (*0-7855-4670-7*, Pub. by Current Dist) St Mut.

Datta, Dhirendra M. The Philosophy of Mahatma Gandhi. LC 53-9213. 168p. reprint ed. pap. 52.10 (*0-8357-4744-1*, 203766500009) Bks Demand.

An Asterisk (*) at the beginning of an entry indicates that the title is appearing for the first time.

Datta, Dilip K. Finite Math for Liberal Arts. 304p. (Orig.). (C). 1995. pap. text 15.00 (*0-9638605-2-6*) RI Desktop.
— Math Education at Its Best: The Potsdam Model. LC 93-85952. 235p. 1993. pap. 9.95 (*0-9638605-1-8*) RI Desktop.
Datta, Dipak B. A Comprehensive Introduction to Membrane Biochemistry. (Illus.). 625p. (Orig.). 1987. write for info. (*0-938057-00-6*); pap. text. write for info. (*0-938057-01-4*) Floral Pub.
— With the Hues of Autumn. (Illus.). 150p. 1989. 14.95 (*0-938057-02-2*) Floral Pub.
Datta, K. B. & Mohan, B. M. Orthogonal Functions in Systems & Control. 288p. 1995. text 68.00 (*981-02-1889-3*) World Scientific Pub.
Datta, Kankabati, tr. see Nasrin, Taslima.
Datta, Kavita & Jones, Gareth A. Housing & Finance in Developing Countries. LC 98-24258. (Studies in Development & Society). xxiii, 270 p. 1999. 85.00 (*0-415-17242-X*) Routledge.
Datta, M., et al, eds. Environmental Aspects of Electrochemical Technology. LC 97-194404. (Proceedings Ser.: Vol. 96-21). (Illus.). 296p. 1997. 44.00 (*1-56677-171-4*) Electrochem Soc.
— High Rate Metal Dissolution Processes. LC 95-61592. (Proceedings Ser.: Vol. 95-19). (Illus.). 348p. 1996. 44.00 (*1-56677-114-5*) Electrochem Soc.
Datta, M., et al. Electrochemical Microfabrication: Second International Symposium. (Proceedings Ser.: Vol. 94-32). 422p. 1995. 65.00 (*1-56677-091-2*) Electrochem Soc.
Datta, Madhav, jt. ed. see Osaka, Tetsuya.
***Datta, Manjula.** Bilinguality & Literacy. 244p. 2000. 74.95 (*0-8264-4840-2*); pap. 28.95 (*0-8264-4839-9*) Continuum.
Datta-Mitra, Jayati. Fiscal Management in Adjustment Lending. (World Bank Operations Evaluation Study Ser.). 190p. 1997. pap. 22.00 (*0-8213-3965-6*, 13965) World Bank.
Datta, Moitri. Farewell Sweet Monsoon: A Memoir. (Illus.). iii, 199p. 1996. 24.95 (*0-9654238-0-8*) Upadhya Pubns Intl.
Datta-Munshi, J. S. & Dutta, Hiran M. Fish Morphology: Horizon of New Research. (Illus.). 326p. (C). 1996. text 128.00 (*90-5410-289-6*, Pub. by A A Balkema) Ashgate Pub Co.
Datta Munshi, J. S., jt. auth. see Hughes, G. M.
Datta, Nilanjana S. The Trgveda as Oral Literature. LC 98-915910. 236 p. 1999. write for info. (*81-85151-80-6*) Advent Bks Div.
Datta, P., tr. see Barkow, N. I., ed.
Datta, P., tr. see Dolgin, I. M., ed.
Datta, P., tr. see Kodrat'ev, K. Ya., et al, eds.
Datta, P. K. & Burnell-Gray, J. S., eds. Surface Engineering, Vol. II. 2nd ed. (Process Technology Ser.). 1997. write for info. (*0-85404-752-2*) Am Chemical.
— Surface Engineering, Vol. III. 2nd ed. (Engineering Applications Ser.). 1997. write for info. (*0-85404-757-3*) Am Chemical.
— Surface Engineering Casebook: Solutions to Corrosion & Wear-Related Failures. 352p. 1996. 179.95 (*1-85573-260-2*) Technomic.
Datta, P. K. & Gray, J. S., eds. Surface Engineering, 3 vols., Vol. I: Fundamentals of Coatings. 370p. 1993. 105.00 (*0-85186-665-4*, Q) CRC Pr.
— Surface Engineering, 3 vols., Vol. II: Engineering Applications. 342p. 1993. 105.00 (*0-85186-675-1*, R8667) CRC Pr.
— Surface Engineering, 3 vols., Vol. III: Process Technology & Surface Analysis. 312p. 1993. 105.00 (*0-85186-685-9*, R8668) CRC Pr.
Datta, P. S. Ethnic Peace Accords in India. (C). 1995. 28.00 (*7-7069-8879-5*, Pub. by Vikas) S Asia.
Datta, Prabhat. Regionalisation of Indian Politics. (C). 1993. write for info. (*81-207-1493-8*) Sterling Pubs.
Datta, Prabhat K. Politics of Region & Religion in India. (C). 1991. 18.00 (*81-85024-83-9*, Pub. by Uppal Pub Hse) S Asia.
Datta, Pradip Kumar. Carving Blocs: Communal Ideology in Early Twentieth-Century Bengal. 320p. 1999. 29.95 (*0-19-564379-8*) OUP.
Datta, R. K. Indus Valley Civilization. 1996. 18.00 (*1-886106-69-X*, 669X) Science Pubs.
***Datta-Ray, B. & Baishya, Prabin.** Sociological Constraints to Industrial Development in North East India. LC 98-915418. 273 p. 1998. write for info. (*81-7022-733-X*) Concept.
Datta-Ray, B., et al. Dynamics of a Tribal Society: A Micro-Study LC 93-903374. xvi, 315 p. 1993. write for info. (*81-85565-27-9*, Pub. by Uppal Pub Hse) S Asia.
Datta, Rekha. Why Alliances Endure: The United States-Pakistan Alliance. LC 94-902399. (C). 1994. 22.00 (*81-7003-169-9*, Pub. by S Asia Pubs) S Asia.
***Datta, Rupa.** Family Involvement in Education: A National Portrait, Highlights. 12p. 1999. pap. 3.25 (*0-16-049858-9*) USGPO.
Datta, S. C. Five Eminent Women. (C). 1993. 24.00 (*81-7041-689-2*, Pub. by Anmol) S Asia.
Datta, S. K. Pathogenesis-Related Proteins in Plants. LC 99-12438. 304p. 1999. boxed set 129.95 (*0-8493-0697-3*) CRC Pr.
— Soil Conservation & Land Management. 337p. (C). 1976. text 250.00 (*0-89771-592-6*, Pub. by Intl Bk Distr) St Mut.
Datta, S. K. Soil Conservation & Land Management. 330p. 1989. pap. 350.00 (*81-7089-259-7*, Pub. by Intl Bk Distr) St Mut.
Datta, S. K., ed. see American Society of Mechanical Engineers Staff.
Datta, Sanjay. The Obstetric Anesthesia Handbook, Vol. 2E. 2nd ed. LC 95-788. (Illus.). 368p. (C). (gr. 13). 1995. pap. text 46.95 (*0-8151-2349-3*, 24719) Mosby Inc.
Datta, Satya, ed. Third World Urbanization: Reappraisals & New Perspectives. 282p. (Orig.). 1990. pap. 38.50 (*91-86362-12-7*) Coronet Bks.
Datta, Satya B. Capital Accumulation & Worker's Struggle. (C). 1990. 29.60 (*81-7074-038-X*, Pub. by KP Bagchi) S Asia.
— Capital Accumulation & Workers Struggle in Indian Industrialization: The Case of the Tata Iron & Steel Company, 1900-1970. 295p. (Orig.). 1986. pap. text 48.00 (*91-7146-457-3*) Coronet Bks.
Datta, Sudhin & Lohse, David J. Polymeric Compatibilizers: Uses & Benefits in Polymer Blends. LC 96-14531. 542p. 1996. 139.00 (*1-56990-194-5*) Hanser-Gardner.
Datta, Supriyo. Electronic Transport in Mesoscopic Systems. (Cambridge Studies in Semiconductor Physics & Microelectronic Engineering Ser.: No. 3). (Illus.). 393p. 1997. pap. text 36.95 (*0-521-59943-1*) Cambridge U Pr.
Datta, T. A Treatise on Children's Disease. (C). 1984. 40.00 (*0-7855-4653-7*, Pub. by Current Dist) St Mut.
Datta, V. N. Maulana Azad. 1990. 31.00 (*81-85054-98-3*, Pub. by Manohar) S Asia.
Datta, V. N. & Gleghorn, B. E., eds. A Nationalist Muslim & Indian Politics. LC 75-902114. 352p. 1974. 14.00 (*0-333-90023-5*) S Asia.
Datta, V. N. & Mittal, S. C., eds. Sources on National Movement, Vol. 1: January 1919-September 1920, Protest, Disturbance & Defiance. 1985. 24.00 (*0-8364-1499-3*, Pub. by Allied Pubs) S Asia.
Datta, Venita. Birth of a National Icon: The Literary Avant-Garde & the Origins of the Intellectual in France. LC 98-39033. (Illus.). 256p. (C). 1999. text 57.50 (*0-7914-4207-1*); pap. text 18.95 (*0-7914-4208-X*) State U NY Pr.
Dattaraya. Avadhuta Gita of Dattatreya. Ashokananda, Swami, tr. from SAN. 1978. pap. 4.95 (*81-7120-037-0*, Pub. by Ramakrishna Math) Vedanta Pr.
Dattareya. Avadhuta Gita: The Song of the Ever-Free. Chetanananda, Swami, tr. from SAN. 138p. 1985. pap. 4.95 (*81-7120-004-4*, Pub. by Advaita Ashrama) Vedanta Pr.
***Dattatreya.** Dattatreya's Song of the Avadhut. Abhayananda, Swami, tr. from SAN. LC 99-54114. (Classics of Mystical Literature Ser.). Orig. Title: Dattatreya: The Song of the Avadhut. 172p. 2000. pap. 14.95 (*0-914557-15-7*) Atma Bks.
Dattatreya, Ravi, jt. ed. see Konishi, Atsuo.
Dattatreya, Ravi E. The Structured Note Market: The Definitive Guide for Investors, Traders & Issuers. LC 96-175050. 250p. 1995. text 65.00 (*1-55738-826-1*, Irwn Prfssnl) McGraw-Hill Prof.
Dattatreya, Ravi E., ed. Fixed Income Analytics: State-of-the-Art Debt Analysis & Valuation Modeling. (Institutional Investor Publications). 1991. 69.95 (*1-55738-163-1*, Irwn Prfssnl) McGraw-Hill Prof.
Dattatreya, Ravi E. & Fabozzi, Frank J. Active Total Return Management of Fixed-Income Portfolios. 2nd rev. ed. 350p. 1995. 70.00 (*1-55738-565-3*, Irwn Prfssnl) McGraw-Hill Prof.
Dattatreya, Ravi E. & Hotta, Kensuke, eds. Advanced Interest Rate & Currency Swaps: State-of-the-Art Products, Strategies & Risk Management Applications. 450p. 1993. text 65.00 (*1-55738-444-4*, Irwn Prfssnl) McGraw-Hill Prof.
Dattatreya, Ravi E., et al. Interest Rate & Currency Swaps: The Markets, Products & Applications. 225p. 1993. text 65.00 (*1-55738-468-1*, Irwn Prfssnl) McGraw-Hill Prof.
Dattatreya, Ravi E., jt. auth. see Konishi, Atsuo.
***Dattatri, Kayshav.** C++ Effective Object-Oriented Software Construction. 2nd ed. LC 99-42728. 755p. 1999. pap. text 49.99 (*0-13-086769-1*) P-H.
Dattatri, Kayshav. C++ Effective Object-Oriented Software Construction, Concepts, Principles, Industrial Strategies, & Practices. 704p. 1997. pap. 44.99 (*0-13-104118-5*) P-H.
Dattel, Eugene R. The Sun That Never Rose: The Inside Story of Japan's Failed Attempt at Global Financial Dominance. LC 94-171527. 250p. 1994. text 27.50 (*1-55738-562-9*, Irwn Prfssnl) McGraw-Hill Prof.
D'Attellis, Carlos E. & Fernandez-Berdaguer, Elana M., eds. Wavelet Theory & Harmonic Analysis in Applied Sciences. LC 97-184. (Applied & Numerical Harmonic Analysis Ser.). 400p. 1997. 65.00 (*0-8176-3953-5*) Birkhauser.
D'Attellis, Carlos E. & Fernandez-Berdaguer, Elena M. Wavelet Theory & Harmonic Analysis in Applied Sciences. LC 97-184. 1997. write for info. (*3-7643-3953-5*) Birkhauser.
D'Attilio, Anthony, jt. auth. see Radwin, George E.
Dattilio, Daniel J. Fort Clatsop: The Story Behind the Scenery. LC 86-81743. (Illus.). 48p. (Orig.). 1986. pap. 7.95 (*0-88714-011-4*) KC Pubns.
Dattilio, F. M., jt. ed. see Freeman, Arthur.
Dattilio, Frank M., ed. Case Studies in Couple & Family Therapy: Systemic & Cognitive Perspectives. LC 97-40877. (Family Therapy Ser.). 486p. 1998. lib. bdg. 47.00 (*1-57230-297-6*, C0297) Guilford Pubns.
***Dattilio, Frank M. & Bevilacqua, Louis.** Comparative Treatments for Relationship Dysfunction. LC 99-88867. (Series on Comparative Treatments for Psychological Disorders). 2000. write for info. (*0-8261-1324-9*) Springer Pub.
Dattilio, Frank M. & Freeman, Arthur, eds. Cognitive-Behavioral Strategies in Crisis Intervention. LC 94-8645. 412p. 1994. lib. bdg. 42.95 (*0-89862-221-2*) Guilford Pubns.
***Dattilio, Frank M. & Freeman, Arthur, eds.** Cognitive-Behavioral Strategies in Crisis Intervention. 2nd ed. 459p. 2000. lib. bdg. 46.95 (*1-57230-579-7*, C0579) Guilford Pubns.
***Dattilio, Frank M. & Jongsma, Arthur E.** The Family Therapy Treatment Planner. (Practice Planners Ser.). 272p. 2000. 175.00 incl. disk (*0-471-34769-8*); pap. 39.95 (*0-471-34768-X*) Wiley.
Dattilio, Frank M. & Padesky, Christine A. Cognitive Therapy with Couples. LC 90-52991. 150p. 1990. pap. 21.95 (*0-943158-49-4*, CTCBP) Pro Resource.
Dattilio, Frank M. & Salas-Auvert, Jesus A. Panic Disorder: Assessment & Treatment Through a Wide-Angle Lens. LC 99-27032. 2000. 38.50 (*1-891944-35-5*) Zeig Tucker.
***Dattilo, John.** Facilitation Techniques in Therapeutic Recreation. LC 99-69164. (Illus.). 512p. 2000. text 35.95 (*1-892132-13-3*, FAC115) Venture Pub PA.
Dattilo, John. Inclusive Leisure Services: Responding to the Rights of People with Disabilities. LC 94-61217. 414p. (C). 1994. text 33.95 (*0-910251-68-1*, INC72) Venture Pub PA.
***Dattilo, John.** Leisure Education Program Planning: A Systematic Approach. 2nd rev. ed. LC 99-62854. 355p. (C). 1999. text 31.95 (*1-892132-05-2*, LPP108) Venture Pub PA.
Dattilo, John & Murphy, William D. Behavior Modification in Therapeutic Recreation: An Introductory Learning Manual. LC 87-51016. 174p. 1987. pap. text 19.95 (*0-910251-21-5*) Venture Pub PA.
— Leisure Education Program Planning: A Systematic Approach. LC 91-66103. 485p. 1991. 34.95 (*0-910251-49-5*) Venture Pub PA.
***Dattner, Fabian, et al.** Three Spirits of Leadership: Seeking the United Voice of the Entrepeneur, the Corporation, & the Community. 2000. pap. text 19.95 (*1-875680-69-1*) Woodslane.
Dattoli, G. & Renieri, A. Free Electron Lasers, 1996: Proceedings of the Eighteenth International Free Electron Laser Conference, Rome, Italy, August 26-31, 1996. LC 97-34236. 594p. 1997. 273.00 (*0-444-82819-2*) Elsevier.
Dattoli, G., et al. Lecture Notes on the Free Electron Laser Theory & Related Topics. 400p. (C). 1993. text 86.00 (*981-02-0565-1*); pap. text 48.00 (*981-02-0566-X*) World Scientific Pub.
Datye, Hemant, jt. ed. see Daniel, J. C.
Datyner, Arved. Surfactants in Textile Processing. (Surfactant Science Ser.: Vol. 14). (Illus.). 232p. 1983. text 165.00 (*0-8247-1812-7*) Dekker.
Datz, Frederick L. Gamuts in Nuclear Medicine. 3rd ed. LC 94-231304. 512p. (C). (gr. 13). 1994. pap. text 46.95 (*0-8016-8097-2*, 08097) Mosby Inc.
— Handbook of Nuclear Medicine. 2nd rev. ed. LC 93-14365. (Handbooks in Radiology Ser.). Orig. Title: Nuclear Medicine. (Illus.). 294p. (C). (gr. 13). 1993. reprint ed. pap. text 49.95 (*0-8016-7700-9*, 07700) Mosby Inc.
Datz, Frederick L., jt. ed. see Taylor, Andrew, Jr.
Datz, I. M. Planning in a Military Context: An Army Perspective. 1998. 38.00 (*81-259-0438-7*, Pub. by Vikas) S Asia.
Datz, Stephen R. The Buyer's Guide: An Analysis of Selected U. S. Stamps. 176p. (Orig.). 1992. pap. 14.95 (*0-88219-026-1*) General Trade.
***Datz, Stephen R.** The Buyers Guide: Get the Most for Your Stamp Collecting Dollar. 2nd ed. (Illus.). 171p. 2000. pap. 14.95 (*0-88219-031-8*, Pub. by General Trade) IPG Chicago.
— Catalogue of Errors on U. S. Postage Stamps 2001. 10th rev. ed. LC 97-80544. (Illus.). 200p. 2000. pap 14.95 (*0-87341-942-1*, ER00) Krause Pubns.
Datz, Stephen R. Collecting Stamps: Instant Expert, Vol. 1. LC 96-197007. (Instant Expert Ser.). 150p. (Orig.). 1996. pap. 14.00 (*1-887110-01-1*) Allian Pubng.
— On the Road: The Quest for Stamps. 168p. (Orig.). 1991. pap. 9.95 (*0-88219-025-3*) General Trade.
— Stamp Collecting: Discover the Fun of the World's Most Popular Hobby! 1999. pap. text 14.95 (*0-88219-030-X*) General Trade.
— Stamp Investing. LC 98-138665. (Illus.). 166p. 1997. pap. 14.95 (*0-88219-029-6*, General Philatelic) General Trade.
— Top Dollar Paid: The Complete Guide to Selling Your Stamps. (Illus.). 176p. (Orig.). 1989. pap. 14.95 (*0-88219-022-9*) General Trade.
***Datz, Stephen R.** 2000 Catalogue of Errors on U. S. Postage Stamps. 9th ed. LC 97-80544. (Illus.). 180p. 1999. pap. 14.95 (*0-87341-771-2*) Krause Pubns.
Datz, Stephen R. The Wild Side: Philatelic Mischief, Murder & Intrigue. 164p. 1990. pap. 9.95 (*0-88219-024-5*) General Trade.
Datz, Stephen R., ed. see Sine, Richard L.
Dau-Schmidt, Kenneth G. & Ulen, Thomas S., eds. Law & Economics Anthology: An Anthology. LC 98-228634. 580p. 1998. pap. 29.95 (*0-87084-208-0*) Anderson Pub Co.
Dau, W. H. Woman Suffrage in the Church. 23p. 1997. reprint ed. pap. 1.75 (*1-891469-11-8*) Repristination.
Dau, W. H., tr. see Walther, Carl F.
Daub, Edward E. Kanji for Understanding Technical Japanese. LC 94-24047. (Technical Japanese Supplements Ser.). (ENG & JPN.). 216p. 1995 pap. 30.00 (*0-299-14704-5*) U of Wis Pr.
Daub, Edward E., et al. Basic Technical Japanese. LC 90-50082. 800p. (C). 1990. text 59.95 (*0-299-12730-3*) U of Wis Pr.
— Comprehending Technical Japanese. LC 74-5900. 440p. 1975. 44.95 (*0-299-06680-0*) U of Wis Pr.
Daub, Edward E., jt. auth. see Davis, James L.
Daub, G. William. Basic Chemistry. 7th ed. 1995. pap. text, student ed. 32.00 (*0-13-378530-0*) P-H.
Daub, G. William & Seese, William S. Basic Chemistry. 7th ed. LC 95-32224. 652p. (C). 1995. 82.00 (*0-13-373630-X*) P-H.
Daub, Merv. Gael Force: A Century of Football at Queen's. (Illus.). 304p. 1996. 49.95 (*0-7735-1509-7*, Pub. by McG-Queens Univ Pr); pap. 22.95 (*0-7735-1519-4*, Pub. by McG-Queens Univ Pr) CUP Services.
Daub, Mervin. Canadian Economic Forecasting: In a World Where All's Unsure. 236p. 1987. 65.00 (*0-7735-0621-7*, Pub. by McG-Queens Univ Pr) CUP Services.
***Daub, Mervin & Buchan, P. Bruce.** Getting down to Business: A History of Business Education at Queen's, 1889-1999. 152p. 1999. 55.00 (*0-7735-2007-4*) McG-Queens Univ Pr.
Daub, Suzanne, ed. see Cennamo, James.
Daub, William G. In Preparation for College Chemistry. 5th ed. LC 94-154335. 352p. 1993. pap. text 46.00 (*0-13-120627-3*) P-H.
Daubach, Gunther. Computer Dictionary: Woerterbuch der Computerei. 9th ed. (ENG & GER.). 121p. 1990. 65.00 (*0-8288-0241-6*, M15291) Fr & Eur.
— Worterbuch der Computerei. 9th ed. (ENG & GER.). 121p. 1990. lib. bdg. 75.00 (*0-8288-3599-3*) Fr & Eur.
Daube, David. Appeasement or Resistance & Other Essays on New Testament Judaism. 1987. 40.00 (*0-520-06158-6*, Pub. by U CA Pr) Cal Prin Full Svc.
— Collected Works of David Daube: New Testament & Rabbinic Judaism. Carmichael, Calum M., ed. (Studies in Comparative Legal History: Vol. 2). 1000p. (C). Date not set. text 60.00 (*1-882239-04-0*) Robbins Collection.
— Collected Works of David Daube: Talmudic Law. Carmichael, Calum M., ed. & tr. by. LC 92-61641. (Studies in Comparative Legal History: Vol. 1). (ARC, ENG, GER, GRE & HEB., Illus.). 527p. (C). 1992. text 40.00 (*1-882239-00-8*) Robbins Collection.
— Collected Works of David Daube: Talmudic Law, Set. Carmichael, Calum M., ed. & tr. by. LC 92-61641. (Studies in Comparative Legal History). (ARC, ENG, GER, GRE & HEB., Illus.). 527p. (C). 1998. text. write for info. (*1-882239-01-6*) Robbins Collection.
— The Exodus Pattern in the Bible, No. 2. LC 78-9920. 94p. 1979. reprint ed. lib. bdg. 35.00 (*0-313-21190-6*, DAEX, Greenwood Pr) Greenwood.
— The New Testament & Rabbinic Judaism. 496p. 1994. pap. 24.95 (*1-56563-141-2*) Hendrickson MA.
— The New Testament & Rabbinic Judaism. LC 73-2191. (Jewish People; History, Religion, Literature Ser.). 1979. reprint ed. 42.95 (*0-405-05257-X*) Ayer.
Daube, David, jt. auth. see Carmichael, Calum.
Daube, Jasper R., ed. Clinical Neurophysiology. LC 95-31428. (Contemporary Neurology Ser.: No. 46). (Illus.). 560p. 1996. text 150.00 (*0-19-513652-7*) OUP.
Daube, Jasper R., et al. Medical Neurosciences: An Approach to Anatomy, Pathology, & Physiology by Systems & Levels. 2nd ed. 1985. pap. text 27.00 (*0-685-03086-5*, Little Brwn Med Div) Lppncott W & W.
Daube, Jean-Michel. Lexique Bilingue des Techniques Commerciales, Anglais-Francais/Francais-Anglais. (ENG & FRE.). write for info. (*0-7859-9324-X*) Fr & Eur.
— Lexique Bilingue du Commerce Internationale, Anglais-Francais-Francais-Anglais. (ENG & FRE.). 208p. 1996. 19.95 (*0-7859-9321-5*) Fr & Eur.
Daubechies, I. Ten Lectures on Wavelets. LC 92-13201. (CBMS-NSF Regional Conference Series in Applied Mathematics: No. 61). xix, 357p. 1992. pap. text 49.50 (*0-89871-274-2*) Soc Indus-Appl Math.
— Wavelets: A Selected Collection of Published Papers. (Series in Approximations & Decomposition). 500p. 1997. text 78.00 (*981-02-2409-5*) World Scientific Pub.
Daubechies, Ingrid, ed. Different Perspectives on Wavelets. LC 93-33264. (Proceedings of Symposia in Applied Mathematics Ser.: No. 47). 205p. 1993. text 34.00 (*0-8218-5503-4*, PSAPM/47) Am Math.
Dauben, Joseph W. Abraham Robinson: The Creation of Non-Standard Analysis: Personal & Mathematical Odyssey. LC 94-32715. 540p. 1995. text 65.00 (*0-691-03745-0*, Pub. by Princeton U Pr) Cal Prin Full Svc.
— Abraham Robinson: The Creation of Nonstandard Analysis, a Personal & Mathematical Odyssey. 579p. 1995. pap. text 29.95 (*0-691-05911-X*, Pub. by Princeton U Pr) Cal Prin Full Svc.
— Georg Cantor: His Mathematics & Philosophpy of the Infinite. (Illus.). 413p. (C). 1990. pap. text 24.95 (*0-691-02447-2*, Pub. by Princeton U Pr) Cal Prin Full Svc.
— Georg Cantor: His Mathematics & Philosophy of the Infinite. LC 77-23435. 418p. reprint ed. pap. 129.60 (*0-7837-2245-1*, 205733300004) Bks Demand.
***Dauben, Joseph W. & Lewis, A., eds.** The History of Mathematics from Antiquity to the Present: A Selective Annotated Bibliography. rev. ed. 2000. audio compact disk 49.00 (*0-8218-0844-3*) Am Math.
Dauben, William G. Organic Reactions, Vol. 29. LC 79-642486. 480p. (C). 1983. reprint ed. 99.95 (*0-471-87490-6*) Wiley.
Dauben, William G., ed. Organic Reactions, Vol. 17. (Organic Reactions Ser.). 352p. 1969. 98.95 (*0-471-19615-0*) Wiley.
— Organic Reactions, Vol. 18. (Organic Reactions Ser.). 475p. 1970. 98.95 (*0-471-19618-5*) Wiley.
Dauben, William G., ed. Organic Reactions, Vol. 19. (Organic Reactions Ser.). 434p. 1972. 98.95 (*0-471-19619-3*) Wiley.
— Organic Reactions, Vol. 20. (Organic Reactions Ser.). 494p. 1973. 98.95 (*0-471-19621-5*) Wiley.
— Organic Reactions, Vol. 24. 431p. 1976. 98.95 (*0-471-19625-8*) Wiley.
— Organic Reactions, Vol. 28. (Organic Reactions Ser.). 347p. 1982. 99.95 (*0-471-86141-3*) Wiley.
— Organic Reactions, Vol. 30. (Organic Reactions Ser.). 592p. 1984. 99.95 (*0-471-89013-8*) Wiley.

— Organic Reactions, Vol. 31. LC 42-20265. (Organic Reaction Mechanisms Ser.: No. 2-201). 416p. 1984. 99.95 (*0-471-88671-8*) Wiley.

— Organic Reactions, Vol. 32. (Organic Reactions Ser.). 544p. 1984. 99.95 (*0-471-88101-5*) Wiley.

Daubendiek, Bertha A., ed. see Newnan, Edna S.

Daubeny, Ulric. Orchestral Wind Instruments, Ancient & Modern. (Select Bibliographies Reprint Ser.). 1977. 18.95 (*0-8369-5597-8*) Ayer.

— Orchestral Wind Instruments, Ancient & Modern. 1977. lib. bdg. 59.95 (*0-8490-2380-7*) Gordon Pr.

— Orchestral Wind Instruments, Ancient & Modern. 147p. 1990. reprint ed. lib. bdg. 59.00 (*0-7812-9113-5*) Rprt Serv.

Dauber, Andrew, ed. see Gilbertson, Michelle.

Dauber, Cori E. Cold War Analytical Structures & the Post Post-War World: A Critique of Deterrence Theory. LC 92-28475. (Political Communication Ser.). 224p. 1993. 52.95 (*0-275-94419-0*, C4419, Praeger Pubs) Greenwood.

Dauber, Heinrich, jt. ed. see Fox, Jonathan.

Dauber, Kenneth. The Idea of Authorship in America: Democratic Poetics from Franklin to Melville. LC 89-40530. 288p. (Orig.). reprint ed. pap. 89.30 (*0-608-09903-1*, 206924100003) Bks Demand.

— Rediscovering Hawthorne. LC 76-45893. 248p. reprint ed. 76.90 (*0-8357-9510-1*, 201403000088) Bks Demand.

Dauber, Maximilien, jt. auth. see De Bruycker, Daniel.

Dauber, Maximilien, jt. auth. see Deltenre, Chantal.

Dauber, Nick. How to Prepare for the CPA: Certified Public Accountant Exam. 6th ed. LC 97-44962. 400p. 1998. pap. 18.95 (*0-7641-0185-4*) Barron.

Dauber, Nicky A., et al. The Vest-Pocket CPA. 2nd ed. LC 96-21189. 576p. (C). 1996. text 39.95 (*0-13-462300-2*); pap. text 15.95 (*0-13-462318-5*) P-H.

Dauber, Philip M. The Three Big Bangs. (C). 1997. pap. 14.00 (*0-201-15495-1*) Addison-Wesley.

Dauber, Roslyn & Cain, Melinda, eds. Women & Technological Change in Developing Countries. LC 80-21653. (AAAS Selected Symposium Ser.: No. 53). 266p. 1980. pap. text 38.50 (*0-89158-791-8*) Westview.

Dauber, W., jt. auth. see Feneis, H.

Dauber, Wolfgang, jt. auth. see Feneis, Heinz.

D'Auberge, Alfred. The Alfred d'Auberge Piano Course, Bk. 2. 48p. 1961. pap. 6.95 (*0-7390-0786-6*, 504) Alfred Pub.

D'Auberge, Alfred. It's Recorder Time: Alfred Edition. 1968. pap. 3.50 (*0-88284-814-3*) Alfred Pub.

D'Auberge, Alfred & Manus, Morton. Alfred's Basic Guitar Method, Bk. 1. 1966. pap. 6.50 (*0-88284-790-2*) Alfred Pub.

D'Auberge, Alfred & Manus, Morton. Alfred's Basic Guitar Method, Bk. 1. (Basic Guitar Method Ser.). 1995. audio compact disk 9.95 (*0-7390-0661-4*, 14045) Alfred Pub.

— Alfred's Basic Guitar Method, Bk.2. (Alfred's Basic Guitar Method Ser.). 48p. 1959. pap. 6.95 (*0-7390-0657-6*, 306) Alfred Pub.

— Alfred's Basic Guitar Method, Bk.2. (Alfred's Basic Guitar Method Ser.). 1997. pap. 16.90 incl. audio compact disk (*0-7390-0658-4*, 14960) Alfred Pub.

Daubert, Darlene M., jt. auth. see Brownstein, Oscar L.

Daubert, J. Claude, et al, eds. Prevention of Tachyarrhythmias with Cardiac Pacing. LC 96-46589. (Illus.). 224p. 1996. 39.50 (*0-87993-651-7*) Futura Pub.

Daubert, James R. & Rothert, Eugene A., Jr. Horticultural Therapy for the Mentally Handicapped. (Illus.). 118p. (C). 1981. pap. 10.00 (*0-939914-04-2*) Chi Horticult.

Daubert, James R., jt. auth. see Rothert, Eugene A.

Daubert, Madeline J. Financial Management for Small & Medium-Sized Libraries. LC 93-1076. (Illus.). 270p. 1993. pap. text 38.00 (*0-8389-0618-4*) ALA.

— Money Talk: Accounting Fundamentals for Special Librarians. 47p. 1995. pap. 85.00 (*0-87111-445-3*) SLA.

Daubert, T. E. & Danner, R. P. Physical & Thermodynamic Properties of Pure Chemicals, No. 6. 600p. 1996. ring bd. 175.00 (*1-56032-491-0*) Taylor & Francis.

— Physical & Thermodynamic Properties of Pure Chemicals, Suppl. 1. 416p. 1991. ring bd. 155.00 (*1-56032-155-5*) Hemisp Pub.

— Physical & Thermodynamic Properties of Pure Chemicals, Suppl. 3. 1993. ring bd. 175.00 (*1-56032-281-0*) Hemisp Pub.

— Physical & Thermodynamic Properties of Pure Chemicals, Suppl. 4. 1994. ring bd. 175.00 (*1-56032-307-8*) Hemisp Pub.

— Physical & Thermodynamic Properties of Pure Chemicals, Suppl. 5. 440p. 1995. ring bd. 175.00 (*1-56032-333-7*) Hemisp Pub.

— Physical & Thermodynamic Properties of Pure Chemicals, Supplement 2. 736p. 1992. ring bd. 175.00 (*1-56032-270-5*) Hemisp Pub.

Daubert, T. E. & Foster, Diane, eds. Physical & Thermodynamic Properties of Pure Chemicals: Data Compilation, 4 vols. 1100p. 1989. 412.00 (*0-89116-948-2*) Hemisp Pub.

Daubert, Todd & Nelson, Pauline. Fractions: An Integrated Unit. (ECS Thematic Math Unit Ser.). (Illus.). 128p. (Orig.). 1996. pap., teacher ed. 16.95 (*1-57022-052-2*) ECS Lrn Systs.

— Geometry: An Integrated Unit. (ECS Thematic Math Unit Ser.). (Illus.). 128p. (Orig.). 1995. pap. 15.95 (*1-57022-049-2*) ECS Lrn Systs.

— Money. (Activity Book for Math Ser.). (Illus.). 112p. (Orig.). 1995. pap. 14.95 (*1-57022-045-X*) ECS Lrn Systs.

Daubert, Todd, jt. auth. see Nelson, Pauline.

D'Aubigne, Agrippa. His Life, to His Children - Sa Vie a Ses Enfants. Nothnagle, John, tr. from FRE. & intro. by. LC 88-20491. 201p. 1989. reprint ed. pap. 62.40 (*0-608-02684-0*, 206333700004) Bks Demand.

— Les Tragiques, 4 tomes. Garnier, M. & Plattard, Jean, eds. (Soc. des Textes Francais Modernes Ser.). 84.50 (*0-685-34180-1*) Fr & Eur.

D'Aubigne, J. H. Cromwell, the Protector. 1992. 17.99 (*0-87377-975-4*) GAM Pubns.

— History of the Reformation. (Illus.). 904p. 1993. reprint ed. pap. 19.95 (*0-923309-14-4*) Hartland Pubns.

D'Aubigne, Merle. The Reformation in England. 1977. pap. 39.99 (*0-85151-488-X*) Banner of Truth.

— The Reformation in England, 2 vols., 1. 1977. pap. 21.99 (*0-85151-486-3*) Banner of Truth.

— The Reformation in England, 2 vols., 2. 1977. pap. 21.99 (*0-85151-487-1*) Banner of Truth.

D'Aubigne, Theodore A. Oeuvres. deluxe ed. (Pleiade Ser.). (FRE.). 1664p. 1969. 110.00 (*0-8288-3418-0*, F28320) Fr & Eur.

Daubitz, Paul. Complete Guide to Buying a Telephone System. 152p. (C). 1985. text. write for info. (*0-89006-230-7*) Artech Hse.

— The Complete Guide to Buying a Telephone System. LC 86-71825. 160p. reprint ed. pap. 49.60 (*0-7837-5845-6*, 204556400006) Bks Demand.

Daublon, Georges, jt. auth. see Baker, Keith F.

***Daubney, Kate.** Now Voyager: A Film Score Guide, 1. LC 99-88601. (Film Score Guides Ser.: Vol. 1). 128p. 2000. lib. bdg. 45.00 (*0-313-31253-2*, Greenwood Pr) Greenwood.

Daubree, Cecile, jt. auth. see Azam, Jean-Paul.

Dauch, Richard E. & Troyanovich, Jack. Passion for Manufacturing: Real World Advice from Dick Dauch - The Man Who Engineered the Manufacturing Renaissance at Chrysler. LC 92-85522. (Illus.). 274p. 1993. 39.00 (*0-87263-436-1*) SME.

Dauchet, M. & Nivat, Maurice, eds. CAAP '88. (Lecture Notes in Computer Science Ser.: Vol. 299). viii, 304p. 1988. 39.00 (*0-387-19021-X*) Spr-Verlag.

Dauchin, Pierre. Dictionnaire des Unites et Valeurs Approximatives. (FRE.). 180p. 1992. pap. 49.95 (*0-7859-7945-X*, 2714428754) Fr & Eur.

Daud, Abraham I. The Exalted Faith. Weiss, Gershon, ed. Samuelson, Norbert M., tr. LC 83-49341. (HEB.). 408p. 1986. 95.00 (*0-8386-3185-1*) Fairleigh Dickinson.

Daudel, D., et al, eds. Structure & Dynamics of Molecular Systems, No. I. 1985. text 140.50 (*90-277-1977-2*) Kluwer Academic.

Daudel, Raymond. Quantum Theory of Chemical Reactivity. LC 73-75762. 1973. pap. text 88.00 (*90-277-0420-1*) Kluwer Academic.

Daudel, Raymond, et al, eds. Quantum Theory of Chemical Reactions. 1982. lib. bdg. 88.00 (*90-277-1467-3*) Kluwer Academic.

— Quantum Theory of Chemical Reactions: Collision Theory, Reaction Path, Static Indices, Vol. 1. 1979. text 155.00 (*90-277-1047-3*) Kluwer Academic.

— Quantum Theory of Chemical Reactions: Solvent Effect, Reaction Mechanisms, Photochemical Processes, Vol. 11. 340p. 1980. lib. bdg. 112.00 (*90-277-1182-8*) Kluwer Academic.

— Structure & Dynamics of Molecular Systems, No. II. 1986. text 158.50 (*90-277-2246-3*) Kluwer Academic.

Daudel, Raymond & Pullman, Bernard, eds. The World of Quantum Chemistry: Proceedings, First International Congress of Quantum Chemistry, Menton, France, July 4-10, 1973. LC 73-91429. 1974. text 176.50 (*90-277-0421-X*) Kluwer Academic.

Daudel, Raymond & Sandorfy, Camille. Semiempirical Wave-Mechanical Calculations Polyatomic Molecules: A Current Review. LC 74-140525. (Yale Series in the Sciences). (Illus.). 147p. reprint ed. pap. 45.60 (*0-608-11851-6*, 201679700005) Bks Demand.

Daudel, Raymond, et al. Quantum Chemistry. LC 82-23688. (Illus.). 574p. reprint ed. pap. 178.00 (*0-8357-4319-5*, 203711800007) Bks Demand.

Daudel, Sylvain, et al. Yield Management: Applications to Air Transport & Other Service Industries. 150p. 1994. pap. 39.00 (*2-908537-10-9*, Pub. by Inst Air Transport) Bks Intl VA.

Daudelin, Jean & Dosman, Edgar. Adjusting the Sights: A New Policy for a Changing Hemisphere. (Changing Americas Ser.). 256p. 1999. text 65.00 (*0-88629-299-9*) McG-Queens Univ Pr.

Daudelin, Marilyn W., jt. auth. see Seibert, Kent W.

***Dauderstadt, Ulrike Anna.** A Thermal Accelerometer. (Illus.). 156p. 1999. pap. 42.50 (*90-407-1885-7*, Pub. by Delft U Pr) Coronet Bks.

Daudert, Charles. The Bridge Monkey: Murder in Heidelberg. LC 98-71421. 250p. 1998. 22.00 (*0-945732-01-5*, 2015) Hansa-Hewlett.

— In the Wake of the Northern Lights. LC 88-80455. 360p. 1988. 19.95 (*0-945732-00-7*) Hansa-Hewlett.

— The Temptation of St. Rosalie: Portrait of a Black Slave Owner. unabridged ed. LC 99-71564. (Illus.). 386p. 1999. 24.00 (*0-945732-02-3*) Hansa-Hewlett.

Daudet. Les Contes du Lundi. unabridged ed. (FRE.). pap. 5.95 (*2-87714-290-6*, Pub. by Bookking Intl) Distribks Inc.

— Lettres de Mon Moulin. (FRE.). (C). 1985. pap. 8.95 (*0-8442-1828-6*, VF1828-6) NTC Contemp Pub Co.

— Lettres de Mon Moulin. unabridged ed. (FRE.). pap. 6.95 (*2-87714-135-7*, Pub. by Bookking Intl) Distribks Inc.

— Le Petit Chose. unabridged ed. (FRE.). pap. 7.95 (*2-87714-195-0*, Pub. by Bookking Intl) Distribks Inc.

— Tartarin de Tarascon. (FRE.). (C). 1968. pap. 7.95 (*0-8442-1959-2*, VF1959-2) NTC Contemp Pub Co.

Daudet, Alphonse. Adventures Prodigieuses De Tartarin De Tarascon. (FRE.). 256p. 1987. pap. 10.95 (*0-7859-2061-7*, 2070378241) Fr & Eur.

— L' Arlesienne. 11.00 (*0-685-34888-1*) Fr & Eur.

— L' Arlesienne. (FRE.). 170p. 1986. pap. 24.95 (*0-7859-4665-9*) Fr & Eur.

— La Belle-Nivernaise, & Other Stories. LC 77-130056. (Short Story Index Reprint Ser.). 1977. 17.95 (*0-8369-3643-4*) Ayer.

— La Chevre de M. Seguin.Tr. of M. Seguin's Goat. (FRE., Illus.). 48p. 1998. boxed set 11.95 incl. audio (*2-921997-56-8*, Pub. by Coffragants) Penton Overseas.

— La Chevre de Monsieur Seguin. (FRE., Illus.). 32p. 1989. pap. 9.95 (*0-7859-4668-3*) Fr & Eur.

— Contes Choisis. (FRE., Illus.). 186p. 1977. 10.95 (*0-8288-9183-4*, F60002) Fr & Eur.

— Les Contes du Lundi. (FRE.). 1962. pap. 10.95 (*0-8288-9188-5*, F59800) Fr & Eur.

— Les Contes du Lundi. 344p. 1969. 13.95 (*0-686-55587-2*) Fr & Eur.

— Fromont Jeune et Risler Aine. (FRE.). 306p. 1953. 8.95 (*0-8288-9184-2*, F59830) Fr & Eur.

— La Legende des Siecles: Fragments. (FRE., Illus.). 31p. 1977. 13.95 (*0-7859-1174-X*, 2203131241) Fr & Eur.

— Letters from My Mill & Letters to an Absent One. LC 72-37266. (Short Story Index Reprint Ser.). 1980. reprint ed. 20.95 (*0-8369-4077-6*) Ayer.

— Lettres de Mon Moulin. (Illus.). write for info. (*0-318-52036-2*, 848); 428.00 (*0-685-34889-X*) Fr & Eur.

— Lettres de Mon Moulin. (FRE.). 1984. pap. 11.95 (*0-7859-1988-0*, 2070375331) Fr & Eur.

— Lettres de Mon Moulin. (Folio Ser.: No. 1533). (FRE., Illus.). 1962. 9.95 (*2-07-037533-1*) Schoenhof.

— Monday Tales. LC 78-113654. (Short Story Index Reprint Ser.). 1977. 21.95 (*0-8369-3383-4*) Ayer.

— Le Petit Chose. (FRE.). 447p. 1977. pap. 11.95 (*0-7859-2213-X*, 207036979X) Fr & Eur.

— Le Petit Chose. (FRE.). 347p. 1989. pap. 10.95 (*0-7859-4666-7*) Fr & Eur.

— Le Petit Chose. (Folio Ser.: No. 979). (FRE.). 420p. 1948. pap. 10.95 (*2-07-036979-X*) Schoenhof.

— Le Roi Pecheur. (FRE.). 78p. 1988. 13.95 (*0-7859-1202-9*, 2876230321) Fr & Eur.

— Les Rois en Exil. (FRE.). 1940. pap. 13.95 (*0-7859-5493-7*) Fr & Eur.

— Sapho. (FRE.). 247p. 1992. pap. 28.95 (*0-7859-4667-5*) Fr & Eur.

— Sappho. Wilkins, Eithne, tr. from FRE. LC 88-60593. 183p. 1988. reprint ed. pap. 14.95 (*0-948166-12-6*, Pub. by Soho Bk Co) Dufour.

— Le Secret de Maitre Cornille. (FRE., Illus.). 32p. 1964. 14.95 (*0-8288-9187-7*, F60050) Fr & Eur.

— Sortileges. (FRE., Illus.). 125p. 1991. 24.95 (*0-7859-1204-5*, 2878580184) Fr & Eur.

— Soutien De Famille. (FRE.). 460p. 1898. 14.95 (*0-8288-9191-5*, F59870) Fr & Eur.

— Tartarin de Tarascon. (Coll. Prestige). 1965. 27.95 (*0-685-11580-1*) Fr & Eur.

— Tartarin de Tarascon. (FRE., Illus.). 228p. 1991. pap. 14.95 (*0-7859-4669-1*) Fr & Eur.

— Tartarin de Tarascon. (Folio Ser.: No. 1824). (FRE.). pap. 7.95 (*2-07-037824-1*) Schoenhof.

— Tartarin de Tarascon. unabridged ed. (FRE.). Date not set. reprint ed. pap. 6.95 (*2-87714-338-4*, Pub. by Bookking Intl) Distribks Inc.

— Tartarin sur les Alpes. 8.95 (*0-686-55601-1*) Fr & Eur.

Daudet, Leon. Oeuvres, Vol. 1. (Pleiade Ser.). (FRE.). 1986. 120.00 (*0-8288-3471-7*, M10355) Fr & Eur.

— Oeuvres, Vol. 2. (Pleiade Ser.: No. 2). (FRE.). 1990. 120.00 (*0-8288-3472-5*, F98140) Fr & Eur.

— Le Voyage de Shakespeare. (FRE.). 384p. 1969. pap. 10.95 (*0-7859-1776-4*, 2070365387) Fr & Eur.

Daudet, Y., jt. auth. see Debbasch, J.

Daudin, H. Cuvier Et Lamarck: Les Classes Zoologiques et L'Idee de Serie Animale, 1790-1830, 2 vols., Set. (FRE.). 798p. 1983. pap. text 44.00 (*2-903928-02-9*) Gordon & Breach.

Daudin, H. Cuvier et Lamarck: Les Classes Zoologiques et l'idee de Serie Animale (1790-1830), Tome II. (FRE.). 798p. 1983. pap. text 44.00 (*2-903928-04-5*) Ed des Arch.

Daudin, H. De Linne A Lamarck: Methodes de la Classification et Idee de Serie en Botanique et En Zoologie. (FRE.). 264p. 1984. pap. text 32.00 (*2-903928-05-3*) Gordon & Breach.

Daudistel, Howard, et al. Criminal Justice: Situations & Decisions. (C). 1979. write for info. (*0-318-53476-2*); write for info. (*0-03-039426-0*) Harcourt Coll Pubs.

Daudon, M., jt. ed. see Dao, N. Quy.

Dauenhauer, Bernard, ed. Textual Fidelity & Textual Disregard. LC 89-27808. (American University Studies: Comparative Literature: Ser. III, Vol. 33). XVIII, 182p. 1990. text 40.95 (*0-8204-1221-X*) P Lang Pubng.

Dauenhauer, Bernard P. Citizenship in a Fragile World. 250p. (C). 1996. pap. text 25.95 (*0-8476-8223-4*); lib. bdg. 66.00 (*0-8476-8222-6*) Rowman.

— Elements of Responsible Politics. (Contributions to Phenomenology Ser.). 304p. (C). 1991. lib. bdg. 155.50 (*0-7923-1329-1*, Pub. by Kluwer Academic) Kluwer Academic.

— Paul Ricoeur: The Promise & Risk of Politics. LC 98-37915. (Twentieth Century Political Thinkers Ser.: No. 100). 320p. 1998. pap. 24.95 (*0-8476-9237-X*); text 68.00 (*0-8476-9236-1*) Rowman.

— The Politics of Hope. (Critical Social Thought Ser.). 200p. 1986. 49.50 (*0-7102-0823-5*, 08235, Routledge Thoemms) Routledge.

— Silence: The Phenomenon & Its Ontological Significance. LC 80-7683. 223p. 1980. reprint ed. pap. 69.20 (*0-7837-6099-X*, 205914500008) Bks Demand.

***Dauenhauer, Nora M.** Life Woven with Song. LC 99-6845. (Sun Tracks Ser.). 160p. 2000. pap. 16.95 (*0-8165-2006-2*) U of Ariz Pr.

Dauenhauer, Nora M. & Dauenhauer, Richard, eds. Haa Kusteeyi, Our Culture: Tingit Life Stories. LC 94-28657. (Classics of Tlingit Oral Literature Ser.: Vol. 3). (Illus.). 600p. 1994. pap. 29.95 (*0-295-97401-X*); text 50.00 (*0-295-97400-1*) U of Wash Pr.

— Haa Shuka, Our Ancestors. (Classics of Tlingit Oral Literature Ser.: Vol. I). (Illus.). 520p. 1987. pap. 24.95 (*0-295-96495-2*) U of Wash Pr.

— Haa Tuwunaagu Yis, for Healing Our Spirit. (Classics of Tlingit Oral Literature Ser.: Vol. II). (Illus.). 664p. 1990. 35.00 (*0-295-96849-4*); pap. 22.50 (*0-295-96850-8*) U of Wash Pr.

Dauenhauer, Richard. Phenologies. (Orig.). 1988. pap. 6.00 (*0-914476-90-4*) Thorp Springs.

Dauenhauer, Richard & Binham, Philip, eds. Snow in May: An Anthology of Modern Finnish Writing 1945-1972. LC 74-4967. (Illus.). 389p. 1978. 40.00 (*0-8386-1583-X*) Fairleigh Dickinson.

Dauenhauer, Richard, jt. ed. see Dauenhauer, Nora M.

Dauer, Edward A., ed. see Institute of Medicine, Forum on Blood Safety Staff.

Dauer, Ernst A. Comparative Operating Experience of Consumer Installment Financing Agencies & Commercial Banks, 1929-41. (Financial Research Program II: Studies in Consumer Installment Financing: No. 10). 239p. 1944. reprint ed. 62.20 (*0-87014-126-0*) Natl Bur Econ Res.

Dauer, Karen T. Down on the Farm. LC 93-60298. (Illus.). 150p. (Orig.). 1993. pap. 11.95 (*0-9630213-2-X*) Winsted Pubns.

Dauer, Lesley. The Fragile City. LC 96-3208. (Bluestem Award Ser.). 72p. (C). 1996. 24.00 (*1-878325-17-5*); pap. 11.00 (*1-878325-16-7*) Bluestem Press.

Dauer, Manning J. The Adams Federalists. LC 68-17645. (Illus.). 320p. reprint ed. pap. 99.20 (*0-8357-5093-0*, 202580700046) Bks Demand.

Dauer, Manning J., ed. Florida's Politics & Government. 2nd ed. LC 84-7303. 518p. (Orig.). (C). 1984. pap. 29.95 (*0-8130-0797-6*) U Press Fla.

Dauer, Rebecca M. Accurate English: A Complete Course in Pronunciation. 256p. (C). 1992. pap. 31.53 (*0-13-007253-2*) P-H.

Daug, jt. auth. see Feldman, Arthur M.

***Daugavietis, Pamela H., ed.** Women's Voices, Women's Visions: A Book of Days for the New Millennium. (Illus.). 224p. 1999. 16.95 (*0-9672723-4-3*) Innernet Affirm.

Daugbjerg, Carsten. Policy Networks under Pressure: Pollution Control, Policy Reform & the Power of Farmers. (Illus.). 232p. 1998. text 59.95 (*1-84014-140-9*, Pub. by Ashgate Pub) Ashgate Pub Co.

D'Auge, Bernard, jt. auth. see Maillefer, Francois-Elie.

Dauge, M. Elliptic Boundary Value Problems on Corner Domain. (Lecture Notes in Mathematics Ser.: Vol. 1341). viii, 259p. 1988. 43.95 (*0-387-50169-X*) Spr-Verlag.

D'Augelli, Anthony R. & Patterson, Charlotte J., eds. Lesbian, Gay & Bisexual Identities over the Lifespan: Psychological Perspectives. 472p. 1996. reprint ed. pap. 27.50 (*0-19-510899-X*) OUP.

D'Augelli, Anthony R., jt. ed. see Patterson, Charlotte J.

Daugeras, Dominique & Janiaud-Powell, Patricia. La Correspondence Commerciale Anglaise. (ENG & FRE.). 157p. 1992. 24.95 (*0-7859-0968-0*, 2091760730) Fr & Eur.

Daughaday, Charles H., ed. & intro. see Stuart, Jesse H.

Daugharty, J. Whistle: A Novel. 224p. 1999. pap. 13.00 (*0-06-093091-8*) HarpC.

Daugharty, Janice. Dark of the Moon. Howle, Jane, ed. 275p. 1994. 19.00 (*1-880909-17-0*) Baskerville.

Daugharty, Janice. Earl in the Yellow Shirt: A Novel. LC 96-44628. 272p. 1997. 22.00 (*0-06-018750-6*) HarpC.

Daugharty, Janice. Earl in the Yellow Shirt: Novel, A. LC 96-44628. 272p. (J). 1998. pap. 12.00 (*0-06-092898-0*) HarpC.

— Going Through the Change. LC 94-9464. 200p. 1994. 19.95 (*0-86538-081-3*) Ontario Rev NJ.

— Like A Sister: A Novel. LC 99-15621. 208p. 1999. 23.00 (*0-06-019360-3*) HarpC.

***Daugharty, Janice.** Like A Sister: A Novel. 208p. 2000. pap. 13.00 (*0-06-093179-5*) HarpC.

Daugharty, Janice. Pawpaw Patch: A Novel. 1996. write for info. (*0-614-96290-0*) HarpC.

— Whistle: A Novel. LC 97-42166. 224p. 1998. 22.00 (*0-06-017551-6*, Pub. by Harper SF) HarpC.

Daughen. Heart God Hears. 1997. pap. 7.95 (*0-9655471-0-8*) Gospel Net Minist.

Daughenbaugh, Leonard. Sierra Mountaineering. (Illus.). 1990. 32.50 (*0-939919-11-7*) Bear Flag Bks.

Daugherity, Reed. Passionate Purpose: Awakening the Inner Fire. LC 97-76829. 140p. 1998. pap. 14.95 (*1-885221-75-4*) BookPartners.

Daugherty. Fluid Mechanics Engineering Applications. 8th ed. 1986. 37.25 (*0-07-015442-2*) McGraw.

Daugherty. Worlds & Words. (C). Date not set. pap. write for info. (*0-395-68565-6*); pap., teacher ed. write for info. (*0-395-68566-4*) HM.

Daugherty, jt. auth. see Camp.

Daugherty, Beth R. & Barrett, Eileen, eds. Virginia Woolf: Texts & Contexts: Selected Papers from the Fifth Annual Conference on Virginia Woolfe. LC 96-18435. (Selected Papers from the Fifth Annual Conference). 325p. 1996. pap. 37.50 (*0-944473-28-8*) Pace Univ Pr.

— Virginia Woolf: Texts & Contexts: Selected Papers from the Fifth Annual Conference on Virginia Woolfe. LC 96-18435. (Selected Papers from the Fifth Annual Conference). 325p. 1996. 69.50 (*0-944473-27-X*) Pace Univ Pr.

D

An Asterisk (*) at the beginning of an entry indicates that the title is appearing for the first time.

***Daugherty, Beth Rigel.** Approaches to Teaching Woolf's To the Lighthouse. (Approaches to Teaching World Literature Ser.: Vol. 71). 200p. 2001. pap. write for info. (*0-87352-766-6*) Modern Lang.

***Daugherty, Beth Rigel, ed.** Approaches to Teaching Woolf's To the Lighthouse. (Approaches to Teaching World Literature Ser.: Vol. 71). 200p. 2001. 37.50 (*0-87352-765-8*) Modern Lang.

Daugherty, Billy J. Be Courageous. 32p. (Orig.). 1993. pap. 0.50 (*1-56267-075-1*) Victory Ctr OK.
— Be on Fire for the Lord. (Orig.). 1991. pap. 0.50 (*1-56267-008-5*) Victory Ctr OK.
— Be Strong in the Lord. 32p. (Orig.). 1993. pap. 0.50 (*1-56267-080-8*) Victory Ctr OK.
— The Breakfast of Champions (Early Morning Prayer) 32p. (Orig.). (YA). 1996. pap. 0.50 (*1-56267-113-8*) Victory Ctr OK.
— Building Quality Relationships. 32p. (Orig.). (YA). 1996. pap. 0.50 (*1-56267-058-1*) Victory Ctr OK.
— Building Stronger Marriages. 172p. (Orig.). 1991. pap. 7.99 (*0-89274-858-3*, HH-858) Harrison Hse.
— Care Group Lessons, Bk. 1. 29p. 1985. pap. text 5.00 (*1-56267-000-X*) Victory Ctr OK.
— Care Group Lessons, Bk. 2. 29p. 1985. pap. text 5.00 (*1-56267-001-8*) Victory Ctr OK.
— Care Group Lessons, Bk. 3. 29p. 1985. pap. text 5.00 (*1-56267-002-6*) Victory Ctr OK.
— Care Group Lessons, Bk. 4. 29p. 1986. pap. text 5.00 (*1-56267-003-4*) Victory Ctr OK.
— Care Group Lessons, Bk. 5. 29p. 1988. pap. text 5.00 (*1-56267-004-2*) Victory Ctr OK.
— Care Group Lessons, 11 bks., Bk. 6. 29p. 1991. pap. text 5.00 (*1-56267-053-0*) Victory Ctr OK.
— Care Group Lessons, 11 bks., Bk. 7. 29p. 1991. pap. text 5.00 (*1-56267-054-9*) Victory Ctr OK.
— Care Group Lessons, 11 bks., Bk. 8. 29p. 1992. pap. text 5.00 (*1-56267-074-3*) Victory Ctr OK.
— Care Group Lessons, 11 bks., Bk. 9. 29p. 1993. pap. text 5.00 (*1-56267-090-5*) Victory Ctr OK.
— Care Group Lessons, 11 bks., Bk. 10. 29p. 1997. pap. text 5.00 (*1-56267-180-4*) Victory Ctr OK.
— Care Group Lessons, 11 bks., Bk. 11. 29p. 1998. pap. text 5.00 (*1-56267-185-5*) Victory Ctr OK.
— Death Is Not the End. 32p. (Orig.). 1993. pap. 0.50 (*1-56267-095-6*) Victory Ctr OK.
— Delivered from Evil. 32p. (Orig.). 1992. pap. 0.50 (*1-56267-089-1*) Victory Ctr OK.
— The Demonstration of the Gospel. 75p. (Orig.). 1991. pap. 4.50 (*1-56267-030-1*) Victory Ctr OK.
— Diligence Produces Results. (Orig.). 1991. pap. 0.50 (*1-56267-035-2*) Victory Ctr OK.
— Don't Be Offended! 32p. 1996. pap. 0.25 (*1-56267-168-5*) Victory Ctr OK.
— Escaping Fatal Attractions. 32p. (Orig.). (YA). 1995. pap. 0.50 (*1-56267-119-7*) Victory Ctr OK.
— Faith Power. pap. 4.99 (*0-89274-100-7*, ABD003) Harrison Hse.
— Getting over the Moody Blues. 32p. 1996. pap. 0.25 (*1-56267-096-4*) Victory Ctr OK.
— The Goal. 32p. 1992. pap. 0.25 (*1-56267-078-6*) Victory Ctr OK.
— God Is Not Mad at You. 32p. (Orig.). (YA). 1995. pap. 0.50 (*1-56267-112-X*) Victory Ctr OK.
— God's Protecting Angels. 32p. (Orig.). (YA). 1995. pap. 0.50 (*1-56267-040-9*) Victory Ctr OK.
— God's Word to You, "Fear Not!" 32p. 1996. pap. 0.25 (*1-56267-107-3*) Victory Ctr OK.
— Healing, Help & Hope. 32p. (Orig.). 1993. pap. 0.50 (*1-56267-093-X*) Victory Ctr OK.
— How to Know God's Will: Mini Book. 28p. 1991. pap. 0.50 (*1-56267-048-4*) Victory Ctr OK.
— Juggling Your Priorities. 32p. (Orig.). (YA). 1996. pap. 0.50 (*1-56267-106-5*) Victory Ctr OK.
— Killing the Giant of Ministry Debt: How God Enabled One Church to Come Out of a $3.3 Million Debt to Buy Land & Build Facilities Worth $16 Million on a Cash Basis. 86p. 1996. pap. 2.95 (*1-56267-128-6*) Victory Ctr OK.
— Led by the Spirit: How God Guides & Provides. LC 93-74611. 1994. pap. 9.99 (*0-88419-364-0*) Creation House.
— Living in God's Abundance. 126p. 1999. pap. 6.95 (*1-56267-184-7*) Victory Ctr OK.
— Mercy & Grace. 32p. (Orig.). 1993. pap. 0.50 (*1-56267-083-2*) Victory Ctr OK.
— Overcoming Strife--The AIDS Virus of the Spirit. 32p. (Orig.). 1993. pap. 0.50 (*1-56267-084-0*) Victory Ctr OK.
— Overcoming the Storms of Life. 32p. 1991. pap. 0.50 (*1-56267-006-9*) Victory Ctr OK.
— Possessing God's Promises. 32p. (Orig.). 1992. pap. 0.50 (*1-56267-082-4*) Victory Ctr OK.
— Possibility Living. 32p. (Orig.). 1993. pap. 0.50 (*1-56267-086-7*) Victory Ctr OK.
— Praise & Thanksgiving. 32p. (Orig.). 1992. pap. 0.50 (*1-56267-070-0*) Victory Ctr OK.
— Principles of Prayer. LC 98-119430. 265p. 1997. pap. 9.99 (*1-56267-099-9*) Victory Ctr OK.
— Renewing Your Mind. 32p. (Orig.). (YA). 1995. pap. 0.50 (*1-56267-167-7*) Victory Ctr OK.
— Seven Keys to Family Power. 32p. (Orig.). 1993. pap. 0.50 (*1-56267-079-4*) Victory Ctr OK.
— Soaring with Eagles. 32p. (Orig.). 1993. pap. 0.50 (*1-56267-091-3*) Victory Ctr OK.
— The Spirit of Faith. 32p. (Orig.). 1993. pap. 0.50 (*1-56267-087-5*) Victory Ctr OK.
— Taking Control of Your Thoughts. 32p. (Orig.). (YA). 1996. pap. 0.50 (*1-56267-059-X*) Victory Ctr OK.
— Victory over Sin. 32p. (Orig.). 1993. pap. 0.50 (*1-56267-072-7*) Victory Ctr OK.
— The Warnings of God. 32p. (Orig.). 1993. pap. 0.50 (*1-56267-073-5*) Victory Ctr OK.
— What Is the Fear of the Lord? 32p. (Orig.). 1991. pap. 0.50 (*1-56267-005-0*) Victory Ctr OK.
— You Are Valuable. 32p. 1991. pap. 0.50 (*1-56267-017-4*) Victory Ctr OK.
— You Can Be Healed. 114p. (Orig.). 1991. pap. 7.99 (*0-89274-876-1*, HH876) Harrison Hse.
— You Can Start Over. 32p. (Orig.). 1991. pap. 0.50 (*1-56267-018-2*) Victory Ctr OK.
— You Have a Destiny. 32p. 1996. pap. 0.25 (*1-56267-169-3*) Victory Ctr OK.
— You Will Increase. 29p. 1991. pap. 0.50 (*1-56267-046-8*) Victory Ctr OK.

***Daugherty, Billy Joe.** Breaking the Chains of Bondage. 111p. 1999. pap. 8.00 (*1-56267-130-8*) Victory Ctr OK.
— How to Overcome a Life-Threatening Illness. 1999. pap. 0.25 (*1-56267-170-7*) Victory Ctr OK.
— How to Turn Your Scars into Stars. 32p. 1999. pap. 0.25 (*1-56267-165-0*) Victory Ctr OK.
— Recovering What the Devil Has Stolen. 32p. 1999. pap. 0.25 (*1-56267-049-2*) Victory Ctr OK.
— What to Do When You Don't Know What to Do. 32p. 1999. pap. 0.25 (*1-56267-189-8*) Victory Ctr OK.

Daugherty, Billy Joe. When Life Throws You a Curve: Divine Strategies for Handling Whatever Life Throws You. 152p. 1998. pap. 9.99 (*1-57778-061-2*, Pub. by Albury Pub) Appalach Bk Dist.

***Daugherty, Billy Joe & Daugherty, Sharon.** Heaven Is on Its Feet. 155p. 2000. pap. 8.00 (*1-56267-076-X*) Victory Ctr OK.

Daugherty, Brighton H. Hurricane & Other Winds of Hawaii. (Illus.). 62p. 1986. pap. 6.95 (*0-937101-00-1*) Bright Morning.

Daugherty, Don G., jt. auth. see Talley, Harry E.

Daugherty, Duane A. A Manager's Guide to the New OSHA: Blueprints for Effective Training & Written Programs. LC 95-46554. (AMA Management Briefing Ser.). 1995. write for info. (*0-8144-2360-4*) AMACOM.

***Daugherty, Edward R.** Random Processes for Image & Signal Processing. (Imaging Science & Engineering Ser.). 616p. 1999. 79.95 (*0-7803-3495-7*) IEEE Standards.

Daugherty, F. Mark, ed. Sacred Choral Music in Print: 1996 Supplement. LC 85-15368. (Music-in-Print Ser.: Vol. 1u). 225p. 1996. lib. bdg. 95.00 (*0-88478-039-2*) Musicdata.

Daugherty, F. Mark & Simon, Susan H., eds. Sacred Choral Music in Print: 1992 Supplement. LC 92-27658. (Music-in-Print Ser.: Vol. 1t). 1992. lib. bdg. 95.00 (*0-88478-029-5*) Musicdata.
— Secular Choral Music in Print: 1991 Supplement. LC 91-15287. (Music-in-Print Ser.: Vol. 2S). 200p. 1991. 95.00 (*0-88478-027-9*) Musicdata.
— Secular Choral Music in Print: 1993 Supplement. LC 93-28494. (Music-in-Print Ser.: Vol. 2). 210p. 1993. 95.00 (*0-88478-031-7*) Musicdata.

Daugherty, F. Mark, jt. ed. see Eslinger, Gary S.

Daugherty, F. Mark, jt. ed. see Simon, Susan H.

Daugherty, Franklin. Isle of Joy. 1996. 23.00 (*1-881320-78-2*, Black Belt) Black Belt Communs.
— Postmodern Times. LC 87-71793. 280p. (YA). 1988. 14.95 (*0-944284-00-0*) T C Deleon.

Daugherty, Greg. You Can Write for Magazines. LC 98-48930. (You Can Write It! Ser.). 128p. 1999. pap. 12.99 (*0-89879-902-3*, 10599, Wrtrs Digest Bks) F & W Pubns Inc.

Daugherty, Harry M. The Inside Story of the Harding Tragedy. (Select Bibliographies Reprint Ser.). 1977. reprint ed. 28.95 (*0-8369-5833-0*) Ayer.

Daugherty, Helen Ginn & Kammeyer, Kenneth C. W. An Introduction to Population. 2nd ed. LC 95-6657. 343p. 1995. lib. bdg. 43.00 (*0-89862-616-1*, 2616) Guilford Pubns.

Daugherty, J. S. & Powell, R. E. Sheet-Metal Pattern Drafting & Shop Problems. 4th rev. ed. 196p. (C). 1975. pap. text 25.29 (*0-02-665680-9*) Glencoe.

Daugherty, Jack E. Assessment of Chemical Exposures: Calculation Methods for Environmental Professionals. LC 97-34697. 456p. 1997. lib. bdg. 75.00 (*1-56670-216-X*) Lewis Pubs.

Daugherty, Jack E. Industrial Environmental Management: A Practical Handbook. 572p. 1996. 79.00 (*0-86587-515-4*) Gov Insts.

Daugherty, Jackson. History of the Daugherty Family in America. 2nd rev. ed. Andersson, Mari, ed. (Illus.). 200p. (Orig.). 1996. pap. 75.00 (*0-9619043-1-3*) Starquest Pub Co.

Daugherty, Jackson T. History of the Daugherty Family in America. LC 87-82013. (Illus.). 200p. 1987. reprint ed. pap. 62.00 (*0-7837-8749-9*, AU0045300001) Bks Demand.

Daugherty, James. Andy & the Lion. LC 88-28803. (Illus.). 72p. (J). (ps-3). 1989. pap. 5.99 (*0-14-050277-7*, PuffinBks) Peng Put Young Read.
— The Landing of the Pilgrims. LC 80-21430. (Landmark Ser.). (Illus.). 160p. (J). (gr. 5-9). 1981. reprint ed. pap. 5.99 (*0-394-84697-4*, Pub. by Random Bks Yng Read) Random.
— The Magna Charta. (Illus.). 181p. (YA). (gr. 5 up). 1998. reprint ed. pap. 10.95 (*0-9643803-5-8*) Beautiful Feet.

***Daugherty, James.** Of Courage Undaunted: Across the Continent with Lewis & Clark. (Illus.). 168p. (YA). (gr. 6-12). 1999. reprint ed. pap. 16.95 (*1-893103-02-1*) Beautiful Feet.

Daugherty, James H. Landing of the Pilgrims. (Landmark Bks.). (J). 1978. 11.09 (*0-606-02153-1*, Pub. by Turtleback) Demco.

Daugherty, James Henry. Andy & the Lion: A Tale of Kindness Remembered, or, the Power of Gratitude. (Picture Puffin Ser.). (J). 1966. 10.19 (*0-606-03973-2*, Pub. by Turtleback) Demco.

Daugherty, Jean. Magic Toy Shop: Memories to Cherish. (Illus.). 48p. 1998. pap. 14.95 (*0-9654732-2-8*) Signature NY.

***Daugherty, Leo J.** Fighting Techniques of a U. S. Marine, 1941-1945. (Illus.). 96p. 2000. 17.95 (*0-7603-0930-2*, 130533AP, Pub. by MBI Pubg) Motorbooks Intl.

Daugherty, Linda. The Little Mermaid. (J). 1995. 6.00 (*0-87602-330-8*) Anchorage.

Daugherty, Lyman H. The Upper Triassic Flora of Arizona. LC 41-9472. (Carnegie Institution of Washington Publication Ser.: No. 526). 150p. reprint ed. pap. 46.50 (*0-7837-5945-2*, 204574400007) Bks Demand.

***Daugherty, Marc.** The Soul Is a Wilderness. 1999. pap. write for info. (*1-58235-261-5*) Watermrk Pr.

Daugherty, Marc R. The Dark Garden. 1997. pap. 56.95 (*1-57553-650-1*) Watermrk Pr.

Daugherty, Mark, ed. Classical Vocal Music in Print: 1995 Supplement. LC 76-29568. (Vol. 4T: No. 4T). 279p. 1995. 95.00 (*0-88478-035-X*) Musicdata.
— Organ Music in Print: 1990 Supplement. LC 90-5438. (Music in Print Ser.: Vol. 3S). 284p. 1990. lib. bdg. 95.00 (*0-88478-026-0*) Musicdata.

***Daugherty, Mike.** Monitoring & Managing Microsoft Exchange 2000. (Illus.). 320p. 2000. pap. 32.95 (*1-55558-232-X*, Digital DEC) Buttrwrth-Heinemann.

Daugherty, Paul. Fair Game. LC 99-35770. 288p. 1999. text 24.95 (*1-882203-58-5*) Orange Frazer.

Daugherty, R. D. Early Man in the Columbia No. 24: Intermontane Province. (Publications of the Department of Anthropology, University of Utah: No. 24). (Illus.). 128p. (C). 1956. reprint ed. pap. text 14.38 (*1-55567-475-5*) Coyote Press.

Daugherty, Raymond P. & Leukefeld, Carl. Reducing the Risks for Substance Abuse: A Lifespan Approach. LC 98-29801. (Prevention in Practice Library). (Illus.). 192p. (C). 1998. pap. text 22.50 (*0-306-45899-3*, Kluwer Plenum) Kluwer Academic.
— Reducing the Risks for Substance Abuse: A Lifespan Approach. LC 98-29801. (Prevention in Practice Library). (Illus.). 192p. (C). 1998. 39.50 (*0-306-45898-5*, Plenum Trade) Perseus Pubng.

Daugherty, Richard. National Curriculum Assessment: A Review of Policy, 1987-1994. LC 94-46733. 152p. 1995. 85.00 (*0-7507-0254-0*, Falmer Pr); pap. 29.95 (*0-7507-0255-9*, Falmer Pr) Taylor & Francis.
— Science in Geography Series, 4 vols. Incl. Vol 2. Data Collection. (Illus.). 78p. 1974. pap. text 6.95 (*0-19-913066-3*); (C). 1974. write for info. (*0-318-54891-7*) OUP.

Daugherty, Richard, jt. ed. see Williams, Michael.

Daugherty, Richard A., jt. ed. see Rawling, Eleanor M.

***Daugherty, Richard F.** Special Education: A Summary of Legal Requirements, Terms & Trends. LC 00-31202. 140p. 2000. 49.00 (*0-89789-726-9*, Bergin & Garvey) Greenwood.

Daugherty, Richard F. & Cockerill, Charles P. Nevada Education Law. 266p. 1998. 32.00 (*1-56534-072-8*) Ed Law Assn.

Daugherty, Robert. Chillyblast: A Narrative: American Autobiography. 85p. 1995. lib. bdg. 69.00 (*0-7812-8495-3*) Rprt Serv.

Daugherty, Robert L., et al. Fluid Mechanics with Engineering Applications. 8th ed. LC 84-10050. 640p. (C). 1984. text 83.50 (*0-07-015441-4*) McGraw.

Daugherty, Robin T. Splint Woven Basketry. LC 86-80913. (Illus.). 160p. 1986. pap. 17.95 (*0-934026-22-X*) Interweave.
— Splint Woven Basketry. LC 99-21360. (Illus.). 1999. pap. 17.95 (*0-8069-9518-1*) Sterling.

Daugherty, Sharon. Avoiding Deception. LC 97-198387. 176p. (Orig.). 1997. pap. 8.99 (*1-56267-157-X*) Victory Ctr OK.
— Closeted Screams: A Service Provider Handbook for Same-Sex Domestic Violence Issues. 250p. (Orig.). 1992. pap. text 20.00 (*0-9633940-0-2*) Smith-Flesher Soria.
— Walking in the Fruit of the Spirit. expanded rev. ed. 210p. 1998. pap. 10.00 (*1-56267-181-2*) Victory Ctr OK.
— Walking in the Spirit. 128p. 1991. 5.99 (*0-89274-502-9*, HH-502) Harrison Hse.

Daugherty, Sharon, jt. auth. see Daugherty, Billy Joe.

Daugherty, Sharon F., 2nd. The Guidebook to Transsexual Transition. 1995. write for info. (*0-9644134-0-X*) NHBGDA.

Daugherty, Terry L., jt. auth. see Carr, Sharon L.

Daugherty, Thomas B., jt. auth. see Camp, William G.

Daugherty, Tracy. The Boy Orator: A Novel. LC 98-38959. 264p. 1998. 19.95 (*0-87074-433-X*) SMU Press.
— The Woman in the Oil Field: Stories. LC 96-26734. 192p. 1996. 22.50 (*0-87074-402-X*); pap. 12.95 (*0-87074-403-8*) SMU Press.

Daugherty, Tracy E. College Students Tell It Like It Is: What College Is Really Like. LC 83-51572. (Illus.). 192p. 1984. pap. 7.95 (*0-9613096-0-1*) Sara Pubns.
— Narrative Techniques in the Novels of Fanny Burney. (Studies in the Romantic Age: Vol. 1). 225p. (C). 1989. text 37.00 (*0-8204-0664-3*) P Lang Pubng.

Daugherty, William E. A Psychological Warfare Casebook. LC 58-2297. 904p. reprint ed. pap. 200.00 (*0-608-30769-6*, 200384800037) Bks Demand.

Daughety, Andrew F., ed. Cournot Oligopoly: Characterization & Application. (Illus.). 456p. 1989. text 89.95 (*0-521-36176-1*) Cambridge U Pr.

Daughety, Andrew F., jt. ed. see McMullen, B. Starr.

Daughters, Andrew. Gospel Treasury, Cycle C. (Orig.). 1988. pap. 9.95 (*1-55673-065-9*, 8862) CSS OH.

Daughters, Charles G. Wells of Discontent. Bruchey, Stuart & Carosso, Vincent P., eds. LC 78-18959. (Small Business Enterprise in America Ser.). (Illus.). 1979. reprint ed. lib. bdg. 30.95 (*0-405-11463-X*) Ayer.

Daughters, Kenneth. N. T. Church Government. 1989. pap. 5.50 (*0-937396-82-6*) Walterick Pubs.

Daughters of Bilitis. The Ladder, 9 vols. LC 75-12330. (Homosexuality Ser.). 1975. reprint ed. 361.95 (*0-405-07371-2*) Ayer.

Daughters of St. Paul Staff. Basic Catechism. LC 80-149. 264p. 1999. pap. 7.95 (*0-8198-0623-4*) Pauline Bks.
— Bells of Conquest - St. Bernard of Clairvaux. LC 68-28105. (Encounter Ser.). 79p. (J). (gr. 4-9). 1987. 3.00 (*0-8198-0228-X*) Pauline Bks.
— Devotion to St. Anthony. 46p. pap. 1.75 (*0-8198-1848-8*) Pauline Bks.
— Devotion to St. Joseph. 46p. pap. 1.75 (*0-8198-1851-8*) Pauline Bks.
— Father Damien of Molokai. 13p. 1979. pap. 0.95 (*0-8198-0640-4*) Pauline Bks.
— God Loves Me. 160p. (J). (gr. 1-6). 1982. pap., teacher ed. 4.50 (*0-8198-3031-3*); pap. text 2.50 (*0-8198-3032-1*) Pauline Bks.
— The Holy Mass Coloring Book. rev. ed. (Illus.). 16p. (J). (gr. 1-4). 1993. pap. 1.95 (*0-8198-3343-6*) Pauline Bks.
— I Learn About Jesus. rev. ed. LC 72-91979. (Illus.). 145p. (J). (ps-4). 1995. 12.95 (*0-8198-0246-8*) Pauline Bks.
— I Learn About Jesus. rev. ed. LC 72-91979. (Illus.). 145p. (J). 1995. pap. 8.95 (*0-8198-0247-6*) Pauline Bks.
— I Pray with Jesus. deluxe rev. ed. (Illus.). 177p. (J). (gr. 1-5). 1991. 12.95 (*0-8198-3630-3*); 12.95 (*0-8198-3631-1*) Pauline Bks.
— I Pray with Jesus. rev. ed. (Illus.). 177p. (J). (gr. 1-5). 1991. 8.95 (*0-8198-3629-X*) Pauline Bks.
— I Pray with Jesus Gift Box. (Illus.). 177p. (J). (gr. 1-5). 18.95 (*0-8198-3633-8*) Pauline Bks.
— Into the Woods & Other Favorite Verses. LC 73-89937. (Illus.). 91p. 1974. 5.50 (*0-8198-0281-6*) Pauline Bks.
— No Place for Defeat. (Encounter Ser.). 96p. (J). (gr. 3-9). 1987. 3.00 (*0-8198-0241-7*); pap. 2.00 (*0-8198-5100-0*) Pauline Bks.
— Novena Prayers to St. Theresa, the Little Flower. 22p. (J). 1985. pap. 1.25 (*0-8198-5123-X*) Pauline Bks.
— Patron Saints. 70p. pap. 1.95 (*0-8198-5859-5*) Pauline Bks.
— Preparing to Receive Jesus. 1978. 2.75 (*0-8198-0548-3*); pap., teacher ed. 7.50 (*0-8198-0549-1*); student ed. 1.95 (*0-8198-0550-5*) Pauline Bks.
— Saints of the Americas Coloring Book. Flanagan, Anne J., ed. (Illus.). 18p. (Orig.). (J). (gr. 1-4). 1993. pap. 0.95 (*0-8198-4768-2*) Pauline Bks.
— St. Paul Family Catechism. 368p. 1983. pap. 4.95 (*0-8198-7330-6*) Pauline Bks.
— Yes Is Forever. LC 79-22266. (Encounter Ser.). (Illus.). 109p. 1982. 3.00 (*0-8198-8700-5*, EN0260) Pauline Bks.

Daughters of St. Paul Staff, compiled by. Moments for Prayer. 52p. 1979. pap. 1.50 (*0-8198-4753-4*) Pauline Bks.
— Queen of Apostles Prayerbook. 384p. 1991. vinyl bd. 12.95 (*0-8198-6201-0*) Pauline Bks.

Daughters of St. Paul Staff, ed. I Pray with Jesus Gift Box. (Illus.). 177p. (J). (gr. 1-5). 18.95 (*0-8198-3632-X*) Pauline Bks.
— I Pray with Jesus Gift Box. deluxe ed. (Illus.). 177p. (J). (gr. 1-5). 24.95 (*0-8198-3635-4*) Pauline Bks.
— I Pray with Jesus Gift Box. deluxe ed. (Illus.). 177p. (J). (gr. 1-5). 24.95 (*0-8198-3634-6*) Pauline Bks.

Daughters of St. Paul Staff, tr. see Luzi, Marina.

Daughters of St. Paul Staff, tr. see Paltro, Piera.

Daughters of St. Paul Staff, tr. see Ricciardi, Antonio.

Daughters of the American Revolution-Georgia. Index of the Rolls of Honor (Ancestor's Index) in the Lineage Books of the National Society of the Daughters of the American Revolution, 4 vols. in 2. 1734p. 1988. reprint ed. 75.00 (*0-8063-0509-6*, 1330) Genealog Pub.

Daughters of the American Revolution Staff. Genealogical Guide Vols. 1-84: Master Index of Genealogy in the Daughters of the American Revolution Magazine (1892-1950) Published with Supplement to Genealogical Guide Volumes 85-89 (1950-1955) LC 93-80321. 169p. 1994. reprint ed. 20.00 (*0-8063-1399-4*, 1335) Genealog Pub.

Daughters of the Republic of Texas District VIII S. A Pinch of This & a Handful of That: Historic Recipes of Texas, 1830-1900. 200p. 1988. 16.95 (*0-89015-649-2*) Sunbelt Media.

Daughters of the Republic of TX District VIII Staf. Seconds of a Pinch of This & a Handful of That. 192p. 1994. 15.95 (*0-89015-970-X*) Sunbelt Media.

Daughters, Robert, jt. ed. see Rojas, Eduardo.

Daughtery. Basic Business & Economic Education. 4th ed. (GB - Basic Business Ser.). 1990. mass mkt. 37.95 (*0-538-60236-8*) S-W Pub.

Daughtery, Sean T. The Body's Precocious Balance. Date not set. pap. 16.95 (*1-881168-42-5*) Red Danceflr.

Daughtery, William E., jt. auth. see Johns Hopkins University Operations Research Offic.

Daughtrey. General Business, Units 1-6. 12th ed. (GB - Basic Business Ser.). 1981. mass mkt., wbk. ed. 17.95 (*0-538-07151-6*) S-W Pub.

Daughtrey & Ristau. Introduction to Business. (GB - Basic Business Ser.). 1986. mass mkt., wbk. ed. 17.95 (*0-538-07162-1*) S-W Pub.
— Introduction to Business: The Economy & You. (GB - Basic Business Ser.). 1985. mass mkt. 17.95 (*0-538-07161-3*) S-W Pub.
— Introduction to Business: The Economy, Tests. (GB - Basic Business Ser.). 1985. pap. 4.95 (*0-538-07163-X*) S-W Pub.

D

An Asterisk (*) at the beginning of an entry indicates that the title is appearing for the first time.

Daughtrey, et al. Introduction to Business: International. 2nd ed. (GB - Basic Business Ser.). 1992. 152.95 (*0-538-63712-9*) S-W Pub.

— Introduction to Business: Leadership. 2nd ed. (GB - Basic Business Ser.). 1992. 152.95 (*0-538-63713-7*) S-W Pub.

— Introduction to Business: Marketing. 2nd ed. (GB - Basic Business Ser.). 1992. 152.95 (*0-538-63715-3*) S-W Pub.

— Introduction to Business: The Economy & You. 2nd ed. (GB - Basic Business Ser.). 1990. pap., wbk. ed. 15.95 (*0-538-61218-5*); mass mkt. 47.95 (*0-538-61217-7*) S-W Pub.

— Introduction to Business: The Economy & You, Units 7-11. 2nd ed. (GB - Basic Business Ser.). 1990. pap., wbk. ed. 15.95 (*0-538-61219-3*) S-W Pub.

— Introduction to Business, the Economy. 2nd ed. (GB - Basic Business Ser.). 1992. 5.95 (*0-538-61220-7*) S-W Pub.

Daughtrey, Margery & Chase, A. R. Ball Field Guide to Diseases of Greenhouse Ornamentals. LC 91-35939. (Illus.). 224p. (C). 1992. pap. text 66.95 (*0-9626796-3-1*, B007) Ball Pub.

Daughtrey, Margery & Semel, Maurie. Herbaceous Perennials: Diseases & Insect Pests. (Illus.). 25p. 1992. reprint ed. pap. 9.75 (*1-57753-258-9*, 160IB207) Corn Coop Ext.

Daughtrey, Margery L., et al. Compendium of Flowering Potted Plant Diseases. LC 95-78639. (Disease Compendium Ser.). (Illus.). 128p. 1995. pap. 42.00 (*0-89054-202-3*) Am Phytopathol Soc.

Daughtry, Herbert D., Sr. My Beloved Community: Selected Sermons & Speeches. 1998. 59.95 (*0-86543-589-8*); pap. 18.95 (*0-86543-590-1*) Africa World.

Daughtry, Herbert D. No Monoply on Suffering: Blacks & Jews in Crown Heights & Elsewhere. LC 97-7987. 287p. 1997. 24.95 (*0-86543-586-3*) Africa World.

Daughtry, Philip. Celtic Blood: Selected Poems 1968-1994. LC 94-69076. 104p. (Orig.). 1995. pap. 9.95 (*1-883197-05-8*) New Native Pr.

Daugirdas, John T. STD: Sexually Transmitted Diseases, Including HIV - AIDS. 3rd rev. ed. 1992. 14.95 (*0-9629279-1-0*) Medtext.

Daugirdas, John T. & Ing, Todd, eds. Handbook of Dialysis. 2nd ed. LC 93-19710. (Illus.). 656p. 1994. pap. text 44.00 (*0-316-17383-5*) Lppncott W & W.

Daugirdas, John T., et al. Handbook of Dialysis. 3rd ed. 750p. pap. text 39.95 (*0-316-17381-9*) Lppncott W & W.

Daugulis, A. J., jt. auth. see Goosen, Mattheus F.

***D'Augustine, Jamie, et al.** Customer Value Measurement: Gaining Strategic Advantage. Henderson, Craig, ed. 132p. 1999. spiral bd. 495.00 (*1-928593-15-1*) Am Prodtv Qual.

D'Augustine, Jamie, et al. The 21st Century Call Center Rep. Henderson, Craig, ed. (Illus.). 126p. 1998. spiral bd. 495.00 (*1-928593-11-9*) Am Prodtv Qual.

Dauija, jt. auth. see Ash.

Daula, Thomas V., jt. auth. see Berner, J. Kevin.

D'Aulaire, Edgar P., jt. auth. see D'Aulaire, Ingri.

D'Aulaire, Edgar Parim, see Parim D'Aulaire, Ingri & Parim D'Aulaire, Edgar.

D'Aulaire, Edgar Parin, jt. auth. see D'Aulaire, Ingri.

D'Aulaire, Ingri. Benjamin Franklin. (Illus.). 48p. (J). (gr. k-6). 1998. pap. 12.95 (*0-9643803-9-0*) Beautiful Feet.

Daulaire, Ingri. Benjamin Franklin. 1950. 18.15 (*0-606-03515-X*, Pub. by Turtleback) Demco.

D'Aulaire, Ingri. D'Aulaires' Trolls. (J). 1993. 13.20 (*0-606-05221-6*, Pub. by Turtleback) Demco.

Daulaire, Ingri. Ingri & Edgar Parin d'Aulaires' Book of Greek Myths. 1962. 22.05 (*0-606-00875-6*, Pub. by Turtleback) Demco.

D'Aulaire, Ingri & D'Aulaire, Edgar. Abraham Lincoln. (Illus.). 64p. (J). (ps-3). 1987. pap. 10.95 (*0-440-40690-0*) Dell.

D'Aulaire, Ingri & D'Aulaire, Edgar P. Columbus. (Illus.). 57p. (J). (ps-5). 1996. reprint ed. pap. 12.95 (*0-9643803-3-1*) Beautiful Feet.

— D'Aulaires' Book of Greek Myths. LC 62-15877. (Illus.). 192p. (J). 1962. 29.95 (*0-385-01583-6*) Doubleday.

— D'Aulaires' Norse Gods & Giants. (Illus.). (J). (gr. 3-7). 1967. 16.95 (*0-385-04908-0*, 260155) Doubleday.

— George Washington. (Illus.). 64p. (J). (gr. k-6). 1996. pap. 12.95 (*0-9643803-1-5*) Beautiful Feet.

D'Aulaire, Ingri & D'Aulaire, Edgar P. Leif the Lucky. LC 94-74546. (Illus.). 64p. (J). (gr. k-6). 1995. pap. 13.95 (*0-9643803-0-7*) Beautiful Feet.

D'Aulaire, Ingri & D'Aulaire, Edgar Parin. D'Aulaire's Book of Greek Myths. (Illus.). 192p. (J). (gr. 4-7). 1992. pap. 18.95 (*0-440-40694-3*, YB BDD) BDD Bks Young Read.

D'Aulaire, Ingri Parim, see Parim D'Aulaire, Ingri.

Dauler, Margaret, jt. auth. see Wilson, Margaret D.

Dauler Wilson, Margaret. Ideas & Mechanism: Essays on Early Modern Philosophy. LC 98-35153. 540p. 1999. 75.00 (*0-691-00470-6*, Pub. by Princeton U Pr) Cal Prin Full Svc.

— Ideas Mechanism: Essays on Early Modern Philosophy. LC 98-35153. 540p. 1999. pap. 31.95 (*0-691-00471-4*, Pub. by Princeton U Pr) Cal Prin Full Svc.

Daules, Shann. Macau. LC 90-63332. (China Guides Ser.). (Illus.). 158p. 1992. reprint ed. pap. 12.95 (*0-8442-9797-6*, Passprt Bks) NTC Contemp Pub Co.

Dault, Gary M., ed. see Fairley, Barker.

***Daum, Berthold.** Success With Electronic Business. (Illus.). 288p. (C). 2000. pap. text 39.95 (*0-201-67482-3*) Addison-Wesley.

Daum, E. Woerterbuch Deutsches-Russiches. 5th ed. (GER & RUS.). 719p. 1990. 45.00 (*0-7859-7538-1*, 3324001692) Fr & Eur.

— Woerterbuch Russisch-Deutsch. 21st ed. (GER & RUS.). 960p. 1990. 45.00 (*0-7859-7539-X*, 3324000904) Fr & Eur.

Daum, Edmund, jt. auth. see Schenk, Werner.

Daum, Edmund, ed. see Schenk, Werner.

Daum, Frederic, ed. Extrahepatic Biliary Atresia. LC 83-15108. (Gastroenterology Ser.: No. 1). (Illus.). 275p. reprint ed. pap. 85.30 (*0-7837-0842-4*, 204115500019) Bks Demand.

Daum, Fredric, jt. auth. see Brandt, Lawrence J.

Daum, Kent Michael, jt. auth. see Rutstein.

Daum, Michelle. The Can-Do Eating Plan for Overweight Kids & Teens: Helping Kids Control Weight, Look Better & Feel Great. LC 96-25742. 192p. 1997. pap. 10.00 (*0-380-78008-9*, Avon Bks) Morrow Avon.

Daum, P. A. Ups & Downs of Life in the Indies. Beekman, E. M., ed. Sturtevant, Elsje & Sturtevant, Donald, trs. from DUT. LC 86-16807. (Library of the Indies). 216p. 1987. lib. bdg. 30.00 (*0-87023-551-6*) U of Mass Pr.

Daum, P.A. Ups & Downs of Life in the Indies: A Novel of the East Indies. (Library of the Indies). 336p. 1999. pap. 14.95 (*962-593-512-6*) Tuttle Pubng.

Daum, Rhoda, jt. auth. see Walzer, Robert.

Daum, Terry. Terry-Thomas Tells Tales: An Autobiography. 1993. pap. 11.95 (*0-86051-795-0*, Robson-Parkwest) Parkwest Pubns.

Daum, Terry, jt. auth. see Thomas, Terry.

Daum, V. & Schenk. Dictionary of Russian Verbs (Russian-English) (ENG & RUS.). 750p. 1980. 110.00 (*0-569-08093-2*) St Mut.

Daumal, Rene. A Fundamental Experiment. Shattuck, Roger, tr. from FRE. 66p. (Orig.). 1987. pap. 5.95 (*0-937815-10-1*) Hanuman Bks.

— Mont Analogue. (Imaginaire Ser.). (FRE.). 175p. 1981. pap. 11.95 (*2-07-022877-0*) Schoenhof.

Daumal, Rene. Night of Serious Drinkng. 1979. 8.95 (*0-394-50766-5*) Random.

Daumal, Rene. The Powers of the Word. Polizzotti, Mark, tr. from FRE. 192p. (Orig.). 1991. pap. 12.95 (*0-87286-259-3*) City Lights.

— Rasa, or Knowledge of the Self. Levi, Louise L., tr. from FRE. LC 81-22389. 128p. 1982. 12.95 (*0-8112-0824-9*, Pub. by New Directions) Norton.

— Rene Daumal's Mugle & the Silk: And the Silk. Powrie, Phil, tr. from FRE. LC 97-25495. (Studies in French Literature: Vol. 4). 100p. 1997. text 59.95 (*0-7734-8580-5*) E Mellen.

— You've Always Been Wrong. Vosteen, Thomas, tr. from FRE.Tr. of Tu T'es Toujours Trompe. 168p. 2000. pap. 13.95 (*1-878972-32-4*, Pub. by Exact Change) Consort Bk Sales.

— You've Always Been Wrong. Vosteen, Thomas, tr. LC 94-37337. (French Modernist Library).Tr. of Tu T'es Toujours Trompe. (ENG & FRE., Illus.). xxvii, 133p. 1995. text 30.00 (*0-8032-1699-8*) U of Nebr Pr.

Dauman, R., jt. ed. see Aran, J. M.

Daumas, Eugene & Mazollier, J. Die Pferde der Sahara & die Arabischen Pferde in Syrien, 2 vols. in 1. (Documenta Hippologica Ser.). xii, 342p. 1988. reprint ed. write for info. (*3-487-08135-0*) G Olms Pubs.

Daumas, M. Le Cheval de Cesar. (FRE.). 324p. 1991. pap. text 31.00 (*2-88124-822-5*) Gordon & Breach.

Daumas, Maurice. Histoire de la Science. write for info. (*0-318-52022-2*); write for info. (*0-8288-7687-8*, M5187) Fr & Eur.

— Histoire Generale des Techniques, 3 tomes. Incl. Tome I. Origines de la Civilisation Technique. 66.80 Tome II. Premieres Etapes du Machinsisme. 66.80 Tome III. Expansion du Machinisme. 66.80 write for info. (*0-318-52026-5*) Fr & Eur.

Daumas, Maurice, ed. Histoirie Generale des Techniques, 3 vols. (FRE.). 670p. 1962. 125.00 (*0-7859-4558-X*) Fr & Eur.

Daumeister, W., ed. Electron Microscopy at Molecular Dimensions. (Proceedings in Life Sciences Ser.). (Illus.). 300p. 1980. 86.95 (*0-387-10131-4*) Spr-Verlag.

Daumier, Honore. Daumier: One Hundred Twenty Great Lithographs. Ramus, Charles, ed. LC 77-83928. (Illus.). 158p. 1978. pap. 10.95 (*0-486-23512-2*) Dover.

— Daumier & Music. (Music Reprint Ser.). 1992. lib. bdg. 35.00 (*0-306-76054-1*) Da Capo.

— Drawings of Daumier. Longstreet, Stephen, ed. (Master Draughtsman Ser.). (Illus.). (Orig.). 1964. pap. 4.95 (*0-87505-156-1*) Borden.

— Lawyers & Law Courts. (Illus.). 1967. 12.50 (*0-87505-152-9*) Borden.

Daun, Ake. Swedish Mentality. Teeland, Jan, tr. from ENG. LC 95-14585. 240p. 1996. 45.00 (*0-271-01501-2*); pap. 18.95 (*0-271-01502-0*) Pa St U Pr.

***Daun, Ake & Jansson, Soren, eds.** Europeans: Essays on Culture & Identity. 280p. 2000. 75.00 (*91-89116-06-2*, Pub. by Nordic Acad Pr) Intl Spec Bk.

Daunce, Edward. A Briefe Discourse of the Spanish State, with a Dialogue Intituled Philobasilis. LC 72-6281. (English Experience Ser.: No. 73). 52p. 1968. reprint ed. 20.00 (*90-221-0073-1*) Walter J Johnson.

***Dauncey, Guy.** Earthfuture: Stories from a Sustainable World. 176p. 2000. pap. 14.95 (*0-86571-407-X*, Pub. by New Soc Pubs) Consort Bk Sales.

***Dauncey, Guy & Mazza, Patrick.** Stormy Weather: 101 Solutions to Global Climate Change. 256p. 2000. pap. 18.95 (*0-86571-421-5*, Pub. by New Soc Pubs) Consort Bk Sales.

Dauncey, Hugh, ed. see Hare, Geoff.

DauNe, Michele. Molecular Biophysics: Structures & Dynamics. Duffin, W. J., tr. from FRE. LC 98-36756. (Illus.). 522p. (C). 1999. pap. text 49.95 (*0-19-857782-6*) OUP.

Dauner, Duane C. Health Care Solution: Understanding the Crisis & the Cure. LC 93-60944. 1993. 21.95 (*0-9636281-9-4*) CA Assn Hosp.

Dauns, John. Modules & Rings. LC 93-49759. (Illus.). 460p. (C). 1994. text 80.00 (*0-521-46258-4*) Cambridge U Pr.

Dauns, John & Hofmann, Karl H. Representation of Rings by Sections. LC 52-42839. (Memoirs Ser.: No. 1/83). 180p. 1983. reprint ed. pap. 17.00 (*0-8218-1283-1*, MEMO/1/83) Am Math.

Daunt, J. G., ed. see International Conference on Low Temperature Physic.

Daunt, Patrick. Meeting Disability: A European Response. 224p. 1992. pap. text 24.95 (*0-304-32386-1*) Continuum.

Daunt, Patrick, jt. ed. see Mittler, Peter.

Daunter, M. Teri. The Spiritual Dance of Life: Where Two Worlds Meet. LC 94-96592. 220p. 1995. pap. 16.00 (*0-9643646-9-7*) Mobius Pubng.

— The Spiritual Dance of Life: Where Two Worlds Meet. LC 94-96592. (Illus.). 220p. 1995. 20.00 (*0-9643646-8-9*) Mobius Pubng.

Daunton. Charity, Self-Interest & Welfare in the English Past. 262p. 1996. text 59.95 (*0-312-16074-7*) St Martin.

Daunton, M. J. Royal Mail: The Post Office since 1840. (Illus.). 388p. (C). 1985. text 45.00 (*0-485-11280-9*, Pub. by Athlone Pr) Humanities.

***Daunton, M. J. & Halpern, Rick.** Empire & Others: British Encounters with Indigenous Peoples, 1600-1850 LC 98-50783. 1999. 24.95 (*0-8122-1699-7*) U of Pa Pr.

Daunton, Martin. Progress & Poverty: An Economic & Social History of Britain 1700-1850. (Illus.). 636p. 1995. text 85.00 (*0-19-822282-3*); pap. text 24.00 (*0-19-822281-5*) OUP.

Daunton, Martin, ed. Housing the Workers: A Comparative History, 1850-1914. 240p. 1990. text 45.00 (*0-7185-1315-0*) St Martin.

***Daunton, Martin J. & Hilton, Matthew, eds.** Material Politics: Consumers, Citizenship & Political Cultures. (Leisure, Consumption & Culture Ser.). (Illus.). 256p. 2001. 65.00 (*1-85973-466-9*, Pub. by Berg Pubs); pap. 19.50 (*1-85973-471-5*, Pub. by Berg Pubs) NYU Pr.

Daunton, N. G., et al, eds. Mechanisms of Motion-Induced Vomiting. (Journal: Brains, Behavior & Evolution: Vol. 23, No. 1-2). (Illus.). 80p. 1983. pap. 45.25 (*3-8055-3790-5*) S Karger.

Dauoud, Mohamed. Soft Matter Physics. LC 98-39229. 330p. 1999. 79.95 (*3-540-64852-6*) Spr-Verlag.

Dauphin, Sue. Parkinson's Disease: The Mystery, the Search & the Promise. LC 92-93912. (Illus.). 229p. 1995. pap. 16.95 (*0-9620354-1-6*) Pixel Pr.

— Understanding Sjogren's Syndrome. enl. ed. LC 93-85164. (Illus.). 245p. (Orig.). 1993. pap. 16.95 (*0-9620354-2-4*) Pixel Pr.

Dauphin-Tanguy, Genevieve, jt. ed. see Granda, Jose J.

Dauphinais, Denise & Wilcox, Robert. Sierra Leone: A Pre-Election Technical Assessment, November 1995. ii, 24p. 1996. pap. text 4.00 (*1-879720-27-2*) Intl Fndt Elect.

***Dauphinais, G. William & Price, Colin.** Straight from the CEO: The World's Top Business Leaders Reveal Ideas That Every Manager Can Use. 320p. 1999. per. 14.00 (*0-684-85195-4*, Fireside) S&S Trade Pap.

Dauphinais, G. William & Price, Colin. Straight from the CEO: World's Top Business Leaders Reveal Ideas That Every Manager Can Use. LC 97-32090. 288p. 1998. 25.00 (*0-684-84608-X*) S&S Trade.

***Dauphinais, G. William, et al.** Wisdom of the CEO: 29 Global Leaders Tackle Today's Most Pressing Business Challenges. 384p. 2000. 27.95 (*0-471-35762-6*) Wiley.

***Dauphinais, Marc.** The Incredible Internet Guide to Diet & Nutrition. Flowers, James R., Jr., ed. (Incredible Internet Guide Ser.). (Illus.). 360p. 2000. pap. 15.95 (*1-889150-14-2*, Pub. by Facts on Demand) Natl Bk Netwk.

— The Incredible Internet Guide to Online Investing & Money Management. Flowers, James R., ed. 320p. 2000. pap. 17.95 (*1-889150-16-9*, Pub. by Facts on Demand) Natl Bk Netwk.

Dauphinee, Joan E., et al. Nursing Management of Multiple Birth Families: Preconception Through Postpartum. LC 96-40371. 1997. write for info. (*0-86525-076-6*) March of Dimes.

Dauphinee, Rosanne C. Eat Well & Live Cookbook, Vol. I. 60p. 1995. reprint ed. spiral bd. 9.95 (*0-9648668-0-3*) Majestic Hse.

— Eat Well & Live Cookbook, Vol. II. 94p. 1998. reprint ed. spiral bd. 9.95 (*0-9648668-1-1*) Majestic Hse.

Dauprat, Louis-Francois. Method for Cor Alto & Cor Basse. deluxe ed. Roth, Viola et al, trs. from ENG. LC 93-74474.Tr. of Methode de Cor-Alto et Cor-Basse. (Illus.). 502p. 1994. lthr. 350.00 (*0-929309-03-0*) Birdalone Bks.

— Method for Cor Alto & Cor Basse. limited ed. Roth, Viola et al, trs. from ENG. LC 93-74474.Tr. of Methode de Cor-Alto et Cor-Basse. (Illus.). 502p. 1994. lib. bdg. 150.00 (*0-929309-02-2*) Birdalone Bks.

Daura, Maiwa A. Islam: The Seed of Slavery. 1996. pap. text. write for info. (*0-927936-91-7*) Vincom Pubng Co.

Dauraul. Witches & Sorcerers. pap. 2.95 (*0-8065-0286-X*, Citadel Pr) Carol Pub Group.

Daurella, Paco. Musa: Profile & Background of a Man's Life. Bacalski, Robert, tr. from SPA. LC 90-42185. 177p. (C). 1991. text 41.95 (*0-8204-1363-1*) P Lang Pubng.

D'Aurevilly. Oeuvres Romanesques Completes, 2 tomes, Vol. 1. deluxe ed. Petit, ed. (Pleiade Ser.). (FRE.). 73.95 (*2-07-010048-0*) Schoenhof.

— Oeuvres Romanesques Completes, 2 tomes, Vol. 2. deluxe ed. Petit, ed. (Pleiade Ser.). (FRE.). 73.95 (*2-07-010049-9*) Schoenhof.

D'Aurevilly, Barbey. Les Diaboliques. unabridged ed. (FRE.). pap. 7.95 (*2-87714-210-8*, Pub. by Bookking Intl) Distribks Inc.

— Les Diaboliques - She Devils. rev. ed. Irwin, Robert, ed. Boyd, Ernest, tr. from FRE. (Empire of the Senses Ser.). 254p. 1997. pap. 11.99 (*1-873982-27-5*, Pub. by Dedalus) Subterranean Co.

D'Aurevilly, Jules B. Une Vieille Maitresse: Un Pretre Marie: L'Ensorceles. (FRE.). 1981. pap. 52.95 (*0-7859-3035-3*) Fr & Eur.

***d'Auria, Giuliano, et al.** Property Rights & the Environment. (IEA Studies on the Environment: No. 13). 55p. 1999. pap. 15.95 (*0-255-36471-7*, Pub. by Inst Economic Affairs) Coronet Bks.

D'Auria, John, jt. auth. see Saphier, Jon.

Daurio, Beverley, ed. Hard Times: New Fiction. pap. 12.95 (*0-920544-75-4*, Pub. by Mercury Bk) LPC InBook.

Daus, Beryl, ed. see Sechrest, Dale K. & Collins, William C.

Daus, Carol. Past Imperfect: How Tracing Your Family Medical History Can Save Your Life. LC 98-32131. 240p. 1999. pap. 12.95 (*1-891661-03-5*, 1035, Offbeat) Snta Monica.

Daus, Carol & Karavasil, Josephine. Houses & Homes Around the World. LC 86-2073. 1986. 15.25 (*0-87518-336-0*, Dillon Silver Burdett) Silver Burdett Pr.

Daus, Peter. Topical Diagnosis in Neurology: Anatomy, Physiology, Sight, Symptoms. 3rd ed. (Illus.). 348p. 1997. pap. 35.00 (*0-86577-711-X*) Thieme Med Pubs.

Dausch, D. & Honegger, H. Timolol Ophthalmic Solution in the Treatment of Glaucoma. LC 78-72505. 1978. 3.00 (*0-911910-95-6*) Merck-Sharp-Dohme.

***Dauscher, Russell R.** Biblical Butts. 99p. 2000. pap. 17.95 (*0-7541-0935-6*, Pub. by Minerva Pr) Unity Dist.

D'Ausilio, Rosanne. Wake up Your Call Center: How to Be a Better Call Center Agent. rev. ed. LC 99-14112. 1999. pap. 44.95 (*1-55753-169-2*) Purdue U Pr.

Dausmann, Guenther J., ed. Holographic & Diffractive Techniques. (Europto Ser.: Vol. 2951). 192p. 1996. 85.00 (*0-8194-2355-6*) SPIE.

Daussant, J. Seed Portions. LC 82-71240. 1983. text 146.00 (*0-12-204380-4*) Acad Pr.

Dauster, F. & Lyday, Leon F. En un Acto: Diez Piezas Hispanoamericanas. 2nd ed. (C). 1983. mass mkt. 20.95 (*0-8384-1229-7*) Heinle & Heinle.

Dauster, F. & Lyday, Leon F. En un Acto: Diez Piezas Hispanoamericanas. 3rd ed. (C). 1990. pap. 37.95 (*0-8384-1865-1*) Heinle & Heinle.

Dauster, Frank. The Double Strand: Five Contemporary Mexican Poets. LC 86-14653. 208p. 1987. 26.00 (*0-8131-1618-X*) U Pr of Ky.

— Xavier Villaurrutia. (Twayne's World Authors Ser.). 1971. pap. text 7.95 (*0-8290-1960-X*); lib. bdg. 17.95 (*0-686-82929-8*) Irvington.

Dauster, Frank, ed. Perspectives on Contemporary Spanish American Theatre. LC 55-58217. (Bucknell Review Ser.: Vol. XL, No. 2). 160p. 1997. 24.00 (*0-8387-5345-0*) Bucknell U Pr.

Daute, Horst. The Macmillan Book of Bonsai. (Gardening Guides Ser.). (Illus.). 128p. 1986. pap. 9.95 (*0-02-062660-6*) Macmillan.

***Dauten, Dale.** The Gifted Boss. 2000. pap. write for info. (*0-688-17770-0*, Quil) HarperTrade.

Dauten, Dale. The Gifted Boss: How to Find, Create & Keep Great Employees. LC 98-54390. 128p. 1999. 20.00 (*0-688-16877-9*, Wm Morrow) Morrow Avon.

— Less of the Same: A Guide for the Bored, the Unappreciated, & the Unemployed. 1996. 22.00 (*0-614-15442-1*, Wm Morrow) Morrow Avon.

— The Max Strategy: How a Businessman Got Stuck at an Airport & Learned to Make His Career Take Off. 116p. 1998. text 20.00 (*0-7881-5974-7*) DIANE Pub.

Dauten, Dale A. The Max Strategy: How a Businessman Got Stuck at an Airport & Learned to Make His Career Take Off. LC 95-14308. 160p. 1996. 19.95 (*0-688-14402-0*, Wm Morrow) Morrow Avon.

***Dautenhahn, Kerstin.** Human Cognition & Social Agent Technology. LC 99-39726. (Advances in Consciousness Research Ser.: Vol. 19). xxiv, 448p. 2000. pap. 59.95 (*1-55619-435-8*) J Benjamins Pubng.

Dautenhahn, Kerstin, et al, eds. Socially Intelligent Agents: Papers from the 1997 Fall Symposium. (Technical Reports). 124p. 1997. spiral bd. 25.00 (*1-57735-039-1*) AAAI Pr.

Dauterman, Carl C. Sevres Porcelain: Makers & Marks of the Eighteenth Century. (Illus.). 264p. 1986. 45.00 (*0-87099-227-9*, 0-8109-6473-2) Metro Mus Art.

Dautermann. Using ISETL 3.0: A Language for Learning. 1992. pap. 23.00 (*0-314-01327-X*) Wadsworth Pub.

— Using ISETL 3.0: A Language for Learning Mathematics. 1992. text 26.00 (*0-314-01326-1*) West Pub.

Dautermann, Carl C. & Watson, F. J. Wrightsman Collection: Furniture, Snuffboxes, Silver, Porcelain, Vols. 3 & 4. LC 66-10181. (Illus.). 860p. 1970. 100.00 (*0-87099-105-1*) Metro Mus Art.

Dautermann, Jennie. Writing at Good Hope: A Study of Negotiated Composition in a Community of Nurses. LC 96-38040. (ATTW Studies in Technical Communication). 250p. 1997. text 73.25 (*1-56750-316-0*) Ablx Pub.

Dautermann, Jennie. Writing at Good Hope: A Study of Negotiated Composition in a Community of Nurses. LC 96-38040. (ATTW Studies in Technical Communication). 250p. 1997. pap. 24.95 (*1-56750-317-9*) Ablx Pub.

Dauthy, Mircea E. Fruit & Vegetable Processing. LC 96-144320. (Agriculture Services Bulletin: 119). 390p. 1995. pap. 50.00 (*92-5-103657-8*) Food & Agri Org UN.

Dautov, Sh. A. & Aizenberg, L. A. Differential Forms Orthogonal to Holomorphic Functions or Forms, & Their Properties. LC 83-2696. (Translations of Mathematical Monographs: Vol. 56). 165p. 1983. text 52.00 (*0-8218-4508-X*, MMONO/56) Am Math.

Dautray, R. Mathematical Analysis & Numerical Methods for Science & Technology: Functional & Variational Methods, Vol. 2. (Illus.). 580p. 1988. 139.95 (*0-387-19045-7*) Spr-Verlag.

An Asterisk (*) at the beginning of an entry indicates that the title is appearing for the first time.

Dautray, R. & Lions, J. L. Mathematical Analysis & Numerical Methods for Science & Technology, Vol. 1. (Illus.). 670p. 1990. 139.95 (*0-387-50207-6*) Spr-Verlag.

— Mathematical Analysis & Numerical Methods for Science & Technology: Evolution Problems II - the Navier-Stokes & Transport Equations & Numerical Methods, Vol. 6. Craig, A., tr. from FRE. (Illus.). 500p. 1993. 145.00 (*0-387-50206-8*) Spr-Verlag.

***Dautray, R. & Lions, J. L.** Mathematical Analysis & Numerical Methods for Science & Technology Vol. 1: Physical Origins & Classical Methods. 695p. 2000. pap. 49.95 (*3-540-66097-6*) Spr-Verlag.

— Mathematical Analysis & Numerical Methods for Science & Technology Vol. 2: Functional & Variational Methods. (Illus.). 560p. 2000. pap. 49.95 (*3-540-66098-4*) Spr-Verlag.

Dautray, R. & Lions, J. L. Mathematical Analysis & Numerical Methods for Science & Technology Vol. 3: Spectral Theory & Applications, 6 vols. Amson, J. C., tr. from FRE. (Illus.). 536p. 1990. 139.95 (*0-387-50208-4*) Spr-Verlag.

***Dautray, R. & Lions, J. L.** Mathematical Analysis & Numerical Methods for Science & Technology Vol. 3: Spectral Theory & Applications. (Illus.). 515p. 2000. pap. 49.95 (*3-540-66099-2*) Spr-Verlag.

Dautray, R. & Lions, J. L. Mathematical Analysis & Numerical Methods for Science & Technology Vol. 4: Integral Equations & Numerical Methods, 6 vols. Amson, J. C., tr. from FRE. (Illus.). 488p. 1990. 149.95 (*0-387-50209-2*) Spr-Verlag.

***Dautray, R. & Lions, J. L.** Mathematical Analysis & Numerical Methods for Science & Technology Vol. 4: Integral Equations & Numerical Methods. (Illus.). 465p. 2000. pap. 49.95 (*3-540-66100-X*) Spr-Verlag.

Dautray, R. & Lions, J. L. Mathematical Analysis & Numerical Methods for Science & Technology Vol. 5: Evolution Problems I. Craig, A., tr. from FRE. (Illus.). 728p. 1992. 149.95 (*0-387-50205-X*) Spr-Verlag.

***Dautray, R. & Lions, J. L.** Mathematical Analysis & Numerical Methods for Science & Technology Vol. 5: Evolution Problems I. (Illus.). 710p. 2000. pap. 49.95 (*3-540-66101-8*) Spr-Verlag.

— Mathematical Analysis & Numerical Methods for Science & Technology Vol. 6: Evolution Problems II. (Illus.). 485p. 2000. pap. 49.95 (*3-540-66102-6*) Spr-Verlag.

Dautrich, Kenneth. How the News Media Fail American Voters: Causes, Consequences & Remedies. LC 98-33369. 11p. 1999. 49.50 (*0-231-11176-2*) Col U Pr.

Dautrich, Kenneth & Hartley, Thomas H. How the News Media Fail American Voters: Causes, Consequences & Remedies. LC 98-33369. 5p. 1999. 19.50 (*0-231-11177-0*) Col U Pr.

D'Autume, Antoine & Cartelier, Jean, eds. Is Economics Becoming a Hard Science? LC 96-603. (Illus.). 328p. (C). 1997. 90.00 (*1-85898-469-6*) E Elgar.

Dauve, Jan L., jt. auth. see Rhodes, V. James.

Dauven, Jean. The Powers of Hypnosis. (Illus.). 254p. 1980. pap. 5.95 (*0-8128-1391-X*, Scrbrough Hse) Madison Bks UPA.

Dauvergne, Peter. Shadows in the Forest: Japan & the Politics of Timber in Southeast Asia. LC 96-50982. (Politics, Science, & the Environment Ser.). (Illus.). 336p. 1997. 50.00 (*0-262-04160-X*); pap. text 24.50 (*0-262-54087-8*) MIT Pr.

***Dauvergne, Peter, ed.** Weak & Strong States in Asia-Pacific Societies. 220p. 1999. pap. 29.95 (*1-86373-983-1*, Pub. by Allen & Unwin Pty) Paul & Co Pubs.

Dauvillier, Jean. Le Mariage en Droit Canonique Oriental. LC 80-2357. reprint ed. 35.00 (*0-404-18905-9*) AMS Pr.

Dauw, Dean C. God & Sex. (God & Sex Trilogy Ser.). 600p. (C). 1993. 24.95 (*1-884094-00-7*); pap. 19.95 (*1-884094-01-5*) Ft Dearborn.

— God & Sex, Secrets of Christ. LC 97-216735. (God & Sex Trilogy Ser.). 400p. 1996. pap. 19.95 (*1-884094-05-8*) Ft Dearborn.

— God & Sex, Too: The Novel. (God & Sex Trilogy Ser.). 400p. 1994. pap. 19.95 (*1-884094-04-X*) Ft Dearborn.

— God & Sex, Too: The Novel. LC 95-102700. (God & Sex Trilogy Ser.). 362p. 1996. 24.95 (*1-884094-03-1*) Ft Dearborn.

— The God & Sex Trilogy, 3 vols., Set. 1400p. 1993. 59.00 (*1-884094-07-4*) Ft Dearborn.

— New Educational Methods for Increasing Religious Effectiveness. pap. 1.00 (*0-8199-0389-2*, L38532, Frncscn Herld) Franciscan Pr.

— Secrets of Christ: Novel. LC 97-216735. (God & Sex Trilogy Ser.). 400p. 1995. pap. 19.95 (*1-884094-06-6*) Ft Dearborn.

— Stranger in Your Bed: A Guide to Emotional Intimacy. LC 78-23444. 120p. 1979. text 25.95 (*0-88229-472-5*) Burnham Inc.

— Up Your Career. 4th rev. ed. (Illus.). 200p. (C). 1997. pap. 24.95 (*1-884094-12-0*) Ft Dearborn.

Dauwalder, David, jt. auth. see Wayne, Stan.

Dauwalder, David P., jt. auth. see Wayne, F. Stanford.

Dauwalder, J. P., et al. Controversial Issues in Behavior Modification. (Annual Series of European Research in Behavior Therapy: Vol. 11). viii, 312p. 1988. 51.50 (*90-265-0854-9*) Swets.

Dauwalder, Jean-Pierre, ed. Psychology & Promotion of Health. LC 93-46517. (Swiss Monographs in Psychology: Vol. 2). (Illus.). 250p. 1994. pap. text 36.00 (*0-88937-089-3*) Hogrefe & Huber Pubs.

D'Auxiron, Claude F. Principes de Tout Gouvernement, 2 vols., Set. (Economistes Francais du XVIIIe Siecle Ser.). 1990. reprint ed. pap. 68.00 (*3-601-00145-4*) Periodicals Srv.

D'Auzac, J., et al, eds. Physiology of Rubber Tree Latex, 2 vols. 488p. 1988. 265.00 (*0-8493-4893-5*, SB291, CRC Reprint) Franklin.

Dauzat, A. Dictionnaire Etymologique et Historique Du Francais. (FRE.). 872p. 1993. 39.95 (*0-7859-9832-2*) Fr & Eur.

Dauzat, Albert. Dictionnaire Etymologique des Noms de Famille et Prenoms de France. (FRE.). 626p. 1985. 34.95 (*0-8288-9498-1*) Fr & Eur.

— Dictionnaire Etymologique des Noms des Lieux en France. 2nd ed. (FRE.). 786p. 1979. 85.00 (*0-8288-9499-X*, EM74) Fr & Eur.

— Larousse Dictionnaire des Noms de Familles et Prenoms. 6th ed. (FRE.). 652p. 1970. 45.00 (*0-7859-8603-0*, 203340207x) Fr & Eur.

— Nouveau Dictionnaire Etymologique: New Etymological Dictionary. 6th ed. (FRE.). 805p. 1991. pap. 33.95 (*0-7859-4627-6*) Fr & Eur.

— La Vie du Langage. 311p. reprint ed. write for info. (*0-318-71336-5*) G Olms Pubs.

Dauzat, Albert, et al. Dictionnaire Etymologique des Noms de Rivieres et de Montagnes en France. (FRE.). 1982. pap. 95.00 (*0-7859-4817-1*, M6101) Fr & Eur.

Dauzat, Albert, jt. auth. see Larousse Staff.

Dauzat, M., tr. see Fruhwald, Franz X. & Blackwell, D. Eric, eds.

Dauzere-Peres, Stephane & Lasserre, Jean-Bernard. An Integrated Approach in Production Planning & Scheduling. LC 94-7929. (Lecture Notes in Economics & Mathematical Systems Ser.: Vol. 411). 1994. write for info. (*0-387-57905-2*) Spr-Verlag.

Davalo, Eric & Naim, Patrick. Neural Networks. Sumner, F. H., ed. Rawsthorne, A., tr. (Computer Science Ser.). (Illus.). 157p. (C). 1991. pap. text 35.00 (*0-333-54996-1*, Pub. by Macmillan Ed) Scholium Intl.

D'Avalon, Suzanne. How to Feed a Vegetarian: Help for Non-Vegetarian Cooks. 128p. (Orig.). 1996. pap. 12.95 (*0-9650941-0-3*) Placidly Amid.

Davalos, Felipe. Hijos de la Primavera (Children of the Spring) (SPA.). 237p. (YA). 1994. 19.99 (*968-16-4434-4*, Pub. by Fondo) Continental Bk.

Davalos, Felipe, ed. see Mapa, Araceli C.

Davane, G. V. Perspectives in the Vedic & the Classical Sanskrit Heritage. (C). 1995. 30.00 (*81-246-0031-7*, Pub. by DK Pubs Ind) S Asia.

— Various Interpretations of the Rbhu-Hymns in the Rgveda. (C). 1991. 22.00 (*81-7030-292-7*) S Asia.

***Davaney, Sheila G.** Pragmatic Historicism: A Theology for the Twenty-first Century. LC 99-57803. (C). 2000. pap. text 20.95 (*0-7914-4694-8*) State U NY Pr.

— Pragmatic Historicism: A Theology for the Twenty-first Century. LC 99-57803. (C). 2000. text 62.50 (*0-7914-4693-X*) State U NY Pr.

Davaney, Sheila G., ed. Changing Conversations. LC 96-39546. 272p. (C). 1996. 70.00 (*0-415-91432-9*) Routledge.

— Feminism & Process Thought: The Harvard Divinity School-Claremont Center for Process Studies Symposium Papers. LC 81-3942. (Symposium Ser.: Vol. 6). 144p. 1984. lib. bdg. 69.95 (*0-88946-903-2*) E Mellen.

— Theology at the End of Modernity. LC 91-13306. 288p. (C). 1991. pap. 25.00 (*1-56338-017-X*) TPI PA.

Davaney, Sheila G., jt. ed. see Chopp, Rebecca S.

***Davani, Darush & Guest, Clark C., eds.** Proceedings of the 1997 International Conference on Simulation in Engineering Education (ICSEE '97) Held in Phoenix, Arizona - January, 1997. (Simulation Ser.: Vol. 29, No. 2). 232p. 1998. 100.00 (*1-56555-104-4*, SS-29-2) Soc Computer Sim.

Davankov, Vadim A., et al. Ligand Exchange Chromatography. 240p. 1988. 127.00 (*0-8493-6775-1*, QD79, CRC Reprint) Franklin.

Davanloo, Habib. Unlocking the Unconscious: Selected Papers of Habib Davanloo, MD. 344p. 1995. pap. 110.00 (*0-471-95611-2*) Wiley.

Davanloo, Habib, ed. Basic Principles & Techniques in Short-Term Dynamic Psychotherapy. LC 94-72557. 584p. 1994. pap. text 50.00 (*1-56821-354-9*) Aronson.

Davanne, A. La Photographie, 2 vols. Bunnell, Peter C. & Sobieszek, Robert A., eds. LC 76-23052. (Sources of Modern Photography Ser.). (FRE., Illus.). 1979. lib. bdg. 53.95 (*0-405-09615-1*) Ayer.

DaVanzo, Julie, ed. Russia's Demographic "Crisis" LC 98-105872. (Illus.). 65p. 1996. pap. text 9.00 (*0-8330-2446-9*, CF-124-CRES) Rand Corp.

DaVanzo, Julie & Hawes-Dawson, Jennifer. Surveying Immigrant Communities: Policy Imperatives & Technical Challenges. LC 94-38284. 178p. 1994. pap. 15.00 (*0-8330-1594-X*) Rand Corp.

D'Avanzo, Mario. The Literary Art of the Bible: A Commentary. 266p. (C). 1988. pap. text 24.95 (*0-89641-172-9*) American Pr.

D'Avanzo, Mario L. A Cloud of Other Poets: Robert Frost & the Romantics. 250p. (Orig.). (C). 1991. pap. text 24.00 (*0-8191-7998-1*) U Pr of Amer.

— Keat's Metaphors for the Poetic Imagination. LC 67-17149. 244p. reprint ed. pap. 75.70 (*0-608-15089-4*, 202619500048) Bks Demand.

Davar, Adi, et al. The Journal of the Research & Historical Preservation Committee. 70p. (Orig.). 1996. pap. 5.00 (*1-883345-01-4*) FEZANA.

***Davar, Bhargavi V.** Mental Health of Indian Women: A Feminist Agenda. LC 98-46659. 292p. 1999. 35.00 (*0-7619-9300-2*) Sage.

Davar, Bhargavi V. & Bhat, Parameshwar R. Psychoanalysis As a Human Science: Beyond Foundationalism. LC 94-39606. 212p. 1995. text 22.50 (*0-8039-9196-7*) Sage.

Davaras, Costis, jt. ed. see Betancourt, Philip P.

Davarseisvili, A. G., jt. ed. see Celidze, V. G.

Davati, Mir M., tr. see Shirazi, Naser M.

Davats, V. & Lvov, N. Russkaia Armiia Na Chuzhbine: The Russian Army in Exile (1920-1923) LC 85-62402. (RUS.). 124p. 1985. 9.50 (*0-911971-18-1*) Effect Pub.

***Davatz, Barbara.** As Time Goes By: Portraits 1982, 1988, 1997. (Illus.). 128p. 2000. 39.95 (*3-905509-25-3*, Pub. by Patrick Frey) Dist Art Pubs.

Davau, Maurice. Dictionnaire Bordas. (FRE.). 49.95 (*0-8288-9324-1*, M6102) Fr & Eur.

Davau, Maurice, et al. Dictionnaire du Francais Vivant.Tr. of Dictionary of Living French. (FRE.). 1360p. 1972. pap. 49.95 (*0-8288-6379-2*, M-6102) Fr & Eur.

Davault, Doris B. Devault - Davault, 1750s-1996. (Illus.). 219p. 1996. write for info. (*0-934426-67-8*) NAPSAC Reprods.

Dave, et al. I Made This Jar . . . The Life & Works of the Enslaved African-American Potter, Dave. LC 98-3600. 1998. 20.00 (*0-938983-12-1*) McKissick.

Dave, G., jt. ed. see Munawar, M.

Dave, G. L. Emerging Dimension's in Accounting. 4p. 1993. pap. 180.00 (*81-07-23307-7*, Pub. by Scientific Pubs) St Mut.

Dave, Jagdish. Colloquial Gujarati. (gr. 13). 1995. pap. 39.95 incl. audio (*0-415-09198-5*, Pub. by Tavistock) Routldge.

— Colloquial Gujarati: A Complete Language Course. LC 94-3969. 288p. (gr. 13). 1995. pap. 24.99 (*0-415-09196-9*) Routledge.

— Colloquial Gujarati: A Complete Language Course. LC 94-3969. (C). (gr. 13). 1995. audio 29.99 (*0-415-09197-7*) Routledge.

Dave, Jitendra V. & Furukawa, P. M. Scattered Radiation in the Ozone Absorbtion Bands at Selected Levels of a Terrestrial, Rayleigh Atmosphers. (Meteorological Monograph: Vol. 7, No. 29). (Illus.). 353p. 1966. 27.00 (*0-933876-21-1*); pap. 25.00 (*0-933876-22-X*) Am Meteorological.

Dave, Mark. Learn C++ on the Macintosh. (C). 1996. pap. text. write for info. (*0-201-47945-1*) Addison-Wesley.

Dave, Nalini V. Vedanta & Management: Relevance of Vedantic Concepts in Modern Management Practices. LC 97-900218. (C). 1997. 18.00 (*81-7100-902-6*, Pub. by Deep & Deep Pubns) S Asia.

Dave, Raju S. & Loos, Alfred C. Processing of Composites. LC 99-27337. (Progress in Polymer Processing Ser.). 1999. write for info. (*1-56990-226-7*) Hanser-Gardner.

Davel, C. J. & Jordaan, R. A. Law of Persons Students' Textbook. 244p. 1994. pap. 26.50 (*0-7021-3273-X*, 15607, Pub. by Juta & Co) Gaunt.

Davel, C. J., jt. auth. see Jordaan, R. A.

Davel, T., jt. auth. see Jordaan, A.

Davelaar, E. J. Regional Economic Analysis of Innovation & Incubation. 349p. 1991. text 91.95 (*1-85628-139-6*, Pub. by Avebry) Ashgate Pub Co.

Daveline, Dan, ed. Accounting Practices & Procedures for Property/Casualty Insurance Companies. rev. ed. 176p. 1998. ring bd. 75.00i (*0-89382-521-2*, APP-PM97) Nat Assn Insurance.

***Daven, Mark.** Extreme Entrepreneur. 2000. pap. 17.95 (*1-891984-19-5*, Pub. by Entrepreneur) Natl Bk Netwk.

D'Avenant, Charles. Essay upon the Government of the English Plantations on the Continent of America, 1701. Wright, Louis B., ed. LC 76-141118. (Research Library of Colonial Americana). 1972. reprint ed. 20.95 (*0-405-03334-6*) Ayer.

D'Avenant, William. Dramatic Works, 5 vols. (BCL1-PR English Literature Ser.). 1992. reprint ed. lib. bdg. 450.00 (*0-7812-7239-4*) Rprt Serv.

Davenant, William. The Shorter Poems & Songs from the Plays & Masques. Gibbs, A. M., ed. 1972. 39.00 (*0-19-812434-1*) OUP.

— The Works of Sir William Davenant, 2 vols., Set. LC 67-31454. 1018p. 1972. 60.95 (*0-405-08433-1*, Pub. by Blom Pubns) Ayer.

— The Works of Sir William Davenant, 2 vols., Vol. 1. LC 67-31454. 1972. 30.95 (*0-405-08434-X*, Pub. by Blom Pubns) Ayer.

— The Works of Sir William Davenant, 2 vols., Vol. 2. LC 67-31454. 1972. 30.95 (*0-405-08435-8*, Pub. by Blom Pubns) Ayer.

Davenas, Alain, ed. Solid Rocket Propulsion Technology. 620p. 1992. 290.00 (*0-08-040999-7*, Pergamon Pr) Elsevier.

Davenas, J. Clusters Physics Materials. 1986. lib. bdg. 292.50 (*90-247-3279-4*, Pub. by M Nijhoff) Kluwer Academic.

D'Avenes, Prisse. Rare Masterpieces of Arab & Islamic Art. 1840. 149.95 (*0-86685-373-1*) Intl Bk Ctr.

Daveney, Sheila G. Changing Conversations. LC 96-39546. 272p. (C). 1996. pap. 23.99 (*0-415-91433-7*) Routledge.

***Davenhauer, Frank.** PowerPoint 2000: Module II. Nigro, Linnea & DeFlippo, Kathleen, eds. (Illus.). 205p. (C). 1999. pap. write for info. (*0-7423-0301-2*) ComputerPREP.

Davenhill, Rachael & Patrick, Matthew. Rethinking Clinical Audit: Psychotherapy Services in the NHS. LC 97-47788. 208p. (C). 1998. pap. 24.99 (*0-415-16208-4*) Routledge.

— Rethinking Clinical Audit: Psychotherapy Services in the NHS. LC 97-47788. 208p. (C). 1998. 75.00 (*0-415-16207-6*) Routledge.

D'Aveni, Richard A. Hypercompetition: Managing the Dynamics of Strategic Maneuvering. 500p. 1994. 35.00 (*0-02-906938-6*) Free Pr.

D'Aveni, Richard A. & Gunther, Robert. Hypercompetitive Rivalries: Competing in Highly Dynamic Environments. LC 95-24077. 288p. 1995. pap. 25.00 (*0-02-874112-9*) Free Pr.

Davenier, Christine. Leon & Albertine. Barth, Dominic, tr. LC 97-25399. (Illus.). 32p. (J). (ps-1). 1998. 15.95 (*0-531-30072-2*) Orchard Bks Watts.

D'Avennes, E. Prisse. Atlas of Egyptian Art. LC 98-100431. (Illus.). 167p. 1997. pap. 34.50 (*977-424-427-3*, Pub. by Am Univ Cairo Pr) Col U Pr.

D'Avennes, Prisse. L' Art Arabe d'Apres les Monuments du Kaire depuis le 7th Siecle Jusqu'a la Fin du 18th, 4 vols., Set. 1973. reprint ed. lib. bdg. 3672.50 (*90-277-9005-1*) Kluwer Academic.

Davenport. Birth of the New South Africa. LC 98-133636. (Illus.). 104p. 1997. text 30.00 (*0-8020-4190-6*); pap. text 16.95 (*0-8020-8054-5*) U of Toronto Pr.

— A Color Atlas of Removable Partial Dentures. (C). (gr. 13). 1988. 55.00 (*0-7234-1620-6*) Mosby Inc.

— Process Innovation. 220p. 1992. pap. 29.95 (*0-07-103382-3*) McGraw.

— True Value. LC 98-45840. 1999. text 32.95 (*0-7879-4015-1*) Jossey-Bass.

Davenport, contrib. by. Basic Criminal Law. (C). 2002. 44.67 (*0-13-079771-5*, Macmillan Coll) P-H.

Davenport & Sellwood. Science Challenge, Bk. 1. Date not set. pap. text. write for info. (*0-582-07008-2*, Pub. by Addison-Wesley) Longman.

Davenport, et al. Calculus Labs Using Maple V. LC 96-14567. (C). 1995. pap. text 18.00 (*0-673-99814-2*) Addson-Wesley Educ.

Davenport, A. B. A History & Genealogy of the Davenport Family in England & America, 1086-1850. (Illus.). 398p. 1989. reprint ed. pap. 59.50 (*0-8328-0455-X*); reprint ed. lib. bdg. 67.50 (*0-8328-0454-1*) Higginson Bk Co.

— Supplement to the Eighteen Fifty-One Davenport Genealogy, Continued to 1876. (Illus.). 437p. 1989. reprint ed. pap. 65.50 (*0-8328-0457-6*); reprint ed. lib. bdg. 72.50 (*0-8328-0456-8*) Higginson Bk Co.

Davenport, A. G., jt. ed. see Riera, J. D.

Davenport, A. J. & Gordon, J. G., II, eds. X-Ray Methods in Corrosion & Interfacial Electrochemistry. LC 92-70073. (Proceedings Ser.: Vol. 92-1). 350p. 1992. 42.00 (*1-56677-000-9*) Electrochem Soc.

Davenport, A. N. James Watt & the Patent System. (History of Science & Technology Ser.). 40p. 1989. pap. 14.50 (*0-7123-0752-4*, Pub. by SRIS) L Erlbaum Assocs.

Davenport, Alfred. Camp & Field Life of the Fifth New York Volunteer Infantry. 485p. 1989. reprint ed. 32.50 (*0-942211-77-4*) Olde Soldier Bks.

— Fifth New York Volunteer Infantry, Duryee Zouaves. 485p. Date not set. reprint ed. lib. bdg. 37.50 (*0-913419-05-2*, J M C & Co) Amereon Ltd.

Davenport, Alicia B., jt. auth. see Hirsch, Jeffrey L.

Davenport, Allen & Devyr, Ainge. The Life & Literary Pursuits of Allen Davenport. Thompson, Dortothy, ed. (Chartism, Working-Class Politics in the Industrial Revolution Ser.). 308p. 1987. lib. bdg. 26.00 (*0-8240-5595-0*) Garland.

Davenport, Alma. The History of Photography: An Overview. LC 99-26953. (Illus.). 216p. 1999. pap. 19.95 (*0-8263-2076-7*) U of NM Pr.

Davenport, Andrew. Merry Christmas, Teletubbies! (Teletubbies Ser.). (Illus.). 32p. (J). (ps-k). 1999. 9.99 (*0-439-10596-X*, Pub. by Scholastic Inc) Penguin Putnam.

***Davenport, Anne.** Measure of a Different Greatness: The Intensive Infinite, 1250-1650 LC 99-29174. (Studien und Texte zur Geistesgeschichte des Mittelalters). 1999. write for info. (*90-04-11481-5*) Brill Academic Pubs.

***Davenport, B. T.** Soldiering at Marfa, Texas, 1911-1945. 213p. 1999. pap. write for info. (*0-7392-0195-6*, PO3184) Morris Pubng.

Davenport, Barbara L., jt. auth. see Howe, Edward.

Davenport, Basil, ed. Portable Roman Reader. (Portable Library: No. 56). 656p. 1977. pap. 16.95 (*0-14-015056-0*, Penguin Bks) Viking Penguin.

Davenport, Basil, et al. The Science Fiction Novel: Imagination & Social Criticism. 3rd ed. LC 58-7492. 128p. 1969. reprint ed. 15.00 (*0-911682-02-3*); reprint ed. pap. 8.00 (*0-911682-13-9*) Advent.

Davenport, Beatrix C., ed. see Morris, Gouverneur.

Davenport, Benjamin R. Blood Will Tell. LC 78-38645. (Black Heritage Library Collection). (Illus.). 1977. reprint ed. 25.95 (*0-8369-9003-X*) Ayer.

— The Crime of Caste in Our Country: Bullets, 1861-Ballots 1892. 1977. text 27.95 (*0-8369-9248-2*, 9102) Ayer.

Davenport, Betty L. Hands on Rigid Heddle Weaving. LC 86-83426. (Illus.). 112p. 1987. pap. 12.95 (*0-934026-25-4*) Interweave.

Davenport, Brian A., jt. auth. see Blacker, Coit D.

Davenport, Carol L. The Insider's Guide to Smoking & Dining in Manhattan. (Illus.). 140p. (Orig.). 1995. pap. 9.95 (*0-9647624-1-2*) Kato Enter.

Davenport, Carol L., ed. The Insider's Guide to Smoking & Dining in Los Angeles, Vol. 1. (Illus.). 100p. (Orig.). 1995. pap. 9.95 (*0-9647624-2-0*) Kato Enter.

Davenport, Charles. Farm Income Tax Manual: Supplement to 1998 Edition. (Farm Income Tax Manual Series). 208p. 1999. pap. write for info. (*0-327-00904-7*, 6534616) LEXIS Pub.

— Farm Income Tax Manual: 1990 Edition. 1185p. 1990. pap. text. write for info. (*0-87473-698-6*, 65341-10, MICHIE) LEXIS Pub.

— Farm Income Tax Manual: 1991 Supplement. 142p. 1992. pap. text. write for info. (*0-87473-796-6*, 65344-10, MICHIE) LEXIS Pub.

— Farm Income Tax Manual: 1997 Edition. 1300p. 1997. pap. text 105.00 (*1-55834-784-4*, 65345-15, MICHIE) LEXIS Pub.

***Davenport, Charles.** Farm Income Tax Manual: 1999 Edition. 1375p. 1999. 120.00 (*0-327-10018-4*, 6534517) LEXIS Pub.

Davenport, Charles. Farm Income Tax Manual, 1996 Edition. 1485p. 1996. pap. 120.00 (*1-55834-211-7*, 65345-14) LEXIS Pub.

D

An Asterisk (*) at the beginning of an entry indicates that the title is appearing for the first time.

— Farm Income Tax Manual, 1998 Edition. 1352p. 1998. pap. write for info. (*0-327-00625-0*, 6534516) LEXIS Pub.

— Selected Readings on Tax Policy: 25 Years of Tax Notes LC 98-160190. xiii, 484p. 1997. write for info. (*0-918255-67-8*) Tax Analysts.

Davenport, Charles B. Heredity in Relation to Eugenics. LC 73-180571. (Medicine & Society in America Ser.). (Illus.). 320p. 1972. reprint ed. 24.95 (*0-405-03946-8*) Ayer.

— Race Crossing in Jamaica. LC 77-106833. 516p. 1970. reprint ed. lib. bdg. 75.00 (*0-8371-3455-2*, DRC&, Greenwood Pr) Greenwood.

Davenport, Christian, ed. Paths to State Repression: Human Rights Violations & Contentious Politics. LC 99-59363. 272p. 1999. pap. 24.95 (*0-8476-9391-0*) Rowman.

***Davenport, Christian, ed.** Paths to State Repression: Human Rights Violations & Contentious Politics. LC 99-59363. 272p. 1999. 69.00 (*0-8476-9390-2*) Rowman.

***Davenport, Clay, et al.** Baseball Prospectus 2001 Edition. 2000. pap. 21.95 (*1-57488-214-7*) Brasseys.

Davenport, David A. The Equity Manager Search: Strategies & Techniques for Plan Sponsors. LC 90-32723. 224p. 1990. 59.95 (*0-89930-518-0*, DMB/, Quorum Bks) Greenwood.

Davenport, David P. The Census of Montgomery County, New York, 1855: An Index. LC 89-84656. 314p. 1989. lib. bdg. 38.00 (*1-56012-102-5*, 97) Kinship Rhinebeck.

— The Census of Schenectady, New York, 1855: An Index. LC 89-80272. 228p. 1989. lib. bdg. 41.00 (*1-56012-101-7*, 94) Kinship Rhinebeck.

— The Census of Schoharie County, New York, 1855: An Index. LC 92-188010. 350p. 1988. lib. bdg. 47.00 (*1-56012-089-4*, 89) Kinship Rhinebeck.

— Matched Mortality & Population Schedules of the 1860 Census of Albany City & County, NY. LC 93-182178. 133p. 1988. lib. bdg. 27.00 (*1-56012-083-5*, 82) Kinship Rhinebeck.

— Population Persistence & Migration in Rural New York, 1855-1860. (Studies in Historical Demography). 264p. 1990. text 15.00 (*0-8240-3769-3*) Garland.

Davenport, Don. Acorn Guide to Northwest Illinois. LC 93-27179. 148p. 1994. pap. 9.95 (*1-879483-14-9*) Prairie Oak Pr.

Davenport, Don. Country Roads of Wisconsin. (Country Roads of... Ser.). (Illus.). 144p. 1996. pap. 10.95 (*1-56626-166-X*, 6166X, Cntry Rds Pr) NTC Contemp Pub Co.

***Davenport, Don.** Country Roads of Wisconsin: Drives, Day Trips & Weekend Excursions. LC 99-40606. (Country Road Ser.). 160p. 2000. pap. 12.95 (*0-658-00243-0*, 002430, Cntry Rds Pr) NTC Contemp Pub Co.

Davenport, Don. The Green Bay Packers: Titletown Trivia Teasers. 2nd ed. LC 97-13602. (Illus.). 144p. 1999. pap. 8.95 (*1-879483-55-6*) Prairie Oak Pr.

— In Lincoln's Footsteps: A Historical Guide to the Lincoln Sites in Illinois, Indiana & Kentucky. LC 90-64143. (Illus.). 224p. 1991. pap. 12.95 (*1-879483-00-9*) Prairie Oak Pr.

— Natural Wonders of Wisconsin. 2nd ed. LC 99-462599. (Natural Wonders of... Ser.). 160p. 1999. pap. 14.95 (*1-56626-091-4*, 60914) NTC Contemp Pub Co.

— Natural Wonders of Wisconsin: A Guide to Parks, Preserves & Wild Places. (Natural Wonders Ser.). (Illus.). 180p. 1995. pap. 9.95 (*1-56626-081-7*, Cntry Rds Pr) NTC Contemp Pub Co.

Davenport, Donald J. Street Art. (Illus.). 56p. 1996. 22.50 incl. VHS (*0-9606640-0-9*) Video Educ Art.

Davenport, Donna S., jt. auth. see Pipes, Randolph B.

Davenport, Edith E. Benton. David Benton & Nancy Pitts, Their Ancestors & Descendants, 1620-1920. (Illus.). 101p. 1997. reprint ed. pap. 17.00 (*0-8328-7509-0*); reprint ed. lib. bdg. 27.00 (*0-8328-7508-2*) Higginson Bk Co.

Davenport, Elisabeth, jt. auth. see Cronin, Blaise.

Davenport, Elizabeth, jt. auth. see Snyder, Herbert.

Davenport, Elizabeth O., jt. auth. see Davenport, George L.

Davenport-Ennis, Nancy. New Home Selling Strategies: A Handbook for Success. 206p. (Orig.). 1992. pap. 24.95 (*0-7931-0354-1*, 1909-0601, Real Estate Ed) Dearborn.

Davenport, F. M. Primitive Traits in Religious Revivals: A Study in Mental & Social Evolution. 1977. lib. bdg. 59.95 (*0-8490-2478-1*) Gordon Pr.

***Davenport, Fionn.** Lonely Planet Sicily. (Travel Guides Ser.). (Illus.). 2888p. 2000. pap. 15.95 (*1-86450-099-9*) Lonely Planet.

Davenport, Frances Gardiner. The Economic Development of a Norfolk Manor, 1085-1585. LC 67-16349. (Reprints of Economic Classics Ser.). (Illus.). x, 105, ciip. 1967. reprint ed. 30.00 (*0-678-05041-4*) Kelley.

— Economic Development of a Norfolk Manor, 1086-1565. (Illus.). 106p. 1967. reprint ed. 32.50 (*0-7146-1297-9*, Pub. by F Cass Pubs) Intl Spec Bk.

Davenport, Frances Gardiner, ed. European Treaties Bearing on the History of the United States & Its Dependencies to 1815, Vol. 2. 1990. 18.50 (*0-8446-1148-4*) Peter Smith.

Davenport, Frances Gardiner, ed. European Treaties Bearing on the History of the United States & Its Dependencies to 1815, Vol. 4. 1990. 18.50 (*0-8446-6841-9*) Peter Smith.

Davenport, Frances Gardiner, jt. auth. see Andrews, C. M.

Davenport, Francis Garvin. Ante-Bellum Kentucky: A Social History, 1800-1860. LC 83-10871. 238p. 1983. reprint ed. lib. bdg. 59.75 (*0-313-24113-9*, DAAN, Greenwood Pr) Greenwood.

— The Myth of Southern History: Historical Consciousness in Twentieth-Century Southern Literature. LC 76-112600. 224p. reprint ed. pap. 69.50 (*0-8357-3253-3*, 203947400013) Bks Demand.

Davenport, Francis Garvin, ed. European Treaties Bearing on the History of the United States & Its Dependencies to 1815, Vol. 3. 1990. 18.50 (*0-8446-6840-0*) Peter Smith.

Davenport, Frederick M. Primitive Traits in Religious Revivals. LC 72-163669. reprint ed. 34.50 (*0-404-01929-3*) AMS Pr.

Davenport, Gay & Urrutia, Benjamin, trs. The Logia of Yeshua. 96p. 1998. pap. 10.00 (*1-887178-70-8*, Pub. by Counterpt DC) HarpC.

Davenport, George L. & Davenport, Elizabeth O. The Genealogies of the Families of Cohasset. LC 84-61011. (Illus.). 707p. 1984. reprint ed. 55.00 (*0-89725-051-6*, 1227) Picton Pr.

Davenport, Gloria M. Working with Toxic Older Adults: A Guide to Coping with Difficult Elders. LC 98-45133. (Life Styles & Issues in Aging Ser.). (Illus.). 312p. 1998. 39.95 (*0-8261-1223-4*) Springer Pub.

Davenport, Gregory J. Wilderness Survival. LC 97-24515. (Illus.). 192p. 1998. pap. 14.95 (*0-8117-2985-0*) Stackpole.

Davenport, Guy. The Cardiff Team. LC 96-24208. 192p. 1996. 22.95 (*0-8112-1335-8*, Pub. by New Directions) Norton.

— Da Vinci's Bicycle. LC 97-4441. (Classic Ser.). 202p. 1997. pap. 11.95 (*0-8112-1350-1*, NDP842, Pub. by New Directions) Norton.

— Eclogues: Eight Stories. LC 93-18477. (Poetry & Fiction Ser.). 256p. (C). 1993. reprint ed. pap. 12.95 (*0-8018-4695-1*) Johns Hopkins.

— 50 Drawings. deluxe ed. (Illus.). 64p. 1996. 300.00 (*1-891472-06-2*) Dim Gray.

— Flowers & Leaves. 114p. 1991. pap. 9.50 (*0-917453-22-0*) Bamberger.

— The Geography of the Imagination: Forty Essays. LC 97-17831. 400p. 1997. pap. 18.95 (*1-56792-080-2*) Godine.

— Hunter Gracchus: And Other Papers on Literature & Art. (Illus.). 352p. 1997. pap. 16.50 (*1-887178-55-4*, Pub. by Counterpt DC) HarpC.

— The Lark. deluxe ed. (Illus.). 16p. 1993. 85.00 (*1-891472-05-4*) Dim Gray.

— Objects on a Table: Harmonious Disarray in Art & Literature. LC 98-35507. (Illus.). 144p. 1998. 27.50 (*1-887178-85-6*, Pub. by Counterpt DC) HarpC.

***Davenport, Guy.** Objects on a Table: Harmonious Disarray in Art & Literature. 136p. 1999. pap. text 17.50 (*1-58243-035-7*, Pub. by Counterpt DC) HarpC.

Davenport, Guy. A Table of Green Fields. LC 93-18677. 160p. 1993. 21.95 (*0-8112-1251-3*, Pub. by New Directions) Norton.

— Tatlin: Six Stories. LC 81-48197. (Illus.). 271p. 1982. reprint ed. pap. 84.10 (*0-608-04050-9*, 206478600011) Bks Demand.

— Twelve Stories. LC 97-28155. (Illus.). 240p. 1997. pap. 14.00 (*1-887178-44-9*, Pub. by Counterpt DC) HarpC.

***Davenport, Guy.** Will McBride: Coming of Age. (Illus.). 112p. 1999. 45.00 (*0-89381-853-4*) Aperture.

Davenport, Guy, tr. from GRE. Seven Greeks. LC 95-4227. 256p. (Orig.). 1995. pap. 16.95 (*0-8112-1288-2*, NDP799, Pub. by New Directions) Norton.

Davenport, Guy, ed. see Agassiz, Louis.

Davenport, Guy, ed. & intro. see Henry, O.

Davenport, Guy, tr. see Heraclitus & Diogenes.

Davenport, H. The Higher Arithmetic. 7th rev. ed. (Illus.). 240p. (C). 2000. text 74.95 (*0-521-63269-2*); pap. text 27.95 (*0-521-63446-6*) Cambridge U Pr.

— Multiplicative Number Theory. (Graduate Texts in Mathematics Ser.: Vol. 74). 177p. 1980. 39.00 (*0-387-90533-2*) Spr-Verlag.

Davenport, H. B. Tales of the Elk: And Other Stories. 122p. 1992. reprint ed. pap. 7.95 (*1-881413-01-2*) Thomas In-Prints.

Davenport, Henry B., Jr. Davenport Genealogy of the Davenport Family & Connections. (Illus.). 99p. 1997. reprint ed. pap. 18.50 (*0-8328-8220-8*); reprint ed. lib. bdg. 28.50 (*0-8328-8219-4*) Higginson Bk Co.

Davenport, Herbert J. The Economics of Alfred Marshall. LC 65-19648. (Reprints of Economic Classics Ser.). 481p. 1965. reprint ed. 49.50 (*0-678-00095-6*) Kelley.

— The Economics of Enterprise. LC 66-21668. (Reprints of Economic Classics Ser.). xvi, 544p. 1968. reprint ed. 49.50 (*0-678-00424-2*) Kelley.

— Outlines of Economic Theory. LC 67-29500. (Reprints of Economic Classics Ser.). xxi, 381p. 1968. reprint ed. 45.00 (*0-678-00389-0*) Kelley.

— Value & Distribution: A Critical & Constructive Study. LC 64-17406. (Reprints of Economic Classics Ser.). xi, 582p. 1964. reprint ed. 49.50 (*0-678-00036-0*) Kelley.

***Davenport, Hester.** Their Faithful Handmaid: Fanny Burney at the Court of King George III. (Illus.). 256p. 2000. 34.95 (*0-7509-1881-0*) Sutton Publng.

Davenport-Hines, R. P., ed. Business in the Age of Depression & War. 326p. 1990. text 49.50 (*0-7146-3387-9*, Pub. by F Cass Pubs) Intl Spec Bk.

— Speculators & Patriots: Essays in Business Biography. 224p. 1986. 32.00 (*0-7146-3301-1*, Pub. by F Cass Pubs) Intl Spec Bk.

Davenport-Hines, R. P. & Jones, G., eds. End of Insularity: Essays in Comparative Business History. 138p. 1989. text 35.00 (*0-7146-3352-6*, Pub. by F Cass Pubs) Intl Spec Bk.

— Enterprise, Management & Innovation in British Business, 1914-1980. (Illus.). 128p. 1988. text 30.00 (*0-7146-3348-8*, Pub. by F Cass Pubs) Intl Spec Bk.

Davenport-Hines, R. P. & Jones, Geoffrey, eds. British Business in Asia since 1860. (Illus.). 320p. (C). 1989. text 69.95 (*0-521-33527-2*) Cambridge U Pr.

Davenport-Hines, R. P. & Liebenau, Jonathan, eds. Business in the Age of Reason. 224p. 1995. 35.00 (*0-7146-3306-2*, Pub. by F Cass Pubs) Intl Spec Bk.

Davenport-Hines, R. P. & Slinn, Judy. Glaxo: A History to Nineteen Sixty-Two. 422p. (C). 1993. text 125.00 (*0-521-41539-X*) Cambridge U Pr.

Davenport-Hines, R. T., ed. Capital, Enterpreneurs & Profits. 305p. 1990. text 49.50 (*0-7146-3386-0*, Pub. by F Cass Pubs) Intl Spec Bk.

Davenport-Hines, Richard. Auden. LC 95-31796. (Illus.). 416p. 1996. 4.99 (*0-679-42633-7*) Pantheon.

— Auden: A Biography. (Vintage Ser.). (Illus.). 448p. 1999. pap. 15.00 (*0-679-74785-0*) Vin Bks.

Davenport-Hines, Richard. Gothic: Four Hundred Years of Excess, Horror, Evil & Ruin. LC 98-40556. (Illus.). 448p. 1999. 35.00 (*0-86547-544-X*) N Point Pr.

***Davenport-Hines, Richard.** Gothic: Four Hundred Years of Excess, Horror, Evil & Ruin. (Illus.). 448p. 2000. pap. 15.00 (*0-86547-590-3*) N Point Pr.

Davenport, Horace W. ABC of Acid-Base Chemistry: The Elements of Physiological Blood-Gas Chemistry for Medical Students & Physicians. rev. ed. LC 79-88230. 132p. 1974. pap. text 10.00 (*0-226-13703-1*) U Ch Pr.

— Doctor Dock: Teaching & Learning Medicine at the Turn of the Century. (Illus.). 250p. 1987. text 45.00 (*0-8135-1190-9*) Rutgers U Pr.

— An Eagle-Feather: The Short Life of Albert Moser, M.D., A Footnote to the Life of Walter B. Cannon. (Countway Library Associates Historical Publication Ser.: No. 2). (Illus.). 41p. 1974. 2.50 (*0-686-05841-0*) F A Countway.

— A History of Gastric Secretion & Digestion: Experimental Studies to 1975. (Illus.). 432p. 1992. text 79.00 (*0-19-507393-2*) OUP.

— Not Just Any Medical School: The Science, Practice & Teaching of Medicine at the University of Michigan, 1850-1941. LC 99-6221. 400p. 1999. text 52.50 (*0-472-11076-4*, 11076) U of Mich Pr.

— Physiology of the Digestive Tract. 5th ed. (Illus.). 1982. 32.95 (*0-8151-2330-2*) Mosby Inc.

***Davenport, J.** Baltic Regional Coinage (1250-1780 AD) (Illus.). 105p. 2000. pap. 20.00 (*1-886720-10-X*) S J Durst.

Davenport, J. German Church & City Talers (1600-1700) (Illus.). 1976. lib. bdg. 38.00 (*0-932106-14-5*) S J Durst.

— German Secular Tales, 1600-1700. 1976. lib. bdg. 50.00 (*3-921302-12-9*) S J Durst.

— Talers of the Austrian Noble Houses. (Illus.). 1972. pap. 12.00 (*0-932106-44-7*) S J Durst.

Davenport, J. H. On the Integration of Agebraic Function. (Lecture Notes in Computer Science Ser.: Vol. 102). 197p. 1981. pap. 23.00 (*0-387-10290-6*) Spr-Verlag.

Davenport, J. H., ed. Eurocal '87. (Lecture Notes in Computer Science Ser.: Vol. 378). viii, 499p. 1989. 55.00 (*0-387-51517-8*) Spr-Verlag.

Davenport, J. S. German Talers Seventeen Hundred to Eighteen Hundred. 1979. 45.00 (*0-932106-56-0*) S J Durst.

Davenport, James. Grove Family of Halesowen. (Illus.). 84p. 1997. reprint ed. pap. 16.00 (*0-8328-8852-4*); reprint ed. lib. bdg. 26.00 (*0-8328-8851-6*) Higginson Bk Co.

Davenport, James H. Davenport: James & Elizabeth Davenport of Tennessee: Their Descendants, & Some Speculation Regarding Their Ascendants. (Illus.). 327p. 1995. reprint ed. pap. 49.50 (*0-8328-4908-1*); reprint ed. lib. bdg. 59.50 (*0-8328-4907-3*) Higginson Bk Co.

Davenport, James W., jt. auth. see Wylie, David M.

Davenport, Jennifer A. The House in the Woods: And Other Stories of Men & Women on the Knobby Landscape of Life. (Illus.). 232p. (Orig.). 1996. pap. 12.95 (*0-9649552-0-2*) Blue Arc.

Davenport, John, Jr. An Apologetical Reply to a Book Called: An Answer to the Unjust Complaint of W.B. (English Experience Ser.: No. 792). 1977. reprint ed. lib. bdg. 40.00 (*90-221-0792-2*) Walter J Johnson.

— A Just Complaint Against an Unjust Doer, Mr. J. Paget. LC 76-57376. (English Experience Ser.: No. 793). 1977. reprint ed. lib. bdg. 20.00 (*90-221-0793-0*) Walter J Johnson.

— Letters of John Davenport, Puritan Divine. Calder, Isabel M., ed. 1937. 100.00 (*0-685-69794-0*) Elliots Bks.

Davenport, John S. East Baltic Regional Coinage. 104p. 1996. pap. 15.00 (*1-889172-20-0*) Numismatic Intl.

— Talers of the Austrian Noble Houses. 64p. 1988. pap. 4.00 (*1-889172-14-6*) Numismatic Intl.

Davenport, John T., tr. see Pandita, Sakya.

Davenport, John W. Baseball Graphics. LC 79-52663. 1979. pap. 7.95 (*0-934794-00-6*) First Impressions.

— Baseball's Pennant Races: A Graphic View. LC 81-67611. (Illus.). 1981. 19.95 (*0-934794-03-0*); pap. 12.95 (*0-934794-02-2*) First Impressions.

— Berkshire-Bennington Locater. 112p. 1988. pap. 10.95 (*0-934794-05-7*) First Impressions.

— Cape & Islands Locater. (Illus.). 144p. (Orig.). 1989. pap. 12.95 (*0-934794-06-5*) First Impressions.

— Graphics for the Dot-Matrix Printer. write for info. (*0-318-58697-5*) S&S Trade.

Davenport, Julia C. Sanctuary Explorations: A User's Guide to the Monterey Bay. Welch, Dorris, ed. (Illus.). 44p. 1997. pap. 7.95 (*0-9662619-0-9*) UC Santa Cruz Inst Marine.

— Sanctuary Explorations: Access Guide to Monterey Bay National Marine Sanctuary. Welch, Dorris, ed. (Illus.). 1997. pap. 7.95 (*0-9658776-4-7*) Cntrl Coast Pr.

Davenport, Kiana. Shark Dialogues. Goerner, Lee, ed. 512p. 1994. 22.00 (*0-689-12191-1*, Pub. by Ctrl Bur voor Schimmel) Macmillan.

— Shark Dialogues. LC 95-737. 1995. pap. 13.95 (*0-452-27458-3*, Plume) Dutton Plume.

Davenport, Kiana. Song of the Exile. LC 99-14224. 368p. 1999. 24.95 (*0-345-42539-1*) Ballantine Pub Grp.

***Davenport, Kiana.** Song of the Exile. 368p. 2000. pap. 14.00 (*0-345-43494-3*) Ballantine Pub Grp.

Davenport, Linda. Supply Belcher: The Collected Works. LC 56-5. 144p. 1996. text 72.00 (*0-8153-2427-8*) Garland.

Davenport, Linda G. Divine Song on the Northeast Frontier: Maine's Sacred Tunebooks, 1800-1830. LC 95-9756. (Composers of North America Ser.: No. 18). 440p. 1996. 75.00 (*0-8108-3025-6*) Scarecrow.

Davenport, Lyn. The Guardian 2. (Orig.). 1997. mass mkt. 6.50 (*1-56333-505-0*) Masquerade.

Davenport, Marc. Dear Mr. President: One Hundred Earthsaving Letters. 224p. (Orig.). 1991. pap. 12.95 (*0-8065-1269-5*, Citadel Pr) Carol Pub Group.

— Visitors from Time: The Secret of the UFO's. rev. ed. LC 94-36813. 266p. 1994. reprint ed. pap. 18.95 (*1-883729-02-5*) Greenleaf Tenn.

Davenport, Marc, ed. see Stearn, Jess & Geller, Larry.

Davenport, Marcia. The Constant Image. 1998. lib. bdg. 31.95 (*1-56723-035-0*) Yestermorrow.

— East Side West Side. 1994. lib. bdg. 24.95 (*1-56849-419-X*) Buccaneer Bks.

— East Side, West Side. LC 78-74647. 1979. reprint ed. lib. bdg. 22.00 (*0-8376-0428-1*) Bentley Pubs.

— Mozart. 1976. 30.95 (*0-8488-0976-9*) Amereon Ltd.

— Mozart. 440p. 1979. mass mkt. 5.95 (*0-380-45534-X*, Avon Bks) Morrow Avon.

— My Brother's Keeper. LC 78-74646. 1979. reprint ed. 24.00 (*0-8376-0429-X*) Bentley Pubs.

— Of Lena Geyer. 1976. 30.95 (*0-8488-0795-2*) Amereon Ltd.

— Of Lena Geyer. 1998. lib. bdg. 30.95 (*1-56723-036-9*) Yestermorrow.

— Too Strong for Fantasy. LC 92-53723. (Illus.). 504p. (C). 1992. reprint ed. text 49.95 (*0-8229-3834-0*) U of Pittsburgh Pr.

— The Valley of Decision. LC 78-74648. 1979. reprint ed. lib. bdg. 18.00 (*0-8376-0427-3*) Bentley Pubs.

— The Valley of Decision. LC 88-33758. 640p. 1989. reprint ed. pap. 19.95 (*0-8229-5805-8*) U of Pittsburgh Pr.

Davenport, Marge. Afloat & Awash in the Old Northwest. (Illus.). 224p. (Orig.). 1988. pap. 9.95 (*0-938274-04-X*) Paddlewheel.

— Best of the Old Northwest. LC 80-83780. (Illus.). (Orig.). 1981. pap. 7.95 (*0-938274-00-7*) Paddlewheel.

— Cooking with Honey: The Natural Way to Health & Better Eating. Cady, L. B., ed. (Illus.). (Orig.). 1991. pap. 13.55 (*0-938274-05-8*) Paddlewheel.

— Fabulous Folks of the Old Northwest. LC 85-73153. (Illus.). (Orig.). 1986. pap. 9.95 (*0-938274-03-1*) Paddlewheel.

— Northwest Glory Days. (Illus.). 208p. (Orig.). 1983. pap. 6.95 (*0-938274-02-3*) Paddlewheel.

— Wild Berry Magic: Pick the Berries. (Illus.). (Orig.). 1981. pap. 3.95 (*0-938274-01-5*) Paddlewheel.

Davenport, Marilyn A., et al. Children of Divorce. LC 92-35959. (Workshop Models for Family Life Education Ser.). 96p. 1993. pap. 16.95 (*0-87304-265-4*) Manticore Pubs.

Davenport, Mark, jt. auth. see O'Connor, Jerry.

Davenport, May. Blow Away Seaweeds. LC 89-92456. 265p. (YA). (gr. 7-12). 1994. 29.95 (*0-943864-60-7*) Davenport.

Davenport, May, et al. Comic Tales Anthology No. 1: Watch Out, the Tide. LC 86-91602. 84p. (YA). (gr. 7-12). 1987. pap. 4.95 (*0-943864-27-5*) Davenport.

Davenport, May, ed. see Kruse, Donald W.

Davenport, May, ed. see Ropes, Linda.

Davenport, May, ed. see Ross, Andrea.

Davenport, Megan, jt. auth. see O'Connell, Caroline.

Davenport, Michael L. Finding Happiness Sitting on Your Butt Going Backwards. (Illus.). (Orig.). 1996. pap. 24.95 (*0-9639300-2-8*) Mouse Hse Bks.

— The Nuts & Bolts Guide to Rigging: A Step by Step Handbook for Empaches, Kaschper, Pocock, Schgenbrod & Vespoli. LC 92-91056. 306p. 1992. 28.95 (*0-9639300-0-1*) Mouse Hse Bks.

Davenport, Mike & Hannahs, S. J. Introducing Phonetics & Phonology. LC 98-22273. (Arnold Publication Ser.). (Illus.). 208p. 1998. text 70.00 (*0-340-66218-2*); pap. text 19.95 (*0-340-66217-4*) OUP.

Davenport, Mike, jt. ed. see Hannahs, S. J.

Davenport Museum of Art (Davenport, Iowa) Staff, jt. auth. see Burke, Marcus B.

Davenport, Neil, tr. see Diemberger, Kurt & Mantovani, Roberto.

Davenport, Neil F., tr. see Massa, Renato.

Davenport, Neil F., tr. see Massa, Renato, et al.

Davenport, Nicholas. The Honour of St. Valery: The Story of an English Manor House. LC 79-314545. 157 p. 1978. 15.95 (*0-85967-463-0*) Scolar Pr.

Davenport, Noa, et al. Mobbing: Emotional Abuse in the American Workplace. (Illus.). 216p. 1999. pap. 14.95 (*0-9671803-0-9*, Pub. by Civil Society) BookMasters.

Davenport, Penny. Natural Way: Colds & Flu. 128p. 1995. pap. 5.95 (*1-85230-630-0*, Pub. by Element MA) Penguin Putnam.

Davenport, Peter, ed. Archaeology in Bath 1976-1985: Excavations at Orange Grove, Swallow Street, the Crystal Palace, Abbey Street. (Illus.). 170p. 1991. pap. 36.00 (*0-947816-28-3*, Pub. by Oxford Univ Comm Arch) David Brown.

Davenport, Philip. Construction Claims. 240p. 1995. pap. 40.00 (*1-86287-180-9*, Pub. by Federation Pr) Gaunt.

Davenport, Philip & Harris, Christina. Unjust Enrichment. 142p. 1997. 44.00 (*1-86287-255-4*, Pub. by Federation Pr) Gaunt.

Davenport, Raymond J. Davenport's Art Reference & Price Guide, 1996-1997. 8th rev. ed. 2000p. 1995. 165.00 (*0-9616110-7-3*) Davenport Pub.

***Davenport, Raymond J., ed.** Davenport's Art Reference & Price Guide, 1999-2000. 1872p. 1999. 195.00 (*0-931036-83-6*) Gordon s Art.

Davenport, Reuben B. The Death-Blow to Spiritualism: Being the True Story of the Fox Sisters. LC 75-36836. (Occult Ser.). 1976. reprint ed. 21.95 (*0-405-07949-4*) Ayer.

Davenport, Richard. Outline of Animal Development. LC 78-62548. (Life Sciences Ser.). (Illus.). 1979. text. write for info. (*0-201-01814-4*) Addison-Wesley.

Davenport, Rita. De Grazia & Mexican Cookery. LC 82-80299. 86p. 1999. pap. 12.95 (*0-87358-307-8*) Northland AZ.

Davenport, Robert. Related at Birth. 1994. pap. 12.00 (*0-517-88079-2*) Crown Pub Group.

— Rich & Famous Baby Name Book Vol. 1: Ten Thousand Celebrity Names for Your Baby. 1994. mass mkt. 4.99 (*0-312-95407-7*) St Martin.

— The Works of Robert Davenport. Bullen, Arthur H., ed. LC 68-24819. 362p. 1972. 30.95 (*0-405-08436-6*, Pub. by Blom Pubns) Ayer.

Davenport, Robert R. Davenport Genealogy: History & Genealogy of the Ancestors & Descendants of the Rev. John Davenport. 332p. 1982. text 38.00 (*1-885943-00-8*) Historic Trust.

— Hereditary Society Blue Book: 1994 Edition. 318p. 1994. 25.00 (*0-8063-1398-6*, 1355) Genealog Pub.

— Hereditary Society Blue Book, 1995. (Illus.). 320p. 1995. text 45.00 (*1-885943-02-4*) Historic Trust.

— Hereditary Society Blue Book (1996) 320p. 1996. lib. bdg. 38.00 (*1-885943-04-0*) Historic Trust.

— Hereditary Society Blue Book (1997) 1997. lib. bdg. 48.00 (*1-885943-05-9*) Historic Trust.

— Heredity Society Blue Book (1994) (Illus.). 320p. 1994. text 24.95 (*1-885943-01-6*) Historic Trust.

— Roots of the Rich & Famous. LC 98-38969. (Illus.). 144p. 1998. pap. 10.95 (*0-87833-217-0*) Taylor Pub.

Davenport, Robert R., ed. Hereditary Society: Blue Book, 1998. (Illus.). 320p. 1998. 45.00 (*1-885943-06-7*) Historic Trust.

— Hereditary Society: Blue Book, 1999. (Illus.). 320p. 1999. 45.00 (*1-885943-07-5*) Historic Trust.

— Hereditary Society: Blue Book, 2000. (Illus.). 320p. Date not set. text 45.00 (*1-885943-08-3*) Historic Trust.

Davenport, Robert R., ed. see Metcalf, Bryce.

Davenport, Robertson D. & Snyder, Edward L., eds. Cytokines in Transfusion Medicine: A Primer. LC 97-35729. 1997. text 129.00 (*1-56395-080-4*) Am Assn Blood.

Davenport, Russell W., jt. auth. see Fortune Magazine Editors.

Davenport, Sheila. Canal & River Cruising: The IWA Manual. (C). 1990. text 65.00 (*0-906754-49-6*, Pub. by Fernhurst Bks) St Mut.

Davenport, Stephen G. Anatomy & Physiology in Focus: Laboratory Workbook. 473p. (C). 1993. pap. write for info. (*0-9637670-0-3*) Link Pub.

Davenport, T. C., ed. Rheology of Lubricants. (Illus.). 148p. 1973. 39.75 (*0-85334-473-6*) Elsevier.

Davenport, T. H. Innovacion de Procesos. (SPA.). 344p. 1996. pap. 31.50 (*84-7978-270-6*, Pub. by Ediciones Diaz) IBD Ltd.

— South Africa: A Modern History. 4th ed. 658p. 1991. text 60.00 (*0-8020-5940-6*); pap. text 27.50 (*0-8020-6880-4*) U of Toronto Pr.

Davenport, T. R. South Africa: A Modern History. LC 77-375725. 447p. reprint ed. pap. 127.40 (*0-608-16873-4*, 2056136) Bks Demand.

— South Africa: A Modern History. 3rd rev. ed. LC 85-223940. 716p. 1987. reprint ed. pap. 200.00 (*0-7837-1230-8*, 204136700020) Bks Demand.

Davenport, T. R., jt. auth. see Elphick, Richard.

***Davenport, T. R. H.** South Africa: A Modern History. 2000. pap. 29.65 (*0-312-23376-0*) St Martin.

Davenport, Teresa J. Florida Rules of Evidence Code with Objections. 3rd ed. LC 98-232602. 232p. 1998. 25.95 (*1-55681-605-7*) Natl Inst Trial Ad.

Davenport, Terilyn A. Minor League: Step-by-Step Guide to Understanding Investment Basics. LC 94-65046. 320p. (Orig.). 1996. 29.95 (*1-884573-08-8*); pap. 19.95 (*1-884573-11-8*) S-By-S Pubns.

— Starting Out: Step-by-Step Guide for Teens Succeeding in the '90s. LC 93-87661. 320p. (Orig.). (YA). (gr. 11 up). 1994. 29.95 (*1-884573-09-6*); pap. 19.95 (*1-884573-10-X*) S-By-S Pubns.

Davenport, Thom. Parent Talk. (YouthSearch: Small-Group Resources Ser.: Vol. 10). 64p. 1996. pap. 5.95 (*0-687-05532-6*) Abingdon.

Davenport, Thomas H. Information Ecology: Mastering the Information & Knowledge Environment. 1997. 29.95 (*0-614-28016-8*) OUP.

***Davenport, Thomas H.** Mission Critical: Realizing the Promise of Enterprise Systems. 2000. 29.95 (*0-87584-906-7*, HBS Pr) Harvard Busn.

Davenport, Thomas H. Process Innovation: Reengineering Work Through Information Technology. LC 92-21959. 337p. (C). 1993. 34.95 (*0-87584-366-2*) Harvard Busn.

***Davenport, Thomas H.** Working Knowledge: How Organizations Manage What They Know. 2000. pap. text 16.95 (*1-57851-301-4*) Harvard Busn.

Davenport, Thomas H. & Prusak, Laurance. Information Ecology: Mastering the Information & Knowledge Environment. LC 96-45169. (Illus.). 272p. 1997. 29.95 (*0-19-511168-0*) OUP.

Davenport, Thomas H. & Prusak, Lawrence. Working Knowledge: How Organizations Manage What They Know. LC 97-10781. 224p. 1998. 29.95 (*0-87584-655-6*, HBS Pr) Harvard Busn.

Davenport, Tim, jt. auth. see Malehorn, Merlin K.

Davenport, Tom & Carden, Gary. From the Brothers Grimm: A Contemporary Retelling of American Folktales & Classic Stories. LC 92-30828. (Illus.). 105p. (J). (gr. 2-12). 1993. pap. 9.00 (*0-917846-20-6*, 95526) Highsmith Pr.

***Davenport, Tom & Marchand, Donald A.** Mastering Information Management: The Complete MBA Companion in Information Management. 416p. 2000. pap. 34.00 (*0-273-64352-5*) F T P-H.

Davenport, Tom, et al. The Guide to Making Grimm Movies. (Illus.). 48p. (Orig.). 1993. pap. write for info. (*1-888522-01-1*) Davenport Films.

Davenport, Tony, jt. auth. see Penn, Sarah.

Davenport, W. A. The Art of the Gawain-Poet. LC 85-24527. 233p. (C). 1978. pap. 17.50 (*0-485-12050-X*, Pub. by Athlone Pr) Humanities.

— Chaucer: Complaint & Narrative. (Chaucer Studies: No. XIV). 211p. (C). 1988. 75.00 (*0-85991-277-9*) Boydell & Brewer.

— Chaucer & His English Contemporaries: Prologue & Tale in the Canterbury Tales. LC 98-2627. 256p. 1998. pap. 19.95 (*0-312-21439-1*) St Martin.

— Fifteenth-Century English Drama: The Early Moral Plays & Their Literary Relations. 162p. 1970. 75.00 (*0-85991-091-1*) Boydell & Brewer.

Davenport, W. G., jt. auth. see Biswas, Asit K.

Davenport, W. G., jt. ed. see Biswas, A.K.

Davenport, Wilbur B. & Root, William L. An Introduction to the Theory of Random Signals & Noise. LC 87-22594. 408p. 1987. 59.95 (*0-87942-235-1*, PCO2253) Inst Electrical.

Davenport, William H. Pi'o: An Enquiry into the Marriage of Brothers & Sisters & Other Close Relatives in Old Hawai'i. LC 93-45520. 104p. lib. bdg. 32.50 (*0-8191-9395-X*) U Pr of Amer.

Davenport, William H., et al. Social Organization & Cultural Aesthetics: Essays in Honor of William H. Davenport. Donner, William W. & Flanagan, James G., eds. LC 97-19969. 160p. 1997. 48.00 (*0-7618-0783-7*); pap. 26.50 (*0-7618-0784-5*) U Pr of Amer.

Davenport, William H., jt. auth. see Cox, J. Halley.

Davenport, Zoe. Animals. LC 94-20821. (Words for Everyday Ser.). (Illus.). 16p. (J). (ps-2). 1995. 5.95 (*0-395-71537-7*) Ticknor & Flds Bks Yng Read.

Daventry, Paula. Sasakawa, the Warrior for Peace: Global Philanthropist. (Illus.). 143p. 1981. pap. 9.00 (*0-08-028126-5*, Pergamon Pr) Elsevier.

Daver, B. M., et al. A Handbook of Plastic Surgery for the General Surgeon. (Illus.). 254p. 1995. pap. text 21.95 (*0-19-563635-X*) OUP.

***Daver, B. M., et al.** Handbook of Plastic Surgery for the General Surgeon. 2nd ed. (Illus.). 272p. 2000. text 34.50 (*0-19-565137-5*) OUP.

Daver, Roberta A. Bankers & Diplomats in China, 1917-1925: The Anglo-American Relationship. 324p. 1981. 35.00 (*0-7146-3118-3*, Pub. by F Cass Pubs) Intl Spec Bk.

Daverio, John. Robert Schumann: Herald of a New Poetic Age. LC 96-23177. (Illus.). 624p. 1997. 45.00 (*0-19-509180-9*) OUP.

Daverio, John J. Nineteenth-Century Music & the German Romantic Ideology. (Illus.). 274p. 1993. 45.00 (*0-02-870675-7*, Schirmer Books) Mac Lib Ref.

Daverman, Elizabeth, tr. see Du Perron, E.

Davern, Frank. The Sportsman's Guide to Recipes. Wirkkala, Stephanie, ed. (Illus.). 104p. 1996. pap. 9.95 (*1-889694-00-2*) Wolf Pr.

Davern, Linda, et al. Inclusion in Secondary Schools: Bold Initiatives Challenging Change. Sage, Daniel D., ed. LC 98-116070. xi, 256p. (C). 1997. pap. text 29.95 (*1-887943-12-9*) Nat Prof Res.

D'Averoigne, Lanthe. The New Carolingian Modelbook: Counted Embroidery Patterns from Before 1600. LC 95-70710. 214p. 1995. pap. text 24.95 (*0-9642082-2-9*) Outlaw Pr.

Daves, Bryan R., ed. Defense & Foreign Affairs Handbook, 1987-88. 1338p. 1987. 185.00 (*0-9605932-5-X*) Intl Strtgc Stds Assn.

Daves, Charles W., ed. The Uses & Misuses of Tests. LC 84-47982. (Jossey-Bass Social & Behavioral Science Ser.). 155p. reprint ed. pap. 48.10 (*0-7837-0166-7*, 204046300017) Bks Demand.

Daves, Jada L. And the Tardy Bell Rings. 192p. 1995. text 19.95 (*0-7872-1517-1*) Kendall-Hunt.

Daves, Marvin L. Cardiac Roentgenology: Shadows of the Heart. LC 81-10424. (Illus.). 608p. reprint ed. pap. 188.50 (*0-8357-6765-5*, 203542600095) Bks Demand.

Daveson, Mons. Land of Tomorrow. large type ed. (Linford Romance Library). 280p. 1984. pap. 16.99 (*0-7089-6031-6*) Ulverscroft.

— Sugar Country. large type ed. 1991. pap. 16.99 (*0-7089-6973-9*) Ulverscroft.

***Davet, Pierre & Rouxel, Francis.** Detection & Isolation of Soil Fungi.Tr. of Detection et Isolement des Champignons du Sol. (Illus.). 214p. 2000. pap. text 49.50 (*1-57808-125-4*) Science Pubs.

Davey. Abracadabra Violin Duets. 32p. (J). (gr. k-3). 1998. pap. 9.95 (*0-7136-3240-2*, Pub. by A & C Blk) Midpt Trade.

— Abracadabra Violin Repertoire. 32p. (J). (gr. k-3). 1998. pap. 8.95 (*0-7136-3241-0*, Pub. by A & C Blk) Midpt Trade.

— Violin Extra: Extra Book I, Bk. 1. 32p. (J). 1998. pap. 4.95 (*0-7136-5544-5*, Pub. by A & C Blk) Midpt Trade.

— Violin Extra: Extra Book 2, Bk. 2. 32p. (J). (gr. k-3). 1998. pap. 6.95 (*0-7136-5545-3*, Pub. by A & C Blk) Midpt Trade.

Davey. Worrying: Perspectives on Theory, Assessment & Treatment. 328p. pap. 51.00 (*0-471-96803-X*) Wiley.

***Davey, et al, eds.** Tree Biotechnology Towards the Millennium. 396p. 1999. pap. 160.00 (*1-897676-68-9*, Pub. by Nottingham Univ Pr) St Mut.

Davey, Adrian G., et al. National System Planning for Protected Areas. LC 98-173115. (Best Practice Protected Area Guidelines Ser.). x, 71 p. 1998. write for info. (*2-8317-0399-9*, Pub. by IUCN) Island Pr.

Davey, A. R. Winter in Paradise Square. 496p. 1996. text 35.00 (*0-340-63774-9*, Pub. by Hodder & Stought Ltd) Trafalgar.

Davey, A. R. Winter in Paradise Square. 601p. 1997. mass mkt. 10.95 (*0-340-66602-1*, Pub. by Hodder & Stought Ltd) Trafalgar.

Davey, Andrew & Moyle, John T. Ward's Anaesthetic Equipment. 4th ed. (Illus.). 399p. 1997. text 95.00 (*0-7020-2169-5*, Pub. by W B Saunders) Saunders.

Davey, Andy. The Care & Conservation of Georgian Houses: A Maintenance Manual of Edinburgh New Town. 4th ed. LC 94-25926. (Illus.). 320p. 1999. pap. text 79.95 (*0-7506-1860-4*, Butterwrth Archit) Buttrwrth-Heinemann.

Davey, B. A., jt. auth. see Priestly, H. A.

Davey, B. J. Rural Crime in the Eighteenth Century. 167p. 1995. pap. 18.95 (*0-85958-618-9*, Pub. by Univ of Hull Pr) Paul & Co Pubs.

Davey, B. R., jt. ed. see Prpic, K. J.

Davey, Basiro. Immunology: A Foundation Text. 184p. (C). 1990. text 48.00 (*0-13-456138-4*) P-H.

— Immunology: A Foundation Text. 1991. pap. text 66.00 (*0-471-93212-4*) Wiley.

Davey, Basiro, ed. Birth to Old Age: Health in Transition. 2nd ed. LC 94-27569. (Health & Disease Ser.: Bk. 5). 224p. (Orig.). 1995. pap. text 31.95 (*0-335-19207-6*) OpUniv Pr.

Davey, Basiro, et al, eds. Health & Disease: A Reader. 2nd ed. LC 94-2470. 384p. 1995. pap. 36.95 (*0-335-19209-2*) OpUniv Pr.

— Health & Disease: A Reader. 2nd ed. LC 94-2470. 384p. 1995. 112.00 (*0-335-19326-9*) Taylor & Francis.

Davey, Basiro & Halliday, Tim, eds. Human Biology & Health: An Evolutionary Approach. 2nd rev. ed. LC 93-49558. (Health & Disease Ser.: Bk. 4). 192p. 1994. pap. 31.95 (*0-335-19253-X*) OpUniv Pr.

Davey, Basiro & Popay, Jennie, eds. Dilemmas in Health Care. rev. ed. LC 92-44760. (Health & Disease Ser.: Bk. 7). 1993. pap. 35.95 (*0-335-19119-3*) OpUniv Pr.

Davey, Basiro & Seale, Clive, eds. Experiencing & Explaining Disease. LC 95-44211. (Health & Disease Ser.: Bk. 8). 224p. 1996. pap. 29.95 (*0-335-19208-4*) OpUniv Pr.

Davey, Brian A., jt. auth. see Clark, David M.

***Davey, Chris.** The Aviator's Apprentice. Phelps, Janice, ed. (Turner Logs Ser.). (Illus.). 448p. 2000. 18.95 (*0-9676050-3-2*) Lucky Pr.

Davey, Cyril. John Wesley & the Methodists. 49p. (Orig.). 1985. 2.98 (*0-687-20434-8*) Abingdon.

— Mad about Mission: The Story of Thomas Coke. 127p. 1987. pap. 3.95 (*0-310-55242-7*, 19024P) Zondervan.

Davey, Elieen. Northern Cyprus: A Traveller's Guide. (Illus.). 256p. 1994. 19.95 (*1-85043-747-5*, Pub. by I B T) St Martin.

Davey, Frank. Margaret Atwood: A Feminist Poetics. LC 85-103362. 178p. 1984. pap. 13.95 (*0-88922-217-7*, Pub. by Talonbks) Genl Dist Srvs.

— Post-National Arguments: The Politics of the Anglophone-Canadian Novel Since 1967. LC 93-93081. 277p. 1993. text 45.00 (*0-8020-2785-7*) U of Toronto Pr.

— Reading Canadian Reading. 1997. pap. 11.95 (*0-88801-130-X*, Pub. by Turnstone Pr) Genl Dist Srvs.

— Selected Poems: The Arches. LC 81-91052. 112p. 1980. pap. 11.95 (*0-88922-174-X*, Pub. by Talonbks) Genl Dist Srvs.

— Tish, Nos. 1-19. 440p. pap. 26.95 (*0-88922-077-8*, Pub. by Talonbks) Genl Dist Srvs.

Davey, Frank, jt. auth. see Bailey, Anne E.

Davey, Frank, jt. auth. see Jaeger, Peter.

Davey, Fred. The Growth Factor. 1991. 1.99 (*0-87152-583-0*, D3999) Warner Pr.

Davey, Frederick, jt. ed. see Cooper, Alan K.

Davey, Graham. Cognitive Processes & Pavlovian Conditioning in Humans. fac. ed. LC 86-19036. 308p. 1987. reprint ed. pap. 95.50 (*0-7837-8282-9*, 204906300009) Bks Demand.

— Phobias: A Handbook of Theory, Research & Treatment. LC 96-32895. 470p. 1997. 179.95 (*0-471-96983-4*) Wiley.

Davey, Graham, ed. see Cullen, Chris.

Davey, Graham C. Ecological Learning Theory. 300p. 1989. 60.00 (*0-415-01189-2*); pap. 29.95 (*0-415-01190-6*) Routledge.

Davey, Graham C., ed. Animal Models of Human Behavior: Conceptual, Evolutionary, & Neurobiological Perspectives. fac. ed. LC 82-13714. (Illus.). 382p. pap. 118.80 (*0-7837-7362-5*, 204717100005) Bks Demand.

Davey, Graham C. & Tallis, Frank, eds. Worrying Perspectives on Theory, Assessment, & Treatment. LC 93-21368. (Clinical Psychology Ser.). 328p. 1994. 175.50 (*0-471-94114-X*) Wiley.

***Davey, Graham C. L., ed.** Phobias: A Handbook of Theory, Research & Treatment. 470p. 2000. pap. 95.00 (*0-471-49220-5*) Wiley.

Davey, Gwenda B. & Seal, Graham, eds. The Oxford Companion to Australian Folklore. (Illus.). 398p. 1993. text 55.00 (*0-19-553057-8*) OUP.

***Davey, H. E.** Brush Meditation: A Japanese Way to Mind & Body Harmony. LC 99-26561. 144p. 1999. pap. 14.95 (*1-880656-38-8*, Pub. by Stone Bridge Pr) Consort Bk Sales.

Davey, H. E. Unlocking the Secrets of Aiki-Jujutsu. LC 97-2289. (Illus.). 256p. (Orig.). 1997. pap. 17.95 (*1-57028-121-1*, 81211H, Mstrs Pr) NTC Contemp Pub Co.

***Davey, H. E. & Kameoka, Ann.** The Japanese Way of the Flower: Ikabana As Moving Meditation. 2000. pap. 16.95 (*1-880656-47-7*) Stone Bridge Pr.

Davey, Henry. History of English Music. 3rd ed. LC 69-15620. (Music Ser.). 1969. reprint ed. lib. bdg. 55.00 (*0-306-71133-8*) Da Capo.

Davey, Herbert. The Law Relating to the Mentally Defective. (Historical Foundations of Forensic Psychiatry & Psychology Ser.). 568p. 1980. reprint ed. lib. bdg. 55.00 (*0-306-76070-3*) Da Capo.

Davey, Howard & Vos, Ed. Financial Management & Decision Making. 3rd ed. 573p. 1993. pap. 93.00 (*0-409-79043-5*, NZ, MICHIE) LEXIS Pub.

Davey, Jane, tr. see Salvayre, Lydie.

Davey, John. Burnout: Stress in the Ministry. 164p. 1996. pap. 14.95 (*0-85244-339-0*, 6311, Pub. by Gracewing) Morehouse Pub.

— Mining Coal. (Junior Reference Ser.). (Illus.). 64p. (J). (gr. 6 up). 1976. 15.95 (*0-7136-1596-6*) Dufour.

Davey, Joseph D. The New Social Contract: America's Journey from a Welfare State to a Police State. LC 95-3326. 208p. 1995. 65.00 (*0-275-95123-5*, Praeger Pubs); pap. 18.95 (*0-275-95239-8*, Praeger Pubs) Greenwood.

— The Politics of Prison Expansion: Winning Elections by Waging War on Crime. LC 97-49278. 168p. 1998. 55.00 (*0-275-96209-1*, Praeger Pubs) Greenwood.

***Davey, Judith A. & Victoria University of Wellington. Institute of Policy Studies.** Tracking Social Change in New Zealand: From Birth to Death IV. LC 98-214999. (Illus.). 1998. 30.00 (*0-908935-28-5*) Vict U Well IPS.

Davey, Julia A. La Caridad. LC 90-24739. (Orig.). 1991. pap. 14.95 (*0-87949-329-1*) Ashley Bks.

Davey, Keith. The Rainmaker: A Passion for Politics. (Illus.). 356p. 1986. 24.95 (*0-7737-2090-1*) Genl Dist Srvs.

— The Rainmaker: A Passion for Politics. (Illus.). 416p. 1988. pap. 14.95 (*0-7737-5138-6*) Genl Dist Srvs.

Davey, Ken. Building Conservation Contracts & Grant Aid: A Practical Guide. LC 91-23020. 1991. write for info. (*0-442-31466-3*) Chapman & Hall.

— Building Conservation Contracts & Grant Aid: A Practical Guide. (Illus.). 240p. (C). 1991. 70.00 (*0-419-17140-1*, E & FN Spon) Routledge.

Davey, Ken & Graffam, Joe, eds. The Experience of Disability: Social Construction & Imposed Limitation. 206p. 1995. pap. 40.00 (*0-909184-15-1*, Pub. by Deakin Univ) St Mut.

Davey, Kenneth, ed. Urban Management: The Challenge of Growth. 320p. 1996. 77.95 (*1-85972-063-3*, Pub. by Avebry) Ashgate Pub Co.

Davey, Kenneth J. Elements of Urban Management. LC 93-19385. (Urban Management Program, Urban Management & Land Ser.). 70p. 1993. pap. 22.00 (*0-8213-2424-1*, 12424) World Bank.

— Elements of Urban Management. LC 93-19385. (Urban Management Program, Urban Management & Land Ser.). 76p. 1994. pap. 22.00 (*0-8213-2457-8*, 12457) World Bank.

— Financing Regional Government: International Practices & Their Relevance to the Third World. LC 82-11132. (Wiley Series on Public Administration in Developing Countries). 205p. reprint ed. pap. 63.60 (*0-608-15875-5*, 203075300070) Bks Demand.

Davey, Kevin. English Imaginaries: Anglo-British Approaches to Modernity. 224p. 1998. pap. 18.50 (*0-85315-867-3*, Pub. by Lawrence & Wishart) NYU Pr.

— English Imaginaries: Anglo-British Approaches to Modernity. 224p. 1999. pap. 21.50 (*0-85315-868-1*, Pub. by Lawrence & Wishart) NYU Pr.

Davey, Lawrence & Schuldenfrei, R. Going after Feta. LC 93-87377. (Illus.). 335p. 1994. pap. 11.95 (*0-9641459-0-1*) N Austin Pubng.

Davey, Michael R., jt. ed. see Gartland, Kevan M. A.

Davey, Michael R., ed. see Krishef, Curtis H.

Davey, Neil K. & Tripp, Susan G. Garrett Collection: Japanese Art. 326p. 1994. 120.00 (*1-872357-07-5*, Pub. by P Wilson) Scala Books.

Davey, Nigel & Parry-Wingfield, Maurice. Ray: Partnership Taxation. 4th ed. 1996. pap. write for info. (*0-406-08183-2*, RPT4, MICHIE) LEXIS Pub.

— Ray - Partnership Taxation Supplement: The New Rules for Simplified Assessing. (Orig.). 1994. pap. 35.00 (*0-406-04527-5*, MICHIE) LEXIS Pub.

Davey, P., jt. ed. see Spens, Michael.

Davey, Peter. Abracadabra Viola: Way to Learn. 48p. (J). 1998. pap. 7.95 (*0-7136-5629-8*, Pub. by A & C Blk) Midpt Trade.

— Abracadabra Violin: Way to Learn, Bk. 1. 48p. (J). (gr. k-3). 1998. pap. 6.95 (*0-7136-5543-7*, Pub. by A & C Blk) Midpt Trade.

— Arts & Crafts Architecture. (Illus.). 256p. 1997. pap. 39.95 (*0-7148-3711-3*, Pub. by Phaidon Press) Phaidon Pr.

— Piano Accompaniments, Bk. 1. 64p. (J). 1998. pap. 10.95 (*0-7136-3728-5*, Pub. by A & C Blk) Midpt Trade.

Davey, Ralph G. Dewey's Celebrity Balloons. (Illus.). 36p. 1994. pap. text 6.00 (*1-880215-22-5*) Deweys GNB.

Davey, Richard J. & McMican, Ann, eds. Collected Questions & Answers. 4th ed. 79p. (C). 1994. pap. text 28.00 (*1-56395-036-7*) Am Assn Blood.

Davey, Rick, jt. auth. see Massey, Don.

***Davey, Robert A.** A Spy Affair. 384p. 2001. pap. write for info. (*1-57197-239-0*, Pub. by Pentland Pr) Assoc Pubs Grp.

Davey, Samuel. Darwin, Carlyle & Dickens. LC 77-116791. (English Literature Ser.: No. 33). 1970. reprint ed. lib. bdg. 75.00 (*0-8383-1033-8*) M S G Haskell Hse.

Davey-Smith, George. Clinical Meta-Analysis. 150p. 2000. text 64.95 (*0-471-96706-8*) Wiley.

Davey, Thomas. A Generation Divided: German Children & the Berlin Wall. LC 87-13497. (Illus.). xii, 155p. 1987. text 37.95 (*0-8223-0729-4*) Duke.

***Davey, V. S., et al, eds.** Nondestructive Examination of Underwater Welded Structures: Revision of Document IIS/IIW - 1033-89 'Information on Practices for Underwater Nondestructive Testing' 76p. 1999. pap. 117.00 (*1-85573-427-3*) Am Educ Systs.

D

***Davey, William.** Bitter Rainbow & Other Poems. 88p. 2000. pap. 14.95 (*1-897722-79-6*, Pub. by Alyscamps Pr) Gotham.

Davey, William. Lost Adulteries & Other Stories. 174p. 1997. pap. 14.95 (*1-897722-39-7*, Pub. by Alyscamps Pr) Gotham.

— The Trial of Pythagoras & Other Poems. LC 97-162439. 101p. (Orig.). 1996. pap. 14.95 (*1-897722-44-3*, Pub. by Alyscamps Pr) Gotham.

Davezac, Bertrand. Greek Icons after the Fall of Constantinople: The Roger Cabal Collection. LC 94-42321. 1995. pap. 19.95 (*0-939594-33-1*, Menil Collection) Menil Found.

Davezac, Bertrand, ed. Four Icons in the Menil Collection. LC 90-19433. (Collection Monographs). (Illus.). 135p. (C). 1992. pap. 25.00 (*0-939594-21-8*) Menil Found.

Davezies, Laurent, jt. auth. see Besnainou, Denis.

Davi. Getting Through To the Man You Love. 1999. pap. write for info. (*0-312-24576-9*) St Martin.

Davi, Ann M. The Real Paradise. (C). 1989. text 59.00 (*1-85821-044-5*, Pub. by Pentland Pr) St Mut.

Davia, Howard R. Fraud 101: Techniques & Strategies for Detection. 272p. 2000. 39.95 (*0-471-37309-5*) Wiley.

***Davia, Howard R., et al.** Accountant's Guide to Fraud Detection & Control. 2nd ed. LC 99-88273. 312p. 2000. text 59.95 (*0-471-35378-7*) Wiley.

Daviau, Donald, et al, eds. The Correspondence of Stefan Zweig with Raoul Auernheimer & Richard Beer-Hofmann. LC 83-70922. (GERM Ser.: Vol. 20). (Illus.). xii, 110p. 1983. 29.95 (*0-938100-22-X*) Camden Hse.

***Daviau, Donald G., ed.** Austria in Literature. LC 99-86608. (Studies in Austrian Literature, Culture & Thought). 2000. pap. 30.50 (*1-57241-065-5*) Ariadne CA.

Daviau, Donald G., ed. Austrian Writers & the Anschluss: Understanding the Past, Overcoming the Past. (Studies in Austrian Literature, Culture, & Thought). 388p. 1991. 42.00 (*0-929497-16-3*) Ariadne CA.

— Major Figures of Nineteenth-Century Austrian Literature. LC 97-43722. (Studies in Austrian Literature, Culture & Thought). 572p. 1998. 59.95 (*1-57241-047-7*) Ariadne CA.

Daviau, Donald G., ed. Jura Soyfer & His Time. LC 95-14687. (Studies in Austrian Literature, Culture, & Thought). (ENG & GER.). 395p. 1995. 45.00 (*1-57241-005-1*) Ariadne CA.

— Major Figures of Austrian Literature: The Interwar Years, 1918-1938. LC 95-1998. (Studies in Austrian Literature, Culture, & Thought). 588p. 1995. 59.95 (*0-929497-60-0*) Ariadne CA.

— Major Figures of Modern Austrian Literature. (Studies in Austrian Literature, Culture, & Thought). 481p. 1988. 39.95 (*0-929497-00-7*) Ariadne CA.

— Major Figures of Turn-of-the-Century Austrian Literature. LC 90-893. (Studies in Austrian Literature, Culture & Thought). lx, 488p. 1990. 45.00 (*0-929497-30-9*) Ariadne CA.

Daviau, Donald G. & Buelow, George J. The Ariadne Auf Naxos of Hugo von Hofmannsthal & Richard Strauss. LC 74-14835. (University of North Carolina Studies in Comparative Literature: No. 80). 282p. reprint ed. pap. 87.50 (*0-7837-2074-2*, 204234800004) Bks Demand.

Daviau, Michele. Houses & Their Furnishings in Bronze Age Palestine: Domestic Activity Areas & Artifact Distribution in the Middle & Late Bronze Ages. (Journal for the Study of the Old Testament Supplement Monographs Ser.: No. 8). (Illus.). 489p. 1993. 90.75 (*1-85075-355-5*, Pub. by Sheffield Acad) CUP Services.

Davich, Victor N. The Best Guide to Meditation. LC 97-36555. (Best Guide Ser.: No. 1). (Illus.). 320p. 1998. pap. 16.95 (*1-58063-010-3*) Renaissance.

David. Batman Forever. 1995. 17.00 (*1-57042-273-7*) Warner Bks.

— Cases in Strategic Management. 7th ed. LC 98-47061. (Illus.). 525p. 1998. 61.00 (*0-13-080783-4*) P-H.

***David.** Charts & Coastal Views of Captain Cook's Voyages, Vol. 1. 1998. 288.95 (*0-904180-23-9*) Ashgate Pub Co.

— Charts & Coastal Views of Captain Cook's Voyages, Vol. 2. 1998. 253.95 (*0-904180-31-X*) Ashgate Pub Co.

David. Concept's Strategic Management. 7th ed. LC 98-47067. (Illus.). 351p. 1998. pap. text 59.00 (*0-13-080784-2*) P-H.

— Craniomaxillofacial Trauma. 1995. text 205.00 (*0-443-04414-7*, W B Saunders Co) Harcrt Hlth Sci Grp.

***David.** Dream of Lost. 1999. mass mkt. 6.99 (*0-8125-7646-2*) Tor Bks.

David. Expert Systems for Managers, Vol. 1. (C). 1996. text. write for info. (*0-201-05924-X*) Addison-Wesley.

— Expert Systems for Managers, Vol. 2. (C). 1996. text. write for info. (*0-201-05925-8*) Addison-Wesley.

— Macclesfield Collection of Egyptian Antiquities. (Modern Egyptology Ser.). 1980. 49.95 (*0-85668-129-6*, Pub. by Aris & Phillips) David Brown.

— McAllister's Baby. large type ed. 1997. per. 3.25 (*0-373-15718-5*) Harlequin Bks.

— Order Statistics. 2nd ed. 360p. 1995. pap. text 129.95 (*0-471-13728-6*) Wiley.

— Recent Advances in Pediatrics. 15th ed. 1997. pap. text 60.00 (*0-443-05849-0*, W B Saunders Co) Harcrt Hlth Sci Grp.

— Recent Advances in Pediatrics. 16th ed. (C). 1997. pap. text 60.00 (*0-443-05960-8*, W B Saunders Co) Harcrt Hlth Sci Grp.

— Strategic Management: Concepts & Cases. 7th ed. 525p. 1998. 100.00 (*0-13-080785-0*) P-H.

David & Cohen, Bernard. Eczema in Children: A Guide for Parents. Oski, Frank A., ed. (Pediatrics Ser.). (Illus.). 24p. 1999. pap. 2.95 (*1-885274-09-2*) Health InfoNet Inc.

David, jt. auth. see Bacharach.

David, jt. auth. see Geithman.

David, jt. auth. see Kann, Robert A.

David, jt. auth. see White.

David & Alfred Smart Museum of Art Staff. Get Out: Nine Artists from Midway Studios, University of Chicago. LC 98-217543. 17 p. 1998. write for info. (*0-935573-24-0*) D & A Smart Museum.

— Robert Laurent & American Figurative Sculpture, 1910-1960: Selections from the John N. Stern Collection & The David & Alfred Smart Museum of Art. Born, Richard A., tr. (Illus.). 64p. (Orig.). 1994. pap. text. write for info. (*0-935573-15-1*) D & A Smart Museum.

David, A. Ben. SAFAD: The Transition Period from the Termination of the British Mandate until the Implementation of the State of Israel Postal Service. (Illus.). 140p. (C). 1995. 25.00 (*0-9647395-0-X*) WPIC.

David, A. Rosalie. The Ancient Egyptians: Religious Beliefs & Practices. (Religious Beliefs & Practices Ser.). 250p. 1982. pap. 19.95 (*0-7100-0878-3*, Routledge Thoemms) Routledge.

— The Ancient Egyptians: The Philosophy of Structuralism & Post-Structuralism. 1982. pap. 19.95 (*0-415-04536-3*) Routledge.

***David, A. Rosalie.** Experience of Ancient Egypt. LC 99-30521. 1999. 49.99 (*0-415-03263-6*) Routledge.

David, A. Rosalie. Handbook to Life in Ancient Egypt. LC 97-35824. (Illus.). 382p. (YA). 1998. 45.00 (*0-8160-3312-9*) Facts on File.

David, Abraham, ed. A Hebrew Chronicle from Prague, c. 1615. Weinberger, Leon J. & Ordan, Dena, trs. LC 92-26939. (Judaic Studies). 136p. (C). 1993. text 24.95 (*0-8173-0596-3*) U of Ala Pr.

***David, Adam.** Lost & Found in the Land of Seduction. 2000. pap. 9.95 (*1-55279-026-6*) Picasso Publ.

David, Al. A Complete Introduction to Conures. (Illus.). 128p. (Orig.). 1987. pap. 8.95 (*0-86622-296-0*, CO-014S) TFH Pubns.

— A Complete Introduction to Garden Ponds. rev. ed. (Complete Introduction to...Ser.). (Illus.). 96p. (Orig.). 1997. pap. 8.95 (*0-86622-298-7*, CO-017S) TFH Pubns.

— Tarantulas: A Complete Introduction. (Complete Introduction to...Ser.). (Illus.). 62p. (Orig.). 1987. pap. 8.95 (*0-86622-353-3*, CO-024S) TFH Pubns.

— Turtles As a New Pet. (Illus.). 64p. (Orig.). 1990. pap. 6.95 (*0-86622-621-4*, TU-013) TFH Pubns.

David, Alfred. The Strumpet Muse: Art & Morals in Chaucer's Poetry. LC 76-11939. 290p. reprint ed. pap. 89.90 (*0-7837-1747-4*, 205728100024) Bks Demand.

David, Alfred & Meek, Mary E. The Twelve Dancing Princesses & Other Fairy Tales. LC 73-16517. (Illus.). 320p. (J). (gr. 1-6). 1974. pap. 14.95 (*0-253-20173-X*, MB-173) Ind U Pr.

David, Alfred, ed. see Chaucer, Geoffrey.

David, Alfred E. Teaching with the Norton Anthology of English literature: A Guide for Instructors. 6th ed. pap. 5.00 (*0-393-96291-1*) Norton.

David, Almitra. Between the Sea & Home. LC 93-7200. 96p. 1993. pap. 10.95 (*0-933377-22-3*, Pub. by Eighth Mount Pr); lib. bdg. 21.95 (*0-933377-23-1*, Pub. by Eighth Mount Pr) Consort Bk Sales.

— Impulse to Fly. LC 98-67098. 77p. 1998. pap. 10.95 (*0-9660459-1-2*, Pub. by Perugia Pr) SPD-Small Pr Dist.

David, Andrew. The Voyage of HMS Herald, 1852-1861. (The Miegunyah Press Ser.: No. 2:3). (Illus.). 576p. 1995. 69.95 (*0-522-84390-5*, Pub. by Melbourne Univ Pr) Paul & Co Pubs.

David, Anthony S., jt. ed. see Amador, Xavier F.

David, Anthony S., jt. ed. see Ron, Maria A.

David, Antony E., jt. auth. see David, Rosalie.

David, Arie E. The Strategy of Treaty Termination: Lawful Breaches & Retaliations. LC 74-82748. 342p. reprint ed. pap. 106.10 (*0-7837-4556-7*, 208049300006) Bks Demand.

David, Arthur, tr. see Maimonides.

***David, Aryeh Ben.** Around the Shabbat Table: A Guide to Fulfilling & Meaningful Shabbat Table Conversations. LC 99-41841. 300p. 2000. 30.00 (*0-7657-6124-6*) Aronson.

David, Avraham. To Come to the Land: Immigration & Settlement in Sixteenth-Century Eretz-Israel. LC 98-25424. (Judaic Studies). 360p. 1999. text 49.95 (*0-8173-0935-7*) U of Ala Pr.

David, B., et al, eds. Echinoderms Through Time: Proceedings of the 8th International Echinoderm Conference, Dijon, France, 6-10 September 1993. (Illus.). 992p. (C). 1995. text 175.00 (*90-5410-514-3*, Pub. by A A Balkema) Ashgate Pub Co.

David Ben Abraham. The Hebrew-Arabic Dictionary of the Bible, Known As Kitab Jami al-Alfaz (Agron), 2 vols., Set. Skoss, Solomon L., ed. LC 78-63565. (Yale Oriental Series: Researches: Nos. 20-21). (ARA & HEB.). reprint ed. 97.50 (*0-404-60290-8*) AMS Pr.

David, Bernard J. Milestone Planning for Successful Ventures: Mac. LC 94-29642. 1996. pap., teacher ed. 55.00 (*0-89426-861-9*) Course Tech.

David, Beverly R. Mark Twain & His Illustrators, 1869-1875, Vol. I. LC 85-51269. (Illus.). xii, 268p. 1986. 45.00 (*0-87875-307-9*) Whitston Pub.

David, C., jt. ed. see Egorov, I. K.

***David, C. A.** C. A. David's Greenville of Old, Vol. II. Case, Suzanne J. & Marchant, Sylvia Lanford, eds. LC 98-71488. (Illus.). 140p. 2000. pap. 20.00 (*0-9700666-0-0*) Historic Grnvlle Fdn.

David, C. Cook. Bible Promises. (My Jesus Pocket Bks.). pap. 0.79 (*1-55513-337-1*) Chariot Victor.

— Birth of Jesus: Pencil Fun Book. (J). 1969. pap. text 0.89 (*1-55513-155-7*) Chariot Victor.

— Child Is Born: Pencil Fun Book. (Illus.). pap. text 8.90 (*1-55513-174-3*) Chariot Victor.

— Elisha God's Helper: Pencil Fun Book. (J). Date not set. pap. text 0.89 (*1-55513-269-3*) Chariot Victor.

— God's Promise to Abraham: Pencil Fun Book. pap. 0.79 (*1-55513-126-3*) Chariot Victor.

— Jesus Lives: Pencil Fun Book. Date not set. pap. text 0.89 (*1-55513-156-5*) Chariot Victor.

— Joseph's Carpenter Shop: Pencil Fun Book. pap. 0.79 (*1-55513-152-2*) Chariot Victor.

— Noah's Ark: Pencil Fun Book. Date not set. pap. text 0.89 (*1-55513-159-X*) Chariot Victor.

David C. Cook Publishing Co., Staff. Praise. (J). Date not set. pap. text 7.90 (*1-55513-207-3*) Cook.

David, C. J. Lattice Bracelets Beadwork, Bk. II. 58p. 1997. 11.95 (*0-9655049-1-3*) Am Supply Co.

— Lattice Bracelets Beadwork Book I. David, Kristen, ed. (Illus.). 50p. 1996. spiral bd. 9.95 (*0-9655049-0-5*) Am Supply Co.

David, C. S., ed. H-2 Antigens: Genes, Molecules, Function. LC 87-35977. (NATO ASI Series A, Life Sciences: Vol. 144). (Illus.). 868p. 1988. 155.00 (*0-306-42804-0*, Plenum Trade) Perseus Pubng.

David, Carole. Impala. Sloate, Daniel, tr. from FRE. LC 97-70436. 128p. 1997. pap. 10.00 (*1-55071-065-6*) Guernica Editions.

David, Catherine. The Beauty of Gesture: The Invisible Keyboard of Piano & T'ai Chi. LC 95-52654.Tr. of La Beaute du Geste. 166p. (Orig.). 1996. pap. 12.95 (*1-55643-219-4*) North Atlantic.

— Documenta X: The Book. LC 98-180481. (Illus.). 800p. 1997. 65.00 (*3-89322-911-6*, Pub. by Edition Cantz) Dist Art Pubs.

— Simone Signoret. Sampson, Sally, tr. LC 92-35037. (Illus.). 225p. 1993. 22.95 (*0-87951-491-4*, Pub. by Overlook Pr) Penguin Putnam.

— Simone Signoret. (Illus.). 225p. 1995. pap. 12.95 (*0-87951-581-3*, Pub. by Overlook Pr) Penguin Putnam.

David, Charles Alexander, et al. Greenville of Old Vol. 1: Newspaper Stories of C. A. David, Early 1900's. Case, Suzanne J. & Marchant, Sylvia Lanford, eds. LC 98-71488. 1998. 15.00 (*1-884416-24-1*) A Press.

David, Charles-Philippe & Levesque, Jacques, eds. The Future of NATO: Enlargement, Russia & European Security. 232p. 65.00 (*0-7735-1850-9*); pap. 22.95 (*0-7735-1872-X*) McG-Queens Univ Pr.

David, Charles-Philippe, et al. Foreign Policy Failure in the White House: Reappraising the Fall of the Shah & the Iran-Contra Affair. LC 93-2807. 198p. (Orig.). (C). 1993. pap. text 24.50 (*0-8191-9076-4*); lib. bdg. 52.50 (*0-8191-9075-6*) U Pr of Amer.

David, Charles W. Robert Curthose, Duke of Normandy. LC 78-63356. (Crusades & Military Orders Ser.: Second Series). (Illus.). 296p. reprint ed. 49.50 (*0-404-17007-2*) AMS Pr.

David, Chella S., jt. auth. see Ferrone, Soldano.

David, Christina C. & Otsuka, Keijiro, eds. Modern Rice Technology & Income Distribution in Asia. 475p. 1994. pap. text 27.50 (*1-55587-431-2*); lib. bdg. 55.00 (*1-55587-404-5*) L Rienner.

David, Comandante, jt. auth. see Marcos, Subcomandante.

***David Cook Publishers Staff.** Problems in Society/Making Choices/Friendship: 13 Bible-Based Sessions. 2000. pap. 18.99 (*0-7814-5517-0*) Cook.

David, Courtney. Celtic Image. (Illus.). 128p. 1997. pap. 16.95 (*0-7137-2482-X*, Pub. by Blandford Pr) Sterling.

David, Cynthia. Women on the Brink of Divorce: A Guide to Self-Help Books. LC 95-15693. 272p. 1995. 19.00 (*0-917846-54-0*) Highsmith Pr.

David, Cyrille, et al, eds. Tax Treatment of Financial Instruments: A Survey to France, Germany, The Netherlands & the United Kingdom. LC 93-42437. (Series on International Taxation: Vol. 14). 1993. write for info. (*90-6544-666-4*) Kluwer Law Intl.

***David, D. J. & Misra, Ashok.** Relating Materials Properties to Structure: Handbook & Software for Polymer Calculations & Materials. LC 99-63892. 712p. 1999. pap. text 149.95 (*1-56676-797-0*) Technomic.

David, D. J. & Staley, H. B. Analytical Chemistry of Polyurethanes. LC 78-12430. (High Polymer Ser.: Vol. 16, Pt. 3). 639p. 1979. reprint ed. lib. bdg. 56.50 (*0-88275-753-9*) Krieger.

David, D. J., et al. Craniofacial Deformities. (Illus.). x, 147p. 1989. 235.00 (*0-387-96969-1*, 2655) Spr-Verlag.

David, Daniel Narsai. Names: Names You Just Won't Find in the Other Books. LC 97-69592. 200p. 1999. pap. 9.95 (*0-88739-173-7*) Creat Arts Bk.

***David, Deborah & Frediani, Paul.** Sex Flex: The Guide to Enhanced Intimacy & Communication for Couples. (Illus.). 160p. 2000. pap. 16.95 (*1-57826-079-5*, Pub. by Hatherleigh) Norton.

David, Deirdre. Rule Britannia: Women, Empire, & Victorian Writing. (Illus.). 256p. 1996. pap. text 16.95 (*0-8014-8277-1*) Cornell U Pr.

***David, Dennis.** Dennis "Hurricane" David. 2000. 32.95 (*1-902304-46-2*, Pub. by Grub St) Seven Hills Bk.

David Der-Wei Wang, jt. ed. see Widmer, Ellen.

David, Dick, tr. see Ginzburg, Natalia.

David, Eduardo. Gay Mexico: The Men of Mexico. 3rd ed. LC 98-222413. (Illus.). 288p. 1998. pap. 21.95 (*0-942777-27-1*) Orchid Hse.

David, Edward, jt. auth. see Rebmann, Andrew.

David, Elaine. A Teacher's Guide to Teaching BASIC in the Elementary Schools. 1982. 5.95 (*0-318-01731-8*) E David Assoc.

David, Elizabeth. Elizabeth David Classics: Mediterranean Food, French Country Cooking, Summer Food. LC 97-52206. (Illus.). 688p. 1998. 14.98 (*0-9643600-6-3*) Biscuit Bks.

— English Bread & Yeast Cookery. LC 95-13020. (Illus.). 626p. 1994. 14.98 (*0-9643600-0-4*) Biscuit Bks.

— French Provincial Cooking. LC 99-195317. 524p. 1999. pap. 14.95 (*0-14-118153-2*) Viking Penguin.

— Italian Food. LC 99-200031. 376p. 1999. pap. 13.95 (*0-14-118155-9*) Viking Penguin.

— An Omelette & a Glass of Wine. 1989. pap. 14.95 (*0-14-046846-3*) Viking Penguin.

— An Omelette & a Glass of Wine. LC 96-37821. (Cook's Classic Library). 320p. 1997. reprint ed. pap. 14.95 (*1-55821-571-9*) Lyons Pr.

— South Wind Through the Kitchen: The Best of Elizabeth David. LC 98-28790. (Illus.). 400p. 1998. 25.00 (*0-86547-535-0*) N Point Pr.

***David, Elizabeth.** South Wind Through the Kitchen: The Best of Elizabeth David. (Illus.). 400p. 1999. pap. 14.00 (*0-86547-575-X*) N Point Pr.

— Summer Cooking. (Illus.). 240p. pap. 24.95 (*0-14-046997-4*, Pub. by Pnguin Bks Ltd) Trafalgar.

David, Elizabeth H. I Played Their Accompaniments. (Music Book Index Ser.). 245p. 1992. reprint ed. lib. bdg. 79.00 (*0-685-66151-2*) Rprt Serv.

David, Ella M., jt. auth. see Holmes, Thomas E.

David, Ella M., jt. ed. see Holmes, Thomas H.

David, Ephraim. Old Age in Sparta. ii, 178p. 1991. pap. 42.00 (*90-256-1013-7*, Pub. by AM Hakkert) BookLink Distributors.

— Sparta Between Empire & Revolution, 404-243 B.C. rev. ed. Connor, W. R., ed. LC 80-2646. (Monographs in Classical Studies). 1981. lib. bdg. 30.00 (*0-405-14033-9*) Ayer.

***David, Esther.** By the Sabarmati. LC 99-937344. (Illus.). 1999. write for info. (*0-14-027843-5*) Penguin Books.

David, F., et al, eds. Fluctuating Geometries in Statistical Mechanics & Field Theory: Proceedings of the Les Houches Summer School, Session LXII, 2 August-9 September 1994. (Houches Summer School Proceedings Ser.: Vol. 62). 1126p. 1996. 301.50 (*0-444-82294-1*, North Holland) Elsevier.

David, F. N. A First Course in Statistics. 2nd rev. ed. 1971. 24.95 (*0-85264-206-7*) Lubrecht & Cramer.

— Games, Gods, & Gambling: A History of Probability & Statistical Ideas. LC 97-46416. 275p. 1998. pap. 9.95 (*0-486-40023-9*) Dover.

David, F. N., et al. Symmetric Function & Allied Tables. 278p. 1966. lib. bdg. 32.50 (*0-85264-702-6*) Lubrecht & Cramer.

David, Felicien. Melodies Orientales & Other Piano Works. (Music Reprint Ser.). 100p. 1982. 13.95 (*0-306-76214-5*) Da Capo.

David-Fox, Michael. Revolution of the Mind: Higher Learning among the Bolsheviks, 1918-1929. LC 96-47757. (Studies of the Harriman Institute). (Illus.). 256p. 1996. text 42.50 (*0-8014-3128-X*) Cornell U Pr.

***David-Fox, Michael & Peteri, Gyorgy, eds.** Academia in Upheaval: Origins, Transfers & Transformations of the Communist Academic Regime in Russia & East Central Europe. LC 00-20484. 352p. 2000. 69.95 (*0-89789-708-X*, H708, Bergin & Garvey) Greenwood.

David, G. Hungarian-Turkish & Turkish-Hungarian Dictionary for Tourists. 575p. 1991. 40.00 (*963-205-270-6*, Pub. by Akade Kiado) St Mut.

— Wavelets & Singular Integrals on Curves & Surfaces. 107p. 1992. 35.95 (*0-387-53902-6*) Spr-Verlag.

David, Gail, ed. Female Heroism in the Pastoral. LC 90-23907. (Gender & Genre in Literature Ser.: Vol. 2). 288p. 1991. text 15.00 (*0-8240-7107-7*, 1329) Garland.

David, Gary. Creativity Is Forever. 1992. pap. 32.95 (*0-8403-9876-X*) Kendall-Hunt.

— A Log of Deadwood: A Postmodern Epic of the South Dakota Gold Rush. LC 93-6715. 148p. 1993. 9.95 (*1-55643-156-2*) North Atlantic.

— The Possibilities of Blue Sky. (Salt River Poetry Ser.). 80p. 1989. pap. write for info. (*1-882021-02-9*) Summer.

— Tierra Zia. (Illus.). 40p. 1996. pap. 9.00 (*1-878888-19-6*) Nine Muses Books.

David, Gary, ed. see Bois, J. Samuel.

David, Georges, ed. see International Symposium on Artificial Insemination.

David, Gerard B. The Art Signature File. 6th ed. (Illus.). 900p. 1998. 59.95 (*1-884939-06-6*); pap. 49.95 (*1-884939-10-4*) Antoine Versailles.

David, Gerhard. Hochstfrequenz-Charakterisierung von Monolithisch Integrierten Mikrowellenbauelementen und Schaltungen Durch Zweidimensionale Elektrooptische Feldverteilungsmessungen.Tr. of High Frequency Characterization of MMIC's Using 2D Electrooptic Field Mapping. (GER., Illus.). 165p. 1997. pap. text 20.00 (*0-9659306-0-2*, 010697) G David.

David, Geza, jt. auth. see Fodor, Pal.

David, Guy & Semmes, Stephen. Analysis of & on Uniformly Rectifiable Sets. LC 93-36311. (Mathematical Surveys & Monographs: Vol. 38). 356p. 1993. text 111.00 (*0-8218-1537-7*, SURV/38) Am Math.

David, Guy R. & Semmes, Stephen W. Fractured Fractals & Broken Dreams: Self-Similar Geometry Through Metric & Measure. (Oxford Lecture Series in Mathematics & Its Applications: No. 7). (Illus.). 222p. 1998. text 68.00 (*0-19-850166-8*) OUP.

David, Gwenda, tr. see Strasser, Otto.

David, H. A. The Method of Paired Comparisons. rev. ed. 1963. pap. 17.95 (*0-85264-013-7*) Lubrecht & Cramer.

David, H. A. & David, H. T., eds. Statistics, an Appraisal: Proceedings of a Conference Marking the 50th Anniversary of the Statistical Laboratory, Iowa State University, Ames, IA, June 13-15, 1983. LC 84-4669. (Illus.). 674p. 1984. reprint ed. pap. 200.00 (*0-608-00010-8*, 206077600006) Bks Demand.

***David, H. A. & Edwards, A. W. F.** Annotated Readings in the History of Statistics. annot. ed. LC 00-41977. (Series in Statistics). 2000. pap. write for info. (*0-387-98844-0*) Spr-Verlag.

David, H. A. & Moeschberger, Melvin L. The Theory of Competing Risks. 1978. 25.00 (*0-85264-249-0*) Lubrecht & Cramer.

An Asterisk (*) at the beginning of an entry indicates that the title is appearing for the first time.

David, H. T., jt. ed. see David, H. A.

David, Hans. The New Bach Reader: A Life of Johann Sebastian Bach in Letters & Documents. LC 97-41850. 512p. 1998. 35.00 (*0-393-04558-7*) Norton.

David, Hans T. J. S. Bach's Musical Offering: History, Interpretation, & Analysis. LC 72-165391. 190p. (C). 1972. reprint ed. pap. 6.95 (*0-486-22768-5*) Dover.

— The New Bach Reader. 608p. 1999. pap. 18.95 (*0-393-31956-3*) Norton.

David, Hans T., jt. auth. see Rau, Albert G.

David, Harris. A Society of Signs? LC 95-31320. 256p. (C). 1996. 75.00 (*0-415-11128-5*); pap. 22.99 (*0-415-11129-3*) Routledge.

David, Henry P., ed. From Abortion to Contraception: A Resource to Public Policies & Reproductive Behavior in Central & Eastern Europe from 1917 to the Present. LC 98-51634. (Illus.). 408p. 1999. lib. bdg. 95.00 (*0-313-30587-0*, GR0587, Greenwood Pr) Greenwood.

David, Henry P., et al, eds. Born Unwanted: Developmental Effects of Denied Abortion. LC 88-16651. 144p. 1988. 26.95 (*0-8261-6080-8*) Springer Pub.

David, Herbert A., ed. Order Statistics. 2nd ed. LC 80-6928. (Probability & Mathematical Statistics Ser.). 384p. 1981. 198.50 (*0-471-02723-5*) Wiley.

David, Herbert A., jt. ed. see Armitage, Peter.

David, Hugh. Stephen Spender: A Portrait with Background. LC 93-158897. xii, 308p. 1992. write for info. (*0-434-17506-4*) Buttrwrth-Heinemann.

David Hume Institute Staff. Fraud on the European Budget: Hume Papers in Public Policy 4.3. 96p. 1997. pap. 18.00 (*0-7486-0883-4*, Pub. by Edinburgh U Pr) Col U Pr.

David Hume Institute Staff, jt. auth. see Roberts, Colin J.

David, Irene R. & Buckley, Mary, eds. Weaving New Visions: Art Therapy in Collaboration with Allied Professions. 178p. (Orig.). pap. 20.00 (*1-882147-50-2*) Am Art Therapy.

David, Irwin T., et al. How to Evaluate & Improve Internal Controls in Government Units. LC 81-83910. (Illus.). 111p. 1981. pap. 18.00 (*0-686-84336-3*); pap. 16.00 (*0-686-84337-1*) Municipal.

David, Isabelle. Lebanese Cookery: An Easy Way. LC 77-539. (Illus.). 160p. 1982. 8.95 (*0-9607824-0-0*) GaryDavid Prods.

David, Ismar. The Passover Haggadah: A Family Haggadah for Passover. 112p. 1998. pap. 10.95 (*0-9666561-0-5*) Shunammite Pr.

David, J. & Curie, Marie Sklodowska, eds. Cancer Care: Prevention, Treatment & Palliation. (Illus.). 444p. 1994. pap. text 54.25 (*1-56593-288-9*, 0612) Singular Publishing.

David, J., jt. auth. see Battlin, Margaret P.

David, J. C., jt. auth. see Hawksworth, D. L.

***David, J. F.** Peter's Redemption: A Novel about Power, Political Intrigue & Change in the Catholic Church of the 21st Century. 307p. 1999. pap. 15.95 (*0-9668228-1-1*) Caritas Commns.

David, Jack, ed. Brave New Wave. 226p. (C). 1978. pap. text 10.00 (*1-55022-041-1*, Pub. by ECW) Genl Dist Srvs.

David, Jack & Lecker, Robert, eds. Canadian Poetry. 320p. 1982. pap. 5.95 (*0-7736-7036-X*); pap. 5.95 (*0-7736-7037-8*) Genl Dist Srvs.

David, Jack & Redfern, Jon, eds. Short Short Stories. 202p. (C). 1986. pap. 12.00 (*0-920763-98-7*, Pub. by ECW) Genl Dist Srvs.

David, Jack, jt. auth. see Baynard, Caroline.

David, Jack, jt. ed. see Lecker, Robert.

David, Jairus R. Aseptic Processing & Packaging of Food: A Food Industry Perspective. LC 95-21370. (Contemporary Food Science Ser.). 272p. 1996. boxed set 149.95 (*0-8493-8004-9*, 8004) CRC Pr.

David, James F. Footprints of Thunder. 1997. mass mkt. 6.99 (*0-614-27806-6*); mass mkt. 6.99 (*0-8125-2402-0*, Pub. by Tor Bks) St Martin.

— Fragments. LC 96-53979. 384p. 1997. text 25.95 (*0-312-86313-6*) St Martin.

— Fragments. 1998. mass mkt. 6.99 (*0-8125-7147-9*, Pub. by Tor Bks) St Martin.

***David, James F.** Ship of the Damned. 384p. 2000. 24.95 (*0-312-87203-8*, Pub. by Forge NYC) St Martin.

David, Jane L. Redesigning an Education System: Early Observations from Kentucky. 42p. (Orig.). 1993. pap. text 15.00 (*1-55877-204-9*) Natl Governor.

David, Jane L. & Cohen, Michael. State Actions to Restructure Schools: The First Steps. 51p. (Orig.). 1990. pap. text 7.50 (*1-55877-101-8*) Natl Governor.

David, Jane L. & Goren, Paul D. Transforming Education: Overcoming Barriers. Feinstein, Gerry, ed. 48p. (Orig.). 1993. pap. text 15.00 (*1-55877-216-2*) Natl Governor.

David, Jay, pseud. Growing Up Black, from Slave Days to the Present: 25 African-Americans Reveal the Trials & Triumphs. LC 92-135054. 1992. 17.35 (*0-606-06430-3*) Turtleback.

David, Jay, pseud. Growing up Jewish: An Anthology. 1997. 17.10 (*0-606-13452-2*, Pub. by Turtleback) Demco.

— The New York Yankees. LC 97-1326. 1997. pap. 9.95 (*0-688-15505-7*, Wm Morrow) Morrow Avon.

— Songs of Wisdom: Quotes from Great African-Americans of the 20th Century. LC 99-36058. 192p. 2000. 20.00 (*0-688-16497-8*) Morrow Avon.

— The Stay-at-Home Entrepreneur: 125 Ways to Earn Money While Raising Your Family. LC 99-208422. 192p. 1999. pap. 12.00 (*0-380-79742-9*, Avon Bks) Morrow Avon.

David, Jay, pseud, ed. Growing Up Black. rev. ed. 288p. 1992. pap. 12.00 (*0-380-76632-9*, Avon Bks) Morrow Avon.

— Growing Up Jewish. LC 95-26106. 240p. 1997. pap. 12.00 (*0-380-73019-7*, Avon Bks) Morrow Avon.

***David, Jay, pseud, ed.** Growing up Jewish: An Anthology. 249p. 1999. reprint ed. text 22.00 (*0-7881-6704-9*) DIANE Pub.

David, Jean M., et al, eds. Second Generation Expert Systems. LC 93-19194. 1993. 119.95 (*0-387-56192-7*) Spr-Verlag.

David, Jean-Michel. The Roman Conquest of Italy. Nevill, Antonia, tr. LC 96-17076. 224p. (C). 1996. 57.95 (*0-631-20321-4*) Blackwell Pubs.

— The Roman Conquest of Italy. Nevill, Antonia, tr. LC 96-17076. 224p. 1997. pap. 22.95 (*0-631-20325-7*) Blackwell Pubs.

David, Jo. How to Trace Your Jewish Roots: Discovering Your Unique History. LC 98-52019. (Illus.). 224p. 1998. pap. 12.95 (*0-8065-2042-6*) Carol Pub Group.

David, Jo, et al. The Book of the Jewish Life. LC 97-15824. (Illus.). 160p. (J). (gr. 5-8). 1997. pap. text 12.00 (*0-8074-0628-7*, 121712) UAHC.

David, Joe. The Fire Within. LC 81-65447. 245p. 1981. 10.95 (*0-939360-00-4*) Bks for All Times.

— Glad You Asked! LC 86-70613. 141p. (Orig.). 1986. pap. 5.95 (*0-939360-02-0*) Bks for All Times.

— Teacher of the Year. LC 96-85521. 196p. 1997. pap. 9.95 (*0-939360-03-9*) Bks for All Times.

David, Joel. Fields of Vision: Critical Applications in Recent Philippine Cinema. LC 96-946086. 176p. 1997. pap. text 14.00 (*971-550-174-5*, Pub. by Ateneo de Manila Univ Pr) UH Pr.

— Wages of Cinema: Film in Philippine Perspective LC 98-947543. xv, 223 p. 1998. write for info. (*971-542-168-7*) U of Philippines Pr.

David, Jonathan. Jesus Is His Name. LC 92-17694. 58p. (Orig.). 1992. pap. 6.95 (*1-877971-01-4*) Mid Atl Reg Pr.

David, Joyce B. What You Should Know If You're Accused of a Crime. rev. ed. 32p. (Orig.). 1989. pap. 4.00 (*0-9617121-1-2*) Balaban Pub.

David, Judy, jt. auth. see Galinsky, Ellen.

David, Judy, jt. ed. see Mitchell, Ann.

David, Jules. American Political & Economic Penetration of Mexico, 1877-1920. Bruchey, Stuart & Bruchey, Eleanor, eds. LC 76-5001. (American Business Abroad Ser.). 1976. lib. bdg. 40.95 (*0-405-09269-5*) Ayer.

David, Jules, ed. Perspectives in American Diplomacy. (Individual Publications). 1979. lib. bdg. 26.95 (*0-405-09162-1*) Ayer.

David, Julia, tr. see Heidegger, Martin.

David, Justine. To Hold an Eagle. (Intimate Moments Ser.). 1993. mass mkt. 3.39 (*0-373-07497-2*, 5-07497-6) Silhouette.

David, Karen. Numerology Asks: Who Do You Think You Are Anyway? rev. ed. 167p. 1982. reprint ed. pap. text 9.95 (*0-87500-009-6*) RKM Pub Co.

David, Kati. A Child's War: World War II Through the Eyes of Children. LC 88-34463. 212p. 1989. 17.95 (*0-941423-24-7*) FWEW.

— A Child's War: World War II Through the Eyes of Children. 224p. 1990. pap. 7.95 (*0-380-71109-5*, Avon Bks) Morrow Avon.

David, Kay. And Daddy Makes Three. 1997. per. 3.99 (*0-373-07784-X*, 1-07784-1) Silhouette.

— Are You My Mommy? (Count on a Cop) (Harlequin Super Romance Ser.: No. 822). 1999. mass mkt. 4.25 (*0-373-70823-8*, Harlequin) Harlequin Bks.

— Baby of the Bride. (Intimate Moments Ser.). 1996. per. 3.99 (*0-373-07706-8*, 1-07706-4) Silhouette.

— Desperate. (Intimate Moments Ser.). 1995. per. 3.75 (*0-373-07624-X*, 1-07624-9) Silhouette.

— The Ends of the Earth. 1998. per. 4.25 (*0-373-70798-3*) Harlequin Bks.

— Hero in Hiding. (Intimate Moments Ser.). 1996. mass mkt. 3.99 (*0-373-07725-4*, 1-07725-4) Silhouette.

— Lone-Star Lawman. 1998. per. 4.25 (*0-373-07845-5*, 1-07845-0) Silhouette.

— The Man from High Mountain. (Superromance Ser.: Bk. 848). 1999. per. 4.25 (*0-373-70848-3*, 1-70848-6) Harlequin Bks.

***David, Kay.** Obsession. (Superromance Ser.: Bk. 945). 2000. mass mkt. 4.50 (*0-373-70945-5*, 1-70945-0) Harlequin Bks.

— Two Sisters: (Twins) (Superromance Ser.: No. 888). 2000. per. 4.50 (*0-373-70888-2*, 1-70888-2, Harlequin) Harlequin Bks.

David, Kenneth, ed. The New Wind: Changing Identities in South Asia. (World Anthropology Ser.). xvi, 537p. 1977. 61.55 (*90-279-7959-6*) Mouton.

David, Kenneth & Williams, Trefor, eds. Health Education in Schools. 2nd ed. 288p. (C). 1987. pap. 38.00 (*0-06-318376-5*, Pub. by P Chapman) St Mut.

David, Kenneth, jt. auth. see Terpstra, Vern.

David, Kenneth, jt. ed. see Charlton, Tony.

David, Kenneth C. Don't Know Much About the Bible. LC 98-16744. 512p. 1998. 25.00 (*0-688-14884-0*, Wm Morrow) Morrow Avon.

David, Kenneth S. Eisenhower: Soldier of Democracy. 564p. 1999. reprint ed. 14.95 (*1-56852-059-X*, Konecky & Konecky) W S Konecky Assocs.

David, Kristen, ed. see David, C. J.

David, Larry, jt. auth. see Seinfeld, Jerry.

David, Lawrence. Beetle Boy. LC 97-18961. (Illus.). 32p. (YA). (gr. 1 up). 1999. 15.95 (*0-385-32549-5*) Doubleday.

***David, Lawrence.** Chicken Run: Classic Edition. (Illus.). (J). 2000. 9.99 (*0-525-46420-4*) Viking Penguin.

David, Lawrence. The Good Little Girl. (Illus.). 32p. (J). (gr. 1 up). 1998. 15.95 (*0-385-32614-9*) BDD Bks Young Read.

***David, Lawrence.** The Good Little Girl. (Illus.). 32p. (J). (gr. 1 up). 2000. pap. 6.99 (*0-440-41520-9*, Yearling) BDD Bks Young Read.

— The Land of Hungry Armadillos. LC 99-54078. (Illus.). 32p. (J). (gr. 1-4). 2000. 15.95 (*0-385-32698-X*) BDD Bks Young Read.

David, Lawrence. Need. 1996. mass mkt. 6.99 (*0-312-95922-2*) St Martin.

— Peter Claus & the Naughty List. LC 98-54644. (J). 1999. write for info. (*0-385-32654-8*) Doubleday.

***David, Lawrence.** Superhero Max. LC 99-88212. (Illus.). (J). 2001. write for info. (*0-385-32746-3*) BDD Bks Young Read.

— The Window Song. 56p. 2000. pap. 7.00 (*0-8059-4965-8*) Dorrance.

David, Lelyveld. Aligarh's First Generation: Muslim Solidarity in British India. (Oxford India Paperbacks). (Illus.). 416p. (C). 1996. pap. text 18.95 (*0-19-563665-1*) OUP.

David, Leonard, jt. auth. see Borg, Nicholas.

David, Leonard, jt. auth. see Sacknoff, Scott.

David, Lester. Good Ted, Bad Ted: The Two Faces of Edward M. Kennedy. LC 92-39544. 1993. 21.95 (*1-55972-167-7*, Birch Ln Pr) Carol Pub Group.

— Jacqueline Kennedy Onassis: The Woman She Has Become. LC 93-45492. 1994. 19.95 (*1-55972-234-7*) Carol Pub Group.

David, Linda. Children's Books: Published by William Darton & His Sons. (Illus.). 85p. 1992. pap. 10.00 (*1-879598-11-6*) IN Univ Lilly Library.

***David, Lisa R. & Schneider, Andrew M.** Surgeon's Guide to Staging, Grading & Classifications. (Illus.). 255p. 2001. text. write for info. (*0-7216-8807-1*, W B Saunders Co) Harcrt Hlth Sci Grp.

***David, Loay M.** Visual Diagnosis Self-Tests on STDS (Sexually Transmitted Diseases) (Visual Diagnosis Self-Tests Ser.). (Illus.). 2000. pap. text 19.95 (*1-873413-97-1*) Merit Pub Intl.

David, Lockwood. Kilvert, the Victorian: A New Selection from Kilvert's Diaries. 340p. 1996. pap. 25.00 (*1-85411-094-2*, Pub. by Seren Bks) Dufour.

David, Luke. Chuckie Visits the Eye Doctor. (Rugrats Ser.). (Illus.). 24p. (J). (ps-3). 1999. pap. 3.50 (*0-689-82670-2*, 076714003507, Simon Spot) Litle Simon.

***David, Luke.** Oh, Brother! (Rugrats Ser.). (Illus.). (J). (ps-3). 1999. per. 3.50 (*0-671-02871-5*) S&S Trade.

David, Luke. Oh, Brother!, Vol. 1. (Rugrats Ser.: Vol. 9). (Illus.). 24p. (J). (ps-2). 1999. pap. 3.50 (*0-689-82440-8*, 076714003507, Simon Spot) Litle Simon.

***David, Luke.** Rugrats vs. the Monkeys. (Rugrats Ser.). (Illus.). 22p. (J). (ps-2). 1998. pap. 3.25 (*0-689-82142-5*) S&S Childrens.

David, Luke. Sight for Sore Eyes. (Rugrats Ser.: Vol. 8). (Illus.). 24p. (J). (ps-2). 1999. pap. 3.50 (*0-689-82262-6*) S&S Childrens.

— Tommy's New Playmate. (Rugrats Ser.). (Illus.). 24p. (J). (ps-3). 1998. pap. 3.25 (*0-689-82141-7*) S&S Childrens.

***David, Luke.** Twin Trouble. (Rugrats Ser.: Vol. 11). (Illus.). 24p. (J). (ps-2). 1999. pap. 3.50 (*0-689-82624-9*, 076714003507, Simon Spot) Litle Simon.

David, Luke & Cardona, Jose M. Bonjour, Babies! (Rugrats Chapter Bks.: No. 4). (Illus.). 64p. (J). (gr. 2-5). 1999. pap. 3.99 (*0-689-82894-2*, Simon Spot) Litle Simon.

David, M. Handbook of Applied Advanced Geostatistical Ore Reserve Estimation. (Developments in Geomathematics Ser.: Vol. 6). 232p. 1988. 124.50 (*0-444-42918-2*, North Holland) Elsevier.

— World's Best Dirty Limericks. (Illus.). 192p. 1982. 8.95 (*0-8184-0324-1*) Carol Pub Group.

David, M. & Lezine, I. Early Child Care in France. (International Monographs on Early Child Care). xvi, 148p. 1975. text 129.00 (*0-677-05210-3*) Gordon & Breach.

David M. Kennedy Center for International Studied. Citizen Diplomacy: Responding to Questions about America. rev. ed. Andrus, Amy L., ed. LC 95-38762. 223p. (C). 1995. pap. text 15.00 (*0-912575-15-8*, BYU DMK Ctr Intl) Brigham.

— International Opportunities: A Career Guide for Students. LC 93-44288. 116p. (Orig.). 1993. pap. 10.95 (*0-912575-13-1*, BYU DMK Ctr Intl) Brigham.

David, Margaret T. Light & Dark. large type ed. 721p. 1994. 27.99 (*0-7505-0612-1*, Pub. by Mgna Lrg Print) Ulverscroft.

David, Marian A. Correspondence & Disquotation: An Essay on the Nature of Truth. 216p. 1994. text 49.95 (*0-19-507924-8*) OUP.

David, Marilee. The New Voice Pedagogy. LC 94-30743. 220p. 1995. 47.50 (*0-8108-2943-6*) Scarecrow.

***David, Mark.** Coaching Illustrated: A Proven Approach to Real-World Management. Jamson, Deme & Fellner, Richard, eds. LC 98-93996. (Illus.). 88p. 1999. per. 17.99 (*1-893778-00-2*, H100-15) Mark David.

David, Martin & Smeeding, Timothy, eds. Horizontal Equity, Uncertainty & Economic Well-Being. LC 85-5879. (National Bureau of Economic Research Studies in Income & Wealth: No. 50). xii, 536p. 1985. lib. bdg. 66.00 (*0-226-13726-0*) U Ch Pr.

David, Martin H., ed. see National Conference on Regulatory Reform Staff.

David, Martin H., ed. see National Research Council Staff.

David-Menard, Monique. Hysteria from Freud to Lacan: Body & Language in Psychoanalysis. Porter, Catherine, tr. from FRE. LC 89-42870. 240p. 1989. 45.00 (*0-8014-2100-4*) Cornell U Pr.

***David, Michael M.** Advanced ANSI SQL Data Modeling & Structure Processing. LC 99-33463. 244p. 1999. 85.00 (*1-58053-038-9*) Artech Hse.

David, Miriam. Negotiating the Glass Ceiling: Careers of Senior Women in the Academic World. 216p. 1998. 85.00 (*0-7507-0837-9*, Falmer Pr) Taylor & Francis.

David, Miriam, et al. Mothers & Education, Inside Out? Exploring Family-Education Policy & Experience. LC 93-15. 256p. 1993. text 39.95 (*0-312-09596-1*) St Martin.

— Mother's Intuition: Choosing Secondary Schools. LC 94-17289. 174p. 1994. 85.00 (*0-7507-0286-9*, Falmer Pr) Taylor & Francis.

David, Miriam E. Parents, Gender, & Education Reform. LC 92-31272. (Family Life Ser.). 1993. pap. 22.95 (*0-7456-0637-7*) Blackwell Pubs.

David, Miriam E., ed. The Fragmenting Family: Does It Matter? (Choices in Welfare Ser.: No. 44). (Illus.). 95p. 1998. pap. 18.95 (*0-255-36436-9*, Pub. by Inst Economic Affairs) Coronet Bks.

David, Nat. Heartdance. (Illus.). 100p. (Orig.). 1989. 24.00 (*0-9622016-0-X*); pap. 12.00 (*0-9622016-1-8*) Doublestar Pr.

David-Neel, Alexandra. Immortality & Reincarnation: Wisdom for the Forbidden Journey. Graham, Jon, tr. LC 97-2446. 176p. 1997. pap. 12.95 (*0-89281-619-8*) Inner Tradit.

— Initiations & Initiates in Tibet. Rothwell, Fred, tr. from FRE. LC 93-3372.Tr. of Initiations Lama Iques. (Illus.). 240p. 1993. reprint ed. pap. 8.95 (*0-486-27579-5*) Dover.

— Magic & Mystery in Tibet. (Illus.). 321p. 1971. pap. 8.95 (*0-486-22682-4*) Dover.

— Magic & Mystery in Tibet. LC 93-38172. (Collector's Library of the Unknown). (Illus.). 320p. 1994. reprint ed. write for info. (*0-8094-8406-4*) Time-Life.

— My Journey to Lhasa. LC 93-16631. (Illus.). 346p. 1993. pap. 17.00 (*0-8070-5903-X*) Beacon Pr.

— Secret Oral Teachings in Tibetan Buddhist Sects. 1967. pap. 8.95 (*0-87286-012-4*) City Lights.

David-Neel, Alexandra & Yongden, Lama. The Superhuman Life of Gesar of Ling. Bolle, Kees W., ed. LC 77-79120. (Mythology Ser.). 1978. reprint ed. lib. bdg. 37.95 (*0-405-10532-0*) Ayer.

David, Nicholas & Driver, Jonathan. The Next Archaeology Workbook. LC 89-40406. (Illus.). 118p. (C). 1989. pap. text 19.95 (*0-8122-1293-2*) U of Pa Pr.

David, Nicholas, jt. auth. see Bricker, Harvey M., Jr.

David, Nicholas, jt. auth. see Daniels, Steve.

David, Norina. The Detroit Actors' & Performing Artists' Resource Guide & Log Directory, 2 bks. in 1. 510p. 1996. pap. 30.00 (*0-9656452-1-5*); spiral bd. 45.00 (*0-9656452-0-7*) A Emmanuel.

***David, Norman.** Jazz Arranging. 196p. (C). 1998. pap. text 33.45 (*1-880157-60-8*) Ardsley.

David O. McKay Library Staff, jt. auth. see Upper Snake River Valley Family History Center Staff.

David, P. Dynamics of Collective Phenomena in Nuclear & Subnuclear Long Range Interactions in Nuclei. 572p. 1988. text 125.00 (*9971-5-0598-3*) World Scientific Pub.

David-Parez, E., ed. Recipes of the Philippines. (Illus.). 170p. 1982. 6.50 (*0-318-36301-1*) Asia Bk Corp.

David, Patricia J. Through the Bible: A Complete Old & New Testament Bible Study Study Guide. (Illus.). 253p. 1994. spiral bd., wbk. ed. 14.95 (*0-89827-130-4*, BKC77) Wesleyan Pub Hse.

— Through the Bible: A Comprehensive, Sequential Bible Survey Study & Reference Resource. LC 96-135446. (Illus.). 385p. 1995. 24.95 (*0-89827-131-2*, BKC78) Wesleyan Pub Hse.

David, Patrick & Vogel, Gernot. The Snakes of Sumatra: An Annotated Checklist & Key with Natural History Notes. LC 97-151757. (Illus.). 264p. (Orig.). 1996. pap. 39.95 (*3-930612-08-9*, Pub. by Edition Chimaira) Bibliomania.

***David, Paul, et al, eds.** Advances in Modeling Innovation Diffusion. (Illus.). 448p. 2000. text 65.00 (*0-19-505468-7*) OUP.

David, Paul A. Behind the Diffusion Curve: Theoretical & Applied Contributions to the Microeconomics of Technology Adoption. (Underground Classics in Economics Ser.). 150p. (C). 2000. pap. 25.00 (*0-8133-7483-9*) Westview.

— Technical Choice Innovation & Economic Growth: Essays on American & British Experience in the Nineteenth Century. LC 74-76583. 344p. reprint ed. pap. 98.10 (*0-608-12227-0*, 2024448) Bks Demand.

***David, Paul A. & Steinmueller, W. Edward, eds.** Information Technology & the Productivity Paradox. 208p. 1998. text 48.00 (*90-5702-100-5*, Harwood Acad Pubs) Gordon & Breach.

David, Paul T. Barriers to Youth Employment, Vol. 1. LC 74-1678. (Children & Youth Ser.). 1974. reprint ed. 17.95 (*0-405-05957-4*) Ayer.

— Party Strength in the United States, 1872-1970. LC 77-183897. (Illus.). 324p. reprint ed. pap. 100.50 (*0-7837-4343-2*, 204405300012) Bks Demand.

David, Paul T. & Ceaser, James W. Proportional Representation in Presidential Nominating Politics. LC 79-4387. 314p. reprint ed. pap. 97.40 (*0-8357-2708-4*, 203982100013) Bks Demand.

David, Paul T. & Everson, David H., eds. The Presidential Election & Transition, 1980-1981. LC 82-19145. 304p. 1983. 31.95 (*0-8093-1109-7*) S Ill U Pr.

David, Paul T. & Pollock, Ross. Executives for Government: Central Issues of Federal Personnel Administration. LC 76-48706. 196p. 1977. reprint ed. lib. bdg. 55.00 (*0-8371-9335-4*, DAEG, Greenwood Pr) Greenwood.

David, Paul T., et al. The Politics of National Party Conventions. rev. ed. 394p. 1984. reprint ed. pap. text 29.00 (*0-8191-4002-3*) U Pr of Amer.

***David, Penny.** Garden Lost in Time: The Mystery of the Ancient Gardens of Aberglasney. (Illus.). 2000. 34.95 (*0-297-82484-8*) Weidenfeld & Nicolson.

David, Peter. Aquaman: Time & Tide. (Illus.). 96p. 1996. mass mkt. 9.95 (*1-56389-259-6*, Pub. by DC Comics) Time Warner.

D

An Asterisk (*) at the beginning of an entry indicates that the title is appearing for the first time.

***David, Peter.** Babylon 5: Out of the Darkness. 2000. mass mkt. 6.50 (0-345-42720-3) Ballantine Pub Grp.

David, Peter. Babylon 5: In the Beginning. 1998. mass mkt. 5.99 (0-345-42452-2, Del Rey) Ballantine Pub Grp.

— Babylon 5: Thirdspace TV Tie-in. 1998. mass mkt. 5.99 (0-345-42454-9, Del Rey) Ballantine Pub Grp.

— Body & Soul. Ryan, Kevin, ed. (Alien Nation Ser.: No. 3). 288p. (Orig.). 1993. mass mkt. 5.50 (0-671-73601-9) PB.

— But I Digress' LC 93-80099. 256p. 1994. pap. 14.95 (0-87341-286-9, DV01) Krause Pubns.

— Captain's Table: Once Burned, Vol. 5. (Star Trek: The Captain's Table Ser.: No. 5). 1998. mass mkt. 6.50 (0-671-02078-1) PB.

***David, Peter.** Chomper, No. 11. (Dinotopia Ser.: Vol. 11). 144p. (YA). (gr. 3-7). 1999. pap. 3.99 (0-679-89109-9, Pub. by Random Bks Yng Read) Random.

David, Peter. Dark Allies. (Star Trek Ser.: Vol. 8). 256p. 1999. per. 6.50 (0-671-02080-3) PB.

— Demora. (Star Trek Ser.: No. 76). 1995. mass mkt. 5.99 (0-671-52047-4) PB.

— Double or Nothing No. 5: Double Helix (Vol. 5) (Star Trek: The Next Generation Ser.: No. 54). 277p. 1999. per. 6.50 (0-671-03478-2, Star Trek) PB.

— End Game. (Star Trek: Bk. 4). 304p. 1997. per. 3.99 (0-671-01398-X, Star Trek) PB.

— The Escape, No. 2. (Star Trek Ser.: No. 02). 1995. mass mkt. 5.50 (0-671-52096-2) PB.

***David, Peter.** Excalibur: Restoration. (Star Trek: Bk. 3). 304p. 2000. 19.95 (0-671-04243-2, Star Trek) PB.

— Excalibur Book One: Requiem. (Star Trek Ser.: Vol. 9). 304p. 1909. mass mkt. 6.99 (0-671-04238-6) S&S Trade.

— Excalibur Book Two: Renaissance. (Star Trek Ser.: Vol. 10). 304p. 1909. mass mkt. 6.99 (0-671-04239-4, Star Trek) PB.

David, Peter. Fire on High, No. 6. (Star Trek: Bk. 6). 272p. 1998. mass mkt. 6.50 (0-671-02037-4, Star Trek) PB.

— House of Cards. (Star Trek: Bk. 1). 168p. 1997. per. 3.99 (0-671-01395-5, Star Trek) PB.

— Imzadi. (Star Trek: The Next Generation Ser.). 1998. mass mkt. 3.99 (0-671-02610-0) PB.

— Imzadi. Stern, Dave, ed. (Star Trek: The Next Generation Ser.). 352p. 1993. reprint ed. mass mkt. 5.99 (0-671-86729-6) PB.

***David, Peter.** Imzadi II: Triangle. LC 98-221234. (Star Trek: The Next Generation Ser.: Vol. 2). 375p. 1998. 23.00 (0-671-02532-5) PB.

— Imzadi II: Triangle. (Star Trek: The Next Generation Ser.: Vol. 2). 375p. 1999. reprint ed. per. 6.50 (0-671-02538-4, Star Trek) PB.

— Imzadi Star Trek Continuity. 1999. 12.99 (0-671-02165-6) S&S Trade.

David, Peter. Incredible Hulk: Future Imperfect. LC 96-159933. 96p. 1994. pap. 12.95 (0-7851-0029-6) Marvel Entrprs.

— Incredible Hulk: Ghosts of the Past. 112p. 1997. pap. text 12.95 (0-7851-0261-2) Marvel Entrprs.

— Incredible Hulk: What Savage Beast. 1996. mass mkt. 5.99 (1-57297-135-5) Blvd Books.

— Into the Void. (Star Trek: Bk. 2). 1997. per. 3.99 (0-671-01396-3, Star Trek) PB.

— Last Avengers Story. (Illus.). 96p. 1996. pap. text 12.95 (0-7851-0218-3) Marvel Entrprs.

— Legions of Fire: The Long Night of Centauri Prime. 4th ed. 1999. mass mkt. 6.50 (0-345-42718-1, Del Rey) Ballantine Pub Grp.

— Line of Fire. (Star Trek Ser.). (J). 1993. 9.09 (0-606-05622-X, Pub. by Turtleback) Demco.

— Martyr. (Star Trek: Bk. 5). 282p. 1998. mass mkt. 6.50 (0-671-02036-6, Star Trek) PB.

— The Maze. LC 98-66418. (Dinotopia Ser.). (YA). (gr. 5-8). 1998. pap. 3.99 (0-679-88264-2) Random.

— New Frontier. (Star Trek: Bks. 1-4). 688p. 1998. per. 15.00 (0-671-01978-3, Star Trek) PB.

— Onslaught: Eye of the Storm, Vol. 4. (Illus.). 96p. 1997. pap. text 9.95 (0-7851-0283-3) Marvel Entrprs.

***David, Peter.** Psi-Man: Mind-Force Warrior. Vol. 1. (Illus.). 208p. 2000. mass mkt. 5.99 (0-441-00705-8) Ace Bks.

— Psi-Man No. 2: Deathscape. (PSI-Man Ser.: No. 2). 192p. 2000. mass mkt. 5.99 (0-441-00710-4) Ace Bks.

— Psi-Man No. 3: Main Street D. O. A. Vol. 3. 192p. 2000. mass mkt. 5.99 (0-441-00717-1) ACE.

— Psi-Man No. 4: The Chaos Kid. (PSI-Man Ser.: Vol. 4). 192p. 2000. mass mkt. 5.99 (0-441-00745-7) Ace Bks.

— Psi-Man No. 5: Stalker. (PSI-Man Ser.: Vol. 5). 192p. 2000. mass mkt. 5.99 (0-441-00758-9) Ace Bks.

— Psi-Man No. 6: Haven. (PSI-Man Ser.: Vol. 6). (Illus.). 192p. 2000. mass mkt. 5.99 (0-441-00764-3) Ace Bks.

David, Peter. Q-in-Law. Stern, Dave, ed. (Star Trek Ser.: No. 18). 272p. 1991. mass mkt. 5.99 (0-671-73389-3, Star Trek) PB.

— Q-Squared. (Star Trek Ser.: No. 37). 448p. 1995. per. 6.50 (0-671-89151-0, Star Trek) PB.

— The Quiet Place. abr. ed. (Star Trek Ser.). 1999. per. 6.50 (0-671-02079-X) PB.

— Return of the Heroes. (Marvel's Finest' Collection). 128p. 1998. pap. 14.95 (0-7851-0705-3) Marvel Entrprs.

— The Rift. Stern, Dave, ed. (Star Trek Ser.: No. 57). 288p. 1991. mass mkt. 4.99 (0-671-74796-7) PB.

— The Rift. 1991. pap. 4.99 (0-685-51957-0) PB.

— A Rock & a Hard Place. Stern, Dave, ed. (Star Trek: The Next Generation Ser.: No. 10). 256p. 1991. mass mkt. 5.50 (0-671-74142-X) PB.

— The Siege. (Star Trek: Deep Space Nine Ser.: No. 2). 288p. 1993. mass mkt. 5.50 (0-671-87083-1) PB.

David, Peter. Star Trek: New Frontier, Set. abr. ed. 1997. audio 22.00 (0-671-57625-9) S&S Audio.

David, Peter. Star Trek: Who Killed Captain Kirk? Kahan, Bob, ed. 176p. 1993. mass mkt. 16.95 (1-56389-096-8) DC Comics.

— Starfleet Academy: Worf's Mission. (Star Trek Ser.: No. 2). 128p. (J). (gr. 3-8). 1993. 3.99 (0-671-87085-8, Minstrel Bks) PB.

— Strike Zone. (Star Trek: The Next Generation Ser.: No. 5). 1991. per. 5.99 (0-671-74647-2) PB.

— Supergirl. Kahan, Bob, ed. LC 98-152435. (Illus.). 224p. 1998. pap. text 14.95 (1-56389-410-6, Pub. by DC Comics) Time Warner.

— Survival. (Star Trek: The Next Generation Starfleet Academy Ser.: No. 3). (Illus.). 128p. (J). (gr. 3-6). 1993. 3.99 (0-671-87086-6, Minstrel Bks) PB.

— Survival. (Star Trek Next Generation Starfleet Acad Ser.). 1993. 9.09 (0-606-06019-7, Pub. by Turtleback) Demco.

— The Two-Front War. (Star Trek: Bk. 3). 304p. 1997. per. 3.99 (0-671-01397-1, Star Trek) PB.

— Vendetta. (Star Trek: No. 2). 1991. per. 5.99 (0-671-74145-4) PB.

— Vendetta. Stern, Dave, ed. (Star Trek). 416p. 1991. mass mkt. 5.99 (0-671-73305-2) PB.

— Worf's First Adventure. (Star Trek: The Next Generation Starfleet Academy Ser.: No. 1). 128p. (J). (gr. 3-6). 1993. pap. 3.99 (0-671-87084-X, Minstrel Bks) PB.

— Worf's First Adventure. (Star Trek Ser.). (J). 1993. 9.09 (0-606-05621-1, Pub. by Turtleback) Demco.

— Wrath of the Prophets, Vol. 20. (Deep Space Nine Ser.). 1997. per. 5.99 (0-671-53817-9, Star Trek) PB.

David, Peter & Englehart, Steve. The Incredible Hulk: The Beauty & the Beast. (Illus.). 176p. 1998. pap. 16.95 (0-7851-0659-6) Marvel Entrprs.

David, Peter & Howell, Richard. Soulsearchers & Company Vol. 1: On the Case. (Illus.). 152p. (Orig.). 1996. pap. 12.95 (0-9653109-1-4, Claypool Comics) Boffin Bks.

David, Peter, et al. Best of Marvel, 1997. (Illus.). 224p. 1998. pap. 19.95 (0-7851-0582-4) Marvel Entrprs.

David, Peter, see Peters, David, pseud.

David, Peter, jt. auth. see De Lancie, John.

David, Peter, jt. auth. see De Lancie, John Q.

David, Peter, jt. auth. see Doohan, James.

David, Peter, jt. auth. see Keyes, J. Gregory.

David, Peter, jt. auth. see Marz, Ron.

David, Peter, jt. ed. see Kirklin, Perry W.

David, Peter, jt. ed. see Lee, Stan.

David, Reginald E. Hawaii's Birds. 4th rev. ed. (Illus.). 112p. 1996. pap. 9.95 (1-889708-00-3) HI Audubon Soc.

David, Rene. Arbitration in International Trade. LC 84-5700. 494p. 1985. 132.00 (90-6544-164-6) Kluwer Law Intl.

— Random Testing of Digital Circuits: Theory & Application. LC 98-2765. (Illus.). 496p. 1998. text 185.00 (0-8247-0182-8) Dekker.

David, Rene & Brierly, John E. Major Legal Systems in the World Today: An Introduction to the Comparative Study of Law. 2nd ed. LC 78-67751. 1978. reprint ed. pap. 24.95 (0-02-907610-2) Free Pr.

David, Richard. Janus of Poets: An Essay on the Dramatic Value of Shakespeare's Poetry Both Good & Bad. (Select Bibliographies Reprint Ser.). 1977. 20.95 (0-8369-5253-7) Ayer.

— Janus of Poets: Being an Essay on the Dramatic Value of Shakespeare's Poetry Both Good & Bad. LC 75-115397. reprint ed. 21.50 (0-404-01939-0) AMS Pr.

David, Richard W., ed. see Shakespeare, William.

David, Robert J., et al. Moving Forward from the Past: Early Writings & Current Reflections of Middle School Founders. LC 98-19634. 1998. pap. write for info. (1-56090-154-3) Natl Middle Schl.

David Rockefeller Center for Latin American Studie, jt. auth. see Suarez-Orozco, Marcelo M.

David, Ron. Arabs & Israel for Beginners. (Illus.). 210p. 1993. pap. 12.95 (0-86316-161-8) Writers & Readers.

***David, Ron.** Paradise Explained: A Reader's Road Map to the Novels of Toni Morrison. 256p. 2000. pap. 14.95 (0-375-70732-8) Random Ref & Info.

David, Ronald B. Child & Adolescent Neurology. 3rd ed. LC 96-49799. (Neurology Psychiatry Access Ser.). (Illus.). 656p. (C). (gr. 13). 1997. text 64.95 (0-8151-2320-5, 26884) Mosby Inc.

David, Rosalie. The Ancient Egyptians: Beliefs & Practices. 2nd ed. LC 97-39681. 1998. pap. 24.95 (1-898723-72-9, Pub. by Sussex Acad Pr) Intl Spec Bk.

***David, Rosalie.** Conversations with Mummies: New Light on the Lives of the Ancient Egyptians. (Illus.). 192p. 2000. 40.00 (0-688-17143-5, Wm Morrow) Morrow Avon.

David, Rosalie. Growing up in Ancient Egypt. LC 91-40264. (Growing up in Ser.). (Illus.). 32p. (J). (gr. 3-5). 1997. pap. 4.95 (0-8167-2718-X) Troll Communs.

— Handbook to Life in Ancient Egypt. LC 99-10264. (Illus.). 400p. 1999. pap. 17.95 (0-19-513215-7) OUP.

— The Pyramid Builders of Ancient Egypt: A Modern Investigation of Pharaoh's Workforce. 304p. (C). 1997. pap. 25.99 (0-415-15292-5) Routledge.

David, Rosalie & David, Antony E. A Biographical Dictionary of Ancient Egypt. LC 95-36539. (Illus.). 208p. 1996. pap. 17.95 (0-8061-2822-4) U of Okla Pr.

David, Ruth A., jt. auth. see Stearns, Samuel D.

David, S., ed. Seminaire de Theorie des Nombres, Paris, 1990-1991. (Progress in Mathematics Ser.: Vol. 108). vii, 279p. 1992. 92.00 (0-8176-3684-6) Birkhauser.

— Seminaire de Theorie des Nombres, Paris, 1991-1992. (Progress in Mathematics Ser.: Vol. 116). (Illus.). vii, 302p. 1993. 103.50 (0-8176-3741-9) Birkhauser.

David, S. A. & Vitek, J. M., eds. International Trends in Welding Science & Technology: Proceedings of the Third International Conference on Trends in Welding Research Held June 1-5, 1992, in Gatlinburg, TN. LC 93-70230. (Illus.). 1185p. 1993. reprint ed. pap. 200.00 (0-608-02628-X, 206328600004) Bks Demand.

David, S. A., jt. ed. see Abbaschian, G. J.

David, Sara. Single Girls! Nice Guys Do Answer Personal Ads: How to Find Excitement, New Friends Maybe Even Love & Marriage - Through the Personal Ads. LC 88-70572. 128p. (Orig.). 1989. pap. 8.95 (0-929034-00-7) Palmtree Pr.

David Sarafan, Inc., Staff, ed. see Sarafan, David.

David, Saul. Military Blunders. LC 98-6806. (Illus.). 384p. 1998. pap. 11.95 (0-7867-0504-3) Carroll & Graf.

— Mutiny at Salerno: An Injustice Exposed. (Illus.). 241p. (C). 1995. 29.95 (1-85753-146-9, Pub. by Brasseys) Brasseys.

David, Saul. Prince of Pleasure: The Prince of Wales & the Making of the Regency. LC 98-46754. (Illus.). 496p. 1999. 30.00 (0-87113-739-9) Grove-Atltic.

***David, Saul.** Prince of Pleasure: The Prince of Wales & the Making of the Regency. 496p. 2000. pap. 15.00 (0-8021-3703-2, Pub. by Grove-Atltic) Publishers Group.

David, Scott & Perior, Tim. The Eye & the Eagle. 246p. 1991. pap. 8.00 (0-9631946-0-7) Frontline Intl.

David, Serge. The Molecular & Supramolecular Chemistry of Carbohydratas: Chemical Introduction to the Glycosciences. Beau, Rosemary G., tr. LC 97-18604. (Illus.). 330p. 1998. text 95.00 (0-19-850047-5) OUP.

— The Molecular & Supramolecular Chemistry of Carbohydrates: A Chemical Introduction to the Glycosciences. Beau, Rosemary G., tr. LC 97-18604. (Illus.). 330p. 1998. pap. text 45.00 (0-19-850046-7) OUP.

David, Sharon. I Heard It Through the Grapevine: Marvin Gaye: The Biography. (Illus.). 192p. 1992. 29.95 (1-85158-317-3, Pub. by Mainstream Pubng) Trafalgar.

David Shepard Associates Inc. Staff. The New Direct Marketing: How to Implement a Profit-Driven Database Marketing Strategy. 450p. 1990. text 60.00 (1-55623-317-5, Irwn Prfssnl) McGraw-Hill Prof.

David, Sheri I. With Dignity: The Search for Medicare & Medicaid, 132. LC 84-27941. (Contributions in Political Science Ser.: No. 12). 194p. 1985. 49.95 (0-313-24720-X, DWD/, Greenwood Pr) Greenwood.

David, Sinnou. Number Theory: Seminaire de Theorie des Nombres de Paris 1993-94. (London Mathematical Society Lecture Note Ser.: No. 235). 223p. 1996. pap. text 44.95 (0-521-58549-X) Cambridge U Pr.

David, Sinnou, ed. Number Theory 1992-3: Seminaire de Theorie des Nombres. (London Mathematical Society Lecture Note Ser.: No. 215). 301p. (C). 1995. pap. text 47.95 (0-521-55911-1) Cambridge U Pr.

David, Steven R. Choosing Sides: Alignment & Realignment in the Third World. LC 90-5297. 264p. 1991. reprint ed. pap. 81.90 (0-608-05946-3, 206628300008) Bks Demand.

— Defending Third World Regimes from Coups d'Etat. 100p. (Orig.). 1985. pap. text 14.00 (0-8191-4644-7) U Pr of Amer.

— Third World Coups d'Etat & International Security. LC 86-45451. 208p. 1987. reprint ed. pap. 64.50 (0-608-05947-1, 206628400008) Bks Demand.

David, Steven R. & Digeser, Peter. The United States & the Law of the Sea Treaty. (Pew Case Studies in International Affairs). 50p. (Orig.). (C). 1990. pap. text 3.50 (1-56927-418-5) Geo U Inst Dplmcy.

David, Stuart. How to Be a Successful Lettering Artist. (Illus.). 1987. 15.95 (0-88108-029-2); pap. 12.50 (0-88108-031-4) Art Dir.

— How to Become a Professional Calligrapher. (Illus.). 80p. 1985. pap. 11.95 (0-8008-3959-5) Taplinger.

***David, Susan L., ed.** National Conference on Drug Abuse Prevention Research 1996: Presentations, Papers & Recommendations. (Illus.). 182p. 2000. reprint ed. pap. text 35.00 (0-7567-0050-7) DIANE Pub.

David, T. J. Food & Food Additive Intolerance in Childhood. 2nd ed. (Illus.). 384p. (Orig.). 1997. pap. text 54.95 (0-86542-663-5) Blackwell Sci.

— Recent Advances in Paediatrics. 17th ed. (C). 1999. text 65.00 (0-443-06184-X) Church.

— Symptoms of Disease in Childhood. LC 95-7187. 281p. 1995. write for info. (0-86542-970-7) Blackwell Sci.

— Symptoms of Disease in Childhood. LC 95-7187. 1995. 49.95 (0-632-03635-4) Blackwell Sci.

David, T. J., ed. Recent Advances in Paediatrics, Vol. 12. (Illus.). 244p. 1993. pap. write for info. (0-443-04871-1) Church.

— Recent Advances in Paediatrics, Vol. 13. 13th ed. 233p. 1995. pap. text 69.95 (0-443-05100-3) Church.

— Recent Advances in Paediatrics 11. 11th ed. (Illus.). 224p. (Orig.). 1993. pap. text 51.00 (0-443-04753-7) Church.

— Recent Advances in Paediatrics 9. 9th ed. (Illus.). 239p. 1990. text 51.00 (0-443-04304-3) Church.

— Recent Advances in Paediatrics 10. (Illus.). 246p. (Orig.). 1992. pap. 45.95 (0-443-04520-8) Church.

David, T. P. Mother, Daughter, Sister: Journeys of the Spirit. LC 98-75061. 125p. 1998. 18.95 (1-57860-069-3) Guild Pr IN.

David, Thomas. Miracle Medicines of the Rainforest: A Doctor's Revolutionary Work with Cancer & AIDS Patients. Beasley, J. Michal, tr. from GER. LC 97-22873. (Illus.). 144p. 1997. pap. 19.95 (0-89281-746-1) Inner Tradit.

David, Thomas, jt. auth. see Lemke, Elisabeth.

David, Thomas G. & Weinstein, Carol S., eds. Spaces for Children: The Built Environment & Child Development. (Illus.). 346p. (C). 1987. 71.00 (0-306-42423-1, Plenum Trade) Perseus Pubng.

***David, Thomas L.** Voicing & Comping for Jazz Vibraphone: Four-mallet Studies for the Modern Vibist. 40p. 1999. pap. 12.95 incl. audio compact disk (0-7935-8854-5) H Leonard.

David, Tirone E., ed. Surgery for Mechanical Complications of Myocardial Infarction. LC 93-23998. (Illus.). 252p. 1993. 156.00 (1-879702-67-3, R) CRC Pr.

David, Tirone E. & Cheng, Davy C. Perioperative Care in Cardiac Anesthesia & Surgery. LC 98-50222. (Vademecum Ser.). 1999. spiral bd. 45.00 (1-57059-527-5) Landes Bioscience.

David, Tony. A Complete Introduction to Budgerigars. (Complete Introduction to...Ser.). (Illus.). 128p. (Orig.). 1987. pap. 8.95 (0-86622-286-3, CO008S) TFH Pubns.

David, Tricia. Child Protection & Early Years Teachers: Coping with Child Abuse. LC 92-16386. 1992. pap. 31.95 (0-335-09894-0) OpUniv Pr.

— Under Five, under Educated? 1990. pap. 30.95 (0-335-09262-4) OpUniv Pr.

David, Tricia, ed. Educational Provision for Our Youngest Children: European Perspectives. 176p. 1993. pap. 34.00 (1-85396-204-X, Pub. by P Chapman) Taylor & Francis.

David, Tricia, et al. Effective Teaching in the Early Years. 32p. 1993. pap. 5.50 (0-948080-86-8, Trentham Bks) Stylus Pub VA.

David, Trisha. Borrowed-One Bride. (Australians Ser.). 192p. 1998. per. 4.50 (0-373-82577-3, 1-82577-7) Harlequin Bks.

— Bride 2000 Bride Two Thousand. (Romance Ser.: Bk. 3585). 186p. 2000. per. 3.50 (0-373-03585-3, 1-03585-6) Harlequin Bks.

— Falling for Jack: Daddy Boom. (Romance Ser.: No. 3558). 1999. per. 3.50 (0-373-03558-6, 1-03558-3, Harlequin) Harlequin Bks.

— Falling for Jack: Daddy Boom. large type ed. (Larger Print Ser.: No. 404). 1999. per. 3.50 (0-373-15804-1, 1-15804-7, Harlequin) Harlequin Bks.

— Une Famille pour Lucy. (Azur Ser.: Vol. 751). (FRE.). 1999. mass mkt. 3.50 (0-373-34751-0, 1-34752-5) Harlequin Bks.

***David, Trisha.** Marriage for Maggie. 288p. 2000. 26.99 (0-263-16441-1, Pub. by Mills & Boon) Ulverscroft.

David, Trisha. Marrying William. (Romance Ser.: No. 449). 1999. mass mkt. 3.50 (0-373-17449-7, 1-17449-9) Harlequin Bks.

— McAllister's Baby. 1997. per. 3.25 (0-373-03472-5, 1-03472-7) Harlequin Bks.

— McTavish & Twins. (Romance Ser.: No. 3494). 1998. per. 3.50 (0-373-03494-6, 1-03494-1) Harlequin Bks.

— McTavish & Twins. large type ed. (Kids & Kisses Ser.). 1998. per. 3.50 (0-373-15740-1, Harlequin) Harlequin Bks.

***David, Trisha.** Noblesse Oblige. (Azur Ser.: No. 805). (FRE.). 2000. mass mkt. 3.99 (0-373-34805-3, 1-34805-1, Harlequin French) Harlequin Bks.

David, V. M., tr. see Entelis, S. G., et al.

David, Vernon J. Macrocosm: Unified Energy Matter Gravity Life. LC 92-90127. (Illus.). 1992. write for info. (0-9632581-0-9) David Pub KS.

David, W. K. Secrets of Wise Men, Chemists & Great Physicians: A Book of Rare Formulas, Recipes & Prescriptions. (Alternative Medicine Ser.). 1991. lib. bdg. 79.95 (0-8490-4306-9) Gordon Pr.

— Secrets of Wise Men, Chemists & Great Physicians: Formulas, Recipes & Prescriptions. 1991. lib. bdg. 250.00 (0-87700-994-5) Revisionist Pr.

David, Ward S. Ask Not for Victory. Grant, Wilda L., ed. (Illus.). 234p. (Orig.). (YA). (gr. 8-12). 1991. pap. 9.95 (0-9630883-3-5) W S David.

David, Wendy. From Metal to Music. (Changes Ser.). (J). (gr. 2-3). 1997. pap. 6.95 (0-516-26068-5) Childrens.

David, Wendy, et al. Safe Without Sight: Crime Prevention & Self-Defense Strategies for People Who Are Blind. Croft, Diane, ed. (Illus.). 88p. 1998. pap. write for info. (0-939173-12-3) Natl Braille Pr.

— Safe Without Sight: Crime Prevention & Self-Defense Strategies for People Who Are Blind. braille ed. Croft, Diane, ed. (Illus.). 88p. 1998. pap. write for info. (0-939173-13-1) Natl Braille Pr.

David, Wenzel, jt. auth. see Kurt, Busiek.

David, Werner. Managing Company-Wide Communication. LC 94-74698. (Illus.). 244p. 1995. mass mkt. 32.50 (0-412-56420-3) Chapman & Hall.

David, Wilfred L. Conflicting Paradigms in the Economics of Developing Nations. LC 86-16906. 236p. 1986. 55.00 (0-275-92108-5, C2108, Praeger Pubs) Greenwood.

— The Conversation of Economic Development: Historical Voices, Interpretations, & Reality. LC 97-10367. 272p. (C). (gr. 13). 1997. text 80.95 (0-7656-0116-8) M E Sharpe.

— The IMF Policy Paradigm: The Macroeconomics of Stabilization, Structural Adjustment, & Development. LC 85-6533. 140p. 1985. 49.95 (0-275-90082-7, C0082, Praeger Pubs) Greenwood.

— Political Economy of Economic Policy: The Quest for Human Betterment. LC 88-9961. 283p. 1988. 65.00 (0-275-93015-7, C3015, Praeger Pubs) Greenwood.

David, Wilfred L., ed. Public Finance, Planning & Economic Development: Essays in Honor of Ursula Hicks. LC 73-77734. (Illus.). 349p. 1973. 42.50 (0-8290-0201-4) Irvington.

David, William K. Secrets of Wise Men, Chemists & Great Physicians. 125p. 1993. reprint ed. spiral bd. 13.00 (0-7873-0238-4) Hlth Research.

— Secrets of Wise Men, Chemists & Great Physicians (1889) 130p. 1996. reprint ed. pap. 12.95 (1-56459-757-1) Kessinger Pub.

David, Young, tr. see Rilke, Rainer Maria.

David, Zdenek V., ed. see Dillon, Kenneth J.

David, Zdenek V., ed. see Dorr, Steven R.

David, Zdenek V., ed. see Kim, Hong N.

David, Zdenek V., ed. see Mayerchak, Patrick M.

David, Zdenek V., ed. see Pitschmann, Louis A.

An Asterisk (*) at the beginning of an entry indicates that the title is appearing for the first time.

Davida, George, et al, eds. Information Security: First International Workshop, ISW '97 Tatsunokuchi, Ishikawa, Japan, September 1997, Vol. 139. LC 98-18045. (Lecture Notes in Computer Science: Vol. 1396). xii, 357p. 1998. pap. 59.00 (3-540-64382-6) Spr-Verlag.

Davidann, Jon T. A World of Crisis & Progress: The American YMCA In Japan, 1890-1930. LC 97-40391. (Illus.). 208p. 1998. 37.50 (0-934223-43-2) Lehigh Univ Pr.

Davidar, E. R. C. Cheetal Walk: Living in the Wilderness. LC 97-914014. (Illus.). 1997. write for info. (0-19-564145-0) OUP.

Davide, F., jt. ed. see Natale, C. D.

Davidek, J., et al, eds. Chemical Changes During Food Processing. (Developments in Food Science Ser.: No. 21). 452p. 1990. 262.50 (0-444-98845-9) Elsevier.

Davidek, Jiri, ed. Toxic Compounds of Foods. 280p. 1995. lib. bdg. 184.00 (0-8493-4623-1) CRC Pr.

Davidge, R. W. Mechanical Behavior of Ceramics. LC 77-90206. (Illus.). 173p. (C). 1988. reprint ed. text 55.00 (1-878907-04-2, RAN) TechBooks.

Davidhazi, Peter, jt. ed. see Klein, Holger M.

Davidhazy, Andrew, et al, eds. Ultrahigh- & High-Speed Photography & Image-Based Motion Measurement, Vol. 3173. LC 98-143986. 526p. 1997. 99.00 (0-8194-2595-8) SPIE.

Davidhizar, Ruth Elaine, jt. auth. see Giger, Joyce Newman.

Davidian, David, intro. Addressing Turkish Genocide Apologists, April 6 - June 16, 1989, Vol. V: On UNIX (R) UseNet World Wide Computer Network. 480p. (Orig.). 1989. pap. text. write for info. (0-318-65522-5) SDP Armenia.

— Addressing Turkish Genocide Apologists, February 4 - June 3, 1988, Vol. I: On UNIX (R) UseNet World Wide Computer Network. 411p. (Orig.). 1989. pap. text. write for info. (0-318-65518-7) SDP Armenia.

— Addressing Turkish Genocide Apologists, June 3 - August 17, 1988, Vol. II: On UNIX (R) UseNet World Wide Computer Network. 304p. (Orig.). 1989. pap. text. write for info. (0-318-65519-5) SDP Armenia.

— Addressing Turkish Genocide Apologists, November 23 - December 23, 1988: On UNIX (R) UseNet World Wide Computer Network, Vol. IV. 179p. (Orig.). 1989. pap. text. write for info. (0-318-65521-7) SDP Armenia.

— Addressing Turkish Genocide Apologists, October 11 - November 21, 1988, Vol. III: On UNIX (R) UseNet World Wide Computer Network. 326p. (Orig.). 1989. pap. text. write for info. (0-318-65520-9) SDP Armenia.

Davidian, H., jt. auth. see Sartorius, N.

Davidian, H. H. The Rhododendron Species Vol. II: Elepidotes (Arboreum-Lactaeum) LC 81-23232. (Illus.). 392p. 1989. 54.95 (0-88192-109-2) Timber.

— The Rhododendron Species Vol. III: Elepidotes Continued (Neriiflorum - Thomsonii, Azaleastrum & Camtschaticum) LC 81-23232. (Illus.). 429p. 1992. 54.95 (0-88192-168-8) Timber.

— The Rhododendron Species Vol. IV: Azaleas. (Illus.). 184p. 1995. 54.95 (0-88192-311-7) Timber.

Davidian, John E. & Todres, Jacob L. Reducing Personal Income Tax: A Guide to Deductions & Credits. 1988. ring bd. 70.00 (0-318-23689-3) NY Law Pub.

— Reducing Personal Income Taxes: A Guide to Deductions & Credits. 700p. 1988. ring bd. 80.00 (0-317-05397-3, 00605) NY Law Pub.

Davidian, Marie. Nonlinear Models for Repeated Measurement Data. 360p. (gr. 13). 1995. boxed set 65.95 (0-412-98341-9, Chap & Hall CRC) CRC Pr.

Davidian, Richard D. Learn a New Language: A Creative Guide. 1988. write for info. (0-318-63667-0) Andrews U CIR.

Davidian, Steven. On the Need for, & Derivation of a Comprehensive Behavioral Theory, & a Subset, Organization Theory. (Illus.). viii, 300p. (C). 1998. pap. text 24.95 (0-9664417-0-2, CBT001) Zebra Skim.

Davidian, Zaven N. Economic Disparities among Nations: A Threat to Survival in a Globalized World. LC 94-906884. 336p. 1994. 26.00 (0-19-563475-6) OUP.

Davidkov, Ivan. Fires of the Sunflower. Osers, Ewald, tr. LC 88-81866. (Illus.). 65p. 1988. pap. 16.95 (0-948259-48-5, Pub. by Forest Bks) Dufour.

Davidman, Joy. Letter to a Comrade. LC 75-144744. (Yale Series of Younger Poets: No. 37). reprint ed. 18.00 (0-404-53837-1) AMS Pr.

— Smoke on the Mountain: An Interpretation of the Ten Commandments. LC 85-7622. 144p. 1985. pap. 16.95 (0-664-24680-X) Westminster John Knox.

Davidman, Leonard & Davidman, Patricia. Teaching with a Multicultural Perspective: A Practical Guide. LC 92-38387. 288p. (C). 1994. pap. text 33.25 (0-8013-0835-6, 78902) Longman.

Davidman, Leonard & Davidman, Patricia T. Teaching with a Multicultural Perspective: A Practical Guide. 2nd ed. LC 96-10445. 336p. (C). 1996. pap. 48.00 (0-8013-1748-7) Longman.

Davidman, Lyn & Tenebaum, Shelly, eds. Feminist Perspectives on Jewish Studies. LC 94-16445. 288p. 1995. 35.00 (0-300-06028-9) Yale U Pr.

Davidman, Lynn. Feminist Perspectives on Jewish Studies. 288p. 1996. pap. 17.00 (0-300-06867-0) Yale U Pr.

***Davidman, Lynn.** Motherloss. LC 99-53072. 293p. 2000. 24.95 (0-520-22319-5, Pub. by U CA Pr) Cal Prin Full Svc.

Davidman, Lynn. Tradition in a Rootless World: Women Turn to Orthodox Judaism. 1993. pap. 16.95 (0-520-07545-5, Pub. by U CA Pr) Cal Prin Full Svc.

Davidman, Lynn, jt. auth. see Reinharz, Shulamit.

Davidman, Patricia, jt. auth. see Davidman, Leonard.

Davidman, Patricia T., jt. auth. see Davidman, Leonard.

Davidmann, Manfred. Reorganising the National Health Service: An Evaluation of the Griffiths Report. (C). 1988. text 50.00 (0-85192-046-2) St Mut.

— Work & Pay: Incomes & Differentials. (C). 1988. text 50.00 (0-85192-031-4) St Mut.

Davido, Roseline d. The Childhood Hand That Disturbs Projective Test: A Diagnostic & Therapeutic Drawing Test. LC 93-23677. 200p. 1994. 59.95 (0-275-94417-4, Praeger Pubs) Greenwood.

Davidoff. Handbook of the Spinal Cord, Vol. 1. 560p. 1983. text 275.00 (0-8247-1708-2) Dekker.

Davidoff, Donald M. Contact: Customer Service in the Hospitality & Tourism Industry. LC 93-31853. 272p. (C). 1993. pap. text 56.00 (0-13-808916-7) P-H.

Davidoff, Doris S. & Davidoff, Philip G. Worldwide Tours: A Travel Agents Guide to Selling Tours. 80p. (C). 1990. pap. text 19.20 (0-13-964891-7) P-H.

Davidoff, Doris S., jt. auth. see Davidoff, Philip G.

Davidoff, Frank, et al, eds. Digital Video 1. (Illus.). 114p. 1982. reprint ed. pap. text 25.00 (0-940690-02-0) Soc Motion Pic & TV Engrs.

Davidoff, Frank, et al. Who Has Seen a Blood Sugar? Reflections on Medical Education. LC 96-2019. 232p. 1996. 25.00 (0-943126-47-9) Amer Coll Phys.

Davidoff, Frank, jt. ed. see Lee, Richard V.

Davidoff, Howard & Minars, David A. Tax Penalties & Interest Handbook, 1990-1991. 1991. ring bd., suppl. ed. 40.00 (0-318-68638-4, MICHIE) LEXIS Pub.

Davidoff, Howard, jt. auth. see Minars, David A.

Davidoff, Judith, ed. see Davidoff, Sydney.

Davidoff, Judith M. Beginning Well: Framing Fictions in Late Middle English Poetry. LC 83-49344. 248p. 1988. 35.00 (0-685-16465-9) Fairleigh Dickinson.

— Beginning Well: Framing Fictions in Late Middle English Poetry. 1989. 38.50 (0-8386-3208-4) Fairleigh Dickinson.

***Davidoff, Jules B.** Brain & Behaviour: Critical Concepts in Psychology. LC 99-89477. 2000. write for info. (0-415-13499-4) Routledge.

***Davidoff, Leonore.** Family Story. LC 98-23156. (Women & Men in History Ser.). 312p. (C). 1998. 69.95 (0-582-30351-6) Addison-Wesley.

Davidoff, Leonore. Worlds Between: Historical Perspectives on Gender & Class. LC 95-16491. (Illus.). 286p. (C). 1995. pap. 20.99 (0-415-91488-4) Routledge.

— Worlds Between: Historical Perspectives on Gender & Class. LC 95-16491. (Illus.). 286p. (C). (gr. 13). 1995. 75.00 (0-415-91487-6) Routledge.

Davidoff, Leonore & Hall, Catherine. Family Fortunes: Men & Women of the English Middle Class, 1780-1850. LC 86-30874. (Women in Culture & Society Ser.). (Illus.). 576p. 1987. 42.00 (0-226-13732-5) U Ch Pr.

— Family Fortunes: Men & Women of the English Middle Class, 1780-1850. LC 86-30874. (Women in Culture & Society Ser.). (Illus.). 576p. 1990. pap. text 22.00 (0-226-13733-3) U Ch Pr.

Davidoff, Leonore & Westover, Belinda, eds. Our Work, Our Lives, Our Words. LC 86-14046. 240p. 1986. pap. 23.00 (0-389-20656-3, N8214) B&N Imports.

***Davidoff, Leonore, et al, eds.** Retrospect & Prospect. (Gender & History Ser.). 232p. 2000. pap. 26.95 (0-631-21998-6) Blackwell Pubs.

Davidoff, Linda & Williams, Cynthia. Executive Orders: A New Strategy to Use Public Agencies to Increase Voter Registration. 45p. 1985. 5.95 (0-89788-091-9) CPA Washington.

Davidoff, Linda L. Introduction to Psychology. 3rd ed. 736p. (C). 1986. text 65.25 (0-07-015570-4) McGraw.

Davidoff, Martin. Satellite Experimenter's Handbook. LC 83-71699. 1990. pap. 20.00 (0-87259-318-5) Am Radio.

Davidoff, Martin R. The Radio Amateur's Satellite Handbook. LC 98-189103. 1998. write for info. (0-87259-658-3) Am Radio.

Davidoff, Philip. Sales & Marketing, Travel & Tourism. 296p. (C). 1983. pap. text 29.00 (0-13-787813-3) P-H.

— Tourism Geography. 512p. (C). 1989. pap. text 54.00 (0-13-925397-1) P-H.

Davidoff, Philip, et al. Apollo Reservations & Ticketing. LC 93-39910. (C). 1994. text 29.50 (0-256-15638-7, Irwn McGrw-H) McGrw-H Hghr Educ.

Davidoff, Philip G. & Davidoff, Doris S. Air Fares & Ticketing. 250p. 1987. pap. text 18.00 (0-935920-39-0, Ntl Pubs Blck) P-H.

— Air Fares & Ticketing. 3rd ed. LC 94-40705. 300p. (C). 1995. pap. text 66.00 (0-13-324484-9) P-H.

— Sales & Marketing for Travel & Tourism. (Illus.). 296p. 1983. pap. text 19.75 (0-935920-09-9, Ntl Pubs Blck) P-H.

— Sales & Marketing for Travel & Tourism. 2nd ed. LC 93-17461. 304p. 1994. pap. text 64.00 (0-13-786518-X) P-H.

Davidoff, Philip G., et al. Tourism Geography. (Illus.). 650p. (Orig.). 1988. pap. text 27.50 (0-935920-48-X, Ntl Pubs Blck) P-H.

— Tourism Geography Workbook. 144p. (C). 1992. pap. text 28.00 (0-13-923152-8) P-H.

Davidoff, Philip G., jt. auth. see Davidoff, Doris S.

Davidoff, Phillip G., et al. Tourism Geography. 2nd ed. LC 94-47027. 544p. (C). 1995. pap. text 83.00 (0-13-148735-3) P-H.

Davidoff, Robert A. Migraine: Manifestations, Pathogenesis, & Management. LC 94-16409. (Contemporary Neurology Ser.: No. 42). (Illus.). 400p. (C). 1994. text 85.00 (0-8036-2360-7) OUP.

Davidoff, Sydney. Suite for Viola da Gamba & Harpsichord. Davidoff, Judith & Earle, Eugenia, eds. (Contemporary Instrumental Ser.: No. 4). i, 14p. 1991. pap. text 10.00 (1-56571-040-1) PRB Prods.

Davidor, Y. Genetic Algorithms & Robotics. 180p. (C). 1991. text 32.00 (981-02-0217-2) World Scientific Pub.

Davidor, Y., et al, eds. Parallel Problem Solving from Nature - Evolutionary Computation: Proceedings of the International Conference on Evolutionary Computation, Held jointly with the Third Conference on Parallel Problem Solving from Nature, PPSN III, Jerusalem, Israel, October 9-14, 1994. (Lecure Notes in Computer Science Ser.: Vol. 866). xv, 642p. 1994. 93.95 (3-540-58484-6) Spr-Verlag.

Davidov, Corinne & Dawes, Ginny R. The Bakelite Jewelry Book. (Illus.). 156p. 1988. 45.00 (0-89659-867-5) Abbeville Pr.

— Victorian Jewelry: Unexplored Treasures. (Illus.). 156p. 1991. 35.00 (1-55859-135-4) Abbeville Pr.

Davidov, Judith F. Women's Camera Work: Self/Body/Other in American Visual Culture. LC 97-34684. (New Americanists Ser.). 1997. write for info. (0-8223-2054-1) Duke.

— Women's Camera Work: Self/Body/Other in American Visual Culture. LC 97-34684. (New Americanists Ser.). 494p. 1998. pap. 24.95 (0-8223-2067-3) Duke.

Davidov, M., tr. see Luzhkov, Y. M.

Davidovic, Milorad & Ikonic, Zoran, eds. Contemporary Studies in Condensed Matter Physics: Proceedings of the Symposium on Condensed Matter Physics (SFKM '97), Kladovo, Yugoslavia, September-October 1997. (Solid State Phenomena Ser.: Vols. 61 & 62). (Illus.). 370p. 1998. text 162.00 (3-908450-34-9, Pub. by Scitec Pubns) Enfield Pubs NH.

Davidovich, Adina. Religion As a Province of Meaning: The Kantian Foundations of Modern Theology. LC 93-28255. (Harvard Theological Studies: Vol. 37). 362p. (Orig.). (C). 1996. pap. 19.00 (0-8006-7090-6) TPI PA.

Davidovich, Boris L. Serbian Diaries. 1996. pap. 14.95 (0-85449-222-4, Pub. by Gay Mens Pr) LPC InBook.

Davidovich, Gene. Agricultural Reform in the U. S. S. R. Contract & Lease Farming Implications for Perestroika. Gallant, Jonathan, ed. (Illus.). 126p. (Orig.). 1989. pap. 75.00 (1-55831-112-2) Delphic Associates.

— Mathematical Models of Soviet Foreign Trade Optimization. Dawson, Melissa, ed. 247p. (Orig.). 1989. pap. text 75.00 (1-55831-106-8) Delphic Associates.

Davidovitch, David. The Ketuba: Jewish Marriage Contracts Through the Ages. LC 82-1247. (Illus.). 120p. 1985. 39.95 (0-915361-21-3) Lambda Pubs.

Davidovits, Joseph. The Book of Stone: Alchemy & Pyramids, Vol. I. 2nd ed. James, Andrew C. & James, Jacqueline, trs. from FRE. (Illus.). 252p. 1984. reprint ed. pap. text 11.95 (2-902933-09-6) Geopolymer Inst.

Davidow, Jenny. Embracing Your Subconscious: Bringing All Parts of You Into Creative Partnership. (Illus.). 250p. (Orig.). 1996. pap. 12.95 (1-880732-13-0) Tidal Wave Pr.

Davidow, Joel. Antitrust Guide for International Business Transactions. 2nd ed. (Corporate Practice Ser.: No. 35). 1995. 95.00 (1-55871-319-0) BNA.

Davidow, Joie. Infusions of Healing: A Treasury of Mexican-American Herbal Medicine. LC 99-34047. 304p. 1999. per. 12.00 (0-684-85416-3, Fireside) S&S Trade Pap.

Davidow, Joie, jt. ed. see Santiago, Esmeralda.

Davidow, Leonard S., ed. Plutarch's Lives. 30.00 (0-8196-2860-3) Biblo.

Davidow, M. The Abacus Made Easy. 2nd large type ed. 110p. (J). (gr. 2-12). 1975. 13.10 (0-317-01865-5, 4-00100-00) Am Printing Hse.

Davidow, Mike. Life Without Landlords. 32p. 1973. pap. 0.40 (0-87898-100-4) New Outlook.

— Perestroika: Its Rise & Fall. 1993. pap. 8.95 (0-7178-0703-7) Intl Pubs Co.

Davidow, Robert P., ed. Natural Rights & Natural Law: The Legacy of George Mason. (George Mason Lectures). (Illus.). 270p. (Orig.). 1986. pap. text 21.25 (0-8026-0001-8); lib. bdg. 46.50 (0-8026-0000-X) Univ Pub Assocs.

Davidow, William & Uttal, Bro. Total Customer Service: Uttal,&William. unabridged ed. 1990. audio 1[illegible].00 (1-55994-273-8, CPN 1867) HarperAudio.

Davidow, William H. Marketing High Technology An Insider's View. 224p. 1986. 35.00 (0-02-907990-X) Free Pr.

Davidow, William H. & Malone, Michael S. The Virtual Corporation: Customization & Instantaneous Response in Manufacturing & Service: Lessons from the World's Most Advanced Companies. LC 92-52569. 304p. 1992. 23.00 (0-88730-593-8, HarpBusn) HarpInfo.

— The Virtual Corporation: Structuring & Revitalizing the Corporation for the 21st Century. LC 92-52569. 304p. 1993. reprint ed. pap. 14.00 (0-88730-657-8, HarpBusn) HarpInfo.

Davidow, William H. & Uttal, Bro. Total Customer Service: The Ultimate Weapon. LC 89-45033. 256p. 1990. reprint ed. pap. 13.00 (0-06-092009-2, Perennial) HarperTrade.

Davidowitz, Samuel. Poems for the Insomniac. 1998. pap. write for info. (1-57553-666-8) Watermrk Pr.

Davidowitz, Steve, jt. auth. see Havens, Richie.

Davidowitz, Steven. Betting Thoroughbreds: A Professional's Guide for the Horseplayer. 2nd rev. ed. 288p. 1997. pap. 16.95 (0-452-27042-1, Plume) Dutton Plume.

— Master Handicapping. 1987. 19.95 (0-525-24291-0, Dutt); pap. 8.95 (0-525-48139-7, Dutt) Dutton Plume.

Davids, Adelbert, ed. The Empress Theophano: Byzantium & the West at the Turn of the First Millennium. (Illus.). 360p. (C). 1995. text 69.95 (0-521-45296-1) Cambridge U Pr.

Davids, C. A., tr. from PLI. Psalms of the Early Buddhists. (C). 1937. 73.50 (0-86013-076-2, Pub. by Pali Text) Elsevier.

Davids, C. A. & Norman, K. R., trs. from PLI. Poems of Early Buddhist Nuns: Therigatha. (C). 1989. pap. 14.00 (0-86013-289-7, Pub. by Pali Text) Elsevier.

Davids, C. A., ed. see Robertson, George C.

Davids, C. A., jt. tr. see Davids, T. W.

Davids, C. A. F. Rhys, jt. ed. see Davids, T. W. Rhys.

Davids, C. A. F. Rhys, jt. tr. see Aung, S. Z.

Davids, C. Rhys. Gotama, the Man. LC 78-72409. reprint ed. 25.00 (0-404-17273-3) AMS Pr.

— The Milinda Question: An Inquiry into Its Place in the History of Buddhism with a Theory As to Its Author. LC 78-72411. reprint ed. 22.50 (0-404-17275-X) AMS Pr.

— Outlines of Buddhism: A Historical Sketch. LC 78-72412. reprint ed. 18.50 (0-404-17276-8) AMS Pr.

— Wayfarer's Words, 3 vols. LC 78-72414. reprint ed. 125.00 (0-404-17600-3) AMS Pr.

— What Was the Original Gospel in 'Buddhism'? LC 78-72416. reprint ed. 17.00 (0-404-17277-6) AMS Pr.

Davids, C. Rhys, ed. Khuddaka-Nikaya: The Minor Anthologies of the Pali Canon, 4 vols. reprint ed. 105.00 (0-404-17640-2) AMS Pr.

Davids, C. Rhys, intro. Stories of the Buddha. LC 78-72444. reprint ed. 30.00 (0-404-17316-0) AMS Pr.

Davids, Carolina A. The Birth of Indian Psychology & Its Development in Buddhism. LC 78-72405. reprint ed. 37.50 (0-404-17267-9) AMS Pr.

— Buddhism: A Study of the Buddhist Norm. LC 78-72408. reprint ed. 25.00 (0-404-17269-5) AMS Pr.

— Buddhism: Its Birth & Dispersal. rev. ed. LC 78-72407. reprint ed. 25.00 (0-404-17268-7) AMS Pr.

— A Manual of Buddhism for Advanced Students. LC 78-72410. reprint ed. 32.50 (0-404-17274-1) AMS Pr.

— Psalms of the Early Buddhists, 2 vols., Set. LC 78-72413. reprint ed. 67.50 (0-404-17590-2) AMS Pr.

Davids, Caroline A. Outlines of Buddhism: A Historical Sketch. 126p. 1934. reprint ed. text 22.00 (0-685-13700-7) Coronet Bks.

— Sakya: or Buddhist Origins. 444p. 1931. reprint ed. text 32.50 (0-685-13679-5) Coronet Bks.

***Davids, Clarence, Sr.** Out of the Air & onto the Ground: The Clarence Davids Story. LC 99-63451. 160p. 1999. pap. 10.99 (1-57921-188-7) WinePress Pub.

Davids, Hollace & Davids, Paul. The Fires of Pele: Mark Twain's Legendary Lost Journal. (Illus.). 56p. (Orig.). (YA). 1986. pap. 9.95 (0-939031-00-0) Pictorial Legends.

Davids, Hollace, jt. auth. see Davids, Paul.

Davids, Jens-Ulrich & Stinshoff, Richard, eds. The Past in the Present: Proceedings, 5th British & Cultural Studies Conference, Oldenburg, Germany, 1994. LC 96-10166. (Studien zur Germanistik & Anglistik: Bd. 10). 162p. 1996. pap. 35.95 (0-8204-2993-7, DA566) P Lang Pubng.

Davids, Jules, ed. American Diplomatic & Public Papers: The Sino-Japanese War to the Russo-Japanese War, 1894-1905, 14 vols., Set. LC 81-9058. (Series 3). 4500p. 1982. lib. bdg. 1050.00 (0-8420-2185-X) Scholarly Res Inc.

— American Diplomatic & Public Papers, the United States & China: The United States, China & the Imperial Rivalries, 1861-93, 18 vols., Set. LC 79-12914. (Series 2). 1979. lib. bdg. 1350.00 (0-8420-2136-1) Scholarly Res Inc.

Davids, Karel & Lucassen, Jan, eds. A Miracle Mirrored: The Dutch Republic in European Perspective. (Illus.). 559p. (C). 1996. text 80.00 (0-521-46247-9) Cambridge U Pr.

Davids, Keith, jt. auth. see Williams, Mark.

Davids, Ken. Espresso: Ultimate Coffee. LC 92-32837. (One Hundred One Productions Ser.). (Illus.). 160p. (Orig.). 1993. pap. 12.95 (1-56426-557-9, One Hund One Prods) Cole Group.

Davids, Kenneth. Coffee: A Guide to Buying, Brewing & Enjoying. 4th ed. (One Hundred One Productions Ser.). (Illus.). 254p. (Orig.). 1994. pap. 12.95 (1-56426-555-2, One Hund One Prods) Cole Group.

— Home Coffee Roasting. 2nd ed. 256p. 1996. pap. 14.95 (0-312-14111-4) St Martin.

Davids, L. Robert. Minor League Baseball Stars, Vol. III. 184p. 1992. pap. 9.95 (0-910137-49-8) Soc Am Baseball Res.

Davids, L. Robert, ed. Baseball Historical Review. (Illus.). 112p. 1981. 6.00 (0-910137-15-3) Soc Am Baseball Res.

— The Baseball Research Journal, 1975. 2nd ed. (Illus.). 112p. 1983. pap. 3.00 (0-910137-02-1) Soc Am Baseball Res.

— Baseball Research Journal, 1976. 2nd ed. (Illus.). 128p. 1983. pap. 4.00 (0-910137-03-X) Soc Am Baseball Res.

— The Baseball Research Journal, 1978. 2nd ed. (Illus.). 116p. 1983. pap. 4.00 (0-910137-05-6) Soc Am Baseball Res.

— The Baseball Research Journal, 1981. (Illus.). 188p. (Orig.). 1981. 5.00 (0-910137-17-X) Soc Am Baseball Res.

— Minor League Baseball Stars. rev. ed. (Illus.). 128p. 1984. 5.00 (0-910137-12-9) Soc Am Baseball Res.

— Minor League Baseball Stars, Vol. II. (Illus.). 158p. 1985. pap. 5.00 (0-910137-13-7) Soc Am Baseball Res.

Davids, Lewis E. Dictionary of Insurance. 7th rev. ed. LC 89-36094. 516p. 1990. pap. text 17.95 (0-8226-3000-1) Littlefield.

— Instant Business Dictionary: 3,200 Words, Phrases & Abbreviations Most Commonly Used in Business. LC 78-150232. 320p. 1992. 6.95 (0-911744-07-X) Career Pub IL.

Davids, Mrs. C. A., tr. from PLI. Buddhist Psychological Ethics. 3rd ed. (C). 1974. reprint ed. 46.00 (0-86013-062-2, Pub. by Pali Text) Elsevier.

Davids, Mrs. C. A., jt. tr. see Aung, S. Z.

Davids, Mrs. C. A. F. Rhys & Woodward, F. L., trs. from PLI. The Book of the Kindred Sayings, 5 vols., 1. (C). 1989. 38.00 (0-86013-004-5, Pub. by Pali Text) Elsevier.

— The Book of the Kindred Sayings, 5 vols., 2. (C). 1990. 28.50 (0-86013-007-X, Pub. by Pali Text) Elsevier.

— The Book of the Kindred Sayings, 5 vols., 3. (C). 1975. 30.00 (0-86013-010-X, Pub. by Pali Text) Elsevier.

D

— The Book of the Kindred Sayings, 5 vols., 5. (C). 1990. 38.00 (*0-86013-012-6*, Pub. by Pali Text) Elsevier.

— The Book of the Kindred Sayings, 5 vols., Set. (C). 155.00 (*0-86013-256-0*, Pub. by Pali Text) Elsevier.

— The Book of the Kindred Sayings, 5 vols., Vol. 4. (C). 1980. 38.00 (*0-86013-011-8*, Pub. by Pali Text) Elsevier.

Davids, Paul. The Fountain of Youth. (Illus.). 56p. (Orig.). (YA). (gr. 5-9). pap. text 9.95 (*0-939031-01-9*) Pictorial Legends.

— The Glove of Darth Vader. (Star Wars: No. 1). (YA). (gr. 4 up). 1996. pap. 4.99 (*0-553-54282-6*) BDD Bks Young Read.

— The Glove of Darth Vader. (Star Wars: No. 1). (YA). (gr. 4 up). 1992. 9.09 (*0-606-00535-8*, Pub. by Turtleback) Demco.

— The Lost City of the Jedi. (Star Wars: No. 2). (YA). (gr. 4 up). 1992. 9.09 (*0-606-00543-9*, Pub. by Turtleback) Demco.

— Mission from Mount Yoda. (Star Wars: No. 4). 128p. (YA). (gr. 4-7). 1993. pap. 4.50 (*0-553-15890-2*) Bantam.

Davids, Paul. Mission from Mount Yoda. (Star Wars: No. 4). (YA). (gr. 4 up). 1993. 9.09 (*0-606-02755-6*, Pub. by Turtleback) Demco.

Davids, Paul. Mission from Mount Yoda. (Star Wars: No. 4). (YA). (gr. 4 up). 1999. 9.50 (*0-7607-0447-3*, Pub. by Turtleback) Demco.

— Prophets of the Dark Side. LC 94-137284. (Star Wars: No. 6). 128p. (YA). (gr. 4-7). 1993. pap. 4.50 (*0-553-15892-9*) Bantam.

— Prophets of the Dark Side. (Star Wars: No. 6). (YA). 1993. 9.09 (*0-606-05557-6*, Pub. by Turtleback) Demco.

— Queen of the Empire. (Star Wars: No. 5). 128p. (YA). (gr. 4-7). 1993. pap. 4.50 (*0-553-15891-0*) Bantam.

— Queen of the Empire. (Star Wars: No. 5). (YA). (gr. 4 up). 1993. 9.09 (*0-606-02849-8*, Pub. by Turtleback) Demco.

— Zorba the Hutt's Revenge. (Star Wars: No. 3). (YA). (gr. 4-5). 1992. 9.09 (*0-606-00544-7*, Pub. by Turtleback) Demco.

Davids, Paul & Davids, Hollace. The Glove of Darth Vader. (Star Wars: No. 1). 128p. (YA). (gr. 4 up). 1992. pap. 3.99 (*0-553-15887-2*, Starfire BDD) BDD Bks Young Read.

— The Lost City of the Jedi. LC 92-668025. (Star Wars: No. 2). 128p. (YA). (gr. 4-7). 1992. pap. 4.50 (*0-553-15888-0*, Starfire BDD) BDD Bks Young Read.

***Davids, Paul & Davids, Hollace.** The Lost City of the Jedi. (Star Wars: No. 2). (Illus.). 94p. (YA). (gr. 4 up). 1999. reprint ed. pap. text 10.00 (*0-7881-6480-5*) DIANE Pub.

Davids, Paul & Davids, Hollace. Star Wars, 6 bks. large type ed. Incl. Glove of Darth Vader. large type ed. LC 97-21961. 112p. (J). (gr. 4 up). 1997. lib. bdg. 19.93 (*0-8368-1989-6*); Lost City of the Jedi. large type ed. LC 97-21972. 112p. (J). (gr. 4 up). 1997. lib. bdg. 19.93 (*0-8368-1990-X*); Mission from Mount Yoda. large type ed. LC 97-21971. 112p. (J). (gr. 4 up). 1997. lib. bdg. 19.93 (*0-8368-1992-6*); Prophets of the Dark Side. large type ed. LC 97-21436. 112p. (J). (gr. 4 up). 1997. lib. bdg. 18.60 (*0-8368-1994-2*); Queen of the Empire. large type ed. LC 97-21970. 112p. (J). (gr. 4 up). 1997. lib. bdg. 18.60 (*0-8368-1993-4*); Zorba the Hutt's Revenge. large type ed. LC 97-21969. 112p. (J). (gr. 4 up). 1997. lib. bdg. 19.93 (*0-8368-1991-8*); (Star Wars Ser.). Set lib. bdg. 111.60 (*0-8368-1988-8*) Gareth Stevens Inc.

— Zorba the Hutt's Revenge. (Star Wars: No. 3). 128p. (YA). (gr. 4-7). 1992. pap. 4.50 (*0-553-15889-9*) Bantam.

Davids, Paul, jt. auth. see Davids, Hollace.

Davids, Peter H. Commentary on James. (New International Greek Testament Commentaries). 226p. 1982. 28.00 (*0-8028-2388-2*) Eerdmans.

— I Peter. (New International Commentary on the Old Testament Ser.). 288p. 1990. 30.00 (*0-8028-2516-8*) Eerdmans.

— James. (New International Biblical Commentary Ser.). 172p. 1989. pap. 11.95 (*0-943575-13-3*) Hendrickson MA.

— More Hard Sayings of the New Testament. LC 91-22655. (Hard Sayings Ser.). 300p. (Orig.). 1991. pap. 12.99 (*0-8308-1747-6*, 1747) InterVarsity.

Davids, Peter H., jt. ed. see Martin, Ralph P.

Davids, Rhys. Buddhism: Its History & Literature. 1972. lib. bdg. 250.00 (*0-87968-510-7*) Krishna Pr.

— Buddhist Birth Stories: or Jataka Tales: The Oldest Collection of Folklore Extant. Dorson, Richard M., ed. Williams, Thomas, tr. LC 77-70620. (International Folklore Ser.). 1977. reprint ed. lib. bdg. 40.95 (*0-405-10090-6*) Ayer.

— Buddhist Suttas. 1972. lib. bdg. 250.00 (*0-87968-511-5*) Krishna Pr.

— Poems of Cloister & Jungle, a Buddhist Anthology. 1972. 59.95 (*0-8490-0849-2*) Gordon Pr.

***Davids, Rhys.** Sacred Writings of the Buddhists, 3 vols. 1998. pap. 347.50 (*81-7041-664-7*, Pub. by Print Hse) St Mut.

Davids, Rhys. Sakya: or Buddhist Origins. 1972. lib. bdg. 200.00 (*0-87968-512-3*) Krishna Pr.

— Vinaya Texts, 3 vols, Set. 1972. lib. bdg. 900.00 (*0-87968-513-1*) Krishna Pr.

Davids, Rhys T., tr. see Fausboll, V., ed.

Davids, Richard C. The Man Who Moved a Mountain. LC 75-99609. (Illus.). 272p. 1972. pap. 12.99 (*0-8006-1237-X*, 1-1237, Fortress Pr) Augsburg Fortress.

Davids, Robert L., ed. Baseball Research Journal 1980. (Illus.). 180p. 1980. pap. 5.00 (*0-910137-16-1*) Soc Am Baseball Res.

— Baseball Research Journal 1981. (Illus.). 188p. 1981. 5.00 Soc Am Baseball Res.

— International Affairs Yearbook, 1976. 2nd ed. (Illus.). 128p. 1983. pap. 4.00 Soc Am Baseball Res.

— 1978. 2nd ed. (Illus.). 116p. 1983. pap. 4.00 Soc Am Baseball Res.

— 1975. 2nd ed. (Illus.). 112p. 1983. pap. 3.00 Soc Am Baseball Res.

— 1979. 2nd ed. (Illus.). 1983. reprint ed. pap. 5.00 Soc Am Baseball Res.

Davids, T. Rhys. Buddhism: Being a Sketch of the Life & Teachings of Gautama, the Buddha. LC 78-72417. reprint ed. 28.00 (*0-404-17278-4*) AMS Pr.

— Early Buddhism (1908) 90p. 1998. reprint ed. pap. 9.95 (*0-7661-0490-7*) Kessinger Pub.

Davids, T. W. & Davids, C. A., trs. from PLI. Dialogues of the Buddha, 3 vols., 1. (C). 1977. 37.00 (*0-86013-033-9*, Pub. by Pali Text) Elsevier.

— Dialogues of the Buddha, 3 vols., 2. (C). 1977. 37.00 (*0-86013-034-7*, Pub. by Pali Text) Elsevier.

— Dialogues of the Buddha, 3 vols., 3. (C). 1977. 34.50 (*0-86013-035-5*, Pub. by Pali Text) Elsevier.

— Dialogues of the Buddha, 3 vols., Set. (C). 1977. 103.90 (*0-86013-258-7*, Pub. by Pali Text) Elsevier.

Davids, T. W. & Stede, William. Pali-English Dictionary. (C). 1993. text 56.00 (*81-208-1144-5*, Pub. by Motilal Bnarsidass) S Asia.

— Pali-English Dictionary. (C). 1925. 40.00 (*0-86013-059-2*, Pub. by Pali Text) Elsevier.

***Davids, T. W. Rhys.** Buddhism: Its History & Literature. 1998. 34.00 (*81-85294-08-9*, Pub. by Orient Pubns) S Asia.

— Buddhist India. 347p. 1999. 33.50 (*81-215-0910-6*, Pub. by M Manoharial) Coronet Bks.

Davids, T. W. Rhys. Buddhist India. (C). 1993. reprint ed. 16.00 (*81-208-0424-4*, Pub. by Motilal Bnarsidass) S Asia.

***Davids, T. W. Rhys.** The History & Literature of Buddhism. 2nd ed. 136p. 1999. 20.00 (*81-215-0927-0*, Pub. by M Manoharial) S Asia.

***Davids, T. W. Rhys & Davids, C. A. F. Rhys, eds.** Dialogues of the Buddha Vol. I, II, III: Translated from the Pali of the Digha Nikaya. 334, 382, 274p. 1999. 450.00 (*81-208-1668-4*, Pub. by Motilal Bnarsidass); pap. 300.00 (*81-208-1669-2*, Pub. by Motilal Bnarsidass) St Mut.

Davids, Thomas W. Buddhist India. LC 78-38349. (Select Bibliographies Reprint Ser.). 1977. reprint ed. 30.95 (*0-8369-6766-6*) Ayer.

Davidse, Kristin, ed. see Simon-Vandenbergen, Anne-Marie, et al.

Davidsen, Leif. The Sardine Deception. Nunnally, Tiina & Murray, Steven T., trs. from DAN. LC 86-2094.Tr. of Uhellige Alliancer. 199p. 1986. pap. 6.95 (*0-940242-15-X*) Fjord Pr.

Davidsen-Nielsen, Marianne, jt. auth. see Leick, Nini.

Davidsen-Nielsen, Niels. Tense & Mood in English: A Comparison with Danish. (Topics in English Linguistics Ser.: No. 1). x, 224p. (C). 1990. lib. bdg. 65.40 (*3-11-012581-1*) Mouton.

Davidsen-Nielsen, Niels, jt. auth. see Bache, Carl.

Davidsen, Ole. The Narrative Jesus: A Semiotic Reading of Mark's Gospel. 416p. (Orig.). (C). 1993. 33.00 (*87-7288-423-1*, Pub. by Aarhus Univ Pr) David Brown.

Davidshofer, Charles O., jt. auth. see Murphy, Kevin R.

Davidson. After the Fact, Vol. 1. 4th ed. 224p. 1999. pap. 21.55 (*0-07-229427-2*) McGraw.

— After the Fact, Vol. 2. 4th ed. 288p. 1999. pap. 21.55 (*0-07-229428-0*) McGraw.

— Alice: Story of Jesus/Blind Man. 1997. 5.95 (*0-7667-1734-8*) Gibson.

— Alice: Story of Samson. 1997. 5.95 (*0-7667-1732-1*) Gibson.

— Alice: Story of Zacchaeus. (Illus.). (J). (ps-3). 1997. 5.95 (*0-7667-1735-6*) Gibson.

Davidson. American Journey: The Quest for Liberty. 1992. text. write for info. (*0-13-390477-6*) P-H.

— American Journey Quest Library SNC. 1992. text 53.20 (*0-13-390568-3*) P-H.

Davidson. American Record Nation of a Nation, 1. 1995. 54.00 (*0-07-912103-9*) McGraw.

***Davidson.** Business Law: Telecourse. 7th ed. (SWC-Business Law Ser.). (C). 2000. pap. 16.25 (*0-324-04297-3*) Thomson Learn.

Davidson. Complete Idiot's Guide to Managing Your Time. 1996. 14.95 (*0-02-861378-3*) Macmillan.

— Deer Avenger. 1998. 15.00 (*0-671-31707-5*) S&S Trade.

— A Dictionary of Angels. 1994. 19.95 (*0-318-14563-4*) Free Pr.

— Discovering Africa's Past. Date not set. pap. text. write for info. (*0-582-22049-1*, Pub. by Addison-Wesley) Longman.

— Employment in Minnesota, Issue 2. 3rd ed. 141p. 1998. ring bd. write for info. (*0-327-00682-X*, 8187222) LEXIS Pub.

— Exploring Earth: Introduction to Physical Geography. (C). 1997. write for info. (*0-13-715954-4*, Macmillan Coll) P-H.

— Florida Criminal Defense Trial Manual, No. 98-3. 170p. 1998. ring bd. write for info. (*0-327-00698-6*, 8062126) LEXIS Pub.

— Florida Criminal Defense Trial Manual 99-1, 5 vols. 190p. 1999. ring bd. 48.00 (*0-327-01165-3*, 8062127) LEXIS Pub.

— Florida Criminal Defense Trial Manual 99-2, 5 vols., Set. 156p. 1999. ring bd. write for info. (*0-327-01510-1*, 8062128) LEXIS Pub.

— Florida Criminal Sentencing, No. 98-4. 510p. 1998. ring bd. write for info. (*0-327-00700-1*, 8061019) LEXIS Pub.

— How To Build the High Performance. 1998. 17.95 (*0-949398-65-9*, 861766Q, Pub. by Graffiti) Motorbooks Intl.

— The Joy of Simple Living: Over 1,500 Ways to Make Your Life Easy & Content - at Home & at Work. 480p. 2000. pap. 15.95 (*1-57954-104-6*) Rodale Pr Inc.

— Minnesota Family Practice Manual, 2 vols., Issue 51. Gorlin, ed. 150p. 1998. ring bd. write for info. (*0-327-00540-8*, 8176831) LEXIS Pub.

— Minnesota Limitations Manual, No. 10. 60p. 1998. ring bd. write for info. (*0-327-00320-0*, 83042-14) LEXIS Pub.

— Nation of Nations. 4th ed. 2000. 55.00 (*0-07-231502-4*) McGraw.

— Nation of Nations, Vol. 1. 2nd ed. 1994. student ed. 17.50 (*0-07-015636-0*) McGraw.

— Nation of Nations, Vol. I. 3rd ed. 752p. 1997. pap. 52.50 (*0-07-015796-0*) McGraw.

— Nation of Nations, Vol. I. 3rd ed. 1997. pap. 18.13 (*0-07-015797-9*) McGraw.

— Nation of Nations, Vol. I. 4th ed. 2000. 42.00 (*0-07-231507-5*) McGraw.

— Nation of Nations, Vol. 2. 2nd ed. 1994. student ed. 17.50 (*0-07-015637-9*) McGraw.

— Nation of Nations, Vol. II. 3rd ed. 816p. 1997. pap. 52.50 (*0-07-015799-5*) McGraw.

— Nation of Nations, Vol. II. 3rd ed. 1997. pap. 18.13 (*0-07-015800-2*) McGraw.

— Nation of Nations, Vol. 2. 4th ed. 2000. 42.00 (*0-07-231509-1*) McGraw.

— A Nation of Nations, vols. 2nd ed. 576p. 1998. pap. 25.63 (*0-07-303385-5*) McGraw.

***Davidson.** Nursery Management: Administration & Culture. 4th ed. LC 99-25857. (Illus.). 529p. 1999. 93.00 (*0-13-857996-2*) P-H.

Davidson. Picture Puzzle Book. 1995. pap. 10.95 (*0-201-48008-5*) Addison-Wesley.

— Pre-Colonial West Africa. LC 97-48911. 272p. (C). 1998. 74.00 (*0-582-31852-1*) Addison-Wesley.

— Radiation. 110p. 1986. pap. 8.50 (*0-85207-180-9*, Pub. by C W Daniel) Natl Bk Netwk.

— Search for Common Ground. LC 97-66310. 256p. 1997. 19.95 (*0-87973-925-8*) Our Sunday Visitor.

— Spect Properties/Inorganic & Organometallic Compounds, Vol. 10. 1990. 153.00 (*0-85186-093-1*) CRC Pr.

— Spect Properties/Inorganic & Organometallic Compounds, Vol. 12. 1991. 175.00 (*0-85186-920-3*) CRC Pr.

— Spect Properties/Inorganic & Organometallic Compounds, Vol. 14. 1989. 274.00 (*0-85186-123-7*) CRC Pr.

— Spect Properties/Inorganic & Organometallic Compounds, Vol. 15. 1989. 274.00 (*0-85186-133-4*) CRC Pr.

— Spect Properties/Inorganic & Organometallic Compounds, Vol. 16. 1989. 263.00 (*0-85186-143-1*) CRC Pr.

— Spect Properties/Inorganic & Organometallic Compounds, Vol. 18. Ebswor, E. A. V., ed. 1988. 286.00 (*0-85186-163-6*) CRC Pr.

— Spect Properties/Inorganic & Organometallic Compounds, Vol. 22. Ebswor, E. A. V., ed. 1989. 362.00 (*0-85186-203-9*) CRC Pr.

— Spectroscopic Properties of Inorganic & Organometallic Compounds, Vol. 26. 1993. 341.00 (*0-85186-474-0*) CRC Pr.

— Spectroscopic Properties of Inorganic & Organometric Materials, Vol. 24. 1991. 331.00 (*0-85186-223-3*) CRC Pr.

— Story Club Class Set 1. 1994. 139.75 (*0-201-50837-0*) Addison-Wesley.

— Story Club Class Set 2. 1994. 139.74 (*0-201-50838-9*) Addison-Wesley.

Davidson & Crocker. Business Law: Principles & Cases. 2nd ed. 1987. pap. text 20.00 (*0-534-07513-4*) Brooks-Cole.

Davidson & Ebswor, E. A. V. Spect Properties/Inorganic & Organometallic Compounds, Vol. 17. 1988. 286.00 (*0-85186-153-9*) CRC Pr.

— Spect Properties/Inorganic & Organometallic Compounds, Vol. 21. 1989. 330.00 (*0-85186-193-8*) CRC Pr.

— Spect Properties/Inorganic & Organometallic Compounds, Vol. 23. 1990. 362.00 (*0-85186-213-6*) CRC Pr.

Davidson & Frame, J. Davidson. Project Management Competence: Building Key Skills for Individuals, Teams, & Organizations. LC 99-31823. 256p. 1999. text 34.95 (*0-7879-4662-1*) Jossey-Bass.

Davidson & Gambell. Investment in Southeast Asia. LC 98-153948. 1997. 44.95 (*981-00-8745-4*) Buttrwrth-Heinemann.

Davidson & Knowles. Business Law: Principles & Cases. 6th ed. (Miscellaneous Catalogs Ser.). 1997. mass mkt., student ed. 17.95 (*0-538-86858-9*) S-W Pub.

— Business Law: Principles & Cases in the Legal Environment. 6th ed. LC 97-15970. (Miscellaneous/ Catalogs Ser.). (C). 1997. pap. 107.95 (*0-538-86856-2*) S-W Pub.

Davidson & Moore. Marriage & Family. 1996. pap. text, student ed. 20.00 (*0-205-18432-4*) Allyn.

Davidson, et al. Business & The Law - Telecourse Guide. 2nd ed. (SWC-Business Law). 1993. mass mkt. 26.50 (*0-534-93283-5*) S-W Pub.

— Comprehensive Business Law. (LA - Business Law Ser.). 1987. mass mkt. 71.50 (*0-534-07536-3*) S-W Pub.

Davidson, jt. auth. see Batastini.

Davidson, James West. United States: A History of the Republic. LC 81-114142. 1981. 21.28 (*0-13-937995-9*) P-H.

Davidson & Associates Inc. Staff. Multicultural Tales from Around the World, Vol. I. (Story Club Ser.: Vol. 1). (J). (gr. 4-7). 1994. pap. text 14.56 (*0-201-57578-7*) Addison-Wesley.

Davidson & Associates Inc Staff. Multicultural Tales from Around the World, Vol. II. (Story Club Ser.: Vol. 2). (J). (gr. 4-7). 1994. pap. text 14.56 (*0-201-57579-5*) Addison-Wesley.

Davidson & Associates Inc. Staff. Story Club Readers, Nos. 1 & 2. (J). 1994. pap., teacher ed. 12.14 (*0-201-57580-9*) Addison-Wesley.

Davidson & Associates Staff. Fisher-Price ABC's Version 1.0, 1. 1995. 26.44 (*5-554-25721-6*) Davidson & Assocs.

— SAT & PSAT. 13th ed. 1999. pap. 12.00 incl. disk (*0-02-861080-6*, Arco) Macmillan Gen Ref.

Davidson, A. Joy Kogawa's Obasan. (Canadian Fiction Studies: No. 30). 120p. (C). 1994. pap. text 14.95 (*1-55022-179-5*, Pub. by ECW) Genl Dist Srvs.

Davidson, A. B. A Key to the Exercises in the Introductory Hebrew Grammar. Mauchline, John, ed. (Introductory Hebrew Grammar Ser.). 192p. 1993. 29.95 (*0-567-01006-6*, Pub. by T & T Clark) Bks Intl VA.

— The Theology of the Old Testament. Salmond, S. D., ed. 572p. 1904. pap. 27.95 (*0-567-27206-0*, Pub. by T & T Clark) Bks Intl VA.

Davidson, A. L., jt. auth. see Erskine, A. A.

Davidson, A. S. Samuel Walters - Marine Artist: Fifty Years of Sea, Sail & Steam. 1992. 195.00 (*0-947764-46-1*, Pub. by Jones-Sands) St Mut.

Davidson, Abraham A. Early American Modernist Painting 1910-1935. LC 94-14968. (Illus.). 342p. 1994. reprint ed. pap. 19.95 (*0-306-80595-2*) Da Capo.

— Ralph Albert Blakelock. 1996. 65.00 (*0-271-01504-7*) Pa St U Pr.

Davidson, Adele K., ed. see Sicher, Lydia.

Davidson, Al. Penny Lane: A History of Antique Mechanical Toy Banks. Long, Ida & Long, Earnest A., eds. (Illus.). 272p. 1987. 70.00 (*0-9604406-0-7*) Deborah Davidson.

— Penny Lane: A History of Antique Toy Banks. deluxe ed. Long, Ida & Long, Earnest A., eds. (Illus.). 272p. 1987. 70.00 (*0-9604406-1-5*) Deborah Davidson.

Davidson, Alan. The Oxford Companion to Food. (Illus.). 908p. 1999. 60.00 (*0-19-211579-0*) OUP.

Davidson, Alan & Davidson, Robert. How Good Parents Raise Great Kids: The Six Essential Habits of Highly Successful Parents. 336p. (Orig.). 1996. mass mkt. 12.99 (*0-446-67137-1*, Pub. by Warner Bks) Little.

Davidson, Alan & McGurn, James. EnCycleopedia: The International Buyer's Guide to Alternatives in Cycling. LC 97-38325. (Illus.). 146p. 1998. pap. 19.95 (*0-87951-854-5*, Pub. by Overlook Pr) Penguin Putnam.

— Encyclopedia, 1999: The International Buyer's Guide to Alternatives in Cycling. LC 98-16780. (Illus.). 168p. 1998. pap. 19.95 (*0-87951-884-7*, Pub. by Overlook Pr) Penguin Putnam.

***Davidson, Alan & McGurn, Jim.** Encyclopedia 2001. 2000. pap. 23.95 (*1-58567-086-3*, Pub. by Overlook Pr) Penguin Putnam.

Davidson, Alan, jt. auth. see McGregor-Lowndes, Myles.

Davidson, Alan, tr. see Dumas, Alexandre.

Davidson, Alan J. & Hartman, David S., eds. Radiology of the Kidney & Urinary Tract. 2nd ed. (Illus.). 864p. 1993. text 159.00 (*0-7216-3552-0*, W B Saunders Co) Harcrt Hlth Sci Grp.

Davidson, Alan J., et al. Radiology of the Kidney & Genitourinary Tract. 3rd ed. Bralow, Lisette, ed. LC 98-9758. (Illus.). 832p. (C). 1998. text. write for info. (*0-7216-7144-6*, W B Saunders Co) Harcrt Hlth Sci Grp.

Davidson, Alastair. From Subject to Citizen: Australian Citizenship in the Twentieth Century. LC 96-24270. 355p. 1997. pap. text 24.95 (*0-521-45973-7*) Cambridge U Pr.

— From Subject to Citizen: Australian Citizenship in the Twentieth Century. LC 96-24270. (Illus.). 355p. (C). 1997. text 64.95 (*0-521-45367-4*) Cambridge U Pr.

— Globalization & Citizenship in the Asia-Pacific. LC 98-25636. 260p. 1999. text 69.95 (*0-312-21798-6*) St Martin.

— The Invisible State: The Formation of the Australian State. (Studies in Australian History). 349p. (C). 1991. text 69.95 (*0-521-36658-5*) Cambridge U Pr.

Davidson, Alex & Dence, Michael, eds. The Brundtland Challenge & the Cost of Inaction. 159p. 1988. 17.95 (*0-88645-076-4*, Pub. by Inst Res Pub) Ashgate Pub Co.

Davidson, Alexander. Two Models of Welfare: The Origins & Development of the Welfare State in Sweden & New Zealand, 1888-1988. (Acta Universitatis Upsaliensis Ser.: No. 108). 437p. (Orig.). 1989. pap. 47.50 (*91-554-2486-4*) Coronet Bks.

Davidson, Alice J. David & the Big Giant. LC 98-138318. (My Bible Friends Board Bks.). (Illus.). 12p. (J). 1997. 3.99 (*0-310-97326-0*) Zondervan.

— David y el Gran Gigante. (SPA.). 1998. 3.99 (*0-8297-2485-0*) Vida Pubs.

— Esther & the Good King. (Bible Friends Ser.). (Illus.). 12p. (J). (ps). Date not set. bds. 3.99 (*0-310-97600-6*) Zondervan.

— Happy Easter! LC 99-162664. (My Bible Friends Ser.). (Illus.). 1998. 3.99 (*0-310-97488-7*, Zondervan Gifts) Zondervan.

— Hosanna! LC 99-163656. (My Bible Friends Ser.). (Illus.). 1998. 3.99 (*0-310-97489-5*, Zondervan Gifts) Zondervan.

— Jonah & the Big Fish. LC 97-184138. (My Bible Friends Board Bks.). (Illus.). 12p. (J). 1997. 3.99 (*0-310-97323-6*) Zondervan.

— Jonas y el Gran Pez. (SPA.). (J). 1998. 3.99 (*0-8297-2484-2*) Zondervan.

— Joseph & the Splendid Coat. LC 98-182163. (My Bible Friends Board Bks.). (Illus.). (J). 1998. 3.99 (*0-310-97325-2*) Zondervan.

— Little Donkey's Day with Jesus. (J). (ps-3). 1997. 3.99 (*0-310-97169-1*) Zondervan.

— Little Lamb & Good Shepherd. (J). (ps-3). 1997. 3.99 (*0-310-97170-5*) Zondervan.

— The Lord's Prayer. (Alice in Bibleland Storybooks). (Illus.). (J). (gr. 3 up). 1989. 5.95 (*0-8378-1868-0*) Gibson.

— Maria y la Tumba Vacia. (SPA.). 1998. 3.99 (*0-8297-2488-5*) Vida Pubs.

— Mary & the Empty Tomb. LC 98-182179. (My Bible Friends Ser.). (Illus.). 12p. 1998. 3.99 (*0-310-97455-0*, Zondervan Gifts) Zondervan.

An Asterisk (*) at the beginning of an entry indicates that the title is appearing for the first time.

— Moses & the Pharaoh. LC 98-182174. (My Bible Friends Board Bks.). (Illus.). 12p. (J). 1998. 3.99 (*0-310-97456-9*, Zondervan Gifts) Zondervan.
— My Bible Friend's: Mary & the Baby Jesus. LC 98-138317. (My Bible Friends Board Books). (Illus.). 12p. (J). 1997. bds. 3.99 (*0-310-97327-9*) Zondervan.
— Noah & the Big Boat. LC 97-184124. (My Bible Friends Board Bks.). (Illus.). 12p. (J). 1997. 3.99 (*0-310-97322-8*) Zondervan.
— Noe y el Gran Barco. (SPA.). 1998. 3.99 (*0-8297-2487-7*) Vida Pubs.
— Prayers & Graces. (Alice in Bibleland Storybooks). (Illus.). 32p. (J). (gr. 3 up). 1986. 5.95 (*0-8378-5078-9*) Gibson.
— Psalms & Proverbs. (Alice in Bibleland Storybooks). (Illus.). 32p. (J). (gr. 3 up). 1984. 5.95 (*0-8378-5069-X*) Gibson.
— Samson & His Strength. (My Bible Friends Board Bks.). (Illus.). 1998. 3.99 (*0-310-97324-4*) Zondervan.
— The Story of Baby Jesus. (Alice in Bibleland Storybooks). (Illus.). 32p. (J). (gr. 3 up). 1985. 5.95 (*0-8378-5072-X*) Gibson.
— The Story of Baby Moses. (Alice in Bibleland Storybooks). (Illus.). 32p. (J). (ps-3). 1985. 5.95 (*0-8378-5071-1*) Gibson.
— The Story of Creation. (Alice in Bibleland Storybooks). (Illus.). 32p. (J). (gr. 3 up). 1984. 5.95 (*0-8378-5066-5*) Gibson.
— The Story of Daniel & the Lion. (Alice in Bibleland Storybooks). (Illus.). 32p. (J). (gr. 3 up). 1986. 5.95 (*0-8378-5079-7*) Gibson.
— The Story of David & Goliath. (Alice in Bibleland Storybooks). (Illus.). 32p. (J). (gr. 3 up). 1985. 5.95 (*0-8378-5070-3*) Gibson.
— The Story of Easter. (Alice in Bibleland Storybooks). (Illus.). 32p. (J). (gr. 3 up). 1988. 5.95 (*0-8378-1839-7*) Gibson.
— The Story of Esther. (Alice in Bibleland Storybooks). (Illus.). (J). (gr. 3 up). 1990. 5.95 (*0-8378-1851-6*) Gibson.
— The Story of Exodus. (Alice in Bibleland Storybooks). (Illus.). (J). (gr. 3 up). 1990. 5.95 (*0-8378-1849-4*) Gibson.
— The Story of Isaac & Rebeckah. (Alice in Bibleland Storybooks). (Illus.). (J). (gr. 3 up). 1990. 5.95 (*0-8378-1852-4*) Gibson.
— The Story of Jesus & His Disciples. (Alice in Bibleland Storybooks). (Illus.). (J). (gr. 3 up). 1990. 5.95 (*0-8378-1860-5*) Gibson.
— The Story of Jonah. (Alice in Bibleland Storybooks). (Illus.). 32p. (J). (gr. 3 up). 1984. 5.95 (*0-8378-5068-1*) Gibson.
— The Story of Joshua. (Alice in Bibleland Storybooks). (Illus.). (J). (gr. 3 up). 1990. 5.95 (*0-8378-1850-8*) Gibson.
— Story of Noah. (Alice in Bibleland Storybooks). (Illus.). 32p. (J). (gr. 3 up). 1984. 5.95 (*0-8378-5067-3*) Gibson.
— The Story of Paul. (Alice in Bibleland Storybooks). (Illus.). (J). (gr. 3 up). 1990. 50.95 (*0-8378-1853-2*) Gibson.
— The Story of Ruth & Naomi. (Alice in Bibleland Storybooks). (Illus.). (J). (gr. 3 up). 1990. 5.95 (*0-8378-1855-9*) Gibson.
— The Story of the Good Samaritan. (Alice in Bibleland Storybooks). (Illus.). (J). (gr. 3 up). 1990. 5.95 (*0-8378-1854-0*) Gibson.
— The Story of the Loaves & Fishes. (Alice in Bibleland Storybooks). (Illus.). 32p. (J). (ps-3). 1985. 5.95 (*0-8378-5073-8*) Gibson.
— The Story of the Lost Sheep. (Alice in Bibleland Storybooks). (Illus.). (J). (gr. 3 up). 1990. 5.95 (*0-8378-1865-6*) Gibson.
— The Story of the Prodigal Son. (Alice in Bibleland Storybooks). (Illus.). (J). (gr. 3 up). 1990. 5.95 (*0-8378-1848-6*) Gibson.
— The Story of the Tower of Babel. (Alice in Bibleland Storybooks). (Illus.). (J). (gr. 3 up). 1990. 5.95 (*0-8378-1866-4*) Gibson.
— Zacchaeus & the Tall Tree. (Bible Friends Ser.). (Illus.). 12p. (J). (ps). bds. 3.99 (*0-310-97578-6*) Zondervan.
***Davidson, Alice Joyce.** Baby Blessings Bible. (Baby Blessings Ser.). (Illus.). 22p. (J). 2000. 12.99 (*0-7847-1189-5*, 04329) Standard Pub.
— Basket Bed for Baby Moses. (Baby Blessings Ser.). (Illus.). 14p. (J). (ps-k). 2000. 7.99 (*0-7847-1141-0*) Standard Pub.
— Five Little Loaves & Two Little Fish. (Baby Blessings Ser.). (Illus.). 14p. (J). (ps-3). 2000. bds. 7.99 (*0-7847-1142-9*, 04322) Standard Pub.
— God Loves Baby. (Baby Blessings Ser.). (Illus.). 2000. 12.99 (*0-7847-1187-9*, 04327) Standard Pub.
— How Many Sheep? A Bible Counting Book. (Baby Blessings Ser.). (Illus.). 12p. (J). 2000. bds. 7.99 (*0-7847-1138-0*, 04318) Standard Pub.
Davidson, Alice Joyce. Jesus & the Children. 1999. 3.99 (*0-310-97601-4*) Zondervan.
***Davidson, Alice Joyce.** Story of Joseph & His Rainbow Coat. 1999. 5.95 (*0-7667-1733-X*) Gibson.
Davidson, Alison. Metal Power: The Soul Life of the Planets. Brown, Tom, ed. LC 91-76081. 112p. (Orig.). 1991. pap. 8.95 (*0-945685-11-4*) Borderland Sciences.
Davidson, Alison, jt. auth. see Veggi, Athon.
***Davidson, Alistair & Gellman, Harvey.** Riding the Tiger: How to Outsmart the Computer That is After Your Job, How Not to Bankrupt Your Organization with Information Management, How Good Clients Get Exceptional Results. LC 99-21663. (Illus.). 278p. 1999. pap. 16.95 (*1-57112-099-8*) Park Ave.
Davidson, Alistair, et al. Riding the Tiger. 336p. 1998. pap. 15.00 (*0-00-638507-9*) HarpC.
Davidson, Alistair, jt. ed. see Wright, Steve.

Davidson, Alma M. & Pineda, Leonardo A. Kapampangan Newspaper Reader. LC 91-75539. (Philippine Language Ser.). 105p. 1992. 43.00 (*0-931745-77-2*) Dunwoody Pr.
Davidson, Alvie L. Florida Land: Records of the Tallahassee & Newmansville General Lane Office, 1825-1892. (Illus.). xii, 305p. (Orig.). 1997. pap. 23.00 (*1-55613-233-6*, D083) Heritage Bk.
Davidson, Amanda. Tapestry Cats & Dogs. (Illus.). 128p. 1998. pap. 16.95 (*0-7153-0776-2*, Pub. by D & C Pub) Sterling.
— Tapestry Cats & Dogs: Twenty-Five Complete Projects. (Illus.). 128p. 1995. 24.95 (*0-7153-0167-5*, Pub. by D & C Pub) Sterling.
— Teddy's Christmas Cut-Out. (Illus.). 16p. (J). (gr. 4-7). 1990. pap. 2.50 (*0-8167-2197-1*) Troll Communs.
— Teddy's Countdown to Christmas. (Illus.). 16p. (J). (gr. 4-7). 1990. pap. 2.50 (*0-8167-2198-X*) Troll Communs.
Davidson, Andrea. Tiger's Den. (Intrigue Ser.). 1992. per. 2.89 (*0-373-22203-3*, 1-22203-3) Harlequin Bks.
Davidson, Andrea L. Embrace the Dawn: One Woman's Story of Triumph over Epilepsy. LC 88-92687. (Illus.). 144p. (Orig.). 1989. pap. 10.95 (*0-9621761-1-7*) Sylvan Creek Pr.
Davidson, Andrew P. In the Shadow of History: The Passing of Lineage Society. 344p. (C). 1996. text 44.95 (*1-56000-230-1*) Transaction Pubs.
Davidson, Andrew S. & Herskovitz, Michael D. Mortgage-Backed Securities: Investment Analysis & Advanced Valuation Techniques. 300p. 1993. text 65.00 (*1-55738-440-1*, Irwn Prfssnl) McGraw-Hill Prof.
— The Mortgage-Backed Securities Workbook: Hands-on Analysis, Valuation, & Strategies For Investment Decision Making. 224p. 1996. pap. 50.00 (*1-55738-915-2*, Irwn Prfssnl) McGraw-Hill Prof.
Davidson, Andrew S., et al. Collateralized Mortgage Obligations: Analysis, Valuation & Portfolio Strategy. 1994. text 75.00 (*1-55738-499-1*, Irwn Prfssnl) McGraw-Hill Prof.
Davidson, Angela. Samples & Motifs in Cross Stitch. (Illus.). 1999. pap. 6.95 (*1-85391-681-1*) Tuttle Pubng.
Davidson, Angus, tr. see Berto, Giuseppe.
Davidson, Angus, tr. see Ginzburg, Natalia.
Davidson, Angus, tr. see Moravia, Alberto, pseud.
Davidson, Ann. Alzheimer's, A Love Story: One Year in My Husband's Journey. LC 96-51668. 224p. 1997. 19.95 (*1-55972-418-8*, Birch Ln Pr) Carol Pub Group.
— Modified Radical & Other Cancer Poems. 32p. (Orig.). 1990. pap. 5.00 (*0-9627007-0-3*) Monday Pr CA.
Davidson, Ann, et al, eds. Second Harvest: More Life Stories of the Twentieth Century. 352p. (Orig.). 1988. pap. 8.00 (*0-945131-00-3*) Terrace Pr.
Davidson, Ann L. Making & Molding Identity in Schools: Student Narratives on Race, Gender, & Academic Engagement. LC 95-47050. (SUNY Series in Power, Social Identity, & Education). 257p. (C). 1996. pap. text 19.95 (*0-7914-3082-0*) State U NY Pr.
Davidson, Ann L. & Phelan, Patricia J. Renegotiating Cultural Diversity in American Schools. LC 93-22720. 272p. (C). 1993. text 44.00 (*0-8077-3288-5*) Tchrs Coll.
Davidson, Ann L., jt. auth. see Phelan, Patricia.
***Davidson, Anthony.** Wayne Gretzky. (Illus.). 256p. 1999. 14.99 (*1-55263-098-6*) Key Porter.
Davidson, Apollon. The Russians & the Anglo-Boer War, 1899-1902. LC 98-173354. 1998. pap. text 35.00 (*0-7981-3804-1*) Human & Rousseau.
Davidson, Arnold, ed. see Hadot, Pierre.
Davidson, Arnold E. Conrad's Endings: A Study of the Five Major Novels. Litz, A. Walton, ed. LC 84-8508. (Studies in Modern Literature: No. 39). 134p. reprint ed. pap. 41.60 (*0-8357-1587-6*, 207044200090) Bks Demand.
— Coyote Country: Fictions of the Canadian West. LC 93-43231. (New Americanists Ser.). 168p. 1994. text 49.95 (*0-8223-1453-3*); pap. text 16.95 (*0-8223-1469-X*) Duke.
— Seeing in the Dark No. 35: Margaret Atwood's Cat's Eye. LC 98-140673. (Canadian Fiction Studies). 120p. 1997. pap. 14.95 (*1-55022-312-7*, Pub. by ECW) Genl Dist Srvs.
Davidson, Arnold E., ed. Studies on Canadian Literature: Introductory & Critical Essays. LC 90-6529. v, 371p. 1991. pap. 19.75 (*0-87352-380-6*, T125P); lib. bdg. 37.50 (*0-87352-199-4*, T125C) Modern Lang.
Davidson, Arnold I. Foucault & His Interlocutors. LC 96-50315. 272p. 1998. pap. 17.95 (*0-226-13714-7*) U Ch Pr.
Davidson, Arnold I., ed. Foucault & His Interlocutors. LC 96-50315. 325p. 1997. 30.00 (*0-226-13713-9*) U Ch Pr.
Davidson, Art. Discover Alaska: An Introduction to America's Last Frontier. LC 91-31722. (Illus.). 64p. (Orig.). 1995. pap. 10.95 (*0-88240-412-1*, Alaska NW Bks) Gr Arts Ctr Pub.
— Endangered Peoples. LC 93-22026. (Sierra Club Guides Ser.). (Illus.). 176p. 1994. pap. 20.00 (*0-87156-423-8*, Pub. by Sierra) Random.
— In the Wake of the Exxon Valdez: The Devastating Impact of the Alaska Oil Spill. LC 89-29294. (Illus.). 224p. 1990. 24.00 (*0-87156-614-1*, Pub. by Sierra) Random.
***Davidson, Art.** Minus 148 Degrees. 3rd ed. 1999. pap. text 14.95 (*0-89886-687-1*) Mountaineers.
Davidson, Art. Minus 148 Degrees: First Winter Ascent of Mt. McKinley. 2nd enl. rev. ed. (Illus.). 254p. 1987. pap. 14.95 (*0-938567-00-4*) Mountaineers.
— Wilderness Homestead. (Alaska Christmas Ser.: No. I). (Illus.). 16p. 1991. 55.00 (*0-9630863-3-2*); pap. 20.00 (*0-9630863-2-4*) Limner Pr.
Davidson, Art, ed. see Wolfe, Art.
Davidson, Arthur T. The Racial Equation: Pontius Pilate Plus Judus Iscariot Equals Crucification. 1986. write for info. (*0-933389-00-0*) Northeastern Pub.

***Davidson, Astrid.** Como Conquistar Su Propia Aceptacion: La Guia Que Transformara Su Vida. (SPA.). 123p. 1999. pap. 10.00 (*0-9664420-2-4*) Healing Pr.
— Ejercision Para Conquistar Su Propia Aceptacion. (SPA.). 23p. 1999. pap. 5.00 (*0-9664420-6-7*) Healing Pr.
Davidson, Astrid. Embracing Self-Acceptance. 160p. 1998. pap. 12.00 (*0-9664420-0-8*) Healing Pr.
— The Self-Acceptance Workbook. 21p. 1999. pap. 5.00 (*0-9664420-1-6*) Healing Pr.
Davidson, Audrey. Substance & Manner: Studies in Music & the Other Arts. (Illus.). 1977. pap. 4.95 (*0-930276-00-0*) Hiawatha Pr.
Davidson, Audrey E. Holy Week & Easter Ceremonies & Dramas from Medieval Sweden. (Early Drama, Art & Music Monograph: No. 13). 1990. pap. 12.95 (*0-918720-37-0*); boxed set 22.95 (*0-918720-35-2*) Medieval Inst.
Davidson, Audrey E., ed. The Ordo Virtutum of Hildegard of Bingen: Critical Studies. (Early Drama, Art & Music Monograph: No. 18). 1992. pap. 13.00 (*1-879288-18-4*); boxed set 25.00 (*1-879288-17-6*) Medieval Inst.
Davidson, Audrey E., et al. Performing Medieval Music Drama. LC 97-41852. 1997. pap. 5.00 (*1-879288-96-6*) Medieval Inst.
Davidson, Audrey E., tr. see Steel, Matthew & Batch, Nicholas, eds.
Davidson, Avram. The Adventures of Doctor Eszterhazy. (Illus.). 1991. 24.50 (*0-913896-28-4*) Owlswick Pr.
— The Avram Davidson Treasury. Silverberg, Robert & Davis, Grania, eds. LC 98-23556. 447p. 1998. 27.95 (*0-312-86729-8*, Pub. by Tor Bks) St Martin.
***Davidson, Avram.** The Avram Davidson Treasury Silverberg, Robert & Davis, Granis, eds. 448p. 1999. pap. 17.95 (*0-312-86731-X*, Pub. by Tor Bks) St Martin.
Davidson, Avram. The Investigations of Avram Davidson. Davis, Grania & Lupoff, Richard A., eds. LC 98-44012. 1999. text 24.95 (*0-312-19931-7*) St Martin.
— The Redward Edward Papers. LC 74-27578. 208p. 1978. 25.00 (*0-89366-265-8*) Ultramarine Pub.
— Strange Seas & Shores. 1993. reprint ed. lib. bdg. 18.95 (*0-89968-337-1*, Lghtyr Pr) Buccaneer Bks.
Davidson, Avran & Davis, Grania. The Boss in the Wall: A Treatise on the House Devil. 1998. pap. 12.00 (*0-9648320-9-7*) Tachyon Pubns.
***Davidson, B. LeRoy.** Lewisias. LC 99-53481. (Illus.). 238p. 2000. 34.95 (*0-88192-447-4*) Timber.
Davidson, Basil Risbridger. Africa in History. rev. expanded ed. 480p. 1995. per. 16.00 (*0-684-82667-4*) S&S Trade.
— African Civilization Revisited: From Antiquity to Modern Times. rev. ed. LC 88-83120. Orig. Title: The African Past. 460p. (C). 1990. pap. 18.95 (*0-86543-124-8*) Africa World.
— African Civilization Revisited: From Antiquity to Modern Times. 2nd rev. ed. LC 88-83120. Orig. Title: The African Past. 460p. (C). 1990. 39.95 (*0-86543-123-X*) Africa World.
— The African Slave Trade. enl. rev. ed. 304p. 1988. pap. 15.95 (*0-316-17438-6*) Little.
— Afrika i DFet Tjudonde Seklet. (Afrikabiblioteket Ser.: Nr. 2). 306p. 1991. write for info. (*91-7106-316-1*, Pub. by Nordic Africa) Transaction Pubs.
— The Black Man's Burden: Africa & the Curse of the Nation State. LC 92-38427. 368p. 1993. pap. 15.00 (*0-8129-2210-7*, Times Bks) Crown Pub Group.
— The Fortunate Isles. LC 88-83119. (Illus.). 300p. (C). 1989. 35.95 (*0-86543-121-3*); pap. 11.95 (*0-86543-122-1*) Africa World.
— Kap Verde - De Lyckliga Oarna. (Afrikabiblioteket Ser.: Nr. 1). 232p. 1990. write for info. (*91-7106-301-3*, Pub. by Nordic Africa) Transaction Pubs.
— Lost Cities of Africa. rev. ed. 366p. 1988. pap. 16.95 (*0-316-17431-9*) Little.
— Modern Africa. 2nd ed. LC 82-14941. (Illus.). 289p. (C). 1989. pap. text 17.50 (*0-582-01900-1*, 78284) Longman.
— Modern Africa. 3rd ed. LC 93-3815. 320p. (C). 1995. pap. text 31.88 (*0-582-21288-X*, 76250, Pub. by Addison-Wesley) Longman.
— The People's Cause: A History of Guerrillas in Africa. LC 81-201497. (Longman Studies in African History). (Illus.). 222p. reprint ed. pap. 68.90 (*0-8357-6590-3*, 203598500097) Bks Demand.
— Scenes from the Anti-Nazi War. LC 81-81696. 294p. reprint ed. pap. 91.20 (*0-7837-3920-6*, 204376800010) Bks Demand.
Davidson, Basil Risbridger & Bronda, Antonio. Crossroads in Africa. 99p. 1980. 33.50 (*0-85124-245-6*, Pub. by Spkesman); pap. 17.95 (*0-85124-246-4*, Pub. by Spkesman) Coronet Bks.
Davidson, Basil Risbridger, jt. auth. see Bourgeois, Jean-Louis.
Davidson, Basil Risbridger, jt. ed. see Cliffe, Lionel.
Davidson, Ben, jt. ed. see Barker, Philip J.
Davidson, Benjamin. The Analytical Hebrew & Chaldee Lexicon. (ENG & HEB.). 784p. 1981. 27.95 (*0-913573-03-5*) Hendrickson MA.
— The Analytical Hebrew & Chaldee Lexicon. (ENG & HEB.). 896p. 1993. reprint ed. 29.99 (*0-310-39891-6*) Zondervan.
Davidson, Bernice, et al. Paintings from the Frick Collection. (Illus.). 146p. 1991. 49.50 (*0-8109-3710-7*, Pub. by Abrams) Time Warner.
Davidson, Bernice F. Raphael's Bible: A Study of the Vatican Logge. LC 84-43088. (College Art Association Monographs: Vol. 39). (Illus.). 198p. 1985. 40.00 (*0-271-00388-X*) Pa St U Pr.
***Davidson, Betsy.** Twyla Tulip & Her Talking Toes: A Friendship Story. (Illus.). 17p. 1999. pap. 5.95 (*1-57543-080-0*) Mar Co Prods.
Davidson, Bill. Spencer Tracy, Tragic Idol. 1989. mass mkt. 5.99 (*0-8217-3738-4*, Zebra Kensgtn) Kensgtn Pub Corp.

Davidson, Bill, jt. auth. see Davis, Stan M.
Davidson, Bob. Hillary & Tenzing Climb Everest. (Great Twentieth Century Expeditions Ser.). (Illus.). 32p. (YA). (gr. 5 up). 1993. lib. bdg. 13.95 (*0-87518-534-7*, Dillon Silver Burdett) Silver Burdett Pr.
Davidson, Bruce. Brooklyn Gang: Summer 1959. (Illus.). 96p. 1998. 60.00 (*0-944092-50-0*) Twin Palms Pub.
— Bruce Davidson: Brooklyn Gang. limited ed. (Illus.). 96p. 1998. 750.00 (*0-944092-51-9*) Twin Palms Pub.
***Davidson, Bruce.** Bruce Davidson: Portraits. (Illus.). 72p. 1999. text 35.00 (*0-89381-851-8*) Aperture.
Davidson, Bruce, photos by. Central Park. LC 95-76135. (Illus.). 40p. 1995. 60.00 (*0-89381-625-6*) Aperture.
Davidson, C. Machine Vision for Neural Networks. 1993. text. write for info. (*0-442-01476-7*, VNR) Wiley.
***Davidson, C. L. & Mjhor, Ivar A.** Advances in Glass-Ionomer Cements. LC 99-22881. 18p. 1999. write for info. (*0-86715-360-1*) Quint Pub Co.
Davidson, C. Melvin, jt. auth. see Askin, Leon.
Davidson, C. T. Upon This Rock, 3 vols., 1. 692p. 1973. 19.95 (*0-934942-16-1*) White Wing Pub.
— Upon This Rock, 3 vols., 2. 692p. 1973. 14.95 (*0-934942-17-X*) White Wing Pub.
— Upon This Rock, 3 vols., 3. 692p. 1973. 17.95 (*0-934942-18-8*) White Wing Pub.
Davidson, C. T., jt. auth. see Willing, Ora M.
Davidson, Carl. The New Radicals in the Multiversity: A 1968 Manifesto of Students for a Democratic Society. (Sixties Ser.). 64p. (Orig.). 1990. reprint ed. pap. 9.00 (*0-88286-177-8*); reprint ed. lib. bdg. 24.95 (*0-88286-178-6*) C H Kerr.
— Recent Developments in the Theory of Involuntary Unemployment. LC 90-21175. 171p. 1990. text 24.00 (*0-88099-105-4*); pap. text 14.00 (*0-88099-106-2*) W E Upjohn.
Davidson, Carol M. Bram Stoker's Dracula: Sucking Through the Century,1897-1997. LC 98-101620. 432p. 1997. mass mkt. 22.00 (*1-55002-279-2*) DUN.
Davidson, Caroline, et al. Uncivilizing: A Collection of Poetry. LC 98-115127. 112p. 1998. 9.99 (*1-895837-17-0*) Insomniac.
***Davidson, Carolyn.** The Bachelor Tax. (Historical Ser.: No. 496). 2000. per. 4.99 (*0-373-29096-9*, 1-29096-4, Harlequin) Harlequin Bks.
Davidson, Carolyn. The Forever Man. 1997. per. 4.99 (*0-373-28985-5*, 1-28985-9) Harlequin Bks.
— Gerrity's Bride. LC 96-705. 296p. 1995. per. 4.50 (*0-373-28898-0*, 1-28898-4) Harlequin Bks.
— Loving Katherine. (Harlequin Historical Ser.: No. 325). 1996. per. 4.99 (*0-373-28925-1*, 1-28925-5) Harlequin Bks.
— The Midwife. (Historical Ser.). 1999. per. 4.99 (*0-373-29075-6*, 1-29075-8) Harlequin Bks.
— Runaway. (Historical Ser.). 1998. per. 4.99 (*0-373-29016-0*, 1-29016-2) Harlequin Bks.
***Davidson, Carolyn.** Tanner Stakes His Claim. (Historical Ser.: Vol. 513). 299p. 2000. per. 4.99 (*0-373-29113-2*) Harlequin Bks.
Davidson, Carolyn. The Tender Stranger. 304p. 1999. per. 4.99 (*0-373-29056-X*, 1-29056-8, Harlequin) Harlequin Bks.
— The Wedding Promise. (Historical Ser.: Vol. 431). 1998. per. 4.99 (*0-373-29031-4*, 1-29031-1) Harlequin Bks.
— Word-a-Holic Quiz Book: Guess the Real Words You Won't Believe. LC 95-9431. 128p. 1995. pap. 5.95 (*0-8069-0702-9*) Sterling.
***Davidson, Carolyn, et al.** One Christmas Wish: Wish upon a Star; Christmas Wishes; More Than a Miracle. (Historical Ser.: Bk. 531). 2000. mass mkt. 4.99 (*0-373-29131-0*, 1-29131-9) Harlequin Bks.
Davidson, Carolyn, jt. auth. see Banks, Pat.
Davidson, Cassie, jt. auth. see Davidson, Karl.
Davidson, Catherine T. The Priest Fainted: A Novel. LC 97-36726. 1998. 23.00 (*0-8050-5539-8*) H Holt & Co.
— The Priest Fainted: A Novel. 272p. 1999. pap. 12.00 (*0-8050-6109-6*, Pub. by H Holt & Co) VHPS.
Davidson, Cathy N. The Experimental Fictions of Ambrose Bierce: Structuring the Ineffable. LC 83-16844. 176p. reprint ed. pap. 54.60 (*0-7837-6876-1*, 204670600003) Bks Demand.
— Ideology & Genre: The Rise of the Novel in America. 28p. 1987. reprint ed. pap. 4.95 (*0-912296-88-7*) Am Antiquarian.
— New Melville, Vol. 66, No. 1. 1994. pap. 10.00 (*0-8223-6407-7*) Duke.
— Revolution & the Word: The Rise of the Novel in America. (Illus.). 336p. 1988. pap. text 13.95 (*0-19-505653-1*) OUP.
— 36 Views of Mount Fuji: On Finding Myself in Japan. 320p. 1994. pap. 13.95 (*0-452-27240-8*, Plume) Dutton Plume.
Davidson, Cathy N., ed. No More Separate Spheres. (Best from American Literature Ser.: Vol. 70, No. 3). 275p. 1998. pap. 12.00 (*0-8223-6462-X*) Duke.
— Reading in America: Literature & Social History. LC 88-35821. 320p. 1989. pap. text 16.95 (*0-8018-3800-2*) Johns Hopkins.
Davidson, Cathy N. & Wagner-Martin, Linda, eds. The Oxford Companion to Women's Writing in the United States. 1056p. 1995. 60.00 (*0-19-506608-1*) OUP.
— The Oxford Companion to Women's Writing in the United States. 1021p. 1999. reprint ed. text 45.00 (*0-7881-6143-1*) DIANE Pub.
Davidson, Cathy N., jt. auth. see Bamberger, William L.
Davidson, Cathy N., jt. ed. see Moon, Michael.
Davidson, Cathy N., jt. ed. see Wagner-Martin, Linda.
Davidson, Chandler. Race & Class in Texas Politics. (Illus.). 372p. 1990. pap. text 17.95 (*0-691-02539-8*, Pub. by Princeton U Pr) Cal Prin Full Svc.

D

An Asterisk (*) at the beginning of an entry indicates that the title is appearing for the first time.

Davidson, Chandler, ed. Minority Vote Dilution. LC 84-10883. 298p. 1989. pap. 14.95 (0-88258-176-7) Howard U Pr.

Davidson, Chandler, jt. ed. see Grofman, Bernard N.

Davidson, Charles. Studies in the English Mystery Plays. LC 68-752. (Studies in Drama: No. 39). 1969. reprint ed. lib. bdg. 75.00 (0-8383-0536-9) M S G Haskell Hse.

Davidson, Charles & Diamant, Lincoln. Stamping Our History: The Story of the United States Portrayed on Its Postage Stamps. 1990. 49.95 (0-8184-0532-5) Carol Pub Group.

Davidson, Charles S. & Diamant, Lincoln. Stamping Our History: The Story of the United States Portrayed on Its Postage Stamps. 2nd ed. (Illus.). 272p. 1995. pap. 24.95 (0-8065-1691-7, Citadel Pr) Carol Pub Group.

Davidson, Christine. Best Places to Stay in Florida. 5th ed. (Best Places to Stay Ser.). (Illus.). 512p. 1999. pap. 18.00 (0-395-86941-2) HM.

***Davidson, Christine.** Best Places to Stay in Florida. 6th ed. (Best Places to Stay Ser.). (Illus.). 2000. pap. text 19.00 (0-618-00534-X) HM.

Davidson, Christine. Staying Home Instead: How to Be There for Your Kids While Balancing Your Life (And Your Checkbook) LC 97-45097. 227p. 1998. pap. text 21.95 (0-7879-3940-4) Jossey-Bass.

Davidson, Clarissa S. God's Man: The Story of Pastor Niemoeller. LC 78-10131. 242p. 1979. reprint ed. lib. bdg. 55.00 (0-313-21065-9, DAGM, Greenwood Pr) Greenwood.

Davidson, Clay, ed. see Simpson, George L., III.

Davidson, Clayton W., III, ed. see Huggard, John P.

Davidson, Cliff I. Clean Hands: Clair Patterson's Crusade Against Environmental Lead Contamination. LC 98-21167. 1998. 39.00 (1-56072-568-0) Nova Sci Pubs.

Davidson, Cliff I. & Ambrose, Susan A. The New Professor's Handbook: A Guide to Teaching & Research in Engineering & Science. 216p. (C). 1994. pap. text 24.95 (1-882982-01-0) Anker Pub.

Davidson, Clifford. From Creation to Doom: The York Cycle of Mystery Plays. LC 83-45273. (Studies in the Middle Ages: No. 5). (Illus.). 1984. 39.50 (0-404-61435-3) AMS Pr.

— The Guild Chapel Wall Paintings at Stratford-upon-Avon. LC 86-47844. (Studies in the Renaissance: No. 22). 1988. 46.50 (0-404-62292-5) AMS Pr.

— Material Culture & Medieval Drama. LC 98-54791. (Early Drama, Art, & Music Monographic Ser. : Vol. 25). 11p. 1999. pap. 15.00 (1-58044-021-5) Medieval Inst.

— On Tradition: Essays on the Use & Valuation of the Past. LC 91-57959. (Studies in the Middle Ages: No. 20). (Illus.). 250p. 1992. 45.00 (0-404-64160-1) AMS Pr.

— Star Poems & Other Poems. LC 76-27932. (Illus.). 1976. pap. 5.00 (0-87423-021-7) Westburg.

— Technology, Guilds, & Early English Drama. LC 96-32689. (Early Drama, Art & Music Monograph). 1996. pap. 15.00 (1-879288-80-X); boxed set 35.00 (1-879288-79-6) Medieval Inst.

— Visualizing the Moral Life. LC 88-47809. (AMS Studies in the Middle Ages: No. 16). 1989. 39.50 (0-404-61446-9) AMS Pr.

Davidson, Clifford, ed. Drama & the Classical Heritage: Comparative & Critical Essays. LC 91-57957. (Ancient & Classical Studies: No. 1). 1993. 47.50 (0-404-64301-9) AMS Pr.

— Fools & Folly. (EDAM Monograph: Vol. 22). 1996. pap. 15.00 (1-879288-70-2); boxed set 35.00 (1-879288-69-9) Medieval Inst.

— The Iconography of Heaven. LC 96-124468. (EDAM Monograph: Series 21). 1994. pap. 15.00 (1-879288-49-4); boxed set 30.00 (1-879288-48-6) Medieval Inst.

— Illustrations of the Stage & Acting in England to 1580. (Early Drama, Art & Music Monograph: No. 17). 1992. pap. 19.95 (0-918720-48-6); boxed set 39.95 (0-918720-47-8) Medieval Inst.

— The Saint Play in Medieval Europe. (Early Drama, Art & Music Monograph: No. 8). 1987. pap. 15.95 (0-918720-78-8); boxed set 25.95 (0-918720-77-X) Medieval Inst.

Davidson, Clifford, ed. Torquato Tasso's Aminta Englisht: The Henry Reynolds Translation of 1628. LC 72-78233. (North American Mentor Texts & Studies: No. 1). (Illus.). 80p. 1972. pap. 16.50 (0-87423-007-1) Westburg.

Davidson, Clifford, ed. A Tretise of Miraclis Pleyinge. (Early Drama, Art & Music Monograph: Vol. 19). 1993. pap. 15.00 (1-879288-32-X); boxed set 36.00 (1-879288-31-1) Medieval Inst.

— Word, Picture & Spectacle. (Early Drama, Art & Music Monograph: No. 5). 1984. pap. 10.95 (0-918720-50-8); boxed set 17.95 (0-918720-51-6) Medieval Inst.

Davidson, Clifford, et al, eds. Drama in the Middle Ages: Comparative & Critical Essays. LC 81-68995. (Studies in the Middle Ages: No. 4). 400p. 1982. reprint ed. 39.50 (0-404-61434-5) AMS Pr.

— Drama in the Middle Ages: Comparative & Critical Essays, Second Series. LC 90-1191. (Studies in the Middle Ages: No. 18). 1991. 47.50 (0-404-61448-5) AMS Pr.

— Drama in the Renaissance: Comparative & Critical Essays. LC 83-45277. (Studies in the Renaissance: No. 12). 1986. 39.50 (0-404-62282-8) AMS Pr.

— Drama in the Twentieth Century: Comparative & Critical Essays. LC 83-45289. (Studies in Modern Literature: No. 11). (Illus.). 1984. 39.50 (0-404-61581-3) AMS Pr.

— Emblem, Iconography, & Drama. 1994. pap. 12.00 (1-879288-57-5) Medieval Inst.

Davidson, Clifford & Alexander, Jennifer. The Early Art of Coventry, Stratford-upon-Avon, Warwick, & Lesser Sites in Warwickshire: A Subject List of Extant & Lost Art Including Items Relevant to Early Drama. (Early Drama, Art & Music Monograph: No. 4). 1985. pap. 15.95 (0-918720-64-8); boxed set 24.95 (0-918720-63-X) Medieval Inst.

***Davidson, Clifford & Happe, Peter.** The Worlde & the Chylde. LC 99-43610. (Early Drama, Art & Music Monograph Ser.: Vol. 26). 1999. pap. 15.00 (1-58044-052-5) Medieval Inst.

***Davidson, Clifford & Happe, Peter, eds.** The Worlde & the Chylde. LC 99-43610. (Early Drama, Art & Music Monograph Ser: Vol. 26). (Illus.). 130p. (C). 1999. 30.00 (1-58044-051-7) Medieval Inst.

Davidson, Clifford & Nichols, Ann E., eds. Iconoclasm vs. Art & Drama. (Early Drama, Art & Music Monograph: No. 11). 1988. pap. 17.95 (0-918720-98-2); boxed set 27.95 (0-918720-97-4) Medieval Inst.

Davidson, Clifford & Seiler, Thomas H., eds. The Iconography of Hell. (Early Drama, Art & Music Monograph: No. 17). 1992. boxed set 30.00 (1-879288-01-X) Medieval Inst.

Davidson, Clifford & Stroupe, John H., eds. Early & Traditional Drama: Africa, Asia, & the New World. 1994. pap. 12.00 (1-879288-43-5) Medieval Inst.

— Iconographic & Comparative Studies in Medieval Drama. 1991. pap. 10.95 (0-918720-49-4) Medieval Inst.

— Medieval Drama on the Continent of Europe. (C). 1993. pap. 12.00 (1-879288-37-0) Medieval Inst.

Davidson, Clifford, jt. ed. see Campbell, Thomas P.

Davidson, Clifford, jt. ed. see King, Pamela M.

Davidson, Conrad E. Commercials: A One-Act Play. (Illus.). 24p. (Orig.). 1990. pap. 3.25 (0-88680-322-5) I E Clark.

Davidson, Cynthia. Eleven Authors in Search of a Building. LC 96-34532. 1997. pap. text 29.95 (1-885254-45-8, Pub. by Monacelli Pr) Penguin Putnam.

— The Over-Fifty Insurance Survival Guide: How to Know What You Need, Get What You Want & Avoid Rip-offs. 1994. pap. 16.95 (1-56343-070-3) Silver Lake.

Davidson, Cynthia, ed. Anybody. LC 97-8118. (Illus.). 287p. 1997. pap. text 35.00 (0-262-54088-6) MIT Pr.

***Davidson, Cynthia, ed.** Anymore. LC 00-35159. (Illus.). 292p. 2000. pap. 35.00 (0-262-54110-6) MIT Pr.

Davidson, Cynthia, ed. Anytime. (Illus.). 300p. 1999. pap. text 35.00 (0-262-54102-5) MIT Pr.

— Legacies for the Future: Contemporary Architecture in Islamic Societies. LC 98-61186. (Illus.). 176p. 1999. pap. 27.50 (0-500-28087-8, Pub. by Thames Hudson) Norton.

Davidson, D. & Aldersmith, H. The Great Pyramid: Its Divine Message. (Illus.). 568p. (Orig.). 1998. reprint ed. spiral bd. 65.00 (1-885395-48-5) Book Tree.

— The Great Pyramid: Its Divine Message. 568p. (Orig.). 1992. reprint ed. pap. 45.00 (1-56459-116-6) Kessinger Pub.

Davidson, D. & Harman, G., eds. Semantics of Natural Language. 2nd ed. LC 73-76427. (Synthese Library: No. 40). 779p. 1973. pap. text 72.50 (90-277-0310-8, D Reidel) Kluwer Academic.

Davidson, D. & Hintikka, K. J., eds. Words & Objections: Essays on the Work of W. V. Quine. (Synthese Library: No. 21). 380p. 1975. pap. text 64.50 (90-277-0602-6, D Reidel) Kluwer Academic.

Davidson, D. A., jt. ed. see Bridges, Edwin M.

Davidson, D. C. Astrology: How to Cast Your Horoscope. 235p. 1979. 9.95 (0-583-13082-8) Asia Bk Corp.

— Spectacles, Lorgnettes & Monocles. 1989. pap. 25.00 (0-85263-957-0, Pub. by Shire Pubns) St Mut.

— Spectacles, Lorgnettes & Monocles. (Shire Album Ser.: No. 227). (Illus.). 32p. 1989. pap. text 5.50 (0-85263-975-9, Pub. by Shire Pubns) Lubrecht & Cramer.

Davidson, D. D. & Magoon, Orville T., eds. Stresses in Concrete Armor Units. LC 90-698. 421p. 1990. pap. text 6.00 (0-87262-760-8) Am Soc Civil Eng.

Davidson, D. D., jt. ed. see Magoon, Orville T.

Davidson, D. Kirk. Selling Sin: The Marketing of Socially Unacceptable Products. LC 96-3621. 240p. 1996. 59.95 (0-89930-994-1, Quorum Bks) Greenwood.

Davidson, D. L. & Lenman, J. A. Neurological Therapeutics. 350p. 1981. pap. 64.95 (0-8464-1216-0) Beekman Pubs.

Davidson, Dale, jt. auth. see Standard, Charles.

Davidson, Dan & Davidson, Dave. A Cup of Devotion with God. LC 98-66305. (Illus.). 80p. 1998. pap. 5.99 (0-89221-426-0) New Leaf.

— The Fragrance of Christmas: Secrets for a Season of Christmas Spirit. LC 98-66304. (Illus.). 80p. 1998. pap. 5.99 (0-89221-425-2) New Leaf.

Davidson, Dan, ed. see Lekic, Maria D., et al.

Davidson, Dan A. Energy: Breakthroughs to New Free Energy Devices History & Current Status of Developed Free Energy Devices. 2nd ed. (Illus.). 121p. (Orig.). 1990. pap. 19.95 (0-9626321-0-4) Rivas Pub.

— Energy: Free Energy, The Aether & Electrification. 53p. 1992. pap. 15.00 (0-9626321-3-9) Rivas Pub.

— Energy: T-Field Energy Research - Recent Free Energy Information. 2nd ed. (Illus.). 60p. 1990. 15.00 (0-9626321-1-2) Rivas Pub.

— Shape Power. LC 97-203507. (Illus.). 176p. (Orig.). 1997. pap. 19.95 (0-9626321-5-5) Rivas Pub.

Davidson, Dan A., compiled by. The Theta Device & Other Free Energy Patents. 82p. 1991. pap. 15.00 (0-9626321-2-0) Rivas Pub.

Davidson, Dan E., ed. see American Councils for International Education Staff.

Davidson, Daniel. Business Law: Principles & Cases in the Legal Environment. 5th ed. (Business Law Ser.). (C). 1996. mass mkt., student ed. 25.95 (0-538-84554-6) S-W Pub.

— Image. 1992. pap. 7.00 (84-87467-15-6, Pub. by Zasterle Pr) SPD-Small Pr Dist.

— Product. 40p. 1991. 6.00 (0-938979-37-X) EG Bksellers.

Davidson, Daniel & Knowles, Brenda E. Business Law: Principles & Cases in the Legal Environment. 6th ed. (Miscellaneous/Catalogs Ser.). (C). 1997. mass mkt., student ed. 20.95 (0-538-86857-0) S-W Pub.

***Davidson, Daniel, et al.** Business Law: Principles & Cases in the Legal Environment. 7th ed. (SWC-Business Law Ser.). 2000. 108.95 (0-324-04080-6) Sth-Wstrn College.

Davidson, Daniel, jt. auth. see Mandel, Tom.

Davidson, Daniel S. Aboriginal Australian & Tasmanian Rock Carvings & Paintings. LC 36-32912. (American Philosophical Society, Philadelphia. Memoirs Ser.: Vol. 5). 175p. reprint ed. pap. 54.30 (0-8357-5012-4, 200035300025) Bks Demand.

— A Preliminary Consideration of Aboriginal Australian Decorative Art. LC 38-6677. (American Philosophical Society, Philadelphia. Memoirs Ser.: Vol. 9). 163p. reprint ed. pap. 50.60 (0-608-11231-3, 200035800025) Bks Demand.

Davidson, Daniel V., et al. Business Law: Principles & Cases. 5th ed. LC 95-32750. (C). 1995. pap. 71.95 (0-538-84553-8) S-W Pub.

— Business Law: Principles & Cases. LC 83-23863. (SWC-Business Law). 1024p. (C). 1984. pap. 37.75 (0-534-01456-9) PWS Pubs.

— Business Law: Principles & Cases. 4th ed. LC 92-26530. (SWC-Business Law). 1199p. 1993. mass mkt. 73.50 (0-534-93280-0) S-W Pub.

Davidson, Dante, jt. auth. see Tyler, Alison.

Davidson, Dave. Biplane Adventures. 112p. 25.00 (0-614-13198-7, 21-10468) EAA Aviation.

Davidson, Dave, jt. auth. see Davidson, Dan.

Davidson, David. Overlords. LC 98-92924. (Illus.). 256p. 1998. pap. 14.95 (0-9664135-0-4) Daves Tree.

Davidson, David, ed. Poetry & Revolution: An Anthology of British & Irish Verse, 1625-1660. LC 97-44267. 716p. 1998. text 135.00 (0-19-818441-7) OUP.

Davidson, David, jt. auth. see Blot, David.

Davidson, David M. & Blot, David. Write from the Start. 2nd ed. LC 93-43511. 144p. (J). 1994. mass mkt. 15.00 (0-8384-4848-8) Heinle & Heinle.

Davidson, Deborah & Peloquin, Suzanne. Making Connections with Others: A Handbook on Interpersonal Practice. 168p. 1998. pap. text 35.00 (1-56900-100-6, 1142) Am Occup Therapy.

Davidson, Denise, et al, eds. 1998 Security Transactions: Taxation of Your Stock & Bond Transactions. 56p. 1998. pap. text 9.95 (0-8080-0316-X) CCH INC.

Davidson, Diane. Deadly Gamble: A Toni Underwood Mystery. 256p. (Orig.). 1997. pap. 11.99 (1-883061-12-1) Rising AZ.

— Deadly Rendezvous: A Toni Underwood Mystery. LC 93-87607. (Orig.). 1994. pap. 9.99 (1-883061-02-4) Rising AZ.

Davidson, Diane, ed. see Moberg, L. Ernest, et al.

Davidson, Diane, ed. & illus. see Shakespeare, William.

Davidson, Diane Mott. Catering to Nobody. 1998. pap. 5.99 (0-449-45833-4) Fawcett.

— Catering to Nobody. 1998. pap. 5.99 (0-449-45882-2) Fawcett.

— Catering to Nobody. LC 98-51455. 1999. write for info. (1-57490-204-0) T T Beeler.

— Catering to Nobody. LC 89-78086. 310p. 1992. reprint ed. mass mkt. 5.99 (0-449-22046-X) Fawcett.

— The Cereal Murders. LC 93-17746. 368p. 1994. mass mkt. 6.50 (0-553-56773-X) Bantam.

— The Cereal Murders. large type ed. LC 99-15867. 1999. write for info. (1-56895-743-2) Wheeler Pub.

— Dying for Chocolate. LC 91-44720. (Culinary Mystery Ser.). (Illus.). 352p. 1993. mass mkt. 6.50 (0-553-56024-7) Bantam.

— The Grilling Season. 432p. 1998. reprint ed. mass mkt. 6.50 (0-553-57466-3) Bantam.

— Killer Pancake. LC 95-10852. 368p. 1996. mass mkt. 6.50 (0-553-57204-0) Bantam.

— Killer Pancake. large type ed. (Cloak & Dagger Ser.). 527p. 1996. lib. bdg. 21.95 (0-7862-0635-7) Thorndike Pr.

— The Last Suppers. LC 94-18886. 304p. 1995. mass mkt. 6.50 (0-553-57258-X, Crimeline) Bantam.

***Davidson, Diane Mott.** The Last Suppers. large type ed. LC 99-11187. 1999. 23.95 (1-56895-640-1) Wheeler Pub.

Davidson, Diane Mott. The Main Corpse. large type ed. LC 96-49135. (Large Print Bks.). 1997. 25.95 (1-56895-409-3) Wheeler Pub.

— The Main Corpse. 384p. 1997. reprint ed. mass mkt. 6.50 (0-553-57463-9, Crimeline) Bantam.

— Prime Cut. LC 98-47822. 1998. 26.95 (1-56895-588-X) Wheeler Pub.

— Prime Cut. 336p. 2000. reprint ed. mass mkt. 6.50 (0-553-57467-1) Bantam.

***Davidson, Diane Mott.** Tough Cookie. LC 99-46457. 304p. 2000. 23.95 (0-553-10723-2) Bantam.

— Tough Cookie. 2000. 30.95 (1-56895-892-7) Wheeler Pub.

Davidson, Dianne. Women on the Warpath: Feminists of the First Wave. LC 98-177873. 1997. pap. 29.95 (1-875560-91-2, Pub. by Univ of West Aust Pr) Intl Spec Bk.

Davidson, Don, ed. see Brenneman, Tim.

Davidson, Donald. The Big Ballad Jamboree. Ellison, Curtis W. & Pratt, William, eds. LC 95-25543. 295p. 1996. 27.00 (0-87805-853-2) U Pr of Miss.

— The Big Ballad Jamboree. 2nd ed. Ellison, Curtis W. & Pratt, William, eds. 295p. 1998. reprint ed. pap. 17.00 (1-57806-098-2) U Pr of Miss.

— Essays on Actions & Events. 320p. 1980. pap. text 24.00 (0-19-824637-4) OUP.

— Inquiries into Truth & Interpretation. 312p. 1984. pap. text 26.00 (0-19-875046-3) OUP.

— Regionalism & Nationalism in the United States: The Attack on Leviathan. 388p. (C). 1991. pap. 24.95 (0-88738-372-6) Transaction Pubs.

— Rivers of America: The Tennessee. Date not set. lib. bdg. 25.95 (0-8488-1969-1) Amereon Ltd.

— Still Rebels, Still Yankees, & Other Essays. fac. ed. LC 70-168395. (Library of Southern Civilization). 304p. 1972. reprint ed. pap. 94.30 (0-7837-7772-8, 204752800007) Bks Demand.

— The Tennessee Vol. 1: The Old River, Frontier to Secession, Vol. 1. LC 91-62454. (Southern Classics Ser.). (Illus.). 342p. (C). 1991. reprint ed. pap. 14.95 (1-879941-01-5) J S Sanders.

— The Tennessee Vol. 2: The New River: Civil War to TVA, Vol. 2. LC 91-62454. (Southern Classics Ser.). (Illus.). 395p. 1992. reprint ed. pap. 14.95 (1-879941-08-2) J S Sanders.

Davidson, Donald, ed. British Poetry of the Eighteen Nineties. reprint ed. 69.00 (0-403-08915-8) Somerset Pub.

Davidson, Donald & Suppes, Patrick C. Decision Making: An Experimental Approach. LC 77-13439. 122p. 1977. reprint ed. lib. bdg. 49.75 (0-8371-9854-2, DAVD, Greenwood Pr) Greenwood.

Davidson, Donald C. The William Wyles Collection: Author-Title Catalog; Subject Catalog, 5 vols., Set. LC 70-19247. 1970. lib. bdg. 1125.00 (0-8371-3268-1, WWA/, Greenwood Pr) Greenwood.

Davidson, Donald E. British Poetry of the Eighteen Nineties. 1988. reprint ed. lib. bdg. 59.00 (0-7812-0087-3) Rprt Serv.

Davidson, Donald W. America's Landfall: The Historic Lighthouses of Cape Cod, Nantucket & Martha's Vineyard. rev. ed. LC 96-67225. (Illus.). 184p. 2000. 16.00 (1-883684-09-9) Peninsula MA.

Davidson, Donald W., ed. see Hough, Henry B.

Davidson, Donna. Lord Langcliffe's Lady. (Zebra Regency Romance Ser.). 288p. 1998. mass mkt. 4.99 (0-8217-5903-5, Zebra Kensgtn) Kensgtn Pub Corp.

— The Seductive Smuggler. 256p. 1997. mass mkt. 4.99 (0-8217-5689-3, Zebra Kensgtn) Kensgtn Pub Corp.

Davidson, Donna, et al. An Evening at Almack's. 288p. 1997. mass mkt. 4.99 (0-8217-5757-1, Zebra Kensgtn) Kensgtn Pub Corp.

Davidson, Doris. The Three Kings. large type ed. (Magna Large Print Ser.). 553p. 1997. 27.99 (0-7505-1115-X, Pub. by Mgna Lrg Print) Ulverscroft.

— Time Shall Reap. large type ed. (Magna Large Print Ser.). 1994. 27.99 (0-7505-0654-7, Pub. by Mgna Lrg Print) Ulverscroft.

Davidson, Doud P. Along the Endless Strip. 225p. (Orig.). (YA). 1992. pap. text 5.95 (0-9630884-2-4) Team Effort.

Davidson, Dustine, jt. auth. see Ward, Dale.

Davidson, E. Formatting Letters & Reports: A Computer User's Guide. Manber, Beverly, ed. LC 91-76254. (Fifty-Minute Ser.). 90p. (Orig.). 1992. pap. 10.95 (1-56052-130-9) Crisp Pubns.

Davidson, E. H., ed. see Poe, Edgar Allan.

Davidson, Edward. World War II: The Personalities. LC 98-111572. (Illus.). 192p. 1998. 29.95 (1-85409-396-7, Pub. by Arms & Armour) Sterling.

***Davidson, Edward & Manning, Dale.** Chronology of World War Two. (Illus.). 288p. 1999. 29.95 (0-304-35309-4, Pub. by Cassell) Sterling.

Davidson, Edward H. Poe: A Critical Study. LC 57-12965. 310p. reprint ed. pap. 96.10 (0-7837-3834-X, 204365500010) Bks Demand.

Davidson, Edward H. & Scheick, William J. Paine, Scripture, & Authority: The Age of Reason As Religious & Political Ideal. LC 92-55135. 1994. 29.50 (0-934223-29-7) Lehigh Univ Pr.

Davidson, Eleanor J. Business Writing at Work. LC 93-29856. 272p. (C). 1993. text 25.00 (0-256-14220-3, Irwn Prfssnl) McGraw-Hill Prof.

Davidson, Elizabeth H. Establishment of the English Church in Continental American Colonies. (Duke University. Trinity College Historical Society. Historical Papers: No. 20). reprint ed. 30.00 (0-404-51770-6) AMS Pr.

Davidson, Elizabeth W., ed. Pathogenesis of Invertebrate Microbial Diseases. LC 81-65007. 576p. 1981. text 65.00 (0-86598-014-4) Rowman.

***Davidson, Ellen.** Goodnight Around the World. Wise, Noreen, ed. (Illus.). 32p. (J). (ps up). 2000. pap. 5.95 (1-58584-352-0) Huckleberry CT.

— I Miss You. Wise, Noreen, ed. 32p. (YA). (ps). 2000. pap. 5.95 (1-58584-354-7) Huckleberry CT.

— Princess Justina Albertina. Wise, Noreen, ed. (Book-a-Day Collection). (Illus.). 32p. (YA). (ps up). 2000. pap. 5.95 (1-58584-366-0) Huckleberry CT.

— Ruby's Hair. Wise, Noreen, ed. (Book-a-Day Collection). (Illus.). 32p. (YA). 2000. pap. 5.95 (1-58584-368-7) Huckleberry CT.

Davidson, Ellen, jt. auth. see Schniedwind, Nancy.

Davidson, Ellis. Gods & Myths of Northern Europe. 256p. 1965. pap. 12.95 (0-14-013627-4) Viking Penguin.

Davidson, Emily, jt. ed. see Santelli, Robert.

***Davidson, Eric A.** You Can't Eat GNP: Economics as Though Ecology Mattered. (Illus.). 272p. 2000. text 24.00 (0-7382-0276-2, Pub. by Perseus Pubng) HarpC.

Davidson, Ernest R. Modern Electronic Structure Theory & Applications in Organic Chemistry. LC 97-27046. 200p. 1997. 28.00 (981-02-3168-7) World Scientific Pub.

Davidson, Eugene. The Death & Life of Germany: An Account of the American Occupation. LC 99-35479. 456p. 1999. pap. 19.95 (0-8262-1249-2) U of Mo Pr.

— The Making of Adolf Hitler: The Birth & Rise of Nazism. LC 96-37316. (Illus.). 448p. 1997. pap. 19.95 (0-8262-1117-8) U of Mo Pr.

D

— The Nuremberg Fallacy. expanded ed. LC 98-8048. 352p. 1998. pap. 19.95 (*0-8262-1201-8*) U of Mo Pr.

*__Davidson, Eugene.__ Reflections on a Disruptive Decade: Essays from the Sixties. 248p. 2000. 29.95 (*0-8262-1297-2*) U of Mo Pr.

Davidson, Eugene. The Trial of the Germans: An Account of the Twenty-Two Defendants Before the International Military Tribunal at Nuremberg. LC 97-21795. 696p. 1997. pap. 24.95 (*0-8262-1139-9*) U of Mo Pr.

— The Unmaking of Adolf Hitler. (Illus.). 536p. (C). 1996. 29.95 (*0-8262-1045-7*) U of Mo Pr.

Davidson, Eugene A., et al, eds. Glycoconjugates: Proceedings of the Eighth International Symposium, Houston, Texas, September 8-13, 1985, 2 vols., Set. LC 85-12353. 720p. 1985. 130.00 (*0-275-90200-5*, C02000, Praeger Pubs) Greenwood.

— Glycoconjugates: Proceedings of the Eighth International Symposium, Houston, Texas, September 8-13, 1985, 2 vols., Vol. 1. LC 85-12353. 1985. 85.00 (*0-275-90201-3*, C02011, Praeger Pubs) Greenwood.

— Glycoconjugates: Proceedings of the Eighth International Symposium, Houston, Texas, September 8-13, 1985, 2 vols., Vol. 2. LC 85-12353. 1985. 85.00 (*0-275-90202-1*, C02022, Praeger Pubs) Greenwood.

Davidson, Fiona M., et al, eds. Teaching Political Geography, Vol. 1. (Illus.). 135p. 1998. pap. 16.95 (*1-884136-15-X*) NCFGE.

Davidson, Florence & Davidson, Miriam. Changing Childhood Prejudice: The Caring Work of the Schools. LC 94-18559. 256p. 1994. 59.95 (*0-89789-395-6*, Bergin & Garvey) Greenwood.

Davidson, Florence E., jt. auth. see Blackman, Margaret B.

Davidson, Fran, jt. auth. see Pelo, Ann.

Davidson, Frank P., et al. Macro-Engineering: Mit Brunel Lectures on Global Infrastructure LC 98-202039. (Horwood Series in Engineering Science). 206p. 1997. write for info. (*1-898563-33-0*, Pub. by Horwood Pub) Paul & Co Pubs.

Davidson, Fraser. The Wages Act. 1986. 142p. (C). 1986. 140.00 (*1-85185-047-3*, Pub. by Blackstone Pr) St Mut.

Davidson, Fred. Principles of Statistical Data Handling. LC 95-41821. 319p. 1996. pap. 23.50 (*0-7619-0103-5*); text 49.95 (*0-7619-0102-7*) Sage.

Davidson, Frederic M., ed. Selected Papers on Photorefractive Materials. LC 93-34008. (Milestone Ser.: Vol. MS 86). 1993. pap. 45.00 (*0-8194-1393-3*) SPIE.

— Selected Papers on Photorefractive Materials. LC 93-34008. (Milestone Ser.: Vol. MS 86/HC). 1993. 55.00 (*0-8194-1394-1*) SPIE.

Davidson, Frena G. The Alzheimer's Sourcebook for Caregivers: A Practical Guide for Getting Through the Day. 240p. 1993. 23.95 (*1-56565-080-8*, Anodyne) Lowell Hse.

— The Alzheimer's Sourcebook for Caregivers: A Practical Guide for Getting Through the Day. 228p. 1994. pap. 15.00 (*1-56565-146-4*) Lowell Hse.

— The Alzheimer's Sourcebook for Caregivers: A Practical Guide for Getting Through the Day. rev. ed. 252p. 1996. pap. 16.00 (*1-56565-483-8*) Lowell Hse.

*__Davidson, Frena G.__ Caregivers Sourcebook. (Illus.). 240p. 2000. pap. 16.95 (*0-7373-0136-8*, 01388W) NTC Contemp Pub Co.

Davidson, G. Spectgroscopic Properties of Inorganic & Organometallic Compounds, Vol. 27. 474p. 1994. 341.00 (*0-85186-981-5*, R6981) CRC Pr.

Davidson, G., ed. see Ebswor.

Davidson, Garber A., ed. see Hartley, James J.

Davidson, George. The Tracks & Landfalls of Bering & Chirikof on the Northwest Coast of America. 44p. 1994. 16.95 (*0-87770-112-1*) Ye Galleon.

Davidson, George, jt. auth. see Maurer, Matthew M.

Davidson, George T., Jr. A Village Pastor Looks Back: A History of the First Christian Church of Freedom, New Hampshire. 1993. pap. 10.00 (*0-945069-02-2*) Freedom Pr Assocs.

Davidson, Gladys R. The Minor Objects. (Corinth Ser.: Vol. 12). (Illus.). xvi, 366p. 1987. reprint ed. 60.00 (*0-87661-122-6*) Am Sch Athens.

Davidson, Glen, ed. The Hospice: Development & Administration. 2nd ed. LC 84-19211. (Death Education, Aging & Health Care Ser.). (Illus.). 300p. (C). 1985. 59.95 (*0-89116-370-0*) Hemisp Pub.

Davidson, Glen W. Understanding Mourning: A Guide for Those Who Grieve. LC 84-14527. 112p. (Orig.). 1984. pap. 9.99 (*0-8066-2080-3*, 10-6805, Augsburg) Augsburg Fortress.

Davidson, Glen W., et al. The Emmet F. Pearson Collection of Disinfected Mail. (Pearson Museum Ser.). (Illus.). 70p. 1992. 15.00 (*0-931369-23-1*) Southern IL Univ Sch.

Davidson, Gordon, jt. auth. see McLaughlin, Corinne.

Davidson, Gordon, jt. auth. see McLaughlin, Corrine.

Davidson, Gordon C. The North West Company. (BCL1 - History - Canada Ser.). 349p. 1991. reprint ed. lib. bdg. 89.00 (*0-7812-6371-9*) Rprt Serv.

Davidson, Grace G. Early Records of Georgia: Wilkes County, 2 vols. 830p. pap. 70.00 (*0-8063-4669-8*) Clearfield Co.

Davidson, Grace G. Historical Collections of the Georgia Chapters Daughters of the American Revolution. 348p. 1998. pap. 30.00 (*0-8063-4568-3*) Clearfield Co.

— Historical Collections of the Georgia Chapters Daughters of the American Revolution Vol. 2: Records of Richmond County, Georgia. 402p. 1995. reprint ed. pap. 35.00 (*0-8063-4581-0*, 9312) Clearfield Co.

Davidson, Graeme, et al, eds. The Oxford Companion to Australian History. (Illus.). 800p. 1999. 75.00 (*0-19-553597-9*) OUP.

*__Davidson, Greg.__ The Everything Magic Book: Everything You Need to Amaze, Baffle & Entertain Your Friends. (Illus.). 304p. 2000. pap. 12.95 (*1-58062-418-9*) Adams Media.

Davidson, Greg & Davidson, Paul. Economics for a Civilized Society. rev. ed. LC 96-10884. 244p. (gr. 13). 1996. text 74.95 (*1-56324-893-X*) M E Sharpe.

— Economics for a Civilized Society. 2nd rev. ed. LC 96-10884. 244p. (C). (gr. 13). 1996. pap. text 34.95 (*1-56324-894-8*) M E Sharpe.

Davidson, Gustav. All Things Are Holy. limited ed. LC 78-146980. (Living Poets' Library). (Illus.). pap. 2.50 (*0-686-01280-1*) Dragons Teeth.

— A Dictionary of Angels: Including the Fallen Angels. (Illus.). 387p. 1994. per. 19.95 (*0-02-907052-X*) Free Pr.

Davidson, H. F., jt. auth. see Certon, M. J.

Davidson, H. R. Katherine Briggs: Story-Teller. LC 96-75145. (Illus.). 210p. 1996. 27.95 (*0-7188-2659-0*, Lutterworth-Parkwest) Parkwest Pubns.

— Myths & Symbols in Pagan Europe: Early Scandinavian & Celtic Religions. (Illus.). 270p. (C). 1988. pap. text 17.95 (*0-8156-2441-7*) Syracuse U Pr.

Davidson, H. W., et al. Manufactured Carbon. 1968. 61.00 (*0-08-012667-7*, Pub. by Pergamon Repr) Franklin.

Davidson, Harold A. Ansley. "Our Ansley Family" Record of the Lives & Times of the Early Members of the Ansley House in America, with Ancestral Tables Covering a Number of the Family Groups of Their Descendants. (Illus.). 97p. 1997. reprint ed. pap. 18.00 (*0-8328-7289-X*); reprint ed. lib. bdg. 28.00 (*0-8328-7288-1*) Higginson Bk Co.

Davidson, Harriet. T. S. Eliot. LC 98-7717. (Longman Critical Readers Ser.). 224p. (C). 1998. pap. 34.60 (*0-582-06153-9*) Longman.

— T. S. Eliot. LC 98-7717. (Longman Critical Reader Ser.). (C). 1999. text 62.95 (*0-582-06154-7*) Longman.

— T. S. Eliot & Hermeneutics: Absence & Interpretation in "The Waste Land" LC 84-21757. 143p. 1985. text 25.00 (*0-8071-1208-9*) La State U Pr.

Davidson, Harry X. Somebody's Trying to Kill You Vol. I: Psychodynamics of White Racism & Black Pathology. 2nd rev. ed. 137p. pap. write for info. (*0-9644417-1-3*) H R Davidson.

Davidson, Harry X., et al. Somebody's Trying to Kill You Vol. II: The Economics of Death. Lewis, R. H., ed. 158p. pap. 15.00 (*0-9644417-0-5*) H R Davidson.

Davidson, Helene B. The Man in a Country Boy. (Illus.). 185p. (Orig.). 1997. per. 14.95 (*0-9656698-0-7*) H B Davidson.

Davidson, Henry M. Good Christian Men. LC 70-142616. (Essay Index Reprint Ser.). 1977. reprint ed. 21.95 (*0-8369-2390-1*) Ayer.

Davidson, Herbert A. Alfarabi, Avicenna & Averroes on Intellect: Their Cosmologies, Theories of Active Intellect & Theories of the Human Intellect. 384p. 1992. text 65.00 (*0-19-507423-8*) OUP.

— The Philosophy of Abraham Shalom: A Fifteenth-Century Exposition & Defense of Maimonides. LC 65-63470. (University of California Publications, Near Eastern Studies: Vol. 5). 119p. reprint ed. pap. 36.90 (*0-608-10009-9*, 201482000090) Bks Demand.

— Proofs for Eternity, Creation & the Existence of God. 430p. 1996. 49.95 (*0-614-21187-5*, 989) Kazi Pubns.

Davidson, Herbert A., ed. see Averroes.

Davidson, Herbert A., ed. see Averrois.

Davidson, Hilda. Battle God of the Vikings. (C). 1990. 35.00 (*0-7855-5098-4*, Pub. by W Sessions) St Mut.

Davidson, Hilda E. The Lost Beliefs of Northern Europe. LC 92-40808. 240p. (C). (gr. 13). 1993. pap. 22.99 (*0-415-04937-7*) Routledge.

— Roles of the Northern Goddess. LC 97-18309. (Illus.). 224p. (C). 1998. 85.00 (*0-415-13610-5*); pap. 22.99 (*0-415-13611-3*) Routledge.

— The Sword in Anglo-Saxon England: Its Archaeology & literature. (Illus.). 286p. 1998. reprint ed. pap. 35.00 (*0-85115-716-5*) Boydell & Brewer.

Davidson, Hilda E., ed. see Saxo.

*__Davidson, Hilda Ellis & Blacker, Carmen, eds.__ Women & Tradition. 278p. 2000. write for info. (*0-89089-739-5*) Carolina Acad Pr.

*__Davidson, Hilda Ellis & Chaudhri, Anna.__ Supernatural Enemies. 2000. write for info. (*0-89089-711-5*) Carolina Acad Pr.

*__Davidson, Hillary.__ Frommer's Toronto 2001. (Illus.). 2000. pap. 14.99 (*0-7645-6173-1*) IDG Bks.

Davidson, Hollye, jt. auth. see Busch, Julia.

Davidson, Hollye, jt. auth. see Busch, Julia M.

Davidson, Homer L. Build Your Own Test Equipment. 1991. 22.95 (*0-07-015559-3*) McGraw.

— Build Your Own Test Equipment. (Illus.). 300p. 1991. 25.95 (*0-8306-8475-1*, 3475); pap. 17.95 (*0-8306-3475-4*) McGraw-Hill Prof.

— Care & Repair of Lawn & Garden Tools. 272p. 1992. 26.95 (*0-8306-3898-9*, 3753); pap. 14.95 (*0-8306-3897-0*, 3753) McGraw-Hill Prof.

*__Davidson, Homer L.__ Consumer Electronics Components Handbook: How to Identify, Locate, & Test Consumer Electronic Components. LC 98-3964. 1998. 79.95 (*0-07-015807-X*) McGraw.

Davidson, Homer L. Consumer Electronics Troubleshooting & Repairing Handbook. LC 99-19660. 1168p. 1999. 79.00 (*0-07-015809-6*) McGraw.

— Electronic Troubleshooting & Repair Handbook. LC 95-9908. 1008p. 1995. 69.00 (*0-07-015676-X*) McGraw-Hill Prof.

— The Illustrated Home Electronics Fix-it Book. 2nd ed. (Illus.). 432p. 1988. 25.95 (*0-8306-7883-2*); pap. 18.95 (*0-8306-2883-5*) McGraw-Hill Prof.

— Microwave Oven Repair. 2nd ed. (Illus.). 368p. 1991. 29.95 (*0-8306-6457-2*, 3457); pap. 19.95 (*0-8306-3457-6*) McGraw-Hill Prof.

— Practical Microwave Oven Repair. (Illus.). 364p. (Orig.). 1984. pap. 15.95 (*0-8306-1667-5*) McGraw-Hill Prof.

— Radio Receiver Projects You Can Build. 352p. 1994. pap. 21.95 (*0-07-015641-7*) McGraw.

— Radio Receiver Projects You Can Build. 1993. 28.95 (*0-8306-4189-0*); pap. 18.95 (*0-8306-4190-4*) McGraw-Hill Prof.

*__Davidson, Homer L.__ SMD Electronics Projects. Heusel, Kim, ed. LC 00-100354. (Illus.). 296p. 2000. pap. 29.95 (*0-7906-1211-9*) Prompt Publns.

Davidson, Homer L. Troubleshooting & Repairing Audio & Video Cassette Players & Recorders. 432p. 1992. pap. 24.95 (*0-07-157756-4*) McGraw.

— Troubleshooting & Repairing Audio & Video Cassette Players & Recorders. LC 92-9559. 432p. 1992. 29.95 (*0-8306-4259-5*, 3795); pap. 19.95 (*0-8306-4258-7*, 3795) McGraw-Hill Prof.

— Troubleshooting & Repairing Audio Equipment. 2nd ed. LC 92-32380. 1993. write for info. (*0-8306-3808-3*); pap. 19.95 (*0-8306-3807-5*) McGraw-Hill Prof.

— Troubleshooting & Repairing Audio Equipment. 3rd ed. (Illus.). 528p. 1996. pap. 24.95 (*0-07-015756-1*) McGraw.

— Troubleshooting & Repairing Camcorders. 2nd ed. (Illus.). 524p. 1996. 34.95 (*0-07-015759-6*) McGraw.

— Troubleshooting & Repairing Cars. (Illus.). 576p. 1990. 35.95 (*0-8306-8337-2*); pap. 22.95 (*0-8306-3337-5*) McGraw-Hill Prof.

— Troubleshooting & Repairing Compact Disc Players. (Illus.). 368p. 1989. 26.95 (*0-8306-9107-3*, 3107); pap. 18.95 (*0-8306-3107-0*, 3107) McGraw-Hill Prof.

— Troubleshooting & Repairing Compact Disc Players. 3rd ed. (Illus.). 518p. 1996. 44.95 (*0-07-015761-8*); pap. 29.95 (*0-07-015762-6*) McGraw.

— Troubleshooting & Repairing Consumer Electronics Without a Schematic. 2nd ed. LC 96-37281. (Illus.). 528p. 1996. 44.95 (*0-07-015764-2*); pap. 24.95 (*0-07-015765-0*) McGraw.

— Troubleshooting & Repairing Microwave Ovens. 4th ed. (Illus.). 544p. 1996. 44.95 (*0-07-015766-9*); pap. 29.95 (*0-07-015767-7*) McGraw.

— Troubleshooting & Repairing Power Tools. (Illus.). 350p. 1990. pap. 17.95 (*0-8306-3347-2*) McGraw-Hill Prof.

— Troubleshooting & Repairing Solid-State TVs. (Illus.). 480p. 1986. pap. 18.95 (*0-8306-2707-3*, 2707P) McGraw-Hill Prof.

— Troubleshooting & Repairing Solid-State TVs. 2nd ed. 624p. 1992. 36.95 (*0-8306-3894-6*); pap. 24.95 (*0-8306-3893-8*) McGraw-Hill Prof.

— Troubleshooting & Repairing Solid-State TVs. 3rd ed. (Illus.). 619p. 1996. 44.95 (*0-07-015753-7*); pap. 24.95 (*0-07-015754-5*) McGraw.

— Troubleshooting Consumer Audio Circuits. LC 99-64767. 1999. pap. text 34.95 (*0-7906-1165-1*) Prompt Publns.

Davidson, Homer L. & Zwick, George. TV Repair for Beginners. 5th ed. LC 97-25446. (Illus.). 376p. 1997. pap. 24.95 (*0-07-015806-1*) McGraw.

— TV Repair for Beginners. 5th ed. LC 97-25446. (Illus.). 376p. 1998. 44.95 (*0-07-015805-3*) McGraw.

Davidson, Howard. Just Ask: A Handbook for Instructors of Students Being Treated for Mental Disorders. 174p. 1993. pap., teacher ed. 12.95 (*1-55059-058-8*) Temeron Bks.

Davidson, Howard A., et al. Establishing Ombudsman Programs for Children & Youth: How Government's Responsiveness to Its Young Citizens Can Be Improved. LC 93-49628. 220 p. 1993. write for info. (*0-89707-960-4*) Amer Bar Assn.

Davidson, Howard A., jt. auth. see Horowitz, Robert M.

Davidson, Howard S. Schooling in a "Total Institution" Critical Perspectives on Prison Education. LC 94-36221. (Critical Studies in Education & Culture). 248p. 1995. pap. 24.95 (*0-89789-426-X*, Bergin & Garvey) Greenwood.

Davidson, Howard S., ed. Schooling in a "Total Institution" Critical Perspectives on Prison Education. LC 94-36221. (Critical Studies in Education & Culture). 248p. 1995. 65.00 (*0-89789-347-6*, Bergin & Garvey) Greenwood.

Davidson, Hugh M. Blaise Pascal. (World Authors Ser.: No. 701). 165p. 1983. 23.95 (*0-8057-6548-4*, Twayne) Mac Lib Ref.

— The Origins of Certainty: Means & Meanings in Pascal's "Pensees" LC 78-12768. 1993. 16.00 (*0-226-13716-3*) U Ch Pr.

— The Origins of Certainty: Means & Meanings in Pascal's Pensees. LC 78-12768. 170p. reprint ed. pap. 52.70 (*0-608-09443-9*, 205424300005) Bks Demand.

— Pascal & the Arts of the Mind. LC 92-40937. (Cambridge Studies in French: No. 46). 284p. (C). 1993. text 69.95 (*0-521-33193-5*) Cambridge U Pr.

Davidson, Hugh M., ed. see Pascal, Blaise.

Davidson, I. & Hennessen, W., eds. Reduction of Animal Usage in the Development & Control of Biological Products. (Developments in Biological Standardization Ser.: Vol. 64). (Illus.). x, 330p. 1986. pap. 61.00 (*3-8055-4460-X*) S Karger.

Davidson, I., jt. auth. see McGrath, G.

Davidson, I. A., jt. ed. see Foex, P.

Davidson, Iain, jt. auth. see Noble, William.

*__Davidson, Ingemar J.A., ed.__ Kidney & Pancreas Transplantation: Detailed Surgical Procedures & Management Protocols. 2nd ed. (Vademecum Ser.). 228p. 1999. spiral bd. 45.00 (*1-57059-646-8*) Landes Bioscience.

Davidson, Israel. Parody in Jewish Literature. LC 77-163670. (Columbia University. Oriental Studies: No. 2). reprint ed. 37.50 (*0-404-50492-2*) AMS Pr

Davidson, J. Farm Machinery: Practical Hints for Handy-Men. LC 99-32979. 1999. pap. text 12.95 (*1-55821-951-X*) Lyon Press.

— An Introduction to TCP-IP. (Illus.). 110p. 1997. 29.95 (*0-387-96651-X*) Spr-Verlag.

Davidson, J., ed. see Chekhov, Anton.

*__Davidson, J. Brownlee.__ Farm Motors: Practical Hints for Handy-Men. (Illus.). 2000. pap. 12.95 (*1-58574-007-1*) Lyons Pr.

Davidson, J. Kenneth, Sr. & Moore, Nelwyn B. Marriage & Family: Change & Continuity. 2nd ed. LC 95-39047. 704p. 1996. 79.00 (*0-205-16747-0*) Allyn.

Davidson, J. Kenneth & Moore, Nelwyn B. Marriage & Family: Change & Continuity, Examination Copy. 864p. (C). 1996. write for info. (*0-205-18408-1*, H8408-0) Allyn.

Davidson, J. L. Prophets of Deceit. 1960. 5.25 (*0-88027-016-0*) Firm Foun Pub.

Davidson, J. L., et al, eds. Diamond Materials V. LC 98-234758. (Proceedings Ser.: Vol. 97-32). 696p. 1998. 96.00 (*1-56677-185-4*) Electrochem Soc.

Davidson, J. M. Russian Grammar. (Grammar Card Guides Ser.). (ENG & RUS.). 1964. pap. 3.95 (*0-8120-5072-X*) Barron.

Davidson, J. M., jt. ed. see Abatangelo, G.

Davidson, J. Scott. The Inter-American Court of Human Rights. 180p. 1992. text 82.95 (*1-85521-234-X*, Pub. by Dartmth Pub) Ashgate Pub Co.

— The Inter-American Human Rights System. LC 96-36538. (Illus.). 408p. 1997. text 87.95 (*1-85521-776-7*, Pub. by Dartmth Pub) Ashgate Pub Co.

Davidson, Jack W., jt. auth. see Cahoon, James P.

Davidson, James. The Complete Home Lighting Book: Contemporary Interior & Exterior Lighting for the Home. LC 96-45709. (Illus.). 224p. 1997. 39.95 (*0-87951-766-2*, Pub. by Overlook Pr) Penguin Putnam.

— Courtesans & Fishcakes: The Consuming Passions of Classical Athens. LC 99-26020. (Illus.). 416p. 1999. pap. 15.00 (*0-06-097766-3*) HarpC.

*__Davidson, James.__ Econometric Theory. LC 99-45659. (Illus.). 524p. 1999. text 69.95 (*0-631-17837-6*); pap. text 34.95 (*0-631-21584-0*) Blackwell Pubs.

— Garden Lighting: Contemporary Exterior Lighting. (Illus.). 2000. 27.95 (*0-7063-7778-8*) Ward Lock Ltd UK.

Davidson, James. In Touch with Your Breasts: The Answers to Women's Questions about Breast Care. (Illus.). 160p. (YA). Date not set. pap. 9.95 (*1-56796-128-2*) WRS Group.

— Mobilizing Social Movement Organization: The Formation, Institionalization & Effectiveness of Economical Urban Ministries. (Monographs: No. 6). 1985. pap. 8.00 (*0-932566-05-7*) Soc Sci Stud Rel.

*__Davidson, James.__ One Mykonos: Being Ancients, Being Islands, Being Giants, Being Gay. LC 00-29458. 160p. 2000. text 19.95 (*0-312-26214-0*) St Martin.

Davidson, James. Stochastic Limit Theory. (Advanced Texts in Econometrics Ser.). (Illus.). 562p. 1994. pap. text 48.00 (*0-19-877403-6*) OUP.

Davidson, James, ed. Courtesans & Fishcakes: The Consuming Passions of Classical Athens. LC 98-4496. 400p. 1998. text 25.95 (*0-312-18559-6*) St Martin.

Davidson, James & Ninebrenner, Jan. In Touch with Your Breasts. LC 94-30838. 112p. 1994. pap., teacher ed. 19.95 (*1-56796-048-0*) WRS Group.

Davidson, James, et al. American Catholic Laity in a Changing Church. LC 88-60114. 198p. (Orig.). (C). 1989. pap. 15.95 (*1-55612-247-0*) Sheed & Ward WI.

Davidson, James D. & Mogg, Rees. The Sovereign Individual: How to Survive & Thrive During the Collapse of the Welfare State. LC 96-48244. 400p. 1997. 24.50 (*0-684-81007-7*) Simon & Schuster.

Davidson, James D. & Rees-Mogg, Lord William. The Great Reckoning. (Illus.). 592p. 1993. pap. 14.00 (*0-671-79722-0*, Touchstone) S&S Trade Pap.

*__Davidson, James D. & Rees-Mogg, Lord William.__ The Sovereign Individual: How to Survive & Thrive During the Collapse of the Welfare State - Mastering the Transition to the Information Age. 448p. 1999. per. 15.00 (*0-684-83272-0*) S&S Trade.

Davidson, James G. Jesus Christ: Conception to Crucifixion. 229p. 1995. pap. text, write for info. (*0-9648691-0-1*) Marcotech Res.

Davidson, James H., tr. see French Oil & Gas Industry Association Staff, et al, eds.

Davidson, James L. & Henshall, Audrey S. The Chambered Cairns of Caithness. 1991. text 70.00 (*0-7486-0256-9*, Pub. by Edinburgh U Pr) Col U Pr.

Davidson, James L., jt. auth. see Henshall, Audrey S.

Davidson, James W. The Island of Formosa: Past & Present. (Illus.). 816p. (C). 1989. 65.00 (*0-19-584951-5*) OUP.

— The Island of Formosa: Past & Present. LC 77-86949. (Illus.). reprint ed. 67.50 (*0-404-16704-7*) AMS Pr.

— The Logic of Millennial Thought: Eighteenth-Century New England. LC 75-43315. (Yale Historical Publications: Miscellany: No. 112). 320p. reprint ed. pap. 99.20 (*0-8357-8734-6*, 203370300087) Bks Demand.

— Nation of Nations: A Concise Narrative of the American Republic, Vol. 2. abr. ed. 560p. (C). 1995. pap. 25.94 (*0-07-015740-5*) McGraw.

— Nation of Nations: A Narrative History of the American Republic. 3rd ed. LC 97-1197. 1408p. 1997. pap. 70.31 (*0-07-015794-4*) McGraw.

— Nation of Nations Vol. 1: A Concise Narrative of the American Republic, Vol. 1. abr. ed. LC 95-13161. 560p. (C). 1995. pap. 25.94 (*0-07-015739-1*) McGraw.

Davidson, James W. & Gienapp, William E. Nation of Nations: A Concise Narrative of the American Republic, Vol. 1. abr. ed. (C). 1995. pap. text 16.50 (*0-07-015742-1*) McGraw.

Davidson, James W. & Lytle, Mark H. After the Fact: The Art of Historical Detection, 2 vols. 3rd ed. 480p. (C). 1992. 29.69 (*0-07-015609-3*); text 18.75 (*0-07-015610-7*); text 18.75 (*0-07-015611-5*) McGraw.

D

An Asterisk (*) at the beginning of an entry indicates that the title is appearing for the first time.

***Davidson, James W. & Lytle, Mark H.** After the Fact: The Art of Historical Detection. 4th ed. LC 99-16991. 448p. 1999. pap. 32.50 (*0-07-229426-4*) McGraw.

Davidson, James W. & Rugge, John. The Complete Wilderness Paddler. LC 82-40021. 288p. 1983. pap. 13.00 (*0-394-71153-X*) Vin Bks.

— Great Heart: The History of a Labrador Adventure. LC 96-900976. (Illus.). 400p. 1997. pap. 22.95 (*0-7735-1657-3*, Pub. by McG-Queens Univ Pr) CUP Services.

— Great Heart: The History of a Labrador Adventure. Turner, Philip, ed. (Illus.). 400p. 1996. reprint ed. pap. 16.00 (*1-56836-168-8*, Kodansha Globe) Kodansha.

***Davidson, James W. & Rugge, John.** Great Heart: The History of a Labrador Adventure. unabridged deluxe ed. LC 00-105500. (Illus.). 400p. 2000. reprint ed. lib. bdg. 35.00 (*1-885283-21-0*) Advent Library.

Davidson, James W., et al. Nation of Nations: A Concise Narrative of the American Republic, Brief Edition, Vol. 1. (C). 1995. pap., student ed. 15.63 (*0-07-015750-2*) McGraw.

— Nation of Nations: A Concise Narrative of the American Republic, Brief Edition, Vol. 2. (C). 1995. pap., student ed. 15.63 (*0-07-015751-0*) McGraw.

— Nation of Nations: A Narrative History of the American Republic, 2 vols., 1. 2nd ed. LC 93-30481. (C). 1994. pap. 42.50 (*0-07-015635-2*) McGraw.

— Nation of Nations: A Narrative History of the American Republic, 2 vols., Vol. 2. 2nd ed. LC 93-30481. (C). 1994. text. write for info. (*0-07-015639-5*) McGraw.

— Nation of Nations Vol. 1: A Concise Narrative of the American Republic, Vol. 1. LC 95-13161. 1104p. (C). 1995. pap. 39.69 (*0-07-015741-3*) McGraw.

— Nation of Nations Vol. 1: A Concise Narrative of the American Republic, Vol. 1. LC 95-13161. 1070p. (C). 1995. 46.25 (*0-07-015738-3*) McGraw.

— Nation of Nations, a Concise Narrative of the American Republic: A Concise Narrative of the American Republic. 2nd ed. LC 98-21631. 1120p. 1999. pap. 31.00 (*0-07-303375-8*, McGrw-H College) McGrw-H Hghr Educ.

Davidson, James West. The American Nation: Beginnings to 1877. LC 96-206817. (Illus.). (J). 1997. write for info. (*0-13-411083-8*) P-H.

Davidson, James West, et al. The American Nation. LC 99-233976. (Illus.). write for info. (*0-13-434908-3*) P-H.

Davidson, Jane, tr. see Dumas, Alexandre.

Davidson, Jane I. Children & Computers Together in the Early Childhood Classroom. Whitney, Jay, ed. 256p. 1988. pap., teacher ed. 12.00 (*0-8273-3342-0*) Delmar.

— Emergent Literacy & Dramatic Play in Early Education. 320p. (C). 1995. pap. 48.95 (*0-8273-5721-4*) Delmar.

— Emerging Literacy Through Play. (Early Childhood Education Ser.). 64p. (C). 1996. teacher ed. 12.00 (*0-8273-5722-2*) Delmar.

Davidson, Jane P. The Bone Sharp: The Life of Edward Drinker Cope. (Illus.). x, 237p. (Orig.). 1997. pap. 25.00 (*0-910006-53-9*) Acad Nat Sci Phila.

Davidson, Janelle. Ashland, an Oregon Oasis: An Oregon Documentary. Webber, Bert, ed. LC 95-33529. (Illus.). 160p. 1995. pap. 12.95 (*0-936738-89-8*) Webb Research.

Davidson, Janet, jt. ed. see Sternberg, Robert J.

Davidson, Jean. The Divided Heart. large type ed. (Romance Ser.). 1994. pap. 16.99 (*0-7089-7606-9*, Linford) Ulverscroft.

— Guilt by Association. large type ed. (Linford Mystery Library). 432p. 1997. pap. 16.99 (*0-7089-5167-8*) Ulverscroft.

— Manhattan Magic. large type ed. 1990. pap. 16.99 (*0-7089-6928-3*, Linford) Ulverscroft.

— That Italian Summer. large type ed. (Linford Romance Library). 1991. pap. 16.99 (*0-7089-7048-6*) Ulverscroft.

— Troubled Waters. large type ed. 1991. pap. 16.99 (*0-7089-6974-7*) Ulverscroft.

Davidson, Jeff. The Complete Idiot's Guide to Assertiveness. LC 97-73152. 368p. 1997. pap. 16.95 (*0-02-861964-1*) Macmillan Gen Ref.

— Complete Idiot's Guide to Reaching Your Goals. LC 97-80961. 368p. 1997. 16.95 (*0-02-862114-X*) Macmillan Gen Ref.

— Get a Life! Living & Working at a Comfortable Pace in a High-Speed World. (Smart Tapes Ser.). 28p. (YA). (gr. 10 up). 1997. pap. text 19.95 incl. audio (*1-55678-066-4*, 3290) Learn Inc.

— Market Yourself & Your Career. 2nd ed. LC 99-20339. 1999. pap. 12.95 (*1-58062-119-8*) Adams Media.

***Davidson, Jeff.** 10 Minute Guide to Managing Your Time. (10 Minute Guides Ser.). 176p. 2000. pap. text 10.95 (*0-02-863886-7*, Alpha Ref) Macmillan Gen Ref.

Davidson, Jeff, jt. auth. see Connor, Dick.

Davidson, Jeff, jt. auth. see Earle, Richard.

Davidson, Jeff M. Security Measures - for Professionals, Patients, Hospitals & Data Protection: Index of New Information. 160p. 1994. 47.50 (*0-7883-0214-0*); pap. 44.50 (*0-7883-0215-9*) ABBE Pubs Assn.

Davidson, Jeffrey L. Political Partnerships: Neighborhood Residents & Their Council Members. LC 79-13107. (City & Society Ser.: No. 5). 231p. 1979. reprint ed. pap. 71.70 (*0-608-01452-4*, 205949600001) Bks Demand.

Davidson, Jeffrey P. Blow Your Own Horn: How to Market Yourself & Your Career. 1988. 10.95 incl. audio (*0-671-66385-2*, Sound Ideas) S&S Trade.

Davidson, Jeffrey P. Marketing for the Home-Based Business. 2nd ed. LC 98-26818. 256p. 1999. pap. text 10.95 (*1-58062-078-7*) Adams Media.

Davidson, Jeffrey P., jt. auth. see Connor, Dick.

Davidson, Jeffrey P., jt. auth. see Vlcek, Donald J., Jr.

Davidson, Jennifer. Stop Smelling My Rose! (Illus.). 128p. 1997. pap. 11.95 (*0-9661092-0-1*) Redgrove Pr.

— TIPS - Thinking Skills in the Music Classroom. (TIPS Ser.). 24p. 1994. pap. text 6.00 (*1-56545-027-2*, 1100) MENC.

Davidson, Jennifer, jt. ed. see Stauffer, Sandra.

Davidson, Jessica. Using the Cuisenaire Rods: A Photo-Text Guide for Teachers. (Illus.). 150p. (J). (gr. 1-8). 1983. pap. text 16.95 (*0-914040-04-9*) Cuisenaire.

Davidson, Jim. Lyrebird Rising: Louise Hanson-Dyer of l'Oiseau-Lyre, 1884-1962. (Illus.). 578p. 1994. 35.00 (*0-931340-72-1*, Amadeus Pr) Timber.

— Mine Work: A Novel. LC 99-6251. 312p. 1999. pap. 17.95 (*0-87421-275-8*) Utah St U Pr.

— You Can Be the Best: Most Requested Selections from the Author's Nationally Acclaimed Radio Series. LC 91-76202. 256p. 1991. pap. 9.95 (*0-9630963-3-8*) Cont Educ Srvs.

Davidson, Jiton, ed. see Haskins, Scott D.

Davidson, Joan & Lloyd, Richard, eds. Conservation & Agriculture. LC 77-697. (Illus.). 280p. reprint ed. pap. 86.80 (*0-608-17665-6*, 203037900069) Bks Demand.

Davidson, Joan, et al. No Time to Waste: Poverty & the Global Environment. (Illus.). 224p. (C). 1992. 39.95 (*0-85598-182-2*, Pub. by Oxfam Pub); pap. 15.95 (*0-85598-183-0*, Pub. by Oxfam Pub) Stylus Pub VA.

Davidson, Joan, jt. auth. see Dankelman, Irene.

Davidson, Jody J. Snow Child. 1999. pap. 3.00 (*1-57514-339-9*, 1182) Encore Perform Pub.

Davidson, Joe. Art of the Cigar Label. 252p. 1995. 29.98 (*1-55521-436-3*) Bk Sales Inc.

— Fruit Crate Art. 1990. 14.98 (*1-55521-664-1*) Bk Sales Inc.

Davidson, Joe & Davidson, Sue. Smoker's Art. (Illus.). 252p. 1997. 34.98 (*0-7858-0866-3*) Bk Sales Inc.

Davidson, Joel. The New Solar Electric Home: The Photovoltaics How-To Handbook. (Illus.). 416p. 1987. pap. 18.95 (*0-937948-09-8*) aatec Pubns.

Davidson, Joel R. The Unsinkable Fleet: The Politics of U. S. Navy Expansion in World War II. LC 96-13714. (Illus.). 264p. 1996. 29.95 (*1-55750-156-4*) Naval Inst Pr.

Davidson, John. Complete Poems, 2 vols. 1977. 600.00 (*0-87968-917-X*) Gordon Pr.

— Fleet Street Eclogues 1893: A Second Series of Fleet Street Eclogues 1896, 2 vols. in 1. LC 93-26579. (Decadents, Symbolists, Anti-Decadents Ser.). 260p. 1993. 49.50 (*1-85477-139-6*) Continuum.

***Davidson, John.** Hockey for Dummies. 2nd ed. (For Dummies Ser.). (Illus.). 384p. 2000. pap. 19.99 (*0-7645-5228-7*) IDG Bks.

Davidson, John. In a Music-Hall 1891; Ballads & Songs 1894, 2 vols. in 1. LC 93-26578. (Decadents, Symbolists, Anti-Decadents Ser.). 296p. 1993. 49.50 (*1-85477-138-8*) Continuum.

— Natural Creation & the Formative Mind. (Illus.). 240p. 1992. pap. 16.95 (*1-85230-197-X*, Pub. by Element MA) Penguin Putnam.

— Natural Creation or Natural Selection? (Illus.). 240p. 1992. pap. 16.95 (*1-85230-240-2*, Pub. by Element MA) Penguin Putnam.

— Natural Fertility Awareness. 108p. 1994. pap. 11.95 (*0-85207-275-2*, Pub. by C W Daniel) Natl Bk Netwk.

— Radiation: What It Is, How It Affects Us & What We Can Do about It. 96p. (Orig.). pap. 12.95 (*0-8464-4279-5*) Beekman Pubs.

— The Secret of the Creative Vacuum. 432p. (Orig.). pap. 35.95 (*0-8464-4287-6*) Beekman Pubs.

— The Secret of the Creative Vacuum. 189p. (Orig.). 1989. pap. 25.95 (*0-85207-202-3*, Pub. by C W Daniel) Natl Bk Netwk.

— Selected Poems & Prose of John Davidson. Sloan, John, ed. 236p. 1995. text 55.00 (*0-19-818335-6*) OUP.

— The Stroll: Inner City Subcultures. (Illus.). 165p. 1986. pap. 9.95 (*0-920053-65-3*, Pub. by NC Ltd) U of Toronto Pr.

— Subtle Energy. 288p. (Orig.). pap. 23.95 (*0-8464-4296-5*) Beekman Pubs.

— Subtle Energy. 190p. (Orig.). 1987. pap. 15.95 (*0-85207-184-1*, Pub. by C W Daniel) Natl Bk Netwk.

— The Web of Life. 408p. (Orig.). pap. 29.95 (*0-8464-4312-0*) Beekman Pubs.

— The Web of Life. 191p. (Orig.). 1988. pap. 19.95 (*0-85207-199-X*, Pub. by C W Daniel) Natl Bk Netwk.

Davidson, John & Casady, Cort. The Singing Entertainer: A Contemporary Study of the Art & Business of Being a Professional. 244p. 1979. pap. 14.95 (*0-88284-194-7*, 1488) Alfred Pub.

Davidson, John & Davidson, Lucie. Natural Fertility Awareness. rev. ed. (Illus.). 136p. 1994. pap. 17.95 (*0-8464-4337-6*) Beekman Pubs.

Davidson, John & Steinbreder, John. Hockey for Dummies. LC 97-80182. (For Dummies Ser.). (Illus.). 408p. 1997. pap. 19.99 (*0-7645-5045-4*) IDG Bks.

Davidson, John & Tidman, Marjorie, eds. Cooperative Peace Strategies. 244p. 1992. 19.95 (*0-909991-43-X*) Bahai.

***Davidson, John & Von Bertele, Otto.** Process Pumps Selection: A Systems Approach. 2nd ed. 202p. 2000. 112.00 (*1-86058-180-3*) Prof Eng Pubng.

Davidson, John, jt. auth. see Gretzky, Wayne.

Davidson, John E. Deterritorializing the New German Cinema. LC 98-26980. 224p. 1999. 29.95 (*0-8166-2982-X*) U of Minn Pr.

Davidson, John F., et al, eds. Progress in Chemical Fibrinolysis & Thrombolysis, Vol. 3. LC 78-643573. (Illus.). 631p. reprint ed. pap. 195.70 (*0-7837-7144-4*, 204715000003) Bks Demand.

Davidson, John F. & Harrison, O. Fluidised Particles. LC 63-22979. (Illus.). 185p. reprint ed. pap. 52.80 (*0-608-11545-2*, 2050790) Bks Demand.

Davidson, John H., Jr., jt. auth. see Delogu, Orlando E.

***Davidson, John K.** Clinical Diabetes Mellitus: A Problem Oriented Approach. 3rd ed. LC 99-42914. (Illus.). 928p. 1999. 189.00 (*0-86577-840-X*) Thieme Med Pubs.

Davidson, John K., ed. Clinical Diabetes Mellitus. 2nd ed. (Illus.). 848p. 1991. text 175.00 (*0-86577-370-X*) Thieme Med Pubs.

Davidson, John M. Eminent English Liberals in & Out of Parliament. LC 70-37521. (Essay Index Reprint Ser.). 1977. reprint ed. 20.95 (*0-8369-2542-4*) Ayer.

Davidson, Jon P., et al. Exploring Earth. LC 96-32914. 477p. 1996. pap. text 73.33 (*0-13-463936-7*) P-H.

***Davidson, Jonathan.** Face to Face with Social Anxiety Disorder: Management. (LEA/DLN Mental Health Professionals Video Reference Library). 1999. VHS 89.95 (*0-8058-3453-2*) L Erlbaum Assocs.

***Davidson, Jonathan & Peters, Jim.** Voice over IP Fundamentals. 500p. 1999. pap. 50.00 (*1-57870-168-6*) Cisco Press.

Davidson, Jonathan R. & Foa, Edna B., eds. Posttraumatic Stress Disorder: DSM-IV & Beyond. LC 92-7052. 262p. 1992. text 35.00 (*0-88048-502-7*, 8502) Am Psychiatric.

***Davidson, Jonathan R. T. & Connor, Kathryn M.** Herbs for the Mind: What Science Tells Us about Nature's Remedies for Depression, Stress, Memory Loss & Insomnia. 260p. 2000. lib. bdg. 29.95 (*1-57230-572-X*, C0572) Guilford Pubns.

— Herbs for the Mind: What Science Tells Us about Nature's Remedies for Depression, Stress, Memory Loss & Insomnia. LC 00-26341. (Illus.). 260p. 2000. pap. text 14.95 (*1-57230-476-6*, C0476) Guilford Pubns.

Davidson, Joseph & Strang, Thomas, eds. PracticeCards for Golfers: Problem Solving Instructional Cards for Use on the Practice Range & Practice Green. (PracticeCard Ser.). (Illus.). 128p. 1992. 19.95 (*0-9633090-0-5*) PracticeCard.

Davidson, Josephine. The Old Testament: Ten Plays for Readers' Theater. LC 92-90957. (Illus.). 189p. (Orig.). (J). (gr. 6-8). 1992. pap. text. write for info. (*0-9628252-1-2*) Right Bk.

Davidson, Josephine & Shelley, Phyllis. Jesus & People with Disabilities. (Illus.). (Orig.). (YA). (gr. 6-8). 1995. pap. text. write for info. (*0-9628252-2-0*) Right Bk.

Davidson, Judith & Koppenhaver, David. Adolescent Literacy: What Works & Why. 2nd ed. LC 92-13812. (Reference Library of Social Science). 352p. 1993. text 66.00 (*0-8153-0877-9*); pap. text 24.95 (*0-8153-0920-1*, SS0850) Garland.

Davidson, Judy K., jt. auth. see Batastini, Peggy H.

Davidson, Julia O. Privatisation & Employment Relations: The Case of the Water Industry. Elger, Tony & Fairbrother, Peter, eds. LC 92-45067. (Employment & Work Relations in Context Ser.). 224p. 1993. 110.00 (*0-7201-2150-7*) Continuum.

Davidson, Julia O. Prostitution, Power & Freedom. LC 98-43995. 240p. 1998. text 49.50 (*0-472-09695-8*, 09695) U of Mich Pr.

***Davidson, Julia O.** Prostitution, Power & Freedom. LC 98-43995. 240p. 1998. pap. text 19.95 (*0-472-06695-1*, 06695) U of Mich Pr.

Davidson, Julia O., jt. auth. see Layder, Derek.

Davidson, Julian M., jt. ed. see Davidson, Richard J.

Davidson, Karen L. Our Latter-Day Hymns: The Stories & the Messages. LC 88-1067. ix, 486p. 1988. 21.95 (*0-87579-137-9*) Deseret Bk.

Davidson, Karen Lynn, jt. ed. see Carmack, Noel A.

Davidson, Karl. Four Hundred Twenty-Seven Ways to Make Your World a Better Place! 160p. (Orig.). 1992. pap. 5.95 (*0-9630884-4-0*) Team Effort.

— Karl's One Hundred One Handy Handouts. 220p. 1991. student ed. 44.95 (*0-9630884-0-8*) Team Effort.

— Ways to Make A's. (Illus.). 127p. (Orig.). 1992. pap. 8.95 (*0-9630884-3-2*) Team Effort.

Davidson, Karl & Davidson, Cassie. Miles of Smiles. (Illus.). 96p. (Orig.). 1992. pap. text 7.95 (*0-9630884-1-6*) Team Effort.

***Davidson, Kate.** Cognitive Therapy for Personality Disorders. 161p. 2000. pap. 27.00 (*0-7506-4488-5*) Buttrwrth-Heinemann.

Davidson, Kate M., jt. auth. see Blackburn, Ivy-Marie.

Davidson, Kathryn & Glassman, Elizabeth. Transfixed by Light. Newhall, Beaumont, ed. & selected by by. LC 81-80810. 46p. (C). 1981. pap. 7.50 (*0-939594-00-5*, Menil Collection) Menil Found.

Davidson, Kay. Carl Sagan: A Life. LC 99-36206. 576p. 1999. 30.00 (*0-471-25286-7*) Wiley.

Davidson, Kay W., ed. Social Work in Health Care: A Handbook for Practice. LC 89-24535. 517p. (C). 1990. text 19.95 (*0-86656-846-8*); pap. text 49.95 (*0-86656-907-3*) Haworth Pr.

***Davidson, Keay.** Carl Sagan: A Life. 2000. pap. 17.95 (*0-471-39536-6*) Wiley.

Davidson, Keay. Tornadoes: Chaos from the Sky. 1996. pap. 14.00 (*0-614-97659-6*, Pocket Books) PB.

— Twister: The Science of Tornadoes & the Making of Adventure Movie. (Illus.). 224p. 1996. pap. 14.00 (*0-671-00029-2*) PB.

— Twister: The Science of Tornadoes & the Making of Adventure Movie. (J). 1996. per. 3.99 (*0-671-00396-8*) PB.

Davidson, Keay, jt. auth. see Smoot, George.

Davidson, Ken & Pennigstore, Werner. Insuring Environmental Risks. 122p. (C). 1986. 110.00 (*0-948691-13-1*, Pub. by Witherby & Co) St Mut.

Davidson, Kenneth M. Megamergers: Corporate America's Billion-Dollar Takeovers. LC 85-4025. 432p. 1985. 35.00 (*0-88730-058-8*, HarpBusn) HarpInfo.

Davidson, Kenneth R. C*-Algebras by Example. LC 96-20184. (Fields Institute Monographs: Vol. 6). 309p. 1996. text 59.00 (*0-8218-0599-1*, FIM/6) Am Math.

Davidson, Kris, et al, eds. Physics of Luminous Blue Variables. (C). 1989. text 186.00 (*0-7923-0443-8*) Kluwer Academic.

Davidson, L. S. & Ward, John O., trs. The Sorcery Trial of Alice Kyteler (1324) 104p. 1993. pap. 8.95 (*0-86698-171-3*, P21) Pegasus Pr.

Davidson, Lance. The Ultimate Reference Book: The Wit's Thesaurus. 688p. (Orig.). 1994. pap. 15.00 (*0-380-76957-3*, Avon Bks) Morrow Avon.

Davidson, Lance S. Ludicrous Laws & Mindless Misdemeanors. LC 98-2672. 256p. 1998. pap. 14.95 (*0-471-13897-5*) Wiley.

Davidson, Larry D., ed. see Wenger, Virginia.

Davidson, Lawrence. Islamic Fundamentalism, Vol. 109. LC 97-37511. (Greenwood Press Guides to Historic Events of the Twentieth Century Ser.). 224p. 1998. 39.95 (*0-313-29978-1*, Greenwood Pr) Greenwood.

Davidson, Len. Funky Neon. LC 99-14282. (Illus.). 192p. 1999. 59.95 (*0-7643-0857-2*) Schiffer.

Davidson, Les. Using the Magic of Word Power to Multiply Real Estate Sales. 1973. 49.50 (*0-685-01591-2*) Exec Reports.

Davidson, Let. Wisdom at Work: Awakening of Consciousness in the Workplace. 192p. 1998. pap. 15.95 (*0-943914-86-8*) Larson Pubns.

Davidson, Levette J. Guide to American Folklore. LC 74-97313. 132p. 1970. reprint ed. lib. bdg. 55.00 (*0-8371-2552-9*, DAAF, Greenwood Pr) Greenwood.

Davidson, Levette J., ed. Poems of the Old West. LC 68-58824. (Granger Index Reprint Ser.). 1977. 27.95 (*0-8369-6012-2*) Ayer.

Davidson, Liam. The White Woman. LC 94-228352. 1995. pap. text 14.95 (*0-7022-2680-7*, Pub. by Univ Queensland Pr) Intl Spec Bk.

Davidson, Linda, ed. Creative Ideas for Lent, Vol. 3. 110p. (Orig.). 1996. pap. 14.95 (*1-877871-93-1*, 2541) Ed Ministries.

— Creative Ideas for Pentecost. 74p. 1994. pap. 10.95 (*1-877871-63-X*, 2514) Ed Ministries.

Davidson, Linda, et al, eds. The Miracles of St. James. Dunn, Maryjane et al, trs. from LAT. LC 96-14801. (Illus.). 150p. (Orig.). 1996. pap. 17.50 (*0-934977-38-0*) Italica Pr.

Davidson, Linda K. & Dunn, Maryjane. The Pilgrimage to Compostela in the Middle Ages: A Book of Essays. LC 96-5338. (Medieval Casebooks Ser.: Vol. 17). (Illus.). 240p. 1996. text 39.00 (*0-8153-1638-0*, H1829) Garland.

Davidson, Linda K., jt. auth. see Dunn, Maryjane.

***Davidson, Linda Kay.** Pilgrimage: An Encyclopedia. 2001. lib. bdg. 65.00 (*1-57607-004-2*) ABC-CLIO.

Davidson, Linda S., ed. Creative Ideas for Advent, Vol. 3. (Orig.). 1990. pap. 12.95 (*1-877871-00-1*) Ed Ministries.

— Creative Ideas for Epiphany. 84p. 1991. pap. 10.95 (*1-877871-24-9*, 2512) Ed Ministries.

— Creative Ideas for Thanksgiving. 72p. (Orig.). 1989. pap. 10.95 (*0-940754-75-4*) Ed Ministries.

Davidson, Linda S., jt. ed. see Davidson, Robert G.

Davidson, Lionel. Kolymsky Heights. 1995. mass mkt. 6.50 (*0-312-95661-4*) St Martin.

— Kolymsky Heights. large type ed. LC 94-40736. 1994. 25.95 (*1-56895-158-2*) Wheeler Pub.

— Menorah Men. 1996. mass mkt. 5.99 (*0-312-95815-3*, Pub. by Tor Bks) St Martin.

— The Night of Wenceslas. 1996. mass mkt. 6.99 (*0-312-95876-5*) St Martin.

— The Rose of Tibet. 1996. mass mkt. 6.50 (*0-312-95833-1*, Pub. by Tor Bks) St Martin.

Davidson, Lisa. Madam, Your Daughter Is Molting. 74p. (Orig.). 1994. pap. 7.00 (*0-944920-10-1*) Bellowing Ark Pr.

Davidson, Lisa, tr. see Cheneviere, Alain.

Davidson, Lisa, tr. see Wallens, Gerard de & Pomarede, Vincent.

Davidson, Lloyd & Florida Association of Legal Secretaries Staff. The Manual for Florida Legal Secretaries, 1984-1994, 3 vols., Set. 108p. 1997. ring bd. 180.00 (*0-409-26252-8*, 80876-10, MICHIE) LEXIS Pub.

Davidson, Lloyd T. Florida Criminal Sentencing Law. 1994. suppl. ed. 45.00 (*0-685-73745-4*, MICHIE) LEXIS Pub.

— Florida Criminal Sentencing Law, 2 vols., Set. 900p. Date not set. ring bd. 180.00 (*0-409-26191-2*, 80605-10, MICHIE) LEXIS Pub.

— Florida Zoning Law Manual, 1980-1994, 3 vols., Set. 1200p. 1995. ring bd. 270.00 (*0-409-26121-1*, 80823-10, MICHIE) LEXIS Pub.

***Davidson, Louise.** Uncertainty, International Money, Employment & Theory: The Collected Writings of Paul Davidson. 1999. text 90.00 (*0-312-22191-6*) St Martin.

Davidson, Louise, ed. see Breeding, Robert L.

Davidson, Lucie, jt. auth. see Davidson, John.

Davidson, Lucy & Linnoila, Markku, eds. Risk Factors for Youth Suicide. (Death Education, Aging & Health Care Ser.). 275p. 1990. 57.95 (*1-56032-138-5*) Hemisp Pub.

Davidson, M. The Stars & the Mind: A Study of the Impact of Astronomical Development on Human Thought. 1972. 59.95 (*0-8490-1121-3*) Gordon Pr.

Davidson, M. G., jt. auth. see Sterling, C. L.

Davidson, Malcolm, et al, eds. BSAVA Manual of Small Animal Clinical Pathology. (Illus.). 230p. 1998. pap. text 92.95 (*0-905214-41-2*, Pub. by BSAVA) Iowa St U Pr.

Davidson, Margaret. Five True Dog Stories. (FRE.). (J). pap. 4.99 (*0-590-73687-6*) Scholastic Inc.

— Five True Dog Stories. 48p. (J). (gr. 4-7). 1989. pap. 2.95 (*0-590-42401-7*) Scholastic Inc.

— Five True Horse Stories. 64p. (J). (gr. 4-7). 1989. pap. 2.99 (*0-590-42400-9*) Scholastic Inc.

— Frederick Douglass Fights for Freedom. 80p. (J). (gr. 2-5). 1989. pap. 2.50 (*0-590-42218-9*, Apple Paperbacks) Scholastic Inc.

An Asterisk (*) at the beginning of an entry indicates that the title is appearing for the first time.

***Davidson, Margaret.** Helen Keller. (Illus.). 1999. pap. 11.70 (*0-8085-5141-8*) Econo-Clad Bks.

Davidson, Margaret. Helen Keller. LC 71-150016. (Scholastic Biography Ser.). (Illus.). 95p. (J). (gr. 2-5). 1989. pap. 2.99 (*0-590-42404-1*) Scholastic Inc.

— Helen Keller. (J). 1969. 8.09 (*0-606-03807-8*, Pub. by Turtleback) Demco.

— Helen Keller's Teacher. 160p. (Orig.). (J). (gr. 4-7). 1992. pap. 3.99 (*0-590-44652-5*, Apple Paperbacks) Scholastic Inc.

— I Have a Dream: The Story of Martin Luther King. 128p. (Orig.). (J). (gr. 4-7). 1991. pap. 3.99 (*0-590-44230-9*) Scholastic Inc.

— Louis Braille. (FRE.). (J). pap. 5.99 (*0-590-71110-5*) Scholastic Inc.

— Louis Braille: The Boy Who Invented Books for the Blind. (Illus.). 80p. (J). (gr. 2-5). 1991. pap. 3.50 (*0-590-44350-X*) Scholastic Inc.

— Louis Braille: The Boy Who Invented Books for the Blind. LC 73-39630. (J). 1971. 8.70 (*0-606-03851-5*, Pub. by Turtleback) Demco.

— Louis Braille, l'Enfant de la Nuit. (Folio - Cadet Rouge Ser.: No. 225). (FRE., Illus.). 103p. (J). (gr. 3-7). 1990. pap. 10.95 (*2-07-031225-9*) Schoenhof.

— Story of Alex Bell. (J). 1996. pap. 3.95 (*0-440-91270-9*) BDD Bks Young Read.

— The Story of Benjamin Franklin: Amazing American. 96p. (J). (gr. k-6). 1988. pap. 3.99 (*0-440-40021-X*, YB BDD) BDD Bks Young Read.

Davidson, Margaret. Story of Benjamin Franklin, Amazing American. (J). 1988. 9.19 (*0-606-03928-7*, Pub. by Turtleback) Demco.

Davidson, Margaret. The Story of Jackie Robinson: Bravest Man in Baseball. 96p. (J). (gr. k-6). 1987. pap. 3.99 (*0-440-40019-8*, YB BDD) BDD Bks Young Read.

Davidson, Margaret. Story of Jackie Robinson, Bravest Man in Baseball. (Dell Yearling Biography Ser.). (J). 1988. 8.70 (*0-606-03930-9*, Pub. by Turtleback) Demco.

Davidson, Margaret. Story of Thomas Alva Edison: The Wizard of Menlo Park. 64p. (J). (gr. 2-5). 1990. pap. 3.50 (*0-590-42403-3*) Scholastic Inc.

Davidson, Margaret & Bokoske, Sharon. Dolphins! (Step into Reading Ser.: A Step 2 Book). (Illus.). 47p. (J). (gr. 1-3). 1993. pap. 3.99 (*0-679-84437-6*, Pub. by Random Bks Yng Read) Random.

Davidson, Margaret & Wilson, Roger. Nine True Dolphin Stories.Tr. of Neuf Histoires Vraies de Dauphins. (FRE.). (J). mass mkt. 4.99 (*0-590-71188-1*) Scholastic Inc.

Davidson, Margaret, jt. ed. see Maunder, Elwood R.

Davidson, Margaret G. A Guide for Newspaper Stringers. (Communication Textbook Ser.). 232p. 1990. 69.95 (*0-8058-0764-0*); pap. 36.00 (*0-8058-0765-9*) L Erlbaum Assocs.

Davidson, Marilyn J. The Black & Ethnic Minority Woman Manager: Cracking the Concrete Ceiling. LC 97-202965. 192p. 1997. pap. 34.95 (*1-85396-299-6*, Pub. by P Chapman) Taylor & Francis.

Davidson, Marilyn J. & Burke, Ronald J., eds. Women in Management: Current Research Issues. 352p. 1994. 75.00 (*1-85396-235-X*, Pub. by P Chapman); pap. 39.95 (*1-85396-289-9*, Pub. by P Chapman) Taylor & Francis.

Davidson, Marilyn J. & Cooper, Cary L. European Women in Business Management. 199p. 1993. pap. 57.00 (*1-85396-138-8*, Pub. by P Chapman) Taylor & Francis.

— Shattering the Glass Ceiling: The Woman Manager. 192p. 1992. pap. 29.95 (*1-85396-132-9*, Pub. by P Chapman) Taylor & Francis.

Davidson, Marilyn J. & Cooper, Cary L., eds. Working Women: An International Survey. LC 84-3645. (Illus.). 314p. 1984. pap. 97.40 (*0-608-05256-6*, 206579400001) Bks Demand.

***Davidson, MarJoe.** Angel in Disguise: Bridging This World to the Other Side. Orig. Title: My Life Is on Hold. 160p. 2000. reprint ed. 12.95 (*0-9639866-9-4*, Pub. by MDees Pubng) New Leaf Dist.

Davidson, MarJoe. My Life Is on Hold: One Family's Struggle with Terminal Illness. large type ed. LC 94-96007. 160p. (Orig.). 1994. pap. 13.00 (*0-9639866-1-9*) MDees Pubng.

Davidson, Mark. Watchwords: A Dictionary of What's Right, Wrong & Risky in Today's American English Usage. 496p. (C). 1997. pap. text 30.00 (*1-891037-03-X*) Copley Ridge Pr.

— Watchwords: A Dictionary of What's Right, Wrong & Risky in Today's American English Usage. unabridged ed. 496p. 1998. pap. 30.00 (*1-893260-01-1*) Harrison Pubg.

Davidson, Mark G., et al. Differential Operators & Highest Weight Representations. LC 91-27804. (Memoirs Ser.: No. 94/455). 102p. 1991. pap. 20.00 (*0-8218-2509-7*, MEMO/94/455) Am Math.

Davidson, Marl. Barbie Doll Structures & Furniture. LC 98-186079. (Illus.). 144p. 1997. 24.95 (*0-87588-504-7*) Hobby Hse.

Davidson, Marlon. The Pig Barn. (Illus.). 78p. 1997. pap. 9.95 (*0-926147-09-9*) Loonfeather.

Davidson, Martha. Picture Collections in Mexico: A Guide to Picture Sources in the United Mexican States. LC 87-28475. (Illus.). 346p. 1988. 70.00 (*0-8108-2074-9*) Scarecrow.

Davidson, Martin. Texture: How to Draw It, How to Paint It. 144p. 1992. 17.98 (*1-55521-790-7*) Bk Sales Inc.

Davidson, Martin & Levy, Adam. Decisive Weapons: The Technology That Transformed Warfare. LC 97-74401. (Illus.). 160p. 1997. 25.95 (*0-563-38768-8*, BBC-Parkwest) Parkwest Pubns.

Davidson, Martin P. The Consumerist Manifesto: Advertising in Postmodern Times. LC 91-33798. (Comedia Bk.). 224p. (C). 1992. pap. 24.99 (*0-415-04620-3*, A7210) Routledge.

Davidson, Mary F. The Dye Pot. 3rd rev. ed. 1981. pap. text 4.00 (*0-686-10137-5*) M F Davidson.

— Dye Pot. 4th rev. ed. 1990. pap. text 6.00 (*0-317-99817-X*) M F Davidson.

Davidson, Maxwell J. Angels at Qumran: A Comparative Study of 1 Enoch 1-36, 72-108 & Sectarion Writings from Qumran. (Journal for the Study of the Pseudepigrapha Supplement Ser.: No. 11). 386p. (C). 1992. 85.00 (*1-85075-332-6*, Pub. by Sheffield Acad) CUP Services.

Davidson, Mayer. Diabetes Vol. II: A Guide for Patients. (Endocrinology Ser.). 1996. pap. text 2.95 (*1-885274-32-7*) Health InfoNet Inc.

— Diabetes - Type I: A Guide for Patients. (Endocrinology Ser.). (Illus.). 32p. (Orig.). 1996. pap. 2.95 (*1-885274-64-5*) Health InfoNet Inc.

Davidson, Mayer, ed. Diabetes in Children: A Guide for the Family. (Pediatric Ser.). (Illus.). 32p. (Orig.). 1996. pap. text 2.95 (*1-885274-31-9*) Health InfoNet Inc.

Davidson, Mayer B. Diabetes Mellitus: Diagnosis & Treatment. 2nd ed. LC 85-20167. (Wiley Medical Publications). (Illus.). 603p. reprint ed. pap. 187.00 (*0-8357-3063-8*, 203931900012) Bks Demand.

— Diabetes Mellitus: Diagnosis & Treatment. 4th ed. Zorab, Richard, ed. LC 97-50320. (Illus.). 544p. 1998. pap. text 65.00 (*0-7216-6403-2*, W B Saunders Co) Harcrt Hlth Sci Grp.

Davidson, Meagan. The Song Within. 416p. 1998. mass mkt. 5.50 (*0-7860-0402-9*) Kensgtn Pub Corp.

Davidson, Megan. Road to the Isle. 384p. 1995. mass mkt. 4.99 (*0-8217-0131-2*, Zebra Kensgtn) Kensgtn Pub Corp.

— The Song Within. 384p. 1998. mass mkt. 4.99 (*0-8217-5824-1*, Zebra Kensgtn) Kensgtn Pub Corp.

Davidson, Michael. Analogy of the Ion. 1988. 4.00 (*0-935724-33-8*) Figures.

***Davidson, Michael.** The Arcades. 72p. 1999. 10.00 (*1-882022-35-1*, Pub. by O Bks) SPD-Small Pr Dist.

Davidson, Michael. Ghostlier Demarcations: Modern Poetry & the Material Word. LC 96-34563. (Illus.). 273p. 1997. 37.50 (*0-520-20739-4*, Pub. by U CA Pr) Cal Prin Full Svc.

— The Landing of Rochambeau: Poems. 80p. 1985. pap. 7.00 (*0-930901-26-6*) Burning Deck.

— Magical Display: The Art of Photomicrography. (Illus.). 128p. 1998. pap. 24.95 (*0-945798-83-0*) Amber Lotus.

— Post Hoc. (Orig.). 1990. pap. 7.50 (*0-939691-04-3*) Avenue B.

— Post Hoc. limited ed. (Orig.). 1990. pap. 18.00 (*0-685-35601-9*) Avenue B.

— Some Boys. 201p. 1997. reprint ed. pap. 14.95 (*0-85449-259-3*, Pub. by Gay Mens Pr) LPC InBook.

Davidson, Michael, et al. Leningrad: American Writers in the Soviet Union. LC 90-23186. (Illus.). 160p. 1991. pap. 9.95 (*1-56279-005-6*) Mercury Hse Inc.

Davidson, Michael J. Guide to Military Criminal Law. LC 98-46460. 1999. 27.95 (*1-55750-155-6*) Naval Inst Pr.

***Davidson, Michele, ed.** Exhibitions: Tales of Sex in the City. 2000. pap. 15.95 (*1-55152-078-8*) Arsenal Pulp.

Davidson, Mike. Flathead Fever. (Illus.). (J). 1996. pap. 16.95 (*0-949398-25-X*, Pub. by Graffiti) Motorbooks Intl.

— The Grand Strategist: The Revolutionary New Management System. 88p. 1995. 18.95 (*0-8050-4612-7*) H Holt & Co.

— Painting Ancient & Medieval Warriors with Mike Davidson. LC 98-86530. (Illus.). 64p. (Orig.). 1999. pap. 14.95 (*0-7643-0648-0*) Schiffer.

— Painting Miniature Military Figures. LC 94-66368. (Illus.). 80p. (Orig.). 1994. pap. 14.95 (*0-88740-625-4*) Schiffer.

— Painting Napoleonic Miniatures. (Illus.). 80p. 1996. pap. 16.95 (*0-7643-0129-2*) Schiffer.

— Painting World War II Minatures. LC 97-80075. (Illus.). 80p. 1997. pap. 16.95 (*0-7643-0371-6*) Schiffer.

— The Transformation of Management. LC 95-25906. 256p. 1995. text 29.95 incl. audio compact disk (*0-7506-9774-1*) Buttrwrth-Heinemann.

— The Transformation of Management. 256p. 1996. pap. text 21.95 (*0-7506-9814-4*) Buttrwrth-Heinemann.

Davidson, Miles H. Columbus Then & Now: A Life Reexamined. LC 96-49447. (Illus.). 640p. 1997. 39.95 (*0-8061-2934-4*) U of Okla Pr.

Davidson, Miriam. Convictions of the Heart: Jim Corbett & the Sanctuary Movement. LC 88-4796. 187p. 1988. 30.95 (*0-8165-1034-2*); pap. 7.50 (*0-8165-1107-1*) U of Ariz Pr.

***Davidson, Miriam.** Lives on the Line: Dispatches from the U. S. - Mexican Border. LC 00-8566. 200p. 2000. 35.00 (*0-8165-1997-8*) U of Ariz Pr.

— Lives on the Line: Dispatches from the U. S. - Mexican Border. LC 00-8566. (Illus.). 200p. 2000. pap. 17.95 (*0-8165-1998-6*) U of Ariz Pr.

Davidson, Miriam, jt. auth. see Davidson, Florence.

Davidson, Morris I. Growing up in Hartford, Connecticut 1908-1928. (Illus.). 44p. (Orig.). 1990. pap. 4.00 (*0-916897-12-5*) Andrew Mtn Pr.

Davidson, Myra. Pillows, Curtains, & More: Coordinated Projects to Sew. (Illus.). 160p. 1993. 19.95 (*0-8019-8389-4*) NP-Chilton.

Davidson, Nadine N. Travel with Others Without Wishing They'd Stayed Home. 1998. pap. 16.95 (*0-9658194-3-4*) Prince Pub.

Davidson, Naida M. African-American Sites & Insights: A Guide to Places to Go & People to Know, 1994. 125p. (Orig.). 1993. pap. 7.95 (*0-9638924-0-1*) Grace Commun.

Davidson, Neil. Cooperative Learning in Mathematics. 416p. (J). 1996. pap. 32.00 (*0-201-23299-5*) Addison-Wesley.

***Davidson, Neil.** The Origins of Scottish Nationhood. LC 99-89799. 2000. write for info. (*0-7453-1609-2*, Pub. by Pluto GBR) Stylus Pub VA.

Davidson, Neil & Galloway, Richard P., eds. Procuctive Use of Saline Land. 124p. (Orig.). 1993. pap. 99.00 (*1-86320-078-9*) St Mut.

Davidson, Neil & Worsham, Toni, eds. Enhancing Thinking Through Cooperative Learning. 320p. (C). 1992. text 48.00 (*0-8077-3158-7*); pap. text 20.95 (*0-8077-3157-9*) Tchrs Coll.

Davidson, Neil, jt. ed. see Brody, Celeste M.

Davidson, Neil, ed. see McLean, Daniel W.

Davidson, Neil, ed. see Olson, James D.

Davidson, Neil, ed. see Roer, Kathleen M.

Davidson, Neil B., ed. see Roer, Kathleen M.

Davidson, Neil B., ed. see Stein, Robert.

Davidson, Nicholas, tr. see Christen, Yves.

Davidson, Nicholas, tr. see De Bonald, Louis.

Davidson, Nicole. Crash Landing. 192p. (YA). 1995. mass mkt. 3.99 (*0-380-78153-0*, Avon Bks) Morrow Avon.

— Demon's Beach. 160p. (Orig.). (J). (gr. 7-12). 1992. pap. 3.50 (*0-380-76644-2*, Avon Bks) Morrow Avon.

— Dying to Dance. 192p. (Orig.). (J). (gr. 7). 1996. pap. 3.99 (*0-380-78152-2*, Avon Bks) Morrow Avon.

— Fan Mail. 176p. (Orig.). (YA). 1993. pap. 3.50 (*0-380-76995-6*, Avon Bks) Morrow Avon.

— Final Cruise Vol. 3: Farewell Kiss. (Final Cruise Ser.: Vol. 3). 208p. (Orig.). (YA). (gr. 5 up). 1995. mass mkt. 3.99 (*0-380-72246-1*, Avon Bks) Morrow Avon.

— Night Terrors. 192p. (Orig.). (YA). 1994. mass mkt. 3.99 (*0-380-72243-7*, Avon Bks) Morrow Avon.

— The Stalker. 176p. (Orig.). 1992. pap. 3.50 (*0-380-76645-0*, Avon Bks) Morrow Avon.

— Surprise Party. 192p. (Orig.). (J). (gr. 5). 1993. pap. 3.50 (*0-380-76996-4*, Avon Bks) Morrow Avon.

— Winterkill. 192p. (Orig.). (YA). 1991. mass mkt. 3.99 (*0-380-75965-9*, Avon Bks) Morrow Avon.

Davidson, Nita A., et al. Managing Insects & Mites with Spray Oils. (Illus.). 48p. 1991. pap. 6.50 (*1-879906-07-4*, 3347) ANR Pubns CA.

Davidson, Noel. As Our Heads Are Bowed: Lives transformed through the Ministry of Ian Paisley. 222p. (Orig.). 1998. pap. text 11.99 (*1-84030-023-X*) Ambassador Prodns Ltd.

— How Sweet the Sound: The Story of John Newton & William Cooper. (Illus.). 270p. 1997. pap. 11.99 (*1-84030-005-1*) Emerald House Group Inc.

— Only the Best Will Do: The Eddie Stobart Story. 1999. pap. text 9.99 (*1-84030-043-4*) Ambassador Prodns Ltd.

— Some Party in Heaven. 1997. pap. 8.99 (*1-898787-53-0*) Emerald House Group Inc.

— Something Worth Living For. 136p. 1997. pap. 7.99 (*1-898787-45-X*) Emerald House Group Inc.

— This is for Real: George Bates. 1999. pap. text 7.99 (*0-907927-84-X*) Ambassador Prodns Ltd.

Davidson, Norma. Letters from California: He Married Me for My Drapes. LC 96-71030. 352p. 1997. pap. 14.95 (*0-88739-113-3*) Creat Arts Bk.

Davidson, Norman. Astronomy & the Imagination: A New Approach to Man's Experience of the Stars. 238p. 1990. pap. 12.95 (*0-7102-1179-1*, 1251, Routledge Thoemms) Routledge.

— Sky Phenomena: A Guide to Naked-Eye Observation of the Stars: with Sections on Poetry in Astronomy, Constellation Mythology, & the Southern Hemisphere Sky. LC 92-43572. (Renewal of Education Ser.). 1993. pap. 19.95 (*0-940262-56-8*, Lindisfarne) Anthroposophic.

Davidson, Ogunlade R. & Karekezi, Stephen, eds. Renewable Energies in Africa. LC 97-5701. (African Energy Policy Research Network Ser.). (Illus.). 240p. (C). 1997. text 65.00 (*1-85649-089-0*, Pub. by Zed Books) St Martin.

***Davidson, Olga M.** Comparative Literature & Classical Persian Poetics: Seven Essays. LC 99-47021. (Bibliotheca Iranica Ser.: No. 4). 220p. 1999. pap. text 17.95 (*1-56859-098-9*) Mazda Pubs.

Davidson, Olga M. Poet & Hero in the Persian Book of Kings. (Myth & Poetics Ser.). 208p. 1994. text 42.50 (*0-8014-2780-0*) Cornell U Pr.

Davidson, Orlando R., et al. The Deadeyes: The Story of the 96th Infantry Division. (Divisional Ser.: No. 20). (Illus.). 310p. 1981. reprint ed. 49.95 (*0-89839-051-6*) Battery Pr.

Davidson, Osha G. The Best of Enemies: From Prejudice to Friendship in the Post Civil-Rights South. LC 95-45543. 320p. 1996. 25.00 (*0-684-19759-6*) S&S Trade.

— Broken Heartland: The Rise of America's Rural Ghetto. 224p. 1990. text 24.95 (*0-02-907055-4*) Free Pr.

— Broken Heartland: The Rise of America's Rural Ghetto. expanded ed. LC 96-12117. 240p. (C). 1996. pap. 13.95 (*0-87745-554-6*) U of Iowa Pr.

***Davidson, Osha G.** The Enchanted Braid: Coming to Terms with Nature on the Coral Reef. LC 97-39797. 288p. 1998. 24.95 (*0-471-17727-X*) Wiley.

Davidson, Osha G. Under Fire. 1995. pap. 13.95 (*0-8050-3210-X*) H Holt & Co.

— Under Fire: The NRA & the Battle for Gun Control. LC 92-30814. 320p. 1995. 25.00 (*0-8050-1904-9*) H Holt & Co.

— Under Fire: The NRA & the Battle for Gun Control. expanded ed. LC 98-24998. 328p. 1998. pap. 19.95 (*0-87745-646-1*) U of Iowa Pr.

Davidson, P. Michael & Branen, Alfred Larry, eds. Antimicrobials in Foods. 2nd ed. LC 93-16039. (Food Science & Technology Ser.: Vol. 57). (Illus.). 664p. 1993. text 250.00 (*0-8247-8906-7*) Dekker.

Davidson, P. Michael, jt. ed. see Branen, Alfred L.

Davidson, Pamela. Ivanov Reference Guide: A Reference Guide. (Reference Guide to Literature Ser.). 1996. 60.00 (*0-8161-1825-6*, G K Hall & Co) Mac Lib Ref.

***Davidson, Pamela, ed.** Russian Literature & Its Demons. LC PG2987.D45R87. (Studies in Slavic Literature, Culture & Society : Vol. 6). (Illus.). 556p. 2000. 85.00 (*1-57181-758-1*) Berghahn Bks.

Davidson, Patricia. From Here to There. 1995. pap. 9.50 (*0-914040-88-X*) Addison-Wesley.

— Idea Book: For Cuisenaire Rods at the Primary Level. (Illus.). 164p. (J). (ps-2). 1977. pap. text 17.95 (*0-914040-18-9*) Cuisenaire.

— Spatial Problem Solving. 6p. 1995. pap. 9.50 (*0-201-48027-1*) Addison-Wesley.

Davidson, Patricia, text. One Hundred Eleventh Annual Exhibition - "9" (Illus.). 29p. (Orig.). 1992. pap. 5.00 (*0-930495-18-7*) San Fran Art Inst.

Davidson, Patricia & Sellon, Jeffrey. Picture Puzzles with Cuisenaire Rods. 64p. (J). (gr. 1-6). 1979. pap. text 9.50 (*0-914040-77-4*) Cuisenaire.

Davidson, Patricia & Willcitt, Robert E. Spatial Problem Solving: With Cuisenaire Rods. 64p. (J). (gr. 4-9). 1984. pap. text 9.50 (*0-914040-99-5*) Cuisenaire.

Davidson, Patricia & Willcutt, Robert E. Multiplication & Division with Rod Patterns & Graph Paper. (Illus.). 64p. (J). (gr. 3-8). 1980. pap. text 9.50 (*0-914040-82-0*) Cuisenaire.

Davidson, Patricia S. Idea Book. 15p. 1995. pap. 17.95 (*0-201-48033-6*) Addison-Wesley.

Davidson, Patricia S. & Willcutt, Robert E. Multiplication & Division Tables. 1995. pap. 9.50 (*0-201-48021-2*) Addison-Wesley.

— Spatial Problem Solving with Paper Folding & Cutting. 64p. (J). (gr. 4-12). 1984. pap. text 9.50 (*0-914040-36-7*) Cuisenaire.

Davidson, Paul. Chronic Muscle Pain Syndrome. (J Hook Ser.). 1991. pap. 5.99 (*0-425-13054-1*); mass mkt. 5.99 (*0-425-12775-3*) Berkley Pub.

— Collect Writings Davidson, Set. (C). 1991. text 200.00 (*0-8147-1837-X*) NYU Pr.

— Collected Writings Davidson, Vol. 1. (C). 1991. text 100.00 (*0-8147-1835-3*) NYU Pr.

— Collected Writings Davidson, Vol. 2. (C). 1991. text 100.00 (*0-8147-1836-1*) NYU Pr.

— Controversies in Post Keynesian Economics. 144p. 1991. text 80.00 (*1-85278-366-4*); pap. text 20.00 (*1-85278-375-3*) E Elgar.

— Post Keynesian Macroeconomic Theory: A Foundation for Successful Economic Policies for the Twenty-First Century. 320p. 1994. 95.00 (*1-85278-835-6*); pap. 30.00 (*1-85278-836-4*) E Elgar.

Davidson, Paul, ed. Can the Free Market Pick Winners? What Determines Investment. LC 93-35885. 208p. (C). (gr. 13). 1993. text 70.95 (*1-56324-306-7*); pap. text 35.95 (*1-56324-307-5*) M E Sharpe.

— Trading Arrangements in the Pacific Rim: ASEAN & APEC, 2 vols. LC 96-219375. 1995. ring bd. 375.00 (*0-379-00855-6*) Oceana.

***Davidson, Paul.** Fibromyalgia: Relief from Chronic Muscle Pain. 107p. 1999. 69.95 incl. audio (*0-9653493-2-2*) HlthRd Prods.

Davidson, Paul & Ciambella, Franca. Investment in Southeast Asia: Laws & Policy. 360p. 1996. text 74.95 (*981-00-6798-4*) Buttrwrth-Heinemann.

***Davidson, Paul & Kregal, Jan A., eds.** Full Employment & Price Stability in a Global Economy. LC 98-55206. 288p. (C). 1999. 95.00 (*1-85898-989-2*) E Elgar.

Davidson, Paul & Kregel, Jan. Economic Problems of the 1990s: Europe, the Developing Countries & the United States. 256p. 1991. text 95.00 (*1-85278-459-8*) E Elgar.

Davidson, Paul & Kregel, Jan A., eds. Employment, Growth, & Finance: Economic Reality & Economic Growth. LC 94-5164. 256p. 1994. 95.00 (*1-85898-061-5*) E Elgar.

— Improving the Global Economy: Keynesianism & the Growth in Output & Employment. LC 97-25021. 384p. 1997. 100.00 (*1-85898-541-2*) E Elgar.

***Davidson, Paul, et al.** Antique Collector's Directory of Period Detail. 224p. 2000. 29.95 (*0-7641-5167-3*) Barron.

Davidson, Paul, et al. Wildwater West Virginia. 336p. 1995. pap. 14.95 (*0-89732-156-1*) Menasha Ridge.

Davidson, Paul, jt. auth. see Davidson, Greg.

Davidson, Paul, jt. auth. see Dotterer, Betty.

Davidson, Paul, jt. auth. see Jackson, Craig.

Davidson, Penny. Enjoying American History: Teacher's Guide for Mining the Rich Vein of Ideas in Wild Jake Hiccup: The History of America's First Frontiersman. LC 91-19499. (Illus.). 80p. (Orig.). 1992. pap. 8.95 (*1-56412-002-3*) Hse Nine Muses.

***Davidson, Peter.** Finesse 'Em: How to Get What You Want Without a Sledgehammer. LC 99-64522. 150p. 2000. pap. 17.95 (*1-58501-013-8*, Pub. by CeShore Pubg) Natl Bk Netwk.

Davidson, Peter, ed. The Complete Works of George Orwell, 20 vols. LC 84-170. 1987. write for info. (*0-15-135101-5*) M Secker & Warburg.

Davidson, Peter & Van der Weel, Adriaan, eds. A Selection of the Poetry of Sir Constantijn Huygens (1596-1687) (Orig.). (C). 1996. pap. 39.50 (*90-5356-180-3*, Pub. by Amsterdam U Pr) U of Mich Pr.

Davidson, Peter, ed. see Fanshawe, Richard.

Davidson, Peter, ed. see Scott, Sir Walter.

Davidson, Peter, jt. ed. see Stevenson, Jan.

Davidson, Phebe. The Artists' Colony. LC 96-11184. 60p. 1996. pap. 14.95 (*0-7734-2684-1*, Mellen Poetry Pr) E Mellen.

— Caribbean Scrapbook. 28p. 1998. pap. 5.00 (*1-889806-17-X*) Devils Millhopper.

— Conversations with the World: American Women Poets & Their Work. 263p. 1998. pap. 14.95 (*0-9623879-9-1*) Trilogy Bks.

D

— Dreameater: Poems by Phebe Davidson. (Illus.). 64p. 1998. 15.00 (0-937158-10-0); pap. 10.00 (0-937158-09-7) Del Valley.

***Davidson, Phebe.** Reaching for Air. LC 00-39424. 72p. 2000. pap. text 14.95 (0-7734-1264-6) E Mellen.

Davidson, Phebe. Uses of the Spirit: Religious Impulse in Selected Autobiographies of American Women, 1630-1893. LC 93-5973. (Studies in Women & Religion: Vol. 33). 228p. 1993. text 89.95 (0-7734-9354-9) E Mellen.

Davidson, Phebe, ed. Film & Literature - Points of Intersection. LC 97-11113. 192p. 1997. text 79.95 (0-7734-8612-7) E Mellen.

— New Readings of Spiritual Narrative from the Fifteenth to the Twentieth Century: Secular Force & Self-Disclosure. LC 95-6141. (Studies in Religion & Society: Vol. 31). 132p. 1995. 69.95 (0-7734-8878-2) E Mellen.

Davidson, Phebe, ed. see Groth, Patricia C.

Davidson, Phil, tr. see Piaget, Jean & Garcia, Rolando, eds.

Davidson, Phillip B. Vietnam at War: The History Nineteen Forty-Six to Nineteen Seventy-Five. (Illus.). 864p. 1991. pap. 22.50 (0-19-506792-4) OUP.

***Davidson, Phillip L.** Healthcare Information Systems '99. LC 99-33558. (Best Practices Ser.). 592p. 1999. boxed set 79.95 (0-8493-9963-7) CRC Pr.

Davidson, Phillip L. SWAT (Special Weapons & Tactics) (Illus.). 148p. 1979. 32.95 (0-398-03890-2) C C Thomas.

Davidson, Phyllis I., jt. auth. see Koch, Richard T.

***Davidson Press Staff.** New Testament, 1vol. 2000. pap. text 30.00 (1-891833-13-8) Davidson Pr.

— New Testament with Psalms & Proverbs, 1vol. 2000. 60.00 (1-891833-12-X) Davidson Pr.

Davidson, R. S. & Collins, L. J. The Measurement & Analysis of Gear Noises. (Technical Papers: Vol. P185). (Illus.). 22p. 1938. pap. text 30.00 (1-55589-378-3) AGMA.

Davidson, R. Theodore. Chicano Prisoners: The Key to San Quentin. (Illus.). 196p. (C). 1983. reprint ed. pap. text 11.95 (0-88133-050-7) Waveland Pr.

Davidson, Ralph & Erskine, Angus, eds. Poverty, Deprivation & Social Work. 175p. 1992. 39.95 (1-85302-043-5) Taylor & Francis.

Davidson, Ralph H. & Lyon, William F. Insect Pests of Farm, Garden & Orchard. 8th ed. LC 86-23421. 656p. 1987. pap. 77.95 (0-471-01124-X) Wiley.

Davidson, Ralph K. Price Discrimination in Selling Gas & Electricity. LC 78-64222. (Johns Hopkins University. Studies in the Social Sciences. Thirtieth Ser. 1912: 1). 192p. 1982. reprint ed. 36.50 (0-404-61325-X) AMS Pr.

Davidson, Randy. Overcoming Math Anxiety. 2nd ed. LC 99-38594. 144p. (C). 1999. pap. text 23.00 (0-321-06918-8) Addison-Wesley.

Davidson, Rebecca, ed. see Williams, John A.

***Davidson, Rene H.** The Shiren. LC 99-91082. 1999. 25.00 (0-7388-0608-0); pap. 18.00 (0-7388-0609-9) Xlibris Corp.

Davidson, Richard. Furniture: Antiques Checklist. Miller, Judith & Miller, Martin, eds. (Illus.). 192p. 1991. 15.95 (0-85533-889-X, Pub. by Millers Pubns) Antique Collect.

— The Gentleman from Hyde Park. 6p. (Orig.). 1982. pap. 0.75 (0-934776-04-0) Bard Pr.

— Ribbon of Smoke & Stars. 20p. 1980. write for info. (0-318-64135-6) Poets Pr.

Davidson, Richard, jt. auth. see Ekman, Paul.

Davidson, Richard J. Neuropsychological Perspectives on Affective & Anxiety Disorders. LC 98-186024. 224p. 1998. write for info. (0-86377-971-9, Pub. by Psychol Pr) Taylor & Francis.

Davidson, Richard J., ed. Anxiety, Depression & Emotion: The First Wisconsin Symposium on Emotion. (Series in Affective Science). (Illus.). 288p. 2000. 59.95 (0-19-513358-7) OUP.

Davidson, Richard J. & Davidson, Julian M., eds. Psychobiology of Consciousness. LC 79-316. 508p. 1980. 80.00 (0-306-40138-X, Plenum Trade) Perseus Pubng.

Davidson, Richard J. & Hugdahl, Kenneth, eds. Brain Asymmetry. 650p. 1994. 75.00 (0-262-04144-8, Bradford Bks) MIT Pr.

— Brain Asymmetry. (Illus.). 752p. 1996. reprint ed. pap. text 45.00 (0-262-54079-7, Bradford Bks) MIT Pr.

Davidson, Richard J., jt. ed. see Fox, Nathan A.

Davidson, Richard M. Typology in Scripture: A Study of Hermeneutical Tupos Structures. (Andrews University Seminary Doctoral Dissertation Ser.: Vol. 2). 510p. (Orig.). 1981. pap. 19.99 (0-943872-34-0) Andrews Univ Pr.

Davidson, Robert. A Beginner's Guide to the Old Testament. 160p. (C). 1992. pap. 40.00 (0-7855-6847-6, Pub. by St Andrew) St Mut.

— A Beginner's Guide to the Old Testament. 160p. 1993. pap. 11.50 (0-7152-0637-0) St Mut.

— Broadband Networks: A Manager's Guide. LC 95-49740. 264p. 1996. pap. 29.95 (0-471-13885-1) Wiley.

— Eagle Transforming: The Art of Robert Davidson. LC 94-6768. (Illus.). 174p. 1994. 39.95 (0-295-97371-4) U of Wash Pr.

— Ecclesiastes & Song of Solomon. 172p. 1993. pap. 22.00 (0-7152-0537-4) St Mut.

***Davidson, Robert.** Fighting Back: A Battered Woman's Desperate Struggle to Survive. 352p. 2000. mass mkt. 6.99 (0-449-00542-9, Ballantine) Ballantine Pub Grp.

Davidson, Robert. Jeremiah Vols. 1-2: With Lamentations, Vol. 1. 176p. 1993. pap. 22.00 (0-7152-0526-9, Pub. by St Andrew) St Mut.

— Jeremiah Vols. 1-2: With Lamentations, Vol. 2. 224p. 1993. pap. 22.00 (0-7152-0529-3, Pub. by St Andrew) St Mut.

— The Vitality of Worship: A Commentary on the Book of Psalms. LC 98-16156. 496p. 1998. pap. 32.00 (0-8028-4246-1) Eerdmans.

— Wisdom & Worship. LC 90-39210. 160p. (Orig.). (C). 1990. pap. 13.00 (0-334-02461-7) TPI PA.

Davidson, Robert, ed. After the Watergaw: A Collection of New Poetry from Scotland Inspired by Water. 112p. 1994. pap. 21.00 (1-84017-024-7) St Mut.

— Genesis, Chapters 1-11. LC 72-93675. (Cambridge Bible Commentary on the New English Bible, New Testament Ser.). 118p. (Orig.). 1973. pap. text 20.95 (0-521-09760-6) Cambridge U Pr.

Davidson, Robert & Muller, Nathan. The Guide to Sonet. 1991. 31.95 (0-936648-29-5) Telecom Bks.

Davidson, Robert & Scottish Cultural Press Staff. Total Immersion. LC 99-206342. 1990. pap. 21.00 (1-898218-95-1) St Mut.

Davidson, Robert, jt. auth. see Davidson, Alan.

Davidson, Robert, ed. see Dollar, Alan.

Davidson, Robert C. & Busman, Denise. Acute Myocardial Infarction (Heart Attack) Grin, Oliver D. & Bouwman, Dorothy L., eds. (Patient Education Ser.). (Illus.). 30p. (Orig.). 1992. pap. text 4.00 (0-929689-47-X) Ludann Co.

Davidson, Robert Franklin. Philosophies Men Live By. 2nd ed. 442p. (C). 1974. text 40.00 (0-03-011851-4) Harcourt Coll Pubs.

Davidson, Robert G. Art of Worship. 20p. 1987. pap. 5.50 (0-940754-45-2) Ed Ministries.

— Being an Effective Teacher. 20p. 1987. pap. 5.50 (0-940754-42-8) Ed Ministries.

— Biblical Arts Festival. 1988. pap. 5.75 (0-940754-48-7, 5404) Ed Ministries.

— Conversation Time. 100p. 1997. pap. 12.95 (1-57438-014-1, 5525) Ed Ministries.

— Dynamics of Communicating. 20p. (Orig.). 1987. pap. 5.50 (0-940754-46-0) Ed Ministries.

— Gathering the Pieces. 88p. (Orig.). (gr. 7-12). 1985. pap. 9.95 (0-940754-30-4) Ed Ministries.

— God Doesn't Make Junk. (YA). (gr. 9-12). 1990. pap. 8.00 (0-940754-93-2, 8242) Ed Ministries.

— Growing with Discipline. (Leadership Ser.). 1987. pap. 5.50 (0-940754-43-6, 4012) Ed Ministries.

— Held in High Value. 65p. (Orig.). (gr. 7-12). 1986. pap. 9.95 (0-940754-34-7) Ed Ministries.

— Learning Through Art & Drama. 20p. (Orig.). 1987. pap. 5.50 (0-940754-47-9) Ed Ministries.

— Mark: What Is He Saying? 88p. 1998. pap. 7.95 (1-57438-025-7, 6621) Ed Ministries.

— Using the Story. (Leadership Ser.). 1987. pap. 5.50 (0-940754-44-4, 4013) Ed Ministries.

— What Do They Expect of Me? 80p. (gr. 7-12). 1986. pap. 9.95 (0-940754-32-0) Ed Ministries.

— Youth Programming Workbook. 40p. (Orig.). (YA). 1989. pap. 8.50 (0-940754-67-3) Ed Ministries.

Davidson, Robert G., ed. Creative Ideas for Advent, Vol. 1. 114p. 1980. pap. 12.95 (0-940754-06-1) Ed Ministries.

— Creative Ideas for Advent, Vol. 2. 100p. 1986. pap. 12.95 (0-940754-35-5) Ed Ministries.

— Creative Ideas for Lent, Vol. 1. 120p. (Orig.). 1985. pap. 12.95 (0-940754-25-8) Ed Ministries.

Davidson, Robert G. & Davidson, Linda S., eds. Creative Ideas for Advent, Vol. 4. (Creative Ideas for Advent Ser.). 130p. 1998. pap. 14.95 (1-57438-028-1, 2543) Ed Ministries.

— Creative Ideas for Lent, Vol. 2. 110p. (Orig.). 1989. pap. 12.95 (0-940754-62-2) Ed Ministries.

Davidson, Robert L. Handbook of Water-Soluble Gums & Resins. LC 79-24007. (Illus.). 671p. reprint ed. pap. 200.00 (0-8357-3966-X, AU0040000005) Bks Demand.

— Small Business Incorporation Kit. LC 92-14054. 160p. 1992. pap. 16.95 (0-471-57652-2) Wiley.

— The Small Business Partnership Kit. 160p. 1992. pap. 19.95 (0-471-57654-9) Wiley.

Davidson, Robert L., jt. ed. see Bland, William F.

Davidson, Robert P. Broadband Networking ABCs for Managers: ATM, BISDN, Cell-Frame Relay Sonet. 176p. 1994. pap. 29.95 (0-471-61954-X) Wiley.

Davidson, Robert P. & Muller, Nathan J. Internetworking LANs: Operation, Design & Management. (Telecommunications Ser.). 754p. 1992. text 95.00 (0-89006-598-5) Artech Hse.

Davidson, Robyn. Ancestors. large type ed. 451p. 1991. 24.95 (1-85089-408-6, Pub. by ISIS Lrg Prnt) Transaction Pubs.

— Desert Places. 1997. pap. 9.95 (0-14-015762-X); pap. 13.95 (0-14-026797-2) Viking Penguin.

— From Alice to Ocean: Alone Across the Outback. 1992. 50.00 (0-201-63216-0) Addison-Wesley.

— Tracks. LC 95-192552. 1995. pap. 12.00 (0-679-76287-6) Random.

Davidson, Roger. Whitehall & the Labour Problem in Late Victorian & Edwardian Britain: A Study in Official Statistics & Social Control. LC 84-21424. 294p. 1985. 32.50 (0-7099-0832-6, Pub. by C Helm) Routldge.

Davidson, Roger & White, Phil, eds. Information & Government. 224p. 1989. 18.00 (0-85224-554-8, Pub. by Edinburgh U Pr) Col U Pr.

Davidson, Roger H. The Politics of Comprehensive Manpower Legislation. LC 72-10874. (Policy Studies in Employment & Welfare: No. 15). 128p. reprint ed. pap. 39.70 (0-608-11886-9, 202309200032) Bks Demand.

— The Postreform Congress. LC 91-61134. 384p. (Orig.). (C). 1991. pap. text 22.00 (0-312-05673-7) St Martin.

Davidson, Roger H., ed. Congress & the Presidency: Invitation to Struggle. (Annals Ser.: Vol. 499). 1988. 26.00 (0-8039-3105-0); pap. 17.00 (0-8039-3106-9) Sage.

Davidson, Roger H., et al, eds. Masters of the House: Congressional Leadership over Two Centuries. LC 98-11326. (Transforming American Politics Ser.). 360p. (C). 1998. pap. text 30.00 (0-8133-6895-2, Pub. by Westview) HarpC.

Davidson, Roger H. & Levitan, Sar A. Antipoverty Housekeeping: The Administration of the Economic Opportunity Act. LC 68-65876. (Policy Papers in Human Resources & Industrial Relations Ser.: No. 9). (Orig.). 1968. pap. 5.00 (0-87736-109-6) U of Mich Inst Labor.

Davidson, Roger H. & Oleszek, Walter J. Congress & Its Members. 4th ed. LC 93-27786. 484p. 1993. 42.95 (0-87187-767-8) Congr Quarterly.

— Congress & Its Members. 6th ed. LC 97-27766. 490p. (YA). 1997. text 46.95 (1-56802-336-7); text 41.50 (1-56802-343-X) Congr Quarterly.

***Davidson, Roger H. & Oleszek, Walter J.** Congress & Its Members. 7th ed. LC 99-36620. 525p. 1999. 49.95 (1-56802-519-X); pap. 38.95 (1-56802-433-9) CQ Pr.

Davidson, Roger H., jt. auth. see Baker, Richard A.

Davidson, Roger H., jt. ed. see Longley, Lawrence D.

Davidson, Roger H., jt. ed. see Pfiffner, James P.

Davidson, Roger H., jt. ed. see Thurber, James A.

Davidson, Ronald. High Jinks at the Hot Pool: Mirror Reflects the Life of a City LC 94-189030. 239p. 1994. write for info. (1-86368-090-X) Intl Spec Bk.

— Physics of Non-Neutral Plasmas. (C). 1992. pap. 49.95 (0-201-57830-1) Addison-Wesley.

Davidson, Ronald C. Mathematical Methods for Introductory Physics with Calculus. 3rd ed. LC 94-5656. (C). 1994. pap. text 29.50 (0-03-009128-4, Pub. by SCP) Harcourt.

Davidson, Ronald M., jt. ed. see Goodman, Steven D.

Davidson, Ronald R. "Bushwacked by Bushmasters" Waco, the Raw Truth. LC 95-94001. 208p. (Orig.). 1995. pap. 19.95 (0-9645223-0-6) Watchman Davidson.

Davidson, Roy W. Documents on Contemporary Dervish Communities. 28p. 1990. pap. 9.00 (0-86304-015-2, Pub. by Octagon Pr) ISHK.

Davidson, Russell & MacKinnon, James G. Estimation & Inference in Econometrics. (Illus.). 896p. (C). 1993. text 65.00 (0-19-506011-3) OUP.

***Davidson, Ruth.** I, the Lord, Have Seen Thy Sorrow: An LDS Guide to Dealing with the Pain of Infidelity. 240p. 1999. pap. 14.95 (1-890828-18-1, Pub. by Camden Ct) Origin Bk Sales.

Davidson, S. I. & Jay, B., eds. Recent Advances in Ophthalmology 8. (Illus.). 214p. 1992. text 62.95 (0-443-04373-6) Church.

Davidson, S. S., jt. auth. see Ratnatunga, P. D.

Davidson, Sabrina M. Daughters of Deborah. LC 94-34513. 1995. pap. 14.95 (1-885275-52-8) C J Howie.

Davidson, Sandra. The Enchanting. 256p. 1997. mass mkt. 4.99 (0-8217-5762-8, Zebra Kensgtn) Kensgtn Pub Corp.

***Davidson, Sandra.** Timeless Winter. 1999. mass mkt. 5.99 (0-8217-6438-1, Zebra Kensgtn) Kensgtn Pub Corp.

Davidson, Sandra, et al. Timeless Spring. 1. 352p. 1999. mass mkt. 5.50 (0-8217-6148-X) Kensgtn Pub Corp.

Davidson, Sandra, jt. ed. see Winfield, Betty H.

***Davidson, Sara.** Cowboy: A Love Story. LC 98-30753. 288p. 2000. pap. 13.00 (0-06-093135-3) HarpC.

— Cowboy: A Love Story. 288p. 1999. 24.00 (0-06-099582-3, Cliff Street) HarperTrade.

— Cowboy: A Love Story. LC 98-30753. 288p. 1999. 24.00 (0-06-019326-3, Cliff Street) HarperTrade.

Davidson, Sara. Cowboy: A Love Story. large type ed. LC 99-31991. 1999. write for info. (1-56895-758-0) Wheeler Pub.

***Davidson, Sara.** Cowboy: A Love Story, Set. 1999. audio 18.00 (0-694-52135-3, 394875, Pub. by HarperAudio) Lndmrk Audiobks.

Davidson, Sara. Loose Change: 3 Women of the 60s. LC 96-37040. 381p. 1997. pap. 14.95 (0-520-20910-9, Pub. by U CA Pr) Cal Prin Full Svc.

Davidson, Sara, jt. auth. see Hudson, Rock.

Davidson, Sarah A., jt. ed. see Blegen, Theodore C.

Davidson, Scooter T. & Anthony, Valerie. Great Women in the Sport of Kings: America's Top Women Jockeys Tell Their Stories. LC 98-31881. 168p. 1999. 27.95 (0-8156-0565-X) Syracuse U Pr.

Davidson, Scott. Human Rights. LC 92-40622. (Law & Political Change Ser.). 224p. 1993. 99.00 (0-335-15769-6); pap. 39.00 (0-335-15768-8) OUP.

Davidson-Shaddox, Brenda. Mountains, Meadows & Mushrooms: A Guide to Cooking with Wild Mushrooms. (Illus.). 107p. 1992. pap. 10.95 (0-9631719-1-7) C R Shaddox.

Davidson-Shaddox, Brenda, ed. Stoneflower Literary Journal, Vol. 2. (Illus.). 92p. (Orig.). 1997. per. 8.00 (0-9631719-3-3) C R Shaddox.

***Davidson, Sherry.** Alcoholocaust: Breaking the Family Curse. 409p. 1999. pap. write for info. (0-9673116-3-2) WordPro Pr.

Davidson, Sidney & Weil, Roman L. Handbook of Cost Accounting. 756p. (C). 1989. text 79.95 (0-13-376039-1, Pub. by P-H) S&S Trade.

Davidson, Sol M. Wild Jake Hiccup: The History of America's First Frontiersman. unabridged ed. LC 91-19499. (Illus.). 160p. (J). (gr. 3-10). 1992. 19.95 (1-56412-003-1); pap. 14.95 (1-56412-004-X) Hse Nine Muses.

Davidson, Sonia. All about Worms. (Allen Photographic Guides Ser.). (Illus.). 24p. 2000. pap. 10.95 (0-85131-709-X, Pub. by J A Allen) Trafalgar.

Davidson Sr., Kenneth J. & Moore, Newlyn B., eds. Exploring Human Sexuality: An Anthology. LC 99-35447. 400p. (C). 2000. pap. text. write for info. (1-891487-33-7) Roxbury Pub Co.

Davidson, Stephanie G. 101 Ways to Have a Great Day at Work. LC 99-216192. 112p. 1998. pap. 7.95 (1-887166-41-6) Sourcebks.

Davidson, Stephen M. & Somers, Stephen A. Remaking Medicaid: Managed Care for the Public Good. LC 98-18333. 1998. 45.95 (0-7879-4042-9) Jossey-Bass.

Davidson, Stephen M., et al. The Physician-Manager Alliance: Building the Healthy Health Care Organization. (Health Ser.). 288p. 1996. 36.95 (0-7879-0215-2) Jossey-Bass.

Davidson, Steve. In the Medic's House: Poems of Desert Storm. 32p. 1992. pap. 5.00 (1-877603-39-2) Pecan Grove.

Davidson, Steven & Lukow, Gregory, eds. The Administration of Television Newsfilm & Videotape Collections: A Curatorial Manual. LC 97-70587. (Illus.). 247p. 1997. pap. 41.00 (0-9649097-0-7) Nat Ctr Film Vid.

Davidson, Sue. Changing the Game: The Stories of Tennis Champions Alice Marble & Althea Gibson. LC 96-51698. (Women Who Dared Ser.). (Illus.). 192p. (Orig.). (YA). (gr. 6-12). 1997. pap. 10.95 (1-878067-88-5) Seal Pr WA.

— Getting the Real Story: Nellie Bly & Ida B. Wells. LC 91-38041. (Illus.). 160p. (Orig.). (YA). (gr. 6-12). 1992. pap. 8.95 (1-878067-16-8) Seal Pr WA.

— A Heart in Politics: Jeannette Rankin & Patsy T. Mink. LC 94-11066. (Women Who Dared Ser.). (Illus.). 160p. (Orig.). (YA). (gr. 6-12). 1994. pap. 9.95 (1-878067-53-2) Seal Pr WA.

— Steeples on the Riverbend. 352p. 1991. write for info. (0-942407-16-4) Father & Son.

Davidson, Sue, jt. auth. see Davidson, Joe.

Davidson, Sue, jt. auth. see NiCarthy, Ginny.

Davidson, Sue, ed. see Pinzer, Maimie.

Davidson, Susan E., ed. A Piece of the Moon World: Paul Klee in Texas Collections. LC 94-4876. 1994. pap. 14.95 (0-939594-31-5, Menil Collection) Menil Found.

Davidson, Susan J. It's Only Life: Rhythmic Forays into Politics & Human Nature. 44p. 1992. pap. 7.50 (0-9633629-0-9) S J Davidson.

Davidson, Sydney. The Plant Accounting Regulations of the Federal Power Commission: A Critical Analysis. Brief, Richard P., ed. LC 77-87296. (Development of Contemporary Accounting Thought Ser.). 1978. reprint ed. lib. bdg. 23.95 (0-405-10936-9) Ayer.

Davidson, T. Rousseau & Education According to Nature. 1972. 59.95 (0-8490-0976-6) Gordon Pr.

Davidson, Terence M. Aging-Face Surgery with Emphasis on Face-Lift. 2nd ed. LC 98-21889. (Self-Instructional Package Ser.). (Illus.). 179p. (Orig.). 1998. reprint ed. pap. text 25.00 (1-56772-066-8, 5506510) AAO-HNS.

— Endoscopic Sinus Surgery. 2nd rev. ed. LC 98-36304. (Self-Instructional Package Ser.). (Illus.). 164p. 1998. pap. text 25.00 (1-56772-068-4, 5506515) AAO-HNS.

***Davidson, Terence M.** MOHs. LC 99-47753. (Self-Instructional Package Ser.). (Illus.). 121p. 1999. pap. text 25.00 (1-56772-028-5, 5506360) AAO-HNS.

Davidson, Terence M. Scar Revision. 4th rev. ed. LC 98-14945. (Self-Instructional Package Ser.). (Illus.). 113p. (Orig.). 1998. pap. text 25.00 (1-56772-063-3, 5506035) AAO-HNS.

Davidson, Terence M., ed. Clinical Manual of Otolaryngology. 2nd ed. LC 91-3857. (Clinical Manual Ser.). (Illus.). 267p. 1992. text 29.50 (0-07-105399-9, RF56) McGraw-Hill HPD.

Davidson, Terence M., et al. The Principles & Dynamics of Local Skin Flaps. 4th rev. ed. LC 98-3832. (Self-Instructional Package Ser.). (Illus.). 110p. 1998. pap. text 25.00 (1-56772-062-5) AAO-HNS.

Davidson, Theodore, ed. Polymers in Electronics. LC 83-25782. (ACS Symposium Ser.: No. 242). 616p. 1984. lib. bdg. 87.95 (0-8412-0823-9) Am Chemical.

— Polymers in Electronics. LC 83-25782. (ACS Symposium Ser.: Vol. 242). 616p. 1984. reprint ed. pap. 191.00 (0-608-03123-2, 206357600007) Bks Demand.

Davidson, Theodore F., jt. auth. see Sondley, F. A.

Davidson, Thomas. Aristotle & Ancient Educational Ideals. (Notable American Authors Ser.). 1992. reprint ed. lib. bdg. 75.00 (0-7812-2620-1) Rprt Serv.

— Collected Works. 1990. reprint ed. lib. bdg. 75.00 (0-7812-2616-3, 1504); reprint ed. write for info. (0-318-67680-X); reprint ed. write for info. (0-318-67681-8); reprint ed. write for info. (0-318-67682-6); reprint ed. write for info. (0-318-67683-4); reprint ed. write for info. (0-318-67684-2); reprint ed. write for info. (0-318-67685-0); reprint ed. write for info. (0-318-67686-9) Rprt Serv.

— Education of the Greek People, & Its Influence on Civilization. LC 74-136402. (BCL Ser. I). reprint ed. 32.50 (0-404-01944-7) AMS Pr.

— The Education of the Greek People & Its Influence on Civilization. 1988. reprint ed. lib. bdg. 75.00 (0-7812-0205-1) Rprt Serv.

— The Education of the Greek People & Its Influence on Civilization. (Notable American Authors Ser.). 1992. reprint ed. lib. bdg. 75.00 (0-7812-2621-X) Rprt Serv.

— The Education of the Greek People & Its Influence on Civilization. 1977. reprint ed. 29.00 (0-403-07980-2) Scholarly.

— The Education of the Wage Earner. (Notable American Authors Ser.). 1992. reprint ed. lib. bdg. 90.00 (0-7812-2624-4) Rprt Serv.

— History of Education. LC 74-121286. (BCL Ser. I). reprint ed. 20.00 (0-404-01945-5) AMS Pr.

— A History of Education. (Notable American Authors Ser.). 1992. reprint ed. lib. bdg. 75.00 (0-7812-2623-6) Rprt Serv.

— The Parthenon Frieze & Other Essays. (Notable American Authors Ser.). 1992. reprint ed. lib. bdg. 75.00 (0-7812-2617-1) Rprt Serv.

D

An Asterisk (*) at the beginning of an entry indicates that the title is appearing for the first time.

— Philosophy of Goethe's Faust. LC 68-24963. (Studies in German Literature: No. 13). (C). 1969. reprint ed. lib. bdg. 75.00 (*0-8383-0933-X*) M S G Haskell Hse.
— The Place of Art in Education. (Notable American Authors Ser.). 1992. reprint ed. lib. bdg. 75.00 (*0-7812-2618-X*) Rprt Serv.
— Prolego-mena to In Memoriam. (Notable American Authors Ser.). 1992. reprint ed. lib. bdg. 75.00 (*0-7812-2619-8*) Rprt Serv.
— Rousseau & Education According to Nature. LC 70-136373. reprint ed. 32.50 (*0-404-01977-3*) AMS Pr.
— Rousseau & Education According to Nature. (Notable American Authors Ser.). 1992. reprint ed. lib. bdg. 75.00 (*0-7812-2622-8*) Rprt Serv.
— Rousseau & Education According to Nature. LC 70-108469. 1970. reprint ed. 15.00 (*0-403-00427-6*) Scholarly.
***Davidson, Thomas.** 7 Steps for Organizational & School Violence Management. 240p. 2000. pap. 15.95 (*1-58374-016-3*) Chicago Spectrum.
Davidson, Thomas E. Free Blacks on the Lower Eastern Shore of Maryland: The Colonial Period, 1662-1775. 2nd ed. (Manuscript Ser.: No. 42). 116p. 1991. spiral bd. 11.00 (*1-878399-45-4*) Div Hist Cult Progs.
Davidson, Thomas E., jt. auth. see Rountree, Helen C.
Davidson, Todd & Donchez, Bob. Legends of Lehigh-Lafayette: College Football's Most-Played Rivalry. LC 95-92244. 256p. 1995. 39.95 (*0-9640341-1-5*) Successful Concepts.
Davidson, Toni. Intoxication: An Anthology of Stimulant-Based Writing. 213p. 1998. pap. 13.99 (*1-85242-558-X*) Serpents Tail.
***Davidson, Toni.** Scar Culture. 256p. 2000. pap. 14.00 (*0-393-32089-8*) Norton.
Davidson, Victor. Principles & Applications of Quinoproteins. LC 92-26045. (Illus.). 472p. 1992. text 199.00 (*0-8247-8764-1*) Dekker.
Davidson, W. S., II, et al. Alternative Treatments for Troubled Youth: The Case of Diversion from the Justice System. (Crime & Justice Ser.). (Illus.). 308p. (C). 1990. 65.00 (*0-306-43421-0*, Plenum Trade) Perseus Pubng.
Davidson, Warren R., jt. auth. see Smith, G. Elliot.
Davidson, Wilburt C. Davidson's Compleat Pediatrician. 9th ed. Arena, Jay M., ed. LC 78-98492. 806p. reprint ed. pap. 200.00 (*0-608-12668-3*, 205599500043) Bks Demand.
Davidson, William. Brother Goose. 1942. pap. 5.25 (*0-87129-743-4*, B34) Dramatic Pub.
— Cardinal Cross. 18p. 1963. 8.00 (*0-86690-179-5*, D1054-014) Am Fed Astrologers.
— Houseplants. 96p. 1988. 25.00 (*1-85283-225-8*, Pub. by Boxtree) St Mut.
Davidson, William, et al. Retailing Management. 6th ed. LC 87-10555. 896p. 1988. text 92.95 (*0-471-85094-2*) Wiley.
— Vision Fulfilling: The Story of Rural & Small Community Work of the Episcopal Church in the 20th Century. LC 97-27225. 320p. 1997. 25.95 (*0-8192-1732-8*); pap. 19.95 (*0-8192-1733-6*) Morehouse Pub.
Davidson, William F. The Free Will Baptists in America, 1727-1984. 462p. (C). 1985. text 16.95 (*0-89265-093-1*) Randall Hse.
Davidson, William L. The Stoic Creed. Vlastos, Gregory, ed. LC 78-19341. (Morals & Law in Ancient Greece Ser.). 1979. reprint ed. lib. bdg. 33.95 (*0-405-11535-0*) Ayer.
Davidson, William R., et al. Retailing Management. LC 83-23378. (Illus.). 796p. reprint ed. pap. 200.00 (*0-7837-3505-7*, 205783800008) Bks Demand.
Davidson, William V. Historical Geography of the Bay Islands, Honduras: Anglo-Hispanic Conflict in the Western Caribbean. (Illus.). 1974. 35.00 (*0-686-96890-5*); pap. 15.00 (*0-87651-207-4*) Southern U Pr.
Davidson, William V. & Parsons, James J., eds. Historical Geography of Latin America: Papers in Honor of Robert C. West. LC 80-120352. (Geoscience & Man Ser.: Vol. 21). (Illus.). 170p. 1980. pap. 14.00 (*0-938909-20-7*) Geosci Pubns LSU.
Davidson, Wilma & McCloskey, Susan. Writing a Winning College Application Essay: Peterson's Practically Painless Guide. 136p. (Orig.). (YA). (gr. 10-12). 1996. pap. 9.95 (*1-56079-601-4*) Petersons.
Davidsson, A., jt. auth. see Holm, G.
***Davidsson, Marcy Foley, et al.** Illuminating Physical Experience. Johnson, Donald, ed. 252p. 2000. per. 15.00 (*0-9631452-4-X*) Komax.
Davie, Bruce. Formal Specification & Verification in VLSI Design. 1991. text 75.00 (*0-7486-0159-7*, Pub. by Edinburgh U Pr) Col U Pr.
Davie, Bruce, et al. Switching in IP Networks: IP Switching, Tag Switching & Related Technologies. LC 98-4558. 256p. 1998. pap. 44.95 (*1-55860-505-3*, 900070) Morgan Kaufmann.
***Davie, Bruce S. & Rekhter, Yakov.** MPLS: Technology & Applications. (Networking Ser.). 300p. 2000. pap. 44.95 (*1-55860-656-4*) Morgan Kaufmann.
Davie, Bruce S., jt. auth. see Peterson, Larry L.
Davie, Cedric T. Musical Structure & Design. (Illus.). 181p. 1966. pap. 6.95 (*0-486-21629-2*) Dover.
Davie, Cedric T. & McVicar, George, eds. Oxford Scottish Song Book. 1969. 12.00 (*0-19-330270-5*); pap. 12.00 (*0-19-330271-3*); pap. 3.50 (*0-19-330272-1*) OUP.
Davie, Donald. Articulate Energy: An Inquiry into the Syntax of English Poetry. 1988. reprint ed. lib. bdg. 59.00 (*0-7812-0488-7*) Rprt Serv.
— Articulate Energy: An Inquiry into the Syntax of English Poetry. LC 77-158901. 1971. reprint ed. 45.00 (*0-403-01316-X*) Scholarly.
— Church, Chapel, & the Unitarian Conspiracy: Essays in Dissent. 54p. 1996. 45.00 (*1-85754-123-5*, Pub. by Carcanet Pr) Paul & Co Pubs.
— Collected Poems. (Phoenix Poets Ser.). 480p. 1991. pap. 17.95 (*0-226-13761-9*); lib. bdg. 48.00 (*0-226-13760-0*) U Ch Pr.
— Ezra Pound. LC 81-21857. viii, 134p. (C). 1993. pap. 4.95 (*0-226-13753-8*) U Ch Pr.
— Poems & Melodrama. LC 97-143398. 128p. pap. 14.95 (*1-85754-290-8*, Pub. by Carcanet Pr) Paul & Co Pubs.
— Purity of Diction in English Verse & Articulate Energy. 380p. 1995. pap. 9.95 (*1-85754-121-9*, Pub. by Carcanet Pr) Paul & Co Pubs.
— Slavic Excursions: Essays on Russian & Polish Literature. LC 90-34525. 312p. 1990. pap. text 17.00 (*0-226-13759-7*) U Ch Pr.
— Slavic Excursions: Essays on Russian & Polish Literature. LC 90-34525. 312p. 1996. lib. bdg. 36.00 (*0-226-13758-9*) U Ch Pr.
— To Scorch or Freeze: Poems About the Sacred. (Phoenix Poets Ser.). 62p. 1988. pap. 9.95 (*0-226-13755-4*); lib. bdg. 29.00 (*0-226-13754-6*) U Ch Pr.
— Trying to Explain. (Poets on Poetry Ser.). 224p. 1979. pap. 13.95 (*0-472-06310-3*, 06310) U of Mich Pr.
***Davie, Donald.** Two Ways Out of Whitman: American Essays. Davie, Doreen, ed. 352p. 2000. pap. 29.95 (*1-85754-460-9*, Pub. by Carcanet Pr) Paul & Co Pubs.
Davie, Donald. Under Briggflatts: A History of Poetry in Great Britain, 1960-1988. LC 89-5111. 262p. 1989. 29.95 (*0-226-13756-2*) U Ch Pr.
***Davie, Donald.** With the Grain: Essays on Thomas Hardy & Modern British Poetry. 288p. 1999. pap. 29.95 (*1-85754-394-7*, Pub. by Carcanet Pr) Paul & Co Pubs.
Davie, Donald, ed. The New Oxford Book of Christian Verse. 368p. 1988. pap. 14.95 (*0-19-282157-1*) OUP.
— Russian Literature & Modern English Fiction: A Collection of Critical Essays. LC 65-18337. (Patterns of Literary Criticism Ser.). 250p. reprint ed. pap. 77.50 (*0-608-18558-2*, 202005200016) Bks Demand.
Davie, Donald, ed. & tr. see Pasternak, Boris.
Davie, Doreen, ed. see Davie, Donald.
Davie, E. W. & Kakishita, E., eds. Blood Coagulation, Fibrinolysis & Platelets. (Illus.). 240p. 1996. pap. 79.00 (*4-431-70165-6*) Spr-Verlag.
Davie, Elspeth. Creating a Scene. 304p. (Orig.). 1984. pap. 11.95 (*0-7145-0731-8*) Riverrun NY.
— Spark & Other Stories. 288p. (Orig.). 1983. pap. 11.95 (*0-7145-0538-2*) Riverrun NY.
Davie, Ethel O. Talent & Courage: Outstanding West Virginia Women in the 1990s. 125p. 1992. pap. write for info. (*0-9634513-0-8*) E O Davie.
Davie, G. S. The Garden of Fragrance: Being a Complete Translation of the Bostan of Sadi. 325p. 1996. reprint ed. pap. 24.95 (*1-56459-520-X*) Kessinger Pub.
Davie, George. Crisis of Democratic Intellect. 1989. 29.95 (*0-85224-648-X*, Pub. by Polygon) Subterranean Co.
— The Passion for Ideas. 1994. 16.00 (*0-7486-6147-6*, Pub. by Polygon) Subterranean Co.
***Davie, George Elder.** The Democratic Intellect: Scotland & Her Universities in the Nineteenth Century. 392p. 2000. pap. text 25.00 (*0-7486-1274-2*) Col U Pr.
Davie, Grace. Religion in Britain: Since Nineteen Forty-Five. (Making Contemporary Britain Ser.). (Illus.). 240p. 1994. pap. 27.95 (*0-631-18444-9*) Blackwell Pubs.
***Davie, Grace.** Religion in Modern Europe: A Memory Mutates. (European Societies Ser.). 240p. 2000. pap. 26.00 (*0-19-924124-4*); text 60.00 (*0-19-828065-3*) OUP.
Davie, Grace, jt. ed. see Cook, Malcolm.
Davie, J. T. & Morrison, R. Recursive Descent Compiling. LC 81-6778. (Computers & Their Applications Ser.). 195p. 1982. pap. text 39.95 (*0-470-27361-5*) P-H.
Davie, Jane L. Transforming State Education Agencies to Support Education Reform. 56p. (Orig.). 1994. pap. text 15.00 (*1-55877-198-0*) Natl Governor.
Davie, Jody S. Women in the Presence: Constructing Community & Seeking Spirituality in Mainline Protestantism. LC 95-14736. 184p. 1995. text 35.00 (*0-8122-3286-0*); pap. text 14.95 (*0-8122-1514-1*) U of Pa Pr.
Davie, John, ed. see Austen, Jane.
Davie, John, ed. & notes see Austen, Jane.
Davie, John, tr. see Euripides.
Davie, John L. His Honor, the Buckaroo: The Autobiography of John L. Davie. rev. ed. LC 87-91072. (Illus.). 239p. (YA). (gr. 9-12). 1988. pap. 9.95 (*0-943077-12-5*) Pub J Herzberg.
Davie, Judith F., jt. auth. see Wright, Kieth C.
Davie, Mark. Half-Serious Rhymes: The Narrative Poetry of Luigi Pulci. LC 98-188873. 240p. 1997. 47.50 (*0-7165-2601-8*, Pub. by Irish Acad Pr) Intl Spec Bk.
Davie, Martin. British Quaker Theology since 1895. LC 97-13395. 316p. 1997. text 99.95 (*0-7734-8611-9*) E Mellen.
Davie, Maurice, ed. Refugees in America: Committee for the Study of Recent Immigration from Europe. LC 74-1513. (Illus.). 453p. 1974. reprint ed. lib. bdg. 79.50 (*0-8371-7390-6*, DARA, Greenwood Pr) Greenwood.
Davie, Michael. Titanic: The Death & Life of a Legend. LC 86-46021. 272p. 1987. 19.95 (*0-317-58565-7*) Knopf.
Davie, Sandy, jt. auth. see Lauffer, Butch.
Davie, Sandy, ed. see Van der Zande, Irene & Santa Cruz Toddler Center Staff.
Davies. Babies, Believers & Baptism. 1994. pap. 1.25 (*0-9505476-9-7*, Pub. by Evangelical Pr) P & R Pubng.
— Best of Sherlock Holmes. (Classics Library). 304p. 1998. pap. 3.95 (*1-85326-744-9*, 7449WW, Pub. by Wrdsworth Edits) NTC Contemp Pub Co.
— Biology 110: Anatomy. 110p. (C). 1998. pap. text, lab manual ed. 12.75 (*0-536-01289-X*) Pearson Custom.
— A Corpus of Inscribed Egyptian Funerary Cones, Vol. 1. (Plates Ser.). 65p. 1957. 50.00 (*0-900416-12-2*, Pub. by Aris & Phillips) David Brown.
***Davies.** Digital Imaging for Photographers. 4th ed. 224p. 2000. pap. text 39.95 (*0-240-51590-0*) Buttrwrth-Heinemann.
Davies. Efficiency In Research: Development & Production. 1993. 89.00 (*0-85186-457-0*) CRC Pr.
— Elusive Liberty. 1999. text 22.95 (*0-312-18093-4*) St Martin.
— Essay Writing in German. LC 96-43634. 1997. pap. 19.95 (*0-7190-3888-X*); text 69.95 (*0-7190-3887-1*) St Martin.
Davies. Essential Social Worker. 240p. 1994. pap. 29.95 (*1-85742-101-9*) Ashgate Pub Co.
Davies. Essential Vascular Surgery. 1999. text 38.00 (*0-7020-2326-4*, W B Saunders Co) Harcrt Hlth Sci Grp.
— Essentials of Medical Terminology. LC 97-42612. 416p. (C). 1997. pap. 33.95 (*0-314-12811-5*) Delmar.
Davies. History of Music in Wales. 59.95 (*1-85928-401-9*) Ashgate Pub Co.
Davies. How to Read Faces. 1987. pap. 9.95 (*0-85030-804-6*, Pub. by Aqrn Pr) Harper SF.
— Industrial Biotechnology in Europe. (C). 1986. text. write for info. (*0-86187-648-2*) St Martin.
— Magic of Physics. (C). 1998. write for info. (*0-201-62608-X*) Addison-Wesley.
— Making Adverts. 1991. pap. text. write for info. (*0-582-05943-7*, Pub. by Addison-Wesley) Longman.
— Modeling Marine Systems, Vol. 2. 456p. 1990. boxed set 249.00 (*0-8493-4222-8*, GC10) CRC Pr.
— Psychiatric Nursing Value Package. 1991. 71.25 (*0-86720-311-0*) Jones & Bartlett.
— Public Health, Preventive Medicine & Social Services. 6th ed. LC 96-218055. write for info. (*0-340-61373-4*, Pub. by E A) Routldge.
Davies. Receovered Memories. text. write for info. (*0-471-49131-4*) Wiley.
— Recovered Memories. pap. text. write for info. (*0-471-49132-2*) Wiley.
— Retail Management. pap. text. write for info. (*0-471-48912-3*) Wiley.
Davies. Soviet History in the Yeltsin Era. LC 96-29714. 272p. 1997. text 69.95 (*0-312-17372-5*) St Martin.
Davies. Understanding Marketing. 304p. 1997. pap. 40.00 (*0-13-490467-2*) P-H.
Davies. War of the Mines: Cambodia, Landmines & the Impoverishment of a Nation. LC 94-2724. 172p. (C). 119.95 (*0-7453-0859-7*, Pub. by Pluto GBR) Stylus Pub VA.
— War of the Mines: Cambodia, Landmines & the Impoverishment of a Nation. (Illus.). 172p. (C). pap. 42.95 (*0-7453-0860-0*, Pub. by Pluto GBR) Stylus Pub VA.
***Davies.** Witchcraft Magic & Cult 1736-5. 320p. 1999. text 79.95 (*0-7190-5655-1*) St Martin.
Davies & Austin. Vitamin C: Its Chemistry & Biochemistry. 1991. 39.00 (*0-85186-333-7*) CRC Pr.
Davies & Coxo. Key Texts in Multidimensional Scaling. 1982. text 51.95 (*0-435-82254-3*) Ashgate Pub Co.
Davies & Creaser. Analytical Application of Spectroscopy II. 1991. 154.00 (*0-85186-403-1*) CRC Pr.
Davies & Francis. Invisible Crimes. LC 99-11218. 497p. 1999. text 69.95 (*0-312-22182-7*) St Martin.
Davies & Morley. County Borough Elections in England, Vol. 2. 145.95 (*1-84014-247-2*) Ashgate Pub Co.
Davies, et al. Computer-Aided Drawing & Design (Illus.). 328p. (Orig.). (C). (gr. 13). Date not set. pap. text 50.95 (*0-412-34230-8*) Chapman & Hall.
Davies, jt. auth. see Casper.
Davies, jt. auth. see Collins.
Davies, jt. auth. see Gilmore, Rachna.
Davies, jt. auth. see Rees.
Davies, jt. auth. see Warman, Adrian R.
Davies, ed. see Chamfort.
Davies, P. D. O., ed. Clinical Tuberculosis. 2nd ed. (An Arnold Publication). (Illus.). 744p. 1999. text 125.00 (*0-412-80340-2*, Pub. by E A) OUP.
Davies, A. C. The Science & Practice of Welding Vol. 1: Welding Science & Technology. 10th ed. (Illus.). 361p. (C). 1993. pap. text 29.95 (*0-521-43565-X*) Cambridge U Pr.
— The Science & Practice of Welding Vol. 2: The Practice of Welding. 10th ed. (Illus.). 535p. (C). 1993. text 95.00 (*0-521-43404-1*); pap. text 39.95 (*0-521-43566-8*) Cambridge U Pr.
Davies, A. C., jt. auth. see Schwarz, W.
Davies, A. E. & Billson, A. L. Key Topics in Pediatrics. 300p. (Orig.). 1994. pap. 52.50 (*1-872748-56-9*, Pub. by Bios Sci) Coronet Bks.
Davies, A. Emil. Investments Abroad. Wilkins, Mira, ed. LC 76-29984. (European Business Ser.). 1977. reprint ed. lib. bdg. 20.95 (*0-405-09749-2*) Ayer.
Davies, A. G. Organotin Chemistry. LC 97-194256. 340p. 1997. 270.00 (*3-527-29049-4*, Wiley-VCH) Wiley.
Davies, A. H., tr. see Engel, Klaus.
Davies, A. M., et al, eds. Orthopedic Imaging: Techniques & Applications. LC 97-49118. (Medical Radiology Ser.). (Illus.). 350p. 1998. 189.00 (*3-540-63187-9*) Spr-Verlag.
Davies, A. Mervyn. Life & Times of Warren Hastings: Maker of British India. (C). 1988. reprint ed. 72.50 (*81-212-0144-6*, Pub. by Gian Publng Hse) S Asia.
Davies, A. N. Raj in Charge. (Illus.). (J). pap. 6.95 (*0-14-038159-7*, Pub. by Pnguin Bks Ltd) Trafalgar.
Davies, A. T., ed. Sallust: Catiline. (Bristol Latin Texts Ser.). (LAT.). 128p. 1987. reprint ed. pap. 18.95 (*0-86292-258-5*, Pub. by Brist Class Pr) Focus Pub-R Pullins.
Davies, A. T. & Sutherland, D. G., eds. Superstrings & Supergravity. (Scottish Universities Summer School in Physics, a NATO Advanced Study Institute Ser.: No. 28). (Illus.). 554p. 1986. 189.00 (*0-905945-11-5*) IOP Pub.
Davies, Adrain & Fennessy, Phil. Electronic Imaging for Photographers. 2nd ed. (Illus.). 160p. 1996. pap. text 39.95 (*0-240-51441-6*, Focal) Buttrwrth-Heinemann.
***Davies, Adrian.** Corporate Governance. LC 98-47107. 1999. 74.95 (*0-566-08074-5*) Ashgate Pub Co.
Davies, Adrian. The Digital Imaging, A to Z. LC 97-48315. 100p. 2000. pap. text 14.95 (*0-240-51500-5*, Focal) Buttrwrth-Heinemann.
***Davies, Adrian.** The Encyclopedia of Photography. (Illus.). 2000. 24.95 (*0-7624-0704-2*) Running Pr.
— The Quakers in English Society, 1655-1725. LC 99-45356. (Oxford Historical Monographs). 280p. 2000. 65.00 (*0-19-820820-0*) OUP.
Davies, Adrian. The Strategic Role of Marketing: Understanding Why Marketing Should Be Central to Your Business Strategy. LC 95-7927. 1995. write for info. (*0-07-707854-3*) McGraw.
Davies, Adrian & Fennessy, Phil. Digital Imaging for Photographers. 3rd ed. LC 98-27210. (Illus.). 192p. 1998. pap. text 39.95 incl. cd-rom (*0-240-51538-2*, Focal) Buttrwrth-Heinemann.
Davies, Alan. Active Twenty-Four Hours. (Roof Bks.). 100p. (Orig.). 1984. pap. 5.00 (*0-937804-11-8*) Segue NYC.
— Candor. LC 90-62685. 1990. 9.00 (*1-882022-08-4*) O Bks.
***Davies, Alan.** Introduction to Applied Linguistics: From Practice to Theory. (Illus.). 2000. pap. 25.50 (*0-7486-1258-0*, Pub. by Edinburgh U Pr) Col U Pr.
Davies, Alan. Mnemonotechnics. 28p. (Orig.). 1982. pap. 5.50 (*0-937013-12-9*) Potes Poets.
— The Native Speaker in Applied Linguistics. 192p. 1992. pap. text 18.00 (*0-7486-0296-8*, Pub. by Edinburgh U Pr) Col U Pr.
— Rave. 1994. pap. 7.95 (*0-937804-55-X*) Segue NYC.
— Signage. LC 87-60108. (Roof Bks.). 150p. (Orig.). 1987. pap. 10.95 (*0-937804-24-X*) Segue NYC.
Davies, Alan, ed. A an Av Es. 28p. (Orig.). 1981. pap. 5.50 (*0-937013-04-8*) Potes Poets.
Davies, Alan & Davies, M. M. Winterford. 1994. 7.00 (*84-87467-20-2*, Pub. by Zasterle Pr) SPD-Small Pr Dist.
Davies, Alan & Nefsky, Marilyn F. How Silent Were the Churches? Canadian Protestantism & the Jewish Plight During the Nazi Era. LC 98-232717. 195p. 1997. pap. 27.95 (*0-88920-309-1*) W Laurier U Pr.
Davies, Alan H. Old Carmarthen. 96p. 1985. 30.00 (*0-86383-171-0*, Pub. by Gomer Pr) St Mut.
Davies, Alan M., ed. Modeling Marine Systems, Vol. I. 312p. 1989. boxed set 195.00 (*0-8493-4221-X*, GC10) CRC Pr.
Davies, Alan M., jt. ed. see Lynch, Daniel R.
Davies, Alan T. Antisemitism in Canada: History & Interpretation. 312p. (C). 1992. pap. 39.95 (*0-88920-221-4*) W Laurier U Pr.
— Infected Christianity: A Study of Modern Racism. 176p. (C). 1988. text 60.00 (*0-7735-0651-9*, Pub. by McG-Queens Univ Pr) CUP Services.
Davies, Alastair, ed. An Annotated Critical Bibliography of Modernism, No. 1. LC 82-13864. (Harvester-Barnes & Noble Annotated Critical Bibliographies Ser.). 276p. (C). 1982. text 53.50 (*0-389-20303-3*, N7138) B&N Imports.
Davies, Alfred T. John Calvin: Many Sided Genius. LC 83-45609. reprint ed. 37.50 (*0-404-19827-9*) AMS Pr.
Davies, Alice I., text. 16th & 17th - Century Dutch & Flemish Paintings in the Springfield Museum of Fine Arts. (Illus.). 160p. 1993. 26.95 (*0-916746-17-8*) Springfield Lib & Mus.
***Davies, Alistair & Sinfield, Alan.** British Culture of the Postwar: An Introduction to Literature & Society, 1945-1999. LC 00-35276. (Illus.). 2000. write for info. (*0-415-12811-0*) Routledge.
Davies, Alun E. The Welsh Language & Welsh Dissertations. 384p. 1997. 60.00 (*0-7083-1210-1*, Pub. by Univ Wales Pr) Paul & Co Pubs.
Davies, Andrew. B. Monkey. LC 97-452. 224p. (J). 1998. pap. 11.45 (*0-7868-8249-2*, Pub. by Hyperion) Time Warner.
***Davies, Andrew.** Double Standards in Isaiah: Re-Evaluating Prophetic Ethics & Divine Justice. LC 99-86720. (Biblical Interpretation Ser.). 224p. 2000. 70.00 (*90-04-11581-1*) Brill Academic Pubs.
Davies, Andrew. Leisure, Gender & Poverty: Working-Class Culture in Salford & Manchester, 1900-1939. (Themes in the Twentieth Century Ser.). 192p. 1992. pap. 40.95 (*0-335-15637-1*) OpUniv Pr.
Davies, Andrew & Roydhouse, Eric, eds. Halsbury's Statutes of England & Wales. write for info. (*0-406-04753-7*, HS4ASET, MICHIE) LEXIS Pub.
Davies, Andrew & Vergriete, Patrice. Integrating Distressed Urban Areas. LC 98-180300. 172p. 1998. pap. 22.00 (*92-64-16062-0*, 04 98 03 1 P, Pub. by Org for Econ) OECD.
Davies, Andrew C. Telecommunications & Politics: The Decentralised Alternative. 290p. 1993. 99.00 (*1-85567-144-1*) Bks Intl VA.
Davies, Angela, ed. see Schivelbusch, Wolfgang.
Davies, Angela, tr. see Schivelbusch, Wolfgang.
Davies, Angela F., jt. auth. see Adinolfi, Matteo.
Davies, Ann. How to Make Hand-Hooked Rag Rugs. (Illus.). 48p. (Orig.). 1996. pap. 11.95 (*0-85532-807-X*, 807, Pub. by Srch Pr) A Schwartz & Co.
— Inspirational Thoughts on the Tarot. 1983. 15.00 (*0-938002-05-8*) Builders of Adytum.
***Davies, Ann.** Rag Rugs. (Illus.). 96p. 2000. spiral bd. 29.95 (*1-86126-229-9*, Pub. by Crolwood) Trafalgar.
Davies, Ann. Rag Rugs: Ancient & Modern Rug-Making Tech. (Illus.). 88p. 1995. pap. 14.95 (*0-8050-2812-9*) H Holt & Co.
***Davies, Ann.** Rag Rugs: Ancient & Modern Rug-Making Tech. 96p. 1999. pap. text 14.95 (*1-85368-860-6*) New5 Holland.

D

An Asterisk (*) at the beginning of an entry indicates that the title is appearing for the first time.

Davies, Ann. This Is Truth about the Self. 3rd ed. 1984. 4.00 (0-938002-03-1) Builders of Adytum.

Davies, Ann & Tennant, Emma. Hooked Rugs. LC 95-46737. (Illus.). 128p. 1996. 29.95 (0-8069-1338-X) Sterling.

Davies, Anne, et al. Making Themes Work. (Building Connections Ser.). 88p. (Orig.). 1993. pap., teacher ed. 14.00 (1-895411-60-2) Peguis Pubs Ltd.

Davies, Anne, jt. auth. see Politano, Colleen.

Davies, Anne, jt. auth. see Smith, Ardy.

Davies, Anthony & Voluntary Service Overseas Staff. Managing for a Change: How to Run Community Development Projects. LC 98-184810. xi, 164p. 1997. pap. 18.95 (1-85339-399-1, Pub. by Intermed Tech) Stylus Pub VA.

Davies, Anthony & Wells, Stanley, eds. Shakespeare & the Moving Image: The Plays on Film & Television. LC 93-42524. (Illus.). 278p. (C). 1994. pap. text 20.95 (0-521-43573-0) Cambridge U Pr.

Davies, Arwel, jt. auth. see Arrowsmith, Sue.

Davies, B. J., jt. auth. see Ding, Qiulin.

Davies, Barry. The Complete Encyclopedia of the SAS. (Illus.). 1998. text 39.95 (1-85227-707-6, Pub. by Virgin Bks) London Brdge.

***Davies, Barry.** Joining the SAS. (Illus.). 214p. 1999. 22.95 (0-9666771-4-5) Lewis Intl Inc.

Davies, Barry. Royal Blood. 256p. 1997. mass mkt. 23.95 (1-85227-624-X, Pub. by Virgin Bks) London Brdge.

— S. A. S. Encyclopedia of Survival. (Illus.). 256p. 1999. 39.95 (0-9666771-5-3) Lewis Intl Inc.

— SAS: The Illustrated History. (Illus.). 224p. 1997. pap. text 19.95 (0-7535-0197-X, Pub. by Virgin Bks) London Brdge.

— SAS (Britain's Special Air Service) The Illustrated History. (Illus.). 224p. 1998. pap. text 20.00 (0-7881-5790-6) DIANE Pub.

— SAS Escape, Evasion & Survival Manual. LC 97-116903. (Illus.). 276p. 1996. pap. 19.95 (0-7603-0302-9) MBI Pubg.

— SAS Self-Defense. (Gem Ser.). (J). 1997. pap. 8.00 (0-00-472096-2) Collins SF.

— Survival Is a Dying Art. 1987. pap. text 16.95 (0-9512298-0-X) Collins.

***Davies, Barry & Beynon, Par.** Survival Is a Dying Art. (Illus.). 233p. 1999. pap. 16.95 (0-9666771-3-7) Lewis Intl Inc.

***Davies, Barry & Vignali, Claudio.** Marketing Planning: Strategy, Tactics & Implementation. 352p. (Orig.). 2000. pap. 50.00 (0-273-62862-3) F T P H.

Davies, Basil & Davies, Cennard. Welsh, Vol. 1. (Self-Instructional Language Courses). 258p. pap. 135.00 incl. audio (0-88432-209-2, AFWE10) Audio-Forum.

Davies, Ben. Bali & Java. (Illustrated Travel Guides from Thomas Cook Ser.). (Illus.). 192p. (Orig.). 1994. pap. 14.95 (0-8442-9081-5, 90815, Passprt Bks) NTC Contemp Pub Co.

***Davies, Ben.** Passport's Illustrated Guide to Bali & Java. 2nd ed. (Passport's Illustrated Travel Guides from Thomas Cook Ser.). 192p. 2000. pap. 14.95 (0-658-00152-3, 001523) NTC Contemp Pub Co.

— Passport's Illustrated Guide to Thailand. 2nd ed. (Passport's Illustrated Travel Guides from Thomas Cook Ser.). 192p. 2000. pap. 14.95 (0-658-00155-8, 001558) NTC Contemp Pub Co.

Davies, Ben, ed. California Deering's 1998 Midyear Pamphlet, 2 vols. Date not set. pap. 55.00 (0-327-06100-6, 57605-11) LEXIS Pub.

Davies, Benedict G. Egyptian Historical Inscriptions of the Nineteenth Dynasty. (Documenta Mundi: No. 2). 363p. 1997. 92.50 (91-7081-158-X, Pub. by P Astroms) Coronet Bks.

Davies, Benedict G., tr. from EGY. Egyptian Historical Records of the Later Eighteenth Dynasty, Fascicle IV. 88p. 1992. pap. 16.50 (0-85668-579-8, Pub. by Aris & Phillips) David Brown.

— Egyptian Historical Records of the Later Eighteenth Dynasty, Fascicle V. 1994. pap. 16.50 (0-85668-578-X, Pub. by Aris & Phillips) David Brown.

— Egyptian Historical Records of the Later Eighteenth Dynasty, Fascicle VI. 1994. pap. 16.50 (0-85668-577-1, Pub. by Aris & Phillips) David Brown.

Davies, Betsy, ed. see Hunt, Donna.

Davies, Betty. Shadows in the Sun: The Experiences of Sibling Bereavement in Childhood. LC 98-43019. (Series in Death, Dying, & Bereavement). 1998. pap. 49.00 (0-87630-911-2); pap. text 29.95 (0-87630-912-0) Brunner-Mazel.

Davies, Betty, et al. Fading Away: The Experience of Transition in Families with Terminal Illness. (Death, Value & Meaning Ser.). 140p. 1995. pap. 27.95 (0-89503-127-2) Baywood Pub.

Davies, Bill. Electric Motors & Mechanical Devices: For Hobbyists & Engineers. (Practical Robitics Ser.). (Illus.). 337p. Date not set. 24.95 (0-9681830-1-8, Pub. by Werd Tech) Mondo-tronics.

— Practical Robotics. unabridged ed. LC 98-106773. (Illus.). 330p. Date not set. 39.95 (0-9681830-0-X, Pub. by Werd Tech) Mondo-tronics.

Davies, Bleddwyn & Challis, David. Matching Resources to Needs in Community Care. 350p. 1986. text 91.95 (1-85742-113-2, Pub. by Arena) Ashgate Pub Co.

Davies, Bleddyn, et al. Community Care in England & France: Reforms & the Improvement of Equity & Efficiency. LC 98-71404. 250p. 1998. text 65.95 (1-84014-584-6, Pub. by Ashgate Pub) Ashgate Pub Co.

Davies, Bleddyn, jt. auth. see Challis, David.

Davies, Bob & Rentzel, Lori. Coming Out of Homosexuality: New Freedom for Men & Women. LC 93-41902. 202p. (Orig.). 1994. pap. 10.99 (0-8308-1653-4, 1653) InterVarsity.

Davies, Bob, jt. auth. see Worthen, Anita.

Davies, Brenda. The 7 Healing Chakras: Unlocking Your Body's Energy Centers. (Illus.). 240p. 1999. pap. text 14.95 (1-56975-168-4) Ulysses Pr.

Davies, Brenda, reader. The Rainbow Journey: Seven Steps to Self Healing. abr. ed. 1998. pap. text 16.95 incl. audio (1-85998-973-X) Trafalgar.

Davies, Brenda, ed. see Davies, Robertson.

Davies, Brent & Ellison, Linda. Managing the Effective Primary School. 160p. 1994. pap. 47.50 (0-582-22868-9, Pub. by Addison-Wesley) Trans-Atl Phila.

Davies, Brent & Ellison, Linda. School Leadership for 21st Century: Competency & Knowledge Approach. LC 96-2156. 1997. pap. write for info. (0-415-13366-1) Routledge.

— Strategic Direction & Development of the School. LC 98-7082. 192p. 1998. pap. 24.99 (0-415-18917-9) Routledge.

Davies, Brent & West-Burnham, John, eds. Reengineering & Total Quality in Schools: How to Reform & Restructure Your School to Meet the Challenge of the Future. 208p. 1996. pap. 54.50 (0-273-62410-5, Pub. by F T P-H) Trans-Atl Phila.

Davies, Brian. Exploring Chaos: Theory & Experiment. 256p. 1999. text 45.00 (0-7382-0090-5, Pub. by Perseus Pubng) HarpC.

— An Introduction to the Philosophy of Religion. 2nd ed. LC 92-18488. 270p. 1993. pap. text 17.95 (0-19-289235-5) OUP.

— Philosophy of Religion: A Guide to the Subject. Date not set. pap. text 32.95 (0-225-66822-X, Pub. by G Chapman) Bks Intl VA.

— The Thought of Thomas Aquinas. 408p. 1993. reprint ed. pap. text 28.00 (0-19-826753-3) OUP.

***Davies, Brian, ed.** Philosophy of Religion: A Guide & Anthology. 670p. 2000. pap. 24.95 (0-19-875194-X) OUP.

Davies, Brian, ed. Philosophy of Religion: A Guide to the Subject. LC 98-38312. 400p. 1999. pap. text 29.95 (0-87840-695-6) Georgetown U Pr.

Davies, Brian & Burrows, Graham. An Introduction to Clinical Psychiatry. 4th ed. 200p. 1991. pap. 24.95 (0-522-84328-X, Pub. by Melbourne Univ Pr) Paul & Co Pubs.

Davies, Brian & Delamont, Sara. Discourse & Reproduction: A Festschrift for Basil Beinstein. Atkinson, Paul et al, eds. LC 94-23554. 320p. 1995. text 67.50 (1-881303-04-7) Hampton Pr NJ.

— Discourse & Reproduction: Essays in Honor of Basil Bernstein. Atkinson, Paul et al, eds. LC 94-23554. 320p. 1995. pap. text 28.50 (1-881303-05-5) Hampton Pr NJ.

Davies, Brian, ed. see Anselm of Canterbury.

Davies, Brian, ed. see Aquinas, Thomas, Saint.

Davies, Brian, jt. ed. see Evans, John.

Davies, Brian, ed. see Fergusson, David A.

Davies, Brian, ed. see Kennedy, Philip.

Davies, Brian, ed. see O'Donnell, John.

Davies, Brian F., jt. auth. see Nicolson, Robert B.

Davies, Brian L. German Uniforms of the Third Reich, 1933-1945. (Illus.). 224p. 1997. pap. 19.95 (1-85409-420-3, Pub. by Arms & Armour) Sterling.

Davies, Brian M. Public Health, Preventive Medicine & Social Services. 6th ed. 368p. 1995. pap. text 29.95 (1-56593-503-9, 1164) Singular Publishing.

***Davies, Bronwyn.** A Body of Theory, 1990-1999. LC 99-53859. 200p. 2000. 62.00 (0-7425-0321-6) AltaMira Pr.

— A Body of Writing, 1990-1999. LC 99-53859. 191p. 2000. 24.95 (0-7425-0322-4) AltaMira Pr.

Davies, Bronwyn. Frogs, Snails, Feminist Tales: Preschool Children & Gender. 176p. (Orig.). pap. 18.95 (0-04-520007-6, Pub. by Allen & Unwin Pty) Paul & Co Pubs.

***Davies, Bronwyn.** Inscribing Body Landscape Relationships. LC 99-55137. 288p. 2000. pap. 24.95 (0-7425-0320-8) AltaMira Pr.

— Inscribing Body Landscape Relationships. LC 99-55137. 288p. 2000. 62.00 (0-7425-0319-4) AltaMira Pr.

Davies, Bronwyn. Post Structuralist Theory & Classroom Practice. 127p. (C). 1995. pap. 60.00 (0-7300-1728-1, Pub. by Deakin Univ) St Mut.

Davies, Bronwyn & Corson, David. Oral Discourse & Education. LC 97-30202. (Encyclopedia of Language & Education Ser.). 1997. lib. bdg. write for info. (0-7923-4639-4) Kluwer Academic.

Davies, Bronwyn & Green, Judith L. Shards of Glass: Children Reading & Writing Beyond Gendered Identity. LC 93-11086. (Language & Social Processes Ser.). 228p. 1993. pap. text 20.95 (1-881303-18-7) Hampton Pr NJ.

Davies, Bryan & Day, Jenny. Vanishing Waters. LC 98-143329. (Illus.). 502p. 1998. pap. 79.95 (1-919713-11-5, U Pr W Africa) Intl Scholars.

Davies, Bryan R. & Walker, Keith F., eds. The Ecology of River Systems. (Biologicae Monographiae). 1986. text 389.50 (90-6193-540-7) Kluwer Academic.

Davies, C. Andreyev, Leonid Photographs by a Russian Writer: An Undiscovered Portrait of Pre-Revolutionary Russia. (C). 1990. 170.00 (0-7855-4428-3, Pub. by Collets) St Mut.

— Housing for Life: A Guide to Housing Management Practices. (Illus.). 168p. (Orig.). pap. text 39.95 (0-419-12070-X, E & FN Spon) Routledge.

— Inhaled Particles & Vapours: Proceedings International Symposium British Occupational Hygiene Society, Oxford 3-60. LC 61-10786. 1961. 221.00 (0-08-013131-X, Pub. by Pergamon Repr) Franklin.

Davies, C. C. Private Correspondence of Lord Mccartney. (Camden Third Ser.). 63.00 (0-86193-077-0) David Brown.

Davies, C. R. Single Ply Roofing - Advantages & Concerns RICS Occasional Paper. (C). 1989. text 45.00 (0-7855-5974-4, Pub. by Surveyors Pubns) St Mut.

Davies, Carole B. Black Women, Writing & Identity: Migrations of the Subject. LC 93-44335. 232p. (C). 1994. pap. 25.99 (0-415-10087-9, B3145) Routledge.

Davies, Carole B. & Graves, Anne A., eds. Ngambika: Studies of Women in African Literature. LC 85-71385. 298p. (C). 1986. 59.95 (0-86543-017-9); pap. 18.95 (0-86543-018-7) Africa World.

Davies, Carole B. & Ogundipe-Leslie, Molara, eds. Moving Beyond Boundaries Vol. 1: International Dimensions of Black Women's Writing. LC 94-31075. 252p. (C). 1995. text 55.00 (0-8147-1237-1); pap. text 19.50 (0-8147-1238-X) NYU Pr.

— Moving Beyond Boundaries Vol. 2: International Dimensions of Black Women's Writing. 320p. (C). 1995. text 55.00 (0-8147-1239-8); pap. text 19.50 (0-8147-1240-1) NYU Pr.

Davies, Catherine. Contemporary Feminist Fiction in Spain: The Work of Monserrat Roig & Rosa Montero. Flower, John, ed. (New Directions in European Writing Ser.). 224p. 1994. 39.50 (1-85973-086-8) Berg Pubs.

— A Place in the Sun? Women Writers in Twentieth Century Cuba. LC 97-36970. 256p. 1998. 65.00 (1-85649-541-8); pap. 25.00 (1-85649-542-6) Humanities.

— Spanish Women's Writing, 1849-1996. LC 98-11468. (Women in Context Ser.: Vol. 5). 11p. 1998. 85.00 (0-485-91006-3, Pub. by Athlone Pr); pap. 29.95 (0-485-92006-9, Pub. by Athlone Pr) Humanities.

Davies, Catherine, ed. Women Writers in Twentieth-Century Spain & Spanish America. LC 92-46176. 224p. 1993. text 89.95 (0-88946-423-5) E Mellen.

Davies, Catherine, jt. auth. see Jones, Anny B.

Davies, Catherine, jt. ed. see Jones, Anny B.

Davies, Cecil. The Plays of Ernst Toller: A Revelation. (Contemporary Theatre Studies: Vol. 10). 685p. 1996. text 55.00 (3-7186-5614-0, ECU70, Harwood Acad Pubs); pap. text 25.00 (3-7186-5615-9, ECU32, Harwood Acad Pubs) Gordon & Breach.

***Davies, Cecil.** The Volksbuhne Movement: A History. (Contemporary Theatre Studies: Vol. 33). (Illus.). 224p. 1999. text 47.00 (90-5755-089-X, Harwood Acad Pubs) Gordon & Breach.

Davies, Celia. Gender & the Professional Predicament in Nursing. LC 94-40172. 240p. 1995. pap. 31.95 (0-335-19402-8) OpUniv Pr.

Davies, Celia, ed. Rewriting Nursing History. 226p. 1980. 44.00 (0-389-20153-7, N6982) B&N Imports.

***Davies, Celia & Beach, Abigail.** Interpreting Professional Self-Regulation: A History of the United Kingdom Central Council for Nursing, Midwifery & Health Visiting. LC 00-27211. 2000. write for info. (0-415-23033-0) Routledge.

Davies, Cennard, jt. auth. see Davies, Basil.

Davies, Ceri. Welsh Literature & the Classical Tradition. 220p. 1996. 39.95 (0-7083-1321-3, Pub. by Univ Wales Pr) Paul & Co Pubs.

***Davies, Ceri.** Welsh Literature & the Classical Tradition. 196p. 1999. pap. 19.95 (0-7083-1499-6, Pub. by Univ Wales Pr) Paul & Co Pubs.

Davies, Charles E. The Blood-Red Arab Flag: An Investigation into Qasimi Piracy 1797-1820. 500p. 1997. 80.00 (0-85989-509-2, Pub. by Univ Exeter Pr) Northwestern U Pr.

Davies, Charles E., ed. Global Interests in the Arab Gulf. LC 92-18276. 1992. text 55.00 (0-312-08574-5) St Martin.

Davies, Charlotte A. Reflexive Ethnography: A Guide to Researching Selves & Others. LC 98-29216. 1999. write for info. (0-415-15190-2); pap. 24.99 (0-415-15191-0) Routledge.

— Welsh Nationalism in the Twentieth Century: The Ethnic Option & the Modern State. LC 88-28832. 153p. 1989. 55.00 (0-275-93116-1, C3116, Praeger Pubs) Greenwood.

***Davies, Chris.** British & American Hit Singles, 1946-1997. 520p. 1998. pap. text 29.95 (0-7134-8275-3, Pub. by B T B) Branford.

Davies, Chris. What Is English Teaching? 160p. 1996. pap. 29.95 (0-335-19478-8) OpUniv Pr.

Davies, Chris, jt. ed. see Pointon, Anne.

Davies, Christie. Ethnic Humor Around the World: A Comparative Analysis. LC 88-46026. (Illus.). 416p. 1996. pap. 19.95 (0-253-21081-X) Ind U Pr.

— Jokes & Their Relation to Society. LC 98-27688. (Humor Research Ser.). 234p. 1998. 122.80 (3-11-016104-4) De Gruyter.

Davies, Christopher E. Divided by a Common Language: A British/American Dictionary Plus. LC 97-94724. (Illus.). 192p. 1998. pap. 12.95 (0-9660945-7-3) Mayflower Pr.

Davies, Christopher S., jt. auth. see Holz, Robert K.

***Davies, Clare C., et al.** The Creative Jeweler: Inspirational Projects Using Semi-Precious & Everyday Materials. LC 99-67513. (Illus.). 160p. 2000. pap. 21.95 (0-87341-556-6, CRJE) Krause Pubns.

Davies, Colin. British Pavilion: Sevile Exposition 1992 Nicholas Grimshaw & Partners. (Architecture in Detail Ser.). (Illus.). 60p. (C). 1993. pap. 29.95 (0-7148-2747-9, Pub. by Phaidon Press) Phaidon Pr.

— Hopkins: The Work of Michael Hopkins & Partners. 240p. (C). 1993. text 69.95 (0-7148-2782-7, Pub. by Phaidon Press) Phaidon Pr.

Davies, Colin, jt. ed. see Lambot, Ian.

Davies, Colin G. Squires: Tax Planning for Groups of Companies. 1996. ring bd. write for info. (0-406-99148-0, STPGASET, MICHIE) LEXIS Pub.

Davies, Cynthia J., ed. see Harvey, Byron, III, et al.

Davies, Cyril, et al. Organization for Program Management. LC 78-27660. 252p. reprint ed. pap. 78.20 (0-608-17664-8, 203037800069) Bks Demand.

Davies, D. Counselling Psychological Serv. LC 96-54224. (Counselling in Context Ser.). 1997. write for info. (0-335-19165-7); pap. 25.95 (0-335-19164-9) OpUniv Pr.

— Infection & Immunity. LC 99-167629. 1998. pap. 24.95 (0-7484-0788-X) Taylor & Francis.

— Introduction to Corporate Finance. Davis, Peter R., ed. 395p. (C). 1990. pap. 125.00 (0-85297-210-5, Pub. by Chartered Bank) St Mut.

Davies, D. Arthur, frwd. Forty Years of Progress & Achievement: A Historical Review of WMO. (WMO Ser.: No. 721). (Illus.). 205p. 1990. 95.00 (92-63-10721-1, Pub. by Wrld Meteorological) St Mut.

Davies, D. B., et al. Soil Management. 5th ed. (Illus.). 288p. 1993. 34.95 (0-85236-238-2, Pub. by Farming Pr) Diamond Farm Bk.

Davies, D. C., ed. Alzheimer's Disease: Towards an Understanding of the Aetiology & Pathogenesis. (Current Problems in Neurology Ser.: Vol. 11). 140p. 1989. 54.95 (0-86196-166-8, Pub. by J Libbey Med) Bks Intl VA.

Davies, D. G., ed. see International Conference on Modelling under Uncert.

Davies, D. Garfield & Jahn, Anthony J. The Singer's & Actor's Voice: An Essential Guide to Its Care. LC 98-22187. (Illus.). 160p. 1999. pap. text 24.95 (0-7506-3640-8) Buttrwrth-Heinemann.

Davies, D. H., ed. Zambia in Maps. LC 73-653626. (Graphic Perspectives in Developing Countries Ser.). 128p. (C). 1972. 37.95 (0-8419-0081-7, Africana) Holmes & Meier.

Davies, D. M. Davies's Textbook of Adverse Drug Reactions. 5th ed. (Illus.). 992p. 1999. text 225.00 (0-412-82480-9, Pub. by E A) OUP.

Davies, D. P. Against the Tide. Stephens, Meic, ed. (Changing Wales Ser.). 44p. 1998. pap. 11.95 (0-8464-4714-2) Beekman Pubs.

Davies, D. R. Reinhold Niebuhr: Prophet from America. (Select Bibliographies Reprint Ser.). 1977. 16.95 (0-8369-5324-X) Ayer.

Davies, D. R., jt. ed. see Casey, R.

Davies, D. S., jt. auth. see Brown, S. S.

Davies, D. W. Dutch Influences on English Culture, 1558-1625. LC 64-18226. (Folger Guides to the Age of Shakespeare Ser.). 1964. pap. 4.95 (0-918016-13-4) Folger Bks.

— Scott E. Haselton & His Abbey Garden Press. (Illus.). 26p. 1985. 25.00 (0-87093-182-2) Dawsons.

Davies, D. W., et al, eds. Advances in Cryptology - EUROCRYPT '91: Proceedings of the Workshop on the Theory & Application of Cryptographic Techniques Brighton, U. K., April 8-11, 1991. (Lecture Notes in Computer Science Ser.: Vol. 547). x, 556p. 1991. pap. 52.00 (0-387-54620-0) Spr-Verlag.

Davies, D. W. & Price, W. L. Security for Computer Networks: An Introduction to Data Security in Teleprocessing & Electronic Funds Transfer. 2nd ed. LC 89-14760. 398p. 1989. 260.00 (0-471-92137-8) Wiley.

Davies, D. W., ed. see Williams, Roger.

Davies, Dale. ABC of Marital Success. (Illus.). 192p. 1987. write for info. (0-942307-00-3) Adebara & Honeycomb.

— The Hidden Facts. 128p. 1987. 9.95 (0-942307-01-1) Adebara & Honeycomb.

Davies, Daniel M. The Life & Thought of Henry Gerhard Appenzeller (1858-1902) Missionary to Korea. LC 87-11041. (Studies in the History of Missions). 512p. lib. bdg. 119.95 (0-88946-069-8) E Mellen.

Davies, Dave. Grammar? No Problem! Scanlon, Kelly, ed. LC 98-68153. 140p. 1997. pap. 12.95 (1-57294-080-8, 12-0032) SkillPath Pubns.

— Kink: An Autobiography. LC 96-24545. (Illus.). 258p. (J). 1997. 22.45 (0-7868-6149-5, Pub. by Hyperion) Time Warner.

— Kink: An Autobiography. (Illus.). 288p. (J). 1998. reprint ed. pap. 13.45 (0-7868-8269-7, Pub. by Hyperion) Time Warner.

— Letters & Memos Just Like That! LC 97-67311. (Self-Study Sourcebook Ser.). 164p. 1997. pap. 15.95 (1-57294-095-6, 13-0037) SkillPath Pubns.

Davies, David. The Case of Labourers in Husbandry Stated & Considered in Three Parts. 200p. 1974. 45.00 (0-678-00863-9) Kelley.

— The Evergreen Tree. 1971. 3.75 (0-910330-18-2) Grant Dahlstrom.

— Finance & Accountancy for Managers. 160p. (C). 1990. 85.00 (0-85292-436-4, Pub. by IPM Hse) St Mut.

— Finance & Accounting for Managers. 108p. (C). 1994. pap. 36.00 (0-85292-527-1, Pub. by IPM Hse) St Mut.

***Davies, David.** Managing Financial Information. 192p. 2000. pap. 41.95 (0-8464-5111-5) Beekman Pubs.

Davies, David, et al, eds. Velazquez in Seville. LC 96-60915. (Illus.). 172p. 1996. 50.00 (0-300-06949-9) Yale U Pr.

Davies, David & Matheson, Carl, eds. The Philosophy of Literature: An Anthology. 400p. 2000. pap. 24.95 (1-55111-177-2) Broadview Pr.

Davies, David & Vines, Mike. Antique & Classic Airplanes. (Illus.). 127p. 13.95 (0-614-13197-9, 21-37702) EAA Aviation.

Davies, David B. The Art of Managing Finance. 3rd ed. LC 97-5060. 1997. write for info. (0-07-709178-7) McGraw.

Davies, David G. U. S. Taxes & Tax Policy. LC 85-31414. 336p. 1986. pap. text 19.95 (0-521-31769-X) Cambridge U Pr.

Davies, David G., ed. The Economic Evaluation of Projects: Papers from a Curriculum Development Workshop. LC 95-19178. (EDI Learning Resources Ser.). 140p. 1996. pap. 22.00 (0-8213-3325-9, 13325) World Bank.

Davies, David H., jt. auth. see Pincus, Alexis G.

Davies, David H., jt. ed. see Pincus, Alexis G.

An Asterisk (*) at the beginning of an entry indicates that the title is appearing for the first time.

Davies, David S. Sherlock Holmes & the Hentzau Affair. 160p. 1991. 25.00 (*0-86025-274-4*, Pub. by I Henry Pubns) Empire Pub Srvs.

***Davies, David Stuart.** The Scroll of the Dead: A Sherlock Holmes Adventure. 147p. 1998. pap. 19.50 (*1-899562-47-8*, Calabash Pr) Ash-Tree.

— The Shadow of the Rat: A Sherlock Holmes Adventure. 162p. 1999. 30.00 (*1-899562-70-2*, Calabash Pr) Ash-Tree.

— Sherlock Holmes - The Last Act! 68p. 1999. pap. 15.00 (*1-899562-77-X*, Calabash Pr) Ash-Tree.

— The Tangled Skein. 171p. 1998. pap. 19.50 (*1-899562-46-X*, Calabash Pr) Ash-Tree.

— The Tangled Skein. large type ed. 320p. 2000. pap. 20.99 (*1-85389-997-6*, Dales) Ulverscroft.

Davies, David T. Aromatic Heterocyclic Chemistry. (Oxford Chemistry Primers Ser.: No. 2). (Illus.). 96p. (C). 1992. pap. text 12.95 (*0-19-855660-8*) OUP.

— Nelson's Navy: English Fighting Ships, 1793-1815. LC 96-44275. (Illus.). 208p. 1997. 27.95 (*0-8117-1118-8*) Stackpole.

— Will Precedents & Inheritance Tax. 4th ed. 320p. 1991. boxed set 94.00 (*0-406-11783-7*, UK, MICHIE) LEXIS Pub.

Davies, David W., jt. auth. see Abbott, Edwin A.

Davies, Denny. In Pictures Glen Canyon - Lake Powell: The Continuing Story. LC 92-70429. (Illus.). 48p. (Orig.). 1992. pap. 7.95 (*0-88714-066-1*) KC Pubns.

— In Pictures Glen Canyon - Lake Powell: The Continuing Story. Morales, Brigitte, tr. (GER., Illus.). 48p. (Orig.). 1992. pap. 8.95 (*0-88714-726-7*) KC Pubns.

— In Pictures Glen Canyon - Lake Powell: The Continuing Story. Le Bras, Yvon, tr. (FRE., Illus.). 48p. (Orig.). 1992. pap. 8.95 (*0-88714-727-5*) KC Pubns.

— In Pictures Glen Canyon - Lake Powell: The Continuing Story. Petzinger, Saori, tr. (JPN., Illus.). 48p. (Orig.). 1992. pap. 8.95 (*0-88714-728-3*) KC Pubns.

— In Pictures Glen Canyon - Lake Powell: The Continuing Story. Lee, Frances Y., tr. (CHI., Illus.). 48p. (Orig.). 1993. pap. 8.95 (*0-88714-729-1*) KC Pubns.

Davies, Denys J., tr. see An-Nawawi, Shaykh M.

Davies, Derek. Ecuador. (Traveler's Companion Ser.). (Illus.). 240p. 1998. pap. text 22.95 (*0-7627-0251-6*) Globe Pequot.

Davies, Derek, jt. auth. see Bond, Michael.

Davies, Derek, jt. auth. see Carroll, Donald.

Davies, Derek, jt. auth. see Stone, Merlin.

Davies, Devi. Cinnabar or Coral: Poems, Proverbs, Invocation & Awakening, Haiko - Epilogue. Wekerle, Ingrid, ed. LC 87-81963. (Illus.). 64p. 1987. 10.00 (*0-9618994-0-9*) I M Wekerle.

Davies, Diana. Another Way: An Alternative Path to Health & Personal Growth. Brinkerhoff, Audrey, ed. LC 85-73905. (Illus.). 320p. (Orig.). 1986. pap. 9.95 (*0-937251-00-3*) Another Way.

— Another Way's Guide to Growing Your Blue Ribbon Body. Brinkerhoff, Audrey, ed. (Illus.). 128p. (Orig.). 1986. pap. 6.95 (*0-937251-01-1*) Another Way.

— Dear Russ & Rebecca: Letters to Parents & Others Interested in Natural Childbirth. Teasdale, Carrie, ed. 320p. (Orig.). 1986. pap. 9.95 (*0-251-93704-6*) Another Way.

Davies, Dilys. Alliums: The Ornamental Onions. (Illus.). 168p. 1993. pap. 22.95 (*0-88192-241-2*) Timber.

— Insomnia: Your Questions Answered. (Element Guide Ser.). 128p. 1999. pap. 9.95 (*1-86204-296-9*, Pub. by Element MA) Penguin Putnam.

***Davies, Dominic.** Therapeutic Perspectives on Working with Lesbian, Gay & Bisexual Clients. 2000. pap. text 33.95 (*0-335-20333-7*) OpUniv Pr.

Davies, Dominic & Neal, Charles, eds. Pink Therapy: A Guide for Counsellors & Therapists Working with Lesbian, Gay, & Bisexual Clients. LC 95-26372. 256p. 1996. pap. 33.95 (*0-335-19145-2*) OpUniv Pr.

— Pink Therapy: A Guide for Counsellors & Therapists Working with Lesbian, Gay, & Bisexual Clients. LC 95-26372. 256p. 1996. 97.95 (*0-335-19657-8*) OpUniv Pr.

***Davies, Dominic & Neal, Charles, eds.** Therapeutic Perspectives on Working with Lesbian, Gay & Bisexual Clients. LC 99-30665. 187p. 2000. 110.00 (*0-335-20334-5*, Pub. by OpUniv Pr) Taylor & Francis.

Davies, Don. Parent Involvement in the Public Schools: Proposals, Issues, Opportunities. 24p. 1985. pap. 5.95 (*1-56602-005-0*) Research Better.

Davies, Don & Armstrong, Malcom. Psychological Factors in Competitive Sport. 180p. 1989. pap. 34.95 (*1-85000-607-5*, Falmer Pr) Taylor & Francis.

Davies, Donald. Commencement of Laytime. 2nd ed. 254p. 1992. 90.00 (*1-85044-441-2*) LLP.

— Commencement of Laytime. 2nd ed. 1992. 95.00 (*1-85044-147-2*) LLP.

Davies, Donald W. & Barber, Derek L. Communication Networks for Computers. LC 73-2775. (Wiley Series in Computing). (Illus.). 593p. reprint ed. pap. 183.90 (*0-8357-4563-5*, 203746500008) Bks Demand.

Davies, Dorian S., jt. auth. see Gittins, Rob.

***Davies, Doug.** Exploring IBM RS/6000 Computers: The Instant Insider's Guide to IBM's UNIX Workstations & Servers. 10th ed. (Exploring IBM Ser.). 395p. 2000. pap. 39.95 (*1-885068-42-5*, Pub. by Maximum Pr) IPG Chicago.

Davies, Doug & Hoskins, Jim. Exploring IBM RS-6000 Computers: The Instant Insiders Guide to IBM's UNIX Workstations & Servers. 9th ed. LC 98-51241. (Exploring IBM Ser.). (Illus.). 394p. 1999. pap. 39.95 (*1-885068-27-1*) Maximum Pr.

Davies, Doug, jt. auth. see Hoskins, Jim.

Davies, Douglas. Child Development: A Practitioner's Guide. LC 98-43264. (Social Work Practice with Children & Families Ser.). 412p. 1999. lib. bdg. 42.00 (*1-57230-429-4*) Guilford Pubns.

Davies, Douglas, et al. Church & Religion in Rural England. (Illus.). 304p. 1991. pap. text 29.95 (*0-567-29201-0*, Pub. by T & T Clark) Bks Intl VA.

Davies, Douglas J. Death, Ritual, & Belief: The Rhetoric of Funerary Rites. LC 97-19557. 240p. 1997. 75.00 (*0-304-33821-4*); pap. 24.95 (*0-304-33822-2*) Continuum.

— Frank Byron Jevons, 1858-1936: An Evolutionary Realist. LC 89-77805. (Illus.). 472p. 1991. lib. bdg. 109.95 (*0-88946-925-3*) E Mellen.

— Themes & Issues in Christianity. Drury, Clare, ed. LC 96-52966. (World Religions). 224p. 1997. pap. 26.95 (*0-304-33849-4*) Continuum.

— Themes & Issues in Christianity. Drury, Clare, ed. LC 96-52966. (World Religions). 224p. 1997. 79.50 (*0-304-33848-6*) Continuum.

Davies, Douglas J., ed. Mormon Identities in Transition. LC 96-1635. (Religious Studies). 256p. 1996. text 55.00 (*0-304-33686-6*) Continuum.

***Davies, Douglas James.** The Mormon Culture of Salvation: Force, Grace & Glory. LC 00-29310. 2000. pap. write for info. (*0-7546-1330-5*) Ashgate Pub Co.

Davies, Duncan & McCarthy, Callum. Introduction to Technological Economics. LC 67-30538. (Illus.). 212p. reprint ed. pap. 65.80 (*0-608-17346-0*, 202980300065) Bks Demand.

Davies, Duncan, et al. The Telling Image: The Changing Balance Between Pictures & Words in a Technological Age. (Science, Technology, & Society Ser.: No. 5). (Illus.). 210p. 1990. 59.00 (*0-19-858339-7*) OUP.

Davies, E., jt. auth. see Dummer, G. W.

Davies, E., jt. auth. see Miller, M. R.

Davies, E. B. Spectral Theory & Differential Operators. (Cambridge Studies in Advanced Mathematics: No. 42). 192p. (C). 1995. text 64.95 (*0-521-47250-4*) Cambridge U Pr.

— Spectral Theory & Differential Operators. (Cambridge Studies in Advanced Mathematics: No. 42). 192p. 1996. pap. text 25.95 (*0-521-58710-7*) Cambridge U Pr.

***Davies, E. Brian & Safarov, Yuri, eds.** Spectral Theory & Geometry. (London Mathematical Society Lecture Note Ser.: Vol. 273). 340p. (C). 1999. pap. text 44.95 (*0-521-77749-6*) Cambridge U Pr.

Davies, E. J. Conduction & Induction Heating. (Power Ser.: No. 11). 450p. 1990. 109.00 (*0-86341-174-6*, PO011) INSPEC Inc.

Davies, E. R. Machine Vision: Theory, Algorithms, Practicalities. 2nd ed. (Signal Processing & Its Applications Ser.). (Illus.). 784p. 1996. text 49.95 (*0-12-206092-X*) Acad Pr.

Davies, E. T. An Introduction to Knots. (C). 1987. 65.00 (*0-85174-406-0*) St Mut.

***Davies, Earle.** One Love. 1998. text 35.00 (*0-233-99443-2*, Pub. by Andre Deutsch) Trafalgar.

— One Love. 1999. pap. 15.95 (*0-233-99450-5*, Pub. by Andre Deutsch) Trafalgar.

Davies, Ebenezer. American Scenes & Christian Slavery. LC 70-123671. reprint ed. 39.50 (*0-404-00026-6*) AMS Pr.

Davies, Ebenezer T. Episcopacy & the Royal Supremacy in the Church of England in the XVI Century. LC 78-13202. 137p. 1979. reprint ed. lib. bdg. 49.50 (*0-313-20626-0*, DAER, Greenwood Pr) Greenwood.

Davies, Ed, et al. Douglas DC-3: 60 Years & Counting. LC 95-76183. 160p. 1995. pap. 24.95 (*0-9637543-4-3*) Aero Vintage.

Davies, Edward, II. Anthracite Aristocracy: Leadership & Social Change in the Hard Coal Regions of Northeastern Pennsylvania, 1800-1930. LC 85-2947. 277p. 1985. 32.00 (*0-87580-107-2*) N Ill U Pr.

Davies, Edward. The Art of War & Englands Traynings. LC 68-54633. (English Experience Ser.: No. 37). 1968. reprint ed. 45.00 (*90-221-0037-5*) Walter J Johnson.

Davies, Elaine M. Lovell White Durrant: Guide to Corporation Tax. 307p. 1995. pap. 50.00 (*1-85941-037-5*, Pub. by Cavendish Pubng) Gaunt.

Davies, Elam & Buchanan, John M. Sermons for the City: Fourth Presbyterian Church - Chicago, Illinois. LC 96-69158. 112p. (Orig.). 1996. pap. 12.95 (*1-57736-008-7*) Providence Hse.

Davies, Eleanor. Prophetic Writings of Lady Eleanor Davies. Cope, Esther S., ed. (Women Writers in English 1350-1850 Ser.). (Illus.). 400p. (C). 1995. text 65.00 (*0-19-507875-6*, 4537) OUP.

— Prophetic Writings of Lady Eleanor Davies. Cope, Esther S., ed. (Women Writers in English 1350-1850 Ser.). (Illus.). 400p. (C). 1995. pap. 26.00 (*0-19-508717-8*, 74) OUP.

Davies, Elisabeth & Dingle, John, eds. Immunopharmacology of Joints & Connective Tissue. (Illus.). 288p. 1994. text 79.00 (*0-12-206345-7*) Acad Pr.

Davies, Elizabeth W. The Legal Status of British Dependent Territories: The West Indies & North Atlantic Region. (Illus.). 410p. (C). 1995. text 95.00 (*0-521-48188-0*) Cambridge U Pr.

Davies, Elspeth. Dr. Kitchiner & the Cook's Oracle. 91p. (C). 1989. text 60.00 (*1-872795-83-8*, Pub. by Pentland Pr) St Mut.

— The Years of the Barbarians. 210p. (C). 1989. text 50.00 (*0-946270-49-X*, Pub. by Pentland Pr) St Mut.

Davies, Elwyn. Mild Majesty. 164p. (C). 1987. 30.00 (*0-86383-450-7*, Pub. by Gomer Pr) St Mut.

Davies, Emily. The Higher Education of Women. 248p. 1988. 40.00 (*1-85285-008-6*); pap. 15.00 (*1-85285-009-4*) Hambledon Press.

— Higher Education of Women. LC 77-37688. reprint ed. 30.00 (*0-404-56742-8*) AMS Pr.

— Thoughts on Some Questions Relating to Women, 1860-1908. LC 73-14557. reprint ed. 34.50 (*0-404-56741-X*) AMS Pr.

Davies, Erica. 20 Mares Field Gardens: A Guide to the Freud Museum. 1998. pap. 25.00 (*1-85242-536-9*) Serpents Tail.

Davies, Eryl. Condemned Forever! 1987. pap. 3.99 (*0-85234-241-1*, Pub. by Evangelical Pr) P & R Pubng.

***Davies, Eryl.** Heaven is a Far Better Place. 1999. pap. text 13.99 (*0-85234-423-6*) Evangelical Pr.

Davies, Eryl. Inventions. LC 94-24434. (DK Pockets Ser.). (Illus.). 128p. (YA). (gr. 7 up). 1995. pap. 6.95 (*1-56458-889-0*) DK Pub Inc.

— Transport: On Land, Road & Rail. (Timelines Ser.). (Illus.). 48p. (J). (gr. 5-8). 1992. 24.00 (*0-531-14376-7*) Watts.

— Truth under Attack: Cults & Contemporary Religions. 1995. pap. 16.99 (*0-85234-341-8*, Pub. by Evangelical Pr) P & R Pubng.

Davies, Eryl W. Numbers. 378p. 1995. pap. 19.95 (*0-551-02835-1*, Pub. by Sheffield Acad) CUP Services.

— Prophecy & Ethics: Isaiah & the Ethical Traditions of Israel. (JSOT Supplement Ser.: No. 16). 185p. 1981. 57.50 (*0-905774-26-4*, Pub. by Sheffield Acad) CUP Services.

Davies, Euros & Roderick, Arthur, eds. Lampeter Yesterday. 88p. 1994. pap. 20.95 (*0-8464-4705-1*) Beekman Pubs.

Davies, Evan. The Book of Dulwich. 1977. 45.00 (*0-86023-003-1*) St Mut.

Davies, Evan, ed. see Michaux, Louis A.

Davies, Evelyn, et al. Task Reading. (Illus.). 128p. (C). 1990. pap. text 15.95 (*0-521-35810-8*) Cambridge U Pr.

***Davies, F. G. & Verdcourt, B.** Flora of Tropical East Africa: Sapindaceae. 114p. 1998. 21.00 (*90-6191-380-2*, Pub. by A A Balkema) Ashgate Pub Co.

Davies, F. R. Contract: Concise College Texts. 5th ed. (C). 1986. 90.00 (*0-7855-4243-4*, Pub. by Witherby & Co) St Mut.

Davies, F. S. & Albrigo, L. G. Citrus. (Crop Production Science in Horticulture Ser.: 2). (Illus.). 272p. 1994. pap. text 45.00 (*0-85198-867-9*) OUP.

Davies, Frank. Kidding Around Miami: What to Do, Where to Go, & How to Have Fun in Miami. LC 00-503364. (Kidding Around Ser.). (Illus.). 144p. (J). (gr. 1-5). 1997. pap. 7.95 (*1-56261-372-3*) Avalon Travel.

Davies, Frank & Maddocks, Graham. Bloody Red Tabs: General Officer Casualties of the Great War, 1914-18. (Illus.). 225p. 1995. 29.95 (*0-85052-463-6*, Pub. by Leo Cooper) Trans-Atl Phila.

***Davies, Fred.** Film, History & the Holocaust. (Illus.). 200p. 2000. (*0-85303-379-X*); pap. (*0-85303-392-7*) Intl Spec Bk.

Davies, Freda. Let Heaven Fall. large type ed. (Linford Mystery Large Print Ser.). 400p. 1998. pap. 17.99 (*0-7089-5288-7*, Linford) Ulverscroft.

Davies, Frederick H., tr. see Goldoni, Carlo.

Davies, G. Copyright & the Public Interest. LC 95-113290. (IIC Studies Ser.). 221p. 1994. pap. 115.00 (*3-527-28638-1*, Wiley-VCH) Wiley.

Davies, G., ed. Properties & Growth of Diamond. (EMIS Datareviews Ser.: No. 9). xx, 435p. 1994. boxed set 245.00 (*0-85296-875-2*, EM009) INSPEC Inc.

Davies, G., et al, eds. Humic Substances: Structures, Properties & Uses. (Special Publication Ser.: No. 228). 259p. 1999. 119.00 (*0-85404-704-2*, Pub. by Royal Soc Chem) Spr-Verlag.

— Perceiving & Remembering Faces. LC 81-66698. 1981. text 157.00 (*0-12-206220-5*) Acad Pr.

Davies, G., jt. ed. see Coutie, M. G.

Davies, G., tr. see Eck, A. & Gillin, J. C., eds.

Davies, G. A., ed. Separation Processes in Hydrometallurgy. 502p. 1987. text 169.00 (*0-470-20883-X*) P-H.

***Davies, G. F.** Dynamic Earth: Plates, Plumes & Mantle Convection. LC 98-51722. (Illus.). 464p. (C). 2000. 90.00 (*0-521-59067-1*); pap. 39.95 (*0-521-59933-4*) Cambridge U Pr.

Davies, G. H., et al. Biotransformations in Preparative Organic Chemistry: The Use of Isolated Enzymes & Whole Cell Systems in Synthesis. (Best Synthetic Methods Ser.). 300p. 1989. text 122.00 (*0-12-206230-2*) Acad Pr.

Davies, G. I., ed. Ancient Hebrew Inscriptions: Corpus & Concordance. 597p. (C). 1991. text 135.00 (*0-521-40248-4*) Cambridge U Pr.

Davies, G. I., tr. see Calvin, John.

Davies, G. I., tr. see Smelik, K.A.D.

Davies, G. N. Cost & Benefit of Fluoride in the Prevention of Dental Caries. (Offset Publications: No. 9). 1974. pap. text 20.00 (*92-4-170009-2*, 1120009) World Health.

Davies, Gareth. From Opportunity to Entitlement: The Transformation & Decline of Great Society Liberalism. LC 95-46919. 246p. (C). 1996. 35.00 (*0-7006-0757-9*) U Pr of KS.

— From Opportunity to Entitlement: The Transformation & Decline of Great Society Liberalism. LC 95-46919. 246p. 1999. reprint ed. pap. 17.95 (*0-7006-0994-6*) U Pr of KS.

Davies, Gary. Trade Marketing Strategy. 1993. 88.00 (*1-85396-213-9*, Pub. by P Chapman) Taylor & Francis.

Davies, Gary, jt. ed. see McGoldrick, Peter.

Davies, Geoff. Practical Primary Drama. 63p. (C). 1983. pap. text 17.50 (*0-435-18236-6*) Heinemann.

Davies, Geoffrey. Forensic Science. 2nd ed. LC 85-28688. 388p. 1986. text 75.00 (*0-8412-0918-9*, Pub. by Am Chemical); pap. text 46.00 (*0-8412-0919-7*, Pub. by Am Chemical) OUP.

— General Chemistry. 5th ed. 499p. (C). 1989. pap. text, wbk. ed. 25.00 (*0-89801-017-9*) NE Univ Pub.

Davies, Geoffrey, jt. ed. see Ghabbour, Elham A.

Davies, Geoffrey M. Office Diagnosis & Management of Chronic Obstructive Pulmonary Disease. LC 81-8386. (Illus.). 142p. reprint ed. pap. 44.10 (*0-608-15989-1*, 205674000084) Bks Demand.

Davies, George J., ed. Rehabilitation of the Surgical Knee. (Illus.). 100p. (Orig.). 1984. pap. 25.00 (*0-930269-00-4*) CyPr NY.

Davies, George J., jt. auth. see Ellenbecker, Todd S.

***Davies, Gilbert W.** Harpooned History. LC 99-94029. (Illus.). 151p. (C). 1999. pap. 8.95 (*1-887200-07-X*) HiSt ink Bks.

— Harpooned History II: 150 Original Cartoon Gags. LC 00-132002. (Illus.). 150p. 2000. pap. 8.95 (*1-887200-08-8*) HiSt ink Bks.

Davies, Gilbert W. State the State: More Than 2,500 Questions & Answers from Alabama to Wyoming. LC 94-75126. 118p. (C). 1994. pap. 7.95 (*0-9634413-4-5*) HiSt ink Bks.

— The Torn Pages of History: Anything But History. LC 96-75247. 130p. (C). 1996. pap. 6.95 (*1-887200-02-9*) HiSt ink Bks.

Davies, Gilbert W. & Frank, Florice M. Gold Rush Signs in California's Mother Lode Country. LC 98-70067. (Illus.). 203p. 1998. pap. 21.95 (*1-887200-04-5*) HiSt ink Bks.

— Historical & Commemorative Signs, Plaques & Monuments in Siskiyou County, California. LC 94-75588. (Illus.). 138p. (Orig.). (C). 1994. pap. 14.95 (*0-9634413-6-1*) HiSt ink Bks.

— Historical & Commemorative Signs, Plaques, Markers & Monuments in Shasta County, California. LC 96-75076. (Illus.). 174p. (Orig.). (C). 1996. pap. 15.85 (*1-887200-00-2*) HiSt ink Bks.

— Name the Nation: More Than 2,000 Questions & Answers from Afghanistan to Zimbabwe. LC 95-75157. 138p. (C). 1995. pap. 7.95 (*0-9634413-8-8*) HiSt ink Bks.

— Thirty Country Road Loop Trips in Northern California: North of Sacramento. LC 94-76970. (Illus.). 220p. (Orig.). (C). 1995. pap. 14.95 (*0-9634413-7-X*) HiSt ink Bks.

Davies, Gilbert W. & Frank, Florice M., eds. Forest Service Animal Tales: More Than 200 True Stories. LC 98-70116. (Illus.). 412p. (Orig.). 1998. pap. 22.95 (*1-887200-05-3*) HiSt ink Bks.

— Forest Service Humor: More Than 300 True Stories. LC 96-75239. (Illus.). 544p. 1996. pap. 24.95 (*1-887200-01-0*) HiSt ink Bks.

— Forest Service Memories: Past Lives & Times in the United States Forest Service. LC 97-70410. (Illus.). 624p. 1997. pap. 26.95 (*1-887200-03-7*) HiSt ink Bks.

— Fort Jones (CA), 1852-1858 Military Notes. LC 93-61398. (Illus.). 380p. 1993. pap. 16.95 (*0-9634413-2-9*) HiSt ink Bks.

— Memorable Forest Fires: Two Hundred Stories by U. S. Forest Service Retirees. LC 95-75176. (Illus.). 506p. (C). 1995. pap. 21.95 (*0-9634413-9-6*) HiSt ink Bks.

— Memories from the Land of Siskiyou: Past Lives & Times in Siskiyou County. LC 93-78430. (Illus.). 460p. (C). 1993. pap. 24.95 (*0-9634413-1-0*) HiSt ink Bks.

— Photographic Images of the Klamath National Forest in Siskiyou & Humboldt Counties - a Historical Journey. LC 94-75404. (Illus.). 132p. (C). 1994. pap. 14.95 (*0-9634413-5-3*) HiSt ink Bks.

— Stories of the Klamath National Forest: The First 50 Years, 1905-1955. LC 92-73759. (Illus.). 436p. 1992. pap. 16.95 (*0-9634413-0-2*) HiSt ink Bks.

Davies, Gili. The Very Best Flavour of Wales. 1997. pap. 29.95 (*0-8464-4802-5*) Beekman Pubs.

Davies, Gill. Book Commissioning & Acquisition. 192p. (C). 1994. pap. 29.99 (*0-415-13671-7*) Routledge.

***Davies, Gill.** Create Your Own Stage Effects. (Illus.). 160p. 1999. pap. text 24.95 (*0-8230-8811-1*) Watsn-Guptill.

— Create Your Own Stage Production Company. (Illus.). 160p. 2000. pap. 24.95 (*0-8230-7714-4*) Watsn-Guptill.

Davies, Gill. Crocodile Is Green. (Illus.). 14p. (J). (ps). 1997. bds. 4.98 (*1-85854-592-7*) Brimax Bks.

— Fish Wear Scales. (Illus.). 14p. (J). (ps). 1997. bds. 4.98 (*1-85854-593-5*) Brimax Bks.

— Going Out. (Now I Am Big Ser.). (Illus.). 24p. (J). (ps-1). 1996. 3.49 (*1-85854-366-5*) Brimax Bks.

***Davies, Gill.** Greedy Little Dino. (Squish Pops Ser.). 6p. (J). (ps). 2001. 4.99 (*1-57584-733-7*, Pub. by Rdrs Digest) S&S Trade.

— Here Comes Noddy. (Squeaky Fun Ser.). (Illus.). 14p. (J). (ps-k). 2000. bds. 7.99 (*1-57584-681-0*, Pub. by Rdrs Digest) S&S Trade.

Davies, Gill. I Can Count. (Now I Am Big Ser.). (Illus.). 24p. (J). (ps-1). 1997. 3.49 (*1-85854-596-X*) Brimax Bks.

— I Can Tell the Time. (Illus.). 24p. (J). (ps-1). 1997. 4.98 (*1-85854-493-9*) Brimax Bks.

— I Can't Sleep. (Illus.). 32p. (J). (ps-2). 1996. 8.00 (*1-85854-377-0*) Brimax Bks.

— I Know My Alphabet. (Now I Am Big Ser.). (Illus.). 24p. (J). (ps-1). 1997. 3.49 (*1-85854-597-8*) Brimax Bks.

— I Like Night-Time. (Illus.). 14p. (J). (ps). Date not set. bds. 4.98 (*1-85854-594-3*) Brimax Bks.

— A Little Bit Scary. (Illus.). 48p. (J). (gr. k-4). 1997. 9.00 (*1-85854-527-7*) Brimax Bks.

***Davies, Gill.** Mr. Plod's New Whistle. (Squeaky Fun Ser.). (Illus.). 14p. (J). (ps-k). 2000. bds. 7.99 (*1-57584-682-9*, Pub. by Rdrs Digest) S&S Trade.

— Rude Little Dino. (Squish Pops Ser.). (Illus.). 6p. (J). (ps). 2001. 4.99 (*1-57584-734-5*, Pub. by Rdrs Digest) S&S Trade.

Davies, Gill. Santa's Sleigh. (Christmas Window Bks.). (Illus.). 14p. (J). (ps up). 1997. bds. 4.98 (*1-85854-667-2*) Brimax Bks.

— Staging a Pantomime. (Illus.). 128p. 1996. pap. write for info. (*0-7136-4120-7*, Pub. by A & C Blk) Midpt Trade.

— Teddy at the Farm. (My Big Little Fat Bks.). (Illus.). 20p. (J). (ps). 1996. bds. 3.49 (*1-85854-401-7*) Brimax Bks.

D

— Today Is Very Windy. (Illus.). 14p. (J). (ps). Date not set. bds. 4.98 (*1-85854-595-1*) Brimax Bks.
— A Very Special Night. (Christmas Window Bks.). (Illus.). 14p. (J). (ps up). 1997. bds. 4.98 (*1-85854-668-0*) Brimax Bks.
Davies, Gill & Hurlock, Fiona. Gorf's Pond. (Illus.). 32p. (J). (ps-2). 1996. 8.00 (*1-85854-376-2*) Brimax Bks.
Davies, Gill & Longfoot, Stephanie. Off to School. (Not I Am Big Ser.). (Illus.). 24p. (J). (ps-1). 1996. 3.49 (*1-85854-368-1*) Brimax Bks.
— Sharing. (Now I Am Big Ser.). (Illus.). 24p. (J). (ps-1). 1996. 3.49 (*1-85854-369-X*) Brimax Bks.
Davies, Gill, jt. auth. see Longfoot, Stephanie.
***Davies, Gilli, ed.** The Red Book Eat Well in Wales: Restaurants, Pubs, Cafes, Hotels, Guesthouses & Farmhouses, Millennium Edition. (Illus.). 216p. 2000. pap. 16.95 (*1-900477-06-8*, Pub. by U Wales Pr) Paul & Co Pubs.
Davies, Glenn N. Faith & Obedience in Romans: A Study in Romans 1-4. (JSNT Supplement Ser.: Vol. 39). 232p. 1990. 70.00 (*1-85075-233-8*, Pub. by Sheffield Acad) CUP Services.
Davies, Glenys, ed. Polytheistic Systems. 1991. pap. text 35.00 (*0-7486-0135-X*, Pub. by Edinburgh U Pr) Col U Pr.
Davies, Glyn. A History of Money: From Ancient Times to the Present Day. 733p. pap. 29.95 (*0-7083-1351-5*, Pub. by Univ Wales Pr) Paul & Co Pubs.
— Practical Data Handling Bk. A: Activities for Stages 1 & 2, Bk. A. 162p. 1993. pap., teacher ed. 35.00 (*0-340-55389-8*, Pub. by Hodder & Stought Ltd) Lubrecht & Cramer.
Davies, Glyn & Oates, John, eds. Colobine Monkeys: Their Evolutionary Ecology. (Illus.). 429p. (C). 1995. text 85.00 (*0-521-33153-6*) Cambridge U Pr.
Davies, Glyn A. Virtual Work in Structural Analysis. LC 81-15926. 341p. reprint ed. pap. 105.80 (*0-7837-0192-6*, 204048800017) Bks Demand.
Davies, Godfrey. Early Stuarts, 1603-1660. 2nd ed. (Oxford History of England Ser.: Vol. 9). (Illus.). 482p. 1937. text 65.00 (*0-19-821704-8*) OUP.
Davies, Godfrey & Keeler, Mary F. Bibliography of British History: Stuart Period, 1603-1714. 2nd ed. (Bibliography of British History Ser). 1971. 130.00 (*0-19-821371-9*) OUP.
Davies, Gordon. Painting in Acrylics. (Illus.). 128p. 1990. pap. 22.50 (*0-85532-684-0*, 684-0, Pub. by Srch Pr) A Schwartz & Co.
— Working with Acrylics. (Leisure Arts Ser.: No. 25). (Illus.). 32p. pap. 4.95 (*0-85532-535-6*, 535-6, Pub. by Srch Pr) A Schwartz & Co.
Davies, Gordon, ed. Shallow Impurities in Semiconductors. 502p. 1991. text 191.00 (*0-87849-619-X*, Pub. by Trans T Pub) Enfield Pubs NH.
Davies, Gordon, et al, eds. Defects in Semiconductors Sixteen. 1634p. 1992. text 433.00 (*0-87849-628-9*, Pub. by Trans T Pub) Enfield Pubs NH.
Davies, Gordon & Nazare, Maria H., eds. Defects in Semiconductors 19: ICDS-19. (Materials Science Forum Ser.: Vols. 258-263). 1932p. (C). 1998. text 480.00 (*0-87849-786-2*, Pub. by Scitec Pubns) Enfield Pubs NH.
Davies, Gordon & Samways, Brian, eds. Teleteaching: Proceedings of the IFIP TC3 Third Teleteaching Conference. LC 93-8819. (IFIP Transactions Ser.: Vol 29). (Illus.). 960p. 1993. pap. 200.00 (*0-444-81585-6*, North Holland) Elsevier.
Davies, Gordon, jt. auth. see Collis, Betty.
Davies, Gordon F. Israel in Egypt: A Reading Exodus 1-2. (Journal for the Study of the Old Testament Supplement Ser.: No. 135). 204p. (C). 1992. 57.50 (*1-85075-337-7*, Pub. by Sheffield Acad) CUP Services.
Davies, Gordon F., et al. Erza & Nehemiah. LC 98-24496. (Berit Olam Ser.). 148p. 1999. 29.95 (*0-8146-5049-X*) Liturgical Pr.
***Davies, Graham.** Drug Education: Teacher's Ed. (PSE in Focus Ser.). (Illus.). 128p. (YA). 2000. pap., teacher ed. 110.00 (*0-7487-5276-5*, Pub. by S Thornes Pubs) Trans-Atl Phila.
Davies, Graham, et al, eds. Psychology, Law & Criminal Justice: International Developments in Research & Practice. LC 95-22785. xx, 606p. 1995. lib. bdg. 152.30 (*3-11-013858-1*) De Gruyter.
Davies, Graham & Hussey, Michael, eds. New Technology in Language Learning: Proceedings of the 1989 Man & the Media Symposium. LC 92-27589. (Illus.). 127p. 1992. 32.00 (*3-631-44890-2*) P Lang Pubng.
Davies, Graham I. Hosea. (New Century Bible Ser.). 315p. 1992. pap. 24.50 (*0-551-02445-3*, Pub. by Sheffield Acad) CUP Services.
— Hosea. (Old Testament Guides Ser.: No. 25). 110p. 1993. pap. 12.50 (*1-85075-393-8*, Pub. by Sheffield Acad) CUP Services.
Davies, Graham I. Megiddo. LC 86-213062. (Cities of the Biblical World Ser.). (Illus.). 128p. (Orig.). reprint ed. pap. 39.70 (*0-8357-4360-8*, 203718800007) Bks Demand.
Davies, Graham M. & Logie, Robert H., eds. Memory in Everyday Life. LC 93-14511. (Advances in Psychology Ser.: Vol. 100). 568p. 1993. 191.50 (*0-444-88997-3*, North Holland) Elsevier.
Davies, Grant. Twenty Training Workshops for Improving Management Performance. 386p. 1992. 139.95 (*0-566-07279-3*, Pub. by Gower) Ashgate Pub Co.
Davies Group Staff, ed. see Johnson, D. L.
Davies Group Staff, ed. & illus. see Aichele, Ronald G.
Davies Group Staff, ed. & illus. see Colorado State University Staff.
Davies Group Staff, ed. & illus. see Martin, John M.
Davies Group Staff, ed. & illus. see O'Toole, Thomas.
Davies, Gwendolyn, jt. afterword by see Gerson, Carole.
Davies, Gwynne H. Overcoming Food Allergies: You Don't Have to Live with It. 128p. 1997. pap. text 9.99 (*1-85398-088-9*, Pub. by Ashgrove Pr) Words Distrib.
— You Don't Have to Live with Arthritis. 96p. (Orig.). 1998. pap. 10.95 (*1-85398-108-7*, Pub. by Ashgrove Pr) Words Distrib.
Davies, Gwynne H. & Morgan-Wynne, John E. The Last Seven Days: The Story of Jesus & Holy Week. LC 99-28534. (Regent's Study Guide Ser.). 224p. 1999. pap. 16.00 (*1-57312-292-0*) Smyth & Helwys.
Davies, H. Beginner's French Dictionary. (Beginner's Language Dictionaries Ser.). (Illus.). 128p. (J). (gr. 4 up). 1989. pap. 10.95 (*0-7460-0016-2*) EDC.
— Beginner's French Dictionary. (Beginner's Language Dictionaries Ser.). (Illus.). 128p. (J). (gr. 4 up). 1999. lib. bdg. 18.95 (*0-88110-346-2*) EDC.
— Beginner's German Dictionary. (Beginner's Language Dictionaries Ser.). (Illus.). 128p. (gr. 4 up). 1989. pap. 10.95 (*0-7460-0018-9*) EDC.
— Beginner's German Dictionary. (Beginner's Language Dictionaries Ser.). (Illus.). 128p. (gr. 4 up). 1999. lib. bdg. 18.95 (*0-88110-347-0*) EDC.
— Beginner's Italian Dictionary. (Beginner's Language Dictionaries Ser.). (Illus.). 128p. (YA). (gr. 4-7). 1992. pap. 10.95 (*0-7460-0764-7*, Usborne) EDC.
— Beginner's Italian Dictionary. (Beginner's Language Dictionaries Ser.). (Illus.). 128p. (J). (gr. 4 up). 1999. lib. bdg. 20.95 (*0-88110-423-X*, Usborne) EDC.
— Beginner's Spanish Dictionary. (Beginner's Language Dictionaries Ser.). (SPA., Illus.). 128p. (gr. 4 up). 1989. pap. 10.95 (*0-7460-0020-0*) EDC.
— Beginner's Spanish Dictionary. (Beginner's Language Dictionaries Ser.). (SPA., Illus.). 128p. (YA). (gr. 4 up). 1999. lib. bdg. 18.95 (*0-88110-348-9*) EDC.
Davies, H. E. Davies Memoir: A Genealogical & Biographical Monograph on the Family & Descendants of John Davies of Litchfield, Ct. 138p. 1995. reprint ed. pap. 19.50 (*0-8328-4768-2*); reprint ed. lib. bdg. 29.50 (*0-8328-4767-4*) Higginson Bk Co.
Davies, H. Oladipo. Nigeria: The Prospects for Democracy. (B. E. Ser.: No. 176). 1961. 30.00 (*0-8115-3086-8*) Periodicals Srv.
Davies, H. T., jt. auth. see Crombie, I. K.
Davies, H. W. & Healey, Patsy. British Planning Practice & Planning Education in the 1970's & 1980's. (C). 1983. 29.00 (*0-7855-3847-X*, Pub. by Oxford Polytechnic) St Mut.
Davies, Hazel W., ed. State of Play: Four Playwrights of Wales. (Illus.). 444p. 1998. pap. 49.95 (*0-8464-4933-1*) Beekman Pubs.
Davies, Helen. Beginner's Irish Dictionary. (ENG & IRI., Illus.). 128p. (J). (gr. 1-8). 1990. pap. 13.95 (*0-7171-1763-4*, Pub. by Gill & MacMill) Irish Bks Media.
Davies, Helen & Jensen, Mike. Alzheimers: The Answers You Need. 140p. (Orig.). 1997. per. 10.95 (*0-943873-46-0*) Elder Bks.
Davies, Henry W. & Grace, Harvey. Music & Worship. LC 74-24067. reprint ed. 29.50 (*0-404-12894-7*) AMS Pr.
Davies, Hereward. Channel Crossing. 115p. 1986. 25.00 (*0-7223-1990-8*, Pub. by A H S Ltd) St Mut.
Davies, Hilary. In a Valley of This Restless Mind. LC 98-134166. 80p. 1998. pap. 17.95 (*1-870612-97-3*, Pub. by Enitha Pr) Dufour.
— The Shanghai Owner of the Bonsai Shop. 84p. (Orig.). 1991. pap. 16.95 (*1-870612-56-6*, Pub. by Enitha Pr) Dufour.
***Davies, Horton.** Bread of Life & Cup of Joy: Newer Ecumenical Perspectives on the Eucharist. 284p. 1999. pap. 26.00 (*1-57910-209-3*) Wipf & Stock.
Davies, Horton. A Church Historian's Odyssey: A Memoir. LC 93-430. 1993. pap. 10.00 (*1-55635-018-X*) Pickwick.
— The English Free Churches. 2nd ed. LC 85-7684. 208p. 1985. reprint ed. lib. bdg. 59.50 (*0-313-20838-7*, DAEF, Greenwood Pr) Greenwood.
— Great South African Christians. LC 70-104242. 190p. 1970. reprint ed. lib. bdg. 35.00 (*0-8371-3916-3*, DAGC, Greenwood Pr) Greenwood.
— Like Angels from a Cloud: The English Metaphysical Preachers, 1588-1645. LC 86-10613. 515p. 1986. reprint ed. pap. 159.70 (*0-608-03169-0*, 206362200007) Bks Demand.
— Mirror of the Ministry in Modern Novels. LC 70-111824. (Essay Index Reprint Ser.). 1977. 21.95 (*0-8369-1601-8*) Ayer.
— The Vigilant God: Providence in the Thought of Augustine, Aquinas, Calvin, & Barth. LC 92-13701. 170p. (C). 1992. text 35.95 (*0-8204-1496-4*) P Lang Pubng.
— Worship & Theology in England, Vols. 1-3. 1996. pap. 150.00 (*0-8028-0890-5*) Eerdmans.
— Worship & Theology in England Vol. 1: From Cranmer to Baxter, 1534-1690, Vol. 1. 1108p. 1996. pap. 50.00 (*0-8028-0891-3*) Eerdmans.
— Worship & Theology in England Vol. 2: From Watts & Wesley to Martineau 1690-1900. 762p. 1996. pap. 50.00 (*0-8028-0892-1*) Eerdmans.
— Worship & Theology in England Vol. 3: The Ecumenical Century, 1900 to the Present. 799p. 1996. pap. 50.00 (*0-8028-0893-X*) Eerdmans.
— The Worship of the American Puritans, 1629-1730. LC 90-47784. (Illus.). X, 292p. (C). 1991. text 49.95 (*0-8204-1222-8*) P Lang Pubng.
— The Worship of the American Puritans, 1629-1730. 2nd ed. (Illus.). 327p. 1999. reprint ed. pap. 16.95 (*1-57358-099-6*) Soli Deo Gloria.
— The Worship of the English Puritans. LC 97-222200. 300p. 1997. reprint ed. pap. 15.95 (*1-57358-043-0*) Soli Deo Gloria.
Davies, Horton, ed. The Communion of Saints: Prayers of the Famous. 168p. 1996. pap. text 12.00 (*0-8028-4303-4*) Eerdmans.
— The Communion of Saints: Prayers of the Famous. LC 90-35714. 168p. reprint ed. pap. 52.10 (*0-7837-6557-6*, 204612200011) Bks Demand.
***Davies, Horton & Davies, Marie-Helene.** French Huguenots in English-Speaking Lands. LC 99-28014. 160p. (C). 2000. pap. text 22.95 (*0-8204-4542-8*) P Lang Pubng.
Davies, Horton & Davies, Marie-Helene. Holy Days & Holidays: The Medieval Pilgrimage to Compostela. LC 80-69875. (Illus.). 256p. 1982. 37.50 (*0-8387-5018-4*) Bucknell U Pr.
Davies, Hugh. Sculpture by Bill Woodrow: Natural Produce, an Armed Response. LC 85-81552. (Illus.). 20p. 1985. 5.00 (*0-934418-21-X*) Mus Contemp Art.
***Davies, Hugh.** The Titanium Professional: Building Exciting & Resilient Careers. 208p. 2000. pap. 19.95 (*1-875680-85-3*, Pub. by Business & Professional) IPG Chicago.
***Davies, Hugh, compiled by.** Catalogue of a Collection of Early French Books in the Library of C. Fairfax Murray. 1200p. 1999. reprint ed. 100.00 (*1-57898-177-8*) Martino Pubng.
Davies, Hugh, pref. Selections from the Permanent Collection of the San Diego Museum of Contemporary Art. LC 90-61679. (Illus.). 120p. (C). 1990. text 35.00 (*0-934418-36-5*) Mus Contemp Art.
Davies, Hugh & Forsha, Lynda. Jene Highstein. LC 86-82610. (Illus.). 44p. 1986. pap. 12.95 (*0-934418-26-8*) Mus Contemp Art.
Davies, Hugh & Yard, Sally. Francis Bacon. LC 85-6044. (Modern Masters Ser.). (Illus.). 128p. 1985. 35.00 (*0-89659-447-5*) Abbeville Pr.
— Francis Bacon. LC 85-6044. (Modern Masters Ser.). (Illus.). 128p. 1991. pap. 14.95 (*1-55859-245-8*) Abbeville Pr.
Davies, Hugh M. Richard Long. LC 89-63456. (Illus.). 24p. 1989. 12.00 (*0-934418-33-0*) Mus Contemp Art.
Davies, Hugh M. & Farrell, Anne. Learning from La Jolla: Robert Venturi Remakes a Museum in the Precinct of Irving Gill. LC 96-79507. (Illus.). 1997. 45.00 (*0-934418-48-9*); pap. 22.95 (*0-934418-47-0*) Mus Contemp Art.
Davies, Hugh M. & Forsha, Lynda. Robert Cumming: Cone of Vision. LC 92-62592. (Illus.). 83p. 1993. pap. 20.00 (*0-934418-40-3*) Mus Contemp Art.
Davies, Hugh M. & Onorato, Ronald J. Sitings: Aycock, Fleischner, Miss, Trakas. Yard, Sally, ed. LC 86-80303. (Illus.). 150p. (Orig.). 1986. per. 19.50 (*0-934418-25-X*) Mus Contemp Art.
Davies, Hugh M., et al. Blurring the Boundaries: Installation Art 1969-96. Farrell, Anne, ed. LC 94-75415. (Illus.). 184p. 1996. 65.00 (*0-934418-44-6*) Mus Contemp Art.
— John Baldessari: National City. LC 96-76793. (Illus.). 60p. 1997. pap. 24.95 (*0-934418-49-7*) Mus Contemp Art.
Davies, Hugh M., jt. auth. see Baza, Larry T.
Davies, Hugh S. & Watson, George, eds. The English Mind: Studies in the English Moralists Presented to Basil Wiley. LC 64-21539. 310p. reprint ed. pap. 88.40 (*0-608-10003-X*, 2050742) Bks Demand.
***Davies, Hugh William, compiled by.** Catalogue of a Collection of Early German Books in the Library of C. Fairfax Murray. 2 in 1. 925p. 1998. reprint ed. 95.00 (*1-57898-093-3*) Martino Pubng.
Davies, Hunter. The Beatles: The Classic. rev. ed. 516p. 1996. pap. 14.00 (*0-393-31571-1*) Norton.
— The Glory Game: A Year in the Life of Tottenham Hotspur. 350p. 1993. text 22.95 (*1-85158-376-9*, Pub. by Mainstream Pubng) Trafalgar.
— The Teller of Tales: In Search of Robert Louis Stevenson. (Literary Roads Ser.). (Illus.). 352p. (Orig.). 1996. 40.00 (*1-56656-205-8*); pap. 16.00 (*1-56656-204-X*) Interlink Pub.
***Davies, Hunter.** Wainwright: The Biography. 368p. 1998. pap. 15.95 (*0-14-027010-8*, Pub. by Pnguin Bks Ltd) Trafalgar.
Davies, Hunter. William Wordsworth: The Only Full Length Popular Biography. LC 97-163922. (Illus.). 384p. 1997. pap. 17.95 (*0-7509-1482-3*, Pub. by Sutton Pub Ltd) Intl Pubs Mktg.
Davies, Huw T., et al, eds. Controlling Costs: Strategic Issues in Health Care Management. LC 99-72983. 250p. 1999. text 65.95 (*0-7546-1110-8*, Pub. by Ashgate Pub) Ashgate Pub Co.
[D]avies, Huw T., et al, eds. Managing Quality: Strategic Issues in Health Care Management. LC 99-72982. 248p. 1999. text 69.95 (*0-7546-1004-7*, Pub. by Ashgate Pub) Ashgate Pub Co.
Davies, Hywel M. Transatlantic Brethren: Rev. Samuel Jones (1735-1814) & His Friends: Baptists in Wales, Pennsylvania & Beyond. LC 94-30666. 368p. 1995. 49.50 (*0-934223-32-7*) Lehigh Univ Pr.
Davies, Hywel M., et al. Information Systems Strategies for Public Financial Management. LC 93-6962. (Discussion Paper Ser.: No. 193). 61p. 1993. pap. 22.00 (*0-8213-2380-6*, 12380) World Bank.
Davies, I. M., jt. ed. see Truman, A.
***Davies, Ian.** Teaching the Holocaust. 160p. 2000. 74.95 (*0-304-70591-8*); pap. 24.95 (*0-304-70592-6*) Continuum.
***Davies, Ian, et al.** Good Citizenship & Educational Provision. LC 99-28038. 160p. 1999. 74.00 (*0-7507-0960-X*, Pub. by Falmer Pr UK); pap. 25.95 (*0-7507-0959-6*, Pub. by Falmer Pr UK) Taylor & Francis.
Davies, Idris. The Angry Summer: A Poem of 1926. (Illus.). xxxii, 74p. 1993. write for info. (*0-7083-1080-X*, Pub. by Univ Wales Pr) Paul & Co Pubs.
— I Was Born in Rhymney. 68p. 1990. 17.95 (*0-8464-4639-1*) Beekman Pubs.
Davies, Ioan. African Trade Unions. LC 76-44461. 1977. reprint ed. 35.00 (*0-8371-9081-9*, DAATU, Greenwood Pr) Greenwood.
— Cultural Studies & Beyond: Fragments of Empire. LC 94-42065. 224p. (C). 1995. pap. 24.99 (*0-415-03837-5*) Routledge.
— Cultural Studies & Beyond: Fragments of Empire. LC 94-42065. 224p. (C). (gr. 13). 1995. 80.00 (*0-415-03836-7*) Routledge.
Davies, Iolo. A Certaine Schoole: A History of Cowbridge Grammar School. 392p. (C). 1989. 65.00 (*0-7855-6869-7*, Pub. by D Brown & Sons Ltd) St Mut.
Davies, Iwan. Textbook on Commercial Law. xli, 541p. 1992. pap. 48.00 (*1-85431-195-6*, Pub. by Blackstone Pr) Gaunt.
Davies, J. Anna of All the Russias: The Life of Anna Akhmatova, 1889-1966. 148p. (C). 1988. 90.00 (*0-569-09086-5*, Pub. by Collets) St Mut.
— Introducing the Christian Faith. 1994. pap. 0.99 (*0-946462-11-9*, Pub. by Evangelical Pr) P & R Pubng.
— Introducing Truth & Reality. 1994. pap. text 0.99 (*0-946462-35-6*, Pub. by Evangelical Pr) P & R Pubng.
— Kobon. (Descriptive Grammars Ser.). 264p. 1986. pap. 72.50 (*0-7099-0878-4*, Pub. by C Helm) Routldge.
Davies, J., et al. Guide to the Study of Soil Ecology. 1973. text 13.12 (*0-13-370973-6*); pap. text 12.40 (*0-13-370965-5*) P-H.
Davies, J. A. Selective Hydrocarbon Activation: Principles & Progress. 568p. 1990. 220.00 (*0-471-18724-0*, Wiley-VCH) Wiley.
Davies, J. Alans & Coy, John. Economics from Square One. LC 77-409712. 278 p. 1969. write for info. (*0-04-330130-4*) Allen & Unwin Pty.
Davies, J. C. Mr. Fish & the Alabama Claims: A Chapter in Diplomatic History. LC 71-95065. (Select Bibliographies Reprint Ser.). 158p. 1972. reprint ed. lib. bdg. 18.00 (*0-8290-0485-8*) Irvington.
Davies, J. Clarence, ed. Comparing Environmental Risks: Tools for Setting Government Priorities. LC 95-44579. 157p. 1996. text 27.00 (*0-915707-79-9*) Resources Future.
Davies, J. Clarence & Mazurek, Jan. Pollution Control in the United States: Evaluating the System. LC 97-49246. (Illus.). 319p. 1998. 48.00 (*0-915707-87-X*); pap. text 32.95 (*0-915707-88-8*) Resources Future.
— Regulating Pollution: Does the U. S. System Work? (Illus.). 50p. 1998. pap. text 20.00 (*0-7881-4805-2*) DIANE Pub.
— Regulating Pollution: Does the U. S. System Work? LC 97-7159. (Illus.). 50p. 1997. pap. 9.95 (*0-915707-85-3*) Resources Future.
Davies, J. D. Gentlemen & Tarpaulins: The Officers & Men of the Restoration Navy. (Oxford Historical Monographs). 288p. 1991. 79.00 (*0-19-820263-6*) OUP.
Davies, J. E., ed. The Bone-Biomaterial Interface. 352p. 1991. text 140.00 (*0-8020-5941-4*) U of Toronto Pr.
Davies, J. Eric, ed. Spectroscopic & Computational Studies of Supramolecular Systems. LC 92-26743. (Topics in Inclusion Science Ser.: Vol. 4). 320p. 1992. text 185.00 (*0-7923-1958-3*) Kluwer Academic.
Davies, J. Eric, jt. ed. see Atwood, Jerry L.
Davies, J. G. Pilgrimage Yesterday & Today: Why? Where? How? 1988. 27.00 (*0-334-02254-1*) TPI PA.
Davies, J. G., ed. The New Westminster Dictionary of Liturgy & Worship. LC 86-9219. (Illus.). 560p. 1986. 39.95 (*0-664-21270-0*) Westminster John Knox.
Davies, J. G. & University of Birmingham Staff. Looking to the Future: Papers Read at an International Symposium On Prospects For Worship, Religious Architecture & Socio-religious Studies, 1976. LC 77-369107. 171p. 1976. write for info. (*0-7044-0234-3*) Univ of Birmingham.
Davies, J. G., et al. A Shaker Dance Service Reconstucted. 1984. pap. 3.00 (*0-941500-34-9*) Sharing Co.
Davies, J. Glyn. Welsh Metrics. LC 78-72625. (Celtic Language & Literature Ser.: Goidelic & Brythonic). reprint ed. 27.50 (*0-404-17547-3*) AMS Pr.
Davies, J. H. & Long, A. R., eds. Physics of Nanostructures. (Scottish Universities Summer School in Physics, a NATO Advanced Study Institute Ser.: No. 38). (Illus.). 356p. 1993. pap. 50.00 (*0-7503-0169-4*) IOP Pub.
***Davies, J. I., et al, eds.** Low Surface Brightness Universe: IAU Colloquium 171, Vol. 170. (ASP Conference Series Proceedings). (C). 1999. text 52.00 (*1-886733-92-9*) Astron Soc Pacific.
Davies, J. K. Democracy & Classical Greece. LC 83-45337. (Illus.). 284p. 1978. pap. 14.95 (*0-8047-1226-3*) Stanford U Pr.
— Democracy & Classical Greece. 2nd ed. LC 93-795. 328p. 1993. pap. 16.50 (*0-674-19607-4*) HUP.
Davies, J. Kenneth & Ovard, Glen F. Economics & the American System. LC 74-166320. (The Lippincott Social Studies Program Ser.). xiii, 656p. 1970. write for info. (*0-397-40171-X*) Lppncott W & W.
Davies, J. M. Blake's Milton Designs: The Dynamics of Meaning. LC 92-32678. (Locust Hill Literary Studies: No. 7). (Illus.). 347p. (C). 1993. lib. bdg. 40.00 (*0-933951-40-X*) Locust Hill Pr.
— Bridging the Gap: Literary Theory in the Classroom. LC 94-17926. (Locust Hill Literary Studies: No. 17). 373p. (C). 1994. lib. bdg. 38.00 (*0-933951-60-4*) Locust Hill Pr.
Davies, J. M., et al. The Impact of an Oil Spill in Turbulent Waters: The Braer : Proceedings of a Symposium Held at the Royal Society of Edinburgh, 7-8 September 1995. LC 98-128432. (Illus.). 1997. write for info. (*0-11-495798-3*) Statnry Office.
Davies, J. S. Amino Acid & Peptides, Vol. 24. 286p. 1993. 200.00 (*0-85186-224-1*, R6224) CRC Pr.
— Amino Acids, Peptides, & Proteins Vol. 25. 424p. 1994. 205.00 (*0-85186-234-9*, R6234) CRC Pr.

D

Davies, J. S., ed. Amino Acids & Peptides. 800p. 1985. ring bd. write for info. (*0-412-26950-3*, NO. 6569, Chap & Hall CRC) CRC Pr.

Davies, J. W. Communication for Engineering Students. 144p. (C). 1996. pap. text 34.80 (*0-582-25648-8*) Addison-Wesley.

Davies, J. W., ed. Molecular Plant Virology: Replication & Gene Expression, Vol. II. 240p. 1985. 138.00 (*0-8493-6291-1*, QR351, CRC Reprint) Franklin.

— Molecular Plant Virology: Virus Structure & Assembly & Nucleic Acid-Protein Interactions, Vol. I. 240p. 1985. 138.00 (*0-8493-6290-3*, QR351, CRC Reprint) Franklin.

Davies, Jack. Legislative Law & Process in a Nutshell. 2nd ed. LC 86-7768. (Nutshell Ser.). 346p. (C). 1986. reprint ed. pap. 21.00 (*0-314-21437-2*) West Pub.

Davies, Jack, jt. auth. see Davies, Jamie.

Davies, Jacqueline. Computing Fundamentals: Pagemaker. (Illus.). 160p. (C). 1990. pap. text 12.95 (*0-201-19828-2*) Addison-Wesley.

Davies, Jacqueline, jt. auth. see Bickenbach, Jerome E.

Davies, James. Life & Death. LC 76-356587. (Elementary Go Ser.: Vol. 4). 1975. pap. 12.95 (*4-87187-013-8*, G13) Ishi Pr Intl.

— Ways of Thinking. LC 91-18025. (American University Studies: Philosophy: Ser. V, Vol. 131). 258p. 1991. 44.95 (*0-8204-1692-4*) P Lang Pubng.

— When Men Revolt & Why. LC 96-38938. 360p. (Orig.). 1997. pap. text 24.95 (*1-56000-939-X*) Transaction Pubs.

Davies, James & Bozulich, Richard. An Introduction to Go. 1984. pap. 4.95 (*4-87187-030-8*, G30) Ishi Pr Intl.

Davies, James, jt. auth. see Ishida Akira, Seven-Dan.

Davies, James, jt. auth. see Kosugi Kiyoshi, Six-Dan.

Davies, James, jt. auth. see Ogawa, Tomoko.

Davies, James A. Characterization in Dickens. 1988. 52.50 (*0-389-20588-5*, N8146) B&N Imports.

— John Forster: A Literary Life. LC 83-3792. (Illus.). 328p. (C). 1983. text 45.00 (*0-389-20391-2*, N7269) B&N Imports.

— A Leap in the Dark: A Welsh Airman's Adventures in Occupied Europe, WW II. (Illus.). 256p. 1994. 29.95 (*0-85052-314-1*, Pub. by Leo Cooper) Trans-Atl Phila.

— A Leap in the Dark: A Welsh Airman's Adventures in Occupied Europe, WW II. large type ed. (Illus.). 352p. 1995. 27.99 (*0-7089-3425-0*) Ulverscroft.

Davies, James A., ed. A Reference Companion to Dylan Thomas. LC 97-24572. 392p. 1998. lib. bdg. 89.50 (*0-313-28774-0*, Greenwood Pr) Greenwood.

Davies, James A., jt. ed. see Ratcliff, Donald.

Davies, James B. & MacDonald, Glenn M. Information in the Labour Market: Job-Worker Matching & Its Implications for Education in Ontario. (Ontario Economic Council Research Studies: No. 29). 200p. (Orig.). 1984. pap. 10.95 (*0-8020-3403-9*) U of Toronto Pr.

Davies, James C. Baronial Opposition to Edward Second: Its Character & Policy. 644p. 1967. reprint ed. 37.50 (*0-7146-1466-1*, BHA-01466, Pub. by F Cass Pubs) Intl Spec Bk.

— Human Nature in Politics: The Dynamics of Political Behavior. LC 77-13870. (Illus.). 403p. 1978. reprint ed. lib. bdg. 75.00 (*0-8371-9870-4*, DAHN, Greenwood Pr) Greenwood.

Davies, James S. ISO 9000 Management Systems Manual. LC 96-48236. (Illus.). 218p. 1997. 60.00 (*0-07-015768-5*) McGraw.

Davies, James W. Empire of the Gods: The Liberation of Eros. (New Perspectives in Philosophical Scholarship Series: Texts & Issues: Vol. 8). XI, 374p. 1997. text 58.95 (*0-8204-3057-9*) P Lang Pubng.

Davies, Jamie & Davies, Jack. Sparkling Harvest: The Seasons of the Vine. LC 96-50166. (Illus.). 144p. 1997. 45.00 (*0-8109-1247-3*, Pub. by Abrams) Time Warner.

***Davies, Jan & Westhorpe, Rod.** All about Anaesthesia. (Illus.). 192p. 2001. pap. 22.95 (*0-19-551089-5*) OUP.

Davies, Jane D. Le Compagnon du Petit Prince: Cahier d'Exercises sur le Texte de Saint-Exupery. (FRE.). 120p. (C). 1975. 24.00 (*0-15-550448-7*) Harcourt Coll Pubs.

***Davies, Janet.** A Pocket Guide. 160p. 1999. pap. (*0-7083-1516-X*, Pub. by Univ Wales Pr) Paul & Co Pubs.

Davies, Janet, ed. The Mercator Media Guide, Vol. 2. 273p. 1997. pap. 25.00 (*0-7083-1381-7*, Pub. by Univ Wales Pr) Paul & Co Pubs.

Davies, Janet L. & Janosik, Ellen H. Mental Health & Psychiatric Nursing: A Caring Approach. 768p. 1991. 62.50 (*0-86720-442-7*) Jones & Bartlett.

Davies, Janet L., jt. auth. see Janosik, Ellen H.

Davies, Jean S., et al. Pittsford's Second Century, 1872-1997. (Illus.). 768p. 1999. 50.00 (*0-914659-85-5*) Phoenix Pub.

Davies, Jennifer. The Victorian Kitchen. LC 91-72390. (Illus.). 192p. 1992. reprint ed. pap. 18.95 (*0-563-36281-2*, BBC-Parkwest) Parkwest Pubns.

Davies, Jill. Herbs & Herb Gardens. (Album Ser.: No. 111). (Illus.). 32p. 1989. pap. 4.75 (*0-85263-656-3*, Pub. by Shire Pubns) Parkwest Pubns.

— Star Gazing for Cats: Jill Davies Wood Engravings. (Illus.). 48p. 1995. 9.95 (*1-885061-11-0*) Adventure Pubns.

Davies, Jill & Dickerson, John. Nutrient Content of Food Portions. (Royal Society of Chemistry Publications). 64p. 1991. 37.00 (*0-85186-426-0*, R6426, CRC Reprint) Franklin.

Davies, Jill, jt. auth. see Coultate, Tom.

Davies, Jill M., et al. Safety Planning with Battered Women: Complex Lives Difficult Choices. LC 97-45282. (Series on Violence Against Women). 1998. 46.00 (*0-7619-1224-X*); pap. 21.95 (*0-7619-1225-8*) Sage.

Davies, Jill R. Garlic: Allium Sativum: A Step-by-Step Guide. (In a Nutshell Ser.). 2000. 7.95 (*1-86204-559-3*, Pub. by Element MA) Penguin Putnam.

— Hawthorn: Cratageus Oxycanthia: A Step-by-Step Guide. LC 99-28109. (In a Nutshell Ser.). 2000. 7.95 (*1-86204-557-7*, Pub. by Element MA) Penguin Putnam.

— Healing Herbs: Echinacea. LC 99-18448. (In a Nutshell Ser.). 64p. 1999. text 7.95 (*1-86204-503-8*, Pub. by Element MA) Penguin Putnam.

— Healing Herbs: Ginko Biloba. LC 99-14121. (In a Nutshell Ser.). 64p. 1999. text 7.95 (*1-86204-504-6*, Pub. by Element MA) Penguin Putnam.

— Healing Herbs: Ginseng. LC 99-18449. (In a Nutshell Ser.). 64p. 1999. text 7.95 (*1-86204-505-4*, Pub. by Element MA) Penguin Putnam.

— Marigold: Calendula Officinalis: A Step-by-Step Guide. (In a Nutshell Ser.). 2000. 7.95 (*1-86204-558-5*, Pub. by Element MA) Penguin Putnam.

— St. John's Wort. LC 99-18450. (In a Nutshell Ser.). 64p. 1999. text 7.95 (*1-86204-506-2*, Pub. by Element MA) Penguin Putnam.

— Saw Palmetto: Serenoa Serrulata: A Step-by-Step Guide. (In a Nutshell Ser.). 2000. 7.95 (*1-86204-556-9*, Pub. by Element MA) Penguin Putnam.

Davies, Jill Rosemary, jt. auth. see Nice, Jill.

Davies, Jill Rosemary, jt. auth. see Ryan, Joseph.

Davies, Jim. Specification & Proof in Real Time CSP. (Distinguished Dissertations in Computer Science Ser.: No. 6). (Illus.). 198p. (C). 1993. text 54.95 (*0-521-45055-1*) Cambridge U Pr.

Davies, Jim, jt. auth. see Woodcock, Jim.

Davies, Jody M. & Frawley, Mary G. Treating the Adult Survivor of Childhood Sexual Abuse: A Psychoanalytic Perspective. LC 93-34377. 304p. 1994. pap. 45.00 (*0-465-06633-X*, Pub. by Basic) HarpC.

Davies, John. At the Edge of Town. 76p. (C). 1981. 30.00 (*0-85088-923-5*, Pub. by Gomer Pr) St Mut.

— Cardiff & the Marquesses of Bute. (Studies in Welsh History). xii, 335p. 1981. 29.95 (*0-7083-0761-2*, Pub. by Univ Wales Pr) Paul & Co Pubs.

— Christians, Politics & Violent Revolution. LC 75-42517. 224p. reprint ed. pap. 69.50 (*0-608-12643-8*, 202511800042) Bks Demand.

— Dirt Roads. LC 98-128335. 72p. 1998. pap. 17.95 (*1-85411-184-1*, Pub. by Seren Bks) Dufour.

— A Discovery of the True Causes Why Ireland Was Never Entirely Subdued & Brought under Obedience of the Crown of England until the Beginning of His Majesty's Happy Reign (1612) Myers, James P., Jr., ed. LC 87-25595. 256p. 1988. reprint ed. pap. 79.40 (*0-7837-9192-5*, 204989300004) Bks Demand.

— Educating Students in a Media-Saturated Culture. LC 95-61804. 310p. 1997. pap. text 39.95 (*1-56676-365-7*) Scarecrow.

***Davies, John.** A Fever in the Blood. large type ed. 352p. 1999. pap. 20.99 (*1-85389-962-3*, Dales) Ulverscroft.

Davies, John. Flight Patterns. 78p. 1991. pap. 16.95 (*1-85411-044-6*, Pub. by Seren Bks) Dufour.

Davies, John. Hanes Cymru: A History of Wales in Welsh. pap. 19.95 (*0-14-012570-1*, Pub. by Pnguin Bks Ltd) Trafalgar.

Davies, John. A History of Wales. 736p. 1995. pap. 16.95 (*0-14-014581-8*, Penguin Bks) Viking Penguin.

— Making of Wales. 1999. pap. text 22.95 (*0-7509-2176-5*) A Sutton.

— Newnes Radio Engineer's Pocket Book. (Illus.). 280p. 1995. text 29.95 (*0-7506-1738-1*) Buttrwrth-Heinemann.

— Orchestra: or a Poem of Dancing. 1988. reprint ed. lib. bdg. 49.00 (*0-7812-0025-3*) Rprt Serv.

— Orchestra: or a Poem of Dancing. LC 70-161962. 1947. reprint ed. 45.00 (*0-403-01333-X*) Scholarly.

— Poems. Krueger, Robert, ed. (Oxford English Texts Ser.). (Illus.). 522p. 1975. text 85.00 (*0-19-812716-2*) OUP.

***Davies, John.** See Naples & Die. 368p. 1999. 20.99 (*1-85389-979-8*) Ulverscroft.

Davies, John. A Tahitian & English Dictionary. LC 75-35188. reprint ed. 42.50 (*0-404-14217-6*) AMS Pr.

— Wittes Pilgrimage, (by Poeticall Essaies) Through a World of Amorous Sonnets, Etc. LC 79-84099. (English Experience Ser.: No. 919). 172p. 1979. reprint ed. lib. bdg. 20.00 (*90-221-0919-4*) Walter J Johnson.

— Works in Verse & Prose, 3 vols., Set. (BCL1-PR English Literature Ser.). 1992. reprint ed. lib. bdg. 270.00 (*0-7812-7197-5*) Rprt Serv.

— The Writing School-Master. LC 76-57376. (English Experience Ser.: No. 794). 1977. reprint ed. lib. bdg. 20.00 (*90-221-0794-9*) Walter J Johnson.

Davies, John, et al, eds. Political Policing in Wales. 1984. 20.00 (*0-7855-1463-5*, Pub. by NCCL) St Mut.

— Surface Analytical Techniques for Probing Biomaterial Processes. LC 96-6084. 192p. 1996. boxed set 134.95 (*0-8493-8352-8*) CRC Pr.

***Davies, John & Carr, Joseph.** Newnes Radio & RF Engineers Pocket Book. 608p. 2000. 29.95 (*0-7506-4600-4*, Newnes) Buttrwrth-Heinemann.

Davies, John & Jenkins, Mike, eds. Valleys. (Illus.). 141p. 1984. pap. 10.95 (*0-907476-31-7*) Dufour.

Davies, John & Parr, Martin. John Davies & Martin Parr: Sguardigardesani. (Illus.). 96p. 1999. pap. 35.00 (*88-8158-223-6*, Pub. by Charta) Dist Art Pubs.

Davies, John & Thomas, J. E. A Select Bibliography of Adult Continuing Education. 300p. (C). 1988. 140.00 (*0-900559-78-0*, Pub. by Natl Inst Adult Continuing Educ) St Mut.

Davies, John A. The Reins of Life. 176p. (C). 1990. 40.00 (*0-85131-449-X*, Pub. by J A Allen) St Mut.

Davies, John B. The Myth of Addiction: An Application of the Psychological Theory of Attribution to Illicit Drug Use. xii, 180p. 1992. text 71.00 (*3-7186-5197-1*, Harwood Acad Pubs); pap. text 43.00 (*3-7186-5243-9*, Harwood Acad Pubs) Gordon & Breach.

— The Psychology of Music. LC 77-92339. 240p. 1978. 37.50 (*0-8047-0980-7*) Stanford U Pr.

Davies, John B., jt. ed. see Shewan, David.

Davies, John D. & Garner, Philip. At the Crossroads: Special Educational Needs & Teacher Education. LC 97-202414. 256p. 1997. pap. 25.95 (*1-85346-447-3*, Pub. by David Fulton) Taylor & Francis.

Davies, John Dwyfor. Managing Special Needs in Mainstream Schools: The Role of the Senco. 1998. 28.95 (*1-85346-526-7*) Taylor & Francis.

Davies, John H. The Physics of Low-Dimensional Semiconductors: An Introduction. LC 97-88. (Illus.). 456p. 1998. pap. text 44.95 (*0-521-48491-X*) Cambridge U Pr.

— The Physics of Low-Dimensional Semiconductors: An Introduction. LC 97-88. (Illus.). 456p. (C). 1998. text 100.00 (*0-521-48148-1*) Cambridge U Pr.

Davies, John K. Satellite Astronomy: The Principles & Practice of Astronomy from Space. 232p. 1988. text 52.95 (*0-470-21174-1*) P-H.

— Wealth & the Power of Wealth in Classical Athens. rev. ed. Connor, W. R., ed. LC 80-2647. (Monographs in Classical Studies). 1981. lib. bdg. 26.95 (*0-88143-019-6*) Ayer.

Davies, John K. & MacDonald, Gordon. Quality Evidence, & Effectiveness in Health Promotion. LC 98-22995. 240p. (C). 1998. pap. 24.99 (*0-415-17967-X*) Routledge.

— Quality, Evidence, & Effectiveness in Health Promotion. LC 98-22995. (Illus.). 248p. (C). 1998. 85.00 (*0-415-17966-1*) Routledge.

Davies, John L. Geographical Variation in Coastal Development. 2nd ed. Clayton, K. M., ed. LC 79-41082. (Geomorphology Texts Ser.: No. 4). (Illus.). 220p. reprint ed. pap. 68.20 (*0-608-18740-2*, 203033800068) Bks Demand.

Davies, John L., ed. Working Men's College, 1854-1904. LC 75-144594. reprint ed. 32.00 (*0-404-01978-1*) AMS Pr.

Davies, John L., ed. 1066. 39.00 (*1-56696-113-0*) Jackdaw.

Davies, John L. & Gurr, Ted R., eds. Preventive Measures: Building Risk Assessment & Crisis Early Warning Systems. LC 98-28589. (Illus.). 304p. 1998. 65.00 (*0-8476-8873-9*); pap. 24.95 (*0-8476-8874-7*) Rowman.

Davies, John M. The Essential Guide to Database Marketing. LC 92-15223. 1992. 28.00 (*0-685-57488-1*) McGraw.

***Davies, John Phillip.** US Elections Today: New Edition of Elections USA. LC 99-43123. 237p. 1999. text 59.95 (*0-7190-4507-X*, Pub. by Manchester Univ Pr) St Martin.

Davies, John S., ed. English Chronicle, of the Reigns of Richard Second, Henry Fourth, Henry Fifth, Henry Sixth, Written Before the Year 1471. LC 73-166036. (Camden Society, London. Publications, First Ser.: No. 64). reprint ed. 55.00 (*0-404-50164-8*) AMS Pr.

Davies, John W., jt. auth. see Butler, David.

Davies, Jon. The Christian Warrior in the Twentieth Century. LC 94-18253. (Illus.). 182p. 1994. text 79.95 (*0-7734-9034-5*) E Mellen.

***Davies, Jon.** Death Burial & Rebirth in Religions of Antiquity. LC 98-49845. (Religion in the First Christian Centuries Ser.). 1999. pap. 24.99 (*0-415-12991-5*); text 75.00 (*0-415-12990-7*) Routledge.

Davies, Jon, ed. Ritual & Remembrance: Responses to Death in Human Societies. (Individual Titles in Religion Ser.). 284p. 1994. pap. 28.50 (*1-85075-469-1*, Pub by Sheffield Acad) CUP Services.

Davies, Jon, et al, eds. The Family: Is It Just Another Lifestyle Choice? (Choice in Welfare Ser.: No. 15). 109p. 1993. pap. 19.95 (*0-255-36276-5*, Pub by Inst Economic Affairs) Coronet Bks.

Davies, Jon, et al, eds. Words Remembered, Texts Renewed: Essays in Honour of John F. A. Sawyer. (JSOT Supplement Ser.: No. 195). 533p. 1995. 90.00 (*1-85075-542-6*, Pub. by Sheffield Acad) CUP Services.

Davies, Jon & Loughlin, Gerard, eds. Sex These Days: Essays on Theology, Sexuality & Society. (Studies in Theology & Sexuality). 223p. 1997. 65.00 (*1-85075-662-7*, Pub. by Sheffield Acad) CUP Services.

— Sex These Days: Essays on Theology, Sexuality & Society. (Studies in Theology & Sexuality: Vol. 1). 223p. 1997. pap. 19.95 (*1-85075-804-2*, Pub. by Sheffield Acad) CUP Services.

Davies, Jon & Wollaston, Isabel, eds. The Sociology of Sacred Texts. (SAT Title Ser.). 193p. 1993. 58.00 (*1-85075-404-7*, Pub. by Sheffield Acad) CUP Services.

Davies, Jonathan. Florence & Its University During the Early Renaissance. LC 98-18524. (Education & Society in the Middle Ages & Renaissance Ser.: No. 8). xii, 232p. 1998. 86.00 (*90-04-11003-8*) Brill Academic Pubs.

— Given in Evidence. (Illus.). 265p. 1996. pap. 10.95 (*0-340-63231-3*, Pub. by Hodder & Stought Ltd) Trafalgar.

Davies, Jonathan I. & Burstein, David, eds. The Opacity of Spiral Disks: Proceedings of NATO Advanced Research Workshop on the Opacity of Spiral Disks Held 1994, Cardiff, Wales. LC 95-33174. (NATO ASI Ser.: Ser. C). 379p. (C). 1995. text 191.50 (*0-7923-3638-0*) Kluwer Academic.

Davies, Joseph E., jt. auth. see Lee, Thomas.

Davies, Joy. Noodles & Pasta. LC 99-12434. (Illus.). 144p. (YA). (gr. 11). 1999. 19.95 (*0-7370-0031-7*) T-L Custom Pub.

Davies, Juanita J., jt. auth. see Collins, C. Edward.

Davies, Jude & Smith, Carol R. Gender, Ethnicity, & Sexuality in Contemporary American Film. 160p. 1998. pap. 22.00 (*1-85331-174-X*, Pub. by Edinburgh U Pr) Col U Pr.

Davies, Judy, jt. auth. see Doiron, Ray.

Davies, Julia, et al. The Challenge to Western Management Development: International Alternatives. 256p. 1989. 57.50 (*0-415-00100-5*, A3107) Routledge.

Davies, Julian. The Caroline Captivity of the Church: Charles I & the Remoulding of Anglicanism, 1625-1641. (Oxford Historical Monographs). 424p. 1992. 98.00 (*0-19-820311-X*) OUP.

— A Compendium of Ockham's Teachings: A Translation of the Tactus de Principiis Theologiae. (Text Ser.). 120p. 1998. pap. text 14.00 (*1-57659-129-8*) Franciscan Inst.

Davies, Julian, compiled by. Displaced People & Refugee Studies: A Resource Guide. 232p. 1990. 68.00 (*0-905450-76-0*, Pub. by H Zell Pubs) Seven Hills Bk.

Davies, Julian A., et al, eds. Selective Hydrocarbon Activation: Principles & Progress. 568p. 1990. 155.00 (*0-89573-713-2*, Wiley-VCH) Wiley.

Davies, Julian A., tr. Ockham on Aristotle's Physics: A Translation of Ockham's Brevis Summa Libri Physicorum. 170p. 1989. pap. 12.00 (*1-57659-060-7*) Franciscan Inst.

Davies, Julian A., et al. Synthetic Coordination Chemistry: Theory of Practice. 500p. 1996. text 104.00 (*981-02-2084-7*) World Scientific Pub.

Davies, Julian E., jt. ed. see Demain, Arnold L.

Davies, Julie. Coordinating History Across the Primary School. LC 99-173999. (Subject Leaders Handbks.). 139p. 1998. pap. 23.95 (*0-7507-0691-0*, Falmer Pr) Taylor & Francis.

Davies, Julie, ed. Developing a Curriculum Leadership Role in Key Stage 2: A Handbook for Students & Newly Qualified Teachers. LC 95-7262. 208p. 1995. 85.00 (*0-7507-0424-1*, Falmer Pr); pap. 29.95 (*0-7507-0425-X*, Falmer Pr) Taylor & Francis.

Davies, June W. Golden Destiny. large type ed. 1994. 27.99 (*0-7089-3184-7*) Ulverscroft.

Davies, K. Advances in Separation Processes. (Institution of Chemical Engineers Symposium Ser.: No. 118). 168p. 1990. 95.00 (*1-56032-077-X*) Hemisp Pub.

— Ionospheric Radio. (Electromagnetic Waves Ser.: No. 31). 580p. 1990. boxed set 92.00 (*0-86341-186-X*, EW031) INSPEC Inc.

— Namibia: Profile of Agricultural Potential. 1993. pap. 35.00 (*0-85954-363-3*, Pub. by Nat Res Inst) St Mut.

— The SADC Region: Profile of Agricultural Potential. 1993. pap. 40.00 (*0-85954-353-6*, Pub. by Nat Res Inst) St Mut.

Davies, K. E., ed. Genome Analysis: A Practical Approach. (Practical Approach Ser.). (Illus.). 208p. (C). 1988. pap. 45.00 (*1-85221-110-5*); text 74.00 (*1-85221-109-1*) OUP.

— Human Genetic Disease Analysis: A Practical Approach. 2nd ed. LC 92-48251. (Practical Approach Ser.). (Illus.). 140p. 1993. pap. text 55.00 (*0-19-963308-8*) OUP.

Davies, K. G., ed. Documents of the American Revolution, 1778-1783 Vols. 1 to 14: Transcript Volumes. 7,780p. 1981. 750.00 (*0-7165-2085-0*, Pub. by Irish Acad Pr) Intl Spec Bk.

— Documents of the American Revolution, 1778-1783 Vols. 15-21: Calendar Volumes. Date not set. write for info. (*0-614-16250-5*, Pub. by Irish Acad Pr) Intl Spec Bk.

Davies, Karen. At Home in Manhattan: Modern Decorative Arts, 1925 to the Depression. (Illus.). 120p. (Orig.). 1983. pap. 15.00 (*0-89467-028-X*) Yale Art Gallery.

— Women, Time & the Weaving of the Strands of Everyday Life. (Illus.). 258p. 1990. text 67.95 (*0-566-07163-0*, Pub. by Avebry) Ashgate Pub Co.

Davies, Kate. Daniel in the Lion's Den. (Bible Pop-Ins Ser.). 10p. (J). 1997. bds. 4.99 (*1-884628-28-1*, Flyng Frog) Allied Pub MD.

— Jonah & the Big Fish. (Bible Pop-Ins Ser.). 10p. (J). 1997. bds. 4.99 (*1-884628-30-3*, Flyng Frog) Allied Pub MD.

— Moses in the Bulrushes. (Bible Pop-Ins Ser.). 10p. (J). 1997. bds. 4.99 (*1-884628-29-X*, Flyng Frog) Allied Pub MD.

— Noah & the Ark. (Bible Pop-Ins Ser.). 10p. (J). 1997. bds. 4.99 (*1-884628-31-1*, Flyng Frog) Allied Pub MD.

Davies, Kath. Amelia Earhart Flies Around the World. LC 93-29954. (Great Twentieth Century Expeditions Ser.). (Illus.). 32p. (J). (gr. 4 up). 1994. lib. bdg. 13.95 (*0-87518-531-2*, Dillon Silver Burdett) Silver Burdett Pr.

Davies, Kath, et al, eds. Out of Focus: Writings on Women & the Media. 256p. pap. 11.95 (*0-7043-4059-3*, Pub. by Womens Press) Trafalgar.

Davies, Katherine. Enlightenment Comes in the Dark. 96p. 1983. 9.50 (*0-87516-521-4*) DeVorss.

— Enlightenment Comes in the Dark. 96p. 1994. pap. 6.50 (*0-87516-674-1*) DeVorss.

Davies, Kay & Oldfield, Wendy. First Step Science, 8 bks. Incl. My Apple. LC 94-7107. (Illus.). 32p. (J). (gr. 1 up). 1994. lib. bdg. 21.27 (*0-8368-1114-3*); My Boat. LC 94-7108. (Illus.). 32p. (J). (gr. 1 up). 1994. lib. bdg. 21.27 (*0-8368-1115-1*); My Drum. LC 94-7109. (Illus.). 32p. (J). (gr. 1 up). 1994. lib. bdg. 21.27 (*0-8368-1116-X*); (Illus.). (J). Set lib. bdg. 148.87 (*0-8368-1189-5*) Gareth Stevens Inc.

— Rain. LC 95-6005. (See for Yourself Ser.). (Illus.). 30p. (J). (ps-4). 1995. lib. bdg. 21.40 (*0-8172-4043-8*) Raintree Steck-V.

— Snow & Ice. LC 95-6007. (See for Yourself Ser.). (Illus.). 30p. (J). (ps-4). 1995. lib. bdg. 19.97 (*0-8172-4042-X*) Raintree Steck-V.

— Sun. LC 95-6006. (See for Yourself Ser.). (Illus.). 30p. (J). (ps-4). 1995. lib. bdg. 21.40 (*0-8172-4040-3*) Raintree Steck-V.

— Wind. LC 95-6008. (See for Yourself Ser.). (Illus.). 30p. (J). (ps-4). 1995. lib. bdg. 21.40 (*0-8172-4041-1*) Raintree Steck-V.

Davies, Kay E. & Tilghman, Shirley M., eds. Gene Expression & Its Control. (Genome Analysis Ser.: Vol. 2). (Illus.). 118p. (C). 1991. text 49.00 (*0-87969-359-2*) Cold Spring Harbor.

— Genes & Phenotypes. (Genome Analysis Ser.: Vol. 3). 174p. (C). 1991. text 49.00 (*0-87969-402-5*) Cold Spring Harbor.

— Genetic & Physical Mapping. (Genome Analysis Ser.: Vol. 1). (Illus.). 250p. (C). 1991. text 49.00 (*0-87969-358-4*) Cold Spring Harbor.

D

— Genome Maps & Neurological Disorders. LC 93-70643. (Genome Analysis Ser.: Vol. 6). (Illus.). 133p. reprint ed. pap. 41.30 (*0-608-09128-6*, 206976000006) Bks Demand.
— Regional Physical Mapping. (Genome Analysis Ser.: Vol. 5). (Illus.). 200p. (C). 1993. text 25.00 (*0-87969-413-0*) Cold Spring Harbor.
— Strategies for Physical Mapping. LC 92-70761. (Genome Analysis Ser.: Vol. 4). 165p. 1992. 16.00 (*0-87969-412-2*, QH445) Cold Spring Harbor.
Davies, Kay E. & Warren, Ephen T., eds. Genome Rearrangement & Stability. LC 93-72455. (Genome Analysis Ser.: No. 7). (Illus.). 175p. Date not set. reprint ed. pap. 54.30 (*0-608-20713-6*, 207181100002) Bks Demand.
Davies, Keith. Executive Guide to the UNIX System. 350p. 1990. boxed set 38.00 (*0-13-294588-5*) P-H.
— Law of Compulsory Purchase & Compensation. 4th ed. 400p. 1984. pap. 48.00 (*0-406-57188-0*, U.K., MICHIE) LEXIS Pub.
— Law of Compulsory Purchase & Compensation. 5th ed. 327p. 1994. 210.00 (*0-85459-922-3*, Pub. by Tolley Pubng) St Mut.
— Local Government Law. 350p. 1983. pap. 50.00 (*0-406-25267-X*, UK, MICHIE) LEXIS Pub.
Davies, Keith A. Landowners in Colonial Peru. (Latin American Monographs: No. 61). (Illus.). 247p. 1984. text 22.50 (*0-292-74639-3*) U of Tex Pr.
Davies, Ken. Better Shot. 1992. 50.00 (*1-870948-64-5*, Pub. by Quiller Pr) St Mut.
Davies, Kenneth G. The North Atlantic World in the Seventeenth Century. LC 74-78994. (Europe & the World in the Age of Expansion Ser.: No. 4). 380p. 1974. pap. 117.80 (*0-7837-2967-7*, 205748700006) Bks Demand.
***Davies, Kevin.** Comp. 110p. 2000. pap. 12.50 (*1-890311-08-1*, Pub. by Edge Bks) SPD-Small Pr Dist.
Davies, Kevin. Pause Button. 80p. 1992. pap. 8.95 (*0-921331-10-X*, Pub. by Tsunami Edits) Barnholden.
***Davies, Kevin.** The Sequence: The Race to Crack the Genetic Code. 2001. 25.00 (*0-7432-0479-4*) Free Pr.
Davies, Kevin & White, Michael James Denham. Breakthrough: The Race to Find the Breast Cancer Gene. LC 95-30911. 310p. 1996. 24.95 (*0-471-12025-1*) Wiley.
Davies, Kevin, et al. Modern Medicine for the MRCP. 135p. 1996. pap. text 19.95 (*0-7020-2112-1*, Pub. by W B Saunders) Saunders.
***Davies, Kim.** Me, Amazon Woman: What Every Woman Needs to Know about LCIS Breast Cancer. LC 00-103196. 208p. 2000. pap. 18.95 (*1-886289-24-7*) Three Pyramids.
Davies, Kirk. Earth's Final Hours. 330p. (Orig.). 1982. pap. 19.95 (*0-9609174-0-3*) Pacific Inst.
Davies, Kirk L., jt. ed. see Gittins, Richard A.
Davies, Larry. Sowing Seeds of Faith . . . Vol. 1: Messages of Hope in a World Gone Bonkers! (Illus.). 176p. Date not set. 8.00 (*0-9656688-0-0*) ABM Enterprises.
Davies, Larry E. When a Used Car Salesman Becomes a Preacher . . . There Must Be a God! Saliter, Ann B., ed. (Sowing Seed of Faith in a World Gone Bonkers Ser.: Vol. 2). (Illus.). 192p. 1998. pap., mass mkt. 12.95 (*0-9656688-1-9*) ABM Enterprises.
Davies, Laurence. Cesar Franck & His Circle. LC 77-4231. (Music Reprint Ser.). (Illus.). 1977. reprint ed. lib. bdg. 45.00 (*0-306-77410-0*) Da Capo.
Davies, Laurence, jt. auth. see Watts, Cedric T.
Davies, Laurence, ed. see Conrad, Joseph.
Davies, Lawrence E. A World War II Diary by Lawrence E. Davies the West Coast Correspondent for the New York Times. LC 94-75079. 216p. (C). 1994. pap. 12.95 (*0-9634413-3-7*) HiSt ink Bks.
Davies, Leah G. Drug Abuse Prevention Program Leader Guide. 56p. (J). 1993. pap. write for info. (*0-9621054-5-7*) Bur For At-Risk.
— Kelly Bear Activities. LC 92-70013. (Illus.). 40p. (J). (ps-3). 1992. pap. 4.50 (*0-9621054-4-9*) Bur For At-Risk.
— Kelly Bear Behavior. LC 88-82603. (Illus.). 28p. (Orig.). (J). (ps-3). 1988. pap. 4.50 (*0-9621054-1-4*) Bur For At-Risk.
— Kelly Bear Drug Awareness. (Illus.). 40p. (J). (ps-3). 1993. pap. 4.50 (*0-9621054-6-5*) Bur For At-Risk.
— Kelly Bear Feelings. rev. ed. LC 88-82577. (Illus.). 28p. (J). (ps-3). 1988. pap. 4.50 (*0-9621054-0-6*) Bur For At-Risk.
— Kelly Bear Health. LC 89-85159. (Illus.). 28p. (Orig.). (J). (ps-3). 1989. pap. 4.50 (*0-9621054-2-2*) Bur For At-Risk.
Davies, Leonard E. Anatomy of Cross-Examination. LC 93-24745. 1993. 90.00 (*0-13-105883-5*) Aspen Law.
Davies, Leslie. Efficiency in Research, Development & Production: The Statistical Design & Analysis of Chemical Experiments. 180p. 1993. 52.00 (*0-85186-137-7*) CRC Pr.
Davies, Leslie G. & Gibb, Allan A. Recent Research in Entrepreneurship: The Third International EIASM Workshop. (Avebury Business School Library). 369p. 1991. text 101.95 (*1-85628-135-3*, Pub. by Avebury) Ashgate Pub Co.
Davies, Lewis. Freeways: A Journey West on Route 66. LC 98-122578. 172p. 1998. 19.95 (*0-9521558-5-0*, Pub. by Parthian Bks) Dufour.
— A Key to the British Species of Simulidae (Diptera) in the Larval, Pupal & Adult Stages. 1968. 60.00 (*0-900386-12-6*) St Mut.
— Tree of Crows. LC 97-189756. 102p. 1997. pap. 9.95 (*0-9521558-3-4*) Dufour.
— Work, Sex & Rugby. 174p. 1993. pap. 9.95 (*0-9521558-0-X*) Dufour.
***Davies, Lewis & Smith, Arthur, eds.** Mama's Baby (Papa's Maybe) New Welsh Short Fiction. 500p. 2000. pap. 15.95 (*1-902638-03-4*, Pub. by Parthian) Dufour.
Davies, Linda. Nest of Vipers. large type ed. LC 95-8921. (Large Print Bks.). 1995. 25.95 (*1-56895-222-8*) Wheeler Pub.
Davies, Linda & Shragge, Eric, eds. Bureaucracy & Community. LC 90-81638. 180p. 1996. 45.99 (*0-921689-57-8*, Pub. by Black Rose); pap. 19.99 (*0-921689-56-X*, Pub. by Black Rose) Consort Bk Sales.
Davies, Linda, jt. ed. see Burmeister-Brown, Susan.
Davies, Liz, jt. auth. see Blackburn, Mattie.
Davies, Lucy & Fini, Mo. Arts & Crafts of South America. 160p. 1995. 35.00 (*0-8118-0812-2*) Chronicle Bks.
— Arts & Crafts of South America. (Illus.). 160p. 1998. pap. text 23.00 (*0-7881-5692-6*) DIANE Pub.
Davies, Luke. Candy. LC 97-48390. 304p. 1998. pap. 12.95 (*0-345-42387-9*) Ballantine Pub Grp.
Davies, Lynn. Equity & Efficiency? School Management in an International Context. 200p. 1990. pap. 34.95 (*1-85000-659-8*, Falmer Pr) Taylor & Francis.
Davies, M. Butterworths Tutorials: Torts. 320p. 1992. pap. 36.00 (*0-409-30411-5*, Austral, MICHIE) LEXIS Pub.
— Torts. 2nd ed. (Master Ser.). 352p. 1995. pap. write for info. (*0-409-31072-7*, MICHIE) LEXIS Pub.
Davies, M. & Sidoli, Mara, eds. Jungian Child Psychotherapy: Individuation in Childhood. 304p. 1988. pap. 30.00 (*0-946439-47-8*, Pub. by H Karnac Bks Ltd) Other Pr LLC.
Davies, M. C. Land Reclamation: An End to Dereliction? 422p. 1991. mass mkt. 139.95 (*1-85166-658-3*) Elsevier.
Davies, M. C. & Schlosser, F. Ground Improvement GEO systems: Densification & Reinforcement. LC 97-210292. 508p. 1997. 143.00 (*0-7277-2605-6*) Am Soc Civil Eng.
Davies, M. J. Colour Atlas of Cardiovascular Pathology. (Illus.). 175p. 1986. text 95.00 (*0-19-921047-0*) OUP.
Davies, M. J., jt. ed. see Adams, J. N.
Davies, M. K. & Giles, T., eds. ACE Inhibitors in Heart Failure: Advancing Clinical Practice. (Journal Ser.: Vol. 87, Suppl. 1, 1996). (Illus.). iv, 44p. 1996. pap., suppl. ed. 21.75 (*3-8055-6272-1*) S Karger.
Davies, M. M., jt. auth. see Davies, Alan.
Davies, M. S., et al. A Directory of Clothing Research. 136p. 1968. 60.00 (*0-7855-7195-7*) St Mut.
Davies, Maire M. The Breastfeed Book. 128p. 1998. pap. 28.00 (*0-7112-0677-5*, Pub. by F Lincoln) St Mut.
— Fake, Fact & Fantasy: Children's Interpretations of Television Reality. LC 96-9530. (Communication Ser.). 270p. (C). 1996. text 59.95 (*0-8058-2046-9*); pap. text 27.50 (*0-8058-2047-7*) L Erlbaum Assocs.
Davies, Malcolm. Punishing Criminals: Developing Community-Based Intermediate Sanctions, 41. LC 93-9315. (Contributions in Criminology & Penology Ser.: No. 41). 192p. 1993. 55.00 (*0-313-28033-9*, DPY/, Greenwood Pr) Greenwood.
Davies, Malcolm, ed. Poetarum Melicorum Graecorum Fragmenta, Vol. I: Alcman, Stesichorus, Ibycus. (GRE & LAT.). 350p. 1991. text 100.00 (*0-19-814046-0*) OUP.
Davies, Malcolm, et al. Criminal Justice. LC 95-13898. 400p. (C). 1995. text 87.00 (*0-582-24769-1*, 15738) Gaunt.
Davies, Malcolm, et al. Criminal Justice. LC 95-13898. 400p. (C). 1995. pap. 48.00 (*0-582-24768-3*, 15738) Longman.
Davies, Malcolm, et al. Penological Esperanto & Sentencing Parochialism: A Comparative Study of the Search for Non-Prison Punishments. (Illus.). 240p. 1996. 87.95 (*1-85521-772-4*, Pub. by Dartmth Pub) Ashgate Pub Co.
Davies, Mansel, jt. auth. see Sutton, Leslie.
Davies, Margaret. Asking the Law Question. 308p. 1994. pap. 45.00 (*0-455-21242-2*, Pub. by LawBk Co) Gaunt.
— Delimiting the Law: Postmodernism & the Politics of Law. LC 97-103514. 160p. 1996. 59.95 (*0-7453-1100-8*, Pub. by Pluto GBR) Stylus Pub VA.
— Delimiting the Law: Postmodernism & the Politics of Law. LC 97-103514. (Law & Social Theory Ser.). 160p. (C). 1996. pap. 18.95 (*0-7453-0769-8*, Pub. by Pluto GBR) Stylus Pub VA.
Davies, Margaret. Matthew. (Readings Ser.). 224p. 1993. 57.50 (*1-85075-392-X*, Pub. by Sheffield Acad); pap. 19.50 (*1-85075-432-2*, Pub. by Sheffield Acad) CUP Services.
Davies, Margaret. The Pastoral Epistles. (New Testament Guides Ser.: Vol. 14). 127p. 1996. pap. 12.50 (*1-85075-743-7*, Pub. by Sheffield Acad) CUP Services.
Davies, Margaret. Pastoral Epistles: I & II Timothy & Titus. 1997. pap. text 17.00 (*0-7162-0504-1*) Epworth Pr.
Davies, Margaret. Pembrokeshire Children in History. 126p. (C). 1983. text 40.00 (*0-85088-566-3*, Pub. by Gomer Pr) St Mut.
— Rhetoric & Reference in the Fourth Gospel. (JSNT Supplement Ser.: No. 69). 412p. 1992. 85.00 (*1-85075-345-8*, Pub. by Sheffield Acad) CUP Services.
Davies, Margaret, jt. auth. see Sanders, E. P.
Davies, Margaret, jt. ed. see Rogerson, John W.
Davies, Margaret G. Enforcement of English Apprenticeship: A Study in Applied Mercantilism, 1563-1642. LC 56-5174. (Economic Studies: No. 97). 329p. 1956. 22.50 (*0-674-25450-3*) HUP.
Davies, Margaret L. & Davies, T. A. The Bible: Medicine & Myth. 264p. 1993. pap. 36.00 (*1-85183-053-7*) St Mut.
Davies, Margery W. Woman's Place Is at the Typewriter: Office Work & Office Workers, 1870-1930. 256p. 1984. reprint ed. pap. 22.95 (*0-87722-368-8*) Temple U Pr.
Davies, Margery W., jt. ed. see Jacobs, Francine H.
Davies, Marie-Helene. Laughter in a Genevan Gown: The Works of Frederick Buechner, 1970-1980. LC 83-14205. 208p. reprint ed. pap. 64.50 (*0-608-14489-4*, 202531900043) Bks Demand.
— Reflections of Renaissance England: Life, Thought, & Religion Mirrored in Illustrated Pamphlets. LC 85-32028. (Princeton Theological Monographs: No. 1). 1986. pap. 18.00 (*0-915138-68-9*) Pickwick.
Davies, Marie-Helene, jt. auth. see Davies, Horton.
Davies, Marion. Lore of the Sacred Horse. (Illus.). 219p. (Orig.). 1995. pap. 21.95 (*1-898307-17-2*) Holmes Pub.
— Magical Lore of Cats. (Illus.). (Orig.). 1995. pap. 21.95 (*1-898307-66-0*, Pub. by Capall Bann Pubng) Holmes Pub.
— Sacred Celtic Animals. (Orig.). 1998. pap. 22.95 (*1-898307-75-X*, Pub. by Capall Bann Pubng) Holmes Pub.
— The Times We Had. 1985. mass mkt. 6.99 (*0-345-32739-X*) Ballantine Pub Grp.
***Davies, Mark.** Government Ethics & Law Enforcement: Toward Global Guidelines. El-Ayouty, Yassin J. & Ford, Kevin, eds. LC 99-56464. 344p. 2000. 65.00 (*0-275-96592-9*, Praeger Pubs) Greenwood.
Davies, Mark. Malcolm X: Another Side of the Movement. Gallin, Richard, ed. (History of the Civil Rights Movement Ser.). (Illus.). 128p. (J). (gr. 5 up). 1990. lib. bdg. 12.95 (*0-382-09925-7*) Silver Burdett Pr.
— Malcolm X: Another Side of the Movement. Gallin, Richard, ed. (History of the Civil Rights Movement Ser.). (Illus.). 128p. (YA). (gr. 5 up). 1990. pap. 7.95 (*0-382-24063-4*) Silver Burdett Pr.
— Malcolm X: Another Side of the Movement. (History of the Civil Rights Movement Ser.). (J). 1990. 13.15 (*0-606-04739-5*, Pub. by Turtleback) Demco.
Davies, Mark N. & Green, Patrick R. Perception & Motor Control in Birds: An Ecological Approach. LC 93-33022. 1994. 262.95 (*0-387-52855-5*) Spr-Verlag.
Davies, Mark Y. A., jt. ed. see Auxier, Randall E.
Davies, Martin. Aldus Manutius: Printer & Publisher of Renaissance Venice. LC 90-49669. (Illus.). 64p. 1995. pap. 17.95 (*0-89236-344-4*, Pub. by J P Getty Trust) OUP.
***Davies, Martin.** Aldus Manutius: Printer & Publisher of Renaissance Venice. (Medieval & Renaissance Tests & Studies: Vol. 214). (Illus.). 64p. 1999. pap. 15.00 (*0-86698-256-6*, MR214) MRTS.
— The Blackwell Encyclopedia of Social Work. 480p. 2000. 84.95 (*0-631-21450-X*); pap. 34.95 (*0-631-21451-8*) Blackwell Pubs.
Davies, Martin. The Earlier Italian Schools. (National Gallery Publications). (Illus.). 1990. pap. 28.00 (*0-300-06139-0*) Yale U Pr.
— Early Netherlandish School. (Illus.). 1991. pap. 22.50 (*0-300-06184-6*) Yale U Pr.
— The Essential Social Worker: An Introduction to Professional Practice in the 1990s. 3rd ed. 240p. 1994. 59.95 (*1-85742-100-0*, Pub. by Arena) Ashgate Pub Co.
— How to Apply for a Legal Aid Franchise. 134p. 1993. pap. 36.00 (*1-85431-303-7*, Pub. by Blackstone Pr) Gaunt.
— Legal Marketing. (Legal Practice Course Guides Ser.). 120p. 1995. pap. 26.00 (*1-85431-376-2*, Pub. by Blackstone Pr) Gaunt.
— Romanesque Architecture: A Bibliography. LC 93-820. (Illus.). 340p. 1993. 95.00 (*0-8161-1826-4*, Hall Reference) Macmillan.
Davies, Martin, ed. The Blackwell Companion to Social Work. LC 96-14974. 320p. (C). 1996. 82.95 (*0-631-19876-8*); pap. 28.95 (*0-631-19877-6*) Blackwell Pubs.
— Incunabula: Studies in Fifteenth Century Printed Books Presented to Lotte Hellinga. (British Library Studies in the History of the Book). (Illus.). 416p. 1999. write for info. (*0-7123-4507-8*, Pub. by B23tish Library) U of Toronto Pr.
Davies, Martin & Dickey, Anthony. Shipping Law. lxxii, 431p. 1990. 89.50 (*0-455-20936-7*, Pub. by LawBk Co) Gaunt.
— Shipping Law. 1995. 120.00 (*0-455-21355-0*, Pub. by LawBk Co); pap. 75.00 (*0-455-21356-9*, Pub. by LawBk Co) Gaunt.
Davies, Martin & Ravelli, Louise, eds. Advances in Systemic Linguistics: Recent Theory & Practice. 300p. 1992. text 69.00 (*0-86187-070-0*, Pub. by P P Pubs) Cassell & Continuum.
Davies, Martin & Stone, Tony, eds. Folk Psychology: The Theory of Mind Debate. (Readings in Mind & Language Ser.). (Illus.). 350p. (C). 1995. pap. 30.95 (*0-631-19515-7*) Blackwell Pubs.
— Mental Simulation: Evaluations & Applications. (Readings in Mind & Language Ser.). 350p. (C). 1995. 64.95 (*0-631-19872-5*); pap. 30.95 (*0-631-19873-3*) Blackwell Pubs.
Davies, Martin, jt. ed. see Coltheart, Max.
Davies, Martin, ed. see Mortimer, Eunice.
Davies, Martin L. Identity or History? Marcus Herz & the End of the Englightenment. LC 95-15885. (Kritik Ser.). (Illus.). 360p. 1995. text 39.95 (*0-8143-2434-7*) Wayne St U Pr.
Davies, Mary E., et al. So--You Want to Be an Innkeeper. 3rd ed. LC 95-37028. (Illus.). 240p. 1996. pap. 14.95 (*0-8118-1226-X*) Chronicle Bks.
Davies, Meirion. Glynogwr & Gilfach Goch: A History. 229p. (C). 1989. 65.00 (*0-905928-14-8*, Pub. by D Brown & Sons Ltd) St Mut.
Davies, Meredith. Manual of Childhood Infections. (C). 1996. pap. text 41.00 (*0-7020-1832-5*) Harcourt.
Davies, Merton & Murray, Bruce C. The View from Space: Photographic Exploration of the Planets. LC 75-16887. 1973. pap. text 20.00 (*0-231-08330-0*) Col U Pr.
Davies, Michael. Altar & Throne Vol. 1: The Rising in the Vendee. (Illus.). 140p. 1997. pap. write for info. (*1-890740-00-4*) Remnant Pr.
— Apologia Pro Marcel Lefebvre, Vol. 1. 3rd ed. 461p. 1992. reprint ed. pap. text 13.95 (*0-935952-00-4*) Angelus Pr.
— Apologia Pro Marcel Lefebvre, Vol. 2. 393p. 1983. pap. text 10.95 (*0-935952-11-X*) Angelus Pr.
— Apologia Pro Marcel Lefebvre: The Historical Defense of Abp. Marcel Lefebvre & the Society of Saint Pius X, Vol. 3. 468p. 1999. pap. 14.95 (*0-935952-19-5*) Angelus Pr.
— Archbishop Lefebvre & Religious Liberty. 32p. 1990. pap. 1.50 (*0-89555-143-8*) TAN Bks Pubs.
— Atlas of Coronary Artery Disease. LC 98-12094. 240p. 1998. text 125.00 (*0-397-58750-3*) Lppncott W & W.
— The Barbaraians Have Taken Over. (Illus.). 60p. 1985. pap. 4.45 (*0-935952-14-4*) Angelus Pr.
— Belief in the Sea-Government Policy & Development of British Merchant Shipping & Shipbuilding. 356p. 1992. 124.00 (*1-85044-422-6*) LLP.
— The Catholic Sanctuary: And the Second Vatican Council. LC 96-61969. 40p. 1997. pap. 2.00 (*0-89555-547-6*, 1336) TAN Bks Pubs.
— Cranmer's Godly Order. 2nd rev. ed. (Liturgical Revolution Ser.). (Illus.). 390p. 1995. text 25.95 (*0-912141-24-7*) Roman Cath Bks.
— The Davies Report: The Great Battle in Swansea. 140p. 1994. pap. 6.95 (*1-85506-366-2*) Bks Intl VA.
— The Goldfish Bowl: The Church since Vatican II. 3rd ed. 40p. 1993. reprint ed. pap. text 3.95 (*0-935952-87-X*) Angelus Pr.
Davies, Michael. I Am with You Always. rev. ed. 101p. 1997. pap. 10.00 (*0-911845-09-7*) Neumann Pr.
— I Am with You Always. 2nd rev. ed. 101p. 1997. 15.00 (*0-911845-08-9*) Neumann Pr.
Davies, Michael. Liturgical Revolution Vol. 2: Pope John's Council. 2nd ed. 331p. 1992. reprint ed. pap. text 10.95 (*0-935952-04-7*) Angelus Pr.
— Liturgical Revolution Vol. 3: Pope Paul's New Mass. 3rd ed. 673p. 1992. reprint ed. pap. text 19.95 (*0-935952-02-0*) Angelus Pr.
— Liturgical Shipwreck - 25 Years of the New Mass. 42p. 1995. pap. 1.50 (*0-89555-535-2*) TAN Bks Pubs.
Davies, Michael. Mass Facing the People. (Illus.). 43p. 1991. pap. 6.00 (*0-911845-25-9*) Neumann Pr.
Davies, Michael. Medical Law. 374p. 1996. pap. 48.00 (*1-85431-504-8*, Pub. by Blackstone Pr) Gaunt.
— Medjugorje: After Fifteen Years. 2nd rev. ed. 95p. 1998. pap. 9.00 (*1-890740-01-2*) Remnant Pr.
— The New Mass. 48p. 1992. reprint ed. pap. text 3.95 (*0-935952-22-5*) Angelus Pr.
— On Communion in the Hand & Similar Frauds. Michael, Matto, ed. 52p. 1998. 5.50 (*1-890740-03-9*) Remnant Pr.
— Open Lesson to a Bishop. 1980. pap. 2.00 (*0-89555-142-X*) TAN Bks Pubs.
Davies, Michael. A Privilege of the Ordained. (Illus.). 1990. reprint ed. pap. 6.00 (*0-911845-21-6*) Neumann Pr.
Davies, Michael. The Reign of Christ the King. LC 92-61180. 36p. (Orig.). 1992. pap. 1.25 (*0-89555-474-7*) TAN Bks Pubs.
— The Roman Rite Destroyed. 2nd rev. ed. (Illus.). 54p. 1992. pap. 3.95 (*0-935952-10-1*) Angelus Pr.
Davies, Michael. Saint John Fisher. (Illus.). 137p. Date not set. 16.00 (*0-911845-86-0*) Neumann Pr.
Davies, Michael. A Short History of the Roman Mass. LC 96-61302. 50p. 1997. pap. 2.00 (*0-89555-546-8*, 1337) TAN Bks Pubs.
— Textbook on Medical Law. 2nd ed. LC 99-168472. 416p. 1998. pap. 48.00 (*1-85431-842-X*) Gaunt.
— The Tridentine Mass: The Mass That Will Not Die. 6th ed. 120p. 1985. reprint ed. pap. 4.45 (*0-935952-03-9*) Angelus Pr.
***Davies, Michael, ed.** The Wisdom of Adrian Fortescue. (Illus.). 424p. 1999. 35.95 (*0-912141-53-0*) Roman Cath Bks.
Davies, Michael, et al. The Great Debate of '98: Questioning the Status of the New Order Mass. Matt, Michael, ed. 65p. 1998. pap. 5.50 (*1-890740-04-7*) Remnant Pr.
Davies, Michael C. BNA's 1994 Source Book on Collective Bargaining & Employee Relations. LC KF3408.Z9B84. 302p. reprint ed. pap. 93.70 (*0-608-00755-2*, 206154700010) Bks Demand.
Davies, Michael J. & Dean, Roger T. Radical-Mediated Protein Oxidation: From Chemistry to Medicine. LC 97-28433. (Illus.). 456p. 1998. text 95.00 (*0-19-850097-1*) OUP.
Davies, Michael J., jt. auth. see Sheppard, Mary N.
Davies, Michele. Healing Sylvia: Childhood Sexual Abuse & the Construction of Identity. 176p. 1995. 79.95 (*0-7484-0175-X*); pap. 24.95 (*0-7484-0176-8*) Taylor & Francis.
Davies, Mike. Woodcarving: Techniques & Designs. (Illus.). 144p. 1998. 27.99 (*0-9658248-3-7*) GUILDcom.
Davies, Mike, et al. U. K. Gaap: Generally Accepted Accounting Practic in the United Kingdom. 5th ed. 1500p. 1997. 100.00 (*1-56159-189-0*) Groves Dictionaries.
Davies, Miranda & Jansz, Natania, eds. Women Travel: A Rough Guide Special. 3rd ed. (Illus.). 800p. 1999. 19.95 (*1-85828-459-7*, Pub. by Rough Guides) Penguin Putnam.
Davies, Miranda E. Women & Violence: Realities & Responses Worldwide. 264p. (C). 1994. text 25.00 (*1-85649-146-3*, Pub. by Zed Books) St Martin.
Davies, Miranda E., ed. Third World-Second Sex: Women's Struggles & National Liberation, 1. (Illus.). (C). 1983. pap. 22.50 (*0-86232-029-1*, Pub. by St Martin); text 59.95 (*0-86232-017-8*, Pub. by St Martin) St Martin.
Davies-Morel, Mina C. G. Equine Artificial Insemination. LC 98-33256. (CABI Publishing Ser.). 416p. 1999. text 135.00 (*0-85199-315-X*) OUP.
— Equine Reproductive Physiology, Breeding & Stud Management. LC 99-17676. (CABI Publishing Ser.). (Illus.). 478p. 1999. pap. text 45.00 (*0-85199-372-9*) OUP.
***Davies, Morgan.** To Be Where I Have Been. 378p. 2000. 11.95 (*1-930498-00-4*) HedgehogCasino.

An Asterisk (*) at the beginning of an entry indicates that the title is appearing for the first time.

Davies, Morton R., et al, eds. Serving the State: Global Public Administration Education & Training. LC 98-2532. (Policy Studies Organization). 224p. 1998. text 72.95 (*1-84014-074-7*, Pub. by Ashgate Pub) Ashgate Pub Co.

Davies, Moya L., tr. see O'Sullivan, Maurice.

Davies, N. Europe: A History. LC 97-32889. 1392p. 1998. pap. 24.00 (*0-06-097468-0*) HarpC.

— Power Chess Program Book 1. 1999. pap. text 19.95 (*0-7134-8415-2*) B T B.

Davies, N. B. Dunnock Behaviour & Social Evolution. (Oxford Series in Ecology & Evolution). (Illus.). 286p. 1992. pap. text 45.00 (*0-19-854675-0*) OUP.

Davies, N. B., jt. auth. see Krebs, J. R.

Davies, Nancy M. The Stock Market Crash of 1929. LC 92-23310. (American Events Ser.). (Illus.). 96p. (YA). (gr. 6 up). 1994. lib. bdg. 14.95 (*0-02-726221-9*, New Dscvry Bks) Silver Burdett Pr.

***Davies-Netzley, Sally Ann.** Gendered Capital: Entrepreneurial Women in American Society. LC 00-34729. (Studies in Entrepreneurship). 2000. write for info. (*0-8153-3869-4*) Garland.

***Davies, Nic.** Dolphin. (Natural World Ser.). (Illus.). (J). 2000. 9.95 (*0-7398-3125-9*) Raintree Steck-V.

Davies, Nicholas. Diana: A Princess & Her Troubled Marriage. (Illus.). 320p. 1992. 21.95 (*1-55972-115-4*, Birch Ln Pr) Carol Pub Group.

— Diana: The Lonely Princess. LC 95-26379. (Illus.). 288p. 1996. 22.50 (*1-55972-360-2*, Birch Ln Pr) Carol Pub Group.

— Diana: The Lonely Princess. LC 97-32278. (Illus.). 304p. 1997. mass mkt. 6.99 (*0-8065-8013-5*, Citadel Pr) Carol Pub Group.

— The Princess Who Changed the World. 1998. 27.95 (*1-85782-204-8*, Pub. by Blake Publng) Seven Hills Bk.

— Princess Who Changed the World. 256p. 1998. mass mkt. 7.99 (*1-85782-380-X*) Blake Publng.

— Queen Elizabeth II: A Woman Who Is Not Amused. LC 93-46668. 1994. 24.95 (*1-55972-217-7*, Birch Ln Pr) Carol Pub Group.

— Queen Elizabeth II: A Woman Who Is Not Amused. rev. ed. (Citadel Stars Ser.). (Illus.). 544p. 1996. mass mkt. 6.99 (*0-8065-8001-1*, Citadel Pr) Carol Pub Group.

— Queen Elizabeth II: A Woman Who Is Not Amused. rev. ed. (Illus.). 544p. 1998. mass mkt. 6.99 (*0-8065-8015-1*, Citadel Pr) Carol Pub Group.

***Davies, Nicholas.** William: King for the 21st Century. (Illus.). 2000. 26.00 (*1-85782-394-X*, Pub. by Blake Publng) Seven Hills Bk.

Davies, Nicholas. William: The Inside Story of the Man Who Will Be King. LC 99-18177. 112p. 1999. pap. 13.95 (*0-312-20683-6*) St Martin.

***Davies, Nick.** Cuckoos, Cowbirds & Other Cheats. 2000. 24.95 (*0-12-206060-1*) Acad Pr.

Davies, Nick. White Lies: Rape, Murder & Justice, Texas Style. 432p. 1993. mass mkt. 4.99 (*0-380-71845-6*, Avon Bks) Morrow Avon.

Davies, Nicola. Big Blue Whale. LC 96-42327. (Read & Wonder Bks.). (Illus.). 32p. (J). (gr. 1-4). 1997. 15.99 (*1-56402-895-X*) Candlewick Pr.

***Davies, Nicola.** Big Blue Whale. (Illus.). 32p. (J). (gr. 1-4). 2000. pap. 19.99 (*0-7636-1282-0*, Pub. by Candlewick Pr) Penguin Putnam.

— Dolphin: Habitats, Life Cycles, Food Chains, Threats. LC 00-27460. (Natural World Ser.). (Illus.). (J). 2000. 27.12 (*0-7398-2766-9*) Raintree Steck-V.

— Everything Happens on Mondays. 64p. (J). (gr. 4). 1995. pap. 9.95 (*0-8464-4835-1*) Beekman Pubs.

Davies, Nicola. Shampoo & Seawater. (J). 1998. pap. write for info. (*0-8464-4913-7*) Beekman Pubs.

Davies, Nicola & Cox, Sandra. Connections, Nos. 1-4. (C). 1985. write for info. (*0-7855-2622-6*, Pub. by Gomer Pr); teacher ed. 24.00 (*0-86383-104-4*, Pub. by Gomer Pr); pap. 20.00 (*0-86383-109-5*, Pub. by Gomer Pr); pap. 20.00 (*0-86383-114-1*, Pub. by Gomer Pr); pap. 20.00 (*0-86383-119-2*, Pub. by Gomer Pr); pap. 20.00 (*0-86383-124-9*, Pub. by Gomer Pr) St Mut.

Davies, Nigel. Ancient Kingdoms of Mexico. 1991. pap. 13.95 (*0-14-013587-1*) Viking Penguin.

— The Ancient Kingdoms of Peru. LC 98-128168. 220p. 1998. pap. 13.95 (*0-14-023381-4*) Viking Penguin.

— Los Antiguos Reinos de Mexico (The Ancient Kingdom of Mexico) (SPA.). 248p. 1988. pap. 12.99 (*968-16-2801-2*, Pub. by Fondo) Continental Bk.

— The Aztec Empire: The Toltec Resurgence. LC 87-40210. (Civilization of the American Indian Ser.: Vol. 187). (Illus.). 352p. 1987. 45.00 (*0-8061-2098-3*) U of Okla Pr.

— The Aztecs: A History. LC 80-12141. (Illus.). 384p. 1980. reprint ed. pap. 21.95 (*0-8061-1691-9*) U of Okla Pr.

— The Chess Player's Battle Manual: Equip Yourself for Competitive Play. (Illus.). 144p. 1998. pap. text 19.95 (*0-7134-7043-7*, Pub. by B T B) Branford.

— The Incas. (Illus.). 288p. 1995. 34.95 (*0-87081-360-9*) Univ Pr Colo.

***Davies, Nigel.** The Power Chess Program Bk. 2: The Ultimate Chess Workout. (Chess Bks). (Illus.). 256p. 1999. pap. text 18.95 (*0-7134-8420-9*) B T B.

Davies, Nigel, et al. Middleware '98: IFIP International Conference on Distributed Systems Platforms & Open Distributed Processing. LC 98-43175. 1998. write for info. (*1-85233-088-0*) Spr-Verlag.

Davies, Norah & Pratt, Jon, eds. Minnesota Nonprofit Directory. 420p. (Orig.). 1988. pap. 24.75 (*0-929080-04-1*) MN Council Nonprofits.

Davies, Norman. Europe: A History. LC 96-42032. (Illus.). 1424p. 1996. text 39.95 (*0-19-520912-5*) OUP.

— God's Playground: A History of Poland, 2 vols., Set. LC 81-10241. (Illus.). 1330p. 1984. pap. text 62.00 (*0-231-04327-9*) Col U Pr.

— God's Playground, a History of Poland Vol. 1: The Origins to 1795. 605p. 1984. pap. text 31.00 (*0-231-05351-7*) Col U Pr.

— God's Playground, A History of Poland Vol. 2: 1795 to the Present. LC 81-10241. 725p. 1982. text 110.50 (*0-231-05352-5*) Col U Pr.

— God's Playground, a History of Poland Vol. 2: 1795 to the Present. 725p. 1984. pap. text 31.00 (*0-231-05353-3*) Col U Pr.

— Heart of Europe: A Short History of Poland. LC 83-22003. (Illus.). 536p. 1986. pap. text 16.95 (*0-19-285152-7*) OUP.

— The Isles: A History. (Illus.). 1222p. 2000. 45.00 (*0-19-513442-7*) OUP.

— Poland Past & Present: Select Bibliography of Works in English. (Illus.). 175p. 1976. lib. bdg. 26.00 (*0-89250-010-7*) Orient Res Partners.

— The Tomb of Rekh-Mi-Re at Thebes: Metropolitan Museum of Art Egyptian Expedition Publications, 2 vols., Vol. 11. LC 75-168403. (Metropolitan Museum of Art Publications in Reprint). (Illus.). 374p. 1980. reprint ed. 52.95 (*0-405-02267-0*) Ayer.

Davies, Norman De Garis. The Tomb of Ken-Amun at Thebes: Metropolitan Museum of Art Egyptian Expedition Publications, 2 Vols., Vol. 5. LC 78-168401. (Metropolitan Museum of Art Publications in Reprint). (Illus.). 208p. 1972. reprint ed. 39.00 (*0-685-00518-6*) Ayer.

— The Tomb of Nefer-Hotep at Thebes: Metropolitan Museum of Art Egyptian Expedition Publications, 2 vols in 1, Vol. 9. LC 71-168402. (Metropolitan Museum of Art Publications in Reprint). (Illus.). 192p. 1972. reprint ed. write for info. (*0-685-00519-4*) Ayer.

Davies, Oliver. Celtic Christianity in Early Medieval Wales. 193p. 1997. pap. 50.00 (*0-7083-1359-0*, Pub. by Univ Wales Pr); pap. 25.00 (*0-7083-1287-X*, Pub. by Univ Wales Pr) Paul & Co Pubs.

— Celtic Spirituality. LC 99-41570. (CWS Ser.: No. 97). 592p. 1999. pap. 29.95 (*0-8091-3894-8*) Paulist Pr.

— Celtic Spirituality: Classics of Western Spirituality. LC 99-41570. (CWS Ser.: No. 97). 592p. 1999. 39.95 (*0-8091-0505-5*) Paulist Pr.

— God Within: The Mystical Tradition of Northern Europe. 256p. 1988. pap. 9.95 (*0-8091-3041-6*) Paulist Pr.

— Roman Mines in Europe. Finley, Moses I., ed. LC 79-4966. (Ancient Economic History Ser.). (Illus.). 1979. reprint ed. lib. bdg. 44.95 (*0-405-12354-X*) Ayer.

Davies, Oliver, ed. Promise of Good Things - The Apostolic Fathers. (Spirituality of the Fathers Ser.). 120p. (Orig.). 1993. pap. 7.95 (*1-56548-019-8*) New City.

Davies, Oliver & Bowie, Fiona, eds. Celtic Christian Spirituality: An Anthology of Mythology & Modern Sources. 224p. 1995. pap. 19.95 (*0-8264-0835-4*) Continuum.

— Discovering Welshness. 181p. 1992. pap. 27.00 (*0-86383-722-0*, Pub. by Gomer Pr) St Mut.

Davies, Oliver, ed. & tr. see Eckhart, Meister.

Davies, Oliver, tr. see Von Balthasar, Hans U.

Davies, Owen. Witchcraft, Magic & Culture, 1736-1951. 320p. 1999. pap. 27.95 (*0-7190-5656-X*) St Martin.

Davies, Owen, ed. The Omni Book of Medicine. 1984. mass mkt. 3.95 (*0-8217-1364-7*, Zebra Kensgtn) Kensgtn Pub Corp.

Davies, Owen, jt. auth. see Cetron, Marvin.

Davies, Owen, jt. auth. see Cetron, Marvin J.

Davies, Owen L., ed. The Design & Analysis of Industrial Experiments. 2nd ed. LC 77-12563. 653p. reprint ed. pap. 200.00 (*0-608-13232-2*, 202525900043) Bks Demand.

Davies, P. A., ed. see European Geophysical Society Staff.

Davies, P. C. Es Espacio y el Tiempo en el Universo. (Breviarios Ser.). (SPA.). pap. 9.99 (*968-16-1310-4*, Pub. by Fondo) Continental Bk.

— Quantum Mechanics. (Student Physics Ser.). 12800p. (Orig.). (C). 1984. pap. text 13.95 (*0-7100-9962-2*, Routledge Thoemms) Routledge.

Davies, P. C., ed. The New Physics. (Illus.). 526p. (C). 1992. pap. 38.95 (*0-521-43831-4*) Cambridge U Pr.

Davies, P. C. & Broown, J., eds. The Ghost in the Atom: A Discussion of the Mysteries of Quantum Physics. (Canto Book Ser.). (Illus.). 169p. (C). 1993. pap. 10.95 (*0-521-45728-9*) Cambridge U Pr.

Davies, P. C. & Brown, J., eds. Superstrings: A Theory of Everything? (Canto Book Ser.). (Illus.). 244p. (C). 1992. pap. 12.95 (*0-521-43775-X*) Cambridge U Pr.

Davies, P. J., jt. auth. see Camoin, G. F.

Davies, P. M. Right in the Middle: Selective Trunk Activity in the Treatment of Adult Hemiplegia. (Illus.). 288p. 1996. 49.00 (*0-387-51242-X*) Spr-Verlag.

— Steps to Follow: A Guide for the Treatment of Adult Hemiplegia. (Illus.). 335p. 1996. 46.00 (*0-387-13436-0*) Spr-Verlag.

Davies, P. R. Daniel. (Old Testament Guides Ser.: No. 24). 133p. 1985. pap. 12.50 (*1-85075-002-5*, Pub. by Sheffield Acad) CUP Services.

Davies, P. Spencer & Sunderland, N. Perspectives in Experimental Biology: Zoology & Botany, 2 pts. 1090p. 1976. 477.00 (*0-08-019939-9*, Pub. by Pergamon Repr) Franklin.

Davies, Pamela & Gothefors, Leif. Bacterial Infections in the Fetus & Newborn Infant. (Major Problems in Clinical Pediatrics Ser.: Vol. 26). (Illus.). 350p. 1984. text 98.00 (*0-7216-1185-0*, W B Saunders Co) Harcrt Hlth Sci Grp.

Davies, Pamela A. & Rudd, P. T. Neonatal Meningitis. (Clinics in Developmental Medicine Ser.: No. 132). (Illus.). 185p. 1995. text 52.95 (*0-901260-96-7*) Cambridge U Pr.

Davies, Pat, ed. Adults in Higher Education: International Perspectives on Access & Participation. LC 95-1109. 250p. 1995. 49.95 (*1-85302-286-1*) Taylor & Francis.

Davies, Patricia M. Starting Again: Early Rehabilitation after Traumatic Brain Injury. LC 94-9131. (Illus.). 442p. 1994. write for info. (*0-387-55934-5*) Spr-Verlag.

— Steps to Follow Updated: The Comprehensive Treatment of Patients with Hemiplegia. 2nd expanded rev. ed. (Illus.). xx, 516p. 2000. pap. 54.00 (*3-540-60720-X*) Spr-Verlag.

Davies, Patrick, jt. auth. see Cummings, E. Mark.

Davies, Paul. About Time: Einstein's Unfinished Revolution. 304p. 1995. 24.00 (*0-671-79964-9*) S&S Trade.

— About Time: Einstein's Unfinished Revolution. (Illus.). 320p. 1996. per. 14.00 (*0-684-81822-1*, Touchstone) S&S Trade Pap.

— Are We Alone? Philosophical Implications of the Discovery of Extraterrestrial Life. 176p. 1996. pap. 12.00 (*0-465-00419-9*, Pub. by Basic) HarpC.

***Davies, Paul.** Beckett & Eros: Death of Humanism. 2000. text 55.00 (*0-312-23407-4*) St Martin.

Davies, Paul. Dropping the Chase: The Enigmas of the Goddess. 32p. 1995. pap. 6.95 (*1-55022-257-0*, Pub. by ECW) Genl Dist Srvs.

— Exactly 12 Cents & Other Convictions. LC 95-188251. (Illus.). 48p. 1995. pap. 8.95 (*1-55022-230-9*) LPC InBook.

— The Fifth Miracle: The Search for the Origin & Meaning of Life. LC 98-33421. 304p. 1999. 25.00 (*0-684-83799-4*) S&S Trade.

— The Fifth Miracle: The Search for the Origin & Meaning of Life. 304p. 2000. per. 14.00 (*0-684-86309-X*) S&S Trade.

— God & the New Physics. 256p. 1984. pap. 12.00 (*0-671-52806-8*, Touchstone) S&S Trade Pap.

— Grace: A Story. LC 96-148108. 80p. 1996. pap. 11.95 (*1-55022-275-9*, Pub. by ECW) Genl Dist Srvs.

Davies, Paul. The Ideal Real: Beckett's Fiction & Imagination. LC 92-55028. (C). 1994. 39.50 (*0-8386-3517-2*) Fairleigh Dickinson.

Davies, Paul. The Indispensable Guide to C. LC 95-139439. 766p. (C). 1995. pap. text 52.50 (*0-201-62438-9*) Addison-Wesley.

***Davies, Paul.** The Indispensable Guide to Calculus. 2nd ed. (C). 2000. pap. text. write for info. (*0-201-61909-1*) Addison-Wesley.

Davies, Paul. Jamie Drum's Massive Recovery. 80p. (YA). (gr. 4 up). pap. 6.95 (*1-901881-15-6*, Pub. by Element MA) Penguin Putnam.

— Joe Ironstone: A Drama for Radio. LC 98-160078. 32p. 1997. pap. 5.00 (*1-55022-335-6*, Pub. by ECW) LPC InBook.

— The Last Three Minutes: Conjectures about the Ultimate Fate of the Universe. 176p. 1996. pap. 10.00 (*0-465-03851-4*, Pub. by Basic) HarpC.

— The Mind of God: The Scientific Basis for a Rational World. 256p. 1993. pap. 12.00 (*0-671-79718-2*, Touchstone) S&S Trade Pap.

— Music in the Nachtwachen. LC 90-27765. (American University Studies: Germanic Languages & Literature: Ser. I, Vol. 94). 191p. (C). 1991. text 35.95 (*0-8204-1559-6*) P Lang Pubng.

— Oblique Litanies: Nine Conversations & an Afterthought. 48p. (Orig.). 1992. pap. 12.00 (*1-55022-157-4*, Pub. by ECW) Genl Dist Srvs.

— Other Worlds. LC 97-209250. 208p. 1997. pap. 12.95 (*0-14-013877-3*) Viking Penguin.

— Romanticism & Esoteric Tradition: Studies in Imagination. LC 97-47417. (Studies in Imagination). 204p. 1998. pap. 18.95 (*0-940262-88-6*, 2075, Lindisfarne) Anthroposophic.

***Davies, Paul.** The Truth. LC 99-232513. 206p. 1999. pap. write for info. (*1-895837-66-9*) Insomniac.

Davies, Paul. The Wreck of the Apollo. 32p. 1994. pap. 5.95 (*1-55022-228-7*, Pub. by ECW) Genl Dist Srvs.

Davies, Paul, et al, eds. European Community Labour Law: Principles & Perspectives: Liber Amicorum Lord Wedderburn of Charlton. 360p. 1997. text 75.00 (*0-19-826010-5*) OUP.

Davies, Paul & Freedland, Mark. Labour Law. 2nd ed. (Law in Context Ser.). 1008p. (C). 1994. pap. text, per. 39.95 (*0-297-78090-5*) Northwestern U Pr.

— Labour Law: Text & Materials. 2nd ed. (Law in Context Ser.). xlii, 964p. 1984. reprint ed. text 45.00 (*0-297-78089-1*) W S Hein.

— Labour Legislation & Public Policy: A Contemporary History. LC 92-43630. (Clarendon Law Ser.). 726p. 1993. text 75.00 (*0-19-876060-4*, Clarendon Pr); pap. text 35.00 (*0-19-876288-7*, Clarendon Pr) OUP.

Davies, Paul & Gibbons, Bob. Field Guide to Wild Flowers of Southern Europe. (Illus.). 320p. 1993. pap. 24.95 (*1-85223-659-0*, Pub. by Crolwood) Trafalgar.

Davies, Paul & Gribbin, John. The Matter Myth: Dogmatic Discoveries That Challenge Our Understanding of Physical Reality. (Illus.). 320p. (Orig.). 1992. per. 13.00 (*0-671-72841-5*, Touchstone) S&S Trade Pap.

Davies, Paul, jt. auth. see Gibbons, Bob.

Davies, Paul H. The Complete Guide to Close-Up & Macro Photography. LC 99-202844. (Illus.). 160p. 1999. 29.95 (*0-7153-0800-9*, Pub. by D & C Pub) Sterling.

***Davies, Paul S.** Norms of Nature: Naturalism & the Nature of Functions. LC 00-55403. (Life & Mind Ser.). 2001. write for info. (*0-262-04187-1*) MIT Pr.

***Davies, Penelope J. E.** Death & the Emperor: Roman Imperial Funerary Monuments, from Augustus to Marcus Aurelius. LC 99-55506. (Illus.). 288p. (C). 2000. write for info. (*0-521-63236-6*) Cambridge U Pr.

***Davies, Pete.** The Devil's Flu: The World's Deadliest Influenza Epidemic & the Scientific Hunt for the Virus That Caused It. 320p. 2000. pap. 14.00 (*0-8050-6622-5*, Owl) H Holt & Co.

— Inside the Hurricane: Face to Face with Nature's Deadliest Storms. LC 00-29562. 288p. 2000. write for info. (*0-8050-6574-1*) H Holt & Co.

Davies, Pete. Twenty-Two Foreigners In Funny Shorts: The Intelligent Fan's Guide to Soccer & World Cup '94. LC 93-41274. 1994. pap. 10.00 (*0-679-77493-9*) Random.

***Davies, Peter.** Antique Kilims of Anatolia. 2000. 55.00 (*0-393-73047-6*) Norton.

Davies, Peter. Artificial Intelligence: Its Role in the Information Industry. 129p. 1991. 39.50 (*0-938734-50-4*) Info Today Inc.

— A Corner of Paradise. 2nd large type ed. 153p. 1993. 19.95 (*1-85695-130-8*, Pub. by ISIS Lrg Prnt) Transaction Pubs.

— The Farms of Home. (Illus.). 216p. 1994. 34.95 (*0-233-98838-6*, Pub. by Andre Deutsch) Trafalgar.

— The Historical Dictionary of Golfing Terms: From 1500 to the Present. LC 92-27571. (Illus.). 192p. 1996. pap. 16.95 (*0-935576-44-4*) Kesend Pub Ltd.

— Josef Herman. 112p. (C). 1989. 69.00 (*1-872971-50-4*, Pub. by Redcliffe Pr Ltd) St Mut.

***Davies, Peter.** The National Front & France: Ideology, Discourse, & Power. LC 98-42868. 278p. 1999. 90.00 (*0-415-15866-4*) Routledge.

— 70 Activities for Tutor Groups. LC 99-24994. 200p. 1999. pap. 78.95 (*0-566-08000-1*, Pub. by Ashgate Pub) Ashgate Pub Co.

Davies, Peter, ed. Human Rights. 144p. 1989. 39.95 (*0-415-02609-1*, A3377) Routledge.

Davies, Peter & Finch, Caleb E., eds. Molecular Neuropathology of Aging. LC 87-15673. (Banbury Report Ser.: No. 27). (Illus.). 484p. 1988. text 80.00 (*0-87969-227-8*) Cold Spring Harbor.

Davies, Peter & Kennedy, Angus J., eds. Rewards & Punishments in the Arthurian Romances & Lyric Poetry of Medieval France. 1987. 75.00 (*0-85991-250-7*) Boydell & Brewer.

Davies, Peter & Kenny, Michael. Michael Kenny. LC 97-3962. (Illus.). 96p. 1997. text 56.95 (*1-85928-410-8*, Pub. by Scolar Pr) Ashgate Pub Co.

— Michael Kenny. limited ed. LC 97-3962. (Illus.). 96p. 1997. text 250.00 (*1-85928-411-6*, Pub. by Scolar Pr) Ashgate Pub Co.

Davies, Peter & Thornborough, Anthony. F-111 Aardvark. (Illus.). 192p. 1997. 49.95 (*1-86126-079-2*, Pub. by Crolwood) Motorbooks Intl.

Davies, Peter, jt. ed. see Finch, Caleb E.

Davies, Peter, jt. ed. see Maclure, Stuart.

Davies, Peter A., ed. Mixing & Dispersion in Stably Stratified Flows. LC 99-229769. (Institute of Mathematics & Its Applications Conference Ser.; New Ser.: 68). (Illus.). 660p. 1999. text 225.00 (*0-19-850015-7*) OUP.

Davies, Peter D. O. & Ormerod, Peter. Case Presentation in Clinical Tuberculosis. LC 99-22798. (An Arnold Publication). (Illus.). 320p. 1999. pap. text 49.50 (*0-340-74159-7*, Pub. by E A) OUP.

***Davies, Peter E.** Gray Ghosts, Us Navy & Marine Corps F-4 Phantoms. (Illus.). 192p. 2000. 49.95 (*0-7643-1021-6*) Schiffer.

Davies, Peter E. & Thornborough, Anthony M. The Harrier Story. LC 96-70726. (Illus.). 288p. 1997. 39.95 (*1-55750-357-5*) Naval Inst Pr.

Davies, Peter H. The Ugliest House in the World. 240p. 1998. pap. 12.00 (*0-395-92480-4*) HM.

— The Ugliest House in the World: Stories. LC 97-12873. 192p. 1997. 20.00 (*0-395-78629-0*) HM.

***Davies, Peter Ho.** Equal Love. LC 99-46755. 192p. 2000. pap. 12.00 (*0-618-00699-0*, Mariner Bks) HM.

***Davies, Peter J.** Beethoven in Person: His Deafness, Other Illnesses & Death. Vol. 59. 2001. write for info. (*0-313-31587-6*) Greenwood.

Davies, Peter J. Mozart in Person: His Character & Health, 14. LC 88-25091. (Contributions to the Study of Music & Dance Ser.: No. 14). 299p. 1989. 57.95 (*0-313-26340-X*, DVM/, Greenwood Pr) Greenwood.

Davies, Peter J., ed. Plant Hormones: Physiology, Biochemistry & Molecular Biology. rev. ed. LC 94-45154. Orig. Title: Plant Hormones & Their Role in Plant Growth & Development. 836p. (C). 1995. lib. bdg. 330.00 (*0-7923-2984-8*) Kluwer Academic.

— Plant Hormones & Their Role in Plant Growth & Development. (C). 1987. pap. text 105.00 (*90-247-3498-3*); lib. bdg. 323.50 (*90-247-3497-5*) Kluwer Academic.

Davies, Peter M., et al, eds. Sex, Gay Men, & AIDS. LC 93-16012. (Social Aspects of AIDS Ser.). 1993. 85.00 (*0-7507-0095-5*, Falmer Pr); pap. 27.95 (*0-7507-0096-3*, Falmer Pr) Taylor & Francis.

Davies, Peter M., ed. see Aggleton, Peter, et al.

Davies, Peter N. Fyffes & the Banana: Musa Sapientum: A Centenary History 1888-1988. LC 89-18553. (Illus.). 240p. (C). 1990. text 39.95 (*0-485-11382-1*, Pub. by Athlone Pr) Humanities.

Davies, Peter N., jt. auth. see Chida, Tomohei.

Davies, Peter S.W. & Cole, T. J., eds. Body Composition Techniques in Health & Disease. (Society for the Study of Human Biology Symposium Ser.: 36). (Illus.). 292p. (C). 1995. text 64.95 (*0-521-46179-0*) Cambridge U Pr.

Davies, Peter V. Glanures Occitanes Recueillies dans Trois Livres d'Heures, Vols. XIVe-XVe. 112p. 1993. 40.00 (*0-85261-348-2*, Pub. by Univ of Glasgow) St Mut.

Davies, Peter W. Current Issues in Business Ethics. LC 96-25690. (Professional Ethics Ser.). 224p. (C). 1997. pap. 25.99 (*0-415-12450-6*) Routledge.

Davies, Peter W., jt. auth. see Quinn, John J.

Davies, Phil. Scenic Driving Minnesota. LC 97-10979. (Illus.). 208p. (Orig.). 1997. pap. 14.95 (*1-56044-557-2*) Falcon Pub Inc.

Davies, Phil & Walsh, Dermot. Alcohol Problems & Alcohol Control in Europe. 320p. 1983. 31.95 (*0-89876-090-9*) Gardner Pr.

D

***Davies, Philip.** U. S. Elections Today. 2nd ed. LC 99-43123. (Politics Today Ser.). 1999. pap. 22.50 (*0-7190-4508-8*, Pub. by Manchester Univ Pr) St Martin.

Davies, Philip H. British Secret Services: An Annotated Bibliography. (International Organizations Ser.: Vol. 13). 188p. (C). 1996. text 59.95 (*1-56000-231-X*) Transaction Pubs.

Davies, Philip J., ed. An American Quarter Century: U. S. Politics from Vietnam to Clinton. LC 95-3503. 1995. text 79.95 (*0-7190-4514-2*, Pub. by Manchester Univ Pr) St Martin.

Davies, Philip J. & Waldstein, Fredric A., eds. Political Issues in America Today: The 1990's Revisited. 2nd ed. (Politics Today Ser.). 272p. 1996. text 69.95 (*0-7190-4225-9*); text 24.95 (*0-7190-4226-7*, Pub. by Manchester Univ Pr) St Martin.

Davies, Philip J., jt. ed. see White, John K.

Davies, Philip R. The Damascus Covenant: An Interpretation of the 'Damascus Document' (Journal for the Study of the Old Testament Supplement Ser.: No. 25). 267p. 1983. 75.00 (*0-905774-50-7*, Pub. by Sheffield Acad); pap. 24.50 (*0-905774-51-5*, Pub. by Sheffield Acad) CUP Services.

— In Search of Ancient Israel. 2nd ed. (Journal for the Study of the Old Testament Supplement Ser.: Vol. 148). 166p. 1995. pap. 14.95 (*1-85075-737-2*, Pub. by Sheffield Acad) CUP Services.

— In Search of Ancient Israel: A Study in Biblical Origins. (JSOT Supplement Ser.: No. 148). 172p. (C). 1992. 52.00 (*1-85075-380-6*, Pub. by Sheffield Acad) CUP Services.

— Priests, Prophets & Scribes: Essays on the Formation & Heritage of Second Temple Judaism in Honour of Joseph Blenkinsopp. Ulrich, Eugene et al, eds. (Journal for the Study of the Old Testament Supplement Ser.: No. 149). (Illus.). 274p. 1992. 75.00 (*1-85075-375-X*, Pub. by Sheffield Acad) CUP Services.

— The Prophets: A Sheffield Reader. (Biblical Seminar Ser.: No. 42). 388p. 1996. pap. 19.95 (*1-85075-788-7*, Pub. by Sheffield Acad) CUP Services.

— Scribes & Schools: The Canonization of the Hebrew Scriptures. LC 97-39684. (Library of Ancient Israel Ser.). 224p. 1998. 24.00 (*0-664-22077-0*) Westminster John Knox.

— Second Temple Studies: 1. Persian Period. (Journal for the Study of the Old Testament Supplement Ser.: No. 117). 192p. (C). 1991. 57.50 (*1-85075-315-6*, Pub. by Sheffield Acad) CUP Services.

Davies, Philip R. Whose Bible Is It Anyway? (JSOT Supplement Ser.: Vol. 204). 150p. 1995. 52.50 (*1-85075-569-8*, Pub. by Sheffield Acad); pap. 16.50 (*1-85075-749-6*, Pub. by Sheffield Acad) CUP Services.

Davies, Philip R & Clines, D. J., eds. Among the Prophets: Language, Image & Structure in the Prophetic Writings. (JSOT Supplement Ser.: No. 144). 218p. 1993. 60.00 (*1-85075-361-X*, Pub. by Sheffield Acad) CUP Services.

Davies, Philip R. & Clines, David J., eds. The World of Genesis: Persons, Places, Perspectives. LC 98-121908. (JSOTS Ser.: Vol. 257). 179p. 1998. 57.50 (*1-85075-875-1*, Pub. by Sheffield Acad) CUP Services.

Davies, Philip R. & White, Richard T., eds. A Tribute to Geza Vermes: Essays on Jewish & Christian Literature & History. (JSOT Supplement Ser.: No. 100). 406p. 1990. 90.00 (*1-85075-253-2*, Pub. by Sheffield Acad) CUP Services.

Davies, Philip R., jt. auth. see Fritz, Volkmar.

Davies, Philip R., jt. ed. see Fritz, Volkmar.

Davies, Philippa. Total Confidence: A Complete Guide to Self Assurance & Personal Success. 208p. 1995. pap. 14.95 (*0-7499-1434-3*, Pub. by Piatkus Bks) London Brdge.

— Your Total Image: How to Communicate Success. 192p. 1996. pap. text 14.95 (*0-7499-1641-9*, Pub. by Piatkus Bks) London Brdge.

Davies, Phillip L., jt. auth. see Rose, Richard.

Davies, Phillips G. Welsh in Wisconsin. LC 82-10283. (Ethnic Ser.). (Illus.). 40p. 1982. pap. 3.95 (*0-87020-214-6*, WEWI) State Hist Soc Wis.

Davies, Phillips G., tr. see Griffiths, T. Solomon.

Davies, Phyllis. Grief: Climb Toward Understanding: Self-Help When You Are Struggling. 5th rev. ed. (Illus.). 320p. 1998. pap. 19.95 (*0-941343-39-1*) Sunnybank.

— When Someone Dies: What You Can Do. (Illus.). 48p. (Orig.). 1997. pap. 6.50 (*0-941343-32-4*) Sunnybank.

— When Someone Is Seriously Ill or Injured: What You Can Do. (Illus.). 36p. (Orig.). 1997. pap. 6.50 (*0-941343-31-6*) Sunnybank.

Davies, Powell A. Without Apology: Collected Meditations on Liberal Religion by A. Powell Davies. Church, Forrester F., ed. LC 98-10394. 104p. 1998. pap. 12.00 (*1-55896-366-9*, Skinner Hse Bks) Unitarian Univ.

Davies, R. A. & Lloyd, K. M., eds. Index Kewensis, Supplement Nineteen: 1986-1990. 360p. 1991. 195.00 (*0-19-854676-9*) OUP.

Davies, R. A. & Lloyd, K. M., eds. Kew Index for 1986: Names of Seed-Bearing Plants, Ferns, & Fern Allies at the Rank of Family & Below Published During 1986 with Some Omissions from Earlier Years. 200p. 1987. pap. text 32.50 (*0-19-854227-5*) OUP.

Davies, R. A., jt. compiled by see Challis, K. M.

Davies, R. D., ed. see International Astronomical Union Staff.

Davies, R. E. Aeroflot: An Airline & Its Aircraft. (Great Airlines of the World Ser.). (Illus.). 96p. 1992. 37.50 (*0-9626483-1-0*) Paladwr Pr.

— Airlines of Asia since 1920. (Illus.). 572p. 1997. 65.00 (*1-888962-02-X*) Paladwr Pr.

— Airlines of Latin America since 1919. 2nd ed. (Illus.). 698p. 1997. reprint ed. 65.00 (*1-888962-03-8*) Paladwr Pr.

— Airlines of the United States since 1914. 2nd ed. (Illus.). 760p. 1998. reprint ed. 65.00 (*1-888962-08-9*) Paladwr Pr.

— Charles Lindbergh: An Airman, His Aircraft, & His Great Flights. (Illus.). 56p. 1997. 30.00 (*1-888962-04-6*) Paladwr Pr.

— Delta: An Airline & Its Aircraft. (Great Airlines of the World Ser.). (Illus.). 112p. 1990. 25.00 (*0-9626483-0-2*) Paladwr Pr.

— Fallacies & Fantasies of Air Transport History. (Illus.). 240p. 1994. 25.00 (*0-9626483-5-3*) Paladwr Pr.

— A History of the World's Airlines. LC 82-72843. (Airlines History Project Ser.). (Illus.). 608p. 1983. reprint ed. 57.50 (*0-404-19325-0*) AMS Pr.

— Lufthansa: An Airline & Its Aircraft. (Great Airlines of the World Ser.). (Illus.). 96p. 1991. 30.00 (*0-9626483-3-7*) Paladwr Pr.

— Pan Am: An Airline & Its Aircraft. (Great Airlines of the World Ser.). (Illus.). 96p. 1987. 25.00 (*0-9626483-2-9*) Paladwr Pr.

— Rebels & Reformers of the Airways. LC 86-26243. (Illus.). 440p. 1987. 30.00 (*0-87474-354-0*) Paladwr Pr.

— Saudia: An Airline & Its Aircraft. (Illus.). 64p. 1995. 30.00 (*0-9626483-7-X*) Paladwr Pr.

— Supersonic (Airliner) Non-Sense: A Case Study in Applied Market Research. (Illus.). 192p. 1998. 30.00 (*1-888962-09-7*) Paladwr Pr.

— Transbrasil: An Airline & Its Aircraft. (Great Airlines of the World Ser.). (Illus.). 64p. 1997. 30.00 (*1-888962-01-1*) Paladwr Pr.

Davies, R. E., ed. Pan Am's First Lady: The Diary of Betty Stettinius Trippe. 322p. 1996. 30.00 (*1-888962-00-3*) Paladwr Pr.

Davies, R. E. & Quastler, I. E. Commuter Airlines of the United States. LC 94-19849. (Illus.). 480p. 1994. text 56.00 (*1-56098-404-X*) Smithsonian.

Davies, R. E., ed. see Culbert, Tom & Dawson, Andy.

Davies, R. E., ed. see Provan, John.

Davies, R. G. Outlines of Entomology. 7th ed. (Illus.). 350p. (gr. 13). 1988. pap. text 46.95 (*0-412-26680-6*) Chapman & Hall.

Davies, R. L. & Hall, Peter G. Issues in Urban Society LC 79-315015. (Geography & Environmental Studies). 299,p. 1978. write for info. (*0-14-080935-X*) Penguin Books.

Davies, R. L. & Rogers, David S., eds. Store Location & Assessment Research. LC 83-21614. 386p. 1984. 495.00 (*0-471-90381-7*) Wiley.

Davies, R. L., jt. auth. see Howard, E. B.

***Davies, R. R.** The Age of Conquest: Wales 1063-1415. (Oxford History of Wales Ser.: Vol. 2). 544p. 2000. pap. text 26.00 (*0-19-820878-2*) OUP.

Davies, R. R. Conquest, Coexistence, & Change: Wales, 1063-1415. (Oxford History of Wales Ser.: Vol. II). (Illus.). 544p. 1991. reprint ed. pap. 26.00 (*0-19-820198-2*) OUP.

***Davies, R. R.** The First English Empire: Power & Identities in the British Isles, 1093-1343. (Illus.). 200p. 2000. 24.95 (*0-19-820849-9*) OUP.

Davies, R. R. The Revolt of Owain Glyn Dwr. (Illus.). 414p. 1997. reprint ed. pap. 18.95 (*0-19-285336-8*) OUP.

Davies, R. T., ed. Medieval English Lyrics. 384p. 1988. pap. 16.95 (*0-8101-0075-4*) Northwestern U Pr.

Davies, R. Trevor. Four Centuries of Witch-Belief. LC 74-180026. 1972. reprint ed. 30.95 (*0-405-08437-4*) Ayer.

Davies, R. Trevor, ed. Medieval English Lyrics. LC 72-8279. (Granger Index Reprint Ser.). 1977. reprint ed. 23.95 (*0-8369-6386-5*) Ayer.

Davies, R. W. Soviet Economic Development from Lenin to Khrushchev. LC 97-27997. (New Studies in Economic & Social History: Vol. 34). 124p. (C). 1998. text 39.95 (*0-521-62260-3*); pap. text 11.95 (*0-521-62742-7*) Cambridge U Pr.

Davies, R. W., ed. From Tsarism to the New Economic Policy: Continuity & Change in the Economy of the U. S. S. R. LC 90-56047. 432p. 1991. pap. text 24.95 (*0-8014-9919-4*) Cornell U Pr.

— Soviet Investment for Planned Industrialisation, 1929-1937, Policy & Practice: Selected Papers from the Second World Congress for Soviet & East European Studies. (Orig.). 1985. pap. 12.00 (*0-933884-32-X*) Berkeley Slavic.

Davies, R. Wayne & Morris, Brian J., eds. Molecular Biology of the Neuron. (The Molecular & Cellular Neurobiolgy Ser.). (Illus.). 416p. 1998. text 95.00 (*1-85996-240-8*) OUP.

Davies, Ray. Waterloo Sunset. 256p. 2000. 13.00 (*0-7868-8454-1*, Pub. by Hyprn Ppbks) Little.

— Waterloo Sunset: Stories. LC 99-18688. 288p. 1999. 22.95 (*0-7868-6535-0*, Pub. by Hyperion) Time Warner.

— X-Ray. 1999. pap. 19.95 (*0-525-93697-1*) NAL.

— X-Ray: The Unauthorized Autobiography. LC 95-17328. 420p. 1995. 24.95 (*0-87951-611-9*, Pub. by Overlook Pr) Penguin Putnam.

— X-Ray: The Unauthorized Autobiography. 420p. 1996. pap. 15.95 (*0-87951-664-X*, Pub. by Overlook Pr) Penguin Putnam.

Davies, Ray J., jt. auth. see Bird, Frank E., Jr.

Davies, Reginald T. The Golden Century of Spain, 1501-1621. LC 83-45426. reprint ed. 49.50 (*0-404-20073-7*) AMS Pr.

Davies, Rex & McDermott, David. Forty-Five Activities for Developing a Learning Organization. 232p. 1994. 149.95 (*0-566-07321-8*, Pub. by Gower) Ashgate Pub Co.

— Mind-Opening Training Games: Activities to Help Groups Learn How to Learn, Tap Their Right-Brain Power & "Think Outside the Box" 205p. 1996. pap. 69.95 (*0-07-913053-4*) McGraw.

Davies, Rex, jt. auth. see Gilgrist, David.

Davies, Rhian. Never So Pure a Sight - Yr. Eneth Ddisglair Annwyl Morfydd Owen (1891-1918) a Life in Pictures. LC 95-128052. 136p. 1994. pap. 27.00 (*0-86383-936-3*, Pub. by Gomer Pr) St Mut.

— Never So Pure a Sight, Morfydd Owen, 1891-1918: A Life in Pictures. (Illus.). 136p. 1994. pap. 26.95 (*0-8464-4658-8*) Beekman Pubs.

Davies, Rhona & Johnson, Peter R. The Uzi & the Stone: Images of Gaza. (Illus.). 256p. (Orig.). 1991. pap. 19.95 (*1-55059-025-1*) Temeron Bks.

Davies, Rhys. Print of a Hare's Foot. LC 99-192172. 183p. 1999. pap. 17.95 (*1-85411-180-9*, Pub. by Seren Bks) Dufour.

— Ram with Red Horns. LC 96-223091. 180p. 1997. pap. 16.95 (*1-85411-165-5*, Pub. by Seren Bks) Dufour.

***Davies, Richard.** Introductory Java for Scientists & Engineers. LC 98-49587. 294p. (C). 1999. pap. 45.00 (*0-201-39813-3*) Addison-Wesley.

Davies, Richard, ed. The Maverick Spirit: Building the New Nevada. LC 98-21144. (History & Humanities Ser.). (Illus.). 296p. 1998. pap. 17.95 (*0-87417-327-2*) U of Nev Pr.

Davies, Richard, jt. auth. see Casper, Scott E.

Davies, Richard, jt. auth. see Radice, Roberto.

Davies, Richard, jt. ed. see Dale, Angela.

Davies, Richard, tr. see Reale, Giovanni.

Davies, Richard E. Handbook for Doctor of Ministry Projects: An Approach to Structured Observation Ministry. (Illus.). 238p. (Orig.). (C). 1984. pap. text 19.75 (*0-8191-3764-2*) U Pr of Amer.

Davies, Richard L. Stress in Social Work. LC 98-101763. 250p. 1997. pap. write for info. (*1-85302-390-6*, Pub. by Jessica Kingsley) Taylor & Francis.

Davies, Richard O. America's Obsession: Sports & Society since 1945. Nash, Gerald D. & Etulain, Richard W., eds. (Books on America since 1945). 192p. (C). 1994. pap. text 22.00 (*0-03-073332-4*, Pub. by Harcourt Coll Pubs) Harcourt.

— Main Street Blues: The Decline of Small-Town America. LC 97-51225. (Urban Life & Landscape Ser.). 248p. 1998. text 50.00 (*0-8142-0781-2*, DAVMAI); pap. text 21.95 (*0-8142-0782-0*, DAVMAX) Ohio St U Pr.

Davies, Richard W. The Industrialization of Soviet Russia Vol. 4: The Soviet Economy in Turmoil, 1929-1930. LC 88-21318. (Illus.). 600p. 1989. 82.00 (*0-674-82655-8*) HUP.

— The Socialist Offensive: The Collectivization of Soviet Agriculture, 1929-1930. LC 79-15263. (Industrialization of Soviet Russia Ser.: Vol. 1). (Illus.). 512p. 1980. 46.50 (*0-674-81480-0*) HUP.

— The Soviet Collective Farm, 1929-1930. LC 79-15273. (Industrialization of Soviet Russia Ser.: Vol. 2). 226p. 1980. 29.00 (*0-674-82600-0*) HUP.

Davies, Richard W., ed. The Soviet Union. 2nd ed. 240p. (C). 1989. pap. text 18.95 (*0-04-445215-2*) Routledge.

— The Soviet Union. 2nd ed. 240p. (C). (gr. 13). 1989. text 59.95 (*0-04-445205-5*) Routledge.

Davies, Richard W., et al, eds. The Economic Transformation of the Soviet Union, 1913-1945. (Illus.). 413p. (C). 1993. text 69.95 (*0-521-45152-3*) Cambridge U Pr.

— The Economic Transformation of the Soviet Union, 1913-1945. (Illus.). 413p. (C). 1994. pap. text 24.95 (*0-521-45770-X*) Cambridge U Pr.

Davies, Richard W., jt. auth. see Wheatcroft, Stephen G.

Davies, Robert. Reptile & the Amphibian Problem Solver: Practical & Expert Advice on Keeping Snakes & Lizards. 1997. 29.95 (*1-56465-194-0*) Tetra Pr.

— South African Strategy Towards Mozambique in the Post-Nkomati Period. (Research Report Ser.: No. 73). 71p. 1985. write for info. (*91-7106-238-6*, Pub. by Nordic Africa) Transaction Pubs.

— VW Beetle: The Complete Story. (Illus.). 200p. 1996. 35.95 (*1-85223-953-0*, Pub. by Crol wood) Motorbooks Intl.

Davies, Robert, ed. Life of Marmaduke Rawdon of York. (Camden Society, London. Publications, First Ser.: No. 85). reprint ed. 55.00 (*0-404-50185-0*) AMS Pr.

Davies, Robert, jt. auth. see Murray, Susan.

Davies, Robert A. Tracks in Oregon. pap. 10.00 (*0-9622738-3-X*) Mr Cogito Pr.

Davies, Robert A., jt. auth. see Gogol, John M.

Davies, Robert A., ed. see Gray, Patrick W.

Davies, Robert A., ed. see Napora, Joe.

Davies, Robert A., ed. see Russell, Norman H.

Davies, Robert B. Peacefully Working to Conquer the World: Singer Sewing Machine in Foreign Markets, 1854-1920. Bruchey, Stuart & Bruchey, Eleanor, eds. LC 76-5000. (American Business Abroad Ser.). 1976. 39.95 (*0-405-09270-9*) Ayer.

Davies, Robert J. & Ollier, Susan. Allergy: The Facts. (Illus.). 208p. 1989. 19.95 (*0-19-261439-8*) OUP.

Davies, Robert W. The Development of the Soviet Budgetary System. LC 78-23596. 373p. 1979. reprint ed. lib. bdg. 75.00 (*0-313-21191-4*, DADS, Greenwood Pr) Greenwood.

Davies, Robertson. Animal U. (Illus.). 36p. (J). (ps-5). 1995. pap. 9.95 (*1-880812-23-1*) S Ink WA.

— Conversations with Robertson Davies. Davis, J. Madison, ed. LC 88-39305. (Literary Conversations Ser.). 307p. reprint ed. pap. 95.20 (*0-608-08717-3*, 206928500003) Bks Demand.

— The Cornish Trilogy: The Rebel Angels; What's Bred in the Bone; The Lyre of Orpheus. LC 91-50242. 1200p. 1992. pap. 22.95 (*0-14-015850-2*, Penguin Bks) Viking Penguin.

— The Cunning Man. 480p. 1996. pap. 13.95 (*0-14-024830-7*, Viking) Viking Penguin.

— The Cunning Man. large type ed. LC 95-16353. 1995. pap. 23.95 (*1-56895-230-9*) Wheeler Pub.

— The Cunning Man: A Novel. 352p. 1994. write for info. (*0-7710-2581-5*) McCland & Stewart.

— The Deptford Trilogy. 864p. 1990. pap. 19.95 (*0-14-014755-1*, Penguin Bks) Viking Penguin.

— Fifth Business. 272p. 1977. pap. 12.95 (*0-14-016794-3*, Viking) Viking Penguin.

***Davies, Robertson.** For Your Eye Alone: The Letters of Robertson Davies. Grant, Judith Skelton, ed. 2001. 29.95 (*0-670-89291-2*, Viking) Viking Penguin.

Davies, Robertson. Happy Alchemy: On the Pleasures of Music & the Theatre. LC 98-5622. 384p. 1998. 27.95 (*0-670-88019-1*) Viking Penguin.

— Happy Alchemy: On the Pleasures of Music & the Theatre. 1999. pap. 14.95 (*0-14-027562-2*) Viking Penguin.

Davies, Robertson. Happy Alchemy: Writings on the Theatre & Other Lively Arts. Surridge, Jennifer & Davies, Brenda, eds. 360p. 1997. 32.50 (*0-7710-2585-8*) McCland & Stewart.

Davies, Robertson. High Spirits. LC 83-47878. (Penguin Short Fiction). 208p. 1983. pap. 12.95 (*0-14-006505-9*, Penguin Bks) Viking Penguin.

— Leaven of Malice. 272p. 1980. pap. 11.95 (*0-14-016789-7*, Penguin Bks) Viking Penguin.

Davies, Robertson. The Lyre of Orpheus. 480p. 1990. pap. 13.95 (*0-14-011433-5*, Penguin Bks) Viking Penguin.

Davies, Robertson. The Manticore. 312p. 1977. pap. 12.95 (*0-14-016793-5*, Penguin Bks) Viking Penguin.

— The Merry Heart: Reflections on Reading, Writing & the World of Books. 1998. pap. 14.95 (*0-14-026391-8*); pap. 14.95 (*0-14-027586-X*) Viking Penguin.

— The Merry Heart & Happy Alchemy. 1997. write for info. (*0-7710-2588-2*) McCland & Stewart.

— The Mirror of Nature. (Illus.). 132p. 1996. pap. text 12.95 (*0-8020-7939-3*) U of Toronto Pr.

— The Mirror of Nature. LC 83-196795. (Alexander Lectures: No. 1982). (Illus.). 144p. reprint ed. pap. 44.70 (*0-8357-6359-5*, 203571300096) Bks Demand.

— A Mixture of Frailties. 384p. 1980. pap. 12.95 (*0-14-016791-9*, Penguin Bks) Viking Penguin.

— Murther & Walking Spirits. 368p. 1992. reprint ed. pap. 13.95 (*0-14-016884-2*, Penguin Bks) Viking Penguin.

— The Rebel Angels. 336p. 1982. pap. 8.99 (*0-14-006271-8*, Penguin Bks) Viking Penguin.

— The Salterton Trilogy. 1990. pap. write for info. (*0-318-66792-4*, Penguin Bks) Viking Penguin.

— The Salterton Trilogy. 784p. 1991. pap. 19.95 (*0-14-015910-X*, Penguin Bks) Viking Penguin.

— What's Bred in the Bone. 348p. 1986. pap. 13.95 (*0-14-009711-2*, Penguin Bks) Viking Penguin.

— World of Wonders. 320p. 1977. pap. 12.95 (*0-14-016796-X*, Penguin Bks) Viking Penguin.

Davies, Robin & Awdry, Reverend Wilbert V. Henry & the Tunnel. LC 99-163935. (My First Thomas Ser.). (Illus.). (J). 1997. write for info. (*0-434-80116-X*) Buttrwrth-Heinemann.

Davies-Rodgers, Ellen. Education: Then, Now & Yon. 1971. 5.00 (*0-685-84988-0*) Plantation.

— The Great Book: Calvary Protestant Episcopal Church. Memphis, Tennessee 1832-1972. 1973. 30.00 (*0-685-84989-9*) Plantation.

— Heirs Through Hope: The Episcopal Diocese of West Tennessee. LC 83-50733. 1983. 30.00 (*0-317-05919-X*) Plantation.

— The Holy Innocents: The Story of a Historic Church & Country Parish. (Illus.). 1966. 12.00 (*0-685-84990-2*) Plantation.

— The Romance of the Episcopal Church in West Tennessee. 1964. 12.00 (*0-685-84991-0*) Plantation.

Davies, Rodney. Doubles: The Enigma of the Second Self. 192p. 1999. 22.95 (*0-7090-6118-8*, Pub. by R Hale Ltd) Seven Hills Bk.

— Dowsing: The Art of Finding Hidden Things. (Illus.). 144p. (Orig.). 1991. pap. 7.95 (*1-85538-073-0*, Pub. by Aqrn Pr) Harper SF.

— Fortune-Telling by Palmistry: A Practical Guide to the Art of Hand Analysis. (Illus.). 144p. (Orig.). 1988. pap. 7.95 (*0-85030-599-3*) Sterling.

— Fortune-Telling with Numbers: Knowing Yourself & Your Fate Through Numerology. (Illus.). 112p. (Orig.). 1988. pap. 7.95 (*0-85030-486-5*) Sterling.

— Lazarus Syndrome: Burial Alive & Other Horrors of the Undead. (Illus.). 224p. 1999. 22.95 (*0-7090-6304-0*, Pub. by R Hale Ltd) Seven Hills Bk.

— Personal Secrets: Your True Character Unveiled. (Illus.). 176p. 1991. pap. 6.95 (*1-85538-044-7*, Pub. by Aqrn Pr) Harper SF.

— The Psychic Development Workbook: How to Awaken & Use Your ESP. LC 97-201762. (Illus.). 128p. 1997. reprint ed. pap. 14.95 (*0-8069-9765-6*) Sterling.

— Supernatural Vanishings: Otherworldly Disappearances. LC 95-46883. (Illus.). 192p. 1996. pap. 10.95 (*0-8069-4896-5*) Sterling.

Davies, Roger L., jt. ed. see Bender, Ralf.

Davies, Roger W. Old Llanelli. (Illus.). 97p. (C). 1985. text 39.00 (*0-86383-139-7*, Pub. by Gomer Pr) St Mut.

— Old Pembrokeshire. (Illus.). 100p. (C). 1989. text 55.00 (*0-86383-506-6*, Pub. by Gomer Pr) St Mut.

— Old Pembrokeshire & Carmarthenshire. 132p. 1991. 22.95 (*0-8464-4688-X*) Beekman Pubs.

— Old Pembrokeshire & Carmarthenshire. 132p. (C). 1991. 45.00 (*0-86383-726-3*, Pub. by Gomer Pr) St Mut.

Davies-Rogers, Ellen. Our Ancestors. 1986. write for info. (*0-318-59202-9*) Plantation.

— A Tree Is Lighted. LC 84-90673. (Illus.). 1984. 5.00 (*0-317-19588-3*) Plantation.

Davies, Rosalyn A. & Luxon, Linda M., eds. Handbook of Vestibular Rehabilitation. LC 97-8265. (Illus.). 200p. (Orig.). 1997. pap. 49.95 (*1-56593-847-X*, 1654) Thomson Learn.

An Asterisk (*) at the beginning of an entry indicates that the title is appearing for the first time.

Davies, Rosemary. Fabulous Foliage Plants. (Illus.). 128p. pap. 12.95 (*1-86447-029-1*, Pub. by Hyland Hse) Seven Hills Bk.

— Guide to Garden Nurseries of New South Wales. (Illus.). 168p. 1996. pap. 14.95 (*0-86840-318-0*, Pub. by New South Wales Univ Pr) Intl Spec Bk.

Davies, Rosemary & Massam, Katherine. Guide to Garden Nurseries of Victoria. LC 97-158212. (Illus.). 168p. 1996. pap. 14.95 (*0-86840-079-3*, Pub. by New South Wales Univ Pr) Intl Spec Bk.

Davies, Ross, ed. Retail Planning Policies in Western Europe. LC 94-49065. 320p. (C). (gr. 13). 1995. pap. 81.95 (*0-415-10997-3*) Thomson Learn.

Davies, Ross E., jt. auth. see Kosma, Montgomery N.

Davies, Ross L. Marketing Geography with Special Reference to Retailing. 320p. 1977. pap. 15.95 (*0-416-70700-9*, 6079) Routledge.

Davies, Rowland. Journal of the Very Rev. Rowland Davies, from March 8, 1688-9, to September 29, 1690. Caulfield, Richard, ed. LC 71-163674. (Camden Society, London. Publications, First Ser.: No. 68). reprint ed. 49.50 (*0-404-50168-0*) AMS Pr.

Davies, Roy. Intelligent Information Systems: Progress & Prospects. (Artificial Intelligence Ser.). 240p. 1986. text 52.95 (*0-470-20726-4*) P-H.

— Nautilus: The Story of Man under the Sea. LC 94-69301. (Illus.). 256p. 1995. 36.95 (*1-55750-615-9*) Naval Inst Pr.

Davies, Rupert E. Methodism. 2nd ed. 1976. pap. text 18.25 (*0-7162-0280-8*) Epworth Pr.

Davies, Rupert E., jt. ed. see Flew, Robert N.

Davies, Russell. Secret Sins: Sex, Violence & Society in Carmarthenshire 1870-1920. LC 97-141783. 334p. 1997. pap. 29.95 (*0-7083-1367-1*, Pub. by Univ Wales Pr) Paul & Co Pubs.

Davies, S. Declaration of Love. 1998. pap. text 2.99 (*0-85234-408-2*) P & R Pubng.

Davies, S. G., ed. Organotransition Metal Chemistry: Applications to Organic Synthesis. (Organic Chemistry Ser.: Vol. 2). (Illus.). 428p. 1983. text 190.00 (*0-08-026202-3*, CRC Reprint); pap. text 48.00 (*0-08-030714-0*, CRC Reprint) Franklin.

Davies, S. R. Spreadsheets in Structural Design. (C). 1996. 94.95 (*0-582-22698-8*) Longman.

Davies, Sally. When William Went Away. LC 98-14271. 32p. (J). (gr. k-3). 1998. 15.95 (*1-57505-303-9*, Carolrhoda) Lerner Pub.

— Why Did We Have to Move Here? LC 96-44995. (Illus.). 32p. (J). (gr. k-3). 1997. 14.95 (*1-57505-046-3*, Carolrhoda) Lerner Pub.

***Davies, Sam.** County Borough Election Results, England & Wales, 1919-1938 Vol. 1: Barnsley-Bournemouth. Moores, John D., ed. LC 99-12017. (Illus.). 600p. 1999. text 102.95 (*1-84014-246-4*, Pub. by Ashgate Pub) Ashgate Pub Co.

Davies, Samuel. Collected Poems. Davis, Richard B., ed. LC 68-17019. 288p. 1968. 50.00 (*0-8201-1011-6*) Schol Facsimiles.

— The Sermons of Samuel Davies, 3 vols. Incl. Vol. 1. Sermons of Samuel Davies. Sprague, William B., intro. 667p. 1993. reprint ed. 40.00 (*1-877611-67-0*); Vol. 2. Sermons of Samuel Davies. 672p. 1994. reprint ed. 40.00 (*1-877611-94-8*); Vol. 3. Sermons of Samuel Davies. 660p. 1995. reprint ed. 40.00 (*1-57358-026-0*); 1995. 120.00 (*1-57358-029-5*) Soli Deo Gloria.

Davies, Samuel & Morley, Bob. County Borough Election Results, England & Wales, 1919-1938. LC 99-12017. 1999. write for info. (*1-84014-261-8*) Ashgate Pub.

Davies, Sandi J., ed. see Minion, Ronald R.

Davies, Sandi J., jt. ed. see Minion, Ronald.

Davies, Sarah. Popular Opinion in Stalin's Russia: Terror, Propaganda & Dissent, 1934-1941. (Illus.). 256p. (C). 1997. text 59.95 (*0-521-56214-7*) Cambridge U Pr.

Davies, Saunders, tr. see Lauer, Hans E.

Davies, Scott F., jt. auth. see Sarosi, George A.

Davies, Shann, ed. see Malmstrom, Karin & Nash, Nancy.

Davies, Sharon, jt. auth. see Jost, Timothy.

Davies, Sioned. The Four Branches of the Mabinogi. 86p. 1993. pap. 11.95 (*0-8464-4775-4*) Beekman Pubs.

— The Four Branches of the Mabinogi. 86p. 1993. pap. 20.00 (*1-85902-005-4*, Pub. by Gomer Pr) St Mut.

Davies, Sioned & Jones, Nerys A., eds. The Horse in Celtic Culture: Medieval Welsh Perspectives. LC 97-122254. (Illus.). 190p. 1997. pap. 29.95 (*0-7083-1414-7*, Pub. by Univ Wales Pr) Paul & Co Pubs.

Davies, Stan, jt. auth. see Allen, Peter J.

Davies, Stanley P. Social Control of the Mentally Deficient. LC 75-17215. (Social Problems & Social Policy Ser.). (Illus.). 1976. reprint ed. 35.95 (*0-405-07486-7*) Ayer.

Davies, Stephanie. Costume Language: A Dictionary of Dress Terms. (Illus.). 192p. (Orig.). 1995. pap. 22.50 (*0-89676-138-X*, Costume & Fashion Pr) QSMG Ltd.

Davies, Stephen. Art & Its Messages: Meaning, Morality, & Society. LC 96-43905. 1997. pap. 13.95 (*0-271-01683-3*) Pa St U Pr.

— Definitions of Art. LC 90-55756. 256p. 1991. pap. text 15.95 (*0-8014-9794-9*) Cornell U Pr.

— The Diffusion of Process Innovations. LC 78-15143. 207p. reprint ed. pap. 59.00 (*0-608-13315-9*, 2025580) Bks Demand.

— Musical Meaning & Expression. LC 93-39890. (Illus.). 400p. (C). 1994. text 57.50 (*0-8014-2930-7*); pap. text 22.50 (*0-8014-8151-1*) Cornell U Pr.

Davies, Stephen & Morgan, Elaine. Cruising Guide to Southeast Asia Vol. 1: The South China Sea, Philippines, Gulf of Thailand to Singapore. (Illus.). 224p. (C). 1998. pap. 125.00 (*0-85288-296-3*, Pub. by Laurie Norie & Wilson Ltd) St Mut.

— Cruising Guide to Southeast Asia Vol. 2: Papua New Guinea, Indonesia, Singapore, Malacca Strait to Phuket. (Illus.). 260p. (C). 1999. pap. 125.00 (*0-85288-378-1*, Pub. by Laurie Norie & Wilson Ltd) St Mut.

Davies, Stephen & Stewart, Alan. Nutritional Medicine: The Drug-Free Guide to Better Family Health. 640p. (Orig.). 1990. pap. 12.95 (*0-380-70733-0*, Avon Bks) Morrow Avon.

— Nutritional Medicine: The Drug-Free Guide to Better Family Health. Stanway, Andrew, ed. 543p. (Orig.). 1987. pap. 24.00 (*0-330-28833-4*, Pub. by Pan) Trans-Atl Phila.

Davies, Stephen, et al. Industrial Organization in the European Union: Structure, Strategy, & the Competitive Mechanism. LC 96-570. (Illus.). 304p. 1996. text 79.00 (*0-19-828973-1*, Clarendon Pr) OUP.

Davies, Stephen, jt. auth. see Morgan, Elaine.

Davies, Stephen, jt. ed. see Ashford, Nigel.

Davies, Stevan L. Jesus the Healer: Possession, Trance, & the Origins of Christianity, Vol. 1. 226p. (C). 1995. 22.95 (*0-8264-0794-3*) Continuum.

— New Testament Fundamentals. rev. ed. LC 93-48825. (Illus.). 256p. 1994. pap. 17.95 (*0-944344-41-0*) Polebridge Pr.

— The Revolt of the Widows: The Social World of the Apocryphal Acts. LC 80-11331. 150p. 1980. 18.95 (*0-8093-0958-0*) S Ill U Pr.

Davies, Steve, ed. & intro. see Bronte, Anne.

Davies, Steveie. John Donne. 1990. 22.50 (*0-7463-0733-0*, Pub. by Northcote House) Trans-Atl Phila.

***Davies, Steven.** Alex Cox: Film Anarchist. (Illus.). 176p. 2000. pap. 21.95 (*0-7134-8670-8*) B T B.

Davies, Steven Paul, jt. auth. see Pulver, Andrew.

Davies, Stevie. Arms & the Girl. pap. 13.95 (*0-7043-4309-6*, Pub. by Womens Press) Trafalgar.

— Closing the Book. pap. 13.95 (*0-7043-4388-6*, Pub. by Womens Press) Trafalgar.

— Emily Bronte. LC 88-10916. (Key Women Writers Ser.). 192p. 1988. 27.50 (*0-253-30105-X*) Ind U Pr.

— Emily Bronte. Armstrong, Isobel & Loughrey, Bryan, eds. (Writers & Their Work Ser.). 1998. pap. 17.00 (*0-7463-0834-5*) Northcote House.

— Emily Bronte: Heretic. LC 95-132724. 274p. 1997. pap. 17.95 (*0-7043-4401-7*, Pub. by Womens Press) Trafalgar.

— The Feminine Reclaimed: The Idea of Woman in Spenser, Shakespeare & Milton. LC 85-22482. 288p. 1986. 32.50 (*0-8131-1589-2*) U Pr of Ky.

— Four Dreamers & Emily. LC 97-16648. 272p. 1997. text 21.95 (*0-312-16844-6*) St Martin.

— Henry Vaughan. 213p. 1995. pap. 17.95 (*1-85411-143-4*, Pub. by Seren Bks) Dufour.

— Henry Vaughan. 213p. 1996. 32.00 (*1-85411-142-6*, Pub. by Seren Bks) Dufour.

— John Donne. (Writers & Their Work Ser.). 95p. 1996. pap. text 15.00 (*0-7463-0738-1*, Pub. by Northcote House) U Pr of Miss.

— Primavera. pap. 11.95 (*0-7043-4299-5*, Pub. by Womens Press) Trafalgar.

***Davies, Stevie.** Unbridled Spirits. 1998. 35.00 (*0-7043-5082-3*, Pub. by Womens Press) Trafalgar.

— Unbridled Spirits: Women of the English Revolution, 1640-1660. 368p. 2000. pap. 17.95 (*0-7043-4489-0*, Pub. by Womens Press) Trafalgar.

Davies, Stevie, ed. see Bronte, Charlotte, et al.

Davies, Susan, ed. Dear Kathleen, Dear Manning: The Correspondence of Manning Clark & Kathleen Fitzpatrick, 1949-1990. 184p. 1997. 24.95 (*0-522-84703-X*, Pub. by Melbourne Univ Pr) Paul & Co Pubs.

Davies, Susan E. & Haney, Eleanor H., eds. Redefining Sexual Ethics: A Sourcebook of Essays, Stories & Poems. LC 91-33864. 400p. (Orig.). 1991. pap. 24.95 (*0-8298-0912-0*) Pilgrim OH.

Davies, Susan E. & Sister Paul Teresa Hennessee, eds. Ending Racism in the Church. LC 98-20658. 150p. (Orig.). 1998. pap. 12.95 (*0-8298-1238-5*) Pilgrim OH.

***Davies, Susan G.** The Survivor's Guide to Coping with Loss: How Friends & Family Can Help a Grieving Loved One. Relova, Lia, ed. & illus. by. 80p. 1999. pap. 25.00 (*0-9676252-3-8*) Pumpkin.

Davies, Susan S. 15 Ways to Nourish Your Faith. LC 98-14609. (Illuminaiton Book Ser.). (Illus.). 80p. 1998. pap. 5.95 (*0-8091-3790-9*, 3790-9) Paulist Pr.

Davies, Susanna. Versatile Livelihoods: Strategic Adaptation to Food Insecurity in the Malian Sahel. LC 95-8216. 304p. 1996. text 85.00 (*0-312-12684-4*) St Martin.

Davies, Susanna, jt. auth. see Buchanan-Smith, Margaret.

Davies, Susanne, jt. ed. see Cook, Sandy.

Davies, Susanne, jt. ed. see Philips, David.

Davies, T. Protection of Industrial Power Systems. 2nd ed. LC 96-2720. (Illus.). 272p. 1998. pap. text 49.95 (*0-7506-2662-3*) Buttrwrth-Heinemann.

Davies, T. & Craig, T. K., eds. ABC of Mental Health. (Illus.). 82p. 1998. pap. text 30.00 (*0-7279-1220-8*, Pub. by BMJ Pub) Login Brothers Bk Co.

Davies, T., jt. ed. see Manolis, G. D.

Davies, T. A., jt. auth. see Davies, Margaret L.

Davies, T. D., et al, eds. Seasonal Snowpacks: Processes of Compositional Change. (NATO ASI Series G: Ecological Sciences: Vol. 28). (Illus.). 488p. 1991. 230.95 (*0-387-51760-X*) Spr-Verlag.

Davies, T. Witton. Magic, Black & White, Charmes & Counter Charmes, Divination & Demonology among the Hindus, Hebrews, Arabs & Egyptians. 130p. 1972. reprint ed. spiral bd. 13.50 (*0-7873-0239-2*) Hlth Research.

— Magic, Divination & Demonology among the Hebrews & Their Neighbors. 1898. 150p. 1993. reprint ed. pap. 14.75 (*1-56459-412-2*) Kessinger Pub.

Davies, Taffy. The New Star. (Illus.). 32p. (J). (gr. k). 1997. 12.95 (*0-687-08750-3*) Abingdon.

Davies, Terry, ed. see Goodman, Vera.

Davies, Thomas. Dramatic Miscellanies - on Several Plays of Shakespeare, 3 vols. LC 73-163675. reprint ed. 155.00 (*0-404-01990-0*) AMS Pr.

— Memoirs of the Life of David Garrick, 2 vols., Set. Jones, Stephen, ed. LC 73-82825. 1972. 60.95 (*0-405-08438-2*) Ayer.

— Memoirs of the Life of David Garrick, 2 vols., Vol. 1. Jones, Stephen, ed. LC 73-82825. 1972. 30.95 (*0-405-08439-0*) Ayer.

— Memoirs of the Life of David Garrick, 2 vols., Vol. 2. Jones, Stephen, ed. LC 73-82825. 1972. 30.95 (*0-405-08440-4*) Ayer.

— Memoirs of the Life of David Garrick: Interspersed with Characters & Anecdotes of His Theatrical Contemporaries, 2 vols., Set. (Anglistica & Americana Ser.: No. 132). 1972. reprint ed. 128.70 (*3-487-04224-X*) G Olms Pubs.

Davies, Thomas, ed. Allegheny County, Pennsylvania Court Rules. 400p. (Orig.). 1996. per. 52.50 (*1-57786-025-X*) Legal Communs.

— Bucks County, PA Court Rules. 320p. (Orig.). 1996. per. 52.50 (*1-57786-019-5*) Legal Communs.

— Chester County (PA) Court Rules. 200p. (Orig.). 1997. per. 52.50 (*1-57786-059-4*) Legal Communs.

— Montgomery County, PA Court Rules. 272p. (Orig.). 1996. per. 52.50 (*1-57786-037-3*) Legal Communs.

— 1997 Pennsylvania Tax Handbook. 604p. (Orig.). 1996. per. write for info. (*1-57786-077-2*) Legal Communs.

— 1997 Westmoreland County (PA) Court Rules. 176p. 1997. per. 52.50 (*1-57786-001-2*) Legal Communs.

— Philadelphia County (PA) Court Rules. 664p. (Orig.). 1996. pap., per. 52.50 (*1-57786-012-8*) Legal Communs.

— Westmoreland County (PA) Court Rules. 176p. (Orig.). 1996. per. 52.50 (*1-57786-000-4*) Legal Communs.

Davies, Thomas & Garzarelli, Tammy, eds. 1997 Pennsylvania State Rules. (Orig.). Date not set. per. 59.00 (*1-57786-044-6*) Legal Communs.

Davies, Thomas D. Concise Tables for Sight Reduction. LC 84-45259. (Illus.). 65p. (Orig.). 1984. reprint ed. pap. 30.00 (*0-7837-9070-8*, 204981900003) Bks Demand.

Davies, Thomas L. May I Call You Brother? Messages from "A Course in Miracles" LC 95-92300. 128p. (Orig.). 1995. pap. 10.00 (*0-9646896-0-X*) Awaken The Genius.

Davies, Thomas M. Indian Integration in Peru: A Half Century of Experience, 1900-1948. LC 73-80965. 220p. reprint ed. pap. 68.20 (*0-8357-8682-X*, 205683900092) Bks Demand.

Davies, Thomas W. Magic, Divination & Demonclogy among the Hebrews & Their Neighbors. 1970. 15.00 (*0-87068-051-X*) Ktav.

Davies, Thomas W., ed. Flash Reaction Processes Proceedings of the NATO Advanced Research Workshop on Flash Reaction Processes, Istanbul, Turkey, May 6-8, 1994. LC 94-46546. (NATO ASI, Series E, Applied Sciences: No. 282). 1995. text 202.50 (*0-7923-3323-3*) Kluwer Academic.

Davies-Tight, Sharon L. The Menu. (My Animal-Free Kitchen Ser.). 187p. 1996. 15.95 (*1-885099-04-5*) Rainbow Sunshine.

— My Animal-Free Kitchen! deluxe ed. 184p. 1996. reprint ed. pap. 22.95 (*1-885099-00-2*) Rainbow Sunshine.

— My Animal-Free Kitchen! Small Edition. 2nd ed. 184p. 1996. pap. 15.95 (*1-885099-01-0*) Rainbow Sunshine.

— Sharon Lee's Original Animal-Free Salad Dressings! 48p. 1993. pap. 8.95 (*1-885099-02-9*) Rainbow Sunshine.

Davies, Tim, tr. see Bech, Henning.

Davies, Tom. I Conker. 308p. 1994. pap. 29.95 (*0-8464-4765-7*) Beekman Pubs.

— I, Conker... 308p. 1994. pap. 60.00 (*1-85902-100-X*) St Mut.

— Road to the Stars: A European Pilgrimage. 1999. pap. text 12.95 (*0-281-05149-6*) Society Prom Christ Know.

***Davies, Tom.** Through Fields of Gold: A Pilgrimage from Berlin to Rome. 2001. 30.00 (*0-281-05293-X*, Pub. by Society Prom Christ Know) Intl Pubs Mktg.

Davies, Tom. Wild Skies & Celtic Paths. 1999. pap. text 12.95 (*0-281-05190-9*) Society Prom Christ Know.

Davies, Tony. Humanism. LC 96-17602. (New Critical Idiom Ser.). 160p. (C). 1996. 50.00 (*0-415-13478-1*); pap. 12.99 (*0-415-11052-1*) Routledge.

Davies, Tony & Wood, Nigel, eds. A Passage to India. LC 93-42009. (Theory in Practice Ser.). 1994. pap. 29.95 (*0-335-15712-2*) OpUniv Pr.

— The Waste Land. LC 93-20998. (Theory in Practice Ser.). 1994. 29.95 (*0-335-15716-5*) OpUniv Pr.

Davies, Trefor, jt. ed. see Cremer, Herbert W.

***Davies, Trish.** The Balkan Cookbook. 96p. 2000. 14.95 (*1-84215-107-X*) Anness Pub.

Davies, Tristan. Lost Slipper & the Curse of the Ramsbottoms. (Wallace & Gromit Comic Strip Bks.). 1998. pap. text 9.95 (*0-8417-3035-0*) Advent Med Kits.

***Davies, Tristan.** Wallace & Gromit: Anoraknophobia. 1999. pap. 8.95 (*0-340-72834-5*) Hodder & Stought Ltd.

Davies, Tristan. Wallace & Gromit & the Lost Slipper. 1997. 16.95 (*0-8417-2026-6*) Adlers Foreign Bks.

Davies, Tristan, ed. Soundings from the Parish Pump: A Celebration of Little Local Difficulties from the Weekend Section of the Daily Telegraph. (Illus.). 160p. 1997. 19.95 (*1-86105-073-9*, Robson-Parkwest) Parkwest Pubns.

Davies, Tristan, ed. Soundings from the Parish Pump: A Celebration of Little Local Difficulties from the Weekend Section of The Daily Telegraph. 160p. 1999. pap. 11.95 (*1-86105-147-6*, Pub. by Robson Bks) Parkwest Pubns.

Davies, Uri, jt. auth. see Lehn, Walter.

Davies, V. J. & Tomasin, K. Construction Safety Handbook. 2nd ed. LC 97-106230. 316p. 1996. 96.00 (*0-7277-2519-X*) Am Soc Civil Eng.

Davies, Valentine. It Happens Every Spring. 1995. reprint ed. lib. bdg. 24.95 (*1-56849-665-6*) Buccaneer Bks.

— Miracle on 34th Star. LC 98-72387. (Illus.). 144p. (ps-3). 1998. 9.99 (*1-57866-027-0*) Galahad Bks.

— The Miracle on 34th Street. LC 47-4221. 120p. 1947. 13.95 (*0-15-160239-5*) Harcourt.

— The Miracle on 34th Street. (Illus.). (J). (gr. k up). 1984. 16.95 (*0-15-254526-3*, Harcourt Child Bks) Harcourt.

— The Miracle on 34th Street. LC 84-3742. (Illus.). 128p. (ps-3). 1987. pap. 13.00 (*0-15-254528-X*, Voyager Bks) Harcourt.

— The Miracle on 34th Street. 160p. 1994. pap. 9.95 (*0-15-600198-5*) Harcourt.

— Miracle on 34th Street. 76p. 1996. pap. 5.60 (*0-87129-707-8*, M96) Dramatic Pub.

— The Miracle on 34th Street. reprint ed. lib. bdg. 17.95 (*0-88411-934-3*) Amereon Ltd.

— The Miracle on 34th Street. 128p. 1992. reprint ed. lib. bdg. 17.95 (*0-89968-313-4*, Lghtyr Pr) Buccaneer Bks.

— Miracle on 34th Street, Gift Edition. (Illus.). 146p. 1991. pap. 9.95 (*0-15-660455-8*, Harvest Bks) Harcourt.

Davies, Vanessa. Abortion & Afterwards. 224p. (Orig.). 1997. pap. 12.50 (*1-85398-018-8*, Pub. by Ashgrove Pr) Words Distrib.

Davies, Vanessa. Betrayal of Trust: Women Understanding & Overcoming Their Experience of Childhood Sexual Abuse. 212p. 1995. pap. text 21.95 (*1-85398-059-5*, Pub. by Ashgrove Pr) Words Distrib.

Davies, Vanessa, jt. auth. see Sheridan, Nina.

Davies, Victor, jt. auth. see Cowie, Victor.

***Davies, Vikki.** Ancient Lexigraming the Lost "Word History" Schulte, Marcia, ed. 68p. 2000. spiral bd. 18.95 (*0-9679323-0-0*) Vikki Davies.

Davies, Vivian. Egypt Uncovered. LC 97-62390. (Illus.). 224p. 1998. 29.95 (*1-55670-818-1*) Stewart Tabori & Chang.

— Trading in Metals Futures & Options. (Illus.). 192p. Date not set. write for info. (*1-85573-150-9*, Pub. by Woodhead Pubng) Am Educ Systs.

***Davies, W. D.** Christian Engagements with Judaism. LC 99-29534. 352p. 1999. 29.00 (*1-56338-268-7*) TPI PA.

Davies, W. D. Christian Origins & Judaism. LC 73-2192. (Jewish People; History, Religion, Literature Ser.). 1978. reprint ed. 24.95 (*0-405-05258-8*) Ayer.

Davies, W. D. The Gospel & the Land: Early Christianity & Jewish Territorial Doctrine. (Biblical Seminar Ser.: No. 25). 520p. 1994. reprint ed. pap. 43.00 (*1-85075-478-0*, Pub. by Sheffield Acad) CUP Services.

Davies, W. D. Invitation to the New Testament. (Biblical Seminar Ser.: Vol. 19). 540p. 1993. pap. 43.00 (*1-85075-411-X*, Pub. by Sheffield Acad) CUP Services.

— Paul & Rabbinic Judaism: Some Rabbinic Elements in Pauline Theology. 456p. 1980. reprint ed. pap. 28.00 (*1-888961-06-6*) Sigler Pr.

— Paul & Rabbinic Judaism: Some Rabbinic Elements in Pauline Theology. 456p. 1998. reprint ed. 44.00 (*1-888961-07-4*) Sigler Pr.

— System Identification for Self-Adaptive Control. LC 70-128756. 394p. reprint ed. pap. 122.20 (*0-608-30572-3*, 202254000027) Bks Demand.

Davies, W. D. & Allison, Dale C. Matthew 19-28, Vol. 3. Emerton, J. A., ed. (International Critical Commentary Ser.). 800p. 1997. 69.95 (*0-567-08518-X*, Pub. by T & T Clark) Bks Intl VA.

— Matthew 1-17, Vol. 1. (International Critical Commentary Ser.). 780p. 1997. 69.95 (*0-567-09481-2*, Pub. by T & T Clark) Bks Intl VA.

Davies, W. D. & Finkelstein, Louis, eds. The Cambridge History of Judaism Vol. 1: Introduction, The Persian Period. LC 77-85704. 495p. 1984. text 110.00 (*0-521-21880-2*) Cambridge U Pr.

— The Cambridge History of Judaism Vol. 2: The Hellenistic Age. (Illus.). 756p. 1990. text 120.00 (*0-521-21929-9*) Cambridge U Pr.

Davies, W. D., jt. ed. see Karsa, David R.

Davies, W. H. Young Emma. 166p. 1991. 22.95 (*1-85089-506-6*, Pub. by ISIS Lrg Prnt) Transaction Pubs.

Davies, W. J. & Jones, H. G., eds. Abascisic Acid: Physiology & Biochemistry. (Environmental Plant Biology Ser.). 280p. 1991. 125.00 (*1-872748-65-1*, Pub. by Bios Sci) Coronet Bks.

Davies, W. Keith, jt. auth. see Longworth, Norman.

Davies, W. Martin. Experience & Content: Consequences of a Continuum Theory. (Avebury Series in Philosophy). 360p. 1997. text 87.95 (*1-85972-342-X*, Pub. by Avebry) Ashgate Pub Co.

Davies, W. Paul, jt. auth. see Gooding, Mike J.

Davies, W. V. Egyptian Hieroglyphs. (Reading the Past Ser.: Vol. 6). (C). 1988. pap. 13.95 (*0-520-06287-6*, Pub. by U CA Pr) Cal Prin Full Svc.

Davies, W. V., jt. auth. see James, T. G.

Davies, Walford. Dylan Thomas. 2nd ed. (Writers of Wales Ser.). vi, 68p. 1990. pap. write for info. (*0-7083-1066-4*, Pub. by Univ Wales Pr) Paul & Co Pubs.

— Dylan Thomas: Open Guides to Literature. LC 86-794. 128p. 1986. 102.50 (*0-335-15092-6*); pap. 27.95 (*0-335-15083-7*) OpUniv Pr.

Davies, Walford, ed. Let's Sing Together. 1987. pap. 40.00 (*0-946095-13-2*, Pub. by Gresham Bks) St Mut.

Davies, Wallace E. Patriotism on Parade: The Story of Veterans' & Hereditary Organizations in America, 1783-1900. LC 55-11951. (Historical Studies: No. 66). 402p. 1955. 27.50 (*0-674-65800-0*) HUP.

***Davies, Warnock.** Partner Risk. 2000. 34.95 (*1-55753-210-9*) Purdue U Pr.

Davies, Wendy. Closing the Borders. (Global Issues Ser.). (Illus.). 64p. (J). (gr. 6-7). 1995. lib. bdg. 25.69 (*1-56847-335-4*) Raintree Steck-V.

— The International Debt Crisis. (World Issues Ser.: Set I). 48p. (J). 1988. lib. bdg. 25.27 (*0-86592-076-1*) Rourke Enter.

D

— Patterns of Power in Early Wales: O'Donnell Lectures Delivered in the University of Oxford, 1983. (Illus.). 128p. 1990. 39.95 (*0-19-820153-2*) OUP.

— We Cry for Our Land: Farm Workers in South Africa. (Illus.). 64p. (C). 1990. pap. 8.95 (*0-85598-143-1*, Pub. by Oxfam Pub) Stylus Pub VA.

Davies, Wendy & Astill, Grenville. The East Brittany Survey: Fieldwork & Field Data. LC 94-17879. 1995. 131.95 (*1-85928-125-7*, Pub. by Scolar Pr) Ashgate Pub Co.

Davies, Wendy & Fouracre, Paul, eds. Property & Power in the Early Middle Ages. 336p. (C). 1995. text 59.95 (*0-521-43419-X*) Cambridge U Pr.

Davies, William. The Setting of the Sermon on the Mount. LC 64-630. 563p. reprint ed. pap. 160.50 (*0-608-12451-6*, 2024449) Bks Demand.

Davies, William D. Choctaw Verb Agreement & Universal Grammar. 1985. lib. bdg. 127.50 (*90-277-2065-7*) Kluwer Academic.

— Jewish & Pauline Studies. LC 82-48620. 431p. reprint ed. pap. 133.70 (*0-608-15819-4*, 20312790074) Bks Demand.

Davies, William H. Captive Lion & Other Poems. 1921. 39.50 (*0-685-89738-9*) Elliots Bks.

Davies, Wynne. An Introduction to Welsh Ponies & Cob. (Illus.). 144p. text 19.95 (*1-873580-07-X*, Pub. by Whittet Bks) Diamond Farm Bk.

— Welsh Champions. 63p. 1990. pap. 21.00 (*0-85131-396-5*, Pub. by J A Allen) St Mut.

— Welsh Cob Champions. 1990. pap. 21.00 (*0-85131-410-4*, Pub. by J A Allen) St Mut.

— The Welsh Mountain Pony. 134p. 1990. 52.00 (*0-85131-571-2*, Pub. by J A Allen) Trafalgar.

Davies, Wynne, ed. The Welsh Cob. (Illus.). 160p. 1998. 75.90 (*0-85131-721-9*, Pub. by J A Allen) Trafalgar.

— Welsh Pony Champions. 80p. 1990. pap. 30.00 (*0-85131-458-9*, Pub. by J A Allen) St Mut.

Davies, Zoe, jt. auth. see Pilliner, Sarah.

Daviess, Maria T. Seven Times Seven. Baxter, Annette K., ed. LC 79-8786. (Signal Lives Ser.). (Illus.). 1980. reprint ed. lib. bdg. 37.95 (*0-405-12834-7*) Ayer.

Daviess, Maria T. History of Mercer & Boyle Counties (Kentucky) (Illus.). 175p. 1998. reprint ed. pap. 21.50 (*0-8063-4774-0*, 9317) Clearfield Co.

Daviet, J. P. Un Destin International: La Compagnie de Saint-Gobain, 1830-1939. (FRE.). 724p. 1988. pap. text 60.00 (*2-88124-220-0*) Gordon & Breach.

Davignon, J., et al, eds. Atherosclerosis X: Proceedings of the 10th International Symposium on Atherosclerosis, Montreal, October 9-14, 1994. LC 95-12158. (International Congress Ser.: No. 1066). 1106p. 1995. 357.00 (*0-444-82007-8*, Excerpta Medica) Elsevier.

D'Avignon, Jacques. Propagation Programs: A Review of Current Forecasting Software. Grove, Bob, ed. (Illus.). 48p. (Orig.). 1992. 9.95 (*0-944543-06-5*) Grove Enterp.

Davil, Gerardo N. Cambio y Desarrollo en Puerto Rico: La Transformacion Ideologic del Partido Popular Democratico. (SPA.). 214p. 1985. 6.50 (*0-8477-2435-2*) U of PR Pr.

Davila, Arlene M. Sponsored Identities: Cultural Politics in Puerto Rico. LC 97-1942. (Puerto Rican Studies). 288p. 1997. 59.95 (*1-56639-548-8*); pap. 19.95 (*1-56639-549-6*) Temple U Pr.

Davila, Carlos & Miller, Rory, eds. Business History in Latin America: The Experience of Seven Countries. LC 99-231813. 4p. 1998. pap. 19.95 (*0-85323-723-9*, Pub. by Liverpool Univ Pr) Intl Spec Bk.

Davila Cox, Emma. Este Inmenso Comercio. (SPA., Illus.). 364p. 1996. pap. 12.95 (*0-8477-0250-2*) U of PR Pr.

Davila, Denise, jt. auth. see Kopp, Jaine.

***D'Avila-La Tourette, Victor-Antoine.** Simplicity & Great Food from a Monastery Kitchen. 2000. 27.95 (*0-7679-0609-8*) Broadway BDD.

D'Avila-Latourrette. Desert Wisdom. 1999. write for info. (*0-385-49041-0*) Doubleday.

***D'Avila-Latourrette.** Fresh from a Monastery Garden: An A-to-Z Treasury of Delectable Vegetable Recipes. LC 98-10356. (Illus.). 320p. 1998. 25.00 (*0-385-49039-9*) Doubleday.

***D'Avila-Latourrette, Victor-Antoine.** From a Monastery Kitchen. LC 99-88796. 2000. 6.99 (*0-517-20639-0*) Random Hse Value.

D'Avila-Latourrette, Victor-Antoine. From a Monastery Kitchen: The Classic Natural Foods Cookbook. LC 96-2748. 176p. 1997. 24.00 (*0-7648-0029-9*, Liguori Triumph) Liguori Pubns.

***D'Avila-Latourrette, Victor-Antoine.** In Celebration of the Seasons: Recipes from a Monastery Kitchen. LC 99-55364. (Illus.). 234p. 2000. 24.95 (*0-7648-0571-1*, Liguori Triumph) Liguori Pubns.

— A Monastic Year: Reflections from a Monastery. LC 99-51380. 172p. 2000. 9.99 (*1-56955-177-4*, Charis) Servant.

D'Avila-Latourrette, Victor-Antoine. A Monastic Year: Reflections from a Monastery. (Illus.). 184p. 1996. 14.95 (*0-87833-923-X*) Taylor Pub.

— Table Blessings: Mealtime Prayers Throughout the Year. LC 94-71884. (Illus.). 176p. 1994. pap. 12.95 (*0-87793-538-6*) Ave Maria.

— This Good Food: Contemporary French Vegetarian Recipes from a Monastery Kitchen. (Illus.). 222p. 1994. reprint ed. pap. 13.95 (*0-87951-551-1*, Pub. by Overlook Pr) Penguin Putnam.

— This Good Food: French Vegetarian Recipes from a Monastery Kitchen. LC 92-25544. (Illus.). 240p. 1993. 22.95 (*0-87951-483-3*, Pub. by Overlook Pr) Penguin Putnam.

— Twelve Months of Monastery Soups: International Favorites. LC 97-42099. (Illus.). 208p. 1998. pap. 16.00 (*0-7679-0180-0*) Broadway BDD.

— Twelve Months of Monastery Soups: International Favorites. LC 96-10865. 208p. 1996. 25.00 (*0-89243-931-9*, Liguori Triumph) Liguori Pubns.

Davila-Lizardi, Luis A., ed. see McQuade, J. Stanley.

Davila, Maria D. Castro De, see Castro De Davila, Maria D.

Davila, Patricio & Zaragoza, Diana, eds. Arqueologia de San Luis Potosi. 298p. 1991. pap. 11.00 (*968-6487-69-7*, IN035) UPLAAP.

Davila-Rubero. Razonamiento Matematico y Comunicacion. (SPA.). 482p. 1996. pap. write for info. (*0-929441-81-8*) Pubns Puertorriquenas.

***Davila, Sergio.** Una No Es Ninguna. (SPA.). 2000. pap. 6.99 (*0-8297-2885-6*) Vida Pubs.

Davila-Villers, David R., ed. NAFTA on Second Thought: A Plural Evaluation. LC 98-9552. 152p. 1998. 49.00 (*0-7618-1057-9*); pap. 27.50 (*0-7618-1058-7*) U Pr of Amer.

Davilier, Charles. Le Cabinet Du Duc D'Aumont: A Facsimile of the 1870 Edition Recording the Auction of 1782. Munhall, Edgar, ed. (Reprint Series of Historical Auction Catalogues). (FRE., Illus.). 256p. 1986. reprint ed. text 50.00 (*0-317-93172-5*) Acanthus Pr.

Davilla, James J. & Soltan, Arthur M. French Aircraft of the First World War. LC 96-52092. (Illus.). 500p. 1997. 89.95 (*0-9637110-4-0*) Flying Machines.

Davin, Anna. Growing up Poor. LC 95-219623. 1997. pap. 19.50 (*1-85489-063-8*, Pub. by Rivers Oram) NYU Pr.

Davin, D. M. Crete. (Official History Ser.: Vol. 14). (Illus.). 565p. 1997. reprint ed. 54.95 (*0-89839-265-9*) Battery Pr.

Davin, Dan, ed. Classic New Zealand Short Stories. (Classic Short Stories Ser.). 288p. 1998. pap. text 16.95 (*0-19-558384-1*) OUP.

Davin, Delia. Internal Migration in Contemporary China. LC 98-28378. xii, 177 p. 1998. text 65.00 (*0-312-21718-8*) St Martin.

— Mao Zedong. LC 98-111033. (New Pocket Biographies Ser.). (Illus.). 128p. 1998. pap. 9.95 (*0-7509-1531-5*, Pub. by Sutton Pub Ltd) Intl Pubs Mktg.

Davin, Donna, jt. ed. see Chugh, Y. Paul.

***Davin, Eric Leif.** Pioneers of Wonder: Conversations with the Founders of Science Fiction. LC 99-37717. 414p. 1999. 24.95 (*1-57392-702-3*) Prometheus Bks.

Davin, Nicholas F. The Irishman in Canada. 714p. 1998. reprint ed. pap. 45.00 (*1-58211-071-9*, 097638) Quintin Pub RI.

Davin, Patricia A., et al. Female Sexual Abusers: Three Views. (Illus.). 256p. (J). (gr. 3-6). 1999. pap. 22.00 (*1-884444-54-7*, WPO70) Safer Soc.

Davin-Power, Maurice. Shadows in the Sun. (Irish Play Ser.). 1980. pap. 2.95 (*0-912262-64-8*) Proscenium.

Davino, Joe. Batter Up: A Hall of Fame Cookbook. 1997. 22.95 (*1-888170-04-2*) Advent Quest.

Davinroy, Paul V. Dusty & the Grand Canyon. 40p. (J). (gr. k-2). 1996. pap. 8.00 (*0-8059-3898-2*) Dorrance.

Davinson, Donald E. Academic Libraries in the Enterprise Culture. LC 89-21175. (Viewpoints in Library & Information Science: Vol. 2). 46p. 1989. reprint ed. pap. 30.00 (*0-7837-9257-3*, 204999700004) Bks Demand.

— The Periodicals Collection. 2nd ed. LC 78-17873. 243 p. 1978. 18.00 (*0-89158-833-7*) Westview.

Davinson, Patricia & Oliver, Andrew, Jr. Ancient Greek & Roman Jewelry. 214p. 1984. 45.00 (*0-913696-31-5*) Bklyn Mus.

Davio, John, jt. auth. see Arrathoon, Leigh.

Davio, John, jt. auth. see Arrathoon, Leigh A.

Davio, John, ed. see Arrathoon, Leigh A.

Davio, Marc, et al. Digital Systems with Algorithm Implementation. LC 82-2710. (Wiley-Interscience Publications). 523p. reprint ed. pap. 162.20 (*0-7837-4513-3*, 204429200001) Bks Demand.

Davion, Victoria & Wolf, Clark, eds. The Idea of Political Liberalism: Essays on Rawls. LC 99-36523. (Studies in Social, Political, & Legal Philosophy). 272p. 1998. pap. 18.95 (*0-8476-8794-5*); text 62.95 (*0-8476-8793-7*) Rowman.

Davis. Administrative Law, Vol. 1. LC 93-78055. 1993. 150.00 (*0-316-17667-2*, Aspen Law & Bus) Aspen Pub.

— Administrative Law, Vol. 2. LC 93-78055. 1993. 150.00 (*0-316-17668-0*, Aspen Law & Bus) Aspen Pub.

— Administrative Law, Vol. 3. LC 93-78055. 1994. write for info. (*0-316-17669-9*, Aspen Law & Bus) Aspen Pub.

— Adventures in Physics. 1999. pap. text 27.00 (*0-697-33535-6*) McGraw.

— Aphasia. 356p. 1999. 59.00 (*0-205-29834-6*, Longwood Div) Allyn.

— Autocad Training Manual. LC 98-41444. 183p. 1998. spiral bd. 33.60 (*0-13-763013-1*, Prentice Hall) P-H.

— A Basic Guide to Equestrian. (Official United States Olympic Committee Sports Ser.). (Illus.). 128p. 1995. pap. 7.95 (*1-882180-29-1*) Griffin CA.

— Between Jihad & Salaam. 1999. pap. 17.95 (*0-312-21781-1*) St Martin.

— Bone Wars. 1998. per. 5.99 (*0-671-87880-8*) PB.

— Business Research. 4th ed. (Business Statistics Ser.). 1995. pap., teacher ed. 56.25 (*0-534-24613-3*) PWS Pubs.

— Business Research for Decision Making with InfoTrac. 4th ed. (Business Statistics Ser.). 1998. pap. 61.25 (*0-534-36336-9*) Brooks-Cole.

***Davis.** C++ for Dummies Deluxe Compiler Kit. (For Dummies Ser.). 400p. 1999. pap. 39.99 incl. cd-rom (*0-7645-0609-9*) IDG Bks.

Davis. Celluloid Mirrors. LC 98-127540. (C). 1996. pap. text 22.00 (*0-15-501568-0*, Pub. by Harcourt Coll Pubs) Harcourt.

***Davis.** The Christmas Quilt. 288p. 2000. 18.99 (*1-55853-814-3*) Rutledge Hill Pr.

Davis. Cinema. 2nd ed. 238p. 1998. pap. text 30.40 (*0-536-01314-4*) Pearson Custom.

— College Physics. (C). 1912. text 68.00 (*0-03-076116-6*) Harcourt.

— Computer Security & Privacy for Dummies. LC 96-76246. (For Dummies Ser.). 360p. 1996. pap. 19.99 (*1-56884-635-5*) IDG Bks.

— Computing Fundamentals. (C). 1991. pap. text. write for info. (*0-201-57992-8*) Addison-Wesley.

— Comrade or Brother? The History of the British Labour Movement 1789-1951. LC 93-6223. 226p. (C). 59.95 (*0-7453-0760-4*, Pub. by Pluto GBR); pap. 19.95 (*0-7453-0761-2*, Pub. by Pluto GBR) Stylus Pub VA.

— Confederate States of America. 2000. 35.00 (*0-02-874088-2*) Free Pr.

— Counselling & Communication in Health Care. 1991. pap. text 70.00 (*0-471-92965-4*) Wiley.

— Davis Picture Book. (J). 1998. 14.00 (*0-671-88337-2*) S&S Bks Yung.

***Davis.** Discovery. 2000. 15.00 (*0-07-238466-2*) McGraw.

Davis. Economics. 1997. pap. text, teacher ed. write for info. (*0-13-598160-3*) Allyn.

— Ethics in Nursing. (International Journal of Nursing Studies: Vol. 22). 1986. pap. 27.50 (*0-08-033969-7*, Pergamon Pr) Elsevier.

— Exploring Biology. 1996. lab manual ed. write for info. (*0-8016-6625-2*) Mosby Inc.

— Forest Management. 4th ed. 2000. 110.93 (*0-07-032694-0*) McGraw.

— Fundamentals of Gastroenterology. 1999. pap. text. write for info. (*0-7216-5203-4*, W B Saunders Co) Harcrt Hlth Sci Grp.

— Fundamentals Operations Management. 3rd ed. 1998. 12.74 (*0-07-289247-1*) McGraw.

— Getting Rich Investing in Tomorrow. 1994. 25.00 (*0-02-529755-4*) Macmillan.

— Graphing Calculator Guide: Functions & Graphics. (Math). 1995. mass mkt. 19.25 (*0-534-19801-5*) PWS Pubs.

— Human Sexuality. (C). 1998. pap. text, teacher ed., suppl. ed. 28.00 (*0-15-503605-X*) Harcourt Coll Pubs.

— Human Sexuality. (C). 2000. text 59.00 (*0-15-501277-0*); pap. text, student ed. 22.00 (*0-15-503603-3*) Harcourt Coll Pubs.

— Human Sexuality: Test Bank. (C). 2000. pap. text, teacher ed., suppl. ed. 31.00 (*0-15-503604-1*, Pub. by Harcourt Coll Pubs) Harcourt.

— I Hate to Go to Bed. LC 98-22331. 36p. (J). 1999. 14.00 (*0-15-201920-0*, Harcourt Child Bks) Harcourt.

— Instructor's Manual College Physics. (C). 1912. pap. text, teacher ed. write for info. (*0-03-097156-X*) Harcourt Coll Pubs.

— Intro to Music Therapy. 2nd ed. LC 98-29454. 1998. 44.78 (*0-697-38860-3*, Dshkn McG-Hill) McGrw-H Hghr Educ.

— Introduction to Agricultural Statistics. LC 99-42442. (Agriculture Ser.). 271p. (C). 1999. pap. 42.95 (*0-7668-1155-7*) Delmar.

— Introduction to Environmental Engineering. 2nd ed. 1991. 27.50 (*0-07-015912-2*) McGraw.

— Introduction to Phlebotomy: Instructor's Guide. (Medical Lab Technician Ser.). 1994. teacher ed. 12.00 (*0-8273-5564-5*) Delmar.

— Journeys Writing. 1999. pap. text, teacher ed. 13.93 (*0-13-226903-1*) P-H.

— Journeys Writing, Vol. 1. 128p. 1998. pap. 27.73 (*0-13-181546-6*) P-H.

— Lasers in Otolaryngology. (Illus.). 224p. 1990. text 135.00 (*0-7216-3124-X*, W B Saunders Co) Harcrt Hlth Sci Grp.

— Linear Circuit Analysis. LC 97-30067. (Electrical Engineering Ser.). (C). 1998. 101.95 (*0-534-95095-7*) PWS Pubs.

— Linear System Analysis. (Electrical Engineering Ser.). 2001. mass mkt. 74.95 (*0-534-95086-8*) PWS Pubs.

— Magazine Journalism Today. 260p. 1988. pap. 46.95 (*0-7506-0728-9*) Buttrwrth-Heinemann.

— Plan Graphics. 5th ed. (Landscape Architecture Ser.). 1997. pap. 39.95 (*0-442-02481-9*, VNR) Wiley.

— PPM for Manufacturing. 4th ed. 96p. 1995. teacher ed. 21.00 (*0-8273-6711-2*) Delmar.

— Quantative Environmental Science. 2001. 69.25 (*0-07-235053-9*) McGraw.

— Readings in Human Sexuality. (C). 2000. pap. text 23.50 (*0-15-504117-7*) Harcourt.

— Real Voices. LC 96-9726. 320p. 1997. text 35.00 (*0-312-16475-0*) St Martin.

— Requirements Management: Best Practices. (C). Date not set. pap. text 35.00 (*0-13-632985-5*) P-H.

— Scared Stiff C. 2001. Price not set. (*0-15-202305-4*) Harcourt.

— The Shadow of Evil: Where Is God in a Violent World. 132p. 1996. pap. text, per. 19.95 (*0-7872-1981-9*) Kendall-Hunt.

— Social Psychology. 4th ed. 240p. 2000. pap. 16.56 (*0-07-236583-8*) McGraw.

— Social Psychology 1999-2000 Edition. 3rd ed. 1999. pap., student ed. 16.56 (*0-07-040087-3*) McGraw.

— Spon's Architects & Builders. 1997. 107.95 (*0-419-18910-6*, E & FN Spon) Routledge.

— Study Guide College Physics. (C). 1912. pap. text, teacher ed. 16.75 (*0-03-097157-8*) Harcourt.

— Terribly Tasteless. 1999. pap. 4.95 (*0-312-79202-6*) St Martin.

— Tertulia. (C). 1995. 51.50 incl. audio (*0-03-010349-5*) Harcourt.

— Tertulia. (C). 1994. pap. text, teacher ed. 33.75 (*0-03-012968-0*) Harcourt Coll Pubs.

— Tertulia: Conversational Skills. (C). 1995. pap. text 50.00 (*0-03-098568-4*) Harcourt Coll Pubs.

— Western Literature Vol. 2: Five Novels. 2000. pap. text 61.20 (*0-312-13279-4*) St Martin.

***Davis.** Western Public Lands & Environment. 2nd ed. 2000. pap. 24.00 (*0-8133-3768-2*, Pub. by Westview) HarpC.

Davis, et al, eds. Factors Influencing Sludge Utilization Practices in Europe. (Illus.). 124p. 1986. text 54.95 (*1-85166-007-0*) Elsevier.

— North of Eden: An Anthology of Alaskan Writings. 128p. (Orig.). 1995. pap. 7.95 (*0-9647550-0-9*) Loose Affil.

Davis & Anderson. Recreational Folk Dance. LC 99-173065. 148p. (C). 1998. spiral bd. 26.95 (*0-7872-5145-3*, 41514501) Kendall-Hunt.

Davis & Cass. Administrative Law: 1994 Supplement. 1994. 125.00 (*0-316-17683-4*, Aspen Law & Bus) Aspen Pub.

Davis & Heunis. Linear Stochastic Systems. 2nd ed. (Stochastic Modeling Ser.). (Illus.). 256p. (C). (gr. 13). 1997. 54.95 (*0-412-31740-0*) Chapman & Hall.

Davis & Langdon, eds. Spon's Architects' & Builders' Price Book 1998. 944p. (C). (gr. 13). 1997. pap. 120.00 (*0-419-23060-2*) Thomson Learn.

Davis & Moran. Functions & Graphs: Precalculus. (Mathematics Ser.). 1996. teacher ed. 19.25 (*0-534-19793-0*) Brooks-Cole.

Davis & Signell. Music: A Multicultural Experience. 2nd ed. 384p. (C). 1998. per. 39.95 (*0-7872-5270-0*, 41527001) Kendall-Hunt.

Davis & Zitelli, Basil J. Atlas of Pediatric Physical Diagnosis. 3rd ed. LC 96-46308. (Illus.). 912p. (C). (gr. 13), 1997. text 110.00 (*0-8151-9930-9*, 27081) Mosby Inc.

Davis, et al. AMER PEOPL CREATG BRF V1. 2nd abr. ed. 448p. (C). 1996. text 29.06 (*0-673-99527-5*) Addson-Wesley Educ.

— Differential Equations. LC 99-18101. 641p. 1999. 93.33 (*0-13-736539-X*) P-H.

— Foundations of Psychiatry. (Illus.). 336p. 1990. text 52.00 (*0-7216-1341-1*, W B Saunders Co) Harcrt Hlth Sci Grp.

— Guide & Key to Alabama Trees. 5th ed. 144p. (C). 1999. spiral bd. 29.95 (*0-7872-5790-7*, 41579001) Kendall-Hunt.

— Western Tradition. 1994. pap. text, teacher ed. 5.00 (*0-312-08123-5*) St Martin.

Davis, jt. auth. see Donatelle.

Davis, jt. auth. see McCurley.

Davis, jt. auth. see Meier.

Davis, jt. auth. see Mitchell.

Davis, jt. auth. see Moore.

Davis, jt. auth. see Moran.

Davis, jt. auth. see Morse.

Davis, jt. auth. see Norris.

Davis, jt. auth. see Roberts, Willo Davis.

Davis, jt. auth. see Smith.

Davis, jt. auth. see Umstattd, William D.

Davis, jt. compiled by see Mitchell.

Davis, ed. see Everest Staff.

Davis, tr. see Hennig, Willi.

Davis, Lloyd D., jt. auth. see Artiaga, Lucio.

Davis, M. C., et al. A Catalogue of the Pre-1850 Books in the Cecil Roth Collection. LC 96-154499. 119p. 1994. write for info. (*0-902454-08-0*) Brotherton Library.

Davis, A. Drug Treatment in Intestinal Helminthiasis. 1973. pap. text 16.00 (*92-4-156036-3*, 1150035) World Health.

— Violin Sonata. 32p. 1995. pap. 11.95 (*0-7935-4502-1*, 50482386) H Leonard.

Davis, A., ed. Metsudah Shabbat Siddur. 1998. pap. 14.95 (*0-88125-623-4*) Ktav.

Davis, A., et al, eds. Symptom Analysis & Physical Diagnosis. 2nd ed. 328p. 1985. text 42.00 (*0-08-029870-2*); pap. text 25.95 (*0-08-029869-9*) Elsevier.

Davis, A., jt. auth. see Kennedy, Eberhard C.

Davis, A., jt. ed. see Birtwistle, G. M.

Davis, A., tr. see Rabe, Thomas.

Davis, A. C. & Brandenberger, R. Formation & Interactions of Topological Defects: Proceedings of a NATOASI Held in Cambridge, England, August 21-September 3, 1994. (NATO ASI Ser.: Vol. 349). (Illus.). 406p. (C). 1995. text 125.00 (*0-306-45116-6*, Kluwer Plenum) Kluwer Academic.

Davis, A. C., III, jt. auth. see Shvyrkov, V.

Davis, A. C., jt. ed. see Scott, P. H.

Davis, A. J. Great Harmonia: The Seer (1852) 402p. 1998. reprint ed. pap. 22.50 (*0-7661-0497-4*) Kessinger Pub.

Davis, A. J., ed. History of Clarion County, with Illustrations & Biographical Sketches of Some of Its Prominent Men & Pioneers. (Illus.). 736p. 1997. reprint ed. lib. bdg. 77.50 (*0-8328-6401-3*) Higginson Bk Co.

Davis, A. M. The Origin of the National Banking System. Bruchey, Stuart, ed. LC 80-1142. (Rise of Commercial Banking Ser.). 1981. reprint ed. lib. bdg. 26.95 (*0-405-13644-7*) Ayer.

***Davis, A. P.** CITES Bulb Checklist. 131p. 1999. pap. 20.00 (*1-900347-39-3*, Pub. by Royal Botnic Grdns) Balogh.

Davis, Aaron P. & Royal Botanic Gardens Kew Staff. The Genus Galanthus: A Botanical Magazine Monograph. LC 98-56148. (Illus.). 333p. 1999. 39.95 (*0-88192-431-8*) Timber.

Davis, Aarron. The Luger Handbook. LC 97-215928. 112p. 1997. pap. 9.95 (*0-87341-501-9*, LH01) Krause Pubns.

Davis, Abraham L., ed. The U. S. Supreme Court & the Uses of Social Science Data. LC 73-8983. 150p. (C). 1975. pap. text 10.95 (*0-8422-0338-9*) Irvington.

Davis, Abraham L. & Graham, Barbara L. The Supreme Court, Race, & Civil Rights. LC 95-12923. 512p. (C). 1995. 68.00 (*0-8039-7219-9*); pap. 31.50 (*0-8039-7220-2*) Sage.

Davis, Ada R. Advanced Practice Nurses: Education, Roles, Trends. (Nursing Ser.). 232p. 1997. pap. 41.25 (*0-7637-0370-2*) Jones & Bartlett.

An Asterisk (*) at the beginning of an entry indicates that the title is appearing for the first time.

Davis, Ada R., et al, compiled by. Home Health Care: An Annotated Bibliography, 16. LC 91-46848. (Bibliographies & Indexes in Gerontology Ser.: No. 16). 168p. 1992. lib. bdg. 49.95 (*0-313-28334-6*, DHH, Greenwood Pr) Greenwood.

Davis, Adelaide B., jt. auth. see Davis, James R.

Davis, Adele, jt. ed. see Keys, Jean.

Davis, Adelle. Let's Get Well. 480p. 1972. mass mkt. 7.99 (*0-451-15463-0*, Sig) NAL.

— Let's Have Healthy Children. 1995. reprint ed. lib. bdg. 28.95 (*1-56849-622-2*) Buccaneer Bks.

— You Can Get Well. 1975. pap. 2.95 (*0-87904-033-5*) Lust.

Davis-Adeshote, Jeanette. Black Survival in White America: From Past History to the Next Century. Blakeley, Gwendolynne A., ed. LC 94-79897. 128p. (Orig.). (C). 1995. pap. 10.95 (*0-9638672-3-7*) Bryant & Dillon.

Davis, Adrian. Hearing in Adults. 950p. 1994. 310.00 (*1-56593-243-9*, 0566) Singular Publishing.

Davis, Akie. Black Man's Version to Exhale. large type ed. Middleton, Jennie, ed. 165p. 1998. per. 13.95 (*0-9662369-0-4*, 2000) Fanon Prodns.

Davis, Al, jt. auth. see Warner, Evie.

Davis, Al, ed. see Dorn, Edward G., II.

Davis, Al, ed. see Dorn, Edward & Dorn, Cecilia.

***Davis, Alan.** Alone with the Owl. (Minnesota Voices Project Ser.: Vol. 97). 2000. pap. 14.95 (*0-89823-203-1*, Pub. by New Rivers Pr) Consort Bk Sales.

Davis, Alan. Clandestine vs. the X-Men. (Illus.). 240p. 1997. pap. text 24.95 (*0-7851-0557-3*) Marvel Entrprs.

— The Fun Also Rises Travel Guide International: The Most Fun Places to Be at the Right Time. Thompson, Chuck, ed. LC 99-73373. 255p. 1999. pap. 19.95 (*0-9666352-1-3*) Greenline Pubns.

— The Fun Also Rises Travel Guide North America: The Most Fun Places to Be at the Right Time. 260p. 1999. pap. text 17.95 (*0-9666352-0-5*) Greenline Pubns.

— Justice League of America: The Nail. LC 99-232465. (Illus.). 160p. 1998. pap. 12.95 (*1-56389-480-7*) DC Comics.

— Rumors from the Lost World: A Collection of Stories. (Minnesota Voices Project Ser.: Vol. 54). 112p. (Orig.). 1993. pap. 9.95 (*0-89823-142-6*) New Rivers Pr.

Davis, Alan & White, Michael James Denham, eds. American Fiction Vol. 8: The Best Unpublished Short Stories by Emerging Writers. LC 96-67816. 300p. (Orig.). 1997. pap. 19.95 (*0-89823-172-8*) New Rivers Pr.

— American Fiction Vol. 10: The Best Unpublished Short Stories by Emerging Writers. LC 96-67816. 259p. 1998. pap. 19.95 (*0-89823-192-2*, Pub. by New Rivers Pr) Consort Bk Sales.

Davis, Alan, jt. auth. see Stecher, Brian M.

Davis, Alan, jt. ed. see White, Michael C.

Davis, Alan F., et al. The American People: Creating a Nation & a Society, 2 vols. 2nd abr. ed. 768p. (C). 1996. text 41.25 (*0-673-99526-7*) Addson-Wesley Educ.

Davis, Alan J. Second Chance: White Pastor - Black Church. LC 90-62236. (Illus.). 184p. (Orig.). 1990. pap. 10.00 (*0-913428-70-1*) Landfall Pr.

Davis, Alan M. 201 Principles of Software Development. LC 94-47075. 1995. 24.95 (*0-07-015840-1*) McGraw.

Davis, Alan M., BTG Inc. Staff & Weidner, Marilyn D. Software Requirements: Objects, Functions & States. 2nd rev. ed. 521p. (C). 1993. 80.00 (*0-13-805763-X*) P-H.

Davis, Alan R., ed. Maps: Craft Essays, Fiction, Poetry. (Illus.). (Orig.). 1986. pap. 6.00 (*0-9617312-0-6*) MoonsQuilt Pr.

Davis, Albert B. Leechtime: Novel. LC 88-27629. 184p. 1989. 17.95 (*0-8071-1494-4*) La State U Pr.

— Marquis at Bay: Novel. LC 91-29369. 336p. 1992. 24.95 (*0-8071-1737-4*) La State U Pr.

Davis, Albert H. History of Ellsworth. (Illus.). 244p. 1998. reprint ed. lib. bdg. 34.50 (*0-8328-7020-X*) Higginson Bk Co.

Davis, Albert R. Tao Yuan-ming (AD 365-427) His Works & Their Meaning, Vol. 1. LC 84-104289. 279p. 1983. reprint ed. pap. 86.50 (*0-608-02387-6*, 206302900001) Bks Demand.

— Tao Yuan-ming (AD 365-427) His Works & Their Meaning, Vol. 2. LC 84-104289. 229p. 1983. reprint ed. pap. 71.00 (*0-608-02388-4*, 206302900002) Bks Demand.

Davis, Albert R. & Rawls, Walter C., Jr. The Magnetic Blueprint of Life. 2nd ed. (Illus.). 150p. 1988. reprint ed. pap. 15.00 (*0-911311-15-7*) Acres USA.

— The Magnetic Effect. 6th ed. (Illus.). 128p. 1990. reprint ed. pap. 15.00 (*0-911311-17-3*) Acres USA.

— Magnetism & Its Effects on the Living System. 9th ed. LC 74-84423. (Illus.). 132p. 1988. reprint ed. pap. 15.00 (*0-911311-14-9*) Acres USA.

— The Rainbow in Your Hands. 7th ed. (Illus.). 101p. 1988. reprint ed. pap. 10.00 (*0-911311-16-5*) Acres USA.

***Davis, Alex & Jenkins, Lee M., eds.** Locations of Modernism: Region & Nation in British & American Modernist Poetry. 309p. (C). 2000. text Price not set. (*0-521-78032-2*) Cambridge U Pr.

Davis, Alexander. Henry Moore Bibliography, 5 vols. (Illus.). 2632p. 1997. 500.00 (*0-906909-14-7*, Pub. by Lund Humphries) Antique Collect.

Davis, Alexander J. Pleasure Grounds: Andrew Jackson Downing & Montgomery Place. (Illus.). 96p. 1988. 19.95 (*0-912882-65-4*) Sleepy Hollow.

— Rural Residences. (Architecture & Decorative Art Ser.). 1980. reprint ed. 110.00 (*0-306-71165-6*) Da Capo.

— Sketches of Montgomery Place. (Illus.). 9.95 (*0-912882-74-3*) Sleepy Hollow.

Davis, Alice. Basic Colloquial Maithili: A Maithili-Nepali-English Vocabulary with Notes. (ENG & NEP.). 1987. 75.00 (*0-8288-1625-5*, F33950) Fr & Eur.

Davis, Alice T. Making of a Teacher: Fifty Years in Social Work. LC 81-17807. (Illus.). 208p. reprint ed. pap. 64.50 (*0-7837-5364-0*, 204512800005) Bks Demand.

Davis, Alison. Beloved Companions: Letters on a Way of Wonder. LC 96-94254. 165p. (Orig.). 1996. pap. 12.95 (*0-9619499-6-1*) Little River Pr.

— Hampton Remembers: A Small Town in New England, 1885-1950. 2nd rev. ed. LC 98-91561. (Illus.). 173p. 1998. pap. 15.00 (*0-9619499-7-X*) Little River Pr.

— A Sense of Wonder: A Spiritual Guidebook. 2nd ed. LC 84-81421. 96p. (Orig.). 1987. reprint ed. pap. 7.95 (*0-9619499-5-3*) Little River Pr.

Davis, Allan & Woodman, Harold D. Conflict & Consensus in Modern American History, Vol. I. 9th ed. 476p. (C). 1996. pap. text 30.76 (*0-669-41696-7*) HM Trade Div.

— Conflict & Consensus in Modern American History, Vol. II. 9th ed. LC 96-76888. 576p. (C). 1996. pap. text 30.76 (*0-669-41697-5*) HM Trade Div.

***Davis, Allen F.** American Heroine: The Life & Legend of Jane Adams. LC 99-57842. (Illus.). 368p. 2000. pap. 16.95 (*1-56663-296-X*, Pub. by I R Dee) Natl Bk Netwk.

Davis, Allen F., ed. For Better or Worse: The American Influence in the World, 51. LC 80-1048. (Contributions in American Studies: No. 51). (Illus.). 195p. 1981. 57.95 (*0-313-22342-4*, DBO, Greenwood Pr) Greenwood.

***Davis, Allen F., ed.** The Peoples of Philadelphia: A History of Ethnic Groups & Lower-Class Life, 1790-1940. LC 98-20934. (Pennsylvania Paperbacks Ser.). 312p. 1998. pap. 17.50 (*0-8122-1670-9*) U of Pa Pr.

Davis, Allen F. & Woodman, Harold D. Conflict & Consensus in American History, 2 vols. 6th ed. (C). 1983. pap. text. write for info. (*0-318-57819-0*) HM Trade Div.

— Conflict & Consensus in American History, 2 vols., 1. 6th ed. (C). 1983. pap. text 30.76 (*0-669-06751-2*) HM Trade Div.

— Conflict & Consensus in American History, 2 vols., 2. 6th ed. (C). 1983. pap. text 30.76 (*0-669-06750-4*) HM Trade Div.

— Conflict & Consensus in American History, 2 vols., I. 7th ed. LC 87-81344. (C). 1988. pap. text 30.76 (*0-669-12802-3*) HM Trade Div.

— Conflict & Consensus in American History, 2 vols., II. 7th ed. LC 87-81344. 1988. pap. text 16.00 (*0-685-19350-0*) HM Trade Div.

Davis, Allen F. & Woodman, Harold D., eds. Conflict & Consensus. 8th ed. 454p. (C). 1992. pap. text 30.76 (*0-669-24990-4*); pap. text 30.76 (*0-669-26908-5*) HM Trade Div.

Davis, Allen F., jt. auth. see Watts, J. F.

Davis, Allen F., jt. ed. see Bryan, Mary L.

Davis, Allison. The Motivation of the Under-Privileged Worker. (Reprint Series in Social Sciences). (C). 1993. reprint ed. pap. text 1.90 (*0-8290-2672-X*, S-62) Irvington.

— Psychology of the Child in the Middle Class. LC 60-15158. (Horace Mann Lectures). 80p. reprint ed. pap. 30.00 (*0-608-30575-8*, 201787500010) Bks Demand.

Davis, Allison, et al. Deep South: A Social Anthropological Study of Caste & Class. LC 41-23645. (CAAS Community Classics Ser.: Vol. 1). 567p. 1988. pap. 17.50 (*0-934934-27-4*) CAAS Pubns.

— Deep South: A Social Anthropological Study of Caste & Class. LC 41-23645. (CAAS Community Classics Ser.: Vol. 1). 567p. 1988. 25.95 (*0-934934-26-6*) CAAS Pubns.

Davis, Almond H. The Female Preacher: Memoir of Salome Lincoln, Afterwards the Wife of Elder Junia S. Mowry. LC 72-2599. (American Women Ser.: Images & Realities). (Illus.). 168p. 1978. reprint ed. 16.95 (*0-405-04489-5*) Ayer.

Davis-Almond, L. A. & Almond, Larry H. The Jolly Art of Junking: Finding Treasure in the Trash & Other Fun Places. (Illus.). 80p. 1997. pap. 5.95 (*1-890905-07-0*) Day to Day.

***Davis, Althea T.** Early Black American Leaders in Nursing: Architects for Integration & Equality. LC 98-52865. (National League for Nursing Ser.). 243p. 1999. 30.00 (*0-7637-1009-1*) Jones & Bartlett.

Davis, Alva L., et al, eds. A Compilation of the Work Sheets of the Linguistic Atlas of the United States & Canada & Associated Projects. 2nd ed. LC 78-100481. (Midway Reprint Ser.). 106p. 1973. reprint ed. pap. text 5.75 (*0-226-13806-2*) U Ch Pr.

Davis, Alvis O. Black Men Not Looking for Sex: Why They Commit Forever. LC 94-61196. 216p. (Orig.). 1995. pap. 12.95 (*0-9627656-4-3*) Zevon Pubns.

— The Cold Reality: How to Get & Keep a Black Man in a Relationship. Weisser, Paul, ed. 105p. (Orig.). 1990. pap. text 9.95 (*0-9627656-0-0*) Zevon Pubns.

— How to Have a Super Relationship! Anytime! Anywhere! Cooley, Carletta, ed. 73p. (Orig.). 1995. pap. 5.00 (*0-9627656-7-8*) Zevon Pubns.

— It Won't Hurt to Know: What White Men Think about Black Women Sexually, What Black Women Think about White Men Sexually, What Black Men & White Women Think about Each Other. Morgan, Helen, ed. (Illus.). 202p. (Orig.). 1987. pap. text 6.00 (*0-9627656-2-7*) Zevon Pubns.

Davis, Amanda. Black Holes. LC 96-53487. (Exploring Space Ser.). (J). (gr. k-4). 1997. lib. bdg. 18.00 (*0-8239-5061-1*, PowerKids) Rosen Group.

***Davis, Amanda.** Circling the Drain. 208p. 2000. pap. 13.00 (*0-688-17909-6*, Perennial) HarperTrade.

Davis, Amanda. Circling the Drain: Stories. LC 99-10760. 208p. 1999. 23.00 (*0-688-16780-2*, Wm Morrow) Morrow Avon.

— Comets & Asteroids. LC 96-53485. (Exploring Space Ser.). (J). 1997. lib. bdg. 18.00 (*0-8239-5059-X*, PowerKids) Rosen Group.

— Extraterrestrials: Is There Life in Outer Space? LC 96-53486. (Exploring Space Ser.). 24p. (J). (ps-3). 1997. lib. bdg. 18.00 (*0-8239-5058-1*, PowerKids) Rosen Group.

— Our Solar System. LC 96-53488. (Exploring Space Ser.). (Illus.). 24p. (J). (gr. k-4). 1997. lib. bdg. 18.00 (*0-8239-5060-3*, PowerKids) Rosen Group.

— Space Ships. LC 96-54498. (Exploring Space Ser.). (J). (gr. k-4). 1997. lib. bdg. 18.00 (*0-8239-5063-8*, PowerKids) Rosen Group.

— Space Stations: Living & Working in Space. LC 96-54497. (Exploring Space Ser.). (J). (gr. k-4). 1997. lib. bdg. 18.00 (*0-8239-5062-X*, PowerKids) Rosen Group.

***Davis, Amelia.** The First Look. 168p. 2000. 34.95 (*0-252-02602-0*); pap. 16.95 (*0-252-06925-0*) U of Ill Pr.

Davis, Amy, et al, eds. Interpharm Guide to FDA Pre-Approval & Post-Approval GMP Inspections. 1994. ring bd. 249.00 (*0-935184-67-8*) Interpharm.

Davis, Amy & Anisfeld, Michael H., eds. Complaint Handling: Worldwide Regulations for Healthcare Manufacturers. LC 97-143866. 66p. (Orig.). 1996. pap. 119.00 (*1-57491-033-7*) Interpharm.

Davis, Amy & Dejong, Marja G. Complaint Handling: Worldwide Regulations for Healthcare Manufacturing. 2nd rev. ed. 1998. pap. 119.00 (*1-57491-092-2*) Interpharm.

Davis, Amy, jt. ed. see Anisfeld, Michael.

Davis, Amy L, ed. see Collins, Shawn.

***Davis, Andrew.** Craft. (Illus.). 80p. 2000. pap. 15.00 (*0-930829-47-6*) Lumen Inc.

— God Bless Mr. Devil. Aikens, Susan, ed. LC 99-67880. 253p. 2000. 22.95 (*0-9675811-0-9*, 2000) Moonscape Pubng.

Davis, Andrew. Other Theatres: A History of Experimental Theatre in Britain. 272p. 1987. 53.00 (*0-389-20706-3*, N8264); pap. 16.00 (*0-389-20707-1*, N8265) B&N Imports.

Davis, Andrew & Pettitt, Deirdre, eds. Developing Understanding in Primary Mathematics: Key Stages 1 & 2. 174p. 1994. 85.00 (*0-7507-0357-1*, Falmer Pr); pap. 27.95 (*0-7507-0358-X*, Falmer Pr) Taylor & Francis.

Davis, Andrew J. Answers to Ever Recurring Questions from the People: A Sequel to the Penetralia. 417p. 1996. reprint ed. spiral bd. 23.00 (*0-7873-0248-1*) Hlth Research.

— Answers to Ever-Recurring Questions from the People (1926) 420p. 1998. reprint ed. pap. 29.95 (*0-7661-0676-4*) Kessinger Pub.

— Arabula: The Divine Guest. 403p. 1996. reprint ed. spiral bd. 23.00 (*0-7873-0247-3*) Hlth Research.

— Death & the after Life. 210p. 1996. spiral bd. 14.50 (*0-7873-0240-6*) Hlth Research.

— The Diakka, & Their Earthly Victims. 102p. 1996. reprint ed. spiral bd. 11.00 (*0-7873-0259-7*) Hlth Research.

— The Events in the Life of a Seer. 5th ed. 488p. 1996. reprint ed. pap. 21.00 (*0-7873-0258-9*) Hlth Research.

— The Fountain with Jets of New Meanings. 252p. 1996. reprint ed. spiral bd. 16.50 (*0-7873-0257-0*) Hlth Research.

— The Great Harmonia Vol. I: The Physician. 466p. 1998. reprint ed. pap. 24.50 (*0-7873-0254-6*) Hlth Research.

— The Great Harmonia Vol. II: The Teacher. 396p. 1996. reprint ed. pap. 24.50 (*0-7873-0249-X*) Hlth Research.

— The Great Harmonia Vol. III: The Seer. 268p. 1996. reprint ed. pap. 24.50 (*0-7873-0243-0*) Hlth Research.

— The Great Harmonia Vol. IV: Concerning Physiological Vices & Virtues & the Seven Phases of Marriage: The Reformer. 446p. 1996. reprint ed. pap. 24.50 (*0-7873-0245-7*) Hlth Research.

— The Great Harmonia Vol. V: The Thinker. 419p. 1996. reprint ed. pap. 24.50 (*0-7873-0251-1*) Hlth Research.

— The Harbinger of Health, Containing Medical Prescriptions for the Human Body & Mind. 428p. 1996. reprint ed. spiral bd. 28.50 (*0-7873-0256-2*) Hlth Research.

— The Harmonial Philosophy. 428p. 1996. reprint ed. spiral bd. 24.50 (*0-7873-0246-5*) Hlth Research.

— The Limits of Educational Assessment. (Journal of Philosophy of Education Ser.: Vol. 32). 224p. 1999. pap. 29.95 (*0-631-21020-2*, Pub. by Blckwll Scitfc UK) Blackwell Pubs.

— The Magic Staff: An Autobiography of Andrew Jackson Davis. 5th ed. 552p. 1998. reprint ed. pap. 24.50 (*0-7873-0241-4*) Hlth Research.

— Memoranda of Persons, Places, & Events: Embracing Authentic Facts, Visions, Impressions, Discoveries, in Magnetism, Clairvoyance, Spiritualism. 488p. 1996. reprint ed. spiral bd. 21.00 (*0-7873-0242-2*) Hlth Research.

— The Penetralia: Being Harmonial Answers to Important Questions. 516p. 1997. reprint ed. pap. 24.50 (*0-7873-0253-8*) Hlth Research.

— The Philosophy of Death. 8p. 1993. reprint ed. spiral bd. 8.00 (*0-7873-1063-8*) Hlth Research.

— The Philosophy of Spiritual Intercourse Being an Explanation of Modern Mysteries (1853) 150p. 1998. reprint ed. pap. 19.95 (*0-7661-0366-8*) Kessinger Pub.

— The Present Age & Inner Life: A Sequel to Spiritual Intercourse. 281p. 1996. reprint ed. spiral bd. 21.00 (*0-7873-0244-9*) Hlth Research.

— The Principles of Nature, Her Divine Revelations, (&) a Voice to Mankind, 2 vols. 34th ed. 800p. 1996. reprint ed. pap. 62.50 (*0-7873-0255-4*) Hlth Research.

— The Temple: Concerning Diseases of the Brain & Nerves. 487p. 1996. reprint ed. spiral bd. 24.50 (*0-7873-0250-3*) Hlth Research.

— Views of Our Heavenly Home. 290p. 1996. reprint ed. spiral bd. 21.00 (*0-7873-0252-X*) Hlth Research.

Davis, Andrew M. Currency & Banking in the Province of the Massachusetts-Bay, 2 vols., Set, Vols. 1-2. LC 68-55700. (Library of Money & Banking History). (Illus.). 1970. reprint ed. 95.00 (*0-678-00637-7*) Kelley.

— Journey of Moncacht-Ape. 1968. reprint ed. 9.95 (*0-87770-009-5*) Ye Galleon.

Davis, Andrew M., ed. Colonial Currency Reprints, 1682-1751, 4 vols., Set. LC 64-14707. (Reprints of Economic Classics Ser.). 1964. reprint ed. 195.00 (*0-678-00041-7*) Kelley.

***Davis, Andrew N.** ISO 14001: Meeting Business Goals Through an Effective Environmental Management System. LC 99-182814. 72p. 1998. write for info. (*0-87622-777-9*) Aspen Pub.

Davis, Andrew N. & Schaffman, Paul. The Home Environmental Checklist: 50 Environmental Questions to Ask When Buying, Selling or Maintaining a Home. LC 96-17749. 256p. 1995. pap. 19.95 (*0-8050-4177-X*, Owl) H Holt & Co.

Davis, Andy. The Beatles Files. (Illus.). 160p. 1998. 19.99 (*1-85833-857-3*) Quadrillion Pubng.

***Davis, Andy.** Beatles Files. (Illus.). 160p. 2000. 14.98 (*1-58663-100-4*) M Friedman Pub Grp Inc.

Davis, Angela. If They Come in the Morning: Voices of Resistance. (Illus.). 256p. 1971. 29.95 (*0-89388-022-1*) Okpaku Communications.

— If They Come in the Morning: Voices of Resistance. (Illus.). 256p. 1992. pap. 17.95 (*0-89388-217-8*) Okpaku Communications.

***Davis, Angela.** The Prison Industrial Complex. 1999. cd-rom 14.98 (*1-902593-22-7*, Pub. by AK Pr) SPD-Small Pr Dist.

Davis, Angela Y. Angela Davis: An Autobiography. LC 88-8232. (Illus.). 408p. 1988. reprint ed. pap. 14.95 (*0-7178-0667-7*) Intl Pubs Co.

— Blues Legacies & Black Feminism: Gertrude "Ma" Rainey, Bessie Smith & Billie Holiday. LC 97-33021. (Illus.). 427p. 1998. 27.50 (*0-679-45005-X*) Pantheon.

— Blues Legacies & Black Feminists. 1999. 15.00 (*0-679-77126-3*) Discovery.

— Violence Against Women & the Ongoing Challenge to Racism. (Freedom Organizing Pamphlet Ser.). 20p. (Orig.). (C). 1987. pap. 3.95 (*0-913175-11-0*) Kitchen Table.

— Woman, Culture & Politics. 1989. 17.95 (*0-318-41492-9*) Random.

— Women, Culture, & Politics. 1990. pap. 12.00 (*0-679-72487-7*) Vin Bks.

— Women, Race & Class. LC 82-40414. 288p. (C). 1983. pap. 12.00 (*0-394-71351-6*) Vin Bks.

Davis, Anita. Reading Instruction Essentials. 2nd ed. (Illus.). 280p. (C). 1999. pap. text 24.95 (*0-89641-323-3*) American Pr.

Davis, Anita & Hall, Ed Y. Harriet Quimby - America's First Lady of the Air: A Biography for Intermediate Readers. (Aviation History Ser.: Vol. 5). (Illus.). 96p. (YA). (gr. 5-12). 1998. lib. bdg., mass mkt. 10.95 (*1-885354-06-1*) Honoribus Pr.

Davis, Anita & Preston, Katharine. Discoveries: Significant Contributions of Deaf Women & Men. (Illus.). 96p. (Orig.). 1996. pap. text 14.95 (*1-884362-14-1*) Butte Pubns.

Davis, Anita P. LSAT TestBuster. 250p. 2000. pap. 19.95 (*0-87891-144-8*) Res & Educ.

Davis, Anita P. & Hall, Ed Y. Harriet Quimby America's First Lady of the Air: An Activity Book for Children. (Aviation History Ser.). (Illus.). 40p. (Orig.). (J). (gr. 4-8). 1993. wbk. ed. 4.95 (*0-9622166-5-8*) Honoribus Pr.

Davis, Anita P., jt. auth. see Bell, Robert.

Davis, Ann. The Logic of Ecstasy: Canadian Mystical Painting, 1920-1940. (Illus.). 216p. 1992. text 60.00 (*0-8020-5916-3*) U of Toronto Pr.

Davis, Ann. The Logic of Ecstasy: Canadian Mystical Painting, 1920-1940. (Illus.). 216p. 1992. pap. text 24.95 (*0-8020-6861-8*) U of Toronto Pr.

Davis, Ann, ed. Guide to Reprints, 1998: An International Bibliography of Scholarly Reprints. 1998. 170.00 (*0-918086-24-8*) Guide to Reprints.

Davis, Ann, jt. ed. see Brook, Eve.

Davis, Ann B. Alice's Brady Bunch Cookbook. LC 94-29393. (Illus.). 256p. 1994. spiral bd. 12.95 (*1-55853-307-9*) Rutledge Hill Pr.

Davis, Ann E., et al. Schizophrenics in the New Custodial Community: Five Years after the Experiment. LC 74-11383. (Illus.). 242p. reprint ed. pap. 75.10 (*0-608-09665-2*, 206978000006) Bks Demand.

Davis, Ann K., jt. auth. see Albers, Henry H.

Davis, Ann S., ed. Guide to Reprints: An International Bibliography of Scholarly Reprints. 950p. 1994. text 160.00 (*0-918086-20-5*) Guide to Reprints.

— Guide to Reprints: 1981 Edition, 2 vols. rev. ed. LC 66-29279. 974p. 1981. 75.00 (*0-918086-07-8*) Guide to Reprints.

— Guide to Reprints: 1983 Edition. 87.50 (*0-918086-09-4*) Guide to Reprints.

— Guide to Reprints, 1985. LC 66-29279. 1985. 95.00 (*0-918086-11-6*) Guide to Reprints.

— Guide to Reprints 1986. LC 66-29279. 1986. 110.00 (*0-918086-12-4*) Guide to Reprints.

— Guide to Reprints 1987. LC 66-29279. 1987. 125.00 (*0-317-61574-2*) Guide to Reprints.

Davis, Anne, jt. auth. see Baker, Susan S.

Davis, Anne B., jt. auth. see Kalkman, Markian E.

Davis, Anne C. Come, Go with Me: Following Christ's Example of Ministry & Witness. 116p. 1997. per. 6.95 (*1-56309-193-3*, W973107) Womans Mission Union.

Davis, Anne J., et al. Ethical Dilemmas & Nursing Practice. 4th ed. LC 96-41638. 275p. (C). 1997. pap. text 36.95 (*0-8385-2283-1*, A-2283-8) Appleton & Lange.

***Davis, Annette B.** Wine Sense Diet. LC 99-57590. 2000. 29.95 (*0-89526-256-8*, Gateway Editions) Regnery Pub.

D

Davis, Annie. The Little Book of Miracles: Testimonies of God's Grace. 112p. 1998. pap. 6.99 (*1-884369-83-9*) McDougal Pubng.

Davis, Anthony C. Tolley's Taxation in Corporate Insolvency. 288p. 1991. 105.00 (*0-85459-536-8*, Pub. by Tolley Pubng) St Mut.

— Tolley's Taxation in Corporate Insolvency. 290p. (C). 1995. 195.00 (*0-85459-573-2*, Pub. by Tolley Pubng) St Mut.

Davis, Anthony C. & Jackson, Jeffrey. Yo, Little Brother: Basic Rules of Survival for Young African American Males. 120p. (YA). (gr. 7 up). 1998. pap. 14.95 (*0-913543-58-6*) African Am Imag.

***Davis, Anthony E.** The Year 2000 Problem & the Legal Profession: Managing the Risks. LC 98-74372. 41p. 1998. write for info. (*1-57073-632-4*) Amer Bar Assn.

***Davis, Anthony R.** Linking by Types in the Hierarchical Lexicon. LC 99-43705. (Studies in Constraint-Based Lexicalism (SCBL): No. 4). 280p. 1999. 64.95 (*1-57586-223-9*, Pub. by CSLI); pap. 22.95 (*1-57586-224-7*, Pub. by CSLI) Cambridge U Pr.

Davis, Archie K. Boy Colonel of the Confederacy: The Life & Times of Henry King Burgwyn, Jr. LC 84-26958. (Illus.). 424p. 1998. reprint ed. pap. 19.95 (*0-8078-4709-7*) U of NC Pr.

Davis, Ardie. Great Barbecue Sauce Book. LC 98-42434. (Illus.). 160p. 1999. pap. 15.95 (*0-89815-944-X*) Ten Speed Pr.

Davis, Arnold R. & Miller, Donald C. Science Games. (J). (gr. 1-6). 1974. pap. 4.99 (*0-8224-6303-2*) Fearon Teacher Aids.

Davis, Art, et al, eds. Athletic Drug Reference '95. 1995. 9.95 (*1-881011-04-6*) Clean Data.

Davis, Arthur. Elvis Presley: Quote Unquote. (Illus.). 79p. 1998. text 22.00 (*0-7881-5770-1*) DIANE Pub.

Davis, Arthur, ed. George Grant & the Subversion of Modernity: Art, Philosophy, Religion, Politics & Education. 288p. 1996. text 60.00 (*0-8020-0668-X*); pap. text 19.95 (*0-8020-7622-X*) U of Toronto Pr.

Davis, Arthur K. Farewell to Earth Vol. I: The Collected Writings of Arthur K. Davis. LC 91-39085. 500p. 1991. 45.00 (*0-912362-09-X*) Adamant Pr.

— Farewell to Earth Vol. II: Selected Writings of Arthur K. Davis. LC 91-39085. 785p. 1993. 60.00 (*0-912362-10-3*) Adamant Pr.

— Folk-Songs of Virginia. LC 79-163676. reprint ed. 37.50 (*0-404-01987-0*) AMS Pr.

— Matthew Arnold's Letters: A Descriptive Checklist. LC 68-14092. 478p. reprint ed. pap. 148.20 (*0-608-11327-1*, 201142400078) Bks Demand.

— Thorstein Veblen's Social Theory. Zuckerman, Harriet & Merton, Robert K., eds. LC 79-8989. (Dissertations on Sociology Ser.). 1980. lib. bdg. 46.95 (*0-405-12961-0*) Ayer.

Davis, Arthur K. & Brady, James P. Farewell to Earth: Edging into Mainstream, Vol. III. (Illus.). 275p. 2000. write for info. (*0-912362-19-7*) Adamant Pr.

Davis, Arthur P. From the Dark Tower: Afro-American Writers, 1900 to 1960. LC 73-88969. 306p. (C). 1974. 29.50 (*0-88258-004-3*) Howard U Pr.

— From the Dark Tower: Afro-American Writers, 1900 to 1960. LC 73-88969. 306p. (C). 1981. pap. 14.95 (*0-88258-058-2*) Howard U Pr.

Davis, Arthur P., et al. The New Cavalcade, 2 vols., Set. 1990. pap. 60.00 (*0-88258-135-X*) Howard U Pr.

— The New Cavalcade II. 1992. pap. 32.95 (*0-88258-134-1*) Howard U Pr.

Davis, Arthur P., ed. see Redding, J. Saunders & Joyce, Joyce A.

Davis, Artice M., ed. Circuit Analysis Exam File. LC 85-25346. (Exam File Ser.). 314p. 1986. pap. 19.50 (*0-910554-53-6*) Engineering.

Davis, Ascar A. First Baptist Church History, Gadsden, Alabama, 1855- 1985. 256p. 1987. write for info. (*0-942407-01-6*) Father & Son.

Davis, Ascher. My Grandma the Monster. (Illus.). 32p. (J). reprint ed. pap. 2.95 (*0-88961-099-1*, Pub. by Womens Pr) LPC InBook.

Davis, Asiyih, jt. auth. see Runyon, Cheryl C.

Davis, Aubrey. Bone Button Borscht. (Illus.). 32p. (J). 1995. pap. 5.95 (*1-55074-326-0*) Kids Can Pr.

Davis, Aubrey. Bone Button Borscht. unabridged ed. (Illus.). 32p. (J). (gr. k-4). 1997. 14.95 (*1-55074-224-8*, Pub. by Kids Can Pr) Genl Dist Srvs.

Davis, Aubrey. The Enormous Potato. (Illus.). 136p. (J). 1997. pap. 5.95 (*1-55074-669-3*) Kids Can Pr.

Davis, Audrey B. Circulation Physiology & Medical Chemistry in England, 1650-1680. (Illus.). 263p. 1973. 17.50 (*0-87291-059-8*) Coronado Pr.

— Medicine & Its Technology: An Introduction to the History of Medical Instruments, 7. LC 80-25202. (Contributions in Medical History Ser.: No. 7). (Illus.). 285p. 1981. 69.50 (*0-313-22807-8*, DMT/, Greenwood Pr) Greenwood.

Davis, Audrey B. & Merzbach, Uta C. Early Auditory Studies: Activities in the Psychology Laboratories of American Universities. LC 75-619025. (Smithsonian Studies in History & Technology: No. 31). (Illus.). 46p. reprint ed. pap. 30.00 (*0-608-30836-6*, 200423000042) Bks Demand.

Davis, Audrey C. Metaphysical Techniques That Really Work. 144p. 1996. pap. text 12.95 (*0-87554-597-1*, B939) Valley Sun.

Davis, Aviva. A Quick Guide to Decorating Your Home Yourself. (Illus.). 35p. (Orig.). 1995. pap. 12.95 (*0-9647085-0-7*) Expo Group.

Davis, Avram. The Way of Flame: A Guide to the Forgotten Mystical Tradition of Jewish Meditation. LC 95-46074. 1996. pap. 10.00 (*0-06-061753-5*) Harper SF.

— The Way of Flame: A Guide to the Forgotten Mystical Tradition of Jewish Meditation. LC 99-36860. 176p. 1999. pap. 15.95 (*1-58023-060-1*) Jewish Lights.

Davis, Avram, ed. Meditation from the Heart of Judaism: Today's Teachers Share Their Practices, Techniques & Faith. LC 97-35827. 256p. 1997. 21.95 (*1-879045-77-X*) Jewish Lights.

— Meditation from the Heart of Judaism: Today's Teachers Share Their Practices, Techniques & Faith. 256p. 1999. pap. 16.95 (*1-58023-049-0*) Jewish Lights.

Davis, Avram & Shendelman, Sara. Traditions: The Complete Book of Prayers, Rituals, & Blessings for Every Jewish Home. LC 98-203049. (Illus.). 256p. (J). 1998. 21.45 (*0-7868-6381-1*, Pub. by Hyperion) Time Warner.

Davis, Avrohom. The Metsudah Chumash-Rashi on Exodus, Vol. 2. Date not set. 23.95 (*0-88125-414-2*) Ktav.

— The Metsudah Chumash-Rashi on Levitcus, Vol. 3. Date not set. 23.95 (*0-88125-493-2*) Ktav.

— The Metsudah Chumash-Rashi on Numbers, Vol. 4. 1995. 23.95 (*0-88125-514-9*) Ktav.

— Metsudah Five Meggilahs. Date not set. 14.95 (*0-88125-510-6*) Ktav.

— Metsudah Haggadah. Date not set. 10.95 (*0-88125-480-0*) Ktav.

— Metsudah Siddur. 1995. pap. 10.95 (*0-88125-552-1*) Ktav.

— Metsudah Tehillim. 1995. 14.95 (*0-88125-576-9*); pap. 9.95 (*0-88125-513-0*) Ktav.

Davis, Avrohom & Kleinkaufman, Avrohom. The Metsudah Chumash-Rashi on Bereishis. Date not set. 23.95 (*0-88125-389-8*) Ktav.

— The Metsudah Chumash-Rashi on Devarim Deutoronomy, Vol. 5. 1996. 23.95 (*0-88125-529-7*) Ktav.

Davis, B. & Stevens. Cell Structure & Function. (Integrated Medical Sciences Ser.). (C). 2000. pap. 22.95 (*1-889325-25-2*, Pub. by Fence Crk Pubng) Blackwell Sci.

Davis, B., et al. German Expressionist Prints & Drawings, 2 vols. (Illus.). 846p. 1989. 268.00 (*3-7913-0959-5*, Pub. by Prestel) te Neues.

Davis, B. D. Principles of Botany. (Illus.). 78p. (C). 1998. 18.00 (*1-887052-06-2*) SOS Pubns NJ.

Davis, B. L. Glossary Glossary Glossary: Value & Goal Program & Kit. 8p. 1995. pap., teacher ed., student ed. 10.00 (*0-9640982-5-3*) B L Davis.

— Value & Goal Program & Kit: Christian Edition. 83p. 1995. pap., teacher ed., student ed. 19.50 (*0-9640982-7-X*) B L Davis.

— Value & Goal Program & Kit with Glossary. rev. ed. 65p. 1995. reprint ed. pap. text, teacher ed. 19.00 (*0-9640982-2-9*) B L Davis.

Davis, B. L., ed. see Dan, Lea.

Davis, B. W. Warren, Jackson & Allied Families: Being the Ancestry of Jesse Warren & Betsey Jackson. (Illus.). 207p. 1992. reprint ed. pap. 32.50 (*0-8328-2759-2*); reprint ed. lib. bdg. 42.50 (*0-8328-2758-4*) Higginson Bk Co.

Davis, B. Walker. Which Mrs. Turner? LC 99-70434. 352p. 1999. 25.95 (*1-57197-172-6*) Pentland Pr.

Davis, Bailey F. Amherst County, Virginia, Wills, 1761-1865. 472p. 1985. 37.50 (*0-89308-302-X*) Southern Hist Pr.

— The Deeds of Amherst County, Virginia, 1808-1852, Books S-2, Vol. 3. 420p. 1985. 37.50 (*0-89308-363-1*) Southern Hist Pr.

— Lynchburg, Virginia, & Nelson County, Virginia: Wills, Deeds & Marriages, 1807-1831. 252p. 1985. reprint ed. 30.00 (*0-89308-289-9*) Southern Hist Pr.

Davis, Bailey F. The Deeds of Amherst County, Virginia, 1808-1852, Books L-R Vol. 2. 384p. 1985. 35.00 (*0-89308-301-1*) Southern Hist Pr.

Davis, Barbara. Field Guide to Birds of the Desert Southwest. LC 96-48172. (Gulf's Field Guide Ser.). 320p. 1997. pap. 21.95 (*0-88415-278-2*, 5278) Gulf Pub.

— Precious Angels: A True Story of Two Slain Children & a Mother Convicted of Murder, 1 vol. LC 99-187309. 1999. mass mkt. 6.99 (*0-451-40853-5*, Onyx) NAL.

— Suffer the Little Children. 320p. 1999. mass mkt. 6.50 (*0-7860-0664-1*) Kensgtn Pub Corp.

Davis, Barbara, ed. Remaking Cities: Proceedings of the 1988 International Conference in Pittsburgh. LC 89-60853. (Illus.). 200p. 1989. pap. 12.95 (*0-8229-6906-8*) U of Pittsburgh Pr.

Davis, Barbara & Newland, Joseph N. Henry Art Gallery, University of Washington, 1927-1986. LC 86-22916. (Illus.). 80p. 1986. 29.95 (*0-935558-20-9*) Henry Art.

Davis, Barbara, et al. American Catholic Schools for the 21st Century Vol. 1: Reflections on the Future of American Catholic Elementary Schools. Kealey, Robert J., ed. LC 98-144517. 43p. 1996. pap. 8.00 (*1-55833-182-4*) Natl Cath Educ.

Davis, Barbara, jt. auth. see Skalias, La Vonne.

Davis, Barbara, ed. see Mochnick, Beth R.

Davis, Barbara, ed. see Rollins, Mary R.

Davis, Barbara, ed. see Shannon, Patricia J. & Dyster, Floy.

Davis, Barbara, ed. see Wilson, Kyndra.

Davis, Barbara A., ed. see Bain, William J. & Bain, Mildred C.

Davis, Barbara Brewer, jt. auth. see Towner-Larsen, Susan.

Davis, Barbara G. Tools for Teaching. LC 93-19500. (Higher Education-Adult & Continuing Education Ser.). 457p. 1993. text 36.95 (*1-55542-568-2*) Jossey-Bass.

Davis, Barbara G., et al. The Evaluation of Composition Instruction. LC 80-68774. 230p. (Orig.). (C). 1981. pap. 7.50 (*0-918528-11-9*) Edgepress.

— The Evaluation of Composition Instruction. 2nd ed. 256p. (Orig.). (C). 1987. 27.00 (*0-8077-2850-0*) Tchrs Coll.

— The Evaluation of Composition Instruction. 2nd ed. LC 87-9348. 251p. (Orig.). 1987. reprint ed. pap. 77.90 (*0-608-02762-6*, 206382800007) Bks Demand.

Davis, Barbara J. In the Way: A Novel of Love & Loss. 2nd ed. (Illus.). 320p. 1994. pap. 14.95 (*0-9632975-2-X*) Sampo Pub.

Davis, Barbara K. Read All Your Life: A Subject Guide to Fiction. LC 89-42709. 296p. 1989. lib. bdg. 39.95 (*0-89950-370-5*) McFarland & Co.

Davis, Barbara K. & Sommer, Barry. You Can Choose Your Own Life: A Decision-Making Program for Students. 56p. 1992. pap., teacher ed. 26.40 (*0-89106-057-X*) Consulting Psychol.

— You Can Choose Your Own Life: Stories for Decision Making. 112p. (J). (gr. 6-8). 1992. pap., student ed. 8.80 (*0-89106-058-8*) Consulting Psychol.

Davis, Bart. Atlantic Run. McCarthy, Paul, ed. 304p. (Orig.). 1993. mass mkt. 5.50 (*0-671-76904-9*, Pocket Star Bks) PB.

— Conspiracy of Eagles. 1995. mass mkt. 5.99 (*0-671-76099-8*) PB.

— Destroy the Kentucky. McCarthy, Paul, ed. 416p. (Orig.). 1992. mass mkt. 5.50 (*0-671-69664-5*) PB.

— Full Fathom Five. (Orig.). 1995. mass mkt. 5.99 (*0-671-76102-1*) PB.

— Raise the Red Dawn. 352p. 1991. mass mkt. 4.95 (*0-671-69663-7*, Pocket Star Bks) PB.

— The Voyage of the Storm. 1995. mass mkt. 5.99 (*0-671-76905-7*) PB.

***Davis, Bart O.** A Desktop Guide to Restoring Dignity & Leadership: How to Restore the Dignity & Leadership That Have Been Engineered Out of the Workforce; a How-to Manual for First-Time Supervisors & a Refresher for Leaders. LC 99-490064. 85p. 1999. pap. 14.95 (*0-9672130-0-2*) B&K Solutions.

Davis, Bea. Cam Jansen & the Mystery of the Dinosaur Bones: A Study Guide. (Novel-Ties Ser.). (J). (gr. 1-3). 1986. pap. text, teacher ed., student ed. 15.95 (*0-88122-068-X*) Lrn Links.

Davis, Beatrice G. All of a Kind Family: A Study Guide. (Novel-Ties Ser.). (J). (gr. 3-6). 1984. pap. text, teacher ed., student ed. 15.95 (*0-88122-072-8*) Lrn Links.

— The Lion, the Witch & the Wardrobe: A Study Guide. (Novel-Ties Ser.). (J). (gr. 3-5). 1985. pap. text, teacher ed., student ed. 15.95 (*0-88122-078-7*) Lrn Links.

— Westing Game: A Study Guide. (Novel-Ties Ser.). (J). (gr. 5-7). 1984. pap. text, teacher ed., lab manual ed. 15.95 (*0-88122-096-5*) Lrn Links.

Davis, Beatrice G., et al. Black Boy. (Novel-Ties Ser.). (YA). (gr. 9-12). 1984. pap. text, teacher ed., student ed. 15.95 (*0-88122-105-8*) Lrn Links.

Davis, Becke. The Foliage Garden: Creating Tapestries of Color, Shape, & Texture. LC 99-167171. (Illus.). 144p. 1998. 27.50 (*1-56799-696-5*, Friedman-Fairfax) M Friedman Pub Grp Inc.

— Garden Blueprints. (Illus.). 128p. 1998. 25.00 (*1-56799-447-4*, Friedman-Fairfax) M Friedman Pub Grp Inc.

***Davis, Belinda.** Home Fires Burning: Food, Politics & Everyday Life in World War I Berlin. LC 99-32578. 424p. 2000. pap. 24.95 (*0-8078-4837-9*) U of NC Pr.

***Davis, Belinda J.** Home Fires Burning: Food, Politics & Everyday Life in World War I Berlin. LC 99-32578. (Illus.). 2000. lib. bdg. 55.00 (*0-8078-2526-3*) U of NC Pr.

Davis, Benjamin G. Economics: An Integrated Approach. LC 96-47277. (Illus.). 329p. (C). 1997. pap. text 60.00 (*0-13-082810-6*) P-H.

Davis, Benjamin J. Communist Councilman from Harlem. LC 90-21426. (Illus.). 248p. 1991. reprint ed. pap. 6.95 (*0-7178-0680-4*) Intl Pubs Co.

***Davis, Benjamin O., Jr.** Benjamin O. Davis, Jr., American: An Autobiography. 480p. 2000. pap. 17.95 (*1-56098-395-7*) Smithsonian.

Davis, Bernard. Food & Beverage Management. 3rd ed. 416p. 1998. pap. 29.95 (*0-7506-3286-0*) Buttrwrth-Heinemann.

Davis, Bernard B. & Wood, W. Gibson, eds. Homeostatic Function & Aging. LC 85-18437. (Aging Ser.: Vol. 30). 222p. 1985. reprint ed. pap. 68.90 (*0-608-00404-9*, 206111800007) Bks Demand.

Davis, Bernard D. Storm over Biology: Essays on Science, Sentiment, & Public Policy. LC 85-63388. 330p. 1986. 31.95 (*0-87975-324-2*) Prometheus Bks.

Davis, Bernard D., ed. The Genetic Revolution: Scientific Prospects & Public Perceptions. LC 91-11019. (Illus.). 320p. 1991. pap. 16.95 (*0-8018-4239-5*) Johns Hopkins.

Davis, Bernard D., et al. Microbiology. 4th ed. LC 89-2338. (Illus.). 1237p. 1990. reprint ed. pap. 200.00 (*0-608-07243-5*, 206746800009) Bks Demand.

Davis, Bertam H. A Proof of Eminence: The Life of Sir John Hawkins. LC 72-75389. 466p. reprint ed. pap. 144.50 (*0-608-30311-9*, 201581400097) Bks Demand.

Davis, Bertha S., jt. auth. see Marshall, Jeffrey L.

Davis, Bertram H. Johnson Before Boswell. LC 72-12309. 222p. 1973. reprint ed. lib. bdg. 59.50 (*0-8371-6691-8*, DAJA, Greenwood Pr) Greenwood.

— Thomas Percy: A Scholar-Cleric in the Age of Johnson. LC 88-38842. (Illus.). 346p. (C). 1989. text 46.95 (*0-8122-8161-6*) U of Pa Pr.

Davis, Bertran E., ed. see Vincenet, Johannes.

Davis, Beth G. & Lass, Bonnie. Elementary Reading: Strategies That Work. LC 95-42255. 208p. (C). 1996. pap. text 26.00 (*0-205-15961-3*) Allyn.

Davis, Betsy S., jt. auth. see Ingersoll, Barbara D.

Davis, Betty J. The Storytellers in Marguerite de Navare's Heptameron. LC 77-93406. (French Forum Monographs: No. 9). 203p. (Orig.). 1978. pap. 10.95 (*0-917058-08-9*) French Forum.

Davis, Beverly, ed. see Jones, Lynne.

Davis, Beverly J. Chant of the Centuries. rev. ed. (Illus.). 240p. 1984. teacher ed. 4.00 (*0-87443-065-8*); text 32.00 (*0-87443-064-X*) Benson.

Davis, Bill. Computer & Information Systems: An Introduction, Text & Student Study Guide. 1996. 42.00 (*0-314-21808-4*) West Pub.

— A Fool for Forensics. 224p. (Orig.). 1996. pap. text 16.67 (*0-931054-47-8*) Clark Pub.

— From an Earthly to a Heavenly Image. 88p. 1997. pap. 9.00 (*0-8059-4090-1*) Dorrance.

***Davis, Bill.** Gardner's Guide to Traditional Animation Techniques: A Beginner's Guide to Creating Land Drawn Architecture. Ford, Bonney, ed. (Illus.). 224p. 1999. pap. write for info. (*0-9661075-5-1*) G Gardner Co.

Davis, Bill. Management, Information & Systems: An Introduction to Business Information Systems Student Note-Taking Guide. Date not set. student ed. 15.00 (*0-314-22005-4*) West Pub.

— Shipwrecks of the Atlantic: Montauk to Cape May, New Jersey. Barrett, Linda, ed. (Fisherman Library). (Illus.). 248p. (Orig.). (C). 1991. pap. text 18.95 (*0-923155-12-0*) Fisherman Lib.

— They Call Me Bill: Musings of an Enlightened Curmudgeon. LC 97-65226. 144p. 1997. 15.95 (*1-887750-56-8*) Rutledge Bks.

Davis, Bill & Tree, C. The Kennedy Library. LC 80-53154. (Illus.). 128p. 1980. pap. 9.95 (*0-916838-36-6*) Schiffer.

Davis, Bill, et al. Derivatives: Measuring Growth. 275p. 1993. pap. text. write for info. (*0-318-72200-3*) Addison-Wesley.

— Integrals: Measuring Accumulated Growth. 275p. (C). 1993. pap. text. write for info. (*0-318-72201-1*) Addison-Wesley.

Davis, Bill C. Mass Appeal. 1982. pap. 5.25 (*0-8222-0738-9*) Dramatists Play.

— Wrestlers. 1987. pap. 5.25 (*0-8222-1278-1*) Dramatists Play.

Davis, Billie. The Dynamic Classroom. LC 86-83084. (Sunday School Staff Training Ser.). 141p. 1987. pap., teacher ed. 2.95 (*0-88243-798-4*, 02-0798) Gospel Pub.

— Ensenando a Enfrentar los Crisis. (SPA.). 352p. 1995. pap. 9.99 (*0-8297-0512-0*) Vida Pubs.

— Renewing Hope: Helps for Helping Others. LC 95-79628. 176p. (Orig.). 1995. pap. 3.95 (*0-88243-327-X*) Gospel Pub.

***Davis, Billy.** Beat the Drum! This Old Man. LC 00-24932. (Rockin' Rhythm Band Board Books Ser.). (Illus.). 12p. (J). (ps-1). 2000. bds. 7.95 (*0-439-19262-5*) Scholastic Inc.

— Shake the Maracas! Row, Row, Row Your Boat. LC 00-24931. (Rockin' Rhythm Band Board Books Ser.). (Illus.). 12p. (J). (ps-1). 2000. bds. 7.95 (*0-439-19261-7*) Scholastic Inc.

— Tap the Tambourine! Old MacDonald. (Rockin' Rhythm Band Board Books Ser.). (Illus.). 12p. (J). (ps-1). 2000. 7.95 (*0-439-19260-9*, Cartwheel) Scholastic Inc.

***Davis, Billy & Taylor, Jane.** Ring the Bells! Twinkle, Twinkle, Little Star. LC 00-24933. (Rockin' Rhythm Band Board Books Ser.). (Illus.). 12p. (J). (ps-1). 2000. bds. 7.95 (*0-439-19263-3*) Scholastic Inc.

***Davis, Bob.** Ephesians. (Bible Commentary Ser.). 166p. 1999. pap. 9.95 (*0-9671507-1-X*) Apply Within.

— Galatians. (Bible Commentary Ser.). 208p. 1999. pap. 9.95 (*0-9671507-0-1*) Apply Within.

— Hum-Hum: A Lesson in Love & Acceptance. (Walk in Wisdom Ser.). 24p. 1999. pap. 1.95 (*0-9671507-4-4*) Apply Within.

Davis, Bob. Physical Education & the Study of Sport. 2nd ed. 448p. (C). 1994. text 26.95 (*0-7234-1972-8*) Mosby Inc.

— Prosperity: Coming Twenty-Year Boom & What it Mean. LC 97-44858. 1998. 27.50 (*0-8129-2819-9*, Times Bks) Crown Pub Group.

— Prosperity: The Coming Twenty Year Boom & What It Means to You. 324p. 1999. pap. 14.00 (*0-8129-3200-5*, Times Bks) Crown Pub Group.

***Davis, Bob.** The Purpose of Suffering. 19p. 1999. pap. 1.95 (*0-9671507-2-8*) Apply Within.

Davis, Bob. Whatever Happened to High School History? 278p. pap. 19.95 (*1-55028-486-X*, Pub. by J Lorimer) Formac Dist Ltd.

***Davis, Bob.** When Things Go Wrong. (Walk in Wisdom Ser.). 22p. 1999. pap. 1.95 (*0-9671507-3-6*) Apply Within.

Davis, Bob, jt. auth. see Dorsman, Jerry.

Davis, Bob J. & Walter, C. K. Contract Railroad Rates. Hattwick, Richard E., ed. 175p. 1984. pap. 25.00 (*0-931497-01-9*) WIU CBER.

Davis, Bobby J. The Armour of Prayer. 65p. pap. write for info. (*0-9649866-1-2*) Miracle Faith.

— First Fruits & Tithes: Are They the Same & Do They Apply Today? 36p. 1999. pap. write for info. (*0-9649866-2-0*) Miracle Faith.

Davis, Bobby J. Help Heal the Wounds. LC 95-80866. 95p. (Orig.). 1995. pap. write for info. (*0-9649866-0-4*) Miracle Faith.

Davis, Bobbye J., jt. ed. see Brantley, Clarice P.

Davis, Bonnie, jt. auth. see Spangler, Randal.

Davis, Bonnie K. Phlebotomy: A Client-Based Approach. (Medical Lab Technician Ser.). (Illus.). 176p. (C). 1996. mass mkt. 35.95 (*0-8273-5453-3*) Delmar.

***Davis, Borbie.** Grammar as Rhetoric: Mastering Synactic Structure. 288p. (C). 2000. per. 61.95 (*0-7872-7125-X*) Kendall-Hunt.

Davis, Boyd H. & Brewer, Jeutonne P. Electronic Discourse: Linguistic Individuals in Virtual Space. LC 97-11131. (SUNY Series in Computer-Mediated Communication). 217p. (C). 1997. text 50.50 (*0-7914-3475-3*); pap. text 16.95 (*0-7914-3476-1*) State U NY Pr.

Davis, Boyd H. & O'Cain, Raymond K., eds. First Person Singular: Papers from the Conference on an Oral Archive for the History of American Linguistics (Charlotte NC, March 9-10, 1979) (Studies in the History of Linguistics Sciences : No. 21). xiv, 239p. (C). 1980. 59.00 (*90-272-4502-9*) J Benjamins Pubng Co.

D

An Asterisk (*) at the beginning of an entry indicates that the title is appearing for the first time.

Davis, Brad, ed. Promises Worth Keeping: Adventure Implementation Manual: (Nineteen Ninety-Nine 50-Day Spiritual Adventure Ser.). 1998. pap. 119.00 (*1-57849-116-9*) Mainstay Church.

— Promises Worth Keeping: Your Basic Guide to the 50-Day Spiritual Adventure. 1998. pap. 6.00 (*1-57849-126-6*) Mainstay Church.

Davis, Brad, ed. see Asimakoupoulos, Greg.

Davis, Brad, ed. see Campbell, Pam.

Davis, Brad, ed. see Koupoulos, Greg A.

Davis, Bradley H. Mastering Joker Wild Video Poker: How to Play As an Expert & Walk Away a Winner. LC 90-82847. 144p. (Orig.). 1990. pap. 14.95 (*0-9626766-5-9*) Applied Tech Pr.

***Davis, Brandon, et al.** 3D Studio Max 3 Effects Magic with CD-ROM. 325p. 2000. pap. 45.00 incl. cd-rom (*0-7357-0867-3*) New Riders Pub.

***Davis, Brangien.** What's Real, What's Ideal: Overcoming a Negative Body Image. 1999. pap. text 6.95 (*1-56838-258-8*) Hazelden.

Davis, Brangien. What's Real, What's Ideal: Overcoming a Negative Body Image. LC 98-29941. (Teen Health Library of Eating Disorder Prevention). (Illus.). 64p. (YA). (gr. 7-12). 1999. lib. bdg. 17.95 (*0-8239-2771-7*, EDREID) Rosen Group.

Davis, Brenda. Spirited Woman Devotional: 2000 Edition, Vol. 1. LC 99-37520. 1999. 14.99 (*0-88419-660-7*) Creation House.

Davis, Brendan. The Economics of Automatic Testing. 2nd ed. 352p. 1992. 60.00 (*0-07-707568-4*) McGraw.

— Economics of Automatic Testing. 2nd ed. 1994. 65.00 (*0-07-707792-X*) McGraw.

Davis, Brent. The Spelling Bee. 304p. 1996. 23.00 (*1-881320-66-9*, Black Belt) Black Belt Communs.

— Teaching Mathematics: Toward a Sound Alternative. Kincheloe, Joe, ed. LC 96-1697. (Critical Education Practice Ser.: Vol. 7). (Illus.). 360p. 1996. text 52.00 (*0-8153-2297-6*); pap. text 24.95 (*0-8153-2298-4*) Garland.

***Davis, Brent, et al.** Engaging Minds: Learning & Teaching in a Complex World. LC 00-27199. 224p. 2000. pap. write for info. (*0-8058-3785-X*) L Erlbaum Assocs.

Davis, Brenta G., et al. Clinical Laboratory Science: Strategies for Practice. (Illus.). 1024p. 1988. text 57.50 (*0-397-50860-3*) Lppncott W & W.

Davis, Brett. Bone Wars: Fossil Robbers from Outer Space--Sitting Bull to the Rescue. 1998. mass mkt. 53.91 (*0-671-71326-4*) Baen Bks.

— Hair of the Dog. 288p. 1997. per. 5.99 (*0-671-87762-3*) Baen Bks.

— Two Tiny Claws: Old Fossils Never Die... 1999. mass mkt. 5.99 (*0-671-57785-9*) Baen Bks.

Davis, Brian. Badges & Insignia of the Third Reich 1933-1945. 144p. 1999. pap. text 19.95 (*1-85409-512-9*) Arms & Armour.

— Gardener's Essential Plant Guide. LC 97-31339. (Illus.). 432p. 1997. 19.99 (*1-57145-601-5*, Laurel Glen Pub) Advantage Pubs.

— The Plant Selector: Over 1500 Garden Plants to Help You Pick Winning Combinations. LC 98-120900. (Illus.). 240p. 1998. 27.95 (*0-7063-7567-X*, Pub. by WrLock) Sterling.

Davis, Brian, ed. The Poetry of the Canadian People, 1720 to 1920, Vol. 1. (Illus.). 288p. (Orig.). 1995. pap. 10.95 (*0-919600-50-6*, Pub. by NC Ltd) U of Toronto Pr.

— The Poetry of the Canadian People 1900-1950, Vol. 2. (Illus.). 224p. 1978. pap. 12.95 (*0-919600-97-2*, Pub. by NC Ltd) U of Toronto Pr.

Davis, Brian L. Badges & Insignia of the Third Reich, 1933-1945. LC 83-131573. 1983. 17.95 (*0-7137-1130-2*) Blandford Pr.

— Flags of the Third Reich I No. 2: Waffen SS. (Men-at-Arms Ser.: No. 274). (Illus.). 48p. 1994. pap. 11.95 (*1-85532-446-6*, 9241, Pub. by Ospry) Stackpole.

— Flags of the Third Reich, No. 3: Party & Police Units. (Men-at-Arms Ser.: No. 278). (Illus.). 48p. 1994. pap. 11.95 (*1-85532-459-8*, 9250, Pub. by Ospry) Stackpole.

— Flags of the Third Reich 2: Waffen-SS. (Illus.). 48p. pap. 12.95 (*1-85532-431-8*, Pub. by Ospry) Stackpole.

— Qaddafi, Terrorism, & the Origins of the U. S. Attack on Libya. LC 89-16095. 213p. 1990. 45.00 (*0-275-93302-4*, C3302, Praeger Pubs) Greenwood.

***Davis, Brian L.** Uniforms & Insignia of the Luftwaffe, 1940-1945, Vol. 2. 320p. 1999. pap. 24.95 (*1-85409-498-X*) Arms & Armour.

Davis, Brian L. Uniforms & Insignia of the Luftwaffe: 1933-1940, 2. 1999. pap. text 24.95 (*1-85409-497-1*) Arms & Armour.

Davis, Brian L., et al, eds. Successful Manager's Handbook: Development Suggestions for Today's Managers. rev. ed. LC 98-128785. (Illus.). 808p. 1996. reprint ed. pap. 54.95 (*0-938529-03-X*, Pub. by Personnel Decisions) Bookmen Inc.

Davis, Brian T. & Davis, Kathy M. Tales of Black Fish Bear: Mystery of the Tides. (Illus.). 32p. (J). (ps-3). 1997. pap. 7.99 (*1-891166-00-X*, 1) Black Fish.

Davis, Bridget C. & Harrison, Ronald H. Hydrotherapy in Practice. (Illus.). 183p. 1988. pap. text 35.00 (*0-443-03062-6*) Church.

Davis, Britton. The Truth about Geronimo. Quaife, Milo M., ed. LC 75-37958. (Illus.). xxxii, 265p. 1976. reprint ed. pap. 10.95 (*0-8032-5840-2*, Bison Books) U of Nebr Pr.

Davis, Bruce. Charles Christopher Hill: Three Decades. 26p. 1995. pap. 15.00 (*0-9649724-0-9*) Cirrus Gallery.

— Geographic Information Systems: A Visual Approach. 392p. (C). 1996. pap. 47.95 (*1-56690-098-0*) Thomson Learn.

— How to Involve Parents in a Multicultural School. LC 95-4383. 1995. pap. 8.95 (*0-87120-247-6*) ASCD.

— Made in L. A. The Prints of Cirrus Editions. (Illus.). 368p. 65.00 (*0-87587-173-9*) LA Co Art Mus.

— The Magical Child Within You. LC 82-84601. 128p. (Orig.). 1995. reprint ed. pap. 7.95 (*0-89087-422-0*) Celestial Arts.

— Mannerist Prints: International Style in the Sixteenth Century. LC 88-12674. (Illus.). 336p. 1988. text 29.95 (*0-87587-147-X*) LA Co Art Mus.

— Master Drawings in the Los Angeles County Museum of Art. LC 97-73596. (Illus.). 244p. 1998. 60.00 (*1-55595-152-X*, Pub. by Hudson Hills) Natl Bk Netwk.

Davis, Bruce & Wright, Genny. Hugs & Kisses. LC 77-5283. (Illus.). 96p. 1978. pap. 4.50 (*0-89480-106-6*, 307) Workman Pub.

Davis, Bruce, jt. auth. see Feinblatt, Ebria.

Davis, Bruce A. Biogenic Monamines & Their Metabolites in the Urine, Plasma & Cerebrospinal Fluid of Normal, Psychiatric, & Neurological Subjects. LC 96-20558. (Illus.). 464p. 1990. 252.00 (*0-8493-4611-8*, RC455, CRC Reprint) Franklin.

Davis, Bruce H. Nature's Window - Charles Frace. Frace, Elke et al, eds. LC 91-71713. (Illus.). 168p. 1992. 65.00 (*1-880044-00-5*) Am Masters Found.

— Nature's Window - Charles Frace. deluxe ed. Frace, Elke et al, eds. LC 91-71713. (Illus.). 168p. 1992. 125.00 (*1-880044-01-3*) Am Masters Found.

Davis, Bruce L., compiled by. Criminological Bibliographies: Uniform Citations to Bibliographies, Indexes, & Review Articles of the Literature of Crime Study in the United States. LC 78-59442. 182p. 1978. lib. bdg. 49.95 (*0-313-20545-0*, DCR/) Greenwood.

Davis, Bryan. Jesus' Baptism & Temptation. LC 97-136034. 1997. pap. 1.99 (*0-570-07530-0*, 59-1503) Concordia.

***Davis, Bryn D.** Caring for People in Pain. LC 99-36130. 2000. pap. write for info. (*0-415-18891-1*) Routledge.

— Caring for People in Pain. LC 99-36130. (Essentials for Nurses Ser.). 264p. (C). 2000. text. write for info. (*0-415-18890-3*) Routledge.

Davis, Bryn D., ed. Research into Nurse Education. 208p. 1983. pap. 22.00 (*0-7099-0825-3*, Pub. by C Helm) Routldge.

Davis, Buddy. When Dragons' Hearts Were Good. LC 99-64018. 40p. 1999. boxed set 12.99 (*0-89051-259-0*) Master Bks.

Davis, Buddy & Davis, Kay. Special Wonders of the Sea World. LC 99-70078. (Special Wonders Ser.). (Illus.). 80p. 1999. boxed set 12.99 (*0-89051-253-1*) Master Bks.

— Special Wonders of the Wild Kingdom. LC 99-70079. (Special Wonders Ser.). (Illus.). 80p. 1999. boxed set 12.99 (*0-89051-254-X*) Master Bks.

Davis, Buddy, et al. Great Alaskan Dinosaur Adventure: Real Life Journey Through the Frozen Past. LC 98-66309. 144p. 1998. pap. text 10.99 (*0-89051-232-9*) Master Bks.

Davis, Burke. Black Heroes of the American Revolution. LC 75-42218. (Illus.). 80p. (J). (gr. 5 up). 1976. 14.95 (*0-15-208560-2*, Harcourt Child Bks) Harcourt.

— Black Heroes of the American Revolution. LC 91-8921. (Illus.). 80p. (YA). (gr. 5 up). 1992. pap. 5.00 (*0-15-208561-0*, Harcourt Child Bks) Harcourt.

— Black Heroes of the American Revolution. (J). 1991. 10.20 (*0-606-02522-7*, Pub. by Turtleback) Demco.

— The Campaign That Won America: The Story of Yorktown. (Illus.). 319p. 1979. reprint ed. pap. 4.95 (*0-915992-01-9*) Eastern National.

— Civil War: Strange & Fascinating Facts. 256p. 1988. 7.99 (*0-517-37151-0*) Random Hse Value.

— Gray Fox: Robert E. Lee & the Civil War. (Illus.). 480p. 1992. 9.99 (*0-517-34772-5*) Random Hse Value.

— Gray Fox: Robert E. Lee & the Civil War. rev. ed. LC 98-27652. (Illus.). 488p. 1998. pap. 18.95 (*1-58080-069-6*, Pub. by Burford Bks) Natl Bk Netwk.

***Davis, Burke.** Jeb Stuart: The Last Cavalier. LC 99-89611. (Illus.). 488p. 2000. pap. 18.95 (*1-58080-075-0*) Burford Bks.

Davis, Burke. Jeb Stuart, the Last Cavalier. LC 87-32017. (Illus.). 470p. 1992. 10.99 (*0-517-18597-0*) Random Hse Value.

— Marine! The Life of Chesty Puller. 400p. (YA). 1991. mass mkt. 6.99 (*0-553-27182-2*) Bantam.

— Sherman's March. Stone, Jeff & Reidy, Carolyn, eds. LC 87-45927. (Vintage Civil War Library). 356p. 1988. reprint ed. pap. 14.00 (*0-394-75763-7*) Random.

— The Southern Railway: Road of the Innovators. LC 84-15343. 317p. reprint ed. pap. 98.30 (*0-7837-0288-4*, 204060900018) Bks Demand.

— They Called Him Stonewall: A Life of Lieutenant General T. J. Jackson, C. S. A. LC 87-32655. (Illus.). 480p. 1988. 9.99 (*0-517-66204-3*) Random Hse Value.

— They Called Him Stonewall: A Life of Lieutenant General T. J. Jackson, C. S. A. LC 99-21661. (Classics of War Reprint Ser.). (Illus.). 488p. 1999. reprint ed. pap. 18.95 (*1-58080-029-7*) Burford Bks.

— To Appomattox: Nine April Days, 1865. 444p. 1989. reprint ed. pap. 4.25 (*0-915992-17-5*) Eastern National.

— War Bird: The Life & Times of Elliott White Springs. LC 87-5934. (Illus.). 308p. reprint ed. pap. 95.50 (*0-608-10496-5*, 207112500009) Bks Demand.

Davis, Burtron H. & Hettinger, William P., Jr., eds. Heterogeneous Catalysis: Selected American Histories. LC 83-8745. (ACS Symposium Ser.: No. 222). 532p. lib. bdg. 54.95 (*0-8412-0778-X*) Am Chemical.

— Heterogeneous Catalysis: Selected American Histories. LC 83-8745. (ACS Symposium Ser.: Vol. 222). 549p. 1983. reprint ed. pap. 170.20 (*0-608-03072-4*, 206352500007) Bks Demand.

Davis, Byron P., ed. see O'Connor, Michol.

Davis, C. Bibliography of Cicadulina, Homoptera, Cicadellidae Vectors of Maize Streak & Related Viruses. 1991. pap. 25.00 (*0-85954-288-2*, Pub. by Nat Res Inst) St Mut.

— Mannheim Steamroller: Fresh Aire 3. 64p. 1988. otabind 12.95 (*0-7935-2749-X*, 00357476) H Leonard.

***Davis, C.** Teacher's Pack on Experiments in Materials Science. 64p. 1998. pap. text, teacher ed. 40.00 (*1-86125-059-2*, Pub. by Inst Materials) Ashgate Pub Co.

Davis, C., et al, eds. The Geometric Vein: The Coxeter Festschrift. (Illus.). 512p. 1982. 144.95 (*0-387-90587-1*) Spr-Verlag.

Davis, C. H. The History of Wallingford, Connecticut: From Its Settlement in 1670 to the Present, Including Meriden & Cheshire. (Illus.). 956p. 1988. reprint ed. lib. bdg. 96.50 (*0-8328-0017-1*, CT0025) Higginson Bk Co.

Davis, C. K., tr. see De Espronceda, Jose.

Davis, C. N., et al. The Official Military Atlas of the Civil War: Atlas to Accompany the Official Records of the Union & Confederate Armies. 1979. 72.95 (*0-405-18842-0*, 19368) Ayer.

Davis, C. Thomas. Incorporation & Business Guide for Oregon: How to Form Your Own Corporation. 4th ed. (Oregon Legal Ser.). 120p. 1992. pap. 14.95 (*0-88908-834-9*) Self-Counsel Pr.

— Incorporation Forms for Oregon. (Legal Ser.). 120p. 1992. pap. 14.95 (*0-88908-835-7*) Self-Counsel Pr.

Davis, Calvin. Love in Opposing Colors: An Unsanctioned Romance. LC 93-93664. 170p. write for info. (*0-9639770-0-8*) T Z Leether Pubs.

Davis, Calvin C. The History of Midway-the Real Story. 400p. 1995. pap. 36.95 (*0-9645044-0-5*) C C Davis.

Davis, Calvin D. The United States & the Second Hague Peace Conference: American Diplomacy & International Organization, 1899-1914. LC 75-17353. ix, 398p. 1976. text 51.95 (*0-8223-0346-9*) Duke.

Davis, Camron. Gameboy Survival Guide: 1999 Edition. 1999. pap. text 12.95 (*1-884364-38-1*) Sandwich Islands.

Davis, Candace. Treasury of Scottie Dog Collectibles: Identification & Values. 1998. pap. text 19.95 (*1-57432-060-2*, 5057) Collector Bks.

Davis, Candace Sten & Baugh, Patricia. A Treasury of Scottie Dog Collectibles Bk. II: Identification & Values. 2nd ed. 176p. 1999. pap. text 19.95 (*1-57432-151-X*) Collector Bks.

Davis, Carl & Drackley, James. The Development, Nutrition, & Management of the Young Calf. (Illus.). 308p. 1998. text 62.95 (*0-8138-2980-1*) Iowa St U Pr.

Davis, Carl J. The Name & Way of the Lord: Old Testament Themes, New Testament Christology. LC 96-144621. (JSNT Supplement Ser.: No. 129). 227p. 1996. 65.00 (*1-85075-604-X*, Pub. by Sheffield Acad) CUP Services.

Davis, Carl S. & Schmidt, Marlin R., eds. Differential Treatment of Drug & Alcohol Abusers. LC 76-54203. 1977. 19.95 (*0-88280-048-5*) ETC Pubns.

***Davis, Carla Norman.** French Made Fun, Vol. 1, Bk. 1. 1999. teacher ed. 20.00 (*1-930272-06-5*) Queen Enter.

— French Made Fun, Vol. 1, Bk. 1. (J). (gr. 1-3). 1999. wbk. ed. 15.00 (*1-930272-04-9*) Queen Enter.

— French Made Fun, Vol. 1, Bk. 2. 1999. 22.00 (*1-930272-07-3*) Queen Enter.

— French Made Fun, Vol. 1, Bk. 2. (J). (gr. 4-5). 1999. wbk. ed. 15.00 (*1-930272-05-7*) Queen Enter.

— German Made Fun, Vol. 1, Bk. 1. 1999. teacher ed. 20.00 (*1-930272-10-3*) Queen Enter.

— German Made Fun, Vol. 1, Bk. 1. (J). (gr. 1-3). 1999. wbk. ed. 15.00 (*1-930272-08-1*) Queen Enter.

— German Made Fun, Vol. 1, Bk. 2. 1999. teacher ed. 22.00 (*1-930272-11-1*) Queen Enter.

— German Made Fun, Vol. 1, Bk. 2. (J). (gr. 4-5). 1999. wbk. ed. 15.00 (*1-930272-09-X*) Queen Enter.

— Japanese Made Fun, Vol. 1, Bk. 1. 1999. teacher ed. 20.00 (*1-930272-14-6*) Queen Enter.

— Japanese Made Fun, Vol. 1, Bk. 1. (J). (gr. 1-3). 1999. wbk. ed. 15.00 (*1-930272-12-X*) Queen Enter.

— Japanese Made Fun, Vol. 1, Bk. 2. 1999. teacher ed. 22.00 (*1-930272-15-4*) Queen Enter.

— Japanese Made Fun, Vol. 1, Bk. 2. (J). (gr. 4-5). 1999. wbk. ed. 15.00 (*1-930272-13-8*) Queen Enter.

— Spanish Made Fun, Vol. 1, Bk. 1. 1999. teacher ed. 20.00 (*1-930272-02-2*) Queen Enter.

— Spanish Made Fun, Vol. 1, Bk. 1. (J). (gr. 1-3). 1999. wbk. ed. 15.00 (*1-930272-00-6*) Queen Enter.

— Spanish Made Fun, Vol. 1, Bk. 2. 1999. teacher ed. 22.00 (*1-930272-03-0*) Queen Enter.

— Spanish Made Fun, Vol. 1, Bk. 2. (J). (gr. 4-5). 1999. wbk. ed. 15.00 (*1-930272-01-4*) Queen Enter.

Davis, Carlton F. Global Sundy School Hebrew & Greek Comprehensive Study Guide Dictionary. 130p. 1998. 19.95 (*0-9665096-0-9*) ELPIs-Notlrac.

Davis, Carlton G., jt. ed. see Coppedge, Robert O.

***Davis, Carol & Reese, Esther D.** Mirror's Edge. (Quantum Leap Ser.: No. XVIII). 2000. mass mkt. 6.99 (*0-425-17351-8*) Berkley Pub.

Davis, Carol & University of Hull Staff. Women's Conversations in a Minangkabau Market: Toward an Understanding of the Social Context of Economic Transactions. LC 98-147218. (Occasional Papers in Economic & Social History). 28p. 1997. write for info. (*0-85958-903-X*) Univ of Hull Pr.

Davis, Carol, jt. auth. see Moore, Tim.

***Davis, Carol A.** Safe As Houses. (Orig.). 1999. pap. 14.95 (*1-899344-47-0*, Pub. by Do-Not Pr) Dufour.

Davis, Carol A. Shrouded. LC 97-178267. (Bloodlines Ser.). 224p. 1997. pap. 14.95 (*1-899344-17-9*, Pub. by Do-Not Pr) Dufour.

Davis, Carol M. Complementary Therapies in Rehabilitation: Holistic Approaches for Prevention & Wellness. LC 96-44699. 352p. 1996. pap. 35.00 (*1-55642-281-4*, 42814) SLACK Inc.

— Patient Practitioner Interaction: An Experiential Manual for Developing the Art of Health Care. 3rd ed. LC 98-3498. (Illus.). 352p. 1998. pap. text 32.00 (*1-55642-400-0*, 44000) SLACK Inc.

— Patient Practitioner Interaction: Instructor's Manual. 3rd ed. 26p. 1998. pap. text, teacher ed. Price not set. (*1-55642-401-9*, 44019) SLACK Inc.

***Davis, Carole, et al.** Thematic Unit Kites: Primary. (Illus.). 80p. 2000. pap., teacher ed. 9.95 (*1-57690-367-2*, TCM 2367) Tchr Create Mat.

Davis, Carole B. & Fido, Elaine, eds. Out of the Kumbla: Womanist Perspectives on Caribbean Literature. LC 88-70199. 450p. 1989. 49.95 (*0-86543-042-X*); pap. 15.95 (*0-86543-043-8*) Africa World.

Davis, Carole M. & Graham, Dorothy. Planning Your Career: A Workshop Series for Women. 138p. (Orig.). 1981. pap., teacher ed. 12.00 (*1-55719-106-9*); pap., student ed. 9.50 (*1-55719-102-6*) U NE CPAR.

Davis, Carole M., et al. A Study of the Knowledge & Use of Hospice by Health Care Professionals in Omaha. 48p. (Orig.). 1984. pap. 3.50 (*1-55719-093-3*) U NE CPAR.

Davis, Carole M., jt. auth. see Burch, Genevieve.

Davis, Carole M., jt. auth. see DiMartino, David R.

Davis, Carole M., jt. auth. see Rood, Lois S.

Davis, Caroline. The Kingdom of the Horse: A Comprehensive Guide to the Horse & the Major Breeds. LC 98-11554. (Illus.). 1998. 34.95 (*0-87605-037-2*) Howell Bks.

***Davis, Caroline.** The Young Equestrian: Professional Instruction for Ambitious Riders. (Illus.). 178p. 2000. 29.95 (*1-55209-495-2*); pap. 19.95 (*1-55209-484-7*) Firefly Bks Ltd.

Davis, Caroline, jt. auth. see Bayley, Lesley.

Davis, Caroline F. The Evidential Force of Religious Experience. 278p. 1989. text 70.00 (*0-19-824436-3*) OUP.

— The Evidential Force of Religious Experience. 280p. 1999. pap. text 19.95 (*0-19-825001-0*) OUP.

Davis, Carolyn, jt. auth. see Davis, Don.

Davis, Carolyn O. Hopi Quilting: Stitched Traditions from an Ancient Community. Dart, Allen, ed. (Illus.). 128p. 1997. pap. 27.95 (*0-9635092-3-3*) Sanpete Pubns.

— Pioneer Quiltmaker: The Story of Dorinda Moody Slade, 1808-1895. Rooker, Margaret & Lynn, Stacey, eds. LC 90-62945. (Illus.). 80p. 1990. pap. 17.95 (*0-918080-75-4*) Treas Chest Bks.

— A Quilt for the Promised Valley. Di Donato, Lisa, ed. (Illus.). 64p. (Orig.). 1996. pap. 17.95 (*0-9635092-2-5*) Sanpete Pubns.

— Quilted All Day: The Prairie Journals of Ida Chambers Melugin. 128p. 1993. pap. 21.95 (*0-9635092-0-9*) Sanpete Pubns.

— Treasured Earth: Hattie Cosgrove's Mimbres Archaeology in the American Southwest. (Illus.). 216p. (Orig.). 1995. pap. 24.95 (*0-9635092-1-7*) Sanpete Pubns.

Davis, Carrie. The Naturally Sweet Baker. LC 97-17377. 1997. 25.00 (*0-02-861257-4*) Macmillan.

Davis, Casey W. Oral Biblical Criticism: The Influence of the Principles of Orality on the Literary Structure of Paul's Epistle to the Philippians. LC 99-179315. (JSNTS Ser.: Vol. 172). 196p. 1999. 57.50 (*1-85075-972-3*, Pub. by Sheffield Acad) CUP Services.

Davis, Catherine L. Talking with God. LC 96-46385. 1997. write for info. (*1-56476-608-X*, Victor Bks) Chariot Victor.

Davis, Catherine L., ed. see Richardson, Arleta.

Davis, Cathy. Baby Bible Devotions. (Illus.). 36p. (J). (ps). 1996. 11.99 (*0-7814-0304-9*, Chariot Bks) Chariot Victor.

— Faithful Friend. LC 98-182381. (Count Your Blessings: No. 1). 96p. 1998. 4.99 (*1-56476-690-X*, Victor Bks) Chariot Victor.

— A Place Called Home. LC 98-182366. (Count Your Blessings Ser.: No. 1). 96p. 1998. 4.99 (*1-56476-691-8*, Victor Bks) Chariot Victor.

Davis, Cathy, ed. Count Your Blessings Devotional. LC 98-182383. 384p. 1997. write for info. (*1-56476-693-4*, Victor Bks) Chariot Victor.

— A Place Called Heaven. LC 98-182281. (Count Your Blessings Ser.: No. 3). 96p. 1998. 4.99 (*1-56476-692-6*, Victor Bks) Chariot Victor.

Davis, Cathy, ed. see Biehl, Bobb.

Davis, Cathy, ed. see Evans, Debra.

***Davis, Cathy Durbin.** Big Dog Winnie. LC 99-67734. (Illus.). 40p. (J). 1999. 19.95 (*0-943335-18-3*) Marblehead Pub.

Davis, Cathy H. & Domina, Lyle. Structured Programming: PL-1 with PL-C. LC 87-12473. (Illus.). 704p. (C). 1995. pap. text 57.00 (*0-03-003723-9*) OUP.

Davis Caves Construction, Inc. Staff. Earth Sheltered Designs. rev. ed. Davis, Ruthanne & Davis, Martyn, eds. (Illus.). 90p. pap. 17.00 (*0-9700296-0-8*) Davis Caves Constr.

***Davis, Cecelia G.** The Ring of Fire. 254p. 1999. pap. 15.95 (*0-7414-0206-8*) Buy Books.

***Davis, Charles.** Allegiances: A Novel. LC 99-63299. 384p. 1999. 24.95 (*0-9675563-0-9*) Merriman Pr.

Davis, Charles. Ground Water Monitoring. (Applied Environmental Statistics Ser.). 2000. ring bd. 89.95 (*1-58488-077-5*, Chap & Hall CRC) CRC Pr.

***Davis, Charles.** The Letters & Diaries of a Combat Rifleman. 2000. pap. 18.00 (*0-8059-5047-8*) Dorrance.

Davis, Charles. Religion & the Making of Society: Essays in Social Theology. (Studies in Ideology & Religion: No. 4). 223p. (C). 1993. text 59.95 (*0-521-44310-5*); pap. text 19.95 (*0-521-44789-5*) Cambridge U Pr.

— Spirituality for the Vulnerable. LC 89-61233. 120p. 1990. reprint ed. pap. 8.95 (*1-55612-273-X*) Sheed & Ward WI.

— A Way of Life. Newman, Nancy K., ed. 132p. (Orig.). 1989. pap. 5.00 (*0-685-26555-2*) CMC Pr FL.

Davis, Charles, ed. American Numismatic Literature. LC 92-80471. 230p. 1992. 85.00 (*0-88000-147-X*) Quarterman.

D

— Database Management: How Much Power Is Enough?: Proceedings of the 1989 Clinic on Library Applications of Data Processing. 1991. 20.00 (*0-87845-082-3*) U of Ill Grad Sch.

— Western Public Lands & Environmental Politics. LC 96-48499. 224p. (C). 1997. pap. text 25.00 (*0-8133-2970-1*, Pub. by Westview) HarpC.

Davis, Charles & Davis, Linda. Mississippi. LC 98-19618. (America the Beautiful Ser.). 144p. (YA). (gr. 5-8). 1999. write for info. (*0-516-20688-5*) Childrens.

Davis, Charles & Lester, James P., eds. Hazardous Waste Politics & Policy. 208p. (Orig.). 1985. pap. 15.00 (*0-918592-84-4*) Pol Studies.

Davis, Charles & Varey, J. E., eds. Los Corrales de Comedias y los Hospitales De Madrid 1574-1615: Estudio y Documentos. (Fuentes Para la Historia del Teatro en Espana Ser.).Tr. of Theaters & Hospitals of Madrid 1574-1615. 360p. 1997. 54.00 (*1-85566-040-7*, Pub. by Tamesis Bks Ltd) Boydell & Brewer.

— Los Corrales de Comedias y los Hospitales de Madrid: 1615-1849: Estudio y Documentos, Vol. 2. (Fuentes Para la Historia del Teatro en Espana Ser.: Vol. 21). (SPA.). 300p. 1997. 69.00 (*1-85566-029-6*, Pub. by Tamesis Bks Ltd) Boydell & Brewer.

— Los Aposentos Laterales del Corral de la Cruz, 1582-1680: Estudio y Documentos. (Fuentes Para la Historia del Teatro en Espana Ser.: No. 0959-9487). (SPA.). 250p. 2001. 60.00 (*1-85566-061-X*) Boydell & Brewer.

Davis, Charles, jt. auth. see Gorfinkel, Claire.

Davis, Charles, ed. see De Armona, Jose A.

Davis, Charles, jt. ed. see Varey, J. E.

Davis, Charles A. Handbook for New College Teachers & Teaching Assistants. 60p. (Orig.). (C). 1992. pap. 8.00 (*0-9636197-0-5*) Davis & Assocs.

— Poems in the Key of Life. (Illus.). 64p. 1994. pap. 6.95 (*0-9636197-1-3*) Davis & Assocs.

Davis, Charles A., ed. Welding & Brazing of Carbon Steels, 2 bks., Bk. 1: Arc Welding. LC 76-44372. (Metalworking & Manufacturing Processes Ser.). (Illus.). 172p. 1976. reprint ed. pap. 53.40 (*0-608-08528-6*, 201948000001) Bks Demand.

— Welding & Brazing of Carbon Steels, 2 bks., Bk. 2, High-Deposition-Rate & Special-Application. LC 76-44372. (Metalworking & Manufacturing Processes Ser.). (Illus.). 139p. 1976. reprint ed. pap. 43.10 (*0-608-08529-4*, 201948000002) Bks Demand.

Davis, Charles A., ed. see American Society for Metals Staff.

Davis, Charles B. Adventures & Letters of Richard Harding Davis. (American Newspapermen 1790-1933 Ser.). (Illus.). iii, 417p. 1974. reprint ed. 34.95 (*0-8464-0024-3*) Beekman Pubs.

— Borderland of Society. LC 79-140328. (Short Story Index Reprint Ser.). 1977. reprint ed. 18.95 (*0-8369-3720-1*) Ayer.

— Lodger Overhead, & Others. LC 71-121533. (Short Story Index Reprint Ser.). (Illus.). 1977. 24.95 (*0-8369-3489-X*) Ayer.

— Stage Door. LC 74-122693. (Short Story Index Reprint Ser.). 1977. 20.95 (*0-8369-3526-8*) Ayer.

— Tales of the Town. LC 78-167447. (Short Story Index Reprint Ser.). 1977. reprint ed. 23.95 (*0-8369-3973-5*) Ayer.

Davis, Charles E. Creatures at My Feet. 1999. pap. text 8.95 (*0-87358-739-1*, Rising Moon Bks) Northland AZ.

— The Great Chase: A Novel. 1995. pap. 9.95 (*1-55503-814-X*, 01112023) Covenant Comms.

Davis, Charles E. & Lester, James P., eds. Dimensions of Hazardous Waste Politics & Policy, 200. LC 87-17792. (Contributions in Political Science Ser.: No. 200). 273p. 1988. 65.00 (*0-313-25989-5*, LHZ/, Greenwood Pr) Greenwood.

Davis, Charles G. American Sailing Ships. (Antiques Series: Transportation). (Illus.). 240p. 1984. reprint ed. pap. 7.95 (*0-486-24658-2*) Dover.

— Built-up Ship Model. (Illus.). 256p. 1989. pap. 6.95 (*0-486-26174-3*) Dover.

— The Ship Model Builder's Assistant. (Illus.). 208p. 1988. reprint ed. pap. 7.95 (*0-486-25584-0*) Dover.

— Ship Models: How to Build Them. 1990. 19.25 (*0-8446-6280-1*) Peter Smith.

— Ship Models: How to Build Them. 192p. 1986. reprint ed. pap. 7.95 (*0-486-25170-5*) Dover.

— The Ways of the Sea. (Illus.). 185p. (YA). 1994. pap. 13.95 (*0-941567-51-6*) South St Sea Mus.

Davis, Charles H. & Lundeen, Gerald W. Illustrative Computer Programming for Libraries: Selected Examples for Information Specialists, 39. 2nd ed. LC 81-1128. (Contributions in Librarianship & Information Science Ser.: No. 39). (Illus.). 129p. 1981. 42.95 (*0-313-22151-0*, DAD/) Greenwood.

Davis, Charles H. & Rush, James E. Guide to Information Science. LC 78-75240. (Illus.). 305p. 1979. lib. bdg. 49.95 (*0-313-20982-0*, DGI/, Greenwood Pr) Greenwood.

Davis, Charles H., et al. Pascal Programming for Libraries: Illustrative Examples for Information Specialists, 6. LC 87-32293. (Contributions in Librarianship & Information Science Ser.: No. 60). 376p. 1988. lib. bdg. 79.50 (*0-313-22979-1*, DPC) Greenwood.

— Pascal Programming for Libraries: Illustrative Examples for Information Specialists, 60. LC 87-32292. (Contributions in Librarianship & Information Science Ser.: No. 60). 122p. 1988. 45.00 (*0-313-25259-9*) Greenwood.

Davis, Charles H., jt. auth. see Bullen, Andrew H.

Davis, Charles H., jt. ed. see Sutton, Brett.

Davis, Charles L. Working-Class Mobilization & Political Control: Venezuela & Mexico. LC 88-23314. 224p. 1989. 29.95 (*0-8131-1670-8*) U Pr of Ky.

Davis, Charles M. Every Person's Guide to Practical Y2K Preparation: Common Sense Guidance to Protect Your Family, Your Money, Your Home & Your Community from the Year 2000 Computer Bug. (Illus.). 60p. (Orig.). 1999. pap. 7.95 (*1-928533-01-9*) Red Setter.

***Davis, Charles N. & Spilchal, Sigman L.** Access Denied: Freedom of Information in the Information Age. LC 00-40728. (Illus.). 219p. 2000. 44.95 (*0-8138-2567-9*) Iowa St U Pr.

Davis, Charles R. Organization Theories & Public Administration. LC 95-53000. 160p. 1996. 52.95 (*0-275-95576-1*, Praeger Pubs) Greenwood.

— World War II: My Trip Abroad with the United States Army 66th Ordinance in Europe & North Africa. LC 92-74402. 160p. 1993. lib. bdg. 19.95 (*0-9630768-1-7*) Heritage Oak.

Davis, Charles T. Black Is the Color of the Cosmos: Essays on Afro-American Literature & Culture, 1942-81. Gates, Henry Louis, Jr., ed. 376p. 1989. pap. 19.95 (*0-88258-166-X*) Howard U Pr.

— The Manufacture of Paper. LC 72-5042. (Technology & Society Ser.). (Illus.). 625p. 1972. reprint ed. 37.95 (*0-405-04694-4*) Ayer.

— The New Standard San Francisco Bartenders Workbook, No. 1. Walter, Robert L., ed. (Illus.). 270p. (Orig.). (C). 1998. pap. text 26.50 (*0-9621628-0-9*, 6969) Fubar Pr.

Davis, Charles T. & Gates, Henry Louis, Jr., eds. The Slave's Narrative. (Illus.). 384p. 1991. reprint ed. pap. text 19.95 (*0-19-506656-1*) OUP.

Davis, Charlotte & Bean, Dawn. Three Month Curriculum for the Beginning Synchronized Swimming Class. 55p. (Orig.). pap. text 10.00 (*0-911543-08-2*) US Synch Swim.

Davis, Cherie M., ed. see Kinzie, Patti L.

Davis, Cheryl, jt. auth. see Bullis, Michael.

Davis, Chet, et al. Burpee: Flowering Gardens. (Illus.). 320p. 1997. 19.98 (*0-7651-9329-9*) Smithmark.

Davis, Chip. My Little Christmas Tree: And Other Christmas Bedtime Stories. LC 98-138707. (J). 1997. 29.95 (*0-9656909-0-3*) American Gramaphone.

Davis, Chris. Death by Fire. 412p. 1998. pap. text 6.00 (*0-7881-5788-4*) DIANE Pub.

— Death by Fire. 3rd ed. LC PS3554.D3957 1995. (Illus.). 412p. 1995. mass mkt. 5.99 (*0-9644444-7-X*) BZ Bks NY.

Davis, Christina, et al. A Networking Tool. 1993. text 10.95 (*0-9634153-0-1*) Prod Busn Srv.

***Davis, Christina DiStefano.** Totally Surrounded. (International Adventures Ser.: Vol. 7). 160p. 2000. reprint ed. pap. 8.99 (*1-57658-165-9*) YWAM Pub.

***Davis, Christine.** For Every Cat an Angel. (Illus.). 32p. 2001. 9.95 (*0-9659225-1-0*) Lighthearted.

Davis, Christine. For Every Dog an Angel. LC 98-100073. (Illus.). 32p. 1997. 9.95 (*0-9659225-0-2*) Lighthearted.

***Davis, Christopher.** Death in Abeyance: Illness & Therapies among the Tabwa of Zaire/Congo. 288p. 2000. pap. text 23.00 (*0-7486-1305-6*) Col U Pr.

Davis, Christopher. Dog Horse Rat. 1999. pap. write for info. (*0-14-011731-8*, Viking) Viking Penguin.

— The Patriot: Poems by Christopher Davis. LC 97-49513. 104p. 1998. pap. 14.95 (*0-8203-1991-0*) U of Ga Pr.

— The Tyrant of the Past & the Slave of the Future. LC 89-4996. (Orig.). (C). 1989. 15.00 (*0-89672-199-X*); pap. 8.50 (*0-89672-200-7*) Tex Tech Univ Pr.

Davis, Christopher & Charemza, Wojciech W., eds. Models of Disequilibrium & Shortage in the Centrally Planned Economies. 350p. (C). (gr. 13). 1989. text 215.95 (*0-412-28420-0*) Chapman & Hall.

Davis, Christopher A. The Structure of Paul's Theology: The Truth Which Is the Gospel. LC 94-48472. (Biblical Press Ser.: Vol. 36). 452p. 1995. text 109.95 (*0-7734-2422-9*, Mellen Biblical Pr) E Mellen.

Davis, Christopher C. Lasers & Electro-Optics: Fundamentals & Engineering. (Illus.). 741p. (C). 1996. text 139.95 (*0-521-30831-3*); pap. text 49.95 (*0-521-48403-0*) Cambridge U Pr.

Davis, Christopher K., jt. auth. see Wilcox, Donald P.

***Davis, Chuck.** Port Coquitlam: Where the Rivers Meet. (Illus.). 196p. 2000. 39.95 (*1-55017-221-2*) Harbour Pub Co.

Davis, Cinda-Sue, et al, eds. The Equity Equation: Fostering the Advancement of Women in the Sciences, Mathematics, & Engineering. (Higher & Adult Education Ser.). 400p. 1996. 38.95 (*0-7879-0213-6*) Jossey-Bass.

Davis, Cindy. Yup'ik Eskimo Dictionary. (ESK.). viii, 758p. (C). 1984. pap. 35.00 (*0-933769-21-0*) Alaska Native.

Davis, Clara. Azusa Street Revival. 144p. 1996. mass mkt. 5.99 (*0-88368-467-5*) Whitaker Hse.

— The Move of God: Azusa Street to Now. 80p. (Orig.). 1983. pap. 2.95 (*0-88144-016-7*, CPS-016) Christian Pub.

Davis, Clarence B., et al, eds. Railway Imperialism, 26. LC 89-26025. (Contributions in Comparative Colonial Studies: No. 26). 248p. 1991. 59.95 (*0-313-25966-6*, DRY/, Greenwood Pr) Greenwood.

Davis, Clark. After the Whale: Melville in the Wake of Moby-Dick. LC 94-43179. (Illus.). 256p. (C). 1995. text 34.95 (*0-8173-0774-5*) U of Ala Pr.

***Davis, Clark.** Company Men. LC 99-38677. (Studies in Industry & Society). 2000. 39.95 (*0-8018-6274-4*) Johns Hopkins.

Davis, Clinton T., jt. ed. see Newman, Harry.

Davis, Clive M., et al, eds. Sexuality-Related Measures: A Compendium. 270p. (C). 1988. pap. text 39.50 (*0-9620581-0-6*) Graphic Pub.

Davis, Clive M., et al. Handbook of Sexuality-Related Measures. LC 98-19732. 920p. 1998. 61.00 (*0-8039-7111-7*) Sage.

Davis, Clyde B. Rivers of America: The Arkansas. Date not set. lib. bdg. 25.95 (*0-8488-1970-5*) Amereon Ltd.

Davis, Colin. Elie Wiesel's Secretive Texts. LC 94-8400. 224p. 1994. 49.95 (*0-8130-1303-8*) U Press Fla.

***Davis, Colin.** Ethical Issues in Twentieth-Century French Fiction: Killing the Other. LC 99-27402. 2000. text 59.95 (*0-312-22396-X*) St Martin.

Davis, Colin. Levinas: An Introduction. LC 96-46628. 1996. pap. 17.00 (*0-268-01314-4*) U of Notre Dame Pr.

— Michel Tournier: Philosophy & Fiction. (Oxford Modern Languages & Literature Monographs). 232p. 1988. 75.00 (*0-19-815152-7*) OUP.

***Davis, Colin & Fallaize, Elizabeth.** French Fiction in the Mitterrand Years: Memory, Narrative, Desire. (Oxford Studies in Modern European Culture). 176p. 2000. pap. 19.95 (*0-19-815955-2*); text 72.00 (*0-19-815956-0*) OUP.

Davis, Colin G., ed. see Hudson, MacIntyre.

Davis, Colin J. Power at Odds: The 1922 National Railroad Shopmen's Strike. LC 96-35702. 272p. 1997. text 49.95 (*0-252-02312-9*); pap. text 19.95 (*0-252-06612-X*) U of Ill Pr.

Davis, Colin J., jt. ed. see Brown, Edwin L.

***Davis, Corbett A., Jr.** The Deadly Reef. LC 99-66264. 184p. 2000. 19.95 (*1-56167-554-7*) Am Literary Pr.

Davis, Corinne D., jt. auth. see Chino, Allan F.

Davis, Cortney. Details of Flesh. LC 97-6686. 96p. (Orig.). 1997. 23.95 (*0-934971-58-7*); pap. 11.95 (*0-934971-57-9*) Calyx Bks.

Davis, Cortney & Schaefer, Judy, eds. Between the Heartbeats: Poetry & Prose by Nurses. LC 95-30297. 256p. 1995. pap. 14.95 (*0-87745-517-1*); text 27.95 (*0-87745-516-3*) U of Iowa Pr.

Davis, Courtney. Art of Celtia. (Illus.). 128p. 1995. pap. 16.95 (*0-7137-2307-6*, Pub. by Blandford Pr) Sterling.

— Book of Celtic Saints. LC 96-154922. (Illus.). 128p. 1996. 29.95 (*0-7137-2396-3*, Pub. by Blandford Pr) Sterling.

***Davis, Courtney.** Celtic & Old Norse Designs. LC 00-31614. (Pictorial Archive Ser.). (Illus.). (J). 2000. write for info. (*0-486-41229-6*) Dover.

Davis, Courtney. The Celtic Art Source Book. (Illus.). 128p. 1989. pap. 16.95 (*0-7137-2144-8*, Pub. by Blandford Pr) Sterling.

— Celtic Borders & Decorations. (Illus.). 96p. 1992. pap. 12.95 (*0-7137-2330-0*, Pub. by Blandford Pr) Sterling.

— Celtic Designs & Motifs. (Illus.). 48p. 1991. pap. 5.95 (*0-486-26718-0*) Dover.

— Celtic Designs Stained Glass Coloring Book. 1993. pap. 3.95 (*0-486-27456-X*) Dover.

— Celtic Illumination: The Irish School. LC 97-61610. (Illus.). 96p. 1998. pap. 15.95 (*0-500-28039-8*, Pub. by Thames Hudson) Norton.

— Celtic Initials & Alphabets. LC 99-164232. (Illus.). 96p. 1998. 24.95 (*0-7137-2665-2*, Pub. by Blandford Pr) Sterling.

***Davis, Courtney.** Celtic Initials & Alphabets. 96p. 1999. pap. text 12.95 (*0-7137-2804-3*) Strlng Pub CA.

Davis, Courtney. Celtic Iron-On Transfer Patterns. 48p. 3.95 (*0-486-26059-3*) Dover.

— Celtic Mandalas. (Illus.). 96p. 1994. pap. 16.95 (*0-7137-2375-0*, Pub. by Blandford Pr) Sterling.

— Celtic Ornament: Art of the Scribe. (Illus.). 96p. 1998. pap. 12.95 (*0-7137-2547-8*, Pub. by Blandford Pr) Sterling.

— Saint Patrick: A Visual Celebration. 128p. 1999. 29.95 (*0-7137-2674-1*) Blandford Pr.

***Davis, Courtney.** A Treasury of Celtic Design. (Illus.). 60p. 1999. pap. 11.95 (*0-09-478730-1*, Pub. by Constable & Co) Trafalgar.

Davis, Courtney. Key Patterns & Animals: A Celtic Art Workbook. 68p. 1999. pap. 9.95 (*0-7137-2744-6*, Pub. by Blandford Pr) Sterling.

— King Arthur's Return: Legends of the Round Table & Holy Grail Retraced. 128p. 1997. pap. 16.95 (*0-7137-2428-5*, Pub. by Blandford Pr) Sterling.

— Knotwork & Spirals: A Celtic Art Workbook. 68p. 1999. pap. 9.95 (*0-7137-2743-8*, Pub. by Blandford Pr) Sterling.

Davis, Courtney & James, David. The Celtic Image. (Illus.). 128p. 1996. 27.95 (*0-7137-2480-3*, Pub. by Blandford Pr) Sterling.

Davis, Craig R. Beowulf & the Demise of Germanic Legend in England. LC 95-43555. (Albert Bates Lord Studies in Oral Tradition: No. 17). 256p. 1996. text 53.00 (*0-8153-2354-9*, H1987) Garland.

Davis, Creath. How to Win in a Crisis. 224p. 1987. pap. 7.70 (*0-310-23191-4*, 6323P) Zondervan.

Davis, Cullom, et al. Oral History: From Tape to Type. LC 77-4403. 151p. reprint ed. pap. 46.90 (*0-608-14976-4*, 202569600045) Bks Demand.

Davis, Curtis C. Revolution's Godchild: The Birth, Death, & Regeneration of the Society of the Cincinnati in North Carolina. LC 76-7967. 319p. reprint ed. pap. 98.90 (*0-7837-2071-8*, 204234500004) Bks Demand.

Davis, Cushman K. Law in Shakespeare. 2nd ed. LC 72-163677. reprint ed. 34.50 (*0-404-01988-9*) AMS Pr.

— The Law in Shakespeare, 1883. LC 98-32333. 1999. 60.00 (*1-886363-75-7*) Lawbk Exchange.

— Treatise on International Law Including American Diplomacy. xiii, 368p. 1982. reprint ed. 45.00 (*0-8377-0441-3*, Rothman) W S Hein.

Davis, Cynthia J. & West, Kathryn. Women Writers in the United States: A Timeline of Literary, Cultural & Social History. 504p. (C). 1996. 55.00 (*0-19-509053-5*) OUP.

Davis, Cynthia L. Peace Be Still: Inner Healing for Racial Harmony. (Illus.). 75p. 1997. pap. 5.00 (*0-9659539-0-4*) Unications Pub.

***Davis, Cynthia Legette.** I Know How You Feel: Hope & Encouragement Even in Your Darkest Moments. 100p. 2001. pap. 10.00 (*0-9659539-2-0*) Unications Pub.

Davis, Cyprian. The History of Black Catholics in the United States. 360p. 1995. pap. 19.95 (*0-8245-1495-5*) Crossroad NY.

Davis, Cyprian, jt. auth. see Hayes, Diana.

Davis, D, ed. see Levey, Marc M.

***Davis, D. Diane.** Breaking Up (at) Totality: A Rhetoric of Laughter. LC 99-32609. (Rhetorical Philosophy & Theory Ser.). 2000. pap. 15.95 (*0-8093-2229-3*) S Ill U Pr.

Davis, D. G. American Spoken English: Introductory Basics in 57 Languages - No Foreign Accent. rev. ed. 265p. 1997. pap. 10.00 (*0-929350-28-6*) Am Spoken English.

— American Spoken English in Real Life - Fast Natural, Urgent Survival, Foreign Accent Begone! The Phonology of General American Colloquial, Vol. 1. 300p. (Orig.). 1994. pap. 25.00 (*0-929350-01-4*) Am Spoken English.

— American Spoken English in Real Life, Basic Course: Learning to Understand Americans Talking Naturally & to Talk So They Readily Understand You, Vol. 2. 119p. (Orig.). 1993. pap. 10.00 incl. audio (*0-929350-02-2*) Am Spoken English.

— American Spoken English-Phonetic Dictionary (Sounds & Utterances) For Learning to Understand Americans Talking Naturally & Speak So They Easily Understand You. 176p. (Orig.). 1996. pap. 25.00 (*0-929350-30-8*) Am Spoken English.

***Davis, D. Layten & Nielsen, Mark T., eds.** Tobacco: Production, Chemistry & Technology. LC 98-51589. 480p. 1999. text 164.95 (*0-632-04791-7*, Pub. by Blckwell Science) Iowa St U Pr.

Davis, D. M. Gordon & Getz: The South African Law of Insurance. 4th ed. 668p. 1993. 106.00 (*0-7021-2802-3*, Pub. by Juta & Co) Gaunt.

Davis, D. W., et al. Biological Control & Insect Pest Management. 112p. 1979. pap. 7.00 (*0-931876-34-6*, 1911) ANR Pubns CA.

Davis, D. Webster, jt. auth. see Jackson, Giles B.

Davis, Dale. Differential Diagnosis of Arrhythmias. 2nd ed. Biello, Lisa, ed. (Illus.). 288p. 1997. pap. text 31.50 (*0-7216-4477-5*, W B Saunders Co) Harcrt Hlth Sci Grp.

— How to Quickly & Accurately Master ECG Interpretation. 2nd ed. (Illus.). 402p. 1991. pap. text 38.00 (*0-397-51106-X*) Lppncott W & W.

Davis, Dale. Quick & Accurate 12-Lead ECG Interpretation. 3rd ed. 480p. text 38.00 (*0-7817-2327-2*) Lppncott W & W.

Davis, Dale, jt. auth. see Standard, Charles.

Davis, Dale A. Develop & Market Your Creative Ideas. 2nd ed. LC 96-8709. (Successful Business Library). 188p. 1996. pap. 15.95 (*1-55571-383-1*, Oasis Pr) PSI Resch.

Davis, Dale A., jt. auth. see McKinney, Thomas H.

Davis, Dale Ralph. 2nd Samuel. 1999. pap. text 12.99 (*1-85792-335-9*) Christian Focus.

Davis, Dales, jt. auth. see Thiessen, Frank J.

Davis, Dan. Creative Comping. 119p. 1995. 29.95 (*0-8497-5506-9*, WG104) Kjos.

Davis, Dan M., jt. auth. see Consolmagno, Guy J.

Davis, Daniel. Practical Treatise upon the Authority & Duty of Justices of the Peace in Criminal Prosecutions. iv, 687p. 1994. reprint ed. 67.50 (*0-8377-2040-0*, Rothman) W S Hein.

Davis, Daniel C., et al, eds. Mechanical Behavior of Advanced Materials: Proceedings International Mechanical Engineering Congress & Exposition 1998, Anaheim, CA. LC 98-74433. (MD Ser.: Vol. 84). 362p. 1998. 200.00 (*0-7918-1609-5*) ASME.

Davis, Daniel J. Parables of Matthew. LC 98-74304. (Covenant Bible Studies). 120p. 1998. pap. 5.95 (*0-87178-013-5*, 8135) Brethren.

Davis, Daniel J. & Davis, Julie A. Hazardous Materials Reference Book: Cross-Index. LC 96-111779. (Industrial Health & Safety Ser.). 491p. 1995. text 54.95 (*0-442-01965-3*, VNR) Wiley.

Davis, Daniel J. & Davis, Julie A. Hazardous Materials Reference Book: Cross-Index. 491p. 1995. 65.95 (*0-471-28681-8*, VNR) Wiley.

Davis, Daniel J., et al. Firefighter's Hazardous Materials Reference Book & Index. 2nd ed. LC 92-33266. 1333p. 1992. text 134.95 (*0-442-01346-9*, VNR) Wiley.

Davis, Daniel J., et al. Firefighter's Hazardous Materials Reference Book & Index. 2nd ed. 1333p. 1992. 165.00 (*0-471-28535-8*, VNR) Wiley.

***Davis, Daniel L.** The Aggressive Adolescent: Clinical & Forensic Issues. LC 99-37681. 170p. (C). 1999. pap. text 24.95 (*0-7890-0910-2*) Haworth Pr.

— The Aggressive Adolescent: Clinical & Forensic Issues. LC 99-37681. 158p. (C). 2000. lib. bdg. 39.95 (*0-7890-0863-7*) Haworth Pr.

Davis, Daniel L., jt. auth. see Ben-Porath, Yossef S.

Davis, Daniel M., jt. auth. see Consolmagno, Guy J.

Davis, Daniel S., et al. Accidental Releases of Air Toxics: Prevention, Control & Mitigation. LC 89-8858. (Pollution Technology Review Ser.: No. 170). (Illus.). 649p. 1990. 86.00 (*0-8155-1210-4*) Noyes.

***Davis, Darien J.** Avoiding the Dark: Essays on Race & the Forging of National Culture in Modern Brazil. (Research in Migration & Ethnic Relations Ser.). 280p. 1999. text 69.95 (*1-84014-874-8*, Pub. by Ashgate Pub) Ashgate Pub Co.

Davis, Darien J., ed. Slavery & Beyond: The African Impact on Latin America & the Caribbean. (Jaguar Books on Latin America: No. 5). 328p. 1994. 55.00 (*0-8420-2484-0*) Scholarly Res Inc.

— Slavery & Beyond: The African Impact on Latin America & the Caribbean. (Jaguar Books on Latin America: No. 5). 328p. 1995. pap. 18.95 (*0-8420-2485-9*) Scholarly Res Inc.

Davis, Darin, et al. Mirth of Yore: Cartoons of Fantasy. LC 90-70743. 96p. (Orig.). 1990. pap. 7.95 (*0-9627030-0-1*, 1001) Starlance Pubns.

Davis, Darrel, ed. see Curris, Constantine.

An Asterisk (*) at the beginning of an entry indicates that the title is appearing for the first time.

Davis, Darrel W. Micro-Ledger: Problem Booklet for IBM--Version 2.2. 58p. 1991. pap. text 5.95 (*1-57094-038-X*) S E Warner Sftware.

Davis, Darrell W. Picturing Japaneseness: Monumental Style, National Identity, Japanese Film. (Film & Culture Ser.). 1996. 55.00 (*0-231-10230-5*); pap. 19.50 (*0-231-10231-3*) Col U Pr.

Davis, Daryl. Klan-Destine Relationships: A Black Man's Odyssey in the Ku Klux Klan. LC 97-66564. (Illus.). xxv, 315p. 1998. 23.95 (*0-88282-159-8*) New Horizon NJ.

***Davis, Dave D.** Jolly Beach & the Preceramic Occupation of Antigua, West Indies. (Publications in Anthropology: VCol. 84). (Illus.). 140p. 2000. pap. 18.00 (*0-913516-20-1*) Yale U Anthro.

Davis, Dave D., ed. Perspectives on Gulf Coast Prehistory. LC 84-3686. (Ripley P. Bullen Monographs in Anthropology & History: No. 5). (Illus.). 390p. 1984. 49.95 (*0-8130-0756-9*) U Press Fla.

***Davis, David.** Cajun Night before Christmas; Gaston the Green-Nosed Alligator. (Illus.). 32p. (J). (gr. k-3). 1998. 9.95 incl. audio (*1-56554-189-8*) Pelican.

Davis, David. GIS for Everyone: Exploring Your Neighborhood & Your World with a Geographic Information System. 156p. 1999. pap. 19.95 (*1-879102-49-8*) ESR Inst.

— Interactive Research in Drama in Education. LC 98-128416. 150p. 1997. pap. 14.95 (*1-85856-078-0*, Trentham Bks) Stylus Pub VA.

— A Redneck Night Before Christmas. LC 97-14421. (Illus.). 32p. (J). (ps-3). 1997. 14.95 (*1-56554-293-2*) Pelican.

***Davis, David.** Valley of Trouble. 1999. pap. 11.99 (*1-56043-336-1*, Treasure Hse) Destiny Image.

Davis, David, ed. see Garvin, Kevin.

Davis, David A. & Walker, Theodore D. Plan Graphics. 5th ed. LC 98-51606. 224p. 1999. pap. 49.95 (*0-471-29221-4*) Wiley.

Davis, David A., jt. auth. see Walker, Theodore D.

Davis, David B. Antebellum American Culture: An Interpretive Anthology. LC 96-31036. 1997. pap. 19.95 (*0-271-01646-9*) Pa St U Pr.

— From Homicide to Slavery: Studies in American Culture. 320p. 1988. reprint ed. pap. text 24.95 (*0-19-505418-0*) OUP.

— Homicide in American Fiction, 1798-1860: A Study in Social Values. 364p. 1968. pap. text 16.95 (*0-8014-9066-9*) Cornell U Pr.

— The Problem of Slavery in Western Culture. 528p. 1988. pap. text 17.95 (*0-19-505639-6*) OUP.

— Revolutions: Reflections on American Equality & Foreign Liberations. LC 89-48924. (William E. Massey Sr. Lectures in the History of American Civilization). 144p. 1990. text 26.50 (*0-674-76805-1*) HUP.

— The Slave Power Conspiracy & the Paranoid Style. fac. ed. LC 79-96257. (Walter Lynwood Fleming Lectures in Southern History). 109p. 1969. reprint ed. pap. 33.80 (*0-7837-7729-9*, 204748500007) Bks Demand.

— Slavery in the Colonial Chesapeake. (Foundations of America Ser.). (Illus.). 42p. (Orig.). 1986. pap. 9.95 (*0-87935-115-2*) Colonial Williamsburg.

Davis, David B. & Mintz, Steven, eds. Boisterous Sea of Liberty: A Documentary History of America from Discovery Through the Civil War. LC 98-7332. (Illus.). 608p. 1998. 30.00 (*0-19-511669-0*) OUP.

Davis, David Brion. The Problem of Slavery in the Age of Revolution, 1770-1823. LC 98-19513. 576p. 1999. pap. 24.95 (*0-19-512671-8*) OUP.

Davis, David Brion & Mintz, Steven, eds. The Boisterous Sea of Liberty: A Documentary History of America from Discovery through the Civil War. LC 98-7332. (Illus.). 608p. 2000. pap. 18.95 (*0-19-511670-4*) OUP.

Davis, David C., et al, eds. Service Parts Management Reprints. LC 82-72118. 123p. 1982. pap. 10.00 (*0-935406-19-0*) Am Prod & Inventory.

Davis, David E., Jr. Thus Spake David E. Collected Wit & Wisdom of the Most Influential Automotive Journalist of Our Time. LC 98-54772. (Illus.). 242p. 1999. 29.95 (*1-879094-55-X*) Momentum Bks.

Davis, David E., ed. Handbook of Census Methods for Terrestrial Vertebrates. 424p. 1982. boxed set 261.95 (*0-8493-2970-1*, QL752) CRC Pr.

Davis, David E., tr. see Kozameh, Alicia.

Davis, David F., ed. see Dibble, Peter C.

Davis, David F., ed. see Miller, Eric & Miller, Walden.

Davis, David F., jt. ed. see Woodcock, Alexander E.

Davis, David H. American Environmental Politics. LC 97-24488. (Illus.). 272p. (C). 1998. pap. text 37.95 (*0-8304-1518-1*) Thomson Learn.

— Energy Politics. 3rd ed. LC 81-51846. 323p. (C). 1982. pap. text 14.00 (*0-312-25205-6*) St Martin.

— Energy Politics. 4th ed. LC 92-81533. (Illus.). 321p. (C). 1992. pap. 31.95 (*0-312-07232-5*) St Martin.

Davis, David, Memorial Institute of International. Neutral States & the European Community. Harden, Sheila, ed. 176p. 1994. 49.00 (*1-85753-024-1*, Pub. by Brasseys) Brasseys.

***Davis, David R.** Trucker's Night Before Christmas. LC 99-30580. (Illus.). 32p. (J). (gr. k-3). 1999. 14.95 (*1-56554-656-3*) Pelican.

Davis, David S., jt. auth. see Vinson, Donald E.

Davis, David W., jt. auth. see Brown, Lisa E.

***Davis, Dawn.** If You Can Stand the Heat: Tales from Chefs & Restaurateurs. LC 99-26563. (Illus.). 336p. 1999. pap. 16.95 (*0-14-028158-4*, Penguin Bks) Viking Penguin.

Davis, Daylelynn. Balloon Catcher. LC 97-77479. 1998. pap. 5.95 (*0-9652894-3-5*) GA Publng.

Davis, Dayna. All White Dogs Love Mud. (Illus.). 14p. (J). (gr. 1-5). pap. write for info. (*0-9660350-1-1*) Suzalooz Pr.

— Watching Hi Sleep: Poems by Dayna Davis. 15p. 1997. write for info. (*0-9660350-0-3*) Suzalooz Pr.

Davis, Dean, ed. see Sherman, Robert G.

Davis, Deane C. Deane C. Davis: An Autobiography. Graff, Nancy P., ed. LC 91-52770. (Illus.). 400p. 1990. 24.95 (*0-933050-91-7*) New Eng Pr VT.

— Nothin' But the Truth: More Yankee Yarns. LC 82-80343. (Illus.). 224p. 1982. 10.95 (*0-933050-10-0*) New Eng Pr VT.

Davis, Debbie. Lilly White. 1999. pap. 9.95 (*0-9640801-7-6*, 8017-6) Jireh Pubns.

Davis-Debeuneure, Linda, jt. auth. see Makris, Barbara L.

Davis, Deborah. Children of God: The Inside Story. LC 83-26025. 1983. write for info. (*0-310-27840-6*) Zondervan.

***Davis, Deborah.** The Consumer Revolution in Urban China LC 98-43811. (Studies on China: Vol. 22). 399p. 1999. 55.00 (*0-520-21639-3*, Pub. by U CA Pr) Cal Prin Full Svc.

Davis, Deborah. Katharine the Great: Katharine Graham & Her Washington Post Empire. LC 91-19941. (Illus.). 344p. 1991. 21.95 (*0-941781-14-3*); pap. 14.95 (*0-941781-13-5*) IMA NYC.

— Loving & Letting Go: Parents Who Decide Against Medical Intervention. (Illus.). 64p. (Orig.). 1992. pap. 5.95 (*1-56123-060-X*, LLGC) Centering Corp.

— My Brother Has AIDS. 192p. (J). (gr. 4-8). 1994. 15.00 (*0-689-31922-3*) Atheneum Yung Read.

— The Secret of the Seal. (Illus.). 64p. (J). (gr. 2 up). 1994. pap. 3.99 (*0-679-86566-7*, Pub. by Random Bks Yng Read) Random.

Davis, Deborah. Secret of the Seal. 1994. 9.19 (*0-606-07083-4*, Pub. by Turtleback) Demco.

Davis, Deborah & Harrell, Stevan, eds. Chinese Families in the Post-Mao Era. LC 92-23163. (Studies on China: Vol. 17). (C). 1993. 60.00 (*0-520-07797-0*, Pub. by U CA Pr); pap. 19.95 (*0-520-08222-2*, Pub. by U CA Pr) Cal Prin Full Svc.

Davis, Deborah & Vogel, Ezra, eds. Chinese Society on the Eve of Tiananmen: The Impact of Reform. (Contemporary China Ser.: No. 7). (Illus.). 390p. 1990. 40.00 (*0-674-12534-7*, DAVCHS) HUP.

Davis, Deborah & Vogel, Ezra F., eds. Chinese Society on the Eve of Tiananmen: The Impact of Reform. (Harvard Contemporary China Ser.: No. 7). (Illus.). 390p. 1990. pap. 20.00 (*0-674-12535-5*) HUP.

Davis, Deborah, jt. auth. see Hegde, M. N.

Davis, Deborah, jt. auth. see Ramsay, Young S.

Davis, Deborah, ed. see Massey, Grace C.

***Davis, Deborah C. & Humphrey, Keren M.** College Counseling: Issues & Strategies for a New Millennium. LC 00-21361. 2000. write for info. (*1-55620-220-2*) Am Coun Assn.

***Davis, Deborah D.** Aleatory. 12p. 1999. pap. 4.00 (*0-9674487-7-8*) Good SAMAR.

Davis, Deborah L. Empty Cradle, Broken Heart: Surviving the Death of Your Baby. rev. expanded ed. 280p. 1996. pap. 16.95 (*1-55591-302-4*) Fulcrum Pub.

Davis, Deborah S., ed. The Consumer Revolution in Urban China. LC 98-43811. Vol. 22. 399p. 1999. pap. 22.00 (*0-520-21640-7*, Pub. by U CA Pr) Cal Prin Full Svc.

***Davis, Dee.** Decoupage: A Practical Guide to the Art of Decorating Surfaces with Paper Cutouts. LC 94-60348. (Illus.). 144p. 2000. pap. 17.95 (*0-500-28203-X*, Pub. by Thames Hudson) Norton.

— Everything in Its Time. 2000. mass mkt. 5.99 (*0-515-12874-0*, Jove) Berkley Pub.

***Davis, Dee & Cooper, Gail B.** The Decoupage Gallery: A Collection of over 450 Color & 550 Black-&-White Design Motifs. (Illus.). 176p. 2000. pap. 19.95 (*0-8230-1289-1*) Watsn-Guptill.

Davis, DeeAnne, et al. New Voices 1 from Aunt Lute. LC 95-13818. 152p. (Orig.). 1995. pap. 10.95 (*1-879960-38-9*); lib. bdg. 20.95 (*1-879960-39-7*) Aunt Lute Bks.

Davis, Deena, ed. Discipleship Journal's 101 Best Small-Group Ideas. 160p. 1996. pap. 11.00 (*0-89109-950-6*) NavPress.

Davis, Deena, ed. see Haidle, David & Haidle, Helen.

Davis, Deirdre. Side Dishes Creative & Simple: Vegetable & Fruit Accompaniments for All Occasions. Martin, Rux, ed. LC 96-37468. (Illus.). 208p. 1997. pap. 14.95 (*1-57630-027-7*, Chapters Bks) HM.

Davis, Delbert D. The Giant Panda: A Morphological Study of Evolutionary Mechanisms. LC 64-8995. (Chicago Natural History Museum, Fieldiana; Zoology Memoirs Ser.: Vol. 3). 339p. reprint ed. pap. 105.10 (*0-608-14431-2*, 205183100008) Bks Demand.

***Davis, Dena S. & Zoloth, Laurie, eds.** Notes from a Narrow Ridge: Religion & Bioethics. 302p. 1999. pap. 24.95 (*1-55572-052-8*); lib. bdg. 55.00 (*1-55572-077-3*) Univ Pub Group.

Davis, Denise. Health, Wellness & Restoration: The Complete Guide for Restoring Your Health the Natural Way. (Illus.). 175p. 1998. 23.60 (*0-9668415-0-6*) Denise D.

Davis, Denise, ed. see Mehale, Alilali G.

Davis, Denise E., jt. auth. see Andrews, Joan.

Davis, Denise E., jt. auth. see Andrews, Joan M.

Davis, Dennis. Build Your Own Canoe. (Illus.). 160p. 1997. 29.95 (*1-86126-053-9*, Pub. by Crolwood) Trafalgar.

***Davis, Dennis.** Democracy & Deliberation. 204p. 1999. pap. 35.00 (*0-7021-5141-6*, Pub. by Juta & Co) Gaunt.

Davis, Dennis, et al. Fundamental Rights in the Constitution: Commentary & Cases: a Commentary on Chapter 3 on Fundamental Rights of the 1993 Constitution & Chapter 2 of the 1996 Constitution. LC 98-126548. 773p. 1997. write for info. (*0-7021-3636-0*) Juta & Co.

Davis, Dennis, jt. auth. see Kraus, Sidney.

Davis, Dennis A. Threats Pending, Fuses Burning: Managing Workplace Violence. LC 96-40266. 216p. 1997. 27.95 (*0-89106-102-9*, 7750, Davies-Black Pub) Consulting Psychol.

Davis, Dennis D. Practical Problems in Mathematics for Manufacturing. 4th ed. LC 95-5979. (Practical Problems in Mathematics Ser.). (C). 1995. mass mkt. 21.95 (*0-8273-6710-4*) Delmar.

Davis, Dennis K., jt. auth. see Baran, Stanley J.

Davis, Dennis M. & Clapp, Steve. The Third Wave & the Local Church. 175p. (Orig.). 1983. pap. 8.00 (*0-914527-54-1*) C-Four Res.

Davis, Denys, jt. auth. see Algotsson, Sharne.

Davis, Derek. Original Intent: Chief Justice Rehnquist & the Course of American Church-State Relations. LC 90-27447. 222p. 1991. 32.95 (*0-87975-649-7*) Prometheus Bks.

Davis, Derek, ed. The Role of Government in Monitoring & Regulating Religion in Public Life. LC 92-74168. 273p. (Orig.). (C). 1993. pap. 9.95 (*0-929182-18-9*); text 24.95 (*0-929182-17-0*) Baylor U J M Dawson.

Davis, Derek, jt. ed. see Weeks, Kent M.

Davis, Derek, jt. ed. see Wood, James E., Jr.

***Davis, Derek H.** Religion & the Continental Congress, 1774-1789: Contributions to Original Intent. LC 99-26044. (Illus.). 304p. 2000. text 39.95 (*0-19-513355-2*) OUP.

***Davis, Derek H., ed.** Genesis & the Millennium: An Essay on Religious Pluralism in the Twenty-First Century by Bill Moyers. LC 99-69672. 75p. 2000. pap. 6.95 (*0-929182-62-6*) Baylor U J M Dawson.

Davis, Derek H., ed. Journal of Church & State Index, 1994-1998, Vols. 36-40. LC 64-1440. 149p. 1999. pap. text 5.00 (*0-929182-57-X*) Baylor U J M Dawson.

— The Separation of Church & State Defended: Selected Writings of James E. Wood, Jr. LC 95-75329. 375p. 1995. 24.95 (*0-929182-23-5*); pap. 10.95 (*0-929182-24-3*) Baylor U J M Dawson.

Davis, Derek H. & Hankins, Barry, eds. Welfare Reform & Faith-Based Organizations. LC 98-67934. 350p. 1999. 27.95 (*0-929182-54-5*); pap. 13.95 (*0-929182-55-3*) Baylor U J M Dawson.

Davis, Derek R. Scenes of Madness: A Psychiatrist at the Theatre. LC 95-18951. 224p. (C). 1995. pap. 27.99 (*0-415-13173-1*) Routledge.

Davis, Deta S. Computer Applications in Music: A Bibliography, Supplement 1. (Computer Music & Digital Audio Ser.: Vol. 10). 600p. (C). 1993. 79.95 (*0-89579-267-2*) A-R Eds.

***Davis, Devra L. & Saldiva, Paulo H. N.** Urban Air Pollution Risks to Children: A Global Environmental Health Indicator. 20p. 1999. pap. 5.00 (*1-56973-427-5*) World Resources Inst.

Davis, Diane. Algo Anda Mal en Mi Casa: Un Libro Acerca de las Peleas de los Padres. Jones, Cynthia, tr.Tr. of Something Is Wrong at My House. (SPA., Illus.). 40p. (J). (ps-6). 1998. pap. 5.95 (*1-884734-40-5*) Parenting Pr.

— Political Power & Social Theory, Vol. 12. 1998. 78.50 (*0-7623-0270-4*) Jai Pr.

— Reaching Out to Children with FAS - FAE: A Handbook for Teachers, Counselors, & Parents Who Live & Work with Children Affected by Fetal Alcohol Syndrome & Fetal Alcohol Effects. LC 94-11953. 224p. 1994. pap. text 27.95 (*0-87628-857-3*) Ctr Appl Res.

— Something Is Wrong at My House: A Book about Parents' Fighting. LC 84-62129. (Illus.). 40p. (J). (ps-6). 1985. pap. 5.95 (*0-943990-10-6*); lib. bdg. 15.95 (*0-943990-11-4*) Parenting Pr.

— Working with Children from Violent Homes: Ideas & Techniques. 37p. 1988. pap. text 7.95 (*0-941816-22-2*) ETR Assocs.

Davis, Diane, ed. Political Power & Social Theory, Vol. 11. 1997. 78.50 (*0-7623-0242-9*) Jai Pr.

Davis, Diane, et al, eds. Political Power & Social Theory, Vol. 1. 334p. 1980. 78.50 (*0-89232-115-6*) Jai Pr.

— Political Power & Social Theory, Vol. 3. 352p. 1982. 78.50 (*0-89232-204-7*) Jai Pr.

— Political Power & Social Theory, Vol. 4. 302p. 1984. 78.50 (*0-89232-330-2*) Jai Pr.

Davis, Diane & Kimeldorf, Howard, eds. Political Power & Social Theory, Vol. 6. 374p. 1987. 78.50 (*0-89232-741-3*) Jai Pr.

— Political Power & Social Theory, Vol. 7. 320p. 1989. 78.50 (*0-89232-895-9*) Jai Pr.

— Political Power & Social Theory, Vol. 8. 295p. 1994. 78.50 (*1-55938-042-X*) Jai Pr.

— Political Power & Social Theory, Vol. 9. 221p. 1995. 78.50 (*1-55938-111-6*) Jai Pr.

— Political Power & Social Theory, Vol. 10. 1996. 78.50 (*0-7623-0037-X*) Jai Pr.

Davis, Diane, jt. auth. see Peled, Einat.

Davis, Diane, ed. see Tiner, John.

Davis, Diane, ed. see Zeitlin, Maurice.

Davis, Diane E. Urban Leviathan: Mexico City in the Twentieth Century. LC 93-23069. (Illus.). 464p. 1994. 69.95 (*1-56639-150-4*); pap. 27.95 (*1-56639-151-2*) Temple U Pr.

Davis, Diane M. Passports to Adventure: A World Drive in Model A Fords. (Illus.). 160p. (Orig.). 1994. pap. 15.00 (*0-9641026-0-9*) Peardale Pr.

Davis, Diane W. Heart of the Falcon. 400p. 1990. pap. 3.95 (*0-380-75711-7*, Avon Bks) Morrow Avon.

— Heart of the Raven. 368p. 1989. pap. 3.95 (*0-380-75710-9*, Avon Bks) Morrow Avon.

Davis, Dianne, jt. auth. see Bush-Brown, Albert.

Davis, Dick. Borrowed Ware: Medieval Persian Epigrams. (Poetica Ser.). 120p. 1997. pap. 15.95 (*0-85646-270-5*, Pub. by Anvil Press) Dufour.

— The Covenant: Poems, 1979-1983. 62p. 1984. pap. 13.95 (*0-85646-124-5*, Pub. by Anvil Press) Dufour.

— Devices & Desires: New & Selected Poems, 1967-1987. 128p. 1989. 28.95 (*0-85646-207-1*, Pub. by Anvil Press); pap. 17.95 (*0-85646-208-X*, Pub. by Anvil Press) Dufour.

— Epic & Sedition. LC 98-32324. 222p. 1999. 29.95 (*0-934211-55-8*) Mage Pubs Inc.

— Epic & Sedition: The Case of Ferdowsi's Shahnameh. LC 92-3329. xxxvi, 222p. 1992. text 19.50 (*1-55728-251-X*) Bibliotheca Persica.

— Hold'em Poker Bible. LC 83-72831. 256p. 1983. 14.95 (*0-89227-104-3*) Commonwealth Pr.

— Seeing the World. 56p. 1980. pap. 13.95 (*0-85646-061-3*, Pub. by Anvil Press) Dufour.

— Touchwood. LC 96-220175. 80p. 1997. pap. 15.95 (*0-85646-269-1*) Anvil Press.

Davis, Dick, ed. from PER. Borrowed Ware: Medieval Persian Epigrams. LC 97-26837. (Illus.). 208p. 1997. 24.95 (*0-934211-52-3*) Mage Pubs Inc.

Davis, Dick, ed. see Traherne, Thomas.

Davis, Dick, tr. see Attar, Farid Al-Din.

Davis, Dick, tr. see Ferdowski.

Davis, Dick, tr. see Ginzburg, Natalia.

Davis, Dick, tr. see Pezeshkzad, Iraj.

Davis, Dick, tr. see Yarshater, Ehsan, ed.

Davis, Dolores H. Czechoslovak Coins. 112p. 1972. pap. 3.00 (*1-889172-00-6*) Numismatic Intl.

Davis, Don. Appointment with the Squire: A Novel. 333p. 1995. 24.95 (*1-55750-157-2*) Naval Inst Pr.

— Death Cruise. 1996. mass mkt. 5.99 (*0-312-95786-6*, Pub. by Tor Bks) St Martin.

— Death of an Angel. 336p. 1994. mass mkt. 5.99 (*0-312-95277-5*) St Martin.

— A Father's Rage. (True Crime Library). 1997. mass mkt. 5.99 (*0-312-96095-6*) St Martin.

— Hush Little Babies: The True Story of a Mother Who Murdered Her Own Children. LC 97-227963. (St. Martin's True Crime Library). 1997. mass mkt. 5.99 (*0-312-96485-4*) St Martin.

— Milwaukee Murders, Nightmare in Apartment 213: The True Story. 1991. mass mkt. 6.50 (*0-312-92840-8*) St Martin.

***Davis, Don.** Wheel-Thrown Ceramics. (Illus.). 2000. pap. 24.95 (*1-57990-185-9*, Pub. by Lark Books) Sterling.

Davis, Don. Wheel-Thrown Ceramics: Altering, Trimming, Adding, Finishing. LC 98-13032. 160p. 1998. 27.50 (*1-57990-052-6*, Pub. by Lark Books) Random.

Davis, Don & Carter, David. Mountain Biking. LC 93-24692. (Outdoor Pursuits Ser.). (Illus.). 144p. 1993. pap. 12.95 (*0-87322-452-3*, PDAV0452) Human Kinetics.

Davis, Don & Davis, Carolyn. Sound System Engineering. 2nd ed. (Illus.). 665p. 1986. 62.95 (*0-240-80305-1*, Focal) Buttrwrth-Heinemann.

Davis, Don & Davis, Jay. Bring on the Night. 416p. (Orig.). 1993. mass mkt. 4.99 (*0-8125-1189-1*) Tor Bks.

— Sins of the Flesh. 416p. 1989. mass mkt. 4.50 (*0-8125-1679-6*) Tor Bks.

Davis, Don, jt. auth. see Armstrong, William A.

Davis, Don, jt. auth. see Cernan, Eugene.

Davis, Don, jt. auth. see Cernan, Eugene A.

Davis, Don, jt. auth. see Thomas, Steve.

Davis, Don D. Induced Task Competence & Effects on Problem Solving Behavior. (Illus.). 52p. (Orig.). 1980. pap. text 3.00 (*0-907152-00-7*) Prytaneum Pr.

— The Unique Animal. (Illus.). 336p. 1981. 25.00 (*0-907152-02-3*); pap. 12.95 (*0-907152-01-5*) Prytaneum Pr.

Davis, Don R. Neopseustidae. Heppner, John B., ed. (Lepidopterorum Catalogus Ser.: Vol. 1: Fasc. 7). (Illus.). 8p. (Orig.). 1997. pap. text 4.50 (*0-945417-51-9*) Sci Pubs.

Davis, Dona L. & Low, Setha M., eds. Gender, Health & Illness: A Case of Nerves. 175p. 1989. 63.95 (*0-89116-903-2*) Hemisp Pub.

Davis, Donald. Barking at a Fox-Fur Coat. 206p. 1991. 19.95 (*0-87483-141-5*); pap. 12.95 (*0-87483-140-7*) August Hse.

***Davis, Donald.** I See Asheville, I See France: Back to School with Donald Davis. 2000. pap. 4.95 (*0-87483-606-9*) August Hse.

Davis, Donald. Jack & the Animals: An Appalachian Folktale. LC 94-46966. (Illus.). (J). (ps-2). 1995. 15.95 (*0-87483-413-9*) August Hse.

***Davis, Donald.** Listening for the Crack of Dawn: A Master Storyteller Recalls the Appalachia of His Youth. 2000. reprint ed. pap. 11.95 (*0-87483-605-0*) August Hse.

Davis, Donald. Listening for the Crack of Dawn, a Master Storyteller Recalls the Appalachia of the 1950's & 60's. 1991. 18.05 (*0-606-12397-0*, Pub. by Turtleback) Demco.

— See Rock City: A Story Journey Through Appalachia. 1996. 22.95 (*0-87483-448-1*); pap. text 12.95 (*0-87483-456-2*) August Hse.

— Southern Jack Tales. LC 97-28887. (J). 1997. pap. text 11.95 (*0-87483-500-3*) August Hse.

— Telling Your Own Stories: A Resource for Family Storytelling, Classroom Story Creation, & Personal Journaling. (American Storytelling Ser.). 96p. 1993. pap. 10.00 (*0-87483-235-7*) August Hse.

— Thirteen Miles from Suncrest: A Novel. LC 94-12998. 256p. 1994. 22.95 (*0-87483-379-5*) August Hse.

***Davis, Donald.** Writing as a Second Language: From Experience to Story to Prose. 144p. 2000. pap. 11.95 (*0-87483-567-4*) August Hse.

Davis, Donald, jt. auth. see Davis, Owen, Sr.

Davis, Donald D. Listening for the Crack of Dawn: A Master Storyteller Recalls the Appalachia of the 1950's & 60's. 220p. 1991. pap. 12.95 (*0-87483-130-X*) August Hse.

Davis, Donald D., ed. see Adkins, Winthrop R.

D

Davis, Donald Edward. Where There Are Mountains: An Environmental History of the Southern Appalachians. LC 99-23869. (Illus.). 352p. 1999. 40.00 (*0-8203-2125-7*) U of Ga Pr.

Davis, Donald F. Conspicuous Production: Automobiles & Elites in Detroit, 1899-1933. LC 87-26745. (Technology & Urban Growth Ser.). (Illus.). 320p. (C). 1988. 37.95 (*0-87722-549-4*) Temple U Pr.

Davis, Donald G., Jr., ed. Libraries, Books & Culture. LC 86-14821. 491p. 1986. 15.00 (*0-938729-00-4*) UTX SLIS.

— Reading & Libraries: Proceedings of Library History Seminar VIII, 9-11 May 1990, Bloomington, Indiana. 492p. 1991. 15.00 (*0-938729-01-2*) UTX SLIS.

Davis, Donald G., Jr. & Tucker, John M. American Library History: A Comprehensive Guide to the Literature. LC 89-33480. 494p. 1989. 35.00 (*0-87436-142-7*, 33481, Pub. by ABC-CLIO) Oak Knoll.

Davis, Donald G., Jr., jt. auth. see Taher, Mohamed.

Davis, Donald G., Jr., ed. see Holley, Edward G., et al.

Davis, Donald G., Jr., jt. ed. see Wiegand, Wayne A.

Davis, Donald M. The Nature & Power of Mathematics. LC 92-26744. (Illus.). 488p. (C). 1993. pap. text 27.50 (*0-691-02562-2*, Pub. by Princeton U Pr) Cal Prin Full Svc.

Davis, Donald M., jt. auth. see Carroll, Raymond L.

Davis, Donald R. Generic Revision of the Opostegidae, with a Synoptic Catalog of the World's Species: Lepidoptera: Nepticuloidea. LC 89-600066. (Smithsonian Contributions to Zoology Ser.: No. 478). 101p. reprint ed. pap. 31.40 (*0-8357-6412-5*, 203577300096) Bks Demand.

Davis, Donald R., et al. Solutions to Practice Sets 1-5 to Accompany Hillman, Kochanek, Norgaard "Principles of Accounting," Sixth Edition & Kochanek, Hillman, Norgaard "Financial Accounting," Second Edition. 274p. (C). 1993. 8.75 (*0-15-500307-0*) Dryden Pr.

Davis, Donn M. Survival Skills for the Modern Man. LC 98-5655. (Illus.). 176p. 1998. pap. 14.95 (*0-8092-2973-0*, 297300, Contemporary Bks) NTC Contemp Pub Co.

Davis, Donna R. The Princess & Ballet. (Illus.). 52p. (Orig.). (J). (gr. k-5). 1996. pap. 5.95 (*0-9644890-5-8*) Spirit Bks.

— Tick Tock the Giant Who Hates Time. 20p. (J). (gr. k-5). 1995. pap. text 9.95 (*0-9644890-0-7*) Spirit Bks.

Davis, Dorinne S. Otitis Media: Coping with the Effects in the Classroom. 138p. (C). 1989. 26.20 (*0-9622326-0-2*) The Davis Ctr.

— A Parent's Guide to Middle Ear Infections. Birsner, E. Patricia, ed. LC 94-96116. (Illus.). 128p. (Orig.). 1994. pap. 24.95 (*0-9622326-2-9*) The Davis Ctr.

Davis, Doris. The Mystery of Briar Rose Manor. LC 89-82583. (Illus.). 122p. (YA). 1990. pap. 3.95 (*0-88243-652-X*, 02-0652) Gospel Pub.

Davis, Doris A. Flower of the Nile. Davis, Henry A., ed. (Illus.). 224p. 1998. pap. 13.95 (*0-9665986-0-1*) D A Davis.

Davis, Dorothy. God's Portrait of a Beautiful Woman. 120p. (Orig.). 1996. reprint ed. pap. 6.29 (*0-87227-186-2*, RBP5228) Reg Baptist.

Davis, Dorothy, et al, eds. Llegando a Cristo: Por Que Hago Lo Que Hago? (Happy Heart Ser.: No. 1-882283-09-0). (SPA., Illus.). 48p. (Orig.). pap. 3.00 (*1-882283-03-1*) D M Eichler.

Davis, Dorothy B. The Little Man. rev. ed. (Illus.). 52p. (J). (ps-4). 1966. 2.50 (*0-87178-530-7*, 8307) Brethren.

— The Tall Man. (Illus.). 28p. (J). (ps-4). 1996. reprint ed. 11.95 (*0-87178-831-4*, 8314) Brethren.

Davis, Dorothy B. & Davis, Sara E. The Middle Man. (Illus.). 36p. (J). (ps-2). 1993. 11.95 (*0-87178-570-6*, 8706) Brethren.

Davis, Dorothy E. Your Faith on Trial: The Books of 1 & 2 Peter. (Women's Bible Studies Ser.). 112p. (Orig.). 1998. pap. 6.29 (*0-87227-197-8*, RBP5235) Reg Baptist.

Davis, Dorothy S. Death of an Old Sinner. large type ed. (Nightingale Ser.). 304p. 1989. pap. 14.95 (*0-8161-4791-4*, G K Hall Lrg Type) Mac Lib Ref.

— A Gentleman Called. (Black Dagger Crime Ser.). 200p. 1997. 19.50 (*0-7451-8708-0*, Black Dagger) Chivers N Amer.

— The Habit of Fear. 1989. mass mkt. 3.50 (*0-373-26031-8*) Harlequin Bks.

— The Habit of Fear. large type ed. (General Ser.). 425p. 1989. lib. bdg. 18.95 (*0-8161-4648-9*, G K Hall Lrg Type) Mac Lib Ref.

— Lullaby of Murder. 224p. 1989. reprint ed. spiral bd. 3.50 (*0-373-26021-0*) Harlequin Bks.

— Old Sinners Never Die. large type ed. (Nightingale Series Large Print Bks.). 262p. 1991. pap. 14.95 (*0-8161-5167-9*, G K Hall Lrg Type) Mac Lib Ref.

— Where the Dark Streets Go. 192p. 1986. mass mkt. 2.95 (*0-380-70131-6*, Avon Bks) Morrow Avon.

Davis, Douglas. The Museum Transformed: Design & Culture in the Post-Pompidou Age. (Illus.). 240p. 1990. 29.98 (*1-55859-064-1*) Abbeville Pr.

— The Nature of the Machine. Silverman, Lanny, ed. (Illus.). 32p. (Orig.). 1993. pap. 12.00 (*0-938903-15-2*) Cty of Chicago.

Davis, Douglas, jt. ed. see Gracia, Jorge J.

Davis, Douglas A. Classical Mechanics. 451p. (C). 1986. text 81.00 (*0-15-507630-2*) SCP.

Davis, Douglas A., jt. auth. see Davis, Susan S.

Davis, Douglas D. & Holt, Charles A. Experimental Economics. LC 92-27662. 590p. (C). 1993. text 49.50 (*0-691-04317-5*, Pub. by Princeton U Pr) Cal Prin Full Svc.

***Davis, Drew.** Rx for New Product Success: A Guide to Successful Innovation for Media Executives. (Illus.). 68p. 1999. pap. 17.50 (*0-9656018-6-2*) NMC.

Davis, Drew K., jt. auth. see Balmer, Wayne T.

Davis, Duane. Business Research for Decision Making. 4th ed. (C). 1995. pap. 58.00 (*0-534-24612-5*) Wadsworth Pub.

— Business Research For Decision Making. 5th ed. (Business Statistics Ser.). 1999. 62.00 (*0-534-37106-X*) PWS Pubs.

— Demon Eyes. Bowen, Jerry, ed. LC 96-96111. 227p. (Orig.). 1996. pap. 6.99 (*0-9651311-0-6*) Davis Bks.

— Listen & Play with My Friends & Me Activity Manual. (My Friends & Me Ser.). (J). (ps). 1988. student ed. 33.95 (*0-88671-331-5*, 4631) Am Guidance.

— My Friends & Me Activity Manual. rev. ed. (My Friends & Me Ser.). (J). (ps). 1988. pap. text 72.95 (*0-88671-325-0*, 4601) Am Guidance.

— My Friends & Me Story Book. rev. ed. (My Friends & Me Ser.). (J). (ps). 1988. pap. text 86.95 (*0-88671-326-9*, 4605) Am Guidance.

***Davis, Duane, ed.** Merleau-Ponty's Later Works & Their Practical Implications: The Dehiscence of Responsibility. 340p. 2001. 69.95 (*1-57392-862-3*) Prometheus Bks.

Davis, Duane & Cosenza, Robert. Business Research For Decision Making. LC 84-15412. (Business Statistics Ser.). 561p. (C). 1985. pap. 33.00 (*0-534-04107-8*) PWS Pubs.

Davis, Duane & Cosenza, Robert M. Business Research For Decision Making. 2nd ed. (Business Statistics Ser.). 561p. 1988. pap. 45.75 (*0-534-87213-1*) PWS Pubs.

Davis, Duane & Cosenza, Robert M. Business Research for Decision Making. 3rd ed. LC 92-30553. 622p. 1993. text 47.75 (*0-534-93249-5*) Wadsworth Pub.

Davis, Duane H. The Dehiscence of Responsibility: Merleau Pontys Later Works & Their Practical Implications. (C). Date not set. text. write for info. (*0-391-04041-3*) Humanities.

***Davis, Duke.** Cowboy Poetry Contemporary Verse by Duke Davis. Coggin, Janice & Coggin, H. Mason, eds. (Illus.). 208p. 2000. 20.00 (*0-9662091-4-1*) Cowboy Miner.

Davis, E., ed. Maynaud Features, Acrocyanosis, Cryoimmunoproteins. (Advances in Microcirculation Ser.: Vol. 10). (Illus.). viii, 116p. 1982. 85.25 (*3-8055-2790-X*) S Karger.

— The Microcirculation in Diabetes. (Advances in Microcirculation Ser.: Vol. 8). (Illus.). 1979. 100.00 (*3-8055-2916-3*) S Karger.

— Raynaud Update: Pathophysiology & Treatment. (Advances in Microcirculation Ser.: Vol. 12). (Illus.). vi, 162p. 1985. 120.00 (*3-8055-3992-4*) S Karger.

Davis, E. A., ed. Science in the Making: Scientific Development As Chronicled by Historic Papers in the Philosophical Magazine, with Commentaries & Illustrations, Vol. 1: 1798-1850. 300p. 1995. 99.00 (*0-7484-0219-5*, Pub. by Tay Francis Ltd) Taylor & Francis.

Davis, E. A., et al, eds. Nevill Mott Festschrift: In Celebration of His Eightieth Birthday, a Special Issue of Philosophical Magazine B, Vol. 52, No. 3. 616p. 1985. 46.00 (*0-85066-972-3*) Taylor & Francis.

Davis, E. A. & Cox, S. F., eds. Protons & Muons in Materials Science. 500p. 1996. 126.00 (*0-7484-0478-3*) Taylor & Francis.

Davis, E. A. & Falconer, Isobel. J. J. Thompson & the Discovery of the Electron. LC 97-197570. 256p. 1997. 135.00 (*0-7484-0696-4*, Pub. by Tay Francis Ltd); pap. 45.00 (*0-7484-0720-0*, Pub. by Tay Francis Ltd) Taylor & Francis.

Davis, E. E., jt. auth. see Thomas, M. Donald.

Davis, E. F., et al. Supplying Household Heating Services by High Temperature Circulating Liquids & Vapors. (Research Bulletin Ser.: No. 3). iv, 23p. 1948. pap. 25.00 (*1-58222-049-2*) Inst Gas Tech.

Davis, E. H., jt. auth. see Squier, Ephraim G.

Davis, E. J. Practical Sales Forecasting. 256p. 1989. text 13.95 (*0-07-707080-1*) McGraw.

Davis, E. L., et al, contrib. by. Cultural Resource Reconnaissance of the Live Fire Maneuver Range Assembly & Defense Areas, Ft. Irwin, San Bernardino County, California. fac. ed. (Fort Irwin, Miscellaneous Reports). (Illus.). 180p. (C). 1981. reprint ed. pap. text 19.38 (*1-55567-518-2*) Coyote Press.

Davis, E. L., jt. auth. see Schmitter, W. P.

Davis, E. P. Bank Credit Risk. LC HG4521.. (Working Papers: No. 8). 51p. reprint ed. pap. 30.00 (*0-7837-5946-0*, 204574500007) Bks Demand.

— The Consumption Function in Macroeconomic Models: A Comparative Study. LC HB0172.5.D3. (Bank of England Technical Series. Discussion Papers: No. 1). 78p. reprint ed. pap. 30.00 (*0-608-13129-6*, 201947000011) Bks Demand.

— Industrial Structure & Dynamics of Financial Markets: The Primary Eurobond Market. LC HG0173.. (Bank of England. Discussion Papers: No. 35). 64p. reprint ed. pap. 30.00 (*0-7837-6659-9*, 204627000011) Bks Demand.

— Instability in the Euromarkets & the Economic Theory of Financial Crisis. LC HG0136.D57. (Bank of England, Discussion Papers: No. 43). 61p. reprint ed. pap. 30.00 (*0-7837-7002-2*, 204681500004) Bks Demand.

— International Diversification of Institutional Investors. LC HG8850.. (Bank of England, Discussion Papers: Vol. 44). 60p. 1991. reprint ed. pap. 30.00 (*0-608-02764-2*, 206383000007) Bks Demand.

— Modelling the U. K. Economy in a Stock-Flow Consistent Manner. LC HG1581.D57. (Bank of England. Discussion Papers. Technical Ser.: No. 14). 123p. reprint ed. pap. 38.20 (*0-8357-4084-6*, 203677500005) Bks Demand.

— A Recursive Model of Personal Sector Expenditure & Accumulation. LC HB0141.. (Bank of England. Technical Series. Discussion Papers: No. 6). 100p. reprint ed. pap. 31.00 (*0-608-12168-1*, 202478900038) Bks Demand.

Davis, E. P. & Mayer, C. P. Corporate Finance in the Euromarkets & the Economics of Intermediation. fac. ed. LC HC0010.D545.. (Bank of England, Discussion Papers: No. 45). 44p. 1994. pap. 30.00 (*0-7837-7648-9*, 204740100007) Bks Demand.

Davis, E. P., jt. auth. see Bodie, Zvi.

Davis, E. P., jt. auth. see Colwell, R. J.

Davis, E. Philip. Debt, Financial Fragility & Systemic Risk. (Illus.). 408p. 1995. pap. text 35.00 (*0-19-823331-0*) OUP.

— Pension Funds: Retirement-Income Security & the Development of Financial Systems: An International Perspective. (Illus.). 350p. 1998. reprint ed. pap. text 27.95 (*0-19-829304-6*) OUP.

Davis, Earl & Davis, Stuart, texts. Stuart Davis: Scapes. (Illus.). 127p. 1990. pap. 40.00 (*1-58821-015-4*) Salander OReilly.

Davis, Earl C. Gods' Mighty Mountains: Sermonic Meditations for Spiritual Growth. 1997. pap. 8.95 (*0-7880-0920-6*, Fairway Pr) CSS OH.

— A Theological Practicum: A Training Guide for Christian Service. unabridged ed. 119p. 1999. pap. text 17.95 (*0-9672609-0-6*) Earl Davis.

Davis, Earl H. Hobson of Virginia & North Carolina, Descendants of George & Elizabeth Hobson, Virginia, North Carolina, Ohio & Indiana. 322p. 1997. reprint ed. pap. 49.00 (*0-8328-9152-5*); reprint ed. lib. bdg. 59.00 (*0-8328-9151-7*) Higginson Bk Co.

Davis, Ed. Atlantic City Diary, 1880-1985: A Century of Memories. (Illus.). 172p. reprint ed. pap. 9.95 (*0-9622645-1-2*) Atlantic City News Pub.

— Whispering Leaves. 28p. 1989. 4.00 (*0-945251-02-5*) Great Elm.

Davis, Edith & McGinnis, Esther. Parent Education: A Survey of the Minnesota Program, Vol. 17. LC 76-141544. (University of Minnesota Institute of Child Welfare Monographs: No. 17). (Illus.). 153p. 1975. reprint ed. lib. bdg. 22.50 (*0-8371-5891-5*, CWDP) Greenwood.

Davis, Edith S. Whether White or Black, a Man. LC 77-37590. (Black Heritage Library Collection). (Illus.). 1977. reprint ed. 19.95 (*0-8369-8966-X*) Ayer.

Davis, Edward. Dispute Resolution & Conflict Management in Construction. 1998. 90.00 (*0-419-23700-3*, E & FN Spon) Routledge.

Davis, Edward, jt. compiled by see Norgren, Jill.

Davis, Edward B., ed. The Antievolution Pamphlets of Harry Rimmer. LC 94-42616. (Creationism in Twentieth-Century America Ser.: Vol. 6). (Illus.). 520p. 1995. text 96.00 (*0-8153-1807-3*) Garland.

Davis, Edward B., ed. see Boyle, Robert.

Davis, Edward D. A Half Century of Struggle for Freedom in Florida. LC 82-50932. 1982. write for info. (*0-9610068-0-3*) Drake's Ptg & Pub.

Davis, Edward E. Bruno the Pretzel Man. LC 84-47630. (Illus.). 64p. (J). (gr. 2-5). 1984. 11.50 (*0-06-021398-1*) HarpC Child Bks.

Davis, Edward G. Maryland & North Carolina in the Campaign of 1780-1781, with a Preliminary Notice of the Revolution, in Which the Troops of the Two States Won Distinction. LC 72-14418. (Maryland Historical Society. Fund-Publications: No. 33). reprint ed. 27.50 (*0-404-57633-8*) AMS Pr.

Davis, Edward H. & Morgan, Edward B. The Virginia Creeper Trail: Nature & History along Southwest Virginia's National Recreation Trail. 1997. pap. 9.95 (*1-57072-065-7*) Overmountain Pr.

Davis, Edward J., ed. see Yakimanskaya, I. S.

Davis, Edward L. Entrepreneurship in Vocational Education: A Guide for Program Planning. 6.50 (*0-318-23259-6*, LT 62) Ctr Educ Trng Employ.

Davis, Edward L. & Zelinko, Margaret. Entrepreneurship in Vocational Education: A Guide for Program Planning. 77p. 1982. 6.50 (*0-318-22094-6*, LT62) Ctr Educ Trng Employ.

Davis, Edward M. & Newcomb, William W., eds. Exhibicion de la Coleccion Peruana Danciger. Benavides, Magdalena, tr. from SPA. (Illus.). 1960. pap. 5.00 (*0-87959-024-6*) U of Tex H Ransom Ctr.

— A Preview of the Danciger Peruvian Collection. LC 60-63787. (Illus.). 1960. pap. 5.00 (*0-87959-023-8*) U of Tex H Ransom Ctr.

Davis, Edward T., jt. auth. see Sanders, John L.

Davis, Edward W., jt. ed. see Buckland, Roger.

Davis, Edwin A. Fallen Guidon: The Saga of Confederate General Jo Shelby's March to Mexico. LC 95-12207. (Illus.). 192p. (C). 1995. reprint ed. 27.50 (*0-89096-683-4*); reprint ed. pap. 14.95 (*0-89096-684-2*) Tex A&M Univ Pr.

Davis, Edwin A. & Hogan, William R. Barber of Natchez. LC 54-10885. (Illus.). 278p. 1973. pap. 14.95 (*0-8071-0212-1*) La State U Pr.

Davis, Edwin A., ed. see Barrow, Bennet H.

Davis, Edwin A., jt. ed. see Hogan, William R.

Davis, Edwin G. Customer Relations for Technicians. 128p. 1990. teacher ed. write for info. (*0-318-65457-1*) McGraw.

— Customer Relations for Technicians. 128p. 1990. pap. 22.59 (*0-07-015832-0*) McGraw.

Davis, Edwin H., jt. auth. see Squier, Ephraim G.

Davis, Edwin S. A Public Policy Primer. 74p. (C). 1992. pap. text 18.60 (*0-536-58314-5*) Pearson Custom.

Davis, Eileen. Horse Deductions & Income. 32p. 1998. spiral bd. 7.95 (*0-9655015-1-5*) E L Davis.

Davis, Eileen, ed. see Kopp, Linda.

Davis, E.J. Tank's Choice. 1995. 4.99 (*1-85792-102-X*, Pub. by Christian Focus) Spring Arbor Dist.

Davis, Elaine N. Eve's Fruit. 136p. 1995. pap., per. 10.95 (*1-884289-11-8*, Life Press) Grandmother Erth.

— From Now to the End: An Easy Guide to Revelation Times. LC 98-65935. (Illus.). 159p. 1998. pap. 14.95 (*1-892113-00-7*, 1-892113) Lightside.

— Mothers of Jesus: From Matthew's Genealogy. LC 94-75436. 400p. (Orig.). 1994. pap. 12.95 (*1-884289-05-3*) Grandmother Erth.

Davis, Elaine R. Total Quality Management for Home Care. 368p. 1994. 69.00 (*0-8342-0332-4*, 20332) Aspen Pub.

Davis, Eli. The Quack - A Tale of Diabetics, Rheumatics, Olives. 344p. 1986. pap. 18.00 (*965-09-0115-9*, 73825, Pub. by R Mass Ltd) Lambda Pubs.

— Who Health All Thy Diseases. 351p. 1975. 18.00 (*965-09-0116-7*, 73826, Pub. by R Mass Ltd) Lambda Pubs.

Davis, Eli & Davis, Elise. Jewish Folk Art over the Ages. 2nd rev. ed. (Illus.). 72p. 1977. 26.00 (*965-09-0017-9*, 73827, Pub. by R Mass Ltd) Lambda Pubs.

Davis, Elisabeth B. Using the Biological Literature: A Practical Guide. 2nd expanded rev. ed. LC 95-11639. (Books in Library & Information Sciences: Vol. 57). (Illus.). 440p. 1995. text 85.00 (*0-8247-9477-X*) Dekker.

Davis, Elisabeth B. & Schmidt, Diane. Guide to Information Sources in the Botanical Sciences. 2nd ed. (Reference Sources in Science & Technology Ser.). xxi, 275p. 1995. lib. bdg. 59.00 (*1-56308-075-3*) Libs Unl.

Davis, Elise, jt. auth. see Davis, Eli.

Davis, Eliza T. Surry County Records: Surry County, Virginia, 1652-1684. 156p. 1997. reprint ed. pap. 17.50 (*0-8063-0904-0*, 1378) Clearfield Co.

Davis, Elizabeth. Energetic Pregnancy. LC 88-2978. (Illus.). 156p. 1995. pap. 8.95 (*0-89087-522-7*) Celestial Arts.

— Heart & Hands: A Midwife's Guide to Pregnancy & Birth. 3rd rev. ed. LC 97-40593. 1997. pap. 21.95 (*0-89087-838-2*) Celestial Arts.

— Women, Sex & Desire: Exploring Your Sexuality at Every Stage of Life. LC 95-33256. (Illus.). 224p. 1995. 22.95 (*0-89793-195-5*); pap. 12.95 (*0-89793-194-7*) Hunter Hse.

— Women's Intuition. LC 89-318870. 1989. pap. 7.95 (*0-89087-572-3*) Celestial Arts.

— The Women's Wheel of Life. 256p. 1997. pap. 11.95 (*0-14-019505-X*) Viking Penguin.

Davis, Elizabeth A. Index to the New World Recorded Anthology of American Music. 224p. (C). 1981. pap. text 10.50 (*0-393-95172-3*) Norton.

Davis, Elizabeth A. & Music Library Association Staff. A Basic Music Library: Essential Scores & Sound Recordings. 3rd ed. LC 96-47351. 650p. 1997. write for info. (*0-8389-3461-7*) American Library Association National Library.

***Davis, Elizabeth B.** Myth & Identity in the Epic of Imperial Spain. 2000. 34.95 (*0-8262-1277-8*) U of Mo Pr.

Davis, Elizabeth W. "You Should Meet Them" Your Ancestors & Descendants. LC 83-71329. 1983. write for info. (*0-9611384-0-8*) E W H Davis.

Davis, Ella. Black History Coloring Book Series. (Illus.). 20p. (J). (ps-4). 1999. pap. 1.95 (*1-888185-58-9*) Davis Pubng LA.

— Black History Picture Book Series. (Illus.). 20p. (J). (ps-4). 1999. pap. 3.95 (*1-888185-59-7*) Davis Pubng LA.

— Learn to Read: For Those That Didn't. 1999. pap. 59.95 (*1-888185-60-0*) Davis Pubng LA.

Davis, Ella D. Behavior Booklet. 7p. 1992. pap. text 10.95 (*1-888185-55-4*) Davis Pubng LA.

— A Complete Guide to Setting up a Special Education Program. 16p. 1992. pap. text 19.95 (*1-888185-50-3*) Davis Pubng LA.

— I'm Behaving Now. 24p. (C). 1994. pap. text 25.95 (*1-888185-54-6*) Davis Pubng LA.

— I'm Special - Teach Me to Read: A Guide for Elementary Teachers, Special Education Teachers, Tutors, Aides, Parents, & Guardians to Teach Reluctant Elementary Students & Special Education Students How to Write, Read, & Spell. 1994. pap. text 39.95 (*1-888185-57-0*) Davis Pubng LA.

— My Math Fact Booklet. 14p. (J). (gr. k-6). 1992. pap. text 12.95 (*1-888185-51-1*) Davis Pubng LA.

— My Word Booklet. 6p. (J). (gr. k-6). 1993. pap. text 15.95 (*1-888185-53-8*) Davis Pubng LA.

— Special Education Lesson Plan Booklet. 10p. (C). 1992. pap. text 19.95 (*1-888185-52-X*) Davis Pubng LA.

Davis, Ellen C., ed. see Heyward, Carter.

Davis, Ellen F. Imagination Shaped: Old Testament Preaching in the Anglican Tradition. LC 95-11558. 304p. (Orig.). 1995. pap. 19.00 (*1-56338-121-4*) TPI PA.

***Davis, Ellen F.** Proverbs, Ecclesiastes & the Song of Songs. (Westminster Bible Companion Ser.). 272p. 2000. pap. 21.95 (*0-664-25522-1*, Pub. by Westminster John Knox) Presbyterian Pub.

— Swallowing the Scroll: Textuality & the Dynamics of Discourse in Ezekiel's Prophecy. (JSOT Supplement Ser.: No. 78). 184p. 1989. 57.50 (*1-85075-206-0*, Pub. by Sheffield Acad) CUP Services.

Davis, Elmer. History of the New York Times, 1851-1921. 1988. reprint ed. lib. bdg. 59.00 (*0-7812-0540-9*) Rprt Serv.

— History of the New York Times, 1851-1921. LC 70-144968. (Illus.). 1971. reprint ed. 59.00 (*0-403-00937-5*) Scholarly.

Davis, Elmer H. But We Were Born Free. LC 73-138585. 229p. 1971. reprint ed. lib. bdg. 59.50 (*0-8371-5784-6*, DABF, Greenwood Pr) Greenwood.

— By Elmer Davis. Davis, Robert L., ed. LC 77-117780. (Essay Index Reprint Ser.). 1977. 26.95 (*0-8369-1798-7*) Ayer.

Davis, Elmer H. History of the New York Times, 1851-1921. LC 72-95092. 434p. 1970. reprint ed. lib. bdg. 37.50 (*0-8371-2578-2*, DAHT, Greenwood Pr) Greenwood.

D

An Asterisk (*) at the beginning of an entry indicates that the title is appearing for the first time.

Davis, Elmer H. Not to Mention the War. LC 71-107692. (Essay Index Reprint Ser.). 1977. 23.95 (*0-8369-1602-6*) Ayer.

Davis, Elwin N., ed. see Society for Applied Spectroscopy Staff.

Davis, Emily & Fiddler, Brenda Kirk. Henderson County, Tennessee: A Pictorial History. (Illus.). 368p. 1996. 45.00 (*0-9676742-1-2*) E D Bks.

***Davis, Emily C.** Lake County, Tennessee, Memories: History in Pictures & Newsprint. (Illus.). 344p. 1998. 45.00 (*0-9676742-0-4*) E D Bks.

Davis, Emily Cleveland, see Cleveland Davis, Emily.

***Davis, Emma.** To the Circus. LC 99-70454. (All in a Row, Go! Ser.). (Illus.). 12p. (J). (ps-1). 1999. 9.95 (*0-7613-1037-1*, Copper Beech Bks) Millbrook Pr.

Davis, Emma. To the Zoo: Animal Poems. LC 99-70453. (All in a Row, Go! Ser.). (Illus.). 12p. (J). (ps-1). 1999. 9.95 (*0-7613-1036-3*, Copper Beech Bks) Millbrook Pr.

Davis, Emma L., et al, contrib. by. Cultural Resource Reconnaissance of a Portion of the Live Fire Maneuver Range, Fort Irwin, San Bernardino County, California. fac. ed. (Fort Irwin, Miscellaneous Reports). (Illus.). 103p. (C). 1980. reprint ed. pap. text 11.56 (*1-55567-517-4*) Coyote Press.

***Davis, Eric.** Born to Play: The Eric Davis Story: Life Lessons in Overcoming Adversity on & off the Field. 2000. mass mkt. 6.99 (*0-451-20104-3*, Sig) NAL.

Davis, Eric. Challenging Colonialism: Bank Mi Sr & Egyptian Industrialization, 1920-1941. LC 82-47590. (Princeton Studies on the Near East). 247p. 1983. reprint ed. pap. 76.60 (*0-608-07657-0*, 205997700010) Bks Demand.

— Slick Boys: A Ten-Point Plan to Rescue Your Community by Three Chicago Cops Who Are Making It Happen. LC 98-16933. 240p. 1998. 22.00 (*0-684-83300-X*) S&S Trade.

Davis, Eric & Gavrielides, Nicolas, eds. Statecraft in the Middle East: Historical Memory & Popular Culture. 304p. 1991. 49.95 (*0-8130-1046-2*); pap. 24.95 (*0-8130-1058-6*) U Press Fla.

Davis, Eric & Wiley, Ralph. Born to Play: The Eric Davis Story. LC 98-35636. (Illus.). 278p. 1999. 24.95 (*0-670-88511-8*, Viking) Viking Penguin.

Davis, Erik. Timing is Everything. 1999. pap. 14.00 (*0-609-80474-X*) Crown Pub Group.

***Davis, Erin, et al.** Looking at Microbes: Viewers Guide. (Illus.). (C). 1998. pap. text. write for info. (*0-7637-0760-0*) Jones & Bartlett.

Davis, Ernest. Representations of Commonsense Knowledge. (Representation & Reasoning Ser.). 544p. (C). 1990. text 58.95 (*1-55860-033-7*) Morgan Kaufmann.

— Representing & Acquiring Geographic Knowledge. LC 86-10673. (Research Notes in Artificial Intelligence Ser.). (Illus.). 223p. 1986. pap. text 30.95 (*0-934613-22-2*) Morgan Kaufmann.

Davis, Estelle M., ed. see Davis, Grace Helen.

Davis, Estelle M., ed. & illus. see Davis, Grace H.

Davis, Esther. Sensational Dried Flowers: Make Arrangements So Beautiful They Look Fresh. LC 98-51246. (Illus.). 176p. 1999. text 24.95 (*0-87596-800-7*) Rodale Pr Inc.

Davis, Esther P. Crime Prevention in the 90's. 76p. (YA). (gr. 7-12). 1993. pap. 6.95 (*1-57515-057-3*) PPI Pubng.

— Teens in the '90s. 179p. (YA). (gr. 7-12). 1992. pap. 6.95 (*1-57515-058-1*) PPI Pubng.

Davis, Evia L. African American Awareness for Young Children: A Curriculum. 1998. pap. 11.95 (*0-673-58645-6*) Addison-Wesley.

Davis, F. Hadland. Jami: The Persian Mystic. 103p. (Orig.). 1985. pap. 4.50 (*1-56744-315-X*) Kazi Pubns.

— Myths & Legends of Japan. Date not set. lib. bdg. 28.95 (*0-8488-2096-7*) Amereon Ltd.

— Myths & Legends of Japan. (Illus.). 432p. 1989. reprint ed. pap. 19.50 (*9971-4-9125-7*) Heian Intl.

— Rumi: The Persian Mystic. 107p. (Orig.). (C). 1985. pap. text 3.50 (*1-56744-372-9*) Kazi Pubns.

Davis, F. James. Who Is Black? One Nations's Definition. 216p. 1991. pap. 15.95 (*0-271-00749-4*) Pa St U Pr.

Davis, Fanny. The Ottoman Lady: A Social History from 1718-1918, 70. LC 85-14717. (Contributions in Women's Studies: No. 70). (Illus.). 336p. 1986. 75.00 (*0-313-24811-7*, DOL, Greenwood Pr) Greenwood.

Davis, Fei-Ling. Primitive Revolutionaries of China: A Study of Secret Societies in the Late Nineteenth Century. LC 76-45585. 262p. reprint ed. pap. 74.70 (*0-8357-3503-6*, 2034637) Bks Demand.

Davis, Ferdinand, tr. see Gedalge, Andre.

Davis, Fitzhugh D. Geologic Map of the McCornick Quadrangle, Millard County, Utah. (Map of the Utah Geological Survey Ser.). (Illus.). 13p. 1994. pap. 6.00 (*1-55791-567-9*, M-165) Utah Geological Survey.

Davis, Fitzhugh D., jt. auth. see Doelling, Hellmut H.

Davis, Flora. Moving the Mountain: The Women's Movement in America since 1960. LC 99-11521. 632p. 1999. pap. 21.95 (*0-252-06782-7*) U of Ill Pr.

Davis, Flora, jt. auth. see Raphael, Dana.

Davis, Flora P. & Lane, Lauree. Don't Cry: A Family's Story of Struggle, Hope, Inspiration, & Success. Owensby, Craig, ed. (Illus.). (Orig.). 1995. pap. 12.95 (*0-9649467-0-X*) Naja Press.

Davis-Floyd, R. & Dumit, J., eds. Cyborg Babies: From Techno-Sex to Techno-Tots. LC 97-44516. 368p. 1998. pap. 22.99 (*0-415-91604-6*, D1296) Routledge.

— Cyborg Babies: From Techno-Sex to Techno-Tots. LC 97-44516. 368p. (C). 1998. 80.00 (*0-415-91603-8*, D1292) Routledge.

Davis-Floyd, Robbee E. Birth As an American Rite of Passage. (C). 1993. pap. 17.95 (*0-520-08431-4*, Pub. by U CA Pr) Cal Prin Full Svc.

Davis-Floyd, Robbie. Birth As an American Rite of Passage. 1992. 48.00 (*0-520-07439-4*, Pub. by U CA Pr) Cal Prin Full Svc.

— The Power of Ritual. 1999. write for info. (*0-8052-4155-8*) Schocken.

Davis-Floyd, Robbie & Arvidson, P. Sven. Intuition: The Inside Story. LC 96-37299. 240p. (C). 1997. 70.00 (*0-415-91593-7*); pap. 20.99 (*0-415-91594-5*) Routledge.

Davis-Floyd, Robbie & Sargent, Carolyn F., eds. Childbirth & Authoritative Knowledge: Cross-Cultural Perspectives. LC 96-48263. 505p. 1997. 50.00 (*0-520-20625-8*, Pub. by U CA Pr); pap. 19.95 (*0-520-20785-8*, Pub. by U CA Pr) Cal Prin Full Svc.

Davis-Floyd, Robbie & St. John, Gloria. From Doctor to Healer: The Transformative Journey. LC 97-39343. (Illus.). 293p. (C). 1998. text 50.00 (*0-8135-2519-5*); pap. text 20.00 (*0-8135-2520-9*) Rutgers U Pr.

Davis, Forest K. The Bird of Utica: Life, Thought & Art of Sylvia H. Bliss, 1870-1963. LC 86-20558. 1986. 15.00 (*0-912362-05-7*) Adamant Pr.

— Journey among Mountains. LC 74-175896. 1974. 9.00 (*0-912362-03-0*); pap. 7.00 (*0-912362-04-9*) Adamant Pr.

— Return from Enlightenment. LC 74-155656. 1971. 9.00 (*0-912362-01-4*); pap. 7.00 (*0-912362-02-2*) Adamant Pr.

— Things Were Different in Royce's Day: Royce S. Pitkin As Progressive Educator. A Perspective from Goddard College, 1950-1967. unabridged ed. (Illus.). 325p. 1996. 35.00 (*0-912362-17-0*) Adamant Pr.

Davis, Forrest. The Atlantic System: The Story of Anglo-American Control of the Seas. (History - United States Ser.). 363p. 1993. reprint ed. lib. bdg. 89.00 (*0-7812-4862-0*) Rprt Serv.

Davis, France A. Light in the Midst of Zion: Calvery Missionary Baptist Church & a History of Black Baptists in Utah 1892-1996. (Illus.). 150p. (Orig.). 1997. pap. 10.00 (*0-9656532-1-8*) University Pub.

Davis, Frances. A Fearful Innocence. LC 81-11793. 271p. reprint ed. pap. 84.10 (*0-7837-0499-2*, 204082300018) Bks Demand.

Davis, Frances A. Frank Lloyd Wright: Maverick Architect. (J). 1996. lib. bdg. 23.93 (*0-8225-4953-0*, Lerner Publctns) Lerner Pub.

Davis, Frances A., jt. ed. see Parker, Robert P.

Davis, Francis. The History of the Blues: The Roots, the Music, the People - from Charley Patton to Robert Cray. (Illus.). 320p. (J). 1996. pap. 16.95 (*0-7868-8124-0*, Pub. by Hyperion) Time Warner.

— The History of the Blues: The Roots, the Music, the People-from Charley Patton to Robert Cray. (Illus.). 320p. (J). 1995. 24.45 (*0-7868-6052-9*, Pub. by Hyperion) Time Warner.

— In the Moment: Jazz in the 1980s. 272p. 1996. reprint ed. pap. 13.95 (*0-306-80708-4*) Da Capo.

— Untitled History of Jazz. (Illus.). 384p. 2002. 27.95 (*0-7868-6292-0*, Pub. by Hyperion) Little.

Davis, Frank. Customer Responsive Management: The Flexible Advantage. 1996. pap. text 29.95 (*1-55786-505-1*) Blackwell Pubs.

— Frank Davis Cooks Cajun, Creole, & Crescent City. LC 93-44631. (Illus.). 304p. 1994. 21.95 (*1-56554-055-7*) Pelican.

— Frank Davis Cooks Naturally N'Awlins. LC 89-28333. 272p. 1990. 18.95 (*0-88289-772-1*) Pelican.

— The Frank Davis Seafood Notebook. LC 82-24679. (Illus.). 288p. 1983. 18.95 (*0-88289-309-2*) Pelican.

— One Hundred Years Ago. 1980. pap. 4.95 (*0-910286-79-5*) Boxwood.

Davis, Frank M. I Am the American Negro. LC 70-178471. (Black Heritage Library Collection). 1977. reprint ed. 13.95 (*0-8369-8920-1*) Ayer.

— Livin' the Blues: Memoirs of a Black Journalist & Poet. Tidwell, John E., ed. & intro. by. LC 92-50248. (Studies in American Autobiography). (Illus.). 408p. 1993. 19.95 (*0-299-13500-4*) U of Wis Pr.

Davis, Franklin T., jt. ed. see Wadsworth, Milton E.

Davis, Fred. Definitions of Time & Recovery in Paralytic Polio Convalescence. (Reprint Series in Sociology). (C). 1993. reprint ed. pap. text 1.00 (*0-8290-2640-1*, S-366) Irvington.

— Fashion, Culture & Identity. xii, 238p. 1994. pap. text 12.00 (*0-226-13809-7*) U Ch Pr.

— Fashion, Culture & Identity. LC 91-44012. (Illus.). 238p. 1994. 24.95 (*0-226-13808-9*) U Ch Pr.

— Passage Through Crisis: Polio Victims & Their Families. 256p. (C). 1990. pap. 24.95 (*0-88738-853-1*) Transaction Pubs.

Davis, Fred & Crosby, Kip. The Windows 98 Bible. Collins, Corbin, ed. 994p. (C). 1998. pap. text 34.95 (*0-201-69690-8*, Pub. by Peachpit Pr) Addison-Wesley.

Davis, Frederic E., et al. Newsletter Publishing with PageMaker: Macintosh & IBM Editions. 350p. 1988. pap. 25.00 (*1-55623-064-8*, Irwn Prfssnl) McGraw-Hill Prof.

Davis, Frederick. Suite Polonaise. LC 93-46261. 64p. 1995. pap. 14.95 (*0-7734-2720-1*, Mellen Poetry Pr) E Mellen.

— Windows 95 Bible. 2nd ed. (Illus.). 680p. (C). 1996. pap. text 29.95 (*0-201-88388-0*) Peachpit Pr.

Davis, Frederick E., ed. Contributed Papers & Abstracts for the Conference on Water, Laws & Management: September 17-22, 1989, Tampa, Florida. LC TD0345.C65. (AWRA Special Publication: No. 89-4). (Illus.). 872p. reprint ed. pap. 200.00 (*0-7837-1092-5*, 204162400021) Bks Demand.

Davis-Friedmann, Deborah. Long Lives: Chinese Elderly & the Communist Revolution. 2nd ed. LC 89-64240. (Illus.). 190p. 1991. pap. 12.95 (*0-8047-1808-3*) Stanford U Pr.

Davis, G., retold by. African American: John Henry. (Graphic Learning Multicultural Literature Program Ser.). (ENG & SPA., Illus.). (J). (gr. k-5). 1994. teacher ed. 45.00 (*0-87746-407-3*) Graphic Learning.

— African American Folk Tale: Mr. Knee-High Man. (Graphic Learning Multicultural Literature Program Ser.). (ENG & SPA., Illus.). (J). (gr. k-5). 1994. teacher ed. 45.00 (*0-87746-404-9*) Graphic Learning.

— Asian American: The Way of the Tiger. (Graphic Learning Multicultural Literature Program Ser.). (ENG & SPA., Illus.). (J). (gr. k-5). 1994. teacher ed. 45.00 (*0-87746-425-1*) Graphic Learning.

Davis, G., jt. ed. see Hunting, R. P.

Davis, G. Albyn. A Survey of Adult Aphasia & Related. 2nd ed. LC 92-49840. 384p. (C). 1992. 89.00 (*0-13-878018-8*, Pub. by P-H) S&S Trade.

***Davis, G. H.** The Transports. (Illus.). 240p. 1999. pap. write for info. (*0-930412-25-7*) Bureau Issues.

Davis, G. J. Automotive Reference: A New Approach - to the World of Auto & Related Information. 470p. (Orig.). 1987. 39.95 (*0-937591-01-7*); pap. 24.95 (*0-937591-00-9*) Whitehorse.

— Gas Saver's Reference: A New Approach to the World of Fuel Economy. (Illus.). 134p. (Orig.). 1991. pap. 12.95 (*0-937591-02-5*) Whitehorse.

Davis, G. L. Samuel Davis of Oxford, Mass. & Joseph Davis of Dudley, Mass., & Their Descendants. 618p. 1989. reprint ed. pap. 92.00 (*0-8328-0459-2*); reprint ed. lib. bdg. 100.00 (*0-8328-0458-4*) Higginson Bk Co.

Davis, G. Scott, ed. Religion & Justice in the War over Bosnia. 208p. (C). 1996. 70.00 (*0-415-91519-8*); pap. 18.99 (*0-415-91520-1*) Routledge.

Davis, G. T. Genealogy of the Descendants of Colonel John Davis of Oxford, Connecticut, with a Partial Genealogy of His Ancestors. (Illus.). 338p. 1989. reprint ed. pap. 50.50 (*0-8328-0461-4*); reprint ed. lib. bdg. 58.50 (*0-8328-0460-6*) Higginson Bk Co.

Davis, G. W., ed. Mediterranean-Type Ecosystems: The Function of Biodiversity. LC 94-34429. (Ecological Studies: 109). 1994. write for info. (*3-540-57809-9*) Spr-Verlag.

Davis, G. W. & Richardson, D. M., eds. Mediterranean-Type Ecosystems: The Function of Biodiversity. LC 94-34429. (Ecological Studies: Vol. 109). xix, 352p. 1995. 140.95 (*0-387-57809-9*) Spr-Verlag.

Davis, Gabriel. The Moving Book: A Kid's Survival Guide. LC 95-40604. (Illus.). 128p. (J). 1996. pap. 16.95 (*0-316-17684-2*) Little.

Davis, Gabriele A. Wittig, see Wittig Davis, Gabriele A.

Davis, Gail. The Complete Guide to Vegetarian Convenience Foods. LC 99-20236. 160p. 1999. reprint ed. pap. 12.95 (*0-939165-35-X*) NewSage Press.

— So, Now What Do I Eat? The Complete Guide to Vegetarian Convenience Foods. LC 97-75324. 158p. 1998. pap. 12.95 (*0-9660296-0-7*) Blue Coyote.

— Vegetarian Food for Thought: Quotations & Inspirations. LC 99-14519. (Illus.). 120p. 1999. pap. 14.95 (*0-939165-36-8*) NewSage Press.

Davis, Gale. My Visit to Me-Maw. (Illus.). 18p. (J). (ps-6). 1997. pap. 3.59 (*0-9661299-0-3*) Unika Pubns.

Davis, Garold N. German Thought & Culture in England, 1700-1770. LC 78-629000. (University of North Carolina Studies in Comparative Literature: No. 47). 152p. reprint ed. 47.20 (*0-8357-9703-1*, 201722900006) Bks Demand.

Davis, Garrick, ed. see Hallberg, Edmond C. & Hallberg, Kaylene.

Davis, Garry W. & Iverson, Gregory K., eds. Explanation in Historical Linguistics. LC 92-25765. (Current Issues in Linguistic Theory Ser.: No. 84). xiv, 238p. 1992. 74.00 (*1-55619-139-1*) J Benjamins Pubng Co.

Davis, Gary. Atlantic Coral Reef. LC 96-51021. (Habitats Ser.). 32p. (gr. 2-5). 1997. lib. bdg. 17.30 (*0-516-20375-4*) Childrens.

Davis, Gary. Creativity Is Forever. 4th ed. LC 98-132266. 320p. 1997. per. 34.95 (*0-7872-4524-0*) Kendall-Hunt.

***Davis, Gary.** Creativity Is Forever. 4th ed. 368p. (C). 1999. per. 38.95 (*0-7872-6429-6*, 41642902) Kendall-Hunt.

Davis, Gary. Designing Multimedia Web Sites. LC 96-77069. 456p. 1996. 50.00 incl. cd-rom (*1-56830-308-4*) Hayden.

— Friends: A Novel. LC 94-28700. 1994. pap. 7.95 (*1-55503-716-X*, 019406) Covenant Comms.

— Study Guide & Creativity Exercises to Accompany Creativity Is Forever. 76p. (C). 1995. write for info. (*0-8403-9875-1*) Kendall-Hunt.

— Submarine Wahoo. 1994. pap. 5.95 (*0-382-24753-1*, Crstwood Hse) Silver Burdett Pr.

— Submarine Wahoo. LC 94-7102. (Those Daring Machines Ser.). (J). 1994. pap. 5.95 (*0-382-24765-5*, Crstwood Hse) Silver Burdett Pr.

— Submarine Wahoo. LC 94-7102. (Those Daring Machines Ser.). (J). 1999. lib. bdg. 21.00 (*0-89686-828-1*, Crstwood Hse) Silver Burdett Pr.

— Working at a TV Station. LC 98-6412. (Working Here Ser.). (J). 1998. 23.00 (*0-516-20750-4*) Childrens.

Davis, Gary & Greggory, Catherine. Designing Multimedia for the Web. 1996. 50.00 incl. cd-rom (*0-614-20286-8*, Hayden Sftwre) MCP SW Interactive.

Davis, Gary & Jones, Ralph. The Sound Reinforcement Handbook. 2nd ed. (Illus.). 432p. (Orig.). 1988. per. 34.95 (*0-88188-900-8*, 00500964) H Leonard.

Davis, Gary A. Educational Psychology: Theory & Practice. 704p. (Orig.). (C). 1983. student ed. 5.00 (*0-685-08660-7*) McGraw.

— Teaching Values: An Idea Book for Teachers & Parents. LC 95-90783. 305p. 1996. pap. 21.95 (*1-888115-02-5*) Westwood Pubng.

— Values Are Forever: Becoming More Caring & Responsible. LC 95-90784. 140p. (J). (gr. 4-3). 1996. pap. 15.95 (*1-888115-00-9*) Westwood Pubng.

Davis, Gary A. & Rimm, Sylvia B. Education of the Gifted & Talented. 4th ed. LC 97-17564. 497p. 1997. 79.00 (*0-205-27000-X*) Allyn.

Davis, Gary A., jt. auth. see Colangelo, Nicolas.

Davis, Gary A., jt. auth. see Piasecki, Bruce W.

Davis, Gary W. From Rock to Fireworks. LC 97-25657. (Changes Ser.). (J). (gr. 2-3). 1997. lib. bdg. 24.00 (*0-516-20739-3*) Childrens.

— From Rock to Fireworks. LC 97-25657. (Changes Ser.). (J). (gr. 2-3). 1998. pap. text 6.95 (*0-516-20364-9*) Childrens.

— Working at a TV Station. (Working Here Ser.). (Illus.). 32p. (J). (gr. 2-4). 1999. pap. text 6.95 (*0-516-20378-9*) Childrens.

***Davis, Gayle A.** High Performance Thinking: For Business, Sports & Life. 134p. 1999. pap. 14.95 (*0-9672835-0-7*) Psychology Connections.

Davis, Gene. The Power of Self-Knowledge. 107p. (Orig.). 1992. pap. 9.95 (*0-685-66138-5*) Life Res Found.

— Reversing the Aging Process. 332p. (Orig.). 1987. pap. 29.95 (*0-9618919-0-4*) Life Res Found.

Davis, Genevieve. Beverly Hills: An Illustrated History. (Illus.). 208p. (YA). (gr. 7 up). 1988. 36.95 (*0-89781-238-7*) Am Historical Pr.

Davis, Geoffrey V. South Africa. 2nd rev. ed. LC 96-132941. 496p. 1994. lib. bdg. 99.00 (*1-85109-203-X*) ABC-CLIO.

Davis, Geoffrey V., ed. Beyond the Echoes of Soweto: Five Plays by Matsemela Manaka. (Contemporary Theatre Studies). (Illus.). 160p. 1998. text 41.00 (*90-5702-160-9*, Harwood Acad Pubs) Gordon & Breach.

Davis, Geoffrey V. & Fuchs, Anne, eds. Theatre & Change in South Africa. (Contemporary Theatre Studies: Vol. 12). 366p. 1996. text 58.00 (*3-7186-5650-7*, ECU76, Harwood Acad Pubs); pap. text 20.00 (*3-7186-5651-5*, ECU25, Harwood Acad Pubs) Gordon & Breach.

Davis, Geoffry V., ed. Beyond the Echoes of Soweto: Five Plays by Matsemela Manaka. (Contemporary Theatre Studies). (Illus.). 160p. 1998. pap. text 21.00 (*90-5702-161-7*, Harwood Acad Pubs) Gordon & Breach.

Davis, George. Love Lessons: African Americans & Sex, Romance & Marriage the Nineties. LC 97-28865. 256p. 1998. pap. 12.00 (*0-688-14864-6*, Wm Morrow) Morrow Avon.

— Multiple Choice Questions in Preparation for the AP Economics ("Macro" & "Micro") Examination. 76p. 1992. teacher ed. write for info. (*1-878621-22-X*); student ed. 15.95 (*1-878621-21-1*) D & S Mktg Syst.

— The Posthumous Papers of the Pickwick Club. LC 72-3167. (Studies in Dickens: No. 52). 1972. reprint ed. lib. bdg. 75.00 (*0-8383-1533-X*) M S G Haskell Hse.

Davis, George B. Drafting, Enacting & Maintaining Local Ordinances. 1991. 15.00 (*0-317-05701-4*) MI Municipal.

***Davis, George B.** The Elements of Law: An Introduction to the Study of the Constitutional & Military Law of the United States. 188p. 1999. reprint ed. 60.00 (*1-56169-553-X*, 18184) Gaunt.

Davis, George D. 2020 Vision: Biological Diversity: Saving All the Pieces. (Twenty Twenty Vision: Fulfilling the Promise of the Adirondack Park Ser: Vol. 1). (Illus.). 64p. (Orig.). 1988. pap. 10.00 (*0-9621202-0-0*) Adirondack Council.

Davis, George D., et al. The Lake Baikal Region in the Twenty-First Century: A Model of Sustainable Development or Continued Degradation?: A National Program of Land Use Policies for the Russian Portion of the Lake Baikal Watershed. Birnbaum, Irina, tr. (Comprehensive Land Use Programs Ser.). (ENG & RUS., Illus.). (Orig.). 1993. pap. text. write for info. (*0-9635624-0-1*) Davis NY.

— 2020 Vision: Fulfilling the Promise of the Adirondack Park, 6 vols., Set. (Illus.). (Orig.). 1988. pap. write for info. (*0-9621202-6-X*) Adirondack Council.

***Davis, George H.** Structural Geology of the Colorado Plateau Region of Southern Utah, with Special Emphasis on Deformation Bands. LC 99-45163. (Special Papers). 1999. write for info. (*0-8137-2342-6*) Geol Soc.

Davis, George H. & Coplen, Tyler B. Late Cenozoic Paleohydrogeology of the Western San Joaquin Valley, California, As Related to Structural Movements in the Central Coast Ranges. LC 89-7545. (Geological Society of America Ser.: Vol. 234). (Illus.). 44p. 1989. reprint ed. pap. 30.00 (*0-608-07758-5*, 206784600010) Bks Demand.

Davis, George H. & Reynolds, Steven. Structural Geology of Rocks & Regions. 2nd ed. LC 95-40790. 800p. 1996. text 92.95 (*0-471-52621-5*) Wiley.

Davis, George K. Fundamentals of Macro Economics. (Illus.). 352p. (C). 1995. pap. text 26.95 (*0-9647223-0-5*) Ross Pub OH.

Davis, George M. The Origin & Evolution of the Gastropod Family Pomatiopsidae, with Emphasis on the Mekong River Triculinae. (Monograph: No. 20). (Illus.). 120p. 1979. pap. 5.00 (*0-910006-28-8*) Acad Nat Sci Phila.

Davis, George T. A Navy Second to None: The Development of Modern American Naval Policy. LC 77-110826. (Illus.). 508p. 1971. reprint ed. lib. bdg. 79.50 (*0-8371-3226-6*, DANS, Greenwood Pr) Greenwood.

Davis, George W. Davis. Family History, with Special Emphasis on the Ancestors of the Brothers Philip Christopher Davis, George G. Davis, Joseph G. Davis, James C. Davis & John Edward Davis. 122p. 1997. reprint ed. pap. 21.00 (*0-8328-8230-5*); reprint ed. lib. bdg. 31.00 (*0-8328-8229-1*) Higginson Bk Co.

Davis, Gerald. How to Function in This Economy According to Heaven's Economy. 272p. (Orig.). 1994. pap. 12.00 (*1-880563-08-8*) FAME Pub.

Davis, Gerald, ed. Building Performance: Function, Preservation, & Rehabilitation, STP 901. LC 86-8008. (Special Technical Publication Ser.). (Illus.). 202p. 1986. text 39.00 (*0-8031-0458-8*, STP901) ASTM.

D

Davis, Gerald & Ventre, Francis T., eds. Performance of Buildings & Serviceability of Facilities. LC 90-31703. (Special Technical Publication Ser.: No. 1029). (Illus.). 353p. 1990. text 44.00 (0-8031-1292-0, STP1029) ASTM.

Davis, Gerald L. I Got the Word in Me & I Can Sing It, You Know: A Study of the Performed African-American Sermon. LC 85-2544. (Illus.). 209p. 1985. reprint ed. pap. 64.80 (0-608-05705-3, 206622000007) Bks Demand.

***Davis, Gerald N. & Davis, Norma S.** Behind the Iron Curtain: Recollections of Latter-Day Saints in East Germany, 1945-1989. xiv, 354p. 2000. pap. 11.95 (0-8425-2464-9, BYU Studies) Brigham.

***Davis, Gerald S. & Seward, Elizabeth A.** Medical Management of Pulmonary Diseases. LC 99-37340. (Clinical Guides to Medical Management Ser.). (Illus.). 795p. 1999. text 225.00 (0-8247-6002-6) Dekker.

Davis, Gibbs. Camp Sink or Swim. LC 96-50356. (J). (gr. 1-4). 1997. lib. bdg. 11.99 (0-679-98216-7, Pub. by Random Bks Yng Read) Random.

Davis, Gibbs. Camp Sink or Swim. (Stepping Stone Bks.). 1997. 9.19 (0-606-11186-7, Pub. by Turtleback) Demco.

Davis, Gibbs. Dolley's Detectives. (White House Ghosthunters Ser.: No. 3). (J). 1997. per. 3.99 (0-671-56857-4, Minstrel Bks) PB.

— Merry Christmas, World! (Full House Michelle Ser.: Vol. 23). 96p. (J). (gr. 4-7). 1998. pap. 3.99 (0-671-02098-6, Minstrel Bks) PB.

— Money Madness. (White House Ghosthunters Ser.: No. 1). (J). (gr. 3-7). 1996. per. 3.99 (0-671-56855-8) PB.

— Nest Egg Nightmare. (White House Ghosthunters Ser.: No. 2). (YA). 1997. per. 3.99 (0-671-56856-6) PB.

— The Other Emily. (Illus.). 32p. (J). (gr. k-3). 1990. pap. 4.95 (0-395-54947-7) HM.

— Swann Song. 176p. (YA). (gr. 7 up). 1989. mass mkt. 2.50 (0-380-75609-9, Avon Bks) Morrow Avon.

Davis, Gilbert A. Centennial Celebration. (Illus.). 169p. 1996. reprint ed. pap. 19.50 (0-8328-5128-0); reprint ed. lib. bdg. 29.50 (0-8328-5127-2) Higginson Bk Co.

Davis, Glen. Lotus 1-2-3 Release 6 for Windows, Quick Reference. LC 98-100711. (Quick Reference Guides Ser.). (Illus.). (Orig.). 1996. pap. 12.00 (1-56243-348-2, G-13) DDC Pub.

Davis, Glen & Gosselin. Microsoft Project for Windows 3.1 & Windows 95, Quick Reference. (Orig.). 1996. pap. 12.00 (1-56243-279-6, MP-17) DDC Pub.

Davis, Glen & Baumgarten, Alan. Internet 2, Quick Reference. (Quick Reference Guides Ser.). (Illus.). (Orig.). 1996. pap. 12.00 (1-56243-428-4, I217) DDC Pub.

Davis, Glenn & Roberts, John G. An Occupation Without Troops: America's Japan Lobby & Its Puppets in Japan's Government. (Illus.). 232p. (Orig.). 1996. pap. 12.95 (4-900737-45-3) Tuttle Pubng.

Davis, Glenn, jt. auth. see Martin, Teresa A.

Davis, Glenn B. Choice of Entity: Legal Considerations of Selection. 3rd ed. (Corporate Practice Ser.: No. 50). 1995. 95.00 (1-55871-316-6) BNA.

Davis, Glenn B., jt. auth. see Bradford, W. Murray.

Davis, Glyn, et al. The New Contractualism? LC 98-172799. 270p. 1998. pap. 32.95 (0-7329-4442-2, Pub. by Macmill Educ) Paul & Co Pubs.

D

Davis, Glyn, jt. auth. see Bridgeman, Peter.

Davis, Glyn, jt. auth. see Weller, Patrick.

Davis, Glyn, ed. see Pecar, Branko.

Davis-Goff, Annabel. The Dower House. LC 97-33065. 274p. 1998. text 22.95 (0-312-17028-9) St Martin.

— The Dower House. 1999. pap. 13.95 (0-312-20645-3) St Martin.

Davis, Gordon, ed. see Halim, Jacob.

Davis, Gordon B. Writing the Doctoral Dissertation. 2nd rev. ed. LC 97-11497. 160p. 1997. pap. text 10.95 (0-8120-9800-5) Barron.

Davis, Gordon B., ed. The Blackwell Encyclopedic Dictionary of Management Information Systems. (Blackwell Encyclopedia of Management Ser.). 288p. 1999. reprint ed. pap. 29.95 (0-631-21484-4) Blackwell Pubs.

— The Blackwell Encyclopedic Dictionary of Management of Information Systems. LC 96-30373. (Blackwell Encyclopedia of Management Ser.). 256p. 1997. 110.00 (1-55786-948-0) Blackwell Pubs.

Davis, Gordon B. & Hamilton, Scott. Managing Information: How Information Systems Impact Organizational Strategy. (APICS Ser.). 300p. 1993. 47.50 (1-55623-768-5, Irwn Prfssnl) McGraw-Hill Prof.

Davis, Gordon B. & Litecky, Charles R. Elementary Cobol Programming: A Step By Step Approach. LC 78-140254. x, 164p. 1971. write for info. (0-07-015780-4) McGraw.

Davis, Gordon B. & Naumann, David. Personal Productivity in Information Technology. LC 96-78928. (Illus.). 512p. (C). 1997. pap. 45.00 (0-07-015916-5) McGraw.

Davis, Gordon B., et al. Auditing & EDP Study Guide. 2nd ed. LC HF5667.D39. 246p. reprint ed. pap. 76.30 (0-8357-2651-7, 204017900015) Bks Demand.

Davis, Gordon B., Jr., jt. auth. see Hedrick, David T.

Davis, Grace H. A Garden of Youthful Thoughts & Prayers. Davis, Estelle M., ed. & illus. by. LC 95-70421. 160p. 1995. 12.95 (1-881576-43-4) Providence Hse.

Davis, Grace Helen. Garden of Youthful Thoughts & Prayers. 2nd ed. Davis, Estelle M., ed. LC 98-68211. (Illus.). 160p. 1999. 18.95 (1-57736-111-3) Providence Hse.

Davis, Graeme. Clanbook: Assamite. (Illus.). 72p. 1995. pap., per. 12.00 (1-56504-214-X, 2059(4214)) White Wolf.

— The Word-Order of Aelfric. LC 97-2088. (Studies in British Literature: Vol. 28). 320p. 1997. text 99.95 (0-7734-8649-6) E Mellen.

— World of Darkness: Mummy. 2nd ed. (Vampire Ser.). 1996. pap. text 18.00 (1-56504-206-9) White Wolf.

Davis, Graeme, jt. auth. see Bernhardt, Karl A.

Davis, Graham. Quick Solutions to Great Layouts. (Illus.). 144p. 1993. 28.99 (0-89134-507-8, 30529, North Lght Bks) F & W Pubns Inc.

Davis, Graham A. South African Managed Trade Policy: The Wasting of a Mineral Endowment. LC 93-40568. 168p. 1994. 59.95 (0-275-94814-5, Praeger Pubs) Greenwood.

Davis, Graham De Vahl, see De Vahl Davis, Graham.

Davis, Grahame, jt. ed. see Wack, Amy.

Davis, Granger. Draw Science Fiction. 64p. (J). 1995. pap. 7.95 (1-56565-355-6, 03556W, Pub. by Lowell Hse) NTC Contemp Pub Co.

Davis, Grania & Gellek, Nazli. The Monkey King. LC 98-2676. (Jataka Tales Ser.). (Illus.). (J). 1998. 16.95 (0-89800-293-1) Dharma Pub.

— The Monkey King. LC 98-2676. (Jataka Tales Ser.). (Illus.). 32p. (J). (gr. k-6). 1998. reprint ed. pap. 7.95 (0-89800-292-3) Dharma Pub.

Davis, Grania, jt. auth. see Davidson, Avran.

Davis, Grania, ed. see Davidson, Avram.

Davis, Grant M. & Cummingham, William A. A Primer on Highway Finance. 206p. (Orig.). (C). 1994. pap. text 29.50 (0-8191-9362-3); lib. bdg. 52.00 (0-8191-9361-5) U Pr of Amer.

Davis, Grant M. & Dillard, John E., Jr. Physical Logistics Management. LC 83-10300. (Illus.). 566p. (C). 1983. lib. bdg. 74.50 (0-8191-3342-6) U Pr of Amer.

Davis, Grant M. & Shephard, Eugene H. Motor Carrier Rate Structure: The Need for Basic Revision. LC 78-24194. 132p. 1979. 55.00 (0-275-90345-1, C0345, Praeger Pubs) Greenwood.

Davis, Granville D. The University Council on Education for Public Responsibility, 1961-1975. LC 75-2281. 130p. 1975. pap. 2.75 (0-87060-068-0, OCP 43) Syracuse U Cont Ed.

Davis, Greg & Morgan, Bill. TV Toys & Memorabilia 1960s & 1970s: Identification & Values. 2nd ed. LC 99-194890. 320p. 1998. 24.95 (1-57432-094-7) Collector Bks.

Davis, Gregory H. Technology-Humanism or Nihilism: A Critical Analysis of the Philosophical Basis & Practice of Modern Technology. LC 81-40178. 304p. (Orig.). 1981. pap. text 24.00 (0-8191-1777-3) U Pr of Amer.

Davis, Gregson. Aime Cesaire. LC 96-51158. (Studies in African & Caribbean Literature: Vol. 5). 224p. (C). 1997. text 64.95 (0-521-39072-9) Cambridge U Pr.

— Polyhymnia: The Rhetoric of Horatian Lyric Discourse. LC 90-49630. 293p. 1991. 50.00 (0-520-07077-1, Pub. by U CA Pr) Cal Prin Full Svc.

Davis, Gregson, ed. The Poetics of Derek Walcott: Intercultural Perspectives, Vol. 96, No. 2. 250p. 1997. pap. 12.00 (0-8223-6444-1) Duke.

Davis, Gregson, tr. from FRE. Non-Vicious Circle: Twenty Poems of Aime Cesaire. LC 83-42791. (Illus.). 168p. 1984. 12.95 (0-8047-1207-7) Stanford U Pr.

Davis, Guillermo H. Gramatica Elemental del Griego del Nuevo Testamento: Beginners Grammar of the Greek N.T. McKibben, Jorge F., tr. 240p. 1986. reprint ed. 13.50 (0-311-42008-7) Casa Bautista.

***Davis, Guy.** Barney for Baby: Love & Lullabies. LC 00-10049. (Barney Ser.). (Illus.). 48p. (J). (ps-k). 2000. 7.95 (1-57064-904-9, 97988) Lyrick Pub.

— Barney for Baby: Ring-A-Ling-A-Ding-Dong! LC 00-105014. (Illus.). (J). 2001. 5.95 (1-58668-130-3) Lyrick Studios.

— Barney Says "Night-Night" LC 98-65339. (Barney Ser.). (Illus.). 12p. (J). (ps-k). 1998. bds. 6.95 (1-57064-455-1) Lyrick Pub.

Davis, Guy. Barney's ABC, 123 & More. LC 98-67009. (Barney Ser.). (Illus.). 14p. (J). (ps-k). 1999. 9.95 (1-57064-243-5, Barney Publ) Lyrick Pub.

— Barney's Alphabet Fun. (Barney Ser.). 32p. (J). (ps-k). 1998. pap. text 3.25 (1-57064-257-5) Lyrick Pub.

— Barney's Baby Farm Animals. LC 97-74899. (Barney Ser.). (Illus.). 22p. (J). (ps-k). 1998. 4.95 (1-57064-260-5) Lyrick Pub.

— Barney's Easter Parade. LC 97-74898. (Barney Ser.). (Illus.). 21p. (J). (ps-k). 1998. pap. text 3.25 (1-57064-256-7) Lyrick Pub.

***Davis, Guy.** Barney's Farm Friends. LC 00-105004. (J). (ps). 2001. 3.95 (1-58668-129-X) Lyrick Studios.

— Barney's Favorite Seasons. (Illus.). 16p. (J). (ps-k). 2000. 8.95 (1-57064-715-1, Barney Publ) Lyrick Pub.

— Barney's Happy Halloween. LC 00-100422. (Barney Ser.). (Illus.). 16p. (J). (ps-2). 2000. 5.95 (1-57064-989-8, 97999) Lyrick Pub.

— Barney's Neighborhood. (Barney Ser.). (Illus.). 18p. (J). (ps-k). 1999. 6.95 (1-57064-463-2, Barney Publ) Lyrick Pub.

— Barney's Painting Fun. (Illus.). 32p. (J). (ps-2). 2000. pap. 1.99 (1-57064-728-3, 97979) Lyrick Pub.

— Barney's Peek-A-Boo Halloween! (Barney Ser.). (Illus.). 20p. (J). (ps-k). 1999. bds. 5.95 (1-57064-464-0, Barney Publ) Lyrick Pub.

Davis, Guy. Barney's Treasure Hunt. LC 97-70878. (Barney Ser.). (Illus.). 18p. (J). (ps-1). 1997. bds. 5.95 (1-57064-135-8) Lyrick Pub.

— Barney's Wonderful, Wild & Wacky Race. (Barney Ser.). (Illus.). 24p. (J). (ps-k). 2001. pap. 3.25 (1-57064-710-0, Barney Publ) Lyrick Pub.

***Davis, Guy.** Freddi Fish. (Illus.). 112p. (J). (ps-2). 2000. pap. 2.99 (1-57064-946-4, 73113, Humongous Bks) Lyrick Pub.

— Playtime at Barney's House! LC 00-105008. (Illus.). (J). (ps). 2000. 9.95 (1-58668-051-X) Lyrick Studios.

Davis, Guy. Vampire: The Dark Ages Companion. 1997. 18.00 (1-56504-279-4, 2804) White Wolf.

***Davis, Guy.** Witzy Wonders. LC 00-105057. (Illus.). (J). (ps-1). 2001. 5.95 (1-58668-057-9) Lyrick Studios.

— Witzy's Colors. LC 00-105055. (Illus.). (J). (ps-1). 2000. 4.95 (1-58668-055-2) Lyrick Studios.

— Witzy's Opposites. LC 00-105056. (Illus.). (J). (ps-1). 2001. 4.95 (1-58668-056-0) Lyrick Studios.

Davis, Guy, ed. Barney's Five Senses. (Barney Ser.). (Illus.). 22p. (J). (ps-k). 2000. 4.95 (1-57064-706-2, Barney Publ) Lyrick Pub.

***Davis, Guy, ed.** Barney's We Wish You a Merry Christmas. LC 99-60911. (Barney Ser.). (Illus.). 14p. (J). (ps-k). 1999. 5.95 (1-57064-750-X, Barney Publ) Lyrick Pub.

Davis, Guy & Valentine, June. Baby Bop's Blankey. LC 98-67846. (Barney Ser.). (Illus.). 14p. (J). (ps-k). 1999. bds. 5.95 (1-57064-613-9, Barney Publ) Lyrick Pub.

Davis, Guy, jt. auth. see Reed, Gary.

Davis, Guy, ed. see Bernthal, Mark.

Davis, Guy, ed. see Cooner, Donna.

Davis, Guy, ed. see Dowdy, Linda.

Davis, Guy, ed. see Halfmann, Janet.

Davis, Guy, ed. see Kearns, Kimberly & Amaral, Gayla.

Davis, Guy, ed. see Payne, Sandra J.

Davis, Guy, ed. see Payne, Sandra J., et al.

Davis, Guy, ed. see Valvassori, Maureen.

Davis, Guy, ed. see White, Stephen.

Davis, Gwen. Jade. 432p. 1992. mass mkt. 5.99 (0-446-36301-4) Warner Bks.

— The Pretenders. 1987. mass mkt. 4.95 (0-446-34563-6, Pub. by Warner Bks) Little.

— The Princess & the Pauper: An Erotic Fairy Tale. 288p. 1989. 17.95 (0-316-17499-8) Little.

— Silk Lady. 1989. mass mkt. 5.95 (0-446-35961-0, Pub. by Warner Bks) Little.

— West of Paradise. LC 98-5328. 304p. 1998. text 23.95 (0-312-18678-9) St Martin.

Davis, Gwenn & Joyce, Beverly A. Short Fiction by Women to 1900: A Bibliography of American & British Writers. LC 97-41885. (Bibliographies of Writings by American & British Women to 1900). 1998. 110.00 (0-7201-2094-2) Continuum.

Davis, Gwynn & Cretney, Antonia. Punishing Violence. (Illus.). 248p. (C). 1995. pap. 27.99 (0-415-09840-8, C0342) Routledge.

Davis, Gwynn & Murch, Mervyn. Grounds for Divorce. 192p. 1988. 49.95 (0-19-825220-X) OUP.

Davis, Gwynn, et al. Child Support in Action. 224p. 1998. 60.00 (1-901362-32-9, Pub. by Hart Pub); pap. 30.00 (1-901362-70-1, Pub. by Hart Pub) Northwestern U Pr.

— Simple Quarrels: Negotiations & Adjudication in Divorce. (Illus.). 322p. 1994. text 65.00 (0-19-825777-5) OUP.

Davis, Gwynn, jt. auth. see Cretney, Antonia.

Davis, H. The Appointed State: Quasi-Governmental Organizations & Democracy. LC 97-45701. (Public Policy & Management Ser.). 206p. 1998. pap. 105.95 (0-335-19882-1) OpUniv Pr.

— The Appointed State: Quasi-Governmental Organizations & Democracy. LC 97-45701. (Public Policy & Management Ser.). (Illus.). 192p. 1998. pap. 34.95 (0-335-19881-3) OpUniv Pr.

***Davis, H. A.** Feeling Younger with Homeopathic HGH: For Everyone Who Wants to Stay Young at Any Age. expanded rev. ed. 64p. 2000. pap. 6.95 (1-884820-58-1) SAFE GOODS.

Davis, H. C. & Bridgeman, J. C. Three Minute Declamations for College Men. LC 68-58819. (Granger Index Reprint Ser.). 1977. 20.95 (0-8369-6013-0) Ayer.

Davis, H. Clint. The Dogman of Boggy Bottoms: A Biographical Sketch. 191p. 1994. 19.95 (0-9641802-0-0) Iluztrafix.

Davis, H. Grady. Design for Preaching. LC 58-5749. 308p. 1958. 24.00 (0-8006-0806-2, 1-806, Fortress Pr) Augsburg Fortress.

Davis, H. L. Honey in the Horn. 512p. 1978. mass mkt. 4.95 (0-380-01831-4, 68882, Avon Bks) Morrow Avon.

— Honey in the Horn. 1994. reprint ed. lib. bdg. 32.95 (1-56849-273-1) Buccaneer Bks.

— Honey in the Horn. 400p. 1992. reprint ed. pap. text 19.95 (0-89301-155-X) U of Idaho Pr.

— The Selected Poems of H. L. Davis. 2nd ed. Burmaster, Orvis C., ed. LC 77-83226. (Ahsahta Press Modern & Contemporary Poets of the West Ser.). 72p. 1978. pap. 6.95 (0-916272-07-9) Ahsahta Pr.

***Davis, H. Leigh, ed.** 1,001 More Secret Codes (1996) for the Hottest Video Games. (Illus.). 80p. 2000. reprint ed. pap. text 12.00 (0-7881-9197-7) DIANE Pub.

Davis, H. Scott. New Employee Orientation: A How-to-Do-It Manual for Librarians. LC 93-43416. (How-to-Do-It Manuals for Libraries Ser.: No. 38). 144p. 1994. pap. 45.00 (1-55570-158-2) Neal-Schuman.

Davis, H. T. Statistical Mechanics of Phases, Interfaces & Thin Films. 728p. 1995. 129.00 (0-471-18562-0) Wiley.

Davis, H. T. & Nitsche, J. C., eds. Statistical Thermodynamics & Differential Geometry of Microstructured Materials. LC 93-12274. (IMA Volumes in Mathematics & Its Applications Ser.: Vol. 51). 1993. 58.95 (0-387-94027-8) Spr-Verlag.

***Davis, H. Ted.** Linear Algebra & Linear Operators in Engineering: With Applications in Mathematica. 522p. 2000. 89.95 (0-12-206349-X) Acad Pr.

Davis, H. Ted. Statistical Mechanics of Phases, Interfaces & Thin Films. Evans, D. Fennell, ed. LC 95-14941. (Advances in Interfacial Engineering Ser.). (Illus.). 750p. 1995. 95.00 (1-56081-513-2, Wiley-VCH) Wiley.

Davis, H. Thomas. 40 Km into Lebanon: Israel's 1982 Invasion. (Illus.). 144p. (C). 1995. pap. text 35.00 (0-7881-2334-3) DIANE Pub.

Davis, H. W., rev. Select Charters & Other Illustrations of English Constitutional History: From the Earliest Times to the Reign of Edward the First. 9th rev. ed. LC 85-28220. xix, 528p. 1985. reprint ed. 55.00 (0-8377-2609-3, Rothman) W S Hein.

Davis, H. W., ed. see Batiffol, Louis.

Davis, Hadland F. Myths & Legends of Japan. (Illus.). 432p. 1992. reprint ed. pap. 10.95 (0-486-27045-9) Dover.

Davis, Hallowell, jt. auth. see Stevens, Stanley S.

Davis, Hamilton E. Mocking Justice: Vermont's Biggest Drug Scandal. LC 89-61952. 256p. 1989. reprint ed. pap. 12.95 (0-933050-76-3) New Eng Pr VT.

Davis, Hank. Small-Town Heroes: Images of Minor League Baseball. LC 96-41937. (Illus.). 372p. 1997. 34.95 (0-87745-579-1) U of Iowa Pr.

Davis, Hank & Balfour, Dianne, eds. The Inevitable Bond: Examining Scientist-Animal Interactions. (Illus.). 413p. (C). 1992. text 80.00 (0-521-40510-6) Cambridge U Pr.

Davis, Harmer E., et al. The Testing of Engineering Materials. 4th ed. 480p. (C). 1982. 103.44 (0-07-015656-5) McGraw.

Davis, Harold. JavaScript Advanced: Visual QuickPro Guide. 450p. (C). 2000. pap. 24.99 incl. cd-rom (0-201-35425-X) Peachpit Pr.

— Never Alone: Dating from the Biblical Perspective. 108p. 1993. reprint ed. pap. text 15.00 (0-9638553-0-1) KJAC Pubng.

— The Photographer's Publishing Handbook. 182p. (Orig.). 1991. pap. 19.95 (0-929667-07-7, 10253) Images NY.

— Publishing Your Art As Cards, Posters & Calendars. 2nd ed. Levy, Susan P., ed. 160p. 1993. pap. 19.95 (0-913069-42-6) Consultant Pr.

— Red Hat Linux 6: Visual QuickPro Guide. (Visual Quickpro Guides Ser.). (Illus.). 311p. (C). 1999. pap. 29.99 incl. cd-rom (0-201-35437-3) Peachpit Pr.

— Successful Fine Art Photography. (Illus.). 1992. pap. 21.95 (0-929667-14-X) Images NY.

— Talks My Daddy Never Had with Me: A Loving Father's Perspective for Young Women. (Illus.). 213p. (YA). 1998. pap. 15.00 (0-9638553-7-9) KJAC Pubng.

— Talks My Father Never Had with Me: Helping the Young Black Male Make It to Adulthood. 236p. (Orig.). 1995. pap. text 15.00 (0-9638553-1-X) KJAC Pubng.

— Talks My Father Never Had with Me: Helping the Young Male Reach Adulthood. (Illus.). 160p. (YA). 1997. pap. 15.00 (0-9638553-5-2) KJAC Pubng.

— Talks My Father Never Had with Me: Helping the Young Male Reach Adulthood (Elementary Version) (Illus.). 170p. (J). 1997. pap. 19.00 (0-9638553-6-0) KJAC Pubng.

— Talks My Father Never Had with Me Mentor's Guide: Helping the Young Black Male Make It to Adulthood. 256p. 1998. pap. text 26.00 (0-9638553-2-8) KJAC Pubng.

— Talks My Father Never Had with Me Mentor's Guide: Helping the Young Male Reach Adulthood. 144p. (YA). 1997. pap. 19.00 (0-9638553-4-4) KJAC Pubng.

— Talks My Father Never Had with Me Mentor's Text: Helping the Young Male Make It to Adulthood. 207p. (Orig.). 1996. pap. text 15.00 (0-9638553-3-6) KJAC Pubng.

— Visual Basic 4 Secrets. 800p. 1996. pap. 44.99 incl. cd-rom (1-56884-872-2) IDG Bks.

— Visual Basic 6 Secrets. LC QA76.73.B3D3763 1998. (Secrets Ser.). 936p. 1998. pap. 59.99 incl. cd-rom (0-7645-3223-5) IDG Bks.

Davis, Harold, jt. auth. see Cottingham, Marion.

Davis, Harold E. The Fledgling Province: Social & Cultural Life in Colonial Georgia, 1733-1776. LC 76-2570. 318p. 1976. reprint ed. pap. 98.60 (0-608-02799-5, 206386600007) Bks Demand.

— Henry Grady's New South: Atlanta, a Brave & Beautiful City. LC 89-30565. (Illus.). 268p. 1990. reprint ed. pap. 83.10 (0-608-01666-7, 206232100002) Bks Demand.

— History of Latin America. LC 68-28843. 800p. (gr. 9-12). reprint ed. 200.00 (0-8357-9906-9, 201255200081) Bks Demand.

— Latin American Leaders. LC 68-56189. reprint ed. 57.00 (0-8154-0271-6) Cooper Sq.

— Latin American Thought: A Historical Perspective. LC 78-181564. 279p. reprint ed. pap. 86.50 (0-608-09815-9, 206998300007) Bks Demand.

— Makers of Democracy in Latin America. LC 68-56190. reprint ed. 53.00 (0-8154-0272-4) Cooper Sq.

— Revolutionaries, Traditionalists & Dictators in Latin America. LC 72-77988. 1973. lib. bdg. 46.00 (0-8154-0420-4) Cooper Sq.

Davis, Harold E., ed. Government & Politics in Latin America. LC 58-5649. (Illus.). 545p. reprint ed. pap. 169.00 (0-608-09937-6, 201255100081) Bks Demand.

Davis, Harold E., et al. Latin American Diplomatic History: An Introduction. LC 76-58901. viii, 302p. 1977. pap. text 18.95 (0-8071-0286-5) La State U Pr.

Davis, Harold L. Beulah Land. LC 75-136062. 314p. 1971. reprint ed. lib. bdg. 35.00 (0-8371-5212-7, DABL, Greenwood Pr) Greenwood.

— Honey in the Horn. LC 83-45745. reprint ed. 37.50 (0-404-20074-5) AMS Pr.

— The Winds of Morning. LC 77-138586. 344p. 1972. reprint ed. lib. bdg. 38.50 (0-8371-5785-4, DAWM, Greenwood Pr) Greenwood.

Davis, Harold S., et al. Modern Approaches to School Organization. 1974. pap. text 13.95 (0-8422-0368-0) Irvington.

Davis, Harold T. Introduction to Nonlinear Differential & Integral Equations. 566p. 1962. pap. 13.95 (0-486-60971-5) Dover.

An Asterisk (*) at the beginning of an entry indicates that the title is appearing for the first time.

Davis, Harold T. Studies in Differential Equations. Scott, Sir Walter, ed. LC 56-14277. (Northwestern University Series in Mathematical & Physical Sciences: No. 3). 120p. reprint ed. pap. 37.20 (*0-608-30422-0*, 2006876000060) Bks Demand.

Davis, Harold T. & Nelson, William F. Elements of Statistics with Application to Economic Data. 2nd enl. rev. ed. LC 78-163681. reprint ed. 45.00 (*0-404-01994-3*) AMS Pr.

Davis, Harriet. World on My Doorstep: American Autobiography. 274p. 1995. lib. bdg. 79.00 (*0-7812-8496-1*) Rprt Serv.

Davis, Harriet E., ed. Pioneers in World Order. LC 70-128232. (Essay Index Reprint Ser.). 1977. 21.95 (*0-8369-1913-0*) Ayer.

Davis, Harry. The Art of Tasha Tudor. LC 99-87687. (Illus.). 160p. 2000. 34.95 (*0-316-17493-9*) Little.

— Forever Christmas. (Illus.). 96p. 2000. 18.95 (*0-316-85542-1*) Little.

— Tasha Tudor's Dollhouse: A Lifetime in Miniature. 1999. write for info. (*0-316-17469-6*) Little.

Davis, Harry A. Davis Family (Davies & David) in Wales & America: Genealogy of Morgan David of Pennsylvania. (Illus.). 445p. 1996. reprint ed. pap. 67.00 (*0-8328-5400-X*); reprint ed. lib. bdg. 77.00 (*0-8328-5399-2*) Higginson Bk Co.

Davis, Harry C., ed. Commencement Parts: Valedictories, Salutatories, Orations, Essays, Class Poems, Ivy Orations, Toasts. LC 74-152149. (Granger Index Reprint Ser.). 1977. reprint ed. 31.95 (*0-8369-6252-4*) Ayer.

Davis, Harry F. Fourier Series & Orthogonal Functions. 416p. 1989. pap. 11.95 (*0-486-65973-9*) Dover.

Davis, Harry L. & Silk, Alvin J., eds. Behavioral & Management Science in Marketing. LC 77-18878. 278p. reprint ed. pap. 86.20 (*0-8357-7111-3*, 205560600029) Bks Demand.

Davis, Harwell G. The Legend of Landsee. LC 76-40829. 1976. 10.95 (*0-87397-106-X*, Strode Pubs) Circle Bk Service.

Davis, Hassoldt. Nepal Land of Mystery. 1997. pap. 92.00 (*0-7855-7616-9*) St Mut.

Davis, Hattie C. Cataloochee Valley: Vanished Settlements of the Great Smoky Mountains. (Illus.). 304p. 1997. 29.95 (*1-56664-108-X*) WorldComm.

***Davis, Hattie C.** Civil War Letters & Memories from the Great Smoky Mountains. Howell, Jim & Garza, Amy Ammons, eds. (Illus.). 197p. 1999. pap. 19.95 (*0-9670689-0-8*) H C Davis.

— Reflections of Cataloochee Valley & Its Vanished People from the Great Smoky Mountains. 304p. 1999. pap. write for info. (*0-9670689-1-6*) H C Davis.

Davis, Hazel, jt. auth. see Davis, James.

Davis, Heather C. Baptism by Fire: The True Story of a Mother Who Finds Faith During Her Daughter's Darkest Hour. 272p. 1999. reprint ed. pap. 10.95 (*0-553-37991-7*) Bantam.

Davis, Helen. Lots-a-Dots. LC 87-90414. 1987. 4.98 (*0-916809-16-1*) Scott Pubns MI.

Davis, Helen & Davis, Ren. Atlanta Walks: A Comprehensive Guide to Walking, Running & Bicycling the Area's Scenic & Historic Locals. 2nd rev. ed. (Illus.). 320p. 1998. pap. 14.95 (*1-56145-188-6*) Peachtree Pubs.

Davis, Helen, jt. auth. see Ansons, Alec M.

Davis, Helen, jt. auth. see Davis, Ren.

Davis, Helen C., ed. Constitutions, Electoral Laws, Treaties of States in the Near & Middle East. LC 79-99886. reprint ed. 34.50 (*0-404-01995-1*) AMS Pr.

Davis, Helen D., ed. see Hamilton, Mary.

Davis, Helen E. Tolstoy & Nietzsche. LC 72-119083. (Studies in Comparative Literature: No. 35). 1970. reprint ed. lib. bdg. 75.00 (*0-8383-1079-6*) M S G Haskell Hse.

Davis, Helene. Chemo-Poet & Other Poems. LC 88-31560. 72p. (Orig.). (C). 1989. pap. 9.95 (*0-914086-87-1*) Alice James Bks.

— Nightblind. Kaplan, Peter, ed. 1976. 3.00 (*0-915176-17-3*) Pourboire.

Davis, Henry. A Forgotten Heritage: The Story of the Early American Rifle. 1976. reprint ed. 12.95 (*0-88227-008-7*) Gun Room.

Davis, Henry A. Cash Flow & Performance Measurement: Managing for Value. LC 95-83616. 217p. (Orig.). 1996. pap. 38.00 (*1-885065-07-8*, 096-07) Finan Exec.

— Financial Products for Medium-Sized Companies: Adding Value by Integrating Financial & Total Quality Management. LC 89-84510. (Illus.). 91p. 1989. pap. 20.00 (*0-910586-73-X*, 076-90) Finan Exec.

— Project Finance: Practical Case Studies. 1996. pap. 215.00 (*1-85564-460-6*, Pub. by Euromoney) Am Educ Systs.

Davis, Henry A. & Sihler, William W. Building Value with Capital-Structure Strategies. LC 97-77704. (Illus.). 332p. 1998. pap. 39.75 (*1-885065-11-6*, 098-04) Finan Exec.

Davis, Henry A., jt. auth. see Militello, Frederick C.

Davis, Henry A., ed. see Davis, Doris A.

Davis, Henry B. Electrical & Electronic Technologies: A Chronology of Events & Inventors from 1940 to 1980. LC 84-13957. 321p. 1985. 40.00 (*0-8108-1726-8*) Scarecrow.

Davis, Henry B., Jr. Generals in Khaki. LC 97-69238. (Illus.). 640p. 1998. 50.00 (*1-57197-088-6*) Pentland Pr.

Davis, Henry E. The American Wild Turkey. (Illus.). 328p. 1984. 29.95 (*0-685-62739-X*) Real Turkeys Pubs.

Davis, Henry K. K-Rations, Kilroy, KP, & Kaputt: One GI's War. Moeller, Roger, ed. LC 95-94518. (Illus.). 400p. (Orig.). 1995. pap. 18.95 (*0-9646795-0-7*) M Litchfield.

Davis, Henry M. Use of State High School Examinations As an Instrument for Judging the Work of Teachers. LC 77-176713. (Columbia University. Teachers College. Contributions to Education Ser.: No. 611). reprint ed. 37.50 (*0-404-55611-6*) AMS Pr.

Davis, Henry W. Charlemagne (Charles the Great) The Hero of Two Nations. (Select Bibliographies Reprint Ser.). 1977. reprint ed. 29.95 (*0-8369-9957-6*) Ayer.

Davis, Henry W., jt. auth. see Poole, Reginald L.

Davis, Herbert, ed. see Congreve, William.

Davis, Herbert, ed. see Pope, Alexander.

Davis, Herbert J. The Satire of Jonathan Swift. LC 79-17603. 109p. 1979. reprint ed. lib. bdg. 35.00 (*0-313-22068-9*, DAJS, Greenwood Pr) Greenwood.

Davis, Herbert J., et al, eds. Nineteenth Century Studies. LC 69-10083. 1969. reprint ed. lib. bdg. 19.75 (*0-8371-0057-7*, DANC, Greenwood Pr) Greenwood.

Davis, Herbert J. & Schulte, William D. National Culture & International Management in East Asia. LC 97-16113. 656p. 1997. pap. 24.99 (*1-86152-052-2*) Thomson Learn.

Davis, Herm & Kennedy, Joyce L. College Financial Aid for Dummies. LC 97-72418. (For Dummies Ser.). 432p. 1997. pap. 19.99 (*0-7645-5049-7*) IDG Bks.

— College Financial Aid for Dummies. 2nd ed. (For Dummies Ser.). 456p. 1999. pap. 19.99 (*0-7645-5165-5*, Dummies Trade Pr) IDG Bks.

Davis, Hester A., ed. see Arnold, Morris, et al.

Davis, Hilda R., ed. Children's Church Time No. 2: For Children's Church, Second Sunday School Sessions, & OT. (Education Settings Ser.). 56p. (Orig.). 1992. pap. 19.95 (*0-687-08385-0*) Abingdon.

— Children's Church Time No. 3: For Children's Church, Second Sunday School Sessions, & OT. (Education Settings Ser.). 56p. 1993. pap. 19.95 (*0-687-08386-9*) Abingdon.

— Children's Church Time No. 4: For Children's Church, Second Sunday School Sessions, & OT. (Education Settings Ser.). 56p. 1993. pap. 19.95 (*0-687-08387-7*) Abingdon.

— Children's Church Times Vol. 1: Children's Church, Second Sunday School Sessions, & Other. (Education Settings Ser.). 56p. (Orig.). 1992. pap. 19.95 (*0-687-08384-2*) Abingdon.

— New Bridges . . . A Curriculum for Persons with Disabilities Vol. 2: Spring. 72p. 1996. pap. 12.95 (*0-687-71984-4*) Abingdon.

— New Bridges . . . A Curriculum for Persons with Disabilities Vol. 2: Winter. 72p. 1996. pap. 12.95 (*0-687-71983-6*) Abingdon.

— New Invitation Bridges . . . A Curriculum for Persons with Disabilities Vol. 1: Fall. 72p. 1995. pap. 12.95 (*0-687-71978-X*) Abingdon.

— New Invitation Bridges . . . A Curriculum for Persons with Disabilities Vol. 1: Spring. 72p. 1994. pap. 12.95 (*0-687-71980-1*) Abingdon.

— New Invitation Bridges . . . A Curriculum for Persons with Disabilities Vol. 1: Summer. 72p. 1996. pap. 12.95 (*0-687-71981-X*) Abingdon.

— New Invitation Bridges . . . A Curriculum for Persons with Disabilities Vol. 1: Winter. 72p. 1995. pap. 12.95 (*0-687-71979-8*) Abingdon.

— New Invitation Bridges . . . A Curriculum for Persons with Disabilities Vol. 2: Fall. 72p. 1996. pap. 12.95 (*0-687-71982-8*) Abingdon.

— New Invitation Bridges . . . A Curriculum for Persons with Disabilities Vol. 2: Summer. 72p. 1997. pap. 12.95 (*0-687-71985-2*) Abingdon.

— New Invitation Bridges . . . A Curriculum for Persons with Disabilities Vol. 3: July. 72p. 1997. pap. 12.95 (*0-687-71986-0*) Abingdon.

— New Invitation Bridges . . . A Curriculum for Persons with Disabilities Vol. 3: Spring. 72p. 1997. pap. 12.95 (*0-687-71988-7*) Abingdon.

— New Invitation Bridges . . . A Curriculum for Persons with Disabilities Vol. 3: Summer. 72p. 1998. pap. 12.95 (*0-687-71989-5*) Abingdon.

— New Invitation Bridges . . . A Curriculum for Persons with Disabilities Vol. 3: Winter. 72p. 1997. pap. 12.95 (*0-687-71987-9*) Abingdon.

Davis, Hillary. The International Burrito. 128p. (Orig.). 1994. mass mkt. 10.99 (*0-446-67051-0*, Pub. by Warner Bks) Little.

— Million a Minute: Inside the Mega-Money, High-Tech World of Traders. LC 98-28133. 304p. 1998. 27.00 (*0-88730-941-0*) HarpC.

Davis, Hillary, jt. auth. see Horan, Patricia.

Davis, Hilton. Counselling Parents of Children with Chronic Illness or Disability. 144p. (Orig.). (C). 1993. pap. text 23.00 (*1-85433-091-8*, Pub. by Brit Psychol Soc) P H Brookes.

Davis, Holly. My Birthday/Jesus Birthday. LC 98-11305. (J). 1998. 12.99 (*0-310-21968-X*) Zondervan.

***Davis, Holly.** Nourish: Sustenance for Body & Soul. (Illus.). 192p. 2000. pap. 19.95 (*1-58008-181-9*) Ten Speed Pr.

Davis, Hope H. Great Day Coming: A Memoir of the 1930's. LC 94-31548. 325p. 1994. 24.00 (*1-883642-17-5*) Steerforth Pr.

Davis, Horace B. Nationalism & Socialism: Marxist & Labor Theories of Nationalism to 1917. LC 67-19255. 258p. 1973. pap. 12.00 (*0-85345-293-8*, PB-2938, Pub. by Monthly Rev) NYU Pr.

— Toward a Marxist Theory of Nationalism. LC 77-91740. 294p. 1980. 17.50 (*0-85345-441-8*, Pub. by Monthly Rev); pap. 10.00 (*0-85345-516-3*, Pub. by Monthly Rev) NYU Pr.

Davis, Horace B., ed. see Luxemburg, Rosa.

***Davis, Hossoldt.** The Jungle & the Damned. (Illus.). 334p. 2000. pap. 16.95 (*0-8032-6598-0*) U of Nebr Pr.

Davis, Howard. Chinoiserie: Polychrome Decoration on Staffordshire Porcelain, 1790-1850. (Illus.). 215p. 1991. 45.00 (*0-948695-09-9*, Pub. by Rubicon Pr) David Brown.

— The Culture of Building. LC 98-19051. (Illus.). 400p. 2000. 45.00 (*0-19-511294-6*) OUP.

Davis, Howard, ed. QUANGOs & Local Government: A Changing World. 220p. 1996. pap. 22.00 (*0-7146-4324-6*, Pub. by F Cass Pubs); text 35.00 (*0-7146-4735-7*, Pub. by F Cass Pubs) Intl Spec Bk.

Davis, Howard, jt. auth. see Alexander, Christopher.

Davis, Howard, jt. auth. see Hayden, Jerome D.

Davis, Howard, jt. auth. see Leach, Steve.

Davis, Howard, tr. see Luhmann, Niklas.

Davis, Howard C. And Murder Won. large type ed. (Linford Mystery Library). 320p. 1989. pap. 16.99 (*0-7089-6733-7*, Linford) Ulverscroft.

— The Big Heist. large type ed. (Linford Mystery Large Print Ser.). 336p. 1995. pap. 16.99 (*0-7089-7656-5*, Linford) Ulverscroft.

— Child Witness. large type ed. (Linford Mystery Library). 1994. pap. 16.99 (*0-7089-7632-8*) Ulverscroft.

— Dangerous Twin. large type ed. (Linford Mystery Library). 1990. pap. 16.99 (*0-7089-6843-0*) Ulverscroft.

— Dead Man's Cross. large type ed. (Linford Mystery Library). 1989. pap. 16.99 (*0-7089-6743-4*) Ulverscroft.

— Death in the Scillies. large type ed. (Linford Mystery Library). 304p. 1989. pap. 16.99 (*0-7089-6725-6*, Linford) Ulverscroft.

— Desperate Night. large type ed. (Linford Mystery Library). 1990. pap. 16.99 (*0-7089-6851-1*) Ulverscroft.

— The Gunmen of Gozo. large type ed. (Linford Mystery Library). 1991. pap. 16.99 (*0-7089-7130-X*) Ulverscroft.

— Murder Out of Class. large type ed. (Linford Mystery Library). 1991. pap. 16.99 (*0-7089-7070-2*) Ulverscroft.

— Murder Starts from Fishguard. large type ed. (Linford Mystery Library). 1991. pap. 16.99 (*0-7089-7086-9*) Ulverscroft.

— Perhaps to Kill. large type ed. (Mystery Ser.). 1994. pap. 16.99 (*0-7089-7626-3*, Linford) Ulverscroft.

— Poodle's Grave. large type ed. (Linford Mystery Library). 1989. pap. 16.99 (*0-7089-6750-7*, Linford) Ulverscroft.

— The Selsey Gold. large type ed. (Linford Mystery Library). 1991. pap. 16.99 (*0-7089-7066-4*) Ulverscroft.

— The Third Assassin. large type ed. (Linford Mystery Large Print Ser.). 1994. pap. 16.99 (*0-7089-7637-9*) Ulverscroft.

— The Tortured Boy. large type ed. 384p. 1992. pap. 16.99 (*0-7089-7216-0*) Ulverscroft.

— Trouble in the Bank. large type ed. (Linford Mystery Library). 1991. pap. 16.99 (*0-7089-7082-6*) Ulverscroft.

— The Waxworks Spies. large type ed. (Mystery Library). 352p. 1995. pap. 16.99 (*0-7089-7649-2*, Linford) Ulverscroft.

***Davis, Howard G.** Political Freedom. 256p. 2001. 90.95 (*0-8264-5030-X*) Continuum.

Davis, Howard T., jt. auth. see Hayden, Jerome D.

Davis, Howland & Kelly, Arthur C., eds. A Livingston Genealogical Register: A Sequel to the 1986 "Genealogy" for the Friends of Clermont. LC 97-113871. 720p. 1995. lib. bdg. 55.00 (*1-56012-136-X*, 135) Kinship Rhinebeck.

Davis, Hubert J. Facts, Fancies & Folklore about Snakes. LC 95-41132. (Appalachian Connection Ser.). (Illus.). 40p. (J). (gr. 4 up). 1995. pap. 7.50 (*0-936015-59-4*) Pocahontas Pr.

— What Will the Weather Be? No. 1: A Folk Weather Calendar. LC 88-17869. (Illus.). 36p. (Orig.). (J). (gr. k-12). 1988. pap. 4.95 (*0-936015-11-X*) Pocahontas Pr.

— What Will the Weather Be? No. 2: Animal Signs. LC 90-22327. (Illus.). 56p. (Orig.). (J). (gr. k-12). 1991. pap. 5.95 (*0-936015-12-8*) Pocahontas Pr.

Davis, Hugh. Joshua Leavitt, Evangelical Abolitionist. LC 89-36161. 328p. 1990. text 45.00 (*0-8071-1521-5*) La State U Pr.

— Leonard Bacon: New England Reformer & Antislavery Moderate. LC 98-24710. (Illus.). 392p. 1998. text 60.00 (*0-8071-2287-4*) La State U Pr.

Davis, Hugh J. Intrauterine Devices for Contraception: The IUD. LC 70-157109. 222p. reprint ed. pap. 68.90 (*0-608-15172-6*, 205607100045) Bks Demand.

***Davis, Ian.** My Boys Can Swim: The Official Guy's Guide to Pregnancy. LC 99-32679. 1999. pap. 9.99 (*0-7615-2167-4*) Prima Pub.

Davis, Ian, jt. auth. see Clayton, Andrew.

Davis, Ian, jt. ed. see Gittings, John.

Davis, Ian A. Forty-Four Dynamic ZX-81 Games & Recreations. (Illus.). 1984. pap. 13.95 (*0-13-329144-8*) P-H.

Davis, Ila M. & Stenbock-Ditty, Evelyn. A Gleam of Light: The Trials & Triumphs of a Century of Missionary Work in Morocco. LC 99-182054. (Illus.). 187p. 1998. per. 9.95 (*1-890940-02-X*) Gospel Missionary.

Davis, Inez S. Story of the Church. 1989. pap. 17.50 (*0-8309-0188-4*) Herald Pub Hse.

Davis, Inger P. Adolescents: Theoretical & Helping Perspectives. LC 84-20175. 1985. lib. bdg. 91.00 (*0-89838-165-7*) Kluwer Academic.

***Davis, Irene.** Collectible Paint Advertising & Memorabilia. (Illus.). 160p. 2000. pap. 29.95 (*0-7643-1047-X*) Schiffer.

Davis, Irma & Lehman, Celia. Come Walk with Me Thru the Needle's Eye. (Illus.). 124p. 1991. 5.95 (*0-936369-43-4*) Son-Rise Pubns.

Davis, Iwan. Effective Retention of Title. 183p. 1991. 60.00 (*1-85190-123-X*, Pub. by Tolley Pubng) St Mut.

Davis, J. Aesthetic & Reconstructive Otoplasty. (Illus.). 582p. 1987. 325.00 (*0-387-96308-1*) Spr-Verlag.

***Davis, J.** Garfield Alphabet Soup: Games & Sticker Fun. (Garfield Ser.). (J). 1998. pap. text 4.95 (*2-922148-26-2*) Presses Avent.

Davis, J., et al, eds. Radiative Properties of Hot Dense Matter. 620p. 1985. 104.00 (*9971-978-37-7*) World Scientific Pub.

Davis, J., jt. auth. see Mason, J.

Davis, J., jt. auth. see Shilov, G. Y.

Davis, J., tr. see Sharratt, Nick & Tucker, Stephen.

***Davis, J. B.** How to Become a Millionaire in Your Current Job: Choose Wisely with 401(K) & IRA. LC 99-94278. 208p. 2000. pap. 14.00 (*0-9670511-4-2*, 53) Galaxy Publishing.

Davis, J. Bancroft. Mister Fish & the Alabama Claims: A Chapter in Diplomatic History. (Select Bibliographies Reprint Ser.). 1977. 19.95 (*0-8369-5067-4*) Ayer.

Davis, J. Boyce & Knight, E. Leslie. CVR Fitness: A Basic Guide for Cardio-Vascular-Respiratory Exercise. 4th ed. LC 85-179374. vi, 159 p. 1985. write for info. (*0-8403-3592-X*) Kendall-Hunt.

Davis, J. Bradley. A Kid's Day Out: 84 Ways to Spend Memorable Time with Your Child. 80p. 1992. pap. text 7.95 (*1-881458-01-6*) Crazy Creat.

Davis, J. C., jt. ed. see Van Driel, J. N.

Davis, J. D. & Merriman, D., eds. Observations on the Ecology & Biology of Western Cape Cod Bay, Massachusetts. (Lecture Notes on Coastal & Estuarine Studies: Vol. 11). x, 289p. 1984. pap. 44.00 (*0-387-96084-8*) Spr-Verlag.

Davis, J. David. Finding the God of Noah: The Spiritual Journey of a Baptist Minister from Christianity to the Laws of Noah. LC 96-10548. 1997. 25.00 (*0-88125-535-1*) Ktav.

Davis, J. E. Ye Sylvan Archer, Vol. II. 288p. 60.00 (*1-56416-102-1*) Derrydale Pr.

— Ye Sylvan Archer, Vol. III. 320p. 60.00 (*1-56416-103-X*) Derrydale Pr.

— Ye Sylvan Archer, Vol. V. 384p. 60.00 (*1-56416-106-4*) Derrydale Pr.

Davis, J. Francis, et al. Parenting in a TV Age. (Illus.). 1991. student ed. 21.95 (*1-879419-03-3*, W52/53) Ctr Media Values.

Davis, J. Frank. Road to San Jacinto. 1993. reprint ed. lib. bdg. 75.00 (*0-7812-5964-9*) Rprt Serv.

Davis, J. H., jt. ed. see Stephenson, G. M.

Davis, J. L. Wave Propagation in Electromagnetic Media. (Illus.). xi, 294p. 1989. 87.00 (*0-387-97066-5*) Spr-Verlag.

— Wave Propagation in Solids & Fluids. (Illus.). 400p. 1988. 118.95 (*0-387-96739-7*) Spr-Verlag.

Davis, J. L., jt. auth. see Greig, D. W.

Davis, J. M., ed. Basic Cell Culture: A Practical Approach. (Practical Approach Ser.: No. 146). (Illus.). 322p. 1995. pap. text 60.00 (*0-19-963433-5*) OUP.

Davis, J. M., jt. ed. see Domino, E. F.

Davis, J. Madison. And the Angels Sing. 320p. 1996. 24.00 (*1-877946-70-2*) Permanent Pr.

— Dick Francis. (English Authors Ser.). 200p. (C). 1989. 22.95 (*0-8057-6970-6*, TEAS 464, Twyne) Mac Lib Ref.

***Davis, J. Madison.** The Novelist's Essential Guide to Creating Plot. LC 00-36798. (Novelist's Essential Guide Ser.). 208p. 2000. pap. 14.99 (*0-89879-984-8*, Wrtrs Digest Bks) F & W Pubns Inc.

Davis, J. Madison. Stanislaw Lem. LC 87-17646. (Starmont Reader's Guide Ser.: No. 32). x, 116p. 1990. pap. 17.00 (*1-55742-026-2*) Millefleurs.

Davis, J. Madison, ed. Conversations with Robertson Davies. LC 88-39305. (Literary Conversations Ser.). 321p. 1989. text 39.50 (*0-87805-383-2*) U Pr of Miss.

Davis, J. Madison & Frankforter, A. Daniel, eds. Shakespeare Name & Place Dictionary. 546p. 1996. lib. bdg. 95.00 (*1-884964-17-6*) Fitzroy Dearborn.

— The Shakespeare Name Dictionary. LC 94-13784. 552p. 1995. text 85.00 (*0-8240-6341-4*, H976) Garland.

Davis, J. Madison, ed. see Davies, Robertson.

Davis, J. Madison, jt. ed. see Westlake, Donald E.

***Davis, J. Mark.** From Mind to Market 1999: The Inventors Handbook. 2nd ed. 1999. pap. 29.95 (*0-9663515-0-9*) Key Two Ideas.

Davis, J. Matthew, jt. ed. see Fraser, Gordon S.

Davis, J. Mearle, ed. see International Missionary Council, Department of So.

Davis, J. Merle, ed. Modern Industry & the African. 2nd ed. 450p. 1967. reprint ed. 45.00 (*0-7146-1650-8*, BHA-01650-8, Pub. by F Cass Pubs) Intl Spec Bk.

***Davis, J. Micheal.** Oxygenates in Water: Critical Information & Research Needs. 65p. 2000. reprint ed. pap. text 20.00 (*0-7567-0070-1*) DIANE Pub.

Davis, J. Morton & Ford, Michael T. From Hard Knocks to Hot Stocks: How I Made a Fortune Through Smart Investing & How You Can Too. LC 97-27352. 224p. 1998. 25.00 (*0-688-15322-4*, Wm Morrow) Morrow Avon.

Davis, J. P. How to Pass the Bar Exam. LC 88-34084. 150p. 1990. reprint ed. pap. 495.00 (*0-89941-683-7*, 304660) W S Hein.

***Davis, J. R.** Alloy Digest Sourcebook: Stainless Steels. LC 99-87182. 450p. 2000. write for info. (*0-87170-649-0*) ASM.

Davis, J. R. Instabilities in MOS Devices, Vol. 1. (Electrocomponent Science Monographs). xiv, 178p. 1981. text 142.00 (*0-677-05590-0*) Gordon & Breach.

Davis, J. R., ed. ASM Materials Engineering Dictionary. (Illus.). 555p. 1992. 146.00 (*0-87170-447-1*, 6311) ASM.

— ASM Specialty Handbook: Carbon & Alloy Steels. LC 95-49550. (Specialty Handbook Ser.). 731p. 1995. 198.00 (*0-87170-557-5*, 6611) ASM.

— ASM Specialty Handbook: Tool Materials. (ASM Specialty Handbook Ser.). (Illus.). 501p. 1995. 198.00 (*0-87170-545-1*, 6506) ASM.

***Davis, J. R., ed.** Corrosion: Understanding the Basics. LC 99-57146. 275p. 2000. 129.00 (*0-87170-641-5*, 06691G) ASM.

Davis, J. R., ed. Corrosion of Aluminum & Aluminum Alloys. LC 99-27326. (Illus.). 313p. 1999. 144.00 (*0-87170-629-6*, 6786) ASM.

— Specialty Handbook: Cast Irons. LC 96-31175. 494p. 1996. 198.00 (*0-87170-564-8*, 6613) ASM.

D

Davis, J. S., et al, eds. Assessment of Agricultural Research Priorities. 85p. (Orig.). 1986. pap. 50.00 (*0-949511-31-5*) St Mut.

Davis, J. Stark. All As One. 287p. (Orig.). 1995. pap. 10.00 (*1-56794-083-8*, C-2379) Star Bible.

Davis, J. W., ed. see Topical Conference on Ferritic Alloys for Use in N.

Davis, Jack. Otoplasty: Aesthetic & Reconstructive Techniques. 2nd ed. LC 96-35161. (Illus.). 1525p. 1997. 165.00 (*0-387-94878-3*) Spr-Verlag.

Davis, Jack, et al, eds. Paperbark: A Collection of Black Australian Writings. (Illus.). 369p. 1990. pap. 19.95 (*0-7022-2180-5*, Pub. by Univ Queensland Pr) Intl Spec Bk.

***Davis, Jack & Merritt, Susan.** The Web Design Wow! Book. (Illus.). 224p. 1998. pap. 39.95 incl. cd-rom (*0-201-88678-2*) Peachpit Pr.

***Davis, Jack & Ryan, Dorothy.** Samuel L. Schmucker: The Discovery of His Lost Art. deluxe ed. LC 00-103693. (Illus.). 176p. (C). 2000. pap. write for info. (*0-615-11186-6*) Olde Amer.

— Samuel L. Schmucker: The Discovery of His Lost Art. deluxe ed. LC 00-102706. (Illus.). 176p. (C). 2001. write for info. (*0-615-11181-5*) Olde Amer.

***Davis, Jack, et al.** Flash X Wow! Book. 2000. pap. text 49.99 (*0-201-70909-0*) Peachpit Pr.

Davis, Jack, et al. Plays from Black Australia. (Currency Plays Ser.). (Illus.). xi, 233p. 1989. reprint ed. pap. 24.95 (*0-86819-226-0*, Pub. by Currency Pr) Accents Pubns.

Davis, Jack, jt. auth. see Dayton, Linnea.

Davis, Jack, jt. auth. see Redd, Lorraine.

Davis, Jack, jt. ed. see Queen, Carol.

Davis, Jack E. The Spanish of Argentina & Uruguay: An Annotated Bibliography for 1940-1978. (Janua Linguarum, Series Major: No. 105). 360p. 1982. text 98.50 (*90-279-3339-1*) Mouton.

***Davis, Jack E., ed.** The Civil Rights Movement. 2000. 59.95 (*0-631-22043-7*); pap. 27.95 (*0-631-22044-5*) Blackwell Pubs.

Davis, Jack E., tr. see Leon-Portilla, Miguel.

***Davis, Jack I.** Captain Jack's Basic Navigation. Kaufman, John P. & O'Connor, John P., Jr., eds. LC 98-74176. (Illus.). 155p. 1998. spiral bd. 21.95 (*1-892216-09-4*) Bristol Fash.

Davis, Jack I. Captain Jack's Celestial Navigation. O'Connor, John P., ed. LC 99-73128. (Illus.). 138p. 1999. spiral bd. 24.95 (*1-892216-18-3*) Bristol Fash.

***Davis, Jack I.** Captain Jack's Complete Navigation. Kaufman, John P., ed. (Illus.). 240p. 1999. spiral bd. write for info. (*1-892216-25-6*, 256) Bristol Fash.

Davis, Jack L. Ayia Irini: Period V. (Illus.). xxi, 125p. 1986. write for info. (*3-8053-0841-8*, DM117, Pub. by P Zabern) Eisenbrauns.

Davis, Jack L., ed. see Alcock, Susan E.

Davis, Jackie, jt. auth. see Bakke, Diane.

Davis, Jacqueline E., jt. ed. see Keenan, James P.

Davis, Jacqueline K. Cvx: A Smart Carrier for a New Era. (Institute for Foreign Policy Anaylsis Ser.). 94p. 1998. pap. 15.00 (*1-57488-191-4*) Brasseys.

Davis, Jacqueline P. International Health Data Reference Guide, 1993. 6th ed. (Illus.). 118p. (C). 1994. pap. text 40.00 (*0-7881-0691-0*) DIANE Pub.

— International Health Data Reference Guide, 1995. (Illus.). 140p. (Orig.). 1996. pap. text 40.00 (*0-7881-3244-X*) DIANE Pub.

Davis, Jacquelyn K. Aircraft Carriers & the Role of Naval Power in the Twenty-First Century. LC 93-27011. (National Security Papers: No. 13). 1993. 15.00 (*0-89549-099-4*) Inst Foreign Policy Anal.

— Forward Presence & U. S. Security Policy: Implications for Force Posture, Service Roles, & Joint Planning. LC 94-45022. (National Security Papers: Vol. 16). 1994. write for info. (*0-89549-107-9*) Inst Foreign Policy Anal.

Davis, Jacquelyn K. & Pfaltzgraff, Robert L., Jr. The Atlantic Alliance & U. S. Global Strategy. LC 83-18642. (Special Reports). 44p. 1983. pap. 11.95 (*0-89549-051-X*) Inst Foreign Policy Anal.

— Power Projection & the Long-Range Combat Aircraft: Missions, Capabilities & Alternative Designs. LC 81-82130. (Special Reports). 37p. 1981. 11.95 (*0-89549-033-1*) Inst Foreign Policy Anal.

Davis, Jacquelyn K. & Pfaltzgraff, Robert L. Strategic Defense & Extended Deterrence. LC 86-69. (National Security Papers: No. 4). 56p. 1986. 8.00 (*0-89549-070-6*) Inst Foreign Policy Anal.

Davis, Jacquelyn K. & Sweeney, Michael J. Strategic Paradigms 2025. (IFPA Special Reports Ser.). 120p. 1999. pap. 15.00 (*1-57488-197-3*) Brasseys.

Davis, Jacquelyn K., jt. auth. see Pfaltzgraff, Robert L.

Davis, Jacquelyn K., jt. auth. see Pfaltzgraff, Robert L., Jr.

Davis, James. Does Your Doctor Charge Too Much? The Consumers Guide to Physicians Fees. LC 97-5172. 275p. (Orig.). 1997. pap. 12.95 (*1-885987-02-1*, ME071, Health Info Pr) Practice Mgmt Info.

— Road to San Jacinto. (BCL1-PS American Literature Ser.). 334p. 1993. reprint ed. lib. bdg. 89.00 (*0-7812-6955-5*) Rprt Serv.

***Davis, James.** Rosetta Stone of God. Klemp, Joan et al, eds. LC 00-13244. 293p. 2000. pap. 14.00 (*1-57043-150-7*, Pub. by Eckankar) Assoc Pubs Grp.

Davis, James. Three Hundred Sixty-Five Ways to Manage the Business Called Private Practice. 140p. 1990. 24.95 (*1-878487-10-8*, 9105) Practice Mgmt Info.

Davis, James, ed. Health & Medicine on the Internet: Annual Guide to the World Wide Web. annuals LC 96-78922. (Illus.). 622p. (Orig.). 1998. pap. 19.95 (*1-885987-03-X*, ME078, Health Info Pr) Practice Mgmt Info.

— Medical Diagnosis Codes: A Consumer's Guide to the Classification of Diseases. LC 96-78923. 1375p. 1999. pap. 29.95 (*1-885987-06-4*, ME076, Health Info Pr) Practice Mgmt Info.

Davis, James, et al, eds. Health & Medicine on the Internet: An Annual Guide to the World Wide Web for Health Care Professionals. (Illus.). 600p. (Orig.). 1998. pap. text 29.95 (*1-57066-065-4*, ME121) Practice Mgmt Info.

Davis, James & Davis, Hazel. Presenting William Sleator. (Twayne's Young Adult Authors Ser.: No. 594). 130p. 1991. 21.95 (*0-8057-8215-X*, 594, Twyne) Mac Lib Ref.

Davis, James, jt. auth. see Watkins, James.

Davis, James, jt. ed. see Brandstatter, Hermann.

Davis, James, jt. ed. see Polite, Vernon.

Davis, James A. Education for Positive Mental Health: A Review of Existing Research & Recommendations for Future Studies. LC 64-15607. (Monographs in Social Research: No. 5). 1965. 15.00 (*0-202-09009-4*) Natl Opinion Res.

— Fifty-First Virginia Infantry. (Virginia Regimental Histories Ser.). (Illus.). 1985. 19.95 (*0-930919-13-0*) H E Howard.

— General Social Survey 1972. 1973. write for info. (*0-89138-060-4*) ICPSR.

— General Social Survey 1973. 1974. write for info. (*0-89138-073-6*) ICPSR.

— General Social Survey 1974. LC 75-36289. 1975. write for info. (*0-89138-119-8*) ICPSR.

— Great Aspirations: The Graduate School Plans of America's College Seniors. LC 64-15603. (Monographs in Social Research: No. 1). 1964. 15.00 (*0-202-09004-3*) Natl Opinion Res.

— Living Rooms As Symbols of Status: A Study in Social Judgment. LC 90-42478. (Harvard Studies in Sociology). 250p. 1991. text 30.00 (*0-8240-4324-3*) Garland.

— The Logic of Causal Order. LC 85-62371. (Quantitative Applications in the Social Sciences Ser.: Vol. 55). 96p. (Orig.). 1985. pap. text 10.95 (*0-8039-2553-0*) Sage.

— Okay, Don't Quit: How to Stop Smoking Without Quitting Cold Turkey. LC 91-61454. (Illus.). 130p. (Orig.). 1991. 19.95 (*0-915377-03-9*); pap. 11.95 (*0-915377-02-0*) Trad Pub.

— Studies in Social Change since 1948 Vol. 1: Methodological. (Report Ser.: No. 127-A). 1976. 15.00 (*0-932132-19-7*) Natl Opinion Res.

— Studies in Social Change since 1948 Vol. 2: Substantive. (Report Ser.: No. 127-B). 1976. 15.00 (*0-932132-20-0*) Natl Opinion Res.

— Times Table Secrets. (Illus.). 12p. (J). (gr. 3-5). 1994. 10.00 (*0-9634088-1-X*) Simp Solns.

— Undergraduate Career Decisions: Correlates of Occupational Choice. LC 64-15604. (Monographs in Social Research: No. 2). (Illus.). 1965. 15.00 (*0-202-09007-8*) Natl Opinion Res.

— An Unfair Advantage: The Mental Part of Sports & Business. LC 84-50120. (Illus.). 215p. (Orig.). 1984. 19.95 (*0-915377-00-4*); pap. 13.95 (*0-915377-01-2*) Trad Pub.

— Wisdom & Spirit: An Investigation of 1 Corinthians 1.18-3.20 Against the Background of Jewish Sapiential. (Traditions in the Greco-Roman Period Ser.). 270p. (Orig.). 1984. lib. bdg. 52.00 (*0-8191-4210-7*) U Pr of Amer.

Davis, James A. & Gebhard, Ruth. Great Books & Small Groups. LC 77-24390. 237p. 1977. reprint ed. lib. bdg. 59.50 (*0-8371-9742-2*, DAGB, Greenwood Pr) Greenwood.

Davis, James A. & Hayes, Kim F., eds. Geochemical Processes at Mineral Surfaces. LC 86-22173. (ACS Symposium Ser.: No. 323). (Illus.). ix, 672p. 1986. 109.95 (*0-8412-1004-7*) Am Chemical.

— Geochemical Processes at Mineral Surfaces. LC 86-22173. (ACS Symposium Ser.: Vol. 323). 696p. 1986. reprint ed. pap. 200.00 (*0-608-03527-0*, 206424600008) Bks Demand.

Davis, James A. & Sheatsley, Paul B. Americans View the Military: A 1984 Update. (Report Ser.: No. 132). 135p. 1986. pap. text 10.00 (*0-932132-36-7*) Natl Opinion Res.

Davis, James A. & Smith, Tom W. General Social Survey Cumulative File, 1972-1982. LC 85-117516. 1983. write for info. (*0-89138-917-2*) ICPSR.

— General Social Surveys, 1992-1998: Cumulative Codebook. (National Data Program for the Social Sciences Ser.: No. 16). 1479p. 1999. pap. 36.00 (*0-932132-55-3*) Natl Opinion Res.

— General Social Surveys, 1972-1987: Cumulative Codebook. (National Data Program for the Social Sciences Ser.: No. 8). 650p. 1987. pap. text 15.00 (*0-932132-39-1*) Natl Opinion Res.

Davis, James A. & Smith, Tom W. General Social Surveys, 1972-1991: Cumulative Codebook. (National Data Program for the Social Sciences Ser.: No. 12). vi, 989p. 1991. pap. 15.00 (*0-932132-45-6*) Natl Opinion Res.

Davis, James A. & Smith, Tom W. The NORC General Social Survey: A User's Guide. (Guides to Major Social Science Data Bases Ser.: Vol. 1). 96p. (C). 1991. text 28.00 (*0-8039-4367-9*); pap. text 11.50 (*0-8039-4037-8*) Sage.

Davis, James A., et al. Americans View the Military: Public Opinion in 1982. (Report Ser.: No. 131). 1983. 10.00 (*0-932132-29-4*) Natl Opinion Res.

— General Social Surveys, 1972-1982: Cumulative Codebook. 1982. 15.00 (*0-932132-27-8*) Natl Opinion Res.

Davis, James A., jt. auth. see Stouffer, Samuel A.

Davis, James B. The Coder's Handbook 2000. Swanson, Kathryn, ed. Date not set. text 99.95 (*1-57066-164-2*, 20045) Practice Mgmt Info.

Davis, James B. Reimbursement Manual for the Medical Office. 3rd ed. 316p. 1996. pap. text 49.95 (*1-57066-025-5*, ME064) Practice Mgmt Info.

***Davis, James B.** Reimbursement Manual for the Medical Office. 4th rev. ed. Swanson, Kathryn, ed. 460p. 2000. pap. text 49.95 (*1-57066-147-2*, ME123) Practice Mgmt Info.

Davis, James B., contrib. by. CDT-2: Current Dental Terminology. LC 97-30411. 250p. 1996. pap. text 39.95 (*1-57066-071-9*, 9718) Practice Mgmt Info.

***Davis, James B., et al, eds.** Health & Medicine on the Internet, 2000: Annual Guide to the World Wide Web for Health Care Professionals. 2nd rev. ed. (Illus.). 950p. 1999. pap. 29.95 (*1-57066-144-8*) Practice Mgmt Info.

***Davis, James B. & Lewis, Maxine.** Medicare Compliance Manual 2000. annuals rev. ed. (Illus.). 956p. 2000. ring bd. 129.95 (*1-57066-168-5*, 20047) Practice Mgmt Info.

Davis, James B., jt. ed. see ADP Context Software staff.

Davis, James B., ed. see HCFA Staff.

Davis, James C. The Decline of the Venetian Nobility As a Ruling Class. LC 78-64238. (Johns Hopkins University. Studies in the Social Sciences. Thirtieth Ser. 1912: 2). reprint ed. 37.50 (*0-404-61343-8*) AMS Pr.

— Rise from Want: A Peasant Family in the Machine Age. LC 86-19228. 183p. 1986. pap. 56.80 (*0-608-04821-6*, 206547800004) Bks Demand.

— A Venetian Family & Its Fortune, 1500-1900: The Dona & the Conservation of Their Wealth. LC 74-26309. (American Philosophical Society, Memoirs Ser.: No. 106). (Illus.). 205p. reprint ed. pap. 63.60 (*0-8357-7914-9*, 203634300002) Bks Demand.

Davis, James D. Collectible Novelty Phones: If Mr. Bell Could See Me Now. LC 97-80683. (Illus.). 144p. 1998. pap. 24.95 (*0-7643-0472-0*) Schiffer.

Davis, James E. Frontier Illinois. LC 98-8070. (History of the Trans-Appalachian Frontier Ser.). (Illus.). 432p. 1999. 39.95 (*0-253-33423-3*) Ind U Pr.

***Davis, James E.** Frontier Illinois. 2000. reprint ed. pap. 18.95 (*0-253-21406-8*) Ind U Pr.

Davis, James E. Rules of Order: An Authoritative, Simplified Guide to Parliamentary Procedure. LC 92-895. (Illus.). 180p. 1992. 24.95 (*1-55652-150-2*) Chicago Review.

Davis, James E., ed. Planning a Social Studies Program: Activities, Guidelines, Resources. rev. ed. 203p. 1997. pap. 24.95 (*0-89994-395-0*, 395-0) Soc Sci Ed.

Davis, James E., ed. see Parke, Charles R.

Davis, James E., jt. ed. see Salomone, Ronald E.

Davis, James Earl, jt. ed. see Brown, M. Christopher, II.

Davis, James F. Almanzar. LC 70-144153. (Short Story Index Reprint Ser.). (Illus.). 1977. reprint ed. 19.95 (*0-8369-3768-6*) Ayer.

— A Survey of the Spherical Space Form Problem, Vol. 2. (Mathematical Reports: vol.2, pt. 2). xii, 60p. 1986. text 63.00 (*3-7186-0250-4*) Gordon & Breach.

Davis, James F., et al. Intelligent Systems in Process Engineering. 2nd ed. LC 96-17881. (CCPS Guidelines Ser.). 422p. 1998. 179.00 (*0-8169-0707-2*) Am Inst Chem Eng.

***Davis, James G.** James G. Davis: Paintings. 32p. 2000. 7.00 (*0-934306-26-5*) Springfield.

Davis, James H., Jr. The Happy Island: Images of Childhood in the Eighteenth-Century French Theatre d'Education. (American University Studies: Education: Ser. XIV, Vol. 10). XII, 195p. 1987. text 31.50 (*0-8204-0446-2*) P Lang Pubng.

Davis, James H. Texans in Gray: A Regimental History of the Eighteenth Texas Infantry Walker's Texas Division in the Civil War. LC 93-79082. (Illus.). 210p. 1999. lib. bdg. 24.95 (*0-9630768-8-4*) Heritage Oak.

Davis, James H., jt. ed. see Witte, Erich H.

Davis, James J. Own Court Book of Tennis. 1987. pap. write for info. (*0-318-62750-7*) Davis Turner Pub.

Davis, James K. Assault on the Left: The F. B. I. & the Sixties Antiwar Movement. LC 96-44675. 240p. 1997. 24.95 (*0-275-95455-2*, Praeger Pubs) Greenwood.

— Spying on America: The FBI's Domestic Counterintelligence Program. LC 91-23131. 208p. 1992. 39.95 (*0-275-93407-1*, C3407, Praeger Pubs) Greenwood.

Davis, James L. Unveiling Revelation: The Prophetic Visions of St. John of Patmos. LC 96-77009. 193p. 1998. pap. 19.95 (*0-9635645-5-2*) KMT Pubns.

Davis, James L., contrib. by. Familiar Bird Songs of the Northwest. 1988. audio 10.95 (*0-931686-10-5*) Audubon Soc Portland.

Davis, James L. & Daub, Edward E. Biotechnology. LC 94-42317. (Technical Japanese Supplements Ser.). 1996. pap. 25.00 (*0-299-14714-2*) U of Wis Pr.

Davis, James M. & Webber, Bert. Top Secret: The Details of the Planned World War II Invasion of Japan & How the Japanese Would Have Met It (the Japanese Atomic Bomb)(Documentary) LC 94-44934. (Illus.). 88p. 1994. pap. 9.95 (*0-936738-85-5*) Webb Research.

Davis, James M., Jr., jt. ed. see Kolin, Philip C.

Davis, James N. Liens: Lectures Diverses. (Bridging the Gap Ser.). (FRE.). (C). 1994. mass mkt. 36.95 (*0-8384-4618-3*) Heinle & Heinle.

Davis, James O. The Pastor's Best Friend. LC 97-17775. 240p. 1997. 12.00 (*0-88243-783-6*) Gospel Pub.

Davis, James P. An Experimental Reading of Wordsworth's Prelude: The Poetics of Bimodal Consciousness. LC 95-1669. (Salzburger Studien Ser.). 204p. 1995. text 89.95 (*0-7734-1245-X*) E Mellen.

Davis, James R. Better Teaching, More Learning: Strategies for Success in Post-Secondary Settings. LC 93-9809. (American Council on Education-Oryx Press Series on Higher Education). 392p. 1993. 35.00 (*0-89774-813-1*) Oryx Pr.

— Interdisciplinary Courses & Team Teaching: New Arrangements for Learning. LC 95-19858. 288p. 1995. boxed set 34.95 (*0-89774-887-5*) Oryx Pr.

Davis, James R. & Cushing, Barry E. Accounting Information Systems: A Book of Readings. LC 78-74681. pap. write for info. (*0-201-01099-2*) Addison-Wesley.

Davis, James R. & Davis, Adelaide B. Effective Training Strategies: A Comprehensive Guide to Maximizing Learning in Organizations. LC 98-28368. 442p. 1998. 49.95 (*1-57675-037-X*) Berrett-Koehler.

***Davis, James R. & Davis, Adelaide B.** Managing Your Own Learning. 200p. 2000. pap. 15.95 (*1-57675-067-1*) Berrett-Koehler.

Davis, James R., et al. Accounting Information Systems: A Cycle Approach. 3rd ed. LC 89-25014. 784p. 1990. text 96.95 (*0-471-61560-9*) Wiley.

Davis, James T. Trade Routes & Economic Exchange among the Indians of California. fac. ed. (Reports of the University of California Archaeological Survey: No. 54). (Illus.). 78p. 1961. reprint ed. pap. 9.06 (*1-55567-370-8*) Coyote Press.

Davis, James T., jt. auth. see Treganza, Adam E.

Davis, James V. Trickles from a Dry Well: Select Poems by James V. Davis. Emond, Loves, ed. LC 98-71046. (Illus.). 96p. 1998. 19.95 (*0-9658029-1-4*) Caduceus Pr.

Davis, James W. The American Presidency. 2nd ed. LC 95-7981. 480p. 1995. 79.50 (*0-275-94874-9*, Praeger Pubs); pap. 27.95 (*0-275-94875-7*, Praeger Pubs) Greenwood.

***Davis, James W.** Leadership Selection in Six Western Democracies. 200p. 1999. lib. bdg. 70.00 (*1-57958-111-0*) Fitzroy Dearborn.

Davis, James W. National Conventions in an Age of Party Reform, 91. LC 82-9382. (Contributions in Political Science Ser.: No. 91). 304p. 1983. 65.00 (*0-313-23048-X*, DNC/, Greenwood Pr) Greenwood.

— Nominating National Leaders: A Cross-National Survey. LC 97-52297. 232p. 1998. lib. bdg. 65.00 (*0-313-30147-6*, Greenwood Pr) Greenwood.

— The President As Party Leader. LC 91-35809. (Contributions in Political Science Ser.: No. 295). 240p. 1992. pap. 18.95 (*0-275-94112-4*, B4112, Greenwood Pr) Greenwood.

— The President As Party Leader, 295. LC 91-34997. (Contributions in Political Science Ser.: No. 295). 248p. 1992. 57.95 (*0-313-28007-X*, DVP/, Greenwood Pr) Greenwood.

— Presidential Primaries: Road to the White House, 41. LC 79-54062. (Contributions in Political Science Ser.: No. 41). 395p. 1980. 69.50 (*0-313-22057-3*, DPP/, Greenwood Pr) Greenwood.

***Davis, James W.** Threats & Promises: The Pursuit of International Influence. LC 00-24993. (Illus.). 232p. 2000. 36.00 (*0-8018-6296-5*) Johns Hopkins.

Davis, James W. U. S. Presidential Primaries & the Caucus-Convention System: A Sourcebook. LC 96-32980. 312p. 1997. lib. bdg. 79.50 (*0-313-29629-4*, Greenwood Pr) Greenwood.

***Davis, James W. & DiClerico, Robert E.** Choosing Our Choices: Debating the Presidential Nominating Process. 208p. 2000. 55.00 (*0-8476-9447-X*); pap. 15.95 (*0-8476-9448-8*) Rowman.

Davis, Jan & Hawkins, Kari. Huntsville Tapestry. LC 99-26352. (Illus.). 1999. 49.95 (*1-881096-70-X*) Towery Pub.

Davis, Jan & Lambert, Robert. Engineering in Emergencies: A Practical Guide for Engineers & Relief Workers. 717p. 1995. pap. 35.00 (*1-85339-222-7*, Pub. by Intermed Tech) Stylus Pub VA.

Davis, Jan, et al. Developing & Managing Community Water Supplies: A Guide for Development Workers. (Illus.). 184p. (C). 1993. 39.95 (*0-85598-192-X*, Pub. by Oxfam Pub); pap. 14.95 (*0-85598-193-8*, Pub. by Oxfam Pub) Stylus Pub VA.

Davis, Jan, ed. see Unger, Barbara.

Davis, Jane. Perfect Style with Grammatik. 1994. pap. 29.95 incl. disk (*0-07-015865-7*, Windcrest) TAB Bks.

— Physics Exploration. 172p. (C). 1995. 20.95 (*0-7872-1205-9*) Kendall-Hunt.

— South Africa: A Botched Civilization? Racial Conflict & Identity in Selected South African Novels. LC 96-36986. 216p. 1997. 52.50 (*0-7618-0604-0*); pap. 29.50 (*0-7618-0605-9*) U Pr of Amer.

***Davis, Jane.** The White Image in the Black Mind: A Study of African American Literature, 194. LC 99-36173. (Contributions in Afro-American & African Studies). 184p. 2000. 55.00 (*0-313-30464-5*) Greenwood.

Davis, Jane, ed. Politics & International Relations in the Middle East: Continuity & Change. LC 94-45149. 176p. 1995. 85.00 (*1-85898-234-0*) E Elgar.

Davis, Jane S. Breakthrough: Human-Cat Communication. 256p. (Orig.). 1999. pap. 17.95 (*0-9639544-6-6*) A F A B.

Davis, Janet. Back-up Banjo. 240p. 1981. spiral bd. 17.95 (*0-87166-888-2*, 93771) Mel Bay.

***Davis, Janet.** Back-Up Banjo. 240p. 1999. spiral bd. 36.95 incl. audio compact disk (*0-7866-5116-4*, 93771CDP) Mel Bay.

Davis, Janet. Banjo Handbook. 80p. 1988. pap. 10.95 (*0-87166-402-X*, 94206) Mel Bay.

— Banjo Handbook. 1988. audio 9.98 (*0-87166-403-8*, 94206C) Mel Bay.

— Banjo Handbook. 1993. 18.95 incl. audio (*0-87166-404-6*, 94206P) Mel Bay.

***Davis, Janet.** Banjo Handbook. 80p. 1999. pap. 25.95 incl. audio compact disk (*0-7866-5118-0*, 94206CDP) Mel Bay.

— Christmas Songs for 5-String Banjo. 96p. 1995. pap. 10.95 (*0-7866-0473-5*, 95444); pap. 24.95 incl. audio compact disk (*0-7866-0690-8*, 95444CDP) Mel Bay.

— Famous Banjo Pickin' Tunes. 32p. 2000. pap. 5.95 incl. audio compact disk (*0-7866-5074-5*, 98530BCD) Mel Bay.

D

An Asterisk (*) at the beginning of an entry indicates that the title is appearing for the first time.

Davis, Janet. Splitting the Licks/Banjo - 5 String: Intermediate. 108p. 1985. spiral bd. 12.95 (0-87166-913-7, 93998) Mel Bay.
— Up the Neck. 1993. spiral bd. 12.95 (1-56222-572-3, 94820); audio 9.98 (1-56222-571-5, 94820C) Mel Bay.
— Up the Neck: Banjo: Intermediate to Advanced. 144p. 1993. pap., spiral bd. 20.95 incl. audio (0-7866-1123-5, 94820P) Mel Bay.
— You Can Teach Yourself Banjo. 116p. 1991. pap. 9.95 (1-56222-001-2, 94429); audio 9.98 (1-56222-002-0, 94429C); audio compact disk 15.98 (0-7866-0381-X, 94429CD) Mel Bay.
— You Can Teach Yourself Banjo. 1993. pap. 18.95 incl. audio (1-56222-515-4, 94429P) Mel Bay.
***Davis, Janet.** You Can Teach Yourself Banjo. 116p. 1998. pap. 17.95 incl. audio compact disk (0-7866-4444-3, 94429BCD) Mel Bay.
Davis, Janet. You Can Teach Yourself Dobro. LC 70-6181 /. 134p. 1996. pap. 9.95 (0-7866-0801-3, 95227) Mel Bay.
— You Can Teach Yourself Dobro. 1996. audio 9.98 (0-7866-0802-1, 95227C); audio compact disk 15.98 (0-7866-1440-4, 95227CD) Mel Bay.
Davis, Janet. You Can Teach Yourself Dobro. 134p. 1996. pap. 18.95 incl. audio (0-7866-1235-5, 95227P) Mel Bay.
— You Can Teach Yourself Dobro. 136p. 1998. pap. 17.95 incl. audio compact disk (0-7866-4445-1, 95227BCD) Mel Bay.
Davis, Janet, jt. auth. see Dayley, Beth.
Davis, Jay, Jr. Beginning in Eighteen Sixty-One: A Novel of the War Between the States. LC 94-16389. 192p. (Orig.). 1994. pap. 12.95 (1-56474-108-7) Fithian Pr.
Davis, Jay, jt. auth. see Davis, Don.
Davis, Jay, jt. ed. see Garrod, Andrew.
Davis, Jean. Reaching Maturity, What Are My Options? large type ed. LC 97-93390. 134p. (Orig.). 1997. pap. 12.95 (0-9658233-2-6) Angel Wrks LA.
Davis, Jean E., jt. ed. see Convery, Frank J.
Davis, Jeanne. From Here to There: Stepping Stones. (Illus.). 1991. 9.50 (0-8378-2060-X) Gibson.
— You Are My Friend, Because. (Illus.). 1993. boxed set 8.95 (0-8378-5303-6) Gibson.
***Davis, Jeannie.** Beyond "Hello" A Practical Guide for Excellent Telephone Communication & Quality Customer Service. LC 98-88128. 158p. 1999. 24.95 (0-944918-04-2) Now Hear This.
Davis, Jed. Spinner Fishing for Steelhead, Salmon & Trout. 3rd ed. LC 88-31377. (Illus.). 97p. 1995. pap. 19.95 (0-936608-40-4) F Amato Pubns.
Davis, Jed H. & Evans, Mary J. Theatre, Children & Youth. rev. ed. (Illus.). 360p. 1987. pap. text 40.00 (0-87602-026-0) Anchorage.
Davis, Jeff, jt. auth. see Whitener, Angela.
Davis, Jefferson. Jefferson Davis: Private Letters, 1823-1889. Strode, Hudson, ed. (Illus.). 604p. 1995. reprint ed. pap. 16.95 (0-306-80638-X) Da Capo.
— Jefferson Davis, Constitutionalist: His Letters, Papers & Speeches, 10 vols. Rowland, Dunbar, ed. LC 71-163682. reprint ed. 960.00 (0-404-02000-3) AMS Pr.
— The Messages & Papers of Jefferson Davis & the Confederacy, 2 vols., Set. (American Biography Ser.). 1991. reprint ed. lib. bdg. 180.00 (0-7812-8099-0) Rprt Serv.
— Papers of Jefferson Davis: October 1863-August 1864, Vol. 10. Crist, Lynda L. et al, eds. (Illus.). 1000p. 1999. text 95.00 (0-8071-2412-5) La State U Pr.
— Papers of Jefferson Davis, 1853-1855, Vol. 5. Crist, Lynda L. & Dix, Mary S., eds. LC 76-152704. (Illus.). xlii, 557p. 1985. text 75.00 (0-8071-1240-2) La State U Pr.
— Papers of Jefferson Davis, 1856-1860, Vol. 6. Crist, Lynda L. & Dix, Mary S., eds. LC 76-152704. (Illus.). 840p. 1989. text 80.00 (0-8071-1502-9) La State U Pr.
— Papers of Jefferson Davis, 1849-1852, Vol. 4. Crist, Lynda L., ed. LC 76-152704. (Illus.). 472p. 1982. text 70.00 (0-8071-1037-X) La State U Pr.
— Papers of Jefferson Davis, 1808-1840, Vol. 1. Monroe, Haskell M., Jr. & McIntosh, James T., eds. LC 76-152704. (Illus.). xcii, 594p. 1971. text 80.00 (0-8071-0943-6) La State U Pr.
— Papers of Jefferson Davis, 1861, Vol. 7. Crist, Lynda L. & Dix, Mary S., eds. LC 91-11198. (Illus.). 557p. 1991. text 75.00 (0-8071-1726-9) La State U Pr.
— Papers of Jefferson Davis, 1862, Vol. 8. Crist, Lynda L. et al, eds. LC 95-152704. (Illus.). 720p. 1993. text 85.00 (0-8071-1938-5) La State U Pr.
— Papers of Jefferson Davis, January-September 1863, Vol. 9. Crist, Lynda L. et al, eds. LC 91-11198. (Illus.). 552p. 1997. text 75.00 (0-8071-2087-1) La State U Pr.
— Papers of Jefferson Davis, July 1846-December 1848, Vol. 3. McIntosh, James T., ed. LC 76-152704. (Illus.). xxxiv, 598p. 1981. text 80.00 (0-8071-0786-7) La State U Pr.
— Papers of Jefferson Davis, June 1841-July 1846, Vol. 2. McIntosh, James T., ed. LC 76-152704. (Illus.). xlii, 806p. 1975. text 90.00 (0-8071-0082-X) La State U Pr.
— The Rise & Fall of the Confederate Government, 2 vols. 1990. pap. write for info. (0-306-80420-4) Da Capo.
— The Rise & Fall of the Confederate Government. abr. ed. 1990. 22.50 (0-8446-0074-1) Peter Smith.
— The Rise & Fall of the Confederate Government. 1992. reprint ed. lib. bdg. 49.95 (0-89968-282-0, Lghtyr Pr) Buccaneer Bks.
— The Rise & Fall of the Confederate Government, Vol. 1. (Illus.). 696p. 1990. pap. 17.95 (0-306-80418-2) Da Capo.
— The Rise & Fall of the Confederate Government, Vol. 2. (Illus.). 636p. 1990. pap. 17.95 (0-306-80419-0) Da Capo.
***Davis, Jefferson.** Talkin' Tuna: The Wit & Wisdom of Coach Bill Parcells. (Illus.). 96p. 1999. pap. 8.95 (1-55022-387-9, ECWR & EC) Evangel Concern Wstrn.
***Davis, Jefferson & Podnieks, Andrew.** Hello Hockey Fans from Coast to Coast: Amazing Lists for Trivia Lovers. (Illus.). 170p. 1999. pap. 15.95 (1-55022-386-0, ECWR & EC) Evangel Concern Wstrn.
Davis, Jefferson, ed. see Confederate States of America - Constitutional Con.
Davis, Jefferson J., et al. Georgia Litigation Forms & Analysis, Vols. 1-3. LC 95-80808. 1800p. 1995. text. write for info. (0-7620-0011-2) West Group.
Davis, Jeffery. Children's Television, 1947-1990: Over 200 Series, Game & Variety Shows, Cartoons, Educational Programs & Specials. LC 94-10808. (Illus.). 295p. 1995. lib. bdg. 45.00 (0-89950-911-8) McFarland & Co.
***Davis, Jeffrey G. & Menze, Scott A.** Atlas of Ohio's Frogs & Toads. (Miscellaneous Contributions Ser.: Vol. 6). (Illus.). 35p. (C). 2000. pap. text 5.00 (0-86727-136-1) Ohio Bio Survey.
— Frogs & Toads. LC 00-102480. (In Ohio's Backyard Ser.: Vol. 3). (Illus.). 150p. (J). (gr. 6 up). 2000. 15.00 (0-86727-139-6) Ohio Bio Survey.
***Davis, Jeffrey M.** Fiscal & Macroeconomic Impact of Privatization. LC 00-31909. (Occasional Papers). 2000. pap. write for info. (1-55775-888-3) Intl Monetary.
Davis, Jeffrey M., ed. Macroeconomic Adjustment: Policy Instruments & Issues. LC 92-22870. 90p. 1992. pap. 12.50 (1-55775-303-2) Intl Monetary.
Davis, Jemma. A Spanish Affair. large type ed. (Linford Romance Library). 256p. 1998. pap. 17.99 (0-7089-5233-X, Linford) Ulverscroft.
Davis, Jenell, ed. see Adams, Pamela W.
Davis, Jenell, ed. see Carpenter, Elizabeth & Martin, Rick.
Davis, Jenell L., ed. see Adams, Pamela W.
Davis, Jenell L., ed. see Adams, Pamela W. & Carpenter, Elizabeth.
Davis, Jenell L., ed. see Adams, Pamela W. & Pressley, Sara R.
Davis, Jenell L., ed. & illus. see Adams, Pamela W., et al.
Davis, Jennell L., ed. see Adams, Pamela W. & Pressley, Sara R.
Davis, Jennie, jt. auth. see Buerger, Jane.
Davis, Jenny. Anchovy Breath to Zoo Food: One Hundred Seventy-Five Names I Call My Brother When I'm Mad. (Illus.). 80p. (Orig.). (YA). 1994. pap. 3.50 (0-380-77135-7, Avon Bks) Morrow Avon.
— Checking on the Moon. LC 91-8284. 224p. (J). (gr. 4-7). 1991. 16.95 (0-531-05960-X) Orchard Bks Watts.
— Checking on the Moon. LC 91-8284. 224p. (J). (gr. 6 up). 1991. 17.99 (0-531-08560-0) Orchard Bks Watts.
— Checking on the Moon. 1991. 9.09 (0-606-05199-6, Pub. by Turtleback) Demco.
***Davis, Jenny.** Dear Heart. large type unabridged ed. 111p. 1999. 23.95 (0-7531-5093-X, 15093X, Pub. by ISIS Lrg Prnt) ISIS Pub.
— Sex Education: A Novel. 1995. 9.09 (0-606-08602-1, Pub. by Turtleback) Demco.
Davis, Jeremy & Devinney, Timothy. The Essence of Corporate Strategy: Theory for Modern Decision Making. 376p. 1998. pap. 45.00 (1-86448-300-8, Pub. by Allen & Unwin Pty) Paul & Co Pubs.
Davis, Jeri & Freeman, Michael A., eds. Marketing for Therapists: A Handbook for Success in Managed Care. LC 95-44177. (Psychology Ser.). 208p. (Orig.). 1996. pap. 28.95 (0-7879-0207-1) Jossey-Bass.
Davis, Jerome. Russian Immigrant. LC 69-18770. (American Immigration Collection. Series 1). 1969. reprint ed. 11.95 (0-405-00518-0) Ayer.
***Davis, Jerome.** Waiting to Expire: The Incoherent Ramblings of an Inebriated Soul. unabridged ed. 80p. 1999. pap. 15.00 (0-9670792-0-9, 1) J Davis.
Davis, Jerome, ed. New Russia: Between the First & Second Five-Year Plans. LC 68-22909. (Essay Index Reprint Ser.). 1977. 19.95 (0-8369-0365-X) Ayer.
Davis, Jerra, ed. see Brown, Bernita J.
Davis, Jerry, jt. auth. see Hyland, Terry L.
Davis, Jerry, jt. auth. see Sterba, Michael.
***Davis, Jerry L., et al, eds.** Safe & Effective Secondary Schools: The Boys Town Model. 145p. 2000. pap. 24.95 (0-938510-75-4) Boys Town Pr.
Davis, Jerry S. College Affordability: A Closer Look at the Crisis. LC 97-92262. 60p. (Orig.). (C). 1997. pap. 10.00 (0-9659127-0-1) Sallie Mae Educ.
Davis, Jesse. A Mother Looks at the Gay Child. LC 97-65810. 176p. (Orig.). 1997. pap. 14.95 (1-56184-126-9) New Falcon Pubns.
Davis, Jessica, jt. auth. see Martin, Lexi.
Davis, Jessica M., jt. auth. see Matte, Gerard.
Davis, Jim. La Bonne Vie. (Garfield Ser.). (FRE.). (J). 1988. 18.95 (0-8288-4581-6) Fr & Eur.
— Breitet Sich Aus, 4. 1999. pap. text 10.95 (3-8105-0722-9) W Kruger.
Davis, Jim. La Diete, Jamais! (Garfield Ser.). (FRE.). (J). 1987. 18.95 (0-8288-4582-4) Fr & Eur.
Davis, Jim. The Eighth Garfield Treasury. LC 95-94224. 128p. 1995. pap. 12.00 (0-345-39778-9) Ballantine Pub Grp.
***Davis, Jim.** Eleventh Garfield Fat Cat 3. 1999. pap. 9.95 (0-345-43801-9) Ballantine Pub Grp.
Davis, Jim. La Faim Justifie Les Moyens. (Garfield Ser.). (FRE.). (J). 1985. 18.95 (0-8288-4583-2, F91530) Fr & Eur.
— The Ninth Garfield Fat Cat 3-Pack, Vols 25-27. LC 98-96212. (Garfield Ser.: Vol. 9). (Illus.). 384p. 1998. pap. 9.95 (0-345-42903-6) Ballantine Pub Grp.
Davis, Jim. Faut Pas S'En Faire. (Garfield Ser.). (FRE.). (J). 1984. 18.95 (0-8288-4584-0, F101551) Fr & Eur.
— Die Feldmaus Und Die Stadtmaus. (Lesen Leicht Germacht Ser.).Tr. of Country Mouse & the City Mouse. (J). 1999. pap. text 7.95 (88-8148-247-9) Midwest European Pubns.
Davis, Jim. The Fifth Garfield Treasury. (Illus.). 120p. 1989. pap. 12.00 (0-345-36268-3) Ballantine Pub Grp.
— For You, with Love: Garfisms of Affection. (Illus.). 40p. 1995. 6.95 (0-8362-0565-0) Andrews & McMeel.
— The Fourth Garfield Treasury. 144p. 1987. pap. 12.00 (0-345-34726-9) Ballantine Pub Grp.
— Garfield's Son of Big, Fat Hairy Jokes. (Illus.). 144p. 1994. mass mkt. 3.99 (0-345-38953-0) Ballantine Pub Grp.
— Garfield: Garfield's 20th Anniversary Collection. LC 97-97062. (Illus.). 192p. 1998. pap. 14.95 (0-345-42126-4) Ballantine Pub Grp.
— Garfield: His Nine Lives. 128p. (Orig.). 1984. pap. 16.00 (0-345-32061-1) Ballantine Pub Grp.
— Garfield: Life in the Fat Lane. (Illus.). 128p. 1995. pap. 6.95 (0-345-39776-2) Ballantine Pub Grp.
— Garfield: The Best Things in Life Are Edible. LC 97-116081. (Illus.). 80p. 1995. 4.95 (0-8362-0563-4) Andrews & McMeel.
— Garfield: The Truth about Cats. 64p. 1991. 6.95 (0-345-37226-3) Ballantine Pub Grp.
— Garfield No. 13: Food for Thought, Vol.. 13. Vol 13. 128p. 1987. pap. 6.95 (0-345-34129-5) Ballantine Pub Grp.
— Garfield & the Beast in the Basement. (Planet Reader First Chapter Bks.). (Illus.). 80p. (J). (gr. 2-5). 1998. pap. 2.95 (0-8167-4439-4) Troll Communs.
***Davis, Jim.** Garfield & the Beast in the Basement. (J). 1998. 8.05 (0-606-13411-5, Pub. by Turtleback) Demco.
Davis, Jim. Garfield & the Mysterious Mummy. (Planet Reader First Chapter Bks.). (Illus.). 80p. (J). (gr. 2-4). 1998. pap. 2.95 (0-8167-4438-6) Troll Communs.
***Davis, Jim.** Garfield & the Mysterious Mummy. (J). 1998. 8.05 (0-606-13412-3, Pub. by Turtleback) Demco.
— Garfield & the Teacher Creature. 1999. pap. 2.95 (0-8167-4928-0) Troll Communs.
Davis, Jim. Garfield at Large. Vol. 1. 128p. 1984. pap. 6.95 (0-345-32013-1) Ballantine Pub Grp.
— Garfield at Large. (J). 1980. 12.05 (0-606-03063-8, Pub. by Turtleback) Demco.
***Davis, Jim.** Garfield Beefs Up. 2000. pap. 8.95 (0-345-44109-5) Ballantine Pub Grp.
Davis, Jim. Garfield Bigger & Better No. 30: Bigger & Better, Vol. 30. LC 96-96531. Vol. 30. 128p. 1996. pap. 6.95 (0-345-40770-9) Ballantine Pub Grp.
— Garfield, Bigger Than Life. (J). 1981. 12.05 (0-606-02987-7, Pub. by Turtleback) Demco.
— Garfield Bigger Than Life: His Third Book, Vol. 3. Vol. 3. 128p. 1984. pap. 6.95 (0-345-32007-7) Ballantine Pub Grp.
— Garfield by the Pound, Vol. 22. Vol. 22. 128p. (Orig.). 1992. pap. 6.95 (0-345-37579-3) Ballantine Pub Grp.
— Garfield Chews the Fat, Vol.. 17. LC 88-92024. Vol. 17. 128p. 1989. pap. 6.95 (0-345-35956-9) Ballantine Pub Grp.
***Davis, Jim.** Garfield Crazy about Numbers: Games & Sticker Fun. 1998. pap. text 4.95 (2-922148-27-0) Modus Viv.
Davis, Jim. Garfield Discovers America. (Illus.). 32p. (J). (ps-3). 1994. pap. 6.95 (0-8167-3431-3) Troll Communs.
— Garfield Dishes It out No. 27, Vol. 27. LC 94-96513. Vol. 27. 128p. (Orig.). 1995. pap. 6.95 (0-345-39287-6) Ballantine Pub Grp.
— Garfield Eats His Heart Out. (J). 1983. 12.05 (0-606-02986-9, Pub. by Turtleback) Demco.
— Garfield Eats His Heart Out, Vol. 6. Vol. 6. (Illus.). 128p. 1984. pap. 6.95 (0-345-32018-2) Ballantine Pub Grp.
***Davis, Jim.** Garfield Fat Cat. LC 98-96724. (Illus.). 1999. pap. 9.95 (0-345-43458-7) Ballantine Pub Grp.
Davis, Jim. Garfield Fat Cat, 3 Vols., Vol. 2. LC 94-94383. Vol. 2. (Illus.). 384p. 1994. pap. 9.95 (0-345-39192-6) Ballantine Pub Grp.
— Garfield Fat Cat, Vols., Vol. 3. Vol. 3. 1995. pap. 9.95 (0-345-39493-3) Ballantine Pub Grp.
— Garfield Fat Cat Three Pack, 3 Vols., Vol. 3. Vol. 3. (Illus.). 384p. 1993. pap. 9.95 (0-345-38385-0) Ballantine Pub Grp.
— Garfield Fat Cat Three Pack, 3 Vols., Vol. 4. LC 94-94383. Vol. 4. 4p. 1995. pap. 9.95 (0-345-40238-3) Ballantine Pub Grp.
— Garfield Fat Cat Three Pack, 3 Vols., Vol. 5. Vol. 5. 1996. pap. 9.95 (0-345-40404-1) Ballantine Pub Grp.
— Garfield Fat Cat Three Pack, Vol. 6. LC 94-94383. Vol. 6. 6p. 1996. pap. 9.95 (0-345-40884-5) Ballantine Pub Grp.
— Garfield Fat Cat Three Pack, Vol. 7. Vol. 7. 1997. pap. 9.95 (0-345-41449-7) Ballantine Pub Grp.
***Davis, Jim.** Garfield Feeds the Kitty, Vol. 35. 1999. pap. 6.95 (0-345-43673-3) Ballantine Pub Grp.
Davis, Jim. Garfield Gains Weight. (J). 1981. 12.05 (0-606-02927-3, Pub. by Turtleback) Demco.
— Garfield Gains Weight No. 2, Vol. 2. Vol. 2. 128p. (Orig.). 1984. pap. 6.95 (0-345-32008-5) Ballantine Pub Grp.
— Garfield Gets a Life. 1991. pap. 6.95 (0-345-37375-8) Ballantine Pub Grp.
— Garfield Goes to (Dis)Obedience School. (Illus.). (J). (gr. k-3). 1997. pap. 2.95 (0-8167-4291-X) Troll Communs.
— Garfield Goes to Waist No. 18, Vol. 18. Vol. 18. 128p. 1990. pap. 6.95 (0-345-36430-9) Ballantine Pub Grp.
— Garfield Hams It Up, No. 31. LC 96-95038. Vol. 31. 128p. 1997. pap. 6.95 (0-345-41241-9) Ballantine Pub Grp.
— Garfield Hangs out, No. 19. Vol. 19. (Illus.). 128p. 1990. pap. 6.95 (0-345-36835-5) Ballantine Pub Grp.
— Garfield Hits the Big Time: His 25th Book, Vol. 25. LC 93-90003. Vol. 25. (Illus.). 128p. 1993. pap. 6.95 (0-345-38332-X) Ballantine Pub Grp.
***Davis, Jim.** Garfield Hogs the Spotlight. (Illus.). (J). 2000. 12.34 (0-606-17987-9) Turtleback.
— Garfield Hogs the Spotlight: His 36th Book. LC 99-68499. Vol. 36. (Illus.). 128p. 2000. pap. 6.95 (0-345-43922-8) Ballantine Pub Grp.
Davis, Jim. Garfield Hop, Skip & Jump: Games & Sticker Fun. (Garfield Ser.). (Illus.). (J). 1998. pap. 4.95 (2-922148-29-7) Presses Avent.
— Garfield in Paradise. 64p. 1986. pap. 6.95 (0-345-33796-4) Ballantine Pub Grp.
— Garfield in Paradise. (J). 1986. 12.15 (0-606-01871-9, Pub. by Turtleback) Demco.
— Garfield in the Rough. 64p. 1984. pap. 6.95 (0-345-32242-8) Ballantine Pub Grp.
— Garfield in the Rough. (J). 1984. 12.15 (0-606-00284-7, Pub. by Turtleback) Demco.
— Garfield Insults, Put-Downs & Slams. LC 93-90861. (Illus.). 1994. pap. 3.99 (0-345-38689-2) Ballantine Pub Grp.
— Garfield Keeps His Chins up, Vol.. 23. LC 92-90049. Vol. 23. (Illus.). 128p. (Orig.). 1992. pap. 6.95 (0-345-37959-4) Ballantine Pub Grp.
— Garfield Learning to Tell. 1998. pap. text 9.95 (2-922148-21-1) Modus Viv.
— Garfield Loses His Feet, Vol. 9. Vol. 9. 128p. 1984. pap. 6.95 (0-345-31805-6, Ballantine) Ballantine Pub Grp.
— Garfield Makes It Big. (J). 1985. 12.05 (0-606-00283-9, Pub. by Turtleback) Demco.
— Garfield Makes It Big, Vol. 10. Vol. 10. 128p. 1985. pap. 6.95 (0-345-31928-1) Ballantine Pub Grp.
— Garfield on the Town. 64p. 1983. pap. 6.95 (0-345-31542-1, Ballantine) Ballantine Pub Grp.
— Garfield on the Town. (J). 1983. 12.15 (0-606-03270-3, Pub. by Turtleback) Demco.
— Garfield Out to Lunch. (J). 1986. 12.05 (0-606-01872-7, Pub. by Turtleback) Demco.
— Garfield Out to Lunch, Vol. 12. Vol. 12. (Illus.). 128p. 1986. pap. 6.95 (0-345-33118-4) Ballantine Pub Grp.
***Davis, Jim.** Garfield Predicts! Mini Edition: Fearless Forecasts for a Brave New Millennium. 1999. pap. text 4.95 (0-8362-3282-8) Andrews & McMeel.
Davis, Jim. Garfield Prend Du Poids. (Garfield Ser.). (FRE.). (J). 1984. 18.95 (0-8288-4586-7, F101550) Fr & Eur.
— Garfield Pulls Weight, Vol. 26. LC 93-90469. Vol. 26. 128p. (Orig.). 1994. pap. 6.95 (0-345-38666-3) Ballantine Pub Grp.
— Garfield Rolls on, Vol. 11. Vol. 11. 128p. (Orig.). 1985. pap. 6.95 (0-345-32634-2) Ballantine Pub Grp.
— Garfield Rounds Out, Vol.. 16. Vol. 16. (Illus.). 128p. 1988. pap. 6.95 (0-345-35388-9) Ballantine Pub Grp.
— Garfield Says a Mouthful, Vol. 21. LC 91-91856. Vol. 21. (Illus.). 128p. (Orig.). 1991. pap. 6.95 (0-345-37368-5) Ballantine Pub Grp.
— Garfield Season's Greetings Postcard Book. (Illus.). 1992. pap. 8.95 (0-345-01938-5) Ballantine Pub Grp.
— Garfield Sits Around the House. (J). 1983. 12.05 (0-606-03273-8, Pub. by Turtleback) Demco.
— Garfield Sits Around the House, Vol. 7. Vol. 7. 128p. 1984. pap. 6.95 (0-345-32011-5) Ballantine Pub Grp.
— Garfield Swallows His Pride. (Garfield Ser.: No. 14). 128p. 1987. pap. 6.95 (0-345-34725-0) Ballantine Pub Grp.
— Garfield Takes His Licks, Vol. 24. LC 92-90384. Vol. 24. 128p. (Orig.). 1993. pap. 6.95 (0-345-38170-X) Ballantine Pub Grp.
— Garfield Takes the Cake. (J). 1982. 12.05 (0-606-02926-5, Pub. by Turtleback) Demco.
— Garfield Takes the Cake, Vol. 5. Vol. 5. 128p. 1984. pap. 6.95 (0-345-32009-3) Ballantine Pub Grp.
***Davis, Jim.** Garfield Takes the Cake: Games & Sticker Fun. (Garfield Ser.). (J). 1998. pap. text 4.95 (2-922148-38-6) Presses Avent.
Davis, Jim. Garfield Takes up Space, Vol. 20. Vol. 20. 128p. 1991. pap. 6.95 (0-345-37029-5) Ballantine Pub Grp.
— Garfield Thanksgiving Special. 64p. 1988. pap. 6.95 (0-345-35650-0) Ballantine Pub Grp.
— Garfield, the Easter Bunny? (J) (ps-3). 1997. pap. 6.95 (0-8167-3437-2) Troll Communs.
Davis, Jim. Garfield Thinks Big. LC 97-94053. Vol. 32. 128p. 1997. pap. 6.95 (0-345-41671-6) Ballantine Pub Grp.
Davis, Jim. Garfield Thinks Big, No. 32. 1997. pap. 6.95 (0-345-42671-1) Ballantine Pub Grp.
— Garfield Throws His Weight Around, Vol.. 33. LC 98-96144. (Garfield Ser.: Vol. 33). (Illus.). 1998. pap. 6.95 (0-345-42749-1) Ballantine Pub Grp.
— Garfield, Tiens Bon la Rampe. (Garfield Ser.). (FRE.). (J). 1989. 18.95 (0-8288-4585-9) Fr & Eur.
— Garfield Tips the Scales. (J). 1984. 12.05 (0-606-03274-6, Pub. by Turtleback) Demco.
— Garfield Tips the Scales, Vol.. 8. Vol. 8. 128p. 1986. pap. 6.95 (0-345-33580-5) Ballantine Pub Grp.
— Garfield Tons of Fun, Vol. 29. LC 95-95020. Vol. 29. 128p. 1996. pap. 6.95 (0-345-40386-X) Ballantine Pub Grp.
— The Garfield Treasury. LC 82-90221. 112p. 1984. pap. 11.95 (0-345-32106-5) Ballantine Pub Grp.
— The Garfield Treasury. (J). 1982. 16.80 (0-606-02922-2, Pub. by Turtleback) Demco.
— Garfield Weighs In. 1982. 12.05 (0-606-00281-2, Pub. by Turtleback) Demco.
— Garfield Weighs in, Vol. 4. Vol. 4. 128p. (Orig.). 1984. pap. 6.95 (0-345-32010-7) Ballantine Pub Grp.
— Garfield Worldwide, Vol.. 15. Vol. 15. 128p. 1988. pap. 6.95 (0-345-35158-4) Ballantine Pub Grp.
***Davis, Jim.** Garfield's Big Book of Excellent Excuses. (Illus.). (J). 2000. 8.95 (0-606-18664-6) Turtleback.
Davis, Jim. Garfield's Big Fat Hairy Joke Book. (Illus.). (Orig.). 1994. mass mkt. 3.99 (0-345-38640-X) Ballantine Pub Grp.
— Garfield's Book of Jokes & Riddles. (Illus.). (J). (gr. k-3). 1997. pap. 2.95 (0-8167-4290-1) Troll Communs.
— Garfield's Christmas Tales. 32p. (J). (ps-3). 1995. pap. 4.95 (0-8167-3705-3) Troll Communs.

D

— Garfield's Feline Fantasies. 141p. (Orig.). 1990. pap. 6.95 (*0-345-36902-5*) Ballantine Pub Grp.

— Garfield's Furry Tales. (J). (ps-3). 1994. pap. 6.95 (*0-8167-3432-1*) Troll Communs.

— Garfield's Halloween Adventure. 1985. 12.15 (*0-606-00280-4*, Pub. by Turtleback) Demco.

— Garfield's Haunted House: And Other Spooky Tales. (Illus.). 32p. (J). (ps-3). 1996. pap. 6.95 (*0-8167-3483-6*) Troll Communs.

— Garfield's Insults. 1994. mass mkt. 3.99 (*0-345-80147-4*) Ballantine Pub Grp.

— Garfield's Judgment Day. (Illus.). 64p. 1990. pap. 6.95 (*0-345-36755-3*) Ballantine Pub Grp.

— Garfield's Night Before Christmas. (Illus.). 32p. (J). (ps-3). 1996. pap. 6.95 (*0-8167-3434-8*) Troll Communs.

— Garfield's Stupid Cupid: And Other Silly Stories. (J). (ps-3). 1995. pap. 6.95 (*0-8167-3485-2*) Troll Communs.

— Garfield's Tales of Mystery. (J). (ps-3). 1994. pap. 6.95 (*0-8167-3436-4*) Troll Communs.

— Garfield's Top Ten Tom(cat) Foolery. (Illus.). 48p. 1997. 6.95 (*0-8362-2875-8*) Andrews & McMeel.

— The Great Christmas Contest. (Illus.). 48p. (J). (ps up). 1988. bds. 7.95 (*0-553-34609-1*) Bantam.

***Davis, Jim.** Grip It & Rip It! Mini Edition: Garfield's Guide to Golf. (Illus.). 48p. 1999. pap. text 4.95 (*0-8362-8757-6*) Andrews & McMeel.

Davis, Jim. Hat's Voll Drauf, 8. 1999. pap. text 10.95 (*3-8105-0744-X*) W Kruger.

— Have You Booted Your Computer Today? LC 96-86669. (Illus.). 80p. 1997. 4.95 (*0-8362-2884-7*) Andrews & McMeel.

— Here Comes Garfield. 128p. 1984. pap. 6.95 (*0-345-32012-3*) Ballantine Pub Grp.

***Davis, Jim.** How to Draw Garfield & the Gang. (Illus.). (Orig.). 1999. pap. text 9.90 (*0-613-15823-7*) Econo-Clad Bks.

Davis, Jim. How to Draw Garfield & the Gang. (Illus.). 32p. (Orig.). (J). (gr. 3-7). 1996. pap. 2.95 (*0-8167-4132-8*) Troll Communs.

— I Can't Think Now: I'm Working! (Little Bks.). (Illus.). 80p. 1996. 4.95 (*0-8362-0934-6*) Andrews & McMeel.

— I'd Like Mornings Better If They Started Later. (Main Street Editions Ser.). (Illus.). 48p. 1996. 6.95 (*0-8362-0933-8*) Andrews & McMeel.

— K-Ninner Dog of Doom. (Garfield's Pet Force Ser.: Vol. 3). (J). (gr. 3-7). 1998. pap. text 3.99 (*0-590-05944-0*) Scholastic Inc.

— Langt Zu, 1. 1999. pap. text 10.95 (*3-8105-0716-4*) W Kruger.

— Liegt Im Trend, 9. 1999. pap. text 10.95 (*3-8105-0753-9*) W Kruger.

— Life to the Fullest. LC PN6728.G28D3929 1999. (Garfield Ser.). (Illus.). 128p. 1999. pap. 6.95 (*0-345-43239-8*) Ballantine Pub Grp.

— Menace of the Nutanator. (Garfield's Pet Force Ser.: No. 4). (Illus.). (J). (gr. 3-7). 1998. pap. 3.99 (*0-590-05945-9*) Scholastic Inc.

— Moi, on M'Aime. (Garfield Ser.). (FRE.). (J). 1986. 18.95 (*0-8288-4587-5*, M4211) Fr & Eur.

***Davis, Jim.** Never Accept a Gift with Air Holes: Garfield's Holiday Tips & Quips. LC 99-177992. (Illus.). 48p. 1998. 4.95 (*0-8362-5280-2*) Andrews & McMeel.

Davis, Jim. The Ninth Garfield Treasury. LC 97-93768. (Illus.). 128p. 1997. pap. 12.50 (*0-345-41670-8*) Ballantine Pub Grp.

— Out of Shape Beats No Shape at All. (Little Bks.). (Illus.). 80p. 1996. 4.95 (*0-8362-0935-4*) Andrews & McMeel.

— Outrageous Origin. (Garfield's Pet Force Ser.: Vol. 1). (J). (gr. 3-7). 1998. pap. text 3.99 (*0-590-05908-4*) Scholastic Inc.

— Party Now, Age Later. (Main Street Editions Ser.). (Illus.). 48p. 1996. 6.95 (*0-8362-0931-1*) Andrews & McMeel.

— Pie-Rat's Revenge. (Garfield's Pet Force Ser.: Vol. 2). (Illus.). (J). (gr. 3-7). 1998. pap. text 3.99 (*0-590-05909-2*) Scholastic Inc.

— Qui Dort Dine. (Garfield Ser.). (FRE.). (J). 1988. 18.95 (*0-8288-4588-3*) Fr & Eur.

— Sahnt Ab, 5. 1999. pap. text 10.95 (*3-8105-0737-7*) W Kruger.

— Save the Rivers, Rain Forests & Ravioli. LC 96-86674. (Illus.). 80p. 1997. 4.95 (*0-8362-2876-6*) Andrews & McMeel.

— Schlaft Sich Durch, 2. 1999. pap. text 10.95 (*3-8105-0717-2*) W Kruger.

— Schmust Sich Ran, 7. 1999. pap. text 10.95 (*3-8105-0743-1*) W Kruger.

— The Second Garfield Treasury. 112p. 1985. pap. 12.00 (*0-345-33276-8*) Ballantine Pub Grp.

— Setzt An, 6. 1999. pap. text 10.95 (*3-8105-0738-5*) W Kruger.

— The Seventh Garfield Treasury. LC 93-90045. (Illus.). 120p. 1993. pap. 12.00 (*0-345-38427-X*) Ballantine Pub Grp.

— The Sixth Garfield Treasury. (Illus.). 128p. 1991. pap. 10.95 (*0-345-37367-7*) Ballantine Pub Grp.

***Davis, Jim.** Tenth Garfield Treasury. LC 99-90168. (Illus.). 128p. 1999. pap. 12.50 (*0-345-43674-1*) Ballantine Pub Grp.

Davis, Jim. The Third Garfield Treasury. 112p. 1985. pap. 12.00 (*0-345-32635-0*) Ballantine Pub Grp.

— The Third Garfield Treasury. 1985. 17.10 (*0-606-00446-7*, Pub. by Turtleback) Demco.

— Tiens Bon la Rampe. (Garfield Ser.). (FRE.). (J). 1989. 18.95 (*0-8288-4589-1*) Fr & Eur.

— Ueberlegensgross, 3. 1999. pap. text 10.95 (*3-8105-0721-0*) W Kruger.

— Les Yeux Plus Gros Que le Ventre. (Garfield Ser.). (FRE.). (J). 1985. 18.95 (*0-8288-4590-5*, F91520) Fr & Eur.

Davis, Jim, et al, eds. Cutting Edge: Technology, Information Capitalism & Social Revolution. 302p. 1998. pap. 20.00 (*1-85984-185-6*, Pub. by Verso) Norton.

Davis, Jim & Wallace, Carol M. The Garfield Book of Cat Names. 64p. 1988. pap. 6.95 (*0-345-35082-0*) Ballantine Pub Grp.

Davis, Jim, et al. Garfield's Big Fat Holiday Joke Book. 144p. (Orig.). 1994. mass mkt. 3.99 (*0-345-38955-7*) Ballantine Pub Grp.

— Garfield's Big Fat Scary Joke Book. LC 94-94422. 144p. (Orig.). 1994. mass mkt. 3.99 (*0-345-38954-9*) Ballantine Pub Grp.

Davis, Jimmy H., jt. auth. see Poe, Harry L.

Davis, Jo. Wings: Poetry of the Spirit. Frances, Dee, ed. (Illus.). 43p. 1999. pap. 12.00 (*1-885519-33-8*) DDDD Pubns.

Davis, Joan, jt. ed. see Brown, Iem.

Davis, Joan, ed. see Lay, William O.

Davis, Joanne. Mademoiselle de Scudery & the Looking-Glass Self. LC 92-8710. (Currents in Comparative Romance Languages & Literatures Ser.: Vol. 7). 135p. (C). 1994. text 39.95 (*0-8204-1904-4*) P Lang Pubng.

***Davis, Jodi & Hoffman, Beth.** Quilting. (Quick Starts for Kids! Ser.). (Illus.). 64p. (J). (gr. 3 up). 2000. pap. 8.95 (*1-885593-49-X*) Williamson Pub Co.

Davis, Jodie. Crafting Lamps & Shades: Easy, Inexpensive & Unique Projects to Light Up Your Home. LC 98-84097. (Illus.). 144p. 1998. pap. 21.95 (*0-87341-661-9*, LASH) Krause Pubns.

— Garden-Inspired Quilt Block Designs. LC 96-30336. (Foundation Piecing Library). 128p. 1996. 24.95 (*1-56799-366-4*, Friedman-Fairfax) M Friedman Pub Grp Inc.

***Davis, Jodie.** Hometown Quilts: Paper Piece a Village of Memories. LC 99-66999. (Illus.). 128p. 2000. pap. 21.95 (*0-87341-797-6*, MEMQU) Krause Pubns.

— Make Your Own Teddy Bear & Bear Clothes. (Quick Starts for Kids! Ser.). (Illus.). 64p. (J). (gr. 3 up). 2000. pap. 8.95 (*1-885593-75-9*) Williamson Pub Co.

— Paper Piece a Merry Christmas. LC 00-35510. (Illus.). 96p. 2000. pap. 24.95 (*1-56477-296-9*) Martingale & Co.

— Paper-Pieced Curves. LC 99-87653. (Illus.). 80p. 2000. pap. 21.95 (*1-56477-302-7*, B432, Pub. by Martingale & Co) F & W Pubns Inc.

Davis, Jodie. A Quick-&-Easy Teddy Bear: With Full-Size Patterns for Clothing. (Illus.). 32p. (Orig.). 1991. pap. 2.95 (*0-486-26864-0*) Dover.

— Teach Yourself Cloth Dollmaking: Simple Techniques & Patterns for Dolls & Doll Clothes. (Illus.). 128p. 1995. 24.95 (*1-56799-188-2*, Friedman-Fairfax); pap. 14.95 (*1-56799-159-9*, Friedman-Fairfax) M Friedman Pub Grp Inc.

— Teach Yourself Teddy Bear Making: Simple Techniques & Patterns for Teddy Bears. 1996. 24.95 (*1-56799-256-0*, Friedman-Fairfax) M Friedman Pub Grp Inc.

— Teach Yourself to Make Angels & Fairies: Simple Techniques & Patterns for Cloth Dolls & Their Clothes. LC 96-28957. (Jodie Davis Needle Arts School Ser.). (Illus.). 128p. 1996. 24.95 (*1-56799-370-2*, Friedman-Fairfax) M Friedman Pub Grp Inc.

— Teach Yourself to Make Soft Toys. LC 96-35748. (Jodie Davis Needle Arts School Ser.). 1997. 24.95 (*1-56799-399-0*, Friedman-Fairfax) M Friedman Pub Grp Inc.

— Three-Dimensional Pieced Quilts. LC 94-34910. (Illus.). 152p. 1995. pap. 19.95 (*0-8019-8390-8*) Krause Pubns.

— Victorian Quilt Block Design. (Illus.). 1996. 24.95 (*1-56799-258-7*, Friedman-Fairfax) M Friedman Pub Grp Inc.

— A Year of Cross-Stitch: Patterns for Every Season. LC 95-1794. 1995. 24.95 (*1-56799-217-X*, Friedman-Fairfax); pap. write for info. (*1-56799-213-7*, Friedman-Fairfax) M Friedman Pub Grp Inc.

Davis, Jodie & Schiffer, Linda H. Hearts & Flower Quilt Block Design. LC 96-38477. (Jodie Davis Needle Arts School Ser.). 1997. write for info. (*1-56799-443-1*, Friedman-Fairfax) M Friedman Pub Grp Inc.

— Holiday Quilt Block Designs. LC 97-7242. (Jodie Davis Needle Arts School Ser.). 1997. write for info. (*1-56799-487-3*, Friedman-Fairfax) M Friedman Pub Grp Inc.

— Quilting Made Easy: More Than 150 Patterns & Inspiring Ideas for Creating Beautiful Quilt Blocks. LC 97-52727. (Foundation Piecing Library). 1998. 27.98 (*1-56799-655-8*) Kenan Bks.

Davis, Joe L. The Sons of Ben: Jonsonian Comedy in Caroline England. LC 67-11271. 252p. reprint ed. 78.20 (*0-608-16993-5*, 202760200055) Bks Demand.

Davis, Joe T. Historic Towns of Texas, Vol. I. (Illus.). 288p. 1991. 18.95 (*0-89015-824-X*) Sunbelt Media.

— Historic Towns of Texas, Vol. II. (Illus.). 304p. 1996. 22.95 (*1-57168-044-6*, Eakin Pr) Sunbelt Media.

— Legendary Texians, Vol. I. (Illus.). 192p. 1982. 15.95 (*0-89015-336-1*) Sunbelt Media.

— Legendary Texians, Vol. II. (Illus.). 200p. 1985. 15.95 (*0-89015-473-2*) Sunbelt Media.

— Legendary Texians, Vol. III. (Illus.). 224p. 1987. 15.95 (*0-89015-559-3*) Sunbelt Media.

— Legendary Texians, Vol. IV. (Illus.). 224p. 1989. 15.95 (*0-89015-669-7*) Sunbelt Media.

Davis, Joel. Alternate Realities: How Science Shapes Our Vision of the World. LC 97-26417. (Illus.). 320p. (C). 1997. 27.95 (*0-306-45629-X*, Plenum Trade) Perseus Pubng.

— Mapping the Mind: The Secrets of the Human Brain & How It Works. (Illus.). 384p. 1996. 24.95 (*1-55972-344-0*, Birch Ln Pr) Carol Pub Group.

— Mapping the Mind: The Secrets of the Human Brain & How It Works. (Illus.). 304p. 1999. reprint ed. 33.95 (*0-7351-0091-8*) Replica Bks.

— Mother Tongue: How Humans Create Language. 320p. 1993. 21.95 (*1-55972-206-1*, Birch Ln Pr) Carol Pub Group.

Davis, Joel J. Advertising Research: Theory & Practice. LC 96-45163. 695p. 1996. 79.00 (*0-13-221813-5*) P-H.

Davis, Joel L. Mapping the Code: The Human Genome Project & the Choices of Modern Science. LC 90-12572. 294p. 1991. 19.95 (*0-471-50383-5*) Wiley.

Davis, Joel L. & Eichenbaum, Howard, eds. Olfaction: A Model System for Computational Neuroscience. (Illus.). 320p. 1991. 55.00 (*0-262-04124-3*) MIT Pr.

Davis, Joel L., jt. auth. see Eichenbaum, Howard B.

Davis, Joel L., jt. ed. see Baudry, Michel.

Davis, Joel L., jt. ed. see Koch, Christof.

Davis, John. Antique Garden Ornament. (Illus.). 389p. 1991. 79.50 (*1-85149-098-1*) Antique Collect.

— Baltimore County, Maryland Deed Records, 1755-1767, Vol. 3. LC 96-209695. viii, 408p. (Orig.). 1996. pap. 32.00 (*0-7884-0553-5*, D040) Heritage Bk.

— Baltimore County, Maryland Deed Records, 1767-1775, Vol. 4. LC 96-209695. viii, 367p. 1997. pap. 35.50 (*0-7884-0621-3*, D041) Heritage Bk.

— Chinese Moral Maxims. 30p. 1993. pap. 6.95 (*0-910704-77-5*) Hawley.

— Cleobury Mortimer. (C). 1989. 45.00 (*0-947712-07-0*, Pub. by S A Baldwin) St Mut.

— Cremation: A Christian Perspective. 7.95 (*0-88469-226-4*) BMH Bks.

***Davis, John.** Diamond Approach: An Introduction to the Teachings of A.H. Almaas. LC 98-55925. 192p. 1999. pap. 15.00 (*1-57062-406-2*, Pub. by Shambhala Pubns) Random.

Davis, John. Energy, to Use or Abuse. 192p. 1980. pap. 75.00 (*0-905381-00-9*, Pub. by Gresham Bks) St Mut.

— Exchange. Parkin, Frank, ed. (Concepts in the Social Sciences Ser.). 112p. 1992. 32.50 (*0-335-15584-7*); pap. 9.99 (*0-335-15583-9*) OpUniv Pr.

— Exchange. (Concepts in Social Thought Ser.). 192p. (C). 1992. pap. 12.95 (*0-8166-2181-0*); text 34.95 (*0-8166-2180-2*) U of Minn Pr.

***Davis, John.** History Of Britain, 1885-1939. LC 98-40372. 312p. 1999. text 59.95 (*0-312-22033-2*) St Martin.

Davis, John. History of Britain, 1885-1939. LC 98-40372. 312p. 1999. pap. 19.95 (*0-312-22034-0*) St Martin.

***Davis, John.** How to Enjoy Your Surgery: A Lighthearted Look at Health & Medicine. 128p. 2000. pap. 7.95 (*0-9635865-5-6*) Pinegrove Publishing.

Davis, John. How to Write a Training Manual. 250p. 1992. 74.95 (*0-566-07325-0*, Pub. by Gower) Ashgate Pub Co.

— Inside Rank. (C). 1988. 80.00 (*1-869828-04-6*, Pub. by Moonstone Bks) St Mut.

— The Landscape of Belief: Encountering the Holy Land in Nineteenth-Century American Art & Culture. LC 95-7051. (Series in Nineteenth-Century Art, Culture, & Society). 351p. 1996. text 75.00 (*0-691-04373-6*, Pub. by Princeton U Pr) Cal Prin Full Svc.

— Landscape of Belief: Encountering the Holy Land in Nineteenth-Century American Art & Culture. 286p. 1996. pap. text 29.95 (*0-691-05845-8*, Pub. by Princeton U Pr) Cal Prin Full Svc.

— Real Fishermen Are Never Thin. (Illus.). 123p. (Orig.). 1993. pap. 7.95 (*0-9635865-0-5*) Pinegrove Publishing.

— Real Fishermen Never Lie. (Illus.). 123p. (Orig.). 1993. pap. 7.95 (*0-9635865-1-3*) Pinegrove Publishing.

— Real Fishermen Never Wear Suits. (Illus.). 120p. (Orig.). 1996. pap. 7.95 (*0-9635865-3-X*) Pinegrove Publishing.

— Reforming London: The London Government Problem, 1855-1900. (Oxford Historical Monographs). (Illus.). 320p. 1988. 69.00 (*0-19-822937-2*) OUP.

— Revelation for Our Time: A New Paradigm for the Next Millenium. LC 98-90325. (Illus.). 300p. 1998. pap. 20.00 (*0-9664450-0-7*) Spiritual Unity.

— The Seamans Secrets. LC 92-21729. 136p. 1992. 75.00 (*0-8201-1475-8*) Schol Facsimiles.

— Youth & the Condition of England: Images of Adolescent Conflict. Rock, Paul E. & Downes, David, eds. LC 89-18550. (Conflict & Change in Britain - A New Audit Ser.). 240p. (C). 1990. text 50.00 (*0-485-80001-2*, Pub. by Athlone Pr) Humanities.

Davis, John. Youth & the Condition of England: Images of Adolescent Conflict. Rock, Paul E. & Downes, David, eds. LC 89-18550. (Conflict & Change in Britain - A New Audit Ser.). 240p. (C). 1990. pap. 25.00 (*0-485-80101-9*, Pub. by Athlone Pr) Humanities.

***Davis, John, ed.** Rural Change in Ireland. 228p. 1999. pap. 17.95 (*0-85389-734-4*, Pub. by Inst Irish Studies) Irish Bks Media.

Davis, John & Baldridge, Alan. The Bird Year: A Book for Birders with Special Reference to the Monterey Bay Area. 1987. reprint ed. pap. 9.95 (*0-910286-62-0*) Boxwood.

***Davis, John & Leshko, Jaroslaw.** Smith College Museum of Art: European & American Painting & Sculpture, 1760-1960. (Illus.). 240p. 2000. 50.00 (*1-55595-194-5*, Pub. by Hudson Hills) Natl Bk Netwk.

Davis, John, jt. auth. see Zong, Ping.

Davis, John, ed. see Davis, Mary B.

Davis, John, tr. see Angelopoulos, Angelos T.

Davis, John A., Jr. A Look at the Credit Approval Process. LC 86-23855. (Illus.). 56p. 1986. pap. text 35.00 (*0-936742-36-4*) Robt Morris Assocs.

Davis, John A. Merchants, Monopolists, & Contractors: A Study of Economic Activity & Society in Bourbon Naples 1815-1860. Bruchey, Stuart, ed. LC 80-2802. (Dissertations in European Economic History Ser.). (Illus.). 1981. lib. bdg. 39.95 (*0-405-13986-1*) Ayer.

Davis, John A., Jr. Organizing & Staffing Loan Review. Behr, Joan H., ed. LC 88-33045. (Illus.). 68p. 1989. pap. text 48.00 (*0-936742-63-1*) Robt Morris Assocs.

Davis, John A. Regional Organization of the Social Security Administration. LC 68-59254. (Columbia University. Studies in the Social Sciences: No. 571). reprint ed. 32.50 (*0-404-51571-1*) AMS Pr.

***Davis, John A., ed.** Italy in the Nineteenth Century, 1796-1900. (Short Oxford History of Italy Ser.). 262p. 2000. pap. 19.95 (*0-19-873127-2*); text 65.00 (*0-19-873128-0*) OUP.

Davis, John A. & Ginsborg, Paul, eds. Society & Politics in the Age of the Risorgimento: Essays in Honour of Denis Mack Smith. 301p. (C). 1991. text 69.95 (*0-521-36592-9*) Cambridge U Pr.

Davis, John A., jt. ed. see Mathias, Peter.

Davis, John B. Keynes Philosophical Development. LC 93-50564. 210p. (C). 1995. text 64.95 (*0-521-41902-6*) Cambridge U Pr.

Davis, John B., ed. The Economic Surplus in Advanced Economies. (New Directions in Modern Economics Ser.). 208p. 1992. 85.00 (*1-85278-555-1*) E Elgar.

— New Economics & Its Writing. (History of Political Economy Annual Supplement Ser.). 300p. 1997. lib. bdg. 49.95 (*0-8223-2037-1*) Duke.

— The State of Interpretation of Keynes. LC 94-34751. (Recent Economic Thought Ser.). 272p. (C). 1994. lib. bdg. 113.00 (*0-7923-9508-5*) Kluwer Academic.

Davis, John B., et al, eds. The Handbook of Economic Methodology. LC 97-29958. 592p. 1998. 225.00 (*1-85278-795-3*) E Elgar.

Davis, John B. & O'Boyle, Edward J., eds. The Social Economics of Human Material Need. LC 93-8620. (Political & Social Economy Ser.). 304p. (C). 1994. 41.95 (*0-8093-1921-7*) S Ill U Pr.

Davis, John B., jt. ed. see Bateman, Bradley W.

Davis, John C. Statistics & Data Analysis in Geology. 2nd ed. LC 85-12331. 656p. 1986. text 99.95 (*0-471-08079-9*) Wiley.

Davis, John C. & Herzfeld, Ute C., eds. Computers in Geology: 25 Years of Progress. (International Association for Mathematical Geology: Studies in Mathematical Geology: No. 5). (Illus.). 316p. 1993. text 70.00 (*0-19-508593-0*) OUP.

Davis, John C., jt. ed. see Wakid, Shukri A.

Davis, John D. Baltimore County Maryland Deed Records, 1659-1737. LC 96-209695. 463p. (Orig.). 1996. pap. 35.50 (*0-7884-0485-7*, D038) Heritage Bk.

— Baltimore County, Maryland Deed Records, 1727-1757 1727-1757, Vol. 2. LC 96-209695. 461p. (Orig.). 1996. pap. 35.50 (*0-7884-0503-9*, D039) Heritage Bk.

— Bergen County New Jersey Deed Records 1689-1801. 420p. (Orig.). 1995. pap. 30.00 (*0-7884-0311-7*) Heritage Bk.

— Bucks County Pennsylvania Deed Records, 1684-1763. LC 98-119891. 518p. 1998. pap. 35.50 (*0-7884-0779-1*, D084) Heritage Bk.

— Harrison County, West Virginia, Deed Records, 1785-1810. viii, 502p. (Orig.). 1993. pap. text 34.00 (*1-55613-806-7*) Heritage Bk.

Davis, John D., ed. see Lee, Henry S.

Davis, John E. Contested Ground: Collective Action & the Urban Neighborhood. LC 90-42034. (Illus.). 368p. 1991. 49.95 (*0-8014-2215-9*); pap. text 19.95 (*0-8014-9905-4*) Cornell U Pr.

— Play & Mental Health. 1982. 21.95 (*0-8434-0427-2*, Pub. by McGrath NH) Ayer.

Davis, John E., ed. The Affordable City: Toward a Third Sector Housing Policy. LC 93-705. (Conflicts in Urban & Regional Development Ser.). 320p. 1994. 69.95 (*1-56639-109-1*) Temple U Pr.

Davis, John F. China, During the War & since the Peace, 2 vols., Set. LC 72-79816. (China Library). (Illus.). 1972. reprint ed. lib. bdg. 45.00 (*0-8420-1369-5*) Scholarly Res Inc.

— Chinese Novels. LC 76-43332. 296p. 1976. reprint ed. 50.00 (*0-8201-1278-X*) Schol Facsimiles.

Davis, John F. Chinese Moral Maxims (1910) 50p. 1998. reprint ed. pap. 5.95 (*0-7661-0681-0*) Kessinger Pub.

Davis, John G., jt. auth. see Griffin, William R.

Davis, John H. Jacqueline Bouvier: An Intimate Memoir. LC 96-4332. (Illus.). 224p. 1996. 24.95 (*0-471-12945-3*) Wiley.

— Jacqueline Bouvier: An Intimate Memoir. LC 96-4332. 240p. 1997. pap. 6.99 (*0-471-19356-9*) Wiley.

***Davis, John H.** Jacqueline Bouvier: An Intimate Memoir. 208p. 1998. pap. 12.95 (*0-471-24944-0*) Wiley.

Davis, John H. Mafia Dynasty: The Rise & Fall of the Gambino Crime Family. LC 92-53366. 544p. 1994. mass mkt. 6.99 (*0-06-109184-7*, Harp PBks) HarpC.

***Davis, John H.** Twilight of the Godfathers. 2002. mass mkt. write for info. (*0-06-103042-2*) HarpC.

Davis, John H., jt. auth. see Fried, N. Elizabeth.

Davis, John J. Biblical Numerology: A Basic Study of the Use of Numbers in the Bible. LC 68-19207. 176p. 1968. pap. 10.99 (*0-8010-2813-2*) Baker Bks.

— The Birth of a Kingdom: Studies in I & II Samuel & I Kings I-II. pap. 10.99 (*0-88469-053-9*) BMH Bks.

— Conquest & Crisis: Studies in Joshua, Judges & Ruth. (Illus.). pap. 9.99 (*0-88469-052-0*) BMH Bks.

— Contemporary Counterfeits. 1979. pap. 1.50 (*0-88469-003-2*) BMH Bks.

— Demons, Exorcism & the Evangelical. 1979. pap. 1.50 (*0-88469-043-1*) BMH Bks.

— Evangelical Ethics: Issues Facing the Church Today. 2nd ed. 296p. 1993. pap. 13.99 (*0-87552-223-8*) P & R Pubng.

— Favorite Fish & Seafood Recipes. large type ed. LC 96-109645. (Illus.). 224p. 1995. pap. 13.95 (*0-9635865-2-1*) Pinegrove Publishing.

— Handbook of Basic Bible Texts: Every Key Passage for the Study of Doctrine & Theology. 160p. 1984. pap. 14.99 (*0-310-43711-3*, 12103P) Zondervan.
— Hebrew Language: An Analysis of the Strong Verb. 2p. (C). 1995. 3.50 (*1-887070-00-1*) Stylus Publ.
— Moses & the Gods of Egypt: Studies in Exodus. rev. ed. (Illus.). 1985. pap. 14.99 (*0-88469-177-2*) BMH Bks.
— The Mummies of Egypt. 1986. pap. 10.99 (*0-88469-179-9*) BMH Bks.
— Paradise to Prison: Studies in Genesis. pap. 17.95 (*0-88469-050-4*) BMH Bks.
— Paradise to Prison: Studies in Genesis. 363p. 1998. reprint ed. pap. text 18.50 (*1-879215-35-7*) Sheffield WI.
— The Perfect Shepherd: Studies in the Twenty-Third Psalm. pap. 6.50 (*0-88469-110-1*) BMH Bks.
— Victory of Christ's Kingdom: An Introduction to Post Millennialism. 96p. (Orig.). 1996. pap. 6.00 (*1-885767-22-6*) Canon Pr ID.
— What about Cremation? A Christian Perspective. (Illus.). 128p. 1998. pap. 7.95 (*0-9635865-4-8*) Pinegrove Publishing.

Davis, John J. & Whitcomb, John C. History of Israel. 21.99 (*0-88469-061-X*) BMH Bks.

Davis, John J., ed. see Nixon, David J.

Davis, John L. Houston: A Historical Portrait. (Illus.). 183p. 1983. 29.95 (*0-88426-062-3*) Encino Pr.
— San Antonio: A Historical Portrait. (Illus.). 1978. 29.95 (*0-88426-055-0*) Encino Pr.
— Texans One & All. (Illus.). 67p. 1998. pap. text 14.95 (*0-86701-074-6*) U of Tex Inst Tex Culture.
— The Texas Rangers: Images & Incidents. (Illus.). 1992. 29.95 (*0-86701-052-5*) U of Tex Inst Tex Culture.

***Davis, John Lee.** How to Memorize the Books of the Bible. 32p. 1999. pap. 4.95 (*1-58169-039-8*, Gazelle Pr) Genesis Comm Inc.

Davis, John M. & Maas, James W., eds. The Affective Disorders. LC 83-3731. 445p. reprint ed. pap. 138.00 (*0-8357-7854-1*, 203623100002) Bks Demand.

Davis, John M. & Shires, George T., eds. Host Defenses in Trauma & Surgery. LC 86-17765. (Advances in Host Defense Mechanisms Ser.: Vol. 6). 208p. 1986. reprint ed. pap. 64.50 (*0-608-00442-1*, 206115700007) Bks Demand.

Davis, John M. G. & Jaurand, Marie-Claude, eds. Cellular & Molecular Effects of Mineral & Synthetic Dusts & Fibres. LC 94-20085. (NATO ASI Series H: Cell Biology: Vol. 85). 1994. 238.95 (*0-387-58063-8*) Spr-Verlag.

Davis, John P. Chrysalis. Duarte, Abigail D., ed. LC 96-80487. 144p. (Orig.). 1997. pap. 18.95 (*1-879418-86-X*) Audenreed Pr.

***Davis, John P.** Corporations: A Study of the Origin & Development of Great Business Combinations & of Their Relation to the Authority of the STA. (Business Classics Ser.). 318p. 2000. pap. 34.95 (*1-58798-010-X*); pap. 34.95 (*1-58798-011-8*) Beard Bks.

Davis, John P. Corporations: A Study of the Origin & Development of Great Business Combinations & of Their Relation to the Authority of the State, 2 vols., Set. (Business Enterprises Reprint Ser.). 628p. 1986. reprint ed. lib. bdg. 110.00 (*0-89941-443-5*, 303820) W S Hein.
— The Union Pacific Railway. LC 73-2501. (Big Business; Economic Power in a Free Society Ser.). 1979. reprint ed. 20.95 (*0-405-05082-8*) Ayer.

Davis, John R. Britain & the German Zollverein, 1848-66. LC 97-5370. 290p. 1997. text 69.95 (*0-312-17466-7*) St Martin.
— Great Exhibition. 2000. 36.00 (*0-7509-1614-1*) Bks Intl VA.

Davis, John T. Austin City Limits: 25 Years of American Music. LC 99-36010. (Illus.). 192p. 1999. 35.00 (*0-8230-8303-9*) Watsn-Guptill.
— Fictus Adulter: Poet As Actor in the 'Amores' 128p. 1989. pap. 30.00 (*90-5063-019-7*, Pub. by Gieben) J Benjamins Pubng Co.

Davis, John T. & Colson, J. B. Austin: Lone Star Rising. LC 94-14484. (Urban Tapestry Ser.). (Illus.). 320p. 1994. 39.50 (*1-881096-08-4*) Towery Pub.

Davis, John W. Fast Track to Waste-Free Manufacturing: Straight Talk from a Plant Manager. LC 99-17090. (Illus.). 425p. 1999. 45.00 (*1-56327-212-1*) Productivity Inc.
— Paperless Contracting: The EDI Revolution. 177p. Date not set. ring bd. 99.00 (*1-56726-025-X*, B557) Mgmt Concepts.
— Value & Valuation: Axiological Studies in Honor of Robert S. Hartman. LC 72-146661. 362p. reprint ed. 112.30 (*0-608-16857-2*, 202756400055) Bks Demand.

Davis, John W., et al, eds. Contemporary Issues in Biomedical Ethics. LC 78-71406. (Contemporary Issues in Biomedicine, Ethics, & Society Ser.). 336p. 1979. 49.50 (*0-89603-002-4*) Humana.
— Infectious & Parasitic Diseases of Wild Birds. LC 71-88003. 354p. reprint ed. pap. 109.80 (*0-608-14587-4*, 202482300038) Bks Demand.
— Infectious Diseases of Wild Mammals. 2nd ed. LC 81-6064. (Illus.). 446p. (C). 1981. text 54.95 (*0-8138-0445-0*) Iowa St U Pr.

Davis, John W. & Anderson, Roy C., eds. Parasitic Diseases of Wild Mammals. LC 72-103854. (Illus.). 372p. reprint ed. pap. 115.40 (*0-608-17497-1*, 202999900067) Bks Demand.

Davis, John W., jt. ed. see Edwards, Rem B.

***Davis, Johnathan R., et al.** Public Health Systems & Emerging Infections: Assessing the Capabilities of the Public & Private Sectors. 128p. 2000. pap. 23.00 (*0-309-06829-0*) Natl Acad Pr.

***Davis-Johnson, Sandra.** Seven Essentials for Character Discipline: Elementary Classroom Management. LC 00-8748. 2000. pap. write for info. (*0-7619-7643-4*) Corwin Pr.

***Davis, Jon.** Advanced Taxation, 2000 Ed., 5. 1999. 77.95 (*0-324-00948-8*) Sth-Wstrn College.

Davis, Jon. The Hawk. The Road. The Sunlight after Clouds. 1994. pap. 7.00 (*0-937669-53-9*) Owl Creek Pr.
— Local Color. 32p. 1994. pap. 5.00 (*1-889806-08-0*) Devils Millhopper.
— Scrimmage of Appetite. LC 95-24381. 102p. (Orig.). (C). 1995. 24.95 (*1-884836-11-9*); pap. 12.95 (*1-884836-12-7*) U Akron Pr.

Davis, Jonathan. Learn Bridge in a Weekend. LC 93-722. 1993. 16.00 (*0-679-42752-X*) Knopf.

Davis, Jonathan P. Stephen King's America. LC 93-73797. (Illus.). 183p. 1994. 34.95 (*0-87972-647-4*); pap. 14.95 (*0-87972-648-2*) Bowling Green Univ Popular Press.

***Davis, Jonathan R., et al, eds.** Assuring Data Quality & Validity in Clinical Trials for Regulatory Decision Making: Workshop Report. (Illus.). 88p. 1999. pap. 18.00 (*0-309-06594-1*) Natl Acad Pr.

Davis, Joseph, et al. Davis Dispute Resolution Japan. LC 96-32073. 1996. 145.00 (*90-411-0974-9*) Kluwer Law Intl.

Davis, Joseph A. The Compleat Otter. 1999. write for info. (*1-57524-078-5*) Krieger.

Davis, Joseph C. & Walker, Claxton. Wage the Energy War at Home. LC 78-51121. (Illus.). 1978. 14.95 (*0-87523-191-8*) Emerson.

***Davis, Joseph E.** Identity & Social Change. 2000. 44.95 (*0-7658-0034-9*) Transaction Pubs.

Davis, Joseph E. Thought Control, Totalism & the Extension of the Anti-Cult Critique Beyond the "Cults" 1993. pap. text 3.50 (*0-9636937-2-7*) Tabor Hse.

Davis, Joseph L. Sectionalism in American Politics, 1774-1787. LC 76-11310. 251p. reprint ed. pap. 77.90 (*0-608-01964-X*, 206261900003) Bks Demand.

Davis, Joseph N., jt. auth. see Frazee, Barbara.

Davis, Joseph R., ed. ASM Specialty Handbook: Aluminum & Aluminum Alloys. LC 93-41647. (Illus.). 784p. 1993. 198.00 (*0-87170-496-X*, 6610) ASM.
— ASM Specialty Handbook: Stainless Steels. LC 94-23392. (ASM Specialty Handbook Ser.). (Illus.). 576p. 1994. 198.00 (*0-87170-503-6*, 6398) ASM.
— Concise Metals Engineering Data Book. LC 97-75187. 255p. (C). 1997. 78.00 (*0-87170-606-7*, 6557) ASM.
— Metals Handbook Desk Edition. 2nd rev. ed. LC 98-45866. (Illus.). 1521p. 1998. 198.00 (*0-87170-654-7*, 06542G) ASM.

Davis, Joseph S. Wheat & the AAA. LC 76-172868. (FDR & the Era of the New Deal Ser.). 468p. 1973. reprint ed. 59.50 (*0-306-70375-0*) Da Capo.
— The World Between the Wars, 1919-39: An Economist's View. LC 74-6821. 448p. 1975. reprint ed. pap. 138.90 (*0-608-03650-1*, 206447600009) Bks Demand.

Davis, Josephine D., ed. Coloring the Halls of Ivy: Leadership & Diversity in the Academy. LC 94-208547. 200p. (C). 1993. text 31.95 (*0-9627042-9-6*) Anker Pub.

Davis, Joy E., jt. auth. see Edwards, Lawrence.

Davis, Joyce. Between Jihad & Salaam: Profiles in Islam. LC 96-48928. 272p. 1997. text 29.95 (*0-312-16587-0*) St Martin.

Davis, Joyce, ed. see Stephens, Ronald L.

Davis, Joyce E. More Speedwell Families. (Illus.). 616p. 1988. 37.50 (*0-89308-630-4*, TN 112) Southern Hist Pr.

Davis, Judi. Nurturing Young Minds & Bodies. 186p. 1995. pap. text 24.95 (*1-885477-16-3*) Fut Horizons.

Davis, Judi R. Dental Hygienist's Guide Nutritional Care. LC 98-13149. (C). 1998. text. write for info. (*0-7216-6934-4*, W B Saunders Co) Harcrt Hlth Sci Grp.

Davis, Judi R. & Sherer, Kim. Applied Nutrition & Diet Therapy for Nurses. 2nd ed. LC 92-49079. (Illus.). 1178p. 1993. text 62.95 (*0-7216-6785-6*, W B Saunders Co) Harcrt Hlth Sci Grp.
— Applied Nutrition & Diet Therapy for Nurses. 2nd ed. (Illus.). 1994. teacher ed. write for info. (*0-7216-5459-2*, W B Saunders Co) Harcrt Hlth Sci Grp.

Davis, Judi R., et al. The Dental Hygienist's Guide to Nutritional Care. Kaszczuk, Selma, ed. LC 97-31211. (Illus.). 480p. 1998. pap. text 34.95 (*0-7216-5014-7*, W B Saunders Co) Harcrt Hlth Sci Grp.

Davis, Judith. Whose Bar/Bat Mitzvah is This, Anyway. LC 97-36420. 304p. 1998. pap. 13.95 (*0-312-18197-3*) St Martin.

Davis, Judith M., jt. ed. see Akehurst, F. R.

Davis, Judy G., jt. auth. see Davis, William R.

Davis, Judy M. & Meisner, Jane S. Des Moines: Iowa's Commercial Center. LC 98-52518. (Urban Tapestry Ser.). (Illus.). 1999. 49.95 (*1-881096-65-3*) Towery Pub.

Davis, Julia. The Doctor's Favorite Nurse. large type ed. (Linford Romance Library). 256p. 1993. pap. 16.99 (*0-7089-7468-6*) Ulverscroft.
— The Embassy Girls. 2nd ed. (Illus.). 186p. 1992. 15.00 (*0-937058-28-9*) West Va U Pr.
— Nurse in Arabia. large type ed. 240p. 1992. pap. 16.99 (*0-7089-7187-3*, Linford) Ulverscroft.
— Rivers of America: The Shenandoah. Date not set. lib. bdg. 26.95 (*0-8488-1971-3*) Amereon Ltd.
— Sands of Desire. large type ed. (Linford Romance Library). 256p. 1993. pap. 16.99 (*0-7089-7450-3*) Ulverscroft.

Davis, Julia & Fleming, Dolores, eds. The Ambassadorial Diary of John W. Davis: The Court of St. James 1918-1921. 510p. 1993. 20.00 (*0-937058-27-0*) West Va U Pr.

Davis, Julia A. African-American History for Young Readers. 2nd ed. (Illus.). 336p. (J). (gr. 5-9). 1992. 30.00 (*0-9631110-5-1*) Epps-Alford.
— The Children's Picture Book of African American History. (Illus.). 150p. (J). (ps-5). 1992. 20.00 (*0-9631110-3-5*) Epps-Alford.
— Critical Thinking That Empowers Us to Choose Non-Violent Life Skills. 2nd rev. ed. Hutchins, Anita, ed. (Illus.). 250p. 1995. text 25.00 (*0-9631110-9-4*) Epps-Alford.

Davis, Julian & Healey, Patsy. Wokingham: The Implementation of Strategic Planning Policy in a Growth Area in the South East. (C). 1983. 75.00 (*0-7855-3845-3*, Pub. by Oxford Polytechnic) St Mut.

Davis, Julie, et al. It's Our Own Knowledge: Labour, Public Education & Skills Training. Turk, Jim, ed. 133p. 1989. pap. 14.95 (*0-921908-03-2*, Our Schools) J Lorimer.

Davis, Julie, jt. auth. see Prevention Magazine Editors.

Davis, Julie A., jt. auth. see Davis, Daniel J.

Davis, Julie N., jt. auth. see Blos, Sarah I.

Davis, Junior, jt. ed. see Hare, Paul.

Davis, Justin. Love under Cover. (Silhouette Romance Ser.). 1998. 21.95 (*0-373-59923-4*) Silhouette.

Davis, Justine. Badge of Honor. (Intimate Moments Ser.). 1998. per. 4.25 (*0-373-07871-4*, 1-07871-6) Silhouette.
— Clay Yeager's Redemption: Trinity Street West. Intimate Moments Ser.: No. 926). 1999. per. 4.25 (*0-373-07926-5*, 1-07926-8) Silhouette.
— Errant Angel: (Spellbound) (Desire Ser.). 1995. per. 3.25 (*0-373-05924-8*, 1-05924-5) Silhouette.
— Found Father. (Desire Ser.). 1993. pap. 2.89 (*0-373-05772-5*, 5-05772-4) Silhouette.
— Gage Butler's Reckoning. 1998. per. 4.25 (*0-373-07841-2*, 1-07841-9) Silhouette.
— Leader of the Pack. (Intimate Moments Ser.). 1996. per. 3.99 (*0-373-07728-9*, 1-07728-8) Silhouette.
— Left at the Altar. 1994. per. 3.50 (*0-373-07596-0*, 1-07596-9) Harlequin Bks.
— Lover under Cover (Trinity Street West) LC 96-7309. (Intimate Moments Ser.). 250p. 1996. per. 3.99 (*0-373-07698-3*, 1-07698-3) Silhouette.
— A Man to Trust. 1997. per. 3.99 (*0-373-07805-6*, 1-078054) Silhouette.
— The Morning Side of Dawn. 1995. per. 3.75 (*0-373-07674-6*, 1-07674-4) Silhouette.
— The Morning Side of Dawn. large type ed. (Silhouette Romance Ser.). 1997. 20.95 (*0-373-59819-X*) Mac Lib Ref.
— One Last Chance: America Heroes. (Intimate Moments Ser.). 1993. mass mkt. 3.50 (*0-373-07517-0*, 5-07517-1) Silhouette.
— Out of the Dark. (Intimate Moments Ser.). 1995. per. 3.75 (*0-373-07638-X*, 1-07638-9) Silhouette.
— Private Reasons. (Desire Ser.). 1994. mass mkt. 2.99 (*0-373-05833-0*, 5-05833-4) Silhouette.

***Davis, Justine.** The Return of Luke Mcguire. (Intimate Moments Ser.: Bk. 1036). 2000. mass mkt. 4.50 (*0-373-27106-9*, 1-27106-3) Silhouette.

Davis, Justine. The Skypirate. 384p. 1995. mass mkt. 4.99 (*0-451-40491-2*, Topaz) NAL.
— Suspicion's Gate. (Intimate Moments Ser.: No. 423). 1992. mass mkt. 3.39 (*0-373-07423-9*, 5-07423-2) Harlequin Bks.
— Target of Opportunity. (Intimate Moments Ser.). 1993. mass mkt. 3.50 (*0-373-07506-5*, 5-07506-4) Silhouette.
— Upon the Storm. (Desire Ser.: No. 712). 1992. pap. 2.89 (*0-373-05712-1*, 5-05712-0) Harlequin Bks.

***Davis, Justine.** Whole Lot of Love. (Desire Ser.: Vol. 129). 2000. per. 3.99 (*0-373-76281-X*) Silhouette.

Davis, Justine. Wicked Secrets. (Intimate Moments Ser.). 1994. per. 3.50 (*0-373-07555-3*, 5-07555-1) Silhouette.
— The Wrangler's Bride. 1997. per. 4.50 (*0-373-50186-2*, 1-50186-5) Harlequin Bks.

Davis, Justine, jt. auth. see Broadrick, Annette.

Davis, K. Charles. Foul Play & Other Dubious Achievements in Sports. 176p. 1988. mass mkt. 3.95 (*0-446-34802-3*, Pub. by Warner Bks) Little.

Davis, K. E., jt. ed. see Gergen, Kenneth J.

Davis, K. M. & Chang, Y. C. Lectures on Bochner-Riesz Means. (London Mathematical Society Lecture Note Ser.: No. 114). 160p. 1987. pap. text 42.95 (*0-521-31277-9*) Cambridge U Pr.

Davis, K. Rutherford. The Rutherfords in Britain: A History & Guide. LC 89-36154. 288p. 1989. 26.95 (*0-86299-368-7*, Pub. by Sutton Pub Ltd) Intl Pubs Mktg.

Davis, K. U., ed. see Williams, Ruby.

Davis, K. Vernon. Gretchen (Awakens) Eternal Man. Wright, Clarence, Jr., ed. 300p. (Orig.). 1994. pap. 12.95 (*1-878431-06-4*) Artist Profile Pub.
— Gretchen II: Reprogramming Eternal Man. Wright, Clarence, Jr., ed. 300p. (Orig.). 1995. pap. 12.95 (*1-878431-09-9*) Artist Profile Pub.
— Letters to the Wizard. 2nd large type ed. 280p. (YA). 1998. pap. 12.50 (*1-878431-12-9*) Artist Profile Pub.
— Web Surfing Today: (A Guide for the Rest of Us) (Illus.). 300p. 1998. pap. 14.50 (*1-878431-13-7*) Artist Profile Pub.
— Whiskey Tax. large type ed. 280p. (Orig.). 1997. pap. 12.50 (*1-878431-11-0*) Artist Profile Pub.

Davis, Karen. Instead of Chicken, Instead of Turkey: A Poultryless "Poultry" Potpourri. rev. ed. LC 99-44958. (Illus.). 160p. 1999. pap. 12.95 (*1-57067-083-5*) Book Pub Co.
— National Health Insurance: Benefits, Costs, & Consequences. LC 77-91832. (Studies in Social Economics). 182p. 1975. 29.95 (*0-8157-1760-1*); pap. 10.95 (*0-8157-1759-8*) Brookings.
— Prisoned Chickens, Poisoned Eggs: An Inside Look at the Modern Poultry Industry. LC 96-45937. 176p. (Orig.). 1996. pap. 12.95 (*1-57067-032-3*) Book Pub Co.
— Somali Cats: Everything about Purchase, Care, Nutrition, Breeding, Health Care, & Behavior. LC 95-53672. (Complete Pet Owner's Manual Ser.). (Illus.). 112p. 1996. pap. 6.95 (*0-8120-9583-9*) Barron.
— Star Light, Star Bright. LC 92-17120. (J). (ps-2). 1993. 15.00 (*0-671-79455-8*, Green Tiger S&S) S&S Childrens.

Davis, Karen & Rowland, Diane. Medicare Policy: New Directions for Health & Long-Term Care. LC 85-45048. (Illus.). 155p. 1986. reprint ed. pap. 48.10 (*0-608-05948-X*, 206628500008) Bks Demand.

Davis, Karen & Schoen, Cathy. Health & the War on Poverty: A Ten-Year Appraisal. (Studies in Social Economics). 1978. 28.95 (*0-8157-1758-X*) Brookings.

Davis, Karen, et al. Health Care Cost Containment. LC 89-45481. (Studies in Health Care Finance & Administration). 300p. 1990. text 48.00 (*0-8018-3874-6*) Johns Hopkins.
— Health Care Cost Containment, No. 3. LC 89-45481. (Studies in Health Care Finance & Administration). 300p. 1990. pap. text 18.95 (*0-8018-3875-4*) Johns Hopkins.

Davis, Karen, ed. see Blitzer, Robert F. & Gill, Jack C.

Davis, Karen, ed. see Gill, Jack C. & Blitzer, Robert F.

Davis, Karen, ed. see Hackworth, Robert H., et al.

Davis, Karen, ed. see Hackworth, Robert, et al.

Davis, Karen H., ed. see Bogue, Carole.

Davis, Karen H., ed. see Hackworth, Robert & Alwin, Robert H.

Davis, Karen H., ed. see Hackworth, Robert, et al.

Davis, Karen H., ed. see Vitale, Edmund.

Davis, Karen L. American Shorthaired Cats: Everything about Purchase, Care, Nutrition, Health Care, Behavior, & Showing. LC 98-44057. (Complete Pet Owner's Manual Ser.). (Illus.). 104p. 1999. pap. 6.95 (*0-7641-0658-9*) Barron.
— The Exotic Shorthair Cat. LC 96-47263. 1997. pap. 6.95 (*0-8120-9822-6*) Barron.
— Fat Cat, Finicky Cats. LC 97-22431. 144p. 1997. pap. text 9.95 (*0-8120-9853-6*) Barron.
— Turkish Angora Cats. LC 98-20366. (Complete Pet Owner's Manual Ser.). 111p. 1998. pap. 6.95 (*0-7641-0365-2*) Barron.

***Davis, Karen Leigh.** Cat Handbook. LC 99-56277. (Pet Handbooks Ser.). (Illus.). 144p. 2000. pap. 9.95 (*0-7641-1228-7*) Barron.
— Compatible Cats. LC 00-44464. (Illus.). (J). 2001. write for info. (*0-7641-1478-6*) Barron.
— Mixed Breed Cats: A Complete Pet Owner's Manual. LC 99-15226. 104p. 1999. pap. text 6.95 (*0-7641-0805-0*) Barron.

Davis, Karen Leigh. Ragdoll Cats. LC 98-33446. (Complete Pet Owner's Manual Ser.). (Illus.). 104p. 1999. pap. 6.95 (*0-7641-0732-1*) Barron.

Davis, Katharine B. Factors in the Sex Life of Twenty-Two Hundred Women. LC 70-169379. (Family in America Ser.). 456p. 1977. reprint ed. 33.95 (*0-405-03856-9*) Ayer.

Davis, Katherine, ed. see Gentry, Robert R. & Martinez, Patricia Brandon.

***Davis, Katherine Bland & Tankersley, Melissa Maupin.** The Elementary Teacher's Guide to Parent & Student Communication: Sample Comments, Reproducible Contracts, Forms, Letters Home. (Illus.). 96p. 2000. pap., teacher ed. 10.99 (*0-88724-567-6*, CD-2702) Carson-Dellos.
— The Internet in Your Classroom: Teacher Instructions & Student Activities (4-5+) (Illus.). 64p. 2000. pap., teacher ed. 10.99 (*0-88724-566-8*, CD-2701) Carson-Dellos.

D

Davis, Kathi. Introduction to Database Management. (C). 1996. pap. text. write for info. (*0-201-06613-0*) Addison-Wesley.

Davis, Kathleen. Killer Bees. (Illus.). 60p. (J). (gr. 4-7). 1996. pap. text 5.95 (*0-382-39483-6*) Silver Burdett Pr.

Davis, Kathleen, ed. Such Are the Trials: The Civil War Diaries of Jacob Gantz. LC 90-48636. (Illus.). 136p. 1991. 29.95 (*0-8138-0947-9*) Iowa St U Pr.

Davis, Kathleen & Mayes, Dave. Killer Bees. LC 92-46894. (Remarkable Animals Ser.). (Illus.). 60p. (J). (gr. 5 up). 1993. lib. bdg. 13.95 (*0-87518-582-7*, Dillon Silver Burdett) Silver Burdett Pr.

Davis, Kathleen, jt. auth. see Boenig, Robert.

Davis, Kathleen A. Sport Management. 2nd ed. 2000. pap. text 28.00 (*0-697-29508-7*) McGraw.
— Sport Management: Successful Private Sector Business Strategies. 320p. (C). 1994. text. write for info. (*0-697-13995-6*) Brown & Benchmark.

***Davis, Kathryn.** Labrador: A Novel. 240p. 2000. pap. 13.00 (*0-618-07542-9*, Mariner Bks) HM.

Davis, Kathryn. Volleyball. 3rd ed. 144p. (C). 1996. per. 21.95 (*0-7872-2334-4*, 41233401) Kendall-Hunt.

Davis, Kathryn. The Walking Tour: A Novel. LC 99-35547. 272p. 1999. 23.00 (*0-395-94541-0*) HM.

***Davis, Kathryn.** The Walking Tour: A Novel. 288p. 2000. pap. 13.00 (*0-618-08238-7*, Mariner Bks) HM.

***Davis, Kathryn A., ed.** Foreign Language Teaching & Language Minority Education. (Technical Report Ser.: Vol. 19). 152p. 1999. pap. text 20.00 (*0-8248-2239-0*) UH Pr.

Davis, Kathryn A., jt. ed. see Huebner, Thom.

Davis, Kathryn Anne. Language Planning in Multilingual Contexts: Policies, Communities, & Schools in Luxemborg. LC 93-45415. (Studies in Bilingualism (SiBiL): No. 8). xix, 220p. 1994. lib. bdg. 45.00 (*1-55619-539-7*) J Benjamins Pubng Co.

Davis, Kathryn H., ed. Yanks & Some Rebs in Texas, 1890. LC 91-76908. 443p. 1991. pap. 45.00 (*0-911317-50-3*) Ericson Bks.

Davis, Kathryn H. & Ericson, Carolyn R. Shelby County, Texas in the Civil War. 333p. 1993. pap. 35.00 (*0-911317-56-2*) Ericson Bks.

Davis, Kathryn H., jt. auth. see Ericson, Carolyn R.

Davis, Kathryn L. All We Hold Dear. 1996. mass mkt. 6.99 (*0-671-73604-3*) PB.

— The Art of Sports Officiating. LC 95-2559. 128p. 1995. pap. text 25.00 (0-205-15900-1, h59009) Allyn.

— Child of Awe. Marrow, Linda, ed. 480p. 1990. reprint ed. mass mkt. 6.50 (0-671-72550-5) PB.

— Fitness Walking Everyone. (Everyone Ser.). (Illus.). 137p. 1997. pap. text 15.95 (0-88725-237-0) Hunter Textbks.

— Sing to Me of Dreams. Marrow, Linda, ed. 608p. 1992. reprint ed. mass mkt. 5.99 (0-671-68314-4) PB.

— Too Deep for Tears. (Illus.). (J). 1990. mass mkt. 6.99 (0-671-72532-7) PB.

***Davis, Kathryn Lynn.** Somewhere Lies the Moon. LC 99-26701. 530p. 1999. 24.95 (0-671-73605-1) Simon & Schuster.

— Somewhere Lies the Moon. 720p. 2000. reprint ed. mass mkt. 6.99 (0-671-73606-X, Pocket Star Bks) PB.

***Davis, Kathy.** Friends Are Flowers That Never Fade. (Illus.). 64p. 2000. 12.95 (0-7683-2160-3) CEDCO Pub.

— Heartfelt Affection. 1999. 7.95 (1-56245-365-3) Great Quotations.

Davis, Kathy. A Kiss of Sun: A Garden of Quotes for Year Round Warmth. Caton, Patrick, ed. 365p. 1996. 6.50 (1-56245-230-4) Great Quotations.

— A Light Heart Lives Long. Hansen, Debbie, ed. (Illus.). 168p. (Orig.). 1993. pap. 5.95 (1-56245-074-3) Great Quotations.

— A Light Heart Lives Long - Journal. Ryan, Michael, ed. (Illus.). (Orig.). 1993. pap. 8.50 (1-56245-029-8) Great Quotations.

— Proverbs from Around the World, Vol. II. (Great Quotations Ser.). (Illus.). 64p. 1992. 9.95 (1-56245-053-0) Great Quotations.

— Reshaping the Female Body: The Dilemma of Cosmetic Surgery. LC 94-19290. 256p. (C). (gr. 13). 1994. pap. 19.99 (0-415-90632-6, A7456) Routledge.

— Time to Be Happy Is Now. 1999. 12.95 (0-7683-2116-6) CEDCO Pub.

— The Time to Be Happy Is Now: A Book of Inspirations. 64p. 1999. 12.95 (0-7683-2115-8) CEDCO Pub.

Davis, Kathy, ed. Embodied Practices: Feminist Perspectives on the Body. LC 97-67935. (European Journal of Women's Studies Reader). 224p. 1997. 75.00 (0-7619-5362-0); pap. 26.95 (0-7619-5363-9) Sage.

Davis, Kathy, et al. The Gender of Power. 192p. 1991. 55.00 (0-8039-8542-8); pap. 18.95 (0-8039-8543-6) Sage.

Davis, Kathy, jt. auth. see Fisher, Sue.

Davis, Kathy D. Responsible Dog Ownership. LC 93-17581. (Illus.). 224p. 1994. 21.95 (0-87605-801-2) Howell Bks.

— Therapy Dogs: Training Your Dog to Reach Others. (Illus.). 256p. 1992. 25.95 (0-87605-776-8) Howell Bks.

Davis, Kathy M., jt. auth. see Davis, Brian T.

Davis, Katie. Who Hoots? LC 99-6331. (Illus.). 36p. (J). (ps-k). 2000. 14.00 (0-15-202312-7, Harcourt Child Bks) Harcourt.

— Who Hops? LC 97-37175. (Illus.). 36p. (J). (ps-2). 1998. 13.00 (0-15-201839-5) Harcourt.

Davis, Katrina. Toothpick Building Illustrated: With Bridges. (Illus.). 48p. (Orig.). 1980. pap. 5.95 (0-937242-04-7) Scandia Pubs.

Davis, Kay & Oldsfield, Wendy. Animals. LC 91-23413. (Starting Science Ser.). (Illus.). 32p. (J). (gr. 2-5). 1991. pap. 4.95 (0-8114-1528-7) Raintree Steck-V.

Davis, Kay, jt. auth. see Davis, Buddy.

D

Davis, Kaye. Possessions: A Maris Middleton Mystery. LC 97-40375. 240p. (Orig.). 1998. pap. 11.95 (1-56280-192-9) Naiad Pr.

***Davis, Kaye.** Shattered Illusions: A Maris Middleton Mystery. LC 98-48238. (Maris Middleton Mystery Ser.: No. 4). 240p. 1999. pap. 11.95 (1-56280-252-6) Naiad Pr.

Davis, Kaye. Until the End: A Maris Middleton Mystery. LC 98-13221. (Maris Middleton Mystery Ser.: No. 3). 224p. 1999. pap. 11.95 (1-56280-222-4) Naiad Pr.

Davis, Keith & Subler, Craig A. Zeke Berman: Photographs. (Illus.). 12p. (Orig.). 1992. pap. 5.00 (0-914489-10-0) Univ Miss-KC Art.

Davis, Keith, jt. auth. see Newstrom, John W.

Davis, Keith, jt. auth. see Werther, William B., Jr.

Davis, Keith E., ed. Advances in Descriptive Psychology, Vol. 1. 389p. 1981. 40.00 (0-89232-179-2) Descriptive Psych Pr.

Davis, Keith E. & Mitchell, Thomas O., eds. Advances in Descriptive Psychology, Vol. 2. 289p. 1982. 40.00 (0-89232-225-X) Descriptive Psych Pr.

— Advances in Descriptive Psychology, Vol. 3. 311p. 1983. 40.00 (0-89232-293-4) Descriptive Psych Pr.

— Advances in Descriptive Psychology, Vol. 4. 310p. 1985. 40.00 (0-89232-358-2) Descriptive Psych Pr.

Davis, Keith E., jt. ed. see Putman, Anthony O.

Davis, Keith F. An American Century of Photography: From Dry-Plate to Digital: The Hallmark Photographic Collection. 2nd rev. enl. ed. LC 98-54099. (Illus.). 608p. 1999. 95.00 (0-8109-6378-7, Pub. by Abrams) Time Warner.

— Edward Weston: One Hundred Photographs from the Nelson-Atkins Museum of Art & the Hallmark Photographic Collection. 64p. 1982. 10.00 (0-317-60861-4) Hallmark.

— George N. Barnard: Photographer of Sherman's Campaign. (Illus.). 232p. 1990. 40.00 (0-87529-627-0); pap. 25.00 (0-87529-628-9) Hallmark.

— Harry Callahan: New Color--Photographs 1978-1987. (Illus.). 131p. (Orig.). 1988. 34.95 (0-87529-624-6); pap. 19.95 (0-87529-625-4) Hallmark.

— Harry Callahan: Photographs. 64p. 1981. pap. 10.00 (0-87529-606-8) Hallmark.

— The Passionate Observer: Photographs by Carl Van Vechten. (Illus.). 120p. 1993. 40.00 (0-87529-668-8); pap. 25.00 (0-87529-669-6) Hallmark.

— The Photographs of Dorothea Lange. (Illus.). 132p. 1996. 35.00 (0-8109-6315-9, Pub. by Abrams) Time Warner.

— Todd Webb: Photographs of New York & Paris, 1945-1960. 116p. 1986. pap. 16.95 (0-87529-620-3) Hallmark.

— Wanderlust: Work by Eight Contemporary Photographers from the Hallmark Photographic Collection. (Illus.). 92p. (Orig.). 1987. pap. 14.95 (0-87529-621-1) Hallmark.

Davis, Keith F., et al. Clarence John Laughlin: Visionary Photographer. 1990. 40.00 (0-87529-629-7); pap. 25.00 (0-87529-630-0) Hallmark.

Davis, Keith G. Oxalis: A Story of Renewal. (Illus.). 64p. 1998. pap. 16.95 (0-9647751-2-3) Clayton Paige Pubng.

— The Pause: A Christmas Book. 1994. pap. 16.95 (0-9647751-0-7) Clayton Paige Pubng.

Davis, Keith G., ed. The Pause: A Christmas Gift. (Illus.). 38p. (Orig.). 1994. pap. 16.95 (0-9647751-9-0) Clayton Paige Pubng.

Davis, Keith R. & Hammerschmidt, Raymond, eds. Arabidopsis Thaliana As a Model for Plant-Pathogen Interactions. LC 93-71322. (Symposium Ser.). (Illus.). 132p. (Orig.). 1993. pap. 34.00 (0-89054-153-1) Am Phytopathol Soc.

Davis, Kelly. Holiday Cookie Kit. 1998. 29.95 (1-57990-070-4); 29.95 (1-57990-113-1, Pub. by Lark Books) Random.

Davis, Ken. Don't Know Much about Dinosaurs. 48p. pap. 5.95 (0-06-446233-1) HarpC.

— Don't Know Much about Dinosaurs. (Picture Bks.: No. 7). 48p. (J). Date not set. 15.95 (0-06-028619-9); lib. bdg. 15.89 (0-06-028620-2) HarpC Child Bks.

— Don't Know Much about Mummies. 48p. pap. 5.95 (0-06-443645-4) HarpC.

— Don't Know Much about Mummies. (Picture Bks.: No. 8). (Illus.). 48p. (J). (gr. 1-4). Date not set. 15.95 (0-06-028781-0); lib. bdg. 15.89 (0-06-028782-9) HarpC Child Bks.

— Don't Know Much about the 50 States. 64p. pap. 5.95 (0-06-446227-7) HarpC.

— Don't Know Much about the 50 States. (Picture Bks.: No. 1). 64p. 2001. 15.95 (0-06-028607-5); lib. bdg. 15.89 (0-06-028608-3) HarpC Child Bks.

— Don't Know Much about the Kings & Queens of England. 48p. pap. 5.95 (0-06-446229-3) HarpC.

— Don't Know Much about the Kings & Queens of England. (Picture Bks.: No. 3). 48p. 2001. 15.95 (0-06-028611-3); lib. bdg. 15.89 (0-06-028612-1) HarpC Child Bks.

— Don't Know Much about the Pilgrims. 48p. pap. 5.95 (0-06-446228-5) HarpC.

— Don't Know Much about the Pilgrims. (Picture Bks.: No. 2). 48p. 2001. 15.95 (0-06-028609-1); lib. bdg. 15.89 (0-06-028610-5) HarpC Child Bks.

— Don't Know Much about the Pioneers & Indians. 48p. pap. 5.95 (0-06-446232-3) HarpC.

— Don't Know Much about the Pioneers & Indians. (Picture Bks.: No. 6). 48p. (J). Date not set. 15.95 (0-06-028617-2); lib. bdg. 15.89 (0-06-028618-0) HarpC Child Bks.

— Don't Know Much about the Presidents. 48p. pap. 5.95 (0-06-446231-5) HarpC.

— Don't Know Much about the Presidents. (Picture Bks.: No. 5). 48p. (J). Date not set. 15.95 (0-06-028615-6); lib. bdg. 15.89 (0-06-028616-4) HarpC Child Bks.

— Don't Know Much about the Solar System. 48p. pap. 5.95 (0-06-446230-7) HarpC.

— Don't Know Much about the Solar System. (Picture Bks.: No. 4). 48p. 2001. 15.95 (0-06-028613-X); lib. bdg. 15.89 (0-06-028614-8) HarpC Child Bks.

— Don't Know Much Biography, Vol. 1. (Illus.). 80p. (J). (gr. 2-5). 14.89 (0-06-028817-5); 4.25 (0-06-442124-4) HarpC Child Bks.

— Don't Know Much Biography, Vol. 2. (Illus.). 80p. (J). (gr. 2-5). 14.89 (0-06-028818-3); 4.25 (0-06-442125-2) HarpC Child Bks.

— Don't Know Much Biography, Vol. 3. (Illus.). 80p. (J). (gr. 2-5). 14.89 (0-06-028819-1); 4.25 (0-06-442126-0) HarpC Child Bks.

— Don't Know Much Biography, Vol. 4. (Illus.). 80p. (J). (gr. 2-5). 14.89 (0-06-028820-5); 4.25 (0-06-442127-9) HarpC Child Bks.

— Don't Know Much Biography, Vol. 5. (Illus.). 80p. (J). (gr. 2-5). 14.89 (0-06-028821-3); 4.25 (0-06-442128-7) HarpC Child Bks.

— Don't Know Much Biography, Vol. 6. (Illus.). 80p. (J). (gr. 2-5). 14.89 (0-06-028822-1); 4.25 (0-06-442129-5) HarpC Child Bks.

Davis, Ken. Fire up Your Life: Living with Nothing to Hide, Nothing to Prove, Nothing to Lose. 208p. 1995. pap. 10.99 (0-310-48661-0) Zondervan.

— Fired! Vol. 1: Your Proven Guide to Finding a Better Job Faster & Earning More Money Than Ever Before! Lose, John, ed. (Illus.). 144p. (Orig.). 1995. pap. 19.95 (0-9602868-2-9) Intelexxi.

— How to Live with Your Parents Without Losing Your Mind. 160p. (YA). (gr. 7 up). 1988. pap. 10.99 (0-310-32331-2, 11791P) Zondervan.

— How to Speak to Youth...& Keep Them Awake at the Same Time: A Step-by-Step Guide for Improving Your Talks. rev. ed. 176p. 1996. pap. 12.99 (0-310-20146-2) Zondervan.

— I Don't Remember Dropping the Skunk, but I Do Remember Trying to Breathe: Survival Skills for Teenagers. 160p. 1990. pap. 9.99 (0-310-32341-X) Zondervan.

— I'm Not OK, You're Not OK But That's OK. LC 99-39361. 2000. pap. 12.99 (0-310-22757-7) Zondervan.

Davis, Ken & Lambert, Dave. Jumper Fables. 192p. (YA). (gr. 5 up). 1994. pap. 10.99 (0-310-40011-2) Zondervan.

Davis, Ken, jt. ed. see Hommerding, Alan.

Davis, Ken, ed. see Parks, Nancy.

Davis, Kenneth. Families: A Handbook of Concepts & Techniques for the Helping Professional. LC 95-2878. 284p. 1995. 67.95 (0-534-25806-9) Brooks-Cole.

Davis, Kenneth & Webster, Frederick E. Sales Force Management. LC 68-20549. 776p. reprint ed. pap. 200.00 (0-608-13660-3, 205518900011) Bks Demand.

Davis, Kenneth, et al. Alzheimer's Disease - Questions & Answers. (Questions & Answers Ser.). (Illus.). 136p. (Orig.). 1997. pap. text 14.95 (1-873413-36-X) Merit Pub Intl.

Davis, Kenneth C. Administrative Law Treatise, 3 vols. 3rd ed. 1686p. 1994. boxed set 425.00 (0-316-17670-2, 76702, Aspen Law & Bus) Aspen Pub.

— Basic Text on Administrative Law. 3rd ed. LC 71-181451. xvi, 617p. 1972. 19.95 (0-317-00000-4) West Pub.

— Discretionary Justice: A Preliminary Inquiry. LC 80-16898. 233p. 1980. reprint ed. lib. bdg. 69.50 (0-313-22503-6, DADC, Greenwood Pr) Greenwood.

***Davis, Kenneth C.** Don't Know Much About Geography. 400p. 1999. reprint ed. pap. 12.50 (0-380-71379-9, Avon Bks) Morrow Avon.

Davis, Kenneth C. Don't Know Much about Geography: Everything You Need to Know about the World but Never Learned. (Don't Know Much about Bks.). 1992. 17.60 (0-606-06115-0, Pub. by Turtleback) Demco.

***Davis, Kenneth C.** Don't Know Much About History. 496p. 1999. reprint ed. pap. 12.50 (0-380-71252-0, Avon Bks) Morrow Avon.

— Don't Know Much about History: Everything You Need to Know about American History but Never Learned. 1990. 17.60 (0-606-04909-6, Pub. by Turtleback) Demco.

— Don't Know Much about Mixed Boxed, Vol. 2. 1999. pap. 25.00 (0-380-80475-1, Avon Bks) Morrow Avon.

— Don't Know Much About the Bible. LC 98-16744. 560p. 1999. pap. 12.50 (0-380-72839-7, Avon Bks) Morrow Avon.

Davis, Kenneth C. Don't Know Much About the Civil War. LC 95-50352. 480p. 1996. 25.00 (0-688-11814-3, Wm Morrow) Morrow Avon.

***Davis, Kenneth C.** Don't Know Much About the Civil War. 560p. 1999. pap. 12.50 (0-380-71908-8, Avon Bks) Morrow Avon.

Davis, Kenneth C. Don't Know Much about the Civil War: Everything You Need to Know about America's Greatest Conflict but Never Learned. 1997. pap. 12.50 (0-614-27374-9, Avon Bks) Morrow Avon.

Davis, Kenneth Culp. Administrative Law. 1995. 125.00 (0-316-17685-0, Aspen Law & Bus) Aspen Pub.

Davis, Kenneth G. Primero Dios: Alcoholics Anonymous & the Hispanic Community. LC 93-29626. 1994. 29.50 (0-945636-50-4) Susquehanna U Pr.

Davis, Kenneth R. Anabaptism & Asceticism: A Study in Intellectual Origins. fac. ed. LC 73-19593. (Studies in Anabaptist & Mennonite History: No. 16). 367p. 1974. pap. 104.60 (0-7837-7327-7, 2047256) Bks Demand.

Davis, Kenneth R. & Webster, Frederick E., Jr., eds. Readings in Sales Force Management. LC 68-20550. (Illus.). 475p. reprint ed. pap. 147.30 (0-608-10963-0, 201239400081) Bks Demand.

***Davis, Kenneth Ronald.** Anabaptism & Asceticism: A Study in Intellectual Origins. 368p. 1998. pap. 30.00 (1-57910-178-X) Wipf & Stock.

Davis, Kenneth S. FDR, into the Storm, 1937-1940: A History. LC 92-21640. 1993. 35.00 (0-679-41541-6) Random.

— Franklin Delano Roosevelt: The New Deal Years, 1933-1937. LC 85-31704. 756p. 1986. 29.95 (0-394-52753-4) Random.

Davis, Kenneth W. & Lovejoy, Kim B. Writing: Process, Product, & Power. 320p. (C). 1992. pap. text 23.60 (0-13-971011-6) P-H.

Davis, Kent. CDC's Complete Guide to Healthy Travel: The Centers for Disease Control Guidelines for International Travel. 1997. pap. text 14.95 (1-883323-58-4) Open Rd Pub.

Davis, Kent L. Abraham Lincoln: An Most Humble Instrument in the Hands of the Almighty. LC 98-70316. (Illus.). 900p. 1998. lib. bdg. 89.00 (1-888106-87-5, Agreka) Agreka Bks.

Davis, Kevin. Getting into Your Customer's Head: Secrets of Selling Your Competitors Don't Know. LC 95-46877. (Illus.). 320p. 1996. 25.00 (0-8129-2628-5, Times Business) Random.

— Getting into Your Customer's Head: 8 Secret Roles of Selling Your Customers Don't Know. 1999. pap. 15.00 (0-8129-3120-3, Times Bks) Crown Pub Group.

***Davis, Kevin.** Look What Came from Australia. 2000. pap. text 6.95 (0-531-16433-0) Watts.

— Look What Came from England. (Look What Came from Ser.). (Illus.). (J). 2000. pap. 6.95 (0-531-16434-9) Watts.

— Look What Came from Germany. (Look What Came from Ser.). (Illus.). (J). 2000. pap. 6.95 (0-531-16435-7) Watts.

— Look What Came from the United States. (Look What Came from Ser.). (Illus.). (J). 2000. pap. 6.95 (0-531-16436-5) Watts.

Davis, Kevin. The Wrong Man. 360p. (Orig.). 1996. mass mkt. 5.99 (0-380-77815-7, Avon Bks) Morrow Avon.

Davis, Kevin & Harper, Ian, eds. Privitization: The Financial Implications. 192p. 1994. pap. 24.95 (1-86373-540-2, Pub. by Allen & Unwin Pty) Paul & Co Pubs.

Davis, Kevin A. Look What Came from Australia. LC 99-19254. (Look What Came From Ser.). 1999. 21.00 (0-531-11684-0) Watts.

— Look What Came from England. LC 99-19258. (Look What Came from Ser.). 1999. 21.00 (0-531-11686-7) Watts.

— Look What Came from Germany. LC 99-19256. (Look What Came from Ser.). 1999. 21.00 (0-531-11685-9) Watts.

— Look What Came from Greece. LC 99-19257. (Look What Came from Ser.). 1999. write for info. (0-531-11744-8) Watts.

***Davis, Kevin A.** Look What Came from the United States. (Illus.). (J). 2000. 12.40 (0-606-18155-5) Turtleback.

Davis, Kevin A. Look What Came from the United States. LC 99-109255. (Look What Came from Ser.). 1999. 21.00 (0-531-11687-5) Watts.

Davis, Kevin T., jt. auth. see Lewis, Mervyn K.

Davis, Kim, et al. Sails, Steamships & Sea Captains: Early Settlement, Trade & Transportation County, Washington. (Illus.). 150p. (Orig.). 1993. pap. 15.95 (0-929186-02-8) Island Cnty Hist Soc.

Davis, Kim C., jt. auth. see Ritter, Beverly L.

Davis, Kimberly. Adapted Physical Education for Students with Autism. (Illus.). 142p. 1990. pap. 23.95 (0-398-06085-1) C C Thomas.

Davis, Kimberly. Adapted Physical Education for Students with Autism. (Illus.). 142p. (C). 1990. text 36.95 (0-398-05688-9) C C Thomas.

Davis, Kingsley. Final Note on a Case of Extreme Isolation. (Reprint Series in Social Sciences). (C). 1993. reprint ed. pap. text 5.00 (0-8290-3789-6, S-63) Irvington.

— A Structural Analysis of Kinship: Prolegomena to the Sociology of Kinship. Zuckerman, Harriet & Merton, Robert K., eds. LC 79-8990. (Dissertations on Sociology Ser.). 1980. lib. bdg. 41.95 (0-405-12962-9) Ayer.

Davis, Kingsley, ed. Demography Series, 20 vols., Set. 1976. 643.50 (0-405-07980-X) Ayer.

Davis, Kingsley, et al, eds. Below-Replacement Fertility in Industrialized Societies: Causes, Consequences, Policies - Supplement to Population & Development Review, Vol. 12. LC 87-2458. 1987. pap. 14.00 (0-87834-056-4) Population Coun.

Davis, Kingsley & Grossbard-Shechtman, Amyra, eds. Contemporary Marriage: Comparative Perspectives on a Changing Institution. LC 85-62452. 360p. (C). 1986. 20.00 (0-87154-221-8) Russell Sage.

Davis, Kingsley & Moore, Wilbert E. Some Principles of Stratification. (Reprint Series in Social Sciences). (C). 1993. reprint ed. pap. text 5.00 (0-8290-3802-7, S-68) Irvington.

Davis, Kingsley, et al. Below Replacement Fertility in Industrial Societies: Causes, Consequences, Politics. Hoover Institute Staff, ed. 358p. 1987. text 85.00 (0-521-34324-0) Cambridge U Pr.

Davis, Kortright. Serving with Power: Reviving the Spirit of Christian Ministry. LC 99-32696. 224p. 1999. pap. 14.95 (0-8091-3890-5) Paulist Pr.

Davis, Kristin. Financing College: How Much You'll Really Have to Pay & How Much to Get the Money. 2nd rev. ed. LC 98-12361. 308p. (C). 1998. pap. 17.95 (0-938721-56-9) Kiplinger Bks.

Davis, L., jt. auth. see Ray, J.

Davis, L. D. Rotary, Kelly, Swivel, Tongs, & Top Drive. Bork, K. R., ed. (Rotary Drilling Ser.: Unit I, Lesson 4). (Illus.). 164p. (Orig.). (C). 1995. pap. text 16.00 (0-88698-172-7, 2.104101) PETEX.

Davis, L. D., et al, eds. Evolutionary Algorithms. LC 99-18387. (IMA Volumes in Mathematics & Its Applications Ser.: Vol. 111). (Illus.). 308p. 1999. 69.95 (0-387-98826-2) Spr-Verlag.

Davis, L. Edward, pref. The Westminster Confession of Faith: An Authentic Modern Version. 2nd rev. ed. x, 89p. 1985. pap. text. write for info. (0-9614303-1-1) Summertown.

Davis, L. Porter, ed. Smart Structures & Materials, 1998: Passive Damping & Isolation. (Proceedings of SPIE Ser.: Vol. 3327). 494p. 1998. 80.00 (0-8194-2771-3) SPIE.

— Smart Structures & Materials, 1997: Passive Damping & Isolation. LC 97-193069. 350p. 1997. 80.00 (0-8194-2458-7) SPIE.

Davis, L. S. & Johnson, K. N. Forest Management. 3rd ed. 544p. (C). 1987. 97.50 (0-07-032625-8) McGraw.

Davis, L. V., jt. ed. see Ash, S. R.

Davis, Laird. Castle Crags. (Classic Rock Climbs Ser.: Vol. 18). (Illus.). (Orig.). 1997. pap. 8.95 (1-57540-043-X) Falcon Pub Inc.

— Classic Rock Climbs Vol. 15: City of Rocks. LC 98-15006. (Illus.). 52p. (Orig.). 1997. pap. 9.95 (1-57540-040-5) Falcon Pub Inc.

Davis, Lana, ed. see Gould, Theodore A.

Davis, Lana D. Zebina's Kin, the Descendancy of a Puritan People. 171p. (Orig.). 1995. pap. 27.00 (0-7884-0349-4) Heritage Bk.

Davis, Lance & North, Douglass Cecil. Institutional Change & American Economic Growth. LC 70-155584. 291p. reprint ed. pap. 83.00 (0-608-12225-4, 2024447) Bks Demand.

***Davis, Lance E. & Gallman, Robert E.** Evolving Financial Markets & International Capital Flows: Britain, the Americas & Australia, 1865-1914. LC 99-42142. (Japan-U. S. Center Sanwa Monographs on International Financial Markets: No. 3). (Illus.). 888p. (C). 2000. 125.00 (0-521-55352-0) Cambridge U Pr.

Davis, Lance E. & Huttenback, Robert A. Mammon & the Pursuit of Empire: The Political Economy of British Imperialism, 1860-1912. (Interdisciplinary Perspectives on Modern History Ser.). (Illus.). 414p. 1987. text 89.95 (0-521-23611-8) Cambridge U Pr.

Davis, Lance E., et al. In Pursuit of Leviathan: Technology, Innovation, Productivity, & Profits in American Whaling, 1816-1906. LC 96-21263. (National Bureau of Economic Research Long Term Factors in Economic Development Ser.). 550p. 1997. 80.00 (0-226-13789-9) U Ch Pr.

Davis, Lance E., jt. auth. see Cull, Robert J.

Davis, Lance E., jt. auth. see Payne, Peter L.

***Davis, Langdon & E & F N Spon Staff.** Spon's European Construction Costs Handbook. 3rd ed. LC 00-24967. 2000. write for info. (0-419-25460-9, E & FN Spon) Routledge.

An Asterisk (*) at the beginning of an entry indicates that the title is appearing for the first time.

Davis Langdon & Everest Staff. Spon's Architect's & Builder's Price Book, 1997. 22nd ed. 1996. mass mkt. 129.95 (*0-419-22190-5*, E & FN Spon) Routledge.
— Spon's Civil Engineering & Highway Works Price Book, 1997. 11th ed. 1996. mass mkt. 154.95 (*0-419-22200-6*, E & FN Spon) Routledge.
— Spon's Mechanical & Electrical Services Price Book. 28th ed. 1996. mass mkt. 134.95 (*0-419-22210-3*, E & FN Spon) Routledge.
Davis Langdon & Everest Staff, ed. Spon's Architect's & Builder's Price Book, 1992. 117th ed. 1050p. 1991. write for info. (*0-419-17360-9*, E & FN Spon) Routledge.
— Spon's Civil Engineering & Highway Works Price Book, 1992. 6th ed. 850p. 1991. write for info. (*0-419-17380-3*, E & FN Spon) Routledge.
— Spon's European Construction Costs Handbook. 2nd ed. (Illus.). 608p. (C). 1995. 150.00 (*0-419-19650-1*, E & FN Spon) Routledge.
— Spon's Mechanical & Electrical Services Price Book, 1992. 23rd ed. 700p. 1991. write for info. (*0-419-17370-6*, E & FN Spon) Routledge.
Davis Langdon & Everest Staff, jt. auth. see Derek Lovejoy Partnership Staff.
Davis Langdon & Everest Staff, jt. ed. see Lovejoy Derek & Patrners Staff.
Davis, Lanny J. Truth to Tell: Tell It Early, Tell It All, Tell It Yourself; Notes from My White House Education. LC 99-22419. 288p. 1999. 25.00 (*0-684-86278-6*) Free Pr.
— A User's Guide to Computer Contracting: Forms, Techniques, Strategies. LC 84-9667. 1984. 75.00 (*0-15-004368-6*) Harcourt.
Davis, Lanny J., jt. auth. see Allen, Don A.
Davis, Larry. B-52 Stratofortress in Action. (Aircraft in Action Ser.). (Illus.). 50p. 1993. pap. 9.95 (*0-89747-289-6*, 1130) Squad Sig Pubns.
— B-17 in Action. (In Action Ser.: No. 1063). (Illus.). 58p. 1984. pap. 9.95 (*0-89747-152-0*) Squad Sig Pubns.
— B-29 Superfortress in Action. (Aircraft in Action Ser.: No. 165). (Illus.). 58p. 1997. pap. 9.95 (*0-89747-370-1*, 1165) Squad Sig Pubns.
— C-47 Skytrain in Action. (Aircraft in Action Ser.). (Illus.). 58p. 1995. pap. 9.95 (*0-89747-329-9*) Squad Sig Pubns.
— F-84 Thunderjet. (Aircraft in Action Ser.: No. 1061). (Illus.). 50p. 1983. pap. 9.95 (*0-89747-147-4*) Squad Sig Pubns.
— F-4 Phantom II in Action. (Aircraft in Action Ser.: Vol. 65). (Illus.). 58p. 2000. pap. 9.95 (*0-89747-154-7*, 1065) Squad Sig Pubns.
***Davis, Larry.** F-86 Sabre Walk Around. (Walk Around Ser.: Vol. 21). (Illus.). 80p. 2000. pap. 14.95 (*0-89747-409-0*) Squad Sig Pubns.
Davis, Larry. Fifty-Sixth Fighter Group. (Fighter Groups - Squadrons Ser.). (Illus.). 64p. 1991. pap. 10.95 (*0-89747-240-3*, 6172) Squad Sig Pubns.
— Gunships: A Pictorial History of Spooky. (Vietnam Studies Group). (Illus.). 64p. 1982. pap. 10.95 (*0-89747-123-7*, 6032) Squad Sig Pubns.
— P-51 Mustang. (Aircraft Specials Ser.). (Illus.). 64p. 1995. pap. text 11.95 (*0-89747-350-7*) Squad Sig Pubns.
— North American P-51 Mustang: A Photo Chronicle. LC 92-81714. (Illus.). 112p. 1992. pap. 19.95 (*0-88740-411-1*) Schiffer.
— P-51D Walk Around. (Walk Around Ser.: No. 7). (Illus.). 80p. (Orig.). 1996. pap. 14.95 (*0-89747-360-4*, 5507) Squad Sig Pubns.
— P-47 Thunderbolt in Action. (Aircraft in Action Ser.). 50p. 1985. pap. 9.95 (*0-89747-161-X*, 1067) Squad Sig Pubns.
— P-61 Black Widow in Action. (Aircraft in Action Ser.: Vol. 106). (Illus.). 50p. 2000. reprint ed. pap. 9.95 (*0-89747-248-9*, 1106) Squad Sig Pubns.
— P-38 Lightning. (Aircraft in Action Ser.). (Illus.). 50p. 1990. pap. 9.95 (*0-89747-255-1*, 1109) Squad Sig Pubns.
— P-35 "Mini" in Action. (Mini in Action Ser.). (Illus.). 50p. 1994. pap. 5.95 (*0-89747-321-3*) Squad Sig Pubns.
— P-12 - F-4B in Action. (Aircraft in Action Ser.). (Illus.). 50p. 1994. pap. 9.95 (*0-89747-309-4*) Squad Sig Pubns.
— P-26 "Mini" in Action. (Mini in Action Ser.). (Illus.). 50p. 1994. pap. 5.95 (*0-89747-322-1*) Squad Sig Pubns.
***Davis, Larry.** Pioneering Organizations: The Convergence of Individualism, Teamwork & Leadership. LC 00-8278. 2000. 22.95 (*1-890009-84-9*) Exec Excell.
Davis, Larry. Planes, Names & Dames, Vol. 3. (Aircraft Specials Ser.). (Illus.). 80p. 1995. pap. 14.95 (*0-89747-339-6*) Squad Sig Pubns.
— Planes, Names & Dames Vol. 2: Korea Nose Art. (Specials Ser.: Vol. 2). (Illus.). 80p. 1993. pap. 10.95 (*0-89747-291-8*, 6058) Squad Sig Pubns.
— Rural Firefighting Operations Bk. I: The First No-Nonsense Guide to Small Community Fire Protection. (Illus.). 1986. pap. text 24.95 (*0-9615990-0-6*) Intl Soc Fire Serv.
— Rural Firefighting Operations Bk. II: The Encyclopedia of Water Supplies & Water Delivery Techniques. (Illus.). 375p. 1986. pap. text 24.95 (*0-9615990-1-4*) Intl Soc Fire Serv.
— T-6 Texan in Action. (Aircraft in Action Ser.). (Illus.). 50p. 1989. pap. 9.95 (*0-89747-224-1*, 1094) Squad Sig Pubns.
Davis, Larry & Proctor, Enola. Race, Gender, & Class. 368p. (C). 1995. pap. text 63.00 (*0-13-750118-8*) P-H.
Davis, Larry, jt. auth. see Quinn, Daniel.
Davis, Larry, ed. see Colletti, Dominic J.
Davis, Larry E. Black & Single. 2nd ed. 256p. 1997. pap. text 14.95 (*1-879360-50-0*) Noble Pr.
— Black & Single: Meeting & Choosing a Partner Who's Right for You. LC 93-21565. 214p. (Orig.). 1993. pap. 12.95 (*1-879360-29-2*) Noble Pr.
— The Money Trucks. (Illus.). 320p. (Orig.). 1987. pap. 4.95 (*0-941177-22-X*) Castle Pub.
— Working with African American Males: A Guide to Practice. LC 98-40277. 391p. 1999. 46.00 (*0-7619-0471-9*); pap. 21.95 (*0-7619-0472-7*) Sage.
Davis, Larry E., ed. Ethnicity in Social Group Work Practice. LC 84-6628. (Social Work with Groups Ser.: Vol. 7, No. 3). 134p. 1984. text 39.95 (*0-86656-323-7*) Haworth Pr.
***Davis, Larry E. & Kennedy, Peter G. E.** Infectious Diseases of the Nervous System. (Illus.). 576p. 2000. 95.00 (*0-7506-4213-0*) Buttrwrth-Heinemann.
***Davis, Larry Moench.** Armageddon - The Warning & the Promise. LC 99-67669. 139p. 1999. 14.95 (*0-9670193-3-8*) Zions Pubg.
Davis, Larry N., ed. see Radde, Paul O.
Davis, Laura. Allies in Healing: When the Person You Love Was Sexually Abused As a Child, a Support Book for Partners. LC 90-56423. 368p. (Orig.). 1991. pap. 16.00 (*0-06-096883-4*, Perennial) HarperTrade.
— The Courage to Heal: A Guide for Women Survivors of Child Sexual Abuse. LC 89-45646. 480p. 1990. pap., wbk. ed. 22.50 (*0-06-096437-5*, Perennial) HarperTrade.
Davis, Laura & Keyser, Janis. Becoming the Parent You Want to Be: A Sourcebook of Strategies for the First Five Years. LC 96-12035. (Illus.). 544p. 1997. pap. 20.00 (*0-553-06750-8*) Broadway BDD.
Davis, Laura, jt. auth. see Bass, Ellen.
Davis, Laura, ed. see Woolf, Virginia, et al.
Davis, Laurel D. The Blocks & Drilling Line. 3rd ed. Bork, Kathy, ed. & intro. by. LC 96-13442. (Rotary Drilling Ser.: Unit I, Lesson 5). (Illus.). 156p. (C). 1996. pap. text 16.00 (*0-88698-170-0*, 2-10530) PETEX.
Davis, Laurel R. The Swimsuit Issue & Sport: Hegemonic Masculinity in "Sports Illustrated" LC 96-38825. (Series on Sport, Culture, & Social Relations). 168p. (C). 1997. pap. text 17.95 (*0-7914-3392-7*) State U NY Pr.
— The Swimsuit Issue & Sport: Hegemonic Masculinity in "Sports Illustrated" LC 96-38825. (Series on Sport, Culture, & Social Relations). 168p. (C). 1997. text 54.50 (*0-7914-3391-9*) State U NY Pr.
***Davis, Lauren.** Rat Medicine: And Other Unlikely Curatives. 193p. 2000. pap. 14.00 (*0-88962-690-1*, Pub. by Mosaic) Midpt Trade.
***Davis, Laurena.** Grand Junction: Western Colorado in the New Millennium. LC 99-36652. (Illus.). 184p. 1999. 35.00 (*1-58192-003-2*) Community Comm.
Davis, Lawrence B. Immigrants, Baptists & the Protestant Mind in America. LC 72-81264. 240p. reprint ed. pap. 74.40 (*0-8357-9682-5*, 201904000010) Bks Demand.
Davis, Lawrence M. Statistics in Dialectology. LC 90-35856. 104p. 1990. pap. text 16.95 (*0-8173-0510-6*) U of Ala Pr.
Davis, Lee. Bolton & Wodehouse & Kern: The Men Who Made Musical Comedy. (Illus.). 480p. 1993. 29.95 (*0-87008-131-4*) JAS Heineman.
— Bolton & Wodehouse & Kern: The Men Who Made Musical Comedy. (Illus.). 480p. 1995. 29.95 (*0-87008-145-4*) JAS Heineman.
— Catch That Hat! LC 97-8523. (P. B. Bear Ser.). (Illus.). (J). 1997. write for info. (*0-7894-1413-9*) DK Pub Inc.
Davis, Lee. Dinosaur Dinners. (Eyewitness Readers). 0032p. (J). (gr. 1-3). 12.95 (*0-7894-4252-3*) DK Pub Inc.
Davis, Lee. Environmental Disasters. LC 98-29134. (Illus.). 480p. 1998. 45.00 (*0-8160-3265-3*) Facts on File.
— Fly-Away Kite. LC 97-8526. (P. B. Bear Ser.). (Illus.). (J). 1997. write for info. (*0-7894-1411-2*) DK Pub Inc.
***Davis, Lee.** Keyboard Primer. large type ed. Vogl, Peter, ed. (Illus.). 64p. 2000. pap. text 14.95 (*1-893907-38-4*) Cassett & Video.
— Lee Davis. (My First Steps to Reading Ser.). (Illus.). (ps-3). 1999. pap. 0.00 (*0-7894-4593-X*) DK Pub Inc.
Davis, Lee. The Lifesize Animal Opposites Book. LC 94-14988. (Illus.). 32p. (J). (ps). 1994. 12.95 (*1-56458-720-7*) DK Pub Inc.
— Lifesize Animal Opposites Book. (Illus.). 32p. (J). (ps). text 16.95 (*0-590-24372-1*) Scholastic Inc.
— The P. B. Bear Read-Alongs. Incl. What Does P. B. Bear Choose? LC 97-14044. (J). (ps). 1997. (*0-7894-2223-9*); What Is P. B. Bear Doing? LC 97-14042. (J). (ps). 1997. (*0-7894-2224-7*); Where Is P. B. Bear? LC 97-14177. (Illus.). (J). (ps). 1997. pap. (*0-7894-2222-0*); 29.95 (*0-614-31313-9*) DK Pub Inc.
— P. B. Bear's Treasure Hunt. LC 95-5466. (Illus.). 32p. (J). (ps-1). 1995. 12.95 (*0-7894-0214-9*, 5-70627) DK Pub Inc.
***Davis, Lee.** Quality Assurance: ISO 9000 as A Management Tool. LC 98-132811. 1999. 24.00 (*87-16-13361-7*) Mksgaard.
Davis, Lee. Sand Castle Surprise. LC 97-8524. (P. B. Bear Ser.). (Illus.). (J). 1997. write for info. (*0-7894-1412-0*) DK Pub Inc.
— Scandals & Follies: The Rise & Fall of the Great Broadway Revue. LC 99-88656. (Illus.). 480p. 2000. 37.50 (*0-87910-274-8*) Limelight Edns.
— The Snowy Ride. LC 97-10701. (P. B. Bear Ser.). (J). 1997. write for info. (*0-7894-1414-7*) DK Pub Inc.
— Why Is Mommy's Tummy So Big? Questions Children Ask about Growing Up. LC 97-14464. (Why Books Ser.). (J). 1997. write for info. (*0-7894-2175-5*) DK Pub Inc.
Davis, Lee, jt. auth. see Hainstock, Elizabeth G.
Davis, Lee A. Man Made Catastrophes: From the Burning of Rome to the Lockerbie Crash. (Encyclopedia of Disasters Ser.). (Illus.). 320p. 1993. lib. bdg. 40.00 (*0-8160-2035-3*) Facts on File.
Davis, Lee E. Five Steps to Successful Money Management. LC 92-26089. (Orig.). 1993. pap. 6.99 (*0-8054-5356-3*, 4253-56) Broadman.
Davis, Leila. Lover Boy. 176p. 1989. pap. 2.95 (*0-380-75722-2*, Avon Bks) Morrow Avon.
Davis, Leith. Acts of Union: Scotland & the Literary Negotiation of the British Nation, 1707-1830. LC 98-35263. 1999. 39.50 (*0-8047-3269-8*) Stanford U Pr.
Davis, Lela, jt. auth. see Franklin, Rogayle.
Davis, Lennard J. Enforcing Normalcy: Disability, Deafness, & the Body. LC 95-31509. 224p. (C). 1995. pap. 19.00 (*1-85984-007-8*, Pub. by Verso) Norton.
— Factual Fictions: The Origins Of The English Novel. LC 96-38572. 264p. 1997. pap. text 16.50 (*0-8122-1610-5*) U of Pa Pr.
— Factual Fictions: The Origins of the English Novel. LC 82-12815. (Illus.). 255p. reprint ed. pap. 79.10 (*0-8357-6868-6*, 203556600095) Bks Demand.
***Davis, Lennard J.** My Sense of Silence: Memoirs of a Childhood with Deafness. LC 99-6618. (Creative Non-Fiction Ser.). (Illus.). 176p. 2000. 23.95 (*0-252-02533-4*) U of Ill Pr.
Davis, Lennard J. Resisting Novels: Ideology & Fiction. 248p. 1987. 39.50 (*0-416-37820-X*, 9097); pap. 13.95 (*0-416-37830-7*, 9098) Routledge.
Davis, Lennard J., ed. Disability Studies Reader. LC 96-30187. 464p. 1997. pap. 28.99 (*0-415-91471-X*) Routledge.
— Disability Studies Reader. LC 96-30187. 464p. (C). 1997. 90.00 (*0-415-91470-1*) Routledge.
— Shall I Say a Kiss? The Courtship Letters of a Deaf Couple, 1936-1938. LC 98-51831. (Illus.). 144p. 1999. 29.95 (*1-56368-076-9*) Gallaudet Univ Pr.
Davis, Lennard J. & Mirabella, M. Bella, eds. Left Politics & the Literary Profession. (Social Foundations of Aesthetic Forms Ser.). 320p. 1990. text 57.50 (*0-231-06566-3*) Col U Pr.
Davis Lenski, Susan, jt. auth. see Johns, Jerry L.
Davis, Lenwood. A Paul Robeson Handbook: Every. LC 98-152996. 358p. 1998. pap. 14.00 (*1-57502-780-1*, P02156) Morris Pubng.
Davis, Lenwood G. The Black Family in the United States: A Selected Bibliography of Annotated Books, Articles, & Dissertations on Black Families in America. LC 77-89109. 1978. lib. bdg. 35.00 (*0-8371-9851-8*, DBF/, Greenwood Pr) Greenwood.
— Black-Jewish Relations in the United States, 1752-1984: A Selected Bibliography, 1. LC 84-4685. (Bibliographies & Indexes in Afro-American & African Studies: No. 1). 130p. 1984. lib. bdg. 55.00 (*0-313-23329-2*, DBB/) Greenwood.
— Black Women in the Cities, Eighteen Seventy-Two to Nineteen Seventy-Five: A Bibliography of Published Works on the Life & Achievements of Black Women in Cities in the U. S., Nos. 751-752. 2nd ed. 1975. 7.50 (*0-686-20343-7*, Sage Prdcls Pr) Sage.
— Blacks in the American West: A Working Bibliography, No. 984. 2nd ed. 1976. 5.00 (*0-686-20388-7*, Sage Prdcls Pr) Sage.
— Blacks in the State of Ohio, 1800-1976: A Preliminary Survey, Nos. 1208-1209. 1977. 8.50 (*0-686-19690-2*, Sage Prdcls Pr) Sage.
— I Have a Dream: The Life & Times of Martin Luther King, Jr. LC 70-154202. 303p. 1973. reprint ed. lib. bdg. 45.00 (*0-8371-5977-6*, DHD&, Greenwood Pr) Greenwood.
— Sickle Cell Anemia: A Preliminary Survey, Nos. 1042-1043. 2nd ed. 1976. 9.50 (*0-686-20397-6*, Sage Prdcls Pr) Sage.
— Travel Guide to Black Historical Sites & Landmarks in North Carolina. LC 91-70215. (Illus.). 240p. (Orig.). 1991. pap. 9.95 (*1-878177-02-8*) Bandit Bks.
Davis, Lenwood G., compiled by. The Black Aged in the United States: A Selectively Annotated Bibliography, 23. LC 88-32359. (Bibliographies & Indexes in Afro-American & African Studies: No. 23). 251p. 1989. lib. bdg. 75.00 (*0-313-25931-3*, DVB/, Greenwood Pr) Greenwood.
— The Black Family in the United States, 14. rev. ed. LC 86-9926. (Bibliographies & Indexes in Afro-American & African Studies: No. 14). 244p. 1986. lib. bdg. 79.50 (*0-313-25237-8*, DFR/, Greenwood Pr) Greenwood.
— Blacks in the Cities, Nineteen Hundred to Nineteen Seventy Four: A Bibliography, Nos. 787-788. 2nd ed. 1975. 8.00 (*0-686-20353-4*, Sage Prdcls Pr) Sage.
— Daddy Grace: An Annotated Bibliography, 28. LC 91-42599. (Bibliographies & Indexes in Afro-American & African Studies: No. 28). 144p. 1992. lib. bdg. 55.00 (*0-313-26504-6*, DDG/, Greenwood Pr) Greenwood.
— Ecology of Blacks in the Inner City: An Exploratory Bibliography, Nos. 785-786. 1975. 8.00 (*0-686-20352-6*, Sage Prdcls Pr) Sage.
— The Ku Klux Klan: A Bibliography. LC 83-1709. 643p. 1984. lib. bdg. 85.00 (*0-313-22949-X*, DKK/, Greenwood Pr) Greenwood.
— A Paul Robeson Research Guide: A Selected Annotated Bibliography. LC 82-11680. 879p. 1982. lib. bdg. 59.95 (*0-313-22864-7*, DPR/, Greenwood Pr) Greenwood.
Davis, Lenwood G., ed. The Black Family in Urban Areas in the U. S., 1965-1974: A Bibliography of Published Works on the Black Family in Urban Areas in the U. S., Nos. 808-809. 2nd ed. 1975. 8.50 (*0-686-20354-2*, Sage Prdcls Pr) Sage.
— The Woman in American Society: A Selected Bibliography, Nos. 810-811. 2nd ed. 1975. 10.00 (*0-686-20355-0*, Sage Prdcls Pr) Sage.
Davis, Lenwood G. & Daniels, Belinda S., compiled by. Black Athletes in the United States: A Bibliography of Books, Articles, Autobiographies & Biographies on Black Professional Athletes in the United States, 1880 to 1981. LC 81-6334. 265p. 1981. lib. bdg. 65.00 (*0-313-22976-7*, DBL/) Greenwood.
Davis, Lenwood G. & Hill, George. A Bibliographical Guide to Black Studies Programs in the United States: An Annotated Bibliography, 6. LC 85-12722. (Bibliographies & Indexes in Afro-American & African Studies: No. 6). 120p. 1985. lib. bdg. 49.95 (*0-313-23328-4*, DBS/) Greenwood.
Davis, Lenwood G. & Moore, Marsha L., compiled by. Joe Louis: A Bibliography of Articles, Books, Pamphlets, Records, & Archival Materials. LC 83-1732. 232p. 1983. lib. bdg. 42.95 (*0-313-23327-6*, DAJ/, Greenwood Pr) Greenwood.
— Malcolm X: A Selected Bibliography. LC 83-18329. 146p. 1984. lib. bdg. 55.00 (*0-313-23061-7*, DAM/, Greenwood Pr) Greenwood.
Davis, Lenwood G. & Sims, Janet L. Black Artists in the United States: An Annotated Bibliography of Books, Articles, & Dissertations on Black Artists, 1779-1979. LC 79-8576. 138p. 1980. lib. bdg. 45.00 (*0-313-22082-4*, DBA/) Greenwood.
Davis, Lenwood G. & Sims, Janet L., compiled by. Marcus Garvey: An Annotated Bibliography. LC 80-653. 192p. 1980. lib. bdg. 49.95 (*0-313-22131-6*, DMG/, Greenwood Pr) Greenwood.
Davis, Lenwood G., et al. African Americans in Winston-Salem & Forsyth County: A Pictorial History. LC 99-33121. 1999. write for info. (*1-57864-067-9*) Donning Co.
Davis, Lenwood G., et al. Blacks in the American Armed Forces, 1776-1983: A Bibliography, 3. LC 84-15697. (Bibliographies & Indexes in Afro-American & African Studies: No. 3). 198p. 1985. lib. bdg. 62.95 (*0-313-24092-2*, DAV/) Greenwood.
Davis, Leo D. The First Seven Ecumenical Councils: Their History & Theology. LC 86-46356. (Theology & Life Ser.: Vol. 21). 400p. (C). 1987. pap. 19.95 (*0-8146-5616-1*, M Glazier) Liturgical Pr.
Davis, Leo D., tr. see Rahner, Hugo.
***Davis, Leonard.** Asian Journey. 210p. 2000. pap. 16.95 (*1-85756-491-X*, Pub. by Janus Pubng) Paul & Co Pubs.
Davis, Leonard. Children of the East: Childcare Policy & Practice in South East Asia. (Illus.). 72p. 1994. pap. 19.95 (*1-85756-171-6*, Pub. by Janus Pubng) Paul & Co Pubs.
— Hong Kong & the Asylum-Seekers from Vietnam. LC 91-21409. 272p. 1991. text 69.95 (*0-312-06763-1*) St Martin.
— Sex & the Social Worker. 112p. (Orig.). 1994. pap. 14.95 (*1-85756-069-8*, Pub. by Janus Pubng) Paul & Co Pubs.
Davis, Leonard G., et al. Basic Methods in Molecular Biology. 4th ed. (Illus.). 345p. (C). 1995. pap. 75.00 (*0-8385-0642-9*, A0642-7, Apple Lange Med) McGraw.
Davis, Leroy. A Clashing of the Soul: John Hope & the Dilemma of African American Leadership & Black Higher Education in the Early Twentieth Century. LC 97-42440. 448p. 1998. text 50.00 (*0-8203-1987-2*) U of Ga Pr.
Davis, Les. Risk, Vol. 1. LC 97-76976. 304p. 1997. pap. 12.95 (*1-56167-401-X*) Am Literary Pr.
Davis, Lesli I., jt. auth. see Sirotowitz, Sandi A.
Davis, Leslie. All about Alcohol: A Special Report for Young People. rev. ed. 1999. pap. 0.50 (*0-89230-125-2*) Do It Now.
Davis, Leslie, jt. auth. see Sirotowitz, Sandi.
Davis, Leslie A. The Slaughterhouse Province: An American Diplomat's Report on the Armenian Genocide of 1915-17. Blair, Susan K., ed. & intro. by. (Illus.). viii, 216p. 1989. 30.00 (*0-89241-458-8*) Caratzas.
***Davis, Leslie Dorfman.** Serapion Sister: The Poetry of Elizaveta Polonskaja. 2000. 85.00 (*0-8101-1579-4*) Northwestern U Pr.
Davis, Lester A., jt. auth. see McGuire, Sumiye O.
Davis, Liane V., ed. Building on Women's Strengths: A Social Work Agenda for the 21st Century. 338p. 1994. pap. 19.95 (*1-56024-863-7*) Haworth Pr.
— Building on Women's Strengths: A Social Work Agenda for the 21st Century. 338p. 1994. lib. bdg. 49.95 (*1-56024-862-9*) Haworth Pr.
***Davis, Lillie Frances Harrington.** The Letters of Kate Duncan Smith & John Harrington, 1894-1907. 112p. 2000. 22.00 (*0-937194-42-5*, Deepak Heritage Bks) A Deepak Pub.
***Davis, Linda.** Applied College Algebra & Trigonometry. 2nd ed. LC 98-52466. 779p. 1999. 88.00 (*0-13-083754-7*) P-H.
Davis, Linda. How to Be the Happy Wife of an Unsaved Husband. 153p. 1987. mass mkt. 5.99 (*0-88368-189-7*) Whitaker Hse.
— A Purim Story. (Illus.). (J). (ps-3). 1988. 9.95 (*0-87306-454-2*) Feldheim.
Davis, Linda, jt. auth. see Davis, Charles.
Davis, Linda, jt. auth. see Fabre, Jean-Henri.
Davis, Linda, ed. see Liboff, Richard L.
Davis, Linda H. Badge of Courage: The Life of Stephen Crane. LC 98-11870. 384p. 1998. 35.00 (*0-89919-934-8*) HM.
Davis, Linda L. & Davis, Terry M. Portable Gardens. (Illus.). 24p. 1999. pap. 14.95 (*0-9672536-0-8*, 100648) Lindas Creat Cents.
***Davis, Linda P.** Applied College Algebra & Trigonometry with Calculus. 2nd ed. (Illus.). 1152p. (C). 1999. pap. text 91.00 (*0-13-083755-5*) P-H.
Davis, Linda S., ed. see Petersen, Gwen.
Davis, Linda W. Weed Seeds of the Great Plains: A Handbook for Identification. LC 93-15615. (Illus.). 208p. 1993. 25.00 (*0-7006-0651-3*) U Pr of KS.
Davis, Lindsey. The Course of Honor. LC 98-13395. 336p. 1998. 21.50 (*0-89296-674-2*, Pub. by Mysterious Pr) Little.
— A Dying Light in Corduba. (Marcus Didius Falco Mystery Ser.). 436p. 1999. mass mkt. 6.99 (*0-446-60680-4*, Pub. by Warner Bks) Little.

D

An Asterisk (*) at the beginning of an entry indicates that the title is appearing for the first time.

— The Iron Hand of Mars. 1994. mass mkt. 5.99 (*0-345-38024-X*) Ballantine Pub Grp.

— Last Act in Palmyra. 432p. 1997. reprint ed. mass mkt. 6.50 (*0-446-40474-8*, Pub. by Warner Bks) Little.

***Davis, Lindsey.** One Virgin Too Many. 304p. 2000. 23.95 (*0-89296-716-1*) Mysterious Pr.

Davis, Lindsey. Poseidon's Gold. 1995. mass mkt. 5.99 (*0-345-38025-8*) Ballantine Pub Grp.

— Shadows in Bronze. 1992. mass mkt. 4.99 (*0-345-37426-6*) Ballantine Pub Grp.

— Silver Pigs. 256p. 1991. mass mkt. 4.99 (*0-345-36907-6*) Ballantine Pub Grp.

— Three Hands in the Fountain. LC 98-45058. (Marcus Didius Falco Mystery Ser.). 368p. 1999. 23.00 (*0-89296-691-2*, Pub. by Mysterious Pr) Little.

— Three Hands in the Fountain. 432p. 2000. mass mkt. 6.50 (*0-446-60774-6*, Pub. by Warner Bks) Little.

— Time to Depart: A Marcus Didius Falco Mystery Novel. 432p. 1998. pap. 6.50 (*0-446-40528-0*, Mysterious Paperbk); mass mkt. 6.99 (*0-446-60591-3*, Pub. by Warner Bks) Little.

— Time to Depart: A Marcus Didius Falco Mystery Novel. large type ed. LC 96-49065. 674p. 1997. 24.95 (*0-7862-0962-3*) Thorndike Pr.

— Two for the Lions. LC 99-19727. 400p. 1999. 23.95 (*0-89296-693-9*, Pub. by Mysterious Pr) Little.

***Davis, Lindsey.** Two for the Lions. 2000. mass mkt. 6.99 (*0-446-60902-1*) Warner Bks.

Davis, Lindsey. Venus in Copper. 1993. mass mkt. 4.50 (*0-345-37390-1*) Ballantine Pub Grp.

Davis, Lisa. Journeys Within: Source Book of Guided Meditations. (Guidebooks for Growth Together). 144p. (Orig.). 1995. pap. 10.95 (*1-899171-35-5*, Pub. by Findhorn Pr) Words Distrib.

***Davis, Lisa.** Managing Yourself. LC 99-204259. 96p. 1998. pap. text 44.95 (*0-7506-3661-0*) Buttrwrth-Heinemann.

Davis, Lisa. Shortcuts for Smart Managers: Checklists, Worksheets & Action Plans for Managers with No Time to Waste. LC 98-14987. 352p. 1998. 24.95 (*0-8144-0432-4*) AMACOM.

Davis, Lisa, ed. see Brennan, James A.

Davis, Lisa E. & Taran, Isabel C., eds. The Analysis of Hispanic Texts: Current Trends in Methodology. LC 76-45294. (Second York College Colloquium). 1976. pap. 20.00 (*0-916950-17-4*); lib. bdg. 30.00 (*0-916950-03-4*) Biling Rev-Pr.

***Davis, Lisa F.** The Gottschalk Antiphonary: Music & Liturgy in 12th Century Lambach. (Cambridge Studies in Palaeography & Codicology: No. 8). (Illus.). 368p. (C). 2000. 85.00 (*0-521-59249-6*) Cambridge U Pr.

Davis, Liz, jt. auth. see Cohen, Larry.

Davis, Llewellyn B. Going Home to School. rev. ed. 160p. (Orig.). 1991. pap. 12.95 (*1-884098-00-2*) Elijah Co.

Davis, Lloyd. Guise & Disguise: Rhetoric & Characterization in the English Renaissance. 224p. 1993. text 45.00 (*0-8020-2956-6*) U of Toronto Pr.

— Sexuality & Textuality in Henry James: Reading Through the Virginal. (Sexuality & Literature Ser.: Vol. 1). X, 230p. (C). 1989. text 37.50 (*0-8204-0599-X*) P Lang Pubng.

Davis, Lloyd, ed. Contemporary American Poetry: A Checklist. LC 85-11815. (Second Series, 1973-1983). 301p. 1985. 31.00 (*0-8108-1829-9*) Scarecrow.

— Sexuality & Gender in the English Renaissance: An Annotated Edition of Contemporary Documents. LC 97-29382. (Studies in the Renaissance: Vol. 10). 440p. 1998. text 90.00 (*0-8153-2452-9*, H2011) Garland.

— Virginal Sexuality & Textuality in Victorian Literature. LC 91-45286. (SUNY Series, The Body in Culture, History, & Religion). (Illus.). 257p. (C). 1992. pap. text 24.95 (*0-7914-1284-9*) State U NY Pr.

— Virginal Sexuality & Textuality in Victorian Literature. LC 91-45286. (SUNY Series, The Body in Culture, History, & Religion). (Illus.). 257p. (C). 1993. text 74.50 (*0-7914-1283-0*) State U NY Pr.

Davis, Lloyd & McKay, Susan. Structures & Strategies: An Introduction to Academic Writing. 237p. 1996. 59.95 (*0-7329-2929-6*, Pub. by Macmill Educ); pap. 29.95 (*0-7329-2930-X*, Pub. by Macmill Educ) Paul & Co Pubs.

Davis, Lloyd S. & Darby, John T., eds. Penguin Biology. 467p. 1990. text 94.00 (*0-12-206335-X*) Acad Pr.

Davis, Lola A. Towards a New World Religion. 256p. 1983. pap. 16.00 (*0-942494-77-6*) Coleman Pub.

Davis, Lon L., ed. see Buchanan, D. Kirk.

Davis-Long, Trudie & Eader, Edith O. The Jacob Engelbrecht Marriage Ledger of Frederick County, Maryland, 1820-1890. LC 94-67326. 269p. 1994. pap. 17.00 (*0-9642239-0-2*) Paw Prnts.

Davis-Long, Trudie, jt. auth. see Eader, Edith O.

Davis-Long, Trudie, jt. compiled by see Eader, Edith O.

Davis, Lora. Hiking Trails in the Collegiate Peaks Wilderness Area. LC 94-2898. (Illus.). 158p. 1994. pap. 16.95 (*0-87108-847-9*) Pruett.

Davis, Lora. Wyoming's Continental Divide Trail: The Official Guide. LC 98-50584. (Illus.). 304p. 2000. pap. 24.95 (*1-56579-332-3*) Westcliffe Pubs.

***Davis, Lori J.** Paint Shop Pro Solutions: Create, Edit & Prepare Your Graphics. (Solutions Ser.). (Illus.). 288p. 2000. pap. 29.95 (*1-929685-09-2*, Pub. by Muska Lipman) IPG Chicago.

Davis, Lorin R. Fundamentals of Environmental Discharge Modeling. LC 98-50541. (Mechanical Engineering Ser.). 352p. 1999. lib. bdg. 74.95 (*0-8493-9657-3*) CRC Pr.

— Paint Shop Pro Power! 416p. 1999. pap. 39.99 (*0-9662889-2-0*) Muska Lipman.

Davis, Lorraine G., jt. auth. see Donatelle, Rebecca J.

Davis, Lou E., jt. auth. see Carr, Audrey.

Davis, Louise. Special Poems for Special People. 1988. pap. 5.95 (*0-938645-08-0*) In His Steps.

Davis, Lucile. Alabama. LC 98-19621. (America the Beautiful Ser.). (Illus.). 144p. (YA). (gr. 4-10). 1999. lib. bdg. 32.00 (*0-516-20683-4*) Childrens.

— Cesar Chavez. Ferrer, Martin L., tr. from ENG. (Leer y Descubrir Ser.). (FRE.). 24p. (J). (gr. 3-5). 1998. lib. bdg. 15.93 (*1-56065-808-8*, Bridgestone Bks) Capstone Pr.

— Cesar Chavez. (Read-&-Discover Biographies Ser.). (Illus.). 24p. (J). (gr. k-3). 1997. lib. bdg. 13.75 (*0-516-20899-3*) Childrens.

— Charles Lindberg. LC 98-31473. (Photo-Illustrated Biographies Ser.). (Illus.). 1999. 14.00 (*0-7368-0204-5*, Bridgestone Bks) Capstone Pr.

— Charles Lindbergh. 1999. 14.00 (*0-516-21762-3*) Capstone Pr.

— Eleanor Roosevelt. (Read-&-Discover Biographies Ser.). (Illus.). 24p. (J). (gr. k-3). 1997. lib. bdg. 13.75 (*0-516-20902-7*) Childrens.

— Elizabeth Cady Stanton. (Read-&-Discover Biographies Ser.). (J). 1998. 14.00 (*0-516-21271-0*, Bridgestone Bks) Capstone Pr.

***Davis, Lucile.** Florence Nightingale. LC 98-46009. (J). 1999. 19.00 (*0-7368-0205-3*) Capstone PC.

Davis, Lucile. Florence Nightingale. 1999. 14.00 (*0-516-21763-1*) Capstone Pr.

— Ghana. LC 98-3486. (Countries of the World Ser.). (J). 1998. 10.35 (*0-7368-0069-7*, Bridgestone Bks) Capstone Pr.

— Ghana. (Countries of the World Ser.). (J). 1998. 14.00 (*0-516-21351-2*) Childrens.

— Lucretia Mott. (Read-&-Discover Biographies Ser.). (J). 1998. 14.00 (*0-516-21272-9*, Bridgestone Bks) Capstone Pr.

— Malcolm X. (Read-&-Discover Biographies Ser.). (Illus.). 24p. (J). (gr. k-3). 1997. lib. bdg. 13.75 (*0-516-20901-9*) Childrens.

— Mayo Brothers: Doctors to the World. LC 97-35783. (Community Builders Ser.). (J). 1998. 23.00 (*0-516-20965-5*) Childrens.

— The Mayo Brothers: Doctors to the World. (Community Builders Ser.). (Illus.). 48p. (J). (gr. 3-5). 1999. pap. text 6.95 (*0-516-26347-1*) Childrens.

— The Philippines. LC 98-3487. (Countries of the World Ser.). (J). 1998. 14.00 (*0-7368-0071-9*) Bridgeview.

— Philippines. (Countries of the World Ser.). (J). 1998. 14.00 (*0-516-21352-0*) Childrens.

***Davis, Lucile.** Puerto Rico LC 99-26988. (J). 2000. 32.00 (*0-516-21042-4*) Childrens.

— R. J. Reynolds: He Saw the Future. LC 99-59780. (Community Builders Ser.). (J). 2000. write for info. (*0-516-21600-7*) Childrens.

Davis, Lucile. Read & Discover Photo-Illustrated Biographies Complete Set of 22. (Read & Discover Photo-Illustrated Biography Ser.). 1999. pap. text 308.00 (*1-56065-822-3*) Capstone Pr.

— South Korea. (Countries of the World Ser.). (J). 1998. 14.00 (*0-516-21353-9*) Childrens.

***Davis, Lucile.** South Korea: Countries of the World. LC 98-15910. (Countries of the World Ser.). (Illus.). 1999. 15.93 (*0-7368-0070-0*, Bridgestone Bks) Capstone Pr.

Davis, Lucile. Susan B. Anthony. (Read-&-Discover Biographies Ser.). (J). 1998. 14.00 (*0-516-21273-7*, Bridgestone Bks) Capstone Pr.

— Susan B. Anthony: A Photo-Illustrated Biography. LC 97-41651. (Read & Discover Photo-Illustrated Biographies Ser.). 24p. (J). 1998. lib. bdg. 13.75 (*1-56065-750-2*) Capstone Pr.

Davis, Luise. Handbook of Constructed Wetlands in the Mid-Atlantic Region: General Considerations. 54p. 1995. pap. 4.25 (*0-16-052999-9*) USGPO.

Davis, Lydia. Almost No Memory. LC 96-48091. 160p. 1997. text 21.00 (*0-374-10281-3*) FS&G.

— Almost No Memory. LC 97-44249. 208p. 1998. reprint ed. pap. 14.95 (*0-88001-606-X*) HarpC.

— Break It Down. (Illus.). 196p. 1996. pap. 12.99 (*1-85242-421-4*) Serpents Tail.

— The End of the Story. LC 94-14361. 192p. (Orig.). 1995. 20.00 (*0-374-14831-7*) FS&G.

— The End of the Story. (High Risk Bks.). (Illus.). 231p. (Orig.). 1996. 12.99 (*1-85242-420-6*) Serpents Tail.

— Sketches for a Life of Wassily. 32p. 1981. pap. 6.50 (*0-930794-45-1*) Station Hill Pr.

Davis, Lydia, jt. auth. see Jouve, Pierre J.

Davis, Lydia, tr. see Blanchot, Maurice.

Davis, Lydia, tr. see Butor, Michel.

Davis, Lydia, tr. see Giroud, Francoise.

Davis, Lydia, tr. see Hocquard, Emmanuel.

Davis, Lydia, tr. see Jardin, Andre.

Davis, Lydia, tr. see Jouve, Pierre J.

Davis, Lydia, tr. see Leiris, Michel.

Davis, Lydia, tr. see Levy, Justine.

***Davis, Lynn.** Bitter Road. (Mage Ser.). 2000. pap. 17.95 (*1-56504-407-X*) White Wolf.

Davis, Lynn. Bodywork. (Illus.). 120p. 1995. 45.00 (*3-905514-37-0*) Dist Art Pubs.

— On Location III. (Aperture Ser.: Vol. 146). 1997. pap. text 27.95 (*0-89381-697-3*) Aperture.

— Personal Ads, Why Not? Meehan, Trudy, ed. LC 83-60285. (Illus.). 128p. 1983. pap. 9.95 incl. audio (*0-9610742-0-5*) Purcell Prods.

Davis, Lynn & Woodcock, Lindsay. Initiates of the Art. (Mage Ser.). (Illus.). 88p. 1999. pap. 13.95 (*1-56504-437-1*, 4253) White Wolf.

Davis, Lynn A. & Foster, Nelson. A Photographer in the Kingdom: Christian J. Hedemann's Early Images of Hawai'i. 1988. 25.00 (*0-930897-36-6*) Bishop Mus.

Davis, Lynn D., et al. Innovative Materials Development & Testing, Vol. 1: Project Overview. 45p. (C). 1993. pap. text 10.00 (*0-309-05609-8*, SHRP-H-352) SHRP.

Davis, Lynn E. Peacekeeping & Peacemaking after the Cold War. LC 93-24111. 1993. pap. 15.00 (*0-8330-1410-2*, MR-281-RC) Rand Corp.

Davis, Lynn M. Bed & Breakfast & Unique Inns of Virginia: A Pictorial Guide. 3rd ed. LC 88-72026. (Illus.). 116p. (Orig.). 1996. pap. 19.95 (*0-9620996-7-8*) Crystal Springs.

Davis, Lynne, jt. compiled by see Touchon, Judith G.

Davis, M. The Art of Decision-Making. (Illus.). viii, 92p. 1985. 52.95 (*0-387-96228-X*) Spr-Verlag.

***Davis, M.** 1998 Rehabilitation Services Administration Consumer Satisfaction Survey. 102p. 1998. pap. write for info. (*1-888557-91-5*) No Ariz Univ.

Davis, M., et al, eds. Drug Reactions & the Liver. 300p. (C). 1981. pap. 69.00 (*0-8464-1220-9*) Beekman Pubs.

***Davis, M. & Meaney, F. J.** 1998 Rehabilitation Services Administration Consumer Satisfaction Survey. 1998. write for info. (*1-888557-90-7*) No Ariz Univ.

Davis, M., jt. auth. see Cleland, J.

Davis, M. Edward & Meilach, Dona Z. Doctor Discusses Menopause & Estrogens. (Illus.). 1994. pap. 6.00 (*0-910304-26-2*) Budlong.

Davis, M. H., ed. Applied Stochastic Analysis, Vol. 5. (Stochastics Monographs). ix, 572p. 1991. text 278.00 (*2-88124-716-4*) Gordon & Breach.

Davis, M. I., jt. ed. see Brumfitt, J. H.

Davis, M. Jane, ed. Security Issues in the Post-Cold War World. LC 95-39638. 256p. 1996. 90.00 (*1-85898-334-7*) E Elgar.

Davis, M. K. Ingram: Descendants of Winifred Nelms & Joseph Ingram, of Virginia & North Carolina. 39p. 1994. reprint ed. pap. 8.00 (*0-8328-4138-2*) Higginson Bk Co.

Davis, Mackenzie L. Introduction to Environmental Engineering. 2nd ed. (C). 1991. text 96.50 (*0-07-015911-4*) McGraw.

Davis, MacKenzie L., et al. Introduction to Environmental Engineering. 3rd ed. LC 97-21847. (Series in Water Resources & Environmental Engineering). 750p. (C). 1997. text 91.50 (*0-07-015918-1*) McGraw.

Davis, Madeleine & Wallbridge, David. Boundary & Space: An Introduction to the Work of D. W. Winnicott. LC 90-48118. 240p. 1991. pap. 23.95 (*0-87630-641-5*) Brunner-Mazel.

Davis, Madeline D., jt. auth. see Kennedy, Elizabeth L.

Davis, Maggie. The Far Side of Home. 314p. 1992. reprint ed. 21.95 (*1-881454-00-2*); reprint ed. pap. 10.95 (*1-881454-01-0*) Amer Hist Bks.

Davis, Maggie S. Choices of a Growing Woman. LC 81-1083. 144p. 1993. pap. 10.00 (*0-9638813-1-0*) Heartsong Bks.

— A Garden of Whales. LC 92-34411. (Illus.). 32p. (J). (ps-2). 1993. pap. 6.95 (*0-944475-35-3*); text 16.95 (*0-944475-36-1*) Firefly Bks Ltd.

— Glory! to the Flowers: A Celebration. LC 94-74465. (Illus.). 32p. (Orig.). (J). (gr. k-3). 1995. pap. 10.00 (*0-9638813-2-9*) Heartsong Bks.

— Roots of Peace, Seeds of Hope: A Journey for Peacemakers. LC 93-80449. (Illus.). 60p. (J). 1993. pap. 10.00 (*0-9638813-0-2*) Heartsong Bks.

Davis, Malcolm. How to Make Low-Cost Building Blocks: Stabilized Soil Block Technology. (Illus.). 36p. 1993. pap. 12.00 (*1-85339-086-0*, Pub. by Intermed Tech) Stylus Pub VA.

Davis-Manigaulte, Jacqueline, et al. Clothing Connections. (Four-H Ser.). (Illus.). 44p. (J). (gr. 6-12). 1982. pap. 3.75 (*1-57753-193-0*, 329L-22-7) Corn Coop Ext.

Davis Many Voices Staff. Turtle Going Nowhere in the Plenty of Time: Native American Tales from the South- & Midwest/& Maria Posa (Healing Wings) (Illus.). 48p. (Orig.). (J). (gr. 4 up). 1996. pap. 7.95 (*0-87961-244-4*) Naturegraph.

Davis, Marc. Cleveland Indians Facts & Trivia. (Illus.). 160p. 1997. pap. 12.99 (*0-938313-25-8*) E B Houchin.

— Detroit Lions Facts & Trivia. (Illus.). 160p. 1996. pap. 9.99 (*0-938313-19-3*) E B Houchin.

Davis, Marcia Szmania, jt. ed. see Youngkin, Ellis Quinn.

Davis, Margaret. Balcony, Terrace & Patio Gardens. LC 95-48079. (Illus.). 160p. (Orig.). 1997. pap. 17.95 (*1-55591-256-7*) Fulcrum Pub.

— Retire to Your Garden. (Illus.). 80p. 1998. pap. 14.95 (*0-86417-846-8*, Pub. by Kangaroo Pr) Seven Hills Bk.

— What Shall I Do to Inherit Life? 2nd rev. ed. (Illus.). 224p. 1997. pap. 5.95 (*0-923309-40-3*) Hartland Pubns.

Davis, Margaret L. Bullocks Wilshire. LC 95-80640. (Illus.). 120p. (Orig.). 1996. pap. 17.95 (*0-9643119-4-1*) Balcony Pr.

Davis, Margaret Leslie. The Dark Side of Fortune: Triumph & Scandal in the Life of Oil Tycoon Edward L. Doheny. LC 98-7240. (Illus.). 440p. 1998. 35.00 (*0-520-20292-9*, Pub. by U CA Pr) Cal Prin Full Svc.

Davis, Margaret R. Families in a Working World: The Impact of Organizations on the Domestic Life. Steinmetz, Suzanne K., ed. LC 82-446. (Praeger Studies on Changing Issues in the Family). 235p. 1982. 55.00 (*0-275-90779-1*, C0779, Praeger Pubs) Greenwood.

Davis, Margaret R. & Weckler, David A. Organization Design: A Practical Guide. Paris, Janis, ed. LC 95-83228. 151p. (Orig.). 1996. pap. 12.95 (*1-56052-388-3*) Crisp Pubns.

Davis, Margaret T. The Breadmakers Saga. 591p. 1993. pap. 18.95 (*1-873631-27-8*, Pub. by B&W Pub) Firebird Dist.

— Burning Ambition. 256p. 1998. pap. 13.95 (*1-873631-81-2*, Pub. by B&W Pub) Firebird Dist.

— The Dark Side of Pleasure. 278p. 1995. pap. 13.95 (*1-873631-50-2*, Pub. by B&W Pub) Firebird Dist.

— Light & Dark. 452p. 1994. pap. 16.95 (*1-873631-43-X*, Pub. by B&W Pub) Firebird Dist.

— A Sense of Belonging. large type ed. 578p. 1995. 27.99 (*0-7505-0676-8*) Ulverscroft.

— A Woman of Proper. large type ed. (Magna Large Print Ser.). 1994. 27.99 (*0-7505-0613-X*, Pub. by Mgna Lrg Print) Ulverscroft.

Davis, Marge. Sportsmen United: The Story of the Tennessee Conservation League. LC 96-79647. (Illus.). xvi, 354p. (Orig.). 1997. pap. 12.95 (*0-9654561-8-8*) Bench Top Bks.

***Davis, Margie.** The Healing Way: A Journal for Cancer Survivors. 2000. 19.95 (*1-86204-696-4*, Pub. by Element MA) Penguin Putnam.

Davis, Margo & Nilan, Roxanne. The Stanford Album: A Photographic History, 1885-1945. (Illus.). 320p. 1989. 24.95 (*0-8047-1639-0*) Stanford U Pr.

Davis, Marian. Visual Design in Dress. 3rd ed. 386p. (C). 1996. 77.00 (*0-13-112129-4*) P-H.

Davis, Marianna W. Transformational Grammar & Written Sentences. (Janua Linguarum, Series Didactica: No. 2). 1973. pap. text 33.85 (*90-279-2384-1*) Mouton.

Davis, Marianna W., ed. Contributions of Black Women to America. LC 94-25944. 1995. write for info. (*0-8204-2411-0*); pap. write for info. (*0-8204-2641-5*) P Lang Pubng.

Davis, Marianna W. & Graham, Maryemma, eds. Teaching African American Literature: Theory & Practice. (Transforming Teaching Ser.). 256p. (C). 1998. pap. 19.99 (*0-415-91696-8*) Routledge.

— Teaching African American Literature: Theory & Practice. (Transforming Teaching Ser.). 256p. (C). 1998. 70.00 (*0-415-91695-X*) Routledge.

Davis, Marianne, jt. ed. see Davis, Richard.

Davis, Marie. The Lactation Consultant's Clinical Practice Manual. (Illus.). x, 320p. 1998. ring bd. 145.00 (*0-9668111-0-0*) Bright Future.

Davis, Marietta. Caught up into Heaven. LC 99-28209. 185p. 1999. pap. 6.99 (*0-88368-575-2*) Whitaker Hse.

— Scenes Beyond the Grave. Lindsay, Gordon, ed. 1961. per. 4.95 (*0-89985-091-X*) Christ for the Nations.

Davis, Marilyn C. Ohio's Statehouse Is Intriguing! (Illus.). 132p. (Orig.). 1997. pap. 12.95 (*0-9659338-0-6*) M C Davis.

Davis, Marilyn E., ed. & illus. see Benefield, Laurance.

Davis, Marilyn P. Mexican Voices - American Dreams: An Oral History of Mexican Immigration to the United States. LC 90-31640. 464p. 1995. 29.95 (*0-8050-1216-8*); pap. 15.95 (*0-8050-1859-X*, Owl) H Holt & Co.

Davis, Marion. The Magical Lore of Herbs. 1994. pap. 22.95 (*1-898307-14-8*, Pub. by Capall Bann Pubng) Holmes Pub.

Davis, Marjorie McKenzie, see McKenzie Davis, Marjorie.

Davis, Mark. Social Psychology, 98-99. 2nd ed. (Annual Ser.). (Illus.). 240p. 1998. pap. text 12.25 (*0-07-292509-4*, Dshkn McG-Hill) McGrw-H Hghr Educ.

Davis, Mark & Petheram, Harry. Fundamentals of Operations Management. 3rd ed. LC 98-40391. 608p. (C). 1998. text 61.50 (*0-256-22557-5*, Irwn McGrw-H) McGrw-H Hghr Educ.

Davis, Mark, jt. auth. see Aldrich, Gary W.

Davis, Mark D., jt. auth. see Baker, Stewart A.

Davis, Mark E. & Suib, Steven L., eds. Selectivity in Catalysis. LC 92-42872. (Symposium Ser.: No. 517). 406p. 1993. text 110.00 (*0-8412-2519-2*, Pub. by Am Chemical) OUP.

Davis, Mark H. Empathy: A Social Psychological Approach. LC 96-422. (Social Psychology Ser.). (C). 1996. pap. 24.00 (*0-8133-3001-7*, Pub. by Westview) HarpC.

— Markov Models & Optimization. LC 92-39557. 296p. (gr. 13). 1993. ring bd. 78.95 (*0-412-31410-X*, Chap & Hall CRC) CRC Pr.

— Social Psychology, '97-'98. annuals (Annual Ser.). (Illus.). 256p. (C). 1996. pap. text 12.25 (*0-697-35425-3*, Dshkn McG-Hill) McGrw-H Hghr Educ.

— Stochastic Control & Nonlinear Filtering. (Tata Institute Lectures on Mathematics). iv, 109p. 1984. 27.95 (*0-387-13343-7*) Spr-Verlag.

Davis, Mark H., et al, eds. Mathematical Finance. LC 94-44431. (IMA Volumes in Mathematics & Its Applications Ser.: Vol. 65). 1996. 59.95 (*0-387-94439-7*) Spr-Verlag.

Davis, Mark H. & Vinter, Richard. Stochastic Modelling & Control. (Monographs on Statistics & Applied Probability). 350p. (C). 1985. 42.50 (*0-412-16200-8*, 6874) Chapman & Hall.

Davis, Mark M. A T-Cell Primer. (Illus.). 208p. (C). Date not set. text 34.95 (*0-19-509337-2*); pap. text 29.95 (*0-19-509338-0*) OUP.

Davis, Mark S. Grantsmanship for Criminology & Criminal Justice. LC 99-6109. 1999. write for info. (*0-7619-1129-4*) Sage.

Davis, Mark W. & Streufert, Randall K. Gold Occurrences of Colorado. (Resource Ser.: No. 28). (Illus.). 101p. (Orig.). 1990. pap. 14.00 (*1-884216-33-1*) Colo Geol Survey.

Davis, Marsha & Moran, Judy Flagg. Precalculus: Concepts in Context Lab Book. 2nd ed. LC 97-43190. 1998. mass mkt. 34.95 (*0-534-35232-4*) Brooks-Cole.

Davis, Marsha, et al. Precalculus in Context: Functioning in the Real World. (C). 1992. mass mkt. 22.25 (*0-534-19788-4*) PWS Pubs.

Davis, Martha. Assertiveness Training. abr. ed. (Messages Tapes Ser.). 1987. 11.95 incl. audio (*0-934986-36-3*, 17) New Harbinger.

— Leader's Guide to the Relaxation & Stress Reduction Workbook. 4th rev. ed. 104p. 1995. pap. 20.95 (*1-57224-036-9*) New Harbinger.

— Methods of Perceiving Patterns of Small Group Behavior. LC 78-322618. (Illus.). 88p. 1977. pap. text 14.95 (*0-932582-11-7*) Dance Notation.

D

An Asterisk (*) at the beginning of an entry indicates that the title is appearing for the first time.

— Scientific Papers & Presentations. LC 96-28241. (Illus.). 296p. 1996. pap. text 24.95 (*0-12-206370-8*) Morgan Kaufmann.

— Towards Understanding the Intrinsic in Body Movement. LC 74-7857. (Body Movement Perspectives in Research Ser.). (Illus.). 192p. 1980. 34.95 (*0-405-06200-1*) Ayer.

— Understanding Body Movement: An Annotated Bibliography. LC 73-37652. 1676p. 1979. 23.95 (*0-405-00286-6*) Ayer.

Davis, Martha, ed. Anthropological Perspectives of Movement: An Original Anthology. LC 74-9162. (Body Movement Perspectives in Research Ser.). (Illus.). 203p. 1975. reprint ed. text 28.95 (*0-405-06201-X*) Ayer.

— Body Movement: Perspectives in Research, 10 vols. (Illus.). 1975. 84.00 (*0-405-06197-8*) Ayer.

— Interaction Rhythms: Periodicity in Communicative Behavior. LC 81-2936. 372p. 1982. 45.95 (*0-89885-003-7*, Kluwer Acad Hman Sci) Kluwer Academic.

— Psychoanalytic Perspectives of Movement: An Original Anthology. LC 74-9161. (Body Movement Perspectives in Research Ser.). 164p. 1975. reprint ed. 33.95 (*0-405-06199-4*) Ayer.

— Recognition of Facial Expression: An Original Anthology. LC 74-9160. (Body Movement Perspectives in Research Ser.). 252p. 1975. reprint ed. 35.95 (*0-405-06198-6*) Ayer.

Davis, Martha, et al. The Relaxation & Stress Reduction Workbook. 288p. 1995. reprint ed. 9.98 (*1-56731-075-3*, MJF Bks) Fine Comms.

— The Relaxation & Stress Reduction Workbook. 4th ed. LC 94-68249. (Illus.). 276p. 1995. pap. 18.95 (*1-879237-82-2*) New Harbinger.

— The Relaxation & Stress Reduction Workbook. 4th ed. (Illus.). 276p. 1997. reprint ed. pap. text 18.00 (*0-7881-5075-8*) DIANE Pub.

***Davis, Martha, et al.** The Relaxation & Stress Reduction Workbook. 5th ed. 300p. 2000. pap., wbk. ed. 19.95 (*1-57224-214-0*, Pub. by New Harbinger) Publishers Group.

Davis, Martha F. Brutal Need: Law, Lawyers, & the Welfare Rights Movement, 1960-1973. LC 93-1313. 224p. 1993. 35.00 (*0-300-05378-9*) Yale U Pr.

— Brutal Need: Lawyers & the Welfare Rights Movement, 1960-1973. (C). 1995. pap. 13.00 (*0-300-06424-1*) Yale U Pr.

Davis, Martha M. Sarah's Seasons: An Amish Diary & Conversation. LC 97-10556. (Bur Oak Original Ser.). (Illus.). 196p. 1997. 22.95 (*0-87745-596-1*) U of Iowa Pr.

***Davis, Martha Moore.** Sarah's Seasons: An Amish Diary & Conversation. LC 97-10556. (Illus.). 196p. 2000. reprint ed. pap. 11.95 (*0-87745-742-5*) U of Iowa Pr.

Davis, Martha S., jt. auth. see Childress, Steven A.

Davis, Martha S., jt. auth. see Childress, Steven Alan.

***Davis, Martin.** Astrolocality Astrology: A Guide to What It Is & How to Use It. 1999. pap. 20.00 (*1-902405-05-6*) Wessex Astrologer.

Davis, Martin. Bobby Jones: Flicker Book. (Illus.). 74p. 1996. pap. 10.00 (*1-888531-02-9*) Amer Golfer.

— Computability & Unsolvability. (Mathematics Ser.). 288p. 1985. reprint ed. pap. 8.95 (*0-486-61471-9*) Dover.

— A First Course in Functional Analysis. (Notes on Mathematics & Its Applications Ser.). xii, 110p. (Orig.). 1966. pap. text 112.00 (*0-677-01155-5*) Gordon & Breach.

— Greatest of Them All: The Legend of Bobby Jones. 1996. 60.00 (*1-888531-00-2*) Amer Golfer.

***Davis, Martin.** Universal Computer: The Road from Leibniz to Turing. 2000. 25.95 (*0-393-04785-7*) Norton.

Davis, Martin, ed. Solvability, Provability, Definability: The Collected Works of Emil L. Post. LC 93-9347. (Contemporary Mathematicians Ser.). 1993. 109.00 (*0-8176-3579-3*) Spr-Verlag.

— The Undecidable: Basic Papers on Undecidable Propositions, Unsolvable Problems & Computable Functions. LC 65-3996. 446p. 1965. text 64.00 (*0-911216-01-4*) Lppncott W & W.

Davis, Martin & Oughton, David W. Sourcebook on Contract Law. (Sourcebook Ser.). 700p. 1996. pap. 40.00 (*1-85941-048-0*, Pub. by Cavendish Pubng) Gaunt.

Davis, Martin D., et al. Computability, Complexity & Languages: Fundamentals of Theoretical Computer Science. 2nd ed. LC 93-26807. (Computer Science & Scientific Computing Ser.). (Illus.). 609p. 1994. text 52.00 (*0-12-206382-1*) Acad Pr.

Davis, Martyn. Successful Advertising: Key Alternative Approaches. 141p. 1997. 79.50 (*0-304-70096-7*) Continuum.

Davis, Martyn, ed. see Davis Caves Construction, Inc. Staff.

Davis, Marvin. Rank & Rivalry: The Politics of Inequality in Rural West Bengal. LC 82-9747. (Cambridge Studies in Cultural Systems: No. 7). 249p. reprint ed. pap. 71.00 (*0-608-15710-4*, 2031638) Bks Demand.

***Davis, Mary.** Newlywed Games. LC 99-89172. 384p. 2000. mass mkt. 6.99 (*1-57673-268-1*, Pub. by Multnomah Pubs) GL Services.

Davis, Mary. Pet Owner's Guide to the Shetland Sheepdog. (Pet Owner's Guide Ser.). (Illus.). 80p. 1997. 8.00 (*0-948955-24-4*, Pub. by Ringpr Bks) Seven Hills Bk.

— Spur-of-the-Moment Crafts. LC 96-84995. (Illus.). 96p. 1996. 9.99 (*0-89636-327-9*) Accent CO.

— Spur-of-the-Moment Games & Learning Activities. LC 96-84990. 80p. 1996. 9.99 (*0-89636-328-7*) Accent CO.

— Sylvia Pankhurst. LC 99-26258. 1999. write for info. (*0-7453-1523-2*, Pub. by Pluto GBR) LPC InBook.

***Davis, Mary.** Sylvia Pankhurst: A Life in Radical Politics. 160p. 1999. pap. 18.95 (*0-7453-1518-6*, Pub. by Pluto GBR) Stylus Pub VA.

Davis, Mary A. Easy to Knit Doll Socks. (Illus.). 32p. (Orig.). 1995. pap. 6.95 (*0-916809-82-X*) Scott Pubns MI.

Davis, Mary-Ann, jt. auth. see Michelson, Carmen.

Davis, Mary B. Old Growth in the East: A Survey. Davis, John, ed. (Illus.). 150p. (Orig.). 1993. spiral bd. 20.00 (*0-9638402-0-7*) Cenozoic Soc.

Davis, Mary B., ed. Native America in the Twentieth Century: An Encyclopedia. LC 94-768. (Illus.). 832p. 1994. text 100.00 (*0-8240-4846-6*, 452) Garland.

— Native America in the Twentieth Century: An Encyclopedia. LC 94-768. (Illus.). 832p. 1996. pap. text 29.95 (*0-8153-2583-5*) Garland.

Davis, Mary Byrd, ed. Eastern Old-Growth Forests: Prospects for Rediscovery & Recovery. (Illus.). 420p. 1996. pap. text 29.95 (*1-55963-409-X*) Island Pr.

Davis, Mary D. Going off the Beaten Path: An Untraditional Travel Guide. 2nd rev. ed. LC 90-63428. 488p. 1991. pap. 15.95 (*1-879360-01-2*) Noble Pr.

Davis, Mary E. Elephant's Track & Other Stories. LC 78-94714. (Short Story Index Reprint Ser.). 1977. 21.95 (*0-8369-3093-2*) Ayer.

***Davis, Mary J.** My Answer Journal: What Kids Wonder about God & the Bible. 136p. (J). (gr. 4). 1999. pap. 9.99 (*1-885358-72-5*, Lgacy Pr) Rainbow CA.

— My Bible Journal: A Journey Through the Word for Kids. 152p. (J). 1999. pap. 9.99 (*1-885358-70-9*, Lgacy Pr) Rainbow CA.

Davis, Mary J. My Prayer Journal: A Keepsake for Kids Who Love the Lord. 144p. (J). (gr. 4-7). pap. 9.99 (*1-885358-37-7*, LP46841, Lgacy Pr) Rainbow CA.

***Davis, Mary J.** My Wisdom Journal: A Discovering of Proverbs for Kids. 160p. (J). 1999. pap. 9.99 (*1-885358-73-3*, Lgacy Pr) Rainbow CA.

Davis, Mary J., jt. auth. see Legacy Press Staff.

Davis, Mary J., jt. auth. see Owen, David G.

Davis, Mary K. Nat Turner Before the Bar of Judgment: Fictional Treatments of the Southampton Slave Insurrection. LC 98-24707. (Southern Literary Studies). 272p. 1999. text 30.00 (*0-8071-2249-1*) La State U Pr.

Davis, Mary L. Working in Law & Justice. LC 97-42864. (Exploring Careers Ser.). 112p. (YA). (gr. 6-8). 1999. 23.93 (*0-8225-1766-3*, Lerner Publctns) Lerner Pub.

Davis, Mary L. & Pack, Greta. Mexican Jewelry. (Illus.). 278p. 1963. pap. 19.95 (*0-292-75073-0*) U of Tex Pr.

Davis, Mary O. Metanoia: A Transformational Journey. LC 84-71551. 154p. 1984. pap. 7.95 (*0-87516-544-3*) DeVorss.

***Davis, Maryann & Vander Stoep, Ann.** The Transition to Adulthood among Adolescents Who Have Serious Emotional Disturbance. (Illus.). 90p. (C). 2000. reprint ed. pap. text 20.00 (*0-7881-8616-7*) DIANE Pub.

Davis, Maryann, jt. auth. see Clark, Hewitt B.

Davis, Matt. The Baizel Berry Bread. LC 97-5681. (Illus.). 52p. (YA). (gr. 3 up). 1997. 15.00 (*1-890110-14-0*) Cobblestone Ent.

— The Baizel Berry Bread. deluxe rev. ed. LC 97-5681. (Illus.). 56p. (J). (gr. k up). 1998. 15.00 (*1-890110-19-1*, SAN 299-1942) Cobblestone Ent.

Davis, Matthew L. Memoirs of Aaron Burr, with Miscellaneous Selections from His Correspondence, 2 Vols, Set. (Select Bibliographies Reprint Ser.). 1977. 55.95 (*0-8369-5213-8*) Ayer.

***Davis, Maurice W.** An Illustrated Anthology of Lore & Legends of the Klamath River Indians. 2000. 14.95 (*0-87961-258-4*) Naturegraph.

***Davis, Max.** Flat Tires in the Rain: Stepping Through Life's Puddles & Wading Through Its Floods with Power & Grace. LC 00-32840. 2001. write for info. (*0-399-14692-X*) Putnam Pub Group.

Davis, Max. Never Stick Your Tongue Out at Mama & Other Life Transforming Revelations. 160p. 1995. pap. 12.50 (*0-9648462-0-9*) Enhance Pub.

Davis, May H. No Ordinary Clam Book: A Cook Book. LC 83-62033. (Illus.). 103p. 1983. pap. 6.95 (*0-9616663-0-7*) Megan Pubns.

Davis, Meg. Avidly Perplexed. (Illus.). 48p. (Orig.). 1994. pap. 9.95 (*0-933313-22-5*) SUN Gemini Pr.

Davis, Megan A., jt. auth. see Rinear, Sheila L.

Davis, Mel. ALPHanauts. 182p. 1985. 7.25 (*0-89697-246-1*) Intl Univ Pr.

***Davis, Mel & Veranth, John.** High Uinta Trails. LC 99-15804. 1999. pap. text 12.95 (*0-87480-632-1*) U of Utah Pr.

Davis, Mel & Veranth, John. High Uinta Trails: A Hiking & Backpacking Guide to the High Uintas Wilderness. rev. ed. (Illus.). 160p. 1993. reprint ed. pap. 7.50 (*0-915272-37-7*) Wasatch Pubs.

Davis, Mel, ed. see Mitchell, Finis.

***Davis, Melba.** Lion House Desserts. LC 99-86125. (Illus.). 2000. write for info. (*1-57345-550-4*) Deseret Bk.

Davis, Melba, compiled by. Lion House Lite Recipes. LC 95-51135. (Illus.). vii, 160p. 1996. 19.95 (*0-87579-904-3*) Deseret Bk.

Davis, Melba & Lion House Staff. Lion House International Recipes. LC 97-8704. (Illus.). 134p. 1997. 19.95 (*1-57345-245-9*) Deseret Bk.

Davis, Melinda D. Winslow Homer: An Annotated Bibliography of Periodical Literature. LC 75-29243. 138p. 1975. 21.00 (*0-8108-0876-5*) Scarecrow.

Davis, Melissa, ed. see Fueroghne, Dean K.

Davis, Melodie M. Departure. LC 90-32027. 200p. (Orig.). 1991. pap. 7.99 (*0-8361-3549-0*) Herald Pr.

— Why Didn't I Just Raise Radishes? Finding God in the Everyday. LC 93-31064. 176p. (Orig.). 1994. pap. 9.99 (*0-8361-3659-4*) Herald Pr.

— You Know You're a Mother When . . . 112p. 1987. pap. 4.95 (*0-310-44811-5*, 12478P) Zondervan.

***Davis, Melodie M., compiled by.** 366 Ways to Peace: Perpetual Peace Calendar. 384p. 1999. spiral bd. 12.99 (*0-8361-9113-7*) Herald Pr.

Davis, Melody D. The Male Nude in Contemporary Photography. (Visual Studies). (Illus.). 184p. 1991. 59.95 (*0-87722-839-6*) Temple U Pr.

— The Male Nude in Contemporary Photography. (Visual Studies). (Illus.). 184p. (C). 1994. pap. 24.95 (*1-56639-198-9*) Temple U Pr.

Davis, Melvin C. Toning & Tinting Made Easy. (Illus.). 76p. 1996. pap. text 35.00 (*1-874031-24-X*, Pub. by Hove Foto) Watsn-Guptill.

Davis, Meredith. Up & Away! Taking a Flight. LC 96-44026. (Illus.). 24p. (J). (gr. 2-4). 1997. pap. 4.95 (*1-57255-214-X*) Mondo Pubng.

Davis, Meredith, et al. Design As a Catalyst for Learning. LC 97-43361. 147p. 1998. pap. 34.95 (*0-87120-284-0*, 197022) ASCD.

Davis, Michael. Ancient Tragedy & the Origins of Modern Science. LC 87-21275. (Philosophical Explorations Ser.). 193p. (C). 1988. text 21.95 (*0-8093-1390-1*) S Ill U Pr.

— The Autobiography of Philosophy: Roussea's "The Reveries of the Solitary Walker" LC 98-38402. 296p. 1998. 60.00 (*0-8476-9226-4*); pap. 24.95 (*0-8476-9227-2*) Rowman.

— Ethics in the University. LC 98-27141. (Professional Ethics Ser.). 1999. 80.00 (*0-415-18097-X*); pap. 25.99 (*0-415-18098-8*) Routledge.

— The Flower Princess. (Illus.). 32p. (J). (gr. k-12). 1989. write for info. (*0-318-65119-X*) R Bane Ltd.

— Justice in the Shadow of Death: Rethinking Capital & Lesser Punishments. 288p. 1996. pap. text 23.95 (*0-8476-8270-6*); lib. bdg. 62.50 (*0-8476-8269-2*) Rowman.

— The Poetry of Philosophy: On Aristotle's Poetics. LC 99-21188. 203p. 1999. reprint ed. pap. 19.00 (*1-890318-62-0*) St Augustines Pr.

— The Politics of Philosophy: A Commentary on Aristotle's Politics. LC 95-48150. 176p. (C). 1996. pap. text 24.95 (*0-8476-8206-4*); lib. bdg. 57.50 (*0-8476-8205-5*) Rowman.

— Thinking Like an Engineer: Studies in the Ethics of a Profession. (Practical & Professional Ethics Ser.). 256p. 1998. text 49.95 (*0-19-512051-5*) OUP.

— Upon Waking. (Premier Ser.: Vol. 8). (Illus.). 21p. 1997. pap. 5.00 (*0-9654421-6-0*) Mica Press.

Davis, Michael, ed. Human Rights & Chinese Values: Legal, Philosophical & Political Perspectives. 226p. 1995. pap. 21.00 (*0-19-586782-3*) OUP.

Davis, Michael & Elliston, Frederick A., eds. Ethics & the Legal Profession. LC 86-61919. 495p. 1986. pap. 25.95 (*0-87975-331-5*) Prometheus Bks.

Davis, Michael & Snider, Clare J. The Ford Fleet, 1923-1989. LC 94-61026. 221p. (C). 1994. 23.00 (*0-912514-54-X*) Freshwater.

Davis, Michael, et al. Manuals that Work: A Guide for Writers. rev. ed. 128p. 1990. pap. 27.50 (*0-89397-353-X*) Nichols Pub.

Davis, Michael, jt. auth. see Hopper, Christopher.

Davis, Michael, ed. see Benardete, Seth, et al.

Davis, Michael, jt. ed. see Cohen, Elliot D.

Davis, Michael C. Constitutional Confrontation in Hong Kong: Issues & Implications of the Basic Law. LC 89-24264. 204p. 1990. text 59.95 (*0-312-04074-1*) St Martin.

Davis, Michael C., et al. Confidential U. S. State Department Central Files: Internal Affairs, 1930-1939. LC 87-10387. 88 p. 1987. write for info. (*0-89093-886-5*) U Pubns Amer.

Davis, Michael D. Black American Women in Olympic Track & Field: A Complete Illustrated Reference. LC 91-50946. 188p. 1992. lib. bdg. 29.95 (*0-89950-692-5*) McFarland & Co.

Davis, Michael D. & Clark, Hunter R. Thurgood Marshall: Warrior at the Bar, Rebel on the Bench. (Illus.). 304p. 1992. 22.00 (*1-55972-133-2*, Birch Ln Pr) Carol Pub Group.

— Thurgood Marshall: Warrior at the Bar, Rebel on the Bench. LC 93-44236. 1994. pap. 16.95 (*0-8065-1494-9*, Citadel Pr) Carol Pub Group.

— Thurgood Marshall: Warrior at the Bar, Rebel on the Bench. 442p. 1999. reprint ed. 39.95 (*0-7351-0097-7*) Replica Bks.

Davis, Michael D. & Kilgo, Jennifer L. Young Children with Special Needs: A Developmentally Appropriate Approach. LC 97-44676. 270p. 1998. pap. text 40.00 (*0-205-18894-X*) Allyn.

Davis, Michael D., et al. Young Children with Special Needs: A Developmentally Appropriate Approach. 64p. (C). 1998. pap. text, teacher ed. write for info. (*0-205-28533-3*, T8533-6) Allyn.

Davis, Michael H. Business Law in Egypt. 350p. 1983. 123.00 (*90-6544-086-0*) Kluwer Law Intl.

Davis, Michael I. Electron Diffraction in Gases. LC 77-157833. (Illus.). 191p. reprint ed. pap. 59.30 (*0-7837-0929-3*, 204123400019) Bks Demand.

Davis, Michael L. & Hayes, Kathy J. Efficiency & Inefficiency in the Texas Public Schools. 1990. pap. 10.00 (*0-943802-53-9*, 150) Natl Ctr Pol.

Davis, Michael M. Paying Your Sickness Bills. LC 77-180572. (Medicine & Society in America Ser.). 292p. 1972. reprint ed. 21.95 (*0-405-03947-6*) Ayer.

Davis, Michael M., Jr. & Warner, Andrew R. Dispensaries, Their Management & Development: A Book for Administrators, Public Health Workers. Rosenkrantz, Barbara G., ed. LC 76-25658. (Public Health in America Ser.). (Illus.). 1977. reprint ed. lib. bdg. 36.95 (*0-405-09813-8*) Ayer.

Davis, Michael T., jt. auth. see Thomis, Malcolm I.

Davis, Michael W. Computerizing Healthcare Records: Developing Electronic Patient & Medical Records. 200p. (C). 1994. text 60.00 (*1-55738-609-9*, Irwn Prfssnl) McGraw-Hill Prof.

Davis, Michael W., jt. auth. see Schweitzer, Robert.

Davis, Michaela A. Beloved Baby: A Baby's Scrapbook & Journal. Chernoff, Dona, ed. (Illus.). 64p. 1995. 18.00 (*0-671-52269-8*, PB Hardcover) PB.

Davis, Micheal H., jt. auth. see Miller, Arthur R.

Davis, Mick. Sopwith Aircraft. (Illus.). 192p. 1999. 44.95 (*1-86126-217-5*, 128159AE) Motorbooks Intl.

Davis, Mick, jt. auth. see Revell, Alex.

Davis, Mike. Beyond Bladerunner: Urban Control, the Ecology of Fear. (Open Magazine Pamphlet Ser.: No. 23). 21p. 1994. 4.00 (*1-884519-00-8*) Open Media.

— Burning Our Illusions Tonight. 1999. pap. write for info. (*0-8050-5107-4*) H Holt & Co.

— City of Quartz: Excavating the Future in Los Angeles. 1992. pap. 15.00 (*0-679-73806-1*) Vin Bks.

— City of Quartz: Excavating the Future of Los Angeles. 384p. (gr. 13). 1990. 30.00 (*0-86091-303-1*, A4994, Pub. by Verso) Norton.

— Ecology of Fear: Los Angeles & the Imagination of Disaster. LC 98-2645. (Illus.). 484p. 1998. 27.50 (*0-8050-5106-6*, Metropol Bks) H Holt & Co.

— Ecology of Fear: Los Angeles & the Imagination of Disaster. LC 98-50270. (Illus.). 496p. 1999. pap. 14.00 (*0-375-70607-0*) Vin Bks.

***Davis, Mike.** General Motors: A Photographic History. (Images of America Ser.). (Illus.). 128p. 1999. pap. 18.99 (*0-7385-0019-4*) Arcadia Publng.

— Late Victorian Holocausts: El Nino Famines & the Making of the Third World. 2000. 27.00 (*1-85984-739-0*, Pub. by Verso) Norton.

— Magical Urbanism: Latinos Reinvent the U. S. Big City. 128p. 2000. 19.00 (*1-85984-771-4*, Pub. by Verso) Norton.

Davis, Mike. 9 to 5 Beats Ten to Life: How to (Re)Enter Society. LC 96-152602. 125p. 1996. 12.00 (*1-56991-041-3*) Am Correctional.

— 99 Surefire Ways to Stay Unemployed. LC 98-5796. (Illus.). 144p. 1998. pap. 12.95 (*1-880090-53-8*) Galde Pr.

***Davis, Mike.** Prisoners of the American Dream: Politics & Economy in the History of the U. S. Working Class. 2000. pap. 20.00 (*1-85984-248-8*) Norton.

Davis, Mike. Prisoners of the American Dream: Politics & Economy in the History of the U. S. Working Class. (Haymarket Ser.). 320p. (C). 1986. pap. 20.00 (*0-86091-840-8*, Pub. by Verso) Norton.

***Davis, Mike.** Sunshine & Noir: Art in L.A., 1960-1997. 1998. 49.95 (*87-90029-19-4*) Louisana.

Davis, Mike & Tell, David, eds. The Technology Century: 100 Years of ESD - The Engineering Society 1895-1995. (Illus.). 262p. 1995. text 25.00 (*1-56378-022-4*) ESD.

Davis, Mike, et al. Urban Revisions: Current Projects for the Public Realm. (Illus.). 195p. 1994. pap. text 29.95 (*0-262-69173-6*) MIT Pr.

Davis, Mildred. Child in My Heart. 1998. pap. 4.95 (*0-9652894-8-6*) GA Publng.

Davis, Miles. Miles: The Autobiography. 448p. 1990. per. 14.00 (*0-671-72582-3*) S&S Trade.

Davis, Miles & Troupe, Quincy. Miles: The Autobiography, Set. unabridged ed. 1995. 15.95 incl. audio (*0-944993-62-1*) Audio Lit.

Davis, Miles A. History of Jerusalem. (Illus.). 103p. 1997. reprint ed. pap. 17.50 (*0-8328-6159-6*); reprint ed. lib. bdg. 27.50 (*0-8328-6158-8*) Higginson Bk Co.

Davis, Millard C. Natural Pathways of New Jersey. LC 98-106742. (Illus.). 272p. (Orig.). 1997. pap. 19.95 (*0-937548-35-9*) Plexus Pub.

Davis, Mitchell. Cook Something. LC 97-3158. (Illus.). 256p. 1997. 19.95 (*0-02-861255-8*) Macmillan.

Davis, Mitchell, jt. auth. see Ginor, Michael.

***Davis, Mitchell P., ed.** Yearbook of Experts, Authorities & Spokespersons: An Encyclopedia of Sources. 17th rev. ed. 880p. 1998. pap. 39.95 (*0-934333-33-5*) Broadcast Inter.

Davis, Mollie E. Under the Man-Fig. 1993. lib. bdg. 75.00 (*0-7812-5873-1*) Rprt Serv.

***Davis, Mollie Evelyn Moore.** Under the Man-Fig. Grider, Sylvia A., ed. LC 99-57287. 323p. 2000. reprint ed. pap. 15.95 (*0-87565-222-0*, Pub. by Tex Christian) Tex A&M Univ Pr.

Davis, Molly. Letters to Our Daughters: Mothers' Words of Love. LC 99-18779. (Illus.). 144p. 1999. 18.00 (*0-7868-6528-8*, Pub. by Disney Pr) Time Warner.

Davis, Molly E. Guidelines for Personal Safety Risk Management: A Manual for Social Work Practicum Students. 3rd ed. 40p. (C). 1995. reprint ed. pap. text 10.00 (*0-9660108-2-5*) I H C Bks.

Davis, Monica. On the Receiving End: A Collection of Works for Realizing the Potential Within Ourselves. LC 97-71575. 144p. (Orig.). 1997. pap. 11.95 (*1-56167-357-9*) Am Literary Pr.

Davis, Morgan, jt. auth. see Stout, Rick.

Davis, Morris. Interpreters for Nigeria: The Third World & International Public Relations. LC 77-2345. 208p. 1977. text 24.95 (*0-252-00552-X*) U of Ill Pr.

— Interpreters for Nigeria: The Third World & International Public Relations. fac. ed. LC 77-2345. 207p. 1994. pap. 64.20 (*0-7837-7620-9*, 204737200007) Bks Demand.

Davis, Morton D. Game Theory: A Nontechnical Introduction. LC 97-16147. 272p. 1997. reprint ed. pap. text 8.95 (*0-486-29672-5*) Dover.

Davis, Moshe. America & the Holy Land Series, 72 vols. (Illus.). 1977. reprint ed. lib. bdg. 2212.50 (*0-405-10220-8*) Ayer.

— With Eyes Toward Zion No. 4: America & the Holy Land, IV. LC 94-28005. 208p. 1995. 59.95 (*0-275-94621-5*, Praeger Pubs) Greenwood.

Davis, Moshe, ed. Call to America to Build Zion: An Original Anthology. LC 77-70723. (America & the Holy Land Ser.). 1977. lib. bdg. 23.95 (*0-405-10306-9*) Ayer.

D

An Asterisk (*) at the beginning of an entry indicates that the title is appearing for the first time.

— Christian Protagonists for Jewish Restoration: An Original Anthology. LC 77-70678. (America & the Holy Land Ser.). 1977. lib. bdg. 23.95 (0-405-10221-6) Ayer.
— Holy Land Missions & Missionaries: An Original Anthology. LC 77-70703. (America & the Holy Land Ser.). (Illus.). 1977. lib. bdg. 23.95 (0-405-10259-3) Ayer.
— Israel: Its Role in Civilization. LC 77-70673. (America & the Holy Land Ser.). 1977. reprint ed. lib. bdg. 34.95 (0-405-10241-0) Ayer.
— The Jerusalem Mission: Under the Direction of the American Christian Missionary Society. (America & the Holy Land Ser.). 1977. reprint ed. lib. bdg. 29.95 (0-405-10233-X) Ayer.
— Pioneer Settlement in the Twenties: An Original Anthology. LC 77-70699. (America & the Holy Land Ser.). 1977. lib. bdg. 23.95 (0-405-10250-X) Ayer.
— Teaching Jewish Civilization: A Global Approach to Higher Education. 400p. (C). 1995. pap. text 20.00 (0-8147-1867-1) NYU Pr.
— Teaching Jewish Civilization: A Global Approach to Higher Education. 400p. (C). 1995. text 50.00 (0-8147-1866-3) NYU Pr.
— With Eyes Toward Zion: Scholars Colloquium on America-Holy Land Studies. LC 77-2493. (America & the Holy Land Ser.). (Illus.). 1977. lib. bdg. 23.95 (0-405-10312-3) Ayer.
— With Eyes Toward Zion No. 2: Themes & Sources in the Archives of the United States, Breat Britain, Turkey & Israel, 2. LC 85-28288. (Illus.). 434p. 1986. 59.95 (0-275-92090-9, C2090, Praeger Pubs) Greenwood.
— World Jewry & the State of Israel. LC 77-72730. (Individual Publications). 1976. lib. bdg. 15.95 (0-405-10305-0) Ayer.
— The Yom Kippur War: Israel & the Jewish People. LC 74-10466. 381p. 1975. 13.95 (0-405-06192-7) Ayer.
— Zionism in Transition. LC 80-67905. 1980. lib. bdg. 23.95 (0-405-13825-3) Ayer.
— Zionism in Transition. 1980. pap. 8.00 (0-930832-61-2) Herzl Pr.

Davis, Moshe & Hovav, Meir, eds. The Living Testify. Kohn, Moshe, tr. (Illus.). 120p. (Orig.). 1994. pap. text 16.95 (965-229-105-6, Pub. by Gefen Pub Hse) Gefen Bks.

Davis, Moshe & Yehoshua, Ben-Arieh, eds. Eyes Toward Zion Vol. 3: Western Societies & the Holy Land, 3. LC 90-14310. 296p. 1991. 69.50 (0-275-93793-3, C3793, Praeger Pubs) Greenwood.

Davis, Moshe, ed. see Adler, Cyrus & Margalith, Aaron M.
Davis, Moshe, ed. see Alvan, Bond.
Davis, Moshe, ed. see Babcock, Maltbie D.
Davis, Moshe, ed. see Badt-Strauss, Bertha.
Davis, Moshe, ed. see Barclay, James T.
Davis, Moshe, ed. see Bartlett, Samuel C.
Davis, Moshe, jt. ed. see Ben-Arieh, Yehoshua.
Davis, Moshe, ed. see Bliss, Frederick J.
Davis, Moshe, ed. see Bloomgarden, Yehoash.
Davis, Moshe, ed. see Browne, John R.
Davis, Moshe, ed. see Cox, Samuel S.
Davis, Moshe, ed. see Cresson, Warder.
Davis, Moshe, ed. see Crossman, Richard H.
Davis, Moshe, ed. see De Hass, Frank S.
Davis, Moshe, ed. see Field, Frank M.
Davis, Moshe, ed. see Fosdick, Harry E.
Davis, Moshe, ed. see Fulton, John.
Davis, Moshe, ed. see Gilmore, Albert F.
Davis, Moshe, ed. see Gordon, Benjamin L.
Davis, Moshe, ed. see Holmes, John H.
Davis, Moshe, ed. see Hoofien, Sigfried.
Davis, Moshe, ed. see Intercollegiate Zionist Association of America Sta.
Davis, Moshe, ed. see Isaacs, Samuel H.
Davis, Moshe, ed. see Israel, John & Lundt, Henry.
Davis, Moshe, ed. see Johnson, Sarah B.
Davis, Moshe, ed. see Kallen, Horace M.
Davis, Moshe, ed. see Krimsky, Joseph.
Davis, Moshe, ed. see Kyle, Melvin G.
Davis, Moshe, ed. see Lipsky, Louis.
Davis, Moshe, ed. see Lynch, William F.
Davis, Moshe, ed. see Macalister, Robert A.
Davis, Moshe, ed. see McCrackan, William D.
Davis, Moshe, ed. see Merrill, Selah.
Davis, Moshe, ed. see Miller, Ellen C.
Davis, Moshe, ed. see Minor, Clorinda.
Davis, Moshe, ed. see Morris, Robert.
Davis, Moshe, ed. see Morton, Daniel O.
Davis, Moshe, ed. see Odenheimer, William H.
Davis, Moshe, ed. see Olin, Stephen.
Davis, Moshe, ed. see Palmer, Edward H.
Davis, Moshe, ed. see Paton, Lewis B.
Davis, Moshe, ed. see Prime, William C.
Davis, Moshe, ed. see Rifkind, Simon H., et al.
Davis, Moshe, ed. see Rix, Herbert.
Davis, Moshe, ed. see Robinson, Edward.
Davis, Moshe, jt. ed. see Salo, Baron W. & Baron, Jennette M.
Davis, Moshe, ed. see Schaff, Philip.
Davis, Moshe, ed. see Smith, Ethan.
Davis, Moshe, ed. see Smith, George A., et al.
Davis, Moshe, ed. see Sneersohn, Haym Z.
Davis, Moshe, ed. see Szold, Henrietta.
Davis, Moshe, ed. see Talmage, Thomas.
Davis, Moshe, ed. see Taylor, Bayard.
Davis, Moshe, ed. see Thompson, George, et al.
Davis, Moshe, ed. see Van Dyke, Henry.
Davis, Moshe, ed. see Vester, Bertha H.
Davis, Moshe, ed. see Wallace, Edwin S.
Davis, Moshe, ed. see Ware, William.
Davis, Moshe, ed. see Worsley, Israel.
Davis, Moya, jt. auth. see Owen, Diane.

Davis, Muller. Illinois Practice of Family Law. LC 95-60038. xlvi, 1075 p. 1995. write for info. (0-314-05967-9) West Pub.

Davis, Muriel. Practical Illustrations of Bible Truths: Ideas for Children, Youth & Adults. LC 89-4006. 80p. 1989. pap. 5.99 (0-87227-131-5, RBP5161) Reg Baptist.

Davis, Murray S. Smut: Erotic Reality-Obscene Ideology. LC 82-16061. 342p. (C). 1998. pap. 17.95 (0-226-13792-9) U Ch Pr.
— What's So Funny? The Comic Conception of Culture & Society. LC 93-10217. (Illus.). 400p. 1993. 29.95 (0-226-13810-0) U Ch Pr.

Davis, Murt, jt. auth. see Allen, Clifford G., Jr.
Davis Museum & Cultural Center Staff, ed. see Acton, David, et al.
Davis, Nadine A., ed. see LCC-ST Staff.

Davis, Nanciellen. Ethnicity & Ethnic Group Persistence in an Acadian Village in Maritime Canada. LC 83-45352. (Immigrant Communities & Ethnic Minorities in the U. S. & Canada Ser.: No. 4). (Illus.). 1985. 38.50 (0-404-19405-2) AMS Pr.

***Davis, Nancy.** Bridal Style. (Illus.). 252p. 1999. 40.00 (0-88363-477-5) H L Levin.

Davis, Nancy. Bridal Style: Concise Edition. 1997. 24.50 (0-88363-597-6) H L Levin.
— Handle with Care: Preserving Your Heirlooms. (Illus.). 31p. 1991. pap. 2.95 (0-938551-02-7) Rochester Mus & Sci Ctr.

***Davis, Nancy.** Stories That Teach & Heal: Therapeutic Stories for Parents & Educators to Use with Children. (Illus.). 2001. pap. 26.95 (1-885473-36-2) Wood N Barnes.

***Davis, Nancy, ed.** Pojo's Unofficial Big Book of Pokeman: The Ultimate Player & Collector's Guide. (Pokemon Ser.). 2000. pap. 19.95 (1-57243-361-2) Triumph Bks.

Davis, Nancy & Hart, Kathy. Coastal Carolina Cooking. LC 85-22265. (Illus.). xvii, 179p. 1986. pap. 15.95 (0-8078-4152-8) U of NC Pr.

Davis, Nancy & Marcey, Marcella. Therapeutic Stories That Teach & Heal. (Illus.). 604p. 1996. pap. 69.00 (0-9653088-1-2, 002) Nancy Davis.

Davis, Nancy, et al. Therapeutic Stories to Heal Abused Children. rev. ed. (Illus.). 516p. 1988. ring bd. 59.00 (0-9653088-0-4, 001) Nancy Davis.

Davis, Nancy, ed. see Blatner, David.
Davis, Nancy, ed. see Castro, Elizabeth.
Davis, Nancy, ed. see Dalin, Anne.
Davis, Nancy, ed. see Davis, Phyllis & Craig, Deborah.
Davis, Nancy, ed. see Henderson, Chuck.
Davis, Nancy, ed. see Hester, Nolan.
Davis, Nancy, ed. see Langer, Maria.
Davis, Nancy, ed. see Williams, Robin.

Davis, Nancy D., et al, eds. Lesbian Therapists & Their Therapy: From Both Sides of the Couch. LC 96-13471. (Women & Therapy Ser.: Vol. 18, No. 2). 80p. 1996. pap. 9.95 (1-56023-082-7, Harrington Park) Haworth Pr.
— Lesbian Therapists & Their Therapy: From Both Sides of the Couch. LC 96-13471. (Women & Therapy Ser.: Vol. 18, No. 2). 80p. 1996. 39.95 (1-56024-800-9, Haworth Pastrl) Haworth Pr.

Davis, Nancy M. Eskimos. (Davis Teaching Units Ser.: Vol. 2, No. 11). (Illus.). 32p. (Orig.). (J). (ps-5). 1986. pap. 4.95 (0-937103-06-3) DaNa Pubns.

Davis, Nancy M. & Moon, Teresa S. Indians. (Davis Teaching Units Ser.: Vol. 2, No. 1). (Illus.). 33p. (Orig.). (J). (ps-5). 1986. pap. 4.95 (0-937103-03-9) DaNa Pubns.

Davis, Nancy M., et al. April & Easter. (Davis Teaching Units Ser.: Vol. 1, No. 8). (Illus.). 45p. (Orig.). (J). (ps-2). 1986. pap. 5.95 (0-937103-10-1) DaNa Pubns.
— Colors. (Davis Teaching Units Ser.: Vol. 2, No. 6). (Illus.). (Orig.). (J). (ps-2). 1986. pap. 4.95 (0-937103-13-6) DaNa Pubns.
— Fall & September. (Davis Teaching Units Ser.: Vol. 1, No. 1). (Illus.). 25p. (Orig.). 1986. pap. 4.95 (0-937103-00-4) DaNa Pubns.
— February & Valentines. (Davis Teaching Units Ser.: Vol. 1, No. 6). (Illus.). 29p. (Orig.). (J). (ps-2). 1986. pap. 4.95 (0-937103-07-1) DaNa Pubns.
— November & Thanksgiving. (Davis Teaching Units Ser.: Vol. 1, No. 3). (Illus.). 31p. (Orig.). (J). (ps-2). 1986. pap. 4.95 (0-937103-02-0) DaNa Pubns.
— Numbers. (Davis Teaching Units Ser.: Vol. 2, No. 5). (Illus.). 26p. (Orig.). (J). (ps-2). 1986. pap. 4.95 (0-937103-14-4) DaNa Pubns.

Davis, Nancy M, et al. October & Halloween. (Davis Teaching Units Ser.: Vol. 1, No. 2). (Illus.). 28p. (Orig.). (J). (ps-4). 1986. pap. 4.95 (0-937103-01-2) DaNa Pubns.

Davis, Nancy M., et al. Patriotism. (Davis Teaching Units Ser.: Vol. 2, No. 12). (Illus.). 34p. (Orig.). (J). (ps-5). 1986. pap. 4.95 (0-937103-19-5) DaNa Pubns.
— St. Patrick's. (Davis Teaching Units Ser.: Vol. 1, No. 7). (Illus.). 29p. (Orig.). (J). (ps-4). 1986. pap. 4.95 (0-937103-08-X) DaNa Pubns.
— Spring & May. (Davis Teaching Units Ser.: Vol. 1, No. 9). (Illus.). 46p. (Orig.). (J). (ps-4). 1986. pap. 5.95 (0-937103-11-X) DaNa Pubns.
— Winter. (Davis Teaching Units Ser.: Vol. 1, No. 5). (Illus.). 29p. (J). (ps-2). 1986. pap. 4.95 (0-937103-05-5) DaNa Pubns.

Davis, Nancy Y. The Zuni Enigma. LC 99-38955. (Illus.). 352p. 2000. text 26.95 (0-393-04788-1) Norton.

Davis, Nancy Y. & Davis, William E., eds. Adventures Through Time: Readings in Anthropology of Cook Inlet, Alaska: Proceedings of a Symposium. LC 96-85078. (Illus.). 284p. (Orig.). (C). 1996. pap. text 39.95 (1-878462-02-4) Cook Inlet Hist Soc.

Davis, Nanette J. From Crime to Choice: The Transformation of Abortion in America, 60. LC 85-8018. (Contributions in Women's Studies: No. 60). (Illus.). 290p. 1985. 55.00 (0-313-24929-6, DCC/, Greenwood Pr) Greenwood.
— Youth Crisis: Growing up in the High-Risk Society. LC 98-24558. 392p. 1999. 69.50 (0-275-95939-2, Praeger Pubs) Greenwood.
— Youth Crisis: Growing Up in the High-Risk Society. LC 98-24558. 392p. 1999. pap. 29.95 (0-275-96443-4, Praeger Pubs) Greenwood.

Davis, Nanette J., ed. Prostitution: An International Handbook on Trends, Problems, & Policies. LC 92-27880. 424p. 1993. lib. bdg. 89.50 (0-313-25754-X, DIR/, Greenwood Pr) Greenwood.

Davis, Nanette J. & Anderson, Bo. Social Control: The Production of Deviance in the Modern State. LC 83-136. 364p. 1983. text 22.95 (0-8290-0727-X) Irvington.
— Social Control: The Production of Deviance in the Modern State. LC 83-136. 364p. (C). 1986. reprint ed. pap. text 14.95 (0-8290-2010-1) Irvington.

Davis, Nanette J. & Stasz, C. Social Control of Deviance. 2nd ed. 384p. (C). 1990. 41.88 (0-07-015930-0) McGraw.

Davis, Natalie Z. Fiction in the Archives: Pardon Tales & Their Tellers in Sixteenth-Century France. LC 87-17951. (Illus.). 240p. 1987. pap. 13.95 (0-8047-1799-0) Stanford U Pr.
— The Return of Martin Guerre. (Illus.). 176p. 1983. 33.95 (0-674-76690-3) HUP.
— The Return of Martin Guerre. LC 83-277. (Illus.). 176p. 1993. pap. text 13.50 (0-674-76691-1) HUP.
— Society & Culture in Early Modern France: Eight Essays by Natalie Zemon Davis. LC 74-82777. (Illus.). xx, 364p. 1975. 49.50 (0-8047-0868-1); pap. 17.95 (0-8047-0972-6) Stanford U Pr.
— Women on the Margins: Three Seventeenth-Century Lives. LC 97-13765. (Illus.). 360p. (C). 1995. 24.95 (0-674-95520-X) Belknap Pr.

***Davis, Natalie Zemon.** The Gift in Sixteenth-Century France. LC 00-8913. 2000. pap. write for info. (0-299-16884-0) U of Wis Pr.
— The Gift in Sixteenth-Century France. 2000. 50.00 (0-299-16880-8) U of Wis Pr.
— Slaves on Screen. 180p. 2000. pap. write for info. (0-679-31023-1) Random.
— Slaves on Screen: Film & Historical Vision. LC 00-39687. (Illus.). 176p. 2000. 22.95 (0-674-00444-2) HUP.

Davis, Natalie Zemon. Women on the Margins: Three Seventeenth-Century Lives. (Illus.). 400p. 1997. text 16.00 (0-674-95521-8) HUP.

Davis, Nathan. Carthage & Her Remains. 680p. 1985. 300.00 (1-85077-033-6, Pub. by Darf Pubs Ltd) St Mut.
— Jazz Photo Album. 224p. (C). 1995. pap. text 28.95 (0-7872-1760-3) Kendall-Hunt.
— Writings in Jazz. 5th ed. 288p. (C). 1996. per. 29.95 (0-7872-1895-2, 41189501) Kendall-Hunt.

Davis, Nathan T. African American Music: A Philosophical Look at African American Music in Society. LC 96-140416. 176p. (C). 1995. pap. text 31.20 (0-536-58496-6, ML3556) Pearson Custom.

Davis, Nathaniel. Long Walk to Church: A Contemperary History of Russian Orthodoxy. (C). 1994. pap. 32.00 (0-8133-2277-4, Pub. by Westview) HarpC.

Davis, Nathaniel, ed. Afro-American Reference: An Annotated Bibliography of Selected Resources, 9. LC 85-21942. (Bibliographies & Indexes in Afro-American & African Studies: No. 9). 288p. 1985. lib. bdg. 85.00 (0-313-24930-X, DRS/) Greenwood.

***Davis, Neal.** Motorcycle Journeys Through Northern Mexico. (Motorcycle Journeys Ser.). (Illus.). 221p. 1999. pap. 19.95 (1-884313-20-5, MJNM) Whitehorse NH.

Davis, Neil. Alaska Science Nuggets. LC 82-80679. (Illus.). 233p. (Orig.). 1989. pap. 14.95 (0-912006-38-2) U of Alaska Pr.
— Battling Against Success. (Illus.). 259p. 1997. 26.95 (0-9632596-7-9); pap. 16.95 (0-9632596-6-0) McRoy & Blackburn.
— Caught in the Sluice: Tales from Alaska's Gold Camps. (Illus.). 169p. 1994. 19.95 (0-9632596-2-8); pap. 13.95 (0-9632596-1-X) McRoy & Blackburn.
— The College Hill Chronicles: How the University of Alaska Came of Age. LC 93-16969. 1993. 30.00 (1-883309-01-8) U AK Fnd.

***Davis, Neil M.** Medical Abbreviations: 14,000 Conveniences at the Expense of Communications & Safety. 9th rev. ed. LC 98-93615. (Illus.). 11p. 1999. pap. 17.95 (0-931431-09-3) N M Davis.

***Davis, Nick.** Cuckoos, Cowbirds & Other Cheats. 333p. 2000. 29.95 (0-85661-135-2) Acad Pr.

Davis, Nick. Stories of Chaos: Reason & Its Displacement in Early Modern English Narrative. LC 98-23107. (Illus.). 17p. 1998. text 67.95 (1-84014-649-4, Pub. by Ashgate Pub) Ashgate Pub Co.

Davis, Nigel, jt. auth. see Meinhardt, Peter.
Davis, Niki, jt. auth. see Somekh, Bridget.

Davis, Nina C. Autobiography As Burla in the Guzman de Alfarache. LC 91-55272. 160p. 1991. 29.50 (0-8387-5221-7) Bucknell U Pr.

Davis, Nolan. Ain't Got Time to Die. 320p. (Orig.). 1993. mass mkt. 3.95 (0-87067-395-5) Holloway.

Davis, Norah D., jt. auth. see McNerney, Colleen.
Davis, Norah D., ed. see Roca, Roberto, et al.

Davis, Norbert. The Adventures of Max Latin. 272p. 1988. 8.95 (0-89296-932-6) Mysterious Pr.

***Davis, Norma.** Just Before Sunset. 2000. 17.00 (0-8059-5046-X) Dorrance.

Davis, Norma, tr. see Kempowski, Walter.

Davis, Norma S. A Lark Ascends: Florence Kate Upton, Artist & Illustrator. LC 91-38840. (Illus.). 240p. 1992. 34.50 (0-8108-2511-2) Scarecrow.

***Davis, Norma S.** A Song of Joys: The Biography of Mahonri Mackintosh Young: Sculptor, Painter, Etcher. LC 99-50114. (Illus.). 300p. 1999. write for info. (0-8425-2453-3, Pub. by Brigham) U Ch Pr.

Davis, Norma S., jt. auth. see Davis, Gerald N.

***Davis, Norman.** Jailbirds & Stool Pigeons Vol. 1: Crime Stories of the West. (Illus.). 144p. 1999. pap. 12.95 (0-88839-431-4) Hancock House.

Davis, Norman. Journeys to the Past. 1980. 9.95 (0-910286-83-3); pap. 6.95 (0-910286-78-7) Boxwood.

Davis, Norman, ed. Non-Cycle Plays & Fragments. (SS 1 Ser.). 1970. 19.50 (0-19-722401-6) OUP.
— Paston Letters & Papers of the 15th Century, Pt. 2. (Illus.). 698p. 1977. text 115.00 (0-19-812555-0) OUP.
— Zero Tolerance: Policing a Free Society. 2nd ed. (Choice in Welfare Ser.: No. 35). 152p. 1998. pap. 22.50 (0-255-36432-6, Pub. by Inst Economic Affairs) Coronet Bks.

Davis, Norman, ed. The Paston Letters: A Selection in Modern Spelling. (Oxford World's Classics Ser.). (Illus.). 320p. 1999. pap. 10.95 (0-19-283640-4) OUP.

Davis, Norman, et al. A Chaucer Glossary. 206p. 1979. pap. text 19.95 (0-19-811171-1) OUP.

Davis, Norman, ed. see Sweet, Henry.

Davis, Norman R. & Salisbury, Jaci. Wedding Cake Ensembles: Cakes for All Seasons. LC 99-159770. (The Sweet Life Ser.). 112p. 1997. write for info. (1-891199-00-5) Sweet Life.

***Davis, Noy S., ed.** Guidelines for the Screening of Persons Working with Children, the Eldery, & Individuals with Disabilities in Need of Support. 52p. (C). 1999. pap. text 20.00 (0-7881-8550-0) DIANE Pub.

Davis, O. B. Introduction to Biblical Literature. 2nd ed. LC 88-2801. 279p. (C). 1988. pap. text 18.00 (0-86709-227-0, 0227, Pub. by Boynton Cook Pubs) Heinemann.

Davis, O. J., Jr., jt. ed. see Mehlinger, Howard D.

Davis, O. K. Gramblings Gridiron Glory: Eddie Robinson & the Tigers' Success Story. (Illus.). 101p. 1985. pap. 7.95 (0-9610262-0-0) O K Davis.

Davis, O. L., Jr., ed. NCSS in Retrospect. LC 95-71964. (Bulletin Ser.: No. 92). 118p. (Orig.). 1996. pap. 14.95 (0-87986-068-5) Nat Coun Soc Studies.

Davis, O. L., jt. ed. see Smith Crocco, Margaret.

Davis, O. Preston. Remembrances of a Time Gone By: Growing Up in the South Carolina Low Country, 1910-1922. LC 94-9219. 1994. 15.00 (0-87152-480-5) Reprint.

Davis-O'Brien, Linda. As Good As Gold: Grand Prize Recipes from America's Cooking Contests. LC 92-96945. 224p. 1993. spiral bd. 16.95 (0-9634470-0-9) L Davis-OBrien.

Davis, Olena K. And Her Soul Out of Nothing. LC 97-15599. (Brittingham Prize in Poetry Ser.). 94p. 1997. pap. 11.95 (0-299-15714-8) U of Wis Pr.

Davis, Olena K. And Her Soul Out of Nothing. LC 97-15599. (Brittingham Prize in Poetry Ser.). 84p. 1997. 18.95 (0-299-15710-5) U of Wis Pr.

Davis, Olga S. A Time to Be Born. (Illus.). 80p. 1991. pap. 10.00 (1-877603-09-0) Pecan Grove.

Davis, Olive. From the Ohio to the San Joaquin: A Biography of William S. Moss, 1798-1883. LC 90-84139. (Illus.). 261p. (Orig.). (C). 1991. pap. 16.95 (0-9623048-0-8) Heritage West.
— Stockton: Sunrise Port on the San Joaquin. LC 98-74146. (Illus.). 164p. 1998. 28.95 (1-892724-00-6) Am Historical Pr.

Davis, Oliver J., ed. see Osterman, Eurydice.

Davis, Ossie. Just Like Martin. LC 94-30194. 224p. (YA). 1995. pap. 4.99 (0-14-037095-1, PuffinBks) Peng Put Young Read.
— Just Like Martin. (J). (gr. 5-9). 1996. 19.50 (0-8446-6897-4) Peter Smith.
— Just Like Martin. LC 91-4672. 208p. (YA). (gr. 5-9). 1992. pap. 15.00 (0-671-73202-1) S&S Bks Yung.
— Just Like Martin. (YA). 1995. 9.09 (0-606-07756-1, Pub. by Turtleback) Demco.
— Just Like Martin. large type ed. (YA). 1995. 58.00 (0-614-09593-X, L-81852-00) Am Printing Hse.
— Purlie Victorious: A Commemorative. Day, Nora D., ed. LC 94-94236. 124p. 1993. write for info. (0-9638416-0-2); pap. write for info. (0-9638416-1-0) Emmalyn Ent.

Davis, Ossie & Dee, Ruby. With Ossie & Ruby: In This Life Together. LC 98-35621. 512p. 1998. 25.00 (0-688-15396-8, Wm Morrow) Morrow Avon.

***Davis, Ossie & Dee, Ruby.** With Ossie & Ruby: In This Life Together. (Illus.). 496p. 2000. pap. 14.00 (0-688-17582-1) Morrow Avon.

Davis, Otto A., et al. A Theory of the Budgetary Process. (Reprint Series in Social Sciences). (C). 1993. reprint ed. pap. text 5.00 (0-8290-3376-9, PS-375) Irvington.

Davis, Owen, Sr. Instant Java Applets. 240p. 1996. 29.99 (1-56276-386-5, Ziff-Davis Pr) Que.
— Instant Java Applets. 264p. 1998. pap. 299.40 (1-56276-415-2, Ziff-Davis Pr) Que.

Davis, Owen, Sr. & Davis, Donald. Ethan Frome: A Dramatization of the Novel by Edith Wharton. 1954. pap. 5.25 (0-8222-0363-4) Dramatists Play.

Davis, Owen, Sr., ed. see Rogers, Denis.

Davis, Ozora S. Meeting the Master (1917) 160p. 1998. reprint ed. pap. 17.95 (0-7661-0535-0) Kessinger Pub.

Davis, P. Managing Medicines: Public Policy & Therapeutic Drugs. LC 96-37264. 192p. 1997. pap. 30.95 (0-335-19292-0) OpUniv Pr.
— Mirror of Awakening: A Spiritual Visionary's Adventures with Sex, God, & Unspeakable Wonders. Houston, M., ed. LC 92-81050. (Illus.). 186p. (Orig.). 1992. pap. 19.95 (0-9632307-0-0) New Cent Pdns.

Davis, P., et al, eds. Issues & Technology in the Management of Impacted Wildlife: Proceedings of the Fifth National Symposium (1991) (Illus.). 300p. (C). 1991. pap. 35.00 (*0-916055-05-1*) Thorne Eco Inst.

Davis, P. B. Cystic Fibrosis. (Lung Biology in Health & Disease Ser.: Vol. 64). (Illus.). 576p. 1993. text 250.00 (*0-8247-8815-X*) Dekker.

Davis, P. D., et al. Basic Physics & Measurement in Anesthesia. 4th ed. (Illus.). 360p. 2000. pap. text 52.50 (*0-7506-1713-6*) Buttrwrth-Heinemann.

Davis, P. H. & Heywood, V. H. Principles of Angiosperm Taxonomy. 578p. (C). 1991. reprint ed. 57.50 (*81-7019-383-4*, 203836) Krieger.

Davis, P. J. The Lore of Large Numbers. LC 61-13842. (New Mathematical Library: No. 6). 165p. 1961. pap. text 5.00 (*0-88385-606-9*, NML-06) Math Assn.

— The Schwarz Function & Its Applications. (Carus Mathematical Monograph: No. 17). 241p. 1974. text 5.00 (*0-88385-017-6*, CAM-17) Math Assn.

Davis, P. R., ed. Performance under Sub-Optimal Conditions. 104p. 1970. pap. 31.00 (*0-85066-044-0*) Taylor & Francis.

— Slipping, Tripping & Falling Accidents. (Ergonomics Special Issue Ser.: Vol. 28). 168p. 1985. pap. 23.00 (*0-85066-950-2*) Taylor & Francis.

Davis, P. Thomas, jt. auth. see Bergmann, Thomas F.

Davis-Pack, Denise. Foolish Things. 256p. 1997. pap. 10.99 (*0-9660637-1-6*) D D Pack.

— Maxie & Chase. (Illus.). 20p. (J). (gr. k-4). 1997. pap. 5.99 (*0-9660637-0-8*) D D Pack.

Davis, Paige & Juneau, Karen R. Technical Drawing. 2nd ed. LC 99-38883. 206p. (C). 1999. pap. 26.67 (*0-13-025954-3*) P-H.

Davis, Pamela J. & Fletcher, Neville H. Vocal Fold Physiology: Controlling Complexity & Chaos. (Vocal Fold Physiology Ser.). (Illus.). 454p. (Orig.). 1996. pap. 65.00 (*1-56593-714-7*, 1404) Thomson Learn.

Davis, Pat. Badminton. (Play the Game Ser.). (Illus.). 80p. 1998. pap. 10.95 (*0-7063-7688-9*, Pub. by WrLock) Sterling.

— Badminton Rules. 1999. pap. 10.95 (*0-7063-7734-6*, Pub. by WrLock) Sterling.

Davis, Pat, jt. auth. see Hargreaves, Margaret.

Davis, Pat, jt. auth. see Whitman, Charles W.

Davis, Patiricia. Subtle Aromatherapy. 111p. 1992. pap. 17.95 (*0-85207-227-9*, Pub. by C W Daniel) Natl Bk Netwk.

Davis, Patricia. Aromatherapy: An A-Z. enl. rev. ed. 368p. 1999. pap. 23.95 (*0-85207-295-3*, Pub. by C W Daniel) Natl Bk Netwk.

— Aromatherapy an A-Z. 382p. (Orig.). 1991. pap. 29.95 (*0-8464-1537-2*) Beekman Pubs.

— A Change for the Better. 256p. (Orig.). 1993. pap. 26.95 (*0-8464-4174-8*) Beekman Pubs.

— Change for the Better. 104p. 1994. pap. 21.95 (*0-85207-265-1*, Pub. by C W Daniel) Natl Bk Netwk.

— End of the Line: Alexander J. Cassatt & Pennsylvania Railroad. LC 78-977. 1978. 20.00 (*0-88202-181-8*) Watson Pub Intl.

— Subtle Aromatherapy. (Illus.). 256p. (Orig.). pap. 23.95 (*0-8464-4295-7*) Beekman Pubs.

***Davis, Patricia A.** Art of Economic Persuasion: Positive Incentives & German Economic Diplomacy. LC 99-6212. 216p. (C). 2000. text 49.50 (*0-472-10988-X*, 10988) U of Mich Pr.

— Brian's Bird. LC 99-36094. (Concept Book Ser.). (Illus.). 32p. (J). (gr. 1-4). 2000. lib. bdg. 14.95 (*0-8075-0881-0*) A Whitman.

Davis, Patricia A. & Oprendek, Donald V. Making Progress in Russian. LC 71-170354. 327p. (C). 1988. pap., student ed. 33.95 (*0-471-60290-6*) Wiley.

***Davis, Patricia H.** Beyond Nice: Girl's Emerging Spiritual Voices. 2000. pap. 15.00 (*0-8006-3256-7*, Fortress Pr) Augsburg Fortress.

Davis, Patricia H. Counseling Adolescent Girls. (Creative Pastoral Care & Counseling Ser.). 96p. 1996. pap. 15.00 (*0-8006-2905-1*, 1-2905, Fortress Pr) Augsburg Fortress.

Davis, Patricia K. A Midnight Carol: A Novel of How Charles Dickens Saved Christmas. LC 99-15886. 192p. 1999. text 16.95 (*0-312-24523-8*) St Martin.

***Davis, Patricia K.** A Midnight Carol: A Novel of How Charles Dickens Saved Christmas. 2000. reprint ed. pap. 4.99 (*0-312-97698-4*, St Martins Paperbacks) St Martin.

Davis, Patricia M. Cognition & Learning: A Review of the Literature with Reference to Ethnolinguistic Minorities. LC 91-75098. x, 90p. 1991. pap. 6.00 (*0-88312-100-X*) S I L Intl.

Davis, Patricia M., jt. auth. see Larson, Mildred L.

Davis, Patricia M., jt. ed. see Larson, Mildred L.

Davis, Patricia T. A Family Tapestry: Five Generations of the Curwens of Walnut Hill & Their Various Relatives. LC 72-14325. (Illus.). 224p. 1972. lib. bdg. 17.50 (*0-915010-15-1*) Sutter House.

— The Railroad General. 238p. 1994. text. write for info. (*0-9640329-0-2*) Metro Printing.

— Together They Built a Mountain. LC 74-14727. (Illus.). 196p. 1974. 14.95 (*0-915010-00-3*) Sutter House.

Davis, Patrick, jt. auth. see Gilmore, Scott.

***Davis, Patrick A.** The General. 1999. reprint ed. pap. 7.50 (*0-425-16804-2*) Berkley Pub.

Davis, Patrick A. The Passenger. LC 99-25579. 384p. 1999. 24.95 (*0-399-14491-9*, G P Putnam) Peng Put Young Read.

Davis, Patti. Bondage. Rubenstein, Julie, ed. 320p. 1995. mass mkt. 5.99 (*0-671-86954-X*) PB.

— Bondage. 1994. 23.00 (*0-671-86953-1*) S&S Trade.

— A House of Secrets. 256p. 1991. text 18.95 (*1-55972-082-4*, Birch Ln Pr) Carol Pub Group.

— The Way I See It. 304p. (Orig.). 1993. mass mkt. 5.99 (*0-515-11089-2*, Jove) Berkley Pub.

Davis, Patty. A Long Goodbye. LC 97-2994. 1999. 20.00 (*0-679-45092-0*) McKay.

Davis, Patty, ed. see Kuralt, Charles & McGlohan, Loonis.

Davis, Patty, ed. see Kuralt, Charles & McGlohan, Loonis.

Davis, Patty, ed. see Weathers, Lavern R.

Davis, Paul. Castles of Dyfed. 77p. (C). 1987. text 35.00 (*0-86383-382-9*, Pub. by Gomer Pr) St Mut.

— Charles Dickens A to Z: The Essential Reference to His Life & Work. LC 97-26237. (Illus.). 448p. 1998. 50.00 (*0-8160-2905-9*, Checkmark) Facts on File.

***Davis, Paul.** Charles Dickens A to Z: The Essential Reference to His Life & Work. (Illus.). 448p. 1999. pap. 17.95 (*0-8160-4087-7*, Checkmark) Facts on File.

Davis, Paul. Defense Planning for the Post-Cold War Era: Giving Meaning to Flexibility, Adaptiveness, & Robustness of Capability. 228p. 1993. pap. 15.00 (*0-8330-1442-0*, MR-322) Rand Corp.

— Encyclopedia of Invasions & Conquests: From Ancient Times to the Present. LC 96-49452. (Illus.). 443p. 1996. lib. bdg. 65.00 (*0-87436-782-4*) ABC-CLIO.

— The Lives & Times of Ebenezer Scrooge. 296p. (C). 1990. 40.00 (*0-300-04664-2*) Yale U Pr.

Davis, Paul & Rinvolucri, Mario. Dictation: New Methods, New Possibilities. (Cambridge Handbooks for Language Teachers Ser.). 128p. 1989. pap. text 17.95 (*0-521-34819-6*) Cambridge U Pr.

— More Grammar Games: Cognitive, Affective & Movement Activities for EFL Students. (Illus.). 193p. (C). 1995. pap. text 19.95 (*0-521-46630-X*) Cambridge U Pr.

Davis, Paul, et al. Ways of Doing: Students Explore Their Everyday & Classroom Processes. LC 98-44353. (Handbks. for Language Teachers). (Illus.). 181p. 1999. pap. 19.95 (*0-521-58559-7*) Cambridge U Pr.

— Western Literature in Context, 2 vols., Vol. 1. 2280p. 1994. pap. text 50.95 (*0-312-08124-3*) St Martin.

— Western Literature in Context, 2 vols., Vol. 2. 2016p. 1994. pap. 50.95 (*0-312-08125-1*) St Martin.

Davis, Paul B., jt. auth. see Weinberg, Leonard B.

Davis, Paul D. How to Make 50,000 Dollars a Year (or More) As a Freelance Business Writer: The Business of Business Writing, Explained for Beginners. LC 92-1730. 320p. (Orig.). 1992. pap. 14.95 (*1-55958-221-9*) Prima Pub.

Davis, Paul D., jt. auth. see Kenny, Gavin.

Davis, Paul K. Aggregation, Dissaggregation, & the 3:1 Rule in Ground Combat. LC 95-39769. 47p. 1995. pap. 7.50 (*0-8330-2321-7*, MR-638/AF/A/OSD) Rand Corp.

— Encyclopedia of Invasions & Conquests: From Ancient Times to the Present. (Illus.). 448p. 1998. pap. 17.95 (*0-393-31789-7*) Norton.

— Ends & Means: The British Mesopotamian Campaign & Commission. LC 92-55121. 1994. 41.50 (*0-8386-3530-X*) Fairleigh Dickinson.

— Land-Mobile ICBMs: Verification & Breakout. (CISA Working Papers: No. 18). 31p. (Orig.). 1980. pap. 15.00 (*0-86682-017-5*) Ctr Intl Relations.

— 100 Decisive Battles. LC 99-47618. (Illus.). 468p. 1999. lib. bdg. 75.00 (*1-57607-075-1*) ABC-CLIO.

***Davis, Paul K.** 100 Famous Sieges in History. 2001. lib. bdg. 65.00 (*1-57607-195-2*) ABC-CLIO.

Davis, Paul K., ed. New Challenges for Defense Planning: Rethinking How Much Is Enough. LC 94-9770. 750p. 1994. 35.00 (*0-8330-1666-0*, MR-400-RC); pap. 20.00 (*0-8330-1527-3*, MR-400-RC) Rand Corp.

Davis, Paul K. & Bigelow, James H. Experiments in Multiresolution Modeling (MRM) LC 98-33725. (Illus.). xvii, 69p. 1998. pap. text 13.00 (*0-8330-2653-4*, MR-1004-DARPA) Rand Corp.

Davis, Paul K. & Hamilton, Allen L. Encyclopedia of Warrior Peoples & Fighting Groups. LC 98-36079. 304p. 1998. lib. bdg. 75.00 (*0-87436-961-4*) ABC-CLIO.

Davis, Paul K. & Hamilton, Allen Lee. Encyclopedia of Warrior Peoples & Fighting Groups. LC 98-36079. 294 p. 1998. pap. write for info. (*1-57607-046-8*) ABC-CLIO.

Davis, Paul K. & Khalilzad, Zalmay M. A Composite Approach to Air Force Planning. LC 96-27146. (Illus.). 69p. 1996. pap. 13.00 (*0-8330-2433-7*, MR-787-AF) Rand Corp.

***Davis, Paul K., et al.** Analytical Methods for Studies & Experiments on "Transforming the Force" (Illus.). xi, 55p. 1999. pap. 6.00 (*0-8330-2749-2*, DB-278-OSD) Rand Corp.

— Effects of Terrain, Maneuver Tactics & C4ISR on the Effectiveness of Long Range Precision Fires: A Stochastic Multiresolution Model (PEM) Calibrated to High-Resolution. (Illus.). xvii, 93p. 2000. pap. 15.00 (*0-8330-2819-7*, MR-1138-OSD) Rand Corp.

Davis, Paul K., et al. Exploratory Analysis of "the Halt Problem" A Briefing on Methods & Initial Insights. LC 98-119740. (Documented Briefing Ser.). ix, 49 p. 1997. pap. 10.00 (*0-8330-2565-1*) Rand Corp.

— Mitigating Effects of Access Problems in Persian Gulf Contingencies. LC 97-45901. (Illus.). 144p. 1999. pap. 15.00 (*0-8330-2570-8*, MR-915-OSD) Rand Corp.

— Strategic Issues & Options for the Quadrennial Defense Review. LC 98-108907. (Documented Briefing Ser.). (Illus.). 55p. 1997. pap. 6.00 (*0-8330-2498-1*) Rand Corp.

Davis, Paul M. & Fenwick, Amy C. Development & Procurement of Gliders in the Army Air Forces, 1941-1944. (USAF Historical Studies: No. 47). 208p. 1946. reprint ed. pap. text 38.95 (*0-89126-148-6*) MA-AH Pub.

Davis, Paul R. Historic Gower. 1997. pap. 29.95 (*0-8464-4872-6*) Beekman Pubs.

— Historic West Wales. 130p. (C). 1992. 59.00 (*0-7154-0722-8*, Pub. by C Davies Pubs) St Mut.

Davis, Paul W. Differential Equations for Mathematics, Science & Engineering. 592p. (C). 1991. text 84.00 (*0-13-211236-1*) P-H.

Davis, Paxton. Being a Boy. 253p. 1997. pap. 8.95 (*0-89587-168-8*) Blair.

— A Boy No More. 252p. 1997. pap. 8.95 (*0-89587-170-X*) Blair.

— A Boy's War. 296p. 1997. pap. 8.95 (*0-89587-169-6*) Blair.

Davis, Peggy. New Icons. LC 80-5679. (Lucky Heart Bk.). 16p. 1980. reprint ed. pap. 30.00 (*0-7837-9153-4*, 204985300003) Bks Demand.

Davis, Peggy C. Neglected Stories: The Constitution & Family Values. (Illus.). 304p. 1998. pap. text 14.00 (*0-8090-1607-9*) Hill & Wang.

Davis, Peggy Cooper. Neglected Stories: The Constitution & Family Values. LC 97-3898. 1997. 25.00 (*0-8090-7241-6*) Hill & Wang.

Davis, Penny A., jt. auth. see McCurley, Robert L., Jr.

Davis, Percival & Kenyon, Dean H. Of Pandas & People: The Central Question of Biological Origins. (Illus.). 166p. 1989. 17.95 (*0-685-58687-1*) Haughton.

Davis, Percival, jt. auth. see Frair, Wayne.

Davis, Pete & Wallace, Mike. Windows Undocumented File Formats: Working Inside Windows 3.X & Windows '95. 283p. (Orig.). 1997. pap. 39.95 incl. disk (*0-87930-437-5*) C M P Books.

Davis, Pete, et al. Issues & Technology in the Management of Impacted Wildlife: Proceedings of a National Symposium (1987) 177p. 1988. pap. 35.00 (*0-916055-03-5*) Thorne Eco Inst.

Davis, Peter. Ecomuseums: A Sense of Place. LC 99-13881. (Museum Studies Ser.). 1999. 69.95 (*0-7185-0208-6*) Continuum.

— If You Came This Way: A Journey Through the Lives of the Underclass. LC 95-12872. 224p. 1995. 22.95 (*0-471-11074-4*) Wiley.

— In Darkest Hollywood: Exploring the Jungles of Cinema's South Africa. LC 96-17480. (Illus.). 225p. (Orig.). 1996. pap. 19.95 (*0-8214-1162-4*) Ohio U Pr.

— Introduction to the Sociology of Dentistry: A Comparative Perspective. 108p. 1987. pap. 24.95 (*0-908569-40-8*, Pub. by Univ Otago Pr) Intl Spec Bk.

— Managing Medicines: Public Policy & Therapeutic Drugs. LC 96-37264. (State of Health Ser.). 192p. 1997. 116.95 (*0-335-19293-9*) OpUniv Pr.

— Museums & the Natural Environment: The Role of Natural History Museums in Biological Conservation. 208p. 1996. 90.00 (*0-7185-1548-X*) Bks Intl VA.

— Sams Teach Yourself Windows 2000 Server in 21 Days. 2000th ed. 850p. 2000. 29.99 (*0-672-31703-6*) Macmillan.

— Teach Yourself Windows NT Server 4 in 21 Days. LC 98-89972. 1999. pap. text 29.99 (*0-672-31555-6*) Sams.

Davis, Peter, ed. Contested Ground: Public Purpose & Private Interest in the Regulation of Prescription Drugs. (Illus.). 272p. (C). 1996. text 39.95 (*0-19-509120-5*) OUP.

— Intimate Details & Vital Statistics: AIDS, Sexuality & the Social Order in New Zealand. 250p. 1996. pap. 24.95 (*1-86940-139-5*, Pub. by Auckland Univ) Paul & Co Pubs.

***Davis, Peter & Dew, Kevin, eds.** Health & Society in Aotearoa New Zealand. 320p. 2000. pap. text 39.95 (*0-19-558391-4*) OUP.

Davis, Peter & Lewis, Barry. Teach Yourself Windows NT 4 Server 4 in 14 Days. LC 96-71198. 888p. 1997. 35.00 (*0-672-31019-8*) Sams.

Davis, Peter, jt. auth. see Cannon, Teresa.

Davis, Peter, jt. auth. see Jackson, Christine E.

Davis, Peter A. & Postlewait, Thomas, eds. Directory of Doctoral Programs in Theatre Studies, Performance Studies, & Dance: U. S. A. & Canada 1996. 2nd ed. 124p. (C). 1996. pap. text 15.00 (*0-9631991-1-0*) Am Soc Theatre Res.

— Directory of Doctoral Programs in Theatre Studies, Performance Studies & Dance: U. S. A. & Canada, 1999. 3rd ed. 124p. (C). 1998. pap. text 15.00 (*0-9631991-2-9*) Am Soc Theatre Res.

Davis, Peter G. The American Opera Singer: The Lives & Adventures of America's Great Singers in Opera & Concert, from 1825 to the Present. (Illus.). 640p. 1999. pap. 19.95 (*0-385-42174-5*) Doubleday.

Davis, Peter H. Flora of Turkey, Vol. 9. 724p. 1986. 160.00 (*0-85224-516-5*, Pub. by Edinburgh U Pr) Col U Pr.

— Flora of Turkey, Vol. 10. 590p. 1989. 160.00 (*0-85224-559-9*, Pub. by Edinburgh U Pr) Col U Pr.

Davis, Peter H., ed. The Flora of Turkey, 6 vols., 7. 946p. 1982. 160.00 (*0-85224-396-0*, Pub. by Edinburgh U Pr) Col U Pr.

— The Flora of Turkey, 6 vols., Vol. 1. 567p. 1979. 125.00 (*0-85224-159-3*, Pub. by Edinburgh U Pr) Col U Pr.

— The Flora of Turkey, 6 vols., Vol. 2. 580p. 1979. 160.00 (*0-85224-000-7*, Pub. by Edinburgh U Pr) Col U Pr.

— The Flora of Turkey, 6 vols., Vol. 3. 628p. 1979. 160.00 (*0-85224-154-2*, Pub. by Edinburgh U Pr) Col U Pr.

— The Flora of Turkey, 6 vols., Vol. 4. 657p. 1979. 160.00 (*0-85224-208-5*, Pub. by Edinburgh U Pr) Col U Pr.

— The Flora of Turkey, 6 vols., Vol. 5. 890p. 1979. 160.00 (*0-85224-280-8*, Pub. by Edinburgh U Pr) Col U Pr.

— The Flora of Turkey, 6 vols., Vol. 6. 825p. 1979. 160.00 (*0-85224-336-7*, Pub. by Edinburgh U Pr) Col U Pr.

— The Flora of Turkey, Vol. 8. 632p. 1984. 160.00 (*0-85224-494-0*, Pub. by Edinburgh U Pr) Col U Pr.

Davis, Peter J. Shifting Song. (Altertumswissenschaftliche Texte und Studien: Bd. 26). (GER.). iv, 274p. 1993. write for info. (*3-487-09748-6*) G Olms Pubs.

Davis, Peter J., jt. ed. see Cook, D. Ryan.

Davis, Peter J., ed. see Motoyama, Etsuro K.

Davis, Peter R., ed. Industrial Back Pain in Europe. (Ergonomics Special Issue Ser.: Vol. 28, No. 1). 416p. 1984. pap. 23.00 (*0-85066-985-5*) Taylor & Francis.

Davis, Peter R., ed. see Davies, D.

Davis, Peter S., ed. Nursing the Orthopaedic Patient. LC 93-43058. 1995. pap. text 37.95 (*0-443-04461-9*) Church.

Davis, Peter T., ed. Securing Client/Server Computer Networks. (Illus.). 589p. 1999. reprint ed. pap. text 25.00 (*0-7881-6520-8*) DIANE Pub.

Davis, Phil. Beyond the Zone System. 3rd ed. LC 93-17818. (Illus.). 192p. 1993. pap. text 34.95 (*0-240-80193-8*, Focal) Buttrwrth-Heinemann.

— Beyond the Zone System. 4th ed. LC 98-35337. 220p. 1998. pap. text 34.95 (*0-240-80343-4*, Focal) Buttrwrth-Heinemann.

Davis, Philip. The Basic Photo Book. 160p. (C). 1991. text 28.00 (*0-697-11480-5*) Brown & Benchmark.

— Experimental Essays of Bernard Malamud: Malamud's People. LC 94-22867. 204p. 1995. 89.95 (*0-7734-9060-4*) E Mellen.

— History Atlas of North America. (Macmillan Continental History Atlases Ser.). (Illus.). 160p. 1998. 27.95 (*0-02-862582-X*) Macmillan.

— Photography. 7th ed. 448p. (C). 1994. text. write for info. (*0-697-12514-9*) Brown & Benchmark.

Davis, Philip, ed. see Ruskin, John.

Davis Philip, A. G., ed. Calibration of Stellar Ages. 250p. 1988. 25.00 (*0-933485-09-3*) L Davis Pr.

— Finding Charts: Contributions of Van Vleck Obs., Vol. 2. 1985. pap. 15.00 (*0-9607902-6-8*) L Davis Pr.

— Horizontal-Branch & UV-Bright Stars. 146p. 1985. 22.00 (*0-933485-03-4*); pap. 17.00 (*0-933485-02-6*) L Davis Pr.

— New York State Astronomy. 184p. 1992. 32.00 (*0-933485-16-6*) L Davis Pr.

— Spectroscopic & Photometric Classification of Population II Stars. 114p. 1986. 22.00 (*0-933485-05-0*); pap. 17.00 (*0-933485-04-2*) L Davis Pr.

Davis Philip, A. G., et al, eds. CCDs in Astronomy, No. II. 302p. 1990. 27.00 (*0-933485-12-3*) L Davis Pr.

— New Directions in Spectrophotometry. 400p. 1988. 32.00 (*0-933485-08-5*) L Davis Pr.

— Precision Photometry: Astrophysics of the Galaxy. 300p. 1991. 32.00 (*0-933485-13-1*) L Davis Pr.

— Workshop on Databases for Galactic Structure. 240p. 1993. 36.00 (*0-933485-17-4*) L Davis Pr.

Davis Philip, A. G. & Latham, D. W., eds. Stellar Radial Velocities. (IAU Colloquium Ser.: No. 88). 1985. 32.00 (*0-933485-01-8*); pap. 32.00 (*0-933485-00-X*) L Davis Pr.

Davis Philip, A. G. & Lu, Phillip, eds. The Gravitational Force Perpendicular to the Galactic Plane. 182p. 1989. 32.00 (*0-933485-11-5*) L Davis Pr.

Davis Philip, A. G. & Upgren, A. R., eds. Objective - Prism & Other Surveys. 202p. 1991. 32.00 (*0-933485-15-8*) L Davis Pr.

— Star Catalogues: A Centennial Tribute to A. N. Vyssotsky. 100p. 1989. 22.00 (*0-933485-10-7*) L Davis Pr.

Davis Philip, A. G., ed. see Hayes, D. S. & Liebert, J.

Davis, Philip E., ed. Moral Duty & Legal Responsibility: A Philosophical-Legal Casebook. 2nd ed. (Orig.). write for info. (*0-8290-0681-8*) Irvington.

Davis, Philip G. Goddess Unmasked: The Rise of Neopagan Feminist Spirituality. LC 97-47378. 350p. 1998. 29.95 (*0-9653208-9-8*) Spence Pub.

***Davis, Philip G.** Goddess Unmasked: The Rise of Neopagan Feminist Spirituality. LC 97-47378. xii, 420p. 1999. pap. 17.95 (*1-890626-20-1*) Spence Pub.

Davis, Philip J. Circulant Matrices. 2nd ed. LC 94-711743. xv, 250p. 1994. text 27.50 (*0-8284-0338-4*) Chelsea Pub.

— The Companion Guide to the Mathematical Experience, Study Edition. LC 96-101526. 120p. 1995. pap. 14.95 (*0-8176-3849-0*, QA8) Birkhauser.

***Davis, Philip J.** The Education of a Mathematician. LC 00-20739. (Illus.). 368p. 2000. 29.95 (*1-56881-116-0*) AK Peters.

Davis, Philip J. Interpolation & Approximation. LC 75-2568. (Illus.). 393p. (C). 1975. reprint ed. pap. text 10.95 (*0-486-62495-1*) Dover.

— Mathematical Encounters of the Second Kind. LC 96-22131. 1996. write for info. (*3-7643-3939-X*) Birkhauser.

— Mathematical Encounters of the Second Kind. (Illus.). 304p. 1996. 24.95 (*0-8176-3939-X*) Birkhauser.

— The Mathematical Experience. 464p. 1999. pap. 18.00 (*0-395-92968-7*) HM.

— Thomas Gray in Copenhagen: In Which the Philosopher Cat Meets the Ghost of Hans Christian Andersen. LC 95-13243. (Illus.). 192p. 1995. 16.00 (*0-387-94493-1*) Spr-Verlag.

— Thomas Gray, Philosopher Cat. (Illus.). 160p. 1990. pap. 8.95 (*0-15-690100-5*, Harvest Bks) Harcourt.

Davis, Philip J. & Hersh, Reuben. Descartes' Dream: The World According to Mathematics. (Illus.). 400p. 1986. 24.95 (*0-15-125260-2*) Harcourt.

Davis, Philip J. & Park, David, eds. No Way: Essays on the Nature of the Impossible. LC 86-19728. (Trade Ser.). (Illus.). 325p. 1988. pap. text 14.95 (*0-7167-1966-5*) W H Freeman.

Davis, Philip J., et al. The Mathematical Experience. 460p. 1987. 29.95 (*0-8176-3018-X*) Birkhauser.

— The Mathematical Experience. 487p. 1995. student ed. 38.50 (*0-8176-3739-7*) Birkhauser.

Davis, Philip W., ed. Alternative Linguistics: Descriptive & Theoretical Modes. LC 95-50364. (Current Issues in Linguistic Theory Ser.: Vol. 102). vii, 325p. 1996. 69.00 (*1-55619-586-9*) J Benjamins Pubng Co.

D

An Asterisk (*) at the beginning of an entry indicates that the title is appearing for the first time.

Davis, Philip W. & Saunders, Ross. A Grammar of Bella Coola. LC 97-60542. (University of Montana Occasional Papers in Linguistics: No. 13). iii, 188p. (Orig.). 1997. pap. 20.00 (*1-879763-13-3*) U MT UMOPL.

Davis, Phillip M. The Vision Casting Church. Date not set. write for info. (*0-9652262-2-0*) Orman Pr.

Davis, Phillip V. & Speilman, Bethany J. Organ & Tissue Donation & Transplantation: A Humanities Curriculum for Medical Students. 166p. 1997. ring bd. 25.00 incl. cd-rom (*0-931369-32-0*) Southern IL Univ Sch.

Davis, Phillipa, compiled by. Pingouin Book of Classic Knitting Patterns. 80p. (C). 1989. 125.00 (*1-85368-018-4*, Pub. by New5 Holland) St Mut.

Davis, Phyllis. CorelDraw Eight for Windows: Visual QuickStart Guide. 4th ed. 320p. (C). 1998. pap. text 17.95 (*0-201-69661-4*, Pub. by Peachpit Pr) Addison-Wesley.

— CorelDRAW 9 for Windows: Visual Quickstart Guide. 3rd ed. 336p. (C). 1999. pap. 18.99 (*0-201-35451-9*) Addison-Wesley.

— CorelDRAW 7 for Windows 95/NT: Visual QuickStart Guide. LC 97-143364. 272p. (C). 1996. pap. text 17.95 (*0-201-69420-4*) Addison-Wesley.

***Davis, Phyllis.** The GIMP for Linux & Unix. (Visual QuickStart Guides Ser.). (Illus.). 304p. 2000. pap. 19.99 (*0-201-70253-3*) Addison-Wesley.

— WordPerfect 8 for Linux: Visual QuickStart Guide. (Visual QuickStart Guide Ser.). 256p. (C). 1999. pap. text 18.99 (*0-201-70051-4*) Peachpit Pr.

Davis, Phyllis & Craig, Deborah. FrontPage 98 for Windows: Visual QuickStart Guide. 2nd ed. Davis, Nancy, ed. 352p. (C). 1998. pap. text 17.95 (*0-201-69694-0*) Peachpit Pr.

Davis, Phyllis E., jt. auth. see Smith, Genevieve L.

Davis, Phyllis K. The Power of Touch: The Basis for Survival, Health, Intimacy & Emotional Well-Being. 2nd rev. ed. LC 98-55707. xxviii, 238p. (Orig.). 1999. pap. 11.95 (*1-56170-574-8*, 576) Hay House.

Davis, Pia, jt. auth. see Lasdun, James.

Davis Pub Staff. Patrol Administration: Management by Objectives Study Guide. 3rd ed. 204p. 1979. 28.95 (*1-56325-011-X*, DS006) Davis Pub Law.

Davis Publishing Company Staff. Criminal Investigation Study Guide: Based on the Text by Swanson, Territo & Chamelin. 6th ed. 336p. 1996. 28.95 (*1-56325-061-6*) Davis Pub Law.

— Elements of Police Supervision Study Guide. 2nd ed. 176p. (C). 1990. 28.95 (*1-56325-019-5*) Davis Pub Law.

— Environment of the First Line Supervisor Study Guide: Based on the Text by Trojanowicz. Dahl, Robert, ed. 96p. (Orig.). (C). 1990. student ed. 28.95 (*1-56325-017-9*, DS142) Davis Pub Law.

— The Law of Criminal Investigation Study Guide. 96p. (Orig.). (C). 1989. pap. 28.95 (*1-56325-010-1*) Davis Pub Law.

— Police Administration: Structures, Processes & Behaviors Study Guide: Based on the Text by Swanson, Territo & Taylor. 2nd ed. Dahl, Robert, ed. 108p. (C). 1991. 28.95 (*1-56325-000-4*, DS097) Davis Pub Law.

— Police Administration: Structures, Processes & Behaviors Study Guide: Based on the Text by Swanson, Territo & Taylor. 3rd ed. Dahl, Robert, ed. 108p. (C). 1995. 28.95 (*1-56325-057-8*, DS097) Davis Pub Law.

D

— Police Entrance Examinations Handbook. rev. ed. (Illus.). 219p. 1991. reprint ed. pap. 28.95 (*1-56325-004-7*, T46) Davis Pub Law.

— Police Field Operations Study Guide. 3rd ed. 156p. (C). 1997. pap., student ed. 28.95 (*1-56325-012-8*, DS444) Davis Pub Law.

— The Police Manager: Professional Leadership Skills. 3rd ed. 96p. (C). 1989. pap. 28.95 (*1-56325-014-4*, DS036) Davis Pub Law.

— Principles of Police Patrol Study Guide. 208p. (Orig.). 1990. pap. 28.95 (*1-56325-015-2*, DS072) Davis Pub Law.

— Proactive Police Management Study Guide: Based on the Text by Thibault, Lynch & McBride. 4th ed. 214p. 1997. 28.95 (*1-56325-060-8*, DS100) Davis Pub Law.

— What Every Supervisor Should Know Study Guide: Based on the Text by Bittel & Newstrom. 6th ed. Dahl, Robert, ed. 144p. 1990. 28.95 (*1-56325-018-7*) Davis Pub Law.

Davis Publishing Staff. Fundamentals of Criminal Investigation. 6th ed. 245p. (Orig.). 1995. student ed. 28.95 (*1-56325-055-1*) Davis Pub Law.

***Davis Pullen, Jeanie.** Life Teachings: Raising a Child. 112p. 1999. mass mkt. 12.95 (*0-9672660-0-9*, Pub. by Yllow House) Bookmen Inc.

Davis, R. Formaldehyde Toxicology. 180p. 1993. pap. text 106.00 (*2-88124-578-1*) Gordon & Breach.

Davis, R. The Right to Silence. 1996. mass mkt. 13.95 (*0-340-65784-7*, Pub. by Hodder & Stought Ltd) Trafalgar.

Davis, R., tr. see Japan Environmental Council Staff, et al, eds.

Davis, R., tr. see Rabe, Thomas.

Davis, R. A., compiled by. Geology of Holocene Barrier Island Systems. LC 93-46742. 1994. 182.95 (*0-387-56964-2*) Spr-Verlag.

Davis, R. A., ed. Cincinnati Fossils: An Elementary Guide to the Ordivician Rocks & Fossils of the Cincinnati, Ohio, Region. rev. ed. (Illus.). 64p. 1992. reprint ed. pap. text 6.95 (*1-882151-00-3*) Cin Mus Ctr.

Davis, R. A., Jr., ed. Coastal Sedimentary Environments. 2nd rev. ed. (Illus.). xvii, 716p. 1985. 105.00 (*0-387-96097-X*) Spr-Verlag.

Davis, R. A., jt. auth. see Brockwell, P. J.

Davis, R. A., jt. auth. see Rockwell, P. J.

Davis, R. C., jt. ed. see Cutler, W. Gale.

Davis, R. D., et al, eds. Environmental Effects of Organic & Inorganic Contaminants in Sewage Sludge. 1983. text 152.50 (*90-277-1586-6*) Kluwer Academic.

Davis, R. Dean. The Heavenly Court Judgement of Revelation 4-5. 304p. (C). 1992. lib. bdg. 48.00 (*0-8191-8613-9*) U Pr of Amer.

Davis, R. Dell. Ashes & Sparks, Set. LC 89-81718. (Illus.). 172p. 1989. text, boxed set 24.95 incl. audio (*0-9616736-1-3*) J Franklin.

Davis, R. Dowd. Baptist Distinctives: A Pattern for Service. 64p. (Orig.). 1986. pap. 3.95 (*0-913029-11-4*) Stevens Bk Pr.

Davis, R. E. Reassessment of Selected Factors Affecting Siting of Nuclear Power Plants. 119p. 1997. per. 11.00 (*0-16-062816-4*) USGPO.

Davis, R. F. The Heat Treatment of Gearing. (Technical Paper: Vol. P42). (Illus.). 14p. 1933. pap. text 30.00 (*1-55589-318-X*) AGMA.

Davis, R. H. From Alfred the Great to Stephen. 320p. 1991. 55.00 (*1-85285-045-0*) Hambledon Press.

— A History of Medieval Europe: From Constantine to Saint Louis. 2nd ed. (Illus.). 408p. (C). 1988. pap. text 24.38 (*0-582-49400-1*, 70604) Longman.

***Davis, R. H.** The Romances of Blanche la Mare. (FRE.). 176p. 2000. mass mkt. 7.95 (*1-56201-175-8*, Pub. by Blue Moon Bks) Publishers Group.

Davis, R. H., ed. see William of Poitiers.

***Davis, R. H. C.** History of Medieval Europe: From Constantine to St. Louis. 424p. 2000. pap. write for info. (*0-582-41861-5*) Longman.

Davis, R. Hunt, Jr., jt. ed. see Johns, Sheridan.

Davis, R. I. Men's Garments, 1830-1900: A Guide to Pattern Cutting & Tailoring. LC 94-22441. (Illus.). 160p. 1995. pap. 27.00 (*0-88734-648-0*) Players Pr.

— Men's 17th & 18th Century Costume, Cut & Fashion. Landes, William-Alan, ed. LC 99-56138. (Illus.). 224p. 2000. pap. 60.00 (*0-88734-637-5*) Players Pr.

Davis, R. J., jt. ed. see Jackson, N.

Davis, R. K. Productivity Improvements Through TPM: The Philosophy & Application of Total Productive Maintenance. LC 94-31925. 160p. 1995. pap. text 45.00 (*0-13-133034-9*) P-H.

Davis, R. M. Outside the Lines. 1990. write for info. (*0-9617714-3-7*) Cow Hill Pr.

Davis, R. M. & Buford, P. D., eds. Alive in the Spirit. 160p. (Orig.). 1999. mass mkt. 5.99 (*1-56722-207-2*) Word Aflame.

— Bible - Its Origin & Use. 160p. 1993. reprint ed. pap. 5.99 (*1-56722-051-7*) Word Aflame.

— Bible Doctrines - Foundation of the Church. 160p. 1991. reprint ed. pap. 5.99 (*1-56722-050-9*) Word Aflame.

— The Christian Man. 160p. 1995. pap. 5.99 (*1-56722-033-9*) Word Aflame.

— The Christian Parent. 160p. 1991. pap. 5.99 (*1-56722-052-5*) Word Aflame.

— The Christian Woman. 160p. 1991. reprint ed. pap. 5.99 (*1-56722-042-8*) Word Aflame.

— The Christian Youth. 160p. 1995. pap. 5.99 (*1-56722-034-7*) Word Aflame.

— Facing the Issues. 160p. 1992. pap. 5.99 (*1-56722-053-3*) Word Aflame.

— The Holy Spirit. 160p. 1993. pap. 5.99 (*1-56722-054-1*) Word Aflame.

— Life's Choices. 160p. 1994. reprint ed. pap. 5.99 (*1-56722-055-X*) Word Aflame.

***Davis, R. M. & Buford, P. D., eds.** A Look at Stewardship. 160p. 2000. mass mkt. 5.99 (*1-56722-253-6*) Word Aflame.

Davis, R. M. & Buford, P. D., eds. Meet the United Pentecostal Church International. 160p. 1995. pap. 5.99 (*1-56722-056-8*) Word Aflame.

— Spiritual Growth & Maturity. 160p. 1993. reprint ed. pap. 5.99 (*1-56722-060-6*) Word Aflame.

— Spiritual Leadership & Successful Soulwinning. 160p. 1993. reprint ed. pap. 5.99 (*1-56722-061-4*) Word Aflame.

— Strategy for Life for Singles & Young Adults. 160p. 1986. pap. 5.99 (*1-56722-062-2*) Word Aflame.

— Values That Last. 160p. 1992. reprint ed. pap. 5.99 (*1-56722-063-0*) Word Aflame.

— Why? A Study of Christian Standards. 160p. 1991. reprint ed. pap. 5.99 (*1-56722-043-6*) Word Aflame.

— Your New Life. 160p. 1996. reprint ed. pap. 5.99 (*1-56722-064-9*) Word Aflame.

Davis, R. M. & Buford, P.D., eds. Purpose at Sunset. 160p. 1987. reprint ed. pap. 4.99 (*1-56722-057-6*) Word Aflame.

— Salvation - Key to Eternal Life. 160p. 1985. reprint ed. pap. 4.99 (*1-56722-059-2*) Word Aflame.

Davis, R. Mack, jt. auth. see Price, Courtney H.

Davis, R. Michael, et al. Compendium of Lettuce Diseases. LC 97-77193. (Illus.). 104p. 1997. pap. 42.00 (*0-89054-186-8*) Am Phytopathol Soc.

Davis, R. O. & Selvadurai, A. P. Elasticity & Geomechanics. (Illus.). 212p. (C). 1996. text 80.00 (*0-521-49506-7*); pap. text 30.95 (*0-521-49827-9*) Cambridge U Pr.

Davis, R. P., Jr. Aboriginal Settlement Patterns in the Little Tennessee River Valley. LC 90-10911. (Publications in Anthropology: Vol. 54). (Illus.). 381p. 1990. write for info. (*0-87077-005-5*) TVA.

Davis, R. P., Jr., jt. auth. see Ward, H. Trawick.

Davis, R. W., ed. Lords of Parliament Studies, 1714-1914. LC 94-17743. x , 230p. 1995. 45.00 (*0-8047-2476-8*) Stanford U Pr.

— The Origins of Modern Freedom in the West. LC 94-20717. (Making of Modern Freedom Ser.). xvi, 384p. 1995. 49.50 (*0-8047-2474-1*) Stanford U Pr.

Davis, Rachel. My Outlaw. 384p. 1997. mass mkt. 5.99 (*0-8217-5680-X*, Zebra Kensgtn) Kensgtn Pub Corp.

Davis, Rachel & James, Deana. Loving Enemies. 416p. 1996. mass mkt. 5.99 (*0-8217-5418-1*, Zebra Kensgtn) Kensgtn Pub Corp.

Davis, Ralph. Netware 386 Programmer's Guide. 416p. (C). 1991. pap. 26.95 (*0-201-57709-7*) Addison-Wesley.

— Netware 386: Programmer's Guide. (C). 1993. pap. text. write for info. (*0-201-59490-0*) Addison-Wesley.

— The Rise of the Atlantic Economies. Wilson, Charles, ed. (World Economic History Ser.). 340p. 1973. pap. text 17.95 (*0-8014-9143-6*) Cornell U Pr.

Davis, Ralph. Windows 95 Network Programming with MFC. 832p. (C). 1996. pap. 46.95 (*0-201-48930-9*) Addison-Wesley.

Davis, Ralph C., Jr. Fundamentals of Top Management. Chandler, Alfred D., ed. LC 79-7539. (History of Management Thought & Practice Ser.). 1980. reprint ed. lib. bdg. 75.95 (*0-405-12324-8*) Ayer.

Davis, Ramdy A. Tattles the Toothless Rattlesnake. 1998. 10.95 (*0-533-12680-0*) Vantage.

Davis, Randal, jt. auth. see Dalkey, Victoria.

Davis, Randal B. Hybrid Visions: The Multimedia Works of Ken Butler. pap. 2.00 (*0-914435-14-0*) Marylhurst Art.

Davis, Randall P. Carp & Catfish: A Complete Guide to Preparing & Fishing Doughbaits. (Illus.). 75p. (Orig.). 1992. pap. 6.95 (*1-881399-06-0*) Beaver Pond P&P.

Davis, Randall W., jt. ed. see Williams, Terrie M.

Davis, Rankin. Abuse of Process. 1998. mass mkt. 6.99 (*0-425-16150-1*) Berkley Pub.

— Hung Jury. 336p. 1999. pap. 6.99 (*0-425-16674-0*) Berkley Pub.

Davis, Ray & Davis, W. J. The Story of Ray Davis: Gen, USMC, Ret (Medal of Honor) 350p. 1994. 19.95 (*1-885541-00-7*) Marine Bks.

***Davis, Raymond.** Clear Conscience: The Atom Bomb Vs. the Super Holocaust. 1999. 21.95 (*1-56311-445-3*) Turner Pub KY.

Davis, Raymond, tr. The Lives of the Ninth-Century Popes: Liber Pontificalis. 360p. (Orig.). 1996. pap. text 20.95 (*0-85323-479-5*) U of Pa Pr.

Davis, Raymond E., et al. Surveying Theory & Practice. 6th ed. (Illus.). 1120p. (C). 1981. text 81.00 (*0-07-015790-1*) McGraw.

Davis, Raymond G., jt. auth. see Harder, Marvin A.

Davis, Reba, jt. ed. see Davis, Walter.

Davis, Reba B. & Balderson, John L. Word Processing Supervision. 320p. (C). 1984. teacher ed. write for info. (*0-672-98449-0*); text. write for info. (*0-672-98448-2*) Macmillan.

***Davis, Rebecca.** The History of the Washington Mystics. LC 99-18887. (Women's Pro Basketball Today Ser.). 1999. lib. bdg. 21.30 (*1-58341-012-0*, Creat Educ) Creative Co.

Davis, Rebecca & Asay, Roger. Rebecca Davis - Roger Asay: Touching Earth. Stuhr, Joanne, ed. (Illus.). 31p. 1995. pap. 10.00 (*0-911611-03-7*) Tucson Mus Art.

Davis, Rebecca & Sprinkle, Karen. Riverside's History from Its First People to the Present: Third Grade Student Edition. (Illus.). 141p. (J). (gr. 3-6). 1998. pap. text, student ed. 5.00 (*0-935661-29-8*) Riverside Mus Pr.

Davis, Rebecca & Tuntland, Carol. The Textiles Handbook. (Illus.). (C). 1996. pap. 23.95 (*0-916434-11-7*) Plycon Pr.

Davis, Rebecca, tr. see Seike, Kiyosi.

Davis, Rebecca G. Small Gardens: Inspired Plantings for Diminutive Spaces. LC 96-35753. 1997. 25.00 (*1-56799-429-6*) M Friedman Pub Grp Inc.

Davis, Rebecca H. Life in the Iron Mills. Tichi, Cecilia, ed. LC 96-86795. 432p. 1997. text 35.00 (*0-312-16374-6*) St Martin.

— Life in the Iron Mills & Other Stories. 2nd ed. Olsen, Tillie, ed. LC 84-25908. 248p. 1985. pap. 10.95 (*0-935312-39-0*) Feminist Pr.

— Margaret Howth. LC 77-104437. 266p. reprint ed. lib. bdg. 32.50 (*0-8398-0353-2*) Irvington.

— Margaret Howth. 266p. (C). 1986. reprint ed. pap. text 9.95 (*0-8290-1949-9*) Irvington.

— Margret Howth. LC 90-3684. 312p. 1990. reprint ed. 35.00 (*1-55861-030-8*); reprint ed. pap. 11.95 (*1-55861-036-7*) Feminist Pr.

— Silhouettes of American Life. (C). 1972. reprint ed. lib. bdg. 29.50 (*0-8422-8033-2*) Irvington.

— Silhouettes of American Life. (C). 1986. reprint ed. pap. text 6.95 (*0-685-16965-0*) Irvington.

— Silhouettes of American Lives. Rose, Jane, ed. (Masterworks of Literature Ser.). pap. 12.95 (*0-8084-0478-4*) NCUP.

— Waiting for the Verdict. Dingledine, D., ed. LC 68-57520. (Masterworks of Literature Ser.). pap. 12.95 (*0-685-71560-4*) NCUP.

— Waiting for the Verdict. LC 68-57520. (Illus.). 361p. reprint ed. lib. bdg. 52.50 (*0-8398-0354-0*) Irvington.

— With Daring Faith. (Illus.). 188p. (J). 1987. pap. 6.49 (*0-89084-414-3*, 033167) Bob Jones Univ.

— Women & Power in Parliamentary Democracies: Cabinet Appointments in Western Europe, 1968-1992. LC 96-22358. (Women & Politics Ser.). xi, 139p. 1997. text 40.00 (*0-8032-1707-2*) U of Nebr Pr.

Davis, Rebecca J. A Sunnybrook Garden Tale. LC 92-97014. (Illus.). 32p. (J). (gr. 3-5). 1993. lib. bdg. 12.00 (*0-9634032-0-6*) R J Davis.

Davis, Reed M., ed. Moral Reasoning & Statecraft: Essays Presented to Kenneth W. Thompson. (Illus.). 208p. (Orig.). (C). 1988. pap. text 21.00 (*0-8191-7019-4*, Pub. by White Miller Center); lib. bdg. 45.00 (*0-8191-7018-6*, Pub. by White Miller Center) U Pr of Amer.

Davis, Regen. Cat Home Alone: Fifty Ways to Keep Your Cat Happy & Safe While You're Away, Incl. toy. (Illus.). 64p. 1997. pap. 10.95 (*0-8362-3259-3*) Andrews & McMeel.

Davis, Reginald F. & Borns, Nicholas F. Solo Dad Survival Guide. LC 98-26011. 128p. 1998. pap. 12.95 (*0-8092-2925-0*, 292500, Contemporary Bks) NTC Contemp Pub Co.

Davis, Rel. The Existential Pagan: Freedom & Responsibility. LC 98-96550. 192p. 1998. pap. 18.95 (*0-9666380-0-X*) Old Time FL.

Davis, Ren & Davis, Helen. Atlanta's Urban Trails Vol. 2: Country Tours. Mueller, Phyllis, ed. LC 88-8811. (Illus.). 136p. (Orig.). 1988. pap. 9.95 (*0-932419-20-8*) Cherokee.

Davis, Ren, jt. auth. see Davis, Helen.

Davis, Rib. Writing Dialogue for Scripts. unabridged ed. 1998. pap. 15.95 (*0-7136-4802-3*, Pub. by A & C Blk) Midpt Trade.

Davis, Ricardo A. Unspoken Word. Goodman, Sharon L., ed. (Orig.). 1986. pap. text 3.50 (*0-935369-04-X*) In Tradition Pub.

***Davis, Rich.** Wild about Kansas City Barbecue. rev. ed. Orig. Title: All about Bar-B-Q Kansas City - Style. 160p. 2000. pap. 14.95 (*0-925175-31-5*) Pig Out Pubns.

Davis, Rich & Stein, Shifra. All about BarB-Q Kansas City Style. 2nd ed. (Illus.). 160p. 1995. pap. 14.95 (*0-925175-11-0*) Pig Out Pubns.

Davis, Rich, jt. illus. see Meister, Cari.

Davis, Richard. The Adventures & Letters of Richard Harding Davis. (American Biography Ser.). 417p. 1991. reprint ed. lib. bdg. 89.00 (*0-7812-8101-6*) Rprt Serv.

— Anna Bishop: The Adventures of an Intrepid Prima Donna. (Illus.). 314p. 1997. 45.00 (*0-86819-485-9*, Pub. by Currency Pr) Accents Pubns.

— Antics: An Ant Thology. (Illus.). 64p. (Orig.). 1995. pap. 3.95 (*0-9644285-0-4*) R Davis OK.

— A Beginning Singer's Guide. (Illus.). 224p. 1998. 45.00 (*0-8108-3555-X*); pap. 26.50 (*0-8108-3556-8*) Scarecrow.

— Beyond the BS 5750-ISO 9000 Certificate: The Bureaucracy Buster's Guide to Quality Assurance. (C). 1994. 97.50 (*0-946655-83-9*, Pub. by S Thornes Pubs) Trans-Atl Phila.

— Combating Terrorism: Opportunities to Improve Domestic Preparedness Program Focus & Efficiency. (Illus.). 52p. (C). 1999. pap. text 20.00 (*0-7881-7920-9*) DIANE Pub.

***Davis, Richard.** Complete Guide to Film Scoring. (Illus.). 384p. 2000. per. 24.95 (*0-634-00636-3*, Berklee Pr) H Leonard.

— Construction Insolvency. 2nd ed. 615p. 1999. write for info. (*1-902558-17-0*, Pub. by Palladian Law) Gaunt.

Davis, Richard. A Man to Cross Rivers With. LC 99-61619. (Illus.). 272p. 1999. pap. 12.95 (*1-890437-09-3*) Western Reflections.

— Mirror Hate: The Convergent Ideology of Northern Ireland Paramilitaries, 1966-1992. LC 94-27123. 1994. 77.95 (*1-85521-558-6*, Pub. by Dartmth Pub) Ashgate Pub Co.

— The Press & American Politics: The New Mediator. 2nd ed. LC 95-16059. 432p. 1995. pap. text 41.00 (*0-13-185943-9*) P-H.

***Davis, Richard.** The Press & American Politics: The New Mediator. 3rd ed. LC 99-86445. 368p. 2000. pap. text 36.00 (*0-13-026404-0*) P-H.

— Revolutionary Imperialist: William Smith O'Brien, 1803-1864. LC 98-215010. viii, 392 p. 1998. pap. write for info. (*1-901866-20-3*, Pub. by Lilliput Pr) Dufour.

Davis, Richard. Vermin Blond. 208p. 1993. 23.95 (*0-575-05007-1*, Pub. by V Gollancz) Trafalgar.

— The Web of Politics: The Internet's Impact on the American Political System. LC 98-6872. 248p. 1999. text 39.95 (*0-19-511484-1*); pap. text 18.95 (*0-19-511485-X*) OUP.

***Davis, Richard.** Yours, D3. 324p. 2000. pap. 12.95 (*0-9665234-1-5*) Allnce Hse.

Davis, Richard. Yours D3. 1999. 24.95 (*0-9665234-0-7*) Allnce Hse.

Davis, Richard, ed. Defense Budget: Analysis of Operation & Maintenance Accounts for 1985-2001. (Illus.). 78p. (C). 1999. reprint ed. pap. text 20.00 (*0-7881-4377-8*) DIANE Pub.

Davis, Richard & Davis, Marianne, eds. The Rebel in His Family: Selected Papers of William Smith O'Brien. LC 99-175827. (Irish Narrative Ser.). 96p. 1998. pap. 12.95 (*1-85918-181-3*, Pub. by Cork Univ) Intl Spec Bk.

Davis, Richard & Owen, Diana. New Media & American Politics. LC 97-52291. 320p. 1998. 45.00 (*0-19-512060-4*); pap. 19.95 (*0-19-512061-2*) OUP.

Davis, Richard & Robertson, David. Textbook of Neuropathology. 2nd ed. (Illus.). 1176p. 1990. 180.00 (*0-683-02344-6*) Lppncott W & W.

Davis, Richard, et al. Growing up Catholic: An Infinitely Funny Guide for the Faithful, the Fallen & Everyone in Between. LC 83-25394. 144p. 1985. pap. 9.95 (*0-385-19240-1*) Doubleday.

Davis, Richard, jt. auth. see Mirtschin, Peter.

Davis, Richard, jt. auth. see Rajak, Harry.

Davis, Richard A. Beach & Nearshore Sediments & Processes: Selected Papers Reprinted from Journal of Sedimentary Petrology, SEPM Special Publication No. 24, SEPM Eastern Section Field Guide, Sedimentology. LC 89-138157. (SEPM Reprint Ser.: No. 12). (Illus.). 228p. 1987. reprint ed. pap. 70.70 (*0-608-02976-9*, 206344400006) Bks Demand.

— The Black Family in a Changing Black Community: Essays on the Black Underclass. LC 92-27491. (Library of Sociology: Vol. 26). 144p. 1993. text 15.00 (*0-8153-0878-7*, H838) Garland.

Davis, Richard A., Jr. The Evolving Coast. LC 97-127212. (Illus.). 231p. 1996. pap. 19.95 (*0-7167-6021-5*) W H Freeman.

Davis, Richard A. Kuniyoshi (Yasuo) The Complete Graphic Work. (Illus.). 288p. 1991. 125.00 (*1-55660-089-5*) A Wofsy Fine Arts.

— The Myth of Black Ethnicity: Monophylety, Diversity, & the Dilemma of Identity. LC 96-34171. (Illus.). 250p. 1997. pap. 39.50 (*1-56750-293-8*); text 73.25 (*1-56750-292-X*) Ablx Pub.

An Asterisk (*) at the beginning of an entry indicates that the title is appearing for the first time.

Davis, Richard A., tr. see Marx, Karl.
Davis, Richard B. The Abbe Correa in America, 1812-1820: The Contributions of the Diplomat & Natural Philosopher to the Foundations of Our National Life. LC 92-81891. 375p. 1993. reprint ed. pap. text 15.00 (*0-943722-17-9*) Gavea-Brown.
— American Literature Through Bryant. LC 76-79172. (Goldentree Bibliographies Series in Language & Literature). 160p. (C). 1969. pap. text 6.95 (*0-88295-510-1*) Harlan Davidson.
— Butterbean: When Glory Is Just a Whisper. 1994. pap. 15.95 (*0-9623414-8-7*) Smith Collins.
— Butterbean: When Glory's Just a Whisper. LC 94-66257. 227p. 1994. pap. 15.95 (*0-9642202-5-3*) Butterbean Prods.
— Intellectual Life in Jefferson's Virginia, 1790-1830. LC 64-13548. 523p. reprint ed. pap. 162.20 (*0-608-13344-2*, 202555900044) Bks Demand.
— Literature & Society in Early Virginia, 1608-1840. LC 72-89896. (Southern Literary Studies). 356p. 1973. pap. 110.40 (*0-7837-8510-0*, 204931900011) Bks Demand.
Davis, Richard B., ed. see Davies, Samuel.
Davis, Richard C., ed. Rupert's Land: A Cultural Tapestry. (Calgary Institute for the Humanities Ser.). (Illus.). 316p. (C). 1989. 39.95 (*0-88920-976-6*) W Laurier U Pr.
Davis, Richard C., et al. Rational Numbers Study Aid. (J). 1976. pap. 3.00 (*0-87738-039-2*) Youth Ed.
Davis, Richard C., ed. see Forest History Society Editors.
Davis, Richard E. Deer Camp - Oswegatchie River - & Other Places. 130p. (Orig.). 1996. pap. 12.95 (*1-57502-199-4*, P0827) Morris Pubng.
Davis, Richard G. Carl A. Spaatz & the Air War in Europe. LC 92-14889. (General Histories Ser.). 1992. per. write for info. (*0-912799-77-3*); boxed set 47.00 (*0-912799-75-7*) AFH & MP.
— Carl A. Spaatz & the Air War in Europe. (History of Aviation Ser.). (Illus.). 762p. 1994. 49.95 (*1-56098-254-3*) Smithsonian.
Davis, Richard G. Carl A. Spaatz & the Air War in Europe. 830p. 1993. per. 52.00 (*0-16-061356-6*) USGPO.
— Decisive Force: Strategic Bombing in the Gulf War. 87p. 1996. pap. 9.00 (*0-16-061368-X*) USGPO.
Davis, Richard G. Decisive Force: Strategic Bombing in the Gulf War. (Illus.). 85p. 1998. reprint ed. pap. text 25.00 (*0-7881-3814-6*) DIANE Pub.
— Hap: Henry H. Arnold, Military Aviator. LC 97-177027. 40p. 1997. pap. 2.25 (*0-16-049071-5*) USGPO.
Davis, Richard H. About Paris. (C). 1988. pap. text 6.95 (*0-8290-2233-3*) Irvington.
— About Paris. LC 70-96879. reprint ed. lib. bdg. 22.00 (*0-8398-0355-9*) Irvington.
— At a New Mining Camp: Creede of Colorado, 1892. Jones, William R., ed. (Illus.). 32p. 1977. reprint ed. pap. 3.95 (*0-89646-018-5*) Vistabooks.
— Bar Sinister. 1971. 6.00 (*0-403-00017-3*) Scholarly.
— Bar Sinister. LC 69-13877. 108p. 1970. reprint ed. lib. bdg. 45.00 (*0-8371-1965-0*, DABS, Greenwood Pr) Greenwood.
— The Bar Sinister. (BCL1-PS American Literature Ser.). 108p. 1992. reprint ed. lib. bdg. 69.00 (*0-7812-6700-5*) Rprt Serv.
— Cinderella, & Other Stories. LC 70-90579. (Short Story Index Reprint Ser.). 1977. 19.95 (*0-8369-3062-2*) Ayer.
— Cuban & Puerto Rican Campaigns. (Select Bibliographies Reprint Ser.). (Illus.). 1977. 31.95 (*0-8369-5278-2*) Ayer.
— Episodes in Van Bibber's Life. LC 75-101795. (Short Story Index Reprint Ser.). 1977. 16.95 (*0-8369-3183-1*) Ayer.
— The Exiles & Other Stories. 1972. 32.00 (*0-8422-8034-0*) Irvington.
— Gallegher: And Other Stories. (BCL1-PS American Literature Ser.). 236p. 1992. reprint ed. lib. bdg. 79.00 (*0-7812-6701-3*) Rprt Serv.
— Gallegher & Other Stories. (Illus.). reprint ed. 29.50 (*0-404-01997-8*) AMS Pr.
— Gallegher & Other Stories. (Illus.). (C). 1972. reprint ed. 9.50 (*0-8422-8035-9*) Irvington.
— Gallegher & Other Stories. (Illus.). (C). 1986. reprint ed. pap. text 8.45 (*0-8290-1934-0*) Irvington.
— Gallegher & Other Stories. LC 71-131684. (Illus.). 1970. reprint ed. 10.00 (*0-403-00571-X*) Scholarly.
— Lion & the Unicorn. LC 71-94715. (Short Story Index Reprint Ser.). 1977. 19.95 (*0-8369-3094-0*) Ayer.
***Davis, Richard H.** Lives of Indian Images. 331p. 1999. pap. 150.00 (*81-208-1692-7*, Pub. by Motilal Bnarsidass) St Mut.
Davis, Richard H. Lives of Indian Images. LC 96-22196. 350p. 1997. text 39.50 (*0-691-02622-X*, Pub. by Princeton U Pr) Cal Prin Full Svc.
***Davis, Richard H.** Lives Of Indian Images. 1999. pap. text 18.95 (*0-691-00520-6*, Pub. by Princeton U Pr) Cal Prin Full Svc.
Davis, Richard H. Ranson's Folly. LC 79-152938. (Short Story Index Reprint Ser.). (Illus.). 1977. reprint ed. 23.95 (*0-8369-3797-X*) Ayer.
— Ranson's Folly & Other Stories. (Airmont Classics Ser.). (J). (gr. 9 up). 1968. mass mkt. 1.95 (*0-8049-0192-9*, CL-192) Airmont.
— Ritual in an Oscillating Universe: Worshiping Siva in Medieval India. LC 91-3954. (Illus.). 216p. reprint ed. pap. 67.00 (*0-608-07641-4*, 205995800010) Bks Demand.
— Rulers of the Mediterranean. LC 76-38788. (Essay Index Reprint Ser.). 1977. reprint ed. 26.95 (*0-8369-2645-5*) Ayer.
— Soldiers of Fortune. 1976. 19.95 (*0-8488-0258-6*) Amereon Ltd.
— Soldiers of Fortune. LC 74-96880. (Illus.). 348p. reprint ed. lib. bdg. 18.00 (*0-8398-0356-7*) Irvington.
— Soldiers of Fortune. (Illus.). 348p. (C). 1986. reprint ed. pap. text 7.95 (*0-8290-2027-6*) Irvington.
— Soldiers of Fortune. (BCL1-PS American Literature Ser.). 347p. 1992. reprint ed. lib. bdg. 89.00 (*0-7812-6702-1*) Rprt Serv.
— Stories for Boys. LC 73-150472. (Short Story Index Reprint Ser.). 1977. reprint ed. 20.95 (*0-8369-3812-7*) Ayer.
— Van Bibber & Others, Vol. 1. LC 72-5865. (Short Story Index Reprint Ser.). 1977. reprint ed. 23.95 (*0-8369-4208-6*) Ayer.
— Year from a Reporter's Notebook. LC 70-125691. (American Journalists Ser.). (Illus.). 1971. reprint ed. 25.95 (*0-405-01668-9*) Ayer.
— Year from a Reporter's Notebook. (American Biography Ser.). 305p. 1991. reprint ed. lib. bdg. 79.00 (*0-7812-8102-4*) Rprt Serv.
Davis, Richard H., ed. Images, Miracles & Authority in Asian Religious Traditions. LC 98-9211. 272p. (C). 1998. text 65.00 (*0-8133-3463-2*, Pub. by Westview) HarpC.
***Davis, Richard Harding.** Cuba in War Time. (Illus.). 143p. 2000. pap. 10.00 (*0-8032-6625-1*, Bison Books) U of Nebr Pr.
Davis, Richard J. Walk with God. (Illus.). 80p. 1995. pap. 4.95 (*0-9660331-0-8*) Lord & Davis.
Davis, Richard L. Court & Family in Sung China, 960-1279: Bureaucratic Success & Kinship Fortunes for the Shih of Ming-Chou. LC 85-20656. xvi, 354p. 1986. text 46.95 (*0-8223-0512-7*) Duke.
— Domestic Violence: Facts & Fallacies. LC 97-27924. 224p. 1998. 55.00 (*0-275-96126-5*, Praeger Pubs) Greenwood.
— Wind Against the Mountain: The Crisis of Politics & Culture in Thirteenth-Century China. LC 96-25667. (Harvard-Yenching Institute Monographs: No. 42). 335p. 1996. 40.00 (*0-674-95357-6*) HUP.
Davis, Richard L. & Donnini, Frank P. Professional Military Education for Air Force Officers: Comments & Criticisms. LC 91-15110. (Illus.). 136p. 1991. pap. 9.00 (*1-58566-039-6*) Air Univ.
Davis, Richard L. & Robertson, David M., eds. Textbook of Neuropathology. 3rd ed. LC 96-15265. (Illus.). 1296p. 1996. 195.00 (*0-683-02355-1*) Lppncott W & W.
Davis, Richard M. Thesis Projects in Science & Engineering. LC 78-65255. (Illus.). 1979. pap. 8.95 (*0-312-79963-2*) St Martin.
Davis, Richard W. The English Rothschilds. LC 83-10517. (Illus.). 272p. reprint ed. pap. 84.40 (*0-7837-6853-2*, 204668200003) Bks Demand.
Davis, Rick. Totally Useless Office Skills. LC 96-78425. (Illus.). 128p. (Orig.). 1996. pap. 12.95 (*0-9636413-2-8*) Hobblebush Bks.
Davis, Rick, jt. auth. see Thaiss, Christopher.
Davis, Rick, tr. see Ibsen, Henrik.
Davis, Rita. Simple Yet Stunning Quilts. (Illus.). 80p. 1981. pap. 8.95 (*0-942152-07-7*) R C Pubns OR.
Davis, Robert. Academic Thanatos? 96p. (C). 1995. pap. text 19.95 (*0-7872-1363-2*) Kendall-Hunt.
— The Doomsday Kiss. 450p. 1998. 24.95 (*1-890248-02-9*) Horizon Pr MI.
— It's the Little Things: Small Steps Toward Big Success in Public Relations. LC 97-75687. 112p. 1998. pap. 14.95 (*1-887750-80-0*) Rutledge Bks.
— Iz. Seligman, Carole, ed. (Orig.). 1995. pap. 10.00 (*0-9645592-0-X*) Lost Bks Pr.
— Kimura. 224p. (J). 1989. 18.95 (*0-8027-5736-7*) Walker & Co.
— Learning Mathematics: The Cognitive Science Approach to Mathematics Education. LC 84-2853. 400p. 1984. text 73.25 (*0-89391-245-X*) Ablx Pub.
— My Journey into Alzheimer's Disease. 140p. 1989. pap. 7.99 (*0-8423-4645-7*) Tyndale Hse.
— The Plutonium Murders. 392p. 1997. pap. 24.95 (*1-890248-00-2*) Horizon Pr MI.
— World of Hi-Tech Sales: Rules & Realities. (Illus.). 235p. (Orig.). 1996. pap. 20.00 (*0-9656094-0-5*) Wrld of Hi-Tech Sales.
Davis, Robert & Zannis, Mark. The Genocide Machine in Canada: The Pacification of the North. LC 75-306912. (Black Rose Bks.: Vol. D10). 203p. 1973. reprint ed. pap. 63.00 (*0-608-00454-5*, 206127300007) Bks Demand.
Davis, Robert, et al. Marketing Management: Casebook. 3rd ed. (C). 1980. 45.50 (*0-256-02347-6*, Irwn McGrw-H) McGrw-H Hghr Educ.
Davis, Robert, jt. auth. see Dahl, Richard C.
Davis, Robert, jt. auth. see Misner, Ivan.
Davis, Robert A., Sr. Police Sergeants Handbook, Vol. I. 195p. (Orig.). 1968. pap. 28.95 (*1-56325-024-1*, DH011) Davis Pub Law.
Davis, Robert B. Discovery in Mathematics: A Text for Teachers. 274p. 1980. pap. text 16.50 (*0-914040-86-3*) Cuisenaire.
Davis, Robert B., et al, eds. Constructivist Views on the Teaching & Learning of Mathematics. LC 90-45001. (Journal for Research in Mathematics Education Monograph Ser.: No. 4). 210p. 1990. pap. 13.50 (*0-87353-300-3*) NCTM.
Davis, Robert C. Contemporary Literary Criticism: Literary & Cultural Studies. 4th ed. LC 97-37648. 700p. (C). 1998. 74.00 (*0-8013-3002-5*); text. write for info. (*0-8013-3003-3*) Addison-Wesley.
— Final Mutiny: Reinhard Goering, His Life & Art. LC 83-49394. (Stanford German Studies: Vol. 21). 465p. (Orig.). (C). 1987. text 52.50 (*0-8204-0098-X*) P Lang Pubng.
— The Paternal Romance: Reading God-the-Father in Early Western Culture. 200p. (C). 1993. text 32.50 (*0-252-01949-0*); pap. text 14.95 (*0-252-06265-5*) U of Ill Pr.
— Shipbuilders of the Venetian Arsenal: Workers & Workplace in the Preindustrial City. LC 90-43807. (Studies in Historical & Political Science: 109th Series, No. 1 (1991)). (Illus.). 256p. 1991. text 42.50 (*0-8018-4095-3*) Johns Hopkins.
— Shipbuilders of the Venetian Arsenal: Workers & Workplace in the Preindustrial City. LC 90-43807. (Johns Hopkins Studies in Historical & Political Science: Series 109, 1). (Illus.). 280p. reprint ed. pap. 86.80 (*0-608-08800-5*, 206943900004) Bks Demand.
Davis, Robert C., ed. The Fictional Father: Lacanian Readings of the Text. LC 80-26222. 224p. 1981. reprint ed. pap. 69.50 (*0-608-01708-6*, 206236300002) Bks Demand.
— The Grapes of Wrath: A Collection of Critical Essays. 157p. 1982. 15.95 (*0-13-363358-6*) P-H.
Davis, Robert C., et al, eds. Drugs & the Community: Involving Community Residents in Combatting the Sale of Illegal Drugs. LC 92-33880. (Illus.). 328p. (C). 1993. 70.95 (*0-398-05835-0*) C C Thomas.
— Victims of Crime. 2nd ed. LC 96-45872. 295p. 1996. 56.00 (*0-7619-0154-X*); pap. 25.95 (*0-7619-0155-8*) Sage.
Davis, Robert C. & Lurigio, Arthur J. Fighting Back: Neighborhood Antidrug Strategies. LC 95-41798. 176p. (C). 1996. 38.00 (*0-8039-7112-5*); pap. 17.95 (*0-8039-7113-3*) Sage.
Davis, Robert C. & Schleifer, Ronald. Criticism & Culture: The Role of Critique in Modern Literary Theory. 259p. (C). 1992. 87.00 (*0-582-05081-2*); pap. text 37.50 (*0-582-05082-0*, 79203) Longman.
Davis, Robert C., jt. auth. see Brown, Judith C.
Davis, Robert C., jt. ed. see O'Donnell, Patrick.
Davis, Robert C., ed. see Rosenbaum, Dennis P.
Davis, Robert D., jt. auth. see Moon, Robert A.
Davis, Robert E. The Imagical World of Bossons. (Illus.). 238p. 1982. write for info. (*0-9614255-0-4*) R E Davis.
— Organizations, Programs, & Activities of the Geologic Division, U. S. Geological Survey. (Illus.). 40p 1998. reprint ed. pap. 5.00 (*0-89904-902-8*, Ecosystems Resrch) Crumb Elbow Pub.
— Response to Innovation: A Study of Popular Argument about New Mass Media. Loweth, Garth S., ed. LC 75-21430. (Dissertations on Film Ser.). 1976. lib. bdg. 38.95 (*0-405-07533-2*) Ayer.
Davis, Robert F., ed. Diamond Films & Coatings: Developments, Properties, & Applications. LC 92-35011. (Illus.). 421p. 1993. 109.00 (*0-8155-1323-2*) Noyes.
Davis, Robert F., et al, eds. Emergent Process Methods for High-Technology Ceramics. LC 84-6941. (Materials Science Research Ser.: Vol. 17). 856p. 1984. 145.00 (*0-306-41677-8*, Plenum Trade) Perseus Pubng.
Davis, Robert G. John Dos Passos. LC 62-63696. (University of Minnesota Pamphlets on American Writers Ser.: No. 20). 47p. (Orig.). reprint ed. pap. 30.00 (*0-7837-2892-1*, 205756300006) Bks Demand.
— Ten Modern Masters: An Anthology of the Short Story. 3rd ed. 583p. (C). 1972. pap. text, teacher ed. 2.50 (*0-15-590282-2*) Harcourt Coll Pubs.
— Without Benefit of Clergy: A Challenge to Ministers. LC 96-70898. 64p. (Orig.). 1996. pap. 8.95 (*1-57736-016-8*) Providence Hse.
***Davis, Robert G. & Isaacs, Larry D.** Elementary Physical Education: Growing Through Movement. 4th ed. (Illus.). 430p. 2000. pap. text 52.00 (*0-88725-264-8*) Hunter Textbks.
Davis, Robert H. Aloe Vera: A Scientific Approach. LC 96-90679. (Illus.). 321p. 1997. 21.95 (*0-533-12137-X*) Vantage.
— Historical Dictionary of Colombia. 2nd ed. LC 93-29007. (Latin American Historical Dictionaries Ser.: No. 23). (Illus.). 615p. 1993. 70.00 (*0-8108-2636-4*) Scarecrow.
Davis, Robert H., ed. Colombia. annot. ed. LC 90-202925. (World Bibliographical Ser.: No. 112). 228p. 1990. lib. bdg. 60.00 (*1-85109-093-2*) ABC-CLIO.
***Davis, Robert H., et al.** A Dark Mirror: Romanov & Imperial Palace Library Materials in the Holdings of the New York Public Library: A Checklist & Agenda for Research. LC 99-86965. (Slavic, Baltic & Eurasian Resource Ser.). 2000. write for info. (*0-88354-039-8*) N Ross.
Davis, Robert J. Digital & Computer Projects. LC 99-12721. 208p. 1999. 29.95 (*0-7506-7172-6*, Newnes) Buttrwrth-Heinemann.
Davis, Robert K., et al. The Range of Choice in Water Management: A Study of Dissolved Oxygen in the Potomac Estuary. LC 68-27737. 214p. reprint ed. pap. 66.40 (*0-7837-3134-5*, 201982100014) Bks Demand.
Davis, Robert L. Whitman & the Romance of Medicine. LC 96-39258. 205p. 1997. 37.50 (*0-520-20760-2*, Pub. by U CA Pr) Cal Prin Full Svc.
***Davis, Robert L., et al.** Entrevistas: An Introduction to Language & Culture. LC 99-51364. 2000. write for info. (*0-07-230053-1*) McGrw-H Hghr Educ.
Davis, Robert L., ed. see Davis, Elmer H.
Davis, Robert M. Alaska Tales: Flying Is Fun? LC 94-96150. 72p. 1994. pap. text 8.95 (*0-9641998-0-7*) Lapcat Pubns.
— Alaska Tales No. 2: Goin' with the Floes. LC 95-76138. 133p. (Orig.). 1995. pap. 9.95 (*0-9641998-1-5*) Lapcat Pubns.
— Brideshead Revisited: The Past Redeemed. rev. ed. (Twayne's Masterwork Studies: No. 59). 168p. 1990. 23.95 (*0-8057-8092-0*, Twyne); pap. 13.95 (*0-8057-8138-2*, Twyne) Mac Lib Ref.
— Evelyn Waugh & the Forms of His Time. LC 88-16161. (Contexts & Literature Ser.: No. 1). 284p. 1989. reprint ed. pap. 88.10 (*0-7837-9195-X*, 204989700004) Bks Demand.
— Evelyn Waugh, Writer: The Making of a Man of Letters. 342p. 1986. reprint ed. pap. text 13.95 (*0-937664-72-3*) Pilgrim Bks OK.
— A Lower-Middle-Class Education. LC 96-4378. (Illus.). 192p. (C). 1996. 24.95 (*0-8061-2848-8*) U of Okla Pr.
***Davis, Robert M.** Mischief in the Sun: The Making & Unmaking of "The Loved One" LC 97-60171. viii, 136p. (C). 1999. 28.50 (*0-87875-494-6*) Whitston Pub.
Davis, Robert M. Playing Cowboys: Low Culture & High Art in the Western. LC 91-34453. 192p. 1994. pap. 11.95 (*0-8061-2627-2*) U of Okla Pr.
Davis, Robert M., compiled by. A Catalogue of the Evelyn Waugh Collection at the Humanities Research Center: The University of Texas at Austin. LC 80-50840. vi, 369p. 1981. 48.50 (*0-87875-194-7*) Whitston Pub.
Davis, Robert M., ed. see Waugh, Evelyn.
Davis, Robert P. Where a Man Can Go: Major General William Phillips, British Royal Artillery, 1731-1781, 179. LC 99-17842. 240p. 1999. 59.95 (*0-313-31020-3*) Greenwood.
Davis, Robert S., Jr. Cotton, Fire, & Dreams: The Robert Findlay Iron Works (The Macon Confederate Arsenal) & Heavy Industry in Macon, Georgia, 1839-1912. LC 98-5975. 304p. 1998. 29.95 (*0-86554-598-7*, H450) Mercer Univ Pr.
— The Georgia Black Book: Morbid, Macabre, & Disgusting Records of Genealogical Value. (Illus.). 456p. 1992. 42.50 (*0-89308-291-0*, GA 63) Southern Hist Pr.
— Georgia Citizens & Soldiers of the American Revolution. 350p. 1983. reprint ed. pap. 27.00 (*0-89308-411-5*) Southern Hist Pr.
— Georgians in the Revolution: At Kettle Creek (Wilkes Co.) & Burke County. (Illus.). 272p. 1987. 35.00 (*0-89308-350-X*, GA 45) Southern Hist Pr.
Davis, Robert S. Georgians Past: Special Files of Georgia Settlers & Citizens, Subjects & Counties, 1733-1970s LC 98-185001. ii, 225 p. 1997. write for info. (*1-890307-02-5*) Boyd Pub Co.
Davis, Robert S., Jr. The Land Lottery of Georgia & Other Missing Names of Winners in the Georgia Land Lotteries, 1833. 100p. 1991. pap. 20.00 (*0-89308-338-0*, GA 88) Southern Hist Pr.
— Records of Jasper County, Georgia, 1802-1922. 485p. 1990. 40.00 (*0-89308-659-2*, GA 91) Southern Hist Pr.
— Requiem for a Lost City: Sallie Clayton's Memoirs of Civil War Atlanta. LC 99-25581. (Civil War Georgia Ser.). 256p. 1999. 32.95 (*0-86554-622-3*) Mercer Univ Pr.
— Research in Georgia: With a Special Emphasis Upon the Georgia Department of Archives & History. (Illus.). 268p. 1991. pap. 30.00 (*0-89308-199-X*) Southern Hist Pr.
— A Researcher's Library of Georgia History, Genealogy, & Records Sources. (Illus.). 450p. 1987. 42.50 (*0-89308-535-9*, GA 70) Southern Hist Pr.
— A Researcher's Library of Georgia History, Genealogy, & Records Sources, Vol. II. (Illus.). 480p. 1990. 42.50 (*0-89308-683-5*, GA 87) Southern Hist Pr.
— The Wilkes County Papers, Seventeen Seventy-Seven to Eighteen Thirty-Three. 338p. 1979. pap. 28.50 (*0-89308-410-7*) Southern Hist Pr.
Davis, Robert S., Jr., jt. ed. see Lucas, Silas E., Jr.
***Davis, Robin.** Infusions: Making Flavored Oils, Vinegars & Spirits. (Illus.). 64p. 1999. boxed set 18.95 (*0-8118-2289-3*) Chronicle Bks.
Davis, Robin. The Star Wars Cookbook: Wookiee Cookies & Other Galactic Recipes. LC 99-209025. (Star Wars Ser.). (Illus.). 60p. (J). (gr. 4-7). 1998. 15.95 (*0-8118-2184-6*) Chronicle Bks.
***Davis, Robin & White, Marshall.** St. Joseph. (Images of America Ser.). (Illus.). 128p. 1999. pap. 18.99 (*0-7385-0266-9*) Arcadia Publng.
Davis, Robin J. & Butler, Lance S., eds. Make Sense Who May: Essays on Samuel Beckett's Later Works. (Irish Literary Studies: No. 30). (C). 1988. 53.00 (*0-389-20791-8*, N8349) B&N Imports.
Davis, Robin W. An Alphabet of Authors. 88p. 1996. pap. 14.95 (*0-917846-62-1*, 34010, Alleyside) Highsmith Pr.
— An Alphabet of Books: Literature Based Activities for Schools & Libraries. (Illus.). 85p. 1995. pap. 14.95 (*0-917846-38-9*, 33918, Alleyside) Highsmith Pr.
— Art & Children: Using Literature to Expand Creativity. LC 96-18941. (School Library Media Ser.: No. 9). 168p. 1996. pap. 22.50 (*0-8108-3158-9*) Scarecrow.
— Big Books for Little Readers. LC 98-50933. (School Library Media Ser.: No. 19). (Illus.). 136p. 1999. pap. 19.50 (*0-8108-3621-1*) Scarecrow.
— Toddle on Over: Developing Infant & Toddler Literature Programs. LC 97-42216. (Alleyside Press Reading Activities Ser.). (Illus.). 96p. 1998. pap. 16.95 (*1-57950-000-5*, 37681, Alleyside) Highsmith Pr.
***Davis, Robin Works.** Multimedia Storytimes. LC 99-53292. (Illus.). 100p. 2000. pap. text, teacher ed. 15.95 (*1-57950-028-5*, Alleyside) Highsmith Pr.
Davis, Robyn M. Rainbows in the Night. LC 88-92496. (Illus.). 25p. (Orig.). 1988. pap. 8.95 (*0-9621030-0-4*) Pyramid Indps.
Davis, Rod. American Voudou: Journey into a Hidden World. LC 98-21264. (Illus.). 392p. 1998. 29.95 (*1-57441-049-0*) UNTX Pr.
***Davis, Rod.** American Voudou: Journey into a Hidden World. LC 98-21264. (Illus.). 392p. 2000. reprint ed. pap. 19.95 (*1-57441-081-4*, Pub. by UNTX Pr) Tex A&M Univ Pr.
— What You Need to Know Before You Invest. 2nd ed. LC 99-12695. 288p. 1999. pap. 9.95 (*0-7641-1002-0*) Barron.
Davis, Rodney. Real Estate. LC 79-155. (Career Competencies in Marketing Ser.). (Illus.). (gr. 11-12). 1979. text 12.04 (*0-07-015672-7*) McGraw.
Davis, Roger. Concepts Biology Lab Manual. 196p. (C). 1995. pap. text, spiral bd. 34.95 (*0-7872-1122-2*, 41112201) Kendall-Hunt.
Davis, Roger, jt. auth. see Wong, Szuson J.

D

Davis, Roger D., jt. auth. see Millon, Theodore.

Davis, Roger E. The Organists' Manual: Technical Studies & Selected Compositions for the Organ. (C). 1985. 53.50 (*0-393-95461-7*) Norton.

Davis, Roger M. Ultimate Mental Power: The IKO - Meditation Technique. (Illus.). 424p. 1999. pap. 27.95 (*0-939366-09-6*) AKU Pr.

— Youth-Run Organizations: A Youth Development Workshop. rev. ed. (Illus.). 150p. (C). 1999. pap., teacher ed. 99.99 (*0-939366-02-9*); pap., wbk. ed. 18.95 (*0-939366-03-7*) AKU Pr.

— Youth-Run Organizations: A Youth Development Workshop. rev. ed. (Illus.). 200p. (C). 1999. pap. text 49.95 (*0-939366-01-0*) AKU Pr.

Davis, Roger W. Review of Pain Medicine. 148p. 1993. pap. 24.70 (*1-884401-00-7*) Pain Review.

Davis, Rolanda J. Eating to the Glory of God. Mason, Sharon, ed. (Illus.). 160p. 1996. pap. 14.95 (*0-9651904-0-4*) D & R Davis.

Davis, Ron. Women & Horses. (Chapbooks Ser.). (Illus.). (Orig.). 1981. pap. 3.00 (*0-914140-11-6*) Carpenter Pr.

Davis, Ron, ed. How to Be a Smart Investor: Turning a Small Stake into a Big Payoff. unabridged ed. 512p. 1997. 31.96 (*0-9660073-0-1*) Hume Grp.

Davis, Ronald B., ed. Paleolimnology & the Reconstruction of Ancient Environments. (C). 1990. text 257.50 (*0-7923-0571-X*) Kluwer Academic.

Davis, Ronald D. The Gift of Dyslexia: Why Some of the Smartest People Can't Read & How They Can Learn. LC 94-17275. (Illus.). 232p. 1994. 14.95 (*0-929551-23-0*) Ability Workshop Pr.

Davis, Ronald d. The Gift of Dyslexia: Why Some of the Smartest People Can't Read & How They Can Learn, Incl. 3 audio cass. Braun, Eldon M., ed. LC 94-17275. (Illus.). 232p. (Orig.). 1994. 34.95 incl. audio (*0-929551-24-9*) Ability Workshop Pr.

Davis, Ronald D. & Braun, Eldon M. The Gift of Dyslexia: Why Some of the Smartest People Can't Read, & How They Can Learn. LC 96-28849. (Illus.). 258p. 1997. pap. 14.95 (*0-399-52293-X*, Perigee Bks) Berkley Pub.

Davis, Ronald H. ATM for Public Networks. LC 99-31235. (Telecommunications Ser.). (Illus.). 385p. 1999. 59.95 (*0-07-134476-4*) McGraw.

Davis, Ronald L. The Black Experience in Natchez. 236p. 1994. pap. 14.95 (*0-915992-62-0*) Eastern National.

— Duke: The Life & Image of John Wayne. LC 97-42059. (Illus.). 400p. 1998. 24.95 (*0-8061-3015-6*) U of Okla Pr.

— The Glamour Factory: Inside Hollywood's Big Studio System. LC 93-8861. (Illus.). 464p. (Orig.). 1993. 29.95 (*0-87074-357-0*); pap. 14.95 (*0-87074-358-9*) SMU Press.

— Good & Faithful Labor: From Slavery to Sharecropping in the Natchez District, 1860-1890, 100. LC 81-13367. (Contributions in American History Ser.: No. 100). (Illus.). 225p. 1982. 59.95 (*0-313-23134-6*, DFL/) Greenwood.

— A History of Music in American Life, Vol. 2: The Gilded Years, 1865-1920. LC 79-25359. 286p. 1980. lib. bdg. 31.50 (*0-89874-003-7*) Krieger.

— Hollywood Beauty: Linda Darnell & the American Dream. LC 90-50685. 256p. 1991. 24.95 (*0-8061-2327-3*) U of Okla Pr.

— John Ford: Hollywood's Old Master. LC 94-25178. (Oklahoma Western Biographies Ser.: Vol. 10). (Illus.). 383p. 1995. 29.95 (*0-8061-2708-2*) U of Okla Pr.

— John Ford: Hollywood's Old Master. LC 94-25178. (Oklahoma Western Biographies Ser.: Vol. 10). (Illus.). 400p. 1997. pap. 14.95 (*0-8061-2916-6*) U of Okla Pr.

***Davis, Ronald L.** La Scala West: The Dallas Opera under Kelly & Rescigno. (Illus.). 224p. 2000. 49.95 (*0-87074-454-2*) SMU Press.

Davis, Ronald L. Twentieth Century Cultural Life in Texas. (Texas History Ser.). (Illus.). 50p. 1981. pap. text 8.95 (*0-89641-072-2*) American Pr.

***Davis, Ronald L. F.** The Black Experience in Natchez, 1720-1880: A Special History Study. rev. ed. 226p. 1999. pap. text 12.50 (*1-888213-37-X*) Eastern National.

Davis, Ronald M. Health Benefits of Smoking Cessation: A Report of the Surgeon General, 1990. 668p. 1990. per. 27.00 (*0-16-026426-X*) USGPO.

Davis, Ronald W. Ethnohistorical Studies on the Kru Coast. (Liberian Research Working Papers: No. 5). (Illus.). 217p. 1976. 11.50 (*0-916712-04-4*) Arden Assocs.

Davis, Ronald W., et al. Advanced Bacterial Genetics. LC 80-25695. (Manual for Genetic Engineering Ser.). (Illus.). 265p. 1980. pap. 82.20 (*0-608-05183-7*, 206572000001) Bks Demand.

Davis, Roscoe K., jt. auth. see Leitch, Robert A.

Davis, Rose P., compiled by. Zora Neale Hurston: An Annotated Bibliography & Reference Guide, 34. LC 97-37459. (Bibliographies & Indexes in Afro-American & African Studies: 34). 224p. 1997. lib. bdg. 65.00 (*0-313-30387-8*, Greenwood Pr) Greenwood.

Davis, Ross & Bloedel, James R., eds. Cerebellar Stimulation for Spasticity & Seizures. 360p. 1984. 201.00 (*0-8493-6067-6*, RC350, CRC Reprint) Franklin.

Davis, Roswita B. Assorted Lives: A Collection of Poetry. (Orig.). 1995. pap. 14.95 (*0-9632687-5-9*) PenRose Pub.

— Assorted Lives: A Collection of Poetry. (Orig.). 1995. pap. 14.95 (*0-9634687-5-8*) PenRose Pub.

***Davis, Rowland H.** Neurospora: Contributions of a Model Organism. LC 99-42516. (Illus.). 320p. 2000. text 95.00 (*0-19-512236-4*) OUP.

Davis, Rowland H. & Weller, Stephen G. The Gist of Genetics: Guide to Learning & Review. (Life Science Ser.). 264p. (C). 1996. pap. text 25.00 (*0-86720-919-4*) Jones & Bartlett.

Davis, Roy E. An Easy Guide to Ayurveda. 1996. pap. 4.95 (*0-87707-249-3*) CSA Pr.

— An Easy Guide to Meditation. 48p. 1995. 2.00 (*0-87707-244-2*) CSA Pr.

— The Eternal Way: Bhagavad Gita. 1996. 14.95 (*0-87707-248-5*) CSA Pr.

— Life Surrendered in God: Yoga-Sutras. 1995. 14.95 (*0-87707-246-9*) CSA Pr.

— Living in God: Daily Reflections. 1997. 7.95 (*0-87707-276-0*) CSA Pr.

— A Master Guide to Meditation. 1994. 6.95 (*0-87707-238-8*) CSA Pr.

— Miracle Man of Japan: The Life & Work of Masaharu Taniguchi, One of the Most Influential Spiritual Leaders of Our Time. (Illus.). 160p. (Orig.). pap. 3.00 (*0-87707-048-2*) CSA Pr.

— The Self-Revealed Knowledge That Liberates the Spirit. 1997. 7.95 (*0-87707-275-2*) CSA Pr.

***Davis, Roy E.** Spiritual Basis of Real Prosperity. 1999. 7.95 (*0-87707-279-5*) CSA Pr.

Davis, Roy Eugene. Una Guia Maestra para la Meditacion. 1998. pap. text 4.95 (*0-87707-278-7*) CSA Pr.

***Davis, Roy Eugene.** Living in God: 366 Themes for Daily Meditative Contemplation & Spiritual Enrichment (With Life Enhancing Affirmations & Inspirational Quotations) 159p. 1998. 100.00 (*81-208-1543-2*, Pub. by Motilal Bnarsidass); pap. 50.00 (*81-208-1544-0*, Pub. by Motilal Bnarsidass) St Mut.

— The Path of Light: A Guide to 21st Century Discipleship & Spiritual Practice in the Kriya Yoga Tradition. 155p. 1999. pap. 50.00 (*81-208-1657-9*, Pub. by Motilal Bnarsidass) St Mut.

Davis, Roy G. VAXcluster Principles. LC 93-817. (Alpha-VAX-VMS Ser.). (Illus.). 600p. 1993. 64.95 (*1-55558-112-9*, EY-M740E-DP, Digital DEC) Buttrwrth-Heinemann.

— VAXcluster Principles. LC 93-817. 602p. reprint ed. pap. 186.70 (*0-608-08850-1*, 206948900004) Bks Demand.

Davis, Roy M. Paw Paw River Days & Nights. (Illus.). 388p. (Orig.). 1993. pap. 16.95 (*1-883228-03-4*) Invictus MI.

— Paw Paw River Times & People, Vol. I. (Illus.). 360p. (Orig.). 1990. pap. 11.95 (*0-9625866-0-9*) R M Davis.

Davis, Roy W., tr. see Lussu, Emilio.

Davis, Royce. How to Become Rich & Make Your Dreams a Reality, Vol. 1. (Illus.). (Orig.). 1994. pap. 10.00 (*0-9649868-0-9*) New Wrld Vision.

Davis, Ruby, ed. see Clark, Barbara R., et al.

Davis, Russ. Gabbin' 1991. 6.50 (*0-913150-72-X*) Pioneer Pr.

— Grub! Cookin' for Mountain Men. 1992. 6.50 (*1-877704-10-5*) Pioneer Pr.

Davis, Russ, ed. see Brunet, Edward J., et al.

Davis, Russ, ed. see Conte, Alba.

Davis, Russ, ed. see Givens, Richard A.

Davis, Russ, ed. see Kelly, Kathryn.

Davis, Russ, ed. see O'Reilly, James T.

Davis, Russell. The Last Good Moment of Lily Baker. 1991. pap. 5.25 (*0-8222-0635-8*) Dramatists Play.

Davis, Russell, jt. ed. see Greenburg, Martin H.

Davis, Russell B. & Ashabranner, Brent K. The Choctaw Code. LC 93-36392. (Illus.). 152p. (J). (gr. 4-8). 1994. reprint ed. lib. bdg. 17.50 (*0-208-02377-1*, Linnet Bks) Shoe String.

Davis, Russell H. Black Americans in Cleveland. (Illus.). (YA). 1990. pap. 10.00 (*0-87498-075-5*) Assoc Pubs DC.

— Freud's Concept of Passivity. LC 91-3036. (Psychological Issues Monographs: No. 60). 250p. 1993. 37.50 (*0-8236-2032-8*) Intl Univs Pr.

Davis, Russell L. A Guide to Trustee Investment under a Prudent Person Approach. 57p. 1990. pap. 45.00 (*0-409-78899-6*, NZ, MICHIE) LEXIS Pub.

***Davis, Ruth.** The Nursing Home Handbook: A Guide to Living Well. LC 99-28127. 220p. 1999. pap. 10.95 (*1-58062-208-9*) Adams Media.

Davis, Ruth, jt. auth. see Rothwell, Donald R.

***Davis, Ruth Barton.** A Story from Home Featuring... Zoro, a Cat. (Illus.). 40p. (C). 1999. pap. write for info. (*0-9623785-1-8*) Pilgrim Way.

Davis, Ruthanne, ed. see Davis Caves Construction, Inc. Staff.

Davis, S. Hong Kong in Its Geographical Setting. LC 70-179188. (Illus.). reprint ed. 37.50 (*0-404-54818-0*) AMS Pr.

Davis, S., et al, eds. Ground Water Tracers. LC 85-21785. 200p. 1985. 18.75 (*1-56034-020-7*, T206) Natl Grnd Water.

Davis, S. D., et al, eds. Centres of Plant Diversity, Europe, Africa, South West Asia & the Middle East Vol. 1: A Guide & Strategy for Their Conservation. LC 95-152429. (Centres of Plant Diversity: No. 1). 355p. 1994. text 60.00 (*2-8317-0197-X*, Pub. by IUCN) Island Pr.

Davis, S. H., et al, eds. Interactive Dynamics of Convection & Solidification. LC 92-24978. (NATO Advanced Study Institutes Series E, Applied Sciences: Vol. 219). 288p. 1992. text 171.00 (*0-7923-1910-9*) Kluwer Academic.

Davis, S. K. Bible Crossword Puzzle Book. (Quiz & Puzzle Bks.). 112p. (J). (gr. k-3). 1974. mass mkt. 5.99 (*0-8010-2812-4*) Baker Bks.

Davis, S. L. & Prescott, J. R. Aboriginal Frontiers & Boundaries in Australia. 182p. (Orig.). 1992. pap. 24.95 (*0-522-84483-9*, Pub. by Melbourne Univ Pr) Paul & Co Pubs.

Davis, S. N. Banking in Boston. (C). 1989. pap. 30.00 (*0-7855-6990-1*, Pub. by R K Pubns); text 40.00 (*0-902662-64-3*, Pub. by R K Pubns) St Mut.

***Davis, S. O. & Handschin, Bill.** Reinventing Yourself: Life Planning after 50 : Using the Strong & the MBTI. LC 98-201802. (Illus.). 1998. write for info. (*0-89106-118-5*) Consulting Psychol.

Davis, S. Rufus. Theory & Reality: Federal Ideas in Australia, England & Europe. 240p. 1995. pap. 19.95 (*0-7022-2605-X*, Pub. by Univ Queensland Pr) Intl Spec Bk.

Davis, S. S., et al, eds. Delivery Systems for Peptide Drugs. LC 87-11036. (NATO ASI Series A, Life Sciences: Vol. 125). 380p. 1987. 110.00 (*0-306-42496-7*, Plenum Trade) Perseus Pubng.

Davis, S. S., et al, eds. Microspheres & Drug Therapy: Pharmaceutical, Immunological & Medical Aspects. 448p. 1985. 168.25 (*0-444-80577-X*) Elsevier.

Davis, Sally & Lawall, Gilbert. Cicero's Somnium Scipionis. 1988. pap. text 14.88 (*0-582-36751-4*, 72527) Longman.

Davis, Sam. The Architecture of Affordable Housing. LC 94-7469. 1995. 40.00 (*0-520-08758-5*, Pub. by U CA Pr) Cal Prin Full Svc.

— Architecture of Affordable Housing. LC 94-7469. (Illus.). 1997. pap. 24.95 (*0-520-20885-4*, Pub. by U CA Pr) Cal Prin Full Svc.

Davis, Samantha A. Understanding Children Through Astrology: A Uniquely New Approach. 2nd ed. Nguyen, Alina & Powell, Judith L., eds. LC 93-14947. (Illus.). 416p. (Orig.). 1993. pap. 16.95 (*1-56087-072-9*) Top Mtn Pub.

***Davis, Sammy, Jr. & Boyar, Burt.** Sammy: An Autobiography. rev. ed. (Illus.). 480p. 2000. 15.00 (*0-374-29355-4*) FS&G.

Davis, Sammy, Jr., et al. Why Me? 1990. mass mkt. 5.95 (*0-446-36025-2*) Warner Bks.

Davis, Samuel M. Rights of Juveniles: The Juvenile Justice System. 2nd ed. LC 80-12465. (Civil Rights Ser.). (C). 1980. ring bd. 135.00 (*0-87632-104-X*) West Group.

Davis, Samuel M., et al. Children in the Legal System, Cases & Materials On. 2nd ed. LC 97-1582. (University Casebook Ser.). 1021p. 1997. text 40.50 (*1-56662-459-2*) Foundation Pr.

Davis, Samuel P. History of Nevada, Nineteen Thirteen, 2 vols., Set. (Illus.). 1344p. 1984. 195.00 (*0-913814-58-X*) Nevada Pubns.

Davis, Sandra, et al. International Child Abduction - A Practical Guide to the Law. 1995. pap. 56.00 (*0-406-00541-9*, UK, MICHIE) LEXIS Pub.

Davis, Sandra P. That Special Touch. LC 89-92544. (Illus.). 140p. 1990. 39.95 (*0-9625232-0-8*) Special Touch.

Davis, Sandra T. Intellectual Change & Political Development in Early Modern Japan: Ono Azusa, a Case Study. LC 76-14762. 328p. 1977. 38.50 (*0-8386-1953-3*) Fairleigh Dickinson.

Davis, Sandrea S. In Search of the Thingamajig: In the Bible Belt & Beyond. LC 99-177334. (Illus.). 199p. 1999. pap. 9.95 (*0-9667852-0-7*) Funnier Fic.

Davis, Sara D., jt. ed. see Boren, Lynda S.

Davis, Sara E., jt. auth. see Davis, Dorothy B.

***Davis, Sara N., et al, eds.** Coming into Her Own: Encouraging Educational Success in Girls & Women. LC 99-6037. (Jossey-Bass Education Ser.). 416p. 1999. 35.95 (*0-7879-4490-4*) Jossey-Bass.

Davis, Sara N., jt. ed. see Gergen, Mary M.

Davis, Schiff. Young Gun. 1989. mass mkt. 2.95 (*0-8217-2846-6*, Zebra Kensgtn) Kensgtn Pub Corp.

***Davis, Scott.** Brand Asset Management: Driving Profitable Growth Through Your Brands. LC 00-8013. (Business & Management Ser.). 300p. 2000. 34.95 (*0-7879-5077-7*) Jossey-Bass.

Davis, Scott. One Hundred One Self-Defense Techniques of Kung-Fu: Basic to Advanced. (Illus.). 92p. (Orig.). 1993. pap. 16.00 (*0-939427-02-8*) Alpha Pubns OH.

Davis, Scott, ed. American Athletics Annual, 1983. 1983. 10.00 (*0-686-46900-3*) Athletics Cong.

— American Athletics Annual, 1984. 1984. 12.00 (*0-317-11295-3*) Athletics Cong.

***Davis, Scott & Hunts, Holly.** Academic & Career Tech Integration, Vol. 3. Ries, Eric, ed. (Illus.). 36p. 2000. pap. 6.50 (*0-89514-007-1*) ACTE.

Davis, Scott C. Cune: A New Approach to Publishing. 12p. (Orig.). 1995. pap. 3.95 (*1-885942-54-0*) Cune.

— Lost Arrow: And Other True Stories. LC 94-92414. 64p. 1995. 19.95 (*1-885942-75-3*, 753); pap. 9.95 (*1-885942-50-8*, 508) Cune.

***Davis, Scott C.** The Road from Damascus: Syria 1987. 288p. 2000. 32.95 (*1-885942-84-2*); pap. 14.95 (*1-885942-53-2*) Cune.

— Tips for Writers: Simple Steps to Improve Your Communication Skills. 1999. 12.95 (*1-885942-58-3*) Cune.

***Davis, Scott C.** The World of Patience Gromes: Making & Unmaking a Black Community. 287p. 1999. pap. 15.95 (*1-885942-51-6*, 516) Cune.

Davis, Scott C. The World of Patience Gromes: Making & Unmaking a Black Community. LC 88-98. 232p. 1988. 27.50 (*0-8131-1644-9*) U Pr of Ky.

Davis, Scott C., ed. An Ear to the Ground: Presenting Writers from 2 Coasts. (Illus.). 496p. 1997. 34.95 (*1-885942-85-0*, 650); pap. 19.95 (*1-885942-56-7*) Cune.

Davis, Scott E. Career Power. rev. ed. 24p. (C). 1994. reprint ed. pap. text 4.95 (*0-9640932-0-0*); reprint ed. pap. text 19.95 incl. audio (*0-9640932-3-5*) Simsbury Mgmt.

— Como Conseguir el Trabajo Que Usted Quiere! How to Get the Job You Want. Paramo, Constanza G., ed. (SPA.). 36p. (Orig.). 1994. pap. 6.95 (*0-9640932-8-6*) Simsbury Mgmt.

— Listo Al Trabajo: Job Ready. (SPA.). 36p. (Orig.). 1994. pap. 4.95 (*0-9640932-9-4*) Simsbury Mgmt.

***Davis-Seaver, Jane.** Critical Thinking in Young Children. LC 00-32453. (Studies in Education: Vol. 50). 104p. (C). 2000. 59.95 (*0-7734-7749-7*) E Mellen.

Davis, Shannon G., jt. ed. see Kelly, Donald R.

***Davis, Sharon.** Chart-Toppers: The 80's. 400p. 1999. pap. 24.95 (*1-85158-838-8*, Pub. by Mainstream Pubng) Trafalgar.

Davis, Sharon. Every Chart Topper Tells a Story: The Seventies. 488p. 1998. pap. 24.95 (*1-85158-837-X*, Pub. by Mainstream Pubng) Trafalgar.

— So You Want to Be a Foster Parent LC 98-50667. 1998. pap. write for info. (*0-9646184-2-7*) Lucid Pr.

Davis, Sharon & Jaskulski, Tecla, eds. Collaborating for Inclusion, 1995 Report to the President: President's Committee on Mental Retardation. (Illus.). 51p. (Orig.). 1996. pap. text 25.00 (*0-7881-3687-9*) DIANE Pub.

Davis, Sharon, ed. see Billac, Pete.

Davis, Sharon, ed. see Billac, Pete & Ragusa, Shirley.

Davis, Sharon, tr. see Shaughnessy, Joyce.

Davis, Sharon K., ed. see Billac, Pete.

Davis, Sharon P., ed. From Wheat to Flour. (Illus.). 75p. 1998. pap. text 25.00 (*0-7881-4764-1*) DIANE Pub.

Davis, Sheila. The Craft of Lyric Writing. 350p. 1985. 24.99 (*0-89879-149-9*, Wrtrs Digest Bks) F & W Pubns Inc.

— Songwriter's Idea Book. 240p. 1992. 18.99 (*0-89879-519-2*, Wrtrs Digest Bks) F & W Pubns Inc.

— Successful Lyric Writing: A Step-by-Step Course & Workbook. 292p. 1988. pap. 19.99 (*0-89879-283-5*, Wrtrs Digest Bks) F & W Pubns Inc.

Davis, Shelton H. Land Rights & Indigenous Peoples: The Role of the Inter-American Commission on Human Rights. (Cultural Survival Reports: No. 29). 114p. 1988. 19.95 (*0-939521-42-3*); pap. 8.00 (*0-939521-28-8*) Cultural Survival.

— La Tierra de Nuestros Antepasados: Estudio de la Herencia y la Tenencia de la Tierra en el Altiplano de Guatemala. Valladares, Margarita Cruz, tr. LC 97-66660. (Serie Monografica: Vol. 8). (SPA., Illus.). 279p. (Orig.). 1997. pap. 20.00 (*0-910443-13-0*) Plumsock Meso Studies.

Davis, Shelton H. & Hodson, Julie. Witnesses to Political Violence in Guatemala: The Suppression of a Rural Development Movement. Simon, Laurence R., ed. (Impact Audit Ser.: No. 2). (Illus.). 54p. (Orig.). (C). 1984. pap. 5.00 (*0-910281-00-9*) Oxfam Am.

Davis, Shiff. Last Debt at Newton. 192p. 1988. mass mkt. 2.95 (*0-8217-2462-2*, Zebra Kensgtn) Kensgtn Pub Corp.

Davis, Shirley M. Servant Shoes. LC 96-195788. 192p. (Orig.). 1996. pap. 10.95 (*1-883893-46-1*) WinePress Pub.

Davis, Sid. Adding Value to Your Home. Fucci, Joseph, ed. LC 97-75264. (Illus.). 176p. 1999. pap. 14.95 (*1-58011-011-8*) Creative Homeowner.

Davis, Sidney. Your Future in Computer Programming. LC 74-114129. (Arco-rosen Career Guidance Ser.). 144 p. 1971. write for info. (*0-668-02237-X*, Arco) Macmillan Gen Ref.

Davis, Simon, jt. auth. see Smith, Joseph.

***Davis, Simone Weil.** Ad Work: Gender Fictions of the 1920s. LC 99-37024. (New Americanists Ser.). 272p. 2000. pap. 17.95 (*0-8223-2446-6*) Duke.

Davis, Skeeter. Bus Fare to Kentucky: The Autobiography of Skeeter Davis. LC 93-8841. (Illus.). 288p. 1993. 19.95 (*1-55972-191-X*, Birch Ln Pr) Carol Pub Group.

Davis, Skeeter & Pelletier, Cathie. The Christmas Note. (Illus.). 50p. 1997. 18.00 (*0-9660776-0-1*, 001) Nashville Bks.

Davis, Sonia H. The Private Life of H. P. Lovecraft. 38p. (Orig.). 1985. pap. 4.95 (*0-318-04718-7*) Necronomicon.

Davis, Sonny B. A Brotherhood of Arms: Brazil-United States Military Relations, 1945-1977. 288p. 1996. lib. bdg. 39.95 (*0-87081-418-4*) Univ Pr Colo.

Davis, Stan. Future Perfect. 2nd ed. 272p. 1997. pap. 13.00 (*0-201-32795-3*) Addison-Wesley.

— Monster under the Bed. 192p. 1995. per. 11.00 (*0-684-80438-7*, Touchstone) S&S Trade Pap.

Davis, Stan & McCarthy, Ellie. Future Perfect. 2nd anniversary ed. 272p. 1996. 24.00 (*0-201-59045-X*) Addison-Wesley.

Davis, Stan & Meyer, Christopher. Blur: The Speed of Change in the Connected Economy. LC 98-4877. 1998. 25.00 (*0-201-33987-0*) Addison-Wesley.

— Blur: The Speed of Change in the Connected Economy. LC 98-50267. (Illus.). 265p. 1999. mass mkt. 14.00 (*0-446-67533-4*, Pub. by Warner Bks) Little.

***Davis, Stan & Meyer, Christopher.** Future Wealth. LC 99-59014. 224p. 2000. 27.50 (*1-57851-194-1*) Harvard Busn.

Davis, Stan M. & Davidson, Bill. 2020 Vision: Transform Your Business Today to Succeed in Tomorrow's Economy. (Illus.). 224p. 1992. pap. 12.00 (*0-671-77815-3*, Fireside) S&S Trade Pap.

Davis, Stanley, jt. auth. see Goetsch, David L.

Davis, Stanley B., jt. auth. see Goetsch, David L.

Davis, Stanley D., ed. The Hidden Falls Site: Baranof Island, Alaska. (Aurora Ser.: Vol. 5). (Illus.). xiii, 383p. 1989. pap. 28.00 (*1-890396-05-2*) AK Anthropological.

Davis, Stanley M. Managing Corporate Culture. 1990. pap. 14.95 (*0-88730-401-X*, HarpBusn) HarpInfo.

Davis, Stanley N. Hydrogeology. 476p. (C). 1991. reprint ed. 69.95 (*0-89464-638-9*) Krieger.

Davis, Stenley N. Introduction to Ground Water Tracer. (C). 1990. 210.00 (*81-85046-92-1*, Pub. by Scientific) St Mut.

***Davis, Stephanie G.** 9 Steps to Your New Home: A Home Building Guide. (Illus.). viii, 73p. 2000. pap. 6.95 (*0-615-11247-1*) S G Davis.

Davis, Stephen. Australia's Extant & Imputed Traditional Aboriginal Territories: A Map. 1994. 24.95 (*0-522-84608-4*, Pub. by Melbourne Univ Pr) Paul & Co Pubs.

— Bob Marley. rev. ed. LC 90-8241. 286p. 1992. reprint ed. pap. 18.95 (*0-87047-044-2*) Schenkman Bks Inc.

— Faith, Skepticism & Evidence: An Essay in Religious Epistemology. 233p. 1978. 32.50 (*0-8387-2039-0*) Bucknell U Pr.

— George Sugarman, Sculpture. (Illus.). 24p. 1998. pap. 7.50 (*1-885998-11-2*) Hunter College.

D

An Asterisk (*) at the beginning of an entry indicates that the title is appearing for the first time.

— Hammer of the Gods: The Led Zeppelin Saga. LC 97-198253. 400p. 1997. mass mkt. 7.50 (*1-57297-306-4*) Blvd Books.

***Davis, Stephen.** Psychology Major: Career Options & Strategies for Success. LC 99-35067. 160p. 2000. pap. 11.25 (*0-13-083753-9*) P-H.

Davis, Stephen. Walk This Way. LC 97-25598. 448p. 1997. mass mkt. 25.00 (*0-380-97594-7*, Avon Bks) Morrow Avon.

Davis, Stephen, et al, eds. The Trinity: An Interdisciplinary Study of the Doctrine of the Trinity. LC 99-24523. (Illus.). 424p. 2000. 39.95 (*0-19-826993-5*) OUP.

Davis, Stephen, jt. auth. see Aerosmith Staff.

Davis, Stephen, jt. auth. see Fleetwood, Mick.

Davis, Stephen, jt. auth. see Helm, Levon.

Davis, Stephen, jt. auth. see Horvat, Joseph.

Davis, Stephen, ed. see Blue & Gray Magazine Editors.

Davis, Stephen, jt. ed. see Trubowitz, Sidney.

Davis, Stephen A. Mi'kmaq: Peoples of the Maritimes. LC 96-950112. 1998. pap. text 10.95 (*1-55109-180-1*) Nimbus Publ.

Davis, Stephen C. California Gold Rush Merchant: The Journal of Stephen Chapin Davis. Richards, Benjamin B., ed. LC 73-21490. (Illus.). 124p. (C). 1974. reprint ed. lib. bdg. 55.00 (*0-8371-6408-7*, DAGR, Greenwood Pr) Greenwood.

— California Gold Rush Merchant: The Journal of Stephen Chapin Davis. (American Biography Ser.). 124p. 1991. reprint ed. lib. bdg. 59.00 (*0-7812-8103-2*) Rprt Serv.

***Davis, Stephen F.** Psychology. 3rd ed. LC 99-21562. 807p. 1999. 56.00 (*0-13-932583-2*) P-H.

— Psychology 2. 2nd ed. 1999. 55.00 (*0-13-025787-7*) P-H.

Davis, Stephen F. & Palladino, Joseph J. Psychology. (Illus.). 700p. (C). 1994. text 47.00 (*0-02-327851-X*, Macmillan Coll) P-H.

Davis, Stephen F., jt. auth. see Smith, Randolph A.

Davis, Stephen H., jt. ed. see Brown, Robert A.

***Davis, Stephen J.** The Culture of Saint Thecla: A Tradition of Women's Piety in Late Antiquity. (Oxford Early Christian Studies). (Illus.). 280p. 2000. text 70.00 (*0-19-827019-4*) OUP.

Davis, Stephen M. Robin Hood's England. (Guide Ser.). (Illus.). 150p. (Orig.). 1991. pap. 9.95 (*0-9628576-0-2*) Timetraveler.

Davis, Stephen M., et al. Interventional Therapy in Acute Stroke. LC 97-13106. (Illus.). 240p. 1997. 145.00 (*0-86542-377-6*) Blackwell Sci.

Davis, Stephen R. C++ for Dummies. LC 94-76647. (For Dummies Ser.). 432p. 1994. pap. 19.95 (*1-56884-163-9*) IDG Bks.

— C++ for Dummies, 2 vols. large type ed. 476p. 119.00 (*0-614-20549-2*, L-39081-00 APHB) Am Printing Hse.

— C++ for Dummies. 3rd ed. LC 98-85435. (For Dummies Ser.). 432p. 1998. pap. 29.99 incl. cd-rom (*0-7645-0389-8*) IDG Bks.

***Davis, Stephen R.** C++ for Dummies. 4th ed. (For Dummies Ser.). 456p. 2000. pap. 24.99 (*0-7645-0746-X*) IDG Bks.

— C++ Weekend Crash Course. (Illus.). 552p. 2000. pap. text 19.99 (*0-7645-4689-9*) IDG Bks.

Davis, Stephen R. Inside Visual J++ 6.0. 608p. 1997. 44.99 incl. cd-rom (*1-57231-701-9*) Microsoft.

— Windows Networking & Connectivity Guide: How to Survive in a World of Windows, Netware, & DOS. LC 92-28198. 560p. (C). 1992. pap. 32.95 (*0-201-58133-7*) Addison-Wesley.

— Windows 98 Programming for Dummies. 2nd ed. LC 98-84965. 408p. 1998. pap. 29.99 incl. cd-rom (*0-7645-0262-X*) IDG Bks.

Davis, Stephen T. God, Reason, & Theistic Proofs. LC 98-124566. (Reason & Religion Ser.). 224p. 1997. pap. text 26.00 (*0-8028-4450-2*) Eerdmans.

— Philosophy & Theological Discourse. LC 97-3926. (Claremont Studies in the Philosophy of Religion). 260p. 1997. text 59.95 (*0-312-15837-8*) St Martin.

Davis, Stephen T., ed. Encountering Evil: Live Options in Theodicy. LC 80-84647. 1985. pap. 19.95 (*0-8042-0517-5*) Westminster John Knox.

— Encountering Jesus: A Debate on Christology. LC 87-18950. 200p. 1988. pap. 19.95 (*0-8042-0537-X*) Westminster John Knox.

Davis, Stephen T., et al, eds. The Resurrection: An Interdisciplinary Symposium on the Resurrection of Jesus. 390p. 1999. reprint ed. pap. text 19.95 (*0-19-826985-4*) OUP.

Davis, Steve. Compuserve Complete Handbook & Membership Kit: The Complete Handbook & Membership Kit. 2nd ed. LC 94-68395. 1996. pap. text 24.95 (*0-7615-0417-6*) Prima Pub.

— CompuServe Information Manager for Windows: The Complete Membership Kit & Handbook. LC 93-85788. 1994. pap. 29.95 (*1-55958-455-6*) Prima Pub.

— Grandmaster Meets Chess Amateur. 1995. pap. 15.00 (*0-8050-4224-5*, Pub. by Batsford Chess) H Holt & Co.

***Davis, Steve.** Math Skills Practice & Apply: Grade 4. (Illus.). 128p. 2000. pap. text 10.95 (*1-58037-127-2*, Pub. by M Twain Media) Carson-Dellos.

— Math Skills Practice & Apply: Grade 5. (Illus.). 128p. 2000. pap. text 10.95 (*1-58037-128-0*, Pub. by M Twain Media) Carson-Dellos.

— Math Skills Practice & Apply: Grade 6. (Illus.). 128p. 2000. pap. text 10.95 (*1-58037-129-9*, Pub. by M Twain Media) Carson-Dellos.

— Math Skills Practice & Apply: Grade 7. (Illus.). 128p. 2000. pap. text 10.95 (*1-58037-130-2*, Pub. by M Twain Media) Carson-Dellos.

— Metrics. (Illus.). 64p. 1999. pap. text 8.95 (*1-58037-114-0*, Pub. by M Twain Media) Carson-Dellos.

— Understanding Graphs & Charts. (Illus.). 80p. (YA). (gr. 5). 1998. pap. text 9.95 (*1-58037-037-3*, Pub. by M Twain Media) Carson-Dellos.

Davis, Steve. Usenet Navigator Kit. 272p. 1995. pap. 29.95 (*1-55958-745-8*) Prima Pub.

— Using dBase 4, 2.0 Special Edition. (Illus.). 1034p. (Orig.). 1993. 29.95 (*1-56529-153-0*) Que.

***Davis, Steve.** Using the Internet. (Illus.). 64p. (YA). (gr. 5). 1998. pap. text 8.95 (*1-58037-078-0*, Pub. by M Twain Media) Carson-Dellos.

Davis, Steve. Web Browsing with Netscape Navigator 1.1. 1p. 1995. pap. text 24.95 (*0-7615-0239-4*) Prima Pub.

Davis, Steve, ed. see Molesworth, Ralph.

***Davis, Steven.** Color Perception: Philosophical, Psychological, Artistic & Computational Perspectives. LC 99-39970. (Vancouver Studies in Cognitive Science: Vol. 9). (Illus.). 256p. 1999. text 65.00 (*0-19-513667-5*); pap. text 35.00 (*0-19-513668-3*) OUP.

Davis, Steven, ed. Causal Theories of Mind: Action, Knowledge, Memory, Perception & Reference. LC 83-15082. (Foundations of Communication & Cognition Ser.). x, 421p. 1983. 173.10 (*3-11-007730-2*) De Gruyter.

Davis, Steven & Ogden, John, eds. Everglades: The Ecosystem & Its Restoration. LC 93-44643. (Illus.). 860p. 1994. boxed set 152.95 (*0-9634030-2-8*) St Lucie Pr.

Davis, Steven, ed. see Conference on Montague Grammar, Philosophy, & Linguistics, 1977, State Univ. of NY at Albany, Staff.

***Davis, Steven I.** Bank Mergers: Lessons for the Future. LC 00-42061. 2000. write for info. (*0-312-23552-6*) St Martin.

Davis, Steven I. Leadership in Conflict: The Lessons of History. LC 95-22033. 256p. 1996. text 39.95 (*0-312-12713-8*) St Martin.

— Pragmatics: A Reader. 608p. (C). 1991. pap. text 49.95 (*0-19-505898-4*) OUP.

Davis, Steven I., ed. Connectionism: Theory & Practice. (Vancouver Series in Cognitive Science: Vol. 3). 336p. 1992. text 60.00 (*0-19-507665-6*); pap. text 40.00 (*0-19-507666-4*) OUP.

Davis, Steven J., et al. Job Creation & Destruction. (Illus.). 288p. 1998. reprint ed. pap. text 19.50 (*0-262-54093-2*) MIT Pr.

Davis, Stewart, ed. see Rand, James R.

Davis, Stewart, ed. see Tillman, Ernest C.

Davis, Stuart & Agee, William, texts. Stuart Davis: Motifs & Versions. (Illus.). 107p. 1988. pap. 30.00 (*1-58821-012-X*) Salander OReilly.

Davis, Stuart, jt. text see Davis, Earl.

Davis, Sue. Circumstantial Evidence. (Rainbow Romances Ser.: No. 896). 160p. 1994. 14.95 (*0-7090-4958-7*) Parkwest Pubns.

— Justice Rehnquist & the Constitution. LC 88-23413. 257p. reprint ed. pap. 79.70 (*0-608-06314-2*, 206667600008) Bks Demand.

Davis, Sue A., jt. auth. see Rowe, Alan J.

Davis, Sue C. The Picture Book of Vaseline Glass. LC 98-83237. (Illus.). 160p. 1999. 29.95 (*0-7643-0830-0*) Schiffer.

Davis, Susan. The Healthy Woman: Menopause & Other Things We Don't Talk About. 160p. 1996. pap. 13.95 (*0-87630-806-X*) Brunner-Mazel.

— The Long Reach. LC 92-50343. 208p. (Orig.). 1993. pap. 12.95 (*0-936609-27-3*) QED Ft Bragg.

— When God Lived in a Tent. (My Church Teaches Ser.). (Illus.). (J). (ps-1). 1978. pap. 1.95 (*0-8127-0181-X*) Review & Herald.

Davis, Susan & Meier, Scott T. Elements of Counseling. 2nd ed. 96p. (C). 1993. pap. 10.50 (*0-534-19428-1*) Brooks-Cole.

— The Elements of Counseling. 3rd ed. (Miscellaneous/Catalogs Ser.). 112p. (C). 1996. pap. 19.95 (*0-534-34547-6*) Brooks-Cole.

Davis, Susan, ed. see Lipski, Liz.

Davis, Susan E., ed. Gynecology. LC 95-7923. (New York City Resource Guide Ser.). 1995. write for info. (*0-9643861-0-0*) Wom Hlth Educ.

Davis, Susan E., ed. see Carasa Collective Staff.

Davis, Susan G. Spectacular Nature: Corporate Culture & the Sea World Experience. LC 96-44902. 336p. 1997. 50.00 (*0-520-20031-4*, Pub. by U CA Pr); pap. 18.95 (*0-520-20981-8*, Pub. by U CA Pr) Cal Prin Full Svc.

Davis, Susan J. & Johns, Jerry L. Language Arts for Gifted Middle School Students. (Teaching Resources in the ERIC Database (TRIED) Ser.). (Illus.). 1990. pap. 14.95 (*0-927516-16-0*) ERIC-REC.

Davis, Susan M. The Magnitude of Life. 1998. pap. write for info. (*1-58235-000-0*) Watermrk Pr.

Davis, Susan S. Patience & Power: The Lives of Morrocan Village Women. 200p. 1985. pap. 15.95 (*0-87073-504-7*) Schenkman Bks Inc.

Davis, Susan S. & Davis, Douglas A. Adolescence in a Moroccan Town. LC 88-16897. (Adolescents in a Changing World Ser.). 288p. (C). 1989. text 42.00 (*0-8135-1368-5*) Rutgers U Pr.

Davis, Suzannah. Amores Secretos: Dr. Holt & the Texan. (Deseo Ser.: Vol. 118).Tr. of Secret Loves. (SPA.). 1998. per. 3.50 (*0-373-35248-4*, 1-35248-3) Harlequin Bks.

— Angel Eyes. 416p. (Orig.). 1993. mass mkt. 4.50 (*0-380-76822-4*, Avon Bks) Morrow Avon.

— A Christmas Cowboy. (Desire Ser.). 1995. per. 2.99 (*0-373-05903-5*, 1-05903-9) Silhouette.

— The Cop & the Cradle: Switched at Birth. (Special Edition Ser.: No. 1143). 1997. per. 3.99 (*0-373-24143-7*, 1-24143-9) Harlequin Bks.

— Dance of Deception. 1992. mass mkt. 4.50 (*0-380-76128-9*, Avon Bks) Morrow Avon.

— Devil's Deception. 400p. 1990. pap. 3.95 (*0-380-75673-0*, Avon Bks) Morrow Avon.

— Devil's Moon. 400p. 1991. pap. 3.95 (*0-380-76127-0*, Avon Bks) Morrow Avon.

— Dr. Holt & the Texan. 1997. per. 3.50 (*0-373-76067-1*, 1-76067-7) Silhouette.

— Gabriel's Bride. 1996. per. 3.50 (*0-373-76041-8*, 1-76041-2) Silhouette.

— Heatcrazed! (Love & Laughter Ser.). 1997. per. 3.50 (*0-373-44016-2*, 1-44016-3) Harlequin Bks.

— Little Boy Blue: Switched at Birth. (Special Edition Ser.: No. 1149). 1998. per. 3.99 (*0-373-24149-6*, 1-24149-6) Silhouette.

— The Master's Bride. 416p. (Orig.). 1993. mass mkt. 4.50 (*0-380-76821-6*, Avon Bks) Morrow Avon.

— Matrimonio de Conveniencia: The Rancher & the Redhead. (Deseo Ser.). (SPA.). 1996. per. 3.50 (*0-373-35163-1*, 1-35163-4) Harlequin Bks.

— Outlaw Heart. 352p. 1989. pap. 3.95 (*0-380-75672-2*, Avon Bks) Morrow Avon.

— The Rancher & the Redhead. (Desire Ser.). 1995. per. 3.25 (*0-373-05947-7*, 1-05947-6) Silhouette.

— Sueno de Felicidad. (SPA.). 1997. per. 3.50 (*0-373-35185-2*, 1-35185-7) Harlequin Bks.

— Untamed Glory. 368p. 1988. pap. 3.95 (*0-380-75397-9*, Avon Bks) Morrow Avon.

Davis, Sydney G. & Tregear, Mary. Man Kok Tsui Archaeological Site 30, Lantau Island, Hong Kong. LC DS0796.H47D3. 54p. reprint ed. pap. 30.00 (*0-608-11791-9*, 201769700007) Bks Demand.

Davis, Sydney W. & New, Gregory R. Abridged 13 Workbook: For Small Libraries Using Dewey Decimal Classification Abridged Edition 13. 2nd rev. ed. LC 97-27055. 71p. 1997. pap. 20.00 (*0-910608-61-X*) OCLC Forest Pr.

Davis, T. & Namson, Jay S., eds. Geologic Transect Across the Western Transverse Ranges, Southern California. (Illus.). 74p. (Orig.). 1986. pap. 7.00 (*1-878861-24-7*) Pac Section SEPM.

Davis, T. A. Was Jesus Really Like Us? 189p. (Orig.). Date not set. pap. 7.95 (*0-923309-25-X*) Hartland Pubns.

Davis, T. D. The Rocks Wept. 218p. (YA). (gr. 6 up). 1998. pap. 18.95 (*0-9641861-8-7*) Redhawk Pubng.

Davis, T. D. & Haissig, B. E. Biology of Adventitious Root Formation. LC 93-46186. (Basic Life Sciences Ser.: Vol. 62). (Illus.). 358p. (C). 1994. text 105.00 (*0-306-44627-8*, Kluwer Plenum) Kluwer Academic.

***Davis, T. F.** Destruction of a Dream. LC 99-97061. 2000. pap. 14.95 (*0-533-13384-X*) Vantage.

Davis, T. Frederick. History of Jacksonville, Florida & Vicinity 1513 to 1924. 3rd ed. (Illus.). 513p. (YA). (gr. 8 up). 1990. reprint ed. 22.50 (*0-935259-06-6*) San Marco Bk.

Davis, T. J. A Rumor of Revolt: The "Great Negro Plot" in Colonial New York. LC 90-34785. 336p. (C). 1990. reprint ed. pap. 19.95 (*0-87023-725-X*) U of Mass Pr.

Davis, T. K. Davis Family: A History of the Descendants of Wm. Davis & His Wife, Mary Means. (Illus.). 248p. 1992. reprint ed. pap. 39.00 (*0-8328-2649-9*); reprint ed. lib. bdg. 49.00 (*0-8328-2648-0*) Higginson Bk Co.

Davis, T. L. Autobiography of Denis Zachaire. 1993. pap. 6.95 (*1-55818-142-3*) Holmes Pub.

— Home to Texas. LC 97-60886. 304p. (Orig.). (C). 1997. pap. 13.00 (*0-9656536-6-8*) F&S Press.

— Shadow Soldier. LC 97-90015. 312p. 1997. 19.95 (*0-9656536-4-1*) F&S Press.

Davis, T. L., et al. Tectonic Influence on Sedimentation, Early Cretaceous, East Flank Powder River Basin, Wyoming & South Dakota. Goldberg, J. H. & Raese, Jon W., eds. LC 82-17894. (Colorado School of Mines Quarterly Ser.: Vol. 77, No. 4). (Illus.). 61p. 1983. pap. text 12.00 (*0-686-82131-9*) Colo Sch Mines.

Davis, T. Neil. Alaska Science Nuggets. LC 82-80679. (Illus.). 233p. (Orig.). 1982. 15.95 (*0-915360-02-0*); pap. 9.95 (*0-685-05558-2*) Geophysical Inst.

— The Aurora Watcher's Handbook. LC 91-43080. (Illus.). x, 262p. 1992. 35.00 (*0-912006-59-5*); pap. 20.00 (*0-912006-60-9*) U of Alaska Pr.

— Energy - Alaska. LC 83-51414. (Illus.). 530p. 1984. 19.95 (*0-912006-07-2*) U of Alaska Pr.

Davis, T. Patrick. New Methods of Rectification: Lincoln. LC 83-71861. 154p. 1985. 16.50 (*0-86690-254-6*, D2440-014) Am Fed Astrologers.

— Pronunciation Guide for Astrology. 16p. 1973. 4.50 (*0-86690-180-9*, D1055-014) Am Fed Astrologers.

Davis, T. W. Rhys. On the Ancient Coins & Measures of Ceylon. (Illus.). 1975. pap. 10.00 (*0-916710-24-6*) Obol Intl.

Davis, Tarring S. & Schenk, Lucile, eds. History of Blair County, 2 vols. in 1, Set. (Illus.). 1527p. 1995. reprint ed. lib. bdg. 56.00 (*0-8328-5104-3*) Higginson Bk Co.

Davis, Ted S. Constant Processes. (Illus.). 1978. 29.50 (*0-685-19863-4*) Constant Soc.

Davis, Tenney L., compiled by. The Chemistry of Powder & Explosives. unabridged ed. 500p. 1943. reprint ed. 25.00 (*0-945001-17-7*) GSG & Assocs.

Davis, Tenney L., tr. see Bacon, Roger.

Davis, Tenny L. Chemistry of Powder & Explosives. 512p. 1972. reprint ed. 18.00 (*0-913022-00-4*) Angriff Pr.

Davis, Terence. The Gothick Taste. LC 75-10733. (Illus.). 168p. 1972. 55.00 (*0-8386-1746-8*) Fairleigh Dickinson.

***Davis, Teresa R.** National Household Survey on Drug Abuse: Population Estimates (1997) (Illus.). 123p. (C). 1999. pap. text 30.00 (*0-7881-8223-4*) DIANE Pub.

— National Household Survey on Drug Abuse: Population Estimates (1998) (Illus.). 125p. 2000. pap. text 30.00 (*0-7881-8745-7*) DIANE Pub.

Davis, Terrell. The Memoirs of Terrell Davis. (Illus.). 320p. (YA). 1999. mass mkt. 6.50 (*0-06-109882-5*) HarpC Child Bks.

— Td: Dreams in Motion. LC 98-34498. (Illus.). 224p. 1998. 23.00 (*0-06-019282-8*) HarpC.

***Davis, Terry.** The History of the Houston Comets. LC 99-18888. (Women's Pro Basketball Today Ser.). 1999. lib. bdg. 21.30 (*1-58341-013-9*, Creat Educ) Creative Co.

Davis, Terry. Presenting Chris Crutcher. large type ed. LC 97-14505. 144p. (gr. 6 up). 1997. 24.95 (*0-8057-8223-0*, Twayne) Mac Lib Ref.

— Rock & Roll. 1992. 16.95 (*0-385-30732-2*) Doubleday.

— Roll Tide! The Alabama Crimson Tide Story. LC 98-36408. (College Sports Today Ser.). (Illus.). 32p. (YA). (gr. 4 up). 1999. lib. bdg. 21.30 (*0-88682-975-5*, Creat Educ) Creative Co.

Davis, Terry, jt. auth. see Shadley, Eugene W.

Davis, Terry M., jt. auth. see Davis, Linda L.

Davis, Thadious, jt. ed. see Harris, Trudier.

Davis, Thadious, ed. & intro. see Larsen, Nella.

Davis, Thadious M. Nella Larsen, Novelist of the Harlem Renaissance: A Woman's Life Unveiled. LC 93-32515. (Illus.). 520p. (C). 1996. pap. 17.95 (*0-8071-2070-7*) La State U Pr.

Davis, Thadious M., jt. ed. see Harris, Trudier.

Davis, Theresa J. Confessions on Hearing from God. 32p. 1995. pap. 1.00 (*0-9648625-0-6*) DWD Publns.

Davis, Theresa M. Caramel Raindrops Vol. 2: Poetry by Theresa Mims Davis. 2nd ed. Pancho, Eric & Wilson, Julius C., Jr., eds. LC 97-92232. (Illus.). 62p. 1997. reprint ed. pap. 7.00 (*0-9659420-0-7*) Davis-Knock Out.

***Davis, Thomas.** Sustaining the Forest, the People, & the Spirit. LC 99-13229. (C). 2000. text 54.50 (*0-7914-4415-5*) State U NY Pr.

— Sustaining the Forest, the People & the Spirit. LC 99-13229. (C). 2000. pap. text 17.95 (*0-7914-4416-3*) State U NY Pr.

Davis, Thomas, et al. A First Course in Membrane Processes. 1997. write for info. (*0-614-30063-0*) Electrosyn Co.

Davis, Thomas, tr. see Madero, Francisco I.

Davis, Thomas A. Horse Owners & Breeders Tax Handbook. 928p. 1997. 63.50 (*0-318-12777-6*) Am Horse Coun.

— Questions That Demand Answers. 160p. (Orig.). 1988. pap. 6.95 (*0-923309-10-1*) Hartland Pubns.

— Tax Tips for Horse Owners. 16p. 1997. 10.00 (*0-317-04924-0*) Am Horse Coun.

Davis, Thomas B. Defense of the Ruffians: A Dialogue with Conscience. 14p. 1997. pap. 3.00 (*0-88053-007-3*, M-13) Macoy Pub.

Davis, Thomas B. & Ricon, Amado. The Political Plans of Mexico. LC 87-10568. 704p. 1987. lib. bdg. 68.50 (*0-8191-6426-7*) U Pr of Amer.

Davis, Thomas D. Philosophy: An Introduction Through Original Fiction, Discussion & Readings. 3rd ed. 256p. (C). 1993. pap. 27.50 (*0-07-015933-5*) McGraw.

***Davis, Thomas E. & Osborn, Cynthia J.** The Solution-Focused School Counselor: Shaping Professional Practice. LC 99-55849. 1999. pap. 16.95 (*1-56032-862-2*) Taylor & Francis.

Davis, Thomas J. The Clearest Promises of God: The Development of Calvin's Eucharistic Teaching. LC 91-58297. (Studies in Religious Tradition: No. 1). 1995. 52.50 (*0-404-62531-2*) AMS Pr.

— God in My Grief: The Music of Grace When Loss Lives On. LC 98-36320. 120p. 1998. pap. 14.00 (*0-8170-1291-5*) Judson.

Davis, Thomas L. & Namson, Jay S., eds. Structural Evolution of the Western Transverse Ranges. (Illus.). 156p. (Orig.). 1987. pap. 8.00 (*1-878861-23-9*) Pac Section SEPM.

Davis, Thomas L., jt. ed. see Weimer, Paul.

Davis, Thomas M. Edward Taylor's Elegy on Deacon David Dewey. 15p. 1986. pap. 2.95 (*0-912296-85-2*) Am Antiquarian.

— A Reading of Edward Taylor. LC 90-50935. 240p. 1992. 40.00 (*0-87413-428-5*) U Delaware Pr.

Davis, Thomas O. Prose Writings. 1977. text 18.95 (*0-8369-8153-7*, 8293) Ayer.

Davis, Thomas W. The Corps Roots the Loudest: A History of VMI Athletics. fac. ed. LC 85-13446. 351p. reprint ed. pap. 108.90 (*0-7837-8292-6*, 204907400009) Bks Demand.

Davis, Thomas W., et al. Computer-Aided Analysis of Electrical Networks. LC 72-80234. (Illus.). 446p. reprint ed. pap. 138.30 (*0-608-10241-5*, 201504400092) Bks Demand.

Davis, Thomas X., tr. see William of St. Thierry.

***Davis-Thompson, Esther.** Motherlove: Reinventing a Good & Blessed Future for Our Children. LC 99-11524. 160p. (Orig.). 1999. pap. 12.00 (*1-880913-38-0*) Innisfree Pr.

— Raising up Queens: Loving Our Daughters Loud & Strong. LC 00-26798. (Illus.). 160p. 2000. pap. write for info. (*1-880913-46-1*) Innisfree Pr.

Davis-Thompson, Helen. Let's Celebrate Kwanzaa: An Activity Book for Young Readers. (Illus.). 32p. (J). (ps-5). 1993. pap. 5.95 (*0-936073-07-1*) Gumbs & Thomas.

Davis, Thulani. Maker of Saints. 256p. 1996. 21.50 (*0-684-81225-8*) S&S Trade.

Davis Tibbitts, Alison. James K. Polk. LC 98-29554. (United States Presidents Ser.). 128p. (YA). (gr. 5 up). 1999. lib. bdg. 20.95 (*0-7660-1037-6*) Enslow Pubs.

***Davis, Tim.** Dailies. 128p. 2000. pap. 12.50 (*0-935724-77-X*, Pub. by Figures) SPD-Small Pr Dist.

Davis, Tim. Mice of the Herring Bone. LC 92-11425. (Illus.). 106p. (J). 1992. pap. 6.49 (*0-89084-626-X*, 058537) Bob Jones Univ.

***Davis, Tim.** Mice of the Herring Bone, 2 vols. 2000. pap. 14.98 (*0-89084-907-2*) Bob Jones Univ.

Davis, Tim. Mice of the Nine Lives. LC 94-26128. (Illus.). 86p. (J). (gr. 1-5). 1994. pap. 6.49 (*0-89084-755-X*, 080556) Bob Jones Univ.

***Davis, Tim.** Mice of the Nine Lives, 2 vols. 2000. pap. 14.98 (*1-57924-089-5*) Bob Jones Univ.

Davis, Tim. Mice of the Seven Seas. LC 95-36840. 138p. (J). 1995. pap. 6.49 (*0-89084-845-9*, 092312) Bob Jones Univ.
— Mice of the Westing Wind, Bk. 2. LC 98-14559. (Illus.). 120p. (gr. 2-3). 1998. pap. 6.49 (*1-57924-067-4*) Bob Jones Univ.
— Mice of the Westing Wind Book One. LC 98-14559. (Illus.). 120p. (J). 1998. pap. 6.49 (*1-57924-065-8*) Bob Jones Univ.
Davis, Tim. Tales from Dust River Gulch. LC 96-38576. 102p. (J). 1997. pap. 6.49 (*0-89084-896-3*, 102517) Bob Jones Univ.
***Davis, Tim.** Tales from Dust River Gulch, 2 vols. 2000. pap. 14.98 (*0-89084-956-0*) Bob Jones Univ.
Davis, Tim, jt. auth. see Kinnard, Roy.
***Davis, Timothy C., et al.** Sports & the Law: A Modern Anthology. LC 99-65466. 635p. 1999. 35.00 (*0-89089-734-4*) Carolina Acad Pr.
***Davis, Todd.** New Big Book of U. S. Presidents: Fascinating Facts about Each & Every President. (Illus.). (J). 2001. 9.98 (*0-7624-0849-9*) Running Pr.
Davis, Todd M., ed. Open Doors, 1996-97: Report on International Educational Exchange. annuals 224p. 1997. pap. 42.95 (*0-87206-243-0*) Inst Intl Educ.
Davis, Todd M. & Murrell, Patricia H. Turning Teaching into Learning: The Role of Student Responsibility in the Collegiate Experience. Fife, Jonathan D., ed. & frwd. by. (ASHE-ERIC Higher Education Reports: No. 93-8). 97p. (Orig.). 1994. pap. 24.00 (*1-878380-29-X*) GWU Grad Schl E&HD.
Davis, Todd S. Criminal Thawts. 46p. (Orig.). 1996. pap. 3.00 (*0-9635398-2-5*) Tertium Non Data.
— Sun Plus Moon Rendezvous. 51p. 1993. pap. 3.00 (*0-9635398-0-9*); audio 5.00 (*0-9635398-1-7*) Tertium Non Data.
Davis, Todd S. & Margolis, Kevin D. Brownfields: A Comprehensive Guide to Redeveloping Contaminated Property. LC 97-71739. xxii, 703 p. 1997. write for info. (*1-57073-439-9*) Amer Bar Assn.
Davis, Tom. From the Tundra to Texas: The Art of Ken Carlson. 192p. 1994. 60.00 (*0-9632969-4-9*) Collect Covey.
— Just Goldens. LC 96-32598. (Illus.). 141p. 1996. 35.00 (*1-57223-041-X*, 041X) Willow Creek Pr.
— Just Goldens: Half-Pint Edition. LC 98-52366. (Half-Pint Ser.). (Illus.). 96p. 1999. 12.95 (*1-57223-218-8*, 2188) Willow Creek Pr.
— The Long & the Short. LC 94-69062. (Illus.). 40p. (Orig.). 1994. pap. text 5.95 (*1-884778-05-4*) Old Mountain.
— The Patrol Order. (Illus.). 104p. 1994. pap. text 7.95 (*1-884778-02-X*) Old Mountain.
— Pickaberry Pig. LC 95-70168. (Illus.). 32p. (J). 1995. pap. text 6.95 (*1-884778-10-0*) Old Mountain.
— Thomas Davis, Selections from His Prose & Poetry. LC 75-28810. (Illus.). 392p. reprint ed. 57.50 (*0-404-13803-9*) AMS Pr.
— What Would You Like on Your Mashed Potatoes? (Illus.). 124p. 1993. pap. text 10.00 (*1-884778-00-3*) Old Mountain.
— Why Dogs Do That: A Collection of Curious Canine Behaviors. LC 98-30019. (Illus.). 96p. 1998. 13.95 (*1-57223-139-4*) Willow Creek Pr.
Davis, Tom & Spartas, Dale C. The Little Book of Flyfishing. LC 97-1342. (Illus.). 112p. 1997. 14.95 (*1-57223-106-8*, 1068) Willow Creek Pr.
Davis, Tom, ed. see Goldsmith, Oliver.
***Davis, Tom I.** The Little Spokane. 64p. 2000. pap. 10.00 (*0-9668612-7-2*) Lost Horse.
Davis, Tony. Houseplants. LC 99-187949. (Easy-Step Ser.). 64p. (Orig.). 1998. pap. 4.95 (*0-8069-7055-3*) Sterling.
Davis, Townsend. Weary Feet, Rested Souls: A Guided History of the Civil Rights Movement. (Illus.). 432p. 1999. pap. 16.95 (*0-393-31819-2*, Norton Paperbks) Norton.
— Weary Feet, Rested Souls: A Guided History Through the Civil Rights Movement. LC 97-6749. 448p. 1998. 27.50 (*0-393-04592-7*) Norton.
Davis, Tracy. First Love & Others. 32p. (Orig.). 1996. pap. 4.95 (*1-880743-07-8*) Dead Metaphor.
— Scent of Spring. large type ed. 1990. pap. 16.99 (*0-7089-6874-0*) Ulverscroft.
Davis, Tracy C. Actresses As Working Women: Their Social Identity in Victorian England. (Gender & Performance Ser.). (Illus.). 224p. (C). 1991. pap. 25.99 (*0-415-06353-1*, A6161) Routledge.
***Davis, Tracy C.** The Economics of the British Stage: 1800-1914. LC 00-20381. (Illus.). 466p. (C). 2000. text Price not set. (*0-521-57115-4*) Cambridge U Pr.
Davis, Tracy C. George Bernard Shaw & the Socialist Theatre. LC 93-49613. 216p. 1994. pap. 18.95 (*0-275-93764-X*, Praeger Pubs) Greenwood.
— George Bernard Shaw & the Socialist Theatre, 56. LC 93-49613. (Contributions in Drama & Theatre Studies: No. 56). 216p. 1994. 59.95 (*0-313-27611-0*, Greenwood Pr) Greenwood.
Davis, Tracy C. & Donkin, Ellen, eds. Women & Playwriting in Nineteenth-Century Britain. LC 98-38099. (Illus.). 290p. (C). 1999. text 59.95 (*0-521-57413-7*); pap. text 21.95 (*0-521-65982-5*) Cambridge U Pr.
***Davis, Travis.** Special Edition Using Microsoft Systems Management Server 2.0. 700p. 2000. pap. 59.99 (*0-7897-2302-6*) Que.
Davis, Treva. Spice of Life Cookbook. (Illus.). vii, 159p. (Orig.). 1995. pap., spiral bd. 14.95 (*0-9654972-0-8*) Spice of Life Inc.
Davis, Treva L., jt. auth. see Gucciardi, Joan.
Davis, Troy D. Dublin's American Policy: Irish-American Diplomatic Relations, 1945-1952. LC 97-40218. 232p. 1998. text 54.95 (*0-8132-0907-2*); pap. text 24.95 (*0-8132-0915-3*) Cath U Pr.
Davis, Troy H. Turn down an Empty Glass. 1997. pap. write for info. (*1-57553-603-X*) Watermrk Pr.
Davis-Turner, Wanda. Sex Traps. LC 97-215180. 140p. 1997. pap. 9.99 (*1-56043-193-8*, Treasure Hse) Destiny Image.
— Sex Traps Workbook. 48p. 1997. pap. 7.99 (*1-56043-300-0*, Treasure Hse) Destiny Image.
Davis-Turner, Wanda A. I Stood in the Flames. 154p. (Orig.). 1996. pap. 9.99 (*1-56043-275-6*, Treasure Hse) Destiny Image.
Davis, Uri. Citizenship & the State: A Comparative Study of Citizenship Legislation in Israel, Jordan, Palestine, Syria & Lebanon. 224p. 1997. 40.00 (*0-86372-218-0*, Pub. by Garnet-Ithaca) LPC InBook.
— Israel: An Apartheid State. LC 87-14744. (Illus.). 240p. (C). 1987. pap. 15.00 (*0-86232-318-5*, Pub. by Zed Books); text 39.95 (*0-86232-317-7*, Pub. by Zed Books) St Martin.
Davis, Uri, tr. see El-Asmar, Fouzi.
Davis, Ursula. Cinema: The Hidden Persuader. 232p. (C). 1996. text 39.60 (*0-536-59297-7*) Pearson Custom.
Davis, Val. Flight of the Serpent. 288p. 1998. mass mkt. 5.50 (*0-553-57803-0*) Bantam.
— Track of the Scorpion. 336p. 1997. mass mkt. 5.50 (*0-553-57728-X*) Bantam.
— Wake of the Hornet. 304p. 2000. mass mkt. 5.99 (*0-553-57804-9*) Bantam.
Davis, Valerie. Mud Between My Toes: Poems for the Womanist. 100p. 1992. pap. 9.95 (*1-880299-02-X*) Woman to Woman.
Davis, Valerie, ed. Arizona Annotated Service, 1998 Edition: AZ Expanded AS. annot. rev. ed. 752p. 1998. pap. write for info. (*0-327-06075-1*, 40593-14) LEXIS Pub.
— Arizona Rules of Court Annotated, 1998 Edition: AZ, '98 Rules Edition. annot. rev. ed. 1208p. 1998. pap. write for info. (*0-327-06074-3*, 40585-13) LEXIS Pub.
Davis, Valerie, jt. auth. see Hilda, Attride.
Davis, Valerie B. In Search of Warriors Dark & Strong. (Illus.). 90p. (Orig.). Date not set. pap. 14.95 (*0-9645689-1-8*) Pubn Designers.
Davis, Vance A. & Blashaw, Brian. Unbroken Promises: A True Story of Courage & Belief. 280p. 1995. 22.95 (*1-887266-00-3*) White Mesa Pubs.
Davis, Varina. Jefferson Davis: Ex-President of the Confederate States of America, a Memoir by His Wife, 2 Vols., Set. (Select Bibliographies Reprint Ser.). 1977. reprint ed. 104.95 (*0-8369-6611-2*) Ayer.
Davis, Varina H. Jefferson Davis, a Memoir by His Wife, I. LC 90-6596. (Illus.). 1808p. (C). 1990. reprint ed. 48.95 (*1-877853-06-2*); reprint ed. pap. 24.95 (*1-877853-03-8*) Nautical & Aviation.
— Jefferson Davis, a Memoir by His Wife, II. LC 90-6596. (Illus.). 1808p. (C). 1990. reprint ed. 48.95 (*1-877853-07-0*); reprint ed. pap. 24.95 (*1-877853-04-6*) Nautical & Aviation.
— Jefferson Davis, a Memoir by His Wife, Set, Vols. I & II. LC 90-6596. (Illus.). 1808p. (C). 1990. reprint ed. 98.00 (*1-877853-05-4*); reprint ed. pap. 49.90 (*1-877853-08-9*) Nautical & Aviation.
Davis, Verna Burger, see Burger Davis, Verna.
Davis, Verdell. Let Me Grieve, but Not Forever. LC 97-5643. Orig. Title: Riches Stored in Secret Places. 160p. 1997. 12.99 (*0-8499-1425-6*) Word Pub.
Davis, Vernon. Financial Survival. rev. ed. 310p. 1990. pap. 14.95 (*1-878431-03-X*) Artist Profile Pub.
Davis, Victoria. Innocence: Universal Expressions of Childhood. LC 00-25549. (Illus.). 96p. 2000. 10.95 (*1-57223-213-7*) Willow Creek Pr.
Davis, Vincent, ed. The Post-Imperial Presidency. LC 79-67064. 190p. 1980. 49.95 (*0-275-90466-0*, C0466, Praeger Pubs) Greenwood.
— The Post-Imperial Presidency. LC 79-67064. 190p. 1980. pap. text 21.95 (*0-87855-747-4*) Transaction Pubs.
***Davis, Viola.** Help from My Subconcious Mind. 250p. 1999. pap. 6.99 (*1-893181-27-8*, Simon & Northrop) Le Gesse Stevens.
Davis, Virginia. Anima Speaking. 120p. 1994. pap. 8.95 (*1-882550-04-8*) Quiet Lion Pr.
— Simply Ridiculous. unabridged ed. (Illus.). 32p. (J). (ps-2). 1995. 14.95 (*1-55074-107-1*, Pub. by Kids Can Pr) Genl Dist Srvs.
— William Waynflete: Bishop & Educationalist. (Studies in the History of Medieval Religion: Vol. VI). (Illus.). 205p. (C). 1993. 75.00 (*0-85115-349-6*, Boydell Pr) Boydell & Brewer.
Davis, Virginia H., ed. see Howe, Henry.
Davis, Virginia I. Crafts: A Basic Survey. 336p. (C). 1988. text. write for info. (*0-697-00621-2*) Brown & Benchmark.
Davis, Virginia L. Tidewater Virginia Families. 730p. 1998. reprint ed. 75.00 (*0-8063-1283-1*) Genealog Pub.
Davis, Virginia Lee Hutcheson. Tidewater Virginia Families: Generations Beyond: Adding the Families of Alsobrook, Bibb, Edwards, Favor, Gray, Hux, Ironmonger, Laker, Southern, Taylor, & Woolfolk. LC 98-72719. 221 p. 1998. 45.00 (*0-8063-1578-4*) Genealog Pub.
Davis, Vivian I., et al. Portable Writing Lab. 352p. (C). 1990. pap. text 22.75 (*0-15-570779-5*) Harcourt Coll Pubs.
Davis, W. Jodi Sextet. 1995. pap. text 20.00 (*0-7935-4830-6*, 00000770) H Leonard.
Davis, W., et al, eds. The Control of Tumour Growth & Its Biological Bases. (Developments in Oncology Ser.). 1984. text 256.50 (*0-89838-603-9*) Kluwer Academic.
Davis, W., ed. see MacLennan, Robert, et al.
***Davis, W. Alan & Agarwal, Krishna.** Radio Frequency Circuit Design. 340p. 2001. 84.95 (*0-471-35052-4*) Wiley.
Davis, W. Church. Davis. Ancestry & Posterity of Joseph Davis (1773-1865) of Norway, New York, & His Wife Elizabeth Hallock Davis. 172p. 1997. reprint ed. pap. 27.00 (*0-8328-8228-3*); reprint ed. lib. bdg. 37.00 (*0-8328-8227-5*) Higginson Bk Co.
Davis, W. E. Black Dragon. large type ed. LC 97-3982. 324p. 1997. 21.95 (*0-7862-1054-0*) Thorndike Pr.
— Drastic Park: A Gil Beckman Mystery. LC 97-17231. (Gil Beckman Mystery Ser.). 208p. 1997. pap. 8.99 (*0-89107-962-9*) Crossway Bks.
— Drastic Park: A Gil Beckman Mystery. large type ed. LC 98-9954. 1998. 22.95 (*0-7862-1403-1*) Thorndike Pr.
— Victim of Circumstance, No. 2. LC 95-10851. (Gil Beckman Mystery Ser.: Bk. 2). 208p. 1995. pap. 8.99 (*0-89107-843-6*) Crossway Bks.
Davis, W. E., jt. ed. see Vermeer, A.
Davis, W. Eugene. The Celebrated Case of Esther Waters: The Collaboration of George Moore & Barrett H. Clark on "Esther Waters: A Play" LC 84-15380. 168p. (Orig.). 1985. pap. text 20.50 (*0-8191-4222-0*); lib. bdg. 48.00 (*0-8191-4221-2*) U Pr of Amer.
Davis, W. Eugene & Gerber, Helmut E., eds. Thomas Hardy: An Annotated Bibliography of Writings about Him, Vol. II. LC 72-7514. (Annotated Secondary Bibliography Series on English Literature in Transition, 1880-1920). 735p. 1983. 55.00 (*0-87580-091-2*) N Ill U Pr.
Davis, W. Eugene, jt. ed. see Gerber, Helmut E.
Davis, W. G. Isaac: The Ancestry of Mary Isaac. (Illus.). 400p. 1991. reprint ed. pap. 61.00 (*0-8328-2153-5*); reprint ed. lib. bdg. 71.00 (*0-8328-2152-7*) Higginson Bk Co.
— Lunt: The Ancestry of Abel Lunt. (Illus.). 269p. 1991. reprint ed. pap. 42.00 (*0-8328-2085-7*); reprint ed. lib. bdg. 52.00 (*0-8328-2084-9*) Higginson Bk Co.
Davis, W. H. The Freewill Question. 98p. 1971. pap. text 50.50 (*90-247-5101-2*, Pub. by M Nijhoff) Kluwer Academic.
Davis, W. Hardy. Aiming for the Jugular in New Orleans. LC 75-16561. 1976. 21.95 (*0-87949-035-7*) Ashley Bks.
Davis, W. Hersey. Greek Papyri of the First Century. 84p. 1980. pap. 10.00 (*0-89005-332-4*) Ares.
Davis, W. Howard, jt. auth. see Fonseca, Raymond J.
Davis, W. J. Chosin Marine: Breakout from North Korea. 134p. 1985. pap. 11.00 (*1-885541-04-X*) Marine Bks.
— The Federal Reserve System: Legal or Illegal? 1982. lib. bdg. 250.00 (*0-87700-357-2*) Revisionist Pr.
— From Hanoi-Gate to Higgins: A Planned Raid to Save POWS in Hanoi. 143p. 1989. pap. 11.00 (*1-885541-03-1*) Marine Bks.
— How to Wage Peace: A Framework for the Future. 122p. 1989. pap. 11.00 (*1-885541-06-6*) Marine Bks.
— Tet Marine: An Autobiography. 185p. 1987. pap. 11.00 (*1-885541-02-3*) Marine Bks.
— Worldwide Marine: Answers to Combat Questions. 167p. 1987. pap. 11.00 (*1-885541-05-8*) Marine Bks.
Davis, W. J., jt. auth. see Davis, Ray.
Davis, W. J., jt. auth. see Marshall, S. L.
Davis, W. L., Jr. Screenplay Companion: A Workbook for Screenwriters. 2nd rev. ed. (Illus.). 110p. (C). 1996. pap. 18.95 (*0-9639177-1-4*) Write-Side Prods.
Davis, W. M. Davis: Genealogy of the Clinton H. Davis Family, Short Sketch of the Lost Creek 7th Day Baptist Church. 100p. 1994. reprint ed. pap. 19.00 (*0-8328-4148-X*); reprint ed. lib. bdg. 29.00 (*0-8328-4147-1*) Higginson Bk Co.
— The Way to Get What You Want. 1941. pap. 3.50 (*0-88027-022-5*) Firm Foun Pub.
Davis, W. S. Davis Trans 03183/03161. 2nd ed. 1981. trans. 14.50 (*0-201-03577-4*) Addison-Wesley.
— Info Processg Sys Fortrn. 1981. 18.25 (*0-201-13296-6*) Addison-Wesley.
— Information Processing Systems & BASIC: Getting Started. 1981. 20.75 (*0-201-13297-4*) Addison-Wesley.
— Stdnt Wkbk Information Processing. 2nd ed. 1981. pap. text, student ed. 6.25 (*0-201-03185-X*) Addison-Wesley.
Davis, W. W. El Gringo: New Mexico & Her People. LC 82-2735. (Illus.). 432p. 1982. pap. 7.95 (*0-8032-6558-1*, Bison Books) U of Nebr Pr.
— Hart. History of the Hart Family of Warminster, Bucks County, Pennsylvania, to Which is Added the Genealogy of the Family from the First Settlement in America. (Illus.). 159p. 1997. reprint ed. pap. 25.00 (*0-8328-9022-7*); reprint ed. lib. bdg. 35.00 (*0-8328-9021-9*) Higginson Bk Co.
— History of Bucks County, from the Discovery of the Delaware to the Present Time (1905), 3 vols. 2nd enl. rev. ed. Ely, Warren S. & Jordan, John W., eds. (Illus.). 1997. reprint ed. lib. bdg. 155.00 (*0-8328-6394-7*) Higginson Bk Co.
— History of Bucks County, Pennsylvania. (Illus.). 929p. 1993. reprint ed. lib. bdg. 92.50 (*0-8328-3212-X*) Higginson Bk Co.
— History of Doylestown, Old & New, from Its Settlement to the Close of the 19th Century, 1745-1900. (Illus.). 389p. 1997. reprint ed. lib. bdg. 45.00 (*0-8328-6409-9*) Higginson Bk Co.
Davis, Wade. One River: Explorations & Discoveries in the Amazon Rain Forest. 544p. 1997. per. 16.00 (*0-684-83496-0*) S&S Trade Pap.
— One River: Explorations & Discoveries in the Amazon Rain Forest. (Illus.). 537p. 1996. 27.00 (*0-684-80886-2*) Simon & Schuster.
— Passage of Darkness: The Ethnobiology of the Haitian Zombie. LC 87-40537. (Illus.). xxi, 344p. (C). 1988. 39.95 (*0-8078-1776-7*); pap. 19.95 (*0-8078-4210-9*) U of NC Pr.
— Rain Forest: Ancient Realm of the Pacific Northwest. 128p. 1999. 35.00 (*1-890132-24-1*) Chelsea Green Pub.
— The Serpent & the Rainbow. 304p. 1997. per. 13.00 (*0-684-83929-6*) S&S Trade Pap.
— Shadows in the Sun. LC 99-33453. 304p. 1999. pap. 13.00 (*0-7679-0402-8*) Bantam.
— Shadows in the Sun: Travels to Landscapes of Spirit & Desire. LC 98-34097. 260p. 1998. 22.95 (*1-55963-354-9*) Island Pr.
***Davis, Wade & Osborne, Graham.** Rainforest: Ancient Realm of the Pacific Northwest. (Illus.). 128p. 2000. pap. 21.95 (*1-890132-79-9*) Chelsea Green Pub.
Davis, Wally. The Corvette Cartoon Book. (Illus.). 96p. (Orig.). 1991. pap. 5.95 (*0-938417-02-9*) Copouts Ink.
— Desperately Seeking Crime Crushers. (Illus.). 96p. (Orig.). 1986. pap. 4.95 (*0-938417-00-2*) Copouts Ink.
— The Laugh Factor: Stress Management for Law Enforcement. (Illus.). 116p. (Orig.). 1987. pap. 9.95 (*0-938417-01-0*) Copouts Ink.
***Davis, Walter & Davis, Reba, eds.** The Heritage of Clarke County, Alabama. (Heritage of Alabama Ser.: Vol. 13). 320p. 2001. 50.00 (*1-891647-40-7*) Herit Pub Consult.
Davis, Walter A. The Act of Interpretation: A Critique of Literary Reason. LC 77-13803. 194p. reprint ed. pap. 60.20 (*0-608-09444-7*, 205424400005) Bks Demand.
***Davis, Walter A.** Deracination: Historicity, Hiroshima, & a Humanism Without Guarantees. (C). 2001. pap. text 22.95 (*0-7914-4834-7*) State U NY Pr.
— Deracination: Historicity, Hiroshima, & a Humanism Without Guarantees. (C). 2001. text 68.50 (*0-7914-4833-9*) State U NY Pr.
Davis, Walter A. Get the Guests: Psychoanalysis, Modern American Drama, & the Audience. LC 93-38608. (Wisconsin Project on American Writers Ser.). 304p. 1994. pap. 19.95 (*0-299-14154-3*) U of Wis Pr.
— Inwardness & Existence: Subjectivity in - & Hegel, Heidegger, Marx, & Freud. LC 88-40428. 440p. (C). 1989. pap. text 24.95 (*0-299-12014-7*) U of Wis Pr.
Davis, Walter A., compiled by. Early Records of the Town of Lunenburg, Including That Part Which Is Now Fitchburg, 1719-1764, Town & Selectmen's Records: Vital Statistics. 384p. 1995. reprint ed. lib. bdg. 42.50 (*0-8328-4641-4*) Higginson Bk Co.
***Davis, Walter C.** The Proprietor's Records of the Town of Lunenburg, Massachusetts: Including Fitchburg & a Portion of Ashby 1729-1833. 392p. 2000. reprint ed. pap. 30.00 (*0-7884-1456-9*, 1456) Heritage Bk.
Davis, Walter Goodwin. Massachusetts & Maine Families: In the Ancestry of Walter Goodwin Davis (1885-1966), 3 vols., Set. LC 95-81293. 2096p. 1996. reprint ed. 135.00 (*0-8063-1496-6*) Genealog Pub.
— Massachusetts & Maine Families in the Ancestry of Walter Goodwin Davis (1885-1966) Vol. I: Allanson-French. 746p. 1996. text 50.00 (*0-8063-1495-8*) Genealog Pub.
— Massachusetts & Maine Families in the Ancestry of Walter Goodwin Davis (1885-1966) Vol. II: Gardner-Moses. 732p. 1996. text 50.00 (*0-8063-1494-X*) Genealog Pub.
— Massachusetts & Maine Families in the Ancestry of Walter Goodwin Davis (1885-1966) Vol. III: Neal-Wright. 732p. 1996. text 50.00 (*0-8063-1493-1*) Genealog Pub.
Davis, Walter R. Idea & Art in Elizabethan Fiction. LC 68-56307. 311p. reprint ed. pap. 96.50 (*0-8357-8915-2*, 203339600085) Bks Demand.
— Thomas Campion. LC 87-11. (Twayne's English Authors Ser.: No. 450). 208p. (C). 1987. 26.95 (*0-8057-6949-8*) Macmillan.
Davis, Walter T., Jr. Shattered Dream: America's Search for Its Soul. LC 94-10248. 208p. (Orig.). (C). 1994. pap. 16.00 (*1-56338-095-1*) TPI PA.
Davis, Walter W. Eastern & Western History, Thought, & Culture, 1600-1815. 822p. (Orig.). (C). 1993. text 85.00 (*0-8191-8823-9*); pap. text 58.50 (*0-8191-8824-7*) U Pr of Amer.
Davis, Warren J. Japan, the Air Menace of the Pacific. LC 73-111751. (American Imperialism: Viewpoints of United States Foreign Policy, 1898-1941 Ser.). 1970. reprint ed. 16.95 (*0-405-02010-4*) Ayer.
***Davis, Wayne.** John Stone & the Choctaw Kid, Vol. 1. large type ed. LC 99-38420. 404p. 1999. 24.95 (*0-7838-8728-0*) Macmillan Gen Ref.
Davis, Wayne, ed. Graphics Interface Proceedings, 1996. 260p. 1998. pap. text 45.00 (*1-55860-424-3*) Morgan Kaufmann.
Davis, Wayne, ed. see Booth, Kellogg S. & Fournier, Alain.
Davis, Wayne A. Implicature: Intention, Convention, & Principle in the Failure of Gricean Theory. LC 98-3021. (Cambridge Studies in Philosophy). 176p. (C). 1998. text 49.95 (*0-521-62319-7*) Cambridge U Pr.
Davis, Wayne H. & Roca, Philippe. Bluebirds & Their Survival. (Illus.). 168p. 1995. pap. 17.00 (*0-8131-0846-2*) U Pr of Ky.
Davis, Wayne H., jt. auth. see Barbour, Roger W.
Davis, Wayne T., jt. auth. see Air & Waste Management Association Staff.
Davis, Wayne T., ed. see Air & Waste Management Association Staff.
Davis, Wendy. City Park. LC 97-28741. (Habitats Ser.). 1997. 24.00 (*0-516-20741-5*) Childrens.
— City Park. LC 97-28741. (Habitats Ser.). (J). (gr. 2-3). 1998. pap. text 6.95 (*0-516-20370-3*) Childrens.
Davis, Wendy. From Metal to Music. LC 96-47178. (Changes Ser.). (J). (gr. 2-3). 1997. lib. bdg. 24.00 (*0-516-20707-5*) Childrens.
Davis, Wendy. From Tree to Paper. (J). (gr. k-2). 1995. pap. 8.95 incl. audio (*0-7608-0487-7*); pap. 4.95 (*1-56801-494-5*) Sundance Pub.
— From Tree to Paper, Big Book. (J). (gr. k-2). 1995. pap. 17.95 (*1-56801-426-0*) Sundance Pub.
— Limestone Cave. LC 97-26985. (Habitats Ser.). 1997. 24.00 (*0-516-20742-3*) Childrens.

D

An Asterisk (*) at the beginning of an entry indicates that the title is appearing for the first time.

— Limestone Cave. (Habitats Ser.). (J). (gr. 2-3). 1998. pap. text 6.95 (*0-516-20371-1*) Childrens.

Davis, Wendy & Knight, Bertram T. Working at a Marine Institute. LC 98-13206. (Working Here Ser.). 32p. (J). (ps-5). 1998. 23.00 (*0-516-21223-0*) Childrens.

— Working at a Marine Institute. (Working Here Ser.). (Illus.). 32p. (J). (gr. 2-4). 1999. pap. text 6.95 (*0-516-26453-2*) Childrens.

Davis, Wendy A. Douglas Fir. LC 96-51027. (Habitats Ser.). (J). 1997. lib. bdg. 24.00 (*0-516-20712-1*) Childrens.

— Douglas Fir. (Habitats Ser.). (J). (gr. 2-5). 1997. pap. 6.95 (*0-516-26064-2*) Childrens.

Davis-Weyer, Caecilia, ed. Early Medieval Art 300-1150: Sources & Documents. (Medieval Academy Reprints for Teaching Ser.). 182p. 1986. reprint ed. pap. text 12.95 (*0-8020-6628-3*) U of Toronto Pr.

Davis-White, Jeanne, ed. Polish Arrivals at the Port of Baltimore, 1880-1884. 168p. 1994. pap. 5.95 (*1-887124-09-8*, PG 109) Historyk Pr.

***Davis-White, Jeanne S.** People of Polonia: The 1910 Census Ward Two Baltimore City, Maryland, Pt. II. 1999. pap. 8.95 (*1-887124-16-0*) Historyk Pr.

Davis-White, Jeanne S., ed. People of Polonia: The 1910 Census, 5 vols. 1993. pap. 31.95 (*1-887124-04-7*, HP 105A) Historyk Pr.

— People of Polonia Vol. 1: The 1910 Census: Anne Arundel & Baltimore County. 97p. 1993. pap. 4.95 (*1-887124-05-5*, PG 105) Historyk Pr.

— People of Polonia Vol. 2: The 1910 Census: Baltimore City - Ward One. 193p. 1993. pap. 7.95 (*1-887124-06-3*, PG 106) Historyk Pr.

— People of Polonia Vol. 3: The 1910 Census: Baltimore City - Ward 3. 84p. 1993. pap. 3.95 (*1-887124-07-1*, PG 107) Historyk Pr.

— People of Polonia Vol. 4, Pt. 1 (A-M) The 1910 Census: Ward Two. 278p. 1995. pap. 6.95 (*1-887124-08-X*, PG 108) Historyk Pr.

Davis, Whitney. Drawing the Dream of the Wolves: Homosexuality, Interpretation, & in Freud's "Wolf Man" LC 95-4117. (Theories of Representation & Difference Ser.). (Illus.). 352p. 1995. 39.95 (*0-253-32919-1*); pap. 16.95 (*0-253-20988-9*) Ind U Pr.

— Masking the Blow: The Scene of Representation in Late Prehistoric Egyptian Art. (California Studies in the History of Art: No. XXX). (C). 1992. 65.00 (*0-520-07488-2*, Pub. by U CA Pr) Cal Prin Full Svc.

— Replications: Archaeology, Art History, Psychoanalysis. Quinn, Richard W., ed. 1996. 70.00 (*0-271-01523-3*); pap. 29.95 (*0-271-01524-1*) Pa St U Pr.

Davis, Whitney, intro. Gay & Lesbian Studies in Art History. LC 93-49027. (Journal of Homosexuality). (Illus.). 225p. 1994. 49.95 (*1-56024-661-8*); pap. 22.95 (*1-56023-054-1*, Harrington Park) Haworth Pr.

Davis, Whitney, et al. Pacing the World: Construction in the Sculpture of David Rabinowitch. LC 96-30954. (Illus.). 310p. 1996. 50.00 (*0-916724-93-X*, Pub. by Harvard Art Mus); pap. 35.00 (*0-916724-91-3*, Pub. by Harvard Art Mus) HUP.

Davis, Will. Start Your Own Business for One Thousand Dollars or Less. 280p. 1994. pap. 17.95 (*0-936894-70-9*, 610063-01) Dearborn.

Davis, William. Battle at Bull Run. (Illus.). 336p. 1995. 19.95 (*0-8117-0202-2*) Stackpole.

— Bench & Bar of the Commonwealth of Massachusetts, 2 vols. (American Constitutional & Legal History Ser). 1299p. 1974. reprint ed. lib. bdg. 145.00 (*0-306-70612-1*) Da Capo.

— Civil War Journal: The Leaders. Pohanka, Brian C., ed. LC 97-6861. (Illus.). 512p. 1997. 29.95 (*1-55853-437-7*) Rutledge Hill Pr.

— Concise History of the Civil War. (Civil War Ser.). 60p. 1994. pap. 4.95 (*0-915992-64-7*) Eastern National.

— The First Battle of Manassas. (Civil War Ser.). (Illus.). 48p. 1995. pap. 4.95 (*0-915992-76-0*) Eastern National.

— Great Myths of Business: Everything You Think You Know Is Wrong. 1997. 19.95 (*0-7494-2253-X*) Kogan Page Ltd.

— History of the Judiciary of Massachusetts. LC 74-8535. (American Constitutional & Legal History Ser.). xxiv, 446p. 1974. reprint ed. lib. bdg. 55.00 (*0-306-70613-X*) Da Capo.

— The Lucky Generation: A Positive View of the 21st Century. 320p. 1996. mass mkt. 13.95 (*0-7472-4744-7*, Pub. by Headline Bk Pub) Trafalgar.

— Study Guide for Operating Systems: A Systematic View. 4th ed. 208p. (C). 1991. pap. text 17.00 (*0-201-56703-2*) Addison-Wesley.

— Three Roads to the Alamo: The Lives & Fortunes of David Crockett, James Bowie, & William Barret Travis. (Illus.). 816p. 1999. pap. 18.00 (*0-06-093094-2*) HarpC.

Davis, William, photos by. If Mountains Die: A New Mexico Memoir. LC 94-2243. (Illus.). 1994. reprint ed. pap. 19.95 (*0-393-31159-7*) Norton.

Davis, William, et al. The Encyclopedia of Dollhouse Decorating Techniques. (Illus.). 160p. 1997. 24.95 (*0-7624-0095-1*) Running Pr.

Davis, William, jt. auth. see Tree, Christina.

Davis, William A. Maydays & Mermaids. 152p. 1983. 10.00 (*0-89540-133-9*, SB-133) Sun Pub.

Davis, William A., jt. auth. see Schultes, Richard E.

Davis, William B. Revealing the End of the World: To the Children of Light. LC 97-60418. 80p. (Orig.). 1997. pap. 7.99 (*1-57921-014-7*) WinePress Pub.

Davis, William B. & Schmidly, David J. The Mammals of Texas. rev. ed. (Illus.). 328p. 1995. pap. 17.95 (*1-885696-00-0*) TX Prks & Wldlife.

Davis, William B., et al. An Introduction to Music Therapy: Theory & Practice. 400p. (C). 1995. text. write for info. (*0-697-33997-1*) Brown & Benchmark.

***Davis, William C.** American Frontier: Pioneers, Settlers & Cowboys, 1800-1899. LC 98-37720. 1999. pap. text 19.95 (*0-8061-3129-2*) U of Okla Pr.

Davis, William C. Battle at Bull Run: A History of the First Major Campaign of the Civil War. LC 76-42322. (Illus.). xiv, 328p. 1981. pap. 14.95 (*0-8071-0867-7*) La State U Pr.

— The Battle of New Market. LC 82-18705. (Illus.). xiii, 280p. 1983. pap. 14.95 (*0-8071-1078-7*) La State U Pr.

— The Battle of New Market. LC 92-31082. (Illus.). 288p. 1993. 18.95 (*0-8117-0576-5*) Stackpole.

— The Battlefields of the Civil War. LC 96-11782. (Illus.). 256p. 1996. pap. 19.95 (*0-8061-2882-8*, 2882) U of Okla Pr.

— Battlefields of the Civil War. LC 99-23238. (Rebels & Yankees Ser.). (Illus.). 256p. 1999. 24.98 (*1-57145-194-3*, Thunder Bay) Advantage Pubs.

— Battles of the Civil War. 1999. 9.99 (*1-84100-278-X*) Quadrillion Media.

— Breckinridge: Statesman, Soldier& Symbol. LC 73-77658. (Southern Biography Ser.). (Illus.). 688p. (C). 1982. pap. 16.95 (*0-8071-1805-2*) La State U Pr.

***Davis, William C.** Brothers in Arms: The Lives & Experiences of the Men Who Fought the Civil War--In Their Own Words. 2000. 14.99 (*0-7858-1203-2*) Bk Sales Inc.

Davis, William C. The Cause Lost: Myths & Realities of the Confederacy. LC 87-46161. (Modern War Studies). (Illus.). 228p. 1996. 24.95 (*0-7006-0809-5*) U Pr of KS.

— Civil War Parks: The Story Behind the Scenery. LC 83-83006. (Illus.). 64p. (Orig.). 1984. pap. 7.95 (*0-916122-95-6*) KC Pubns.

— Civil War Parks: The Story Behind the Scenery. Sommer, Sigrid, tr. (GER.). 64p. (Orig.). 1993. pap. 8.95 (*0-88714-777-1*) KC Pubns.

— Commanders of the Civil War. LC 99-26422. (Rebels & Yankees Ser.). (Illus.). 256p. 1999. 24.98 (*1-57145-192-7*, Thunder Bay) Advantage Pubs.

— Duel Between the First Ironclads. LC 75-11071. (Illus.). xii, 220p. 1981. pap. 14.95 (*0-8071-0868-5*) La State U Pr.

— Duel Between the First Ironclads. 2nd ed. LC 93-26867. (Illus.). 240p. 1994. 18.95 (*0-8117-0536-6*) Stackpole.

— Fighting Men of the Civil War. LC 99-28865. (Rebels & Yankees Ser.). (Illus.). 256p. 1999. 24.98 (*1-57145-193-5*, Thunder Bay) Advantage Pubs.

— First Blood: Fort Sumter to Bull Run. LC 82-17014. (Civil War Ser.). (Illus.). 176p. 1983. lib. bdg. 25.93 (*0-8094-4705-3*) Time-Life.

Davis, William C. Fort Sumter to Gettysburg: Compact Edition. (Civil War Times Illustrated Ser.: Vol. 1). 1376p. 1998. 19.98 (*1-57912-012-1*) Blck Dog & Leventhal.

Davis, William C. Generals of the Civil War. 1999. 9.99 (*1-84100-277-1*) Quadrillion Media.

— Gettysburg: The Story Behind the Scenery. LC 83-80606. (Illus.). 48p. (Orig.). 1983. pap. 7.95 (*0-916122-89-1*) KC Pubns.

— A Government of Our Own: The Making of the Confederacy. LC 94-15205. (Illus.). 550p. 1994. 27.95 (*0-02-907735-4*) Free Pr.

— A Government of Our Own: The Making of the Confederacy. (Illus.). 576p. 1997. pap. 19.95 (*0-8071-2177-0*) La State U Pr.

— Historic Site Studies in Churchill County, Nevada. LC 99-166343. 136p. 1998. pap. 15.95 (*1-56167-429-X*) Am Literary Pr.

— The Illustrated History of the Civil War: The Soldiers, Generals, Weapons & Battles of the Civil War. (Illus.). 264p. 1997. 24.98 (*0-7624-0172-9*, Courage) Running Pr.

— Jefferson Davis: The Man & His Hour. LC 90-56352. 816p. (C). 1996. pap. 22.95 (*0-8071-2079-0*) La State U Pr.

***Davis, William C.** Lincolns Men: How President Lincoln Became Father to an Army & a Nation. 336p. 2000. per. 14.00 (*0-684-86294-8*) S&S Trade.

Davis, William C. Lincoln's Men: How President Lincoln Became Father to an Army & a Nation. LC 98-8069. 352p. 1999. 25.00 (*0-684-83337-9*) Free Pr.

— The Orphan Brigade: The Kentucky Confederates Who Couldn't Go Home. LC 82-18700. (Illus.). xvi, 318p. 1983. pap. 17.95 (*0-8071-1077-9*) La State U Pr.

— The Orphan Brigade: The Kentucky Confederates Who Couldn't Go Home. 2nd ed. LC 93-16359. (Illus.). 352p. 1993. reprint ed. 19.95 (*0-8117-1182-X*) Stackpole.

***Davis, William C.** Rebels & Yankees: Naval Battles of the Civil War. 2000. 24.98 (*1-57145-246-X*, Thunder Bay) Advantage Pubs.

Davis, William C. Soldiers of the Civil War. 1999. 9.99 (*1-84100-276-3*) Quadrillion Media.

— Three Roads to the Alamo: The Saga of Davy Crockett, Jim Bowie, & William Travis. LC 97-43815. (Illus.). 816p. 1998. 35.00 (*0-06-017334-3*) HarpC.

— Touched by Fire: A National Historical Society Photographic Portrait of the Civil War. (Illus.). 664p. 1997. 29.98 (*1-57912-001-6*) Blck Dog & Leventhal.

— Vicksburg to Appomattox. (Civil War Times Illustrated Ser.: Vol. 2). 1376p. 1998. 19.98 (*1-57912-013-X*) Blck Dog & Leventhal.

— Warnings from the Far South: Democracy vs. Dictatorship in Uruguay, Argentina & Chile. LC 95-7017. 256p. 1995. 65.00 (*0-275-95021-2*, Praeger Pubs) Greenwood.

— A Way Through the Wilderness: The Natchez Trace & the Civilization of the Southern Frontier. (Illus.). 416p. 1996. pap. 16.95 (*0-8071-2132-0*) La State U Pr.

Davis, William C., ed. The Confederate General Vol. 1: Adams-Cobb. (Confederate General Ser.). (Illus.). 288p. 1991. 34.95 (*0-918678-63-3*) Natl Hist Soc.

***Davis, William C., ed.** Fire-Eater Remembers: The Confederate Memoir of Robert Barnwell Rhett. LC 00-8864. 192p. 2000. 24.95 (*1-57003-348-X*) U of SC Pr.

Davis, William C., ed. Monoclonal Antibody Protocols. LC 95-13504. (Methods in Molecular Biology Ser.: Vol. 45). (Illus.). 274p. 1995. 79.50 (*0-89603-308-2*) Humana.

Davis, William C., ed. Diary of a Confederate Soldier: John S. Jackman of the Orphan Brigade. LC 90-12431. 174p. 1997. pap. 12.95 (*1-57003-164-9*) U of SC Pr.

Davis, William C., et al, eds. Civil War Journal: The Legacies. (Illus.). 480p. 1999. 29.95 (*1-55853-439-3*) Rutledge Hill Pr.

— Civil War Journal Vol. 2: The Battles. LC 97-6861. (Illus.). 480p. 1998. 29.95 (*1-55853-438-5*) Rutledge Hill Pr.

Davis, William C. & Hoffman, Julie, eds. The Confederate General Vol. 3: Gordon, George - Jordan, Thomas. 221p. 1991. 34.95 (*0-918678-65-X*) Natl Hist Soc.

Davis, William C. & Hoffman, Julie, eds. The Confederate General Vol. 4: Kelly, J. H. to Payne, W. H. F. 225p. 1991. 34.95 (*0-918678-66-8*) Natl Hist Soc.

Davis, William C. & Hoffman, Julie, eds. The Confederate General Vol. 5: Peck to Steele. 1991. 34.95 (*0-918678-67-6*) Natl Hist Soc.

— The Confederate General Vol. 6: Steuart, G. H. - Zollicoffer, F. K. 250p. 1992. 34.95 (*0-918678-68-4*) Natl Hist Soc.

Davis, William C. & Pritchard, Russ A. Fighting Men of the Civil War. LC 97-40733. 256p. 1998. 19.95 (*0-8061-3060-1*) U of Okla Pr.

Davis, William C. & Swentor, Meredith L., eds. Bluegrass Confederate: The Headquarters Diary of Edward O. Guerrant. LC 99-32046. 584p. 1999. 49.95 (*0-8071-2411-7*) La State U Pr.

Davis, William C & Wiley, Bell I. Civil War Times Illustrated Photographic History of the Civil War: Vicksburg to Appomattox, Vol. 2. LC 94-30567. (Illus.). 1376p. 1994. 39.98 (*1-884822-09-6*) Blck Dog & Leventhal.

Davis, William C. & Wiley, Bell I., eds. The Civil War Times Illustrated Photographic History of the Civil War, 2, 2. LC 94-30567. (Illus.). 1376p. 39.98 (*1-884822-08-8*) Blck Dog & Leventhal.

Davis, William C., jt. auth. see Mother Earth News Editors.

Davis, William E. The Alaska Gallery at the Anchorage Museum of History & Art: A Guidebook. LC 89-86013. (Illus.). 90p. (Orig.). 1990. pap. 6.00 (*1-878462-00-8*) Cook Inlet Hist Soc.

Davis, William E., Jr. History of the Nuttall Ornithological Club, 1873 - 1986. (Memoirs of the Nuttall Ornithological Club Ser.: No. 11). (Illus.). 179p. 1987. 20.00 (*1-877973-33-5*) Nuttall Ornith.

Davis, William E., Jr. & Jackson, Jerome J., eds. Contributions to the History of North American Ornithology. (Memoir Ser.: No. 12). (Illus.). 501p. 1995. 40.00 (*1-877973-36-X*) Nuttall Ornith.

Davis, William E., jt. ed. see Davis, Nancy Y.

***Davis, William H.** Beginner's Grammar of the Greek New Testament. 270p. 1999. pap. 23.00 (*1-57910-260-3*) Wipf & Stock.

Davis, William H. Seventy-Five Years in California: Recollections & Remarks by One Who Visited These Shores in 1831, & Again in 1833 & Except When Absent on Business Was a Resident from 1838 until 1909. (American Biography Ser.). 345p. 1991. reprint ed. lib. bdg. 79.00 (*0-7812-8104-0*) Rprt Serv.

Davis, William J. Massachusetts Wildlife Viewing Guide. LC 96-36433. (Illus.). 96p. (Orig.). 1997. pap. 8.95 (*1-56044-426-6*) Falcon Pub Inc.

Davis, William J., jt. auth. see Pankey, Lindsey D.

Davis, William J., ed. see Johnson, A. R.

Davis, William K., et al. Laboratory Exercises for General Botany. 4th ed. (Illus.). 110p. (C). 1981. pap. text 10.95 (*0-89641-067-6*) American Pr.

— Laboratory Exercises for General Zoology. 3rd ed. (Illus.). 131p. 1980. pap. text 10.95 (*0-89641-030-7*) American Pr.

Davis, William Morris. Coral Reef Problem. reprint ed. 37.50 (*0-404-01998-6*) AMS Pr.

— The Coral Reef Problem. LC 75-45469. 612p. 1977. reprint ed. 62.00 (*0-88275-383-5*) Krieger.

Davis, William N., jt. ed. see Whitaker, Leighton C.

Davis, William O. Shipwrecks off Central New Jersey Coast. 1987. write for info. (*0-318-62717-5*) Wm O Davis.

Davis, William R., et al, eds. Cornelius Lanczos Collected Published Papers with Commentaries, 6 vols. LC 98-67928. (Illus.). 3456p. 1999. lib. bdg. 120.00 (*0-929493-01-X*, LAN99, Pub. by NCSU Physics) CES Mail.

Davis, William R. & Davis, Judy G. Roger's Rules of Public Relations. (Illus.). 100p. (Orig.). 1984. pap. 9.95 (*0-915113-01-5*) Bizarre Butterfly.

Davis, William R., jt. auth. see Berk, S. L.

Davis, William S. BASIC: Getting Started. 69p. 1981. pap. text 8.76 (*0-201-03258-9*) Addison-Wesley.

— Computer & Business Information Processing. 2nd ed. LC 82-6864. (Illus.). 448p. 1983. pap. text. write for info. (*0-201-11118-7*); trans. write for info. (*0-318-56792-X*) Addison-Wesley.

— Computer for Business: Student Workbook. 2nd ed. LC 82-6864. (Illus.). 448p. 1983. pap. text, student ed. 5.50 (*0-201-11121-7*) Addison-Wesley.

— Computers & Business Information Processing. LC 80-10946. 448p. (C). 1981. pap. text 16.00 (*0-201-03161-2*) Addison-Wesley.

— Computers Business Information. LC 80-10946. 448p. (C). 1981. pap. text 6.25 (*0-201-03713-0*) Addison-Wesley.

— Computing Fundamentals: Concepts. 2nd ed. (Illus.). 182p. (C). 1989. pap. text 15.00 (*0-201-19826-6*) Addison-Wesley.

— Computing Fundamentals: Lotus 1-2-3. (Computing Fundamentals Ser.). (Illus.). 160p. (C). 1989. pap. text. write for info. (*0-201-19824-X*) Addison-Wesley.

— Computing Fundamentals: WordPerfect 5.0. (Computing Fundamentals Ser.). (Illus.). 160p. (C). 1989. pap. text 12.95 (*0-201-19823-1*) Addison-Wesley.

— Day in Old Athens. LC 60-16707. (Illus.). (J). (gr. 7 up). 1965. pap. 17.00 (*0-8196-0111-X*) Biblo.

— Day in Old Rome. LC 61-24993. (Illus.). (YA). (gr. 7 up). 1963. pap. 24.00 (*0-8196-0106-3*) Biblo.

— Falaise, the Blessed Voice. (YA). (gr. 7 up). 1999. pap. 20.00 (*0-8196-1206-5*) Biblo.

— FORTRAN: Getting Started. 1980. pap. text 6.25 (*0-201-03104-3*) Addison-Wesley.

— A Friend of Caesar. 1995. pap. 25.00 (*0-8196-1200-6*) Biblo.

— Gilmon of Redford. 1999. pap. 20.00 (*0-8196-1203-0*) Biblo.

— Influence of Wealth in Imperial Rome. 1910. pap. 25.00 (*0-8196-1202-2*) Biblo.

— Life in Elizabethian Days. 1988. pap. 25.00 (*0-8196-1201-4*) Biblo.

— Life on a Medieval Barony. (Illus.). 414p. 1990. pap. 25.00 (*0-8196-2061-0*) Biblo.

— Operating Systems: A Systematic View. 2nd ed. (Illus.). 448p. 1983. text. write for info. (*0-201-11116-0*) Addison-Wesley.

— Operating Systems: A Systematic View. 3rd ed. LC 86-10898. 539p. (C). 1987. text 47.50 (*0-201-11185-3*) Addison-Wesley.

— Operating Systems: A Systematic View. 4th ed. (Illus.). 672p. (C). 1991. 77.00 (*0-201-56701-6*) Addison-Wesley.

— Readings in Ancient History Vol. I: Greece & the East. 1999. 20.00 (*0-8196-1225-1*) Biblo.

— Readings in Ancient History Vol. II: Rome & the West. 1999. 20.00 (*0-8196-1226-X*) Biblo.

— Systems Analysis & Design: A Structured Approach. 432p. (C). 1983. text 33.50 (*0-201-10271-4*) Addison-Wesley.

— Systems Analysis & Design: A Systematic View. 2nd ed. (Illus.). 480p. (C). 1992. pap. text. write for info. (*0-201-55711-8*) Addison-Wesley.

— Tools & Techniques for Structured Systems Analysis & Design. LC 83-4629. 208p. 1983. pap. text 15.96 (*0-201-10274-9*) Addison-Wesley.

— The Whirlwind. 1998. pap. 20.00 (*0-8196-1209-X*) Biblo.

Davis, William S. & Fisher, Richard H. Cobol: An Introduction to Structured Logic & Modular Program Design. 1979. pap. text 31.25 (*0-201-01431-9*) Addison-Wesley.

Davis, William S. & McCormack, Allison. Information Age. LC 78-55817. 1979. text. write for info. (*0-201-01101-8*) Addison-Wesley.

Davis, William S. & Schreiner, Paul. Computing Fundamentals: dBase III Plus. (Computing Fundamentals Ser.). (Illus.). 192p. (C). 1990. pap. text 12.95 (*0-201-19825-8*) Addison-Wesley.

Davis, William S. & Yen, David C. The Information System Consultant's Handbook: Systems Analysis & Design. LC 98-28765. 800p. 1998. boxed set 104.95 (*0-8493-7001-9*) CRC Pr.

Davis, William S., et al. Calculus & Mathematica, Part II. (C). 1991. text. write for info. (*0-201-18740-X*) Addison-Wesley.

— Computing Fundamentals: Productivity Tools PC & MS-DOS, Wordperfect 5.0, Lotus 1-2-3, dBase III PLUS. (Computing Fundamentals Ser.). (Illus.). 608p. (C). 1990. pap. text 32.25 (*0-201-19820-7*) Addison-Wesley.

— Mastering Microcomputers. LC 92-41337. (C). 1993. pap. text 46.00 (*0-8053-1170-X*) Behjamin-Cummings.

— Mastering Microcomputers: Applications & Core Concepts. (Illus.). 640p. (C). 1992. pap. text. write for info. (*0-201-55583-2*) Addison-Wesley.

Davis, William T. Genealogical Register of Plymouth Families. (Ancient Landmarks of Plymouth Ser.: Pt. II). 363p. 1997. reprint ed. 25.00 (*0-8063-0655-6*, 1385) Genealog Pub.

Davis, William T., ed. Records of the Town of Plymouth (1636-1705, 1705-1743, 1743-1783), 3 vols. in 1. 1193p. 1995. reprint ed. pap. 75.00 (*0-8063-4562-4*, 9124) Clearfield Co.

Davis, William V. Critical Essays on Robert Bly. (Critical Essays on American Literature Ser.). 200p. 1992. 49.00 (*0-8161-7316-8*, Twyne) Mac Lib Ref.

— One Way to Reconstruct the Scene. LC 79-22810. (Younger Poets Ser.: No. 75). 1980. 18.00 (*0-300-02481-9*); pap. 11.00 (*0-300-02503-3*) Yale U Pr.

— Robert Bly: The Poet & His Critics. (LCENG Ser.). xii, 120p. 1994. 55.00 (*1-879751-79-8*) Camden Hse.

Davis, William V., ed. Miraculous Simplicity: Essays on R. S. Thomas. LC 92-24609. 288p. 1993. text 26.00 (*1-55728-265-X*) U of Ark Pr.

Davis, William W. The Fries Rebellion, Seventeen Ninety Eight to Seventeen Ninety Nine. LC 78-90171. (Mass Violence in America Ser.). (Illus.). 1977. reprint ed. 22.95 (*0-405-01305-1*) Ayer.

***Davis, William W.** A Genealogical & Personal History of Bucks County, Pennsylvania, 2 vols. Ely, Warren S. & Jordan, John W., eds. LC 74-18311. (Illus.). 732p. 1999. reprint ed. pap. 75.00 (*0-8063-0641-6*) Clearfield Co.

Davis, William W. El Gringo. LC 72-9438. (Far Western Frontier Ser.). (Illus.). 436p. 1973. reprint ed. 26.95 (*0-405-04968-4*) Ayer.

— History of Whiteside County, Illinois, 2 vols., Set. (Illus.). 1458p. 1993. reprint ed. lib. bdg. 139.00 (*0-8328-3466-1*) Higginson Bk Co.

D

Davis, Wilma S., ed. The Federal Census of 1860 for Monroe County, Ohio. 594p. 1996. pap. 34.50 (*0-89725-274-8*, 1751) Picton Pr.

Davis, Wilson, jt. auth. see Brown, Allan E.

Davis, Winborn. Introduction to Health Care Administration - New Century Edition. rev. ed. LC 99-184339. 1999. 97.50 (*0-929442-41-5*, 2201PP) Prof Prnting & Pub.

***Davis, Winborn.** Supervision in Healthcare Facilities. (Illus.). 138p. (C). 1999. pap. 30.00 (*0-929442-54-7*) Prof Prnting & Pub.

Davis, Winston. Dojo: Magic & Exorcism in Modern Japan. LC 79-64219. (Illus.). xx, 324p. 1980. 47.50 (*0-8047-1053-8*); pap. 16.95 (*0-8047-1131-3*) Stanford U Pr.

— Japanese Religion & Society: Paradigms of Structure & Change. LC 90-24745. 327p. (C). 1992. pap. text 21.95 (*0-7914-0840-X*) State U NY Pr.

— The Moral & Political Naturalism of Baron Kato Kiroyuki. LC 96-13847. (Japan Research Monographs: Vol. 13). 1996. pap. 15.00 (*1-55729-052-0*) IEAS.

Davis, Zachary S. & Frankel, Benjamin, eds. The Proliferation Puzzle: Why Nuclear Weapons Spread & What Results. LC 93-28873. (Illus.). 357p. (C). 1994. pap. text 32.50 (*0-7146-4108-1*, Pub. by F Cass Pubs) Intl Spec Bk.

Davision. Abnormal Psychology: Instructors Free Copy. 6th ed. 1993. text 67.95 (*0-471-31161-8*) Wiley.

***Davismoon, Stephen, ed.** Fragments & Silence, Part 2. (Illus.). 130p. 1999. pap. text 21.00 (*90-5755-113-6*, Harwood Acad Pubs) Gordon & Breach.

— The Suspended Song Part1. (Illus.). 108p. 1999. pap. text 21.00 (*90-5755-112-8*, Harwood Acad Pubs) Gordon & Breach.

Davison. Abnormal Psychology 7th ed. 288p. 1997. pap., student ed. 34.95 (*0-471-18099-8*) Wiley.

— Abnormal Psychology. 8th ed. LC 99-44837. 720p. 2000. text 97.95 (*0-471-31811-6*) Wiley.

Davison. Near Net Shape Manufacturing of Advanced Ceramics. LC 97-132553. 142p. 1995. 2750.00 (*1-56965-227-9*, GB163) BCC.

— Progress in Surface Science, 8 vols., Vol. 1. 1977. pap. 15.25 (*0-08-021765-6*, Pergamon Pr) Elsevier.

Davison, jt. auth. see Barnes.

Davison, A. C. & Hinkley, D. V. Bootstrap Methods & Their Application. LC 96-30064. (Series in Statistical & Probabilistic Mathematics: No. 1). (Illus.). 592p. (C). 1997. text 110.00 (*0-521-57391-2*); pap. text 42.95 (*0-521-57471-4*) Cambridge U Pr.

Davison, Alan. The Minotaur's Tale. (Illus.). 80p. (Orig.). 1992. pap. 11.95 (*1-878574-42-6*) Dark Horse Comics.

— Residential Care: The Provision of Quality Care in Residential & Educational Group Care Setting. 432p. 1995. 83.95 (*1-85742-309-7*, Pub. by Arena) Ashgate Pub Co.

***Davison, Alan.** Spiral Dreams. (Illus.). 2000. pap. 12.50 (*1-899866-36-1*) Slab-O-Concrete Pubns.

Davison, Alan, ed. see Sing, Phia.

Davison, Alan J., jt. ed. see Anderson, Ewan W.

Davison, Alan R. The Adventures of Captain Harvey: A Modern Odyssey. (Illus.). xii, 340p. 1997. pap. 14.95 (*0-9661441-0-4*) Shield Pubs.

— El Corno Emplumado-The Plumed Horn: A Voice of the Sixties. 130p. (C). 1994. pap. text 14.95 (*0-9643576-0-7*) Textos toledanos.

Davison, Alec & Gordon, Peter. Games & Simulations in Action. 200p. 1978. text 9.95 (*0-7130-0150-X*, Pub. by Woburn Pr) Intl Spec Bk.

Davison, Alex M., et al. Oxford Textbook of Clinical Nephrology, 3 vols. 2nd ed. LC 98-121868. (Illus.). 3,166p. 1997. text 495.00 (*0-19-262413-X*) OUP.

***Davison, Alex M., et al.** Oxford Textbook of Clinical Nephrology. 2nd ed. 1998. text 275.00 (*0-19-268581-3*) OUP.

Davison, Alice & Green, Georgia, eds. Linguistic Complexity & Text Comprehension: Readability Issues Reconsidered. 312p. (C). 1988. text 59.95 (*0-89859-541-X*) L Erlbaum Assocs.

Davison, Andrew. Secularism & Revivalism in Turkey: A Hermeneutic Reconsideration. LC 97-49379. (Yale Series in Hermeneutics). 288p. 1998. 37.50 (*0-300-06936-7*) Yale U Pr.

Davison, Andrew, ed. Humour the Computer. LC 95-3065. 226p. 1995. pap. text 13.95 (*0-262-54075-4*) MIT Pr.

Davison, Andrew J. & Elliott, Richard M., eds. Molecular Virology: A Practical Approach. LC 93-7052. (Practical Approach Ser.). (Illus.). 344p. 1993. pap. text 55.00 (*0-19-963357-6*); spiral bd. 95.00 (*0-19-963358-4*) OUP.

Davison, Archibald. Choral Conducting. LC 40-27315. 85p. reprint ed. pap. 30.00 (*0-7837-2246-X*, 205733400004) Bks Demand.

— Protestant Church Music in America. 1972. 59.95 (*0-8490-0905-7*) Gordon Pr.

Davison, Archibald T. Bach & Handel, the Consummation of the Baroque in Music. LC 51-10950. 84p. reprint ed. pap. 30.00 (*0-8357-5942-3*, 200601100054) Bks Demand.

Davison, Archibald T. & Apel, Willi, eds. Historical Anthology of Music, 2 vols. Incl. Vol. 1. Oriental, Medieval, & Renaissance Music. rev. ed. LC 49-4339. (Illus.). 269p. 1949. 41.50 (*0-674-39300-7*); Vol. 2. Baroque, Rococo, & Pre-Classical Music. LC 49-4339. (Illus.). 313p. 1950. 41.50 (*0-674-39301-5*); LC 49-4339. write for info. (*0-318-53071-6*) HUP.

Davison, Archibald T. & Wolff, Christoph. Bach & Handel: The Consummation of the Baroque in Music. (Music Reprint Ser.). 77p. 1986. reprint ed. 18.50 (*0-306-76258-7*) Da Capo.

Davison, Bev. Creative Physical Activities & Equipment. LC 98-11615. (Illus.). 128p. 1998. pap. text 16.00 (*0-88011-779-6*, BDAV0779) Human Kinetics.

Davison, Bob. Tales of a Water Bailiff. large type ed. (Magna Large Print Ser.). 303p. 1996. 27.99 (*0-7505-1004-8*, Pub. by Mgna Lrg Print) Ulverscroft.

Davison, Brian H., et al, eds. Eighteenth Symposium on Biotechnology for Fuels & Chemicals. (ABAB Symposium Ser.: No. 63-65). (Illus.). 912p. 1997. 200.00 (*0-89603-504-2*) Humana.

Davison, Brian H., jt. auth. see Finkelstein, Mark.

Davison, Brian H., jt. ed. see Finkelstein, Mark.

Davison, Brian H., jt. ed. see Wyman, Charles E.

***Davison, Caroline.** Home Inspirations: Over 60 Decorative Projects for Every Room in the Home. (Illus.). 2000. 24.95 (*0-7548-0267-1*, Lorenz Bks) Anness Pub.

Davison, Charles. The Founders of Seismology. Albritton, Claude C., Jr., ed. LC 77-6518. (History of Geology Ser.). 1978. reprint ed. lib. bdg. 26.95 (*0-405-10440-5*) Ayer.

***Davison, Claire.** Winter Range. 272p. 2000. 23.00 (*0-312-26140-3*, Picador USA) St Martin.

Davison, Claire, tr. see Audisio, Gabriel.

***Davison, David M., et al.** Integrating Science & Mathematics in the Elementary Curriculum. (Fastback Ser.: No. 444). 35p. 1999. pap. 3.00 (*0-87367-644-0*, FB# 444) Phi Delta Kappa.

Davison, E. M. & McKee, E. B., eds. Annals of Old Wilkinsburg & Vicinity, the Village, 1788-1888. (Illus.). 549p. 1995. reprint ed. lib. bdg. 57.50 (*0-8328-5112-4*) Higginson Bk Co.

Davison, Edward L. Some Modern Poets, & Other Critical Essays. LC 68-16926. (Essay Index Reprint Ser.). 1977. reprint ed. 20.95 (*0-8369-0366-8*) Ayer.

Davison, Ellen K. Scotland County, Missouri, U. S. A., Community at Large: A Focus on Lawn Ridge, Historical, Biographical, Pictorial. LC 93-72626. (Illus.). 224p. 1993. lib. bdg. 39.50 (*0-9638069-0-4*) E K Davison.

Davison, Ellen S. Forerunners of Saint Francis & Other Studies. Richards, Gertrude R., ed. LC 77-85270. reprint ed. 49.50 (*0-404-16120-0*) AMS Pr.

Davison, Emma. Catwalk. 518p. 1995. mass mkt. 8.95 (*0-340-61352-1*, Pub. by Hodder & Stought Ltd) Trafalgar.

Davison, Frank, tr. see Alain-Fournier.

Davison, Frederick L., II. Black Thoroughbred the Only Success Formula for Colored People. 320p. (Orig.). 1991. pap. 13.95 (*0-9628544-0-9*) Blk Thoroughbred.

— Black Thoroughbred the Only Success Formula to Make Colored People the New Leaders of the World, Part II. 680p. (Orig.). 1995. 30.00 (*0-9628544-1-7*) Blk Thoroughbred.

***Davison, Frederick Leroy, II.** The Preacher's Wife Sings. 350p. 2000. pap. 13.95 (*0-9628544-3-3*) Blk Thoroughbred.

— A Song for Love. 350p. 2000. pap. 13.95 (*0-9628544-2-5*) Blk Thoroughbred.

Davison, Frieda P., ed. Honaker Family in America. unabridged ed. LC 98-71053. (Illus.). xvii, 1437p. 1998. 66.50 (*0-9664219-1-4*) Honaker Family.

***Davison, G. & Skuse, D. R., eds.** Advances in Additives for Water-Based Coatings. 98p. 1999. 120.00 (*0-85404-754-9*, Pub. by Royal Soc Chem) Spr-Verlag.

Davison, G. W. & Chew Yen Fook. A Photographic Guide to Birds of Peninsular Malaysia & Singapore. (Eco-Travel Guides Ser.). (Illus.). 144p. 1998. pap. 15.95 (*0-88359-036-0*, Pub. by R Curtis Pubng) Chelsea Green Pub.

Davison, Geoffrey W. Birds of Borneo. (Eco-Travel Guides Ser.). (Illus.). 144p. 1998. pap. 15.95 (*0-88359-039-5*, RCB-0395P, Pub. by R Curtis Pubng) Chelsea Green Pub.

Davison, George E. Bible Quest: The Two Daddy Papers, Etc., Vol. I. LC 91-62718. (Illus.). 631p. (Orig.). 1991. 35.00 (*0-9625315-1-0*); pap. 25.00 (*0-9625315-0-2*) New Faith Pub.

Davison, Gerald. The Handbook of Marks Chinese Porcelain. (Illus.). 192p. 1994. 60.00 (*0-906610-20-6*) Antique Collect.

Davison, Gerald C. & Neale, John M. Abnormal Psychology. 6th rev. ed. 32p. 1995. pap. text, student ed. 12.95 (*0-471-14067-8*) Wiley.

— Abnormal Psychology. 7th ed. LC 97-21696. 800p. 1997. text 96.95 (*0-471-11122-8*) Wiley.

Davison, Gerald C., jt. auth. see Goldfried, Marvin R.

***Davison, Graeme.** The Use & Abuse of Australian History. 336p. 2000. pap. 29.95 (*1-86448-720-8*, Pub. by Allen & Unwin Pty) Paul & Co Pubs.

Davison, Gwen. Clem's Cracker Barrel. 48p. 1989. 7.95 (*0-942407-03-2*) Father & Son.

Davison, Holly. Mayan Birthday Decoding Kit: Decoder, Guidebook & Galactic Signature Pad. (Illus.). 72p. 1998. pap. 20.00 (*1-892102-03-X*) Design Mat.

Davison, J. Kenneth, ed. see Massachusetts General Hospital, Dept. of Anesthesi & Harvard Medical School Staff.

Davison, James. Prisoners of Our Past: A Critical Look at Self-Defeating Attitudes Within the Black Community. LC 92-38064. 1993. 17.95 (*1-55972-176-6*, Birch Ln Pr) Carol Pub Group.

***Davison, James E.** The Bible Book of the Month. 80p. 1999. pap. 10.95 (*1-57895-039-2*) Curriculm Presbytrn KY.

— Living Water: A Guide to Baptism for Presbyterians. LC 00-37626. 50p. 2000. pap. 5.95 (*0-664-50145-1*, Pub. by Geneva Press) Presbyterian Pub.

Davison, James E. The Year of the Bible - Leader's Manual, Vol. 1. rev. ed. Basham, Beth, ed. 92p. 1996. pap. 19.95 (*1-57895-002-3*) Bridge Resources.

— The Year of the Bible - Participant's Book, Vol. 1. rev. ed. Basham, Beth, ed. 54p. 1996. pap. 5.95 (*1-57895-003-1*) Bridge Resources.

Davison, James F. & Grundstein, Nathan D., eds. Cases & Readings on Administrative Law. LC 72-108388. 777p. 1971. reprint ed. lib. bdg. 145.00 (*0-8371-3811-6*, DAAL, Greenwood Pr) Greenwood.

Davison, James N. Newllano: History of the Llano Movement. 98p. 1994. pap. 7.95 (*0-9646846-5-9*) Dogwood TX.

Davison, Jan & Lewis, Maxine. Working with Insurance & Managed Care Plans: A Guide for Getting Paid. (Illus.). 470p. (Orig.). 1995. reprint ed. pap. text 44.95 (*1-57066-081-6*, Me117) Practice Mgmt Info.

Davison, Jan, jt. auth. see Lewis, Maxine.

Davison, Jean. Gender, Ethnicity & Lineage in Southern Africa. LC 96-30267. 6p. (C). 1996. text 79.00 (*0-8133-2759-8*, Pub. by Westview) HarpC.

— Voices from Mutira: Change in the Lives of Rural Gikuyu Women, 1910-1995. 2nd ed. 271p. 1995. pap. text 19.95 (*1-55587-602-1*) L Rienner.

Davison, Jeffrey P. Marketing Your Community. LC 86-62165. 125p. (Orig.). 1986. pap. 40.00 (*1-55657-000-7*) Pub Tech Inc.

Davison-Jenkins, Dominic J. Irrigation & Water Supply Systems of Vijayanagara. LC 97-901692. (C). 1997. 88.00 (*81-7304-031-1*, Pub. by Manohar) S Asia.

Davison, John. Gangsta: The Sinister Spread of Yardie Gun Crime. (Illus.). 208p. 1997. pap. 15.95 (*1-901250-02-4*, Pub. by V1ision Pprbcks) Trafalgar.

— Gangsta: The Sinister Spread of Yardie Gun Culture. 200p. 1999. pap. 14.95 (*1-883319-84-6*) Frog Ltd CA.

Davison, Jon & Dowson, Jane. Learning to Teach English in the Secondary School. LC 97-15889. (Learning to Teach Subjects in the Secondary School Ser.). 352p. (C). 1997. pap. 24.99 (*0-415-15677-7*) Routledge.

***Davison, Jon & Moss, John.** Issues in English Teaching. LC 99-41105. (Issues in Subject Teaching Ser.). 264p. 2000. pap. write for info. (*0-415-20665-0*) Routledge.

***Davison, Judith A.** Legal & Ethical Considerations for Dental Hygienists & Assistants. (Illus.). 320p. 1999. text. write for info. (*1-55664-422-1*) Mosby Inc.

Davison, Julian. Balinese Architecture. (Asia's Cultural Attractions Ser.). (Illus.). 32p. 2000. 9.95 (*962-593-194-5*) Tuttle Pubng.

— Balinese Flora & Fauna. (Asia's Cultural Attractions Ser.). (Illus.). 32p. 2000. 9.95 (*962-593-197-X*) Tuttle Pubng.

— Balinese Temples. (Asia's Cultural Attractions Ser.). (Illus.). 32p. 2000. 9.95 (*962-593-196-1*) Tuttle Pubng.

Davison, June & Schaub, Ardella. Piano Progress - Primary Book. Podolsky, Leo, ed. 1982. 5.50 (*0-913650-42-0*, V032PMBP) Wrner Bros.

— Piano Progress for the Partially Sighted, Bk. 2A. Podolsky, Leo, ed. 1967. 5.00 (*0-913650-15-3*) Wrner Bros.

— Piano Progress for the Partially Sighted, Bk. 2B. Podolsky, Leo, ed. 1967. 4.00 (*0-913650-16-1*) Wrner Bros.

— Piano Progress for the Partially Sighted, Bk. 3A. Podolsky, Leo, ed. 1974. 6.00 (*0-913650-17-X*) Wrner Bros.

— Piano Progress for the Partially Sighted, Bk. 3B. Podolsky, Leo, ed. 1974. 6.95 (*0-913650-18-8*) Wrner Bros.

— Piano Progress for the Partially Sighted, Bk. IA. Podolsky, Leo, ed. 1972. 5.00 (*0-913650-13-7*) Wrner Bros.

— Piano Progress for the Partially Sighted, Bk. IB. Podolsky, Leo, ed. 1972. 5.00 (*0-913650-14-5*) Wrner Bros.

Davison, Katherine. Moon Magic: Stories from Asia. LC 92-44504. (Middle-Grade Fiction Ser.). (Illus.). 48p. (J). (gr. 2-5). 1993. lib. bdg. 19.95 (*0-87614-751-1*, Carolrhoda) Lerner Pub.

Davison, Kenneth & Kerr, Alan, eds. Contemporary Themes in Psychiatry: A Tribute to Sir Martin Roth. 519p. 1989. pap. text 47.50 (*0-902241-28-1*, 4128, Pub. by Royal Coll Psych) Parkwest Pubns.

Davison, Kenneth E. The Presidency of Rutherford B. Hayes, 3. LC 79-176289. (Contributions in American Studies: No. 3). 266p. 1972. 69.50 (*0-8371-6275-0*, DPH/, Greenwood Pr) Greenwood.

Davison, L. W. & Shahinpoor, Mohsen, eds. High-Pressure Shock Compression of Solids, Vol. III. LC 97-22862. (High-Pressure Shock Compression of Condensed Matter Ser.). (Illus.). 336p. 1997. 89.00 (*0-387-98292-2*) Spr-Verlag.

Davison, L. W., et al. High-Pressure Shock Compression of Solids IV: Response of Highly Porous Solids to Shock Compression. LC 97-3757. 1997. 79.95 (*0-387-94995-X*) Spr-Verlag.

Davison, L. W., jt. ed. see Aifantis, E. C.

Davison, Lee & Grady, D. E. High Pressure Shock Compression of Solids II: Dynamic Fracture & Fragmentation. Shahinpoor, Mo, ed. LC 94-37843. (High Pressure Shock Compression of Condensed Matter Ser.). (Illus.). 536p. 1995. 149.95 (*0-387-94402-8*) Spr-Verlag.

Davison, Leslie, jt. auth. see McLean, Gary.

Davison, Leslie, jt. auth. see Sangster, William E.

Davison, Liam. Soundings. (Orig.). 1993. pap. 14.95 (*0-7022-2462-6*, Pub. by Univ Queensland Pr) Intl Spec Bk.

***Davison, Liam.** Spirit of Rural Australia. (Illus.). 160p. 1999. 49.95 (*1-86436-493-9*, Pub. by New Holland) BHB Intl.

Davison, Linda J. Chameleons: Their Care & Breeding. LC Ql666. 112p. 1997. pap. 19.95 (*0-88839-353-9*) Hancock House.

Davison, M., jt. auth. see Duns, J.

Davison, Marc. All Area Access: A Personal Management Guide for the Unsigned Artist. 384p. 1997. per. 24.95 (*0-7935-8134-6*, HL00330295) H Leonard.

Davison, Marguerite P. A Handweaver's Pattern Book. rev. ed. (Illus.). 1996. 30.00 (*0-9603172-0-1*) M P Davison.

— A Handweaver's Source Book. (Illus.). 128p. 1953. pap. text 20.00 (*0-9603172-1-X*) M P Davison.

Davison, Mark L. Multidimensional Scaling. LC 91-30195. 256p. (C). 1992. reprint ed. lib. bdg. 44.95 (*0-89464-662-1*) Krieger.

Davison, Michael. Ancient Rome. (Illus.). 1996. pap. 4.95 (*0-89659-092-5*) Abbeville Pr.

Davison, Michael & McCarthy, Dianne. The Matching Law: A Research Review. 296p. 1987. 59.95 (*0-89859-923-7*) L Erlbaum Assocs.

Davison, Ned. Eduardo Barrios. LC 70-120478. (Twayne's World Authors Ser.). 1970. lib. bdg. 20.95 (*0-8057-2112-6*) Irvington.

Davison, Neil R. James Joyce, "Ulysses", & the Construction of Jewish Identity: Culture, Biography, & "the Jew" in Modern Europe. 330p. (C). 1998. pap. text 18.95 (*0-521-63620-5*) Cambridge U Pr.

— James Joyce, "Ulysses", & the Construction of Jewish Identity: Culture, Biography & "the Jew" in Modernist Europe. 317p. (C). 1996. text 59.95 (*0-521-55181-1*) Cambridge U Pr.

Davison, P. H., ed. see Shakespeare, William.

Davison, Patricia. Lobedu. LC 96-45308. (Heritage Library of African Peoples: Set 4). (Illus.). 64p. (YA). (gr. 7-12). 1996. lib. bdg. 16.95 (*0-8239-1989-7*, D1989-7) Rosen Group.

Davison, Patricia, tr. see Stevens, Jan Romero.

Davison, Peter. The Breaking of the Day & Other Poems. LC 75-21578. (Yale Series of Younger Poets: No. 60). reprint ed. 18.00 (*0-404-53860-6*) AMS Pr.

***Davison, Peter.** Breathing Room: New Poems. LC 00-23277. 80p. 2000. 23.00 (*0-375-41104-6*) Knopf.

Davison, Peter. Dark Houses. LC 77-117946. 1971. pap. 4.00 (*0-912604-07-7*) Halty Ferguson.

— The Fading Smile: From Beauty to Truth in Boston, 1955-1960. LC 93-43945. (Illus.). 368p. 1994. 24.00 (*0-679-40658-1*) Knopf.

— The Fading Smile: Poets in Boston from Robert Lowell to Sylvia Plath, 1955-1960. 345p. 1996. pap. 14.00 (*0-393-31358-1*) Norton.

— Glenans Guides: Yacht Handling under Sail. (Pevensey Island Guides Ser.). (Illus.). 128p. 1995. pap. 19.95 (*0-7153-0298-1*, Pub. by D & C Pub) Sterling.

— The Poems of Peter Davison. 336p. 1997. pap. 17.50 (*0-679-76589-1*) Knopf.

— The Poems of Peter Davison, 1957-1995. 1995. 25.00 (*0-679-44180-8*) Knopf.

— Songs of the British Music Hall. (Illus.). 224p. 1971. pap. 21.95 (*0-8256-0099-5*, OK64007, Oak) Music Sales.

Davison, Peter, et al, eds. Content & Taste: Religion & Myth. LC 77-90615. (Literary Taste, Culture & Mass Communication Ser.: Vol. 7). 338p. 1978. lib. bdg. write for info. (*0-85964-042-6*) Chadwyck-Healey.

— The Cultural Debate Pt. 1. LC 77-90622. (Literary Taste, Culture & Mass Communication Ser.: Vol. 13). 250p. 1978. lib. bdg. write for info. (*0-85964-048-5*) Chadwyck-Healey.

— The Cultural Debate Pt. 11: Name & Subject Index. LC 77-90623. (Literary Taste, Culture & Mass Communication Ser.: Vol. 14). 261p. 1978. lib. bdg. write for info. (*0-85964-049-3*) Chadwyck-Healey.

— Culture & Mass Culture. LC 77-90608. (Literary Taste, Culture & Mass Communication Ser.: Vol. 1). 348p. 1978. lib. bdg. write for info. (*0-85964-036-1*) Chadwyck-Healey.

— Literature & Society. LC 77-90613. (Literary Taste, Culture & Mass Communication Ser.: Vol. 5). 281p. 1978. lib. bdg. write for info. (*0-85964-040-X*) Chadwyck-Healey.

— Mass Media & Mass Communication. LC 77-90610. (Literary Taste, Culture & Mass Communication Ser.: Vol. 2). 348p. 1978. write for info. (*0-85964-037-X*) Chadwyck-Healey.

— The Sociology of Literature. LC 77-90614. (Literary Taste, Culture & Mass Communication Ser.: Vol. 6). 370p. 1978. lib. bdg. write for info. (*0-85964-041-8*) Chadwyck-Healey.

— Theatre & Song. LC 77-90616. (Literary Taste, Culture & Mass Communication Ser.: Vol. 8). 279p. 1978. lib. bdg. write for info. (*0-85964-043-4*) Chadwyck-Healey.

— Use of Literacy: Media. LC 77-90618. (Literary Taste, Culture & Mass Communication Ser.: Vol. 9). 299p. 1978. lib. bdg. 100.00 (*0-85964-044-2*) Chadwyck-Healey.

— The Writer & Politics. LC 77-90620. (Literary Taste, Culture & Mass Communication Ser.: Vol. 11). 285p. 1978. 99.00 (*0-85964-046-9*) Chadwyck-Healey.

Davison, Peter, ed. see Orwell, George.

Davison, Peter, ed. see Shakespeare, William.

Davison, Peter Hobley. The Book Encompassed: Studies in Twentieth-Century Bibliography. LC 98-34393. 1998. 29.95 (*1-884718-63-9*) Oak Knoll.

Davison, Philip. The Crooked Man. 214p. 1998. pap. 17.95 (*0-224-04304-8*, Pub. by Jonathan Cape) Trafalgar.

Davison, Ray. Camus: The Challenge of Dostoevsky. LC 98-185100. 208p. 1997. 70.00 (*0-85989-531-9*, Pub. by Univ Exeter Pr); pap. 19.95 (*0-85989-532-7*, Pub. by Univ Exeter Pr) Northwestern U Pr.

Davison, Richard. Dressage Priority Points. (Illus.). 96p. 1996. 16.95 (*0-87605-932-9*) Howell Bks.

Davison, Richard A., jt. ed. see Bryer, Jackson R.

Davison, Richard R., et al. Design & Use of Superior Asphalt Binders. 5th ed. (Illus.). 184p. (Orig.). (C). 1994. pap. text 50.00 (*0-7881-0193-5*) DIANE Pub.

Davison, Roderic H. Essays in Ottoman & Turkish History, 1774-1923: The Impact of the West. 299p. 1996. 40.00 (*0-614-21110-7*, 261) Kazi Pubns.

— Essays in Ottoman & Turkish History, 1774-1923: The Impact of the West. (Modern Middle East Ser.: No. 16). 299p. (C). 1990. text 40.00 (*0-292-72064-5*) U of Tex Pr.

An Asterisk (*) at the beginning of an entry indicates that the title is appearing for the first time.

— Reform in the Ottoman Empire, 1856-1876. LC 73-148618. 503p. (C). 1973. reprint ed. 95.00 (0-87752-135-2) Gordian.
— Turkey: A Short History. LC 97-175733. 207p. 1997. pap. 25.00 (0-906719-14-3, Pub. by Eothen) Paul & Co Pubs.
— Turkey: A Short History. 3rd ed. 235p. 1998. pap. 27.95 (0-906719-22-4, Pub. by Eothen) Paul & Co Pubs.
Davison, Ron E. Circles. 89p. 1999. pap. 12.95 (1-890667-08-0, Hand-In-Hand Bks) Introspect Bks.
Davison, Ron W. Quiet Evolution. 2nd ed. v, 76p. 1997. pap. 12.95 (1-890667-01-3) Introspect Bks.
Davison, Ronald. Synastry: Understanding Human Relationships Through Astrology. 335p. 1983. 21.95 (0-943358-05-1) Aurora Press.
Davison, Ronald C. Astrology: The Classic Guide to Understanding Your Horoscope. LC 64-10326. (Illus.). 180p. (Orig.). 1988. reprint ed. pap. 10.95 (0-916360-37-7) CRCS Pubns CA.
— The Technique of Prediction: The New Complete System of Secondary Directing. (Illus.). 152p. 1999. pap. 19.95 (0-8464-4952-8) Beekman Pubs.
Davison, S. G., ed. Progress in Surface Science, Vol. 10, No. 1. (Illus.). 164p. 1981. pap. 31.00 (0-08-027154-5, Pergamon Pr) Elsevier.
— Progress in Surface Science, Vol. 11. LC 77-141188. 378p. 1983. 115.00 (0-08-030875-9, 17, Pergamon Pr) Elsevier.
— Progress in Surface Science, Vol. 12. 436p. 1984. 120.00 (0-08-030876-7, Pergamon Pr) Elsevier.
— Progress in Surface Science, Vol. 13. LC 77-141188. 355p. 1985. 120.00 (0-08-030886-4, Pergamon Pr) Elsevier.
— Progress in Surface Science, Vol. 14. LC 77-141188. 423p. 1985. 120.00 (0-08-030887-2, Pergamon Pr) Elsevier.
— Progress in Surface Science, Vol. 15. 494p. 1985. 120.00 (0-08-030894-5, Pub. by PPL) Elsevier.
— Progress in Surface Science, Vol. 16. 1985. 120.00 (0-08-030904-6, Pub. by PPL) Elsevier.
— Progress in Surface Science, Vol. 17. LC 77-141188. 328p. 1986. 126.00 (0-08-030905-4, Pub. by PPL) Elsevier.
— Progress in Surface Science, Vol. 18. LC 77-141188. 541p. 1986. 126.00 (0-08-030906-2, Pub. by PPL) Elsevier.
Davison, Sandra, jt. auth. see Abramowski, Dwain.
Davison, Sandra, jt. auth. see Newton, Roy G.
***Davison, Simon, et al.** Pocket Guide to Psoriasis. LC 99-53651. (Illus.). 72p. 2000. pap. 29.95 (0-632-05208-2) Blackwell Sci.
Davison, Stanley S. Leadership of the Reclamation Movement, 1875-1902. Bruchey, Stuart, ed. LC 78-53545. (Development of Public Land Law in the U. S. Ser.). (Illus.). 1979. lib. bdg. 26.95 (0-405-11365-X) Ayer.
Davison, Steven G., et al. Chesapeake Waters: Four Centuries of Controversy, Concern, & Legislation. 2nd ed. LC 97-28122. (Illus.). 288p. 1997. 29.95 (0-87033-501-4, Tidewtr Pubs) Cornell Maritime.
Davison, Sven M. Blockbuster: How to Make a Big Studio Picture from Script to Projector & Other Trivial Asides. 567p. pap. 7.95 (0-9666149-7-6) Bedouin Pr.
— Blockbuster: How to Make a Big Studio Picture from Script to Projector & Other Trivial Asides. LC 98-93099. 567p. 1999. 22.95 (0-9666149-9-2) Bedouin Pr.
Davison, Sydney G. & Steslicka, Maria. Basic Theory of Surface States. (Monographs on the Physics & Chemistry of Materials). (Illus.). 240p. 1992. 69.00 (0-19-851990-7) OUP.
— Basic Theory of Surface States. LC 96-14123. (Monographs on the Physics & Chemistry of Materials: Vol. 46). (Illus.). 236p. 1996. reprint ed. pap. text 29.95 (0-19-851896-X, Clarendon Pr) OUP.
Davison, Tim. The Lawer Book. 3rd ed. (C). 1993. text 14.95 (0-906754-78-X, Pub. by Fernhurst Bks) St Mut.
Davison, Tim, jt. auth. see Craig, John.
Davison, Tim, jt. auth. see Judkins, Steve.
Davison, Tim, jt. auth. see Smith, Andy.
Davison, Todd. Life after Psychotherapy. 192p. 1997. 30.00 (1-56821-849-4) Aronson.
— Trust the Force: Change Your Life Through Attitudinal Healing. LC 95-18420. 320p. 1995. 35.00 (1-56821-594-0) Aronson.
Davison, W. Phillips. The Berlin Blockade: A Study in Cold War Politics. Zuckerman, Harriet & Merton, Robert K., eds. LC 79-8992. (Dissertations on Sociology Ser.). (Illus.). 1980. reprint ed. lib. bdg. 44.95 (0-405-12963-7) Ayer.
Davison, W. Phillips & Gordenker, Leon, eds. Resolving Nationality Conflicts: The Role of Public Opinion Research. LC 80-15128. 242p. 1980. 55.00 (0-275-90467-9, C0467, Praeger Pubs) Greenwood.
Davison, Zeta C., jt. auth. see Reed, Carroll E.
Daviss, Bennett, jt. auth. see Wilson, Kenneth G.
Davisson, Charles, tr. see Unger, Georg.
Davisson, Darrell. Using dBase III on the IBM PC. write for info. (0-318-59638-5) S&S Trade.
Davisson, L. D. & Longo, G., eds. Adaptive Signal Processing. (CISM International Centre for Mechanical Sciences Ser.: No. 324). (Illus.). x, 203p. 1992. 52.95 (0-387-82333-6) Spr-Verlag.
Davisson, Linda C. Psychosocial Methods of Pain Management: An Interdisciplinary Team Approach. (Illus.). 134p. 1996. 26.50 (1-877735-40-X, 2302PP) Prof Prnting & Pub.
Davisson, Lisa, tr. see Unger, Georg.

Davisson, Russell L. The Davissons, Twelve Generations: 1630-1992 Davidson-Davison-Davisson Families. (Illus.). 228p. 1993. 29.95 (0-87012-498-6) McClain.

After 43 years of research, the history & genealogy of the descendants of Daniel & Margaret (Low) Davison trace 12 generations of Davidson-Davison-Davisson families. Illustration by Pierre Bergem embellish this work. Fully indexed. *Publisher Paid Annotation.*

Davisson, William I. & Harper, James E. European Economic History: The Ancient World. LC 75-172518. (Illus.). (C). 1972. 36.50 (0-89197-153-X) Irvington.
Davitt, Carol. Marketing Your Remodeling Services: Putting the Pieces Together. LC 93-31673. (Illus.). 128p. (Orig.). 1993. pap. 20.00 (0-86718-388-8) Home Builder.
— Remodeling Your Home: An Insider's Guide. Tennyson, Doris M., ed. LC 95-37194. (Illus.). 140p. (Orig.). 1996. pap. 21.95 (0-86718-411-6) Home Builder.
Davitt, Joan K., jt. auth. see Kaye, Lenard W.
Davitt, M., jt. compiled by see Macdonald, I.
***Davitt, Maury C.** College Ready Parents' Guide. 40p. 1999. pap. 7.95 (0-9669867-0-9) Student Res.
Davitt, Michael. Boer Fight for Freedom. LC 72-5540. (Black Heritage Library Collection). 1977. reprint ed. 66.95 (0-8369-9137-0) Ayer.
— Selected Poems: Rogha Danta, 1968-1984. 143p. 1987. pap. 12.95 (1-85186-029-0) Dufour.
— Within the Pale: The True Story of Anti-Semitic Persecutions in Russia. LC 74-27976. (Modern Jewish Experience Ser.). 1975. reprint ed. 28.95 (0-405-06705-4) Ayer.
Davitt, Thomas E. The Basic Values in Law: A Study of the Ethics-Legal Implications of Psychology & Anthropology. LC 68-24357. 1968. pap. 15.00 (0-87462-451-7) Marquette.
— Ethics in the Situation. LC 72-121300. 1978. pap. 15.00 (0-87462-450-9) Marquette.
Davitz, Joel R. & Davitz, Lois J. A Guide for Evaluating Research Plans in Psychology & Education. LC 67-25063. 52p. reprint ed. pap. 30.00 (0-608-11143-0, 200546500054) Bks Demand.
Davitz, Joel R. & Davitz, Lois L. Evaluating Research Proposals: A Guide for the Behavioral Sciences. LC 95-11841. 57p. (C). 1995. pap. text 15.00 (0-13-348566-8) P-H.
Davitz, Joel R., et al. Terminology & Concepts in Mental Retardation. LC 61-62621. (TC Series in Special Education). 135p. reprint ed. pap. 41.90 (0-608-18422-5, 203014500067) Bks Demand.
Davitz, Joel R., jt. auth. see Davitz, Lois L.
Davitz, Joel R., jt. auth. see Leiderman Davitz, Lois.
Davitz, Lois J., jt. auth. see Davitz, Joel R.
Davitz, Lois L. Baby Hunger: Every Woman's Longing for a Baby. LC 83-51386. 144p. (Orig.). 1984. 7.95 (0-86683-810-4, 8402) Harper SF.
Davitz, Lois L. & Davitz, Joel R. 20 Tough Questions Teenagers Ask & 20 Tough Answers. LC 98-18813. 144p. 1998. pap. 9.95 (0-8091-3807-7) Paulist Pr.
Davitz, Lois L., jt. auth. see Davitz, Joel R.
Davletshina, Tatyana A. Industrial Fire Safety Guidebook. LC 97-51236. (Illus.). 531p. 1998. 145.00 (0-8155-1420-4) Noyes.
Davletshina, Tatyana A. & Cheremisinoff, Nicholas P. Fire & Explosion Hazards Handbook of Industrial Chemicals. LC 98-22341. 484p. 1998. 145.00 (0-8155-1429-8) Noyes.
Davock, Marcia. Cruising Guide to Tahiti & the French Society Islands. Wilensky, Julius M., ed. LC 85-50922. (Illus.). 272p. (Orig.). 1985. pap. 34.95 (0-918752-04-3) Wescott Cove.
— Cruising Guide to the Turquoise Coasts of Turkey. Wilensky, Julius M., ed. LC 89-40171. (Illus.). 352p. (Orig.). 1989. pap. 39.95 (0-918752-09-4) Wescott Cove.
Davol, Howard, et al. Quick Desk Reference to Mental Health Treatment Goals: Targeted Treatment Goals for Behavioral Healthcare. 262p. 1996. ring bd. 29.99 (0-9659932-0-5) Behav Therapy.
Davol, Marguerite. Black, White, Just Right! LC 93-19932. (Albert Whitman Concept Bks.). (Illus.). 32p. (J). (gr. 1-3). 1993. lib. bdg. 14.95 (0-8075-0785-7) A Whitman.
Davol, Marguerite W. Batwings & the Curtain of Night. LC 96-42482. (Illus.). 32p. (J). (ps-3). 1997. 15.95 (0-531-30005-6); lib. bdg. 16.99 (0-531-33005-2) Orchard Bks Watts.
— Heart of the Wood. LC 91-3374. (J). (ps-3). 1992. pap. 15.00 (0-671-74778-9) S&S Bks Yung.
— How Snake Got His Hiss: An Original Tale. LC 94-45917. (Illus.). 32p. (J). (ps-2). 1996. 14.95 (0-531-09468-5); lib. bdg. 15.99 (0-531-08768-9) Orchard Bks Watts.
***Davol, Marguerite W.** Loudest, Fastest, Best Drummer in Kansas. LC 99-29513. 32p. (J). (gr. k-4). 2000. 15.95 (0-531-30191-5); lib. bdg. 16.99 (0-531-33191-1) Orchard Bks Watts.
Davol, Marguerite W. Papa Alonzo Leatherby: A Collection of Tall Tales from the Best Storyteller in Carroll County. LC 94-19372. (Illus.). 80p. (J). (gr. 3-7). 1995. per. 14.00 (0-689-80278-1) S&S Bks Yung.
— Papa Alonzo Leatherby: The Best Storyteller in Carroll County. LC 94-19372. (Illus.). (J). 14.00 (0-671-86580-3) S&S Bks Yung.
— The Paper Dragon. LC 95-32166. (Illus.). 60p. (J). (gr. k-3). 1997. 17.00 (0-689-31992-4) Atheneum Yung Read.
Davoli, Barbara. Saved by the Bell. 24p. (J). (ps-2). 1997. pap. write for info. (0-7814-3025-9, Chariot Bks) Chariot Victor.
***Davoll, Barbara.** Bedtime Snuggles with Christopher. (Illus.). (J). 2000. 11.99 (0-8024-5395-3) Moody.
Davoll, Barbara. The Christopher Churchmouse Birthday Collection. (Christopher Churchmouse Classics Ser.). (Illus.). (J). (ps-2). 1993. 16.99 (1-56476-191-6, #6-3191, Victor Bks) Chariot Victor.
— The Christopher Churchmouse Treasury. (Christopher Churchmouse Classics Ser.). (Illus.). (Orig.). (J). (ps-2). 1992. pap. 16.99 (0-89693-078-5, 6-1078, Victor Bks) Chariot Victor.
— A Churchmouse Birthday. (Christopher Churchmouse Classics Ser.). (Illus.). 24p. (J). 1994. audio 11.99 Chariot Victor.
— A Churchmouse Birthday. (Christopher Churchmouse Classics Ser.). (Illus.). 24p. (J). (ps-2). 1994. 8.99 (1-56476-277-7, 6-3277, Victor Bks) Chariot Victor.
— A Churchmouse Christmas. (J). 1994. 11.99 (7-900882-15-4, Chariot Bks) Chariot Victor.
***Davoll, Barbara.** A Churchmouse Christmas. (J). 1999. 9.99 (0-8024-5394-5) Moody.
Davoll, Barbara. Fire in the Bramblewood. (Tales from Schroon Lake Ser.: No. 4). (Illus.). (J). 7.99 (0-8024-1036-7, 669) Moody.
— Flood of Friends. (Christopher Churchmouse Classics Ser.). (Illus.). (J). (ps-2). 1990. 8.99 (0-89693-538-8, 6-1538, Victor Bks) Chariot Victor.
— Grandpa's Secret. (Christopher Churchmouse Classics Ser.). (Illus.). 24p. (J). 1993. 8.99 (1-56476-161-4, 6-3161, Victor Bks) Chariot Victor.
***Davoll, Barbara.** High Adventure in Paris, Vol. 3. (J). 1999. 7.99 (0-8024-5398-8) Moody.
Davoll, Barbara. Hobo Holiday. (Tales from Schroon Lake Ser.: No. 1). (Illus.). (J). 7.99 (0-8024-1033-2, 670) Moody.
— Una Inundacion de Amigos. (Cristobal Raton de Iglesia Ser.).Tr. of Flood of Friends. (SPA.). 23p. (J). 1990. 3.99 (1-56063-300-X, 490378) Editorial Unilit.
— La Lengua Mentirosa.Tr. of Tattletale Tongue. (SPA.). (J). 1990. 6.99 (1-56063-123-6, 490375) Editorial Unilit.
— The Little Mouse Library, 6 bks., Set. LC 96-205260. (Illus.). 60p. (J). 1996. bds. 10.99 (1-56476-568-7, 6-3568, Victor Bks) Chariot Victor.
— A Load of Trouble. (Christopher Churchmouse Classics Ser.). (Illus.). 24p. (J). (ps-2). 1988. pap. 8.99 (0-89693-407-1, 6-1407, Victor Bks) Chariot Victor.
— A Load of Trouble. (Christopher Churchmouse Classics Ser.). (Illus.). 24p. (J). (ps-3). 1999. 7.99 (0-8024-4932-8) Moody.
— A Pack of Lies. (Christopher Churchmouse Classics Ser.). (Illus.). 24p. (J). (ps-2). 1989. 8.99 (0-89693-497-7, 6-1497, Victor Bks) Chariot Victor.
— The Potluck Supper. (Christopher Churchmouse Classics Ser.). (Illus.). 24p. (J). (ps-2). 1988. 8.99 (0-89693-406-3, 6-1406, Victor Bks) Chariot Victor.
— The Problem with Prickles. (Tales from Schroon Lake Ser.: No. 3). (Illus.). (J). 7.99 (0-8024-1035-9, 571) Moody.
— Rainy Day Rescue. (Christopher Churchmouse Classics Ser.). (Illus.). 24p. (J). (ps-2). 1988. 8.99 (0-89693-408-X, 6-1408, Victor Bks) Chariot Victor.
— Rainy Day Rescue. (Christopher Churchmouse Classics Ser.). (Illus.). 24p. (J). (ps-3). 1999. 7.99 (0-8024-4933-6) Moody.
— Rescate en un Dia de Lluvia.Tr. of Rainy Day Rescue. (SPA.). 24p. (J). 1983. pap. 6.99 (1-56063-124-4, 490376) Editorial Unilit.
— Saved by the Bell. (Christopher Churchmouse Classics Ser.). (Illus.). 24p. (J). (ps-2). 1988. 8.99 (0-89693-403-9, 6-1403, Victor Bks) Chariot Victor.
— Saved by the Bell. (Christopher Churchmouse Classics Ser.). (Illus.). 24p. (J). (ps-3). 1999. 7.99 (0-8024-4934-4) Moody.
— The Shiny Red Sled. (Christopher Churchmouse Classics Ser.). (Illus.). 24p. (J). (ps-2). 1989. 8.99 (0-89693-498-5, 6-1498, Victor Bks) Chariot Victor.
— A Short Tail. (Christopher Churchmouse Classics Ser.). (Illus.). 24p. (J). (ps-2). 1989. 8.99 (0-89693-499-3, 6-1499, Victor Bks) Chariot Victor.
— Una Sorpresa Dominical: Cristobal Raton de Iglesia. (Cristobal Raton de Iglesia Ser.).Tr. of Sunday Surprise: Christopher Church Mouse. (SPA.). 23p. (J). 1990. 3.99 (1-56063-299-2, 490377) Editorial Unilit.
— A Sticky Mystery. (Christopher Churchmouse Classics Ser.). (Illus.). 24p. (J). (ps-2). 1989. 8.99 (0-89693-485-3, 6-1485, Victor Bks) Chariot Victor.
***Davoll, Barbara.** Stowaways, Vol. 2. (J). 1999. 7.99 (0-8024-5397-X) Moody.
Davoll, Barbara. A Sunday Surprise. 24p. (J). (ps-2). 1997. pap. write for info. (0-7814-3024-0, Chariot Bks) Chariot Victor.
— A Sunday Surprise. (Christopher Churchmouse Classics Ser.). (Illus.). 24p. (J). (ps-3). 1999. 7.99 (0-8024-4935-2) Moody.
— Tattletale Tongue. (Illus.). (J). (ps-2). 1990. 8.99 (0-89693-537-X, 6-1537, Victor Bks) Chariot Victor.
***Davoll, Barbara.** To London to See the Queen, Vol. 4. (New Christopher Churchmouse Adventures Ser.). (Illus.). (J). 1999. 7.99 (0-8024-5399-6) Moody.
— The Unplanned Voyage, Vol. 1. (J). 1999. 7.99 (0-8024-5396-1) Moody.
Davoll, Barbara. A Visit from Rudy Beaver. (Tales from Schroon Lake Ser.: No. 2). (Illus.). (J). 7.99 (0-8024-1034-0, 672) Moody.
— The White Trail. (Christopher Churchmouse Classics Ser.). (Illus.). 24p. (J). (ps-2). 1988. 8.99 (0-89693-404-7, 6-1404, Victor Bks) Chariot Victor.
Davoll, Barbara & Hockerman, Dennis. The Camping Caper. (Christopher Churchmouse Ser.). (Illus.). 24p. (J). (ps-2). 1993. 11.99 incl. audio (1-56476-162-2, 6-3162, Victor Bks) Chariot Victor.
— A Flood of Friends. (Christopher Churchmouse Ser.). (J). (ps-2). 1990. 11.99 incl. audio (0-89693-137-4, 3-2137, Victor Bks) Chariot Victor.
— A Load of Trouble. (Christopher Churchmouse Ser.). (Illus.). 24p. (J). (gr. 4-7). 1988. 11.99 incl. audio (0-89693-618-X, 3-1618, Victor Bks) Chariot Victor.
— A Pack of Lies. (Christopher Churchmouse Ser.). (Illus.). 24p. (J). (ps-2). 1989. 11.99 incl. audio (0-89693-030-0, 3-1202, Victor Bks) Chariot Victor.
— Rainy Day Rescue. (Christopher Churchmouse Ser.). (Illus.). 24p. (J). (ps-2). 1988. 11.99 incl. audio (0-89693-619-8, 3-1619, Victor Bks) Chariot Victor.
— Saved by the Bell. (Christopher Churchmouse Ser.). (Illus.). 24p. (J). (ps-2). 1988. 11.99 incl. audio (0-89693-614-7, 3-1614, Victor Bks) Chariot Victor.
— The Shiny Red Sled. (Christopher Churchmouse Ser.). (Illus.). 24p. (J). (ps-2). 1989. 11.99 incl. audio (0-89693-031-9, 3-1203, Victor Bks) Chariot Victor.
— A Sunday Surprise. (Christopher Churchmouse Ser.). (Illus.). 24p. (J). (ps-2). 1988. 11.99 incl. audio (0-89693-616-3, 3-1616, Victor Bks) Chariot Victor.
Davoll, Barbara & Wyrtzen, Don. A Churchmouse Christmas: A Musical for Children. 1994. suppl. ed. 7.00 (0-614-01708-4, L-9173C); suppl. ed. 15.00 (0-614-01709-2, MC-88SF); pap. 5.99 (0-8341-9116-4, MC-88); sl. 45.00 (0-614-01710-6, MM-9173) Lillenas.
— A Churchmouse Christmas: A Musical for Children. 1994. pap., suppl. ed. 6.99 (0-8341-9208-X, MC-88A) Lillenas.
Davor. Fundamentals of Graphics. (C). 1998. text. write for info. (0-201-53232-8) Addison-Wesley.
Davoust, E. P. Danger de Mort. (C). 1984. 30.00 (0-7175-1227-4, Pub. by S Thornes Pubs) St Mut.
Davoust, Eugene-Pierre. Resistance? Defendu, Mademoiselle! 4.25 (0-8219-1034-5) EMC-Paradigm.
D'Avray, David. Death & the Prince: Memorial Preaching Before 1350. 328p. 1994. 65.00 (0-19-820396-9) OUP.
Davril, Anselme, ed. The Monastic Ritual of Fleury: Orleans, Bibliotheque Municipale MS 123 (101) (Henry Bradshaw Society Ser.: No. CV). (Illus.). 200p. 1990. 45.00 (0-9501009-9-4, Henry Bradshaw Soc) Boydell & Brewer.
— The Winchcombe Sacramentary: Orleans, Bibliotheque Municipale, 127 (105) (Henry Bradshaw Society Ser.: No. 109). (Illus.). 461p. (C). 1995. 55.00 (1-870252-07-1, Henry Bradshaw Soc) Boydell & Brewer.
Davrout, L., tr. see Wieger, L.
***Davson, Christopher.** I Merlin: An Historical Recreation. (Illus.). 411p. 2000. 32.50 (1-85776-480-3, Pub. by Book Guild Ltd) Trans-Atl Phila.
Davson-Galle, Peter. The Possibility of Relative Truth. LC 97-77551. (Avebury Series in Philosophy). 198p. 1998. text 59.95 (1-84014-115-8, Pub. by Ashgate Pub) Ashgate Pub Co.
Davson, H. Physiology of the Eye. 5th ed. (Illus.). 750p. 1990. 85.00 (0-08-037907-9, Pub. by PPI) McGraw.
Davson, Hugh & Segal, Malcolm B., eds. Physiology of the Cerebrospinal Fluids & Blood-Brain Barriers. LC 95-8041. (Illus.). 832p. 1995. boxed set 314.95 (0-8493-4472-7, 4472) CRC Pr.
Davson, Hugh, et al. An Introduction to the Blood-Brain Barrier. LC 92-49384. 1992. 120.00 (0-8493-7761-7, QP375) CRC Pr.
Davson, Victor L., et al. Things That Are Broken or Unfinished: The Art of Doug Kenney. (Illus.). 48p. (Orig.). 1996. write for info. (0-614-23698-3) Aljira.
Davutoglu, Ahmet. Alternative Paradigms: The Impact of Islamic & Western Weltanschauungs on Political Theory. LC 92-46275. 1993. 62.50 (0-8191-9046-2); pap. 36.00 (0-8191-9047-0) U Pr of Amer.
Davy, Aidan, jt. auth. see McPhail, Kathryn.
Davy, B. Essential Injustice Vol. XXIII: When Legal Institutions Cannot Resolve Environmental & Land Use Disputes. LC 96-47985. (Illus.). 536p. 1997. 81.00 (3-211-82951-2) Spr-Verlag.
Davy, Charles, ed. Footnotes to the Film. LC 75-124004. (Literature of Cinema, Ser. 1). 1970. reprint ed. 24.95 (0-405-01610-7) Ayer.
Davy, Charles, tr. see Steiner, Rudolf.
Davy, Elizabeth & Davy, Karen. TOEFL Reading & Vocabulary Workbook. 2nd ed. 256p. 1992. per. 11.95 (0-13-926965-7, Arc) IDG Bks.
Davy, F. Brian, ed. Asian Fisheries Directory. 130p. 1989. per. write for info. (971-10-2257-5, Pub. by ICLARM) Intl Spec Bk.
— Resource Allocation to Fisheries Research in Asia. (Asian Fisheries Society Spec. Publications: No. 7). 172p. 1993. per. write for info. (971-8709-35-5, Pub. by ICLARM) Intl Spec Bk.
Davy, G. N., jt. auth. see Dallmayr, Fred.
Davy, Georges. La Foi Juree. LC 74-25746. (European Sociology Ser.). 390p. 1975. reprint ed. 31.95 (0-405-06501-9) Ayer.
Davy, Gudron & Davy, John. Hope, Evolution & Change: Selected Essays by John Davy. (Social Ecology Ser.). 274p. 1985. pap. 12.95 (0-9507062-7-2, 1037, Pub. by Hawthorn Press) Anthroposophic.
Davy, Gudron & Voors, Bons. Lifeways: Working with Family Questions. (Lifeways Ser.). (Illus.). 328p. 1990. pap. text 15.95 (0-9507062-4-8, 793, Pub. by Hawthorn Press) Anthroposophic.
Davy, Humphrey. Salmonia. 305p. 45.00 (1-56416-123-4) Derrydale Pr.
Davy, Humphry. Humphry Davy on Geology: The 1805 Lectures for the General Audience. Siegfried, Robert & Dott, Robert H., eds. LC 79-5022. (Illus.). 217p. reprint ed. pap. 67.30 (0-608-09930-9, 206926800003) Bks Demand.
— Salmonia. (Illus.). 273p. 1970. boxed set 10.75 (0-88395-004-9) Freshet Pr.
Davy, J. R. & Dew, P. M., eds. Abstract Machine Models for Highly Parallel Computers. (Illus.). 350p. 1995. text 85.00 (0-19-853796-4) OUP.
Davy, John. West Indies Before & since Emancipation Compromising the Windward & Leeward Islands' Military Command. 1971. reprint ed. 49.50 (0-7146-1935-3, Pub. by F Cass Pubs) Intl Spec Bk.

D

An Asterisk (*) at the beginning of an entry indicates that the title is appearing for the first time.

***Davy, John & Ellis, Susan.** Counselling Skills in Palliative Care. LC 00-35626. 2000. pap. write for info. (*0-335-20313-2*, Pub. by OpUniv Pr) Taylor & Francis.

Davy, John, et al. The Marriage of Sense & Thought: Imaginative Participation in Science. LC 96-29674. (Renewal in Science Ser.). 160p. 1997. pap. 16.95 (*0-940262-82-7*, Lindisfarne) Anthroposophic.

Davy, John, jt. auth. see Davy, Gudron.

Davy, John, ed. see Bockemuhl, Jochen, et al.

Davy, Joseph B. Stock Ranges of Northwestern California: Notes on the Grasses & Forage Plants & Range. (Illus.). 81p. (YA). (gr. 10-12). 1998. reprint ed. pap. 16.00 (*0-933421-52-4*) Redwood Seed.

***Davy, Karen.** On Your Mark. 2nd ed. LC 99-33870. 2000. write for info. (*0-201-47174-4*) Addison-Wesley.

— On Your Mark. 2nd ed. LC 99-33871. 2000. 15.67 (*0-201-66394-5*) Addison-Wesley.

Davy, Karen, jt. auth. see Davy, Elizabeth.

Davy, Keith. Come Together: Disciplemating. (Inter Acta Ser.). (Illus.). 6p. (C). 1994. teacher ed., ring bd. 1.25 (*1-885702-85-X*, 741-069t, Inter Acta); student ed., ring bd. 3.25 (*1-885702-84-1*, 741-069s, Inter Acta) WSN Pr.

— The Turning Point: Convictions. (Inter Acta Ser.). (Illus.). 6p. (C). 1994. teacher ed., ring bd. 1.25 (*1-885702-97-3*, 741-070t, Inter Acta); student ed., ring bd. 3.25 (*1-885702-96-5*, 741-070s, Inter Acta) WSN Pr.

— Under the Influence: Spirit Power. rev. ed. (Inter Acta Ser.). (Illus.). 6p. (C). 1996. teacher ed., ring bd. 1.25 (*0-614-14269-5*, 741-012t, Inter Acta); student ed., ring bd. 3.25 (*1-57334-015-4*, 741-012s, Inter Acta) WSN Pr.

— Walk This Way: Spirit-Filled Life. (Inter Acta Ser.). (Illus.). 6p. (C). 1994. teacher ed., ring bd. 1.25 (*1-885702-03-5*, 741-011t, Inter Acta); student ed., ring bd. 3.25 (*1-885702-02-7*, 741-011s, Inter Acta) WSN Pr.

Davy, Martin. The Life of Francis Bacon. 120p. 1996. reprint ed. pap. 16.95 (*1-56459-640-0*) Kessinger Pub.

Davy, Merv, ed. Hengan. (C). 1989. 40.00 (*0-907566-71-5*, Pub. by Dyllansow Truran) St Mut.

Davy, Richard. European Detente: A Reappraisal. (Royal Institute of International Affairs Ser.). (Illus.). 288p. (C). 1992. text 60.00 (*0-8039-8688-2*) Sage.

Davydoff, A. Russian Sketches: Memoirs. 303p. 1985. pap. 85.00 (*0-7855-0846-5*) St Mut.

Davydov, A. A. Qualitative Theory of Control Systems. LC 94-30834. (Translations of Mathematical Monographs: Vol. 141). 147p. 1994. text 75.00 (*0-8218-4590-X*, MMONO/141) Am Math.

Davydov, A. S. Solitons in Molecular Systems. 2nd ed. (Mathematics & Its Applications, Soviet Ser.). 426p. (C). 1990. text 257.50 (*0-7923-1029-2*) Kluwer Academic.

— Solutions in Molecular Systems. 1985. text 208.00 (*90-277-1854-7*) Kluwer Academic.

Davydov, A. S. & Loktev, V. M., eds. High-Tc Superconductivity: Experiment & Theory. (Research Reports in Physics). (Illus.). 209p. 1992. 79.95 (*0-387-55152-2*) Spr-Verlag.

Davydov, E., et al. Kinetic Peculiarities of Solid Phase Reactions. LC 98-12082. 160p. 1998. 150.00 (*0-471-98374-8*) Wiley.

Davydov, I. A., et al. Local Properties of Distributions of Stochastic Functionals. Nazaikinski, V. E. & Shishkova, M. S., trs. from RUS. LC 97-44426. (Translations of Mathematical Monographs Ser.). 184p. 1997. text 75.00 (*0-8218-0584-3*) Am Math.

Davydov, Isay. Creation & Evolution. LC 97-93280. (RUS., Illus.). 384p. 1997. 25.00 (*0-9630594-1-6*) Intl Sci Ctr.

***Davydov, Joseph.** God Exists: New Light on Science & Creation. LC 00-24815. (Illus.). 302p. 2000. pap. 24.95 (*1-887563-51-2*, Pub. by Schreiber Pub) Natl Bk Netwk.

Davydov, Joseph. Six Biblical Days. LC 97-74692. (RUS., Illus.). 16p. 1997. 4.00 (*0-9630594-3-2*) Intl Sci Ctr.

Davydov, M. Oncology Reviews Vol. 4, Pt. 4.3: Review of Soviet Literature on the Problem of Esophageal Cancer for 1980-1990, Vol. 4. (Soviet Medical Reviews Ser.: Section F). 98p. 1992. pap. text 96.00 (*3-7186-5360-5*, Harwood Acad Pubs) Gordon & Breach.

***Davydov, O. D. & Oreshkin, V. A.** Liberalization of Russian Foreign Trade: Problems & Prospects. LC 99-49278. 2000. write for info. (*0-8232-1969-0*) Fordham.

Davydov, Oleg D. Inside Out: The Radical Transformation of Russia's Foreign Trade, 1992-1997. LC 98-9579. viii, 224p. 1998. 29.95 (*0-8232-1830-9*) Fordham.

Davydov, V. V. Dictionary of Psychology. (RUS.). 448p. 1983. 29.95 (*0-8288-2210-7*, M15381) Fr & Eur.

Davydova, Ilona. English, Set. 1990. pap. text 179.00 incl. audio (*0-9675296-0-3*) Express Method.

Davys, Mary. The Reform'd Coquet. LC 72-170558. (Foundations of the Novel Ser.: Vol. 42). 1972. lib. bdg. 61.00 (*0-8240-0554-6*) Garland.

— The Reform'd Coquet, Familiar Letters Betwixt a Gentleman & a Lady & the Accomplished Rake. Bowden, Martha F., ed. LC 99-13687. (Eighteenth-Century Novels by Women Ser.). 304p. 1999. pap. 16.95 (*0-8131-0969-8*) U Pr of Ky.

***Davys, Mary.** The Reform'd Coquet, Familiar Letters Betwixt a Gentleman & a Lady & the Accomplished Rake. Bowden, Martha F., ed. LC 99-13687. (Eighteenth-Century Novels by Women Ser.). 304p. 1999. 45.00 (*0-8131-2127-2*) U Pr of Ky.

Daw, Carl P., Jr. A Year of Grace: Hymns for the Church Year. LC 90-80709. 167p. (C). 1990. 14.95 (*0-916642-41-0*, 935) Hope Pub.

Daw, Carl P., Jr., ed. Breaking the Word. 210p. 1994. 19.95 (*0-89869-210-5*) Church Pub Inc.

Daw, Kurt. Acting Shakespeare & His Contemporaries: Thought into Action. LC 97-52067. 156p. 1997. pap. 19.95 (*0-325-00054-9*) Heinemann.

Daw, Kurt & Matthews, Julia. A Guide to Scenes & Monologues from Shakespeare's Stage. LC 97-52066. 1998. pap. 13.95 (*0-325-00015-8*) Heinemann.

Daw, M. S. & Schluter, M. A., eds. Atomic Scale Calculations of Structure in Materials Vol. 193: Symposium Proceedings Ser. 359p. 1990. text 17.50 (*1-55899-082-8*) Materials Res.

Daw, Nigel W. Visual Development. (Perspectives in Vision Research Ser.). (Illus.). 242p. (C). 1995. text 54.00 (*0-306-45023-2*, Kluwer Plenum) Kluwer Academic.

Daw, Stephen. Music of Johann Sebastian Bach: The Choral Works. LC 78-68624. (Illus.). 240p. 1981. 36.50 (*0-8386-1682-8*) Fairleigh Dickinson.

Dawa-Samdup, Kazi, tr. from TIB. Shrichakrasambhara Tantra: A Buddhist Tantra. 255p. 1984. reprint ed. lib. bdg. 29.50 (*0-88181-000-2*) Canon Pubns.

Dawa, Tashi. A Soul in Bondage: Stories from Tibet. 234p. (Orig.). 1992. pap. 8.95 (*0-8351-2096-1*) China Bks.

***Dawahare, Michael D.** Civil Society & Lebanon: Toward A Hermeneutic Theory of the Public Sphere in Comparative Studies. LC 00-9931. 2000. write for info. (*1-58112-400-7*, Brown Walker Pr) Dissertation.

***Dawar, Tamim A.** Deutsche Direktinvestitionen In Australien: Eine Evaluation der Theoretischen Erklarungsansatze und der Standortattraktivitat Des Produktions - Und Investitionsstandortes Australien. (GER., Illus.). 312p. 1999. 57.00 (*3-631-34533-X*) P Lang Pubng.

Dawbarn, David & Allen, Shelley J., eds. Neurobiology of Alzheimer's Disease. LC 98-138325. (The Molecular & Cellular Neurobiolgy Ser.). (Illus.). 336p. 1998. text 87.00 (*1-872748-14-7*) OUP.

***Dawbarn, David & Allen, Shelley J., eds.** Neurobiology of Alzheimer's Disease. 2nd ed. (The Molecular & Cellular Neurobiology Ser.). (Illus.). 464p. 2000. pap. text 59.50 (*0-19-852459-5*) OUP.

***Dawber, Diane.** Lifting the Bull: Overcoming Chronic Back Pain, Fibromyalgia & Environmental Illness. 176p. 1999. pap. write for info. (*1-55082-199-7*) Quarry Pr.

Dawber, Diane. My Underwear's Inside Out: The Care & Feeding of Young Poets. (Illus.). 64p. (J). 1991. 14.95 (*1-55082-010-9*, Pub. by Quarry Pr); pap. 8.95 (*1-55082-011-7*, Pub. by Quarry Pr) LPC InBook.

***Dawber, Diane.** Reading to Heal: A Guide to the Best Alternative & Complementary Nutritional Health Books. (Illus.). 96p. 1999. pap. 6.95 (*1-55082-229-2*) Quarry Pr.

Dawber, Keith & Redshaw, Dai. Sustainable Energy: Options for New Zealand. LC 96-154728. (Illus.). 208p. (C). 1996. pap. 24.95 (*0-908569-95-5*, Pub. by Univ Otago Pr) Intl Spec Bk.

Dawber, Michael. Dawber's Guide to the Kawarthas & Haliburton Highlands. 288p. 1996. pap. 14.95 (*1-55082-144-X*, Pub. by Quarry Pr) LPC InBook.

— Up Your Kilt: Ashley MacIsaac & the Gay Men's Music Movement. (Illus.). 240p. 1998. pap. 15.95 (*1-55082-217-9*, Pub. by Quarry Pr) LPC InBook.

Dawber, Michael, jt. auth. see Fitsell, Bill.

Dawber, P. G. Vectors & Vector Operators. (Student Monographs in Physics). (Illus.). 64p. 1987. pap. 15.00 (*0-85274-585-0*) IOP Pub.

***Dawber, R. & Powell, J.** An Atlas of Hair Diseases. (Encyclopedia of Visual Medicine Ser.). (Illus.). 140p. 2001. write for info. (*1-84214-013-2*) Prthnon Pub.

Dawber, R. P. Cutaneous Cryosurgery. 2nd ed. 184p. 1998. write for info. (*1-85317-430-0*, Pub. by Martin Dunitz) Mosby Inc.

Dawber, R. P., jt. auth. see Gray, John.

Dawber, R. P. R., jt. ed. see Baran, Robert.

Dawber, Rodney. Diseases of the Hair & Scalp. 3rd ed. LC 96-45303. (Illus.). 640p. 1997. text 199.95 (*0-86542-866-2*) Blackwell Sci.

Dawber, Rodney & Van Neste, Dominique. Hair & Scalp Disorders: Common Presenting Signs, Differential Diagnosis & Treatment. (Illus.). 208p. 1995. text 76.00 (*0-397-51421-2*) Lppncott W & W.

Dawber, Rodney, et al. Cutaneous Cryosurgery: Principles & Clinical Practice. 1992. 70.00 (*1-85317-082-8*, M Dunitz) Scovill Paterson.

Dawber, Thomas R. The Framingham Study: The Epidemiology of Atherosclerotic Disease. LC 80-11189. 269p. reprint ed. pap. 83.40 (*0-7837-2247-8*, 205733500004) Bks Demand.

Dawdy, Doris O. George Montague Wheeler: The Man & the Myth. LC 93-12998. (Illus.). 140p. (C). 1993. text 24.95 (*0-8040-0973-2*) Swallow.

Dawe. Math & Dosage Calculations for Health Occupations: Instructor's Guide. 1999. teacher ed. 12.21 (*0-02-800678-X*) Glencoe.

— Sometimes Gladness: Collected Poems, 1954-1992. 4th ed. 1993. pap. text. write for info. (*0-582-90879-5*, Pub. by Addison-Wesley) Longman.

Dawe, ed. Sophoclis: Antigone. (GRE.). 1996. pap. 18.95 (*3-8154-1811-9*, T1811, Pub. by B G Teubner) U of Mich Pr.

— Sophoclis: Oedipus Coloneus. (GRE.). 1996. pap. 19.95 (*3-8154-1814-3*, T1814, Pub. by B G Teubner) U of Mich Pr.

— Sophoclis: Philoctetes. (GRE.). 1996. pap. 19.95 (*3-8154-1815-1*, T1815, Pub. by B G Teubner) U of Mich Pr.

— Sophoclis: Trachiniae. (GRE.). 1996. pap. 19.95 (*3-8154-1816-X*, T1816, Pub. by B G Teubner) U of Mich Pr.

Dawe, Bruce, ed. Imago: Literary Magazine. (C). 1990. 40.00 (*0-7855-6625-2*, Pub. by Pascoe Pub) St Mut.

Dawe, C. M. Programming for Computer Science. 1994. pap. 35.00 (*3-540-19811-3*) Spr-Verlag.

— Prolog for Computer Science. 189p. 1994. 29.00 (*0-387-19811-3*) Spr-Verlag.

Dawe, Charles W. & Dornan, Edward A. One to One. 5th ed. LC 96-2758. 460p. (C). 1997. pap. text 48.00 (*0-673-98068-5*) Addson-Wesley Educ.

Dawe, Charles W., jt. auth. see Dornan, Edward A.

Dawe, Charles W., jt. ed. see Dornan, Edward A.

Dawe, Chris M., jt. auth. see Balzer, Wolfgang.

Dawe, Clyde J., ed. The Chromosome: Structural & Functional Aspects. (In Vitro Journal Back Volumes: Vol. 1). 107p. 1965. 15.00 (*0-317-36060-4*) Soc In Vitro Biol.

Dawe, Donald G. & Carman, John B., eds. Christian Faith in a Religiously Plural World. LC 78-50927. 208p. (Orig.). reprint ed. pap. 64.50 (*0-8357-2671-1*, 204020700015) Bks Demand.

Dawe, Fiona & Goddard, Eileen. Smoking-Related Behavior & Attitudes: A Report on Research Using the ONS OMNIB. LC 98-133888. 1997. 25.00 (*0-11-620948-8*, HM094888, Pub. by Statnry Office) Bernan Associates.

Dawe, Gerald. Heart of Hearts. 48p. 1995. pap. 12.95 (*1-85235-153-5*) Dufour.

— The Lundy's Letter. 50p. 1985. pap. 10.95 (*0-904011-84-4*) Dufour.

***Dawe, Gerald.** Morning Train. 52p. 2000. 25.95 (*1-85235-260-4*, Pub. by Gallery Pr); pap. 13.95 (*1-85235-259-0*, Pub. by Gallery Pr) Dufour.

Dawe, Gerald. New Younger Irish Poets. 176p. 1991. pap. 14.95 (*0-85640-460-8*) Dufour.

— Sunday School. 48p. 1991. pap. 10.95 (*1-85235-063-6*) Dufour.

Dawe, Gerald, ed. Younger Irish Poets. 176p. 1982. pap. 12.95 (*0-685-25870-X*, Pub. by Blackstaff Pr) Dufour.

— Younger Irish Poets. 176p. 1982. pap. 12.95 (*0-85640-261-3*) Dufour.

Dawe, Gerald, ed. see Fiacc, Padraic.

Dawe, Karen. The Beach Book & the Beach Bucket. (Hand in Hand with Nature Ser.). (Illus.). 64p. (J). (gr. k-5). 1998. pap. 7.95 (*0-921051-08-5*) Somerville Hse.

— The Beach Book & the Beach Bucket. LC 87-40648. (Illus.). 64p. (J). (gr. k-5). 1988. pap. 7.95 (*0-89480-590-8*, 1590) Workman Pub.

— The Pond Book & the Tadpole Tank. (Hand in Hand with Nature Ser.). (Illus.). 80p. (J). (gr. k-5). 1998. pap. 14.95 (*1-895897-18-1*) Somerville Hse.

— The Pond Book & the Tadpole Tank. LC 95-3289. (Illus.). 80p. (J). (gr. 2-6). 1999. pap. 14.95 (*1-56305-921-5*, 3921) Workman Pub.

Dawe, Karen, jt. auth. see Dawe, Neil.

Dawe, Margaret. Nissequott. LC 92-44444. 304p. 1994. pap. 10.95 (*0-8112-1260-2*, NDP775, Pub. by New Directions) Norton.

Dawe, Michael. Red Deer: An Illustrated History. (Illus.). 1989. 27.95 (*0-89781-261-1*) Am Historical Pr.

***Dawe, Neil.** Hummingbird Book & Feeder. (Illus.). 64p. 2000. pap. 16.99 (*1-58184-026-8*) Somerville Hse.

Dawe, Neil & Dawe, Karen. The Bird Book & the Bird Feeder. LC 88-40225. (Illus.). 64p. (J). (gr. k-7). 1999. pap. 12.95 (*0-89480-614-9*, 1614) Workman Pub.

***Dawe, R. D.** Philogelos. 2000. 34.50 (*3-519-01595-1*) B G Teubner.

Dawe, R. D., ed. see Sophocles.

Dawe, Renee A. Math & Dosage Calculations for Health Occupations. (Illus.). 240p. (gr. 6-12). 1993. text, student ed. 29.90 (*0-02-800677-1*) Glencoe.

Dawe, Roger D. Sophocles: The Classical Heritage. Briggs, Ward, ed. LC 95-53958. (Classical Heritage Ser.: Vol. 04). 344p. 1996. reprint ed. text 55.00 (*0-8153-0334-3*, H1455) Garland.

***Dawei, Fei.** Cai Guo-Qiang. LC 00-100980. (Illus.). 120p. 2000. 27.50 (*0-500-97493-4*, Pub. by Thames Hudson) Norton.

***Dawes.** Everyday Irrationality. 2000. 26.00 (*0-8133-6552-X*, Pub. by Westview) HarpC.

Dawes. Psychology's Myths & Misconceptions. 19.95 (*0-465-06700-X*, Pub. by Basic) HarpC.

Dawes, jt. auth. see Cunningham.

Dawes, Andy, ed. Understanding Conflict & Promoting Peace: Contributions from South Africa: A Special Issue of Peace & Conflict, Vol. 3, No. 3. 71p. 1997. pap. 20.00 (*0-8058-9856-5*) L Erlbaum Assocs.

Dawes, Bain. Cargo Handlers: Liability & Insurance. (C). 1982. 70.00 (*0-906297-22-2*, Pub. by ICHCA) St Mut.

Dawes, Brian. International Business: A European Perspective. 328p. 1999. pap. 52.50 (*0-7487-1860-5*, Pub. by S Thornes Pubs) Trans-Atl Phila.

Dawes, Charles G. The Banking System of the United States & Its Relation to the Money & Business of the Country. Bruchey, Stuart, ed. LC 80-1143. (Rise of Commercial Banking Ser.). 1981. reprint ed. lib. bdg. 15.95 (*0-405-13645-5*) Ayer.

— Journal As Ambassador to Great Britain. (History - United States Ser.). 442p. 1993. reprint ed. lib. bdg. 99.00 (*0-7812-4863-9*) Rprt Serv.

***Dawes, Chip.** OCP: Oracle8i DBA SQL & PL/SQL Study Guide. (Illus.). 2000. 49.99 (*0-7821-2682-0*) Sybex.

***Dawes, Chip, et al.** Ocp: Oracle8i DBA Certification Kit with CD-ROM. 2000. pap. 109.97 incl. cd-rom (*0-7821-2685-5*) Sybex.

Dawes, Christopher. Laser Welding. LC 92-19179. 176p. 1993. 50.00 (*0-07-016123-2*) McGraw.

Dawes, Claiborne. A Different Drummer: Thoreau & Will's Independence Day. LC 97-78303. (Illus.). 32p. (J). (gr. 2-5). 1998. pap. 7.95 (*1-57960-039-5*) Disc Enter Ltd.

Dawes, Clinton J. Marine Algae of the West Coast of Florida. LC 73-22107. (Illus.). 272p. 1990. pap. 20.00 (*0-87024-258-X*) U of Miami Pr.

— Marine Botany. 2nd ed. LC 97-10372. 328p. 1998. 90.00 (*0-471-19208-2*) Wiley.

Dawes County History Book Committee, ed. History of Dawes County, Nebraska. (Illus.). 340p. 1985. 50.00 (*0-88107-035-1*) Curtis Media.

Dawes, Dana C., ed. see Burke, Kathleen, et al.

Dawes, E. A. Microbial Energetics. (Tertiary Level Biology Ser.). (Illus.). 192p. (C). 1985. text 39.95 (*0-412-01041-0*, 9444, Chap & Hall NY); pap. text 29.50 (*0-412-01051-8*, 9445, Chap & Hall NY) Chapman & Hall.

Dawes, E. A., jt. ed. see Drews, G.

Dawes, E. A., jt. ed. see Kyslik, P.

Dawes, Edna. A Hidden Heart of Fire. large type ed. (Linford Romance Library). 320p. 1985. pap. 16.99 (*0-7089-6097-9*) Ulverscroft.

Dawes, Edwin A. Charles Bertram: The Court Conjurer. (Illus.). 360p. 1997. 60.00 (*0-916638-85-5*) Meyerbooks.

Dawes, Edwin A., ed. Novel Biodegradable Microbial Polymers. (Nato Advanced Science Institutes, Applied Sciences Ser.: Series E). (C). 1990. text 236.50 (*0-7923-0949-9*) Kluwer Academic.

Dawes, Elizabeth & Baynes, Norman H., trs. from GRE. Three Byzantine Saints. LC 96-31502. 275p. 1996. pap. 13.95 (*0-913836-44-3*) St Vladimirs.

Dawes, Elizabeth A., tr. see Comnena, Anna.

Dawes, G. S., et al, eds. Fetal Autonomy & Adaptation. LC 90-12458. (Illus.). 200p. 1990. reprint ed. pap. 62.00 (*0-608-01632-2*, 206221700002) Bks Demand.

Dawes, Geri-Lynn, ed. see Christopher, Maurine.

Dawes, Ginny R., jt. auth. see Davidov, Corinne.

Dawes, Graham, jt. auth. see Cunningham, Ian.

Dawes, Greg. Aesthetics & Revolution: Nicaraguan Poetry, 1979-1990. 224p. (C). 1992. 29.95 (*0-8166-2146-2*) U of Minn Pr.

Dawes, Gregory W. The Body in Question: Metaphor & Meaning in the Interpretation of Ephesians 5:21-33. LC 97-50049. (Biblical Interpretation Ser.). xiv, 264p. 1998. 90.50 (*90-04-10959-5*) Brill Academic Pubs.

***Dawes, Gregory W., ed.** The Historical Jesus: A Foundational Anthology. 320p. 2000. pap. 24.95 (*0-664-22262-5*, Pub. by Westminster John Knox) Presbyterian Pub.

Dawes, Greyham. Tolley's Charity Accountability & Compliance. 1998. pap. write for info. (*1-86012-917-X*, Pub. by Tolley Pubng) St Mut.

Dawes, Ian W. & Sutherland, Ian W. Microbial Physiology. 2nd ed. (Basic Microbiology Ser.). (Illus.). 304p. 1991. pap. 44.95 (*0-632-02463-1*) Blackwell Sci.

Dawes, J., et al, eds. Selecting an Ada Compilation System. (Ada Companion Ser.). 183p. (C). 1991. text 59.95 (*0-521-40498-3*) Cambridge U Pr.

Dawes, John. John Dawes's Book of Water Gardens. (Illus.). 192p. 1989. 35.95 (*0-86622-662-1*, H-1104) TFH Pubns.

Dawes, John. The Pond Owner's Problem Solver. (Illus.). 208p. 29.95 (*1-56465-196-7*) Tetra Pr.

— Tropical Aquarium Fish: A Step-by-Step Guide to Setting up & Maintaining a Freshwater or Marine Aquarium. (Illus.). 96p. 2000. pap. 14.95 (*1-85368-579-8*) New5 Holland.

Dawes, Kathleen A., ed. see Dawes, Walter A.

Dawes, Kawame. Resisting the Anomie. LC 95-163927. 112p. 1995. pap. 10.95 (*0-86492-147-0*, Pub. by Goose Ln Edits) Genl Dist Srvs.

***Dawes, Kwame.** Midland: Poems. 104p. 2000. 24.95 (*0-8214-1355-4*); pap. 12.95 (*0-8214-1356-2*) Ohio U Pr.

Dawes, Kwame. Natural Mysticism: Towards a New Reggae Aesthetic. 216p. 1998. pap. 24.95 (*1-900715-22-8*, Pub. by Peepal Tree Pr) Paul & Co Pubs.

Dawes, Kwame, compiled by. Wheel & Come Again: An Anthology of Reggae Poetry. LC 98-124583. 216p. 1998. pap. 18.95 (*1-900715-13-9*, Pub. by Peepal Tree Pr) Paul & Co Pubs.

***Dawes, Kwame, ed.** Talk Yuh Talk: Interviews with Anglophone Caribbean Poets. 288p. 2000. 49.50 (*0-8139-1945-2*); pap. 17.50 (*0-8139-1946-0*) U Pr of Va.

Dawes, Kwame, ed. Wheel & Come Again: An Anthology of Reggae Poetry. 184p. 1999. pap. 17.95 (*0-86492-199-3*, Pub. by Goose Ln Eds) Genl Dist Srvs.

***Dawes, Martin.** Evidence-Based Practice: A Primer for Health Care Professionals. LC 99-29502. 2000. write for info. (*0-443-06126-2*, W B Saunders Co) Harcrt Hlth Sci Grp.

Dawes, Mike. Flytier's Companion. (Illus.). 160p. (Orig.). 1989. pap. 19.95 (*0-88317-148-1*) Stoeger Pub Co.

— The Flytier's Manual. 160p. 1985. pap. 19.95 (*0-88317-130-9*) Stoeger Pub Co.

Dawes, Nigel. Shiatsu for Beginners: A Step-by-Step Guide: Achieve Overall Health & Well-Being with Finger-Pressure Massage. (Illus.). 144p. 1995. pap. 16.95 (*0-7615-0132-0*) Prima Pub.

Dawes, Peter. Trade Secrets: How to Start & Run an Import/Export Business. 320p. Date not set. pap. write for info. (*0-471-64389-0*) Wiley.

Dawes, Richard. Dog Lover's Companion. 1997. 9.99 (*1-85833-729-1*, Pub. by CLib Bks) Whitecap Bks.

Dawes, Robert A., Jr. The Dragon's Breath: Hurricane at Sea. LC 95-12441. (Illus.). 222p. 1995. 32.95 (*1-55750-153-X*) Naval Inst Pr.

Dawes, Robert C., jt. auth. see Young, Peter S.

Dawes, Robin, ed. see Brother Lawrence.

Dawes, Robyn. House of Cards: Psychology & Psychotherapy Built on Myth. 338p. 1994. 22.95 (*0-02-907205-0*) Free Pr.

Dawes, Robyn M. House of Cards. 352p. 1996. 17.95 (*0-684-83091-4*) S&S Trade.

— Rational Choice in an Uncertain World. 346p. (C). 1988. pap. text 28.00 (*0-15-575215-4*, Pub. by Harcourt Coll Pubs) Harcourt.

Dawes, Rufus R. A Full Blown Yankee of the Iron Brigade: Service with the Sixth Wisconsin Volunteers. LC 98-47486. (Illus.). 368p. 1999. pap. 16.95 (*0-8032-6618-9*, Bison Books) U of Nebr Pr.

— Service with the Sixth Wisconsin Volunteers. 367p. 1996. reprint ed. 35.00 (*0-89029-079-2*) Morningside Bkshop.

D

Dawes, Susan. When Mom's Happy, Everyone's Happy: A Guide for Improving Self-Identity & Relationships. McBride, Kirsten, ed. (Illus.). 180p. 1997. pap. write for info. (*0-9660242-0-6*) Cardinal Hse.
Dawes, Walter A. Bold Challenge. (Illus.). 103p. (Orig.). 1980. pap. 5.95 (*0-938792-14-8*) New Capernaum.
— Christianity Four Thousand Years Before Jesus. Dawes, Kathleen A., ed. (Illus.). 63p. (Orig.). 1982. pap. 4.95 (*0-938792-17-2*) New Capernaum.
— The Ghost of Old Capernaum. (Illus.). 358p. (Orig.). 1980. reprint ed. pap. text 19.95 (*0-938792-00-8*) New Capernaum.
— Hidden Gospel. Dawes, Kathleen A., ed. 175p. (Orig.). 1988. pap. 10.00 (*0-938792-21-0*) New Capernaum.
— Impact: The Religion of the Twenty-First Century. (Illus.). 79p. (Orig.). 1980. pap. text 8.95 (*0-938792-05-9*) New Capernaum.
Dawes, William, jt. auth. see Seidenberg, Robert.
Dawes, William R., Jr., et al. Hardening Semiconductor Components Against Radiation & Temperature. LC 89-8752. (Illus.). 328p. 1990. 109.00 (*0-8155-1212-0*) Noyes.
Dawg, Dinker. On the Other Side of the Rainbow. (Illus.). 128p. 1997. 14.00 (*1-887750-66-5*) Rutledge Bks.
Dawg, Dreamer. Pets Welcome: A Guide to Hotels, Inns & Resorts That Welcome You & Your Pet. 1997. pap. text 14.95 (*1-888820-05-5*) Millennium Calif.
Dawick, John. Pinero: A Theatrical Life. (Illus.). 384p. 1993. 39.95 (*0-87081-302-1*) Univ Pr Colo.
Dawid, Annie. York Ferry. LC 92-53146. 179p. (Orig.). (C). 1992. pap. text 10.95 (*0-943433-10-X*) Cane Hill Pr.
***Dawid, H.** Adaptive Learning by Genetic Algorithms: Analytical Results & Applications to Economic Models. 2nd enl. rev. ed. LC 99-14480. (Illus.). xiv, 200p. 1999. 69.95 (*3-540-65607-3*) Spr-Verlag.
Dawid, Herbert. Adaptive Learning by Genetic Algorithms: Analytical Results & Applications to Economic Models, Vol. 441. LC 96-9861. (Lecture Notes in Economics & Mathematical Systems Ser.). 166p. 1996. pap. 52.00 (*3-540-61513-X*) Spr-Verlag.
Dawidoff, Nicholas. The Catcher Was a Spy: The Mysterious Life of Moe Berg. LC 93-41324. 480p. 1994. 24.00 (*0-679-41566-1*) Pantheon.
— The Catcher Was a Spy: The Mysterious Life of Moe Berg. 1995. pap. 13.00 (*0-679-76289-2*) Vin Bks.
— In the Country of Country. 384p. 1998. pap. 14.00 (*0-375-70082-X*) Vin Bks.
— In the Country of Country: People & Places in American Music. LC 96-34682. 372p. 1997. 25.00 (*0-679-41567-X*) Pantheon.
Dawidoff, Robert. The Education of John Randolph. 352p. 1979. pap. text 6.95 (*0-393-95287-8*) Norton.
— The Genteel Tradition & the Sacred Rage: High Culture vs. Democracy in Adams, James, & Santayana. LC 91-30746. (Cultural Studies of the United States). xxvi, 218p. (C). 1992. text 19.95 (*0-8078-2017-2*) U of NC Pr.
— Making History Matter. LC 99-17037. (Illus.). 304p. 2000. 64.50 (*1-56639-748-0*); pap. 22.95 (*1-56639-749-9*) Temple U Pr.
Dawidoff, Robert, jt. ed. see Sullivan, Thomas Richard.
Dawidoff, Robert, intro. see Santayana, George.
Dawidowicz, L. S., et al, eds. For Max Weinreich on His Seventieth Birthday: Studies in Jewish Language, Literature & Society. 1964. 126.95 (*3-11-000037-7*) Mouton.
Dawidowicz, Lucy, ed. Holocaust Reader. LC 75-33740. pap. 19.95 (*0-87441-236-6*) Behrman.
Dawidowicz, Lucy S. The Golden Tradition: Jewish Life & Thought in Eastern Europe. LC 96-8858. (Modern Jewish History Ser.). 502p. 1996. reprint ed. pap. 17.95 (*0-8156-0423-8*, DAGTP) Syracuse U Pr.
— Holocaust & the Historians. LC 80-29175. (Illus.). 197p. 1981. pap. 15.50 (*0-674-40567-6*) HUP.
— The War Against the Jews, 1933-1945. 512p. 1986. pap. 17.95 (*0-553-34532-X*) Bantam.
Dawidowicz, Lucy S. & Goldstein, Leon J. Politics in a Pluralist Democracy. LC 74-9630. 100p. 1974. reprint ed. lib. bdg. 59.75 (*0-8371-7599-2*, DAPD, Greenwood Pr) Greenwood.
***Dawidowski, Christian.** Die geschwachte Moderne: Robert Musils episches Fruhwerk im Spiegel der Epochendebatte. 2000. 47.95 (*3-631-35980-2*) P Lang Pubng.
Dawids, Steen, ed. Polymers: Their Properties & Blood Compatibility. (Developments in Hematology & Immunology Ser.). (C). 1989. text 251.00 (*0-7923-0491-8*) Kluwer Academic.
— Test Procedures for the Blood Compatibility of Biomaterials. LC 92-41726. 1993. text 255.50 (*0-7923-2107-3*) Kluwer Academic.
Dawids, Steen & Bantjes, A., eds. Blood Compatible Materials & Their Testing. (Developments in Hematology & Immunology Ser.). 1986. text 256.50 (*0-89838-813-9*) Kluwer Academic.
Dawidziak, Mark. The Barter Theatre Story. LC 82-22667. 1982. 8.50 (*0-913239-03-8*) Appalach Consortium.
— Night Stalking: A Twentieth Century Anniversary Kolchak Companion. (Illus.). 160p. (Orig.). 1991. pap. 14.95 (*0-685-50339-9*) Retro Vision.
— The Nightstalker Companion: A 25th Anniversary Tribute. LC 97-67156. (Illus.). 208p. 1997. pap. 17.95 (*0-938817-44-2*) Pomegranate Pr.
Dawis, Carol. Obsessions. (Quantam Leap Ser.: No. 13). 320p. 1997. pap. 6.50 (*1-57297-241-6*) Blvd Books.
Dawis, Rene V. & Fruehling, Rosemary T. Psychology: Realizing Human Potential. 8th ed. LC 94-20886. 1994. text 34.95 (*1-56118-341-5*) Paradigm MN.
— Psychology: Realizing Human Potential. 8th ed. LC 94-20886. 1995. text, teacher ed. 14.00 (*1-56118-343-1*); text, student ed. 12.95 (*1-56118-342-3*) Paradigm MN.
Dawis, Rene V. & Lofquist, Lloyd H. A Psychological Theory of Work Adjustment: An Individual Differences Model & Its Applications. LC 83-23381. (Illus.). 256p. reprint ed. pap. 79.40 (*0-8357-7665-4*, 205699300097) Bks Demand.
Dawis, Rene V., jt. auth. see Lofquist, Lloyd H.
Dawis, Rene V., jt. ed. see Lubinski, David.
Dawisha, Karen. International Politics of Eurasia. 1997. pap. text 199.50 (*1-56324-373-3*) M E Sharpe.
Dawisha, Karen & Parrott, Bruce. Russia & the New States of Eurasia: The Politics of Upheaval. LC 93-20994. 457p. (C). 1994. pap. text 22.95 (*0-521-45895-1*) Cambridge U Pr.
Dawisha, Karen & Parrott, Bruce, eds. Conflict, Cleavage & Change in Central Asia & the Caucasus. (Democratization & Authoritarianism in Post-Communist Societies Ser.: Vol. 4). 441p. (C). 1997. text 64.95 (*0-521-59246-1*) Cambridge U Pr.
— Democratic Changes & Authoritarian Reactions in Russia, Ukraine, Belarus & Moldova. (Democratization & Authoritarianism in Post-Communist Societies Ser.: Vol. 3). 404p. (C). 1997. text 64.95 (*0-521-59245-3*) Cambridge U Pr.
— Politics, Power & the Struggle for Democracy in South-East Europe. (Democratization & Authoritarianism in Post-Communist Societies Ser.: Vol. 2). 492p. (C). 1997. text 64.95 (*0-521-59244-5*) Cambridge U Pr.
Dawkins. Blink Watchmaker Software Evolution for DOS 3.5. 1990. pap. text 23.50 (*0-393-99546-1*) Norton.
Dawkins, Barbara, jt. auth. see Pellegrino, Mark J.
Dawkins, Cecil. The Live Goat. LC 75-138781. 1971. 25.00 (*0-06-010998-X*) Ultramarine Pub.
— The Quiet Enemy. LC 95-14566. 1995. pap. 12.95 (*0-8203-1785-3*) U of Ga Pr.
Dawkins, Cecilia, jt. auth. see Logan, Barbara.
Dawkins, David. Economics, Politics & Education. 142p. (C). 1986. 80.00 (*0-7300-0398-1*, Pub. by Deakin Univ) St Mut.
Dawkins, David, ed. Power & Politics in Education. (Deakin Studies in Education Ser.: No. 6). 220p. 1991. 75.00 (*1-85000-889-2*, Falmer Pr); pap. 34.95 (*1-85000-890-6*, Falmer Pr) Taylor & Francis.
***Dawkins, Dorothy.** Inspirational Poems. 1999. pap. write for info. (*1-58235-304-2*) Watermrk Pr.
Dawkins, H. C. & Field, D. R. A Long-Term Surveillance System for British Woodland Vegetation. 1978. 45.00 (*0-85074-038-X*) St Mut.
Dawkins, H. Colyear & Philip, Michael S. Tropical Moist Forest Silviculture & Management: A History of Success & Failure. LC 97-51764. (A CAB International Publication). 386p. 1998. text 110.00 (*0-85199-255-2*) OUP.
Dawkins, Holly V., ed. see Institute of Medicine, Committee on Technological.
Dawkins, Jane. Letters from Pemberley: The First Year. LC 98-56074. 200p. 1999. pap. 12.00 (*1-893337-00-6*) Chicken Soup.
Dawkins, John, ed. see Granowsky, Alvin.
Dawkins, Keith D., et al. Lecture Notes on Cardiology. 4th ed. (Illus.). 288p. 1997. pap. text 29.95 (*0-86542-864-6*) Blackwell Sci.
Dawkins, Kristin. Gene Wars: The Politics of Biotechnology. LC 96-39684. (Open Media Pamphlet Ser.: Vol. 3). 64p. (Orig.). 1997. pap. 4.95 (*1-888363-48-7*) Seven Stories.
Dawkins, Kristin & Brecher, Jeremy. NAFTA, GATT & the World Trade Organization: The New Rules of Corporate Conquest. (Open Magazine Pamphlet Ser.: No. 29). 21p. 1994. 4.00 (*1-884519-04-0*) Open Media.
Dawkins, Marian S. Through Our Eyes Only? The Search for Animal Consciousness. LC 92-32995. (Illus.). 208p. 1998. reprint ed. text 38.00 (*0-7167-4501-1*) OUP.
— Through Our Eyes Only? The Search for Animal Consciousness. (Illus.). 202p. 1998. reprint ed. pap. text 15.95 (*0-19-850320-2*) OUP.
— Unravelling Animal Behvr. 2nd ed. (C). 1995. pap. text 30.94 (*0-582-21875-6*, Pub. by Addison-Wesley) Longman.
Dawkins, Marian S., jt. auth. see Manning, Aubrey.
***Dawkins, Marvin P. & Kinloch, Graham C.** African American Golfers During the Jim Crow Era. LC 99-34486. 200p. 2000. 49.95 (*0-275-95940-6*) Greenwood.
Dawkins, Mary M., ed. see Pfeiffer, Philip A.
Dawkins, Peter. Zoence - The Science of Life: Discovering the Sacred Spaces of Your Life. LC 98-24636. Orig. Title: Zoence, Science of Life: An Introduction to the Basic Principles & Practice of Zoence. (Illus.). 160p. 1999. pap. 14.95 (*1-57863-042-8*) Weiser.
***Dawkins, Peter, et al, eds.** How Big Business Performs Private Performance & Public Policy. 208p. 2000. pap. 35.00 (*1-86448-867-0*, Pub. by Allen & Unwin Pty) Paul & Co Pubs.
Dawkins, R. M. Modern Greek in Asia Minor. xii, 695p. write for info. (*0-318-70906-6*) G Olms Pubs.
— The Nature of the Cypriot Chronicle of Leontios Makhairas. 32p. 1980. pap. 6.00 (*0-89005-334-0*) Ares.
Dawkins, R. M., ed. see Machairas, Leontios.
Dawkins, Richard. The Blind Watchmaker: Why the Evidence of Evolution Reveals a Universe Without Design. 1988. 18.25 (*0-393-99341-8*) Norton.
— The Blind Watchmaker: Why the Evidence of Evolution Reveals a Universe Without Design. LC 96-229669. 364p. 1996. pap. 14.95 (*0-393-31570-3*) Norton.
— Climbing Mount Improbable. 352p. 1997. pap. 14.95 (*0-393-31682-3*) Norton.
— Growing-Up in the Universe. Date not set. text. write for info. (*0-393-03696-0*) Norton.
— River Out of Eden. 176p. 1996. pap. 13.00 (*0-465-06990-8*) HarpC.
— The Selfish Gene. 2nd ed. 366p. 1990. pap. text 12.95 (*0-19-286092-5*) OUP.
Dawkins, Richard. Unweaving the Rainbow: Science, Delusion & the Appetite for Wonder. 336p. 1998. 26.00 (*0-395-88382-2*) HM.
***Dawkins, Richard.** Unweaving the Rainbow: Science, Delusion & the Appetite for Wonder. (Illus.). 352p. 2000. pap. 14.00 (*0-618-05673-4*, Mariner Bks) HM.
Dawkins, Richard & Dennett, Daniel Clement. The Extended Phenotype: The Long Reach of the Gene. 2nd rev. ed. LC 98-44794. (Popular Science Ser.). 324p. 1999. pap. 16.95 (*0-19-288051-9*) OUP.
Dawkins, Richard & Ridley, Mark. Oxford Surveys in Evolutionary Biology, Vol. 3: 1986. (Illus.). 256p. 1987. 65.00 (*0-19-854199-6*) OUP.
Dawkins, Richard & Ridley, Mark, eds. Oxford Surveys in Evolutionary Biology, Vol. 2: 1985. (Illus.). 232p. 1986. 59.00 (*0-19-854174-0*) OUP.
Dawkins, Richard M. Forty-Five Stories from the Dodekanese. Dorson, Richard M., ed. LC 80-742. (Folklore of the World Ser.). 1981. reprint ed. lib. bdg. 99.95 (*0-405-13308-1*) Ayer.
— Modern Greek in Asia Minor. LC 78-67703. (Folktale Ser.). reprint ed. 49.50 (*0-404-16077-8*) AMS Pr.
Dawkins, Richard M., ed. from GRE. More Greek Folktales. LC 74-9218. 178p. 1974. reprint ed. lib. bdg. 35.00 (*0-8371-7631-X*, DAMGF, Greenwood Pr) Greenwood.
***Dawkins, Terrod.** Coming Apart at the Seams: Biblically Unravelling the Evils of Greek Fraternities & Sororities. 400p. 1999. spiral bd. 12.50 (*0-9674563-0-4*) Reprove Rebuke.
Dawkins, Wayne. Black Journalists: The NABJ Story. LC 92-83827. 208p. (Orig.). 1993. pap. 12.95 (*0-9635720-0-8*) August Pr.
— Black Journalists: The NABJ Story. 2nd expanded rev. ed. LC 96-95514. 288p. (Orig.). 1997. pap. 14.00 (*0-9635720-4-0*) August Pr.
Dawley, Alan. Class & Community: The Industrial Revolution in Lynn. LC 75-29049. (Studies in Urban History). (Illus.). 315p. 1976. 34.00 (*0-674-13390-0*) HUP.
— Class & Community: The Industrial Revolution in Lynn. LC 75-29049. (Studies in Urban History). (Illus.). 315p. 1976. pap. 18.00 (*0-674-13395-1*) HUP.
***Dawley, Alan.** Class & Community: The Industrial Revolution in Lynn. 25th ed. 320p. 2000. pap. 18.95 (*0-674-00431-0*) HUP.
Dawley, Alan. Struggles for Justice: Social Responsibility & the Liberal State. (Illus.). 538p. 1991. text 36.50 (*0-674-84580-3*) Belknap Pr.
— Struggles for Justice: Social Responsibility & the Liberal State. (C). 1991. text 27.95 (*0-685-48479-3*) HUP.
— Struggles for Justice: Social Responsibility & the Liberal State. (Illus.). 576p. (C). 1993. pap. text 17.50 (*0-674-84581-1*) HUP.
Dawley, Alan, jt. ed. see Buhle, Paul.
Dawley, David. A Nation of Lords: The Autobiography of the Vice Lords. 2nd ed. (Illus.). 202p. (C). 1992. pap. text 12.50 (*0-88133-628-9*) Waveland Pr.
Dawley, Donald L. What Auditors Should Know about Data Processing. LC 83-17879. (Research for Business Decisions Ser.: No. 63). (Illus.). 250p. reprint ed. pap. 77.50 (*0-8357-1483-7*, 207037400088) Bks Demand.
Dawley, Gloria, jt. auth. see Dawley, Joseph.
***Dawley, Harold H., Jr.** Friendship: How to Make & Keep Friends. 163p. 2000. reprint ed. pap. 12.95 (*0-9617202-5-5*) Wellness Inst.
Dawley, Harold H., Jr. SmokeFree - How to Stop Smoking in Nine Easy Steps. (Illus.). 127p. (Orig.). 1987. pap. 9.95 (*0-9617202-0-4*) Wellness Inst.
— SmokeFree - Worksite Smoking Control, Discouragement, & Cessation. (Illus.). 90p. (Orig.). 1987. pap. 14.95 (*0-9617202-1-2*) Wellness Inst.
***Dawley, Harold H., Jr. & General, Dale A.** Freedom from Fear: A Guide to Conquering Your Fears & Phobias. 214p. 2000. reprint ed. 12.95 (*0-9617202-7-1*) Wellness Inst.
***Dawley, Harold H., Jr. & Wenrich, W. W.** Achieving Assertive Behavior: A Guide to Assertive Training. 121p. 2000. pap. 12.95 (*0-9617202-8-X*) Wellness Inst.
Dawley, Joseph & Dawley, Gloria. Seeing & Painting the Colors of Nature: An Impressionist's View. (Illus.). 144p. 1993. pap. 18.95 (*0-8230-4762-8*) Watsn-Guptill.
Dawley, Muriel & McLaughlin, Roberta, eds. American Indian Songs. 40p. 1990. pap. 5.50 (*0-7390-0747-5*, 12000) Alfred Pub.
***Dawley, Powel Mills.** The Story of the General Theological Seminary: A Sesquicentennial History. 390p. 1999. pap. 30.00 (*1-57910-306-5*) Wipf & Stock.
Dawley, William G., jt. auth. see Trammell, Mary M.
Dawn, C. Ernest. From Ottomanism to Arabism: Essays on the Origins of Arab Nationlism. LC 72-88953. 224p. reprint ed. pap. 69.50 (*0-608-11705-6*, 202025500016) Bks Demand.
Dawn, Carroll. Nom de Code: Casanova. (Rouge Passion Ser.). (FRE.). 1997. pap. 3.50 (*0-373-37430-5*, 1-37430-5) Harlequin Bks.
Dawn, D. MCQ in Obstetrics Gynecology & Contraception. (C). 1985. 35.00 (*0-7855-4656-1*, Pub. by Current Dist) St Mut.
— Obstetric & Gynecology Oral Practice Handbook. (C). 1984. 45.00 (*0-7855-4657-X*, Pub. by Current Dist) St Mut.
— T. B. of Obstetrics & Neonatology. 12th ed. (C). 1990. 130.00 (*0-7855-4658-8*, Pub. by Current Dist) St Mut.
Dawn, Jesse A. Never Old - The Ultimate Success Story: Secrets of Perpetual Youth, Health & CE Mindpower Revealed. (Illus.). 264p. (Orig.). 1995. pap. 9.95 (*0-9636589-0-5*) Wrld Changing.
***Dawn, Jesse Anson.** The Rejuvenator's Bible: Winning the Anti-Aging Revolution - Working Ways to Create Perpetual Youth Naturally. LC 99-71085. (Illus.). 238p. 1999. pap. write for info. (*0-9636589-1-3*) Wrld Changing.
Dawn, Marion. Gleaning Up! (Continuing Adventures of Timothy Glean Ser.). 38p. (J). (gr. k-3). 1998. pap. 6.95 (*1-885986-02-5*) Glean Pubns.
Dawn, Marva J. I'm Lonely, Lord - How Long? Meditations on the Psalms. LC 98-22492. 256p. 1998. pap. 14.00 (*0-8028-4471-5*) Eerdmans.
— Is It a Lost Cause? Having the Heart of God for the Church's Children. LC 97-17548. 264p. 1997. pap. 16.00 (*0-8028-4373-5*) Eerdmans.
— Joy in Our Weakness: A Gift of Hope from the Book of Revelation. LC 93-45000. 224p. (Orig.). 1994. pap. 10.99 (*0-570-04638-6*, 12-3218) Concordia.
— Keeping the Sabbath Wholly: Ceasing, Resting, Embracing, Feasting. 234p. (Orig.). (C). 1989. pap. 15.00 (*0-8028-0457-8*) Eerdmans.
— Reaching Out Without Dumbing Down: A Theology of Worship for the Turn-of-the-Century Culture. 327p. (Orig.). 1995. pap. 18.00 (*0-8028-4102-3*) Eerdmans.
***Dawn, Marva J.** A Royal Waste of Time: The Splendor of Worshiping God & Being Church for the World. LC 99-19405. 376p. 1999. pap. 18.00 (*0-8028-4586-X*) Eerdmans.
Dawn, Marva J. Sexual Character: Beyond Technique to Intimacy. LC 93-1216. 192p. (Orig.). (C). 1993. pap. 13.00 (*0-8028-0700-3*) Eerdmans.
— To Walk & Not Faint: A Month of Meditations on Isaiah 40. 2nd ed. 202p. 1997. pap. 15.00 (*0-8028-4290-9*) Eerdmans.
— Truly the Community: Romans 12 & How to Be the Church. 319p. 1997. pap. text 16.00 (*0-8028-4466-9*) Eerdmans.
***Dawn, Marva J. & Peterson, Eugene H.** The Unnecessary Pastor: Rediscovering the Call. Santucci, Peter, ed. 144p. 1999. pap. 14.00 (*0-8028-4678-5*) Eerdmans.
— The Unnecessary Pastor: Rediscovering the Call. Santucci, Peter, ed. 260p. 2000. pap. 12.97 (*1-57383-148-4*) Regent College.
Dawn Sign Press Production Staff, ed. Numbering in American Sign Language: Number Signs for Everyone. LC 98-25013. 142p. 1998. pap. text 19.95 (*0-915035-72-3*) Dawn Sign.
***Dawn, Tara.** Illustrated Illusions. 58p. 2000. pap. 7.50 (*0-9655816-9-1*) Wings of Dawn.
Dawnay, Hugh. Polo Vision. rev. ed. 171p. 1990. 90.00 (*0-85131-539-9*, Pub. by J A Allen) Trafalgar.
Dawne, Diana. Venture's Story: Life & Times of a Guide Dog. (Illus.). 304p. 1997. pap. 19.95 (*0-9644857-3-7*) Wrds & Pict Pr.
Dawood, Adel. Introduction to Reinsurance. 200p. 1992. 210.00 (*0-948691-48-4*, Pub. by Witherby & Co) St Mut.
Dawood, M. Yusoff, jt. auth. see Clarke-Pearson, Daniel.
Dawood, N. J. Aladdin & Other Tales from the Arabian Nights. (Puffin Classics). (J). 1996. 9.09 (*0-606-02968-0*, Pub. by Turtleback) Demco.
— Aladdin & Other Tales from the Arabian Nights. (Illus.). 208p. (YA). (gr. 5-9). 1997. pap. 3.99 (*0-14-036782-9*) Viking Penguin.
— Sinbad the Sailor & Other Stories. (Illus.). 224p. (YA). (gr. 5 up). 1997. pap. 3.99 (*0-14-036769-1*) Viking Penguin.
Dawood, N. J., tr. Tales from the Thousand & One Nights. 416p. (C). 1973. pap. 12.95 (*0-14-044289-8*) Viking Penguin.
Dawood, N. J., tr. & intro. see Wyatt, Thomas.
***Daws & Loose.** Child Psychotherapy: A Report from the Tavistock Clinic. (Psychoanalytic Inquiry Ser.: Vol. 19, No. 2). 1999. pap. 20.00 (*0-88163-925-7*) Analytic Pr.
Daws, Dilys & Boston, Mary, eds. The Child Psychotherapist & Problems of Young People. 340p. 1990. reprint ed. pap. text 31.95 (*0-946439-43-5*, Pub. by H Karnac Bks Ltd) Brunner-Mazel.
Daws, Gavan. A Dream of Islands: Voyages of Self Discovery in the South Seas. 320p. 1991. reprint ed. mass mkt. 4.95 (*0-935180-71-0*) Mutual Pub HI.
— Hawaii, the Islands of Life: The Nature Conservancy. LC 88-18238. (Illus.). 156p. 1988. 24.95 (*0-943823-01-3*) Signature HI.
— Hawaii, 1959-1989: The First Thirty Years of the Aloha State with Memorable Photographs from the Honolulu Advertiser. (Illus.). 228p. 1990. 39.95 (*0-935180-64-8*) Mutual Pub HI.
— Holy Man: Father Damien of Molokai. (Illus.). 308p. 1984. reprint ed. pap. 12.95 (*0-8248-0920-3*) UH Pr.
— The Night of the Dolphins. (C). 1982. 45.00 (*0-86828-156-5*, Pub. by Deakin Univ) St Mut.
— Prisoners of the Japanese: POWs of World War II in the Pacific. 1996. pap. 15.00 (*0-688-14370-9*, Quil) HarperTrade.
— Shoal of Time: A History of the Hawaiian Islands. LC 73-92053. 510p. 1974. reprint ed. pap. 12.95 (*0-8248-0324-8*) UH Pr.
Daws, Gavan & Bushnell, O. A. Illustrated Atlas of Hawaii. LC 74-152566. (Illus.). 1970. pap. 9.95 (*0-89610-034-0*) Island Heritage.
Daws, Gavan & Fujita, Marty. Archipelago: Islands of Indonesia: from the Nineteenth-Century Discoveries of Alfred Russel Wallace to the Fate of Forests & Reefs in the Twenty-First Century. LC 99-22769. 254p. 1999. text 45.00 (*0-520-21576-1*, Pub. by U CA Pr) Cal Prin Full Svc.
Daws, Gavan, jt. auth. see Cooper, George.
Daws, Gavan, jt. auth. see Holzman, Jac.
Daws, Ron. Self-Made Olympian. LC 75-20960. (Illus.). 150p. 1978. pap. 3.95 (*0-89037-103-2*); student ed. 5.95 (*0-89037-104-0*) Anderson World.

D

Daws, Sam & Taylor, Paul G., eds. The United Nations Vol. I & II. LC 98-55701. (International Library of Politics & Comparative Government). 1000p. 1999. 224.95 (*1-85521-738-4*, Pub. by Ashgate Pub) Ashgate Pub Co.

Daws, Sam, jt. auth. see Bailey, Sydney.

Dawsey, Cyrus, Jr. Living Water: True Experiences from the Missionary Field. Dawsey, James M., ed. 200p. (Orig.). Date not set. pap. 11.95 (*0-89896-160-2*) Larksdale.

Dawsey, Cyrus B. Confederados: Old South Immigrants in Brazil. 288p. 1998. pap. text 19.95 (*0-8173-0944-6*) U of Ala Pr.

Dawsey, Darrell. Living to Tell about It: Young Black Men in America Speak. 368p. 1997. pap. 12.95 (*0-385-47314-1*, Anchor NY) Doubleday.

Dawsey, Jack. 21st Century: A Philosophical View of the Millennium. Orig. Title: Israel: The 21st Century. 328p. (Orig.). 1995. pap. 13.95 (*0-9640579-0-5*) J H Dawsey.

Dawsey, James. A Scholar's Guide to Academic Journals in Religion. LC 88-18104. (American Theological Library Association Monograph). 316p. 1989. 34.50 (*0-8108-2135-4*) Scarecrow.

Dawsey, James, jt. auth. see Andelson, Robert V.

Dawsey, James M. The Lukan Voice: Confusion & Irony in the Gospel of Luke. LC 86-19173. 208p. 1986. 24.95 (*0-86554-193-0*, MUP-H178) Mercer Univ Pr.

Dawsey, James M., ed. see Dawsey, Cyrus, Jr.

Dawson. Academic Survival Kit: Batteries not Included! 456p. (C). 1997. per. 52.95 (*0-7872-4285-3*, 41428501) Kendall-Hunt.

— Basic & Clinical Biostats. 3rd ed. 1999. pap. text 36.95 (*0-8385-0510-4*) Appleton & Lange.

— Black Visions. 1997. 27.50 (*0-226-13860-7*) U Ch Pr.

— Dicho Y Hecho Beginning Spanish. 5th ed. 17p. 1997. pap. text 25.00 (*0-471-25305-7*) Wiley.

— Dicho y Hecho. 5th ed. (SPA.). 336p. 1997. pap. text, wbk. ed. 24.00 (*0-471-14017-1*) Wiley.

— Dicho y Hecho 5th ed. 912p. 1997. text, wbk. ed. 104.00 incl. audio (*0-471-18428-4*) Wiley.

— Dicho y Hecho: Beginning Spanish. 5th annot. ed. 1997. pap. text, teacher ed. 25.00 (*0-471-16116-0*) Wiley.

***Dawson.** Dicho y Hecho: Beginning Spanish. 6th ed. 624p. (C). 2000. write for info. (*0-471-32353-5*) Wiley.

Dawson. Dicho y Hecho: Pronunciation. 5th ed. (SPA.). 525p. 1996. pap. text 56.00 incl. audio (*0-471-16225-6*) Wiley.

Dawson. Dicho y Hecho Beginning Spanish Annotated. 5th ed. 576p. 1997. text, teacher ed. 69.95 (*0-471-15860-7*) Wiley.

— Dicho y Hecho Student Text. 5th ed. 560p. 1997. text 81.95 incl. audio compact disk (*0-471-17722-9*) Wiley.

— Hecho. 5th ed. 867p. 1998. text, wbk. ed. 78.00 incl. cd-rom (*0-471-31679-2*) Wiley.

Dawson. Law Today. 1994. pap. text. write for info. (*0-582-05635-7*, Pub. by Addison-Wesley) Longman.

— Lymphokines & Interleukins. 1991. 109.00 (*0-8493-7103-1*, QR185) CRC Pr.

— Science Teaching in the Secondary School. 1994. pap. text. write for info. (*0-582-80129-X*, Pub. by Addison-Wesley) Longman.

— Supplementary Grammar 2. 1988. pap. text. write for info. (*0-582-01406-9*, Pub. by Addison-Wesley) Longman.

— Total Quality & Customer Satisfaction. (C). 1996. pap. text. write for info. (*0-03-098225-1*) Harcourt Coll Pubs.

Dawson. Young People at Leisure. 56.95 (*1-84014-165-4*) Ashgate Pub Co.

Dawson, jt. auth. see Dix.

Dawson, Adele. Herbs - Partners in Life: A Guide to Cooking, Gardening, & Healing with Wild & Cultivated Plants. (Illus.). 288p. 1991. reprint ed. pap. 12.95 (*0-89281-429-2*, Heal Arts VT) Inner Tradit.

***Dawson, Adele G.** Herbs: Partners in Life. (Illus.). 304p. 2000. reprint ed. pap. 16.95 (*0-89281-934-0*) Inner Tradit.

Dawson, Aileen. Bernard Moore. (Illus.). 116p. 1982. pap. 40.00 (*0-903685-12-4*, Pub. by R Dennis) Antique Collect.

***Dawson, Aileen.** Portrait Sculpture in the British Museum: A Catalogue. (Illus.). 240p. 1999. 150.00 (*0-7141-0598-8*, Pub. by British Mus Pr) Antique Collect.

Dawson, Alain H., ed. see Overstreet, Kris.

Dawson, Alain H., ed. see Seabolt, Gene.

Dawson, Alain H., ed. see Stoddard, Bill.

Dawson, Alan. The Official Lite History & Cookbook of the Vietnam War. (Illus.). 160p. 1989. reprint ed. pap. 6.95 (*0-9623992-2-1*) Electric Strawberry.

— The Official Vietnam War Trivia Book. (Illus.). 130p. 1989. pap. 5.95 (*0-9623992-0-5*) Electric Strawberry.

Dawson, Alastair G. Ice Age Earth: Late Quaternary Geology & Climate. (Physical Environment Ser.). (Illus.). 320p. (C). 1991. pap. 29.99 (*0-415-01567-7*, A6545) Routledge.

Dawson, Albert C. & Dawson, Laila M. Vida: Experiencia y Expresion. LC 88-32985. 292p. 1989. pap. 48.95 (*0-471-62402-0*) Wiley.

— Vida: Experiencia y Expresion. Ep. 1989. cd-rom 56.95 (*0-471-50245-6*) Wiley.

Dawson, Albert C., jt. auth. see Dawson, Laila M.

Dawson, Alistair, jt. auth. see Downward, Paul.

***Dawson, Amy.** Weekend Decorator. (Illus.). 192p. 2000. 24.95 (*0-7894-6129-3*) DK Pub Inc.

Dawson, Andre & Bird, Tom. Andre Dawson. (Today's Heroes Ser.). 112p. 1994. pap. 4.99 (*0-310-41181-5*) Zondervan.

Dawson, Andrea, et al. Albania: A Guide & Illustrated Journal. 2nd ed. LC 95-4995. (Bradt Guides Ser.). (Illus.). 216p. 1995. pap. 14.95 (*1-56440-697-0*, Pub. by Bradt Pubns) Globe Pequot.

Dawson, Andrew. The Birth & Impact of the Base Ecclesial Community & Liberative Theological Discourse in Brazil. LC 98-20482. 280p. 1998. pap. 54.95 (*1-57309-314-9*, Cath Scholar Pr) Intl Scholars.

Dawson, Andrew, jt. ed. see Rapport, Nigel.

Dawson, Andrew H. The Land Problem in the Developed Economy. LC 83-24360. 280p. 1984. 50.00 (*0-389-20456-0*, N8017) B&N Imports.

Dawson, Andrew R., jt. auth. see Jones, Ron.

Dawson, Andy, jt. auth. see Culbert, Tom.

Dawson, Anne, jt. auth. see Dawson, Mark.

Dawson, Anthony. Two Faces Economics. 280p. (C). 1996. pap. text 23.50 (*0-582-27451-6*, Pub. by Addison-Wesley) Longman.

Dawson, Anthony B. Hamlet. (Illus.). 261p. 1997. pap. 22.95 (*0-7190-4625-4*) St Martin.

— Indirections: Shakespeare & the Art of Illusion. LC 78-6016. 210p. reprint ed. pap. 65.10 (*0-608-15397-4*, 202932800060) Bks Demand.

Dawson, Anthony B. Tamburlaine: Parts One & Two. 2nd ed. 1997. pap. 8.00 (*0-393-90079-7*) Norton.

Dawson, Arthur. The Stories Behind Sonoma Valley Place Names: From Arrowhead Mountain to Yulupa LC 97-76375. ix, 54p. 1998. write for info. (*0-9661867-4-5*) Kulupi Pr.

Dawson, Atieen. Eighteenth Century French Porcelain. (Illus.). 80p. 1997. 19.95 (*1-85444-075-6*, 0764, Pub. by Ashmolean Mus); pap. 12.95 (*1-85444-076-4*, 0756, Pub. by Ashmolean Mus) A Schwartz & Co.

Dawson, B. M., et al, eds. Image Processing Algorithms & Techniques III. 1992. 20.00 (*0-8194-0811-5*, 1659) SPIE.

Dawson-Balman, Jean. The Gray Divorcee. (Illus.). 110p. 1986. 9.95 (*0-9617725-0-6*) Jeanne d'Art.

Dawson, Barbara, ed. Direct-Reading Colorimetric Indicator Tubes Manual. 2nd ed. (Illus.). 65p. (C). 1993. pap. 28.00 (*0-932627-53-6*, 175-SI-93) Am Indus Hygiene.

Dawson, Barbara J., et al. A Finding Aid to the Esther McCoy Papers. LC 93-72457. vii, 33 p. 1993. write for info. (*1-880193-06-X*) Arch Am Art.

Dawson, Barry. Street Graphics India. LC 98-61183. (Illus.). 112p. 1999. pap. 19.95 (*0-500-28095-9*, Pub. by Thames Hudson) Norton.

Dawson, Beth D. & Trapp, Robert G. Basic & Clinical Biostatistics. 2nd ed. (Illus.). 344p. (C). 1994. pap. text 36.95 (*0-8385-0542-2*, A0542-9, Apple Lange Med) McGraw.

Dawson, Bonnie. Women's Films in Print: An Annotated Guide to Eight Hundred Films Made by Women. LC 74-80642. 1975. pap. 10.00 (*0-912932-02-3*) Booklegger Pubng.

Dawson, Bruce. The Solution Group. LC 93-8758. 190p. (Orig.). 1993. pap. 12.00 (*0-944337-16-3*, 163) New View Pubns.

Dawson, Bruce, jt. auth. see Clay, Roger.

Dawson, Bruce W. UH-1H/V Flight Handbook for U. S. Army Aviators: Study Guide & Quick Reference. rev. ed. Jose, Michael E. & Dawson, Denise C., eds. LC 90-64133. (Illus.). 310p. 1995. 80.00 (*1-878595-00-8*, 1-878595-00-8) Silver Wngs Pubs.

***Dawson, Buck.** Mermaids on Parade: America's Love Affair with It's First Olympic Swimmers. (Illus.). 2000. 23.95 (*1-56072-726-8*, Nova Kroshka Bks) Nova Sci Pubs.

Dawson, Buck. Saga of the All American. 400p. 1991. 27.95 (*1-880236-03-6*) Hoffman FL.

— Stand up & Hook Up. 185p. 1990. 21.95 (*1-880236-01-X*) Hoffman FL.

— When the Earth Explodes! Volcanos & the Environment. LC 97-36650. (Illus.). 200p. 1998. pap. 17.95 (*1-56072-450-1*, Nova Kroshka Bks) Nova Sci Pubs.

Dawson, C., et al. Guide to Trachoma Control. (Nonserial Publication). 56p. 1981. pap. text 9.00 (*92-4-154157-1*, 1150066) World Health.

Dawson, C. C. A Collection of Family Records with Biographical Sketches & Other Memoranda of Those Bearing the Name Dawson. (Illus.). 572p. 1989. reprint ed. pap. 87.00 (*0-8328-0463-0*); reprint ed. lib. bdg. 97.00 (*0-8328-0462-2*) Higginson Bk Co.

Dawson, C. E. Indo-Pacific Pipefishes: Red Sea to the Americas. LC 84-48414. (Illus.). 230p. 1985. 48.00 (*0-917235-00-2*) Gulf Coast Lab.

Dawson, Canon. Heroines of Missionary Adventures, 1. (J). 1979. pap. 4.99 (*0-88019-039-6*) Schmul Pub Co.

— Heroines of Missionary Adventures, 2. (J). 1979. pap. 4.99 (*0-88019-040-X*) Schmul Pub Co.

Dawson, Carl. Lafcadio Hearn & the Vision of Japan. LC 91-44785. (Parallax Ser.). (Illus.). 213p. 1992. reprint ed. pap. 66.10 (*0-608-06705-9*, 206690200009) Bks Demand.

— Living Backwards: A Transatlantic Memoir. 224p. (C). 1995. 24.95 (*0-8139-1633-X*) U Pr of Va.

— November, 1948: A Memoir. 176p. 1990. text 20.00 (*0-8139-1258-X*) U Pr of Va.

— Prophets of Past Time: Seven British Autobiographers, 1880-1914. LC 87-30025. 280p. 1988. reprint ed. pap. 86.80 (*0-608-03725-7*, 206455000009) Bks Demand.

— Victorian Noon: English Literature in 1850. LC 78-13939. 288p. 1979. reprint ed. pap. 89.30 (*0-608-03680-3*, 206450600009) Bks Demand.

Dawson, Carley, tr. see Poulet, Georges.

Dawson, Carol. Body of Knowledge. LC 94-13355. 480p. 1994. 22.95 (*1-56512-054-X*) Algonquin Bks.

— Body of Knowledge. 480p. 1996. pap. 12.00 (*0-671-53572-2*, WSP) PB.

— Meeting the Minotaur. LC 97-4032. 444p. 1997. 22.95 (*1-56512-126-0*, 72126) Algonquin Bks.

— The Mother-in-Law Diaries. LC 98-27774. 294p. 1999. 19.95 (*1-56512-127-9*) Algonquin Bks.

***Dawson, Carol.** The Mother-in-Law Diaries. LC 99-52912. 288p. 2000. reprint ed. per. 12.95 (*0-671-04085-5*, WSP) PB.

Dawson, Charlie K. The Complete Guide to Technical Recruiting. LC 98-89535. 275p. 1999. ring bd. 49.95 (*1-879876-09-4*, 30401) Mgmt Advantage.

— Internal Recruiter's Guide to Successful Technical Recruiting. LC 99-60317. 195p. 1999. spiral bd. 49.95 (*1-879876-10-8*, 30402) Mgmt Advantage.

***Dawson, Charlie K.** Technical Recruiting Success for IT Firms. 220p. 1999. ring bd. 49.95 (*1-879876-11-6*) Mgmt Advantage.

Dawson, Chris. Due North of Montana: A Guide to Flyfishing in Alberta. LC 96-31156. (Illus.). 192p. (Orig.). 1996. pap. 16.95 (*1-55566-180-7*, Sprng Creek Pr) Johnson Bks.

Dawson, Chris, tr. see Gadamer, Hans-Georg.

***Dawson, Christian W.** The Essence of Computing Projects. LC 99-29612. 2000. write for info. (*0-13-021972-X*) P-H.

Dawson, Christopher. Christianity & European Culture: Selections from the Work of Christopher Dawson. Russello, Gerald J., ed. LC 97-38951. 272p. (C). 1998. pap. text 24.95 (*0-8132-0914-5*) Cath U Pr.

— Christianity in East & West. Mulloy, John J., ed. 224p. 1981. pap. 8.95 (*0-89385-015-2*) Sugden.

— Crisis of Western Education. 204p. 1989. 12.95 (*0-940535-27-0*, UP127) Franciscan U Pr.

— Dynamics of World History. Mulloy, John J., ed. 509p. 1978. pap. 12.95 (*0-89385-003-9*) Sugden.

— Historic Reality of Christian Culture: A Way to the Renewal of Human Life. 1960. 49.50 (*0-614-00056-4*) Elliots Bks.

— Mission to Asia. (Medieval Academy Reprints for Teaching Ser.). 228p. 1981. reprint ed. pap. text 13.95 (*0-8020-6436-1*) U of Toronto Pr.

— Progress & Religion. 287p. 1991. pap. 12.95 (*0-89385-038-1*) Sugden.

Dawson, Christopher H. Beyond Politics. LC 74-111825. (Essay Index Reprint Ser.). 1977. 17.95 (*0-8369-1603-4*) Ayer.

— Enquiries into Religion & Culture. LC 68-29200. (Essay Index Reprint Ser.). 1977. 20.95 (*0-8369-0367-6*) Ayer.

— Medieval Essays. LC 68-58785. (Essay Index Reprint Ser.). 1977. 20.95 (*0-8369-0070-7*) Ayer.

— Progress & Religion, an Historical Enquiry. LC 79-104266. 254p. 1970. reprint ed. lib. bdg. 38.50 (*0-8371-3917-1*, DAPR, Greenwood Pr) Greenwood.

— Religion & Culture. LC 77-27183. (Gifford Lectures: 1947). 232p. reprint ed. 35.00 (*0-404-60498-6*) AMS Pr.

— Religion & the Rise of Western Culture. LC 77-27181. (Gifford Lectures: 1948-49). reprint ed. 46.50 (*0-404-60499-4*) AMS Pr.

— Religion & Western. 240p. 1991. pap. 12.50 (*0-385-42110-9*) Doubleday.

— The Spirit of the Oxford Movement. LC 75-30020. reprint ed. 34.50 (*0-404-14025-4*) AMS Pr.

Dawson, Christopher H., ed. The Mongol Mission. LC 78-63334. (Crusades & Military Orders Ser.: Second Series). reprint ed. 44.00 (*0-404-17008-0*) AMS Pr.

Dawson, Clarence W. Return of Montezuma: A Novel. LC 91-29139. 128p. (Orig.). 1991. pap. 10.95 (*0-86534-162-1*) Sunstone Pr.

Dawson, Clayton L. Modern Russian 2. LC 77-5837. (ENG & RUS.). 183p. 1986. reprint ed. pap., wbk. ed. 56.80 (*0-608-04094-0*, 206482600011) Bks Demand.

Dawson, Clayton L. & Humesky, Assya. Modern Russian 2. LC 77-5837. (ENG & RUS.). 493p. 1965. reprint ed. pap. 152.90 (*0-608-04093-2*, 206482500002) Bks Demand.

Dawson, Clayton L., et al. Modern Russian I, 24 cass. 480p. pap. text 255.00 incl. audio (*0-88432-044-8*, AFB101) Audio-Forum.

— Modern Russian II. 479p. pap. text 255.00 incl. audio (*0-88432-056-1*, AFB125) Audio-Forum.

Dawson, Connie & Clarke, Jean I. Growing up Again: Parenting Ourselves, Parenting Our Children. 2nd ed. LC 97-48978. (Illus.). 250p. (Orig.). 1998. reprint ed. pap. 14.95 (*1-56838-190-5*) Hazelden.

Dawson, D. & Gartner, J. Large Deviations, Free Energy Functional & Quasi-Potential for a Mean Field Model of Interacting Diffusions. LC 89-164. (Memoirs Ser.: Vol. 78/398). 94p. 1989. pap. 16.00 (*0-8218-2461-9*, MEMO/78/398) Am Math.

Dawson, D. A., ed. Measure-Valued Processes, Stochastic Partial Differential Equations, & Interacting Systems. LC 93-48193. (CRM Proceedings & Lecture Notes Ser.: Vol. 5). 241p. 1994. pap. 59.00 (*0-8218-6992-2*, CRMP/5) Am Math.

Dawson, D. M., et al. Nonlinear Control of Electric Machinery. LC 98-14952. (Illus.). 464p. 1998. text 175.00 (*0-8247-0180-1*) Dekker.

Dawson, Daniel. The Mexican Adventure. 1976. lib. bdg. 59.95 (*0-8490-2232-0*) Gordon Pr.

— The Mexican Adventure. (Select Bibliographies Reprint Ser.). 1977. reprint ed. 29.95 (*0-8369-6682-1*) Ayer.

Dawson, Darren M., jt. auth. see Qu, Zhihua.

Dawson, David. Allegorical Readers & Cultural Revision in Ancient Alexandria. LC 91-2851. (C). 1992. 55.00 (*0-520-07102-6*, Pub. by U CA Pr) Cal Prin Full Svc.

— Equipping the Saints: 8 Weeks Training for New Believers - Chinese Edition. Cac, Ting W., tr. (CHI.). 116p. 1992. ring bd. 10.00 (*1-56582-049-5*) Christ Renew Min.

— Equipping the Saints No. 1: Chinese Edition. CRM Staff, tr. (CHI.). 242p. 1999. pap. 24.00 (*1-56582-035-5*) Christ Renew Min.

— Equipping the Saints No. 2: Chinese Edition. CRM Staff, tr. (CHI.). 254p. 1990. pap. 24.00 (*1-56582-036-3*) Christ Renew Min.

— Equipping the Saints No. 3: Chinese Edition. CRM Staff, tr. (CHI.). 313p. 1999. pap. 24.00 (*1-56582-037-1*) Christ Renew Min.

— Equipping the Saints No. 4: Chinese Edition. CRM Staff, tr. (CHI.). 262p. 1999. pap. 24.00 (*1-56582-038-X*) Christ Renew Min.

— How to Share Your Testimony Effectively - Chinese Edition. Leung, John, tr. (CHI.). 41p. 1995. pap. 3.00 (*1-56582-040-1*) Christ Renew Min.

— Literary Theory. LC 95-5492. (Guides to Theological Inquiry Ser.). 128p. 1995. pap. 14.00 (*0-8006-2693-1*, 1-2693, Fortress Pr) Augsburg Fortress.

— Survey of the Bible: Chinese Edition. Leung, John, tr. (CHI.). 58p. 1989. pap. 11.50 (*1-56582-030-4*) Christ Renew Min.

Dawson, David, et al. Schizophrenia in Focus: Guidelines for Treatment & Rehabilitation. 190p. 1983. 32.95 (*0-89885-096-7*, Kluwer Acad Hman Sci) Kluwer Academic.

Dawson, David, ed. see Crockett, Pat.

Dawson, David Allan. Text-Linguistics & Biblical Hebrew. (JSOT Supplement Ser.: No. 177). 242p. 1994. 70.00 (*1-85075-490-X*, Pub. by Sheffield Acad) CUP Services.

Dawson, David B. & Lovejoy, Elizabeth. Memphis: New Visions, New Horizons. LC 96-51739. (Urban Tapestry Ser.). 464p. 1997. 44.95 (*1-881096-38-6*) Towery Pub.

Dawson, David C., ed. see Society of General Physiologists, et al.

***Dawson, David L.** Understanding the Trinity. 160p. 1999. pap. text. write for info. (*1-85240-227-X*) SOV5.

Dawson, David L. & MacMillan, Harriet L. Relationship Management of the Borderline Patient: From Understanding to Treatment. LC 93-18886. (Illus.). 240p. 1993. text 30.95 (*0-87630-714-4*) Brunner-Mazel.

Dawson, David L., jt. auth. see Scott-Conner, Carol E.

Dawson, David M. Entrapment Neuropathies. 2nd ed. 1990. 94.95 (*0-316-17743-1*, Little Brwn Med Div) Lppncott W & W.

Dawson, David M. & Sabin, Thomas D., eds. Chronic Fatigue Syndrome. LC 92-49249. 300p. 1993. 74.95 (*0-316-17748-2*, Little Brwn Med Div) Lppncott W & W.

Dawson, David M., et al. Entrapment Neuropathies. 307p. 1983. 49.50 (*0-316-17742-3*, Little Brwn Med Div) Lppncott W & W.

— Entrapment Neuropathies. 3rd ed. LC 98-25819. 448p. 1998. text 99.00 (*0-316-17733-4*) Lppncott W & W.

Dawson, Debra. Good Thyme Herb Blend Cookbook: A User's Guide. (Illus.). 160p. 1993. pap. write for info. (*0-9635515-1-5*) Good Thyme Pr.

Dawson, Deidre. Voltaire's Correspondence: An Epistolary Novel. LC 92-35301. (Age of Revolution & Romanticism Ser.: Vol. 5). (Illus.). XXI, 190p. (C). 1994. text 52.95 (*0-8204-2116-2*) P Lang Pubng.

Dawson, Denise C., ed. see Dawson, Bruce W.

Dawson, Dinky & Alan, Carter. Life on the Road: The Incredible Rock 'n' Roll Adventures of Dinky Dawson. LC 98-87331. 354p. 1998. pap. 19.95 (*0-8230-8344-6*) Watsn-Guptill.

Dawson, Donald A. Cryptanalysis of the Single Rotor Cipher Machine. (Cryptographic Ser.). (Illus.). 217p. (Orig.). 1996. pap. 38.80 (*0-89412-262-2*, C-73) Aegean Park Pr.

— Large Deviations, Free Energy Functional & Quasi-Potential for a Mean Field Model of Interacting Diffusions. LC 89-164. (American Mathematical Society Ser.: Vol. 398). 100p. reprint ed. pap. 31.00 (*0-608-10512-0*, 205279500009) Bks Demand.

Dawson, Donald A. & Perkins, Edwin A. Historical Processes. LC 91-22744. (Memoirs Ser.). 179p. 1991. pap. 25.00 (*0-8218-2508-9*, MEMO/93/454) Am Math.

Dawson, Doug. Capturing Light & Color with Pastel. (Illus.). 144p. (Orig.). 1995. pap. 22.99 (*0-89134-678-3*, North Lght Bks) F & W Pubns Inc.

Dawson, Doyne. The Origins of Western Warfare: Militarism & Morality in the Ancient World. (History & Warfare Ser.). 216p. (C). 1997. pap. 24.00 (*0-8133-3392-X*, Pub. by Westview) HarpC.

Dawson, E. Matthews. The Hidden Meanings of the World's Greatest Stories. 74p. 1997. reprint ed. 12.95 (*0-7661-0047-2*) Kessinger Pub.

Dawson, E. Y. Marine Red Algae of Pacific Mexico: Ceramiales, Dasyaceae, Rhodomelaceae, Part 8. (Illus.). 1963. pap. 15.00 (*3-7682-0209-7*) Lubrecht & Cramer.

Dawson, E. Yale & Foster, Michael S. Seashore Plants of California. LC 81-19690. (California Natural History Guides Ser.: No. 47). (Illus.). 226p. 1982. pap. 11.95 (*0-520-04139-9*, Pub. by U CA Pr) Cal Prin Full Svc.

Dawson, Ed & Govic, Jovan, eds. Cryptography: Policy & Algorithms: International Conference, Brisbane, Queensland, Australia, July 3-5, 1995 Proceedings. LC 95-51353. (Lecture Notes in Computer Science Ser.: Vol. 1029). 327p. 1996. pap. 56.00 (*3-540-60759-5*) Spr-Verlag.

Dawson, Elizabeth. The Bending Reed. large type ed. (Linford Romance Library). 336p. 1985. pap. 16.99 (*0-7089-6062-6*, Linford) Ulverscroft.

Dawson, Elmer J., jt. auth. see Schenck, W. Egbert.

Dawson, Fielding. The Black Mountain Book: A New Edition. LC 90-62149. (Illus.). 256p. 1991. reprint ed. pap. 15.95 (*0-933598-20-3*) NC Wesleyan Pr.

— Delayed: Not Postponed. Owen, Maureen, ed. LC 77-21162. 1978. pap. 6.00 (*0-916382-17-6*) Telephone Bks.

— Krazy Kat & Seventy-Six More: Collected Stories, 1950-1976. LC 82-14641. 378p. (C). 1982. 17.50 (*0-87685-564-8*); pap. 12.50 (*0-87685-563-X*) Black Sparrow.

— Krazy Kat & Seventy-Six More: Collected Stories, 1950-1976. deluxe ed. LC 82-14641. 378p. (C). 1982. 25.00 (*0-87685-565-6*) Black Sparrow.

— The Orange in the Orange: A Novella & Two Stories. LC 94-45314. 172p. (C). 1994. 25.00 (*0-87685-963-5*); pap. 13.50 (*0-87685-962-7*) Black Sparrow.

— Three Penny Lane. LC 80-27344. 150p. (Orig.). 1981. pap. 5.00 (*0-87685-446-3*) Black Sparrow.

D

An Asterisk (*) at the beginning of an entry indicates that the title is appearing for the first time.

— Three Penny Lane. deluxe ed. LC 80-27344. 150p. (Orig.). 1981. 20.00 (*0-87685-447-1*) Black Sparrow.
— Tiger Lilies: An American Childhood. LC 84-4170. vi, 213p. 1984. text 32.95 (*0-8223-0593-3*) Duke.
— The Trick: New Stories. LC 90-23890. (Illus.). 160p. 1991. 25.00 (*0-87685-819-1*); pap. 12.50 (*0-87685-818-3*) Black Sparrow.
— Two Stories by Fielding Dawson. (Illus.). 16p. 1996. pap. 3.00 (*1-885710-18-6*) Geekspeak Unique.
— Virginia Dare: Stories 1976-1981. LC 84-18573. (Illus.). 178p. 1985. 14.00 (*0-87685-618-0*); pap. 10.00 (*0-87685-617-2*) Black Sparrow.
— Will She Understand? New Short Stories. LC 88-2450. (Illus.). 158p. (Orig.). 1988. 20.00 (*0-87685-730-6*) Black Sparrow.
— Will She Understand? New Short Stories. LC 88-2450. (Illus.). 158p. (Orig.). 1988. pap. 10.00 (*0-87685-729-2*) Black Sparrow.
— Will She Understand? New Short Stories, signed ed. deluxe ed. LC 88-2450. (Illus.). 158p. (Orig.). 1988. 30.00 (*0-87685-731-4*) Black Sparrow.
Dawson, Fielding, et al. PlopLop No. 8: An "Antholozine" of Poetry, Prose & Artwork. Andis, Kitrell, ed. (Illus.). 35p. 1996. pap. 5.00 (*1-885710-15-1*) Geekspeak Unique.
Dawson, Frances E., tr. see Steiner, Rudolf.
Dawson, Francis W. Reminiscences of Confederate Service, 1861-1865. LC 79-26720. 214p. 1993. pap. 11.95 (*0-8071-1885-0*) La State U Pr.
Dawson, Frank G. The First Latin American Debt Crisis: The City of London & the 1822-1825 Loan Bubble. 320p. (C). 1990. 40.00 (*0-300-04727-4*) Yale U Pr.
Dawson, Frank G. & Head, Ivan L. International Law, National Tribunals & the Rights of Aliens. LC 76-155828. xvi, 334p. 1976. 45.00 (*0-8156-2152-3*, 306530) W S Hein.
***Dawson, Gary Fisher.** Documentary Theatre in the United States: An Historical Survey & Analysis of Its Content, Form & Stagecraft, 89. LC 98-44418. (Contributions in Drama & Theatre Studies: Vol. 89). 272p. 1999. 65.00 (*0-313-30449-1*) Greenwood.
Dawson, Gaynor W. & Mercer, Basil W. Hazardous Waste Management. LC 85-9313. 532p. 1986. 170.00 (*0-471-82268-X*) Wiley.
Dawson, George. Pleasure of Angling with Rod & Reel. 264p. 45.00 (*1-56416-120-X*) Derrydale Pr.
Dawson, George & Glaubman, Richard. Life Is So Good. LC 99-48834. 288p. 2000. 23.00 (*0-375-50396-X*) Random.
***Dawson, George & Glaubman, Richard.** Life Is So Good. 2000. write for info. (*0-375-75604-3*) Random.
Dawson, George C., jt. auth. see Gordon, Sanford D.
Dawson, George G. Healing: Pagan & Christian. LC 75-23704. reprint ed. 42.50 (*0-404-13256-1*) AMS Pr.
Dawson, George G., jt. auth. see Gordon, Sanford D.
Dawson, George M. Borrowing to Build Your Business: Getting Your Banker to Say "Yes" LC 97-9646. 144p. 1997. pap. 16.95 (*1-57410-073-4*, 6100-0902) Dearborn.
Dawson, George M., ed. see Georgetown Publishing House, Inc. Staff.
Dawson, Geraldine, ed. Autism: Nature, Diagnosis, & Treatment. LC 88-16356. 417p. 1989. lib. bdg. 52.00 (*0-89862-724-9*) Guilford Pubns.
Dawson, Geraldine & Fischer, Kurt W., eds. Human Behavior & the Developing Brain. LC 93-36030. 568p. 1994. lib. bdg. 65.00 (*0-89862-092-9*) Guilford Pubns.
***Dawson, Geralyn.** The Bad Luck Wedding Cake. 1998. per. 6.50 (*0-671-01517-6*) PB.
Dawson, Geralyn. The Kissing Stars. 392p. 1999. mass mkt. 6.50 (*0-671-01518-4*, Pocket Star Bks) PB.
— Simmer All Night. 406p. 1999. per. 6.50 (*0-671-03410-3*) S&S Trade.
***Dawson, Geralyn.** Sizzle All Day. 368p. 2000. mass mkt. 6.50 (*0-671-03448-0*, Sonnet Bks) PB.
Dawson, Geralyn. The Wedding Raffle. 1996. mass mkt. 5.99 (*0-671-00126-4*) PB.
— The Wedding Raffle. 1998. per. 3.99 (*0-671-02574-0*) PB.
— The Wedding Ransom. 1998. per. 6.50 (*0-671-00127-2*) PB.
Dawson, Gerrit. Heartfelt: Finding Our Way Back to God. LC 93-60482. 168p. 1993. pap. 10.00 (*0-8358-0684-7*) Upper Room Bks.
Dawson, Gerrit S. Love Bade Me Welcome: Daily Readings with George Herbert. LC 97-92692. 249p. 1997. 16.00 (*0-9660973-1-9*) Glen Lorien Bks.
— Writing on the Heart: Inviting Scripture to Shape Daily Life. LC 94-61265. 160p. 1995. pap. 10.00 (*0-8358-0713-4*) Upper Room Bks.
Dawson, Gerrit Scott. Heartfelt. 1993. 9.95 (*0-687-60464-8*) Abingdon.
— Writing on the Heart. 1995. pap. 9.95 (*0-687-61442-2*) Abingdon.
Dawson, Glenn E. Explosive Growth: How to Create Task-Oriented Growth Plans for Your Business. LC 94-61373. 132p. (Orig.). 1995. pap. 21.95 (*0-9643938-0-8*) SRG Pubns.
Dawson, Graham. Inflation & Unemployment: Causes, Consequences & Cures. 224p. 1992. 95.00 (*1-85278-119-X*) E Elgar.
— Inflation & Unemployment: Causes, Consequences & Cures. 224p. 1994. pap. 25.00 (*1-85278-658-2*) E Elgar.
— Soldier Heros: British Adventure, Empire, & the Imagining of Masculinity. LC 94-1523. (Illus.). 360p. (C). 1994. pap. 29.99 (*0-415-08882-8*, B2265) Routledge.
***Dawson, Graham & Watson-Brown, Linda.** Market, State & Feminism: The Economics of Feminist Policy. 240p. 2000. write for info. (*1-85898-231-6*) E Elgar.
Dawson, Gregory, jt. auth. see Conradt, Mark.
Dawson, H. B. New York City During the American Revolution. 1972. 59.95 (*0-8490-0727-5*) Gordon Pr.
Dawson, Hal, ed. see Garrett, Charles.
Dawson, Hal, ed. see Garrett, Charles, et al.
Dawson, Hal, ed. see Lagal, Roy.
Dawson, Hal, ed. see Marx, Jenifer.
Dawson, Hal, ed. see Marx, Robert.
Dawson, Helen, jt. auth. see Dunn, Seamus.
Dawson, Helen D. Contraceptives - Oral & Combinations: Index of New Information. 160p. Date not set. 47.50 (*0-7883-1928-0*); pap. 44.50 (*0-7883-1929-9*) ABBE Pubs Assn.
— Contraceptives-Postcoital & the Morning after Pill: Index of New Information. 160p. Date not set. 47.50 (*0-7883-1926-4*); pap. 744.50 (*0-7883-1927-2*) ABBE Pubs Assn.
Dawson, Henry B. Sons of Liberty in New York. LC 71-90172. (Mass Violence in America Ser.). 1975. reprint ed. 13.95 (*0-405-01306-X*) Ayer.
— Westchester County During the American Revolution. (Illus.). 281p. 1997. reprint ed. lib. bdg. 35.00 (*0-8328-6277-0*) Higginson Bk Co.
Dawson-Holt, Hannelore, tr. see Pauli, Eugen.
Dawson-Holt, Hannelore, tr. see Pauli, Philip.
Dawson, I. J. & Stephenson, I. S. Protection of Minority Shareholders. 150p. 1993. 120.00 (*0-85459-816-2*, Pub. by Tolley Pubng) St Mut.
Dawson, Ian K. Findhorn Railway. (C). 1985. 65.00 (*0-85361-284-6*) St Mut.
Dawson, Ibert C., jt. auth. see Dawson, Laila M.
Dawson, Imogen. Clothes & Crafts in the Middle Ages. LC 97-8326. (J). 1998. 22.00 (*0-382-39699-5*, Dillon Silver Burdett); pap. write for info. (*0-382-39700-2*, Dillon Silver Burdett) Silver Burdett Pr.
— Food & Feasts with the Aztecs. (Food & Feasts Ser.). (Illus.). (YA). (gr. 6 up). 1995. pap. 7.95 (*0-382-24977-1*, New Dscvry Bks) Silver Burdett Pr.
— In Aztec Times. LC 96-27291. (Clothes & Crafts Ser.). (J). 1997. pap. 7.95 (*0-382-39696-0*, Dillon Silver Burdett); lib. bdg. 14.95 (*0-382-39695-2*, Dillon Silver Burdett) Silver Burdett Pr.
— In the Middle Ages. LC 93-27200. (Food & Feasts Ser.). (Illus.). 32p. (YA). (gr. 6 up). 1994. lib. bdg. 14.95 (*0-02-726324-X*, New Dscvry Bks) Silver Burdett Pr.
— In the Middle Ages. 32p. 1996. pap. text 7.95 (*0-382-39571-9*) Silver Burdett Pr.
Dawson, Imogene. American Indian Food: Sixty-One Indian Recipes. 25p. (Orig.). 1993. pap. 4.95 (*0-9633533-2-2*) Holitopa.
— Indian Food for the Body, Food for the Soul: Truly, a Book of Art. (Illus.). 276p. (C). 1992. 26.95 (*0-9633533-0-6*) Holitopa.
— Indian Leaves, Lovers, Loneliness: Losing Their Heritage. (Illus.). 55p. 1980. per. 12.95 (*0-9633533-5-7*) Holitopa.
Dawson, Imogene, compiled by. Chata, Choctaw Hymn Book: Uba Isht Taloa Holissa. (CHO., Illus.). 224p. 1990. pap. 7.00 (*0-9633533-1-4*) Holitopa.
Dawson, J., jt. auth. see Moir, C. B.
Dawson, J. A., et al, eds. Progress in Marketing. 224p. 1989. 39.00 (*0-86187-961-9*) St Martin.
Dawson, J. B. Kimberlites & Their Xenoliths. (Minerals & Rocks Ser.: Vol. 15). (Illus.). 252p. 1980. 86.95 (*0-387-10208-6*) Spr-Verlag.
Dawson, J. Brian. Moon Cakes in Gold Mountain: From China to the Canadian Plains. (Illus.). 256p. (Orig.). 1991. pap. 19.95 (*1-55059-026-X*) Temeron Bks.
Dawson, J. Dudley. An Antioch Career: The Memoirs of J. Dudley Dawson. Hotaling, Dan & Soctt, Dorothy O., eds. LC 95-75943. (Orig.). 1995. pap. text 12.95 (*0-9646148-4-7*) Antioch Univ.
Dawson, J. Frank. Place Names in Colorado. 1976. pap. 1.75 (*0-87315-067-8*) Golden Bell.
Dawson, J. L., et al, eds. A Concordance to "The Complete Poems & Plays of T. S. Eliot" (Cornell Concordances Ser.). 1264p. 1995. text 90.00 (*0-8014-1561-6*) Cornell U Pr.
— Perspectives in Asian Cross-Cultural Psychology. x, 198p. 1981. pap. 29.75 (*90-265-0359-8*) Swets.
Dawson, J. L. & SeSaussure, H. W. Census of the City of Charleston, for the Year 1848: Exhibiting the Condition & Prospects of the City. (Illus.). 262p. 1997. reprint ed. lib. bdg. 32.00 (*0-8328-6919-8*) Higginson Bk Co.
Dawson, J. L., jt. ed. see Pickles, J. A.
Dawson, J. William. Modern Ideas of Evolution. 1977. pap. 8.95 (*0-88202-167-2*, Sci Hist) Watson Pub Intl.
Dawson, Jack. What Is Love? 110p. 1993. pap. 15.00 (*0-9635888-0-X*) Loverly Pubs.
Dawson, Jack, tr. see Bernhard, Thomas.
Dawson, James, ed. Subject Guide to Raymond B. Clark's "Maryland & Delaware Genealogist" 53p. (Orig.). 1991. pap. 9.75 (*0-685-57107-6*) Unicorn Bkshop.
Dawson, Jan. Films of Hellmuth Costard. 1979. pap. 5.95 (*0-918432-24-3*) Baseline Bks.
— The Life & Times of Dudsberry. 29p. 1995. pap. 4.95 (*0-9626939-9-5*) Janelle Pubns.
— Teaching Safe Horsemanship: A Guide to English & Western Instruction. LC 97-648. 144p. 1997. 29.95 (*0-88266-972-9*) Storey Bks.
Dawson, Jan & Kluge, Alexander. Alexander Kluge. (Illus.). (Orig.). 1977. pap. 6.95 (*0-918432-03-0*) Baseline Bks.
Dawson, Jan & Wenders, Wim. Wim Wenders. (Illus.). (Orig.). 1977. pap. 8.95 (*0-918432-04-9*) Baseline Bks.
Dawson, Jane I. Eco-Nationalism: Anti-Nuclear Activism & National Identity in Russia, Lithuania, & Ukraine. LC 96-14630. 248p. 1996. text 49.95 (*0-8223-1831-8*); pap. text 16.95 (*0-8223-1837-7*) Duke.
Dawson, Janet. A Credible Threat. (Jeri Howard Mystery Ser.). 1997. mass mkt. 5.99 (*0-449-22357-4*) Fawcett.
— A Credible Threat: A Jeri Howard mystery. 256p. 1996. 21.00 (*0-449-90977-8*) Fawcett.
***Dawson, Janet.** A Killing at the Track. 320p. 2000. mass mkt. 6.99 (*0-449-00531-3*) Fawcett.
Dawson, Janet. Kindred Crimes. 1992. mass mkt. 4.99 (*0-449-22014-1*, Crest) Fawcett.
— Kindred Crimes. large type ed. 336p. 1995. 27.99 (*0-7089-2929-X*) Ulverscroft.
— Nobody's Child. 1996. mass mkt. 5.99 (*0-449-22356-6*) Fawcett.
— Take a Number. (Northern California Mysteries Ser.). 1994. mass mkt. 4.99 (*0-449-22183-0*) Fawcett.
— Till the Old Men Die. (Orig.). 1993. mass mkt. 4.50 (*0-449-22133-4*) Fawcett.
— Where the Bodies Are Buried. LC 98-15756. 1998. 23.50 (*0-449-00198-9*) Fawcett.
— Where the Bodies Are Buried. 1999. mass mkt. 6.50 (*0-449-00322-1*, Crest) Fawcett.
— Witness to Evil. 1998. mass mkt. 6.50 (*0-449-22471-6*, Crest) Fawcett.
— Witness to Evil. 1998. 21.95 (*0-449-91060-1*) Fawcett.
Dawson, Janet, jt. auth. see Bishop, Lilli.
Dawson, Jeff. Gay & Lesbian Online. rev. expanded ed. LC 96-164581. (Illus.). 320p. (C). 1996. pap. text 15.95 (*0-201-88453-4*) Peachpit Pr.
— Gay & Lesbian Online. 2nd expanded rev. ed. LC 97-183162. (Illus.). 400p. (C). 1997. pap. text 16.95 (*0-201-68861-1*) Peachpit Pr.
— Gay & Lesbian Online: Your Indispensible Guide to Cruising the Queer Web. 3rd rev. ed. LC 98-47384. 394p. 1998. pap. 17.95 (*1-55583-489-2*) Alyson Pubns.
— Quentin Tarantino: The Cinema of Cool. LC 95-79935. (Illus.). 224p. 1995. pap. 14.95 (*1-55783-227-7*) Applause Theatre Bk Pubs.
***Dawson, Jeff, ed.** Gay & Lesbian Online: Your Indispensable Guide to Cruising the Queer Web. 4th ed. 544p. 2000. pap. 17.95 (*1-55583-581-3*, Pub. by Alyson Pubns) Consort Bk Sales.
Dawson, Jeff, jt. auth. see Jones, Cleve.
Dawson, Jeffrey R., jt. auth. see Scott, David W.
Dawson, Jerry. Elmer & the Peas: Inspiration, Satire & Humor by an Educated Baptist. LC 97-4251. 152p. 1997. pap. 14.95 (*1-57168-151-5*, 151-5, Eakin Pr) Sunbelt Media.
Dawson, Jill, ed. Kisses on Paper: Love Letters by Women from the 13th Century to the Present. 176p. 1995. 19.95 (*0-571-19864-3*) Faber & Faber.
— School Tales: Stories by Young Women. (Livewire Ser.). (YA). (gr. 6-9). pap. 7.95 (*0-7043-4922-1*, Pub. by Womens Press) Trafalgar.
Dawson, Jim. Doghouse: "Los Angeles under World of 1940s" 288p. 1992. mass mkt. 3.95 (*0-87067-379-3*) Holloway.
***Dawson, Jim.** Marine Biologist. 1999. 19.93 (*0-516-21889-1*) Capstone Pr.
— Mechanical Drafter. 1999. 19.93 (*0-516-21890-5*) Capstone Pr.
Dawson, Jim. Nervous Man Nervous: Big Jay McNeely & the Rise of the Honking Tenor Sax! 160p. 1994. pap. 21.95 (*0-936433-17-5*) Big Nickel.
***Dawson, Jim.** Park Naturalist. LC 99-30637. (Career Exploration Ser.). 48p. (YA). 1999. 19.93 (*0-7368-0332-7*) Capstone Pr.
Dawson, Jim. Who Cut the Cheese? A Cultural History of the Fart. (Illus.). 175p. 1998. pap. 9.95 (*1-58008-011-1*) Ten Speed Pr.
Dawson, Jim & Leigh, Spencer. Memories of Buddy Holly: In the Words of His Friends, His Fans & Himself. 168p. 1996. pap. 19.95 (*0-936433-20-5*) Big Nickel.
Dawson, John. Logical Dilemmas: The Life & Work of Kurt Godel. LC 96-50001. (Illus.). 376p. 1996. 49.95 (*1-56881-025-3*) AK Peters.
— Reconquista de Tu Cuidad.Tr. of Taking Our Cities for God. (SPA.). 1992. pap. 9.99 (*0-88113-023-0*) Caribe Betania.
— Taking Our Cities for God. LC 89-80822. 220p. 1989. pap. 10.99 (*0-88419-241-5*) Creation House.
— What Christians Should Know about Reconciliation. (What Christian Should Know Ser.). 1998. pap. 5.99 (*1-85240-229-6*) Gospel Lght.
***Dawson, John.** What Christians Should Know about Reconciliation. 2nd rev. ed. 56p. (YA). (gr. 10 up). 2000. write for info. (*0-9702590-0-X*) Intl Reconcil Coalitn.
Dawson, John & Phillips, Melanie. Doctors' Dilemmas: Medical Ethics & Contemporary Science. 224p. (Orig.). 1985. pap. 12.95 (*0-416-01121-7*, 9342) Routledge.
Dawson, John, jt. ed. see Dupuis, Marc.
Dawson, John C. Lakanal the Regicide. (Select Bibliographies Reprint Ser.). 1977. 21.95 (*0-8369-5520-X*) Ayer.
Dawson, John C., ed. Flow-of-Funds Analysis: A Handbook for Practitioners. LC 95-26614. (Illus.). 774p. (C). (gr. 13). 1996. text 108.95 (*1-56324-645-7*) M E Sharpe.
Dawson, John E. & Stan, Peter J. Public Expenditures in the United States, 1952-1993. LC 95-8386. 132p. 1995. pap. text 15.00 (*0-8330-1634-2*, MR-555-RC) Rand Corp.
— Public Receipts in the United States, 1952-1994. LC 96-21963. 1996. pap. text 15.00 (*0-8330-2409-4*, MR-589-RC) Rand Corp.
Dawson, John L., ed. see International Association for Cross-Cultural Psych.
***Dawson, John P.** A History of Lay Judges, 1960. LC 98-50812. 1999. reprint ed. 75.00 (*1-886363-69-2*) Lawbk Exchange.
Dawson, John P. Oracles of the Law. 520p. 1968. pap. 40.00 (*0-685-39008-X*, 73-008) U MI Law CLE.
— The Oracles of the Law. LC 78-7. 520p. 1978. reprint ed. lib. bdg. 85.00 (*0-313-20260-5*, DAOL, Greenwood Pr) Greenwood.
— Oracles of the Law. (Michigan Legal Publications). xix, 520p. 1986. reprint ed. lib. bdg. 55.00 (*0-89941-541-5*, 304700) W S Hein.
***Dawson, John P.** Unjust Enrichment: A Comparative Analysis: A Series of Lectures Delivered under the Auspices of the Julius Rosenthal Foundation at Northwestern Univerity School of Law, in April 1950. LC 99-37209. viii, 201p. 1999. reprint ed. 48.00 (*1-57588-523-9*, 323570) W S Hein.
Dawson, John P. Unjust Enrichment - A Comparative Analysis: A Series of Lectures Delivered under the Auspices of the Julius Rosenthal Foundation at Northwestern University School of Law, in April 1950. viii, 201p. 1999. reprint ed. 65.00 (*1-56169-464-9*) Gaunt.
Dawson, John P., et al. Contracts: Appendix UCC Article 2 (Sales) LC 98-12116. 112p. 1998. pap. text. write for info. (*1-56662-595-5*) Foundation Pr.
— Contracts, Cases & Comment. 6th ed. LC 92-45699. (University Casebook Ser.). 1068p. (C). 1993. text 44.95 (*1-56662-053-8*) Foundation Pr.
Dawson, Jonathan & Barwell, Ian. Roads Are Not Enough: New Perspectives on Rural Transport Planning in Developing Countries. (Illus.). 80p. (Orig.). 1993. pap. 21.00 (*1-85339-191-3*, Pub. by Intermed Tech) Stylus Pub VA.
***Dawson, Jonathan & Jeans, Andy.** Looking Beyond Credit. 56p. 1998. pap. 25.00 (*1-85339-423-8*, Pub. by Intermed Tech) Stylus Pub VA.
***Dawson, Jonathon.** Screenwriting: A Manual. (Illus.). 240p. 2000. pap. 19.95 (*0-19-550832-7*) OUP.
Dawson, Joseph G., III. Army Generals & Reconstruction: Louisiana, 1862-1877. LC 81-11735. (Illus.). xvi, 312p. 1994. pap. 14.95 (*0-8071-1960-1*) La State U Pr.
— Doniphan's Epic March: The 1st Missouri Volunteers in the Mexican War. LC 98-55515. (Modern War Studies). (Illus.). 360p. 1999. 35.00 (*0-7006-0956-3*) U Pr of KS.
— The Late Nineteenth Century U. S. Army, 1865-1898: A Research Guide, 3. LC 90-41839. (Research Guides in Military Studies: No. 3). 272p. 1990. lib. bdg. 65.00 (*0-313-26146-6*, DWA/, Greenwood Pr) Greenwood.
Dawson, Joseph G., III, ed. Commanders in Chief: Presidential Leadership in Modern Wars. LC 92-30601. (Modern War Studies). (Illus.). 240p. 1993. 29.95 (*0-7006-0578-9*); pap. 14.95 (*0-7006-0579-7*) U Pr of KS.
— Louisiana Governors: From Iberville to Edwards. LC 89-27333. (Illus.). 360p. 1990. text 50.00 (*0-8071-1527-4*) La State U Pr.
Dawson, Joseph G., 3rd, ed. The Texas Military Experience: From the Revolution Through World War II. LC 95-3321. (Military History Ser.: No. 43). (Illus.). 264p. (C). 1995. 29.50 (*0-89096-655-9*) Tex A&M Univ Pr.
Dawson, Joseph G., III, jt. ed. see Spiller, Roger J.
Dawson, Joseph M. Baptists & the American Republic. Gaustad, Edwin S., ed. LC 79-52584. (Baptist Tradition Ser.). 1980. reprint ed. lib. bdg. 23.95 (*0-405-12451-1*) Ayer.
— A Thousand Months to Remember: An Autobiography. 296p. 1964. 10.00 (*0-918954-03-7*) Baylor Univ Pr.
Dawson, Joy. Algunas de las Maneras en Que Sana Dios.Tr. of Some of the Ways of God in Healing. (SPA.). 128p. 1997. 7.99 (*0-88113-129-6*, B043-1296) Caribe Betania.
— Amistad Intima con Dios.Tr. of Intimate Friendship with God. (SPA.). 112p. (Orig.). 1990. pap. 7.99 (*0-88113-019-2*) Caribe Betania.
— Character of the One Who Says Go: A Pamphlet Dealing with God's Character & Missions. 16p. 1986. pap. 2.99 (*0-927545-08-X*) YWAM Pub.
— How to Pray for Someone near You Who Is Away from God: A Pamphlet Dealing with Prayer for Those Who Don't Know Christ. 13p. 1990. pap. 1.99 (*0-9615534-7-2*) YWAM Pub.
Dawson, Joy. Intercession: Thrilling, Fulfilling. 1997. pap. 11.99 (*1-57658-006-7*) YWAM Pub.
Dawson, Joy. Intercession, Thrilling & Fulfilling. 208p. 1997. 17.99 (*1-57658-003-2*) YWAM Pub.
— Intimate Friendship with God: Through Understanding the Fear of the Lord. LC 86-15526. 156p. (YA). (gr. 10). 1989. pap. 8.99 (*0-8007-9084-7*) Chosen Bks.
— Some of the Ways of God in Healing: How to Get Answers & Directions When You're Suffering. 138p. 1991. pap. 7.99 (*0-927545-14-4*) YWAM Pub.
Dawson, Karen J. & Istok, Athan D. Aquifer Testing: Design & Analysis of Pumping & Slug Tests. 368p. 1991. lib. bdg. 115.00 incl. 5.25 hd (*0-87371-501-2*, L501) Lewis Pubs.
Dawson, Kate, ed. see Ulrich, Laurie Ann.
Dawson, Kathleen, ed. see Oscard, Anne L.
Dawson, Keith. The Call Center Handbook: The Complete Guide to Starting, Running & Improving Your Call Center. 300p. 1996. 34.95 (*0-936648-95-3*, P50008) Telecom Bks.
— The Call Center Handbook: The Complete Guide to Starting, Running & Improving Your Call Center. 2nd rev. ed. 300p. 1998. per. 34.95 (*1-57820-019-9*) Telecom Bks.
***Dawson, Keith.** The Call Center Handbook: The Complete Guide to Starting, Running & Improving Your Call Center. 3rd ed. 300p. 1999. pap. 34.95 (*1-57820-047-4*, Pub. by Telecom Bks) Publishers Group.
— Call Center Savvy. 210p. 1999. pap. 19.95 (*1-57820-050-4*) Telecom Bks.
Dawson, Keith, jt. auth. see Bodin, Madeline.
Dawson, Kenneth M. & Dawson, Sheryl N. Job Search: The Total System. 1988. write for info. (*0-9621405-1-1*) Dawson & Dawson.
— Job Search: The Total System. 2nd ed. LC 95-46091. 335p. 1996. pap. 15.95 (*0-471-14590-4*) Wiley.
— Job Search: The Total System, Set. 1988. student ed. 199.95 (*0-9621405-3-8*) Dawson & Dawson.
Dawson, L. R., jt. ed. see Appelbaum, A.
Dawson, L. R., jt. ed. see Gibson, J. Murray.

D

An Asterisk (*) at the beginning of an entry indicates that the title is appearing for the first time.

Dawson, Laila M. & Dawson, Albert C. Dicho y Hecho: Beginning Spanish. 861p. 1997. text 164.85 incl. cd-rom (0-471-25225-5) Wiley.

Dawson, Laila M. & Dawson, Albert C. Dicho y Hecho: Beginning Spanish. 5th ed. LC 96-19751. (SPA.). 560p. 1996. text 66.95 (0-471-14018-X) Wiley.

Dawson, Laila M. & Dawson, Ibert C. Dicho y Hecho: Text & Cassette. 4th ed. 576p. 1994. text 41.00 incl. audio (0-471-07675-9) Wiley.

Dawson, Laila M., jt. auth. see Dawson, Albert C.

Dawson, Laura R. A Vision for Victory: A Pictorial History of Voorhees College, 1897-1997. LC 96-40189. (Illus.). 1997. write for info. (0-89865-985-X) Donning Co.

Dawson, Lawrence. Locust & Wild Honey. 252p. (Orig.). 1990. pap. 9.95 (0-941995-08-9) Paradigm.

Dawson, Lawrence D. The Death of Reality: How a Conspiracy of Fools Has Laid Claim to the Destiny of a Nation. LC 96-48496. 240p. (Orig.). 1996. pap. 17.95 (0-941995-10-0) Paradigm ID.

Dawson, Lawrence H. Complete Hoyle's Games. (Reference Library). 480p. 1997. pap. 6.95 (1-85326-316-8, 3168WW, Pub. by Wrdsworth Edits) NTC Contemp Pub Co.

Dawson, Lawrence H., ed. see Licht, Hans, pseud.

Dawson, Layla. Daniel Libeskind - The Felix Nussbaum Museum: Museum Without Exit. (Illus.). 64p. 1999. 19.95 (3-7913-2127-7) te Neues.

Dawson, Les. The Blade & the Passion: A Spoof on Romance Novels. large type ed. 20.95 (1-85695-204-5, Pub. by ISIS Lrg Prnt) Transaction Pubs.

— Ghost Brand of the Wishbones. LC 98-22713. 1998. 18.95 (0-7862-1159-8) Thorndike Pr.

— Ghost Brand of the Wishbones. large type ed. LC 99-21836. 1999. pap. 30.00 (0-7862-1171-7) Mac Lib Ref.

Dawson, Leslie Y. Managing Diabetes on a Budget. LC 95-16705. 96p. 1996. pap. 7.95 (0-945448-53-8, 5002-01, Pub. by Am Diabetes) NTC Contemp Pub Co.

Dawson, Linda. Tennis. (Butterfly Bks.). (J). 1990. 8.95 (0-86685-476-2) Intl Bk Ctr.

***Dawson, Lorne L.** Comprehending Cults: The Sociology of New Religious Movements. LC 99-173192. (Illus.). 240p. 1998. pap. text 19.95 (0-19-541154-4) OUP.

Dawson, Lorne L. Reason, Freedom, & Religion: Closing the Gap Between the Humanistic & Scientific Study of Religion. (Toronto Studies in Religion: Vol. 6). X, 247p. 1988. text 46.95 (0-8204-0600-7) P Lang Pubng.

Dawson, Lorne L., ed. Cults in Context: Readings in the Study of New Religious Movements. LC 98-22986. 480p. 1998. pap. 29.95 (0-7658-0478-6) Transaction Pubs.

Dawson, Louis W. Colorado 10th Mountain Huts & Trails: The Official Guide to America's Largest Backcountry Ski Hut System 350 Miles of Trail Connecting with 20 Huts & Inns. 3rd ed. Ohlrich, Warren H., ed. LC 97-62138. (Illus.). 240p. 1998. pap. 19.95 (1-882426-06-1) W H O Pr.

Dawson, Louis W., II. The Northern Peaks, Vol. 1. Couchman, Robert, ed. LC 94-71273. (Dawson's Guide to Colorado's Fourteeners Ser.). (Illus.). 255p. 1994. pap. 19.95 (0-9628867-1-8) Blue Clover.

Dawson, Louis W., 2nd. The Southern Peaks, 2 vols., Set. Couchman, Robert, ed. LC 94-71273. (Dawson's Guide to Colorado's Fourteeners Ser.). (Illus.). 204p. 1998. pap. 19.95 (0-9628867-2-6) Blue Clover.

Dawson, Louis W. Wild Snow: A Historical Guide to North American Ski Mountaineering. (American Alpine Book Ser.). (Illus.). 292p. 1997. 40.00 (0-930410-68-8) Amer Alpine Club.

— Wild Snow: 54 Classic Ski & Snowboard Descents in North America. (American Alpine Book Ser.). (Illus.). 324p. 1998. pap. 24.95 (0-930410-81-5, AAC Pr) Amer Alpine Club.

Dawson, Lutera B. Saltwater Farm. (Illus.). 109p. (Orig.). 1993. pap. 7.95 (0-9637523-0-8) Impatiens Pr.

Dawson, M., jt. ed. see Butler, M.

Dawson, M., jt. ed. see Carling, P. A.

Dawson, M. M. The Ethics of Socrates. LC 74-30274. (Studies in Philosophy: No. 40). 1974. lib. bdg. 75.00 (0-8383-2042-2) M S G Haskell Hse.

Dawson, M. T., et al. Gene Technology. (Introduction to Biotechniques Ser.). 160p. (Orig.). 1994. pap. 47.50 (1-872748-76-7, Pub. by Bios Sci) Coronet Bks.

Dawson, Marcia I. & Okamura, William H., eds. Chemistry & Biology of Synthetic Retinoids. 560p. 1990. lib. bdg. 375.00 (0-8493-4797-1, QP801) CRC Pr.

Dawson, Margaret, tr. see Steiner, Rudolf.

Dawson, Mark & Dawson, Anne. Nantucket Recipes from the Fog Island Cafe. (Illus.). 128p. 1996. 14.95 (0-939218-16-X) Chapman Billies.

Dawson, Martha E. Hampton University: A National Treasure. 224p. 1995. 29.95 (0-931761-36-0) Beckham Pubns.

Dawson, Mary, ed. Mirror, Mirror on the Easel: Caesar Cirigliano. LC 98-211629. (Illus.). 192p. 1998. 40.00 (1-85756-393-X, Pub. by Janus Pubng) Paul & Co Pubs.

Dawson, Mary R., jt. ed. see Genoways, Hugh H.

Dawson, Mathew Q. Partisanship, Politics & Partners: America's 'French Party,' 1796-1800, 387. LC 99-22145. 387. 264p. 2000. 62.95 (0-313-31046-7, Greenwood Pr) Greenwood.

Dawson, Melissa, ed. see Davidovich, Gene.

Dawson, Melissa, ed. see Popescu, Ludmila.

Dawson, Michael. Healing the Cause: A Path to Forgiveness. (Illus.). 160p. (Orig.). 1994. pap. 12.95 (0-905249-91-7, Pub. by Findhorn Pr) Words Distrib.

— A Late Roman Cemetery at Bletsoe. (Bedfordshire Archaeological Monograph Ser.: No. 1, 1994). (Illus.). 68p. 1994. pap. 22.00 (1-85351-174-9, Pub. by Oxbow Bks) David Brown.

Dawson, Michael, jt. ed. see Eccleston, Bernard.

Dawson, Michael, jt. ed. see Maidment, Richard A.

Dawson, Michael C. Behind the Mule: Race & Class in African-American Politics. LC 93-44088. 248p. 1994. text 45.00 (0-691-08770-9, Pub. by Princeton U Pr) Cal Prin Full Svc.

Dawson, Michael E., et al, eds. Startle Modification: Implications for Neuroscience, Cognitive Science, & Clinical Science. LC 98-39368. (Illus.). 400p. (C). 1999. text 85.00 (0-521-58046-3) Cambridge U Pr.

Dawson, Michael E., jt. auth. see Grings, William W.

Dawson, Michael R. Understanding Cognitive Science. LC 98-13849. (Illus.). 320p. 1998. 59.95 (0-631-20894-1); pap. 29.95 (0-631-20895-X) Blackwell Pubs.

Dawson, Mike. AS/400: A Systems Programmer's Guide. Ranade, Jay, ed. LC 97-14727. (IBM Ser.). (Illus.). 304p. 1997. text 49.95 incl. disk (0-07-913239-1) McGraw.

***Dawson, Mike.** The AS/400 Owner's Manual for V4. (Illus.). 464p. 1999. spiral bd. 59.00 (1-58347-001-8) Midrange Comput.

Dawson, Mike. The AS/400 Owner's Manual. LC 97-182834. (Illus.). 344p. (Orig.). 1997. spiral bd. 49.00 (1-883884-40-3, 568) Midrange Comput.

Dawson, Mike & Manto, Mike. OPNQRYF by Example. LC 99-6049. Orig. Title: Desktop Guide to OPNQRYF. 160p. 1999. pap. 39.95 (1-58304-039-0) News Four-Hund.

Dawson, Miles M. Ethical Religion of Zoroaster. LC 73-90100. (BCL Ser. I). reprint ed. 34.50 (0-404-01999-4) AMS Pr.

***Dawson, Millie.** All the Day Long: Missionaries Reaching Tribes in the Amazon. LC 99-66556. 272p. 2000. pap. 14.99 (1-57921-254-9) WinePress Pub.

Dawson, Moses. Life of Harrison. 1993. reprint ed. lib. bdg. 89.00 (0-7812-5354-3) Rprt Serv.

***Dawson, Nancy.** Hormone-Refractory Prostate Cancer: Current Issues & Treatment Options LC 99-70505. 45 p. 1999. write for info. (0-924428-11-2) Phys Sci Pub.

Dawson, Nancy A & Vogelzang, Nicholas J., eds. Prostate Cancer. 300p. 1994. 129.95 (0-471-58834-2, Wiley-Liss) Wiley.

Dawson, Nelson L., ed. Brandeis & America. LC 89-30929. 176p. 1989. text 22.50 (0-8131-1690-2) U Pr of Ky.

***Dawson, Norma Ann, ed.** Making a Difference: Stories by & about Lawyers Who Have. 76p. 1999. pap. 10.95 (0-7414-0008-1) Buy Books.

Dawson, P. & Clauss, W., eds. Advances in X-Ray Contrast: Collected Papers. 114p. 1998. 50.00 (0-7923-8741-4) Kluwer Academic.

Dawson, P. & Dawson, W. Contrast Media in Practice: Questions & Answers. LC 93-33120. 256p. 1993. 70.95 (0-387-57187-6) Spr-Verlag.

Dawson, P. M., contrib. by. Bodleian Manuscript Shelley, No. e.4. LC 86-4746. (Bodleian Shelley Manuscripts Ser.: Vol. III). 880203p. 1988. text 134.00 (0-8240-6979-X) Garland.

Dawson, P. M. S., ed. see Shelley, Percy Bysshe.

Dawson, Pam. Aran Island Knitting. 32p. pap. 11.95 (0-85532-688-3, 688-3, Pub. by Srch Pr) A Schwartz & Co.

— Art of Painting On Silk, Vol. 3: Fashions. 3rd ed. 128p. 1989. pap. 22.50 (0-85532-628-X, 628-X, Pub. by Srch Pr) A Schwartz & Co.

— Art of Painting On Silk, Vol. 4: Potpourri, Vol. 4. 96p. 1989. pap. 22.50 (0-85532-646-8, 646-8, Pub. by Srch Pr) A Schwartz & Co.

— Filet Crochet. (Craft Library). 48p. pap. 5.50 (0-85532-620-4, 620-4, Pub. by Srch Pr) A Schwartz & Co.

— Traditional Island Knitting. Dace, Rosalind, ed. (Illus.). 144p. 1989. pap. 19.95 (0-85532-657-3, Pub. by Srch Pr) A Schwartz & Co.

— Traditional Island Knitting: A Classic Collection of Unique Hand-Knitting Designs. 2nd ed. (Illus.). 144p. 1998. pap. 22.95 (0-85532-873-8, 8738, Pub. by Srch Pr) A Schwartz & Co.

Dawson, Pam, ed. The Art of Painting on Silk, Vol. 2. 2nd ed. 96p. 1991. pap. 19.95 (0-85532-623-9, 623-9, Pub. by Srch Pr) A Schwartz & Co.

— How to Paint on Silk. (Craft Library). 48p. pap. 5.50 (0-85532-626-3, 626-3, Pub. by Srch Pr) A Schwartz & Co.

Dawson, Pam, et al. Enhancing the Abilities of Persons with Alzheimer's & Related Dementias: A Nursing Perspective. LC 93-12113. 184p. 1993. 32.95 (0-8261-7790-5) Springer Pub.

Dawson, Pam, jt. auth. see Riches, Gordon.

Dawson, Pam, ed. see Henge, Renate.

Dawson, Pam, ed. see Messent, Jan.

Dawson, Patricia, jt. auth. see Hall, Michael E.

Dawson, Patricia L. Forged by the Knife: The Experience of Surgical Residency from the Perspective of a Woman of Color. LC 99-35331. 1999. 24.00 (0-940880-63-6, 0-940880); pap. 15.00 (0-940880-64-4, 0-940880) Open Hand.

Dawson, Patricia N. Iowa History & Culture: A Bibliography of Materials Published Between 1952 & 1986. LC 88-34452. 370p. 1989. reprint ed. pap. 114.70 (0-608-06843-8, 206704100009) Bks Demand.

***Dawson, Patrick.** The Montana Cowboy. 2nd ed. (Illus.). 276p. 1999. text 60.00 (0-922029-67-9, Pub. by Stoecklein Pub) Gr Arts Ctr Pub.

Dawson, Patrick. Mr. Rodeo: The Big Bronco Years of Leo Cremer. 170p. 1986. pap. 25.00 (0-937959-05-7) Cayuse Pr MT.

— Technology & Quality: Change in the Workplace. 180p. 1996. pap. 21.95 (0-415-12302-X) Thomson Learn.

Dawson, Patrick, ed. see Anderson, Douglas T. & Tribble, Mike.

Dawson, Paul R., jt. ed. see Shen Shan-Fu.

***Dawson, Paul Robert.** My Amazing Human Body Explorer. LC 00-29469. (Illus.). (J). 2000. pap. write for info. (0-7894-6707-0) DK Pub Inc.

Dawson, Pauline. The Peacekeepers of Kashmir: The U. N. Military Observer Group in India & Pakistan. 300p. 1996. text 49.95 (0-312-07589-8) St Martin.

Dawson, Percy G., et al. Early English Clocks. (Illus.). 552p. 1982. 99.50 (0-902028-59-6) Antique Collect.

Dawson, Peter. Angel Peak: Western Stories. large type ed. LC 00-24234. (G. K. Hall Western Ser.). 275p. 2000. 24.95 (0-7838-0312-5, G K Hall Lrg Type) Mac Lib Ref.

— The Big Outfit. large type ed. LC 93-7033. 269p. 1993. lib. bdg. 17.95 (1-56054-698-0) Thorndike Pr.

— Claiming of the Deerfoot. LC 00-23524. (Western Trio Ser.). 201p. 2000. 30.00 (0-7862-2101-1) Mac Lib Ref.

— Dark Riders of Doom. LC 95-50437. (Five-Star Western Ser.). 230p. 1996. 16.95 (0-7862-0626-8) Thorndike Pr.

— Dark Riders of Doom. large type ed. LC 97-18661. 366p. 1997. 18.95 (0-7862-0628-4) Thorndike Pr.

— Dead Man Pass. large type ed. LC 94-5474. 317p. 1994. lib. bdg. 18.95 (1-56054-701-4) Thorndike Pr.

— Devil on Angel Peak: the Western Stories. LC 99-19830. 250p. 1999. 30.00 (0-7862-1572-0) Thorndike Pr.

— Gunsmoke Graze. large type ed. LC 92-25152. 345p. 1993. reprint ed. lib. bdg. 18.95 (1-56054-525-9) Thorndike Pr.

— High Country. 1995. 17.50 (0-7451-4623-6, Gunsmoke) Chivers N Amer.

— Man on the Buckskin. large type ed. LC 95-13844. 269p. 1995. 18.95 (0-7862-0479-6) Thorndike Pr.

— Rattlesnake Mesa. LC 97-27718. 284p. 1997. lib. bdg. 17.95 (0-7862-0753-1) Five Star.

— Rattlesnake Mesa. large type ed. LC 98-30792. 1999. 30.00 (0-7862-0776-0) Thorndike Pr.

— Renegade Canyon. 1998. 17.50 (0-7540-8021-8, Gunsmoke) Chivers N Amer.

— Renegade Canyon. large type ed. LC 93-35501. (Large Type Ser.). 294p. 1993. lib. bdg. 17.95 (1-56054-704-9) Thorndike Pr.

— Ruler of the Range. large type ed. LC 97-330. (Western Ser.). 252p. 1997. 18.95 (0-7862-1077-X) Thorndike Pr.

— Run to Gold Rock. large type ed. LC 92-44605. (General Ser.). 306p. 1993. lib. bdg. 20.95 (0-8161-5733-2, G K Hall Lrg Type) Mac Lib Ref.

***Dawson, Peter.** Treachery at Rock Point. LC 98-48261. 1999. 22.95 (0-7838-8493-1) Macmillan Gen Ref.

Dawson, Peter, jt. auth. see Kessler, Daniel B.

Dawson, Peter E., ed. Evaluation, Diagnosis & Treatment of Occlusal Problems. 2nd ed. (Illus.). 632p. (C). (gr. 13). 1988. text 145.00 (0-8016-2788-5, 02788) Mosby Inc.

Dawson, Peter H., ed. Quadrupole Mass Spectrometry: And Its Applications. LC 95-21857. (AIP-AVS Classics Ser.). (Illus.). 373p. (C). 1994. reprint ed. pap. text 69.95 (1-56396-455-4, AIP Pr) Spr-Verlag.

Dawson, Peter H. & Clauss, W. Contrast Media in Practice: Questions & Answers. 2nd ed. LC 98-44436. (Illus.). 265p. 1999. pap. 80.00 (3-540-64759-7) Spr-Verlag.

Dawson, Philip. Canberra: In the Wake of a Legend. Marshall, N., ed. LC 97-153935. (Illus.). 176p. 1997. 38.95 (0-85177-707-4, Pub. by Brasseys) Brasseys.

— Provincial Magistrates & Revolutionary Politics in France, 1789-1795. LC 74-182816. (Historical Monographs: No. 66). (Illus.). 436p. 1972. 30.00 (0-674-71960-3) HUP.

Dawson, Phoebe. Joshua Finds a Friend. (Child of Destiny Ser.). (Illus.). 24p. (J). (gr. k-5). 1998. 9.95 (1-889018-47-3) Micah Pubg.

Dawson, R. M., et al. Data for Biochemical Research. 3rd ed. (Illus.). 592p. 1989. pap. text 85.00 (0-19-855299-8) OUP.

Dawson, R. MacGregor & Dawson, W. F. Democratic Government in Canada. 5th rev. ed. 1989. pap. text 13.95 (0-8020-6703-4) U of Toronto Pr.

Dawson, Ralph E., III & Dawson, Shirley. Cherokee-English Interlinear First Epistle of John of the New Testament: First Epistle of John of the New Testament. 2nd ed. (CHR & ENG.). 25p. (C). 1996. reprint ed. pap. 5.00 (0-940392-11-9) Indian U Pr OK.

Dawson, Raymond, ed. The Legacy of China. LC 90-83185. (C & T Asian Language Ser.). 460p. (C). 1990. reprint ed. pap. 18.95 (0-88727-152-9) Cheng & Tsui.

Dawson, Raymond, tr. The Analects. LC 92-46274. (World's Classics Ser.). 146p. (C). 1993. pap. 8.95 (0-19-283091-0) OUP.

Dawson, Raymond, tr. & intro. see Qian, Sima.

Dawson, Richard. Challenging Technology. rev. ed. Doyle, Connie, ed. (Design & Make Ser.). (Illus.). 33p. (J). (gr. 3-6). 1994. reprint ed. 5.95 (1-884461-06-9) NES Arnold.

***Dawson, Richard.** My Baby Brother: A Fill-In & Keep Book. (Illus.). 32p. (J). 2000. pap. 3.99 (0-330-36970-9) Mcm Child Bks.

— My Baby Sister: Fill-In & Keep Book. (Illus.). 32p. (J). 2000. pap. 3.99 (0-330-36971-7) Mcm Child Bks.

Dawson, Rita, jt. auth. see Ellis, Oma.

Dawson, Robert. Ansel Adams, New Light: Essays on His Legacy & Legend. LC 92-74384. (Untitled Ser.: No. 55). (Illus.). 96p. 1993. pap. 16.95 (0-933286-61-9) Frnds Photography.

— The Present State of Australia. (Discovery of the Pacific & Australia Ser.). (Illus.). 488p. 1998. reprint ed. pap. 240.00 (1-85297-003-0, Pub. by Archival Facs) St Mut.

Dawson, Robert & Brechin, Gray A. Farewell, Promised Land: Waking from the California Dream. LC 98-24030. 253p. 1999. 60.00 (0-520-21123-5, Pub. by U CA Pr); pap. 35.00 (0-520-21124-3, Pub. by U CA Pr) Cal Prin Full Svc.

***Dawson, Robert, et al.** A Doubtful River. LC 99-42383. (Environmental Arts & Humanities Ser.). (Illus.). 2000. 49.95 (0-87417-349-3) U of Nev Pr.

Dawson, Robert M. The Government of Canada. 4th rev. ed. LC JL0015.D3. (Canadian Government Ser.: No. 2). 622p. reprint ed. pap. 192.90 (0-8357-8150-X, 203404200088) Bks Demand.

Dawson, Robert M., ed. Development of Dominion Status, 1900-1936. 466p. 1965. reprint ed. 35.00 (0-7146-1467-X, BHA-01467, Pub. by F Cass Pubs) Intl Spec Bk.

Dawson, Robert M. & Dawson, W. Democratic Government in Canada. LC 71-163808. 193p. reprint ed. pap. 59.90 (0-608-16908-0, 202641500049) Bks Demand.

Dawson, Roger. The Confident Decision Maker: How to Make the Right Business & Personal Decisions Every Time. 1995. pap. 12.00 (0-688-14228-1, Quil) HarperTrade.

***Dawson, Roger.** Secrets of Power Negotiating: Inside Secrets from a Master Negotiator. 2nd ed. LC 99-11389. 320p. 1999. 24.99 (1-56414-399-6) Career Pr Inc.

— Secrets of Power Negotiating: Inside Secrets from a Master Negotiator. 2nd ed. 320p. 2000. pap. 15.99 (1-56414-498-4) Career Pr Inc.

— Secrets of Power Negotiating for Sales People: Inside Secrets from a Master Negotiator. LC 99-29739. 256p. 1999. 24.99 (1-56414-428-3) Career Pr Inc.

Dawson, Roger. Secrets of Power Persuasion: Everything You'll Ever Need to Get Anything You'll Ever Want. 320p. (C). 1992. text 27.95 (0-13-799354-4, Busn); pap. text 14.95 (0-13-799362-5, Busn) P-H.

— 13 Secrets of Power Performance. 320p. (C). 1997. pap. text 14.95 (0-13-671497-8) P-H.

Dawson Rogers Smith, Jean. Two Exiles from Florence: Selected Essays. 200p. 1999. pap. 9.95 (1-882063-48-1) Cottage Pr MA.

Dawson, Ron. Nature Bound Pocket Field Guide. 1990. pap. text 13.99 (0-8163-1072-6) Pacific Pr Pub Assn.

Dawson, Ron, et al. First Aid Procedures & Lifesaving Techniques & Outback Skills & Survival Techniques. 56p. 1995. spiral bd. write for info. (0-9647141-0-8) Ron L Dawson.

***Dawson, Ross.** Developing Knowledge-Based Client Relationships. LC 99-45024. 240p. 1999. pap. text 19.95 (0-7506-7185-8) Buttrwrth-Heinemann.

***Dawson, Roy.** ExCet Psychology. (ExCet Teacher Certification Ser.). (C). 1999. per. 10.00 (1-58197-120-6) XAM.

Dawson, Roy. FTCE Psychology. (C). 1998. per. 10.00 (1-58197-087-0) XAM.

***Dawson, Roy.** PRAXIS Psychology. (Praxis Ser.). (C). 2000. per. 10.00 (1-58197-025-0) XAM.

Dawson, S. CP Violation: The BNL Summer Study. 392p. 1991. text 101.00 (981-02-0480-9) World Scientific Pub.

***Dawson, Sally.** Search for Electroweak Symmetry Breaking. 2000. pap. 38.00 (981-02-4213-1) World Scientific Pub.

Dawson, Sam & Reddy, Vishu, eds. Powder Coating Applications. fac. ed. LC 89-64306. (Manufacturing Update Ser.). (Illus.). 300p. 1990. reprint ed. pap. 93.00 (0-7837-8188-1, 204789300008) Bks Demand.

Dawson, Samuel A. Freedom of the Press: A Study of the Legal Doctrine of "Qualified Privilege" 120p. 1982. reprint ed. 30.00 (0-8377-0516-9, Rothman) W S Hein.

Dawson, Sandra. Analyzing Organizations. 2nd ed. 304p. (C). 1992. text 45.00 (0-333-57645-4) NYU Pr.

Dawson, Sandra & Imperial College of Science Technology Staff. Managing in the NHS. LC 96-164689. xii, 265 p. 1995. write for info. (0-11-321878-8) Sterling.

Dawson, Saranne. Deception & Desire. (American Romance Ser.). 1993. per. 3.39 (0-373-16480-7, 1-16480-5) Harlequin Bks.

— The Enchanted Land. 368p. (Orig.). 1998. mass mkt. 5.50 (0-505-52245-4, Love Spell) Dorchester Pub Co.

— Expose. LC 96-3689. (Intrigue Ser.). 248p. 1996. per. 3.50 (0-373-22356-0, 1-22356-9) Harlequin Bks.

— From the Mist. 368p. 1997. mass mkt. 5.50 (0-505-52207-1, Love Spell) Dorchester Pub Co.

— Greenfire. 400p. (Orig.). 1994. mass mkt. 4.99 (0-505-51985-2, Love Spell) Dorchester Pub Co.

— Heart of the Wolf. 400p. (Orig.). 1993. mass mkt. 4.99 (0-505-51901-1, Love Spell) Dorchester Pub Co.

— Her Other Half. (Intrigue Ser.). 1995. per. 2.99 (0-373-22307-2, 1-22307-2) Harlequin Bks.

— In Self Defense. (Intrigue Ser.). 1994. per. 2.99 (0-373-22286-6, 1-22286-6) Harlequin Bks.

— Lawman Lover. (Intrigue Ser.: No. 503). 1999. per. 3.99 (0-373-22503-2, 1-22503-6) Harlequin Bks.

— The Magic of Two. (Love Spell Ser.). 368p. 1999. mass mkt. 5.50 (0-505-52308-6, Love Spell) Dorchester Pub Co.

— Prince of Thieves. 368p. 1998. mass mkt. 5.50 (0-505-52288-8, Love Spell) Dorchester Pub Co.

— Runaway Heart. (Intrigue Ser.). 1998. per. 3.99 (0-373-22472-9, 1-22472-4) Harlequin Bks.

— Secrets of the Wolf. 368p. 1998. mass mkt. 5.50 (0-505-52260-8, Love Spell) Dorchester Pub Co.

***Dawson, Saranne.** The Sorceress & the Savage. 368p. 2000. pap. 5.50 (0-505-52379-5, Love Spell) Dorchester Pub Co.

— Spell Bound. 368p. (Orig.). 1996. mass mkt. 5.50 (0-505-52152-0) Dorchester Pub Co.

Dawson, Saranne. Star-Crossed. 400p. (Orig.). 1994. mass mkt. 4.99 (0-505-51982-8, Love Spell) Dorchester Pub Co.

***Dawson, Saranne.** Starlight, Starbright. 368p. 1999. mass mkt. 5.50 (0-505-52346-9, Love Spell) Dorchester Pub Co.

Dawson, Saranne. Twilight Magic. (American Romance Ser.). 1993. per. 3.50 (0-373-16504-8, 1-16504-2) Harlequin Bks.

***Dawson, Saranne.** Twilight Magic. 2000. mass mkt. 4.50 (0-373-82243-X, 1-82243-6) Harlequin Bks.

An Asterisk (*) at the beginning of an entry indicates that the title is appearing for the first time.

Dawson, Sheryl N., jt. auth. see Dawson, Kenneth M.

Dawson, Shirley, jt. auth. see Dawson, Ralph E., III.

Dawson Smith, Barbara. Seduced by a Scoundrel. 320p. 1999. mass mkt. 6.50 (*0-312-97272-5*, St Martins Paperbacks) St Martin.

Dawson, Sophie. The Art & Craft of Papermaking: Step-by-Step Instructions for Creating Distinctive Handmade Paper. LC 96-42365. (Illus.). 144p. 1997. reprint ed. pap. 18.95 (*1-887374-24-8*, Pub. by Lark Books) Random.

— A Hand Papermaker's Sourcebook. (Illus.). 104p. 1995. pap. 26.95 (*1-55821-389-9*) Lyons Pr.

Dawson, Stephen, jt. auth. see Clegg, John.

Dawson, Stephen, jt. ed. see Clegg, John.

Dawson, Steve & Slooten, Elizabeth. Down-under Dolphins: The Story of Hector's Dolphin. (Illus.). 48p. (Orig.). (YA). 1996. pap. 19.95 (*0-908812-50-7*, Pub. by Canterbury Univ) Accents Pubns.

Dawson, Steve C. The Story of Liberty. 98p. (Orig.). 1993. pap., student ed. 9.95 (*0-938558-27-7*) Maranatha.

Dawson, Stuart. Effective Tutorial Teaching: A Guide for University & College Tutors. 80p. 1999. pap. 19.95 (*1-877133-58-2*) Univ Otago Pr.

Dawson, Terence, jt. ed. see Young-Eisendrath, Polly.

Dawson, Terence J. Kangaroos: Biology of the Largest Marsupials. (Comstock Bk.). (Illus.). 208p. 1995. pap. text 27.50 (*0-8014-8262-3*) Cornell U Pr.

Dawson, Terry, jt. auth. see Kirch, Olaf.

Dawson, Terry, ed. see Jones, W. Lawson.

Dawson, Thomas. The Good Huswifes Jewell & the Second Part of the Good Huswifes Jewel. LC 77-6868. (English Experience Ser.: No. 865). 1977. reprint ed. lib. bdg. 65.00 (*90-221-0865-1*) Walter J Johnson.

Dawson, Thomas A., jt. auth. see Deacon, Jeanette.

Dawson, Thomas H. Offshore Structural Engineering. (Illus.). 352p. 1983. text 74.00 (*0-13-633206-4*) P-H.

***Dawson, Tim P. & Neal, J. S.** Manual of Practical Neuropathology Techniques. (Illus.). 256p. 2000. pap. 75.00 (*0-7506-9086-0*) Buttrwrth-Heinemann.

***Dawson, Tony.** Principles & Practice of Modern Management. 406p. 2000. 32.95 (*1-872807-97-6*, Pub. by Tudor Business Pubg Ltd) Intl Spec Bk.

Dawson, Tony. Wilderness. 350p. 1999. reprint ed. 30.00 (*0-943698-05-7*) Papyrus Letterbox.

Dawson United Methodist Women's Staff. A Standing Invitation: To Gracious Southern Living. Cowart, Lynette & Tuck, Mary, eds. (Illus.). 400p. 1990. 16.95 (*0-9627311-0-2*) Dawson United Methodist.

Dawson, Virginia. Engines & Innovation: Lewis Laboratory & American Propulsion Technology. 286p. 1991. pap. text 17.00 (*0-16-030742-2*) USGPO.

Dawson, Virginia. Nature's Enigma: The Problem of the Polyp in the Letters of Bonnet, Trembley & Reaumur. LC 86-72886. (Memoirs Ser.: Vol. 174). (Illus.). (C). 1987. 20.00 (*0-87169-174-4*, M174-DAV) Am Philos.

Dawson, Virginia D. The Lamp. (Illus.). 48p. 1981. 28.00 (*0-88014-030-5*) Mosaic Pr OH.

Dawson, W., jt. auth. see Dawson, P.

Dawson, W., jt. auth. see Dawson, Robert M.

Dawson, W., jt. auth. see Smith, G. E.

Dawson, W. A. Pile Driving: Construction Guide. 30p. 1981. 10.00 (*0-7277-0093-6*, Pub. by T Telford) RCH.

Dawson, W. F. Christmas: Its Origin & Associations. LC 89-63012. (Illus.). 366p. 1990. reprint ed. lib. bdg. 48.00 (*1-55888-842-X*) Omnigraphics Inc.

Dawson, W. F., jt. auth. see Dawson, R. MacGregor.

Dawson, W. W. & Enoch, Jay M., eds. Foundations of Sensory Science. (Illus.). 615p. 1984. 244.00 (*0-387-12967-7*) Spr-Verlag.

Dawson, Warren R. The Beginnings: Egypt & Assyria. LC 75-23650. (Clio Medica Ser.: No. 1). reprint ed. 29.50 (*0-404-58901-4*) AMS Pr.

Dawson, Warren R., jt. auth. see Frazer, James George.

Dawson, Warren R., tr. see Capart, Jean.

Dawson, William B., jt. auth. see Hoffman, Robert M.

Dawson, William F. Procedure in the Canadian House of Commons. LC 63-3048. (Canadian Government Ser.: No. 12). 284p. reprint ed. pap. 88.10 (*0-8357-4153-2*, 203692700007) Bks Demand.

Dawson, William H. Bismarck & State Socialism: An Exposition of the Social & Economic Legislation of Germany since 1804. LC 79-106366. 1970. reprint ed. 8.00 (*0-403-00192-7*) Scholarly.

— Germany under the Treaty. (Select Bibliographies Reprint Ser.). 1977. reprint ed. 22.95 (*0-8369-9958-4*) Ayer.

— Social Insurance in Germany, 1883 to 1911. LC 78-32002. (Illus.). 283p. 1979. reprint ed. lib. bdg. 65.00 (*0-8371-5446-4*, DASI, Greenwood Pr) Greenwood.

Dawson, William J. Makers of English Fiction. 3rd ed. LC 74-142617. (Essay Index Reprint Ser.). 1977. 20.95 (*0-8369-2043-0*) Ayer.

Dawson, William L. The Birds of California. 1992. reprint ed. lib. bdg. 75.00 (*0-7812-5023-4*) Rprt Serv.

— Birds of Ohio, 2 vols. 1993. reprint ed. lib. bdg. 150.00 (*0-7812-5355-1*) Rprt Serv.

Dawson, Winnie. Dare to Journal: From Self-Discovery to Transformation. (Illus.). xi, 158p. 1998. pap. 14.95 (*0-9666064-1-8*) MedSearch Inc.

Dawson, Zo E. South Africa. LC 95-16714. (Postcards From Ser.). 32p. (J). (gr. 2-3). 1995. lib. bdg. 21.40 (*0-8172-4015-2*) Raintree Steck-V.

Dawson, Zoe. Canada. LC 95-16223. (Postcards From Ser.). (J). 1995. lib. bdg. 21.40 (*0-8172-4014-4*) Raintree Steck-V.

— Canada. LC 95-16223. (Postcards from Ser.). (Illus.). 32p. (J). (gr. 2-4). 1996. pap. text 4.95 (*0-8172-4235-X*) Raintree Steck-V.

— China. LC 95-8099. (Postcards from Ser.). 32p. (J). (gr. 2-3). 1995. lib. bdg. 21.40 (*0-8172-4007-1*) Raintree Steck-V.

— China. LC 95-8099. (Postcards From Ser.). (Illus.). 32p. (J). (gr. 2-4). 1996. pap. text 4.95 (*0-8172-4228-7*) Raintree Steck-V.

— Japan. LC 95-10035. (Postcards from Ser.). 32p. (J). (gr. k-3). 1995. lib. bdg. 21.40 (*0-8172-4011-X*) Raintree Steck-V.

— Japan. LC 95-10035. (Postcards From Ser.). (Illus.). 32p. (J). (gr. 2-4). 1996. pap. text 4.95 (*0-8172-4232-5*) Raintree Steck-V.

— Postcards from Brazil. LC 95-10301. (Postcards From Ser.). (J). 1995. lib. bdg. 21.40 (*0-8172-4013-6*) Raintree Steck-V.

— Postcards from Brazil. LC 95-10301. (Postcards from... Ser.). (Illus.). 32p. (J). (gr. 2-4). 1995. pap. 4.95 (*0-8172-4234-1*) Raintree Steck-V.

— South Africa. LC 95-16714. (Postcards From Ser.). (Illus.). 32p. (J). (gr. 2-4). 1996. pap. text 4.95 (*0-8172-4236-8*) Raintree Steck-V.

Dawtrey, Liz, ed. Equality & Inequality in Education Policy: A Reader. LC 94-28786. (Equality & Difference Ser.). 1994. text 74.95 (*1-85359-250-1*); pap. text 29.95 (*1-85359-249-8*) Taylor & Francis.

Dawtry, Liz, et al, eds. Investigating Modern Art. LC 95-50877. (Illus.). 208p. 1996. 50.00 (*0-300-06796-8*); pap. 20.00 (*0-300-06797-6*) Yale U Pr.

Dawud, Abdul A. Muhammad in the Bible. 263p. (C). 1993. pap. 16.50 (*1-56744-487-3*) Kazi Pubns.

Dawydiak, Orysia, jt. auth. see Sims, David E.

Dax, D. F. An Easy Guide to Modern Spells: A Handbook of Practical Magick. LC 97-92722. (Illus.). v, 101p. 1997. pap. 11.95 (*1-891530-02-X*) Centaur Bks.

— Star Magick: A Complete Guide to Astrological Sorcery. LC 97-92724. (Illus.). v, 118p. 1997. pap. 12.95 (*1-891530-05-4*) Centaur Bks.

Dax, Eric C. The Cunningham Dax Collection: Selected Works of Psychiatric Art. (Illus.). 112p. 1998. pap. 24.95 (*0-522-84768-4*, Pub. by Melbourne Univ Pr) Paul & Co Pubs.

Dax, Scott L. Antibacterial Chemotherapeutic Agents. LC 96-83762. 350p. 1996. pap. write for info. (*0-7514-0289-3*) Kluwer Academic.

Dax, Scott L. Chemotherapeutic Antibacterial Agents. LC 94-47608. 1995. 59.95 (*0-412-04161-8*) Chapman & Hall.

Day. Angela Carter: The Rational Glass. LC 97-47412. 220p. 1998. pap. 24.95 (*0-7190-5316-1*, Pub. by Manchester Univ Pr); text 79.95 (*0-7190-5315-3*, Pub. by Manchester Univ Pr) St Martin.

— Angels. 1995. pap. 10.99 (*1-57081-771-5*) At-A-Glance Consumer.

— Biopsy Pathology of Oesophagus, Stomach & Duodenum. 2nd ed. (Biopsy Pathology Ser.). 416p. 1996. 125.00 (*0-412-63570-4*, Pub. by E A) OUP.

— China & Soviet Union. 2nd ed. Date not set. pap. text. write for info. (*0-582-90265-7*, Pub. by Addison-Wesley) Longman.

— Claiming a Continent. 1998. pap. 13.95 (*0-207-19670-2*) HarpC.

***Day.** Dictionary for Clinical Trials. LC 99-11151. 228p. 1999. 124.95 (*0-471-98611-9*); pap. 34.95 (*0-471-98596-1*) Wiley.

Day. Ethics In Media Communication. 3rd ed. (Mass Communication). 1999. pap. 50.95 (*0-534-56187-X*) Wadsworth Pub.

— Geotechnical Foundations in Engineering. LC 99-20164. 1999. 90.00 (*0-07-134138-2*) McGraw.

— How to Talk about Women & Still Be Politically Correct. 1994. pap. 7.99 (*1-57081-769-3*) At-A-Glance Consumer.

— In Circles of Fear & Desire. 1993. 19.95 (*0-226-13890-9*) U Ch Pr.

Day. Liberty & Justice. 240p. 1994. 53.95 (*0-7512-0305-X*) Ashgate Pub Co.

Day. Management Principles for the Advancement Professional. LC 97-39246. 289p. 1998. 59.00 (*0-8342-1040-1*) Aspen Pub.

— Natural Remedies. (Threshold Picture Guide Ser.: No. 35). (Illus.). 24p. 1996. pap. 12.00 (*1-872082-79-3*) Half Halt Pr.

— Perfect Man: He's Quiet, He's Sweet, & If He Gives You Any Grief, You Can Bite His Head Off. 1994. pap. 7.99 (*1-57081-768-5*) At-A-Glance Consumer.

— Power Vision: Featuring New High Definition 3D Images. 1995. pap. 10.99 (*1-57081-654-9*) At-A-Glance Consumer.

— Power Vision II: Featuring New High Definition 3D Images. 1995. pap. 10.99 (*1-57081-832-0*) At-A-Glance Consumer.

— Textbook of Clinical Trials. 2000. text Price not set. (*0-471-98787-5*) Wiley.

— Think Tanks. Date not set. text. write for info. (*0-582-20905-6*, Pub. by Addison-Wesley) Longman.

— Typography: Its History & Use. 3.00 (*0-318-19216-0*) Quill & Scroll.

— William Tyndale. 1998. 24.95 (*0-8057-7037-2*, Twyne) Mac Lib Ref.

— With Wolves. 1995. pap. 10.99 (*1-57081-880-0*) At-A-Glance Consumer.

— World of Whales & Dolphins. 1995. pap. 10.99 (*1-57081-881-9*) At-A-Glance Consumer.

Day, ed. Microeconomics: Concepts & Applications. (C). 1988. pap. text, student ed. 11.00 (*0-673-38117-X*) Addson-Wesley Educ.

Day & Dean. Visual Genetics Basic. 1996. student ed. 39.95 (*0-7637-0148-3*) Jones & Bartlett.

— Visual Genetics Enhanced. 1996. student ed. 59.95 incl. cd-rom (*0-7637-0149-1*) Jones & Bartlett.

— Visual Genetics Faculty Version. 1996. 395.00 incl. cd-rom (*0-7637-0150-5*) Jones & Bartlett.

Day & Devereux. Liquid Crystal Displays & Devices. (Optical & Quantum Electronics Ser.). (Illus.). 400p. 1997. write for info. (*0-412-64440-1*, Chap & Hall NY) Chapman & Hall.

Day & Swan. Journeys Reading, Vol. 3. 1998. pap. text 39.80 (*0-13-230640-9*) P-H.

Day & Underwood. Quantitative Analysis. 6th ed. 1991. pap. text, lab manual ed. 38.00 (*0-13-747403-2*) P-H.

Day, jt. auth. see Burr.

Day, A. Colin. Compatible FORTRAN. LC 78-2483. 115p. reprint ed. pap. 32.80 (*0-608-15711-2*, 2031639) Bks Demand.

— Roget's Thesaurus of the Bible. 1996. 20.00 (*0-06-061743-8*) Harper SF.

— Using Ventura Publisher. (Illus.). 160p. 1989. pap. 21.00 (*0-19-853817-0*) OUP.

— Using Ventura Publisher 2.0: (Including the Professional Extension) (Illus.). 208p. 1990. pap. 24.95 (*0-19-853831-6*) OUP.

Day, A. Colin, jt. auth. see Roget, Peter M.

Day, A. Grove. Coronado's Quest: Discovery of the American Southwest. 322p. 1987. reprint ed. mass mkt. 5.95 (*0-935180-37-0*) Mutual Pub HI.

— Eleanor Dark. LC 75-23369. (Twayne's World Authors Ser.). (C). 1976. lib. bdg. 20.95 (*0-8057-6224-8*) Irvington.

— Great California Stories. LC 90-37672. viii, 268p. 1991. pap. 13.95 (*0-8032-6583-2*, Bison Books) U of Nebr Pr.

— Hawaii: Fiftieth Star. 204p. 1993. mass mkt. 4.95 (*0-935180-44-3*) Mutual Pub HI.

— Hawaii & Its People. 341p. 1993. mass mkt. 4.95 (*0-935180-50-8*) Mutual Pub HI.

— Hawai'i & Points South. 292p. 1992. mass mkt. 4.95 (*0-935180-01-X*) Mutual Pub HI.

— James A. Michener. 2nd ed. (United States Authors Ser.: No. 60). 1977. 24.95 (*0-8057-7184-0*) Macmillan.

— Mad about Islands: Novelists of a Vanished Pacific. 320p. 1987. 13.95 (*0-935180-46-X*); pap. 9.95 (*0-935180-47-8*) Mutual Pub HI.

— Mark Twain in Hawaii: Roughing It in the Sandwich Islands. 144p. 1990. reprint ed. mass mkt. 4.95 (*0-935180-93-1*) Mutual Pub HI.

— The Sky Clears: Poetry of the American Indians. LC 83-1576. 204p. 1983. lib. bdg. 59.75 (*0-313-23883-9*, Greenwood Pr) Greenwood.

Day, A. Grove, ed. The Lure of Tahiti. LC 86-62756. 324p. 1987. mass mkt. 5.95 (*0-935180-31-1*) Mutual Pub HI.

Day, A. Grove & Bowmann, Sylvia E. James Michener. LC 64-13956. (Twayne's United States Authors Ser.). 168p. (C). 1964. lib. bdg. 20.95 (*0-8290-1704-6*) Irvington.

Day, A. Grove & Kirtley, Bacil F., eds. Horror in Paradise: Grim & Uncanny Tales from Hawaii & the South Seas. LC 86-60370. 285p. 1986. mass mkt. 6.95 (*0-935180-23-0*) Mutual Pub HI.

Day, A. Grove & Stroven, Carl, eds. Best South Sea Stories. LC 64-12430. 312p. 1985. reprint ed. mass mkt. 6.95 (*0-935180-12-5*) Mutual Pub HI.

— A Hawaiian Reader. LC 59-14048. 380p. 1985. reprint ed. mass mkt. 6.95 (*0-935180-07-9*) Mutual Pub HI.

— A Hawaiian Reader, Vol. II. 352p. 1998. mass mkt. 6.95 (*1-56647-207-5*) Mutual Pub HI.

— True Tales of Hawaii & the South Seas. 342p. 1993. mass mkt. 4.95 (*0-935180-22-2*) Mutual Pub HI.

Day, A. Grove, jt. auth. see Buenzle, Fred J.

Day, A. Grove, ed. see Becke, Louis.

Day, A. Grove, ed. see London, Jack.

Day, A. Grove, ed. see Stevenson, Robert Louis.

Day, A. Grove, ed. see Twain, Mark, pseud.

Day, Abby. How to Get Research Published in Journals. 130p. 1996. 65.95 (*0-566-07886-4*, Pub. by Gower) Ashgate Pub Co.

— How to Get Research Published in Journals. LC 96-21609. 200p. 1996. pap. 33.95 (*0-566-07767-1*, Pub. by Gower) Ashgate Pub Co.

Day, Adrian. Thirty Minutes to Financial Freedom. 3rd ed. 91p. 1989. 19.95 (*0-945332-15-7*) Agora Inc MD.

Day, Adrienne. A Gentle Taming. 384p. (Orig.). 1994. mass mkt. 4.50 (*0-380-77411-9*, Avon Bks) Morrow Avon.

— In Search of a Song, Vol. 4. Spiegel, Richard A. & Fisher, Barbara, eds. (Illus.). 27p. (Orig.). (J). (gr. 3 up). 1983. pap. 2.00 (*0-934830-29-0*) Ten Penny.

— Rebellious Bride. 352p. (Orig.). 1995. mass mkt. 4.99 (*0-380-77413-5*, Avon Bks) Morrow Avon.

Day, Aidan, jt. ed. see Ricks, Christopher.

Day, Aidan, ed. see Tennyson, Alfred Lord.

Day, Aiden. Romanticism. LC 95-8288. (New Critical Idiom Ser.). 240p. (C). 1995. pap. 12.99 (*0-415-08578-8*) Routledge.

Day, Alan. Digital Building. LC 96-51638. 192p. 1997. pap. text 42.95 (*0-7506-1897-3*) Buttrwrth-Heinemann.

***Day, Alan.** Directory of European Union Political Parties. 216p. 2000. 60.00 (*0-9536278-6-1*, Pub. by John Harper Pub); pap. 25.00 (*0-9536278-5-3*, Pub. by John Harper Pub) Turpin Dist.

Day, Alan. England. LC 94-147566. (World Bibliographical Ser.). 612p. 1993. lib. bdg. 134.75 (*1-85109-040-1*) ABC-CLIO.

— The Falkland Islands, South Georgia & the South Sandwich Islands. LC 96-192577. (World Bibliographical Ser.). 252p. 1996. lib. bdg. 69.00 (*1-85109-236-6*) ABC-CLIO.

— Inside the British Library. LC 99-203802. 297p. 1998. 85.00 (*1-85604-280-4*, LAP2804, Pub. by Library Association) Bernan Associates.

Day, Alan, ed. The Annual Register, 1997: A Record of World Events. 239th ed. 600p. 1998. 175.00 (*1-886994-13-7*, 111531) Wrldwide Govt.

Day, Alan, et al, eds. Walford's Guide to Reference Material Vol. 2: Social & Historical Sciences, Philosophy & Religion. 7th ed. 1156p. 1997. 269.00 (*1-85604-223-5*, LAP2235, Pub. by Library Association) Bernan Associates.

Day, Alan, ed. see Chalcraft, Anthony, et al.

Day, Alan E. Archaeology: A Reference Handbook. LC 77-21938. 319p. reprint ed. pap. 98.90 (*0-7837-5292-X*, 204504600005) Bks Demand.

— The British Library: A Guide to Its Structure, Publications, Collections, & Services. LC 90-165596. 200p. reprint ed. pap. 62.00 (*0-608-02481-3*, 206312400004) Bks Demand.

— Discovery & Exploration Vol. 1: A Reference Handbook: Old World. LC 80-119195. 295p. reprint ed. pap. 91.50 (*0-7837-5295-4*, 204504900001) Bks Demand.

— History: A Reference Handbook. fac. ed. LC 76-28410. 352p. 1977. reprint ed. pap. 109.20 (*0-7837-8200-4*, 204795800008) Bks Demand.

— The New British Library. LC 94-34695. 279p. Date not set. reprint ed. pap. 86.50 (*0-608-20733-0*, 207183100002) Bks Demand.

Day, Alan F. A Social Study of Lawyers in Maryland, 1660-1775. (Outstanding Studies in Early American History). 350p. 1990. reprint ed. 35.00 (*0-8240-6177-2*) Garland.

Day, Alan J., ed. The Annual Register, 1996: A Record of World Events. 228th ed. 608p. 1997. 185.00 (*1-886994-09-9*, 110774) Wrldwide Govt.

Day, Alan J. & Hoffman, Verena, eds. The Annual Register, 1993: A Record of World Events. LC 94-17979. 635p. 1994. 170.00 (*0-582-23449-2*, Pub. by Addison-Wesley) Longman.

Day, Alastair. Lease & Finance Evaluation: Applications for Successful Financing Alternatives. 105p. 1996. pap. 225.00 (*1-85564-535-1*, Pub. by Euromoney) Am Educ Systs.

Day, Albert M. Making a Living in Conservation: A Guide to Outdoor Careers. LC 70-162449. 96p. 1971. write for info. (*0-8117-0964-7*) Stackpole.

Day, Alen. St. Helena, Ascension & Tristan Da Cunha. LC 97-180595. Vol. 197. 286p. 1997. lib. bdg. 76.00 (*1-85109-272-2*) ABC-CLIO.

***Day, Alexandra.** Boswell Wide Awake. LC 98-75733. (Illus.). 32p. (J). (ps-1). 1999. 15.00 (*0-374-39973-5*) FS&G.

Day, Alexandra. A Bouquet. (Illus.). 24p. 1996. 8.95 (*1-883211-07-7*) Laughing Elephant.

***Day, Alexandra.** Carl. 2001. text. write for info. (*0-374-31088-2*) FS&G.

Day, Alexandra. Carl Goes Shopping. LC 88-46216. (Illus.). 32p. (J). (ps-3). 1989. 12.95 (*0-374-31110-2*) FS&G.

— Carl Goes to Daycare. LC 93-17256. 32p. (J). (ps-3). 1993. 12.95 (*0-374-31093-9*) FS&G.

— Carl Goes to Daycare. 32p. (J). (ps-k). 1995. bds. 5.95 (*0-374-31145-5*) FS&G.

— Carl Makes a Scrapbook. (Illus.). 32p. 1994. 12.95 (*0-374-31129-3*) FS&G.

— Carl Pops Up. (J). 1994. 14.95 (*0-671-87105-6*, Green Tiger S&S) S&S Childrens.

— Carlito en el Parque una Tarde: Carl's Afternoon in the Park. LC 91-43926. (SPA., Illus.). 32p. (J). (gr. 2 up). 1992. bds. 12.95 (*0-374-31100-5*) FS&G.

— Carl's Afternoon in the Park. LC 91-12501. (Illus.). 32p. (J). (ps-3). 1991. 12.95 (*0-374-31109-9*) FS&G.

— Carl's Baby Journal. 48p. (J). 1996. pap. 10.95 (*0-374-31152-8*) FS&G.

— Carl's Birthday. LC 94-61974. (Illus.). 32p. (J). (ps-3). 1995. 12.95 (*0-374-31144-7*) FS&G.

— Carl's Birthday. 32p. (J). (ps). 1997. bds. 5.95 (*0-374-31150-1*) FS&G.

— Carl's Christmas. LC 90-55164. (Illus.). 32p. (J). (ps-3). 1990. bds. 12.95 (*0-374-31114-5*) FS&G.

— Carl's Masquerade. 32p. (J). 1992. 12.95 (*0-374-31094-7*) FS&G.

— Children from the Golden Age. (J). pap. 14.95 (*0-671-75200-6*) S&S Bks Yung.

Day, Alexandra. Crealo Si Se Puede. (SPA., Illus.). 172p. 1997. pap. text 20.98 (*968-13-2905-8*) Edit Diana.

Day, Alexandra. Follow Carl! LC 97-76928. (Illus.). 32p. (J). (ps-3). 1998. 12.95 (*0-374-34380-2*) FS&G.

— Frank & Ernest on the Road. (Illus.). 48p. (J). (ps-3). 1994. 14.95 (*0-590-45048-4*, Scholastic Hardcover) Scholastic Inc.

— Frank & Ernest Play Ball. LC 89-10312. (Illus.). 40p. (J). (gr. k-3). 1990. 12.95 (*0-590-42548-X*) Scholastic Inc.

— Good Dog, Carl. (J). 1998. pap. 8.00 (*0-671-76958-8*) S&S Bks Yung.

Day, Alexandra. Good Dog, Carl. (Illus.). 36p. (J). (ps-k). 1996. mass mkt. 5.95 (*0-689-80748-1*) S&S Childrens.

Day, Alexandra. Good Dog, Carl. 1997. per. 4.99 (*0-689-81771-1*) S&S Trade.

— Good Dog, Carl. (J). 1987. 10.95 (*0-310-57040-9*, 16104) Zondervan.

— Good Dog Carl. LC 91-25274. (Illus.). 36p. (Orig.). (J). (ps up). 1991. pap. 12.00 (*0-671-75204-9*, Green Tiger S&S) S&S Childrens.

— Good Dog Carl. (Orig.). 1997. 10.19 (*0-606-13437-9*, Pub. by Turtleback) Demco.

***Day, Alexandra & Edens, Cooper.** Darby, the Special Order Pup. LC 99-42632. (Illus.). 32p. (J). (ps-3). 2000. 15.99 (*0-8037-2496-9*, Dial Yng Read) Peng Put Young Read.

Day, Alexandra, jt. auth. see Day, Carl.

Day, Alexandra, jt. auth. see Edens, Cooper.

Day, Alice T. Remarkable Survivors: Insights into Successful Aging among Women. (Illus.). 340p. (C). 1991. pap. text 26.00 (*0-87766-491-9*) Urban Inst.

Day, Andrew P., jt. auth. see Mayne, Philip.

D

Day, Angelique. The Ordnance Survey Memoirs of Ireland Vol. 13: Antrim IV: The Glens. McWilliams, Patrick, ed. (Illus.). 150p. 1991. pap. 15.99 (*0-85389-392-6*, Pub. by Inst Irish Studies) Irish Bks Media.

Day, Angelique & McWilliams, Patrick, eds. The Ordnance Survey Memoirs of Ireland Vol. 1: County Armagh. LC 91-154915. (Illus.). 150p. 1990. pap. 15.99 (*0-85389-341-1*, Pub. by Inst Irish Studies) Irish Bks Media.

— The Ordnance Survey Memoirs of Ireland Vol. 2: County Antrim I: Newtownabbey & District. (Illus.). 150p. 1990. pap. 15.99 (*0-85389-347-0*, Pub. by Inst Irish Studies) Irish Bks Media.

— The Ordnance Survey Memoirs of Ireland Vol. 3: County Down I: South Down. (Illus.). 150p. 1990. pap. 15.99 (*0-85389-358-6*, Pub. by Inst Irish Studies) Irish Bks Media.

— The Ordnance Survey Memoirs of Ireland Vol. 4: Fermanagh I: Enniskillen & Upper Loch Erne. (Illus.). 150p. 1990. pap. 15.99 (*0-85389-360-8*, Pub. by Inst Irish Studies) Irish Bks Media.

— The Ordnance Survey Memoirs of Ireland Vol. 5: Tyrone I: South West & South Tyrone (Omagh) (Illus.). 150p. 1990. pap. 15.99 (*0-85389-362-4*, Pub. by Inst Irish Studies) Irish Bks Media.

— The Ordnance Survey Memoirs of Ireland Vol. 6: Londonderry 1: Magherafelt & District. (Illus.). 150p. 1990. pap. 15.99 (*0-85389-364-0*, Pub. by Inst Irish Studies) Irish Bks Media.

— The Ordnance Survey Memoirs of Ireland Vol. 7: Down II: North Down & the Ards. (Illus.). 150p. 1991. pap. 15.99 (*0-85389-374-8*, Pub. by Inst Irish Studies) Irish Bks Media.

— The Ordnance Survey Memoirs of Ireland Vol. 8: Antrim II: Lisburn & South Antrim. (Illus.). 150p. 1991. pap. 15.99 (*0-85389-376-4*, Pub. by Inst Irish Studies) Irish Bks Media.

— The Ordnance Survey Memoirs of Ireland Vol. 9: Antrim II: Larne & Island Magee. (Illus.). 150p. 1991. pap. 15.99 (*0-85389-378-0*, Pub. by Inst Irish Studies) Irish Bks Media.

— The Ordnance Survey Memoirs of Ireland Vol. 10: Antrim III: Larne & Island Magee. (Illus.). 150p. 1991. pap. 15.99 (*0-85389-389-6*, Pub. by Inst Irish Studies) Irish Bks Media.

— The Ordnance Survey Memoirs of Ireland Vol. 11: Londonderry III: Roe Valley Lower (Magilligan) (Illus.). 150p. 1991. pap. 15.99 (*0-85389-390-X*, Pub. by Inst Irish Studies) Irish Bks Media.

— The Ordnance Survey Memoirs of Ireland Vol. 12: Down III: Mid-Down. (Illus.). 150p. 1991. pap. 15.99 (*0-85389-391-8*, Pub. by Inst Irish Studies) Irish Bks Media.

— The Ordnance Survey Memoirs of Ireland Vol. 14: Fermanagh II: Lower Lough Erne. (Illus.). 150p. 1991. pap. 15.99 (*0-85389-393-4*, Pub. by Inst Irish Studies) Irish Bks Media.

— The Ordnance Survey Memoirs of Ireland Vol. 15: Londonderry IV: Roe Balley Upper (Dungiven) (Illus.). 150p. 1991. pap. 15.99 (*0-85389-394-2*, Pub. by Inst Irish Studies) Irish Bks Media.

— The Ordnance Survey Memoirs of Ireland Vol. 16: County Antrim V: Giant's Causeway & Ballymoney. (Illus.). 125p. 1991. pap. 15.99 (*0-85389-388-8*, Pub. by Inst Irish Studies) Irish Bks Media.

— The Ordnance Survey Memoirs of Ireland Vol. 17: Down IV: East Down & Lecale. (Illus.). 150p. 1992. pap. 15.99 (*0-85389-439-6*, Pub. by Inst Irish Studies) Irish Bks Media.

Day, Angelique & McWilliams, Patrick, eds. The Ordnance Survey Memoirs of Ireland Vol. 18: County Londonderry V: Maghera & Tamlaght O'Crilly. (Illus.). 144p. 1993. pap. 18.50 (*0-85389-441-8*, Pub. by Inst Irish Studies) Irish Bks Media.

— The Ordnance Survey Memoirs of Ireland Vol. 19: County Antrim VI: Southwest Antrim. (Illus.). 138p. 1993. pap. 18.50 (*0-85389-458-2*, Pub. by Inst Irish Studies) Irish Bks Media.

Day, Angelique & McWilliams, Patrick, eds. The Ordnance Survey Memoirs of Ireland Vol. 20: Tyrone II: Mid & East Tyrone (Cookstown & Dungannon) (Illus.). 150p. 1993. pap. 18.50 (*0-85389-460-4*, Pub. by Inst Irish Studies) Irish Bks Media.

Day, Angelique & McWilliams, Patrick, eds. The Ordnance Survey Memoirs of Ireland Vol. 21: County Antrim VII. (Illus.). 150p. 1990. pap. 15.99 (*0-85389-462-0*, Pub. by Inst Irish Studies) Irish Bks Media.

— The Ordnance Survey Memoirs of Ireland Vol. 22: County Londonderry VI: Northeast Londonderry. (Illus.). 122p. 1993. pap. 18.50 (*0-85389-464-7*, Pub. by Inst Irish Studies) Irish Bks Media.

— The Ordnance Survey Memoirs of Ireland Vol. 24: County Antrim IX: North Antrim Coast & Rathlin. (Illus.). 134p. 1994. pap. 18.50 (*0-85389-468-X*, Pub. by Inst Irish Studies) Irish Bks Media.

— The Ordnance Survey Memoirs of Ireland Vol. 25: Londonderry VII: North-West Londonderry. (Illus.). 125p. 1994. pap. 18.50 (*0-85389-510-4*, Pub. by Inst Irish Studies) Irish Bks Media.

— The Ordnance Survey Memoirs of Ireland Vol. 26: County Antrim X: East Antrim (Glynn, Inver, Kilroot & Templecorran) (Illus.). 132p. 1996. pap. 18.50 (*0-85389-512-0*, Pub. by Inst Irish Studies) Irish Bks Media.

— The Ordnance Survey Memoirs of Ireland Vol. 27: County Londonderry VIII: East Londonderry. (Illus.). 130p. 1994. pap. 18.50 (*0-85389-514-7*, Pub. by Inst Irish Studies) Irish Bks Media.

— The Ordnance Survey Memoirs of Ireland Vol. 28: County Londonderry IX: West Londonderry. (Illus.). 127p. 1995. pap. 18.50 (*0-85389-516-3*, Pub. by Inst Irish Studies) Irish Bks Media.

— The Ordnance Survey Memoirs of Ireland Vol. 29: County Antrim XI: Antrim Town & Ballyclare. (Illus.). 157p. 1995. pap. 18.50 (*0-85389-518-X*, Pub. by Inst Irish Studies) Irish Bks Media.

— The Ordnance Survey Memoirs of Ireland Vol. 30: County Londonderry X: Mid-Londonderry. (Illus.). 132p. 1995. pap. 18.50 (*0-85389-520-1*, Pub. by Inst Irish Studies) Irish Bks Media.

— The Ordnance Survey Memoirs of Ireland Vol. 31: County Londonderry XI: South Londonderry. (Illus.). 144p. 1995. pap. 18.50 (*0-85389-550-3*, Pub. by Inst Irish Studies) Irish Bks Media.

— The Ordnance Survey Memoirs of Ireland Vol. 32: County County Antrim XII: Ballynure & District. (Illus.). 141p. 1995. pap. 18.50 (*0-85389-552-X*, Pub. by Inst Irish Studies) Irish Bks Media.

— The Ordnance Survey Memoirs of Ireland Vol. 33: County Londonderry XII: Coleraine & Mouth of the Bann. (Illus.). 173p. 1995. pap. 18.50 (*0-85389-554-6*, Pub. by Inst Irish Studies) Irish Bks Media.

— The Ordnance Survey Memoirs of Ireland Vol. 34: County Londonderry XIII: Clondermot & the Waterside. (Illus.). 133p. 1996. pap. 18.50 (*0-85389-556-2*, Pub. by Inst Irish Studies) Irish Bks Media.

— The Ordnance Survey Memoirs of Ireland Vol. 35: County County Antrim XIII: Templepatrick & District. (Illus.). 160p. 1996. pap. 18.50 (*0-85389-560-0*, Pub. by Inst Irish Studies) Irish Bks Media.

— The Ordnance Survey Memoirs of Ireland Vol. 36: County Londonderry XIV: Faughanvale. (Illus.). 120p. 1996. pap. 18.50 (*0-85389-558-9*, Pub. by Inst Irish Studies) Irish Bks Media.

— The Ordnance Survey Memoirs of Ireland Vol. 37: County Antrim XIV: Carrickfergus. (Illus.). 195p. 1996. pap. 18.50 (*0-85389-563-5*, Pub. by Inst Irish Studies) Irish Bks Media.

— The Ordnance Survey Memoirs of Ireland Vol. 38: County Donegal: North-East Donegal. LC 91-154915. (Illus.). 152p. 1997. pap. 18.50 (*0-85389-564-3*, Pub. by Inst Irish Studies) Irish Bks Media.

— The Ordnance Survey Memoirs of Ireland Vol. 39: County Donegal II: West & South Donegal. (Illus.). 199p. 1997. pap. 18.50 (*0-85389-659-3*, Pub. by Inst Irish Studies) Irish Bks Media.

Day, Angelique & McWilliams, Patrick, eds. The Ordnance Survey Memoirs of Ireland Vol. 40: Counties Cavan, Leitrim, Louth, Mnaghan & Sligo. (Illus.). 150p. 1998. pap. 18.50 (*0-85389-661-5*, Pub. by Inst Irish Studies) Irish Bks Media.

Day, Angell. English Secretary. LC 67-10122. 1967. reprint ed. 50.00 (*0-8201-1012-4*) Schol Facsimiles.

Day, Ann, jt. auth. see Lunn, Kenneth.

Day, Anne L. & Myles, Carolyn. Training Resources for the Produce Industry. 92p. 1992. ring bd. write for info. (*0-9632546-0-X*) U Fresh Fruit & Veg.

Day, Anthony. Kaleidoscope: Five Views of Life. LC 95-15476. 48p. 1995. 10.95 (*0-944957-55-2*) Rivercross Pub.

Day, Archibald A. The Origins of Latin Love-Elegy. 148p. 1983. reprint ed. lib. bdg. 36.50 (*3-487-04307-6*) G Olms Pubs.

Day, Arden D. & Ludeke, Kenneth L. Plant Nutrients in Desert Environments. LC 92-32705. (Adaptations of Desert Organisms Ser.). 1993. 118.00 (*3-540-55695-8*); 104.95 (*0-387-55695-8*) Spr-Verlag.

Day, Arthur G. Books about Hawaii: Fifty Basic Authors. LC 77-7997. 139p. reprint ed. pap. 43.10 (*0-7837-1309-6*, 204145700020) Bks Demand.

— Coronado's Quest: The Discovery of the Southwestern States. LC 81-13443. 419p. 1982. reprint ed. lib. bdg. 65.00 (*0-313-23207-5*, DACO, Greenwood Pr) Greenwood.

Day, Ashley M., jt. auth. see Bryan-Day, Lisa.

Day, Barbara. Fast Facts on Fast Food for Fast People. 4th rev. ed. 84p. 1995. per. 4.95 (*0-9631538-6-2*) An Apple a Day.

— High Energy Eating: Sport Nutrition for Active People. 2nd rev. ed. 112p. 1995. student ed., per. 17.95 (*0-9631538-5-4*) An Apple a Day.

***Day, Barbara.** The Velvet Philosophers. 344p. 2000. 55.00 (*1-870626-37-0*, Pub. by Claridge Pr); 32.95 (*1-870626-42-7*, Pub. by Claridge Pr) Paul & Co Pubs.

Day, Barbara, ed. Czech Plays: Modern Czech Drama. LC 94-127607. 256p. 1998. pap. 19.95 (*1-85459-074-X*, Pub. by N Hern Bks) Consort Bk Sales.

***Day, Barbara & Kappa Delta Pi (Honor Society) Staff.** Teaching & Learning in the New Millennium. LC 99-52741. 174p. 1999. 20.00 (*0-912099-36-4*) Kappa Delta Pi.

Day, Barbara, jt. auth. see Wagner, Tricia.

Day, Barbara, jt. auth. see Wilt, Pamela C.

Day, Barry. This Wooden "O" Shakespeare's Globe Reborn Achieving an American's Dream. LC 98-2549. (Illus.). 354p. 1988. pap. 22.50 (*0-87910-267-5*) Limelight Edns.

***Day, Barry, compiled by.** Noel Coward: A Life in Quotes. (Illus.). 116p. 2000. 19.95 (*1-900512-84-X*, Pub. by Metro Bks) Trafalgar.

Day, Barry, ed. Noel Coward: The Complete Lyrics. LC 98-17414. (Illus.). 356p. 1998. 65.00 (*0-87951-896-0*, Pub. by Overlook Pr) Penguin Putnam.

Day, Barry, ed. see Coward, Noel.

Day, Bernie. The Unconscious Agendas. LC 97-74313. 208p. 1997. per. 22.95 (*0-7872-4248-9*) Kendall-Hunt.

Day, Beth. Glacier Pilot. LC 57-6781. (Illus.). 1976. reprint ed. pap. 5.95 (*0-89174-009-0*) Comstock Edns.

Day, Beth. Grizzlies in Their Backyard. LC 94-910037. (Illus.). 192p. 1994. pap. 14.95 (*1-895811-16-3*) Heritage Hse.

***Day, Betty H. & Wortman, William A.** Literature in English: A Guide for Librarians in the Digital Age. LC 00-24213. (ACRL Publications in Librarianship). 2000. write for info. (*0-8389-8081-3*) Assn Coll & Res Libs.

Day, Bill. Day-Ja Vu. (Illus.). 195p. 1988. pap. 9.95 (*0-937247-07-3*) Detroit Pr.

Day-Bivins, Pat & Smith, Philip D. The Rabbit & the Promise Sign. LC 97-74229. (Illus.). 32p. (J). (gr. k-5). 1998. 15.95 (*1-886864-08-X*) Goldn Anchor Pr.

Day-Bivins, Pat, jt. auth. see Smith, Philip D.

Day, Bradford M., ed. The Checklist of Fantastic Literature in Paperbound Books. LC 74-15961. (Science Fiction Ser.). 128p. 1977. reprint ed. 15.95 (*0-405-06326-1*) Ayer.

— The Supplemental Checklist of Fantastic Literature. LC 74-15962. (Science Fiction Ser.). 160p. 1976. reprint ed. 13.95 (*0-405-06327-X*) Ayer.

Day, Bradford M., et al, eds. Bibliography of Adventure: Mundy, Burroughs, Rohmer, Haggard. rev. ed. LC 77-84282. (Lost Race & Adult Fantasy Ser.). 1978. lib. bdg. 19.95 (*0-405-11019-7*) Ayer.

Day, Brant. Not in the Wind. (Illus.). 32p. (J). 1995. 12.95 (*0-910523-14-2*) Grandin Bk Co.

Day, Brenda. Beautiful Cross-Stitch from Classic Quilts Designs. LC 95-47446. (Illus.). 128p. 1996. 27.95 (*0-8069-1342-8*) Sterling.

***Day, Brian A., et al.** Communication for Environmental Action: Lessons from International Initiatives. (Illus.). 2000. pap. write for info. (*0-89492-108-8*) Acad Educ Dev.

Day, Bruce, jt. auth. see Thomas, Mack.

Day, C., et al, eds. Radiation from Black Holes, Future Missions to Primitive Bodies & Middle Atmospheric Fine Structures: Proceedings of the E1.1, B.5 & C2.4 Symposia of COSPAR Scientific Commissions E, B & C Held During the Thirtieth COSPAR Scientific Assembly, Hamburg, Germany, 11-21 July 1994. (Advances in Space Research Ser.: No. 19). 196p. (Orig.). 1997. pap. 110.00 (*0-08-043097-X*, Pergamon Pr) Elsevier.

Day, C. M. History of the Eastern Townships: Province of Quebec, Civil & Descriptive, in Three Parts. (Illus.). 475p. 1996. reprint ed. lib. bdg. 52.00 (*0-8328-5158-2*) Higginson Bk Co.

Day, C. R. The Music & Musical Instruments of Southern India & the Deccan. 1990. reprint ed. 12.50 (*81-85395-24-1*, Pub. by Low Price) S Asia.

Day, C. R. The Music & Musical Instruments of Southern India & the Deccan. 1996. reprint ed. 11.00 (*81-86142-91-6*, Pub. by Low Price) S Asia.

Day, Carl & Day, Alexandra. My Puppy's Record Book. (Illus.). 32p. (J). (ps-3). 1994. 9.95 (*0-374-36151-7*) FS&G.

Day, Caroline. Study of Some Negro-White Families in the U. S. LC 76-106857. (Illus.). 126p. 1971. reprint ed. lib. bdg. 38.50 (*0-8371-3479-X*, DNF&) Greenwood.

Day, Catharina. Ireland. 4th ed. (Cadogan Guides Ser.). (Illus.). 676p. 1995. pap. text 19.95 (*1-86011-088-6*, Pub. by Cadgn Bks) Globe Pequot.

***Day, Catharina.** North of Ireland. 2nd ed. (Country Guides Ser.). 2000. pap. text 14.95 (*1-86011-970-0*) Cadgn Bks.

Day, Catharina. Southwest Ireland. 2nd ed. 1999. pap. text 17.95 (*1-86011-911-5*) Cadogan Pubns.

***Day, Catharina.** Take the Kids Ireland. (Take the Kids Ser.). (Illus.). 2000. pap. 19.95 (*1-86011-993-X*) Cadgn Bks.

***Day, Cecil B., Jr.** Day by Day: The Story of Cecil B. Day & His Simple Formula for Success. (Illus.). 2000. 20.95 (*0-8246-0425-3*) Jonathan David.

***Day, Charles E.** Profiting from Teleservices: An Operational Guide to Call Center Technologies. (Illus.). 528p. 2000. pap. 65.00 (*0-07-016430-4*) McGraw.

Day, Charles E., ed. High-Density Lipoproteins. LC 81-4379. (Illus.). 710p. reprint ed. pap. 200.00 (*0-7837-0805-X*, 204112000019) Bks Demand.

Day, Charles S., jt. ed. see Holt, Stephen S.

Day, Cherie H. Life on Intertidal Rocks: A Guide to Marine Life of the Rocky North Atlantic Coast. (Illus.). 62p. 1987. pap. 3.00 (*0-912550-15-5*) Nature Study.

Day, Cherie H., et al. Beyond/Within: A Collection of Rengay. (Illus.). xii, 46p. 1997. pap. 9.95 (*0-9659589-0-6*) Sundog Press.

Day, Chet, jt. auth. see Bass, Stanley S.

Day, Chris & Morre, Roger. Staff Development in the Secondary School: Management Perspectives. 320p. 1987. 49.95 (*0-7099-0895-4*, Pub. by C Helm); pap. 17.00 (*0-7099-4539-6*, Pub. by C Helm) Routldge.

Day, Chris & Poster, Cyril. Partnership in Educational Management. 224p. (C). 1988. lib. bdg. 55.00 (*0-415-00588-4*) Routledge.

Day, Chris, jt. auth. see Allison, Keith.

Day, Christine E. The Belle Books. (Illus.). 104p. (J). (gr. k-6). 1997. write for info. (*0-9659669-6-8*) Belle Bks.

Day, Christine L. What Older Americans Think: Interest Groups & Aging Policy. (Illus.). 179p. (C). 1990. text 32.50 (*0-691-07825-4*, Pub. by Princeton U Pr) Cal Prin Full Svc.

Day, Christine R., ed. see Williams, Tennessee.

Day, Christopher. Developing Teachers: The Challenge of Lifelong Learning. LC 99-218328. 224p. 1999. 85.00 (*0-7507-0748-8*, Falmer Pr); pap. 26.95 (*0-7507-0747-X*, Falmer Pr) Taylor & Francis.

— The Homeopathic Treatment of Small Animals. 129p. 1998. pap. 21.95 (*0-85207-216-3*, Pub. by C W Daniel) Natl Bk Netwk.

— The Jacaltec Language. (Language Science Ser.: No. 12). 136p. 1973. pap. text 59.25 (*90-279-2676-X*) Mouton.

— The Jacaltec Language. (Language Science Monographs: Vol. 12). viii, 136p. 1973. pap. text 16.00 (*0-87750-176-9*) Res Inst Inner Asian Studies.

***Day, Christopher.** Leading Schools in Times of Change. LC 99-50029. 2000. pap. write for info. (*0-335-20582-8*) Taylor & Francis.

Day, Christopher. Places of the Soul: Architecture & Environmental Design As Healing Art. 1990. 22.95 (*0-85030-880-1*, Pub. by Aqm Pr) Harper SF.

Day, Christopher, et al. Leadership & Curriculum in the Primary School: The Roles of Senior & Middle Management. LC 93-10937. 1993. write for info. (*1-85396-214-7*) Chapman & Hall.

— Managing Primary Schools: A Professional Development Approach. 224p. (C). 1986. pap. 36.00 (*0-06-318306-4*, Pub. by P Chapman) St Mut.

Day, Christopher, jt. auth. see Allison, Keith.

Day, Christopher, jt. ed. see Poster, Cyril D.

Day, Christopher E. Homeopathic Treatment of Small Animals. 224p. (Orig.). pap. 29.95 (*0-8464-4232-9*) Beekman Pubs.

Day, Christopher W., et al, eds. Insights into Teachers' Thinking & Practice. 250p. 1990. pap. 39.95 (*1-85000-661-X*, Falmer Pr) Taylor & Francis.

— Research on Teacher Thinking: Understanding Professional Development. 256p. 1993. pap. 33.95 (*0-7507-0178-1*, Falmer Pr) Taylor & Francis.

Day, Christopher W. & Norman, John L., Jr., eds. Issues in Educational Drama. (Curriculum Series for Teachers Monograph). 197p. 1984. 65.00 (*0-905273-66-4*, Falmer Pr); pap. 34.95 (*0-905273-65-6*, Falmer Pr) Taylor & Francis.

Day, Christopher W., et al. Appraisal & Professional Development in Primary Schools. 256p. 1987. 99.95 (*0-335-15542-1*) OpUniv Pr.

Day, Clarence. The Best of Clarence Day. 29.95 (*0-88411-528-3*) Amereon Ltd.

— Life with Father. 25.95 (*0-88411-527-5*) Amereon Ltd.

— Life with Father. 1981. reprint ed. lib. bdg. 25.95 (*0-89966-430-X*) Buccaneer Bks.

— Life with Father. 1993. reprint ed. lib. bdg. 27.95 (*1-56849-156-5*) Buccaneer Bks.

— The Simian World. 107p. Date not set. 16.95 (*0-8488-2242-0*) Amereon Ltd.

Day, Clarence, Jr. This Simian World. (Illus.). 64p. 1998. pap. 2.00 (*0-486-29965-1*) Dover.

Day, Clarence A. Ezekiel Holmes: Father of Maine Agriculture. 1968. pap. 8.95 (*0-89101-015-7*) U Maine Pr.

Day, Clarence B. The Philosophers of China. 1978. pap. 5.95 (*0-8065-0622-9*, Citadel Pr) Carol Pub Group.

Day, Clive. The Distribution of Industrial Occupations in England, 1841-1861. (Connecticut Academy of Arts & Sciences Ser., Trans.: Vol. 28). 1927. pap. 75.00 (*0-685-44360-4*) Elliots Bks.

Day, Colin A. Roget's Theaurus of the Bible. 944p. 1998. pap. 20.00 (*0-06-061774-8*, Pub. by Harper SF) HarpC.

Day Communications Staff, ed. see Marshall, Nelson.

Day, Cyrus L. Art of Knotting & Splicing. 1980. 32.95 (*0-87021-083-1*) Naval Inst Pr.

— Knots & Splices. (Illus.). 64p. 1989. pap. 6.95 (*0-07-156378-4*) McGraw.

— Knots & Splices. rev. ed. (Illus.). 64p. 1989. pap. text 6.95 (*0-87742-252-4*) Intl Marine.

Day, D. A., jt. ed. see Douce, Roland.

Day, Dan. Ever Been Irritated? (Uplook Ser.). 31p. 1972. pap. 0.99 (*0-8163-0070-4*, 05630-9) Pacific Pr Pub Assn.

Day, Dan. How to Change Your Behavior. (Lifestyle Ser.). 30p. 1986. pap. 0.99 (*0-8163-0654-0*) Pacific Pr Pub Assn.

Day, Dan. Hurting. (Uplook Ser.). 1978. pap. 0.99 (*0-8163-0088-7*, 08889-8) Pacific Pr Pub Assn.

Day, Dave. Setting up Radio Control Helicopters. (R-C Handbook Ser.). (Illus.). 61p. 1988. pap. text 12.95 (*0-85242-975-4*, Pub. by Nexus) Motorbooks Intl.

Day, David. The Animals Within. 1984. 6.95 (*0-920806-61-9*, Pub. by Penumbra Pr) U of Toronto Pr.

— The Bevin Boy: A History of the Use of Young Boys in British Mines During WWII. large type ed. 21.95 (*1-85695-162-6*, Pub. by ISIS Lrg Prnt) Transaction Pubs.

— Contraband & Controversy: The Customs History of Australia from 1901. (Illus.). 616p. 1996. 59.95 (*0-644-33151-8*, 9416566, Pub. by AGPS Pr) Intl Spec Bk.

— Contraband & Controversy: The Customs History of Australia from 1901. deluxe limited ed. (Illus.). 616p. 1996. 194.95 (*0-644-35545-X*, 9428965, Pub. by AGPS Pr) Intl Spec Bk.

— The King of the Woods. LC 93-9410. (Illus.). 32p. (J). (ps-2). 1993. lib. bdg. 13.95 (*0-02-726361-4*, Mac Bks Young Read) S&S Childrens.

— Menzies & Churchill at War. (Illus.). 288p. 1994. pap. 28.00 (*0-19-553559-6*) OUP.

— A Preaching Workbook. LC 99-229396. 168p. 1998. pap. 15.95 (*1-901443-15-9*) Intl Pubs Mktg.

— Reluctant Nation: Australia & the Allied Defeat of Japan, 1942-1945. (Illus.). 384p. 1992. text 49.95 (*0-19-553242-2*) OUP.

— The Search for King Arthur. LC 95-24119. (Illus.). 176p. 1995. 24.95 (*0-8160-3370-6*) Facts on File.

— The Sleeper. 32p. 1990. 14.95 (*0-385-25253-6*) Doubleday.

— Smugglers & Sailors: The Customs History of Australia 1788-1901. 1992. lib. bdg. 253.50 (*0-644-25239-1*, Pub. by Aust Gov Pub) Accents Pubns.

— Tolkien: The Illustrated Encyclopedia. 1996. per. 20.00 (*0-684-83979-2*) S&S Trade.

— Tolkien Beastiary. 286p. 1995. 19.99 (*0-517-12077-1*) Random Hse Value.

— A Tolkien Bestiary. LC 79-9961. 287 p. 1979. 19.95 (*0-345-28283-3*) Ballantine Pub Grp.

— Tolkien's Ring. (Illus.). 224p. 1994. write for info. (*0-261-10298-2*, Pub. by HarpC) Trafalgar.

— Utah's Favorite Hiking Trails. LC 97-92587. (Illus.). 368p. 1998. pap. 14.95 (*0-9660858-0-9*) Rincon Pub.

Day, David, ed. Brave New World: Dr. H. V. Evatt & Australian Foreign Policy, 1941-1949. 1996. pap. 22.95 (*0-7022-2608-4*, Pub. by Univ Queensland Pr) Intl Spec Bk.

An Asterisk (*) at the beginning of an entry indicates that the title is appearing for the first time.

— Tolkien: The Illustrated Encyclopedia. (Illus.). 288p. 1991. text 29.95 (*0-02-533431-X*) Macmillan.

Day, David, jt. auth. see Astley, Jeff.

Day, David, jt. auth. see Jackson, Albert.

Day, David, jt. ed. see Goffin, Stacie.

Day, David A. Construction 2e. 2nd ed. LC 90-29315. (Series of Practical Construction Guides). 464p. 1991. 130.00 (*0-471-88840-0*) Wiley.

Day, David H. A Treasure Hard to Attain: Images of Archaeology in Popular Film with a Filmography. LC 96-12630. 176p. 1997. 37.50 (*0-8108-3171-6*) Scarecrow.

Day, David H., jt. auth. see Nichols, Herbert L., Jr.

Day, Deborah O., jt. ed. see Parnell, Teresa F.

***Day, Dianne.** Beacon Street Mourning: A Fremont Jones Mystery. LC 00-28190. 288p. 2000. 22.95 (*0-385-48610-3*) Doubleday.

Day, Dianne. The Bohemian Murders: A Fremont Jones Mystery. LC 96-40172. 256p. 1997. 21.95 (*0-385-47923-9*) Doubleday.

***Day, Dianne.** The Bohemian Murders: A Fremont Jones Mystery. LC 99-51849. 1999. 25.95 (*1-57490-217-2*) T T Beeler.

Day, Dianne. The Bohemian Murders: A Fremont Jones Mystery. 288p. 1998. reprint ed. mass mkt. 5.99 (*0-553-57412-4*, Crimeline) Bantam.

— Death Train to Boston. LC 99-12258. 272p. 1999. 21.95 (*0-385-48609-X*) Doubleday.

— Emperor Norton's Ghost. 336p. 1999. mass mkt. 5.99 (*0-553-58078-7*) Bantam.

— Emperor Norton's Ghost. LC 98-2809. 320p. 1998. 21.95 (*0-385-48608-1*) Doubleday.

— Fire & Fog. 288p. 1997. mass mkt. 5.99 (*0-553-56922-8*, Crimeline) Bantam.

— The Strange Files of Fremont Jones. 272p. 1996. mass mkt. 5.99 (*0-553-56921-X*, Crimeline) Bantam.

— The Strange Files of Fremont Jones. large type ed. (Niagara Large Print Ser.). 341p. 1996. 29.50 (*0-7089-5824-9*) Ulverscroft.

Day, Dick, jt. auth. see McDowell, Josh.

Day, Donald. The Autobiography of Will Rogers. 1976. 28.95 (*0-89190-330-5*) Amereon Ltd.

Day, Donald, jt. auth. see Rogers, Will.

Day, Donald, jt. ed. see Boatright, Mody C.

Day, Donald, ed. see Houston, Samuel.

Day, Donald, ed. see Rogers, Will.

Day, Donald D. This I Believe. 224p. 1972. pap. 1.95 (*0-9600500-1-9*) Three D Pubs.

Day, Donald L. & Kovacs, Diane K., eds. Computers, Communication & Mental Models. LC 97-197228. 96p. 1997. pap. 29.95 (*0-7484-0543-7*, Pub. by Tay Francis Ltd) Taylor & Francis.

Day, Donna G. Historic Inns & Famous Homes of Maryland: A Guide to Historic B&Bs in the Free State. 100p. 1997. pap. 6.95 (*1-885457-10-3*) Eastwind MD.

Day, Dorothy. Dorothy Day. Garvey, Michael, ed. LC 95-6227. (Modern Spirituality Ser.). 96p. 1996. pap. 4.95 (*0-87243-219-X*) Templegate.

Day, Dorothy. Dorothy Day: Selected Writings. Ellsberg, Robert, ed. LC 92-25801. 416p. 1992. reprint ed. pap. 18.00 (*0-88344-802-5*) Orbis Bks.

— From Union Square to Rome. 1978. 19.95 (*0-405-10815-X*) Ayer.

— Loaves & Fishes. LC 97-23637. 221p. 1997. reprint ed. pap. 13.00 (*1-57075-156-0*) Orbis Bks.

— Long Loneliness - Reissue. LC 81-4727. (Illus.). 304p. 1997. pap. 15.00 (*0-06-061751-9*, RD363, Pub. by Harper SF) HarpC.

— The Meditations of Dorothy Day. LC 97-60413. (Illus.). 128p. 1997. pap. 9.95 (*0-87243-227-0*) Templegate.

— On Pilgrimage. LC 99-23525. 266p. 1999. pap. 16.00 (*0-8028-4629-7*) Eerdmans.

— Therese. 178p. 1979. pap. 12.95 (*0-87243-090-1*) Templegate.

Day, Dorothy R. Naturalization in Caldwell County, Texas. 110p. (Orig.). 1989. pap. 10.50 (*0-9624711-0-0*) D R Day.

Day, Douglas. The Prison Notebooks of Ricardo Flores Magon. 1991. 21.95 (*0-15-174598-6*) Harcourt.

Day, Douglas, ed. see Faulkner, William.

Day, Doyle. Our Day Family, 1597-1990. ix, 356p. 1990. 40.00 (*0-944619-51-7*) Gregath Pub Co.

Day, Dwayne A., et al, eds. Eye in the Sky: The Story of the Corona Spy Satellites. LC 97-19238. (History of Aviation Ser.). (Illus.). 320p. 1998. 29.95 (*1-56098-830-4*) Smithsonian.

***Day, Dwayne A., et al, eds.** Eye in the Sky: The Story of the CORONA Spy Satellites. (History of Aviation Ser.). (Illus.). 1999. pap. 17.95 (*1-56098-773-1*) Smithsonian.

Day, E. W. One Thousand Years of Hubbard History, 866 to 1895. (Illus.). 512p. reprint ed. pap. 76.50 (*0-8328-0688-9*); reprint ed. lib. bdg. 84.50 (*0-8328-0687-0*) Higginson Bk Co.

Day, Edmund E. Education for Freedom & Responsibility: Selected Essays. Konvitz, Milton R., ed. LC 78-142618. (Essay Index Reprint Ser.). 1977. reprint ed. 20.95 (*0-8369-2391-X*) Ayer.

Day, Edmund E. & Thomas, Woodlief. The Growth of Manufactures, 1899-1923. LC 75-22811. (America in Two Centuries Ser.). 1976. reprint ed. 19.95 (*0-405-07682-7*) Ayer.

Day, Elaine M. & Shapson, Stan M. Studies in Immersion Education. LC 95-49679. (Language & Education Library: Vol. 11). 160p. 1996. 89.00 (*1-85359-356-7*, Pub. by Multilingual Matters); pap. 29.95 (*1-85359-355-9*, Pub. by Multilingual Matters) Taylor & Francis.

Day, Elyn. A Bed of Roses: Premier. (Special Edition Ser.). 1993. mass mkt. 3.50 (*0-373-09846-4*, 5-09846-2) Silhouette.

Day, Eugene D., ed. Advanced Immunochemistry. 2nd ed. 716p. 1990. pap. 225.00 (*0-471-56768-X*) Wiley.

Day, Faye & Geistfeld, Annette. Books Too Good to Miss. (Illus.). 53p. 1984. pap. 7.50 (*0-912773-04-9*) One Hund Twenty Creat.

— Productive Thinking Activities. 56p. (Orig.). 1985. pap. 6.25 (*0-912773-11-1*) One Hund Twenty Creat.

— Tales Too Good To Miss. (Illus.). 44p. 1983. pap. 7.50 (*0-912773-03-0*) One Hund Twenty Creat.

Day, Filomena T. & Milo, Jack. The Maine Food & Fun Guide. annuals 250p. (Orig.). 1995. pap. 24.95 (*0-9635054-0-8*) Better Day Vent.

Day, Frances A. Latina & Latino Voices in Literature for Children & Teenagers. LC 96-44895. 228p. 1997. pap. text 28.00 (*0-435-07202-1*, 07202) Heinemann.

Day, Frances A. Multicultural Voices in Contemporary Literature: A Resource for Teachers. LC 94-26262. (Illus.). 244p. 1994. pap. text 26.00 (*0-435-08826-2*, 08826) Heinemann.

***Day, Frances Ann.** Lesbian & Gay Voices: An Annotated Bibliography & Guide to Literature for Children & Young Adults. LC 00-21074. 296p. 2000. 35.00 (*0-313-31162-5*, GR1162, Greenwood Pr) Greenwood.

Day, Francis. Fishes Vol. I: Fauna of British India Including Ceylon & Burma. (Illus.). xviii, 548p. 1989. reprint ed. 25.00 (*1-55528-160-5*, Pub. by Today Tomorrow) Scholarly Pubns.

Day, Frank. Edmund Wilson: A Reference Guide. (Modern Critics & Critical Schools Ser.: Vol. 15). 300p. text 43.00 (*0-8240-0689-5*, H977) Garland.

Day, Frank P. Rockbound. LC 73-81763. (Literature of Canada, Poetry & Prose in Reprint Ser.). 324p. reprint ed. pap. 100.50 (*0-608-12841-4*, 202360900033) Bks Demand.

— Rockbound. rev. ed. 328p. 1989. pap. 12.95 (*0-8020-6723-9*) U of Toronto Pr.

Day, Frederick J. & Tran, Huong. Regulation of Wireless Communication Systems. LC 97-15293. 353p. 1997. text 89.00 (*0-86587-586-3*) Gov Insts.

***Day, G. W.** Technical Digest Nineteen Ninety Eight: Symposium on Optical Fiber Measurements. 195p. 1998. pap. 16.00 (*0-16-060882-1*) USGPO.

***Day, G. W., et al, eds.** Technical Digest - Symposium on Optical Fiber Measurements, 1998. 187p. (C). 1999. pap. text 35.00 (*0-7881-8374-5*) DIANE Pub.

Day, Gary. Literature & Culture in Modern Britain, Vol. 2. (C). 1997. pap. text 28.00 (*0-582-07550-5*) Addison-Wesley.

— Re-Reading Leavis: Culture & Literary Criticism. LC 96-24143. 256p. 1996. text 49.95 (*0-312-16419-X*) St Martin.

Day, Gary, ed. The British Critical Tradition: A Re-Evaluation. LC 91-29661. 208p. 1992. text 39.95 (*0-312-07481-6*) St Martin.

— Readings in Popular Culture: Trivial Pursuits? LC 89-34357. (Insights Ser.). 290p. 1990. text 45.00 (*0-312-03550-0*) St Martin.

Day, Gary & Docherty, Brian, eds. British Poetry from the 1950s to the 1990s: Politics & Art. LC 96-44311. 220p. 1997. text 39.95 (*0-312-17250-8*) St Martin.

— British Poetry, 1900-50: Aspects of Tradition. LC 94-33036. 1995. text 45.00 (*0-312-12406-6*) St Martin.

Day, Gary, jt. auth. see Bloom, Clive.

Day, Geoffrey. From Fiction to the Novel. 192p. 1987. 47.50 (*0-7102-0911-8*, 09118, Routledge Thoemms) Routledge.

Day, George. Return with Honor. (Illus.). 288p. 1991. pap. 28.50 (*0-912173-16-5*) Champlin Museum.

Day, George, et al, eds. The Interface of Marketing & Strategy. LC 90-4678. (Strategic Management, Policy & Planning Ser.: Vol. 4). 453p. 1990. 73.25 (*0-89232-809-6*) Jai Pr.

Day, George E. A Practical Treatise on the Domestic Management & Most Important Diseases of Advanced Life. Kastenbaum, Robert J., ed. LC 78-22198. (Aging & Old Age Ser.). 1979. reprint ed. lib. bdg. 19.95 (*0-405-11815-5*) Ayer.

Day, George F. The Uses of History in the Novels of Vardis Fisher. (Vardis Fisher Ser.). 1974. lib. bdg. 250.00 (*0-87700-225-8*) Revisionist Pr.

Day, George S. The Market Driven Organization: Understanding, Attracting & Keeping Valuable Customers. LC 99-16155. (Illus.). 304p. 1999. 28.00 (*0-684-86467-3*) Free Pr.

— Market Driven Strategy: Processes for Creating Value. 420p. 1990. 35.00 (*0-02-907211-5*) Free Pr.

***Day, George S.** Market Driven Strategy: Processes for Creating Value. LC 99-30544. (Illus.). 432p. 1999. 35.00 (*0-684-86536-X*) Free Pr.

Day, George S. Wharton on Dynamic Competetive Strategies. LC 96-53177. 480p. 1997. 29.95 (*0-471-17207-3*) Wiley.

***Day, George S., et al, eds.** Wharton on Managing Emerging Technologies. LC 99-56131. (Illus.). 464p. 2000. 34.95 (*0-471-36121-6*) Wiley.

Day, George S., jt. auth. see Aaker, David A.

Day, Gerald W. Genoa's Response to Byzantium, 1155-1204: Commercial Expansion & Factionalism in a Medieval City. LC 87-29517. 208p. 1988. 24.95 (*0-252-01496-0*) U of Ill Pr.

Day, Glenn R., jt. auth. see Likes, Robert C.

Day, Gordon M. In Search of New England's Native Past: Selected Essays by Gordon M. Day. Foster, Michael K. & Cowan, William, eds. LC 98-1154. (Native Americans of the Northeast Ser.). 392p. 1998. 70.00 (*1-55849-150-3*); pap. 19.95 (*1-55849-151-1*) U of Mass Pr.

— Western Abenaki Dictionary Vol. 1: Abenaki-English, Vol. 1. (Mercury Ser.: CES No. 128). 612p. 1994. pap. 34.95 (*0-660-14024-1*, Pub. by CN Mus Civilization) U of Wash Pr.

— Western Abenaki Dictionary Vol. 2: English-Abenaki. (Mercury Ser.: CES No. 129). (FRE, ENG & ALG.). 612p. 1995. pap. 34.95 (*0-660-14030-6*, Pub. by CN Mus Civilization) U of Wash Pr.

Day, Graham & Thomas, Dennis, eds. Contemporary Wales Vol. 8: An Annual Review of Economic & Social Research, Vol. 8. 316p. 1996. pap. 16.95 (*0-7083-1327-2*, Pub. by Univ Wales Pr) Paul & Co Pubs.

Day, Graham, jt. auth. see Thurbin, Patrick.

***Day, Greg.** Metamorphose. 1998. 44.95 (*3-925442-84-3*) Janssen.

Day, H. Curries of India. 64p. 1982. 6.95 (*0-318-36284-8*) Asia Bk Corp.

— Yoga Illustrated Dictionary. (Illus.). 186p. 1986. 8.95 (*0-318-37201-0*) Asia Bk Corp.

Day, H. James, contrib. by. Assay for Ristocetin Cofactor: Proposed Guideline (1993) 1993. 75.00 (*1-56238-226-8*, H41-P) NCCLS.

— Determination of von Willebrand Factor Antigen: Proposed Guideline, 1993) 1993. 75.00 (*1-56238-225-X*, H39-P) NCCLS.

— Procedure for the Determination of Fibrinogen in Plasma: Approved Guidelines (1994) 1994. 75.00 (*1-56238-221-7*, H30-A) NCCLS.

Day, Heather F. Protestant Theological Education in America: A Bibliography. LC 85-18300. (American Theological Library Association Monograph: No. 15). 523p. 1985. 45.00 (*0-8108-1842-6*) Scarecrow.

Day, Heather F., jt. auth. see Galbraith, Leslie R.

Day, Henry N. The Art of Discourse: A System of Rhetoric. LC 98-19071. 1998. write for info. (*0-8201-1513-4*) Schol Facsimiles.

Day-Hickman, Barbara A. Napoleonic Art: Nationalism & the Spirit of Rebellion in France, 1815-1848. LC 97-35761. (Illus.). 176p. 1998. 55.00 (*0-87413-615-6*) U Delaware Pr.

Day, Holliday D. The Shape of Space, George Sugarman. Allen, Jane A., ed. (Illus.). 144p. (Orig.). 198 . pap. 14.95 (*0-936364-06-8*) Joslyn Art.

Day, Holliday T. Power: Its Myths & Mores in American Art, 1961-1991. LC 91-71454. (Illus.). 160p. 1991. pap. 27.50 (*0-936260-57-2*); lib. bdg. 47.50 (*0-253-31658-8*) Ind Mus Art.

Day, Holliday T., ed. Indianapolis Museum of Art Collections Handbook. LC 88-80317. (Illus.). 189p. (Orig.). 1988. pap. 10.00 (*0-936260-20-3*) Inc Mus Art.

***Day, Holliday T., et al.** Crossroads of American Sculpture. (Illus.). 2000. write for info. (*0-936260-72-6*) Ind Mus Art.

Day, Holliday T., jt. auth. see Coleman, Floyd.

Day, Holliday T., jt. auth. see Danoff, I. Michael.

Day, Horace & Grob, Gerald N., eds. The Opium Habit, with Suggestions As to the Remedy. LC 80-1224. (Addiction in America Ser.). 1981. reprint ed. lib. bdg. 31.95 (*0-405-13580-7*) Ayer.

Day, Howard W., jt. ed. see Schiffman, Peter.

Day, I. & Humphries, S., eds. Genetics of Common Diseases: Future Therapeutic & Diagnostic Possibilities. (UCL Molecular Pathology Ser.). 300p. 1997. 157.50 (*1-85996-041-3*) Bios Sci.

***Day, Ian N. M.** Genetics of Common Diseases: Future Therapeutic & Diagnostic Possibilities. 328p. 1999. 110.00 (*0-12-220436-0*) Acad Pr.

***Day, Irene Frances.** The Moroccan Cookbook. LC 99-26996. (Illus.). 160p. 1999. pap. 12.95 (*1-56554-700-4*) Pelican.

***Day, Ivan, ed.** Eat, Drink & Be Merry: British at Table 1600-2000. (Illus.). 144p. 2000. 37.50 (*0-85667-519-9*, Pub. by P Wilson) Antique Collect.

Day, J. Database Management. 400p. 1999. write for info. (*1-58076-122-4*) Que Educ & Trng.

Day, J. Psalms. (Old Testament Guides Ser.: No. 15). 159p. 1990. pap. 12.50 (*1-85075-703-8*, Pub. by Sheffield Acad) CUP Services.

Day, J. D., et al. Color Atlas of Microneurosurgical Approaches: Cranial Base & Intracranial Midline. LC 97-199400. (Illus.). 320p. 1997. text 199.00 (*0-86577-630-X*) Thieme Med Pubs.

Day, J. D., jt. ed. see Pryor, J. B.

Day, J. Diaz, et al. Microsurgical Dissection of the Cranial Base. 176p. 1996. text 116.00 (*0-443-07550-6*) Church.

Day, J. Edward. Farming for Fun. 170p. 1994. pap. 12.00 (*0-87012-527-3*) McClain.

J. Edward Day is a retired lawyer & previously President Kennedy's postmaster general. Before he retired, he & his wife bought a neglected farm including a 15-year old house in central Maryland. Developing the farm became a full-time hobby with a large herd of beef cattle, llamas & an extensive orchard. Follow J. Edward Day, his family & friends as they discover the unexpected world of hobby farming. Farming for Fun includes helpful hints for the amateur farmer. ***Publisher Paid Annotation.***

–My Appointed Round: 929 Days As Postmaster General. 160p. 1965. reprint ed. 8.00 (*0-87012-149-9*) McClain. The funniest-&-wisest book ever written about the post office. By the father of the zip code, President Kennedy's postmaster general, this book is rollicking humor with political revelations. A wonderful gift for friends who work, or have worked, for the post office. Third Printing, 1973. ***Publisher Paid Annotation.***

–An Unlikely Sailor. 148p. 1990. pap. 10.95 (*0-9626033-0-9*) McClain.

1992 was the fiftieth anniversary of the year in which it became inevitable that the United States would be a major participant in World War II. The history of the navy's crucial role in World War II is not complete without recognizing the part played by the PC 597 & the DE 222 (antisub-marines). ***Publisher Paid Annotation.***

Day, J. H., ed. Estuarine Ecology: With Particular Reference to Southern Africa. 419p. (C). 1981. 233.00 (*90-6191-205-9*, Pub. by A A Balkema) Ashgate Pub Co.

Day, J. Laurence, jt. auth. see Seelye, H. Ned.

Day, J. P. The Banner of David. 276p. 1998. pap. 29.95 (*0-8464-4791-6*) Beekman Pubs.

— The Banner of David. 276p. 1992. pap. 30.00 (*0-86383-754-9*, Pub. by Gomer Pr) St Mut.

— Liberty & Justice. 256p. 1986. 49.95 (*0-7099-4523-X*, Pub. by C Helm) Routldge.

— The Tenth String. 1997. pap. 38.95 (*0-8464-4741-X*) Beekman Pubs.

— The Tenth String. 1997. pap. 39.00 (*1-85902-364-9*, Pub. by Gomer Pr) St Mut.

Day, James. The Vanishing Vision: The Inside Story of Public Television. LC 94-40304. (Illus.). 453p. 1995. 34.95 (*0-520-08659-7*, Pub. by U CA Pr) Cal Prin Full Svc.

— Vaughan Williams. (Master Musicians Ser.). (Illus.). 368p. 1998. 69.00 (*0-19-816632-X*) OUP.

— Vaughan Williams. 3rd ed. (Master Musicians Ser.). (Illus.). 358p. 1998. pap. text 26.00 (*0-19-816631-1*) OUP.

Day, James A., jt. ed. see Duquet, William.

Day, James A., ed. see Olympic Scientific Congress (1984: Eugene, OR) Sta.

Day, James M. Human Development Across the Life Span: Educational & Psychological Applications. Mosher, Ralph L. & Youngman, Deborah J., eds. LC 98-44538. 296p. 1999. 65.00 (*0-275-96457-4*, Praeger Pubs) Greenwood.

— Maps of Texas, 1527-1900. 597p. 1997. reprint ed. 65.00 (*1-57898-054-2*) Martino Pubng.

Day, James M. & Laufer, William, eds. Crimes, Values, & Religion - Toward a Comprehensive View. LC 86-28783. 280p. (C). 1987. text 73.25 (*0-89391-411-8*) Ablx Pub.

Day, James M., et al. Indian Tribes of Texas. (Illus.). 178p. 1971. 24.95 (*0-87244-000-1*) Texian.

— What Every American Should Know about the Mid East & Oil. LC 98-35458. 1998. 16.95 (*0-9640104-7-X*) Bridger Hse.

Day, James M, ed. see Parker, Morris B.

Day, James M., jt. ed. see Winfrey, Dorman H.

Day, Jane. Changing Lives: Voices from a School That Works. (Illus.). 188p. (Orig.). (C). 1994. pap. text 27.50 (*0-8191-9419-0*) U Pr of Amer.

— Rock Art of the Western Canyon. 1988. pap. 10.95 (*0-916278-66-2*) Denver Mus.

Day, Jane S. The Fall of the Aztec Empire. (Illus.). 128p. 1993. pap. 14.95 (*1-879373-43-2*) Roberts Rinehart.

Day, Jane S., jt. ed. see Seaman, Gary.

Day, Jane S., jt. ed. see Stanford, Dennis J.

Day, Jane Stevenson. Precolumbian Art: From the Collection of Paul L. & Alice C. Baker. (Illus.). 90p. 1996. pap. 20.00 (*0-911611-05-3*) Tucson Mus Art.

Day, Jared N. Urban Castles: Tenement Housing & Landlord Activism in New York City 1890-1943. LC 99-25052. (History of Urban Life Ser.). (Illus.). 315p. 1999. pap. 18.50 (*0-231-11403-6*) Col U Pr.

***Day, Jared N., ed.** Urban Castles: Tenement Housing & Landlord Activism in New York City, 1890-1943. LC 99-25052. (Illus.). 315p. 1999. 47.50 (*0-231-11402-8*) Col U Pr.

Day, Jean. Blackbeard, Terror of the Seas. Campbell, Douglas & Rumley, Mildred M., eds. LC 96-95347. (Illus.). 126p. (Orig.). 1997. pap. 10.50 (*1-890238-44-9*) Golden Age Pr.

— The I & the You. 111p. (Orig.). 1993. pap. 11.00 (*0-937013-41-2*) Potes Poets.

— The Literal World. unabridged ed. LC 98-137442. 112p. 1998. pap. 12.95 (*1-891190-01-6*, Pub. by Atelos) SPD-Small Pr Dist.

— A Young Recruit. LC 88-90722. (Roof Bks.). 75p. (Orig.). 1988. pap. 6.00 (*0-937804-30-4*) Segue NYC.

Day, Jean & Day, Robert. Banker Ponies: An Endangered Species. (Illus.). 150p. 1997. pap. 10.50 (*1-890238-45-7*) Golden Age Pr.

Day, Jeanne D. & Borkowski, John G., eds. Intelligence & Exceptionality: New Directions for Theory, Assessment & Instructional Practices. LC 87-11405. 256p. 1987. text 73.25 (*0-89391-394-4*) Ablx Pub.

Day, Jeanne D., jt. ed. see Borkowski, John D.

Day, Jeff & Schiff, David, eds. Walls, Walks & Patios. LC 97-68497. (Illus.). 192p. 1997. pap. 14.95 (*1-880029-97-9*) Creative Homeowner.

Day, Jeff, ed. see Cory, Steve.

Day, Jennifer. Children Believe Everything You Say: Creating Self-Esteem with Children. LC 96-37510. 128p. 1997. pap. 10.95 (*1-85230-958-X*, Pub. by Element MA) Penguin Putnam.

— Creative Visualization with Children: A Practical Guide. LC 94-25015. 1994. pap. 12.95 (*1-85230-469-3*, Pub. by Element MA) Penguin Putnam.

Day, Jennifer C. Population Projections of the United States by Age, Sex, Race, & Hispanic Origin: 1995 to 2050. (Illus.). 127p. (Orig.). 1997. pap. text 45.00 (*0-7881-3837-5*) DIANE Pub.

Day, Jenny, jt. auth. see Davies, Bryan.

D

An Asterisk (*) at the beginning of an entry indicates that the title is appearing for the first time.

Day, Jeremiah. An Examination of President Edwards' Inquiry on the Freedom of the Will. LC 75-3125. reprint ed. 32.50 (*0-404-59125-6*) AMS Pr.

Day, Jerry B. Color Scanning Technique. LC 97-19529. 304p. (C). 1997. pap. text 29.95 (*0-13-357211-0*) P-H.

Day, Jim. The Black Giant: History of East Texas Oil Field & Oil Industry Sludgery. (Illus.). 160p. 1999. pap. 11.95 (*1-893157-01-6*) Bridger Hse.

Day, Jishnu, jt. auth. see Dey, Mira.

***Day, Joan & Hanson, Terry, contrib. by.** Managing the Electronic Library. LC 98-36368. xxiii, 191p. 1999. 75.00 (*1-85739-184-5*) Bowker-Saur.

Day, Joan & Tylecote, Ronald F. Industrial Revolution in Metals. 318p. 1991. 75.00 (*0-901462-82-9*, Pub. by Inst Materials) Ashgate Pub Co.

Day, JoAnne. The Complete Book of Stencilcraft. 224p. 1987. reprint ed. pap. 10.95 (*0-486-25372-4*) Dover.

Day, Joanne C. Cut & Use Stencil Early Amer. 81st ed. 1975. pap. 5.95 (*0-486-20231-3*) Dover.

Day, JoAnne C. Cut & Use Stencil-Pennsylvania Dutch. 1976. pap. text 5.95 (*0-486-20574-6*) Dover.

Day, JoAnne C. Early American Stencils: 54 Cut-&-Use Stencils. 1990. 16.50 (*0-8446-5179-6*) Peter Smith.

Day, JoAnne C., ed. Decorative Silhouettes of the Twenties for Designers & Craftsmen. LC 73-89255. (Pictorial Archive Ser.). (Illus.). 160p. (Orig.). 1975. pap. 6.95 (*0-486-23152-6*) Dover.

Day, Jocelyn. Glitter Girl. large type ed. (Romance Ser.). 384p. 1993. 27.99 (*0-7089-2966-4*) Ulverscroft.

— Tarnished Rainbow. large type ed. (Romance Ser.). 352p. 1993. 27.99 (*0-7089-2950-8*) Ulverscroft.

Day, John. Being There: The Way to God, Love, Meaning & Life. 150p. 1992. pap. 9.95 (*0-685-61435-2*) J Day Pubs.

— An Economic History of Athens under Roman Domination. LC 72-7887. (Greek History Ser.). 1977. reprint ed. 25.95 (*0-405-04781-9*) Ayer.

— Living with Diabetes I: The British Diabetic Association Guide for those Treated with Insulin. LC 98-23733. 240p. 1998. pap. 38.50 (*0-471-97274-6*) Wiley.

— Molech: A God of Human Sacrifice in the Old Testament. (University of Cambridge Oriental Publications: No. 41). 125p. (C). 1990. text 49.95 (*0-521-36474-4*) Cambridge U Pr.

— Money & Finance in the Age of Merchant Capitalism. LC 98-25561. 240p. 1999. 59.95 (*0-631-16462-6*) Blackwell Pubs.

— 95 Years with John "Jack" Day: The Orphan Nobody Wanted. LC 97-73382. (Illus.). 266p. 1997. 24.95 (*1-878044-55-9*) Mayhaven Pub.

Day, John, ed. King & Messiah in Israel & the Ancient Near East: Proceedings of the Oxford Old Testament Seminar. LC 99-158505. (JSOTS Ser.: Vol. 270). 528p. 1998. 90.00 (*1-85075-946-4*, Pub. by Sheffield Acad) CUP Services.

Day, John, et al, eds. Wisdom in Ancient Israel. 325p. (C). 1998. reprint ed. pap. text 22.95 (*0-521-62489-4*) Cambridge U Pr.

Day, John & Chettle, Henry. Blind Beggar of Bednal Green. (Tudor Facsimile Texts. Old English Plays Ser.: No. 143). reprint ed. 59.50 (*0-404-53443-0*) AMS Pr.

Day, John, ed. see Day, Price.

Day, John, ed. see Smith, William Robertson.

Day, John, tr. see Ladurie, Emmanuel L.

Day, John C. Managing the Lower Rio Grande: An Experience in International River Development. LC 70-129457. (University of Chicago, Department of Geography, Research Paper Ser.: No. 125). (Illus.). 289p. reprint ed. pap. 89.60 (*0-8357-3720-9*, 203644200003) Bks Demand.

— PFS: First Choice Workbook. (C). 1989. text 31.50 (*0-673-38780-1*) Addson-Wesley Educ.

Day, John C., jt. auth. see Software Publishing Corp. Staff.

Day, John F. Bloody Ground. fac. ed. LC 79-57571. (Illus.). 352p. 1994. pap. 109.20 (*0-7837-7589-X*, 204734200007) Bks Demand.

Day, John G. Eight Days of Desert Storm. 288p. 1991. 19.95 (*1-880361-13-2*) Premier Pubns.

Day, John G. & McLellan, Mark R., eds. Cryopreservation & Freeze-Drying Protocols. LC 94-44732. (Methods in Molecular Biology Ser.: No. 38). (Illus.). 254p. 1995. 79.50 (*0-89603-296-5*) Humana.

Day, John J., ed. see Roberts, Charles A., et al.

Day, John L. & British Diabetic Association Staff. The BDA Handbook for Non-Insulin Dependent Diabetes. LC 97-22984. 132p. 1998. pap. 40.00 (*0-471-97275-4*) Wiley.

Day, John T., et al, eds. Word, Church, & State: Tyndale Quincentenary Essays. LC 97-38531. 344p. (C). 1998. text 39.95 (*0-8132-0902-1*) Cath U Pr.

Day, John W., et al. Estuarine Ecology. LC 87-27031. 576p. 1989. 135.00 (*0-471-06263-4*) Wiley.

Day, Jon. Let's Make Magic: Over Forty Tricks You Can Do. LC 92-53093. (Illus.). 96p. (J). (gr. 2-6). 1992. pap. 12.95 (*1-85697-806-0*, Kingfisher) LKC.

***Day, Jonathan S.** Traditional Hopi Kachinas: A New Generation of Carvers. (Illus.). 136p. 2000. 21.95 (*0-87358-761-8*); pap. 14.95 (*0-87358-740-5*) Northland AZ.

Day, Julia. Between Earth & Sky. (Illus.). 1999. pap. 19.95 (*1-86163-050-6*, Pub. by Capall Bann Pubng) Holmes Pub.

***Day, Julia.** Patchwork of Magic: Living in a Pagan World. 1998. pap. 19.95 (*1-898307-21-0*, Pub. by Capall Bann Pubng) Holmes Pub.

Day, Julie. Come Back for Light Refreshments after the Service: A Play. LC 98-232330. 63 p. 1997. write for info. (*0-573-60130-5*) French.

Day, Kate P. Only When They're Little: The Story of an Appalachian Family. LC 85-3893. 1985. 11.95 (*0-913239-25-9*) Appalach Consortium.

***Day, Kathleen.** Mist on the Mountain. 255p. 1999. pap. 13.95 (*0-9675071-0-3*) Daybreak Lake.

Day, Ken G., et al, eds. Grand Larceny: Reclaiming Stolen Histories. 72p. 1994. pap. text 7.00 (*0-9641855-0-4*) L A Works.

Day, Ken W. Concrete Mix Design, Quality Control & Specifications. (Illus.). 384p. (C). 1994. 90.00 (*0-419-18190-3*, E & FN Spon) Routledge.

***Day, Ken W.** Concrete Mix Design, Quality Control & Specifications. 2nd ed. LC 98-51602. 1999. text 100.00 (*0-419-24330-5*) Routledge.

Day, Kenneth. Alvis: The Story of the Red Triangle. 3rd ed. LC 96-78556. (Illus.). 424p. 1996. 65.00 (*0-85429-975-0*) Haynes Manuals.

Day, Kenneth, et al. Behaviour Problems in Mental Handicap: An Annotated Bibliography 1970-1985. LC BF0435.. 152p. reprint ed. pap. 47.20 (*0-7837-0999-4*, 204130500020) Bks Demand.

Day, Kevin, jt. auth. see Potter, Michael.

Day, Kimberly. The Cat Who Went Back in Time. (Illus.). 24p. (J). (gr. 2-3). 1998. pap. 7.00 (*0-8059-4269-6*) Dorrance.

Day, Kristen, jt. auth. see Cohen, Uriel.

Day, Kristin, jt. ed. see De Peyster, Ann.

Day, Lal B. Bengal Peasant Life. LC 76-44747. reprint ed. 55.00 (*0-404-15946-X*) AMS Pr.

— Folk-Tales of Bengal. LC 78-67727. (Folktale Ser.). reprint ed. 37.50 (*0-404-16138-3*) AMS Pr.

Day, Lance & McNeil, Ian, eds. Biographical Dictionary of the History of Technology. 864p. (C). (gr. 13). 1998. pap. 65.00 (*0-415-19399-0*, D6030) Routledge.

Day, Lance, jt. ed. see McNeil, Ian.

Day, Lara. My Brother & I. (Foundations Ser.). 15p. (J). (ps). 1992. pap. text 4.50 (*1-56843-054-X*) EMG Networks.

— My Brother & I: Big Book. (Foundations Ser.). 15p. (J). (ps). 1992. pap. text 23.00 (*1-56843-004-3*) EMG Networks.

Day, Laura. Practical Intuition: How to Harness the Power of Your Instinct & Make It Work for You. abr. ed. 1996. audio 18.00 (*0-694-51748-8*, CPN 2644) HarperAudio.

Day, Laura. Practical Intuition: How to Harness the Power of Your Instinct & Make It Work for You. LC 97-19482. 208p. 1997. reprint ed. pap. 14.00 (*0-7679-0034-0*) Broadway BDD.

— Practical Intuition for Success: A Step-by-Step Program to Increase Your Wealth Today. 216p. 1998. text 22.00 (*0-7881-5812-0*) DIANE Pub.

— Practical Intuition for Success: Let Your Interests Guide You To the Career of Your Dreams. 256p. 1999. pap. 13.00 (*0-06-093022-5*, Perennial) HarperTrade.

Day, Laura. Practical Intuition for Success: Trust Your Gut & Increase Your Bottom Line in Ten Days. abr. ed. 1997. audio 18.00 (*0-694-51864-6*, CPN 2675) HarperAudio.

Day, Laura. Practical Intuition in Love: Start a Journey through Pleasure to the Love of Your Life. LC 98-34520. 256p. 1998. 23.00 (*0-06-017578-8*) HarpC.

— Practical Intuition in Love: Start a Journey Through Pleasure to the Love of Your Life. LC 99-89316. 256p. 2000. pap. 12.95 (*0-06-093110-8*) HarpC.

***Day, Laura.** Practical Intuition in Love: Start a Journey Through Pleasure to the Love of Your Life, Set. 1998. audio 18.00 (*0-694-51980-4*) HarperAudio.

— Practical Intuition/Business. 22.00 (*0-375-50026-X*) Villard Books.

Day, Lauren. Are We There Yet? (Rockett's World Ser.: No. 3). 128p. (J). (gr. 3-7). 1999. mass mkt. 3.99 (*0-439-08209-9*, Pub. by Scholastic Inc) Penguin Putnam.

***Day, Lauren.** What Kind of Friend Are You? (Rockett's World Ser.: No. 2). 128p. (J). (gr. 3-7). 1999. pap. 3.99 (*0-439-06312-4*, Pub. by Scholastic Inc) Penguin Putnam.

— Where Do You Belong?, Vol. 5. (Rockett's World Ser.: Vol. 5). 128p. (J). (gr. 4-7). 2000. pap. 3.99 (*0-439-08694-9*) Scholastic Inc.

Day, Lauren. Who Can You Trust? (Rockett's World Ser.: No. 1). 128p. (J). (gr. 3-7). 1999. pap. 3.99 (*0-439-04405-7*, Pub. by Scholastic Inc) Penguin Putnam.

Day, Leslely, ed. see D'Agati, Vivette D., et al.

Day, Lesley, ed. see Benumof, Jonathan L.

Day, Lesley, ed. see Bibbo, Marluse.

Day, Lesley, ed. see Chung, David C. & Lam, Arthur M.

Day, Lesley, ed. see Dewan, David M.

Day, Lesley, ed. see Ferry, Judith A. & Harris, Nancy L.

Day, Lesley, ed. see Foster, Christopher S. & Bostwick, David G.

Day, Lesley, ed. see Henry, John B.

Day, Lesley, ed. see Katzenstein, Anna-Luise A., et al.

Day, Lesley, ed. see Longnecker, David E. & Murphy, Frank L.

Day, Lesley, ed. see Martin, John T. & Warner, Mark A.

Day, Lesley, ed. see Ro, Jae Y., et al.

Day, Lesley, ed. see Taylor, David H., et al.

Day, Lesley, ed. see Virmani, Renu, et al.

Day, Lesley, ed. see Waldman, Steven D. & Winnie, Alon P.

Day, Lesley, ed. see Wenig, Bruce M., et al.

Day, Lesley, ed. see Whitehead, Richard.

Day, Lesley, ed. see Wigglesworth, Jonathan S.

Day, Leslie, ed. see Gambling, David R. & Douglas, M. Joanne.

Day, Leslie, ed. see Murphy, William M.

Day, Leslie P., jt. auth. see Smith, Robert H.

Day Lewis, Cecil. The Complete Poems of C. Day Lewis. LC 91-68076. 752p. (C). 1992. 65.00 (*0-8047-2070-3*) Stanford U Pr.

— The Complete Poems of C. Day Lewis. 768p. 1995. 65.00 (*0-8047-2073-8*); pap. 24.95 (*0-8047-2585-3*) Stanford U Pr.

— The Lyric Impulse. LC 65-16682. (Charles Eliot Norton Lectures, 1964-1965). 174p. reprint ed. pap. 54.00 (*0-7837-4103-0*, 205792600011) Bks Demand.

— The Poetic Image. LC 83-45427. reprint ed. 29.50 (*0-404-20075-3*) AMS Pr.

— Revolution in Writing. LC 75-37952. (Studies in English Literature: No. 33). 1976. lib. bdg. 75.00 (*0-8383-2115-1*) M S G Haskell Hse.

— Tangled Web. 1976. 19.95 (*0-8488-0977-7*) Amereon Ltd.

Day Lewis, Cecil, ed. English Lyric Poems Fifteen Hundred to Nineteen Hundred. LC 61-7707. (Goldentree Books in English Literature). (Orig.). 1961. pap. text 14.95 (*0-89197-146-7*) Irvington.

Day Lewis, Cecil & Lehman, John, eds. The Chatto Book of Modern Poetry: Nineteen Fifteen to Nineteen Fifty-Five. LC 77-25967. 287p. 1978. reprint ed. lib. bdg. 35.00 (*0-313-20099-8*, DLCB, Greenwood Pr) Greenwood.

Day Lewis, Cecil & Lehmann, John, eds. The Chatto Book of Modern Poetry: Nineteen Fifteen to Nineteen Fifty-Five. reprint ed. 29.00 (*0-403-03067-6*) Somerset Pub.

Day Lewis, Cecil, ed. see Owen, Wilfred.

Day Lewis, Cecil, tr. see Virgil.

Day, Lewis F. Pattern Design. LC 99-45781. 318p. 1999. pap. text 9.95 (*0-486-40709-8*) Dover.

— Penmanship of the XVI, XVII & XVIII Centuries. LC 78-58919. (Illus.). 1979. reprint ed. pap. 7.95 (*0-8008-6277-5*) Taplinger.

***Day-Lewis, Tamasin.** The Art of the Tart: Savory & Sweet. LC 00-32800. (Illus.). 2001. write for info. (*0-375-50492-3*) Random.

Day-Lewis, Tamasin. West of Ireland Summers--A Cookbook: Recipes & Memories from an Irish Childhood. (Illus.). 160p. 1999. pap. 19.95 (*1-57098-280-5*) Roberts Rinehart.

Day, Lillian. Paganini of Genoa. 318p. 1990. reprint ed. lib. bdg. 79.00 (*0-7812-9101-1*) Rprt Serv.

Day, Lincoln H. The Future of Low Birth-Rate Populations. (Illus.). 208p. (C). 1995. pap. 25.99 (*0-415-12704-1*, C0605) Routledge.

— The Future of Low Birthrate Populations. LC 91-46078. (Illus.). 208p. (C). (gr. 13 up). 1992. 757.00 (*0-415-08034-7*) Routledge.

Day, Lincoln H. & Xia, Ma, eds. Migration & Urbanization in China. LC 93-29350. (Studies in Chinese Environment & Development Ser.). 264p. (C). (gr. 13). 1994. text 73.95 (*1-56324-338-5*, East Gate Bk) M E Sharpe.

Day, Linda. Three Faces of a Queen: Characterization in the Book of Esther. (JSOT Supplement Ser.: No. 186). 254p. 1995. 75.00 (*1-85075-517-5*, Pub. by Sheffield Acad) CUP Services.

Day, Linda S. The Teacher's Craft File. 3rd rev. ed. Day, Robert O., ed. (Illus.). 68p. 1998. ring bd. 12.95 (*1-890905-06-2*) Day to Day.

Day, Linda S., jt. auth. see Day, Robert O.

Day, Loraine & Jones, Tony. La Place - Une Femme, Ernaux: Critical Monographs in English. 96p. 1993. pap. 32.00 (*0-85261-262-1*, Pub. by Univ of Glasgow) St Mut.

Day, Lorraine. AIDS: What the Government Isn't Telling You. LC 91-75346. (Illus.). 301p. 1991. pap., per. 22.95 (*0-9630940-0-9*) Rockford Pr.

Day, Louis. Ethics in Media Communications: Cases & Controversies. 2nd ed. (Mass Communication Ser.). 480p. (C). 1996. 32.50 (*0-534-50716-6*) Wadsworth Pub.

Day, Louis A. Ethics in Media Communications: Cases & Controversies. 365p. (C). 1991. mass mkt. 28.50 (*0-534-14784-4*) Wadsworth Pub.

Day, Lucille. Self-Portrait with Hand Microscope. 52p. 1982. pap. 9.95 (*0-917658-18-3*) BPW & P.

Day, Lucille L. Fire in the Garden. LC 96-78254. (Muchos Somos Ser.: Vol. 23). 63p. (Orig.). 1997. pap. 9.95 (*0-914370-72-3*) Mothers Hen.

***Day, Lucille Lang.** A Wild One: Poems. LC 00-130149. 100p. 2000. pap. 12.95 (*0-9670224-3-6*) Scar Tana.

Day, Lynda R. Making a Way to Freedom: A History of African Americans on Long Island. LC 97-40816. 1997. write for info. (*1-55787-149-3*) Hrt of the Lakes.

Day, M., jt. ed. see Fry, J. C.

Day, M. F., jt. ed. see Campbell, K. S.

Day, M. H., ed. Human Evolution. (Symposia of the Society for the Study of Human Biology Ser.: Vol. 11). 162p. 1973. 36.00 (*0-85066-061-0*) Taylor & Francis.

Day, Mabel, ed. The English Text of the Ancrene Riwle: British Museum MS. Cotton NeroA.xiv. (EETS Original Ser.: Vol. 225). 1963. reprint ed. 30.00 (*0-19-722225-0*, Pub. by EETS) Boydell & Brewer.

Day, Mabel & Steele, R., eds. Charles of Orleans: The English Poems, 2 vols., Vols. 1 & 2. (EETS Original Ser.). 1970. reprint ed. 30.00 (*0-19-722215-3*, Pub. by EETS) Boydell & Brewer.

Day, Malcolm. The World of Castles & Forts. LC 96-31619. (World of Ser.). (Illus.). 45p. (YA). (gr. 1-4). 1996. lib. bdg. 19.95 (*0-87226-278-2*, 62782B, P Bedrick Books) NTC Contemp Pub Co.

Day, Marcus. Aliens. LC 98-26844. (Illus.). 128p. 1999. pap. 14.95 (*0-8092-2770-3*, 277030, Pub. by Lowell Hse) NTC Contemp Pub Co.

— Aliens: Encounters with the Unexplained. (Illus.). 128p. 1997. pap. 12.99 (*1-85833-662-7*, Pub. by CLib Bks) Whitecap Bks.

***Day, Marele.** The Case of the Chinese Boxes. 2000. pap. 5.95 (*1-86448-671-6*, Pub. by Allen & Unwin Pty) IPG Chicago.

Day, Marele. The Disappearances of Madalena Grimaldi: A Claudia Valentine Mystery. abr. ed. LC 95-48782. 224p. 1996. 19.95 (*0-8027-3277-1*) Walker & Co.

— Lambs of God. 336p. 1999. reprint ed. pap. 12.95 (*1-57322-722-6*, Riverhd Trade) Berkley Pub.

— The Last Tango of Delores Delgado. 192p. 1993. pap. 9.95 (*1-86373-323-X*, Pub. by Allen & Unwin Pty) IPG Chicago.

— The Life & Crimes of Harry Lavender. large type ed. (Bolinda Large Print Ser.). 1997. 24.95 (*1-86340-566-6*) T T Beeler.

Day, Marie. Dragon in the Rocks: A Story Based on the Childhood of the Early Paleontologist, Mary Anning. (Illus.). 32p. (J). (ps up). 1994. pap. 5.95 (*1-895688-38-8*, Pub. by Greey dePencier) Firefly Bks Ltd.

— Quennu & the Cave Bear. (Illus.). 32p. (J). (gr. k-5). 1999. 17.95 (*1-895688-86-8*, Pub. by Owl Bks) Firefly Bks Ltd.

— Quennu & the Cave Bear. (Illus.). 32p. (J). (gr. 1-5). 1999. pap. 6.95 (*1-895688-87-6*, Pub. by Owl Bks) Firefly Bks Ltd.

Day, Mark. Yuletide Lost. 1981. 5.20 (*0-89536-484-0*, 2506) CSS OH.

Day, Mark, jt. auth. see Day, Peggy.

Day, Marlena. Trails, Trails & Tidepools in Pails: Over One Hundred Fun & Easy Nature Activities for Families & Teachers to Share with Babies & Young Children. 2nd ed. LC 94-65875. 112p. 1994. reprint ed. pap. text 9.95 (*0-9632753-1-3*) Child Nature Inst.

Day, Marlena & Nature Institute Staff. Cantos, Caminos y Juegos Para Ninos: Mas de 100 Actividades en la Naturaleza Para Ninos Pequenos. Moore, Rhonda & Campos, Patricia, trs. (SPA., Illus.). 112p. (J). (gr. k-3). 1998. pap. 12.95 (*0-9632753-6-4*) Child Nature Inst.

Day, Marlis. Why Johnny Died. 192p. 1999. pap. 11.95 (*1-56315-184-7*, Pub. by SterlingHse) Natl Bk Netwk.

***Day, Martha.** Home Baking. (Illus.). 2000. 14.95 (*0-7548-0290-6*, Lorenz Bks) Anness Pub.

— Perfect Pie. (Illus.). 2000. 11.95 (*0-7548-0351-1*, Lorenz Bks) Anness Pub.

Day, Martin, jt. auth. see Beech, Len.

Day, Martyn. Environmental Action: A Citizen's Guide. LC 97-22286. 416p. 1998. 69.95 (*0-7453-1191-1*, Pub. by Pluto GBR) Stylus Pub VA.

***Day, Martyn, ed.** Environmental Action: A Citizen's Guide. 416p. 1998. pap. 21.95 (*0-7453-1190-3*, Pub. by Pluto GBR) Stylus Pub VA.

Day, Martyn, jt. auth. see Pugh, Charles.

Day, Maurice. Party Games for Three's to Eight's: And Easy Cakes Too! 195p. 1995. pap. 8.95 (*0-572-01580-1*, Pub. by Foulsham UK) Assoc Pubs Grp.

Day, Meredith. Add to Excellent Without Drugs. 1997. pap. text 12.95 (*0-933025-62-9*) Blue Bird Pub.

Day, Michael. Fight for the Tiger: One Man's Fight to Save the Wild Tiger from Extinction. (Illus.). 448p. 1996. 29.95 (*0-7472-1548-0*, Pub. by Headline Bk Pub); pap. 13.95 (*0-7472-5147-9*, Pub. by Headline Bk Pub) Trafalgar.

Day, Michael, ed. Preparing Teachers of Art. 154p. 1997. pap. text 22.00 (*1-890160-01-6*, 271) Natl Art Ed.

Day, Michael & Neff, Ken. Troubleshooting Netware for the 386. 873p. (Orig.). 1995. pap. 34.95 (*1-55851-223-3*, M&T Bks) IDG Bks.

Day, Michael, jt. ed. see Alexander, Kay.

Day, Michael, tr. see St. Therese of Lisieux.

Day, Michael, tr. & intro. see St. Therese of Lisieux.

Day, Michael H. Guide to Fossil Man. 3rd rev. ed. LC 77-10517. 1997. reprint ed. lib. bdg. 24.00 (*0-226-13888-7*) U Ch Pr.

— Guide to Fossil Man. 4th ed. LC 86-5548. xvi, 448p. (C). 1986. 54.00 (*0-226-13889-5*) U Ch Pr.

Day, Milly & Holzapfel, Richard N. Prepare to Be Healed: Gaining Emotional & Spiritual Independence. LC 95-76714. 1995. 11.95 (*0-88494-988-5*) Bookcraft Inc.

Day, N. E., jt. auth. see Breslow, N. E.

Day, N. R. Your Faith Is Growing! 51p. (Orig.). 1981. pap. 6.95 (*0-940754-10-X*) Ed Ministries.

Day, N. Raymond. David's Faithfulness. 85p. (Orig.). 1979. pap. 7.95 (*0-940754-02-9*) Ed Ministries.

Day, Nancy. Abortion: Debating the Issue. LC 94-40697. (Issues in Focus Ser.). (Illus.). 128p. (YA). (gr. 6 up). 1995. lib. bdg. 20.95 (*0-89490-645-3*) Enslow Pubs.

— Advertising: Information or Manipulation? LC 98-35032. (Issues in Focus Ser.). 128p. (YA). (gr. 6 up). 1999. lib. bdg. 20.95 (*0-7660-1106-2*) Enslow Pubs.

— Animal Experimentation: Cruelty or Science? LC 93-46996. (Issues in Focus Ser.). (Illus.). 128p. (YA). (gr. 6 up). 1994. lib. bdg. 20.95 (*0-89490-578-3*) Enslow Pubs.

***Day, Nancy.** Animal Experimentation: Cruelty Or Science? rev. ed. LC 99-49334. (Issues in Focus Ser.). (Illus.). 128p. (YA). (gr. 6 up). 2000. lib. bdg. 20.95 (*0-7660-1244-1*) Enslow Pubs.

Day, Nancy. Censorship: Freedom of Expression? LC 99-24215. (Frontline Ser.). (Illus.). 112p. (YA). (gr. 7-10). 2000. 25.26 (*0-8225-2628-X*, Lerner Publctns) Lerner Pub.

***Day, Nancy.** The Death Penalty for Teens: A Pro/Con Issue. (Hot Pro/Con Issues Ser.). (Illus.). 64p. (YA). (gr. 6 up). 2000. lib. bdg. 19.95 (*0-7660-1370-7*) Enslow Pubs.

Day, Nancy. The Horseshoe Crab. LC 92-9772. (Remarkable Animals Ser.). (Illus.). 60p. (J). (gr. 4 up). 1992. text 13.95 (*0-87518-545-2*, Dillon Silver Burdett) Silver Burdett Pr.

— Sensational TV: Trash or Journalism? LC 95-35675. (Issues in Focus Ser.). (Illus.). 112p. (YA). (gr. 6 up). 1996. lib. bdg. 20.95 (*0-89490-733-6*) Enslow Pubs.

— Violence in Schools: Learning in Fear. LC 95-40198. (Issues in Focus Ser.). (Illus.). 128p. (YA). (gr. 6 up). 1996. lib. bdg. 20.95 (*0-89490-734-4*) Enslow Pubs.

D

***Day, Nancy.** Your Travel Guide to Ancient Egypt. LC 99-36810. (Passport to History Ser.). (Illus.). 112p. (J). (gr. 5-9). 2000. lib. bdg. 26.60 (*0-8225-3075-9*, Lerner Publctns) Lerner Pub.
— Your Travel Guide to Ancient Greece. LC 99-36804. (Passport to History Ser.). (Illus.). 112p. (J). (gr. 4-7). 2000. lib. bdg. 26.60 (*0-8225-3076-7*, Lerner Publctns) Lerner Pub.
— Your Travel Guide to Civil War America. LC 99-37097. (Passport to History Ser.). (Illus.). 112p. (J). (gr. 4-7). 2000. lib. bdg. 26.60 (*0-8225-3078-3*, Lerner Publctns) Lerner Pub.
— Your Travel Guide to Colonial America. LC 99-38137. (Passport to History Ser.). (Illus.). 112p. (J). (gr. 4-7). 2000. lib. bdg. 26.60 (*0-8225-3079-1*, Lerner Publctns) Lerner Pub.
— Your Travel Guide to Renaissance Europe. LC 99-36805. (Passport to History Ser.). (Illus.). 112p. (J). 2000. lib. bdg. 26.00 (*0-8225-3080-5*, Lerner Publctns) Lerner Pub.
— Your Travel Guide to the Ancient Mayan Civilization. LC 99-38688. (Passport to History Ser.). (Illus.). 112p. (J). (gr. 4-7). 2000. lib. bdg. 26.60 (*0-8225-3077-5*, Lerner Publctns) Lerner Pub.
Day, Nancy, ed. see Mammen, Lori.
***Day, Nancy R.** A Kitten's Year. LC 99-21162. (Illus.). 32p. (J). (ps-4). 2000. 14.95 (*0-06-027230-9*); lib. bdg. 14.89 (*0-06-027231-7*) HarpC.
Day, Nancy R. The Lion's Whiskers: An Ethiopian Folktale. LC 94-14453. (Illus.). 32p. (J). (gr. k-3). 1995. 14.95 (*0-590-45803-5*) Scholastic Inc.
Day, Nancy S., ed. see Mammen, Lori.
Day, Nicholas B. & American Society of Civil Engineers Staff. Pipeline Route Selection for Rural & Cross-Country Pipelines. LC 98-26052. (ASCE Manuals & Reports on Engineering Practice). 95p. 1998. 49.00 (*0-7844-0345-7*) Am Soc Civil Eng.
Day, Nicolas, jt. auth. see Simpson, Ken.
Day, Nora D., ed. see Davis, Ossie.
Day, Noreha Y. Kancil & the Crocodiles: A Tale from Malaysia. (Illus.). 32p. (J). (gr. 4 up). 1996. mass mkt. 16.00 (*0-689-80954-9*) S&S Bks Yung.
Day, Nundo L. The Geographical Dictionary of Ancient & Medieval India. 1990. reprint ed. 17.50 (*81-85395-93-4*, Pub. by Low Price) S Asia.
Day-Oliver, Deborah. Clinical Coding Compendium. rev. ed. 415p. (C). 1994. pap. text 54.00 (*1-884103-00-6*) Hlth Data Concepts.
Day, P., ed. Electronic Structure & Magnetism of Inorganic Compounds, Vols. 1-6. Incl. Vol. 2. 1971-72 Literature. LC 72-78529. 1973. 37.00 (*0-85186-261-6*); Vol. 3. 1972-73 Literature. LC 72-78529. 1974. 43.00 (*0-85186-271-3*); Vol. 4. 1973-74 Literature. LC 72-78529. 1976. 45.00 (*85186-281-0*); Vol. 5. 1974-75 Literature. LC 72-78529. 1977. 54.00 (*0-85186-291-8*); Vol. 6. LC 72-78529. 1979. 70.00 (*0-85186-610-7*); Vol. 1. 1970-71 Literature. 1972. 32.00 (*0-85186-251-9*); LC 72-78529. write for info. (*0-318-50468-5*) Am Chemical.
***Day, P., ed.** Proceedings of the Royal Institution of Great Britain, Vol. 70. (Illus.). 360p. 1999. text 130.00 (*0-19-850539-6*) OUP.
Day, P., ed. see NATO Advanced Study Institute Staff.
Day, P. C. Helical Gears in Retrospect & Prospect. (Technical Papers: Vol. P42A). (Illus.). 11p. 1934. pap. text 30.00 (*1-55589-387-2*) AGMA.
Day, P. C. & Schmitter, W. P. Speed Increasing Gears & Their Technical Differences From Reducing Gears. (Technical Papers: Vol. P123). (Illus.). 18p. 1935. pap. text 30.00 (*1-55589-404-6*) AGMA.
Day, P. D. & Nall, S. E. Town Planning Appeals: A Citizen's Guide. 84p. (C). 1990. pap. 35.00 (*0-86439-075-0*, Pub. by Boolarong Pubns) St Mut.
Day, Pamela, et al. Ours to Keep: A Guide for Building a Community Assessment Strategy for Child Protection. 256p. 1998. pap. text 18.95 (*0-87868-702-5*, 7025, CWLA Pr) Child Welfare.
Day, Patricia, et al, eds. State, Politics, & Health: Essays for Rudolf Klein. LC 95-36573. 1995. 58.95 (*1-55786-868-9*) Blackwell Pubs.
***Day, Patrick.** Voice & Vision Vol. 2: History of Broadcasting in New Zealand. 432p. 2000. 42.00 (*1-86940-233-2*, Pub. by Auckland Univ) Paul & Co Pubs.
Day, Paul. The Burns Book. (Illus.). 96p. 1990. reprint ed. pap. 19.95 (*0-933224-09-5*) Bold Strummer Ltd.
Day, Paul. In His Footsteps: A New Testament Expedition. pap. 11.95 (*1-57734-323-9*, 01113712) Covenant Comms.
Day, Paul, jt. auth. see Bacon, Tony.
Day, Paul R. Book of Mormon Expedition. 1996. pap., student ed. 8.95 (*1-55503-862-X*, 01112112) Covenant Comms.
— Doctrine & Covenants Expedition. 1996. pap. 9.95 (*1-57734-031-0*, 01112538) Covenant Comms.
Day, Paul W. John Mulgan. (Twayne's World Authors Ser.). (C). 1969. lib. bdg. 20.95 (*0-8057-2638-1*) Irvington.
Day, Peggy & Day, Mark. RVer's Best Guide to the Oregon Coast. (Illus.). 176p. 1997. pap. 12.95 (*1-57188-070-4*) F Amato Pubns.
Day, Peggy J. Microsoft Project 4.0 for Windows & the Macintosh: Setting Project Management Standards. 320p. 1994. pap. 34.95 (*0-471-28610-9*, VNR) Wiley.
Day, Peggy J. Microsoft Project 4.0 for Windows & the Macintosh: Setting Project Management Standards - Version 4. (Illus.). 296p. 1994. pap. 34.95 (*0-442-01767-7*, VNR) Wiley.
Day, Peggy R. Thanks & Hurrah! The Pilgrims' Feast. (Illus.). 28p. (J). (ps-3). 1991. pap. 5.98 (*1-879997-06-1*) Mystic Child Studio.
Day, Peggy R., compiled by. And I Will Be Your God: Bible Verses for Quiet Time. 2nd rev. ed. (Illus.). 32p. 1994. 5.98 (*1-879997-10-X*) Mystic Child Studio.
Day-Perroots, Due, jt. auth. see Flack, Bruce C.
Day, Peter. The Liturgical Dictionary of Eastern Christianity. 344p. 1994. 82.50 (*0-86012-216-6*, Pub. by Srch Pr) St Mut.
Day, Peter, ed. Emission & Scattering Techniques: Studies of Inorganic Molecules, Solids, & Surfaces. 400p. 1981. text 155.50 (*90-277-1317-0*) Kluwer Academic.
— Exploring the Universe: Essays on Science & Technology from the Royal Institution. LC 97-223552. (Illus.). 224p. (C). 1997. 35.00 (*0-19-850085-8*) OUP.
— Killers in the Brain: Essays in Science & Technology from the Royal Institution. (Illus.). 184p. 1999. text 24.95 (*0-19-850540-X*) OUP.
— Proceedings of the Royal Institution of Great Britain, Vol. 67. (Illus.). 344p. 1996. text 110.00 (*0-19-855938-0*) OUP.
— Proceedings of the Royal Institution of Great Britain, Vol. 68. (Illus.). 386p. 1997. text 125.00 (*0-19-850084-X*) OUP.
— Proceedings of the Royal Institution of Great Britain, Vol. 69. (Illus.). 348p. 1999. text 125.00 (*0-19-850366-0*) OUP.
— Search for Extraterrestrial Life Vol. 69: Proceedings of the Royal Institution. LC 98-8015. (Illus.). 180p. 1998. text 35.00 (*0-19-850414-4*) OUP.
— Unveiling the Microcosmos: Essays on Science & Technology from the Royal Institution. (Illus.). 182p. 1996. pap. 19.95 (*0-19-855937-2*) OUP.
Day, Peter & Catlow, Richard, eds. Bicycling to Utopia: Essays on Science & Technology from the Royal Instituion. LC 96-130686. (Illus.). 180p. 1995. pap. text 24.95 (*0-19-855895-3*) OUP.
— The Candle Revisited: Essays on Science & Technology. (Illus.). 170p. 1994. pap. 16.95 (*0-19-855835-X*) OUP.
— Proceedings of the Royal Institution, Vol. 65. (Illus.). 274p. 1994. text 59.00 (*0-19-855836-8*) OUP.
— Proceedings of the Royal Institution of Great Britain, Vol. 66. (Illus.). 302p. 1995. 80.00 (*0-19-855896-1*) OUP.
Day, Peter, jt. auth. see Cheetham, A. K.
Day, Peter, jt. ed. see Cheetham, A. K.
Day, Peter R. Perspectives on Later Life. 200p. 1994. pap. 34.95 (*1-871177-44-8*, Pub. by Whiting & Birch) Paul & Co Pubs.
***Day, Phyllis J.** The New History of Social Welfare. 3rd ed. LC 99-24028. 469p. (C). 1999. 61.00 (*0-205-29691-2*) Allyn.
Day, Phyllis J., et al. Social Working: Exercises General Practice. 2nd ed. LC 99-46797. 301p. (C). 1999. pap. text 31.00 (*0-205-29131-7*, Longwood Div) Allyn.
Day, Price. The Spillway: Columns from the Baltimore Sun 1956-1960. Day, John, ed. LC 97-92529. (Illus.). xv, 413p. (Orig.). 1997. pap. write for info. (*0-9659749-0-1*) Day & Slevin.
Day, Priscilla A. & Weaver, Hilary N., eds. Health & the American Indian. LC 99-12963. 88p. 1999. 49.95 (*0-7890-0658-8*) Haworth Pr.
Day, R., jt. ed. see Braunschweig, B.
Day, R. A. Integration of Graphics & OSI Standards. LC 93-41289. 1994. 34.95 (*0-387-57015-2*) Spr-Verlag.
Day, R. A., Jr. & Underwood, Arthur L., Jr. Quantitative Analysis. 6th ed. 768p. 1991. 72.80 (*0-13-747155-6*, 520104) P-H.
— Quantitative Analysis: Solutions to Problems. 5th ed. 180p. (C). 1986. pap. text 12.95 (*0-317-40029-0*) P-H.
***Day, R. Alan.** Family First: A Biblical & Practical Study. 180p. 1999. pap. write for info. (*0-7392-0367-3*, PO3573) Morris Pubng.
Day, R. E. Papers of Sir William Johnson, 9 vols., Set. 1993. reprint ed. lib. bdg. 675.00 (*0-7812-5171-0*) Rprt Serv.
Day, R. H., jt. ed. see McKenzie, Beryl.
Day, R. L. The Effect of Secondary Ettringite Formation on the Durability of Concrete: A Literature Analysis. 126p. 1992. 25.00 (*0-89312-169-X*, RD108T) Portland Cement.
Day, R. O., jt. auth. see Quinn, D. I.
Day, R. Pat. Growing into Greatness. (Illus.). (Orig.). 1988. pap. text 9.95 (*0-9621772-0-2*) R P Day.
Day, Rachel, jt. auth. see Barrington Hofer, Grace.
***Day, Ralph L., ed.** Journal of Consumer Satisfaction, Dissatisfaction & Complaining Behavior, Vol. 12. 1999. 15.00 (*0-922279-12-8*) CSDCBI.
Day, Ralph L. & Hunt, H. Keith, eds. Journal of Consumer Satisfaction, Dissatisfaction & Complaining Behavior, Vol. 1. 1988. pap. 15.00 (*0-922279-01-2*) CSDCBI.
— Journal of Consumer Satisfaction, Dissatisfaction & Complaining Behavior, Vol. 2. 1989. pap. 15.00 (*0-922279-02-0*) CSDCBI.
— Journal of Consumer Satisfaction, Dissatisfaction & Complaining Behavior, Vol. 3. 1990. pap. 15.00 (*0-922279-03-9*) CSDCBI.
— Journal of Consumer Satisfaction, Dissatisfaction & Complaining Behavior, Vol. 4. 228p. 1991. pap. 15.00 (*0-922279-04-7*) CSDCBI.
— Journal of Consumer Satisfaction, Dissatisfaction & Complaining Behavior, Vol. 5, 1992. 232p. 1992. pap. 15.00 (*0-922279-05-5*) CSDCBI.
— Journal of Consumer Satisfaction, Dissatisfaction & Complaining Behavior, Vol. 6. 279p. 1993. pap. 15.00 (*0-922279-06-3*) CSDCBI.
— Journal of Consumer Satisfaction, Dissatisfaction & Complaining Behavior, Vol. 7. 270p. 1994. pap. 15.00 (*0-922279-07-1*) CSDCBI.
— Journal of Consumer Satisfaction, Dissatisfaction & Complaining Behavior, Vol. 8. 238p. 1995. pap. 15.00 (*0-922279-08-X*) CSDCBI.
— Journal of Consumer Satisfaction, Dissatisfaction & Complaining Behavior, Vol. 9. 239p. 1996. pap. 15.00 (*0-922279-09-8*) CSDCBI.
— Journal of Consumer Satisfaction, Dissatisfaction & Complaining Behavior, Vol. 10. 1997. pap. 15.00 (*0-922279-10-1*) CSDCBI.
Day, Ralph L. & Hunt, Keith, eds. Journal of Consumer Satisfaction, Dissatisfaction & Complaining Behavior, Vol. 11. 1998. pap. 15.00 (*0-922279-11-X*) CSDCBI.
Day, Randal D., jt. ed. see Peters, H. Elizabeth.
Day, Randall D. Research & Theory In Family Science. (Psychology). 661p. 1994. mass mkt. 40.00 (*0-534-21780-X*) Brooks-Cole.
Day, Rebecca, jt. auth. see Merrick, Catherine.
Day, Reed B. The Cumberland Road: A History of the National Road. (Illus.). 42p. 1997. per. 7.95 (*1-55856-227-3*, 279) Closson Pr.
— Legal Issues Surrounding Safe Schools. 90p. 1994. text 30.00 (*1-56534-066-3*) Ed Law Assn.
— The Whiskey Insurrection. 33p. 1992. per. 6.00 (*1-55856-117-X*, 104) Closson Pr.
Day, Rhonda, ed. see Garcia, Joseph G.
Day, Richard. Do-It-Yourself Plumbing... It's Easy with Genova. Kellogg, Jeanette & Williams, Robert M., eds. (Illus.). 142p. (C). 1991. pap. text 12.95 (*0-9616509-0-7*) Genova Products.
— Psychology 1A6 Student Handbook. 5th ed. 212p. (C). 1996. pap. text, spiral bd. 19.95 (*0-7872-2792-7*, 41279201) Kendall-Hunt.
Day, Richard. Two Dog River. 298p. 1995. pap. 12.95 (*0-9664659-0-3*) Sutton Pubg.
Day, Richard, jt. auth. see Hopper, Bill.
Day, Richard B. Cold War Capitalism: The View from Moscow, 1945-1975. LC 95-9029. 376p. (C). (gr. 13). 1995. text 77.95 (*1-56324-660-0*); pap. text 40.95 (*1-56324-661-9*) M E Sharpe.
Day, Richard B., et al, eds. Democratic Theory & Technological Society. LC 88-4442. 370p. (C) (gr. 13). 1988. text 70.95 (*0-87332-448-X*) M E Sharpe.
Day, Richard B., ed. & tr. see Bukharin, Nikolai I.
Day, Richard B., ed. & tr. see Preobrazhenskii, Evgenii A.
Day, Richard E. Beacon Lights of Grace: Twelve Biographical Vignettes. LC 71-148210. (Biography Index Reprint Ser.). 1977. 19.95 (*0-8369-8057-3*) Ayer.
Day, Richard E., jt. auth. see Pound, Arthur.
Day, Richard H. Complex Economic Dynamics Vol. 1: An Introduction to Dynamical Systems & Market Mechanisms. LC 93-30291. 340p. 1994. 45.00 (*0-262-04141-3*) MIT Pr.
— Complex Economic Dynamics Vol. 2: An Introduction to Macroeconomic Dynamics. (Studies in Dynamical Economic Science). (Illus.). 400p. 1999. 49.50 (*0-262-04172-3*) MIT Pr.
Day, Richard H., ed. Economic Analysis & Agricultural Policy. LC 82-15341. 386p. 1982. reprint ed. pap. 119.70 (*0-608-00147-3*, 206092800006) Bks Demand.
Day, Richard H., et al, eds. The Markets for Innovation, Ownership & Control: Proceedings of the International Conference, Saltsjobaden, Sweden, June 12-15, 1988. LC 93-14648. (Studies in Economic Decision, Organization & Behavior: Vol. 2). 456p. 1993. 166.50 (*0-444-89675-9*, North Holland) Elsevier.
Day, Richard H. & Singh, Inderjit. Economic Development As an Adaptive Process: The Green Revolution in the Indian Punjab. LC 76-9173. 336p. reprint ed. pap. 95.80 (*0-608-17507-2*, 2030589) Bks Demand.
Day, Richard H. & Smith, Vernon L., eds. Experiments in Decision, Organization & Exchange. LC 93-14647. (Studies in Economic Decision, Organization & Behavior: Vol. 1). (Illus.). 388p. 1993. 130.00 (*0-444-89777-1*, North Holland) Elsevier.
Day, Richard H., jt. ed. see Kamrany, Nake M.
Day, Richard R., ed. New Ways in Teaching Reading. LC 93-60127. 300p. 1993. pap. 22.95 (*0-939791-45-5*) Tchrs Eng Spkrs.
Day, Richard R. & Bamford, Julian. Extensive Reading in the Second Language Classroom. LC 97-24481. (Language Education Ser.). (Illus.). 256p. (C). 1998. text 54.95 (*0-521-56073-X*); pap. text 20.95 (*0-521-56829-3*) Cambridge U Pr.
Day, Robert. The Four Wheel Drive Quartet. LC 85-82497. 39p. (Orig.). 1986. 11.95 (*0-913123-08-0*); pap. 5.95 (*0-913123-09-9*) Galileo.
— The Last Cattle Drive. LC 83-16887. 224p. 1983. reprint ed. 25.00 (*0-7006-0243-7*); reprint ed. pap. 9.95 (*0-7006-0344-1*) U Pr of KS.
— Speaking French in Kansas & Other Stories. (Illus.). 112p. (Orig.). 1989. per. 8.95 (*1-878434-14-4*) Cottonwood KS.
Day, Robert, jt. auth. see Arnold, Matthew.
Day, Robert, jt. auth. see Day, Jean.
Day, Robert A. How to Write & Publish a Scientific Paper. 5th ed. LC 98-7718. (Illus.). 240p. 1998. pap. text 24.50 (*1-57356-165-7*) Oryx Pr.
— How to Write & Publish a Scientific Paper. 5th ed. LC 98-7718. (Illus.). 296p. 1998. text 34.95 (*1-57356-164-9*) Oryx Pr.
— Scientific English: A Guide for Scientists & Other Professionals. 2nd ed. LC 95-370. (Illus.). 160p. 1995. pap. 19.95 (*0-89774-989-8*) Oryx Pr.
Day, Robert A., ed. see Smollett, Tobias George.
Day, Robert O. The Enoch Train Pioneers: Trek of the First Two Handcart Companies. (Illus.). 388p. 1999. pap. 19.95 (*1-890905-01-1*) Day to Day.
— The Mormon Battalion, the Lord's Faithful. 2nd rev. ed. (Illus.). 364p. 1998. pap. 19.95 (*1-890905-09-7*) Day to Day.
— Say Me a Say...Play Me a Play. (Illus.). 90p. 1988. reprint ed. pap. 12.95 (*1-890905-05-4*) Day to Day.
Day, Robert O. & Day, Linda S. FB & the Gang. 2nd ed. (Illus.). 61p. 1988. reprint ed. ring bd. 12.95 (*1-890905-02-X*) Day to Day.
Day, Robert O., ed. see Day, Linda S.
Day, Robert W. Forensic Geotechnical & Foundation Engineering. LC 98-18043. 460p. 1998. 79.95 (*0-07-016444-4*) McGraw.
***Day, Robert W.** Geotechnical Engineer's Portable Handbook. LC 99-48908. 560p. 1999. pap. text 59.95 (*0-07-135111-6*) McGraw.
***Day, Roger.** The Christmas Carol Collection. 127p. 1999. pap. text 12.95 (*0-7119-7772-0*, AM953304) Music Sales.
Day, Roger. The Pianist's Picture Chords. (Illus.). 32p. 1978. pap. 8.95 (*0-86001-528-9*, AM21429) Music Sales.
Day, Roger, jt. auth. see Jones, Graham A.
Day, Roger W. Decline to Glory: A Reassessment of the Life & Times of Lady Hester Stanhope. 416p. 1997. pap. 29.95 (*3-7052-0153-0*, Pub. by Univ of West Aust Pr) Intl Spec Bk.
Day, Ron. Computer Studies for Australian Primary Schools. (C). 1992. pap. text. write for info. (*0-201-55618-9*) Addison-Wesley.
Day, Ronald G. Quality Function Deployment: Linking a Company with Its Customers. LC 93-4479. 245p. 1993. 48.00 (*0-87389-202-X*, H0749) ASQ Qual Pr.
Day, Ronnie, ed. see Morriss, Mack.
Day, S., tr. see Lechner, G. & Naunheimer, H.
Day, S. A., et al. Bibliographic Checklist of the Non-Marine Algae of Australia. (Flora of Australia: Supplementary Ser.: Vol. 4). (Illus.). 276p. (Orig.). 1995. pap. 49.95 (*0-642-22788-8*, Pub. by CSIRO) Accents Pubns.
Day, S. B. Cancer, Stress & Death. 2nd ed. LC 86-570. 392p. (C). 1986. text 59.50 (*0-306-42187-9*, Kluwer Plenum) Kluwer Academic.
Day, S. B., jt. auth. see Lambo, T. A.
Day, Samantha. The Three of Us. (Romance Ser.). 1994. per. 2.99 (*0-373-03297-8*, 1-03297-8) Harlequin Bks.
Day, Samuel H., Jr. Crossing the Line: From Editor to Activist to Inmate - A Writer's Journey. LC 90-84431. (Illus.). 258p. (Orig.). 1991. pap. 12.00 (*1-879175-01-0*) Prog Found.
Day, Samuel H., Jr., ed. see Nukewatch Staff.
Day, Sandy. The Pollution Prevention Guide: A Common Sense Approach to Environmental Management. Date not set. pap. 6.95 (*0-9650267-1-X*) SanDay Servs.
Day, Sara, ed. Heart of the Circle: Photographs by Edward S. Curtis of Native American Women. LC 96-28464. (Illus.). 128p. 1997. pap. 34.95 (*0-7649-0006-4*) Pomegranate Calif.
Day, Sara, jt. auth. see Hutson, James H.
Day, Sara, ed. see Library of Congress Carson, Marian S., Collection, et al.
Day, Sara, ed. see Oliphant, Pat & Katz, Harry.
Day-Schmal, Linda. Soul-Birthing: How to Choose, Attract & Influence the Soul of Your Baby Before Conception or Birth. (Illus.). 240p. 1998. pap. 14.95 (*0-9651546-9-6*) Med Bear.
Day-Schmal, Linda, ed. see Engels-Lora, Gabriela.
Day-Schmal, Linda, ed. see Peter, Edwin A.
Day, Sherman. Historical Collections of the State of Pennsylvania. (Illus.). 708p. (Orig.). 1995. reprint ed. pap. 42.50 (*0-7884-0267-6*) Heritage Bk.
***Day, Sherman.** Historical Collections of the State of Pennsylvania: A Copious Selection of the Most Interesting Facts, Traditions, Biographical Sketches, Anecdotes, Etc. Relating to Its History & Antiquities ... 708p. 1999. reprint ed. pap. 49.95 (*0-8063-4858-5*) Clearfield Co.
Day, Sherman. Historical Collections of the State of Pennsylvania: Containing a Copious Selection of the Most Interesting Facts, Traditions, Biographical Sketches, Anecdotes, Etc., Relating to the History & Antiquities...with Topographical Descriptions of Every County. (Illus.). 705p. 1995. reprint ed. lib. bdg. 74.00 (*0-8328-5099-3*) Higginson Bk Co.
Day, Shirley. Luna & the Big Blur: A Story for Children Who Wear Glasses. (Illus.). 32p. (J). (ps-3). 1995. 11.95 (*0-945354-66-5*) Am Psychol.
***Day, Shirley J., ed.** Writers & Heroines: Essays on Women in French Literature. 177p. 1999. 32.95 (*3-906761-61-4*, Pub. by P Lang) P Lang Pubng.
Day, Shirley J., ed. Writers & Heroines: Essays on Women in French Literature. LC 98-33248. 177p. 1998. pap. 32.95 (*0-8204-4214-3*) P Lang Pubng.
***Day, Shirley Jones.** The Search for Lyonnesse: Women's Fiction in France, 1670-1703. LC 99-38633. 340p. (C). 1999. pap. text 52.95 (*0-8204-4242-9*) P Lang Pubng.
***Day, Sophie, et al.** Lilies of the Field: Marginal People Who Live for the Moment. LC 98-30158. (Studies in the Ethnographic Imagination). 272p. 1998. text 63.00 (*0-8133-3531-0*, Pub. by Westview) HarpC.
Day, St. John V. Papers on the Great Pyramid. 127p. 1996. reprint ed. spiral bd. 12.00 (*0-7873-0260-0*) Hlth Research.
Day, Stacey B. Biogenesis of Ethics: Unbeing of Earthly Incarnation & Other Essays. (Illus.). 220p. 2000. 55.00 (*0-934314-26-8*) Intl Found Biosocial Dev.
— Biologos & Biopsychosocial Synthesis: The SAMA Foundation Lectures, Calabar, West Africa, 1982. LC 84-82409. 130p. 1985. 35.00 (*0-934314-75-6*) Intl Found Biosocial Dev.
— Creative Health & Health Enhancement: Individual Initiative & Responsibility for Self Health & Wellness. LC 81-81300. (Monograph on Health Communications & Biopsychosocial Health). (Illus.). 1982. lib. bdg. 150.00 (*0-934314-07-1*, SBD/HES82SKI) Intl Found Biosocial Dev.
— Death & Attitudes Towards Death. LC 72-76821. Orig. Title: Proceedings A Symposium of the Bell Museum, Univ. of Minn. Med. School. 94p. (Orig.). 1984. reprint ed. 10.00 (*0-934314-76-4*) Intl Found Biosocial Dev.
— Developing Health in the West African Bush: A Fulbright Memoir, 2 pts., Set. (Illus.). 335p. (C). 1995. text 33.75 (*0-930329-96-1*) Kabel Pubs.
— The Idle Thoughts of a Surgical Fellow: Being An

An Asterisk (*) at the beginning of an entry indicates that the title is appearing for the first time.

Account of Experimental Surgical Studies 1956-1966. LC 68-31066. (Illus.). 344p. (C). 1984. 25.00 (*0-934314-99-3*) Intl Found Biosocial Dev.

— Letters of Owen Wangensteen to a Surgical Fellow - With a Memoir. LC 96-78241. (Illus.). 240p. 1996. 59.50 (*0-934314-25-X*, B10-10) Intl Found Biosocial Dev.

— Man & Mu: The Cradle of Becoming & Unbecoming: Desiderata for Human Science. LC 97-72905. (Illus.). 200p. (Orig.). (C). 1998. lib. bdg. 39.50 (*0-934314-00-4*) Intl Found Biosocial Dev.

— Selected Poems & Embers of a Medical Life. LC 98-75410. (Illus.). 200p. 1999. lib. bdg. 35.00 (*0-934314-03-9*) Intl Found Biosocial Dev.

— The Surgical Treatment of Ischaemic Heart Disease with an Account of the Coronary & Intercoronary Circulation in Man & Animals. (Illus.). 200p. 2000. 55.00 (*0-934314-24-1*, MOYNIHAN 1960) Intl Found Biosocial Dev.

Day, Stacey B., ed. Image of Science & Society. (Biosciences Communications Ser.: Vol. 3, No. 1). 1977. 16.75 (*3-8055-2690-3*) S Karger.

— Some Systems of Biological Communication: Journal: Biosciences Communications, Vol. 3, Nos. 5 & 6. (Illus.). 1977. 49.75 (*3-8055-2817-5*) S Karger.

— What Is a Scientist? Memorial Issue for Professor Oscar Bodansky. (Journal: Biosciences Communications: Vol. 4, No. 5). 1978. pap. 16.75 (*3-8055-2967-8*) S Karger.

Day, Stacey B., et al, eds. Cancer Invasion & Metastasis: Biologic Mechanisms & Therapy. LC 77-83695. (Progress in Cancer Research & Therapy Ser.: No. 5). (Illus.). 540p. reprint ed. pap. 167.40 (*0-7837-7099-5*, 204692800004) Bks Demand.

Day, Stacey B., et al. Czech Caesura - Golden Prague & the Black Years: Notes from Diaries 1970-1990. LC 98-70219. (Illus.). 250p. 2001. lib. bdg. write for info. (*0-934314-01-2*, CZ99PRHA) Intl Found Biosocial Dev.

***Day, Sterling B.** Turkon, a Stripling Young Warrior. (Illus.). 51p. 2000. pap. write for info. (*0-7541-0967-4*, Pub. by Minerva Pr) Unity Dist.

Day, Susan. Early Childhood Education: Developmental-Experiential Learning. 4th ed. LC 93-37977. 640p. (C). 1994. pap. text 66.33 (*0-02-327923-0*, Macmillan Coll) P-H.

Day, Susan & McMahan, Elizabeth, eds. The Writer's Resource: Readings for Composition. 4th ed. LC 93-23204. 576p. (C). 1994. pap. 34.06 (*0-07-016176-3*) McGraw.

Day, Susan, et al. The Elements of Writing about Literature & Film. LC 87-21904. 130p. 1988. pap. text 15.00 (*0-02-327954-0*, Macmillan Coll) P-H.

Day, Susan, et al. Keeping in Touch: English Skills Program , Apple Version. 656p. (C). 1987. pap. text, teacher ed. 527.00 incl. disk (*0-02-327952-4*, Pub. by P-H) S&S Trade.

— Reading & the Writing Process. 2nd ed. LC 93-10711. 640p. (C). 1993. pap. text 44.00 (*0-02-327901-X*, Macmillan Coll) P-H.

Day, Susan, jt. auth. see McMahan, Elizabeth.

Day, Susan X. & McMahan, Elizabeth. The Practical Writer's Guide. LC 96-7026. 466p. 1996. pap. text 40.00 (*0-205-17386-1*) Allyn.

— The Practical Writer's Guide with Readings. LC 96-1201. 546p. 1996. pap. text 42.00 (*0-205-17389-6*) Allyn.

Day, Susan X., et al. The Practical Writer's Guide: Examination Copy. 496p. (C). 1996. pap. text. write for info. (*0-205-26429-8*, T6429-9) Allyn.

— The Practical Writer's Guide with Additional Readings: Examination Copy. 576p. (C). 1996. pap. text. write for info. (*0-205-26430-1*, T6430-7) Allyn.

Day, Terence P. Great Tradition & Little Tradition in Theravada Buddhist Studies. LC 87-15228. (Studies in Asian Thought & Religion: Vol. 7). 248p. (C). 1987. lib. bdg. 89.95 (*0-88946-057-4*) E Mellen.

Day, Thomas. Why Catholics Can't Sing: The Culture of Catholicism & the Triumph of Bad Taste. 248p. 1992. pap. 14.95 (*0-8245-1153-0*) Crossroad NY.

Day, Thomas, ed. see Lotti, Antonio.

Day, Thomas F. The Voyage of Detroit. 2nd rev. ed. LC 97-61366. (Illus.). 200p. 1997. reprint ed. pap. write for info. (*0-9659506-0-3*) Eastern Offset.

Day, Thomas I. Dietrich Bonhoeffer on Christian Community & Common Sense. LC 82-25900. (Toronto Studies in Theology: Vol. 11). 248p. 1983. lib. bdg. 89.95 (*0-88946-752-8*) E Mellen.

Day, Thomas J. Sewer Management Systems. LC 99-42171. 400p. 2000. 90.00 (*0-471-31799-3*) Wiley.

***Day, Timothy.** A Century of Recorded Music: Listening to Musical History. (Illus.). 304p. 2000. 30.00 (*0-300-08442-0*) Yale U Pr.

Day, Trevor. Guide to Sex. (Teach Yourself Ser.). (Illus.). 288p. 1998. pap. 10.95 (*0-8442-0023-9*, 00239, Teach Yrslf) NTC Contemp Pub Co.

— Light. LC 97-5991. (Science Projects Ser.). (J). 1998. 24.26 (*0-8172-4943-5*) Raintree Steck-V.

— Oceans. LC 98-18110. (Ecosystem Ser.). 1999. 45.00 (*0-8160-3647-0*) Facts on File.

— The Random House Book of One Thousand One Questions & Answers about the Human Body. LC 93-6386. 160p. (J). (gr. 4-7). 1994. pap. 15.00 (*0-679-85432-0*, Pub. by Random Bks Yng Read) Random.

***Day, Trevor, et al.** Youch! Real-life Monsters up Close. LC 99-47355. (J). (gr. 4-6). 2000. 16.00 (*0-689-83416-0*) S&S Trade.

Day, U. N. The Government of the Sultanate. 154p. (C). 1993. reprint ed. 32.50 (*81-215-0519-4*, Pub. by M Manoharial) Coronet Bks.

Day, Valerie. A Fruitful Vessel: A Journey to Fruitfulness. (Illus.). 65p. 1997. pap. 8.50 (*0-9653688-7-4*) P & P Ent.

Day, Veronique, tr. see Hindman, Sandra.

Day, Veronique P., tr. see Hindman, Sandra.

***Day, Vicki & Cabral, Nola.** My Favorite Things. (Illus.). 44p. 1999. pap. 12.95 (*0-936459-45-X*) Stained Glass.

Day, Victoria, jt. auth. see Hicks, Roger.

Day, Vox, jt. auth. see Bethke, Bruce.

Day, W. & Atkin, R. K., eds. Wheat Growth & Modeling. LC 85-3691. (NATO ASI Series A, Life Sciences: Vol. 86). 420p. 1985. 95.00 (*0-306-41933-5*, Plenum Trade) Perseus Pubng.

Day, W., jt. ed. see Hashimoto, Y.

Day, W. A. A Commentary on Thermodynamics. (Tracts in Natural Philosophy Ser.). 110p. 1987. 79.95 (*0-387-96615-3*) Spr-Verlag.

— Heat Conduction Within Linear Thermoelasticity. LC 85-11455. (Tracts in Natural Philosophy Ser.: Vol. 30). viii, 82p. 1985. 65.95 (*0-387-96156-9*) Spr-Verlag.

***Day, W. A.** A True History of Company I, 49th Regiment, North Carolina Troops. (Army of Northern Virginia Ser.: Vol. 9). 143p. 1998. reprint ed. 25.00 (*0-935523-62-6*) Butternut & Blue.

Day, W. G., ed. see Pepys, Samuel.

Day, Walter A. Twin Galaxies Official Video Game & Pinball Book of World Records: The Official Book of Records Listing the High Scores on Arcade Video Games, Pinball, Home Video Games, & Network Games. LC 96-72617. (Illus.). 250p. (Orig.). 1998. pap. 19.95 (*1-887472-25-8*) Sunstar Pubng.

Day, William. Bridge from Nowhere Vol. II: The Photonic Origin of Matter. LC 96-67391. x, 102p. (Orig.). (C). 1996. pap. 12.95 (*0-9625455-1-1*) Rhombics.

Day, William D. A Place in the Race. 1998. pap. 11.27 (*1-57502-782-8*, P02165) Morris Pubng.

Day, William H. Maximizing Small Business Profits: With Precision Management. LC 78-9407. 1979. 13.95 (*0-13-566257-5*, Spectrum IN); pap. 6.95 (*0-13-566240-0*, Spectrum IN) Macmillan Gen Ref.

Day, William P. In the Circles of Fear & Desire: A Study of Gothic Fantasy. LC 84-28004. 220p. reprint ed. pap. 68.20 (*0-608-09445-5*, 205424500005) Bks Demand.

Day, William Patrick. In the Circles of Fear & Desire: A Study of Gothic Fantasy. LC 84-28004. xi, 208 p. 1985. 25.00 (*0-226-13891-7*) U Ch Pr.

Day, William V. God Bless: A Collection of Essays by William V. Day. (Illus.). vii, 167p. 1998. pap. 15.95 (*0-9665690-0-8*) St Barnabas Found.

Daya, Sr. The Guru & the Disciple. 1976. pap. 4.95 (*0-911564-26-8*) Vedanta Ctr.

Daya, Salim. Recurrent Spontaneous Abortion. 1999. 179.95 (*0-8493-5852-3*) CRC Pr.

Dayal, Edison. Food, Nutrition & Hunger in Bangladesh. 242p. 1997. 69.95 (*1-85972-582-1*, Pub. by Avebry) Ashgate Pub Co.

Dayal, Indira, jt. auth. see Murti, Isana.

Dayal, Ishwar. Reappraising Management Education: Perspectives for the Future. (Illus.). 127p. 1998. 16.00 (*81-7099-677-5*, Pub. by Mittal Pubs Dist) Nataraj Bks.

Dayal, John & Bose, Ajoy. The Shah Commission Begins: India under Emergency. 1978. 13.50 (*0-8364-0179-4*) S Asia.

***Dayal, Lakshmeshwar.** State & the People: Political History of Government in India. LC 99-931670. 1998. 38.50 (*81-7099-702-X*, Pub. by Mittal Pubns) S Asia.

Dayal, Maheshwar. Renewable Energy: Environment & Development. (Illus.). 256p. 1990. text 30.00 (*81-220-0150-5*, Pub. by Konark Pubs Pvt Ltd) Advent Bks Div.

Dayal, R. Chytrids of India. LC 97-905303. 316p. 1997. pap. 350.00 (*81-7533-038-4*, Pub. by Print Hse) St Mut.

Dayal, R., ed. Advances in Zoosporic Fungi. 291p. 1996. pap. 400.00 (*81-7533-002-3*, Pub. by Print Hse) St Mut.

Dayal, R. & Kiran, Usha. Zoosporic Fungi of India. (C). 1988. 44.00 (*81-210-0228-1*, Pub. by Inter-India Pubns) S Asia.

***Dayal, Rajeshwar.** Life of Our Times. LC 98-907278. 1998. 36.00 (*81-250-1546-9*, Pub. by Orient Longman Ltd) S Asia.

Dayal, Ravi, ed. We Fought Together for Freedom: Chapters from the Indian National Movement. 284p. 1998. reprint ed. pap. text 14.50 (*0-19-564537-5*) OUP.

Dayal, S. D. LDL Online - Laying down the Law Computer-Assisted Legal Research. 184p. 1995. pap. write for info. (*0-409-31165-0*, MICHIE) LEXIS Pub.

Dayal, Veneeta. Locality in WH Quantification: Questions & Relative Clauses in Hindi. LC 96-17891. (Studies in Linguistics & Philosophy). 264p. 1996. text 104.00 (*0-7923-4099-X*) Kluwer Academic.

Dayal, Yogeshwar. Endocrine Pathology of the Gut & Pancreas. (Illus.). 328p. 1991. lib. bdg. 202.00 (*0-8493-5993-7*, RC280) CRC Pr.

Dayalan, D. Early Temples of Tamilnadu. (C). 1992. 58.00 (*81-85151-55-5*, Pub. by Harman Pub Hse) S Asia.

Dayan, A. D., et al, eds. Immunotoxicity of Metals & Immunotoxicology. LC 90-14178. (Illus.). 330p. (C). 1990. text 114.00 (*0-306-43679-5*, Kluwer Plenum) Kluwer Academic.

Dayan, A. D., jt. ed. see Walker, S. R.

Dayan, Chaim M., ed. see Hadakov, Mordechai I.

Dayan, Daniel. Media Events: The Live Broadcasting of History. (Illus.). 320p. 1994. pap. 19.50 (*0-674-55956-8*) HUP.

Dayan, Daniel & Katz, Elihu. Media Events: The Live Broadcasting of History. (Illus.). 320p. (C). 1992. 43.00 (*0-674-55955-X*) HUP.

Dayan, Joan. Haiti, History & the Gods. 1998. pap. text 16.95 (*0-520-21368-8*, Pub. by U CA Pr) Cal Prin Full Svc.

Dayan, Moshe. Diary of the Sinai Campaign. (Quality Paperbacks Ser.). (Illus.). 236p. 1991. reprint ed. pap. 12.95 (*0-306-80451-4*) Da Capo.

— Moshe Dayan: Story of My Life. (Illus.). 640p. 1992. reprint ed. pap. 17.95 (*0-306-80497-2*) Da Capo.

Dayan, Peter. Mallarme's "Divine Transportation" Real & Apparent Sources of Literary Value. (Oxford Modern Languages & Literature Monographs). 288p. 1987. 55.00 (*0-19-815841-6*) OUP.

Dayanand. All the Secrets of Palmistry for Profession & Popularity. (C). 1992. 10.00 (*0-8364-2857-9*, Pub. by UBS Pubs Dist) S Asia.

— Palmistry, How to Master It? A Gist of Indian & Western Systems of Hand Reading. (C). 1994. 10.00 (*81-7386-116-1*, Pub. by DK Pubs Ind) S Asia.

Dayananda, M. A., et al, eds. Diffusion in High Technology Materials. 400p. 1988. text 106.00 (*0-87849-561-4*, Pub. by Trans T Pub) Enfield Pubs NH.

Dayananda, M. A., ed. see Metallurgical Society of AIME Staff.

Dayananda, M. A., ed. see Norman L. Peterson Memorial Symposium on Oxidation.

Dayand. Designers Handbook of Designers. (Illus.). 192p. Date not set. 34.95 (*1-883915-06-6*, 858562) RC Pubns.

Dayantis. Thermodynamics of Polymer Solutions. 300p. 1998. write for info. (*0-12-207550-1*) Acad Pr.

***Dayao, Dinna Louise C., ed.** Asian Business Wisdom: Lessons from the Region's Best & Brightest Business Leaders. 250p. 2000. 29.95 (*0-471-83756-3*) Wiley.

Dayar, T. & Gudukbay, U., eds. Advances in Computer & Information Sciences '98: Proceedings of the 13th International Symposium on Computer & Information Sciences. LC 98-72490. (Concurrent Systems Engineering Ser.: Vol. 53). 800p. Date not set. 107.00 (*90-5199-405-2*) IOS Pr.

Dayaratnam, P. Brick & Reinforced Brick Structures. 108p. (C). 1987. 14.00 (*81-204-0249-9*, Pub. by Oxford IBH) S Asia.

***Daybell, Chad C.** An Errand for Emma. 1999. pap. 11.95 (*1-55517-422-1*) CFI Dist.

Daydi-Tolson, Santiago. Voces y Ecos en la Poesia de Jose Angel Valente. LC 83-51783. (SPA.). 182p. 1984. pap. 25.00 (*0-89295-034-X*) Society Sp & Sp-Am.

Daydi-Tolson, Santiago, ed. Five Poets of Aztlan. LC 83-71140. 224p. 1985. 26.00 (*0-916950-41-7*); pap. 16.00 (*0-916950-42-5*) Biling Rev-Pr.

— Vicente Aleixandre: A Critical Appraisal. LC 81-65036. (Studies in Literary Analysis). 330p. (C). 1981. pap. text 20.00 (*0-916950-20-4*); lib. bdg. 30.00 (*0-916950-21-2*) Biling Rev-Pr.

Daye & Morris. North Carolina Law of Torts: 1992 Supplement. 1992. write for info. (*0-87473-976-4*, 61171-10, MICHIE) LEXIS Pub.

Daye, Alexandra. All the Missing Pieces. LC 98-85978. 325p. 1998. 25.00 (*0-7388-0013-9*); pap. 15.00 (*0-7388-0029-5*) Xlibris Corp.

Daye, Charles E. & Morris, Mark W. North Carolina Law of Torts. 722p. 1991. 85.00 (*0-87473-757-5*, MICHIE); 85.00 (*0-87473-751-6*, 61170-10, MICHIE); 85.00 (*0-327-00993-4*, 61170, MICHIE) LEXIS Pub.

— North Carolina Law of Torts. 1995. suppl. ed. 40.00 (*0-614-25254-7*, 61171-13, MICHIE) LEXIS Pub.

***Daye, Charles E. & Morris, Mark W.** North Carolina Law of Torts. 2nd ed. 950p. 1999. write for info. (*0-327-04935-9*, 6117011) LEXIS Pub.

Daye, Charles E. & Morris, Mark W. North Carolina Law of Torts: 1998 Cumulative Supplement. LC 91-61407. 210p. 1998. write for info. (*0-327-00219-0*, 61171-16) LEXIS Pub.

— North Carolina Law of Torts with 1992 Supplement. 722p. 1991. 75.00 (*0-685-48592-7*, MICHIE) LEXIS Pub.

***Daye, Charles E., et al.** Housing & Community Development. 3rd ed. LC 99-65808. 1999. boxed set 70.00 (*0-89089-736-0*) Carolina Acad Pr.

Daye, Charles E., et al. Housing & Community Development: Cases & Materials. LC 89-62028. 536p. 1991. lib. bdg. 45.00 (*0-89089-370-5*) Carolina Acad Pr.

Daye, Douglas D. Tactics & Mindsets: A Source Book on Asian Crime & Culture. 464p. 1996. boxed set 84.95 (*0-8493-8116-9*, 8116) CRC Pr.

Daye, Sharon J. Middle-Class Blacks in Britain: A Racial Fraction of a Class Group or a Class Fraction of a Racial Group? LC 93-29486. 1994. text 69.95 (*0-312-10638-6*) St Martin.

***Dayee, Frances S.** Babysitting. rev. ed. (Illus.). (J). 2000. write for info. (*0-531-11745-6*) Watts.

Dayem, Rifaat A. Mobile Data & Wireless LAN Technologies. LC 97-156866. 336p. (C). 1997. 69.00 (*0-13-839051-7*) P-H.

— PCs Networking. LC 97-172305. 256p. (C). 1997. 63.00 (*0-13-616574-5*) P-H.

Dayfoot, Arthur C. A History of Protestant Churches in the West Indies. LC 98-17620. 448p. 1998. 49.95 (*0-8130-1626-6*) U Press Fla.

D'Aygalliers, A. Wautier. Ruysbroeck the Admirable. 372p. 1996. reprint ed. pap. 24.95 (*1-56459-558-7*) Kessinger Pub.

Dayger, Kendra. Review of Mainstream CFIDS Research in the U. S. A., 1990 - June 1992. 271p. 1992. pap. 21.00 (*0-317-05542-9*) CFIDS Rochester.

Dayhaw, Laurence-T. Rockett's World. (Rockett's World Ser.: No. 4). 128p. (J). (gr. 4-7). 1999. pap. 4.99 (*0-439-08210-2*, Pub. by Scholastic Inc) Penguin Putnam.

***Dayhaw, Laurence-T.** Rockett's World Mixed Floor Display. 1999. pap. text 71.82 (*0-439-13487-0*) Scholastic Inc.

Dayhoff, J. Advanced Neural Networks & Molecular Manual. (Management Information Systems Ser.). 1991. text. write for info. (*0-442-01392-2*, VNR) Wiley.

Dayhoff, Judith, jt. ed. see Omidvar, Omid.

Dayhoff, M. O., ed. Atlas of Protein Sequence & Structure, Vol. 5, Suppl. No. 1. LC 65-29342. 1973. pap. 5.00 (*0-912466-04-9*) Natl Biomedical.

— Atlas of Protein Sequence & Structure, Vol. 5, Suppl. No. 3. LC 65-29342. 1979. pap. 25.00 (*0-912466-07-3*) Natl Biomedical.

Dayhoff, Margaret O., et al. Nucleic Acid Sequence Database, Vol 1. LC 81-84122. (Illus.). xiv, 214p. (Orig.). 1981. pap. text 25.00 (*0-686-79304-8*) Natl Biomedical.

***Dayhoff, Signe A.** Diagonally-Parked in a Parallel Universe: Working Through Social Anxiety. LC 99-90673. (Illus.). 408p. 2000. pap. 19.95 (*0-9671265-0-9*) Effect Plus.

Dayhoff, Signe A. Get the Job You Want: Successful Strategies for Selling Yourself in the Job Market. LC 90-32748. 208p. (Orig.). 1990. pap. 14.95 (*0-931790-94-8*) Brick Hse Pub.

Daykin, Frank. Islands. (Orig.). 1991. 20.00 (*1-880551-01-2*) Silver Hill.

— Words Without Song. (Orig.). 1992. pap. text 20.00 (*1-880551-02-0*) Silver Hill.

Daykin, Norma. Health & Work under Capitalism: An International Perspective. LC 99-19219. 258p. 1999. text 55.00 (*0-312-22342-0*) St Martin.

Dayle, Jeri. Sock Crafts. LC 98-17189. 24p. (J). 1999. pap. 3.25 (*0-679-88643-5*, Pub. by Random Bks Yng Read) Random.

Dayley, Beth & Davis, Janet. If I Were a Model Mother. 1992. pap. 1.98 (*0-88290-446-9*) Horizon Utah.

Dayley, Jon & Crum, Beverly. Western Shoshoni Grammar. 300p. (C). 1994. pap. text 24.95 (*0-9639749-0-4*) Boise St U Dept Anthrop.

Dayley, Jon P. Tumpisa (Panamint) Shoshone Grammar. (Publications in Linguistics: Vol. 115). (Illus.). 536p. 1990. pap. 60.00 (*0-520-09752-1*, Pub. by U CA Pr) Cal Prin Full Svc.

***Dayley, Wendall.** Archipelago. 1999. write for info. (*1-58235-252-6*) Watermrk Pr.

Daymon, Joy J. Rabbit Pancakes: A Century of Family Recipes. LC 95-92066. (Illus.). 434p. 1995. spiral bd. 24.95 (*0-9645110-0-2*) J Daymon.

Daymond, Margaret. South African Feminisms: Writing, Theory & Criticism, 1990-1994. Bowen, Barbara C., ed. (Gender & Genre in Literature Ser.: Vol. 5). 392p. 1996. text 70.00 (*0-8153-1626-7*) Garland.

Daymond, Margaret, ed. see Colenso, Frances E.

Daymond, Margaret J., et al. Momentum: On Recent South African Writing. 336p. 1984. pap. 24.95 (*0-86980-377-8*, Pub. by Univ Natal Pr) Intl Spec Bk.

Daymond, Scott, jt. auth. see Wood, Frank.

***Daynard, Jodi.** The Place Within: Portraits of the American Landscape by Contemporary Writers. 268p. 2000. reprint ed. text 23.00 (*0-7881-9119-5*) DIANE Pub.

Daynard, Jodi. The Place Within: Portraits of the American Landscape by 20 Contemporary Writers. 224p. 1996. 23.00 (*0-393-03999-4*) Norton.

Daynell, Elphinstone. Why the Sun & the Moon Live in the Sky, 001. 32p. 1968. 16.00 (*0-395-29609-9*) HM.

Daynes. To Govern a Nation, Vol. 1. LC 97-65177. 500p. 1997. pap. 39.95 (*0-312-15413-5*) St Martin.

Daynes, jt. auth. see Sussman.

***Daynes, Byron W. & Sussman, Glen.** The American Presidency & the Social Agenda. LC 00-39139. 2001. write for info. (*0-13-082632-4*) Aspen Law.

Daynes, Byron W., jt. ed. see Tatlovich, Raymond.

Daynes, Gary. Making Villains, Making Heroes: Joseph R. McCarthy, Martin Luther King, Jr. & the Politics of American Memory. Bruchey, Stuart et al, eds. LC 97-38427. (Studies in American Popular History & Culture). 284p. 1997. text 63.00 (*0-8153-2992-X*) Garland.

Daynes, R. & Krueger, G. R. Experimental & Clinical Photoimmunology, Vol. 2. LC 82-14695. 208p. 1983. 120.00 (*0-8493-5371-8*, CRC Reprint) Franklin.

Daynes, Raymond A. & Krueger, Gerald, eds. Experimental & Clinical Photoimmunology, Vol. III. 256p. 1985. 132.00 (*0-8493-5372-6*, QR182, CRC Reprint) Franklin.

Dayrell, Elphinstone. Folk Stories from Southern Nigeria, West Africa. LC 77-76488. 158p. 1969. reprint ed. lib. bdg. 35.00 (*0-8371-1125-0*, DAS&) Greenwood.

— Why the Sun & the Moon Live in the Sky. (Illus.). 32p. (J). (gr. k-3). 1990. pap. 6.95 (*0-395-53963-3*) HM.

— Why the Sun & the Moon Live in the Sky: An African Folktale. (J). 1968. 11.15 (*0-606-04586-4*, Pub. by Turtleback) Demco.

Dayringer, Richard. Dealing with Depression: Five Pastoral Interventions. LC 94-33088. (Illus.). 182p. 1995. pap. 14.95 (*1-56024-967-6*, Harrington Park) Haworth Pr.

— God Cares for You. large type ed. (Large Print Inspirational Ser.). 216p. (Orig.). 1986. pap. 14.95 (*0-8027-2561-9*) Walker & Co.

— The Heart of Pastoral Counseling: Healing Through Relationship. rev. ed. LC 97-28387. (Illus.). 205p. (C). 1998. 39.95 (*0-7890-0172-1*, Haworth Pastrl); pap. 19.95 (*0-7890-0421-6*, Haworth Pastrl) Haworth Pr.

***Dayringer, Richard.** Life Cycle: Psychological & Theological Perceptions. LC 99-37919. 177p. 1999. 49.95 (*0-7890-0171-3*, Haworth Pastrl); pap. 22.95 (*0-7890-0905-6*, Haworth Pastrl) Haworth Pr.

Dayringer, Richard, ed. Pastor & Patient: A Handbook for Clergy Who Visit the Sick. LC 80-70247. 292p. 1995. reprint ed. pap. 45.00 (*1-56821-512-6*) Aronson.

Dayringer, Richard & Eicher, Byron. Dealing with Depression: Five Pastoral Interventions. LC 94-33088. (Illus.). 175p. 1995. lib. bdg. 39.95 (*1-56024-933-1*) Haworth Pr.

Days, Drew S., et al. Justice Enjoined: The State of the Judiciary in Kenya. 90p. 1992. pap. text. write for info. (*1-881055-00-0*) RFK Mem Ctr HR.

***Dayton, Arwen.** Sovereign's Hold. (Illus.). 200p. 2000. pap. 11.00 (*1-883573-16-5*) Pride & Imprints.

Dayton, C. Mitchell. Latent Class Scaling Analysis. LC 98-43854. (University Papers Ser.). 1999. pap. 13.95 (*0-7619-1323-8*) Sage.

An Asterisk (*) at the beginning of an entry indicates that the title is appearing for the first time.

Dayton, C. Mitchell & Stunkard, Clayton L. Statistics for Problem Solving. LC 79-140955. viii, 290p. 1971. write for info. (*0-07-016182-8*) McGraw.

Dayton, Chip R. Kiss Outtakes, Vol. 1. Conte, Robert V., ed. LC 97-6243. (Illus.). 144p. 1998. pap. 24.95 (*1-890313-04-1*, RCTP9801) Studio Chikara.

Dayton, Cornelia H. Women Before the Bar: Gender, Law, & Society in Connecticut, 1639-1789. LC 95-20116. (Published for the Institute of Early American History & Culture Ser.). (Illus.). 400p. (C). 1995. text 59.95 (*0-8078-2244-2*); pap. text 19.95 (*0-8078-4561-2*) U of NC Pr.

Dayton, Daug. Information Technology Audit Handbook. LC 96-40197. 352p. (C). 1997. text 69.95 (*0-13-614314-8*) P-H.

Dayton, Delbert H., jt. ed. see Cooper, Max D.

Dayton, Donald W. Discovering an Evangelical Heritage. 184p. 1988. pap. 9.95 (*0-943575-06-0*) Hendrickson MA.

— Theological Roots of Pentecostalism. 200p. 1991. pap. 14.95 (*0-943575-79-6*) Hendrickson MA.

— Theological Roots of Pentecostalism. 208p. 1987. pap. 19.95 (*0-310-39371-X*, 10386P) Zondervan.

Dayton, Donald W. & Johnston, Robert K., eds. The Variety of American Evangelicalism. 291p. 1997. pap. 25.00 (*1-57910-054-6*) Wipf & Stock.

Dayton, Donald W., ed. see Dieter, Melvin E.

Dayton, Donald W., ed. see Kaufman, Paul L.

Dayton, Doug. Selling Microsoft: Sales Secrets from Inside the World's Most Successful Company. LC 98-8651. 272p. 1998. pap. text 9.95 (*1-58062-052-3*) Adams Media.

— Total Market Domination: 10 Steps for Supercharging Your Sales & Marketing. LC 98-52735. (Illus.). 331p. 1999. 24.95 (*1-58062-113-9*) Adams Media.

Dayton, Ed & Engstrom, Ted W. La Mejor Forma de Planear Su Dia. (Serie Guia de Bolsillo - Pocket Guides Ser.).Tr. of Best Way to Plan Your Day. (SPA.). 1991. 2.79 (*1-56063-032-9*, 498059) Editorial Unilit.

Dayton, Edson C. Dayton. Record of a Family Descent from Ralph Dayton & Alice Goldhatch Tritton, Married June 16, 1617, Ashford, County. Kent: Genealogical & Biographical Account of One Branch of the Dayton Family in America. (Illus.). 96p. 1997. reprint ed. pap. 18.00 (*0-8328-8242-9*); reprint ed. lib. bdg. 28.00 (*0-8328-8241-0*) Higginson Bk Co.

Dayton, Edward R. Tools for Time Management: Time-Saving Tools for Managing Your Life. rev. ed. 224p. 1983. pap. 8.95 (*0-310-23221-X*, 10675P) Zondervan.

— What Ever Happened to Commitment? 224p. 1984. pap. 6.99 (*0-310-23161-2*, 10748P) Zondervan.

Dayton, Eldorous L. Give 'Em Hell Harry: An Informal Biography of the Terrible Tempered Mr. T. LC 56-9833. 256p. reprint ed. pap. 79.40 (*0-608-13475-9*, 202270700029) Bks Demand.

Dayton, Eric, ed. Art & Interpretation. 560p. 1999. pap. 37.95 (*1-55111-190-X*) Broadview Pr.

Dayton, H. L. Su Dinero: Frustracion O Libertad?Tr. of Your Money: Frustration or Feedom?. (SPA.). 186p. 7.99 (*1-56063-946-6*, 498576) Editorial Unilit.

Dayton, Howard. Your Money Counts. 1997. pap. 9.99 (*0-8423-8592-4*) Tyndale Hse.

Dayton, Howard L. Getting Out of Debt. abr. ed. (Pocket Guides Ser.). 80p. 1986. pap. 3.99 (*0-8423-1004-5*) Tyndale Hse.

Dayton Hudson Corporation Staff. With Warmest Regards. LC 95-40775. 1995. 4.25 (*0-8092-3214-6*) NTC Contemp Pub Co.

Dayton, John E. The Discovery of Glass: Experiments in the Smelting of Rich "Dry" Iron Ores, & the Reproduction of Bronze Age-Type Cobalt Blue As a Slag. (Peabody Museum of Archaeology & Ethnology American School of Prehistoric Research Ser.: Vol. 41). (Illus.). 72p. 1991. pap. 16.95 (*0-685-38743-7*, DAYDIS) HUP.

— The Discovery of Glass: Experiments in the Smelting of Rich "Dry" Silver Ores & the Reproduction of Bronze Age - Type Cobalt Blue Glass As a Slag. LC 90-62664. (American School of Prehistoric Research Bulletins Ser.: Vol. 41). (Illus.). 72p. 1993. pap. 18.00 (*0-87365-544-3*) Peabody Harvard.

Dayton, Julia. World Bank HIV/AIDS Interventions: Ex-Ante & Ex-Post Evaluation. LC 98-23816. (Discussion Paper Ser.: No. 389). 44p. 1998. pap. 22.00 (*0-8213-4251-7*, 14251) World Bank.

Dayton, Kenneth. The Stages of Giving. (Conversations with Leaders Ser.). 6p. Date not set. pap. 9.00 (*0-929556-21-6*) Ind Sector.

Dayton, Laura. Lower Body Solutions: Middle Age Fat - Stubborn "Pear" Shapes - 50 Pounds Plus - Lose It All. (Illus.). 160p. 1998. pap. 24.95 (*0-9662752-2-5*) Dayton Pubns.

Dayton, Linnea. Adobe Illustrator: A Visual Guide to the Macintosh. (Illus.). 144p. (C). 1995. pap. text 28.95 (*0-201-40723-X*) Addison-Wesley.

Dayton, Linnea & Davis, Jack. Photoshop 5.0/5.5 Wow! Book. 368p. 1999. pap. write for info. incl. cd-rom (*0-201-35371-7*, Pub. by Peachpit Pr) Addison-Wesley.

— The Photoshop 4 for Macintosh: Windows Edition. 336p. 1997. pap. text 44.95 (*0-201-68857-3*) Peachpit Pr.

— The Photoshop 4 Wow! Macintosh Edition. LC 98-136922. 336p. 1997. pap. text 44.95 (*0-201-68856-5*) Peachpit Pr.

Dayton, Linnea, et al. The CorelDraw Wow! Book. Woodward, Jeanne, ed. (Illus.). 256p. 1999. pap. 44.95 incl. cd-rom (*0-201-88632-4*) Peachpit Pr.

Dayton, Linnea, jt. auth. see Gosney, Michael.

Dayton, Mark B. Securing Minnesota's Financial Future: Fiscal Arrangements in Other States. (Illus.). 94p. (Orig.). (C). 1995. pap. text 30.00 (*0-7881-0996-0*) DIANE Pub.

— Securing Minnesota's Financial Future: Property Tax Reform in the 1990s. (Illus.). 206p. (Orig.). (C). 1995. pap. text 40.00 (*0-7881-0997-9*) DIANE Pub.

Dayton, Martin. The Case for Intravenous EDTA Chelation Therapy. 1995. pap. 12.00 (*0-9664838-0-4*) Martin Dayton.

Dayton, Neil A. New Facts on Mental Disorders. Grob, Gerald N., ed. LC 78-22558. (Historical Issues in Mental Health Ser.). (Illus.). 1980. reprint ed. lib. bdg. 37.95 (*0-405-11912-7*) Ayer.

Dayton, O. William. Athletic Training & Conditioning. rev. ed. LC GV0341.D35. 397p. reprint ed. pap. 123.10 (*0-8357-5831-1*, 205567000029) Bks Demand.

Dayton, Rick. The Epson Connection, Macintosh. LC 84-22261. x, 260 p. 1985. 16.95 (*0-8359-1753-3*) P-H.

Dayton, Rick. Macintosh Microsoft BASIC. write for info. (*0-318-58183-3*) P-H.

Dayton, Ruth W. Greenbrier (W. Va.) Pioneers & Their Homes. (Illus.). 383p. 1997. reprint ed. pap. 36.50 (*0-8063-4668-X*, Pub. by Clearfield Co) ACCESS Pubs Network.

— Pioneers & Their Homes on Upper Kanawha. (Illus.). 378p. 1991. reprint ed. pap. 22.00 (*1-55613-516-5*) Heritage Bk.

— Pioneers & Their Homes on Upper Kanawha [West Virginia]. (Illus.). 320p. 1998. reprint ed. pap. 38.00 (*0-8063-4815-1*) Clearfield Co.

Dayton, Tian. Daily Affirmations for Forgiving & Moving On: Powerful Inspiration for Personal Change. 375p. (Orig.). 1992. pap. 7.95 (*1-55874-215-8*) Health Comm.

— Daily Affirmations for Parents: How to Nurture Your Children & Renew Yourself During the Ups & Downs of Parenthood. 366p. (Orig.). 1991. pap. 6.95 (*1-55874-151-8*) Health Comm.

— Drama Games: Techniques for Self-Development. 104p. 1989. 7.95 (*1-55874-021-X*) Health Comm.

— The Drama Within: Psychodrama & Experiential Therapy. LC 94-16374. 275p. (Orig.). 1994. pap. 14.95 (*1-55874-296-4*, 2964) Health Comm.

— Heartwounds: The Role of Unresolved Trauma & Grief on Relationships. LC 97-34760. 230p. 1997. pap. 11.95 (*1-55874-510-6*) Health Comm.

***Dayton, Tian.** It's My Life! A Power Journal for Teens: A Workout for Your Mind. (YA). 2000. pap. 11.95 (*1-55874-833-4*) Health Comm.

Dayton, Tian. The Quiet Voice of Soul: How to Find Meaning in Ordinary Life. 180p. (Orig.). 1995. pap. 9.95 (*1-55874-339-1*, 3391) Health Comm.

— The Soul's Companion: Connecting with the Soul Through Daily Meditations. 392p. (Orig.). 1995. pap. 8.95 (*1-55874-358-8*, 3588) Health Comm.

***Dayton, Tian.** Trauma & Addiction: Why We Hurt Ourselves & How to Stop. LC 00-23354. 250p. 2000. pap. 12.95 (*1-55874-751-6*, Simcha Press) Health Comm.

Dayton, Wilbur T., et al. Marriage: The Biblical Perspective. 84p. 1984. pap. 5.99 (*0-89827-022-7*, BKZ65) Wesleyan Pub Hse.

Daytrade Technologies Staff. Trader 2000: A Complete Online Training Manual. Centala, Sandy, ed. (Illus.). 62p. (Orig.). 1998. pap. 345.00 incl. VHS (*0-9669326-0-9*) Trader Two-Thous.

Dayus, Kathleen. All My Days. 1989. pap. 7.95 (*0-86068-076-2*) Random.

— The Best of Times. large type ed. (Reminiscence Ser.). 23.95 (*1-85695-136-7*, Pub. by ISIS Lrg Prnt) Transaction Pubs.

— Her People: Memoirs of Growing up in Birmingham. large type ed. (Reminiscence Ser.). 23.95 (*1-85695-190-1*, Pub. by ISIS Lrg Prnt) Transaction Pubs.

— Where There's Life. large type ed. (Reminiscence Ser.). 22.95 (*1-85695-131-6*, Pub. by ISIS Lrg Prnt) Transaction Pubs.

Daza, Esteban. Esteban Daza: The Fantasias for Vihuela. Griffiths, John, ed. (Recent Researches in Music of the Renaissance Ser.: Vol. RRR54). (Illus.). xviii, 81p. 1982. pap. 35.00 (*0-89579-166-8*, RRR54) A-R Eds.

Daza, Nora V. The Best of the Maya Cookfast, Pt. II. 130p. 1981. 24.95 (*0-318-36303-8*) Asia Bk Corp.

— Let's Cook with Nora. (Illus.). 279p. 1979. 15.95 (*0-318-36296-1*) Asia Bk Corp.

***Daza, Ricardo.** Looking for Mies. (Illus.). 200p. 2000. pap. 24.95 (*3-7643-6238-3*, Pub. by Birkhauser) Princeton Arch.

***Dazai, Osamu.** Blue Bamboo: Japanese Tales of Fantasy. 2001. pap. 11.00 (*4-7700-2610-2*) Kodansha.

Dazai, Osamu. Crackling Mountain & Other Stories. O'Brien, James, tr. LC 89-50024. 256p. 1989. 16.95 (*0-8048-1565-8*) Tuttle Pubng.

— No Longer Human. Keene, Donald, tr. from JPN. & intro. by. LC 58-9509. 192p. 1973. pap. 10.95 (*0-8112-0481-2*, NDP357, Pub. by New Directions) Norton.

— The Setting Sun. rev. ed. Keene, Donald, tr. from JPN. LC 56-13350. (Illus.). 1968. reprint ed. pap. 9.95 (*0-8112-0032-9*, NDP258, Pub. by New Directions) Norton.

Dazat, Olivier, jt. auth. see Dag'Naud, Alain.

***Dazed & Confused Magazine Editors.** Dazed & Confused: Inside Out. 1999. 59.95 (*1-86154-138-4*) Booth-Clibborn.

— Star Cult: The Dazed & Confused Collected Interviews. (Illus.). 2000. 39.95 (*0-7148-3955-8*) Phaidon Pr.

D'Azeglio, Massimo. The Challenge of Barletto. unabridged ed. LC 96-42813. 258p. 1996. pap. 20.00 (*0-911876-07-3*) Greenvale.

Dazet, Chris A., jt. auth. see Schwartz, Brett C.

D'Azevedo, Warren L., ed. The Traditional Artist in African Societies. LC 79-160126. (Illus.). 478p. reprint ed. pap. 148.20 (*0-608-09331-9*, 205407700002) Bks Demand.

D'Azevedo, Warren L., jt. ed. see Sturtevant, William C.

Daziel, Bradford D. Sarton Selected: An Anthology of the Novels, Journals, & Poetry of May Sarton. 1991. 22.95 (*0-393-02968-9*) Norton.

Dazord, P. & Weinstein, Alan. Symplectic Geometry, Groupoids & Integrable Systems. (Mathematical Sciences Research Institute Publications: Vol. 20). (Illus.). 328p. 1991. 76.95 (*0-387-97526-8*) Spr-Verlag.

D'Azzo, John & Houpis, Constantine. Linear Control System Analysis & Design: Conventional & Modern, Solutions Manual. 4th ed. 1995. pap. text. write for info. (*0-07-016322-7*) McGraw.

D'Azzo, John J. & Houpis, Constantine H. Linear Control System Analysis & Design: Conventional & Modern. 4th ed. LC 94-25299. (Electrical & Computer Engineering Ser.). 800p. (C). 1995. 98.13 (*0-07-016321-9*) McGraw.

DBCC Staff. The Communication Program at DBCC: A Handbook. 92p. (C). 1997. per. 9.95 (*0-7872-3909-7*, 41390901) Kendall-Hunt.

Dbe, Shobha. Selective Memory: Stories from My Life. LC 98-908655. 531p. 1998. 21.00 (*0-14-027784-6*) Viking Penguin.

DBM Editors. New Beginnings: Your Guide to Retirement & Lifetime Action Planning. 192p. 1995. pap. 11.95 (*1-880030-41-1*) DBM Pub.

DC Comics Editors. Batman. 1995. 8.98 (*1-57042-296-6*) Warner Bks.

DC Comics Staff. Batman: Contagion. Kahan, Bob, ed. LC 96-159684. (Illus.). 264p. 1996. pap. 12.95 (*1-56389-293-6*, Pub. by DC Comics) Time Warner.

— Batman Picture Book: Book 2. (J). 1997. pap. write for info. (*0-316-17799-7*) Little.

DC Comics Staff. Batman 3. (J). 1995. pap. write for info. (*0-316-15441-5*) Little.

DC Comics Staff. DC/Marvel: Crossover Classic II, Vol. 1. (Illus.). 224p. 1998. pap. text 14.95 (*1-56389-399-1*, Pub. by DC Comics) Time Warner.

***DC Comics Staff.** Gangland. Chiarello, Mark, ed. (Illus.). 112p. (YA). 2000. pap. 12.95 (*1-56389-608-7*, Pub. by DC Comics) Time Warner.

DC Comics Staff. The Greatest Batman Stories Ever Told. Gold, Mike, ed. 350p. 1989. mass mkt. 15.95 (*0-446-39123-9*, Pub. by Warner Bks) Little.

— The Greatest Batman Stories Ever Told: Catwoman & the Penguin. (Illus.). (Orig.). 1992. mass mkt. 14.99 (*0-446-39427-0*, Pub. by Warner Bks) Little.

— The Greatest Joker Stories Ever Told. Gold, Mike, ed. 288p. 1989. mass mkt. 14.95 (*0-446-39125-5*, Pub. by Warner Bks) Little.

— MAD: The Half-Wit & Wisdom of Alfred E. Neuman. LC 97-151527. (Illus.). 96p. 1997. 8.95 (*0-446-91200-X*, Pub. by Warner Bks) Little.

— Starman: Times Past. 176p. 1999. pap. text 17.95 (*1-56389-492-0*, Pub. by DC Comics) Time Warner.

— Superman: Bizarro World. Kahan, Bob, ed. (Illus.). 128p. 1996. pap. 9.95 (*1-56389-260-X*, Pub. by DC Comics) Time Warner.

— Superman: The Wedding & Beyond. LC 98-142457. (Illus.). 192p. 1998. pap. text 14.95 (*1-56389-392-4*, Pub. by DC Comics) Time Warner.

***DC Comics Staff.** Superman: They Saved Luthor's Brain. (Illus.). 160p. (J). 2000. pap. text 14.95 (*1-56389-601-X*, Pub. by DC Comics) Time Warner.

DC Comics Staff. Superman Picture Book: Book 2. (J). 1997. pap. write for info. (*0-316-17805-5*) Little.

— Superman Puzzle & Game Book. 160p. (YA). (gr. 4-7). 1995. 3.99 (*0-8125-7733-7*, Pub. by Tor Bks) St Martin.

— Zero Hour: Crisis in Time. Kahan, Bob, ed. LC 94-215739. (Illus.). 160p. 1994. pap. 9.95 (*1-56389-184-0*) DC Comics.

DC Comics Staff, ed. Green Candles. 1997. per. 10.00 (*0-671-00467-0*, PB Trade Paper) PB.

— History of Violence. 1997. per. 10.00 (*0-671-00466-2*, PB Trade Paper) PB.

DC Comics Staff, et al. Batman: Dark Legends. LC 96-208578. (Illus.). 176p. 1996. pap. 14.95 (*1-56389-266-9*, Pub. by DC Comics) Time Warner.

***DCC Inc. Staff.** A LifeCare Digest for Employers: Preventing Violence in the Workplace. 4p. 1999. pap. 1.95 (*1-58559-067-3*) DCC Inc.

***DCC Inc., Staff.** A LifeCare Digest on Balancing Work & Life. 4p. 1999. pap. 1.95 (*1-58559-060-6*) DCC Inc.

— A LifeCare Digest on Birthing Options. 7p. 2000. pap. 2.50 (*1-58559-027-4*) DCC Inc.

— A LifeCare Digest on Blended Families. 4p. 1999. pap. 1.95 (*1-58559-040-1*) DCC Inc.

***DCC Inc. Staff.** A LifeCare Digest on Breastfeeding - What You Need to Know Before Your Baby Arrives. 4p. 1999. pap. 1.95 (*1-58559-028-2*) DCC Inc.

— A LifeCare Digest on Business Etiquette: England. 1999. pap. 1.50 (*1-58559-064-9*) DCC Inc.

***DCC Inc., Staff.** A LifeCare Digest on Career Change. 8p. 2000. pap. 2.50 (*1-58559-072-X*) DCC Inc.

— A LifeCare Digest on Choosing Your Child's Medical Provider. 8p. 1999. pap. 2.50 (*1-58559-058-4*) DCC Inc.

***DCC Inc. Staff.** A LifeCare Digest on Coping after a Tornado. 3p. 1999. pap. 1.75 (*1-58559-065-7*) DCC Inc.

— A LifeCare Digest on Coping with Hurricanes. 4p. 1999. pap. 1.95 (*1-58559-061-4*) DCC Inc.

— A LifeCare Digest on Coping with Job Loss. 3p. 1999. pap. 1.75 (*1-58559-068-1*) DCC Inc.

— A LifeCare Digest on Formula Feeding. 4p. 2000. pap. 1.95 (*1-58559-034-7*) DCC Inc.

— A LifeCare Digest on Helping Children Cope with School Violence. 4p. 1999. pap. 1.95 (*1-58559-069-X*) DCC Inc.

***DCC Inc., Staff.** A LifeCare Digest on Kinship Care & Stepparent Adoption. 7p. 1999. pap. write for info. (*1-58559-059-2*) DCC Inc.

***DCC Inc. Staff.** A LifeCare Digest on Mergers & Acquisitions. 1999. pap. 1.50 (*1-58559-066-5*) DCC Inc.

— A LifeCare Digest on Preventing Workplace Violence. 4p. 1999. pap. 1.95 (*1-58559-063-0*) DCC Inc.

***DCC Inc., Staff.** A LifeCare Digest on Relocating with Children. 8p. 1999. pap. 2.50 (*1-58559-057-6*) DCC Inc.

***DCC Inc. Staff.** A LifeCare Digest on Stress Management. 4p. 1999. pap. 1.95 (*1-58559-062-2*) DCC Inc.

***DCC Inc., Staff.** A LifeCare Guide to ADD/ADHD. 16p. 1999. pap. 10.95 (*1-58559-016-9*) DCC Inc.

***DCC Inc. Staff.** A LifeCare Guide to Alzheimer's Disease & Related Dementia. 100p. 1999. pap. 14.95 (*1-58559-036-3*) DCC Inc.

DCC Inc., Staff. A LifeCare Guide to Backup Child Care Options. 7p. 1999. pap. 3.95 (*1-58559-007-X*) DCC Inc.

— A LifeCare Guide to Care Options. 1999. pap. 14.95 (*1-58559-004-5*) DCC Inc.

— A LifeCare Guide to Child Care Centers. 7p. 1999. pap. 3.95 (*1-58559-008-8*) DCC Inc.

— A LifeCare Guide to Child Care Options. 5p. 1999. pap. 2.95 (*1-58559-009-6*) DCC Inc.

***DCC Inc., Staff.** A LifeCare Guide to Child Development: Birth to Three Years. 20p. 1999. pap. 9.95 (*1-58559-026-6*) DCC Inc.

***DCC Inc. Staff.** A LifeCare Guide to College Admissions. 76p. 2000. pap. 12.95 (*1-58559-070-3*) DCC Inc.

— A LifeCare Guide to College Financial Aid. 52p. 2000. pap. 12.95 (*1-58559-071-1*) DCC Inc.

— A LifeCare Guide to Early Intervention. 12p. 1999. pap. 10.95 (*1-58559-015-0*) DCC Inc.

— A LifeCare Guide to Elementary & Secondary Education. 78p. 2000. pap. 12.95 (*1-58559-010-X*) DCC Inc.

— A LifeCare Guide to Family Child Care. 5p. 2000. pap. 2.95 (*1-58559-038-X*) DCC Inc.

***DCC Inc., Staff.** A LifeCare Guide to Parenting Your Toddler. 68p. 1999. pap. 11.95 (*1-58559-013-4*) DCC Inc.

DCC Inc., Staff. A LifeCare Guide to Reducing Child Care Costs. 5p. 1999. pap. 3.95 (*1-58559-006-1*) DCC Inc.

***DCC Inc. Staff.** A LifeCare Guide to Retirement & Estate Planning. 84p. 2000. pap. 15.95 (*1-58559-035-5*) DCC Inc.

— A LifeCare Guide to Summer Care. 46p. 2000. pap. 9.95 (*1-58559-037-1*) DCC Inc.

DCC Inc., Staff. A LifeCare Guide to Visiting & Interviewing Potential Providers. 20p. 1999. pap. 10.95 (*1-58559-005-3*) DCC Inc.

DCCCD (Forshee) Staff. Telecourse Study Guide to Government by Consent: A Texas Perspective. 320p. (C). 1995. per. 19.95 (*0-8403-8440-8*) Kendall-Hunt.

DCCCD (Lee) Staff. Telecourse Guide for Government by Consent. 5th ed. 320p. (C). 1997. pap. text 32.95 (*0-7872-3760-4*, 41376001) Kendall-Hunt.

— Telecourse Study Guide No. 1: People, Parties, & Politics. 3rd ed. 320p. (C). 1994. per. 16.95 (*0-8403-8441-6*) Kendall-Hunt.

— Telecourse Study Guide II: Executive, Legislative & Judicial. 3rd ed. 320p. (C). 1994. per. 18.95 (*0-8403-8442-4*) Kendall-Hunt.

DCCCD Staff. Study Guide 1: People . . . Politics. 4th ed. 320p. (C). 1995. per. 25.95 (*0-7872-1763-8*, 41176301) Kendall-Hunt.

— Study Guide 2: Executive . . . Judicial. 4th ed. 320p. (C). 1995. per. 20.95 (*0-7872-1764-6*) Kendall-Hunt.

Dchiff, Dave, ed. see Feirer, Mark.

D'Costa. Escape to Last Man Peak. Date not set. pap. text. write for info. (*0-582-76575-7*, Pub. by Addison-Wesley) Longman.

— Over Our Way. rev. ed. LC 95-122360. 1995. pap. text. write for info. (*0-582-22580-9*, Pub. by Addison-Wesley) Longman.

— Sprat Morrison. Date not set. pap. text. write for info. (*0-582-05207-6*, Pub. by Addison-Wesley) Longman.

D'Costa, Anthony P. The Global Restructuring of the Steel Industry: Innovations, Institutions, & Industrial Change. LC 98-27603. 9p. 1999. 99.99 (*0-415-14827-8*) Routledge.

D'Costa, Estelle & Zambelli, Grace. Changing Tides Training System: A Child-Parent Bereavement Program. (Illus.). 235p. (J). (ps up). 1998. pap. 125.00 incl. VHS (*0-9622089-2-2*) Ctr Hospice Care.

D'Costa, Gavin. Christian Uniqueness Reconsidered: The Myth of a Pluralistic Theology of Religions. LC 90-41981. (Faith Meets Faith Ser.). 1990. pap. 17.00 (*0-88344-686-3*) Orbis Bks.

***D'Costa, Gavin.** The Meeting of Religions & the Trinity. (Faith Meets Faith Ser.). 192p. 2000. pap. 20.00 (*1-57075-303-2*) Orbis Bks.

D'Costa, Gavin. Resurrection Reconsidered. 240p. (Orig.). 1996. pap. 18.99 (*1-85168-113-2*, 577, Pub. by Onewrld Pubns) Penguin Putnam.

D'Costa, Jean & Lalla, Barbara, eds. Voices in Exile: Jamaican Texts of the 18th & 19th Centuries, Vol. 1. LC 87-13267. (Illus.). 176p. 1989. text 32.50 (*0-8173-0382-0*) U of Ala Pr.

D'Costa, Jean, jt. auth. see Lalla, Barbara.

D'Costa, Roland. Executorship & Administration. (Practice Notes Ser.). 98p. 1994. pap. write for info. (*0-7520-0039-X*, Pub. by Cavendish Pubng) Gaunt.

D'Costa, Wilfred, jt. auth. see Desai, A. R.

D'Cruz, Ivan. Echocardiographic Anatomy. 563p. (C). 1996. pap. text 115.00 (*0-8385-2037-5*, A2037-8, Apple Lange Med) McGraw.

D'Cruz, Joe. Strategy Tools: AC Matrix. 1995. student ed. write for info. (*0-201-83976-8*) Addison-Wesley.

D'Cruz, Joseph. Strategy Tools: AC Matrix Professional Version. 1995. write for info. (*0-201-83977-6*) Addison-Wesley.

D'Cruz, Joseph R. & Rugman, Alan M. New Compacts for Canadian Competitiveness. (Illus.). 61p. (C). 1993. pap. text 35.00 (*1-56806-690-2*) DIANE Pub.

D'Cruz, Joseph R., jt. auth. see Rugman, Alan.

D'Cruz, Joseph R., jt. auth. see Rugman, Alan M.

D

D'Cruze, Shani. Crimes of Outrage: Sex, Violence, & Victorian Working Women. LC 98-14886. 288p. 1998. 38.00 (*0-87580-242-7*); pap. 16.50 (*0-87580-578-7*) N Ill U Pr.

DDC Publishing Staff. Access 97: Day 3. (One-Day Course Ser.). 1998. pap. text 22.00 (*1-56243-580-9*) DDC Pub.

— Accounting Internet Skills. 1999. pap. text 18.00 (*1-56243-840-9*) DDC Pub.

— Advanced Internet Research. 1999. pap. text 18.00 (*1-56243-831-X*) DDC Pub.

***DDC Publishing Staff.** Aprendiendo Office 2000. (SPA.). 1999. pap. 29.00 (*1-56243-809-3*) DDC Pub.

DDC Publishing Staff. Claris Works 4 & 5 for Macintosh. (Quick Reference Guide Ser.). 1998. pap. text. write for info. (*1-56243-595-7*, 639) DDC Pub.

— Conducting Internet Research. 1999. pap. text 18.00 (*1-56243-830-1*) DDC Pub.

— DDC Floor Stand Box One. 1994. pap. write for info. (*1-56243-217-6*) DDC Pub.

— Excel 97: Day 2. (One-Day Course Ser.). 1998. pap. text 22.00 (*1-56243-577-9*) DDC Pub.

— Exploring the Web. 1999. pap. text 18.00 (*1-56243-829-8*) DDC Pub.

— For Bargain Hunters. 1998. pap. 10.00 (*1-56243-697-X*) DDC Pub.

— HTML 4.0 Fundamentals. 1999. pap. text 18.00 (*1-56243-834-4*) DDC Pub.

— HTML 4.0 Intermediate. 1999. pap. text 18.00 (*1-56243-835-2*) DDC Pub.

— Intermediate Microsoft Access 97: Day 2 With 3.5" Disk. (One-Day Course Ser.). (Illus.). 132p. 1998. pap. 22.00 (*1-56243-579-5*) DDC Pub.

— Internet Explorer 4.0. (Visual Reference Basics Ser.). 1998. pap. text 15.00 (*1-56243-591-4*, G37) DDC Pub.

— Internet in an Hour for Beginners. LC 98-216632. 1998. pap. text 18.00 (*1-56243-603-1*, HR3) DDC Pub.

— Internet in an Hour for Managers. 1998. pap. text 18.00 (*1-56243-602-3*, HR2) DDC Pub.

— Internet in an Hour for Sales People. LC 99-162111. 1998. pap. text 18.00 (*1-56243-604-X*, HR4) DDC Pub.

— Internet in an Hour for Students. 1998. pap. text 18.00 (*1-56243-601-5*, HR1) DDC Pub.

— Laptops & Mobile Computing. 1994. spiral bd. 12.00 (*1-56243-136-6*, LM-18) DDC Pub.

— Learning Access 2000. 1999. 32.00 (*1-56243-733-X*) DDC Pub.

— Learning Access 2000. 1999. 31.00 (*1-56243-704-6*) DDC Pub.

— Learning Corel Wordperfect Suite 8. LC 99-168703. (Learning Ser.). 1998. pap. text 27.00 (*1-56243-590-6*, Z28) DDC Pub.

— Learning Excel 5. (Fast-Teach Learning Ser.). 1993. spiral bd. 27.00 (*1-56243-124-2*, E-9) DDC Pub.

— Learning Excel 2000. 1999. 32.00 (*1-56243-734-8*) DDC Pub.

***DDC Publishing Staff.** Learning Excel 2000. (Illus.). 382p. 1999. 31.00 (*1-56243-705-4*) DDC Pub.

— Learning Microsoft Windows 2000. 1999. pap. 29.00 (*1-56243-748-8*) DDC Pub.

— Learning Office 2000. 1999. 32.00 (*1-56243-736-4*) DDC Pub.

DDC Publishing Staff. Learning Office 2000. 1999. 32.00 (*1-56243-638-4*) DDC Pub.

— Learning PowerPoint 2000. 1999. 32.00 (*1-56243-735-6*) DDC Pub.

— Learning PowerPoint 2000. 1999. 31.00 (*1-56243-706-2*) DDC Pub.

— Learning the Internet. 1996. 29.00 (*1-56243-346-6*, Z-15HC); pap. text 27.00 (*1-56243-345-8*, Z-15) DDC Pub.

— Learning the Internet. 2nd ed. LC 99-168428. (Learning Ser.). 1998. pap. text 27.00 (*1-56243-593-0*, Z30) DDC Pub.

— Learning the Internet for Business. (Learning Ser.). 1998. pap. text 27.00 (*1-56243-587-6*, Z27) DDC Pub.

— Learning Word 2000. 1999. 32.00 (*1-56243-732-1*) DDC Pub.

— Learning Word 2000. 1999. 31.00 (*1-56243-703-8*) DDC Pub.

— Learning WordPerfect 6.0 for Windows. (Fast-Teach Learning Ser.). 1993. spiral bd. 27.00 (*1-56243-125-0*, Z-9) DDC Pub.

— Legal Community Internet Skills. 1999. pap. text 18.00 (*1-56243-839-5*) DDC Pub.

— Lotus for Windows 4.0. 1993. pap. 12.00 (*1-56243-138-2*, 03013) DDC Pub.

— Mastering Java. 1999. pap. text 50.00 (*1-56243-841-7*) DDC Pub.

— Mastering Java Threads. 1999. pap. text 45.00 (*1-56243-842-5*) DDC Pub.

— Mastering JavaScript Part 1. 1999. pap. text 18.00 (*1-56243-836-0*) DDC Pub.

— Mastering JavaScript Part 2. 1999. pap. text 18.00 (*1-56243-837-9*) DDC Pub.

— Microsoft Access 97. LC 97-209730. (Quick Reference Guide Ser.). 230p. spiral bd. 27.00 (*1-56243-470-5*, G-28) DDC Pub.

— Microsoft Excel 97. LC 97-226283. (Quick Reference Guide Ser.). spiral bd. 27.00 (*1-56243-456-X*, G-27) DDC Pub.

— Microsoft Excel 2000. 1999. pap. text 15.00 (*1-56243-783-6*) DDC Pub.

— Outlook 97: Day 2. (One-Day Course Ser.). 1998. pap. text 22.00 (*1-56243-582-5*, DC32) DDC Pub.

— Outlook 98 Visual Reference Basics. 1999. pap. 17.00 (*1-56243-690-2*) DDC Pub.

— PageMaker 5 Mac & IBM. LC 94-171352. 1994. spiral bd. 12.00 (*1-56243-134-X*, PM18) DDC Pub.

— Paradox 4.5 for Windows. LC 95-106438. 1993. spiral bd. 12.00 (*1-56243-122-6*, PW18) DDC Pub.

— PowerPoint for Windows 4.0 Quick Reference Guide. LC 94-216277. 1994. spiral bd. 12.00 (*1-56243-178-1*, OPPW4) DDC Pub.

— PowerPoint 97: Day 2. (One-Day Course Ser.). 1998. pap. text 22.00 (*1-56243-581-7*, DC31) DDC Pub.

— Promoting Your Web Site. 1999. pap. text 18.00 (*1-56243-833-6*) DDC Pub.

— Quattro Pro 5 for Windows. 1993. spiral bd. 12.00 (*1-56243-137-4*, OQPW5) DDC Pub.

— Quick Reference Guide: UNIX. 1992. pap. 12.00 (*1-56243-075-0*, U-17) DDC Pub.

— Quick Reference Guide for Powerpoint 97. (Quick Reference Guide Ser.). 15.00 (*1-56243-466-7*, Z22HC) DDC Pub.

— Quick Reference Guide WordPerfect 7 for Windows 95. 1996. pap. text 12.00 (*1-56243-347-4*, G-12) DDC Pub.

— Real Estate Internet Skills. 1999. pap. text 18.00 (*1-56243-838-7*) DDC Pub.

— Romance & Relationships. (Internet-in-an-Hour Ser.). 1999. pap. text 10.00 (*1-56243-772-0*) DDC Pub.

— Short Course for Windows 98. (Short Course Ser.). pap. text 25.00 (*1-56243-586-8*) DDC Pub.

— Using the Internet in Business. 1999. pap. text 18.00 (*1-56243-832-8*) DDC Pub.

— Windows 98 Visual Reference Guide. (Visual Reference Basics Ser.). Date not set. pap. text 15.00 (*1-56243-584-1*, G36) DDC Pub.

— Windows 98. (Quick Reference Guides Ser.). pap. text 12.00 (*1-56243-583-3*, G35) DDC Pub.

— Word for Windows 6.0. LC 94-171500. 1993. spiral bd. 12.00 (*1-56243-140-4*, OWDW6) DDC Pub.

— Word 97: Day 2. (One-Day Course Ser.). 1998. pap. text 22.00 (*1-56243-575-2*, DC25) DDC Pub.

— Word 97: Day 3. (One-Day Course Ser.). 1998. pap. text 22.00 (*1-56243-576-0*, DC26) DDC Pub.

— WordPerfect for Windows 6.0. 1993. spiral bd. 12.00 (*1-56243-139-0*, OWPW6) DDC Pub.

— Works for Windows 3.0. LC 94-171312. 1993. spiral bd. 12.00 (*1-56243-141-2*, OWKW3) DDC Pub.

DDC Publishing Staff & Robbins, Curt. Internet Fundamentals: Learning Cyberspace Skills. (One-Day Course Ser.). (Illus.). 149p. 1999. pap. 16.00 (*1-56243-826-3*) DDC Pub.

— Intro to the Internet & Online Services: Navigating Cyberspace & AOL. (One-Day Course Ser.). (Illus.). 78p. 1999. pap. 18.00 (*1-56243-827-1*) DDC Pub.

— Navigating the Web: Mastering Internet Hypermedia. (One-Day Course Ser.). (Illus.). 148p. 1999. pap. 18.00 (*1-56243-828-X*) DDC Pub.

DDC Staff. Entertainment & Leisure, 1. 1998. pap. text 10.00 (*1-56243-696-1*) DDC Pub.

— Excel 97: Day 3. (One-Day Course Ser.). 1998. pap. 22.00 (*1-56243-578-7*) DDC Pub.

— For Seniors Only: Student Workbook, 1. 1998. pap. 10.00 (*1-56243-695-3*) DDC Pub.

— Learning Communication Skills Through Word-Processing. (DDC Learning Ser.). 1998. 29.00 (*1-56243-627-9*) DDC Pub.

— Learning English Skills Through Word-Processing. (Learning Series Texts). 1998. pap. 27.00 (*1-56243-624-4*) DDC Pub.

— Learning Word-Processing & Typing with Word 97 for Kids. (Learning Series Texts). (J). 1998. pap. 27.00 (*1-56243-623-6*) DDC Pub.

— Visual Reference Basics for Windows 98. 1998. pap. 17.00 (*1-56243-609-0*) DDC Pub.

De A Samarasinghe, S. W. & Coughlan, Reed, eds. Economic Dimensions of Ethnic Conflict. LC 91-28654. 200p. 1992. text 55.00 (*0-312-07571-5*) St Martin.

De Abajian, James T. Blacks in Selected Newspapers, Censuses & Other Sources: An Index to Names & Subjects. 1982. 430.00 (*0-8161-1322-X*, G K Hall & Co) Mac Lib Ref.

— Blacks in Selected Newspapers, Censuses & Other Sources: An Index to Names & Subjects, Supplement 1. 1987. suppl. ed. 380.00 (*0-8161-1525-7*, G K Hall & Co) Mac Lib Ref.

De Aberle, S. B. The Pueblo Indians of New Mexico: Their Land, Economy & Civil Organization. LC 49-2640. (American Anthropological Association Memoirs Ser.: No. 70). 1974. reprint ed. 25.00 (*0-527-00569-X*) Periodicals Srv.

De Abreu, Carlos. Opening the Doors to Hollywood: How to Sell Your Idea, Story, Screenplay, Manuscript. LC 97-14390. 1997. pap. 15.00 (*0-609-80110-4*) Random Hse Value.

De Abreu, Carlos & Smith, Howard J. Opening the Doors to Hollywood: How to Sell Your Idea, Story Book, Screenplay. LC 94-68044. 416p. 1995. 21.95 (*1-884025-04-8*) Custos Morum.

De Abreu, Carlos, jt. auth. see Pennington, Janice.

***De Abreu, Joao C.** Chapters of Brazil's Colonial History 1500-1800. Brakel, Arthur, tr. (Library of Latin America). 272p. 1998. reprint ed. pap. 13.95 (*0-19-510302-5*) OUP.

De Acha, Eduardo. A la Ofensiva. LC 94-72068. (Coleccion Cuba y sus Jueces). (SPA.). 82p. (Orig.). 1994. pap. 9.95 (*0-89729-746-6*) Ediciones.

— Algunos Analisis: (El Terreriamo, Derecho Internacional) (SPA.). 104p. (Orig.). 1987. pap. 9.00 (*0-89729-436-X*) Ediciones.

— Discursos Breves. LC 91-71432. (Coleccion Cuba y sus Jueces). (SPA.). 96p. (Orig.). 1991. pap. 9.00 (*0-89729-603-6*) Ediciones.

— El Estado de Derecho - el Ladron Nunca Adquiere el Dominio - el Crimen. LC 93-74345. (Coleccion Cuba y sus Jueces). (SPA.). 96p. (Orig.). 1994. pap. 9.95 (*0-89729-716-4*) Ediciones.

— Fusilados. (Coleccion Cuba y sus Jueces). (SPA.). 78p. 1989. pap. 9.00 (*0-89729-540-4*) Ediciones.

— El Hombre Medio. LC 92-70964. (Coleccion Cuba y sus Jueces). (SPA.). 64p. (Orig.). 1992. pap. 9.00 (*0-89729-639-7*) Ediciones.

— La Inocencia de los Balseros. (SPA.). 1995. pap. 9.95 (*0-89729-768-7*) Ediciones.

— Marxismo y Derecho. LC 84-72917. (Coleccion Cuba y sus Jueces). 158p. (Orig.). 1985. pap. 9.95 (*0-89729-364-9*) Ediciones.

— Ni Caida, Ni Cambios. LC 93-72350. (Coleccion Cuba y sus Jueces). (SPA.). 85p. (Orig.). 1993. pap. 9.95 (*0-89729-702-4*) Ediciones.

— Una Nota de Derecho Penal. LC 82-71757. (SPA.). 184p. (Orig.). 1982. 12.95 (*0-89729-314-2*) Ediciones.

— Un Paso Al Frente. LC 92-75090. (Coleccion Cuba y sus Jueces). (SPA.). 80p. (Orig.). 1992. pap. 9.95 (*0-89729-664-8*) Ediciones.

— Pesimismo. LC 83-82918. (SPA.). 112p. (Orig.). 1984. pap. 5.00 (*0-89729-340-1*) Ediciones.

— La Revolucion. LC 88-82485. (Coleccion Cuba y sus Jueces). (SPA.). 88p. (Orig.). 1989. pap. 9.00 (*0-89729-508-0*) Ediciones.

De Acosta, Mercedes. Here Lies the Heart. LC 75-13709. (Homosexuality Ser.). 1975. reprint ed. 32.95 (*0-405-07360-7*) Ayer.

De Aghion, Beatriz Armendariz, see Armendariz de Aghion, Beatriz.

De Aguiar, Ricardo W., tr. see Furtado, Celso.

De Aguilar, Maria M. Ramillete de Recuerdos: Poesias. LC 92-73336. (Coleccion Espejo de Paciencia). (SPA., Illus.). 96p. (Orig.). 1992. pap. 12.00 (*0-89729-651-6*) Ediciones.

De Aguilar, Ruth M., tr. see Huidobro, Matias M.

de Aguilar, Ruth M., tr. see Molina, Silvia.

de Aguilar, Ruth M., tr. see Romero, Jose R.

de Aguilar, Ruth M., tr. see Taibo, Paco I., 2nd.

De Aguirre, Jose A. Escape Via Berlin: Eluding Franco in Hitler's Europe. LC 90-25136. (Basque Ser.). 400p. 1991. 34.95 (*0-87417-167-9*) U of Nev Pr.

De Alarcao. Roman Portugal: Complete Work, 3 vols. 1992. pap. 125.00 (*0-85668-393-0*, Pub. by Aris & Phillips) David Brown.

— Roman Portugal Vol. 1: Introduction. 1982. 49.95 (*0-85668-444-9*, Pub. by Aris & Phillips); pap. 50.00 (*0-85668-289-6*, Pub. by Aris & Phillips) David Brown.

— Roman Portugal Vol II Fasc1: Porto, Braganza & Viseu. 1987. pap. 35.00 (*0-85668-390-6*, Pub. by Aris & Phillips) David Brown.

— Roman Portugal Vol II Gazetteer Fasc 3: Evora, Faron& Lagos. 1987. pap. 35.00 (*0-85668-392-2*, Pub. by Aris & Phillips) David Brown.

— Roman Portugal Vol II Gazetteer Fasc2: Coimbra & Lisbon. 1987. pap. 35.00 (*0-85668-391-4*, Pub. by Aris & Phillips) David Brown.

De Alarcao, J. Roman Portugal: Complete Work, 3 vols. 1992. 250.00 (*0-85668-290-X*, Pub. by Aris & Phillips) David Brown.

De Alarcon, Hernando Ruiz, see Ruiz de Alarcon, Hernando.

De Alarcon, Juan Ruiz, see Ruiz De Alarcon, Juan.

De Alarcon, Pedro A. Capitan Veneno, No. 37. (SPA.). 150p. 1978. write for info. (*0-8288-8575-3*) Fr & Eur.

— The Nail & Other Stories. Fedorchek, Robert M., tr. from SPA. LC 97-2143. (Illus.). 136p. 1997. 29.50 (*0-8387-5361-2*) Bucknell U Pr.

— El Sombrero de Tres Picos: El Capitan Veneno. Rubio-Jimenez, Jesus, tr. (Nueva Austral Ser.: No. 228). (SPA.). 1991. pap. text 19.95 (*84-239-7228-3*) Elliots Bks.

— Three-Cornered Hat. 23.95 (*0-8488-0903-3*) Amereon Ltd.

De Alarcon, Pedro Antonio. The Nun & Other Stories. Fedorchek, Robert M., tr. from SPA. LC 98-39220. (Illus.). 184p. 1999. 35.00 (*0-8387-5415-5*) Bucknell U Pr.

De Alarcon, Ruiz. Obras - Ruiz de Alarcon, Vol. I. (SPA.). 36.99 (*968-16-4974-5*, Pub. by Fondo) Continental Bk.

— Obras - Ruiz de Alarcon, Vol. II. (SPA.). 36.99 (*968-16-0238-2*, Pub. by Fondo) Continental Bk.

— Obras - Ruiz de Alarcon, Vol. III. (SPA.). 36.99 (*968-16-0239-0*, Pub. by Fondo) Continental Bk.

De Alba, Alicia Gaspar, see Gaspar De Alba, Alicia.

De Alba, Alicia Gaspar, see Gaspar de Alba, Alicia.

de Alba, Jose G. Moreno, see Moreno de Alba, Jose G.

De Alba, Jose G. Moreno, see Moreno De Alba, Jose G.

***De Alberdi, Lita.** Channeling: What It Is & How to Do It. LC 99-49279. 176p. 2000. pap. 12.95 (*1-57863-145-9*) Weiser.

De Albuquerque, Afonso. Caesar of the East. Villiers, J. & Earle, T. F., eds. (Hispanic Classics Ser.). 320p. (C). 1991. 59.95 (*0-85668-487-2*, Pub. by Aris & Phillips); pap. 28.00 (*0-85668-488-0*, Pub. by Aris & Phillips) David Brown.

De Albuquerque, Klaus, jt. auth. see McElroy, Jerome L.

De Alcala-Zamora, Pedro. Alcala-Zamora, Diccionario Frances-Espanol, Espanol-Frances. (FRE & SPA.). 960p. 1982. pap. 28.95 (*0-7859-5110-5*, S50399) Fr & Eur.

de Alcantara, Cynthia Hewitt, see Hewitt de Alcantara, Cynthia, ed.

De Alcantara, L. P. Mathematical Logic & Formal Systems. (Lecture Notes in Pure & Applied Mathematics Ser.: Vol. 94). (Illus.). 320p. 1985. pap. text 155.00 (*0-8247-7330-6*, 7330-6) Dekker.

***De Alcantara, Pedro.** The Alexander Technique: A Skill for Life. 1999. pap. 29.95 (*1-86126-286-8*, Pub. by Crolwood) Trafalgar.

De Alcantara, Pedro. Indirect Procedures: A Musician's Guide to the Alexander Technique. LC 96-19698. (Illus.). 330p. 1997. pap. text 24.95 (*0-19-816569-2*) OUP.

De, Alcega Juan. Tailor's Pattern Book 1589. 256p. 1999. pap. 40.00 (*0-89676-234-3*) QSMG Ltd.

De Alcuaz, Marie. Red Grooms, Michael C. McMillen: A Collaboration. LC 87-83038. (Illus.). 32p. (Orig.). 1987. pap. 1.00 (*0-936429-09-7*) LA Municipal Art.

De Alcuaz, Marie, ed. see McDonald, Robert.

De Alcuaz, Marie, ed. see Starrels, Josine I.

De Aldama, A. M. Formula of the Institute: Notes for a Commentary. Echaniz, Ignacio, tr. from SPA. (Modern Scholarly Studies about the Jesuits, in English Translations Series II: No. 10). x, 107p. 1990. 16.95 (*0-912422-55-6*); pap. 9.95 (*0-912422-56-4*) Inst Jesuit.

— Introductory Commentary on the Constitutions. Owen, A. J., tr. from SPA. LC 89-80527. (Modern Scholarly Studies about the Jesuits, in English Translations Series II: No. 9). xx, 319p. 1989. 22.95 (*0-912422-92-0*); pap. 16.95 (*0-912422-93-9*) Inst Jesuit.

De Aldama, Antonio M. The Constitutions of the Society of Jesus Pt. VI: Jesuit Religious Life. LC 95-79974. (Modern Scholarly Studies about the Jesuits, in English Translation: Series II, Vol. 13). xii, 147p. (Orig.). 1995. pap. 14.95 (*1-880810-13-1*) Inst Jesuit.

— The Constitutions of the Society of Jesus Pt. VIII: Union among Jesuits. O'Keefe, Martin, ed. Echaniz, Ignacio, tr. from SPA. LC 98-70331. (Series II: Vol. 15). Orig. Title: La Vida Religiosa en la Compania de Jesus. xv, 169p. 1998. pap. 18.95 (*1-880810-32-8*) Inst Jesuit.

***De Aldama, Antonio M.** The Constitutions of the Society of Jesus Pt. IX: The Superior General. O'Keefe, Martin, ed. Delius, Ramon E. & Echaniz, Ignacio, trs. from SPA. LC 99-72093. (Series II: Vol. 16). Orig. Title: Comentario a la IX Parte de las Constituciones. xiii, 213p. 1999. pap. 18.95 (*1-880810-35-2*) Inst Jesuit.

De Aldecoa, Ignacio. Parte de Una Historia (Part of a Story) (SPA.). 1996. pap. 14.95 (*0-679-76849-1*) Vin Bks.

De Alessi, Louis. Some Economic Aspects of Government Ownership & Regulation: Essays From Economia Pubblica. LC 82-84249. (LEC Occasional Paper). 40p. 1983. pap. 3.00 (*0-916770-12-5*) Law & Econ U Miami.

De Alessi, Michael. Fishing for Solutions. (IEA Studies on the Environment: No. 11). 88p. 1998. pap. 19.95 (*0-255-36444-X*, Pub. by Inst Economic Affairs) Coronet Bks.

De Almansa, Andres & De Mendoza, Andres. Two Royall Entertainments, Lately Given to Charles, Prince of Great Britaine, by Philip the Fourth of Spaine. LC 77-6847. (English Experience Ser.: No. 842). 1977. reprint ed. lib. bdg. 15.00 (*90-221-0842-2*) Walter J Johnson.

De Almanza, Adelina, tr. see Sanchez, Daniel R.

De Almeida, A. Betamio & Viseu, T., eds. Dams & Safety Management at Downstream Valleys: Proceedings of the International NATO Workshop, Lisbon, Portugal, 13-15 November 1996. (Illus.). 256p. (C). 1997. text 91.00 (*90-5410-916-5*, Pub. by A A Balkema) Ashgate Pub Co.

De Almeida, A. T., et al, eds. Autonomous Robotic Systems. LC 98-17839. (Lecture Notes in Control & Information Sciences: Vol. 236). x, 423p. 1998. pap. 79.00 (*1-85233-036-8*) Spr-Verlag.

De Almeida, A. T., jt. ed. see Casals, A.

De Almeida, Abraao. Homossexualismo.Tr. of Homosexuality. (POR.). 64p. 1991. 1.95 (*0-8297-1713-7*) Vida Pubs.

— O Deus Dos Pobres.Tr. of Liberation Theo.: God of ... Poor. (POR.). 160p. 1990. pap. 7.95 (*0-8297-1666-1*) Vida Pubs.

De Almeida, Anibal T., ed. Integrated Electricity Resource Planning: Proceedings of the NATO Advanced Research Workshop on Models for Integrated Resource Planning, Espinho, Portugal, June 28-July 2, 1993. LC 94-6393. (NATO Advanced Study Institutes Series E, Applied Sciences: Vol. 261). 536p. (C). 1994. text 361.00 (*0-7923-2764-0*) Kluwer Academic.

De Almeida, Anibal T. & Rosenfeld, Arthur H., eds. Demand-Side Management & Electricity End-Use Efficiency. (C). 1988. text 321.00 (*90-247-3698-6*) Kluwer Academic.

De Almeida, Anna & Campari, Joao S. Sustainable Settlement in the Brazilian Amazon. (World Bank Publication). 300p. (C). 1996. text 32.95 (*0-19-521104-9*) OUP.

De Almeida, Anna L. Ozorio, see Ozorio de Almeida, Anna L.

***De-Almeida, Cristina & Clark-Langager, Sarah A.** Review/Preview: Faculty of Art Exhibition, Western Gallery, Western Washington University, September 30 to November 18, 1998. LC 99-22279. 1999. write for info. (*1-878237-04-7*) WWU Western Gallery.

De Almeida, Darcy F., ed. Science Policy Research: Implications & Applications. 1991. text 39.00 (*0-86187-130-8*, Pub. by P P Pubs) Cassell & Continuum.

De Almeida, Hermione. Critical Essays on John Keats. (Critical Essays on British Literature Ser.). 352p. 1990. 49.00 (*0-8161-8851-3*, G K Hall & Co) Mac Lib Ref.

— Romantic Medicine & John Keats. 432p. 1990. text 75.00 (*0-19-506307-4*) OUP.

De Almeida, Miguel V. The Hegemonic Male: Masculinity in a Portuguese Town. LC 96-18532. (New Directions in Anthropology Ser.: Vol. 4). (Illus.). 224p. 1996. 55.00 (*1-57181-888-X*); pap. 16.50 (*1-57181-891-X*) Berghahn Bks.

***De Almeida, Miguel V.** Memoirs of a Militia Sergeant. Holloway, Thomas H. & Sussekind, Flora, eds. Sousa, Ronald W., tr. from POR. LC 98-48751. 208p. 2000. 30.00 (*0-19-511549-X*); pap. 14.95 (*0-19-511550-3*) OUP.

De Almeida Prado, Bento L. Enciclopedia del Whisky: Encyclopedia of Whiskey. (SPA.). 216p. 1978. 35.00 (*0-8288-5224-3*, S37337) Fr & Eur.

De Almeida-Val, V. M., jt. auth. see Val, A. L.

De Almeida-Val, V. M., jt. ed. see Val, A. L.

D

De Alonso, Irma T., ed. Trade, Industrialization & Integration in Twentieth Century Central America. LC 93-23678. 304p. 1994. 69.50 (*0-275-94804-8*, Praeger Pubs) Greenwood.

De Alonso, Irma Tirado, see Tirado de Alonso, Irma, ed.

***De Alteriis, Martin.** Consumer Price Index: Impact of Commodity Analysts[0012] Decisionmaking Needs to Be Assessed. (Illus.). 160p. (C). 2000. pap. text 30.00 (*0-7881-8812-7*) DIANE Pub.

De, Alva Bartolome. Guide to Confession Large & Small in the Mexican Language, 1634. LC 99-18502. 1999. 40.00 (*0-8061-3145-4*) U of Okla Pr.

De Alvarez, Leo P., tr. see Machiavelli, Niccolo.

De Alvarez, Leo Paul S. The Machiavellian Enterprise: A Commentary on the Prince. LC 98-54214. 205p. 1999. 32.00 (*0-87580-247-8*) N Ill U Pr.

De Alvarez, Russell R., ed. The Kidney in Pregnancy. LC 76-13184. (Wiley Clinical Obstetrics & Gynecology Ser.). 249p. reprint ed. 77.20 (*0-8357-9919-0*, 201519000095) Bks Demand.

— Textbook of Gynecology. LC 76-10816. 562p. reprint ed. pap. 174.30 (*0-608-13674-3*, 205541800022) Bks Demand.

De Alverga, Alex P. Forest of Visions: Ayahuasca, Amazonian Spirituality, & the Santo Daime Tradition. LC 98-47847. (Illus.). 240p. 1999. pap. 14.95 (*0-89281-716-X*) Inner Tradit.

De Amescua, Mira. Esclavo Del Demonio. (SPA.). 141p. 1977. 6.95 (*0-8288-7182-5*, S9149) Fr & Eur.

De Amezua, Agustin G., ed. see de Vega, Lope.

De Amicis, E. Morocco: Its People & Places. 396p. 1984. 220.00 (*1-85077-055-7*, Pub. by Darf Pubs Ltd) St Mut.

De Amicis, Edmondo. Holland & Its People. Tilton, Caroline, tr. from ITA. LC 72-3433. (Essay Index Reprint Ser.). 1977. reprint ed. 40.95 (*0-8369-2887-3*) Ayer.

— Spain & the Spaniards, 2 vols. 1976. lib. bdg. 250.00 (*0-8490-2639-3*) Gordon Pr.

— Studies of Paris. LC 72-3348. (Essay Index Reprint Ser.). 1977. reprint ed. 21.95 (*0-8369-2888-1*) Ayer.

De Amigo, Cantigas, jt. auth. see Fowler, Barbara H.

De Anda, Diane. The Ice Dove & Other Stories. LC 96-50200. (Illus.). 64p. (YA). (gr. 3-7). 1997. pap. 7.95 (*1-55885-189-5*, Pinata Bks) Arte Publico.

— The Immortal Rooster: And Other Stories. LC 99-10498. 112p. (J). (gr. 4-7). 1999. pap. 9.95 (*1-55885-278-6*) Arte Publico.

***De Anda, Diane & Becerra, Rosina M.** Violence: Diverse Populations & Communities. LC 00-44872. (Illus.). 2000. write for info. (*0-7890-1163-8*) Haworth Pr.

De Anda, Miriam Curet, see Curet De Anda, Miriam.

De Anda, Roberto M., ed. Chicanas & Chicanos in Contemporary. LC 94-48278. 209p. 1995. pap. text 48.00 (*0-02-327982-6*, Macmillan Coll) P-H.

De Andia, Ysabel. L' Union a Dieu Chez Denys L'Areopagite. (Philosophia Antiqua Ser.: Vol. 71). (FRE.). 528p. 1996. 178.00 (*90-04-10656-1*) Brill Academic Pubs.

De Andrade, Camilo, jt. auth. see Hardin, Jerry W.

De Andrade, Camilo, tr. see Hardin, Jerry W.

De Andrade, Eugenio. Another Name for Earth - O Outro Nome da Terra. Levitin, Alexis, tr. from POR. LC 95-72726. (ENG & POR.). 128p. (Orig.). 1997. pap. 12.95 (*0-936609-37-0*) QED Ft Bragg.

***De Andrade, Eugenio.** Close to Speech. Levitin, Alexis, tr. from POR. 128p. 1999. pap. 12.95 (*1-881168-08-5*) Red Danceflr.

De Andrade, Eugenio. Inhabited Heart: The Selected Poems of Eugenio de Andrade. Levitin, Alexis, ed. LC 84-61570. (Translation Ser.: No. 8). (Illus.). 81p. (Orig.). 1985. pap. 10.00 (*0-912288-24-8*, PTS 8) Perivale Pr.

— Materia Solar-Solar Matter. Levitin, Alexis, tr. from POR. LC 94-26801. (ENG & POR.). 128p. (Orig.). 1994. pap. 12.95 (*0-936609-34-6*) QED Ft Bragg.

— The Shadow's Weight. Levitin, Alexis, tr. from POR. LC 96-75501.Tr. of O Peso da Sombra. (ENG & POR.). 145p. (Orig.). 1996. pap. text 7.50 (*0-943722-23-3*) Gavea-Brown.

De Andrade, Lucia M. & Santos, Leinad Ayer O., eds. Hydroelectric Dams on Brazil's Xingu River & Indigenous Peoples. Wright, Robin, tr. from POR. LC 90-47242. (Cultural Survival Reports: No. 30). (Illus.). 192p. (Orig.). 1990. pap. 19.95 (*0-939521-40-7*) Cultural Survival.

De Andrade, Mario. Antologia da Poesia Negra de Expressao Portuguese, Precedida de Cultura Negro-Africana e Assimilacao. (B. E. Ser.: No. 30). (POR.). 1958. 25.00 (*0-8115-2981-9*) Periodicals Srv.

— Literatura Africana de Expressao Portuguesa Vol. 1: Poesia. (B. E. Ser.: No. 31). (POR.). 1967. 35.00 (*0-8115-2982-7*) Periodicals Srv.

— Literatura Africana de Expressao Portuguesa Vol. 2: Prosa. (B. E. Ser.: No. 32). (POR.). 1968. 35.00 (*0-8115-2983-5*) Periodicals Srv.

De Andrande, Mario. Hallucinated City: Paulicea Desvairada. Tomlins, Jack E., tr. LC 68-20547. (POR.). 118p. 1968. reprint ed. pap. 36.60 (*0-7837-9663-3*, 205929700005) Bks Demand.

De Andreis. Guide des Maisons d'Hotes de Charmes en France (Bed & Breakfast a la francaise)1995.Tr. of (Bed & Breakfast a la francaise)1995. 1995. pap. text 45.00 (*0-7859-9040-2*) Fr & Eur.

De Andreis, Marco & Calogero, Francesco. The Soviet Nuclear Weapon Legacy. (SIPRI Research Reports: No. 10). (Illus.). 142p. 1995. text 45.00 (*0-19-829192-2*); pap. text 21.00 (*0-19-829197-3*) OUP.

De Angeli, Marguerite. Copper-Toed Boots. LC 88-34417. (Great Lakes Bks.). (Illus.). 94p. (J). (gr. 1-6). 1996. pap. 15.95 (*0-8143-2654-4*) Wayne St U Pr.

— The Door in the Wall. (J). 1996. pap. 4.99 (*0-440-91164-8*) BDD Bks Young Read.

— The Door in the Wall. (J). (gr. 3-6). 1995. 18.75 (*0-8446-6834-6*) Peter Smith.

De Angeli, Marguerite. The Door in the Wall. (J). 1977. 9.60 (*0-606-03234-7*, Pub. by Turtleback) Demco.

De Angeli, Marguerite. The Door in the Wall. 1998. 9.60 (*0-606-13344-5*, Pub. by Turtleback) Demco.

— The Door in the Wall. (Illus.). 128p. (J). (gr. 5-9). 1998. reprint ed. mass mkt. 4.99 (*0-440-22779-8*, LLL BDD) BDD Bks Young Read.

— The Door in the Wall: Story of Medieval London. LC 64-7025. (Illus.). 128p. (J). (gr. 3-6). 1989. 16.95 (*0-385-07283-X*) Doubleday.

— The Door in the Wall: Story of Medieval London. 128p. (J). 1990. reprint ed. pap. 4.99 (*0-440-40283-2*) Dell.

— Henner's Lydia. LC 97-52821. (Illus.). 74p. (J). (ps-3). 1998. pap. 14.99 (*0-8361-9093-9*) Herald Pr.

***De Angeli, Marguerite.** Skippack School. LC 99-14584. (Illus.). 88p. (J). 1999. pap. 14.99 (*0-8361-9124-2*) Herald Pr.

— Thee, Hannah! LC 99-52422. (Illus.). 112p. (J). 2000. pap. 15.99 (*0-8361-9106-4*) Herald Pr.

De Angeli, Marguerite. Yonie Wondernose. LC 97-18919. (Illus.). 48p. (J). (gr. 2-6). 1997. pap. 14.99 (*0-8361-9083-1*) Herald Pr.

de Angeli Walls, Nina, see Walls, Nina de Angeli.

***De Angelis, April.** April De Angelis: Plays One. 320p. 2000. pap. 18.00 (*0-571-19709-4*) Faber & Faber.

— A Warwickshire Testimony. 96p. 2000. pap. 13.00 (*0-571-20355-8*) Faber & Faber.

De Angelis, Barbara. Are You the One for Me? Knowing Who's Right & Avoiding Who's Wrong. 448p. (YA). 1993. mass mkt. 6.99 (*0-440-21575-7*, Island Bks) Dell.

— Are You the One for Me? Knowing Who's Right & Avoiding Who's Wrong. 368p. 1994. pap. 12.95 (*0-440-50670-0*) Dell.

— Are You the One for Me? - Real Moments. LC 97-75442. 656p. 1998. reprint ed. 9.98 (*1-56731-241-1*, MJF Bks) Fine Comms.

— Confidence: Finding It & Living It. LC 95-11222. 128p. 1995. 12.95 (*1-56170-318-4*, 177) Hay House.

— How to Make Love All the Time. 288p. 1988. pap. 10.95 (*0-440-50077-X*, Dell Trade Pbks) Dell.

— How to Make Love All the Time. 432p. 1991. mass mkt. 6.50 (*0-440-20893-9*) Dell.

— Inspirations about Love. Kramer, Jill, ed. LC 94-46388. 176p. (Orig.). 1996. pap. 5.95 (*1-56170-278-1*, 179) Hay House.

De Angelis, Barbara, et al. Love, Passion & Soul. abr. ed. (Quest love Ser.: Vol. 1). 1998. 12.00 incl. audio (*0-671-57895-2*, Sound Ideas) S&S Trade.

De Angelis, Barbara. 101 Ways to Transform Your Love Life. Kramer, Jill, ed. 101p. (Orig.). 1996. pap. 5.95 (*1-56170-277-3*, 178) Hay House.

— 101 Ways to Romance. 1998. pap. 9.95 (*1-56170-494-6*) Hay House.

— Passion. LC 97-51854. 112p. 1998. 14.95 (*0-385-31435-3*) Delacorte.

— Passion. 112p. 1999. pap. 9.95 (*0-440-50815-0*) Dell.

— Real Moments. 288p. 1995. reprint ed. pap. 12.95 (*0-440-50729-4*, Dial Pr) Dell.

— Real Moments for Lovers. 1997. pap. 8.95 (*0-614-17748-0*) Delacorte.

— Real Moments for Lovers. 112p. 1997. pap. 8.95 (*0-440-50778-2*) Dell.

— The Real Rules. LC 97-144759. 1997. mass mkt. 4.99 (*0-440-22448-9*, Island Bks) Dell.

***De Angelis, Barbara.** Secrets about Life Every Woman Should Know: Ten Principles for Total Emotional & Spiritual Fulfillment. 2000. mass mkt. 6.99 (*0-7868-8993-4*) Hyperion.

De Angelis, Barbara. Secrets about Life Every Woman Should Know: Ten Principles for Total Spiritual & Emotional Fulfillment. LC 99-21882. 261p. 1999. 22.95 (*0-7868-6468-0*, Pub. by Hyperion) Time Warner.

— Secrets about Men Every Woman Should Know. 400p. 1991. mass mkt. 6.50 (*0-440-20841-6*) Dell.

— Secrets about Men Every Woman Should Know. 304p. 1992. pap. 11.95 (*0-440-50538-0*, Dell Trade Pbks) Dell.

De Angelis, Carl, jt. ed. see Steen, Sara J.

De, Angelis Catherine D. John Hopkins University School of Medicine Curriculum for the Twenty-First Century. LC 98-41891. (Illus.). 256p. 1998. 55.00 (*0-8018-5977-8*) Johns Hopkins.

***De Angelis, Catherine D.** John Hopkins University School of Medicine Curriculum for the Twenty-First Century. 2000. pap. 21.50 (*0-8018-6350-3*) Johns Hopkins.

De Angelis, Erminio. Ceramic Tile Repair & Regrouting. 43p. 1994. pap. 139.00 incl. VHS (*0-944352-14-6*) Cleaning Cons.

De Angelis, Frank T. The Polytheism of the Bible & the Mystery of Lucifer. 2nd rev. ed. Strickfaden, William et al, eds. LC 97-91766. (Illus.). (C). 1997. pap. 15.95 (*0-9657834-6-4*) Spartacus Pubns.

De Angelis, Gina. Gregory Hines - Performer. LC 99-17790. (Illus.). 144p. (YA). (gr. 5 up). 1999. pap. 9.95 (*0-7910-5198-6*) Chelsea Hse.

***De, Angelis Gina.** Hernan Cortes & the Conquest of Mexico. LC 99-35232. (Explorers of the New World Ser.). (Illus.). 64p. 1999. write for info. (*0-7910-5516-7*) Chelsea Hse.

De Angelis, Gina & Marvis, B. Black Cowboys. LC 97-24823. (African-American Achievers Ser.). 124p. (YA). (gr. 5 up). 1997. pap. 8.95 (*0-7910-2590-X*); lib. bdg. 19.95 (*0-7910-2589-6*) Chelsea Hse.

De Angelis, Gina, ed. see Da Angelious, Therese.

De Angelis, Lissa, jt. auth. see Adderly, Brenda.

***De Angelis, M.** Keynesianism, Social Conflict & Political Economy. LC 99-55733. 2000. 65.00 (*0-312-23146-6*) St Martin.

De Angelis, Manlio F. U. S. Foreign Aid Programs. 1996. text 22.00 (*0-86531-277-X*) Westview.

De Angelis, Michele A. & Lentz, Thomas W. Architecture in Islamic Painting: Permanent & Impermanent Worlds. Walsh, Peter L., ed. (Illus.). 31p. 1982. pap. 7.50 (*0-916724-51-4*, 4514) Harvard Art Mus.

De Angelis, Paul, ed. see Abe, Kobo.

De Angelis, Paul, ed. see App, Urs.

De Angelis, Paul, ed. see Delany, Sarah L., et al.

De Angelis, Paul, ed. see Dubcek, Alexander & Hochman, Jiri.

De Angelis, Paul, ed. see Edgeworth, Anthony & Norman, Geoffrey.

De Angelis, Paul, ed. see Morris, Ivan.

De Angelis, Paul, ed. see Pan, Lynn.

De Angelis, Paul, ed. see Sakaiya, Taichi.

De Angelis, Paul, ed. see Suyin, Han.

De Angelis, Paul, ed. see Yamazaki, Ikue.

De Angelis, Therese. Native Americans & the Spanish. LC 97-7498. (Indians of North America Ser.). (Illus.). 10p. (YA). (gr. 5-13). 1997. pap. 9.95 (*0-7910-4465-3*) Chelsea Hse.

— Wonders of the Ancient World. LC 98-35808. (Costume, Tradition, & Culture Ser.). (Illus.). 64p. (YA). 1998. 16.95 (*0-7910-5170-6*) Chelsea Hse.

De Angelis, V. & Sampietri, C. State of the Art Regarding the Problem of Residual Stresses in Welds of LMFBR. 467p. 1995. 70.00 (*92-826-8906-9*, CR-NA-15895-ENC, Pub. by Comm Europ Commun) Bernan Associates.

De Angulo, Gui. The Old Coyote of Big Sur: The Life of Jaime de Angulo. (Illus.). 472p. (Orig.). 1995. pap. 26.00 (*1-879042-03-7*) Stonegarden Pr.

De Angulo, Gui, ed. see Angulo, Jaime de.

De Angulo, Jaime. Indians in Overalls: And Two Other Achumawi Tales. 1996. pap. text 8.95 (*0-87286-312-3*) City Lights.

De Angulo, Jamie. Indian Tales. LC 97-69086. (Illus.). 256p. 1997. pap. text 13.00 (*0-86547-523-7*) N Point Pr.

De Anhalt, Nedda G. A Buena Hora Mangos Verdes. Hiriart, Rosario, ed. (Cocodrilo Verde Ser.). (SPA.). 119p. 1998. pap. 15.00 (*1-887175-05-9*) ECV NY.

De Anton, G. Haberkamp. Langenscheidts Handworterbucher: Deutsch-Spanisch. (SPA.). 640p. 1997. pap. write for info. (*3-468-04346-5*) Langenscheidt.

De Anton, G. Haberkamp, jt. auth. see Haensch, Guenther.

De Antoni, F., et al, eds. COMPSTAT 1986: Proceedings in Computational Statistics. (Illus.). xv, 512p. 1986. 84.00 (*0-387-91286-X*) Spr-Verlag.

De, Anuradha. Public Report of Basic Education in India. LC 99-932760. (Illus.). 168p. 1999. pap. text 8.95 (*0-19-564870-6*) OUP.

De Anza College Staff, jt. auth. see Peck, Willys I.

De Appendini, Kirsten A. & Bislev, Sven. Economic Integration in NAFTA & the EU: Deficient Institutionality. LC 98-38453. (Illus.). 270p. 1999. text 79.95 (*0-312-21864-8*) St Martin.

De Aquino, Fran. Gravitational-Electromagnetic Field Theory. 1992. 18.50 (*0-533-10098-4*) Vantage.

— Psychic Interaction. 1994. 18.50 (*0-533-11114-5*) Vantage.

De Aragon, Alvaro Cubillo, see Cubillo De Aragon, Alvaro.

De Aragon Andujar, Gloria, tr. see Bunting, Eve.

De Aragon Andujar, Gloria, tr. see Ehlert, Lois.

De Aragon Andujar, Gloria, tr. see Paulsen, Gary.

De Aragon, Ray J. Beyond Man's Powers. (Illus.). 105p. (Orig.). pap. 5.95 (*0-932906-19-2*) Pan-Am Publishing Co.

— Dodo the Bird & Other Stories. (Illus.). 105p. (Orig.). (J). (gr. 1-12). pap. 5.95 (*0-932906-21-4*) Pan-Am Publishing Co.

— Don Juan & Dulcinea's. 105p. (Orig.). pap. 5.95 (*0-932906-18-4*) Pan-Am Publishing Co.

— Grey Eminence of Taos. 105p. (Orig.). pap. 5.95 (*0-932906-20-6*) Pan-Am Publishing Co.

— Padre Martinez & Bishop Lamy. 3rd ed. LC 78-70565. (History Ser.). (Illus.). (C). 1978. pap. 7.95 (*0-932906-00-1*) Pan-Am Publishing Co.

— Los Penitentes. (Illus.). 105p. (Orig.). 1988. pap. 5.95 (*0-932906-16-8*) Pan-Am Publishing Co.

De Aragon, Uva, jt. ed. see Perez, Lisandro.

De Arantes, E. R., jt. ed. see Tasso, C.

De Araoz, J., et al. Principles & Practices of Cholera Control. (Public Health Papers: No. 40). 139p. 1970. pap. text 13.00 (*92-4-130040-X*, 1110040) World Health.

De Araujo, C. B. & De Oliveira, F. A. Nonlinear & Quantum Optics: Proceedings of the Third School of Ja Swieca. 1994. text 75.00 (*981-02-1089-2*) World Scientific Pub.

De Araujo, Carlos P., et al. Ferroelectric Thin Films: Synthesis & Basic Properties. (Ferroelectricity & Related Phenomena Ser.). 600p. 1996. text 139.00 (*2-88449-189-9*) Gordon & Breach.

de Araujo, Carlos Paz, see Paz de Araujo, Carlos

***de Araujo, Fernando Dantas, et al, eds.** Plantas do Nordeste (Plants of the Northeast) Anais do I Workshop Geral (Proceedings of the First General Workshop) (POR.). 150p. 1999. pap. 30.00 (*1-900347-79-2*, Pub. by Royal Botnic Grdns) Balogh.

De Arce, G. H. Why Israel? A Year-2000 Celebration. (Illus.). 352p. 1997. pap. 18.50 (*0-9662446-0-5*) HDA Literary.

De Arellano, E. Ramirez, see Ramirez de Arellano, E., ed.

De Arellano, Enrique R., et al, eds. Operator Theory for Complex & Hypercomplex Analysis: A Conference on Operator Theory & Complex & Hypercomplex Analysis, December 12-17, 1994, Mexico City, Mexico, Vol. 212. LC 97-28599. (Contemporary Mathematics Ser.: Vol. SALINAS). 298p. 1997. pap. 65.00 (*0-8218-0677-7*) Am Math.

De Armas, Armando. Mala Jugada. De Fana, Angel, ed. (SPA., Illus.). 130p. 1996. pap. 15.00 (*1-890829-07-2*) DFana Editions.

De Armas, F. A. The Invisible Mistress: Aspects of Feminism & Fantasy in the Golden Age. (Biblioteca Siglo De Oro Ser.). 1976. pap. 10.00 (*84-399-5958-3*) Biblio Siglo.

De Armas, Frederick A. Cervantes, Raphael & the Classics. LC 97-30167. (Studies in Latin American & Iberian Literature: No. 12). (Illus.). 224p. (C). 1998. text 59.95 (*0-521-59302-6*) Cambridge U Pr.

— The Return of Astraea: An Astral-Imperial Myth in Calderon. LC 86-7758. (Studies in Romance Languages: No. 32). 272p. 1986. reprint ed. pap. 84.40 (*0-608-02129-6*, 206277800004) Bks Demand.

— A Star-Crossed Golden Age: Myth & the Spanish Comedia. LC 97-39644. (Illus.). 248p. 1998. 39.50 (*0-8387-5376-0*) Bucknell U Pr.

De Armas, Frederick A., ed. Heavenly Bodies: The Realms of La Estrella de Sevilla. LC 95-42784. 296p. 1996. 45.00 (*0-8387-5308-6*) Bucknell U Pr.

— The Prince in the Tower: Perceptions of la Vida es Sueno. LC 92-54454. (C). 1993. 39.50 (*0-8387-5252-7*) Bucknell U Pr.

De Armas, Frederick A., et al, eds. Critical Perspectives on Calderon de la Barca. LC 80-53823. 183p. (Orig.). reprint ed. pap. 56.80 (*0-608-14801-6*, 202557100045) Bks Demand.

De Armas, Jose R. & Steele, Charles W. Cuban Consciousness in Literature, 1923-1974. LC 78-53265. (Coleccion Antologias). 1978. pap. 12.00 (*0-89729-166-2*) Ediciones.

De Armas, Jose R., tr. see Conde, Carmen.

De Armona, Jose A. Memorias Cronologicas Sobre el Origen de la Representacion de Comedias en Espana, Ano 1785. Davis, Charles et al, eds. (Fuentes Para la Historia del Teatro en Espana, Series C: Vol. XIV). (Illus.). 350p. 1999. 54.00 (*1-85566-045-8*, Pub. by Tamesis Bks Ltd) Boydell & Brewer.

De Armond, A. L. Winning Lotto Analysis Secrets: With Lotto Software Reviews & Source Directory. 124p. 1992. per. 12.95 (*0-9630841-0-0*) Castor-Pollux.

De Armond, Elizabeth. Tiny Tired Twins. (Illus.). 16p. (J). (ps). 1998. pap. 5.95 (*0-9655442-5-7*) Busn Word.

***De Armond, Garry E.** The Flower Caper. 32p. (J). 2000. pap. 9.99 (*0-9676287-0-9*) G De Armond.

De Armond Marchant, Alexander N. Boundaries of the Latin American Republics: An Annotated List of Documents, 1493-1943. (Latin America Ser.). 1979. lib. bdg. 59.95 (*0-8490-2876-0*) Gordon Pr.

***De Armond, R. N.** A Voyage in a Dory: Sitka to Tacoma by Oars, Sail & Towrope. LC 99-63925. (Illus.). 1999. pap. 13.95 (*1-929292-00-7*) Arrowhead Pr AK.

De Armond, Robert N., jt. compiled by see Atwood, Evangeline.

De Armond, Steve, jt. auth. see Kunzle-Watson, Karin.

De Arredondo, Gonzalo. Vida Rimada de Fernan Gonzalez. De Mercedes, ed. (Exeter Hispanic Text Ser.: No. 44). (SPA.). 120p. Date not set. pap. text 17.95 (*0-85989-269-7*, Pub. by Univ Exeter Pr) Northwestern U Pr.

De Arredondo, Gonzalo, see De Arredondo, Gonzalo.

De Arrigoitia, Luis. Pensamiento y Forma en la Prosa de Gabriela Mistral. LC 89-33662. 408p. (Orig.). 1989. pap. 18.50 (*0-8477-3613-X*) U of PR Pr.

De Arrigoitia, Luis, jt. auth. see Gallego, Laura.

De Arteaga, W. Apagando el Espiritu.Tr. of Quenching the Spirit. (SPA.). 12.99 (*0-7899-0387-3*, 550057) Editorial Unilit.

de Assis, Joaquim Maria Machado, see Machado de Assis, Joaquim Maria.

***de Assis, Sebastian.** Teachers of the World, Unite! LC 00-133080. 96p. 2000. pap. 10.95 (*0-9700722-0-1*) Educational Ctr.

de Assuncao, Celio Santos, see Assuncao, Celio Santos de.

De Asua, Luis J., et al, eds. Control Mechanisms in Animal Cells: Specific Growth Factors. fac. ed. LC 79-5293. (Illus.). 406p. pap. 125.90 (*0-7837-7225-4*, 204707300005) Bks Demand.

De Avellaneda y Arteaga, Gertrudis G. Sab & Autobiography. Scott, Nina M., ed. & tr. by. from SPA. LC 92-21961. (Texas Pan American Ser.). 185p. (C). 1993. pap. 14.95 (*0-292-70442-9*) U of Tex Pr.

De Avendano y Loyola, Fray A. Relation of Two Trips to Peten: Made for the Conversion of the Heathen Ytzaex & Cehaches. Comparato, Frank E., ed. Bowditch, Charles P. & Rivera, Guillermo, trs. LC 86-80968. 84p. (Orig.). 1987. pap. 20.00 (*0-911437-06-1*) Labyrinthos.

De Avila, Edie. The Great Wine Adventure. (Illus.). 128p. (Orig.). 1997. pap. 10.95 (*0-940987-01-5*) Port Royal Pubns.

— The Great Wine Puzzle Book, Vol. 1. (Illus.). 127p. (Orig.). 1986. pap. 9.95 (*0-940987-00-7*) Port Royal Pubns.

De Avila, Elizabeth, ed. see Maxwell, Jane, et al.

De Avila, Elizabeth, ed. see Werner, David B.

De Avila, Lisa, tr. see Burns, A. August, et al.

***de Avillez Pereira, Miguel.** Antitrust & New Media. LC 99-86511. (AIJA Law Library). 2000. write for info. (*90-411-1347-9*) Kluwer Law Intl.

De Avinon, Juan. Sevillana Medicina, Burgos, 1545. Naylor, Eric W., ed. (Medieval Spanish Medical Texts Ser.: No. 8). (SPA.). 6p. 1987. 10.00 incl. fiche (*0-940639-03-3*) Hispanic Seminary.

De Ayala, Pero L. El Libro de Caca de las Aves. Cummins, John G., ed. 1986. 51.00 (*0-7293-0258-X*, Pub. by Tamesis Bks Ltd) Boydell & Brewer.

***de Ayala, Pero Lopez.** Rimado de Palacio. Martinez, H. Salvador, ed. (Iberica Ser.: Vol. 35). (SPA.). 456p. 2000. 72.95 (*0-8204-4916-4*) P Lang Pubng.

De Ayala, Ramon Perez, see Perez De Ayala, Ramon.

D

An Asterisk (*) at the beginning of an entry indicates that the title is appearing for the first time.

De Azara, Don Felix. Apuntamientos para la Historia Natural de los Quadrupedos del Paraguay y Rio de la Plata, 2 vols. Sterling, Keir B., ed. LC 77-81077. (Biologists & Their World Ser.). (SPA.). 1978. reprint ed. lib. bdg. 57.95 (*0-405-10645-9*) Ayer.

De Azcarate, Pablo. League of Nations & National Minorities: An Experiment. (Studies in the Administration of International Law & Organization: No. 5). 1969. reprint ed. 25.00 (*0-527-00883-4*) Periodicals Srv.

— Mission in Palestine, 1948 to 1952. LC 66-30659. 1966. 3.00 (*0-916808-07-6*) Mid East Inst.

De Azcarraga, J. A. & Izquierdo, J. M. Lie Groups, Lie Algebras, Cohomology & Some Applications in Physics. (Monographs on Mathematical Physics). (Illus.). 473p. (C). 1996. text 110.00 (*0-521-46501-X*) Cambridge U Pr.

De Azcarraga, Jose A. & Izquierdo, Jose M. Lie Groups, Lie Algebras, Cohomology & Some Applications in Physics. (Monographs on Mathematical Physics). (Illus.). 473p. (C). 1998. reprint ed. pap. text 49.95 (*0-521-59700-5*) Cambridge U Pr.

De Azua, Felix. Diary of a Humiliated Man. Jones, Julie, tr. LC 96-26942. 282p. 1996. pap. 15.95 (*1-57129-029-X*) Brookline Bks.

De Azvedo, Carlos. Baroque Organ-Cases of Portugal. (Illus.). 130p. (Orig.). 1972. 60.00 (*0-913746-23-1*) Organ Lit.

De, B., tr. The Tabaqat-I-Akbari. 1990. reprint ed. 25.00 (*81-85418-03-9*, Pub. by Low Price) S Asia.

De Baar, Mirjam, et al, eds. Choosing the Better Part: Anna Maria Van Schurman (1607-1678), Vol. 146. Richards, Lynne, tr. LC 95-40131. (Archives Internationales d'Histoire des Idees Ser.). 196p. (C). 1996. lib. bdg. 132.50 (*0-7923-3799-9*) Kluwer Academic.

De Bac, C., et al, eds. Chronically Evolving Viral Hepatitis. LC 92-2366. (Archives of Virology Ser.: Suppl. 4). (Illus.). 250p. 1992. 188.95 (*0-387-82350-6*) Spr-Verlag.

De Bac Vacher, Eugene. The Boy Who Loved Music. large type ed. Lay, Eldonna, ed. (East County Childhoods Ser.: Vol. 3). (Illus.). 29p. (Orig.). (J). (gr. 3 up). 1995. pap. 2.50 (*0-9619184-6-2*) E P Lay Assocs.

De Bac Vacher, Eugene, jt. auth. see Vacher, Josephine A.

De Baca Fabiola, Cabeza, see Cabeza de Baca, Fabiola.

De Baca Gilbert, Fabiola C. Historic Cookery. (Illus.). 48p. 1997. reprint ed. pap. 4.95 (*0-941270-99-8*) Ancient City Pr.

***De Baca, Vincent C., ed.** La Gente: Hispano Life & History in Colorado. 294p. 1999. pap. 24.50 (*0-87081-538-5*) Univ Pr Colo.

De Bacan, Alvaro. Relation of the Expongnable Attempt & Conquest of the Ylande of Tercera. LC 76-57352. (English Experience Ser.: No. 772). 1977. reprint ed. lib. bdg. 20.00 (*90-221-0772-8*) Walter J Johnson.

De Backer, Aloys & Sommervogel, Carlos. Bibliotheque de la Compagnie de Jesus, 9 vols. 9000p. 1998. 1100.00 (*1-57898-070-4*) Martino Pubng.

De Backer, Philippe, jt. auth. see Farkas, Charles M.

De Backker, Vera. En Cuerpo y Alma. (SPA., Illus.). 32p. (J). 1993. pap. 5.95 (*0-8120-1743-9*) Barron.

***De Backker, Vera.** Coco the Koala, 3 bks. Incl. Coco Makes Music. (Illus.). 32p. (J). (ps up). 2000. lib. bdg. 21.27 (*0-8368-2730-9*); Coco the Koala. De Backker, Vera. (Illus.). 32p. (J). (ps up). 2000. lib. bdg. 21.27 (*0-8368-2729-5*); Coco's Surprise. (Illus.). 32p. (J). (ps up). 2000. lib. bdg. 21.27 (*0-8368-2731-7*); (Illus.). (J). (ps up). 2000. Set lib. bdg. 63.81 (*0-8368-2728-7*) Gareth Stevens Inc.

De Badajoz, Diego Sanchez, see Sanchez de Badajoz, Diego.

De Baecque, Antoine. The Body Politic: Corporeal Metaphor in Revolutionary France, 1770-1800. LC 96-44516. (Mestizo Spaces Ser.). 1997. write for info. (*0-8047-2815-1*); pap. 19.95 (*0-8047-2817-8*) Stanford U Pr.

De Baecque, Antoine, jt. auth. see Toubiana, Serge.

De Baerdemaeker, J. & Vandewalle, J., eds. Control Applications in Post Harvest & Processing Technology: 1st IFAC/CIGR/EURAGENG/ISHS Workshop, Ostend, Belguim, June 1-2, 1995. (IFAC Postprint Ser.). 330p. 1995. pap. 84.00 (*0-08-042598-4*, Pergamon Pr) Elsevier.

De Baets, M., et al, eds. Myasthenia Gravis: European Conference on Myasthenia Gravis, Maastricht, 1st, June 1987. (Monographs in Allergy: Vol. 25). (Illus.). viii, 160p. 1988. 109.75 (*3-8055-4736-6*) S Karger.

De Baets, Marc H. & Oosterhuis, Hans J., eds. Myasthenia Gravis. LC 92-49515. 288p. 1993. lib. bdg. 198.00 (*0-8493-6343-8*, RC935) CRC Pr.

De Bairacli, Juliette, et al. Nature's Children. expanded rev. ed. LC 96-84258. (Herbals by Our Foremothers Ser.). (Illus.). 196p. 1997. reprint ed. pap. 11.95 (*0-9614620-8-6*) Ash Tree.

De Bairacli Levy, Juliette. Common Herbs for Natural Health. expanded ed. LC 96-84261. (Herbals by Our Foremothers Ser.). (Illus.). 236p. 1997. reprint ed. pap. 11.95 (*0-9614620-9-4*) Ash Tree.

De Bakker, H. Major Soils & Soil Regions in the Netherlands. (Illus.). 1978. text 148.50 (*90-6193-590-3*) Kluwer Academic.

De Bakker, J. W., ed. Languages for Parallel Architectures: Design, Semantics, Implementation Models. LC 89-14705. (Illus.). 289p. reprint ed. pap. 89.60 (*0-7837-5872-3*, 204559200006) Bks Demand.

De Bakker, J. W., et al, eds. Current Trends in Concurrency. (Lecture Notes in Computer Science Ser.: Vol. 224). xii, 716p. 1986. 74.00 (*0-387-16488-X*) Spr-Verlag.

— A Decade of Concurrency: Reflections & Perspectives. LC 94-15490. (Lecture Notes in Computer Science Ser.: Vol. 803). 1994. 93.95 (*0-387-58043-3*) Spr-Verlag.

— Foundations of Object-Oriented Languages: REX School Workshop, Noordwijkerhout, The Netherlands, May 28-June 1, 1990 Proceedings. (Lecture Notes in Computer Science Ser.: Vol. 489). x, 442p. 1991. 44.95 (*0-387-53931-X*) Spr-Verlag.

— Linear Time, Branching Time & Partial Order in Logics & Models for Concurrency. (Lecture Notes in Computer Science Ser.: Vol. 354). viii, 713p. 1989. 74.00 (*0-387-51080-X*) Spr-Verlag.

— PARLE: Parallel Architectures & Languages Europe. (Lecture Notes in Computer Science Ser.: Vol. 258). xii, 480p. 1987. pap. 49.00 (*0-387-17943-7*) Spr-Verlag.

— PARLE: Parallel Architectures & Languages Europe. Vol. 259. xii, 464p. 1987. pap. 49.00 (*0-387-17945-3*) Spr-Verlag.

— Real-Time: Theory in Practice: REX Workshop, Mook, The Netherlands, June 3-7, 1991: Proceedings. LC 92-14687. (Lecture Notes in Computer Science Ser.: Vol. 600). viii, 723p. 1992. 106.95 (*0-387-55564-1*) Spr-Verlag.

— Semantics: Foundations & Applications: REX Workshop, Beekbergen, the Netherlands, June 1-4, 1992: Proceedings. LC 93-16725. (Lecture Notes in Computer Science Ser.: Vol. 666). 1993. 93.95 (*0-387-56596-5*) Spr-Verlag.

— Stepwise Refinement of Distributed Systems: Models, Formalisms, Correctness; REX Workshop Mook, The Netherlands May 29-June 2, 1989 Proceedings. (Lecture Notes in Computer Science Ser.: Vol. 430). x, 808p. 1990. 100.00 (*0-387-52559-9*) Spr-Verlag.

De Bakker, J. W. & Rutten, J. Ten Years of Concurrency Semantics: Selected Papers of the Amsterdam Concurrency Group. LC 92-19669. 420p. 1992. text 109.00 (*981-02-1041-8*) World Scientific Pub.

De Bakker, Jaco & De Vink, Erik. Control Flow Semantics. LC 95-47439. (Foundations of Computing Ser.). (Illus.). 608p. 1996. 57.50 (*0-262-04154-5*) MIT Pr.

De Balboa, Silvestre. Espejo de Paciencia. Aparicio, Angel, ed. (SPA.). 1970. pap. 9.00 (*0-89729-011-9*) Ediciones.

De Banegas, Marianne N., tr. see Chunko, Shelby E. & Madsen, Jane M.

De Bango, Guillermo. Campanas Al Viento. 384p. (Orig.). 1992. pap. 18.00 (*0-9631736-1-8*) Ediciones Cambio.

De Banville, Theodore. Poesies de Theodore De Banville, "Les Cariatides" LC 75-41015. 1976. reprint ed. 39.50 (*0-404-14504-3*) AMS Pr.

de Bar-sur-Aube, Bertrand. Song of Girart of Vienne. Newth, Michael A., tr. from FRO. LC 99-17134. (Medieval & Renaissance Texts & Studies: Vol. 196). 200p. 1999. 24.00 (*0-86698-238-8*, MR 196) MRTS.

***de Baranano, Kosme.** Picasso: A Dialogue with Ceramics. LC 99-192323. (Illus.). 234p. 1998. pap. 60.00 (*84-89413-36-3*, Pub. by Fundacion Bancaja) U of Wash Pr.

De Barandiaran, Jose M. & Duvert, Michel, eds. Dictionnaire Ilustre de Mythologie Basque. (FRE.). 1993. write for info. (*0-7859-8708-8*, 8479173297) Fr & Eur.

De Barbadillo, J. J., et al, eds. Mechanical Alloying for Structural Applications: Proceedings of the 2nd International Conference on Structural Applications of Mechanical Alloying, September 20-22, 1993, Vancouver, British Columbia, Canada. LC 93-79328. (Illus.). 482p. 1993. reprint ed. pap. 149.50 (*0-608-02614-X*, 206327200004) Bks Demand.

De Bari, Vito. His Glorious Passion. 216p. 1997. pap. 16.00 (*0-8059-4214-9*) Dorrance.

De Barjac, Huguette & Sutherland, Donald J., eds. Bacterial Control of Mosquitoes & Black Flies: Biochemistry, Genetics, & Applications of Bacillus Thuringiensis Israelensis & Bacillus Sphaericis. LC 89-70095. 352p. (C). 1990. pap. text 48.00 (*0-8135-1546-7*) Rutgers U Pr.

***De Baroid, Ciaran.** Ballymurphy & the Irish War. 2nd ed. 320p. 2000. 69.95 (*0-7453-1514-3*, Pub. by Pluto GBR); pap. 22.50 (*0-7453-1509-7*, Pub. by Pluto GBR) Stylus Pub VA.

De Barold, Claran. Bally Murphy & the Irish War. (C). pap. 23.00 (*0-7453-0445-1*, Pub. by Pluto GBR) Stylus Pub VA.

De Barran, Alicia C., jt. ed. see Finch, Henry.

De Barros, Paul. Jackson Street after Hours: The Roots of Jazz in Seattle. (Illus.). 256p. (Orig.). 1993. pap. 22.95 (*0-912365-92-7*) Sasquatch Bks.

De Barros, Philip, et al. Archaeological Investigations at Franciscan Plaza: San Juan Capistrano, California, Phase I. (Illus.). 461p. (C). 1990. reprint ed. pap. text 47.50 (*1-55567-604-9*) Coyote Press.

— Archaeological Investigations at Franciscan Plaza: San Juan Capistrano, California, Phase II. (Illus.). 307p. (C). 1990. reprint ed. pap. text 32.50 (*1-55567-605-7*) Coyote Press.

De Barrosa Du Bocacho, Manuel M. Coisas Do Coiso e Da Coisa: Sonetos Eroticos e Satiricos. 2nd ed. (Coleccao Poesia Ser.: Vol. 3). (POR.). 96p. 1997. boxed set 10.00 (*1-889358-04-5*) Peregrinacao.

De Barry, Anton. Investigations of the Brand Fungi & the Diseases of Plants Caused by Them with Reference to Grain & Other Useful Plants. Heffner, R. M. et al, trs. (Phytopathological Classics Ser.). 93p. 1969. 22.00 (*0-89054-012-8*) Am Phytopathol Soc.

De Barry Barnett, Edward. Explosives. 1980. lib. bdg. 350.00 (*0-8490-3154-0*) Gordon Pr.

De Barsy, Carlotta. The Great Dream Book. 215p. 1996. reprint ed. spiral bd. 16.00 (*0-7873-0261-9*) Hlth Research.

— The Great Dream Book: Standard Explanations with Accurate List of Lucky Numbers (1899) 216p. 1996. reprint ed. pap. 15.95 (*1-56459-874-8*) Kessinger Pub.

De Bartha, Georges, jt. auth. see Duncan, Alastair.

De Barthe, Joe. Life & Adventures of Frank Grouard. Stewart, Edgar I., ed. LC 58-11651. (Illus.). 298p. reprint ed. 92.40 (*0-8357-9731-7*, 201620900002) Bks Demand.

De Bartolomeis, P., et al, eds. Manifolds & Geometry. (Symposia Mathematica Ser.: No. 36). (Illus.). 329p. (C). 1996. text 69.95 (*0-521-56216-3*) Cambridge U Pr.

De, Barun & Samaddar, Ranabir, eds. State Development & Political Culture: Bangladesh & India. LC 97-901390. (C). 1997. 52.00 (*81-241-0455-7*, Pub. by Har-Anand Pubns) S Asia.

De Bary, Brett, tr. see Karatani, Kojin.

De Bary Nee, Brett, jt. auth. see Nee, Victor G.

De Bary, W. Theodore. The Trouble with Confucianism. 152p. 1996. pap. text 13.00 (*0-674-91016-8*) HUP.

***De Bary, W. Theodore & Lufrano, Richard J.** Sources of Chinese Tradition Vol. II. 2nd ed. (Illus.). 696p. 1999. 49.50 (*0-231-11270-X*) Col U Pr.

De Bary, W. Theodore, jt. ed. see Lee, Peter H.

De Bary, William T. Asian Values & Human Rights: A Confucian Communitarian Perspective. LC 97-46726. 1998. write for info. (*0-674-04955-1*) HUP.

***De Bary, William T.** Asian Values & Human Rights: A Confucian Communitarian Perspective. (Wing-TSit Chan Memorial Lectures). 2000. pap. text 14.95 (*0-674-00196-6*) HUP.

De Bary, William T. Confucianism & Human Rights. Tu Wei-Ming, ed. LC 97-14687. 1997. pap. 19.50 (*0-231-10937-7*) Col U Pr.

— Confucianism & Human Rights. Weiming, Tu, ed. LC 97-14687. 408p. 1997. 42.00 (*0-231-10936-9*) Col U Pr.

— Learning for One's Self: Essays on the Individual in Neo-Confucian Thought. 1991. text 64.50 (*0-231-07426-3*) Col U Pr.

***De Bary, William T.** Sources of Chinese Tradition. 2nd ed. 2000. pap. 24.00 (*0-231-10939-3*) Col U Pr.

De Bary, William T. Sources of Korean Tradition Vol. 1: From Early Times Through the Sixteenth Century. Lee, Peter H., ed. LC 96-17701. 432p. 1997. 52.00 (*0-231-10566-5*) Col U Pr.

De Bary, William T. The Trouble with Confucianism. (Tanner Lectures on Human Values). 152p. (C). 1996. pap. 25.95 (*0-674-91015-X*) HUP.

De Bary, William T. & Bloom, Irene, eds. Approaches to the Asian Classics. (Companions to Asian Studies). 400p. 1995. pap. 20.50 (*0-231-07005-5*) Col U Pr.

De Bary, William T. & Chaffee, John W. Neo-Confucian Education: The Formative Stage. (Studies on China: Vol. 9). 1989. 90.00 (*0-520-06393-7*, Pub. by U CA Pr) Cal Prin Full Svc.

De Bary, William T., jt. auth. see Saikaku, Ihara.

De Bary, William T., ed. see Conference on Oriental Classics in General Educati.

De Bary, William T., ed. see Keene, Donald.

De Basily, Lascelle. Memoirs of a Lost World. LC 75-29793. (Special Projects Ser.: No. 15). 308p. 1975. 9.95 (*0-8179-9287-1*) Hoover Inst Pr.

De Basily, Nicolas. Memoirs. LC 70-175450. (Publication Ser.: No. 125). 201p. 1973. 8.95 (*0-8179-6251-4*) Hoover Inst Pr.

De Bassompierre, Guy. Changing the Guard in Brussels: An Insider's View of the EC Presidency, 135. LC 88-23580. (Washington Papers: No. 135). 179p. 1988. 55.00 (*0-275-93186-2*, C3186, Praeger Pubs); pap. 18.95 (*0-275-93187-0*, B3187, Praeger Pubs) Greenwood.

De Bastide, Jean-Francois. The Little House: An Architectural Seduction. El-Khoury, Rodolfe, tr. from FRE. (Illus.). 112p. (Orig.). 1996. pap. 14.95 (*1-56898-017-5*) Princeton Arch.

De Batist, M. & Jacobs, P., eds. The Geology of Siliciclastic Shelf Seas. (Geological Society Special Publication Ser.: No. 117). (Illus.). viii, 346p. 1996. 110.00 (*1-897799-71-3*, 358, Pub. by Geol Soc Pub Hse) AAPG.

De Baubeta, Pat O., jt. ed. see Coulthard, Malcolm.

de Baubeta, Patricia A. Odber, see Odber de Baubeta, Patricia A.

de Baubeta, Patricia A. Odber, see Coulthard, Malcolm & Odber de Baubeta, Patricia A., eds.

De Bauw, Robert, jt. auth. see Dore, Julia.

***de Bay, Philip & Bolton, James.** Garden Mania: The Ardent Gardener's Compendium of Design & Decoration. (Illus.). 400p. 2000. pap. 35.00 (*0-609-80728-5*) C Potter.

de Bazancourt, Baron. Secrets of the Sword. LC 98-67196. (Illus.). 258p. 1998. reprint ed. pap. 19.95 (*1-884528-18-X*) Laureate Pr.

De Beau Chesne, John & Baildon, John. A Booke Containing Divers Sortes of Hands, As Well As the English & French Secretarie. LC 77-6875. (English Experience Ser.: No. 867). 1977. reprint ed. lib. bdg. 20.00 (*90-221-0867-8*) Walter J Johnson.

De Beauclair, Inez. Ethnographic Studies: The Collected Papers of Inez De Beauclair. (Illus.). xvii, 587p. 1986. 85.00 (*0-89986-366-3*) Oriental Bk Store.

De Beaucorps, Monique & Ergmann, Raoul. Great Masters of European Painting. LC 98-15728. (Illus.). 560p. 1998. 75.00 (*0-8109-4131-7*, Pub. by Abrams) Time Warner.

De Beaufort, Raphael L., ed. & tr. see Sand, George.

De Beaufort, Simon. Yellow Earth, Green Jade: Constants in Chinese Political Mores. (Harvard Studies in International Affairs: No. 41). 90p. 1984. reprint ed. pap. text 13.50 (*0-8191-4059-7*) U Pr of Amer.

De Beaufort Wijnholds, Onno, et al, eds. A Framework for Monetary Stability: Paper & Proceedings of an International Conference Organized by De Nederlandsche Bank & the Center for Economic Research at Amsterdam, The Netherlands, October 1993. LC 93-45987. (Financial & Monetary Policy Studies). 352p. (C). 1994. lib. bdg. 137.50 (*0-7923-2667-9*) Kluwer Academic.

De Beaugrande. Linguistic Theory. 1991. text. write for info. (*0-582-08210-2*, Pub. by Addison-Wesley) Longman.

De Beaugrande, Robert. Critical Discourse: A Survey of Literary Theorists. LC 87-19462. 496p. 1988. pap. 39.50 (*0-89391-453-3*); text 78.50 (*0-89391-441-X*) Ablx Pub.

— New Foundations for a Science of Text & Discourse. (Advances in Discourse Processes Ser.: Vol. 61). (Illus.). 300p. 1997. pap. 42.50 (*1-56750-279-2*) Ablx Pub.

— New Foundations for a Science of Text & Discourse. (Advances in Discourse Processes Ser.: Vol. 61). (Illus.). 300p. 1997. text 78.50 (*1-56750-278-4*) Ablx Pub.

— Text, Discourse & Process - Toward a Multidisciplinary Science of Texts. (Advances in Discourse Processes Ser.: Vol. 4). 368p. 1980. text 78.50 (*0-89391-033-3*) Ablx Pub.

De Beaugrande, Robert, et al, eds. Language, Discourse & Translation in the West & Middle East: Selected & Revised Papers from the Language & Translation Conference, Irbid, Jordan, 1992. LC 94-33138. (Benjamins Translation Library: No. 7). xii, 256p. 1994. lib. bdg. 65.00 (*1-55619-685-7*) J Benjamins Pubng Co.

De Beaugrande, Robert, et al. Advances in Discourse Processes: Language Policy & Language Education in Emerging Nations, No. 63. LC 98-43127. 1999. 78.50 (*1-56750-413-2*) Ablx Pub.

— Advances in Discourse Processes: Language Policy & Language Education in Emerging Nations, Vol. 63. 1999. pap. 39.50 (*1-56750-414-0*) Ablx Pub.

De Beaumarchais, Jean-Pierre. Le Mariage de Figaro. (FRE.). 1965. pap. 9.95 (*0-8288-9336-5*, F46096) Fr & Eur.

De Beaumarchais, Jean-Pierre, et al. Dictionary of French Language Literature: Dictionnaire des Litteratures de Langue Francaise, 4. (ENG & FRE.). 3000p. 1994. 700.00 (*0-8288-1562-3*, M6181) Fr & Eur.

De Beaumarchais, Pierre. Correspondance, 3 vols. Morton, Brian N., ed. (FRE.). 250p. 1969. write for info. (*0-318-51967-4*) Fr & Eur.

De Beaumarchais, Pierre A. The Marriage of Figaro. Sahlins, Bernard, ed. & tr. by. LC 94-26337. (Plays for Performance Ser.). (FRE.). 112p. 1994. pap. 7.95 (*1-56663-065-7*, Pub. by I R Dee); lib. bdg. 15.95 (*1-56663-066-5*, Pub. by I R Dee) Natl Bk Netwk.

De Beaumarchais, Pierre Augustin. The Barber of Seville. Sahlins, Bernard, tr. LC 98-30443. (Plays for Performance Ser.). 112p. 1998. pap. 7.95 (*1-56663-203-X*, Pub. by I R Dee); lib. bdg. 15.95 (*1-56663-202-1*, Pub. by I R Dee) Natl Bk Netwk.

De Beaumarchais, Pierre-Augustin C. The Barber of Seville: or the Futile Precaution: A New English Translation. Pestureau, Gilbert et al, trs. from FRE. LC 97-33294. (Studies in the History & Interpretation of Music: Vol. 56). 160p. 1997. text 69.95 (*0-7734-8548-1*) E Mellen.

— Correspondance, 3 vols. Morton, Brian N., ed. (FRE.). 250p. 1969. pap. 24.95 (*0-7859-5280-2*); pap. 24.95 (*0-685-73257-6*); pap. 24.95 (*0-685-73258-4*) Fr & Eur.

— Le Mariage de Figaro - La Mere Coupable. (Folio Ser.: No. 1527). (FRE.). 1984. pap. 14.95 (*2-07-037527-7*) Schoenhof.

— Theatre Complet, Parades, Lettres Relatives a Son Theatre. Allem, Maurice & Courant, Paul N., eds. (Bibliotheque de la Pleiade Ser.). (FRE.). 876p. 1934. 85.00 (*0-7859-1074-3*, 2070100529) Fr & Eur.

de Beaumont, De Leprince, see De Leprince de Beaumont.

De Beaumont, Gustave. Marie, or Slavery in the United States. LC 98-31234. 282p. 1998. pap. 15.95 (*0-8018-6064-4*) Johns Hopkins.

— Marie: or Slavery in the United States: A Novel of Jacksonian America. Chapman, Barbara, tr. from FRE. LC 58-11693. 252p. 1958. reprint ed. pap. 30.00 (*0-608-01658-6*, 2062310) Bks Demand.

De Beaumont, Gustave A. Marie, or Slavery in the United States: A Novel of Jacksonian America. Chapman, Barbara, tr. from FRE. xx, 252p. 1958. 35.00 (*0-8047-0545-3*) Stanford U Pr.

De Beaumont, Madame. Beauty & the Beast. (Talking Mother Goose Ser.). (Illus.). 26p. (J). (ps). 1987. 9.95 incl. audio (*0-934323-66-6*) Alchemy Comms.

De Beauplan, Sieur, jt. auth. see Le Vasseur, Guillaume.

De Beauport, Elaine & Diaz, Aura S. The Three Faces of Mind: Developing Your Mental, Emotional & Behavioral Intelligences. LC 96-22709. (Illus.). 1996. pap. 24.95 (*0-8356-0748-8*, Quest) Theos Pub Hse.

De Beauregard, Diane C. The Blue Planet: Seas & Oceans. Bogard, Vicki, tr. from FRE. LC 89-8912. (Young Discovery Library). (Illus.). 38p. (J). (gr. k-5). 1989. 5.95 (*0-944589-22-7*, 022) Young Discovery Lib.

De Beauregard, Diane Costa, see Costa de Beauregard, Diane.

De Beauregard, Olivier Costa, see Costa de Beauregard, Olivier.

De Beauregard Robinson, Gilbert. The Foundations of Geometry. 4th ed. LC 48-3776. (Mathematical Expositions Ser.: No. 1). 184p. reprint ed. pap. 57.10 (*0-608-30912-5*, 202051500018) Bks Demand.

De Beausobre, Isaac. Histoire Critique de Manichee et du Manicheisme. Feldman, Burton & Richardson, Robert D., eds. LC 78-60880. (Myth & Romanticism Ser.). 1510p. 1984. text 15.00 (*0-8240-3552-6*) Garland.

De Beausobre, Julia. Flame in the Snow. 1996. pap. 12.95 (*0-87243-223-8*) Templegate.

De Beausorbe, Iulia, tr. see Marcarius Starets of Optina & Macarius, Staretz.

De Beck, Jansen. Singing Bowls Package. 110p. pap. 27.95 incl. audio compact disk (*90-74597-30-0*, Pub. by Binkey Kok) Weiser.

De Beck, John. Appleworks Simplified: An Individualized Instruction Program Manual. (Orig.). 1986. pap. 13.95 (*0-89420-248-0*, 222060); audio 151.50 (*0-89420-249-9*, 222030) Natl Book.

D

An Asterisk (*) at the beginning of an entry indicates that the title is appearing for the first time.

De Becker, Eric V. Survey of Some Japanese Tax Laws. LC 78-78358. (Studies in Japanese Law & Government). 181p. 1979. reprint ed. lib. bdg. 72.50 (*0-313-26984-X*, U6984, Greenwood Pr) Greenwood.

De Becker, Gavin. The Gift of Fear: Survival Signals That Protect Us from Violence. 1998. mass mkt. 6.99 (*0-440-22619-8*) Dell.

— The Gift of Fear: Survival Signals That Protect Us from Violence. 372p. 1999. pap. 11.95 (*0-440-50883-5*) Dell.

— The Gift of Fear: Survival Signals That Protect Us from Violence. LC 96-51051. 352p. (gr. 8). 1997. 22.95 (*0-316-23502-4*) Little.

— The Gift of Fear: Survival Signals That Protect Us from Violence. 1998. pap. write for info. (*0-316-23577-6*) Little.

***De Becker, Gavin.** Protecting the Gift: Keeping Children & Teenagers Safe (And Parents Sane) 368p. 2000. pap. 11.95 (*0-440-50900-9*, Dell Trade Pbks) Dell.

De Becker, Gavin. Protecting the Gift: Keeping Children & Teenagers Safe (and Parents Sane) LC 99-22006. 336p. 1999. 22.95 (*0-385-33309-9*) Doubleday.

— Thinking Caps. 1999. pap. write for info. (*0-316-23515-6*) Little.

De Becker, Joseph E. Elements of Japanese Law: Studies in Japanese Law & Government. LC 78-78345. 467p. 1979. reprint ed. lib. bdg. 95.00 (*0-313-26991-2*, U6991, Greenwood Pr) Greenwood.

De Becker, Joseph E., tr. from JPN. Annotated Civil Code of Japan, Vol. 1. LC 78-78346. (Studies in Japanese Law & Government). 197p. 1979. lib. bdg. 72.50 (*0-313-27115-1*, U7115) Greenwood.

— Annotated Civil Code of Japan, Vol. 2. LC 78-78346. (Studies in Japanese Law & Government). 197p. 1979. lib. bdg. 72.50 (*0-313-27116-X*, U7116) Greenwood.

— Annotated Civil Code of Japan, Vol. 3. LC 78-78346. (Studies in Japanese Law & Government). 197p. 1979. lib. bdg. 45.00 (*0-313-27117-8*, U7117) Greenwood.

— Annotated Civil Code of Japan, Vol. 4. LC 78-78346. (Studies in Japanese Law & Government). 181p. 1979. lib. bdg. 50.00 (*0-313-27118-6*, U7118) Greenwood.

***De Becque, Antoine & Toubiana, Serge.** Truffaut. LC 00-25926. (Illus.). 462p. 2000. pap. 18.95 (*0-520-22524-4*, Pub. by U CA Pr) Cal Prin Full Svc.

De Bedrossian, Nydia & Bedrossian, Analia. Familias Sanas en un Mundo en Fermo.Tr. of Healthy Families in a Sick World. (SPA.). 96p. 1997. pap. text 7.99 (*0-311-12111-X*) Casa Bautista.

De Beeck, Bart Op, see Callewaert, Winand M.

De Beeck, Bart Op, see Callewaert, Winand M. & Op De Beeck, Bart.

De Beeck, Bart Op, see Callewaert, Winand M.

De Beeck, Bart Op, see Callewaert, Winand M. & Op De Beeck, Bart.

De Beeck, Bart Op, see Callewaert, Winand M.

De Beeck, Bart Op, see Callewaert, Winand M. & Op De Beeck, Bart.

De Beeck, Bart Op, see Callewaert, Winand M.

De Beer, A. S. Mass Media for the Nineties: The South African Handbook of Mass Communication. LC 93-215629. 426 p. 1993. write for info. (*0-627-01837-8*) J L Van Schaik.

— Mass Media, Towards the Millennium: The South African Handbook of Mass Communication. 2nd ed. LC 98-143264. vii, 530 p. 1998. write for info. (*0-627-02324-X*) J L Van Schaik.

De Beer, Carel, jt. auth. see Jackson, Melvin H.

De Beer, Cedric. The South African Disease: Apartheid Health & Health Services. LC 86-70877. 240p. 1986. 19.95 (*0-86543-038-1*); pap. 7.95 (*0-86543-039-X*) Africa World.

De Beer, E. S., ed. see Locke, John.

De Beer, Francis. We Saw Brother Francis. 145p. 1983. 9.00 (*0-8199-0803-7*, Frncscn Herld) Franciscan Pr.

De Beer, Gabriella. Contemporary Mexican Women Writers: Five Voices. LC 96-1302. (Texas Pan American Ser.). (Illus.). 304p. 1996. pap. 15.95 (*0-292-71586-2*); text 35.00 (*0-292-71585-4*) U of Tex Pr.

De Beer, Gavin. Early Travellers in the Alps. (Illus.). 1967. 8.95 (*0-8079-0041-9*); pap. 4.95 (*0-8079-0042-7*) October.

De Beer, Gavin R. Charles Darwin: Evolution by Natural Selection. LC 74-1779. (British Men of Science Ser.). 290p. 1976. reprint ed. lib. bdg. 69.50 (*0-8371-7378-7*, DECD, Greenwood Pr) Greenwood.

— The Development of the Vertebrate Skull. LC 85-1081. (Illus.). xxiv, 730p. 1995. reprint ed. lib. bdg. 66.00 (*0-226-13958-1*) U Ch Pr.

— The Development of the Vertebrate Skull. LC 85-1081. (Illus.). xxiv, 760p. 1998. reprint ed. pap. text 27.00 (*0-226-13960-3*) U Ch Pr.

— Sir Hans Sloane & the British Museum. LC 74-26258. (History, Philosophy & Sociology of Science Ser.). (Illus.). 1975. reprint ed. 24.95 (*0-405-06586-8*) Ayer.

De Beer, Gavin R., ed. see Locke, John.

De Beer, Hans. Ahoy There, Little Polar Bear. LC 88-42533. (Illus.). 32p. (J). (gr. k-3). 1988. 13.95 (*1-55858-028-X*, Pub. by North-South Bks NYC); pap. 6.95 (*1-55858-389-0*, Pub. by North-South Bks NYC) Chronicle Bks.

— Ahoy There, Little Polar Bear. (JPN., Illus.). 32p. (J). (gr. k-3). 1997. 15.95 (*4-924684-46-5*, Pub. by North-South Bks NYC) Chronicle Bks.

— Ahoy There, Little Polar Bear. (Illus.). 14p. (J). (ps). 1999. bds. 6.95 (*0-7358-1079-6*, Pub. by North-South Bks NYC) Chronicle Bks.

De Beer, Hans. Ahoy There, Little Polar Bear. (J). 1995. 12.15 (*0-606-08683-8*, Pub. by Turtleback) Demco.

De Beer, Hans. Ahoy There, Little Polar Bear: A Pop-Up Book. (Illus.). 12p. (J). (gr. k-3). 1995. 15.95 (*1-55858-438-2*, Pub. by North-South Bks NYC) Chronicle Bks.

— Al Mar, al Mar, Osito Polar. (J). 1995. 13.00 (*0-606-08684-6*, Pub. by Turtleback) Demco.

— Al Mar, Al Mar, Osito Polar. Roffe, Mercedes, tr. LC 95-13132. (SPA., Illus.). 32p. (J). (gr. k-3). 1995. pap. 6.95 (*1-55858-504-4*, Pub. by North-South Bks NYC) Chronicle Bks.

— Al Mar, Al Mar, Osito Polar. Antreasyan, Agustin, tr. (SPA., Illus.). 14p. (J). (ps). 1998. bds. 6.95 (*0-7358-1091-5*, Pub. by North-South Bks NYC) Chronicle Bks.

— Bernard Bear's Amazing Adventure. Martens, Marianne, tr. LC 94-34843. (Illus.). 32p. (J). (gr. k-3). 1994. 14.95 (*1-55858-294-0*, Pub. by North-South Bks NYC); lib. bdg. 14.88 (*1-55858-295-9*, Pub. by North-South Bks NYC) Chronicle Bks.

***De Beer, Hans.** Donde Vas Osito Polar. 1998. pap. text 11.00 (*84-264-3611-0*) Lectorum Pubns.

— Der Kleine Eisbar und der Angsthase.Tr. of Little Polar Bear & the Brave Little Hare. (GER., Illus.). (J). (gr. k-3). pap. 15.95 (*3-314-00675-6*, Pub. by North-South Bks NYC) Chronicle Bks.

De Beer, Hans. Der Kleine Eisbar und der Angsthase.Tr. of Little Polar Bear & the Brave Little Hare. (GER., Illus.). (J). 1996. 12.95 (*3-314-00000-6*, Pub. by North-South Bks NYC) Chronicle Bks.

— Kleiner Eisbar, Komm Bald Wieder!Tr. of Ahoy There, Little Polar Bear!. (GER., Illus.). 32p. (J). (gr. k-3). 1994. 13.95 (*3-314-00316-1*, Pub. by North-South Bks NYC) Chronicle Bks.

De Beer, Hans. Kleiner Eisbar, Lass Mich Nicht Allein!Tr. of Little Polar Bear & the Husky Pup. (GER., Illus.). (J). (ps-3). pap. 15.95 (*3-314-00955-0*, Pub. by North-South Bks NYC) Chronicle Bks.

De Beer, Hans. Little Polar Bear. LC 86-33208. (Illus.). 32p. (J). (gr. k-3). 1987. 15.95 (*1-55858-024-7*, Pub. by North-South Bks NYC) Chronicle Bks.

— Little Polar Bear. LC 86-33208. (Illus.). 32p. (J). (gr. k-3). 1994. pap. 6.95 (*1-55858-358-0*, Pub. by North-South Bks NYC) Chronicle Bks.

— Little Polar Bear. (JPN., Illus.). 32p. (J). (gr. k-3). 1997. 15.95 (*4-924684-43-0*, Pub. by North-South Bks NYC) Chronicle Bks.

— Little Polar Bear. (Illus.). 14p. (J). (ps). 1999. bds. 6.95 (*0-7358-1080-X*, Pub. by North-South Bks NYC) Chronicle Bks.

De Beer, Hans. Little Polar Bear. 1994. 12.15 (*0-606-08803-2*, Pub. by Turtleback) Demco.

De Beer, Hans. Little Polar Bear: A Pop-Up Book. (Illus.). 32p. (J). (gr. k-3). 1993. 15.95 (*1-55858-226-6*, Pub. by North-South Bks NYC) Chronicle Bks.

***De Beer, Hans.** Little Polar Bear: Mini Book & Audio Package. (Illus.). (J). (gr. k-3). 2000. 11.95 incl. audio (*0-7358-1275-6*, Pub. by North-South Bks NYC) Chronicle Bks.

De Beer, Hans. Little Polar Bear: Mini Pop-Up Book. (Illus.). 16p. (J). (ps-2). 1997. 7.95 (*1-55858-711-X*, Pub. by North-South Bks NYC) Chronicle Bks.

— Little Polar Bear Address Book. (Illus.). 120p. (J). 1990. 7.95 (*1-55858-080-8*, Pub. by North-South Bks NYC) Chronicle Bks.

— Little Polar Bear & the Brave Little Hare. LC 92-9803. (Illus.). 48p. (J). (gr. 1-3). 1994. pap. 5.95 (*1-55858-357-2*, Pub. by North-South Bks NYC) Chronicle Bks.

— Little Polar Bear & the Brave Little Hare. LC 98-17134. (Illus.). 32p. (J). (gr. k-3). 1998. 15.95 (*0-7358-1011-7*, Pub. by North-South Bks NYC); lib. bdg. 15.88 (*0-7358-1012-5*, Pub. by North-South Bks NYC) Chronicle Bks.

***De Beer, Hans.** Little Polar Bear & the Brave Little Hare. (Illus.). 32p. (gr. k-3). 2000. pap. 6.95 (*0-7358-1332-9*) North-South Bks NYC.

De Beer, Hans. Little Polar Bear & the Husky Pup. LC 99-17369. (Illus.). 32p. (J). (ps-3). 1999. lib. bdg. 15.88 (*0-7358-1155-5*, Pub. by North-South Bks NYC) Chronicle Bks.

***De Beer, Hans.** Little Polar Bear & the Husky Pup. LC 99-17369. (Illus.). 32p. (J). (ps-3). 1999. 15.95 (*0-7358-1154-7*, Pub. by North-South Bks NYC) Chronicle Bks.

— Little Polar Bear Big Book. (Illus.). 32p. (J). (gr. k-3). 1999. pap. 19.95 (*0-7358-1216-0*, Pub. by North-South Bks NYC) Chronicle Bks.

De Beer, Hans. Little Polar Bear Birthday Book. (Illus.). 120p. (J). 1990. 7.95 (*1-55858-081-6*, Pub. by North-South Bks NYC) Chronicle Bks.

— Little Polar Bear Finds a Friend. LC 89-43727. (Illus.). 32p. (J). (gr. k-3). 1990. 15.95 (*1-55858-092-1*, Pub. by North-South Bks NYC) Chronicle Bks.

— Little Polar Bear Finds a Friend. LC 89-43727. (Illus.). 32p. (J). (gr. k-3). 1996. pap. 6.95 (*1-55858-607-5*, Pub. by North-South Bks NYC) Chronicle Bks.

De Beer, Hans. Little Polar Bear Finds a Friend. (JPN., Illus.). 32p. (J). (gr. k-3). 1997. 15.95 (*4-924684-56-2*, Pub. by North-South Bks NYC) Chronicle Bks.

De Beer, Hans. Little Polar Bear Mini Book. LC 86-33208. (Illus.). 32p. (J). (gr. k-3). 1989. pap. 6.95 (*1-55858-030-1*, Pub. by North-South Bks NYC) Chronicle Bks.

— Little Polar Bear, Take Me Home! LC 96-25525. (Illus.). 32p. (J). (gr. k-3). 1996. 15.95 (*1-55858-630-X*, Pub. by North-South Bks NYC); lib. bdg. 15.88 (*1-55858-631-8*, Pub. by North-South Bks NYC) Chronicle Bks.

***De Beer, Hans.** Little Polar Bear with Doll. (Illus.). (ps-k). 2000. bds. 12.95 (*0-7358-1237-3*) North-South Bks NYC.

De Beer, Hans. El Osito Polar. LC 94-40894.Tr. of Polar Bear. (SPA., Illus.). 26p. (J). (gr. k-3). 1995. pap. 6.95 (*1-55858-390-4*, Pub. by North-South Bks NYC) Chronicle Bks.

— El Osito Polar. Antreasyan, Agustin, tr.Tr. of Polar Bear. (SPA., Illus.). 14p. (J). (ps). 1998. bds. 6.95 (*0-7358-1092-3*, Pub. by North-South Bks NYC) Chronicle Bks.

— El Osito Polar.Tr. of Polar Bear. (J). 1995. 12.40 (*0-606-08736-2*) Turtleback.

***De Beer, Hans.** El Osito Polar Libro Grande.Tr. of Little Polar Bear Big Bear. (SPA., Illus.). 32p. (J). (gr. k-3). 1999. pap. 19.95 (*0-7358-1217-9*, Pub. by North-South Bks NYC) Chronicle Bks.

— El Osito Polar y el Conejito Valiente. Antreasyan, Agustin, tr. (SPA., Illus.). 32p. (J). (gr. k-3). 2000. 15.95 (*0-7358-1004-4*); pap. 6.95 (*0-7358-1005-2*) North-South Bks NYC.

De Beer, Hans. El Osito Polar y Su Nueva Amiga. LC 94-40894.Tr. of Polar Bear & His New Friend. (SPA., Illus.). 32p. (J). (gr. k-3). 1996. pap. 6.95 (*1-55858-639-3*, Pub. by North-South Bks NYC) Chronicle Bks.

De Beer, Hans. Piuma E il Coniglietto Fifone.Tr. of Little Polar Bear & the Brave Little Hare. (ITA., Illus.). (J). 15.95 (*88-8203-045-8*, Pub. by North-South Bks NYC) Chronicle Bks.

— Piuma Nel Paese delle Tigri.Tr. of Little Polar Bear, Take Me Home!. (ITA., Illus.). 32p. (J). (gr. k-3). 15.95 (*88-8203-020-2*, Pub. by North-South Bks NYC) Chronicle Bks.

— Pluma e il Cucciolo di Husky.Tr. of Little Polar Bear & the Husky Pup. (ITA., Illus.). (J). (ps-3). pap. 15.95 (*88-8203-183-7*, Pub. by North-South Bks NYC) Chronicle Bks.

— Plume au Pays des Tigres.Tr. of Little Polar Bear, Take Me Home!. (FRE., Illus.). (J). 15.95 (*3-314-21007-8*, Pub. by North-South Bks NYC) Chronicle Bks.

De Beer, Hans. Plume en Bateau. (FRE., Illus.). 32p. (J). (gr. k-3). 1992. 13.95 (*3-314-20647-X*, Pub. by North-South Bks NYC) Chronicle Bks.

De Beer, Hans. Plume et la Station Polaire.Tr. of Little Polar Bear & the Brave Little Hare. (FRE., Illus.). (J). (gr. 1-3). pap. 15.95 (*3-314-21162-7*, Pub. by North-South Bks NYC) Chronicle Bks.

— Plume et le Chien de Traineau.Tr. of Little Polar Bear & the Husky Pup. (FRE., Illus.). (J). (ps-3). pap. 15.95 (*3-314-21211-9*, Pub. by North-South Bks NYC) Chronicle Bks.

De Beer, Hans, ed. Business Ethics in Progress? (Studies in Economic Ethics & Philosophy). (Illus.). ix, 224p. 1994. 71.95 (*0-387-57758-0*) Spr-Verlag.

De Beer, John, jt. auth. see Killen, Patricia O.

***de Beer, Joop & Deven, F.** Diversity in Family Formation: The Demographic Transition in Belgium & the Netherlands. LC 00-42029. (European Studies of Population). 2000. write for info. (*0-7923-6461-9*) Kluwer Academic.

De Beer, Peter H., jt. auth. see Leonard, Robert J.

De Beer, Pieter, jt. auth. see Braster, Patrick.

De Beer, Shane R. Russian for the Business Traveler. LC 93-31834. (Foreign Language Business Dictionaries Ser.). (ENG & RUS.). 600p. 1994. pap. 11.95 (*0-8120-1784-6*) Barron.

De Begona, Mauricio. Cristo Yanqui. LC 82-84253. (SPA.). 777p. (Orig.). 1984. pap. 19.00 (*0-89729-321-1*) Ediciones.

De Behar, Lisa B. A Rhetoric of Silence & Other Selected Writings. LC 95-34481. (Approaches to Semiotics Ser.: No. 122). (C). 1995. lib. bdg. 152.35 (*3-11-014425-5*) Mouton.

De Beistegui, Miguel. Heidegger & the Political. LC 96-48677. (Thinking the Political Ser.). 216p. (C). 1997. 70.00 (*0-415-13063-8*); pap. 20.99 (*0-415-15064-6*) Routledge.

De Beistegui, Miguel, jt. auth. see Sparks, Simon.

De Beixedon, S. Yvette. Lovers & Survivors: A Partner's Guide to Living with & Loving a Sexual Abuse Survivor. 225p. 1995. pap. 14.95 (*1-885003-09-9*) R D Reed Pubs.

de Bellaing, Vefa. Dictionnaire des Compositeurs de Musique en Bretagne. (FRE.). 280p. 1992. pap. 75.00 (*0-7859-8243-4*, 2908261111) Fr & Eur.

De Bellefonds, C. Robert Benjamin Dictionnaire Francais. (FRE.). 572p. 1997. 39.95 (*0-320-00458-9*) Fr & Eur.

— Robert Junior Illustre (8-12 Ans) (FRE.). 1153p. 1997. 49.95 (*0-320-00429-5*) Fr & Eur.

De Belleroche, J., jt. ed. see Coulton, G. R.

***De Bellis, Jack.** The John Updike Encyclopedia. LC 99-89163. 2000. lib. bdg. write for info. (*0-313-29904-8*, Greenwood Pr) Greenwood.

De Bellis, Jack, compiled by. John Updike: A Bio-Bibiliography, 1967-1993, 17. LC 93-28538. (Bibliographies & Indexes in American Literature Ser.: No. 17). 360p. 1994. lib. bdg. 59.95 (*0-313-28861-5*, Greenwood Pr) Greenwood.

De Bellis, Robert, et al, eds. Thanatology Curriculum-Medicine. LC 88-2934. (Loss, Grief & Care Ser.: Vol. 2, Nos. 1 & 2). (Illus.). 132p. 1988. text 4.95 (*0-86656-738-0*) Haworth Pr.

De Bello, Rosario. Gina's Saturday Adventure. LC 93-5845. (Illus.). 32p. (J). (ps-3). 1994. pap. 4.95 (*0-8091-6612-7*) Paulist Pr.

— Rachel & the Rabbi Jesus. 1989. pap. 2.95 (*0-8091-6580-5*) Paulist Pr.

De Belot, Raymond. The Struggle for the Mediterranean, 1939-1945. Field, James A., Jr., tr. LC 51-12459. 306p. reprint ed. pap. 94.90 (*0-608-12665-9*, 205599300043) Bks Demand.

De Benavente, Luis Quinones, see Quinones De Benavente, Luis.

De Boysson-Bardies, Benedict, see De Boysson-Bardies, Benedict.

De Benedictis, Daniel J., see Ene, Dan, pseud.

De Beneditti, P. G., ed. Theoretical Approaches to Quantitative Pharmacophore Modeling - Biological Activity Relationships. (Theoretical & Computational Chemistry Ser.: Vol. 7). 1999. write for info. (*0-444-82675-0*) Elsevier.

De Benitez, Ana M. Cocina Prehispanica. (ENG & SPA., Illus.). 1977. pap. 35.95 (*968-414-015-0*) Adlers Foreign Bks.

De Bennetot, Arlette Cotton, see Cotton de Bennetot, Arlette.

***De Benneville, James S.** The Haunted House: More Samurai Tales of the Tokugawa II. 276p. 2000. text 110.00 (*0-7103-0696-2*) Col U Pr.

— The Kwaidan of the Lady of Tamiya: Samurai Tales of the Tokugawa I. 286p. 2000. text 110.00 (*0-7103-0700-4*) Col U Pr.

De Benneville, James S. Tales of the Samurai. 480p. 1987. pap. 19.95 (*0-7103-0233-9*, 02339) Routledge.

De Benoist, Alain. The Study of Intelligence & the IQ Controversy: A Bibliographical Introduction. 224p. (C). 1998. pap. text 20.00 (*0-941694-61-5*) Inst Study Man.

De Bens, Elsa & Knoche, Manfred, eds. Electronic Mass Media in Europe Prospects & Developments. (C). 1987. lib. bdg. 218.00 (*90-277-2567-5*) Kluwer Academic.

De Beracasa Gonzales, Bertha, tr. see Angelisanti, Pio Raffaele.

De Berard, F. B. Famous Tales of Barbarians & Savages. LC 72-5688. (Black Heritage Library Collection). 1977. reprint ed. 29.95 (*0-8369-9138-9*) Ayer.

De Berardinis, Olivia. "Let Them Eat Cheesecake" The Art of Olivia. Beren, Joel, ed. (Illus.). 108p. 1993. 29.95 (*0-929643-06-2*) Ozone Prodns.

— Olivia. 1996. 100.00 (*0-9622646-3-6*) R Bane Ltd.

De Berceo, Gonzalo. El Duelo de la Virgen, Los Himnos, Los Loores de Nuestra Senora, Los Signos del Juicio Final (Vol. III of the Oras Completas) Dutton, Brian, ed. (Monagrafias A Ser.: Vol. XVIII). (SPA.). 163p. (Orig.). (C). 1975. pap. 51.00 (*0-900411-96-1*, Pub. by Tamesis Bks Ltd) Boydell & Brewer.

— Milagros de Nuestra Senora. Devoto, Daniel, ed. 3.50 (*0-685-11394-9*) Fr & Eur.

— Miracles of Our Lady. Mount, Richard T. & Cash, Annette G., trs. LC 97-2119. (Illus.). 176p. 1997. 24.95 (*0-8131-2019-5*) U Pr of Ky.

— Poemas: Edicion Facsimil del Manuscrito (Siglo XIV) (Real Academia Ediciones Ser.). (SPA.). 1993. 750.00 (*84-600-3319-8*) Elliots Bks.

— El Sacrificio de la Misa, La Vida de Sante Oria el Martirio de San Lorenzo. Dutton, Brian, ed. (Monagrafias A Ser.: Vol. LXXX). (SPA.). 208p. (Orig.). (C). 1981. pap. 51.00 (*0-7293-0099-4*, Pub. by Tamesis Bks Ltd) Boydell & Brewer.

De Berdt, Dennys. Letters of Dennys De Berdt, 1757-70. (Select Bibliographies Reprint Ser.). 1977. reprint ed. 19.95 (*0-8369-5931-0*) Ayer.

De Berg, Mark, see Berg, Mark de.

De Bergerac. La Mort d'Aggripine. Gossip, ed. (Exeter French Texts Ser.: Vol. 44). (FRE.). 113p. Date not set. pap. text 19.95 (*0-85989-182-8*, Pub. by Univ Exeter Pr) Northwestern U Pr.

De Bergerac, Olivia. Dolphin Within. 192p. 1999. pap. 13.00 (*0-684-86850-4*) S&S Trade.

— Dolphin Within: Awakening Human Potential. 1998. pap. text 11.95 (*0-7318-0688-3*) Simon & Schuster.

De Berker, D. A., et al. Handbook of Diseases of the Nails & Their Management. LC 94-46339. 1995. pap. 59.95 (*0-86542-907-3*) Blackwell Sci.

De Bernado Ares, Jose M. Historiology, Research & Didactics: Elaboration & Transmission of Historical Knowledge. Saint-Saen, Alain, ed. (Iberian Studies in History, Literature & Culture). (SPA.). 159p. 1996. 69.95 (*1-883255-87-2*) Intl Scholars.

De Bernard, B., jt. ed. see Pecile, A.

De Bernardez-Clark, Eliana, jt. ed. see Georgiou, George.

De Bernardo, Mark A. Avoiding Legal Liability: The 25 Most Common Employer Mistakes in Addressing Drug Abuse. 40p. 1996. pap. 28.00 (*1-889437-05-0*) Inst Drug-Free Wrkpl.

— Drug & Alcohol Abuse Prevention & the ADA: An Employer's Guide. 125p. (Orig.). 1992. pap. 32.00 (*1-889437-02-6*) Inst Drug-Free Wrkpl.

— Drug Testing in the Workplace: Basic Issues, Answers, & Options for Employers. (Employer Guide Ser.: Vol. 4). 16p. (Orig.). 1994. pap. 4.50 (*1-889437-13-1*) Inst Drug-Free Wrkpl.

— Employee Assistance Programs: An Employer's Development & Implementation Guide. (Employer Guide Ser.: Vol. 2). 16p. (Orig.). 1994. pap. 4.50 (*1-889437-11-5*) Inst Drug-Free Wrkpl.

— Employee Drug Education & Awareness & Supervisor Training: An Employer's Development & Implementation Guide. 2nd ed. (Employer Guide Ser.: Vol. 3). 16p. 1994. reprint ed. pap. 4.50 (*1-889437-12-3*) Inst Drug-Free Wrkpl.

— Guide to Dangerous Drugs. (Illus.). 16p. 1995. pap. 2.40 (*1-889437-08-5*) Inst Drug-Free Wrkpl.

— Policy on Drug & Alcohol Abuse Prevention: An Employer's Development & Implementation Guide. (Employer Guide Ser.: Vol. 1). 16p. (Orig.). 1994. pap. 4.50 (*1-889437-10-7*) Inst Drug-Free Wrkpl.

— What Every Employee Should Know about Alcohol Abuse: Answers to 25 Good Questions. 20p. 1996. pap. 2.30 (*1-889437-07-7*) Inst Drug-Free Wrkpl.

— What Every Employee Should Know about Drug Abuse: Answers to 20 Good Questions. 16p. 1995. reprint ed. pap. 1.80 (*1-889437-06-9*) Inst Drug-Free Wrkpl.

— Workplace Drug Testing: An Employer's Development & Implementation Guide. 107p. 1994. pap. 35.00 (*1-889437-03-4*) Inst Drug-Free Wrkpl.

D

An Asterisk (*) at the beginning of an entry indicates that the title is appearing for the first time.

***De Bernardo, Mark A. & De Logy, Nancy N.** Guide to State & Federal Drug-Testing Laws. 8th ed. (Orig.). 1999. pap. 295.00 (*1-889437-21-2*) Inst Drug-Free Wrkpl.

De Bernardo, Mark A. & Delogu, Nancy N. Guide to State & Federal Drug-Testing Laws. 7th ed. (Orig.). 1998. pap. 225.00 (*1-889437-20-4*) Inst Drug-Free Wrkpl.

De Bernieres, Louis. Corelli's Mandolin: A Novel. Desser, Robin, ed. 1995. pap. 13.00 (*0-679-76397-X*) Knopf.

— Senor Vivo & the Coca Lord: A Novel. LC 97-35626. 1998. pap. 13.00 (*0-375-70014-5*) Vin Bks.

— The Troublesome Offspring of Cardinal Guzman. LC 98-26442. 480p. 1998. pap. 14.00 (*0-375-70015-3*) Vin Bks.

— The War of Don Emmanuel's Nether Parts: A Novel. LC 97-6740. 1997. pap. 13.00 (*0-375-70013-7*) Vin Bks.

De Bersaques, J., ed. Clinical & Experimental Dermatology: Festschrift to Professor Kint. (Journal Ser.: Vol. 189, Supplement 2, 1994). (Illus.). iv, 72p. 1994. pap. 33.25 (*3-8055-6099-0*) S Karger.

— Symposium sur les Tumeurs Cutanees des Enfants: Gent. November, 1978. (Journal: Dermatologica: Vol. 161, Suppl. 1, 1980). (Illus.). iv, 160p. 1981. pap. 15.75 (*3-8055-2238-X*) S Karger.

De Bertier De Sauvigny, Guillaume. Bourbon Restoration. Case, Lynn M., tr. LC 67-17175. 514p. reprint ed. 159.40 (*0-8357-9746-5*, 205110900079) Bks Demand.

De Bertier de Sauvigny, Guillaume & Pinkney. History of France. rev. enl. ed. 25.95 (*0-88295-425-3*) Forum Pr IL.

De Bertier De Sauvigny, Guillaume & Pinkney, David H. History of France. enl. rev. ed. Friguglietti, James, tr. LC 82-20978. (Illus.). 446p. (C). 1983. pap. text 21.95 (*0-88273-425-3*) Forum Pr IL.

De Bertodan, Teresa. Daily Readings with Mother Teresa. 1994. pap. 9.00 (*0-00-627810-8*) Harper SF.

de Bertoldi, Marco, ed. Science of Composting. 1996. write for info. (*0-7514-0383-0*) Kluwer Academic.

De Besse, B. French (Definitions) - English New Technical Terminology: Office Terminology Recommended by the French Government. 368p. 1982. pap. 73.00 (*2-903988-00-5*) IBD Ltd.

De Betancourt, Ethel Rios. Marmol, Bronce y Barro. LC 81-10286. (Illus.). 499p. 1984. 20.00 (*0-8477-0874-8*) U of PR Pr.

De Betanzos, Juan. Narrative of the Incas. Hamilton, Roland & Buchanan, Dana, eds. & trs. by. from SPA. (Illus.). 352p. 1996. pap. 17.95 (*0-292-75559-7*); text 40.00 (*0-292-75560-0*) U of Tex Pr.

De Bettignies, Henri C. Trade & Investment in the Asia-Pacific Region. LC 95-24872. (Research in the Asian-Pacific Business with the INSEAD Euro-Asia Centre: Vol. 1). 240p. 1997. pap. 60.00 (*1-86152-232-0*) Thomson Learn.

De Bettignies, Henri-Claude. Business Transformation in China. (Henri-Claude de Bettignies Ser.). 240p. 1997. 49.50 (*0-415-12322-4*) Thomson Learn.

— The Changing Business Environment in the Asia-Pacific Region. (Henri-Claude de Bettignies Ser.). 240p. 1997. 76.95 (*0-415-12320-8*) Thomson Learn.

***de Beuckelaer, Gerard M.** It's Broken, Let's Fix It: The Zeitgeist & Modern Entreprise. LC 00-33825. (Illus.). 2000. write for info. (*3-540-67325-3*) Spr-Verlag.

De Beucken, Jean. Vincent Van Gogh - A Portrait. (FRE., Illus.). lib. bdg. 14.95 (*0-8288-4000-8*) Fr & Eur.

De Bevere, Maurice & de Goscinny, Rene. Jesse James. (Lucky Luke Ser.). (Orig.). (Illus.). 48p. (Orig.). (J). (gr. 5-9). 1996. pap. 8.95 (*1-887911-54-5*) Fantsy Flight.

— The Stage Coach. (Lucky Luke Ser.: No. 1). (Illus.). 48p. (J). (gr. 2-7). 1996. reprint ed. pap. 8.95 (*1-887911-52-9*) Fantsy Flight.

De Bevoise, Ken. Agents of Apocalypse: Epidemic Disease in the Colonial Philippines. LC 94-19328. 274p. 1995. text 39.50 (*0-691-03486-9*, Pub. by Princeton U Pr) Cal Prin Full Svc.

***De Bevoise, M. B., tr.** Era of the Individual: A Contribution to a History of Subjectivity. 2000. pap. 22.50 (*81-208-1697-8*, Pub. by Motilal Bnarsidass) S Asia.

De Beyer, Joy, jt. auth. see Kronick, Richard.

De Beze, Claude. Revolution in Siam, 1688: The Memoir of Father de Beze. Hutchinson, E. W., tr. LC 72-5773. 230p. reprint ed. pap. 71.30 (*0-8357-6666-7*, 203533400094) Bks Demand.

De-Bhaldraithe, Eoin, jt. tr. see Costello, Hilary.

De Bhaldraithe, Tomas. English-Irish Dictionary: With Terminological Additions & Corrections. (ENG & IRI.). 1990. reprint ed. pap. 47.50 (*1-85791-035-4*) Colton Bk.

De Bias, Doug. Coming of Age in Babylon: Finding Your Own Reality. LC 97-69920. (Illus.). 161p. (C). 1998. pap. 12.00 (*0-9660657-4-3*) New Spring.

De Bie, Catherine F. Multiplication & Division Made Easy. Weigand, Betty, ed. (Illus.). 72p. (Orig.). (J). 1990. pap. 10.95 (*0-9627585-0-7*) M & D Made Easy.

De Biedma, Jaime G. Longing: Selected Poems. Nolan, James, tr. from SPA. 180p. (Orig.). 1993. pap. 9.95 (*0-87286-277-1*) City Lights.

De Bierre, Julia, jt. auth. see Bain, James.

De Bilio, Beth. Vendetta Con Brio. LC 72-9881. (Black Bat Mystery Ser). 1973. 5.95 (*0-672-51791-4*, Bobbs) Macmillan.

De Billinghurst, Carmen A. Spanish Vocabulary & Verbs. 504p. 1997. 6.95 (*0-02-861722-3*) Macmillan.

De Biran, Pierre Maine, see Maine De Biran, Pierre.

De Biro, Elizabeth. Hungarian Cooking. 25.95 (*0-87557-098-4*) Saphrograph.

De Bit, Ralph M. A Textbook of the Sacred Science: The Philosophy & Metaphysics for the School of the Sacred Science. 334p. 1997. reprint ed. pap. 24.95 (*0-7661-0022-7*) Kessinger Pub.

De Blase, Betty E. Survivor of a Tarnished Ministry. 176p. (Orig.). 1983. pap. text 6.95 (*0-913621-00-5*) Truth CA.

De Blasi, Marlena. Regional Foods of Northern Italy: Recipes & Remembrances. LC 97-14389. (Illus.). 288p. 1997. 26.95 (*0-7615-0905-4*) Prima Pub.

— Regional Foods of Southern Italy. LC 99-13218. (Illus.). 304p. 1999. 28.95 (*0-670-88384-0*) Viking Penguin.

De Blasis, Celeste. A Season of Swans, Vol. 3. 1990. pap. 5.95 (*0-685-47608-1*) Bantam.

De Blassie, Richard R. & Anderson, John. Helping the Troubled. 179p. 1981. pap. 3.95 (*0-8189-1163-8*) Alba.

De Bli, H. J. A Physical Geography of the Global Environment. 2nd ed. 664p. 1997. pap. text 77.95 (*0-471-24779-0*) Wiley.

De Blieux, Dianna. Alone Within. 127p. mass mkt. 4.99 (*1-55197-044-9*) Picasso Publ.

De Blij. Earth & Goode's World Atlas. 2nd ed. 1998. pap. text 59.00 (*0-471-31917-1*) Wiley.

De Blij. Human Geography: Culture & Society. 224p. 1996. pap. 12.95 (*0-471-10566-X*) Wiley.

— Regions. 9th ed. pap. text, teacher ed. write for info. (*0-471-35744-8*) Wiley.

— Regions. 9th ed. 194p. 1999. pap., student ed. 30.95 (*0-471-35748-0*) Wiley.

— Regions Take Note!, Set. 9th ed. 1999. text 57.00 (*0-471-36095-3*) Wiley.

— Regions Update with Base Maps. 8th ed. 1998. text 56.00 (*0-471-34590-3*) Wiley.

***De Blij, H. J. & Murphy, Alexander B.** Human Geography: Culture, Society, & Space. 6th ed. LC 98-34843. 560p. 1998. pap. 81.95 (*0-471-24208-X*) Wiley.

De Blij, Harm. Harm de Blij's Geography Book: A Leading Geographer's Fresh Look at Our Changing World. 336p. 1995. 22.95 (*0-471-11687-4*) Wiley.

***De Blij, Harm.** My Wartime Encounter with Geography. (Illus.). 180p. 2000. 29.50 (*1-85776-457-9*, Pub. by Book Guild Ltd) Trans-Atl Phila.

De Blij, Harm J. Africa South. LC 62-14295. 409p. reprint ed. 126.80 (*0-8357-9445-8*, 201477000093) Bks Demand.

— Dar es Salaam: A Study in Urban Geography. LC 63-18014. 101p. reprint ed. pap. 31.40 (*0-608-13057-5*, 201476900093) Bks Demand.

— Human Geography: Culture, Society, & Space. LC 81-7506. (Illus.). 668p. reprint ed. pap. 200.00 (*0-7837-3495-6*, 205782800008) Bks Demand.

***De Blij, Harm J.** Human Geography: Culture, Society & Space. 6th ed. LC 98-34843. 560p. 1999. text 81.95 (*0-471-35595-X*) Wiley.

De Blij, Harm J. Mombasa: An African City. LC 68-17731. 182p. reprint ed. pap. 56.50 (*0-608-13054-0*, 201485400093) Bks Demand.

— Nature on the Rampage. LC 94-23115. 224p. 1994. 29.97 (*0-89599-048-2*); pap. text 19.95 (*0-89599-049-0*) Smithsonian Bks.

— Regions: Take Note! 9th ed. 1999. pap. text 14.95 (*0-471-35742-1*) Wiley.

De Blij, Harm J. Teach Assist IM Regions. 9th ed. pap. text. write for info. (*0-471-35749-9*) Wiley.

De Blij, Harm J. & Martin, Esmond B. African Perspectives. 1981. 27.50 (*0-416-31790-1*, NO.3023) Routledge.

De Blij, Harm J., et al. The Earth: An Introduction to Its Physical & Human Geography. 4th ed. 480p. 1994. text 83.95 (*0-471-00336-0*) Wiley.

De Blij, Harm J., jt. auth. see Muller, Peter O.

De Block, P. The African Species of Ixora Vol. 9: Rubiaceae-Pavetteae. (Illus.). 218p. 1998. 60.00 (*90-72619-37-4*, Pub. by Natl Botanic Grdn Belgium) Balogh.

De Blois, Lukas & Van Der Spek, R. J. An Introduction to the Ancient World. LC 96-38099. (Illus.). 352p. 1997. pap. 25.99 (*0-415-12774-2*) Routledge.

— An Introduction to the Ancient World. LC 96-38099. (Illus.). 352p. (C). 1997. 80.00 (*0-415-12773-4*) Routledge.

De Board, Robert. The Psychoanalysis of Organizations: A Psychoanalytic Approach to Behaviour in Groups & Organizations. 158p. 1978. pap. 14.95 (*0-422-76530-9*, NO. 2731, Pub. by Tavistock) Routldge.

De Board, Robert & Grahame, Kenneth. Counselling for Toads: A Psychological Adventure. LC 97-17524. (Illus.). 160p. (C). 1998. pap. 14.99 (*0-415-17429-5*) Routledge.

De Bode & Broere. Grandad I'll Always Remember. (J). 1997. write for info. (*0-237-51755-8*) EVN1 UK.

— It's Always Me They're After. (J). 1997. write for info. (*0-237-51754-X*) EVN1 UK.

De Bodinat, Henri. Influence in the Multinational Corporation: The Case of Manufacturing. Bruchey, Stuart, ed. LC 80-567. (Multinational Corporations Ser.). 1980. lib. bdg. 36.95 (*0-405-13364-2*) Ayer.

De Boe, David C. Sponsors' Handbook: Junior Historian & Walter Prescott Webb Historical Society. rev. ed. iv, 86p. (J). 1990. pap. text 10.00 (*0-87611-120-7*) Tex St Hist Assn.

De Boe, David C., et al. Teaching Texas History: An All-Level Resource Guide. 2nd rev. ed. vii, 153p. 1990. reprint ed. pap. text 15.95 (*0-87611-091-X*) Tex St Hist Assn.

De Boef, Walter, et al. Cultivating Knowledge: Genetic Diversity, Farmer Experimentation & Crop Research. 192p. 1993. 47.50 (*1-85339-207-3*, Pub. by Intermed Tech); pap. 21.00 (*1-85339-204-9*, Pub. by Intermed Tech) Stylus Pub VA.

De Boef, Walter, jt. auth. see Almekinder, Connie.

De Boer, A. G., ed. Drug Absorption Enhancement: Concepts, Possibilities, Limitations, & Trends. LC 93-38330. (Drug Targeting & Delivery Ser.: Vol. 3). 430p. 1994. text 146.00 (*3-7186-5492-X*) Gordon & Breach.

De Boer, A. G. & Sutanto, Win, eds. Drug Transport Across the Blood-Brain Barrier: In Vitro & In Vivo Techniques. 236p. 1997. text 62.00 (*90-5702-032-7*, Harwood Acad Pubs) Gordon & Breach.

de Boer-Ashworth, Elizabeth, see Boer-Ashworth, Elizabeth de.

De Boer, C., jt. auth. see Chretien de Troyes.

De Boer, E. & Viergever, Max A., eds. Mechanics of Hearing. 1983. text 126.50 (*90-247-2878-9*) Kluwer Academic.

De Boer, Esther. Mary Magdalene: Beyond the Myth. Bowden, John, tr. from DUT. LC 97-27069. Orig. Title: Maria Magdalena: De Mythe Voorbij; Op Zoek Naar Wie Zij Werkelijkis. 176p. (Orig.). 1997. pap. 15.00 (*1-56338-212-1*) TPI PA.

de Boer, F. R., ed. see Hafner, J., et al.

De Boer, G. F., ed. Avian Leukosis. (Developments in Veterinary Virology Ser.). (C). 1987. text 161.50 (*0-89838-872-4*) Kluwer Academic.

***De Boer, J. & Dubouloz, M., eds.** Handbook of Disaster Medicine. (Illus.). 550p. 2000. 122.50 (*90-6764-316-5*, Pub. by Uppsala Universitet) Coronet Bks.

de Boer, J. A., jt. auth. see Vlaardingerbroek, Marinus T.

De Boer, John J. Teaching Secondary English. LC 76-100155. 427p. 1970. reprint ed. lib. bdg. 75.00 (*0-8371-3426-9*, DETS, Greenwood Pr) Greenwood.

de Boer, Karin. Thinking in the Light of Time: Heidegger's Encounter with Hegel. LC 99-38489. (C). 2000. text 73.50 (*0-7914-4505-4*); pap. text 24.95 (*0-7914-4506-2*) State U NY Pr.

De Boer, Leobert E., ed. Workshop on the Conservation of the Orangutan. LC 82-7722. (Illus.). 353p. 1982. text 249.00 (*90-6193-702-7*) Kluwer Academic.

De Boer, Martinus. The Defeat of Death: Apocalyptic Eshcatology in 1 Corinthians 15 & Romans 5. (Journal for the Study of the New Testament, Supplement Ser.: Vol. 22). 278p. 1998. 56.50 (*1-85075-089-0*) CUP Services.

De Boer, Martinus C., ed. From Jesus to John: Essays on New Testament Christology in Honour of Marinus de Jonge. (JSNT Supplement Ser.: Vol. 84). 358p. 1993. 85.00 (*1-85075-422-5*, Pub. by Sheffield Acad) CUP Services.

De Boer, Marvin E., ed. Destiny by Choice: The Inaugural Addresses of the Governors of Texas. LC 91-15794. (Illus.). 496p. 1992. text 50.00 (*1-55728-232-3*) U of Ark Pr.

De Boer, P., jt. ed. see Searle, A. G.

De Boer, P. L., et al, eds. Tide: Influenced Sedimentary Environments & Facies. (C). 1987. text 236.50 (*90-277-2622-1*) Kluwer Academic.

De Boer, Paul M. Price Effects in Input-Output Relations: A Theoretical & Empirical Study for the Netherlands 1949-1967. (Lecture Notes in Economics & Mathematical Systems Ser.: Vol. 201). (Illus.). 140p. 1982. 29.00 (*0-387-11550-1*) Spr-Verlag.

***de Boer, R.** Theory of Porous Media: Highlights in Historical Development & Current State. LC 99-51452. (Illus.). xvi, 618p. 2000. 95.00 (*3-540-65982-X*) Spr-Verlag.

De Boer, S. P., et al. Biographical Dictionary of Soviet Dissidents. 1982. lib. bdg. 382.00 (*90-247-2538-0*) Kluwer Academic.

De Boer, T. W. & De Bruyne, R. H. Schelpen Van de Friese Waddeneilanden. (DUT., Illus.). 292p. 1991. 40.00 (*90-73348-21-8*, Pub. by Backhuys Pubs) Balogh.

De Boer, Theodore. The Rationality of Transcendence: Studies in the Philosophy of Emmanuel Levinas. (Amsterdam Studies in Jewish Thought: Vol. 4). x, 191p. 1997. lib. bdg. 60.00 (*90-5063-217-3*, Pub. by Gieben) J Benjamins Pubng Co.

De Boer, Tjitze J. The History of Philosophy in Islam. LC 70-131638. 216p. 1903. reprint ed. 55.00 (*0-403-00525-6*) Scholarly.

De Boisdeffre, Pierre. Pierre Loti: Ses Maisons. (FRE., Illus.). 200p. 1996. pap. 54.95 (*2-86808-099-5*) Intl Scholars.

De Boislandelle, Mahe. Dictionnaire Gestion: Vocabulaire, Outils, Concepts. (FRE.). 1998. 95.00 (*0-320-00383-3*) Fr & Eur.

De Boismont, Alexandre-Jacques-Francois Brierre, see Brierre De Boismont, Alexandre-Jacques-Francois.

De Boissieu, Christian, jt. ed. see Fair, Donald E.

De Boissieu, Marc, et al, eds. Aperiodic, '97: Proceedings of the International Conference on Aperiodic Crystals l'Alpe d'Huez, France 27-31 August, 1997. 750p. 1998. 158.00 (*981-02-3371-X*) World Scientific Pub.

De Bolla, Peter. Harold Bloom. (Critics of the Twentieth Century Ser.). 208p. 1988. text 47.50 (*0-415-00899-9*); pap. text 13.95 (*0-415-00900-6*) Routledge.

De Bolt, Alice, ed. see Shapiro, Shelby.

De Bolt, Nancy. "Starlight, Starlight" The Complete One-to-One Activity Program. LC 98-88464. (Illus.). 75p. 1997. pap. 18.00 (*0-9662054-1-3*) Goshen Care.

De Bolt, Nancy & Kastner, Mary E. "I'm in Here!" Strategies for One-to-One Activities. (Illus.). 77p. 1989. pap. 18.00 (*0-9662054-0-5*) Goshen Care.

De Bona, Maurice, Jr. Atheist Reality & the Brain. LC 95-69709. (Illus.). 60p. 1995. pap. 6.00 (*0-916698-02-5*) Desserco Pub.

— God Rejected: A Summary of Atheistic Thought. LC 75-46088. (Illus.). 125p. (C). 1976. 6.95 (*0-916698-00-9*); pap. 4.95 (*0-916698-01-7*) Desserco Pub.

De Bonald, Louis. On Divorce. Davidson, Nicholas, tr. 120p. (C). 1991. text 34.95 (*0-88738-439-0*) Transaction Pubs.

***De Bondt, Gabe J.** Financial Structure & Monetary Transmission in Europe: A Cross-Country Study. LC 99-87209. 176p. 2000. 75.00 (*1-84064-316-1*) E Elgar.

De Bondt, Werner F. Earnings Forecasts & Share Price Reversals. (Orig.). 1992. pap. text 20.00 (*0-943205-13-1*) RFICFA.

De Bonis, V. Stabilization Policy in an Exchange Rate Union: Transmission, Coordination & Influence on the Union Cohesion. 172p. 1994. 61.95 (*3-7908-0789-3*) Spr-Verlag.

De Bonneville, Francoise. The Book of the Bath. LC 98-65882. (Illus.). 208p. 1998. 60.00 (*0-8478-2134-X*, Pub. by Rizzoli Intl) St Martin.

De Bono, Edward. Atlas of Management Thinking. 1990. pap. 30.00 (*0-14-013776-9*) Intl Ctr Creat Think.

De Bono, Edward. Conflicts: A Better Way to Resolve Them. 1990. 25.00 (*0-317-90564-3*) Intl Ctr Creat Think.

— CoRT Thinking Program: CoRT 1 - Breadth. 80p. 1987. teacher ed. 12.50 (*0-685-17432-8*, Pergamon Pr) Elsevier.

— De Bono's Thinking Course. rev. ed. LC 94-17592. 208p. 1994. 26.95 (*0-8160-3175-4*) Facts on File.

— De Bono's Thinking Course. rev. ed. (Illus.). 224p. 1994. pap. 30.00 (*0-8160-3178-9*) Intl Ctr Creat Think.

— Decision Mate. 3.95 (*0-9615400-1-X*) Intl Ctr Creat Think.

— Edward de Bono Super Mind Pack: Expand Your Thinking Powers with Strategic Games & Mental Exercise. LC 99-182732. 96p. 1998. 29.95 (*0-7894-1973-4*) DK Pub Inc.

— Edward De Bono's Mind Pack. LC 95-19318. (Illus.). 72p. 1995. 29.95 (*1-56458-864-5*, 6-70435) DK Pub Inc.

— Edward de Bono's Mind Pack. LC 95-19318. 1995. 24.95 (*0-7894-0382-X*) DK Pub Inc.

De Bono, Edward. Edward de Bono's Smart Thinking. abr. ed. 1994. 10.95 (*1-55927-239-2*) Audio Renaissance.

De Bono, Edward. The Five-Day Course in Thinking. 162p. 1992. pap. 30.00 (*0-14-013789-0*) Intl Ctr Creat Think.

De Bono, Edward. Future Positive. 1990. pap. 30.00 (*0-14-022293-6*) Intl Ctr Creat Think.

De Bono, Edward. The Happiness Purpose. 272p. 1992. pap. 30.00 (*0-14-013786-6*) Intl Ctr Creat Think.

***De Bono, Edward.** How You Can Be More Interesting. 2000. write for info. (*1-893224-06-6*, Pub. by New Millenn Enter) Login Pubs Consort.

De Bono, Edward. I Am Right You Are Wrong. 320p. 1992. reprint ed. pap. 12.95 (*0-14-012678-3*, Penguin Bks) Viking Penguin.

De Bono, Edward. Lateral Thinking. 1990. pap. 30.00 (*0-14-013779-3*) Intl Ctr Creat Think.

De Bono, Edward. Lateral Thinking: Creativity Step by Step. LC 89-46085. 304p. 1990. pap. 15.00 (*0-06-090325-2*, CN325, Perennial) HarperTrade.

— Masterthinker. (Illus.). 1990. student ed. 99.95 incl. audio (*0-9615400-3-6*) Intl Ctr Creat Think.

De Bono, Edward. Masterthinker's Handbook. 160p. 1990. pap. 30.00 (*0-14-014594-X*) Intl Ctr Creat Think.

De Bono, Edward. New Think. 224p. 1985. mass mkt. 4.95 (*0-380-01426-2*, Avon Bks) Morrow Avon.

***De Bono, Edward.** New Thinking for the New Millennium. 2000. 22.95 (*1-893224-05-8*) New Millenn Enter.

De Bono, Edward. Opportunities. 1990. 25.00 (*0-317-90563-5*) Intl Ctr Creat Think.

De Bono, Edward. Po Beyond Yes & No. 1990. pap. 30.00 (*0-14-013782-3*) Intl Ctr Creat Think.

— The Power of Focused Thinking. 1991. student ed. 99.95 incl. audio (*0-9615400-6-0*) Intl Ctr Creat Think.

De Bono, Edward. Practical Thinking. 1990. 25.00 (*0-317-90560-0*) Intl Ctr Creat Think.

— Serious Creativity: Using the Power of Lateral Thinking to Create New Ideas. LC 91-58498. 288p. 1992. 23.00 (*0-88730-566-0*, HarpBusn) HarpInfo.

De Bono, Edward. Six Thinking Hats. 216p. pap. 30.00 (*0-14-013784-X*) Intl Ctr Creat Think.

***de Bono, Edward.** Six Thinking Hats: An Essential Approach to Business Management from the Creator of Lat. Thinking. 192p. 1999. pap. 14.95 (*0-316-17831-4*, Back Bay) Little.

De Bono, Edward. Sur Petition (Going Beyond Competition) Creating Value Monopolies When Everyone Else is Merely Competing. 224p. 1992. 22.00 (*0-88730-543-1*, HarpBusn) HarpInfo.

— Tactics: The Art & Science of Success. 192p. 1984. 17.95 (*0-316-17790-3*) Little.

— Teach Your Child How to Think. 320p. 1994. pap. 13.95 (*0-14-023830-1*, Penguin Bks) Viking Penguin.

— Teaching Thinking. 1990. 25.00 (*0-317-90562-7*) Intl Ctr Creat Think.

— Teaching Thinking. (Illus.). 272p. 1992. pap. 12.95 (*0-14-013785-8*, Penguin Bks) Viking Penguin.

— Thinking: Skills for Success. 128p. (C). 1990. pap. text 14.95 (*1-56118-048-3*) Paradigm MN.

— Thinking Skills for Success. 128p. (C). 1990. pap., teacher ed. 9.95 (*1-56118-049-1*) Paradigm MN.

— Wordpower. 1990. 25.00 (*0-317-90561-9*) Intl Ctr Creat Think.

De Bont, L. G., jt. auth. see Stegenga, B.

De Bont, Petra. Sulfidation Behaviour of Co & Mo in Y-Type Zeolite. (Illus.). 176p. 1998. pap. 44.50 (*90-407-1646-3*, Pub. by Delft U Pr) Coronet Bks.

De Boo, Max. Enquiring Children, Challenging Teaching. LC 98-4043. (Enriching the Primary Curriculum - Child, Teacher, Context Ser.). 1998. 85.00 (*0-335-20097-4*); pap. 21.95 (*0-335-20096-6*) OpUniv Pr.

De Boodt, M. F., et al. Soil Colloids & Their Associations in Aggregates. LC 89-71019. (NATO ASI Ser.: Vol. 215). (Illus.). 616p. 1990. 155.00 (*0-306-43419-9*, Kluwer Plenum) Kluwer Academic.

De Boor, C. Approximation Theory. LC 86-10846. (Proceedings of Symposia in Applied Mathematics Ser.: Vol. 36). 131p. 1986. pap. 30.00 (*0-8218-0098-1*, PSAPM/36) Am Math.

De Boor, C. A Practical Guide to Splines. (Applied Mathematical Sciences Ser.: Vol. 27). (Illus.). 1994. 59.95 (*0-387-90356-9*) Spr-Verlag.

De Boor, C. W., jt. auth. see Conte, S. D.

D

An Asterisk (*) at the beginning of an entry indicates that the title is appearing for the first time.

*__De Boor, Carl.__ A Practical Guide to Splines. 2nd ed. LC 99-42676. (Applied Mathematical Sciences Ser.). 2000. write for info. (*0-387-98922-6*) Spr-Verlag.

De Boor, Carl, et al. Box Splines: Applied Mathematical Sciences Ser. (Vol. 98). (Illus.). 200p. 1993. write for info. (*3-540-94101-0*) Spr-Verlag.

— Box Splines: Applied Mathematical Sciences Ser. LC 93-5263. (Vol. 98). (Illus.). 200p. 1993. 49.95 (*0-387-94101-0*) Spr-Verlag.

De Boor, Carl G., ed. see Nicephorus.

De Boor, Helmut & Wisniewski, Roswitha. Mittelhochdeutsche Grammatik. 208p. 1997. text 14.00 (*3-11-015742-X*) De Gruyter.

De Booy, Theodoor N. Virgin Islands, Our New Possessions & the British Islands. LC 72-109318. (Illus.). 292p. 1970. reprint ed. lib. bdg. 35.00 (*0-8371-3584-2*, BVI&, Greenwood Pr) Greenwood.

De Borhegyi, Stephen F. & Boyd, E. El Santuario de Chimayo. (Illus.). 32p. 1987. pap. 3.95 (*0-941270-09-2*) Ancient City Pr.

De Borja Moll Casasnovas, Francesc. Catalan-Castilian Spanish, Castilian Spanish-Catalan Dictionary: Diccionari Catala-Castella I Castella-Catala. 7th ed. (CAT & SPA.). 1991. write for info. (*0-7859-5038-9*) Fr & Eur.

De Borms, C. T., jt. auth. see Bailly, H. C.

De Boron, Robert. Joseph of Arimathea. pap. 10.95 (*0-85440-426-0*, 1506, Pub. by R Steiner Pr) Anthroposophic.

De Borrero, Beatriz Botero, see Botero de Borrero, Beatriz.

De Borrero, Martha O. Botero, see Botero de Borrero, Beatriz & Botero de Borrero, Martha O.

De Borst, R., et al, eds. Computational Modelling of Concrete Structures: Proceedings of the Euro-C Conference 1998, Badgastein, 31 March-3 April, 1998, 2 vols. (Illus.). 578p. (C). 1998. text 132.00 (*90-5410-946-7*, Pub. by A A Balkema) Ashgate Pub Co.

De Boschere, Jean. La Fleur et Son Parfun. (FRE., Illus.). 168p. 1995. pap. 54.95 (*2-86808-003-0*) Intl Scholars.

De Bot, Kees, et al, eds. Foreign Language Research in Cross-Cultural Perspective. LC 91-6804. (Studies in Bilingualism: Vol. 2). xii, 275p. 1991. pap. 29.95 (*1-55619-541-9*) J Benjamins Pubng Co.

De Bot, Kees, jt. ed. see Bongaerts, Theo.

*__De Botton, Alain.__ The Consolations of Philosophy. LC 99-52188. (Illus.). 288p. 2000. 22.95 (*0-679-44276-6*) Pantheon.

De Botton, Alain. How Proust Can Change Your Life: Not a Novel. LC 96-47106. (Illus.). 160p. 1997. 19.95 (*0-679-44275-8*) Pantheon.

— How Proust Can Change Your Life: Not a Novel. 208p. 1998. pap. 12.00 (*0-679-77915-9*) Vin Bks.

— Kiss & Tell. 1995. 21.00 (*0-614-96270-6*, Picador USA) St Martin.

— Kiss & Tell. 272p. 1997. pap. 13.00 (*0-312-15561-1*) St Martin.

— On Love. LC 92-24888. 240p. 1993. pap. 10.00 (*0-8021-3409-2*, Grove) Grove-Atltic.

— The Romantic Movement. 336p. 1996. pap. 13.00 (*0-312-14403-2*, Picador USA) St Martin.

De Bougainville, Hyacinthe. Journal de la Navigation Autour du Globe de la Fregate Thetis et de la Corvette l'Esperance Atlas. (Discovery of the Pacific & Australia Ser.). (FRE., Illus.). 72p. 1998. reprint ed. pap. 720.00 (*1-85297-004-9*, Pub. by Archival Facs) St Mut.

De Bougainville, Louis-Antoine. Voyage au Tour du Monde par le Fregate du Roi la Boudeuse. (FRE.). 1982. pap. 16.95 (*0-7859-1958-9*, 2070373851) Fr & Eur.

De, Bougraff Esteban W. Smith & Wollensky Quintessential Steak Book. LC 99-38897. 1999. text 27.50 (*1-56799-797-X*, Friedman-Fairfax) M Friedman Pub Grp Inc.

De Boulainvilliers, H. The Life of Mahomet. 416p. 1983. 250.00 (*1-85077-005-0*, Pub. by Darf Pubs Ltd) St Mut.

De Boulogne, Duchenne. The Mechanism of Human Facial Expression. Cuthbertson, R. Andrew, tr. (Studies in Emotion & Social Interaction). (Illus.). 304p. (C). 1990. text 64.95 (*0-521-36392-6*) Cambridge U Pr.

De Bourbon Busset, Jacques. L' Amour Durable. (Journal Ser.: Vol. III). (FRE.). 448p. 1973. pap. 10.95 (*0-7859-1752-7*, 2070364275) Fr & Eur.

— Les Aveux Infideles. (FRE.). 1972. pap. 10.95 (*0-7859-2196-6*, 207036268X) Fr & Eur.

— Lettre a Laurence. (FRE.). 118p. 1989. pap. 10.95 (*0-7859-2110-9*, 2070381080) Fr & Eur.

— Le Lion Bat la Campagne. (FRE.). 276p. 1986. pap. 11.95 (*0-7859-2027-7*, 2070377121) Fr & Eur.

— La Nature Est un Talisman, Journal I. (FRE.). 1978. pap. 10.95 (*0-7859-1866-3*, 2070369943) Fr & Eur.

De Bourgoing, Pascale. Colors. LC 91-13134. (First Discovery Book). (Illus.). 24p. (J). (ps-3). 1991. pap. 11.95 (*0-590-45236-3*, Cartwheel) Scholastic Inc.

— Egg. LC 91-25021. (First Discovery Book). (Illus.). 24p. (J). (ps-3). 1992. 11.95 (*0-590-45266-5*, Cartwheel) Scholastic Inc.

— Fruit. (First Discovery Book). (Illus.). 24p. (J). 1991. pap. 11.95 (*0-590-45233-9*, Cartwheel) Scholastic Inc.

— Ladybug & Other Insects. LC 91-15294. (First Discovery Book). (Illus.). 24p. (J). (ps-3). 1991. 11.95 (*0-590-45235-5*, Cartwheel) Scholastic Inc.

— Tree. (First Discovery Book). (Illus.). 24p. (J). (ps-3). 1992. 11.95 (*0-590-45265-7*, Cartwheel) Scholastic Inc.

— Vegetable in the Garden. (First Discovery Book). (Illus.). 24p. (J). (ps-2). 1994. 11.95 (*0-590-48326-9*, Cartwheel) Scholastic Inc.

— Weather. LC 91-14614. (Illus.). 24p. (J). (ps-3). 1991. 11.95 (*0-590-45234-7*, Cartwheel) Scholastic Inc.

*__De Bourgoing, Pascale & Jeunesse, Gallimard.__ Dogs. LC 98-22870. (First Discovery Book). (Illus.). 24p. (J). (ps-2). 1999. 12.95 (*0-590-87608-2*) Scholastic Inc.

de Bousingen, Denis Durand, see Rogers, Arthur.

de Bousingen, Denis Durand, see Rogers, Arthur & Durand de Bousingen, Denis.

De Bouw, R., et al, eds. European Communities Oil & Gas Technological Development Projects: Third Status Report. (C). 1987. lib. bdg. 184.00 (*0-86010-976-3*, Pub. by Graham & Trotman) Kluwer Academic.

De Boysson-Bardies, Benedict. How Language Comes to Children: From Birth to Two Years. DeBevoise, M.B., tr. from FRE. LC 98-17956. (ENG & ACE., Illus.). 256p. (J). 1999. 27.50 (*0-262-02453-5*, Bradford Bks) MIT Pr.

De Boysson-Bardies, Benedict, et al, eds. Developmental Neurocognition - Speech & Face Processing in the First Year of Life: Proceedings of the NATO Advanced Research Workshop. LC 93-9598. (NATO Advanced Study Institutes Series D, Behavioural & Social Sciences: No. 69). 516p. (C). 1993. text 285.50 (*0-7923-2188-X*) Kluwer Academic.

De Bra, Lemuel. Ways That Are Wary. LC 79-101796. (Short Story Index Reprint Ser.). 1977. 20.95 (*0-8369-3184-X*) Ayer.

De Brabander, Guido L. Regional Specialization, Employment & Economic Growth in Belgium from 1846 to 1970. Bruchey, Stuart, ed. LC 80-2797. (Dissertations in European Economic History Ser.). (Illus.). 1981. lib. bdg. 30.95 (*0-405-13981-0*) Ayer.

De Brahm, William G. The Atlantic Pilot. De Vorsey, Louis, ed. LC 73-18036. (Floridiana Facsimile & Reprint Ser.). (Illus.). 112p. 1974. reprint ed. 16.95 (*0-8130-0366-0*) U Press Fla.

*__de Brakelond, Jocelin.__ Chronicle of the Abbey of Bury St. Edmunds. Greenway, Diana & Sayers, Jane, trs. (Illus.). 182p. 1998. pap. 11.95 (*0-19-283895-4*) OUP.

*__De Brandao, Fiama H.__ Landscape Being Born: Selected Poems. 200p. 2000. pap. 10.95 (*1-892295-77-6*) Green Integer.

De Brandt. The Nature Log. 1998. pap. 7.95 (*1-885061-54-4*) Adventure Pubns.

De Branges, L., et al, eds. Topics in Operator Theory. (Operator Theory Ser.: Vol. 48). 464p. 1990. 139.00 (*0-8176-2532-1*) Birkhauser.

De Brantome, Pierre. Les Dames Galantes. (FRE.). 704p. 1981. pap. 13.95 (*0-7859-2219-9*, 207037260X) Fr & Eur.

— Recueil des Dames: Poesies et Tombeaux. Vaucheret, Jacques, ed. (FRE.). 1991. lib. bdg. 185.00 (*0-7859-3897-4*) Fr & Eur.

De Brasunas, Anton & Stansbury, E. E., eds. Symposium on Corrosion Fundamentals: A Series of Lectures Presented at the University of Tennessee Corrosion Conference at Knoxville on March 1-3, 1955. LC 56-13073. 261p. reprint ed. pap. 81.00 (*0-608-11397-2*, 202221200025) Bks Demand.

De Brath, Stanley, tr. see Geley, Gustave.

De Brath, Stanley, tr. see Richet, Charles.

De Bray, Emile F. A Frenchman in Search of Franklin: De Bray's Arctic Journal, 1852-54. Barr, William, ed. & tr. by. from FRE. 400p. 1992. text 35.00 (*0-8020-2813-6*) U of Toronto Pr.

De Breath, Stanley. Psychic Philosophy As the Foundation of a Religion of Natural Law, 1921. 880p. 1998. reprint ed. pap. 27.50 (*0-7661-0491-5*) Kessinger Pub.

*__de Breffny, Brian, ed.__ The Irish World: The History & Cultural Achievements of the Irish People. 2nd ed. LC 00-101039. (Illus.). 296p. 2001. reprint ed. pap. 34.95 (*0-500-28241-2*, Pub. by Thames Hudson) Norton.

De Bremaecker, Jean-Claude. Geophysics: The Earth's Interior. LC 90-48558. 352p. (C). 1991. reprint ed. lib. bdg. 51.95 (*0-89464-536-6*) Krieger.

De Bremont Anna, Contesse. Oscar Wilde & His Mother. LC 72-2155. (English Biography Ser.: No. 31). 1972. reprint ed. lib. bdg. 75.00 (*0-8383-1457-0*) M S G Haskell Hse.

De Bresson, Chris. Understanding Technological Change. (Illus.). 272p. 1987. 48.99 (*0-920057-26-8*, Pub. by Black Rose); pap. 19.99 (*0-920057-27-6*, Pub. by Black Rose) Consort Bk Sales.

De Bretteville, Sheila L., jt. auth. see Nodal, Al.

De Brinkerhoff, Woo, ed. see Steiger, David G. & Steiger, E. Janet.

De Brissac, Elvire. Grabuge et l'Indomptable Amelie. (Folio - Cadet Rouge Ser.: No. 212). (FRE., Illus.). 144p. (J). (gr. 3-7). 1990. pap. 11.95 (*2-07-031212-7*) Schoenhof.

de Brissac, Gilles & Van Zuylen, Gabrielle. Apremont: A French Folly. LC 99-30843. (Small Books of Great Gardens Ser.). 79p. 1999. text 18.95 (*0-86565-204-X*) Vendome.

De Brissiere. Caribbean Cookery. pap. 11.95 (*0-87557-100-X*) Saphrograph.

De Britto, Marisa M. J. Michaelis S. O. S. Ingles, Guia Pratico de Gramatica. 386p. 1995. 24.95 (*0-7859-9312-6*) Fr & Eur.

De Brodtkorb, Milka K. Non-Metaliferous Strata Bound. 332p. (gr. 13). 1989. mass mkt. 97.95 (*0-442-20522-8*) Chapman & Hall.

De Broe, M. E. Clinical Nephrotoxins: Renal Injury from Drugs & Chemical. LC 97-11284. 528p. 1997. lib. bdg. 265.00 (*0-7923-3611-9*) Kluwer Academic.

*__De Broe, M. E. & Helbert, M. J. F., eds.__ Biology of Tubulo-Interstitial Cells, No. 6. (Experimental Nephrology Ser.: Vol. 7, Nos. 5-6). (Illus.). iv, 146p. 1999. pap. 39.25 (*3-8055-6977-7*) S Karger.

De Broe, Marc E., ed. Aluminum & Renal Failure. (C). 1990. lib. bdg. 226.00 (*0-7923-0347-4*) Kluwer Academic.

— Prevention in Nephrology. (Developments in Nephrology Ser.). 120p. 1991. text 102.00 (*0-7923-0951-0*) Kluwer Academic.

De Broe, Marc E., et al, eds. Bio-Incompatibility & Dialysis. (Contributions to Nephrology Ser.: Vol. 62). (Illus.). viii, 152p. 1988. 111.50 (*3-8055-4695-5*) S Karger.

De Broe, Marc E. & Van de Vyver, F. L., eds. Bone & Renal Failure. (Contributions to Nephrology Ser.: Vol. 64). (Illus.). vi, 182p. 1988. 29.75 (*3-8055-4738-2*) S Karger.

De Broglie, Louis. Heisenberg's Uncertainties & the Probabilistic Interpretation of Wave Mechanics: With Critical Notes of the Author. 320p. (C). 1990. lib. bdg. 175.00 (*0-7923-0929-4*, Pub. by Kluwer Academic) Kluwer Academic.

— Revolution in Physics: A Non-Mathematical Survey of Quanta. Niemeyer, Ralph W., tr. LC 76-95113. 310p. 1970. reprint ed. lib. bdg. 65.00 (*0-8371-2582-0*, BRRP, Greenwood Pr) Greenwood.

De Bromhead, Toni. Looking Two Ways: Documentary Film's Relationship with Reality & Cinema. 148p. (C). 1996. pap. 30.00 (*87-89825-13-6*, Pub. by Intervention Pr) Smyrna.

De Brossard, Sebastien. Dictionnaire de la Musique. 3rd fac. ed. (FRE.). 400p. 1992. pap. 225.00 (*0-7859-8049-0*, 2826608851) Fr & Eur.

*__De Brouwer, Gordon.__ Asia Pacific Financial Deregulation. LC 99-22498. (Pacific Trade & Development Conference Ser.). 1999. pap. write for info. (*0-415-20843-2*) Routledge.

De Brouwer, Gordon. Financial Integration in East Asia. LC 98-33985. (Trade & Development Ser.). (Illus.). 240p. (C). 1999. text 54.95 (*0-521-65148-4*) Cambridge U Pr.

*__De Brouwer, Gordon, et al.__ Asia Pacific Financial Deregulation. LC 99-22498. 1999. write for info. (*0-415-20842-4*) Routledge.

De Broux, Jane, jt. auth. see Demco, Inc. Staff.

De Bruijn. Transesophageal Echocardiography. 1991. 133.00 (*0-316-17816-0*, Little Brwn Med Div) Lppncott W & W.

De Bruijn, J. T. Persian Sufi Poetry: An Introduction to the Mystical Use of Classical Perisan Poems. LC 97-217472. 228p. 1997. 65.00 (*0-7007-0674-7*, Pub. by Curzon Pr Ltd) Paul & Co Pubs.

— Persian Sufi Poetry: An Introduction to the Mystical Use of Classical Persian Poems. LC 97-217472. (Curzon Sufi Ser.: No. 1). 228p. (C). 1997. pap. 25.00 (*0-7007-0312-8*, Pub. by Curzon Pr Ltd) Paul & Co Pubs.

de Bruijn, Jan, jt. ed. see Van Der Kooi, Cornelis.

de Bruijn, Jan, ed. see van der Wall, Ernestine, et al.

De Bruijn, Jeanne & Cyba, Eva, eds. Gender & Organizations - Changing Perspectives: Theoretical Considerations & Empirical Findings. LC 95-109060. 200p. 1995. pap. 25.00 (*90-5383-312-9*, Pub. by VU Univ Pr) Paul & Co Pubs.

De Bruijn, N. G. Asymptotic Methods in Analysis. 224p. (C). 1981. reprint ed. pap. 7.95 (*0-486-64221-6*) Dover.

De Bruijn, Norbert P. & Clements, Fiona M., eds. Intraoperative Use of Echocardiography. LC 91-6368. (Society of Cardiovascular Anesthesiologists Monograph Ser.). (Illus.). 242p. 1991. reprint ed. pap. 75.10 (*0-608-07230-3*, 206745500009) Bks Demand.

De Bruijne, G. A., jt. ed. see Baud, I. S. A.

De Bruin, A., et al, eds. Health Interview Surveys: Towards International Harmonization of Methods & Instruments. LC 96-201281. (Regional Publications, European Ser.: Vol. 58). 161p. (Orig.). 1996. pap. 35.10 (*92-890-1322-2*, 1310058) World Health.

De Bruin-Cousins, A. M., tr. see Thiel, J. H.

De Bruin, E. J., jt. ed. see Mulder, C. L.

De Bruin, Jacqualyn. Apples & Tigers: Collected Poems. LC 98-92083. 80p. 1998. 19.95 (*0-9667253-0-1*) Linden Cottage.

De Bruin, Louise, ed. see Casey, Mary.

De Bruin, Ronald. Digital Video Broadcasting: Technology, Standards, & Regulations. LC 98-51785. 1998. 79.00 (*0-89006-743-0*) Artech Hse.

De Bruin, Sandra. Actor's Interview Log: Where Am I Going? Where Have I Been? 101p. 1998. spiral bd. 9.95 (*0-9668522-0-6*) Break-A-Leg Bks.

*__De Brun, Julio & Luders, Rolf, eds.__ Macroeconomic Policy & the Exchange Rate. LC 99-32276. (Illus.). xii, 292p. 1999. pap. 19.95 (*0-9656930-5-8*) Intl Ctr Economic.

De Brunhoff, Barbara. Basile et les Papillons. 29p. (J). (gr. k-5). 1990. 27.95 (*0-7859-8792-4*) Fr & Eur.

de Brunhoff, Jean. ABC de Babar. 46p. (J). (gr. k-5). 1978. 24.95 (*0-7859-8776-2*) Fr & Eur.

— Babar & His Children. Haas, Merle, tr. Orig. Title: Babar en famille. (Illus.). (J). (ps). 1966. 14.00 (*0-394-80577-1*, Pub. by Random Bks Yng Read) Random.

— Babar au Cirque. (Illus.). 16p. (J). 1974. 4.95 (*0-686-54121-9*, FC241) Fr & Eur.

— Babar en Famille.Tr. of Babar & His Children. 26p. (J). 1975. 15.95 (*0-7859-0672-X*, FC589) Fr & Eur.

— Babar et le Crocodile. 16p. (J). 1975. 4.95 (*0-7859-0673-8*, FC242) Fr & Eur.

— Babar et le Pere Noel.Tr. of Babar & Father Christmas. 29p. (J). 1975. 15.95 (*0-7859-0674-6*, FC582) Fr & Eur.

— Babar Retrouve Ses Amis. (J). (gr. k-5). 1994. pap. 17.95 (*0-7859-8790-8*) Fr & Eur.

*__de Brunhoff, Jean.__ Bonjour, Babar! (Illus.). 288p. (J). (ps-3). 2000. 29.95 (*0-375-81060-9*, Pub. by Random Bks Yng Read) Random.

de Brunhoff, Jean. Le Couronnement de Babar. 16p. (J). 1975. 4.95 (*0-7859-0930-3*, FC251) Fr & Eur.

— L' Enfance de Babar. 16p. (J). 1975. 4.95 (*0-686-54127-8*) Fr & Eur.

— Histoire de Babar, le Petite Elephant. (Illus.). 32p. (J). 18.95 (*0-686-54129-4*, FC593) Fr & Eur.

— The Story of Babar. (Illus.). (J). (ps). 1966. 14.00 (*0-394-80575-5*, Pub. by Random Bks Yng Read) Random.

— The Story of Babar. (Illus.). (J). (ps). 1967. lib. bdg. 13.99 (*0-394-90575-X*, Pub. by Random Bks Yng Read) Random.

— Travels of Babar. (Illus.). (J). (ps). 1966. 14.00 (*0-394-80576-3*, Pub. by Random Bks Yng Read) Random.

— Les Vacances de Zephyr. 40p. (J). 1983. 24.95 (*0-7859-8797-5*) Fr & Eur.

— Vive le Roi Babar. 20p. (J). 1976. 4.95 (*0-7859-0675-4*, FC253) Fr & Eur.

— Le Voyage de Babar. (FRE & SPA., Illus.). (J). bds. 15.95 (*0-685-11626-3*) Fr & Eur.

— Le Voyage de Babar. 27p. (J). 1975. 15.95 (*0-7859-0676-2*, FC581) Fr & Eur.

de Brunhoff, Jean & de Brunhoff, Laurent. Babar a la Ferme. 48p. (J). (gr. k-5). 1990. 17.95 (*0-7859-8778-9*) Fr & Eur.

— Babar a la Fete. 48p. (J). (gr. k-5). 1990. 17.95 (*0-7859-8779-7*) Fr & Eur.

— Babar a la Maison. 48p. (J). (gr. k-5). 1990. 17.95 (*0-7859-8780-0*) Fr & Eur.

— Babar a la Ville. 48p. (J). (gr. k-5). 1990. 17.95 (*0-7859-8781-9*) Fr & Eur.

— Babar en Foret. 48p. (J). (gr. k-5). 1990. 17.95 (*0-7859-8782-7*) Fr & Eur.

— Babar en Vacances. 48p. (J). (gr. k-5). 1990. 17.95 (*0-7859-8783-5*) Fr & Eur.

— Babar Fait Ses Courses. (Illus.). 48p. (J). (gr. k-5). 1991. 17.95 (*0-7859-8788-6*) Fr & Eur.

— Babar Visite Son Royaume. 48p. (J). (gr. k-5). 1991. 17.95 (*0-614-02958-9*) Fr & Eur.

— Le Grand Album de Babar. 142p. (J). (gr. k-5). 1982. 39.95 (*0-7859-8793-2*) Fr & Eur.

de Brunhoff, Jean & Lokvig, Tor. Le Livre Anime de Voyage de Babar. (J). (gr. k-5). 1991. pap. 39.95 (*0-7859-8795-9*) Fr & Eur.

de Brunhoff, Laurent. L' Anniversaire de Babar. 28p. (J). 1975. 17.95 (*0-7859-0677-0*, M11806) Fr & Eur.

— Les Aventures de Babar. 18p. (J). 1977. 15.95 (*0-686-54134-0*) Fr & Eur.

— Babar: Le Livre des Couleurs. (J). (gr. k-5). 1985. 24.95 (*0-7859-8777-0*) Fr & Eur.

— Babar a Celesteville. 16p. (J). 1974. 4.95 (*0-7859-0678-9*, F12062) Fr & Eur.

— Babar a la Fete de Celesteville. (J). (gr. k-5). 1975. pap. 17.95 (*0-614-02957-0*) Fr & Eur.

— Babar a la Mer. (FRE.). (J). (gr. 2-3). 15.95 (*0-685-11023-0*) Fr & Eur.

*__de Brunhoff, Laurent.__ Babar a New York. (FRE., Illus.). (ps up). 1999. 13.95 (*2-01-002552-0*) Distribks Inc.

de Brunhoff, Laurent. Babar a New York. (FRE., Illus.). (J). (gr. 4-6). 1975. bds. 15.95 (*0-7859-5281-0*, 2010025520) Fr & Eur.

— Babar & the Ghost. LC 85-11841. (Step into Reading Ser.: A Step 2 Book). (Illus.). 48p. (J). (ps-3). 1986. pap. 3.99 (*0-394-87908-2*, Pub. by Random Bks Yng Read) Random.

— Babar & the Ghost. (Step into Reading Ser.: A Step 2 Book). (J). (gr. 1-3). 1986. 8.70 (*0-606-00847-0*, Pub. by Turtleback) Demco.

*__de Brunhoff, Laurent.__ Babar & the Succotash Bird. LC 00-21031. (Illus.). 38p. (J). 2000. 16.95 (*0-8109-5700-0*, Pub. by Abrams) Time Warner.

de Brunhoff, Laurent. Babar Artiste Peintre. (FRE.). (J). (gr. 2-3). 1991. 15.95 (*0-7859-5285-3*, 209201417X) Fr & Eur.

— Babar au Cirque. (J). (gr. 2-3). pap. 15.95 (*0-685-33966-1*, FC241) Fr & Eur.

— Babar aux Sports d'Hiver. (Illus.). 20p. (J). 1976. 4.95 (*0-7859-0679-7*, FC250) Fr & Eur.

— Babar Aviateur. 16p. (J). 1974. 4.95 (*0-7859-0680-0*, M5989) Fr & Eur.

— Babar Campeur. 16p. (J). 1974. 4.95 (*0-686-54138-3*) Fr & Eur.

— Babar Chez le Docteur. (FRE.). (J). (gr. 2-3). 15.95 (*0-685-28425-5*) Fr & Eur.

— Babar dans l'Ile aux Oiseaux. 29p. (J). 15.95 (*0-7859-0681-9*, F2002) Fr & Eur.

*__de Brunhoff, Laurent.__ Babar Dans L'Ile Aux Oiseaux. (FRE., Illus.). (ps up). 1999. 14.95 (*2-01-002547-4*) Distribks Inc.

de Brunhoff, Laurent. Babar en Amerique. 23p. (J). 1975. 15.95 (*0-686-54140-5*) Fr & Eur.

— Babar en Amerique. (FRE., Illus.). (J). (ps up). 1999. 13.95 (*2-01-002553-9*) Hachette.

— Babar en Ballon. (FRE.). (J). (gr. 2-3). 15.95 (*0-685-28422-0*) Fr & Eur.

*__de Brunhoff, Laurent.__ Babar En Famille. (FRE., Illus.). (ps up). 1999. 13.95 (*2-01-002516-4*) Distribks Inc.

de Brunhoff, Laurent. Babar en Promenade. (FRE.). (J). (gr. 2-3). 15.95 (*0-685-11026-5*) Fr & Eur.

— Babar et ce coquin d'Arthur. (FRE., Illus.). (J). (gr. 4-6). bds. 15.95 (*0-685-11027-3*) Fr & Eur.

— Babar et la Vieille Dame. (J). (gr. 2-3). pap. 15.95 (*0-7859-0614-2*, FC254) Fr & Eur.

— Babar et le Docteur.Tr. of Babar & the Doctor. 16p. (J). 1975. 4.95 (*0-686-54141-3*) Fr & Eur.

— Babar et le Fantome. 32p. (J). (gr. k-5). 1981. pap. 17.95 (*0-7859-8784-3*) Fr & Eur.

*__de Brunhoff, Laurent.__ Babar Et Le Pere Noel. (FRE., Illus.). (ps up). 1999. 13.95 (*2-01-002549-0*) Distribks Inc.

de Brunhoff, Laurent. Babar et le Prof. Grifaton. (FRE.). (J). (gr. 2-4). 15.95 (*0-685-28434-4*) Fr & Eur.

*__de Brunhoff, Laurent.__ Babar Et Le Professeur Grifton. (FRE., Illus.). (ps-3). 1999. 13.95 (*2-01-002550-4*) Distribks Inc.

— Babar et le Wouly-Wouly. (FRE., Illus.). (ps up). 1999. 13.95 (*2-01-004209-3*) Distribks Inc.

D

An Asterisk (*) at the beginning of an entry indicates that the title is appearing for the first time.

de Brunhoff, Laurent. Babar et le Wouly-Wouly. 26p. (J). 15.95 (*0-7859-0682-7*, M11805) Fr & Eur.
— Babar et les Quatre Voleurs. 28p. (J). (gr. k-5). 1979. pap. 17.95 (*0-7859-8785-1*) Fr & Eur.
— Babar et Moi. (J). (gr. k-5). 1987. 24.95 (*0-7859-8786-X*) Fr & Eur.
— Babar et Sa Famille. 26p. (J). 1976. 4.95 (*0-686-54143-X*) Fr & Eur.
— Babar et Sa Petite Fille Isabelle. (J). (gr. k-5). 1988. 24.95 (*0-7859-8787-8*) Fr & Eur.
— Babar et Ses Amis a la Ferme. 48p. (J). (gr. k-5). 19.95 (*0-7859-8805-X*) Fr & Eur.
— Babar et Ses Amis a la Fete. 48p. (J). (gr. k-5). 19.95 (*0-7859-8806-8*) Fr & Eur.
— Babar et Ses Amis a la Maison. 48p. (J). 19.95 (*0-7859-8804-1*) Fr & Eur.
— Babar et Ses Amis a la Ville. 48p. (J). (gr. k-5). 19.95 (*0-7859-8809-2*) Fr & Eur.
— Babar et Ses Amis a L'Ecole. 48p. (J). (gr. k-5). 19.95 (*0-7859-8802-5*) Fr & Eur.
— Babar et Ses Amis au Spectacle. 48p. (J). 19.95 (*0-7859-8803-3*) Fr & Eur.
— Babar et Ses Amis en Foret. 48p. (J). (gr. k-5). 19.95 (*0-7859-8811-4*) Fr & Eur.
— Babar et Ses Amis en Vacances. 48p. (J). (gr. k-5). 19.95 (*0-7859-8808-4*) Fr & Eur.
— Babar et Ses Amis Font les Courses. 48p. (J). (gr. k-5). 19.95 (*0-7859-8810-6*) Fr & Eur.
— Babar et Ses Amis Visitent le Royaume. 48p. (J). (gr. k-5). 19.95 (*0-7859-8807-6*) Fr & Eur.
— Babar et ses Enfants. (FRE.). (J). (gr. 2-3). 15.95 (*0-685-28436-0*) Fr & Eur.
— Babar Fait Du Ski. (FRE.). (J). (gr. 2-3). 14.95 (*0-685-11029-X*) Fr & Eur.
— Babar Jardinier. (FRE.). (J). (gr. 2-3). 15.95 (*0-685-11030-3*) Fr & Eur.
— Babar le Livre des Chiffres. (J). (gr. k-5). 1986. 24.95 (*0-7859-8789-4*) Fr & Eur.
de Brunhoff, Laurent. Babar Learns to Cook. (Random House Pictureback Ser.). (J). 1989. 8.45 (*0-606-12173-0*, Pub. by Turtleback) Demco.
de Brunhoff, Laurent. Babar les 500 Premiers Mots. 48p. (J). (gr. k-5). 19.95 (*0-7859-8812-2*) Fr & Eur.
— Babar Patissier. 16p. (J). 1975. 4.95 (*0-686-54144-8*) Fr & Eur.
— Babar Raconte Flore Reporter. 48p. (J). (gr. k-5). 19.95 (*0-7859-8813-0*) Fr & Eur.
— Babar Raconte Halte a la Pollution. 48p. (J). (gr. k-5). 19.95 (*0-7859-8816-5*) Fr & Eur.
— Babar Raconte la Course a la Lune. 48p. (J). (gr. k-5). 19.95 (*0-7859-8820-3*) Fr & Eur.
— Babar Raconte l'Affaire de la Couronne. 48p. (J). (gr. k-5). 19.95 (*0-7859-8818-1*) Fr & Eur.
— Babar Raconte l'Arrivee du Bebe Elephant. 48p. (J). (gr. k-5). 19.95 (*0-7859-8815-7*) Fr & Eur.
— Babar Raconte le Fantome. 48p. (J). (gr. k-5). 19.95 (*0-7859-8819-X*) Fr & Eur.
— Babar Raconte le Meilleur Ami des Elephants. 48p. (J). (gr. k-5). 19.95 (*0-7859-8823-8*) Fr & Eur.
— Babar Raconte le Pianiste. 48p. (J). (gr. k-5). 19.95 (*0-7859-8822-X*) Fr & Eur.
— Babar Raconte le Plus Beau Cadeau du Monde. 48p. (J). (gr. k-5). 19.95 (*0-7859-8821-1*) Fr & Eur.
— Babar Raconte Que la Fete Continue. 48p. (J). (gr. k-5). 19.95 (*0-7859-8824-6*) Fr & Eur.
— Babar Raconte un Diner Chez Rataxes. 48p. (J). (gr. k-5). 19.95 (*0-7859-8817-3*) Fr & Eur.
— Babar Raconte Zephir Fait le Singe. 48p. (J). (gr. k-5). 19.95 (*0-7859-8814-9*) Fr & Eur.
— Babar s'Amuse Avec les Lettres et les Chiffres. 48p. (J). (gr. k-5). 19.95 (*0-614-02959-7*) Fr & Eur.
— Babar Saves the Day. LC 76-11684. (Pictureback Ser.). (Illus.). 32p. (J). (ps-3). 1976. pap. 3.25 (*0-394-83341-4*, Pub. by Random Bks Yng Read) Random.
— Babar Sur la Planete Molle. (J). (gr. k-5). 1980. pap. 17.95 (*0-7859-8791-6*) Fr & Eur.
— Babar the King. (Illus.). (J). (ps-3). 1966. 14.00 (*0-394-80580-1*, Pub. by Random Bks Yng Read) Random.
— Babar's Castle. Haas, Merle, tr. (Illus.). (J). (ps). 1994. lib. bdg. 5.99 (*0-394-90586-5*, Pub. by Random Bks Yng Read) Random.
— Babar's Little Circus Star. LC 87-14149. (Step into Reading Ser.: A Step 1 Book). (J). (ps-1). 1988. 9.19 (*0-606-03720-9*, Pub. by Turtleback) Demco.
de Brunhoff, Laurent. Babars Myst. unabridged ed. LC 78-741042. (J). 1989. audio 9.95 (*1-55994-030-1*, CPN 1583, Caedmon) HarperAudio.
— Chateau de Babar. (FRE., Illus.). (ps-3). 1999. 13.95 (*2-01-002515-6*) Distribks Inc.
de Brunhoff, Laurent. Chateau du Roi Babar. (FRE.). (J). (gr. 3-8). 15.95 (*0-685-11078-8*) Fr & Eur.
— Le Couronnement de Babar. (FRE.). (J). (gr. 2-3). 4.95 (*0-685-28420-4*) Fr & Eur.
— Enfance de Babar. (FRE.). (J). (gr. 2-3). 4.95 (*0-685-28421-2*) Fr & Eur.
— La Fete de Celesteville. (J). (gr. 4-6). 15.95 (*0-685-33969-6*) Fr & Eur.
— Histoire de Babar.Tr. of Story of Babar. (FRE.). (J). (gr. 2-4). 15.95 (*0-685-28435-2*) Fr & Eur.
— Je Parle Allemand avec Babar. (FRE., Illus.). (J). (gr. 4-6). 15.95 (*0-685-11271-3*) Fr & Eur.
— Je Parle Anglais avec Babar. (FRE., Illus.). (J). (gr. 4-6). 15.95 (*0-685-11272-1*) Fr & Eur.
— Je Parle Espagnol avec Babar. (FRE., Illus.). (J). (gr. 4-6). 15.95 (*0-685-11273-X*) Fr & Eur.
— Je Parle Italien avec Babar. (FRE.). (J). (gr. 4-6). 7.95 (*0-685-11274-8*) Fr & Eur.
— Une Journee de Babar. 8p. (J). (gr. k-5). 1985. 14.95. (*0-7859-8794-0*) Fr & Eur.
— Meet Babar & His Family. LC 73-2445. (Illus.). 32p. (J). (ps-1). 1973. pap. 3.25 (*0-394-82682-5*, Pub. by Random Bks Yng Read) Random.
— La Petite Boite Babar: Le Feu, l'Eau, l'Air, la Terre. 192p. (J). (gr. k-5). 1980. 39.95 (*0-7859-8796-7*) Fr & Eur.
— Le Roi Babar.Tr. of Babar the King. (FRE.). (J). (gr. 4-6). 1975. 15.95 (*0-685-11533-X*) Fr & Eur.
***de Brunhoff, Laurent.** Roi Babar. (FRE., Illus.). (ps up). 1999. 13.95 (*2-01-002517-2*) Distribks Inc.
de Brunhoff, Laurent. Vive le Roi Babar. (FRE.). (J). (gr. 2-3). 4.95 (*0-685-28423-9*) Fr & Eur.
— Voyage De Babar. (FRE., Illus.). (J). (ps up). 1999. 13.95 (*2-01-002518-0*) Hachette.
de Brunhoff, Laurent, jt. auth. see de Brunhoff, Jean.
De Bruycker, Daniel & Dauber, Maximilien. Africa. (Tintin's Travel Diaries). (Illus.). 76p. (J). (gr. 5 up). 1994. pap. 6.95 (*0-8120-1864-8*) Barron.
De Bruycker, Daniel, et al. China. Walker, Maureen, tr. from FRE. (Tintin's Travel Diaries).Tr. of Carnets de Route de Tintin: La Chine. (Illus.). 76p. (J). (gr. 5 up). 1994. pap. 7.95 (*0-8120-1865-6*) Barron.
De Bruyn, Clive. Practical Beekeeping. (Illus.). 288p. 1997. 50.00 (*1-86126-049-0*, Pub. by Crowood) Trafalgar.
De Bruyn, Frans. The Literary Genres of Edmund Burke: The Political Uses of Literary Form. 330p. 1996. text 72.00 (*0-19-812182-2*) OUP.
de Bruyn, Gareth M., ed. see Kasturi, Rajeev & Nagpal, Arvind.
De Bruyn, Gerd. Contemporary Architecture in Germany, 1970-1996: 50 Buildings. LC 97-35742. (Illus.). 1997. pap. 19.95 (*0-8176-5737-1*) Birkhauser.
De Bruyn, Guenter. Jubelschreie. Trauergesaenge. (GER.). 208p. 1994. pap. 13.50 (*3-596-12154-X*, Pub. by Fischer Tasch) Intl Bk Import.
De Bruyn, Lucy. Mob: Rule & Riots. 1984. 39.00 (*0-7212-0611-5*, Pub. by Regency Pr GBR) St Mut.
De Bruyn, Maria. Altering the Image of AIDS. 96p. 1994. pap. 16.00 (*90-5383-259-9*, Pub. by VU Univ Pr) Paul & Co Pubs.
***de Bruyn, Sander M.** Economic Growth & the Environment: An Empirical Analysis. LC 99-87761. 260p. 2000. 116.50 (*0-7923-6153-9*) Kluwer Academic.
De Bruyn, Theodore. Pelagius's Commentary on St. Paul's Epistle to the Romans. LC 92-33697. (Early Christian Studies). 246p. 1993. text 65.00 (*0-19-814399-0*) OUP.
De Bruyn, Theodore, tr. & intro. see Pelagius.
De Bruyne, Bernard, jt. auth. see Pijls, Nico H.
De Bruyne, Bernard, jt. auth. see Pijls, Nico H. J.
De Bruyne, Jacques & Pountain, Christopher J. A Comprehensive Spanish Grammar. (Reference Grammars Ser.). 640p. (C). 1995. 77.95 (*0-631-16803-6*); pap. 34.95 (*0-631-19087-2*) Blackwell Pubs.
De Bruyne, R. H., jt. auth. see De Boer, T. W.
De Buck, A. Egyptian Reading Book I: Exercises & Middle Egyptian Texts. 128p. 1982. pap. 25.00 (*0-89005-213-1*) Ares.
De Buck, A., ed. Egyptian Readingbook: Exercises & Middle Egyptian Texts. 4th ed. (ENG & EGY., Illus.). ix, 128p. 1977. pap. text 27.50 (*90-6258-107-2*, Pub. by Netherlands Inst) Eisenbrauns.
De Buck, Adriaan. Egyptian Coffin Texts, Vol. 2. 1972. lib. bdg. 12.00 (*0-226-07946-5*) U Ch Pr.
— Egyptian Coffin Texts, Vol. 4. 1972. lib. bdg. 10.00 (*0-226-07947-3*) U Ch Pr.
— Egyptian Coffin Texts, Vol. 6. 1972. lib. bdg. 18.00 (*0-226-07944-9*) U Ch Pr.
De Buck, P. Treasures of the Tsar: Court Culture of Peter the Great from the Kremlin. LC 96-210315. (Illus.). 296p. 1996. 40.00 (*90-6918-161-4*, Pub. by Boymans Mus) U of Wash Pr.
De Buenosaires, Oscar. Bossa Nova & Samba: History, People, Lyrics, Recordings, Scores, Books. 132p. 1999. pap. 16.00 (*0-929928-22-9*, 32) Fog Pubns.
***De Buenosaires, Oscar.** CineLatinoamericano y Argentino: Latin American & Argentine Cinema. (SPA.). 202p. 2000. pap. text 20.00 (*0-929928-23-7*) Fog Pubns.
De Buenosaires, Oscar. Tango: A Bibliography: Books, History, People, Words. (Book's Fingerprints Ser.: No. 7). (Illus.). 108p. (Orig.). 1991. pap. 13.00 (*0-929928-08-3*) Fog Pubns.
— Two to Tango: Bibliography - Discography with an Introduction. 133p. (Orig.). 1997. lib. bdg. 16.00 (*0-929928-20-2*) Fog Pubns.
De Buffon, Georges-Louis. Histoire Naturelle. (FRE.). 1984. pap. 12.95 (*0-7859-1996-1*, 2070375692) Fr & Eur.
***De Burca, Grainne.** Constituition of the European Union. (Law in Context Ser.). 2000. pap. 39.95 (*0-406-90579-7*) LEXIS Pub.
***De Burca, Grainne & Scott, Joanne, eds.** Constitutional Change in the EU from Uniformity to Flexibility? 288p. 2000. 60.00 (*1-84113-103-2*, Pub. by Hart Pub) Intl Spec Bk.
De Burca, Grainne, jt. auth. see Craig, Paul.
De Burca, Grainne, jt. ed. see Craig, Paul.
***De Burca, Marcus.** The GAA (Gaelic Athletic Association) A History. 2nd rev. ed. (Illus.). 352p. 1999. 39.95 (*0-7171-2914-4*, Pub. by Gill & MacMill) Irish Bks Media.
De Bure, Gilles & Braunstein, Chloe, texts. Roger Tallon. (Illus.). 128p. 1999. pap. text 23.50 (*2-906571-87-3*, Pub. by Editions Dis Voir) Dist Art Pubs.
***De Burge, Gilles.** Golden Age of Magazine Illustration 60's/70's. 1999. 44.95 (*2-909450-42-2*) Collectionneur.
De Burgh Daly, M. Peripheral Arterial Chemoreceptors & Respiratory-Cardiovascular Integration. LC 96-9435. (Monographs of the Physiological Society: No. 46). (Illus.). 756p. 1997. text 225.00 (*0-19-857675-7*) OUP.
***De Burgh, Hugo, ed.** Investigative Journalism: Context & Practice. LC 99-43659. 336p. (C). 2000. text 85.00 (*0-415-19053-3*) Routledge.
De Burgh Norman, John E. & Bramley, Paul, eds. Textbook & Color Atlas of the Temporomandibular Joint: Diseases, Disorders, Surgery. (Illus.). 260p. (C). (gr. 13). 1990. 179.00 (*0-8151-6429-7*, 20272) Mosby Inc.
De Burgh, W. J. The Old North Road. 188p. pap. 18.95 (*0-85564-243-2*, Pub. by Univ of West Aust Pr) Intl Spec Bk.
De Burgoa, Francisco. Palestra Historial: De Virtudes, y Exemplares Apostolicos. (SPA.). 280p. 1997. 31.00 (*968-842-617-2*, UN043) UPLAAP.
De Burgoa, Francisco & Juice Gallery Staff. Geografica Descripcion de la Parte Septentrional, del Polo Artico de la America, Tomos I-II. (SPA.). 485p. 1997. 61.80 (*968-842-618-0*, UN044) UPLAAP.
De Burgos, Julia. Cancion de la Verdad Sencilla. LC 82-71883. (Vortice Ser.). (SPA., Illus.). 64p. (Orig.). 1982. pap. 6.95 (*0-940238-66-7*) Ediciones Huracan.
— Poema en Veinte Surcos. LC 83-82116. (Illus.). 64p. (Orig.). 1982. pap. 6.75 (*0-940238-23-3*) Ediciones Huracan.
— Roses in the Mirror: Translated Poems of Julia De Burgos. Lucca, Carmen D., ed. & tr. by. from SPA. 140p. (Orig.). (C). 1992. pap. 8.00 (*0-9623968-1-8*) Poets Refuge.
— Song of the Simple Truth: The Complete Poems of Julia de Burgos, Obra Completa Poetica. Agueros, Jack, tr. from SPA. LC 94-39149. (ENG & SPA.). 524p. (Orig.). 1997. pap. 21.95 (*1-880684-24-1*) Curbstone.
de Burton, Maria A. Ruiz, see Ruiz de Burton, Maria A.
De Busk, Robert. Cardiac Rehabilitation: A Guide for Patients. Rapaport, Elliott, ed. (Cardiology Ser.). (Illus.). 32p. (Orig.). 1996. pap. 2.95 (*1-885274-39-4*) Health InfoNet Inc.
De Bussche, Willy Van, see Van De Bussche, Willy.
De Busscher, Pierre-Olivier, ed. Gay Studies from the French Cultures: Voices from France, Belgium, Brazil, Canada, & the Netherlands. LC 93-10686. (Journal of Homosexuality: Vol. 25, Nos. 1-3). (Illus.). 352p. 1993. lib. bdg. 7.95 (*1-56024-436-4*) Haworth Pr.
— Gay Studies from the French Cultures: Voices from France, Belgium, Brazil, Canada & the Netherlands. LC 93-10686. (Journal of Homosexuality Ser.: Vol. 25, Nos. 1-3). (Illus.). 352p. 1993. pap. text 19.95 (*1-56023-043-6*) Haworth Pr.
De Bussy, Carvel. Count Stephen Tisza, Minister of Hungary: Letters (1914-1916) LC 90-48815. (American University Studies: History: Ser. IX). (Illus.). XXIV, 214p. (C). 1991. text 46.95 (*0-8204-1412-3*) P Lang Pubng.
***De Bussy, Carvel.** Prague Sunset. LC 98-74966. 240p. 1998. text 33.50 (*0-88033-419-3*, 521, Pub. by East Eur Monographs) Col U Pr.
De Bussy, Carvel, ed. Memoirs of Alexander Spitmuller, Freherr Von Harmersbach. 327p. 1987. text 64.50 (*0-88033-124-0*, Pub. by East Eur Monographs) Col U Pr.
De Bussy, Carvel, tr. see Markus, Georg.
De Bussy, Carvel, tr. see Von Habsburg, Otto.
De Bustamante, I. Díaz, jt. auth. see Navarro, R. Lacasa.
De Butteville, Guignard. Genealogie des Guignard. 259p. 1998. reprint ed. pap. 39.50 (*0-8328-9659-4*); reprint ed. lib. bdg. 49.50 (*0-8328-9658-6*) Higginson Bk Co.
De Buys, William. Enchantment & Exploitation: The Life & Hard Times of a New Mexico Mountain Range. LC 85-5833. (Illus.). 394p. 1985. pap. 16.95 (*0-8263-0820-1*) U of NM Pr.
De Buzon, F., ed. see Descartes, Rene.
De Buzzaccarini, Vittoria. Men's Coats. (Twentieth Century-Histories of Fashion Ser.). (Illus.). 135p. 1996. 29.95 (*0-89676-209-2*, Costume & Fashion Pr) QSMG Ltd.
De Buzzaccarini, Vittoria & Minici, Isabella Z. Buttons & Sundries. (Twentieth Century-Histories of Fashion Ser.). (Illus.). 143p. 1996. 29.95 (*0-89676-201-7*, Costume & Fashion Pr) QSMG Ltd.
De By, Rolf A., et al, eds. Transaction Management Support for Cooperative Applications. LC 97-43180. 222p. 1998. text 137.50 (*0-7923-8100-9*) Kluwer Academic.
De C. Clarke, E., et al. Elements of Practical Geology for Australian Students. 4th ed. 1994. 19.95 (*0-85564-028-6*, Pub. by Univ of West Aust Pr) Intl Spec Bk.
De Cadalso, Jose. Escritos Autobiograficos Y Epistolario. Glendinning, Nigel & Harrison, Nicole, eds. (Textos B Ser.: Vol. XXV). (SPA.). 225p. (C). 1979. 51.00 (*0-7293-0076-5*, Pub. by Tamesis Bks Ltd) Boydell & Brewer.
De Cadenas Vicent, Vincente. Diccionario Heraldico. 2nd ed. (SPA.). 340p. 1989. pap. write for info. (*0-7859-5090-7*) Fr & Eur.
De Cadenet, J.J., jt. auth. see Castro, Rene.
De Cahue, Joana. Diccionari Practic de Sinonims Catalans: Mots i Frases. 2nd ed.Tr. of Practical Catalan Dictionary of Synonyms, Words & Phrases. (CAT.). 640p. 1979. write for info. (*0-7859-5112-1*) Fr & Eur.
De Callatay, Armand M. Natural & Artificial Intelligence New Expanded Edition: Misconceptions about Brains & Neural Networks. enl. ed. LC 92-12713. 560p. 1992. pap. 108.50 (*0-444-89502-7*, North Holland) Elsevier.
De Callatay, Vincent & Dollfus, Audouin. Atlas of the Planets. LC 76-350431. 160p. reprint ed. pap. 49.60 (*0-8357-5844-3*, 202638100049) Bks Demand.
***De Callieres, Francois.** On the Manner of Negotiating with Princes. LC 99-87273. 128p. 2000. 16.00 (*0-618-05512-6*) HM.
De Caluwe, Rita. Fuzzy & Uncertain Object-Oriented Databases Concepts & Data Models, Advances in Fuzzy Systems-Applications, Vol. 13. LC 97-28478. 250p. 1997. text 32.00 (*981-02-2893-7*) World Scientific Pub.
de Camacho Schimidt, Aurora, tr. see Poniatowska, Elena.
De Camara, Idalia F. Dictados para Transcripcion. 317p. 1985. pap. 6.00 (*0-8477-2607-X*) U of PR Pr.
De Camera, Mary P. Fall into Darkness. (YA). (gr. 8 up). 1977. per. 1.95 (*0-671-00984-2*, Archway) PB.
De Camoens, Luis V. The Lusiads. 1975. 300.00 (*0-87968-318-X*) Gordon Pr.
De Camp, Catherine C., jt. auth. see De Camp, L. Sprague.
De Camp, David, ed. see Georgetown University Round Table on Languages & L.
De Camp, L. Sprague. The Ancient Engineers. 1987. mass mkt. 5.99 (*0-345-32029-8*, Del Rey) Ballantine Pub Grp.
— The Bones of Zora. 1983. 17.00 (*0-685-14034-2*) Phantasia Pr.
— The Hand of Zei. (Illus.). 200p. 1981. 20.50 (*0-913896-20-9*) Owlswick Pr.
— Heroes & Hobgoblins. (Illus.). 1981. 25.00 (*0-937986-33-X*) D M Grant.
— The Incorporated Knight. 1991. per. 3.95 (*0-671-72045-7*) Baen Bks.
— Lost Continents: The Atlantis Theme in History, Science & Literature. (Illus.). 348p. 1970. reprint ed. pap. 9.95 (*0-486-22668-9*) Dover.
— The Ragged Edge of Science. LC 79-92640. (Illus.). 254p. 1980. 16.00 (*0-913896-06-3*) Owlswick Pr.
— The Reluctant King. 256p. 1996. per. 6.99 (*0-671-87746-1*) Baen Bks.
— Rubber Dinosaurs & Wooden Elephants: Essays on Literature, Film & History. LC 95-5348. (I. O. Evans Studies in the Philosophy & Criticism of Literature: No. 26). 144p. 1996. pap. 19.00 (*0-89370-454-7*) Millefleurs.
— The Tritonian Ring. LC 76-56969. (Illus.). 1977. reprint ed. 12.50 (*0-913896-09-8*) Owlswick Pr.
— The Undesired Princess & the Enchanted Bunny. (J). 1990. mass mkt. 4.99 (*0-671-69875-3*) Baen Bks.
De Camp, L. Sprague & De Camp, Catherine C. Footprints on Sand: A Literary Sampler. (Illus.). 349p. 1981. 18.00 (*0-911682-25-2*) Advent.
— The Incorporated Knight. 1987. 17.00 (*0-932096-46-8*) Phantasia Pr.
De Camp, L. Sprague & Drake, David. Lest Darkness Fall & To Bring the Light. 368p. 1996. mass mkt. 5.99 (*0-671-87736-4*) Baen Bks.
De Camp, L. Sprague & Pratt, Fletcher. The Complete Compleat Enchanter. 544p. (Orig.). 1989. mass mkt. 5.99 (*0-671-69809-5*) Baen Bks.
De Camp, L. Sprague, et al. Dark Valley Destiny: The Life of Robert E. Howard. LC 83-15635. 402p. 1983. 40.00 (*0-89366-247-X*) Ultramarine Pub.
De Campoli, Ginseppe. Strength of Structural Materials: Understanding Basic Structural Design. LC 84-3569. 478p. 1988. reprint ed. lib. bdg. 44.50 (*0-471-89082-0*) Krieger.
De Campos Guimaraes, J. P. Integrated Rural Development in Asia. Ramachandran, H., ed. 1991. text 34.00 (*81-7022-334-2*, Pub. by Concept) S Asia.
De Cande, R. La Musique. (FRE.). 550p. 75.00 (*0-686-56978-4*, M-6105) Fr & Eur.
De Cande, Roland. Nouveau Dictionnaire de la Musique. (FRE.). 680p. 1983. text 165.00 (*0-7859-7623-X*, 2020065754) Fr & Eur.
***De Candido, Keith R. A.** Diplomatic Implausability. (Star Trek : No. 61). 2001. mass mkt. 6.99 (*0-671-78554-0*, Star Trek) PB.
De Candole, James. Czechoslovakia Too Velvet a Revolution? (C). 1991. 55.00 (*0-907967-22-1*, Pub. by Inst Euro Def & Strat) St Mut.
De Candolle, A. P. Collection de Memoires pour servir a l'Histoire du Regne Vegetal et plus specialement pour servir de complement a quelques parties du Prodromus Regni Vegetabilis. (Illus.). 1972. 225.00 (*3-7682-0728-5*) Lubrecht & Cramer.
De Candolle, Alphonse. Histoire des Sciences et des Savants Depuis Deux Siecles. Cohen, I. Bernard, ed. LC 80-2116. (Development of Science Ser.). (Illus.). 1981. lib. bdg. 55.95 (*0-405-13836-9*) Ayer.
De Candolle, Augustin P. & Sprengel, Kurt. Elements of the Philosophy of Plants: Containing the Principles of Scientific Botany. Sterling, Keir B., ed. LC 77-81123. (Biologists & Their World Ser.). (Illus.). 1978. reprint ed. lib. bdg. 44.95 (*0-405-10719-6*) Ayer.
De Cantempre, Thomas. The Life of Lutgard of Aywieres. King, Margot H., tr. (Translation Ser.). 207p. 1991. pap. write for info. (*0-920669-09-3*, Pub. by Peregrina Pubng) Cistercian Pubns.
— The Life of Margaret of Ypres. 2nd ed. King, Margot H., tr. & intro. by. LC 97-18324. (Translations Ser.: Vol. 15). (LAT & ENG., Illus.). 91p. 1999. pap. 9.00 (*0-920669-50-6*, Pub. by Peregrina Pubng) Cistercian Pubns.
De Cantempre, Thomas, jt. auth. see De Vitry, Jacques.
De Cantimpre, Thomas. The Life of Christina the Astonishing: English Translation. 2nd ed. King, Margot H., tr. & intro. by. (Translation Ser.). 57p. 1997. pap. 8.00 (*0-920669-01-8*, Pub. by Peregrina Pubng) Cistercian Pubns.
De Capite, Frances. Student Study Guide to a Basic Course in American Sign Language. 1986. spiral bd. 9.95 (*0-932666-33-7*) T J Pubs.
De Capriles, Miguel A. Modern Financial Accounting, 1001-1088. 166p. 1962. reprint ed. pap. 5.00 (*0-8377-0505-3*, Rothman) W S Hein.
***De Capua, Sarah.** Niagara Falls. LC 99-42013. (Rookie Read-About Geography Ser.). (J). 2001. write for info. (*0-516-22016-0*) Childrens.
De Capua, A. G. German Baroque Poetry: Interpretive Readings. LC 73-152521. 221p. reprint ed. 68.60 (*0-8357-9595-0*, 201010500068) Bks Demand.

An Asterisk (*) at the beginning of an entry indicates that the title is appearing for the first time.

De Capua, Sarah. J. C. Watts: Character Counts. LC 97-50394. (Community Builders Ser.). (Illus.). 48p. (J). (gr. 3-5). 1999. pap. text 6.95 (*0-516-26346-3*) Childrens.

De-Cardenas, Raul. A Family Remembrance. Presbyter's Peartree Staff, tr. from SPA. 78p. 1993. pap. text 4.95 (*1-885901-10-0*) Presbyters Peartree.

De Carias, Maria R. La Cocina Dominicana: Edicion Para Coleccionistas. 2nd ed. Carias, Guillo, ed. Orig. Title: Dominican Cookbook. (SPA., Illus.). 240p. 1993. reprint ed. 23.95 (*0-9635548-1-6*) Pilon FL.

— Dominican Cookbook: Collector's Edition. 2nd rev. ed. Carias, Guillo, ed.Tr. of La Cocina Dominicana. (Illus.). 240p. 1993. 23.95 (*0-9635548-0-8*) Pilon FL.

De Caritat, Patrice, jt. auth. see Reimann, Clemens.

De Caritat, Patrice, jt. auth. see Saether, Ola M.

De Carle, Donald. Clock & Watch Repairing. 2nd ed. (Illus.). 309p. 1983. 25.00 (*0-7091-9436-6*, Pub. by R Hale Ltd) Antique Collect.

— Complicated Watches & Their Repair. (Illus.). 174p. 1978. 34.50 (*0-7198-0090-0*; Pub. by NAG Press) Antique Collect.

— Practical Clock Repairing. 2nd ed. (Illus.). 243p. 1987. 35.00 (*0-7198-0000-5*, Pub. by NAG Press) Antique Collect.

De Carle, Donald. Practical Watch Adjusting. (Illus.). 162p. 21.95 (*0-7198-0050-1*, Pub. by R Hale Ltd) Seven Hills Bk.

De Carle, Donald. Practical Watch Adjusting. (Illus.). 242p. 1987. reprint ed. 29.50 (*0-7198-0051-X*, Pub. by NAG Press) Antique Collect.

— Practical Watch Repairing. 3rd ed. 1986. 35.00 (*0-7198-0030-7*, Pub. by NAG Press) Antique Collect.

***De Carle, Donald.** Watchmaker's & Model Engineer's Lathe: A User's Manual. 5th ed. (Illus.). 240p. 1999. 29.95 (*0-7090-6200-1*, Pub. by R Hale Ltd) Seven Hills Bk.

De Carli, A., ed. Low Cost Automation: Components, Instruments, Techniques & Applications: Selected Papers from the IFAC Symposium, Milan, Italy, 8-10 November 1989. (IFAC Symposia Ser.: 9015). (Illus.). 528p. 1990. 246.00 (*0-08-037866-8*, Pergamon Pr) Elsevier.

De Carli, A. & Masada, E., eds. Motion Control for Intelligent Automation: Preprints of the IFAC Workshop, Perugia, Italy, 27-29 October 1992. LC 92-41311. (IFAC Pre-Print Ser.). 434p. 1993. pap. 118.50 (*0-08-042058-3*, Pergamon Pr) Elsevier.

***De Carli, James, et al.** Professional ASP Data. 500p. 2000. pap. 49.99 (*1-86100-392-7*) Wrox Pr Inc.

De Carlo, Andrea. Yucatan. Weaver, William, tr. from ITA. 1990. 21.95 (*0-15-199895-7*) Harcourt.

De Carlo, Donald T. & Gruenfeld, Deborah H. Stress in the American Workplace: Alternatives for the Working Wounded. LC 89-13187. 188p. (Orig.). 1989. pap. 19.95 (*0-934753-34-2*) LRP Pubns.

De Carlo, Donald T. & Minkowitz, Martin. Workers Compensation Insurance & Law Practice: The Next Generation. LC 89-12856. 367p. 1989. 55.00 (*0-934753-36-9*) LRP Pubns.

De Carlo, Giovanni. How to Play Kena: Whispers from the Incas. (Illus.). 70p. 1999. pap. 25.00 (*0-7392-0202-2*, PO3203) Morris Pubng.

— La Sekta Carta. (SPA.). 62p. 1999. pap. 10.00 (*0-7392-0255-3*, PO3084A) Morris Pubng.

— Uno, el Duende de los Numeros Libro 1: Conociendo a los Numeros. Giovanni De Carlo Inc. Staff, ed. (SPA., Illus.). 70p. (J). 1999. pap. 15.00 (*0-7392-0186-7*, PO3158) Morris Pubng.

***De Carlo, Mark.** Current Topics in Muscoskeletal Medicine: A Case Study Approach. 200p. (C). 2000. pap. text 24.00 (*1-55642-434-5*) SLACK Inc.

De Carmoy, Guy. Foreign Policies of France, Nineteen Forty-Four to Nineteen Sixty-Eight. Halperin, Elaine P., tr. LC 71-85446. 1994. lib. bdg. 16.50 (*0-226-13991-3*) U Ch Pr.

De Carmoy, Guy. Western Europe in World Affairs: Continuity, Change, & Challenge. LC 85-28147. 241p. 1986. 49.95 (*0-275-92057-7*, C2057, Praeger Pubs) Greenwood.

De Caro, Andrea T. Fountain in Spring: Poetry. Bonventura, Enzo, tr. (ENG & ITA.). 23p. 1978. pap. 5.00 (*0-89304-658-2*) Cross-Cultrl NY.

De Caro, Connie, tr. see Casanova, Carlamaria.

De Caro, Connie M. Sicily the Trampled Paradise: Revisited. LC 98-7778. (Sicilian Studies). 1998. 12.00 (*1-881901-15-7*) LEGAS.

De Caro, Francis A., compiled by. Women & Folklore: A Bibliographic Survey. LC 83-12837. 170p. 1983. lib. bdg. 52.95 (*0-313-23821-9*, DWF/, Greenwood Pr) Greenwood.

De Caro, Frank. Folklife in Louisiana Photography: Images of Tradition. LC 90-40451. (Illus.). 213p. 1991. 24.95 (*0-8071-1633-5*) La State U Pr.

— The Folktale Cat. LC 93-20022. (Illus.). 183p. 1993. pap. 14.95 (*0-87483-303-5*) August Hse.

De Caro, Frank, ed. Louisiana Sojourns: Travelers' Tales & Literary Journeys. LC 97-50292. (Illus.). 432p. 1998. 39.95 (*0-8071-2239-4*); pap. 22.95 (*0-8071-2240-8*) La State U Pr.

De Caro, G., et al, eds. The Physiology of Thirst & Sodium Appetite. LC 86-4982. (NATO ASI Series A, Life Sciences: Vol. 105). 586p. 1986. 125.00 (*0-306-42265-4*, Plenum Trade) Perseus Pubng.

De Carr, F. Rene Van, see Van De Carr, F. Rene.

De Carrico, J., jt. auth. see Nattinger, J. R.

De Carrion De Los Condes, Santob. The Moral Proverbs of Santob de Carrion: Jewish Wisdom in Christian Spain. LC 87-45532. 208p. 1987. reprint ed. pap. 64.50 (*0-608-07158-7*, 206738300009) Bks Demand.

De Cartagena, Juntadel A., ed. Acuerdo de Cartagena. LC 97-73092. 210p. 1997. reprint ed. 75.00 (*1-57588-223-X*, 311320) W S Hein.

De Cartagena, Teresa. The Writings of Teresa De Cartagena. Seidenspinner-Nunez, Dayle, tr. LC 97-37484. (Library of Medieval Women). 1998. pap. 17.95 (*0-85991-446-1*, DS Brewer) Boydell & Brewer.

De Carvajal, M. Tragedia Josephina. Gillet, S. E., ed. (Elliott Monographs: Vol. 28). 1974. reprint ed. 35.00 (*0-527-02631-X*) Periodicals Srv.

De Carvalho Azevedo, Marcello. Basic Ecclesial Communities in Brazil: The Challenge of a New Way of Being Church. fac. ed. Drury, John, tr. LC 87-141. (Studies in Ethics Ser.). 318p. 1987. reprint ed. pap. 98.60 (*0-7837-7800-7*, 204755600007) Bks Demand.

— The Consecrated Life: Crossroads & Directions. Cook, Guillermo, tr. from POR. LC 95-12272. 196p. (Orig.). 1995. pap. 17.00 (*1-57075-003-3*) Orbis Bks.

— The Consecrated Life: Crossroads & Directions. Cook, Guillermo, tr. LC 95-12272. 159p. (Orig.). reprint ed. pap. 49.30 (*0-608-20239-8*, 207149800012) Bks Demand.

***De Carvalho, Maria Eulina P.** Rethinking Family-School Relations: A Critique of Parental Involvement in Schooling. LC 00-26748. (Sociocultural, Political & Historical Studies in Education). 176p. 2000. write for info. (*0-8058-3496-6*) L Erlbaum Assocs.

De Carvalho, Mario. God Strolling in the Cool of the Evening: A Novel. Rabassa, Gregory, tr. from POR. LC 97-16093. (Pegasus Prize for Literature Ser.). 272p. 1997. 26.95 (*0-8071-2235-1*) La State U Pr.

***de Carvalho, Miriam Dreysse Passos.** Szene vor Dem Palast: Die Theatralisierung des Chors im Theater einar Schleefs. (Theaomai - Studien Zu Den Performativen Kunsten Ser.). (Illus.). 252p. 1999. 45.95 (*3-631-34617-4*) P Lang Pubng.

De Carvalho, R., ed. Cosmology & Large-Scale Structure in the Universe. (ASP Conference Series Proceedings: Vol. 24). 225p. 1992. 34.00 (*0-937707-43-0*) Astron Soc Pacific.

***De Carvalho, Roberto.** Prehistory. (Art & Civilization Ser.). (Illus.). 40p. (J). (gr. 3-7). 2000. 16.95 (*0-87226-615-X*, 6615XB, P Bedrick Books) NTC Contemp Pub Co.

De Casal, Julian. Poesias Completas y Pequenos Poemas en Prosa en Orden Cronologico. Figueroa, Esperanza, ed. LC 93-71467. (Coleccion Clasicos Cubanos). (SPA., Illus.). 400p. (Orig.). 1993. pap. 39.00 (*0-89729-688-5*) Ediciones.

De Casas, Celso A. Pelon Drops Out. LC 79-84473. (Illus.). 1979. pap. 5.95 (*0-89229-006-4*) TQS Pubns.

De Caso, Jacques. David d'Angers: Sculptural Communication in the Age of Romanticism. Johnson, Dorothy, tr. (Illus.). 210p. 1992. text 55.00 (*0-691-04078-8*, Pub. by Princeton U Pr) Cal Prin Full Svc.

De Cassagnac, Adolphe G. Geschichte der Arbeitenden und Burgerlichten Classen. (GER.). xxxviii, 332p. 1977. reprint ed. write for info. (*3-487-06333-6*) G Olms Pubs.

De Casseres, Benjamin. Forty Immortals. 370p. 1977. 26.95 (*0-8369-2845-8*) Ayer.

— Works, 3 vols. 1976. 900.00 (*0-87968-467-4*) Gordon Pr.

De Castell, Suzanne, et al, eds. Literacy, Society, & Schooling. (Illus.). 352p. 1986. pap. text 29.95 (*0-521-31340-6*) Cambridge U Pr.

De Castell, Suzanne & Bryson, Mary, eds. Radical In(ter)ventions: Identity, Politics, & Difference/s in Educational Praxis. LC 97-4953. (SUNY Series, Identities in the Classroom). 301p. (C). 1997. text 59.50 (*0-7914-3561-X*); pap. text 19.95 (*0-7914-3562-8*) State U NY Pr.

De Castell, Suzanne, et al. Mosaicos. 2nd ed. 465p. 1997. 66.67 (*0-13-237587-7*) P-H.

De Castella, Robert & Friedberg, Ardy. Marathon: The Anatomy of a Race Mile by Mile. 1989. text 17.95 (*0-07-016199-2*) McGraw.

De Castells, Matilda O. & Castells, Ricardo. Student Activitity MNL Mosaicos: Spanish As a World Language. 1994. pap. text, student ed. 35.20 (*0-13-064718-7*) P-H.

De Castells, Matilda O. & Lionetti, Harold E. La Lengue Espanola: Grammatica y Cultura. 3rd ed. (SPA.). 592p. (C). 1983. text 47.20 (*0-13-524489-7*) P-H.

De Castells, Matilda O., et al. Mosaicos: Spanish As a World Language. LC 93-27189. 576p. 1993. text 72.00 (*0-13-064700-4*) P-H.

De Castilla, Constanza. The Book of Devotions (Libro de Devociones y Oficios) Wilkins, Constance L., ed. LC 98-121818. 147p. 1998. pap. text 24.95 (*0-85989-487-8*, Pub. by Univ Exeter Pr) Northwestern U Pr.

De Castillejo, Irene C. Knowing Woman: A Feminine Psychology. 192p. 1997. reprint ed. pap. 14.95 (*1-57062-204-3*, Pub. by Shambhala Pubns) Random.

De Castillejo, Irene Claremont, see Claremont de Castillejo, Irene.

De Castillo, et al. Quiero Ser Libre.Tr. of I Want to Be Free. (SPA.). 212p. 1994. pap. 15.00 (*968-39-0356-8*) Hazelden.

De Castillo, Bernal D. Cortez & the Conquest of Mexico by the Spaniards in 1521. LC 88-581. xii, 165p. (J). (gr. 5 up). 1988. reprint ed. lib. bdg. 22.50 (*0-208-02221-X*, Linnet Bks) Shoe String.

De Castillo, E. Drake. Illustrationes Florae Insularum Maris Pacifici. 1977. reprint ed. 200.00 (*3-7682-1130-4*) Lubrecht & Cramer.

De Castillo, Maria E., et al. Libre de Addiciones.Tr. of Free from Addictions. (SPA.). 248p. pap. 15.00 (*968-39-0507-2*) Hazelden.

De Castillo Solorzano, Alonso. Fiestas Del Jardin. (Textos y Estudios Clasicos De las Literaturas Hispanicas Ser.). viii, 559p. 1973. reprint ed. write for info. (*3-487-04673-3*) G Olms Pubs.

de Castle, Robert L. van, see Van de Castle, Robert L.

De Castro, A. F. & Almeida, W. F., eds. Cholera on the American Continents. LC 93-61303. (Illus.). 136p. 1993. pap. 37.50 (*0-944398-12-X*) ILSI.

de Castro, Ana A. Jarreta, see De Mattos Bicudo, Carlos E. & Jarreta de Castro, Ana A.

De Castro, C. Fernandez. The Life of the Very Noble King of Castile & Leon, Saint Ferdinand III. LC 86-83054. (Illus.). 280p. (Orig.). (J). (gr. 8). 1987. pap. 13.95 (*1-877905-09-7*) Am Soc Defense TFP.

de Castro, Concepcion Obon, see Obon de Castro, Concepcion.

De Castro, Diane R., jt. auth. see Harvey, Ruth B.

De Castro, Dom J. Life of Dom John de Castro, the Fourth Vice-Roy of India Wherein Are Seen the Portuguese's Voyages to the East Indies, Their Discoveries & Conquest There. (C). 1994. 68.00 (*81-206-0900-X*, Pub. by Asian Educ Servs) S Asia.

De Castro, Guillen. Mocedades Del Cid. (SPA.). 246p. 1963. 10.50 (*0-8288-7053-5*) Fr & Eur.

— Mocedades Del Cid. (SPA.). 269p. 1968. 11.95 (*0-8288-7176-0*, S29015) Fr & Eur.

De Castro, J., et al. Regional Opioid Analgesia. (Developments in Anesthesiology & Critical Care Ser.). (C). 1990. text 385.50 (*0-7923-0162-5*) Kluwer Academic.

De Castro, Jean & Ronsard, Pierre De. Jean De Castro: Chansons, Odes, et Sonetz de Pierre Ronsard. Brooks, Jeanice, ed. (Recent Researches in Music of the Renaissance Ser.: Vol. RRR97). (Illus.). xxvi, 179p. 1994. pap. 60.00 (*0-89579-289-3*, RRR97) A-R Eds.

De Castro, Jose Rodriguez, see Rodriguez De Castro, Jose.

De Castro, Josue. The Geopolitics of Hunger. rev. ed. LC 74-2140. 524p. reprint ed. pap. 162.50 (*0-7837-6990-3*, 204680200004) Bks Demand.

***de Castro Lobo, Padre J.** Mass in D Minor. (Music Archive Publications Ser.: Series E, Vol. 3). 147p. 1999. text 34.00 (*90-5755-027-X*, Harwood Acad Pubs) Gordon & Breach.

De Castro, M. D. Luque, see Valcarcel, M. & Luque de Castro, M. D.

De Castro, Martha. El Arte en Cuba: Historia del Arte Cubano Colonial y Moderno. (SPA.). 1970. pap. 15.00 (*0-89729-118-2*) Ediciones.

De Castro, Percio B. De la Penisula Hacia Latinoamerica: El Naturalismo Social en Emlia Pardo-Bazan, Eugenio Cambaceres y Aluisio de Azevedo. LC 92-39170. (American University Studies: Comparative Literature: Ser. III, Vol. 51). IX, 156p. (C). 1993. text 39.95 (*0-8204-2105-7*) P Lang Pubng.

de Castro, Rafael Fernandez, see Pastor, Robert A. & Fernandez de Castro, Rafael, eds.

De Castro, Rogelio, tr. see Bruni, Mary-Ann S.

de Castro, Vicki, jt. auth. see House, Susan T.

De Castro y de Cardenas, Fernando R. Genealogia, Heraldica E Historia De Nuestras Familias. LC 89-85775. (Coleccion Cuba y sus Jueces). (SPA.). 184p. (Orig.). 1990. pap. 19.00 (*0-89729-510-2*) Ediciones.

De Castroverde, Waldo. El Circulo de la Muerte. LC 84-80921. (Coleccion Caniqui). (SPA.). 153p. (Orig.). 1984. pap. 8.95 (*0-89729-349-5*) Ediciones.

De Cataldo Neuburger, Luisella & Valentini, Tiziana. Women & Terrorism. Hughes, Leo M., tr. from ITA. LC 95-13884. 256p. 1996. text 49.95 (*0-312-12716-2*) St Martin.

De Catanzaro, C. J. Symeon, the New Theologian: The Discourses. LC 80-82414. (Classics of Western Spirituality Ser.). 416p. 1988. pap. 22.95 (*0-8091-2230-8*) Paulist Pr.

De Catanzaro, Christine D. & Rainer, Werner. Anton Cajetan Adlgasser (1729-77) A Thematic Catalogue of His Works. LC 96-40067. (Thematic Catalogues Ser.). 2000. 54.00 (*0-945193-78-5*) Pendragon NY.

De Caterina, R. & Schmidt, E. B., eds. Fish Oil & Vascular Disease. LC 92-49797. (Topics in Cardiovascular Diseases Ser.). 1992. write for info. (*3-540-19792-3*); 65.00 (*0-387-19792-3*) Spr-Verlag.

De Caulhiaco, Guigonis. Inventarium Sive Chirurgia Magna, Vol. 1. McVaugh, Michael R., ed. (Studies in Ancient Medicine: Vol. 14, I). (Illus.). xviii, 486p. 1996. 207.00 (*90-04-10706-1*, NLG385) Brill Academic Pubs.

De Caunes, Antoine. Good--but Hot. 224p. 1992. pap. 13.95 (*1-872180-29-9*, Pub. by Fourth Estate) Trafalgar.

De Caus, Salomon. Institution Harmonique. fac. ed. (Monuments of Music & Music Literature in Facsimile Ser., Series II: Vol. 81). 1969. lib. bdg. 55.00 (*0-8450-2281-4*) Broude.

De Caussade, Jean-Pierre. Abandonment to Divine Providence. 128p. 1993. pap. 11.00 (*0-385-45871-7*) Doubleday.

— Daily Readings with Jean-Pierre de Caussade. LLewelyn, Robert, ed. (Daily Readings Ser.). 1986. pap. 4.95 (*0-87243-145-2*) Templegate.

— The Joy of Full Surrender. rev. ed. Helms, Hal M., ed. LC 85-63858. (Living Library). 201p. 1986. pap. 10.95 (*0-941478-49-1*, 930-022, Pub. by Paraclete MA) BookWorld.

— The Sacrament of the Present Moment. LC 81-48206. 128p. 1989. pap. 12.00 (*0-06-061811-6*, Pub. by Harper SF) HarpC.

— Self-Abandonment to Divine Providence: Abandonment to Divine Providence. Thorold, Algar, tr. from FRE. LC 86-51602. 450p. 1993. reprint ed. pap. 18.00 (*0-89555-312-0*) TAN Bks Pubs.

De, Ceballos Alfonso Rodriguez. Cathedral of Santiago: De Compostela. 1999. pap. 25.00 (*1-85759-218-2*) Scala Books.

De Cecco, John P., ed. Bashers, Baiters & Bigots: Homophobia in American Society. LC 84-19121. 203p. 1995. pap. text 14.95 (*0-918393-02-7*, Harrington Park) Haworth Pr.

— Gay Personality & Sexual Labeling. LC 84-22578. 106p. 1985. pap. text 9.95 (*0-918393-01-9*, Harrington Park) Haworth Pr.

— Gay Relationships. LC 87-11958. 290p. (Orig.). 1987. pap. 19.95 (*0-918393-33-7*, Harrington Park); text 49.95 (*0-86656-637-6*) Haworth Pr.

— Homophobia: An Overview. LC 84-8959. (Journal of Homosexuality: Vol. 10, Nos. 1-2). 198p. (C). 1984. text 39.95 (*0-86656-356-3*) Haworth Pr.

De Cecco, John P., jt. ed. see Parker, David A.

De Cecco, John P., ed. see Shively, Michael G.

De Cecco, Marcello, et al, eds. Managing Public Debt: Index-Linked Bonds in Theory & Practice. LC 96-32705. (Illus.). 240p. (C). 1997. 95.00 (*1-85898-491-2*) E Elgar.

De Cecco, Marcello & Giovannini, Alberto, eds. A European Central Bank. (Illus.). 392p. (C). 1989. pap. text 25.95 (*0-521-37623-8*) Cambridge U Pr.

De Cerreino, Allison L. & Keynan, Alex. Scientific Cooperation, State Conflict: The Roles of Scientists in Mitigating International Discord. LC 98-43898. (Annals Ser.). 1998. pap. 60.00 (*1-57331-203-7*) NY Acad Sci.

De, Cerreno Allison L. C. Scientific Cooperation, State Conflict: The Roles of Scientists in Mitigating International Discord. (Annals of the New York Academy of Science Ser.). 280p. 1999. pap. 22.50 (*0-8018-6304-X*) Johns Hopkins.

De Certaines, J. D. Magnetic Resonance Spectroscopy of Biofluids: A New Tool in Clinical Biology. 292p. 1989. text 104.00 (*981-02-0062-5*) World Scientific Pub.

De Certeau. The Possession of Loudun. LC 99-88078. (Illus.). 264p. 1993. pap. text 15.00 (*0-226-10035-9*); lib. bdg. 40.00 (*0-226-10034-0*) U Ch Pr.

De Certeau, Michel. The Capture of Speech & Other Political Writings. Conley, Tom, tr. & afterword by by. LC 97-43050. 192p. 1998. pap. 19.95 (*0-8166-2769-X*); text 49.95 (*0-8166-2768-1*) U of Minn Pr.

— La Fable Mystique. 1992. pap. text 14.95 (*0-226-13999-9*); lib. bdg. 34.95 (*0-226-13998-0*) U Ch Pr.

— Heterologies: Discourse on the Other. Massumi, Brian, tr. LC 85-16457. 277p. 1986. pap. 18.95 (*0-8166-1404-0*) U of Minn Pr.

— Invention du Quotidien Tome 1: Arts de Faire. (Folio Essais Ser.: No. 146). (FRE.). 1990. pap. 12.95 (*2-07-032576-8*) Schoenhof.

— The Mystic Fable: The Sixteenth & Seventeenth Centuries. Smith, Michael B., tr. 384p. 1995. pap. text 22.00 (*0-226-10037-5*) U Ch Pr.

— The Mystic Fable: The Sixteenth & Seventeeth Centuries. Smith, Michael B., tr. (Religion & Postmodernism Ser.). (Illus.). 384p. 1992. 37.50 (*0-226-10036-7*) U Ch Pr.

— The Practice of Everyday Life. Rendall, Steven F., tr. from FRE. LC 83-18070. 260p. 1984. pap. 16.95 (*0-520-06168-3*, Pub. by U CA Pr) Cal Prin Full Svc.

— The Writing of History. Conley, Tom, tr. from FRE. 368p. (C). 1992. pap. 18.00 (*0-231-05575-7*) Col U Pr.

De Certeau, Michel & Giard, Luce. Culture in the Plural. Conley, Tom, tr. from FRE. LC 97-25361. 1998. write for info. (*0-8166-2766-5*); pap. write for info. (*0-8166-2767-3*) U of Minn Pr.

de Cerval, M. Dictionnaire Internationale des Bijoux. (FRE.). 1998. 295.00 (*0-320-00185-7*) Fr & Eur.

De Cervantes Saavedra, Miguel. The Adventures of Don Quixote De La Mancha. Smollett, Tobias George, tr. from SPA. LC 85-2447. 845p. 1986. pap. 18.00 (*0-374-51943-9*) FS&G.

— Adventures of Don Quixote de la Mancha. (J). 1950. 14.05 (*0-606-03005-0*, Pub. by Turtleback) Demco.

— Aventuras de Don Quijote: Relatos Ilustrados. (SPA.). 9.00 (*84-241-5412-6*) E Torres & Sons.

— Cuatro Entremeses. (Fondo 2000 Ser.). (SPA.). pap. 2.99 (*968-16-5045-X*, Pub. by Fondo) Continental Bk.

— Don Quichotte. (FRE.). 1933. 95.00 (*0-8288-3456-3*, M3290) Fr & Eur.

— Don Quichotte, Vol. I. (FRE.). 1996. pap. 8.95 (*2-87714-316-3*, Pub. by Bookking Intl) Distribks Inc.

— Don Quichotte, Vol. II. (FRE.). 1996. pap. 8.95 (*2-87714-317-1*, Pub. by Bookking Intl) Distribks Inc.

— Don Quichotte de la Mancha, Tome I. (FRE.). 634p. 1988. pap. 16.95 (*0-7859-2078-1*, 2070379000) Fr & Eur.

— Don Quichotte de la Mancha, Tome II. (FRE.). 621p. 1988. pap. 16.95 (*0-7859-2079-X*, 2070379019) Fr & Eur.

— Don Quijote. Raffel, Burton, tr. from SPA. 752p. 1996. pap. 19.95 (*0-393-31509-6*) Norton.

***De Cervantes Saavedra, Miguel.** Don Quijote: A New Translation, Backgrounds & Contexts, Critism. Raffel, Burton, tr. from SPA. LC 98-8066. 1999. pap. 17.50 (*0-393-97281-X*) Norton.

De Cervantes Saavedra, Miguel. Don Quijote de la Mancha, 2 vols. (SPA.). pap. 16.95 (*84-376-0118-5*, Pub. by Ediciones Catedra) Continental Bk.

— Don Quijote de la Mancha. Blecua, Alberto, ed. (SPA.). pap. text. write for info. (*84-239-1950-1*) Elliots Bks.

— Don Quijote de la Mancha. (SPA.). pap. 17.95 (*84-239-0150-5*, Pub. by Espasa Calpe) Continental Bk.

— Don Quijote de la Mancha. 1184p. 1989. pap. write for info. (*0-7859-5151-2*) Fr & Eur.

— Don Quijote de la Mancha. (Clasicos Ser.). (SPA.). 860p. 1997. pap. write for info. (*0-929441-91-5*) Pubns Puertorriquenas.

***De Cervantes Saavedra, Miguel.** Don Quijote De La Mancha. LC 98-189797. Vol. 150. (SPA.). 1162p. 1998. pap. text 15.95 (*84-239-9599-2*) Espasa Calpe.

De Cervantes Saavedra, Miguel. Don Quijote de la Mancha, 2 vols., Set. deluxe ed. (SPA., Illus.). 952p. 1989. 850.00 (*84-239-4133-7*) Elliots Bks.

— Don Quijote de la Mancha, Vol. I. unabridged ed. (SPA.). pap. 7.95 (*84-410-0004-2*, Pub. by Bookking Intl) Distribks Inc.

D

— Don Quijote de la Mancha, Vol. 2. 592p. 1990. pap. 15.95 (0-7859-5999-8, 8437601185) Fr & Eur.

— Don Quijote de la Mancha, Vol. II. unabridged ed. (SPA.). pap. 7.95 (84-410-0005-0, Pub. by Bookking Intl) Distribks Inc.

— Don Quixote. (Illustrated Classics Collection 5). 64p. 1994. pap. 4.95 (0-7854-0776-6, 40547) Am Guidance.

— Don Quixote. Motteux, Peter A., tr. 928p. 1991. 23.00 (0-679-40758-8) Everymns Lib.

***De Cervantes Saavedra, Miguel.** Don Quixote. LC 97-47415. 1998. 24.45 (0-679-60286-0) Modern Lib NY.

De Cervantes Saavedra, Miguel. Don Quixote. 1965. mass mkt. 7.95 (0-451-52507-8, Sig) NAL.

— Don Quixote. Harrison, Michael, ed. (Oxford Illustrated Classics Ser.). (Illus.). 96p. (YA). 1999. pap. 12.95 (0-19-274182-9) OUP.

— Don Quixote. (Now Age Illustrated V Ser.). (Illus.). 64p. (J). (gr. 4-12). 1979. pap. text 2.95 (0-88301-387-8); student ed. 1.25 (0-88301-411-4) Pendulum Pr.

— Don Quixote. Cohen, John M., tr. 944p. 1999. pap. 8.95 (0-14-044010-0) Peng Put Young Read.

— Don Quixote. (Classics Library). 928p. 1997. pap. 3.95 (1-85326-036-3, 0363WW, Pub. by Wrdsworth Edits) NTC Contemp Pub Co.

— Don Quixote. LC 92-52995. (Illus.). 32p. (J). (gr. 2 up). 1993. 13.95 (1-56402-174-2) Candlewick Pr.

— Don Quixote. abr. ed. Marshall, Michael J., ed. (Core Classics Ser.: Vol. 6). (Illus.). 264p. (J). (gr. 4-6). 1999. pap. 7.95 (1-890517-10-0) Core Knowledge.

— Don Quixote. abr. ed. Starkie, Walter, tr. 1957. mass mkt. 6.99 (0-451-62684-2, Ment) NAL.

— Don Quixote. 1981. reprint ed. lib. bdg. 37.95 (0-89966-383-4) Buccaneer Bks.

— Don Quixote de la Mancha. 1976. 21.95 (0-8488-0438-4) Amereon Ltd.

— Don Quixote de la Mancha. Riley, E. C., ed. & tr. by. (Oxford World's Classics Ser.). 1,110p. 1998. pap. 7.95 (0-19-283483-5) OUP.

— Don Quixote de la Mancha. Jarvis, Charles, tr. from SPA. LC 99-461935. 1,128p. 1999. 20.00 (0-19-210032-7) OUP.

— Don Quixote Readalong. (Illustrated Classics Collection 5). 64p. 1994. pap. 14.95 incl. audio (0-7854-0792-8, 40549) Am Guidance.

— Eight Interludes. Smith, Dawn, tr. 288p. 1996. pap. 7.95 (0-460-87751-8, Everyman's Classic Lib) Tuttle Pubng.

— Entremeses. (SPA.). pap. 12.95 (84-376-0346-3, Pub. by Ediciones Catedra) Continental Bk.

— Entremeses. 7th ed. (SPA.). 288p. 1989. pap. 11.95 (0-7859-5159-8) Fr & Eur.

— The Exemplary Novels. Price, ed. (Complete Exemplary Novels Ser.: Vol. 2). 1992. pap. 22.00 (0-85668-494-5, Pub. by Aris & Phillips) David Brown.

— Exemplary Novels, 4 vols., Set. Cervantes, Carmen M. et al, eds. 1992. 175.00 (0-85668-557-7, Pub. by Aris & Phillips) David Brown.

— The Exemplary Novels, Vol. I. Cervantes, Carmen M., ed. 1992. 59.95 (0-85668-555-0, Pub. by Aris & Phillips) David Brown.

— The Exemplary Novels, Vol. I. Williams, ed. 1992. pap. 25.00 (0-85668-556-9, Pub. by Aris & Phillips) David Brown.

— The Exemplary Novels, Vol. 3. Thacker, ed. 1992. 59.95 (0-85668-495-3, Pub. by Aris & Phillips); pap. 22.00 (0-85668-496-1, Pub. by Aris & Phillips) David Brown.

— The Exemplary Novels, Vol. 4. Jones Staff & Macklin, eds. 1992. 59.95 (0-85668-497-X, Pub. by Aris & Phillips); pap. 22.00 (0-85668-498-8, Pub. by Aris & Phillips) David Brown.

— Exemplary Stories. Lipson, Lesley, tr. & intro. by. (Oxford World's Classics Ser.). 352p. 1998. pap. 8.95 (0-19-283243-3) OUP.

— Exemplary Stories. Jones, C. A., tr. (Classics Ser.). 256p. 1986. pap. 10.95 (0-14-044248-0, Penguin Classics) Viking Penguin.

De Cervantes Saavedra, Miguel. Exploits of Don Quixote. abr. ed. LC 73-750927. 1970. audio 14.00 (0-694-50198-0, SWC 1289, Caedmon) HarperAudio.

— La Gitanilla Rinconete y Corta. (SPA.). 1999. 13.00 (84-481-0625-3, McGrw-H College) McGrw-H Hghr Educ.

— El Hidalgo de la Mancha: Aventuras de Don Quijote, 001. Quilter, Daniel, ed. (ENG & SPA.). 235p. (C). 1973. pap. 21.24 (0-395-13390-4) HM.

De Cervantes Saavedra, Miguel. History of Don Quixote de la Mancha, 4 vols. Shelton, Thomas, tr. LC 09-3440. (Tudor Translations, First Ser.: Nos. 13-16). reprint ed. 230.00 (0-404-51880-X) AMS Pr.

— El Ingenioso Hidalgo Don Quijote de la Mancha. (SPA.). 1989. 7.95 (0-8288-2561-0) Fr & Eur.

— El Ingenioso Hidalgo Don Quijote de la Mancha. Parr, James A. & Fajardo, Salvador, eds. (Spanish Classical Texts Ser.). (SPA.). 984p. 1998. text 28.95 (1-889818-11-9) Pegasus Pr.

— El Ingenioso Hidalgo Don Quijote de la Mancha. (Clasicos Esenciales Ser.). (SPA.). (C). 1998. pap. 9.95 (84-294-4559-5) Santillana.

***De Cervantes Saavedra, Miguel.** El Ingenioso Hidalgo Don Quijote de la Mancha, Pts. I & II. unabridged ed. Lathrop, Tom, ed. (Documentacion Cervantina Ser.: Nos. 16). 423p. 1999. pap. 16.00 (0-936388-87-0) Juan de la Cuesta.

De Cervantes Saavedra, Miguel. Interludes of Cervantes. Morley, Sylvanus G., tr. LC 69-13852. 223p. 1969. reprint ed. lib. bdg. 59.50 (0-8371-0976-0, CEIN, Greenwood Pr) Greenwood.

— Nouvelles Exemplaires. (FRE.). 640p. 1981. pap. 13.95 (0-7859-1929-5, 2070372561) Fr & Eur.

— Novelas Ejemplares. (SPA.). 7.95 (84-241-5613-7) E Torres & Sons.

— Novelas Ejemplares. (SPA.). pap. 8.95 (968-432-190-2, Pub. by Porrua) Continental Bk.

— Novelas Ejemplares, No. 29. (SPA.). 234p. 1981. write for info. (0-8288-8551-6) Fr & Eur.

— Novelas Ejemplares, Vol. II. unabridged ed. (SPA.). pap. 7.95 (84-410-0041-7, Pub. by Bookking Intl) Distribks Inc.

— Novelas Ejemplares, I. Sevilla Arroyo, Florencio, ed. (Nueva Austral Ser.: Vol. 199). (SPA.). 1991. pap. text 19.95 (84-239-7199-6) Elliots Bks.

— Novelas Ejemplares, II. Sevilla Arroyo, Florencio, ed. (Nueva Austral Ser.: Vol. 200). (SPA.). 1991. pap. text 19.95 (84-239-7200-3) Elliots Bks.

— Ombras Completas. write for info. (0-318-63624-7) Fr & Eur.

— Poesia. (SPA.). 125p. 1972. 8.95 (0-8288-7169-8, S7742) Fr & Eur.

— The Portable Cervantes. Putnam, Samuel, tr. LC 76-44354. (Portable Library: No. 57). 854p. 1976. pap. 22.99 (0-14-015057-9, Penguin Bks) Viking Penguin.

— Rinconete & Cortadillo. pap. 5.95 (0-8283-1453-5) Branden Bks.

— Rinconete & Cortadillo, Level 2. (Leer en Espanol Ser.). (SPA.). (C). 1998. pap. 5.95 (84-294-4039-9) Santillana.

— Rudian Dichoso: Pedro de Urdemalas. 392p. 1986. pap. 12.95 (0-7859-5162-8) Fr & Eur.

— El Rufian Dichoso. (SPA.). 125p. 1977. 7.95 (0-8288-7058-6) Fr & Eur.

— Selections from Don Quixote (Selecciones de Don Quijote de la Mancha) A Dual-Language Book. Appelbaun, Stanley, tr. & intro. by. LC 99-12617. (SPA & ENG.). 256p. 1999. pap. text 9.95 (0-486-40666-0) Dover.

— Six Exemplary Novels. De Onis, Harriet, ed. 1961. pap. 5.95 (0-8120-0159-1) Barron.

— Spanish Englishwoman: The Glass Graduate & the Power of Blood. Ife, B. W., ed. Price, R. M., tr. (Complete Exemplary Novels Ser.: Vol. 2). 1992. 49.95 (0-85668-493-7, Pub. by Aris & Phillips) David Brown.

— Three Exemplary Novels. Putnam, Samuel, tr. LC 81-20235. Orig. Title: Novelas Ejemplares. (Illus.). 232p. 1982. reprint ed. lib. bdg. 38.50 (0-313-23346-2, CETN, Greenwood Pr) Greenwood.

De Cervantes Saavedra, Miguel. Wishbone Classic: Don Quixote, No. 1. LC 97-128638. (Wishbone Classics Ser.: Vol. 1). (Illus.). 128p. (J). (gr. 3-7). 1996. mass mkt. 4.25 (0-06-106416-5) HarpC.

De Cervantes Saavedra, Miguel & Cervantes, Carmen M. Novelas Ejemplares, Vol. I. unabridged ed. (SPA.). pap. 7.95 (84-410-0040-9, Pub. by Bookking Intl) Distribks Inc.

De Cervantes Saavedra, Miguel & De Riquer, Martin. Don Quijote de la Mancha: Spanish Edition. (SPA.). 1138p. 1997. pap. text 24.95 (84-08-01882-5) Planeta.

De Cervera, Alejo. The Statute of Limitations in American Conflicts of Law. LC 65-23494. 189p. (C). 1966. 4.00 (0-8477-3001-8) U of PR Pr.

De Cesare, Angelo. Anthony the Perfect Monster. (J). (ps-2). 1996. 7.99 (0-614-15834-6) Random.

De Cesare, R. Songs for the Italian Class - Songbook. (C). 1984. 40.00 (0-8442-8063-1, Pub. by S Thornes Pubs) St Mut.

— Songs for the Russian Class - Songbook & Cassette. (C). 1984. text 125.00 (0-8442-4271-3, Pub. by S Thornes Pubs) St Mut.

De Cesare, R., jt. auth. see DeCesare, Ruth.

De Cesaris, Janet, tr. see Beneti Jornet, Josep M.

***De Chabaneix, Gilles, photos by.** The Secret Gardens of Paris. LC 00-101384. (Illus.). 176p. 2000. 45.00 (0-500-51017-2, Pub. by Thames Hudson) Norton.

De Chabaneix, Gilles, jt. auth. see D'Arnoux, Alexandra.

De Chadarevain, Soraya & Kamminga, Harmke. Molecularising Biology & Medicine: New Practices & Alliances, 1930s to 1970s. (Studies in the History of Science, Technology & Medicine Ser.: Vol. 6). 350p. 1998. text 70.00 (3-7186-5908-5, Harwood Acad Pubs) Gordon & Breach.

De Chair, Somerset, ed. & tr. see Bonaparte, Napoleon.

***De Cham Marivaux, Pierre Carlet.** La Dispute. 96p. 1999. pap. 10.95 (1-84002-108-X, Pub. by Theatre Comm) Consort Bk Sales.

De Chambonnieres, Jacques. Les Pieces de Clavessin. fac. ed. (Monuments of Music & Music Literature in Facsimile, I Ser.: Vol. 3). 1967. lib. bdg. 60.00 (0-8450-2003-X) Broude.

De Chambrun, Adolphe. The Executive Power in the United States: A Study of Constitutional Law. LC 74-75460. xvii, 288p. 1974. reprint ed. 55.00 (0-912004-13-4) Gaunt.

De Chambrun, Clara L. The Making of Nicholas Longworth: Annals of an American Family. (Select Bibliographies Reprint Ser.). 1977. reprint ed. 29.95 (0-8369-5882-9) Ayer.

De Chambrun, Rene. France During the German Occupation, 1940-1944: A Bibliographical Supplement. (Publication Ser.: No. 337). 52p. (C). 1986. pap. text 3.98 (0-8179-8372-4) Hoover Inst Pr.

— Mission & Betrayal, 1940-1945: Working with Franklin Roosevelt to Help Save Britain & Europe. LC 92-35463. (Publication Ser.: Vol. 414). (Illus.). 228p. (C). 1993. text 33.95 (0-8179-9221-9); pap. text 18.95 (0-8179-9222-7) Hoover Inst Pr.

De Chamerlat, Christian A. Falconry & Art. (Illus.). 256p. 1995. boxed set 60.00 (0-905743-73-3, Pub. by Stacey Intl) Intl Bk Ctr.

De Chamfort, Sebastien R. Maximes et Pensees: Caracteres et Anecdotes. (FRE.). 448p. 1982. pap. 11.95 (0-7859-1953-8, 2070373568) Fr & Eur.

De Champlain, Samuel. Voyages of Samuel de Champlain, 1604-1618. (BCL1 - History - Canada Ser.). 374p. 1991. reprint ed. lib. bdg. 89.00 (0-7812-6351-4) Rprt Serv.

De Chant, Barry. Bonzo's Complete Book of Skits, Vol. 1. LC 97-73580. (Illus.). 128p. 1997. pap. 14.00 (0-9659211-0-7) Bonzo Prodns.

De Chant, John M. Devilbirds: The Story of the United States Marine Corps Aviation in World War II. LC 79-16257. 1982. reprint ed. 30.00 (0-89201-050-9) Zenger Pub.

de Chantal Radimilahy, Marie. Mahilaka: An Archaeological Investigation of an Early Town in Northwestern Madagascar. LC 99-159010. 293p. 1998. write for info. (91-506-1313-8) Uppsala Universitet.

De Chardin, Pierre T. Activation de l'Energie. 428p. 1963. 24.95 (0-8288-7425-5) Fr & Eur.

— Oeuvres Completes: Le Phenomene Humaine, Vol. 1. (FRE.). 1987. pap. 12.95 (0-7859-2670-4) Fr & Eur.

De Chardin, Teilhard. Building the Earth. 35th anniversary ed. (Illus.). 1965. pap. 16.95 (0-87193-078-1) Dimension Bks.

***De Chardin, Teilhard.** Building the Earth. 35th deluxe ed. 2000. boxed set 50.00 (0-87193-320-9) Dimension Bks.

De Charmant, Anne. Art & the Garden: Travels in the Contemporary Mindscape, Profile No. 57. 96p. 1998. pap. 44.95 (0-471-97745-4) Wiley.

De Charmant, Anne, ed. Art & the Garden. (Art & Design Ser.: Vol. 57). (Illus.). 96p. 1997. pap. 29.95 (1-85490-529-5) Academy Ed UK.

De Charms, George. The Tabernacle of Israel. 293p. 1985. 9.00 (0-910557-12-8) Acad New Church.

De Charms, R. Personal Causation: The Internal Affective Determinants of Behavior. 416p. 1983. pap. text 49.95 (0-89859-336-0) L Erlbaum Assocs.

De Charriere, Isabella A. Four Tales by Zelide. LC 75-140327. (Short Story Index Reprint Ser.). 1977. 20.95 (0-8369-3719-8) Ayer.

De Chary, Pauline, tr. see Von Klarwill, Victor, ed.

***de Chassey, Eric.** Impressionists. 1998. pap. text 12.95 (2-86656-136-8) Scala Edit.

De Chastellux, Francois J. Travels in North-America, in the Years 1780-1782, 2 vols., 1. LC 67-29046. (Eyewitness Accounts of the American Revolution Ser.). 1968. reprint ed. 39.95 (0-405-01135-0) Ayer.

— Travels in North-America, in the Years 1780-1782, 2 vols., Set. LC 67-29046. (Eyewitness Accounts of the American Revolution Ser.). 1968. reprint ed. 20.95 (0-405-01109-1) Ayer.

— Travels in North-America, in the Years 1780-1782, 2 vols., Vol. 2. LC 67-29046. (Eyewitness Accounts of the American Revolution Ser.). 1968. reprint ed. 20.95 (0-405-01127-X) Ayer.

De Chateaubriand, Francois-Rene. Atala & Rene. Putter, Irving, tr. 1952. pap. 14.95 (0-520-00223-7, Pub. by U CA Pr) Cal Prin Full Svc.

— La Briere. (FRE.). 1985. pap. 24.95 (0-7859-3045-0) Fr & Eur.

— The Martyrs. Wight, O. W., ed. & tr. by. from FRE. LC 76-15294. 1976. reprint ed. 48.00 (0-86527-275-1) Fertig.

— Memoires d'Outre-Tombe. deluxe ed. Levaillant, Maurice & Moulnier, eds. (Bibliotheque de la Pleiade Ser.). (FRE.). 1280p. 1989. 150.00 (0-7859-1096-4, 2070101274) Fr & Eur.

De Chateaubriand, Rene. Atala: Edition Critique. 208p. 1952. 7.95 (0-8288-9091-9, F58720) Fr & Eur.

— Essai sur les Revolutions. (FRE.). 1978. 105.00 (0-8288-3458-X, M5082) Fr & Eur.

— Le Genie du Christianisme, 2 vols., 1. Reboul, Pierre, ed. 512p. 1966. 10.95 (0-8288-9092-7, F58501) Fr & Eur.

— Le Genie du Christianisme, 2 vols., 2. Reboul, Pierre, ed. 512p. 1966. 10.95 (0-318-52011-7, F58502) Fr & Eur.

— Memoires de Ma Vie. (FRE.). 141p. 1976. 15.95 (0-8288-9093-5, M2225) Fr & Eur.

— Napoleon. (FRE.). 1969. 10.95 (0-8288-9094-3) Fr & Eur.

— Paul et Virginie. (FRE.). 1984. pap. 10.95 (0-7859-1181-2, 2253012556) Fr & Eur.

— Rene. Canal, Denis, ed. (FRE.). 165p. 1991. pap. write for info. (0-7859-4664-0) Fr & Eur.

— La Vie de Rance. (FRE.). 379p. 1986. pap. 11.95 (0-7859-2048-X, 2070377695) Fr & Eur.

De Chateaubriand, Rene & Letessier, Fernand. Atala: Avec: Rene, Le Dernier Abencerage. (FRE.). 512p. 1958. 10.95 (0-8288-9096-X, F58476) Fr & Eur.

De Chateaubriand, Rene & Mourot, Jean. Itineraire de Paris a Jerusalem. 448p. 1968. 10.95 (0-8288-9097-8, F58522) Fr & Eur.

De Chazeau, Eunice. Born Permeable. Adams, Joseph D., ed. LC 91-67822. xii, 68p. (Orig.). 1992. pap. 5.00 (1-880016-09-5) Road Pubs.

***De Chazournes, Laurence B. & Sands, Philippe, eds.** International Law, the World Court & Nuclear Weapons. LC 98-44355. 400p. (C). 1999. 90.00 (0-521-65242-1); pap. 39.95 (0-521-65480-7) Cambridge U Pr.

De Chazournes, Laurence B., jt. auth. see Salman, Salman M. A.

De Chazournes, Laurence Boisson, see Salman, Salman M. A. & Boisson De Chazournes, Laurence, eds.

De Chernatony, Leslie. Creating Powerful Brands. 2nd ed. 384p. 1998. pap. text 37.95 (0-7506-2240-7) Buttrwrth-Heinemann.

***De Chernatony, Leslie.** From Brand Vision to Brand Value: Strategically Building & Substaining Brands. 352p. 2001. pap. 37.95 (0-7506-4614-4, Focal) Buttrwrth-Heinemann.

De Chernatony, Leslie. User's Guide to the VAX-VMS System. 1991. 45.00 (0-07-707220-0) McGraw.

De Chernatony, Leslie, ed. Brand Management. LC 98-2547. (International Library of Management). 375p. 1998. text 153.95 (1-85521-961-1, Pub. by Dartmth Pub) Ashgate Pub Co.

De Chernatony, Leslie & McDonald, Malcolm H. Creating Powerful Brands: The Strategic Route to Success in Consumer, Industrial & Service Markets. (Illus.). 280p. 1992. pap. 36.95 (0-7506-0660-6) Buttrwrth-Heinemann.

De Chiara, J. Time-Saver Standards for Interior Design & Space PLanning. (Illus.). 1004p. 1991. 150.00 (0-07-016299-9) McGraw.

De Chiara, Joseph. Time-Saver Standards for Building Types. 3rd ed. 1472p. 1990. 150.00 (0-07-016279-4) McGraw.

***De Chiara, Joseph.** Time-Saver Standards for Building Types. 4th ed. (Illus.). 2000. 150.00 (0-07-016387-1) McGraw.

De Chiara, Joseph, et al, eds. Time-Saver Standards for Housing & Residential Development. 2nd ed. LC 94-5366. 1114p. 1992. 119.50 (0-07-016301-4) McGraw.

De Chirico, Giorgio. Hebdomeros. (Illus.). 144p. pap. write for info. (0-7206-0877-5, Pub. by P Owen Ltd) Dufour.

— Hebdomeros & Other Writings. Ashbery, John et al, trs. from FRE. 280p. (Orig.). 1992. pap. 15.95 (1-878972-06-5) Exact Change.

— The Memoirs of Giorgio de Chirico. Crosland, Margaret, tr. from ITA. & intro. by. (Illus.). 262p. 1994. reprint ed. pap. 13.95 (0-306-80568-5) Da Capo.

De Choisy, Abbe. Journal of a Voyage to Siam, 1685-1686. Smithies, Michael, tr. (Oxford in Asia Hardback Reprints Ser.). (Illus.). 314p. (C). 1994. text 69.00 (967-65-3026-3) OUP.

De Choisy, Abbe. The Transvestite Memoirs: And the Story of the Marquise-Marquis de Banneville. Scott, R. H., tr. & intro. by. LC 94-218096. (Illus.). 142p. 1994. pap. 18.95 (0-7206-0915-1, Pub. by P Owen Ltd) Dufour.

De Chrapowicki, Maryla. Spectro Biology. 62p. 1996. reprint ed. spiral bd. 10.00 (0-7873-0262-7) Hlth Research.

De Christoforo, Ron. Grease. 1998. per. 5.99 (0-671-02456-6) PB.

De Chungara, Domitila B. & Viezzer, Moema. Let Me Speak! Testimony of Domitila, a Woman of the Bolivian Mines. Ortiz, Victoria, tr. LC 77-91757. 235p. 1979. pap. 15.00 (0-85345-485-X, Pub. by Monthly Rev) NYU Pr.

***De Cico, Eta, et al.** Activities for Using the Internet in Primary Schools. (Illus.). 192p. 1999. pap. 49.95 (0-7494-2989-5, Kogan Pg Educ) Stylus Pub VA.

De Cieza De Le On, Pedro, et al. The Discovery & Conquest of Peru: Chronicles of the New World Encounter. LC 98-20158. (Latin America in Translation - En Traduccion - Em Traducao Ser.). 1998. write for info. (0-8223-2127-0); pap. 21.95 (0-8223-2146-7) Duke.

De Cillia, Rudolf, et al, eds. Fremdsprachendidaktik und Uebersetzungswissenschaft: Beitraege Zum VERBAL-Workshop 1994 Unter Mitarbeit von Heinz Kiko. (Sprache im Kontext Ser.: Band 1). (GER., Illus.). 358p. 1997. pap. 57.95 (3-631-30148-0) P Lang Pubng.

De Civrieux, Marc. Watunna: An Orinoco Creation Cycle. 2nd ed. Guss, David M., ed. & tr. by. from SPA. LC 97-20813. (Illus.). 232p. 1997. reprint ed. pap. 12.95 (0-292-71589-7) U of Tex Pr.

De Claisse-Walford, Nancy L. Reading from the Beginning: The Shaping of the Hebrew Psalter. LC 97-41067. (C). 1997. text 30.00 (0-86554-567-7, MUP/H439) Mercer Univ Pr.

De Clam, DuPaty. Theorie und Praktik der Hoheren Reitkunst, 2 bde. (Illus.). 650p. 1987. write for info. (3-487-08282-9) G Olms Pubs.

De Claramonte, Andres. El Ataud Para el Vivo y el Talamo Para el Muerto. Lopez-Vasquez, Alfredo R., ed. (Textos B Ser.: No. 37). 159p. (C). 1994. pap. 45.00 (1-85566-019-9, Pub. by Tamesis Bks Ltd) Boydell & Brewer.

— El Secreto en la Mujer. Lopez-Vasquez, Alfredo R., ed. (Textos B Ser.: No. 35). (SPA.). 238p. (C). 1991. 35.00 (1-85566-009-1, Pub. by Tamesis Bks Ltd) Boydell & Brewer.

De Claremont, Lewis. Ancient Book of Formulas. 9.95 (0-685-05341-5) Wehman.

— Seven Keys to Power. 9.95 (0-685-22105-9) Wehman.

De Clari, Robert. The Conquest of Constantinople. (Medieval Academy Reprint for Teaching Ser.: Vol. 36). 150p. 1996. reprint ed. pap. text 13.95 (0-8020-7823-0, D164) U of Toronto Pr.

De Clarivaux, Bernard. Predigten des Hl. Bernhard in Altfranzosischer Uebertragung. xx, 442p. 1979. reprint ed. write for info. (3-487-06877-X) G Olms Pubs.

De Cleir, Piaras V. Polymers in Injection Molding. LC 85-51316. 170p. (C). 1991. reprint ed. pap. 52.00 (0-938648-25-X) T-C Pr CA.

De Clerck, F. & Hirschfeld, J., eds. Finite Geometries & Combinatorics. (London Mathematical Society Lecture Note Ser.: No. 191). 422p. (C). 1993. pap. text 49.95 (0-521-44850-6) Cambridge U Pr.

De Clercq, E., jt. ed. see Jeffries, D. J.

De Clercq, Erik, ed. Advances in Antiviral Drug Design, Vol. 1. 329p. 1993. 109.50 (1-55938-155-8) Jai Pr.

— Advances in Antiviral Drug Design, Vol. 2. 1996. 109.50 (1-55938-693-2) Jai Pr.

— Advances in Antiviral Drug Design, Vol. 3. Date not set. 109.50 (0-7623-0201-1) Jai Pr.

De Clercq, Erik & Walker, R. T., eds. Antiviral Drug Development: A Multidisciplinary Approach. (NATO ASI Series A, Life Sciences: Vol. 143). (Illus.). 314p. 1988. 85.00 (0-306-42796-6, Plenum Trade) Perseus Pubng.

de Clercq, Jan, jt. auth. see Balladelli, Micky.

De Clercq, Michel, et al. Emergency Psychiatry & Mental Health Policy: An International Point of View. LC 98-34614. 284p. 1998. write for info. (0-444-50015-4, Excerpta Medica); pap. write for info. (0-444-50016-2, Excerpta Medica) Elsevier.

D

An Asterisk (*) at the beginning of an entry indicates that the title is appearing for the first time.

De Clercq, Peter. At the Sign of the Oriental Lamp, the Musschenbroek Workshop in Leiden, 1660-1750, No. 53. 326p. 1997. pap. 35.00 (*90-5235-104-X*, Pub. by Erasmus Pub) Balogh.

De Clermont-Tonnerre, Alban & Andre-Levy, Michel. Zero Coupon Bonds: Bond Stripping. 150p. 1995. 79.95 (*1-873446-31-4*, Pub. by IFR Pub) Am Educ Systs.

De Cleyre, Voltairine. Selected Works. Havel, H., ed. (Notable American Authors Ser.). 1992. reprint ed. lib. bdg. 75.00 (*0-7812-2625-2*) Rprt Serv.

— Selected Works of Voltairine De Cleyre. Berkman, Alexander & Havel, H., eds. (Great Women Ser.). 484p. 1972. reprint ed. lib. bdg. 250.00 (*0-87700-191-X*) Revisionist Pr.

— Written in Red: Selected Poems. (Poets of Revolt Ser.: No. 2). 56p. 1991. pap. 5.00 (*0-88286-121-2*); lib. bdg. 20.00 (*0-88286-146-8*) C H Kerr.

De Clifford, Norman F. Egypt the Cradle of Ancient Masonry (1902) (Illus.). 744p. 1996. reprint ed. pap. 50.00 (*1-56459-524-2*) Kessinger Pub.

De Cock, F. & Legrand, C., eds. Desing of Axially Loaded Piles - European Practice: Proceedings of an ERTC-3 Seminar, Brussels, 17-18 April 1997. (Illus.). 396p. (C). 1997. text 107.00 (*90-5410-873-8*, Pub. by A A Balkema) Ashgate Pub Co.

De Cock, Kevin, jt. auth. see Greenwood, B. M.

De Cogan, Anne, jt. auth. see De Cogan, Donard.

De Cogan, Donard. Transmission Line Matrix (Tlm) Techniques for Diffusion Applications. 224p. 1998. text 70.00 (*90-5699-129-9*) Gordon & Breach.

De Cogan, Donard & De Cogan, Anne. Applied Numerical Modelling for Engineers. LC 96-49957. (Textbooks in Electrical & Electronic Engineering Ser.: No. 6). (Illus.). 284p. 1997. text 105.00 (*0-19-856438-4*); pap. text 50.00 (*0-19-856437-6*) OUP.

De Cola, Lee, jt. auth. see Balzani, Vincenzo.

De Comeau, Alexander. Monk's Magic. Reginald, R. & Melville, Douglas, eds. LC 77-84213. (Lost Race & Adult Fantasy Ser.). 1978. reprint ed. lib. bdg. 24.95 (*0-405-10968-7*) Ayer.

De Commynes, Philippe. Memoires Sur Louis the Eleventh. (FRE.). 598p. 1979. pap. 12.95 (*0-7859-2216-4*, 207037078X) Fr & Eur.

De Comte Pourtales, Guy. Richard Wagner - the Story of an Artist: Music Book Index. 409p. 1993. reprint ed. lib. bdg. 99.00 (*0-7812-9716-8*) Rprt Serv.

De Conciliis, Anthony J. & Kinsella, John F. Every Decision You Make Is a Spiritual One. LC 95-2309. (Illumination Bks.). (Illus.). 80p. (Orig.). 1995. pap. 3.95 (*0-8091-3562-0*) Paulist Pr.

De Conde, Alexander. A History of American Foreign Policy, Vol. II: Global Power, 1900 to Present. 3rd ed. LC 78-143911. 448p. 1979. pap. text 36.54 (*0-02-327980-X*, Macmillan Coll) P-H.

De Conde, Alexander, ed. Encyclopedia of American Foreign Policy, 3 vols., Set. LC 78-5453. 1978. text 295.00 (*0-684-15503-6*, Scribners Ref) Mac Lib Ref.

— Isolation & Security: Ideas & Interests in 20th Century American Foreign Policy. LC 57-13022. 218p. reprint ed. 67.60 (*0-8357-9108-4*, 201789700010) Bks Demand.

De Condillac, Etienne Bonnot, see Bonnot de Condillac, Etienne.

De Conick, April D. Seek to See Him: Ascent & Vision Mysticism in the Gospel of Thomas. (Supplements to Vigiliae Christianae Ser.: Vol. 33). xiv, 211p. 1996. 89.50 (*90-04-10401-1*) Brill Academic Pubs.

De Coninck, Franky. European Air Law: New Skies for Europe. 336p. 1992. pap. 54.00 (*2-908537-07-9*, Pub. by Inst Air Transport) Bks Intl VA.

De Coninck, J. & Dunlop, F., eds. Wetting Phenomena. (Lecture Notes in Physics Ser.: Vol. 354). viii, 112p. 1990. 40.00 (*0-387-52338-3*) Spr-Verlag.

De Coninck-Smith, Ning, et al, eds. Industrious Children: Work & Childhood in the Nordic Countries, 1850-1990. LC 98-167587. 211p. 1997. 32.00 (*87-7838-269-6*, Pub. by Odense Univ) Intl Spec Bk.

De Conno, F. Managing Cancer Pain. LC 96-32806. 1996. pap. text 29.00 (*0-7923-4202-X*) Kluwer Academic.

De Constant, D'Estaurnelles. America & Her Problems. Paul, H. B., ed. LC 73-13127. (Foreign Travelers in America, 1810-1935 Ser.). 570p. 1974. reprint ed. 42.95 (*0-405-05449-1*) Ayer.

De Contenson, Marie-Laure, et al. Gustave Moreau: Between Epic & Dream. LC 99-73863. (Illus.). 308p. 1999. 60.00 (*0-691-00734-9*, Pub. by Princeton U Pr) Cal Prin Full Svc.

De Cooker, Chris, ed. International Administration: Law & Practice. (C). 1990. ring bd. 345.00 (*0-7923-0465-9*) Kluwer Academic.

De Cooman, Gert, ed. see Ruan, D. & Kerre, Etienne E.

De Coppet, Daniel, ed. Understanding Rituals. LC 92-5657. (European Association of Social Anthropologists Ser.). (Illus.). 144p. (C). 1992. pap. 25.99 (*0-415-06121-0*, A9650) Routledge.

De Coppet, Daniel, et al, eds. Cosmos & Society in Oceania: Their Interrelations or Their Coalescence in Melanesia. (Explorations in Anthropology Ser.). 416p. 1995. 53.00 (*1-85973-037-X*, Pub. by Berg Pubs); pap. 22.50 (*1-85973-042-6*, Pub. by Berg Pubs) NYU Pr.

***De Cordoba, Vincent.** Is 'Peckerhead' Hyphenated? Building the International Space Station. 175p. 1999. pap. 15.95 (*0-7414-0125-8*) Buy Books.

De Cordova, Chris. The Tessellations File. (Orig.). pap., teacher ed. 10.95 (*0-906212-80-4*, Pub. by Tarquin Pubns) Parkwest Pubns.

De Cordova, Loretta P. Five Centuries in Puerto Rico: Portraits & Eras. 2nd rev. ed. LC 93-86378. (Illus.). 120p. 1993. reprint ed. pap. 19.95 (*0-89825-006-4*) Pub Resces PR.

De Cordova, Loretta Phelps, see Phelps De Cordova, Loretta.

De Cornare, Oreste. Sergio Leone: The Great American Dream of Legendary America. (Illus.). 1997. 39.95 (*88-7301-094-6*, Pub. by Gremese Intl) Natl Bk Netwk.

De Cornulier, Benoit. Meaning Detachment. (Pragmatics & Beyond Ser.: Vol. I:7). vi, 124p. 1980. pap. 29.00 (*90-272-2502-8*) J Benjamins Pubng Co.

De Corrales, Jeanne Frankel, see Frankel de Corrales, Jeanne.

De Corso, S. M., jt. ed. see Clark, J. S.

De Corte, E., et al, eds. Learning & Instruction: European Research in an International Context, Vol. 1. (Studia Paedagogica: No. 8). 490p. (Orig.). 1987. pap. 57.50 (*90-6186-206-X*, Pub. by Leuven Univ) Coronet Bks.

De Corte, E. & Weinert, F. International Encyclopedia of Development & Instructional Psychology. LC 96-17900. (Resources in Education Ser.: 6). (Illus.). 1002p. 1996. 219.75 (*0-08-042980-7*, Pergamon Pr) Elsevier.

De Corte, E. & Weinert, Franz E. International Encyclopedia of Development & Instructional Psychology. 1996. write for info. (*0-08-042706-5*, Pergamon Pr) Elsevier.

De Corte, Erik, et al, eds. Computer-Based Learning Environments & Problem Solving. LC 92-19166. (NATO ASI Series F: Computer & Systems Sciences, Special Programme AET: Vol. 84). xvi, 488p. 1992. 119.95 (*0-387-55048-8*) Spr-Verlag.

— Learning & Instruction: A Publication of the European Association of Learning & Instruction. (Illus.). 330p. 1987. 217.00 (*0-08-034769-X*) Franklin.

— Learning & Instruction: European Research in an International Context, Vols. 2.1 & 2.2. 712p. 1990. 206.25 (*0-08-040252-6*, Pergamon Pr) Elsevier.

De Corte, Erik, jt. ed. see Vosniadou, Stella.

De Corte, Frans, jt. auth. see Haute, Peter.

De Cos, Patricia A. A Selected & Annotated Bibliography on California's Central Valley by Geographic & Subject Theme. 86p. 1996. pap. write for info. (*1-58703-054-3*) CA St Libry.

***de Cos, Patricia L.** Educating California's Immigrant Children: An Overview of Bilingual Education. 69p. 1999. pap. write for info. (*1-58703-108-6*, CRB-99-009) CA St Libry.

— Readiness for Kindergarten: What Does It Mean? 51p. 1997. pap. write for info. (*1-58703-077-2*, CRB-97-014) CA St Libry.

De Cosse, Cy, Inc. Staff. A Portfolio of Deck Ideas: Your Practical Guide to Great Deck Design. LC 93-8175. (Illus.). 96p. 1993. pap. 9.95 (*0-86573-922-6*) Creat Pub Intl.

De Cosson, Emilius A. Fighting the Fuzzy-Wuzzy: Days & Nights of Service with Sir Gerald Graham's Field Force at Suakin. (Illus.). 368p. 1990. 37.50 (*1-85367-066-9*, 5505) Stackpole.

De Costa, Denise. Anne Frank & Etty Hillesum: Inscribing Spirituality & Sexuality. Hoyinck, Mischa F. & Chesal, Robert E., trs. LC 97-49649. (Illus.). 304p. (C). 1998. text 50.00 (*0-8135-2549-7*); pap. text 20.00 (*0-8135-2550-0*) Rutgers U Pr.

de Costa, Dolores Guiral, see Guiral de Costa, Dolores, intro.

De Costa, Elena. Collaborative Latin American Popular Theatre: From Theory to Form, from Text to Stage. LC 91-17087. (American University Studies: Romance Languages & Literature: Ser. II, Vol. 179). 175p. (C). 1992. text 36.95 (*0-8204-1653-3*) P Lang Pubng.

De Costa, L. A., jt. ed. see Latham, D.

***De Costa, Rene.** Humor in Borges. LC 99-47070. (Humor in Life & Letters Ser.). 128p. 2000. 24.95 (*0-8143-2888-1*) Wayne St U Pr.

De Costa, Rene. The Poetry of Pablo Neruda. LC 78-18008. (Illus.). 225p. 1979. 24.00 (*0-674-67980-6*) HUP.

— The Poetry of Pablo Neruda. (Illus.). 225p. 1979. pap. 14.95 (*0-674-67981-4*) HUP.

De Coster, Jean. German, French & English Dictionary for Automotive Engineering. 3rd rev. ed. (ENG, FRE & GER.). 620p. 1990. 250.00 (*0-8288-0051-0*, M14314) Fr & Eur.

— Worterbuch fur Kraftfahrzeugtechnik. 3rd rev. ed. (ENG, FRE & GER.). 1990. lib. bdg. 250.00 (*0-8288-3841-0*, M14314) Fr & Eur.

De Coteau Orie, Sandra. Did You Hear Wind Sing Your Name? LC 94-31102. (Illus.). 32p. (J). (ps-3). 1995. 14.95 (*0-8027-8350-3*); lib. bdg. 15.85 (*0-8027-8351-1*) Walker & Co.

— Did You Hear Wind Sing Your Name? An Oneida Song of Spring. LC 94-31102. (Illus.). 32p. (J). (ps-3). 1996. pap. 6.95 (*0-8027-7485-7*) Walker & Co.

De Coteau, Sandra. Did You Hear Wind Sing Your Name?; An Oneida Song of Spring. LC 94-31102. 1996. 12.40 (*0-606-10781-9*) Turtleback.

De Cou-Landberg, Michelle. The Global Classroom: A Thematic Multicultural Model for the K-6 & ESL Classroom. LC 93-48788. 144p. 1994. pap. text 28.58 (*0-201-52759-6*) Addison-Wesley.

— The Global Classroom: A Thematic Multicultural Model for the K-6 & ESL Classroom. LC 93-48788. 1994. pap. text 28.58 (*0-201-52960-2*) Addison-Wesley.

De Coubertin, Pierre. Textes Choisis, 3 vols., Set. xxxviii, 2252p. write for info. (*3-296-18000-1*) G Olms Pubs.

De Coulanges, Fustel. The Ancient City. 1972. 59.95 (*0-87968-624-3*) Gordon Pr.

***De Coulanges, Fustel.** Family, Kin & City-State: The Racial Underpinning of Ancient Greece & Rome. Jamieson, J. W., ed. & rev. by. 108p. 1999. pap. 18.00 (*1-878465-34-1*) Scott-Townsend Pubs.

De Coulanges, Numa D. The Ancient City: A Classic Study of the Religious & Civil Institutions of Ancient Greece & Rome. LC 79-3703. 1980. reprint ed. pap. 16.95 (*0-8018-2304-8*) Johns Hopkins.

De Coulon, Frederic. Signal Theory & Processing. LC 85-73435. (Artech House Communications & Electronic Defense Library). (Illus.). 630p. reprint ed. pap. 195.30 (*0-8357-5586-X*, 203521700093) Bks Demand.

***De Cource-Smale, Percy W.** The Instruments & Art of the Orchestra. 134p. 2000. reprint ed. lib. bdg. 59.00 (*0-7812-9358-8*) Rprt Serv.

De Courcelles, Dominique. La Parole de L'Ange: L'Ecriture at le Corps. LC 91-19568. (Reading Plus Ser. Vol. 9). XII, 291p. (C). 1992. text 61.95 (*0-8204-1639-8*) P Lang Pubng.

De Courcey, Philip. Standing Room Only. Knutson, Tomm, ed. 240p. 1999. pap. 12.99 (*1-889893-12-9*) Emerald House Group Inc.

De Courcy, G., tr. see Revesz, Geza.

De Courcy, G. I., tr. see Ringbom, Nils-Eric.

De Courcy, J. W. The Liffey in Dublin. LC 97-101754. (Illus.). 512p. 1996. 49.95 (*0-7171-2423-1*, Pub. by Gill & MacMill) Irish Bks Media.

De Courcy, Pol Potier, see Potier De Courcy, Pol.

De Courtivron, Gael. Collectible Coca-Cola Toy Trucks. (Illus.). 240p. 1995. 24.95 (*0-89145-606-6*, 3874) Collector Bks.

De Courtivron, Isabelle, jt. ed. see Chadwick, Whitney.

De Coussemaker, Edmond. L' Art Harmonique aux XIIe et XIIIe Siecles. (FRE., Illus.). 550p. 1964. reprint ed. lib. bdg. 85.00 (*0-8450-2501-5*) Broude.

De Coussemaker, Edmond, ed. Drames liturgiques du moyen age, texte et musique. (FRE & LAT., Illus.). 370p. 1964. reprint ed. lib. bdg. 85.00 (*0-8450-1004-2*) Broude.

De Coussemaker, Edmond, ed. see De La Halle, Adam.

De Covarrubias Horozco, Sebastian. Tesoro de la Lengua Castellana, O Espanola. (SPA.). 1927. 25.00 (*0-87535-020-8*) Hispanic Soc.

De Craemer, Willy. The Jamaa & the Church: A Bantu Catholic Movement in Zaire. (Oxford Studies in African Affairs). 202p. 1977. text 95.00 (*0-19-822708-6*) OUP.

De Crauzat, E. Steinlen: The Graphic Work. (FRE., Illus.). 248p. 1983. reprint ed. 95.00 (*0-915346-71-0*) A Wofsy Fine Arts.

De Crebillon, M. The Opportunities of a Night. Sutton, Eric, tr. LC 70-174388. 1972. reprint ed. 23.95 (*0-405-08401-3*) Ayer.

De Crenne, Helisenne. The Torments of Love. Neal, Lisa, ed. & tr. by. Rendall, Steven, tr. LC 95-4101. (C). 1996. pap. 18.95 (*0-8166-2789-4*); text 47.95 (*0-8166-2788-6*) U of Minn Pr.

De Crescenzi, M. & Piancastelli, M. N. Electron Scattering & Related Spectroscopies. 300p. 1996. text 68.00 (*981-02-2300-5*) World Scientific Pub.

De Crespigny, Lachlan & Dredge, Rhonda. Which Tests for My Unborn Baby? Ultrasound & Other Prenatal Tests. 2nd ed. LC 97-180922. (Illus.). 196p. 1997. pap. 21.95 (*0-19-553954-0*) OUP.

De Crespigny, Rafe. Generals of the South: The Foundation & Early History of the Three Kingdoms State of Wu. (Faculty of Asian Studies Monographs: Vol. 16). (Illus.). 742p. 1997. pap. text 60.00 (*0-7315-0901-3*, Pub. by Aust Nat Univ) UH Pr.

— Northern Frontier: The Policies & Strategy of the Later Han Empire. (Faculty of Asian Studies Monographs: Vol. 4). (Illus.). 650p. 1997. pap. text 60.00 (*0-86784-410-8*, Pub. by Aust Nat Univ) UH Pr.

De Crespigny, Rafe, ed. China This Century. 2nd ed. (Illus.). 368p. 1992. pap. text 29.95 (*0-19-585164-1*) OUP.

De Crespigny, Rafe, tr. Emperor Huan & Emperor Ling: Being the Chronicle of Later Han for the Years 157 to 189 A.D. As Recorded in Chapters 54 to 59 of the Zizhi Tongjian of Sima Guang, 2 vols. (Faculty of Asian Studies Monographs: Vol. 12). 630p. 1997. pap. 60.00 (*0-7315-0655-3*, Pub. by Aust Nat Univ) UH Pr.

De Crespigny, Rafe, tr. To Establish Peace: Being the Chronicle of Later Han for the Years 189 to 220 A.D. (Faculty of Asian Studies Monographs: Vol. 21). (Illus.). 690p. 1997. pap. text 60.00 (*0-7315-2537-X*, Pub. by Aust Nat Univ) UH Pr.

***de Crespigny, Rose C.** Norton Vyse: Psychic. Adrian, Jack, ed. (Occult Detectives Library: Vol. 2). xx, 104p. 1999. 34.50 (*1-899562-73-7*) Ash-Tree.

De Crespo, Patria C., jt. auth. see Falcon, Luis N.

De Crevecoeur, J. Hector. More Letters from the American Farmer: An Edition of the Essays in English Left Unpublished by Crevecoeur. Moore, Dennis D., ed. LC 93-23005. 736p. (C). 1995. text 75.00 (*0-8203-1599-0*) U of Ga Pr.

De Crevecoeur, Michel-Guillaume Jean. La Culture des Pommes de Terre. (Works of Michel-Guillaume Jean De Crevecoeur Ser.). 1990. reprint ed. lib. bdg. 90.00 (*0-7812-2454-3*) Rprt Serv.

— Letters from an American Farmer. (Works of Michel-Guillaume Jean de Crevecoeur Ser.). 1990. reprint ed. lib. bdg. 79.00 (*0-685-44765-0*) Rprt Serv.

— Sketches of Eighteenth Century America. (Works of Michel-Guillaume Jean De Crevecoeur Ser.). 1990. reprint ed. lib. bdg. 79.00 (*0-685-44773-1*) Rprt Serv.

— Voyage dans la Haute Pennsylvanie et dans l'Etat de New York. (Works of Michel-Guillaume Jean De Crevecoeur Ser.). 1990. reprint ed. lib. bdg. 79.00 (*0-7812-2455-1*) Rprt Serv.

— The Works of Michel-Guillaume Jean de Crevecoeur. 1990. reprint ed. lib. bdg. 63.00 (*0-685-27750-7*) Rprt Serv.

De Crevecoeur, St. John. Sketches of Eighteenth Century America. Boudin, H. L. et al, eds. LC 72-85505. 1972. reprint ed. 29.95 (*0-405-08406-4*) Ayer.

De Cristoforo, R. J. The Band Saw Book, with Twenty Projects. (Illus.). 288p. (Orig.). 1989. 25.95 (*0-8306-0289-5*) McGraw-Hill Prof.

— The Drill Press Book. (Illus.). 288p. 1991. pap. 16.95 (*0-8306-3609-9*) McGraw-Hill Prof.

— Gifts from the Woodshop. (Illus.). 256p. 1991. pap. 15.95 (*0-8306-3591-2*) McGraw-Hill Prof.

— The Jig Saw Book, with Forty Projects. (Illus.). 352p. 1989. 27.95 (*0-8306-9269-X*) McGraw-Hill Prof.

— Jigs, Fixtures, & Shop Accessories. LC 93-12801. (Illus.). 259p. 1993. 28.95 (*0-8306-4210-2*); pap. 16.95 (*0-8306-4211-0*) McGraw-Hill Prof.

— Popular Science Complete Book of Power Tools. LC 98-11509. (Popular Science Ser.). 672p. 1998. 24.98 (*1-57912-026-1*) Blck Dog & Leventhal.

— The Portable Router Book. (Illus.). 352p. (Orig.). 1987. 24.95 (*0-8306-0869-9*) McGraw-Hill Prof.

— The Portable Router Book. 2nd ed. (Orig.). 1993. pap. 16.95 (*0-8306-4461-X*); pap. 19.95 (*0-07-016337-5*) McGraw-Hill Prof.

— The Table Saw Book. 352p. 1987. pap. 22.95 (*0-07-157042-X*) McGraw.

— The Table Saw Book. (Illus.). 352p. 1987. pap. 16.95 (*0-8306-2789-8*) McGraw-Hill Prof.

— Woodworking for Beginners. (Illus.). 304p. 1992. pap. 15.95 (*0-8306-3829-6*, 4117) McGraw-Hill Prof.

De Cristoforo, Violet K. May Sky: There's Always Tomorrow: A History & Anthology of Haiku. LC 96-49284. 200p. 1996. 29.95 (*1-55713-253-4*) Sun & Moon CA.

De Crombrugghe, Benoit & New York Academy of Medicine Staff. Molecular & Developmental Biology of Cartilage. LC 96-1721. (Annals of the New York Academy of Sciences Ser.). 367p. 1996. pap. 110.00 (*1-57331-011-5*) NY Acad Sci.

De Croy-Roeulx, R. Cameras: Macchine Fotografiche. (Bella Cosa Ser.). (ITA., Illus.). 144p. 1997. pap. 12.95 (*0-8118-1471-8*) Chronicle Bks.

De Cruz, Peter. Comparative Law in a Changing World. 509p. 1995. pap. 45.00 (*1-85941-137-1*, Pub. by Cavendish Pubng) Gaunt.

***De Cruz, Peter.** Comparative Law in a Changing World. 2nd ed. LC 99-168452. 512p. 1999. pap. 49.00 (*1-85941-432-X*, 18113, Pub. by Cavendish Pubng) Gaunt.

De Cruz-Saenz, Michele S. Romancero Tradicional de Costa Rica. (Ediciones Criticas Ser.: Vol. 3). 138p. 1986. pap. 12.50 (*0-936388-23-4*) Juan de la Cuesta.

— Spanish Traditional Ballads from Aragon. LC 95-9256. (Illus.). 264p. 1995. 36.50 (*0-8387-5304-3*) Bucknell U Pr.

De Cruz, Stephen, jt. auth. see Lyon, C. M.

De Cuba, Roland, jt. auth. see Howe, Kate.

***de Cuellar, Jose Tomas.** The Magic Lantern: Having a Ball & Christmas Eve. Glantz, Margo, ed. Carson, Margaret A., tr. LC 99-59209. (Library of Latin America). 208p. 2000. 30.00 (*0-19-511502-3*) OUP.

— The Magic Lantern: Having A Ball & Christmas Eve. Glantz, Margo, ed. Carson, Margaret A., tr. LC 99-59209. (Library of Latin America). 208p. 2000. pap. 14.95 (*0-19-511503-1*) OUP.

De Cuenca, Pilar. Cinco Ciento Palabras Nuevas Para Ti. Alvarez, Ines, tr. LC 81-13766. (Bilingual Picturebacks Ser.).Tr. of Five Hundred Words to Grow on. (SPA., Illus.). 32p. (J). (ps-3). 1982. pap. 3.25 (*0-394-85145-5*, Pub. by Random Bks Yng Read) Random.

De Cuenca, Pilar, tr. see Berenstain, Stan & Berenstain, Jan.

De Cuenca, Pilar, tr. see Eastman, P. D.

de Cumptich, Roberto de Vicq, see De Vicq de Cumptich, Roberto.

De Cunzo, Lu A. & Herman, Bernard L., eds. Historical Archaeology & the Study of American Culture. 1996. 39.95 (*0-912724-36-6*) Winterthur.

De Cusa, Nicholas. De Ludo Globi. Trinkaus, Pauline W., tr. (Janus Ser.).Tr. of Game of Spheres. 136p. 1986. lib. bdg. 25.00 (*0-89835-068-9*) Abaris Bks.

De Cusatis, Casimer, jt. auth. see Das, Pankaj K.

De Custine, Astolphe M. Lettres de Russie (La Russie en 1839) (FRE.). 1975. pap. 11.95 (*0-7859-1807-8*, 2070366898) Fr & Eur.

De Custine, Marquis. Zaprisky O Rossik: The Notes about Russia. 2nd ed. Kustanovich, K., ed. (RUS.). 160p. (Orig.). pap. 15.00 (*0-940294-07-9*) Silver Age Pub.

De Cuyper, H. & Buyse, G., eds. Biological Psychiatry: Marching Backwards into the Future. 152p. (Orig.). 1989. pap. 47.50 (*90-6186-333-3*, Pub. by Leuven Univ) Coronet Bks.

De Cygne, Patrice. Seeds of Our Being. large type ed. LC 98-70635. (Illus.). 60p. 1998. pap. 14.00 (*0-943907-08-X*) Bruce Finson.

De, D. J. The Prevention of Food Adulteration Act 1954 with Central & State Rules & Notification. (C). 1988. 180.00 (*0-7855-3701-5*) St Mut.

— The Prevention of Food Adulteration Act with Central & State Rules & Notifications. (C). 1989. 180.00 (*0-7855-4796-7*) St Mut.

De Dalla Torre, Karl W. & Harms, Hermann G. Register Zu "Genera Siphonogamarum Ad Systema Englerianum Conscripta" (GER.). 570p. 1958. reprint ed. 50.00 (*3-201-00721-8*, Pub. by Akademische Druck-und) Balogh.

De Dalmases, Candido. Francis Borgia: Grandee of Spain, Jesuit, Saint. Buckley, Cornelius M., tr. from SPA. LC 91-71124. (Modern Scholarly Studies about the Jesuits, in English Translations Series II: No. 11). x, 251p. 1991. 27.95 (*0-912422-60-2*); pap. 17.95 (*0-912422-61-0*) Inst Jesuit.

De Dampierre, Florence. The Best of Painted Furniture. LC 86-43192. (Illus.). 200p. 1995. pap. 34.95 (*0-8478-1886-1*, Pub. by Rizzoli Intl) St Martin.

— The Book of Chairs. 1998. write for info. (*0-517-70813-2*) C Potter.

De Dan, Francine G., ed. see Pappadopoulos, George.

De Dan, Rose, ed. see Pappadopoulos, George.

De Iongh, Daniel Crena, see Crena De Iongh, Daniel.

D

De Darco, Alfredo. The Hoax- Files. LC 98-13142. 128p. (J). 1998. pap. 4.50 (*0-689-82185-9*) S&S Childrens.
De Daruvar, Ives. The Tragic Fate of Hungary: A Country Carved up Alive at Trianon. (Illus.). boxed set 10.00 (*0-912404-03-5*) Alpha Pubns.
De Datta, Surajit K. Principles & Practices of Rice Production. LC 86-21370. 640p. 1987. reprint ed. lib. bdg. 72.50 (*0-89874-994-8*) Krieger.
De Davila, E. Paradise in Mexico: Cuernavaca. 1976. lib. bdg. 59.95 (*0-8490-2408-0*) Gordon Pr.
De Davila, Maria D. Castro, see Castro De Davila, Maria D.
De Deckker, P. & Williams, W. D., eds. Limnology in Australia. (Monographiae Biologicae). 1986. text 278.50 (*90-6193-578-4*) Kluwer Academic.
De Deckker, P. T., ed. see Pritchard, George.
De Deguileville, Guillaume. The Pilgrimage of the Life of Man, Pts. 1-3. Furnivall, F. J. & Locock, K. B., eds. (EETS, ES Ser.: Nos. 77, 83, & 92). 1974. reprint ed. 90.00 (*0-527-00279-8*) Periodicals Srv.
— The Pylgremage of the Sowle. Lydgate, J., tr. LC 74-28845. (English Experience Ser.: No. 726). 1975. reprint ed. 10.00 (*90-221-0726-4*) Walter J Johnson.
De Deguilleville, Guillaume. The Booke of the Pylgremage of the Sowle. Cust, Katherine I., ed. Caxton, William, tr. from FRE. LC 78-180445. (Illus.). xix, 91 p. 1973. reprint ed. 21.50 (*0-404-56612-X*) AMS Pr.
De Del Rio, Amelia A. Del Yunque a los Pirineos. (SPA.). 1982. pap. 8.00 (*84-499-5836-9*) Edit Mensaje.
— Leon Felipe: El Hombre y el Poeta. (SPA.). 1980. pap. 7.80 (*84-499-4047-8*) Edit Mensaje.
— Puertorriquenos en Nueva York. (SPA.). 1970. pap. 5.50 (*0-86515-015-X*) Edit Mensaje.
De del Rio, Amelia A., ed. Flores del Romancero, II. LC 73-93965. (SPA.). 202p. (C). 1983. pap. 5.50 (*0-8477-3502-8*) U of PR Pr.
De Denzi, Riccardo & Luise, Marco, eds. Audio & Video Digital Radio Broadcasting Systems & Techniques: Proceedings of the Sixth Tirrenia International Workshop on Digital Communications, Tirrenia, Italy, 5-9 September, 1993. LC 93-49576. 404p. 1994. 194.50 (*0-444-81580-5*) Elsevier.
De Deus Gois, Joao. A New Millennium Catechism. LC 98-230806. 32p. 1998. pap. text 1.00 (*0-7648-0277-1*) Liguori Pubns.
De Deus, J. Dias, see Costa Ramos, S. & Dias de Deus, J., eds.
De Devitiis, Guido & Mariani, Luciano. Reference Grammar: English Grammar of Communication. 312p. 75.00 (*0-7859-8865-3*) Fr & Eur.
De Deyn. Ethics of Animal & Human Experimentation. 388p. 79.00 (*0-86196-429-2*, Pub. by J Libbey Med) Bks Intl VA.
— Textbook of Spect in Neurology & Psychiatry. 564p. text 166.00 (*0-86196-542-6*, Pub. by J Libbey Med) Bks Intl VA.
De Diaz-Limaco, Jane H. Peru in Focus: A Guide to the People, Politics & Culture. (In Focus Guides Ser.). (Illus.). 100p. 1998. pap. 12.95 (*1-56656-232-5*) Interlink Pub.
De Diego, Vicente Garcia, see Garcia de Diego, Vicente.
De Diesbach, Ghislain. Proust. 1997. write for info. (*0-679-42070-3*) Pantheon.
— The Toys of Princes. Howard, Richard, tr. from FRE. & intro. by. LC 92-81006. 200p. (Orig.). (C). 1992. pap. 12.95 (*0-9627987-2-X*) Turtle Point Pr.
De Diez Canseco, Maria R. Conflicts over Coca Fields in 16th-Century Peru. Marcus, Joyce, ed. Silva, Jorge E., tr. (Memoirs Series, Studies in Latin American Ethnohistory & Archaeology: No. 21, Vol. 4). xii, 316p. 1988. pap. 19.50 (*0-915703-13-0*) U Mich Mus Anthro.
de Diez Canseco, Maria Rostworowski, see Rostworowski de Diez Canseco, Maria.
De Dijin, Herman. Discount Travel Handbook: Save Money on Every Vacation or Business Trip You Take. Abbott, Mary L., ed. & intro. by. LC 95-62144. (Illus.). 250p. (Orig.). 1996. pap. 14.95 (*0-9644216-3-1*) Vacation Pubns.
De Dijn, Herman. Spinoza: The Way to Wisdom. LC 95-46211. (Series in the History of Philosophy). 300p. 1996. 34.95 (*1-55753-081-5*); pap. 19.95 (*1-55753-082-3*) Purdue U Pr.
De Dillmont, Therese. The Complete Encyclopedia of Needlework. 3rd ed. LC 95-70675. (Illus.). 704p. 1996. pap. 15.95 (*1-56138-702-9*) Running Pr.
— The Complete Encyclopedia of Needlework. 3rd ed. (Illus.). 704p. 1998. 14.98 (*0-7624-0388-8*, Courage) Running Pr.
— Masterpieces of Irish Crochet Lace: Technique, Patterns, Instructions. (Illus.). 64p. 1986. reprint ed. pap. 3.95 (*0-486-25079-2*) Dover.
De Dios, Angel C., jt. ed. see Facelli, Julio C.
De Dios Ortuzar, Juan & Willumsen, Luis G. Modelling Transport. 2nd ed. 454p. 1996. pap. 75.00 (*0-471-96534-0*) Wiley.
De Dios Ortuzars, Juan, et al. Travel Behaviour Research: Updating the State of Play. LC 98-40466. 1998. 122.50 (*0-08-043360-X*) Elsevier.
De Doelder, Hans & Tiedemann, Klaus, eds. Criminal Liability of Corporations: La Criminalisation Du Comportement Collectif. LC 95-45922. 1996. 146.50 (*90-411-0165-9*) Kluwer Law Intl.
De Dombal, F. T. Medical Informatics: The Essentials. LC 96-205533. 144p. 1996. pap. text 37.50 (*0-7506-2162-1*, Focal) Buttrwrth-Heinemann.
De Dombal, F. T., et al, eds. Inflammatory Bowel Disease: Some International Data & Reflections. 2nd ed. (Illus.). 764p. (C). 1994. text 135.00 (*0-19-262401-6*, 2290) OUP.
De Dombal, F. T., jt. ed. see Rozen, P.
De Domenico, Giovanni & Wood, Elizabeth C. Beard's Massage. 4th ed. Biblis, Margaret, ed. LC 96-14136. 256p. 1997. pap. text 34.00 (*0-7216-6234-X*, W B Saunders Co) Harcrt Hlth Sci Grp.
De Dominicis, Claudio. Italian Immigrants in the Archives of the Apostolic Delegation of the United States: Inventory. (Pastoral Ser.). 45p. 1991. pap. 7.50 (*0-934733-55-4*) CMS.
De Domitrovic, Zalocar, et al. Taxonomic & Ecological Studies of the Parana River Diatom Flora (Argentina) (Bibliotheca Diatomologica Ser.: Band 34). (Illus.). iv, 122p. 1997. 42.00 (*3-443-57025-9*, Pub. by Gebruder Borntraeger) Balogh.
De, Domizio Durini Lucrezia. Joseph Beuys Art Of Cooking. 1999. pap. text 45.00 (*88-8158-166-3*) Charta.
De Domizio, Lucrezia. The Felt Hat: Joseph Beuys a Life Told. (Illus.). 280p. 1997. pap. 24.95 (*88-8158-06-5*, 720401, Pub. by Charta) Dist Art Pubs.
De Domizio, Lucrezia, et al, texts. The Art World Through the Lens of Buby Durini. (Illus.). 254p. 1997. pap. 49.95 (*88-8158-106-X*, 720402, Pub. by Charta) Dist Art Pubs.
De Doncker, R. W., et al. Microprocessor Control for Motor Drives & Power Converters. Stefanovic, V. R. & Nelms, R. M., eds. LC 92-31625. (Tutorial Course Ser.). 1992. 60.00 (*0-7803-9965-X*) Inst Electrical.
— Microprocessor Control for Motor Drives & Power Converters: Presented October 3 at the 1993 IEEE Industry Applications Society Annual Meeting, Toronto, Ontario, Canada, 3rd ed. Stefanovic, V. R. & Nelms, R. M., eds. LC 93-30691. 1993. pap. 60.00 (*0-7803-9969-2*) Inst Electrical.
De Donk, Van. Orwell in Athens. LC 95-75769. 1995. 82.00 (*90-5199-219-X*) IOS Press.
***De Donno, Benito.** Glimpses of Reality. 312p. 1999. 32.00 (*0-9684877-0-X*) Kno1wledge Pubns.
De Dos, Dirk. Hans Memling: The Complete Oeuvre. LC 94-3048. (Illus.). 448p. 1994. 145.00 (*0-8109-3649-6*) Abrams.
De Dreu, Carsten K. & Van De Vliert, Evert, eds. Using Conflict in Organizations. 240p. 1997. 75.00 (*0-7619-5090-7*); pap. 26.95 (*0-7619-5091-5*) Sage.
***De Dreuille, Mayeul.** Seeking the Absolute Love: The Founders of Christian Monasticism. LC 99-74245. (Illus.). 145p. 2000. pap. 16.95 (*0-8245-1830-6*, Herdr & Herdr) Crossroad NY.
De Dueck, Elena R., jt. auth. see Cabrera, Sandra Z.
***de Dues Gois, Joao.** Un Nuevo Milenio: Preguntas y Respuestas. (SPA.). 32p. 1998. pap. 1.00 (*0-7648-0278-X*, Libros Liguori) Liguori Pubns.
De Duffer, Beatriz L., tr. see McGee, Robert S.
***De Dumas, Adrienne J.** Miyon & the Mountain Spirit. (J). (gr. k-3). 1999. pap. 6.95 (*0-533-13057-3*) Vantage.
De Durand-Forest, J. & Berdan, F., comments. Matricula de Tributos: or Codice de Moctezuma. fac. ed. (Codices Selecti C Ser.: Vol. LXVIII). 1980. 159.00 (*3-201-01130-4*, Pub. by Akademische Druck-und) Balogh.
De Duras. Ourika. Little, ed. (Exeter French Texts Ser.: Vol. 84). (FRE.). 109p. Date not set. pap. text 19.95 (*0-85989-394-4*, Pub. by Univ Exeter Pr) Northwestern U Pr.
De Duras, Claire. Ourika: An English Translation. Fowles, John, tr. from FRE. & frwd. by. (MLA Texts & Translations Ser.: No. 3b). xxxiii, 47p. (Orig.). 1994. pap. 5.95 (*0-87352-780-1*, P003P) Modern Lang.
— Ourika: The Original French Text. DeJean, Joan, ed. & intro. by. Waller, Margaret, intro. (MLA Texts & Translations Ser.: No. 3a). (FRE.). xxviii, 45p. (Orig.). 1994. pap. 5.95 (*0-87352-779-8*, Q003P) Modern Lang.
De Duras, Madame. Ourika: Madame de Duras. rev. ed. Little, Roger, ed. 160p. 1998. pap. 23.95 (*0-85989-573-4*, Pub. by Univ Exeter Pr) Northwestern U Pr.
de Duue, Thierry. Basic Forms. (Illus.). 160p. 1999. 22.95 (*3-8238-1001-4*) te Neues.
De Duve, Christian. Vital Dust: Life As a Cosmic Imperative. (Illus.). 384p. 1995. pap. 16.00 (*0-465-09045-1*, Pub. by Basic) HarpC.
De Duve, Thierry. Clement Greenberg: Between the Lines. 160p. 1996. pap. 32.95 (*2-906571-53-9*, Pub. by Editions Dis Voir) Dist Art Pubs.
— Kant after Duchamp. LC 95-38235. (Illus.). 500p. 1996. 49.50 (*0-262-04151-0*) MIT Pr.
— Kant after Duchamp. (Illus.). 500p. 1998. reprint ed. pap. text 25.00 (*0-262-54094-0*) MIT Pr.
— Pictorial Nominalism: On Marcel Duchamp's Passage from Painting to the Readymade, Vol. 51. Polan, Dana B., tr. (Theory & History of Literature Ser.). (FRE., Illus.). 244p. (Orig.). 1991. pap. 17.95 (*0-8166-1565-9*) U of Minn Pr.
De Duve, Thierry, ed. The Definitively Unfinished Marcel Duchamp. (Illus.). 550p. 1991. 62.00 (*0-262-04117-0*) MIT Pr.
De Duve, Thierry, et al. Jeff Wall. LC 96-196857. (Contemporary Artists Ser.). (Illus.). 160p. (Orig.). 1996. pap. 29.95 (*0-7148-3349-5*, Pub. by Phaidon Press) Phaidon Pr.
De Eguilaz y Yanguas, Leopold. Glosario Etimologico De las Palabras Espanolas. xxiv, 591p. 1970. reprint ed. write for info. (*0-318-71620-8*) G Olms Pubs.
De Elia, Thomas, et al. Argentina: The Great Estancias. LC 95-8168. (Illus.). 228p. 1995. 60.00 (*0-8478-1905-1*, Pub. by Rizzoli Intl) St Martin.
De Elia, Tomas. Evita: An Intimate Portrait of Eva Peron. Queiroz, Juan P., ed. LC 96-40201. (Illus.). 192p. 1997. 40.00 (*0-8478-2028-9*, Pub. by Rizzoli Intl) St Martin.
De Elosua, Juan. Business Dictionary Spanish-English-French-German-Italian. 7th ed. 862p. 1997. 64.00 (*84-88717-04-0*, Pub. by Lid Edit Empres) IBD Ltd.
De Elvira, A. Ruiz, see Ruiz De Elvira, A.
De Erauso, Catalina. Lieutenant Nun: Memoir of a Basque Transvestite in the New World. Stepto, Michele & Stepto, Gabriel, trs.Tr. of Historia de la Monja Alferez. 1997. pap. 12.00 (*0-8070-7073-4*) Beacon Pr.
De Escalante, Joel B. Expresiones y Reflexiones: Expressions & Reflections. (ENG & SPA., Illus.). x, 112p. (C). 1998. pap. text 7.50 (*0-9662808-0-6*) Legion Hispanica.
De Espana, Rafael, ed. Directory of Spanish & Portuguese Film-Makers & Films. LC 94-17610. 264p. 1994. lib. bdg. 75.00 (*0-313-29459-3*, Greenwood Pr) Greenwood.
De Espronceda, Jose. The Student of Salamanca: El Estudiante de Salamanca. Cardwell, R. A., ed. Davis, C. K., tr. from SPA. (Hispanic Classics Ser.). (C). 1991. 59.95 (*0-85668-501-1*, Pub. by Aris & Phillips); pap. 22.00 (*0-85668-502-X*, Pub. by Aris & Phillips) David Brown.
De Fabregues, Jean. Edith Stein: Philosopher, Carmelite Nun, Holocaust Martyr. LC 93-2771. 103p. 1993. reprint ed. pap. 6.95 (*0-8198-2333-3*) Pauline Bks.
De Faire, Ulf & Theorell, Torres. Life Stress & Coronary Heart Disease. 130p. 1984. 18.50 (*0-87527-201-0*) Green.
De Fajardo, Vilma, ed. see Rodriquez, Judith.
De Falco, ed. Iamblichi: Theologumena Arithmeticae. rev. ed. (GRE.). 1975. pap. 33.50 (*3-519-01446-7*, T1446, Pub. by B G Teubner) U of Mich Pr.
De Falla, Emily M. CGL Insurance Coverage for Clean up of Hazardous Substances: A Research Guide. LC 89-2095. Vol. 9. ii, 71p. 1989. lib. bdg. 32.50 (*0-89941-684-5*, 305820) W S Hein.
De Fallois. Simenon. pap. 8.95 (*0-685-36579-4*, F126930) Fr & Eur.
De Fana, Angel, ed. see Albertini, J. A.
De Fana, Angel, ed. see De Armas, Armando.
De Fana, Angel, ed. see De Juan, Eduardo.
De Fana, Angel, ed. see Fibla, Alberto.
De Fana, Angel, ed. see Garcia, Haydee & Garcia, De Julio G.
De Fana, Angel, ed. see GrauSierra, Alberto E.
De Fana, Angel, ed. see Lopez, Haudee V.
De Fana, Angel, ed. see Rodriguez, Marisol S.
De Faria Coutinho, Eduardo. The Synthesis Novel in Latin America: A Study on Joao Guimaraes Rosa's Grande Sertao - Veredas. LC 91-10289. (North Carolina Studies in the Romance Languages & Literatures: No. 237). 174p. reprint ed. pap. 54.00 (*0-608-20074-3*, 207134600011) Bks Demand.
De Faye, Eugene. Gnostiques et Gnosticisme: Etude Critique Des Documents Du Gnosticisme Chretien Aux Deuxieme et Troisieme Siecles. LC 77-84699. reprint ed. 55.00 (*0-404-16106-5*) AMS Pr.
***De, Fazio John.** Stardumb. 1999. 15.00 (*1-891273-01-9*) DAP Assocs.
***De Fazio, Teresa.** Studying in Australia: A Guide for International Students. 216p. 2000. pap. 17.95 (*1-86448-886-7*, Pub. by Allen & Unwin Pty) Paul & Co Pubs.
De Federico De Onis, Ensayo. Disciplina y Rebeldia. 51p. 1915. 0.75 (*0-318-14255-4*) Hispanic Inst.
De Federico de Onis, Ensayos, et al. Antonia Merce - la Argentina. 50p. 0.80 (*0-318-14238-4*) Hispanic Inst.
De Felice, Eugene A., jt. ed. see Kostis, John B.
De Felice, F. & Clarke, C. J. Relativity on Curved Manifolds. (Monographs on Mathematical Physics). 459p. (C). 1990. text 125.00 (*0-521-26639-4*) Cambridge U Pr.
— Relativity on Curved Manifolds. (Monographs on Mathematical Physics). 460p. (C). 1992. pap. text 44.95 (*0-521-42908-0*) Cambridge U Pr.
De Felice, Frank, ed. A Primer on Business Finance. LC 73-20489. 1974. 37.75 (*0-8422-5132-4*) Irvington.
De Felice, Renzo. Fascism: An Informal Introduction to Its Theory & Practice. LC 76-13006. (Issues in Contemporary Civilization Ser.). 128p. reprint ed. pap. 39.70 (*0-608-12072-3*, 202415500035) Bks Demand.
— Interpretations of Fascism. Everett, Brenda H., tr. LC 76-30590. 264p. reprint ed. pap. 81.90 (*0-7837-2249-4*, 205733700004) Bks Demand.
— Jews in an Arab Land: Libya, 1835-1970. Roumani, Judith, tr. LC 84-11851. 436p. reprint ed. pap. 135.20 (*0-7837-0088-1*, 204036300016) Bks Demand.
De Fenelon, Marquis. The Adventures of Telemachus, the Son of Ulysses. Brack, O. M., Jr., ed. Smollett, Tobias George, tr. LC 95-45479. (Works of Tobias Smollett). 1997. 50.00 (*0-8203-1820-5*) U of Ga Pr.
De Feo. Andrea Pozzo. (ITA., Illus.). 255p. 1997. 129.95 (*88-435-4225-7*, Pub. by Art Bks Intl) Partners Pubs Grp.
De Ferdinandy, Magdalena, tr. see Ferdinandy, Miguel De.
De Ferdinandy, Miguel. El Emperador Carlos V. 234p. (C). 1964. 3.50 (*0-8477-0826-8*); pap. 3.00 (*0-8477-0827-6*) U of PR Pr.
— En Torno al Pensar Historico, 2 bks., I. (C). write for info. (*0-8477-0829-2*) U of PR Pr.
— En Torno al Pensar Historico, 2 bks., II. (C). write for info. (*0-8477-0830-6*) U of PR Pr.
— En Torno al Pensar Historico, 2 bks., Set. (C). pap. 2.70 (*0-8477-0828-4*) U of PR Pr.
— Mito e Historia. (SPA.). 320p. 1995. pap. 17.95 (*0-8477-0214-6*) U of PR Pr.
De Fernando, Alonso. Mateo y los Reyes Magos. (SPA.). 1996. 24.95 (*84-372-2198-6*) Santillana.
***de Ferranti, Hugh.** Japanese Musical Instruments. (Images of Asia Ser.). (Illus.). 128p. 2000. 16.95 (*0-19-590500-8*) OUP.
De Ferrari, Gabriella. Gringa Latina: A Woman of Two Worlds. Baker, Deborah, ed. LC 95-26306. (Globe Ser.). 176p. 1996. pap. 14.00 (*1-56836-145-9*, Kodansha Globe) Kodansha.
de Ferreira, Antonia. The Comedy of Bristo or the Pimp (Comidia do Fanchono ou de Bristo) Martyn, John R. C., tr. (Carleton Renaissance Plays in Translation Ser.). 120p. 1990. pap. 8.00 (*0-919473-72-5*, Pub. by Dovehouse) Sterling.
De Figueiredo, D. G. Ekeland Variational Principle with Applications & Detours. (Tata Institute Lectures on Mathematics). 1989. 27.95 (*0-387-51179-2*, 3880) Spr-Verlag.
De Figuerdo, Antonio, jt. auth. see Norman, Jill.
De Figueroa, Yesmin A. & Berrios, Angel. Biologia Animal: Manual de Laboratorio. 2nd ed. 142p. (C). 1985. text 24.95 (*1-881375-06-4*) Libreria Univ.
De Filippe, Filippo, ed. An Account of Tibet: The Travels of Ippolito Desideri 1712-1727. (C). 1995. 58.00 (*81-206-1019-9*, Pub. by Asian Educ Servs) S Asia.
De Filippi, Joseph, jt. auth. see Contant, Clement.
De Filippo, Carol L. & Sims, Donald G., eds. New Reflections on Speechreading. LC HV2471.. (Volta Review: Vol. 90, No. 5, Sept. 1988). 319p. 1988. reprint ed. pap. 98.90 (*0-7837-9094-5*, 204984400003) Bks Demand.
De Filippo, Eduardo. De Filippo: Four Plays. Ardito, Carlo & Tinniswood, Peter, trs. (Methuen World Dramatists Ser.). 362p. (C). 1992. pap. write for info. (*0-413-66620-4*, A0657, Methuen Drama) Methn.
— The Nativity Scene. Molino, Anthony & Feinberg, Paul, trs. from ITA. LC 97-136703. (Drama Ser.: No. 8). 150p. 1992. pap. 12.00 (*0-920717-80-2*) Guernica Editions.
— Saturday, Sunday, Monday: A Play in Three Acts. Waterhouse, Keith & Hall, Willis, trs. from ITA. 87p. 1974. 16.95 (*0-435-23200-2*) Boulevard.
De Filippo, Judy. Lifeskills 1, No. 1. 2nd ed. 112p. 1991. pap. text 11.75 (*0-201-53366-9*) Addison-Wesley.
— Lifeskills 3, No. 3. 2nd ed. 112p. 1991. pap. text 11.75 (*0-201-53368-5*) Addison-Wesley.
— Lifeskills 2, No. 2. 2nd ed. 112p. 1991. pap. text 11.75 (*0-201-53367-7*) Addison-Wesley.
De Fina, Allan. When a City Leans Against the Sky. LC 94-79159. (Illus.). 64p. (J). (gr. 5 up). 1997. pap. 8.95 (*1-56397-137-2*, Wordsong) Boyds Mills Pr.
De Finetti, Bruno. Theory of Probability: A Critical Introductory Treatment, Vol. 1. Machi, Antonio & Smith, Adrian, trs. LC 73-10744. (Wiley Series in Probability & Mathematical Statistics). (Illus.). 320p. reprint ed. pap. 99.20 (*0-8357-6297-1*, 203505800001) Bks Demand.
— Theory of Probability Vol. 2: A Critical Introductory Treatment. LC 73-10744. (Illus.). 393p. reprint ed. pap. 121.90 (*0-8357-8634-X*, 203505800002) Bks Demand.
De Fiori, Vittorio E. Mussolini, the Man of Destiny: Studies in Fascism: Ideology & Practice. Pei, Mario A., tr. from ITA. LC 78-63673. (Illus.). 288p. 1982. reprint ed. 34.50 (*0-404-16933-3*) AMS Pr.
De Firmian, Nick. Modern Chess Openings. 14th ed. 736p. 1999. 40.00 (*0-8129-3083-5*, Times Bks); pap. 30.00 (*0-8129-3084-3*, Times Bks) Crown Pub Group.
De Fleur, Melvin L. & Larsen, Otto N. The Flow of Information: An Experiment in Mass Communication. 347p. 1986. pap. 24.95 (*0-88738-675-X*) Transaction Pubs.
De Fliert, E. Van, see Van De Fliert, E.
De Flora, A., jt. ed. see Magnani, M.
De Fluvia i Escorsa, Armand. Diccionari Heraldic. (CAT.). 142p. 1987. pap. 12.95 (*0-7859-6396-0*, 8486387302) Fr & Eur.
De Fonseca, Jose N. An Historical & Archeological Sketch of the City of Goa. 1986. reprint ed. 22.00 (*0-8364-1739-9*, Pub. by Manohar) S Asia.
De Fonseka, Triset. Easy Cooking with Herbs & Spices with 250 Exotic Recipes. 1993. spiral bd. 14.95 (*0-9634997-7-7*) Tris Pubs.
De Fontaubert, A. Charlotte, et al. Biodiversity in the Seas: Implementing the Convention on Biological Diversity in Marine & Coastal Habitats LC 97-189459. (Environmental Policy & Law Paper Ser.). v, 82 p. 1996. write for info. (*2-8317-0338-7*) Elsevier.
De Fontbrune, Jean-Charles. Nostradamus Two: Into the Twenty-First Century. LC 84-25342. (Illus.). 176p. 1995. pap. 10.95 (*0-8050-0599-4*, Owl) H Holt & Co.
— Las Nuevas Profecias Nostradamus Hasta el Ano 2025. pap. text 22.95 (*84-270-2098-8*) E Martinez Roca.
de Fontenay, A., et al. Telecommunication Demand Modelling: An Integrated View. (Contributions to Economic Analysis Ser.: Vol. 187). xxii,480p. 1990. 172.50 (*0-444-88539-0*) Elsevier.
De Fontnouvelle, Pierre, tr. see De Margerie, Bertrand.
De Forbonnais, Francois Veron, see Veron de Forbonnais, Francois.
De Ford, Miriam A. They Were San Franciscans. LC 70-117781. (Essay Index Reprint Ser.). 1977. 24.95 (*0-8369-1914-9*) Ayer.
De Ford, Miriam A. & Jackson, Joan S. Who Was When? A Dictionary of Contemporaries. 3rd ed. LC 76-2404. 184p. 1976. 53.00 (*0-8242-0532-4*) Wilson.
De Ford, Ruth I., ed. see Ferretti, Giovanni.
De Ford, Sara & Lott, Clarinda H. Forms of Verse: British & American. 1987. pap. text 7.95 (*0-8290-2114-0*) Irvington.
De Foreest, Rosalie A. That's Not Alice. (Illus.). 16p. (J). (gr. 1-3). 1998. pap. 6.00 (*0-8059-4522-9*) Dorrance.
De Forest, Elizabeth K. The Gardens & Grounds at Mount Vernon: How George Washington Planned & Planted Them. (Illus.). 116p. pap. 5.95 (*0-931917-08-5*) Mt Vernon Ladies.
De Forest, Izette. The Leaven of Love. (Psychoanalysis: Examined & Re-Examined Ser.). 220p. 1983. reprint ed. lib. bdg. 27.50 (*0-306-76234-X*) Da Capo.
— The Leaven of Love: A Development of the

D

Psychoanalytic Theory & Technique of Sandor Ferenczi. LC 65-14585. 224p. reprint ed. pap. 69.50 (*0-608-11147-3*, 201021300068) Bks Demand.

De Forest, J. W. The De Forests of Avesnes (& of New Netherland) A Hugenot Thread in American Colonial History, 1494-1900. 307p. 1989. reprint ed. pap. 49.00 (*0-8328-0467-3*); reprint ed. lib. bdg. 59.00 (*0-8328-0466-5*) Higginson Bk Co.

De Forest, John W. The Bloody Chasm. LC 72-38011. (Black Heritage Library Collection). 1977. reprint ed. 29.95 (*0-8369-8979-1*) Ayer.

— The Bloody Chasm. (Collected Works of John W. De Forest). 1988. reprint ed. lib. bdg. 79.00 (*0-7812-1164-6*) Rprt Serv.

De Forest, John W. The Collected Works, 17 vols., Set. (Collected Works of John W. De Forest). 1988. reprint ed. lib. bdg. 1343.00 (*0-7812-1151-4*) Rprt Serv.

De Forest, John W. The Collected Works of John W. De Forest, 17 vols., Set. Incl. Bloody Chasm. reprint ed. 69.00 (*0-403-04572-X*); Deforests of Avesnes. 1992. reprint ed. 69.00 (*0-403-04574-6*); Downing Legends. reprint ed. 59.00 (*0-403-04575-4*); European Acquaintance. reprint ed. 59.00 (*0-403-04563-0*); History of the Indians of Connecticut. reprint ed. 69.00 (*0-403-00426-8*); Honest John Vane. reprint ed. 69.00 (*0-403-04568-1*); Irene, the Missionary. reprint ed. 69.00 (*0-403-04571-1*); Justine's Lovers. reprint ed. 69.00 (*0-403-04570-3*); Kate Beaumont. reprint ed. 69.00 (*0-403-04566-5*); Lover's Revolt. reprint ed. 69.00 (*0-403-04573-8*); Miss Ravenel's Conversion from Secession to Loyalty. reprint ed. 69.00 (*0-403-03090-0*); Oriental Acquaintance. reprint ed. 59.00 (*0-403-04562-2*); Overland. reprint ed. 69.00 (*0-403-04565-7*); Playing the Mischief. reprint ed. 69.00 (*0-403-04569-X*); Poems: Medley & Palestina. 1902. reprint ed. 69.00 (*0-403-04576-2*); Seacliff. reprint ed. 59.00 (*0-403-04564-9*); Wetherel Affair. reprint ed. 69.00 (*0-403-04567-3*); 995.00 (*0-403-03455-8*) Somerset Pub.

— The De Forests of Avesnes. (Collected Works of John W. De Forest). 1988. reprint ed. lib. bdg. 79.00 (*0-7812-1166-2*) Rprt Serv.

— The Downing Legends. (Collected Works of John W. De Forest). 1988. reprint ed. lib. bdg. 59.00 (*0-7812-1167-0*) Rprt Serv.

— European Aquaintance. (Collected Works of John W. De Forest). 1988. reprint ed. lib. bdg. 59.00 (*0-7812-1155-7*) Rprt Serv.

— History of the Indians of Connecticut. (Collected Works of John W. De Forest). 1988. reprint ed. lib. bdg. 79.00 (*0-7812-1152-2*) Rprt Serv.

— History of the Indians of Connecticut from the Earliest Known Period to 1850. 536p. 1991. reprint ed. pap. 49.00 (*0-685-59062-3*); reprint ed. lib. bdg. 79.00 (*1-878592-36-X*) Native Amer Bk Pubs.

— Honest John Vane. (Collected Works of John W. De Forest). 1988. reprint ed. lib. bdg. 59.00 (*0-7812-1160-3*) Rprt Serv.

— Irene, the Missionary. (Collected Works of John W. De Forest). 1988. reprint ed. lib. bdg. 79.00 (*0-7812-1163-8*) Rprt Serv.

— Justine's Lovers. (Collected Works of John W. De Forest). 1988. reprint ed. lib. bdg. 79.00 (*0-7812-1162-X*) Rprt Serv.

— Kate Beaumont. (Collected Works of John W. De Forest). 1988. reprint ed. lib. bdg. 59.00 (*0-7812-1158-1*) Rprt Serv.

— A Lover's Revolt. (Collected Works of John W. De Forest). 1988. reprint ed. lib. bdg. 59.00 (*0-7812-1165-4*) Rprt Serv.

***De Forest, John W.** Miss Ravenel's Conversion from Secession to Loyalty. LC 99-36933. (Penguin Classics Ser.). 544p. 2000. pap. 14.95 (*0-14-043757-6*, Penguin Bks) Viking Penguin.

De Forest, John W. Miss Ravenel's Conversion from Secession to Loyalty. (Collected Works of John W. De Forest). 1988. reprint ed. lib. bdg. 59.00 (*0-7812-1153-0*) Rprt Serv.

— Miss Ravenel's Conversion from Secession to Loyalty. LC 98-20846. xxi, 466p. 1998. reprint ed. pap. 20.00 (*0-8032-6615-4*, DEFMIX) U of Nebr Pr.

— Oriental Acquaintance. (Collected Works of John W. De Forest). 1988. reprint ed. lib. bdg. 59.00 (*0-7812-1154-9*) Rprt Serv.

— Overland. (Collected Works of John W. De Forest). 1988. reprint ed. lib. bdg. 59.00 (*0-7812-1156-5*) Rprt Serv.

— Playing the Mischief. (Collected Works of John W. De Forest). 1988. reprint ed. lib. bdg. 59.00 (*0-7812-1161-1*) Rprt Serv.

— Poems: Medley & Palestina. (Collected Works of John W. De Forest). 1988. reprint ed. lib. bdg. 59.00 (*0-7812-1168-9*) Rprt Serv.

— Seacliff. (Collected Works of John W. De Forest). 1988. reprint ed. lib. bdg. 59.00 (*0-7812-1157-3*) Rprt Serv.

De Forest, John W. A Union Officer in the Reconstruction. Croushore, James H. & Potter, David M., eds. LC 96-29715. 248p. 1997. pap. 12.95 (*0-8071-2183-5*) La State U Pr.

De Forest, John W. Volunteer's Adventures: A Union Captain's Record of the Civil War. Croushore, James H., ed. LC 95-50684. (Illus.). 256p. (C). 1996. reprint ed. pap. 11.95 (*0-8071-2084-7*) La State U Pr.

— The Wetherel Affair. (Collected Works of John W. De Forest). 1988. reprint ed. lib. bdg. 79.00 (*0-7812-1159-X*) Rprt Serv.

— Witching Times. Appel, Alfred, Jr., ed. (Masterworks of Literature Ser.). 1967. 19.95 (*0-8084-0332-X*); pap. 14.95 (*0-8084-0333-8*) NCUP.

De Forest, Louis E. Bainbridge. Ancestry of William Seaman Bainbridge. 164p. 1997. reprint ed. 35.00 (*0-8328-7334-9*); reprint ed. pap. 25.00 (*0-8328-7335-7*) Higginson Bk Co.

De Foret, Nancy C. Charon's Daughter. (Illus.). 1977. 12.50 (*0-87140-628-4*, Pub. by Liveright); pap. 5.95 (*0-87140-116-9*, Pub. by Liveright) Norton.

***De Fornel, F.** Evanescent Waves: From Newtonian Optics to Atomic Optics. (Springer Series in Optical Sciences). (Illus.). xii, 282p. 2000. 82.95 (*3-540-65845-9*) Spr-Verlag.

De Forto, Rocco Z. Philosophy in Medicine, Science & Health: Subject Analysis Index with Reference Bibliography. LC 84-47864. 150p. 1987. 47.50 (*0-88164-402-1*); pap. 44.50 (*0-88164-403-X*) ABBE Pubs Assn.

De Forto, Rocco Zio, see Zio De Forto, Rocco.

De Fossa, Johann. Johann de Fossa: The Collected Works. Ennulat, Egbert M., ed. (Recent Researches in Music of the Renaissance Ser.: Vols. RRR28-29). (Illus.). xi, 218p. 1978. pap. 70.00 (*0-89579-102-1*) A-R Eds.

De Fossard, Esta. Reading in Focus: Learning to Get the Message Module A, Module B & Module C, Module C. 3rd ed. 352p. (C). 1989. mass mkt. 23.25 (*0-538-70050-5*, EG40CB2) S-W Pub.

— Reading in Focus: Learning to Get the Message Module A, Module B & Module C, Module A. 3rd ed. 352p. (C). 1989. mass mkt. 23.25 (*0-538-70048-3*, EG40CB) S-W Pub.

— Reading in Focus: Learning to Get the Message Module A, Module B & Module C, Module B. 3rd ed. 352p. (C). 1989. mass mkt. 23.25 (*0-538-70049-1*, EG40CB1) S-W Pub.

De Foucauld, Charles. Come, Let Us Sing a Song Unknown. 1979. pap. 8.95 (*0-87193-080-3*) Dimension Bks.

De Foucault, Bruno. Les Plants et Leurs Noms: Essai de Phytonomie Structurale. (Dissertationes Botanicae Ser.: Band 201). (Illus.). iv, 64p. 1993. 30.00 (*3-443-64113-X*, Pub. by Gebruder Borntraeger) Balogh.

— Les Vegetations Herbacees Basses Amphibes: Systemique, Structuralisme, Synsystematique. (Dissertationes Botanicae Ser.: Band 121). (FRE., Illus.). 150p. 1988. pap. 42.00 (*3-443-64033-8*, Pub. by Gebruder Borntraeger) Balogh.

De Fouloy, Christian D. Glossaire des Termes de la Communaute Europeene: Glossary of EC Terms & Acronyms. (FRE, GER, ITA & SPA.). 421p. 1992. 195.00 (*0-7859-0556-1*, 270131030X) Fr & Eur.

— Glossary of NAFTA Terms. LC 94-16407. (Nijhoff Law Specials Ser.). 152p. 1994. pap. text 60.00 (*0-7923-2719-5*) Kluwer Academic.

— The Practical U.S. Resource Guide to the European Union. LC 98-235197. 280 p. 1998. 75.00 (*90-411-0641-3*) Kluwer Law Intl.

De Fouloy, Christian D., ed. The European Strasbourg Register 1994. 352p. (C). 1994. pap. text 95.50 (*0-7923-2726-8*, Pub. by M Nijhoff) Kluwer Academic.

***De Fournival, Richard.** Master Richard's "Bestiary of Love" & "Response" Beer, Jeanette, tr. (Illus.). 168p. 1999. reprint ed. pap. 16.95 (*1-55753-175-7*, NotaBell) Purdue U Pr.

***De Fouw, Hart & Svoboda, Robert Edwin.** Light on Relationships: The Synastry of Indian Astrology. LC 00-29010. (Illus.). 288p. 2000. pap. 18.95 (*1-57863-148-3*) Weiser.

De Fraeye, Mark. Window on Taiwan. (Illus.). 224p. 1999. 65.00 (*90-5325-109-X*, Pub. by Pet-Pandora) Weatherhill.

De Franca, George. Pelvic Locomotor Dysfunction. 256p. text. write for info. (*0-443-08839-X*) Church.

De Franca, Geroge G. & Franca, Geroge G. De. Pelvic Locomotor Dysfunction: A Clinical Approach. LC 95-47220. (Illus.). 464p. 1996. 69.00 (*0-8342-0756-7*, 20756) Aspen Pub.

De France, Claudine. Du Film: Ethnographique a l'Anthropologie Filmique. (FRE.). 250p. 1994. pap. text 31.00 (*2-88449-006-X*) Gordon & Breach.

De France, J. F., jt. ed. see Chronister, R. B.

de Franceschi, Giulia, ed. Trattoria Italia: A Gastronomic Tour of Italy. (Illus.). 240p. 1999. 35.00 (*0-8478-2174-9*, Pub. by Rizzoli Intl) St Martin.

De Franceschi, Marisa. Pillars of Lace: The Anthology of Italian-Canadian Women Writers. 290p. 1998. pap. 18.00 (*1-55071-055-9*) Guernica Editions.

— Surface Tension. 322p. 1994. pap. 13.00 (*0-920717-94-2*) Guernica Editions.

De Francesco, Grete. The Power of the Charlatan. Beard, Miriam, tr. from GER. LC 79-8609. reprint ed. 31.50 (*0-404-18471-5*) AMS Pr.

De Francesco, Scott. Scandinavian Cultural Radicalism: Literary Commitment & the Collective Novel in the 1930's. LC 90-5877. (American University Studies: General Literature: Ser. XIX, Vol. 7). XII, 152p. (C). 1990. text 39.50 (*0-8204-1263-5*) P Lang Pubng.

De Franchis, Francesco. English/Italian Legal Dictionary, Vol. 1. (ENG & ITA.). 1545p. 1984. 295.00 (*0-8288-0396-X*, F11373) Fr & Eur.

— Italian-English Legal Dictionary. (ENG & ITA.). 1472p. 1996. 295.00 (*0-7859-9289-8*) Fr & Eur.

De Franchis, Roberto, ed. Portal Hypertension II: Definitions, Methodology & Therapeutic Strategies, 2. 336p. 1995. 75.00 (*0-86542-614-7*) Blackwell Sci.

De Francis, F. Law Dictionary Italian-English. 2nd ed. (ENG & ITA.). 1467p. 1996. 208.00 (*88-14-05001-5*, Pub. by Giuffre) IBD Ltd.

De Francis, John. Colonialism & Language Policy in Viet Nam. 1977. 50.80 (*90-279-7643-0*) Mouton.

De Francis, John, tr. see Ma, Ho-t'ien.

De Francis, John F. Chinese-English Glossary of the Mathematical Sciences. LC 64-16997. (CHI & ENG.). 286p. reprint ed. pap. 88.70 (*0-608-30412-3*, 200467000045) Bks Demand.

De Franciscis, Maria E. Italy & the Vatican: The 1984 Concordat Between Church & State. (Studies in Modern European History: Vol. 2). XII, 349p. (C). 1989. text 52.95 (*0-8204-0863-8*) P Lang Pubng.

De Francisco, Cesar P., ed. see World Congress of Psychiatry Staff.

***de Franciscus, A.** Pompeii: Monuments Past & Present. (Illus.). 56p. 2000. pap. 21.95 (*88-8162-075-8*, Pub. by Vision Srl) J P Getty Trust.

De Freine, Sean, jt. auth. see O'Donnell, Jim.

De Freitas, Chrystal. Keys to Your Child's Healthy Sexuality. LC 97-50485. (Barron's Parenting Keys Ser.). 192p. 1998. pap. 6.95 (*0-7641-0298-2*) Barron.

De Freitas, Eura. Metamorphosis A-Z. (Illus.). 56p. 1996. pap. 7.50 (*1-885778-15-5*) Seaburn.

De Freitas Treen, Maria. The Admiral & His Lady Columbus & Filipa of Portugal. (Illus.). 1989. 17.95 (*0-8315-0191-X*) Speller.

De Friederichsen, Kay H. Las Profundas Verdades de la Biblia. Orig. Title: God's Word Made Plain. (SPA.). 256p. 1958. mass mkt. 5.99 (*0-8254-1248-X*, Edit Portavoz) Kregel.

De Fries, Heinrich, ed. Junge Baukunst in Deutschland. (Bauhaus Ser.). 1990. reprint ed. 55.00 (*3-601-00291-4*) Periodicals Srv.

De Frisching, Sacha. America. (Let's Learn about Ser.). (Illus.). 32p. (J). (gr. 4 up). 1991. pap. 5.95 (*0-8442-7629-4*, Passprt Bks) NTC Contemp Pub Co.

— France. (Let's Learn about Ser.). (Illus.). 32p. (J). (gr. 4 up). 1992. pap. 5.95 (*0-8442-1403-5*, Passprt Bks) NTC Contemp Pub Co.

— Germany. (Let's Learn about Ser.). (Illus.). 32p. (J). (gr. 4 up). 1993. pap. 5.95 (*0-8442-2162-7*, Passprt Bks) NTC Contemp Pub Co.

— Italy. (Let's Learn about Ser.). (Illus.). 32p. (J). (gr. 4 up). 1992. pap. text 5.95 (*0-8442-8061-5*, Passprt Bks) NTC Contemp Pub Co.

— Let's Learn about Spain. (Let's Learn about Ser.). (Illus.). 32p. (J). (gr. 4 up). 1991. pap. 5.95 (*0-8442-7631-6*, Passprt Bks) NTC Contemp Pub Co.

De Fuentes, Patricia. Conquistadors: First-Person Accounts of the Conquest of Mexico. LC 93-13383. 1993. pap. 18.95 (*0-8061-2562-4*) U of Okla Pr.

de Fulleda, Carmen A. Caceres, see De Hernandez, Cecilia & Caceres de Fulleda, Carmen A.

De Funiak, William Q. & Vaughn, Michael J. Principles of Community Property. 2nd ed. LC 72-101099. 575p. reprint ed. pap. 178.30 (*0-608-13694-8*, 205534700017) Bks Demand.

De Fur, Sharon & Patton, James R. Transition & School-Based Services: Interdisciplinary Perspectives for Enhancing the Transition Process. LC 98-47362. 1999. pap. 31.00 (*0-89079-806-0*) PRO-ED.

De Furia, Guy. Facilitator's Guide. (Interpersonal Trust Surveys Ser.). 1997. 59.95 (*0-7879-0899-1*) Jossey-Bass.

— Interpersonal Trust Surveys Organizational Instrument. 1997. pap. 3.95 (*0-7879-0900-9*) Jossey-Bass.

— Other Instrument. (Interpersonal Trust Surveys Ser.). 1997. pap. 3.95 (*0-7879-0898-3*) Jossey-Bass.

De Furia, Steve & Scacciaferro, Joe. The MIDI Book: Using MIDI & Related Interfaces. (Syntharts Ser.). 104p. (Orig.). 1986. pap. 14.95 (*0-88188-515-0*, 00605600) H Leonard.

De Furia, Steve, jt. auth. see Scacciaferro, Joe.

De Fusco, Andrea. Robert Frost. LC 98-48267. (Literary Companion Ser.). 127p. 1999. pap. 77.76 (*1-56510-998-8*) Greenhaven.

***De Fusco, Andrea.** Robert Frost. LC 98-48267. (Literary Companion Ser.). 224p. (gr. 7-12). 1999. lib. bdg. 27.95 (*1-56510-999-6*) Greenhaven.

De Gaetano, Yvonne, et al. Kaleidoscope: A Multicultural Approach for the Primary School Classroom. LC 96-6537. 269p. 1997. pap. text 26.00 (*0-02-328002-6*) Macmillan.

De Galba, Marti J., jt. auth. see Martorell, Joanot.

De Galindez, Jesus, jt. auth. see Ireland, Gordon.

De Galindez, Suarez J. The Era of Trujillo: Dominican Dictator. LC 72-79292. 326p. reprint ed. pap. 101.10 (*0-608-13676-X*, 205540300017) Bks Demand.

De Galve, Gelvira. Two Hearts, One Soul: The Correspondence of the Condesa de Galve, 1688-96. Dodge, Meredith D. & Hendricks, Rick, eds. & trs. by. LC 92-36895. 288p. 1993. reprint ed. pap. 89.30 (*0-608-07280-X*, 206750800009) Bks Demand.

De Galvez, Bernardo. Instructions for Governing the Interior Provinces of New Spain, 1786. Worcester, Donald E., ed. LC 67-24723. (Quivira Society Publications, Vol. 12). 1967. reprint ed. 19.95 (*0-405-00086-3*) Ayer.

De Galway, A. O. Tigran Petrosian - World Champion. 1965. pap. 45.00 (*0-08-011012-6*, Pergamon Pr) Elsevier.

De Gamboa, Pedro S. History of the Incas. Markham, Clements R., ed. (Hakluyt Society Works: No. 2, Vol. 22). (Illus.). 1969. reprint ed. 60.00 (*0-8115-0342-9*) Periodicals Srv.

de Gamboa, Pedro Sarmiento, see Sarmiento de Gamboa, Pedro.

De Gamez, Tana & Steiner, Roger. Simon & Schuster International Dictionary Spanish - English. LC 97-72124. 1632p. 1997. 49.95 (*0-02-862013-5*) Macmillan.

De Gandt, Francois. Force & Geometry in Newton's Principle. Wilson, Curtis, tr. LC 94-39315.Tr. of Force et Geometrie. (ENG & FRE.). 297p. 1995. text 49.50 (*0-691-03367-6*, Pub. by Princeton U Pr) Cal Prin Full Svc.

De Garay, Susan, jt. ed. see Verniero, Joan.

De Garayalde, Giovanna. Jorge Luis Borges: Sources & Illumination. 1978. 19.00 (*0-900860-61-8*, Pub. by Octagon Pr) ISHK.

De Garcia, Carmen I. Raffucci, see Raffucci de Garcia, Carmen I.

De Garcia, Karen Batchelor, see Batchelor De Garcia, Karen.

De Garine, Igor, ed. Social Aspects of Obesity. 304p. 1995. pap. text 28.00 (*2-88449-186-4*) Gordon & Breach.

— Social Aspects of Obesity, Vol. 1. 314p. 1995. text 55.00 (*2-88449-185-6*) Gordon & Breach.

De Garis, Brian, ed. Campus in the Community: The University of Western Australia 1963-1987. 3.95 (*0-85564-283-1*, Pub. by Univ of West Aust Pr) Intl Spec Bk.

De Garis, Brian K. Portraits of the South West: Aborigines, Women & the Environment. (Orig.). pap. 29.95 (*1-875560-12-2*, Pub. by Univ of West Aust Pr) Intl Spec Bk.

***De Garis, Hugo.** The Artilect War. 250p. 1999. spiral bd. 15.00 (*0-9673693-0-4*) M Janson.

***de Garmo, Joan Askew.** "Belle Haven II" The End of an Era. 2nd ed. Miller, Joanne, ed. (Illus.). 100p. 1999. pap. 14.00 (*1-879418-64-9*) Audenreed Pr.

De Gasparin, Agenor. Uprising of a Great People: The United States in 1861 to Which Is Added a Word of Peace Between England & the United States. Booth, Mary L., tr. LC 75-95066. (Select Bibliographies Reprint Ser.). 1977. 29.95 (*0-8369-5068-2*) Ayer.

De Gast, Robert. The Churches & Chapels of San Miguel De Allende. (Illus.). 96p. 1997. 19.95 (*0-9655420-0-9*) E & R Pubns.

— The Doors of San Miguel de Allende. LC 94-20415. (Illus.). 96p. 1994. 19.95 (*1-56640-990-X*) Pomegranate Calif.

— Five Fair Rivers: Sailing the James, York, Rappahannock, Potomac & Patuxent. LC 94-47377. (Illus.). 160p. 1995. 19.95 (*0-8018-5079-7*) Johns Hopkins.

— The Lighthouses of the Chesapeake. (Illus.). 176p. (C). 1993. reprint ed. pap. 24.95 (*0-8018-4765-6*) Johns Hopkins.

— Unreal Estate: The Eastern Shore. LC 91-47048. (Illus.). 96p. 1993. pap. 29.95 (*0-8018-4591-2*); text 59.95 (*0-8018-4412-6*) Johns Hopkins.

***De Gast, Robert, photos by.** Behind the Doors of San Miguel de Allende. (Illus.). 96p. 2000. boxed set 19.95 (*0-7649-1341-7*, A544) Pomegranate Calif.

De Gasztold, Carmen B. Creature's Choir. (FRE., Illus.). (J). (gr. 3-8). 29.95 (*0-8288-9331-4*, F140841) Fr & Eur.

De Gategno, Paul J. Ivanhoe: The Mask of Chivalry. LC 93-29454. (Twayne's Masterworks Ser.: No. 125). 136p. 1994. pap. 13.95 (*0-8057-8379-2*) Macmillan.

De Gauffecourt, Jean-Vincent C. Traite de la Relieure des Livres. 134p. 1987. 60.00 (*0-614-16152-5*) Oak Knoll.

— Traite de la Relieure des Livres. Benaiteau, Claude, tr. (ENG & FRE.). 140p. 1987. reprint ed. 100.00 (*0-935072-13-6*) W T Taylor.

De Gaulle, Charles. The Army of the Future. LC 74-5925. 179p. 1977. reprint ed. lib. bdg. 35.00 (*0-8371-7525-9*, GAAF, Greenwood Pr) Greenwood.

— La Discorde Chez l'Ennemi. 283p. 1971. 34.95 (*0-7859-5242-X*) Fr & Eur.

— Discours et Messages, 5 tomes. Incl. Tome I. Pendant la Guerre (Juin 1940-Janv. 1946) 31.95 Tome II. Dans l'Attente (Fev. 46-Avr. 58) 39.95 Tome III. Vers le Renouveau (Mai 58-Juill. 62) 39.95 Tome IV. Pour l'Effort (Aout 62-Dec. 65) 39.95 Tome V. Vers le Terme (Jano. 66-Avril 69) 39.95 write for info. (*0-318-51981-X*) Fr & Eur.

— Discours et Messages Tome I: Pendant la Guerre (Juin 1940-Janv. 1946) (FRE.). 750p. 1970. write for info. (*0-7859-5245-4*) Fr & Eur.

— Discours et Messages Tome II: Dans l'Attente Feb. '46-Apr. '58. 750p. 1970. write for info. (*0-7859-5244-6*) Fr & Eur.

— Discours et Messages Tome III: Vers le Renouveau (Mai '58-Juill. '62) (FRE.). 480p. 1970. 39.95 (*0-7859-5246-2*) Fr & Eur.

— Discours et Messages Tome V: Vers le Terme (Jano. '66-Apr. '69) 750p. 1970. 39.95 (*0-7859-5247-0*) Fr & Eur.

— Discours et Messages, Tome IV: Pour l'Effort (Aout 62-Dec. 65) (FRE.). 486p. 1970. 39.95 (*0-7859-1217-7*, F101753) Fr & Eur.

— The Edge of the Sword. LC 75-26731. 128p. 1975. reprint ed. lib. bdg. 35.00 (*0-8371-8366-9*, GAES, Greenwood Pr) Greenwood.

— Le Fil de l'Epee. 207p. 1971. 28.95 (*0-7859-5240-3*) Fr & Eur.

— La France et Son Armee. (FRE.). 1969. write for info. (*0-7859-5241-1*) Fr & Eur.

— Memoires de Guerre, 3 tomes. Incl. Tome I. Appel (1940-1942) 1961. 39.95 Tome II. Unite (1942-1944) 1961. 39.95 Tome III. Salut (1944-1946) 1961. 39.95 (FRE.). 897p. 1961. Set pap. 69.95 (*0-318-52050-8*) Fr & Eur.

— Memoires de Guerre, 1954-61 Tome I: L'Appel (1940-1942) 320p. 1970. 39.95 (*0-7859-5248-9*) Fr & Eur.

— Memoires de Guerre, 1954-61 Tome II: L'Unite (1942-1944) (FRE.). 497p. 1979. pap. 15.95 (*0-8288-9375-6*, F101791) Fr & Eur.

— Memoires de Guerre, 1954-61 Tome III: Le Salut (1944-1946) 1959. 59.95 (*0-7859-5249-7*) Fr & Eur.

— Memoires D'Espoir, 2 tomes. Incl. Tome I. Renouveau, 1958-1962. 39.95 Tome II. Effort (1962) 39.95 write for info. (*0-318-52053-2*) Fr & Eur.

De Gaultier, Jules. From Kant to Nietzsche. LC 70-134080. (Essay Index Reprint Ser.). 1977. 21.95 (*0-8369-2157-7*) Ayer.

***De Gaury, Gerald.** Arabia Phoenix: An Account of a Visit to Ibn Saud, Chieftain of the Outer Wahabis & Powerful King of Arabia. 170p. 2000. text 110.00 (*0-7103-0677-6*) Col U Pr.

D

De Gaury, Gerald. Rulers of Mecca. LC 78-63458. (Pilgrimages Ser.). (Illus.). 1982. reprint ed. 44.00 (*0-404-16517-6*) AMS Pr.

De Gay, Jane, jt. auth. see Goodman, Lizbeth.

De Gay, Jane, jt. ed. see Goodman, Lizbeth.

De Gaydou, Nelda B., tr. see Kesler, Jay.

De Geest, Gerrit, jt. ed. see Bouckaert, Boudewijn.

De Geest, W. & Putseys, Y. Proceedings of the International Conference on Sentential Complementation. (Linguistic Models Ser.). x, 280p. (Orig.). (C). 1984. pap. 61.55 (*3-11-013113-7*) Mouton.

De Geigel, Alma Simounet, see Handschuh, Jeanne & Simounet de Geigel, Alma.

De Geijn, Robert A. Van, see Van De Geijn, Robert A.

De Gelder, Willem. A Dutch Homesteader on the Prairies: Letters of Willem de Gelder 1910-13. LC 73-85658. 109p. reprint ed. pap. 33.80 (*0-608-16685-5*, 202638200049) Bks Demand.

De Gennard, Lorraine, ed. see Anderson, Martin.

De Gennaro, Lorraine, ed. see Anderson, Martin.

De Gennaro, Ralph, et al. Earth Budget: Making Our Tax Dollars Work for the Environment. (Illus.). 208p. (Orig.). 1993. pap. 30.00 (*0-913890-98-7*) Friends of Earth.

De Gennes, J. L., et al, eds. Latent Dyslipoproteinemias & Atherosclerosis. LC 83-43038. (Illus.). 334p. 1984. reprint ed. pap. 103.60 (*0-7837-9569-6*, 206031800005) Bks Demand.

De Gennes, P. G. Superconductivity of Metals & Alloys. LC 99-60033. 288p. 1999. pap. text 35.00 (*0-7382-0101-4*, Pub. by Perseus Pubng) HarpC.

De Gennes, P. G. & Radoz, J. Fragile Objects: Soft Matter, Hard Science & the Thrill of Discovery. LC 96-17039. (Illus.). 189p. 1996. 24.00 (*0-387-94774-4*) Spr-Verlag.

De Gennes, Pierre-Gilles. Introduction to Polymer Dynamics. (Lezioni Lincee Lectures). (Illus.). 65p. (C). 1990. pap. text 19.95 (*0-521-38849-X*) Cambridge U Pr.

— Simple Views on Condensed Matter. (Series in Modern Condensed Matter Physics: No. 4). 428p. 1992. text 86.00 (*981-02-0909-6*); pap. text 48.00 (*981-02-0910-X*) World Scientific Pub.

— Simple Views on Condensed Matter. LC 98-6463. (Series in Modern Condensed Matter Physics: Vol. 8). 490p. 1998. 58.00 (*981-02-3270-5*); pap. 28.00 (*981-02-3271-3*) World Scientific Pub.

De Gennes, Pierre Gilles, see Gilles De Gennes, Pierre.

De Geoffroy, J. G. & Wignall, T. K. Designing Optimal Strategies for Mineral Exploration. LC 85-19383. (Illus.). 380p. (C). 1985. 126.00 (*0-306-41977-7*, Plenum Trade) Perseus Pubng.

De Geoffroy, J. G., jt. auth. see Wignall, T. K.

De George, Fernande M., jt. ed. see De George, Richard T.

De George, R. T. & Scanlan, James P., eds. Marxism & Religion in Eastern Europe. LC 75-33051. (Sovietica Ser.: No. 36). 199p. 1975. text 126.50 (*90-277-0636-0*, D Reidel) Kluwer Academic.

De George, Richard T. Business Ethics. 4th ed. 591p. (C). 1994. pap. text 50.00 (*0-02-328020-4*, Macmillan Coll) P-H.

— Competing with Integrity in International Business. LC 92-39089. 256p. 1993. pap. text 25.95 (*0-19-508226-5*) OUP.

— The Nature & Limits of Authority. LC 85-8128. viii, 312p. 1985. 29.95 (*0-7006-0269-0*); pap. 14.95 (*0-7006-0270-4*) U Pr of KS.

— Patterns of Soviet Thought: The Origins & Development of Dialectical & Historical Materialism. LC 66-17026. (Ann Arbor Paperbacks Ser.: No. AA-160). 308p. reprint ed. pap. 95.50 (*0-608-10899-5*, 205105600074) Bks Demand.

De George, Richard T. & De George, Fernande M., eds. The Structuralists. 1984. pap. 5.95 (*0-385-00930-5*) Doubleday.

De Villiers, Gerald, see De Villiers, Gerald, ed.

De Geus, Arie. The Living Company. LC 96-48384. 224p. 1997. 24.95 (*0-87584-782-X*) Harvard Busn.

***de Geus, Ee Lco.** Sometimes I Just Stutter, Vol. 31. 1999. pap. 2.00 (*0-933388-42-X*) Stuttering Fnd Am.

De Geus, Marius. Ecological Utopias: Modelling the Sustainable Society. 320p. 1998. pap. 24.95 (*90-5727-019-6*, Pub. by Intl Bks) Paul & Co Pubs.

De Geyndt, Willy. Social Development & Absolute Poverty in Asia & Latin America. LC 96-27954. (World Bank Technical Papers: No. 328). 56p. 1996. pap. 22.00 (*0-8213-3695-9*, 13695) World Bank.

De Geyndt, Willy L. Managing the Quality of Health Care in Developing Countries. LC 94-36278. (Technical Papers: No. 258). 92p. 1995. pap. 22.00 (*0-8213-3092-6*, 13092) World Bank.

De Ghelderode, Michel. Andre Breton, Quelques Aspects de l'Ecrivain. (FRE.). 190p. 1986. 29.95 (*0-7859-1201-0*, 2871320284) Fr & Eur.

De Ghellinck, Joseph. Litterature Latine au Moyen-Age, 2 vols. in 1. 383p. 1975. reprint ed. write for info. (*3-487-02339-3*); reprint ed. write for info. (*0-318-71345-4*); reprint ed. write for info. (*0-318-71346-2*) G Olms Pubs.

De Gherman, Mabel G., tr. see Bagby, Daniel G.

De Gheyn, Jacob. The Exercise of Armes. 248p. 1989. 25.00 (*0-947898-45-X*) Stackpole.

— The Exercise of Armes: All 117 Engravings from the Classic 17th-Century Military Manual. LC 99-31221. (Illus.). 127p. 1999. pap. 12.95 (*0-486-40442-0*) Dover.

De Ghielderode, Michel. Ghelderode: Seven Plays, Vol. 1. Incl. Barabbas. 1960. Blind Men. 1960. Chronicles of Hell. 1960. Lord Halewyn. 1960. Pantagleize. 1960. Three Actors & Their Drama. 1960. Women at the Tomb. 1960. (Mermaid Dramabook Ser.). 304p. (Orig.). 1960. Set pap. 4.95 (*0-8090-0719-3*) Hill & Wang.

De Giacomo, Giuseppe, ed. Cognitive Robotics: Papers from the AAAI Fall Symposium. (Technical Reports: Vol. FS-98-02). (Illus.). 144p. 1998. spiral bd. 25.00 (*1-57735-076-6*) AAAI Pr.

De Giacomo, Piero. Finite Systems & Infinite Interactions: The Logic of Human Interaction & Its Application to Psychotherapy. LC 92-49931. 1992. write for info. (*0-9626184-7-0*, Bramble Bks) Bramble Co.

De Giancarla, Quiroga. Aurora. LC 98-45337. 156p. 1999. pap. 12.95 (*1-879679-12-4*, Pub. by Women Translation) Consort Bk Sales.

***De Gibergues, Emmanuel.** Keep It Simple: The Busy Catholic's Guide to Growing Closer to God. abr. ed. Orig. Title: Simplicity According to the Gospel. 176p. 2000. pap. 11.95 (*1-928832-11-3*) Sophia Inst Pr.

***De, Giorgi Manolo.** Art Design, 77. 1999. 35.00 (*88-85322-40-9*) Birkhauser.

De Giovanni, Francisco & Newell, Martin L., eds. Infinite Groups 1994: Proceedings of the International Conference, Held in Ravello, Italy, May 23-27, 1994. LC 95-38030. xvi, 336p. (C). 1995. lib. bdg. 112.95 (*3-11-014332-1*) De Gruyter.

De Girolami Cheney, Liana, ed. Pre-Raphaelitism & Medievalism in the Arts. LC 92-5491. (Illus.). 328p. 1992. lib. bdg. 99.95 (*0-7734-9491-X*) E Mellen.

De Girolamo, G., et al. Epidemiology of Mental Disorders & Psychosocial Problems: Personality Disorders. World Health Organization Staff, ed. (CHI & FRE.). xi, 66p. 1993. pap. text 17.00 (*92-4-156160-2*, 1151407) World Health.

De Girolamo, G., jt. auth. see Warner, R.

De Giustino, David. Reader in Euro Integratn. LC 96-45451. 296p. (C). 1997. pap. text 20.63 (*0-582-29200-X*, Pub. by Addison-Wesley) Longman.

***De Givenchy, Hubert.** Audrey Hepburn. (Illus.). 2001. 25.00 (*0-7893-0513-5*) Universe.

De Givray, Claude, ed. see Truffaut, Francois.

De Glanville, Ranulph. Translation of Glanville: A Treatise on the Laws & Customs of the Kingdom of England. Beames, John, tr. from LAT. xl, 362p. 1980. reprint ed. 45.00 (*0-8377-0313-1*, Rothman) W S Hein.

De Gobineau, Arthur. The Inequality of Human Races. Collins, Adrian, tr. LC 97-42324. (FRE.). xiv, 218p. 1999. pap. 12.95 (*0-86527-430-4*) Fertig.

De Gobineau, Arthur J. Mademoiselle Irnois & Other Stories. Smith, Annette, ed. & tr. by. Smith, David, ed. 1988. 50.00 (*0-520-05946-8*, Pub. by U CA Pr) Cal Prin Full Svc.

De Goes, John. 3D Game Programming with C++ Gold Book. LC 99-43502. 1999. pap. 49.99 (*1-57610-400-1*) Coriolis Grp.

De Gois, Damiao. Lisbon in the Renaissance. Ruth, Jeffrey S., tr. from LAT. & intro. by. LC 96-25081. (Historical Travel Ser.). (Illus.). 88p. (Orig.). 1996. pap. 14.00 (*0-934977-36-4*) Italica Pr.

De Golia, Jack. Everglades: The Story Behind the Scenery. LC 78-71200. (Illus.). 64p. (Orig.). 1978. pap. 7.95 (*0-916122-55-7*) KC Pubns.

— Fire, a Force of Nature: The Story Behind the Scenery. LC 89-45021. (Illus.). 48p. (Orig.). 1989. pap. 7.95 (*0-88714-038-6*) KC Pubns.

De Goncourt, Edmond & De Goncourt, Jules. Madame Gervaisais. (Folio Ser.: No. 1347). (FRE.). pap. 9.95 (*2-07-037347-9*) Schoenhof.

De Goncourt, Edmond L. La Faustin. Monkshood, G., tr. from FRE. 1976. reprint ed. 40.00 (*0-86527-267-0*) Fertig.

— Madame Saint-Huberty d'Apres Sa Correspondence et Ses Papiers de Famille. 319p. 1990. reprint ed. lib. bdg. 79.00 (*0-7812-9104-6*) Rprt Serv.

De Goncourt, Edmond L. & De Goncourt, Jules. Sister Philomene. Ensor, L., tr. 292p. 1975. reprint ed. 39.50 (*0-86527-304-9*) Fertig.

De Goncourt, Jules, jt. auth. see De Goncourt, Edmond.

De Goncourt, Jules, jt. auth. see De Goncourt, Edmond L.

De Gongora, Luis. Gongora: Soledades. Polack, Philip, ed. & tr. by. (Modern Language Ser.). (SPA.). 160p. (C). 1997. pap. text 18.95 (*1-85399-533-9*, Pub. by Brist Class Pr) Focus Pub-R Pullins.

De Gongora y Argote, Luis. Las Obras, 2 vols. in 3. (Illus.). 1358p. reprint ed. write for info. (*0-318-71621-6*) G Olms Pubs.

— Obras Poeticas. (SPA.). 1970. reprint ed. 12.00 (*0-87535-008-9*) Hispanic Soc.

De Gongora y Argote, Luis & Smith, Michael. Selected Shorter Poems. LC 95-219534. 166p. 1995. pap. 16.95 (*0-85646-250-0*, Pub. by Anvil Press) Dufour.

De Gonzalez, Fe Acosta, see Acosta de Gonzalez, Fe.

De Gonzalez, Nelly S. Bibliographic Guide to Gabriel Garcia Marquez, 1986-1992, 42. LC 93-45321. (Bibliographies & Indexes in World Literature Ser.: Vol. 42). 464p. 1994. lib. bdg. 99.50 (*0-313-28832-1*, Greenwood Pr) Greenwood.

De Gonzalez, Nelly S., tr. see Taulman, James E.

De Gonzalez, Nelly Sfeir, see Sfeir De Gonzalez, Nelly, ed.

de Goot, J. A. M., jt. auth. see Slooteweg, Pieter Johannes.

De Gopal, Chandra. Fundamentals of Agronomy. (C). 1989. pap. 11.00 (*81-204-0416-5*, Pub. by Oxford IBH) S Asia.

De Gordonio, Bernardo. Lilio de Medicina. Wasick, Cynthia M., ed. (Medieval Spanish Medical Texts Ser.: No. 25). (SPA.). 14p. 1989. 10.00 incl. fiche (*0-942260-93-7*) Hispanic Seminary.

De Gorgey, Maria, ed. Polish Cuisine: Traditional Recipes in Polish & English. (Hippocrene Bilingual Cookbks.). (ENG & POL.). 146p. 1999. 11.95 (*0-7818-0738-7*) Hippocrene Bks.

De Gorgey, Maria, tr. see Mostowy, Jan G.

De Gorgey, Maria G. Lithuanian Cookbook. LC 98-8285. 176p. 1998. 24.95 (*0-7818-0610-0*) Hippocrene Bks.

De Gorog, Lisa. From Sibelius to Sallinen: Finnish Nationalism & the Music of Finland, 16. LC 89-11733. (Contributions to the Study of Music & Dance Ser.: No. 16). 261p. 1989. 59.95 (*0-313-26740-5*, DSS/, Greenwood Pr) Greenwood.

De Gorog, Ralph, ed. Dictionnaire Inverse de l'Ancien Francais. LC 81-18874. (Medieval & Renaissance Texts & Studies: Vol. 4). (FRE.). 272p. 1982. 32.00 (*0-86698-010-5*, MR4) MRTS.

De Gorostiza, Fernandez, jt. auth. see Rossello, Elena.

De Gortari, J. C., ed. Heat & Mass Transfer in Energy Systems & Environmental Effects. 550p. 1995. 120.00 (*1-56700-061-4*) Begell Hse.

de Gortari, Raul Salinas, see Salinas de Gortari, Raul.

de Goscinny, Rene. Asterix: La Galere D'Obelix. (FRE.). 48p. (J). 1996. 24.95 (*0-7859-9352-5*) Fr & Eur.

— Asterix - Obelix & Company, No. 22. (Illus.). (J). pap. text 9.95 (*0-340-25307-X*) Intl Lang.

— Asterix & Cleopatra, No. 4. (Asterix Ser.). (Illus.). (J). 1976. pap. text 9.95 (*0-340-17220-7*) Intl Lang.

— Asterix & the Big Fight. (Asterix Ser.: No. 9). (Illus.). (J). 1976. pap. text 9.95 (*0-340-19167-8*) Intl Lang.

— Asterix & the Cauldron, No. 17. (Asterix Ser.). (Illus.). (J). 1976. pap. text 9.95 (*0-340-22711-7*) Intl Lang.

— Asterix & the Chieftain's Shield, No. 18. (Asterix Ser.). (Illus.). (J). 1977. pap. text 9.95 (*0-340-22710-9*) Intl Lang.

— Asterix & the Golden Sickle, No. 15. (Asterix Ser.). (Illus.). (J). 1976. pap. text 9.95 (*0-340-21209-8*) Intl Lang.

— Asterix & the Great Crossing, No. 16. (Asterix Ser.). (Illus.). (J). 1976. pap. text 9.95 (*0-340-21589-5*) Intl Lang.

— Asterix & the Laurel Wreath, No. 13. (Asterix Ser.). (Illus.). (J). 1976. pap. text 9.95 (*0-340-20699-3*) Intl Lang.

— Asterix & the Roman Agent. (Asterix Ser.: No. 10). (Illus.). (J). 1976. pap. text 9.95 (*0-340-19168-6*) Intl Lang.

— Asterix & the Soothsayer, No. 14. (Asterix Ser.). (Illus.). (J). 1976. pap. text 9.95 (*0-340-20697-7*) Intl Lang.

— Asterix at the Olympic Games. (Asterix Ser.: No. 12). (Illus.). (J). 1976. pap. text 9.95 (*0-340-19169-4*) Intl Lang.

— Asterix aux Jeux Olympiques. (FRE.). (J). (gr. 7-9). 1990. 24.95 (*0-8288-5109-3*, FC884) Fr & Eur.

— Asterix Chez les Bretons. (FRE.). (J). (gr. 7-9). 1990. 24.95 (*0-8288-5108-5*, FC880) Fr & Eur.

— Asterix Chez les Helvetes. (FRE., Illus.). (J). (gr. 7-9). 1990. 24.95 (*0-8288-5110-7*, FC889) Fr & Eur.

— Asterix en Hispanie. (FRE., Illus.). (J). (gr. 7-9). 1990. 24.95 (*0-8288-5111-5*, FC887) Fr & Eur.

— Asterix et Cleopatre. (FRE.). (J). (gr. 7-9). 1990. 24.95 (*0-8288-5112-3*, FC878) Fr & Eur.

— Asterix et la Serpe d'or. (FRE., Illus.). (J). (gr. 3-8). 1990. 24.95 (*0-8288-4939-0*) Fr & Eur.

— Asterix et le Chaudron. (FRE., Illus.). (J). (gr. 7-9). 1990. 24.95 (*0-8288-5113-1*, FC885) Fr & Eur.

— Asterix et les Goths. (FRE.). (J). (gr. 7-9). 1990. 24.95 (*0-8288-5114-X*, FC875) Fr & Eur.

— Asterix et les Normands. (FRE.). (J). (gr. 7-9). 1990. 24.95 (*0-8288-5115-8*, FC881) Fr & Eur.

— Asterix Gladiateur. (FRE.). (J). (gr. 7-9). 1990. 24.95 (*0-8288-5116-6*, FC876) Fr & Eur.

— Asterix in Britain, No. 3. (Asterix Ser.). (Illus.). (J). 1976. pap. text 9.95 (*0-340-17221-5*) Intl Lang.

— Asterix in Spain, No. 2. (Asterix Ser.). (Illus.). (J). 1976. pap. text 9.95 (*0-340-18326-8*) Intl Lang.

— Asterix in Switzerland. (Asterix Ser.: No. 8). (Illus.). (J). 1976. pap. text 9.95 (*0-340-19270-4*) Intl Lang.

— Asterix la Zizanie. (FRE., Illus.). (J). (gr. 7-9). 1990. 24.95 (*0-8288-5117-4*, FC888) Fr & Eur.

— Asterix le Gaulois. (FRE.). (J). (gr. 7-9). 1990. 24.95 (*0-8288-5118-2*, FC873) Fr & Eur.

— Asterix Legionnaire. (FRE.). (J). (gr. 7-9). 1990. 24.95 (*0-8288-5119-0*, FC882) Fr & Eur.

— Asterix the Gladiator. (Asterix Ser.: No. 6). (Illus.). (J). 1976. pap. text 9.95 (*0-340-18320-9*) Intl Lang.

— Asterix the Legionary. (Asterix Ser.: No. 7). (Illus.). (J). 1976. pap. text 9.95 (*0-340-18321-7*) Intl Lang.

— Le Bouclier Arverne. (FRE.). (J). (gr. 7-9). 1990. 24.95 (*0-8288-5120-4*, FC883) Fr & Eur.

— Le Combat des Chefs. (FRE.). (J). (gr. 7-9). 1990. 24.95 (*0-8288-5121-2*, FC879) Fr & Eur.

— Le Devin. (FRE.). (J). (gr. 7-9). 1990. 24.95 (*0-8288-5122-0*, FC890) Fr & Eur.

— The Mansion of the Gods. (Asterix Ser.: No. 11). (Illus.). (J). 1976. pap. text 9.95 (*0-340-19269-0*) Intl Lang.

— Obelix & Company. (Adventures of Asterix Ser.). (Illus.). 44p. (J). 1995. reprint ed. pap. 9.95 (*0-917201-70-1*, Pub. by Dargaud) Distribks Inc.

— La Serpe d'Or. (J). (gr. 7-9). 1990. 24.95 (*0-8288-5126-3*, FC874) Fr & Eur.

— Le Tour de Gaulle. (FRE.). (J). (gr. 3-8). 1990. 19.95 (*0-8288-4909-9*) Fr & Eur.

de Goscinny, Rene & Uderzo, A. Asterix Aetepekioe en Oayammie. (GRE.). (J). 1992. 24.95 (*0-7859-1040-9*, 9602202661) Fr & Eur.

— Asterix & Maestria. (GER.). (J). 1992. 24.95 (*0-7859-1025-5*, 3770400291) Fr & Eur.

— Asterix & Son. (J). 1992. 19.95 (*0-7859-1047-6*, 0-340-330082) Fr & Eur.

— Asterix & the Banquet. (J). 1992. 19.95 (*0-7859-1042-5*, 0-340-231742) Fr & Eur.

— Asterix & the Black Gold. (J). 1992. 19.95 (*0-7859-1046-8*, 0-340-27476X) Fr & Eur.

— Asterix & the Great Divide. (J). 1992. 19.95 (*0-7859-1045-X*, 0-340-259884) Fr & Eur.

— Asterix & the Magic Carpet. (J). 1992. 19.95 (*0-7859-1048-4*, 0-340-409576) Fr & Eur.

— Asterix Apud Brittannos. (LAT.). (J). 1992. 24.95 (*0-7859-1029-8*, 3770400593) Fr & Eur.

— Asterix Atque Olla Cypria. (LAT.). (J). 1992. 24.95 (*0-7859-1033-6*, 3770400666) Fr & Eur.

— Asterix aux Jeux Olympiques. (FRE.). (J). 1992. 19.95 (*0-7859-0986-9*, 2205003208) Fr & Eur.

— Asterix Certamen Principum. (LAT.). (J). 1992. 24.95 (*0-7859-1027-1*, 3770400577) Fr & Eur.

— Asterix Chez les Bretons. (FRE.). (J). 1992. 19.95 (*0-7859-1075-1*, 220500185X) Fr & Eur.

— Asterix Chez les Helvetes. (FRE.). (J). 1992. 19.95 (*0-7859-0989-3*, 2205005162) Fr & Eur.

— Asterix Chez Rahazade. (FRE.). (J). 1992. 19.95 (*0-7859-1016-6*, 2864970201) Fr & Eur.

— Asterix Clipeus Arvernus. (LAT.). (J). 1992. 24.95 (*0-7859-1077-8*, 377040064X) Fr & Eur.

— Asterix en Corse. (FRE.). (J). 1992. 19.95 (*0-7859-0991-5*, 2205006940) Fr & Eur.

— Asterix en Hispania. (SPA.). (J). 1992. 24.95 (*0-7859-1039-5*, 8475100287) Fr & Eur.

— Asterix et Cleopatra. (LAT.). (J). 1992. 24.95 (*0-7859-1026-3*, 3770400569) Fr & Eur.

— Asterix et Cleopatre. (FRE.). (J). 1992. 19.95 (*0-7859-0981-8*, 2205001574) Fr & Eur.

— Asterix et Hispanie. (FRE.). (J). 1992. 24.95 (*0-7859-0988-5*, 2205003941) Fr & Eur.

— Asterix et la Surprise de Cesar. (FRE.). (J). 1992. 24.95 (*0-7859-0993-1*, 2205030044) Fr & Eur.

— Asterix et le Chaudron. (FRE.). (J). 1992. 19.95 (*0-7859-0987-7*, 2205003364) Fr & Eur.

— Asterix et les Normands. (FRE.). (J). 1992. 19.95 (*0-7859-0983-4*, 2205001906) Fr & Eur.

— Asterix et Normanni. (LAT.). (J). 1992. 24.95 (*0-7859-1031-X*, 3770400615) Fr & Eur.

— Asterix Gladiateur. (FRE.). (J). 1992. 19.95 (*0-7859-0980-X*, 2205001345) Fr & Eur.

— Asterix in Belgium. (J). 1992. 19.95 (*0-7859-1044-1*, 0-340-257350) Fr & Eur.

— Asterix in Corsica. (J). 1992. 19.95 (*0-7859-1043-3*, 240741) Fr & Eur.

— Asterix in Hispania. (LAT.). (J). 1992. 24.95 (*0-7859-1034-4*, 3770400674) Fr & Eur.

— Asterix la Rosa y la Espada. (SPA.). (J). 1992. 24.95 (*0-7859-1038-7*, 8474199123) Fr & Eur.

— Asterix la Rose et le Glaive. (FRE.). (J). 1992. 24.95 (*0-7859-1017-4*, 2864970538) Fr & Eur.

— Asterix le Gaulois. (FRE.). (J). 1992. 19.95 (*0-7859-0979-6*, 2205000969) Fr & Eur.

— Asterix Legionnaire. (FRE.). (J). 1992. 19.95 (*0-7859-0984-2*, 2205002309) Fr & Eur.

— Asterix Olympius. (LAT.). (J). 1992. 24.95 (*0-7859-0959-1*, 0-377-040658) Fr & Eur.

— Asterix Orientalis. (LAT.). (J). 1992. 24.95 (*0-7859-1035-2*, 3770400682) Fr & Eur.

— Le Bouclier Arverne. (FRE.). 1992. 19.95 (*0-7859-0985-0*, 2205002686) Fr & Eur.

— Le Combat des Chefs. (FRE.). 1992. 19.95 (*0-7859-0982-6*, 2205001701) Fr & Eur.

— Comment Obelix est Tombe dans la Marmite. (FRE.). (J). 1992. 24.95 (*0-7859-1050-6*, 0-340-517727) Fr & Eur.

— Le Coup de Menhir. (FRE.). (J). 1992. 24.95 (*0-7859-0992-3*, 2205030041) Fr & Eur.

— Le Coup de Menhir. (FRE.). 64p. (J). 1993. lib. bdg. 19.95 (*0-7859-3652-1*, 2865030051) Fr & Eur.

— Le Domaine des Dieux. (FRE.). 1992. 24.95 (*0-7859-0990-7*, 2205005820) Fr & Eur.

— Filius Asterix. (LAT.). (J). 1992. 24.95 (*0-7859-1032-8*, 3770400623) Fr & Eur.

— Le Fils d'Asterix. (FRE.). (J). 1992. 24.95 (*0-7859-1015-8*, 2864970112) Fr & Eur.

— Fossa Alta. (LAT.). 1992. 24.95 (*0-7859-1028-X*, 3770400585) Fr & Eur.

— Le Grand Fosse. (FRE.). 1992. 24.95 (*0-7859-1014-X*, 2864970007) Fr & Eur.

— Der Grosse Graben. (GER.). (J). 1992. 24.95 (*0-7859-1022-0*, 3770400259) Fr & Eur.

— How Obelix Fell into the Magic Potion When He Was a Little Boy. (J). 1992. 24.95 (*0-7859-1049-2*, 0-340-511273) Fr & Eur.

— Obelix & Co. 1992. 24.95 (*0-7859-1041-7*, 0-340-227095) Fr & Eur.

— Obelix GMBH Co. (GER.). 1992. 24.95 (*0-7859-1021-2*, 3770400232) Fr & Eur.

— Odyssea Astergis. (LAT.). 1992. 24.95 (*0-7859-1030-1*, 3770400607) Fr & Eur.

— Die Odyssee. (GER.). 1992. 24.95 (*0-7859-1023-9*, 3770400267) Fr & Eur.

— L' Odyssee d'Asterix. (FRE.). (J). 1992. 24.95 (*0-7859-1076-X*, 286497004X) Fr & Eur.

— Operation Getafix. 1992. 24.95 (*0-7859-1051-4*, 0-340-529458) Fr & Eur.

— Der Sohn des Asterix. (GER.). (J). 1992. 24.95 (*0-7859-1024-7*, 3770400275) Fr & Eur.

— Tumultus de Asterige. (LAT.). 1992. 24.95 (*0-7859-1036-0*, 3770400690) Fr & Eur.

— Uderzo de Flamberge a Asterix. (FRE.). 64p. (J). 1993. 24.95 (*0-7859-3653-X*, 2865030077) Fr & Eur.

de Goscinny, Rene & Uderzo, M. El Adivino. (SPA., Illus.). (J). 24.95 (*0-8288-6082-3*, S26630) Fr & Eur.

— Der Arvernerschild. (GER., Illus.). (J). 24.95 (*0-8288-4914-5*) Fr & Eur.

— Asterix: Comment Obelix est Tombe dans la Marmite du Druide Quand Il Etait Petit. (FRE.). (J). 1990. 24.95 (*0-8288-8597-4*) Fr & Eur.

— Asterix: How Obelix Fell into the Magic Cauldron When He Was a Little Boy. (J). 1990. 24.95 (*0-8288-8594-X*) Fr & Eur.

— Asterix als Gladiator. (GER., Illus.). (J). (gr. 7-10). 1992. 24.95 (*0-8288-4923-4*) Fr & Eur.

D

An Asterisk (*) at the beginning of an entry indicates that the title is appearing for the first time.

— Asterix als Legionar. (GER., Illus.). (J). (gr. 7-10). 1992. 24.95 (*0-8288-4924-2*) Fr & Eur.
— Asterix & Caesar's Gift. (Illus.). (J). (gr. 7-10). 1990. 24.95 (*0-8288-4915-3*) Fr & Eur.
— Asterix & Cleopatra. (Illus.). (J). (gr. 7-10). 1990. 24.95 (*0-8288-4916-1*) Fr & Eur.
de Goscinny, Rene & Uderzo, M. Asterix & Operation Getafix. (J). 1990. 24.95 (*0-8288-8570-2*) Fr & Eur.
de Goscinny, Rene & Uderzo, M. Asterix & Son. (J). 1990. 24.95 (*0-8288-8568-0*) Fr & Eur.
— Asterix & the Banquet. (J). 1990. 24.95 (*0-8288-8590-7*) Fr & Eur.
— Asterix & the Big Fight. (Illus.). (J). (gr. 7-10). 1990. 24.95 (*0-8288-4917-X*) Fr & Eur.
— Asterix & the Black Gold. (J). 1990. 24.95 (*0-8288-8592-3*) Fr & Eur.
— Asterix & the Chieftain's Shield. (Illus.). (J). (gr. 7-10). 1990. 24.95 (*0-8288-4918-8*) Fr & Eur.
— Asterix & the Goths. (Illus.). (J). (gr. 7-10). 1990. 24.95 (*0-8288-4919-6*) Fr & Eur.
— Asterix & the Great Divide. (J). 1990. 24.95 (*0-8288-8567-2*) Fr & Eur.
— Asterix & the Laurel Wreath. (Illus.). (J). (gr. 7-10). 1990. 24.95 (*0-8288-4920-X*) Fr & Eur.
— Asterix & the Magic Carpet. (J). 1990. 24.95 (*0-8288-8569-9*) Fr & Eur.
— Asterix & the Normans. (Illus.). (J). (gr. 7-10). 1990. 24.95 (*0-8288-4921-8*) Fr & Eur.
— Asterix & the Roman Agent. (Illus.). (J). (gr. 7-10). 1990. 24.95 (*0-8288-4922-6*) Fr & Eur.
— Asterix apud Gothos. (LAT., Illus.). (J). (gr. 7-10). 1990. lib. bdg. 24.95 (*0-8288-4925-0*) Fr & Eur.
— Asterix at the Olympic Games. (Illus.). (J). (gr. 7-10). 1990. 24.95 (*0-8288-4926-9*) Fr & Eur.
— Asterix auf Korsika. (GER., Illus.). (J). (gr. 7-10). 1990. lib. bdg. 24.95 (*0-8288-4927-7*) Fr & Eur.
— Asterix bei den Briten. (GER., Illus.). (J). (gr. 7-10). 1990. lib. bdg. 24.95 (*0-8288-4928-5*) Fr & Eur.
— Asterix bei den Olympischen Spielen. (GER., Illus.). (J). (gr. 7-10). 1990. lib. bdg. 24.95 (*0-8288-4929-3*) Fr & Eur.
— Asterix bei den Schweizern. (GER., Illus.). (J). (gr. 7-10). 1990. lib. bdg. 24.95 (*0-8288-4930-7*) Fr & Eur.
— Asterix chez les Belges. (FRE., Illus.). (J). (gr. 7-10). 1990. 24.95 (*0-8288-4931-5*) Fr & Eur.
— Asterix Chez Rahazade. (FRE.). (J). 1990. 24.95 (*0-8288-8572-9*) Fr & Eur.
— Asterix der Gallier. (GER., Illus.). (J). (gr. 7-10). 1990. lib. bdg. 24.95 (*0-8288-4932-3*) Fr & Eur.
— Asterix el Galo. (SPA., Illus.). (J). (gr. 7-10). 24.95 (*0-8288-4933-1*) Fr & Eur.
— Asterix en Bretana. (SPA., Illus.). (J). (gr. 7-10). 1990. lib. bdg. 24.95 (*0-8288-4934-X*) Fr & Eur.
— Asterix en Corcega. (SPA., Illus.). (J). (gr. 7-10). 1990. lib. bdg. 24.95 (*0-8288-4935-8*) Fr & Eur.
— Asterix en Corse. (FRE., Illus.). (J). (gr. 7-10). 1990. 24.95 (*0-8288-4936-6*) Fr & Eur.
— Asterix en Helvecia. (SPA., Illus.). (J). (gr. 7-10). 1990. lib. bdg. 24.95 (*0-8288-4937-4*) Fr & Eur.
— Asterix en los Juegos Olimpicos. (SPA., Illus.). (J). (gr. 7-10). 1990. lib. bdg. 24.95 (*0-8288-4938-2*) Fr & Eur.
— Asterix et la Rose et le Glaive. (FRE.). (J). 1990. 24.95 (*0-8288-8573-7*) Fr & Eur.
— Asterix Gallus. (LAT., Illus.). (J). (gr. 7-10). 1990. lib. bdg. 24.95 (*0-8288-4941-2*) Fr & Eur.
— Asterix Gladiador. (SPA., Illus.). (J). (gr. 7-10). 1990. lib. bdg. 24.95 (*0-8288-4942-0*) Fr & Eur.
— Asterix Gladiator. (LAT., Illus.). (J). 1990. 24.95 (*0-8288-4943-9*) Fr & Eur.
— Asterix in Belgium. (J). 1990. 24.95 (*0-8288-8591-5*) Fr & Eur.
— Asterix in Britain. (Illus.). (J). 1990. 24.95 (*0-8288-4944-7*) Fr & Eur.
— Asterix in Corsica. (J). 1990. 24.95 (*0-8288-8566-4*) Fr & Eur.
— Asterix in Spain. (Illus.). (J). 1990. 24.95 (*0-8288-4945-5*) Fr & Eur.
— Asterix in Spanien. (GER., Illus.). (J). 1990. lib. bdg. 24.95 (*0-8288-4946-3*) Fr & Eur.
— Asterix in Switzerland. (Illus.). (J). 1990. lib. bdg. 24.95 (*0-8288-4947-1*) Fr & Eur.
— Asterix iter Gallicum. (LAT., Illus.). (J). 1990. lib. bdg. 24.95 (*0-8288-4948-X*) Fr & Eur.
— Asterix Legionario. (SPA., Illus.). (J). 1990. lib. bdg. 24.95 (*0-8288-4949-8*) Fr & Eur.
— Asterix, Obelix & Company. (J). 1990. 24.95 (*0-8288-8565-6*) Fr & Eur.
— Asterix the Gaul. (Illus.). (J). 1990. 24.95 (*0-8288-4950-1*) Fr & Eur.
— Asterix the Gladiator. (Illus.). (J). 1990. 24.95 (*0-8288-4951-X*) Fr & Eur.
— Asterix the Legionary. (Illus.). (J). 1990. 24.95 (*0-8288-4952-8*) Fr & Eur.
— Asterix und die Goten. (GER., Illus.). (J). 1990. lib. bdg. 24.95 (*0-8288-4953-6*) Fr & Eur.
— Asterix und Kleopatra. (GER., Illus.). (J). 1990. lib. bdg. 24.95 (*0-8288-4954-4*) Fr & Eur.
— Asterix vs Caesar. (J). 1990. 24.95 (*0-8288-8593-1*) Fr & Eur.
— Asterix y Cleopatra. (SPA., Illus.). (J). 1990. lib. bdg. 24.95 (*0-8288-4955-2*) Fr & Eur.
— Asterix y el Caldero. (SPA., Illus.). (J). 1990. lib. bdg. 24.95 (*0-8288-4956-0*) Fr & Eur.
— Asterix y los Godos. (SPA., Illus.). (J). 1990. lib. bdg. 24.95 (*0-8288-4957-9*) Fr & Eur.
— Asterix y los Normandos. (SPA., Illus.). (J). 1990. lib. bdg. 24.95 (*0-8288-4958-7*) Fr & Eur.
— Le Cadeau de Cesar. (FRE., Illus.). (J). 1990. 24.95 (*0-8288-4959-5*) Fr & Eur.
— The Caldron. (Illus.). (J). 1990. 24.95 (*0-8288-4960-9*) Fr & Eur.
— La Cizana. (SPA., Illus.). (J). 24.95 (*0-8288-4961-7*) Fr & Eur.
— El Combate de los Jefes. (SPA., Illus.). (J). 24.95 (*0-8288-4962-5*) Fr & Eur.
— Le Domaine des Dieux. (FRE., Illus.). (J). (gr. 7-9). 1990. 24.95 (*0-8288-5123-9*, FC886) Fr & Eur.
— Les Douze Travaux d'Asterix. (FRE., Illus.). (J). 1990. 24.95 (*0-8288-4964-1*) Fr & Eur.
— El Escudo Arverno. (SPA., Illus.). (J). 24.95 (*0-8288-4965-X*) Fr & Eur.
— Falx Aurea. (LAT., Illus.). (J). 24.95 (*0-8288-4966-8*) Fr & Eur.
— Fils d'Asterix. (FRE.). (J). 1990. 24.95 (*0-8288-8571-0*) Fr & Eur.
— Das Geschenk Casars. (GER., Illus.). (J). 24.95 (*0-8288-4967-6*) Fr & Eur.
— The Golden Sickle. (Illus.). (J). 1990. 24.95 (*0-8288-4968-4*) Fr & Eur.
— Die Goldene Sichel. (GER., Illus.). (J). 24.95 (*0-8288-4969-2*) Fr & Eur.
— La Gran Travesia. (SPA., Illus.). (J). 24.95 (*0-8288-5124-7*) Fr & Eur.
— Le Grand Fosse. (FRE.). (J). 1990. 24.95 (*0-8288-8595-8*) Fr & Eur.
— La Grande Traversee. (FRE., Illus.). (J). 1990. 24.95 (*0-8288-4970-6*) Fr & Eur.
— The Great Crossing. (Illus.). (J). 1990. 24.95 (*0-8288-4971-4*) Fr & Eur.
— Die Grosse Uberfahrt. (GER., Illus.). (J). 24.95 (*0-8288-4972-2*) Fr & Eur.
— La Hoz de Oro. (SPA., Illus.). (J). 24.95 (*0-8288-4973-0*) Fr & Eur.
— Der Kampf der Hauptlinge. (GER., Illus.). (J). 24.95 (*0-8288-4974-9*) Fr & Eur.
— Der Kupferkessel. (GER., Illus.). (J). 24.95 (*0-8288-4975-7*) Fr & Eur.
— Los Laureles del Cesar. (SPA., Illus.). (J). 24.95 (*0-8288-4976-5*) Fr & Eur.
— Les Lauriers de Cesar. (FRE., Illus.). (J). 1990. 24.95 (*0-8288-4977-3*) Fr & Eur.
— Die Lorbeeren des Casar. (GER., Illus.). (J). 24.95 (*0-8288-4978-1*) Fr & Eur.
— The Mansions of the Gods. (Illus.). (J). 1990. 24.95 (*0-8288-4979-X*) Fr & Eur.
— Die Normannen. (GER., Illus.). (J). 24.95 (*0-8288-4980-3*) Fr & Eur.
— Obelix et Compagnie. (FRE., Illus.). (J). 1990. 24.95 (*0-8288-5479-3*) Fr & Eur.
— Odyssee d'Asterix. (FRE.). (J). 1990. 24.95 (*0-8288-8596-6*) Fr & Eur.
— El Regalo del Cesar. (SPA., Illus.). (J). 24.95 (*0-8288-4900-5*) Fr & Eur.
— La Residencia de los Dioses. (SPA., Illus.). (J). 24.95 (*0-8288-4901-3*) Fr & Eur.
— Der Seher. (GER., Illus.). (J). 24.95 (*0-8288-5125-5*) Fr & Eur.
— La Serpe d'Or. (FRE., Illus.). (J). 1990. 19.95 (*0-8288-4904-8*) Fr & Eur.
— The Soothsayer. (Illus.). (J). 1990. 24.95 (*0-8288-4905-6*) Fr & Eur.
— Streit um Asterix. (GER., Illus.). (J). 24.95 (*0-8288-4906-4*) Fr & Eur.
— Tour de France. (GER., Illus.). (J). 1990. 24.95 (*0-8288-4907-2*) Fr & Eur.
— Le Tour de Gaulle. (FRE., Illus.). (J). 24.95 (*0-8288-4908-0*) Fr & Eur.
— Die Trabantenstadt. (GER., Illus.). (J). 24.95 (*0-8288-4910-2*) Fr & Eur.
— La Vuelta a la Galia. (SPA., Illus.). (J). 24.95 (*0-8288-4911-0*) Fr & Eur.
— La Zizanie. (FRE., Illus.). (J). 1990. 24.95 (*0-8288-4912-9*) Fr & Eur.
de Goscinny, Rene, jt. auth. see De Bevere, Maurice.
De Gosson, Maurice. Maslov Classes, Metaplectic Representation & Lagrangian Quantization. 188p. 1997. pap. 105.00 (*3-527-40087-7*) Wiley.
De Gosson, Maurice. Maslov Classes, Metapletic Representation & Lagrangian Quantization. LC 97-154820. 188p. 1997. pap. 89.20 (*3-05-501714-5*) Wiley.
De Gourcuff, Alain. Imperial Palaces in the Vicinity of St. Petersburg: Watercolours, Paintings & Engravings. 1997. 265.00 (*2-909838-01-3*) A Gourcuff.
— View of the Palaces of Tsarskoe-Selo. 1998. 60.00 (*2-909838-35-8*) A Gourcuff.
De Gourmont. Angels of Perversity. pap. 9.95 (*0-946626-72-3*, Pub. by Dedalus) Subterranean Co.
De Gourmont, Remy. Book of Masks. Lewis, J., tr. LC 67-26745. (Essay Index Reprint Ser.). 1977. 18.95 (*0-8369-0490-7*) Ayer.
— The Book of Masks: Symbolist Writing in France of the Fin de Siecle. Mangravite, Andrew, ed. & tr. by. from FRE. Hale, Terry et al, trs. from FRE. (Atlas Arkhive Ser.: Vol. 2). (Illus.). 256p. (Orig.). 1995. pap. 19.99 (*0-947757-81-3*, Pub. by Atlas Pr) Serpents Tail.
— Philosophic Nights in Paris. Goldberg, Irving D., tr. LC 68-8465. (Essay Index Reprint Ser.). 1977. 19.95 (*0-8369-1293-4*) Ayer.
— Le Probleme du Style. LC 78-64031. (Des Imagistes: Literature of the Imagist Movement Ser.). reprint ed. 27.00 (*0-404-17109-5*) AMS Pr.
— Remy De Gourmont, Selections from All His Works. Aldington, Richard, ed. & tr. by. from FRE. LC 77-10269. (Illus.). reprint ed. 49.50 (*0-404-16321-1*) AMS Pr.
De Goutiere, Anthony. Wonders Within Gemstones: The Elusive Beauty of Gemstone Inclusions. (Illus.). 135p. 1996. 49.95 (*0-9641733-2-8*) Gemwrld Intl.
***De Gouy, Louis P.** The Derrydale Fish Cookbook. LC 00-43111. (Illus.). 2000. pap. write for info. (*1-58667-009-3*) Derrydale Pr.
— The Derrydale Game Cookbook. LC 00-43110. (Illus.). 2000. pap. write for info. (*1-58667-008-5*) Derrydale Pr.
De Gouy, Louis P. The Pie Book: 419 Recipes. LC 73-88331. 384p. 1974. reprint ed. pap. 7.95 (*0-486-22997-1*) Dover.
— The Soup Book. LC 73-88332. 428p. 1974. reprint ed. pap. 8.95 (*0-486-22998-X*) Dover.
De Goyon de la Plombanie, Henri. La France Agricole et Marchande, 2 vols. (Economistes Francais du XVIIIe Siecle Ser.). 1990. reprint ed. pap. 120.00 (*3-601-00141-1*) Periodicals Srv.
De Graaf, A. M. Dios Crea al Mundo (Historias Biblicas)Tr. of God Makes the World. (SPA.). (J). 3.49 (*0-7899-0523-X*, 496640) Editorial Unilit.
— Noe y e. Arca (Historias Biblicas)Tr. of Noah & the Ark. (SPA.). (J). 3.49 (*0-7899-0524-8*, 496641) Editorial Unilit.
— La Primera Navidad (Historias Biblicas)Tr. of First Christmas. (SPA.). (J). 3.49 (*0-7899-0526-4*) Editorial Unilit.
— La Torre de Babel.Tr. of Tower of Babel. (SPA.). (J). 3.49 (*0-7899-0525-6*, 496642) Editorial Unilit.
De Graaf, Anne. Abraham. (Little Children's Bible Books Ser.). (Illus.). 38p. (J). 1999. 5.99 (*0-8054-1897-0*) Broadman.
— Bread Upon the Waters. LC 95-484. (Hidden Harvest Ser.: Bk. 1). 352p. 1995. pap. 9.99 (*1-55661-618-X*) Bethany Hse.
— Children & Jesus. (Little Children's Bible Bks.). (Illus.). 38p. (J). (ps-1). 1999. 5.99 (*0-8054-2072-X*) Broadman.
— The Children's Bible Story Book. (Illus.). 408p. (J). (ps-6). 1991. 19.99 (*0-8407-7652-7*) Tommy Nelson.
— Daniel. (Little Children's Bible Books Ser.). (Illus.). 38p. (J). 1999. 5.99 (*0-8054-1898-9*) Broadman.
— David. (Little Children's Bible Books Ser.). (Illus.). 38p. (J). 1999. 5.99 (*0-8054-1899-7*) Broadman.
— Does God See the Wind? (Tiny Triumphs Ser.). (Illus.). 22p. (J). 1997. pap. text 2.95 (*0-687-07149-6*) Abingdon.
— Double Ugh! (Tiny Triumphs Ser.). (Illus.). 22p. (J). 1997. pap. text 2.95 (*0-687-07139-9*) Abingdon.
— The First Christmas. (Little Children's Bible Bks.). (Illus.). 38p. (J). 1998. 5.99 (*0-8054-1784-2*) Broadman.
— God Makes the World. (Little Children's Bible Bks.). (Illus.). 38p. (J). 1998. 5.99 (*0-8054-1782-6*) Broadman.
— Jesus' Stories. (Little Children's Bible Bks.). (Illus.). 38p. (J). (ps-1). 1999. 5.99 (*0-8054-2071-1*) Broadman.
— Jonah. (Little Children's Bible Bks.). (Illus.). 38p. (J). (ps-1). 1999. 5.99 (*0-8054-2070-3*) Broadman
***De Graaf, Anne.** Joseph. (Little Children's Bible Bks.). (Illus.). 38p. (J). (ps-1). 2000. 5.99 (*0-8054-2175-0*) Broadman.
De Graaf, Anne. Moses. (Little Children's Bible Books Ser.). (Illus.). 38p. (J). (gr. k-1). 1999. 5.99 (*0-8054-1900-4*) Broadman.
— Noah & the Ark. (Little Children's Bible Bks.). (Illus.). 38p. (J). 1998. 5.99 (*0-8054-1781-8*) Broadman.
— Sam's Son. (Little Children's Bible Bks.). (Illus.). 38p. (J). (ps-1). 1999. 5.99 (*0-8054-2069-X*) Broadman.
— The Tower of Babel. (Little Children's Bible Bks.). (Illus.). 38p. (J). 1998. 5.99 (*0-8054-1783-4*) Broadman.
— Where the Fire Burns: A Novel, Vol. 2. LC 97-21026. (Hidden Harvest Ser.). 352p. 1997. pap. 9.99 (*1-55661-619-8*) Bethany Hse.
— The Wolf Who Wasn't. (Tiny Triumphs Ser.). (Illus.). 22p. (J). 1997. pap. text 2.95 (*0-687-07109-7*) Abingdon.
***de Graaf, Anne.** Gideon. (Little Children's Bible Bks.). (Illus.). 38p. (J). (ps-1). 2000. 5.99 (*0-8054-2177-7*) Broadman.
— Jesus' Miracles. (Little Children's Bible Bks.). (Illus.). 38p. (J). (ps-1). 2000. 5.99 (*0-8054-2178-5*) Broadman.
— Joshua. (Little Children's Bible Bks.). (Illus.). 38p. (J). (ps-1). 2000. 5.99 (*0-8054-2176-9*) Broadman.
— Out of the Red Shadow. LC 99-6418. (Hidden Harvest Ser.: Vol. 3). 352p. 1999. pap. 10.99 (*1-55661-620-1*) Bethany Hse.
De Graaf, C. N. & Viergever, Max A., eds. Information Processing in Medical Imaging. LC 87-36058. (Illus.). 640p. 1988. 125.00 (*0-306-42807-5*, Plenum Trade) Perseus Pubng.
de Graaf, E. A. & Vermeer, A. Down Syndrome Behind the Dykes: Research in the Netherlands. Heymans, H. A. et al, eds. LC 99-194698. 208p. 1999. pap. 34.90 (*90-5383-610-1*, Pub. by VU Univ Pr) Paul & Co Pubs.
De Graaf, Frank. Marine Tropical Aquarium Guide. (Illus.). 282p. 1982. 17.95 (*0-87666-805-8*, PL-2017) TFH Pubns.
De Graaf, H. C. & Klaassen, F. M. Compact Transistor Modelling for Circuit Design. (Illus.). 352p. 1990. 149.95 (*0-387-82136-8*, 3363) Spr-Verlag.
De Graaf, J., jt. auth. see Van Eijndhoven, S. J.
De Graaf, N. R., jt. auth. see Parren, M. P.
De Graaf, Robin A. In Vivo NMR Spectroscopy: Principles & Techniques. LC 98-17777. 530p. 1998. 275.00 (*0-471-98365-9*) Wiley.
De Graaf, S. G. El Pueblo de la Promesa, Vol. I. (SPA.). 415p. pap. 16.00 (*1-55883-065-0*, 6700-2510C) Libros Desafio.
— El Pueblo de la Promesa, Vol. II. (SPA.). 419p. pap. 16.00 (*1-55883-066-9*, 6700-2520C) Libros Desafio.
— El Pueblo de la Promesa, Vol. III. (SPA.). 413p. pap. 16.00 (*1-55883-067-7*, 6700-2530C) Libros Desafio.
— El Pueblo de la Promesa, Vol. IV. (SPA.). 248p. pap. 12.00 (*1-55883-068-5*, 6700-2540C) Libros Desafio.
De Graaf, T. J. Cosmic Mutons & Neutrinos. write for info. (*0-318-55151-9*, Pergamon Pr) Elsevier.
De Graaf, Willibrord & Maier, Robert, eds. Sociogenesis Reexamined: With 7 Figures. LC 94-1169. 1994. write for info. (*0-387-94276-9*) Spr-Verlag.
De Graaff. Rodents of Southern Africa. deluxe ed. 1981. write for info. (*0-409-09830-2*) Buttrwrth-Heinemann.
de Graaff, Van, see Van de Graaff.
De Graaff, W., jt. auth. see Reijnen, Gijsbertha C.
De Graca Carvalho, Maria, et al, eds. Combustion Technologies for a Clean Environment: Selected Proceedings of the First International Conference, Vilamoura, Portugal, September 3-6, 1991. LC 93-46756. 830p. 1995. text 138.00 (*2-88124-619-2*) Gordon & Breach.
***de Graciansky, Pierre-Charles, et al, eds.** Mesozoic & Cenozoic Sequence Stratigraphy of European Basins. (Special Publications: Vol. 60). (Illus.). 800p. 1999. 175.00 (*1-56576-043-3*) SEPM.
De Grado, Jesus A., ed. Microtubule Proteins. 288p. 1989. lib. bdg. 219.00 (*0-8493-5527-3*, QP552) CRC Pr.
De Grae, Paul. Traditional Irish Guitar. (Illus.). 106p. 1997. pap. text 19.95 (*1-900428-01-6*, OS00130, Pub. by Ossian) Music Sales.
***de Graef, Marc.** Magnetic Imaging & Its Applications to Materials. (Experimental Methods in the Physical Sciences Ser.: Vol. 36). 300p. 2000. 155.00 (*0-12-475983-1*) Acad Pr.
De Graef, Ortwin. Serenity in Crisis: A Preface to Paul de Man, 1939-1960. LC 92-14721. (Texts & Contexts Ser.). 242p. 1993. text 45.00 (*0-8032-1694-7*) U of Nebr Pr.
De Graef, Ortwin, et al, eds. Sense & Transcendence: Essays in Honour of Herman Servotte. (Symbolae; Facultatis Litterarum Lovaniensis Series A: Vol. 17). 325p. (Orig.). 1995. pap. 87.50 (*90-6186-667-7*, Pub. by Leuven Univ) Coronet Bks.
de Graf, H. J., et al. Regional Opportunities for Sustainable Development: Theory, Methods & Applications. LC 99-24909. (Ecological Economics Ser.). 1999. write for info. (*0-7923-5693-4*) Kluwer Academic.
De Graff Ajami, Barbara, ed. see Afif, Kaissar A.
De Graff, Anne. Boss of the Table Manners. (Tiny Triumphs Ser.). (Illus.). 22p. (J). 1997. pap. text 2.95 (*0-687-07119-4*) Abingdon.
— The New Ears. (Tiny Triumphs Ser.). (Illus.). 22p. (J). 1997. pap. text 2.95 (*0-687-07129-1*) Abingdon.
— Please Wonderful Mommy. (Tiny Triumphs Ser.). (Illus.). 22p. (J). 1997. pap. text 2.95 (*0-687-07099-6*) Abingdon.
De Graff, J. The Economics of Coffee. (C). 1991. text 350.00 (*0-89771-626-4*, Pub. by Intl Bk Distr) St Mut.
De Graff, Michel, ed. Language Creation & Language Change: Creolization, Diachrony, & Development. LC 98-35937. (Learning, Development & Conceptual Change Ser.). (Illus.). 586p. 1999. 65.00 (*0-262-04168-5*) MIT Pr.
De Graffenried, Doug, jt. auth. see Durhan, Ron.
De Graffenried, Gaines. Texas Collector. 1988. 21.95 (*0-87244-080-X*) Texian.
De Grahl, Wolfgang. The Grey Parrot. (Illus.). 256p. 1989. 23.95 (*0-86622-094-1*, H-1088) TFH Pubns.
— Papageien, Lebensweise, Art und Zucht. (GER., Illus.). 287p. 1985. lib. bdg. 35.00 (*3-8001-7150-3*, Pub. by Eugen Ulmer) Balogh.
De Grainville, Jean B. The Last Man: Or, Omegarus & Syderia, a Romance in Futurity, 2 vols. LC 77-84246. (Lost Race & Adult Fantasy Ser.). 1978. reprint ed. lib. bdg. 39.95 (*0-405-10992-X*) Ayer.
De Gramont, Alexandre, tr. see Camus, Albert.
De Grana, Lydia Diaz. El Supervisor Universitario de la Practica Docente. 120p. 1975. pap. 3.00 (*0-8477-2707-6*) U of PR Pr.
***De Grand, Alexander.** The Hunchback's Tailor: Giovanni Giolitti & Liberal Italy from the Challenge of Mass Politics to the Rise of Fascism, 1882-1922. LC 00-25126. (Italian & Italian American Studies). 320p. 2000. 66.00 (*0-275-96874-X*, C6874) Greenwood.
De Grand, Alexander. Italian Fascism: Its Origins & Development. 3rd ed. LC 99-47948. (Illus.). 198p. 2000. pap. text 15.95 (*0-8032-6622-7*, Bison Books) U of Nebr Pr.
De Grand, Alexander J. In Stalin's Shadow: Angelo Tasca & the Crisis of the Left in Italy & France, 1910-1945. 1986. 32.00 (*0-87580-116-1*) N Ill U Pr.
— Italian Fascism: Its Origins & Development. 2nd ed. LC 88-27847. xiv, 184p. 1989. reprint ed. pap. text 14.00 (*0-8032-6578-6*, Bison Books) U of Nebr Pr.
— The Italian Left in the Twentieth Century: A History of the Socialist & Communist Parties. LC 87-46371. 198p. 1989. 9.95 (*0-253-33107-2*) Ind U Pr.
— The Italian Nationalist Association & the Rise of Fascism in Italy. LC 77-24633. 250p. reprint ed. pap. 77.50 (*0-8357-3796-9*, 203652300003) Bks Demand.
***de Grand Pre, Donn.** Barbarians Inside the Gates: The Black Book of Bolshevism. (Illus.). 465p. 2000. 40.00 (*0-945001-79-7*) GSG & Assocs.
De Grandis, Francesca. Be A Goddess: A Guide to Magical Celtic Spells for Self-Healing, Prosperity & Great Sex. LC 97-43302. 336p. 1998. pap. 14.00 (*0-06-251505-5*, Pub. by Harper SF) HarpC.
De Grandmont, Eloi. First Secrets & Other Poems, Vol. 1. 112p. pap. 7.00 (*0-919349-29-3*) Guernica Editions.
De Grandpre, L. Voyage in the Indian Ocean & to Bengal, 1789-1790, 2 vols., Set. (C). 1995. reprint ed. 64.00 (*81-206-1031-8*, Pub. by Asian Educ Servs) S Asia.
De Grandpre, Pierre. Histoire de la Litterature Francaise du Quebec, 1534-1900, Vol. 1. (FRE.). 368p. 1967. 39.95 (*0-8288-7691-6*) Fr & Eur.
De Grasse Tyson, Neil. Just Visiting This Planet: Merlin Answers More Questions about Everything under the Sun, Moon, & Stars. LC 97-47122. (Illus.). 352p. 1998. pap. 12.95 (*0-385-48837-8*) Doubleday.
De Grassi, Alex. Alex De Grassi Collection. 72p. 1992. otabind 19.95 (*0-7935-0303-5*, 00660186) H Leonard.

D

De Grauwe, Paul. The Economics of Monetary Integration. 3rd ed. LC 97-12128. (Illus.). 248p. 1997. text 78.00 (*0-19-877550-4*); pap. text 26.00 (*0-19-877549-0*) OUP.

***De Grauwe, Paul.** Economics of Monetary Integration. 4th ed. 200p. 2000. pap. 29.95 (*0-19-877632-2*) OUP.

De Grauwe, Paul. International Money: Post-War Trends & Theories. 2nd ed. (Illus.). 288p. 1996. text 68.00 (*0-19-877514-8*); pap. text 26.00 (*0-19-877513-X*) OUP.

De Grauwe, Paul, et al, eds. Inflation & Wage Behaviour in the European Monetary System. (Illus.). 360p. 1997. text 85.00 (*0-19-828986-3*) OUP.

De Grauwe, Paul & Lavrac, Vladimir, eds. Inclusion of Central European Countries in the European Monetary Union. LC 98-47716. 11p. 1998. write for info. (*0-7923-8385-0*) Kluwer Academic.

De Grauwe, Paul, et al. Exchange Rate Theory: Chaotic Models of Foreign Exchange Markets. LC 92-25472. 328p. 1993. 58.95 (*0-631-18016-8*) Blackwell Pubs.

De Grauwe, Paul, jt. ed. see Argy, Victor.

De Gravelles, Charles, ed. see Favorite, Malaika.

De Grazia, Alfred. Apportionment & Representative Government. LC 83-12719. 180p. 1983. reprint ed. lib. bdg. 39.75 (*0-313-23375-6*, DGRA, Greenwood Pr) Greenwood.

— The Babe: Child of Boom & Bust in Old Chicago, Umbilicus Mundi. 489p. 1992. pap. 22.00 (*0-685-59570-6*) Metron Pubns.

— The Burning of Troy: Essays on Catastrophe & Chronology. (Quantavolution Ser.: No. 12). 300p. (Orig.). 1984. pap. 17.00 (*0-940268-07-8*) Metron Pubns.

— Chaos & Creation: An Introduction to Quantavolution in Human & Natural History. (Quantavolution Ser.). (Illus.). xiii, 336p. 1981. 22.00 (*0-940268-00-0*) Metron Pubns.

— A Cloud over Bhopal: Causes, Consequences, & Constructive Solutions. 145p. 1992. pap. 20.00 (*0-940268-27-2*) Metron Pubns.

— A Cloud over Bhopal-Causes, Consequences. 145p. 1985. 12.95 (*0-318-37222-3*) Asia Bk Corp.

— Cosmic Heretics: A Personal History of Attempts to Establish & Resist Theories of Quantavolution & Catastrophe in the Natural & Human Sciences, 1962-1983. (Quantavolution Ser.). 396p. 1984. pap. 23.00 (*0-940268-08-6*) Metron Pubns.

— The Disastrous Love Affair of Moon & Mars. (Quantavolution Ser.). 278p. (Orig.). 1984. pap. 17.00 (*0-940268-09-4*) Metron Pubns.

— Divine Succession: A Science of Gods Old & New. (Quantavolution Ser.). 204p. 1983. pap. 14.00 (*0-940268-05-1*) Metron Pubns.

— The Fall of Spydom: Memoir of a Case of Espionage, with Reflections & Digressions upon Catastrophism, Pandemic Paranoia, Computers, War Games, Mythology, & Swiss Savoir-faire. 403p. 1992. pap. 19.00 (*0-940268-26-4*) Metron Pubns.

— God's Fire: Moses & the Management of Exodus. (Quantavolution Ser.). (Illus.). 340p. 1983. pap. 20.00 (*0-940268-03-5*) Metron Pubns.

— Homo Schizo I: Human & Cultural Hologenesis. (Quantavolution Ser.). 278p. 1983. pap. 16.00 (*0-940268-01-9*) Metron Pubns.

— Homo Schizo II: Human Nature & Behavior. (Quantavolution Ser.). 240p. 1983. pap. 15.00 (*0-940268-02-7*) Metron Pubns.

— Kalos: What Is to Be Done with Our World? 533p. 1973. 17.00 (*0-940268-13-2*) Metron Pubns.

— Lately Tortured Earth: Exoterrestrial Forces & Quantavolutions in the Earth Sciences. (Quantavolution Ser.). 516p. 1983. 28.00 (*0-940268-06-X*) Metron Pubns.

— Lectures to the Chinese on American Society. 268p. 1993. pap. 12.00 (*0-385-04773-8*) Metron Pubns.

— Passage of the Year: Seventy-Three Poems. 133p. 1967. 9.00 (*0-940268-10-8*) Metron Pubns.

— Public & Republic. LC 84-22449. 271p. 1985. reprint ed. lib. bdg. 65.00 (*0-313-24679-3*, DEPR, Greenwood Pr) Greenwood.

— The Student: At Chicago in Hutchins' Hey-Day. 364p. 1992. pap. 21.00 (*0-940268-25-6*) Metron Pubns.

— Supporting Art & Culture: One-Thousand One Questions on Policy. 1992. 12.00 (*0-940268-30-2*) Metron Pubns.

— Taste of War: Soldiering in World War II. 490p. 1992. pap. 22.00 (*0-685-59571-4*) Metron Pubns.

— Twentieth Century Fire Sale: Poetry by Alfred de Grazia. 268p. 1996. pap. 15.00 (*0-614-25794-8*) Metron Pubns.

De Grazia, Alfred & Milton, Earl R. Solaria Binaria: Origins & History of the Solar System. (Quantavolution Ser.). (Illus.). 292p. 1984. pap. 21.00 (*0-940268-04-3*) Metron Pubns.

De Grazia, Alfred, et al. Eight Bads - Eight Goods. 1995. 12.50 (*0-8446-5181-8*) Peter Smith.

De Grazia, Alfred, tr. see Michels, Robert.

De Grazia, Anne-Marie. Le Pigeon d'Argile: The Clay Pigeon. 104p. 1984. pap. 14.00 (*0-940268-99-X*) Metron Pubns.

***De Grazia, Don.** American Skin: A Novel. LC 99-48500. 304p. 2000. per. 13.00 (*0-684-86222-0*) S&S Trade.

De Grazia, Edward & Newman, Roger K. Banned Films: Movies, Censors & the First Amendment. 532p. 1982. 39.95 (*0-8352-1509-1*); pap. 29.95 (*0-8352-1511-3*) Bowker.

De Grazia, Emilio. A Canticle for Bread & Stones. Howe, Ray, ed. LC 97-71025. 312p. 1997. lib. bdg. 14.95 (*1-883477-19-0*) Lone Oak MN.

— Seventeen Grams of Soul. LC 94-72988. (Illus.). 185p. (Orig.). 1995. pap. 9.95 (*1-883477-07-7*) Lone Oak MN.

De Grazia, Margreta. Shakespeare Verbatim: The Reproduction of Authenticity & the 1790 Apparatus. (Illus.). 256p. 1991. text 80.00 (*0-19-811778-7*, 2094) OUP.

De Grazia, Margreta, et al, eds. Subject & Object in Renaissance Culture. (Cambridge Studies in Renaissance Literature & Culture: No. 8). 416p. (C). 1996. text 64.95 (*0-521-45471-9*) Cambridge U Pr.

— Subject & Object in Renaissance Culture. (Cambridge Studies in Renaissance Literature & Culture). (Illus.). 416p. 1996. pap. text 24.95 (*0-521-45589-8*) Cambridge U Pr.

De Grazia, Raffaele. Clandestine Employment: The Situation in the Industrialised Market Economy Countries. vii, 118p. 1984. pap. 15.75 (*92-2-103355-4*) Intl Labour Office.

De Grazia, Sebastian. Country with No Name. 1999. pap. 17.00 (*0-679-74422-3*) Knopf.

— A Country with No Name: Tales from the Constitution. LC 96-31782. 1997. 27.50 (*0-679-41977-2*) Pantheon.

— Machiavelli in Hell. LC 92-50594. 1994. pap. 18.00 (*0-679-74342-1*) Vin Bks.

De Grazia, Victoria. How Fascism Ruled Women: Italy, 1922-1945. LC 91-8901. (Illus.). 384p. 1991. 45.00 (*0-520-07456-4*, Pub. by U CA Pr); pap. 17.95 (*0-520-07457-2*, Pub. by U CA Pr) Cal Prin Full Svc.

De Grazia, Victoria & Furlough, Ellen, eds. The Sex of Things: Gender & Consumption in Historical Perspective. (Illus.). 443p. 1996. 50.00 (*0-520-20034-9*, Pub. by U CA Pr); pap. 19.95 (*0-520-20197-3*, Pub. by U CA Pr) Cal Prin Full Svc.

De Gree, Melvin. Brickhouse Dreams: Young Benjamin E. Mays. (Illus.). 140p. (Orig.). (J). (gr. 3-10). 1992. pap. 11.95 (*0-9632895-0-0*) Trail of Success.

De Greene, Kenyon B., ed. A Systems-Based Approach to Policymaking. LC 93-538. 384p. (C). 1993. text 150.00 (*0-7923-9336-8*) Kluwer Academic.

De Gregoire, Abbe Henri. An Enquiry Concerning the Intellectual & Moral Faculties & Literature of Negroes. Warden, D. B., tr. (B. E. Ser.: No. 70, Pt. 2). 65.00 (*0-8115-3020-5*) Periodicals Srv.

De Greiff, Pablo, ed. Drugs & the Limits of Liberalism: Moral & Legal Issues. LC 98-48115. 224p. 1998. 29.95 (*0-8014-3561-7*) Cornell U Pr.

De Greiff, Pablo, see Gracia, Jorge J. E. & De Greiff, Pablo, eds.

De Greiff, Pablo, see Gracia, Jorge J. & De Greiff, Pablo.

De Greiff, Pablo, see De Greiff, Pablo, ed.

De Greiff, Pablo, jt. auth. see Gracia, Jorge J.

De Greiff, Pablo, jt. ed. see Gracia, Jorge J. E.

De Greve, J. P., et al, eds. Stellar Atmospheres: Theory & Observations: Lectures Held at the Astrophysics School IX, Organized by the European Astrophysics Doctoral Network (EADN) in Brussels, Belgium, 10-19 September, 1996. LC 97-41178. (Lecture Notes in Physics Ser.: Vol. 497). xiii, 352p. 1997. text 86.00 (*3-540-63477-0*) Spr-Verlag.

de Grey, Aubrey D. N. J. The Mitochondrial Free Radical Theory of Aging. LC QP86.D4 1999. (Molecular Biology Intelligence Unit Ser.: Vol. 9). 212p. 1999. 99.00 (*1-57059-564-X*) Landes Bioscience.

De Grillot, Givry. Witchcraft, Magic & Alchemy. Locke, J. Courtney, tr. from FRE. (Illus.). 395p. 1971. reprint ed. pap. 12.95 (*0-486-22493-7*) Dover.

De Grip, Andries, jt. ed. see Borghans, Lex.

***De Groat, Diane.** Annie Pitts, Burger Kid. LC 00-24304. (Illus.). (J). 2000. write for info. (*1-58717-016-7*); 14.95 (*1-58717-015-9*) SeaStar.

— Happy Birthday to You, You Belong in a Zoo. LC 98-44722. 32p. (J). 1999. 14.93 (*0-688-16545-1*, Wm Morrow) Morrow Avon.

De Groat, Diane. Happy Birthday to You, You Belong in a Zoo. LC 98-44722. (Illus.). 32p. (J). (ps-3). 1999. 15.00 (*0-688-16544-3*, Wm Morrow) Morrow Avon.

De Groat, Diane. Jingle Bells, Homework Smells. 1924. pap. write for info. (*0-688-17545-7*, Wm Morrow) Morrow Avon.

De Groat, Diane. Roses Are Pink, Your Feet Really Stink. 1997. 10.15 (*0-606-11812-8*, Pub. by Turtleback) Demco.

***De Groat, Diane.** Trick or Treat, Smell My Feet. LC 97-32916. (Illus.). 32p. (J). (gr. k-3). 1998. 15.00 (*0-688-15766-1*, Wm Morrow) Morrow Avon.

De Groat, Diane, jt. auth. see Lowry, Lois.

De Groat, Diane, jt. auth. see Nixon, Joan Lowery.

De Groen, Alma. Rivers of China. 69p. 1990. pap. 5.60 (*0-87129-013-8*, R43) Dramatic Pub.

***De Groen, Frances.** Xavier Herbert: A Biography. LC 98-225941. 1p. 1998. 39.95 (*0-7022-3021-9*, Pub. by Univ Queensland Pr) Intl Spec Bk.

De Groff. Legal Status Pupils. LC 98-181053. 1998. lib. bdg. 118.00 (*90-411-0521-2*) Kluwer Law Intl.

De Grolier, Eric, ed. Glossogenetics: The Origin & Evolution of Language, Vol. 1. LC 83-232. (Models of Scientific Thought Ser.: Vol. 6). (Illus.). xii, 546p. 1983. text 102.00 (*3-7186-0158-3*) Gordon & Breach.

De Grood, David H. The Appearance of Reality: Essays in Contemporary Philosophy. ix, 220p. (Orig.). 1985. pap. write for info. (*90-6032-270-3*) B R Gruner.

De Groof, Jan, et al. Democracy & Governance in Higher Education. LC 98-9778. (Legislating for Higher Education in Europe Ser.). 1998. 105.00 (*90-411-0575-1*) Kluwer Academic.

De Groot, Patch Testing: Test Concentrations & Vehicles for 3700 Chemicals. 2nd ed. 334p. 1994. text 188.50 (*0-444-81911-8*) Elsevier.

De Groot, A. C., et al, eds. Unwanted Effects of Cosmetics & Drugs Used in Dermatology. 3rd rev. ed. 782p. 1993. 307.00 (*0-444-89775-5*) Elsevier.

De Groot, Adriaan. Methodology: Foundations of Inference & Research in the Behavioral Sciences. (Psychological Studies: No. 6). 1969. text 43.10 (*90-279-6250-2*) Mouton.

De Groot, Adriaan D. Thought & Choice in Chess. 2nd ed. (Psychological Studies: No. 4). 1978. text 89.25 (*3-11-000286-8*) Mouton.

De Groot, Annette M. & Kroll, Judith F., eds. Tutorials in Bilingualism: Psycholinguistic Perspectives. LC 96-47320. 368p. 1997. pap. text 39.95 (*0-8058-1951-7*) L Erlbaum Assocs.

— Tutorials in Bilingualism: Psycholinguistic Perspectives. LC 96-47320. 368p. 1997. text 79.95 (*0-8058-1950-9*) L Erlbaum Assocs.

De Groot, C. & Tommola, H., eds. Aspect Bound: A Voyage into the Realm of Germanic, Slavonic & Finno-Ugrian Aspectology. viii, 283p. 1984. pap. 65.40 (*90-6765-031-5*) Mouton.

De Groot, C. Hofstede. Beschreibendes und Kritisches Verzeichnis der Werke der Hervorragendsten Hollandischen Maler des XVIIJh, 3 vols. (Catalogue Raisonne of the Works of the Most Eminent Dutch Painters of the Seventeenth Century). 1028p. 1976. lib. bdg. write for info. (*0-85964-027-2*) Chadwyck-Healey.

— Beschreibendes und Kritisches Verzeichnis der Werke der Hervorragendsten Hollandischen Maler des XVIIJh, Vols. 9 & 10. (Catalogue Raisonne of the Works of the Most Eminent Dutch Painters of the Seventeenth Century). 180p. 1976. lib. bdg. write for info. (*0-85964-025-6*) Chadwyck-Healey.

— A Catalogue Raisonne of the Works of the Most Eminent Dutch Painters of the Seventeenth Century, 2 vols. Hawke, E. G., ed. 5100p. 1976. reprint ed. write for info. (*0-89887-167-0*); reprint ed. write for info. (*0-85964-023-X*); reprint ed. write for info. (*0-85964-024-8*) Chadwyck-Healey.

De Groot, Casper. Predicate Structure in a Functional Grammar of Hungarian. (Functional Grammar Ser.). 248p. (Orig.). (C). 1989. pap. 53.60 (*90-6765-435-3*) Mouton.

De Groot, Cornelus. Netherlands Labor & Co-Determination Law in an EEC Perspective. 312p. 1990. pap. 63.00 (*90-6544-525-0*) Kluwer Law Intl.

De Groot, Dennis. God's Backyard. 79p. pap. 11.95 (*1-56212-039-5*) CRC Pubns.

De Groot, Gerard A., ed. see Van Genugten, Willem J. M.

De Groot, Gerard J. Douglas Haig Eighteen Sixty-One to Nineteen Twenty-Eight. 1988. 34.95 (*0-04-440192-2*) Routledge.

***De Groot, Gerard J.** The First World War. LC 00-30891. (Twentieth Century Wars Ser.). 2000. write for info. (*0-312-23752-9*) St Martin.

De Groot, Gerard J. Liberal Crusader: The Life of Sir Archibald Sinclair. LC 92-39141. (C). 1993. text 45.00 (*0-8147-1849-3*) NYU Pr.

***De Groot, Gerard J.** A Noble Cause. (Modern Wars in Perspective Ser.). 391p. (C). 1999. pap. 30.73 (*0-582-28717-0*) Longman.

— A Noble Cause. (Modern Wars in Perspective Ser.). 400p. (C). 1999. 79.95 (*0-582-28718-9*) Longman.

De Groot, Gerard J. Student Protest. LC 98-7586. 1998. 69.95 (*0-582-35619-9*) Addison-Wesley.

De Groot, Gertjan & Schrover, Marlou, eds. Women Workers & Technological Change in Europe in the Nineteenth & Twentieth Century. 208p. 1995. 85.00 (*0-7484-0260-8*); pap. 29.95 (*0-7484-0261-6*) Taylor & Francis.

De Groot, H., jt. auth. see Sies, Helmut.

***de Groot, Henri L. F.** Growth, Unemployment & Deindustrialization. LC 99-45150. 336p. 2000. 100.00 (*1-84064-263-7*) E Elgar.

De Groot, J. Correlative Neuroanatomy of Computed Tomography & Magnetic Resonance Imaging. LC 83-22175. (Illus.). 260p. reprint ed. pap. 80.60 (*0-7837-2698-8*, 204307700006) Bks Demand.

De Groot, J. K., et al. Solicitors Checklists. 2nd ed. 312p. 1993. pap. write for info. (*0-409-30324-0*, MICHIE) LEXIS Pub.

De Groot, John. Papa: The Legendary Lives of Ernest Hemingway, a Play in Two Acts. limited ed. Trusky, Tom, ed. (Hemingway Western Studies). (Illus.). 112p. 1989. 75.00 (*0-932129-07-2*) Heming W Studies.

De Groot, John H. Shakespeare's - 'The Old Faith' LC 68-57315. (Essay Index Reprint Ser.). 1977. 20.95 (*0-8369-0368-4*) Ayer.

De Groot, Klaas. Bioceramics of Calciumphosphate. 152p. 1983. 94.00 (*0-8493-6456-6*, RK655, CRC Reprint) Franklin.

De Groot, Laila. Posture & Motility in Preterm Infants: A Clinical Approach. 160p. 1994. pap. 25.00 (*90-5383-239-4*, Pub. by VU Univ Pr) Paul & Co Pubs.

De Groot, M. B., et al, eds. Geosynthetics: Applications, Design & Construction: Proceedings of the First European Geosynthetics Conference, EUROGEO 1, Maastricht, Netherlands, 30 September-02 October 1996. (Illus.). 1086p. (C). Date not set. text 149.00 (*90-5410-836-3*, Pub. by A A Balkema) Ashgate Pub Co.

De Groot, Mart, jt. ed. see Sterken, Christiaan.

De Groot, P. F. Seismic Reservoir Characterization Employing Factual & Simulated Wells. (Illus.). 200p. (Orig.). 1995. pap. 67.50 (*90-407-1163-1*, Pub. by Delft U Pr) Coronet Bks.

De Groot, Roy A. Auberge Flow Hearth Ckbk. 464p. 1992. pap. 14.95 (*0-88001-278-1*) HarpC.

— Auberge Of The Flowering Hearth. 444p. 1996. reprint ed. pap. 17.00 (*0-88001-504-7*) HarpC.

De Groot, Roy A., jt. auth. see Nadrchal, J.

De Groot, S. R. & Suttorp, L. G. Foundations of Electrodynamics. LC 75-166303. 547p. reprint ed. pap. 169.60 (*0-608-17400-9*, 205640200067) Bks Demand.

De Groot, S. R., et al. Relativistic Kinetic Theory: Principles & Applications. 418p. 1980. 207.50 (*0-444-85453-3*, North Holland) Elsevier.

De Groot, Sjany. I Will Never Give Up. 1997. 24.95 (*0-9658776-1-2*) Cntrl Coast Pr.

De Groot, W. Herman. Sulphonation Technology in the Detergent Industry. 296p. (C). 1991. text 169.50 (*0-7923-1202-3*) Kluwer Academic.

De Groot, Walter P., tr. see Altenkamper, Henner & Eldenburg, Matthias.

De Groot, Wim A., ed. Advanced Sensors & Monitors for Process Industries & the Environment, Vol. 3535. 336p. 1999. 80.00 (*0-8194-2996-1*) SPIE.

De Groot, Wim A., jt. ed. see Nordstrom, Robert J.

De Groot, Wouter T. Environmental Science Theory: Concepts & Methods in a One-World, Problem-Oriented Paradigm. LC 92-28733. (Studies in Environmental Science: Vol. 52). 584p. 1992. 257.50 (*0-444-88993-0*) Elsevier.

De Groote, H. F. Lectures on the Complexity of Bilinear Problems. (Lecture Notes in Computer Science Ser.: Vol. 245). (Illus.). v, 135p. 1987. 26.00 (*0-387-17205-X*) Spr-Verlag.

De Groote, P., et al, eds. Typed Lambda Calculi & Applications: Third International Conference on Typed Lambda Calculi & Applications, TLCA '97, Nancy, France, April 2-4, 1997, Proceedings. (Lecture Notes in Computer Science Ser.: Vol. 1210). viii, 405p. 1997. pap. 67.00 (*3-540-62688-3*) Spr-Verlag.

De Grosbois, Paul. Un Mal Etrange. (Novels in the Roman Plus Ser.). (FRE.). 160p. (YA). (gr. 8 up). 1991. pap. 8.95 (*2-89021-167-3*, Pub. by La Courte Ech) Firefly Bks Ltd.

De Gross, Monalisa. Steal Away. (J). 1999. write for info. (*0-7868-0161-1*) Hyperion.

De Grott, Anton C. Adverse Reactions to Cosmetics. Lackie, Gordon L., ed. (Illus.). 241p. 1989. text 75.00 (*0-685-74191-5*) Scholium Intl.

De Grove, Olivia. Manhattan Lullaby. 206p. 1990. pap. 5.95 (*0-7736-7258-3*) Genl Dist Srvs.

De Gruchy, Graham. Architecture in Brisbane. 160p. (C). 1990. 141.00 (*0-86439-078-5*, Pub. by Boolarong Pubns); pap. 120.00 (*0-7855-7016-0*, Pub. by Boolarong Pubns) St Mut.

De Gruchy, John, ed. Dietrich Bonhoeffer: Witness to Jesus Christ. (Making of Modern Theology Ser.). 320p. 1991. pap. 20.00 (*0-8006-3404-7*, 1-3404) Augsburg Fortress.

De Gruchy, John & Villa-Vicencio, Charles, eds. Doing Theology in Context Vol. 1: South African Perspectives. 225p. (Orig.). 1994. pap. 21.00 (*0-88344-989-7*) Orbis Bks.

De Gruchy, John, jt. ed. see Prozesky, Martin.

De Gruchy, John, jt. ed. see Rumscheidt, H. Martin.

De Gruchy, John W. Christianity & Democracy: A Theology for a Just World Order. (Cambridge Studies in Ideology & Religion: No. 7). 308p. (C). 1995. pap. text 22.95 (*0-521-45841-2*) Cambridge U Pr.

— Cry Justice: Prayers, Meditations, & Readings from South Africa. LC 86-667. (Illus.). 261p. 1986. reprint ed. pap. 81.00 (*0-7837-9812-1*, 206054100005) Bks Demand.

De Gruchy, John W., ed. Bonhoeffer for a New Day: Theology in a Time of Transition. LC 97-8918. 352p. (Orig.). 1997. pap. 30.00 (*0-8028-4284-4*) Eerdmans.

— The Cambridge Companion to Dietrich Bonhoeffer. LC 98-35990. (Companions to Religion Ser.). 281p. (C). 1999. pap. 19.95 (*0-521-58781-6*); text 54.95 (*0-521-58258-X*) Cambridge U Pr.

De Gruchy, John W. & Villa-Vicencio, Charles, eds. Apartheid Is a Heresy. LC 83-8935. 204p. (Orig.). reprint ed. pap. 63.30 (*0-8357-4361-6*, 203718900007) Bks Demand.

— Doing Theology in Context: South African Perspectives. LC 95-116363. (Theology & Praxis Ser.). 248p. reprint ed. pap. 76.90 (*0-608-20266-5*, 207152500012) Bks Demand.

De Gruchy, John W., ed. see Bonhoeffer, Dietrich.

De Gruchy, John W., jt. ed. see Clements, Keith.

De Gruchy, John W., ed. see London Missionary Society Staff.

De Gruchy, John W., jt. ed. see Villa-Vicencio, Charles.

De Grucy, Clare, jt. auth. see Martin, Lillien J.

De Gruijter, D. N. & Van der Kamp, Leo J. Statistical Models in Psychological & Educational Testing. x, 294p. 1984. pap. 59.00 (*90-265-0517-5*) Swets.

De Grummond, Jane L. Renato Beluche: Smuggler, Privateer, & Patriot, 1780-1860. LC 82-14969. 316p. 1983. pap. 98.00 (*0-7837-8506-2*, 204931400011) Bks Demand.

De Grummond, Nancy T. An Encyclopedia of the History of Classical Archaeology. LC 94-29838. 1400p. 1996. lib. bdg. 225.00 (*0-313-22066-2*, Greenwood Pr) Greenwood.

De Grummond, Nancy T., ed. Encyclopedia of the History of Classical Archaeology, 2 vols. 1400p. 1997. lib. bdg. 200.00 (*1-884964-80-X*) Fitzroy Dearborn.

— An Encyclopedia of the History of Classical Archaeology: A-K, Vol. 1. LC 94-29838. 680p. 1996. lib. bdg. 225.00 (*0-313-30204-9*, Greenwood Pr) Greenwood.

— An Encyclopedia of the History of Classical Archaeology: L-Z, Vol. 2. LC 94-29838. 704p. 1996. lib. bdg. 225.00 (*0-313-30205-7*, Greenwood Pr) Greenwood.

***De Grummond, Nancy Thomson & Ridgway, Brunilde Sismondo.** From Pergamon to Sperlonga: Sculpture & Context. LC 00-37775. (Hellenistic Culture & Society Ser.). 2000. write for info. (*0-520-22327-6*) U CA Pr.

De Gubernatis, Angelo. La Mythologie des Plantes: Ou les Legendes du Regne Vegetal. Bolle, Kees W., ed. LC 77-79128. (Mythology Ser.). 1978. reprint ed. lib. bdg. 57.95 (*0-405-10539-8*) Ayer.

— Zoological Mythology or the Legends of Animals, 2 vols. Bolle, Kees W., ed. LC 77-79129. (Mythology Ser.). 1978. reprint ed. lib. bdg. 75.95 (*0-405-10540-1*) Ayer.

De Gucht, Karel & Keukeleire, Stephan. Time & Tide Wait for No Man: The Changing European Geopolitical Landscape. LC 91-9196. 256p. 1991. 59.95 (*0-275-94062-4*, C4062, Praeger Pubs) Greenwood.

De Guchteneire, P. F. & Mochmann, Ekkehard. Data Protection & Data Access: Royal Netherlands. 274p. pap. 47.00 (*0-444-85714-1*, North Holland) Elsevier.

De Guchtenfire, Paul, ed. Inventory of Social Science Information & Documentation Services. 4th ed. (World Social Science Information Directories Ser.). 392p. 1993. pap. 71.95 (*0-631-18965-3*) Blackwell Pubs.

De Guevara, Juan V. Los Celos Hacen Estrellas. Varey, J. E. et al, eds. (Textos B Ser.: Vol. IV). (SPA., Illus.). 277p. (Orig.). (C). 1970. pap. 51.00 (*0-900411-06-6*, Pub. by Tamesis Bks Ltd) Boydell & Brewer.

De Guibert, Joseph. The Jesuits: Their Spiritual Doctrine & Practice. Young, W. J., tr. LC 64-21430. (Modern Scholarly Studies about the Jesuits, in English Translations Series II: No. 1). xxviii, 692p. (C). 1964. pap. 29.95 (*0-912422-09-2*) Inst Jesuit.

De Guise, Elizabeth. Lions Shadow. 1980. pap. 1.50 (*0-373-58006-1*) Harlequin Bks.

De Gutierrez, Carmelina G. Muneca de Trapo: Poesias Infantiles. LC 92-81948. (Coleccion Espejo de Paciencia). (SPA., Illus.). 59p. (Orig.). (J). 1992. pap. 6.00 (*0-89729-642-7*) Ediciones.

De Gutierrez, Edith A. The Movement Against Teaching English in Schools of Puerto Rico. LC 86-30763. 176p. (Orig.). 1987. pap. text 22.00 (*0-8191-6088-1*); lib. bdg. 40.50 (*0-8191-6087-3*) U Pr of Amer.

De Guttry, Andrea & Ronzitti, Natalino, eds. The Iran-Iraq War (1980-1988) & the Law of Naval Warfare: A Collection of Documents & Related Commentaries on Naval Practice. 800p. (C). 1993. text 390.00 (*1-85701-013-2*, Pub. by Grotius Pubns Ltd) St Mut.

***de Guzman, C. C. & Siemonsma, J. S., eds.** Spices. (Plant Resources of South-East Asia Ser.: No. 13). (Illus.). 400p. 1999. 112.50 (*90-5782-046-3*, Pub. by Backhuys Pubs) Balogh.

De Guzman, Daniel. Direct French Conversation, Bk. 2. (C). 1999. pap. 11.67 (*0-13-214743-2*, Macmillan Coll) P-H.

De Guzman, Fernan Perez, see Perez de Guzman, Fernan.

De Guzman, Guillermo N. El Tesoro de los Suenos (The Treasure of Dreams) (SPA., Illus.). (YA). 1994. pap. 6.99 (*968-16-4227-9*, Pub. by Fondo) Continental Bk.

De Guzman-Ladion, Herminia. Healing Wonders of Herbs: Guide to the Effective Use of Medicinal Plants LC 87-115425. 158p. 1985. write for info. (*971-10-1901-9*, Pub. by New Day Pub) S Asia.

***De Guzman, Miguel.** The Countingbury Tales: Fun with Mathematics. LC 99-41241. 130p. 1999. pap. 18.00 (*981-02-4033-3*) World Scientific Pub.

De Guzman, Videa P. Syntactic Derivation of Tagalog Verbs. LC 78-11029. (Oceanic Linguistics Special Publication Ser.: No. 16). 432p. reprint ed. pap. 134.00 (*0-8357-8535-1*, 203483800091) Bks Demand.

***De Guzman, Videa P., et al.** Studies in Grammatical Analysis: Morphology, Syntax & Semantics in Honor of Stanley Starosta. LC 00-33777. (Oceanic Linguistics Special Publications). 2000. pap. write for info. (*0-8248-2105-X*) UH Pr.

De Guzman, Videa P, jt. auth. see Ramos, Teresita V.

***De Gyvez, Jose Pineda & Pradham, Dhiraj K., eds.** Integrated Circuit Manufacturability: The Art of Process & Design Integration. LC 98-6335. 336p. 1998. 99.95 (*0-7803-3447-7*, PC4481-QOE) Inst Electrical.

de Gyvez, Jose Pineda, see Pineda de Gyvez, Jose.

De Haan, Barthold Berens, see Berens de Haan, Barthold.

De Haan, Cornelis, jt. auth. see Oram, Peter A.

De Haan, D., jt. ed. see Brouwer, D.

De Haan, Ellen H. Aging in Place: The Development of Naturally-Occurring Retirement Communities. LC 97-51689. 32p. (C). 1998. pap. write for info. (*0-941301-41-9*) CAI.

De Haan, Ferdinand. The Interaction of Modality & Negation: A Typological Study. rev. ed. Horn, Laurence, ed. LC 97-20279. (Outstanding Dissertations in Linguistics Ser.). 270p. 1997. text 65.00 (*0-8153-2892-3*) Garland.

De Haan, Francisca. Gender & the Politics of Office Work in the Netherlands, 1860-1940. LC 99-160157. 224p. 1998. 47.50 (*90-5356-304-0*, Pub. by Amsterdam U Pr) U of Mich Pr.

De Haan, Ger. Conditions on Rules. 248p. 1981. pap. 75.40 (*90-70176-08-4*) Mouton.

De Haan, H. H. Alternatives in Industrial Development: Sugar Processing in India. (Alternatives in Development Ser.: No. 1). 190p. (C). 1988. text 26.00 (*0-8039-9566-0*) Sage.

De Haan, H. J., ed. New Developments in Improved Oil Recovery. (Geological Society Special Publication Ser.: No. 84). (Illus.). 286p. 1995. 108.00 (*1-897799-22-5*, 231, Pub. by Geol Soc Pub Hse) AAPG.

De Haan, Henk, et al, eds. Sustainable Rural Development. LC 97-72077. (Illus.). 224p. 1997. text 64.95 (*1-85972-595-3*, Pub. by Avebry) Ashgate Pub Co.

De Haan, J. P. Rigging Equipment & Outfit of Seagoing Ships, Pt. 1. 464p. 1957. 330.00 (*0-85950-070-5*) St Mut.

***De Haan, Jakob.** The History of the Bundesbank: Lessons for the European Central Bank. LC 99-46623. (International Studies in Money & Banking). 224p. 2000. 90.00 (*0-415-21723-7*) Routledge.

De Haan, Jakob, jt. auth. see Eijffinger, Sylvester C.

De Haan, M. R. Broken Things: Why We Suffer. rev. ed. 96p. 1988. pap. 7.99 (*0-929239-00-8*) Discovery Hse Pubs.

— Hebrews. LC 88-20592. 1978. pap. 7.95 (*0-310-23371-2*, 9506P) Zondervan.

— Pentecost & After: Studies in the Book of Acts. LC 96-10337. (M. R. De Haan Classic Library). (Illus.). 192p. 1996. pap. 10.99 (*0-8254-2482-8*) Kregel.

— The Romance of Redemption: Studies in the Book of Ruth. (M. R. De Haan Classic Library). 184p. 1996. pap. 10.99 (*0-8254-2480-1*) Kregel.

— The Second Coming of Jesus. LC 96-32046. (M. R. De Haan Classic Library). 176p. 1997. pap. 10.99 (*0-8254-2483-6*) Kregel.

— Signs of the Times: Studies in the Prophetic Scriptures. LC 96-32045. (M. R. De Haan Classic Library). 184p. 1997. pap. 10.99 (*0-8254-2484-4*) Kregel.

— Studies in Hebrews. (M. R. De Haan Classic Library). 216p. 1996. pap. 10.99 (*0-8254-2479-8*) Kregel.

***De Haan, M. R.** Studies in Revelation. LC 98-26807. (M. R. De Haan Classic Library). 312p. 1998. pap. text 12.99 (*0-8254-2485-2*) Kregel.

De Haan, Stefan, tr. see Peppercorn, Lisa M.

De Haan-van Beek, To. New Dimensions in Tatting. 87p. 1994. pap. 14.00 (*0-916896-52-8*) Lacis Pubns.

De Haan, Willem. The Politics of Redress. 224p. 1990. text 49.95 (*0-04-445441-4*) Routledge.

De Haas, Elsa. Antiquities of Bail: Origin & Historical Development in Criminal Cases to the Year 1275. LC 72-163693. reprint ed. 20.00 (*0-404-02067-4*) AMS Pr.

De Haas, Frank. Bolt Action Rifles. 3rd ed. LC 73-163105. (Illus.). 528p. (Orig.). 1995. pap. 24.95 (*0-87349-168-8*, BAR3, DBI Bks) Krause Pubns.

De Haas, Frans A. John Philoponus' New Definition of Prime Matter: Aspects of Its Background in Neoplatonism & the Ancient Commentary Tradition. LC 96-38326. (Philosophia Antiqua Ser.). xxiv, 340p. 1996. 110.00 (*90-04-10446-1*) Brill Academic Pubs.

De Haas, Margaret, ed. see Wilson, Edward O.

De Haas, Paul & Lovejoy, Surya. The Prosperity Handbook: Winning the Money Game. 150p. 1994. 34.95 (*0-566-07447-8*, Pub. by Gower) Ashgate Pub Co.

De Haas, Wim. A Formal Theory of Vowel Coalescence: A Case Study of Ancient Greek. (Publications in Language Sciences: No. 30). x, 222p. 1989. pap. 50.00 (*90-6765-397-7*) Mouton.

De Haene, R., ed. see International Meeting on the Use of Computers in R.

De Hahn, H. Direct Sticking Measurements in Muon Catalyzed Fusion. 116p. (Orig.). 1994. pap. 47.50 (*90-6275-993-9*, Pub. by Delft U Pr) Coronet Bks.

De Halacsy, E. Conspectus Florae Graecae & Supplementum Prim, 4 vols. in 2, Set. 1969. 480.00 (*3-7682-7192-7*) Lubrecht & Cramer.

De Halleux, Andre. Philoxene de Mabbog: Sa Vie, Ses Ecrits, Sa Theologie. LC 82-45812. (Orthodoxies & Heresies in the Early Church Ser.). reprint ed. 64.50 (*0-404-62387-5*) AMS Pr.

De Hamel, Christopher. The British Library Guide to Manuscript Illumination: History & Techniques. (British Library Guides Ser.). (Illus.). 92p. 1998. pap. 19.95 (*0-8020-8173-8*) U of Toronto Pr.

— A History of Illuminated Manuscripts. 2nd ed. (Illus.). 272p. 1997. pap. 35.00 (*0-7148-3452-1*, Pub. by Phaidon Press) Phaidon Pr.

— A History of Illuminated Manuscripts. 2nd ed. LC 95-150977. (Illus.). 240p. (C). 1994. reprint ed. text 55.00 (*0-7148-2949-8*, Pub. by Phaidon Press) Phaidon Pr.

— Scribes & Illuminators. (Medieval Craftsmen Ser.). (Illus.). 72p. 1992. pap. text 19.95 (*0-8020-7707-2*) U of Toronto Pr.

De Hammais, Pierre, ed. A Guide to the Cthulhu Cult. (Illus.). 72p. (Orig.). 1996. pap. 8.00 (*1-887797-06-8*) Tynes Cowan.

De Handlo, Robertus & Hanboys, Johannes. The Rules & the Summa. Lefferts, Peter M., ed. & tr. by. LC 90-415133. (Greek & Latin Music Theory Ser.). (Illus.). x, 403p. 1990. text 50.00 (*0-8032-7934-5*) U of Nebr Pr.

De Haro, M. L. & Varea, C. Thermodynamics & Statistical Mechanics, Lectures: Proceedings of the 21st Meeting in Statistical Physics. 216p. 1992. text 95.00 (*981-02-1221-6*) World Scientific Pub.

— Thermodynamics & Statistical Mechanics on Statistical Physics: Proceedings of the 22nd Winter Meeting. 264p. 1994. text 95.00 (*981-02-1527-4*) World Scientific Pub.

De Haro, M. L., et al. Lectures on Thermodynamics & Statistical Mechanics: Proceedings of the XX Winter Meeting on Statistical Physics, Mexico, 8-11 January 1991. 300p. (C). 1991. text 74.00 (*981-02-0736-0*) World Scientific Pub.

De Haro, MiLopez & Varea, C. Lectures on Thermodynamics & Statistical Mechanics: Nineteenth Winter Meeting on Statistical Physics. 228p. 1990. text 92.00 (*981-02-0243-1*) World Scientific Pub.

De Haro, Ramon G. Marriage & the Family in the Documents of the Magisterium: A Course in the Theology of Marriage. May, William E., tr. LC 93-78531. 350p. 1993. 24.95 (*0-89870-459-6*) Ignatius Pr.

De Hart, Allen. Adventuring in Florida. rev. ed. LC 91-12430. (Sierra Club Guides to the Natural Areas of the United States Ser.). (Illus.). 448p. (Orig.). 1995. pap. 15.00 (*0-87156-373-8*) Sierra.

***De Hart, Allen.** Hiking North Carolina's Mountains-to-Sea Trail. (Illus.). 392p. 2000. pap. 18.95 (*0-8078-4887-5*) U of NC Pr.

De Hart, Allen. Hiking South Carolina Trails: Hikes along the Chattanooga Trail, Cowpens Battlefield Trail, Old Walled City Trail, Table Rock Trail, & Many Others. 4th ed. LC 98-24364. (Illus.). 352p. 1998. pap. 12.95 (*0-7627-0223-0*) Globe Pequot.

— North Carolina Hiking Trails. 3rd rev. ed. LC 87-31848. (Illus.). 512p. 1996. pap. 18.95 (*1-878239-48-1*) AMC Books.

— Trails of the Triad: 100 Hikes in the Winston-Salem/Greensboro/High Point Area. LC 96-53451. (Illus.). (Orig.). 1997. pap. 11.95 (*0-89587-161-0*) Blair.

— Trails of the Triangle: 170 Hikes in the Raleigh/Durham/Chapel Hill Area. LC 96-39789. (Illus.). (Orig.). 1997. pap. 11.95 (*0-89587-160-2*) Blair.

— West Virginia Hiking Trails: Hiking the Mountain State. 2nd rev. ed. LC 97-4398. Orig. Title: Hiking the Mountain State. (Illus.). 416p. 1997. pap. 16.95 (*1-878239-56-2*) AMC Books.

De Hart, Jane S. Defining the Nation. 1997. 29.95 (*0-226-14118-7*) U Ch Pr.

De Hart, Jane S., jt. auth. see Kerber, Linda K.

De Hart, Jane S., jt. auth. see Mathews, Donald G.

De Hartog, Jan. The Artist. Date not set. lib. bdg. 19.95 (*0-8488-0980-7*) Amereon Ltd.

— The Captain. LC 88-23866. (Great War Stories Ser.). (Illus.). 431p. 1988. reprint ed. 24.95 (*0-933852-83-5*) Nautical & Aviation.

— The Distant Shore. 1976. 24.95 (*0-8488-0981-5*) Amereon Ltd.

— The Inspector. 21.95 (*0-88411-069-9*) Amereon Ltd.

— Little Ark. Date not set. lib. bdg. 20.95 (*0-8488-2099-1*) Amereon Ltd.

— The Lost Sea. 1976. 22.95 (*0-8488-0982-3*) Amereon Ltd.

— The Outer Buoy. large type ed. (Ulverscroft Large Print Ser.). 480p. 1997. 27.99 (*0-7089-3771-3*) Ulverscroft.

— The Peculiar People. large type ed. LC 92-46333. (General Ser.). 509p. 1993. reprint ed. lib. bdg. 17.95 (*1-56054-670-0*) Thorndike Pr.

— The Spiral Road. 30.95 (*0-88411-071-0*) Amereon Ltd.

— Star of Peace. large type ed. 560p. 1986. 27.99 (*0-7089-8314-6*, Charnwood) Ulverscroft.

de Harven, Emile. Aerodrame: Teacher's guide. text 10.00 (*0-88436-338-4*) EMC-Paradigm.

— Aerodrame: Textbook. pap. text 9.95 (*0-88436-176-4*) EMC-Paradigm.

— Caminos Peligrosos: Textbook. text 9.95 (*0-88436-259-0*) EMC-Paradigm.

— Chemins Dangereux: Teacher's guide. text, teacher ed. 10.00 (*0-88436-339-2*) EMC-Paradigm.

— Chemins Dangereux: Textbook. text 9.95 (*0-88436-260-4*) EMC-Paradigm.

— Gefahrliche Wege: Textbook. pap. text 9.95 (*0-88436-256-6*) EMC-Paradigm.

— Suivez la Piste: Teacher's guide. text, teacher ed. 5.95 (*0-88436-342-2*) EMC-Paradigm.

de Harven, Emile, jt. auth. see EMC-Paradigm Publishing Staff.

de Harven, Emile, jt. auth. see EMC Publishing Company Staff.

de Harven, Emile, jt. auth. see EMC Staff.

De Haseth, James A., ed. Fourier Transform Spectroscopy: Eleventh International Conference. LC 98-70838. (AIP Conference Proceedings Ser.: Vol. 430). (Illus.). xvii, 753p. 1998. 225.00 (*1-56396-746-4*) Am Inst Physics.

De Hass, Frank S. Buried Cities Recovered: Explorations in Bible Lands. Davis, Moshe, ed. LC 77-70774. (America & the Holy Land Ser.). (Illus.). 1977. lib. bdg. 44.95 (*0-405-10242-9*) Ayer.

De Hass, Margaret R., jt. auth. see Goldrein, Iain S.

De Hass, Wills. History of the Early Settlement & Indian Wars of Western Virginia: Embracing an Account of the Various Expeditions in the West, Previous to 1795... 416p. 1997. reprint ed. pap. 37.50 (*0-8063-4695-7*) Clearfield Co.

De Haven. Funny Papers. Date not set. pap. 12.00 (*0-8050-5743-9*, Owl) H Holt & Co.

De Haven-Smith, Lance, ed. see Boswell, Michael, et al.

De Haven, Tom. Chill Series, Bk. 1. LC 96-83225. (Illus.). 192p. (J). (gr. 7 up). 1996. 18.00 (*0-689-31967-3*) Atheneum Yung Read.

— Derby Dugan's Depression Funnies. 290p. 1995. 23.00 (*0-8050-4445-0*) H Holt & Co.

— Derby Dugan's Depression Funnies. 1997. pap. 12.00 (*0-8050-5356-5*) H Holt & Co.

— Derby Dugan's Depression Funnies. large type ed. (Niagara Large Print Ser.). 328p. 1997. pap. 29.50 (*0-7089-5858-3*, Linford) Ulverscroft.

— Joe Gosh. (Millennium Science Fiction Ser.). (Illus.). (YA). (gr. 7 up). 1988. 15.95 (*0-8027-6824-5*) Walker & Co.

De Havilland, Olivia. Autobiography. 1989. write for info. (*0-318-65586-1*) HarperTrade.

***de Haymes, Maria V., et al.** Latino Poverty in the New Century: Inequities, Challenges & Barriers. LC 00-38853. (Illus.). 176p. 2000. pap. 24.95 (*0-7890-1161-1*) Haworth Pr.

de Haymes, Maria Vidal, see Vidal de Haymes, Maria.

De Heathcote, Niels, jt. auth. see McKie, Douglas.

De Heer, Cornelis, tr. see Lesky, Albin.

***De Heer, Jolene & Grussing, Bob.** James. LC 00-23634. 2000. write for info. (*1-56212-540-0*) CRC Pubns.

De Heer, Robert. Realty Bluebook: Financing, Contract Clauses, Tax Information, Risk Management Checklists. 31st ed. 672p. 1995. pap. 20.95 (*0-7931-1539-6*, 1965-1031, Real Estate Ed) Dearborn.

— Realty Bluebook: Financing, Contract Clauses, Tax Information, Risk Management Checklists. 32nd ed. 672p. 1997. pap. text 27.95 (*0-7931-2659-2*, 1965-1032, Real Estate Ed) Dearborn.

— Risk Management. LC 94-28023. 128p. 1994. pap. text 59.00 (*0-7931-1155-2*, 152019-01, Real Estate Ed) Dearborn.

— Risk Management. 2nd ed. LC 98-9249. 1998. 59.00 (*0-7931-2899-4*) Dearborn.

De Heer, Rolf. Bad Boy Bubby. 94p. (C). 1995. pap. text 17.95 (*0-86819-426-3*, Pub. by Currency Pr) Accents Pubns.

De Hemes-Hernandez, Palau. Diario de Zenobia, No. 2. (SPA.). 400p. 1995. pap. 14.95 (*0-8477-3660-0*) U of PR Pr.

De Hemingford, Walter. Chronicon Domini Walteri de Hemingburgh, Vulgo Heminford Nuncupati, 2 vols. (English Historical Society Publications: Vol. 6). 1972. reprint ed. 100.00 (*0-8115-1523-0*) Periodicals Srv.

De Hemptinne, Xavier. Non-Equilibrium Statistical Thermodynamics Applied to Fluid Dynamics & Laser Physics. 300p. 1992. text 59.00 (*981-02-0926-6*) World Scientific Pub.

De Hennezel, Marie. Intimate Death: How the Dying Teach Us How to Live. Janeway, Carol B., tr. LC 96-32774. 208p. 1998. pap. 12.00 (*0-679-76859-9*) Knopf.

De Heredia, Jose-Maria. The Odes of Bello, Olmedo, & Heredia. Hills, Elijah J., tr. 1977. lib. bdg. 59.95 (*0-8490-2365-3*) Gordon Pr.

— The Trophies: Sonnets. Sewall, Frank, tr. 1977. lib. bdg. 59.95 (*0-8490-2769-1*) Gordon Pr.

De Heredia, Juan F. Cronica de Morea. (Dialect Ser.). Date not set. write for info. (*0-942260-49-X*) Hispanic Seminary.

De Heredia, Margarita A., tr. see Dewey, Melvil.

De Heriarte, Maurico. Descricam Do Estado Do Maranham, Para, Corupa, Rio das Amazonas. fac. ed. (POR., Illus.). 152p. 1964. 30.00 (*3-201-00244-5*, Pub. by Akademische Druck-und) Balogh.

De Hernandez, Cecilia & Caceres de Fulleda, Carmen A. Excavaciones Arqueologicas en Guaduero-Cundinamarca. (SPA., Illus.). 90p. 1989. pap. 8.50 (*1-877812-21-8*, BR019) UPLAAP.

De Hernandez, Hilda Rivera, see Rivera de Hernandez, Hilda.

De Herr, Robert. Realty Bluebook Financial Tables. 520p. 1994. pap. 11.95 (*0-7931-1016-5*, 1965-1129, Real Estate Ed) Dearborn.

De Herrenschwand, Jean F. De l'Economie Politique Moderne. 1990. reprint ed. 58.00 (*3-601-00157-8*) Periodicals Srv.

***De Herrera, Chris.** Chris De Herrera's Windows CE: Maximizing Your Capabilities. 500p. 2000. 29.99 (*0-672-31759-1*, Waite Grp Pr) Sams.

De Herrera, Nancy C. The Socialite & the Holy Man: An Unlikely Spiritual Odyssey. rev. ed. Charles, Rodney, ed. LC 98-60184. (Illus.). 500p. 1999. pap. 17.95 (*1-887472-48-7*) Sunstar Pubng.

De Herrera Tordesillas, Antonio. General History of the Vast Continent & Islands of America, Commonly Called the West-Indies, from the First Discovery Thereof, 6 vols., Set. 2nd ed. Stevens, John, tr. LC 70-169482. (Illus.). reprint ed. write for info. (*0-404-07310-7*) AMS Pr.

De Hertogh, A. & Le Nard, M., eds. Physiology of Flower Bulbs: A Comprehensive Treatise on the Physiology & Utilization of Ornamental Flowering Bulbous & Tuberous Plants. 812p. 1992. 307.00 (*0-444-87498-4*) Elsevier.

De Hesse, Phillip. Chirotherapy. 71p. 1996. reprint ed. spiral bd. 9.00 (*0-7873-0263-5*) Hlth Research.

De Hesse-Wartegg, Chevalier. Tunis Land & People. (C). 1988. 145.00 (*1-85077-201-0*, Pub. by Darf Pubs Ltd) St Mut.

De Heusch, Luc. The Drunken King, or, The Origin of the State. Willis, Roy, tr. LC 81-47569. (African Systems of Thought Ser.). (Illus.). 288p. 1982. 35.00 (*0-253-31832-7*) Ind U Pr.

— Sacrifice in Africa: A Structuralist Approach. O'Brien, Linda & Morton, Alice, trs. LC 84-48487. (African Systems of Thought Ser.). 240p. 1985. 30.00 (*0-253-35038-7*) Ind U Pr.

De Hillerin, Jean. Lumiere de Fifty Chef d'Oeuvres. (FRE., Illus.). 206p. 1963. lib. bdg. 50.00 (*0-8288-3988-3*) Fr & Eur.

De Hinojosa, Ida N., tr. see Georgiady, Nicholas P. & Romano, Louis G.

De Hita, Arcipreste. Libro Del Buen Amor. (SPA.). 162p. 1979. 9.95 (*0-8288-7052-7*, S29007) Fr & Eur.

De Hita, Arcipreste, see Arcipreste de Hita.

De Hodenc, Raoul. Le Roman des Eles', & the Anonymous: 'Ordene de Chevalerie' Two Early French Didactic Poems. Busby, Keith, tr. & intro. by. (Utrecht Publications in Comparative Literature: Vol. 17). x, 175p. 1983. 59.00 (*90-272-2192-8*) J Benjamins Pubng Co.

— Le Roman des Eles, & the Anonymous: 'Ordene de Chevalerie' Two Early Old french DIdactic Poems. Busby, Keith, tr. & intro. by. (Utrecht Publications in General & Comparative Literature: Vol. 17). x, 175p. 1983. pap. 32.95 (*90-272-2202-9*) J Benjamins Pubng Co.

De Hoffmann, Edmond, et al. Mass Spectrometry. LC 96-6746. 352p. 1996. pap. 74.95 (*0-471-96697-5*) Wiley.

De Hojeda, Diego. Christiada: Introduction & Text. Corcoran, Mary H., ed. LC 35-9384. (Catholic University of America. Studies in Romance Languages & Literatures: No. 11). reprint ed. 62.50 (*0-404-50311-X*) AMS Pr.

De Holczer, Joseph L. How Will I Die? Glines, Mary, ed. LC 95-95283. 270p. (Orig.). 1995. pap. 12.95 (*0-9648107-0-0*) Maruschka Bks.

De Honnecourt, Villard. The Sketchbook of Villard de Honnecourt. Bowie, Theodore, ed. LC 82-15540. (Illus.). 144p. (C). 1982. lib. bdg. 43.75 (*0-313-23747-6*, VISK, Greenwood Pr) Greenwood.

De Hoog, Ruth H. Contracting Out for Human Services: Economic, Political, & Organizational Perspectives. LC 83-24292. (SUNY Series in Urban Public Policy). 186p. (C). 1985. pap. text 24.95 (*0-87395-894-2*) State U NY Pr.

De Hooge, Romein. Famous Etchings: Les Indes Orientales. 104p. 1981. 170.00 (*0-7855-7291-0*) St Mut.

De Hoogh, Andre. Obligations Erga Omnes & International Crimes: A Theoretical Inquiry into the Implementation & Enforcement of the International Responsibility of States. 1996. 180.50 (*90-411-0232-9*) Kluwer Law Intl.

De Hoogh, Eugenia. La Lechera y Su Cubeta (The Milkmaid & Her Pail) (Fabulas Bilingues Ser.). (ENG & SPA.). (J). 1987. 10.15 (*0-606-01305-9*, Pub. by Turtleback) Demco.

D

— El Muchacho Que Grito el Lobo! The Boy Who Cried Wolf. (Bilingual Ser.). 1987. 10.15 (*0-606-01265-6*, Pub. by Turtleback) Demco.

— Poniendo el Cascabel Al Gato (Belling the Cat) (Bilingual Ser.). (ENG & SPA.). (J). 1977. 10.15 (*0-606-01429-2*, Pub. by Turtleback) Demco.

De Hoop, Helen. Linguistics in the Netherlands. Coerts, Jane, ed. (AVT Publications: Vol. 14). x, 230p. 1997. pap. 55.00 (*1-55619-221-5*) J Benjamins Pubng Co.

De Hoop, Raymond. Genesis 49 in Its Literary & Historical Context. LC 97-47628. (Oudtestamentische Studin Ser.: No. 39). (Illus.). 510p. 1997. 165.75 (*90-04-10913-7*) Brill Academic Pubs.

De Horowitz, Rosario G. Librarianship: A Third World Perspective, 59. LC 87-17741. (Contributions in Librarianship & Information Science Ser.: No. 59). 150p. 1988. 47.95 (*0-313-25507-5*, HLY/, Greenwood Pr) Greenwood.

De Hossen & Vitek. Computational Materials Science. 1999. text. write for info. (*0-08-042130-X*, Pergamon Pr) Elsevier.

De Hosson, Fred C., comment. Transfer Pricing for Intangibles. 92p. 1990. pap. 35.00 (*90-6544-425-4*) Kluwer Law Intl.

De Hostos, Adolfo. Tesauro de Datos Historicos, Vol. II. (SPA.). 978p. Date not set. 30.00 (*0-8477-0896-9*) U of PR Pr.

— Tesauro de Datos Historicos, Vol. 4. (SPA.). 976p. 1994. 30.00 (*0-8477-0199-9*) U of PR Pr.

— Tesauro de Datos Historicos, Vol. 5. (SPA.). 832p. 1995. 30.00 (*0-8477-0890-X*) U of PR Pr.

— Tesauro de Datos Historicos - Oficina del Indice Historico de PR, Vol. II. 1992. 30.00 (*0-8477-0897-7*) U of PR Pr.

— Tesauro de Datos Historicos de Puerto Rico, Vol. I. (SPA.). 932p. 1990. 30.00 (*0-8477-0889-6*) U of PR Pr.

De Hostos, Eugenio M. America & Hostos. 1976. lib. bdg. 59.95 (*0-8490-1411-5*) Gordon Pr.

— Ciencia de la Pedagogia. 321p. 1991. 12.95 (*0-8477-3663-6*); pap. 8.50 (*0-8477-3662-8*) U of PR Pr.

— Diario De Hostos, 1986-1869: Obras Completas. LC 87-25566. (SPA.). 290p. 1990. 12.95 (*0-8477-3607-5*); pap. 8.50 (*0-8477-3608-3*) U of PR Pr.

— Literatura de Hostos: Critica, Vol. I, Tomo III. (Hosto's Works). (SPA.). 624p. 1995. pap. 8.50 (*0-8477-3680-6*) U of PR Pr.

— Literatura de Hostos: Cuento, Teatro & Poesia, Vol. 1, Tomo II. (Hostos' Complete Works). 1993. 13.50 (*0-8477-3671-7*); pap. 8.50 (*0-8477-3670-9*) U of PR Pr.

— La Peregrinacion de Bayoan. annot. rev. ed. Lopez, Julio C., ed. LC 87-25566. 420p. 1988. 20.00 (*0-8477-3603-2*); pap. 13.00 (*0-8477-3604-0*) U of PR Pr.

— La Tela de Arana. (Hostos Ser.). 285p. 1997. 12.95 (*0-8477-3683-0*) U of PR Pr.

***De Hostos, Eugenio M., et al.** Tratado de Moral LC 99-17039. (Obras Completas (Edicion Critica) Ser.). 1999. write for info. (*0-8477-3609-1*) U of PR Pr.

De Houthulst, Willy C. Days on the Wing: Being the War Memoirs of Major the Chevalier Willy Coppens De Houthulst D.S.O., M.C., Etc., Etc. Gilbert, James B., ed. Insall, A. J., tr. LC 79-7242. (Flight: Its First Seventy-Five Years Ser.). (Illus.). 1980. reprint ed. 28.95 (*0-405-12157-1*) Ayer.

D

De Houwer, Annick, jt. ed. see Gillis, Steven.

De Hoveden, Roger. Annals of Roger De Hoveden, 2 vols. Riley, H. T., tr. LC 68-57865. (Bohn's Antiquarian Library). reprint ed. 87.50 (*0-404-50060-9*) AMS Pr.

De Hoyos, Angela. Woman, Woman. 2nd ed. LC 85-73350. 70p. (Orig.). 1996. pap. 7.00 (*1-55885-156-9*) Arte Publico.

De Hoyos, Angela, ed. Mujeres Grandes Anthology, No. 2. 64p. (Orig.). 1995. pap. 6.00 (*0-913983-15-2*) M & A Edns.

— Mujeres Grandes Anthology: Premier Issue. 63p. 1993. pap. 6.00 (*0-913983-11-X*) M & A Edns.

De Hoyos, Angela, ed. see Galvan, Alicia Z.

De Hoyos, Art. The Cloud of Prejudice: A Case-Study in Modern Anti-Masonry. 170p. 1992. reprint ed. pap. 14.95 (*1-56459-287-1*) Kessinger Pub.

De Hunter, Elena Mellado, see Mellado De Hunter, Elena.

De Huszar, George B., ed. Persistent International Issues. LC 79-142645. (Essay Index Reprint Ser.). 1977. reprint ed. 23.95 (*0-8369-2772-9*) Ayer.

De Huszar, George B., ed. see Bastiat, Frederic.

De Ibanez Y Garcia, Luis. History of the Mariana, Caroline & Palau Islands, 1887. Driver, Marjorie G., tr. from SPA. (Educational Ser.: No. 12). (Illus.). 192p. (Orig.). 1992. pap. text 6.95 (*1-878453-10-6*) Univ Guam MAR Ctr.

De Ibarbourou, Juana. Elegia. (Illus.). 55p. (C). 1968. 3.00 (*0-8477-3206-1*) U of PR Pr.

De Illanes, N. Elsevier's Dictionary of Drug Traffic Terms in English, Spanish, Portuguese, French & German. LC 96-38066. (ENG, FEM, GEH, POR & SPA.). 576p. 1997. 234.50 (*0-444-81937-1*) Elsevier.

De Irizarry, Estelle R. English the Laboratory Way. 97p. 1965. pap. 1.00 (*0-8477-3316-5*) U of PR Pr.

De Ishtar, Zohl. Daughters of the Pacific. 256p. 1995. pap. 19.95 (*1-875559-32-9*) LPC InBook.

De Iturralde, Mary S. Needlepoint the Sport of Queens. (Illus.). 46p. 1942. pap. 4.95 (*0-87012-066-2*) McClain. Reviews needlepoint for various periods. The author points out the good periods of needlepoint design & discusses ways to incorporate them into patterns prepared today. Second Printing, 1968. ***Publisher Paid Annotation.***

De J. Hart, Robert A. Forest Gardening: Cultivate an Edible Landscape. LC 96-31188. (Illus.). 256p. 1997. pap. 17.95 (*0-930031-84-9*) Chelsea Green Pub.

De J. Jackson, J. R. Romantic Poetry by Women: A Bibliography, 1770-1835. LC 92-35190. 514p. (C). 1993. text 75.00 (*0-19-811239-4*, 14309, Clarendon Pr) OUP.

De Jaager, Gerald. The Best Management Resources: Developing Management Skills: A Self-Directed Approach, Bk. 2. LC 84-51544. 373p. (C). 1985. 80.00 (*0-916001-01-6*) Seiler-Doar.

— The Management Skills Inventory: Developing Management Skills: A Self-Directed Approach, Bk. 1. LC 84-51543. 78p. (Orig.). (C). 1985. pap. 20.00 (*0-916001-00-8*) Seiler-Doar.

De Jaegar, Nick C., jt. ed. see Williams, Richard A.

De Jaegher, Paul, ed. An Anthology of Christian Mysticism. 186p. 1977. pap. 12.95 (*0-87243-073-1*) Templegate.

De Jager, A., et al, eds. Restoring & Maintaining the Productivity of West African Soils: Key to Sustainable Development. LC 96-13376. (Miscellaneous Fertilizer Studies: No. 14). (Illus.). 108p. (Orig.). 1996. pap. write for info. (*0-88090-112-8*) Intl Fertilizer.

De Jager, C., ed. The Brightest Stars. (Geophysics & Astrophysics Monographs: No. 19). 472p. 1980. pap. text 85.50 (*90-277-1110-0*); lib. bdg. 182.50 (*90-277-1109-7*) Kluwer Academic.

— Highlights of Astronomy, Vol. 2. LC 71-159657. (International Astronomical Union Highlights Ser.). 793p. 1971. text 288.00 (*90-277-0189-X*) Kluwer Academic.

— Transactions of the International Astronomical Union: Reports on Astronomy, Vol. 14a. LC 30-10103. 566p. 1970. lib. bdg. 129.50 (*90-277-0154-7*) Kluwer Academic.

— Transactions of the International Astronomical Union: Reports on Astronomy, Vol. 15a. LC 73-81827. 762p. 1973. lib. bdg. 269.50 (*90-277-0340-X*) Kluwer Academic.

De Jager, C. & Nieuwenhuijzen, H., eds. Image Processing Techniques in Astronomy. LC 75-23032. (Astrophysics & Space Science Library: No. 54). xi, 418p. 1975. lib. bdg. 141.50 (*90-277-0650-6*) Kluwer Academic.

— Instabilities in Evolved Super & Hypergiants: Proceedings of the International Colloquium, Amsterdam, the Netherlands, 26 February - 1 March 1991. (Verhandelingen der Koninklijke Nederlandse Akademie van Wetenschappen, Afd. Natuurkunde Ser.: No. 36). 200p. pap. 49.50 (*0-444-85736-2*) Elsevier.

De Jager, C. & Smith, E. Advertising & the Law. 162p. 1995. write for info. (*0-409-02223-3*, MICHIE) LEXIS Pub.

De Jager, C. & Svestka, Z., eds. Progress in Solar Physics. 1986. text 273.50 (*90-277-2180-7*) Kluwer Academic.

De Jager, C., ed. see Biderberg Conference Staff.

De Jager, C., ed. see International Astronomical Union Staff.

De Jager, C., ed. see Symposium, University of Utrecht Staff.

De Jager, C. P., jt. auth. see Dijkstra, Jeanne.

De Jager, C. W. & Ketel, T. J., eds. SPIN '96: Proceedings of the 12th International Symposium on High-Energy Spin Physics Amsterdam, The Netherlands 10-14 September, 1996. LC 97-172236. 904p. 1997. 144.00 (*981-02-3052-4*) World Scientific Pub.

De Jager, E. M., see Jager, E. M. De.

De Jager, E. M., jt. auth. see Van Groesen, E.

De Jager, E.M. The Theory of Singular Perturbations. 1996. write for info. (*0-614-17899-1*, North Holland) Elsevier.

De Jager, Marjoli, tr. see Djebar, Assia.

De Jager, Marjolijin, tr. see Beyala, Calixthe.

De Jager, Marjolijin, tr. see Liking, Werewere.

De Jager, Marjolijn, ed. see Diop, Cheikh Anta.

De Jager, Marjolijn, tr. see Bergerot, Franck & Merlin, Arnaud.

De Jager, Marjolijn, tr. see Djebar, Assia.

De Jager, Marjolijn, tr. see Leal, Brigitte, et al.

De Jager, Marjolijn, tr. see Liking, Werewere.

De Jager, Marjolijn, tr. see Mudimbe, V. Y.

De Jager, Patrick. Design of "the Fancier" An Instrument for Fabrication & Analysis of Nanostructures Combining Ion & Electron Regulation. 325p. 1997. pap. 57.50 (*90-407-1478-9*, Pub. by Delft U Pr) Coronet Bks.

***De Jager, Peter & Bergeon, Richard.** Countdown Y2K: Business Survival Planning for the Year 2000. 2nd ed. LC 98-42269. 368p. 1998. pap. 29.99 (*0-471-32734-4*) Wiley.

De Jager, Peter & Smith, Donald. The Bug Stops Here!!! A Collection of Both Humor & Hubris Relating to the Biggest, Dumbest, Most Idiotic Blunders in the. Bray, Bonnie, ed. (Illus.). 192p. 1999. pap. 12.95 (*0-9671745-0-3*) Petrus & Assocs.

De Jalon, Javier Garcia, see Garcia de Jalon, Javier.

De Jantscher, Milka Casanegra, see Bird, Richard M. & Casanegra De Jantscher, Milka, eds.

De Janvry, Alain. The Agrarian Question & Reformism in Latin America. LC 81-4147. (Illus.). 352p. 1981. pap. text 17.95 (*0-8018-2532-6*) Johns Hopkins.

De Janvry, Alain & Subbarao, K. Agricultural Price Policy & Income Distribution in India. 128p. 1987. 15.95 (*0-19-561952-8*) OUP.

De Janvry, Alain, et al. Mexico's Second Agrarian Reform: Household & Community Responses, 1990-1994. LC 97-8991. (Transformations of Rural Mexico Ser.: No. 1). 1997. pap. 16.00 (*1-878367-30-7*) UCSD Ctr US-Mex.

De Janvry, Alain, jt. auth. see Sadoulet, Elisabeth.

De Jaramillo-Arango, Maria J., tr. see Ruiz, Hip-olito, et al.

De Jardin, Jean-Louis. Dynamic Kerr Effects. (Contemporary Chemical Physics Ser.). 248p. 1995. text 53.00 (*981-02-1910-5*) World Scientific Pub.

De-Jasay, Anthony. Against Politics: On Government, Anarchy & Politics. LC 97-8448. 256p. (C). 1997. 85.00 (*0-415-17067-2*) Routledge.

De Jasay, Anthony. Before Resorting to Politics. LC 95-40189. (Shaftesbury Papers: No. 5). 80p. 1996. pap. 13.00 (*1-85898-226-X*) E Elgar.

— Choice, Contract, Consent: A Restatement of Liberalism. 124p. (Orig.). (C). 1991. pap. 26.50 (*0-255-36246-3*, Pub. by Inst Economic Affairs) Coronet Bks.

— Social Contract, Free Ride: A Study of the Public Goods Problem. 264p. 1991. pap. 26.00 (*0-19-823912-2*) OUP.

— The State. LC 97-37267. 1998. 17.00 (*0-86597-170-6*); pap. 9.00 (*0-86597-171-4*) Liberty Fund.

De Jean, Baptiste. Collins Watch Guide: Seashore. (Illus.). 1997. pap. 11.95 (*0-00-220088-0*, Pub. by HarpC) Trafalgar.

De, Jephan, jt. auth. see Lamarche, Caroline.

De Jersey, Katherine & Taves, Isabella. Appointment with Destiny: Real-Life Case Histories. 224p. 1995. 17.95 (*1-885142-14-5*) J & B Editions.

— Destiny Times Six. 1970. 18.95 (*0-86690-414-X*, D2357-014) Am Fed Astrologers.

De Jersey, Philip. Celtic Coinage in Britain. (Archaeology Ser.: No. 72). (Illus.). 56p. 1996. pap. 10.50 (*0-7478-0325-0*, Pub. by Shire Pubns) Parkwest Pubns.

— Coinage in Iron Age Armorica. (Studies in Celtic Coinage: No. 2). (Illus.). 266p. 1994. pap. 30.00 (*0-947816-39-9*, Pub. by Oxford Univ Comm Arch) David Brown.

De Jesus Aquino, Consuelo. The Wings of Hope. 48p. 1998. pap. 7.95 (*1-56167-420-6*) Am Literary Pr.

de Jesus, Armando Rovira, see Rovira de Jesus, Armando.

De Jesus, Carolina M. Bitita's Diary: The Childhood Memoirs of Carolina Maria de Jesus. Levine, Robert M., ed. Oliveira, Emanuelle & Vinkler, Beth J., trs. LC 97-26341. (Latin American Realities Ser.). (ENG & POR.). 178p. (C). (gr. 13). 1997. 60.95 (*0-7656-0211-3*); pap. 24.95 (*0-7656-0212-1*) M E Sharpe.

— I'm Going to Have a Little House: The Second Diary of Carolina Maria de Jesus. Arrington, Melvin S., Jr. & Levine, Robert M., trs. LC 96-53134. (Engendering Latin America Ser.). (Illus.). xiv, 189p. 1997. pap. 15.00 (*0-8032-7599-4*); text 40.00 (*0-8032-2583-0*) U of Nebr Pr.

— The Unedited Diaries of Carolina Maria De Jesus. Levine, Robert M. & Meihy, Jose C., eds. Naro, Nancy P. & Mehrtens, Cristina, trs. LC 98-4396. (Illus.). 224p. (C). 1999. text 50.00 (*0-8135-2569-1*); pap. text 20.00 (*0-8135-2570-5*) Rutgers U Pr.

De Jesus D'Elbee, Jean. Creo en el Amor: Conferencias de un Retiro. Pompeii, Maria T., tr. from FRE. Orig. Title: Croire a l'Amour. (SPA.). 192p. 1998. pap. 9.95 (*0-8189-0792-4*) Alba.

De Jesus, Francisco. Narrative of the Spanish Marriage Treaty. Gardiner, Samuel R., tr. LC 72-168133. (Camden Society, London, Publications, First Ser.: No. 101). reprint ed. 82.50 (*0-404-50201-6*) AMS Pr.

De Jesus Hernandez-Gutierrez, Manuel & Foster, David, eds. Literatura Chicana, 1965-1995: An Anthology in Spanish, English, & Calo. LC 96-24202. 520p. 1997. reprint ed. text 100.00 (*0-8153-2077-9*); reprint ed. pap. text 27.95 (*0-8153-2080-9*) Garland.

De Jesus, Jose. VisualAge for Java Primer. (Advances in Object Technology Ser.: No. 21). 336p. 1999. pap. 44.95 (*0-521-64417-8*) Cambridge U Pr.

De Jesus, Joy L., ed. Growing up Puerto Rican: 20 Puerto Rican Authors Write in Fiction & Essay about Childhood. 352p. 1997. 24.00 (*0-688-13740-7*, Wm Morrow) Morrow Avon.

De Jesus, Raquel. Design Guidelines for Montesorri School. (Publications in Architecture & Urban Planning: No. R87-2). (Illus.). iii, 80p. 1988. 12.00 (*0-938744-55-0*) U of Wis Ctr Arch-Urban.

De Jesus, Socorro & Blot, David. Read a Lot & Write Even More. rev. ed. 90p. (C). 1987. pap. text 5.00 (*0-317-93603-4*) D Blot Pubns.

De Jesus, Teresa. Camino de Perfeccion. Mancho Duque, Maria J., ed. (Nueva Austral Ser.: Vol. 246). (SPA.). 1991. pap. text 24.95 (*84-239-7246-1*) Elliots Bks.

— De Repente-All of a Sudden: Poems by Teresa de Jesus. Proser, Maria A. et al, trs. LC 77-15118. 91p. 1977. pap. 7.95 (*0-915306-14-X*) Curbstone.

— Libro de las Fundaciones. Garcia de la Concha, Victor, ed. (Nueva Austral Ser.: Vol. 205). (SPA.). 1991. pap. text 24.95 (*84-239-7205-4*) Elliots Bks.

De Jeu, W. H. Physical Properties of Liquid Crystalline Materials. x, 134p. 1980. text 209.00 (*0-677-04040-7*) Gordon & Breach.

De Jeu, W. H., jt. auth. see Vertegon, G.

De Jim, Strange. Visioning. LC 79-66208. (Illus.). 112p. (Orig.). 1979. pap. 5.95 (*0-9605308-0-0*) Ash-Kar Pr.

De, Jin H., jt. auth. see Zhou, Zhong Y.

De Joinville, Jean, jt. auth. see De Villehardouin, Geoffroi.

De Joly, Robert. Memoirs of a Speleologist: The Adventurous Life of a Famous French Cave Explorer. Kurz, Peter, tr. LC 75-31836. (Illus.). 185p. (Orig.). 1975. 10.95 (*0-914264-08-7*); pap. 5.95 (*0-914264-09-5*) Cave Bks MO.

De Jomini, Antoine H. The Art of War. LC 96-32213. 416p. 1996. pap. 19.95 (*1-85367-249-1*) Stackpole.

De Jones, Anita D. Pasion Primera. (SPA.). 80p. 1998. 9.95 (*0-9665989-0-3*) M Iannone.

De Jong. Quadralingual Economics Dictionary. 150.00 (*0-8288-9437-X*) Fr & Eur.

De Jong, Albert F. Traditions of the Magi: Zoroastrianism in Greek & Latin Literature. LC 97-14806. (Religions in the Graeco-Roman World Ser.: No. 133). xii, 596p. 1997. 184.50 (*90-04-10844-0*) Brill Academic Pubs.

De Jong, Arthur J. Reclaiming a Mission: New Direction for the Church-Related College. LC 90-32554. 181p. reprint ed. pap. 56.20 (*0-7837-5556-2*, 204533100005) Bks Demand.

De Jong, Ben, tr. see Jackins, Harvey.

De Jong, C. D. Principles & Applications of Permanent GPS Arrays. (Illus.). 116p. 1997. pap. 39.50 (*90-407-1492-4*, Pub. by Delft U Pr) Coronet Bks.

De Jong, Constance. I. T. I. L. O. E. 24p. (Orig.). 1983. pap. 3.00 (*0-917061-15-2*) Top Stories.

De Jong, Daan. Sociolinguistic Aspects of French Liaison. (Topics in Sociolinguistics Ser.). (Orig.). (C). pap. write for info. (*90-6765-489-2*) Mouton.

De Jong, Dola. The Tree & the Vine. LC 95-38608. 152p. 1996. reprint ed. pap. 9.95 (*1-55861-141-X*); reprint ed. lib. bdg. 27.95 (*1-55861-140-1*) Feminist Pr.

De Jong, E. W. Exchange Rate Determination & Optimal Economic Policy under Various Exchange Rate Regimes. (Lecture Notes in Economics & Mathematical Systems Ser.: Vol. 359). (Illus.). viii, 270p. 1991. pap. 39.00 (*0-387-54021-0*) Spr-Verlag.

De Jong, E. W., jt. auth. see Westbroek, P.

De Jong, Eelke D., jt. ed. see Delsen, Lei.

De Jong, Ester J., jt. auth. see Glenn, Charles L.

De Jong, F. A. & Radtke, Bernd. Islamic Mysticism Contested: Thirteen Centuries of Controversies & Polemics. LC 99-11737. (Islamic History & Civilization Ser.). 900p. 1999. write for info. (*90-04-11300-2*) Brill Academic Pubs.

De Jong, Frank P. & Van Hout-Wolters, Bernadette H. Process-Oriented Instruction: Verbal & Pictorial Aid & Comprehension Strategies. LC 94-205367. 200p. 1994. pap. 32.50 (*90-5383-256-4*, Pub. by VU Univ Pr) Paul & Co Pubs.

De Jong, Frans, ed. see Oosterling, Henk.

De Jong, Frits J., et al, eds. Quadrilingual Economics Dictionary. 1981. lib. bdg. 234.00 (*90-247-2243-8*) Kluwer Academic.

De Jong, G. Population Genetics & Evolution. (Illus.). 305p. 1988. 99.00 (*0-387-18452-X*) Spr-Verlag.

De Jong, Gerald F. The Reformed Church in China, 1842-1951. LC 92-18046. (Historical Series of the Reformed Church in America: Vol. 22). 1992. pap. 25.00 (*0-8028-0661-9*) Eerdmans.

De Jong-Gierveld, J. & Hox, J. J. Operationalization & Research Strategy. 288p. 1990. 47.75 (*90-265-0982-0*) Swets.

***de Jong, Gjalt & Nooteboom, Bart.** The Causal Structure of Long-Term Supply Relationships: An Empirical Test of a Generalized Transaction Cost Theory. 168p. 2000. 79.95 (*0-7923-7837-7*) Kluwer Academic.

***De Jong, Gordon F. & Klein, Pamela M.** Educational Attainment of PA's Young Workers: What's It Worth. 15p. 1999. pap. 20.00 (*1-58036-138-2*) Penn State Data Ctr.

De Jong, Henry W., ed. The Structure of European Industry. (C). 1988. pap. text 70.50 (*90-247-3690-0*); lib. bdg. 153.00 (*90-247-3689-7*) Kluwer Academic.

De Jong, Henry W., jt. ed. see Shepherd, William G.

De Jong, Huib L., jt. auth. see Bem, Sacha.

De Jong, Irene J. Homer: Critical Assessments, 4 vols. LC 98-11375. (Illus.). 1328p. (C). 1999. 700.00 (*0-415-14527-9*) Routledge.

— Narrative in Drama: The Art of the Euripidean Messenger-Speech. LC 91-19528. (Supplements to Mnemosyne Ser.: No. 116). ix, 214p. 1991. 74.50 (*90-04-09406-7*) Brill Academic Pubs.

De Jong, Irene J. & Sullivan, J. P., eds. Modern Critical Theory & Classical Literature. LC 93-4053. (Mnemosyne, Bibliotheca Classica Batava Ser.: No. 130). 1993. 134.50 (*90-04-09571-3*) Brill Academic Pubs.

De Jong, J. W. A Brief History of Buddhist Studies in Europe & America. 184p. 1998. pap. 19.95 (*4-333-01762-9*, Pub. by Kosei Pub Co) Tuttle Pubng.

De Jong, J. W., ed. Myocardial Energy Metabolism. (Developments in Cardiovascular Medicine Ser.). (C). 1988. text 195.50 (*0-89838-394-3*) Kluwer Academic.

De Jong, J. W. & Ferrari, R., eds. The Carnitine System: A New Therapeutical Approach to Cardiovascular Diseases, No. 162. LC 94-46324. (Developments in Cardiovascular Medicine Ser.: Vol. 162). 400p. 1995. text 184.00 (*0-7923-3318-7*) Kluwer Academic.

De Jong, John H. A. L., jt. ed. see Verhoeven, Ludo T.

De Jong-Keesing, Elisabeth. Inayat Khan: A Biography. (Illus.). 302p. 1974. pap. 11.00 (*0-7189-0243-2*) Omega Pubns NY.

De Jong, Louis. The Netherlands & Nazi Germany. (Erasmus Lectures). 80p. 1990. 19.95 (*0-674-60805-4*) HUP.

De Jong, M., ed. Religion & Anglo-American Women. 150p. 1991. pap. text 29.00 (*2-88124-519-6*) Gordon & Breach.

De Jong, M. & Du Plessis, J. C. Praktykshandleiding Oor Die Invordering van Skuld. (AFR.). 384p. 1995. pap. write for info. (*0-409-02277-2*, MICHIE) LEXIS Pub.

De Jong, Mayke. In Samuel's Image: Child Oblation in the Early Medieval West. (Studies in Intellectual History: Vol. 70). xvi, 360p. 1995. 112.50 (*90-04-10483-6*) Brill Academic Pubs.

De Jong, Meindert. Along Came a Dog. 1958. 10.05 (*0-606-00303-7*, Pub. by Turtleback) Demco.

De Jong, Meindert. The Easter Cat. 1991. 9.05 (*0-606-12270-2*, Pub. by Turtleback) Demco.

De Jong, Meindert. House of Sixty Fathers. (J). 1987. 10.05 (*0-606-02140-X*, Pub. by Turtleback) Demco.

— Shadrach. (J). 1953. 9.60 (*0-606-00572-2*, Pub. by Turtleback) Demco.

De Jong, Nicolas J. & Moore, Marven E. Shipbuilding on Prince Edward Island: Enterprise in a Maritime Setting, 1787-1920. LC 96-185699. (Mercury Ser.: History No. 46). (Illus.). 418p. 2000. pap. 34.95 (*0-660-14021-7*, Pub. by CN Mus Civilization) U of Wash Pr.

De Jong, Norman, ed. Christian Approaches to Learning Theory - Freedom & Discipline: Major Papers Delivered at the Third Annual Conference, Trinity Christian College, Palos Heights, Illinois, November 1-2, 1985, Vol. III. LC 84-20884. 118p. (Orig.). (C). 1987. pap. text 21.00 (*0-8191-6280-9*) U Pr of Amer.

De Jong, Peter R. & Marmor, Theodore R., eds. Social Policy & the Labour Market: Issues at Stake Across the World. LC 97-72076. (International Studies on Social Security). (Illus.). 448p. 1997. text 83.95 (*1-84014-156-5*, Pub. by Avebry) Ashgate Pub Co.

De Jong, Philip R., et al. Form & Reform of the Dutch Social Security System. 82p. 1990. pap. 29.00 (*90-6544-480-7*) Kluwer Law Intl.

De Jong, Philip R., jt. auth. see Aarts, Leo J.

De Jong, Philip R., jt. ed. see Marmor, Theodore R.

***de Jong, Rudolf E.** A Grammar of the Bedouin Dialects of the Northern Sinai Littoral: Bridging the Linguistic Gap between the Eastern & Western Arab World. 692p. 2000. 154.00 (*90-04-11868-3*) Brill Academic Pubs.

De Jong, Ruth. Basic English Vocabulary Builder Activity Book: Beginning. 96p. 1994. 5.25 (*0-8442-9010-6*, Natl Textbk Co); pap. 9.25 (*0-8442-9009-2*, Natl Textbk Co) NTC Contemp Pub Co.

De Jong, Sjouke, ed. NATO's Reserve Forces, No. 5. (Brassey's Atlantic Commentaries Ser.). 114p. 1992. pap. 16.50 (*0-08-041340-4*, Pub. by Brasseys) Brasseys.

De Jong, T. & Maeder, Andre, eds. Star Formation. (Symposia of the International Astronomical Union Ser.: No. 75). 1977. lib. bdg. 104.50 (*90-277-0796-0*) Kluwer Academic.

De Jong, Ton & Sarti, Luigi, eds. Design & Production of Multimedia & Simulation-Based Learning Material. LC 94-26572. (Diverse Ser.). 272p. (C). 1994. lib. bdg. 119.00 (*0-7923-3020-X*) Kluwer Academic.

de Jong, W., jt. ed. see Ganten, D.

De Jong, W. A., jt. ed. see Van den Berg, P. J.

De Jong, Willem R. The Semantics of John Stuart Mill. (Synthese Historical Library: No. 23). 382p. 1982. text 162.50 (*90-277-1408-8*) Kluwer Academic.

De Jong, William. Preventing Alcohol-Related Problems on Campus: Impaired Driving: A Guide for Program Coordinators. (Illus.). 58p. (C). 1997. pap. text 20.00 (*0-7881-4731-5*) DIANE Pub.

De Jonge, Alex. The Life & Times of Gregorii Rasputin. (Illus.). 363p. 1989. pap. 10.95 (*0-88184-484-5*) Carroll & Graf.

De Jonge, C. R. H., jt. ed. see Mijs, W. J.

de Jonge, H. J. Erasmi Opera Omnia, Vol. IX-2. viii, 292p. 1983. 292.50 (*0-444-86605-1*, North Holland) Elsevier.

De Jonge, Joanne. More Object Lessons from Nature. (Objects Lesson Ser.). 160p. (Orig.). (gr. 10). 1991. pap. 7.99 (*0-8010-3004-8*) Baker Bks.

— Object Lessons from Nature. (Object Lessons Ser.). (Illus.). 128p. (YA). (gr. 10). 1989. pap. 7.99 (*0-8010-2989-9*) Baker Bks.

— Object Lessons from Pebbles & Paper Clips. (Object Lessons Ser.). 176p. (Orig.). (J). (gr. 10). 1995. pap. 7.99 (*0-8010-5041-3*) Baker Bks.

— Precious Moments: Very Shy Angel. LC 97-24113. (Precious Moments for Children Ser.). (Illus.). 128p. (J). (gr. 2 up). 1998. 14.99 (*0-8010-4295-X*) Baker Bks.

***De Jonge, Joanne.** Precious Moments Christmas Play. LC 99-29927. (Illus.). 32p. (J). (gr. k-4). 1999. 9.99 (*0-8010-4424-3*) Baker Bks.

— Precious Moments Easter. LC BT481.D385 1998. (Precious Moments for Children Ser.). 32p. (J). 2000. 9.99 (*0-8010-4418-9*) Baker Bks.

De Jonge, Marinus. God's Final Envoy: Early Christianity & Jesus' Own View of His Mission. LC 98-25620. 168p. 1998. pap. 18.00 (*0-8028-4482-0*) Eerdmans.

— Jesus: Stranger from Heaven & Son of God. Steely, John E., ed. LC 77-9984. (Society of Biblical Literature. Sources for Biblical Study Ser.: No. 11). 246p. reprint ed. 76.30 (*0-8357-9575-6*, 201753200007) Bks Demand.

De Jonge, Marinus & Tromp, Johannes. The Life of Adam & Eve & Related Literature. (GAP Ser.: Vol. 4). 104p. 1997. pap. 14.95 (*1-85075-764-X*, Pub. by Sheffield Acad) CUP Services.

De Jonge, P. Philological & Historical: Commentary on Ammianus Marcellinus XIX. De Waard-Dekking, P., tr. from DUT. (Ammianus Marcellinus Ser.). ix, 279p. 1982. 47.00 (*90-6088-072-2*, Pub. by Boumas Boekhuis) Gen Publ ON.

— Philological & Historical Commentary on Ammianus Marcellinus XV. 82p. 1972. 30.00 (*0-318-41852-5*, Pub. by Egbert Forsten) Hodlder & Stoughton.

— Philological & Historical Commentary on Ammianus Marcellinus XVI. (Ammianus Marcellinus Ser.). xii, 304p. 1972. 60.00 (*90-6088-035-8*, Pub. by Boumas Boekhuis) Gen Publ ON.

— Philological & Historical Commentary on Ammianus Marcellinus XVII. (Ammianus Marcellinus Ser.). xi, 404p. 1977. 61.50 (*90-6088-052-8*, Pub. by Boumas Boekhuis) Gen Publ ON.

— Philological & Historical Commentary on Ammianus Marcellinus XVIII. (Ammianus Marcellinus Ser.). xii, 308p. 1980. 49.50 (*90-6088-065-X*, Pub. by Boumas Boekhuis) Gen Publ ON.

— Sprachlicher und Historischer Kommenter zu Amianus Marcellinus XIV. (GER.). 148p. 1972. 38.00 (*0-318-41850-9*, Pub. by Egbert Forsten) Hodlder & Stoughton.

De Jonge, Peter, jt. auth. see Patterson, James.

De Jongh. Our Common Journey LC 99-20787. 1999. pap. 25.00 (*1-85649-739-9*) St Martin.

***De Jongh, Brian.** The Companion Guide to Mainland Greece. 576p. 2000. pap. 24.95 (*1-900639-35-1*) Boydell & Brewer.

De Jongh, Brian. The Companion Guide to Mainland Greece. rev. ed. Gandon, John, ed. (Illus.). 600p. 1996. pap. 24.95 (*1-900639-08-4*) Boydell & Brewer.

DE JONGH, CAPTAIN. Our Common Journey LC 99-20787. 1999. text 65.00 (*1-85649-738-0*) St Martin.

De Jongh, D. M., tr. see Beth, E. W.

de Jongh, Edith. The Royal Three Quarters of the Town of Charlotte Amalie: A Study of Architectural Details & Forms That Have Endured from 1837. (Illus.). 158p. (Orig.). 1988. pap. 15.95 (*0-926330-02-0*) Mapes Monde.

De Jongh, Elena M. An Introduction to Court Interpreting: Theory & Practice. 362p. (Orig.). (C). 1992. pap. text 37.50 (*0-8191-8611-2*); lib. bdg. 65.00 (*0-8191-8610-4*) U Pr of Amer.

De Jongh, Ferry, jt. auth. see Jansen, Paul.

De Jongh, James L. We Wish to Plead Our Own Cause: Black-Owned Book Publishing in the United States, 1817-1987. 1993. pap. 15.95 (*0-931761-09-3*) Beckham Pubns.

De Jongh-Kearl, Susan, tr. see Beth, E. W.

De Jongh, L. J., ed. Magnetic Properties of Layered Transition Metal Compounds. (C). 1989. text 268.50 (*0-7923-0238-9*) Kluwer Academic.

— Physics & Chemistry of Metal Cluster Compounds: Model Systems for Small Metal Particles. LC 93-49928. (Physics & Chemistry of Materials with Low-Dimensional Structures Ser.: Vol.18). 320p. (C). 1994. text 204.50 (*0-7923-2715-2*) Kluwer Academic.

De Jongh, Nicholas. Not in Front of the Audience: Homosexuality on Stage. (Illus.). 232p. (Orig.). (C). 1992. pap. 24.99 (*0-415-03363-2*, A5626) Routledge.

De Jongh Osborne, Lilly. Four Keys to El Salvador. LC 83-1506. (Illus.). 221p. 1983. reprint ed. lib. bdg. 59.50 (*0-313-22968-6*, OSFK, Greenwood Pr) Greenwood.

De Jongste, H., see Ridderbos, Herman N. & Jongste, H. De.

De Jongste, H., tr. see Dooyeweerd, Herman.

De Jongste, H., Jr., tr. see Ridderbos, Herman N.

***De Jorio, Andrea.** Gesture in Naples & Gesture in Classical Antiquity: A Translation of Andrea de Jorio's La Mimica Degli Antichi Investigata Nel Gestire Napoletano (Gestural Expression of the Ancients in the Light of Neapolitan Gesturing) Kendon, Adam, tr. from ITA. LC 99-33806. (Illus.). 518p. 2000. 49.95 (*0-253-33657-0*) Ind U Pr.

De Jose Y Palleja, J., jt. auth. see Gibert, Buch.

De Jouvenel, Bertrand. Economics & the Good Life. Hale, Dennis & Landy, Marc, eds. 308p. 1999. pap. 24.95 (*0-7658-0428-X*) Transaction Pubs.

— The Ethics of Redistribution. LC 89-27759. 118p. (C). 1990. reprint ed. pap. 5.00 (*0-86597-085-8*); reprint ed. text 12.00 (*0-86597-084-X*) Liberty Fund.

— The Nature of Politics: Selected Essays of Bertrand de Jouvenal. Hale, Dennis & Landy, Marc K., eds. 276p. (C). 1992. pap. 24.95 (*1-56000-607-2*) Transaction Pubs.

— On Power: Its Nature & the History of Its Growth. Huntington, J. F., tr. from FRE. LC 80-24721. 421p. 1981. reprint ed. lib. bdg. 45.50 (*0-313-22515-X*, JOOP, Greenwood Pr) Greenwood.

— On Power: The Natural History of Its Growth. Huntington, J. F., tr. LC 93-1656. 466p. 1993. 25.00 (*0-86597-112-9*); pap. 8.50 (*0-86597-113-7*) Liberty Fund.

***De Jouvenel, Bertrand.** The Pure Theory of Politics. LC 00-20493. 2000. pap. write for info. (*0-86597-265-6*) Liberty Fund.

— Sovereignty: An Inquiry into the Political Good. Huntington, J. F., tr. LC 97-30874. (ENG & FRE.). 1998. 23.00 (*0-86597-172-2*) Liberty Fund.

***De Jouvenel, Bertrand.** Sovereignty: An Inquiry into the Political Good. Huntington, J. F., tr. LC 97-30874. (ENG & FRE.). 1998. pap. 10.00 (*0-86597-173-0*) Liberty Fund.

De Jovine, F. Anthony. The Young Hero in American Fiction: A Motif for Teaching Literature. LC 79-130792. x, 171p. 1971. write for info. (*0-390-26013-4*) McGrw-H Primis Cstm.

De Juan, Eduardo. Jardin de Heroes: Relato Autobiografico del Horror en las Prisoner Castristas. De Fana, Angel, ed. (SPA., Illus.). 346p. 1997. pap. 19.95 (*1-890829-02-1*) DFana Editions.

De Juan, Marcelino E. Diccionario Empresarial. 3rd ed. (SPA.). 560p. 1990. 85.00 (*0-7859-5344-2*, 8485378865) Fr & Eur.

De Juan, Maribel, tr. see Wilson, Angus.

De Julio, Maryann. German Folk Arts of New York State. (Illus.). 32p. 1985. pap. 6.00 (*0-939072-04-1*) Albany Hist & Art.

— Quilts from Montgomery County, New York. (Illus.). 24p. (Orig.). 1981. pap. 3.00 (*0-9608694-0-9*) Montgomery Hist.

— Rhetorical Landscapes: The Poetry & Art Criticism of Jacques Dupin. LC 91-73987. (Armstrong Monographs: No. 76). (Illus.). 115p. (Orig.). 1992. pap. 13.95 (*0-917058-80-1*) French Forum.

De Julio, Maryann, tr. & intro. see Sarsini, Monica.

De Jusus. History of Economics. (C). 1997. text 26.00 (*0-673-19208-3*) Addison-Wesley.

De Juvigny, F. Leonard, jt. auth. see Fair, Donald E.

De Juvigny, F. Leonard, jt. auth. see Wadsworth, J. E.

De Kadt, E., ed. see Conference on Blood Viscosity in Heart Disease, Th.

De Kadt, Emanuel, jt. ed. see Zuckerman, Elaine.

De Kadt, Emanuel J. British Defence Policy & Nuclear War. 144p. 1964. 24.00 (*0-7146-1550-1*, Pub. by F Cass Pubs) Intl Spec Bk.

De Kalb, Howard F. Twisted Earth: Reflections on Patterns People & Places. (Illus.). 160p. 1990. pap. 19.95 (*0-9623271-0-7*) Lytel Eorthe.

De, Kalyan K. Shraddhenjali. 2870p. 1993. pap. 9.95 (*1-57087-030-6*) Prof Pr NC.

De Kam, M. D., jt. auth. see Some, L. M.

de Kamer, H. Maas-van, see Maas-van de Kamer, H.

***De Kare-Silver, Michael.** E-Shock: The Electronic Shopping Revolution; Strategies for Retailers & Manufacturers. LC 98-37350. (Illus.). 288p. 1999. 27.95 (*0-8144-0497-9*) AMACOM.

De Kare-Silver, Michael. Strategy in Crisis: Why Business Urgently Needs a Completely New Approach. LC 97-34292. 320p. 1998. text 42.50 (*0-8147-1899-X*) NYU Pr.

De Kat, Lian. Crocodile Tears. Van Deventer, Eric, tr. from DUT. LC 97-25412. (Illus.). 25p. (J). 1998. 10.95 (*1-57379-071-0*, K1004) High-Scope.

De Kay, Eckford J. The De Kay Family in America. rev. ed. LC 95-79180. 304p. 1995. pap. 28.00 (*0-9638253-1-3*) Acorn Pr CA.

— Heraldry in the Episcopal Church: How Ecclesiastical Coats of Arms Depict the History of the Church. LC 93-72719. 152p. 1993. pap. 12.95 (*0-9638253-0-5*) Acorn Pr CA.

de Kay, James T. The Battle of Stonington: Torpedoes, Submarines, & Rockets in the War of 1812. LC 90-6265. (Illus.). 224p. 1997. pap. 14.95 (*0-940160-73-0*) Parnassus Imprints.

— Left-Handed Book. LC 66-23271. (Illus.). 64p. 1966. pap. 3.50 (*0-87131-156-9*) M Evans.

— Left-Handed Kids. LC 89-36893. (Illus.). 96p. (J). 1989. pap. 5.95 (*0-87131-591-2*) M Evans.

— Meet Christopher Columbus. LC 88-19068. (Step-up Biographies Ser.). (Illus.). 72p. (J). (gr. 2-4). 1989. reprint ed. pap. 3.99 (*0-394-81963-2*, Pub. by Random Bks Yng Read) Random.

***de Kay, James T.** Meet Martin Luther King, Jr. (Illus.). (J). 2001. pap. 5.99 (*0-375-80395-5*) Random Bks Yng Read.

— Meet Martin Luther King Jr. 1999. pap. text 11.10 (*0-8335-3924-8*) Econo-Clad Bks.

de Kay, James T. Monitor: The Story of the Legendary Civil War Ironclad & the Man Whose Invention Changed the Course of History. large type ed. LC 98-4978. 228p. 1998. 25.95 (*0-7838-8441-9*, G K Hall & Co) Mac Lib Ref.

— The Natural Superiority of the Left-Hander. LC 79-15824. (Illus.). 128p. 1979. pap. 3.95 (*0-87131-307-3*) M Evans.

de Kay, James T. & Huffaker, Sandy. The World's Greatest Left-Handers. LC 85-1474. (Illus.). 128p. 1985. pap. 5.95 (*0-87131-449-5*, 0578-170) M Evans.

De Kee, D. Perturbation Methods, Instability, Catastrophe & Chaos. LC 99-14412. 1999. 76.00 (*981-02-3726-X*) World Scientific Pub.

De Kee, D. & Chhabra, R. P. Transport Processes in Bubbles, Drops, & Particles. 275p. 1991. 84.95 (*0-89116-999-7*) Hemisp Pub.

De Kee, D. & Kaloni, Purna N., eds. Recent Developments in Structured Continua, Vol. 2. LC 86-13264. (Pitman Research Notes in Mathematics Ser.: Vol. 229). 360p. 1990. reprint ed. pap. 111.60 (*0-608-03594-7*, 206441700002) Bks Demand.

De Kee, D., jt. auth. see Stastna, J.

De Kee, Daniel, jt. ed. see Siginer, Dennis A.

De Keijzer, Arne, jt. auth. see Burstein, Daniel.

De Keijzer, Arne J. China: Business Strategies for the '90s. LC 92-70169. 277p. (Orig.). 1992. pap. 24.95 (*1-881896-00-5*) Pacific View Pr.

De Keijzer, Arne J., jt. auth. see Posner, Arlene.

De Keizer, R. J., jt. ed. see Sanders, E. A.

De Keizer, Robert, et al, eds. Handbook of Ocular Immunology. 304p. 1998. 88.00 (*90-70430-36-3*) Aeolus Pr VA.

De Kemeseye, Johannes. Roll of the Household Expenses of Richard De Swinfield Bishop of Hereford During Part of the Years 1289 & 1290, 2 vols. Webb, John, ed. (Camden Society, London. Publications, First Ser.: Nos. 59 & 62). reprint ed. 115.00 (*0-404-50207-5*) AMS Pr.

De Kerbrech, F. Faverot. Methodische Dressur des Reitpferdes nach den Letzten Anweisungen von Baucher. 122p. 1981. write for info. (*3-487-08226-8*) G Olms Pubs.

De Kerbrech, R. P. The Shaw Saville Line. 1990. 69.00 (*0-9516038-3-3*, Pub. by Ship Pictorial Pubng) St Mut.

De Kerchove, Rene. International Maritime Dictionary. 2nd ed. (ENG, FRE & GER.). 1018p. 1993. reprint ed. 75.00 (*0-8288-0429-X*, M8066) Fr & Eur.

De Kerckhove, Derrick. Connected Intelligence: The Arrival of the Web Society. 224p. pap. 22.95 (*1-895897-87-4*) Somerville Hse.

— The Skin of Culture: Essays on Media & Technology from the Word of Derrick de Kerchkhove. Dewdney, Christopher, ed. 248p. pap. (*1-895897-45-9*) Somerville Hse.

De Kerckhove, Ferry, tr. see Wallerstein, Immanuel, ed.

De Kerdhove, D., ed. The Alphabet & the Brain. (Illus.). 490p. 1988. 135.00 (*0-387-18122-9*) Spr-Verlag.

De Kerf, E. A., jt. auth. see Bauerle, G. G.

de Kerkhof, Petrus C. Maria van, see Van de Kerkhof, Petrus C. Maria.

de Kernion, George C., jt. auth. see Arthur, Stanley C.

De Kersauson, Olivier. The Sea Never Changes: My Singlehanded Trimaran Race Around the World. Anderson, Alison, tr. from FRE. (Illus.). 212p. 1992. pap. 17.95 (*0-924486-22-8*) Sheridan.

De Ketchiva, Paul. Confessions of a Croupier. 1978. lib. bdg. 59.95 (*0-8490-1663-0*) Gordon Pr.

De Keukeleire, D., jt. auth. see Verzele, M.

De Keyzer, Carl. Carl De Keyzer: East of Eden. (Illus.). 128p. 1996. 45.00 (*90-5544-064-7*, 610631, Pub. by Ludion) Dist Art Pubs.

De Kieffer, Donald, jt. auth. see De Villiers, Les

De Kiewiet, Cornelius W. The Anatomy of South African Misery. LC 83-5635. (Whidden Lectures for 1956). 88p. (C). 1983. reprint ed. lib. bdg. 55.00 (*0-313-23960-6*, DEAN, Greenwood Pr) Greenwood.

De Kiley, Dan. The Peter Pan Syndrome. 320p. 1984. mass mkt. 5.99 (*0-380-68890-5*, Avon Bks) Morrow Avon.

***De Kind, Richard E. L. B.** Houses in Herculaneum: A New View on the Town Planning & the Building of Insulae III & IV. (Circumvesuviana: Vol. 1). 355p. 2000. 80.00 (*90-5063-517-2*) J Benjamins Pubng Co.

De Kleer, Johan, et al. Non-Monotonic Reasoning. (Lecture Notes in Computer Science Ser.: Vol. 346). xiv, 237p. 1988. 37.00 (*0-387-50701-9*) Spr-Verlag.

De Kleer, Johan, jt. auth. see Forbus, Kenneth D.

De Kleer, Johan, jt. ed. see Weld, Daniel S.

De Klemm, Cyrille. Guidelines for Cites Implementation Legislation. 88p. 1993. 15.00 (*2-8317-0116-3*, Pub. by IUCN) Island Pr.

De, Klerck Bram. Brothers Camping: Images & Devotion: Religious Painting in the Sixteenth-Century Lombardy. 1999. 49.50 (*90-5356-383-0*, Pub. by Amsterdam U Pr) U of Mich Pr.

De Klerk. Illustrated Math Dictionary for Australian Schools. Date not set. pap. text. write for info. (*0-582-87045-3*, Pub. by Addison-Wesley) Longman.

***De Klerk, F. W.** F.W. de Klerk, the Autobiography: The Last Trek - A New Beginning. (Illus.). 416p. 2000. pap. 19.95 (*0-330-36960-1*, Pub. by Pan Macmillan) Trans-Atl Phila.

De Klerk, Nico, jt. ed. see Hertogs, Daan.

De Klerk, Theo. Writing VAX-VMS Applications Using Pascal. (VAX-VMS Ser.). (Illus.). 700p. 1991. pap. text 54.95 (*1-55558-067-X*, EY-F592E-DP, Digital DEC) Buttrwrth-Heinemann.

De Klerk, Vivian, ed. Focus on South Africa. LC 95-51026. (Varieties of English Around the World General Ser.: No. G 15). iv, 328p. 1996. lib. bdg. 74.00 (*1-55619-446-3*) J Benjamins Pubng Co.

De Kloet, E. Ron, et al, eds. Methods in Neurosciences Vol. 22: Neurobiology of Steroids. (Illus.). 552p. 1994. text 104.00 (*0-12-185292-X*) Acad Pr.

De Kluiver, Harm-Jan & Van Gerven, Walter, eds. The European Private Company? 234p. 1995. pap. 55.00 (*90-6215-466-2*, Pub. by Maklu Uitgev) Gaunt.

De Kluyver, Cornelis A. Strategic Thinking: An Executive Perspective. LC 99-25828. 150p. 1999. pap. 29.40 (*0-13-020995-3*) P-H.

De Knight, Freda. Ebony Cookbook: A Date with a Dish. LC 72-13963. 390p. 1962. 17.95 (*0-87485-003-7*) Johnson Chicago.

De Knop, Paul, et al. Youth in Sports Clubs: Towards a Youth-Friendly Approach. LC 95-189256. 200p. 1994. pap. 29.50 (*90-5487-071-0*, Pub. by VUB Univ Pr) Paul & Co Pubs.

De Knop, Paul, jt. auth. see Standeven, Joy.

De Kok, Luit J. Responses of Plant Metabolism to Air Pollution & Global Change. Linington, S., ed. (Illus.). xx, 520p. 1998. 145.00 (*90-73348-95-1*) Balogh.

De Koker, A. P. Silke on South African Income Tax, Vol. 1. write for info. (*0-7021-1935-0*, R546,06, Pub. by Juta & Co) Gaunt.

— Silke on South African Income Tax, Vol. 2. write for info. (*0-7021-1936-9*, R546,06, Pub. by Juta & Co) Gaunt.

De Koker, A. P. & Lategan, T. Value-Added Tax, Vol. 1. write for info. (*0-409-07802-6*, R275,88) Buttrwrth-Heinemann.

— Value-Added Tax, Vol. 2. write for info. (*0-409-07804-2*, R275,88) Buttrwrth-Heinemann.

De Koker, A. P., jt. auth. see Urquhart, G. A.

De Koninck, Jean-Marie & Levesque, Claude, eds. Number Theory - Theorie des Nombres: Proceedings of the International Number Theory Conference Held at Universite Laval in 1987. xxii, 1002p. (C). 1989. lib. bdg. 179.95 (*3-11-011791-6*) De Gruyter.

De Koninck, Randolphe. Le Recul de la Foret au Viet Nam. LC 98-700029. (FRE.). x, 110p. 1997. pap. 17.95 (*0-88936-845-7*, Pub. by IDRC Bks) Stylus Pub VA.

***De Koninck, Rodolphe.** Deforestation in Viet Nam. 100p. 1999. pap. 16.95 (*0-88936-869-4*, Pub. by IDRC Bks) Stylus Pub VA.

De Koning, J. Checklist of Vernacular Plant Names in Mozambique/Registo de Nomes Vernaculos de Plantas en Mozambique. (Wageningen Agricultural University Papers: No. 93-2). (Illus.). 260p. 1993. pap. 73.00 (*90-6754-268-7*, Pub. by Backhuys Pubs) Balogh.

De Koning, K., ed. Model-Based Reasoning about Learner Behavior. LC 97-77019. 240p. Date not set. 81.00 (*90-5199-368-4*, 368-4) IOS Press.

De Koning, Korrie, ed. Participatory Research & Health. LC 95-41659. 256p. (C). 1996. text 65.00 (*1-85649-351-2*, Pub. by Zed Books) St Martin.

De Koning, Neil. Guiding the Faith Journey: A Map for Spiritual Leaders. LC 96-14885. 110p. (Orig.). 1996. pap. 5.75 (*1-56212-178-2*) CRC Pubns.

De Koning-Stapel, Hanne V. Silk Quilts: From the Silk Road to the Quilter's Studio. LC 99-18765. 192p. 1999. 29.95 (*0-8442-2081-7*, 20817, Quilt Dgst Pr) NTC Contemp Pub Co.

De Koning, Wim J., et al, eds. Chinese Herbs in Animal Nutrition. 250p. 1999. 220.00 (*1-897676-82-4*, Pub. by Nottingham Univ Pr) St Mut.

De, Kooning Mil. Stephane Beel Architect. 1999. 45.00 (*90-5544-243-7*) Ludion.

De Kooning, Willem. Collected Writings. 200p. (Orig.). 1988. 5.95 (*0-937815-13-6*) Hanuman Bks.

De Kooning, Willem, photos by. Willem De Kooning: Drawing Seeing/Seeing Drawing. (Illus.). 128p. 1998. bds. 60.00 (*0-9657280-8-0*) Arena Editions.

de Koros, Alexander Soma, see Soma de Koros, Alexander.

***de Kort, A. F., et al.** Train Movement Analysis at Railway Stations: Procedures & Evaluation of Wakob's Approach. (TRAIL Studies in Transport). 65p. 1999. pap. 18.00 (*90-407-1855-5*, Pub. by Delft U Pr) Coronet Bks.

D

De Kort, I., jt. ed. see Ridder, J. W. A.

De Korte, John. Chemistry 152-154 Lab Manual. (C). 1997. pap. text 12.05 (1-56870-272-8) RonJon Pub.

De Koster, Katie. Brave New World. LC 98-48266. (Literary Companion to British Literature Ser.). 127p. 1999. pap. 17.45 (1-56510-834-5) Greenhaven.

— Euthanasia. LC 99-24454. (Opposing Viewpoints Digests Ser.). 96p. 1999. pap. 14.95 (1-56510-870-1); lib. bdg. 23.70 (1-56510-871-X) Greenhaven.

— Readings on a Brave New World. LC 98-48266. (Literary Companion Ser.). 224p. 1999. lib. bdg. write for info. (1-56510-835-3) Greenhaven.

***De Koster, Katie.** Readings on "Fahrenheit 451" LC 99-38379. (Literary Companion Ser.). 224p. (gr. 9-12). 2000. pap. 17.45 (1-56510-856-6) Greenhaven.

— Readings on "Fahrenheit 451" LC 99-38379. (Literary Companion Ser.). 127p. (YA). (gr. 9-12). 2000. lib. bdg. 27.95 (1-56510-857-4) Greenhaven.

— Readings on J. R. R. Tolkien. LC 99-34336. (Literary Companion Ser.). 224p. (YA). (gr. 9-11). 2000. pap. 17.45 (0-7377-0244-3) Greenhaven.

— Readings on J. R. R. Tolkien. LC 99-34336. (Literary Companion Ser.). 127p. (YA). (gr. 9-12). 2000. lib. bdg. 27.45 (0-7377-0245-1) Greenhaven.

De Koster, Katie. Readings on the Adventures of Huckleberry Finn. LC 97-43630. (Literary Companion Ser.). (YA). (gr. 9-12). 1998. pap. 16.20 (1-56510-818-3); lib. bdg. 26.20 (1-56510-819-1) Greenhaven.

De Koster, Katie, ed. Mark Twain. (Literary Companion Ser.). 1996. lib. bdg. 26.20 (1-56510-471-4) Greenhaven.

De Koster, Katie, ed. Mark Twain. LC 95-51236. (Literary Companion Ser.). 1996. pap. 16.20 (1-56510-470-6) Greenhaven.

De Koster, Katie, ed. Rape on Campus. (At Issue Ser.). 120p. (C). 1995. pap. text 11.20 (1-56510-263-0) Greenhaven.

De Koster, Katie, ed. Readings on Ernest Hemingway. LC 96-21137. (Literary Companion Ser.). 190p. (YA). (gr. 9-12). 1996. pap. 16.20 (1-56510-462-5); lib. bdg. 26.20 (1-56510-463-3) Greenhaven.

De Koster, Katie, ed. Thornton Wilder. LC 98-9891. (Literary Companion Ser.). 189p. (YA). (gr. 9 up). 1998. pap. 16.20 (1-56510-814-0); lib. bdg. 26.20 (1-56510-815-9) Greenhaven.

De Koster, Katie, jt. ed. see Leone, Bruno.

De Koster, Lester. Work: The Meaning of Your Life. 95p. 1982. 4.95 (0-934874-04-2) Chr Lib Pr.

De Koster, M. B. Capacity Oriented Analysis & Design of Production Systems. (Lecture Notes in Economics & Mathematical Systems Ser.: Vol. 323). xii, 245p. 1989. 39.30 (0-387-50692-6) Spr-Verlag.

De Koven, Anna. Women in Cycles of Culture. 333p. 1977. 23.95 (0-8369-2787-7) Ayer.

De Kretser, D. M., ed. Molecular Biology of the Male Reproductive System. (Illus.). 483p. 1993. text 99.00 (0-12-209030-6) Acad Pr.

De Kretser, David, jt. ed. see Burger, Henry.

De Kretser, David M., et al, eds. The Pituitary & Testis: Clinical & Experimental Studies. (Monographs on Endocrinology: Vol. 25). (Illus.). 200p. 1983. 100.00 (0-387-11874-8) Spr-Verlag.

***De Kretser, Michelle.** The Rose Grower. 448p. 2000. 25.00 (0-7867-0733-X, Pub. by Carroll & Graf) Publishers Group.

***De Kretser, Michelle, ed.** Brief Encounters: Stories of Love, Sex & Travel. 296p. 1998. pap. 12.95 (0-86442-529-5) Lonely Planet.

De Kroes, J. L. & Stoop, J. A., eds. First World Congress on Safety of Transportation: 26-27 November 1992 Proceedings. (Illus.). 706p. 1993. 125.00 (90-6275-891-6, Pub. by Delft U Pr) Coronet Bks.

de Kroon, Cohen Van, see Van der Kroon, Cohen.

De Kroon, H., jt. ed. see Groenendael, J. Van.

De Kroon, Hans & Van Groenendael, J. The Ecology & Evolution of Clonal Plants. (Illus.). 453p. 1997. pap. 68.00 (90-73348-73-0, Pub. by Backhuys Pubs) Balogh.

De Kruif, Paul. Microbe Hunters. LC 67-34588. 337p. 1966. pap. 7.95 (0-15-659413-7, Harvest Bks) Harcourt.

De Kruijf, H. A. M., et al, eds. Manual on Aquatic Ecotoxicology. (C). 1990. reprint ed. 58.00 (0-8364-2736-X, Pub. by Allied Pubs) S Asia.

De Kruijff, J. Spraakmakende Musici. 350p. 1997. pap. write for info. (90-5410-690-5) Ashgate Pub Co.

De Kumar, Branab. Roles of Sense & Thought in Knowledge. (C). 1992. 16.00 (81-7074-117-3, Pub. by KP Bagchi) S Asia.

De Kunffy, Charles. The Athletic Development of the Dressage Horse: Manege Patterns. (Illus.). 224p. 1992. 28.00 (0-87605-896-9) Howell Bks.

— The Ethics & Passions of Dressage. Carnes, Elizabeth A., ed. LC 93-33153. (Illus.). 128p. 1993. 20.95 (0-939481-33-2) Half Halt Pr.

— Training Strategies for Dressage Riders. (Illus.). 240p. 1994. 30.00 (0-87605-972-8) Howell Bks.

De L. Milosz, O. V. Fourteen Poems by O. V. de L. Milosz. Rexroth, Kenneth, tr. (FRE.). 68p. 1984. pap. 7.00 (0-914742-71-X) Copper Canyon.

De L. Rush, A., ed. Ruling Families of Arabia: Documentary Records of the Dynasties of Saudi Arabia, Jordan, Kuwait, Bahrain, Qatar, UAE & Oman, 12 vols. (Illus.). 7500p. 1991. reprint ed. lib. bdg. 2495.00 (1-85207-310-1, Pub. by Archive Editions) N Ross.

De L. Ryals, Clyde & Fielding, Kenneth J., eds. The Collected Letters of Thomas & Jane Welsh Carlyle Vol. 25: January to December 1850. 288p. 1997. lib. bdg. 49.95 (0-8223-1986-1) Duke.

— The Collected Letters of Thomas & Jane Welsh Carlyle Vol. 26: January to December, 1851. 344p. 1998. 54.95 (0-8223-2104-1) Duke.

De La Balze, Felipe. Remaking the Argentine Economy. 150p. 1995. pap. text 14.95 (0-87609-171-0) Coun Foreign.

De La Barca, Frances Calderon, see Calderon de la Barca, Frances.

de la Barquera Arroyo, Elvia C. Sanchez, see Sanchez de la Barquera Arroyo, Elvia C.

De la Barra, Tomas. Integrated Land Use & Transport Modelling. (Cambridge Urban & Architectural Studies: No. 12). (Illus.). 196p. (C). 1989. text 69.95 (0-521-24318-1) Cambridge U Pr.

De la Barre, Francois P. The Woman As Good As the Man: Or the Equality of Both Sexes. LC 88-10808. 160p. (C). 1988. 28.95 (0-8143-1953-X) Wayne St U Pr.

De La Barre, Poullain. The Equality of the Two Sexes: (De l'Egalite des Deux Sexes) Frankforter, A. Daniel & Morman, Paul, trs. from FRE. LC 89-33547. (Studies in the History of Philosophy: Vol. 11). (FRE.). 248p. 1989. lib. bdg. 89.95 (0-88946-303-4) E Mellen.

De la Barrera Y Leirado, Cayetano A. Catalogo Bibliografico y Biografico del Teatro Antiguo Espanol: Desde Sus Origenes Hasta Mediados del Siglo SVIII. (SPA.). 727p. (Orig.). (C). 1968. pap. 51.00 (0-900411-02-3, Pub. by Tamesis Bks Ltd) Boydell & Brewer.

— Catalogo Bibliografico y Biografico Del Teatro Antiguo Espanol Desde Sus Origenes Hasta Mediados Del Siglo XVIII. (SPA.). 1968. 100.00 (84-249-1914-9) Elliots Bks.

De La Bathie, H. Perrier. Flora of Madagascar: Orchids. Humbert, H., ed. Beckman, Steven D., tr. from FRE. LC 82-90881. (Illus.). 542p. 1982. 65.00 (0-9609434-0-4) S D Beckman.

De La Baume, Cecile. Crush: An Erotic Novel. Deofleurs, Ramona, tr. 144p. 1999. reprint ed. pap. text 11.00 (0-8021-3595-1, Grove) Grove-Atltic.

De la Bedoyere, C. Simple Handmade Jewellery: Over Two Hundred Easy-to-Make Designs. (Illus.). 80p. (Orig.). 1993. pap. 17.50 (0-85532-749-9, 749-9, Pub. by Srch Pr) A Schwartz & Co.

De la Bedoyere, Charlotte. How to Grow Natural Herbs & Spices for Culinary Use. (Illus.). 64p. 1994. pap. 16.95 (0-85532-751-0, 751-0, Pub. by Srch Pr) A Schwartz & Co.

De la Bedoyere, Charlotte, tr. Clay Modelling for Everyone: Sculpture, Pottery & Jewellery Without a Wheel. 112p. (Orig.). pap. 16.95 (0-85532-631-X, 631-x, Pub. by Srch Pr) A Schwartz & Co.

***de la Bedoyere, Guy.** Battles over Britain: The Archaeology of the Air War. (Illus.). 176p. 2000. pap. 24.99 (0-7524-1485-2, Pub. by Tempus Pubng) Arcadia Publng.

— A Companion to Roman Britain. (Illus.). 256p. 1999. 37.50 (0-7524-1457-7, Pub. by Tempus Pubng) Arcadia Publng.

de la Bedoyere, Guy. The English Heritage Book of Roman Towns. 152p. 1992. 75.00 (0-7134-6893-9) B&N Imports.

— The Golden Age of Roman Britain. (Illus.). 208p. 1999. 37.50 (0-7524-1417-8, Pub. by Tempus Pubng) Arcadia Publng.

— Hadrian's Wall: History & Guide. (Illus.). 160p. 1998. pap. 16.99 (0-7524-1407-0, Pub. by Tempus Pubng) Arcadia Publng.

— Samian Ware. (Archaeology Ser.: No. 55). (Illus.). 68p. 1989. pap. 10.50 (0-85263-930-9, Pub. by Shire Pubns) Parkwest Pubns.

***de la Bedoyere, Guy.** Voices of Imperial Rome. (Illus.). 256p. 2000. pap. 24.99 (0-7524-1497-6, Pub. by Tempus Pubng) Arcadia Publng.

de la Bedoyere, Guy, ed. Particular Friends: The Correspondence of Samuel Pepys & John Evelyn. (Illus.). 354p. 1998. pap. 29.95 (0-85115-697-5, Boydell Pr) Boydell & Brewer.

de la Bedoyere, Guy, ed. see Evelyn, John.

***De La Bedoyere, Michael.** Francis of Assisi: The Man Who Found Perfect Joy. LC 98-52838. Orig. Title: Francis: A Biography of the Saint of Assisi. 348p. (Orig.). 1999. reprint ed. pap. 17.95 (0-918477-89-1) Sophia Inst Pr.

De La Bedoyere, Michael. SaintMaker: The Remarkable Life of St. Francis de Sales. 358p. 1998. reprint ed. pap. 17.95 (0-918477-86-7) Sophia Inst Pr.

De la Bedoyere, Quentin. How to Get Your Own Way in Business. 250p. 1990. text 56.95 (0-566-02826-3, Pub. by Gower) Ashgate Pub Co.

— Managing People & Problems. 160p. 1988. text 39.95 (0-566-02697-X, Pub. by Gower) Ashgate Pub Co.

— Managing People & Problems. (Gower Audio Manual Ser.). 64p. 1989. pap. text 61.95 (0-566-02763-1, Pub. by Gower) Ashgate Pub Co.

De La Bere, Imogen. The Last Deception of Palliser Wentwood. LC 99-27155. 1999. text 23.95 (0-312-20329-2) St Martin.

De La Billardiere, Jean J. Icones Plantarum Syriae Rariorum: Descriptionibus & Observationibus Illustratar 1791-1812. (Illus.). 1968. 100.00 (3-7682-0540-1) Lubrecht & Cramer.

— Novae Hollandiae Plantarum Specimen, 1894-06: 1894-06, 2 vols. in 1. 1966. 156.00 (3-7682-0344-1) Lubrecht & Cramer.

— Sertum Austro-Caledonicum. (Illus.). 1968. reprint ed. 130.00 (3-7682-0541-X) Lubrecht & Cramer.

De La Blanca, N. P. & Vidal, E. Pattern Recognition & Image Analysis: Selected Papers from the 4th Spanish Symposium. (World Scientific Series on Machine Perception & Artificial I: No. 1). 400p. 1992. text 114.00 (981-02-0881-2) World Scientific Pub.

De la Boetie, Etienne. The Politics of Obedience: The Discourse of Voluntary Servitude. Kurz, Harry, tr.Tr. of De la Servitude Volontaire. (FRE.). 100p. 1975. 44.99 (1-55164-089-9, Pub. by Black Rose) Consort Bk Sales.

— The Politics of Obedience: The Discourse of Voluntary Servitude. LC 96-79525.Tr. of De la Servitude Volontaire. 100p. 1996. pap. 15.99 (1-55164-088-0, Pub. by Black Rose) Consort Bk Sales.

— The Politics of Obedience: The Discourse of Voluntary Servitude.Tr. of De la Servitude Volontaire. 1984. lib. bdg. 79.95 (0-87700-648-2) Revisionist Pr.

— The Politics of Obedience: The Discourse of Voluntary Servitude. Kurz, Harry, tr. from FRE.Tr. of De la Servitude Volontaire. 88p. 1975. reprint ed. 19.95 (0-919618-58-8, Pub. by Black Rose) Consort Bk Sales.

De la Brana, Ramon A. Siglas y Abreviaturas Latinas Con Su Significado Por Orden Alfabetico de un Catalogo de las Abreviaturas Que Se Usan en los Documentos Pontificios. 216p. 1978. reprint ed. write for info. (3-487-06454-5) G Olms Pubs.

de la Brede Montesquieu, Baron. The Persian Letters. Healy, George R., tr. from FRE. LC 99-36814. 320p. (C). 1999. reprint ed. pap. 9.95 (0-87220-490-1); reprint ed. lib. bdg. 34.95 (0-87220-491-X) Hackett Pub.

De La Bretonne, Nicholas E. Restif, see Restif De La Bretonne, Nicholas E.

De la Brosse, Olivier. Diccionario del Cristianismo. 2nd ed. (SPA.). 1104p. 1987. write for info. (0-7859-5088-5) Fr & Eur.

De La Bruyere, Jean. Les Caracteres. (Folio Ser.: No. 693). (FRE.). 1962. pap. 9.95 (2-07-036693-6) Schoenhof.

— Les Caracteres. unabridged ed. (FRE.). pap. 7.95 (2-87714-156-X, Pub. by Bookking Intl) Distribks Inc.

— Les Caracteres de Theophrastre, traduits du grec avec Les Caracteres, ou Les Moeurs de ce siecle. Garagon, ed. (Class. Garnier Ser.). pap. 24.95 (0-685-34227-1) Fr & Eur.

— Les Caracteres de Theophrastre, traduits du grec avec Les Caracters, ou Les Moeurs de ce siecle. Garpon, ed. (Coll. Prestige). 49.95 (0-685-34228-X) Fr & Eur.

— Characters. Van Laun, Henri, tr. from FRE. LC 89-23836. 494p. 1992. reprint ed. lib. bdg. 47.50 (0-86527-394-4) Fertig.

— Maximes et Pensees. 9.95 (0-686-54264-9) Fr & Eur.

— Oeuvres Completes. Benda, Julien, ed. (FRE.). 768p. 1978. lib. bdg. 95.00 (0-7859-3760-9, 2070102947) Fr & Eur.

— Oeuvres Completes. Benda, ed. (Pleiade Ser.). (FRE.). 1935. 64.95 (2-07-010294-7) Schoenhof.

De La Bruyere, Jean & Pignarre, Robert. Les Caracteres: Avec: Caracteres de Theophraste. (FRE.). 668p. 1962. 10.95 (0-7859-0065-9, M1573) Fr & Eur.

De La Cabada, Juan. Maria la Voz y Otras Historias (Maria the Voice) 2nd ed. (SPA.). 184p. 1984. pap. 7.99 (968-16-1631-6, Pub. by Fondo) Continental Bk.

De la Camara, Maria, tr. see Matute, Ana M.

***De La Campa, Roman.** Cuba on My Mind: Journeys to a Severed Nation. 192p. 2000. 23.00 (1-85984-790-0, Pub. by Verso) Norton.

De La Campa, Roman. Late Imperial Culture. Kaplan, E. Ann et al, eds. LC 94-44394. (Postmodern Occasions Ser.). 240p. (C). 1995. pap. 19.00 (1-85984-050-7, C0470, Pub. by Verso) Norton.

De La Campa, Roman & Kaplan, Anne E. Ghostly Demarcations: A Symposium on Jacques Derrida's Spectres of Marx. Sprinker, Michael, ed. pap. 60.00 (1-85984-709-9) Verso.

***De la Campa, Romban.** Latin Americanism. LC 98-56167. (Cultural Studies of the Americas). 1999. pap. 18.95 (0-8166-3117-4) U of Minn Pr.

De la Carrera, Rosalina. Success in Circuit Lies: Diderot's Communicational Practice. LC 91-2608. 256p. 1991. 35.00 (0-8047-1923-3) Stanford U Pr.

De La Casa, Enrique C. La Novela Antioquena. 100p. 2.00 (0-318-14294-5) Hispanic Inst.

De La Cerda, Diego. The Last American. LC 97-69235. 256p. 1998. pap. 16.95 (1-57197-084-3) Pentland Pr.

De la Chapelle, A., ed. Human Gene Mapping Eight: Eighth International Workshop on Human Gene Mapping, Helsinki, Finland, August 1985. (Journal: Cytogenetics & Cell Genetics: Vol. 40, No. 1-4, 1985). (Illus.). vi, 824p. 1985. pap. 139.25 (3-8055-4248-8) S Karger.

De La Colina, Jose & Turrent, Tomas P. Objects of Desire: Conversations with Luis Bunuel. Lenti, Paul, tr. from SPA. LC 92-82642. (Illus.). 280p. 1993. 24.00 (0-941419-68-1) Marsilio Pubs.

De la Colina, Jose & Turrent, Tomas P. Objects of Desire: Conversations with Luis Bunuel. Lenti, Paul, tr. from SPA. LC 92-82642. (Illus.). 280p. 1994. pap. 12.95 (0-941419-69-X) Marsilio Pubs.

De La Colombiere, Claude, jt. auth. see Saint-Jure, Jean B.

De La Concepcion Valdes, Gabriel, jt. auth. see Manzano, Juan F.

De la Concha, Victor Garcia, see Garcia de la Concha, Victor, ed.

***De la Costa, Fernando, et al.** Paseo Pintoresco por la Isla de Cuba. 2nd rev. ed. Cuban National Heritage Staff, ed. LC 99-67187. (Coleccion Arte Cubano). (SPA., Illus.). 480p. 1999. pap. 29.95 (0-89729-900-0) Ediciones.

De la Costa, Horacio, ed. The Trial of Rizal. 202p. 1997. pap. text 15.00 (971-550-208-3, Pub. by Ateneo de Manila Univ Pr) UH Pr.

De La Court, Pieter. The True Interest & Political Maxims of the Republic of Holland. LC 78-38278. (Evolution of Capitalism Ser.). 520p. 1972. reprint ed. 37.95 (0-405-04117-9) Ayer.

De La Cova, Antonio. U. S. Cuba Relations: The Reagan Years. Kvederas, Robert, ed. 250p. 1991. write for info. (0-944273-08-4) U S Cuba Pr.

De La Croix, Aurele, ed. see De LaFayette, Jean M.

De la Croix, Horst, et al. Gardner's Art Through the Ages Vol. 2: Renaissance & Modern Art. 9th ed. (Illus.). 605p. (C). 1991. pap. text 26.00 (0-685-40570-2) Harcourt.

De La Croix, Otto. Naturliche Reitkunst. 1989. write for info. (3-487-08306-X) G Olms Pubs.

De la Cruz Aymes, Maria, et al. A Catholic Response to the Asian Presence. 126p. (Orig.). 1990. pap. 10.00 (1-55833-057-7) Natl Cath Educ.

De la Cruz, Bartolomei. Protection Against Anti-Union Discrimination. vii, 123p. 1976. 18.00 (92-2-101348-0) Intl Labour Office.

De la Cruz, Ben. Business Information Market 2002: The Strategic Outlook. 10th rev. ed. Jaros, Tony et al, eds. (Illus.). 241p. 1998. 2495.00 (0-88709-071-0) Simba Info Inc.

— Information Publishing: Business-Professional Markets & Media 1999 Edition. (Illus.). 362p. 1999. 1895.00 (0-88709-063-X) Simba Info Inc.

— Web Online Services, 99-2003: Market Analysis & Forecast. Kopp, Linda, ed. 355p. 1999. 1895.00 (0-88709-054-0) Simba Info Inc.

— Web/Online Services: 99-03 Review, Trends & Forecast. 9th ed. Kopp, Linda, ed. (Illus.). 355p. 1999. 1895.00 (0-88709-133-4) Simba Info Inc.

— Web/Online Services 99-2003. 9th rev. ed. Courtmanche, John & Krasilovsky, Peter, eds. (Illus.). 355p. 1999. 1895.00 (0-88709-154-7) Simba Info Inc.

De la Cruz, Ben, et al. Web Advertising, 2000: Market Analysis & Forecast. (Illus.). 2000p. 1999. 1695.00 (0-88709-119-9) Simba Info Inc.

De la Cruz, Ben, jt. auth. see Kopp, Linda.

De la Cruz, Enrique B., et al, eds. Confrontations, Crossings, & Convergence: Photographs of the Philippines & the United States, 1898-1998. (Illus.). 96p. 1998. pap. text 15.00 (0-934052-27-1) UCLA Asian Am Studies Ctr.

De La Cruz, Felix, jt. ed. see Lubs, Herbert A.

***De la Cruz, Irving & Thaler, Les.** Inside MAPI. (Illus.). 2000. reprint ed. cd-rom 39.95 (0-9701158-0-6) Inside MAPI.

De la Cruz, Juana I. Autos y Loas. (Obras Completas de Sor Juana Ines de la Cruz: Vol. III). (SPA.). 740p. 22.99 (968-16-4511-1, Pub. by Fondo) Continental Bk.

— Comedias, Sainetes y Prosa. (Obras Completas de Sor Juana Ines de la Cruz: Vol. IV). (SPA.). 551p. 22.99 (968-16-4471-9, Pub. by Fondo) Continental Bk.

— Lirica Personal. (Obras Completas de Sor Juana Ines de la Cruz: Vol. I). (SPA.). 639p. 1994. reprint ed. 22.99 (968-16-3016-5, Pub. by Fondo) Continental Bk.

— Sonetos y Villancicos. (Fondo 2000 Ser.). (SPA.). pap. 2.99 (968-16-5047-6, Pub. by Fondo) Continental Bk.

— Villancicos y Letras Sacras. (Obras Completas de Sor Juana Ines de la Cruz: Vol. II). (SPA.). 551p. 22.99 (968-16-4472-7, Pub. by Fondo) Continental Bk.

De la Cruz, Juana Inez. Selected Sonnets. Sider, Sandra, tr. (Translation Ser.). 47p. 1991. pap. write for info. (0-920669-11-5, Pub. by Peregrina Pubng) Cistercian Pubns.

De la Cruz, M. V. & Markwald, R. R. Living Morphogenesis of the Heart. LC 99-158844. (Cardiovascular Molecular Morphogenesis Ser.). (Illus.). 232p. 1998. 95.00 (0-8176-4037-1) Birkhauser.

De la Cruz, Maria Victoria & Markwald, Roger R. Living Morphogenesis of the Heart. LC 99-158844. (Cardiovascular Molecular Morphogenesis Ser.). xviii, 233 p. 1998. write for info. (3-7643-4037-1) Birkhauser.

***De la Cruz, Martin.** Aztec Herbal: The Classic Codex of 1552. 2000. pap. 8.95 (0-486-41130-3) Dover.

De la Cruz, Martin. Codice de la Cruz Badiano (Codez de la Cruz Badiano) (Book of Indigenous Medicinal Herbs), 2 vols. 2nd ed. (SPA., Illus.). 260p. 1991. pap. 99.99 (968-16-3607-4, Pub. by Fondo) Continental Bk.

De la Cruz, Pablo & Lumholtz, Carl. The Art of the Beautiful: Decorative Art of the Huichol Indians. large type ed. Finson, Bruce, ed. LC 94-72977. (Huichol Shamanic Library: No. 2). (Illus.). 60p. 1994. pap. 20.00 (0-943907-14-4) Bruce Finson.

De la Cruz, Pablo, jt. auth. see Lumholtz, Carl.

de la Cruz, San Juan, see San Juan de la Cruz.

De La Cruz, Sor J. Poems, Protest & a Dream. Peden, Margaret Sayers, tr. LC 96-30638. 304p. 1997. pap. 12.95 (0-14-044703-2, Penguin Classics) Viking Penguin.

De la Cruz, Sor Juana Ines. The Answer - La Respuesta: Including a Selection of Poems. Arenal, Electa & Powell, Amanda, trs. from SPA. LC 93-41115. 196p. (C). 1994. 35.00 (1-55861-076-6); pap. 12.95 (1-55861-077-4) Feminist Pr.

— Obras Completas. (SPA.). pap. 19.95 (968-432-650-5, Pub. by Porrua) Continental Bk.

De la Cuesta, Barbara. The Gold Mine. Miller, Yvette E., ed. LC 88-9296. (Discoveries Ser.). 160p. 1988. pap. 14.95 (0-935480-27-7) Lat Am Lit Rev Pr.

— If There Weren't So Many of Them You Might Say They Were Beautiful. LC 91-75856. (Illus.). 64p. (Orig.). 1991. pap. 12.00 (0-913559-17-2) Birch Brook Pr.

— Westerly, an Integrated Focus for Nursing Home Activity: Finding an Integrative Focus for a Nursing Home Activity Program. (Illus.). 157p. (C). 1993. 19.50 (1-877735-45-0, 2256PP) Prof Prnting & Pub.

De La Cuesta, Felipe A. Grammar of the Mutsun Language: Spoken at the Mission of San Juan Bautiste, Alta, CA. fac. ed. (Shea's Library of American Linguistics: No. VIII). (SPA.). 96p. 1961. reprint ed. pap. text 10.94 (1-55567-510-7) Coyote Press.

— Grammar of the Mutsun Language Spoken at the Mission of San Juan Bautista, Alta California. fac. ed. (Shea's Library of American Linguistics: No. IV). (SPA.). 48p. (C). 1961. reprint ed. pap. text 5.31 (1-55567-508-5) Coyote Press.

De La Cuesta, Felipe Arroyo, see Arroyo De La Cuesta, Felipe.

De la Cuesta, Leonel A., ed. see Instituto de Estudios Cubanos Staff.

De la Cuesta, Leonel A., ed. see Maso, Calixto C.

De la Cueva, Juan. El Infamador. Los Siete Infantes de Lara. Cebrian, Jose, ed. (Nueva Austral Ser.: Vol. 252). (SPA.). 1991. pap. text 24.95 (*84-239-7252-6*) Elliots Bks.

De La Dehesa, Guillermo. Privatization in Eastern & Central Europe. (Occasional Paper Ser.: No. 34). 36p. 1991. pap. 10.00 (*1-56708-033-2*) Grp of Thirty.

De la Dehesa, Guillermo. Le Recent Afflux de Capitaux Prives dans les Pays en Developpement Est-Il Durable? LC HG3891.D44. (Conference Per Jacobsson Ser.: Vol. 1994). (FRE.). 54p. reprint ed. pap. 30.00 (*0-608-08750-5*, 206938900004) Bks Demand.

— The Recent Surge in Private Capital Flows to Developing Countries: Is It Sustainable? LC HG3891.D44. (Per Jacobsson Lecture Ser.: Vol. 1994). 50p. reprint ed. pap. 30.00 (*0-608-08748-3*, 206938700004) Bks Demand.

— La Reciente Afluencia Masiva de Capital Privado Hacia los Paises en Desarrollo: Es Viable? LC HG3891.D44. (Conferencia Per Jacobsson Ser.: Vol. 1994). (SPA.). 56p. reprint ed. pap. 30.00 (*0-608-08749-1*, 206938800004) Bks Demand.

De La Dehesa, Guillermo & Kenen, Peter B. EMU Prospects. (Occasional Paper Ser.: No. 50). 40p. (Orig.). 1995. pap. 10.00 (*1-56708-048-0*) Grp of Thirty.

De La Dehesa, Guillermo & Krugman, Paul. EMU & the Regions. (Occasional Paper Ser.: No. 39). 66p. 1992. pap. 15.00 (*1-56708-084-7*) Grp of Thirty.

De La Derna, Victor. The Gourmet's Tour of Spain: Thirty Great Spanish Restaurants & Their Favorite Recipes. 1992. write for info. (*0-8212-1918-9*) Little.

De La Encina, J. Egloga de Placida y Vitoriano. (SPA.). 125p. 1970. 3.50 (*0-8288-7168-X*) Fr & Eur.

De La Fage, Juste-Adrien. Histoire Generale de la Musique et de la Danse, 2 vols. in 1. xvi, 1063p. 1978. reprint ed. write for info. (*3-487-06554-1*) G Olms Pubs.

De La Faille, Harold B., jt. ed. see Kater, Louis.

De La Faille, J. B. Van Gogh's Complete Works on Paper, 2 vols. rev. ed. (ENG & FRE., Illus.). 1992. 295.00 (*1-55660-126-3*) A Wofsy Fine Arts.

— Vincent Van Gogh - The Works: Catalogue Raisonne. (Illus.). 704p. 1970. 275.00 (*1-55660-811-X*) A Wofsy Fine Arts.

De la Falaise, Maxime. Seven Centuries of English Cooking. LC 92-2350. 256p. 1992. pap. 15.95 (*0-8021-3296-0*, Grove) Grove-Atltic.

De La Fayette, Marie-Madeleine. Histoire de Madame Henriette d'Angleterre. 187p. 1980. pap. 24.95 (*0-7859-4645-4*) Fr & Eur.

— La Princesse de Cleves. 1958. write for info. (*0-318-63581-X*) Fr & Eur.

— La Princesse de Cleves. (Folio Ser.: No. 778). 1958. pap. 9.95 (*2-07-036778-9*) Schoenhof.

— La Princesse de Cleves. unabridged ed. (FRE.). pap. 7.95 (*2-87714-160-8*, Pub. by Bookking Intl) Distribks Inc.

— Romans et Nouvelles. 468p. 1967. 27.50 (*0-7859-0689-4*) Fr & Eur.

— Romans et Nouvelles: Avec: La Princesse de Cleves, La Comtesse de Tende, La Princesse de Montpensier, Zaide. Magne, Emile, ed. (FRE., Illus.). 488p. 1961. pap. 24.95 (*0-7859-1496-X*, 2705001638) Fr & Eur.

— The Secret History of Henrietta, Princess of England: First Wife of Philippe, Duc D'Orleans; Together with, Memoirs of the Court of France for the Years 1688-1689. Shelmerdine, J. M., tr. & intro. by. LC 92-29820. 1993. lib. bdg. 40.00 (*0-86527-409-6*) Fertig.

— Vie de la Princesse d'Angleterre. 264p. 1967. 29.95 (*0-8288-9925-8*) Fr & Eur.

De La Fontainerie, Fidela, tr. see De La Salle, John B.

De La Forge, Louis. Traite de l'Esprit de l'Homme et de Ses Facultes ou Fonctions et de Son Union avec le Corps. (Historia Philosophiae Ser.). xliv, 455p. 1984. reprint ed. write for info. (*3-487-07476-1*) G Olms Pubs.

— Treatise on the Human Mind (1664) Clarke, Desmond M., ed. & tr. by. LC 98-106454. 264p. 1997. text 147.00 (*0-7923-4778-1*) Kluwer Academic.

de la Fuente, Angel. Mathematical Methods & Models for Economists. LC 98-52086. (Illus.). 848p. (C). 2000. text 90.00 (*0-521-58512-0*); pap. text 39.95 (*0-521-58529-5*) Cambridge U Pr.

***de la Fuente, Ariel.** Children of Facundo: Caudillo & Gaucho Insurgency During the Argentine State Formation Process. (Illus.). 248p. 2000. lib. bdg. 54.95 (*0-8223-2582-9*) Duke.

— Children of Facundo: Caudillo & Gaucho Insurgency During the Argentine State-Formation Process. (Illus.). 248p. 2000. pap. 18.95 (*0-8223-2596-9*) Duke.

De La Fuente, Beatriz, see Benson, Elizabeth P. & Fuente, Beatriz de la, eds.

De La Fuente, Jose. Gene Transfer in Aquatic Organisms. LC 97-41836. (Biotechnology Intelligence Unit (SV) Ser.). 129p. 1997. 119.00 (*1-57059-516-X*) Landes Bioscience.

De La Fuente, Jose, ed. Gene Transfer in Aquatic Organisms. LC 97-41836. (Biotechnology Intelligence Unit (SV) Ser.). (Illus.). 129p. 1998. 112.00 (*3-540-63652-8*) Spr-Verlag.

de la Fuente, Jose Iturriaga, see Iturriaga de la Fuente, Jose, ed.

De La Fuente, Julio, jt. auth. see Malinowski, Bronislaw.

De la Fuente, Patricia, ed. Chicano Four: Two. (Riversedge Chapbks.). (ENG & SPA., Illus.). 96p. (C). 1981. pap. 6.00 (*0-938884-03-4*) U TX Pan Am Pr.

De La Fuente, Patricia, ed. Chicano Two: Two. (Illus.). 64p. 1982. 5.95 (*0-938884-02-6*) U TX Pan Am Pr.

De La Fuente, Patricia, ed. see Burciaga, Jose A.

De La Fuente, Patricia, ed. see Ochoa, Esperanza.

***de la Fuente, Roman.** Psicologia Medica. 2nd rev. ed. 547p. 1999. 14.99 (*968-16-3934-0*) Fondo CA.

De La Fuente, Tomas. Diccionario Biblico Elemental.Tr. of Basic Bible Dictionary. (SPA.). 208p. 1996. pap. 8.99 (*0-311-03648-1*) Casa Bautista.

De La Fuente, Vincent M. Behavior of Adolescents: Health, Risks, Violence & Sex: Index of New Information. 1998. 47.50 (*0-7883-1816-0*); pap. 44.50 (*0-7883-1817-9*) ABBE Pubs Assn.

De La Fuye, Allotte. Jules Vernes: Sa Vie, Son Oeuvre. 10.95 (*0-685-37140-9*, F75540) Fr & Eur.

De la Garza, Beatriz. The Candy Vendor's Boy & Other Stories. LC 93-29313. 178p. 1994. pap. 9.95 (*1-55885-106-2*) Arte Publico.

— Pillars of Gold & Silver. LC 97-22161. 260p. (YA). (gr. 5 up). 1997. pap. 9.95 (*1-55885-206-9*, Pinata Bks) Arte Publico.

De la Garza, Phyllis. The Apache Kid. LC 95-61658. (Great West & Indian Ser.: No. 64). (Illus.). 232p. 1995. 28.95 (*0-87026-094-4*) Westernlore.

***De la Garza, Phyllis.** Bounty Hunter's Daughter. 256p. 2000. mass mkt. 4.50 (*0-8439-4741-1*, Leisure Bks) Dorchester Pub Co.

De La Garza, Phyllis. Bounty Hunter's Daughter. LC 98-10087. 256p. 1998. 18.95 (*0-7862-0996-8*) Mac Lib Ref.

— Camels West. (YA). (gr. 9 up). 1999. pap. 10.00 (*0-88092-443-8*) Royal Fireworks.

De La Garza, Phyllis. Chacho. (Illus.). (J). (gr. 4). 1993. 3.95 (*0-88336-763-7*) New Readers.

De La Garza, Phyllis. Charissa of the Overland. 284p. (YA). (gr. 6 up). 1999. pap. 9.99 (*0-88092-370-9*, 3709) Royal Fireworks.

De la Garza, Phyllis. Death Rides the Denver Stage. LC 99-19831. 1999. 20.00 (*0-7862-1331-0*) Five Star.

***De la Garza, Phyllis.** Death Rides the Denver Stage. large type ed. 2000. 20.00 (*0-7838-8399-4*, G K Hall Lrg Type) Mac Lib Ref.

De La Garza, Phyllis, et al. Bounty Hunter's Daughter. large type ed. LC 99-12622. 343p. 1999. 30.00 (*0-7862-1035-4*) Thorndike Pr.

De La Garza, Rodolfo, jt. auth. see Desipio, Louis.

De La Garza, Rodolfo O. Chicano Political Elite Perceptions of the Undocumented Worker: An Empirical Analysis. (Research Reports: No. 31). 24p. (Orig.). (C). 1981. ring bd. 5.00 (*0-935391-30-4*, RR-31) UCSD Ctr US-Mex.

De la Garza, Rodolfo O. & DeSipio, Louis. Ethnic Ironies: Latino Politics in the 1992 Elections. LC 95-47095. 225p. (C). 1996. pap. 24.00 (*0-8133-3012-2*, Pub. by Westview) HarpC.

De la Garza, Rodolfo O. & Velasco, Jesus-Augustin, eds. Bridging the Border: Transforming Mexico - U. S. Relations. LC 97-19263. (Illus.). 208p. 1997. pap. 26.95 (*0-8476-8439-3*); text 68.50 (*0-8476-8438-5*) Rowman.

De la Garza, Rodolfo O., jt. auth. see DeSipio, Louis.

De La Garza, Rodolfo O., jt. ed. see DeSipio, Louis.

De La Garza, Rodolfo O., ed. see Toma's Rivera Center Staff.

De La Garza, Rodolfo O., ed. & pref. see Tomas's Rivera Center Staff.

De la Garza, Velda. Cocina Mexicana Saludable: Recetas Autenticas con Bajo Contenido de Grasa. Hachfeld, Linda, ed. Rancho Park Publishing Staff, tr. from ENG. LC 97-71661.Tr. of Healthy Mexican Cooking. (SPA., Illus.). 256p. (Orig.). 1997. pap. 15.95 (*0-9620471-8-X*, 165) Appletree MN.

De La Garza, Velda. Healthy Mexican Cooking: Authentic Low Fat Recipes. Hachfeld, Linda & Winchester, Faith, eds. LC 95-80011. (Illus.). 256p. (Orig.). 1995. pap. 15.95 (*0-9620471-5-5*, 160) Appletree MN.

***de La Grange, Clementine.** From the Known to the Unknown: From the Memoirs of Baroness de La Grange. Jones, Alice Goen, ed. Buckley, Thomas, tr. from FRE. (Illus.). 105p. 2000. pap. write for info. (*0-9607054-5-7*) Trinity City Hist Soc.

De La Grange, Henry L. & Blaukopf, Herta. Mahler's 7th Symphony: A Symposium. Zychowicz, James L., ed. 148p. 1991. pap. 15.95 (*0-89579-391-1*) A-R Eds.

De La Grange, Henry-Louis. Gustav Mahler Vol. 2: Vienna: The Years of Challenge, 1897-1904. LC 94-18322. (Illus.). 912p. 1995. 45.00 (*0-19-315159-6*) OUP.

***De La Grange, Henry-Louis.** Gustav Mahler Vol. 3: Vienna: Triumph & Disillusion (1904-1907), (Illus.). 1024p. 2000. 55.00 (*0-19-315160-X*) OUP.

De La Gueriniere, Francois R. Reitkunst Oder Grundliche Anweisung Zur Kenntnis der Pferde, Deren Erziehung, Unterhaltung, Abrichtung, Nach Ihrem Verschiedenen Gebrauch und Bestimmung. (Documenta Hippologica Ser.). (GER., Illus.). xxx, 332p. 1996. reprint ed. write for info. (*3-487-08288-8*) G Olms Pubs.

— School of Horsemanship. Boucher, Tracy, tr. 482p. (C). 1993. 175.00 (*0-85131-575-5*, Pub. by J A Allen) Trafalgar.

De la Halle, Adam. Le Jeu de Robin et Marion. Schwam-Baird, Shira I., ed. & tr. by. Scheuermann, Milton G., ed. LC 93-27318. (Library of Medieval Literature: Vol. 94A). 192p. 1993. text 20.00 (*0-8153-0756-X*) Garland.

— Oeuvres Completes. fac. ed. De Coussemaker, Edmond, ed. (FRE., Illus.). 516p. 1970. lib. bdg. 85.00 (*0-8450-1003-4*) Broude.

De La Halle, Adam. The Play of Madness: A Translation of "Jeu de la Feuillee" Mermier, Guy R., tr. from FRE. LC 96-37492. (Studies in Humanities: Vol. 22). XXIX, 127p. (C). 1997. text 38.95 (*0-8204-2860-4*) P Lang Pubng.

De la Harpe, Jean-Baptiste. The Historical Journal of the Establishment of the French in Louisiana. Conrad, Glenn R., ed. Koenig, Virginia & Cain, Joan, trs. (U. S. L. History Ser.: No. 3). 150p. 1985. 15.00 (*0-940984-24-5*) Univ LA Lafayette.

De la Harpe, P., ed. see Gromov, Mikheal.

***De La Harpe, Pierre.** Topics in Geometric Group Theory. LC 00-20271. 1999. lib. bdg. 45.00 (*0-226-31719-6*) U Ch Pr.

***De la Harpe, Pierre.** Topics in Geometric Group Theory. LC 00-20271. (Lectures in Mathematics). 1999. pap. text 20.00 (*0-226-31721-8*) U Ch Pr.

De La Haye, Amy. The Cutting Edge: 50 Years of British Fashion, 1947-1997. LC 96-49423. (Illus.). 224p. 1997. 49.95 (*0-87951-763-8*, Pub. by Overlook Pr) Penguin Putnam.

De La Haye, Amy. Defining Dress. pap. 14.99 (*0-7190-5329-3*, Pub. by Manchester Univ Pr); text 45.00 (*0-7190-5328-5*, Pub. by Manchester Univ Pr) St Martin.

De La Haye, Amy & Dingwall, Cathie. Surfers, Soulies, Skinheads & Skaters: Street Style from the Forties to the Nineties. 160p. 1996. 40.00 (*0-87951-689-5*, Pub. by Overlook Pr) Penguin Putnam.

De La Haye, Amy & Tobin, Shelly. Chanel: The Couturiere at Work. LC 96-18132. (Illus.). 136p. 1996. pap. 24.95 (*0-87951-639-9*, Pub. by Overlook Pr) Penguin Putnam.

De La Haye, Amy, jt. auth. see Mendes, Valerie.

De La Haye, Yves, ed. see Marx, Karl & Engels, Friedrich.

De La Hey, Amy. Chanel: The Couturiere at Work. LC 94-27235. 136p. 1994. 35.00 (*0-87951-570-8*, Pub. by Overlook Pr) Penguin Putnam.

De la Hey, Carolyn. Love the Eternal Link. 1999. pap. 21.00 (*1-85072-038-X*, Pub. by W Sessions) St Mut.

De La Higuera, Colin, jt. auth. see Miclet, Laurent.

De La Hodde, Lucien. The Cradle of Rebellion. Bradburn, J., tr. from FRE. (History of Political Violence Ser.). 1985. reprint ed. lib. bdg. 65.00 (*0-527-41195-7*) Periodicals Srv.

De la Huerta, Christian & Chuen, Lam Kam. Coming Out Spiritually: The Next Step. LC 99-12008. 256p. 1999. 14.95 (*0-87477-966-9*, Tarcher Putnam) Putnam Pub Group.

De La Huerta, Garcia. Raquel. (SPA.). 169p. 1970. 9.95 (*0-8288-7097-7*, S20233) Fr & Eur.

De la Hunt, Thomas J. Perry County, a History. (Illus.). 359p. 1992. reprint ed. lib. bdg. 41.00 (*0-8328-2548-4*) Higginson Bk Co.

De La Iglesia, Felix, jt. auth. see Feuer, George.

De La Iglesia, Felix A. Molecular Biochemistry of Human Diseases, Vol. 1. Feuer, George, ed. LC 84-7156. 240p. 1985. 133.00 (*0-8493-6205-9*, RC627, CRC Reprint) Franklin.

De La Iglesia, Felix A., jt. ed. see Welling, Peter G.

***De la Jara, Ana Maria, et al.** La Ciudad que Queremos. (SPA.). 60p. 1999. write for info. (*92-806-3501-8*) U N I C E.

De La Lama, Luis. The Heart of the Serpent: Mystical Journeys to the Core of Life. LC 93-60379. 192p. 1993. pap. 17.95 (*1-883381-42-8*) White Dragon.

De La Lama, Luisa. The Power Planets: A Manual for Human Empowerment. LC 93-60378. 225p. 1993. pap. 17.95 (*1-883381-20-7*) White Dragon.

***De la Lance, Mennessier & Rene, Gabriel.** Essai de Bibliographie Hippique... Sur Le Cheval et La Cavalerie, 2 vols. 1500p. 1999. reprint ed. 175.00 (*1-57898-178-6*) Martino Pubng.

De La Luz, Antonio. La Empresa y la Funcion de Personal. 358p. 1982. 7.50 (*0-8477-2620-7*); pap. 6.00 (*0-8477-2609-6*) U of PR Pr.

De La Luz Uribe, Maria. Dona Pinones. (Illus.). 48p. 1981. 5.95 (*980-257-024-9*, Pub. by Ediciones Ekare) Kane-Miller Bk.

De La Maiza, Maria Sainz, see Foster, C. Stephen & Sainz De La Maiza, Maria.

De la Mare, Giles, ed. see De La Mare, Walter.

De La Mare, Peter. Electrophilic Halogenation: Reaction Pathways Involving Attack by Electrophilic Halogens on Unsaturated Compounds. LC 75-13451. (Cambridge Chemistry Texts Ser.). 243p. reprint ed. pap. 69.30 (*0-608-12215-7*, 2024444) Bks Demand.

De la Mare, Walter. The Lord Fish. LC 96-26253. (Candlewick Treasures Ser.). (Illus.). 128p. (J). (gr. 3-9). 1997. 11.99 (*0-7636-0134-9*) Candlewick Pr.

De La Mare, Walter. Memoirs of a Midget. large type ed. 579p. 1997. reprint ed. lib. bdg. 24.00 (*0-939495-11-2*) North Bks.

— Memoirs of a Midget. 454p. 1998. reprint ed. lib. bdg. 24.00 (*1-58287-003-9*) North Bks.

De la Mare, Walter. The Return. LC 97-23292. (Dover Horror Classics Ser.). (Illus.). 224p. 1997. reprint ed. pap. text 7.95 (*0-486-29688-1*) Dover.

***De La Mare, Walter.** Short Stories 1895 - 1926. De la Mare, Giles, ed. 498p. 2000. 29.95 (*1-900357-03-8*, Pub. by Giles Mare Pubs) Trafalgar.

De la Mare, Walter. The Turnip. LC 92-6191. (Illus.). 32p. (J). 1992. 18.95 (*0-87923-934-4*) Godine.

De la Mare, Walter, ed. Red Riding Hood Dance. unabridged ed. LC 72-751562. (J). 1972. audio 11.00 (*0-89845-527-8*, CDL5 1331, Caedmon) HarperAudio.

De La Mare, Walter J. Collected Poems. LC 79-670359. 480p. 1979. pap. 25.95 (*0-571-11382-6*) Faber & Faber.

— De La Mare Walter. (Pocket Poet Ser.). 1962. pap. 3.95 (*0-8023-9044-7*) Dufour.

— 1880s: Essays. LC 73-158497. 1971. reprint ed. 39.00 (*0-403-01295-3*) Scholarly.

— Lewis Carroll. (English Literature Ser.: No. 33). 1972. reprint ed. lib. bdg. 75.00 (*0-8383-1489-9*) M S G Haskell Hse.

— Pleasures & Speculations. LC 76-90630. (Essay Index Reprint Ser.). 1977. 23.95 (*0-8369-1255-1*) Ayer.

— The Return. Reginald, R. & Menville, Douglas A., eds. LC 75-46266. (Supernatural & Occult Fiction Ser.). 1976. reprint ed. lib. bdg. 25.95 (*0-405-08124-3*) Ayer.

— Rhymes & Verses: Collected Poems for Young People. LC 88-45278. (Illus.). 370p. (J). (gr. 2-4). 1995. 15.95 (*0-8050-0847-0*, Bks Young Read); pap. 7.95 (*0-8050-0848-9*, Bks Young Read) H Holt & Co.

— The Riddle & Other Stories. 1993. reprint ed. lib. bdg. 18.95 (*0-89968-423-8*, Lghtyr Pr) Buccaneer Bks.

— Riddle & Other Tales. 300p. 1976. 23.95 (*0-8488-0983-1*) Amereon Ltd.

— Rupert Brooke & the Intellectual Imagination. LC 72-3166. (English Literature Ser.: No. 33). 1972. reprint ed. lib. bdg. 75.00 (*0-8383-1515-1*) M S G Haskell Hse.

— Songs of Childhood. 184p. 1985. reprint ed. 25.00 (*0-89609-257-7*) Roth Pub Inc.

— Wind Blows Over. LC 71-113655. (Short Story Index Reprint Ser.). 1977. 23.95 (*0-8369-3384-2*) Ayer.

De La Mater, R. G. The Application of Gear Reducers to Oil Well Pumping Service. (Technical Papers: Vol. P194). (Illus.). 25p. 1939. pap. text 30.00 (*1-55589-408-9*) AGMA.

De la Maza, E. R. & Turrent, D. R. Mexican Lepidoptera: Eurytelinae I. (Sociedad Mexicana de Lepidopterologia Special Publication Ser.: No. 4). (Illus.). 44p. (Orig.). 1985. pap. 25.00 (*0-911836-16-0*) Entomological Repr.

De La Maza, L. M. & Peterson, E. M., eds. Medical Virology, No. 8. (Illus.). 342p. 1989. 85.00 (*0-306-43361-3*, Plenum Trade) Perseus Pubng.

De la Maza, L. M. & Peterson, E. M., eds. Medical Virology, Vol. 10. (Illus.). 312p. (C). 1991. text 114.00 (*0-306-44010-5*, Kluwer Plenum) Kluwer Academic.

De La Maza, Luis M. & Jo Baron, Ellen. Color Atlas of Diagnostic Microbiology. LC 98-130864. (Illus.). 224p. (C). (gr. 13). 1997. text 71.00 (*0-8151-0621-1*, 24752) Mosby Inc.

De La Mere. Selected Poems. (York Notes Ser.). 1992. pap. text. write for info. (*0-582-79289-4*, Pub. by Addison-Wesley) Longman.

De La Mesangere, Pierre & Wees, J. Dustin. Book of Days: Plates from Le Bon Genre. (Illus.). 80p. 1986. pap. 10.00 (*1-55660-183-2*) A Wofsy Fine Arts.

De La Mettrie, Julien O. Man a Machine: Man a Plant. Watson, Richard & Rybalka, Maya, trs. from FRE. LC 94-29259. (Hackett Classics Ser.). 96p. (C). 1994. pap. text 8.95 (*0-87220-194-5*); lib. bdg. 29.95 (*0-87220-195-3*) Hackett Pub.

— Oeuvres Philosophiques, 2 vols. in 1. vii, 623p. 1988. reprint ed. write for info. (*3-487-02811-5*) G Olms Pubs.

De la Meza, L. M. & Peterson, E. M., eds. Medical Virology, No. 9. LC 89-657524. (Illus.). 270p. 1990. 85.00 (*0-306-43700-7*, Plenum Trade) Perseus Pubng.

De la Morandiere, H. Dictionary Networks, Telecommunications, English to French. (ENG & FRE.). 142p. 1997. 125.00 (*0-320-00469-4*) Fr & Eur.

De la Mota Oreja, Ignacio H. Diccionario de la Communicacion, 2 vols., Set. (ENG & SPA.). 744p. 1988. 110.00 (*0-7859-3686-6*, 8428316074) Fr & Eur.

De La Mothe, Gordon. Reconstructing the Black Image. (Illus.). 152p. 1993. pap. 18.95 (*0-948080-61-2*, Trentham Bks) Stylus Pub VA.

De La Mothe, John. C. P. Snow & the Struggle of Modernity. (Illus.). 288p. 1992. 65.00 (*0-7735-0914-3*, Pub. by McG-Queens Univ Pr) CUP Services.

De la Mothe, John. Evolutionary Economics & the New International Political Economy. Paquet, Gilles, ed. LC 95-47989. (Science, Technology & the International Political Economy Ser.). 1996. 69.95 (*1-85567-156-5*) St Martin.

De La Mothe, John & Ducharme, Louis, eds. Science & Technology under Free Trade. 250p. 1990. text 39.00 (*0-86187-728-4*) St Martin.

***De La Mothe, John & Paquet, Gilles.** Information, Innovation & Impacts. LC 99-47412. (Economics of Science, Technology & Innovation Ser.). 1999. write for info. (*0-7923-8692-2*) Kluwer Academic.

De La Mothe, John & Paquet, Gilles. Local & Regional Systems of Innovation. LC 98-39380. (Economics of Science, Technology, & Innovation Ser.). 1998. 120.00 (*0-7923-8287-0*) Kluwer Academic.

De la Motte, Dean. Approaches to Teaching Stendhal's the Red & the Black. LC 98-54245. 1999. 37.50 (*0-87352-747-X*) Modern Lang.

De la Motte, Dean & Haig, Stirling. Approaches to Teaching Stendhal's the Red & the Black LC 98-54245. (Approaches to Teaching World Literature Ser.). 1998. 18.00 (*0-87352-748-8*) Modern Lang.

De la Motte, Dean & Przyblyski, Jeannene M., eds. Making the News: Modernity & the Mass Press in Nineteenth-Century France. LC 98-38552. (Studies in Print Culture & the History of the Book). (Illus.). 400p. 1999. 70.00 (*1-55849-176-7*); pap. 22.95 (*1-55849-177-5*) U of Mass Pr.

De La Motte, Fouque. Undine. Barkow, Ben, ed. (European Classics). (Illus.). 224p. 1997. reprint ed. pap. 11.95 (*0-946626-57-X*, Pub. by Dedalus) Subterranean Co.

De La Motte Fouque, Friedrich. Eginhard und Emma; Vaterlandische Schauspiele; Die Pilgerfahrt. Lorenz, Christoph, ed. (Werke II. Abteilung: Bd. 3). 685p. 1997. reprint ed. 125.00 (*3-487-10327-3*) G Olms Pubs.

— Der Parcival. Lorenz, Christoph, ed. (Werke II. Abteilung: Bd. 6). 630p. 1997. 125.00 (*3-487-10329-X*) G Olms Pubs.

De La Motte-Haber, Helga, jt. auth. see Flesch, Martin.

De La Motte-Haber, Helga, ed. see Kreutz, Gunter.

De la Motte, Helga & Steiner, Wendy. Christina Kubisch: Cross-Examination (Sound + Light) Longhauser, Elsa, ed. LC 95-81454. (Illus.). 16p. 1996. pap. 20.00 (*1-58442-026-X*) Galleries at Moore.

De la Motte, Helga, see De la Motte, Helga.

De La Noceda, Joaquin Garcia, see Garcia de La Noceda, Joaquin.

***De-la-Noy, Michael.** Eddy: The Life of Edward Sackville-West. (Orig.). 1999. pap. 25.95 (*1-900850-20-6*, Pub. by Arcadia Bks) Dufour.

De-la-Noy, Michael. George IV. LC 99-207033. (Pocket Biographies Ser.). 1998. pap. 9.95 (*0-7509-1821-7*, Pub. by Sutton Pub Ltd) Intl Pubs Mktg.

D

— The King That Never Was: The Story of Frederick, Prince of Wales. LC 96-143766. (Illus.). 240p. 1996. 39.95 (*0-7206-0981-X*, Pub. by P Owen Ltd) Dufour.

— Scott of the Antarctic. LC 98-111034. (Get a Life...Pocket Biographies Ser.). (Illus.). 128p. 1997. pap. 9.95 (*0-7509-1512-9*, Pub. by Sutton Pub Ltd) Intl Pubs Mktg.

De la Nuez Caballero, Sebastian, ed. Contemporary Poetry from the Canary Islands. Bourne, Louis, tr. LC 90-71092. 275p. 1993. pap. 27.00 (*0-948259-73-6*, Pub. by Forest Bks) Dufour.

De La Nuez, Manuel. Edurardo Marquina. LC 76-5796. (Twayne's World Authors Ser.). 162p. (C). 1976. text 20.95 (*0-8057-6238-8*) Irvington.

De La Orta, David. Ricky Martin: La Historia Verdadera. (SPA.). 1997. pap. 8.98 (*968-409-983-5*) Diana-Etna Inc.

De La Osa, L. Lopez, ed. see International Symposium on Vulvar Cancer Staff.

De la Paix, Yvonne. Just the Perfect Name: The Complete Baby Name Book. 320p. mass mkt. 6.95 (*0-89529-723-X*, Avery) Penguin Putnam.

De La Para, Marco A. Daedalus in the Belly of the Beast - Dedalo en el Vientre de la Bestia. (InterAmericas Ser.: No. 1). 16p. (Orig.). 1992. 5.00 (*0-9633741-1-7*) RI Study of Man.

De la Parra, Marco A. Secret Holy War of Santiago de Chile. LC 93-19641. (Emerging Voices: New International Fiction Ser.). 328p. 1994. 29.95 (*1-56656-127-2*); pap. 12.95 (*1-56656-123-X*) Interlink Pub.

— The Theatre of Marco Antonio de la Parra: Translations & Commentary. Thomas, Charles P., tr. LC 93-8865. (Taft Memorial Fund & University of Cincinnati Studies in Latin American, Chicano & U. S. Latino Theatre: Vol. 2). (SPA.). XIX, 364p. (C). 1995. text 62.95 (*0-8204-2141-3*) P Lang Pubng.

de la Parra, Marco Antonio, jt. auth. see Dorfman, Ariel.

De La Parra, Pimm J. U2 Live: A Concert Documentary. (Illus.). 176p. pap. 24.95 (*0-7119-3666-8*, OP 47526) Omnibus NY.

— U2 Live: A Concert Documentary. 192p. 1998. pap. 26.95 (*0-7119-6655-9*, OP48024) Omnibus NY.

De la Parra, Teresa. Iphigenia: The Diary of a Young Lady Who Wrote Because She Was Bored. Acker, Bertie, tr. from POR. LC 93-17895. (Texas Pan American Ser.).Tr. of Ifigenia. (Illus.). 372p. (C). 1994. pap. 19.95 (*0-292-71571-4*); text 37.50 (*0-292-71570-6*) U of Tex Pr.

— Mama Blanca's Memoirs. De Onis, Harriet, tr. (Latin American Literature Ser.). 216p. (C). 1992. pap. 14.95 (*0-8229-5910-0*); text 49.95 (*0-8229-3835-9*) U of Pittsburgh Pr.

De La Pasture, Edmee E. Messalina of the Suburbs. LC 75-106286. (Short Story Index Reprint Ser.). 1977. 19.95 (*0-8369-3323-0*) Ayer.

***De la Paz, Luis.** El Otro Lado. LC 99-67260. (Coleccion Caniqui). (SPA.). 133p. 1999. pap. 13.00 (*0-89729-914-0*) Ediciones.

De la Paz, Luis. Un Verano Incesante. LC 96-83142. (Coleccion Caniqui). (SPA.). 123p. (Orig.). 1996. pap. 12.00 (*0-89729-793-8*) Ediciones.

De La Paz, Myrna J. Abadeha: The Philippine Cinderella. (Illus.). 28p. (J). (gr. k-7). 1991. 13.95 (*0-9629255-0-0*) Pazific Queen.

De La Paz, Orlando, et al. How to Draw the Hunchback of Notre Dame. LC 97-138006. (Disney Classic Ser.). 21p. (Orig.). (YA). (gr. 3 up). 1997. pap. 8.95 (*1-56010-199-7*, DC08) W Foster Pub.

De La Pedraja, Rene. Latin American Merchant Shipping in the Age of Global Competition, 209. LC 98-30493. (Contributions in Economics & Economic History Ser.: Vol. 209). 200p. 1999. 59.95 (*0-313-30840-3*, Greenwood Pr) Greenwood.

— Oil & Coffee: Latin American Merchant Shipping from the Imperial Era to the 1950s, 206. LC 98-21665. (Contributions in Economics & Economic History: Vol. 206). 208p. 1998. 59.95 (*0-313-30839-X*, Greenwood Pr) Greenwood.

De La Pedraja Toman, Rene. A Historical Dictionary of the U. S. Merchant Marine & Shipping Industry since the Introduction of Steam. LC 93-39354. 768p. 1994. lib. bdg. 125.00 (*0-313-27225-5*, Greenwood Pr) Greenwood.

— The Rise & Decline of U. S. Merchant Shipping in the Twentieth Century. LC 92-17754. (Twayne's Evolution of American Business Ser.: No. 8). 200p. (C). 1992. pap. 14.95 (*0-8057-9827-7*, Twyne); text 26.95 (*0-8057-9826-9*, Twyne) Mac Lib Ref.

de la Pena, Alvaro Ruiz, see Palacio Valdes, Armando.

De la Pena, Augustin. The Psychobiology of Cancer: Automatization & Boredom in Health & Disease. 240p. 1983. 49.95 (*0-275-90968-9*, C0968, Praeger Pubs) Greenwood.

De la Pena, Guillermo. A Legacy of Promises: Agriculture, Politics, & Ritual in the Morelos Highlands of Mexico. (Texas Pan American Ser.). 299p. (C). 1982. text 25.00 (*0-292-74630-X*) U of Tex Pr.

De La Pena, Jose E. A Victim of Despotism, Mexico City, 1839, a Translation: Introduction & Footnotes by Roger Borroel. Borroel, Roger, ed. Luna, Elena, tr. from SPA. LC 96-60691. (Illus.). 51p. (Orig.). 1996. pap. text 9.98 (*0-9624727-7-8*) LaVillita Pubns.

— With Santa Anna in Texas: A Personal Narrative of the Revolution. expanded ed. Perry, Carmen, ed. & tr. by. from SPA. LC 75-16269. (Illus.). 248p. (C). 1997. pap. 16.95 (*0-89096-527-7*) Tex A&M Univ Pr.

De la Pena, L., ed. see Brody, T. A.

De La Pena, L., ed. see Brody, Thomas A.

De La Pena, Luis. Albert Einstein: Navegante Solitario (Solitary Navigator) (Ciencia para Todos Ser.). (SPA., Illus.). 125p. 1990. reprint ed. pap. 5.99 (*968-16-2566-8*, Pub. by Fondo) Continental Bk.

De La Pena, Luis & Cetto, Ana M. The Quantum Dice: An Introduction to Stochastic Electrodynamics. LC 95-40168. (Fundamental Theories of Physics Ser.: Vol. 75). 528p. (C). 1996. text 235.50 (*0-7923-3818-9*) Kluwer Academic.

De La Pena McCook, Kathleen. Opportunities in Library & Information Science. (Opportunities in... Ser.). (Illus.). 160p. pap. 11.95 (*0-8442-4671-9*, 46719, Natl Textbk Co) NTC Contemp Pub Co.

— Opportunities in Library & Information Science. (Opportunities in... Ser.). (Illus.). 160p. 1996. 14.95 (*0-8442-4670-0*, 46700, Natl Textbk Co) NTC Contemp Pub Co.

De la Pena, Terri. Faults: A Novel. LC 99-29300. 288p. 1999. pap. 11.95 (*1-55583-478-7*, Pub. by Alyson Pubns) Consort Bk Sales.

— Latin Satins. LC 94-15169. 220p. (Orig.). 1994. pap. 10.95 (*1-878067-52-4*) Seal Pr WA.

***De la Pena, Terri.** Margins: A Novel. (Djuna Bks.). 336p. 2000. pap. 12.95 (*1-58005-039-5*) Seal Pr WA.

De la Pena, Terri, jt. auth. see Chin-Lee, Cynthia.

De La Pena, Victor & Gine, E. Decoupling: From Dependence to Independence. LC 98-30322. (Probability & Its Applications Ser.). 392p. 1999. 79.95 (*0-387-98616-2*) Spr-Verlag.

De la Penn, M. & Rumboli, M. Collins Illustrated Checklist: Birds of Southern South America & Antarctica. (Illus.). 224p. 1998. 35.95 (*0-00-220077-5*, Pub. by HarpC) Trafalgar.

De La Perouse, Jean F. Life in a California Mission: Monterey in 1786. (Illus.). 112p. 1989. pap. 10.95 (*0-930588-39-8*) Heyday Bks.

De La Perriere, Guillaume. Le Theatre des Bons Engins with la Morosophie. Saunders, Alison, ed. (Emblem Ser.). 468p. 1993. 83.95 (*0-85967-979-9*, Pub. by Scolar Pr) Ashgate Pub Co.

de la Pina, Terri, jt. auth. see Chin-Lee, Cynthia.

De La Platiere, Marie J. Roland, see Roland De La Platiere, Marie J.

de la Plombanie, Henri De Goyon, see De Goyon de la Plombanie, Henri.

De La Poix de Fremenville, Edme. Dictionnaire Ou Traite de la Police Generale des Villes, Bou. (FRE.). 1989. 95.00 (*0-7859-8167-5*, 2-86971-149-2) Fr & Eur.

De La Portilla, Marta. Digalo en Espanol: Review Grammar for Communication. (Illus.). (C). 1988. pap. text 27.60 (*0-13-211178-0*) P-H.

***De La Portilla, Nicolas.** The Diary of Lt. Col. Nicolas de la Portilla (1836) March 18th - April 23rd. Borroel, Roger, ed. (Illus.). 50p. 1999. pap. 5.99 (*1-928792-04-9*) LaVillita Pubns.

De la Potterie, Ignace. The Hour of Jesus: The Passion & Resurrection of Jesus According to John. 233p. (Orig.). 1990. pap. 12.95 (*0-8189-0575-1*) Alba.

— Mary in the Mystery of the Convenant. Buby, Bertrand, tr. LC 91-43114. 306p. (Orig.). 1992. pap. 15.95 (*0-8189-0632-4*) Alba.

De La Primaudaye, Peter P. The French Academie. (Anglistica & Americana Ser.: No. 112). 812p. 1971. reprint ed. 193.70 (*3-487-04228-2*) G Olms Pubs.

***De La Puebla, Manuel.** La Lucha con el Angel. (SPA.). 54p. 1998. lib. bdg. 6.00 (*1-881708-19-5*) Edcnes Mairena.

De la Puebla, Manuel. Reparos del Espejo: Versos Apocrifos de Sor Juana Ines de la Cruz. (Aqui y Ahora Ser.). 69p. 1997. pap. 6.95 (*0-8477-0288-X*) U of PR Pr.

***De la Puebla, Manuel, ed.** Arpas en Vuelo: Veinte Poetas Puertorrique Nos del Siglo XX. 192p. 1999. pap. 12.50 (*1-881708-22-5*) Edcnes Mairena.

De La Puebla, Manuel, ed. Ecologia y Poesia. (SPA., Illus.). 154p. 1998. pap. 9.95 (*1-881708-18-7*) Edcnes Mairena.

— La Espina del Sueno 6 Poetas Puertorriquenas. (SPA., Illus.). 150p. 1997. pap. 9.95 (*1-881708-17-9*) Edcnes Mairena.

De la Puebla, Manuel, ed. Rosa de Cien Petalos Poemas a la Madre. (SPA., Illus.). 136p. 1998. pap. 9.95 (*1-881708-20-9*) Edcnes Mairena.

De La Puebla, Manuel, ed. El Sueno Desvelado Sor Juana Ines de la Cruz. (SPA.). 164p. (C). 1995. lib. bdg. 9.95 (*1-881708-11-X*) Edcnes Mairena.

De la Puebla, Manuel, ed. Tiempo de Marejada Imagen Poetica del Siglo XX. (SPA., Illus.). 159p. 1996. pap. 9.95 (*1-881708-14-4*) Edcnes Mairena.

De La Puebla, Manuel, ed. Ventana Al Mar: Poesia de Espana y Las Americas. 294p. 1992. pap. 9.95 (*1-881708-21-7*) Edcnes Mairena.

De La Puebla, Manuel, ed. & intro. see Marti, Jose.

De La Puente, J. A., jt. auth. see Crespo, A.

De La Puente, J. A., jt. ed. see Boullart, L.

De La Puente, J. A., ed. see IFAC Workshop on Distributed Computer Control Syst.

De La Puente, J. A., jt. ed. see Sahraoui, A. E.

De la Puente, Rene. Poesias Inmortales para Toda Ocasion. (SPA.). 1997. pap. 16.98 (*968-13-2529-X*) Edit Diana.

De la Questa, Barbara & Dowd, Nancy. Sunlight on the Moon: An Anthology of Poems & Stories by Some Who Love the Mentally Ill. LC 98-89158. 120 P. ;p. 1998. write for info. (*0-9668739-0-4*) Ctr Appalachian.

De La Ramee, Louise. Cecil Castlemaine's Gage, Lady Marabout's Troubles & Other Stories. LC 75-121534. (Short Story Index Reprint Ser.). 1977. 23.95 (*0-8369-3490-3*) Ayer.

— La Strega - Other Stories. LC 72-101797. (Short Story Index Reprint Ser.). 1977. 18.95 (*0-8369-3185-8*) Ayer.

De la Ramee, Marie Louise, see Ouida, pseud.

De La Rey, E. Mars: The Law of Insolvency in South Africa. 8th ed. 824p. 1988. 107.00 (*0-7021-2176-2*, Pub. by Juta & Co) Gaunt.

De La Rey, E., et al. Student's Guide to the Insolvency Law of South Africa. 5th ed. 277p. 1990. pap. write for info. (*0-7021-2518-0*, Pub. by Juta & Co) Gaunt.

De La Riva, Bonvesin. I Volgari de Bonvesin de la Riva: Testi Del Ms. Berlinese. Gokcen, Adnan, ed. (Studies in Italian Culture: Vol. 18). (Illus.). LVII, 224p. (C). 1996. text 54.95 (*0-8204-2746-2*) P Lang Pubng.

De la Rocha, Mercedes Gonzalez, see Gonzalez de la Rocha, Mercedes, ed.

De La Roche, Catherine, jt. auth. see Dickinson, Thorold.

De La Roche, Elisa. Teatro Hispano! Three Major New York Companies. rev. ed. LC 95-14987. (Studies in American Popular History & Culture). 224p. 1995. text 68.00 (*0-8153-1986-X*) Garland.

De La Roche, Mazo. Jalna. large type ed. (Whiteoak Chronicles Ser.). 1973. 27.99 (*0-85456-679-1*) Ulverscroft.

— The Master of Jalna. large type ed. (Whiteoak Chronicles Ser.). 1973. 27.99 (*0-85456-682-1*) Ulverscroft.

— Renny's Daughter. large type ed. (Whiteoak Chronicles Ser.). 1973. 27.99 (*0-85456-686-4*) Ulverscroft.

— Sacred Bullock & Other Stories. LC 76-101798. (Short Story Index Reprint Ser.). 1977. 17.95 (*0-8369-3186-6*) Ayer.

— Wakefield's Course. large type ed. (Whiteoak Chronicles Ser.). 1973. 12.00 (*0-85456-684-8*) Ulverscroft.

— The Whiteoak Brothers. large type ed. (Whiteoak Chronicles Ser.). 1973. 27.99 (*0-85456-678-3*) Ulverscroft.

— Whiteoaks. large type ed. (Whiteoak Chronicles Ser.). 1973. 27.99 (*0-85456-680-5*) Ulverscroft.

***De la Rochere, Dutheil & Hennard, Martine.** Origin & Originality in Rushdie's Fiction. LC 99-35311. xxxvi, 232p. (C). 1999. pap. text 41.95 (*0-8204-4241-0*) P Lang Pubng.

***de la Rochere, Martine Hennard Dutheil.** Origin & Originality in Rushdie's Fiction. xxxvi, 232p. 1999. pap. 41.95 (*3-906762-63-7*, Pub. by P Lang) P Lang Pubng.

De la Ronciere, Charles M. L' Europe du Moyen Age Tome III: Fin du XIIIe Siecle-Fin du XVe Siecle. 328p. 1969. 65.00 (*0-7859-5257-8*) Fr & Eur.

— Religion Paysanne et Religion Urbaine et Toscane (c. 1280-1450) (Collected Studies: No. CS 458). (Illus.). 350p. 1994. 117.95 (*0-86078-445-2*, Pub. by Variorum) Ashgate Pub Co.

De La Ronciere, Delort, et al. L' Europe du Moyen Age: Coll. U. Histoire Medievale, 3 tomes. Incl. Tome II. Fin du IXe Siecle - Fin du XVe Siecle. 22.95 (*0-8288-9657-7*, F20411); write for info. (*0-318-52003-6*) Fr & Eur.

De La Roque, Guillaume. Dictionnaire de l'Allemand des Affaires. (FRE & GER.). 475p. 1989. pap. 16.95 (*0-7859-7854-2*, 2253045799) Fr & Eur.

— Dictionnaire de l'Anglais des Affaires. (ENG & FRE.). 446p. 1988. pap. 16.95 (*0-7859-7853-4*, 2253045780) Fr & Eur.

— Dictionnaire de l'Espagnol des Affaires. (FRE & SPA.). 447p. 1988. pap. 16.95 (*0-7859-7855-0*, 2253045802) Fr & Eur.

De La Rosa, Angeles. Recetas de Todo Mexico.Tr. of All Mexicorecipes. 240p. (Orig.). 1997. pap. text 5.98 (*968-15-0841-6*) Ed Mex.

***de la Rosa, Carlos L. & Nocke, Claudia C.** A Guide to the Carnivores of Central America. LC 99-29963. (Illus.). 272p. 1999. 50.00 (*0-292-71604-4*); pap. 27.95 (*0-292-71605-2*) U of Tex Pr.

De la Rosa, Clarisa, tr. see Francia, Silvia.

De la Rosa, Clarisa, tr. see Koningslow, Andrea W.

De La Rosa, Mario R., et al, eds. Conducting Drug Abuse Research with Minority Populations: Advances & Issues. LC 98-36242. 297p. 1998. 69.95 (*0-7890-0530-1*) Haworth Pr.

de la Rosa, Samuel, et al. Manual Compartiendo la Fe: Faith-Sharing Manual. (SPA.). 96p. 1996. pap. 8.95 (*0-88177-185-6*, DR185) Discipleship Res.

De La Rosa, Sheila. Ghost Files: Creepy . . . but True? LC 97-65952. (Disney Adventures Ser.). 112p. (J). (gr. 2-5). 1997. pap. 3.95 (*0-7868-4181-8*, Pub. by Disney Pr) Time Warner.

de la Rossa Cortes, Alberto, ed. see De Maio, Jim.

de la Rubia, Tomas Diaz, see Diaz de la Rubia, Tomas.

De la Rue, Colin, ed. Liability for Damage to the Marine Environment. 268p. 1993. 110.00 (*1-85044-535-4*) LLP.

De La Rue, Richard M., jt. ed. see Marsh, John H.

de La Rupelle, Guy. Motorcycle Vagabonding in Japan. (Motorcycle Journey Ser.). (Illus.). 255p. 1999. pap. 19.95 (*1-884313-16-7*, GUY) Whitehorse NH.

De La Salle. Le Reconfort de Madame de Fresne. Hill, ed. (FRE.). 76p. Date not set. pap. text 19.95 (*0-85989-185-2*, Pub. by Univ Exeter Pr) Northwestern U Pr.

De La Salle, John B. Collection of Various Short Treatises. Burke, Daniel, ed. Battersby, William J., tr. from FRE. LC 92-74037. (Lasallian Sources, the Complete Works of John Baptist de La Salle: Vol. 3). (Illus.). xii, 99p. 1993. 15.00 (*0-944808-08-5*); pap. 10.00 (*0-944808-07-7*) Lasallian Pubns.

— The Conduct of the Christian Schools. Mann, William, ed. De La Fontainerie, Fidela & Arnandez, Richard, trs. from FRE. LC 95-69329. (Lasallian Sources, the Complete Works of John Baptist de La Salle: Vol. 6). (Illus.). xvi, 287p. 1996. 30.00 (*0-944808-13-1*); pap. 25.00 (*0-944808-14-X*) Lasallian Pubns.

— Explanation of the Method of Interior Prayer. Mouton, Donald, ed. Arnandez, Richard, tr. from FRE. LC 93-74361. (Lasallian Sources, the Complete Works of John Baptist de La Salle: Vol. 5). (Illus.). xiv, 169p. 1995. 20.00 (*0-944808-09-3*); pap. 12.00 (*0-944808-10-7*) Lasallian Pubns.

— The Letters of John Baptist de La Salle. Loes, Augustine, ed. Molloy, Colman, tr. from FRE. LC 87-83220. (Lasallian Sources, the Complete Works of John Baptist de La Salle: Vol. 1). (Illus.). xviii, 301p. 1988. 20.00 (*0-944808-00-X*); pap. 15.00 (*0-944808-01-8*) Lasallian Pubns.

— Meditations by John Baptist de La Salle. Loes, Augustine et al, eds. Arnandez, Richard, tr. from FRE. LC 94-70440. (Lasallian Sources, the Complete Works of John Baptist de La Salle: Vol. 4). (Illus.). xviii, 506p. 1994. 25.00 (*0-944808-11-5*) Lasallian Pubns.

— Meditations by John Baptist de La Salle. Loes, Augustine et al, eds. Arnandez, Richard, tr. from FRE. LC 94-70440. (Lasallian Sources, the Complete Works of John Baptist de La Salle: Vol. 4). (Illus.). xviii, 506p. 1994. pap. 20.00 (*0-944808-12-3*) Lasallian Pubns.

— The Rules of Christian Decorum & Civility. Wright, Gregory, ed. Arnandez, Richard, tr. from FRE. LC 90-60706. (Lasallian Sources, the Complete Works of John Baptist de La Salle: Vol. 2). (Illus.). xxiv, 153p. 1990. pap. 15.00 (*0-944808-05-0*) Lasallian Pubns.

— The Rules of Christian Decorum & Civility. Wright, Gregory, ed. Arnandez, Richard, tr. from FRE. LC 90-60706. (Lasallian Sources, the Complete Works of John Baptist de La Salle: jVol. 2). (Illus.). xxiv, 153p. 1990. 23.00 (*0-944808-04-2*) Lasallian Pubns.

de la Saussure, Ferdinand. Course in General Linguistics. Harris, Roy, tr. LC 86-4322. 256p. 1986. pap. 11.00 (*0-8126-9023-0*) Open Court.

De la Selva, Ma E., jt. auth. see Traversari, Gabriel.

De la Selva, Salomon. Tropical Town & Other Poems. Sirias, Silvo, ed. & intro. by. LC 98-3282. 1998. pap. 12.95 (*1-55885-235-2*) Arte Publico.

De la Selva, Teresa. De la Alquimia a la Quimica. (Ciencia para Todos Ser.). (SPA.). pap. 6.99 (*968-16-3740-2*, Pub. by Fondo) Continental Bk.

De la Sema, A. & Gyenes, Juan. Embajadas de Espana. (SPA., Illus.). 198p. 1993. 249.50 (*84-239-5278-9*) Elliots Bks.

De La Serna, Ramon G. Hombre de Alambre: Novela Para Armar, Textos B, 38. Saitz, Herlinda C., ed. (Textos B Ser.: Vol. 38). (SPA., Illus.). 156p. (C). 1994. 60.00 (*1-85566-023-7*) Boydell & Brewer.

De la Serna, Ramon Gomez, see Gomez de la Serna, Ramon.

De La Serna, Victor. The Gourmet's Tour of Spain. 1991. write for info. (*0-8212-1784-4*) Little.

De La Serre, Francoise, et al, eds. French & British Foreign Policies in Transition: The Challenge of Adjustment. LC 89-17946. (International Issues - Questions Internationales Ser.). 276p. 1990. 19.50 (*0-85496-597-1*) Berg Pubs.

De La Sizeranne, Robert. Celebrities of the Italian Renaissance in Florence & in the Louvre. Jeffery, J. E., tr. LC 73-93354. (Essay Index Reprint Ser.). 1977. 26.95 (*0-8369-1302-7*) Ayer.

de la Solana, Alberto Gutierrez, see Gutierrez de la Solana, Alberto.

De La Soledad, Rosalia & San Juan De Novas, Maria J. Ibo: Yorubas en Tierras Cubanas. LC 87-83226. (Coleccion Ebano y Canela). (SPA., Illus.). 284p. (Orig.). 1988. pap. 19.95 (*0-89729-468-8*) Ediciones.

De la Sota, Ann. Amazing Animals. (BrainBooster Ser.). (Illus.). 32p. (J). (gr. 3 up). 1986. 6.95 (*0-88679-457-9*) Educ Insights.

De la Taille, Jean. Dramatic Works. Hall, Kathleen M. & Smith, C. N., eds. (Renaissance Library). (FRE.). 212p. (C). 1972. text 36.50 (*0-485-13804-2*, Pub. by Athlone Pr) Humanities.

De la Teja, Jesus, ed. see Seguin, Juan N.

De la Teja, Jesus F. San Antonio de Bexar: A Community on New Spain's Northern Frontier. (Illus.). 224p. 1996. pap. 18.95 (*0-8263-1751-0*) U of NM Pr.

De La Teja, Jesus F., ed. see Castaneda, Carlos E., et al.

De La Teja, Jesus F., ed. see Foik, Paul J. & Castaneda, Carlos E.

De la Tessonerie. L' Art de Regner. Chaplin, ed. (Exeter French Texts Ser.: No. 86). (FRE.). 155p. Date not set. pap. text 19.95 (*0-85989-396-0*, Pub. by Univ Exeter Pr) Northwestern U Pr.

De La Torre. Managing Global Corporation. 2nd ed. 672p. 2000. pap. 63.75 (*0-07-234798-8*) McGraw.

De La Torre, Adela & Pesquera, Beatriz M., eds. Building with Our Own Hands: Directions in Chicana Studies. (C). 1993. 55.00 (*0-520-07089-5*, Pub. by U CA Pr); pap. 17.95 (*0-520-07090-9*, Pub. by U CA Pr) Cal Prin Full Svc.

De la Torre, Augusto & Kelly, Margaret R. Regional Trade Arrangements. LC 91-45766. (Occasional Paper Ser.: No. 93). v, 54p. 1992. pap. 15.00 (*1-55775-227-3*) Intl Monetary.

De la Torre, Bartholomew R. Thomas Buckingham & the Contingency of Futures: The Possibility of Human Freedom. LC 86-40336. (Mediaeval Studies: No. 25). 328p. 1987. text 46.00 (*0-268-01861-8*) U of Notre Dame Pr.

***de la Torre, Carlos.** Populist Seduction in Latin America: The Ecuadorian Experience. LC 99-58922. (Research in International Studies : No. 32). 192p. 2000. pap. text 22.00 (*0-89680-210-8*, Ohio U Ctr Intl) Ohio U Pr.

De la Torre, Carolina. Psicologia Latinoamericana. (SPA.). 160p. 1995. pap. write for info. (*0-929441-75-3*) Pubns Puertorriquenas.

De la Torre, Cristina, tr. see Montero, Rosa.

De la Torre, Cristina, tr. see Riera, Carme.

De La Torre, Jack C. Cerebrovascular Pathology in Alzhheimer's Disease. 532p. 1999. pap. text 29.95 (*0-8018-6214-0*) Johns Hopkins.

De La Torre, Jack C. & Hachinski, Vladimir, eds. Cerebrovascular Pathology in Alzheimer's Disease. LC 97-213174. (Annals of the New York Academy of Sciences Ser.: No. 826). 523p. 1997. 160.00 (*1-57331-086-7*); pap. 160.00 (*1-57331-087-5*) NY Acad Sci.

De La Torre, Joe, ed. see Wohlers, Bob, et al.

D

An Asterisk (*) at the beginning of an entry indicates that the title is appearing for the first time.

De La Torre, Jose, Jr. Exports of Manufactured Goods from Developing Countries: Marketing Factors & the Role of Foreign Enterprise. Bruchey, Stuart & Bruchey, Eleanor, eds. LC 76-5002. (American Business Abroad Ser.). (Illus.). 1976. 20.95 (*0-405-09271-7*) Ayer.

***de la Torre, Josefina.** Poemas de la Isla. Reyes, Carlos, tr. (SPA.). 122p. 2000. 24.00 (*0-910055-59-9*, Pub. by East Wash Univ) U of Wash Pr.

***de la Torre, Josephina.** Poemas de la Isla (The Island Poems) Reyes, Carlos, tr. (SPA & ENG.). 90p. 2000. pap. 15.95 (*0-910055-58-0*, Pub. by East Wash Univ) U of Wash Pr.

De La Torre, Lillian. The Exploits of Dr. Sam Johnson, Detector. (Library of Crime Classics). 200p. 1987. pap. 5.95 (*0-930330-63-3*) Intl Polygonics.

— The Return of Dr. Sam Johnson, Detector. 200p. 1985. pap. 4.95 (*0-930330-34-X*) Intl Polygonics.

De la Torre, Marta, ed. La Conservation des Sites Archeologiques dans la Region Mediterraneenne: Une Conference Internationale Organisee par le Getty Conservation Institute et le J. Paul Getty Museum, Mai 1995. (Illus.). 176p. 1997. pap. 50.00 (*0-89236-487-4*, Pub. by J P Getty Trust) OUP.

De La Torre, Marta, et al. The Conservation of Archaeological Sites in the Mediterranean Region: Report on an International Conference, 6-12 May 1995. LC 97-19117. (Illus.). 164p. 1998. pap. 50.00 (*0-89236-486-6*, Pub. by J P Getty Trust) OUP.

De la Torre, Monica & Gower, Terence. Appendices, Illustrations & Notes. (Illus.). 64p. 1999. pap. 15.00 (*1-889195-35-9*) Smart Art Pr.

De La Torre, Rafael, jt. auth. see Segura, Jordi.

De la Torre, Rogelio. Gotas de Presente. (SPA.). 1972. pap. 9.00 (*0-89729-065-8*) Ediciones.

De La Torre, Teodoro, contrib. by. Popular History of Philosophy. 411p. 1998. 18.00 (*0-89555-481-X*) TAN Bks Pubs.

De la Torre Villar, Ernesto. La Independencia de Mexico (The Independence of Mexico) (SPA.). 304p. 1992. pap. 14.99 (*968-16-3882-4*, Pub. by Fondo) Continental Bk.

De La Touche, Louise M. The Book of Infinite Love. O'Connell, E. Patrick, tr. from FRE. LC 79-90488. 1992. reprint ed. pap. 5.00 (*0-89555-129-2*) TAN Bks Pubs.

— The Little Book of the Work of Infinite Love. LC 79-90490. 1988. reprint ed. pap. 3.00 (*0-89555-130-6*) TAN Bks Pubs.

— The Sacred Heart & the Priesthood. LC 79-90487. 1981. reprint ed. pap. 9.00 (*0-89555-128-4*) TAN Bks Pubs.

***De La Tour Du Pin, Madame.** Memoirs: Laughing & Dancing Our Way to the Precipice. Harcourt, Felice, tr. from FRE. 472p. 1999. pap. 16.00 (*1-86046-548-X*, Pub. by Harvill Press) FS&G.

De La Tour, Kevin, tr. see Vieira, Waldo.

De la Tour, Richard, jt. auth. see De la Tour, Shatoiya.

***De la Tour, Shatoiya & De la Tour, Richard.** The Herbalist's Garden. 240p. 2001. pap. 24.95 (*1-58017-294-6*) Storey Bks.

De La Tour, Simone, ed. see Vieira, Waldo.

De La Tour, Simone, tr. see Vieira, Waldo.

De La Trinite, ed. see Maritain, Jacques.

De la Valdene, Guy. For a Handful of Feathers. LC 95-11907. 240p. 1995. 18.00 (*0-87113-618-X*, Atlntc Mnthly) Grove-Atltic.

De La Valdene, Guy. For a Handful of Feathers. LC 95-11907. 224p. 1997. reprint ed. pap. 12.00 (*0-87113-697-X*, Atlntc Mnthly) Grove-Atltic.

De la Valdene, Guy. Making Game: An Essay on Woodcock. 2nd ed. LC 88-63675. (Illus.). 192p. 1990. 24.95 (*0-944439-14-4*) Clark City Pr.

De la Vallee, Elisabeth R., tr. see Larre, Claude.

De la Vallee Poussin, Louis. Abhidharmakosabhasyam, 4 vols. Pruden, Leo M., tr. from FRE. LC 87-71231. 1600p. (C). 1990. text 300.00 (*0-89581-913-9*) Asian Humanities.

De La Vars, Lauren P., jt. ed. see Benzel, Kathryn N.

***De La Vega.** Avanzando Text. 1998. pap. text, wbk. ed. 54.00 (*0-471-28270-7*) Wiley.

De La Vega, Aurelio. Hans Burkhardt: Basel. (Illus.). 32p. 1983. pap. 15.00 (*1-880566-01-X*) J Rutberg Fine Arts.

De la Vega, Eida, tr. see Brandt, Amy.

De la Vega, Eida, tr. see Derby, Sally.

De La Vega, Eida, tr. see Hoffman, Eric.

De la Vega, Eida, tr. see Rice, Judith Anne.

De La Vega, Eida, tr. see Seuss, Dr., pseud.

De La Vega, Garcilaso. The Florida of the Inca. Varner, John G. & Varner, Jeannette, eds. 708p. 1951. pap. 24.95 (*0-292-72434-9*) U of Tex Pr.

— Poesia. (SPA.). 132p. 1977. 4.95 (*0-8288-7127-2*) Fr & Eur.

— Poesia Castellana Completa. unabridged ed. (SPA.). pap. 5.95 (*84-410-0010-7*, Pub. by Bookking Intl) Distribks Inc.

De la Vega, Garcilaso. Poesia Completa. Alcina, Juan F., ed. (Nueva Austral Ser.: No. 96). (SPA.). 1991. pap. text 24.95 (*84-239-1896-3*) Elliots Bks.

***De La Vega, Garcilaso.** Poesia Renacentista. (SPA.). 1999. 13.00 (*84-481-0619-9*, McGrw-H College) McGrw-H Hghr Educ.

De La Vega, Garcilaso. Royal Commentaries of the Incas & General History of Peru. Livvermore, Harold V., tr. LC 65-13518. (Texas Pan-American Ser.). 954p. 1966. reprint ed. pap. 200.00 (*0-608-08368-2*, 202512900002) Bks Demand.

De la Vega, Garcilaso. Royal Commentaries of the Incas, & General History of Peru. Pt. 1. LC 65-13518. (Texas Pan American Ser.). 722p. reprint ed. pap. 200.00 (*0-608-08701-7*, 206922400001) Bks Demand.

De La Vega, Garcilaso. Royal Commentaries of the Incas & General History of Peru, Pts. 1 & 2. Livermore, Harold V., tr. LC 65-13518. (Texas Pan-American Ser.). 671p. 1966. reprint ed. pap. 200.00 (*0-608-08367-4*, 202512900001) Bks Demand.

de la Vega, Inca Carcilaso, see Carcilaso de la Vega, Inca.

De La Vega, John. Mexican Real Estate: Law & Practices Affecting Private U. S. Ownership. LC 75-27888. 78p. reprint ed. pap. 30.00 (*0-608-15686-8*, 203148800074) Bks Demand.

De la Vega, Olimpia, tr. see Purcell, Julia A., et al.

De la Vega, Reena. To Myself Be True: A Simple Book to Empower Women. LC 98-86000. (Illus.). xvi, 118p. 1998. pap. 14.95 (*0-9663675-8-8*) Bridges Pub.

de la Vega, Roberto. Eucharist Through the Centuries. LC 99-191274. 474p. 1998. 0.00 (*0-9651601-2-2*) Circle Pr CT.

De la Vega, Sara L. & Salazar, Carmen. Avanzando: Gramatica Espanola y Lectura. 4th ed. LC 97-20639. 448p. 1997. pap. 55.95 (*0-471-16707-X*) Wiley.

de la Vieja, M. Teresa Lopez, see Lopez de la Vieja, M. Teresa.

De La Villeguerin, Erik. Dictionnaire Fiduciaire Financier. 2nd ed. (FRE.). 1991. write for info. (*0-7859-8140-3*, 2-86521-156-8) Fr & Eur.

De La Villeguerin, Yves-Robert. Jurisprudence Sociale Dictionnaire Fiduciaire. 3rd ed. (FRE.). 428p. 1988. pap. 85.00 (*0-7859-8139-X*, 2865210871) Fr & Eur.

De La Villguerin, Erik. Dictionnaire de la Comptabilite. 4th ed. (FRE.). 1431p. 1993. pap. 165.00 (*0-7859-8143-8*, 2865212181) Fr & Eur.

De Laat, A., jt. ed. see Van Steenberghe, D.

De Labac, jt. auth. see Teilhard De Chardin, Pierre.

De Labillardiere, Jacques-Julien H. Voyage in Search of La Perouse, Performed by Order of the Constituent Assembly, During the Years 1701-1704. (Bibliotheca Australiana Ser.: No. 67). (Illus.). 560p. 1971. reprint ed. lib. bdg. 87.50 (*90-6072-086-5*, Pub. by Nico Israel) Lubrecht & Cramer.

De Laborde, Leon. Journey Through Arabia Petraea, to Mount Sinai, & the Excavated City of Petra, the Edom of the Prophecies. (Illus.). xxviii, 331p. reprint ed. write for info. (*0-318-71526-0*) G Olms Pubs.

De Labriolle, Piere C. La Crise Montaniste: Bibliotheque de la Fondation Thiers, fasc. XXXI. LC 82-45816. (Orthodoxies & Heresies in the Early Church Ser.). reprint ed. 57.50 (*0-404-62389-1*) AMS Pr.

De LaBrosse, Olivier, jt. ed. see Henry, Antonin M.

De La'Cancela, Victor, et al. Community Health Psychology: Empowerment for Diverse Communities. LC 97-21660. 288p. (C). 1998. 80.00 (*0-415-91426-4*); pap. 23.99 (*0-415-91427-2*) Routledge.

De Lacerda, Luiz D. & Salomons, W. Mercury from Gold & Silver Mining: A Chemical Time Bomb? Allan, R. & Fsrstner, U., eds. LC 97-35099. (Environmental Science Ser.). (Illus.). 190p. 1997. 79.95 (*3-540-61724-8*) Spr-Verlag.

De Lacerda, Roberto S., jt. auth. see Player, Steve.

De Lacey & O'Leary, trs. from COP. Fragmentary Coptic Hymns from the Wadi N Natrum: Part One Translation. 1973. reprint ed. pap. 4.00 (*0-89979-016-X*) British Am Bks.

De Laclos, Choderlos. Les Liaisons Dangereuses. Dowson, Ernest C., tr. from ENG. LC 98-6220. (New York Public Library Collector's Edition Ser.). (Illus.). 496p. 1998. 18.50 (*0-385-48733-9*) Doubleday.

— Les Liaisons Dangereuses. 448p. (C). 1987. pap. 17.99 (*0-415-09447-X*) Routledge.

De Laclos, Choderlos. Les Liaisons Dangereuses. Stone, P. W., tr. (Classics Ser.). 400p. 1961. pap. 9.95 (*0-14-044116-6*, Penguin Classics) Viking Penguin.

De Laclos, Choderlos, see Laclos, Choderlos de.

De Laclos, Pierre-Ambroise. Dangerous Acquaintances. Aldington, Richard, tr. LC 83-45443. reprint ed. 37.50 (*0-404-20149-0*) AMS Pr.

— Oeuvres Completes. Versini, Etienne, ed. (FRE.). 1979. lib. bdg. 125.00 (*0-7859-3841-9*) Fr & Eur.

De Laet, S. J., jt. ed. see UNESCO Staff.

De Laet, Siegfried J. Portorium: Etude Sur L'Organisation Douaniere Chez les Romains, Surtout a L'Epoque Du Haut-Empire. LC 75-7312. (Roman History Ser.). (FRE.). 1975. reprint ed. 42.95 (*0-405-07194-9*) Ayer.

***De Laeter.** Inorganic Mass Spectrometry. 400p. (C). 2000. write for info. (*0-471-34539-3*) Wiley.

De Lafayette, J. Maximillien. Comprehensive Guide to the Best College & Universities in the U. S. Copeland, Carole, ed. (Illus.). 136p. 1990. pap. 28.00 (*0-939877-01-5*) ACUPAE.

— Directory of U. S. Colleges & Universities Legally Empowered to Grant Academic Degrees. Chen, John H. et al, eds. 1990. 30.00 (*0-939877-07-4*) ACUPAE.

— How Foreign Students Can Earn an American University Degree Without Leaving Their Country. Chen, John H., ed. (Illus.). 144p. 1989. 30.00 (*0-939877-10-4*) ACUPAE.

De LaFayette, Jean M. The Best & Worst Non-Traditional & Alternative Colleges & Universities in the United States. 3rd ed. Chen, John H., ed. (Black List of Alternative Schools in the United States Ser.). 160p. 1991. 30.00 (*0-939877-14-7*) ACUPAE.

De Lafayette, Jean M. The Black List of United States Non-Traditional & Alternative Colleges & Universities: Fake & Fictitious Colleges, Universities & Degrees in the United States. 3rd rev. ed. Chen, John H. et al, eds. (Illus.). 162p. 1991. 30.00 (*0-939877-33-3*) ACUPAE.

De LaFayette, Jean M. Comparative Study of Penal Codes As Applied in France & Great Britain. rev. ed. De La Croix, Aurele & Gaillard, Francois, eds. 450p. 1991. 30.00 (*0-939877-42-2*) ACUPAE.

— Credentials, Academic Equivalency & New Trends in Higher Education Worldwide. Chen, John H. & Crawford, Judith, eds. (Illus.). 160p. 1990. 30.00 (*0-939877-25-2*) ACUPAE.

— The Dating Phenomenon in the United States: Great Expectations Or Justified Deceptions. Wells, Marna R. et al, eds. (Illus.). 245p. 1991. 40.00 (*0-939877-45-5*) ACUPAE.

— Dictionary of Academic Terminology Worldwide. Naffah, Aurele & Chen, John H., eds. (Illus.). 160p. 1991. 30.00 (*0-939877-19-8*) ACUPAE.

— Directory of United States Postsecondary Education: U. S. Register of Nationally Accredited, State Approved Institutions & Colleges Without Official Recognition. Copeland, Carole et al, eds. (Illus.). 138p. (Orig.). 1990. pap. 30.00 (*0-939877-34-1*) ACUPAE.

De Lafayette, Jean M. Directory of United States Traditional & Alternative Colleges & Universities. rev. ed. Naffah, Aurele & Kebabjian, Garo, eds. (Non-Traditional & Alternative Higher Learning in the United States Ser.). (Illus.). 550p. 1990. pap. 33.00 (*0-939877-12-0*) ACUPAE.

De LaFayette, Jean M. General Index of the Worldwide Encyclopedia of Postsecondary Education. Chen, John H. et al, eds. (Illus.). 160p. 1990. 30.00 (*0-939877-21-X*) ACUPAE.

De Lafayette, Jean M. How to Convert Your Knowledge & Life Experience into Academic Degrees: How to Obtain Your College Degree Through the Evaluation of Personal & Professional Experiences. 3rd rev. ed. Crawford, Judith & Wells, Marna R., eds. (Illus.). 164p. 1991. 30.00 (*0-939877-11-2*) ACUPAE.

De LaFayette, Jean M. How to Protect Yourself from Your Ex-Wife's Lawsuits: Divorce & Lawyers in America Today. Wells, Marna R. et al, eds. (Illus.). 165p. 1991. write for info. (*0-939877-45-7*) ACUPAE.

— How to Understand International Law. rev. ed. Wells, Marna R. & De Sade, Bertrand, eds. (Illus.). 550p. 1991. 50.00 (*0-939877-43-0*) ACUPAE.

De Lafayette, Jean M. How Your Portfolio Can Earn You an Accredited College Degree Without Setting Foot on Campus. 3rd ed. Crawford, Judith & Wells, Marna R., eds. (Illus.). 166p. 1991. 30.00 (*0-939877-30-9*) ACUPAE.

— International Rating of Countries in Higher Education & Comparative Study of Curricula, Degrees & Qualifications Worldwide: The International Directory on Higher Learning Worldwide. rev. ed. Crawford, Judith et al, eds. (Postsecondary Education Worldwide Ser.). (Illus.). 162p. 1991. pap. 30.00 (*0-939877-18-X*) ACUPAE.

De LaFayette, Jean M. International Register of World's Universities. ACUPAE Group Staff & Crawford, Judith, eds. (Illus.). 144p. 1990. 30.00 (*0-939877-17-1*) ACUPAE.

— International Study & Analysis of Academic Life & Its Impact on Foreign Students & Scholars. (Illus.). 160p. 1990. pap. 30.00 (*0-939877-22-8*) ACUPAE.

— Lafayette's Encyclopedic Dictionary of Higher Education Worldwide. Naffah, Aunele & Crawford, Judith, eds. (Comparative Lexicon of Postsecondary Education in 140 Countries Ser.). (Illus.). 160p. 1991. 30.00 (*0-939877-26-0*) ACUPAE.

— The National Rating & Rank Order of Colleges & Universities in the U. S. Profile & Rating of Leading American Colleges & Universities. Crawford, Judith et al, eds. (Illus.). 154p. 1990. 30.00 (*0-939877-09-0*) ACUPAE.

— National Register of Social Prestige & Academic Ratings of American Colleges & Universities. Naffah, Aurele et al, eds. (Illus.). 136p. 1990. 28.00 (*0-939877-05-8*) ACUPAE.

— New Concise Dictionary of Law for Beginners. Akoneck, Oya, ed. 226p. 1990. 30.00 (*0-939877-44-9*) ACUPAE.

De Lafayette, Jean M. The Nine Language Universal Dictionary: How to Write It & Say It in Arabic, English, French, German, Italian, Japanese, Portuguese, Russian, Spanish. rev. ed. ACUPAE Group Staff & NASCU Staff, eds. (Illus.). 186p. (Orig.). 1991. pap. 30.00 (*0-939877-28-7*) ACUPAE.

De LaFayette, Jean M. What Foreigners Should Know about Liberal American Women: A Socio-Psychological Study of the Feminism Revolution in the United States since 1960 to Present. Wells, Marna R. et al, eds. (Illus.). 256p. 1991. 30.00 (*0-939877-47-3*) ACUPAE.

— What People from 140 Countries Think about American Men & Women: The United States Today - People, Society, Life. From A to Z. Naffah, Aurele et al, eds. (United States at Your Fingerprints Ser.). (Illus.). 226p. (Orig.). 1991. pap. 30.00 (*0-939877-35-X*) ACUPAE.

— What People from 140 Countries Think about American Men & Women: The United States Today - People, Society, Life from A to Z. rev. ed. Naffah, Aurele et al, eds. (United States at Your Fingerprints Ser.). (Illus.). 162p. 1991. pap. 30.00 (*0-685-48212-X*) ACUPAE.

— Worldwide Comparative Study & Evaluation of Postsecondary Education. Chen, John H. & Naffah, Aurele, eds. (Illus.). 160p. 1991. 30.00 (*0-939877-20-1*) ACUPAE.

De Lafayette, Jean M. & De LaFayette, Jean M. National Directory of Recognized Alternative & Non-Traditional Colleges & Universities in the United States: National Guide to the Best Alternative Post-Secondary Education Programs in the U.S. 3rd ed. Crawford, Judith et al, eds. (Lafayette's Encyclopedia of Non-Traditional Higher Education in the United States Ser.). (Illus.). 160p. 1991. pap. 30.00 (*0-939877-16-3*) ACUPAE.

De LaFayette, Jean M., jt. auth. see De Lafayette, Jean M.

De Lafayette, Madame. The Princess of Cleves. Lyons, John, ed. (Critical Editions Ser.). (C). 1993. pap. text 12.50 (*0-393-96333-0*) Norton.

— The Princess of Cleves: Novel. Mitford, Nancy, tr. from FRE. & intro. by. LC 88-12472. (Classics Ser.: Vol. 660). 240p. 1988. pap. 12.95 (*0-8112-1070-7*, NDP660, Pub. by New Directions) Norton.

— The Princesse de Cleves. 8th ed. Buss, Robin, tr. & intro. by. 192p. 1992. pap. 10.95 (*0-14-044587-0*, Penguin Classics) Viking Penguin.

De Lafontaine, Henry C. The King's Musick: A Transcript of Records Relative to Music & Musicians. LC 70-169648. 522p. 1973. reprint ed. lib. bdg. 59.50 (*0-306-70269-X*) Da Capo.

De Lafora, Nicholas. Frontiers of New Spain. Kinnaird, Lawrence, ed. LC 67-24724. (Quivira Society Publications, Vol. 13). 1967. reprint ed. 19.95 (*0-405-00087-1*) Ayer.

De Laforcade, Geoffroy, tr. see Noiriel, Gerard.

De Lagarde, Paul. Onomastica Sacra. x, 368p. 1966. reprint ed. write for info. (*0-318-70777-2*) G Olms Pubs.

De Lagny, Germain. Knout & the Russians: or The Muscovite Empire, the Czar, & His People. LC 74-115528. (Russia Observed, Series I). 1970. reprint ed. 21.95 (*0-405-03020-7*) Ayer.

De Lagrange, Joseph L. Oeuvres. xliii, 8063p. 1973. reprint ed. write for info. (*3-487-04710-1*) G Olms Pubs.

De Lagrave, Jean-Paul. Voltaire's Man in America: A Political Biography of Fleury Mesplet. LC 98-142171. 488p. Date not set. pap. 25.99 (*1-55207-007-7*, Pub. by R Davies Pub) Genl Dist Srvs.

De Laguarigue, Jean-Luc, photos by. The Houses of Old Cuba. LC 99-70935. (Illus.). 199p. 1999. 45.00 (*0-500-01953-3*, Pub. by Thames Hudson) Norton.

De Laguna, Asela R., ed. Imagenes & Identidades: El Puertorriqueno en la Literatura. LC 85-80192. (SPA.). 322p. 1985. pap. 13.50 (*0-940238-77-2*) Ediciones Huracan.

— Images & Identities: The Puerto Rican in Two World Contexts. 275p. (C). 1985. 39.95 (*0-88738-060-3*); pap. 24.95 (*0-88738-617-2*) Transaction Pubs.

De Laguna, Asela Rodriguez-Seda, see Rodriguez-Seda de Laguna, Asela.

De Laguna, Frederica. The Archaeology of Cook Inlet, Alaska. LC 74-5832. reprint ed. 67.50 (*0-404-11637-X*) AMS Pr.

— Archeology of the Yakutat Bay Area, Alaska. (Bureau of American Ethnology Bulletins Ser.). 245p. 1995. lib. bdg. 89.00 (*0-7812-4192-8*) Rprt Serv.

— The Arrow Points to Murder. 2nd ed. LC 99-94106. 285p. 1999. reprint ed. pap. write for info. (*0-9651157-3-9*) Kachemak Cntry.

— Fog on the Mountain. 1997. pap. text 14.95 (*0-9651157-2-0*) Kachemak Cntry.

— The Prehistory of Northern North America As Seen from the Yukon. LC 76-43687. (Society for American Archaeology Memoirs Ser.: No. 3). reprint ed. 65.00 (*0-404-15520-0*) AMS Pr.

— Story of a Tlingit Community: A Problem in the Relationship between Archeological, Ethnological, & Historical Methods. (Illus.). vii, 254p. 1990. reprint ed. pap. 29.00 (*1-878592-04-1*); reprint ed. lib. bdg. 49.00 (*1-878592-05-X*) Native Amer Bk Pubs.

***De Laguna, Frederica.** Travels among the Dena: Exploring Alaska's Yukon Valley. LC 99-54538. (Illus.). 368p. 2000. 29.95 (*0-295-97902-X*) U of Wash Pr.

De Laguna, Frederica. Voyage to Greenland: A Personal Initiation into Anthropology. (Illus.). 285p. (C). 1995. reprint ed. pap. text 13.50 (*0-88133-854-0*) Waveland Pr.

De Laguna, Frederica, ed. Selected Papers from the "American Anthropologist" 1888-1920. 930p. 1976. pap. 10.00 (*0-685-10026-X*) Am Anthro Assn.

— The Story of a Tlingit Community: A Problem in the Relationship Between Archeological, Ethnological & Historical Methods. (Bureau of American Ethnology Bulletins Ser.). 254p. 1995. lib. bdg. 89.00 (*0-7812-4172-3*) Rprt Serv.

— Tales from the Dena: Indian Stories from the Tanana, Koyukuk, & Yukon Rivers. LC 94-41285. (Illus.). 304p. 1995. 29.95 (*0-295-97429-X*) U of Wash Pr.

De Laguna, Frederica, jt. auth. see Birket-Smith, Kaj.

De Laguna, Theodore. Introduction to the Science of Ethics. LC 72-4166. (Select Bibliographies Reprint Ser.). 1977. reprint ed. 25.95 (*0-8369-6887-5*) Ayer.

De Lahunta, Alexander & Habel, Robert E. Applied Veterinary Anatomy. (Illus.). 330p. 1986. text 52.00 (*0-7216-1431-0*, W B Saunders Co) Harcrt Hlth Sci Grp.

De Lahunta, Alexander, jt. auth. see Evans, Howard E.

De Lailhacar, Christine. The Mestizo As Crucible: Andean Indian & African Poets of Mixed Origin As Possibility of Comparative Poetics. (Studies in Modern Poetry: Vol. 5). X, 318p. (C). 1996. text 54.95 (*0-8204-2891-4*) P Lang Pubng.

De Laine, Marlene. Ethnography: Theory & Applications in Health Research. (Illus.). 369p. (C). 1997. pap. text 55.00 (*0-8036-0393-2*) Davis Co.

De Lajarte, Theodore D. Bibliotheque Musicale Du Theatre De l'Opera, 2 vols., Set. 724p. 1969. reprint ed. write for info. (*0-318-71361-6*) G Olms Pubs.

De Lajonquiere, Etienne E. Lunet, see Lunet De Lajonquiere, Etienne E.

De Lamadrid, J. G., jt. auth. see Argabright, Loren N.

De Lamadrid, Jesus G., jt. auth. see Argabright, Loren N.

De Lamar, Marie & Rothstein, Elisabeth. Records of Washington County, Georgia. LC 84-73076. 184p. 1985. reprint ed. 18.50 (*0-8063-1110-X*) Genealog Pub.

de LaMarche, Olivier. Olivier de la Marche, Le Chevalier Delibere (The Resolute Knight) Carroll, Carleton W., ed. Hawley Wilson, Lois, tr. (Medieval & Renaissance Texts & Studies: Vol. 199). (Illus.). 368p. 1999. 30.00 (*0-86698-241-8*, MR 199) MRTS.

De Lamarck, P. M. Encyclopedie Methodique Botanique: (1783-1817), 13 vols., Set. 7000p. 1987. 5000.00 (*0-7855-2029-5*, Pub. by Scientific) St Mut.

D

An Asterisk (*) at the beginning of an entry indicates that the title is appearing for the first time.

De Lamartine, Alphonse. Graziella. write for info. (*0-318-63474-0*) Fr & Eur.

— Graziella. (FRE.). 1979. pap. 10.95 (*0-7859-2894-4*) Fr & Eur.

— Graziella. (Folio Ser.: No. 1085). (FRE.). 8.95 (*2-07-037085-2*) Schoenhof.

— Meditations. pap. 9.95 (*0-685-23882-2*) Fr & Eur.

— Meditations. Letessier, Fernand, ed. (Coll. Prestige). 49.95 (*0-685-34927-6*); pap. 28.50 (*0-685-34926-8*) Fr & Eur.

— Meditations Poetiques: Nouvelles Meditations Poetiques. Poesies Diverses. (Poesie Ser.). (FRE.). 480p. 1981. pap. 15.25 (*2-07-032200-9*) Schoenhof.

— Meditations Poetiques: Poesies Diverse. (FRE.). 1981. pap. 17.95 (*0-7859-2782-4*) Fr & Eur.

— Oeuvres Poetiques Completes. Guyard, Jean, ed. (FRE.). 1963. lib. bdg. 145.00 (*0-7859-3920-2*) Fr & Eur.

— Poetical Meditations - Meditations Poetiques. Hittle, Gervase, tr. from FRE. LC 92-43538. (Studies in French Literature: Vol. 14). 248p. 1993. text 89.95 (*0-7734-9221-6*) E Mellen.

De Lamartine, Alphorse. A Pilgrimage to the Holy Land. Lombard, Charles M., ed. LC 78-14368. 512p. 1978. reprint ed. 75.00 (*0-8201-1323-9*) Schol Facsimiles.

De Lamartine, M. Alphonse, tr. Narrative of the Residence of Fatalla Sayeghir among the Wandering Arabs of the Great Desert. LC 97-126280. (Folios Archive Library). 216p. 1997. 19.95 (*1-85964-088-5*, Pub. by Garnet-Ithaca) LPC InBook.

De Lancey, Edward F., ed. see Jones, Thomas.

***De Lancie, John.** I, Q. 256p. 2000. 6.99 (*0-671-02444-2*, Star Trek) PB.

***De Lancie, John & Cool, Tom.** Solider of Light, 1. 317p. 1999. 23.00 (*0-671-03595-9*, Pocket Books) PB.

De Lancie, John & David, Peter. I, Q. (Star Trek Ser.). 249p. 1999. 23.00 (*0-671-02443-4*, Star Trek) PB.

***De Lancie, John & David, Peter.** I, Q. (Star Trek Ser.). 1999. per. 23.00 (*0-7434-0079-8*, Star Trek) PB.

— I, Q. (Star Trek). 2000. mass mkt. 6.50 (*0-671-03581-9*, Star Trek) PB.

***De Lancie, John Q. & David, Peter.** I, Q. abr. ed. (Star Trek: The Next Generation Ser.). 1999. audio 18.00 (*0-671-04378-1*) S&S Audio.

De Landa, Diego. Landa's Relacion de las Cosas de Yucatan. Tozzer, Alfred M., ed. LC 83-45906. reprint ed. 48.00 (*0-404-20150-4*) AMS Pr.

— Relacion de las Cosas de Yucatan. Tozzer, Alfred M., tr. (Harvard University Peabody Museum of Archaeology & Ethnology Papers). 1974. reprint ed. 72.00 (*0-527-01245-9*) Periodicals Srv.

— Yucatan Before & after the Conquest. Gates, William, ed. LC 77-91231. (Illus.). 162p. 1998. reprint ed. pap. 6.95 (*0-486-23622-6*) Dover.

De Landa, Manuel. A Thousand Years of Nonlinear History. LC 96-38752. 288p. 1998. 24.50 (*0-942299-31-0*) Zone Bks.

— A Thousand Years of Nonlinear History. LC 96-38752. (Illus.). 333p. 2000. reprint ed. pap. 16.00 (*0-942299-32-9*, Pub. by Zone Bks) MIT Pr.

De Landsheere, Gilbert. Dictionary of Educational Evaluation & Research: Dictionnaire de l'Evaluation et de la Recherche en Education. (ENG & FRE.). 352p. 1979. 99.50 (*0-8288-4793-2*, M6108) Fr & Eur.

***De Landtsheer, Christ'l & Feldman, Ofer, eds.** Beyond Public Speech & Symbols: Explorations in the Rhetoric of Politicians & the Media. LC 99-37521. 312p. 2000. 69.50 (*0-275-96732-8*, C6732, Praeger Pubs) Greenwood.

De Landtsheer, Christ'l, jt. ed. see Feldman, Ofer.

De Lange, Adriaan M. The Influence of Political Bias in Selected Essays on George Orwell. LC 92-13097. 160p. 1992. 69.95 (*0-7734-9541-X*) E Mellen.

***de Lange, Frits.** Waiting for the Word: Dietrich Bonhoeffer on Speaking about God. LC 99-49037. 159p. 2000. pap. 19.00 (*0-8028-4532-0*) Eerdmans.

De Lange, Gerda G., jt. ed. see Grubb, R.

De Lange, Harry, jt. auth. see Goudzwaard, Bob.

De Lange, Margreet. The Muzzled Muse: Literature & Censorship in South Africa. LC 97-6145. (Utrecht Publications in General & Comparative Literature Ser.: Vol. 32). xiii, 181p. 1997. pap. 24.95 (*1-55619-432-3*); lib. bdg. 59.00 (*1-55619-431-5*) J Benjamins Pubng Co.

De Lange, N. R. M., tr. see Yehoshua, Abraham B.

De Lange, Nicholas. Atlas of the Jewish World. (Cultural Atlas Ser.). (Illus.). 240p. 1984. 45.00 (*0-87196-043-5*) Facts on File.

— Greek Jewish Texts from the Cairo Genizah: Reconstructing the History of the Greek Jews in the Middle Ages. LC 96-112753. (Texte und Studien zum Antiken Judentum: No. 51). 430p. 1995. 225.00 (*3-16-146438-9*, Pub. by JCB Mohr) Coronet Bks.

***De Lange, Nicholas.** An Introduction to Judaism. LC 99-27938. (Illus.). 266p. 2000. 54.95 (*0-521-46073-5*); pap. 19.95 (*0-521-46624-5*) Cambridge U Pr.

***De Lange, Nicholas, ed.** Ignaz Maybaum: A Reader. (European Judaism Ser.: Vol. 3). 256p. 2000. 69.95 (*1-57181-720-4*) Berghahn Bks.

De Lange, Nicholas, ed. An Illustrated History of the Jewish People. (Illus.). 448p. 1997. 36.00 (*0-15-100302-5*) Harcourt.

De Lange, Nicholas, tr. see Oz, Amos.

De Lange, O. L. & Raab, R. E. Operator Methods in Quantum Mechanics. (Illus.). 392p. 1992. 95.00 (*0-19-853961-4*) OUP.

De Lange, P. J. Samuel Butler: Critic & Philosopher. LC 68-716. (English Biography Ser.: No. 31). 1969. reprint ed. lib. bdg. 75.00 (*0-8383-0537-7*) M S G Haskell Hse.

De Lange, S., et al, eds. Cardiac Anaesthesia: Problems & Innovations. (Developments in Critical Care, Medicine, & Anesthesiology Ser.). 1986. text 140.00 (*0-89838-794-9*) Kluwer Academic.

De Lange, Simon B., tr. see Prokofieff, Sergei O.

De Lange, Simon B., tr. see Smit, Jorgen.

de Lange, Simon Blaxland, tr. see Urieli, Baruch & Muller Wiedemann, Hans.

De Lange, Wiesje. A Trek for Trinie. 116p. 1995. pap. text 9.95 (*965-229-124-2*, Pub. by Gefen Pub Hse) Gefen Bks.

de Lange, William. A History of Japanese Journalism: The Kisha Club as the Last Obstacle to a Mature Japanese Press. 240p. (C). 1997. text 45.00 (*1-873410-68-9*, Pub. by Curzon Pr Ltd) UH Pr.

***de Langen, K. J.** Advanced Low-Voltage & High-Speed Techniques for BiCMOS, CMOS & Bipolar Operational Amplifiers. (Illus.). 272p. 1999. pap. 55.00 (*90-407-1846-6*, Pub. by Delft U Pr) Coronet Bks.

De Langlais, Xavier. Roman du Roi Arthur. 229p. 1965. 19.95 (*0-8288-7418-2*) Fr & Eur.

De Langre, Jacques. Sea Salt's Hidden Powers. 2nd ed. (Illus.). 101p. 1993. 8.00 (*0-916508-42-0*) Happiness Pr.

De Langre, Jacques & De Langre, Yvette. Brown Rice Cookbook: Traditional World-Wide Western Recipes. (Illus.). 32p. (Orig.). 1984. pap. 4.00 (*0-916508-21-8*) Happiness Pr.

De Langre, Jacques, jt. auth. see Ohsawa, Georges.

De Langre, Yvette, jt. auth. see De Langre, Jacques.

De Lannoy, ed. Philostrati, Flavii. (GRE.). 1977. 32.50 (*3-322-00878-9*, T1592, Pub. by B G Teubner) U of Mich Pr.

De Lannoy, Jacques-Dominique, jt. auth. see Feyereisen, Pierre.

De Laplace, Marquis, jt. auth. see Simon, Pierre.

De Laplante, Michele, ed. see Smarandache, Florentin.

De Lapp, Lynn R. Putting the Pieces Together: A Status Report on Integrated Child & Family Services. 62p. (Orig.). (C). 1994. pap. text 20.00 (*0-7881-0688-0*) DIANE Pub.

De Lara, L. Gutierrez & Pinchon, Edgcumb. Mexican People: Their Struggle for Freedom. LC 75-111730. (American Imperialism: Viewpoints of United States Foreign Policy, 1898-1941 Ser.). 1977. reprint ed. 25.95 (*0-405-02033-3*) Ayer.

De Lara, L. Gutierrez, see Gutierrez De Lara, L.

***De Largo, Frances.** Sisters Connecting: Spiritual Bonding Between Women. LC 98-88777. 128p. (Orig.). 2000. pap. 9.95 (*1-58501-017-0*, Pub. by CeShore Pubg) Natl Bk Netwk.

De Larivey, Pierre. Les Esprits. Stone, Donald, Jr., ed. LC 78-3473. (Texts from the Romance Languages Ser.: No. 6). (FRE.). 260p. 1978. 11.00 (*0-674-26175-5*) HUP.

— Les Tromperies. Cameron, Keith & Wright, Paul, eds. (Exeter French Texts Ser.: Vol. C). (FRE.). 99p. 1997. pap. 21.95 (*0-85989-539-4*, Pub. by Univ Exeter Pr) Northwestern U Pr.

De Larkin, E. Martin, Jr. The Touch of Love (from the 'Sixties) Owens, S. P., ed. (Illus.). 57p. (Orig.). 1979. pap. text. write for info. (*0-9603844-0-5*) Hse of Larkin.

De Larosa, Sheila. Encyclopedia of Weird. LC 96-43486. 1997. pap. text 9.95 (*0-8125-5536-8*, Pub. by Tor Bks) St Martin.

— Encyclopedia of Weird. 1998. 10.09 (*0-606-13368-2*, Pub. by Turtleback) Demco.

De Larosi Ere, Jacques. Promoting Private Investment: The Role of Multilateral Development Banks, Vol. 199. LC 96-51280. (Per Jacobsson Lecture). 1997. pap. write for info. (*0-8157-1773-3*) Brookings.

De Larosiere, Jacques. Financer le Developpement dans un Monde Domine par les Mouvements de Capitaux Prives: Le Defi Pose aux Banques Multilaterales de Developpement par la Collaboration avec le Secteur Prive. LC HG3879.P4. (Conference Per Jacobsson Ser.: Vol. 1996). (FRE., Illus.). 51p. reprint ed. pap. 30.00 (*0-608-08781-5*, 206942000004) Bks Demand.

— Financing Development in a World of Private Capital Flows: The Challenge for Multilateral Development Banks in Working with the Private Sector. LC HG3879.P4. (Per Jacobsson Lecture Ser.: Vol. 1996). (Illus.). 45p. reprint ed. pap. 30.00 (*0-608-08780-7*, 206941900004) Bks Demand.

De Larra, Mariano J. Articulos de Costumbres. Diaz Larios, Luis F., ed. (Nueva Austral Ser.: Vol. 99). (SPA.). 1991. pap. text 24.95 (*84-239-1899-8*) Elliots Bks.

— Macias. Lorenzo-Rivero, Luis, ed. (Nueva Austral Ser.: Vol. 155). (SPA.). 1991. pap. text 15.95 (*84-239-1955-2*) Elliots Bks.

— Macias. 224p. 1990. pap. 10.95 (*0-7859-5170-9*) Fr & Eur.

De Larrard, Francois. Concrete Mixture Proportioning: A Scientific Approach. LC 98-39234. (Modern Concrete Technology Ser.). 1999. 110.00 (*0-419-23500-0*, E & FN Spon) Routledge.

De las Casas, Bartolome. Del Unico Modo de Atraer a Todos los Pueblos a la Verdadera Religion (The Only Way to Bring People to the True Religion) 2nd ed. (SPA.). 479p. 1992. reprint ed. pap. 10.99 (*968-16-3845-X*, Pub. by Fondo) Continental Bk.

De Las Casas, Bartolome. Devastation of the Indies: A Brief Account. 144p. 1992. pap. 11.95 (*0-8018-4430-4*) Johns Hopkins.

De las Casas, Bartolome. Historia de las Indias (History of the Indies), Vol. 1. 2nd ed. (SPA.). 519p. 1992. reprint ed. 24.99 (*968-16-0994-8*, Pub. by Fondo) Continental Bk.

— Historia de las Indias (History of the Indies), Vol. 2. 2nd ed. (SPA.). 613p. 1992. reprint ed. 24.99 (*968-16-0995-6*, Pub. by Fondo) Continental Bk.

— Historia de las Indias (History of the Indies), Vol. 3. 2nd ed. (SPA.). 525p. 1992. reprint ed. 24.99 (*968-16-0996-4*, Pub. by Fondo) Continental Bk.

De Las Casas, Bartolome. In Defense of the Indians: The Defense of the Most Reverend Lord, Don Fray Bartolome de Las Casas, of the Order of Preachers, Last Bishop of Chiapa, Against the Persecutors & Slanderers of the People of the New World Discovered Across the Seas. rev. ed. Poole, Stafford, tr. LC 92-60321. 410p. 1992. pap. 18.00 (*0-87580-556-6*) N Ill U Pr.

— A Short Account of the Destruction of the Indies. Griffin, Nigel, tr. (Illus.). 192p. 1999. pap. text 6.67 (*0-14-044562-5*) Addson-Wesley Educ.

De Las Casas, Cristobal. Vocabulario de las Dos Lenguas Toscana y Castellana. 500p. reprint ed. write for info. (*0-318-71602-X*) G Olms Pubs.

— Vocabulario des las Dos Lenguas Toscana y Castellana. 500p. reprint ed. write for info. (*0-318-71623-2*) G Olms Pubs.

De Las Casas, Walter M. Tributes. 56p. 1993. pap. 5.95 (*0-9670601-0-9*) Walter De Las Casas.

De Lasa, H. I., et al, eds. Chemical Reactor Technology for Environmentally Safe Reactors & Products. LC 92-36591. (NATO Advanced Study Institutes Series E, Applied Sciences: No. 225). 1992. text 340.50 (*0-7923-2032-8*) Kluwer Academic.

De Laslzo, Violet S., ed. see Jung, C. G.

De Lasry, Benaim. Two Romances: A Study & Edition of Two Medieval Spanish Romances. 234p. 1982. 17.50 (*0-936388-09-9*) Juan de la Cuesta.

De Laszlo, Mary. Breaking the Rules. 480p. 1997. pap. 11.95 (*0-7472-5198-3*, Pub. by Headline Bk Pub) Trafalgar.

***De Laszlo, Mary.** Dancing on Her Own. 568p. 2000. 31.99 (*0-7089-4203-2*) Ulverscroft.

De Laszlo, Violet S., ed. & intro. see Jung, C. G.

De Latassa y Ortin, Felix. Bibliortecas Antiquas y Nuevas, 3 vols. lxvi, 1720p. reprint ed. write for info. (*0-318-71624-0*) G Olms Pubs.

De Latis, Charles, tr. see Galdos, Benito P.

De Latte, Carl. Christ & His Seven Churches: What the Message to the Seven Churches of Revelation Means to Us Today. 154p. 1999. pap. 8.99 (*1-884369-96-0*, Fairmont Bks) McDougal Pubng.

De Laubenfels, David J. Mapping the World's Vegetation: Regionalization of Formations & Flora. LC 75-25934. (Syracuse Geographical Ser.: No. 4). (Illus.). 266p. reprint ed. pap. 82.50 (*0-8357-3123-5*, 203938400012) Bks Demand.

De Laurence, L. W. Albertus Magnus: Egyptian Secrets, White & Black Art for Man & Beast. 208p. 1996. pap. 17.50 (*0-7873-0264-3*) Hlth Research.

— Cave of the Oracle (1916) 180p. 1999. reprint ed. pap. 17.95 (*0-7661-0732-9*) Kessinger Pub.

— Clairvoyance & Thought-Transference, Auto Trance & Spiritualism, Psychometry & Telepathy. 123p. 1994. reprint ed. pap. 14.95 (*1-56459-455-6*) Kessinger Pub.

— Great Book of Magical Art, Hindu Magic & East Indian Occultism & the Book of Secret Hindu, Ceremonial, & Talismanic Magic. 650p. 1997. reprint ed. pap. 45.00 (*0-7661-0118-5*) Kessinger Pub.

— Human Heart Shown As a Temple of God & the Holy Spirit: Or a Workshop of the Devil & Evil Spirits. 68p. 1999. reprint ed. pap. 16.95 (*0-7661-0828-7*) Kessinger Pub.

— Illustrated Key to the Tarot: The Veil of Divination Illustrating the Greater & Lesser America. 176p. 1997. reprint ed. pap. 14.95 (*0-7661-0040-5*) Kessinger Pub.

— Lesser Key of Solomon. 15.95 (*0-685-22016-8*) Wehman.

— Medical Hypnosis. 292p. 1999. reprint ed. pap. 17.95 (*0-7661-0746-9*) Kessinger Pub.

— Oracle Mystery of Life & Destiny (1931) 194p. 1999. reprint ed. pap. 17.95 (*0-7661-0736-1*) Kessinger Pub.

— Sacred Book of Death Hindu Spiritism Soul Transition & Soul Reincarnation. 400p. 1998. reprint ed. pap. 33.00 (*0-7661-0462-1*) Kessinger Pub.

De Laurence, L. W., contrib. by. Bible Defended: The Holy Scriptures Upheld (1902) 194p. 1998. reprint ed. pap. 16.95 (*0-7661-0711-6*) Kessinger Pub.

***De Laurence, L. W., ed.** Lesser Key of Solomon. 90p. 1999. reprint ed. pap. 12.95 (*0-7661-0776-0*) Kessinger Pub.

— Raphael's Ancient Manuscript of Talismanic Magic (1916) 108p. 1999. reprint ed. pap. 12.95 (*0-7661-0773-6*) Kessinger Pub.

De Lauretis, Teresa. Alice Doesn't: Feminism, Semiotics, Cinema. LC 83-48189. 232p. 1984. 35.00 (*0-253-30467-9*); pap. 14.95 (*0-253-20316-3*, MB-316) Ind U Pr.

— The Practice of Love: Lesbian Sexuality & Perverse Desire. LC 93-44453. 352p. 1994. 36.95 (*0-253-31681-2*); pap. 15.95 (*0-253-20878-5*) Ind U Pr.

— Technologies of Gender: Essays on Theory, Film & Fiction. LC 86-46317. (Theories of Representation & Difference Ser.). 166p. 1987. 27.50 (*0-253-35853-1*); pap. 9.95 (*0-253-20441-0*, MB-441) Ind U Pr.

De Lauretis, Teresa, ed. Feminist Studies-Critical Studies. LC 85-45981. (Theories of Contemporary Culture Ser.). 232p. 1986. 32.00 (*0-253-32171-9*); pap. 10.95 (*0-253-20386-4*, MB-386) Ind U Pr.

De Laussat, Pierre-Clement. Louisiana, Napoleon & the United States: An Autobiography of Pierre-Clement de Laussat (1756-1835) LC 89-32164. (Illus.). 226p. (Orig.). (C). 1989. pap. text 22.00 (*0-8191-7448-3*); lib. bdg. 39.00 (*0-8191-7447-5*) U Pr of Amer.

De Lautreamont, Comte. Maldoror. Wernham, Guy, tr. LC 66-12289. 1965. pap. 12.95 (*0-8112-0082-5*, NDP207, Pub. by New Directions) Norton.

— Maldoror & Poems. Knight, Paul, tr. from FRE. & intro. by. 288p. 1988. pap. 11.95 (*0-14-044342-8*, Penguin Classics) Viking Penguin.

— Maldoror & the Complete Works. Lykiard, Alexis, tr. from FRE. 352p. 1998. pap. 15.95 (*1-878972-12-X*) Exact Change.

De Lautreamont, Isidore. Les Chants de Maldoror. (FRE.). 382p. 1992. pap. 12.95 (*0-7859-4683-7*) Fr & Eur.

— Oeuvres Completes. Nouveau, Germain, ed. (FRE.). 1460p. 1973. pap. 17.95 (*0-7859-4682-9*) Fr & Eur.

De Lavalle, Jose A., ed. see Reid, James & Apesteguia, Raul.

De Lavardin, Jacques, jt. ed. see Drysdall, Denis L.

De Laveleye, Emile. Primitive Property. Marriott, G. R., tr. from FRE. xlvii, 356p. 1985. reprint ed. 48.00 (*0-8377-0817-6*, Rothman) W S Hein.

De Lavergne, Gabriel. Love Letters of a Portugese Nun. 48p. 1998. mass mkt. 7.95 (*1-86046-034-8*) Harvill Press.

De Lawrence, L. W. Hypnotism: A Complete System of Method, Application & Use (1900) 188p. 1996. reprint ed. pap. 17.95 (*1-56459-925-6*) Kessinger Pub.

De Lay, Stephen G. Somewhere Beyond . . . The Vile Side. (Illus.). 124p. (Orig.). 1988. 6.95 (*0-9621271-0-8*) Wretched Pubns.

De Le, Vergne. Orleans Digest of Laws (with Moreau Lislet Notes) 1971. 45.00 (*0-87511-022-3*) Claitors.

De Leal, Magdalena L., jt. auth. see Deere, Carmen.

***De l'Ecotais, Emmanuelle.** Man Ray: Photography & Its Double. Lottmann, Herbert, ed. (Illus.). 260p. 1998. 65.00 (*3-927258-66-0*) Gingko Press.

De Ledesman, Charles, et al. Malaysia, Singapore,& Brunei: The Rough Guide. LC 97-216133. 645p. 1997. pap. 18.95 (*1-85828-232-2*) Viking Penguin.

***De Leenheer, A. P., et al.** Modern Chromatographic Analysis of Vitamins. 3rd rev. expanded ed. LC 00-28152. (Chromatographic Science Ser.). (Illus.). 2000. write for info. (*0-8247-0316-2*) Dekker.

De Leeun, Adele, ed. Legends & Folklore of Holland. (Illus.). 157p. (YA). (gr. 4 up). 1999. 12.50 (*0-7818-0743-3*) Hippocrene Bks.

De Leeuw, Adele & De Leeuw, Cateau. Remembered with Love: Letters to My Sister : Biographical Sketches. LC 81-86639. 148 p. 1982. 10.95 (*0-912650-03-6*) Brookdale Pr.

De Leeuw, Ben. Digital Cinematography. LC 97-10925. 1997. 1.95 (*0-12-208876-X*) Acad Pr.

— Digital Cinematography. LC 97-10925. (Illus.). 265p. 1997. pap. text 40.00 (*0-12-208875-1*) Morgan Kaufmann.

De Leeuw, Cateau, jt. auth. see De Leeuw, Adele.

De Leeuw, Eric & De Leeuw, Manya. Read Better, Read Faster: The Essential Guide to Greater Reading Efficiency. 1990. pap. 15.95 (*0-14-013476-X*, Pub. by Pnguin Bks Ltd) Trafalgar.

De Leeuw, Hendrik, et al. Fireproof Children Education Kit. (Illus.). 308p. (J). (gr. k-6). 1990. ring bd. 59.95 (*0-9626076-1-4*) Natl Fire Serv Support Systs.

de Leeuw, Jan, jt. auth. see Kreft, Ita G.

De Leeuw, Manya, jt. auth. see De Leeuw, Eric.

De Leeuw, P. W. & Guinee, P. A., eds. Laboratory Diagnosis in Neonatal Calf & Pig Diarrhea: Current Topics in Veterinary Medicine & Animal Science, No. 13. 210p. 1981. text 101.50 (*90-247-2527-5*) Kluwer Academic.

De Leeuw, Ronald. Van Gogh Museum. LC 98-197977. (Illus.). 312p. 1999. 60.00 (*90-400-9928-6*) Waandrs.

***de leeuw, W. C. & Van Liere, R., eds.** Data Visualization 2000: Proceedings of the Joint Eurographics & IEEE-TCVG Symposium on Visualization in Amsterdam, The Netherlands, May 29-31, 2000. (Eurographics Ser.). (Illus.). xi, 296p. 2000. pap. 69.95 (*3-211-83515-6*) Spr-Verlag.

De Leevw, Adolph L. Rambling Through Science. LC 72-315. (Essay Index Reprint Ser.). 1977. reprint ed. 23.95 (*0-8369-2788-5*) Ayer.

De Leiris, Joel, jt. ed. see Hearse, David J.

De Lellis, Ronald A. Advances in Immunohistochemistry. (C). (gr. 13). 1984. 87.00 (*0-89352-215-5*) Mosby Inc.

De Lemos, Claudia, jt. ed. see Camaioni, Luigia.

De Lempicka-Foxhall, Baroness K. Passion by Design: The Art & Times of Tamara de Lempicka. (Illus.). 192p. 1987. 35.00 (*0-89659-760-1*) Abbeville Pr.

De Lempicka-Foxhall, Kizette. Passion by Design: The Art & Times of Tamara de Lempicka. (Illus.). 192p. 1998. pap. 19.95 (*0-7892-0503-3*) Abbeville Pr.

De Leo, D., et al, eds. Suicide Prevention. LC 97-232. 254p. 1998. lib. bdg. write for info. (*0-7923-4468-5*) Kluwer Academic.

De Leo, Vincent Z., jt. auth. see Buckner, Allen Z.

De Leon. Tejanos & the Numbers Game: A Socio-Historical Interpretation from the Federal Censuses, 1850-1900. LC 88-20773. 130p. 1989. 24.95 (*0-8263-1118-0*) U of NM Pr.

De Leon, Arnold, jt. auth. see Calvert, Robert A.

De Leon, Arnoldo. Comunidad Tejana, 1836-1900. (SPA.). pap. 12.99 (*968-16-2603-6*, Pub. by Fondo) Continental Bk.

— Ethnicity in the Sunbelt: A History of Mexican Americans in Houston. (Mexican American Studies). 255p. 1989. 32.00 (*0-939709-06-6*) Univ Houston Mex Amer.

— Mexican Americans in Texas: A Brief History. 2nd ed. LC 98-54219. (Illus.). 200p. (C). 1999. pap. text 15.95 (*0-88295-948-4*) Harlan Davidson.

— San Angelenos: Mexican Americans in San Angelo, Texas. (Illus.). 176p. (Orig.). (C). 1985. pap. 12.95 (*0-938036-05-X*) Mulberry Ave Bks.

— The Tejano Community, 1836-1900. LC 97-16564. (Illus.). 310p. 1997. pap. 14.95 (*0-87074-419-4*) SMU Press.

— They Called Them Greasers: Anglo Attitudes toward Mexicans in Texas, 1821-1900. LC 82-24850. 167p. (C). 1983. pap. 10.95 (*0-292-78054-0*) U of Tex Pr.

De Leon, Arnoldo & Stewart, Kenneth L. Tejanos & the Numbers Game: A Socio-Historical Interpretation from the Federal Censuses, 1850-1900. LC 88-20773. (Illus.). 131p. 1989. reprint ed. pap. 40.70 (*0-608-07858-1*, 205404100011) Bks Demand.

De Leon, Arnoldo, jt. auth. see Griswold del Castillo, Richard.

An Asterisk (*) at the beginning of an entry indicates that the title is appearing for the first time.

De Leon, D. La Familia Moderna.Tr. of Modern Family. (SPA.). 140p. pap. 6.99 (*0-7899-0291-5*, 497510) Editorial Unilit.
De Leon, Daniel. Abolition of Poverty. 8th ed. 1969. pap. text 0.50 (*0-935534-00-8*) NY Labor News.
— The Ballot & the Class Struggle. 8th ed. 1971. pap. text 0.50 (*0-935534-04-0*) NY Labor News.
— The Burning Question of Trades Unionism. 1977. pap. 0.50 (*0-935534-32-6*) NY Labor News.
— Capitalism Means War! 3rd ed. 1970. pap. 0.50 (*0-935534-33-4*) NY Labor News.
— Diez Secretos Para Desarrollar Tu Potencial. 1998. pap. text 8.99 (*0-88113-463-5*) Caribe Betania.
— Marxian Science & the Colleges. 3rd ed. 96p. 1944. 2.00 (*0-935534-19-9*) NY Labor News.
— Marxian Science & the Colleges. 3rd ed. 96p. 1966. pap. 0.75 (*0-935534-20-2*) NY Labor News.
— Reform or Revolution. 1977. pap. 0.50 (*0-935534-37-7*) NY Labor News.
— Los Siete Pecados Capitales de un Padre. 1996. 8.99 (*0-88113-410-4*) Caribe Betania.
— Socialism vs. Anarchism. 1970. pap. 0.50 (*0-935534-39-3*) NY Labor News.
— A Socialist in Congress: His Conduct & Responsibilities. 5th ed. 1962. pap. 0.50 (*0-935534-41-5*) NY Labor News.
— Socialist Landmarks. 2nd ed. 1977. pap. 1.50 (*0-935534-29-6*) NY Labor News.
— Socialist Reconstruction of Society. 20th ed. 1977. pap. 0.50 (*0-935534-42-3*) NY Labor News.
— The Vatican in Politics. 4th ed. 1962. pap. text 0.50 (*0-935534-31-8*) NY Labor News.
De Leon, Daniel & National Executive Committee - Socialist Labor Par. Two Pages from Roman History. 3rd ed. LC 87-61305. 104p. (Orig.). 1988. pap. 2.50 (*0-935534-45-8*) NY Labor News.
De Leon, David. Everything Is Changing: Contemporary U. S. Movements in Historical Perspective. LC 87-7323. 302p. 1988. 69.50 (*0-275-92892-6*, C2892, Praeger Pubs); pap. 17.95 (*0-275-92893-4*, B2893, Praeger Pubs) Greenwood.
De Leon Felipe, Poesias. Versos y Oraciones de Caminante, Libro II. 104p. 1.10 (*0-318-14316-X*) Hispanic Inst.
De Leon, Fidel. Espanol: Material para el Hispano.Tr. of Spanish for Native Speakers. (SPA.). 240p. (Orig.). (YA). 1996. pap. text 21.00 (*0-9654848-0-7*) Nuevos Horizontes.
De Leon, Fray L. La Perfecta Casada. San Jose, Lera J., ed. (Nueva Austral Ser.: Vol. 275). (SPA.). pap. text. write for info. (*0-318-69901-X*) Elliots Bks.
— La Perfecta Casada, No. 51. (SPA.). 152p. 1980. 20.95 (*0-8288-8555-9*) Fr & Eur.
— Poesias Completas. Escuela Salmantina. (Nueva Austral Ser.: Vol. 41). (SPA.). 1991. pap. text 24.95 (*84-239-1841-6*) Elliots Bks.
De Leon, Fray Luis. De Los Nombres de Cristo. unabridged ed. (SPA.). 187p. 1999. pap. 5.95 (*84-410-0006-9*, Pub. by Bookking Intl) Distribks Inc.
De Leon Freyre, Ponce, et al. Fifteen Hundred Seudonimos Modernos de la Literatura Espanola (1900-1942) 1990. reprint ed. 30.00 (*0-8115-3820-6*) Periodicals Srv.
De Leon, George. Community As Method: Therapeutic Communities for Special Populations & Special Settings. LC 96-26292. 328p. 1997. 69.50 (*0-275-94818-8*) Greenwood.
***De Leon, George.** The Therapeutic Community: Theory, Model & Method. LC 99-89660. 2000. write for info. (*0-8261-1349-4*) Springer Pub.
De Leon, Joanne, jt. auth. see Fomula, Liana Elena.
De Leon, Jorge G., tr. see McCaughrean, Geraldine.
De Leon, Juana P., jt. ed. see Rivera, Esteban R.
De Leon, Luis. Poesia. (SPA.). 129p. 1977. 11.95 (*0-8288-7120-5*, S7942) Fr & Eur.
— Poesias. (SPA.). 200p. 1953. 6.95 (*0-8288-7135-3*) Fr & Eur.
de Leon, Luis, see Luis de Leon, Fray.
De Leon, M. J., ed. An Atlas of Alzheimer's Disease. LC 99-32886. (Encyclopedia of Visual Medicine Ser.). (Illus.). 120p. 1999. 98.00 (*1-85070-912-2*) Prthnon Pub.
De Leon, M. Ponz. Familial & Hereditary Tumors. LC 94-13711. (Recent Results in Cancer Research Ser.: Vol. 136). 1994. 137.00 (*0-387-57633-9*) Spr-Verlag.
De Leon, Napoleon B. To the Spice Islands: A Novel of the Discoverers. LC 93-37080. 1994. 23.95 (*0-15-156296-2*) Harcourt.
De Leon, Pablo M. Sabotage in Air Transport Regulation. LC 92-18237. 282p. (C). 1992. lib. bdg. 118.00 (*0-7923-1795-5*) Kluwer Academic.
De Leon, Pablo M., ed. Air Transport Law & Policy in the 1990s: Controlling the Boom. 176p. (C). 1991. lib. bdg. 93.00 (*0-7923-1328-3*) Kluwer Academic.
De Leon, Pablo M. Mendes, see Masson-Zwaan, Tanja L., ed.
De Leon, Pablo M. Mendes, see Masson-Zwaan, Tanja L. & Mendes de Leon, Pablo M., eds.
De Leon Paiva, Anton P. In Search of the Wise One: A Sacred Journey. Clark, Mary, tr. from SPA. (Illus.). 128p. (Orig.). 1996. pap. 9.95 (*1-885394-16-0*) Bluestar Communs.
— The Wisdom of the Ancient One: An Inca Initiation. LC 94-40696. 121p. 1995. pap. 9.95 (*1-885394-09-8*) Bluestar Communs.
De Leon Pinelo, Antonio. Report Made in the Royal Council of the Indies. Comparato, Frank E., ed. Stone, Doris Z., tr. LC 84-81818. 1986. reprint ed. pap. 10.00 (*0-911437-05-3*) Labyrinthos.
De Leon, Ponce. El Arte de la Conversacion - el Arte de la Composicion. 5th ed. (C). 1991. 38.95 (*0-8384-3749-4*) Heinle & Heinle.
De Leon, Teadoro Bonzales, see Bonzales De Leon, Teadoro, pref.
De Leon, Thomas C. Belles, Beaux & Brains of the Sixties. LC 74-3937. (Women in America Ser.). (Illus.). 476p. 1974. reprint ed. 40.95 (*0-405-06084-X*) Ayer.
De Leonardis, David J. The Ethical Implications of Unity & the Divine in Nicholas of Cusa. LC 97-26585. (Cultural Heritage & Contemporary Change Series I: Vol. 10). 1997. pap. 17.50 (*1-56518-112-3*) Coun Res Values.
De Leone, Renato. High Performance Algorithms & Software in Nonlinear Optimization. LC 98-47443. (Applied Optimization Ser.). 1998. 192.00 (*0-7923-5483-4*) Kluwer Academic.
De Lepper, Marion J., ed. The Added Value of Geographical Information Systems in Public & Environmental Health. (GeoJournal Library). 370p. (C). 1995. lib. bdg. 169.00 (*0-7923-1887-0*) Kluwer Academic.
De Leprince de Beaumont. Belle et la Bete. (Folio - Cadet Bleu Ser.: No. 188).Tr. of Beauty & the Beast. (FRE., Illus.). 87p. (J). (gr. 1-5). 1989. pap. 11.95 (*2-07-031188-0*) Schoenhof.
De Lerin, Olivia S., tr. see Hustad, Donald P.
De Lerma, Dominique-Rene. Bibliography of Black Music: Afro-American Idioms, Vol. 2. LC 80-24681. (Encyclopedia of Black Music Ser.). 220p. 1981. lib. bdg. 65.00 (*0-313-23144-3*, DBI/02, Greenwood Pr) Greenwood.
— Bibliography of Black Music: Reference Materials, Vol. 1. LC 80-24681. (Encyclopedia of Black Music Ser.). 124p. 1981. lib. bdg. 55.00 (*0-313-21340-2*, DBI/01, Greenwood Pr) Greenwood.
— Bibliography of Black Music: Theory, Education, & Related Studies, Vol. 4. LC 80-24681. (Encyclopedia of Black Music Ser.). 254p. 1984. lib. bdg. 65.00 (*0-313-24229-1*, DBI/04, Greenwood Pr) Greenwood.
— Charles Edward Ives Eighteen Seventy-Four to Nineteen Fifty-Four: A Bibliography of His Music. LC 72-99083. 224p. reprint ed. 69.50 (*0-8357-9359-1*, 201538500093) Bks Demand.
— Igor Fedorovitch Stravinsky, 1882-1971: A Practical Guide to Publications of His Music. LC 74-79152. 168p. reprint ed. pap. 52.10 (*0-8357-5569-X*, 203519600093) Bks Demand.
— Reflections on Afro-American Music. With Contributions from Richard L. Abrams & Others. LC 72-619703. 279p. reprint ed. pap. 86.50 (*0-608-17124-7*, 202730100055) Bks Demand.
De Lery, Jean. History of a Voyage to the Land of Brazil Otherwise Called America. Whatley, Janet, tr. LC 90-33487. (Illus.). 266p. 1993. pap. 17.95 (*0-520-08274-5*, Pub. by U CA Pr) Cal Prin Full Svc.
***De les Gavarres, Angel.** Therese, the Little Child of God's Mercy: Her Spiritual Itinerary in the Light of Her Autobiographical Manuscripts. LC 99-30251. 1999. pap. 20.00 (*0-935216-69-3*) ICS Pubns.
De Lesdain. From Pekin to Sikkim: Through the Ordos, the Gobi Desert & Tibet. (C). 1995. reprint ed. 44.00 (*81-206-1046-6*, Pub. by Asian Educ Servs) S Asia.
De Lespinay, Philippe. Vintage Slot Cars. LC 99-25560. (Illus.). 96p. 1999. pap. text 14.95 (*0-7603-0566-8*) MBI Pubg.
De Lesseps, Ferdinand M. The Suez Canal: Letters & Documents Descriptive of Its Rise & Progress in 1854-56. LC 74-83185. (Islam & Mideast Ser.). 1976. reprint ed. 31.00 (*0-8420-1748-8*) Scholarly Res Inc.
De Lesseps, Jean. Travels in Kamtschatka, During the Years 1787 & 1788. LC 72-115557. (Russia Observed, Series I). 1970. reprint ed. 35.95 (*0-405-03043-6*) Ayer.
De Lestrieux, Elisabeth. The Art of Gardening in Pots. (Illus.). 207p. 1990. 49.50 (*1-85149-131-7*) Antique Collect.
De Leval, Georges, ed. Seizures & Overindebtedness in the European Union, Vol. CPES 1. LC 96-52726. (Civil Procedure in Europe Ser.). 1997. 186.00 (*90-411-0152-7*) Kluwer Law Intl.
***De Levie, Robert.** Aqueous Acid-Base Equilibria & Titrations. LC 99-39054. 96p. 1999. write for info. (*0-19-850617-1*) OUP.
— How to Use Excel in Analytical Chemistry: And General Scientific Data Analysis. LC 98-50543. (Illus.). 400p. (C). 1999. 100.00 (*0-521-64282-5*) Cambridge U Pr.
De Levie, Robert. How to Use Excelr in Analytical Chemistry: And General Scientific Data Analysis. (Illus.). 400p. (C). 1999. pap. 44.95 (*0-521-64484-4*) Cambridge U Pr.
— Principles of Quantitative Chemical Analysis. LC 96-75572. (C). 1996. text 69.25 (*0-07-016362-6*) McGraw.
— A Spreadsheet WorkBook for Quantitative Chemical Analysis. (C). 1992. spiral bd. 20.25 (*0-07-016274-3*) McGraw.
De Ley, Gerd, ed. African Proverbs. (Illus.). 135p. 1998. 17.50 (*0-7818-0691-7*) Hippocrene Bks.
— International Dictionary of Proverbs. 500p. 1998. 29.50 (*0-7818-0620-8*) Hippocrene Bks.
— International Dictionary of Proverbs. Darbo, Peter & Potter, David, trs. LC 97-28158. 500p. 1998. pap. 19.95 (*0-7818-0531-7*, 656) Hippocrene Bks.
— 1,000 Dutch Proverbs. LC 98-12002. 131p. 1998. pap. 11.95 (*0-7818-0616-X*) Hippocrene Bks.
De Ley, Herbert. The Movement of Thought: An Essay on Intellect in Seventeenth-Century France. LC 84-16128. 184p. 1985. text 24.95 (*0-252-01165-1*) U of Ill Pr.
De Leyn, P. Patterns & Site of Adenosine Triphosphate Catabolism in Lung Tissue. No. 67. 114p. (Orig.). 1993. pap. 47.50 (*90-6186-550-6*, Pub. by Leuven Univ) Coronet Bks.
De Lezcano. Fantasy Book, Vol. 1. (C). 1997. pap., student ed. 16.25 (*0-07-026329-9*) McGrw-H Hghr Educ.
— Fantasy Book, Vol. 2. (C). 1997. pap., student ed. 16.25 (*0-07-026332-9*) McGrw-H Hghr Educ.
— Fantasy Book, Vol. 3. (C). 1997. pap., student ed. 16.25 (*0-07-026335-3*) McGrw-H Hghr Educ.
De Li, Andres. Reportorio de los Tiempos. Delbrugge, Laura, ed. LC 99-39595. (Monografias A Ser.). 168p. 1999. 55.00 (*1-85566-067-9*) Boydell & Brewer.
De Liano, Ignacio G. Dali. LC 83-61925. (Illus.). 128p. 1993. 27.50 (*0-8478-0522-0*, Pub. by Rizzoli Intl) St Martin.
De Libera, Alain, jt. auth. see Hoenen, Maarten J.
De Liefde, Jacob. Great Dutch Admirals. (Illus.). 1977. 30.95 (*0-8369-2603-X*) Ayer.
De-Light, Dominique & Thomas, Polly. Trinidad & Tobago. (Rough Guide Ser.). (Illus.). 288p. 1998. pap. text 16.95 (*1-85828-379-5*, Pub. by Rough Guides) Penguin Putnam.
De Ligne. Les Enlevments, Ou la Vie de Chateau en 1785. Guy, ed. (Exeter French Texts Ser.: Vol. 54). (FRE.). 80p. Date not set. pap. text 19.95 (*0-85989-206-9*, Pub. by Univ Exeter Pr) Northwestern U Pr.
— Oeuvres Choisies du Prince de Ligne: Nouvelle Anthologie Critique. Guy, Basil, ed. (Stanford French & Italian Studies: No. 13). (FRE.). xlvi, 282p. 1978. pap. 56.50 (*0-915838-28-1*) Anma Libri.
De Ligne, Charles-Joseph. Coup d'Oeil at Beloeil & a Great Number of European Gardens. Guy, Basil, ed. & tr. by. LC 89-30766. (Illus.). 304p. 1991. 110.00 (*0-520-04668-4*, Pub. by U CA Pr) Cal Prin Full Svc.
De Ligt, L. Fairs & Markets in the Roman Empire: Economic & Social Aspects of Periodic Trade in a Pre-Industrial Society. (Dutch Monographs on Ancient History & Archaeology: Vol. XI). x, 315p. 1993. 94.00 (*90-5063-146-0*, Pub. by Gieben) J Benjamins Pubng Co.
de Liguori, Alfonso Maria & Ulanov, Barry. The Way of Saint Alphonsus Liguori: Selected Writings on the Spiritual Life. rev. ed. LC 98-47863. 1999. pap. 18.95 (*0-7648-0382-4*, Liguori Triumph) Liguori Pubns.
De Liguori, Alphonsus. The Sermons of St. Alphonsus Liguori for All the Sundays of the Year. LC 82-50894. 408p. 1992. reprint ed. pap. 16.50 (*0-89555-163-4*) TAN Bks Pubs.
De Lillo, Nicholas. A First Course in Computer Science with ADA. 13th ed. 704p. (C). 1992. text 44.95 (*0-256-12538-4*, Irwn McGrw-H) McGrw-H Hghr Educ.
De Lillo, Nicholas J. A First Course in Computer Science with ADA. LC 92-10700. 560p. (C). 1992. text 44.95 (*0-256-12364-0*, Irwn McGrw-H) McGrw-H Hghr Educ.
De Lillo, S., et al. Field Theory & Collective Phenomena. LC 96-145539. 616p. 1995. text 95.00 (*981-02-1279-8*) World Scientific Pub.
De Lima, Agnes. Our Enemy, the Child. LC 78-89172. (American Education: Its Men, Institutions, & Ideas. Series 1). 1975. reprint ed. 23.95 (*0-405-01410-4*) Ayer.
de Lima, Antonia Pedroso, jt. ed. see De Pina-Cabral, Joao.
De Lima, Arthur. Echoes of Oritumbe. 282p. 1986. 30.00 (*0-7223-1974-6*, Pub. by A H S Ltd) St Mut.
— Oritumbre. 194p. 1987. 35.00 (*0-7223-1539-2*, Pub. by A H S Ltd) St Mut.
De Lima Greene, Alison, ed. see Agee, William C.
De Lima, Hilda. Cuentos De Horror P/ Ninos.Tr. of Scary Stories for Kids. (SPA., Illus.). 132p. (Orig.). (J). (gr. 4-7). 1997. pap. text 7.98 (*968-403-948-4*) Selector.
De Lima, Sara N., ed. see Aspen Reference Group Staff.
***De Lint, Charles.** The Buffalo Man. (Illus.). 48p. 1999. pap. 12.00 (*1-892284-50-2*) Subtrmean Pr.
De Lint, Charles. The Dreaming Place. LC 90-488. (Dragonflight Ser.). (Illus.). 144p. (YA). (gr. 7 up). 1990. lib. bdg. 14.95 (*0-689-31571-6*) Atheneum Yung Read.
— Dreams Underfoot. 480p. 1994. mass mkt. 4.99 (*0-8125-1621-4*, Pub. by Tor Bks) St Martin.
***De Lint, Charles.** Drinking down Moon. 1999. mass mkt. write for info. (*0-8125-3411-5*) Tor Bks.
— Forests of the Heart. 2000. pap. write for info. (*0-312-87568-1*) St Martin.
— Forests of the Heart. LC 00-27679. 400p. 2000. 27.95 (*0-312-86519-8*, Pub. by Tor Bks) St Martin.
De Lint, Charles. Greenmantle. LC 98-6195. 384p. 1998. pap. 14.95 (*0-312-86510-4*) St Martin.
— Into the Green. 384p. 1993. 19.95 (*0-312-85672-5*, Pub. by Tor Bks) St Martin.
— Into the Green. 256p. 1995. mass mkt. 4.99 (*0-8125-2249-4*, Pub. by Tor Bks) St Martin.
— The Ivory & the Horn. 320p. write for info. (*0-614-09437-2*); 21.95 (*0-614-09438-0*) Tor Bks.
— The Ivory & the Horn. 320p. 1995. 21.95 (*0-312-85573-7*) Tor Bks.
— The Ivory & the Horn. 320p. 1996. pap. write for info. (*0-614-05537-7*); mass mkt. 5.99 (*0-8125-3408-5*, Pub. by Tor Bks) St Martin.
***De Lint, Charles.** Jack Giant Killer. 1999. mass mkt. write for info. (*0-8125-3410-7*) Tor Bks.
De Lint, Charles. Jack of Kinrowan. 480p. 1995. pap. 6.99 (*0-8125-3898-6*, Pub. by Tor Bks) St Martin.
— Jack of Kinrowan. 1999. pap. 14.95 (*0-312-86959-2*, Pub. by Tor Bks) St Martin.
— The Little Country. 608p. 1993. mass mkt. 5.99 (*0-8125-2248-6*, Pub. by Tor Bks) St Martin.
— Memory & Dream. 448p. 1995. mass mkt. 6.99 (*0-8125-3407-7*, Pub. by Tor Bks) St Martin.
— Moonheart. 496p. 1994. pap. 13.95 (*0-312-89004-4*) Orb NYC.
De Lint, Charles. Moonheart. 1992. mass mkt. write for info. (*0-8125-1622-2*) Tor Bks.
— Moonlight & Vines. 480p. 1999. mass mkt. 6.99 (*0-8125-6549-5*, Pub. by Tor Bks) St Martin.
De Lint, Charles. Moonlight & Vines: A Newford Collection. LC 98-44610. 384p. 1999. 24.95 (*0-312-86518-X*, Pub. by Tor Bks) St Martin.
— Paperjack. (Illus.). 72p. 1992. boxed set 190.00 (*0-941826-21-X*) Cheap St.
***De Lint, Charles.** Shelf Talker. 1998. mass mkt. write for info. (*0-8125-8924-6*) Tor Bks.
De Lint, Charles. Someplace to Be Flying. LC 97-37443. 380p. 1998. text 24.95 (*0-312-85849-3*) St Martin.
— Someplace to Be Flying. LC 97-37433. 560p. 1999. mass mkt. 6.99 (*0-8125-5158-3*, Pub. by Tor Bks) St Martin.
— Spiritwalk. 416p. 1993. mass mkt. 4.99 (*0-8125-1620-6*, Pub. by Tor Bks) St Martin.
***De Lint, Charles.** Summerborn Legacy. 2000. mass mkt. 4.50 (*0-380-76201-3*) Morrow Avon.
— Svaha. 2000. text 14.95 (*0-312-87650-5*) St Martin.
De Lint, Charles. Svaha. 320p. 1994. reprint ed. pap. 4.50 (*0-8125-3409-3*, Pub. by Tor Bks) St Martin.
— Trader. LC 96-30646. 352p. 1997. 24.95 (*0-312-85847-7*, Pub. by Tor Bks) St Martin.
— Trader, Vol. 1. 1998. mass mkt. 6.99 (*0-8125-5157-5*, Pub. by Tor Bks) St Martin.
— Yarrow. LC 97-24803. 288p. 1997. pap. 12.95 (*0-312-86393-4*) St Martin.
De Lint, Charles, et al. Destination Unknown. Crowther, Peter, ed. (Orig.). 1997. pap. 14.99 (*1-56504-941-1*, 11941, Borealis) White Wolf.
De Lisa, Jeannette, ed. Buddy Guy: Slippin In. 136p. 1995. pap. text 22.95 (*0-89724-657-8*, GF0666) Wrner Bros.
— John P. Kee & the New Life Community Choir: A Special Christmas Gift. 56p. (YA). 1997. pap. 16.95 (*1-57623-973-X*, PF9715) Wrner Bros.
De L'Isle-Adam, Auguste de Villiers, see Villiers De L'Isle-Adam, Auguste de.
De L'Isle-Adam, Villers. Eve of the Future Eden. Rose, Marilyn G., tr.Tr. of L'Eve future. 260p. 1981. pap. 15.00 (*0-87291-207-8*) Coronado Pr.
— Eve of the Future Eden. Rose, Marilyn G., tr. from FRE.Tr. of L'Eve future. 260p. (C). 1981. 30.00 (*0-87291-150-0*) Coronado Pr.
De Lisle, Carol R., ed. see Williams, Andrew M.
De Lisle, Charles-Rene-Marie Leconte, see Leconte De Lisle, Charles-Rene-Marie.
De Lisle, Harold F. The Natural History of Monitor Lizards. LC 95-3063. 240p. 1996. 53.50 (*0-89464-897-7*) Krieger.
De Lisle, James, ed. Appraisal, Market Analysis, & Public Policy in Real Estate: Essays in Honor of James A. Graaskamp. LC 93-16953. 512p. (C). 1994. lib. bdg. 133.50 (*0-7923-9344-9*) Kluwer Academic.
***De Lisle, Leanda & Stanford, Peter.** The Catholics & Their Houses (in Britain) (Illus.). 116p. 2000. reprint ed. text 30.00 (*0-7881-9231-0*) DIANE Pub.
De Lisle, Mark. Navy Seal Exercises: Total Body Workout. Wolf, R. J., ed. (Illus.). 116p. (Orig.). 1996. reprint ed. pap. text 19.95 (*0-9654093-0-9*) Cutting Edge Fit.
— The Navy SEAL Workout. LC 97-38946. (Illus.). 160p. 1998. pap. 14.95 (*0-8092-2902-1*, 290210, Contemporary Bks) NTC Contemp Pub Co.
De Liso, Nicola, jt. auth. see Antonelli, Gilberto.
***de Lissovoy, Noah.** Spark. 32p. 1999. pap. 4.00 (*1-893032-16-7*, Pub. by Jensen Daniels) SPD-Small Pr Dist.
De Little, Rodney J. The Windmills of England. (Illus.). 192p. 59.50 (*0-9529930-0-7*) Colwood Pr.
***de Llover, Claudia Cordova & Eisenthal, Zitta Waleska, eds.** Trajectory of the "Message to the Men of the New Earth" & of the Messenger. Napoli, Giuseppe & Elmo, Francis, trs. from SPA. 216p. 2000. pap. write for info. (*0-936707-07-0*) Action Life Pubns.
De Loaiza, Robert, tr. see Ferry, Luc.
de Loarte, Gaspar, et al. Meditations, 1596-98. LC 77-379708. (English Recusant Literature Ser.). 102 p. 1977. write for info. (*0-85967-397-9*) Ashgate Pub Co.
De Loeper, Nathalie. Dicomarche: Dictionnaire Pratique du Marche. (FRE.). 504p. 1991. pap. 59.95 (*0-7859-8599-9*, 201016699x) Fr & Eur.
De Logy, Nancy N., jt. auth. see De Bernardo, Mark A.
De Lollis, Nicholas J. Adhesives: Adherends, Adhesion. LC 79-13871. 352p. 1980. lib. bdg. 40.50 (*0-88275-981-7*) Krieger.
De Lolme, J. L. & Machelon, Jean-Pierre. The Constitution of England & les Idees Politiques De J.L. De Lolme: 1741-1806, 2 vols. Mayer, J. P., ed. LC 78-67366. (European Political Thought Ser.). (ENG & FRE.). 1980. reprint ed. lib. bdg. 55.95 (*0-405-11714-0*) Ayer.
De Lolme, Jean L. The Constitution of England or an Account of the English Government: In Which It Is Compared Both with the Republican Form of Government & the Other Monarchies in Europe. xxvi, 556p. 1998. reprint ed. 175.00 (*1-56169-434-7*) Gaunt.
De Lombez, Ambroise. A Treatise on Interior Peace. Seton, Elizabeth A., tr. from FRE. LC 95-45564. 200p. (Orig.). 1996. pap. 10.95 (*0-8189-0715-0*) Alba.
De Lomellini, C. A. Antimacassars. 64p. (C). 1988. 25.00 (*0-947612-03-3*, Pub. by Rivelin Grapheme Pr) St Mut.
— Dreams of Samarkand. (C). 1988. 30.00 (*0-904524-30-2*, Pub. by Rivelin Grapheme Pr) St Mut.
De Lone, Susan T. Love, Loss & Healing: A Woman's Guide to Transforming Grief. Columbus, Marge, ed. (Illus.). 232p. 1998. pap. 14.95 (*1-889531-01-4*) Sibyl Pubns.
De Long, David, ed. Frank Lloyd Wright & the Living City. LC 99-510600. (Illus.). 336p. 1999. 65.00 (*88-8118-392-7*, Pub. by Skira IT) Abbeville Pr.
De Long, David G., ed. Frank Lloyd Wright: Designs for an American Landscape, 1922-1932. LC 95-30509. (Illus.). 208p. 1996. 45.00 (*0-8109-3981-9*, Pub. by Abrams) Time Warner.
De Long, Janice A. & Schewdt, Rachel E. Core Collection for Small Libraries: An Annotated Bibliography of Books for Children & Young Adults. LC 96-42267. 240p. 1997. 29.50 (*0-8108-3252-6*) Scarecrow.
De Long, Patrick D. Art in the Humanities. 2nd ed. (C). 1970. pap. text 20.50 (*0-13-046979-3*) P-H.
De Long-Tonelli, Beverly J., tr. see Teitelboim, Volodia.

D

An Asterisk (*) at the beginning of an entry indicates that the title is appearing for the first time.

De Longchamps, Joanne. The Hungry Lions, 25-- LC 74-19783. 60p. 1975. reprint ed. lib. bdg. 49.50 (*0-8371-7806-1*, DEHL, Greenwood Pr) Greenwood.
— Torn by Light: Selected Poems. Griffin, Shaun T., ed. LC 92-40531. (Western Literature Ser.). (Illus.). 176p. 1993. 24.95 (*0-87417-218-7*); pap. 13.95 (*0-87417-217-9*) U of Nev Pr.
***De Loo, Tessa.** The Twins. Levitt, Ruth, tr. from DUT. LC 00-20009. 320p. 2000. 25.00 (*1-56947-200-9*) Soho Press.
De Looff, L. A. Information Systems Outsourcing Decision Making: A Managerial Approach. LC 96-37736. (Series in Information Technology Management). (Illus.). 288p. (C). 1997. pap. text 39.95 (*1-878289-40-3*) Idea Group Pub.
De Loor, G. P., ed. Radar Remote Sensing, Vol. 1. (Remote Sensing Reviews Ser.: Vol. 1, No. 1). 186p. 1983. pap. text 195.00 (*3-7186-0132-X*) Gordon & Breach.
De Loore, B. C., et al, eds. Late Stages of Stellar Evolution: Computational Methods in Astrophysical Hydrodynamics: Proceedings of the Astrophysical School II Organized by the European Astrophysics Doctoral Network at Ponte de Lima, Portugal, 11-23 September 1989. (Lecture Notes in Physics Ser.: Vol. 373). viii, 390p. 1991. 26.95 (*0-387-53620-5*) Spr-Verlag.
De Loore, Camiel W. Structure & Evolution of Single & Binary Stars. (Astrophysics & Space Science Library). 480p. (C). 1992. pap. text 113.00 (*0-7923-1844-7*) Kluwer Academic.
De Loore, Camiel W., et al, eds. Luminous Stars & Associations in Galaxies. 1986. pap. text 82.50 (*90-277-2273-0*); lib. bdg. 194.00 (*90-277-2272-2*) Kluwer Academic.
De Loore, Camiel W. & Doom, C. Structure & Evolution of Single & Binary Stars. LC 92-10276. (Astrophysics & Space Science Library). 480p. (C). 1992. lib. bdg. 188.00 (*0-7923-1768-8*) Kluwer Academic.
De Loore, Camiel W., jt. ed. see Conti, Peter S.
De Loore, Camiel W., jt. ed. see Lamers, Henny G.
De Loos, Onesime-Henri & Chaumette, Pierre G. La Diademe Des Sages, Ou Demonstration de la Nature Inferieure: Dans Lequel on Trouvera une Analyse Raisonnee Du Livre Des Erreurs et De la Verite & Clef Des Erreurs et De la Verite, Vol. VI. Amadou, Robert, ed. (FRE.). xvi, 246p. reprint ed. write for info. (*0-318-71417-5*) G Olms Pubs.
De Loos, W. S. & Op den Velde, W., eds. Psychotrauma. (Psychotherapy & Psychosomatics Ser.: Vol. 57, No. 4, 1992). (Illus.). iv, 72p. 1992. pap. 22.75 (*3-8055-5662-4*) S Karger.
De Looze, Laurence. Pseudo-Autobiography in the Fourteenth Century: Juan Ruiz, Guillaume de Machaut, Jean Froissart, & Geoffrey Chaucer. LC 96-45075. 232p. 1997. 49.95 (*0-8130-1507-3*) U Press Fla.
De Lope, Manuel. El Libro de Piel de Tiburon. 1996, pap. text 11.95 (*84-204-4853-2*) Santillana.
De Lopez, Awilda P. & Ortiz, Ernesto R. En la Calle Estabas: La Vida En una Institucion de Menores. 2nd ed. 137p. 1985. 5.00 (*0-8477-2493-X*) U of PR Pr.
De Lore, Marvin D. Men--Research on Their Attitudes, Lifestyles & Relations: Index of New Information. (Illus.). 160p. Date not set. 44.50 (*0-7883-1922-1*); pap. 44.50 (*0-7883-1923-X*) ABBE Pubs Assn.
De Lorenzo, David L., ed. see Gallaudet, Edward M.
De Lorenzo, Leonardo. My Complete Story of the Flute. rev. ed. LC 92-8525. (Instrument, the Performer, the Music Ser.). (Illus.). 675p. 1992. reprint ed. pap. 35.00 (*0-89672-285-6*) Tex Tech Univ Pr.
De Lorenzo, Lois. Gold Fever: The Art of Panning & Sluicing. LC 79-90416. (Illus.). 80p. 1989. 5.95 (*0-935182-00-4*) Gem Guides Bk.
De Lorenzo, Yusuf T., tr. see Al-Ghazali, Muhammad.
De Lorenzo, Yusuf T., tr. see Ghazali, Muhammad.
De Lorme, Roland L., jt. auth. see Scott, James W.
De Lorre, C. & Willis, A., eds. Wolf-Rayet Stars: Observations, Physics, Evolution. 1982. pap. text 93.00 (*90-277-1470-3*); lib. bdg. 187.00 (*90-277-1469-X*) Kluwer Academic.
***De Lorris, Guillame & De Meun, Jean.** The Romance of the Rose. Horgan, Frances, tr. (Oxford World's Classics Ser.). 374p. 1999. pap. 13.95 (*0-19-283948-9*) OUP.
De Lorris, Guillaume. Roman de la Rose. Nichols, Stephen G., Jr., ed. LC 67-25114. (Medieval French Literature Ser.). (FRE.). (C). 1967. pap. text 9.95 (*0-89197-496-2*) Irvington.
De Lorris, Guillaume & Clopinel, J. The Romance of the Rose, 3 vols. Ellis, Frederick S., tr. LC 74-154119. reprint ed. 155.00 (*0-404-09640-9*) AMS Pr.
De Lorris, Guillaume & De Meun, Jean. Roman de la Rose. 293p. 1983. 9.95 (*0-8288-7437-9*) Fr & Eur.
— Roman de la Rose. (Folio Ser.: No. 1518). (FRE.). pap. 13.95 (*2-07-037518-8*) Schoenhof.
— The Romance of the Rose. 3rd ed. Dahlberg, Charles, tr. from FRE. LC 95-11748. 510p. 1996. pap. text 18.95 (*0-691-04456-2*, Pub. by Princeton U Pr) Cal Prin Full Svc.
De Lorris, Guillaume & De Meur, Jean. Roman de la Rose, 5 tomes. Langlois, E., ed. 199.00 (*0-685-34019-8*) Fr & Eur.
De Lorris, Guillaume, jt. auth. see Chaucer, Geoffrey.
De Lory, Peter. The Wild & the Innocent: A Story & Photographs. (CMP Bulletin Ser.). (Illus.). 48p. (Orig.). 1987. pap. 10.00 (*0-9619038-2-1*) Cal Mus Photo.
De los Angeles Pozas, Maria. Industrial Restructuring in Mexico: Corporate Adaptation, Technological Innovation, & Changing Patterns of Industrial Relations in Monterrey. (Monographs: No. 38). 110p. (C). 1993. pap. 13.95 (*1-878367-15-3*, MN-38) UCSD Ctr US-Mex.
De Los Condes, Santob De Carrion, see De Carrion De Los Condes, Santob.
De los Mar, Richard. Dark Migrations. 48p. (Orig.). 1993. pap. 7.95 (*1-879934-17-5*) St Andrews NC.
De Los Montero, Patricia Espinosa, see Espinosa De Los Montero, Patricia.
De Los Reyes, Isabelo. El Folk-Lore Filipino. Dizon, Salud C. & Imson, Maria E., trs. 660p. (Orig.). 1995. pap. text 25.00 (*971-542-038-9*, Pub. by U of Philippines Pr) UH Pr.
De los Reyes, Paulina. The Rural Poor: Agrarian Changes & Survival Strategies in Chile 1973-1989. (Uppsala Studies in Economic History: No. 34). 196p. (Orig.). 1992. pap. 47.50 (*91-554-2961-0*) Coronet Bks.
De Los Rios, Emilio. Atlas of Therapeutic Proctology. 185p. 1984. text 165.00 (*0-7216-3036-7*, W B Saunders Co) Harcrt Hlth Sci Grp.
De los Rios, Fernando, tr. see Rousseau, Jean-Jacques.
De Los Rios, Francisco Giner, see Giner de Los Rios, Francisco.
de los Rios, Giner. Por Tierras De Espana. (C). 1995. pap. text 8.00 (*0-03-017105-9*) Harcourt Coll Pubs.
De los Rios, Luis B. La Arquitectura del Humo: Una Reconstruccion del "Romancero Gitano" de Fredrico Garcia Lorca. LC 86-50074. (Series A: Monagrafias, CXVII). (SPA.). 1986. 58.00 (*0-7293-0232-6*, Pub. by Tamesis Bks Ltd) Boydell & Brewer.
De Los Rios, Maria M. La Termoluminiscencia en el Fechamiento de Sitios Arqueologicos. 191p. 1989. pap. 6.50 (*968-6068-07-4*, IN004) UPLAAP.
De Los-Santos. English-Navajo Children's Picture Dictionary. LC 91-53028. 1995. 19.95 (*0-912586-72-9*) Dine College Pr.
De los Santos, Marisa. From the Bones Out. LC 99-50918. (James Dickey Contemporary Poetry Ser.). 90p. 2000. 15.95 (*1-57003-322-6*); pap. 9.95 (*1-57003-323-4*) U of SC Pr.
De Lotbiniere-Harwood, Susanne. Re-Belle et Infidele/The Body Bilingual: Translation As a Re-Writing in the Feminine. (ENG & FRE.). 176p. pap. 12.95 (*0-88961-166-1*, Pub. by Womens Pr) LPC InBook.
De Lotbiniere-Harwood, Susanne, tr. see Gauvin, Lise.
De Loubriel, Estela C. La Formacion Del Pueblo Puertorriqueno. (SPA.). 585p. 1989. 23.95 (*0-8477-0887-X*) U of PR Pr.
— The Formation of the Puerto Rican People: Catalonians, Balearic Islanders & Valencianos. (Puerto Rico Ser.). 1979. lib. bdg. 59.95 (*0-8490-2920-1*) Gordon Pr.
De Lourdes Cabrera, Yvette. Decima in Puerto Rico: Historical Survey & Analysis of the Ten Line Stanza Composition As an Expression of the Puerto Rican Spirit. (Puerto Rico Ser.). 1979. lib. bdg. 59.95 (*0-8490-2905-8*) Gordon Pr.
De Lubac, Henri. At the Service of the Church: Henri Lubac Reflects on the Circumstances That Occasioned His Writings. Englund, Anne, tr. from FRE. LC 92-71933. (Communio Bk.). 411p. 1993. pap. 19.95 (*0-89870-414-6*) Ignatius Pr.
***De Lubac, Henri.** Augustinianism & Modern Theology. (Milestones in Catholic Theology Ser.). 288p. 2000. pap. text 29.50 (*0-8245-1802-0*, Pub. by Crossroad NY) Natl Bk Netwk.
De Lubac, Henri. Catholicism: Christ & the Common Destiny of Man. rev. ed. Sheppard, Lancelot C. & Englund, Elizabeth, trs. from FRE. LC 88-80752. 443p. 1988. pap. 17.95 (*0-89870-203-8*) Ignatius Pr.
— Christian Faith. Arnandez, Richard, tr. from FRE. LC 84-80903. Orig. Title: La Foi Chretienne. (Illus.). 353p. (Orig.). 1986. pap. 18.95 (*0-89870-053-1*) Ignatius Pr.
— The Discovery of God. (Resourcement Ser.). 231p. 1996. pap. 18.00 (*0-8028-4089-2*) Eerdmans.
— The Drama of Atheist Humanism. Sebanc, Mark, tr. from FRE. LC 92-75066. (Communio Bk.). 539p. (Orig.). 1995. pap. 24.95 (*0-89870-443-X*) Ignatius Pr.
— Medieval Exegesis, Vol. 1. Sebanc, Mark, tr. from FRE. LC 97-32802. (Ressourcement Ser.). 467p. 1998. pap. 45.00 (*0-8028-4145-7*) Eerdmans.
— The Motherhood of the Church. Englund, Sergia, tr. from FRE. LC 81-83857.Tr. of Les/Eglises particulieres & La maternite de l'eglise. 363p. (Orig.). 1983. pap. 14.95 (*0-89870-014-0*) Ignatius Pr.
— Mystery of the Supernatural. Sheed, Rosemary, tr. LC 97-42442. 300p. 1998. pap. 27.50 incl. audio (*0-8245-1699-0*, Crsrd) Crossroad NY.
— Paradoxes of Faith. Simon, Paule et al, trs. LC 86-62928. Orig. Title: Paradoxes, Nouveaux Paradoxes. (FRE.). 236p. (Orig.). 1986. pap. 11.95 (*0-89870-132-5*) Ignatius Pr.
***De Lubac, Henri.** The Sources of Revelation. 242p. 2000. pap. 29.95 (*0-8245-1871-3*, Pub. by Crossroad NY) Natl Bk Netwk.
De Lubac, Henri. The Splendor of the Church. LC 86-82080. 382p. 1986. pap. 16.95 (*0-89870-120-1*) Ignatius Pr.
— Theology in History. LC 93-78537. 615p. 1996. pap. text 29.95 (*0-89870-472-3*) Ignatius Pr.
De Lubicz, Isha S. The Opening of the Way: A Practical Guide to the Mystical Teachings of Ancient Egypt. 214p. 1995. pap. 14.95 (*0-89281-572-8*) Inner Tradit.
De Lubicz Milosz, Oscar V. The Noble Traveller: The Life & Selected Writings of Oscar V. de Lubicz Milosz. Gascoyne, David et al, trs. from FRE. LC 84-25029. (Illus.). 504p. (Orig.). 1985. 24.95 (*0-940262-15-0*, Lindisfarne); pap. 14.95 (*0-940262-16-9*, Lindisfarne) Anthroposophic.
De Lubicz, R. A. Schwaller, see Schwaller De Lubicz, R. A.
De Luca, A. & Varricchio, S. Finiteness & Regularity in Semigroups & Formal Languages. Brauer, W. et al, eds. LC 98-42554. (Monographs in Theoretical Computer Science. A Series of EATCS). 190p. 1998. 44.95 (*3-540-63771-0*) Spr-Verlag.
De Luca, Anthony R. Personality, Power, & Politics: The Historical Significance of Napoleon, Bismarck, Lenin, & Hitler. 133p. 1983. pap. 13.95 (*0-87073-617-5*) Schenkman Bks Inc.
De Luca, Araldo, photos by. Alexandria: The Site & the History. LC 93-25746. (Illus.). 126p. (C). 1993. text 37.50 (*0-8147-7986-7*) NYU Pr.
De Luca, Diana. Botanica Erotica: Arousing Body, Mind & Spirit. LC 98-20823. (Illus.). 144p. 1998. 24.00 (*0-89281-790-9*, Heal Arts VT) Inner Tradit.
***De Luca, Erri.** Sea Of Memory. Beth Archer, Brombert, tr. LC 99-28848. 118p. 1999. 22.00 (*0-88001-678-7*) HarpC.
De Luca, Giuseppe, jt. auth. see Moses, Julian M.
De Luca, J. English-French Dictionary of Telecommunications. 401p. 1988. pap. 114.00 (*2-225-81063-X*, Pub. by Masson) IBD Ltd.
De Luca, Joanne. English-French Dictionary of Telecommunications & the Internet. (ENG & FRE.). 400p. 1997. pap. 150.00 incl. cd-rom (*0-7859-9502-1*) Fr & Eur.
De Luca, Joanne, jt. auth. see Lopiano-Misdom, Janine.
De Luca, Johanne. Dictionary of Telecommunications: Dictionnaire des Telecommunications: Anglais-Francais. (ENG & FRE.). 408p. 1988. pap. 125.00 (*0-8288-0180-0*, M972) Fr & Eur.
De Luca, L. & Bruni, Mary-Ann S. Unemployment & Labour Market Flexibility: Italy. (Illus.). xiv, 214p. (Orig.). 1993. pap. 27.00 (*92-2-108266-0*) Intl Labour Office.
De Luca, Sara. Dancing the Cows Home: A Wisconsin Girlhood. LC 95-42676. (Midwest Reflections Ser.). x, 232p. 1996. 24.95 (*0-87351-324-X*); pap. 15.95 (*0-87351-325-8*) Minn Hist.
De Luca, Teresa. A Distant Thunder. 624p. 1991. mass mkt. 5.95 (*0-380-71086-2*, Avon Bks) Morrow Avon.
De Luca, Vincent A. Words of Eternity: Blake & the Poetics of the Sublime. (Illus.). 280p. 1991. text 42.50 (*0-691-06874-7*, Pub. by Princeton U Pr) Cal Prin Full Svc.
***De Lucas, A.** Assessment of RELAP5/MOD3.2 Against a Main Steam Isolation Valve Closure at Trillo 1 Nuclear Power Plant. 45p. 2000. pap. 4.50 (*0-16-059100-7*) USGPO.
De Lucca, J. L. Economics Dictionary. 900p. write for info. (*0-444-82448-0*) Elsevier.
— Elsevier's Dictionary of Insurance & Risk Prevention. (ENG, FRE, GER, POR & SPA.). 430p. 1992. 295.00 (*0-8288-9257-1*) Fr & Eur.
De Lucca, J. L., compiled by. Elsevier's Dictionary of Climatology & Meteorology: In English, French, Spanish, Italian, Portuguese & German. LC 94-6656. (ENG, FRE, GER, ITA & POR.). 334p. 1994. 210.50 (*0-444-81532-5*) Elsevier.
— Elsevier's Dictionary of Insurance & Risk Prevention. LC 92-31429. (ENG, FRE, GER, POR & SPA.). 442p. 1992. 210.50 (*0-444-89614-7*) Elsevier.
De Lucca, Robert, tr. see Bruno, Giordano.
De Lucca, Robert, tr. see Weeks, Christopher, ed.
De Lucchi, Lorna, tr. An Anthology of Italian Poems, 13th-19th Century. LC 66-30496. (ENG & ITA.). 1922. pap. 21.00 (*0-8196-0198-5*) Biblo.
De Luce, Judith & Wilder, H. T., eds. Language in Primates: Perspectives & Implications. (Language & Communication Ser.: Vol. 11). (Illus.). xi, 198p. 1983. 92.95 (*0-387-90798-X*); pap. 36.00 (*0-387-90799-8*) Spr-Verlag.
De Lucrezia, Domizio. Felt Hat: Joseph Beuys a Life Told. LC 98-153285. 1997. pap. 24.95 (*88-8158-065-9*, Pub. by Charta) Dist Art Pubs.
De Lue, Willard. The Story of Walpole, Massachusetts, 1724-1924. 374p. 1993. reprint ed. lib. bdg. 41.00 (*0-8328-3141-7*) Higginson Bk Co.
De Luise, Fulvia & Farinetti, Giuseppe. Felicita Socratica. (Europaea Memoria Ser.: Bd. 5). 323p. 1997. 65.00 (*3-487-10251-X*) G Olms Pubs.
De Luna, A. Bayes. Textbook of Clinical Electrocardiography. 1987. pap. text 155.50 (*0-89838-835-X*); lib. bdg. 253.50 (*0-89838-826-0*) Kluwer Academic.
De Luna, A. Bayes, et al, eds. Sudden Cardiac Death. (C). 1990. lib. bdg. 196.50 (*0-7923-0716-X*) Kluwer Academic.
De Luna, A. J., ed. Therapeutics in Cardiology. (Developments in Cardiovascular Medicine Ser.). 700p. (C). 1988. text 325.00 (*0-89838-981-X*) Kluwer Academic.
de Luna, Antonio Baybes, see Baybes de Luna, Antonio.
de Luna, Antonio Bayes, see Bayes de Luna, Antonio.
De Luna, M., jt. ed. see Yabes-Almirante, C.
De Luna, Phyllis K. Public Versus Private Power During the Truman Administration: A Study of Fair Deal Liberalism. (Modern American History Ser.: Vol. 1). XII, 253p. (C). 1998. text 49.95 (*0-8204-3144-3*) P Lang Pubng.
De Luxan, Diego P. Expedition into New Mexico Made by Antonio De Espejo 1582-1583. Hammond, George P., ed. LC 67-24713. (Quivira Society Publications, Vol. 1). 1967. reprint ed. 19.95 (*0-405-00088-X*) Ayer.
De Ly, Filip. International Business Law & Lex Mercatoria. LC 92-15827. 362p. 1992. 142.75 (*0-444-88971-X*, North Holland) Elsevier.
De Lynam, Alicia Garcia. When the World Was New. (Illus.). 32p. (J). 1999. 11.99 (*0-8054-1880-6*) Broadman.
***De, Lynn.** Principles of Spiritualism: The Only Introduction You'll Ever Need. (Illus.). 160p. 1999. pap. 11.00 (*0-7225-3813-8*) Thorsons PA.
De Lys, Claudia. How the World Weds: The Story of Marriage, Adultery, & Divorce. LC 97-15329. 279p. 1997. reprint ed. lib. bdg. 44.00 (*0-7808-0268-3*) Omnigraphics Inc.
De Maar, Harko G. History of Modern English Romanticism. LC 72-141657. (Studies in Poetry: No. 38). 1969. reprint ed. lib. bdg. 75.00 (*0-8383-0538-5*) M S G Haskell Hse.
— A History of Modern English Romanticism. (BCL1-PR English Literature Ser.). 246p. 1992. reprint ed. lib. bdg. 79.00 (*0-7812-7026-X*) Rprt Serv.
De Mably, Gabriel B. Lettres a Madame la Marquise de Pompadour sur l'Opera. LC 76-43925. (Music & Theatre in France in the 17th & 18th Centuries Ser.). reprint ed. 39.50 (*0-404-60169-3*) AMS Pr.
De Macedo, Jorge B., jt. ed. see Bliss, Christopher.
De Machaut, Guillaume, see Guillaume de Machaut.
De Madariaga, Isabel. Catherine the Great: A Short History. LC 90-43666. 244p. (C). 1991. 37.50 (*0-300-04845-9*) Yale U Pr.
— Catherine the Great: A Short History. (Illus.). 244p. (C). 1993. reprint ed. pap. 17.00 (*0-300-05427-0*) Yale U Pr.
— Russia in the Age of Catherine the Great. LC 80-21993. 710p. reprint ed. pap. 200.00 (*0-8357-8763-X*, 203370400087) Bks Demand.
De Madariaga, Salvador. Americans. LC 68-29229. (Essay Index Reprint Ser.). 1977. reprint ed. 17.95 (*0-8369-0661-6*) Ayer.
— Bolivar. LC 79-16763. (Illus.). 711p. 1979. reprint ed. lib. bdg. 95.00 (*0-313-22029-8*, MABO, Greenwood Pr) Greenwood.
— Genius of Spain, & Other Essays on Spanish Contemporary Literature. LC 68-22927. (Essay Index Reprint Ser.). 1977. 18.95 (*0-8369-0662-4*) Ayer.
— Latin America Between the Eagle & the Bear. LC 75-25494. 192p. 1976. reprint ed. lib. bdg. 55.00 (*0-8371-8423-1*, MALAM, Greenwood Pr) Greenwood.
— Mujeres Espanolas. (Nueva Austral Ser.: Vol. 198). (SPA.). 1991. pap. text 24.95 (*84-239-7198-8*) Elliots Bks.
— Poesia. (Nueva Austral Ser.: Vol. 89). (SPA.). 1991. pap. text 24.95 (*84-239-1889-0*) Elliots Bks.
— The World's Design. 1938. 30.00 (*0-686-17395-3*) R S Barnes.
De Magalhaes De Gandavo, P. Histories of Brazil, 2 Vols. in 1. (Cortes Society Ser.). 1969. reprint ed. 50.00 (*0-527-19725-4*) Periodicals Srv.
De Magalhaes, Jose Calvet, see Calvet De Magalhaes, Jose.
De Magnon, Leonor V. The Rebel. Lomas, Clara, ed. LC 93-3607. 297p. 1994. pap. 12.00 (*1-55885-056-2*) Arte Publico.
De Mailles, Jacques. History of Bayard the Good. LC 79-8370. reprint ed. 48.00 (*0-404-18353-0*) AMS Pr.
De Mailly Nesle, Solange. Astrology: History, Symbols, & Signs. (Illus.). 197p. (Orig.). 1985. pap. 14.95 (*0-89281-105-6*) Inner Tradit.
De Maio, Gerald, jt. auth. see Kushner, Harvey W.
***De Maio, Jim.** Helping not Fixing: A Manual for People Who Want to Let Go & Love. de la Rossa Cortes, Alberto, ed. 169p. (Orig.). 1999. pap. 12.15 (*958-96668-0-9*) A De Maio.
De Maistre, Joseph. An Examination of the Philosophy of Bacon: Wherein Different Questions of Rational Philosophy Are Treated. Lebrun, Richard A., ed. & tr. by. 400p. 1998. text 75.00 (*0-7735-1727-8*, Pub. by McG-Queens Univ Pr) CUP Services.
— St Petersburg Dialogues: Or Conversations on the Temporal Government of Providence. Lebrun, Richard A., ed. 448p. 1993. 70.00 (*0-7735-0982-8*, Pub. by McG-Queens Univ Pr) CUP Services.
De Maistre, Joseph M., tr. Letters on the Spanish Inquisition. LC 77-24949. 184p. 1977. reprint ed. 50.00 (*0-8201-1293-3*) Schol Facsimiles.
De Maistre, Joseph-Marie. Oeuvres Completes, 14 vols. in 7. Set. clx, 7056p. 1983. reprint ed. write for info. (*3-487-07361-7*) G Olms Pubs.
De Maistre, Xavier. Voyage Around My Room: Selected Works of Xavier de Maistre. Sartarelli, Stephen, tr. from FRE. LC 94-17834. 192p. (Orig.). 1994. pap. 14.00 (*0-8112-1280-7*, NDP791, Pub. by New Directions) Norton.
De Majo, Gian F. Gian Francesco de Majo: Ifigenia in Tauride (1764) Corneilson, Paul, ed. Shiff, Jonathan, tr. (Recent Researches in Music of the Classic Era Ser.: Vol. RRC46). (Illus.). lxx, 379p. 1996. pap. 150.00 (*0-89579-375-X*) A-R Eds.
De Maleissye Melun, Judith. God is Good: Bedtime Morals for Children, Vol. 2. 64p. (J). 1999. pap. 8.95 (*1-893551-02-4*) Seabird Pubg.
— God is Good: Bedtime Morals for Children, Vol. 3. 64p. (J). 1999. pap. 8.95 (*1-893551-03-2*) Seabird Pubg.
— God is Good: Bedtime Morals for Children, Vol. 4. 64p. (J). 1999. pap. 8.95 (*1-893551-04-0*) Seabird Pubg.
De Mallac, Guy. Gandhi's Seven Steps to Global Change. LC 90-6883. (Peacewatch Editions Ser.). 96p. 1990. pap. 7.95 (*0-943734-16-9*) Ocean Tree Bks.
De Mallac, Guy, ed. & tr. see Tolstoy, Leo.
***De Mallet Burgess, Thomas & Skilbeck, Nicholas.** Singing & Acting Handbook: Games & Exercises for Performer. LC 99-29440. 224p. 1999. pap. 19.99 (*0-415-16658-6*) Routledge.
— The Singing & Acting Handbook: Games & Exercises for the Performer. 224p. 2000. 60.00 (*0-415-16657-8*) Routledge.
De Malpas Grey Egerton, Philip, ed. see Grey De Wilton, Arthur G.
De Malynes, Gerard. The Center of the Circle of Commerce: Or a Refutation of a Treatise Intituled "The Circle of Commerce" LC 66-21687. (Reprints of Economic Classics Ser.). 139p. 1973. reprint ed. 29.50 (*0-678-00296-7*) Kelley.
— Consuetudo, Vel Lex Mercatoria, or the Ancient

Law-Merchant. LC 79-84121. (English Experience Ser.: No. 940). 524p. 1979. reprint ed. lib. bdg. 85.00 (*90-221-0940-2*) Walter J Johnson.

— Englands View, in the Unmasking of Two Paradoxes: With a Replication unto the Answer of Maister John Bodine. LC 79-38254. (Evolution of Capitalism Ser.). 208p. 1972. reprint ed. 18.95 (*0-405-04126-8*) Ayer.

— The Maintenance of Free Trade: According to the Three Essential Parts of Traffic. LC 73-115927. (Reprints of Economic Classics Ser.). 105p. 1971. reprint ed. lib. bdg. 29.50 (*0-678-00644-X*) Kelley.

De Man, Adrianus P., jt. auth. see Van Den Bosch, F. A.

De Man, Hanneke. Boymans van Beuningen Museum. (Illus.). 128p. 1993. 35.00 (*1-870248-95-3*) Scala Books.

De Man, Hendrik. Clothmaking in Medieval Ghent. (Illus.). 224p. 1999. 37.50 (*0-88477-028-1*) Intl General.

De Man, Henri. Joy in Work. Stein, Leon, ed. LC 77-70513. 1977. reprint ed. lib. bdg. 23.95 (*0-405-10182-1*) Ayer.

— The Psychology of Marxian Socialism. Paul, Eden & Paul, Cedar, trs. 518p. (C). 1984. pap. 29.95 (*0-87855-992-2*) Transaction Pubs.

De Man, Paul. Aesthetic Ideology. Warminski, Andrzej, ed. LC 96-16240. (Theory & History of Literature Ser.: Vol. 65). 196p. (C). 1996. pap. 19.95 (*0-8166-2204-3*) U of Minn Pr.

— Blindness & Insight: Essays in the Rhetoric of Contemporary Criticism. rev. ed. (Theory & History of Literature Ser.: Vol. 7). 309p. (C). 1983. pap. 17.95 (*0-8166-1135-1*) U of Minn Pr.

— Critical Writings, 1953-1978. (Theory & History of Literature Ser.: Vol. 66). 246p. (Orig.). 1989. pap. 19.95 (*0-8166-1696-5*) U of Minn Pr.

— The Resistance to Theory. LC 85-28820. (Theory & History of Literature Ser.: Vol. 33). 156p. (Orig.). 1986. pap. 14.95 (*0-8166-1294-3*) U of Minn Pr.

— The Rhetoric of Romanticism. LC 84-3213. 327p. 1984. text 64.50 (*0-231-05526-9*) Col U Pr.

— The Rhetoric of Romanticism. LC 84-3213. 327p. 1986. pap. text 20.50 (*0-231-05527-7*) Col U Pr.

— Romanticism & Contemporary Criticism: The Gauss Seminar & Other Papers. Burt, E. S. et al, eds. 232p. 1993. text 35.95 (*0-8018-4460-6*) Johns Hopkins.

— Vision y Ceguera. 460p. 1991. pap. 30.50 (*0-8477-3614-8*) U of PR Pr.

— Wartime Journalism, 1939-43. Hamacher, Werner et al, eds. LC 88-17234. x, 399p. 1988. pap. text 30.00 (*0-8032-6576-X*) U of Nebr Pr.

De Man Paul Staff. Romanticism & Contemporary Criticism: The Gauss Seminar & Other Papers. Burt, E. S. et al, eds. LC 92-23340. 224p. (C). 1996. reprint ed. pap. text 15.95 (*0-8018-4461-4*) Johns Hopkins.

De Manchicourt, Pierre. Pierre de Manchicourt: Twenty-Nine Chansons. Baird, Margery A., ed. (Recent Researches in Music of the Renaissance Ser.: Vol. RRR11). (Illus.). xix, 88p. 1972. pap. 35.00 (*0-89579-038-6*) A-R Eds.

De Mandeville, Bernard. A Treatise of the Hypochondriack & Hysterick Passions. LC 75-16717. (Classics in Psychiatry Ser.). 1976. reprint ed. 25.95 (*0-405-07445-X*) Ayer.

De Mandeville, Jean. Reisen. (Deutsche Volksbucher in Faksimiledrucken, Reihe A: Pt. 21). xxxiii, 388p. 1991. reprint ed. write for info. (*3-487-09430-4*) G Olms Pubs.

De Mandiargue, Andre Pieyre, see Pieyre de Mandiargue, Andre.

De Mandiargues, Andre P. La Marge. (FRE.). 1981. pap. 10.95 (*0-7859-4152-5*) Fr & Eur.

***De Mandiargues, Andre Pieyre.** Portrait of an Englishman in His Chateau. Fletcher, J., tr. 1999. pap. text 12.99 (*1-873982-93-3*) Dedalus.

De Manhar, Nurho. The Zohar: Bereshith. 4th rev. ed. LC 75-160173. (Secret Doctrine Reference Ser.). 432p. 1995. 25.00 (*0-913510-65-3*) Wizards.

De Mantaras, Ramon L. Approximate Reasoning Models. 1990. text 49.95 (*0-470-21608-5*) P-H.

De Manzoni, D., jt. auth. see Cordiano, C.

***de Marbot, Baron.** The Exploits of Baron de Marbot. Summerville, Christopher, ed. 320p. 2000. pap. 12.95 (*0-7867-0801-8*, Pub. by Carroll & Graf) Publishers Group.

De Marchi, A., ed. Frequency Standards & Metrology. (Illus.). 450p. 1989. 102.95 (*0-387-50818-X*) Spr-Verlag.

De Marchi, Attilio. Il Culto Privato di Roma Antica, 2 vols. LC 75-10641. (Ancient Religion & Mythology Ser.). (ITA., Illus.). 1976. reprint ed. 57.95 (*0-405-07011-X*) Ayer.

De Marchi, John. Fatima: The Full Story. 264p. 1986. 8.25 (*0-911988-70-X*, 37328) AMI Pr.

De Marchi, Neil, ed. Post-Popperian Methodology of Economics: Recovering Practice. 400p. (C). 1992. lib. bdg. 120.50 (*0-7923-9241-8*) Kluwer Academic.

De Marchi, Neil & Blaug, Mark, eds. Appraising Economic Theories: Studies in the Methodology of Research Programs. 592p. 1991. 120.00 (*1-85278-515-2*) E Elgar.

De Marchi, Neil & Morgan, Mary S., eds. Higgling: Transactors & Their Markets in the History of Economics. (Illus.). 420p. 1994. text 49.95 (*0-8223-1530-0*) Duke.

De Marchi, Neil, jt. auth. see Hirsch, Abraham.

De Marco, Donald, jt. ed. see Bradley, Gerald V.

De Marco, Guido & Bartolo, Michael. A Second Generation United Nations: For Peace & Freedom in the 21st Century. LC 96-8014. 152p. 1996. 93.50 (*0-7103-0558-3*, Pub. by Kegan Paul Intl) Col U Pr.

***De Marco, Guido & Bartolo, Michael.** A Second Generation United Nations: For Peace & Freedom in the 21st Century, Second Edition. 2nd ed. 152p. 2000. text 93.50 (*0-7103-0698-9*) Col U Pr.

De Marco, Guy. Ships in Bottles. LC 84-52714. (Illus.). 64p. 1985. pap. 6.95 (*0-88740-033-7*) Schiffer.

de Marco, Neil. Children's Atlas of World History. LC 99-29940. 96p. 1999. 19.95 (*0-87226-603-6*, 66036B, P Bedrick Books) NTC Contemp Pub Co.

De Mare, Eric. The Canals of England. (Illus.). 128p. 1996. reprint ed. pap. 17.95 (*0-86299-418-7*, Pub. by Sutton Pub Ltd) Intl Pubs Mktg.

De Mare, G. R. Mercury Photosensitization. write for info. (*0-318-56739-3*) Elsevier.

De Maret, Pierre, jt. auth. see Childs, S. Terry.

De Margerie, Bertrand. Christ for the World. Carroll, Malachy, tr. from FRE.Tr. of Christ Pour le Monde. 528p. pap. 3.95 (*0-8199-0485-6*, Frncscn Herld) Franciscan Pr.

— Heart of Mary, Heart of the Church. 80p. 1992. 2.00 (*1-56036-041-0*, 44913) AMI Pr.

— Intro to the History of Exegesis Vol. I: The Greek Fathers. De Fontnouvelle, Pierre, tr. from FRE. LC 94-31340. 290p. 1995. pap. text 29.95 (*1-879007-05-3*) St Bedes Pubns.

— Introduction to the History of Exegesis Vol. 2: The First Latin Fathers. 161p. 1996. pap. 29.95 (*1-879007-13-4*) St Bedes Pubns.

De Margerie, Diane. Marcel Proust. (Maison D'Ecrivain Collection). (FRE., Illus.). 1995. pap. 49.95 (*0-614-14006-4*) Intl Scholars.

De Maria, Gary. The Closet. LC 80-11677. (Illus.). 160p. (Orig.). 1980. pap. 5.95 (*0-89407-020-7*) Strawberry Hill.

De Maria, M. & Grilli, M., eds. Restructuring of Physical Sciences in Europe & the U. S., 1945-1960. 832p. (C). 1989. text 166.00 (*9971-5-0740-4*) World Scientific Pub.

De Maria, Richard. Communal Love at Oneida: A Perfectionist Vision of Authority, Property & Sexual Order. LC 78-60958. (Texts & Studies in Religion: Vol. 2). xiii, 248p. 1978. pap. 69.95 (*0-88946-986-5*) E Mellen.

De Maria, Robert. Brothers. 352p. 1984. pap. 3.95 (*0-345-90232-7*) Ballantine Pub Grp.

— The Life of Samuel Johnson: A Critical Biography. LC 92-23302. (Blackwell Critical Biographies Ser.: Vol. 2). 354p. 1994. pap. 25.95 (*1-55786-664-3*) Blackwell Pubs.

De Maria, Rusel. Boogerman Official Game Secrets. 1995. pap. 12.95 (*1-55958-796-2*) Prima Pub.

— Monty Python's Complete Waste of Time: An Official Compendium of Answers to Ruddy Questions... LC 95-69171. 1995. pap. text 14.95 (*0-7615-0139-8*) Prima Pub.

De Marin, Maria V. & Marin, Reymundo. La Historia de los Estados Unidos: La Diversidad de sus Pueblos. (SPA., Illus.). 564p. (Orig.). (C). 1995. pap. 24.50 (*0-927065-04-5*) Marin Chula Vista.

De Marinis, Fabrizio. Velvet: History, Techniques, Fashions. (Illus.). 202p. (Orig.). 1996. pap. 35.00 (*0-9627985-1-7*) Idea Bks.

De Marinis, Marco. The Semiotics of Performance. O'Healy, Aine, tr. LC 92-38671. (Advances in Semiotics Ser.). 1993. 39.95 (*0-253-31686-3*) Ind U Pr.

***De Mario, Govia.** Yo-Yo Tricks: Strategy Guide. 1999. pap. 12.99 (*0-7615-2202-6*) Prima Pub.

De Mark, Judith Boyce, ed. Essays in 20th Century New Mexico History. LC 93-25178. (Illus.). 255p. 1994. pap. 18.95 (*0-8263-1483-X*) U of NM Pr.

De Marliave, Olivier. Petit Dictionnaire de Mythologies Basque et Pyreneene. (FRE.). 295p. 1993. pap. 55.00 (*0-7859-7973-5*, 2726601103) Fr & Eur.

De Marly, Diana. Christian Dior. LC 90-4061. (Illus.). 100p. 1990. pap. 24.95 (*0-8419-1278-5*) Holmes & Meier.

— Dress in North America Vol. 1: The New World, 1492-1800. LC 90-4905. (Illus.). x, 236p. 1991. 59.95 (*0-8419-1199-1*) Holmes & Meier.

De Marmon, P., tr. see Bergeret, L. F.

De Marolles, Chantal. The Farmer's Three Sons. (I Love to Read Collection). (Illus.). 48p. (J). (ps-3). 1992. lib. bdg. 12.79 (*0-89565-816-X*) Childs World.

De Marolles, Michel. Tableaux du Temple des Muses, Repr. of 1655 Ed. LC 75-27876. (Renaissance & the Gods Ser.: Vol. 31). (Illus.). 1976. lib. bdg. 36.00 (*0-8240-2080-4*) Garland.

— Traite du Poeme Epique, pour l'Intelligence de l'Eneide de Virgile. x, 123p. 1974. reprint ed. write for info. (*3-487-05265-2*) G Olms Pubs.

De Mars, Douglas. Masked Avenger. 64p. 1986. pap. 5.00 (*0-941452-18-2*) Acheron Pr.

De Marsily, Ghislain. Quantitative Hydrogeology. 1986. pap. text 63.00 (*0-12-208916-2*) Acad Pr.

De Marsy, Francois-Marie. Dictionnaire Abrege de Peinture et D'Architecture. (FRE.). 1972. write for info. (*0-7859-8043-1*, 2-8266-0228-4) Fr & Eur.

De Martel, Gerard. Reoertiure Des Textes Katubs Rekatufs Au Livre De Ruth (viie - xve s.) (C). 1990. pap. text 201.00 (*0-7923-0917-0*) Kluwer Academic.

De Martinez, Bernice B. Bass, see Sims, William E. & Bass De Martinez, Bernice B.

De Martinez, Luz M., tr. see Hooker, Irene H. & Brindle, Susan A.

De Martinez, Maria C. Childrens Games & Songs in Puerto Rico. (Puerto Rico Ser.). 1979. lib. bdg. 59.95 (*0-8490-2883-3*) Gordon Pr.

— Popular Poetry in Puerto Rico: Origins & Themes. (Puerto Rico Ser.). 1979. lib. bdg. 69.95 (*0-8490-2986-4*) Gordon Pr.

De Martini, Francesco, et al. Quantum Interferometry. 320p. 1994. text 121.00 (*981-02-1517-7*) World Scientific Pub.

De Martino, S., et al, eds. New Perspectives in the Physics of Mesoscopic Systems: Quantum-Like Descriptions & Macroscopic Coherence Phenomena Caserta, Italy 18-20 April, 1996. 350p. 1997. 78.00 (*981-02-3236-5*) World Scientific Pub.

De Marval-McNair, Nora, ed. Jose Ortega y Gasset: Proceedings of the Espectador Universal International Interdisciplinary Conference, 34. LC 87-330. (Contributions in Philosophy Ser.: No. 34). 200p. 1987. 55.00 (*0-313-25896-1*, MMO/) Greenwood.

De Master, Evangeline M. Not Yet: A Story of Faith & Hope John Meyer. (Illus.). (Orig.). 1995. pap. write for info. (*0-9643883-0-8*) Meyer-DeMaster.

de Matos, Maria A. Pinto, see Pinto de Matos, Maria A.

De Matteis, Francesco & Smith, Lewis L., eds. Molecular & Cellular Mechanisms of Toxicity. LC 95-16810. 240p. 1995. boxed set 199.95 (*0-8493-9229-2*, 9229) CRC Pr.

de Mattos, A. Teixeira, tr. see Couperus, Louis.

De Mattos, Alexander T., tr. see De Tocqueville, Alexis.

De Mattos, Alexander T., tr. see Leblanc, Maurice.

De Mattos, Alexander T., tr. see Maeterlinck, Maurice.

De Mattos Bicudo, Carlos E. & Jarreta de Castro, Ana A. Desmidioflorula Paulista Vol. IV: Generos Closterium, Spinoclosterium. (Bibliotheca Phycologica Ser.: Vol. 95). (POR., Illus.). iv, 191p. 1994. 53.00 (*3-443-60022-0*, Pub. by Gebruder Borntraeger) Balogh.

De Maulde, L. & LaClaviere, R. The Women of the Renaissance: A Study of Feminism. 1976. lib. bdg. 69.95 (*0-8490-2835-3*) Gordon Pr.

De Maupeou, Patrick, jt. auth. see Giraudy, Daniele.

de Maurier, Daphne, jt. auth. see Center for Learning Network Staff.

De Mauro, Tullio. Ludwig Wittgenstein: His Place in the Development of Semantics. (Foundations of Language Supplementary Ser.: No. 3). 62p. 1967. text 100.50 (*90-277-0029-X*) Kluwer Academic.

De Mauro, Tullio & Formigari, Lia, eds. Leibniz, Humbold, & the Origins of Comparativism: Proceedings of the International Conference, Rome, 25-28 September 1986. LC 89-17687. (Studies in the History of the Language Sciences: No. 49). vii, 329p. 1990. 97.00 (*90-272-4532-0*) J Benjamins Pubng Co.

De Mause, Alan. Beginning Jazz Guitar. (Illus.). 64p. 1984. pap. 12.95 (*0-8256-2360-X*, AM32505) Music Sales.

— Complete Fingerstyle Jazz Guitar Book. (Complete Bks.). 184p. 1996. pap. 22.95 (*0-7866-0414-X*, MB95434) Mel Bay.

***De Mause, Alan.** Easy Jazz Guitar Solos: Beginning-Intermediate Level. (Value Line Ser.). 24p. 1998. pap. 9.95 incl. audio compact disk (*0-7866-1840-X*, 95700BCD) Mel Bay.

De Mause, Alan. One Hundred One Jazz Guitar Licks. 44p. 1996. 17.95 incl. audio compact disk (*0-7866-2300-4*, 93863BCD) Mel Bay.

De Mause, Alan, contrib. by. Joe Pass: Virtuoso No. 3. 1985. pap., spiral bd. 19.95 incl. audio (*0-7866-0967-2*, 94059P); spiral bd. 12.95 (*0-87166-912-9*, 94059) Mel Bay.

— Joe Pass No. 3: Virtuoso. 1985. audio 10.98 (*1-56222-620-7*, 94059C) Mel Bay.

De Mause, Neil, jt. auth. see Cagon, Joanna.

De, Maya. Bibliography on Employment & Persons with Disabilities. 72p. (C). 1995. pap. text 25.00 (*0-7881-2385-8*) DIANE Pub.

De Mayada, Maruja Del Castillo, see Ackerman, James D. & Del Castillo De Mayada, Maruja.

de McGavock, Catalina J. Actividades Manuales para Ninos.Tr. of Activities & Handwork for Children. (SPA., Illus.). 48p. (J). (gr. 1-7). 1967. pap. 7.50 (*0-311-26601-0*) Casa Bautista.

***De McKissack, Elena A.** Chicano Educational Achievement: Comparing Escuela Tlatelolco, a Chicanocentric School & a Public High School. LC 99-44760. (Latino Communities Ser.). 1999. write for info. (*0-8153-3511-3*) Garland.

De Medeiros, Ana M. Les Visages de L'Autre: Alibis, Masques et Identite dans Alexis ou le Traite du vain Combat, Denier du reve et Memoires d'Hadrien de Marguerite Yourcenar. (Currents in Comparative Romance Languages & Literatures Ser.: Vol. 37). (FRE.). X, 134p. (C). 1996. text 41.95 (*0-8204-2892-2*) P Lang Pubng.

De Medeiros, Selene. This Is How I Love You. 67p. (YA). (gr. 9-12). 1990. per. 6.00 (*0-916418-76-6*) Lotus.

De' Medici, Lorenza. Lorenza's Pasta: 200 Recipes for Family & Friends. Date not set. 0.19 (*0-517-19915-7*) Random Hse Value.

— Pizza. Wertz, Laurie, ed. LC 92-27838. (Williams-Sonoma Kitchen Library). (Illus.). 108p. 1993. lib. bdg. write for info. (*0-7835-0230-3*) Time-Life.

— Pizza. Wertz, Laurie, ed. LC 92-27838. (Williams-Sonoma Kitchen Library). (Illus.). 108p. (J). (gr. 11). 1999. 18.95 (*0-7835-0229-X*) Time-Life.

De Medici, Lorenza. Rennaissance Italy. 1999. pap. write for info. (*0-14-046842-0*) Viking Penguin.

De Medici, Lorenzo. Poesie Volgari, 2 vols. LC 71-172718. (Renaissance Library: No. 2). reprint ed. 34.50 (*0-404-07872-9*) AMS Pr.

***De' Medici Stucchi, Lorenza.** A Passion for Fruit. LC 99-51968. (Illus.). 160p. (J). 2000. 35.00 (*0-7892-0630-7*, Abbeville Kids) Abbeville Pr.

De' Medici Stucchi, Lorenza & Plotkin, Fred. Italy Today The Beautiful Cookbook: Contemporary Recipes Reflecting Simple, Fresh Italian Cooking. LC 96-27506. 256p. 1997. 50.00 (*0-00-225053-5*) HarpC.

De Medina, Maria D., jt. ed. see Bernstein, David E.

De Medina, Pedro. L' Art de Naviguer. LC 92-15326. 264p. 1992. 100.00 (*0-8201-1470-7*) Schol Facsimiles.

De Medrano, Lopez. Involutions on Manifolds. LC 74-139952. (Ergebnisse der Mathematik und Ihrer Grenzgebiete Ser.: Vol. 59). (Illus.). 1971. 59.95 (*0-387-05092-2*) Spr-Verlag.

De Meester, Conrad. The Power of Confidence: Genesis & Structure of the Way of "Spiritual Childhood" of St. Therese of Lisieux. Conroy, Susan, tr. from FRE. LC 98-3989. 443p. 1998. pap. 22.95 (*0-8189-0819-X*) Alba.

— With Empty Hands: The Message of Therese of Lisieux. 122p. 1994. pap. 21.00 (*0-86012-160-7*, Pub. by Srch Pr) St Mut.

De Meester, Conrad, ed. St. Therese of Lisieux: Her Life, Times & Teaching, Centenary Edition. LC 96-52134. Orig. Title: My Vocation Is Love. (Illus.). 300p. 1997. 44.95 (*0-935216-61-8*) ICS Pubns.

De Meijer, A. A., jt. ed. see Geesteranus, R. A.

De Meijere, A., ed. Carbon Rich Compounds I. (Topics in Current Chemistry Ser.: Vol. 196). (Illus.). xxii, 230p. 1997. 175.00 (*3-540-64110-6*) Spr-Verlag.

— Small Ring Compounds in Organic Synthesis III. (Topics in Current Chemistry Ser.: Vol. 144). (Illus.). 210p. 1988. 141.95 (*0-387-18368-X*) Spr-Verlag.

***De Meijere, A., ed.** Small Ring Compounds in Organic Synthesis VI. (Topics in Current Chemistry Ser.: Vol. 207). (Illus.). x, 230p. 2000. 154.00 (*3-540-66471-8*) Spr-Verlag.

De Meijere, A., et al, eds. Carbon Rich Compounds II: Oligoacetylenes. (Topics in Current Chemistry Ser.: Vol. 201). (Illus.). 220p. 1999. 160.00 (*3-540-65301-5*) Spr-Verlag.

De Meijere, A., see Meijere, A. de, ed.

De Meijere, Armin. Strain & Its Implications in Organic Chemistry: Organic Stress & Reactivity. Blechert, Siegfried, ed. (C). 1989. text 260.00 (*0-7923-0176-5*) Kluwer Academic.

De Meijere, Armin, ed. Small Ring Compounds in Organic Synthesis I. (Topics in Current Chemistry Ser.: Vol. 133). (Illus.). 170p. 1986. 93.95 (*0-387-16307-7*) Spr-Verlag.

— Small Ring Compounds in Organic Synthesis II. (Topics in Current Chemistry Ser.: Vol. 135). (Illus.). 160p. 1986. 108.95 (*0-387-16662-9*) Spr-Verlag.

De Meijere, Armin & Dieck, H. Tom, eds. Organometallics in Organic Synthesis. (Illus.). 355p. 1988. 103.95 (*0-387-18592-5*) Spr-Verlag.

De Mejia, Maria Juana, tr. see Witmer, Edith.

De Mejo, Oscar. Journey to Boc Boc: The Kidnapping of a Rock Star. LC 85-45261. (Illus.). 48p. (J). (gr. 3-7). 1987. 12.95 (*0-06-021579-8*) HarpC Child Bks.

— Oscar de Mejo: The Naive Surrealist. (Illus.). 143p. 1992. 49.50 (*0-8109-3209-1*, Pub. by Abrams) Time Warner.

— Oscar de Mejo's ABC. LC 91-28768. (Laura Geringer Bks.). (Illus.). 32p. (J). (ps up). 1992. 17.00 (*0-06-020516-4*); pap. 16.89 (*0-06-020517-2*) HarpC Child Bks.

De Melendez, Robles. A Classroom for All: Teaching Young Children in Multicultural Classrooms, Issues, Concepts & Strategies. LC 96-23105. (Early Childhood Education Ser.). 352p. (C). 1996. mass mkt. 56.95 (*0-8273-7275-2*) Delmar.

De Mello, Anthony. El Amor esa Maravilla. 1997. pap. 2.95 (*950-724-449-2*) Lumen ARG.

— Awakening: Conversations with the Master. LC 98-18327. 372p. 1998. pap. 12.95 (*0-8294-1260-3*) Loyola Pr.

— Awareness. 192p. 1990. pap. 12.00 (*0-385-24937-3*) Doubleday.

De Mello, Anthony. Combatiendo los Miedos. 1997. pap. text 2.98 (*950-724-447-6*) Lumen ARG.

De Mello, Anthony. Contact with God: Retreat Conferences. rev. ed. LC 91-30524. 207p. 1991. pap. 10.95 (*0-8294-0726-X*) Loyola Pr.

— Ejercicios de Superacion. 1997. pap. 2.98 (*950-724-462-X*) Lumen ARG.

— Felicidad Eres Tu. 1997. pap. 2.95 (*950-724-454-9*) Lumen ARG.

— Liberate! 1997. pap. text 2.98 (*950-724-452-2*) Lumen ARG.

— More One Minute Nonsense. LC 92-35241. 161p. 1993. pap. 10.95 (*0-8294-0749-9*) Loyola Pr.

— One Minute Nonsense. LC 92-31735. 180p. (C). 1993. pap. 10.95 (*0-8294-0742-1*) Loyola Pr.

— One Minute Wisdom. LC 85-29003. 224p. 1988. pap. 11.95 (*0-385-24290-5*, Image Bks) Doubleday.

— Praying Body & Soul: Spiritual Living in a Secular World. Berryman, Phillip, tr. LC 97-566. 168p. 1997. pap. 12.95 (*0-8245-1673-7*) Crossroad NY.

— Sadhana: A Way to God. LC 97-29261. (Illus.). 176p. 1998. 18.00 (*0-7648-0170-8*, Liguori Triumph) Liguori Pubns.

— Sadhana: A Way to God, Christian Exercises in Eastern Form. LC 78-70521. (Studies on Jesuit Topics IV: No. 9). xi, 134p. (C). 1978. pap. 7.95 (*0-912422-46-7*) Inst Jesuit.

— Taking Flight: A Book of Story-Meditations. 192p. 1990. pap. 11.95 (*0-385-41371-8*) Doubleday.

— Walking on Water. LC 97-47743. (Illus.). 144p. 1998. pap. 13.95 (*0-8245-1737-7*, Crsrd) Crossroad NY.

— The Way to Love: The Last Meditations of Anthony de Mello. 160p. 1992. 17.00 (*0-385-24938-1*) Doubleday.

— The Way to Love: The Last Meditations of Anthony de Mello. LC 94-23993. 208p. 1995. pap. 6.95 (*0-385-24939-X*) Doubleday.

De Mello, George. Espanol Contemporaneo. 2nd ed. (SPA.). 500p. (C). 1990. pap. text 49.00 (*0-8191-7854-3*) U Pr of Amer.

***De Mello, Luiz E. & Fukusaku, Kiichiro, eds.** Fiscal Decentralisation in Emerging Economies: Governance Issues. (Development Centre Seminars Ser.). 248p. (Orig.). 1999. pap. 53.00 (*92-64-17046-4*, 41 1999 06 1 P, Pub. by Org for Econ) OECD.

De Mello, Luiz S. Homen, see Homen De Mello, Luiz S., ed.

De Mello Vianna, Fernando, ed. see Webster's New World Dictionaries Editors.

De Mello Vianna, Fernando, ed. see Webster's New World Dictionary Staff, et al.

De Mello, W. C. Cell-to-Cell Communication. LC 87-18573. (Illus.). 388p. (C). 1987. text 105.00 (*0-306-42623-4*, Kluwer Plenum) Kluwer Academic.

D

De Mello, Walmor C. & Janse, Michael J., eds. Heart Cell Communication in Health & Disease. LC 97-40862. (Developments in Cardiovascular Medicine Ser.). 312p. 1998. text 153.00 (*0-7923-8052-5*) Kluwer Academic.

De Melo, Carlos A. The Superconducting State in Magnetic Fields: Special Topics & New Trends. LC 98-26899. (Directions in Condensed Matter Physics Ser.). 324p. 1998. pap. 38.00 (*981-02-3566-6*) World Scientific Pub.

De Melo, Dias. Dark Stones. Gavea-Brown Publications Staff, ed. McNab, Gregory, tr. from POR. LC 83-80781. Orig. Title: Piedras Negras. 144p. (Orig.). 1988. pap. 6.50 (*0-943722-05-5*) Gavea-Brown.

De Melo, Jaime & Panagariya, Arvind. The New Regionalism in Trade Policy. LC 92-39285. 32p. 1993. pap. 22.00 (*0-8213-2294-X*, 12294) World Bank.

De Melo, Jaime & Panagariya, Arvind, eds. New Dimensions in Regional Integration. (Illus.). 501p. 1996. pap. text 26.95 (*0-521-55668-6*) Cambridge U Pr.

De Melo, Jaime & Sapir, Andre, eds. Trade Theory & Economic Reform: North, South, & East: Essays in Honor of Bela Balassa. (Illus.). 384p. 1991. 58.95 (*1-55786-256-7*) Blackwell Pubs.

De Melo, Jaime & Tarr, David W. A General Equilibrium Analysis of U. S. Foreign Trade Policy. (Illus.). 300p. 1991. 40.00 (*0-262-04122-7*) MIT Pr.

De Melo, Jaime, jt. auth. see Corbo, V.

De Melo, Jaime, jt. ed. see Connolly, Michael.

De Melo, Martha & Ofer, Gur. Private Service Firms in a Transitional Economy: Findings of A Survey in St. Petersburg. LC 94-4998. (Studies of Economies in Transformation: No. 11). 82p. 1994. pap. 22.00 (*0-8213-2797-6*, 12797) World Bank.

De Melo Neto, Joao Cabral, see Cabral De Melo Neto, Joao.

De Melo, Welington & Van Strien, Sebastian. One-Dimensional Dynamics. LC 93-7846. (Ergebnisse der Mathematik und Ihrer Grenzgebiete Ser.: Vol. 3). 1996. 119.00 (*0-387-56412-8*) Spr-Verlag.

De Mena, Juan. Coplas de los Siete Pecados Mortales: Second & Third Continuations. Rivera, Gladys, ed. 25.50 (*0-916379-16-7*) Scripta.

— Laberinto de Fortuna. Perez Priego, Miguel A., ed. (Nueva Austral Ser.: Vol. 73). (SPA.). 1991. pap. text 12.95 (*84-239-1873-4*) Elliots Bks.

— Laberinto de Fortuna O las Trescientas. (SPA.). 158p. 1968. 15.95 (*0-8288-7118-3*, S30294) Fr & Eur.

— Tratado Sobre el Titulo de Duque. Fainberg, Louise V., ed. (Textos B Ser.: No. 16). (SPA.). 134p. (C). 1976. 41.00 (*0-7293-0009-9*, Pub. by Tamesis Bks Ltd) Boydell & Brewer.

De Mendelssohn, Peter. Japan's Political Warfare. LC 72-4674. (International Propaganda & Communications Ser.). 192p. 1977. reprint ed. 18.95 (*0-405-04758-4*) Ayer.

de Mendez, Amalia Cardos, see Cardos de Mendez, Amalia.

De Mendez, Ana T. Merced, see Merced de Mendez, Ana T.

De Mendiola, Marina P., ed. Bridging the Atlantic: Toward a Reassessment of Iberian & Latin American Cultural Ties. LC 95-47527. (SUNY Series in Latin American & Iberian Thought & Culture). 227p. (C). 1996. text 47.50 (*0-7914-2917-2*); pap. text 15.95 (*0-7914-2918-0*) State U NY Pr.

de Mendiola, Marina Perez, see Perez de Mendiola, Marina.

De Mendoza, Andres, jt. auth. see De Almansa, Andres.

De Mendoza, Antonio Hurtado, see Hurtado de Mendoza, Antonio.

De Meneses, Mary, jt. auth. see Pinnell, Norma N.

De Menezes, Ruth. The Heart's Far Cry. 40p. (Orig.). 1996. pap. 5.00 (*0-614-14290-3*) Claremont CA.

— Love Ascending. 90p. 1987. 7.95 (*0-937495-18-2*) Claremont CA.

— Woman Songs. (Illus.). 94p. 1982. pap. 6.00 (*0-941358-02-X*) Claremont CA.

— You Can Type for Doctors at Home! rev. ed. 72p. 1993. pap. 16.00 (*0-941358-00-3*) Claremont CA.

De Menil, Dominique. Humble Treasures: An Exhibition of Tribal Art from Negro Africa. (Illus.). 26p. 1965. pap. text 5.00 (*0-318-42766-4*) U of St Thomas.

De Menil, Dominique, ed. Jim Love up to Now. LC 80-82000. (Illus.). 1980. pap. 8.00 (*0-914412-16-7*, Inst Arts Catalogues) Menil Found.

De Menil, Dominique, intro. Constant Companions: An Exhibition of Mythological Animals, Demons, & Monsters. (Illus.). 90p. 1986. pap. 5.00 (*0-914412-19-1*, Inst Arts Catalogues) Menil Found.

— Unromantic Agony: An Exhibition. (Illus.). 1965. pap. 6.95 (*0-914412-26-4*, Inst Arts Catalogues) Menil Found.

De Menil, Georges, et al, eds. Economic Policy: A European Forum. (Illus.). 212p. 1997. pap. text 38.95 (*0-631-20475-X*) Blackwell Pubs.

De Menil, Georges, et al. Economic Policy: A European Forum, No. 22. (Illus.). 250p. 1997. pap. text 38.95 (*0-631-20305-2*) Blackwell Pubs.

De Menil, Georges, jt. ed. see Aslund, Anders.

De Menocal, Richard & John Paul, II. The Way of the Cross. LC 96-172523. (Illus.). 63p. 1994. pap. 2.95 (*0-8198-8270-4*) Pauline Bks.

***De Mente, Boye.** The Chinese Have a Word for It: The Complete Guide to Chinese Thought & Culture. LC 00-37455. 2000. 15.95 (*0-658-01078-6*, Passprt Bks) NTC Contemp Pub Co.

De Mente, Boye. Instant Japanese: Everything You Need in 100 Key Words. (ENG & JPN.). 120p. 1998. pap. 5.95 (*4-900737-07-0*, Pub. by Yen Bks) Tuttle Pubng.

— Japan Made Easy. 264p. 1994. pap. 12.95 (*0-8442-8533-1*, Passprt Bks) NTC Contemp Pub Co.

De Mente, Boye L. Bachelor's Japan. rev. ed. LC 91-65060. 160p. (Orig.). 1991. pap. 9.95 (*0-8048-1692-1*) Tuttle Pubng.

— Behind the Japanese Bow: An In-Depth Guide to Understanding & Predicting Japanese Behavior. LC 92-61660. 200p. 1994. pap. 14.95 (*0-8442-8491-2*, 84912, Passprt Bks) NTC Contemp Pub Co.

— Business Guide to Japan: Opening Doors & Closing Deals! LC 89-50662. 125p. (Orig.). 1989. pap. 5.95 (*0-8048-1613-1*) Tuttle Pubng.

— Chinese Etiquette & Ethics in Business. 1993. pap. 14.95 (*0-8442-8525-0*, Passprt Bks) NTC Contemp Pub Co.

— Chinese Etiquette & Ethics in Business. 2nd ed. LC 94-6700. (Etiquette & Ethics Ser.). (CHI., Illus.). 256p. 1994. pap. 16.95 (*0-8442-8524-2*, 85242, NTC Business Bks) NTC Contemp Pub Co.

— Chinese in Plain English. LC 95-67178. (CHI & ENG., Illus.). 176p. 1995. pap. 9.95 (*0-8442-8481-5*) NTC Contemp Pub Co.

— Diner's Guide to Japan: Wining & Dining the Japanese Way. LC 89-51720. (Illus.). 154p. (Orig.). 1990. pap. 5.95 (*0-8048-1641-7*) Tuttle Pubng.

— Discovering Cultural Japan. 176p. (Orig.). 1995. pap. 12.95 (*0-8442-8511-0*, Passprt Bks) NTC Contemp Pub Co.

— Discovering Cultural Japan. 2nd ed. LC 95-67029. (Illus.). 152p. (Orig.). 1995. pap. 13.95 (*0-8442-8483-1*, 84831, Natl Textbk Co) NTC Contemp Pub Co.

— Everything Japanese. 360p. 1992. 27.95 (*0-8442-8513-7*, Passprt Bks) NTC Contemp Pub Co.

— Everything Japanese: The Authoritative Reference on Japan Today. 320p. 1995. pap. 19.95 (*0-8442-8504-8*, 85048, Passprt Bks) NTC Contemp Pub Co.

— How to Do Business with the Japanese. 2nd ed. (Illus.). 294p. 1994. pap. 17.95 (*0-8442-8492-0*, 84920, NTC Business Bks) NTC Contemp Pub Co.

— How to Do Business with the Japanese: A Complete Guide to Japanese Customs & Business Practices. 280p. 1992. pap. 14.95 (*0-8442-8509-9*, NTC Business Bks) NTC Contemp Pub Co.

— Instant Japanese: Everything You Need in 100 Key Words. (JPN.). 120p. 1993. pap. 5.95 (*0-8048-1889-4*) Tuttle Pubng.

— Japan at Night: A Complete Guide to Entertainment & Leisure in Japan. (Illus.). 320p. 1993. pap. 9.95 (*0-8442-8510-2*, Passprt Bks) NTC Contemp Pub Co.

— Japan Made Easy. 2nd ed. LC 95-67030. (Illus.). 264p. 1995. pap. 12.95 (*0-8442-8528-5*, 85285, Passprt Bks) NTC Contemp Pub Co.

— Japanese Business Dictionary. (JPN.). 210p. 1991. pap. 7.95 (*0-8048-1674-3*) Tuttle Pubng.

— Japanese Etiquette & Ethics in Business. 5th rev. ed. 1992. pap. 14.95 (*0-8442-8507-2*, Passprt Bks) NTC Contemp Pub Co.

— Japanese Etiquette & Ethics in Business. 6th ed. LC 93-9084. (Etiquette & Ethics Ser.). (JPN., Illus.). 206p. 1994. pap. 14.95 (*0-8442-8530-7*, 85307, NTC Business Bks) NTC Contemp Pub Co.

— Japanese for the Travel Industry. LC 95-148159. (Illus.). 128p. 1994. pap. 12.95 (*0-8442-8493-9*, 84939) NTC Contemp Pub Co.

— The Japanese Have a Word for It: The Complete Guide to Japanese Thought & Culture. LC 97-34017. (ENG & JPN., Illus.). 400p. 1997. pap. 15.95 (*0-8442-8316-9*) NTC Contemp Pub Co.

— Japanese in Plain English. (JPN & ENG., Illus.). 248p. 1994. pap. 10.95 (*0-8442-8505-6*, 85056, Natl Textbk Co) NTC Contemp Pub Co.

— The Japanese Influence on America: The Impact, Challenge & Opportunity. 192p. 1994. pap. 11.95 (*0-8442-8512-9*, NTC Business Bks) NTC Contemp Pub Co.

— Korean Etiquette & Ethics in Business. 168p. 1992. pap. 14.95 (*0-8442-8522-6*, NTC Business Bks) NTC Contemp Pub Co.

— Korean Etiquette & Ethics in Business. 2nd ed. LC 93-31033. (Etiquette & Ethics Ser.). (KOR., Illus.). 144p. 1994. pap. 16.95 (*0-8442-8523-4*, 85234, NTC Business Bks) NTC Contemp Pub Co.

— Korean in Plain English. (KOR & ENG., Illus.). 224p. 1994. pap. 9.95 (*0-8442-8521-8*, 85218, Passprt Bks) NTC Contemp Pub Co.

— Lover's Guide to Japan: Where the Action Is . . . And How to Get Some! LC 89-50659. 184p. (Orig.). 1989. pap. 5.95 (*0-8048-1589-5*) Tuttle Pubng.

— Made in Japan. 192p. 1991. 17.95 (*0-8442-8506-4*, Passprt Bks) NTC Contemp Pub Co.

— NTC's Dictionary of Japan's Cultural Code Words. (JPN., Illus.). 384p. 1996. pap. 15.95 (*0-8442-8315-0*, 83150, Natl Textbk Co) NTC Contemp Pub Co.

— NTC's Dictionary of Korea's Business: The Complete Guide to Key Words That Express How the Koreans Think, Communicate, & Behave. LC 97-49357. (Illus.). 416p. 1998. 22.95 (*0-8442-8362-2*, 83622) NTC Contemp Pub Co.

— NTC's Dictionary of Mexican Cultural Code Words. (Illus.). 352p. 1996. 18.95 (*0-8442-7959-5*, 79595) NTC Contemp Pub Co.

— Passport's Japan Almanac. (Illus.). 1987. pap. 17.95 (*0-8442-8508-0*, Passprt Bks) NTC Contemp Pub Co.

— Shopper's Guide to Japan: Getting the Most for Your Yen. 128p. 1991. pap. 5.95 (*0-8048-1642-5*) Tuttle Pubng.

— Survival Japanese: How to Communicate Without Fuss or Fear - Instantly. (JPN.). 126p. (Orig.). 1992. pap. 5.95 (*0-8048-1681-6*) Tuttle Pubng.

— There's a Word for It in Mexico: The Complete Guide to Mexican Thought & Culture. LC 98-20592. 368p. 1998. pap. 15.95 (*0-8442-7251-5*, 72515) NTC Contemp Pub Co.

— Women of the Orient. 160p. (Orig.). 1995. pap. 12.95 (*0-8048-1880-0*) Tuttle Pubng.

De Mente, Boye L., et al. Japan's Cultural Code Words. LC 93-84285. (JPN., Illus.). 384p. 1996. 17.95 (*0-8442-8391-6*, 83916, Natl Textbk Co) NTC Contemp Pub Co.

De Meo, Tony. Football's Explosive Multi-Bone Attack. abr. ed. LC 89-78383. (Illus.). 160p. 1990. reprint ed. pap. 15.00 (*0-9624779-1-5*) Harding Pr.

De Mercedes, ed. see De Arredondo, Gonzalo.

De Merritt, Lynne. Growth Management Bibliography. 47p. 1993. pap. 10.00 (*0-86602-292-9*, Sage Prdcls Pr) Sage.

De Mers, Joe. The Return. 448p. 1997. mass mkt. 6.99 (*0-451-40729-6*, Onyx) NAL.

De Mertens, Charles. An Account of the Plague Which Raged at Moscow, 1771. 1977. reprint ed. 19.00 (*0-89250-007-7*) Orient Res Partners.

de Mesa, Blas Fernandez, see Fernandez de Mesa, Blas.

De Mesquita, Bruce B. & Stokman, Frans N., eds. European Community Decision Making: Models, Applications, & Comparisons. LC 93-43875. 256p. (C). 1994. 37.00 (*0-300-05759-8*) Yale U Pr.

De Mestral, A. L. & Gruchalla-Wesierski, T. Extraterritorial Application of Export Control Legislation: Canada & the U. S. A. (C). 1990. lib. bdg. 129.50 (*0-7923-0526-4*) Kluwer Academic.

De Mestre, Neville. The Mathematics of Projectiles in Sport. (Australian Mathematical Society Lecture Ser.: No. 6). 187p. (C). 1990. pap. text 31.95 (*0-521-39857-6*) Cambridge U Pr.

De Meude-Monpas, J. J. Dictionnaire de Musique. (FRE.). 256p. 1982. pap. 95.00 (*0-7859-8047-4*, 2826606662) Fr & Eur.

De Meude-Monpas, Jean J. Dictionnaire de Musique dans Lequel on Simplifie les Expressions et les Definitions Mathematiques et Physiques Qui Ont Rapport a Cet Art. LC 76-43927. (Music & Theatre in France in the 17th & 18th Centuries Ser.). (FRE.). reprint ed. 45.00 (*0-404-60175-8*) AMS Pr.

De Meulemeester, Katie. The TrigTrainer. (Illus.). 1993. pap. text 10.95 (*0-914534-10-6*) Stokes.

De Meun, Jean, jt. auth. see De Lorris, Guillame.

De Meun, Jean, jt. auth. see De Lorris, Guillaume.

De Meur, Jean, jt. auth. see De Lorris, Guillaume.

De Meuron, jt. auth. see Zaugg, Remy.

De Meurville, E., jt. auth. see Creignou, M.

De Mey, Dennis L. Effective Hiring Procedures: A User Friendly Guide to Successful Employment Techniques for the 21st Century. Addeo, Samuel J., ed. & intro. by. 75p. (Orig.). 1996. pap. 44.95 (*0-9642774-6-8*) BSP.

De Mey, J. G., et al, eds. Pharmacology of Cardiac & Vascular Remodelling: Antiproliferative Drugs. 200p. 1991. 47.95 (*0-387-91391-2*) Spr-Verlag.

De Mey, Marc. The Cognitive Paradigm. 1982. lib. bdg. 117.50 (*90-277-1382-0*) Kluwer Academic.

— The Cognitive Paradigm. LC 82-10162. (Illus.). xxvi, 346p. 1992. pap. text 16.95 (*0-226-14259-0*) U Ch Pr.

De Meyer, K. & Biesemans, S., eds. Simulation of Semiconductor Processes & Devices, 1998. xiv, 406p. 1998. 109.00 (*3-211-83208-4*) Spr-Verlag.

***De Meyer, Sandra.** Human Annexin V: Characterization of the Binding to SHBsAG & the Role in HBV Infection. (Acta Biomedica Lovaniensia Ser.: Vol. 195). (Illus.). 163p. 1999. pap. 52.50 (*90-6186-959-5*, Pub. by Leuven Univ) Coronet Bks.

De Meynard, C. Barbier, tr. see Khurdadbeh.

De Meza, Barbara S. Business Letter Handbook: Spanish-English, English-Spanish. (gr. 12 up). 1987. pap. text 8.00 (*0-13-104183-5*, 17765) Prentice ESL.

De Meza, David & Osborne, Michael. Problems in Price Theory. LC 80-16597. (Illus.). xiv, 302p. 1993. pap. text 13.00 (*0-226-14294-9*) U Ch Pr.

De Mezieres, Philippe. Le Livre de la Vertu du Sacrement de Mariage. Williamson, Joan B., ed. LC 92-15499. (FRE.). 442p. 1993. text 59.95 (*0-8132-0767-3*) Cath U Pr.

De Micelis, Marco, jt. notes see Dal Co, Francesco.

De Michele, Vincenzo. Diccionario: Atlas De Mineralogia. 2nd ed. (SPA.). 216p. 1978. 17.50 (*0-8288-5164-6*, S50260) Fr & Eur.

De Micheli, Giovanni. Synthesis & Optimization of Digital Circuits. LC 93-43595. 576p. (C). 1994. 82.19 (*0-07-016333-2*) McGraw.

De Micheli, Giovanni, ed. Hardware/Software Co-Design: Proceedings of the NATO Advanced Study Institute, Tremezzo, Italy, June 19-30, 1995. (NATO ASI Series E: Applied Sciences). 480p. (C). 1996. pap. text 79.00 (*0-7923-3883-9*) Kluwer Academic.

De Micheli, Giovanni & Sami, Mariagiovanna, eds. Hardware/Software Co-Design: Proceedings of the NATO Advanced Study Institute, Tremezzo, Italy, June 19-30, 1995. LC 95-48407. (NATO ASI Series E: Applied Sciences: Vol. 310). 480p. (C). 1996. lib. bdg. 224.00 (*0-7923-3882-0*) Kluwer Academic.

De Micheli, Giovanni, jt. auth. see Ku, David C.

De Michelis, G., ed. see Van Leeuwen, J.

De Michelis, Giorgio, ed. Proceedings of the Third European Conference on Computer-Supported Cooperative Work - ECSCW '93. LC 93-26848. 380p. (C). 1993. lib. bdg. 166.50 (*0-7923-2447-1*) Kluwer Academic.

De Michell, Giovanni, jt. auth. see Benini, Luca.

De Mielche, Paul. Going to the Dog: Therapy Stories for Grown-Ups. 2nd ed. (Illus.). 148p. (Orig.). 1994. pap. 14.95 (*1-883785-02-2*) Paw Print Pub.

De Mier, Fray S. The Memoirs of Fray Servando Teresa de Mier. Rotker, Susana, ed. Lane, Helen, tr. from SPA. LC 97-40671. (Library of Latin America). 304p. 1998. 30.00 (*0-19-510673-3*) OUP.

De Miguel, J. M. Historia de Espana Vol. 13: La Expansion Peninsular y Mediterranea C1212-C1350 el Reino De Navarra, la Corona De Aragon, Portugal. (SPA.). 660p. 1992. 189.50 (*84-239-4824-2*) Elliots Bks.

De Mijolla, Elizabeth. Autobiographical Quests: Augustine, Montaigne, Rousseau, & Wordsworth. LC 93-28201. (C). 1994. 35.00 (*0-8139-1468-X*) U Pr of Va.

De Mille, Agnes. And Promenade Home. LC 79-28690. (Series in Dance). 1980. reprint ed. lib. bdg. 27.50 (*0-306-79614-7*) Da Capo.

— Dance to the Piper & Promenade Home: A Two-Part Autobiography. (Quality Paperbacks Ser.). (Illus.). xii, 643p. 1982. reprint ed. pap. 17.95 (*0-306-80161-2*) Da Capo.

De Mille, Agnes & Gregory, Cynthia, intros. Dance to the Piper, Set. LC 79-28689. (Series in Dance). (Illus.). 342p. 1980. reprint ed. 49.50 (*0-306-79615-5*) Da Capo.

De Mille, Anna G. Henry George, Citizen of the World. Shoemaker, Don C., ed. LC 79-138218. (Illus.). 276p. (C). 1972. reprint ed. lib. bdg. 65.00 (*0-8371-5575-4*, DEHG, Greenwood Pr) Greenwood.

De Mille, James. A Strange Manuscript Found in a Copper Cylinder. LC 74-15964. (Science Fiction Ser.). (Illus.). 291p. 1975. reprint ed. 28.95 (*0-405-06285-0*) Ayer.

De Mille, Richard. My Secret Lover: Lorna Moon. LC 97-48280. (Illus.). 311p. 1998. 25.00 (*0-374-21757-2*) FS&G.

— Put Your Mother on the Ceiling. rev. ed. LC 99-222012. 160p. 1997. 20.00 (*0-939266-28-8*) Gestalt Journal.

De Minon, Miguel Herrero, see Herrero de Minon, Miguel.

De Miquel, Emilio, ed. see Garcia Lorca, Federico.

De Miranda, Celene, ed. see Gilbertson, Roger G.

De Miranda, Francisco. The Diary of Francisco de Miranda: Tour of the United States, 1783-1784. limited ed. Robertson, William S., ed. (SPA.). 1928. 30.00 (*0-686-17414-3*) R S Barnes.

De Miranda, Francisco De Sa, see De Sa De Miranda, Francisco.

De Mitchell, Lisa A., ed. see Bondy, Valerie C.

De Moissac, Jeanne M. Second Skin. LC 99-460582. 88p. 1999. pap. 7.95 (*1-55050-142-9*) Genl Dist Srvs.

De Moivre, A. Doctrine of Chances, or A Method of Calculating the Probabilities of Events in Play. 257p. 1967. reprint ed. 45.00 (*0-7146-1058-5*, BHA-01058, Pub. by F Cass Pubs) Intl Spec Bk.

De Moivre, Abraham. Doctrine of Chances, or A Method of Calculating the Probabilities of Events in Play: Including a Treatise on the Annuities of Lives. 3rd ed. LC 66-23756. 380p. 1967. lib. bdg. 24.95 (*0-8284-0200-0*) Chelsea Pub.

De Mola, Dolores Loret, see Piedra, Joaquin E.

De Mola, Yolanda, tr. see Ferre, Maria I.

De Molina. Damned for Despair. Round, N. G., ed. (Hispanic Classics Ser.). 1986. pap. 25.00 (*0-85668-330-2*, Pub. by Aris & Phillips) David Brown.

De Molina, Gonzalo Argote, see Argote De Molina, Gonzalo.

De Molina, Gwynne. Trickster of Seville & the Stone Guest. Edwards, ed. (Hispanic Classics Ser.). 1986. pap. 25.00 (*0-85668-301-9*, Pub. by Aris & Phillips) David Brown.

de Molina, Jose L. Malo, see Malo de Molina, Jose L.

De Molina, Luis. On Divine Foreknowledge: "Concordia", Pt. IV. LC 88-3887. 320p. 1988. text 45.00 (*0-8014-2131-4*) Cornell U Pr.

***De Molina, Miguel.** Botin de Guerra: Autobiografia. (Espana Plural). (SPA., Illus.). 1998. 33.95 (*84-08-02410-8*) Planeta Edit.

De Molina, Tirso. El Burlador de Sevilla. (SPA.). 144p. 1997. pap. text 4.00 (*1-56328-080-9*) Edit Plaza Mayor.

— El Burlandor de Sevilla y Convidado de Piedra: Del Maestro Tirso de Molina. Parr, James A., ed. (Spanish Classical Texts Ser.). (SPA.). 152p. 1994. pap. 10.95 (*0-86698-162-4*, P20) Pegasus Pr.

— Damned for Despair. Round, Nicholas G., ed. (Hispanic Classics Ser.). 1986. 59.95 (*0-85668-329-9*, Pub. by Aris & Phillips) David Brown.

— Damned for Despair & Don Gill of the Green Breeches. Boswell, Lawrence, tr. 176p. 1992. pap. 14.95 (*0-948230-55-X*, Pub. by Absolute Classics) Theatre Comm.

— Don Juan: The Beguiler from Seville & the Stone Guest. Oppenheimer, Max, Jr., tr. 1976. pap. 8.50 (*0-87291-082-2*) Coronado Pr.

— Poesias Liricas. (SPA.). 228p. 1980. 10.25 (*0-8288-7026-8*) Fr & Eur.

— Revenge of Tamar. Whitworth, Paul, tr. 112p. 1998. pap. 12.95 (*0-948230-94-0*, Pub. by Theatre Comm) Consort Bk Sales.

— Tamar's Revenge: La Venganza de Tamar. Lyon, ed. (Hispanic Classics Ser.). 1988. 59.95 (*0-85668-323-X*, Pub. by Aris & Phillips); pap. 25.00 (*0-85668-324-8*, Pub. by Aris & Phillips) David Brown.

— The Trickster of Seville & the Stone Guest. Edwards, ed. (Hispanic Classics Ser.). 1986. 59.95 (*0-85668-300-0*, Pub. by Aris & Phillips) David Brown.

— La Venganza de Tamar. Paterson, A. K., ed. LC 69-10572. 158p. reprint ed. pap. 45.10 (*0-608-12208-4*, 2024442) Bks Demand.

— La Vida y Muerta de Herodes (The Life & Death of Herod) A Christmas Tragedy & Epiphany: Edited with Berse Translation, Introduction, & Notes. Fornoff, Frederick H., ed. & tr. by. from SPA. LC 91-1716. (Iberica Ser.: Vol. 2). 365p. 1992. 37.95 (*0-8204-1617-7*) P Lang Pubng.

De Molina, Tirso & Zorrilla y Moral, Jose. El Burlador de Sevilla & Don Juan Tenorio. (Classic Collections). (SPA.). (C). 1998. pap. 9.95 (*84-294-4561-7*) Santillana.

De Molinari, Gustavo. The Society of Tomorrow. 1973. 59.95 (*0-8490-1071-3*) Gordon Pr.

de Molino, Cornelia Rosales, see Molino, Cornelia Rosales de.

D

De Molins, Antonio E. Diccionario Biografico y Bibliografico de Escritores y Artistas del Siglo, 2 vols., Set. (SPA., Illus.). lii, 1475p. 1972. reprint ed. write for info. (*3-487-04220-7*) G Olms Pubs.

De Moncrif, Francois A. Adventures of Zeloide & Amanzarifdine. Moncrieff, K. Scott, tr. & intro. by. LC 78-178449. (Short Story Index Reprint Ser.). 1977. reprint ed. 19.95 (*0-8369-4050-4*) Ayer.

De Moncrif, Paradis. The Adventures of Zeloide. Moncrieff, K. Scott, tr. LC 75-172542. 1972. reprint ed. 24.95 (*0-405-08794-2*) Ayer.

de Monfreid. English For Electronics. 1998. 16.00 (*84-7615-445-3*) McGraw.

De Monfreid, Henry. Hashish. large type ed. (Large Print Ser.). 442p. 1992. reprint ed. lib. bdg. 24.00 (*0-939495-33-3*) North Bks.

— Hashish. 268p. 1998. reprint ed. lib. bdg. 24.00 (*1-58287-000-4*) North Bks.

De Monie, Gustaaf. Strategies for Global & Regional Ports: The Case of Caribbean Container & Cruise Ports. LC 99-17113. 1999. write for info. (*0-7923-8431-8*) Kluwer Academic.

De Montalban, Juan Perez, see Perez De Montalban, Juan.

De Montalvo, Soledad. Women, Food & Sex in History, Vol. I. 277p. (Orig.). 1988. pap. 12.00 (*0-910309-47-7*, 5421) Am Atheist.

— Women, Food & Sex in History, Vol. II. 298p. (Orig.). 1989. pap. 12.00 (*0-910309-48-5*, 5422) Am Atheist.

— Women, Food & Sex in History, Vol. III. 319p. (Orig.). 1989. pap. 12.00 (*0-910309-49-3*, 5423) Am Atheist.

— Women, Food & Sex in History, Vol. IV. 300p. (Orig.). 1990. pap. 12.00 (*0-910309-61-2*, 5425) Am Atheist.

De Montano, Marty K. The Butterfly Dance. LC 98-5313. (Tales of the People Ser.). 32p. (J). (ps-5). 2000. 14.95 (*0-7892-0161-5*, Abbeville Kids) Abbeville Pr.

— Coyote in Love with a Star. LC 98-5313. (Tales of the People Ser.). (Illus.). 31p. (J). (ps-2). 1998. 14.95 (*0-7892-0162-3*, Abbeville Kids) Abbeville Pr.

De Montaudouin, Maya. MXM: Man Out of Mutant, a Personal Quest for a Creed to Live By. LC 95-77658. (Illus.). 104p. 1996. pap. 7.95 (*0-9624648-4-8*) Good Earth Pubns.

De Montclos, Jean-Marie P. Vaux-le-Vicomte. (Illus.). 224p. 1997. 40.00 (*1-85759-173-9*) Scala Books.

— Versailles. (Illus.). 424p. 1991. 95.00 (*1-55859-228-8*) Abbeville Pr.

— Versailles. (Illus.). 160p. 1994. 29.98 (*0-89660-052-1*, Artabras) Abbeville Pr.

De Monte, John, ed. A Collection & Portfolio of Golf Humor. 18p. (Orig.). 1984. pap. 3.00 (*0-9605176-2-6*) Raycol Prods.

De Monte, Philippe. The Complete Works of Philippe De Monte, 31 vols. Incl. Canticum Magnificat. Van den Borren, Charles & Van Nuffel, Julius, eds. (Illus.). 1965. reprint ed. pap. 37.50 (*0-8450-1512-5*); Cantiones ad Testudinis Usum Accommodatae. Van den Borren, Charles & Van Nuffel, Julius, eds. 1965. reprint ed. pap. 37.50 (*0-8450-1525-7*); Collectio Decem Carminum Gallicorum, Alias Chansons Francaises 4-5 Vocum. Van den Borren, Charles & Van Nuffel, Julius, eds. (Illus.). 1965. reprint ed. pap. 37.50 (*0-8450-1520-6*); Collectio Decem Motettorum 5-6-7 et 8 Vocum. Van den Borren, Charles & Van Nuffel, Julius, eds. 1965. reprint ed. pap. 37.50 (*0-8450-1515-X*); Liber Quartus Madrigalium Quatuor Vocum. Van den Borren, Charles & Van Nuffel, Julius, eds. (Illus.). 1965. reprint ed. pap. 37.50 (*0-8450-1519-2*); Liber Quartus Motettorum Quinque Vocum. Van den Borren, Charles & Van Nuffel, Julius, eds. (Illus.). 1965. reprint ed. pap. 37.50 (*0-8450-1522-2*); Liber Septimus Motettorum Cum Quinque Vocibus. Van den Borren, Charles & Van Nuffel, Julius, eds. (Illus.). 1965. reprint ed. pap. 37.50 (*0-8450-1517-6*); Madrigalium Spiritualium Liber Primus cum Sex Vocibus. Van Doorslaer, George. 1965. reprint ed. pap. 37.50 (*0-8450-1506-0*); Missa "Ancor Che Col Partire" Van den Borren, Charles & Van Nuffel, Julius, eds. (Illus.). 1965. reprint ed. pap. 37.50 (*0-8450-1508-7*); Missa "Aspice Domine" Van den Borren, Charles & Van Nuffel, Julius, eds. (Illus.). 1965. reprint ed. pap. 37.50 (*0-8450-1526-5*); Missa "Cum Sit Omnipotens Rector Olympi" Van den Borren, Charles & Van Nuffel, Julius, eds. (Illus.). 1965. reprint ed. pap. 37.50 (*0-8450-1524-9*); Missa de "Requiem" Van den Borren, Charles & Van Nuffel, Julius, eds. (Illus.). 1965. reprint ed. pap. 37.50 (*0-8450-1513-3*); Missa "Inclina Cor Meum" Van den Borren, Charles & Van Nuffel, Julius, eds. (Illus.). 1965. reprint ed. pap. 37.50 (*0-8450-1501-X*); Missa "La Dolce Vista" Van den Borren, Charles & Van Nuffel, Julius, eds. (Illus.). 1965. reprint ed. pap. 37.50 (*0-8450-1514-1*); Missa "Nasce la Pena Mia" Van den Borren, Charles & Van Nuffel, Julius, eds. 1965. reprint ed. pap. 37.50 (*0-8450-1510-9*); Missa "O Altitudo Divitiarum" Van den Borren, Charles & Van Nuffel, Julius, eds. (Illus.). 1965. reprint ed. pap. 37.50 (*0-8450-1504-4*); Missa "Quando Lieta Sperai" Van den Borren, Charles & Van Nuffel, Julius, eds. 1965. reprint ed. pap. 37.50 (*0-8450-1523-0*); Missa Quaternis Vocibus. Van den Borren, Charles & Van Nuffel, Julius, eds. (Illus.). 1965. reprint ed. pap. 37.50 (*0-8450-1516-8*); Missa "Quomodo Dilexi" Van den Borren, Charles & Van Nuffel, Julius, eds. (Illus.). 1965. reprint ed. pap. 37.50 (*0-8450-1527-3*); Missa "Reviens Vers Moi" Van den Borren, Charles & Van Nuffel, Julius, eds. 1965. reprint ed. pap. 37.50 (*0-8450-1509-5*); Missa Sex Vocum, Ex Cod. Bibl. Municipalis Norimbergensis. Van den Borren, Charles & Van Nuffel, Julius, eds. (Illus.). 1965. reprint ed. pap. 37.50 (*0-8450-1518-4*); Missa Sine Nomine. Van den Borren, Charles & Van Nuffel, Julius, eds. (Illus.). 1965. reprint ed. pap. 37.50 (*0-8450-1507-9*); Missa "Sine Nomine", 8 Vocum. Van den Borren, Charles & Van Nuffel, Julius, eds. 1965. reprint ed. pap. 37.50 (*0-8450-1529-X*); Missa "Sine Nomine", 5 Vocum. Van den Borren, Charles & Van Nuffel, Julius, eds. 1965. reprint ed. pap. 37.50 (*0-8450-1528-1*); Missa Sine Nomine, No. 2. Van den Borren, Charles & Van Nuffel, Julius, eds. (Illus.). 1965. reprint ed. pap. 37.50 (*0-8450-1503-6*); Missa "Sine Nomine", 6 Vocum. (Illus.). 1965. reprint ed. pap. 37.50 (*0-8450-1530-3*); Missa "Sine Nomine", 6 Vocum. (Illus.). 1965. reprint ed. pap. 37.50 (*0-8450-1531-1*); Missa Super "Cara la Vita Mia" Van den Borren, Charles & Van Nuffel, Julius, eds. 1965. reprint ed. pap. 37.50 (*0-8450-1521-4*); Missa "Ultimi Miei Sospiri" Van den Borren, Charles & Van Nuffel, Julius, eds. 1965. reprint ed. pap. 37.50 (*0-8450-1505-2*); Motettum "O Bone Jesu," Tripartitum. Van Doorslaer, George. (Illus.). 1965. reprint ed. pap. 37.50 (*0-8450-1502-8*); No. 1. Missa Sine Nomine. Van den Borren, Charles & Van Nuffel, Julius, eds. (Illus.). 1965. reprint ed. pap. 37.50 (*0-8450-1511-7*); 2808p. 1965. reprint ed. Set pap. 675.00 (*0-8450-1500-1*) Broude.

De Montebello, Philippe, ed. The Metropolitan Museum of Art Guide. LC 94-9094. 1994. write for info. (*0-87099-711-4*) Metro Mus Art.

De Montebello, Philippe, selected by. The Metropolitan Museum of Art Guide. 2nd ed. (Illus.). 470p. 1995. 19.95 (*0-8109-6486-4*, Pub. by Abrams) Time Warner.

De Montebello, Philippe & Curatorial Staff, eds. The Metropolitan Museum of Art Guide. 2nd ed. LC 94-9094. (Illus.). 470p. 1994. pap. 12.95 (*0-87099-710-6*) Metro Mus Art.

De Monteflores, Carmen. Singing Softly - Cantando Bajito. LC 89-4125. (ENG & SPA.). 208p. 1989. lib. bdg. 18.95 (*0-933216-65-3*) Aunt Lute Bks.

De Monteiro, Longteine & Neustadt, Katherine. The Elephant Walk Cookbook: The Exciting World of Cambodian Cuisine from the Nationally Acclaimed Restaurant. LC 98-28214. 336p. 1998. 35.00 (*0-395-89253-8*) HM.

De Montellano, Bernard R. Ortiz, see Ortiz De Montellano, Bernard R.

de Montellano, Paul R. Ortiz, see Ortiz de Montellano, Paul R., ed.

De Montemayor, Jorge. The Diana. Mueller, Roseanna, tr. from SPA. LC 88-1730. (Spanish Studies: Vol 1). 250p. 1989. lib. bdg. 89.95 (*0-88946-735-8*) E Mellen.

— Los Siete Libros de Diana. Moreno Baez, Enrique, ed. (SPA.). 239p. 1968. pap. 100.00 (*0-614-00214-1*); 100.00 (*0-614-00109-9*) Elliots Bks.

— Los Siete Libros de la Diana. Arribas, Julian, ed. (Illus.). 384p. (C). 1996. 63.00 (*1-85566-044-X*, Pub. by Tamesis Bks Ltd) Boydell & Brewer.

de Montes, Carmen Gil, see Laita, Luis M. & Gil de Montes, Carmen.

De Montes, Fay D. Vida Antes de la Vida. (Coleccion Aprender). (SPA., Illus.). 32p. (Orig.). 1985. pap. 3.00 (*0-89729-359-2*) Ediciones.

De Montesquieu, Charles. The Persian Letters. Betts, C. J., tr. (Classics Ser.). 352p. 1973. pap. 11.95 (*0-14-044281-2*, Penguin Classics) Viking Penguin.

— The Spirit of the Laws. Cohler, Anne M. et al, eds. (Cambridge Texts in the History of Political Thought Ser.). 808p. (C). 1989. text 64.95 (*0-521-36183-4*); pap. text 21.95 (*0-521-36974-6*) Cambridge U Pr.

— The Spirit of the Laws. (Library of Classics: No. 9). 768p. 1970. pap. 16.95 (*0-02-849270-6*) Hafner.

De Montesquieu, Charles-Louis. De l'Espirit des Lois: Les Grands Themes. 1970. 9.95 (*0-686-54781-0*) Fr & Eur.

— De l'Esprit des Lois, 2 vols. 566p. 1973. 19.95 (*0-8288-7485-9*); 19.95 (*0-8288-7486-7*); write for info. (*0-685-74480-9*) Fr & Eur.

— De l'Esprit des Lois. (Coll. Prestige). (FRE.). 510p. 1979. pap. 13.95 (*0-7859-4632-2*) Fr & Eur.

— De l'Esprit des Lois, 2 tomes, Set. Truc, ed. (FRE.). 1962. pap. 7.95 (*0-8288-9966-5*, F48434) Fr & Eur.

— Essai sur le Gout. (FRE.). 176p. 1967. 19.95 (*0-8288-9965-7*, F48400) Fr & Eur.

— Lettres Persanes. Verniere, Paul, ed. (Coll. Prestige). 49.95 (*0-685-34047-3*); pap. 24.95 (*0-685-34046-5*) Fr & Eur.

— Lettres Persanes. 1984. pap. 10.95 (*0-7859-3061-2*) Fr & Eur.

— Oeuvres Completes, 2 tomes, 1. deluxe ed. Caillois, Roger, ed. (Pleiade Ser.). (FRE.). 84.95 (*2-07-010365-X*) Schoenhof.

— Oeuvres Completes, 2 tomes, 2. deluxe ed. Caillois, Roger, ed. (Pleiade Ser.). (FRE.). 88.95 (*2-07-010366-8*) Schoenhof.

— Pensees: Le Spicilege. (FRE.). 1991. pap. 59.95 (*0-7859-3032-9*) Fr & Eur.

— The Spirit of the Laws: A Compendium of the First English Editon with an English Translation of "An Essay on Causes Affecting Mind & Characters", 1737-1743. Carrithers, David W., ed. 1978. pap. 18.95 (*0-520-03455-4*, Pub. by U CA Pr) Cal Prin Full Svc.

De Montesquieu, Charles-Louis & Ehrard, Jean. Considerations sur les Causes de la Grandeur des Romains et de Leur Decadence. (FRE.). 192p. 1990. 8.95 (*0-7859-4652-7*) Fr & Eur.

De Montfaucon, Bernard. Bibliotheca Bibliothecarum Manuscriptorum Nova, 2 vols., Set. cclviii, 1669p. 1982. reprint ed. write for info. (*3-487-07162-2*) G Olms Pubs.

De Montfaucon De Villars, Abbe N. Le Comte de Gabalis. LC 83-63139. (Illus.). 182p. 1984. pap. 10.95 (*0-932785-09-3*) Philos Pub.

— Le Comte de Gabalis. Goscinsky, Michael, ed. & illus. by. LC 83-63139. 182p. 1984. 16.95 (*0-932785-10-7*) Philos Pub.

— Comte de Gabalis: Discourses on the Secret Sciences & Mysteries in Accordance with the Principles of the Ancient Magi & the Wisdom of the Kabalistic Philosophers. 352p. 1992. reprint ed. pap. 27.00 (*1-56459-201-4*) Kessinger Pub.

De Montgolfier, Bernard. Vigner Dictionnaire des Chateaux de France. (FRE.). 250p. pap. 135.00 (*0-686-56837-0*, M-6615) Fr & Eur.

De Montherlant, Henry. Un Assassin Est Mon Maitre. (FRE.). 312p. 1971. pap. 27.95 (*0-8288-9886-3*, F115560) Fr & Eur.

— Aux Fontaines de Desir: La Petite Infante de Castille. (FRE.). 248p. 1954. pap. 15.95 (*0-8288-9631-3*, 2070245756) Fr & Eur.

— Aux Fontaines du Desir. 248p. 1954. 4.95 (*0-686-54803-5*) Fr & Eur.

— Les Bestaires. (FRE.). 1972. pap. 10.95 (*0-8288-3714-7*, F115680) Fr & Eur.

— Le Bestiaire Celeste. 13.95 (*0-8288-9630-5*, F115580) Fr & Eur.

— Bestiaires. (FRE.). 332p. 1972. pap. 10.95 (*0-7859-1629-6*, 2070362698) Fr & Eur.

— Broceliande. (FRE.). 192p. 1956. pap. 10.95 (*0-7859-1289-4*, 2070245861) Fr & Eur.

— Le Cardinal D'Espagne. 1960. 11.50 (*0-685-11063-X*); pap. 10.95 (*0-8288-9632-1*, M6784) Fr & Eur.

— Le Cardinal D'Espagne. (FRE.). 1974. pap. 10.95 (*0-8288-3715-5*, M3784) Fr & Eur.

— Carnets, 4 tomes. Incl. 1942-1943. (FRE.). 236p. 1948. pap. 26.95 (*0-7859-5308-6*); 1932-1934. (FRE.) 224p. 1956. pap. 26.95 (*0-7859-5309-4*); 1930-1932. (FRE.). 216p. 1956. pap. 26.95 (*0-7859-5310-8*); 1968. pap. write for info. (*0-318-51942-9*) Fr & Eur.

— Les Celibataires. 256p. 1972. write for info. (*0-318-63445-7*); pap. 10.95 (*0-8288-3716-3*, F115690) Fr & Eur.

— Celles Qu'on Prend dans ses Bras. pap. 10.95 (*0-8288-9634-8*, F115690) Fr & Eur.

— Celles Qu'on Prend dans Ses Bras. (FRE.). 1983. pap. 10.95 (*0-8288-3717-1*, F115290) Fr & Eur.

— Chant de Mimos, Pasiphae. (Coll. Las Peintres du Livre). (FRE., Illus.). 39.95 (*0-8288-9635-6*, F115610) Fr & Eur.

— Le Chaos et la Nuit. (FRE.). 1973. pap. 10.95 (*0-8288-3718-X*, M3786) Fr & Eur.

— Le Chaos et la Nuit. (Folio Ser.: No. 422). (FRE., Illus.). 8.95 (*2-07-036422-4*) Schoenhof.

— Coups de Soleil: Textes. (FRE.). 344p. 1976. pap. 19.95 (*0-7859-1346-7*, 2070293637) Fr & Eur.

— Demain il fera Jour. (FRE.). 208p. 1949. pap. 10.95 (*0-7859-1287-8*, 2070245691) Fr & Eur.

— Le Demon du Bien. (Jeunes Filles Ser.: Vol. 3). (FRE.). 1972. pap. 10.95 (*0-8288-3719-8*, F115710) Fr & Eur.

— Discours de Reception a l'Academie Francaise. (FRE.). 88p. 1963. pap. 10.95 (*0-7859-1290-8*, 2070245942) Fr & Eur.

— Encore un Instant de Bonheur. LC 91-71902. (FRE.). 144p. 1954. pap. 10.95 (*0-7859-1288-6*, 2070245772) Fr & Eur.

— Essais. (FRE.). 1963. 110.00 (*0-8288-9629-1*, F115200) Fr & Eur.

— L' Etoile du Soir. (FRE., Illus.). 36.95 (*0-8288-9636-4*, F115640) Fr & Eur.

— Le Fichler Parisien. (FRE.). 184p. 1974. pap. 16.95 (*0-7859-1342-4*, 2070289842) Fr & Eur.

— Fils De Personne. 1944. 13.25 (*0-685-35872-0*) Schoenhof.

— Histoire d'amour de la Rose de Sable. 9.95 (*0-685-36981-1*) Fr & Eur.

— L' Infini est du Cote de Malatesta. pap. 9.95 (*0-685-36982-X*) Fr & Eur.

— Les Jeunes Filles. Incl. pap. 8.95 (*2-07-036815-7*; (Folio Ser.: No. 815). (FRE.). write for info. (*0-318-52034-6*) Schoenhof.

— Les Jeunes Filles, Vol. 1. (FRE.). 1978. pap. 10.95 (*0-8288-3720-1*, F115730) Fr & Eur.

— Les Lepreuses, Les Jeunes Filles. (Jeunes Filles Ser.: Vol. 4). (FRE.). 1972. pap. 10.95 (*0-8288-3721-X*, F115740) Fr & Eur.

— Mais Aimons-Nous Ceux Que Nous Aimons? (FRE.). 240p. 1973. 19.95 (*0-7859-0111-6*, M3789) Fr & Eur.

— Maitre de Santiago. 160p. 1972. write for info. (*0-318-63485-6*) Fr & Eur.

— Le Maitre de Santiago. (FRE.). 1972. pap. 10.95 (*0-8288-3722-8*, F115750) Fr & Eur.

— Le Maitre de Santiago. (Folio Ser.: No. 142). (FRE.). 160p. 1972. 6.95 (*2-07-036142-X*) Schoenhof.

— Malatesta. 1973. write for info. (*0-318-63486-4*); pap. 10.95 (*0-8288-3723-6*, M3790) Fr & Eur.

— Malatesta. (Folio Ser.: No. 305). (FRE.). 1973. 6.95 (*2-07-036305-8*) Schoenhof.

— La Maree du Soir: Carnets, 1968-1971. 17.50 (*0-685-36983-8*); pap. 9.95 (*0-686-55525-2*) Fr & Eur.

— Mariette Lydis. (Illus.). 65.75 (*0-685-36997-8*) Fr & Eur.

— Mors et Vita, Service Inutile. pap. 9.50 (*0-685-36984-6*) Fr & Eur.

— La Mort Qui Fait le Trottoir: Don Juan. (FRE.). 1991. pap. 10.95 (*0-8288-3724-4*, F115760) Fr & Eur.

— Moustique. (FRE.). 1987. pap. 8.95 (*0-7859-3419-7*) Fr & Eur.

— Oeuvre Romanesque, 8 vols., Set. 612.50 (*0-685-11433-3*) Fr & Eur.

— Les Olympiques. (FRE.). 1973. pap. 10.95 (*0-8288-3750-3*, M3791) Fr & Eur.

— La Petite Infante de Castille. (FRE.). 1973. pap. 10.95 (*0-8288-3751-1*, M3792) Fr & Eur.

— La Petite Infante de Castille. (Folio Ser.: No. 370). (FRE., Illus.). pap. 6.95 (*2-07-036370-8*) Schoenhof.

— Pitie pour les Femmes. (Jeunes Filles Ser.: Vol. 2). (FRE.). 1972. pap. 10.95 (*0-8288-3752-X*, F115780) Fr & Eur.

— Pitie pour les Femmes. (Folio Ser.: No. 156). (FRE.). 224p. 1972. 8.95 (*2-07-036156-X*) Schoenhof.

— Port-Royal. (FRE.). 1960. write for info. (*0-318-63579-8*) Fr & Eur.

— Port Royal. (FRE.). 1972. pap. 10.95 (*0-8288-3753-8*, F115790) Fr & Eur.

— Port Royal & Notes de Theatre sur le Maitre de Santiago et Port-Royal. (Folio Ser.: No. 253). (FRE.). 192p. 1972. pap. 6.95 (*2-07-036253-1*) Schoenhof.

— Reine Morte. 1957. write for info. (*0-318-63586-0*) Fr & Eur.

— Reine Morte. (Folio Ser.: No. 12). (FRE.). 1957. pap. 6.95 (*2-07-036012-1*) Schoenhof.

— La Reine Morte. (FRE.). 1972. pap. 10.95 (*0-8288-3754-6*, F115800) Fr & Eur.

— La Reine Morte. (FRE.). (C). pap. 9.95 (*0-8442-1840-5*, VF1840-5) NTC Contemp Pub Co.

— La Releve du Matin. (FRE.). 1972. pap. 10.95 (*0-8288-3755-4*, F115810) Fr & Eur.

— Romans, Vol. 1. (FRE.). 1960. lib. bdg. 110.00 (*0-8288-3568-3*, F115180) Fr & Eur.

— Romans, Vol. 2. (FRE.). 1982. lib. bdg. 125.00 (*0-8288-3569-1*, M12083) Fr & Eur.

— Romans et Oeuvres De Fiction Non Theatrales, 1. (Pleiade Ser.). 1960. 72.95 (*0-685-11538-0*) Fr & Eur.

— Romans et Oeuvres De Fiction Non Theatrales, 2. (Pleiade Ser.). 1960. 64.95 (*0-685-01762-1*) Fr & Eur.

— Service Inutile. 9.95 (*0-685-36986-2*) Fr & Eur.

— Le Songe. (FRE.). 1982. pap. 13.95 (*0-8288-3756-2*, F115510) Fr & Eur.

— Le Songe. (Folio Ser.: No. 1458). (FRE.). pap. 10.95 (*2-07-037458-0*) Schoenhof.

— Sur les Femmes. 14.95 (*0-685-36988-9*) Fr & Eur.

— Textes sous une Occupation, 1940-1944. pap. 9.95 (*0-685-36989-7*) Fr & Eur.

— Theatre, 5 vols. (FRE., Illus.). 380p. 1966. 525.00 (*0-8288-9885-5*, F115190) Fr & Eur.

— Theatre. Laprade, Armand, ed. (FRE.). 1472p. 1955. lib. bdg. 115.00 (*0-7859-3768-4*, 2070103749) Fr & Eur.

— Theatre, 5 tomes, Set. 525.00 (*0-685-11587-9*) Fr & Eur.

— Tous Feux Eteints: Carnets 1965, 1966, 1697, Carnets sans Dates et Carnets 1972. (FRE.). 192p. 1975. pap. 19.95 (*0-7859-1343-2*, 2070293025) Fr & Eur.

— La Tragedie Sans Masque: Notes de Theatre. 16.50 (*0-685-36990-0*) Fr & Eur.

— Le Treizieme Cesar. 13.95 (*0-685-36991-9*) Fr & Eur.

— Le Treizieme Cesar. (FRE.). 200p. 1970. pap. 14.95 (*0-7859-1335-1*, 2070272222) Fr & Eur.

— Va Jouer avec Cette Poussiere: Carnets (1958-1964) (FRE.). 1966. 7.95 (*0-8288-9640-2*, F115570) Fr & Eur.

— Ville Dont le Prince Est un Enfant. (Folio Ser.: No. 293). (FRE.). 1963. pap. 9.95 (*2-07-036293-0*) Schoenhof.

— La Ville Dont le Prince Est un Enfant. (FRE.). 1973. pap. 11.95 (*0-8288-3757-0*, M3794) Fr & Eur.

— Voyager Solitaire est un Diable. (FRE.). 212p. 1961. pap. 11.95 (*0-685-74010-2*, 207024590X) Fr & Eur.

De Montherlant, Henry, jt. auth. see Kilmartin, Terence.

De Monthoux, Pierre G. The Moral Philosophy of Management: From Quesnay to Keynes. LC 93-16576. (Studies in Socio-Economics). 328p. (C). (gr. 13). 1993. pap. text 40.95 (*1-56324-377-6*) M E Sharpe.

De Montigny, Gerald A. Social Working: An Ethnography of Front-Line Practice. 276p. 1995. pap. text 19.95 (*0-8020-7726-9*) U of Toronto Pr.

De Montmollin, Olivier. The Archaeology of Political Structure: Settlement Analysis in a Classic Maya Polity. (Illus.). 308p. (C). 1989. text 85.00 (*0-521-36232-6*) Cambridge U Pr.

De Montmort, R. Essai D'analyse sur les Jeux de Hazard. LC 79-1226. (Illus.). 463p. 1980. reprint ed. lib. bdg. 39.50 (*0-8284-0307-4*) Chelsea Pub.

De Montoya, Antonio R. The Spiritual Conquest: Accomplished by the Religious of the Society of Jesus in the Provinces of Paraguay, Parana & Tape. McNaspy, C. J. et al, trs. from SPA. LC 92-75537. (Jesuit Primary Sources in English Translation Ser.: No. 11). 223p. 1993. 24.95 (*1-880810-02-6*); pap. 17.95 (*1-880810-03-4*) Inst Jesuit.

De Montoya, Monica L. Progress, Hunger & Envy: Commercial Agriculture, Marketing & Social Transformation in the Venezuelan Andes. (Stockholm Studies in Social Anthropology: No. 36). (Illus.). 270p. (Orig.). 1996. pap. 67.50 (*91-7153-522-5*) Coronet Bks.

De Montreuil, Gerbert, jt. auth. see Lowe, L. F.

De Montreville, Doris & Crawford, Elizabeth D., eds. Fourth Book of Junior Authors & Illustrators. LC 78-115. 370p. 1978. 45.00 (*0-8242-0568-5*) Wilson.

De Montreville, Doris & Hill, Donna, eds. Third Book of Junior Authors. LC 75-149381. (Illus.). 320p. 1972. 40.00 (*0-8242-0408-5*) Wilson.

De Monvel, Anne B., et al, eds. Recent Developments in Quantum Mechanics: Proceedings of the Brasov Conference, Poiana Brasov 1989, Romania. (C). 1991. text 191.00 (*0-7923-1148-5*) Kluwer Academic.

De Monvel, Anne B. & Marchenko, Vladimir A., eds. Algebraic & Geometric Methods in Mathematical Physics: Proceedings of the Kaciveli Summer School, Crimea, Ukraine, 1993. LC 95-52285. (Mathematical Physics Studies: Vol. 19). 476p. (C). 1996. text 235.50 (*0-7923-3909-6*) Kluwer Academic.

De Monvel, L. Boutet, see Boutet De Monvel, L.

De Monvel, Roger B. Cervantes & the Magicians. LC 72-3201. (Studies in Spanish Literature: No. 36). 1972. reprint ed. lib. bdg. 75.00 (*0-8383-1531-3*) M S G Haskell Hse.

De Mooij, Marieke K. Global Marketing & Advertising: Understanding Cultural Paradoxes. LC 97-4800. 368p. 1997. text 52.00 (*0-8039-5969-9*); pap. text 24.95 (*0-8039-5970-2*) Sage.

***De Mooij, Ruud A.** Environmental Taxation & the Double Dividend. LC 00-34760. (Contributions to Economic Analysis Ser.). 2000. write for info. (*0-444-50491-5*) Elsevier.

De Moor, Bart, jt. ed. see Moonen, Marc.

D

de Moor, Ed, et al, eds. Writing the Self: Autobiographical Writing in Modern Arabic Literature. LC 98-215127. 342p. 1998. 59.95 (0-86356-727-4, Pub. by Saqi) Intl Spec Bk.

De Moor, G., et al, eds. Progress in Standardization in Health Care Informatics. (Studies in Health Technology & Informatics: Vol. 6). 225p. (YA). (gr. 12). 1993. 98.00 (90-5199-114-2, Pub. by IOS Pr) IOS Press.

De Moor, Irene, jt. ed. see Lubke, Roy.

De Moor, J. A. & Wesseling, H. L., eds. Imperialism & War: Essays on Colonial Wars in Asia & Africa. LC 88-22331. (Comparative Studies in Overseas History: Vol. 8). 234p. 1989. text 71.50 (90-04-08834-2) Brill Academic Pubs.

De Moor, J. A., jt. ed. see Mommsen, W. J.

De Moor, J. C. & Finley, Thomas J., eds. A Bilingual Concordance to the Targum of the Prophets Vol. 15: Ezekiel. 450p. 1998. 124.00 (90-04-11015-1) Brill Academic Pubs.

— A Bilingual Concordance to the Targum of the Prophets Vol. 16: Ezekiel. 450p. 1998. 124.00 (90-04-11017-8) Brill Academic Pubs.

— A Bilingual Concordance to the Targum of the Prophets Vol. 17: Ezekiel. 450p. 1998. 124.00 (90-04-11018-6) Brill Academic Pubs.

De Moor, J. C. & Sepmeijer, Floris, eds. A Bilingual Concordance to the Targum of the Prophets Vol. 12: Jeremiah. 450p. 1998. 124.00 (90-04-11012-7) Brill Academic Pubs.

— A Bilingual Concordance to the Targum of the Prophets Vol. 13: Jeremiah. 450p. 1998. 124.00 (90-04-11013-5) Brill Academic Pubs.

— A Bilingual Concordance to the Targum of the Prophets Vol. 14: Jeremiah. 450p. 1998. 124.00 (90-04-11014-3) Brill Academic Pubs.

De Moor, Johannes C., ed. A Bilingual Concordance to the Targum of the Prophets, Vol. 2. (ARC & HEB.). 1995. 149.50 (90-04-10462-3) Brill Academic Pubs.

— Synchronic or Diachronic? A Debate on Method in Old Testament Exegesis. (Oudtestamentische Studi En: No. 34). x, 255p. 1995. 97.50 (90-04-10342-2) Brill Academic Pubs.

De Moor, Johannes C. & Van Staalduine-Sulman, Eveline, eds. A Bilingual Concordance to the Targum of the Prophets Vol. 3: 1 & 2 Samuel (I) 450p. 1996. 124.50 (90-04-10490-9) Brill Academic Pubs.

— A Bilingual Concordance to the Targum of the Prophets Vol. 4: 1 & 2 Samuel (II) 450p. 1996. 111.00 (90-04-10491-7) Brill Academic Pubs.

— A Bilingual Concordance to the Targum of the Prophets Vol. 5: 1 & 2 Samuel (III) 368p. 1996. 121.00 (90-04-10492-5) Brill Academic Pubs.

— A Bilingual Concordance to the Targum of the Prophets Vol. 6: 1 & 2 Kings (I), 3 vols., Set. (ARC & HEB.). 450p. 1997. 118.50 (90-04-10493-3) Brill Academic Pubs.

— A Bilingual Concordance to the Targum of the Prophets Vol. 7: 1 & 2 Kings (II) (ARC & HEB.). 450p. 1997. 118.50 (90-04-10749-5) Brill Academic Pubs.

De Moor, Johannes C. & Watson, Wilfred G. Verse in Ancient Near Eastern Prose. (Alter Orient und Altes Testament Ser.: Vol. 42). xviii, 422p. 1993. text 110.00 (3-7887-1474-3) NeukirchenerV.

De Moor, Johannes C., et al. Intertextuality in Ugarit & Israel. LC 98-6087. (Oudtestamentische Studien). 232p. 1998. 71.00 (90-04-11154-9) Brill Academic Pubs.

***De Moor, Margriet.** Duke of Egypt. 2001. 24.95 (1-55970-546-9, Pub. by Arcade Pub Inc) Time Warner.

— The Virtuoso. Rilke, Ina, tr. LC 99-86847. 200p. 2000. 24.95 (1-58567-003-0, Pub. by Overlook Pr) Penguin Putnam.

De Moor, Oege, jt. auth. see Bird, Richard.

De Moor, Robert. God's Backyard: A Fresh Look at Ecclesiastes. LC 93-27782. 1993. pap. 9.95 (1-56212-038-7) CRC Pubns.

De Mora, Juan Miguel. Tlatelolco T-68: Por Fin Toda la Verdad! 218p. (Orig.). 1997. pap. text 12.98 (968-409-029-3) Edamex.

***de Mora, Stephen, et al, eds.** The Effects of UV Radiation in the Marine Environment. LC 99-15231. (Cambridge Environmental Chemistry Ser.: No. 10). (Illus.). 336p. (C). 2000. 80.00 (0-521-63218-8) Cambridge U Pr.

De Mora, Stephen J. Tributyltin: Case Study of an Environmental Contaminant. (Cambridge Environmental Chemistry Ser.: No. 8). (Illus.). 312p. (C). 1996. text 85.00 (0-521-47046-3) Cambridge U Pr.

De Moraes, Borba & Berrien, William. Manual Bibliografico de Estudos Brasileiros. 1976. lib. bdg. 59.95 (0-8490-2203-7) Gordon Pr.

De Moraes, Ruben B. Bibliographia Brasiliana, 2 vols., Set. rev. ed. LC 82-620036. (Reference Ser.: Vol. 10). (Illus.). 1114p. 1983. lib. bdg. 150.00 (0-87903-109-3) UCLA Lat Am Ctr.

De Moraes, Vinicius. Girl from Ipanema. Barkan, Stanley H., ed. Rabassa, Gregory, tr. (Review Chapbook Ser.: No. 34: Brazillian Poetry 1).Tr. of Port. & Eng.. 1989. 15.00 (0-89304-884-4, CCC157); pap. 5.00 (0-89304-858-5); audio 10.00 (0-89304-883-6) Cross-Cultrl NY.

— Girl from Ipanema: Mini. Barkan, Stanley H., ed. Rabassa, Gregory, tr. (Review Chapbook Ser.: No. 34: Brazillian Poetry I).Tr. of Port. & Eng.. 1989. 15.00 (0-89304-881-X); pap. 5.00 (0-89304-882-8) Cross-Cultrl NY.

De Morais, A. English-Portuguese Dictionary: Dicionario Ingles-Portugues. (ENG & POR.). 1492p. 1982. 39.95 (0-8288-0491-5, M14427) Fr & Eur.

De Morais, O., ed. see Ferreira, J. Albino.

De Moratin, Leandro Fernandez, see Fernandez de Moratin, Leandro.

De Morgan. Ancient Persian Numismatics: Elymais. (Illus.). 62p. 1975. 12.50 (0-915018-15-2) Attic Bks.

De Morgan, Augustus. Budget of Paradoxes, 2 Vols, Set. Smith, David E., ed. (Select Bibliographies Reprint Ser.). 1977. 60.95 (0-8369-5119-0) Ayer.

— An Essay on Probabilities. LC 80-2119. (Development of Science Ser.). (Illus.). 1981. lib. bdg. 33.95 (0-405-13885-7) Ayer.

De Morgan, Augustus, jt. auth. see Smith, David E.

***De Mori, Lori, et al.** Italy Anywhere: Living an Italian Culinary Life Wherever You Call Home. LC 00-28104. (Illus.). 416p. 2000. 29.95 (0-670-88539-8, Viking) Viking Penguin.

De Mori, Renato. Computer Models of Speech Using Fuzzy Algorithms. LC 83-11082. (Advanced Applications in Pattern Recognition Ser.). 508p. 1983. 125.00 (0-306-41381-7, Plenum Trade) Perseus Pubng.

De Mori, Renato, ed. Spoken Dialogs with Computers. LC 97-43104. (Signal Processing & Its Applications Ser.). (Illus.). 720p. 1998. text 99.00 (0-12-209055-1) Acad Pr.

De Mori, Renato, jt. ed. see Laface, P.

De Morier, Everett. Crib Notes for the First Year of Fatherhood: A Survival Guide for New Fathers. LC 98-24290. 224p. 1998. pap. 14.95 (1-57749-073-8, Pub. by Fairview Press) Natl Bk Netwk.

— Crib Notes for the First Year of Marriage: A Survival Guide for Newlyweds. LC 97-7772. 224p. (Orig.). 1997. pap. 14.95 (1-57749-030-4) Fairview Press.

De Morinni, J., tr. see Foch, Ferdinand.

De Mornay, Philippe. A Work Concerning the Trewnesse of the Christian Religion. Sidney, Philip, tr. from FRE. LC 75-45384. 680p. 1976. reprint ed. lib. bdg. 90.00 (0-8201-1166-X) Schol Facsimiles.

De Morris, Clara S. Cesar Chavez, Labor Leader. (Illus.). (J). (gr. 1-4). 1994. pap. 6.35 (0-8136-5272-3); lib. bdg. 17.50 (0-8136-5266-9) Modern Curr.

— Cesar Chavez, Lider Laboral. (SPA., Illus.). (J). (gr. 1-4). 1994. pap. 6.35 (0-8136-5300-2); lib. bdg. 17.55 (0-8136-5294-4) Modern Curr.

***De Moss, Nancy Leigh.** Biblical Portrait of Womanhood: Discovering & Living Out God's Plan for Our Lives. Hawkins, Sandra, ed. 32p. 1999. pap. 1.95 (0-9667124-1-2) Life Action Inc.

de Mota, Clarice Novaes, see Novaes de Mota, Clarice.

De Mota Oreja, Ignacio H. Diccionario de la Communicacion, Vol. 2. (SPA.). 368p. 1988. 59.95 (0-7859-5856-8, 8428316090) Fr & Eur.

De Mott, Benjamin. Created Equal: Reading & Writing about Class in America. 592p. (C). 1997. pap. text, teacher ed. 11.00 (0-06-501317-4) Addson-Wesley Educ.

De Mott, Benjamin. Created Equal: Reading & Writing about Class in America. (Illus.). 560p. (C). 1997. pap. text 47.00 (0-06-501316-6) Addson-Wesley Educ.

De Motte Green, Catherine. The Dynamic Balance Sheet: A German Theory of Accounting. Brief, Richard P., ed. LC 80-1497. (Dimensions of Accounting Theory & Practice Ser.). 1980. lib. bdg. 42.95 (0-405-13491-6) Ayer.

De Mottoni, P., jt. auth. see Li, T. T.

***De Moubray, Amicia & Black, David.** Carpets for the Home. (Illus.). 224p. 1999. 50.00 (0-8478-2200-1, Pub. by Rizzoli Intl) St Martin.

De Moubray, George A. Matriarchy in the Malay Peninsula & Neighbouring Countries. LC 77-87025. 304p. reprint ed. 54.50 (0-404-16810-8) AMS Pr.

De Moulin, Daniel. A History of Surgery: With Emphasis on the Netherlands. (C). 1987. lib. bdg. 225.50 (0-89838-968-2) Kluwer Academic.

— A Short History of Breast Cancer. 1983. lib. bdg. 32.50 (90-247-2814-2) Kluwer Academic.

— A Short History of Breast Cancer. (C). 1989. pap. text 96.00 (0-7923-0524-8) Kluwer Academic.

De Moura Castro, Claudio, ed. Education in the Information Age: What Works & What Doesn't. LC 98-71322. 220p. 1998. pap. text 21.00 (1-886938-33-4) IADB.

De Moura Castro, Claudio & Levy, Daniel C. Myth, Reality & Reform: Higher Education Policy in Latin America. (Inter-American Development Bank Ser.). 122p. 2000. pap. 19.95 (1-886938-60-1) IADB.

De Moura Castro, Claudio, jt. ed. see Espinola, Viola.

De Moux, Maria C. Linajes y Oficios en Tres Entremeses del Siglo de Uro. (Iberian Studies: No. 7). (SPA.). 150p. (Orig.). 1996. pap. text 39.95 (1-889431-08-7) Univ Pr South.

De Mowbray, Stephen A. Key Facts in Soviet History Vol. 1: A Chronology of Major Events in Soviet History since 1917. (Monograph Ser.). 256p. 1990. 45.00 (0-8161-1820-5, Hall Reference) Macmillan.

De Mul, Jos. Romantic Desire in (Post)Modern Art & Philosophy. Reeve, Alan, tr. from DUT. LC 98-41220. (SUNY Series in Postmodem Culture). (Illus.). 320p. (C). 1999. text 59.50 (0-7914-4217-9); pap. text 19.95 (0-7914-4218-7) State U NY Pr.

De Mul, Sjaak. Cognitive Aspects of Electronic Text Processing. Van Oostendorp, Herre, ed. (Advances in Discourse Processes Ser.: Vol. 58). 350p. 1996. text 78.50 (1-56750-235-0) Ablx Pub.

De Mul, Sjaak & Van Oostendorp, Herre, eds. Cognitive Aspects of Electronic Text Processing. LC 96-4090. (Advances in Discourse Processes Ser.: Vol. 58). 329p. 1996. pap. 42.50 (1-56750-236-9) Ablx Pub.

De Mulder, E. F., jt. auth. see McCall, G. J.

De Munch, Victor C. Seasonal Cycles: A Study of Social Change & Continuity in a Sri Lankan Village. (C). 1993. text 19.50 (81-206-0816-X, Pub. by Asian Educ Servs) S Asia.

***De Munck, Victor C.** Culture, Self & Meaning. 113p. 2000. pap. 10.50 (1-57766-137-0) Waveland Pr.

De Munck, Victor C., ed. Romantic Love & Sexual Behavior: Perspectives from the Social Sciences. LC 97-26904. 320p. 1998. 65.00 (0-275-95726-8, Praeger Pubs) Greenwood.

***De Munck, Victor C. & Sobo, Elisa J., eds.** Using Methods in the Field: A Practical Introduction & Casebook. LC 98-9073. (Illus.). 288p. (C). 1998. 65.00 (0-7619-8912-9); pap. 24.95 (0-7619-8913-7) AltaMira Pr.

De Mundo Lo, Sara. Index to Spanish American Collective Biography: The River Plate Countries, Vol. 4. (Reference Publications in Area Studies). 1985. 110.00 (0-8161-8650-2, Hall Reference) Macmillan.

— Julio Cortazar: His Works & His Critics. 280p. 1985. pap. 32.50 (0-932759-00-9) Albatross.

De Mundo Lo, Sara & Garner, Jane, eds. Basic Documents of the Seminar on the Acquisition of Latin American Library Materials, 2 pts. (Orig.). 1985. pap. 7.00 (0-917617-05-3) SALALM.

De Munn, Michael. The Earth Is Good: A Chant in Praise of Nature. LC 97-51345. (Illus.). 32p. (J). (gr. k-4). 1999. 15.95 (0-590-35010-2) Scholastic Inc.

De Munnik, Jeroen F. The Valuation of Interest Rate Derivative Securities. LC 96-6089. (New Advances in Economics Ser.: No. 1). 200p. (C). 1996. 80.00 (0-415-13727-6) Routledge.

De Munter, Agnes, jt. auth. see Snick, Anne.

De Munter, M. & Bauduin, C. Elsevier's Fiscal & Customs Dictionary. 1988. (DUT, ENG, FRE & GER.). 750p. 1987. 324.25 (0-444-42891-7) Elsevier.

De Muralt, Andre. L' Enjeu de la Philosophie Medievale: Etudes Thomistes, Scotistes, Occamiennes & Gregoriennes. LC 90-22455. (Studien und Texte zur Geistesgeschichte des Mittelalters Ser.: No. 24). xvi, 454p. 1993. reprint ed. 142.00 (90-04-09254-4) Brill Academic Pubs.

— The Idea of Phenomenology: Husserlian Exemplarism. Breckon, Garry L., tr. from FRE. & intro. by. (Studies in Phenomenology & Existential Philosophy). 411p. 1989. pap. 19.95 (0-8101-0825-9) Northwestern U Pr.

— L' Idee de la Phenomenologie. xiv, 398p. 1987. reprint ed. write for info. (3-487-07963-1) G Olms Pubs.

***De Murcia, Gilbert & Shall, Sydney, eds.** Poly Adp-Ribosylation Reactions: From DNA Damage & Stress Signalling to Cell Death. (Illus.). 240p. 2000. text 125.00 (0-19-850633-3) OUP.

De Murcia, Santiago, et al. Saldivar Codex No. 4: Santiago de Murcia Manuscript of Baroque Guitar Music. fac. ed. (Saldivar Codex Ser.: Vol. 1). (Illus.). 124p. (Orig.). (C). 1987. pap. text 40.00 (0-9618527-1-2) M Lorimer Pubng.

De Murguia, Valdemar. Capital Flight & Economic Crisis: Mexican Post-Devaluation Exiles in a California Community. (Research Reports: No. 44). 27p. (Orig.). (C). 1986. pap. 5.00 (0-935391-66-5, RR-44) UCSD Ctr US-Mex.

***De Muro, Martin.** Free Cell Games Solutions, Vol. 1. 344p. 1999. pap. 19.95 (0-9676388-1-X) Free Cell Game.

De Murville, M. Couve, ed. The Unsealed Fountain: Essays on the Christian Spiritual Tradition. 155p. (Orig.). 1987. pap. 11.95 (0-86217-243-8, Pub. by Veritas Pubns) St Mut.

De Musset, Alfred. Comedies et Proverbes: Avec: Le Chandelier, Il ne faut Jurer de Rein, Set. Gastinel, Francis, ed. 376p. 1957. 51.95 (0-685-57704-X, F68941) Fr & Eur.

— Comedies et Proverbes: Avec: Louison, On ne Saurait Penser a Tout, Set. Gastinel, Francis, ed. 376p. 1957. 51.95 (0-685-57705-8, F68941) Fr & Eur.

— Confession D'un Enfant Du Siecle. Allem, ed. (Folio Ser.: No. 476). (FRE.). 1962. pap. 9.95 (2-07-036476-3) Schoenhof.

— Correspondance, 1827-1857. (FRE.). 293p. 1977. 89.95 (0-7859-5489-9) Fr & Eur.

— Correspondance, 1827-1857. 300p. reprint ed. 25.00 (0-686-55545-7) Fr & Eur.

— Fantasio & Other Plays. Howard, Richard et al, trs. from FRE. LC 92-44012. (TCG Translations Ser.: Vol. 4). 320p. 1993. pap. 15.95 (1-55936-067-4) Theatre Comm.

— Il Faut qu'une Porte soit Ouverte ou Fermee. 5.95 (0-686-55549-X) Fr & Eur.

— Gamiani. (FRE.). 256p. 1992. pap. 24.95 (0-7859-1554-0, 2859569979) Fr & Eur.

— Lorenzaccio: On Ne Badine Pas avec l'Amour et Autres Pieces. (FRE.). 1988. pap. 16.95 (0-7859-2991-6) Fr & Eur.

— Lorenzaccio. Andre del Sarto. (Folio Ser.: No. 1026). (FRE.). 1978. pap. 9.95 (2-07-037026-7) Schoenhof.

— Musset: Five Plays, No. 5. (Methuen Anthologies Ser.). 1995. pap. 15.95 (0-413-69240-X, A0747) Heinemann.

***De Musset, Alfred.** Musset: Lorenzaccio. Connon, Derek, ed. (Modern Language Ser.). (FRE.). 192p. 1998. pap. text 20.95 (1-85399-516-9, Pub. by Brist Class Pr) Focus Pub-R Pullins.

De Musset, Alfred. Nights.Tr. of Nuit. 48p. 1999. pap. 12.95 (1-892355-02-7) Fifth Season.

— La Nuit de Mai (A Night in May) White, Claire N., tr. from FRE. & intro. by. (Illus.). 28p. (Orig.). 1989. pap. 20.00 (0-930126-27-0) Typographeum.

— Les Nuits. 5.95 (0-686-55550-3) Fr & Eur.

— Oeuvres Completes. 944p. 1963. 25.00 (0-686-55553-8) Fr & Eur.

— Oeuvres Completes, 12 tomes, Set. (Illus.). 850.00 (0-685-34952-7); 1487.50 (0-685-34953-5) Fr & Eur.

— On ne Saurait Penser a Tout. pap. 5.95 (0-686-55555-4) Fr & Eur.

— Premieres Poesies. Poesies Nouvelles. (Poesie Ser.). (FRE.). 1976. pap. 13.95 (2-07-032155-X) Schoenhof.

— Ten Plays. Pellissier, R. & Dey, M., trs. from FRE. LC 87-7426. 506p. 1987. reprint ed. lib. bdg. 49.50 (0-86527-358-8) Fertig.

— Textes Dramatiques Inedits par J. Richer. (FRE.). 213p. 1953. pap. 18.95 (0-7859-5490-2) Fr & Eur.

— Theatre Vol. 1: Les Marrons de Feu; la Nuit Venitienne. (FRE.). 1964. pap. 10.95 (0-7859-2956-8) Fr & Eur.

— Theatre Complet. Jeune, Andre, ed. (FRE.). 1990. lib. bdg. 160.00 (0-7859-3890-7) Fr & Eur.

De Musset, Alfred & Allem, Maurice. Confession D'un Enfant du Siecle. 1962. write for info. (0-318-63464-3) Fr & Eur.

De Musset, Alfred, ed. & tr. see Sices, David.

***De Mylius, Johan, et al, eds.** Hans Christian Andersen: A Poet in Time. (Illus.). 576p. 1999. pap. 42.98 (87-7838-449-4, Pub. by Odense Univ) Intl Spec Bk.

De Nance, William. Dancing on an Edge. 456p. mass mkt. 5.99 (1-55197-075-9) Picasso Publ.

De Nanteuil, Luc. David: Masters of Art. (Illus.). 128p. 1990. 24.95 (0-8109-3201-6, Pub. by Abrams) Time Warner.

***De Natale, Douglas & Ito, Karen L.** International Collaboration in the Arts: A Report on the Ford Foundation Initiative "Internationalizing New Work in the Performing Arts" Phase 1:1995-1998. Levine, Mindy N., ed. (Illus.). 72p. 1999. pap. write for info. (0-9676467-0-7) Arts Intl Inc.

De Navarro, J. M. The Finds from the Site of La Tene: Scabbards & the Swords Found in Them. 498p. 1979. 55.00 (0-19-725909-X) St Mut.

De Navarro, Nicki G., jt. auth. see Ackert, Patricia.

De Navarro, Nikki S. Giroux, see Ackert, Patricia & Giroux De Navarro, Nikki S.

De Nebesky-Wojkowitz, Rene. Oracles & Demons of Tibet. 1974. 300.00 (0-87968-463-1) Gordon Pr.

— Oracles & Demons of Tibet. (Illus.). 666p. 1990. reprint ed. pap. 45.00 (957-9482-19-5) Oriental Bk Store.

De Nebrija, Elio A. El Lexico Castellano de los Vocabularios de Elio Antonio de Nebrija: Concordancia Lematizada, 3 vols. (SPA.). civ, 2117p. 1996. 400.00 (3-487-10096-7) G Olms Pubs.

De Neergaard, Helene Gaillard, see Gaillard de Neergaard, Helene.

De Neeve, P. W. Colonus: Private Farm Tenancy in Roman Italy During the Republic & the Early Principate. viii, 273p. (C). 1984. 64.00 (90-70265-15-X, Pub. by Gieben) J Benjamins Pubng Co.

— Peasants in Peril: Location & Economy in Italy in the Second Century B.C. (Illus.). 44p. (C). 1984. pap. 10.00 (90-70265-26-5, Pub. by Gieben) J Benjamins Pubng Co.

De Negri, Dobrila. Performing Body. (Illus.). 48p. 1998. pap. 19.95 (88-8158-160-4, Pub. by Charta) Dist Art Pubs.

De Nemes, Graciela P. Diario de Zenobia Camprubi Tomo I. (SPA.). 376p. 1991. 16.60 (0-8477-3652-0) U of PR Pr.

De Nerval, Gerard, see Nerval, Gerard De.

De Nettancourt, D., jt. ed. see Magnien, E.

De Neufville, Judith I., ed. The Land Use Policy Debate in the United States. LC 81-13859. (Environment, Development, & Public Policy: Public Policy & Social Services Ser.). 282p. 1981. 49.50 (0-306-40718-3, Plenum Trade) Perseus Pubng.

De Neufville, Richard. Applied Systems Analysis: Engineering Planning & Technology Management. (Illus.). 416p. (C). 1990. text 68.00 (0-07-016372-3) McGraw.

— Applied Systems Analysis: Engineering Planning & Technology Management. 2nd ed. (C). 1990. pap. text, teacher ed. 18.75 (0-07-016373-1) McGraw.

De Neumann, Bernard, ed. Electromagnetic Modelling & Measurements for Analysis & Synthesis Problems. (C). 1991. text 253.00 (0-7923-1265-1) Kluwer Academic.

De Neumann, Bernard, et al, eds. Mathematical Structures for Software Engineering: Based on the Proceedings of a Conference Organized by the Systems & Software Engineering Specialist Group of the Institute of Mathematics & Its Applications Held Manchester Polytechnic in July 1988. (Institute of Mathematics & Its Applications Conference Series, New Ser.: New Series 27). (Illus.). 376p. 1991. text 105.00 (0-19-853627-5, 8993) OUP.

***De Nevers.** Air Pollution Control Engineering. 2nd ed. LC 99-29945. 608p. 1999. 71.88 (0-07-039367-2) McGraw.

De Nevers. Fluid Mechanics for Engineers. 2nd ed. 1991. text, student ed. 27.50 (0-07-016376-6) McGraw.

De Nevers, Klancy, ed. see Hogan, Kathy.

De Nevers, Noel. Air Pollution Control Engineering. LC 94-12074. (Series in Water Resources & Environmental Engineering, Chemical Engineering Ser.). 576p. (C). 1994. 71.88 (0-07-061397-4) McGraw.

— Air Pollution Control Engineering. 1994. pap. text, student ed. write for info. (0-07-061398-2) McGraw.

— Fluid Mechanics for Chemical Engineers. 2nd ed. 612p. (C). 1991. 85.63 (0-07-016375-8) McGraw.

de Newcastle, Guillaume. Methode et Invention Nouvelle de Dresser les Chevaux. reprint ed. 375.00 (88-299-1177-1, Pub. by Piccin Nuova) Gordon & Breach.

De Nicola, Karen B., ed. see Moseley, Romney M., et al.

***de Nicolai-Mazery, Christiane.** The Finest Houses of Paris. LC 00-38145. (Illus.). 208p. 2000. 50.00 (0-86565-217-1) Vendome.

de Nicolas, Antonio T. The Bhagavad Gita. LC 89-77693. (Illus.). 156p. 1990. pap. 12.50 (0-89254-018-4) Nicolas-Hays.

— The Biology of Religion. 29p. 1990. pap. 3.50 (0-914910-96-5) Buddhist Bks.

— Meditations Through the Rg Veda: Four-Dimensional Man. LC 76-39692. 284p. 1976. pap. 12.95 (0-89254-039-7) Nicolas-Hays.

— Powers of Imagining: Ignatius de Loyola: A Philosophical Hermeneutic of Imagining Through the Collected Works of Ignatius de Loyola. LC 85-2739. 390p. (C). 1986. pap. text 19.95 (0-88706-110-9) State U NY Pr.

— St. John of the Cross: Alchemist of the Soul. 288p. (Orig.). 1996. reprint ed. pap. 18.00 (0-87728-859-3) Weiser.

An Asterisk (*) at the beginning of an entry indicates that the title is appearing for the first time.

De Nicolay, Nicolas. The Nauigations into Turkie. Washington, T., tr. LC 68-54638. (English Experience Ser.: No. 48). 322p. 1968. reprint ed. 65.00 (*90-221-0048-0*) Walter J Johnson.

De Nijs, E. Breton. Faded Portraits: A Novel of the East Indies. (Library of the Indies). Orig. Title: Vergeelde Portretten Uit Een Indisch Familie-Album. 176p. 1999. pap. 14.95 (*962-593-511-8*) Tuttle Pubng.

De Nogales, Rafael. The Looting of Nicaragua. LC 70-111726. (American Imperialism: Viewpoints of United States Foreign Policy, 1898-1941 Ser.). 1970. reprint ed. 23.95 (*0-405-02041-4*) Ayer.

De Nooy. The Role of European Ground & Air Forces after the Cold War, Vol. NLSP 27. LC 97-10316. 1997. 62.00 (*90-411-0397-X*) Kluwer Law Intl.

De Nooy, Gert, creator. The Role of European Naval Forces after the Cold War. LC 96-12721. 194p. 1996. pap. 64.00 (*90-411-0227-2*) Kluwer Law Intl.

De Nooy, Gert, ed. The Clausewitzian Dictum & the Future of Wester Military Strategy. LC 97-33971. (Nijhoff Law Specials Ser.: No. 31). 192p. 1997. pap. 53.00 (*90-411-0455-0*) Kluwer Academic.

De Nooy, Juliana. Derrida, Kristeva, & the Dividing Line: An Articulation of Two Theories of Difference. Hart, Jonathan, ed. LC 98-15871. (Comparative Literature & Cultural Studies Ser.: Vol. 5). 352p. 1998. 69.00 (*0-8153-2571-1*, H2078) Garland.

De Norch, Daniel J. The Equine Equation: The Atomic Secrets of Horse Racing Exposed. 335p. 1993. pap. text 75.00 (*1-883429-00-5*) Equine Code.

De Normann, Roderick. For Fuhrer & Fatherland: SS Murder & Mayhem in Wartime Britain. (Illus.). 192p. 1996. 30.95 (*0-7509-1282-0*, Pub. by Sutton Pub Ltd) Intl Pubs Mktg.

De Noronha Goyos, Durval, Jr. Portuguese-English - English-Portuguese Legal Dictionary. 2nd ed. LC 99-194721. (ENG & POR.). 551p. 1994. 70.00 (*85-85548-04-5*) Editora Observ Leg.

De Nostredame, Jehan. Les Vies des Plus Celebres et Anciens Poetes Provencaux. 258p. 1971. reprint ed. write for info. (*0-318-71384-5*) G Olms Pubs.

De Noux, O'Neil. The Big Show. 320p. 1998. pap. 5.95 (*0-9653145-8-8*, Autumn Bks) Pontalba Pr.

— Crescent City Kills. 1992. mass mkt. 4.50 (*0-8217-3752-X*, Zebra Kensgtn) Kensgtn Pub Corp.

De Novas, Maria J. San Juan, see De La Soledad, Rosalia & San Juan De Novas, Maria J.

De Nunez de Villavicencio, Maruxa. Cuentos. (SPA.). 237p. (Orig.). 1987. pap. 9.00 (*84-359-0519-5*, Pub. by Editorial Playor) Ediciones.

De Obaldia, Claire. The Essayistic Spirit: Literature, Modern Criticism, & the Essay. 332p. 1996. text 75.00 (*0-19-815194-2*) OUP.

De Obaldia, Rene. Centenarian. Trocchi, Alexander, tr. from FRE. 192p. pap. 14.95 (*0-7145-0160-3*) Riverrun NY.

de Oca, Elena Montes, see Montes de Oca, Elena.

De Oca, Marco A. Montes, see Montes De Oca, Marco A.

De Odorico, Marco. The Use of Numbers & Quantifications in the Assyrian Royal Inscriptions. (State Archives of Assyria Ser.: Vol. 3). xxxii, 206p. 1995. pap. text 37.50 (*951-45-7125-8*, Pub. by Neo-Assyrian Text) Eisenbrauns.

De Ohiggins, Maria J. A Taste of Old Cuba: More Than 150 Recipes for Delicious, Authentic, & Traditional Dishes. LC 94-10684. (Illus.). 304p. 1994. 27.50 (*0-06-016964-8*) HarperTrade.

De Old, Alan R., jt. auth. see Sheets, Everett.

De Oliv Birchal, Sergio. Entrepreneurship in Nineteenth-Century Brazil: The Formation of a Business Environment. LC 98-34841. 256p. 1999. text 65.00 (*0-312-21716-1*) St Martin.

De Oliveira, Celso L., tr. & intro. see Santareno, Bernardo.

De Oliveira, Claire. La Poesie Allemande de Roumanie: Entre Heteronomie et Dissidence (1944-1990) (Contacts Ser.: Series III, Vol. 32). (FRE.). 400p. 1995. 54.95 (*3-906754-17-0*, Pub. by P Lang) P Lang Pubng.

***de Oliveira-Costa, Angelica & Tegmark, Max, eds.** Microwave Foregrounds. (Conference Series Proceedings: Vol. 181). 377p. 1999. text 52.00 (*1-58381-006-4*) Astron Soc Pacific.

De Oliveira, Evandro, jt. auth. see Sekhar, Laligam N.

De Oliveira, F. A., jt. auth. see De Araujo, C. B.

***de Oliveira, F. M., ed.** Advances in Artificial Intelligence: 14th Brazilian Symposium on Artificial Intelligence, SBIA '98 Porto Alegre, Brazil, November 4-6, 1998, Proceedings. LC 98-44474. 259p. 1998. pap. 49.00 (*3-540-65190-X*) Spr-Verlag.

De Oliveira, Joanyr F. A Igreja Que Desejamos. (POR.). 110p. 1990. pap. 3.95 (*0-8297-1637-8*) Vida Pubs.

De Oliveira, Jocy. Days & Routes Through Maps & Scores. (Illus.). 176p. 1984. 16.95 (*85-7069-001-0*) Lingua Pr.

De Oliveira, Jose A. Audiovestibular Toxicity of Drugs, 2 vols., Vol. 2. 240p. 1989. 152.00 (*0-8493-6960-6*, RF285, CRC Reprint) Franklin.

De Oliveira, Joseph G. Jacinta the Flower of Fatima. 192p. 1982. pap. 3.95 (*0-911988-45-9*, 42207) AMI Pr.

De Oliveira Lima, Manuel. The Evolution of Brazil Compared with That of Spanish & Anglo-Saxon America. Martin, Percy F., ed. LC 74-12766. (Leland Stanford Jr. Univ. Publications: No. 16). 159p. 1975. reprint ed. lib. bdg. 55.00 (*0-8371-7740-5*, OLEB) Greenwood.

De Oliveira, M. Darcy & Tandon, Rajesh, eds. Citoyens du Monde - ou le Renforcement de la Societe Civile Mondiale. (FRE.). 430p. (Orig.). 1995. pap. text 20.00 (*0-9644001-2-X*) CIVICUS.

De Oliveira, Miguel D. & Tandon, Rajesh, eds. Ciudadanos - En Construccion de la Socieded Civil Mundial.Tr. of Citizens: Strengthening Global Civil Society. (SPA.). 681p. (Orig.). 1995. pap. 20.00 (*0-9644001-1-1*) CIVICUS.

De Oliveira, Nicholas, et al. Installation Art. LC 93-86159. (Illus.). 208p. 1994. 49.95 (*1-56098-347-7*) Smithsonian.

De Oliveira, Nicolas, et al. Installation Art. (Illus.). 208p. 1996. pap. 34.95 (*1-56098-704-9*) Smithsonian.

De Oliveira, Plinio C. The Way of the Cross. Parrot, Edward, ed. TFP Publications Dept. Staff, tr. from POR. (Illus.). 64p. (Orig.). 1990. pap. 3.95 (*1-877905-16-X*) Am Soc Defense TFP.

de Oliveira, Plinio Correa, see Correa de Oliveira, Plinio.

De Oliveira, Rosiska D. In Praise of Difference: The Emergence of a Global Feminism. Sharpe, Peggy, tr. from ENG. & pref. by. LC 98-15616. 160p. (C). 1998. text 46.00 (*0-8135-2557-8*); pap. text 19.00 (*0-8135-2558-6*) Rutgers U Pr.

De Oliveira Setubal, Paulo. Domitila: The Romance of an Emperor's Mistress. Richardson, Margaret, tr. 1977. lib. bdg. 59.95 (*0-8490-1730-0*) Gordon Pr.

De Oliveira Slade, Rejane. Portugues Basico para Estrangeiros. 2nd rev. ed. 400p. 1999. pap. text 29.99 (*0-9638790-3-0*) BRAMINAS.

— Portugues Basico para Estrangeiros: Livro de Excercicios. 2nd ed. 250p. 1999. pap. text, wbk. ed. 18.00 (*0-9638790-4-9*) BRAMINAS.

— Portugues Basico para Estrangeiros: Manual Do Professor. 300p. (C). 1994. pap., teacher ed. 20.00 (*0-9638790-1-4*) BRAMINAS.

De Oliveira-Smith, Pamela J. Expeditions. 40p. (Orig.). 1991. pap. 8.98 (*0-9630348-0-4*) Haute Rage.

De Oliveira, Solange R., jt. ed. see McGuirk, Bernard.

De Oliveira, Paulo M. Computing Boolean Statistical Models. 140p. (C). 1991. text 40.00 (*981-02-0238-5*) World Scientific Pub.

De Oliveira, Plinio Correa, see Lee, Hannah S.

De Oliveira, Jose A. Audiovestibular Toxicity of Drugs, 2 vols. 256p. 1989. 152.00 (*0-8493-6959-2*, RF285, CRC Reprint) Franklin.

De Oliveira, Manoel. Angelica. (Illus.). 96p. 1998. pap. 22.50 (*2-906571-75-X*, Pub. by Editions Dis Voir) Dist Art Pubs.

De Olivieri, Matilde Vilarino, see Vilarino De Olivieri, Matilde.

De Onate, Juan. New Laws of the Mines of Spain: Mining in Early New World History. Milford, Homer, ed. LC 99-13096. (SPA.). 96p. 1999. pap. 8.95 (*0-86534-291-1*) Sunstone Pr.

De Onis, Federico. Espana en America. 2nd ed. (SPA.). 843p. (C). 1968. 6.00 (*0-8477-3140-5*) U of PR Pr.

De Onis, Federico & De Torre, Emilio. Canciones Espanolas: Seleccion III y IV.Tr. of Spanish Folk-Songs. (SPA.). 75p. 1952. 2.00 (*0-318-14244-9*) Hispanic Inst.

De Onis, Federico, jt. auth. see Seminario de Estudios Hispanicos Staff.

De Onis, Harriet, ed. see De Cervantes Saavedra, Miguel.

De Onis, Harriet, tr. see Amado, Jorge.

De Onis, Harriet, tr. see Carpentier, Alejo.

De Onis, Harriet, tr. see De la Parra, Teresa.

De Onis, Harriet, tr. see Freyre, Gilberto.

De Onis, Harriet, tr. see Guzman, Martin L.

De Onis, Harriet, tr. see Ortiz, Fernando.

De Onis, Harriet, tr. see Reyes, Alfonso.

De Onis, Jone. The United States As Seen by Spanish American Writers, 1776-1890. 226p. 1952. 4.00 (*0-318-14313-5*) Hispanic Inst.

De Onis, Jose. Melville y el Mundo Hispanico. (UPREX, Estudios Literarios Ser.: No. 38). 143p. (C). 1974. pap. 1.50 (*0-8477-0038-0*) U of PR Pr.

— The United States As Seen by Spanish American Writers, 1776-1890. LC 74-26684. (Cultural Relations Between the U. S. & the Hispanic World Ser.: Vol. 1). 236p. (C). 1975. reprint ed. 50.00 (*0-87752-184-0*) Gordian.

De Oreyegui, P. Buenaventura, jt. auth. see Aberlaitz.

De Oro. Guia Rapida Clipper. 2nd ed.Tr. of Spanishs Guide to Clipper. (SPA.). 1991. 10.95 (*0-7859-3693-9*, 8428317445) Fr & Eur.

De Orozco, Alonso. The Confessions of Blessed Alonso de Orozco. Rotelle, John E., ed. O'Connell, Matthew J., tr. from SPA. LC 91-70265. (Augustinian Ser.: Vol. 23).Tr. of Confesiones. (Illus.). 212p. 1991. pap. text 7.95 (*0-941491-26-9*, 6525) Augustinian Pr.

De Osso, Henry. A Month in the School of the Sacred Heart of Jesus. Chamorro, Grace, tr. LC 96-69118. (Illus.). 166p. 1997. pap. 7.95 (*0-9638041-3-8*) Soc St Teresa.

De Otero, Blas. All My Sonnets/Todos Mis Sonetos. Cobb, Carl W., tr. from SPA. LC 97-10505. (Hispanic Literature Ser.: No. 37).Tr. of Todos Mis Sonetos. (ENG & SPA.). 260p. 1997. text 89.95 (*0-7734-8616-X*) E Mellen.

De Oude, N. T. & Hutzinger, O., eds. Anthropogenic Compounds: Detergents. (Handbook of Environmental Chemistry Ser.: Vol. 3, Pt. F). (Illus.). 456p. 1992. 214.95 (*0-387-53797-X*) Spr-Verlag.

De Pablo, Flora, et al, eds. Current Topics in Developmental Biology Vol. 36: Cellular & Molecular Procedures in Developmental Biology, Vol. 36. (Illus.). 329p. (C). 1997. text 79.95 (*0-12-153136-8*) Morgan Kaufmann.

De Pacheco, Blanca Silvestrini, see Silvestrini De Pacheco, Blanca.

***de Padirac, Bruno.** The International Dimensions of Cyberspace Law. LC 00-34845. (Law of Cyberspace Ser.). 2000. pap. write for info. (*0-7546-2146-4*, Pub. by Ashgate Pub) Ashgate Pub Co.

De Padva, F., jt. auth. see MacFarlane, P. W.

De Palacios, Diego Garcia, see Garcia De Palacios, Diego.

De Palchi, Alfredo. Alfredo de Palchi: Sessions with My Analyst. Salomon, I. L., tr. from ITA. 1971. 8.95 (*0-8079-0167-9*); pap. 4.95 (*0-8079-0168-7*) October.

— Anonymous Constellation - Costellazione Anonima. Raiziss, Sonia, tr. (Xenos Dual-Language Book Ser.). (ENG & ITA.). xiv, 96p. 1997. 23.00 (*1-879378-24-8*); pap. 13.00 (*1-879378-23-X*) Xenos Riverside.

— The Scorpion's Dark Dance (La Buia Danza Di Scorpione) A Xenos Dual-Language Book. Raiziss, Sonia, tr. LC 93-16133. (Xenos Dual-Language Book Ser.). (ENG & ITA., Illus.). xiii, 129p. (Orig.). 1993. pap. 13.00 (*1-879378-05-1*) Xenos Riverside.

De Palerne, Guillaume. The Romance of William of Palerne. Skeat, Walter W., ed. (EETS, ES Ser.: No. 1). 1974. reprint ed. 54.00 (*0-527-00211-9*) Periodicals Srv.

De Palma, Andre, jt. auth. see Anderson, Simon P.

***de Panne, Cornelis van.** Introductory Financial Economics with Spreadsheets. 224p. 1998. text 55.00 (*90-5702-363-6*, Harwood Acad Pubs); pap. text 24.00 (*90-5702-364-4*, Harwood Acad Pubs) Gordon & Breach.

De Paola, Tomie. La Abuelita de Arriba y la Abuelita de Abajo.Tr. of Nana Upstairs & Nana Downstairs. 1998. 10.95 (*958-04-1493-9*, Pub. by Norma SA) Distr Norma.

— Andy That's My Name. LC 73-4593. (Illus.). 32p. (J). (ps-3). 1999. per. 5.99 (*0-689-82697-4*, 076714005990) Aladdin.

De Paola, Tomie. Art Lesson. LC 88-27617. 1997. 11.15 (*0-606-06184-3*, Pub. by Turtleback) Demco.

De Paola, Tomie. The Art Lesson. (Illus.). 32p. (J). (ps-3). 1989. 15.95 (*0-399-21688-X*, G P Putnam) Peng Put Young Read.

— The Art Lesson. (Illus.). 32p. (J). (ps-3). 1994. pap. 5.95 (*0-399-22761-X*, G P Putnam) Peng Put Young Read.

— The Art Lesson. LC 88-27617. (Illus.). 32p. (J). (ps-3). 1997. pap. 5.99 (*0-698-11572-4*, PapStar) Peng Put Young Read.

— The Art Lesson. unabridged ed. (Picture Book Read-Alongs Ser.). (J). (gr. k-2). 1991. pap. 15.98 incl. audio (*0-8072-6003-7*, PRA 809SP) Listening Lib.

— The Baby Sister. LC 94-37218. (Illus.). 32p. (J). (ps-3). 1996. 15.95 (*0-399-22908-6*, G P Putnam) Peng Put Young Read.

***De Paola, Tomie.** The Baby Sister, 1 vol. (Illus.). 32p. (J). (ps-3). 1999. pap. 5.99 (*0-698-11773-5*, PapStar) Peng Put Young Read.

De Paola, Tomie. Baby's First Christmas. (Illus.). 12p. (J). (ps). 1988. bds. 5.95 (*0-399-21591-3*, G P Putnam) Peng Put Young Read.

— Big Anthony: His Story. LC 97-40084. (Illus.). 32p. (J). (ps-3). 1998. lib. bdg. 16.99 (*0-399-23189-7*) Putnam Pub Group.

***De Paola, Tomie.** Big Anthony & the Magic Ring. (Illus.). (ps-3). 1999. pap. 13.40 (*0-88103-359-6*) Econo-Clad Bks.

De Paola, Tomie. Big Anthony & the Magic Ring. LC 78-23631. (Illus.). 32p. (J). (ps-3). 1979. 16.00 (*0-15-207124-5*); pap. 6.00 (*0-15-611907-2*) Harcourt.

De Paola, Tomie. Bill & Pete. (Illus.). 32p. (J). (ps-3). 1996. pap. 5.99 (*0-698-11400-0*, PapStar) Peng Put Young Read.

De Paola, Tomie. Bill & Pete Go down the Nile. LC 86-12258. (Illus.). 32p. (J). (ps-3). 1987. 15.95 (*0-399-21395-3*, G P Putnam) Peng Put Young Read.

— Bill & Pete to the Rescue. LC 97-18684. (Illus.) 48p. (J). (ps-3). 1998. 15.99 (*0-399-23208-7*, G P Putnam) Peng Put Young Read.

— The Bubble Factory. (Illus.). 32p. (J). (ps-2). 1996. pap. 9.95 (*0-448-41349-3*, G & D) Peng Put Young Read.

— Charlie Needs a Cloak. LC 73-16365. (Illus.). 32p. (J). (ps-3). 1982. pap. 5.95 (*0-671-66467-0*) S&S Bks Yung.

— Charlie Needs a Cloak. (J). 1988. 10.90 (*0-606-01691-0*, Pub. by Turtleback) Demco.

— Christopher: The Holy Giant. LC 90-49926. (Illus.). 32p. (J). (ps-3). 1994. lib. bdg. 16.95 (*0-8234-0862-0*) Holiday.

— Christopher: The Holy Giant. (Illus.). 32p. (J). (ps-3). 1994. pap. 6.95 (*0-8234-1169-9*) Holiday.

— La Clase De Dibujo - The Art Lesson. 1996. 11.95 (*84-241-3341-2*) Lectorum Pubns.

— The Cloud Book. LC 74-34493. (Illus.). 32p. (J). (ps-3). 1975. lib. bdg. 15.95 (*0-8234-0259-2*) Holiday.

— The Cloud Book. LC 74-34493. (Illus.). 32p. (J). (ps-3). 1985. pap. 6.95 (*0-8234-0531-1*) Holiday.

— The Clown of God. LC 78-3845. (Illus.). 48p. (J). (ps-3). 1986. 15.00 (*0-15-219175-5*, Harcourt Child Bks) Harcourt.

— The Clown of God. LC 78-3845. (Illus.). 48p. (J). (ps-3). 1989. reprint ed. pap. 6.00 (*0-15-618192-4*, Voyager Bks) Harcourt.

— Country Angel Christmas. LC 94-37433. (Illus.). 32p. (J). (ps-3). 1995. 16.95 (*0-399-22817-9*, G P Putnam) Peng Put Young Read.

— The Days of the Blackbird: A Tale of Northern Italy. LC 96-3371. (Illus.). 32p. (J). (ps-3). 1997. 15.99 (*0-399-22929-9*, G P Putnam) Peng Put Young Read.

— An Early American Christmas. LC 86-3102. (Illus.). 32p. (J). (ps-3). 1987. 16.95 (*0-8234-0617-2*); pap. 6.95 (*0-8234-0979-1*) Holiday.

— Fin M'Coul, the Giant of Knockmany Hill. LC 80-2254. (Illus.). 32p. (J). (ps-3). 1981. pap. 6.95 (*0-8234-0385-8*); lib. bdg. 16.95 (*0-8234-0384-X*) Holiday.

— Flicks. LC 79-87514. (Illus.). (J). (ps-3). 1979. 11.95 (*0-15-228487-7*, Harcourt Child Bks) Harcourt.

— Four Stories for Four Seasons. (Illus.). 48p. (J). (ps-3). 1994. pap. 6.95 (*0-671-88633-9*, Half Moon Paper) S&S Childrens.

— Francis: The Poor Man of Assisi. LC 81-6984. (Illus.). 48p. (J). (ps-3). 1982. reprint ed. pap. 9.95 (*0-8234-0812-4*); reprint ed. lib. bdg. 18.95 (*0-8234-0435-8*) Holiday.

— The Friendly Beasts: An Old English Christmas Carol. (Illus.). 32p. (J). (ps-3). 1998. pap. 6.99 (*0-698-11661-5*, PapStar) Peng Put Young Read.

— Helga's Dowry. LC 76-54953. (Illus.). 32p. (J). (ps-3). 1977. pap. 6.00 (*0-15-640010-3*, Voyager Bks) Harcourt.

***De Paola, Tomie.** Here We All Are. LC 99-46747. (Twenty-Six Fairmount Avenue Book Ser.). (Illus.). 80p. (J). (gr. 2-6). 2000. 13.99 (*0-399-23496-9*, G P Putnam) Peng Put Young Read.

De Paola, Tomie. Hey Diddle Diddle & Other Mother Goose Rhymes. (Illus.). 32p. (J). (ps-k). 1998. pap. 5.99 (*0-698-11640-2*, PapStar) Peng Put Young Read.

— The Hunter & the Animals: A Wordless Picture Book. LC 81-2875. (Illus.). 32p. (J). (gr. k-3). 1981. pap. 6.95 (*0-8234-0428-5*); lib. bdg. 16.95 (*0-8234-0397-1*) Holiday.

— Jamie O'Rourke & the Big Potato: An Irish Folktale. LC 91-10626. (Illus.). 32p. (J). (ps-3). 1992. 15.95 (*0-399-22257-X*, G P Putnam) Peng Put Young Read.

— Jamie O'Rourke & the Big Potato: An Irish Folktale. LC 91-10626. (J). 1997. 11.15 (*0-606-11516-1*, Pub. by Turtleback) Demco.

— Jamie O'Rourke & the Pooka. Frith, Margaret, ed. LC 99-22469. (Illus.). 32p. (J). (ps-3). 2000. 16.99 (*0-399-23467-5*, G P Putnam) Peng Put Young Read.

— Jingle, the Christmas Clown. (Illus.). 40p. (J). (ps-3). 1998. pap. 6.99 (*0-698-11669-0*, PapStar) Peng Put Young Read.

— Kit & Kat. LC 94-15070. (All Aboard Reading Ser.: Level 1). (Illus.). 32p. (J). (ps-1). 1994. pap. 3.99 (*0-448-40748-5*, G & D) Peng Put Young Read.

— Kit & Kat. (All Aboard Reading Ser.). (J). 1994. 9.44 (*0-606-07765-0*) Turtleback.

— The Knight & the Dragon. LC 79-18131. (Illus.). 32p. (J). (ps-3). 1980. 15.95 (*0-399-20707-4*, G P Putnam) Peng Put Young Read.

— The Knight & the Dragon. (Illus.). 32p. (J). (ps-3). 1998. pap. 5.99 (*0-698-11623-2*, PapStar) Peng Put Young Read.

De Paola, Tomie. The Knight & the Dragon. 1980. 11.15 (*0-606-03327-0*, Pub. by Turtleback) Demco.

De Paola, Tomie. The Lady of Guadalupe. LC 79-19610. (Illus.). 48p. (J). (ps-3). 1980. pap. 8.95 (*0-8234-0403-X*); lib. bdg. 16.95 (*0-8234-0373-4*) Holiday.

— The Legend of Old Befana. LC 80-12293. (Illus.). 32p. (J). (gr. 4-7). 1980. pap. 6.00 (*0-15-243817-3*, Voyager Bks) Harcourt.

— The Legend of Old Befana. LC 80-12293. (Illus.). 32p. (J). (ps-3). 1980. 16.00 (*0-15-243816-5*, Harcourt Child Bks) Harcourt.

— The Legend of the Bluebonnet. LC 82-12391. (Illus.). 40p. (J). (ps-3). 1996. pap. 5.99 (*0-698-11359-4*, PapStar) Peng Put Young Read.

— The Legend of the Bluebonnet: An Old Tale of Texas. (J). 1983. 11.15 (*0-606-01690-2*, Pub. by Turtleback) Demco.

— The Legend of the Indian Paintbrush. (J). 1991. 11.15 (*0-606-04963-0*, Pub. by Turtleback) Demco.

— La Leyenda de la Flor de Noche Buena. (SPA., Illus.). (J). (ps-3). 1994. 15.95 (*0-399-22789-X*, G P Putnam) Peng Put Young Read.

— La Leyenda de la Flor de Noche Buena. 1997. 11.15 (*0-606-12751-8*, Pub. by Turtleback) Demco.

— La Leyenda de la Flor "El Conejo" Una Antigua Leyenda de Texas. Orig. Title: The Legend of the Bluebonnet. (SPA.). (J). 1993. 11.15 (*0-606-05402-2*, Pub. by Turtleback) Demco.

— La Leyenda del Pincel Indio. LC 87-20160. Orig. Title: The Legend of the Indian Paintbrush. (SPA., Illus.). 40p. (J). (ps-3). 1996. pap. 6.99 (*0-698-11362-4*, PapStar) Peng Put Young Read.

— La Leyenda del Pincel Indio. Orig. Title: The Legend of the Indian Paintbrush. 1996. 11.15 (*0-606-09522-5*, Pub. by Turtleback) Demco.

— El Libro de las Arenas Movedizas. Mlawer, Teresa, tr. LC 93-18317. (SPA.). 32p. (J). (ps-3). 1993. lib. bdg. 15.95 (*0-8234-1056-0*) Holiday.

— El Libro de las Arenas Movedizas. LC 93-18317. (SPA., Illus.). 32p. (J). (ps-3). 1993. pap. 5.95 (*0-8234-1057-9*) Holiday.

— El Libro de las Nubes. Mlawer, Teresa, tr. LC 93-18316. (SPA., Illus.). 32p. (J). (ps-3). 1993. pap. 6.95 (*0-8234-1055-2*) Holiday.

— El Libro de las Palomitas de Maiz. Mlawer, Teresa, tr. LC 93-18318. (SPA.). 32p. (J). (ps-3). 1993. lib. bdg. 15.95 (*0-8234-1058-7*) Holiday.

— Little Grunt & the Big Egg. (Illus.). (J). (ps-3). 1990. reprint ed. pap. 6.95 (*0-8234-1027-7*) Holiday.

— Little Grunt & the Big Egg: A Prehistoric Fairy Tale. LC 88-17009. (Illus.). 32p. (J). (ps-3). 1990. lib. bdg. 16.95 (*0-8234-0730-6*) Holiday.

— Make Your Own Christmas Cards. (Illus.). 32p. (J). (ps-2). 1998. pap. 8.99 (*0-8431-7444-7*) Putnam Pub Group.

— Mary: The Mother of Jesus. LC 92-54491. (Illus.). 32p. (J). (ps-3). 1995. lib. bdg. 16.95 (*0-8234-1018-8*) Holiday.

— Memo Y Leo, 1. (SPA., Illus.). 32p. (ps-1). 1999. pap. text 6.95 (*980-257-223-3*, Pub. by Ediciones Ekare) Kane-Miller Bk.

— Merry Christmas, Strega Nona. LC 86-4639. (Illus.). 32p. (J). (ps-3). 1986. 16.00 (*0-15-253183-1*, Harcourt Child Bks) Harcourt.

— Merry Christmas, Strega Nona. LC 86-4639. (Illus.). 32p. (J). (ps-3). 1991. pap. 7.00 (*0-15-253184-X*, Harcourt Child Bks) Harcourt.

— Merry Christmas, Strega Nona. (Voyager Bks.). (J). 1986. 12.20 (*0-606-00595-1*, Pub. by Turtleback) Demco.

— Michael Bird-Boy. LC 74-23563. (Illus.). 32p. (J). (gr. 4 up). 1987. 12.95 (*0-317-63504-2*) P-H.

— Michael Bird Boy. LC 74-23563. (Illus.). 32p. (J). (gr. k-4). 1987. 12.95 (*0-671-66468-9*) S&S Bks Yung.

— Michael Bird Boy. LC 74-23563. (Illus.). 32p. (J). (ps-3). 1987. pap. 5.95 (*0-671-66469-7*) S&S Bks Yung.

— The Miracles of Jesus. (Illus.). (J). (ps-3). 1987. pap. 8.95 (*0-8234-1211-3*) Holiday.

D

An Asterisk (*) at the beginning of an entry indicates that the title is appearing for the first time.

— The Mysterious Giant of Barletta. LC 83-18445. (Illus.). 32p. (J). (ps-3). 1988. pap. 6.00 (0-15-256349-0, Voyager Bks) Harcourt.

— The Mysterious Giant of Barletta: An Italian Folktale. LC 83-18445. (Illus.). 32p. (J). (ps-3). 1984. 13.95 (0-15-256347-4) Harcourt.

— Nana Upstairs & Nana Downstairs. LC 77-26698. (Illus.). 32p. (J). (ps-3). 1987. 14.95 (0-399-21417-8, G P Putnam) Peng Put Young Read.

— Nana Upstairs & Nana Downstairs. LC 96-31908. (Illus.). 32p. (J). (ps-3). 1998. 15.99 (0-399-23108-0, G P Putnam) Peng Put Young Read.

*De Paola, Tomie. Nana Upstairs & Nana Downstairs. (Illus.). 32p. (J). (ps-3). 2000. pap. 5.99 (0-698-11836-7, PuffinBks) Peng Put Young Read.

— Nana Upstairs & Nana Downstairs. (J). 1973. 10.19 (0-606-02202-3, Pub. by Turtleback) Demco.

De Paola, Tomie. The Night of Las Posadas. LC 98-36405. (Illus.). 32p. (J). (ps-3). 1999. 15.99 (0-399-23400-4, G P Putnam) Peng Put Young Read.

— Noah & the Ark. (Illus.). 32p. (Orig.). (J). (ps-2). 1984. 12.95 (0-86683-819-8, AY8451) Harper SF.

— Now One Foot, Now the Other. LC 80-22239. (Illus.). 48p. (J). (ps-3). 1981. 13.95 (0-399-20774-0, G P Putnam) Peng Put Young Read.

— Nuestra Senora de Guadalupe. LC 79-19609. (SPA., Illus.). 48p. (J). (ps-3). 1980. pap. 8.95 (0-8234-0404-8); lib. bdg. 16.95 (0-8234-0374-2) Holiday.

— Oliver Button Is a Sissy. LC 78-12624. (Illus.). 43p. (J). (ps-3). 1979. 13.00 (0-15-257852-8, Harcourt Child Bks); pap. 6.00 (0-15-668140-4, Voyager Bks) Harcourt.

— Oliver Button Is a Sissy. (J). 1979. 11.20 (0-606-04494-9, Pub. by Turtleback) Demco.

*De Paola, Tomie. On My Way. LC 00-38229. (26 Fairmount Avenue Bk.). 2001. write for info. (0-399-23583-3) Putnam Pub Group.

De Paola, Tomie. Pancakes for Breakfast. LC 77-15523. (Illus.). 32p. (C). (ps-3). 1978. pap. 5.00 (0-15-670768-3, Voyager Bks) Harcourt.

— Pancakes for Breakfast. LC 77-15523. (Illus.). 32p. (J). (ps-3). 1978. 14.95 (0-15-259455-8, Harcourt Child Bks) Harcourt.

De Paola, Tomie. Pancakes for Breakfast. (J). 1978. 10.20 (0-606-02221-X, Pub. by Turtleback) Demco.

De Paola, Tomie. The Parables of Jesus. (Illus.). 32p. (J). (ps-3). 1987. pap. 8.95 (0-8234-1196-6) Holiday.

— The Parables of Jesus. LC 86-18323. (Illus.). 32p. (J). (ps up). 1987. lib. bdg. 16.95 (0-8234-0636-9) Holiday.

— Patrick: Patron Saint of Ireland. LC 91-19417. (Illus.). 32p. (J). (ps-3). 1992. lib. bdg. 16.95 (0-8234-0924-4) Holiday.

— Patrick: Patron Saint of Ireland. LC 91-19417. (Illus.). 30p. (J). (ps-3). 1992. pap. 6.95 (0-8234-1077-3) Holiday.

— The Popcorn Book. LC 77-21456. (Illus.). 32p. (J). (ps-3). 1978. pap. 6.95 (0-8234-0533-8); lib. bdg. 15.95 (0-8234-0314-9) Holiday.

De Paola, Tomie. Queen Esther. 1985. pap. 5.95 (0-86683-702-7) Harper SF.

De Paola, Tomie. The Quicksand Book. LC 76-28762. (Illus.). 32p. (J). (gr. k-3). 1977. lib. bdg. 15.95 (0-8234-0291-6) Holiday.

— The Quicksand Book. LC 76-28762. (Illus.). 32p. (J). (ps-3). 1977. pap. 6.95 (0-8234-0532-X) Holiday.

— Sing, Pierrot, Sing: A Picture Book in Mime. LC 83-8403. (Voyager Picture Bks.). (Illus.). 32p. (J). (gr. 2 up). 1987. pap. 3.95 (0-15-274989-6, Voyager Bks) Harcourt.

— The Story of the Three Wise Kings. (Illus.). 32p. lib. bdg. 13.99 (0-399-61289-0) Berkley Pub.

— Strega Nona. 1996. 11.95 (84-241-3349-8) Lectorum Pubns.

— Strega Nona. 32p. (J). (ps-k). 1997. 7.99 (0-689-81764-9) Litle Simon.

— Strega Nona. LC 75-11565. (Illus.). 32p. (J). (ps-3). 1975. 15.00 (0-671-66283-X) S&S Bks Yung.

— Strega Nona. LC 75-11565. (Illus.). 32p. (J). (ps-3). 1979. pap. 6.95 (0-671-66606-1) S&S Bks Yung.

— Strega Nona. (Big Bks.). (J). (ps-3). 1992. 19.95 (0-590-72625-0) Scholastic Inc.

De Paola, Tomie. Strega Nona: An Old Tale. (Simon & Schuster Books for Young Readers Ser.). (J). 1975. 12.15 (0-606-02282-1, Pub. by Turtleback) Demco.

De Paola, Tomie. Strega Nona: Her Story. LC 95-22824. (Illus.). 32p. (J). (ps-3). 1996. 15.95 (0-399-22818-7, G P Putnam) Peng Put Young Read.

*De Paola, Tomie. Strega Nona: Her Story. (Illus.). 32p. (J). (gr. k-4). 2000. pap. 5.99 (0-698-11814-6, PuffinBks) Peng Put Young Read.

De Paola, Tomie. Strega Nona Doll. (J). (ps-3). 1995. 10.95 (0-689-80615-9) S&S Childrens.

*De Paola, Tomie. Strega Nona Goes on Vacation. LC 99-41362. (Illus.). 32p. (J). (ps-3). 2000. 16.99 (0-399-23562-0) Putnam Pub Group.

De Paola, Tomie. Strega Nona Meets Her Match. LC 92-8199. (Illus.). 32p. (J). (ps-3). 1993. 15.95 (0-399-22421-1, G P Putnam) Peng Put Young Read.

— Strega Nona Meets Her Match. LC 92-8199. (Illus.). 32p. (J). (ps-3). 1996. pap. 5.95 (0-698-11411-6, PapStar) Peng Put Young Read.

— Strega Nona Meets Her Match. 1993. 11.15 (0-606-10945-5, Pub. by Turtleback) Demco.

— Strega Nona's Magic Lessons. LC 80-28260. (Illus.). 32p. (J). (ps-3). 1982. 16.00 (0-15-281785-9, Harcourt Child Bks) Harcourt.

— Strega Nona's Magic Lessons. LC 80-28260. (Illus.). 32p. (J). (ps-3). 1984. pap. 7.00 (0-15-281786-7, Voyager Bks) Harcourt.

— Tom. LC 92-1022. (Illus.). 32p. (J). (ps-3). 1993. lib. bdg. 15.95 (0-399-22417-3, G P Putnam) Peng Put Young Read.

— Tom. LC 92-1022. (Illus.). 32p. (J). (ps-3). 1997. pap. 5.99 (0-698-11448-5, PapStar) Peng Put Young Read.

De Paola, Tomie. Tom. LC 92-1022. (J). 1997. 11.15 (0-606-11995-7, Pub. by Turtleback) Demco.

De Paola, Tomie. Tomie De Paola's Book of Bible Stories. LC 88-26468. (Illus.). 128p. (J). (gr. 2 up). 1990. 24.95 (0-399-21690-1, G P Putnam) Peng Put Young Read.

— Tomie De Paola's Book of Poems. 25th ed. LC 87-7325. (Illus.). 80p. (J). (gr. 2 up). 1988. 22.95 (0-399-21540-9, G P Putnam) Peng Put Young Read.

*De Paola, Tomie. Tomie de Paola's Mother Goose Favorites. LC 99-52821. (Reading Railroad Bks.). (Illus.). 32p. (J). (ps-3). 2000. pap. 3.49 (0-448-42155-0) Putnam Pub Group.

— Tomie de Paola's Rhyme Time. LC 00-24501. (Illus.). 32p. (J). (ps-3). 2000. pap. 3.49 (0-448-42167-4, G & D) Peng Put Young Read.

De Paola, Tomie. Tony's Bread. (Whitebird Bks.). (Illus.). 32p. (J). (ps-3). 1989. 15.95 (0-399-21693-6, G P Putnam) Peng Put Young Read.

— Tony's Bread. LC 88-7687. (Illus.). 32p. (J). (ps-3). 1996. pap. 5.95 (0-698-11371-3, PapStar) Peng Put Young Read.

— Tony's Bread, an Italian Folktale. LC 88-7687. 1996. 11.15 (0-606-09981-6, Pub. by Turtleback) Demco.

— Too Many Bunnies. (Illus.). 32p. (ps-3). 1997. pap. 2.95 (0-8167-4064-X) Troll Communs.

— 26 Fairmount Avenue. LC 98-12918. (Illus.). 64p. (J). (gr. 2-6). 1999. 13.99 (0-399-23246-X) Putnam Pub Group.

*De Paola, Tomie. 26 Fairmount Avenue. 64p. 2001. pap. text 5.99 (0-698-11864-2) Putnam Pub Group.

De Paola, Tomie. The Unicorn & the Moon. LC 94-20297. (Illus.). (J). 1995. 12.95 (0-382-24659-4, Silver Pr NJ); lib. bdg. 14.95 (0-382-24658-6) Silver Burdett Pr.

— Watch Out for the Chicken Feet in Your Soup. LC 74-8201. (Illus.). 32p. (J). (gr. k-4). 1974. 12.95 (0-685-35587-X); pap. 5.95 (0-685-35588-8) S&S Bks Yung.

— Watch Out for the Chicken Feet in Your Soup. (Illus.). 32p. (J). (ps-3). 1985. pap. 5.95 (0-671-66745-9) S&S Bks Yung.

De Paola, Tomie. Watch Out for the Chicken Feet in Your Soup. (J). 1974. 11.15 (0-606-02345-3, Pub. by Turtleback) Demco.

De Paola, Tomie, ed. The Legend of the Indian Paintbrush. LC 87-20160. 40p. (J). (ps-3). 1988. 15.95 (0-399-21534-4, G P Putnam) Peng Put Young Read.

De Paola, Tomie. Oh, Such Foolishness! LC 78-1622. 96p. (J). (gr. 3-6). 1978. 11.95 (0-397-31807-3) HarpC Child Bks.

— Songs of Praise. 32p. (J). (ps up). 1989. 15.95 (0-15-277108-5) Harcourt.

— Tomie De Paola's Book of the Old Testament. LC 94-22219. 80p. 1995. 18.95 (0-399-22830-6, G P Putnam) Peng Put Young Read.

— Tomie De Paola's Mother Goose. LC 84-26314. 127p. (J). (gr. 2 up). 1985. 24.95 (0-399-21258-2, G P Putnam) Peng Put Young Read.

— Tomie's Little Mother Goose. LC 96-44947. 36p. (J). (ps). 1997. bds. 7.99 (0-399-23154-4, G P Putnam) Peng Put Young Read.

De Paola, Tomie. The Legend of the Bluebonnet: An Old Tale of Texas. LC 82-12391. 32p. (J). (ps-3). 1983. 15.95 (0-399-20937-9, G P Putnam) Peng Put Young Read.

— The Legend of the Poinsettia. LC 92-20459. 32p. (J). (ps-3). 1994. lib. bdg. 15.95 (0-399-21692-8, G P Putnam) Peng Put Young Read.

— The Legend of the Poinsettia. 1997. 11.15 (0-606-12753-4, Pub. by Turtleback) Demco.

— The Miracles of Jesus. LC 86-18297. 32p. (J). (gr. 4-7). 1987. lib. bdg. 16.95 (0-8234-0635-0) Holiday.

De Paola, Tomie. Tomie De Paola's Favorite Nursery Tales. LC 85-28302. 128p. (J). (gr. 2 up). 1986. 24.95 (0-399-21319-8, G P Putnam) Peng Put Young Read.

De Paola, Tomie & Aesop. The Wind & the Sun. LC 74-166457. (A Magic Circle Book Ser.). 23p. (J). 1972. write for info. (0-663-22973-1) Silver.

De Paola, Tomie & Lear, Edward. Bonjour, Mister Satie. LC 90-37633. (Illus.). 32p. (J). (ps-3). 1991. 15.95 (0-399-21782-7, G P Putnam) Peng Put Young Read.

De Paola, Tomie & Martin, Sarah Catherine. The Comic Adventures of Old Mother Hubbard & Her Dog. LC 80-19270. (Illus.). 32p. (J). (ps-3). 1981. 13.95 (0-15-219541-6, Harcourt Child Bks) Harcourt.

— The Comic Adventures of Old Mother Hubbard & Her Dog. LC 80-19270. (Illus.). 32p. (J). (ps-3). 1989. reprint ed. pap. 7.00 (0-15-219542-4, Harcourt Child Bks) Harcourt.

De Paoli, Carlo. The Healing Touch of Massage. LC 95-6209. (Illus.). 144p. 1995. pap. 14.95 (0-8069-1359-2) Sterling.

— Secrets of Sexual Ecstasy: Pathways to Erotic Pleasure. LC 96-75834. (Illus.). 119p. (Orig.). 1996. pap. 15.95 (1-56924-768-4) Marlowe & Co.

De Paoli de Sales, Nanette, tr. see Mester, Cathy S. & Tauber, Robert T.

De Paoli, F. & Macleod, I. M. Distributed Computer Control Systems 1998 (DCCS '98) 15th IFAC Workshop, Como, Italy, 9-11 September 1998. LC 99-11676. 176p. 1999. pap. 60.50 (0-08-043242-5, Pergamon Pr) Elsevier.

De Paoli, Geri & Resler, Nancy D. No Title. Natsoulas, John, ed. (Illus.). 75p. (C). 1998. pap. text. write for info. (1-881572-54-4) J Natsoulas.

De Paoli, Geri, et al. Emmy Lou Packard. (Illus.). 50p. 1998. pap. 30.00 (1-881572-90-0) J Natsoulas.

De Paoli, Geri, jt. auth. see Gelburd, Gail.

De Paolis, Velasio. The Pastoral Care of Migrants in the Directives of the Church. 26p. 1989. 5.00 (0-934733-46-5) CMS.

De Paor. Structural Geology & Personal Computers. LC 96-42328. (Computer Methods in the Geosciences Ser.). 546p. 1996. 154.00 (0-08-042430-9, Pergamon Pr); pap. 48.00 (0-08-043110-0, Pergamon Pr) Elsevier.

De Paor, Eamonn. Jean & the Unicorn. 80p. 1994. pap. 6.95 (0-947962-86-7) Dufour.

De Paor, Liam. A Dictionary of Irish Saints. 320p. 1997. 45.00 (1-85182-190-2, Pub. by Four Cts Pr) Intl Spec Bk.

— Ireland & Early Europe: Essays & Occasional Writings on Art & Culture. LC 97-184713. 208p. 1997. pap. 24.95 (1-85182-298-4, Pub. by Four Cts Pr); boxed set 50.00 (1-85182-297-6, Pub. by Four Cts Pr) Intl Spec Bk.

— Landscapes with Figures. 1998. pap. 30.00 (1-85182-385-9, Pub. by Four Cts Pr); boxed set 45.00 (1-85182-384-0, Pub. by Four Cts Pr) Intl Spec Bk.

— On the Easter Proclamation: And Other Declarations. 128p. 1997. boxed set 30.00 (1-85182-322-0, Pub. by Four Cts Pr) Intl Spec Bk.

— The Peoples of Ireland: From Prehistory to Modern Times. LC 85-52221. 352p. (C). 1990. pap. text 18.50 (0-268-01590-2) U of Notre Dame Pr.

De Paor, Liam, ed. Milestones in Irish History. 56p. (Orig.). 1998. pap. 10.95 (1-85635-217-X, Pub. by Mercier Pr) Irish Amer Bk.

De Paor, Liam, tr. Saint Patrick's World: The Christian Culture of Ireland's Apostolic Age. 352p. 1997. pap. 20.00 (0-268-01757-3) U of Notre Dame Pr.

*de Paor, Louis, ed. Rogha Danta (Selected Poems) Michael Davitt. 120p. 2000. 25.00 (1-85918-247-X, Pub. by Cork Univ); pap. 15.95 (1-85918-248-8, Pub. by Cork Univ) Stylus Pub VA.

De Paor, Maire B. Patrick, the Pilgrim Apostle of Ireland: St. Patrick's Confession & Epistola. LC 98-167668. 313p. 1998. 39.95 (1-85390-304-3) Ignatius Pr.

De Papp Carrington, Ildiko. Controlling the Uncontrollable: The Fiction of Alice Munro. 251p. 1989. text 30.00 (0-87580-149-8) N Ill U Pr.

De Parceveaux, S. Dictionnaire Encylopedique d'Agrometeorologie. (ENG, FRE & SPA.). 328p. 1990. lib. bdg. 75.00 (0-685-48306-1, M6119) Fr & Eur.

— Encyclopedic Dictionary of Agrometeorology: Dictionnaire Encylopedique d'Agrometeorologie. (ENG, FRE & SPA.). 323p. 1990. lib. bdg. 75.00 (0-8288-4040-7, F29051) Fr & Eur.

De Pardieu, Charles-Henri & Weyd, Nathalie. Corporate Acquisitions & Mergers in France: A Practical Guide to the Legal, Financial, & Administrative Implications. LC 93-45396. (European Business Law & Practice Ser.). 128p. (C). 1994. lib. bdg. 98.00 (1-85333-965-2, Pub. by Graham & Trotman) Kluwer Academic.

De Paredes, Ellen S. Atlas of Film-Screen Mammography. 2nd enl. rev. ed. LC 88-20633. (Illus.). 628p. 1992. 150.00 (0-683-06758-3) Lppncott W & W.

De Pascalis, Andrea. Alchemy: The Golden Art. 1996. 32.50 (88-7301-025-3, Pub. by Gremese Intl) Natl Bk Netwk.

De Passalacqua, John L., jt. auth. see Silva-Ruiz, Pedro F.

*De Passe, Derrel B., ed. Traveling the Rainbow: The Life & Art of Joseph E. Yoakum. (Illus.). 224p. 2001. 50.00 (1-57806-311-6); pap. 28.00 (1-57806-248-9) U Pr of Miss.

De Patacsil, Priscila, jt. auth. see Strom, Kay M.

De Pater, A. D. & Pacejka, Hans B. Third Seminar on Advanced Vehicle System Dynamics: Proceedings of the Third ICTS Seminar Held at Amalfi, Italy, May 5-10, 1986. (Supplement to Vehicle System Dynamics Ser.: Vol. 16). x, 366p. 1987. pap. 57.25 (90-265-0676-7) Swets.

De Patta Pillar & Orloci, L. Character-Based Community Analysis: The Theory & an Application Program. (Ecological Computations Ser.: Vol. 5). ix, 270p. 1993. pap. 55.00 (90-5103-085-1, Pub. by SPB Acad Pub) Balogh.

De Paul Univ Staff. Centennial Studies in the History of Chicago's Vincentian University. 192p. 1998. per. 29.95 (0-7872-5100-3) Kendall-Hunt.

De Paul, Vincent. Vincent De Paul Correspondence, Conferences, Documents, Vol. 1. Kilar, Jacqueline, ed. Law, Helen M. et al, trs. from FRE. LC 83-63559. 611p. 1985. 39.00 (0-911782-50-8) New City.

— Vincent De Paul Correspondence, Conferences, Documents, Vol. 2. Poole, Marie J., ed. Law, Helen M. et al, trs. from FRE. 736p. 1990. 39.00 (0-911782-79-6) New City.

— Vincent De Paul Correspondence, Conferences, Documents, Vol. 3. Poole, Marie J., ed. 620p. 1992. 39.00 (1-56548-022-8) New City.

— Vincent De Paul Correspondence, Conferences, Documents, Vol. 4. Poole, Marie J., ed. & tr. by. from FRE. 620p. 1994. lib. bdg. 39.00 (1-56548-063-5) New City.

— Vincent De Paul Correspondence, Conferences, Documents, Vol. 5. Kilar, Jacqueline, ed. Law, Helen M. et al, trs. from FRE. 651p. 1995. 39.00 (1-56548-036-8) New City.

— Vincent De Paul Correspondence, Conferences, Documents, Vol. 6. Poole, Marie, ed. & tr. by. from FRE. Law, Helen M. et al, trs. from FRE. 660p. 1997. lib. bdg. 39.00 (1-56548-085-6) New City.

— Vincent De Paul Correspondence, Conferences, Documents, Vol. 7. Poole, Marie, ed. & tr. by. from FRE. Law, Helen M. et al, trs. from FRE. 660p. 1997. 39.00 (1-56548-102-X) New City.

*De Paul, Vincent. Vincent De Paul Correspondence, Conferences, Documents, Vol. 8. Poole, Marie J. et al, trs. 660p. 1999. 39.00 (1-56548-125-9) New City.

De Paula, F. Clive. Techniques of Business Control. 1973. pap. 12.95 (0-8464-0911-9) Beekman Pubs.

De Paula, Frederic & Zeff, Stephen A. Developments in Accounting: With a Profile of the Author. Brief, Richard P., ed. LC 77-87268. (Development of Contemporary Accounting Thought Ser.). 1978. reprint ed. lib. bdg. 26.95 (0-405-10897-4) Ayer.

De Pauley, William C. Candle of the Lord. LC 75-107693. (Essay Index Reprint Ser.). 1977. 18.95 (0-8369-1496-1) Ayer.

De Pauligny, G. M. Variations on the Theme of Love. 1994. pap. 10.95 (0-533-10769-5) Vantage.

— Variations on the Theme of Love, Vol. II. 1995. pap. 11.95 (0-533-11288-5) Vantage.

— Variations on the Theme of Love, Vol. III. LC 94-90613. 1998. pap. 12.50 (0-533-12522-7) Vantage.

De Paulis, Guido. Avianus - Aviani Index et Lexicus. (Alpha-Omega Ser.: Reihe A, Bd. CLXXXIV). 489p. 1997. 160.00 (3-487-10296-X) G Olms Pubs.

De Paulo, Raymond J. How to Cope with Depression. 1996. pap. 10.00 (0-449-91199-3) Fawcett.

De Pauw & Lauritzen, Erik K. Disaster Planning, Structural Assessment, Demolition & Recycling. LC 93-87224. (Illus.). 192p. (C). 1994. 130.00 (0-419-19190-9, E & FN Spon) Routledge.

De Pauw, Cornelius. A General History of the Americans, of Their Customs, Manners, & Colours. (LC History-America-E). 235p. 1999. reprint ed. lib. bdg. 79.00 (0-7812-4269-X) Rprt Serv.

De Pauw, Gommar A. The Challenge of Peace Through Strength - God's Plan & Our Defense of It: The Stripping of a Bishops' Pastoral Letter. (Illus.). 188p. 1989. 25.00 (1-877787-02-7) CTM Pubns.

— Warning! The New Mass. (Illus.). 100p. 1989. reprint ed. 5.00 (0-318-65212-9) CTM Pubns.

— Weighed & Found Wanting: The American Catholic Bishops & Their Pastoral Letter on War & Peace. 2nd ed. (Illus.). 180p. 1989. write for info. (0-318-65211-0) CTM Pubns.

De Pauw, Gommar A., tr. see Pius, V, pseud.

De Pauw, Gommar A., tr. & illus. see Pius, V, pseud.

De Pauw, John W. Soviet-American Trade Negotiations. LC 78-25883. (Praeger Special Studies). 180p. 1979. 59.95 (0-275-90346-X, C0346, Praeger Pubs) Greenwood.

De Pauw, John W. & Luz, George A., eds. Winning the Peace: The Strategic Implication of Military Civic Action. LC 91-18914. (Illus.). 256p. 1991. 65.00 (0-275-93770-4, C3770, Praeger Pubs) Greenwood.

De Pauw, Linda G. Baptism of Fire. 392p. 1993. pap. 14.95 (0-9634895-0-X) Minerva Ctr.

— Battle Cries & Lullabies: Women in War from Prehistory to the Present. LC 98-21219. (Illus.). 432p. 1998. 24.95 (0-8061-3100-4) U of Okla Pr.

— Founding Mothers: Women of America in the Revolutionary Era, 001. (Illus.). 228p. (J). (gr. 7 up). 1975. 18.00 (0-395-21896-9) HM.

De Pauw, Linda G., ed. House of Representatives Journal, 3 vols., Vol. 3. LC 76-25106. Vol. 3. 466p. 1977. 75.00 (0-8018-1819-2) Johns Hopkins.

— Senate Executive Journal & Related Documents, 3 vols., Vol. 2. LC 73-13443. Vol. 2. 592p. 1974. 65.00 (0-8018-1572-X) Johns Hopkins.

— Senate Legislative Journal, 3 vols., Vol. 3. LC 72-189461. Vol. 3. 800p. 1972. 65.00 (0-8018-1280-1) Johns Hopkins.

De Pauw, Linda Grant, see Grant De Pauw, Linda.

*De Pauw, Linda Grant. Battle Cries & Lullabies: Women in War from Prehistory to the Present. (Illus.). 432p. 2000. pap. 17.95 (0-8061-3288-4) U of Okla Pr.

De Pauw, Linda Grant. Founding Mothers: Women in America in the Revolutionary Era. 1975. 11.05 (0-606-07535-6) Turtleback.

De Paz, Yvette J. Juan Rulfo: Del Paramo a la Esperanza (From Paramo to Hope) 2nd ed. (SPA.). 301p. 1994. pap. 16.99 (968-16-4488-3, Pub. by Fondo) Continental Bk.

De Pazos, Amelia. Past Lives, Universal Energies, & Me. LC 98-94107. (Illus.). 137p. 2000. pap. 10.95 (0-533-12970-2) Vantage.

De Pedro Hernandez, Aquillino. Diccionario de Terminos Religiosos. (SPA.). 312p. 1990. pap. 26.95 (0-7859-5858-4, 8428513775) Fr & Eur.

De Pedro, M. A., et al. Bacterial Growth & Lysis: Metabolism & Structure of the Bacterial Sacculus. LC 92-44630. (FEMS Symposium Ser.: No. 65). (Illus.). 484p. (C). 1993. text 135.00 (0-306-44401-1, Kluwer Plenum) Kluwer Academic.

De Pedrolo, Manuel. Touched by Fire: A Bilingual Edition of Manuel de Pedrolo's "Tocats pel Foc" Griffin, Peter, tr. from CAT. LC 92-44185. (Catalan Studies: Vol. 10). (CAT & ENG.). VIII, 200p. (Orig.). (C). 1993. pap. text 29.95 (0-8204-2133-2) P Lang Pubng.

De Peguilhan, Aimeric, see Aimeric De Peguilhan.

De Peralta, Armando. The Space Between. (Illus.). 92p. 1968. 12.00 (0-938727-02-8) Scorpio Pr.

— We Were Such Fools. LC 97-91847. (Illus.). 105p. 1997. 20.00 (0-938727-24-9) Scorpio Pr.

De Peralta, Armando, et al. Tu' A Moving Collection of Romantic Poetry. Ward, Marilyn A., ed. LC 85-73610. (Illus.). 90p. 1986. 14.95 (0-938727-00-1) Scorpio Pr.

De Peralta, Jose Grave, see Aguiar, Ricardo J.

De Pereda, Jose M. Pedro Sanchez. Gonzalez Herran, Jose M., ed. (Nueva Austral Ser.: Vol. 149). (SPA.). 1991. pap. text 29.95 (84-239-1949-8) Elliots Bks.

— Sotileza. Gullon, German, ed. (Nueva Austral Ser.: Vol. 117). (SPA.). 1991. pap. text 19.95 (84-239-1917-X) Elliots Bks.

de Pereda, Prudencio, tr. see Gerchunoff, Alberto.

De Perouse, Montclos Jean-Marie. Fontainebleau. 1998. 40.00 (1-85759-191-7) Scala Books.

De Persia, Juan. Relaciones de Don Juan de Persia. Alonso Cortes, Narciso, ed. (SPA.). 280p. 1968. 100.00 (0-614-00118-8) Elliots Bks.

An Asterisk (*) at the beginning of an entry indicates that the title is appearing for the first time.

De Petit-Thouars, Abel. Voyage of the Venus: Sojourn in California. Rudkin, Charles N., tr. LC 95-34789. 115p. 1995. pap. 9.95 (*0-87770-553-4*) Ye Galleon.

De Petri, Catharose. Golden Rosycross. Lectorium Rosicrucianum Staff, tr. from DUT. Orig. Title: Het Gouden Rozenkruis. 1991. pap. 11.00 (*90-6732-047-1*) Rosycross Pr.

— Letters (Brieven) 151p. 1997. 22.50 (*90-6732-197-4*) Rosycross Pr.

— The Seal of Renewal.Tr. of Het Zegel der Vernieuwing. (Orig.). 1986. pap. 9.50 (*90-70196-39-5*) Rosycross Pr.

— Seven Voices Speak. Lectorium Rosicrucianum Staff, ed. Orig. Title: Zeven Stemmen Spreken. (DUT.). 79p. 1991. pap. 11.00 (*90-6732-043-9*) Rosycross Pr.

— Transfiguracion. (SPA.). 1987. pap. 7.00 (*90-70196-84-0*) Rosycross Pr.

— Transfiguration. (Rose Ser.: No. 1).Tr. of Transfigurie. 1986. pap. 6.00 (*90-70196-40-9*) Rosycross Pr.

De Petri, Catharose & Van Rijckenborgh, Jan. The Universal Gnosis.Tr. of De/Universele Gnosis. (Orig.). 1986. pap. 16.00 (*90-70196-57-3*) Rosycross Pr.

De Petri, Catharose, jt. auth. see Van Rijckenborgh, Jan.

De Peyster, Ann & Day, Kristin, eds. Ecological Risk Assessment: A Meeting of Policy & Science. LC 98-21948. (Illus.). 205p. 1998. 42.00 (*1-880611-14-7*, SETAC Pr) SETAC.

De Picciotto, Elliot. Makeup for Photography. 3rd ed. (Illus.). 35p. 1993. reprint ed. pap. 17.50 (*0-934420-15-7*) Studio Pr NE.

De Pijper, J. R. Modelling British English Intonation: An Analysis by Resynthesis of British English Intonation. (Netherlands Phonetic Archives Ser.). xii, 150p. 1983. pap. 34.65 (*90-6765-003-X*) Mouton.

De Piles, Roger. Abrege de la Vie des Peintres. 540p. 1969. reprint ed. write for info. (*0-318-71389-6*) G Olms Pubs.

De Pina-Cabral, Joao & Campbell, John L., eds. Europe Observed. 224p. (C). 1992. text 69.95 (*0-333-53824-2*) St Martin.

***De Pina-Cabral, Joao & de Lima, Antonia Pedroso, eds.** Elites: Choice, Leadership & Succession. 256p. 2000. 65.00 (*1-85973-394-8*, Pub. by Berg Pubs); pap. 19.50 (*1-85973-399-9*, Pub. by Berg Pubs) NYU Pr.

De Pina, R. Law Dictionary (Diccionario de Derecho) 11th ed. (SPA.). 514p. 1983. 69.95 (*0-8288-1531-3*, S12345) Fr & Eur.

De Pinna, Simon. Electricity. LC 97-24637. (Science Projects Ser.). (Illus.). 1998. 24.26 (*0-8172-4945-1*) Raintree Steck-V.

— Forces & Motion. LC 97-33987. (Science Projects Ser.). (Illus.). 48 p. (YA). 1998. 24.26 (*0-8172-4962-1*) Raintree Steck-V.

De Pisan, Christine. Lavision-Christine. Towner, Mary L., ed. LC 72-94202. (Catholic University of America. Studies in Romance Languages & Literatures: No. 6). reprint ed. 37.50 (*0-404-50306-3*) AMS Pr.

— The Treasure of the City of the Ladies: or The Book of Three Virtues. Lawson, Sarah, tr. & intro. by. (Classics Ser.). 192p. 1985. pap. 11.95 (*0-14-044453-X*, Penguin Classics) Viking Penguin.

De Pizan, Christine. Book of Fayttes of Arms & of Chyualrye. (EETS, OS Ser.: No. 189). 1972. reprint ed. 63.00 (*0-527-00189-9*) Periodicals Srv.

— The Book of the Body Politic. Forhan, Kate L., ed. & tr. by. LC 93-37130. (Cambridge Texts in the History of Political Thought Ser.). 157p. (C). 1994. pap. text 16.95 (*0-521-42259-0*) Cambridge U Pr.

— The Book of the City of Ladies. LC 97-24021. 1998. pap. 11.95 (*0-89255-230-1*) Persea Bks.

— The Book of the Duke of True Lovers. Fenster, Thelma S. & Margolis, Nadia, trs. from FRE. LC 91-31266. (Illus.). 160p. 1991. 24.95 (*0-89255-163-1*); pap. 11.95 (*0-89255-166-6*) Persea Bks.

— A Medieval Woman's Mirror of Honor: The Treasury of the City of Ladies. Cosman, Madeleine P., ed. Willard, Charity C., tr. from FRO. & intro. by. (Illus.). 265p. 1989. 24.95 (*0-89255-144-5*); pap. 11.95 (*0-89255-135-6*) Persea Bks.

— The Writings of Christine de Pizan. Willard, Charity C., ed. 400p. (Orig.). 1994. 35.00 (*0-89255-180-1*) Persea Bks.

De Planhol, Xavier. An Historical Geography of France. Lloyd, Janet, tr. LC 92-45912. (Cambridge Studies in Historical Geography). (Illus.). 589p. (C). 1994. text 80.00 (*0-521-32208-1*) Cambridge U Pr.

De Plata, Edith M. Mexican Vegetarian Cooking. (Illus.). 128p. (Orig.). 1989. pap. 10.95 (*0-89281-341-5*) Inner Tradit.

De Platt, Lyman. Una Guia Genealogico-Historica de Latinoamerica. (SPA., Illus.). 1978. pap. 20.00 (*0-916552-14-4*) Acoma Bks.

de Plessis, Contessa Villeneuve, see Villeneuve de Plessis, Contessa.

De Plou, Dafne C., tr. see Drakeford, John W.

De Pluvinel, Antoine. Le Maneige Royal. Nelson, Hilda, tr. 170p. 1990. 110.00 (*0-85131-452-X*, Pub. by J A Allen) Trafalgar.

De Podesta, Michael. Understanding the Properties of Matter. 320p. 1996. 80.00 (*1-56032-614-X*) Hemisp Pub.

De Poetterie, Ignace, ed. see Board of St. Paul Editorial Staff.

De Poix, Carol. Jo, Flo & Yolanda. (ENG & SPA., Illus.). 35p. (Orig.). (J). (ps-1). 1973. pap. 4.95 (*0-914996-04-5*) Lollipop Power.

De Poleo, Patty W., jt. auth. see Ferrer, Jami.

De Poli, Giovanni & Piccialli, Aldo, eds. Representations of Musical Signals. (Illus.). 496p. 1991. 57.50 (*0-262-04113-8*) MIT Pr.

De Polignac, Francois. Cults, Territory & the Origins of the Greek City-State. LC 94-46009.Tr. of Naissance de la Cite Grecque. 204p. 1995. pap. text 14.95 (*0-226-67334-0*) U Ch Pr.

— Cults, Territory & the Origins of the Greek City-State. Lloyd, Janet, tr. LC 94-46009.Tr. of Naissance de la Cite Grecque. (ENG & FRE.). 204p. 1995. lib. bdg. 39.95 (*0-226-67333-2*) U Ch Pr.

De Polnay, Peter. Garibaldi: The Legend & the Man. LC 75-22641. (Illus.). 234p. 1976. reprint ed. lib. bdg. 65.00 (*0-8371-8361-8*, DEGA, Greenwood Pr) Greenwood.

De Pomiane, Edouard. Cooking with Pomiane. 246p. 1994. pap. 10.00 (*0-86547-481-8*) N Point Pr.

De Ponce, Blanca N. La Aventura de Estudiar: Programa para Desarrollar Destrezas de Estudio e Informacion en el nivel Elemental e Intermedio. (SPA., Illus.). 100p. (Orig.). (J). (gr. 5-9). 1984. write for info. (*0-318-64879-2*) B Ponce.

De Poncins, Gontran. Kabloona: Among the Inuit. Galantiere, Lewis, tr. from FRE. LC 96-75792. (Rediscovery Ser.). (Illus.). 360p. 1996. pap. 14.95 (*1-55597-249-7*) Graywolf.

De Poncins, Leon. Freemasonry & Judaism: Secrets Powers Behind Revolution. 260p. 1992. pap. 9.95 (*1-881316-90-4*) A&B Bks.

— Freemasonry & the Vatican: A Struggle for Recognition. 224p. 1994. pap. text 9.95 (*1-881316-91-2*) A&B Bks.

— Judaism & the Vatican. 1982. lib. bdg. 250.00 (*0-87700-381-5*) Revisionist Pr.

De Pons, Beatriz. Titeres.Tr. of Puppets. (SPA.). 1991. pap. 5.50 (*0-311-11070-3*) Casa Bautista.

De Pons, Francois R. Travels in South America, 2 vols. LC 71-128420. reprint ed. 145.00 (*0-404-02115-8*) AMS Pr.

De Ponseti, Helena Percas, see Percas de Ponseti, Helena.

De Pont, J. J., ed. European Pancreatic Club EPC, 18th Meeting, Nijmegen, September 1986: Abstracts. (Journal: Digestion: Vol. 35, No. 1). 68p. 1986. pap. 50.50 (*3-8055-4456-1*) S Karger.

— Molecular Aspects of Transport Proteins. LC 92-18220. (New Comprehensive Biochemistry Ser.: Vol. 21). 344p. 1992. 211.25 (*0-444-89562-0*) Elsevier.

De Pontes, M., et al. Natural Gas Conversion IV: Proceedings of the 4th International Natural Gas Conversion Symposium, Kruger Park, South Africa, November 19-23, 1995, Vol. 107. LC 97-327. (Studies in Surface Science & Catalysis). 600p. 297.00 (*0-444-82352-2*) Elsevier.

De Pontfarcy, Y., jt. auth. see Picard, J. M.

De Pontfarcy, Y., jt. auth. see Picard, Jean-Michel.

De Pontgibaud, Chevalier. A French Volunteer of the War of Independence. Douglas, Robert B., ed. & tr. by. LC 73-76558. (Eyewitness Accounts of the American Revolution Ser.). 220p. 1969. reprint ed. 16.95 (*0-405-01171-7*) Ayer.

De Poo, Suzy. Sunny Side Up. 1980. ring bd. 11.95 (*0-9604158-0-7*) Jr League Ft Lauderdale.

De Poorter, Erika. Zeami's Talks on Sarugaku: An Annotated Translation of the Sarugaku Dangi. (Japonica Neerlandica Ser.: Vol. 2). 303p. (C). 1986. 60.00 (*90-70265-30-3*, Pub. by Gieben) J Benjamins Pubng Co.

De Poorter, Erika, ed. As the Twig Is Bent... Essays in Honour of Frits Vos. xxvii, 257p. 1990. 40.00 (*90-5063-054-5*, Pub. by Gieben) J Benjamins Pubng Co.

De Porres, Martin. Simon of Cyrene. 1996. write for info. (*0-9648448-3-4*) CMJ Marian Pubs.

De Portzamparc, Christian. Christian De Portzamparc. LC 97-123572. (Illus.). 168p. 1996. 70.00 (*3-7643-5593-X*, Pub. by Birkhauser) Princeton Arch.

— Genealogy of Forms. 128p. 1996. 60.00 (*2-906571-51-2*, Pub. by Editions Dis Voir) Dist Art Pubs.

De Potter, Patrick, et al, eds. MRI of the Eye & Orbit. LC 94-41374. 320p. 1995. pap. 99.20 (*0-608-05600-6*, 206605800006) Bks Demand.

De Pourtales, Guy. Richard Wagner: The Story of an Artist. May, Lewis, tr. from FRE. LC 76-138173. (Illus.). 1972. reprint ed. lib. bdg. 79.50 (*0-8371-5630-0*, PORW, Greenwood Pr) Greenwood.

De Pous, Miner. Reach Out, Bk 1. 1996. pap., student ed. 19.38 (*0-07-026391-4*) McGraw.

De Prada, Jaun Manuel. La Tempestad. 1999. pap. text 9.95 (*84-08-02840-5*) Planeta.

De Prada, Valentin, et al, eds. Understanding Social Change in the Nineties: Theoretical Approaches & Historiographical Perspectives. LC 95-3346. 520p. 1995. 104.95 (*0-86078-496-7*, Pub. by Variorum) Ashgate Pub Co.

De Prado, R., et al, eds. Weed & Crop Resistance to Herbicides. LC 97-14124. 1997. text 187.00 (*0-7923-4581-9*) Kluwer Academic.

De Pree, Hugh. Business As Unusual: The People & Principles of Herman Miller. 280p. 1986. text 9.95 (*0-87911-005-8*) Herman Miller.

De Pree, Julia. The Ravishment of Persephone: Epistolary Lyric in the Siecle des Lumieres. LC 98-34186. (North Carolina Studies in the Romance Languages & Literatures: No. 258). 130p. 1998. pap. 21.50 (*0-8078-9262-9*) U of NC Pr.

De Pree, Max. Dear Zoe. LC 98-7234. (Illus.). 105p. 1998. pap. 11.00 (*0-8028-4592-4*) Eerdmans.

— Dear Zoe: Letters to My Miracle Grandchild. LC 95-46969. 1996. pap. 10.00 (*0-06-251390-7*) Harper SF.

De Premare, Alfred L. Dictionnaire Arabe-Francais. (ARA & FRE.). 1993. write for info. (*0-7859-8018-0*, 2-7384-1859-7) Fr & Eur.

de Pres, Josquin & Landsman, Mark. Creative Careers in Music. 224p. 2000. pap. text 18.95 (*1-58115-049-0*) Allworth Pr.

De Prisco, Andrew. Mini-Atlas of Dog Breeds. (Illus.). 576p. 1990. 35.95 (*0-86622-091-7*, H-1106) TFH Pubns.

— A New Owner's Guide to Training the Perfect Puppy. (New Owner's Guide to Ser.). (Illus.). 160p. 1996. 12.95 (*0-7938-2758-2*, JG-109) TFH Pubns.

De Prisco, Andrew & Johnson, James B. The Mini-Atlas of Cats of the World. (Illus.). 448p. 1991. text 23.95 (*0-86622-627-3*, TS-152) TFH Pubns.

— The Right Cat for Me. (Illus.). 224p. 1996. 9.95 (*0-7938-1595-9*, KW238) TFH Pubns.

De Prisco, Doris. Cats: Look & Learn. (Illus.). 64p. 1993. pap. 9.95 (*0-7938-0174-5*, KD-001S) TFH Pubns.

De Prospo, R. C. Theism in the Discourse of Jonathan Edwards. LC 84-40406. 296p. 1986. 42.50 (*0-87413-281-9*) U Delaware Pr.

***de Providencia, Joao & Malik, F. B.** Condensed Matter Theories, Vol. 13. 357p. 1998. 97.00 (*1-56072-602-4*) Nova Sci Pubs.

De Prycker, Martin. Asynchronous Transfer: Solution for Broadband. 3rd ed. LC 95-18639. 332p. 1995. 77.00 (*0-13-342171-6*) P-H.

De Puig, Olive. Painting Still Lifes in Oils. LC 95-37550. (Easy Painting & Drawing Ser.). (Illus.). 62p. 1996. 12.95 (*0-8120-9402-6*) Barron.

De Pulford, Nicola. The Book of Spells. (Illus.). 123p. 1998. 18.95 (*0-7641-5098-7*) Barron.

***De Pulford, Nicola.** Spells & Charms: 52 Charms & Spells to Help You Get the Best out of Life. LC 99-35412. 112p. 1999. pap. text 14.95 (*0-8069-9915-2*) Sterling.

***De Puma, Richard.** Corpus Vasorum Antiquorum: United States of America, Vol. 9. Vol. 9. (Illus.). 58p. 2000. 100.00 (*0-89236-608-7*) J P Getty Trust.

De Puma, Richard. Corpus Vasorum Antiquorum, United States of America, Fascicule 31: The J. Paul Getty Museum, Fascicule 6. LC 88-12781. (Illus.). 58p. 1996. 90.00 (*0-89236-293-6*, Pub. by J P Getty Trust) OUP.

De Puma, Richard D. Corpus Speculorum Etruscorum - U. S. A. Vol. 1: Midwestern Collections. LC 86-31135. (Illus.). 244p. reprint ed. pap. 75.70 (*0-608-09055-7*, 206969000001) Bks Demand.

— Corpus Speculorum Etruscorum - U. S. A. Vol. 2: Boston & Cambridge. LC 86-31135. (Illus.). 236p. reprint ed. pap. 73.20 (*0-608-09056-5*, 206969000002) Bks Demand.

De Puma, Richard D. & Small, Jocelyn P., eds. Murlo & the Etruscans: Art & Society in Ancient Etruria. LC 93-14995. (Studies in Classics). (Illus.). 256p. (C). 1994. text 45.00 (*0-299-13910-7*) U of Wis Pr.

De Puma, Richard D., jt. ed. see Begley, Vimala.

De Purucker, G. Clothed with the Sun: The Mystery-Tale of Jesus the Avatara. rev. ed. Small, Emmett & Todd, Helen, eds. Orig. Title: The Story of Jesus. (Illus.). 56p. 1972. pap. 5.00 (*0-913004-06-5*) Point Loma Pub.

— Correlations of Cosmic & Human Constitutions. (Esoteric Teachings Ser.: Vol. IX). 136p. 1987. pap. 9.95 (*0-913004-60-X*) Point Loma Pub.

— Death & the Circulations of the Cosmos, I. (Esoteric Teachings Ser.: Vol. XI). 130p. 1987. pap. 9.95 (*0-913004-62-6*) Point Loma Pub.

— Death & the Circulations of the Cosmos, II. (Esoteric Teachings Ser.: Vol. XII). 150p. 1987. pap. 9.95 (*0-913004-63-4*) Point Loma Pub.

— Dialogues of G. de Purucker, 3 vols., Set. Conger, Arthur L., ed. LC 79-65630. 1420p. 1948. 41.95 (*0-911500-59-6*) Theos U Pr.

— The Doctrine of the Spheres. (Esoteric Teachings Ser.: Vol. VII). 166p. 1987. pap. 9.95 (*0-913004-58-8*) Point Loma Pub.

— The Esoteric or Oriental School: Steps in the Initiatory Cycle. (Esoteric Teachings Ser.: Vol. II). 156p. 1987. pap. 9.95 (*0-913004-53-7*) Point Loma Pub.

— The Esoteric Path: Its Nature & Its Tests. (Esoteric Teachings Ser.: Vol. I). 136p. 1987. pap. 9.95 (*0-913004-52-9*) Point Loma Pub.

— The Esoteric Tradition, 2 vols., Set. 2nd ed. LC 73-81738. 1211p. 1973. reprint ed. 38.95 (*0-911500-65-0*); reprint ed. pap. 26.95 (*0-911500-66-9*) Theos U Pr.

— Fountain-Source of Occultism. Knoche, Grace F., ed. LC 72-92155. 760p. 1974. 29.95 (*0-911500-70-7*); pap. 20.95 (*0-911500-71-5*) Theos U Pr.

— The Four Sacred Seasons. LC 79-63565. 97p. 1979. 11.95 (*0-911500-83-9*); pap. 7.50 (*0-911500-84-7*) Theos U Pr.

— Fundamentals of the Esoteric Philosophy. 590p. 1990. 29.95 (*0-913004-70-7*) Point Loma Pub.

— Fundamentals of the Esoteric Philosophy. 2nd rev. ed. Knoche, Grace F., ed. LC 78-74258. 669p. 1979. 27.95 (*0-911500-63-4*); pap. 18.95 (*0-911500-64-2*) Theos U Pr.

— Galaxies & Solar Systems: Their Genesis, Structure, & Destiny. (Esoteric Teachings Ser.: Vol. IV). 130p. 1987. pap. 9.95 (*0-913004-55-3*) Point Loma Pub.

— Gods, Monads, Life - Atoms. (Esoteric Teachings Ser.: Vol. VIII). 140p. 1987. pap. 9.95 (*0-913004-59-6*) Point Loma Pub.

— Golden Precepts: A Guide to Enlightened Living. 3rd rev. ed. 170p. 1994. 7.00 (*0-913004-02-2*, 913004-02) Point Loma Pub.

— Golden Precepts of Esotericism. 3rd rev. ed. LC 78-74257. 183p. 1979. 13.95 (*0-911500-85-5*); pap. 8.95 (*0-911500-86-3*) Theos U Pr.

— Hierarchies & the Doctrine of Emanations. (Esoteric Teachings Ser.: Vol. V). 136p. 1987. pap. 9.95 (*0-913004-56-1*) Point Loma Pub.

— The Hierarchy of Compassion. (Esoteric Teachings Ser.: Vol. X). 140p. 1987. pap. 9.95 (*0-913004-61-8*) Point Loma Pub.

— In the Temple: Esoteric Teachings on the Four Sacred Seasons. 126p. 1995. pap. 9.95 (*0-913004-91-X*) Point Loma Pub.

— Invisible Worlds & Their Inhabitants. (Esoteric Teachings Ser.: Vol. VI). 130p. 1987. pap. 9.95 (*0-913004-57-X*) Point Loma Pub.

— Mahatmas & Genuine Occultism. rev. ed. Small, Emmett & Todd, Helen, eds. Orig. Title: The Masters & the Path of Occultism. (Illus.). 100p. 1972. pap. 5.00 (*0-913004-07-3*) Point Loma Pub.

— Man in Evolution. 2nd rev. ed. Knoche, Grace F., ed. LC 76-45503. 377p. 1977. pap. 14.95 (*0-911500-55-3*) Theos U Pr.

— Occult Glossary: A Compendium of Oriental & Theosophical Terms. 2nd ed. LC 96-41435. 204p. 1996. reprint ed. 17.95 (*1-55700-050-6*); reprint ed. pap. 11.95 (*1-55700-051-4*) Theos U Pr.

— The Path of Compassion, Set. unabridged ed. LC 86-50300. audio 20.95 (*0-911500-60-X*) Theos U Pr.

— The Path of Compassion: Time-Honored Principles of Spiritual & Ethical Conduct. LC 86-50300. 84p. 1986. pap. 7.95 (*0-911500-69-3*) Theos U Pr.

— Space & the Doctrine of Maya. (Esoteric Teachings Ser.: Vol. III). 118p. 1987. pap. 9.95 (*0-913004-54-5*) Point Loma Pub.

— Studies in Occult Philosophy. LC 73-81739. 762p. 1973. reprint ed. 28.95 (*0-911500-52-9*); reprint ed. pap. 19.95 (*0-911500-53-7*) Theos U Pr.

— What Death Really Is: Questions We All Ask. Small, W. Emmett, ed. 118p. (Orig.). 1986. 6.50 (*0-913004-48-0*) Point Loma Pub.

— Wind of the Spirit. rev. ed. Small, W. Emmett & Todd, Helen, eds. 282p. 1971. reprint ed. pap. 12.00 (*0-913004-00-6*) Point Loma Pub.

— Wind of the Spirit. rev. ed. LC 84-50118. 328p. 1997. reprint ed. pap. 13.95 (*0-911500-68-5*) Theos U Pr.

— Wind of the Spirit. 2nd rev. ed. LC 84-50118. 328p. 1984. reprint ed. 20.95 (*0-911500-67-7*) Theos U Pr.

— Wisdom Practice: Gateway to Enlightenment. Small, Kenneth, ed. 130p. 2000. pap. 10.50 (*0-913004-90-1*) Point Loma Pub.

— Word Wisdom in the Esoteric Tradition. (Study Ser.: No. 2). 1980. pap. 8.00 (*0-913004-35-9*, 913004-35) Point Loma Pub.

De Purucker, G. & Tingley, Katherine. H. P. Blavatsky: The Mystery. rev. ed. Small, W. Emmett & Todd, Helen, eds. (Illus.). 256p. 1974. pap. 10.95 (*0-913004-14-6*) Point Loma Pub.

De Puy, Candace & Dovitch, Dana. Healing Choice: Your Guide to Emotional Recovery After an Abortion. LC 96-47484. 1997. per. 12.00 (*0-684-83196-1*, Fireside) S&S Trade Pap.

***De Puy, Henry F.** A Bibliography of the English Colonial Treaties with the American Indians. fac. ed. (Illus.). 109p. 2000. 50.00 (*1-57898-194-8*) Martino Pubng.

De Puy, Henry F. A Bibliography of the English Colonial Treaties with the American Indians. LC 78-164820. reprint ed. 27.50 (*0-404-07123-6*) AMS Pr.

— A Bibliography of the English Colonial Treaties with the American Indians. 1988. reprint ed. lib. bdg. 59.00 (*0-7812-0049-0*) Rprt Serv.

— A Bibliography of the English Colonial Treaties with the American Indians. LC 78-108471. 1917. reprint ed. 23.00 (*0-403-00425-X*) Scholarly.

De Puy, Henry W. Ethan Allen & the Green Mountain Heroes of '76: With a Sketch of the Early History of Vermont. (Select Bibliographies Reprint Ser.). 1977. 29.95 (*0-8369-5022-4*) Ayer.

De Puytorac, P., et al. Precis de Protistology. (FRE., Illus.). 581p. 1987. pap. text 112.50 (*0-317-68057-9*) Lubrecht & Cramer.

De Qian, Monk. Shaolin Secret Formulas for the Treatment of External Injury. 2nd ed. Zhang Ting-liang & Flaws, Bob, trs. from CHI. 185p. 1995. 18.95 (*0-936185-08-2*) Blue Poppy Pr.

De Quehen, A. H. Editing Poetry from Spenser to Dryden: Papers Given at the Sixteenth Annual Conference on Editorial Problems, University of Toronto, 31 October-1 November, 1980. LC 81-47627. (Conference on Editorial Problems Ser.: No. 16). 1987. 42.50 (*0-404-63666-7*) AMS Pr.

De Quehen, Hugh. Lucy Hutchinson's Lucretius. LC 97-132283. (LAT & ENG.). 270p. (C). 1996. text 42.50 (*0-472-10778-X*, 10778) U of Mich Pr.

De Quehen, Hugh, ed. see Butler, Samuel.

de Queiros, Eca. The City & the Mountains. Campbell, Roy, tr. LC 67-17895. 221p. reprint ed. 68.60 (*0-8357-9480-6*, 200785700067) Bks Demand.

— Maias. LC 99-228033. 640p. 1999. pap. 15.95 (*0-14-044694-X*, PuffinBks) Peng Put Young Read.

de Queiros, Eca. The Yellow Sofa. Vetch, John, tr. from POR. (New Directions Classic Ser.). 112p. (Orig.). 1996. pap. 10.95 (*0-8112-1339-0*, NDP833, Pub. by New Directions) Norton.

De Queiros, Jose M. Alves & Co. Fedorchek, Robert M., tr. from POR. LC 88-22799. 136p. (Orig.). (C). 1988. pap. text 16.50 (*0-8191-7157-3*) U Pr of Amer.

De Queiros Mattoso, Katia M. To Be a Slave in Brazil: 1550-1888. Goldhammer, Arthur, tr. 35p. (C). 1986. text 45.00 (*0-8135-1154-2*) Rutgers U Pr.

— To Be a Slave in Brazil: 1550-1888. Goldhammer, Arthur, tr. 35p. (C). 1986. pap. 18.00 (*0-8135-1155-0*) Rutgers U Pr.

De Queiroz, Kevin. Phylogenetic Systematics of Iguanine Lizards: A Comparative Osteological Study. LC 87-24594. (University of California Publications in Zoology: Vol. 118). 215p. reprint ed. pap. 66.70 (*0-608-00715-3*, 206148900009) Bks Demand.

***de Queiroz, M. S., et al.** Boundary Control of Mechanical Systems. (Control Engineering Ser.). (Illus.). 332p. 2000. 69.95 (*0-8176-4086-X*) Birkhauser.

De Queiroz, Rachel. Dora, Doralina. Loos, Dorothy S., tr. 228p. (Orig.). 1984. mass mkt. 4.50 (*0-380-84822-8*, 84822, Avon Bks) Morrow Avon.

de Queiroz, Ruy J. G. B., tr. see Manzano, Maria.

De Queljoe, David H. Marginal Man in a Colonial Society: Abdoel Moeis' Salah Asuhan. LC 74-620028. (Papers in International Studies: Southeast Asia Ser.: No. 32). 52p. reprint ed. pap. 30.00 (*0-608-10994-0*, 200745100062) Bks Demand.

D

An Asterisk (*) at the beginning of an entry indicates that the title is appearing for the first time.

De Querioz, Eca. The Relic. 2nd ed. Costa, Margaret J., ed. & tr. by. from POR. (European Classics). 281p. 1997. reprint ed. pap. 14.99 (0-946626-94-4, Pub. by Dedalus) Subterranean Co.

***De Quesada, Alejandro M., Jr.** Baseball in Tampa Bay. (Images of America Ser.). 128p. 2000. pap. 18.99 (0-7385-0058-5) Arcadia Publng.

— Cuba. (Images of America Ser.). (Illus.). 128p. 1999. pap. 18.99 (0-7385-0212-X) Arcadia Publng.

De Quesada, Alejandro M., Jr. The Royal Air Force over Florida. LC 98-87572. (Images of America Ser.). 128p. 1998. 16.99 (0-7524-1343-0) Arcadia Publng.

— The Spanish-American War in Tampa Bay. (Images of America Ser.). (Illus.). 128p. 1998. pap. 16.99 (0-7524-0894-1) Arcadia Publng.

— World War II in Tampa Bay. (Images of America Ser.). (Illus.). 128p. 1997. pap. 16.99 (0-7524-0888-7) Arcadia Publng.

***De Quesada, Alejandro M., Jr.** Ybor City. (Images of America Ser.). (Illus.). 128p. 1999. pap. 18.99 (0-7385-0057-7) Arcadia Publng.

***De Quesada, Alejandro M., Jr. & Luisi, Vincent.** Dunedin. (Images of America Ser.). (Illus.). 128p. 1999. pap. 18.99 (0-7385-0059-3) Arcadia Publng.

De Quesada, Gonzalo. War in Cuba, Being a Full Account of Her Great Struggle for Freedoms. LC 79-111731. (American Imperialism: Viewpoints of United States Foreign Policy, 1898-1941 Ser.). 1970. reprint ed. 41.95 (0-405-02047-3) Ayer.

De Quevdo. Poems to Lisi. (Exeter Hispanic Text Ser.: No. 45). (SPA.). 136p. Date not set. pap. text 17.95 (0-85989-274-3, Pub. by Univ Exeter Pr) Northwestern U Pr.

De Quevedo, F. DeQuevedo. Dreams & Discourses: Suenos y Discursos. Britton, ed. (Hispanic Classics Ser.). 1989. pap. 28.00 (0-85668-353-1, Pub. by Aris & Phillips) David Brown.

De Quevedo, Francisco. Dreams & Discourses: Suenos y Discursos. Britton, R. K., ed. (Hispanic Classics Ser.). 1989. 59.95 (0-85668-352-3, Pub. by Aris & Phillips) David Brown.

— Poesia Moral (Polimnia), No. 42. Rey, Alfonso, ed. (Textos B Ser.). 360p. 1999. 72.00 (1-85566-058-X, Pub. by Tamesis Bks Ltd) Boydell & Brewer.

De Quevedo, Francisco, ed. On the Anvil. (C). 1989. 30.00 (0-948268-48-4, Pub. by Dedalus); pap. 15.00 (0-948268-47-6, Pub. by Dedalus) St Mut.

De Quevedo, Francisco, see Quevedo, Francisco de.

De Quevedo Y Villegas, Francisco. Antologia Poetica. 290p. 1989. pap. 16.95 (0-7859-5193-8) Fr & Eur.

De Queyroz, Fernao. The Temporal & Spiritual Conquest of Ceylon, 6 bks. in 2 vols. LC 71-153629. reprint ed. 155.00 (0-404-09630-1) AMS Pr.

De Quille, Dan. The Big Bonanza: An Authentic Account of the Discovery, History & Working of the World-Renowned Comstock Lode of Nevada. LC 71-420448. (Frontier Library). 439p. 1969. write for info. (0-413-27310-5) Routledge.

— A History of the Comstock Silver Lode & Mines, Nevada & the Great Basin Region, Lake Tahoe & the High Sierras. LC 72-9439. (Far Western Frontier Ser.). 162p. 1980. reprint ed. 19.95 (0-405-04969-2) Ayer.

— The Sorceress of Attu. Berkove, Lawrence I., ed. (Illus.). 60p. (Orig.). 1994. pap. 20.00 (0-933691-06-8) U Mich-Dearborn.

De Quincey, Thomas. Biographies of Shakespeare, Pope, Goethe, & Schiller. LC 75-164822. (Illus.). reprint ed. 55.00 (0-404-02079-8) AMS Pr.

— The Collected Writings, 14 vols. Masson, David, ed. LC 68-58566. reprint ed. 975.00 (0-404-02100-X) AMS Pr.

— The Collected Writings, 14 vols., Set. (BCL1-PR English Literature Ser.). 1992. reprint ed. lib. bdg. 1050.00 (0-7812-7508-3) Rprt Serv.

— Confessions of an English Opium Eater. Ward, Aileen, tr. 336p. 1985. mass mkt. 4.95 (0-88184-130-7) Carroll & Graf.

— Confessions of an English Opium Eater. (Green Integer Bks.: No. 35). 350p. 1999. pap. text 11.95 (1-892295-21-0, Pub. by Green Integer) Consort Bk Sales.

— Confessions of an English Opium Eater. Hayter, Alethea, ed. (English Library). 232p. 1971. pap. 10.95 (0-14-043061-X, EL61, Penguin Classics) Viking Penguin.

De Quincey, Thomas. Confessions of an English Opium Eater. (Classics Library). pap. 3.95 (1-85326-096-7, 0967WW, Pub. by Wrdsworth Edits) NTC Contemp Pub Co.

De Quincey, Thomas. Confessions of an English Opium-Eater. 1976. 25.95 (0-8488-1280-8) Amereon Ltd.

— Confessions of an English Opium-Eater. unabridged ed. (Thrift Editions Ser.). 80p. 1995. reprint ed. pap. text 1.00 (0-486-28742-4) Dover.

— Confessions of an English Opium-Eater: And Other Writings. 296p. 1998. pap. 9.95 (0-19-283654-4) OUP.

— Klosterheim. LC 92-37028. 326p. (Orig.). 1992. reprint ed. 55.00 (1-85477-118-3) Continuum.

— Klosterheim. LC 82-8517. (Banquo Bks.). 192p. (Orig.). 1982. reprint ed. pap. 5.95 (0-912800-98-4) Woodbridge Pr.

***De Quincey, Thomas.** Klosterheim: or The Masque. 252p. 2000. pap. 9.95 (0-594-00684-8) Eightn Hundrd.

De Quincey, Thomas. Political Economy & Politics: Collected Writings, Vol. IX. Masson, David, ed. LC 66-21670. (Reprints of Economic Classics Ser.). vii, 444p. 1970. reprint ed. 49.50 (0-678-00680-6) Kelley.

— Reminiscences of the English Lake Poets. LC 83-45741. reprint ed. 31.50 (0-404-20078-8) AMS Pr.

— Reminiscences of the English Lake Poets. (BCL1-PR English Literature Ser.). 355p. 1992. reprint ed. lib. bdg. 89.00 (0-7812-7067-7) Rprt Serv.

— The Uncollected Writings, 2 vols. LC 72-6781. (Essay Index Reprint Ser.). 1977. reprint ed. 38.95 (0-8369-7270-8) Ayer.

— The Uncollected Writings, 2 vols. in 1. (Anglistica & Americana Ser.: No. 144). xx, 714p. 1974. reprint ed. 115.70 (3-487-04887-6) G Olms Pubs.

De Quiros, Beltran. La Otra Cara de la Moneda. LC 83-82388. (Coleccion Caniqui). (SPA.). 62p. (Orig.). 1984. pap. 5.95 (0-89729-342-8) Ediciones.

De, R. N. The Sundarbans. (Illus.). 96p. 1991. pap. 6.95 (0-19-562609-5) OUP.

***De Raad, Boele.** The Big Five Personality Factors. (Illus.). 160p. 2000. 24.50 (0-88937-236-5) Hogrefe & Huber Pubs.

De Raadt, J. D. A New Management of Life. LC 97-52027. (Toronto Studies in Theology: Vol. 75). 152p. 1998. text 69.95 (0-7734-8508-2) E Mellen.

de Rachewiltz, I. Repertory of Proper Names in Yuan Literary Sources, 4 vols. 1996. 210.00 (957-638-380-3) Oriental Bk Store.

De Rachewiltz, Igor. Index to the Secret History of the Mongols. LC 70-183993. (Uralic & Altaic Ser.: Vol. 121). 347p. (Orig.). 1972. pap. text. write for info. (0-87750-166-1) Curzon Pr Ltd.

De Rachewiltz, Igor, ed. see Secen, Sagang.

De Rachewiltz, Mary. Whose World? Selected Poems. 72p. 1998. pap. 10.00 (1-879934-55-8) St Andrews NC.

De Radwan, C. The Secret of Mind Power & How to Use It. 190p. 1996. reprint ed. spiral bd. 14.50 (0-7873-0265-1) Hlth Research.

De Raedt, ed. Advances in Inductive Logic Programming. LC 95-8084. (Frontiers in Artificial Intelligence & Applications: Vol. 32). 333p. (YA). (gr. 12). 1996. 110.00 (90-5199-242-4, 242-4) IOS Press.

De Raeve. Nursing Research: Ethical & Legal. 1996. pap. text 40.95 (0-7020-1888-0, W B Saunders Co) Harcrt Hlth Sci Grp.

De Rafael Rosa, Portada, jt. auth. see Agramonte, Roberto D.

De Raffele, Frank J., Jr. & Hendricks, Edward D. Successful Business Networking. LC 97-77508. 228p. 1998. pap. 19.95 (1-886284-12-1, Pub. by Chandler Hse) Natl Bk Netwk.

De Rais, Gilles. Laughter for the Devil: The Trials of Gilles de Rais, Companion-in-Arms of Joan of Arc (1440) LC 83-20801. 1984. 29.50 (0-8386-3190-8) Fairleigh Dickinson.

De Ramaix, Isabelle, ed. The Illustrated Bartsch Vol. 72-1: Aegidius Sadeler. 1997. 149.00 (0-89835-174-X) Abaris Bks.

De Ramaix, Isabelle, ed. The Illustrated Bartsch Vol. 72-2: Aegidius Sadeler. 1997. lib. bdg. 149.00 (0-89835-175-8) Abaris Bks.

de Ramirez, Susan Berry Brill, see Brill de Ramirez, Susan Berry.

De Ramiro, Yvonne V., tr. see Jimeno, Carlos L., et al.

De Ramirez, Susan B. B. Contemporary American Indian Literatures & the Oral Tradition. LC 98-40233. 272p. 1999. 40.00 (0-8165-1921-8) U of Ariz Pr.

De Rattalma, Marco Frigessi & Treves, Tullio. The United Nations Compensation Commission: A Handbook. LC 99-22913. 1999. 123.00 (90-411-1199-9) Kluwer Law Intl.

De Ravel, Anne, et al, eds. Poesie de Langue Francaise: Anthologie Thematique. (Illus.). 196p. 1985. pap. 14.00 (0-86980-471-5, Pub. by Univ Natal Pr) Intl Spec Bk.

De Raygoza, Mireya C., tr. see Bailey, Mari V., ed.

De Reaumur, Rene A. The Natural History of Ants from an Unpublished Manuscript in the Archives of the Academy of Sciences of Paris. Egerton, Frank N., 3rd, ed. Wheeler, Morton, tr. LC 77-74211. (History of Ecology Ser.). 1978. reprint ed. lib. bdg. 25.95 (0-405-10382-4) Ayer.

De Rebecque, Constant & Benjamin, Henri. Dupolytheisme Romain: Considere dans ses rapports avec la philosophie grecque et la religion chertienne. Bolle, Kees W., ed. LC 77-79118. (Mythology Ser.). (FRE.). 1978. reprint ed. lib. bdg. 65.95 (0-405-10530-4) Ayer.

De Rebeira, Perry, jt. auth. see Saunders, D.

De Recondo, Felix. Felix de Recondo: Paintings & Works on Paper. (Illus.). 24p. 1981. pap. 15.00 (0-8150-0023-5) Wittenborn Art.

De Reeder, P. L., ed. Environmental Programmes of Intergovernmental Organizations. 1978. ring bd. 39.50 (90-01-48002-0) Kluwer Academic.

De Regniers, Beatrice Schenk. May I Bring a Friend? 1964. 10.15 (0-606-01049-1, Pub. by Turtleback) Demco.

De Regniers, jt. auth. see Schenck.

De Regniers, Beatrice S. David & Goliath. LC 95-22025. (Illus.). 32p. (J). (gr. k-3). 1996. 15.95 (0-531-09496-0); lib. bdg. 16.99 (0-531-08796-4) Orchard Bks Watts.

— I Looked in the Mirror. (Illus.). (J). (gr. k-2). 1993. pap. 4.95 (0-88741-921-6) Sundance Pub.

— Jack & the Beanstalk. (J). 1990. 10.15 (0-606-04440-X, Pub. by Turtleback) Demco.

— Jack & the Beanstalk: Retold in Verse for Boys & Girls to Read Themselves. LC 89-18663. (Illus.). 48p. (J). (ps-2). 1990. reprint ed. mass mkt. 4.95 (0-689-71421-1) Aladdin.

— Little Sister & the Month Brothers. LC 75-4594. (Illus.). 48p. (J). (ps-3). 1976. 8.95 (0-8164-3147-7, Clarion Bks) HM.

— May I Bring a Friend? LC 64-19562. (Illus.). 48p. (J). (ps-2). 1971. lib. bdg. 16.00 (0-689-20615-1) Atheneum Yung Read.

***De Regniers, Beatrice S.** May I Bring A Friend. 1999. pap. 13.40 (0-88103-362-6) Econo-Clad Bks.

De Regniers, Beatrice S. May I Bring a Friend? 2nd ed. LC 89-15087. (Illus.). 48p. (J). (gr. k-3). 1989. reprint ed. mass mkt. 4.95 (0-689-71353-3) Aladdin.

— So Many Cats. LC 85-3739. (Illus.). 32p. (J). (ps-3). 1988. pap. 6.95 (0-89919-700-0, Clarion Bks) HM.

De Regniers, Beatrice S. So Many Cats! (J). 1985. 12.15 (0-606-02455-7, Pub. by Turtleback) Demco.

De Regniers, Beatrice S. What Can You Do with a Shoe? limited ed. LC 96-20871. (Illus.). 32p. (J). (ps-2). 1997. mass mkt. 150.00 (0-689-81597-2) S&S Childrens.

De Regniers, Beatrice Schenk, see Schenk De Regniers, Beatrice.

De Regt, L. J. A Parametric Model for Syntactic Studies of a Textual Corpus: Demonstrated on the Hebrew of Deuteronomy 1-30, 2 vols. (Studia Semitica Neerlandica: Vol. 24). (Illus.). ix, 138p. 1988. pap. text 32.00 (90-232-2381-0, Pub. by Van Gorcum) Eisenbrauns.

***De Regt, L. J.** Participants in Old Testament Texts & the Translator: Reference Devices & Their Rhetorical Impact. viii, 125p. 1999. text 70.00 (90-232-3444-8, Pub. by Van Gorcum) Eisenbrauns.

De Regt, L. J., et al, eds. Literary Structure & Rhetorical Strategies in the Hebrew Bible. LC 96-9273. x, 270p. 1996. text 42.50 (1-57506-011-6) Eisenbrauns.

De Reihan, Mireille. Agateware: Pottery Magic. (Illus.). 80p. 1996. pap. 19.95 (0-233-98942-0, Pub. by Andre Deutsch) Trafalgar.

De Reina. Confession de Fe Christiana. Kinder, ed. (Exeter Hispanic Text Ser.: No. 46). (SPA.). 65p. Date not set. pap. text 17.95 (0-85989-315-4, Pub. by Univ Exeter Pr) Northwestern U Pr.

De Remer, Dale. Aircraft Systems for Pilots. LC 91-58613. (Illus.). 450p. 1992. pap. text 25.95 (0-89100-384-3, JS312686) Jeppesen Sanderson.

De Remusat, Charles F. L' Angleterre au XVIIIE Siecle, 2 vols. Mayer, J. P., ed. LC 78-67378. (Angleterre au XVIIIe siecle Ser.). (FRE.). 1980. reprint ed. lib. bdg. 78.95 (0-405-11728-0) Ayer.

— Histoire de la Philosophie en Angleterre de Bacon jusqu'a Locke, 2 vols. LC 79-174312. reprint ed. 95.00 (0-404-05247-9) AMS Pr.

De Reneville, J. D. Aventure de l'Absolu. (Phaenomenologica Ser.: No. 48). 1972. lib. bdg. 121.50 (90-247-1319-6, Pub. by M Nijhoff) Kluwer Academic.

De Rentiis, Dina, jt. ed. see Zimmermann, Margarete.

De Renty, Ivan. The World of Business, English-Spanish, Spanish-English Lexicon: El Mundo de los Negocios, Lexico Espanol-Ingles-Espanol. 2nd ed. 333p. 1981. pap. 29.95 (0-8288-0128-2, S32370) Fr & Eur.

De Renzo, D. J., ed. Advanced Composite Materials Products & Manufacturers. LC 88-4227. (Illus.). 1091p. 1988. 98.00 (0-8155-1155-8) Noyes.

— Corrosion Resistant Materials Handbook. 4th ed. LC 85-4872. (Illus.). 965p. 1986. 195.00 (0-8155-1023-3) Noyes.

De Resende, Andre. Andre de Resende's Poemata Latina (Latin Poems) Martyn, John R., tr. LC 98-24102. (Medieval & Renaissance Studies: Vol. 18). (ENG & LAT.). 568p. 1998. text 119.95 (0-7734-8331-4) E Mellen.

— Biographies of Prince Edward & Friar Pedro by Andre de Resende. Martyn, John R., tr. from POR. LC 97-27257. 232p. 1997. text 89.95 (0-7734-8538-4) E Mellen.

De Retena, Jose M., prologue by. Diccionario Historico Geografico Ilustrado del Pais Vasco, Vol. 3. (SPA.). 384p. 1975. 75.00 (0-7859-4896-1) Fr & Eur.

De Retz, Cardinal. Oeuvres, la Conjuration du Comte de Fiesque et Pamphlets. (Pleiade Ser.). (FRE.). 1256p. 81.95 (2-07-011028-1) Schoenhof.

De Retz, Jean-Francois. Oeuvres. deluxe ed. Hipp, Marie-Therese & Pernot, Michel, eds. (FRE.). 1872p. 1984. 125.00 (0-7859-3863-X, 2070110281) Fr & Eur.

De Reuck, K. M., jt. auth. see Wagner, W.

De Reuck, K. Maiprie, ed. Oxygen. 1991. 61.00 (0-632-01476-8) CRC Pr.

De Reuse, Willem J., jt. ed. see Chelliah, Shobhana L.

De Reuver, Stef. Find the Duckie. LC 95-68963. (Sesame Street Bks.). (J). 1996. 4.99 (0-679-87007-5, Pub. by Random Bks Yng Read) Random.

— Sesame Street Little Theater. (Illus.). (J). 1996. 4.99 (0-679-87185-3, Pub. by Random Bks Yng Read) Random.

— Where's the Ducky? (J). 1996. pap. 4.99 (0-614-15833-8) Random.

De Revere, David W., et al. Chaplaincy in Law Enforcement: What It Is & How to Do It. 140p. 1989. pap. 23.95 (0-398-06091-6) C C Thomas.

— Chaplaincy in Law Enforcement: What It Is & How to Do It. 140p. (C). 1989. text 34.95 (0-398-05558-0) C C Thomas.

De Reyna, Rudy. How to Draw What You See. (Illus.). 176p. 1996. pap. text 14.95 (0-8230-2375-3) Watsn-Guptill.

De Reyna, Rudy, see De Reyna, Rudy.

De Rham, G. Differentiable Manifolds. Smith, F. R., tr. from FRE. (Grundlehren der Mathematischen Wissenschaften Ser.: Vol. 266). (Illus.). 180p. 1984. 118.95 (0-387-13463-8) Spr-Verlag.

De Rhodes, Hanka, tr. see Labbe, Armand J., ed.

***De Ribas, Andres Perez.** History of the Triumphs: Of Our Holy Faith Amongst the Most Barbarous & Fierce Peoples of the New World. Reff, Daniel T., tr. from SPA. LC 98-40196. 744p. 1999. 85.00 (0-8165-1720-7) U of Ariz Pr.

De Ribaupierre, Anik, ed. Transition Mechanisms in Child Development: The Longitudinal Perspective. (Illus.). 352p. (C). 1989. text 74.95 (0-521-37138-4) Cambridge U Pr.

***De Ricci, Seymour.** Census of Caxtons. fac. ed. (Illus.). 196p. 2000. 50.00 (1-57898-225-1) Martino Pubng.

De Ricci, Seymour, jt. auth. see Cohen, Henry.

De Rico, Ul. The Rainbow Goblins. LC 78-55431. (Illus.). 36p. 1994. reprint ed. 19.95 (0-500-27759-1, Pub. by Thames Hudson) Norton.

De Rico, Ul, et al. The White Goblin. LC 96-60140. (Illus.). 36p. (J). 1996. 19.95 (0-500-01724-7, Pub. by Thames Hudson) Norton.

De Ridder, A. J. Design & Construct of Complex Civil Engineering Systems. 420p. (Orig.). 1994. pap. 97.50 (90-407-1027-9, Pub. by Delft U Pr) Coronet Bks.

De Ridder, Chantal, et al, eds. Echinoderm Research: Proceedings of the Second European Conference on Echinoderms, Brussels, 18-21 September 1989. 368p. (C). 1990. text 168.00 (90-6191-141-9, Pub. by A A Balkema) Ashgate Pub Co.

De Ridder, Richard R., jt. auth. see Hofman, Leonard J.

De Ridder-Symoens, Hilde, ed. A History of the University in Europe: Universities in Early Modern Europe 1500-1800, Vol. 2. (Illus.). 718p. (C). 1996. text 100.00 (0-521-36106-0) Cambridge U Pr.

— A History of the University in Europe, Vol. 1: Universities in the Middle Ages. 534p. (C). 1991. text 100.00 (0-521-36105-2) Cambridge U Pr.

De Riedmatten, Henri. Les Actes du Proces de Paul de Samosate: Etude sur la Christologie du IIIe au IVe Siecle. (Paradosis; Etudes de Litterature et de Theologie Ancienne, 6.) LC 82-45822. (Orthodoxies & Heresies in the Early Church Ser.). 1989. reprint ed. 24.50 (0-404-62392-1) AMS Pr.

De Riencourt, Amaury. Lost World: Tibet. 320p. (C). 1990. 110.00 (0-907855-04-0, Pub. by Honeyglen Pub Ltd) St Mut.

— The Soul of China. 326p. (C). 1990. 90.00 (0-907855-08-3, Pub. by Honeyglen Pub Ltd) St Mut.

— The Soul of India. 432p. (C). 1990. 80.00 (0-907855-03-2, Pub. by Honeyglen Pub Ltd) St Mut.

— Woman & Power in History. (C). 1997. reprint ed. pap. text. write for info. (81-207-1992-1) Sterling Pubs.

De Rienzo, Paul, et al. The Ibogaine Story: Report on the Staten Island Project. 1997. pap. 20.00 (1-57027-029-5) Autonomedia.

De Riepen, Magdalena R. La Quimica Hacia la Conquista del Sol. (Ciencia para Todos Ser.). (SPA.). pap. 6.99 (968-16-2397-5, Pub. by Fondo) Continental Bk.

De Riet, Vernon Van, see Van De Riet, Vernon.

De Rijk, L. M. Giraldus Odonis O. F. M.: Opera Philosophica Vol. 1: Logica. Critical Edition from the Manuscripts. LC 97-38198. (Studien und Texte zur Geistesgeschichte des Mittelalters Ser.: No. 60). 536p. 1997. 192.00 (90-04-10950-1) Brill Academic Pubs.

De Rijk, L. M., tr. from GER. Nicholas of Autrecourt: His Correspondence with Master Giles & Bernhard of Arezzo: a Critical Edition from the Two Persian Manuscripts. LC 93-48276. (Studien und Texte zur Geistesgeschichte des Mittelalters Ser.: No. 42). ix, 241p. 1994. 113.50 (90-04-09988-3) Brill Academic Pubs.

De Rijk, L. M. & Spruyt, Joke. Peter of Spain (Petrus Hispanus Portugalensis) Syncategoreumata: First Critical Edition. LC 91-39214. (Studien und Texte zur Geistesgeschichte des Mittelalters Ser.: Vol. 30). (ENG & LAT.). 619p. 1992. 186.00 (90-04-09434-2) Brill Academic Pubs.

De Rijk, L. M. & Weijers, O. Repertorium Commentariorum Medii Aevi in Aristotelem Latinorum Quae in Bibliothecis Neerlandicis Asservantur. (Verhandelingen der Koninklijke Nederlandse Akademie van Wetenschappen, Afd. Letterkunde, Nieuwe Reeks Ser.: No. 109). 65p. 1981. pap. text 22.00 (0-444-85511-4) Elsevier.

De Rijk, L. M., see Rijk, L. M. de.

De Rijk, Lambertus M. Through Language to Reality: Studies on Medieval Semantics & Metaphysics. Bos, E. P., ed. (Collected Studies: No. CS302). (ENG, FRE & GER.). 334p. (C). 1989. reprint ed. text 115.95 (0-86078-250-6, Pub. by Variorum) Ashgate Pub Co.

De Rijke, Maarten. Advances in Intensional Logic. LC 97-27411. (Applied Logic Ser.). 308p. 1997. text 120.50 (0-7923-4711-0) Kluwer Academic.

De Rijke, Maarten, ed. Diamonds & Defaults: Studies in Pure & Applied Intensional Logic. LC 93-17749. (Synthese Library: Vol. 229). 400p. (C). 1993. lib. bdg. 169.50 (0-7923-2342-4, Pub. by Kluwer Academic) Kluwer Academic.

De Rijke, Maarten, jt. ed. see Blackburn, Patrick.

De Rinaldis, Aldo. Neapolitan Painting of the Seicento. LC 75-11055. 1976. reprint ed. lib. bdg. 45.00 (0-87817-177-0) Hacker.

De Rio, Florencio O. Samba: A Bibliography: History, People, Lyrics, Recordings. (Illus.). 110p. (Orig.). 1992. pap. 14.00 (0-929928-11-3) Fog Pubns.

De Rios, Marlene D. Amazon Healer: The Life & Times of an Urban Shaman. 192p. (Orig.). (C). 1992. pap. 10.95 (1-85327-076-8, Pub. by Prism Pr) Assoc Pubs Grp.

— Hallucinogens: Cross-Cultural Perspectives. rev. ed. LC 97-209632. (Illus.). 279p. (C). 1996. reprint ed. pap. text 12.95 (0-88133-916-4) Waveland Pr.

De Riquer, Martin, ed. Diccionario Literario de Obras y Personajes de Todos los Tiempos y Paises, 12 vols., Set. 2nd ed. (SPA.). 11000p. 1972. 1995.00 (0-8288-6364-4, S-12328) Fr & Eur.

De Riquer, Martin & Valvarde, Jose M. Historia de la Literatura Universal: Universal History of Literature, 10 vols., Set. (SPA.). 1295.00 (0-8288-8249-5) Fr & Eur.

De Riquer, Martin, jt. auth. see De Cervantes Saavedra, Miguel.

De Riquer, Martin, ed. & tr. see De Troyes, Chretien.

De Rishanger, William. Chronicle of William De Rishanger, of the Barons' Wars. Halliwell, James O., ed. (Camden Society, London. Publications, First Ser.: No. 15). reprint ed. 50.00 (0-404-50115-X) AMS Pr.

De Ritis, Paul A. Hiroshima. LC 97-30526. 132p. 1997. pap. 14.95 (0-7734-2807-0, Mellen Poetry Pr) E Mellen.

D

An Asterisk (*) at the beginning of an entry indicates that the title is appearing for the first time.

de Rivas Cherif, Cipriano. Portrait of an Unknown Man: Manuel Azana & Modern Spain. Stewart, Paul, tr. LC 94-42956.Tr. of Retrato de un desconocido. 432p. 1995. 59.50 (*0-8386-3584-9*) Fairleigh Dickinson.

De Rivas, Duque. Don Alvaro. (SPA.). 229p. 1975. 10.00 (*0-8288-8561-3*) Fr & Eur.

— Don Alvaro O Fuerza Del Sino - Lanuza. (SPA.). 229p. 1975. 6.95 (*0-8288-7181-7*) Fr & Eur.

— Don Alvaro o la Fuerza del Sino. (SPA.). 172p. 1997. pap. text 4.00 (*1-56328-078-7*) Edit Plaza Mayor.

— Romances, No. 46. (SPA.). 245p. write for info. (*0-8288-8582-6*) Fr & Eur.

— Romances I. (SPA.). 276p. 1966. 12.50 (*0-8288-7116-7*) Fr & Eur.

— Romances II. (SPA.). 279p. 1965. 12.50 (*0-8288-7117-5*) Fr & Eur.

De River, J. Paul. Crime & the Sexual Psychopath. (Illus.). 384p. 1958. 62.95 (*0-398-00436-6*); pap. 47.95 (*0-398-06092-4*) C C Thomas.

— The Sexual Criminal: A Psychoanalytical Study. 2nd ed. (Illus.). 464p. 1999. reprint ed. pap. 18.50 (*0-9650324-2-6*, Pub. by Bloat) LPC InBook.

De Rivera, Flor Pineiro. Un Siglo de Literatura Infantil Puertorriquena: A Century of Puerto Rican Children's Literature. LC 85-8705. (SPA., Illus.). 139p. 1985. 25.00 (*0-8477-3531-1*); pap. 20.00 (*0-8477-3532-X*) U of PR Pr.

De Rivera, Joseph. A Structural Theory of the Emotions. LC 76-53916. (Psychological Issues Monographs: No. 40). 178p. 1977. 32.50 (*0-8236-6171-7*); pap. 27.50 (*0-8236-6170-9*) Intl Univs Pr.

De Rivera, Joseph & Sarbin, Theodore R., eds. Believed-In Imaginings: The Narrative Construction of Reality. LC 98-17312. 345p. 1998. 39.95 (*1-55798-521-9*) Am Psychol.

De Robertis, E. D. & De Robertis, E. M., Jr. Cell & Molecular Biology. 8th ed. LC 86-123. (Illus.). 734p. 1987. text 48.00 (*0-8121-1012-9*) Lppncott W & W.

De Robertis, E. M., Jr., jt. auth. see De Robertis, E. D.

De Robertis, Eduardo D. Synaptic Receptors: Isolation & Molecular Biology. LC 74-80624. (Modern Pharmacology-Toxicology Ser.: No. 4). (Illus.). 405p. reprint ed. pap. 125.60 (*0-7837-0897-1*, 204120200019) Bks Demand.

De Robertis, Francesco M. & Norr, Dieter. Lavoroe Lavoratori Nel Mondo Romano & Zur Sozialen und Rechtlichen Bewertung der Freien Arbeit in Rom. Francesco M. Finley, Moses, ed. LC 79-4967. (Ancient Economic History Ser.). (GER & ITA.). 1979. reprint ed. lib. bdg. 42.95 (*0-405-12355-8*) Ayer.

De Robigne, Bennett M. Trial of D. M. Bennett: Upon the Charge of Depositing Prohibited Matter in the Mail. LC 72-8110. (Civil Liberties in American History Ser.). 202p. 1973. reprint ed. lib. bdg. 27.50 (*0-306-70525-7*) Da Capo.

De Robles Correa, Federico C. Spanish Dictionary of Antonyms & Synonyms: Diccionario Espanol de Sinonimos y Antonimos. 24th ed. (SPA.). 1152p. 1991. 135.00 (*0-7859-4958-5*) Fr & Eur.

De Robles, Sainz & Corriente Cordoba, Federico Carlos. Diccionario de la Literatura, Vol. 1. 3rd ed. (SPA.). 576p. 1982. 65.00 (*0-7859-5708-1*, 8403270747) Fr & Eur.

— El Otro Lope de Vega, No. 114. (SPA.). 150p. 1973. write for info. (*0-8288-8577-X*) Fr & Eur.

De Rocca, A. J. In the Peninsula with a French Hussar: Memoirs of the War of the French in Spain. 192p. 1991. 35.00 (*1-85367-080-4*, 5531) Stackpole.

De Rochambeau, Jean B. Memoirs of the Marshall Count De Rochambeau. LC 74-140880. (Eyewitness Accounts of the American Revolution Ser.). 1976. reprint ed. 14.95 (*0-405-01212-8*) Ayer.

De Roche, Edward F. How School Administrators Solve Problems. LC 84-16021. 316p. 1985. text 27.95 (*0-13-431271-6*, Busn) P-H.

De Roche, Joseph. The Heath Introduction to Poetry. 3rd ed. LC 87-80256. 592p. (C). 1990. pap. text 24.76 (*0-669-14808-3*) HM Trade Div.

De Rochemont, Richard, jt. auth. see Root, Waverley.

De Rochemont, Richard, jt. auth. see Root, Waverly.

De Rocher, F., jt. auth. see Hagiwara, Peter M.

De Rocher, Francoise, jt. auth. see Hagiwara, Peter M.

De Rocher, Francoise, jt. ed. see Hagiwara, Peter M.

De Rocher, Gregory D., tr. The Second Part of the Popular Errors. LC 94-4708. 336p. 1995. text 49.95 (*0-8173-0758-3*) U of Ala Pr.

De Rocher, Gregory D., tr. & anno. see Joubert, Laurent.

De Rodrigo, Victoria Kamhi, see Kamhi de Rodrigo, Victoria.

De Rodrigues, Josefina B., jt. auth. see Rodrigues, Louis J.

De Rodrigues, Josefina Bernet, see Rodrigues, Louis J. & Bernet De Rodrigues, Josefina.

De Rodriguez, Carmela V. Poemas en Prosa. 1978. 2.50 (*84-399-8110-4*) Edit Mensaje.

de Rodriguez, Mercedes Mazquiaran, see Glenn, Kathleen M. & Mazquiaran de Rodriguez, Mercedes, eds.

De Roeck, A. & Wagner, A., eds. Lepton & Photon Interactions at High Energies: Proceedings of the XVIII International Symposium Hamburg, Germany 28 July-1 August, 1997. 700p. 1998. 136.00 (*981-02-3393-0*) World Scientific Pub.

De Roepstorff, A. Vocabulary of Dialects Spoken in the Nicobar & Andaman Isles with a Short Account of the Natives, Their Customs & Habits, & of Previous Attempts at Colonisation. (C). 1987. reprint ed. 19.00 (*81-206-0274-9*, Pub. by Asian Educ Servs) S Asia.

De Roever, W. P., et al, eds. Compositionality: The Significant Difference: International Symposium, COMPOS '97, Bad Malente, Germany, September 8-12, 1997, Revised Lectures. LC 98-55092. (Lecture Notes in Computer Science Ser.). viii, 647p. 1999. pap. 80.00 (*3-540-65493-3*) Spr-Verlag.

De Roin, Gene, ed. see Newton, Raymann.

De Rojas. Celestina. Severin, ed. (Hispanic Classics Ser.). 1987. 59.95 (*0-85668-344-2*, Pub. by Aris & Phillips); pap. 28.00 (*0-85668-345-0*, Pub. by Aris & Phillips) David Brown.

De Rojas, Duque. Don Alvaro. (Clasicos Ser.). (SPA.). 120p. 1997. pap. write for info. (*1-881713-06-7*) Pubns Puertorriquenas.

De Rojo, Alba C. & Castro, Rafael L., eds. Zapata, Iconografia (Zapata, Iconography) 2nd ed. (SPA., Illus.). 144p. 1996. pap. 11.99 (*968-16-5101-4*, Pub. by Fondo) Continental Bk.

De Rola, Stanislas K. Alchemy: The Secret Art. LC 85-50803. (Art & Imagination Ser.). (Illus.). (Orig.). 1986. pap. 15.95 (*0-500-81003-6*, Pub. by Thames Hudson) Norton.

De Rola, Stanislas Klossowski, see Klossowski de Rola, Stanislas.

de Rola, Stanislas Klossowski, see Klossowski De Rola, Stanislas.

de Roland, La Chanson, see La Chanson de Roland.

De Rolf, Shane. Blackboard Jungle. 1998. write for info. (*0-679-88450-5*, Bullseye Bks) Random Bks Yng Read.

— Crayon-Maker. 1998. write for info. (*0-679-88453-X*, Bullseye Bks) Random Bks Yng Read.

— The Cut-Up Sisters. 1998. write for info. (*0-679-88451-3*, Bullseye Bks) Random Bks Yng Read.

De Romanis, Roberto, jt. ed. see Loretelli, Rosamaria.

De Romano, Dora R. Cocine Conmigo. rev. ed. (SPA., Illus.). 678p. 1970. write for info. (*0-9633449-0-0*) D R de Romano.

— Rice & Beans & Tasty Things. Romano, Jaime, ed. (Illus.). 484p. (Orig.). 1986. pap. write for info. (*0-9633449-1-9*) D R de Romano.

De Rome, Denise. BBC's Italianissimo Kit: A Self-Guided Course for Beginners Learning Italian. (ITA.). 288p. 1996. pap. 49.95 incl. audio (*0-8442-8694-X*) NTC Contemp Pub Co.

De Romero, Gabriela, jt. auth. see De Romero, Meilij.

De Romero, Meilij & De Romero, Gabriela. English & Spanish Economic & Legal Vocabulary: Vocabulario Legal y Empresario. (ENG & SPA.). 345p. 1987. pap. 59.95 (*0-8288-0406-0*, S11926) Fr & Eur.

De Romilly, Jacqueline. Great Sophists in Periclean Athens. Lloyd, Janet, tr. 280p. 1992. 85.00 (*0-19-824234-4*) OUP.

— The Great Sophists in Periclean Athens. Lloyd, Janet, tr. 280p. 1998. reprint ed. pap. text 24.95 (*0-19-823807-X*) OUP.

De Romilly, Jacqueline. The Rise & Fall of States According to Greek Authors. (Thomas Spencer Jerome Lectures). (Illus.). 112p. (C). 1991. pap. text 21.95 (*0-472-08152-7*, 08152) U of Mich Pr.

De Romilly, Jacqueline. Thucydides & Athenian Imperialism. Vlastos, Gregory, ed. Thody, Philip, tr. from ENG. LC 78-19381. (Morals & Law in Ancient Greece Ser.). 1979. reprint ed. lib. bdg. 33.95 (*0-88143-072-2*) Ayer.

De Romilly, Nicole & Laude, Jean. Braque Cubism, 1907-1914: Catalogue Raisonne. (Illus.). 308p. 1982. 175.00 (*0-8150-0020-0*) Wittenborn Art.

De Roo. Yearbook Law & Legal Practice in East Asia, 1996, Vol. YEAS 2. 1997. 116.00 (*90-411-0359-7*) Kluwer Law Intl.

De Roo, A. J., et al, eds. Transfrontier Mobility of Law. LC 95-46976. 120p. 1996. pap. 42.00 (*90-411-0170-5*) Kluwer Law Intl.

***De Roo, Annie J. & Jagtenberg, Robert W., eds.** Yearbook Law & Legal Practice in East Asia Vol. 3: 1997-1998. 228p. 1998. 100.00 (*90-411-1038-0*) Kluwer Law Intl.

— Yearbook Law & Legal Practice in East Asia 1999, Vol. 4. 276p. 2000. text 114.00 (*90-411-1349-5*) Kluwer Law Intl.

De Roo, Gert, jt. ed. see Miller, Donald.

De Roo, P. History of America Before Columbus According to Documents & Approved Authors: American Aborigines & European Immigrants, 2 vols., Set. (Caribbean Ser.). 1979. lib. bdg. 250.00 (*0-8490-2934-1*) Gordon Pr.

***De Roo, Peter.** History of America Before Columbus, According to Documents & Approved Authors, 2 vols. (LC History-America-E). 1999. reprint ed. lib. bdg. 180.00 (*0-7812-4322-X*) Rprt Serv.

De Roos, Albert, jt. ed. see Van Der Wall, Ernst E.

De Roos, Johan, jt. ed. see Van Den Hout, Theo P.

De Roover, Dick. Motion Control of a Water Stage: A Design Approach for Speeding up IC Production. (Illus.). 290p. 1997. pap. 59.50 (*90-407-1562-9*, Pub. by Delft U Pr) Coronet Bks.

De Roover, Raymond A. Money, Banking & Credit in Mediaeval Bruges. (Medieval Academy Bks.: No. 51). 1983. reprint ed. 35.00 (*0-910956-25-1*) Medieval Acad.

— Rise & Decline of the Medici Bank, 1397-1494. LC 63-11417. (Studies in Business History: No. 21). (Illus.). 522p. 1963. 30.00 (*0-674-77145-1*) HUP.

De Rooy, F. P. Documentary Credits 1983. 250p. 1984. lib. bdg. 94.00 (*90-6544-075-5*) Kluwer Law Intl.

de Rooy, J. M. van Medenbach, see Van der Maesen, L. J.

De Ropp, Robert S. Self-Completion: Keys to the Meaningful Life. LC 87-82943. (Illus.). 210p. 1988. 15.95 (*0-89556-053-4*) Gateways Bks & Tapes.

— Warrior's Way. 366p. 1992. reprint ed. pap. 18.95 (*0-89556-079-8*) Gateways Bks & Tapes.

De Ropp, Robert S., jt. frwd. see Gold, E. J.

de Rosa, Alessandra, jt. auth. see Murphy, Bruce.

***De Rosa, Loretta.** The Managed Home Care Market Report. 18p. 1998. spiral bd. 47.00 (*0-929156-52-8*) Atlantic Info Services Inc.

De Rosa, Luigi, jt. ed. see Glazier, Ira.

De Rosa, Peter. Rebels: The Irish Rising of 1916. 544p. 1992. pap. 14.00 (*0-449-90682-5*, Columbine) Fawcett.

De Rosa, Tina. Paper Fish. LC 96-19342. 176p. 1996. pap. 9.95 (*1-55861-145-2*); lib. bdg. 20.00 (*1-55861-146-0*) Feminist Pr.

De Rosalia, Antonius, ed. Accius - Lexicon Accianum. (Alpha-Omega, Reihe A Ser.: Bd. LIII). xxiv, 204p. 1982. write for info. (*3-487-07261-0*) G Olms Pubs.

De Rosario. Vocabulario Puertorriqueno. (SPA.). 1966. 10.95 (*0-87751-010-5*) E Torres & Sons.

De Rosario, Vega. El Hombre Que Vion de la Lluvia. (Romance Real Ser.). (SPA.). 192p. 1981. pap. 1.50 (*0-88025-008-9*) Roca Pub.

— Los Malditos Amores. (Romance Real Ser.). (SPA.). 192p. 1981. pap. 1.50 (*0-88025-006-2*) Roca Pub.

De Rosas, Ramon. Concepts for Improvisation: A Comprehensive Guide for Performing & Teaching. 88p. 1997. pap. 24.95 (*0-7935-8213-X*) H Leonard.

De Rosas, Ramon, ed. see Aaron, Hugh.

De Rose, David, ed. see Nedley, Neil.

De Rosen Jervis, Alice, tr. see Landucci, Luca.

De Rosenthal, Gustavus. Journal of a Volunteer Expedition to Sandusky: From May 24 to June 13, 1782. Decker, Peter, ed. LC 77-77111. (Eyewitness Accounts of the American Revolution Ser.). 1969. reprint ed. 16.95 (*0-405-01177-6*) Ayer.

De Rosnay, Joel. The Symbiotic Man: A New Understanding of the Organization of Life & a Vision of the Future. 299p. 2000. 24.95 (*0-07-135744-0*) McGraw.

De Ross, Norma Hernandez, see Hernandez De Ross, Norma.

De Rossanet, Bertrand. Peacemaking & Peacekeeping in Yugoslavia. LC 95-48134. (Nijhoff Law Specials Ser.: Vol. 17). 1996. pap. 87.50 (*90-411-0192-6*) Kluwer Law Intl.

— War & Peace in the Former Yugoslavia. LC 97-38510. (Nijhoff Law Specials Ser.: No. 33). 196p. 1997. pap. 78.00 (*90-411-0499-2*) Kluwer Academic.

De Rosset, Fred, tr. see Nightingale, Earl & Nightingale, Diana.

De Rossi, Danilo E., jt. ed. see Osada, Yoshihito.

***De Rossi, Giovanni Bernardo.** Translation of Dizionario Storico Degli Autori Ebrei E Delle Loro Opere: Dictionary of Hebrew Authors. Heller, Marvin J., tr. from ITA. LC 99-47092. (Jewish Studies: Vol. 19). (HEB & ENG.). 208p. 1999. text 89.95 (*0-7734-7900-7*) E Mellen.

De Rossi, Giuseppe, ed. Radioisotope Study of Salivary Glands. 198p. 1987. 114.00 (*0-8493-6072-2*, RC815, CRC Reprint) Franklin.

De Rothermann, H. F., tr. see Von Rezzori, Gregor.

De Rothschild, Edmund. Edmund De Rothschild: A Gilt-Edged Life. LC 99-159615. (Illus.). 256p. 1998. 45.00 (*0-7195-5471-3*, Pub. by John Murray) Trafalgar.

De Rothschild, Salomon. A Casual View of America: The Home Letters of Salomon de Rothschild, 1859-1861. Diamond, Sigmund, ed. & tr. by. LC 61-14650. 144p. 1961. reprint ed. pap. 30.00 (*0-608-04220-X*, 206496400011) Bks Demand.

De Rouck, A., jt. ed. see Francois, J.

De Rouffignac, Ann E. The Contemporary Peasantry in Mexico: A Class Analysis. LC 85-6317. 224p. 1985. 55.00 (*0-275-90086-X*, C0086, Praeger Pubs) Greenwood.

De Rougemont, Denis. Love in the Western World. Belgion, Montgomery, tr. from FRE. LC 82-48560. (ENG.). 400p. 1983. reprint ed. pap. text 16.95 (*0-691-01393-4*, Pub. by Princeton U Pr) Cal Prin Full Svc.

De Rougemont, Denis, ed. The State of the Union of Europe: Report of the CADMOS Group to the European People. 1979. pap. 56.00 (*0-08-024476-9*, Pub. by Pergamon Repr) Franklin.

De Roussy De Sales, Raoul. Easy French Crossword Puzzles. (Easy...Word Games & Ser.).Tr. of Mots Croises Faciles. (FRE., Illus.). 64p. 1994. pap. 4.95 (*0-8442-1330-6*, 13306, Passprt Bks) NTC Contemp Pub Co.

— French Verb Drills. 2nd ed. (...Verb Drills Ser.). (FRE., Illus.). 160p. 1995. pap. 8.95 (*0-8442-1029-3*, 10293, Passprt Bks) NTC Contemp Pub Co.

De Rouville, Alexander. Imitation of Mary. (Illus.). 1978. 7.50 (*0-89942-330-2*, 330/00) Catholic Bk Pub.

***De Rouvroit, C. L.** The Reeler Mouse as a Model of Brain Development. LC 98-34271. (Advances in Anatomy, Embryology & Cell Biology Ser.: Vol. 150). (Illus.). xi, 108p. 1998. pap. 119.00 (*3-540-64674-4*) Spr-Verlag.

De Roux, Dominique. L' Harmonika-Zug. (FRE.). 1983. pap. 10.95 (*0-7859-4197-5*) Fr & Eur.

De Roux, Xavier & Voillemot, Dominique. Dictionnaire Joly Concurence. (FRE.). 1988. write for info. (*0-7859-8238-8*, 2-907512-00-5) Fr & Eur.

De Rovere, Tiziana. Sacred Fire: Rites of Passage & Rituals of Worship with Angelic Guidance. LC 95-17971. (Illus.). 208p. 1995. pap. 16.95 (*0-89087-760-2*) Celestial Arts.

***De Roy, Tui.** Galapagos: Islands Born of Fire. (Illus.). 160p. 1998. 39.95 (*1-894020-39-1*) Warwick Publ.

De Roy, Tui. Spectacular Galapagos: Exploring an Extraordinary World. (Illus.). 132p. 1999. 75.00 (*0-88363-847-9*, Pub. by H L Levin) Publishers Group.

De Rozekruis Pers Staff, ed. see Schootemeijer, J.

De Rubertis, Barbara. Let's Read Together Set 1: Short Vowel Book Set. (Illus.). 32p. (Orig.). (J). (ps-2). 1996. pap. 24.75 (*1-57565-037-1*) Kane Pr.

— Let's Read Together Set 2: Long Vowel Book Set. (Illus.). 32p. (Orig.). (J). (ps-2). 1997. pap. 24.75 (*1-57565-038-X*) Kane Pr.

***De Rubertis, Barbara.** Lulu's Lemonade. (Illus.). (J). 2000. 10.40 (*0-606-18222-5*) Turtleback.

De Rudder, Chantal, jt. auth. see Maury, Emmerick-Armand.

De Rueda, Lope. Pasos Completos. Martin Martinez, Juan M., ed. (Nueva Austral Ser.: Vol. 135). (SPA.). 1991. pap. text 24.95 (*84-239-1935-8*) Elliots Bks.

De Rueda, Marta F. The Royal Botanical Expedition to the Nuevo Reyno de Granada: Mutis & His Contemporaries. Boyington, Benjamin & Sanders, Gabrielle, eds. (Illus.). 20p. (Orig.). pap. text. write for info. (*1-883592-09-7*) Perm Mission.

De Rueda, Marta F., et al. Barroco de la Nueva Granada: Colonial Art from Columbia & Ecuador. Ffolliot, Ann et al, eds. Fox, Geoffrey, tr. from SPA. LC 92-71535. (Illus.). 80p. (Orig.). 1992. pap. 17.50 (*1-879128-05-5*) Americas Soc.

De Ruffieu, Francois L. The Handbook of Riding Essentials. 112p. 1986. 24.00 (*0-06-015517-5*) HarperTrade.

De Ruffieu, Francois L., jt. auth. see Harris, Susan E.

De Ruggiero, Guido. The History of European Liberalism. Collingwood, R. C., tr. 1977. lib. bdg. 59.95 (*0-8490-1975-3*) Gordon Pr.

De Ruitter, M. M., ed. Advances in Computer Graphics 3. (Eurographic Seminars Ser.). (Illus.). vii, 323p. 1988. 97.95 (*0-387-18788-X*) Spr-Verlag.

De Ruiz, Dana C. To Fly with the Swallows: A Story of Old California. LC 92-14416. (Stories of America Ser.). (Illus.). 53p. (J). (gr. 2-5). 1992. pap. 4.95 (*0-8114-8074-7*); lib. bdg. 25.68 (*0-8114-7234-5*) Raintree Steck-V.

De Ruiz, Dana C. & Larios, Richard. La Causa: The Migrant Farmworkers' Story. LC 92-12806. (Stories of America Ser.). (Illus.). 92p. (J). (gr. 2-5). 1992. pap. write for info. (*0-8114-8071-2*); lib. bdg. 25.68 (*0-8114-7231-0*) Raintree Steck-V.

de Ruiz, Sonia Lombardo, see Lombardo de Ruiz, Sonia.

De Rulhiere, Claude. History or Anecdotes of the Revolution in Russia, in the Year 1762. LC 72-115581. (Russia Observed, Series I). 1970. reprint ed. 17.95 (*0-405-03060-6*) Ayer.

De Rus, ed. see Nash.

De Rutte, Theophile. The Adventures of a Young Swiss in California: The Gold Rush Account of Theophile de Rutte. Paquette, Mary G., ed. & tr. by. from FRE. (Illus.). 128p. 1992. lib. bdg. 40.00 (*0-9617334-2-X*) Sacto Bk Collectors.

De Ruyter, Kitty. As I Have Loved You. LC 94-33538. 1994. 14.95 (*1-55503-707-0*, 019415) Covenant Comms.

— A Mother's Love. LC 98-157402. 1998. pap. 3.95 (*1-57734-225-9*, 01113364) Covenant Comms.

De Ruyter, Peter. Understanding Candida: Treatment & Recipes. 160p. (Orig.). 1989. pap. write for info. (*1-85327-035-0*, Pub. by Prism Pr) Assoc Pubs Grp.

De S. Cameron, Nigel M. Complete in Christ: Rediscovering Jesus & Ourselves. (Biblical Classics Library: Vol. 29). 113p. 1997. reprint ed. mass mkt. 5.99 (*0-85364-849-2*, Pub. by Paternoster Pub) OM Literature.

De, S. K. Bengal's Contribution to Sanskrit Literature & Studies in Bengal Vaisnavism. 150p. 1974. reprint ed. 10.00 (*0-88065-047-8*) Scholarly Pubns.

— Fundamentals of Ear, Nose & Throat Diseases. 1985. 85.00 (*0-7855-0730-2*, Pub. by Current Dist) St Mut.

— History of Sanskrit Poetics. LC 76-911225. 1976. reprint ed. 18.50 (*0-88386-853-9*) S Asia.

De, S. K. & White, J. R., eds. Short Fibre-Polymer Composites. 272p. 1996. boxed set 179.95 (*1-85573-220-3*) Technomic.

De Sa, A. Electronics for Scientists: Physical Principles with Applications to Instrumentation. LC 96-28465. 464p. 1997. pap. 86.00 (*0-13-359480-7*) P-H.

De Sa-Carneiro, Mario. The Great Shadow: And Other Stories. Costa, Margaret J., ed. & tr. by. from POR. (Empire of the Senses Ser.).Tr. of Ceu em Fogo. 249p. 1997. pap. 13.99 (*1-873982-72-0*, Pub. by Dedalus) Hippocrene Bks.

De Sa-Carnejio, Maria. Lucio's Confession. 2nd ed. Costa, Margaret J., tr. from POR. (Decadence Ser.). 121p. 1999. reprint ed. pap. 10.99 (*1-873982-80-1*, Pub. by Dedalus) Hippocrene Bks.

De Sa De Miranda, Francisco. Poesias. cxxxvi, 965p. reprint ed. write for info. (*0-318-71629-1*) G Olms Pubs.

De Sa Rego, Stella, tr. see Debroise, Olivier.

De Sa Rego, Stella, tr. see Ferrez, Gilberto.

De Sabato Swinton, Elizabeth. The Women of the Pleasure Quarter: Japanese Paintings & Prints of the Floating World. LC 95-16908. (Illus.). 196p. 1996. 65.00 (*1-55595-115-5*) Hudson Hills.

De Sabbata, Venzo, ed. Black Hole Physics: Proceedings of the NATO Advanced Study Institute (12th Course of the Int'l. School of Cosmology & Gravitation of the Ettore Majorana Centre for Scientific Culture), Erice, Italy, May 12-22, 1991. 436p. (C). 1992. text 221.50 (*0-7923-1679-7*) Kluwer Academic.

— Cosmology & Particle Physics: Proceedings of the NATO Advanced Study Institute on Cosmology & Particle Physics (13th Course on the International School of Cosmology & Gravitatio of the Ettore Majorana Centre for Scientific Culture), Erice, Italy, May 3-14, 1993. LC 94-8301. (NATO Advanced Study Institutes Series C, Mathematical & Physical Sciences). 352p. (C). 1994. text 204.50 (*0-7923-2768-3*) Kluwer Academic.

— The Origin & Evolution of Galaxies: Proceedings of the Course of the International School of Cosmology & Gravitation, 7th, Erice, Trapani, Scicily, May 11-23, 1981. 222p. 1982. 70.00 (*9971-950-05-7*) World Scientific Pub.

D

De Sabbata, Venzo, et al, eds. Relativistic Astrophysics & Cosmology: Proceedings of the Sir Arthur Eddington Centenary Symposium, Vol. 1. 256p. 1984. 64.00 (*9971-966-99-9*) World Scientific Pub.

De Sabbata, Venzo & Melinkov, V. N., eds. Gravitational Measurements, Fundamental Metrology & Constants. (C). 1988. text 271.50 (*90-277-2709-0*) Kluwer Academic.

De Sabbata, Venzo & Schmutzer, E., eds. Unified Field Theories of More Than Four Dimensions Including Exact Solutions: Proceedings of the 8th Course of the International School Cosmology & Gravitation Erice, Trapani, Siciliy, May 20-June 1, 1982. 458p. 1983. 86.00 (*9971-950-50-2*) World Scientific Pub.

De Sabbata, Venzo & Sivaram, C. Spin & Torsion in Gravitation. 328p. 1994. text 74.00 (*981-02-1766-8*) World Scientific Pub.

De Sabbata, Venzo, jt. auth. see Gasperini, M.

De Sabbata, Venzo, jt. ed. see Audretsch, J.

De Sabbata, Venzo, jt. ed. see Bergmann, Peter.

De Sablet, Philippe. Mathevasion: Exercises Trav aux Pratiques 2e-1re Terminales. (FRE., Illus.). vii, 71p. (Orig.). 1997. pap. 11.95 (*0-9652357-0-X*) Mathevasion.

De Sacy, S. Silvestre & Isaac, Antoine. Principles of General Grammar. LC 90-43612. 168p. 1990. reprint ed. 50.00 (*0-8201-1444-8*) Schol Facsimiles.

De Sacy, S. Sylvestre, ed. see Rousseau, Jean-Jacques.

De Sade, Bertrand, ed. see De LaFayette, Jean M.

***De Sade, Marquis.** Philosophy in the Boudior. 2000. reprint ed. pap. 13.95 (*1-84068-012-1*, Pub. by Creation Bks) Subterranean Co.

De Sade, Marquis, see Marquis De Sade, pseud.

De Saez, Eileen E. Marketing Concepts for Libraries & Information Services. 144p. 1993. 45.00 (*0-85157-448-3*, LAP4483, Pub. by Library Association) Bernan Associates.

De Sahagun, Bernardino. Broken Shields. Aldana, Patricia, tr. from SPA. 32p. (J). 1997. pap. 6.95 (*0-88899-304-8*) Publishers Group.

— The War of Conquest: How It Was Waged Here in Mexico: the Aztecs' Own Story. Anderson, Arthur J. & Dibble, Charles F., trs. LC 78-60241. (Illus.). 112p. reprint ed. pap. 34.80 (*0-8357-4373-X*, 203720200007) Bks Demand.

— What the Aztecs Told Us. Aldana, Patricia, tr. from SPA. 32p. (J). 1997. pap. 6.95 (*0-88899-306-4*) Publishers Group.

De Sahagun, Fray B. The Conquest of New Spain, Fifteen Eighty-Five Revision: Reproductions of the Boston Public Library Manuscript & the Carlos Maria de Bustamante 1840 Edition. Cline, S. L., ed. Cline, Howard F., tr. from SPA. LC 88-20700. 592p. (C). 1989. text 50.00 (*0-87480-311-X*) U of Utah Pr.

De Sain, Carol & Vercimak, Charmaine. Implementing International Drug, Device, & Diagnostic GMPs: A Practical Guide. 273p. 1994. 139.00 (*0-935184-53-8*) Interpharm.

De Saint-Amour, Guillaume. Opera Omnia. (GER.). iv, 506p. 1998. reprint ed. write for info. (*3-487-10562-4*) G Olms Pubs.

***de Saint-Andre, Alix.** The Good Angel Guide: For Reluctant Sinners. Powell, Elfreda, tr. 144p. 2000. pap. 14.95 (*0-285-63529-8*, Pub. by Souvenir Pr Ltd) IPG Chicago.

***de Saint-Cheron, Michael & Wiesel, Elie.** Evil & Exile. 2nd rev. ed. Rothschild, Jon & Gladding, Jody, trs. 240p. 2000. pap. 16.00 (*0-268-02758-7*, Pub. by U of Notre Dame Pr) Chicago Distribution Ctr.

De Saint-Cheron, Philippe, jt. auth. see Wiesel, Elie.

De Saint Didier, Limojon. The Hermetical Triumph: or The Victorious Philosophical Stone. Smith, Patrick, ed. & tr. by. (Alchemical Studies Ser.: Vol. 18). (Illus.). 1999. pap. 9.95 (*1-55818-423-6*, Alchemical) Holmes Pub.

De Saint-Evremond, Charles S. The Letters of Saint Evremond. Hayward, John, ed. LC 72-83506. (Illus.). 436p. 1972. 30.95 (*0-405-08908-2*) Ayer.

— The Letters of Saint Evremond. LC 76-164624. (Select Bibliographies Reprint Ser.). 1977. reprint ed. 27.95 (*0-8369-5907-8*) Ayer.

De Saint-Foix, G., jt. auth. see De Wyzewa, T.

De Saint Germain. Practical Astrology: A Simple Method of Casting Horoscopes, the Language of the Stars, Easily Comprehended. 260p. 1993. reprint ed. pap. 15.95 (*1-56459-371-1*) Kessinger Pub.

De Saint-Germain, Comte C. Practical Astrology: A Simple Method of Casting Horoscope. rev. ed. 224p. 1996. reprint ed. spiral bd. 16.50 (*0-7873-0552-9*) Hlth Research.

— Practical Astrology: A Simple Method of Casting Horoscopes. 1991. lib. bdg. 75.00 (*0-8490-4309-3*) Gordon Pr.

— Practical Hypnotism, Theories & Experiments. 1996. reprint ed. spiral bd. 17.00 (*0-7873-0268-6*) Hlth Research.

— Practical Palmistry. 273p. 1996. reprint ed. spiral bd. 18.00 (*0-7873-0266-X*) Hlth Research.

— The Practice of Palmistry. 410p. 1973. pap. 12.95 (*0-87877-019-4*, P-19) Newcastle Pub.

— The Study of Palmistry for Professional Purposes. 416p. 1973. reprint ed. pap. 27.50 (*0-7873-0267-8*) Hlth Research.

— The Study of Palmistry for Professional Purposes. (Illus.). 415p. 1994. reprint ed. pap. 26.95 (*1-56459-447-5*) Kessinger Pub.

De Saint Lambert. A New Treatise on Accompaniment: With the Harpsichord, the Organ, & with Other Instruments. Powell, John S., ed. & tr. by. from FRE. LC 90-33591. (Publications of the Early Music Institute). 176p. 1991. pap. 15.95 (*0-253-34561-8*) Ind U Pr.

De Saint-Lambert, Jean-Francois. Contes Americains. Little, Roger, ed. (Exeter French Texts Ser.: Vol. IC). (FRE., Illus.). 128p. 1997. pap. 21.95 (*0-85989-544-0*, Pub. by Univ Exeter Pr) Northwestern U Pr.

De Saint Laurent, Thomas. The Book of Confidence. 2nd ed. 95p. 1989. pap. 3.95 (*1-877905-14-3*) Am Soc Defense TFP.

De Saint-Marie, Francois, ed. The Photo Album of St. Therese of Lisieux. Rohrback, Peter-Thomas, tr. LC 62-10909. (Illus.). 226p. 1962. pap. 24.95 (*0-87061-177-1*) Chr Classics.

De Saint-Martin, Louis-Claude. Le Crocodile, Ou la Guerre Du Bien et Du Mal, Arrivee Sous le Regne De Louis the Fifteenth, Vol. IX. Amadou, Robert, ed. 460p. reprint ed. write for info. incl. 3.5 hd (*0-318-71420-5*) G Olms Pubs.

— Des Franzosischen Philosophen Louis-Claude de St. Martin Nachgelessene Werke, Vol. III. 228p. reprint ed. write for info. (*0-318-71431-0*) G Olms Pubs.

— Des Nombres, Vol. X. Amadou, Robert, ed. 117p. reprint ed. write for info. (*0-318-71421-3*) G Olms Pubs.

— Man: His True Nature & Ministry. (Illus.). 512p. 1993. reprint ed. pap. 27.00 (*1-56459-299-5*) Kessinger Pub.

— Oeuvres Completes, 7 vols. in 8. 1975. write for info. (*0-318-71406-X*) G Olms Pubs.

— Oeuvres Postumes, 2 vols. in 1, Vol. 2. Amadou, Robert, ed. xxxii, 892p. reprint ed. write for info. (*0-318-71410-8*) G Olms Pubs.

— Poesies - Ecrits Politiques, Vol. I. Amadou, Robert, ed. viii, 314p. reprint ed. write for info. (*0-318-71409-4*) G Olms Pubs.

— Traductions de Jacob Bohme, 4 vols., Set. Amadou, Robert, ed. reprint ed. write for info. (*0-318-71412-4*) G Olms Pubs.

— Traductions de Jacob Bohme, 4 vols., Vol. V. Amadou, Robert, ed. reprint ed. write for info. (*0-318-71413-2*); reprint ed. write for info. (*0-318-71414-0*); reprint ed. write for info. (*0-318-71415-9*); reprint ed. write for info. (*0-318-71416-7*) G Olms Pubs.

De Saint-Martin, Louis-Claude, et al. Five Christian Principles. 182p. 1985. reprint ed. spiral bd. 14.00 (*0-7873-0269-4*) Hlth Research.

De Saint-Paul, Marc A. Gabon: The Development of a Nation. 220p. 1989. 49.95 (*0-415-03905-3*, A3642) Routledge.

De Saint Phalle, Niki. Niki de Saint Phalle Traces, 1930-1949: Autobiography. (Illus.). 220p. 1999. 24.95 (*2-940033-43-9*, Pub. by Acatos Edit) Antique Collect.

De Saint Phalle, Therese. La Clariere. (FRE.). 1981. pap. 10.95 (*0-7859-4143-6*) Fr & Eur.

— Le Souverain. (FRE.). 1976. pap. 10.95 (*0-7859-4060-X*, 2070367975) Fr & Eur.

— Le Tournesol. (FRE.). 1973. pap. 10.95 (*0-7859-4001-4*) Fr & Eur.

De Saint-Pierre, Bernardin. Empsael et Zoraide. Little, Roger, ed. (Exeter French Texts Ser.: No. 92). (FRE.). 150p. 1995. pap. text 19.95 (*0-85989-464-9*, Pub. by Univ Exeter Pr) Northwestern U Pr.

— Paul et Virginie. (Coll. GF). pap. 8.95 (*0-685-34034-1*) Fr & Eur.

— Paul et Virginie. Trahard, Pierre, ed. (Class. Garnier Ser.). pap. 29.95 (*0-685-34033-3*) Fr & Eur.

— Paul et Virginie. (Folio Ser.: No. 1552). (FRE.). 1964. pap. 12.95 (*2-07-037552-8*) Schoenhof.

— Paul et Virginie. unabridged ed. (FRE.). pap. 5.95 (*2-87714-138-1*, Pub. by Bookking Intl) Distribks Inc.

De Saint-Pierre, Bernardin J. Litterature et Philosophie Melees: Edition Critique, 2 vols. (FRE.). 349p. 1984. pap. 11.95 (*0-7859-1180-4*, 2253007293) Fr & Eur.

— Paul & Virginia. Donovan, John, tr. & intro. by. 1983. 29.95 (*0-7206-0598-9*, Pub. by P Owen Ltd) Dufour.

— Paul & Virginia. Lang, Andrew, tr. from FRE. LC 87-52. 152p. 1987. reprint ed. lib. bdg. 29.50 (*0-86527-363-4*) Fertig.

De Saint Pierre, Michel. Les Aristocrates. (FRE.). 1978. pap. 11.95 (*0-7859-4059-6*) Fr & Eur.

— Dieu, Vous Garde des Femmes! (FRE.). 1973. pap. 10.95 (*0-7859-4003-0*) Fr & Eur.

— Je Reviendrai sur les Ailes de l'Aigle. (FRE.). 1976. pap. 11.95 (*0-7859-4069-3*) Fr & Eur.

— Monsieur de Charette. (FRE.). 1982. pap. 15.95 (*0-7859-4175-4*) Fr & Eur.

— La Passion de l'Abbe Delance. (FRE.). 1980. pap. 11.95 (*0-7859-4139-8*) Fr & Eur.

De Saint-Riquier, Marc. Lexique de l'Homme a Cheval. (FRE.). 39.95 (*0-8288-7976-1*, M4669) Fr & Eur.

De Saint, Sauveur. French Touch: Decoration & Design in the Most Beautiful Homes of France. (Illus.). 240p. 1997. pap. 31.50 (*0-8212-2464-6*, Pub. by Bulfinch Pr) Little.

De Saint Sauveur, Daphne. The French Touch: Decoration & Design in the Most Beautiful Homes of France. (Illus.). 240p. 1989. 50.00 (*0-8212-1712-7*, Pub. by Bulfinch Pr) Little.

De Saint-Simon, Claude H. Memoires. (Folio Ser.: No. 2165). (FRE.). 1990. pap. 16.95 (*2-07-038234-6*) Schoenhof.

De Saint-Trond, Raoul. Gesta Abbatum Trudonensium, Livre IX: Index Verborum. Tombeur, Paul, ed. (GER.). vi, 167p. 1969. write for info. (*0-318-70581-8*) G Olms Pubs.

De Saint-Victor, Niepce. Recherches Photographiques. Bunnell, Peter C. & Sobieszek, Robert A., eds. LC 76-23058. (Sources of Modern Photography Ser.). (FRE.). 1979. reprint ed. lib. bdg. 11.95 (*0-405-09622-4*) Ayer.

De Sainte-Beuve, Charles-Augustin. Port-Royal, 3 tomes, Vol. 1. deluxe ed. (Pleiade Ser.). (FRE.). 1955. 63.95 (*2-07-010495-8*) Schoenhof.

— Port-Royal, 3 tomes, Vol. 2. deluxe ed. (Pleiade Ser.). (FRE.). 1955. 63.95 (*2-07-010496-6*) Schoenhof.

— Port-Royal, 3 tomes, Vol. 3. deluxe ed. (Pleiade Ser.). (FRE.). 1955. 59.95 (*2-07-010497-4*) Schoenhof.

De Sairigne, Catherine. Animals in Winter. Matthews, Sarah, tr. from FRE. LC 87-34086. (Illus.). 38p. (J). (gr. k-5). 1988. 5.95 (*0-944589-05-7*, 057) Young Discovery Lib.

De Salamanca, Cristina Enriques, see McNerney, Kathleen & Enriques De Salamanca, Cristina, eds.

De Salamanca, Gomez. Compendio de Medicina, Biblioteca Universitaria, Salamanca, 2262. Jesus Mancho, M., ed. (Medieval Spanish Medical Texts Ser.: No. 12). (SPA.). 8p. 1987. 10.00 incl. fiche (*0-940639-08-4*) Hispanic Seminary.

De Salas, Francis & Doughter, William N. Spiritual Exercises. (Translation Ser.). 48p. 1993. pap. write for info. (*0-920669-49-2*, Pub. by Peregrina Pubng) Cistercian Pubns.

De Salas y Tovara, Jose P. Lecciones Solemnes a las Obras de Don Luis de Gongora y Argote. (Textos y Estudios Clasicos De las Literaturas Hispanicas Ser.). 488p. 1971. reprint ed. write for info. (*3-487-04168-5*) G Olms Pubs.

De Salazar, Annelise H., jt. auth. see Foreman, Martin.

De Salazar, Francisco Cervantes, see Cervantes de Salazar, Francisco.

de Salazar Tetzaguic, Jesus. Caracteristicas de la Literatura Kaqchikel. 144p. 1995. 9.95 (*84-89451-17-6*) Piedra Santa Editorial.

De Salazar y Torres, A. El Encanto Es la Hermosura y el Hechizo Sin Hechizo/La Segunda Celestina. O'Connor, Thomas A., ed. (Medieval & Renaissance Texts & Studies Ser.: Vol. 128). 224p. 1994. 30.00 (*0-86698-135-7*, MR128) MRTS.

De Salazar y Torres, Agustin, et al. El Encanto es la Hermosura y el Hechizo Sin Hechizo/La Segunda Celestina. O'Connor, Thomas A., ed. (Spanish Classical Texts Ser.: Vol. 2). (SPA.). 224p. 1994. pap. 12.95 (*0-86698-134-9*, P24) Pegasus Pr.

De Sales, Francis. The Art of Loving God: Simple Virtues for the Christian Life. LC 96-8387. Orig. Title: The Spiritual Conferences. 166p. 1998. pap. write for info. (*0-918477-43-3*) Sophia Inst Pr.

— The Catholic Controversy: St. Francis de Sales' Defense of the Faith. Mackey, Henry B., tr. from FRE. LC 89-52138. 413p. 1992. reprint ed. pap. 15.00 (*0-89555-387-2*) TAN Bks Pubs.

— Finding God's Will for You. LC 98-37143. 157p. 1998. pap. 12.95 (*0-918477-83-2*) Sophia Inst Pr.

— Introduction to the Devout Life. 344p. 1997. reprint ed. pap. 24.95 (*0-7661-0074-X*) Kessinger Pub.

— Introduction to the Devout Life: A Popular Abridgment. abr. ed. Bowler, Joseph D. & Fiorelli, Lewis S., eds. LC 90-70232. 354p. (Orig.). 1994. pap. 13.00 (*0-89555-399-6*) TAN Bks Pubs.

— The Sermons of St. Francis de Sales on Prayer. Fiorelli, Lewis S., ed. Visitation Nuns, tr. LC 84-52310. 51p. 1985. pap. 4.00 (*0-89555-258-2*) TAN Bks Pubs.

De Sales, R. Roussy, see Roussy De Sales, R.

De Sales, Raoul De Roussy, see De Roussy De Sales, Raoul.

De Sales, St. Francis. Thy Will Be Done: Letters to Persons in the World. LC 95-13475. 264p. 1995. pap. 12.95 (*0-918477-29-8*) Sophia Inst Pr.

De Salins, Genevieve-Dominique, jt. auth. see Courtillon, Janine.

De Salle, Rob & Lindley, David. The Science of Jurassic Park & the Lost World: Or, How to Build a Dinosaur. (Illus.). 194p. 1998. text 18.00 (*0-7881-5936-4*) DIANE Pub.

De Salles, Antonio A. & Lufkin, Robert B. Minimally Invasive Therapy of the Brain. LC 96-44702. 1996. 189.00 (*0-86577-641-5*) Thieme Med Pubs.

De Salvador Madariaga. On Hamlet. 2nd ed. 145p. 1964. 35.00 (*0-7146-2068-8*, Pub. by F Cass Pubs) Intl Spec Bk.

De Salvatierra, Mario, tr. see Pita, Juana R.

De Salvio, Alfonso. Dante & Heresy. LC 73-2721. (Select Bibliographies Reprint Ser.). 1977. reprint ed. 17.95 (*0-8369-7158-2*) Ayer.

De Salvio, Alfonso, tr. see Bernaldo De Quiros, C.

De Salvio, Alfonso, tr. see Galilei, Galileo.

De Salvo, Donna. Past Imperfect: A Museum Looks at Itself. 1994. 25.00 (*1-56584-166-2*, Pub. by New Press NY) Norton.

— Past Imperfect: A Museum Looks at Itself. LC 93-87113. (Illus.). 79p. 1994. 25.00 (*0-943526-26-4*) Parrish Art.

— Ray Johnson: Correspondences. (Illus.). 224p. 2000. 50.00 (*2-08-013663-1*, Pub. by Flammarion) Abbeville Pr.

— Wide-Point: The Photography of John Chamberlain. LC 93-83245. (Illus.). 44p. 1993. pap. 18.00 (*0-943526-24-8*) Parrish Art.

De Salvo, Donna, et al. Face Value: American Portraits: The Parrish Art Museum. LC 97-190364. (Illus.). 128p. 1995. 35.00 (*2-08-013597-X*, Pub. by Flammarion) Abbeville Pr.

— Success Is a Job in New York . . . The Early Art & Business of Andy Warhol. Blackburn, Sara, ed. LC 89-80466. (Illus.). 92p. (Orig.). 1989. pap. 20.00 (*0-934349-05-3*) Grey Art Gallery Study Ctr.

De San Juan, Juan Huarte, see Huarte de San Juan, Juan.

De San Pedro, Diego. The Castle of Love. LC 51-634. 232p. 1979. reprint ed. 50.00 (*0-8201-1217-8*) Schol Facsimiles.

— Diego de San Pedro's Tractado de Amores de Arnalte y Lucenda: A Critical Edition. Corfis, Ivy A., ed. (Textos B Ser.: Vol. XXVIII). (ENG & SPA., Illus.). 205p. (Orig.). (C). 1985. pap. 51.00 (*0-7293-0205-9*, Pub. by Tamesis Bks Ltd) Boydell & Brewer.

De Sanchez Bustamante y Sirven, Antonio. The World Court. LC 25-23295. xxv, 379p. 1983. reprint ed. lib. bdg. 52.00 (*0-89941-272-6*, 303060) W S Hein.

De Sanchez Hidalgo, Lydia, jt. auth. see Sanchez Hidalgo, Efrain.

De Sancta Maria, Thomas. The Art of Playing the Fantasia. Hultberg, Warren E. & Howell, Almonte C., Jr., trs. from SPA. LC 90-29326. (SPA., Illus.). 850p. 1991. 99.95 (*0-935480-52-8*) Lat Am Lit Rev Pr.

De Sanfilippo, Olga E. Derecho Procesal Penal, 2 Tomos. (SPA.). 400p. 1993. suppl. ed. 60.00 (*0-685-74275-X*, MICHIE) LEXIS Pub.

De Sanfilippo, Olga E. Resumil, see Resumil De Sanfilippo, Olga E.

De Sanna, Jole, ed. see Teha, Carlo.

De Santa Ana, Julio, ed. Separation Without Hope? Essays on the Relation Between the Church & the Poor During the Industrial Revolution & the Western Colonial Expansion. LC 80-12831. 106p. reprint ed. pap. 32.90 (*0-8357-7018-4*, 203357400086) Bks Demand.

De Santa Cruz Mullen, Francis X. Historia de Familias Cubanas VIII. LC 41-2350. (Coleccion Cuba y sus Jueces). (SPA.). 341p. (Orig.). 1986. pap. 49.00 (*0-89729-408-4*) Ediciones.

De Santiago. Portones Del Diablo.Tr. of Gates of Hell. (SPA.). 245p. write for info. (*1-56063-953-9*) Editorial Unilit.

De Santiago, Carmen R. El Desarrollo Constitucional De Puerto Rico: Documentos y Casos. 2nd ed. 567p. 1985. pap. 8.00 (*0-8477-2221-X*) U of PR Pr.

De Santillan, Diego Abad, see Abad de Santillan, Diego.

***De Santillana, Anna Venini, ed.** Venini Glass, 1921-1986. (Illus.). 352p. 2000. 65.00 (*88-8118-651-9*, Pub. by Skira IT) Abbeville Pr.

De Santillana, George, ed. Age of Adventure: The Renaissance Philosophers. LC 71-117839. (Essay Index Reprint Ser.). 1977. reprint ed. 25.95 (*0-8369-1850-9*) Ayer.

De Santillana, Giorgio. The Crime of Galileo. LC 55-7400. (Midway Reprint Ser.). (Illus.). xvi, 366p. 1978. reprint ed. pap. text 22.50 (*0-226-73481-1*) U Ch Pr.

De Santillana, Giorgio & Von Dechend, Hertha. Hamlet's Mill: An Essay on Myth & the Frame of Time. LC 69-13267. (Nonpareil Bks.). (Illus.). 512p. 1977. pap. 20.95 (*0-87923-215-3*) Godine.

De Santillana, Giorgio & Zilsel, Edgar. The Development of Rationalism & Empiricism. LC 74-132777. (International Encyclopedia of Unified Science Ser.: Vol. 2, No. 8). 98p. reprint ed. pap. 30.40 (*0-608-09037-9*, 206967200005) Bks Demand.

De Santis, Alfredo, et al, eds. Advances in Cryptology - EUROCRYPT '94: Workshop on the Theory & Application of Cryptographic Techniques, Perugia, Italy, May 9-12, 1994, Proceedings, Vol. XIII. LC 95-37558. (Lecture Notes in Computer Science Ser.: Vol. 950). 473p. 1995. 75.00 (*3-540-60176-7*) Spr-Verlag.

De Santis, Christopher C. Langston Hughes & the Chicago Defender: Essays on Race, Politics & Culture, 1942-62. LC 94-45656. 240p. 1995. 14.95 (*0-252-06474-7*) U of Ill Pr.

De Santis, Florence S. Gershwin. (Portraits of Greatness Ser.). (Illus.). 96p. 1987. text 12.50 (*0-918367-18-2*) Elite.

De Santis, Franco, jt. ed. see Allegrini, Ivo.

De Santis, Gene. Video Systems Engineering Handbook. 1500p. 1991. 59.95 (*0-8493-7402-2*, QA, CRC Reprint) Franklin.

De Santis, Gustavo, jt. ed. see Livi-Bacci, Massimo.

De Santis, Hugh. Beyond Progress: An Interpretive Odyssey to the Future. LC 95-37971. 328p. 1996. pap. text 15.95 (*0-226-14296-5*); lib. bdg. 42.50 (*0-226-14295-7*) U Ch Pr.

— The Diplomacy of Silence: The American Foreign Service, the Soviet Union, & the Cold War 1933 to 1947. LC 80-16676. 1993. lib. bdg. 23.00 (*0-226-14337-6*) U Ch Pr.

— The Diplomacy of Silence: The American Foreign Service, the Soviet Union, & the Cold War 1933 to 1947. LC 83-4935. 270p. 1995. pap. text 12.00 (*0-226-14338-4*) U Ch Pr.

De Santis, James J. Start an Interdisciplinary Association: A Successful Practice Development Program for Mental Health Professionals. (Illus.). ix, 222p. 1998. ring bd. 159.00 incl. disk (*1-893001-00-8*); ring bd. 159.00 incl. mac hd (*1-893001-01-6*) DeSantis.

De Santis, Jayce. How to Run a Recording Session. LC 97-71345. 116p. 1997. pap. 9.95 (*0-918371-11-2*, HL00330317, MixBooks) Intertec Pub.

De Santis, Richard & Manney, Gerald. Suspended Adolescence: Help for Parents of Chemical Abusers. rev. ed. (Illus.). 70p. 1989. pap. 7.95 (*0-9627723-0-5*) Beech Hill Pubns.

De Santis, Solange. Life on the Line: One Woman's Tale of Work, Sweat & Survival. LC 98-51974. 288p. 1999. 24.95 (*0-385-48977-3*) Doubleday.

***De Santis, Solange.** Life on the Line: One Woman's Tale of Work, Sweat & Survival. 288p. 2000. pap. text 14.00 (*0-385-48978-1*, Anchor NY) Doubleday.

De Santis, Vincent. Gilded Age, 1877-1896. LC 72-96558. (Goldentree Bibliographies Series in American History). (C). 1973. pap. text 6.95 (*0-88295-536-5*) Harlan Davidson.

De Santo, N. G., ed. Cellular Basis of Renal Function: Journal: Renal Physiology & Biochemistry. (Journal: Renal Physiology & Biochemistry: Vol. 16, Nos. 1 & 2, 1993). (Illus.). 92p. 1993. pap. 88.75 (*3-8055-5770-1*) S Karger.

De Santo, Natale G. & Iorio, Luigi, eds. The Heart, Kidney & Renal Failure: 20 Years of Nephrology: International Forum, Montecassino, June 1998. (Mineral & Electrolyte Metabolism Ser.: Vol. 25, Nos. 1-2). (Illus.). 134p. 1999. pap. 39.25 (*3-8055-6859-2*) S Karger.

De Santo, R. S. Concepts of Applied Ecology. (Heidelberg Science Library). 1978. 63.95 (*0-387-90301-1*) Spr-Verlag.

D

An Asterisk (*) at the beginning of an entry indicates that the title is appearing for the first time.

De Santos Otero, Aurelio. Die Handschriftliche Ueberlieferung der Altslavischen Apokryphen, Vol. 1. (Patristische Texte und Studien: Vol 20). (C). 1978. 114.60 (*3-11-007028-6*) De Gruyter.

De Sarker, Dilip. Silkworm: Biology, Genetics & Breeding. 1998. pap. 14.00 (*81-259-0407-7*, Pub. by Vikas) S Asia.

De Sart, Jean. Birds of the Night. LC 93-31749. (Illus.). 48p. (J). (gr. 4-7). 1994. 12.95 (*0-88106-671-0*) Charlesbridge Pub.

De Satnick, Shelly. Bridge for Everyone: A Step by Step Text & Workbook. 160p. 1982. pap. 9.95 (*0-380-81083-2*, Avon Bks) Morrow Avon.

— Everyone's Introduction to Bridge Conventions. 144p. (Orig.). 1984. mass mkt. 6.95 (*0-380-89318-5*, Avon Bks) Morrow Avon.

De, Satyendra Lal. Socio-Economic Change In West Bengal: A Study of the Sunderbans Region. LC 97-914049. 255p. 1997. write for info. (*81-85402-97-3*) Shipra Pubns.

De, Saulles Annette. All about Your Parrot. 32p. 1999. pap. text 3.50 (*0-7641-1192-2*) Barron.

De Saulles, Denys. Home Grown. 1996. 19.98 (*0-88365-937-9*) Galahad Bks.

De Saulles, Janet. Getting to Know Spain. (Getting to Know Ser.). (Illus.). 32p. (J). (gr. 3-7). 1993. pap. 15.95 incl. audio (*0-8120-8127-7*) Barron.

De Saussure, Ferdinand. Course in General Linguistics. Baskin, Wade, tr. (C). 1965. pap. 16.88 (*0-07-016524-6*) McGraw.

— Grundfragen der allgemeinen Sprachwissenschaft. 2nd ed. Bally, Charles & Sechehaye, Riedlinger, eds. Lommel, Herman, tr. (GER.). xvi, 294p. (C). 1983. pap. 24.65 (*3-11-000158-6*) De Gruyter.

— Memoire sur le Systeme Primitif des Voyelles dans les Langues Indo-Europeennes. (FRE.). 302p. 1987. reprint ed. lib. bdg. 65.95 (*3-487-01833-0*) G Olms Pubs.

de Sauvigny, Guillaume De Bertier, see De Bertier De Sauvigny, Guillaume.

De Sauza, James. Brother Anansi & the Cattle Ranch. 1996. 12.15 (*0-606-12899-9*, Pub. by Turtleback) Demco.

De Sauza, James & Rohmer, Harriet. Brother Anansi & the Cattle Ranch (El Hermano Anansi y el Rancho de Ganado) LC 88-37091. (ENG & SPA., Illus.). 32p. (YA). (ps-3). 1996. reprint ed. pap. 7.95 (*0-89239-142-1*) Childrens Book Pr.

De Savigny, Don & Wijeyaratne, Pandu, eds. GIS for Health & the Environment: Proceedings of an International Workshop Held in Colombo, Sri Lanka, 5-10 September 1994. LC 97-701187. ix, 171p. 1995. pap. 17.50 (*0-88936-766-3*, Pub. by IDRC Bks) Stylus Pub VA.

De Savitsch, Eugene. In Search of Complications: An Autobiography. (American Biography Ser.). 352p. 1991. reprint ed. lib. bdg. 79.00 (*0-7812-8341-8*) Rprt Serv.

De Saxce, F. French - English, English - French Accounting Dictionary, Fiscal & Finance: Dictionnaire Comptable, Fiscal et Financier; Francais-Anglais-Francais. (ENG & FRE.). 302p. 1986. 125.00 (*0-8288-0805-8*, M2666) Fr & Eur.

De Saxonia, Albertus. Questiones Subtilissime in Libros Aristotelis de Celo et Mundo. (GER.). 102p. 1986. reprint ed. write for info. (*3-487-07673-X*) G Olms Pubs.

De Sbuzo, Francis H. No. 3 Templeton Place. 301p. 1998. pap. write for info. (*1-86106-879-4*, Pub. by Minerva Pr) Unity Dist.

De Schaps, Hilda W. & Schutz, Albert L. Kosher Yoga: Cabalistic Roots of Western Mysticism. LC 83-60144. 128p. (Orig.). 1983. 12.95 (*0-936596-09-0*) Quantal.

De Schaps, Hilda W., jt. auth. see Schutz, Albert L.

De Schauensee, M. & Phelps, William H., Jr. A Guide to the Birds of Venezuela. LC 76-45903. (Illus.). 528p. 1978. pap. 49.50 (*0-691-08205-7*, Pub. by Princeton U Pr) Cal Prin Full Svc.

De Schauensee, Max. The Collector's Verdi & Puccini, KB46. LC 77-28264. (Keystone Books in Music: No. KB 46). 156p. 1978. reprint ed. lib. bdg. 55.00 (*0-313-20241-9*, SCCV, Greenwood Pr) Greenwood.

De Schauensee, Rodolphe Meyer, see Meyer de Schauensee, Rodolphe.

De Schepper, A. M. Magnetic Resonance Imaging of Bone & Soft Tissue Tumors & Their Mimics. (Series in Radiology - A Clinical Atlas). (C). 1989. text 160.00 (*0-7923-0343-1*) Kluwer Academic.

De Schepper, A. M., et al. Imaging of Soft Tissue Tumors. LC 96-27265. (Illus.). 448p. 1996. 198.00 (*3-540-61392-7*) Spr-Verlag.

De Schepper, Luc. Acupuncture in Practice. (Illus.). 350p. (Orig.). (C). 1994. pap. 39.95 (*0-942501-03-9*) Full of Life.

— Candida Diet Against It: What You Eat Can Help Direct Your Immune System to Help You. 1994. pap. 15.95 (*0-572-01501-1*, Pub. by W Foulsham) Trans-Atl Phila.

— Full of Life: How to Achieve & Maintain Peak Immunity. (Illus.). 221p. 1991. pap. 12.95 (*0-942139-12-7*) Full of Life.

— How to Dine Like the Devil & Feel Like a Saint. (Self-Help - Diet Ser.). (Illus.). 250p. (Orig.). 1993. pap. 17.95 (*0-942501-01-2*) Full of Life.

— Human Condition: Critical. (Self-Help - Health Ser.). (Illus.). 220p. (Orig.). 1993. pap. 12.95 (*0-942501-00-4*) Full of Life.

— Musculo Skeletal Diseases & Homeopathy. 200p. (Orig.). (C). 1994. pap. 39.95 (*0-942501-02-0*) Full of Life.

— The People's Repertory: Your Guide to Jafe, Effective Homeopathic Remedies for First Aid, Cold & Flu, Women's Health, Emotional Upsets. Lennihan, Begabati, ed. (Illus.). 200p. 1998. pap. 9.95 (*0-942501-09-8*) Full of Life.

— What about Men? The Dark & Light Side of the Male. (Illus.). 200p. 1995. pap. 12.95 (*0-942501-04-7*) Full of Life.

***De Schill, Stefan.** Crucial Choices, Crucial Changes: The Resurrection of Psychotherapy. 548p. 2000. 55.95 (*1-57392-812-7*) Prometheus Bks.

de Schonen, jt. auth. see Bisson.

***De Schoutheete, Philippe.** The Case for Europe: Unity, Diversity, & Democracy in the European Union. Butler, Andrew, tr. LC 99-89753. 118p. 2000. 39.95 (*1-55587-898-9*); pap. 15.95 (*1-55587-900-4*) L Rienner.

***De Schreye, Danny, ed.** Logic Programming: Proceedings of the 1999 International Conference on Logic Programming. (Illus.). 450p. 1999. pap. 85.00 (*0-262-54104-1*) MIT Pr.

De Schrijver, Marc. Scintigraphy of Inflammation with Nanometer-Sized Colloidal Tracers. (Developments in Nuclear Medicine Ser.). (C). 1989. text 135.00 (*0-7923-0272-9*) Kluwer Academic.

De Schutter, Georges, jt. ed. see Nuyts, Jan.

De Schweinitz, Edmund A. Life & Times of David Zeisberger, the Western Pioneer & Apostle of the Indians. LC 70-146391. (First American Frontier Ser.). 1971. reprint ed. 42.95 (*0-405-02844-X*) Ayer.

De Seblo, Leon. Sickness & Senility Are Unnecessary. 111p. 1996. reprint ed. spiral bd. 13.50 (*0-7873-0270-8*) Hlth Research.

De Secondat, Charles L. Spirit of Laws, 2 vols. Nugent, Thomas, tr. from FRE. 1991. reprint ed. 85.00 (*0-8377-0864-8*, Rothman) W S Hein.

de Segarra, Teresa Carrero, see Carrero de Segarra, Teresa.

De Segni, Lotario. Vom Elend des Menschlichen Daseins. (Philosophische Texte und Studien: Vol. 24). (GER.). x, 108p. 1990. write for info. (*3-487-09232-8*) G Olms Pubs.

De Segur. Francois le Bossu. (Folio - Junior Ser.: No. 196). (FRE., Illus.). 250p. (J). (gr. 5-10). 1981. pap. 9.95 (*2-07-033196-2*) Schoenhof.

— General Dourakine. (Folio - Junior Ser.: No. 92). (FRE., Illus.). 220p. (J). (gr. 5-10). 1979. pap. 8.95 (*2-07-033092-3*) Schoenhof.

— Nouveaux Contes de Fees pour les Petits. (Folio - Junior Ser.: No. 149). (FRE., Illus.). 216p. (J). (gr. 5-10). 1980. pap. 9.95 (*2-07-033149-0*) Schoenhof.

De Segur, Louis. Memoirs & Recollections of Count Louis Philippe de Segur. LC 73-115584. (Russia Observed, Series I). 1970. reprint ed. 66.95 (*0-405-03061-4*) Ayer.

De Segur, Louis G. Confession: A Little Book for the Reluctant. LC 89-51366. 68p. 1989. reprint ed. pap. 2.00 (*0-89555-385-6*) TAN Bks Pubs.

De Segur, Sophie Comtesse, see Comtesse De Segur, Sophie.

De Segura, Juan. Processo de Cartas de Amores. Place, Edwin B., tr. LC 70-134270. (Northwestern Humanities Ser.: No. 23). 1970. reprint ed. 22.00 (*0-404-50723-9*) AMS Pr.

De Seife, Rodolphe J. The Shar'ia: An Introduction to the Law of the Islam. LC 93-31399. 103p. 1994. 49.95 (*1-880921-39-1*); pap. 34.95 (*1-880921-38-3*) Austin & Winfield.

De Seingalt, Chevalier, jt. auth. see Casanova, Giacomo.

De Seingault, Jacques C. Memoires, 1756-1763 Vol. 2. (FRE.). 1959. 95.00 (*0-8288-3453-9*, M4975) Fr & Eur.

— Memoires, 1725-1756 Vol. 1. (FRE.). 1958. 95.00 (*0-8288-3452-0*, M4974) Fr & Eur.

De Selincourt, Aubrey. The Campaigns of Alexander. (Classics Ser.). 1976. pap. 13.95 (*0-14-044253-7*, Penguin Classics) Viking Penguin.

— Six Great Poets: Chaucer, Pope, Wordsworth, Shelley, Tennyson, the Brownings. 1988. reprint ed. lib. bdg. 49.00 (*0-7812-0106-3*) Rprt Serv.

— Six Great Poets: Chaucer, Pope, Wordsworth, Shelley, Tennyson, the Brownings. reprint ed. 26.00 (*0-403-04283-6*) Somerset Pub.

De Selincourt, Aubrey, tr. Histories-Herodotus. LC 96-195669. 672p. (C). 2000. pap. 10.95 (*0-14-044638-9*) Viking Penguin.

De Selincourt, Aubrey, tr. see Livy.

De Selincourt, Basil. English Secret, & Other Essays. LC 68-16927. (Essay Index Reprint Ser.). 1977. 18.95 (*0-8369-0369-2*) Ayer.

— Towards Peace, & Other Essays, Critical or Constructive. LC 67-30205. (Essay Index Reprint Ser.). 1977. 17.95 (*0-8369-0370-6*) Ayer.

— William Blake. LC 70-173850. (Studies in Blake: No. 3). (Illus.). 1971. reprint ed. lib. bdg. 75.00 (*0-8383-1357-4*) M S G Haskell Hse.

De Selincourt, Ernest. Oxford Lectures on Poetry. LC 67-23202. (Essay Index Reprint Ser.). 1977. 19.95 (*0-8369-0371-4*) Ayer.

De Selincourt, Ernest, ed. see Spenser, Edmund.

De Selincourt, Ernest, ed. see Wordsworth, William.

De Selincourt, Hugh. Nine Tales. LC 79-103506. (Short Story Index Reprint Ser.). 1977. 21.95 (*0-8369-3248-X*) Ayer.

De Sena, Jorge. By the Rivers of Babylon & Other Stories. Patai, Daphne, ed. LC 88-21100. (Fiction Ser.). 155p. 1991. pap. 10.95 (*0-8135-1688-9*) Rutgers U Pr.

— The Evidences: A Bilingual Edition - Poems Translated from the Portuguese. Smith, Phyllis S., tr. LC 94-72085. (Publication Series of the Center for Portuguese Studies: Vol. 6). Orig. Title: As Evidencias. (ENG & POR.). 63p. (C). 1994. pap. text 10.00 (*0-942208-27-7*) Bandanna Bks.

— Metamorphoses. Fagundes, Francisco C. & Houlihan, James, trs. from POR. LC 90-25636. (Illus.). 112p. (Orig.). 1991. pap. 9.95 (*0-914278-55-X*) Copper Beech.

— Sobre Esta Praia: Eight Meditations on the Coast of the Pacific. Griffin, Jonathan, tr. LC 79-114869. (Inklings Ser.: No. 1). (ENG & POR.). 28p. 1979. pap. 5.00 (*0-930012-31-3*) J Mudfoot.

De Senancour, Etienne P. Obermann. (FRE.). 1984. pap. 19.95 (*0-7859-4205-X*, 2070375668) Fr & Eur.

De Senarclens, Pierre. From Yalta to the Iron Curtain: The Great Powers & the Origins of the Cold War. Laidi, Zaki, ed. Pingree, Amanda, tr. LC 95-6809. (Temps Mondial - World Time Ser.).Tr. of De Yalta au Rideau de Fer. (ENG & FRE.). 290p. 1995. 45.00 (*0-85496-809-1*) Berg Pubs.

— Yalta. Singh, Jasmer, tr. from FRE. 224p. 1987. 39.95 (*0-88738-152-9*) Transaction Pubs.

De Sennevoy, Jean Dupotet, see Dupotet de Sennevoy, Jean.

De Serbine Bahrawy, Lisa. The Voice of History: An Exegesis of Selected Short Stories from Ingeborg Bachmann's Das Dreissigste Jahr & Simultan from the Perspective of Austrian History. (American University Studies: Germanic Languages & Literature: Ser. I, Vol. 78). 202p. (C). 1989. text 37.50 (*0-8204-1027-6*) P Lang Pubng.

De Sercey, Patrick. Being Space. LC 89-92387. 300p. (Orig.). (C). 1990. pap. 14.00 (*0-944164-14-5*) Moon Bear Pr.

De Seriere, M. Westendorp, see Deeg, D. J. & Westendorp De Seriere, M., eds.

De Serpa, Allan. The Mexican Contract. LC 84-223722. 148p. 1981. pap. 5.95 (*0-939460-15-7*) Devyn Pr.

De Serpa, Valeria & Robertson, Kirk. Shoes. limited ed. (Illus.). 30p. 1997. 100.00 (*1-891033-06-9*, Rainshadow Editns) Black Rock Pr.

De Serrano, Irma G. The Puerto Rico Teachers' Association & It's Relationship to Teacher Personnel Administration. 427p. 1971. 5.00 (*0-8477-2202-3*); pap. 4.00 (*0-8477-2203-1*) U of PR Pr.

— La Seleccion de Personal en el Servicio Publico de Puerto Rico. 3112p. 1969. 4.50 (*0-8477-2204-X*); pap. 3.50 (*0-8477-2205-8*) U of PR Pr.

De Serres, Alain, jt. auth. see Coppel, Jonathan.

De Serres, Frederick J., ed. Chemical Mutagens: Principles & Methods for Their Detection, Vol. 8. LC 79-640909. 406p. 1983. 85.00 (*0-306-41336-1*, Plenum Trade) Perseus Pubng.

— Chemical Mutagens: Principles & Methods for Their Detection, Vol. 9. LC 79-640909. 320p. 1984. 75.00 (*0-306-41696-4*, Plenum Trade) Perseus Pubng.

— Chemical Mutagens: Principles & Methods for Their Detection, Vol. 10. LC 79-640909. (Illus.). 572p. (C). 1986. text 174.00 (*0-306-42171-2*, Kluwer Plenum) Kluwer Academic.

De Serres, Frederick J. & Hollaender, Alexander, eds. Chemical Mutagens: Principles & Methods for Their Detection, Vol. 7. LC 79-640909. 524p. 1982. 95.00 (*0-306-40771-X*, Plenum Trade) Perseus Pubng.

De Serres, Frederick J., ed. see Ansari, Aftab A.

De Serres, Frederick J., jt. ed. see Bloom, Arthur D.

De Serres, Frederick J., jt. ed. see Hollaender, Alexander.

De Seze, S. & Ryckewaert, A. Traite Maladies des Os et des Articulations Mise a Jour, 1985. (Collection Medico-Chirurgicale). (FRE., Illus.). 168p. 1985. 36.00 (*0-318-04694-6*) S M P F Inc.

***De-Shalit, Avner.** The Environment: Between Theory & Practice. LC 99-57190. 248p. 2000. write for info. (*0-19-829769-6*) OUP.

— The Environment Between Theory & Practice. LC 99-57190. 248p. 2000. pap. write for info. (*0-19-924038-8*) OUP.

De-Shalit, Avner. Why Posterity Matters: Environmental Policies & Future Generations. LC 94-19023. (Environmental Philosophies Ser.). 176p. (C). 1995. pap. 22.99 (*0-415-10019-4*, C0377) Routledge.

De Shalit, Avner, jt. auth. see Avnon, Dan.

De-Shalit, Avner, jt. ed. see Avineri, Shlomo.

De Shazer, Steve. Clues: Investigating Solutions in Brief Therapy. (Professional Bks.). 1988. 23.95 (*0-393-70054-2*) Norton.

— Keys to Solution in Brief Therapy. 1985. 24.00 (*0-393-70004-6*) Norton.

— Patterns of Brief Family Therapy: An Ecosystemic Approach. LC 81-7239. (Family Therapy Ser.). 157p. 1982. lib. bdg. 30.00 (*0-89862-038-4*) Guilford Pubns.

— Putting Difference to Work. 1991. 22.95 (*0-393-70110-7*) Norton.

— Words Were Originally Magic. 320p. (C). 1994. 32.00 (*0-393-70170-0*) Norton.

De Shazer, Steve, jt. ed. see Ray, Wendel A.

De Shazo, Jerry. Soul Talk: Thoughts That Keep on Thinking. Porter, Cynthia J., ed. 150p. (Orig.). 1993. pap. 10.95 (*0-9637611-6-1*) Positive Chngs Hypnosis.

De Shazo, Jerry, ed. see Porter, Patrick K.

De Shell, Jeffrey. S & M: A Novel. 231p. 1997. pap. 11.95 (*1-57366-024-8*) Fiction Coll.

De Shell, Jeffrey, jt. ed. see Mazza, Cris.

De Sherbinin, Julie W. Chekhov & Russian Religious Culture: The Poetics of the Marian Paradigm. LC 97-19248. (Studies in Russian Literature & Theory). 1997. 59.95 (*0-8101-1404-6*) Northwestern U Pr.

De Sherbinin, Michael, ed. World Refugee Survey: 1999. (Illus.). 64p. 1999. 19.00 (*0-936548-01-0*) US Comm Refugees.

De, Shobha. Shooting from the Hip: Selected Writings. LC 94-905942. (C). 1995. 12.50 (*81-86112-30-8*, Pub. by UBS Pubs Dist) S Asia.

De Siano, Frank. Sowing New Seed: Directions for Evangelization Today. LC 94-10551. 176p. 1994. pap. 9.95 (*0-8091-3479-9*) Paulist Pr.

— Visions of the Other: Jewish & Christian Theologians Assess the Dialogue. Fisher, Eugene J., ed. LC 94-18416. (Stimulus Bks.). 175p. 1994. pap. 7.95 (*0-8091-3477-2*) Paulist Pr.

De Sibert, Frederic, tr. see Jones, Proctor.

De Sica, Vittorio. Miracle in Milan. LC 68-30777. (Illus.). 120p. 1968. 16.95 (*0-910278-09-1*) Boulevard.

De Silva. Intelligent Control: Fuzzy Logic Applications. 41p. 1995. lib. bdg., lab manual ed. 0.50 (*0-8493-7984-9*) CRC Pr.

***De Silva, Alvaro, ed.** The Last Letters of Thomas More. LC 00-23125. 225p. 2000. 20.00 (*0-8028-3886-3*) Eerdmans.

De Silva, Alvaro, ed. see Chesterton, G. K.

De Silva, C. W. & Hamza, M. H., eds. Modelling & Simulation. 297p. 1995. 90.00 (*0-88986-222-2*, 210) Acta Pr.

De Silva, C. W. & MacFarlane, A. G. Knowledge-Based Control with Applications to Robots. (Lecture Notes in Control & Information Sciences: Vol. 123). (Illus.). xi, 196p. 1989. 46.95 (*0-387-51143-1*) Spr-Verlag.

De Silva, C. W. & Shoureshi, R., eds. Intelligent Control Systems, 1993. LC 89-49384. 157p. pap. 50.00 (*0-7918-1012-7*) ASME.

De Silva, Cara. In Memory's Kitchen: A Legacy from the Women of Terezin. LC 96-13675. (Illus.). 160p. 1997. 25.00 (*1-56821-902-4*) Aronson.

De Silva, Chandra R. Sri Lanka: A History. Pandley, B. N. & Taylor, David Conrad, eds. 325p. 1987. text 35.00 (*0-7069-3294-3*) Advent Bks Div.

De Silva, Chandra R., jt. ed. see Bartholomeusz, Tessa J.

De Silva, Clarence W. Intelligent Control Fuzzy Logic Applications. LC 94-44558. (Mechatronics Ser.). (Illus.). 368p. 1995. boxed set 104.95 (*0-8493-7982-2*, 7982) CRC Pr.

***De Silva, Clarence W.** Intelligent Machines: Myths & Realities. 344p. (C). 2000. boxed set 89.95 (*0-8493-0330-3*) CRC Pr.

— Vibration Fundamentals & Practice. LC 99-16238. 976p. 1999. boxed set 129.95 (*0-8493-1808-4*, 1808) CRC Pr.

***De Silva, Clarence W.** Vibration Fundamentals & Practice. 378p. (C). 1999. teacher ed., ring bd. write for info. (*0-8493-0084-3*) CRC Pr.

De Silva, Clarence W., jt. auth. see Jain, L. C.

De Silva, Colin. Jungle Tales: All Mankind Is the Jungle. 292p. (Orig.). 1997. pap. 12.95 (*955-619-003-1*, Pub. by Richmond Pubs) East Indies.

De Silva, David A. 4 Maccabees. (Guides to the Apocrypha & Pseudepigrapha Ser.: No. 7). 176p. 1998. pap. text 14.95 (*1-85075-896-4*, Pub. by Sheffield Acad) CUP Services.

De Silva, Donatus, ed. Against All Odds: Breaking the Poverty Trap. LC 89-4258. 186p. 1989. pap. 11.95 (*0-932020-70-4*); text 24.95 (*0-932020-69-0*) Seven Locks Pr.

De Silva, G. Gomez. Elsevier's Concise Spanish Etymological Dictionary. (ENG & SPA.). 560p. 1985. 375.00 (*0-8288-9304-7*, F132080) Fr & Eur.

— Elsevier's International Dictionary of Literature & Grammar. 616p. 1991. 187.25 (*0-444-88064-X*) Elsevier.

— Elsevier's International Dictionary of Literature & Grammar. 604p. 1991. 250.00 (*0-8288-9303-9*) Fr & Eur.

De Silva, Guido G. Breve Dicc. Etimologico de la Lengua Espanola. (SPA.). 39.99 (*968-16-2812-8*, Pub. by Fondo) Continental Bk.

— Elsevier's Concise Spanish Etymological Dictionary. 572p. 1985. 282.75 (*0-444-42440-7*) Elsevier.

De Silva, H. K. & Beumer, W. G. Illustrations & Views of Dutch Ceylon, 1602-1796: A Comprehensive Work of Pictorial Reference with Selected Eye-Witness Accounts. (Illus.). viii, 495p. 1988. text 133.00 (*90-04-08979-9*) Brill Academic Pubs.

De Silva, Henry. Fencing: Skills of the Game. 1997. pap. 19.95 (*1-86126-068-7*, Pub. by Crolwood) Trafalgar.

De Silva, K. M. Reaping the Whirlwind: Ethnic Conflict, Ethnic Politics in Sri Lanka. LC 98-906094. xi, 388 p. 1998. 17.50 (*0-14-027065-5*) Viking Penguin.

— Regional Powers & Small State Security: India & Sri Lanka, 1977-1990. (Woodrow Wilson Center Press Ser.). (Illus.). 400p. 1995. text 48.50 (*0-8018-5149-1*) Johns Hopkins.

— Social Policy & Missionary Organizations in Ceylon, 1840-1855. 318p. 1965. 69.50 (*0-614-01826-9*) Elliots Bks.

— Sri Lanka: A Survey. LC 77-73917. 516p. 1977. reprint ed. pap. 147.10 (*0-608-00535-5*, 2061414) Bks Demand.

De Silva, K. M. & Kiribamune, Sirima. Asian Panorama. 1990. text 50.00 (*0-7069-4959-5*, Pub. by Vikas) S Asia.

De Silva, K. M. & Samarasinghe, S. W., eds. Peace Accords & Ethnic Conflict. 280p. 1993. text 59.00 (*1-85567-079-8*, Pub. by P P Pubs) Cassell & Continuum.

De Silva, K. M. & Wriggins, W. Howard. J. R. Jayewardene of Sri Lanka Vol. 1: A Political Biography: The First Fifty Years. (Illus.). 336p. 1988. text 28.75 (*0-8248-1183-6*) UH Pr.

— J. R. Jayewardene of Sri Lanka Vol. 2: A Political Biography: From 1956 to His Retirement, Vol. 2. (Illus.). 416p. (C). 1995. text 30.25 (*0-8248-1692-7*) UH Pr.

De Silva, Kingsley M. Managing Ethnic Tensions in Multi-Ethnic Societies: Sri Lanka 1880-1985. 450p. (Orig.). (C). 1986. pap. text 42.00 (*0-8191-5398-2*); lib. bdg. 68.50 (*0-8191-5397-4*) U Pr of Amer.

— Problems of Governing Sri Lanka. (Governance in South Asia Ser.). 1993. text 40.00 (*0-685-66298-5*, Pub. by Konark Pubs Pvt Ltd) Advent Bks Div.

De Silva, Lily. The Buddha & Christ As Religious Teachers. 32p. 1992. 2.25 (*955-24-0097-X*, Pub. by Buddhist Pub Soc) Vipassana Res Pubns.

— Nibbana As Living Experience. 56p. 1996. 3.75 (*955-24-0128-3*, Pub. by Buddhist Pub Soc) Vipassana Res Pubns.

— Pali Primer. 152p. 1995. pap. 5.95 (*81-7414-014-X*) Vipassana Res Pubns.

De Silva, Migara, jt. auth. see Girishankar, Navin.

De Silva, P. L., jt. auth. see Kloos, P.

D

De Silva, Padmal & Rachman, Stanley. Obsessive-Compulsive Disorder: The Facts. 2nd ed. (The Facts Ser.). (Illus.). 152p. 1998. pap. 19.95 (*0-19-262860-7*) OUP.

De Silva, Padmasiri. Buddhist & Freudian Psychology. 3rd ed. 221p. 1992. pap. 26.50 (*9971-69-168-X*, Pub. by Sngapore Univ Pr) Coronet Bks.

— Buddhist & Freudian Psychology. 3rd ed. 230p. 1992. 39.50 (*9971-69-167-1*, Pub. by Sngapore Univ Pr) Coronet Bks.

***De Silva, Padmasiri.** An Introduction to Buddhist Psychology. 3rd ed. 176p. 2000. 75.00 (*0-7425-0856-0*); pap. 24.95 (*0-7425-0857-9*) Rowman.

De Silva, S. S., ed. Asian Fisheries Society Commemorative Volume. Date not set. write for info. (*0-614-23057-8*, Pub. by ICLARM) Intl Spec Bk.

— Exotic Aquatic Organisms in Asia. (Asian Fisheries Society Spec. Publications: No. 3). 154p. 1989. per. write for info. (*971-10-2253-2*, Pub. by ICLARM) Intl Spec Bk.

— Fish Nutrition Research in Asia. (Asian Fisheries Society Spec. Publications: No. 4). 166p. 1989. per. write for info. (*971-10-2266-4*, Pub. by ICLARM) Intl Spec Bk.

— Fish Nutrition Research in Asia. (Asian Fisheries Society Spec. Publications: No. 5). 207p. 1991. per. write for info. (*971-8709-03-7*, Pub. by ICLARM) Intl Spec Bk.

— Fish Nutrition Research in Asia. (Asian Fisheries Society Spec. Publications: No. 9). 138p. 1994. per. write for info. (*971-8709-57-6*, Pub. by ICLARM) Intl Spec Bk.

De Silva, Sena S., ed. Reservoir Fisheries of Asia: Proceedings of the 2nd Asian Reservoir Fish Workshop. 295p. 1992. pap. write for info. (*0-88936-590-3*) IDRC Bks.

— Tropical Mariculture. (Illus.). 488p. 1998. boxed set 99.95 (*0-12-210845-0*) Acad Pr.

De Silva-Vigier, Anil. This Moste Highe Prince - John of Gaunt. 452p. (C). 1989. text 85.00 (*1-872795-47-1*, Pub. by Pentland Pr) St Mut.

De Silva, W. P., ed. see Rachman, Stanley J.

De Simone, Andrew, ed. see Weiss, James R.

De Simone, Donald. Railroaded to Resurrection. 204p. 1982. 19.95 (*0-88280-099-X*) ETC Pubns.

De Simone, Gilda. Ending Analysis: Theory & Technique. LC 98-130420. (Illus.). 112p. 1997. pap. 22.00 (*1-85575-126-7*, Pub. by H Karnac Bks Ltd) Other Pr LLC.

De Simone, Paula. The Decorative Painter's Colour Shaper Book: A Creative Guide for the Decorative Artist, Incl. colour shapers. (Illus.). 108p. 1999. pap. 29.99 (*1-56496-558-9*, Quarry Bks) Rockport Pubs.

De Simone, R. & Paolella, G. Interactive Atlas of Transesophageal Color Doppler Echocardiography. 25p. 1997. pap. 325.00 incl. cd-rom (*3-540-14532-X*) Spr-Verlag.

De Singly, Francois. Modern Marriage & Its Cost to Women: A Sociological Look at Marriage in France. Bailey, Malcolm, tr. from FRE. LC 95-42335. 248p. 1996. 38.50 (*0-87413-572-9*) U Delaware Pr.

De Singly, Francois, jt. ed. see Commanille, Jacques.

De Sismondi, J. C. A History of the Italian Republics. 1990. 16.50 (*0-8446-0912-9*) Peter Smith.

de Sismondi, Jean C. Simonde, see Simonde de Sismondi, Jean C.

De Sivry. Traite . . . du Rire. Brooks, Chris, ed. (Exeter French Texts Ser.: Vol. 61). (FRE.). 92p. Date not set. pap. text 19.95 (*0-85989-222-0*, Pub. by Univ Exeter Pr) Northwestern U Pr.

De Smedt, Koenrad, jt. ed. see Dijkstra, Ton.

De Smedt, Marc, compiled by. The Wisdom of Tao. LC 96-21498. (Illus.). 56p. 1996. 8.95 (*0-7892-0241-7*) Abbeville Pr.

— The Wisdom of Zen. (Illus.). 56p. 1996. 8.95 (*0-7892-0240-9*) Abbeville Pr.

De Smet, P. A., et al, eds. Adverse Effects of Herbal Drugs, Vol. 1. 264p. 1992. pap. 72.00 (*0-387-53100-9*) Spr-Verlag.

— Adverse Effects of Herbal Drugs, Vol. 2. (Illus.). 256p. 1993. 78.95 (*0-387-55800-4*) Spr-Verlag.

— Adverse Effects of Herbal Drugs, Vol. 3. (Illus.). xii, 200p. 1996. pap. 74.95 (*3-540-60181-3*) Spr-Verlag.

De Smet, Pierre-Jean. Life, Letters & Travels of Father Pierre Jean de Smet, 4 vols., Set. LC 75-83418. (Religion in America, Ser. 1). 1970. reprint ed. 96.95 (*0-405-00237-8*) Ayer.

— Life, Letters & Travels of Father Pierre Jean de Smet, 4 vols., Vol. 1. LC 75-83418. (Religion in America, Ser. 1). 1976. reprint ed. 24.95 (*0-405-00238-6*) Ayer.

— Life, Letters & Travels of Father Pierre Jean de Smet, 4 vols., Vol. 2. LC 75-83418. (Religion in America, Ser. 1). 1976. reprint ed. 24.95 (*0-405-00239-4*) Ayer.

— Life, Letters & Travels of Father Pierre Jean de Smet, 4 vols., Vol. 3. LC 75-83418. (Religion in America, Ser. 1). 1976. reprint ed. 24.95 (*0-405-00240-8*) Ayer.

— Life, Letters & Travels of Father Pierre Jean de Smet, 4 vols., Vol. 4. LC 75-83418. (Religion in America, Ser. 1). 1976. reprint ed. 24.95 (*0-405-00241-6*) Ayer.

— New Indian Sketches. 146p. 1985. 16.95 (*0-87770-336-1*) Ye Galleon.

— Origin, Progress & Prospects of the Catholic Mission to the Rocky Mountains. 1971. reprint ed. pap. 1.00 (*0-87770-044-3*) Ye Galleon.

De Smet, Robin. Graded Solos for Clarinet. (Illus.). 48p. 1985. pap. 10.95 (*0-8256-1053-2*, AM33598) Music Sales.

— Graded Solos for Trumpet. (Illus.). 48p. 1985. pap. 9.95 (*0-8256-1054-0*, AM33606) Music Sales.

De Smet, Robin, selected by. Christmas Solos for the Bb Saxophone. (Illus.). 48p. 1987. pap. 9.95 (*0-8256-1164-4*, AM65061) Music Sales.

— Christmas Solos for the Clarinet. (Illus.). 48p. 1987. pap. 9.95 (*0-8256-1161-X*, AM65020) Music Sales.

— Christmas Solos for the Flute. (Illus.). 48p. 1987. pap. 7.95 (*0-8256-1160-1*, AM65038) Music Sales.

— Christmas Solos for the Recorder. (Illus.). 48p. 1987. pap. 9.95 (*0-8256-1163-6*, AM65046) Music Sales.

— Early Music for Recorder. (Illus.). 32p. 1984. pap. 9.95 (*0-7119-0499-5*, AM36542) Music Sales.

— Graded Solos for Flute. (Illus.). 48p. 1985. pap. 10.95 (*0-8256-1052-4*, AM33812) Music Sales.

— Irish Music for Recorder. (Illus.). 32p. 1984. pap. 12.95 (*0-7119-0498-7*, AM36542) Music Sales.

De Smet, W. Guides to the Identification of the Microinvertebrates of the Continental Waters of the World Vol. 9: Rotifera 4: The Proalidae (Monogononta) (Illus.). 102p. 1996. 45.00 (*90-5103-119-X*, Pub. by SPB Acad Pub) Balogh.

De Smet, W. H. & Pourriot, R. Guides to the Identification of Microinvertebrates of the Continental Waters of the World Vol. 12: Rotifera: The Dicranophoridae (Monogononta) & the Ituridae. viii, 344p. 1996. pap. 105.00 (*90-5103-135-1*, Pub. by SPB Acad Pub) Balogh.

De Smijter, E., et al. The Future of the European Union in the Light of the 1996 Intergovernmental Conference. (Leuven Law Ser.: Vol. 9). 37p. 1997. pap. 29.50 (*90-6186-849-1*, Pub. by HK Univ Pr) Coronet Bks.

De Smit, Jacob, jt. auth. see Kramer, Nicolas.

De Smith. Constitutional & Administrative Law. 8th ed. LC 98-214268. 736p. pap. 55.00 (*0-14-025816-7*, Pub. by Pnguin Bks Ltd) Trafalgar.

de Smith, Josie, tr. see Hanks, Billie.

de Smith, Josie, tr. see McDowell, Josh.

De Soete, Damiaan, et al. Neutron Activation Analysis. LC 73-122343. (Chemical Analysis Ser.: No. 34). (Illus.). 860p. reprint ed. pap. 200.00 (*0-608-17612-5*, 203046200069) Bks Demand.

De Sola, Anne, ed. see Challes, Robert, et al.

De Sola, Carla. The Spirit Moves: A Handbook of Dance & Prayer. Adams, Doug, ed. & intro. by. LC 77-89743. (Illus.). 152p. 1986. reprint ed. pap. 9.95 (*0-941500-38-1*) Sharing Co.

De Sola Chervin, Ronda. Freed to Love: Healing for Catholic Women. 58p. 1994. pap. 6.95 (*1-887582-00-2*) Chiaro Oscuro Pr.

— The Kiss from the Cross: Saints for Every Kind of Suffering. 220p. 1994. pap. 10.99 (*0-89283-849-3*, Charis) Servant.

— Prayers of the Women Mystics. 260p. (Orig.). 1992. pap. 8.99 (*0-89283-750-0*, Charis) Servant.

De Sola Chervin, Ronda, ed. The Fabric of Our Lives. 200p. 1995. pap. 13.95 (*1-887582-03-7*) Chiaro Oscuro Pr.

De Sola Chervin, Ronda & Conley, Carla C. The Book of Catholic Customs & Traditions: Enhancing Holidays, Special Occasions & Family Celebrations. 184p. 1995. pap. 9.99 (*0-89283-796-9*, Charis) Servant.

De Sola Chervin, Ronda, jt. auth. see Geraghty, Richard.

De Sola-Morales, Ignasi. Differences: Topographies of Contemporary Architecture. Whiting, Sarah, ed. Thompson, Graham, tr. (Writing Architecture Ser.). (Illus.). 120p. 1996. pap. text 18.50 (*0-262-54085-1*) MIT Pr.

De Sola Pinto, Vivian. Sir Charles Sedley, 1639-1701. 1988. reprint ed. lib. bdg. 49.00 (*0-7812-0173-X*) Rprt Serv.

— Sir Charles Sedley, 1639-1701. (Illus.). 1971. reprint ed. 27.00 (*0-403-01150-7*) Scholarly.

De Sola Pinto, Vivian & Rodway, Allan E. The Common Muse: An Anthology of Popular British Ballad Poetry 15th to 20th Century. LC 79-161943. 403p. 1957. reprint ed. 75.00 (*0-403-01331-3*) Scholarly.

De Sola Pinto, Vivian, ed. see Sedley, Charles.

De Sola Pool, David, jt. auth. see Horowitz, George.

De Sola Pool, Ithiel. Forecasting the Telephone: A Retrospective Technology Assessment. LC 82-22637. (Communication & Information Science Ser.). 184p. (C). 1982. text 73.25 (*0-89391-048-1*) Ablx Pub.

— Politics in Wired Nations. Etheredge, Lloyd S., ed. LC 97-51703. 395p. 1997. text 28.95 (*1-56000-344-8*) Transaction Pubs.

— Symbols of Democracy, Series C: Symbols, No. 4. LC 81-6229. (Hoover Institute Studies, Series C: Symbols: No. 4). 80p. 1981. reprint ed. lib. bdg. 59.75 (*0-313-22517-6*, POSD, Greenwood Pr) Greenwood.

— Technologies Without Boundaries: On Telecommunications in a Global Age. 352p. 1990. text 33.95 (*0-674-87263-0*) HUP.

De Sola Pool, Ithiel, jt. auth. see Schramm, Wilbur L.

De Sola Poole, David, tr. see Rabbinical Council of America, ed.

De Sola, Ralph, et al, eds. Abbreviations Dictionary. LC 99-33430. 288p. 1999. 5.95 (*0-395-92691-2*) HM.

De Sole, S. Entwicklung der Drelipore von Coprinus Radiatus (Bolt.) Fr. (Bibliotheca Mycologica Ser.: No. 88). (GER., Illus.). 148p. 1982. pap. 40.00 (*3-7682-1343-9*) Lubrecht & Cramer.

De Solenni, Gino & de Vega, Lope. Lope de Vega's El Brasil Restituido. (ENG & SPA.). 306p. 1929. text 2.60 (*0-318-14282-1*) Hispanic Inst.

De Solla Price, Mark. Living Positively in a World with HIV-AIDS. LC 94-16832. 176p. (Orig.). 1995. pap. 10.00 (*0-380-77623-5*, Avon Bks) Morrow Avon.

De Solms, Marie T., pseud. The Condition of Woman in the United States: A Traveller's Notes. Alger, Abby L., tr. LC 72-2590. (American Women Ser.: Images & Realities). (Illus.). 292p. 1974. reprint ed. 21.95 (*0-405-04447-X*) Ayer.

De Somaize, Antoine B. Le Dictionnaire des Precieuses, 2 vols. in 1. (GER.). lxiv, 704p. 1972. reprint ed. write for info. (*3-487-04417-X*) G Olms Pubs.

De Somogyi, Nick. Shakespeare's Theatre of War. LC 98-26131. 1998. 61.95 (*1-84014-207-3*) Ashgate Pub Co.

De Sonne, Marcia. Digital Audio Broadcasting: 1991 Market & Policy Developments. 100p. 1991. 60.00 (*0-89324-094-X*) Natl Assn Broadcasters.

De Sormo, Maitland C. Noah John Rondeau: Adirondack Hermit. 5th ed. (Illus.). 204p. 1969. reprint ed. pap. 16.00 (*0-932052-74-6*) North Country.

De Sosa, Michael. Taking the Quantum Leap: Using the Sinclair QL Computer. 1985. write for info. (*0-07-016578-5*) McGraw.

De Sota Aburto, Manuel. Diccionario Retana de Autoridades de la Lengua Vasca, 2. 1976. 105.00 (*0-7859-5775-8*) Fr & Eur.

— Diccionario Retana de Autoridades de la Lengua Vasca, 3. (SPA.). 1976. 105.00 (*0-7859-5776-6*) Fr & Eur.

— Diccionario Retana De Autoridades de la Lengua Vasca, Vol. 4. (SPA.). 512p. 1977. 105.00 (*0-7859-6450-9*) Fr & Eur.

***De Soto, Clara.** Beyond Tomorrow. LC 99-91768. 2000. 25.00 (*0-7388-1248-X*); pap. 18.00 (*0-7388-1249-8*) Xlibris Corp.

De Soto, Hermine G. & Anderson, David G., eds. The Curtain Rises: Rethinking Culture, Ideology, & the State in Eastern Europe. LC 92-13577. 368p. (C). 1993. pap. 19.95 (*0-391-03810-9*) Humanities.

***De Soto, Hermine G. & Dudwick, Nora.** Fieldwork Dilemmas: Anthropologists in Postsocialist States. LC 00-8600. 2000. write for info. (*0-299-16374-1*) U of Wis Pr.

***De Soto, Hernando.** The Mystery of Capital: Why Capitalism Succeeds in the West & Fails Everywhere Else. 2000. 27.50 (*0-465-01614-6*, Pub. by Basic) HarpC.

De Soto, Jose M. Vaz, see Vaz De Soto, Jose M.

De Soto, William. The Politics of Business Organizations: Understanding the Role of State Chambers of Commerce. LC 95-36957. 160p. (Orig.). (C). 1995. pap. text 26.50 (*0-7618-0098-0*); lib. bdg. 48.00 (*0-7618-0097-2*) U Pr of Amer.

De Sousa, Geraldo U., jt. auth. see Bergeron, David M.

De Sousa, Jose M. Diccionario de la Informacion, Comunicacio y Periodismo. 6th ed. (SPA.). 584p. 1992. pap. 65.00 (*0-7859-3707-2*, 8428318840) Fr & Eur.

— Diccionario de Ortografia Tecnica. (SPA.). 424p. 1987. 55.00 (*0-7859-4955-0*) Fr & Eur.

— International Dictionary of Siglas & Acronyms: Diccionario Internacional de Siglas y Acronimos. 2nd ed. (SPA.). 552p. 1984. pap. 54.95 (*0-7859-4900-3*) Fr & Eur.

De Sousa, Maria S. Lymphocyte Circulation: Experimental & Clinical Aspects. LC 80-40848. (Illus.). 287p. reprint ed. pap. 89.00 (*0-608-17663-X*, 203037700069) Bks Demand.

De Sousa, Ronald. The Rationality of Emotion. 448p. 1987. 45.00 (*0-262-04092-1*, Bradford Bks) MIT Pr.

— The Rationality of Emotion. 400p. 1990. reprint ed. pap. text 22.50 (*0-262-54057-6*) MIT Pr.

De Sousa Santos, Boaventura. Toward a New Common Sense: Law, Science & Politics in the Paradigmatic Transition. (After the Law Ser.). 614p. (C). 1995. pap. 30.99 (*0-415-90439-0*, A5764) Routledge.

— Toward a New Common Sense: Law, Science & Politics in the Paradigmatic Transition. (After the Law Ser.). 614p. (C). 1995. 90.00 (*0-415-90438-2*, A5760) Routledge.

de Sousa Santos, Maria I. Ramalho, see Materassi, Mario & Ramalho de Sousa Santos, Maria I., eds.

***de Soussa, Jamie.** Isabella. LC 00-130510. (Illus.). 320p. 2000. 26.95 (*1-57197-223-4*) Pentland Pr.

De Souto, Martha S. Group Travel Operations Manual. LC 83-61024. (Travel Management Library). 1985. text 35.95 (*0-916032-20-5*) Delmar.

— Group Travel Operations Manual. 2nd ed. (Travel Management Library). 439p. 1991. teacher ed. 10.00 (*0-8273-3516-4*) Delmar.

— Group Travel Operations Manual. 2nd ed. (Travel Management Library). 439p. (C). 1993. mass mkt. 53.95 (*0-8273-3514-8*) Delmar.

De Souza, Alfred, ed. The Indian City: Poverty, Ecology & Urban Development. 1979. 14.50 (*0-8364-0196-4*) S Asia.

De Souza, Alfred, jt. auth. see Singh, Andre M.

De Souza, Anthony R. & Mather, Cotton, eds. The Capitol Region: Day Trips in Maryland, Virginia, Pennsylvania, & Washington, D.C. LC 92-10412. (Touring North America Ser.). (Illus.). 220p. 1992. pap. 9.95 (*0-8135-1871-7*) Rutgers U Pr.

De Souza, Chris, et al. Textook of Pediatric Otorhinolaryngology - Head & Neck Surgery, Vols. I & II. (Illus.). 888p. 1998. pap. 448.95 (*1-56593-958-1*, 1894) Thomson Learn.

De Souza, Daniel. Under a Crescent Moon. (Masks Ser.). 160p. (Orig.). 1990. pap. 10.95 (*1-85242-142-8*) Serpents Tail.

De Souza, Errol B. & Conn, P. Michael, eds. Methods in Neurosciences: Neurobiology of Cytokines, Vol. 17. (Illus.). 327p. 1993. text 104.00 (*0-12-185283-0*) Acad Pr.

De Souza, Errol B. & Nemeroff, Charles B., eds. Corticotropin-Releasing Factor: Basic & Clinical Studies of Neuropeptides. 368p. 1989. lib. bdg. 259.00 (*0-8493-4550-2*, QP572) CRC Pr.

De Souza, Eunice. Conversations with Indian Poets. (Illus.). 208p. 2000. text 13.95 (*0-19-564782-3*) OUP.

De Souza, Eunice, ed. Nine Indian Women Poets: An Anthology. LC 98-902943. 106p. 1998. text 12.95 (*0-19-564077-2*) OUP.

De Souza, Hildo M. The Adoption of Sustainable Agricultural Technologies: A Case Study in the State of Espirito Santo Brazil. LC 97-74458. (Illus.). 192p. 1997. text 59.95 (*1-84014-160-3*, Pub. by Ashgate Pub) Ashgate Pub Co.

De Souza, Jose Martinez, see Martinez De Souza, Jose.

De Souza, Lorraine & Campling, Jo, eds. Multiple Sclerosis: Approaches to Management. (Therapy in Practice Ser.). 140p. 1990. pap. 23.00 (*0-412-32230-7*, A4411) Chapman & Hall.

De Souza, M. E., ed. Anaerobic Treatment in Tropical Countries: Proceedings of the Seminar Held in Sao Paulo, Brazil, 25-29 August, 1986. LC 82-645900. (Water Science & Technology Ser.: No. 18). (Illus.). 204p. 1987. pap. 68.00 (*0-08-035583-8*, Pergamon Pr) Elsevier.

De Souza, Paulo N. & Silva, J. N. Berkeley Problems in Mathematics. LC 97-34135. (Problem Books in Mathematics). (Illus.). 500p. 1997. pap. 37.50 (*0-387-94933-X*) Spr-Verlag.

— Berkeley Problems in Mathematics. LC 97-34135. (Problem Books in Mathematics). (Illus.). 464p. 1998. 59.95 (*0-387-94934-8*) Spr-Verlag.

***De Souza, Philip.** Piracy in the Greeco-Roman World. (Illus.). 292p. (C). 2000. text 59.95 (*0-521-48137-6*) Cambridge U Pr.

De Souza, Philip, jt. auth. see Langley, Andrew.

De Souza, R. First Communion Days. 96p. (J). (gr. 2-8). 1997. reprint ed. 14.00 (*0-911845-50-X*) Neumann Pr.

De Souza, Teotonio R. Goa to Me. (C). 1994. text 22.50 (*81-7022-504-3*, Pub. by Concept) S Asia.

De Souza, Teotonio R., ed. Essays in Goan History. (C). 1989. 24.00 (*81-7022-263-X*, Pub. by Concept) S Asia.

De Spain, June. The Little Cyanide Cookbook: Delicious Recipes Rich in Vitamin B17. 192p. 1976. pap. text 12.50 (*0-912986-00-X*) Am Media.

De Speville, Bertrand. Hong Kong Policy Initiatives Against Corruption. LC 98-121828. 84p. 1998. pap. 13.00 (*92-64-16010-8*, 41-98-01-1, Pub. by Org for Econ) OECD.

De Spiegeleire, Stephan, ed. see Stiftung Wissenschaft und Politik Staff, et al.

De Spinoza, Benedict. Ethic: Demonstrated in Geometrical Order & Divided into Five Parts, Which Treat (1) of God; (2) of the Nature & Origin of the Mind; (3) of the Nature & Origin of Effects; (4) of Human Bondage; (5) of the Power of the Intellect, or of Human Liberty. White, W. Hale, tr. 400p. 1996. reprint ed. pap. 39.95 (*1-56459-625-7*) Kessinger Pub.

— Ethics Improvement of Understand. 1989. pap. 8.95 (*0-08-795528-8*, Pergamon Pr) Elsevier.

— Ethics (Including the Improvement of the Understanding) LC 88-63467. (Great Books in Philosophy). 304p. 1989. pap. text 9.95 (*0-87975-528-8*) Prometheus Bks.

— Philosophy of Spinoza. 29.95 (*0-8488-1178-X*) Amereon Ltd.

— A Spinoza Reader: The Ethics & Other Works. Curley, Edwin, ed. & tr. by. LC 93-1628. (ENG & LAT., Illus.). 352p. 1994. text 57.50 (*0-691-03363-3*, Pub. by Princeton U Pr); pap. text 17.95 (*0-691-00067-0*, Pub. by Princeton U Pr) Cal Prin Full Svc.

— Tractatus de Intellectus Emendatione. LC 78-94284. (Select Bibliographies Reprint Ser.). 1977. 19.95 (*0-8369-5057-7*) Ayer.

— Works of Spinoza, Vol. 1. unabridged ed. 1990. 24.00 (*0-8446-2986-3*) Peter Smith.

— Works of Spinoza, Vol. 2. unabridged ed. 1990. 24.00 (*0-8446-6839-7*) Peter Smith.

De Spinoza, Benedictus. Algebraic Calculation of the Rainbow. (Illus.). 26p. 1963. reprint ed. text 47.50 (*90-6004-175-5*, Pub. by B De Graaf) Coronet Bks.

***De Spinoza, Benedictus, et al.** Political Treatise. LC 00-33422. 2000. write for info. (*0-87220-544-4*) Hackett Pub.

De Sponde, Jean. Sonnets on Love & Death, v. II. Nugent, Robert, tr. LC 78-12395. 77p. 1979. reprint ed. lib. bdg. 49.50 (*0-313-21126-4*, SPSL, Greenwood Pr) Greenwood.

de St. Aubin, Ed, jt. ed. see McAdams, Dan P.

de St. Croix, F. W. The Fulani of Northern Nigeria: Some General Notes. LC 73-159763. 74 p. 1972. reprint ed. write for info. (*0-576-17120-4*) Gregg Intl.

De St. Jorre, John. Spain. 2nd ed. (Traveler's Companion Ser.). 1997. pap. text 22.95 (*0-7627-0234-6*) Globe Pequot.

De St. Jorre, John, intro. There's a Whip in My Valise - Greta X. 196p. 1995. pap. 19.95 (*1-897767-12-9*, Pub. by Delectus Bks) Xclusiv Distrib.

De St. Jorre, John, jt. auth. see Edgeworth, Anthony.

De Stadler, Leon, ed. see Eyrich, Christopher.

De Stael, Germaine. Corrine, Italy. Goldberger, Avriel, ed. (FRE.). 434p. 1987. text 50.00 (*0-8135-1207-7*) Rutgers U Pr.

— Delphine. Goldberger, Avriel, tr. LC 94-45742. 550p. 1995. pap. 22.95 (*0-87580-567-1*); lib. bdg. 50.00 (*0-87580-200-1*) N Ill U Pr.

— Major Writings of Germaine de Stael. Folkenflik, Vivian, tr. & intro. by. 411p. (C). 1992. pap. text 21.00 (*0-231-05587-0*) Col U Pr.

— Ten Years of Exile. unabridged ed. Goldberger, Avriel H., tr. from FRE. LC 99-23994.Tr. of Dix Annees d'Exil. 250p. 2000. 45.00 (*0-87580-255-9*) N Ill U Pr.

***De Stael, Germaine & Berger, Morroe.** Politics, Literature & National Character. 321p. 2000. pap. 29.95 (*0-7658-0645-2*) Transaction Pubs.

De Stael, Madame. Corinne ou l'Italie. (Folio Ser.: No. 1632). (FRE.). 632p. 1985. pap. 16.95 (*2-07-037632-X*) Schoenhof.

— Correspondance Generale, 3 tomes. Jasinski, ed. Incl. Tome I, Pt. 1. Lettres de Jeunesse de 1777 a Aout, 1788. 20.95 (*0-8288-9660-7*, F73290); Tome II, Pt. 1. Lettres Inedites a Louis de Norbonne. 26.95 (*0-8288-9662-3*, F73292); Tome II, Pt. 2. Lettres Diverses de 1792 a Mai 1794. 31.95 (*0-8288-9663-1*, F73293); Tome III, Pt. 1. Lettres de Mezery et de Coppet (16 Mai 1794-16 Mai 1795) 27.95 (*0-8288-9664-X*, F73294); Tome III, Pt. 2.

D

Lettres d'une Nouvelle Republicaine. 39.95 (*0-8288-9665-8*, F73295); Tome I, Pt. 2. 1788-1791. 20.95 (*0-8288-9661-5*, F73291); write for info. (*0-318-51972-0*) Fr & Eur.

De Staercke, Andre, ed. NATO's Anxious Birth: The Prophetic Vision of the 1940's. LC 84-40609. (Illus.). 220p. 1985. 29.95 (*0-685-10522-9*) St Martin.

De Stefano, G. F., jt. auth. see Hauser, Gertrud.

De Stefano, G. F., jt. ed. see Roberts, D. F.

De Stefano, Josephine, ed. see D'Amato, James J.

De Steiger, Isabel, tr. see Von Eckarthausen, Karl.

De Stoop, Anne. Living in Portugal. (Illus.). 256p. 1995. 50.00 (*2-08-013567-8*, Pub. by Flammarion) Abbeville Pr.

De Strakosch, Maria. Always Victorious. LC 87-73065. (Illus.). 662p. 1991. 29.95 (*0-930422-39-2*) Dennis-Landman.

— A New Beginning. LC 93-71835. (Illus.). 496p. 1994. 29.95 (*0-930422-11-2*) Dennis-Landman.

De Strange, G., jt. auth. see Palmer, Edward H.

De Strange, Jim. The Strange Experience: How to Become the World's Second Greatest Lover. LC 80-69868. (Illus.). 192p. (Orig.). 1980. per. 29.95 (*0-9605308-1-9*) Ash-Kar Pr.

De Strobel, G. Cayrel & Spite, Monique, eds. The Impact of Very High S-N Spectroscopy on Stellar Physics. (C). 1988. pap. text 99.50 (*90-277-2696-5*); lib. bdg. 234.00 (*90-277-2695-7*) Kluwer Academic.

De Sturgeon, Joanna F. Ensenanza Eficiente = Aprendizaje Feliz.Tr. of Effective Learning = Effective Teaching. (SPA.). 240p. 1998. pap. text 13.99 (*0-311-11600-0*) Casa Bautista.

De, Sumitra. Nationalism & Separatism in Bengal. (C). 1992. 32.50 (*0-7069-5964-7*, Pub. by Vikas) S Asia.

De Suria, Tomas. Tomas de Suria & His Voyage with Malaspina, 1791. 91p. 1980. 18.95 (*0-87770-239-X*) Ye Galleon.

De, Sushil K. Early History of the Vaisnava Faith & Movement in Bengal from Sanskrit & Bengal Sources. 700p. 1986. 54.00 (*0-8364-1642-2*, Pub. by Mukhopadhyaya) S Asia.

De Swaan, Abram. The Management of Normality: Critical Essays in Health & Welfare. LC 89-10352. 228p. (C). 1990. pap. text 16.95 (*0-415-03200-8*, A4157) Routledge.

De Swaan, Abram, ed. Social Policy Beyond Borders: Essays on the Global Social Question. 150p. (Orig.). (C). 1994. pap. 34.50 (*90-5356-069-6*, Pub. by Amsterdam U Pr) U of Mich Pr.

***De Swardt-Kraus, Cobus.** Globalisation for Sale: An Analysis of the Interdynamics of Globalisation, Valorisaton & Marginalisation. 272p. 2000. text 110.00 (*0-7103-0666-0*) Col U Pr.

De Swart, H., et al, eds. Automated Reasoning with Analytic Tableaux & Related Methods: International Conference, TABLEAUX'98, Oisterwijk, the Netherlands, May 5-8, 1998. (Lecture Notes in Computer Science: Vol. 1397). x, 325p. 1998. pap. 55.00 (*3-540-64406-7*) Spr-Verlag.

De Swart, Henriette. Adverbs of Quantification: A Generalized Quantifier Approach. LC 93-6928. (Outstanding Dissertations in Linguistics Ser.). 360p. 1993. text 30.00 (*0-8153-1430-2*) Garland.

— Introduction to Natural Language Semantics. LC 98-13781. (CSLI Lecture Notes Ser.: No. 80). 160p. (C). 1998. text 59.95 (*1-57586-139-9*); pap. text 20.95 (*1-57586-138-0*) CSLI.

De Swiet, Michael. Medical Disorders in Obstetric Practice. 3rd ed. 720p. 1995. 149.95 (*0-632-03671-0*, Pub. by Blckwll Scitfc UK) Blackwell Sci.

De Swiet, Michael & Chamerlain, Geoffrey V., eds. Basic Science in Obstetrics & Gynaecology Pt. 1: A Textbook for the MRCOG. 2nd ed. (Illus.). 298p. 1992. pap. text 60.00 (*0-443-04229-2*) Church.

De Sylva, Geoffrey F. John Ruskin's Modern Painters One & Two: A Phenomenological Analysis. Kuspit, Donald, ed. LC 81-13009. (Studies in the Fine Arts - Art Theory: No. 5). 296p. 1981. reprint ed. pap. 91.80 (*0-8357-1233-8*, 207004300063) Bks Demand.

De Szendeffy, John. For Here or to Go? An ESL Reader. LC 97-60204. 152p. 1997. pap. text 15.95 (*0-472-08397-X*, 08397) U of Mich Pr.

De Tagle, Lilian L., tr. see Collyer, Jaime.

De Tagle, Lillian, tr. see Reilly, Tom.

De Tagle, Lillian L., tr. see De Vallbona, Rima.

De Talleyrand-Perigord, Charles M. Rapport Sur l'Instruction Publique, Fait au Nom du Comite de Constitution a l'Assemblee Nationale: 1791 Edition. Stern, Jeffrey, ed. & intro. by. (Classics in Education Ser.). 216p. 1996. reprint ed. 75.00 (*1-85506-311-5*) Bks Intl VA.

De Taranto, Vasco. Tratado de la Epidemia e de la Pestilenc: Biblioteca Nacional de Madrid, I-51. Purificacion Zabia, Maria, ed. (Medieval Spanish Medical Texts Ser.: No. 16). (SPA.). 6p. 1987. 10.00 incl. fiche (*0-940639-12-2*) Hispanic Seminary.

De Tarr, Francis. The French Radical Party: From Herriot to Mendes-France. LC 80-18231. (Illus.). 264p. 1980. reprint ed. lib. bdg. 55.00 (*0-313-22608-3*, DEFR, Greenwood Pr) Greenwood.

De Tejada, Cristina Saenz, see Saenz De Tejada, Cristina.

De Temmerman, G. A-Z of French Food, French to English. (ENG & FRE.). 145p. 1995. pap. write for info. (*0-320-00546-1*) Fr & Eur.

De Tepla, Johannes & Zacensis, Civis. Epistola cum Libello Ackerman und Das Buechlein Ackerman: Nach der Freiburger Hs. 165 und Nach der Stuttgarter Hs HB X 23, 2 vols., Vol. 1. Bertau, Karl, ed. (GER.). 338p. (C). 1994. lib. bdg. 92.35 (*3-11-014019-5*) De Gruyter.

— Epistola cum Libello Ackerman und Das Buechlein Ackerman: Nach der Freiburger Hs. 165 und Nach der Stuttgarter Hs HB X 23, 2 vols., Vol. 2. Bertau, Karl, ed. (GER.). 807p. (C). 1994. lib. bdg. 306.15 (*3-11-014634-7*) De Gruyter.

de Teran, Lisa St. Aubin, see St. Aubin de Teran, Lisa.

De Terra, Hellmut. Yale North India Expedition: Geological Studies in the Northwest Himalaya Between the Kashmir & Indus Valleys. (Connecticut Academy of Arts & Sciences Ser., Trans.: Vol. 8, Article 2). 1935. pap. 100.00 (*0-685-22865-7*) Elliots Bks.

De Tevis, Rose, et al, eds. El Oro y el Futuro Del Pueblo. (Illus.). 155p. 1979. pap. 5.00 (*0-918358-11-6*) Pajarito Pubns.

De-The, G., ed. see International Symposium on Oncogenesis & Herpesvir.

De Thomasis, Antonio. Le Montreal de Mon Enfance. (FRE.). 40p. (J). 1996. 15.99 (*0-88776-343-X*) Tundra Bks.

— Montreal of My Childhood. LC 95-109227. 40p. (J). (gr. 3 up). 1994. 15.95 (*0-88776-342-1*) Tundra Bks.

De Tienne, Kristen B., jt. auth. see Timm, Paul R.

De Tinguy, Anne. Fall of the Soviet Empire. LC 97-74977. Vol. 481. 320p. 1997. lib. bdg. 45.00 (*0-88033-378-2*, 481, Pub. by East Eur Monographs) Col U Pr.

De Tocqueville, Alexis. Alexis de Tocqueville on Democracy, Revolution & Society. Stone, John et al, eds. LC 79-21204. (Heritage of Sociology Ser.). 402p. (C). 1982. pap. text 17.95 (*0-226-80527-1*) U Ch Pr.

— Ancien Regime et la Revolution. (Folio-Histoire Ser.: No. 5). (FRE.). 384p. 1985. pap. 12.95 (*2-07-032299-8*) Schoenhof.

— Correspondence & Conversations of Alexis de Tocqueville with Nassau W. Senior from 1834 to 1859, 2 vols. in 1. 2nd ed. Simpson, M. C., ed. LC 68-30544. 1968. reprint ed. 65.00 (*0-678-00444-7*) Kelley.

— De la Democratie en Amerique, 2 vols., Vol. 1. (Folio-Histoire Ser.: Nos. 12 & 13). (FRE.). 11.95 (*2-07-032354-4*) Schoenhof.

— De la Democratie en Amerique, 2 vols., Vol. 2. (Folio-Histoire Ser.: Nos. 12 & 13). (FRE.). 11.95 (*2-07-032364-1*) Schoenhof.

— Democracy in America. (C). 1997. pap. text. write for info. (*0-321-02605-5*) Addson-Wesley Educ.

— Democracy in America. 1976. 49.95 (*0-89190-572-3*) Amereon Ltd.

— Democracy in America. 320p. 2000. mass mkt. 7.95 (*0-553-21464-0*) Bantam.

— Democracy in America. 1994. 23.00 (*0-679-43134-9*) Everymns Lib.

***De Tocqueville, Alexis.** Democracy in America. Kessler, Sanford, ed. Grant, Stephen D., tr. LC 99-89940. 368p. (C). 2000. lib. bdg. 34.95 (*0-87220-495-2*) Hackett Pub.

— Democracy in America. LC 99-45202. 800p. 2000. pap. 20.00 (*0-06-095666-6*, Perennial) HarperTrade.

— Democracy in America, 2 vols. Bradley, Phillips, ed. (American Past Ser.). 1945. 60.00 (*0-394-42186-8*) Knopf.

De Tocqueville, Alexis. Democracy in America. Bender, Thomas et al, eds. Reeve, Henry et al, trs. LC 80-24544. (Modern Library College Editions). 603p. (C). 1981. pap. 8.44 (*0-07-554273-0*) McGraw.

— Democracy in America. Hacker, Andrew, ed. Reeve, Henry, tr. 1971. pap. 1.50 (*0-671-48795-7*, WSP) PB.

— Democracy in America. 1999. text 39.95 (*0-312-12813-4*) St Martin.

***De Tocqueville, Alexis.** Democracy in America. abr. ed. Kessler, Sanford, ed. Grant, Stephen D., tr. LC 99-89940. 368p. (C). 2000. pap. 9.95 (*0-87220-494-4*) Hackett Pub.

De Tocqueville, Alexis. Democracy in America. Mayer, J. P., ed. Lawrence, George, tr. from FRE. LC 88-45111. 800p. 1988. reprint ed. pap. 20.00 (*0-06-091522-6*, PL 1522, Perennial) HarperTrade.

— Democracy in America, 2 vols., Set. 51.95 (*0-89190-246-5*) Amereon Ltd.

— Democracy in America, 2 vols., Vol. 1. Bradley, Phillips, ed. LC 90-12474. Vol. 1. 452p. 1990. pap. 13.00 (*0-679-72825-2*) Random.

— Democracy in America, 2 vols., Vol. 2. Bradley, Phillips, ed. LC 89-40517. Vol. 2. 578p. 1990. pap. 13.00 (*0-679-72826-0*) Random.

— Journey to America. rev. ed. Mayer, J. P., ed. Lawrence, George, tr. from FRE. LC 80-22556. 424p. 1981. reprint ed. lib. bdg. 38.50 (*0-313-22712-8*, TOJA, Greenwood Pr) Greenwood.

— Journeys to England & Ireland. 224p. 1987. pap. 21.95 (*0-88738-716-0*) Transaction Pubs.

— Journeys to England & Ireland. Mayer, J. P., ed. LC 78-67392. (European Political Thought Ser.). 1980. reprint ed. lib. bdg. 19.95 (*0-405-11745-0*) Ayer.

— Memoir on Pauperism. Drescher, Seymour, tr. from FRE. LC 97-11895. 84p. 1997. pap. 6.95 (*1-56663-168-8*, Elephant Paperbacks); text 15.00 (*1-56663-167-X*) I R Dee.

— Memoir on Pauperism. Drescher, Seymour, tr. from FRE. (Rediscovered Riches Ser.: No. 2). 40p. 1997. pap. 13.95 (*0-255-36394-X*, Pub. by Inst Economic Affairs) Coronet Bks.

— Oeuvres, Vol. 1. Jardin, Jean, ed. (FRE.). 1991. lib. bdg. 175.00 (*0-7859-3896-6*) Fr & Eur.

— Oeuvres, Vol. 2. Jardin, Andre, ed. (FRE.). 1992. lib. bdg. 155.00 (*0-7859-3901-6*) Fr & Eur.

— Oeuvres Tome 1: Voyages, Ecrites Politiques et Academiques... deluxe ed. (Pleiade Ser.). (FRE.). 99.95 (*2-07-011213-6*) Schoenhof.

— Oeuvres Tome 2: De la Democratie en Amerique I et II. deluxe ed. Lamberti, Jean-Claude, ed. (Pleiade Ser.). (FRE.). 1191p. 1992. 99.95 (*2-07-011228-4*) Schoenhof.

***De Tocqueville, Alexis.** Old Regime & Revolution, Vol. 2. 1998. pap. text 9.95 (*0-226-80534-4*); lib. bdg. 40.00 (*0-226-80533-6*) U Ch Pr.

De Tocqueville, Alexis. Old Regime & the French Revolution. Mayer, J. P. & Kerr, A. P., eds. LC 55-10160. 320p. 1955. pap. 12.95 (*0-385-09260-1*, A60, Anchor NY) Doubleday.

— Old Regime & the French Revolution. Gilbert, Stuart, tr. 1990. 22.25 (*0-8446-1973-6*) Peter Smith.

— The Old Regime & the Revolution. Kahan, Alan S., tr. LC 97-43814. 451p. 1998. 32.50 (*0-226-80529-8*) U Ch Pr.

— Recollections: The French Revolution of 1848. Mayer, J. P., ed. & intro. by. 373p. 1986. reprint ed. pap. 21.95 (*0-88738-658-X*) Transaction Pubs.

— The Recollections of Alexis de Tocqueville. Mayer, J. P., ed. De Mattos, Alexander T., tr. LC 78-13685. 331p. 1979. reprint ed. lib. bdg. 37.50 (*0-313-21052-7*, TRRE, Greenwood Pr) Greenwood.

— Souvenirs. (FRE.). 1978. pap. 13.95 (*0-7859-2891-X*, 2070369919) Fr & Eur.

— Tocqueville's America: The Great Quotations. LC 83-60625. 120p. 1983. pap. 7.95 (*0-8214-0753-8*) Ohio U Pr.

De Tocqueville, Alexis & Heffner, Richard D., eds. Democracy in America. abr. ed. 317p. 1999. mass mkt. 4.00 (*0-451-62801-2*) Addson-Wesley Educ.

De Tocqueville, Alexis, et al. The Old Regime & the Revolution. Kahan, Alan S., tr. from FRE. LC 97-43814. 1998. pap. 32.50 (*0-226-80530-1*) U Ch Pr.

De Tocqueville, Herve. The Two Tocquevilles, Father & Son: Herve & Alexis de Tocqueville on the Coming of the French Revolution. Palmer, R. R., ed. & tr. by. LC 86-30244. (Illus.). 261p. 1987. reprint ed. pap. 81.00 (*0-608-07139-0*, 206736500009) Bks Demand.

De Toledano, Ralph & Chambers, Whittaker. Notes from the Underground: The Ralph de Toledano-Whittaker Chambers Letters, 1949-1960. LC 97-27563. 332p. 1997. 24.95 (*0-89526-425-0*) Regnery Pub.

De Toledo, Alfonso. Invencionario. Gericke, Philip O., ed. (Spanish Ser.: No. 75). xxx, 258p. (C). 1992. text 20.00 (*0-940639-78-5*) Hispanic Seminary.

De Toledo, Sylvie & Edler-Brown, Deborah. Grandparents As Parents: A Survival Guide for Raising a Second Family. LC 95-19656. 322p. 1995. lib. bdg. 40.00 (*1-57230-011-6*); lib. bdg. 16.95 (*1-57230-020-5*) Guilford Pubns.

De Tollenaere, F., jt. ed. see Pynenburg, W.

De Tolnay, Charles Q. History & Technique of Old Master Drawings: A Handbook. LC 70-158334. (Illus.). 1972. reprint ed. 75.00 (*0-87817-107-X*) Hacker.

De Tolosan. Memoire sur la Commerce de la France et de ses Colonies. (Economistes Francais du XVIIIe Siecle Ser.). 1990. reprint ed. pap. 30.00 (*3-601-00159-4*) Periodicals Srv.

De Tormes, Lazarillo. La Vida de Lazarillo de Tormes, y de Sus Fortunas y Adversidades. Carrasco, Felix, ed. (Iberica Ser.: Vol. 23). (SPA.). CLVI, 108p. (C). 1998. pap. text 32.95 (*0-8204-3478-7*) P Lang Pubng.

De Tornyay, Rheba & Thompson, Martha A. Strategies for Teaching Nursing. 3rd ed. LC 86-19060. 353p. (C). 1989. mass mkt. 35.50 (*0-8273-4228-4*) Delmar.

De Toro, Fernando. Theatre Semiotics: Text & Staging in Modern Theatre. (Studies in Semiotics). 256p. 1995. text 60.00 (*0-8020-0634-5*); pap. text 18.95 (*0-8020-7589-4*) U of Toronto Pr.

De Toro y Gisbert, Miguel. Dictionnaire de l'Economie du Droit et du Commerce Vol. 2: Francais - Allemand. (ENG & GER.). 546p. 1987. pap. text 12.95 (*0-7859-4870-8*) Fr & Eur.

De Torquemada, Juan. Juan de Torquemada: A Disputation on the Authority of Pope & Council. Tugwell, Simon, ed. Izbicki, Thomas M., tr. from LAT. & intro. by. (Dominican Sources in English Ser.). 85p. 1988. pap. text 4.00 (*0-9511202-3-9*, Pub. by Dominican Sources) Parable.

De Torre, Emilio, jt. auth. see De Onis, Federico.

De Torres, A. R., jt. auth. see Rose, C. L.

De Torres Villarroel, Diego. Vida. Perez Lopez, Manuel M., ed. (Nueva Austral Ser.: Vol. 90). (SPA.). 1991. pap. text 24.95 (*84-239-1890-4*) Elliots Bks.

— Visiones y Visitas Con Don Francisco de Quevedo. Sebold, Russell P., ed. (Nueva Austral Ser.: Vol. 204). (SPA.). 1991. pap. text 24.95 (*84-239-7204-6*) Elliots Bks.

De Tott, Baron. Memoirs of Baron de Tott, 2 vols. LC 73-6303. (Middle East Ser.). 1973. reprint ed. 51.95 (*0-405-05363-0*) Ayer.

De Toulouse-Lautrec, Henri & Joyant, Maurice. The Art of Cuisine. Weiner, Margery, tr. from FRE. LC 95-13390.Tr. of La Cuisine de Monsieur Momo. 1995. 35.00 (*0-8050-4110-9*) H Holt & Co.

De Tourtoulon, Pierre. Philosophy in the Development of Law. Cohen, Morris R., ed. Read, M. M., tr. 1977. lib. bdg. 59.95 (*0-8490-2428-5*) Gordon Pr.

— Philosophy in the Development of Law. (Modern Legal Philosophy Ser.: Vol. 13). lxi, 653p. 1998. reprint ed. 178.00 (*1-56169-392-8*) Gaunt.

— Philosophy in the Development of Law. Read, Martha M., tr. (Modern Legal Philosophy Ser.: Vol. 13). lxii, 654p. 1969. reprint ed. 55.00 (*0-8377-2626-3*, Rothman) W S Hein.

De Tourville, Abbe. Letters of Direction. LC 84-60628. 111p. 1993. reprint ed. pap. 5.95 (*0-8192-1346-2*) Morehouse Pub.

De Tovar, C. Larrucea, see Tovar, A. & Larrucea De Tovar, C.

De, Trenck Charles. Red Chips. 1998. pap. text 17.95 (*962-7160-64-4*) Asia.

De Trenck, Charles, et al. Red Chips: And the Globalization of China's Enterprises. (Illus.). 217p. 1998. pap. text 17.95 (*962-7160-39-3*) U of Wash Pr.

De Treville Lawrence, Robert, III. Jefferson & Wine: Model of Moderation. (Illus.). 396p. 1988. 20.00 (*0-922983-00-3*) Vinifera Wine.

De Trevino, Elizabeth B. El Guero: A True Adventure Story. (Illus.). 112p. (J). (gr. 3 up). 1989. 14.00 (*0-374-31995-2*) FS&G.

— El Guero: A True Adventure Story. (Illus.). 112p. (J). (gr. 3 up). 1991. pap. 3.95 (*0-374-42028-9*) FS&G.

— El Guero: A True Adventure Story. large type ed. (Illus.). (J). 1995. 29.00 (*0-614-09583-2*, L-81892-00) Am Printing Hse.

— I, Juan De Pareja. LC 65-19330. (Sunburst Ser.). 192p. (YA). (ps-3). 1965. 16.00 (*0-374-33531-1*) FS&G.

— I, Juan De Pareja. LC 65-19330. (Sunburst Ser.). 192p. (YA). (gr. 3-7). 1987. pap. 4.95 (*0-374-43525-1*) FS&G.

— I, Juan de Pareja. (J). 1965. 10.05 (*0-606-04126-5*, Pub. by Turtleback) Demco.

— Yo, Juan de Pareja. Borton, Enrique R. Trevino, tr. from ENG.Tr. of I, Juan de Pareja. (SPA.). 192p. (YA). (gr. 12 up). 1994. 16.00 (*0-374-38699-4*) FS&G.

— Yo, Juan de Pareja - I, Juan de Pareja. Borton, Enrique T., tr. (SPA.). 224p. (YA). (gr. 7 up). 1996. pap. 4.95 (*0-374-49292-1*) FS&G.

De Trevino, Elizabeth Borton, see Borton de Trevino, Elizabeth.

De Trevisa, John. On the Properties of Things: John Trevisa's Translation of Bartholomaeus Anglicus, De Proprietatibus Rerum: A Critical Text, Vol. III. 338p. 1988. text 125.00 (*0-19-818530-8*) OUP.

***de Trez, Michel.** First Airborne Task Force: Pictorial History of the Allied Paratroopers in the Invasion of Southern France. (Illus.). 1998. 95.00 (*2-9600176-2-5*) D Day.

De Triana, Rita Vega, see Vega de Triana, Rita.

De Tripitaka Hua, Maestro. Explicacion General Del Sutra En Que El Buda Habla De Amitabha. Buddhist Text Translation Society Staff, tr. 153p. 1979. pap. 8.00 (*0-917512-30-8*) Buddhist Text.

De Troyes, Chretien. Arthurian Romances. Owen, D. D., ed. & tr. by. 550p. 1993. pap. 8.95 (*0-460-87389-X*, Everyman's Classic Lib) Tuttle Pubng.

— Arthurian Romances. Kibler, William W. & Carroll, Carleton W., trs. 528p. 1991. pap. 12.95 (*0-14-044521-8*) Viking Penguin.

— Cliges. Gregory, Stewart & Luttrell, Claude, eds. (Arthurian Studies: No. XXVIII). 429p. (C). 1993. 99.00 (*0-85991-383-X*) Boydell & Brewer.

***De Troyes, Chretien.** Cliges. Cline, Ruth H., tr. from FRO. LC 99-30723. 280p. 1999. 35.00 (*0-8203-2147-8*) U of Ga Pr.

— Cliges. Cline, Ruth H., tr. from FRO. LC 99-30723. (Illus.). 280p. 1999. pap. 15.00 (*0-8203-2142-7*) U of Ga Pr.

De Troyes, Chretien. Cliges. Raffel, Burton, tr. LC 96-52694. 240p. 1997. 30.00 (*0-300-07020-9*); pap. 16.00 (*0-300-07021-7*) Yale U Pr.

— Erec & Enide. Cline, Ruth H., tr. from FRO. LC 99-30721. 280p. 1999. pap. 15.00 (*0-8203-2141-9*) U of Ga Pr.

***De Troyes, Chretien.** Erec & Enide. Cline, Ruth H., tr. from FRO. LC 99-30721. 280p. 1999. 35.00 (*0-8203-2146-X*) U of Ga Pr.

De Troyes, Chretien. Erec et Enide. Gilbert, Dorothy, tr. & intro. by. (C). 1992. 45.00 (*0-520-07345-2*, Pub. by U CA Pr); pap. 16.95 (*0-520-07346-0*, Pub. by U CA Pr) Cal Prin Full Svc.

— Erec et Enide. Raffel, Burton, tr. LC 96-35477. 200p. 1997. 30.00 (*0-300-06770-4*); pap. 16.00 (*0-300-06771-2*) Yale U Pr.

— Lancelot: The Knight of the Cart. Raffel, Burton, tr. from FRO. LC 97-14424. 208p. 1997. pap. 16.00 (*0-300-07121-3*) Yale U Pr.

— Perceval: The Story of the Grail. Bryant, Nigel, tr. (Arthurian Studies Ser.: No. 5). (Illus.). 334p. 1996. reprint ed. pap. 29.95 (*0-85991-224-8*) Boydell & Brewer.

— Perceval O el Cuento del Grial. De Riquer, Martin, ed. & tr. by. (Nueva Austral Ser.: Vol. 227). (SPA.). 1991. pap. text 24.95 (*84-239-7227-5*) Elliots Bks.

— Romans de la Table Ronde: Erec et Enide, Cliges, Lancelot, Yvain (MO) (Folio Ser.: No. 696). (FRE.). pap. 10.95 (*2-07-036696-0*) Schoenhof.

— Yvain, Ou le Chevalier au Lion. Nelson, Jan A., ed. LC 68-22800. (Medieval French Literature Ser.). (Orig.). (C). 1968. pap. 9.95 (*0-89197-477-6*) Irvington.

— Yvain, the Knight of the Lion. LC 86-23346. 224p. 1987. pap. 16.00 (*0-300-03838-0*) Yale U Pr.

— Ywain: The Knight of the Lion. rev. ed. Ackerman, Robert et al, trs. from FRE. 114p. (C). 1992. reprint ed. pap. text 7.50 (*0-88133-716-1*) Waveland Pr.

De Troyes, Chretien & Louis, Rene. Erec et Enide: Traducion en Francais Moderne. (FRE.). 187p. 1980. pap. 24.95 (*0-7859-5236-5*) Fr & Eur.

De Tryon, Charles F., see Montalembert, Charles, pseud.

De Turner, Clorinda M. Torn from the Nest. Carnejo-Polar, Antonio, ed. Polt, John R., tr. LC 97-40726. (Library of Latin America). 224p. 1998. 30.00 (*0-19-511005-6*) OUP.

De Turnhout, Gerard. Gerard de Turnhout Pt. I: Sacred & Secular Songs for Three Voices: Songs to Latin Texts. Wagner, Lavern J., ed. (Recent Researches in Music of the Renaissance Ser.: Vol. RRR9). (Illus.). 107p. 1970. pap. 35.00 (*0-89579-022-X*) A-R Eds.

— Gerard de Turnhout Pt. II: Sacred & Secular Songs for Three Voices: Songs to Latin & French Texts. Wagner, Lavern J., ed. (Recent Researches in Music of the Renaissance Ser.: Vol. RRR10). 101p. 1970. pap. 35.00 (*0-89579-023-8*) A-R Eds.

De Ullmann, Stephan. Epic of the Finnish Nation. 1977. lib. bdg. 59.95 (*0-8490-1780-7*) Gordon Pr.

De Ulloa, Leanor Alvarez, see Ulloa, Justo.

De Ulloa, Leonor A., jt. auth. see Ulloa, Justo.

de Unamuno, Miguel, see Unamuno, Miguel de.

De Urbal, F. J., ed. see Pidal, Ramon M.

D

De Urbel, Justo P. Historia de Espana Vol. 6: Los Comienzos de la Reconquista (711-1038) 660p. 1992. 189.50 (*84-239-4808-0*) Elliots Bks.

De Urbina, Jon O. Some Parameters in the Grammar of Basque. (Studies in Generative Grammar). xii, 266p. (Orig.). (C). 1989. pap. 90.80 (*90-6765-337-3*) Mouton.

De Urbina, Jon Ortiz, jt. ed. see Hualde, Jose Ignacio.

De Urrea. Penitencia de Amor. (Exeter Hispanic Text Ser.: No. 49). (SPA.). 112p. Date not set. pap. text 17.95 (*0-85989-337-5*, Pub. by Univ Exeter Pr) Northwestern U Pr.

De Urrutia y Matos, Bernardo J. Cuba Fomento de la Isla, 1749: Primer Estudio Geo-Economico de la Isla. 2nd ed. (SPA.). 111p. 1993. pap. 13.00 (*0-89729-636-2*) Ediciones.

De Usabel, Frances. American Indian Resource Manual. 150p. (C). 1992. pap. text 27.00 (*1-57337-005-3*) WI Dept Pub Instruct.

***De Usabel, Frances & Swanson, Coral S.** Public Library Services for Youth with Special Needs: A Plan for Wisconsin. (Illus.). 60p. 2000. pap. text 20.00 (*0-7567-0032-9*) DIANE Pub.

de Usabel, Gaizka S. The High Noon of American Films in Latin America. Kirkpatrick, Diane, ed. LC 82-1843. (Studies in Cinema: No. 17). 333p. 1982. reprint ed. pap. 103.30 (*0-8357-1311-3*, 207021000064) Bks Demand.

De V. Booysen, P. & Tainton, N. M., eds. Ecological Effects of Fire in South African Ecosystems. (Ecological Studies, Analysis & Synthesis: Vol. 48). (Illus.). 440p. 1984. 85.95 (*0-387-13501-4*) Spr-Verlag.

de Vaan, J. M. Ich bin eine Schwertklinge des Konigs' Die Sprache des Bel-ibni. (Alter Orient und Altes Testament Ser.: Vol. 242). (GER.). xiv, 549p. 1995. text 109.50 (*3-7887-1536-7*, Pub. by NeukirchenerV) Eisenbrauns.

de Vaca, Alvar Nunez Cabeza, see Nunez Cabeza de Vaca, Alvar.

de Vaca, Alvar Nunez Cabeza, see Johnston, Lissa J. & Nunez Cabeza de Vaca, Alvar.

De Vaca, Cabeza. The Power Within Us. Long, Haniel, ed. & tr. by. (Illus.). 50p. 1976. 75.00 (*0-933861-06-0*) H Berliner.

De Vachon, M., jt. auth. see Levy, G.

De Vahl Davis, Graham. Numerical Methods in Enginering & Science. (Illus.). 288p. 1986. text 70.00 (*0-04-515002-8*); pap. text 24.95 (*0-04-515003-6*) Routledge.

De Valdeavellano, Luis Garcia, see Garcia de Valdeavellano, Luis.

De Valdes, Alfonso. Dialogue of Mercury & Charon. Ricapito, Joseph V., tr. LC 84-48489.Tr. of Dialogo de Mercurio y Charon. 206p. 1986. reprint ed. pap. 63.90 (*0-7837-9647-1*, 205928000005) Bks Demand.

De Valdes, Maria E. The Shattered Mirror: Representations of Women in Mexican Literature. LC 97-16813. (Texas Pan American Ser.). 284p. (C). 1998. 35.00 (*0-292-71591-9*, DEVSHA); pap. 17.95 (*0-292-71590-0*, DEVSHP) U of Tex Pr.

De Valdes, Maria E. & Valdes, Mario J., eds. Approaches to Teaching Garcia Marquez's One Hundred Years of Solitude. LC 90-6555. (Approaches to Teaching World Literature Ser.: No. 31). x, 156p. 1990. pap. 18.00 (*0-87352-536-1*, AP31P); lib. bdg. 37.50 (*0-87352-535-3*, AP31C) Modern Lang.

De Valdez, Delores D., et al. Preparation for Citizenship. 1997. pap., student ed. 10.56 (*0-8114-7987-0*) Raintree Steck-V.

De Vale, Sue C., jt. ed. see Jairazbhoy, Nazir A.

***de Valence.** Building in Value. 416p. 1999. pap. 64.95 (*0-470-35566-2*) Wiley.

De Valencia, Jose. Methode de Flamenco pour la Guitare. Lefferts, Michael, ed. (FRE.). 32p. (Orig.). (C). 1997. pap. text 11.95 (*0-7692-1317-0*, 01010306) Wrner Bros.

De Valencia, Ruby & Volsky, Jeannine S. Design in Venezuelan Petroglyphs. Pampero Foundation Staff, ed.Tr. of Diseno en los Petroglifos Venezolanos; Dessins dans les Petroglighes Venezuelien. (ENG, FRE & SPA., Illus.). 409p. 1989. 100.00 (*980-265-805-7*, Pub. by FUNDACOMUN) Sterling.

De Valenzuela, Fernando, tr. see Kundera, Milan.

De Valinger, Leone, Jr. The Reconstructed 1790 Census of Delaware. (Illus.). 83p. 1954. 9.50 (*0-915156-10-5*, 10) Natl Genealogical.

De Valk, J. P. Integrated Diagnostic Imaging. 386p. 1992. 268.75 (*0-444-81426-4*) Elsevier.

De Valk, J. P., ed. Integrated Diagnostic Imaging: Digital PACS in Medicine. 1992. write for info. (*0-318-69716-5*) Elsevier.

***De Valk, Jeroen.** Chet Baker: His Life & Music. (Illus.). 256p. 2000. pap. 15.95 (*1-893163-13-X*, Pub. by Berkeley Hills) Publishers Group.

De Valk, P. & Wekwete, K. H. Decentralising for Participatory Planning: Comparing the Experience of Zimbabwe & Other Anglophone Countries in Eastern & Southern Africa. (Illus.). 277p. 1990. text 91.95 (*0-566-07113-4*, Pub. by Avebry) Ashgate Pub Co.

De Valk, Peter. African Industry in Decline: The Case of Textiles in Tanzania in the 1980's. (Institute of Social Studies, The Hague Ser.). 384p. 1996. text 69.95 (*0-312-16021-6*) St Martin.

De Vall, Julio G. Heredia y la Libertad. LC 78-57696. 1978. pap. 12.95 (*0-89729-193-X*) Ediciones.

De Valladolid, Alfonso. Text & Concordances of Sermones Contra Iudios e Moros, MS 25H: Biblioteca Publica y Provincial de Soria. Dagenais, John et al, eds. (Spanish Ser.: No. 65). (SPA.). 12p. 1991. 40.00 incl. fiche (*0-940639-59-9*) Hispanic Seminary.

De Vallbona, Rima. Flowering Inferno: Tales of Sinking Hearts. De Tagle, Lillian L., tr. from SPA. LC 93-39645. (Discoveries Ser.). 92p. 1994. pap. 12.95 (*0-935480-64-1*) Lat Am Lit Rev Pr.

De Vallejo, Catharina V. Antologia de la Poesia del Romanticismo Hispanoamericano: (1820-1890) LC 93-70446. (Coleccion Textos). (SPA., Illus.). 406p. (Orig.). 1993. pap. 25.00 (*0-89729-675-3*) Ediciones.

— Elementos Para Una Semiotica Del Cuento Hispanoamericano Del Siglo XX. LC 91-73367. (SPA.). 165p. (Orig.). 1992. pap. 19.95 (*0-89729-614-1*) Ediciones.

— Teoria Cuentistica del Siglo XX: Aproximaciones Hispanicas. LC 88-80976. (Coleccion Textos). (SPA.). 278p. (Orig.). (C). 1989. pap. 15.00 (*0-89729-485-8*) Ediciones.

De Valois, Karen K., jt. auth. see De Valois, Russell L.

De Valois, Ninette. Collected Poems. 80p. 1998. pap. 19.95 (*1-85754-376-9*, Pub. by Carcanet Pr) Paul & Co Pubs.

— Come Dance with Me: A Memoir. LC 79-25045. (Series in Dance). (Illus.). 1980. reprint ed. lib. bdg. 29.50 (*0-306-79616-3*) Da Capo.

— Come Dance with Me: A Memoir 1898-1956. 238p. 1992. pap. 15.95 (*0-946640-62-9*, Pub. by Lilliput Pr) Irish Bks Media.

De Valois, Ninette, jt. auth. see Walker, Kathrine Sorley.

De Valois, Russell L. & De Valois, Karen K. Spatial Vision. (Oxford Psychology Ser.: No. 14). (Illus.). 402p. 1990. reprint ed. pap. text 55.00 (*0-19-506657-X*) OUP.

De Valuy, A. & Borel, B. The French Riviera: A Picture Guide. 1976. lib. bdg. 59.95 (*0-8490-1865-X*) Gordon Pr.

De Van. Verdi, a Theatre of Music: Creating Drama through Music. Roberts, Gilda, tr. from FRE. LC 97-46109. 392p. 1998. pap. text 25.00 (*0-226-14370-8*) U Ch Pr.

De Van Etten, Teresa Pijoan, see Pijoan de Van Etten, Teresa.

De Vaney, Ann, ed. Watching Channel One: The Convergence of Students, Technology, & Private Business. LC 93-28980. (SUNY Series, Education & Culture). 244p. (C). 1994. text 64.50 (*0-7914-1947-9*); pap. text 21.95 (*0-7914-1948-7*) State U NY Pr.

De Vaney, Ann, et al. Technology & Resistance: Decentralized Communications & New Coalitions Around the World. LC 97-17112. (Counterpoints Ser.: No. 59). 192p. (C). 2000. pap. text 24.95 (*0-8204-3795-6*) P Lang Pubng.

De Vany, Arthur S. Inland Waterways: Institutions, Economics & Policy. (C). 1998. pap. 55.00 (*0-8133-3183-8*) Westview.

— Master Optical Techniques. LC 80-24442. (Wiley Series in Pure & Applied Optics). 608p. reprint ed. pap. 188.50 (*0-7837-2368-7*, 204005400006) Bks Demand.

De Vany, Arthur S. & Walls, W. David. The Emerging New Order in Natural Gas: Markets vs. Regulation. LC 94-46198. 240p. 1995. 57.95 (*0-89930-944-5*, Quorum Bks) Greenwood.

De Vany, Arthur S., et al. A Property System Approach to the Electromagnetic Spectrum: A Legal-Economic-Engineering Study. (Cato Papers: No. 10). 87p. 1980. pap. 1.00 (*0-932790-11-9*) Cato Inst.

***De Varennes, Fernand.** Asia-Pacific Human Rights Documents & Resources, Vol. 2. 640p. 1999. 172.25 (*90-411-1318-5*) Kluwer Law Intl.

De Varennes, Fernand. Language, Minorities & Human Rights. LC 96-521. (International Studies in Human Rights: No. 45). 552p. 1996. 192.50 (*90-411-0206-X*) Kluwer Law Intl.

De Vargas, Diego. By Force of Arms: The Journals of Don Diego de Vargas, New Mexico, 1691-93. Kessell, John L. et al, eds. LC 92-4067. (Journals of Don Diego de Vargas). (Illus.). 684p. 1992. reprint ed. pap. 200.00 (*0-608-04114-9*, 206484700011) Bks Demand.

— Remote Beyond Compare: Letters of don Diego de Vargas to His Family from New Spain & New Mexico, 1675-1706. Kessell, John L., ed. LC 88-27651. (Journals of don Diego de Vargas Ser.). (Illus.). 610p. 1989. reprint ed. pap. 189.10 (*0-608-04137-8*, 206487000011) Bks Demand.

***De Vargas, Diego & Kessell, John L.** That Disturbances Cease: The Journals of Don Diego de Vargas, New Mexico, 1697-1700. LC 99-50507. (Journals of Don Diego de Vargas). (Illus.). 2000. 50.00 (*0-8263-2143-7*) U of NM Pr.

De Varona. Cuba. (J). 1996. pap. 15.98 (*0-8050-4371-3*) St Martin.

de Varona, Ana R. Lesbia, see Martin, Rita & Lesbia de Varona, Ana R., eds.

De Varona, Carlos, ed. & tr. see Bustamante, Ines S.

De Varona, Frank. Benito Juarez, President of Mexico. LC 92-19349. (Hispanic Heritage Ser.). (Illus.). 32p. (J). (gr. 2-4). 1993. pap. 4.95 (*1-56294-807-5*); lib. bdg. 19.90 (*1-56294-279-4*) Millbrook Pr.

— Latino Literacy: The Complete Guide to Hispanic American Culture & History. 384p. 1995. 30.00 (*0-8050-3858-2*); pap. 16.95 (*0-8050-3859-0*) H Holt & Co.

— Latino Literacy: The Complete Guide to Hispanic American Culture & History. (Illus.). 192p. 1996. pap. 22.50 (*0-8050-5031-0*) H Holt & Co.

— Miguel Hidalgo y Costilla: Father of Mexican Independence. (Hispanic Heritage Ser.). (J). 1993. 10.15 (*0-606-07870-3*) Turtleback.

— Miguel Hidalgo y Costilla - Father of Mexican Independence. LC 92-36562. (Hispanic Heritage Ser.). (Illus.). 32p. (J). (gr. 2-4). 1993. lib. bdg. 19.90 (*1-56294-370-7*) Millbrook Pr.

— Simon Bolivar: Latin American Liberator. LC 92-19459. (Hispanic Heritage Ser.). (Illus.). 32p. (J). (gr. 2-4). 1993. pap. 4.95 (*1-56294-812-1*); lib. bdg. 19.90 (*1-56294-278-6*) Millbrook Pr.

De, Varona Frank. Simon Bolivar: Latin American Liberator. 1993. pap. text 4.95 (*0-395-68524-9*) HM.

De Varthema, Ludovico. Die Ritterlich und Lobwirdig Rayss. LC 92-23009. 176p. 1992. 55.00 (*0-8201-1477-4*) Schol Facsimiles.

De Varthema, Ludovico, jt. auth. see Hammond, Lincoln D.

De Vattel, Emmerich. Le Droit des Gens ou Principes de la Loi Naturelle, 2 vols. LC 95-77088. (Classics in International Law Reprint Ser.: No. 4, Vol. 1-2). 1995. reprint ed. 240.00 (*1-57588-507-7*) W S Hein.

De Vattel, Emmerich. The Law of Nations. LC 75-31104. 664p. reprint ed. 89.50 (*0-404-13519-6*) AMS Pr.

De Vaucouleurs, Antoinette & Longo, Giuseppe. Catalogue of Visual & Infrared Photometry of Galaxies from 0.5 um to 10 um (1961-1985) Joy, Marshall, ed. (Monographs in Astronomy: No. 5). 210p. (Orig.). 1988. pap. 10.00 (*0-9603796-5-7*) U of Tex Dept Astron.

De Vaucouleurs, Antoinette, jt. auth. see De Vaucouleurs, Gerard H.

De Vaucouleurs, Antoinette, jt. auth. see Longo, Giuseppe.

De Vaucouleurs, Gerard H. & De Vaucouleurs, Antoinette. Second Reference Catalogue of Bright Galaxies. LC 75-44009. (Texas University Monographs in Astronomy: No. 2). 404p. reprint ed. pap. 125.30 (*0-608-18536-1*, 202115300021) Bks Demand.

De Vaucouleurs, Gerard H., et al. Third Reference Catalogue of Bright Galaxies, 3 vols. (Illus.). 1991. 259.95 (*0-387-97552-7*); 98.95 (*0-387-97549-7*) Spr-Verlag.

— Third Reference Catalogue of Bright Galaxies, 3 vols., Vol. 2: Data for Galaxies Between Oh & 12h. (Illus.). viii, 723p. 1991. 109.95 (*0-387-97550-0*) Spr-Verlag.

— Third Reference Catalogue of Bright Galaxies, 3 vols., Vol. 3: Data for Galaxies Between 12h & 24h. (Illus.). viii, 632p. 1991. 109.95 (*0-387-97551-9*) Spr-Verlag.

De Vaul, Diane. Iowa Legacy. (WEP Poetry Ser.: No. 3). (Orig.). 1979. pap. 1.50 (*0-917976-07-X*) Thunder Baas Pr.

De Vault, Christine, jt. auth. see Strong, Bryan.

De Vaus, David. Surveys in Social Work. 4th ed. 424p. 1996. pap. 29.95 (*1-86373-939-4*, Pub. by Allen & Unwin Pty) Paul & Co Pubs.

De Vaus, David A. Surveys in Social Research. LC 85-9146. (Contemporary Social Research Ser.: No. 11). 240p. 1986. text 55.00 (*0-04-312023-7*); pap. text 18.95 (*0-04-312024-5*) Routledge.

— Surveys in Social Research. 2nd ed. 346p. (C). 1990. pap. text 21.95 (*0-04-445722-7*) Routledge.

— Surveys in Social Research. 3rd ed. 400p. (C). 1992. pap. text 24.95 (*1-86373-099-0*, Pub. by Allen & Unwin Pty) Paul & Co Pubs.

De Vaux, Roland. Ancient Israel: Its Life & Institutions. McHugh, John, tr. LC 97-4938. (The Biblical Resource Ser.). 616p. 1997. pap. 30.00 (*0-8028-4278-X*) Eerdmans.

— Die Ausgrabungen von Qumran und en Feschcha: Die Grabungstagebucher. (Novum Testamentum et Orbis Antiquus Series Archaeologic: Vol. 1a). (GER.). 230p. 1996. text 63.00 (*3-7278-1073-4*, Pub. by Presses Univ Fribourg) Eisenbrauns.

De Vaux, Roland & Milik, Jozef T. Discoveries in the Judaean Desert: Qumran Grotte 4-11, Vol. 6. (Illus.). 106p. 1977. text 110.00 (*0-19-826317-1*) OUP.

De Vazquez, Margot Arce, see Arce de Vazquez, Margot.

De Veaux, Scott. The Birth of Bebop: A Social & Musical History. 587p. 1999. pap. 18.95 (*0-520-21665-2*, Pub. by U CA Pr) Cal Prin Full Svc.

De Veaux, Alexis. Don't Explain: A Song of Billie Holiday. 151p. (YA). (gr. 9 up). 1989. reprint ed. pap. 7.95 (*0-86316-132-4*) Writers & Readers.

— An Enchanted Hair Tale. LC 85-45824. (Illus.). 40p. (J). (gr. k-3). 1987. lib. bdg. 14.89 (*0-06-021624-7*) HarpC Child Bks.

— The Woolu Hat. 1997. 15.00 (*0-517-70099-9*); lib. bdg. 16.99 (*0-517-70100-6*) Random.

De Vecchi. Diccionari Catala-Castella i Castella-Catala. (CAT & ENG.). 968p. 1988. 69.95 (*0-7859-5901-7*, 8431501820) Fr & Eur.

De Vecchi, A., jt. ed. see Ponticelli, C.

De Vecchi, Nicolo. Entrepreneurs, Institutions & Economic Change: The Economic Thought of J. A. Schumpeter (1905-1925) Stone, Anne, tr. LC 95-5520. 224p. 1995. 90.00 (*1-85898-209-X*) E Elgar.

De Vecchi, Pieluigi. Michelangelo. (Illus.). 160p. 1998. reprint ed. write for info. (*1-56852-202-9*, Konecky & Konecky) W S Konecky Assocs.

De Vecchi, Pierluigi. Michelangelo: The Vatican Frescoes. 1997. 85.00 (*0-614-28067-2*) Abbeville Pr.

De Vecchi, Pierluigi & Colalucci, Gianluigi. Michelangelo: The Vatican Frescoes: The Complete Works Restored. (Illus.). 272p. 1997. 85.00 (*0-7892-0142-9*) Abbeville Pr.

De Vecchia, Ruth M. Sleep Research & Polysomnography: Index of New Information. rev. ed. 180p. 1997. 47.50 (*0-7883-1596-X*); pap. 44.50 (*0-7883-1597-8*) ABBE Pubs Assn.

De Vee Dixon, Joan. George Rochberg: A Bio-Bibliographic Guide to His Life & Works. LC 92-3452. (Illus.). 1992. lib. bdg. 48.00 (*0-945193-12-2*) Pendragon NY.

De Veen, Jan, jt. auth. see Stock, Elisabeth A.

De Veer, Gerrit. The True & Perfect Description of Three Voyages. LC 93-7016. 500p. 1993. 100.00 (*0-8201-1478-2*) Schol Facsimiles.

— A True & Perfect Description of Three Voyages by the Ships of Holland & Zeland. Phillip, W., tr. LC 75-25746. (English Experience Ser.: No. 274). 164p. 1970. reprint ed. 30.00 (*90-221-0274-2*) Walter J Johnson.

De Vega, H. J. Integrable Quantum Field Theories & Statistical Models: Yang-Baxter & Kac-Moody Algebras. 350p. 1998. text 40.00 (*9971-5-0052-3*) World Scientific Pub.

De Vega, H. J. & Ge, M. L. Quantum Groups, Integrable Statistical Models & Knot: Nankai Lectures on Mathematical Physics Ser. 352p. 1993. text 100.00 (*981-02-1474-X*) World Scientific Pub.

De Vega, H. J. & Sanchez, N. Second Paris Cosmology Colloquium. 560p. 1995. text 136.00 (*981-02-2172-X*) World Scientific Pub.

De Vega, H. J. & Sanchez, N., eds. Field Theory, Quantum Gravity & Strings. (Lecture Notes in Physics Ser.: Vol. 246). vi, 381p. 1986. 48.95 (*0-387-16452-9*) Spr-Verlag.

— Field Theory, Quantum Gravity & Strings II. (Lecture Notes in Physics Ser.: Vol. 280). v, 245p. 1987. 13.95 (*0-387-17925-9*) Spr-Verlag.

— String Theory - Quantum Cosmology & Quantum Gravity Integrable & Conformal Variant Theories: Proceedings of the Paris-Meudon Colloquium, Meudon, France, September 22-26, 1986. 524p. 1987. pap. 58.00 (*9971-5-0299-2*); text 137.00 (*9971-5-0286-0*) World Scientific Pub.

De Vega, H.J. Fourth Paris Cosmology Colloquium: Phrase Transitions in Cosmology Euroconference. LC 98-4709. 1998. 78.00 (*981-02-3438-4*) World Scientific Pub.

de Vega, Lope. Arte Nuevo de Hacer Comedias. (SPA.). 153p. 1981. 9.95 (*0-8288-7163-9*, S9043) Fr & Eur.

— Bella Malmaridada. McGrady, Donald et al, eds. 206p. 1986. pap. 32.00 (*84-599-1505-0*) Biblio Siglo.

— The Best Boy in Spain (El Mejor Mozo de Espana) Gitlitz, David M., tr. from ENG. LC 99-11729. 208p. 2000. pap. 24.00 (*0-927534-85-1*, Pub. by Biling Rev-Pr) SPD-Small Pr Dist.

— La Buena Guarda. (SPA.). 125p. 1964. 7.95 (*0-8288-7162-0*, S9044) Fr & Eur.

— El Caballero de Olmedo. unabridged ed. (SPA.). pap. 5.95 (*84-410-0007-7*, Pub. by Bookking Intl) Distribks Inc.

— El Caballero de Olmedo. 6th ed. 168p. 1991. pap. write for info. (*0-7859-5205-5*) Fr & Eur.

— Carlos V en Francia. Reichenberger, Arnold G., ed. LC 61-6615. (Illus.). 260p. 1962. 24.95 (*0-910278-53-9*) Boulevard.

— El Castigo Sin Venganza. 264p. 1990. pap. 11.95 (*0-7859-5211-X*) Fr & Eur.

— El Castigo Sin Venganza. unabridged ed. (SPA.). pap. 5.95 (*84-410-0063-8*, Pub. by Bookking Intl) Distribks Inc.

— La Corona Tragica de Lope de Vega. LC 81-51027. (SPA., Illus.). 276p. 1982. 17.00 (*0-938972-01-4*) Spanish Lit Pubns.

— La Dama Boba. Zamora Vicente, Alonso, ed. (Nueva Austral Ser.: No. 177). (SPA.). 1991. pap. text 10.95 (*84-239-1977-3*) Elliots Bks.

— Dama Boba - Nina de Plata. 10th ed. 176p. 1990. pap. 10.95 (*0-7859-5185-7*) Fr & Eur.

— Desire's Experience Transformed: A Representative Anthology of Lope de Vega's Lyric Poetry. Cobb, Carl W., tr. & intro. by. LC 91-60466. (ENG & SPA.). 304p. 1991. 40.00 (*0-938972-18-9*) Spanish Lit Pubns.

— The Dog in the Manger (El Perro del Hortelano) 2nd ed. Dixon, Victor, tr. 125p. 1990. pap. 8.95 (*0-919473-74-1*, PDH59, Pub. by Dovehouse) Sterling.

— La Dorotea. (SPA.). 357p. 1946. 9.95 (*0-8288-7108-6*, S31264) Fr & Eur.

— La Dorotea. (SPA.). 496p. 1980. 16.25 (*0-8288-7179-5*) Fr & Eur.

— La Dorotea. (Biblioteca De Cultura Basica Ser.). 625p. 1955. pap. 2.80 (*0-8477-0709-1*) U of PR Pr.

— La Dorotea. Trueblood, Alan S. & Honig, Edwin, eds. LC 84-22371. 363p. reprint ed. pap. 112.60 (*0-7837-6078-7*, 205912400007) Bks Demand.

— Epistolario de Lope de Vega Carpio, 4 vols. De Amezua, Agustin G., ed. (Real Academia Ediciones Ser.). (SPA.). 2058p. 1993. 500.00 (*84-600-7292-4*) Elliots Bks.

— La Estrella de Sevilla. LC 80-66393. (Coleccion Teatro). (SPA.). 167p. (Orig.). 1984. pap. 14.95 (*0-89729-256-1*) Ediciones.

— La Estrella de Sevilla. (SPA.). 125p. 1971. 7.95 (*0-8288-7110-8*, S9064) Fr & Eur.

— La Francesilla. McGrady, Donald, ed. 236p. 1981. pap. 19.00 (*84-499-4456-2*) Biblio Siglo.

— Fuente Ovejuna. Dixon, Victor, ed. (Hispanic Classics Ser.). (Illus.). 223p. 1989. 59.95 (*0-85668-327-2*, Pub. by Aris & Phillips) David Brown.

— Fuente Ovejuna. Colford, William E., tr. 1969. pap. 4.95 (*0-8120-0308-X*) Barron.

— Fuente Ovejuna. Eigenauer, John D., ed. (SPA.). 71p. 1987. pap. text 11.95 (*0-9625734-0-X*) Darien Pub.

***de Vega, Lope.** Fuente Ovejuna. (SPA.). 1999. 13.00 (*84-481-0624-5*, McGrw-H College) McGrw-H Hghr Educ.

de Vega, Lope. Fuente Ovejuna. Dixon, ed. (Hispanic Classics Ser.). 1989. reprint ed. pap. 25.00 (*0-85668-328-0*, Pub. by Aris & Phillips) David Brown.

— Fuenteovejuna. (SPA.). pap. 12.95 (*84-376-0273-4*, Pub. by Ediciones Catedra) Continental Bk.

— Fuenteovejuna. 10th ed. 192p. 1989. pap. write for info. (*0-7859-5152-0*) Fr & Eur.

— Fuenteovejuna, Peribanez y el Comendador de Ocana, el Mejor Alcalde el Rey, el Caballero de Olmedo. (SPA.). pap. 8.95 (*968-432-027-2*, Pub. by Porrua) Continental Bk.

— La Gatomaquia. 232p. 1983. pap. 16.95 (*0-7859-5187-3*) Fr & Eur.

— The Knight of Olmedo: El Caballero de Olmedo. King, Willard F., ed. LC 78-186118. (ENG & SPA.). 214p. reprint ed. pap. 66.40 (*0-7837-1466-1*, 205716100017) Bks Demand.

— Lady Nitwit/La Dama Boda. Oliver, William I., tr. from SPA. LC 98-13215. 182p. (Orig.). 1998. pap. 24.00 (*0-927534-74-6*) Biling Rev-Pr.

— Lope de Vega's "El Desden Vengado" Harlan, Mabel M., ed. & intro. by. xliv, 196p. 1938. 3.60 (*0-318-22347-3*) Hispanic Inst.

— Lope de Vega's "Los Espanoles en Flandes" A Critical Edition. Sauter, Veronica M., ed. LC 95-13285. (Iberica Ser.: No. 17). (Illus.). X, 286p. (C). 1998. text 52.95 (*0-8204-2824-8*) P Lang Pubng.

An Asterisk (*) at the beginning of an entry indicates that the title is appearing for the first time.

— Madness in Valencia & the Witless Lady. 144p. 1996. pap. text 14.95 (*0-948230-66-5*) Theatre Comm.
— El Mejor Alcalde, el Rey. Marin Martinez, Juan M., ed. (Nueva Austral Ser.: No. 118). (SPA.). 1991. pap. text 11.95 (*84-239-1918-8*) Elliots Bks.
— El Mejor Alcalde, el Rey. 16th ed. 144p. 1990. pap. 12.95 (*0-7859-5160-1*) Fr & Eur.
— Los Melindres de Belisa - El Villano en Su Rincon. 5th ed. 1980. pap. 12.95 (*0-7859-5169-5*) Fr & Eur.
— La Moza de Cantaro. Diez Borque, Jose M., ed. (Nueva Austral Ser.: No. 105). (SPA.). 1991. pap. text 24.95 (*84-239-1905-6*) Elliots Bks.
— El Nino Inocente de la Guardia. Farrell, Anthony J., ed. (Textos B Ser.: Vol. XXVII). (ENG & SPA.). 163p. 1985. 41.00 (*0-7293-0215-6*, Pub. by Tamesis Bks Ltd) Boydell & Brewer.
— Paces de los Reyes y Judia de Toledo. (SPA.). 166p. 1971. 7.95 (*0-8288-7173-6*, S9076) Fr & Eur.
— Peregrino en Su Patria. (SPA.). 505p. 1973. 17.95 (*0-8288-7164-7*, S29340) Fr & Eur.
— Peribanez & the Comendador of Ocana. Lloyd, ed. (Hispanic Classics Ser.). 1990. pap. 25.00 (*0-85668-439-2*, Pub. by Aris & Phillips) David Brown.
— Peribanez & the Comendador of Ocana. Lloyd, James, ed. (Hispanic Classics Ser.). (Illus.). 247p. 1990. 59.95 (*0-85668-438-4*, Pub. by Aris & Phillips) David Brown.
— Peribanez y Comendador de Ocana. 18th ed. 200p. 1991. pap. 12.95 (*0-7859-5166-0*) Fr & Eur.
— Peribanez y el Comendador de Ocana. Ruano De La Haza, Jose M., ed. (Nueva Austral Ser.: No. 225). (SPA.). 1991. pap. text 11.95 (*84-239-7225-9*) Elliots Bks.
— Peribanez y el Comendador de Ocana. (SPA.). 221p. 1978. 12.95 (*0-8288-7028-4*, 8437601703) Fr & Eur.
— Peribanez y el Comendador de Ocana. unabridged ed. (SPA.). pap. 5.95 (*84-410-0045-X*, Pub. by Bookking Intl) Distribks Inc.
— Peribanez y el Comendador de Ocana. 2nd ed. (SPA.). 152p. 1997. pap. text 4.00 (*1-56328-071-X*) Edit Plaza Mayor.
— Peribanez y el Comendador de Ocana, No. 43. (SPA.). 221p. 1978. 12.95 (*0-8288-8558-3*) Fr & Eur.
— El Perro del Hortelano. Carreno, Antonio, ed. (Nueva Austral Ser.: No. 221). (SPA.). 1991. pap. text 11.95 (*84-239-7221-6*) Elliots Bks.
— El Perro del Hortelano. 7th ed. 184p. 1991. pap. 12.95 (*0-7859-5202-0*) Fr & Eur.
— Poesia Lirica. 8th ed. 154p. 1984. pap. 7.95 (*0-7859-5188-1*) Fr & Eur.
— Remedio en la Desdicha. (SPA.). 272p. 1975. 15.95 (*0-8288-7184-1*, S19615) Fr & Eur.
— Sembrar en Tierra Buena. (SPA.). 228p. 1968. 10.95 (*0-8288-7152-3*, S18402) Fr & Eur.
— El Sufrimiento Premiado: Comedia Famosa. Dixon, Victor F., ed. (Textos B Ser.: No. 5). (SPA.). 177p. (C). 1967. pap. 41.00 (*0-900411-44-9*, Pub. by Tamesis Bks Ltd) Boydell & Brewer.
— Three Major Plays. Edwards, Gwynne, tr. from SPA. LC 98-26991. (Oxford World's Classics Ser.). 352p. 1999. pap. 11.95 (*0-19-283337-5*) OUP.
— Triunfo de la Fee en los Reynos del Japon. Cummins, J. S., ed. (Textos B Ser.: No. 1). (Illus.). 116p. (Orig.). (C). 1965. pap. 41.00 (*0-900411-40-6*, Pub. by Tamesis Bks Ltd) Boydell & Brewer.
— Villano En Su Rincon. 208p. 1987. pap. 10.95 (*0-7859-5212-8*) Fr & Eur.
— Villano en Su Rincon. (SPA.). 111p. 1969. 7.95 (*0-8288-7143-4*) Fr & Eur.
***de Vega, Lope.** Wit's End: An Adaption of Lope de Vega's "La doma boba" (Iberica Ser.: Vol. 32). 160p. (C). 2000. text 42.95 (*0-8204-4532-0*) P Lang Pubng.
de Vega, Lope, see de Vega, Lope.
de Vega, Lope, see De Solenni, Gino & de Vega, Lope.
de Vega, Lope, see de Vega, Lope.
de Vega, Lope, see Kennedy, Hugh W. & de Vega, Lope.
de Vega, Lope, see de Vega, Lope.
de Vega, Lope, jt. auth. see De Solenni, Gino.
de Vega, Lope, jt. auth. see Kennedy, Hugh W.
De Vega, Manuel & Marscharck, Mark, eds. Models of Visual-Spatial Cognition. (Illus.). 240p. (C). 1996. text 55.00 (*0-19-510084-0*); pap. text 30.00 (*0-19-510085-9*) OUP.
De Vegar, Carol L. The Northumbrian Renaissance: A Study in the Transmission of Style. LC 85-40507. (Illus.). 352p. 1987. 65.00 (*0-941664-11-2*) Susquehanna U Pr.
De Veguar, C. Neuman, see Farrell, R. T. & Neuman de Veguar, C.
De Veitia, Linaje J. Spanish Rule of Trade to the West-Indies. Stevens, John, tr. LC 72-177863. reprint ed. 49.50 (*0-404-06759-X*) AMS Pr.
de Ven, Hans J. Van, see Van de Ven, Hans J.
De Ventos, Xavier R. The Hispanic Labyrinth: Spain's Encounter with Latin America. Newman, Mary A., tr. 357p. (C). 1990. 49.95 (*0-88738-301-7*) Transaction Pubs.
De Ventos, Xavier Rubert, see Rubert de Ventos, Xavier.
De Vere Allen, James. Swahili Origins: Swahili Culture & the Shungwaya Phenomenon. Middleton, John, ed. LC 92-14316. (Eastern African Studies). 288p. (C). 1993. text 39.95 (*0-8214-1030-X*) Ohio U Pr.
— Swahili Origins: Swahili Culture & the Shungwaya Phenomenon. Middleton, John, ed. LC 92-14316. (Eastern African Studies). (Illus.). 288p. (C). 1993. pap. text 19.95 (*0-8214-1044-X*) Ohio U Pr.
De Vere, Joan. In Ruin Reconciled: A Memoir of Anglo-Ireland 1913-1959. 1996. 24.95 (*0-946640-43-2*, Pub. by Lilliput Pr) Irish Bks Media.
De Vere Stacpoole, Henry. The Blue Lagoon Omnibus. rev. ed. 211p. (C). 1981. reprint ed. 10.95 (*0-9605338-0-X*) Blue Lagoon.
De Vere White, Terence. Kevin O'Higgins. rev. ed. 272p. (Orig.). 1986. reprint ed. pap. 13.95 (*0-947962-11-5*, Pub. by Anvil Books Ltd) Irish Bks Media.
De Verger, Ramirez, ed. Sepulvedae, Ionnis Genesii: De Orb Novo Historia. (LAT.). 1992. 105.00 (*3-8154-1887-9*, T1887, Pub. by B G Teubner) U of Mich Pr.
De Vergie, Adrienne & Kell, Mary K. Location Guide to the Manuscripts of Supreme Court Justices. rev. ed. (Legal Bibliography Ser.: No. 24). 146p. 1981. 15.00 (*0-935630-07-4*) U of Tex Tarlton Law Lib.
de Verne, E. R. The Future that Awaits Us. (Illus.). 112p. 1998. pap. 15.00 (*0-8059-4537-7*) Dorrance.
De Verneil, Marie. Attending Secondary School. DuVerlie, Claud, ed. & pref. by. (Special Jeunes Ser.: No. 2). (FRE.). 78p. 1994. teacher ed., spiral bd. 12.50 (*1-887439-04-8*); VHS 70.00 (*1-887439-06-4*) France-TV Mag.
— Attending Secondary School. DuVerlie, Claud, ed. & pref. by. (Special Jeunes Ser.: No. 2). (FRE.). 94p. (YA). (gr. 8 up). 1994. student ed., spiral bd. 12.50 (*1-887439-05-6*) France-TV Mag.
— Attending Secondary School, Set. DuVerlie, Claud, ed. & pref. by. (Special Jeunes Ser.: No. 2). (FRE.). (YA). (gr. 8 up). 1994. 95.00 incl. VHS (*1-887439-07-2*) France-TV Mag.
— From Childhood to Adolescence. DuVerlie, Claud, ed. & pref. by. (Special Jeunes Ser.: No. 1). (FRE.). 90p. 1994. teacher ed., spiral bd. 12.50 (*1-887439-00-5*); VHS 70.00 (*1-887439-02-1*) France-TV Mag.
— From Childhood to Adolescence. DuVerlie, Claud, ed. & pref. by. (Special Jeunes Ser.: No. 1). (FRE.). 97p. (J). (gr. 5-12). 1994. student ed., spiral bd. 12.50 (*1-887439-01-3*) France-TV Mag.
— From Childhood to Adolescence, Set. DuVerlie, Claud, ed. & pref. by. (Special Jeunes Ser.: No. 1). (FRE.). (YA). (gr. 5-12). 1994. 95.00 incl. VHS (*1-887439-03-X*) France-TV Mag.
De Verter, Ruth H. Davis. Our Pioneer Ancestors: Genealogy of the Davis Family, Middlesex County, Virginia & Montgomery County, Kentucky, Vol. 1. (Illus.). 275p. 1997. reprint ed. pap. 42.00 (*0-8328-8234-8*); reprint ed. lib. bdg. 52.00 (*0-8328-8233-X*) Higginson Bk Co.
De Verteuil, Maurice. Maurice's Tropical Fruit Cookbook. 80p. 1979. pap. 2.95 (*0-8200-0806-0*) Great Outdoors.
***De Verteuil, Michael, et al.** Ordo Nobilis. (Ars Magica Ser.). 224p. 2000. pap. 25.95 (*1-887801-82-0*, Atlas Games) Trident MN.
De Verteuil, Michel. Meditating on the Mysteries: The Rosary As Biblical Prayer. 64p. 1998. pap. 7.95 (*1-85390-392-2*, 771, Pub. by Veritas Pubns) Irish Bks Media.
De Vette, Russell B. & Vanderbilt, William R. Coaching Basketball: The Complete Book from Beginning to Championship Play. (Illus.). 254p. (C). 1986. pap. 19.95 (*0-89641-157-5*) American Pr.
De Veubeke, B. M. A Course in Elasticity. (Applied Mathematical Sciences Ser.: Vol. 29). (Illus.). 1979. 70.95 (*0-387-90428-X*) Spr-Verlag.
De Veyra, Manuel E. Doctor in Bataan, 1941-42. (Illus.). 102p. (Orig.). (C). 1992. pap. 10.25 (*971-10-0460-7*, Pub. by New Day Pub) Cellar.
De Vic, Claude. Histoire Generale de Languedoc, 16 vols. LC 78-63203. (Heresies of the Early Christian & Medieval Era Ser.: Second Ser.). reprint ed. 2745.00 (*0-404-16380-7*) AMS Pr.
***De Vicq de Cumptich, Roberto.** Bembo's Zoo: An Animal ABC Book. LC 99-16661. 32p. (J). 2000. 17.95 (*0-8050-6382-X*) H Holt & Co.
De Victoria. O Magnum Mysterium: A Capella. 12p. 1986. pap. 1.10 (*0-7935-5474-8*, 50305150) H Leonard.
De Vidas Levy, Emilie. Sephardic Cookery: Traditional Recipes for a Joyful Table. 150p. (Orig.). 1983. pap. 14.95 (*0-9611294-0-9*) Ctrl Sephardic Jewish Community.
De Vido, Alfredo. House Design: Art & Practice. LC 95-42940. 256p. 1996. 45.00 (*0-471-52980-X*) Wiley.
De Vigenere, Blaise. A Discourse of Fire & Salt: Discovering Many Secret Mysteries, Philosophical, Theological, Alchemical. Stephens, Edward, tr. 1994. pap. 6.95 (*1-55818-297-7*) Holmes Pub.
De Vignay. Les Merveilles de la Terre D'Outremer. Trotter, ed. (FRE.). 196p. Date not set. pap. text 19.95 (*0-85989-348-0*, Pub. by Univ Exeter Pr) Northwestern U Pr.
De Vigny, Alfred. Chatterton. Germain, Sylvie, ed. (Coll. GF). (FRE.). 1964. pap. 7.95 (*0-8288-9666-6*, F75878) Fr & Eur.
— Cinq-Mars. (FRE.). 1980. pap. 15.95 (*0-7859-2896-0*) Fr & Eur.
— Cinq-Mars. (Folio Ser.: No. 1205). (FRE.). pap. 12.95 (*2-07-037205-7*) Schoenhof.
De Vigny, Alfred. Cinq Mars: or A Conspiracy under Louis XIII. Hazlitt, William C., tr. from FRE. 309p. 1986. reprint ed. pap. 27.95 (*0-935005-76-5*) Lincoln-Rembrandt.
De Vigny, Alfred. Les Destinees. Saulnier, V. L., ed. (Textes Litteraires Francais Ser.). (FRE.). pap. 7.95 (*0-8288-9667-4*, F75890) Fr & Eur.
— Lettres a Brizeux. 5.95 (*0-686-55710-7*) Fr & Eur.
— Lettres d'un Dernier Amour: Correspondance Inedit avec Augusta. (FRE.). 152p. 1952. pap. 13.95 (*0-7859-5501-1*) Fr & Eur.
— Memoires Inedits. (FRE.). 480p. 1958. pap. 16.95 (*0-7859-1332-7*, 2070265307) Fr & Eur.
— Moise. Bartfeld, Fernande, ed. (FRE.). 24p. 1967. 7.95 (*0-8288-9669-0*, F75760) Fr & Eur.
— Oeuvres Completes: Cinq-Mars, Servitude et Grandeur Militaires, Etc., Vol. 2. 1404p. 79.95 (*0-686-56465-0*) Fr & Eur.
— Oeuvres Completes: Oeuvres en vers, Theatre en vers, la Defense Obstinee de la Poesie et des Poetes, Etc., Vol. 1. 1032p. 79.95 (*0-686-56464-2*) Fr & Eur.
— Oeuvres Poetiques. (FRE.). 1978. 10.95 (*0-8288-9670-4*, F130070) Fr & Eur.
— Les Poemes. Chuzeville, Jean, ed. 276p. 1953. 12.95 (*0-8288-9668-2*, M2667) Fr & Eur.
— Poemes Antiques et Modernes: Les Destinees. (FRE.). 1973. pap. 14.95 (*0-7859-2773-5*) Fr & Eur.
— Poemes Antiques et Modernes & les Destinees. (Poesie Ser.). (FRE.). 320p. 1973. pap. 11.95 (*2-07-032049-9*) Schoenhof.
— Poesies Choisies. (FRE., Illus.). 96p. 1967. 6.95 (*0-8288-9671-2*, F75785) Fr & Eur.
— Servitude et Grandeur Militaires. Germain, Sylvie, ed. 1965. pap. 7.95 (*0-8288-9672-0*, F75920) Fr & Eur.
— Stello. Germain, Sylvie, ed. (Class. Garnier Ser.). pap. 22.95 (*0-685-37142-5*) Fr & Eur.
— Stello. (FRE.). 1984. pap. 11.95 (*0-7859-3050-7*) Fr & Eur.
— Stello: A Session with Doctor Noir. Massey, Irving, tr. LC 68-48328. 216p. reprint ed. pap. 67.00 (*0-608-12126-6*, 202382800034) Bks Demand.
De Vigo, Johannes. The Most Excellent Works of Chirurgerye Made M. T. Vignon. Traheron, B., tr. LC 68-54639. (English Experience Ser.: No. 67). 540p. 1968. reprint ed. 83.00 (*90-221-0067-7*) Walter J Johnson.
de Vijver, Niels R. van, see van de Vijver, Niels R.
De Vila, Maria Arsuaga, see Arsuaga De Vila, Maria.
***De, Villa Jill Gale.** Philippines Guide. 2nd ed. 2000. pap. text 18.95 (*1-892975-26-2*) Open Rd Pub.
de Villagra, Gaspar Perez. Historia de la Nueva Mexico, 1610: A Critical & Annotated Spanish/English Edition. annot. ed. LC 92-28780. (ENG & SPA.). 367p. 1992. pap. 37.50 (*0-8263-1392-2*) U of NM Pr.
De Villarreal, M. L. Nydia P., see Hoyos de Martens, Veronica & Nydia P. De Villarreal, M. L.
De Villars, Abbe N. Comte De Gabalis. 352p. 1996. reprint ed. pap. 23.00 (*0-7873-0271-6*) Hlth Research
De Villars, Abbe N. De Montfaucon, see De Montfaucon De Villars, Abbe N.
de Villavicencio, Maruxa De Nunez, see De Nunez de Villavicencio, Maruxa.
De Ville, Barry. Data Mining, 2000: Mining Data with Microsoft Ole DB & SQL. 464p. Date not set. pap. 39.95 (*1-55558-242-7*, Digital DEC) Buttrwrth-Heinemann.
De Ville-Colby, Jacqueline. The Expatriates Handbook: Seoul, Korea. (Illus.). 240p. 1995. 9.95 (*1-56591-041-9*, Pub. by Hollym Bks) Weatherhill.
De Ville, J. & Steytler, N. C. Voting in 1999: Choosing an Electoral System. LC 97-160885. 140p. 1996. pap. write for info. (*0-409-02233-0*, MICHIE) LEXIS Pub.
De Ville, Kenneth. Medical Malpractice in Nineteenth Century America. (American Social Experience Ser.: No. 19). (C). 1990. text 50.00 (*0-8147-1832-9*) NYU Pr.
— Medical Malpractice in Nineteenth Century America. (American Social Experience Ser.: No. 19). (C). 1992. pap. text 19.50 (*0-8147-1848-5*) NYU Pr.
De Ville, Paul. The Concertina & How to Play It. (Illus.). 79p. 1905. pap. 6.95 (*0-8258-0159-1*, 0-3311) Fischer Inc NY.
De Ville, Susie, ed. Motorcycle Touring: An International Directory - 1991-92. (Illus.). 360p. 1991. pap., per. 19.95 (*0-9621834-3-1*) Whitehorse NH.
De Ville, Winston. Colonial Louisiana Marriage Contracts: Pointe Coopee, Vol 3. 10.00 (*0-685-01104-6*) Claitors.
***De Ville, Winston.** Gulf Coast Colonials: A Compendium of French Families in Early Eighteenth Century Louisiana, Partially Indexed. 69p. 1999. pap. 12.00 (*0-8063-0093-0*) Clearfield Co.
— Louisiana Troops, 1720-1770. 136p. 1999. pap. 16.50 (*0-8063-4921-2*, Pub. by Clearfield Co) ACCESS Pubs Network.
De Villechenon, Marie-Noelle. Porcelain from the Sevres Museum, 1740-1996. (Illus.). 152p. 1996. 49.95 (*0-85331-689-9*, Pub. by Lund Humphries) Antique Collect.
De Villedieu. Le Potefeuille. Homand, ed. (Exeter French Texts Ser.: Vol. 31). (FRE.). 67p. Date not set. pap. text 19.95 (*0-85989-029-5*, Pub. by Univ Exeter Fr) Northwestern U Pr.
De Villehardouin, Geoffroi. Conqueste de Constantinople. White, Julian E., Jr., ed. LC 68-16196. (Medieval French Literature Ser.). (FRE.). (Orig.). 1968. pap. text 9.95 (*0-89197-102-5*) Irvington.
De Villehardouin, Geoffroi & De Joinville, Jean. Chronicles of the Crusades. Shaw, Margaret R., tr. (Classics Ser.). (Orig.). 1963. pap. 13.95 (*0-14-044124-7*, Penguin Classics) Viking Penguin.
De Villehardouin, Geoffroi, et al. Memoirs of the Crusades. 333. LC 83-1515. (Everyman's Library: History: No. 333). 340p. 1983. reprint ed. lib. bdg. 69.50 (*0-313-23856-1*, VIME, Greenwood Pr) Greenwood.
De Villena, Enrique. The Text & Concordance of Escorial Manuscript f. iv. 1. Arte Cisoria. O'Neill, John, ed. (Spanish Ser.: No. 37). 8p. 1987. 10.00 incl. fiche (*0-942260-98-8*) Hispanic Seminary.
De Villenueve, Jeanne France. Dictionnaire Technique de la Bourse et des Marches. (FRE.). 352p. 1994. 195.00 (*0-7859-8259-0*, 2950495036) Fr & Eur.
De Villepin, M., jt. auth. see Jagoda, A.
De Villers, Marie-Eva. English - French Vocabulary of Administrative Forms. (ENG & FRE.). 141p. 1990. pap. 39.95 (*0-8288-9398-5*) Fr & Eur.
— English-French Vocabulary of the Management of Production, 1981. (ENG & FRE.). 77p. 1981. pap. 19.95 (*0-8288-0620-9*, M4010) Fr & Eur.
— French - English Vocabulary of Government Contracts. (ENG & FRE.). 55p. 1985. pap. 29.95 (*0-8288-9404-3*) Fr & Eur.
— Vocabulaire de L'Informatique de Gestion: English - French. (ENG & FRE.). 33p. 1990. pap. 19.95 (*0-8288-9413-2*) Fr & Eur.
— Vocabulary of the Micro-Computer. (FRE.). 67p. 1990. pap. 29.95 (*0-8288-9403-5*) Fr & Eur.
De Villers, Yves T., jt. auth. see Illouz, Yves-Gerard.
De Villiers, A., ed. Juta - State Library Index to the Government Gazette. 488p. Date not set. 99.00 (*0-7021-2965-8*, Pub. by Juta & Co) Gaunt.
De Villiers, Andries, jt. auth. see De Villiers, Les.
De Villiers, B., jt. ed. see Licht, R.
De Villiers, Bertus. Evaluating Federal Systems. LC 94-44992. 1994. lib. bdg. 155.00 (*0-7923-2818-3*) Kluwer Academic.
De Villiers, Bertus, ed. Birth of a Constitution. LC 95-184452. 444p. 1994. pap. 41.50 (*0-7021-3216-0*, 15626, Pub. by Juta & Co) Gaunt.
— Evaluating Federal Systems. 448p. 1994. pap. 67.50 (*0-7021-3262-4*, 15624, Pub. by Juta & Co) Gaunt.
De Villiers, Bertus & Licht, Robert A. South Africa's Crisis of Constitutional Democracy: Can the U. S. Constitution Help? Van Wyk, David & Schlemmer, Lawrence, eds. LC 93-43191. 200p. 1994. pap. 20.00 (*0-8447-3834-4*, AEI Pr) Am Enterprise.
De Villiers, Bertus, jt. auth. see Licht, Robert A.
***De Villiers, Gerald, ed.** Ravan Twenty Five Years, 1972-1997: A Commemorative Volume of New Writing. LC 98-137290. 176p. 1999. pap. text 16.95 (*0-86975-496-3*, Pub. by Ravan Pr) Ohio U Pr.
De Villiers, J. C., ed. Some Pitfalls & Problems in Neurosurgery. (Progress in Neurological Surgery Ser.: Vol. 13). (Illus.). xii, 208p. 1990. 172.25 (*3-8055-4989-X*) S Karger.
De Villiers, Jill, ed. The Acquisition of WH-Questions: A Special Issue of "Language Acquisition", Vol. 4, Nos. 1 & 2, 1995. 176p. 1995. pap. 40.00 (*0-8058-9947-2*) L Erlbaum Assocs.
De Villiers, Jill G. & De Villiers, Peter A. Language Acquisition. 384p. 1990. 44.00 (*0-674-50931-5*) HUP.
De Villiers, Les. Doing Business with Southern Africa. (Illus.). 240p. 1989. pap. 12.50 (*0-916673-05-7*) Business Bks CT.
— Doing Business with Southern Africa. 2nd ed. (Illus.). 224p. 1991. pap. write for info. (*0-916673-06-5*) Business Bks CT.
De Villiers, Les & De Kieffer, Donald. Doing Business with the U. S. A. (Illus.). 304p. 1984. pap. 12.95 (*0-916673-00-6*) Business Bks CT.
De Villiers, Les & De Villiers, Andries. The Third Eye & Other Animal Riddles. (Illus.). 160p. 1992. pap. write for info. (*0-916673-08-1*) Business Bks CT.
De Villiers, Les, et al. The Travel Guide to South Africa. (Illus.). 256p. (Orig.). 1992. pap. 13.50 (*0-916673-07-3*) Business Bks CT.
De Villiers, Louis S. Blueprint for Better Health: A Dietary Guide to Counteract Disease. 1998. pap. text 17.50 (*0-7981-3748-7*) Human & Rousseau.
De Villiers, M. Dictionnaire du Droit Constitutionnel. (FRE.). 1998. 39.95 (*0-320-00388-4*) Fr & Eur.
***De Villiers, Marq.** Water: The Fate of Our Most Precious Resource. LC 00-21224. 288p. 2000. 25.00 (*0-618-03009-3*) HM.
De Villiers, Marq & Hirtle, Sheila. Into Africa: A Journey Through the Ancient Empires. (Illus.). 400p. 1997. 30.00 (*1-55013-884-7*) Firefly Bks Ltd.
— Into Africa: A Journey Through the Ancient Empires. (Illus.). 400p. 1999. pap. 19.95 (*1-55263-054-4*, Pub. by Key Porter) Firefly Bks Ltd.
De Villiers, Marq, see De Villiers, Marq.
De Villiers, Melius. The Numeral Words. 124p. 1996. reprint ed. spiral bd. 11.50 (*0-7873-0272-4*) Hlth Research.
De Villiers, Michael, jt. auth. see Nielsen, Leslie J.
De Villiers, Peter A., jt. auth. see De Villiers, Jill G.
De Villiers, Pierre, et al. Thirty-Six Chansons by French Provincial Composers, 1529-1550. Miller, Leta E., ed. (Recent Researches in Music of the Renaissance Ser.: Vol. RRR38). (Illus.). xxv, 91p. 1981. pap. 40.00 (*0-89579-157-9*, RRR38) A-R Eds.
De Villiers, T., jt. ed. see Forget, G. Goodman.
De Villiers Van Wisen, Louis & Loots, Cheryl. The Civil Practice of the Supreme Court of South Africa: (Now the High Courts & the Supreme Court of Appeal) 4th ed. LC 97-199461. 1512p. 1997. 177.50 (*0-7021-2990-9*, 15129, Pub. by Juta & Co) Gaunt.
De Villiers, Victor. The Point & Figure Method of Anticipating Stock Price Movements. 1973. pap. 15.00 (*0-685-42039-6*) Windsor.
— The Point & Figure Method of Anticipating Stock Prices. 64p. 1998. pap. 15.00 (*0-930233-64-6*, Pub. by Windsor) Natl Bk Netwk.
***De Villiot, Jean.** Whipped Women. 288p. 2000. mass mkt. 7.95 (*1-56201-190-1*) Blue Moon Bks.
De Vilmorin, Louise. Madame De. Cooper, Duff, tr. from FRE. 64p. 1998. pap. 12.95 (*1-885983-27-1*, Helen Mx) Turtle Point Pr.
De Vincent, George, jt. auth. see Stern, Philip.
De Vincentis-Hayes, Nan. Grammar & Diagramming Sentences. rev. ed. (Straight Forward Advanced English Ser.). 99p. (YA). (gr. 9-12). 1997. pap. 7.95 (*0-931993-75-X*, GP-075) Garlic Pr OR.
— Troublesome Grammar. (Straight Forward Advanced English Ser.). 120p. (YA). (gr. 9-12). 1999. pap. 7.95 (*0-931993-19-9*, GP-019) Garlic Pr OR.
De Vincenzi, Marica. Syntactic Parsing Strategies in Italian: The Minimal Chain Principle. 256p. (C). 1991. lib. bdg. 120.00 (*0-7923-1274-0*) Kluwer Academic.

D

***De Vincenzi, Marica & Lombardo, Vincenzo.** Cross-Linguistic Perspectives on Language Processing. LC 99-88390. (Studies in Theoretical Psycholinguistics). 2000. write for info. (*0-7923-6146-6*) Kluwer Academic.

***De Vincenzo, Sofia.** Sola Busca Tarot. 1998. pap. 9.95 (*1-57281-130-7*) US Games Syst.

De Vinck, C. Poder de los Debiles.Tr. of Power of the Powerless. (SPA.). 1996. pap. 7.99 (*0-8297-0591-0*) Vida Pubs.

De Vinck, Catherine. A Basket of Bread: An Anthology of Selected Poems. LC 96-34565. 200p. (Orig.). 1996. pap. 9.95 (*0-8189-0769-X*) Alba.

— A Book of Eve. 1979. per. 6.00 incl. lp (*0-911726-40-3*, CODE BER) Alleluia Pr.

— A Book of Peace. 44p. 1985. per. 6.75 (*0-911726-47-0*, CODE BPB) Alleluia Pr.

— God of a Thousand Names. LC 93-71939. 122p. 1993. pap. 8.75 (*0-911726-59-4*, GTN) Alleluia Pr.

— A Passion Play. LC 75-26326. 72p. 1975. 12.75 (*0-911726-16-0*, PPC); pap. 8.75 (*0-911726-18-7*, PPB) Alleluia Pr.

— Poems of the Hidden Way. LC 91-76162. 142p. (Orig.). 1991. pap. 9.75 (*0-911726-53-5*, PHW) Alleluia Pr.

— Readings: "John at Patmos" & "A Book of Hours" LC 78-55341. 68p. 1978. 8.75 (*0-911726-32-2*, CODE REC) Alleluia Pr.

— Readings: John at Patmos & A Book of Hours. LC 78-55341. 68p. 1978. pap. 5.75 (*0-911726-33-0*, REB) Alleluia Pr.

— Through the Gateless Gate. LC 96-84270. 170p. (Orig.). 1996. pap. 10.75 (*0-911726-62-4*, TGG) Alleluia Pr.

— A Time to Gather: Selected Poems. LC 67-28572. (Illus.). 72p. 1967. reprint ed. pap. 8.75 (*0-911726-02-0*, ATG) Alleluia Pr.

— The Words of Jesus: With Key Readings from New & Old Testament. deluxe ed. 300p. 1977. boxed set 45.00 (*0-911726-26-8*, WJL) Alleluia Pr.

De Vinck, Catherine, jt. auth. see Catoir, John T.

De Vinck, Christopher. The Book of Moonlight: Why Life Is Good & God Is Generous & Kind. LC 97-31553. 144p. 1998. 15.99 (*0-310-21255-3*) Zondervan.

— Love's Harvest: Family, Faith, Friends. LC 98-9847. 216p. 1998. pap. 14.95 (*0-8245-1749-0*, Crsrd) Crossroad NY.

— Nouwen Then. LC 99-18862. 176p. 1999. 16.99 (*0-310-22462-4*) Zondervan.

— The Power of the Powerless. 2nd ed. 144p. 1995. pap. 10.99 (*0-310-48691-2*) Zondervan.

— Simple Wonders: The Disarming Pleasure of Looking Beyond the Seen. 144p. 1995. pap. 12.99 (*0-310-49891-0*) Zondervan.

De Vinck, Jose. The Quest for the Golden Dove: Thoughts on Love, Human & Divine. gif. ed. LC 93-74756. 96p. 1994. 18.75 (*0-911726-61-6*, QGD) Alleluia Pr.

— Revelations of Women Mystics: From the Middle Ages to Modern Times. 4th ed. LC 84-24485. xiv, 180p. 1984. per. 9.95 (*0-8189-0478-X*, WMB) Alleluia Pr.

— The Virtue of Sex. LC 66-15236. 256p. 1966. 15.75 (*0-911726-14-4*, VOS) Alleluia Pr.

— The Yes Book: An Answer to Life. LC 77-190621. 200p. (C). 1977. 15.75 (*0-911726-12-8*, YBC); pap. 12.75 (*0-911726-11-X*, YBB) Alleluia Pr.

D

De Vinck, Jose, jt. auth. see Raya, Joseph.

De Vinck, Jose, ed. & tr. see St. Bonaventure.

De Vinck, Jose, tr. see St. Bonaventure.

De Vinck, Jose M., ed. see Kucharek, Casimir.

De Vinck, Jose M., ed. see Raya, Joseph.

De Vinck, Jose M., tr. see Contos, Leonidas C.

De Vink, Erik, jt. auth. see De Bakker, Jaco.

De Vinne, Theodore L. The Practice of Typography. LC 68-25308. (Reference Ser.: No. 44). 1972. reprint ed. lib. bdg. 75.00 (*0-8383-0935-6*) M S G Haskell Hse.

De Vinsauf, Geoffrey, et al. Chronicles of the Crusades. Giles, John A. & Johnes, Thomas, trs. LC 73-84862. (Bohn's Antiquarian Library). reprint ed. 56.00 (*0-404-50014-5*) AMS Pr.

De Vio, Tommaso. Cajetan Responds: A Reader in Reformation Controversy. Wicks, Jared, ed. LC 77-22666. 300p. reprint ed. pap. 93.00 (*0-8357-7963-7*, 202950700061) Bks Demand.

De Viri, Anne & Gunderson, Joanna. Indrani & I. LC 65-21134. 1966. 4.95 (*0-87376-004-2*) Red Dust.

***de Virieu, Claire, photos by.** Gardens of Fashion. (Illus.). 208p. (J). 2000. 59.95 (*0-7892-0447-9*, Abbeville Kids) Abbeville Pr.

De Visan, Tancrede. L' Attitude du Lyrisme Contemporain. LC 78-64058. (Des Imagistes: Literature of the Imagist Movement Ser.). reprint ed. 35.00 (*0-404-17112-5*) AMS Pr.

De Visscher, Michel, ed. The Thyroid Gland. LC 78-55803. (Comprehensive Endocrinology Ser.). (Illus.). 551p. reprint ed. pap. 170.90 (*0-7837-7089-8*, 204690300004) Bks Demand.

De Visser, John. Grand River Reflections. (Illus.). 152p. (Orig.). 1995. 32.00 (*1-55046-040-4*, Pub. by Boston Mills) Genl Dist Srvs.

— Muskoka. (Illus.). 120p. 1995. pap. text 24.00 (*1-55046-049-8*, Pub. by Boston Mills) Genl Dist Srvs.

— Toronto. (Illus.). 1976. pap. 12.50 (*0-19-540243-X*) OUP.

— University of Western Ontario. (First Edition Ser.). (Illus.). 112p. 1988. 49.00 (*0-916509-38-9*) Harmony Hse Pub.

***De Visser, John, photos by.** Old Ontario Houses: Traditions in Local Architecture. (Illus.). 224p. 2000. 50.00 (*1-55209-499-5*) Firefly Bks Ltd.

De Visser, John & Ross, Judy. At the Water's Edge. (Illus.). 158p. 1993. 40.00 (*1-55046-082-X*, Pub. by Boston Mills) Genl Dist Srvs.

— Muskoka Souvenir. (Illus.). 80p. 1995. 15.95 (*1-55046-125-7*, Pub. by Boston Mills) Genl Dist Srvs.

De Visser, John & Turner, Larry. The Rideau. (Illus.). 120p. 1995. 28.00 (*1-55046-136-2*, Pub. by Boston Mills) Genl Dist Srvs.

De Visser, John, jt. photos by see DeVisser, John.

De Visser, Marinus W. The Arhats in China & Japan. LC 78-70136. reprint ed. 34.50 (*0-404-17406-X*) AMS Pr.

De Vita, Sharon. All It Takes Is Family. 1997. per. 3.99 (*0-373-24126-7*, 1-24126-4) Silhouette.

— Baby & the Officer. (Romance Ser.). 1998. per. 3.50 (*0-373-19316-5*, 1-19316-8) Silhouette.

— Baby with a Badge. 1998. per. 3.50 (*0-373-19298-3*, 1-19298-8) Silhouette.

— Child of Midnight. 1996. per. 3.99 (*0-373-24013-9*, 1-24013-4) Silhouette.

— L' Enfant du Destin. (Horizon Ser.). 1999. mass mkt. 3.50 (*0-373-39511-6*, 1-39511-0) Harlequin Bks.

— The Lady & the Sheriff. (Silver Creek County Ser.). 1997. per. 3.99 (*0-373-24103-8*, 1-24103-3) Silhouette.

— The Lone Ranger. 1997. per. 3.99 (*0-373-24078-3*, 1-24078-7) Silhouette.

***De Vita, Sharon.** The Marriage Badge: The Blackwell Brothers. 2000. per. 3.50 (*0-373-19443-9*) Silhouette.

— Marriage Basket. (Special Edition Ser.: Vol. 134). 2000. mass mkt. 4.50 (*0-373-24307-3*) Silhouette.

De Vita, Sharon. On Baby Patrol: Bundles of Joy/Lullabies & Love. (Romance Ser.: No. 1276). 1998. per. 3.50 - (*0-373-19276-2*, 1-19276-4) Silhouette.

De Vitis, A. A. Roman Holiday: The Catholic Novels of Evelyn Waugh. LC 71-153314. (BCL Ser. I). reprint ed. 29.50 (*0-404-02119-0*) AMS Pr.

De Vito, Albert. Albert De Vito Piano Course, Bk. 1. 1968. pap. 5.95 (*0-934286-52-3*) Kenyon.

— Chord Approach to Pop Organ Playing Bk. 1. (Illus.). 1965. pap. 6.95 (*0-934286-49-3*) Kenyon.

— Chord Approach to Pop Organ Playing Bk. 2. (Illus.). 1965. pap. 6.95 (*0-934286-50-7*) Kenyon.

— Chord Approach to Pop Piano Playing Bk. 2. (Illus.). 1962. pap. 6.95 (*0-934286-30-2*) Kenyon.

— Chord Approach to Pop Piano Playing Bk. 3. (Illus.). 1963. pap. 6.95 (*0-934286-31-0*) Kenyon.

— Chord Dictionary. LC 75-40685. (Illus.). 1989. pap. 9.95 (*0-934286-01-9*) Kenyon.

— Chord Dictionary for All Keyboard Instruments. 56p. 1986. pap. 9.95 (*0-7935-5298-2*, 50395920) H Leonard.

— Chord Encyclopedia. LC 75-43441. (Illus.). 1980. pap. 16.95 (*0-934286-02-7*) Kenyon.

— Chord Encyclopedia for All Instruments. 96p. 1986. per. 13.95 (*0-7935-5530-2*, 50395910) H Leonard.

— Chord Pianist: Classical Favorites for Piano, Bk. B. (Illus.). 1966. pap. 5.95 (*0-934286-34-5*) Kenyon.

— Chord Pianist: Standard Favorites for Piano, Bk. A. (Illus.). 1966. pap. 5.95 (*0-934286-33-7*) Kenyon.

— Chord Progressions Made Easy for All Organs. (Illus.). 1973. pap. 5.95 (*0-934286-26-4*) Kenyon.

— Chord Progressions Made Easy for Piano. (Illus.). 1973. pap. 5.95 (*0-934286-27-2*) Kenyon.

— Christmas Songs for Piano (Big Note) 1968. pap. 4.95 (*0-934286-53-1*) Kenyon.

— Contrasts for Two Pianos: Set of Two. 1977. pap. 5.95 (*0-934286-58-2*) Kenyon.

— Melodic Organ Pedal Studies. 1969. pap. 4.95 (*0-934286-42-6*) Kenyon.

— Modern Organ Course for All Organs, Bk. 1. 1964. pap. 5.95 (*0-934286-36-1*) Kenyon.

— Modern Organ Course for All Organs, Bk. 2. 1964. pap. 5.95 (*0-934286-37-X*) Kenyon.

— Modern Organ Course for All Organs: Primer. 1964. pap. 4.95 (*0-934286-35-3*) Kenyon.

— Piano Sonata No. I in Db. (Orig.). 1979. pap. 7.50 (*0-934286-12-4*) Kenyon.

— Piano Sonatina. (Illus.). 16p. (Orig.). 1985. pap. 7.50 (*0-934286-65-5*) Kenyon.

— Pocket Dictionary of Music Terms. 48p. 1986. pap. 4.25 (*0-7935-5533-7*, 50395370) H Leonard.

— Popular Organ Classics. 1964. pap. 4.25 (*0-934286-43-4*) Kenyon.

— Popular Piano Classics. 1964. pap. 4.25 (*0-934286-51-5*) Kenyon.

— Progressive Organ Solos, Bk. 2. 1964. pap. 7.95 (*0-934286-39-6*) Kenyon.

— Progressive Organ Solos, Bk. 4. 1965. pap. 7.95 (*0-934286-41-8*) Kenyon.

— Progressive Organ Solos I. 1964. pap. 7.95 (*0-934286-38-8*) Kenyon.

— Seven Novelettes for Piano. 1971. pap. 4.95 (*0-934286-15-9*) Kenyon.

— Your Magical Keyboard. LC 86-80117. (Illus.). 56p. (Orig.). 1986. pap. 8.95 (*0-934286-66-3*) Kenyon.

De Vito, Albert, ed. see Piano Teachers Congress Members.

De Vito, Albert K. Fake It for All Keyboard Instruments. LC 75-40687. (Illus.). 1976. pap. 7.50 (*0-934286-05-1*) Kenyon.

— Playing the Chord Organ & Learning to Read Music. (Illus.). 1974. pap. 5.95 (*0-934286-08-6*) Kenyon.

De Vito, Albert K., ed. see Byman, Isabelle Y.

De Vito, Alfred. Rocks & Minerals: Earth Science Translated. (Illus.). 125p. 1985. pap. 14.95 (*0-942034-04-X*) Creat Ventures IN.

— Teaching with Eggs. (Illus.). 70p. (Orig.). (J). (gr. 3-8). 1982. pap. write for info. (*0-942034-00-7*) Creat Ventures IN.

— Teaching with Quotes. (Illus.). 162p. (Orig.). 1983. pap. 14.95 (*0-942034-01-5*) Creat Ventures IN.

De Vito, Alfred & Krockover, Gerald H. Creative Sciencing: Ideas & Activities for Teachers & Children Grades K to Eight. 1991. pap. 19.95 (*0-673-52008-0*, GoodYrBooks) Addson-Wesley Educ.

De Vito, Michael C. Connecticut's Old Timbered Crossings. (Illus.). 1964. 10.00 (*0-910506-01-9*) De Vito.

De Vito, Michael J. The New York Review, 1905-1908. LC 77-75637. (Monograps: No. 34). (Illus.). 1977. 13.95 (*0-930060-14-8*) US Cath Hist.

De Vitoria, Francisco. Reflection on Homicide & Commentary on Summa Theologiae IIa-IIae Q. 64. Doyle, John P., tr. from LAT. & intro. by. LC 96-51253. (Medieval Philosophical Texts in Translation Ser.: Vol. 34). 280p. (Orig.). 1997. pap. 30.00 (*0-87462-237-9*) Marquette.

De Vitray-Meyerovitch, Eva. Rumi & Sufism. 2nd ed. Fattal, Simone, tr. from FRE. LC 87-62177. (World of Islam Ser.). (FRE., Illus.). 167p. (Orig.). 1987. reprint ed. pap. 13.00 (*0-942996-08-9*) Post Apollo Pr.

De Vitry, Jacques & De Cantempre, Thomas. The Life of Marie d'Oignies & Supplement to the Life. 4th ed. Feiss, Hugh & King, Margot H., trs. (Translations Ser.). 298p. 1998. pap. write for info. (*0-920669-51-4*, Pub. by Peregrina Pubng) Cistercian Pubns.

De Vivanco, Sebastian. Sebastian de Vivanco: Three Masses. Arias, Enrique A., ed. (Recent Researches in Music of the Renaissance Ser.: Vol. RRR31). (Illus.). xi, 87p. 1978. pap. 35.00 (*0-89579-109-9*) A-R Eds.

De Vlaming, Frederiek, ed. Academic Freedom 4: Education & Human Rights. 256p. (C). 1996. text 65.00 (*1-85649-377-6*, Pub. by Zed Books) St Martin.

De Vlieger, Marinus, ed. Handbook of Clinical Ultrasound. LC 78-14458. (Illus.). 988p. reprint ed. pap. 200.00 (*0-608-30218-X*, 205133000095) Bks Demand.

De Voe, James R., ed. Validation of the Measurement Process. LC 77-15555. (ACS Symposium Ser.: No. 63). 1977. 32.95 (*0-8412-0396-2*) Am Chemical.

De Voe, Thomas F. The Market Book Containing a Historical Account of the Public Markets in the Cities of New York, Boston, Philadelphia & Brooklyn Vol. 1: A History of the Public Markets in the City of New York. LC 72-121319. (Library of Early American Business & Industry: No. 40). xiv, 621p. 1970. reprint ed. lib. bdg. 65.00 (*0-678-00685-7*) Kelley.

De Vogel, E. F. Coelogyninae III: The Genus Pholidota. rev. ed. (Orchid Monographs: Vol. 3). (Illus.). 118p. 1988. pap. 38.00 (*90-04-09040-1*, Pub. by Rijksherbarium) Balogh.

De Vogel, E. F. & Turner, H. Coelogyninae (Orchidaceae) IV - Coelogyne Section Tomentosae: Ania, Hancockia, Mischobulbum & Tainia. rev. ed. (Orchid Monographs: Vol. 6). (Illus.). vi, 166p. 1992. pap. 41.00 (*90-71236-12-9*, Pub. by Rijksherbarium) Balogh.

De Vogel, E. F., jt. auth. see Minderhoud, M. E.

De Vogel, E. F., ed. see Ansari, R. & Balakrishnan, N. P.

De Vogel, E. F., ed. see Petterson, B.

De Vogel, E. F., ed. see Schuiteman.

De Vogel, E. F., ed. see Vermeulen, J. J.

De Vogue, Adalbert. Community & Abbot in the Rule of Saint Benedict, Vol. 2. Philippi, Charles & Perkins, Ethel R., trs. from FRE. (Cistercian Studies: 5-2). 506p. 1979. 24.95 (*0-87907-305-5*) Cistercian Pubns.

— Reading Saint Benedict: Reflections on the Rule. Friedlander, Colette, tr. LC 93-27072. (Cistercian Studies: No. 151). 1994. 36.95 (*0-87907-651-8*); pap. 24.95 (*0-87907-751-4*) Cistercian Pubns.

— The Rule of St. Benedict: A Doctrinal & Spiritual Commentary. Hasbrouck, John B., tr. from FRE. (Cistercian Studies: No. 54).Tr. of La/Regle de saint Benoit, VII, Commentaire doctrinal et spirituel. 1983. pap. 25.00 (*0-87907-845-6*) Cistercian Pubns.

— To Desire Eternal Life: Hope Yesterday & Today. Hasbrouck, Jean B., tr. from FRE. LC 98-38342. Orig. Title: Desirer la Vie Eternelle l'Esperance Hier et Aujourd'hui. 86p. 1998. pap. 7.95 (*1-879007-33-9*) St Bedes Pubns.

— To Love Fasting: The Monastic Experience. Houde, John B., tr. from FRE. LC 93-44765. 186p. (Orig.). 1993. pap. 14.95 (*0-932506-87-9*) St Bedes Pubns.

De Vogue, Adalbert, et al. Word & Spirit No. 13: Asceticism Today. LC 81-643362. (Word & Spirit Ser.: No. 13). 154p. 1991. pap. 8.00 (*0-932506-90-9*) St Bedes Pubns.

De Vogue, E. M. The Russian Novelists. LC 74-28331. (Studies in Russian Literature & Life: No. 100). 1974. lib. bdg. 75.00 (*0-8383-1949-1*) M S G Haskell Hse.

De Vogue, Eugene N. The Russian Novelists. Edmands, Jane L., tr. LC 72-1328. (Essay Index Reprint Ser.). 1977. reprint ed. 18.95 (*0-8369-2870-9*) Ayer.

De Voigt, M. J., jt. auth. see Ejiri, Hiroyasu.

De Volpi, Alexander, et al. Born Secret: The H-Bomb, the "Progressive" Case & National Security. (Illus.). 320p. 1981. 42.00 (*0-08-025995-2*, Pergamon Pr) Elsevier.

De Vooght, Marian & Lefevere, Andre. Go Dutch. Lathrop, Thomas, ed. (Illus.). 189p. 1995. pap. text 26.95 (*0-942566-18-1*) LinguaText.

De Voogt, H. J., et al. Urinary Cytology: Phase-Contrast Microscopy & Analysis of Stained Smears. (Illus.). 1977. 114.00 (*0-387-08042-2*) Spr-Verlag.

De Vooys, Sijna. Psychological Element in the English Sociological Novel of the 19th Century. LC 68-2022. (Studies in Fiction: No. 34). 1969. reprint ed. lib. bdg. 75.00 (*0-8383-0539-3*) M S G Haskell Hse.

De Voragine, Jacobus. The Golden Legend. LC 72-88826. (Art Histories Collection). 1980. reprint ed. 57.95 (*0-405-02227-1*) Ayer.

— The Golden Legend: Readings on the Saints, 7 vols. in 4. Ellis, F. S., ed. Caxton, William, tr. LC 76-170839. 1973. reprint ed. write for info. (*0-404-06770-0*) AMS Pr.

— The Golden Legend: Readings on the Saints, 2 vols., 1. Ryan, William G., tr. from LAT. LC 92-30068. 416p. (C). 1993. text 65.00 (*0-691-00865-5*, Pub. by Princeton U Pr) Cal Prin Full Svc.

— The Golden Legend: Readings on the Saints, 2 vols., 2. Ryan, William G., tr. from LAT. LC 92-30068. 416p. (C). 1993. text 65.00 (*0-691-03178-9*, Pub. by Princeton U Pr) Cal Prin Full Svc.

— The Golden Legend: Readings on the Saints, 2 vols., Set. Ryan, William G., tr. from LAT. LC 92-30068. 840p. (C). 1993. text 90.00 (*0-691-00894-9*, Pub. by Princeton U Pr) Cal Prin Full Svc.

— The Golden Legend: Selections. 384p. 1999. pap. 13.95 (*0-14-044648-6*) Viking Penguin.

— The Golden Legend Vol. 1: Readings on the Saints, Vol. 1. Ryan, William G., tr. 410p. 1993. pap. text 17.95 (*0-691-00153-7*, Pub. by Princeton U Pr) Cal Prin Full Svc.

— The Golden Legend Vol. 2: Readings on the Saints, Vol. 2. 410p. 1993. pap. text 17.95 (*0-691-00154-5*, Pub. by Princeton U Pr) Cal Prin Full Svc.

— The Golden Legend Vols. I & II: Readings on the Saints. Ryan, William G., tr. 820p. 1993. pap. text 29.95 (*0-691-00162-6*, Pub. by Princeton U Pr) Cal Prin Full Svc.

De Voragine, James. Seven Sleepers of Ephesus. 1991. pap. 0.50 (*0-89981-125-6*) Eastern Orthodox.

De Vore, R. William, ed. Carnahan Conference on Security Technology, 1988: Proceedings. LC 82-646157. (Illus.). 108p. 1988. pap. 10.00 (*0-89779-071-5*, UKY BU146) OES Pubns.

— Proceedings, Carnahan Conference on Security Technology, 1990. LC 82-646157. (Electronic Crime Countermeasures Ser.). (Illus.). 65p. (Orig.). 1990. pap. 10.00 (*0-89779-076-6*) OES Pubns.

— Proceedings, 1983 International Symposium on Urban Hydrology, Hydraulics & Sediment Control. LC 83-60965. (Illus.). 531p. (Orig.). 1983. pap. 10.00 (*0-89779-056-1*, UKY BU 131) OES Pubns.

— Symposium on Advanced Manufacturing, 1988: Proceedings. LC 86-63797. (Illus.). 150p. 1988. pap. 10.00 (*0-89779-072-3*, UKY BU147) OES Pubns.

De Vore, R. William & Carpenter, Stanley B., eds. Proceedings, 1979 Symposium on Surface Mining Hydrology, Sedimentology, & Reclamation. LC 79-91553. (Illus.). 353p. (Orig.). 1979. pap. 10.00 (*0-89779-024-3*, UKY BU119) OES Pubns.

De Vore, R. William & Graves, Donald H., eds. Proceedings, 1980 Symposium on Surface Mining, Hydrology, Sedimentology, & Reclamation. LC 80-84399. (Illus.). 490p. 1980. 10.00 (*0-89779-044-8*, UKY BU123) OES Pubns.

— Proceedings, 1981 Symposium on Surface Mining, Hydrology, Sedimentology & Reclamation. LC 81-84944. (Illus.). 558p. (Orig.). 1981. 10.00 (*0-89779-050-2*, UKY BU126) OES Pubns.

— Proceedings, 1983 Symposium on Surface Mining, Hydrology, Sedimentology & Reclamation. LC 83-60966. (Illus.). 554p. (Orig.). 1983. pap. 10.00 (*0-89779-058-8*, UKY BU 133) OES Pubns.

De Vore, R. William & Haan, Charles T., eds. International Symposium on Urban Storm Water Management: Proceedings 1978. LC 79-69728. 348p. 1978. pap. text 10.00 (*0-89779-002-2*, UKY BU116) OES Pubns.

De Vore, R. William & Huffsey, R. R. International Symposium on Urban Hydrology, Hydraulic Infrastructures & Water Quality Control, 1985: Proceedings. LC 83-60965. (Illus.). 335p. (Orig.). 1985. pap. 10.00 (*0-89779-063-4*, UKY BU138) OES Pubns.

De Vore, R. William & Huffsey, R. R., eds. International Symposium on Urban Hydrology, Hydraulics & Sediment Control, 1984: Proceedings. LC 83-60965. (Illus.). 284p. (Orig.). 1984. pap. 10.00 (*0-89779-060-X*, UKY BU135) OES Pubns.

— International Symposium on Urban Storm Runoff: Proceedings 1979. LC 79-66289. (Illus.). 365p. (Orig.). 1979. pap. 10.00 (*0-89779-020-0*, UKY BU118) OES Pubns.

De Vore, R. William & Jackson, J. S., eds. Carnahan Conference on Crime Countermeasures, 1980: Proceedings. LC 79-644630. (Illus.). 160p. (Orig.). 1980. pap. 10.00 (*0-89779-030-8*, UKY BU120) OES Pubns.

— Carnahan Conference on Security Technology, 1982: Proceedings. LC 79-644630. (Illus.). 194p. (Orig.). 1982. pap. 10.00 (*0-89779-052-9*, UKY BU127) OES Pubns.

— Carnahan Conference on Security Technology, 1985: Proceedings. LC 82-64615. (Illus.). 181p. 1985. pap. 10.00 (*0-89779-061-8*, UKY BU137) OES Pubns.

— Carnahan Conference on Security Technology, 1986: Proceedings. LC 82-64615. (Illus.). 159p. 1986. pap. 10.00 (*0-89779-065-0*, UKY BU140) OES Pubns.

— Conference on Crime Countermeasures & Security, 1983: Proceedings. LC 82-64615. (Illus.). 118p. 1983. pap. 10.00 (*0-89779-055-3*, UKY BU 130) OES Pubns.

— Proceedings, 1981 Carnahan Conference on Crime Countermeasures. LC 79-644630. (Illus.). 200p. (Orig.). 1981. pap. 10.00 (*0-89779-046-4*, UKY BU124) OES Pubns.

— Security Through Science & Engineering: Proceedings, Third International Conference. LC 80-83300. (Illus.). 313p. 1980. pap. 10.00 (*0-89779-042-1*, UKYBU122) OES Pubns.

De Vore, R. William & Jackson, John S., eds. Carnahan Conference on Crime Countermeasures, 1978: Proceedings. LC 76-63633. 176p. 1978. pap. text 10.00 (*0-89779-000-6*) OES Pubns.

De Vore, R. William & Wood, Don J., eds. Proceedings 1981 International Symposium on Urban Hydrology, Hydraulics & Sediment Control. LC 81-82243. (Illus.). 473p. (Orig.). 1981. pap. 10.00 (*0-89779-047-2*, UKY BU125) OES Pubns.

De Vore, R. William, ed. see Carnahan Conference on Security Technology Staff.

De Vore, R. William, jt. ed. see Graves, Donald H.

De Vore, R. William, ed. see International Carnahan Conference Staff.

De Vore, R. William, ed. see Jackson, J. S.

De Vore, R. William, ed. see Symposium on Advanced Manufacturing Staff.

De Vore, R. William, ed. see Symposium on Mining, Hydrology, Sedimentology & Re.

An Asterisk (*) at the beginning of an entry indicates that the title is appearing for the first time.

De Vore, Russell. Practical Problems in Mathematics for Heating & Cooling Technicians. 2nd ed. (Business Math). 200p. (C). 1991. mass mkt. 14.75 (*0-8273-4062-1*) Delmar.

***De Vore, Sheryl.** Birding Illinois. LC 99-35148. (Illus.). 356p. 2000. pap. text 24.95 (*1-56044-689-7*) Falcon Pub Inc.

De Vorkin, D. H. Race to the Stratosphere. (Illus.). xiii, 406p. 1989. 69.95 (*0-387-96953-5*) Spr-Verlag.

De Vorsey, Louis, Jr. Keys to the Encounter: A Library of Congress Resource Guide for the Study of the Age of Discovery. LC 91-16735. (Illus.). 212p. 1992. pap. 18.00 (*0-8444-0692-9*, 030-000-0234-2) Lib Congress.

De Vorsey, Louis, Jr. & Parker, John, eds. In the Wake of Columbus: Islands & Controversy. LC 85-671. (Illus.). 240p. reprint ed. pap. 74.40 (*0-608-10569-4*, 207118900009) Bks Demand.

De Vorsey, Louis, Jr. & Rice, Marion. The Plantation South: Atlanta to Savannah & Charleston. LC 92-10413. (Touring North America Ser.). (Illus.). 220p. 1992. 25.00 (*0-8135-1872-5*); pap. 9.95 (*0-8135-1873-3*) Rutgers U Pr.

De Vorsey, Louis, ed. see De Brahm, William G.

De Vos. Regsgeskiedenis. 314p. 1991. write for info. (*0-7021-2762-0*, Pub. by Juta & Co); pap. write for info. (*0-7021-2671-3*, Pub. by Juta & Co) Gaunt.

De Vos, Alexis. Endoreversible Thermodynamics of Solar Energy Conversion. (Illus.). 200p. 1992. text 55.00 (*0-19-851392-5*) OUP.

De Vos, Diane C. Basic Principles of Radiographic Exposure. 2nd ed. LC 94-34821. (Illus.). 160p. 1995. pap. 24.50 (*0-683-02458-2*) Lppncott W & W.

***De Vos, Dirk & Van Der Weyden, Rogier.** Rogier Van Der Weyden: The Complete Works. LC 99-23840. (Illus.). 400p. 1999. 145.00 (*0-8109-6390-6*, Pub. by Abrams) Time Warner.

***De Vos, Dominique, et al.** Equality in Law Between Men & Women in the European Community. Verwilghen, Michel & Von Prondzynski, Ferdinand, eds. 246p. 1998. 59.00 (*0-7923-1829-3*) Kluwer Academic.

De Vos, Gail. Tales, Rumors & Gossip: Exploring Contemporary Folk Literature in Grades 7-12. xx, 405p. 1996. lib. bdg. 39.00 (*1-56308-190-3*) Libs Unl.

De Vos, Gail & Altmann, Anna E. New Tales for Old: Folktales as Literary Fictions for Young Adults. LC 99-33150. 250p. 1999. pap. 35.00 (*1-56308-447-3*) Teacher Ideas Pr.

De Vos, George & Romanucci-Ross, Lola. Ethnic Identity: Cultural Continuities & Change. xvi, 396p. (C). 1992. pap. text 14.00 (*0-226-14364-3*) U Ch Pr.

De Vos, George A. Status Inequality: The Self in Culture. (Cross-Cultural Research & Methodology Ser.: Vol. 15). 312p. (C). 1990. text 52.00 (*0-8039-3962-0*) Sage.

De Vos, George A. & Boyer, L. Bryce. Symbolic Analysis Cross Culturally: The Rorschach Test. (C). 1989. 65.00 (*0-520-06086-5*, Pub. by U CA Pr) Cal Prin Full Svc.

De Vos, George A., jt. ed. see Slote, Walter H.

De Vos, J. The Endemic Pleistocene Deer of Create. (Verhandelingen der Koninklijke Nederlandse Akademie van Wetenschappen, Afd. Letterkunde, Nieuwe Reeks Ser.: No. 49(8)). 100p. 1984. pap. text 47.00 (*0-444-85609-9*) Elsevier.

De Vos, L. N. Roll Forming of Gears at Ford Motor Company. (Technical Papers: Vol. P109.19). 13p. 1968. pap. text 30.00 (*1-55589-443-7*) AGMA.

De Vos, Louis, et al. Atlas of Sponge Morphology. LC 90-10099. (Illus.). 128p. (C). 1991. text 45.00 (*1-56098-022-2*) Smithsonian.

De Vos, Maithe. Mots de la Micro: Petit Dictionnaire Micro-Informatique Pour Tous. (FRE.). 224p. 1992. pap. 38.95 (*0-7859-7729-5*) Fr & Eur.

de Vos, Philip. Carnival of the Animals. LC 99-44969. (Illus.). 42p. (YA). (gr. k up). 2000. 16.95 (*1-886910-47-2*, Pub. by Front Str) Publishers Group.

De Vos, Robert, jt. ed. see Brice, Tracy.

De Vos, Robert C., jt. auth. see Chen, Yung-Ping.

De Vos Romulea, M. P. Flora of Southern Africa Series, Vol. 7. (Illus.). 76p. 1983. 23.00 (*0-621-07939-1*, Pub. by Natl Botanical Inst) Balogh.

De Vos, S. M. Household Composition in Latin America. LC 95-22990. (Plenum Series on Demographic Methods & Population Analysis). (Illus.). 248p. (C). 1995. text 44.50 (*0-306-44962-5*, Kluwer Plenum) Kluwer Academic.

De Vos-Schippers, B., jt. ed. see Smook, A. O.

De Vos Van Steenwijk, Alwine. Father Joseph: Champion of the Poor. Fourth World Movement Staff, tr. from FRE. 235p. 1996. pap. 14.00 (*0-934199-03-5*) Fourth Wrld.

— Father Joseph Wresinski: Voice of the Poorest. Sleeth, Charles, tr. from FRE. LC 96-70126.Tr. of Pere Joseph. (Illus.). 188p. 1997. reprint ed. pap. 8.95 (*1-882972-81-3*, 3561) Queenship Pub.

De Vos, W. Verrykingsaanspreeklikheid in die Suid-Afrikaanse Reg. 424p. 1987. write for info. (*0-7021-2002-2*, Pub. by Juta & Co); pap. write for info. (*0-7021-1926-1*, Pub. by Juta & Co) Gaunt.

De Vosjol, Philippa, et al. The Boa Constrictor Manual. (Illus.). 84p. 1998. pap. text 8.50 (*1-882770-41-2*) Adv Vivarium.

De Vosjoli, Philippe. Arachnomania: The General Care & Maintenance of Tarantulas & Scorpions. 79p. 1991. pap. text 8.50 (*1-882770-10-2*, Pub. by Adv Vivarium) IPG Chicago.

— Basic Care of Rough Green Snakes. (Herpetocultural Library). (Illus.). 16p. (Orig.). 1995. pap. 5.00 (*1-882770-31-5*) Adv Vivarium.

— Basic Care of Uromastyx. (Herpetocultural Library). 18p. 1995. pap. 5.00 (*1-882770-32-3*) Adv Vivarium.

— The Box Turtle Manual. LC 95-196662. 1995. pap. text 8.50 (*1-882770-29-3*) Adv Vivarium.

***De Vosjoli, Philippe.** The Care of Land Hermit Crabs. LC 99-33303. (Illus.). 32p. 1999. pap. text 3.00 (*1-882770-50-1*) Adv Vivarium.

De Vosjoli, Philippe. Chameleon Manual. 1999. pap. text 8.95 (*1-882770-45-5*) Adv Vivarium.

— Design & Maintenance of Desert Vivaria. LC 96-6751. (Vivarium Design Ser.). (Illus.). 64p. (Orig.). 1996. pap. 17.00 (*1-882770-33-1*) Adv Vivarium.

— The General Care & Maintenance of Burmese Pythons. 44p. 1991. pap. text 7.50 (*1-882770-07-2*) Adv Vivarium.

— The General Care & Maintenance of Green Anoles. 47p. 1992. pap. text 6.00 (*1-882770-17-X*) Adv Vivarium.

— The General Care & Maintenance of Horned Frogs. 32p. 1990. pap. text 6.00 (*1-882770-00-5*) Adv Vivarium.

— The General Care & Maintenance of Leopard Geckos. 1990. pap. text 6.00 (*1-882770-08-0*) Adv Vivarium.

— General Care & Maintenance of Popular Tortoises. (Illus.). 54p. (Orig.). 1996. pap. text 7.50 (*1-882770-37-4*) Adv Vivarium.

— The General Care & Maintenance of Prehensile-Tailed Skinks. 56p. 1993. pap. text 11.50 (*1-882770-24-2*) Adv Vivarium.

— The General Care & Maintenance of Red-Eared Sliders. 47p. 1992. pap. text 6.00 (*1-882770-12-9*) Adv Vivarium.

— The Green Iguana Manual. 71p. 1992. pap. text 8.50 (*1-882770-18-8*) Adv Vivarium.

— The Leopard Gecko Manual. 1999. pap. text 8.95 (*1-882770-44-7*, Pub. by Adv Vivarium) IPG Chicago.

— The Lizard Keeper's Handbook. (Herpetocultural Library). (Illus.). 176p. (Orig.). 1994. pap. 12.00 (*1-882770-25-0*) Adv Vivarium.

— True Chameleons Pt. II: Notes on Popular Species. 28p. 1990. pap. text 6.00 (*1-882770-05-6*) Adv Vivarium.

De Vosjoli, Philippe & Ferguson, Gary. Care & Breeding of Panther, Jackson's, Veiled & Parson's Chameleons, Vol. 1. LC 96-110864. (Illus.). 128p. (Orig.). 1995. pap. text 12.00 (*1-882770-30-7*) Adv Vivarium.

De Vosjoli, Philippe & Mailloux, Robert. The General Care & Maintenance of Bearded Dragons. 71p. 1997. pap. text 11.50 (*1-882770-40-4*) Adv Vivarium.

De Vosjoli, Philippe, et al. The Ball Python Manual. LC 95-147420. (Illus.). 80p. 1994. pap. text 8.50 (*1-882770-28-5*) Adv Vivarium.

— Care & Breeding of Popular Treefrogs. (Illus.). 80p. (Orig.). 1996. pap. text 8.50 (*1-882770-36-6*) Adv Vivarium.

De Voto, Bernard A. Across the Wide Missouri. LC 83-45742. (Illus.). reprint ed. 94.50 (*0-404-20079-6*) AMS Pr.

***De Voto, Bernard A.** Across the Wide Missouri: The Diary of a Journey from Virginia to Missouri in 1819 & Back Again in 1822, with a Description of the City of Cincinnati. 450p. 1998. pap. 15.00 (*0-395-92497-9*) HM.

De Voto, Bernard A. The Course of Empire. 647p. 1998. pap. 16.00 (*0-395-92498-7*) HM.

— Easy Chair. LC 78-167333. (Essay Index Reprint Ser.). 1977. reprint ed. 23.95 (*0-8369-2433-9*) Ayer.

— Forays & Rebuttals. LC 78-111826. (Essay Index Reprint Ser.). 1977. 30.95 (*0-8369-1604-2*) Ayer.

— Hour. LC 76-106664. 84p. 1970. reprint ed. lib. bdg. 45.00 (*0-8371-3422-6*, DEHO, Greenwood Pr) Greenwood.

— Journals of Lewis & Clark. LC 97-1518. (Illus.). 576p. 1997. pap. 14.00 (*0-395-85996-4*) HM.

— Literary Fallacy. (BCL1-PS American Literature Ser.). 1993. reprint ed. lib. bdg. write for info. (*0-7812-6580-0*) Rprt Serv.

— Mark Twain's America. LC 78-4109. (Illus.). 351p. 1978. reprint ed. lib. bdg. 69.50 (*0-313-20368-7*, DEVMT, Greenwood Pr) Greenwood.

— Minority Report. LC 71-142619. (Essay Index Reprint Ser.). 1977. 23.95 (*0-8369-2105-4*) Ayer.

— The Year of Decision, 1864. 33.95 (*0-88411-292-6*) Amereon Ltd.

De Voto, Bernard A., ed. Letters From the Ear. LC 90-56427. 320p. 1991. reprint ed. pap. 13.00 (*0-06-092105-6*, Perennial) HarperTrade.

De Voto, Bernard A., ed. see Twain, Mark, pseud.

De Voto, J. Taktika: A Manual for Ancient Warfare. (Illus.). viii, 132p. (Orig.). (C). 1993. pap. text 15.00 (*0-89005-517-3*) Ares.

De Voto, J. & Miller, M. C. Fortification of the Roman Camp: Polybius & PS-Hyginus. (Illus.). vi, 120p. (Orig.). (C). 1994. pap. text 15.00 (*0-89005-518-1*) Ares.

De Vree, Johan K., et al. Towards a European Foreign Policy: Legal, Economic, & Political Dimensions. LC 87-5612. 1987. lib. bdg. 147.00 (*90-247-3506-8*) Kluwer Academic.

De Vreee, Freddy, jt. auth. see Restany, Pierre.

De Vriend, H. J., ed. The Old English Herbarium & Medicina de Quadrupedibus. (Early English Text Society Original Ser.: No. 286). 1984. 59.00 (*0-19-722288-9*) OUP.

De Vries, A. Dictionary of Symbols & Imagery. 2nd rev. ed. 516p. 1984. 145.00 (*0-444-10607-3*, North Holland) Elsevier.

De Vries, Andre. Live & Work in Belgium, The Netherlands & Luxembourg. 2nd ed. (Live & Work Abroad Guides Ser.). 288p. (Orig.). 1998. pap. 17.95 (*1-85458-188-0*, Pub. by Vac Wrk Pubns) Seven Hills Bk.

De Vries, Andre & Adams, Greg. Live & Work in Belgium, The Netherlands & Luxembourg. (Live & Work Abroad Guides Ser.). 272p. (Orig.). 1997. pap. 16.95 (*1-85458-076-0*, Pub. by Vac Wrk Pubns) Seven Hills Bk.

De Vries, Anke. Bruises. 176p. (YA). (gr. 9 up). 1997. mass mkt. 4.50 (*0-440-22694-5*) BDD Bks Young Read.

— Bruises. Knecht, Stacey, tr. 174p. (J). (gr. 6-9). 1995. 15.95 (*1-886910-03-0*) Front Str.

— Bruises. 1997. 9.60 (*0-606-12900-6*, Pub. by Turtleback) Demco.

— Feliz Cumpleanos Vivi! Smith, Odette, tr. from DUT.Tr. of Happy Birthday Vivi!. (SPA., Illus.). (J). (ps-1). 1997. 12.99 (*968-16-5418-8*) Fondo CA.

— My Elephant Can Do Almost Anything. LC 95-40267. (Illus.). 28p. (J). (gr. k-3). 1996. 14.95 (*1-886910-06-5*, Front Street) Front Str.

— Piggy's Birthday Dream. LC 97-10027. (Illus.). 32p. (J). 14.95 (*1-886910-21-9*, Front Street) Front Str.

De Vries, B. W. From Pedlars to Textile Barons. (Verhandelingen der Koninklijke Nederlandse Akademie van Wetenschappen, Afd. Letterkunde, Nieuwe Reeks Ser.: No. 141). 340p. pap. 59.50 (*0-444-85687-0*) Elsevier.

De Vries, Barend A. Champions of the Poor: The Economic Consequences of Judeo-Christian Values. LC 97-37200. 336p. 1998. 55.00 (*0-87840-664-6*); pap. 24.95 (*0-87840-665-4*) Georgetown U Pr.

— Remaking the World Bank. LC 87-23406. 184p. (Orig.). 1988. pap. 14.95 (*0-932020-49-6*) Seven Locks Pr.

De Vries, Bert. Umm El-Jimal - A Frontier Town & Its Landscape in Northern Jordan Vol. 1: Fieldwork, 1972-1981. (JRA Supplementary Ser.: Vol. 26). (Illus.). 248p. 1998. 89.50 (*1-887829-26-1*) Jour Roman Arch.

De Vries, Bert, jt. ed. see Rotmans, Jan.

De Vries, Betty. Bible Activities for Everyone. (Illus.). 160p. (gr. k-7). 1999. pap. 6.99 (*0-8010-4429-4*) Baker Bks.

— Search & Solve: Bible Activity Sheets. (Repro Bks Ser.). 128p. (gr. 1-7). 1998. pap. 11.99 (*0-8010-5770-1*) Baker Bks.

De Vries, Betty, et al. Bible Activities for Ever Day. (Illus.). 160p. (gr. k-7). 1999. pap. 6.99 (*0-8010-4430-8*) Baker Bks.

De Vries, Bob. Gotta Have It! It's a Stewardship Thing. (LifeWise Ser.). 1995. pap., teacher ed. 7.95 (*1-56212-084-0*) CRC Pubns.

De Vries, Brian. End of Life Issues: Interdisciplinary & Multidimensional Perspectives. LC 99-14662. (Death & Suicide Ser.). (Illus.). 406p. 1999. text 44.95 (*0-8261-1260-9*) Springer Pub.

De Vries, Brian & Conrad, Bonnie H. Kinship Bereavement in Later (OM35:1) (Death & Bereavement Ser.). 164p. 1997. pap. 18.95 (*0-89503-182-5*, OM35:1) Baywood Pub.

De Vries, C. M. On the Way to Bethlehem. Vilain, Frederic, tr. from DUT. LC 90-43765. (Illus.). 14p. (Orig.). (J). (ps-1). 1990. pap. 2.95 (*0-8198-5415-8*) Pauline Bks.

***De Vries, Clare.** I Am Claudius. 320p. 2000. pap. 14.95 (*1-58234-105-2*) Bloomsbury Pubg.

— I & Claudius: Travels with My Cat. 320p. 1999. 23.95 (*1-58234-054-4*) Bloomsbury Pubg.

De Vries, David, jt. auth. see Swanson, Mark T.

***de Vries, Dirk.** Attitude Life Skills: 32 Powerful Sessions on Real-Life Issues for Teens, 2. 136p. (J). (gr. 8-13). 2000. 14.95 (*1-889108-43-X*) Liv Good News.

De Vries-Evans, Susanna. The Lost Impressionists: Masterpieces from Private Collections. LC 92-80168. (Illus.). 192p. 1992. 40.00 (*1-879373-25-4*) Roberts Rinehart.

De Vries, F. W., et al, eds. Systems Approaches for Agricultural Development: Proceedings of the International Symposium on Systems Approaches for Agricultural Development, 2-6 December 1991, Bangkok, Thailand. LC 92-20496. (System Approaches for Sustainable Agricultural Development Ser.: Vol. 2). 560p. (C). 1992. text 355.00 (*0-7923-1880-3*) Kluwer Academic.

de Vries, F. W. Penning, see Stein, A. & Penning de Vries, F. W.

De Vries, G. J. Miscellaneous Notes on Plato. (Mededelingen der Koninklijke Nederlandse Akademie van Wetenschappen, Afd. Letterkunde Ser.: No. 38(1)). 1975. pap. text 8.75 (*0-7204-8294-1*) Elsevier.

De Vries, H. W., jt. ed. see Rijnberk, Adam.

De Vries, Henri, tr. see Kuyper, Abraham.

De Vries, Hent. Philosophy & the Turn to Religion. LC 99-10359. 1999. 55.00 (*0-8018-5994-8*); pap. 24.95 (*0-8018-5995-6*) Johns Hopkins.

De Vries, Hilary & Bluestein-Davis, Susan. After Midnight: The Life & Death of Brad Davis. (Illus.). 320p. 1998. per. 14.00 (*0-671-79673-9*, PB Trade Paper) PB.

De Vries, Ineke M. & Rubenstein, Michael. How to Combat Sexual Harassment at Work: A Guide to Implementing the European Commission Code of Practice. (Illus.). 104p. (Orig.). (C). 1995. pap. text 35.00 (*0-7881-2399-8*) DIANE Pub.

De Vries, J. Economy of Europe in an Age of Crisis, 1600-1750. LC 75-30438. (Illus.). 295p. 1976. pap. text 19.95 (*0-521-29050-3*) Cambridge U Pr.

— Elements of Toplogical Dynamics. LC 93-7603. (Mathematics & Its Applications Ser.: Vol. 257). 768p. (C). 1993. text 353.00 (*0-7923-2287-8*) Kluwer Academic.

De Vries, J. G., jt. ed. see Terhal, P.

De Vries, J. L., jt. auth. see Jenkins, R.

De Vries, Jan. Arthritis, Rheumatism & Psoriasis. (By Appointment Only Ser.). 124p. 1988. pap. 8.95 (*1-85158-690-3*, Pub. by Mainstream Pubng) Trafalgar.

De Vries, Jan. Cancer & Leukaemia. pap. 11.95 (*1-85158-649-0*, Pub. by Mainstream Pubng) Trafalgar.

De Vries, Jan. The Dutch Rural Economy in the Golden Age, 1500-1700. LC 73-86889. (Yale Series in Economic History). 336p. reprint ed. pap. 104.20 (*0-8357-8707-9*, 203370900087) Bks Demand.

— The Encyclopedia of Energy Healing: A Complete Guide to Using the Major Forms of Healing for Body, Mind & Soul. LC 99-36383. (Illus.). 192p. 1999. 29.95 (*0-8069-9907-1*) Sterling.

— European Urbanization: Fifteen Hundred to Eighteen Hundred. (Illus.). 432p. 1984. 49.95 (*0-674-27015-0*) HUP.

— The Five Senses: Touch, Smell, Taste, Hearing & Vision. 208p. 1998. pap. 15.95 (*1-85158-953-8*, Pub. by Mainstream Pubng) Trafalgar.

— Heroic Song & Heroic Legend. Bolle, Kees W., ed. LC 77-79157. (Mythology Ser.). 1978. reprint ed. lib. bdg. 25.95 (*0-405-10566-5*) Ayer.

***De Vries, Jan.** Inner Harmony: Achieving Physical, Mental & Emotional Well-Being. 1999. pap. text 15.95 (*1-84018-062-5*, Pub. by Mainstream Pubng) Trafalgar.

De Vries, Jan. Melissa Extract: The Natural Remedy for Herpes. (Good Health Guides Ser.). 48p. 1996. pap. 3.95 (*0-87983-719-5*, 37195K, Keats Publng) NTC Contemp Pub Co.

— Menstrual & Pre-Menstrual Tension. (Well Woman Ser.). 160p. 1992. pap. 11.95 (*1-85158-417-X*, Pub. by Mainstream Pubng) Trafalgar.

— Multiple Sclerosis. (By Appointment Only Ser.). 125p. 1985. pap. 13.95 (*0-906391-98-9*, Pub. by Mainstream Pubng) Trafalgar.

— Pregnancy & Childbirth. 144p. 1996. pap. 10.95 (*1-85158-657-1*, Pub. by Mainstream Pubng) Trafalgar.

— Questions & Answers on Family Health. 320p. 1994. pap. 16.95 (*1-85158-587-7*, Pub. by Mainstream Pubng) Trafalgar.

— Stress & Nervous Disorders. (By Appointment Only Ser.). 126p. 1998. pap. 13.95 (*1-85158-651-2*, Pub. by Mainstream Pubng) Trafalgar.

— Traditional Home & Herbal Remedies. (By Appointment Only Ser.). 158p. 1988. pap. 11.95 (*1-85158-012-3*, Pub. by Mainstream Pubng) Trafalgar.

— Viruses, Allergies & the Immune System. (By Appointment Only Ser.). 128p. 1988. pap. 13.95 (*1-85158-176-6*, Pub. by Mainstream Pubng) Trafalgar.

— Water: Healer or Poison? (By Appointment Only Ser.). 123p. 1988. pap. 11.95 (*1-85158-341-6*, Pub. by Mainstream Pubng) Trafalgar.

De Vries, Jan & Van-Der-Woude, Ad. The First Modern Economy: Success, Failure, & Perseverance of the Dutch Economy, 1500-1815. (Illus.). 789p. (C). 1997. text 89.95 (*0-521-57061-1*) Cambridge U Pr.

De Vries, Jan & Woude, Ad van der. The First Modern Economy: Success, Failure, & Perseverance of the Dutch Economy, 1500-1815. 789p. (C). 1997. pap. text 29.95 (*0-521-57825-6*) Cambridge U Pr.

De Vries, Jan, jt. ed. see Freedberg, David.

De Vries, Jan E., et al. Interleukin-10. LC 94-40332. (Molecular Biology Intelligence Unit Ser.). 160p. 1995. text 99.00 (*1-57059-092-3*) Landes Bioscience.

De Vries, Jan V. Architectura. 1973. reprint ed. write for info. (*3-487-05854-5*) G Olms Pubs.

De Vries, Jetty, jt. auth. see Verleun, Jan A.

De Vries, John. Food Safety & Toxicity. LC 95-50844. 368p. 1996. boxed set 74.95 (*0-8493-9488-0*) CRC Pr.

De Vries, John, et al, eds. Toxicology Principles & Applications. 1312p. 1996. boxed set 159.95 (*0-8493-9232-2*, 9232) CRC Pr.

De Vries, L. & Herrmann, T. English-German Technical & Engineering Dictionary. (ENG & GER.). 1153p. 1972. 179.00 (*3-87097-043-X*) IBD Ltd.

De Vries, Leonard. Victorian Inventions. (Illus.). 192p. 1992. pap. 24.95 (*0-7195-5006-8*, Pub. by John Murray) Trafalgar.

De Vries, Linda S., jt. auth. see Govaert, Paul.

De Vries, Louis. Dictionary of Chemistry & Chemical Engineering, Vol. 2. (ENG & GER.). 1972. pap. 350.00 (*0-8288-6367-9*, M-7125) Fr & Eur.

— Woerterbuch der Textilindustrie: Dictionary of Textile Industry, Vol. 2. (GER.). 95.00 (*0-8288-8029-8*, M6948) Fr & Eur.

De Vries, Louis & Kolb, Harold. Dictionary of Chemistry & Chemical Engineering, Vol. 1. 3rd ed. (ENG & GER.). 851p. 1983. 350.00 (*0-8288-0165-7*, M7126) Fr & Eur.

De Vries, Lourens, jt. auth. see Van Enk, Gerrit J.

De Vries, Lyckle. Diamante Gedenkzuilen en Leerzaeme Voorbeelden: Een Bespreking van Johan van Gools "Nieuwe Schouburg" (DUT., Illus.). 280p. 1991. 55.00 (*90-6980-032-2*, Pub. by Egbert Forsten) Hodlder & Stoughton.

— Gerard de Lairesse: An Artist Between Stage & Studio. LC 98-161340. (Illus.). 224p. 1998. pap. text 34.50 (*90-5356-250-8*, Pub. by Amsterdam U Pr) U of Mich Pr.

De Vries, M. J., ed. Design Methodology & Relationships with Science: Proceedings of the NATO Advanced Research Workshop, Eindhoven, the Netherlands, September 29 - October 2, 1992. (NATO Advanced Science Institutes Series C: Mathematical & Physical Sciences). 336p. (C). 1993. lib. bdg. 205.50 (*0-7923-2191-X*, Pub. by Kluwer Academic) Kluwer Academic.

De Vries, Manfred F. Organizational Paradoxes: Clinical Approaches to Management. 2nd ed. LC 94-15858. (Illus.). 240p. (C). (gr. 13). 1994. pap. 16.99 (*0-415-11073-4*, B4781) Thomson Learn.

De Vries, Manfred F. Kets, see Kets de Vries, Manfred F., ed.

De Vries Manfred F.R. Kets Staff & Florent-Treacy, Elizabeth. The New Global Leaders: Richard Branson, Percy Barnevik, & David Simon. LC HD62.4.K484 1999. 224p. 1999. 28.50 (*0-7879-4657-5*) Jossey-Bass.

De Vries, Manfred K. Human Dilemmas in Family Business: Texts & Cases. (Illus.). 336p. 1996. pap. 32.95 (*0-415-11462-4*) Thomson Learn.

De Vries, Margaret G. Balance of Payments Adjustment, 1945 to 1986: The IMF Experience. LC 87-17242. xi, 336p. 1987. pap. 14.50 (*0-939934-93-0*) Intl Monetary.

D

— The IMF in a Changing World, 1945-85. LC 86-2861. 236p. reprint ed. pap. 73.20 (*0-608-17977-9*, 202908700058) Bks Demand.
— The International Monetary Fund, 1972-1978: Cooperation on Trial, 3 vols., 1. LC 85-2352. 627p. reprint ed. pap. 194.40 (*0-608-16282-5*, 202623800001) Bks Demand.
— The International Monetary Fund, 1972-1978: Cooperation on Trial, 3 vols., 2. LC 85-2352. 578p. reprint ed. pap. 179.20 (*0-608-16283-3*, 202623800002) Bks Demand.
— The International Monetary Fund, 1972-1978: Cooperation on Trial, 3 vols., 3. LC 85-2352. 669p. reprint ed. pap. 200.00 (*0-608-16284-1*, 202623800003) Bks Demand.
— The International Monetary Fund, 1972-1978: Cooperation on Trial, 3 vols., Set. LC 85-2352. 1985. 60.00 (*0-939934-43-4*) Intl Monetary.
— The International Monetary Fund, 1972-1978: Cooperation on Trial, 3 vols., Vol. 1: Narrative & Analysis. LC 85-2352. xxiii, 603p. 1985. 25.00 (*0-939934-40-X*) Intl Monetary.
— The International Monetary Fund, 1972-1978: Cooperation on Trial, 3 vols., Vol. 2: Narrative & Analysis (Concluded) LC 85-2352. x, 547p. 1985. 25.00 (*0-939934-41-8*) Intl Monetary.
— The International Monetary Fund, 1972-1978: Cooperation on Trial, 3 vols., Vol. 3: Documents. LC 85-2352. xii, 657p. 1985. 25.00 (*0-939934-42-6*) Intl Monetary.
— The International Monetary Fund, 1966-1971: The System Under Stress, 2 vols., Set. Incl. Vol. 1. Narrative. xxii, 699p. 1976. 11.00 (*0-939934-09-4*); Vol. 2. Documents. viii, 339p. 1976. 6.00 (*0-939934-10-8*); 1976. 15.00 (*0-939934-11-6*) Intl Monetary.

De Vries, Marten J., et al, eds. Intelligent Transportation Systems, Vol. 3207. LC 98-191013. 334p. 1998. 69.00 (*0-8194-2639-3*) SPIE.

De Vries, Marten J., jt. ed. see Chachich, Alan C.

De Vries, Marten W. Extreme Stress & Communities: Impact & Intervention. Hobfoll, Stevan E., ed. LC 95-14392. (Proceedings of the NATO Advanced Research Workshop on 'Stress & Communities' Chateau de Bonas, France, June 14-18, 1994: Vol. 80). 560p. (C). 1995. lib. bdg. 276.00 (*0-7923-3468-X*) Kluwer Academic.

De Vries, Marten W., ed. The Experience of Psychopathology: Investigating Mental Disorders in Their Natural Settings. 447p. (C). 1992. text 130.00 (*0-521-40339-1*) Cambridge U Pr.

De Vries, Mary A. Barron's Business Thesaurus. LC 95-43483. 384p. 1996. pap. 12.95 (*0-8120-9327-5*) Barron.

***De Vries, Mary A.** Complete Desk Reference for Office Professionals. 2000. pap. 20.00 (*0-7352-0184-6*) PH Pr.

De Vries, Mary A. Complete Secretary's Handbook. 7th ed. 436p. (C). 1993. text 24.95 (*0-13-159674-8*) P-H.
— The Elements of Correspondence. 288p. 1996. 12.95 (*0-02-860840-2*) Macmillan.
— Legal Secretary's Complete Handbook. 4th ed. LC 92-8332. 656p. (C). 1992. text 29.95 (*0-13-529876-8*) P-H.
— Professional Secretary's Book of Lists & Tips. 448p. (C). 1994. text 29.95 (*0-13-149345-0*) P-H.
— Vocabulary Book. LC 98-143969. 384p. 1998. mass mkt. 6.99 (*0-451-19268-0*, Sig) NAL.
— Writer's Almanac & Fact Book. 1986. pap. 3.95 (*0-317-38976-9*, Sig) NAL.

***De Vries, Mary Ann.** New Roberts Rules of Order. 1999. pap. 14.55 (*0-613-17400-3*) Econo-Clad Bks.
— The Prentice Hall Office Administrator's Deskbook. LC 00-41667. 2000. write for info. (*0-13-022683-1*) P-H.

De Vries, Michiel S. Calculated Choices in Policy-Making: The Theory & Practice of Impact Assessment. LC 98-38460. 264p. 1999. text 65.00 (*0-312-21984-9*) St Martin.

De Vries, Nanny M., jt. ed. see Best, Jan G.

De Vries, Nellie & Currier, Mary. Bible Activities You Can Do. (Repro Bks Ser.). (Illus.). 160p. (gr. k-7). 1999. pap. 6.99 (*0-8010-4417-0*) Baker Bks.
— More Bible Activities You Can Do. (Repro Bks Ser.). (Illus.). 160p. (J). (gr. k-7). 1999. pap. 6.99 (*0-8010-4416-2*) Baker Bks.

De Vries, P. G. Sampling Theory for Forest Inventory. (Illus.). 420p. 1986. 64.95 (*0-387-17066-9*) Spr-Verlag.

De Vries, Penning, et al. Simulation of Ecophysiological Processes of Growth in Several Annual Crops. 280p. 1989. 56.00 (*90-220-0937-8*, SM 29, Pub. by Pudoc Sci Pubs) Balogh.

De Vries, Pieter, jt. auth. see Zendejas, Sergio.

De Vries, Pieter, jt. ed. see Zendejas, Sergio.

De Vries, R. R., et al, eds. The Role of Micro-Organisms in Non-Infectious Disease. (Argenteuil Symposia Ser.). (Illus.). 208p. 1990. 81.00 (*0-387-19623-4*) Spr-Verlag.

De Vries, R. R., jt. ed. see Van Rood, J. J.

De Vries, Rene, jt. auth. see Ottenhoff, Tom.

De Vries, Robbie. Snowprints: A Grandmother's Glimpses of New Life & Old Art. LC 90-91420. (Lifeprints Ser.: Vol. I). (Orig.). pap. write for info. (*0-9627886-0-0*) R R P de Vries.

De Vries, Robbie R. A Cultural Exchange: American & Chinese Weddings: a High Tea & Linen Shower for Miss Mary Lynn. LC 93-90931. (Lifeprints Ser.: Vol. II). (Illus.). (Orig.). 1993. pap. 12.95 (*0-9627886-1-9*) R R P de Vries.
— A Cultural Exchange: American & Chinese Weddings: A High Tea & Linen Shower for Miss Mary Lynn. 2nd ed. Zhang, Ellen, tr. (Lifeprints Ser.: Vol. III). (CHI., Illus.). 1995. pap. 14.95 (*0-9627886-2-7*) R R P de Vries.

De Vries, Robert C. Family Ties. 121p. pap., teacher ed. 20.10 (*0-930265-76-9*) CRC Pubns.
— Family Ties. (Illus.). 121p. pap., student ed. 11.25 (*0-930265-75-0*) CRC Pubns.

De Vries, Robert C., jt. auth. see Zonnebelt-Smeenge, Susan J.

De Vries, Sherry & De Vries, Wayne. The Fire Escape BBQ: A Cookbook for Grilling Enthusiasts Anywhere. 32p. 1993. pap. 4.95 (*1-883849-00-4*) Nine Hund Forty Six Pr.
— The Rained Out BBQ. 32p. 1993. pap. 4.95 (*1-883849-01-2*) Nine Hund Forty Six Pr.

De Vries-van der Velden, Eva. L' Elite Byzantine Devant l'Avance Turque a l'Epoque de la Guerre Civile de 1341 a 1354. (FRE.). 306p. 1989. 71.00 (*90-5063-026-X*, Pub. by Gieben) J Benjamins Pubng Co.
— Theodore Metochite: Une Reevaluation. (FRE.). x, 276p. (C). 1987. 84.00 (*90-70265-58-3*, Pub. by Gieben) J Benjamins Pubng Co.

de Vries, Vicki, ed. Tennis Etiquette: A Winning Way of Life. Date not set. write for info. (*0-9679796-0-9*) N Koran.

De Vries, W. R. & Dornfield, D. A., eds. Inspection & Quality Control in Manufacturing Systems. (PED Ser.: Vol. 6). 1982. 24.00 (*0-685-06282-1*, H00249) ASME.

De Vries, Wayne, jt. auth. see De Vries, Sherry.

De Vries, William. James: Living on the Edge. LC 94-23551. (Revelation Ser.). 1995. pap., student ed. 4.95 (*1-56212-077-8*) CRC Pubns.

De Vries, Wim. Sonderstab Musik: The Systematic Plundering of the Arts in Nazi-Occupied Europe. (Orig.). (C). 1996. pap. 37.50 (*90-5356-175-7*, Pub. by Amsterdam U Pr) U of Mich Pr.

De Vrijer, R. C., jt. auth. see Klop, J. W.

De Vroom, Bert, jt. ed. see Naschold, Frieder.

De Vroom, Theresia, ed. Netherlandic Secular Plays from the Middle Ages: The "Abele Spelen" & the Farces of the Hulthem Manuscript. LC 96-901017. (Carleton Renaissance Plays in Translation Ser.: No. 29). 225p. 1997. 28.00 (*1-895537-41-X*, Pub. by Dovehouse); pap. 12.00 (*1-895537-35-5*, Pub. by Dovehouse) Sterling.

De Vylder, F., et al, eds. Premium Calculation in Insurance. 1984. text 256.50 (*90-277-1732-X*) Kluwer Academic.

De Vylder, F., et al. Premium Calculation in Insurance. (C). 1984. 690.00 (*0-7855-4060-1*, Pub. by Witherby & Co) St Mut.

De Vylder, F. Etienne. Life Insurance Theory: Actuarial Perspectives. LC 97-30711. 248p. 1997. 110.00 (*0-7923-9995-1*) Kluwer Academic.

De Vylder, Stefan. Allende's Chile: The Political Economy of the Rise & Fall of Unidad Popular, Vol. 7. LC 72-27797. (Cambridge Latin American Studies: No. 25). 221p. reprint ed. pap. 75.00 (*0-8357-5318-2*, 2026338) Bks Demand.

De Vylder, Stefan, jt. auth. see Fforde, Adam.

De Vyver, Jane M. The Artistic Unity of the Russian Orthodox Church: Religion, Liturgy, Icons & Architecture. (Illus.). 80p. (Orig.). 1992. pap. 6.95 (*1-881211-01-0*) Firebird Videos.
— Dancing in the Presence. 2nd rev. ed. (Illus.). 76p. 1994. pap. 9.95 (*1-881211-17-7*) Firebird Videos.
— The Orthodox Church's Vision of Unity. (Illus.). 36p. 1995. pap. 3.50 (*1-881211-24-X*) Firebird Videos.
— Recently Canonized Orthodox Saints: Their Lives & Icons. 2nd rev. ed. (Illus.). 28p. 1994. pap. 4.50 (*1-881211-21-5*) Firebird Videos.
— Visions of Love & Life & Beauty. (Illus.). 76p. 1994. pap. 9.95 (*1-881211-18-5*) Firebird Videos.

De Waal, Alexander. Famine Crimes: Politics & the Disaster Relief Industry in Africa. LC 97-29463. (African Issues Ser.). 256p. Date not set. 39.95 (*0-253-33367-9*); pap. 16.95 (*0-253-21158-1*) Ind U Pr.

***de Waal, Andre.** Power of Performance Management: How Leading Companies Create Sustained Value. 224p. 2001. 39.95 (*0-471-38347-3*) Wiley.

De Waal, Anke Van, see Van De Waal, Anke.

De Waal, Edmund. Bernard Leach. (St. Ives Artists Ser.). (Illus.). 80p. 1998. pap. 19.95 (*1-85437-227-0*, Pub. by Tate Gallery) U of Wash Pr.

***De Waal, Edmund.** New Ceramic Design. (Illus.). 2000. 32.99 (*1-880140-44-6*) Guild.

De Waal, Ester. A Seven Day Journey with Thomas Merton. LC 93-16820. (Illus.). 116p. 1993. reprint ed. pap. 12.99 (*0-89283-789-6*, Charis) Servant.

De Waal, Esther. The Celtic Way of Prayer: The Recovery of the Religious Imagination. LC 96-19712. 256p. 1997. 21.00 (*0-385-48663-4*) Delacorte.
— The Celtic Way of Prayer: The Recovery of the Religious Imagination. 256p. 1999. pap. 10.95 (*0-385-49374-6*) Doubleday.
— Every Earthly Blessing: Rediscovering the Celtic Tradition. LC 99-20291. 160p. 1999. pap. 10.95 (*0-8192-1806-5*, 6096) Morehouse Pub.
— God under My Roof: Celtic Songs & Blessings. LC 85-71565. (Illus.). 40p. 1985. pap. 4.95 (*0-941478-42-4*, 930-029, Pub. by Paraclete MA) BookWorld.
— A Life-Giving Way: A Commentary on the Rule of St. Benedict. 224p. 1995. pap. 19.95 (*0-8146-2358-1*, Liturg Pr Bks) Liturgical Pr.

***De Waal, Esther.** Living with Contradiction: An Introduction to Benedictine Spirituality. LC 97-48801. 176p. 1998. pap. 10.95 (*0-8192-1754-9*) Morehouse Pub.

De Waal, Esther. Seeking God: The Way of St. Benedict. 160p. 1985. pap. 5.95 (*0-8146-1388-8*) Liturgical Pr.

***De Waal, Esther.** Tintern. 48p. 2000. pap. 6.50 (*1-85311-312-3*) Canterbury Press Norwich.

De Waal, Esther, ed. The Celtic Vision. LC 90-34258. (Illus.). 263p. (Orig.). 1990. reprint ed. pap. 12.95 (*0-932506-83-6*) St Bedes Pubns.

De Waal, Esther, jt. ed. see Allchin, A. M.

De Waal, Fans B., jt. ed. see Harcourt Brace Staff.

De Waal, Frans. Bonobo: The Forgotten Ape. LC 96-41095. (Illus.). 234p. 1997. 45.00 (*0-520-20535-9*, Pub. by U CA Pr) Cal Prin Full Svc.
— Chimpanzee Politics: Power & Sex Among Apes. LC 97-44284. (Illus.). 200p. 1998. 29.95 (*0-8018-5839-9*) Johns Hopkins.
— Chimpanzee Politics: Power & Sex Among Apes. LC 88-46075. (Illus.). 232p. 1989. reprint ed. pap. 15.95 (*0-8018-3833-9*) Johns Hopkins.

***De Waal, Frans.** Chimpanzee Politics: Power & Sex Among Apes. rev. ed. (Illus.). 2000. pap. 17.95 (*0-8018-6336-8*) Johns Hopkins.

De Waal, Frans. Good Natured: The Origins of Right & Wrong in Humans & Other Animals. LC 95-46032. (Illus.). 384p. (C). 1996. 24.95 (*0-674-35660-8*) HUP.
— Good Natured: The Origins of Right & Wrong in Humans & Other Animals. (Illus.). 304p. 1996. reprint ed. pap. 14.95 (*0-674-35661-6*) HUP.

De Waal, Frans & Lanting, Frans. Bonobo: The Forgotten Ape. (Illus.). 200p. 1998. pap. 24.95 (*0-520-21651-2*, Pub. by U CA Pr) Cal Prin Full Svc.

De Waal, Frans B. Chimpanzee Cultures. Wrangham, Richard W. et al, eds. LC 94-9080. (Illus.). 448p. 1994. text 46.50 (*0-674-11662-3*, WRACHI) HUP.
— Peacemaking among Primates. LC 88-11067. (Illus.). 320p. 1989. 44.50 (*0-674-65920-1*) HUP.
— Peacemaking among Primates. (Illus.). 320p. 1989. pap. text 17.50 (*0-674-65921-X*) HUP.

De Waal, Frans B. M., jt. ed. see Aureli, Filippo.

De Waal, Franz. Lorenz on Mount Fuji. Date not set. 26.00 (*0-465-04175-2*, Pub. by Basic); pap. write for info. (*0-465-04176-0*) Basic.

De Waal, Franz, jt. auth. see Hart, Stephen.

de Waal, H. Van, see Van de Waal, H.

***De Waal, J., et al.** The Bill of Rights Handbook. 2nd ed. LC 99-213762. 1999. pap. 34.00 (*0-7021-4923-3*, Pub. by Juta & Co) Gaunt.

De Waal, J., et al. The Bill of Rights Handbook, 1998. 1998. 27.50 (*0-7021-4535-1*, Pub. by Juta & Co) Gaunt.

***de Waal, Johan, et al.** The Bill of Rights Handbook. 3rd ed. 620p. 2000. pap. 41.50 (*0-7021-5145-9*, 18663, Pub. by Juta & Co) Gaunt.

De Waal, K. J. & Van Den Brink, W. J., eds. Environmental Technology. (C). 1987. text 389.50 (*90-247-3575-0*) Kluwer Academic.

De Waal, Louise, et al, eds. Rehabilitation of Rivers. LC 98-27224. 350p. 1999. 145.00 (*0-471-95753-4*) Wiley.

De Waal, M. J., et al. Erfreg Studentehandboek. (GER.). 210p. 1992. pap. write for info. (*0-7021-2773-6*, Pub. by Juta & Co) Gaunt.
— Law of Succession Students' Handbook. 2nd ed. 217p. 1996. pap. 27.50 (*0-7021-3626-3*, 15627, Pub. by Juta & Co) Gaunt.
— Succession Student's Handbook. 217p. 1993. pap. write for info. (*0-7021-2915-1*, Pub. by Juta & Co) Gaunt.

De Waal Malefijt, Annemarie. Religion & Culture: An Introduction to Anthropology of Religion. (Illus.). 407p. (C). 1990. reprint ed. pap. text 19.95 (*0-88133-483-9*) Waveland Pr.

De Waal, Ronald B. The Universal Sherlock Holmes, 5 vols., Vol. 1. LC 93-95453. (Illus.). 1440p. 1994. spiral bd. 180.00 (*1-896032-00-1*) Battered Silicon.

De Waal, T., jt. auth. see Willenborg, L.

De Waal, Thomas, jt. auth. see Gall, Carlotta.

De Waal, Victor. The Politics of Reconciliation: Zimbabwe's First Decade. LC 90-81935. 150p. (C). 1990. 39.95 (*0-86543-186-8*); pap. 12.95 (*0-86543-187-6*) Africa World.

De Waard-Dekking, P., tr. see De Jonge, P.

De Waard, Jack & De Waard, Nancy. Surprising Science: 180 Fun & Challenging Science Brain Teasers for Kids: Level 1, Budding Genius, Level 1. 192p. (J). (gr. 3-5). 1996. pap. 9.95 (*0-673-36311-2*, GoodYrBooks) Addson-Wesley Educ.
— Surprising Science: 180 Fun & Challenging Science Brain Teasers for Kids: Level 2, Genius, Level 2. 192p. (J). (gr. 4-6). 1996. pap. 9.95 (*0-673-36312-0*, GoodYrBooks) Addson-Wesley Educ.

De Waard, Jan. A Handbook on Isaiah. LC 97-32827. 1997. text 29.50 (*1-57506-023-X*) Eisenbrauns.

De Waard, Jan & Nida, Eugene A. A Handbook on the Book of Ruth. 2nd ed. LC 94-18833. (UBS Handbook Ser.). Orig. Title: A Translator's Handbook on the Book of Ruth. viii, 99p. 1992. pap. 8.99 (*0-8267-0111-6*, 104855) Untd Bible Soc.

De Waard, Jan & Smalley, William A. A Handbook on the Book of Amos. LC 94-18835. (UBS Handbook Ser.). Orig. Title: A Translator's Handbook on the Book of Amos. viii, 274p. 1979. pap. 14.99 (*0-8267-0131-0*, 102715) Untd Bible Soc.

De Waard, Nancy. Science Puzzlers. (Illus.). 240p. 1997. pap. text 12.95 (*0-673-36378-3*, GoodYrBooks) Addson-Wesley Educ.

De Waard, Nancy, jt. auth. see De Waard, Jack.

de Waarsenburgh, Hans Van, see Van de Waarsenburgh, Hans.

De Waele, Jos. The Propylaia of the Akropolis in Athens: The Project of Mnesikles. (Publications of the Netherlands Institute at Athens: Vol. 1). 106p. 1991. 94.00 (*90-5063-059-6*, Pub. by Gieben) J Benjamins Pubng Co.

De Waelhens, A. La Philosophie et les Experiences Naturelles. (Phaenomenologica Ser.: No. 9). 220p. 1967. pap. text 81.00 (*90-247-0243-7*, Pub. by M Nijhoff) Kluwer Academic.

De Wagenheim, Olga J. El Grito de Lares: Sus Causas & Sus Hombres. LC 84-80158. (Coleccion Semilla). (SPA.). 231p. 1984. pap. 8.25 (*0-940238-75-6*) Ediciones Huracan.
— Puerto Rico's Revolt for Independence: El Grito de Lares. LC 93-15391. (Illus.). 186p. (C). 1993. reprint ed. pap. text 14.95 (*1-55876-071-7*) Wiener Pubs Inc.

De Wagenheim, Olga Jimenez, see Wagenheim, Kal & Jimenez de Wagenheim, Olga, eds.

De Wall, Clement T. Escaping the Mental Straightjacket: Personal Experience as Our Spritual Guide. 250p. 1998. pap. 19.95 (*0-88100-109-0*) Natl Writ Pr.

De Wall, Clement T., see De Wall, Clement T.

De Walle, F. Agriculture & the Environment: Minerals, Manure & Measures. 211p. 1998. 105.00 (*0-7923-4794-3*) Kluwer Academic.

De Walle, F. B., et al, eds. Environmental Condition of the Mediterranean Sea: European Community Countries. LC 93-28722. (Environment & Assessment Ser.: Vol. 5). 540p. (C). 1993. text 223.00 (*0-7923-2468-4*) Kluwer Academic.

de Walle, Mark Van, see Van de Walle, Mark.

De Walle, Nicolas Van, see Bienen, Henry S. & Van De Walle, Nicolas.

De Walle, Nicolas Van, see Van De Walle, Nicolas, ed.

De Wallens, Gerard, see Wallens, Gerard de.

De Wardener, H. E., jt. auth. see MacGregor, G. A.

De Wardner, H. E. The Kidney. 5th ed. (Illus.). 604p. 1985. text 94.00 (*0-443-02841-9*) Church.

De Water, Lois L. Lois: Swiss Roots in Willard Soil. (Illus.). 132p. (Orig.). 1987. pap. 14.95 (*0-9618510-0-7*) Wilderness Valley Pub.

De Waters, Lillian. The Finished Kingdom: A Study of the Absolute. 233p. 1996. reprint ed. spiral bd. 14.00 (*0-7873-0273-2*) Hlth Research.
— The Finished Kingdom: A Study of the Absolute,(1925) 240p. 1996. reprint ed. pap. 13.95 (*1-56459-741-5*) Kessinger Pub.
— Glad Tidings. 316p. 1998. reprint ed. pap. 24.95 (*0-7661-0352-8*) Kessinger Pub.
— The Hidden Truth. 69p. 1996. reprint ed. spiral bd. 11.00 (*0-7873-0277-5*) Hlth Research.
— Journeying Onward (1908) 48p. 1998. reprint ed. pap. 12.95 (*0-7661-0198-3*) Kessinger Pub.
— The Living Way. 20p. 1996. reprint ed. spiral bd. 8.00 (*0-7873-0276-7*) Hlth Research.
— One: A Study of the Absolute. 222p. 1998. reprint ed. pap. 18.95 (*0-7661-0222-X*) Kessinger Pub.
— Science of Ascension: A Study of Our Being. 181p. 1996. reprint ed. spiral bd. 14.50 (*0-7873-0278-3*) Hlth Research.
— Science of Ascension: A Study of Our Being (1929) 190p. 1996. reprint ed. pap. 14.00 (*1-56459-919-1*) Kessinger Pub.
— Thinking Heavenward. 42p. 1996. reprint ed. spiral bd. 9.00 (*0-7873-0275-9*) Hlth Research.
— Thinking Heavenward (1913) 50p. 1996. reprint ed. pap. 7.95 (*1-56459-968-X*) Kessinger Pub.
— Within the Veil: Sequel to Journeying Onward. 57p. 1993. reprint ed. spiral bd. 9.50 (*0-7873-0274-0*) Hlth Research.

De Waurin, Jehan. A Collection of the Chronicles & Ancient Histories of Great Britain, Now Called England, Albina-1431, 3 vols. Hardy, William & Hardy, Edward L., eds. (Rolls Ser.: No. 40). 1972. reprint ed. 210.00 (*0-8115-3576-2*) Periodicals Srv.
— A Collection of the Chronicles & Ancient Histories of Great Britain, Now Called England, Albina-1431, 3 vols., Vol. 1. Hardy, William & Hardy, Edward L., eds. (Rolls Ser.: No. 40). 1972. reprint ed. write for info. (*0-8115-1097-2*) Periodicals Srv.
— Recueil des Croniques et Anchiennes Istories de la Grant: Bretaigne, a Present Nomme Engleterre par...Siegneur du Forestel; Albina-1471, 5 vols., Vol. 1. Hardy, William & Hardy, Edward L., eds. (Rolls Ser.: No. 39). 1974. reprint ed. write for info. (*0-8115-1092-1*) Periodicals Srv.
— Recueil des Croniques et Anchiennes Istories de la Grant: Bretaigne, a Present Nomme Engleterre par...Siegneur du Forestel; Albina-1471, 5 vols., Vol. 2. Hardy, William & Hardy, Edward L., eds. (Rolls Ser.: No. 39). 1974. reprint ed. write for info. (*0-8115-1093-X*) Periodicals Srv.
— Recueil des Croniques et Anchiennes Istories de la Grant: Bretaigne, a Present Nomme Engleterre par...Siegneur du Forestel; Albina-1471, 5 vols., Vol. 3. Hardy, William & Hardy, Edward L., eds. (Rolls Ser.: No. 39). 1974. reprint ed. write for info. (*0-8115-1094-8*) Periodicals Srv.
— Recueil des Croniques et Anchiennes Istories de la Grant: Bretaigne, a Present Nomme Engleterre par...Siegneur du Forestel; Albina-1471, 5 vols., Vol. 4. Hardy, William & Hardy, Edward L., eds. (Rolls Ser.: No. 39). 1974. reprint ed. write for info. (*0-8115-1095-6*) Periodicals Srv.
— Recueil des Croniques et Anchiennes Istories de la Grant: Bretaigne, a Present Nomme Engleterre par...Siegneur du Forestel; Albina-1471, 5 vols., Vol. 5. Hardy, William & Hardy, Edward L., eds. (Rolls Ser.: No. 39). 1974. reprint ed. write for info. (*0-8115-1096-4*) Periodicals Srv.

De Wayne, M. L., ed. Water, Human Values & the Eighties. 100p. 1981. pap. 16.75 (*0-08-028098-6*, Pergamon Pr) Elsevier.

De Weck, A. L., ed. HLA & Allergy. (Monographs in Allergy: Vol. 11). (Illus.). 1977. 41.75 (*3-8055-2639-3*) S Karger.

De Weck, Alain L., ed. Differentiated Lymphocyte Functions. (Progress in Allergy Ser.: Vol. 28). (Illus.). x, 286p. 1981. 126.25 (*3-8055-1834-X*) S Karger.

De Weck, Alain L. & Rundgaard, H., eds. Allergic Reactions to Drugs. (Handbook of Experimental Pharmacology Ser.: Vol. 63). (Illus.). 775p. 1983. 393.00 (*0-387-12399-7*) Spr-Verlag.

De Weck, Alain L., see De Weck, Alain L., ed.

De Weck, Alain L., see Schoenfeld, H. & De Weck, Alain L., eds.

De Weck, Alain L., jt. ed. see Schoenfeld, H.

De Weck, Christine, tr. see Centner, Jacques, et al.

D

An Asterisk (*) at the beginning of an entry indicates that the title is appearing for the first time.

De Weerd, A. W. Atlas of EEG in the First Months of Life. LC 95-14334. (Illus.). 244p. 1995. 259.25 (*0-444-89946-4*) Elsevier.

***de Weert, A., ed.** Environmental Law: Selected Documents & Materials. (Selected Documents Ser.). 1999. pap. 140.00 (*90-5644-014-4*, 18129, Pub. by Global Law Assn) Gaunt.

De Weese, Bob. Backyard Biology. (Science Mini Unit Intermediate Ser.). (Illus.). 16p. (J). (gr. 3-6). 1994. pap. text 5.95 (*1-55799-302-5*, EMC 842) Evan-Moor Edu Pubs.

— Earth, Sun & Moon. (Science Mini Unit Intermediate Ser.). (Illus.). 16p. (J). (gr. 3-6). 1994. pap. text 5.95 (*1-55799-297-5*, EMC 837) Evan-Moor Edu Pubs.

— Hands-on Geology: Land & Water Forms. (Science Mini-Unit Intermediate Ser.). (Illus.). 16p. (J). (gr. 3-6). 1994. pap. text 5.95 (*1-55799-300-9*, EMC 840) Evan-Moor Edu Pubs.

— Making Scientific Comparisons. (Science Mini-Unit Intermediate Ser.: Vol. 7). (Illus.). 16p. (J). (gr. 3-6). 1994. pap. text 5.95 (*1-55799-298-3*, EMC838) Evan-Moor Edu Pubs.

De Weese, Bob. Our Neighbors in Space. Evans, Marilyn, ed. (Science Ser.). (Illus.). 31p. (J). (gr. 4-6). Date not set. pap., wbk. ed. 3.50 (*1-58610-124-2*) Learn Horizon.

De Weese, Bob. Outer Space. (Science Mini-Unit Intermediate Ser.). (Illus.). 16p. (J). (gr. 3-6). 1994. pap. text 5.95 (*1-55799-303-3*, EMC 843) Evan-Moor Edu Pubs.

— Playground Physics. (Science Mini Unit Intermediate Ser.). (Illus.). 16p. (J). (gr. 3-6). 1994. pap. text 5.95 (*1-55799-301-7*, EMC 841) Evan-Moor Edu Pubs.

De Weese, Bob. Science Magic. Evans, Marilyn, ed. (Science Ser.). (Illus.). 31p. (J). (gr. 4-6). Date not set. pap., wbk. ed. 3.50 (*1-58610-123-4*) Learn Horizon.

De Weese, Bob. Solving Science Mysteries. (Science Mini-Unit Intermediate Ser.: Vol. 8). (Illus.). 16p. (J). (gr. 3-6). 1994. pap. text 5.95 (*1-55799-299-1*, ECM839) Evan-Moor Edu Pubs.

De Weese, Bob. United States Geography. Evans, Marilyn, ed. (People & Places Ser.). (Illus.). 31p. (J). (gr. 4-6). Date not set. pap., wbk. ed. 3.50 (*1-58610-131-5*) Learn Horizon.

— United States History Highlights. Evans, Marilyn, ed. (People & Places Ser.). (Illus.). 32p. (J). (gr. 4-6). Date not set. pap., wbk. ed. 3.50 (*1-58610-132-3*) Learn Horizon.

De Weese, Bob, jt. auth. see Moore, Jo Ellen.

De Weese, Bob, ed. see Edwards, Phyllis.

De Weese, Bob, ed. see Melson, Tom.

De Weese, Robert. Phonics Fundamentals, Vol. 1. (Illus.). 240p. (J). (gr. k-1). 1994. pap. text 19.95 (*1-55799-304-1*, EMC 290) Evan-Moor Edu Pubs.

— Phonics Fundamentals, Vol. 2. (Illus.). 240p. (J). (gr. 1-3). 1994. pap. 19.95 (*1-55799-307-6*, EMC 297) Evan-Moor Edu Pubs.

— Spineless Creatures. (Science Primary Mini-Unit Ser.: Vol. 3). (Illus.). 16p. (J). (gr. 1-3). 1994. pap. text 5.95 (*1-55799-291-6*, EMC831) Evan-Moor Edu Pubs.

— What's Inside Your Body? (Science Mini Unit Intermediate Ser.). (Illus.). 16p. (J). (gr. 1-3). 1994. pap. text 5.95 (*1-55799-290-8*, EMC 830) Evan-Moor Edu Pubs.

De Weever, Jacqueline. Chaucer Name Dictionary: A Guide to Astrological, Biblical, Historical, Literary, & Mythological Names in the Works of Geoffrey Chaucer. LC 87-21236. (Illus.). 472p. 1995. pap. text 29.95 (*0-8153-2302-6*, H709) Garland.

— A Chaucer Name Dictionary: Guide to Astrological, Biblical, Historical, Literary, & Mythological Names in the Works of Geoffrey Chaucer. LC 87-21236. 429p. 1988. text 65.00 (*0-8240-8306-7*, H709) Garland.

— Mythmaking & Metaphor in Black Women's Fiction. 200p. 1992. pap. 15.95 (*0-312-06533-7*); text 35.00 (*0-312-06532-9*) St Martin.

— Sheba's Daughters: Whitening & Demonizing the Saracen Woman in Medieval French Epic. LC 98-2622. (Illus.). 288p. 1998. text 52.00 (*0-8153-3018-9*, H2077) Garland.

De Weille, Jan. Quantification of Road User Savings. LC 66-28028. (World Bank Staff Occasional Papers: Vol. 2). (Illus.). 103p. reprint ed. pap. 32.00 (*0-608-18339-3*, 203301600082) Bks Demand.

De Weitte, F. W., ed. Solvay Conference on Surface Science. (Surface Sciences Ser.: Vol. 14). (Illus.). xii, 501p. 1988. 81.95 (*0-387-50450-8*) Spr-Verlag.

De Wesselow, M. R. Donkeys: Their Care & Management. 1969. pap. 20.00 (*0-87556-076-8*) Saifer.

De Wet, Erika. The Constitutional Enforceability of Economic & Social Rights: The Meaning of the German Constitutional Model for South Africa. LC 97-178573. xxi, 161p. 1996. write for info. (*0-409-02287-X*) Buttrwrth-Heinemann.

De Wet, J. C. Kontraktereg en Handelsreg: Kontraktereg, Die Suid-Afrikaanse, Vol. Een. (AFR.). 519p. 1992. write for info. (*0-409-02323-X*, MICHIE); pap. write for info. (*0-409-02324-8*, MICHIE) LEXIS Pub.

De Wet, J. C. & Van Wyk, A. H. Kontraktereg en Handelsreg Herdruk Handelsreg. (AFR.). 852p. 1992. pap. write for info. (*0-409-02325-6*, MICHIE) LEXIS Pub.

De Wet, Johann C. Evaluation of Public Speaking. (Communicamus Ser.: Vol. 6). 113p. (C). 1989. reprint ed. text 29.00 (*0-7021-2368-4*, Pub. by Juta & Co) Intl Spec Bk.

***De Wet, Reza.** De Wet: Plays One. 240p. 2000. pap. 20.95 (*1-84002-145-4*) Theatre Comm.

***De Wever, I., ed.** Introduction to Tumor Biology. (Surgical Oncology Ser.: Vol. 6). 148p. 1999. pap. 46.50 (*90-6186-950-1*, Pub. by Leuven Univ) Coronet Bks.

De Wever, I. & Stas, M., eds. Lipomatous Tumors: Diagnosis & Primary Treatment. (Illus.). 161p. (Orig.). 1997. pap. 47.50 (*90-6186-798-3*, Pub. by Leuven Univ) Coronet Bks.

De Wever, I., jt. ed. see Christiaens, M. R.

De Wevers, Renee, jt. ed. see Lapidus, Gail W.

De Weydenthal, Jan B. The Communists of Poland: An Historical Outline. rev. ed. (Publication Ser.: No. 347). 272p. (C). 1987. pap. text 10.95 (*0-8179-8472-0*) Hoover Inst Pr.

De Wheat, Gaye, jt. auth. see Wheat, Ed.

De Wied, D., jt. ed. see Burbach, J. P.

De Wijk, Rob & Sherwen, Nicholas. NATO on the Brink of a New Millennium: The Battle for Consensus. LC 97-23309. (Atlantic Commentaries Ser.). 176p. 1998. 39.95 (*1-85753-258-9*, Pub. by Brasseys) Brasseys.

De Wijs, Ivo. Donde Esta Paco? (SPA., Illus.). 32p. (J). (ps-2). 1993. pap. 5.95 (*0-8120-1747-1*) Barron.

De Wijze, Louis. Only My Life. LC 96-9443. 224p. 1996. 21.95 (*0-312-14697-3*) St Martin.

De Wilde, J. F. Studies in Begoniaceae, Vol. II. (Wageningen Agricultural University Papers: No. 84-3). 129p. 1985. pap. 31.00 (*90-6754-060-9*, Pub. by Backhuys Pubs) Balogh.

De Wilde, J. J. Studies in Begoniaceae, Vol. I. (Wageningen Agricultural University Papers: No. 83-9). 70p. 1983. pap. 17.00 (*90-6754-053-6*, Pub. by Backhuys Pubs) Balogh.

De Wilde, Jaap. Saved from Oblivion: Interdependency Theory in the First Half of the 20th Century: A Study on the Causality Between War & Complex Interdependence. 298p. 1991. text 77.95 (*1-85521-141-6*, Pub. by Dartmth Pub) Ashgate Pub Co.

De Wilde, Jaap & Wiberg, Hakan. Organized Anarchy in Europe: The Role of States & Intergovernmental Organizations. LC 95-62311. 350p. 1996. text 65.00 (*1-86064-062-1*) St Martin.

De Wilde, Laurent. Monk. 224p. 1998. pap. 13.95 (*1-56924-776-5*) Marlowe & Co.

De Wilde, Philippe. Neural Network Models: An Analysis. (Lecture Notes in Control & Information Sciences: Vol. 210). 153p. 1995. pap. 44.95 (*3-540-19995-0*) Spr-Verlag.

— Neural Network Models: Theory & Projects. 2nd ed. Dickinson, B. W. et al, eds. LC 97-14010. (Communications & Control Engineering Ser.). (Illus.). 200p. 1997. pap. 28.00 (*3-540-76129-2*) Spr-Verlag.

De Wilde, Ton, et al, eds. The Other Policy: The Influence of Policies on Technology Choice & Small Enterprise Development. 512p. (Orig.). 1990. 47.50 (*1-85339-063-1*, Pub. by Intermed Tech) Stylus Pub VA.

De Wilde, W. P., et al, eds. Computer Methods in Composite Materials & Structures VII. (Structures & Materials Ser.). 600p. 2000. 289.00 (*1-85312-825-2*, 8252, Pub. by WIT Pr) Computational Mech MA.

De Wilde, W. P. & Blain, W. R., eds. Composite Materials: Design & Analysis. 552p. 1990. 202.95 (*0-387-52414-2*) Spr-Verlag.

De Wilde, W. P., jt. ed. see Blain, W. R.

De Willink, M. Christina Granara, see Williams, D. & Granara De Willink, M. Christina.

De Winter, Francis. Solar Collectors: Energy Storage & Materials. (Solar Heat Technologies: Fundamentals & Applications Ser.). (Illus.). 1104p. 1991. 95.00 (*0-262-04104-9*) MIT Pr.

De Winter, Francis, ed. see Bereny, Justin A.

De Winter, Jane, jt. auth. see Joutz, Frederick.

De Winter, Leon. The Day Before Yesterday. Rollins, Scott, tr. from DUT. 96p. (Orig.). 1985. pap. 8.00 (*0-931428-15-7*) Vehicle Edns.

De Winter, Lieven & Tursan, Huri. Regionalist Parties in Western Europe. LC 97-40203. (Illus.). 280p. (C). 1998. 90.00 (*0-415-16437-0*) Routledge.

De Winter, M. & Musterd, S. Towards Undivided Cities in Western Europe - Part 4 Brussels: New Challenges for Urban Policy. (Illus.). 51p. 1998. pap. 14.95 (*90-407-1542-4*, Pub. by Delft U Pr) Coronet Bks.

— Towards Undivided Cities in Western Europe - Part 5 Frankfurt: New Challenges for Urban Policy. (Illus.). 49p. 1998. pap. 14.95 (*90-407-1543-2*, Pub. by Delft U Pr) Coronet Bks.

De Winter, Micha. Children: Fellow Citizens: Participation & Commitment. LC 96-41622. 1996. write for info. (*1-85775-179-5*, Radcliffe Med Pr) Scovill Paterson.

De Winter, Patrick M. European Decorative Arts, 1400-1600: An Annotated Bibliography. 1988. 95.00 (*0-8161-8612-X*, Hall Reference) Macmillan.

— The Sacral Treasure of the Guelphs. LC 85-3820. (Illus.). 160p. 1985. pap. 10.00 (*0-910386-81-1*) Cleveland Mus Art.

De Winters, Danielle. Passionate Rebel. large type ed. (Black Satin Romance Ser.). 363p. 1997. 27.99 (*1-86110-033-7*) Ulverscroft.

De Wire, Elinor. Guardians of the Lights. LC 94-42571. (Illus.). 324p. 1995. 27.95 (*1-56164-077-8*); pap. 18.95 (*1-56164-119-7*) Pineapple Pr.

— Guide to Florida Lighthouses. LC 87-16835. (Illus.). 96p. 1987. pap. 14.95 (*0-910923-74-4*) Pineapple Pr.

— Sentries along the Shore. (Illus.). 176p. (Orig.). 1997. pap. 13.95 (*0-9657313-1-6*) Sentinel Pubns.

De Wit, B., et al, eds. Gauge Theories, Applied Supersummetry & Quantum Gravity. (Leuven Notes in Mathematical & Theoretical Physics Ser.: Vol. 6). (Illus.). 366p. (Orig.). 1996. pap. 62.50 (*90-6186-733-9*, Pub. by Leuven Univ) Coronet Bks.

— Supersymmetry & Supergravity 1984: Proceedings of Trieste Spring School, Italy 1984. 500p. 1984. 98.00 (*9971-966-75-1*); pap. 46.00 (*9971-966-76-X*) World Scientific Pub.

— Supersymmetry, Supergravity & Superstrings '86: Proceedings of the Trieste Spring School ICTP Trieste, Italy 7-15 April 1986. 576p. 1987. pap. 49.00 (*9971-5-0145-7*); text 144.00 (*9971-5-0144-9*) World Scientific Pub.

***De Wit, Bob.** Strategy Synthesis: Bridging Conflicting Perspectives (Brief) (ITBP Textbooks Ser.). 255p. 1999. pap. 49.95 (*1-86152-518-4*) Thomson Learn.

De Wit, Bob & Meyer, Ron. Strategy: Process, Content, Context. 2nd ed. 2000. pap., teacher ed. 65.95 (*1-86152-140-5*) Thomson Learn.

— Strategy: Process, Content, Context. 2nd rev. ed. LC 98-213160. 928p. 1998. pap. 26.99 (*1-86152-139-1*) Thomson Learn.

— Strategy: Process, Content, Context: An International Perspective. LC 94-5919. (SWC-Management). 1994. mass mkt. 54.75 (*0-314-03213-4*) West Pub.

De Wit, Bob, jt. auth. see Meyer, Ron.

De Wit, C. Canudas, ed. Advanced Robot Control: Proceedings of the International Workshop on Nonlinear & Adaptive Control: Issues in Robotics Grenoble, November 21-23, 1990. (Lecture Notes in Control & Information Sciences: Vol. 162). ix, 314p. 1991. 73.95 (*0-387-54169-1*) Spr-Verlag.

De Wit, Carlos A. Canudas, see Canudas De Wit, Carlos A.

De Wit, G. Determinants of Self-Employment. (Studies in Empirical Economics). (Illus.). xii, 193p. 1993. 54.95 (*0-387-91451-X*) Spr-Verlag.

De Wit, Han F. Contemplative Psychology. Baird, Marie L., tr. from DUT. LC 91-22624. 200p. (C). 1991. text 19.50 (*0-8207-0228-5*) Duquesne.

— The Spiritual Path: An Introduction to the Psychology of the Spiritual Traditions. Jansen, Henry & Hofland-Jansen, Lucia, trs. from DUT. LC 98-58115. 320p. 1999. 53.00 (*0-8207-0307-9*); pap. 21.95 (*0-8207-0308-7*) Duquesne.

de Wit, J. H., et al, eds. Case Studies in Manufacturing with Advanced Materials, Vol. 1. LC 92-17042. 273p. 1992. 196.50 (*0-444-88468-8*, North Holland) Elsevier.

de Wit, J. H., jt. ed. see Demaid, A.

De Wit, Jan, jt. auth. see Hartup, Willard W.

De Wit, Joop W. Poverty, Policy & Politics in Madras Slums: Dynamics of Survival, Gender & Leadership. LC 96-3336. 308p. 1997. 39.95 (*0-8039-9347-1*) Sage.

De Wit, Maarten J. & Ashwal, Lewis D., eds. Greenstone Belts. LC 95-40313. (Oxford Monographs on Geology & Geophysics: No. 35). (Illus.). 836p. (C). 1997. text 275.00 (*0-19-854056-6*, Clarendon Pr) OUP.

De Wit, Maarten J. & Ransome, Ian G., eds. Inversion Tectonics of the Cape Fold Belt, Karoo & Cretaceous Basins of Southern Africa: Proceedings of the Conference on Inversion Tectonics of the Cape Fold Belt, Cape Town, South Africa 2-6 December 1991. (Illus.). 279p. (C). 1992. text 116.00 (*90-5410-047-8*, Pub. by A A Balkema) Ashgate Pub Co.

De Wit, Margot, et al. Dichotomy Project No. 18: Installation - Performance. (Illus.). 24p. (Orig.). 1989. write for info. (*0-318-65109-2*) M de Wit.

De Wit, P. J. Liquefaction of Cohesive Sediments Caused by Waves. (Studies in Integrated Water Management: Vol. 6). (Illus.). xii, 194p. (Orig.). 1995. pap. 42.50 (*90-407-1139-9*, Pub. by Delft U Pr) Coronet Bks.

De Wit, Reina, tr. see Heng, Cheng.

De Wit, Wim, tr. see Berlage, Hendrik P.

***de With, Witte.** From. 2000. pap. 15.00 (*90-73362-44-X*) Witte De With CFCA.

De Witt, Dave & Wilan, Mary J. Callaloo, Calypso & Carnival: The Cuisines of Trinidad & Tabago. (Illus.). 117p. 1998. pap. text 11.00 (*0-7881-5491-5*) DIANE Pub.

De Witt, David M. Judicial Murder of Mary E. Surratt. (History - United States Ser.). 259p. 1992. reprint ed. lib. bdg. 79.00 (*0-7812-6170-8*) Rprt Serv.

De Witt, Huberts, jt. ed. see Koch, J. H.

De Witt, Ilse, tr. see Hadamovsky, Eugen.

De Witt, Norman J., et al. College Latin. LC 54-4228. (Illus.). 451p. 1954. reprint ed. pap. 139.90 (*0-7837-8853-3*, 204954700001) Bks Demand.

De Witt, Norman W. Epicurus & His Philosophy. LC 72-11234. 388p. 1973. reprint ed. lib. bdg. 65.00 (*0-8371-6639-X*, DEEP, Greenwood Pr) Greenwood.

— St. Paul & Epicurus. LC 54-12314. 211p. reprint ed. pap. 65.50 (*0-8357-7035-4*, 203321700085) Bks Demand.

De Witt, Ralph. Multimodal Transport: Carrier Liability & Documentation. (Lloyd's Shipping Law Library). 500p. 1995. 140.00 (*1-85044-894-9*) LLP.

De Witt, Sorena. String Figures from Around the World, Vol. 2. (Illus.). 32p. (Orig.). (J). (gr. 1-7). 1995. pap. text 5.95 (*0-89346-827-4*) Heian Intl.

De Witte, Bruno, ed. European Community Law of Education. 159p. 1989. pap. 53.00 (*3-7890-1680-2*, Pub. by Nomos Verlags) Intl Bk Import.

***De Witte, Karel.** Organizational Culture. 112p. 2000. pap. 39.95 (*0-86377-997-2*) Psychol Pr.

De Witte, Luc. After the Rehabilitation Centre: A Study into the Course of Functioning after Discharge from Rehabilitation. xii, 240p. 1991. pap. 36.00 (*90-265-1206-6*) Swets.

De Witte, Rozemarijn. Modern Essentials. LC 97-30190. (Illus.). 192p. 1997. 35.00 (*1-57959-000-4*, SOMA) BB&T Inc.

De Woart, Paul, et al, eds. International Law & Development. (C). 1988. lib. bdg. 150.50 (*90-247-3718-4*) Kluwer Academic.

De Wodeham, Adam. Lectura Secunda in Librum Primum Sententiarum, 3 vols. Incl. Vol. I. Lectura Secunda I Sent. Prologus & Distinctio Prima. 354p. 1991. 75.00 (*1-57659-105-0*); Vol. II. Lectura Secunda I Sent. Distinctiones 2-7. 374p. 1991. 75.00 (*1-57659-106-9*); Vol. III. Lectura Secunda I Sent. Distinctiones 8-26. 491p. 1991. 75.00 (*1-57659-107-7*); 125.00 (*1-57659-104-2*) Franciscan Inst.

De Wohl, Louis. Citadel of God: A Novel about Saint Benedict. LC 91-77212. 345p. 1987. pap. 14.95 (*0-89870-404-9*) Ignatius Pr.

— Founded on a Rock: A History of the Catholic Church. LC 81-6557. 249p. 1981. reprint ed. lib. bdg. 59.50 (*0-313-23168-0*, DEFO, Greenwood Pr) Greenwood.

— Lay Siege to Heaven: A Novel of Saint Catherine of Siena. LC 91-72758. 346p. (YA). (gr. 8 up). 1991. reprint ed. pap. 14.95 (*0-89870-381-6*) Ignatius Pr.

— The Quiet Light: A Novel about St. Thomas Aquinas. LC 96-83641. 377p. 1996. pap. text 14.95 (*0-89870-595-9*) Ignatius Pr.

— Restless Flame: Novel St. Augustine. LC 96-78019. 1997. pap. text 12.95 (*0-89870-603-3*) Ignatius Pr.

— Set All Afire: A Novel of Saint Francis Xavier. 2nd rev. ed. LC 90-85368. 280p. (YA). (gr. 8 up). 1991. reprint ed. pap. 12.95 (*0-89870-351-4*) Ignatius Pr.

De Wolf, Charles M. How to Sound Intelligent in Japanese. (Power Japanese Ser.). 128p. 1993. pap. 13.00 (*4-7700-1747-2*) Kodansha.

De Wolf, Charles M., tr. see Fukuda, Hiroko.

***de Wolf, David A.** Essentials of Electromagnetics for Engineering. LC 99-16730. (Illus.). 550p. (C). 2000. 69.95 (*0-521-66281-8*) Cambridge U Pr.

De Wolf Hemmon, Morley. Burgage Tenure in Medieval England. (Harvard Historical Studies: Vol. XX). ix, 234p. 1986. reprint ed. 37.50 (*0-8377-2233-0*, Rothman) W S Hein.

De Wolf, Jan, ed. Bukusu Tales. LC 96-211208. 96p. 1995. pap. text 22.95 (*3-8258-2399-7*) Transaction Pubs.

De Wolf, Peter, ed. Competition in Europe: Essays in Honor of Henk W. de Jong. 308p. (C). 1990. lib. bdg. 129.00 (*0-7923-1050-0*) Kluwer Academic.

De Wolf, R., jt. auth. see Nienhuys-Cheng, S. H.

De Wolf, Richard C. Outline of Copyright Law. xxiv, 330p. 1986. reprint ed. 42.50 (*0-8377-2030-3*, Rothman) W S Hein.

De Wolfe, Elsie. After All: From Colonial Times to the 20th Century. LC 74-3938. (Women in America Ser.). (Illus.). 310p. 1974. reprint ed. 28.95 (*0-405-06085-8*) Ayer.

— The House in Good Taste. fac. ed. LC 75-1839. (Leisure Class in America Ser.). (Illus.). 1975. 43.68 (*0-405-06908-1*) Ayer.

De Wolfe Howe, M. A., intro. Home Letters of General Sherman: (1836-1891) 412p. 1986. reprint ed. pap. 31.95 (*0-935005-75-7*) Lincoln-Rembrandt.

***de Wolfe Howe, Mark, ed.** Touched with Fire: Civil War Letters & Diary of Oliver Wendell Holmes, Jr., 1861-1864. LC 99-55152. (North's Civil War Ser.). (Illus.). 158p. 2000. pap. 19.95 (*0-8232-2017-6*, Pub. by Fordham) BookMasters.

De Wolff, Charles J., jt. ed. see Wallis, Don.

De Wolff, J. The Political Economy of Fiscal Decisions: The Strategic Role of Public Debt. (Contributions to Economics Ser.). (Illus.). xvi, 150p. 1998. pap. 56.00 (*3-7908-1130-0*) Spr-Verlag.

De Wolk, Roland. Northern California's Best Family Campgrounds: 50 Fun, Affordable, Kid-Friendly Sites. (Illus.). 132p. 1997. pap. 16.95 (*0-8118-1270-7*) Chronicle Bks.

De Words-U-Lac, Cyrano. If I Could Live My Life Again... 160p. 1996. pap. 5.99 (*0-88144-182-1*) Christian Pub.

De Words-u-lac, Cyrano. If I Could Live My Life Again: Rhymeos of Life. (Illus.). 212p. (Orig.). 1995. pap. 6.95 (*0-9636177-9-6*) Rhymeo Ink.

— Now I See Why Life Is Like Baseball after All: Rhymeo Game Plans for Baseball Fans. (Illus.). 212p. (Orig.). 1995. pap. 6.95 (*0-9636177-6-1*) Rhymeo Ink.

De Woronin, U. G. Zambezi Trails. LC 79-51772. (Illus.). 1987. 19.95 (*0-930422-17-1*) Dennis-Landman.

De Woskin, Robert, jt. auth. see Maynard, Donald.

De Wulf, Maurice M. Philosophy & Civilization in the Middle Ages. LC 70-88977. 312p. 1970. reprint ed. lib. bdg. 65.00 (*0-8371-2521-9*, WUMA, Greenwood Pr) Greenwood.

de Wyatt, Joyce Cope, see Cope de Wyatt, Joyce.

De Wyzewa, T. & De Saint-Foix, G. W. A. Mozart: Sa Vie Musicale & Son Oeuvre, 2 vols. LC 80-11625. (Music Reprint Ser.). 2274p. 1980. reprint ed. lib. bdg. 125.00 (*0-306-79561-2*) Da Capo.

De-Xin, Yan. Aging & Blood Stasis: A New TCM Approach to Geriatrics. Flaws, Bob, ed. & tr. by. from CHI. Guo-Shun, Tang, tr. from CHI. LC 95-77296. 255p. (Orig.). 1995. pap. 25.95 (*0-936185-63-5*) Blue Poppy Pr.

De Young, C. Coco. A Letter to Mrs. Roosevelt. LC 98-22254. 112p. (YA). (gr. 2-8). 1999. 14.95 (*0-385-32633-5*) BDD Bks Young Read.

De Young, Dirk P. DeJongh & Allied Families: Genealogy & History in Europe & America. 111p. 1997. reprint ed. pap. 18.50 (*0-8328-8258-5*); reprint ed. lib. bdg. 28.50 (*0-8328-8257-7*) Higginson Bk Co.

De Young, Don B. Astronomy & Creation: An Introduction. (Creation Research Society Monographs.: No. 1). (Illus.). 59p. (Orig.). (YA). (gr. 6-12). 1995. pap. 5.45 (*0-940384-17-5*) Creation Research.

De Young, Garry. Abraham Lincoln: Apostle of Freedom. 22p. (Orig.). 1983. pap. 5.00 (*0-936128-04-6*) De Young Pr.

— A Blind Man Speaks Out! 1996. 25.00 (*0-936128-47-X*) De Young Pr.

— Challenge: A Case for Protection of Elders in Kansas. 1995. 25.00 (*0-936128-42-9*) De Young Pr.

— Challenge: A Case to Preserve Juries in Kansas. 1995. 25.00 (*0-936128-43-7*) De Young Pr.

— The Crucible of Life: A Book of Poetry. 1969. pap. 12.00 (*0-936128-27-5*) De Young Pr.

— Environmental Gardening: Gardening in Compliance with the Laws of Nature. 1989. 10.00 (*0-936128-37-2*) De Young Pr.

D

— Garry De Young: Scientist on the Attack. 90p. 1998. 25.00 (*0-936128-94-1*) De Young Pr.

— Garry's Scrap Book: An Account of the De Young Legal Battles. (Illus.). 150p. 1984. 50.00 (*0-936128-07-0*) De Young Pr.

— Letters to War Criminals: The War in the Gulf. 1992. 27.50 (*0-936128-24-0*) De Young Pr.

— The Meaning of Christianity: An Expose of the Religious Rite of Circumcision. 1988. pap. 17.95 (*0-936128-36-4*) De Young Pr.

— Message from God & Other Poems. 1988. pap. 10.00 (*0-936128-21-6*) De Young Pr.

— Naturalists Guide to Self-Hypnosis. 1988. pap. 3.00 (*0-936128-10-0*) De Young Pr.

— Outrage! A Tale of Legal Thievery in Minnesota. 1989. pap. 3.00 (*0-936128-18-6*) De Young Pr.

— Pocket Gopher & Other Poems from the Gopher State. (Illus.). 31p. pap. 7.50 (*0-936128-00-3*) De Young Pr.

— Quest for Justice: Systemic Discrimination in America. 83p. (Orig.). 1984. 15.00 (*0-936128-05-4*) De Young Pr.

— Religion: The Disease. 1993. 25.00 (*0-936128-06-2*) De Young Pr.

— The Silence of the "Good" People. 1989. pap. 17.95 (*0-936128-11-9*) De Young Pr.

— Yankee in a Red Neck Court! 1995. 25.00 (*0-685-67809-1*) De Young Pr.

De Young, Garry, comment. Sex, Church, & the Jungle. 1989. pap. 15.00 (*0-936128-28-3*) De Young Pr.

De Young, Garry, ed. The Wit, Wisdom & Eloquence of Robert G. Ingersoll. 1989. reprint ed. 25.00 (*0-936128-34-8*) De Young Pr.

De Young, Garry, pref. Jefferson's Letters on Religion. 1989. 17.00 (*0-936128-51-8*) De Young Pr.

***De Young, James B.** Homosexuality: Contemporary Claims Examined in the Light of the Bible & Classical Jewish, Greek & Roman Literature & Law. 400p. 2000. pap. text 16.99 (*0-8254-2492-5*) Kregel.

De Young, Jim & Miller, John. London Theatre Walks: Thirteen Walking Tours to London Theatre Sites Past & Present. (Illus.). 224p. 1998. pap. text 14.95 (*1-55783-280-3*) Applause Theatre Bk Pubs.

De Young, Lorie & Winkler, Louanne. Multiplication & Division: Combo. (Math Combo Bks.: No. 02203). (Illus.). 64p. (Orig.). (gr. 3). 1997. pap., wbk. ed. 3.25 (*0-88743-139-9*, 02203) Sch Zone Pub Co.

De Young, Lorie, ed. see Hoffman, J. & Gregorich, B.

De Young, Mary. Quest & Other Poems. 1972. pap. 10.00 (*0-936128-22-4*) De Young Pr.

De Young, Mary W., ed. Drummer Boy. 1990. 45.00 (*0-936128-40-2*) De Young Pr.

De Yturiaga, Jose A. The International Regime of Fisheries, Vol. POOD 30. LC 97-3666. 1997. 114.00 (*90-411-0365-1*) Kluwer Law Intl.

De Yturriaga, Jose Antonio, see Antonio de Yturriaga, Jose.

De Zabaleta, Juan. El Dia de Fiesta por la Manana & El Dia de Fiesta por la Tarde. (SPA.). reprint ed. write for info. (*0-318-71631-3*) G Olms Pubs.

De Zalduondo, Baltazara Colon, see Colon De Zalduondo, Baltazara.

De Zamora, Antonio. Comedias Nuevas. (Textos y Estudios Clasicos De las Literaturas Hispanicas Ser.). 523p. 1975. reprint ed. write for info. incl. 3.5 hd (*3-487-05444-2*) G Olms Pubs.

De Zanger, Andre, jt. auth. see Morgan, Judith.

De Zanger, Arie, jt. auth. see Tennant, S. G. B., Jr.

De Zapata, Celia C., ed. Short Stories by Latin American Women: The Magic & the Real. 2nd ed. LC 89-36298. 224p. 1990. pap. 15.95 (*1-55885-002-3*) Arte Publico.

De Zapata Espinoza, Beatrice. Mama por Estapas Revisada. (SPA.). 1998. pap. 6.99 (*0-8297-1215-1*) Vida Pubs.

De Zardain, Paul F., tr. see Potter, Beatrix & Pomaska, Anna.

De Zavala, Adina. History & Legends of the Alamo & Other Missions. 1993. reprint ed. lib. bdg. 75.00 (*0-7812-5874-X*) Rprt Serv.

— History & Legends of the Alamo & Other Missions in & Around San Antonio. Flores, Richard R., ed. LC 96-19969. 215p. 1997. pap. 12.95 (*1-55885-181-X*) Arte Publico.

De Zayas, Alfred M. Nemesis at Potsdam: The Anglo-Americans & the Expulsion of the Germans. rev. ed. LC 98-68071. (Illus.). 320p. 1998. pap. 23.95 (*0-89725-360-4*, 1899) Picton Pr.

— The Werhrmacht War Crimes Bureau, 1939-1945. LC 88-31596. (Illus.). xx, 364p. 1989. pap. text 20.00 (*0-8032-9908-7*, Bison Books) U of Nebr Pr.

De Zayas, Alfred-Maurice. A Terrible Revenge: The "Ethnic Cleansing" of the East European Germans, 1944-1950. LC 94-5773.Tr. of Anmerkungen zur Vertreibung der Deutschen aus dem Osten. 1994. pap. 15.95 (*0-312-12159-8*) St Martin.

De Zayas, Jose L., tr. see Cadena y Almeida, Luis F.

De Zayas, Maria. The Disenchantments of Love: A Translation of Desenganos Amorosos. Boyer, H. Patsy, tr. from SPA. LC 96-24595. (SUNY Series, Women Writers in Translation). 400p. (C). 1997. text 74.50 (*0-7914-3281-5*); pap. text 24.95 (*0-7914-3282-3*) State U NY Pr.

— The Enchantments of Love: Amorous & Exemplary Novels. Boyer, H. Patsy, tr. from SPA. LC 89-36559. 354p. 1990. 50.00 (*0-520-06671-5*, Pub. by U CA Pr) Cal Prin Full Svc.

De Zayas, Marius. How, When, & Why Modern Art Came to New York. Naumann, Francis M., ed. LC 95-49910. (Illus.). 250p. 1996. 35.00 (*0-262-04153-7*) MIT Pr.

De Zayas, Marous. How, When, & Why Modern Art Came to New York. Naumann, Francis M., ed. LC 95-49910. (Graham Foundation Series in Contemporary Discourse). (Illus.). xiv, 260p. 1998. pap. text 15.00 (*0-262-54096-7*) MIT Pr.

De Zayas y Arancibia, Jose L., jt. auth. see Y Almeida, Luis E.

De Zeeluw, Gerard, jt. ed. see Jungermann, Helmut.

De Zeeuw, Aart J., ed. Advanced Lectures in Quantitative Economics II. (Illus.). 250p. 1993. pap. text 48.00 (*0-12-214685-9*) Acad Pr.

***De Zeeuw, C. I., et al, eds.** Cerebellar Modules. (Progress in Brain Research Ser.). 1999. write for info. (*0-444-50108-8*, Excerpta Medica) Elsevier.

De Zeeuw, Carl, jt. auth. see Panshin, A. J.

De Zeeuw, D. F., ed. Thin-Layer Chromatographic Rf Values of Toxicologically Relevant Substances on Standardized Systems. 223p. 1987. 70.00 (*0-89573-665-9*, Wiley-VCH) Wiley.

de Zeeuw, J., jt. auth. see Berezkin, V. G.

De Zeeuw, M. A. & Lemkowitz, S. M. Environmentally Acceptable Incineration of Chlorinated Chemical Waste. xxxxxx, 144p. (Orig.). 1987. pap. 42.50 (*90-6275-229-2*, Pub. by Delft U Pr) Coronet Bks.

De Zeeuw, Rokus A., et al. Gas chromatographic Retention Indices of Solvents & Other Volatile Substances for Use in Toxicological Analysis. International Association of Forensic Toxicologist, ed. LC 92-49382. (Commission Reports of the Deutsche Forschungsgemeinschaft). (Illus.). 131p. 1992. 74.95 (*3-527-27395-6*, 0930-7958, Wiley-VCH) Wiley.

De Zeeuw, Rokus A., et al. Gas Chromatographic Retention Indices of Toxicologically Relevant Substances on Packed or Capillary Columns with Dimthylsilicone Stationary Phase: Report Xviii of the DFG Commission for Clinical-Toxicological Analysis. 3rd enl. rev. ed. International Association of Forensic Toxicologist, ed. LC 92-49393. (Commission Reports of the Deutsche Forschungsgemeinschaft). (Illus.). 408p. 1992. 165.00 (*3-527-27396-4*, 0930-7958, Wiley-VCH) Wiley.

De Zeeuw, Rokus A., et al. Thin-Layer Chromatographic RF Values of Toxicologically Relevant Substances on Standardized Systems. 2nd enl. rev. ed. International Association of Forensic Toxicologist, ed. 250p. 1992. 92.00 (*1-56081-183-8*, 0930-7958, Wiley-VCH) Wiley.

De Zeeuw, Tim, ed. Structure & Dynamics of Elliptical Galaxies. (C). 1987. pap. text 83.00 (*90-277-2586-1*); lib. bdg. 206.00 (*90-277-2585-3*) Kluwer Academic.

De Zegher, Catherine, ed. Martha Rosler: Positions in the Life World. LC 98-89291. (Illus.). 256p. 1999. 40.00 (*0-262-04174-X*) MIT Pr.

***De Zegher, Catherine, ed.** Untitled Passages by Henri Michaux. (Illus.). 2000. 35.00 (*1-85894-120-2*, Pub. by Merrell Holberton) Rizzoli Intl.

de Zegher, Catherine M. & Vicona, Cecilia. The Precarious: The Art & Poetry of Cecilia Vicuna. Allen, Esther, tr. from SPA. LC 97-61784. (Wesleyan Poetry Ser.). (Illus.). 250p. 1997. 30.00 (*0-8195-6324-2*, Wesleyan Univ Pr) U Pr of New Eng.

De Zegher, F. In Vivo Studies on Growth Hormone Secretion in the Human & Ovine Fetus & Newborn. No. 23. 103p. (Orig.). 1990. pap. 28.50 (*90-6186-368-6*, Pub. by Leuven Univ) Coronet Bks.

De Zendegui, Guillermo. Las Primeras Ciudades Cubanas y Sus Antecedentes Urbanisticos. LC 97-60444. (Coleccion Arte Ser.). (SPA., Illus.). 87p. 1997. pap. 16.00 (*0-89729-836-5*, 836-5) Ediciones.

— Todos Somos Culpables. LC 91-75691. (SPA.). 155p. 1991. 12.00 (*0-89729-620-6*) Ediciones.

De Ziegler, D., jt. ed. see Kupesic, S.

De Zirkoff, Boris. The Dream That Never Dies: Boris de Zirkoff Speaks Out on Theosophy. Small, W. Emmett, ed. (Illus.). 242p. 1983. pap. 12.00 (*0-913004-45-6*) Point Loma Pub.

— Rebirth of the Occult Tradition: How the Secret Doctrine of H. P. Blavatsky was Written. 1990. pap. 7.95 (*0-8356-7535-1*, Quest) Theos Pub Hse.

De Zirkoff, Boris, ed. see Blavatsky, Helena P.

De Zoete, Beryl. Other Mind: A Study of Dance in South India. 1988. reprint ed. lib. bdg. 49.00 (*0-7812-0216-7*) Rprt Serv.

— The Other Mind, a Study of Dance in South India. reprint ed. 69.00 (*0-403-08185-8*) Scholarly.

De Zoete, Beryl, tr. see Svevo, Italo.

De Zoete, Marian. Lipase- & Protease-Catalyzed Transformations with Unnatural Acyl Acceptors. (Illus.). 125p. (Orig.). 1995. pap. 57.50 (*90-407-1135-6*, Pub. by Delft U Pr) Coronet Bks.

De Zoete Wedd, Barclays, jt. auth. see Ricchiuto, Steven R.

De Zorda, Ornella, jt. ed. see Ellis, David.

De Zorzoli, Alicia S., compiled by. Victoria para Mujeres en Crisis: Victory for Women in Crisis. (SPA.). 96p. (Orig.). 1992. pap. 7.50 (*0-311-12104-7*) Casa Bautista.

De Zorzoli, Alicia S., tr. see Conway, Jim & Conway, Sally.

De Zuane, John. Drinking Water Quality. 2nd ed. LC 96-35504. (Illus.). 592p. (C). 1997. text 78.95 (*0-442-02344-8*, VNR) Wiley.

De Zuane, John. Handbook of Drinking Water Quality. 2nd ed. 592p. 1996. 90.00 (*0-471-28789-X*, VNR) Wiley.

De Zulueta, Antonio, tr. see Darwin, Charles.

De Zulueta, Felicity. From Pain to Violence: The Traumatic Roots of Destructiveness. 342p. 1993. pap. 56.00 (*1-56593-253-6*, 0549) Singular Publishing.

De Zutter, Hank. Who Says a Dog Goes Bow-Wow? (Illus.). 32p. (J). 1997. pap. 5.99 (*0-440-41338-9*) Dell.

— Who Says a Dog Goes Bow-Wow? (Dell Picture Yearling Ser.). (J). 1997. 11.19 (*0-606-12089-0*, Pub. by Turtleback) Demco.

De Zwaan, J. W. The Permanent Representatives Committee. LC 95-214946. 336p. 1995. 158.75 (*0-444-82274-7*) Elsevier.

De Zwart, Frank. The Bureaucratic Merry-Go-Round: Manipulating the Transfer of Indian Civil Servants. 250p. (Orig.). (C). 1995. pap. 42.50 (*90-5356-132-3*, Pub. by Amsterdam U Pr) U of Mich Pr.

Dea, Don & Lea, Hugh. World Class Websites. (Foundation Ser.). 65p. 1998. pap. 26.95 (*0-88034-104-1*) Am Soc Assn Execs.

***Dea, Don, et al.** Online Learning Strategies: Association Models for Success. LC 99-32095. (Illus.). 89p. 1999. pap. 28.00 (*0-88034-160-2*) Am Soc Assn Execs.

Dea, Jobe. Forbidden Matter: Home Cares. (Illus.). 50p. 1998. pap. 8.00 (*0-8059-4512-1*) Dorrance.

Dea, Patrick O., ed. A Class of Our Own. 200p. (Orig.). 1994. pap. 13.95 (*1-874597-02-2*, Pub. by New Island Books) Irish Bks Media.

Dea, Phoebe K. & Keyzer, Hendrick. Practical Introductory Quantitative Analysis. rev. ed. (C). 1986. pap. text, student ed. 13.50 (*0-685-29053-0*) Occidental Coll.

Deac, Wilfred P. Road to the Killing Fields: The Cambodian War of 1970-1975. LC 97-13661. (Military History Ser.: Vol. 53). (Illus.). 320p. (C). 1997. text 34.95 (*0-89096-750-4*) Tex A&M Univ Pr.

Deacon. Early Childhood Education. (C). 1998. pap. text 16.36 (*0-395-90259-2*) HM.

Deacon, Alan, et al, eds. Stakeholder Welfare. (Choice in Welfare Ser.: No. 32). 114p. 1996. pap. 19.95 (*0-255-36390-7*, Pub. by Inst Economic Affairs) Coronet Bks.

***Deacon, Andrew.** Weather: Build Your Own Weather Station & Discover the Wonders of Meteorology. (Science Action Bks.). (Illus.). (J). 2000. pap. 19.95 (*0-7624-0812-X*) Running Pr.

Deacon, Bob. The New Eastern Europe: Social Policy Past, Present & Future. 208p. (C). 1992. text 55.00 (*0-8039-8438-3*); pap. text 19.95 (*0-8039-8439-1*) Sage.

Deacon, Bob, ed. Social Policy, Social Justice & Citizenship in Eastern Europe. (Studies in the Social Policy of Eastern Europe & Soviet Union). 1992. 72.95 (*1-85628-243-0*, Pub. by Avebry) Ashgate Pub Co.

Deacon, Carol. Novelty Cakes: 35 Imaginative Cakes for All Occasions. LC 99-230134. (Quick & Easy Ser.). (Illus.). 95p. 1999. pap. 14.95 (*1-85368-735-9*, Pub. by New5 Holland) Sterling.

— Quick & Easy Novelty Cakes: 35 Imaginative Cakes for All Occasions. (Illus.). 96p. 1996. 24.95 (*1-85368-678-6*, Pub. by New5 Holland) Sterling.

— Two-Hour Party Cakes: 30 Cakes to Decorate in Two Hours or Less. (Illus.). 112p. 1999. 21.95 (*1-85974-181-9*) New5 Holland.

Deacon, David, et al. Researching Communications: A Practical Guide to Methods in Media & Cultural Analysis. LC 98-44900. (An Arnold Publication). (Illus.). 448p. 1999. text 75.00 (*0-340-73193-1*) OUP.

Deacon, Desley. Elsie Clews Parsons: Inventing Modern Life. LC 96-36257. 448p. 1997. 29.95 (*0-226-13907-7*) U Ch Pr.

— Elsie Clews Parsons: Inventing Modern Life. (Illus.). 520p. 1999. pap. text 20.00 (*0-226-13908-5*) U Ch Pr.

— Managing Gender: The State, the New Middle Class & Women Workers, 1830-1930. (Illus.). 320p. 1990. text 24.95 (*0-19-554817-5*) OUP.

Deacon, Diane, jt. auth. see Vance, Mike.

Deacon, E. The Descendants of the Family of Deacon of Elstowe & London, & Sketches of Allied Families. (Illus.). 420p. 1989. reprint ed. pap. 66.00 (*0-8328-0465-7*); reprint ed. lib. bdg. 76.00 (*0-8328-0464-9*) Higginson Bk Co.

Deacon, Edward. Bates, Bears & Bunker Hill with a Correction or Two. 90p. 1988. reprint ed. pap. 18.00 (*0-8328-0211-5*); reprint ed. lib. bdg. 28.00 (*0-8328-0210-7*) Higginson Bk Co.

***Deacon, H. J. & Deacon, Janette.** Human Beginnings in South Africa: Uncovering the Secrets of the Stone Age. (Illus.). 224p. 1999. pap. 24.95 (*0-7619-9086-0*) AltaMira Pr.

Deacon, J. W. Modern Mycology. 3rd ed. LC 97-3738. (Illus.). 288p. 1997. pap. text 58.00 (*0-632-03077-1*) Blackwell Sci.

Deacon, James E., jt. ed. see Minckley, Wendell L.

Deacon, Jane, ed. see Organization for Obstetric, Gynecologic & Neonatal.

Deacon, Janette, jt. auth. see Deacon, H. J.

Deacon, Jeanette & Dawson, Thomas A. Voices from the Past: Xam Bushmen & the Bleek & Lloyd Collection. (Illus.). 300p. 1997. pap. 69.95 (*1-86814-247-7*, U Pr W Africa) Intl Scholars.

Deacon, John & Walker, John. Dialogical Discourses of Spirits & Devils, Declaring Their Proper Essence. LC 76-57377. (English Experience Ser.: No. 795). 1977. reprint ed. lib. bdg. 55.00 (*90-221-0795-7*) Walter J Johnson.

Deacon, Joseph. Winding Down a Psychiatric Private Practice. LC 85-7341. (Private Practice Monograph Ser.). 105p. reprint ed. pap. 32.60 (*0-8357-7845-2*, 203622000002) Bks Demand.

Deacon, Lynda & Gocke, Bryan. Understanding Perpetrators: Protecting Children - A Practitioner's Guide to Working Effectively with Child Sexual Abusers. 256p. 1998. pap. 29.95 (*1-86177-021-9*, Pub. by Whiting & Birch) Paul & Co Pubs.

Deacon, Margaret. Scientists & the Sea, 1650-1900: A Study of Marine Science. LC 97-844. 512p. 1997. 87.95 (*1-85928-352-7*, Pub. by Scolar Pr) Ashgate Pub Co.

***Deacon, Mark & Derry, Andrew.** Index Linked Bonds. 160p. (C). 1998. 57.00 (*0-13-889569-4*) P-H.

Deacon, Martin, jt. auth. see Williams, Gail.

Deacon, P., ed. Moratin: El Si de las Ninas. (SPA.). 1995. pap. 18.95 (*1-85399-417-0*, Pub. by Brist Class Pr) Focus Pub-R Pullins.

Deacon, Richard. Kempei Tai: The Japanese Secret Service, Then & Now. 320p. 1990. pap. 14.95 (*0-8048-1653-0*) Tuttle Pubng.

— Napoleon's Book of Fate. Orig. Title: The Book of Fate: Its Origins & Uses. 1977. reprint ed. 10.00 (*0-8065-0564-8*, Citadel Pr); reprint ed. pap. 4.95 (*0-8065-0577-X*, Citadel Pr) Carol Pub Group.

Deacon, Richard & Marian Goodman Gallery Staff. Richard Deacon: Sculptures, 1989-90. LC 91-65064. 1991. write for info. (*0-944219-09-8*) M Goodman Gallery.

Deacon, Robert, et al. Taxing Energy: Oil Severance Taxation & the Economy. 161p. 1990. lib. bdg. 39.95 (*0-945999-69-0*, 6057) Independent Inst.

Deacon, S. Health Surveillance at Work. 1996. pap. 129.00 (*1-85953-000-1*, Pub. by Tech Comm) St Mut.

Deacon, S. Measuring Business Value in Health & Safety. (Financial Times Management Briefings Ser.). 1997. pap. 89.50 (*0-273-63228-0*) F T P-H.

Deacon, S. Measuring Business Value in Health Safety. 1996. pap. 129.00 (*1-85953-095-8*, Pub. by Tech Comm) St Mut.

Deacon, Terrence W. The Symbolic Species: The Co-Evolution of Language & the Brain. (Illus.). 528p. 1998. pap. 15.95 (*0-393-31754-4*) Norton.

— The Symbolic Species: The Co-Evolution of Language & the Human Brain. LC 96-31115. (Illus.). 352p. 1997. 29.95 (*0-393-03838-6*) Norton.

Deaconescu, Marian, ed. Frattini-Like Subgroups of Finite Groups, Vol. 2. (Mathematical Reports: Vol. 2, Pt.4). x, 114p. (Orig.). 1986. text 171.00 (*3-7186-0303-9*) Gordon & Breach.

Deacy, Christopher, jt. ed. see Bowie, Fiona.

Deacy, Susan & Pierce, Karen F. Rape in Antiquity: Sexual Violence in the Greek & Roman Worlds. (Illus.). 266p. 1997. 49.50 (*0-7156-2754-6*, Pub. by Classical Pr) David Brown.

Deaderick, Lucille, ed. Heart of the Valley: A History of Knoxville, Tennessee. (Illus.). 701p. 1976. 11.00 (*0-941199-04-5*) ETHS.

Deaderick, Sam & Turner, Tamara. Gay Resistance: The Hidden History. rev. ed. LC 96-70923. (Illus.). 56p. 1997. pap. 7.00 (*0-932323-03-0*) Red Letter Pr.

***Deadman, Patricia, et al.** Staking Land Claims. (Illus.). 48p. 1999. pap. 10.95 (*0-920159-59-1*) Banff Ctr.

***Deadwood, Hank.** Dynamo. 128p. 2000. pap. 15.00 (*1-58790-002-5*) Regent Pr.

***Deady, Kathleen W.** Egypt. (Countries of the World Ser.). 24p. (J). (ps-3). 2000. lib. bdg. 15.93 (*0-7368-0626-1*, Bridgestone Bks) Capstone Pr.

— England. (Countries of the World Ser.). 24p. (J). (ps-3). 2000. lib. bdg. 15.93 (*0-7368-0627-X*, Bridgestone Bks) Capstone Pr.

— Ireland. LC 00-9729. (Countries of the World Ser.). (Illus.). 2001. write for info. (*0-7368-0814-0*, Bridgestone Bks) Capstone Pr.

— Kansas Facts & Symbols. LC 00-22921. (States & Their Symbols Ser.). (Illus.). 24p. (J). (ps-3). 2000. lib. bdg. 15.93 (*0-7368-0638-5*, Hlltop Bks) Capstone Pr.

— Kentucky Facts & Symbols. LC 00-24708. (States & Their Symbols Ser.). (Illus.). 24p. (J). (ps-3). 2000. lib. bdg. 15.93 (*0-7368-0639-3*, Hlltop Bks) Capstone Pr.

Deady, Matthew P. Pharisee among Philistines: The Diary of Judge Matthew P. Deady, 1871-1892, 2 vols. LC 74-75363. (Illus.). 702p. 1975. boxed set 30.00 (*0-87595-046-9*) Oregon Hist.

Deaett, Mary, et al. 50 Hikes in Vermont: Walks, Hikes, & Overnights in the Green Mountain State. 5th ed. LC 96-48311. (50 Hikes Ser.). (Illus.). 208p. 1997. pap. 14.95 (*0-88150-374-6*, Pub. by Countryman) Norton.

Deaf Action Committee Staff. Abortion Law in the United States Vol. 1-3: From Roe v. Wade to the Present; Historical Development of Abortion Law; Modern Writings on Abortion, Set. Parrish, Jenni, ed. LC 95-30126. (Controversies in Constitutional Law Ser.). 1302p. 1995. text 264.00 (*0-8153-2183-X*) Garland.

— Deaf Perspectives on Sign Writing Video. 1995. pap. 30.00 incl. VHS (*0-914336-71-1*) Ctr Sutton Movement.

Deaf Action Committee Staff & Sutton, Valerie J. Lessons in Sign Writing Video Series, 2 cass.; set. 1996. 75.00 incl. VHS (*0-914336-72-X*) Ctr Sutton Movement.

Deagan. Third Worlds. LC 96-208112. 288p. (C). 1996. 90.00 (*0-415-12218-X*); pap. 25.99 (*0-415-12219-8*) Routledge.

Deagan, Kathleen. Artifacts of the Spanish Colonies of Florida & the Caribbean, 1500-1800: Ceramics, Glassware, & Beads, Vol. 1. LC 86-24772. (Illus.). 208p. 1987. text 39.95 (*0-87474-392-3*) Smithsonian.

Deagan, Kathleen, ed. Puerto Real: The Archaeology of a Sixteenth-Century Spanish Town in Hispaniola. (Ripley P. Bullen & Columbus Quincentennary Ser.). (Illus.). 560p. 1995. 49.95 (*0-8130-1334-8*) U Press Fla.

— Spanish St. Augustine: The Archaeology of a Colonial Creole Community (Monographs) (Studies in Historical Archaeology). 1983. text 79.95 (*0-12-207880-2*) Acad Pr.

Deagan, Kathleen A., ed. America's Ancient City: Spanish St. Augustine, 1565-1763. LC 91-15055. (Spanish Borderlands Sourcebooks Ser.: Vol. 25). 693p. 1991. text 35.00 (*0-8240-2347-1*) Garland.

Deagan, Kathleen A. & MacMahon, Darcie A. Fort Mose: Colonial America's Black Fortress of Freedom. LC 94-42953. (Illus.). 125p. 1995. 29.95 (*0-8130-1351-8*) U Press Fla.

— Fort Mose: Colonial America's Black Fortress of Freedom. LC 94-42953. (Illus.). 125p. 1995. pap. 9.95 (*0-8130-1352-6*) U Press Fla.

Deagan, Virginia G., jt. ed. see Thomes, Sidney P., Jr.

***Deagle, Bill.** Abortion to Armageddon. 108p. 1999. pap. 15.00 (*1-58538-000-8*) Prophecy Club.

— Clay & Iron: Answers to the Endtime Puzzle. 376p. 1999. pap. 20.00 (*1-58538-008-3*) Prophecy Club.

Deagle, Edwin A. The Future of the International Oil Market. (Report Ser.). 56p. 1983. pap. 10.00 (*1-56708-062-6*) Grp of Thirty.

D

Deagle, Edwin A., et al. Energy in the 1980s: An Analysis of Recent Studies. (Occasional Paper Ser.: Vol. 4). 27p. 1981. pap. 5.00 (*1-56708-003-0*) Grp of Thirty.

Deaglio, Enrico. The Banality of Goodness: The Story of Giorgio Perlasca. Conti, Gregory, tr. from ENG. LC 98-13290. 182p. 1998. 18.00 (*0-268-02154-6*) U of Notre Dame Pr.

Deagon, Ann. Carbon 14. LC 74-79483. 72p. 1974. 15.00 (*0-87023-170-7*); pap. 9.95 (*0-87023-171-5*) U of Mass Pr.

— Indian Summer. LC 74-31937. (Illus.). 32p. 1981. pap. 7.50 (*0-87775-146-3*) Unicorn Pr.

— The Pentekontaetia: The Great Fifty Years. (Orig.). 1985. pap. 12.00 (*0-931956-21-8*) Water Mark.

— There Is No Balm in Birmingham. 2nd ed. Date not set. pap. 5.00 (*1-879934-29-9*) St Andrews NC.

Deahl, James. Poetry & Music from Under the Watchful Eye. audio 8.95 (*0-921411-32-4*) Genl Dist Srvs.

— Under the Watchful Eye: Poetry & Discourse. 1995. pap. 8.95 (*0-921411-30-8*) Genl Dist Srvs.

Deahl, James, ed. Poetry Markets for Canadians. 6th ed. 240p. pap. 15.95 (*1-55128-030-2*, Pub. by Mercury Bk) LPC InBook.

Deahl, S. Thomas. Healthline: Using Medline Efficiently in a Busy Clinical Practice. (Informatics Ser.: No. 1). 115p. 1998. pap. 15.00 (*1-893549-04-6*) Biomed Genl.

Deahr, Chris. Eric Learns to Share. (Wizard of the Magic Road Ser.). 1995. 9.15 (*0-606-08739-7*, Pub. by Turtleback) Demco.

— The Secret of Friendship. (Wizard of the Magic Road Ser.). 1996. 9.15 (*0-606-08895-4*, Pub. by Turtleback) Demco.

Deak, Edit. Rope Drawings by Patrick Ireland: An Exhibition. (Illus.). 32p. 1977. pap. 3.00 (*0-934418-04-7*) Mus Contemp Art.

Deak, Etienne & Deak, Simone. Dictionnaire des Americanismes. 8th ed. (FRE.). 823p. 1987. pap. 69.95 (*0-7859-4818-X*, M6103) Fr & Eur.

Deak, F. & Ruddy, F. American International Law Cases, 1783-1978, Vols. 1-31. LC 78-140621. (Series I). 1971. text 2325.00 (*0-379-20075-9*) Oceana.

Deak, Francis & Jessup, Philip C., eds. A Collection of Neutrality Laws, Regulations, & Treaties of Various Countries, 2 vols., Set. LC 39-34164. 850, 860p. 1986. reprint ed. lib. bdg. 120.00 (*0-89941-533-4*, 304680) W S Hein.

Deak, Francis, jt. auth. see Shotwell, James T.

Deak, Frantisek. Symbolist Theater: The Formation of an Avant-Garde. LC 92-35799. (PAJ Bks.). 320p. 1993. pap. text 14.95 (*0-8018-4598-X*) Johns Hopkins.

Deak, George. The Economy & Policy in 20th-Century Hungary: The Role of the National Association of Industrialists. (East European Monographs: No. 288). 224p. 1990. text 37.00 (*0-88033-185-2*, Pub. by East Eur Monographs) Col U Pr.

Deak, Gloria. Discovering America's Southeast: A Sixteenth Century View Based on the Mannerist Engravings of Theodore de Bry. (Illus.). 205p. (Orig.). 1992. pap. 15.00 (*0-942301-20-X*) Birm Pub Lib.

***Deak, Gloria.** Picturing New York: The City fom Its Beginnings to the Year 2000. LC 99-54832. (Illus.). 400p. 2000. 49.95 (*0-231-10728-5*) Col U Pr.

Deak, Gloria G. William James Bennett: Master of the Aquatint View. LC 88-25268. (Illus.). (Orig.). 1988. pap. 17.95 (*0-87104-411-0*) NY Pub Lib.

Deak, Gloria-Gilda. American Views: Prospects & Vistas. LC 76-40041. (Illus.). 134p. 1976. 25.00 (*0-87104-263-0*) NY Pub Lib.

Deak, Istvan. The Lawful Revolution: Louis Kossuth & the Hungarians, 1848-1849. LC 78-22063. Orig. Title: Reluctant Rebels. (Illus.). 415p. 1979. text 29.50 (*0-231-04602-2*) Col U Pr.

***Deak, Istvan, et al, eds.** The Politics of Retribution in Europe: World War II & Its Aftermath. 2000. 55.00 (*0-691-00953-8*, Pub. by Princeton U Pr); pap. 19.95 (*0-691-00954-6*, Pub. by Princeton U Pr) Cal Prin Full Svc.

Deak, Istvan, jt. auth. see Mitchell, Allan.

Deak, JoAnn. How Girls Thrive: An Essential Guide for Educators (And Parents) 94p. 1998. pap. 27.00 (*0-934338-93-0*) NAIS.

Deak, JoAnn, jt. ed. see Aulicino, Christine.

Deak, Judith & Flickinger, Gretchen, eds. Bite of Seattle Cookbook, 8 vols., 1. 210p. write for info. (*0-939449-00-5*) Ink Plus.

— Bite of Seattle Cookbook, 8 vols., 2. 210p. write for info. (*0-939449-01-3*) Ink Plus.

— Bite of Seattle Cookbook, 8 vols., 3. 210p. write for info. (*0-939449-02-1*) Ink Plus.

— Bite of Seattle Cookbook, 8 vols., 4. 210p. write for info. (*0-939449-03-X*) Ink Plus.

— Bite of Seattle Cookbook, 8 vols., 5. 210p. write for info. (*0-939449-04-8*) Ink Plus.

— Bite of Seattle Cookbook, 8 vols., 6. 210p. write for info. (*0-939449-05-6*) Ink Plus.

— Bite of Seattle Cookbook, 8 vols., 7. 210p. write for info. (*0-939449-06-4*) Ink Plus.

— Bite of Seattle Cookbook, 8 vols., 8. 210p. write for info. (*0-939449-07-2*) Ink Plus.

Deak, Maggie & Henry, Kim. Decem Propriae Fabulae Aptac a Fabulis Aesopi - Ten Original Fables Adapted from Aesop's Fables. Schmidt, Mary C., ed. 22p. (J). (gr. 5-6). spiral bd. 3.10 (*0-939507-48-X*, B726) Amer Classical.

Deak, Simone, jt. auth. see Deak, Etienne.

Deak, Tibor & Beuchat, Larry R. Handbook of Food Spoilage Yeasts. LC 95-45244. (Contemporary Food Science Ser.). 224p. 1996. boxed set 149.95 (*0-8493-2703-2*) CRC Pr.

Deak, Zoltan. How the Hungarians Saved Western Civilization. unabridged ed. LC 96-78131. (Illus.). 125p. (Orig.). 1996. pap. 9.95 (*0-9654417-1-7*) Hungarian Herit.

Deakin, Alfred. And Be One People: Alfred Deakin's Federal Story. Macintyre, Stuart, ed. & intro. by. 208p. 1996. 39.95 (*0-522-84646-7*, Pub. by Melbourne Univ Pr) Paul & Co Pubs.

Deakin, Andrew. Outlines of Musical Bibliography: A Catalogue of Early Music & Musical Works Printed or Otherwise Produced in the British Isles. 112p. reprint ed. lib. bdg. 48.50 (*3-487-05925-8*) G Olms Pubs.

Deakin, Brian. Letter Writing in English. 254p. (C). 1986. 50.00 (*81-7002-016-6*, Pub. by Himalayan Bks) St Mut.

— The Youth Labour Market in Britain: The Role of Intervention. (Cambridge Department of Applied Economics Occasional Papers: No. 62). (Illus.). 239p. (C). 1996. text 59.95 (*0-521-55328-8*) Cambridge U Pr.

Deakin, Carol. Wilmington: Treasure on the Atlantic. (Illus.). 176p. 1996. 35.00 (*1-885352-33-6*) Community Comm.

Deakin, Charles D. Clinical Notes for the FRCA. LC 96-5332. 308p. 1997. pap. text 30.00 (*0-443-05386-3*) Church.

***Deakin, Charles D.** Clinical Notes for the FRCA. 2nd ed. LC 99-53893. 1999. write for info. (*0-443-06403-2*) Church.

Deakin, Edward, jt. auth. see Maher, Michael W.

Deakin, Edward B. & Cappell, James J., eds. Bibliography of the Oil & Gas Industry, 1980-1989. 256p. 1990. pap. 25.00 (*0-926969-01-3*) UNTIPA.

Deakin, Edward B., jt. auth. see Maher, Michael W.

Deakin, J. F., ed. The Biology of Depression: Proceedings of a Meeting of the Biological Group of the Royal College of Psychiatrists Held at Manchester University, 1985. LC 87-173519. 231p. reprint ed. pap. 71.70 (*0-8357-7777-4*, 203613700002) Bks Demand.

Deakin, J. F. William, jt. ed. see Reveley, Michael A.

Deakin, Lauren. Japan. (Passport's Illustrated Travel Guides Ser.). (Illus.). 192p. 1996. pap. 14.95 (*0-8442-4828-2*, 48282, Passprt Bks) NTC Contemp Pub Co.

Deakin, Mark, ed. Local Authority Property Management: Initiatives, Strategies, Re-Organisation & Reform. 302p. 1999. text 69.95 (*1-84014-834-9*, Pub. by Ashgate Pub) Ashgate Pub Co.

Deakin, Maureen & Morgovsky, Joel. Modern Dance Reflections. Van Vliet, Barbara, ed. (Illus.). 74p. 1980. pap. 17.95 (*0-9678974-0-8*) Rigel Pr.

Deakin, Motley F., intro. Home Book of the Picturesque: Or American Scenery, Art, & Literature. LC 67-10179. 188p. 1967. reprint ed. 50.00 (*0-8201-1029-9*) Schol Facsimiles.

***Deakin, Nicholas, ed.** Origins of Welfare State in Britain, 8 vols., set. (Illus.). 2600p. (C). 2000. text 980.00 (*0-415-21222-7*) Routledge.

Deakin, Nicholas & Page, Robert. The Costs of Welfare. 288p. 1993. 72.95 (*1-85628-513-8*, Pub. by Avebury) Ashgate Pub Co.

***Deakin, Nicholas & Parry, Richard.** The Treasury & Social Policy: The Contest for Control of Welfare Strategy. LC 99-49498. 2000. text 75.00 (*0-312-23020-6*) St Martin.

***Deakin, Quentin.** Expansion, War & Rebellion: Europe, 1598-1661. (Perspectives in History Ser.). 160p. (C). 2000. pap. 12.95 (*0-521-58616-X*) Cambridge U Pr.

Deakin, Rose & Willmot, Phyllis. Participation in Local Social Services: An Explanatory Study-Discussion Paper. 1979. 30.00 (*0-7855-0570-9*, Pub. by Natl Inst Soc Work) St Mut.

Deakin, Simon & Michie, Jonathan, eds. Contracts, Cooperation & Competition: Studies in Economics, Management & Law. LC 97-19751. (Illus.). 436p. 1998. text 98.00 (*0-19-829266-X*) OUP.

Deakin, Simon, jt. auth. see Morris, Gillian S.

Deakin, Simon F., jt. auth. see Markesinis, Basil S.

Deakin University Press Staff. The Arab-Israeli Conflict. (C). 1988. 45.00 (*0-7300-0596-8*, Pub. by Deakin Univ) St Mut.

— An Australian Casebook of Study Centres in Distance Education. 134p. (C). 1985. 59.00 (*0-7300-0213-6*, Pub. by Deakin Univ) St Mut.

— Central America: Covering Political Unrest in the States of Nicaragua, El Salvador, Guatemala, Honduras & Costa Rica. 66p. (C). 1988. 23.00 (*0-7300-0597-6*, Pub. by Deakin Univ) St Mut.

— Comparative Journalism: Study Guide & Reader 1B. 464p. (C). 1988. 114.00 (*0-7300-0542-9*, Pub. by Deakin Univ) St Mut.

— Computing Fundamentals Study Guide. 132p. (C). 1986. 75.00 (*0-7300-0579-8*, Pub. by Deakin Univ) St Mut.

— Conflict Management: Study Guide 1: Conflict, War & Diplomacy. 177p. (C). 1988. 60.00 (*0-7300-0565-8*, Pub. by Deakin Univ) St Mut.

— Conflict Management: Study Guide 2: Towards the Control of Conflict. 165p. (C). 1988. 60.00 (*0-7300-0566-6*, Pub. by Deakin Univ) St Mut.

— Core Curriculum. 69p. (C). 1985. 38.00 (*0-7300-0313-2*, Pub. by Deakin Univ) St Mut.

— Curriculum Design & Innovation. 168p. (C). 1985. 44.00 (*0-7300-0311-6*, Pub. by Deakin Univ) St Mut.

— Data Structures Study Guide. 160p. (C). 1986. student ed. 57.00 (*0-7300-0580-1*, Pub. by Deakin Univ) St Mut.

— Fantasy & Feminism in Children's Books: Study Guide. Nikolajeva, Maria, ed. 78p. (C). 1995. pap. 34.00 (*0-7300-1676-5*, ECT380, Pub. by Deakin Univ) St Mut.

— Great Powers & Regional Powers. (Asian Defense Policies Ser.: Bk. 1). 173p. (C). 1995. pap. 100.00 (*0-7300-1576-9*, SSS842, Pub. by Deakin Univ) St Mut.

— Guidelines for Academic Staff on Alternative Study Methods for Students with Writing or Typing Disabilities. (C). 1987. 50.00 (*0-7300-0262-4*, Pub. by Deakin Univ) St Mut.

— Health Policy & Administration: Study Guide. 193p. (C). 1990. pap. 90.00 (*0-7300-0714-6*, SSS220, Pub. by Deakin Univ) St Mut.

— Learning to Read Study Guide. 103p. (C). 1986. 45.00 (*0-7300-0390-6*, Pub. by Deakin Univ) St Mut.

— Literacies & the Workplace: A Collection of Original Essays. 1996. pap. 59.95 (*0-7300-1923-3*, Pub by Deakin Univ) St Mut.

— Looking at Literature. 86p. (C). 1986. 75.00 (*0-7300-0404-X*, Pub. by Deakin Univ) St Mut.

— Manual for the Preparation of Assignments on Audio Cassette. 71p. (C). 1987. 24.00 (*0-7300-0261-5*, Pub. by Deakin Univ) St Mut.

— Narrative Exchanges, Unit B. 154p. (C). 1988. 54.00 (*0-7300-0571-2*, Pub. by Deakin Univ) St Mut.

— Narrative Exchanges Reader, Unit B. 172p. (C). 1988. 60.00 (*0-7300-0572-0*, Pub. by Deakin Univ) St Mut.

— Nutrition in Catering: Study Guide. (C). 1991. pap. 75.00 (*0-7300-1240-9*, SHN 795, Pub. by Deakin Univ) St Mut.

— Reading Curriculum (ECT412) 153p. (C). 1985. 70.00 (*0-7300-0319-1*, Pub. by Deakin Univ) St Mut.

— Shakespearean Mythmaking, Unit C. 175p. (C). 1991. pap., student ed. 110.00 (*0-7300-0722-7*, HUL306, Pub. by Deakin Univ) St Mut.

— Situation Reader, Unit A. 89p. (C). 1988. 48.00 (*0-7300-0570-4*, Pub. by Deakin Univ) St Mut.

— Strands of Media Criticism: Study Guide 1A. 102p. (C). 1988. 70.00 (*0-7300-0539-9*, Pub. by Deakin Univ) St Mut.

— The Superpowers: Being a Forty-Five Year Review of the U. S. A. Soviet Union Political Relationship. 95p. (C). 1989. 40.00 (*0-7300-0601-8*, Pub. by Deakin Univ) St Mut.

— Surviving Myths Unit D: Study Guide, Unit D. 164p. (C). 1991. pap. 105.00 (*0-7300-0724-3*, HUL306, Pub. by Deakin Univ) St Mut.

— Taught Not Caught. 128p. (C). 1986. 75.00 (*0-7300-0403-1*, Pub. by Deakin Univ) St Mut.

— The Third Indo-China War. 63p. (C). 1988. 30.00 (*0-7300-0602-6*, Pub. by Deakin Univ) St Mut.

— Women & Social Change: Reader. rev. ed. 287p. (C). 1990. 105.00 (*0-7300-0782-0*, Pub. by Deakin Univ) St Mut.

— Women & Social Change: Study Guide. rev. ed. 236p. (C). 1990. 96.00 (*0-7300-0781-2*, Pub. by Deakin Univ) St Mut.

— Writing in Schools (ECT418) (C). 1989. 71.00 (*0-7300-0633-6*, Pub. by Deakin Univ); student ed. 86.00 (*0-7300-0632-8*, Pub. by Deakin Univ) St Mut.

Deakin University Press Staff, ed. The Action Research Reader. 430p. (C). 1988. 59.00 (*0-7300-0564-X*, Pub. by Deakin Univ) St Mut.

— Applied Nutrition: Study Guide. (C). 1988. pap. text 75.00 (*0-7300-0548-8*, SHN750, Pub. by Deakin Univ) St Mut.

— Applied Nutrition 1: Study Guide. (C). 1987. pap. 75.00 (*0-7300-0464-3*, SHN730, Pub. by Deakin Univ) St Mut.

— The Australian City Unit A: Study Guide - Marvellous Melbourne. 276p. (C). 1986. wbk. ed. 29.00 (*0-7300-0369-8*, Pub. by Deakin Univ) St Mut.

— The Australian City, Unit B: Study Guide & Reader - the Artist & Australian Society. (C). 1987. 126.00 (*0-7300-0499-6*, Pub. by Deakin Univ) St Mut.

— Classical Antiquity Unit A: Study Guide, Unit A. 114p. (C). 1990. pap. 75.00 (*0-7300-0718-9*, HUL305, Pub. by Deakin Univ) St Mut.

— Classroom Processes: Study Guide. 417p. (C). 1989. 120.00 (*0-7300-0650-6*, Pub. by Deakin Univ); 180.00 incl. VHS (*0-7855-6747-X*, Pub. by Deakin Univ) St Mut.

— Contemporary Logo Papers. 68p. (C). 1986. 65.00 (*0-7300-0444-9*, Pub. by Deakin Univ) St Mut.

— Feminist Knowledge As Critique & Construct, Unit B: Research Modules. (C). 1987. 56.00 (*0-7300-0617-4*, Pub. by Deakin Univ) St Mut.

— Food Science 1. (C). 1986. student ed. 90.00 (*0-7300-0700-6*, Pub. by Deakin Univ) St Mut.

— Food Science 2. (C). 1987. student ed. 90.00 (*0-7300-0509-7*, Pub. by Deakin Univ) St Mut.

— Knowledge Making. 91p. (C). 1989. 30.00 (*0-7300-0664-6*, Pub. by Deakin Univ) St Mut.

— Nutrition Education: Study Guide. (C). 1988. pap. 75.00 (*0-7300-0621-2*, SHN770, Pub. by Deakin Univ) St Mut.

— Principles of Nutrition: Study Guide. (C). 1986. pap. 75.00 (*0-7300-0751-0*, SHN710, Pub. by Deakin Univ) St Mut.

— Situations Study Guide, Unit A. 144p. (C). 1988. 51.00 (*0-7300-0569-0*, Pub. by Deakin Univ) St Mut.

— Supernatural & Superhuman Unit B: Study Guide, Unit B. 152p. (C). 1990. pap. 75.00 (*0-7300-0720-0*, HUL305, Pub. by Deakin Univ) St Mut.

— Yirrkala Community School - Case Study. (C). 1985. 24.00 (*0-7300-0316-7*, Pub. by Deakin Univ); 111.00 (*0-7855-6748-8*, Pub. by Deakin Univ) St Mut.

Deakin University Press Staff & Giroux, Henry A. Curriculum Discourse As Post-Modernist Critical Practice. 151p. (C). 1995. pap. 34.00 (*0-7300-0734-0*, ESC802, Pub. by Deakin Univ) St Mut.

Deakin University Press Staff, ed. see Kemmis, Stephen & McTaggart, Robin.

Deakin, Vicki, jt. auth. see Burke, Louise.

Deakins, David. Entrepreneurship & Small Firms. LC 95-50820. 1996. pap. write for info. (*0-07-709068-3*) McGraw.

Deakins, David, et al, eds. Small Firms: Entrepreneurship in the '90s. LC 97-196484. 192p. 1997. 85.00 (*1-85396-361-5*, Pub. by P Chapman) Taylor & Francis.

Deakins, Roger L., tr. see Heywood, Ellis.

Deakins, Suzanne. Crossing the Threshold: From Spiritual Pain to Inner Joy. 200p. 1999. pap. 13.95 (*1-893075-04-4*) Spirit Pr OR.

***Deal.** CCNP Cisco LAN/WAN Switch Configuration Exam Cram. (Networking Ser.). (C). 1999. pap. 15.60 (*0-619-01604-3*) Course Tech.

Deal. Wildlife & Natural Resource Management. (Agriculture Ser.). 1996. pap., teacher ed. 13.95 (*0-8273-6423-7*); pap., teacher ed. 14.95 (*0-8273-6424-5*) Delmar.

— Wildlife & Natural Resource Management. LC 96-20959. (Agriculture Ser.). 336p. 1997. pap. 52.95 (*0-8273-6422-9*) Delmar.

— Wildlife & Natural Resource Management. 32p. 1997. pap. text, teacher ed., wbk. ed. 12.75 (*0-8273-8227-8*) Delmar.

Deal, Alice B., ed. Gravestone Inscriptions in Northampton County Virginia. 2nd rev. ed. xxxiii, 106p. (Orig.). 1984. pap. 12.50 (*0-88490-121-1*) Library of VA.

Deal, B. E., jt. auth. see Helms, C. R.

Deal, Babs H. It's Always Three O'Clock. LC 89-20626. (Library of Alabama Classics). 344p. 1990. reprint ed. pap. 15.95 (*0-8173-0494-0*) U of Ala Pr.

Deal, Barbara J., et al, eds. Current Concepts in Diagnosis & Management of Arrhythmias in Infants & Children. LC 98-9638. (Illus.). 438p. 1998. 95.00 (*0-87993-687-8*) Futura Pub.

Deal, Borden. The Least One. LC 92-13437. (Library of Alabama Classics). 368p. (YA). 1992. pap. 15.95 (*0-8173-0673-0*) U of Ala Pr.

— There Were Also Strangers. 280p. 1986. 15.95 (*0-88282-018-4*) New Horizon NJ.

Deal, Brenda, jt. ed. see Tobar, Andres.

Deal, Carl. Academic Publishing in Chile. (Latin American Information Ser.). 24p. (Orig.). 1996. pap. 10.00 (*0-917617-48-7*) SALALM.

— Academic Publishing in Ecuador. (Latin American Information Ser.: No. 4). 34p. (Orig.). 1994. pap. 14.00 (*0-917617-44-4*) SALALM.

— Academic Publishing in Mexico. (Latin American Information Ser.: No. 2). 18p. (Orig.). 1992. pap. 14.00 (*0-917617-33-9*) SALALM.

Deal, Clifton. Ponds: Planning, Design, Construction. 92p. 1998. pap. 7.50 (*0-16-049350-1*, Agriculture Dept) USGPO.

Deal, Colin. Revelation of the Beast. 118p. (Orig.). 1995. pap. 7.95 (*0-9646960-0-2*) New Life Assembly.

Deal, David, ed. see Clover, Richard.

Deal, Grady A. Dr. Deal's Delicious Detox Diet & Wellness Lifestyle. 240p. 1991. pap. 15.00 (*0-9631405-3-1*) Liv Wellness.

— Dr. Deal's Delicious Detox Diet Weight Loss Wellness Lifestyle. rev. ed. 250p. 1992. pap. 15.95 (*0-9631405-8-2*) Liv Wellness.

Deal, Jacquelyn. Review of Intensive Coronary Care. 5th ed. (C). 1995. pap. text 24.95 (*0-8385-8416-0*) Appleton & Lange.

Deal, James R. A Real Estate Buy-Sell Manual: For Buyers, Sellers, Brokers, Lawyers. 4th ed. 200p. 1994. pap. 19.95 (*1-884949-02-9*) Great Ideas.

Deal, James R. Sample Real Estate Forms: For Buyers, Sellers, Brokers, Lawyers. 4th ed. 130p. 1994. pap. 34.95 (*1-884949-03-7*) Great Ideas.

Deal, James R. What to Serve the Goddess When She Comes for Dinner--An Historical Environmental & Semi-Autobiographical Foodways Book, Goddess Recipes Included. 220p. 1997. pap. 21.95 (*1-884949-10-X*) Great Ideas.

***Deal, Jennifer J., et al.** Choosing Executives: A Research Report on the Peak Selection Simulation. LC 99-23907. (Illus.). 61p. 1999. pap. text 20.00 (*1-882197-51-8*) Ctr Creat Leader.

Deal, Jo. Making Cider. (Illus.). 92p. (Orig.). 1993. reprint ed. pap. 10.95 (*0-9619072-1-5*) G W Kent.

Deal, Joe, photos by. Between Nature & Culture: Photographs of the Getty Center. LC 99-12089. (Illus.). 132p. 1999. 36.00 (*0-89236-549-8*, Pub. by J P Getty Trust) OUP.

***Deal, John R. Grizz.** A Sense of Place: Geospatial Imaging for Everyone. (Illus.). 200p. 2000. pap. 24.95 (*1-879102-82-X*, Pub. by ESR Inst) IPG Chicago.

Deal, Krista. An Archeological Overview of Great Basin National Park, No. 49. (National Park Service, Western Archaeological & Conservation Center Publications in Anthropology). (Illus.). 253p. 1988. reprint ed. pap. text 26.88 (*1-55567-420-8*) Coyote Press.

Deal, Krista C. The Archaeology of the Cava Highway Site, CA-BUT-288, Butte County, California. 272p. (C). 1987. pap. text 28.75 (*1-55567-066-0*) Coyote Press.

Deal, Michael. Pottery Ethnoarchaeology in the Central Maya Highlands. LC 98-12945. 1998. 55.00 (*0-87480-560-0*); pap. 25.00 (*0-87480-561-9*) U of Utah Pr.

Deal, Paula N., ed. see Schnautz, Carmella M.

Deal, Richard A. CCNP Cisco LAN Switch Router Configuration Exam Cram, 1. LC 99-26469. (Exam Cram (Coriolis' Certification Insider Press) Ser.). (Illus.). 715p. 1999. pap. 29.99 (*1-57610-435-4*) Coriolis Grp.

***Deal, Richard A.** CCNP Switching Exam Cram: The Confidence Builder for This Challenging Exam. (Illus.). 2000. pap. write for info. (*1-57610-634-9*) Coriolis Grp.

Deal, S. A Season of Letters. write for info. (*0-943216-01-X*) MoonsQuilt Pr.

Deal, Samuel J., et al. Experimental Microbiology for the Health Sciences. 4th ed. 1976. spiral bd. write for info. (*0-8087-0436-2*) Pearson Custom.

Deal, Shirley H. The Cruising Cook. LC 77-78074. 288p. 1977. ring bd., vinyl bd. 17.95 (*0-930006-00-3*) S Deal Assoc.

Deal, Susan S. The Dark Is a Door. 2nd ed. Burmaster, Orvis C., ed. LC 84-71476. (Ahsahta Press Modern & Contemporary Poets of the West Ser.). 50p. 1984. pap. 6.95 (*0-916272-25-7*) Ahsahta Pr.

D

An Asterisk (*) at the beginning of an entry indicates that the title is appearing for the first time.

— No Moving Parts. 3rd ed. Burmaster, Orvis C., ed. LC 80-67909. (Ahsahta Press Modern & Contemporary Poets of the West Ser.). 60p. 1980. pap. 6.95 (*0-916272-15-X*) Ahsahta Pr.

— Sometimes So Easy. Duggan, Michael, ed. (Illus.). 72p. (Orig.). 1992. pap. 8.00 (*1-878326-03-1*) East Hall Pr.

Deal, Terrence, jt. auth. see Kennedy, Allan.

***Deal, Terrence E.** Corporate Cultures: The Rites & Rituals of Corporate Life. 2000. pap. 15.00 (*0-7382-0330-0*) Perseus Pubng.

— Leadership Paradox: Balancing Logic & Artistry in Schools. 2000. pap. 21.95 (*0-7879-5541-8*) Jossey-Bass.

Deal, Terrence E. & Jenkins, William A. Managing the Hidden Organization: Strategies for Empowering Your Behind-the-Scenes Employees. 384p. (Orig.). 1994. mass mkt. 10.99 (*0-446-39456-4*, Pub. by Warner Bks) Little.

Deal, Terrence E. & Kennedy, Allan A. New Corporate Cultures: Revitalizing the Workplace after Downsizing, Mergers & Reengineering. LC 99-61911. 320p. 1999. text 26.00 (*0-7382-0069-7*, Pub. by Perseus Pubng) HarpC.

Deal, Terrence E. & Key, M. K. Corporate Celebration: Play, Purpose, & Profit at Work. LC 98-4453. 250p. 1998. 24.95 (*1-57675-013-2*) Berrett-Koehler.

Deal, Terrence E. & Peterson, Kent D. The Leadership Paradox: Balancing Logic & Artistry in Schools. LC 93-48709. (Education-Higher Education Ser.). 154p. 1994. text 29.95 (*1-55542-648-4*) Jossey-Bass.

— Shaping School Culture: A Guide for Leaders. LC 98-40112. (Education Ser.). 224p. 1998. 27.95 (*0-7879-4342-8*) Jossey-Bass.

Deal, Terrence E., jt. auth. see Bolman, Lee B.

Deal, Terrence E., jt. auth. see Bolman, Lee G.

Deal, Terrence E., jt. ed. see Baldridge, J. Victor.

Deal, W. Como Vivir Con Conyuge Inconverso (Living with an Unsaved Spouse) (SPA.). 1.79 (*0-685-74920-7*, 497406) Editorial Unilit.

Deal, William. Viviendo con un Conyuge Incredulo. (Serie Enfoque a la Familia - Focus on the Family Ser.).Tr. of Unequally Yoked. (SPA.). 24p. 1994. 1.99 (*1-56063-647-5*, 497406) Editorial Unilit.

Deal, William S. All about Pentecost. 1983. pap. 4.99 (*0-88019-051-5*) Schmul Pub Co.

— Faith, Facts & Feelings. 3rd ed. 1978. pap. 0.95 (*0-686-05527-6*) Crusade Pubs.

— The Furnace of Affliction. 6th ed. 1978. pap. 1.50 (*0-686-05833-X*) Crusade Pubs.

— God's Answer for the Unequally Yoked. LC 80-67387. 1980. pap. 2.95 (*0-89107-182-2*) Crusade Pubs.

— God's Answer for the Unequally Yoked. 1980. pap. 3.99 (*0-685-71180-3*) Schmul Pub Co.

— John Bunyan: The Tinker of Bedford. 1977. pap. 5.99 (*0-685-70975-2*) Schmul Pub Co.

— New Light on the Shepherd Psalm. 1982. pap. 3.95 (*0-317-00334-8*) Crusade Pubs.

— The Other Shepherd. 1982. pap. 1.95 (*0-686-38053-3*) Crusade Pubs.

— Pictorial Introduction to the Bible. 436p. 1997. reprint ed. 19.95 (*1-56563-296-6*) Hendrickson MA.

— Plain Talks on Parenting. 1984. pap. 3.95 (*0-318-18715-9*) Crusade Pubs.

— Plain Talks on Parenting. pap. 5.99 (*0-685-70973-6*) Schmul Pub Co.

— Problems of the Spirit-Filled Life. 1993. pap. 7.99 (*0-88019-298-4*) Schmul Pub Co.

— The Questions of Jesus. unabridged ed. 139p. (Orig.). pap. 6.99 (*0-88019-294-1*) Schmul Pub Co.

— The Sunday School Teacher's Guide. pap., teacher ed. 3.99 (*0-88019-163-5*) Schmul Pub Co.

— What Every Young Christian Should Know. pap. 3.99 (*0-685-70972-8*) Schmul Pub Co.

— Workmen of God. 1975. pap. 0.95 (*0-686-11025-0*) Crusade Pubs.

Deal, William S., ed. A Collection of Preacher Told Tall Tales. pap. 5.99 (*0-685-70971-X*) Schmul Pub Co.

Deal, Zack J., III. Serf & State Peasant Agriculture: Kharkov Province, 1842-1861. Bruchey, Stuart, ed. LC 80-2803. (Dissertations in European Economic History Ser.). (Illus.). 1981. lib. bdg. 47.95 (*0-405-13987-X*) Ayer.

***DeAlba, Alicia Gaspar.** Sor Juana's Second Dream: A Novel. LC 98-58093. 480p. 1999. pap. 24.95 (*0-8263-2092-9*) U of NM Pr.

***DeAlexis, Gheldere.** Alaska & Yukon. (Illus.). 2001. pap. 19.95 (*2-89464-341-1*) Ulysses Travel.

— California. (Illus.). 2001. pap. 21.95 (*2-89464-390-X*) Ulysses Travel.

— Haiti. (Illus.). 2001. pap. 17.95 (*2-89464-394-2*) Ulysses Travel.

— Havana. 2000. pap. 12.95 (*2-89464-320-9*) Ulysses Travel.

— Hawaii. (Illus.). 2000. pap. 21.95 (*2-89464-313-6*) Ulysses Travel.

— Los Angeles. (Illus.). 2000. pap. 14.95 (*2-89464-385-3*) Ulysses Travel.

— Porto. (Illus.). 2000. pap. 12.95 (*2-89464-323-3*) Ulysses Travel.

***Dealey, Carol.** The Care of Wounds. 2nd ed. LC 99-37337. 1999. pap. write for info. (*0-632-05237-6*) Blackwell Sci.

Dealey, J. Q. Growth of American State Constitutions. LC 75-124891. (American Constitutional & Legal History Ser). 308p. 1972. reprint ed. lib. bdg. 39.50 (*0-306-71985-1*) Da Capo.

DeAlteris, Joseph, jt. auth. see Castro, Kathleen M.

DeAlteris, Joseph T. Practical Twinework for Fisherman & Gear Technologists. Castro, Kathleen M., ed. 172p. (Orig.). (C). 1990. 5.00 (*1-882027-02-7*) URI ICMRD.

Dealtry, G. B. & Rickwood, David, eds. Cell Biology Labfax. (Labfax Ser.). (Illus.). 254p. 1992. spiral bd., boxed set 63.00 (*0-12-207890-X*) Acad Pr.

Dealtry, William. The Laborer: A Remedy for His Wrongs. LC 76-89729. (American Labor, from Conspiracy to Collective Bargaining Ser., No. 1). 420p. 1974. reprint ed. 25.95 (*0-405-02116-X*) Ayer.

Dealy, Francis X., Jr. The Power & the Money: Inside the "Wall Street Journal" (Illus.). 288p. 1992. 19.95 (*1-55972-118-9*, Birch Ln Pr) Carol Pub Group.

Dealy, Francis X. Win at Any Cost: The Sell Out of College Athletics. 1990. 18.95 (*1-55972-052-2*, Birch Ln Pr) Carol Pub Group.

Dealy, John M. Rheometers for Molten Plastics: A Practical Guide to Testing & Property Measurement. 300p. (gr. 13). 1981. mass mkt. 93.95 (*0-442-21874-5*) Chapman & Hall.

Dealy, Ross. The Politics of an Erasmian Lawyer: Vasco de Quiroga. (Humana Civilitas Ser.: Vol.3). 33p. (C). 1976. pap. 6.00 (*0-89003-015-4*) Undena Pubns.

Deam, C. C. Flora of Indiana. (Reprints of U. S. Floras Ser.: Vol. 6). (Illus.). 1236p. 1984. lib. bdg. 55.00 (*3-7682-0696-3*) Lubrecht & Cramer.

Deamer, David W. Current Topics in Membranes: 100 Years since Ernest Overton, Vol. 48. (Current Topics in Membranes Ser.). 417p. (C). 1999. text 99.95 (*0-12-153348-4*) Acad Pr.

Deamer, David W. & Fleischaker, Gail R. Origins of Life. 448p. (C). 1994. pap. 42.50 (*0-86720-181-9*) Jones & Bartlett.

Deamer, David W., jt. ed. see Volkov, Alexander G.

Deamer, Robert G. The Black Riders & Other Poems. 1992. 14.95 (*0-7734-0039-7*) E Mellen.

— The Importance of Place in the American Literature of Hawthorne, Thoreau, Crane, Adams, & Faulkner: American Writers, American Culture, & the American Dream. LC 89-13683. (Studies in American Literature: Vol. 7). 232p. 1990. lib. bdg. 89.95 (*0-88946-163-5*) E Mellen.

— Place - Dream & Other Poems. 1991. 14.95 (*0-7734-9671-8*) E Mellen.

— Songs for Sugarloaf. LC 97-17839. 52p. 1997. pap. 14.95 (*0-7734-2818-6*, Mellen Poetry Pr) E Mellen.

— Sugarloaf. LC 95-187688. 1995. 14.95 (*0-7734-2748-1*) E Mellen.

DeAmicis, Bonita. Multiple Intelligences Made Easy: Integrating MI into Your Curriculum. LC 96-30400. 1997. pap. 30.00 (*1-56976-060-8*) Zephyr Pr AZ.

— 3 Cheers for Teaching: A Teacher's Guide to Growing Professionally & Renewing the Spirit. (Illus.). 144p. 1998. pap. 27.00 (*1-56976-094-2*) Zephyr Pr AZ.

Dean. Architect as Stand Designer. 1985. 69.95 (*0-85967-713-3*) Ashgate Pub Co.

Dean. Biology Plants Lab Exercises. 6th ed. 1998. 18.74 (*0-07-234135-1*) McGraw.

— Cold Dead Monday. 1988. pap. text. write for info. (*0-582-68889-2*, Pub. by Addison-Wesley) Longman.

— Core Anatomy: Head & Neck, Vol. 3. (C). 1996. pap. text 23.00 (*0-7020-2042-7*) Harcourt.

— Essentials of the Essay: Writing, Reading & Grammar. 2nd ed. LC 98-3207. 313p. 1998. pap. text 35.00 (*0-205-28691-7*) Allyn.

— Finishes P3. (C). 1995. pap. 25.95 (*0-582-27643-8*, Pub. by Addison-Wesley) Longman.

Dean. Parents Duties Childrens Debts. 196p. 1996. 58.95 (*1-85742-298-8*) Ashgate Pub Co.

Dean. Total Quality. Date not set. pap. text, teacher ed. write for info. (*0-314-03336-X*) West Pub.

Dean & Frownfelter, Donna L. Principles & Practice of Cardiopulmonary Physical Therapy: Clinical Case. 3rd ed. (Illus.). 256p. (C). (gr. 13). 1996. pap. text, student ed. 19.95 (*0-8151-2243-8*, 24873) Mosby Inc.

Dean, Jr. & Rhea, eds. Atmospheric Corrosion of Metals - STP 767. 413p. 1982. 42.50 (*0-8031-0702-1*, STP767) ASTM.

Dean, jt. auth. see Day.

Dean, jt. auth. see Evans.

Dean, jt. auth. see Frownfelter, Donna L.

Dean, A. M., et al. Design & Analysis of Experiments. LC 98-20302. (Springer Texts in Statistics Ser.). 800p. (C). 1999. 84.95 (*0-387-98561-1*) Spr-Verlag.

Dean, Alan. Chaos & Intoxication: Complexity & Adaptation in the Structure of Human Nature. LC 97-2293. (Illus.). 200p. (C). 1997. 80.00 (*0-415-14614-3*); pap. 24.99 (*0-415-14615-1*) Routledge.

***Dean, Alan.** Complex Life: Nonmodernity & the Emergence of Cognition & Culture. LC 99-75539. 149p. 2000. text 61.95 (*0-7546-1049-7*, Pub. by Ashgate Pub) Ashgate Pub Co.

Dean, Alexander & Carra, Lawrence. Fundamentals of Play Directing. 5th ed. 432p. (C). 1989. text 62.00 (*0-03-014843-X*, Pub. by Harcourt Coll Pubs) Harcourt.

Dean, Alyssa. La Belle Vie d'Un Reporter. (Rouge Passion Ser.: No. 488). (FRE.). 1998. mass mkt. 3.50 (*0-373-37488-7*, 1-37488-3) Harlequin Bks.

— Her Desperado. 1999. per. 3.75 (*0-373-25819-4*, Harlequin) Harlequin Bks.

— The Last Hero. LC 96-652. (Temptation Ser.). 217p. 1995. per. 3.25 (*0-373-25651-5*, 1-25651-0) Harlequin Bks.

— Mad about You. LC 95-4600. (Temptation Ser.: No. 524). 218p. 1995. per. 2.99 (*0-373-25624-8*, 1-25624-7) Harlequin Bks.

— Manhunting in Miami. (Temptation Ser.). 1998. per. 3.75 (*0-373-25781-3*, 0-25781-6) Harlequin Bks.

— Mistletoe Mischief. LC 97-13816. (Love & Laughter Ser.: No. 33). 187p. 1997. per. 3.50 (*0-373-44033-2*) Harlequin Bks.

— Rescuing Christine. 1997. per. 3.50 (*0-373-25736-8*, 1-25736-9) Harlequin Bks.

Dean, Alyssa, jt. auth. see St. John, Cheryl.

Dean, Amy. Natural Creativity: Exploring & Using Nature's Raw Material. LC 98-4716. 160p. 1998. pap. 14.95 (*0-87131-852-0*) M Evans.

— Night Light: A Book of Nighttime Meditations. (Illus.). 400p. pap. 10.00 (*0-89486-381-9*, 5030A) Hazelden.

Dean, Amy E. Caring for the Family Soul: Enriching the Family Experience Through Love, Respect, Intimacy... 304p. 1996. pap. 13.00 (*0-425-15448-3*) Berkley Pub.

— Daybreak: 52 Things Nature Teaches Us. LC 96-19225. (Illus.). 160p. 1996. 15.00 (*0-87131-808-3*) M Evans.

— Facing Life's Challenges: Daily Meditations for Overcoming Depression, Grief, & "The Blues" 384p. (Orig.). 1995. pap. 9.00 (*1-56170-145-9*, 140) Hay House.

— First Light: Morning Meditations for Awakening to the Living Planet. 384p. 1997. pap. 10.00 (*0-425-16000-9*) Berkley Pub.

— Growing Older, Growing Better: Daily Meditations for Celebrating Aging. LC 96-46161. 384p. (Orig.). 1997. pap. 12.00 (*1-56170-353-2*, 835) Hay House.

— Lifegoals: Setting & Achieving Goals to Chart the Course of Your Life. Olmos, Dan, ed. LC 90-80051. 256p. (Orig.). 1991. pap. 12.00 (*0-937611-90-5*, 123) Hay House.

— Natural Acts: Reconnecting with Nature to Recover Community, Spirit, & Self. LC 97-2199. (Illus.). 160p. 1997. 15.00 (*0-87131-821-0*) M Evans.

— Overcoming Fears: Creating Safety for You & Your World. Olmos, Dan, ed. LC 93-39153. 380p. 1994. pap. 18.00 (*1-56170-079-7*, 155) Hay House.

— Peace of Mind: Daily Meditations for Easing Stress. LC 94-21563. 384p. 1995. pap. 10.95 (*0-553-35454-X*) Bantam.

***Dean, Amy E.** Pleasant Dreams: Nighttime Meditations for Peace of Mind. LC 99-57405. 128p. 2000. 9.95 (*1-56170-693-0*, L460) Hay House.

Dean, Amy E. Unmarked Trails: Lifepaths for Personal Progress, Spiritual Connection & Moral Courage. 224p. 1999. pap. 14.95 (*0-87131-881-4*, Pub. by M Evans) Natl Bk Netwk.

Dean, Andrea O. Centerbrook, Vol. 2. Vol. 2. (Illus.). 192p. 1996. write for info. (*1-56496-235-0*) Rockport Pubs.

Dean, Anne. David Mamet: Language As Dramatic Action. LC 89-45405. 248p. 1990. 33.50 (*0-8386-3367-6*) Fairleigh Dickinson.

Dean, Anne L. Teenage Pregnancy: The Interaction of Psyche & Culture. LC 97-29816. 280p. 1997. 47.50 (*0-88163-254-6*) Analytic Pr.

Dean, Anne M. Discovery & Invention: The Urban Plays of Lanford Wilson. LC 94-3180. 1994. 29.50 (*0-8386-3548-2*) Fairleigh Dickinson.

Dean, Athena. Consumed by Success: Reaching the Top & Finding God Wasn't There. expanded rev. ed. Logelin, Inger, ed. LC 97-106645. 192p. 1999. pap. 10.99 (*1-883893-22-4*, Pub. by WinePress Pub) BookWorld.

— You Can Do It! A Guide to Christian Self-Publishing. 144p. 1998. pap. 9.99 (*1-883893-82-8*, Pub. by WinePress Pub) BookWorld.

Dean, Athena, jt. ed. see Dean, Chuck.

Dean, Athena, ed. see Neiman, Barbara L.

Dean, Audrey V. Dolls. (Collins Gem Ser.). 1997. pap. 8.00 (*0-00-471006-1*) Collins.

— Learn Lacecraft: More Than 50 Exciting Step-by-Step Projects. (Illus.). 64p. 1998. text 20.00 (*0-7881-5377-3*) DIANE Pub.

Dean, B. Introduction to the Strong Interactions. xiv, 378p. 1976. text 349.00 (*0-677-02750-8*) Gordon & Breach.

Dean, Barbara. Wellspring: A Story from the Deep Country. LC 79-2606. (Illus.). 208p. 1979. pap. text 14.95 (*0-933280-01-7*) Island Pr.

Dean, Becky. Airline Pilot Resume Kit. McLeod, Deanne, ed. 80p. 1998. pap. 29.00 (*1-891726-10-2*) Aviation Info.

Dean, Becky, et al, eds. Major Airline Cargo Series. 48p. 1998. pap. 14.95 (*1-891726-18-8*, AIR Inc) Aviation Info.

Dean, Becky & Waymire, Montina L., eds. 1999 Pilot Resource Guide. 4th ed. 64p. 1999. pap. 24.95 (*1-891726-23-4*, AIR Inc) Aviation Info.

Dean, Becky, et al. Human Resources Interview Series. Waymire, Montina et al, eds. 18p. 1999. pap. 6.95 (*1-891726-21-8*, AIR Inc) Aviation Info.

Dean, Becky, jt. auth. see Darby, Kit.

Dean, Becky, ed. see Black, Rob.

Dean, Becky, ed. see Darby, Kit.

Dean, Becky, ed. see Darby, Kit & Gradwohl, Dan.

Dean, Becky, ed. see Harper, C. Richard & Vereen, H. Stacy.

Dean, Becky, ed. see Norris, Bob.

Dean, Becky, ed. see Williams, Bud.

Dean, Benjamin E. A Virginian in Yankeeland Vol. 1: Introduction to the Yankee Tier. LC 88-72097. (Illus.). 659p. 1989. pap. 25.00 (*0-9621451-0-6*) B E Dean Co.

— A Virginian in Yankeeland Vol. 2: Merriwell Road Through Kangaroo Gate. LC 88-72097. (Illus.). 739p. (Orig.). 1989. pap. 25.00 (*0-9621451-1-4*) B E Dean Co.

— A Virginian in Yankeeland Vol. 3: Of Monkeys, Quinine, & Magnetos....Linked. LC 88-72097. (Illus.). 400p. (Orig.). 1990. pap. 19.00 (*0-9621451-2-2*) B E Dean Co.

— A Virginian in Yankeeland Vol. 4: Some Stars & Stripes Voyages. LC 88-72097. (Illus.). 950p. (Orig.). 1991. pap. 29.95 (*0-9621451-3-0*) B E Dean Co.

— A Virginian in Yankeeland Vol. 5: Quest for Knowledge. LC 88-72097. (Illus.). 800p. (Orig.). 1992. pap. 29.00 (*0-9621451-4-9*) B E Dean Co.

— A Virginian in Yankeeland Vol. 6: Fishy Political Environment. LC 88-72097. (Illus.). 700p. (Orig.). 1994. pap. 28.00 (*0-9621451-5-7*) B E Dean Co.

— A Virginian in Yankeeland Vol. 7: Treachery at Village Hall. LC 88-72097. (Illus.). 700p. (Orig.). 2000. pap. 28.50 (*0-9621451-6-5*) B E Dean Co.

Dean, Beryl. Designing Ecclesiastical Stitched Textiles. (Illus.). 96p. 1993. 35.00 (*0-85532-752-9*, 752-9X, Pub. by Srch Pr) A Schwartz & Co.

Dean, Bessie. Aprendamos el Plan de Dios. Balderas, Eduardo, tr. LC 80-82256. (Books for LDS Children).Tr. of Let's Learn God's Plan. (SPA., Illus.). 64p. (J). (gr. k-3). 1980. pap. text 5.98 (*0-88290-135-4*) Horizon Utah.

— God Hears My Prayers. (Children's Inspirational Coloring Bks.). (Illus.). 24p. (J). (ps-3). 1993. reprint ed. pap. 4.98 (*0-88290-110-9*) Horizon Utah.

— God Loves Me. 1992. 4.98 (*0-88290-108-7*) Horizon Utah.

— I'm Happy When I'm Good. (Children's Inspirational Coloring Bks.). (Illus.). 24p. (J). (ps-3). 1979. pap. 4.98 (*0-88290-109-5*) Horizon Utah.

— It's Fun to Read the Bible: A Storybook to Color. 24p. 1979. pap. 4.98 (*0-88290-112-5*) Horizon Utah.

Dean, Bessie. Lessons Jesus Taught: The Savior's Teachings Retold for Children. (Children's Inspirational Coloring Bks.). (Illus.). 72p. (J). (gr. k-5). 1980. reprint ed. pap. 6.98 (*0-88290-671-2*) Horizon Utah.

Dean, Bessie. Let's Choose the Right. 1993. reprint ed. 3.98 (*0-88290-072-2*, 1337) Horizon Utah.

— Let's Go to Church. LC 76-3995. (Books for LDS Children). (Illus.). 63p. (J). (ps-3). 1993. reprint ed. pap. 3.98 (*0-88290-062-5*) Horizon Utah.

***Dean, Bessie.** Let's Learn about Jesus: The Life of Christ Retold for Children. (Children's Inspirational Coloring Bks.). (Illus.). 72p. (J). (ps-6). 1999. reprint ed. pap. 6.98 (*0-88290-669-0*) Horizon Utah.

Dean, Bessie. Let's Learn God's Plan. LC 78-52114. (Illus.). (J). 1978. pap. 3.98 (*0-88290-092-7*) Horizon Utah.

— Let's Learn of God's Love. LC 79-89367. (Books for LDS Children). (Illus.). 64p. (J). (ps-3). 1979. pap. 3.98 (*0-88290-124-9*) Horizon Utah.

— Let's Learn the First Principles. LC 78-70366. (Books for LDS Children). (Illus.). 64p. (J). (ps-3). 1993. reprint ed. pap. 3.98 (*0-88290-104-4*) Horizon Utah.

— Let's Love One Another. LC 77-74492. (Books for LDS Children). (Illus.). 64p. (J). (ps-3). 1993. reprint ed. pap. 3.98 (*0-88290-077-3*) Horizon Utah.

— Living, Learning & Loving: God Hears My Prayers, Let's Love One Another, Living the Golden Rule, 3 bks., Set. 1994. pap. 12.98 (*0-88290-479-5*) Horizon Utah.

— Living the Articles of Faith. (Illus.). 88p. (J). (gr. k-4). 1988. pap. 7.98 (*0-88290-336-5*) Horizon Utah.

— Living the Golden Rule: A Storybook to Color. 24p. 1979. pap. 4.98 (*0-88290-113-3*) Horizon Utah.

— Paul, God's Special Missionary. (Story Books to Color). 72p. (Orig.). (J). (gr. k-5). 1980. pap. 6.98 (*0-88290-152-4*) Horizon Utah.

— Paul's Letters of Love. (Story Books to Color). (Illus.). 72p. (Orig.). (J). (gr. k-5). 1981. pap. 6.98 (*0-88290-170-2*) Horizon Utah.

***Dean, Bessie.** Stories Jesus Told: The Lord's Parables Retold for Children. rev. ed. (Childrens' Inspirational Coloring Books Ser.). (Illus.). 72p. (J). 1999. pap. 6.98 (*0-88290-670-4*) Horizon Utah.

Dean, Bessie. Stories of Jesus for Children: Lessons Jesus Taught, Let's Learn about Jesus, Stories Jesus Told, 3 bks., Set. (J). 1994. pap. 18.98 (*0-88290-491-4*) Horizon Utah.

— Stories of Paul for Children: Paul, God's Special Missionary, Paul's Letters of Love, 2 bks., Set. (J). 1994. pap. 12.98 (*0-88290-493-0*) Horizon Utah.

— Sundays Are Special: A Storybook to Color. 24p. 1979. pap. 4.98 (*0-88290-111-7*) Horizon Utah.

Dean, Bill. Managing the Potato Production System. LC 92-1676. (Illus.). 203p. 1994. lib. bdg. 49.95 (*1-56022-025-2*) Haworth Pr.

Dean, Blanche, et al. Wildflowers of Alabama & Adjoining States. LC 73-10585. (Illus.). 256p. 1983. pap. 19.95 (*0-8173-0147-X*) U of Ala Pr.

Dean, Blanche E. Birds. (Southern Regional Nature Ser.). (Illus.). pap. 4.95 (*0-87651-018-7*) Southern U Pr.

— Ferns. (Southern Regional Nature Ser.). (Illus.). 1969. pap. 8.00 (*0-87651-019-5*) Southern U Pr.

— Happy Trails. (Southern Regional Nature Ser.). (Illus.). 1969. pap. 4.95 (*0-87651-020-9*) Southern U Pr.

Dean, Bob. The Real World of Buying & Selling Your Home. Denlinger, William W. & Rathman, R. Annabel, eds. LC 84-23045. (Real Estate Ser.). 208p. 1985. pap. 6.95 (*0-87714-119-3*) Denlingers.

Dean, Bradley P., ed. see Thoreau, Henry David.

***Dean, Brian, et al, eds.** Using CNS Autopsy Tissue in Psychiatric Research: A Practical Guide. 188p. 1999. text 95.00 (*90-5702-298-2*, Harwood Acad Pubs) Gordon & Breach.

Dean, Britten. China & Great Britain: The Diplomacy of Commercial Relations, 1860-1864. LC 73-75059. (East Asian Monographs: No. 50). 223p. 1974. pap. 14.00 (*0-674-11725-5*) HUP.

Dean, Britten, tr. & intro. see Nai-Shan, Ch'eng.

Dean, C. Neville & Hinchey, Michael, eds. Teaching & Learning Formal Methods. (International Series in Formal Methods). (Illus.). 272p. 1996. text 49.95 (*0-12-349040-5*) Acad Pr.

Dean, Carole. Just One Kiss. large type ed. (Black Satin Romance Ser.). 288p. 1996. 27.99 (*1-86110-015-9*) Ulverscroft.

— One Tough Cookie. large type ed. (Black Satin Romance Ser.). 312p. 1997. 27.99 (*1-86110-038-8*) Ulverscroft.

Dean, Carolyn. Homeopathic Remedies for 100 Children's Common Ailments. Herman, Phyllis, ed. (Good Health Guides Ser.). 56p. 1995. pap. 3.95 (*0-87983-668-7*, 36687K, Keats Publng) NTC Contemp Pub Co.

— Inka Bodies & the Body of Christ: Corpus Christi in Colonial Cuzco, Peru. LC 98-56544. 264p. 1999. pap. text 18.95 (*0-8223-2367-2*) Duke.

Dean, Carolyn. Menopause Naturally. Herman, Phyllis, ed. (Good Health Guides Ser.). 48p. 1995. pap. 3.95 (*0-87983-681-4*, 36814K, Keats Publng) NTC Contemp Pub Co.

An Asterisk (*) at the beginning of an entry indicates that the title is appearing for the first time.

Dean, Carolyn J. The Body Beyond Imagining: Pornography, Homosexuality, & Other Fantasies in Interwar France LC 99-13320. (Studies on the History of Society & Culture Ser.). 298p. 2000. 30.00 (*0-520-21995-3*, Pub. by U CA Pr) Cal Prin Full Svc.
— The Self & Its Pleasures: Bataille, Lacan, & the History of the Decentered Subject. LC 92-52748. (Illus.). 288p. 1992. text 45.00 (*0-8014-2660-X*); pap. text 17.95 (*0-8014-9954-2*) Cornell U Pr.
— Sexuality & Modern Culture. 130p. 1996. 33.00 (*0-8057-8615-5*, Twyne) Mac Lib Ref.
— Sexuality & Modern Western Culture. 1997. pap. 20.00 (*0-8057-8640-6*, Hall Reference) Macmillan.
Dean, Catherine. Cezanne. (Color Library). (Illus.). 128p. (C). 1994. reprint ed. pap. 14.95 (*0-7148-2682-0*, Pub. by Phaidon Press) Phaidon Pr.
— Klimt. LC 96-216409. (Color Library Ser.). (Illus.). 128p. 1996. pap. text 14.95 (*0-7148-3377-0*, Pub. by Phaidon Press) Phaidon Pr.
Dean, Catherine, ed. see Halverson, Delia.
Dean, Charles, Jr. Sonny Babe Ain't No Monkey. LC 98-90589. (YA). 2000. pap. 8.95 (*0-533-12847-1*) Vantage.
Dean, Chris, jt. ed. see Shepherd, Phil S.
Dean, Christiann. Cooperative Communication Between Home & School: Family Matters Project. 2nd ed. (Cornell Family Matters Ser.: Vol. FMM1). (Illus.). 316p. 1994. reprint ed. ring bd. 36.25 (*1-57753-022-5*, 321FMM1) Corn Coop Ext.
Dean, Christopher. Core Anatomy, Vol. 2. 1995. pap. text 21.00 (*0-7020-2041-9*, W B Saunders Co) Harcrt Hlth Sci Grp.
— The Lady of the Lake in Arthurian Legend. LC 93-17436. 68p. 1993. text 49.95 (*0-7734-9302-6*) E Mellen.
— A Study of Merlin in English Literature from the Middle Ages to the Present Day. LC 92-12081. 388p. 1992. lib. bdg. 99.95 (*0-7734-9532-0*) E Mellen.
Dean, Christopher & Pegington, John. Core Anatomy for Students Vol. 1: The Limbs & Vertebral Column, Vol. 1. (Illus.). 208p. 1995. pap. text 21.00 (*0-7020-2040-0*, W B Saunders Co) Harcrt Hlth Sci Grp.
Dean, Christopher & Whitlock, Quentin. Handbook of Computer-Based Training. 3rd ed. 216p. 1994. pap. 29.95 (*0-7494-1481-2*, Kogan Pg Educ) Stylus Pub VA.
Dean, Christopher & Whitlock, Quentin. Handbook of Computer Based Training. 3rd ed. 1992. 35.00 (*0-88415-088-7*, 5088) Gulf Pub.
Dean, Christopher, jt. ed. see Aiello, Leslie.
Dean, Chuck. Behind Enemy Lines: A Field Manual for God's Army. LC 97-60775. 64p. 1997. pap. 6.99 (*1-57921-027-9*, Pub. by WinePress Pub) BookWorld.
— The Book of Soldiers: The Journey from War to Peace. (Illus.). 1991. pap. write for info. (*0-9622413-2-6*) WinePress Pub.
***Dean, Chuck.** Nam Vet: Making Peace with Your Past. LC 99-62936. 176p. 1999. pap. 10.99 (*1-57921-221-2*, Pub. by WinePress Pub) BookWorld.
— Nam Vet Vol. 11: Making Peace with Your Past. 10.99 (*0-9679371-0-8*) Selah Pubg.
Dean, Chuck. Partner Power: Positive Spouse Support - a Key to Success. (Network Marketing Today Ser.: Vol. II). 112p. (Orig.). 1993. pap. 10.00 (*1-883893-00-3*) WinePress Pub.
Dean, Chuck & Dean, Athena, eds. Hidden Manna. (Illus.). 200p. 1994. pap. 10.00 (*1-883893-02-X*) WinePress Pub.
Dean, Chuck, jt. auth. see Winecoff, Dave.
Dean, Chuck, ed. see Sizemore-Larson, Darlene.
Dean, Chuck, ed. see Smith, Oswald J.
Dean, Chuck, ed. see Yaniv, David.
Dean, Cloisjean N., jt. auth. see Dean, Nicola.
***Dean, Corinna.** Graphic Interiors: Interiors Designed by Graphic Artists. 2000. 50.00 (*1-56496-674-7*) Rockport Pubs.
Dean, Cornelia. Against the Tide: The Battle for America's Coast. LC 98-50755. (Illus.). 280p. 1999. 24.95 (*0-231-08418-8*) Col U Pr.
Dean, D. Hal Leonard Electric Bass Method Bk. 1: With Soundsheet. 1982. pap. 5.95 (*0-7935-4623-0*, 00699280) H Leonard.
— Hal Leonard Electric Bass Method Bk. 2: With Soundsheet. 1982. pap. 5.95 (*0-7935-5124-2*, 00699281) H Leonard.
Dean, D. J. Thermal Design of Electronic Circuit Boards & Packages. 379p. 1997. pap. 344.00 (*0-901150-18-5*) St Mut.
Dean, D. M., et al. Parliament & Locality, 1660-1939. LC 98-196681. 145 p. 1998. write for info. (*0-7486-1027-8*) Edinburgh U Pr.
***Dean, Damon A.** Front Page 2000 for Dummies Quick Reference. LC 99-60742. (For Dummies). (Illus.). 224p. 1999. spiral bd. 12.99 (*0-7645-0499-1*) IDG Bks.
Dean, David. English Shopfronts from Contemporary Source Books, 1792-1840. (Illus.). 1970. 35.00 (*0-85458-270-3*) Transatl Arts.
— Law-Making & Society in Late Elizabethan England: The Parliament of England, 1584-1601. LC 95-47585. (Cambridge Studies in Early Modern British History). 326p. (C). 1996. text 64.95 (*0-521-55108-0*) Cambridge U Pr.
— Museum Exhibition. (Illus.). 192p. (C). 1996. pap. 32.99 (*0-415-08017-7*) Routledge.
Dean, David & Herbener, Thomas E. Cross Sectional Human Anatomy. LC 99-16455. 191p. 2000. 33.00 (*0-683-30385-6*) Lppncott W & W.
Dean, David, jt. auth. see Edson, Gary.
Dean, David, jt. ed. see Edson, Gary.
Dean, David A. Resurrection Hope. 1992. student ed. 2.50 (*1-881909-00-X*) Advent Christ Gen Conf.
Dean, David A. & Griswold, Millie H. Resurrection Hope: Leaders Guide. 1992. teacher ed. 4.50 (*1-881909-01-8*) Advent Christ Gen Conf.
Dean, David J. The Air Force Role in Low-Intensity Conflict. (Illus.). 143p. 1986. pap. 4.00 (*1-58566-014-0*) Air Univ.
Dean, David K., ed. The Year of the Horse: Interesting Information about Horses & Their Riders. (Illus.). 32p. 1996. pap. 5.00 (*0-9640188-4-5*) Mus TX Tech.
Dean, David K., jt. auth. see Johnson, Eileen.
Dean, David M. Defender of the Race: James Theodore Holly, Black Nationalist Bishop. LC 78-26913. 150p. 1995. 40.00 (*0-931186-02-1*) Lambeth Pr.
Dean, Debra A., jt. auth. see Dean, Jeffrey J.
Dean, Debra K. Back to Back. (Harperprints Chapbook Ser.). 24p. 1997. pap. 5.00 (*1-883314-08-9*) NC Writers Network.
— News of Home. LC 98-72186. (New Poets of America Ser.: No. 19). 96p. 1998. pap. 12.50 (*1-880238-66-7*) BOA Edns.
Dean, Dell. Maggie's Mountain. pap. 6.00 (*0-88734-259-0*) Players Pr.
— Mama's Girl: Playscript. LC 93-5664. 20p. (Orig.). 1995. pap. 5.00 (*0-88734-342-2*) Players Pr.
Dean, Dennis, photos by. Do It! or Diet - Moderation Not Deprivation: A System You Can Really Live With - Controlling Weight in the Real World. (Illus.). 124p. 1983. per. 15.00 (*0-9659120-1-9*) Michelle Present.
***Dean, Dennis R.** Gideon Algernon Mantell A Bibliography with Supplementary Essays. LC 98-45596. 1998. 75.00 (*0-8201-1519-3*) Schol Facsimiles.
Dean, Dennis R. Gideon Mantell & the Discovery of Dinosaurs. LC 98-16448. (Studies in Anglo-Saxon England). (Illus.). 288p. (C). 1999. 69.95 (*0-521-42048-2*) Cambridge U Pr.
— James Hutton & the History of Geology. LC 91-55545. (Illus.). 312p. 1992. text 45.00 (*0-8014-2666-9*) Cornell U Pr.
Dean, Dennis R., jt. auth. see Hutton, James.
Dean, Dennis R., ed. see Owen, Richard.
Dean, Diana, ed. see Wordworks Publishing Staff.
***Dean, Donna.** A Merry Heart. LC 99-60757. 80p. 1999. pap. 7.99 (*1-57921-216-6*, Pub. by WinePress Pub) BookWorld.
Dean, Donna H., jt. auth. see King, Elizabeth C.
Dean, Donna M. Warriors Without Weapons: The Victimization of Military Women. LC 97-74015. 168p. 1997. 35.00 (*0-9634895-3-4*) Minerva Ctr.
Dean, Dorothy & Simmons, Rilla. On the Collectible Trail. Weyand, Kenneth C., ed. (Illus.). 92p. (Orig.). 1990. pap. 9.95 (*1-878496-00-X*) Discovery MO.
Dean, Douglas. Prime Time. Bernstein, Harry, ed. 360p. (Orig.). 1988. pap. 5.95 (*0-939477-02-5*) Micro Pro Litera Pr.
Dean, Dudley. Ambush at Rincon. large type ed. (Linford Western Library). 304p. 1989. pap. 16.99 (*0-7089-6716-7*, Linford) Ulverscroft.
— The Broken Spur. large type ed. (Linford Western Library). 304p. 1989. pap. 16.99 (*0-7089-6709-4*, Linford) Ulverscroft.
***Dean, Dudley.** Diamond Deuce. LC 99-41707. 1999. 19.95 (*0-7862-2183-6*) Mac Lib Ref.
— The Diehards. large type ed. LC 99-54771. (G. K. Hall Nightingale Ser.). 2000. pap. 20.95 (*0-7838-8849-X*, G K Hall & Co) Mac Lib Ref.
Dean, Dudley. Gun in the Valley. large type ed. (Linford Western Library). 1989. pap. 16.99 (*0-7089-6766-3*) Ulverscroft.
— Gun the Man Down. large type ed. (Linford Western Library). 258p. 1989. pap. 16.99 (*0-7089-6668-3*, Linford) Ulverscroft.
— History & Genealogy of the Bangs Family in America: Tracing the Descendants, Male & Female from the Pilgrim Ancestor, Edward Bangs of Plymouth & Eastham. (Illus.). 360p. 1988. reprint ed. pap. 54.00 (*0-8328-0177-1*); reprint ed. lib. bdg. 62.00 (*0-8328-0176-3*) Higginson Bk Co.
— The Man from Briondo. large type ed. (Linford Western Library). 288p. 1988. pap. 16.99 (*0-7089-6600-4*, Linford) Ulverscroft.
***Dean, Dudley.** Trail of the Hunter. large type ed. LC 00-39530. 2000. write for info. (*0-7838-9091-5*) Thorndike Pr.
Dean, Elizabeth. Carrie-Ambassador at Large. rev. ed. (Illus.). 269p. 1984. reprint ed. pap. 4.95 (*0-930033-00-0*) Christ Life Revivals.
— Murder Is a Collector's Item. Schantz, Tom & Schantz, Enid, eds. 192p. 1998. reprint ed. pap. 14.00 (*0-915230-19-4*) Rue Morgue.
***Dean, Elizabeth.** Murder Is a Serious Business. 256p. 1999. pap. 14.95 (*0-915230-28-3*) Rue Morgue.
Dean, Elizabeth, et al. Coming Out: Another Fun 'n Games Book for Lesbians. LC 91-32875. (Illus.). 100p. (Orig.). 1991. pap. 8.95 (*0-934678-33-2*) New Victoria Pubs.
Dean, Elizabeth, jt. auth. see Howell, Janet.
Dean, Eric. St. Benedict for the Laity. 88p. 1989. pap. 8.95 (*0-8146-1595-3*) Liturgical Pr.
Dean, Eric T., Jr. Shook over Hell: Post-Traumatic Stress, Vietnam, & the Civil War. LC 97-9737. (Illus.). 352p. 1997. 36.50 (*0-674-80651-4*) HUP.
— Shook over Hell: Post-Traumatic Stress, Vietnam, & the Civil War. 1999. pap. text 16.95 (*0-674-80652-2*) HUP.
Dean, Ernest A. & Woodcock, Gary W. Island Captain: The Autobiography of Mail Boat Captain Ernest Dean of Sandy Point, Abaco, Bahamas. 1997. pap. 14.95 (*0-932265-42-1*) White Sound.
Dean, Evelyn, jt. auth. see Brill, Steve.
Dean, Francis H. America's Army & Air Force Airplanes: Post-World War I to the Present. LC 97-80363. (Illus.). 384p. 1998. 49.95 (*0-7643-0480-1*) Schiffer.
— America's Hundred Thousand: U. S. Production Fighters of World War II. (Illus.). 400p. 1996. 59.95 (*0-7643-0072-5*) Schiffer.
***Dean, Francis H.** America's Navy & Marine Corps Airplanes: 1918 to the Present. LC 98-88429. 416 p. 1999. write for info. (*0-7643-0557-3*) Schiffer.
Dean, Frank E. Trick & Fancy Riding. LC 76-354 66. 269p. reprint ed. pap. 83.40 (*0-608-15452-0*, 202930300060) Bks Demand.
Dean Fry, Karen & Benson, Bob. The Journey Home: A Walk with Bob Benson. LC 96-39991. 136p. 1997. 15.99 (*0-8341-1646-4*) Beacon Hill.
***Dean, G. & Peirce, Ebenezer W.** Life, Experiences & Incidents of Rev. Gardner Dean, with Genealogies of the Gardner, Dean & Hinds Families. 307p. 1999. reprint ed. 56.00 (*0-8328-9935-6*) Higginson Bk Co.
Dean, G. D., jt. auth. see Read, Bryan E.
Dean, G. E. Bible Secrets for Successful Living. LC 98-190472. 357p. 1997. lthr. 4.97 (*1-57748-075-7*) Barbour Pub.
***Dean, G. E.** G. E. Dean's Guide to the Bible: A Genesis to Revelation Tour of God's Word. (Inspirational Library Ser.). 356p. 2000. lthr. 4.97 (*1-57748-666-8*) Barbour Pub.
Dean, G. W., jt. auth. see Chambers, R. J.
***Dean, Gardner & Peirce, Ebenezer W.** Life, Experiences of Rev. Gardner Dean, with Genealogies. 307p. 1999. reprint ed. pap. 46.00 (*0-8328-9936-4*) Higginson Bk Co.
Dean, Gary J. Designing Instruction for Adult Learners. LC 92-30576. 142p. (C). 1994. 22.00 (*0-89464-658-3*) Krieger.
***Dean, Gary J., et al.** Enhancing Organizational Effectiveness in Adult & Community Education. LC 99-88738. (Professional Practices in Adult Education & Human Resource Development Ser.). (Illus.). (C). 1999. text 28.50 (*1-57524-001-7*) Krieger.
Dean, Geoff. Challenging the More Able Language User. LC 98-185499. 1998. pap. 27.95 (*1-85346-517-8*, Pub. by David Fulton) Taylor & Francis.
***Dean, Geoff.** Teaching Reading in Secondary Schools. 2000. pap. 26.95 (*1-85346-661-1*) David Fulton.
Dean, Gloria. The Dean Mountain Story. LC 81-81878. 80p. 1982. pap. 5.50 (*0-915746-20-4*) Potomac Appalach.
Dean, Gordon E. Forging the Atomic Shield: Excerpts from the Office Diary of Gordon E. Dean. Anders, Roger M., ed. LC 86-11385. 341p. reprint ed. pap. 105.80 (*0-608-08604-5*, 206912700003) Bks Demand.
Dean, Graeme, jt. auth. see Clarke, Frank L.
Dean, Gregory D. Step-by-step to Stand-up Comedy. 224p. 2000. pap. 18.95 (*0-325-00179-0*) Heinemann.
Dean, Harry. A Sheltered Life. LC 91-4431. v, 37p. (Orig.). 1991. pap. 5.00 (*0-926487-09-4*) Rowan Mtn Pr.
Dean, Hartley & Melrose, Margaret. Poverty, Riches & Social Citizenship. LC 98-7075. 1998. text 69.95 (*0-312-21684-X*) St Martin.
Dean, Harvey R. & Kittredge, Mary. Changing Education: A Success Story. (Illus.). 240p. 1997. pap. 17.95 (*0-9657261-0-X*) Pitsco.
— Changing Education: A Success Story. (Illus.). 222p. 1997. 21.50 (*0-9657261-1-8*) Pitsco.
Dean, Henry L. & Schuhmacher, Robert W. Biology of Plants: Laboratory Exercises. 6th ed. 304p. (C). 1987. text. write for info. (*0-697-00644-1*, WCB McGr Hill) McGrw-H Hghr Educ.
Dean, Henry L., et al. General Biology. 5th ed. 288p. (C). 1987. text, lab manual ed. write for info. (*0-697-00866-5*, WCB McGr Hill) McGrw-H Hghr Educ.
Dean, Herschel B. Bible Digest Treasures. deluxe ed. (Illus.). 414p. 1988. 19.95 (*0-944035-00-0*) LaMar Pub.
— Golden Treasury of Bible Wisdom. 416p. 1988. im. lthr. 4.97 (*1-55748-047-8*) Barbour Pub.
***Dean, Irene.** Polymer Clay. LC 00-25776. (Weekend Crafter Ser.). (Illus.). 2000. pap. 14.95 (*1-57990-168-9*, Pub. by Lark Books) Sterling.
Dean, J. Analytical Chemistry Handbook. LC 94-47607. 1168p. 1995. 140.00 (*0-07-016197-6*) McGraw.
— Lange's Handbook of Chemistry. 14th ed. (Illus.). 1466p. 1992. 110.00 (*0-07-016194-1*) McGraw.
Dean, J. David. The Fire of Han-Thol: Book One of the Twelve Pearls. LC 97-92641. 446p. 1998. 22.95 (*0-9646604-5-8*) Pandea Pubns.
— Ravennetus. LC 95-74738. 384p. 1996. 21.95 (*0-9646604-4-X*) Pandea Pubns.
Dean, J. R. Down to the Sea. (C). 1987. 35.00 (*0-85174-040-5*) St Mut.
Dean, J. R. & Hitchen, S., eds. Applications of Supercritical Fluids in Industrial Analysis. 1993. 101.00 (*0-8493-7108-2*, TP156) CRC Pr.
Dean, Jack H., et al, eds. Immunotoxicology & Immunopharmacology. LC 85-19607. (Target Organ Toxicology Ser.). 527p. 1985. reprint ed. pap. 163.40 (*0-7837-8353-1*, 204914300010) Bks Demand.
Dean, James. Insurance Company Accounting. 1995. pap. text. write for info. (*0-406-03488-5*, UK, MICHIE) LEXIS Pub.
Dean, James, ed. Six Ecclesiastical Satires. (TEAMS Middle English Text Ser.). 1991. pap. 9.00 (*1-879288-05-2*) Medieval Inst.
Dean, James & Hait, Pam. Paul Calle: An Artist's Journey. Cooper, Dana, ed. LC 92-62400. (Illus.). 152p. 1992. 65.00 (*0-941728-04-8*, 30596) Mill Pond Pr
Dean, James, jt. auth. see Gross, Daniel R.
Dean, James D. & Morris, Charles W. Breaking Out of Plastic Prison: A 10-Step Program to Financial Freedom. LC 97-11015. 192p. 1997. pap. 9.99 (*0-8007-5625-8*) Revell.
Dean, James M. Medieval English Political Writings. LC 96-5082. (Middle English Texts Ser.). (Illus.). 1996. pap. 14.00 (*1-879288-64-8*) Medieval Inst.
— What Type of Financial Institutions Would Be Needed to Incorporate the Northwest Territories into the Canadian Federation? Fiscal Policies for the Future. LC 96-17497. (Canadian Studies: Vol. 18). (Illus.). 232p. 1996. text 89.95 (*0-7734-8813-8*) E Mellen.
— The World Grown Old in Later Medieval Literature. LC 89-63249. (Medieval Academy Bks.: Vol. 101). (Illus.). xi, 379p. 1997. 50.00 (*0-915651-04-1*, MAB 101) Medieval Acad.
Dean, James M. & Waterman, Anthony Michael C. Religion & Economics: Normative Social Theory. LC 98-45101. 5p. 1999. write for info. (*0-7923-8373-7*) Kluwer Academic.
Dean, James M. & Zacher, Christian K., eds. The Idea of Medieval Literature: Essays on Chaucer & Medieval Culture in Honor of Donald R. Howard. LC 91-58041. (Illus.). 360p. 1992. 49.50 (*0-87413-440-4*) U Delaware Pr.
Dean, James M., ed. see Chaucer, Geoffrey.
Dean, James S., Jr., jt. auth. see Benfield, Warren A.
Dean, James W., Jr. Deciding to Innovate: How Firms Justify Advanced Technology. LC 87-17432. 192p. 1987. text 34.95 (*0-88730-189-4*, HarpBusn) HarpInfo.
Dean, James W., Jr. & Evans, James R. Total Quality: Management, Organization, & Strategy. Fenton, ed. LC 94-153049. 300p. (C). 1993. pap. 23.25 (*0-314-02826-9*) West Pub.
Dean, James W., jt. auth. see Bowe, Michael.
Dean, Jan. Finders. LC 94-40544. 176p. (J). (gr. 4-7). 1995. per. 15.00 (*0-689-50612-0*) McElderry Bks.
— The Gardener's Reading Guide. (Illus.). 272p. 1994. reprint ed. pap. 17.95 (*0-8160-3012-X*) Facts on File.
— Industrial Narrow Gauge Railways. (Album Ser.: No. 145). (Illus.). 32p. 1998. pap. 6.25 (*0-85263-752-7*, Pub. by Shire Pubns) Parkwest Pubns.
Dean, Jan, et al. Full House - A Collection. (Illus.). 108p. (C). 1988. 30.00 (*0-947612-10-6*, Pub. by Rivelin Grapheme Pr) St Mut.
Dean, Jean, et al. A Funny Thing Happened on the Way to the Kitchen. Roenicke, Judy & Schmidt, Rosemary J., eds. (Illus.). 304p. 1993. pap. 15.95 (*1-882294-02-5*) Green Gate.
***Dean, Jearlene.** The Sharecropper. 1999. pap. 8.95 (*0-533-12849-8*) Vantage.
Dean, Jeffrey J. & Dean, Debra A. The Amazing Adventures of Abiola. LC 93-30332. (Illus.). 32p. (J). (gr. 6-9). 1994. 12.95 (*0-86543-409-3*); pap. 5.95 (*0-86543-410-7*) Africa World.
— The Amazing Adventures of Abiola, Vol. 3. large type ed. (Selected Children's Multicultural Stories). (Illus.). 32p. (J). (gr. 4-6). 1999. lib. bdg. 12.95 (*1-56674-225-0*) Forest Hse.
***Dean, Jeffrey S.** Salado. (Amerind Foundation New World Studies). 2000. 45.00 (*0-8263-2169-0*) U of NM Pr.
Dean, Jeffrey S., et al, eds. Tree Rings, Environment & Humanity: Proceedings of the International Conference, Tucson, Arizona, 17-21 May 1994. LC 96-25331. (Illus.). 889p. (Orig.). 1996. pap. text 20.00 (*0-9638314-2-9*) Radiocarbon.
Dean, Jennifer K. Deleite del Corazon: Aspectos de la Oracion. Clay, Ele, ed.Tr. of Heart's Cry. (SPA.). 77p. (Orig.). 1992. pap. text 6.95 (*1-56309-088-0*, L934116, New Hope) Womans Mission Union.
— He Restores My Soul: A 40 Day Journey Toward Personal Renewal. LC 99-20298. 192p. 1999. pap. 12.99 (*0-8054-2027-4*) Broadman.
— Heart's Cry: Principles of Prayer. Nelson, Becky, ed. 116p. (Orig.). 1992. pap. text 8.99 (*1-56309-047-3*, N924101, New Hope) Womans Mission Union.
— Power Praying: Prayer That Produces Results. LC 96-61548. 112p. 1996. pap. 9.00 (*1-883893-61-5*, Pub. by WinePress Pub) BookWorld.
— The Praying Life: Living Beyond Your Limits. Nelson, Becky, ed. 96p. (Orig.). 1994. pap. text 8.99 (*1-56309-091-0*, N944105, New Hope) Womans Mission Union.
— Riches Stored in Secret Places: A Devotional Guide for Those Who Hunger after the Deep Things of God. LC 97-167165. 184p. 1997. pap. text 9.99 (*1-56309-203-4*, N974109, New Hope) Womans Mission Union.
Dean, Jennifer K. Secret Place of the Most High: A Journal for Those Who Hunger after the Deep Things of God. 184p. 1997. pap. text 9.99 (*1-56309-204-2*, N974110, New Hope) Womans Mission Union.
Dean, Jennifer K., jt. auth. see Smith, Jack R.
Dean, Jennifer Kennedy. Live a Praying Life: Open Your Life to God's Power & Provision. 1999. pap. 16.99 (*0-9667125-0-1*) Masters Pub Hse.
Dean, Jenny. The Craft of Natural Dyeing. (Illus.). 64p. 1993. pap. 16.95 (*0-85532-744-8*, 7448, Pub. by Srch Pr) A Schwartz & Co.
Dean, Jenny & Casselman, Karen D. Wild Color: The Complete Guide to Making & Using Natural Dyes. (Illus.). 144p. 1999. pap. text 24.95 (*0-8230-5727-5*) Watsn-Guptill.
Dean, Jeremy. Celine Dion: Let's Talk about Love. (Illus.). 72p. 1998. pap. 12.95 (*1-56649-044-8*) Welcome Rain.
— Nirvana: Revealed. (Illus.). 128p. pap. 14.95 (*0-7525-1860-7*, Pub. by Parragon Pub) Music Sales.
***Dean, Jim.** Dogs That Point, Fish That Bite: Outdoor Essays. LC 95-13393. (Chapel Hill Book Ser.). 168p. 2000. pap. 10.95 (*0-8078-4864-6*) U of NC Pr.
Dean, Jim. Dogs That Point, Fish That Bite: Outdoor Essays. LC 95-13393. 168p. (C). 2000. 24.95 (*0-8078-2234-5*) U of NC Pr.
***Dean, Jim.** The Secret Lives of Fishermen: More Outdoor Essays. LC 00-27313. 176p. 2000. 24.95 (*0-8078-2580-8*) U of NC Pr.
Dean, Jimmy. Jimmy Dean on Jimmy Dean. 144p. 1994. per. 14.95 (*0-85965-126-6*, Pub. by Plexus) Publishers Group.
Dean, Joan. Beginning Teaching in the Secondary School. LC 96-33767. (Illus.). 178p. 1996. 87.95 (*0-335-19620-9*) OpUniv Pr.

D

***Dean, Joan.** The Effective School Governor. LC 00-34465. 2001. write for info. (0-415-22351-2) Routledge.
— Improving Children's Learning: Effective Teaching in the Primary School. LC 99-31129. (Educational Management Ser.). 168p. 2000. write for info. (0-415-16896-1) Routledge.

Dean, Joan. Improving the Primary School. LC 98-24878. (Educational Management Ser.). 1998. pap. 25.99 (0-415-16895-3) Routledge.
— Managing the Secondary School. 2nd ed. LC 93-13075. 1994. write for info. (0-415-08770-8) Routledge.
— Professional Development in School. (Developing Teachers & Teaching Ser.). 192p. 1991. pap. 35.95 (0-335-09590-9) OpUniv Pr.

Dean, Joan F. David Hare. (Twayne's English Authors Ser.: No. 480). 168p. (C). 1990. 22.95 (0-8057-6997-8, Twayne) Mac Lib Ref.
— Tom Stoppard: Comedy As a Moral Matrix. LC 80-26400. (Literary Frontiers Editions Ser.). 128p. 1981. text 12.95 (0-8262-0332-9) U of Mo Pr.

Dean, Jodi. Aliens in America: Conspiracy Cultures from Outerspace to Cyberspace. LC 97-44509. (Illus.). 256p. 1998. pap. 15.95 (0-8014-8468-5); text 39.95 (0-8014-3463-7) Cornell U Pr.

***Dean, Jodi.** Cultural Studies & Political Theory. LC 00-9220. 2000. write for info. (0-8014-8578-9) Cornell U Pr.

Dean, Jodi. Solidarity of Strangers: Feminism after Identity Politics. LC 95-13906. 228p. 1996. pap. 17.95 (0-520-20231-7, Pub. by U CA Pr) Cal Prin Full Svc.
— Solidarity of Strangers: Feminism after Identity Politics. LC 95-13906. 228p. (C). 1996. 40.00 (0-520-20230-9, Pub. by U CA Pr) Cal Prin Full Svc.

Dean, Jodi, ed. Feminism & the New Democracy: Resisting the Political. (Philosophy & Social Criticism Ser.: Vol. 5). 256p. (C). 1997. 75.00 (0-8039-7617-8, 76178); pap. 29.95 (0-8039-7618-6, 76186) Sage.

Dean, Joel. The Relation of Cost to Output for a Leather Belt Shop. (Technical Papers: No. 2). 80p. 1941. reprint ed. 20.00 (0-87014-447-2) Natl Bur Econ Res.

Dean, John. Divers Travel Guide to the Caribbean & the Bahamas. (Illus.). 268p. 1987. pap. 19.95 (0-942427-00-9) Travel & Sports SF.
— Games Make Spelling Fun: Activities for Better Spelling. rev. ed. 1973. pap. 5.99 (0-8224-3255-2) Fearon Teacher Aids.

***Dean, John.** The Indiana Torture Slaying: Sylvia Likens' Ordeal & Death. 2nd ed. LC 99-76087. (Illus.). 189p. 1999. pap. 15.55 (0-9604894-7-9) Borf Bks.

Dean, John & Gabilliet, Jean-Paul, eds. European Readings of American Popular Culture: Contributions to the Study of Popular Culture, 50. LC 95-31339. (Contributions to the Study of Popular Culture Ser.: No. 50). 288p. 1996. 69.50 (0-313-29429-1) Greenwood.

Dean, John, et al. Travel & Sports Guide. 3rd ed. Jacobs, Karla & Huysman, Dorthy, eds. 256p. (Orig.). 1989. pap. 2.95 (0-942427-04-1) Travel & Sports SF.

Dean, John A. Lange's Handbook of Chemistry. 15th ed. (Illus.). 1584p. 1998. 120.00 (0-07-016384-7) McGraw-Hill Prof.

Dean, John A. & Rains, Theodore C., eds. Components & Techniques, Vol. 2. LC 76-78830. 378p. pap. 117.20 (0-608-08252-X, 2055081) Bks Demand.
— Flame Emission & Atomic Absorption Spectrometry, Vol. 1. LC 76-78830. 452p. 1969. reprint ed. pap. 140.20 (0-608-08238-4, 205508000001) Bks Demand.
— Flame Emission & Atomic Absorption Spectrometry, Vol. 3: Elements & Matrices. LC 76-78830. 688p. 1975. reprint ed. pap. 200.00 (0-608-08240-6, 202709800003) Bks Demand.
— Flame Emission & Atomic Absorption Spectrometry: Components & Techniques, Vol. 2. LC 76-78830. 378p. 1971. reprint ed. pap. 117.20 (0-608-08239-2, 205508100002) Bks Demand.

Dean, John A., jt. auth. see Shugar, Gershon J.

Dean, John C. Travel & Sports. 4th ed. 300p. 1990. pap. 2.95 (0-942427-05-X) Travel & Sports SF.
— Travel & Sports Guide. (Illus.). 336p. (Orig.). 1988. pap. 9.95 (0-942427-02-5) Travel & Sports SF.

Dean, John F. Writing Well. (J). (gr. 5-12). 1985. pap. 8.99 (0-8224-7530-8) Fearon Teacher Aids.

Dean, John J. Effective Speaking . . . Here's How. 57p. (C). 1990. pap. 30.00 (0-86439-026-2, Pub. by Boolarong Pubns) St Mut.

Dean, John P., et al. A Manual of Intergroup Relations. LC 79-14226. 190p. reprint ed. pap. 58.90 (0-608-08674-6, 206919700003) Bks Demand.

Dean, John R. Extraction Methods for Environmental Analysis. LC 97-48744. 240p. 1998. 110.00 (0-471-98287-3) Wiley.

Dean, John R., et al. Atomic Absorption & Plasma Spectroscopy. 2nd ed. LC 96-47643. (Analytical Chemistry by Open Learning Ser.). 228p. 1997. pap. 55.00 (0-471-97255-X) Wiley.
— Atomic Absorption & Plasma Spectroscopy. 2nd rev. ed. 1999. text 115.00 (0-471-97254-1) Wiley.

Dean, John W. Ward. Memoir of the Rev. Nathaniel Ward . . . With Notices of His Family. 213p. 1998. reprint ed. pap. 31.50 (0-8328-9697-7); reprint ed. lib. bdg. 41.50 (0-8328-9696-9) Higginson Bk Co.

Dean, John W., et al. Arnold. Genealogy of the Family of Arnold in Europe & America, with Brief Notes. (Illus.). 16p. 1996. reprint ed. pap. 5.00 (0-8328-5356-9); reprint ed. lib. bdg. 15.00 (0-8328-5355-0) Higginson Bk Co.

Dean, Johnie, contrib. by. Piano Prayer & Praises. 1987. 8.99 (0-685-68292-7, MB-582) Lillenas.

Dean, Johnny, jt. auth. see Blades, James.

Dean, Jokat. A Sex Godess's Make Up Secrets. 1996. pap. text 23.95 (0-9656869-0-6) King Pub HI.

Dean, Jonathan. Ending Europe's Wars: The Continuing Search for Peace & Security. LC 94-26796. 441p. (C). 1994. 34.95 (0-87078-196-0) Century Foundation.
— Ending Europe's Wars: The Continuing Search for Peace & Security. LC 94-26796. 441p. (C). 1995. pap. 16.95 (0-87078-197-9) Century Foundation.

Dean-Jones, Lesley. Women's Bodies in Classical Greek Science. (Illus.). 306p. 1996. reprint ed. pap. text 21.00 (0-19-815046-6) OUP.

***Dean, Judith.** Karen & Company. LC 99-64157. 160p. 2000. pap. 15.95 (0-88739-296-2) Creat Arts Bk.

Dean, Judith M., et al. Trade Policy Reform in Developing Countries since 1985: A Review of the Evidence. LC 94-39461. (Discussion Paper Ser.: No. 267). 114p. 1994. pap. 22.00 (0-8213-3102-7, 13102) World Bank.

Dean, Julia, photos by. A Year on Monhegan Island. LC 93-24534. (Illus.). 48p. (J). (gr. 2-4). 1995. 14.95 (0-395-66476-4) Ticknor & Flds Bks Yng Read.

Dean, Karen. The Father Keeps His Promises. LC 96-6010. 40p. (Orig.). 1996. pap. 2.99 (0-8341-1588-3) Beacon Hill.
— Mother Always Told Me . . . LC 95-50685. 56p. (Orig.). 1996. pap. 2.99 (0-8341-1622-7) Beacon Hill.

Dean, Karen S. Cammy Takes a Bow. (J). (gr. 3-7). 1988. pap. 2.50 (0-380-75400-2, Avon Bks) Morrow Avon.
— Maggie Adams, Dancer. 1980. pap. 1.75 (0-380-75366-9, Avon Bks) Morrow Avon.
— Maggie Adams, Dancer. 176p. (YA). (gr. 5 up). 1982. pap. 2.50 (0-380-80200-7, Avon Bks) Morrow Avon.

Dean, Kathryn. Politics & the Ends of Identity. (Avebury Series in Philosophy). 312p. 1997. text 83.95 (1-85972-372-1, Pub. by Ashgate Pub) Ashgate Pub Co.

Dean, Kathryn, ed. Population Health Research: Linking Theory & Methods. (Illus.). 256p. (C). 1993. text 62.00 (0-8039-8751-X); pap. text 23.95 (0-8039-8752-8) Sage.

Dean, Kathryn, et al, eds. Self-Care & Health in Old Age: Health & Behaviour Implications for Policy & Practice. LC 85-28015. 368p. 1986. 59.50 (0-7099-0881-4, Pub. by C Helm) Routldge.

Dean, Kelly. Music Theory Made Easy. (Illus.). 96p. 1998. per. 12.95 (0-7935-4254-5, 00841002) H Leonard.

Dean, Ken. Queen: A Visual Documentary. (Illus.). 112p. pap. 21.95 (0-7119-2828-2, OP 46721) Omnibus NY.

Dean, Kenda C., et al. The Godbearing Life: The Art of Soul-Tending for Youth Ministry. LC 98-15998. 192p. 1998. pap. 15.00 (0-8358-0858-0, UR858) Upper Room Bks.

Dean, Kenneth. Lord of the Three in One: The Spread of a Cult in Southeast China. LC 97-46181. 393p. 1998. text 45.00 (0-691-02881-8, Pub. by Princeton U Pr) Cal Prin Full Svc.
— Taoist Ritual & Popular Cults in Southeast China. LC 92-21047. (Illus.). 320p. (C). 1993. text 55.00 (0-691-07417-8, Pub. by Princeton U Pr) Cal Prin Full Svc.
— Taoist Ritual & Popular Cults of Southeast China. 308p. (C). 1993. pap. text 17.95 (0-691-04473-2, Pub. by Princeton U Pr) Cal Prin Full Svc.

Dean, Kenneth & Massumi, Brian. First & Last Emperors: The Absolute State & the Body of the Despot. 1992. pap. 7.00 (0-936756-77-2) Autonomedia.

Dean, Kevin, jt. auth. see Perlman, Meg.

Dean, Lawrie C., jt. auth. see Brown, Margaret K.

Dean, Leonard F., Jr. The History of the Dayton Westside Baptist Preachers. (Illus.). 131p. (Orig.). 1996. pap. 12.95 (0-9655791-0-7) Deliverance.

Dean, Leonard F., ed. Shakespeare: Modern Essays in Criticism. 2nd ed. 486p. (Orig.). (YA). (gr. 9 up). 1967. pap. text 22.95 (0-19-500688-7) OUP.
— Twentieth Century Interpretations of Julius Caesar. LC 69-11355. 1968. 8.95 (0-13-512285-6, Spectrum IN) Macmillan Gen Ref.

Dean, Leonard F., ed. see Erasmus, Desiderius.

Dean, Lois. Fox in a Fix. (J). 1959. 6.00 (0-87602-128-3) Anchorage.

Dean, Loral, jt. auth. see Post, Sandra.

Dean, Lou. Angels in Disguise. 136p. (J). 1995. pap. 7.95 (1-56684-097-X) Evans Bk Dist.
— Osage County Kids: A True Story. 160p. 1999. pap. 11.95 (0-9671208-2-9) Clinescot Pubg.
— Paw Prints in My Soul: A True Story. LC 97-92419. 159p. 1997. pap. 9.95 (1-56684-305-7) Evans Bk Dist.

Dean, Love. The Lighthouses of Hawai'i. LC 90-11214. (Illus.). 224p. 1991. 19.95 (0-8248-1319-7) UH Pr.
— Lighthouses of the Florida Keys. LC 98-20541. (Illus.). 256p. 1998. 24.95 (1-56164-160-X); pap. 18.95 (1-56164-165-0) Pineapple Pr.

Dean, Lucy. Paul Nash as Book Illustrator & Designer: V&A National Art Library, Restaurant Foyer, 16 September-29 November 1998. LC 98-222075. 25 p. 1998. pap. write for info. (1-85177-281-2) V&A Ent.

***Dean, Lynn.** Family Fun Guide: Northern Colorado Edition. Taylor, Susan et al, eds. (Illus.). 80p. 1999. pap. 5.00 (1-881663-11-6) Poudre Canyon Pr.

Dean, Macabee. The Ashmadai Solution. 256p. 1992. pap. 5.95 (965-229-039-4, Pub. by Gefen Pub Hse) Gefen Bks.

Dean, Margaret M. The Jurisprudent Physician: A Physician's Guide to Legal Process & Malpractice Litigation. LC 99-71509. 416p. 1999. pap. 69.99 (0-9670004-0-8) Legis.

***Dean, Mark.** Counter Culture Texas. LC 99-26667. 1999. pap. text 24.95 (1-55622-737-X) Wordware Pub.

Dean, Martin. Collaboration in the Holocaust: Crimes of the Local Police in Belorussia & Ukraine, 1941-44. LC 98-43119. 304p. 1999. text 40.00 (0-312-22056-1) St Martin.

Dean, Mary C., jt. auth. see Schoen, Diane.

Dean, Mary C., ed. see Krueger, Caryl W.

Dean, Melanie A. Borderline Personality Disorder: The Latest Assessment & Treatment Strategies. LC 95-70719. (Condensed Reviews for Professionals Ser.). 96p. (Orig.). (C). 2000. reprint ed. pap. 14.95 (1-887537-09-0) Compact Clinicals.

Dean, Meryll. Japanese Legal System: Text & Materials. LC 98-104298. 653p. 1997. pap. 96.00 (1-85941-192-4, Pub. by Cavendish Pubng) Gaunt.

Dean, Michael. English Grammar Lessons. (Illus.). 172p. (YA). 1993. pap. text (0-19-431358-1); pap. text (0-19-431359-X) OUP.
— Vietnam. (PIER World Education Ser.). 1998. pap., per. 60.00 (1-57858-012-9, 5340) Am Assn Coll Registrars.

Dean, Michael A., et al. Commercial Real Property Lease Practice. California Continuing Education of the Bar Staff, ed. LC 75-26448. (California Practice Bk.: No. 68). (Illus.). 114p. 1990. write for info. (0-88124-342-6, RE-31142) Cont Ed Bar-CA.

***Dean, Michael A., et al.** Office Leasing: Drafting & Negotiating the Lease - 1/98 Update. Blanchette, Janis L., ed. LC 96-83539. (California Commerical Leasing Ser.). 370p. 1998. ring bd. 88.00 (0-7626-0178-7, RE-30892) Cont Ed Bar-CA.

Dean, Michael L. Successful Software Evaluation & Rating: A Quantitative Approach. (Illus.). 250p. (Orig.). 1986. 39.95 (0-87007-996-4); pap. 19.95 (0-87007-997-2) SourceView.

Dean, Michael L. & Elmore, Paul. How to Develop & Publish Profitable Microcomputer Software. (Illus.). 150p. 1985. 33.85 (0-87007-998-0); pap. 15.95 (0-87007-999-9) SourceView.

Dean, Misao. A Different Point of View: Sara Jeannette Duncan. 208p. (C). 1990. text 60.00 (0-7735-0792-2, Pub. by McG-Queens Univ Pr) CUP Services.
— Practising Femininity: Domestic Realism & the Performance of Gender in Early Canadian Fiction. LC 99-165740. (Theory/Culture Ser.). 160p. 1998. text 40.00 (0-8020-4312-7); pap. text 16.95 (0-8020-8138-X) U of Toronto Pr.

Dean, Mitchell. Critical & Effective Histories: Foucault's Methods & Historical Sociology. LC 93-28834. (Illus.). 256p. (C). 1994. pap. 24.99 (0-415-06495-3) Routledge.

Dean, Mitchell, ed. Governing Australia: Studies in Contemporary Rationalities of Government. LC 97-49566. (Reshaping Australian Institutions Ser.). 288p. (C). 1998. pap. text 22.95 (0-521-58671-2) Cambridge U Pr.

Dean, Mitchell & Hindess, Barry, eds. Governing Australia: Studies in Contemporary Rationalities of Government. LC 97-49566. (Reshaping Australian Institutions Ser.). 288p. (C). 1998. text 64.95 (0-521-58357-8) Cambridge U Pr.

Dean-Mo Liu, ed. Porous Ceramic Materials: Fabrication, Characterization, Applications. (Key Engineering Materials Ser.: Vol. 115). (Illus.). 248p. 1996. text 100.00 (0-87849-706-4, Pub. by Trans T Pub) Enfield Pubs NH.

***Dean, Nancy.** Voice Lessons: Classroom Activities to Teach Action, Detail, Imagery, Syntax, & Tone. 124p. 2000. pap. text 19.95 (0-929895-35-5) Maupin Hse.

Dean, Nancy, jt. auth. see Dean, Rodney.

Dean, Nathaniel & Shannon, Gregory E. Computational Support for Discrete Mathematics: DIMACS Workshop, March 12-14, 1992. LC 94-10076. (DIMACS Series in Discrete Mathematics & Theoretical Computer Science: Vol. 15). 399p. 1994. text 77.00 (0-8218-6605-2, DIMACS/15) Am Math.

Dean, Nathaniel, ed. see Conference for African-American Researchers in the Mathematical Sciences Staff.

Dean, Nathaniel, ed. see DIMACS (Group) Staff & NSF Science & Technology Center in Discrete Mathem.

Dean, Nathaniel, ed. see NSF Science & Technology Center in Discrete Mathem.

Dean, Neville. The Essence of Discrete Mathematics. LC 96-8580. 200p. (C). 1996. pap. text 19.95 (0-13-345943-8) P-H.

Dean, Nicola & Dean, Cloisjean N. Fever: A Novel Set in Hana, Maui. LC 98-182407. 179p. 1998. pap. 12.95 (0-9662021-0-4) Puuiki Pr.

Dean, Nora T. Lenape. unabridged ed. 60p. 1979. pap. text 39.95 incl. audio (0-88432-285-8, AFLE10) Audio-Forum.

Dean, O. Handbook of South African Copyright Law. 1987. ring bd. 100.50 (0-7021-1907-5, 15617, Pub. by Juta & Co) Gaunt.

Dean, O. C., Jr., tr. see Becker, Jurgen.

Dean, O. C., Jr., tr. see Jensen, Ann.

Dean, O. C., Jr., tr. see Marxsen, Willi.

Dean, O. C., Jr., tr. see Schmithals, Walter.

Dean, O. C., Jr., tr. see Schnackenburg, Rudolf.

Dean, O. C., Jr., tr. see Schnelle, Udo.

Dean, O. C., tr. see Stegemann, Ekkehard W. & Stegemann, Wolfgang.

Dean of Norwich Staff. Cathedrals & Abbeys of England. (Illus.). 1999. pap. 12.95 (0-7117-1003-1, Pub. by JARR UK) Seven Hills Bk.

Dean, Oida, ed. see McDonald, Archie P.

Dean, Orville A. Facing Chemical Dependency in the Classroom. 1989. pap. 6.95 (1-55874-004-X) Health Comm.

Dean, P. B., jt. auth. see Tabar, Laszlo.

Dean, P. D., et al, eds. Affinity Chromatography: A Practical Approach. (Practical Approach Ser.). 232p. 1985. pap. 45.00 (0-904147-71-1) OUP.

Dean, P. D., jt. auth. see Lowe, Christopher R.

Dean, Pamela. The Dubious Hills. 320p. 1995. 4.99 (0-8125-2362-8, Pub. by Tor Bks) St Martin.
— Juniper, Gentian, & Rosemary. 1999. pap. 14.95 (0-312-85970-8, Pub. by Tor Bks) St Martin.
— Tam Lin. 1992. mass mkt. 4.99 (0-8125-4450-1, Pub. by Tor Bks) St Martin.

Dean, Patricia, ed. see Schervish, Paul G.

Dean, Paul, jt. auth. see Jenkins, Colin.

Dean, Paul M., Jr. The Interrelationship of Tooth Thickness Measurements As Evaluated by Various Measuring Techniques. (Nineteen Eighty-Six Fall Technical Meeting Ser.: Vol. 86FTM5). (Illus.). 12p. 1986. pap. 30.00 (1-55589-469-0, 86FTM5) AGMA.

Dean, Penny Lee. Open Water Swimming. LC 97-38472. (Illus.). 232p. 1998. pap. 18.95 (0-88011-704-4, PDEA0704) Human Kinetics.

Dean, Peter. Teaching & Learning Mathematics. (Illus.). 265p. 1982. text 25.00 (0-7130-0168-2, Pub. by Woburn Pr); pap. text 12.50 (0-7130-4007-6, Pub. by Woburn Pr) Intl Spec Bk.

Dean, Peter B., jt. auth. see Tabar, Lazzlo.

Dean, Peter J., jt. ed. see Stahl, Michael J.

Dean, Phillip H. American Night Cry: A Trilogy. 1990. pap. 5.25 (0-8222-0032-5) Dramatists Play.
— Every Night When the Sun Goes Down. 1976. pap. 5.25 (0-8222-0370-7) Dramatists Play.
— Freeman. 1973. pap. 5.25 (0-8222-0422-3) Dramatists Play.
— Moloch Blues: The Owl Killer & Dink's Blues. 1996. pap. 5.25 (0-8222-1514-4) Dramatists Play.
— Paul Robeson. LC 97-162150. 1997. pap. 5.25 (0-8222-1515-2) Dramatists Play.
— The Sty of the Blind Pig. 1972. pap. 5.25 (0-8222-1091-6) Dramatists Play.
— This Bird of Dawning Singeth All Night Long: One Act Acting Edition. 1971. pap. 3.25 (0-8222-1135-1) Dramatists Play.

***Dean, Ptolemy.** Sir John Soane & the Country Estate. (Illus.). 160p. 1999. text 65.95 (1-84014-293-6, Pub. by Ashgate Pub) Ashgate Pub Co.

Dean, R. Environmental Health Services: A Survey of Administrative & Legal Provisions. (Public Health in Europe Ser.). 220p. 1983. pap. text 19.00 (92-890-1155-6) World Health.

Dean, R., jt. auth. see Colson, H. P.

Dean, R. G. A Seventy-Five Year History of the Texas Section of the Mathematical Association of America 1920-1995. xii, 394p. 1995. 30.00 (0-9645251-0-0) TSMAA.

Dean, R. G. & Dalrymple, R. A. Water Wave Mechanics for Engineers & Scientists. (Advanced Series in Ocean Engineering: Vol. 2). 368p. 1991. text 67.00 (981-02-0420-5); pap. text 32.00 (981-02-0421-3) World Scientific Pub.

Dean, R. G., ed. see McDonald, Archie P.

Dean, R. S., jt. ed. see D'Amato, R. C.

Dean, Ray. Toward the Flame. LC 92-75781. 304p. 1993. 22.95 (1-878398-22-9) Blue Note Pubns.
— Tyrannosaurus Therapy: How to Avoid Emotional Extinction. LC 97-71734. (Illus.). 288p. 1997. 24.95 (1-878398-23-7) Blue Note Pubns.

Dean, Raymond S., jt. ed. see Batchelor, Ervin S., Jr.

Dean, Raymond S., jt. ed. see Gray, Jeffrey W.

Dean, Richard. Basic Monkey Boxing. 64p. 1998. pap. 8.95 (0-901764-68-X, 93217, Pub. by P H Crompton) Midpt Trade.

***Dean, Richard E.** Absite Review Manual 1999. 188p. (C). 1999. pap. text 48.95 (0-9667081-2-1) MSU Lib Comp & Tech.

Dean, Richard E. Training Manual for Enteral Feeding. LC 90-62727. 88p. 1990. pap. 22.95 (0-944496-17-2) Precept Pr.
— Training Manual for Total Parenteral Nutrition. LC 90-62754. 140p. 1990. pap. 22.95 (0-944496-18-0) Precept Pr.

Dean, Richard E., jt. auth. see Apelgren, Keith N.

Dean, Richard H. & O'Neill, James A., Jr., eds. Vascular Disorders of Childhood. LC 82-191. (Illus.). 217p. reprint ed. pap. 67.30 (0-7837-1486-6, 205718100023) Bks Demand.

Dean, Richard H., et al. Current Vascular Surgical Diagnosis & Treatment. 461p. (C). 1995. pap. text 54.95 (0-8385-1351-4, A1351-4, Apple Lange Med) McGraw.

Dean, Robert. Dinner at MME. (Illus.). 1977. 2.50 (0-685-88992-0) Oyez.
— Dinner at MME. deluxe ed. (Illus.). 1977. 12.50 (0-685-88991-2) Oyez.
— The Law of Trade Secrets. l, 629p. 1990. 137.50 (0-455-20806-9, Pub. by LawBk Co) Gaunt.

Dean, Robert A., et al. Safety Flip Chart. rev. ed. 22p. 1993. pap. 7.95 (0-87355-117-6) Natl Sci Tchrs.

Dean, Robert B., ed. Training of Sanitary Engineers in Europe. 198p. 1985. pap. text 16.00 (92-890-1022-3, 1340025) World Health.

Dean, Robert G. Beach Nourishment: Theory & Practice. (Advanced Series in Ocean Engineering). 300p. 1998. text 86.00 (981-02-1547-9); pap. text 43.00 (981-02-1548-7) World Scientific Pub.

Dean, Robert J. Broadman Comments, 1996-97: Jan, Feb, March. 96p. 1996. pap. text 4.99 (0-8054-1745-1, 4217-45) Broadman.
— 13 User-Friendly Bible Study Lessons: Based on the International Sunday School Lesson, June 2000. (Comments Ser.). 2000. pap. 5.99 (0-8054-1300-6) Broadman.
— 13 User-Friendly Bible Study Lessons 2000: March 2000-May 2000. (Comments Ser.). 2000. pap. 5.99 (0-8054-1299-9) Broadman.

Dean, Robert W. The Jukebox & Me. 332p. (Orig.). 1995. per. 29.95 (0-9647890-0-0) Deans Designs.

Dean, Robyn. A Black Cat Named Smokey: On Vacation. LC 92-93502. (Illus.). 64p. (Orig.). (J). (gr. k-3). 1992. pap. 7.95 (0-9633466-0-1) Zyxalon Pr.

Dean, Rodney & Dean, Nancy. Building Family Values: Using the Tools of Bonding & Boundaries. LC 93-41667. 208p. (Orig.). 1994. pap. 10.95 (0-941005-98-4) Chrch Grwth VA.

D

An Asterisk (*) at the beginning of an entry indicates that the title is appearing for the first time.

***Dean, Roger & Kelly, David, eds.** Atherosclerosis: The Role of Gene Expresion, Cell Interactions, & Oxidation. (Illus.). 336p. 2000. text 130.00 (*0-19-850637-6*) OUP.

Dean, Roger, jt. auth. see Smith, Hazel.

Dean, Roger T. New Structures in Jazz & Improvised Music: From the 1960s into the 1980s. 176p. 1991. pap. 41.95 (*0-335-09897-5*) OpUniv Pr.

Dean, Roger T., jt. auth. see Davies, Michael J.

Dean, Rose B., jt. auth. see Cooper, D. Mark.

***Dean, Roy.** Roy Dean-Adam Today. Gerhart, Klaus, ed. (Illus.). 100p. 2000. 49.95 (*1-890377-16-3*) Pohlmann Pr.

Dean, Ruth & Thompson, Melissa. Life in the American Colonies. LC 98-28726. (Way People Live Ser.). (Illus.). 112p. (J). (gr. 4-12). 1998. lib. bdg. 23.70 (*1-56006-376-9*) Lucent Bks.

— Teen Prostitution. LC 97-27452. (Overview Ser.). (Illus.). (YA). (gr. 4-12). 1997. lib. bdg. 22.45 (*1-56006-512-5*) Lucent Bks.

Dean, S. W., ed. see ASTM Committee G-1 on Corrosion of Metals.

Dean, S. W., Jr., jt. ed. see Tonini, D. E.

Dean, Sally A. Fort Irwin Historic Preservation Plan Vol. I: The Management Plan. fac. ed. 93p. (C). 1986. reprint ed. pap. text 10.63 (*1-55567-515-8*) Coyote Press.

— Physical & Chemical Analysis of Sedimentary from 4-MNT-85 Montery County, California. 161p. (C). 1979. pap. text 17.50 (*1-55567-065-2*) Coyote Press.

Dean, Sharon. Winning Marketing Techniques: An Introduction to Marketing for Information Professionals. 1990. student ed. 85.00 (*0-87111-390-2*) SLA.

Dean, Sharon L. Constance Fenimore Woolson: Homeward Bound. LC 95-4332. (Illus.). 256p. (C). 1995. text 28.00 (*0-87049-898-3*) U of Tenn Pr.

Dean, Sheldon W. & Lee, T. S., eds. Degradation of Metals in the Atmosphere. (Special Technical Publication Ser.: No. 965). (Illus.). 455p. 1988. text 55.00 (*0-8031-0966-0*, STP965) ASTM.

Dean-Smith, Margaret. A Guide to English Folk Song Collections. 1988. reprint ed. lib. bdg. 75.00 (*0-7812-0112-8*) Rprt Serv.

Dean, Stacey. Prancing Through the Zodiac Calendar - Almanac - Directory. (Illus.). 50p. (C). 1989. pap. text 9.99 (*0-317-93882-7*) MY Las Vegas.

Dean, Stanley R., ed. Schizophrenia: The First Ten Dean Award Lectures. LC 73-6815. 1973. text 32.50 (*0-8422-7115-5*) Irvington.

Dean, Stephen, compiled by. Planning the Liturgy with Celebration Hymnal. 120p. (C). 1988. 30.00 (*0-85597-437-0*, Pub. by McCrimmon Pub) St Mut.

Dean, Steve. Insider's Guide to Las Vegas: And Surrounding Areas. (Illus.). 250p. (Orig.). 1997. pap. 19.95 (*1-56866-214-9*) Index Pub Grp.

Dean, Steve M. Everybody's Radiation Handbook. 58p. 1989. pap. text 6.95 (*0-9630337-0-0*) Aeon Res.

Dean, Sue. The Traveler: River of Love. (Illus.). 96p. (Orig.). 1995. pap. 10.95 (*1-884385-17-6*) Painted Wheel.

— The Traveler: Shining Wealth. (Illus.). 96p. (Orig.). 1996. pap. 10.95 (*1-884385-18-4*) Painted Wheel.

— The Traveler - Glowing Power. (Illus.). 96p. (Orig.). 1993. pap. 10.95 (*1-884385-15-X*) Painted Wheel.

— The Traveler - Spirit of Play. (Illus.). 96p. (Orig.). 1994. pap. 10.95 (*1-884385-16-8*) Painted Wheel.

Dean, T. & Wickham, C., eds. City & Countryside in Late Medieval & Renaissance Italy. 220p. 1990. 55.00 (*1-85285-035-3*) Hambledon Press.

Dean, Tamara. Network+ Guide to Networks. 800p. per. 61.95 (*0-7600-1145-1*, Pub. by Course Tech) Thomson Learn.

***Dean, Taraneh.** Food Intolerance. 256p. 2000. text 170.00 (*1-85573-497-4*, Pub. by Woodhead Pubng) Am Educ Systs.

***Dean, Tasker.** Roman Games. 224p. 1999. pap. 9.95 (*0-352-33322-7*) Buccaneer Bks.

***Dean, Terry J.** Allis-Chalmers Farms Tractors & Crawlers Data Book. LC 99-51833. (Illus.). 160p. 2000. pap. 11.95 (*0-7603-0770-9*, 129819AP, Pub. by MBI Pubg) Motorbooks Intl.

Dean, Terry J., jt. auth. see Heckart, Ronald J.

Dean, Theresa & Lucadamo, Rhonda. Pocket Full of School Memories. (Illus.). 26p. (J). (ps-8). 1992. 18.95 (*1-881511-00-6*) Pockets Pr.

Dean, Theresa & Whitlock, Sheryl. Clinical Chemistry. (Clinical Laboratory Manual Ser.). (Illus.). 272p. (C). 1996. pap. 31.95 (*0-8273-7197-7*) Delmar.

Dean, Theresa M. Pocket Full of Christmas Memories. (Illus.). 20p. (J). 1993. pap. 19.95 (*1-881511-01-4*) Pockets Pr.

— Pocket Full of Memories Journal. (Illus.). 24p. (J). (gr. 4-7). 1994. pap. 9.95 (*1-881511-03-0*) Pockets Pr.

Dean, Theresa M. Pocket Full of Sports Memories. 20p. 1994. pap. 19.95 (*1-881511-02-2*) Pockets Pr.

Dean, Theresa M. & Lucadamo, Rhonda. Pocket Full of Birthday Memories. (Illus.). 24p. (J). 1997. spiral bd. 19.95 (*1-57102-204-X*, Ideals Child) Hambleton-Hill.

Dean, Theresa M., et al. Pocket Full of Christmas Memories. (Illus.). 20p. (J). 1995. reprint ed. spiral bd. 19.95 (*1-57102-202-3*, Ideals Child) Hambleton-Hill.

— Pocket Full of School Memories. (Illus.). 26p. (J). 1995. reprint ed. spiral bd. 19.95 (*1-57102-200-7*, Ideals Child) Hambleton-Hill.

— Pocket Full of Sports Memories. (Illus.). 20p. (J). 1995. reprint ed. spiral bd. 13.95 (*1-57102-201-5*, Ideals Child) Hambleton-Hill.

Dean, Thomas, ed. Religious Pluralism & Truth: Essays on Cross-Cultural Philosophy of Religion. LC 93-40598. (SUNY Series in Religious Studies). 271p. (C). 1994. pap. text 19.95 (*0-7914-2124-4*) State U NY Pr.

— Religious Pluralism & Truth: Essays on Cross-Cultural Philosophy of Religion. LC 93-40598. (SUNY Series in Religious Studies). 271p. (C). 1995. text 59.50 (*0-7914-2123-6*) State U NY Pr.

Dean, Thomas J. New Venture Formations in United States Manufacturing: The Role of Industry Environments. LC 95-38868. (Studies in Entrepreneurship). (Illus.). 216p. 1995. text 20.00 (*0-8153-2128-7*) Garland.

Dean, Thomas L. & Wellman, Michael P., eds. Planning & Control. 1991. text 53.95 (*1-55860-209-7*) Morgan Kaufmann.

***Dean, Tim.** Beyond Sexuality. LC 99-86743. 1999. pap. text 18.00 (*0-226-13935-2*); lib. bdg. 46.00 (*0-226-13934-4*) U Ch Pr.

***Dean, Trevor.** The Towns of Italy in the Later Middle Ages. LC 99-44268. (Medieval Sources Ser.). 1999. pap. 29.95 (*0-7190-5204-1*) Manchester Univ Pr.

— The Towns of Italy in the Later Middle Ages. LC 99-44268. 2000. text 74.95 (*0-7190-5203-3*) Manchester Univ Pr.

Dean, Trevor & Lowe, K. J., eds. Crime, Society & the Law in Renaissance Italy. 293p. (C). 1994. text 59.95 (*0-521-41102-5*) Cambridge U Pr.

Dean, Trevor, jt. auth. see Chambers, David S.

Dean, Trevor, ed. see Musacchio, Jacqueline & Van Boxel, Piet.

Dean, Vera M. New Patterns of Democracy in India. 2nd ed. LC 79-78516. 267p. 1969. 29.00 (*0-674-61751-7*) HUP.

Dean, Vicky A., ed. CAA Guidance: EPA's Policy & Interpretations, Issue 1, 1. 432p. 1999. pap. 100.00 (*0-444-10004-0*) Elsevier.

Dean, Virgil W., ed. Kansas History: An Annotated Bibliography, 1. LC 91-46959. (Bibliographies of the States of the United States Ser.: No. 1). 616p. 1992. lib. bdg. 75.00 (*0-313-28238-2*, AMSTKS, Greenwood Pr) Greenwood.

Dean, W. E., jt. ed. see Bradbury, J. P.

Dean, W. F., jt. auth. see Scott, M. L.

Dean, W. Richard, et al, eds. The Karoo: Ecological Patterns & Processes. (Illus.). 576p. (C). 1999. text 165.00 (*0-521-55450-0*) Cambridge U Pr.

Dean, W. T., jt. ed. see Zhiyi, Zhou.

Dean, Walter E. & Arthur, Michael A., eds. Stratigraphy & Paleoenvironments of the Cretaceous Western Interior Seaway, U. S. A. (Concepts in Sedimentology & Paleontology Ser.: Vol. 6). (Illus.). 264p. (C). 1998. 83.00 (*1-56576-044-1*) SEPM.

Dean, Ward. Biological Aging Measurement: Clinical Applications. 2nd ed. Weber, Hans U., ed. (Illus.). 472p. 1988. pap. text, per. 59.95 (*0-937777-00-5*) Ctr Bio-Gerontology.

— Biological Aging Measurement: Clinical Applications. 2nd rev. ed. Weber, Hans U. et al, eds. LC 85-63822. (Illus.). 472p. 1988. text 95.00 (*0-937777-01-3*) Ctr Bio-Gerontology.

Dean, Ward & Morgenthaler, John. Smart Drugs & Nutrients: How to Improve Your Memory & Increase Your Intelligence Using the Latest Discoveries in Neuroscience. LC 90-84066. (Smart Drugs Ser.: Vol. 1). (Illus.). 224p. (Orig.). 1991. reprint ed. pap. 12.95 (*0-9627418-9-2*) Smart Pubns CA.

Dean, Ward, et al. GHB: The Natural Mood Enhancer. LC 97-65978. 1998. pap. 16.95 (*0-9627418-6-8*) Smart Pubns CA.

— Smart Drugs II - The New Generation: New Drugs & Nutrients to Improve Your Memory & Increase Your Intelligence, No. II. LC 93-78074. 287p. 1993. pap. 14.95 (*0-9627418-7-6*) Smart Pubns CA.

Dean, Warren. Brazil & the Struggle for Rubber: A Study in Environmental History. (Studies in Environment & History). (Illus.). 256p. 1987. text 54.95 (*0-521-33477-2*) Cambridge U Pr.

— The Industrialization of Sao Paulo, 1880-1945. LC 73-96435. (Latin American Monographs: No. 17). 279p. reprint ed. pap. 86.50 (*0-608-12401-X*, 205214400040) Bks Demand.

— With Broadax & Firebrand: The Destruction of the Brazilian Atlantic Forest. LC 94-5681. (Illus.). 1997. pap. 18.95 (*0-520-20886-2*, Pub. by U CA Pr) Cal Prin Full Svc.

Dean, Warren, jt. ed. see Alden, Dauril.

Dean, Wayne. The Incredible, Spreadable, Magic, Drawing Book. Harryman, Diana L. & Leatherbury, Leven C., eds. (Illus.). 56p. (J). (gr. 3-9). 1983. pap. 9.95 (*0-9616161-0-5*) W Dean Editions.

Dean, Willard H. The Immune System. Wood, Nancy & Embertson, Karen, eds. (Holistic Health Ser.). (Illus.). 68p. 1997. pap. 9.95 (*0-9657169-0-2*) Pathways Pr NM.

Dean, William. American Religious Empiricism. LC 85-27769. (SUNY Series in Religious Studies). 150p. (C). 1986. text 64.50 (*0-88706-280-6*); pap. text 21.95 (*0-88706-281-4*) State U NY Pr.

— The Religious Critic in American Culture. LC 93-42683. 256p. (C). 1994. text 54.50 (*0-7914-2113-9*); pap. text 16.95 (*0-7914-2114-7*) State U NY Pr.

Dean, William G., et al, eds. The Concise Historical Atlas of Canada. (Illus.). 228p. 1998. text 85.00 (*0-8020-4203-1*) U of Toronto Pr.

Dean, William W. A Church at Risk: Lessons for Modern Christians from the Epistle to the Hebrews. 176p. 1990. pap. 9.95 (*0-310-75441-0*) Zondervan.

Dean, Winton. Bizet. (Music Book Index Ser.). 262p. 1993. reprint ed. lib. bdg. 79.00 (*0-7812-9587-4*) Rprt Serv.

— Handel. 1997. pap. 14.95 (*0-393-30358-6*) Norton.

— Handel's Dramatic Oratorios & Masques. (Illus.). 708p. 1990. reprint ed. pap. text 45.00 (*0-19-816184-0*) OUP.

Dean, Winton & Knapp, John M. Handel's Operas 1704-1726. 2nd ed. (Illus.). 792p. 1995. reprint ed. pap. text 35.00 (*0-19-816441-6*) OUP.

Dean, Yvonne. Finishes. 4th ed. (Mitchell's Building Ser.). 144p. (C). 1997. pap. text 60.00 (*0-582-25877-4*) Addison-Wesley.

Deanda. School Planner: A Time Management Program. (CA - Career Development Ser.). 1991. mass mkt. 9.95 (*0-538-61396-3*) S-W Pub.

Deanda, Diane. Controversial Issues in Multiculturalism. LC 96-20611. 256p. 1996. pap. text 35.00 (*0-205-18817-6*) Allyn.

DeAndrea, Matthew, jt. auth. see DeAndrea, William L.

DeAndrea, William. Mysterious Voices. 1997. 27.50 (*0-614-28227-6*) Macmillan USA.

— Night of the Living Yogurt. (Orig.). (J). 1996. 9.09 (*0-606-09685-X*, Pub. by Turtleback) Demco.

— When Dinosaurs Ruled the Basement. LC 95-94497. 1995. 9.09 (*0-606-10056-3*) Turtleback.

Deandrea, William L. Encyclopedia Mysteriosa: A Comprehensive Guide to the Art of Detection in Print, Film, Radio & Television. 405p. 1997. 16.00 (*0-02-861678-2*) Macmillan.

DeAndrea, William L. The Fatal Elixir: A Lobo Blacke-Quinn Booker Mystery. (Lobo Black/Quinn Booker Mystery Ser.). 208p. 1997. 22.95 (*0-8027-3289-5*) Walker & Co.

— The Hog Murders. 1999. pap. text 7.95 (*1-55882-030-2*) Intl Polygonics.

— The Hog Murders. LC 99-25262. 1999. write for info. (*0-7862-1942-4*, Five Star MI) Mac Lib Ref.

— Killed in Fringe Time: A Matt Cobb Mystery. 1995. 21.00 (*1-883402-26-3*) S&S Trade.

Deandrea, William L. Killed in the Fog. 1996. 20.00 (*1-883402-30-1*) S&S Trade.

DeAndrea, William L. Killed in the Fog. LC 96-8453. 1996. 20.50 (*0-684-83054-X*) S&S Trade.

— Killed in the Fog. large type ed. LC 97-9210. (Large Print Book Ser.). 1997. pap. 22.95 (*1-56895-434-4*) Wheeler Pub.

— Killed in the Ratings. 252p. 1986. pap. 4.95 (*0-15-647050-0*, Harvest Bks) Harcourt.

— Killed on the Rocks. 240p. 1991. mass mkt. 4.99 (*0-446-40060-2*, Mysterious Paperbk) Warner Bks.

— The Manx Murders: A Niccolo Benedetti Mystery. 256p. 1994. 20.00 (*1-883402-66-2*) S&S Trade.

— Written in Fire: A Lobo Black/Quinn Booker Mystery. 168p. 1995. 19.95 (*0-8027-3270-4*) Walker & Co.

DeAndrea, William L. & DeAndrea, Matthew. Night of the Living Yogurt. 112p. (Orig.). (J). (gr. 3-7). 1996. pap. 3.99 (*0-380-78358-4*, Avon Bks) Morrow Avon.

— The Pizza That Time Forgot. 128p. (J). (gr. 3-7). 1999. mass mkt. 3.99 (*0-380-79155-2*, Avon Bks) Morrow Avon.

***Deane, Alyssa.** Once & Always. 352p. 2000. mass mkt. 5.99 (*0-8217-6615-5*, Zebra Kensgtn) Kensgtn Pub Corp.

Deane, Andree, jt. auth. see Atkinson, Hilary.

Deane, Anthony N. Nelson's Favourite: HMS Agamemnon, 1781-1809. LC 96-68993. (Illus.). 320p. 1996. 44.95 (*1-55750-620-5*) Naval Inst Pr.

Deane, Barbara. Caring for Your Aging Parents. LC 89-62760. 276p. 1989. pap. 12.00 (*0-89109-578-0*) NavPress.

Deane, Basil. Albert Roussel. LC 80-16642. (Illus.). 188p. 1980. reprint ed. lib. bdg. 55.00 (*0-313-22612-1*, DEAR, Greenwood Pr) Greenwood.

Deane, Bill. Award Voting. 72p. 1988. pap. 6.00 (*0-910137-32-3*) Soc Am Baseball Res.

— Bob Gibson. (Baseball Legends Ser.). (Illus.). 64p. (J). (gr. 3 up). 1994. lib. bdg. 15.95 (*0-7910-1177-1*) Chelsea Hse.

— Following "The Fugitive" An Episode Guide & Handbook to the 1960s Television Series. LC 96-31167. (1960's Television Ser.). (Illus.). 246p. 1996. lib. bdg. 39.95 (*0-7864-0148-6*) McFarland & Co.

***Deane, Bill.** Sports Great Frank Thomas. LC 99-15909. (Sports Great Bks.). (Illus.). 64p. (gr. 4-10). 2000. lib. bdg. 17.95 (*0-7660-1269-7*) Enslow Pubs.

Deane, Bill. Top 10 Baseball Hitters. LC 97-39057. (Sports Top 10 Ser.). (Illus.). 48p. (J). (gr. 4-10). 1998. lib. bdg. 18.95 (*0-7660-1007-4*) Enslow Pubs.

— Top 10 Baseball Home Run Hitters. LC 96-39057. (Sports Top 10 Ser.). (Illus.). 48p. (J). (gr. 4-10). 1997. lib. bdg. 18.95 (*0-89490-804-9*) Enslow Pubs.

— Top 10 Baseball Shortstops. LC 98-44951. (Sports Top 10 Ser.). (Illus.). 48p. (YA). (gr. 4-10). 1999. lib. bdg. 18.95 (*0-7660-1128-3*) Enslow Pubs.

Deane, Bonnie S. Getting Ahead at Work Without Leaving Your Family Behind. 115p. 1997. pap. 12.95 (*0-9658569-0-9*) Sherm Energy.

Deane, Bonnie St. John. Succeeding Sane: Making Room for Joy in a Crazy World. LC 97-35103. 288p. 1998. 22.50 (*0-684-81853-1*) S&S Trade.

Deane, Cecil V. Aspects of Eighteenth-Century Nature Poetry. 145p. 1967. reprint ed. 30.00 (*0-7146-1154-9*, Pub. by F Cass Pubs) Intl Spec Bk.

Deane, Donna. Low Fat Kitchen. (Illus.). 208p. 1998. pap. 18.95 (*1-883792-22-3*, Pub. by LA Times) Sunbelt Pubns.

Deane-Drummond, Celia. Ecology in Jurgen Moltmann's Theology. LC 97-13394. (Texts & Studies in Religion: Vol. 75). 360p. 1997. text 99.95 (*0-7734-8529-5*) E Mellen.

Deane, Edmund. Spadacrene Anglica: Or, the English Spaw-Fountaine in Yorkshire. LC 74-80172 (English Experience Ser.: No. 651). 32p. 1974. reprint ed. 15.00 (*90-221-0651-9*) Walter J Johnson.

Deane, H. W. & Rubin, Betty L., eds. Adrenocortical Hormones: Their Origin, Chemistry, Physiology, & Pharmacology, 3 pts., Pt. 2. (Handbook of Experimental Pharmacology Ser.: Vol. 14). (ENG, FRE & GER., Illus.). 1964. 72.95 (*0-387-03146-4*) Spr-Verlag.

— Adrenocortical Hormones: Their Origin, Chemistry, Physiology, & Pharmacology, 3 pts., Pt. 3. (Handbook of Experimental Pharmacology Ser.: Vol. 14). (ENG, FRE & GER., Illus.). 1968. 144.00 (*0-387-04147-8*) Spr-Verlag.

— Adrenocortical Hormones Pt. 1: Their Origin, Chemistry, Physiology, & Pharmacology, 3 pts. (Handbook of Experimental Pharmacology Ser.: Vol. 14). (ENG, FRE & GER., Illus.). 1962. 232.00 (*0-387-02830-7*) Spr-Verlag.

Deane, Hazel. Powerful Is the Light. (Illus.). 206p. 1987. reprint ed. text 20.00 (*0-685-34706-0*); reprint ed. lib. bdg. 12.95 (*0-685-34705-2*) First Divine Sci Ch Denver.

Deane, Herbert A. The Political & Social Ideas of St. Augustine. LC 63-9809. 356p. (C). 1966. pap. text 25.50 (*0-231-08569-9*) Col U Pr.

Deane, Hugh. Good Deeds & Gunboats: Two Centuries of American-Chinese Encounters. (Illus.). 300p. (C). 1990. 29.95 (*0-8351-2378-2*) China Bks.

***Deane, Hugh.** The Korean War, 1945-1953. 1999. pap. 14.95 (*0-8351-2644-7*) China Bks.

Deane, James P. The Law of Blockade. Kavass, Igor I. & Sprudzs, Adolf, eds. LC 72-76351. (International Military Law & History Ser.: Vol. 5). 218p. 1972. reprint ed. lib. bdg. 39.50 (*0-930342-42-9*, 300230) W S Hein.

Deane, John B. The Worship of the Serpent. 391p. 1996. reprint ed. spiral bd. 23.00 (*0-7873-0279-1*) Hlth Research.

— The Worship of the Serpent. 405p. 1996. reprint ed. pap. 21.50 (*1-56459-898-5*) Kessinger Pub.

— The Worship of the Serpent: Traced Throughout the World & Its Ancient Traditions. 1991. lib. bdg. 88.95 (*0-8490-4989-X*) Gordon Pr.

Deane, John F. Christ, with Urban Fox. 72p. (Orig.). 1998. pap. 12.00 (*1-877727-72-5*) White Pine.

***Deane, John F.** The Coffin Master & Other Stories. 2000. pap. 17.95 (*0-85640-664-3*, Pub. by Blackstaff Pr) Dufour.

Deane, John F. Far Country: Poems. 1992. pap. 35.00 (*1-873790-17-1*, Pub. by Dedalus) St Mut.

***Deane, John F.** In the Name of the Wolf. LC 99-196630. 172p. (Orig.). 2000. pap. 17.95 (*0-85640-640-6*, Pub. by Blackstaff Pr) Dufour.

— Toccata & Fugue: New & Selected Poems. 140p. 2000. pap. 18.95 (*1-85754-467-6*, Pub. by Carcanet Pr) Paul & Co Pubs.

Deane, John F. Upon Foreign Soil. LC 99-191103. (Icarus Ser.). 43 p. 1999. write for info. (*1-901233-50-2*) Dufour.

— Walking on Water. 78p. 1996. pap. 11.95 (*1-873790-53-8*) Dufour.

Deane, John F., jt. auth. see Rancourt, Jacques.

Deane, John F., jt. auth. see Transtromer, Tomas.

Deane, John F., tr. see Koltz, Anise.

Deane, John F., jt. tr. see Transtromer, Tomas.

Deane, Jon F. High Sacrifice. 61p. 1981. pap. 9.95 (*0-85105-382-3*, Pub. by Smyth) Dufour.

Deane, Marion, ed. see Tone, Theobald W.

Deane, Marjorie & Pringle, Robert. Economic Cooperation from the Inside. (Report Ser.). 48p. 1984. pap. 10.00 (*1-56708-063-4*) Grp of Thirty.

***Deane, Michael E.** I Can Breathe Again: Practical Secrets for Breathing Better Naturally for More Energy & Endurance, Right Away!, 1 cass. (YA). 1999. VHS (*1-882899-03-2*) J Miller Designs.

Deane, Michele & ™umber, Margaret. Differentiation. 1998. pap. 34.00 (*0-7487-3788-X*, Pub. by S Thornes Pubs) Trans-Atl Phila.

Deane, Patrick. At Home in Time: Forms of Neo-Augustanism in Modern English Poetry. 272p. 1994. 60.00 (*0-7735-1215-2*, Pub. by McG-Queens Univ Pr) CUP Services.

— History in Our Hands: A Critical Anthology of Writings on Literature, Culture, & Politics from the 1930s. LC 97-49340. 416p. 1998. 85.00 (*0-7185-0143-8*); pap. 19.95 (*0-7185-0144-6*) Bks Intl VA.

— Renga. 37p. 1981. pap. 6.00 (*0-919626-14-9*, Pub. by Brick Bks) Genl Dist Srvs.

Deane, Paul. Grammar in Mind & Brain: Explorations in Cognitive Syntax. LC 92-32127. (Cognitive Linguistics Research Ser.: Vol. 2). (Illus.). iv, 355p. (C). 1992. lib. bdg. 106.15 (*3-11-013183-8*) Mouton.

— Mirrors of American Culture. LC 91-30998. 275p. 1991. 34.50 (*0-8108-2460-4*) Scarecrow.

Deane, Peter. Peter Dean's Guide to Fly-Tying. 1993. pap. 24.95 (*0-88317-172-4*) Stoeger Pub Co.

Deane, Philippe G. The Road Ahead: An Agenda for Canada in the 1990s. 208p. 1990. 24.95 (*0-7737-2401-X*) Genl Dist Srvs.

Deane, Phyllis. The First Industrial Revolution. 2nd abr. ed. LC 78-26388. 328p. 1980. pap. text 21.95 (*0-521-29609-9*) Cambridge U Pr.

Deane, Phyllis & Cole, W. A. British Economic Growth, 1688-1959: Trends & Structure. (Modern Revivals in Economic & Social History Ser.). 376p. 1993. 69.95 (*0-7512-0197-9*, Pub. by Gregg Revivals) Ashgate Pub Co.

Deane, Samuel. History of Scituate, MA from Its First Settlement to 1831. 408p. 1992. reprint ed. lib. bdg. 40.00 (*0-8328-2067-9*) Higginson Bk Co.

— History of Scituate, Massachusetts: From Its First Settlement to 1831. 408p. 1995. reprint ed. pap. 31.50 (*0-8063-4597-7*, 9072) Clearfield Co.

— The New England Farmer: or Georgical Dictionary. LC 72-5043. (Technology & Society Ser.). 543p. 1972. reprint ed. 36.95 (*0-405-04695-2*) Ayer.

Deane, Seamus. Celtic Revivals. LC 86-62902. 199p. 1987. pap. 6.95 (*0-916390-25-X*) Wake Forest.

— Field & Day Anthology of Irish Writing, Vol. 1. Date not set. write for info. (*0-393-03351-1*) Norton.

— Field & Day Anthology of Irish Writing, Vol. 2. Date not set. write for info. (*0-393-03352-X*) Norton.

D

— Field & Day Anthology of Irish Writing, Vol. 3. Date not set. write for info. (*0-393-03353-8*) Norton.
— The French Revolution & Enlightenment in England, 1789-1832. LC 88-1243. 256p. 1988. 40.50 (*0-674-32240-1*) HUP.
— Reading in the Dark. LC 96-49635. 246p. 1997. 23.00 (*0-394-57440-0*) Knopf.
— Reading in the Dark. LC 96-49635. 246p. 1998. pap. 12.00 (*0-375-70023-4*) Vin Bks.
— Reading in the Dark: Reading Group Guide. 1998. 22.50 (*0-676-53733-2*) Random.
— Selected Poems. 78p. 1988. pap. 12.95 (*1-85235-028-8*) Dufour.
— A Short History of Irish Literature. LC 85-52218. (C). 1994. reprint ed. pap. text 17.50 (*0-268-01751-4*) U of Notre Dame Pr.
— Strange Country: Modernity & Nationhood in Irish Writing since 1790. LC 96-24312. (Clarendon Lectures in English Literature). 278p. (C). 1997. text 49.95 (*0-19-818337-2*) OUP.
— Strange Country: Modernity & Nationhood in Irish Writing since 1790. LC 99-194696. (Clarendon Lectures in English Literature). 280p. 1999. reprint ed. pap. text 19.95 (*0-19-818490-5*, Clarendon Pr) OUP.
— The Wizard. 1999. write for info. (*0-375-40042-7*) Knopf.
Deane, Seamus, ed. The Field Day Anthology of Irish Writing: 550-1990, 3 vols., Set. 4500p. 1991. 150.00 (*0-393-03046-6*) Norton.
Deane, Seamus, ed. & intro. see Joyce, James.
Deane, Sheila. Bardic Style in the Poetry of Gerard Manley Hopkins, W. B. Yeats, & Dylan Thomas. LC 89-33155. (Studies in Modern Literature: No. 98). 264p. reprint ed. pap. 81.90 (*0-8357-1950-2*, 207063200011) Bks Demand.
***Deane, Sonia.** The Affair of Doctor Rutland. large type ed. 304p. 1999. pap. 20.99 (*1-85389-895-3*) Ulverscroft.
Deane, Sonia. Bachelor Doctor. large type ed. (Magna Large Print Ser.). 250p. 1996. 27.99 (*0-7505-1002-1*, Pub. by Mgna Lrg Print) Ulverscroft.
— Doctor Accused. large type ed. (Dales Large Print Ser.). 288p. 1998. pap. 19.99 (*1-85389-799-X*, Dales) Ulverscroft.
— Doctor Deceived. large type ed. (Dales Large Print Ser.). 288p. 1998. pap. 19.99 (*1-85389-807-4*, Dales) Ulverscroft.
— Doctor's Forbidden Love. large type ed. (Dales Large Print Ser.). 270p. 1997. pap. 18.99 (*1-85389-728-0*) Ulverscroft.
— Doctor's Romance. large type ed. (Magna Large Print Ser.). (Illus.). 249p. 1996. 27.99 (*0-7505-1001-3*) Ulverscroft.
— Heartache in Harley Street. large type ed. (Dales Large Print Ser.). 279p. 1997. pap. 18.99 (*1-85389-706-X*) Ulverscroft.
***Deane, Sonia.** Nurse Maitland. large type ed. 336p. 1999. pap. 20.99 (*1-85389-961-5*, Dales) Ulverscroft.
— Nurse Trent. large type ed. 384p. 2000. pap. 20.99 (*1-85389-998-4*, Dales) Ulverscroft.
— Portrait of Sister Nicola. 320p. 1999. 20.99 (*1-85389-960-7*) Ulverscroft.
— Private Ward. large type ed. 352p. 1999. pap. 20.99 (*1-85389-896-1*, Dales) Ulverscroft.
***Deane, Stuart.** One by One: A Teacher Considers His Years in the Classroom. (Illus.). 180p. 2000. 15.95 (*1-884540-49-X*) Haleys.
— One by One: A Teacher Considers His Years inthe Classroom. (Illus.). 180p. 2000. 25.95 (*1-884540-53-8*) Haleys.
Deane, Wallace. Fijian Society: Or, The Sociology & Psychology of the Fijians. LC 75-32813. reprint ed. 38.00 (*0-404-14117-X*) AMS Pr.
Deaner, Ellie. From Ellie's Kitchen to Yours. 216p. 1991. pap. 14.95 (*0-9631177-7-7*) Denell Pr.
— So Easy, So Delicious. LC 98-96593. 208p. 1999. 16.95 (*0-9631177-3-4*) Denell Pr.
***Deaner, Janice.** Assam. 400p. 2001. 23.95 (*0-525-94415-X*) NAL.
Deaner, Janice. The Body Spoken. LC 98-14818. 336p. 1999. 25.95 (*0-525-94414-1*, Dutt) Dutton Plume.
***Deaner, Janice.** The Body Spoken: A Novel. 352p. 2000. pap. text 13.95 (*0-452-27973-9*, Plume) Dutton Plume.
Deanes, Charles, jt. auth. see Dixon, Ramon T.
Deanesly, Clare, et al. Badlands: Essential Environmental Law for Property Professionals. (Environmental Law Ser.). 300p. 1993. 105.00 (*1-874698-10-4*, Pub. by Federation Pr) Gaunt.
Deanesly, M. History of the Medieval Church. 9th ed. 292p. (C). 1969. pap. 17.99 (*0-415-03959-2*) Routledge.
Deanesly, Margaret. Augustine of Canterbury. 175p. 1997. pap. 22.95 (*1-901157-25-3*) St Austin.
— History of the Medieval Church, Five Ninety to Fifteen Hundred. 9th ed. (C). 1969. pap. 14.95 (*0-416-18100-7*, NO. 2163) Routledge.
— The Lollard Bible & Other Medieval Biblical Versions. LC 77-84722. reprint ed. 49.50 (*0-404-16125-1*) AMS Pr.
Deanfield, John E. & Sellier, Philippe, eds. Diurnal Distribution in Cardiovascular Disease: Prognosis & Therapy. (Journal: Cardiology: Vol. 85, Suppl. 2, 1994). (Illus.). iv, 32p. 1994. pap. 10.50 (*3-8055-6092-3*) S Karger.
***DeAngeles, Ly.** Witchcraft: Theory & Practice. 2000. pap. 12.95 (*1-56718-782-X*) Llewellyn Pubns.
De'Angeli, Daniel & O'Meara, J. J. The Voyage of Brendan. LC 95-115810. 96p. 1994. 39.50 (*1-85182-165-1*, Pub. by Four Cts Pr); boxed set 225.00 (*1-85182-166-X*, Pub. by Four Cts Pr) Intl Spec Bk.
Deangelis, jt. ed. see Romaniuk, Bohdan R.
Deangelis, Barbara. Ask Barbara: The 100 Most-Asked Questions about Love, Sex, & Relationships. 384p. 1997. mass mkt. 6.99 (*0-440-22428-4*, Island Bks) Dell.
DeAngelis, Barbara. Confidence: Finding It & Living It. 3rd ed. 101p. 1998. reprint ed. pap. 8.95 (*1-56170-528-4*, 177T) Hay House.
DeAngelis, Catherine, ed. An Introduction to Clinical Research. (Illus.). 192p. 1990. text 37.50 (*0-19-506249-3*) OUP.
DeAngelis, Dominick A. The Art of Pizza Making: Trade Secrets & Recipes. LC 92-90099. (Illus.). 100p. (Orig.). 1992. pap. 6.95 (*0-9632034-0-1*) Creat Pizza.
DeAngelis, Donald L. Individual-Based Models & Approaches on Ecology: Concepts & Models. Gross, Louis, ed. (Illus.). 544p. (C). (gr. 13). 1992. ring bd. 78.95 (*0-412-03171-X*, A6480, Chap & Hall CRC) CRC Pr.
DeAngelis, George, et al. The Ford Model A As Henry Built It: Color, Upholstery & Production Facts Book. 4th ed. (Illus.). 234p. 1991. 29.95 (*0-911383-04-2*) Motor Cities.
DeAngelis, George, jt. auth. see Francis, Edward P.
DeAngelis, Gerald G. Testing & Screening for Drugs of Abuse: Techniques, Issues, & Clinical Implications. LC 75-40843. (Illus.). 152p. reprint ed. pap. 47.20 (*0-7837-0839-4*, 204115300019) Bks Demand.
DeAngelis, Gina. Cyber Crimes. (Crime, Justice, & Punishment Ser.). (Illus.). (YA). (gr. 7 up). 1999. lib. bdg. 19.95 (*0-7910-4936-1*) Chelsea Hse.
***DeAngelis, Gina.** Francisco Pizarro & the Conquest of the Inca. LC 00-43076. (Explorers of New Worlds Ser.). (Illus.). 2000. pap. write for info. (*0-7910-6161-2*) Chelsea Hse.
— Francisco Pizarro & the Conquest of the Inca. (Explorers of the New Worlds Ser.). 2000. 17.95 (*0-7910-5951-0*) Chelsea Hse.
DeAngelis, Gina. Hindenburg. (Great Disasters Ser.). (Illus.). 128p. (YA). (gr. 5 up). 2000. write for info. (*0-7910-5272-9*) Chelsea Hse.
***DeAngelis, Gina.** Jackie Robinson. (Overcoming Adversity Ser.). 2000. 19.95 (*0-7910-5897-2*) Chelsea Hse.
— Jackie Robinson. (Overcoming Adversity Ser.). (Illus.). 2000. pap. 9.95 (*0-7910-5898-0*) Chelsea Hse.
— Lucretia Mott: Woman Suffragist. (Women of Achievement Ser.). (Illus.). 112p. (YA). (gr. 5 up). 2000. write for info. (*0-7910-5295-8*); pap. text 9.95 (*0-7910-5296-6*) Chelsea Hse.
— Morgan Freeman. LC 99-18478. (Black Americans of Achievement Ser.). (Illus.). 88p. (YA). (gr. 7 up). 1999. 19.95 (*0-7910-4963-9*) Chelsea Hse.
— Morgan Freeman - Actor. (Black Americans of Achievement Ser.). (Illus.). 144p. (YA). (gr. 5 up). 1999. pap. 9.95 (*0-7910-4964-7*) Chelsea Hse.
— Robin Williams. (Overcoming Adversity Ser.). (Illus.). 128p. 1999. 19.95 (*0-7910-5308-3*) Chelsea Hse.
— Triangle Shirtwaist Company Fire of 1911. (Great Disasters Ser.). (Illus.). 128p. (YA). (gr. 5). 2000. write for info. (*0-7910-5267-2*) Chelsea Hse.
Deangelis, Gina. The Wild West. LC 98-35865. (Costume, Tradition, & Culture Ser.). (Illus.). 64p. 1998. 16.95 (*0-7910-5169-2*) Chelsea Hse.
DeAngelis, Gina, jt. auth. see Marvis, B.
DeAngelis, James, ed. The Grantseeker's Handbook of Essential Internet Sites. 170p. 1996. pap. 75.00 (*1-56925-056-1*, NETG) Capitol Publns.
DeAngelis, James & Licitka, Annette, eds. The School Administrator's Handbook of Internet Sites. 2nd ed. 235p. 1997. pap. 69.00 (*1-56925-084-7*, NET2) Capitol VA.
DeAngelis, James, ed. see Ferguson, Jacqueline.
DeAngelis, James, jt. ed. see Romaniuk, Bohdan R.
DeAngelis, Lissa & Siple, Molly. Recipes for Change: Gourmet Wholefood Cooking for Health & Vitality at Menopause. 1996. 24.95 (*0-614-96796-1*, Dutt) Dutton Plume.
— Recipes for Change: Gourmet Wholefood Cooking for Health & Vitality at Menopause. 416p. 1998. pap. 14.95 (*0-452-27293-9*, Plume) Dutton Plume.
— SOS for PMS: Whole Food Solutions for Premenstrual Syndrome. LC 98-32106. 320p. 1999. pap. 15.95 (*0-452-27965-8*, Plume) Dutton Plume.
DeAngelis, Matthew T. Ghost Writer: Miscellaneous Cartoons by Matthew DeAngelis. (Illus.). 98p. 1998. pap. write for info. (*0-9663902-0-2*) Grifo Ent.
DeAngelis, Paul, ed. see Ohashi, Wataru.
DeAngelis, Richard, jt. auth. see Walter, Martha.
DeAngelis, Robert. The Radiography Workbook. (Illus.). 167p. (C). student ed. 18.95 (*0-943589-00-2*) Health & Allied.
— The Radiography Workbook. 5th rev. ed. (Illus.). 31.95 (*0-943589-18-5*) Health & Allied.
— The Radiography Workbook, No. I. 3rd ed. (Illus.). (C). 1989. 23.95 (*0-943589-11-8*) Health & Allied.
DeAngelis, Robert & Edgar, Michelle. The Radiography Workbook, No. II. 2nd ed. (Illus.). 180p. (C). 24.95 (*0-943589-12-6*) Health & Allied.
— The Radiography Workbook II. (Illus.). 178p. (C). 1988. pap. text 24.95 (*0-943589-01-0*) Health & Allied.
— The Radiography Workbook II. 3rd ed. 1992. 28.95 (*0-943589-14-2*) Health & Allied.
DeAngelis, Robert & Lloyd, Mary F. The Integrated Radiography Workbook. (Illus.). 549p. (C). 1996. pap., wbk. ed. 44.95 (*0-943589-19-3*) Health & Allied.
DeAngelis, Robert W. The Radiography Workbook I. 4th ed. (Illus.). 196p. 1993. 27.95 (*0-943589-15-0*) Health & Allied.
***DeAngelis, Sebastian.** What Is It? (Illus.). 208p. 2000. pap. 19.95 (*0-9679947-0-5*) What is It? Pr.
DeAngelis, Therese. Gregory Hines. (Black Americans of Achievement Ser.). (YA). (gr. 4 up). 1999. pap. 9.95 (*0-7910-4966-3*); lib. bdg. 19.95 (*0-7910-4965-5*) Chelsea Hse.
***DeAngelis, Therese.** Jodie Foster: Actor/Filmmaker. LC 00-24301. (Women of Achievement Ser.). (Illus.). 112p. 2000. pap. text 9.95 (*0-7910-5292-3*) Chelsea Hse.
— Jodie Foster: Actor/Filmmaker. (Women of Achievement Ser.). (Illus.). 112p. (YA). (gr. 5 up). 2000. 19.95 (*0-7910-5291-5*) Chelsea Hse.
DeAngelis, Therese. Louis Farrakhan - Political Activist: Political Activist. LC 98-6101. (Black Americans of Achievement Ser.). (Illus.). 144p. (YA). (gr. 5 up). 1999. 19.95 (*0-7910-4688-5*); pap. 8.95 (*0-7910-4689-3*) Chelsea Hse.
— Native Americans & the Spanish. Porter, Frank W., 3rd, ed. LC 97-7498. (Indians of North America Ser.). (Illus.). 120p. (YA). (gr. 5 up). 1997. lib. bdg. 19.95 (*0-7910-2654-X*) Chelsea Hse.
DeAngelo, Dory & Flynn, Jane F. Kansas City Style: A Social & Cultural History of Kansas City As Seen Through Its Lost Architecture. rev. ed. LC 92-73620. (Illus.). 248p. 1991. 29.95 (*0-9633758-1-4*) Fifield Pub.
Deangelo, Frank. Casinos, U. S. A. A Complete Guide to the Best Hotels, Food, Comps, Gambling & Entertainment. LC 97-50640. (Illus.). 256p. 1997. pap. 14.95 (*0-8184-0591-0*) Carol Pub Group.
DeAngelo, Linda E. The Auditor-Client Contractual Relationship: An Economic Analysis. Dufey, Gunter, ed. LC 81-12923. (Research for Business Decisions Ser.: No. 43). 139p. 1981. reprint ed. pap. 43.10 (*0-8357-1241-9*, 207005700063) Bks Demand.
Deanin, R. D. & Seymour, Raymond B., eds. History of Polymeric Composites: Invited Papers Presented at the American Chemical Society Symposium on the Origin & Development of Polymeric Composites, Anaheim, CA, September, 1986. 391p. 1987. lib. bdg. 115.00 (*90-6764-082-4*, Pub. by VSP) Coronet Bks.
Deanin, Rudolph D. & Crugnola, Aldo M., eds. Toughness & Brittleness of Plastics. LC 76-41267. (Advances in Chemistry Ser.: No. 154). 1976. 54.95 (*0-8412-0221-4*) Am Chemical.
— Toughness & Brittleness of Plastics. LC 76-41267. (Advances in Chemistry Ser.: Vol. 154). 423p. 1976. pap. 131.20 (*0-608-03861-X*, 206430800008) Bks Demand.
Deanin, Rudolph D. & Schott, Nick R., eds. Fillers & Reinforcements for Plastics: A Symposium Co-Sponsored by the ACS Division of Organic Coatings & Plastics Chemistry & the Plastics Institute of America at the 166th Meeting of the American Chemical Society, Chicago, IL, August 27-29, 1973. LC 74-13562. (Advances in Chemistry Ser.: No. 134). (Illus.). 232p. 1974. reprint ed. pap. 72.00 (*0-608-06740-7*, 206693700009) Bks Demand.
Deanne, Ron & Ulmer, Larry. A New Owner's Guide to Pekingese. (New Owner's Guide to Ser.). (Illus.). 160p. 12.95 (*0-7938-2806-6*) TFH Pubns.
Deanovic-Jernej. Serbocroatian-Italian Dictionary: Hrvatsko Ili Srpsko-Talijanski Rjecnik. (ITA & SER.). 1068p. 1988. write for info. (*0-8288-1639-5*, F79210) Fr & Eur.
Deanovich, Connie. Watusi Titanic. 80p. (Orig.). 1996. pap. 12.00 (*0-943221-24-2*) Timken Pubs.
— Zombie Jet. LC 99-29915. 75p. 1999. pap. 13.00 (*1-58195-010-1*, Pub. by Zoland Bks) SPD-Small Pr Dist.
Deans, Candace & Karwan, Kirk, eds. Global Information Systems & Technology: Focus on the Organization & Its Functional Areas. 592p. (C). 1997. text 59.95 (*1-878289-21-7*) Idea Group Pub.
Deans, Candance & Dakin, Shaun. The Thunderbird Guide to International Business Resources on the World Wide Web. LC 96-23146. 142p. 1996. pap. 25.95 (*0-471-16016-4*) Wiley.
Deans, David. The Peatman. 1996. pap. 16.00 (*0-7486-6171-9*, Pub. by Polygon) Subterranean Co.
Deans, David & Beaver, Benjamin. Two Thousand Solutions. unabridged ed. Maxwell, Robert, ed. (Illus.). 40p. 1998. pap. 12.95 (*0-9670207-0-0*) Two Thousand.
Deans, Gordon, et al. Colorectal Disease. (Illus.). 328p. 1998. text 169.50 (*0-19-262704-X*) OUP.
Deans, Mariah T. When the Stars Sing: A Good Night Story. (Kuumba Ser.). (Illus.). 28p. (J). (gr. k-2). 1997. 12.95 (*0-937913-09-X*) W Stery.
Deans, Mary L. Malled. Leonard, Rosa M., ed. 180p. (Orig.). 1990. pap. 7.95 (*0-9624388-1-2*) Flatrock Bks.
Deans, Nora L. Aquatic Life in the John G. Shedd Aquarium: A Guide to Exhibit Animals. (Illus.). 272p. (Orig.). 1983. pap., student ed. 6.95 (*0-9611074-0-5*) Shedd Aquarium.
Deans, Sis. Brick Walls. No. 1000. LC 96-60941. (Illus.). 150p. (YA). 1996. pap. 8.00 (*1-883650-34-8*) Windswept Hse.
— Decisions & Other Stories. (Maine Chapbook for Fiction 1995 Ser.). (Illus.). 72p. (Orig.). 1995. pap. text 8.00 (*0-9618592-3-7*) Maine Writers.
— His Proper Post: A Biography of Gen. Joshua Lawrence Chamberlain. (Illus.). 250p. (YA). (gr. 7-12). 1996. text 25.00 (*1-883926-05-X*); pap. text 18.00 (*1-883926-07-6*) Belle Grv Pub.
Deans, Sis B. Blazing Bear. LC 92-60478. (Illus.). 40p. (J). (gr. 1-6). 1992. pap. 7.95 (*0-932433-94-4*) Windswept Hse.
Deans-Smith, Susan. Bureaucrats, Planters, & Workers: The Making of the Tobacco Monopoly in Bourbon Mexico. 384p. (C). 1992. text 40.00 (*0-292-70786-X*) U of Tex Pr.
Deans, Stanley R. The Radon Transform & Some of Its Applications. rev. ed. LC 92-1004. 308p. (C). 1993. reprint ed. lib. bdg. 58.50 (*0-89464-718-0*) Krieger.
***Deans, Thomas A.** Writing Partnerships: Service-Learning in Composition. 270p. 2000. pap. write for info. (*0-8141-5918-4*, 59184) NCTE.
Dear. Contemporary Authors: New Revision Series, Vol. 47. rev. ed. 1995. 140.00 (*0-8103-5750-X*) Gale.
— Orary Authors. rev. ed. (Contemporary Authors Revised Ser.: Vol. 49). 1995. 140.00 (*0-8103-9340-9*) Gale.
Dear, jt. auth. see Chapman.
Dear, I. C. The Oxford Companion to the Second World War. (Illus.). 1268p. 2000. 65.00 (*0-19-214168-6*) OUP.
Dear, Ian. Enterprise to Endeavour: The J-Class Yachts. 4th ed. LC 99-21010. (Illus.). 160p. 1999. 45.00 (*1-57409-091-7*) Sheridan.
— Escape & Evasion: Prisoner of War Breakouts & the Routes to Safety in World War Two. LC 97-220831. (Illus.). 208p. 1997. 24.95 (*1-85409-293-6*, Pub. by Arms & Armour) Sterling.
— Sabotage & Subversion: Stories from the Files of the SOE & OSS. (Illus.). 240p. 1996. 29.95 (*1-85409-260-X*, Pub. by Arms & Armour) Sterling.
***Dear, Ian.** Sabotage & Subversion: The SOE & OSS at War. (Military Classics). (Illus.). 2000. pap. 9.95 (*0-304-35202-0*) Continuum.
Dear, Ian. Ten Commando, 1942-1945. (Illus.). 208p. 1997. reprint ed. pap. text 20.00 (*0-7881-5011-1*) DIANE Pub.
Dear, Ian & Kemp, Peter, eds. An A-Z of Sailing Terms. 2nd ed. (Oxford Paperback Reference Ser.). (Illus.). 222p. 1999. pap. 12.95 (*0-19-280068-X*) OUP.
Dear, John. Disarming the Heart: Toward a Vow of Nonviolence. rev. ed. LC 93-28739. 192p. 1993. pap. 12.99 (*0-8361-3652-7*) Herald Pr.
***Dear, John.** Jesus the Rebel: Bearer of God's Peace & Justice. LC 99-56804. 240p. 2000. pap. 16.95 (*1-58051-073-6*) Sheed & Ward WI.
Dear, John. Peace Behind Bars: A Peacemaking Priest's Journal from Jail. 320p. (Orig.). 1995. pap. 14.95 (*1-55612-771-5*) Sheed & Ward WI.
— The Sacrament of Civil Disobedience. 300p. (Orig.). (C). 1994. pap. 17.95 (*1-879175-16-9*) Fortkamp.
— Seeds of Nonviolence. 500p. (Orig.). 1992. pap. 19.95 (*1-879175-11-8*) Fortkamp.
***Dear, John.** The Sound of Listening: A Retreat Journal from Thomas Merton's Hermitage. LC 99-29105. 132p. 1999. pap. 13.95 (*0-8264-1189-4*) Continuum.
Dear, John, ed. Apostle of Peace: Essays in Honor of Daniel Berrigan. LC 95-45430. (Illus.). 255p. (Orig.). reprint ed. pap. 79.10 (*0-608-20181-2*, 207143900012) Bks Demand.
Dear, John, ed. see Maguire, Mairead C.
Dear, John, ed. see Nouwen, Henri J. M.
Dear, M. J., et al, eds. Steel City: A Geography of Hamilton & Region. 308p. 1987. pap. 16.95 (*0-8020-6582-1*); text 38.50 (*0-8020-2563-3*) U of Toronto Pr.
Dear, M. J., jt. ed. see Wolch, Jennifer R.
Dear, Michael. The Postmodern Urban Condition. LC 99-43567. 250p. 1999. 64.95 (*0-631-20987-5*) Blackwell Pubs.
— The Postmodern Urban Condition. LC 99-43567. 250p. 1999. pap. 26.95 (*0-631-20988-3*) Blackwell Pubs.
Dear, Michael, et al. The Service Hub Concept in Human Services Planning, Vol. 42-3. (Progress in Planning Ser.: 42). 120p. 1994. pap. 61.00 (*0-08-042543-7*, Pergamon Pr) Elsevier.
Dear, Michael J., et al, eds. Rethinking Los Angeles. LC 96-10037. (Metropolis & Region Ser.: Vol. 2). 380p. 1996. 58.00 (*0-8039-7286-5*); pap. 26.95 (*0-8039-7287-3*) Sage.
Dear, Michael J. & Scott, Allen J. Urbanization & Urban Planning in Capitalist Societies. 1981. pap. 19.95 (*0-416-74650-0*, NO. 6382) Routledge.
Dear, Nick. The Art of Success & in the Ruins. 100p. (C). 1994. pap. 13.95 (*0-413-68230-7*, A0705, Methuen Drama) Methn.
— The Lodger. 112p. 1994. pap. 11.95 (*0-413-68620-5*, A0707, Methuen Drama) Methn.
Dear, Nick, adapted by. Persuasion. (Screenplay Ser.). 1996. pap. 10.95 (*0-413-71170-6*) Methn.
Dear, Nick, jt. auth. see Moliere.
Dear, Pamela S., ed. Contemporary Authors, Vol. 46. rev. ed. 500p. 1995. text 150.00 (*0-8103-5699-6*) Gale.
— Contemporary Authors, 2 Vols., Vol. 47. rev. ed. 500p. 1995. text 150.00 (*0-8103-5751-8*, 000087) Gale.
— Contemporary Authors: A Bio-Bibliographical Guide to Current Writers in Fiction, General Non-Fiction, Poetry, Journalism, Drama, Motion Pictures, Television, & Other Fields. (Contemporary Authors Ser.: Vol. 48). 483p. 1995. text 150.00 (*0-8103-9338-7*) Gale.
— Contemporary Authors: A Bio-Bibliographical Guide to Current Writers in Fiction, General Non-Fiction, Poetry, Journalism, Drama, Motion Pictures, Television, & Other Fields. (Contemporary Authors Ser.: Vol. 50). 467p. 1996. text 150.00 (*0-8103-9341-7*) Gale.
— Contemporary Authors & Cumulative Index: A Bio-Bibliographical Guide to Current Writers in Fiction, General Non-Fiction, Poetry, Journalism, Drama, Motion Pictures, Television, & Other Fields. (Contemporary Authors Ser.: Vol. 49). 449p. 1995. text 150.00 (*0-8103-9339-5*) Gale.
Dear, Pamela S., jt. ed. see Chapman, Jeffery H.
Dear, Paul H., ed. Genome Mapping: A Practical Approach. LC 97-12590. (The Practical Approach Ser.: No. 184). (Illus.). 396p. 1997. pap. text 55.00 (*0-19-963630-3*) OUP.
— Genome Mapping: A Practical Approach. LC 97-12590. (The Practical Approach Ser.: No. 184). (Illus.). 396p. (C). 1997. text 110.00 (*0-19-963631-1*) OUP.
Dear, Peter. Mersenne & the Learning of the Schools. LC 87-23935. (History of Science Ser.). (Illus.). 288p. 1988. 39.95 (*0-8014-1875-5*) Cornell U Pr.
Dear, Peter, ed. The Literary Structure of Scientific Argument: Historical Studies. LC 90-45803. 224p. (C). 1991. text 34.95 (*0-8122-8185-3*) U of Pa Pr.
— The Scientific Enterprise in Early Modern Europe: Readings from Isis. LC 96-42535. 340p. 1996. pap. text 17.95 (*0-226-13947-6*) U Ch Pr.
— The Scientific Enterprise in Early Modern Europe: Readings from Isis. LC 96-42535. 340p. 1997. lib. bdg. 37.50 (*0-226-13946-8*) U Ch Pr.

D

An Asterisk (*) at the beginning of an entry indicates that the title is appearing for the first time.

Dear, Peter R. Discipline & Experience: The Mathematical Way in the Scientific Revolution. LC 95-12996. (Science & Its Conceptual Foundations Ser.). 304p. 1995. pap. text 24.00 (*0-226-13944-1*); lib. bdg. 60.00 (*0-226-13943-3*) U Ch Pr.

— Mersenne & the Learning of the Schools. LC 87-23935. (Cornell History of Science Ser.). 281p. reprint ed. pap. 87.20 (*0-608-20880-9*, 207197900003) Bks Demand.

Dear, Rosemary, tr. see Goldmann, Klaus & Schneider, Wolfgang.

Dearborn. Ethics for the Insurance Professional. 2nd ed. 1996. pap. 23.95 (*0-7931-2276-7*, 5441-0102, R & R Newkirk) Dearborn.

***Dearborn.** General Securities Principal: Principles & Practices. 10th ed. 1999. pap. text 69.00 (*0-7931-3312-2*) Dearborn.

— Passkey for Life Insurance Licensing. 6th ed. 1999. pap. 26.00 (*0-7931-3536-2*) Dearborn.

Dearborn - R&R Newkirk Staff. Virginia Study Manual for Life & Accident & Sickness Insurance. LC 97-173958. 88 p. 1996. write for info. (*0-7931-2488-3*) Dearborn.

Dearborn, David S. Survey in Comfort: A Tool for Archaeoastronomical Studies. (Astronomy & Astrophysics Ser.). (Illus.). 60p. 1985. 50.00 incl. disk (*0-934525-02-1*); pap. 15.00 (*0-934525-01-3*); disk 50.00 (*0-934525-03-X*) West Research.

Dearborn, David S., jt. auth. see Bauer, Brian S.

Dearborn, Dawn. Manchester. LC 99-70092. 256p. 1999. 22.95 (*1-57197-168-8*) Pentland Pr.

Dearborn, Dorothy. True Stories: New Brunswickers at War LC 98-161469. 159p. 1997. write for info. (*1-896270-12-3*) Neptune Pubng.

Dearborn Financial Institute, Inc. Editorial Staff. Direct Participation Programs Limited Principal: Principles & Practices - Questions & Answers. 3rd ed. (Passtrak Ser.: Series 39). 1997. pap. 150.00 (*0-7931-2627-4*) Dearborn.

— General Securities Sales Supervisor: Final Exam - Glossary. (Passtrak Ser.: Series 8). 1996. pap. 49.00 (*0-7931-2377-1*) Dearborn.

— General Securities Sales Supervisor Pt. 1: Principles & Practices - Questions & Answers. 9th ed. (Passtrak Ser.: Series 8). 1996. pap. 140.00 (*0-7931-2375-5*) Dearborn.

— General Securities Sales Supervisor Pt. 2: Principles & Practices - Questions & Answers. 9th ed. (Passtrak Ser.: Series 8). 1996. pap. 140.00 (*0-7931-2376-3*) Dearborn.

— Municipal Securities Principal: License Exam Manual - Questions & Answers. 8th ed. LC 98-131105. (Passtrak Ser.: Series 53). 1997. pap. 165.00 (*0-7931-2535-9*) Dearborn.

— National Commodity Futures: Questions & Answers. 9th ed. (Passtrak Ser.: Series 3). 1997. pap. 40.00 (*0-7931-2339-9*) Dearborn.

Dearborn Financial Institute Staff. Designing Financial Strategies. LC 98-3076. xi, 214p. 1998. pap. 45.00 (*0-7931-2743-2*, 54131301) Dearborn.

***Dearborn Financial Institute Staff.** Diccionario Bilingue de Seguros. (SPA.). 1999. pap. 22.95 (*0-7931-3557-5*) Dearborn.

Dearborn Financial Institute Staff. Diccionario Bilingue de Terminos Bursatiles.Tr. of Securities Dictionary. (SPA.). 526p. 1998. pap. 29.95 (*0-7931-3006-9*, 17001801) Dearborn.

— Estate Planning. 6th ed. LC 98-36523. 355p. 1998. 49.95 (*0-7931-3128-6*, Real Estate Ed) Dearborn.

***Dearborn Financial Institute Staff.** General Securities Representative: Questions & Answers. 10th ed. (PASSTRAK Seven Ser.). (Illus.). 470p. 1999. pap. 54.00 (*0-7931-3346-7*) Dearborn.

— Income Taxation of Financial Products. LC 99-25717. 125p. 1999. pap. 37.00 (*0-7931-3273-8*) Dearborn.

Dearborn Financial Institute Staff. Introduction to Life Underwriting. 11th ed. LC 98-3198. 1998. pap. 26.00 (*0-7931-1552-3*, 54050711) Dearborn.

— License Exam Manual. 18th ed. (Passtrak Ser.). 1998. pap. 24.00 (*0-7931-2806-4*, 36060218) Dearborn.

— License Exam Manual. 18th ed. (Passtrak Ser.). 1998. pap. 35.00 (*0-7931-3004-2*) Dearborn.

— License Exam Manual & Questions & Answers: Uniform Securities Agent State Law Exam. 14th ed. 1998. pap. text 35.00 (*0-7931-3379-3*) Dearborn.

— Life & Health Insurance: License Exam Manual. 4th ed. LC 97-31724. 1997. pap. 29.00 (*0-7931-2736-X*, 5312-0304) Dearborn.

***Dearborn Financial Institute Staff.** Long-Term Care Suitability. LC 00-28250. 2000. pap. 29.00 (*0-7931-3796-9*) Dearborn.

Dearborn Financial Institute Staff. Managed Care: An Agent's Door to the Samll Group Market. LC 98-38592. 131p. 1998. 34.00 (*0-7931-2849-8*, Real Estate Ed) Dearborn.

— Passkey for Health Insurance Licensing. 6th ed. LC 98-46492. 1998. pap. text 26.00 (*0-7931-3233-9*) Dearborn.

— Passtrak Questions & Answers for Life & Health Insurance. 4th ed. (Passtrak Ser.). 1998. pap. 18.00 (*0-7931-2942-7*, 53083904) Dearborn.

— Passtrak Series Vol. 6: Questions & Answers. 18th ed. (Passtrak Ser.). 1998. pap. 24.00 (*0-7931-2807-2*, 36060418) Dearborn.

— Property & Casualty Insurance Principles & Practices. 5th ed. 359p. 1999. pap. 26.00 (*0-7931-2752-1*) Dearborn.

— Questions & Answers. 18th ed. (Passtrak Ser.). 1998. pap. 35.00 (*0-7931-3005-0*) Dearborn.

— Senior Needs Planning. LC 98-26821. 1998. pap. 39.00 (*0-7931-2919-2*) Dearborn.

— Total Needs Planning Text. 6th ed. 1999. pap. text 29.00 (*0-7931-3187-1*) Dearborn.

— Understanding IRAs. LC 98-15130. 96p. 1998. pap. 29.00 (*0-7931-2860-9*, 54591101) Dearborn.

— Uniform Investment Advisor Law/Combined State Law Exam, Questions & Answers 5Th Ed. 5th ed. LC 98-114238. (Passtrak Ser.). 1998. pap. text 85.00 (*0-7931-2584-7*) Dearborn.

***Dearborn Financial Institute Staff.** Variable Universal Life. LC 99-25361. (Illus.). 80p. 1999. pap. 29.00 (*0-7931-3322-X*) Dearborn.

Dearborn Financial Institute Staff, ed. General Securities Representative License Exam Manual: Principles & Practices. 10th ed. LC 99-161456. (Passtrak Ser.). 1998. pap. 54.00 (*0-7931-2796-3*) Dearborn.

— General Securities Representative License Exam Manual: Questions & Answers. 10th ed. (Passtrak Ser.). 1998. pap. 54.00 (*0-7931-2748-3*) Dearborn.

***Dearborn Financial Institution Staff.** General Securities Representative: Questions & Answers. 10th ed. (Passtrak 7 Ser.). 2000. pap. 54.00 (*0-7931-3991-0*) Dearborn.

***Dearborn Financial Pub. Staff.** Life Insurance Suitability. LC 99-48277. (Illus.). 113p. 1999. pap. 29.00 (*0-7931-3295-9*) Dearborn.

Dearborn Financial Pub. Staff, ed. Pensions & Profit Sharing. 7th ed. LC 99-47910. 300p. 2000. pap. text 50.00 (*0-7931-2690-8*, 5415-1407, R & R Newkirk) Dearborn.

— Principles of Retirement Planning. 2nd ed. LC 97-24343. 220p. (Orig.). 1997. pap. text 34.95 (*0-7931-2591-X*, 5442-0102, R & R Newkirk) Dearborn.

***Dearborn Financial Publishing, Inc. Staff.** General Securities Principal: Questions & Answers. 10th ed. (Passtrak Ser.). 399p. 1999. pap. 69.00 (*0-7931-3313-0*) Dearborn.

Dearborn Financial Publishing Staff. 401(K) Plans. 2nd ed. LC 97-20066. 112p. 1997. pap. text 25.95 (*0-7931-2528-6*, 5437-0102) Dearborn.

***Dearborn Financial Publishing Staff.** 401(K) Plans. 3rd ed. LC 99-29089. 133p. 1999. pap. 29.00 (*0-7931-3438-2*) Dearborn.

— Market Conduct for Life Insurance Agents. LC 99-42796. 100p. 1999. pap. 29.00 (*0-7931-3299-1*) Dearborn.

Dearborn Financial Publishing Staff. OneTrak: Compliance Answers for Bankers. LC 94-49129. 189p. 1996. pap. 30.00 (*0-7931-1055-6*, 3925-0101) Dearborn.

Dearborn Financial Publishing Staff. Pass Trak Series 3, National Commodity Futures Exam. 9th ed. LC 96-17902. 1996. pap. 49.00 (*0-7931-2338-0*, 3603-0209) Dearborn.

— Principles of Retirement Planning. 3rd ed. LC 99-23664. 240p. 1999. pap. 37.00 (*0-7931-3427-7*) Dearborn.

— Rollovers. LC 98-48147. 69p. 1999. 37.00 (*0-7931-3098-0*) Dearborn.

Dearborn Financial Publishing Staff. Uniform Securities Agent State Law Exam: License Exam Manual & Questions & Answers. LC 98-131089. (Passtrak Ser.). 1998. pap. text 29.00 (*0-7931-2844-7*) Dearborn.

Dearborn Financial Publishing Staff & Mitchell, Carolyn B. Pass Trak Series 65/66, Uniform Investment Adviser Law/Combined State Law Exam: Principles & Practices, Questions & Answers. 4th rev. ed. LC 95-44598. 1995. pap. 75.00 (*0-7931-1840-9*, 3665-0104) Dearborn.

Dearborn Financial Publishing Staff, jt. auth. see Tromblay, Dan.

Dearborn, George Van Ness. The Psychology of Clothing. (Psychological Monographs General & Applied: Vol. 26). 1974. reprint ed. pap. 55.00 (*0-8115-1425-0*) Periodicals Srv.

Dearborn, Helen E. Town History of Weare, NJ, from 1888. (Illus.). 305p. 1993. reprint ed. lib. bdg. 35.00 (*0-8328-3185-9*) Higginson Bk Co.

Dearborn, Henry. Revolutionary War Journals, 1775-1783. Brown, Lloyd A. & Peckham, Howard H., eds. LC 74-102233. (Select Bibliographies Reprint Ser.). 1977. 31.95 (*0-8369-5118-2*) Ayer.

Dearborn, John J. The History of Salisbury, New Hampshire from Date of Settlement to the Present Time. Adams, James O., ed. (Illus.). 892p. 1988. reprint ed. lib. bdg. 89.50 (*0-8328-0073-2*, NH0020) Higginson Bk Co.

— The History of Salisbury, NH from Date of Settlement to the Present Time. (Illus.). 888p. 1992. reprint ed. lib. bdg. 89.50 (*0-8328-2240-X*) Higginson Bk Co.

Dearborn, Mary V. Love in the Promised Land: The Story of Anzia Yezierska & John Dewey. (Illus.). 350p. 1988. text 29.95 (*0-02-908090-8*) Free Pr.

***Dearborn, Mary V.** Mailer: A Biography. LC 99-32214. (Illus.). 448p. 1999. 30.00 (*0-395-73655-2*) HM.

— Queen of Bohemia: The Life of Louise Bryant. (Illus.). 384p. 1999. 29.95 (*0-7351-0146-9*) Replica Bks.

Dearborn, Mona L. Anson Dickinson: The Celebrated Miniature Painter 1779-1852. LC 83-70635. 224p. 1983. pap. text 7.95 (*0-940748-86-X*) Conn Hist Soc.

Dearborn, Ned. Trapping on the Farm. (Illus.). 30p. 1986. reprint ed. pap. 10.00 (*0-8466-6028-8*, U-28, Shorey Pubns) Shoreys Bkstore.

Dearborn, Ned H. Oswego Movement in American Education. LC 74-89171. (American Education: Its Men, Institutions, & Ideas. Series 1: Its Men, Institutions & Ideas, Ser. 1). 1974. reprint ed. 18.95 (*0-405-01409-0*) Ayer.

***Dearborn-R & R Newkirk Staff.** Ethics for the Insurance Professional. 3rd ed. LC 00-31537. 2000. pap. 26.00 (*0-7931-4118-4*) Dearborn.

Dearborn-R & R Newkirk Staff. Michigan Study Manual for Life & Accident & Sickness Insurance. LC 98-106321. iv, 40 p. 1992. write for info. (*0-7931-0508-0*) Dearborn.

— Passkey for Life Insurance Licensing. 6th ed. LC 98-46603. 1998. pap. text 26.00 (*0-7931-3232-0*) Dearborn.

— Survey of Advanced Sales. 6th ed. LC 96-20652. 7p. 1996. pap. 34.95 (*0-7931-2141-8*, 5408-0406) Dearborn.

***Dearborn Resources Staff.** Science Fun in Chicagoland. (Illus.). (J). 1999. pap. 17.95 (*965-440-961-5*) Dearborn Res.

Dearborn Staff. Individual & Family Markets. 5th ed. 206p. 1992. pap. 26.95 (*0-7931-0432-7*, 5409-1805, R & R Newkirk) Dearborn.

***Dearborn Staff.** Introduction to Trusts. LC 98-48146. 87p. 1999. pap. 37.00 (*0-7931-3176-6*) Dearborn.

Dearborn Staff & R & R Newkirk Staff. Introduction to Financial Products. 300p. 1994. pap. 44.95 (*0-7931-0907-8*, 54430101) Dearborn.

— Introduction to Group Insurance. 4th ed. LC 93-22755. 153p. 1993. pap. 32.95 (*0-7931-0711-3*, 54301304, R & R Newkirk) Dearborn.

Dearborn Staff & R&R Newkirk Staff. Solutions Handbook: For Personal Financial Planning, Business Planning, Employee Benefits & Estate Planning. 500p. 1995. pap. 29.95 (*0-7931-1152-8*, 5606-0201, R & R Newkirk) Dearborn.

Dearborn, Tim. Beyond Duty: A Passion for Christ, a Heart for Mission. 1998. pap. 8.95 (*1-887983-04-X*) MARC.

— Taste & See: Awakening Our Spiritual Senses. LC 96-16318. 137p. (Orig.). 1996. pap. 9.99 (*0-8308-1985-1*, 1985) InterVarsity.

Dearborn Trade Staff. General Securities Representative, 7. 10th ed. (Passtrak Ser.). 1999. pap. text 54.00 (*0-7931-3239-8*) Dearborn.

— General Securities Representative: License Exam Manual. 10th ed. 650p. 1998. pap. 54.00 (*0-7931-3466-8*) Dearborn.

Dearborn Trade Staff & Mitchell, Carolyn B. Study Guide for Modern Real Estate Practice. 14th ed. 1996. pap. 14.95 (*0-7931-2303-8*, 15100214, Real Estate Ed) Dearborn.

Dearden, Carmen D., tr. see Gutierrez, Douglas

Dearden, Ian, jt. auth. see Tronc, Keith.

Dearden, J. & O'Neill, H., eds. Hardenability of Steels. (Illus.). 80p. 1990. pap. 95.00 (*1-85573-009-X*, Pub. by Woodhead Pubng) Am Educ Systs.

***Dearden, James S.** John Ruskin: A Life in Pictures. (Illus.). 261p. 1999. 75.00 (*1-84127-046-6*, Pub. by Sheffield Acad); pap. 39.50 (*1-84127-045-8*, Pub. by Sheffield Acad) CUP Services.

Dearden, Jeannette & Stig-Nielsen, Karin. Spoken Danish, Bk. I. 1976. pap. 90.00 incl. audio (*0-87950-051-4*) Spoken Lang Serv.

Dearden, Jeannette & Stig-Nielsen, Karin. Spoken Danish, Bk. I. 1976. audio 75.00 (*0-87950-050-6*) Spoken Lang Serv.

Dearden, Jeannette & Stig-Nielsen, Karin. Spoken Danish, Bk. I, Units 1-12. 341p. pap. 15.00 (*0-87950-044-1*) Spoken Lang Serv.

— Spoken Danish, Bk. II, Units 13-30. 567p. pap. 20.00 (*0-87950-045-X*) Spoken Lang Serv.

Dearden, M. & Dearden, R. A Modern Course in Biology. 307p. (C). 1969. 6.64 (*0-08-013457-2*, Pergamon Pr) Elsevier.

Dearden, Paul F. The Rhode Island Campaign of 1778: Inauspicious Dawn of Alliance. LC 78-68920. (Illus.). 169p. 1980. 9.95 (*0-917012-17-8*) RI Pubns Soc.

Dearden, Philip & Mitchell, Bruce. Environmental Challenge & Change: A Canadian Perspective. LC 98-131570. (Illus.). 578p. (C). 1998. text 85.00 (*0-19-541014-9*) OUP.

Dearden, R., jt. auth. see Dearden, M.

Dearden, R. F., et al. Educational & the Development of Reason, 3 pts. Incl. Pt. 1. Critique of Current Educationl Aims. 1975. pap. 9.95 (*0-7100-8084-0*); Pt. 2. Reason. 1975. pap. 9.95 (*0-7100-8101-4*); Pt. 3. Education & Reason. 1975. pap. 9.95 (*0-7100-8102-2*); 1975. pap. write for info. (*0-318-55552-2*) Routledge.

Dearden, Richard G., jt. comment see Richard, John D.

Dearden, Stephen, jt. auth. see McDonald, Frank.

Dearden, Steven, jt. auth. see McDonald, Frank.

DeArdo, A. J., ed. see International Conference of the Thermomechanical P.

DeArdo, Anthony J., Jr., ed. see Minerals, Metals & Materials Society Staff.

Deardoff, Kevin, jt. auth. see Byerly, Edwin.

Deardorff, Alan & Stern, Robert. The Michigan Model of World Production Trade: Theory & Application. 296p. 1985. 35.00 (*0-262-04081-6*) MIT Pr.

Deardorff, Alan V. Social Dimensions of U.S. Trade Policy. LC 99-59371. (Studies in International Economics Ser.). 304p. 2000. text 54.50 (*0-472-11099-3*, 11099) U of Mich Pr.

Deardorff, Alan V., et al, eds. New Directions in Trade Theory. (Studies In International Trade Policy). 424p. 1995. text 60.00 (*0-472-10562-0*, 10562) U of Mich Pr.

Deardorff, Alan V. & Stern, Robert M. Measurement of Nontariff Barriers. 152p. (C). 1998. text 47.50 (*0-472-10931-6*, 10931) U of Mich Pr.

Deardorff, Alan V. & Stern, Robert M., eds. Analytical & Negotiating Issues in the Global Trading System. LC 93-39935. (Studies In International Trade Policy). 648p. (C). 1994. text 85.00 (*0-472-10431-4*, 10431) U of Mich Pr.

— Representation of Constituent Interests in the Design & Implementation of U. S. Trade Policies: The Sweetland Conference. LC 98-49952. 344p. (C). 1998. text 57.50 (*0-472-10932-4*, 10932) U of Mich Pr.

— The Stolper-Samuelson Theorem: A Golden Jubilee. (Studies In International Trade Policy). 400p. 1994. text 60.00 (*0-472-10533-7*, 10533) U of Mich Pr.

Deardorff, Barb, et al. Another Kind of War Story: Army Nurses Look Back to Vietnam. (Illus.). 100p. (Orig.). 1993. pap. 9.95 (*0-9636774-0-3*) AKOWS.

***Deardorff, Donald L., II.** Sports: A Reference Guide, 1980-1999. LC 00-20466. (American Popular Culture Ser.). 360p. 2000. lib. bdg. 85.00 (*0-313-30445-9*, GR0445, Greenwood Pr) Greenwood.

Deardorff, James. Celestial Teachings: The Emergence of the True Testament of Jmmanuel (Jesus) 338p. (Orig.). 1990. pap. 12.00 (*0-926524-11-9*) Granite Pub.

Deardorff, James W. Jesus in India. LC 93-45915. 315p. 1995. 64.95 (*1-883255-37-6*); pap. 44.95 (*1-883255-36-8*) Intl Scholars.

— The Problems of New Testament Gospel Origins: A Glasnost Approach. LC 92-20927. 248p. 1992. text 89.95 (*0-7734-9807-9*) E Mellen.

Deardorff, Jennie. Hardin County, Kentucky 1870 Census. 254p. 1994. pap. 23.00 (*1-889221-12-0*) Ancestral Trails.

Deardorff, William W. & Reeves, John. Preparing for Surgery: A Mind-Body Approach to Enhance Healing & Recovery. LC 96-71159. 232p. (Orig.). 1997. pap. 17.95 (*1-57224-071-7*) New Harbinger.

Deardorff, William W., jt. auth. see Belar, Cynthia D.

Deardorff, William W., jt. auth. see Sinel, Michael S.

Dearen, Patrick. A Cowboy of the Pecos. LC 96-42236. 240p. (Orig.). 1996. pap. 12.95 (*1-55622-528-8*, Rep of TX Pr) Wordware Pub.

— Crossing Rio Pecos. LC 95-26692. (Illus.). 208p. (Orig.). 1996. pap. 15.95 (*0-87565-159-3*) Tex Christian.

— The Illegal Man. large type ed. LC 97-35991. (Western Ser.). 363p. 1997. lib. bdg. 19.95 (*0-7862-1238-1*) Thorndike Pr.

— Last of the Old Time Cowboys. LC 98-14583. 1998. pap. text 16.95 (*1-55622-613-6*) Wordware Pub.

— Portraits of the Pecos Frontier. LC 92-29829. 1993. pap. 14.95 (*0-89672-288-0*) Tex Tech Univ Pr.

***Dearen, Patrick.** Portraits of the Pecos Frontier. rev. ed. LC 99-37212. 1999. pap. 19.95 (*0-89672-422-0*) Tex Tech Univ Pr.

Dearen, Patrick. When Cowboys Die. large type ed. 253p. 1995. 19.95 (*0-7838-1514-X*, G K Hall Lrg Type) Mac Lib Ref.

Dearhammer, William G. Unbundling Credit Department Costs. LC 84-16618. (Illus.). 76p. (Orig.). 1984. pap. text 36.00 (*0-936742-19-4*) Robt Morris Assocs.

Dearhammer, William G., et al. Credit Files Manual. LC 86-5257. (Illus.). 64p. (Orig.). 1986. pap. text 41.00 (*0-936742-30-5*) Robt Morris Assocs.

Dearin, Ray D., ed. The New Rhetoric of Chaim Perelman: Statement & Response. LC 88-31489. 266p. (Orig.). (C). 1989. pap. text 24.00 (*0-8191-7309-6*) U Pr of Amer.

***Dearing, Albin P. & Forg, Elisabeth, eds.** Police Combating Violence Against Women: Documentation of the Conference Experts. 271p. 1999. pap. 48.00 (*90-5095-085-X*, 18662, Pub. by Intersentia Uitgevers) Gaunt.

Dearing, Anne. Privileged Gifts: Marriage & Motherhood. 96p. 1987. pap. 3.95 (*0-310-55332-6*, 19035P) Zondervan.

Dearing, Betty V. Dearing Tracks Throughout America. 400p. 1994. lib. bdg. 60.00 (*0-614-00585-X*) B V Dearing.

Dearing, Brian E., jt. auth. see Hartwig, Frederick.

Dearing, C. L. American Highway Policy: Urban Dimension. LC 77-74939. (American Federalism Ser.). (Illus.). 1978. reprint ed. lib. bdg. 29.95 (*0-405-10486-3*) Ayer.

Dearing, Charles L. & Owen, Wilfred. National Transportation Policy. LC 79-28670. (Illus.). 459p. 1980. reprint ed. lib. bdg. 85.00 (*0-313-22301-7*, DENT, Greenwood Pr) Greenwood.

Dearing, Charles L., et al. ABC of the NRA. (Brookings Institution Reprint Ser.). reprint ed. lib. bdg. 34.00 (*0-697-00154-7*) Irvington.

Dearing, James W. Growing a Japanese Science City: Communication in Scientific Research. LC 95-15980. (Nissan Institute/Routledge Japanese Studies Ser.). 248p. (C). (gr. 13). 1995. 90.00 (*0-415-08134-3*) Routledge.

Dearing, James W. & Rogers, Everette M. Agenda Setting. (Communication Concepts Ser.: Vol. 6). 112p. 1996. 37.00 (*0-7619-0562-6*); pap. 16.95 (*0-7619-0563-4*) Sage.

Dearing, Ruthie H., et al. Marketing Women's Health Care. 292p. (C). 1987. 85.00 (*0-87189-633-8*) Aspen Pub.

***Dearing, S.** The Bull Is Not Killed. LC 98-215153. 206p. 1999. 18.95 (*0-7737-3123-7*, Pub. by Stoddart Publ) Genl Dist Srvs.

***Dearing, Sarah.** The Bull Is Not Killed. 216p. 2000. pap. 19.95 (*0-7737-6113-6*) Stoddart Publ.

Dearing, Shirley. Elegantly Frugal Costumes: The Poor Man's Do-It-Yourself Costume Maker's Guide. Zapel, Arthur L. & Middleton, Pat, eds. LC 92-1662. (Illus.). 144p. 1992. pap. 14.95 (*0-916260-88-7*, B125) Meriwether Pub.

Dearing, Vinton A. A Manual of Textual Analysis. LC 82-20947. 108p. 1983. reprint ed. lib. bdg. 49.50 (*0-313-23734-4*, DEMA, Greenwood Pr) Greenwood.

— Works of John Dryden: Plays: King Arthur, Cleomenes, Love Triumphant, the Secular Masque & Others. (Works of John Dryden Ser.). 559p. 1998. 75.00 (*0-520-08766-6*, Pub. by U CA Pr) Cal Prin Full Svc.

Dearing, Vinton A., ed. The Works of John Dryden Vol. XII: Plays: Amboyna, The State of Innocence, Aureng-Zebe. 556p. 1995. 80.00 (*0-520-08247-8*, Pub. by U CA Pr) Cal Prin Full Svc.

Dearing, Vinton A., jt. ed. see Loftis, John.

Dearing, Vinton A., jt. ed. see Miner, Earl.

Dearing/NVCC Staff. The Biology Experience: Laboratory Manual. abr. ed. 152p. (C). 1996. pap. text, spiral bd. 16.50 (*0-8403-9643-0*) Kendall-Hunt.

***Dearl, Elizabeth.** Diamondback. (Taylor Madison Mystery Ser.: Vol. 1). 288p. 2000. mass mkt. 5.99 (*1-929613-33-4*, Mosaic MI) Avid MI.

Dearle, Alan, et al, eds. Advances in Persistent Object Systems: Proceedings of the 4th Workshop. 431p. 1991. pap. text 39.95 (*1-55860-168-6*) Morgan Kaufmann.

D

Dearle, N. B. Dictionary of Official War-Time Organizations. (Economic & Social History of the World War Ser.). 1928. 100.00 (*0-317-27446-5*) Elliots Bks.

Dearle, Norman B. Economic Chronicle of the Great War for Great Britain & Ireland, 1914-1919. (Economic & Social History of the World War Ser.). 1929. 125.00 (*0-686-83531-X*) Elliots Bks.

Dearling. The Illustrated Encyclopedia of Musical Instruments of the World. 1996. 75.00 (*0-02-864667-3*) Mac Lib Ref.

Dearling. Social Welfare. 228p. 1993. pap., wbk. ed. 29.95 (*0-582-21976-0*) Ashgate Pub Co.

***Dearling, Robert.** Encyclopedia of Musical Instruments, 5 vols. (Illus.). 2000. 89.75 (*0-7910-6090-X*) Chelsea Hse.

— Keyboard Instruments & Ensembles. (Encyclopedia of Musical Instruments Ser.). (Illus.). (J). 2000. 17.95 (*0-7910-6094-2*) Chelsea Hse.

Dearling, Robert. The Music of Mozart: The Symphonies. LC 78-68625. (Illus.). 232p. 1982. 36.50 (*0-8386-2335-2*) Fairleigh Dickinson.

***Dearling, Robert.** Non-Western & Absolute Instruments. (Encyclopedia of Musical Instruments Ser.). (Illus.). 2000. 17.95 (*0-7910-6095-0*) Chelsea Hse.

— Percussion & Electronic Instruments. (Encyclopedia of Musical Instruments Ser.). (Illus.). (J). 2000. 17.95 (*0-7910-6093-4*) Chelsea Hse.

— String Instruments. (Encyclopedia of Musical Instruments Ser.). (Illus.). (J). 2000. 17.95 (*0-7910-6092-6*) Chelsea Hse.

— Woodwind & Brass Instruments. (Encyclopedia of Musical Instruments Ser.). (Illus.). (J). 2000. 17.95 (*0-7910-6091-8*) Chelsea Hse.

Dearling, Robert, jt. auth. see Blokker, Roy.

Dearlove, Des, jt. auth. see Clutterbuck, David.

Dearlove, Des, jt. auth. see Crainer, Stuart.

Dearlove, Des. Business the Bill Gates Way: Ten Secrets of the World's Greatest Business Leader. LC 98-52524. (Business Way Ser.). 150p. 1999. pap. 14.95 (*0-8144-7036-X*) AMACOM.

— Business the Richard Branson Way: Ten Secrets of the World's Greatest Brand Builder. LC 98-54706. (Business Way Ser.). 144p. 1999. pap. 14.95 (*0-8144-7035-1*) AMACOM.

— The Ultimate Book of Business Brands: Insights from the World's 50 Greatest Brands. 1999. 19.95 (*1-84112-016-2*) Capstone Pr.

— Ultimate Book of Business Thinking: Harnessing the Power of the World's Great Business Ideas. 1999. pap. text 19.95 (*1-84112-060-X*) Capstone Pub NH.

Dearlove, Des, jt. auth. see Crainer, Stuart.

Dearlove, Desmond, jt. auth. see Clutterbuck, David.

Dearlove, John & Saunders, Peter, eds. The New Introduction to British Politics: Analysing a Capitalist Democracy. 550p. (C). 1991. pap. 43.95 (*0-7456-0600-8*) Blackwell Pubs.

— The New Introduction to British Politics: Analysing a Capitalist Democracy. 2nd ed. 550p. (C). 1991. 93.95 (*0-7456-0599-0*) Blackwell Pubs.

DeArman, J., jt. auth. see Britten, Walter S.

***Dearman, J Andrew.** Religion & Culture in Ancient Israel. (Illus.). 1999. pap. text 24.95 (*1-56563-465-9*) Hendrickson MA.

Dearman, Jill. Queer Astrology: A Guide for Lesbians. LC 98-44573. 208p. 1998. pap. 13.95 (*0-312-19953-8*) St Martin.

— Queer Astrology for Men: An Astrological Guide for Gay Men. 2nd ed. LC 98-37646. (Illus.). 208p. 1998. pap. 13.95 (*0-312-19952-X*) St Martin.

Dearman, Marion, jt. auth. see Howells, John M.

Dearman, Marvene, jt. auth. see Nauman, Ann.

Dearman, Tim. National Radio Pleasure. (Illus.). 176p. (Orig.). 1996. pap. 9.95 (*0-9655724-0-4*) Natl Radio Pleasure.

Dearman, W. R., et al, eds. Engineering Geology of the Earth. 247p. 1990. 52.00 (*5-02-022424-3*, Pub. by A A Balkema) Ashgate Pub Co.

DeArment, Robert K. Alias Frank Canton. LC 95-39758. (Illus.). 448p. 1996. 29.95 (*0-8061-2828-3*) U of Okla Pr.

— Alias Frank Canton. LC 95-39758. (Illus.). 448p. 1997. pap. 18.95 (*0-8061-2900-X*) U of Okla Pr.

— Bat Masterson: The Man & the Legend. LC 78-21383. (Illus.). 456p. 1989. pap. 17.95 (*0-8061-2221-8*) U of Okla Pr.

— George Scarborough: The Life & Death of a Lawman on the Closing Frontier. LC 91-30145. (Illus.). 336p. 1996. pap. 13.95 (*0-8061-2850-X*) U of Okla Pr.

— Knights of the Green Cloth: The Saga of the Frontier Gamblers. LC 81-16196. (Illus.). 432p. 1990. 28.95 (*0-8061-1726-5*); pap. 16.95 (*0-8061-2245-5*) U of Okla Pr.

Dearment, Robert K., jt. auth. see Rasch, Philip J.

DeArment, Robert K., ed. see Rasch, Philip J.

Dearmer, Geoffrey. A Pilgrim's Song: Selected Poems to Mark the Poet's 100th Birthday. 82p. 1994. 29.95 (*0-7195-5242-7*, Pub. by John Murray) Trafalgar.

Dearmer, Percy, et al, eds. Oxford Book of Carols: Music Edition, with Notes. 478p. 1985. pap. 23.95 (*0-19-353315-4*) OUP.

— Songs of Praise. Incl. Music Ed. enl. rev. ed. 932p. 1931. 49.95 (*0-19-231207-3*); write for info. (*0-318-54893-3*) OUP.

***DeArmond, B.** The Wisdom of the Outdoors. 160p. 2000. pap. 6.95 (*1-58334-092-0*, Pub. by Walnut Gr Pr) Midpt Trade.

***Dearmond, Bonnie & Gallery, Jim.** Wisdom of the Outdoors. 2000. pap. 6.95 (*1-58334-097-1*) Walnut Gr Pr.

DeArmond, Dale. The First Man. (Illus.). 38p. (Orig.). 1990. pap. 37.50 (*0-9615529-5-6*) Old Harbor Pr.

— The Raven Charm. LC 98-75289. (Illus.). 51p. (J). (gr. k-4). 1998. 12.95 (*0-9641998-6-6*) Lapcat Pubns.

— Sun Signs from a Polar Star: A Northern Zodiac. (Illus.). 26p. 1993. 120.00 (*1-881655-02-4*); pap. 8.95 (*1-881655-00-8*) Old Harbor Pr.

— Sun Signs from a Polar Star: A Northern Zodiac. limited ed. (Illus.). 26p. 1993. 55.00 (*1-881655-01-6*) Old Harbor Pr.

— Tales from the Four Winds of the North. LC 96-79657. (Illus.). 55p. (Orig.). 1996. pap. 14.95 (*0-9641998-3-1*) Lapcat Pubns.

DeArmond, Dale. The True Story of the Discovery of Gold at Bonanza Creek. LC 97-76103. 49p. 1997. pap. 12.95 (*0-9641998-5-8*) Lapcat Pubns.

DeArmond, Dale. The Seal Oil Lamp. 48p. (J). (gr. k-3). 1997. reprint ed. pap. 7.95 (*0-87156-858-6*) Sierra Club Childrens.

DeArmond, Gillian. Chalice of the Dove. LC 94-45199. 1994. 12.95 (*0-922356-94-7*) Amer West Pubs.

— Violet Flame & Other Meditations. (Illus.). 62p. (Orig.). 1990. pap. 5.95 (*0-922356-19-X*) Amer West Pubs.

DeArmond, Gillian & Viola, Sandra. ETA: A Future Tale. 11.95 (*0-9640104-5-3*) Bridger Hse.

DeArmond, R. N., ed. Klondike Newsman - "Stroller" White. rev. ed. (Illus.). 237p. 1990. pap. 12.95 (*0-945284-03-9*) Lynn Canal Pub.

DeArmond, R. N., jt. auth. see Mayer, Melanie J.

DeArmond, Robert, ed. see Caldwell, Francis E.

DeArmond, Robert N. From Sitka's Past. (Illus.). 272p. (Orig.). 1995. pap. text 25.95 (*0-9644852-1-4*) Sitka Hist Soc.

DeArmond, Stephen J., et al. Structure of the Human Brain: A Photographic Atlas. 3rd ed. (Illus.). 208p. 1989. spiral bd. 29.50 (*0-19-504357-X*) OUP.

Dearne, M. J., jt. auth. see Branigan, K.

Dearness, John L. & Angus, Robert B., Jr. Applied Avionics. 3rd ed. (Illus.). 523p. (C). 1982. teacher ed. 10.00 (*0-942354-02-8*); text 39.00 (*0-942354-01-X*) Bowens Pub Div.

Dearnley, Peter, jt. ed. see Tyrkiel, Eugeneiusz.

***Dearry, Allen & Collman, Gwen, eds.** Children's Environmental Health Research: Indoor Mold & Children's Health. (Illus.). 133p. (C). 2000. pap. text 35.00 (*0-7881-8535-7*) DIANE Pub.

Dears, Donn D. The Entrepreneur as CEO: Building a Business. LC 91-91038. 244p. (Orig.). 1991. 22.95 (*0-9629752-1-4*); pap. 10.95 (*0-9629752-2-2*) WDD Srvcs Corp.

Dearsley, Linda, jt. auth. see Stokes, Doris.

***Dearstyne, Bruce.** Managing Government Records & Information. 264p. 1999. pap. 114.00 (*0-933887-83-3*) ARMA Intl.

Dearstyne, Bruce W. The Archival Enterprise: Modern Archival Principles, Practices, & Management Techniques. LC 92-24279. 309p. reprint ed. pap. 95.80 (*0-608-01444-3*, 206220700002) Bks Demand.

— The Management of Local Government Records: A Guide for Local Officials. LC 88-4004. 156p. 1988. reprint ed. pap. 48.40 (*0-608-04563-2*, 206530200001) Bks Demand.

***Dearstyne, Bruce W.** Managing Historical Records Programs: A Guide for Historical Agencies. (American Association for State & Local History Book Ser.). 240p. 2000. 62.00 (*0-7425-0282-1*); pap. 24.95 (*0-7425-0283-X*) AltaMira Pr.

DeArteaga, William. Quenching the Spirit: Discover the Real Spirit Behind the Charismatic Controversy Spirit. rev. ed. 1996. pap. 12.99 (*0-88419-432-9*) Creation House.

Dearth, Douglas H., jt. auth. see Campen, Alan D.

***Dearth, Kim.** Your Rottweiler's Life. LC 99-39224. (Your ...'s Life Ser.). (Illus.). 303p. 1999. pap. 14.99 (*0-7615-2049-X*) Prima Pub.

***Dearth, Kim D. R.** Your Border Collie's Life: Your Complete Guide to Raising Your Pet from Puppy to Companion. (Your Pet's Life Ser.). (Illus.). 320p. 2000. pap. 14.99 (*0-7615-2536-X*) Prima Pub.

***Deary, Ian J.** Looking down on Human Intelligence. (Oxford Psychology Ser.). (Illus.). 384p. 2000. text 85.00 (*0-19-852417-X*) OUP.

Deary, Ian J., jt. auth. see Matthews, Gerald.

Deary, T. Twist of the Knife. Date not set. pap. text. write for info. (*0-582-39098-2*, Pub. by Addison-Wesley) Longman.

Deary, Terry. Alien Landing. LC 96-181. (Classified Ser.). (Illus.). 96p. (YA). (gr. 5 up). 1996. pap. 5.95 (*0-7534-5004-6*, Kingfisher) LKC.

— Awesome Egyptians. (J). 1997. pap. text 3.99 (*0-590-03168-6*) Scholastic Inc.

— Breakout! LC 96-34094. (Classified Ser.). 96p. (J). (gr. 5 up). 1997. pap. 5.95 (*0-7534-5053-4*) LKC.

— Calamity Kate. LC 82-1326. (Trophy Bk.). (Illus.). 112p. (J). (gr. 3-7). 1991. reprint ed. pap. 3.50 (*0-06-440361-0*, HarpTrophy) HarpC Child Bks.

— The Custard Kid. LC 81-21693. (Trophy Bk.). (Illus.). 96p. (J). (gr. 3-7). 1991. reprint ed. pap. 3.50 (*0-06-440360-2*, HarpTrophy) HarpC Child Bks.

***Deary, Terry.** Greek Legends. (Illus.). 192p. (gr. 6-12). 1999. pap. text 4.50 (*0-439-08618-3*) Scholastic Inc.

Deary, Terry. The Groovy Greeks. (J). 1997. pap. text 3.99 (*0-590-03155-4*) Scholastic Inc.

— Measly Middle Ages. (Horrible History Ser.). (J). (gr. 7-12). 1998. pap. text 3.99 (*0-590-49848-7*) Scholastic Inc.

— The Nuclear Winter Man. LC 96-30163. (Classified Ser.). 96p. (J). (gr. 5 up). 1997. pap. 5.95 (*0-7534-5044-5*) LKC.

— Rotten Romans. (J). 1997. mass mkt. 3.99 (*0-590-73893-3*) Scholastic Inc.

Deary, Terry. Rotten Romans. (J). 1997. pap. text 3.99 (*0-590-03152-X*) Scholastic Inc.

— Shakespeare Stories. (Illus.). 192p. (gr. 6-12). 1999. pap. text 4.50 (*0-439-08387-7*) Scholastic Inc.

Deary, Terry. True Crime Stories. 128p. 1997. pap. 3.99 (*0-14-038588-6*, PuffinBks) Peng Put Young Read.

***Deary, Terry.** True Ghost Stories. large type ed. (Illus.). (J). 1998. pap. 16.95 (*0-7540-6022-5*, Galaxy Child Lrg Print) Chivers N Amer.

— True Horror Stories. large type ed. (J). 2000. pap. write for info. (*0-7540-6092-6*) Chivers N Amer.

— True Monster Stories. 1999. 16.95 (*0-7540-6062-4*) Chivers N Amer.

Deary, Terry. Vanished! LC 96-7209. (Classified Ser.). 96p. (J). (gr. 4-7). 1996. pap. 5.95 (*0-7534-5005-4*, Kingfisher) LKC.

— Vicious Vikings. (Horrible History Ser.). (J). (gr. 7-12). 1998. pap. text 3.99 (*0-590-49849-5*) Scholastic Inc.

Deas, Alston. The Early Ironwork of Charleston. LC 97-7738. (Illus.). 111p. 1997. reprint ed. pap. 19.95 (*0-941936-38-4*) Linden Pub Fresno.

Deas, Michael. The Portraits & Daguerreotypes of Edgar Allan Poe. LC 88-477. 208p. 1989. reprint ed. pap. 64.50 (*0-608-01442-7*, 206220500002) Bks Demand.

Deas, Stewart. In Defence of Hanslick. (Music Book Index Ser.). 114p. 1992. reprint ed. lib. bdg. 69.00 (*0-7812-9499-1*) Rprt Serv.

Dease, Anne. Bits 'n Pieces Quilt. (Illus.). 63p. 1994. 10.95 (*0-922705-48-8*) Quilt Day.

— Dutch Windmills. (Illus.). 56p. (Orig.). 1995. pap. 12.95 (*0-922705-87-9*) Quilt Day.

Dease, Barbara C., jt. auth. see Crockett, M. H.

Deasley, A. R. Search the Scriptures, Old Testament Vol. 4: Deuteronomy. 1970. pap. 1.99 (*0-8341-0031-2*) Beacon Hill.

Deasley, Alex R., jt. ed. see Shelton, R. Larry.

***Deasley, Alex R. G.** Marriage & Divorce in the Bible & the Church. LC 99-87528. 2000. pap. 19.99 (*0-8341-1763-0*) Beacon Hill.

Deasley, Rick, contrib. by. Intros, Improvs, & Interludes, Vol. 1. 52p. 1989. 10.99 (*0-8341-9092-3*, MB-613) Lillenas.

— Intros, Improvs, & Interludes, Vol. 2. 1992. 9.99 (*0-685-68334-6*, MB-637) Lillenas.

Deason, Hilary J. The AAAS Science Book List for Children: A Selected & Annotated List of Science & Mathematics Books for Children in Elementary Schools, & for Children's Collections in Public Libraries. 3rd ed. LC 75-169601. (AAAS Miscellaneous Publications: No. 72-1). 267p. reprint ed. pap. 82.80 (*0-7837-0057-1*, 204030400016) Bks Demand.

Deason, Rhonda, jt. auth. see Sadler, Linda.

Deason, Temd R. & Bold, Harold C. Phycological Studies Vol. 1: Studies of Texas Soil Algae. (University Texas Publication: No. 6022). (Illus.). 70p. 1975. reprint ed. pap. 37.40 (*3-87429-096-4*, 007820, Pub. by Koeltz Sci Bks) Lubrecht & Cramer.

Deason, Wayne O., et al, eds. Proceedings of the Earth Summit Workshop. LC 93-61713. 102p. (Orig.). 1994. pap. 40.00 (*1-884575-00-5*) US Comm Irrigation.

Deason, Wayne O. & Anderson, Susan S., eds. Environmental Enhancement of Water Projects: Proceedings from the 1993 Seminar. LC 94-60399. 288p. (Orig.). 1994. pap. 36.00 (*0-9618257-9-0*) US Comm Irrigation.

Deassis, Machado J., et al. Brazilian Tales. Goldberg, Isaac, tr. 1977. lib. bdg. 59.95 (*0-8490-1551-0*) Gordon Pr.

D'Easum, Dick. Sawtooth Tales. LC 76-24379. (Illus.). 302p. 1977. pap. 93.70 (*0-608-05050-4*, 205971100005) Bks Demand.

Deasy, C. M. Design for Human Affairs. LC 74-5198. (Illus.). 189p. 1974. reprint ed. pap. 58.60 (*0-608-05335-X*, 206504000012) Bks Demand.

Deasy, Irene M. & Andress, Stanford E. The Holy Spirit: Your Divine Companion. unabridged ed. (Illus.). 200p. (Orig.). 1996. pap. 15.95 (*0-9656257-2-9*, I E A F) S E Andress.

Deasy, Irene M., jt. auth. see Andress, Stanford E.

Deasy, Liam. Brother Against Brother LC 99-190899. 126 p. 1998. write for info. (*1-85635-266-8*) Music Sales.

Deasy, Mary. The Hour of Spring. LC 76-6334. (Irish Americans Ser.). 1976. reprint ed. 33.95 (*0-405-09330-6*) Ayer.

Deasy, Patrick B. Microencapsulation & Related Drug Processes. LC 83-26267. (Drugs & the Pharmaceutical Sciences Ser.: Vol. 20). (Illus.). 375p. reprint ed. pap. 116.30 (*0-608-08926-5*, 206956100005) Bks Demand.

Deasy, Richard M., ed. see Staples, William R.

Deasy, Robert P., ed. Immigration Options for Professors & Researchers. 260p. 1994. 57.00 (*1-878677-71-3*, 55.40) Amer Immi Law Assn.

Deasy, Victoria & Relihan, Taun. JC Hears a Wonderful World. large type ed. (Illus.). 50p. (J). (gr. k-2). 1997. 10.00 (*1-891165-01-1*) Sera Pub.

Deasy, Victoria, ed. see Unanaowo, Rhoda.

Death, Chuck & Morton, Colin B. Great Pop Things: The Real History of Rock & Roll from Elvis to Oasis. LC 98-85648. (Illus.). 240p. 1998. pap. 16.95 (*1-891241-08-7*) Verse Chorus Pr.

D'Eath, P. D. Black Holes: Gravitational Interactions. LC 96-4082. (Oxford Mathematical Monographs). (Illus.). 298p. 1996. text 80.00 (*0-19-851479-4*, Clarendon Pr) OUP.

— Supersymmetric Quantum Cosmology. LC 96-228088. (Monographs on Mathematical Physics). (Illus.). 267p. (C). 1996. text 74.95 (*0-521-55287-7*) Cambridge U Pr.

Death, Sarah & Forsas-Scott, Helena, eds. A Century of Swedish Narrative: Essays in Honour of Karin Petherick. 301p. 1994. 55.00 (*1-870041-27-5*, Pub. by Norvik Pr) Dufour.

Death, Sarah, tr. see Benedictsson, Victoria.

Death, Sarah, tr. & frwd. see Bremer, Fredrika.

***Deatherage, C. P.** Steamboating on the Missouri River in the Sixties. 39p. 1998. pap. 4.95 (*0-87770-677-8*) Ye Galleon.

Deatherage, Scott. An Energy Program for the United States: A Critical Analysis of the U. S. Role in Establishing a Program to Increase Renewable Energy Use. LC 97-205629. 165p. 1997. pap. 26.59 (*0-8442-5399-5*, Natl Textbk Co) NTC Contemp Pub Co.

— Modifying Our Policy Toward the People's Republic of China. 256p. 1995. pap. text 25.25 (*0-8442-5839-3*) NTC Contemp Pub Co.

***Deatherage, Scott.** Russia, Friend or Foe: A Critical Analysis of U. S. Foreign Policy Toward Russia. LC 98-212791. x, 196 p. 1998. write for info. (*0-8442-0431-5*) NTC Contemp Pub Co.

Deatherage, Scott, jt. auth. see Goodnight, Lynn.

Deathridge, John. Wagner. (New Grove Composer Biography Ser.). 1997. pap. 16.95 (*0-393-31590-8*) Norton.

Deaton, Jim. Crosscut Saw Reflections in the Pacific Northwest. LC 98-50022. 231p. 1998. pap. 19.95 (*0-87770-675-1*) Ye Galleon.

***Deaton, Jim.** The Kerby Cutoff: A Family. LC 99-15268. 1999. 17.95 (*0-87770-693-X*) Ye Galleon.

Deaton, Agnus & Muellbauer, John. Economics & Consumer Behavior. LC 79-17090. 464p. 1980. pap. text 39.95 (*0-521-29676-5*) Cambridge U Pr.

Deaton, Angus. The Analysis of Household Surveys: A Microeconometric Approach to Development Policy. LC 97-2905. (World Bank Ser.). 432p. 1996. pap. text 39.95 (*0-8018-5254-4*) Johns Hopkins.

— Understanding Consumption. LC 92-30783. (Clarendon Lectures in Economics). (Illus.). 242p. 1993. pap. text 22.00 (*0-19-828824-7*) OUP.

Deaton, Angus & Miller, Ronald. International Commodity Prices, Macroeconomic Performance, & Politics in Sub-Saharan Africa. LC 95-25494. (Princeton Studies in International Finance: Vol. 79). 96p. 1995. pap. 13.50 (*0-88165-251-2*) Princeton U Int Finan Econ.

Deaton, Dennis. Money Wise & Spiritually Rich. LC 98-71543. 1998. pap. 12.95 (*1-57008-424-6*) Bookcraft Inc.

Deaton, Dennis R. The Book on Mind Management. Markland, Cecily, ed. 256p. (Orig.). 1994. text 29.95 (*1-881840-35-2*) TimeMax.

— The Book on Mind Management. Markland, Cecily, ed. 256p. (Orig.). 1994. pap. text 14.95 (*1-881840-34-4*) TimeMax.

— Money: An Owner's Manual: A Personal Guide to Financial Freedom. LC 92-64320. (Illus.). 286p. (Orig.). 1992. pap. 11.95 (*1-881840-25-5*) TimeMax.

Deaton, Donald B., ed. Glossary of Printing Terms. 58p. 1991. 35.00 (*0-318-12163-8*) AATCC.

Deaton, Gail, ed. see Ison, Valeria S.

Deaton, James. Airbrush & Colored Pencil Techniques. Carder, Jennifer, ed. LC 93-84873. (Illus.). 48p. (Orig.). (C). 1993. pap. text 24.95 (*1-883602-03-3*) Atlantic Digital.

***Deaton, James Wright.** Field of Glory. Smith, Billy, ed. & photos by by. (Illus.). 135p. 1999. pap. 5.00 (*0-9675689-0-0*) Theatre.

***Deaton, Michael L. & Winebrake, James J.** Dynamic Modeling of Environmental Systems. LC 99-15368. (Modeling Dynamic Systems Ser.). (Illus.). 216p. 1999. 59.95 incl. cd-rom (*0-387-98880-7*) Spr-Verlag.

Deaton, Oliver, tr. see Becker, Walter Alvin.

Deaton, Robert L. & Berkan, William A. Planning & Managing Death Issues in the Schools: A Handbook. LC 94-21693. 208p. 1995. lib. bdg. 52.95 (*0-313-29525-5*) Greenwood.

Deaton, Wendell R. Exhibitor's Handbook-Mexico. 2nd ed. (Illus.). iv, 126p. (Orig.). (C). 1995. pap. 17.95 (*0-9643371-1-8*) Proteus Pubng.

Deaton, Wendy. Drinking & Drugs in My Family: A Child's Workbook about Substance Abuse in the Family. 64p. (J). 1994. 17.95 (*0-89793-155-6*) Hunter Hse.

— My Own Thoughts & Feelings: A Growth & Recovery Workbook for Young Boys. 64p. (J). (gr. 2-6). 1993. 17.95 (*0-89793-134-3*); pap., student ed. 9.95 (*0-89793-131-9*) Hunter Hse.

— My Own Thoughts & Feelings: A Growth & Recovery Workbook for Young Girls. 64p. (J). (gr. 2-6). 1993. 17.95 (*0-89793-133-5*); pap., student ed. 9.95 (*0-89793-130-0*) Hunter Hse.

— My Own Thoughts on Stopping the Hurt. 64p. (J). (gr. 2-6). 1993. 17.95 (*0-89793-135-1*); pap., student ed. 9.95 (*0-89793-132-7*) Hunter Hse.

— A Separation in My Family: A Child's Workbook about Parental Separation & Divorce. 64p. (J). 1994. 17.95 (*0-89793-154-8*); pap. 9.95 (*0-89793-151-3*) Hunter Hse.

— Someone I Love Died: A Child's Workbook about Loss & Grieving. 64p. (J). 1994. 17.95 (*0-89793-153-X*); pap. 9.95 (*0-89793-150-5*) Hunter Hse.

Deaton, Wendy & Johnson, Kendall. Drinking & Drugs in My Family: A Child's Workbook about Substance Abuse in the Family. 32p. (J). 1994. pap. 9.95 (*0-89793-152-1*) Hunter Hse.

— Living with My Family. 32p. (J). (gr. 4-6). 1991. pap., student ed. 9.95 (*0-89793-084-3*); 17.95 (*0-89793-086-X*) Hunter Hse.

— No More Hurt. 32p. (J). (gr. 4-6). 1991. pap., student ed. 9.95 (*0-89793-083-5*); 17.95 (*0-89793-085-1*) Hunter Hse.

Deaton, Wendy, et al. The Child Sexual Abuse Custody Dispute Annotated Bibliography. LC 94-17097. 96p. 1994. 28.95 (*0-8039-5861-7*) Sage.

Deatrick, W. W., compiled by. Centennial History of Kutztown. (Illus.). 247p. 1997. reprint ed. lib. bdg. 34.50 (*0-8328-6417-X*) Higginson Bk Co.

Deats, Hiram E. Marriage Records of Hunterdon County, New Jersey, 1795-1875. rev. ed. 378p. 1986. lib. bdg. 25.00 (*0-912606-28-2*) Hunterdon Hse.

An Asterisk (*) at the beginning of an entry indicates that the title is appearing for the first time.

Deats, Kim, ed. see Taylor, Ryan M.
Deats-O'Reilly, Diana. Porphyria: The Unknown Disease. 1999. pap. 17.95 (*0-9670365-0-X*) Prophyrin Pr.
Deats, Paul & Robb, Carol S., eds. The Boston Personalist Tradition in Philosophy: Social Ethics & Theology. LC 85-25863. (Illus.). xiv, 295p. 1986. text 28.95 (*0-86554-177-9*, MUP-H167) Mercer Univ Pr.
Deats, Richard. How to Keep Laughing. 107p. 1994. 8.50 (*0-9740972-0-9*, Fellwship Pubns) Fellowship of Recon.
— How to Keep Laughing: Even Though You've Considered All the Facts. 107p. (Orig.). 1994. pap. 8.50 (*0-911810-77-3*, Fellwship Pubns) Fellowship of Recon.
Deats, Richard, et al, eds. Active Nonviolence: A Way of Life, a Strategy for Change. (Illus.). 62p. 1991. 6.00 (*0-911810-78-1*, Fellwship Pubns) Fellowship of Recon.
Deats, Richard, ed. see Nagler, Michael.
Deats, Richard L. Martin Luther King , Jr. - Spirit-Led Prophet: A Biography. LC 99-51952. (Christian Living Ser.). 160p. 1999. pap. 9.95 (*1-56548-097-X*) New City.
Deats, Sara M. Sex, Gender, & Desire in the Plays of Christopher Marlowe. LC 96-40157. 296p. 1997. 43.50 (*0-87413-613-X*) U Delaware Pr.
Deats, Sara M. & Lenker, Lagretta T., eds. Gender & Academe: Feminist Pedagogy & Politics. 370p. (C). 1994. pap. text 23.95 (*0-8476-7970-5*); lib. bdg. 64.50 (*0-8476-7969-1*) Rowman.
Deats, Sara Munson & Lenker, Lagretta Tallent, eds. Aging & Identity: A Humanities Perspective. LC 98-41089. 272p. 1999. 59.95 (*0-275-96479-5*, Praeger Pubs) Greenwood.
Deats, Suzanne. The Life & Art of William Vincent. LC 97-70752. (Illus.). 120p. 1998. 65.00 (*1-889741-14-0*) Internatl Graphics.
Deats, Suzanne, ed. see Lynch, Betty.
Deats, Suzanne, ed. see Vincent, William.
Deatsman, Gerald, ed. see Rezits, David.
DeAugust, Jonathan. Blacksun Rising. 15.00 (*0-9670578-0-9*) LPT One Inc.
Deaux. Social Psychology. 5th ed. (Psychology Ser.). 1987. text, teacher ed. write for info. (*0-534-08228-9*) Brooks-Cole.
Deaux & Wrightsman. Social Psychology. 5th ed. (Psychology Ser.). 1987. student ed. 15.75 (*0-534-08227-0*) Brooks-Cole.
Deaux, jt. auth. see Wrightsman.
Deaux, Kay & Ullman, Joseph C. Women of Steel: Female Blue-Collar Workers in the Basic Steel Industry. LC 83-2434. 197p. 1983. 57.95 (*0-275-90969-7*, C0969, Praeger Pubs) Greenwood.
Deaux, Kay & Wrightsman, Lawrence S. Social Psychology. 5th ed. LC 87-15798. 650p. (C). 1987. mass mkt. 46.00 (*0-534-08226-2*) Brooks-Cole.
Deaux, Kay, et al. Social Psychology in the '80s. 4th ed. LC 83-7379. (Psychology Ser.). 700p. (C). 1984. mass mkt. 33.50 (*0-534-02926-4*) Brooks-Cole.
— Social Psychology in the '90s. 6th ed. 1993. teacher ed. write for info. (*0-534-10401-0*) Brooks-Cole.
— Social Psychology in the '90s. 6th ed. 700p. (C). 1993. text 54.75 (*0-534-10398-7*) Brooks-Cole.
Deauxville, Katherine. The Amethyst Crown. 448p. 1994. mass mkt. 5.99 (*0-8217-4555-7*, Zebra Kensgtn) Kensgtn Pub Corp.
— The Crystal Heart. 320p. 1995. mass mkt. 5.99 (*0-8217-4928-5*, Zebra Kensgtn) Kensgtn Pub Corp.
— Enraptured. (Love Spell Ser.). 400p. 1999. mass mkt. 5.99 (*0-8439-4540-0*) Dorchester Pub Co.
— The Eyes of Love. 1996. pap. 5.99 (*1-57566-035-0*) Kensgtn Pub Corp.
***Deauxville, Katherine, et al.** Masquerade. 400p. 1999. mass mkt. 5.99 (*0-8439-4577-X*, Pub. by Dorchester Pub Co) CMG.
— Strangers in the Night. 368p. 2000. pap. 5.50 (*0-8439-4749-7*, Leisure Bks) Dorchester Pub Co.
Deaver. Ascertaining Bible Authority. 1987. write for info. (*0-88027-115-9*) Firm Foun Pub.
Deaver, B. S., Jr., et al, eds. Future Trends in Superconductive Electronics. LC 78-66638. (AIP Conference Proceedings Ser.: No. 44). (Illus.). 1979. lib. bdg. 22.00 (*0-88318-143-6*) Am Inst Physics.
Deaver, Brenda G., et al. Hiking the Big South Fork. 3rd rev. ed. LC 98-19737. (Illus.). 272p. 1999. pap. 14.95 (*1-57233-031-7*) U of Tenn Pr.
Deaver, Carol. Be Like the Animals. (Illus.). 20p. (Orig.). (J). (ps-1). 1997. pap. 4.95 (*0-9656806-0-6*) Disciple.
Deaver, Gail Macomber. Every Particular Beauty: Crossing from the Depth of Despair to the Summit of Life. LC 99-164356. 126p. 1998. 10.95 (*1-881907-26-0*) Two Bytes Pub.
Deaver, Jeff. The Complete Law School Companion: How to Excel at America's Most Demanding Post- Graduate Curriculum. 2nd rev. ed. LC 91-41666. 240p. 1992. pap. 15.95 (*0-471-55491-X*) Wiley.
***Deaver, Jeffery.** Bloody River Blues. 272p. 2000. (*0-671-04750-7*) PB.
— The Bone Collector. 1997. pap. 6.99 (*0-451-19394-6*) NAL.
Deaver, Jeffery. The Bone Collector. 1997. 22.95 (*0-614-20646-4*, Viking) Viking Penguin.
— The Bone Collector. large type ed. LC 97-47194. (Large Print Bks.). 1998. pap. 23.95 (*1-56895-524-3*) Wheeler Pub.
***Deaver, Jeffery.** The Coffin Dancer. 2000. 15.99 (*0-7435-0548-4*) S&S Audio.
Deaver, Jeffery. The Coffin Dancer. Date not set. pap. 6.99 (*0-671-02606-2*) S&S Trade.
***Deaver, Jeffery.** The Coffin Dancer. LC 98-13537. 352p. 1998. 25.00 (*0-684-85285-3*) S&S Trade.
Deaver, Jeffery. The Coffin Dancer. LC 98-49000. 1998. 26.95 (*1-56895-698-3*) Wheeler Pub.
***Deaver, Jeffery.** Death of a Blue Movie Star. 2000. mass mkt. 6.99 (*0-553-58295-X*) Bantam.
— The Devil's Teardrop: A Novel of the Last Night of the Century. 1999. mass mkt. 7.99 (*0-671-03712-9*) Simon & Schuster.
— The Devil's Teardrop: A Novel of the Last Night of the Century. large type ed. LC 99-26112. 396p. 1999. 24.50 (*0-684-85292-6*) S&S Trade.
— The Devil's Teardrop: A Novel of the Last Night of the Century. 480p. 2000. reprint ed. per. 7.99 (*0-671-03844-3*, Pocket Star Bks) PB.
— The Empty Chair: A Lincoln Rhyme Novel. LC 00-24220. 416p. 2000. 24.50 (*0-684-85563-1*) S&S Trade.
— The Empty Chair: A Novel. 624p. 2000. 24.50 (*0-7432-0424-7*); 24.50 (*0-7432-0162-0*) S&S Trade.
Deaver, Jeffery. The Lesson of Her Death. 528p. 1994. mass mkt. 6.50 (*0-553-56020-4*) Bantam.
— A Maiden's Grave. 419p. 1996. mass mkt. 7.50 (*0-451-18848-9*, Sig) NAL.
***Deaver, Jeffery.** Manhattan Is My Beat. 304p. 2000. mass mkt. 6.99 (*0-553-58176-7*) Bantam.
Deaver, Jeffery. Mistress of Justice. 400p. 1993. mass mkt. 6.50 (*0-553-29733-3*) Bantam.
— Praying for Sleep. 432p. 1994. mass mkt. 7.50 (*0-451-18146-8*, Sig) NAL.
***Deaver, Jeffery.** Shallow Graves. 336p. 2000. mass mkt. 6.99 (*0-671-04748-5*, Pocket Star Bks) PB.
***Deaver, Jeffery.** Speaking in Tongues: A Novel. 400p. 2000. 25.00 (*0-684-87126-2*) Simon & Schuster.
Deaver, Jeffery. Speaking in Tongues: A Novel. 1999. text 21.95 (*0-670-86073-5*, Viking) Viking Penguin.
Deaver, Jeffery, et al. The Coffin Dancer. 532p. 1999. reprint ed. mass mkt. 7.99 (*0-671-02409-4*) PB.
Deaver, Julie R. Chicago Blues. LC 94-38195. 192p. (J). (gr. 4-7). 1995. 15.95 (*0-06-024675-8*) HarpC.
— First Wedding, Once Removed. LC 90-4184. (Charlotte Zolotow Bk.). 224p. (J). (gr. 5-9). 1990. 13.95 (*0-06-021426-0*) HarpC Child Bks.
— Say Goodnight, Gracie. LC 87-45278. (Charlotte Zolotow Bk.). 224p. (YA). (gr. 7 up). 1988. 15.00 (*0-06-021418-X*) HarpC Child Bks.
— Say Goodnight, Gracie. LC 87-45278. (Charlotte Zolotow Bk.). 224p. (YA). (gr. 7 up). 1989. pap. 4.95 (*0-06-447007-5*, HarpTrophy) HarpC Child Bks.
Deaver, Julie R. Say Goodnight, Gracie. (J). 1988. 10.05 (*0-606-04312-8*, Pub. by Turtleback) Demco.
***Deaver, Michael K.** Ronald Reagan & Me. 2000. 25.00 (*0-06-019784-6*) HarpC.
***Deaver, Philip.** Be Our Guest: Perfecting the Art of Customer Service. 208p. 2001. 15.95 (*0-7868-5307-7*) Disney Pr.
— Making Magic Work Inspiring Confidence & Motivating Your Staff. 208p. 2001. 15.95 (*0-7868-5306-9*, Pub. by Disney Pr) Time Warner.
Deaver, Philip F. Silent Retreats. LC 87-14313. (Flannery O'Connor Award for Short Fiction Ser.). 240p. 1988. 19.95 (*0-8203-0981-8*) U of Ga Pr.
Deaver, Robert. Opera Plots Made Easy. 70p. (Orig.). 1985. pap. 7.95 (*0-932665-00-4*) Deaver Intl.
***Deaver, William L.** El Macayo: A Prehistoric Settlement in the Upper Santa Cruz River Valley. 240p. 2000. pap. text 25.00 (*1-879442-74-4*) Stats Res.
Deaver, William L. & Altschul, Jeffrey H. Hohokam & Historic Land Use of the Middle Gila River Valley Uplands: The Florence Army National Guard Survey, Pinal County, Arizona. (Statistical Research Technical Ser.: No. 46). (Illus.). 176p. (Orig.). (C). 1994. per. 15.00 (*1-879442-08-6*) Stats Res.
Deaver, William L., jt. auth. see Ezzo, Joseph A.
Deaver, William L., jt. auth. see Lange, Richard C.
***Deavers, Ken, et al.** A Century of Progress... A Century of Change: American Workplace Report, 1999. Potter, Ed, ed. 93p. 1999. pap. 20.00 (*0-916559-59-9*, 2078) EPF.
DeAvila, Edward A., et al. Mexican-American Schoolchildren: A Neo-Piagetian Analysis. LC 76-11847. 97p. reprint ed. pap. 30.10 (*0-7837-6314-X*, 204602900010) Bks Demand.
DeAvila, Gerardo. El Balance Perfecto. (Serie Guia de Bolsillo - Pocket Guides Ser.).Tr. of Perfect Balance. (SPA.). 155p. 1991. pap. 2.79 (*1-56063-087-6*, 498068) Editorial Unilit.
— Murmuracion: Entretenimiento Social? (Serie Guia de Bolsillo - Pocket Guides Ser.).Tr. of Whining: Social Entertainment?. (SPA.). 88p. 1995. 2.79 (*0-7899-0011-4*, 498078) Editorial Unilit.
Deaville, Alfred S. The Colonial Postal System & Postage Stamps of Vancouver Island & British Columbia Eighteen Forty-Nine to Eighteen Seventy-One. LC 79-67392. 224p. 1980. reprint ed. lib. bdg. 35.00 (*0-88000-111-9*) Quarterman.
Deavor, William T. Deavor. Brief History of the Deavor Family in America. 100p. 1997. reprint ed. pap. 19.00 (*0-8328-8246-1*); reprint ed. lib. bdg. 29.00 (*0-8328-8245-3*) Higginson Bk Co.
Deavors, Sue, ed. see Garrett, Gregory A.
Deavours, C., et al. Cryptology Yesterday, Today & Tomorrow. 450p. 1987. text. write for info. (*0-89006-253-6*) Artech Hse.
Deavours, Cipher. Cryptology: Machines, History, & Methods. LC 89-18065. (Illus.). 518p. 1989. reprint ed. pap. 160.60 (*0-608-00559-2*, 206144200008) Bks Demand.
Deavours, Cipher & Kruh, Louis. Machine Cryptography & Modern Cryptanalysis. 259p. (C). 1985. text. write for info. (*0-89006-161-0*) Artech Hse.
Deavours, Cipher A., et al, eds. Selections from Cryptologia: History, People, & Technology. LC 97-50519. 540p. 1998. 93.00 (*0-89006-862-3*) Artech Hse.
Deavours, Cipher A. & Kruh, Louis. Machine Cryptography & Modern Cryptanalysis. LC 84-73275. (Artech House Telecommunications Library). 274p. 1985. reprint ed. pap. 85.00 (*0-608-00556-8*, 206143900008) Bks Demand.
Deayton-Groom, Virginia. Crime on the Tracks. (Illus.). 60p. (J). 1995. text 14.50 (*0-930329-89-9*) Kabel Pubs.
Deb, A. C., ed. Fundamentals of Biochemistry. (C). 1989. 140.00 (*0-89771-370-2*, Pub. by Current Dist) St Mut.
***Deb, Anjan K.** Powerline Ampacity System: Theory, Modeling & Applications. LC 00-36093. 2000. write for info. (*0-8493-1306-6*) CRC Pr.
Deb, Arun K. Demonstration of Innovative Water Main Renewal Techniques. LC 98-49384. 1999. write for info. (*0-89867-987-7*) Am Water Wks Assn.
Deb, Arun K., et al. Assessment of Existing & Developing Water Main Rehabilitation Practices. (Illus.). 186p. 1990. pap. 47.00 (*0-89867-552-9*, 90572) Am Water Wks Assn.
Deb, D. Flora of Tripura State, Vegetation: Ophioglossaceae-Staphyleaceae, Vol. 1. (International Bioscience Monographs: Vol. 9). (Illus.). 484p. (C). 1981. 50.00 (*0-88065-231-4*) Scholarly Pubns.
— Fundamental of Biochemistry. 4th ed. (C). 1990. 150.00 (*0-7855-4671-5*, Pub. by Current Dist) St Mut.
Deb, D. B. The Flora of Tripura State Vol. 1: Vegetation: Ophioglossaceae-Staphyleaceae. (International Bioscience Ser.: No. 9). 509p. (C). 1981. 70.00 (*0-7855-3243-9*, Pub. by Scientific) St Mut.
— The Flora of Tripura State Vol. 2: Buddlejaceae-Gramineae. xi, 601p. 1983. 59.00 (*0-685-59955-8*) Scholarly Pubns.
Deb, Kalipada. The Challenge of Rural Development: Five Decades of Indian Experience. LC 97-905426. 363p. 1997. pap. 250.00 (*81-7533-062-7*, Pub. by Print Hse) St Mut.
— Chinese Economy: Changes & Challenges in the Post-Mao Era. (C). 1993. write for info. (*81-207-1128-9*) Sterling Pubs.
Deb, Kalipada, ed. Soviet Union to Commonwealth: Transformation & Challenges. 315p. 1996. pap. 250.00 (*81-85880-95-6*, Pub. by Print Hse) St Mut.
Deb, P. C. Bazigars of Punjab: A Socio-Economic Study. 80p. 1987. 11.50 (*0-8364-2024-1*, Pub. by Mittal Pubs Dist) S Asia.
Deb, R. Police & Law Enforcement. 2nd ed. (C). 1989. 125.00 (*0-7855-4795-9*) St Mut.
— Principles of Criminology: Crime & Investigation. (C). 1990. 110.00 (*0-89771-160-2*) St Mut.
Deb, Sandipan, ed. The India Infrastructure Report Vol. I: Policy Imperatives for Growth & Welfare: Executive Summary. (Illus.). 49p. 1998. reprint ed. pap. text 30.00 (*0-7881-2635-0*) DIANE Pub.
— The India Infrastructure Report Vol. II: Policy: The Main Report. (Illus.). 172p. 1998. reprint ed. pap. text 35.00 (*0-7881-3791-3*) DIANE Pub.
— The India Infrastructure Report Vol. III: Policy: Sector Reports. (Illus.). 227p. 1998. reprint ed. pap. text 45.00 (*0-7881-3801-4*) DIANE Pub.
Deb, Satyen & Zunger, Alex, eds. Ternary & Multinary Compounds, Vol. TMC. 1987. text 17.50 (*0-931837-57-X*) Materials Res.
Deb, W. C. Crime Against Humanity. (C). 1992. 18.50 (*81-85565-20-1*, Pub. by Uppal Pub Hse) S Asia.
DeBach, Paul & Rosen, David. Biological Control by Natural Enemies. 2nd ed. (Illus.). 456p. (C). 1991. text 64.95 (*0-521-39191-1*) Cambridge U Pr.
DeBack, Vivien, jt. auth. see Cohen.
DeBaggio, Thomas. Growing Herbs from Seed, Cutting & Root: An Adventure in Small Miracles. (Illus.). 80p. 1994. pap. 9.95 (*0-934026-96-3*) Interweave.
***DeBaggio, Thomas.** Growing Herbs from Seed, Cutting & Root: An Adventure in Small Miracles. rev. ed. (Illus.). 2000. pap. text 14.95 (*1-883010-78-0*) Interweave.
DeBaggio, Thomas & Belsinger, Susan. Basil: An Herb Lover's Guide. (Illus.). 144p. 1996. pap. 19.95 (*1-883010-19-5*) Interweave.
DeBaggio, Thomas, jt. auth. see Tucker, Arthur O.
Debahy, Moses. Dictionary Hebrew Verbs. (ARA & HEB.). 1974. 19.95 (*0-86685-123-2*) Intl Bk Ctr.
***Debaine-Francfort, Corinne.** The Search for Ancient China. LC 99-10996. 160p. 1999. pap. 12.95 (*0-8109-2850-7*, Pub. by Abrams) Time Warner.
Debaisieux, Martine. Proces du Roman: Ecriture et Contrefacon Chez Charles Sorel. LC 89-84499. (Stanford French & Italian Studies: Vol. 63). (FRE.). 196p. 1989. pap. 56.50 (*0-915838-78-8*) Anma Libri.
DeBakey, L., jt. ed. see Manning, P. R.
Debakey, Michael E. New Living Heart. LC 97-365. (Illus.). xvi, 495 p. 1997. pap. text 18.95 (*1-55850-722-1*) Adams Media.
DeBakey, Michael E., et al. The Living Heart Diet. LC 83-10933. (Illus.). 423p. reprint ed. pap. 131.20 (*0-608-09740-3*, 206990300007) Bks Demand.
— The Living Heart Diet: Professional Edition. 424p. 1984. text 33.50 (*0-89004-672-7*) Lppncott W & W.
— The New Living Heart Diet. rev. ed. LC 95-40787. (Illus.). 416p. 1996. per. 16.00 (*0-684-81188-X*, Fireside) S&S Trade Pap.
Debakis, Melissa. Visualizing Labor in American Sculpture: Monuments, Manliness & the Work Ethic, 1880-1935. LC 98-45452. (Studies in American Visual Culture). (Illus.). 304p. (C). 1999. text 80.00 (*0-521-46147-2*) Cambridge U Pr.
DeBallester, Archimandrite P. The Subconscious Orthodoxy of the Spanish Race. Orthodox Christian Educational Society Staff, ed. 8p. (Orig.). 1978. reprint ed. pap. 1.50 (*0-938366-46-7*) Orthodox Chr.
***DeBano, Leonard F., ed.** Biodiversity & the Management of the Madrean Archipelago: The Sky Islands of Southwestern United States & Northwestern Mexico. (Illus.). 669p. (C). 1999. reprint ed. pap. text 50.00 (*0-7881-8386-9*) DIANE Pub.
DeBano, Leonard F., et al. Fire Effects on Ecosystems: It's Effect on Soil & Other Ecosystem Resources. LC 97-35835. 352p. 1998. 125.00 (*0-471-16356-2*) Wiley.
DeBarbadillo, John J. & Snape, Edwin, eds. Sulfide Inclusions in Steel: An International Symposium, 7-8 November, 1974, Port Chester, New York Proceedings. LC 75-19315. (Materials-Metalworking Technology Ser.: No. 6). (Illus.). 508p. reprint ed. pap. 157.50 (*0-608-10709-3*, 205190300013) Bks Demand.
DeBarbadillo, John J., ed. see Minerals, Metals & Materials Society Staff.
Debardat, S. Mapping the Sky: Past Heritage & Future Directions. Eddy, J. A. et al, eds. (C). 1988. pap. text 76.50 (*90-277-2810-0*); lib. bdg. 188.00 (*90-277-2809-7*) Kluwer Academic.
DeBardeleben, Joan. Russian Politics in Transition, 2 Vols. 2nd ed. 288p. (C). 1997. pap. text 27.96 (*0-669-41618-5*) HM Trade Div.
— Soviet Politics in Transition. 188p. (C). 1992. pap. text 32.36 (*0-669-28676-1*) HM Trade Div.
DeBardeleben, Joan, ed. To Breathe Free: Eastern Europe's Environmental Crisis. 266p. 1991. text 34.50 (*0-943875-26-9*); pap. text 12.95 (*0-943875-23-4*) Johns Hopkins.
***DeBarr, Deborah & DeBarr, Tony.** Take This Chance....Just Once: Letters of Today's Lonely. 125p. 2000. 14.95 (*1-893409-03-1*) LY Prods.
DeBarr, Sally, ed. see Curtis, D. Khayman.
DeBarr, Toby. Where Is Lion Yall. 32p. 1997. pap. 10.00 (*1-893409-00-7*) LY Prods.
DeBarr, Toby, ed. see Curtis, D. Khayman.
DeBarr, Toby, ed. see Peterson, Sharon.
DeBarr, Tony, jt. auth. see DeBarr, Deborah.
DeBartolo, Dick. Good Days & Mad: A Hysterical Tour Behind the Scenes at Mad Magazine. (Illus.). 324p. 1998. text 30.00 (*0-7881-5637-3*) DIANE Pub.
— Mad Tales from the School of Hard Yocks. (Illus.). 192p. (Orig.). 1991. mass mkt. 3.99 (*0-446-36203-4*, Pub. by Warner Bks) Little.
DeBartolo, Joseph A. In Further Pursuit of Trivial Pursuit. (Illus.). 444p. (Orig.). 1984. pap. 13.95 (*0-930281-00-4*) Sarsaparilla.
— In Further Pursuit of Trivial Pursuit: Baby Boomers Edition. (Illus.). 450p. 1985. pap. 13.95 (*0-930281-01-2*) Sarsaparilla.
— The Original Chicago Trivia Book. (Illus.). 250p. 1985. pap. 8.95 (*0-930281-03-9*) Sarsaparilla.
Debary, William T. East Asian Civilizations: A Dialogue in Five Stages. (Edwin O. Reischauer Lectures). 184p. 1991. pap. 15.50 (*0-674-22406-X*, DEBEAX) HUP.
— The Message of the Mind in Neo-Confucian Thought. (Neo-Confucian Studies). (Illus.). 292p. 1988. text 64.50 (*0-231-06808-5*) Col U Pr.
— Neo-Confucian Orthodoxy & the Learning of the Mind-&-Heart. LC 81-3809. (Neo-Confucian Studies). 267p. 1981. text 57.50 (*0-231-05228-6*) Col U Pr.
— Neo-Confucian Orthodoxy & the Learning of the Mind-&-Heart. LC 81-3809. (Neo-Confucian Studies). 267p. 1986. pap. text 21.00 (*0-231-05229-4*) Col U Pr.
— Self & Society in Ming Thought. LC 78-101229. (Studies in Oriental Culture: No. 4). 566p. reprint ed. pap. 175.50 (*0-608-17284-7*, 202970200063) Bks Demand.
Debary, William T., ed. The Buddhist Tradition: In India, China & Japan. 448p. 1972. pap. 10.95 (*0-394-71696-5*, V702) Vin Bks.
— Sources of Chinese Tradition, 2 vols., Vol. 1. LC 60-9911. (Records of Civilization: Sources & Studies). 578p. 1964. pap. text 22.00 (*0-231-08602-4*) Col U Pr.
— Sources of Chinese Tradition, 2 vols., Vol. 2. LC 60-9911. (Records of Civilization: Sources & Studies). 322p. 1964. pap. text 20.00 (*0-231-08603-2*) Col U Pr.
— Sources of Japanese Tradition, 2 vols., Vol. 1. LC 58-7167. (Records of Civilization: Sources & Studies). 1964. pap. text 21.00 (*0-231-08604-0*) Col U Pr.
— Sources of Japanese Tradition, 2 vols., Vol. 2. LC 58-7167. (Records of Civilization: Sources & Studies). 1964. pap. text 20.00 (*0-231-08605-9*) Col U Pr.
Debary, William T., et al, eds. A Guide to the Oriental Classics. 3rd ed. (Companions to Asian Studies). 320p. 1989. text 75.00 (*0-231-06674-0*) Col U Pr.
Debary, William T. & Bloom, Irene, eds. Principle & Practicality: Essays in Neo-Confucianism & Practical Learning. LC 78-11530. (Neo-Confucian Series & Studies in Oriental Culture). 1979. pap. text 31.50 (*0-231-04613-8*) Col U Pr.
DeBary, William T. & Bloom, Irene, eds. Sources of Chinese Tradition, Vol. 1. 2nd ed. LC 98-21762. Vol. 1. 998p. 1998. 49.50 (*0-231-10938-5*) Col U Pr.
Debas, H. T., jt. auth. see Jamieson, G. G.
Debate Study Group & Tharchin, Sermey G., compiled by. Logic & Debate Tradition of India, Tibet & Mongolia: History, Reader & Sources. 281p. (Orig.). 1979. pap. 9.50 (*0-918753-00-7*) Mahayana.
Debatin, Bernhard. Die Rationalitaet der Metapher: Eine Sprachphilosophische und Kommunikations - Theoretische Untersuchung. (Grundlagen der Kommunikation und Kognition - Foundations of Communication & Cognition Ser.). (GER.). xii, 381p. (C). 1995. 180.00 (*3-11-014708-4*) De Gruyter.
Debatin, J. F. & Adam, Gerhard, eds. Interventional Magnetic Resonance Imaging. LC 97-21329. (Medical Radiology Ser.). (Illus.). 300p. 1998. 165.00 (*3-540-62587-9*) Spr-Verlag.
Debatin, Jorg F., et al. Ultrafast MRI: Techniques & Applications. LC 97-40499. (Illus.). 270p. 1997. text 90.00 (*3-540-62765-0*) Spr-Verlag.

D

An Asterisk (*) at the beginning of an entry indicates that the title is appearing for the first time.

DeBats, Donald, jt. auth. see Bourke, Paul.

DeBats, Donald A. Elites & Masses: Political Structure, Communications & Behavior in Aute-Bellum GA. LC 90-48477. (Dissertations in Nineteenth-Century American Political & Social History: Vol. 2). 544p. 1990. 35.00 (*0-8240-9799-8*) Garland.

Debatto, David. Healthcare Hiring & Staffing. 200p. 1996. 35.00 (*0-7863-1076-6*, Irwn Prfssnl) McGraw-Hill Prof.

DeBauche, Leslie M. Reel Patriotism: The Movies & World War I. LC 96-45979. (Wisconsin Studies in Film). (Illus.). 224p. 1997. 50.00 (*0-299-15400-9*); pap. 16.95 (*0-299-15404-1*) U of Wis Pr.

DeBaugh, R. Adam. The Least of These: A Christian Social Action Bible Study. 20p. 1994. pap. 2.00 (*1-888493-10-0*) Chi Rho Pr.

DeBaugh, R. Adam, jt. auth. see Miles, Virginia G.

Debavpatnaik, P., jt. auth. see Olander, William.

Debay, Yves. The French Foreign Legion Today Vol. 1, Vol. 10. (Europa Militaria Ser.: No. 10). (Illus.). 64p. 1992. pap. 16.95 (*1-872004-87-3*, Pub. by Windrow & Green) Motorbooks Intl.

***Debay, Yves.** Les Insignes Et Brevets Des Parachutistes Francais: French Paratroop Insignia & Badges. (Illus.). 2000. 39.95 (*2-913903-11-8*, Pub. by Histoire) Combined Pub.

Debay, Yves & Peacock, Lindsay. Heliborne: USMC Helicopter Assault. (Osprey Colour Library). (Illus.). 128p. 1993. 15.95 (*1-85532-311-7*, Pub. by Ospry) Motorbooks Intl.

Debbage, Keith G., jt. auth. see Ioannides, Dimitri.

Debbarma, Sukhendu. Origin & Growth of Christianity in Tripura. (C). 1996. 18.00 (*81-7387-038-1*, Pub. by Indus Pub) S Asia.

Debbasch, J. & Daudet, Y. Lexicon of Political Terms: Lexique des Termes Politiques. 5th ed. (FRE.). 439p. 1988. pap. 49.95 (*0-7859-4781-7*) Fr & Eur.

Debbeche, Patrick, ed. see Ubersfeld, Anne.

Debe, M. K., ed. Optical Probes of Organic Thin Films: Photons-In & Photons-Out. (Progress in Surface Science Ser.: Vol. 24). (Illus.). 285p. 1989. pap. 149.50 (*0-08-036384-9*, Pergamon Pr) Elsevier.

DeBeaumont, M. Horses & Ponies: Breeding & Management. (Illus.). 175p. 1992. pap. 20.00 (*0-87556-620-0*) Saifer.

DeBeauvoir, Simone, see Beauvoir, Simone de.

DeBeer, E. S., ed. see Locke, John.

DeBeer, Lynie, see Mother Goof, pseud.

Debeer, Sara. Open Ears: Musical Adventures for a New Generation. 141p. (J). 1995. pap. text 18.95 (*1-55961-288-6*) Relaxtn Co.

Debeir, Jean-Claude, et al. In the Servitude of Power: Energy & Civilization Through the Ages. Barzman, John, tr. from FRE. LC 90-20794. (Illus.). 368p. (C). 1991. pap. 25.00 (*0-86232-943-4*, Pub. by St Martin) St Martin.

— In the Servitude of Power: Energy & Civilization Through the Ages. Barzman, John, tr. from FRE. LC 90-20794. (Illus.). 368p. (C). 1991. text 55.00 (*0-86232-942-6*, Pub. by Zed Books) St Martin.

Debelak, Don. Entrepreneur Magazine: Bringing a Product to Market. LC 96-36095. (Entrepreneur Magazine Small Business Ser.). 356p. 1997. 39.95 (*0-471-15773-2*) Wiley.

***Debelak, Don.** Infiltration Marketing. 288p. 2000. pap. 12.95 (*1-58062-263-1*) Adams Media.

Debelak, Don. Marketing Magic: Action-Oriented Strategies That Will Help You. 1997. pap. text 9.95 (*1-55850-704-3*) Adams Media.

— Product P. LC 96-36095. (Entrepreneur Magazine Small Business Ser.). 384p. 1997. pap. 19.95 (*0-471-15750-3*) Wiley.

***Debelak, Don.** Streetwise Marketing Plans. LC 00-28870. 352p. 2000. pap. 17.95 (*1-58062-268-2*) Adams Media.

De'Beldomandi, Prosdocimo. Contrapunctus. Herlinger, Jan, ed. LC 83-23367. (Greek & Latin Music Theory Ser.). 109p. 1984. text 40.00 (*0-8032-3669-7*) U of Nebr Pr.

Debelijak, Ales. Twilight of the Idols: The Tragedy of Yugoslavia. Biggins, Michael, tr. LC 94-233172. (Illus.). 86p. (Orig.). 1994. pap. 10.00 (*1-877727-51-2*) White Pine.

Debelius, Helmut, jt. auth. see Baensch, Hans A.

Debelius, Maggie, jt. auth. see Basalla, Susan.

Debeljak, Ales. Anxious Moments. Merrill, Christopher, tr. 78p. 1994. pap. 12.00 (*1-877727-35-0*) White Pine.

— The City & the Child. Merrill, Christopher, tr. from SLV. LC 99-43486. (Terra Incognita Ser.: Vol. 5). 72p. 1999. pap. 14.00 (*1-877727-99-7*, Pub. by White Pine) Consort Bk Sales.

— Dictionary of Silence. Kravanja, Sonja, tr. from SLV. (Witter Bynner Translation Ser.: Vol. 2). 80p. 1999. pap. 15.00 (*0-930829-45-X*) Lumen Inc.

— Modernity's Reluctant Exit: The Institution of Art in Postmodernity. Mestrovic, Stjepan, ed. LC 97-34770. (Postmodern Social Futures Ser.: No. 86). 192p. 1998. 55.00 (*0-8476-8582-9*); pap. 22.95 (*0-8476-8583-7*) Rowman.

Debeljak, Ales, ed. Prisoners of Freedom: Contemporary Slovenian Poetry. LC 92-61137. 180p. (Orig.). (C). 1992. pap. 12.95 (*1-881613-00-3*) Flint Mtn-Pedernal.

Debeljak, Ales, tr. see Jackson, Richard, ed.

Debell, Bob. Conciliation & Mediation in the NHS: A Practical Guide. LC 97-19156. 1997. write for info. (*1-85775-231-7*, Radcliffe Med Pr) Scovill Paterson.

DeBell, Dean S. & Whitesell, Craig D. Diameter-Density Relationships Provide Tentative Spacing Guidelines for Eucalyptus Saligna in Hawaii. (Illus.). 8p. 1997. reprint ed. pap. 1.80 (*0-89904-920-6*, Ecosytems Resrch) Crumb Elbow Pub.

***Debelle, Gury, et al.** Inflation Targeting as a Framework for Monetary Policy. LC 99-209616. (Economic Issues Ser.). 17p. 1998. write for info. (*1-55775-761-5*) Intl Monetary.

DeBellis, Jack. Sidney Lanier: Poet of the Marshes. (Georgia Humanities Council Publications). 56p. 1991. pap. 11.95 (*0-8203-1319-X*) U of Ga Pr.

***DeBellis, John.** That Face. 188p. 2000. 11.95 (*0-9700492-5-0*) Steel Pr Pubng.

DeBellis, Mark. Music & Conceptualization. (Illus.). 175p. (C). 1995. text 59.95 (*0-521-40331-6*) Cambridge U Pr.

Debellis, Robert, et al, eds. Continuing Care: For the Dying Patient, Family & Staff. 5. LC 85-19165. (Foundation of Thanatology Ser.: Vol. 5). 190p. 1985. 59.95 (*0-275-91334-1*, C1334, Praeger Pubs) Greenwood.

DeBellis, Robert, et al, eds. The House Staff & Thanatology. 1982. 18.95 (*0-405-14211-0*) Ayer.

— Medical Care of the Dying Patient. 1982. 33.95 (*0-405-13947-0*) Ayer.

— Psychosocial Aspects of Chemotherapy in Cancer Care: The Patient, Family, & Staff. LC 86-33623. (Loss, Grief & Care Ser.: Vol. 1, No. 3 & 4). 136p. 1987. text 39.95 (*0-86656-627-9*) Haworth Pr.

— Suffering: Psychological & Social Aspects in Loss, Grief, & Care. LC 85-31744. (Loss, Grief & Care Ser.: Vol. 1, Nos. 1 & 2). 196p. 1986. text 49.95 (*0-86656-558-2*) Haworth Pr.

Debello, Paul. Pocket Clinical & Drug Guide. 3rd ed. 672p. (Orig.). (C). 1992. pap. text 25.00 (*0-9627160-2-2*) Tortoise NV.

— Pocket Clinical & Drug Guide. 4th ed. 672p. (Orig.). (C). pap. text 25.00 (*0-9627160-3-0*) Tortoise NV.

DeBello, Thomas, jt. auth. see Dunn, Rita C.

Debelmas, Jacques & Mascle, George. Large-Scale Geologic Structures. (Illus.). 330p. (C). 1998. text 69.00 (*90-5410-776-6*, Pub. by A A Balkema) Ashgate Pub Co.

Debelta, Peter & Martin, Pace. SE Using SQL Server for Programming. Date not set. 49.99 (*0-7897-1522-8*, Que New Media) MCP SW Interactive.

Debenath, Andre & Dibble, Harold L. Handbook of Paleolithic Typology: Lower & Middle Paleolithic of Europe, Vol. I. LC 93-12451. (Illus.). 256p. (C). 1993. pap. text 60.00 (*0-924171-23-5*) U Museum Pubns.

DeBenedette, Valerie. Caffeine. LC 95-51807. (Drug Library Ser.). (Illus.). 104p. (YA). (gr. 6 up). 1996. lib. bdg. 20.95 (*0-89490-741-7*) Enslow Pubs.

DeBenedetti, Charles. The Peace Reform in American History. LC 79-2173. 264p. 1980. reprint ed. 12.95 (*0-253-13095-6*) Ind U Pr.

— The Peace Reform in American History. LC 79-2173. 264p. 1984. reprint ed. pap. 4.95 (*0-253-20320-1*, MB-320) Ind U Pr.

DeBenedetti, Charles, ed. Peace Heroes in 20th-Century America. LC 85-45031. (Illus.). 288p. reprint ed. pap. 89.30 (*0-608-01057-X*, 205936500001) Bks Demand.

DeBenedetti, Charles & Chatfield, Charles. An American Ordeal: The Antiwar Movement of the Vietnam Era. LC 89-21922. (Syracuse Studies on Peace & Conflict Resolution). (Illus.). 512p. 1990. pap. 19.95 (*0-8156-0245-6*) Syracuse U Pr.

— An American Ordeal: The Antiwar Movement of the Vietnam Era. LC 89-21922. (Syracuse Studies on Peace & Conflict Resolution). (Illus.). 532p. 1990. reprint ed. pap. 165.00 (*0-608-06941-8*, 206714900009) Bks Demand.

DeBenedetti, Ellen J. Conflict, Resolution & Diversity. 1993. student ed. write for info. (*0-318-72424-3*) EduPRESS PA.

Debenedetti, Pablo G. Metastable Liquids: Concepts & Principles. LC 96-18027. (Physical Chemistry: Science & Engineering Ser.). 400p. 1997. text 69.50 (*0-691-08595-1*, Pub. by Princeton U Pr) Cal Prin Full Svc.

DeBenedictis, Michel, jt. auth. see Molina, Louis.

Debeneditics, Daniel. Complete Estate Advisor. 1989. mass mkt. 4.95 (*0-671-68375-6*) PB.

DeBenedittis, Peter. Guam's Trial of the Century: News, Hegemony, & Rumor in an American Colony. LC 93-18239. 200p. 1993. 62.95 (*0-275-94516-2*, C4516, Praeger Pubs) Greenwood.

Debenham, Barbara, ed. & intro. see Debenham, Frank.

Debenham, Frank. In the Arctic: Tales Told at Tea-Time. Debenham, Barbara, ed. & intro. by. 1998. pap. 82.50 (*1-85297-049-9*, Pub. by Erskine Press) St Mut.

Debenham, Ian. A Training Officer's Guide to Discussion. (C). 1969. pap. 50.00 (*0-85171-009-3*, Pub. by IPM Hse) St Mut.

Debenham, John. Knowledge Engineering: Unifying Knowledge Base & Database Design. LC 98-9721. (Artificial Intelligence Ser.). xiv, 465p. 1998. 59.95 (*3-540-63765-6*) Spr-Verlag.

Debenham, Warren. Laughter on Record: A Comedy Discography. LC 87-35938. (Illus.). 387p. 1988. 37.00 (*0-8108-2094-3*) Scarecrow.

Debenjak, D. Modern Dictionary Slovene-German-Slovene. deluxe ed. (GER & SLV.). 608p. 1981. 39.95 (*0-8288-4669-3*, M9702) Fr & Eur.

Deber, Raisa B. & Thompson, Gail G., eds. Restructuring Canada's Health Service System: How Do We Get There from Here? 320p. (Orig.). 1992. pap. text 25.00 (*0-8020-6005-6*) U of Toronto Pr.

DeBerardinis, Dell & Fuss, Peggy. Intervention Strategies for Violent-Prone Behavior. LC 95-78362. 217p. 1995. ring bd. 79.95 (*0-914607-38-3*) Master Tchr.

***Deberg, Betty A.** Ungodly Women: Gender & the First Wave of American Fundamentalism. 2000. 19.95 (*0-86554-711-4*, P212) Mercer Univ Pr.

Debergh, P. & Zimmerman, R. H., eds. Micropropagation: Technology & Application. (C). 1991. pap. text 92.50 (*0-7923-0819-0*); lib. bdg. 213.50 (*0-7923-0818-2*) Kluwer Academic.

Deberiot, C. Method for Violin, Pt. 1. 80p. 1986. pap. 8.95 (*0-7935-4363-0*, 50326200) H Leonard.

— Three Duos Concertants Opus 57 for 2 Violins. 28p. 1986. pap. 6.95 (*0-7935-5134-X*) H Leonard.

DeBerry, Clyde E. Blacks in Corrections: Understanding Network Systems in Prison Society. LC 94-209890. 112p. (C). text 32.00 (*1-55605-242-1*); pap. text 16.00 (*1-55605-241-3*) Wyndham Hall.

Deberry, Stephen T. The Externalization of Consciousness & the Psychopathology of Everyday Life, 17. LC 90-36638. (Contributions in Psychology Ser.: No. 17). 232p. 1990. 62.95 (*0-313-27280-8*, DEG, Greenwood Pr) Greenwood.

DeBerry, Stephen T. Quantum Psychology: Steps to a Postmodern Ecology of Being. LC 92-28474. 224p. 1993. 55.00 (*0-275-94171-X*, C4171, Praeger Pubs) Greenwood.

DeBerry, Virginia. Trying to Sleep in the Bed You Made. LC 96-44194. 384p. 1996. text 24.95 (*0-312-15233-7*) St Martin.

***DeBerry, Virginia & Grant, Donna.** Far from the Tree. 352p. 2000. 24.95 (*0-312-20291-1*) St Martin.

DeBerry, Virginia & Grant, Donna. Trying to Sleep in the Bed You Made, Vol. 1. 1997. mass mkt. 6.50 (*0-312-96313-0*) St Martin.

Debertin, David L. Agricultural Production Economics. 623p. (C). 1986. 58.75 (*0-02-328060-3*, Macmillan Coll) P-H.

Debertin, K. & Helmer, R. G. Gamma- & X-Ray Spectrometry with Semiconductor Detectors. x, 400p. 1988. 158.25 (*0-444-87107-1*, North Holland) Elsevier.

Debertin, K. & Mann, W. B. Gamma & X-Ray Spectrometry Techniques & Applications. 1983. pap. 28.00 (*0-08-029159-7*, Pergamon Pr) Elsevier.

Debes, Jo A. Lower Merion Academy: Legend in Learning. 24p. (Orig.). 1997. pap. write for info. (*0-9649368-3-6*) Lower Merion.

DeBessonet, Cary G. A Many-Valued Approach to Deduction & Reasoning for Artificial Intelligence. (International Series in Engineering & Computer Science, VLSI, Computer Architecture, & Digital Screen Processing). 272p. 1991. text 102.00 (*0-7923-9138-1*) Kluwer Academic.

Debets, Reno & Savelkoul, Huub. Human Cytokines & Cytokine Receptors. (Methods in Molecular Biology Ser.: No. 99). (Illus.). 350p. 1999. 109.50 (*0-89603-486-0*); spiral bd. 69.50 (*0-89603-445-3*) Humana.

Debetta, Peter & Lynds, Joe. MS SQL Server 7 Programming How-To. Date not set. 49.99 (*1-57169-126-X*) Sams.

Debetta, Peter, et al. Microsoft SQL Server 6.5 Programming Unleased. (Unleashed Ser.). 900p. 1998. 49.99 (*0-672-31244-1*) Sams.

Debettencourt, Laurie U., jt. auth. see Sabornie, Edward J.

Debettencourt, Laurie U., jt. auth. see Vallecorsa, Ada L.

Debettignies. The Changing Business Environment in the Asia-Pacific Region. 1996. write for info. (*1-86152-310-6*, Pub. by ITBP) Thomson Learn.

Debetz, Barbara. Erotic Focus. 1990. pap. 4.95 (*0-451-16478-4*) NAL.

DeBetz, Barbara. Your Diet Coach. 224p. (Orig.). 1990. pap. 10.95 (*0-685-31174-0*) P-H.

Debevec, Anton, et al, eds. United States Documents in the Propaganda Fide Archives: A Calendar, Vol. 8. 1980. 20.00 (*0-88382-208-3*) AAFH.

— United States Documents in the Propaganda Fide Archives: A Calendar, Vol. 9. 1982. 20.00 (*0-88382-210-5*) AAFH.

***Debevec, John.** Red Dust: A Novel of the Mesabi Iron Range. 253p. 2000. pap. 13.95 (*0-595-00112-2*, Writers Showcase) iUniversecom.

DeBevec, Joseph J. The Iron Ore Miner's Son. DeRevec, Jeff, ed. 157p. 1997. 18.95 (*0-9661137-0-5*) EVC Grp.

Debever, Robert, ed. see Cartan, Elie.

DeBevoise, M. B., tr. see Birnbaum, Pierre.

Debevoise, M. B., tr. see Blay, Michel.

DeBevoise, M. B., tr. see Delacampagne, Christian.

DeBevoise, M. B., tr. see Dupuy, Jean-Pierre.

DeBevoise, M. B., tr. see Renaut, Alain.

DeBevoise, M.B., tr. see De Boysson-Bardies, Benedict.

Debevoise, Neilson C. Political History of Parthia. LC 68-56330. (Illus.). 303p. 1970. reprint ed. lib. bdg. 59.75 (*0-8371-0374-6*, DEPA, Greenwood Pr) Greenwood.

Debevoise, Nielson. The Data Warehouse Method. LC 99-221489. 420p. 1998. pap. 57.00 (*0-13-081306-0*) P-H.

Debi, Asapurna & Majumdar, Gopa. Subarnalata. LC 98-900482. (Modern Indian Novels In Translation Ser.). xxi, 213p. 1997. write for info. (*0-333-92319-7*) Macmillan.

Debi, Mahasveta & Banerjee, Paramita. Our Non-veg Cow & Other Stories. LC 98-903268. x, 115 p. 1998. write for info. (*81-7046-145-6*) Seagull Bks.

Debi, Mahasveta & Bhattacharjee, Nirmal Kanti. The Armenian Champa Tree. LC 98-903404. 54 p. 1998. write for info. (*81-7046-146-4*) Seagull Bks Ltd.

DeBiase, Christina B. Theory & Practice of Dental Health Education. LC 90-13344. (Illus.). 314p. 1991. text 36.00 (*0-8121-1366-7*) Lppncott W & W.

DeBiase, Louis A. How to Break into Politics on a Shoestring. (Illus.). 61p. (Orig.). (J). (gr. 9-12). 1981. pap. 4.95 (*0-686-31571-5*) Louvin Pub.

DeBiaso, Richard A., jt. auth. see Smith, Curtis.

Debiche, Michel G., et al. The Motion of Allochthonous Terranes Across the North Pacific Basin. LC 86-33721. (Geological Society of America Ser.: Vol. 207). (Illus.). 56p. 1987. reprint ed. pap. 30.00 (*0-608-07735-6*, 206782300010) Bks Demand.

Debicki, Andrew & Rozo, Teresa. Paisajes y Recuerdos - Snapshots & Recollections. Harpstrite, Pat & Moorhouse, David M., trs. (ENG & SPA.). 188p. (Orig.). 1994. pap. 15.95 (*1-886480-00-1*) Edici Latidos.

Debicki, Andrew P. Damaso Alonso. LC 74-75876. (Twayne's World Authors Ser.). 1970. lib. bdg. 17.95 (*0-685-42216-X*) Irvington.

— Poetry of Discovery: The Spanish Generation of 1956-1971. LC 82-40171. 248p. 1982. 29.95 (*0-8131-1461-6*) U Pr of Ky.

— Spanish Poetry of the Twentieth Century: Modernity & Beyond. 272p. 1994. pap. 18.00 (*0-8131-0835-7*) U Pr of Ky.

Debicki, Andrew P., ed. Antologia de la Poesia Mexicana Moderna. (Series B: Textos, XX). (SPA.). 305p. (C). 1977. 58.00 (*0-7293-0028-5*, Pub. by Tamesis Bks Ltd) Boydell & Brewer.

Debicki, Andrew P. & Keefe-Ugalde, Sharon, eds. En Homenaje a Angel Gonzalez: Ensayos, Entrevista y Poemas. LC 91-60337. (SPA.). 139p. 1991. pap. 40.00 (*0-89295-063-3*) Society Sp & Sp-Am.

DeBidoli, Emi. Reminiscences of a Vocal Teacher: American Autobiography. 97p. 1995. lib. bdg. 69.00 (*0-7812-8497-X*) Rprt Serv.

Debischop, Eric. Tahiti Nui. Young, Edward, tr. (Illus.). 1959. 15.95 (*0-8392-1109-0*) Astor-Honor.

***DeBitetto, James.** You & Your Puppy: Training & Health Care for Puppy's First Year. (Illus.). 2000. pap. 14.99 (*0-7645-6238-X*) IDG Bks.

DeBitetto, James, jt. auth. see Hodgson, Sarah.

DeBlack, Thomas A., jt. ed. see Adams, Julianne L.

DeBlase, Anthony F. & Martin, Robert E. A Manual of Mammalogy. 2nd ed. 448p. (C). 1980. text. write for info. (*0-697-04591-9*, WCB McGr Hill) McGrw-H Hghr Educ.

DeBlassie, Richard R., ed. Measuring & Evaluating Pupil Progress. LC 74-8974. 210p. 1974. 32.00 (*0-8422-5184-7*) Irvington.

Debler, Walter R. & Yu, Dequan. Fluid Mechanics Fundamentals: Exercise Solutions. 83p. (C). 1991. student ed. 7.00 (*0-9630281-0-3*) Marren Pub.

DeBlieu, Jan. Hatteras Journal. LC 98-14953. 181p. 1998. pap. 12.95 (*0-89587-214-5*) Blair.

— Meant to Be Wild: The Struggle to Save Endangered Species Through Captive Breeding. (Illus.). 305p. 1993. pap. 12.95 (*1-55591-166-8*) Fulcrum Pub.

— Wind: How the Flow of Air Has Shaped Life, Myth, & the Land. LC 98-16851. 320p. 1998. 24.00 (*0-395-78033-0*) HM.

— Wind: How the Flow of Air Has Shaped Life, Myth, & the Land. 294p. 1999. pap. 14.00 (*0-395-95794-X*) HM.

Deblieux, Michael R., jt. auth. see Paterson, Lee T.

Deblieux, Michael R., jt. auth. see Patterson, Lee T.

Deblieux, Mike. Documenting Discipline. Kirchner, Dave, ed. LC 95-75609. (AMI How-to Ser.). 86p. 1995. pap. 12.95 (*1-884926-34-7*, DOCUM) Amer Media.

— Legal Issues for Managers: Essential Skills for Avoiding Your Day in Court. Miller, Karen M., ed. LC 95-80142. (How-to Book Ser.). 120p. (Orig.). 1996. pap. 12.95 (*1-884926-49-5*, BEYON) Amer Media.

— Stopping Sexual Harassment Before It Starts: A Business & Legal Perspective. Kirchner, Dave, ed. LC 97-70154. (How-to Book Ser.). 112p. (Orig.). 1997. pap. 12.95 (*1-884926-75-4*, HARAE) Amer Media.

Deblieux, Mike, jt. auth. see Peterson, Lee.

Deblij. The Earth: An Introduction to Its Physical & Human Geography & Goode World Atlas Set, Set. 4th ed. 1995. text 61.00 (*0-471-13436-8*) Wiley.

— Human Geography: Culture, Society, Space & Goode's World Atlas, set. 5th ed. 1995. text 53.00 (*0-471-15309-5*) Wiley.

— Physical Geography of the Global Environment & Goode World Atlas. 2nd ed. 599p. 1995. pap. text 62.00 (*0-471-13434-1*) Wiley.

— Regions. 8th ed. 1996. text, student ed. 59.00 (*0-471-18501-9*) Wiley.

— Student's Companion to Accompany the Earth: An Introduction to Its Physical & Human Geography. 4th ed. 167p. 1995. pap. 12.95 (*0-471-14219-0*) Wiley.

DeBlij, H. J. Human Geography: Culture, Society & Space. 5th ed. LC 95-35568. 592p. 1995. text 74.95 (*0-471-03914-4*) Wiley.

DeBlij, H. J. & Muller, Peter O. Geography: Realms, Regions & Concepts. 9th ed. LC 99-36716. 656p. 1999. text 83.95 (*0-471-31424-2*) Wiley.

***DeBlij, Harm J.** Nature on the Rampage. Roland, David, ed. (Illus.). 224p. 2000. pap. text 20.00 (*0-7881-9101-2*) DIANE Pub.

Deblinger, Esther & Heflin, Anne H. Cognitive Behavioral Interventions for Treating Abused Children: Treatment Manual. LC 96-9963. (Interpersonal Violence: the Practice Ser.: Vol. 16). 208p. 1996. 48.00 (*0-8039-5928-1*); pap. 21.50 (*0-8039-5929-X*) Sage.

Deblock, Nick J. Elsevier's Dictionary of Public Health. (DUT, ENG, FRE, GER & ITA.). 196p. 1976. 175.00 (*0-8288-9309-8*, M7948) Fr & Eur.

Deblois, Albert D. Micmac Texts. (Mercury Ser.: CES No. 117). 102p. 1994. pap. 11.95 (*0-660-12907-8*, Pub. by CN Mus Civilization) U of Wash Pr.

***Deblois, Bruce M., ed.** Beyond the Paths of Heaven: The Emergence of Space Thought. LC 99-35729. (Illus.). 572p. 1999. pap. write for info. (*1-58566-067-1*) Air Univ.

Deblois, Michael A., jt. auth. see Lindsey, Alfred J.

***DeBlonde, Gautier.** Artists. 136p. 1999. pap. text 29.95 (*1-85437-291-2*) Tate Gallery.

DeBloois, Michael L., ed. Videodisc-Microcomputer Courseware Design. LC 81-22161. 192p. 1982. 37.95 (*0-87778-183-4*) Educ Tech Pubns.

D

Debnam, Betty. Big Ideas in Geography: Mini Page Resource Book. (Illus.). 32p. (J). 1994. pap. 4.95 (*0-8362-4318-8*) Andrews & McMeel.
— Help for Planet Earth: Mini Page Resource Book. (Illus.). 32p. (J). 1995. pap. 4.95 (*0-8362-4316-1*) Andrews & McMeel.
— How the U. S. Government Works: Mini Page Resource Book. (Illus.). 32p. (J). 1994. pap. 4.95 (*0-8362-4322-6*) Andrews & McMeel.
— Love Your Body, Stay Healthy: Mini Page Resource Book. (Illus.). 32p. (J). 1994. pap. 4.95 (*0-8362-4321-8*) Andrews & McMeel.
***Debnam, Betty.** Rookie Cookie Cookbook. (Illus.). 128p. (J). 2000. 6.99 (*0-517-16246-6*) Random Hse Value.
Debnam, Betty. Rookie Cookie Cookbook: Everyday Recipes for Kids. (Illus.). 128p. (Orig.). (J). 1989. pap. 7.95 (*0-8362-4206-8*) Andrews & McMeel.
— Welcome to the White House: A Children's Guide to Where the President Lives. LC 97-216344. (Illus.). 96p. (Orig.). (J). (gr. 1-6). 1997. pap. 8.95 (*0-8362-2153-2*) Andrews & McMeel.
Debnam, Rosemary. Runaway Fred. (Blue Bananas Ser.). (Illus.). (J). 1997. pap. 4.99 (*0-7497-2681-4*) Dell.
Debnath, L. Nonlinear Dispersive Wave Systems. (Advanced Series in Nonlinear Dynamics). 600p. 1992. text 121.00 (*981-02-0948-7*) World Scientific Pub.
— Nonlinear Partial Differential Equations for Scientists & Engineers. LC 97-15710. 532p. 1997. 65.00 (*0-8176-3902-0*) Birkhauser.
***Debnath, L., ed.** Nonlinear Instability Analysis, Vol. II. (Advances in Fluid Mechanics Ser.). 300p. 2000. 145.00 (*1-85312-842-2*, Pub. by WIT Pr) Computational Mech MA.
Debnath, L. & Choudhury, S. R., eds. Nonlinear Instability Analysis. LC 97-65233. (Advances in Fluid Mechanics Ser.: Vol. 12). 336p. 1997. 169.00 (*1-85312-428-1*, 4281) Computational Mech MA.
Debnath, L. & Riahi, D. N., eds. Nonlinear Instability Analysis, Chaos & Turbulence, 2 vols. (Advances in Fluid Mechanics Ser.). 2000. write for info. (*1-85312-731-0*, 7310) Computational Mech MA.
Debnath, L., jt. auth. see Myint-U, T.
Debnath, Lokenath. Integral Transforms & Their Applications. LC 95-10552. 480p. 1995. boxed set 99.95 (*0-8493-9458-9*, 9458) CRC Pr.
— Nonlinear Partial Differential Equations for Scientists & Engineers. LC 97-15710. 1997. write for info. (*3-7643-3902-0*) Birkhauser.
— Nonlinear Water Waves. (Illus.). 544p. 1994. text 138.00 (*0-12-208437-3*) Acad Pr.
***Debnath, Lokenath.** Wavelet Transforms & Time-Frequency Signal Analysis. (Applied & Numerical Harmonic Analysis Ser.). (Illus.). 388p. 2000. 69.95 (*0-8176-4104-1*, Pub. by Birkhauser) Spr-Verlag.
Debnath, Lokenath & Mikusinski, Piotr. Introduction to Hilbert Space: With Applications. 2nd ed. LC 98-17953. (Illus.). xviii, 551p. (C). 1998. 59.95 (*0-12-208436-5*) Acad Pr.
Debnath, Lokenath & Mikusinski, Piotr, eds. Introduction to Hilbert Spaces with Applications. 509p. 1990. text 65.00 (*0-12-208435-7*) Acad Pr.
Debnath, Lokenath & Riahi, Daniel N., eds. Nonlinear Instability Analysis, Chaos & Turbulence, Vol. 1. LC 97-81142. (Advances in Fluid Mechanics Ser.: Vol. 20). 368p. 1999. 185.00 (*1-85312-515-6*, 4156) Computational Mech MA.
***Debnath, Lokenath & Riahi, Daniel N., eds.** Nonlinear Instability Analysis, Chaos & Turbulence, Vol. 25. (Advances in Fluid Mechanics Ser.: Vol. 25). 424p. 2000. 199.00 (*1-85312-730-2*, 7302) Computational Mech MA.
Debnath, Lokenath, jt. auth. see Chandrasekharaiah, D. S.
Debnath, N. C., ed. Computers & Their Applications, ISCA 13th International Conference, March 25-27, 1998, Honolulu, Hawaii, U.S.A: ISCA Proceedings, CATA-98, March 25-27, 1998, Honolulu, Hawaii. 450p. 1998. write for info. (*1-880843-23-4*) Int Soc Comp App.
Debnath, Ruma. Agricultural Development in Nigeria. LC 98-915807. 185p. 1999. write for info. (*81-85163-92-8*) Kalinga.
Debo, Angie. And Still the Waters Run: The Betrayal of the Five Civilized Tribes. 417p. (Orig.). (C). 1940. pap. text 16.95 (*0-691-00578-8*, Pub. by Princeton U Pr) Cal Prin Full Svc.
— Geronimo: The Man, His Time, His Place. LC 76-13858. (Civilization of the American Indian Ser.: No.142). (Illus.). 500p. 1982. pap. 18.95 (*0-8061-1828-8*) U of Okla Pr.
— A History of the Indians of the United States. LC 73-108802. (Civilization of the American Indian Ser.: Vol. 106). (Illus.). 464p. 1984. pap. 18.95 (*0-8061-1888-1*) U of Okla Pr.
— Oklahoma: Foot-Loose & Fancy Free. LC 81-17865. (Illus.). 258p. 1982. reprint ed. lib. bdg. 65.00 (*0-313-23085-4*, DEOK, Greenwood Pr) Greenwood.
— Prairie City: The Story of an American Community. LC 98-15864. (Illus.). 276p. 1998. pap. 12.95 (*0-8061-3094-6*) U of Okla Pr.
— Rise & Fall of the Choctaw Republic. 2nd ed. LC 69-7973. (Civilization of the American Indian Ser.: No. 6). (Illus.). 1975. pap. 16.95 (*0-8061-1247-6*) U of Okla Pr.
— The Road to Disappearance: A History of the Creek Indians. LC 42-1342. (Civilization of the American Indian Ser.). (Orig.). 1979. pap. 17.95 (*0-8061-1532-7*) U of Okla Pr.
Debo, Angie & Sweeney, Edwin R. Great Apache Chiefs - Cochise & Geronimo. LC 96-76475. Orig. Title: Cochise Chirica Hua Apache Chief. (Illus.). 980p. 1996. reprint ed. 17.98 (*1-56731-091-5*, MJF Bks) Fine Comms.
Debo, Ellen W. The Shar-Pei. (Illus.). 256p. 1986. 24.95 (*0-86622-154-9*, PS-818) TFH Pubns.
Debo, Richard K. Revolution & Survival: The Foreign Policy of Soviet Russia, 1917-18. LC 78-9671. 476p. reprint ed. pap. 147.60 (*0-8357-4723-9*, 2037638000091) Bks Demand.
— Survival & Consolidation: The Foreign Policy of Soviet Russia, 1918-1921. 520p. 1992. 70.00 (*0-7735-0828-7*, Pub. by McG-Queens Univ Pr) CUP Services.
Debo, Thomas N. & Reese, Andrew J. Municipal Storm Water Management. 768p. (C). 1995. boxed set 104.95 (*0-87371-981-6*, L981) Lewis Pubs.
DeBoard, Robert. Counselling Skills. 137p. 1991. pap. text 26.95 (*0-7045-0563-0*, Pub. by Gower) Ashgate Pub Co.
DeBock, Ron. Practice What You Preached. LC 93-90373. (Illus.). 231p. 1993. 21.95 (*0-9636750-1-X*); pap. 9.95 (*0-9636750-0-1*) Fireball Pubns.
Deboeck, G. J. & Kohonen, T. K., eds. Visual Explorations in Finance with Self-Organising Maps. LC 98-11388. (Springer Finance Ser.). (Illus.). xiv, 258p. 1998. 96.00 (*3-540-76266-3*) Spr-Verlag.
Deboeck, Guido J., ed. The Trading Edge: Neural, Genetic & Fuzzy Systems for Chaotic & Financial Markets. LC 94-2364. (Finance Editions Ser.). 416p. 1994. 69.95 (*0-471-31100-6*) Wiley.
DeBoer, Anita. Working Together: The Art of Consulting & Communicating. 246p. 1995. pap. text, teacher ed. 22.50 (*1-57035-041-8*, 71WORK) Sopris.
DeBoer, Anita & Fister, Susan. Working Together: Tools for Collaborative Teaching. (Working Together Ser.). 138p. 1995. pap. text 19.50 (*1-57035-046-9*, 70COTEACH) Sopris.
DeBoer, Anita, jt. auth. see Fister, Susan.
DeBoer, Brett, jt. auth. see Jordan, Roy A.
DeBoer, Carolyn J., jt. auth. see Peura, Robin E.
DeBoer, Clara M. Be Jubilant My Feet: African American Abolitionists in the American Missionary Association, 1839-1861. LC 93-33226. (Studies in African American History & Culture). (Illus.). 288p. 1993. text 25.00 (*0-8153-1592-9*) Garland.
— His Truth Is Marching On: African Americans Who Taught the Freedmen for the American Missionary Association 1861-1877. LC 94-26421. (Studies in African American History & Culture). (Illus.). 424p. 1994. text 86.00 (*0-8153-1788-3*) Garland.
Deboer, Cy. Take a Woman's Word for It: The Dictionary According to Women. Carle, Cliff, ed. 144p. 1997. pap. 6.95 (*1-57644-066-4*) CCC Pubns.
DeBoer, David J. Piggyback & Containers: A History of Rail Intermodal on America's Steel Highway. LC 92-39181. 1992. 47.95 (*0-87095-108-4*) Gldn West Bks.
DeBoer, Frederick E., jt. auth. see Bandem, I. Made.
DeBoer, George E. History of Ideas in Science Education: Implications for Practice. 288p. (C). 1990. pap. text 22.95 (*0-8077-3053-X*) Tchrs Coll.
Deboer, Gertrude, tr. see Prins, Piet.
DeBoer, Katie. Automobile Waste Report. 175p. (Orig.). (C). 1994. pap. text 45.00 (*0-7881-0586-8*) DIANE Pub.
DeBoer, Kee & Ahouse, John B. Daniel Pinkham: A Bio-Bibliography, 12. LC 88-157. (Bio-Bibliographies in Music Ser.: No. 12). 246p. 1988. lib. bdg. 49.95 (*0-313-25503-2*, DDP/, Greenwood Pr) Greenwood.
***DeBoer, M. P., et al, eds.** Materials Science of Microelectromechanical Systems (MEMS) Devices II Vol. 605: Materials Research Society Symposium Proceedings. 2000. text 90.00 (*1-55899-513-7*) Materials Res.
DeBoer, Peter B., ed. Educating Christian Teachers for Responsive Discipleship. (Christian Studies Today). 166p. (Orig.). 1993. pap. text 23.50 (*0-8191-9071-3*); lib. bdg. 49.50 (*0-8191-9070-5*) U Pr of Amer.
DeBoer, Peter P. Origins of Teacher Education at Calvin College, 1900-1930: And Gladly Teach. LC 91-27032. (Mellen Studies in Education: Vol. 18). 120p. 1991. lib. bdg. 59.95 (*0-7734-9670-X*) E Mellen.
— The Wisdom of Practice. LC 89-34184. (Studies of Teaching in Christian Elementary & Middle Schools). 170p. (Orig.). (C). 1989. pap. text 19.00 (*0-8191-7485-8*); lib. bdg. 42.00 (*0-8191-7484-X*) U Pr of Amer.
DeBoer, Peter P., ed. Annotated List of "Chicago Tribune" Editorials on Elementary & Secondary Education in the U. S. 1852-1971. LC 92-26145. 324p. 1992. text 99.95 (*0-7734-9595-9*) E Mellen.
DeBoer, Piet, jt. auth. see Hoppenfeld, Stanley.
Deboer, Robby. Losing Jessica. large type ed. LC 94-24146. 547p. 1995. 23.95 (*0-7862-0371-4*) Thorndike Pr.
DeBoer, Warren R. Traces Behind the Esmeraldas Shore: Prehistory of the Santiago-Cayapas Region, Ecuador. LC 95-8371. (SPA., Illus.). 240p. (Orig.). (C). 1996. pap. text 29.95 (*0-8173-0792-3*) U of Ala Pr.
***Debois, J. M.** Selected Topics in Clinical Oncology: An In-Depth Study of 18 Cancers Usually Neglected. LC 00-21826. (Illus.). 2000. write for info. (*0-7923-6195-4*) Kluwer Academic.
Debois, W. E. B. Prayers for Dark People. unabridged ed. 1997. 16.95 incl. audio (*0-9645593-9-0*) MasterBuy Audio Bks.
Debold, Elizabeth. Mother Daughter Revolution: From Good Girls to Great Women. 400p. 1994. pap. 12.95 (*0-553-37418-4*) Bantam.
Debold, Elizabeth, et al. Mother Daughter Revolution: From Betrayal to Power. (Illus.). 1993. 22.95 (*0-201-63277-2*) Addison-Wesley.
DeBold, Kathleen, ed. Out for Office: Campaigning in the Gay '90s. LC 93-80847. 305p. 1994. pap. text 12.95 (*1-883665-01-9*) Gay & Lesbian.
DeBold, Richard C. The Banana Shooter. 302p. 1993. 15.95 (*0-9635185-0-X*); pap. 5.95 (*0-9635185-1-8*) DeBold Line.
Debolski, Tom & Yenne, Bill. The Ultimate Book of Beer Trivia. LC 94-71776. (Illus.). 112p. (Orig.). 1994. pap. 8.95 (*0-912517-07-7*) Bluewood Bks.
DeBolt, Alice & Shapiro, Shalby, eds. The Journal of Holistic Health, Vol. VIII. 1983. write for info. (*0-939410-12-5*) Mandala Holistic.
DeBolt, Alice & Shapiro, Shelby, eds. Journal of Holistic Health, Vol. VII. (Illus.). 120p. 1982. pap. 12.00 (*0-939410-10-9*) Mandala Holistic.
DeBolt, Aurelia J. The Nurse Log. large type ed. (Illus.). 64p. 1998. pap. 9.95 (*0-9664595-0-4*) Minute Pr WA.
DeBolt, Barbara. How to Write a Bestseller in 40 Days or Less: An Agent's Guide to Writing a Novel. 112p. 1989. reprint ed. spiral bd. 9.99 (*1-881542-06-8*) Book World Inc.
DeBolt, Gary P. & Marine-Dershimer, Greta, eds. Teacher Induction & Mentoring: School-Based Collaborative Programs. (SUNY Series, Educational Leadership). 203p. (C). 1992. pap. text 21.95 (*0-7914-1136-2*) State U NY Pr.
DeBolt, Gerald. Debolt's Dictionary of American Pottery Marks Whiteware & Porcelain. 288p. 1993. pap. 17.95 (*0-89145-539-6*, 3435) Collector Bks.
DeBolt, Nancy, ed. see Cunninghis, Richelle N.
DeBolt, Virginia. Write! Cooperative Learning & the Writing Process. (Illus.). 208p. 1993. pap. text 25.00 (*1-879097-20-6*) Kagan Cooperative.
Debon, Claude, ed. see Queneau, Raymond.
DeBon, Margaret, jt. auth. see Klesges, Robert.
Debon, Nicolas, jt. auth. see Pilegard, Virginia Walton.
***Debon, Oliver, et al.** Friends of ED: Flash 5 Dynamic Content Studio. 450p. 2000. pap. 39.99 (*1-903450-06-3*) Wrox Pr Inc.
Deboni, Franco. Venini Glass. LC 97-160487. (Illus.). 296p. 1996. 125.00 (*88-422-0613-X*) Antique Collect.
Deboni, Franco, ed. Authentic Art Deco Jewelry Designs: 700 Illustrations. (Antiques Ser.). (Illus.). 96p. (Orig.). 1998. pap. 6.95 (*0-486-24346-X*) Dover.
DeBonis, Anthony, jt. auth. see Maley, John.
DeBonis, J. Nicholas, jt. auth. see Pincus, J. David.
DeBonis, Steven. Children of the Enemy: Oral Histories of Vietnamese Amerasians & Their Mothers. LC 94-28735. (Illus.). 309p. 1994. lib. bdg. 39.95 (*0-89950-975-4*) McFarland & Co.
DeBonis, Todd, ed. see Anthony, Sensei Mark.
DeBono, Edward. Teach Yourself to Think. 1997. 25.00 (*0-7810-7107-0*, NewStar Pr) NewStar Media.
Debono, Ken. Everything Men Really Know about Women. 200p. (Orig.). 1996. pap. 5.95 (*0-9613901-5-8*, Falcon Bks CA) Ankh Pr CA.
Debono, Ken, ed. see Hoopingarner, Debra D.
Debono, Paul. The Indianapolis ABCs: History of a Premier Team in the Negro Leagues. LC 97-10304. (Illus.). 239p. 1997. boxed set 32.50 (*0-7864-0367-5*) McFarland & Co.
Debono, Roberta. The Snow Wolf. 243p. (Orig.). 1989. pap. 8.95 (*0-9613901-0-7*) Ankh Pr CA.
Debono, Roberta, ed. see Heimburger, Mary S.
Debono, Roberta, ed. see Tennant, Jennie.
Debons, Anthony. Information Science, 2 vols., Set. 1987. text 426.00 (*90-247-2808-8*) Kluwer Academic.
Debons, Anthony, et al. Information Science: An Integrated View. (Professional Librarian Ser.). 200p. (C). 1988. 35.00 (*0-8161-1877-9*, Hall Reference) Macmillan.
Debons, Anthony, ed. see NATO Advanced Study Institute in Information Scien.
Debons, Anthony, jt. ed. see Wise, J. A.
DeBoor, Carl, ed. I. J. Schoenberg: Selected Papers, 2 vols., Set. (Contemporary Mathematicians Ser.). 888p. 1988. 194.50 (*0-8176-3378-2*) Birkhauser.
— I. J. Schoenberg: Selected Papers, 2 vols., Vol. I. (Contemporary Mathematicians Ser.). 424p. 1988. 122.00 (*0-8176-3404-5*) Birkhauser.
— I. J. Schoenberg: Selected Papers, 2 vols., Vol. II. (Contemporary Mathematicians Ser.). 464p. 1988. 122.00 (*0-8176-3405-3*) Birkhauser.
Deborah M. Kolb, & Associates Staff, ed. Negotiation Eclectics: Essays in Memory of Jeffrey Z. Rubin. 362p. (C). 1998. 25.00 (*1-880711-12-5*, Pon Bks); pap. 20.00 (*1-880711-13-3*, Pon Bks) Prog Negot HLS.
Deborah, Potts. Zimbabwe. 2nd rev. ed. LC 94-178378. (World Bibliographical Ser.). 402p. 1994. lib. bdg. 82.50 (*1-85109-195-5*) ABC-CLIO.
Debord, Brigitte, tr. see Herzhaft, Gerard.
Debord, George. Rivers of the Heart. 1989. pap. 9.95 (*0-944627-35-8*) Sand River Pr.
Debord, Guy. Comments on the Society of the Social Spectacle. 2nd ed. 1998. pap. 18.00 (*1-85984-169-4*, Pub. by Verso) Norton.
***Debord, Guy.** Considerations on the Assassination of Gerard Lebovici. unabridged ed. Greene, Robert, tr. (FRE.). 125p. 1999. pap. 15.00 (*0-9662346-2-6*, Pub. by TamTam Bks) SPD-Small Pr Dist.
Debord, Guy. In Girum Imus Nocte et Consumimur Igni: A Film. Forsyth, Lucy, tr. from FRE. (Illus.). 80p. (Orig.). 1990. pap. 15.95 (*0-948688-06-8*, Pub. by Pelagian Pr) AK Pr Dist.
— Panegyric. Brook, James, tr. LC 91-34269. 104p. (gr. 13). 1991. pap. 17.00 (*0-86091-559-X*, A6394, Pub. by Verso) Norton.
— The Society of the Spectacle. 1983. pap. 4.00 (*0-934868-07-7*) Black & Red.
— The Society of the Spectacle. Nicholson-Smith, Donald, tr. from FRE. LC 89-39940. 154p. 1994. 21.95 (*0-942299-80-9*) Zone Bks.
— The Society of the Spectacle. Nicholson-Smith, Donald, tr. from FRE. 154p. 1995. pap. 10.95 (*0-942299-79-5*) Zone Bks.
— Society of the Spectacle Film Scripts. (Illus.) 136p. (Orig.). pap. 12.00 (*0-946061-06-8*) Autonomedia.
Debord, Guy & Chetglov, Ivan. Theory of the Derive: And Other Situationist Texts. 200p. 1997. pap. 22.00 (*84-89698-15-5*) Dist Art Pubs.
Debord, Guy & SanGuinetti, Gianfranco. Veritable Split in the International: Public Circular of the Situationist International. 138p. (Orig.). (C). 1989. pap. 15.95 (*0-9508380-2-0*, Pub. by Chronos Pubns) AK Pr Dist.
Deborde, Sherry. Spring Will Come. 384p. 1987. mass mkt. 3.95 (*0-373-97046-3*) Harlequin Bks.
DeBoskey, Dana S. Coming Home: A Discharge Manual for Families of Persons with a Brain Injury. (Illus.). 80p. (Orig.). 1995. pap. 12.50 (*1-882855-34-5*) HDI Pubs.
— An Educational Challenge: Meeting the Needs of Students with Brain Injury. (Illus.). 120p. (Orig.). 1995. pap. 14.50 (*1-882855-37-X*) HDI Pubs.
— Pain: Making Life Liveable. (Illus.). 80p. (Orig.). 1995. pap. 12.50 (*1-882855-36-1*) HDI Pubs.
— Working after Brain Injury: What Can I Do? (Illus.). 128p. (Orig.). 1995. pap. 12.50 (*1-882855-35-3*) HDI Pubs.
DeBosset, C. P. Proceedings in Parga & the Ionian Islands. (Illus.). 1976. 30.00 (*0-916710-27-0*) Obol Intl.
DeBourg, Austin. Working the Harvest. LC 99-207811. 1998. pap. 8.99 (*1-56043-326-4*, Treasure Hse) Destiny Image.
Debout, D. G., et al. Characterization of the Grayburg Reservoir. University Lands Dune Field, Crane County, Texas. (Reports of Investigations: RI 168). (Illus.). 98p. 1987. pap. 6.50 (*0-318-23677-X*) Bur Econ Geology.
Debouzy, Marianne, ed. In the Shadow of the Statue of Liberty: Immigrants, Workers, & Citizens in the American Republic, 1880-1920. 336p. (C). 1992. text 39.95 (*0-252-01924-5*); pap. text 15.95 (*0-252-06252-3*) U of Ill Pr.
DeBow, jt. auth. see Hughes.
DeBow, John M. Exploring the Natural World. (Illus.). 538p. (C). 1995. lab manual ed. write for info. (*1-890756-06-7*) VisionKeeper.
— Survey of Biology Lecture Outlines. (Illus.). 231p. (C). 1995. wbk. ed. 18.84 (*1-890756-00-8*, 36121-1) VisionKeeper.
***DeBow, Ken & Syer, John C.** Power Politics California. 6th ed. LC 99-42111. 241p. (C). 1999. pap. text 42.00 (*0-321-07043-7*) Addison-Wesley.
Debowski, Sharon S. Archaeological Survey of the Buttes Reservoir, Vol. I. (Archaeological Ser.: No. 93). (Illus.). 228p. 1976. pap. 9.95 (*1-889747-00-9*) Ariz St Mus.
Debowski, Sharon S., et al. Archaeological Survey of the Buttes Reservoir, Vol. 2. 288p. 1976. pap. 9.95 (*1-889747-01-7*) Ariz St Mus.
Deboy, David, jt. auth. see Ekstrom, Peter.
DeBoy, James J., Jr. Getting Started in Adult Religious Education: A Practical Guide. LC 79-88932. 128p. 1979. pap. 6.95 (*0-8091-2222-7*) Paulist Pr.
DeBoy, Jill, ed. see Litton, Burt.
Debra Ann, pseud. WomanHood - A Journey Towards Love: Discover How You Can Become a Woman of Greatness in a World Where the Mold Is Broken. 208p. (Orig.). 1994. pap. 11.95 (*0-9640854-0-2*) M J Beth.
DeBra, D. B. & Gottzein, E. Automatic Control in Aerospace. (IFAC Symposia Ser.: Vol. 9312). 572p. 1993. pap. 112.50 (*0-08-042384-1*, Pergamon Pr) Elsevier.
— Automatic Control in Aerospace, 1992: Selected Papers from the IFAC Symposium, 12th, Ottobrunn, Germany, 7-11 September 1992. LC 93-20882. (IFAC Symposia Ser.: No. 12). 572p. 1993. 203.00 (*0-08-041715-9*, Pergamon Pr) Elsevier.
Debra Sizer-Webb, Whitney. Expanded Ed, Health: Making Life Choices- (CYRT Update) 2nd ed. (Unknown Planning Family). 1999. 4975.00 (*0-538-42985-2*) Thomson Learn.
DeBraak, LaRonna. A Breath of Fresh Air: A Practical Guide for Filtering Out Indoor Air Pollution Utilizing House Plants. McDonald, Ben, ed. (Illus.). 138p. (Orig.). 1991. pap. 12.95 (*0-9630603-0-9*) LaRonna Debraak.
DeBraal, J. Peter. Foreign Ownership of U. S. Agricultural Land Through December 31, 1994. (Illus.). 50p. 1999. reprint ed. pap. text 20.00 (*0-7881-7982-9*) DIANE Pub.
DeBrandt. Bird Log Kids. 1998. pap. 8.95 (*1-885061-55-2*) Adven Amer.
DeBrandt. Nature Log Kids. (J). pap. 11.95 (*1-885061-56-0*) Adventure Pubns.
***Debrandt, Don.** Shakedown. (Angel Ser.: Vol. 5). 192p. 2000. mass mkt. 5.99 (*0-7434-0696-6*) PB.
Debrandt, Don. Steeldriver. 1998. mass mkt. 5.99 (*0-441-00520-9*) Ace Bks.
— Timberjak. 1999. mass mkt. 5.99 (*0-441-00626-4*) Ace Bks.
***Debrandt, Don.** V. I. 2000. mass mkt. 6.99 (*0-441-00716-3*) Ace Bks.
Debray, Elizabeth H., jt. auth. see Orfield, Gary.
Debray, Regis. Against Venice. Wohlstetter, Philip, tr. from FRE. LC 98-49056. (Anti-Voyages Ser.). 100p. 1999. pap. 12.95 (*1-55643-305-0*) North Atlantic.
— Charles de Gaulle: Futurist of the Nation. LC 93-46232. 256p. (C). 1994. pap. 17.00 (*0-86091-452-6*, Pub. by Verso) Norton.
— Media Manifestos: On the Technological Transmission of Cultural Forms. LC 95-51442. 192p. (C). 1996. pap. 19.00 (*1-85984-087-6*, Pub. by Verso) Norton.
— Revolution in the Revolution? Armed Struggle & Political Struggle in Latin America. LC 80-19409. 126p. reprint ed. pap. 39.10 (*0-608-15881-X*, 203076000070) Bks Demand.
— Revolution in the Revolution? Armed Struggle & Political Struggle in Latin America. Ortiz, Bobbye, tr. from FRE. LC 80-19409. 126p. 1980. reprint ed. lib. bdg. 59.50 (*0-313-22669-5*, DERE, Greenwood Pr) Greenwood.
***Debray, Regis.** Transmitting Culture. Rauth, Eric, tr. from FRE. LC 99-87716. 2000. 29.50 (*0-231-11344-7*) Col U Pr.

D

Debre, P. Louis Pasteur. Forster, Elborg, tr. from FRE. LC 97-43686. (Illus.). 560p. 1998. 39.95 (*0-8018-5808-9*) Johns Hopkins.

***Debre, Patrice.** Louis Pasteur. Forster, Elborg, tr. 560p. 2000. pap. 19.95 (*0-8018-6529-8*) Johns Hopkins.

Debreczeny, Paul. The Other Pushkin: A Study of Alexander Pushkin's Prose Fiction. LC 81-85449. xiv, 386p. 1983. 47.50 (*0-8047-1143-7*) Stanford U Pr.

— Social Functions of Literature: Alexander Pushkin & Russian Culture. LC 96-16591. 1997. write for info. (*0-8047-2662-0*) Stanford U Pr.

Debreczeny, Paul, ed. American Contributions to the Ninth International Congress of Slavists (Kiev 1983), Vol. 2: Literature, Poetics, History. 400p. (Orig.). 1983. pap. 29.95 (*0-89357-113-X*) Slavica.

Debreczeny, Paul & Zeldin, Jesse, eds. Literature & National Identity: Nineteenth-Century Russian Critical Essays. LC 77-109598. 214p. reprint ed. pap. 66.40 (*0-8357-6193-2*, 203466600090) Bks Demand.

Debreczeny, Paul, jt. ed. see Anderson, Roger B.

Debreczeny, Paul, tr. see Pushkin, Aleksandr.

DeBresson, Christian, et al. Economic Interdependence & Innovative Activity: An Input-Output Analysis. LC 95-36674. 480p. (C). 1996. 110.00 (*1-85898-388-6*) E Elgar.

Debrett's Peerage, jt. auth. see Ashe, Geoffrey.

Debreu, Gerard. Mathematical Economics: 20 Papers of Gerard Debreu. LC 82-12875. (Econometric Society Monographs). 262p. 1986. pap. text 26.95 (*0-521-33561-2*) Cambridge U Pr.

— Theory of Value: An Axiomatic Analysis of Economic Equilibrium. (Cowles Foundation Monograph Ser.: No. 17). 128p. 1972. reprint ed. pap. 14.00 (*0-300-01559-3*, Y-251) Yale U Pr.

Debreu, Gerard, ed. General Equilibrium Theory, 3 vols., Set. LC 96-12608. (International Library of Critical Writings in Economics: No. 67). 1720p. 1996. 600.00 (*1-85278-417-2*) E Elgar.

DeBrito, Alexandra B. Human Rights & Democratization in Latin America: Uruguay & Chile. LC 97-163590. (Oxford Studies in Democratization). 346p. 1997. text 69.00 (*0-19-828038-6*) OUP.

Debrix, Francois. Re-Envisioning Peacekeeping: The United Nations & the Mobilization of Ideology. LC 99-40977. (Borderlines Ser.: Vol. 13). 240p. 1999. pap. 19.95 (*0-8166-3237-5*, Pub. by U of Minn Pr); lib. bdg. 49.95 (*0-8166-3236-7*, Pub. by U of Minn Pr) Chicago Distribution Ctr.

DeBrizzi, John A. Ideology & the Rise of Labor Theory in America, 14. LC 82-12024. (Contributions in Labor History Ser.: No. 14). 196p. 1983. 52.95 (*0-313-23614-3*, DID/, Greenwood Pr) Greenwood.

Debrock, G., jt. ed. see Scheurer, P. B.

Debrock, Guy. Living Doubt: Essays Concerning the Epistemology of Charles Sanders Pierce. Hulswit, Menno, ed. LC 94-12528. (Synthese Library: Vol. 243). 336p. (C). 1994. lib. bdg. 140.00 (*0-7923-2898-1*, Pub. by Kluwer Academic) Kluwer Academic.

Debroey, Steven. South Africa: To the Sources of Apartheid. LC 88-37221. 626p. (Orig.). (C). 1989. pap. text 44.00 (*0-8191-7319-3*) U Pr of Amer.

— South Africa under the Curse of Apartheid. LC 89-22619. 660p. (C). 1990. lib. bdg. 57.50 (*0-8191-7546-3*) U Pr of Amer.

Debroff, Stacy & Feinberg, Marsha. Mom Central: The Ultimate Family Organizer. (Illus.). 192p. 1998. spiral bd. 22.00 (*1-56836-219-6*) Kodansha.

Debroise, Olivier. Lola Alvarez Bravo: In Her Own Light. Oles, James, tr. from SPA. (Illus.). 88p. 1994. pap. 17.00 (*0-938262-24-6*) Ctr Creat Photog.

***Debroise, Olivier.** Mexican Suite: A History of Photography in Mexico. De Sa Rego, Stella, tr. LC 00-39295. (Illus.). 344p. 2001. 60.00 (*0-292-71611-7*) U of Tex Pr.

Debroise, Olivier, et al. True Poetry: The Art of Maria Izquierdo. (Illus.). 144p. 1997. pap. text 29.95 (*1-879128-15-2*) Americas Soc.

Debroitner, Rita Kirsch, jt. auth. see Hart, Avery.

Debrovner, Charles M., ed. Premenstrual Tension: A Multidisciplinary Approach. LC 81-6659. 111p. 1982. 30.95 (*0-89885-019-3*, Kluwer Acad Hman Sci) Kluwer Academic.

Debrovolsky, jt. auth. see O'Grady.

Debroy, Bibeck. Beyond the Uruguay Round: The Indian Perspective on GATT. LC 96-8983. 280p. 1996. 35.00 (*0-8039-9317-X*) Sage.

Debroy, Bibek. Atharva Veda. (Great Epics of India Ser.: Veda 4). (C). 1992. pap. 3.00 (*0-8364-2774-2*, Pub. by BR Pub) S Asia.

— Foreign Trade Policy Changes & Devaluation: Current Perspective. (C). 1992. 10.00 (*81-7018-709-5*, Pub. by BR Pub) S Asia.

— Rig Veda. (Great Epics of India Ser.: Veda 1). (C). 1992. pap. 3.00 (*0-8364-2778-5*, Pub. by BR Pub) S Asia.

— Sama Veda. (Great Epics of India Ser.: Veda 3). (C). 1992. pap. 3.00 (*0-8364-2779-3*, Pub. by BR Pub) S Asia.

— Yajur Veda. (Great Epics of India Ser.: Veda 2). (C). 1992. pap. 3.00 (*0-8364-2780-7*, Pub. by BR Pub) S Asia.

Debroy, Bibek, ed. Challenges of Globalization. LC 98-908224. 1998. 38.00 (*81-220-0521-7*, Pub. by Konark Pubs Pvt Ltd) S Asia.

— China's External Trade since the Reforms. (C). 1991. 48.00 (*81-7169-107-2*, Pub. by Commonwealth) S Asia.

Debroy, Bibek & Debroy, Dipavali. The Holy Vedas: Rig Veda, Yajur Veda, Sama Veda, & Atharva Veda. (C). 1994. 32.00 (*81-7018-805-9*, Pub. by BR Pub) S Asia.

Debroy, Bibek & Debroy, Dipvali. The Puranas: Skanda Purana, Vamana Purana, Kurma Purana, Matsya Purana, Garuda Purana, Brahmanda Purana, Vayu Purana, Set. (C). 1994. 94.00 (*81-7018-806-7*, Pub. by BR Pub) S Asia.

Debroy, Dipavali. Great Epics of India: Purana, 19 vols., Set. (C). 1992. pap. 26.00 (*0-8364-2776-9*, Pub. by BR Pub) S Asia.

Debroy, Dipavali, jt. auth. see Debroy, Bibek.

Debru, Armelle. Le Corps Respirant: La Pensie Physiologique Chez Galien. Vol. 13. (FRE., Illus.). Viii, 302p. 1996. text (*90-04-10436-4*) Brill Academic Pubs.

Debru, Armelle, ed. Galen on Pharmacology, Philosophy, History & Medicine. LC 97-12154. (Studies in Ancient Medicine: Vol. 16). (Illus.). 300p. Date not set. 140.50 (*90-04-10403-8*) Brill Academic Pubs.

Debruhl, Duneen, ed. see Russ, Wilbert D.

DeBruijn, A., ed. Inter-Noise '81, 2 vols., Vols. 1 & 2. 1981. pap. 60.00 (*0-318-68797-6*) Noise Control.

Debruijn, Ernst A. & Tjaden, Ubbo R. Bioanalysis of Anticancer Drugs. 1999. 120.00 (*0-8493-8977-1*) CRC Pr.

DeBruijne, G. A., jt. ed. see Baud, I. S. A.

DeBruin, Jerry. Creative Hands-On Science Cards & Activities. 336p. (J). (gr. 3-9). teacher ed. 17.99 (*0-86653-538-1*, GA1150) Good Apple.

— Creative, Hands-on Science Experiences. 256p. (J). (gr. k-6). 1980. 17.99 (*0-916456-87-0*, GA 165) Good Apple.

— Look to the Sky. 160p. (J). (gr. 4-12). 1988. student ed. 12.99 (*0-86653-440-7*, GA1051) Good Apple.

— School Yard-Backyard, Cycles of Science. 160p. (J). (gr. 3-9). 1989. 12.99 (*0-86653-489-X*, GA1084) Good Apple.

— Science Fairs with Style. 336p. (J). (gr. 5-12). 1991. 20.99 (*0-86653-606-X*, GA1325) Good Apple.

— Scientists Around the World. (Illus.). 160p. (J). (gr. 4-12). 1987. pap. 12.99 (*0-86653-416-4*, GA1005) Good Apple.

DeBruin-Parecki, Andrea, jt. auth. see Teel, Karen Manheim.

Debruin, Richard. One-Hundred Topographic Maps. 128p. (Orig.). (C). 1970. pap. text 13.35 (*0-8331-1704-1*, 534) Hubbard Sci.

Debruine, jt. auth. see Hohmann.

DeBruine, Tim, jt. auth. see Hohmann, Luke.

Debrunner, jt. auth. see Frauenfelder, Hans.

Debrunner, A., jt. auth. see Blass, F.

Debrunner, Peter G., jt. ed. see Chan, Shirley S.

Debrus, J. & Hirschfeld, A. C., eds. The Fundamental Interaction: Geometrical Trends. LC 88-17661. (Illus.). 258p. 1988. 75.00 (*0-306-42935-7*, Plenum Trade) Perseus Pubng.

Debrus, J. & Hirshfeld, A. C., eds. Geometry & Theoretical Physics. (Illus.). x, 323p. 1991. 59.00 (*0-387-53570-5*) Spr-Verlag.

DeBruyn, Gareth, et al. Advanced ABAP Programming for SAP. LC 98-67614. (SAP R/3 Ser.). (Illus.). 402p. 1999. 69.99 (*0-7615-1798-7*) Prima Pub.

— Getting Started with SAP R/3: An Introductory Guide to R/3 Naviation & Use. LC 98-67822. (Prima Computer Bks.). 281p. 1998. boxed set 24.99 (*0-7615-1904-1*) Prima Pub.

DeBruyn, Gareth M. & Kroes, Ken. Becoming an SAP Consultant. LC 98-67706. (Prima Computer Bks.). 6p. 1999. boxed set 29.99 (*0-7615-1884-3*) Prima Pub.

DeBruyn, Randall, ed. Glory & Praise: Hymnal. 2nd ed. 746p. 1997. 10.50 (*0-915531-65-8*) OR Catholic.

DeBruyn, Robert L. Before You Can Discipline. LC 83-62446. 172p. (Orig.). 1984. 17.95 (*0-914607-03-0*) Master Tchr.

DeBruyn, Robert L. Proactive Leadership in the 21st Century Classroom, School & District. x, 360p. 1997. pap. text 24.95 (*0-914607-44-8*, 1723) Master Tchr.

DeBruyn, Robert L. Understanding & Relating to Parents . . . Professionally. LC 84-62205. 66p. (Orig.). 1985. pap. 4.95 (*0-914607-21-9*) Master Tchr.

***DeBruyn, Robert L.** Understanding & Relating to Parents... Professionally. 69p. 1999. pap. text 5.95 (*0-914607-65-0*, 1450) Master Tchr.

DeBruyn, Robert L. Welcome to Teaching . . . And Our Schools. LC 84-60402. 60p. (Orig.). 1985. pap. 4.95 (*0-914607-05-7*) Master Tchr.

DeBruyn, Robert L. Welcome to Teaching... And Our Schools. 54p. 1997. pap. text 5.95 (*0-914607-49-9*, 1490) Master Tchr.

DeBruyn, Robert L. & Benjamin, James M. Mastering Meetings. LC 83-62444. 107p. (Orig.). 1984. pap. 5.95 (*0-914607-02-2*) Master Tchr.

DeBruyn, Robert L. & Larson, Jack L. You Can Handle Them All. LC 83-62445. 320p. (Orig.). 1984. text 24.95 (*0-914607-04-9*) Master Tchr.

DeBruyn, Robert L., jt. auth. see MacPhee, Tracey H.

DeBruyn, Terry D. Walking with Bears: One Man's Relationship with Three Generations of Wild Bears. LC 99-40861. 288p. 1999. 24.95 (*1-55821-642-1*) Lyons Pr.

DeBruyn, Tracey H. Messages from Management: A Guide to over 300 Manager-Employee Counseling Situations. LC 91-62228. 247p. 1991. pap. 12.95 (*0-914607-33-2*) Master Tchr.

— Preparing Students for the World of Work. LC 88-93071. 70p. 1989. ring bd. 49.95 (*0-914607-26-X*) Master Tchr.

Debruyne, jt. auth. see Rolfes, Sharon R.

Debruyne, F. M., et al, eds. Immunotherapy of Renal Cell Carcinoma: Clinical & Experimental Developments. (Illus.). 144p. 1991. 70.95 (*0-387-52835-0*) Spr-Verlag.

Debruyne, F. M. & Van Kerrebroeck, E. V., eds. Practical Aspects of Urinary Incontinence. (Developments in Surgery Ser.). 1986. text 111.00 (*0-89838-752-3*) Kluwer Academic.

DeBruyne, Linda, jt. auth. see Rolfes, Sharon Rady.

DeBruyne, Linda K., et al. The Fitness Triad: Motivation, Training, & Nutrition. Marshall, ed. 286p. (C). 1990. mass mkt. 36.75 (*0-314-78262-1*) West Pub.

***DEBRUYNE, WHITNEY & Sizer-Webb.** Aids Unit Health Making Life Choices: Skills & Concepts 2nd ed. 1999. 26.25 (*0-538-42832-5*) Thomson Learn.

DeBruzzi, D. J., jt. auth. see Healy, J. J.

DeBry-Pexton, Patricia. Extravagance of Sentiment: Book of Quotations by Women of the French Courts & Salons of the 17th, 18th, & 19th Centuries. Mead, Irene K., tr. from FRE. (Illus.). 128p. (Orig.). 1989. pap. 8.00 (*0-9624039-0-3*, BK-20) DeBry-Pexton.

Debs, Eugene V. Eugene V. Debs Speaks. Tussey, Jean, ed. LC 72-108720. (Illus.). 320p. 1970. reprint ed. pap. 19.95 (*0-87348-132-1*) Pathfinder NY.

— Letters of Eugene V. Debs, 1874-1926, 3 vols., Vols. 1-3. Constantine, J. Robert, ed. (Illus.). 1952p. 1991. text 120.00 (*0-252-01742-0*) U of Ill Pr.

— Walls & Bars. LC 74-172574. (Criminology, Law Enforcement, & Social Problems Ser.: No. 161). 1973. reprint ed. 15.00 (*0-87585-161-4*) Patterson Smith.

***Debs, Eugene V.** Walls & Bars: Prisons Memoirs of Eugene V. Debs. (Illus.). 240p. 2000. 30.00 (*0-88286-249-9*); pap. 16.00 (*0-88286-248-0*) C H Kerr.

Debs, Richard, et al. Financing Eastern Europe. (Report Ser.). 203p. 1991. pap. 30.00 (*1-56708-075-8*) Grp of Thirty.

Debs, Richard A., et al. Finance for Developing Countries. (Report Ser.). 43p. 1987. pap. 10.00 (*1-56708-069-3*) Grp of Thirty.

Debs, Victor, Jr. Missed It by That Much: Baseball Players who Challenged the Record Books. LC 98-7486. (Illus.). 252p. 1998. pap. 29.95 (*0-7864-0508-2*) McFarland & Co.

Debs, Victor, Jr. Stil Standing after All These Years: Twelve of Baseball's Longest Standing Records. LC 96-31885. (Illus.). 264p. 1997. pap. 29.95 (*0-7864-0230-X*) McFarland & Co.

***Debski, Robert & Levy, Mike, eds.** WorldCALL: Global Perspectives on Computer-Assisted Language Learning. LC 99-44145. 364p. 1999. 87.00 (*90-265-1555-3*) Swets.

Debt Crisis Network Staff. From Debt to Development: Alternatives to the International Debt Crisis. rev. ed. 1986. pap. 3.95 (*0-89758-041-9*) Inst Policy Stud.

Debuigne, Gerard. Dictionary of Wines 1991. 4th ed. (FRE.). 400p. 1991. 35.00 (*0-8288-6958-8*, F118400) Fr & Eur.

— Larousse des Plantes Qui Guerissent: Dictionary of Healing Plants. (FRE.). 256p. 1974. 95.00 (*0-8288-6059-9*, M-6104) Fr & Eur.

— Larousse Dictionnaire des Plantes Qui Guerissent. (FRE.). 256p. 1987. pap. 28.95 (*0-7859-7688-4*, 2037300182) Fr & Eur.

Debuisson, Pierrette. Dictionnaire du Francais Regional de Berry-Bourbonnais. (FRE.). 160p. 1993. 39.95 (*0-7859-5660-3*, 2862531405) Fr & Eur.

DeBuono, Barbara A. Healthy Rhode Islanders 2000. (Illus.). 77p. (Orig.). (C). 1995. pap. text 30.00 (*0-7881-1560-X*) DIANE Pub.

DeBurger, James, jt. auth. see Holmes, Ronald M.

DeBurgh, David, tr. see Wirth, Morand.

***DeBurr, Detrick.** Deal Us In! How Black America Can Play & Win in the Digital Economy. 160p. 2000. 24.95 (*0-9701968-0-6*) Anji Pubng.

Debus, Allen. El Hombre y la Naturaleza en el Renacimiento. (Breviarios Ser.). (SPA.). pap. 8.99 (*968-16-1823-8*, Pub. by Fondo) Continental Bk.

Debus, Allen, jt. auth. see Rust, Brian.

Debus, Allen A., et al. Dinosaur Sculpting: A Complete Beginners' Guide from Dragon Attack & Hell Creek Creations. LC 96-94088. (Illus.). 102p. 1996. pap. 19.95 (*0-9651463-0-8*) Hell Creek Creat.

Debus, Allen G. The French Paracelsians: The Chemical Challenge to Medical & Scientific Tradition in Early Modern France. (Illus.). 265p. (C). 1991. text 80.00 (*0-521-40049-X*) Cambridge U Pr.

— Man & Nature in the Renaissance. LC 77-91085. (Cambridge History of Science Ser.). (Illus.). 180p. 1978. pap. text 17.95 (*0-521-29328-6*) Cambridge U Pr.

Debus, Allen G. & Merkel, Ingrid, eds. Hermeticism & the Renaissance. LC 85-45616. (Illus.). 1988. 75.00 (*0-918016-85-1*) Folger Bks.

Debus, Allen G. & Walton, Michael T. Reading the Book of Nature: The Other Side of the Scientific Revolution. LC 97-33101. (Sixteenth Century Essays & Studies: Vol. 41). 268p. 1997. 40.00 (*0-940474-47-6*, SCJP) Truman St Univ.

Debus, Allen G., et al. Experiencing Nature: Proceedings of a Conference in Honor of Allen G. Debus. LC 97-3536. (University of Western Ontario Series in Philosophy of Science). 1997. lib. bdg. 117.50 (*0-7923-4477-4*) Kluwer Academic.

***Debus, Anne.** Das Verfassungsprinzip der Toleranz Unter Besonderer Berucksichtigung der Rechtsprechung des Bundesverfassungsgerichtes. (Illus.). 268p. 1999. 48.95 (*3-631-34456-2*) P Lang Pubng.

Debus, Friedhelm & Seibicke, Wilfried. Reader Zur Namenkunde No. 1: Namentheorie. 450p. 1990. write for info. (*3-487-09290-5*) G Olms Pubs.

— Reader Zur Namenkunde Vol. 1: Toponymie. 1996. write for info. (*3-487-10229-3*) G Olms Pubs.

Debus, Friedhelm. Kleinere Schriften. 1997. write for info. (*3-487-10309-5*) G Olms Pubs.

Debus, Friedhelm & Leirbukt, Oddleif, eds. Studien Zu Deutsch Als Fremdsprache III HEFT 136/97, Bd. 3. (Germanistische Linguistik Ser.: Heft 136/97). (GER.). 170p. 1997. 35.00 (*3-487-10372-9*) G Olms Pubs.

Debus, Friedhelm & Seibicke, Wilfried. Reader Zur Namenkunde No. 2: Anthroponymie. 564p. 1993. write for info. (*3-487-09711-7*) G Olms Pubs.

— Reader Zur Namenkunde No. 3: Toponymie. xxviii, 999p. 1996. write for info. (*3-487-10228-5*) G Olms Pubs.

Debus, Friedhelm, et al. Sprachliche Normen und Normierungsfolgen in der DDR. (Illus.). xviii, 320p. 1986. write for info. (*3-487-07031-6*) G Olms Pubs.

Debus, Friedhlem & Seibicke, Wilfried. Reader Zur Namenkunde Vol. 2: Toponymie. 1996. write for info. (*3-487-10230-7*) G Olms Pubs.

Debus, Karl E., ed. see Association for Library Collections & Technical Se.

Debus, Reinhard. Untersuchungen Zum Wasserhaushalt Von Myrceugenia Exsucca und Temu Divaricatum In Relation Zur Morphologie und Anatomie der Wurzel An Uberflutungsstandorten. (Dissertationes Botanicae Ser.: Band 100). (GER., Illus.). 151p. (C). 1987. pap. 42.00 (*3-443-64012-5*, Pub. by Gebruder Borntraeger) Balogh.

Debus, Stephen. The Birds of Prey of Australia: A Field Guide to Australian Raptors. LC 98-195846. (Illus.). 160p. 1998. pap. text 18.95 (*0-19-550624-3*) OUP.

DeBuse, Lisa D., jt. auth. see Hirsch, Jeffrey L.

DeBusk, Damon K. & Ajuria, Sergio, eds. In-Line Characterization Techniques for Performance & Yeild Enchancement in Microelectronic Manufacturing, Vol. 3215. LC 98-125245. 192p. 1997. 69.00 (*0-8194-2647-4*) SPIE.

DeBusk, Damon K. & Chen, Ray T., eds. Optical Characterization Techniques for High-Performance Microelectronic Device Manufacturing III, Vol. 2877. 228p. 1996. 56.00 (*0-8194-2275-4*) SPIE.

DeBusk, Dianne, jt. auth. see Weiss, Douglass.

DeBusk, Ruth M., jt. auth. see Coughlin, Carol M.

Debussclere, Evelynne B. The Revelation of Evolutionary Events. Mitchell, David, ed. (Illus.). 93p. 1998. pap. 10.00 (*1-888365-10-2*) Assn Waldorf Schls.

Debussy, Claude. Cello Sonata, Violin Sonata & Sonata for Flute, Viola & Harp. 80p. 1993. pap. 8.95 (*0-486-27813-1*) Dover.

***Debussy, Claude.** Children's Corner & Individual Pieces. (Music Scores Ser.). 1998. pap. 7.98 (*963-8303-38-7*) Kone Music.

— Clair de Lune: For the Piano. Orig. Title: Moonlight. 8p. 1986. pap. 3.95 (*0-7935-5301-6*, 50289010) H Leonard.

Debussy, Claude. Complete Preluces, Bks. 1 & 2. 3p. 1989. pap. 6.95 (*0-486-25970-6*) Dover.

— Debussy: Images. 1999. pap. 7.95 (*963-9059-59-5*) Kone Music.

— Debussy: Preludes. 1999. pap. 7.95 (*963-9059-58-7*) Kone Music.

— Debussy Letters. Lesure, Francois, ed. Nichols, Roger, ed. & tr. by. LC 87-385. (Illus.). 384p. 1987. 42.00 (*0-674-19429-2*) HUP.

— Debussy, Prelude to the Afternoon of a Faun. Austin, William W., ed. (Critical Scores Ser.). (C). 1970. pap. text 15.50 (*0-393-09939-3*) Norton.

***Debussy, Claude.** Debussy, Suite Bergamasque Pour Le Piano, 1. 1999. pap. 7.95 (*963-9059-60-9*) Koeneman Res.

— The Essential Horn. 16p. 1995. pap. 7.95 (*0-7935-4646-X*, 50482414) H Leonard.

Debussy, Claude. Etudes, Children's Corner, Images Book II & Other Works for Piano. 176p. 1992. pap. 9.95 (*0-486-27145-5*) Dover.

***Debussy, Claude.** Etudes Piano. 1999. pap. text 7.95 (*963-9059-57-9*) Kone Music.

Debussy, Claude. Images Jeux & the Martyrdom of St. Sebastian (Suite) in Full Score. 400p. 1992. pap. 18.95 (*0-486-27101-3*) Dover.

— La Mer the Sea. 1998. 3.95 (*0-486-29848-5*, 741731Q) Dover.

— Monsieur Croche, Antidilettante. 212p. 1977. 18.95 (*0-8369-2897-0*) Ayer.

— Monsieur Croche, the Dilettante Hater. 212p. 1990. lib. bdg. 69.00 (*0-7812-9059-7*) Rprt Serv.

— Pelleas & Melisande. John, Nicholas, ed. Mac Donald, Hugh, tr. from FRE. (English National Opera Guide Series: Bilingual Libretto, Articles: No. 9). (Illus.). 128p. (Orig.). 1982. pap. 9.95 (*0-7145-3906-6*) Riverrun NY.

Debussy, Claude. Pelleas & Melisande Librettos. 56p. 1986. pap. 4.95 (*0-7935-1547-5*, 50339970) H Leonard.

Debussy, Claude. Pelleas et Melisande in Full Score. (Music Scores to Play & Study Ser.). 416p. 1985. reprint ed. pap. 18.95 (*0-486-24825-9*) Dover.

Debussy, Claude. Petite Suite: 2 Pianos, 4 Hands. 40p. 1986. pap. 4.95 (*0-7935-5111-0*, 50262320) H Leonard.

Debussy, Claude. Piano Music, 1888-1905. 5th ed. 175p. 1974. pap. 7.95 (*0-486-22771-5*) Dover.

***Debussy, Claude.** Prelude a "l'Apres-MIDI d'Un Faune"/Trois Nocturnes. (Miniature Scores Ser.). 1999. pap. 4.95 (*0-486-40865-5*) Dover.

Debussy, Claude. Preludes Bk. 1: The Autograph Score, Book 1. 48p. 1988. pap. 8.95 (*0-486-25549-2*) Dover.

Debussy, Claude. Preludes for Piano, Set, Bks. 1 & 2. 160p. 1991. per. 14.95 (*0-7935-0435-X*, 50480346) H Leonard.

— Reverie: Piano Solo. 8p. 1986. pap. 3.95 (*0-7935-0586-0*, 50281810) H Leonard.

Debussy, Claude. Selected Short Works for Piano Solo: Centennial Edition. 152p. 1993. 10.95 (*0-7935-2966-2*) H Leonard.

— Songs, 1880 to 1904. Benson, Rita, ed. 175p. (Orig.). 1998. pap. 8.95 (*0-486-24131-9*) Dover.

— Songs of Claude Debussy Vol. 1: High Voice. 168p. 1993. per. 18.95 (*0-7935-2987-5*, 00660164) H Leonard.

— Songs of Claude Debussy Vol. 2: Medium Voice. 184p. 1993. per. 18.95 (*0-7935-2962-X*, 00660283) H Leonard.

Debussy, Claude. Suite Pour le Piano. 32p. 1987. pap. 4.95 (*0-7935-5110-2*, 50480159) H Leonard.

Debussy, Claude. Three Great Orchestral Works in Full Score. 279p. 1983. pap. 13.95 (*0-486-24441-5*) Dover.

Debussy, Claude. Twelve Etudes for the Piano: Centennial Edition. 64p. 1994. pap. 7.95 (*0-7935-3158-6*) H Leonard.

Debussy, Claude. Works for Piano Four Hands & Two Pianos, Ser. I. 144p. 1992. pap. 9.95 (*0-486-26974-4*) Dover.

— Works for Piano Four Hands & Two Pianos, Ser. II. 144p. 1992. pap. 8.95 (*0-486-26975-2*) Dover.

D

An Asterisk (*) at the beginning of an entry indicates that the title is appearing for the first time.

Debussy, Claude & Ravel, Maurice. String Quartet by Debussy & Ravel/Claude Debussy: Quartet in G Minor, Op. 10/Maurice Ravel: Quartet in F Major. 112p. 1987. pap. 7.95 (*0-486-25231-0*) Dover.

Debussy, Claude, et al. Three Classics in the Aesthetic of Music. 188p. 1962. pap. 6.95 (*0-486-20320-4*) Dover.

DeBustamante, Rafael C., tr. see MacArthur, John F., Jr.

DeButts, Mary C., ed. Growing up in the 1850s: The Journal of Agnes Lee. LC 84-10452. (Illus.). xx, 151p. 1984. pap. 10.95 (*0-8078-4243-5*) U of NC Pr.

***Debuvitz, William.** College Physics Lab Manual. 320p. (C). 2000. spiral bd. 21.95 (*0-7872-7318-X*) Kendall-Hunt.

***DeBuys, Virginia, ed.** Home Rules & Homework Tools: Your Guide to a Simple Homework System. (Illus.). 54p. 2000. pap. write for info. (*0-9676970-0-X*, Pub. by M S Wendt) Acalogic Inc.

DeBuys, William. Salt Dreams: Land & Water in Low-Down California. LC 99-6422. (Illus.). 400p. 1999. 35.00 (*0-8263-2126-7*) U of NM Pr.

DeBuys, William & Harris, Alex. River of Traps: A Village Life. (Illus.). 238p. (C). 1996. reprint ed. pap. 15.95 (*0-8263-1680-8*) U of NM Pr.

Debye, Kristina E., jt. auth. see Mather, Cynthia L.

Debye, Peter J. The Collected Papers of Peter J. W. Debye. LC 87-36895. xxi, 700p. 1988. reprint ed. 95.00 (*0-918024-58-7*) Ox Bow.

Debyser, Z. Viral DNA Synthesis: HIV-1 Reverse Transcription & DNA Synthesis at the Replication Fork of Bacteriophage T-7. No. 77. 218p. (Orig.). 1994. pap. 52.50 (*90-6186-600-6*, Pub. by Leuven Univ) Coronet Bks.

Dec, Jennifer & Landis, Lauren. Children in Crisis. (Illus.). 28p. 1998. pap. write for info. (*1-888393-01-7*) Save the Children.

Dec, Maryann, ed. see Coyne, Jim.

Dec, Myra & Dec, Sam. Wilderness Tails: A Book to Color, Poetry to Share. 32p. (J). (ps-3). 1993. pap. 3.50 (*0-9638192-0-8*) Quinn Pubng.

Dec, Robert J. After Dark: A Comprehensive Guide to Dining & Evening Entertainment. 3rd ed. (Illus.). Date not set. pap. 4.95 (*0-9671547-0-7*) After Dark Pubns.

Dec, Sam, jt. auth. see Dec, Myra.

D'Eca, Raul, jt. ed. see Hanke, Lewis.

Decade of Indigenous People Staff, jt. auth. see United Nations Staff.

Decahors, Jean E. Dictionnaire Francais-Latin. 1957. write for info. (*0-7859-7782-1*, 2218005301) Fr & Eur.

Decalmer, Peter & Glendenning, Frank. The Mistreatment of Elderly People. 2nd ed. LC 97-66778. 256p. 1997. text 85.00 (*0-7619-5262-4*); pap. text 29.95 (*0-7619-5263-2*) Sage.

Decalmer, Peter & Glendenning, Frank, eds. The Mistreatment of Elderly People. (Illus.). 224p. (C). 1993. text 59.95 (*0-8039-8712-9*); pap. text 19.95 (*0-8039-8713-7*) Sage.

Decalo, Samuel. Burkina Faso. LC 95-114752. (World Bibliographical Ser.). 153p. 1994. lib. bdg. 48.50 (*1-85109-214-5*) ABC-CLIO.

— Cinl-Military Relations in Africa. LC 97-75223. (African Studies Ser.: No. 3). 216p. 1998. pap. 24.95 (*1-890357-03-0*, 299-3643) Fla Acad Pr.

— Civil-Military Relations in Africa. LC 97-75223. (African Studies: Vol. 3). 216p. 1998. 35.00 (*1-890357-04-9*) Fla Acad Pr.

— Coups & Army Rule in Africa: Motivation & Constraints. 2nd ed. 368p. (C). 1990. 47.50 (*0-300-04043-1*) Yale U Pr.

— Historical Dictionary of Benin. 3rd ed. LC 94-17082. (African Historical Dictionaries Ser.: No. 61). (Illus.). 604p. 1995. 94.00 (*0-8108-2905-3*) Scarecrow.

— Historical Dictionary of Chad. 2nd ed. (African Historical Dictionaries Ser.: No. 13). (Illus.). 570p. 1987. 50.00 (*0-8108-1937-6*) Scarecrow.

— Historical Dictionary of Chad. 3rd ed. LC 96-38910. (African Historical Dictionaries Ser.). 1997. 95.00 (*0-8108-3253-4*) Scarecrow.

— Historical Dictionary of Niger. 3rd ed. LC 95-52222. (African Historical Dictionaries Ser.: No. 20). 1996. text 94.50 (*0-8108-3136-8*) Scarecrow.

— Historical Dictionary of Togo. 3rd ed. LC 95-44920. (African Historical Dictionaries Ser.). 420p. 1996. 84.00 (*0-8108-3073-6*) Scarecrow.

— Israel & Africa: Forty Years, 1956-1996. LC 97-75052. (Middle East Ser.: Vol. 1). 206p. 1998. pap. 23.95 (*1-890357-01-4*) Fla Acad Pr.

— Malawi. 2nd rev. ed. LC 96-192626. (World Bibliographical Ser.). 220p. 1995. lib. bdg. 62.00 (*1-85109-238-2*) ABC-CLIO.

— Psychoses of Power: African Personal Dictatorships. 2nd rev. ed. LC 97-75225. (African Studies Ser.: Vol. 3). 320p. 1998. 49.95 (*1-890357-02-2*, SAN 299-3643) Fla Acad Pr.

— The Stable Minority: Civilian Rule in Africa, 1960-1990. LC 97-75050. (Africa Ser.: Vol. 1). 344p. 1998. 47.50 (*1-890357-00-6*) Fla Acad Pr.

Decalo, Samuel, et al. Historical Dictionary of Congo. 448p. 1995. 79.50 (*0-8108-3116-3*) Scarecrow.

DeCalves, Don A., et al. The Narrative of Don Alonso DeCalves, John Van Delure & Capt, James Vanleason. LC 96-27267. 1996. 19.95 (*0-87770-582-8*); pap. 14.95 (*0-87770-583-6*) Ye Galleon.

DeCamp, Graydon. The Grand Old Lady of Vine Street: A History of the Cincinnati Enquirer. Doherty, J. Dennis, ed. (Illus.). 176p. (Orig.). 1991. pap. 14.95 (*0-9630442-0-6*) Cinc Equirer.

DeCamp, Graydon & DeCamp, Sherri. Connoisseur up North: A Food-Lover's Guide to Northern Michigan. (Illus.). 224p. (Orig.). 1996. pap. 17.95 (*0-9651442-0-8*) Bayshore Prtnrs.

DeCamp, J. M. DeCamp: Record of the Descendants of Ezekial & Mary Baker DeCamp of Butler Co. Ohio. (Illus.). 177p. 1991. reprint ed. pap. 24.00 (*0-8328-1898-4*); reprint ed. lib. bdg. 34.00 (*0-8328-1897-6*) Higginson Bk Co.

DeCamp, John W. The Franklin Cover-Up: Child Abuse, Satanism & Murder in Nebraska. LC 92-70074. 324p. 1992. pap. 9.95 (*0-9632158-0-9*) AWT Inc.

DeCamp, Sherri, jt. auth. see DeCamp, Graydon.

DeCamp, Suzanne. Linguistic Minorities of New York City. LC 92-195680. 77p. 1991. pap. 9.00 (*0-88156-114-2*) Comm Serv Soc NY.

— Selected New York City Public School Data, 1993-1994. 9th ed. 116p. 1994. 9.00 (*0-88156-168-1*) Comm Serv Soc NY.

DeCampo, John F., jt. auth. see Lau, Laurence S.

Decamps, H., jt. ed. see Naiman, Robert J.

DeCandido, Keith, jt. ed. see Sherman, Josepha.

DeCandido, Keith R. & Nieto, Jose R. Spider-Man: Venom's Wrath. (Spider-Man Ser.). 352p. 1998. pap. 6.99 (*0-425-16574-4*) Blvd Books.

DeCandido, Keith R., ed. see Gilman, Laura A.

Decandido, Keith R.A. The Xander Years, Vol. 1. (Buffy the Vampire Slayer Ser.: Vol. 8). (YA). (gr. 7 up). 1999. per. 4.99 (*0-671-02629-1*) S&S Trade.

— Young Hercules. (J). 1999. per. 3.99 (*0-671-03554-1*) S&S Childrens.

— Young Hercules, Vol. 2. 145p. (J). 1999. per. 3.99 (*0-671-03552-5*) PB.

DeCandido, Robert. Preservation Planning Program Resource Guides: Collections Conservation. 134p. 1993. pap. 15.00 (*0-918006-67-8*) ARL.

Decaneas, Anthony. Bradford Washburn: Mountain Photography. LC 99-6783. (Illus.). 144p. 1999. 60.00 (*0-89886-689-8*) Mountaineers.

— Bradford Washburn: Mountain Photography. (Illus.). 144p. 2000. pap. 29.95 (*0-89886-690-1*) Mountaineers.

— Pavlia, Portrait of a Greek Village. (Illus.). 128p. (Orig.). 1987. 39.95 (*0-945149-00-X*); pap. 22.95 (*0-945149-01-8*) Panopticon Pr.

DeCapite, Michael. Sitting Pretty. (Illus.). 36p. 1999. pap. 5.95 (*0-9666328-3-4*) CUZ Ed.

— Through the Windshield. LC 98-96545. 457 p. 1998. write for info. (*0-9666592-0-1*) Sparkle St Bks.

***DeCapite, Raymond.** Go Very Highly Trippingly To & Fro/The Stretch Run: Two Novels. 280p. 2000. pap. 14.95 (*0-9666592-1-X*) Sparkle St Bks.

DeCaprio, Annie. A Modern Approach to Business English. LC 73-90044. 1974. pap. text. write for info. (*0-672-96102-4*) Macmillan.

— A Modern Approach to Business Spelling. LC 73-86847. 1974. teacher ed. 5.00 (*0-672-26105-7*, Bobbs); pap. text 10.70 (*0-672-96104-0*, Bobbs) Macmillan.

— A Modern Approach to Business Spelling. 2nd ed. LC 78-3421. 1979. teacher ed. write for info. (*0-672-97207-7*); pap. text. write for info. (*0-672-97206-9*) Macmillan.

DeCaprio, Beth. Guilt-Free Gourmet Secrets Made Simple. Geiskopf-Hadler, Susann, ed. (Illus.). 160p. 1996. pap. 15.95 (*0-9653475-0-8*) Calif Fresh Baking.

DeCapua, Sarah. J. C. Watts: Character Counts. LC 97-50394. (Community Builders Ser.). (J). 1998. 23.00 (*0-516-21130-7*) Childrens.

DeCapua, Sarah, ed. see Alter, Judy.

DeCapua, Sarah, ed. see Collins, Mary.

DeCapua, Sarah, ed. see January, Brendan.

DeCapua, Sarah, ed. see Kalbacken, Joan.

DeCapua, Sarah, ed. see Nelson, Sharlene & Nelson, Ted.

DeCapua, Sarah, ed. see Simon, Charnan.

Decareau, Robert V. Microwave Foods: New Product Development. 213p. 1992. 50.00 (*0-917678-30-3*) Food & Nut Pr.

— Microwaves in the Food Processing Industry. (Food Science & Technology Ser.). 1985. text 94.00 (*0-12-208430-6*) Acad Pr.

Decarie, Therese G. Intelligence & Affectivity in Early Childhood: An Experimental Study of Jean Piaget's Object Concept & Object Relations. LC 65-28439. 230p. (Orig.). 1966. 35.00 (*0-8236-2720-9*) Intl Univs Pr.

Decarie, Therese G., et al. The Infant's Reaction to Strangers. Diamanti, Joyce, tr. from FRE. LC 73-8080. (Illus.). 238p. (Orig.). (C). 1973. 35.00 (*0-8236-2650-4*) Intl Univs Pr.

DeCario, Joseph W. Property Management in California. 2nd ed. (Illus.). (Orig.). 1987. pap. 24.95 (*0-317-61553-X*) JD Pub & Seminars.

DeCarle, Donald. Watch & Clock Encyclopedia. (Illus.). 1959. 35.00 (*0-685-22155-5*) Wehman.

Decarli, A., et al, eds. Statistical Modelling. (Lecture Notes in Statistics Ser.: Vol. 57). ix, 343p. 1989. 70.95 (*0-387-97097-5*) Spr-Verlag.

DeCarlo, Adeline Catherine & Seelman, Anne Daniels. Reflections in the Mirror of Time. Date not set. 10.00 (*1-929342-10-1*) Olde Ridge Bk.

DeCarlo, Elisa. The Devil You Say. 192p. (Orig.). 1993. mass mkt. 4.50 (*0-380-76993-X*, Avon Bks) Morrow Avon.

— Strong Spirits. 160p. (Orig.). 1994. mass mkt. 4.50 (*0-380-77405-4*, Avon Bks) Morrow Avon.

DeCarlo, Emily G. Let It Shine: A Tribute To . . . LC 92-53713. 37p. (Orig.). 1993. pap. 6.95 (*0-936026-31-6*) R&M Pub Co.

DeCarlo, Joseph W. Property Management. LC 96-41969. 368p. (C). 1996. pap. text 39.80 (*0-13-257262-1*) P-H.

— Property Management in California. 6th ed. (Illus.). (Orig.). (C). 1996. pap. 24.95 (*0-937841-01-3*) JD Pub & Seminars.

— Real Estate: Adventures, Principles & Practices. (Orig.). (C). 1993. pap. 14.95 (*0-937841-09-9*) JD Pub & Seminars.

DeCarlo, Montez & Cunningham, Teresa, eds. Our Sacred Identity: The Book of American Indian Names & Their Meanings. (Illus.). 95p. (Orig.). (YA). (gr. 10 up). 1995. pap. 12.95 (*0-9648416-0-6*) Nat Exper.

Decarlo, R. A. & Saeks, R. Interconnected Dynamical Systems. (Electrical Engineering & Electronics Ser.: Vol. 10). (Illus.). 528p. 1981. text 190.00 (*0-8247-5639-3*) Dekker.

***Decarmo.** Core Java Media Frame Work. LC 99-21037. 500p. 1999. pap. text 44.99 (*0-13-011519-3*) P-H.

Decarnin, Camilla, tr. see Holdt, Jacob.

Decaro, Frank. A Boy Named Phyllis: A Surburban Memoir. 1996. 22.95 (*0-201-40967-4*) Addison-Wesley.

— Unmistakably Mackie: The Fashion & Fantasy of Bob Mackie. (Illus.). 144p. 1999. 45.00 (*0-7893-0373-6*, Pub. by Universe) St Martin.

DeCaro, Louis A., Jr. Malcolm & the Cross: The Nation of Islam, Malcolm X, & Christianity. LC 98-19687. 282p. 1998. 29.95 (*0-8147-1860-4*) NYU Pr.

Decaro, Louis A. Malcolm & the Cross: The Nation of Islam, Malcolm X, & Christianity. pap. text 18.50 (*0-8147-1932-5*) NYU Pr.

Decaro, Louis A. On the Side of My People. 1997. pap. text 19.00 (*0-8147-1891-4*) NYU Pr.

Decaro, Louis A., Jr. On the Side of My People: A Religious Life of Malcolm X. (Illus.). 328p. (C). 1995. text 45.00 (*0-8147-1864-7*) NYU Pr.

DeCaro, Louis A., Jr., jt. ed. see Carle, Robert D.

Decarpentry. Piaffer & Passage. LC 98-22033. (Masters of Horsemanship Ser.). 1998. 26.95 (*0-939481-51-0*) Half Halt Pr.

Decarpigny, J. N., jt. ed. see Hamonic, B. F.

***DeCarrico, Jeanette.** The Structure of English: Studies in Form & Function for Language Teaching. 232p. (C). 2000. pap. text 21.95 (*0-472-08602-2*, 08602); pap. text, wbk. ed. 18.95 (*0-472-08631-6*, 08631) U of Mich Pr.

DeCarrico, Jeanette S. The Structure of English: Studies in Form & Function for Language Teaching. (Illus.). 330p. (C). write for info. (*0-472-08652-9*) U of Mich Pr.

DeCarteret, Mark. Review: A Book of Poems. (Illus.). 88p. (Orig.). 1995. pap. 8.95 (*1-886963-01-0*) Kettle of Fish.

DeCarteret, Mark, ed. see Agran, Rick & Crill, Hildred.

DeCarvalho, C. A. Environmental Education in Protected Areas: International Perspectives & Experiences. Filho, Walter L. et al, eds. LC 97-24534. (Illus.). 158p. 1998. pap. 35.00 (*1-85070-004-4*) Prthnon Pub.

DeCarvalho, Roy J. The Founders of Humanistic Psychology. LC 91-444. 232p. 1991. 59.95 (*0-275-94008-X*, C4008, Praeger Pubs) Greenwood.

— The Growth Hypothesis in Psychology: The Humanistic Psychology of Abraham Maslow & Carl Rogers. LC 91-17536. 180p. 1991. pap. 59.95 (*0-7734-9908-3*) E Mellen.

DeCarvalho, Sergio. The Definitive Work on the Origins of Human Lymphomas. LC 84-72903. 148p. 1985. 19.50 (*0-930376-40-4*) Chem-Orbital.

— Immunohomeostatic Disorders: An Inquiry into the Origins of Human Lymphomas. LC 81-82445. 81p. 1982. 11.90 (*0-930376-36-6*) Chem-Orbital.

Decary, F., jt. ed. see Rock, Gail A.

Decary, Francine & Rock, Gail A., eds. Platelet Serology. (Current Studies in Hematology & Blood Transfusion: No. 52). (Illus.). vii, 124p. 1986. 85.25 (*3-8055-4208-9*) S Karger.

Decary, Marie. Amour Reglisse et Chocolat. (Novels in the Roman Jeunesse Ser.). (FRE.). 96p. (J). (gr. 4-7). 1985. pap. 8.95 (*2-89021-051-0*, Pub. by La Courte Ech) Firefly Bks Ltd.

— Au Pays des Toucans Marrants. (Novels in the Roman Jeunesse Ser.). (FRE.). 96p. (J). (gr. 4-7). 1992. pap. 8.95 (*2-89021-170-3*, Pub. by La Courte Ech) Firefly Bks Ltd.

— L' Incroyable Destinee. (Novels in the Roman Plus Ser.). (FRE.). 160p. (YA). (gr. 8 up). 1993. pap. 8.95 (*2-89021-194-0*, Pub. by La Courte Ech) Firefly Bks Ltd.

— Nuisance Publik. (Novels in the Roman Plus Ser.). (FRE., Illus.). 160p. (YA). (gr. 8 up). 1995. pap. 8.95 (*2-89021-249-1*, Pub. by La Courte Ech) Firefly Bks Ltd.

Decasaris, Janet, jt. ed. see Kirschner, Carl.

DeCastell, Suzanne, et al. Language, Authority & Criticism: Readings on the School Textbook. 380p. 1989. 99.95 (*1-85000-365-3*, Falmer Pr); pap. 44.95 (*1-85000-366-1*, Falmer Pr) Taylor & Francis.

DeCastro, Luque, jt. auth. see Valcarcel, M.

Decastro, Norma. Mental Health Nursing. 496p. (C). 1994. pap. text, per. 47.95 (*0-8403-9677-5*) Kendall-Hunt.

DeCastroverde, Waldo. Que la Patria Se Sienta Orgullosa: Memorias de una Lucha Sin Fin. LC 98-85504. (Coleccion Cuba y Sus Jueces Ser.). (SPA., Illus.). 495p. 1999. pap. 29.00 (*0-89729-869-1*) Ediciones.

Decatanzaro. Motivation & Emotion. LC 98-7523. 352p. 1998. 66.00 (*0-13-849159-3*) P-H.

DeCaterina, R., et al, eds. N-3 Fatty Acids & Vascular Disease: Backgound & Pathophysiology - Hyperlipidaemia - Renal Diseases- Ischaemic Heart Disease. 166p. 1995. 49.00 (*0-387-19837-7*) Spr-Verlag.

Decatur Celebration Writers. The Jungle Celebration. (WeWrite Kids! Ser.: No. 29). (Illus.). 44p. (J). (ps-3). 1995. pap. 3.95 (*1-884987-97-4*) WeWrite.

— Spotty's Adventures. (WeWrite Kids! Ser.: No. 26). (Illus.). 43p. (J). (ps-3). 1995. pap. 3.95 (*1-884987-88-5*) WeWrite.

— To Mars & Back. (WeWrite Kids! Ser.: No. 28). (Illus.). 45p. (J). (ps-3). 1995. pap. 3.95 (*1-884987-94-X*) WeWrite.

— Twinkling Decatur Celebration. (WeWrite Kids! Ser.: No. 27). (Illus.). 40p. (J). (ps-3). 1995. pap. 3.95 (*1-884987-91-5*) WeWrite.

Decatur, Stephen. The Private Affairs of George Washington. LC 77-86596. (American Scene Ser.). 1969. reprint ed. 45.00 (*0-306-71416-7*) Da Capo.

Decaudin, ed. see Apollinaire, Guillaume.

Decaudin, M., ed. Anthologie de la Poesie Francaise du XXe Siecle, de Paul Claudel a Rene Char. (Poesie Ser.). (FRE.). 1992. pap. 16.95 (*2-07-032231-9*) Schoenhof.

Decaudin, Michel, jt. auth. see Kihm, Jean J.

Decaudin, Michel, ed. see Apollinaire, Guillaume.

Decaux, Alain. C'Etait le XX Siecle. large type ed. 432p. 1996. pap. 25.99 (*2-84011-164-0*) Ulverscroft.

— Dictionnaire Illustre de l'Histoire de France. 1989. lib. bdg. 85.00 (*0-8288-2495-9*) Fr & Eur.

Decaux, Alain, et al. Dictionnaire d'Histoire de France.Tr. of Dictionary of the History of France. (FRE.). 1981. 225.00 (*0-8288-1487-2*, M14212) Fr & Eur.

DeCava, Judith A. Food Fundamentals: Safety Tips for Healthful Eating. LC 93-80895. 96p. 1994. pap. text 10.00 (*1-882657-07-1*) Health Digest.

Decavalles, Adonis. Ransoms to Time: Selected Poems. LC 82-49314. 144p. 1984. 26.50 (*0-8386-3180-0*) Fairleigh Dickinson.

Decavalles, Adonis, et al, eds. Voice of Cyprus. 1966. 8.50 (*0-8079-0132-6*) October.

Decavalles, Andonis. Odysseus Elytis: From the Golden to the Silver Poem. LC 94-67648. 218p. (Orig.). 1994. pap. text 14.00 (*0-918618-61-4*) Pella Pub.

Decavelles, Andonis. Pandelis Prevelakis & the Value of a Heritage. Stavrou, Theofanis G., ed. Woodhead, Jean H., tr. from GRE. LC 81-81839. (Modern Greek History & Culture Ser.). 1981. 10.00 (*0-935476-08-3*) Nostos Bks.

D'Ecclesia, R. L. & Zenios, S. A., eds. Operations Research Models in Quantitative Finance: Proceedings of 13th Meeting, EURO Working Group for Financial Modeling. University of Cyprus, Nicosia, Cyrus. LC 96-137949. (Contributions to Management Science Ser.). 263p. 1996. 61.00 (*3-7908-0803-2*) Spr-Verlag.

DeCecco, John & Coleman, Eli. Integrated Identity for Gay Men & Lesbians: Psychotherapeutic Approaches for Emotional Well Being. LC 87-342. (Journal of Homosexuality Ser.: Vol. 14, No. 1-2). 343p. 1994. pap. text 24.95 (*0-918393-38-8*, Harrington Park) Haworth Pr.

Dececco, John P. Sex, Cells & Same-Sex Desire: The Biology of Sexual Preference. LC 95-6140. 1995. pap. text 34.95 (*1-56023-060-6*, Harrington Park) Haworth Pr.

DeCecco, John P., ed. Bisexual & Homosexual Identities: Critical Clinical Issues. LC 84-4569. (Journal of Homosexuality: Vol. 9, No. 4). 106p. 1984. text 39.95 (*0-86656-300-8*) Haworth Pr.

DeCecco, John P. & Shively, Michael G., eds. Bisexual & Homosexual Identities: Critical Theoretical Issues. LC 83-26371. (Journal of Homosexuality: Vol. 9, Nos. 2-3). 174p. 1984. text 5.95 (*0-86656-271-0*) Haworth Pr.

DeCecco, John P., jt. ed. see Ross, Michael.

Decell, Florri, jt. auth. see Weston, Marti.

DeCell, Ken, jt. auth. see Lichtman, Allan J.

DeCelle, Kathryn T., jt. auth. see Hearin, Emily S.

December, John. Creating Web Applets with Java. LC 95-72940. 336p. 1996. pap. text 39.99 incl. cd-rom (*1-57521-070-3*) Sams.

— Presenting Java. 224p. 1995. pap. 25.00 (*1-57521-039-8*) Sams.

December, John & Ginsburg, Mark. HTML & CGI Unleashed. 2nd ed. 1400p. 1997. 59.99 (*1-57521-333-8*) Sams.

— HTML 3.2 & CGI Unleashed: Profession Reference Edition. 2nd ed. LC 96-69396. 1376p. 1996. 59.99 (*1-57521-177-7*) Sams.

December, John, jt. auth. see Randall, Neil.

Decenzo. Human Resource Management. 1996. reel tape 263.95 (*0-471-12425-7*) Wiley.

— Human Resources Cases Set. 6th ed. 1999. pap. text 57.00 (*0-471-36926-8*) Wiley.

Decenzo, David A. Human Relations: Personal & Professional Development. LC 96-32428. 478p. (C). 1996. 69.00 (*0-13-502329-7*) P-H.

***DeCenzo, David A. & Robbins, Stephen P.** Human Resource Management: Concepts & Applications. 6th ed. LC 98-40473. 576p. 1998. pap. 74.95 (*0-471-29989-8*) Wiley.

DeCenzo, David A., jt. auth. see Bowers, Mollie H.

DeCenzo, David A., jt. auth. see Robbins, Stephen P.

Decenzo, David A., jt. auth. see Robbins, Stephens P.

DeCerreno, Allison L. Scientific Cooperation, State Conflict: The Roles of Scientists in Mitigating International Discord. LC 98-43898. 1998. 75.00 (*1-57331-202-9*) NY Acad Sci.

DeCesare, Angelo. Anthony, the Perfect Monster. LC 94-26105. (Beginner Bks.). (J). (gr. 2-5). 1996. lib. bdg. 11.99 (*0-679-96845-8*, Pub. by Random Bks Yng Read) Random.

***DeCesare, Angelo.** Flip's Fantastic Journal, 1. LC 99-14586. (J). 1999. 13.99 (*0-525-46262-7*, Dutt) Dutton Plume.

— Flip's Fantastic Journal, 1. 1999. pap. 5.99 (*0-14-056655-4*, PuffinBks) Peng Put Young Read.

DeCesare, Angelo, ed. Walt Disney's Mickey & Friends: Time Twisters. (Look & Find Ser.). (Illus.). 24p. (J). (gr. k-6). 1995. lib. bdg. 14.95 (*1-56674-124-6*, HTS Bks) Forest Hse.

DeCesare, Ruth. Myth, Music & Dance of the American Indian. Feldstein, Sandy et al, eds. (Illus.). 80p. (J). (gr. 4-12). 1988. teacher ed. 12.95 (*0-88284-371-0*, 3518); student ed. 4.95 (*0-88284-372-9*, 3520) Alfred Pub.

— Myth, Music & Dance of the American Indian. Feldstein, Sandy et al, eds. (Illus.). 80p. (J). (gr. 4-12). 1988. teacher ed. 19.95 incl. audio (*0-88284-383-4*, 3534) Alfred Pub.

D

— Myth, Music & Dance of the American Indian: Teachers Handbook. 1997. pap. 21.95 incl. audio compact disk (*0-88284-845-3*, 16415) Alfred Pub.

— Myth, Music & Dance of the American Indian, Songbook. Feldstein, Sandy et al, eds. (Illus.). 24p. (J). (gr. 4-12). 1988. student ed. 6.95 (*0-88284-373-7*, 3519) Alfred Pub.

— Songs of Hispanic Americans. O'Reilly, John & Wilson, Patrick, eds. 64p. (J). (gr. 4-12). 1991. teacher ed. 12.95 (*0-88284-486-5*, 3569); pap., teacher ed. 19.95 incl. audio (*0-88284-488-1*, 3570); pap., student ed. 5.50 (*0-88284-487-3*, 3568) Alfred Pub.

DeCesare, Ruth & De Cesare, R. Songs for the Italian Class. (C). 9.95 incl. audio (*0-8442-8062-3*, Pub. by S Thornes Pubs) St Mut.

Decesaris, Janet A., jt. auth. see Lunn, Patricia Vinning.

DeCesaris, Janet Ann, tr. see Cabre, M. Teresa.

Decety, Jean. Perception & Action: Recent Advances in Cognitive Neuropsychology. LC 99-187262. 1998. pap. text 64.95 (*0-86377-600-0*) Taylor & Francis.

DeCew, Judith W. In Pursuit of Privacy: Law, Ethics, & the Rise of Technology. LC 97-5409. 208p. 1996. text 39.95 (*0-8014-3380-0*); pap. text 15.95 (*0-8014-8411-1*) Cornell U Pr.

DeCew, Judith W. Privacy Protection. pap. 0.00 (*0-691-02324-7*) Princeton U Pr.

Decew, Judith W., jt. ed. see Shapiro, Ian.

Dech, V. N., jt. auth. see Knoring, L. D.

DeChaine, Laura, et al. Stress, Salespeople, Serial Killers, & Seminars: Not Your Ordinary Day at the Office. (Business Playground Ser.). (Illus.). 194p. (Orig.). 1995. pap. 10.95 (*0-9648485-0-3*) Baird Commun.

— The Treatment & Disposal of Clinical Waste: Handbook, No. 3. Favno, Brian P., ed. 120p. 1994. pap. 125.00 (*0-948237-18-X*, Pub. by H&H Sci Cnslts) St Mut.

Dechamps, R. Dictionary of Regional Planning & Development Dictionnaire Multilingue de l'Amenagement du Territoire et du Developpement Locale. (FRE.). 695p. 1997. pap. 88.00 (*2-85608-099-5*, Pub. by La Maison Du Dict) IBD Ltd.

DeChancie, John. Bride of the Castle. 192p. (Orig.). 1994. mass mkt. 4.99 (*0-441-00120-3*) Ace Bks.

— Castle Dreams. 1992. mass mkt. 4.99 (*0-441-09414-7*) Ace Bks.

— Castle Murders. 1991. mass mkt. 4.99 (*0-441-09273-X*) Ace Bks.

— Castle Spellbound. 240p. (Orig.). 1992. mass mkt. 4.99 (*0-441-09407-4*) Ace Bks.

— Castle War! 1990. mass mkt. 4.99 (*0-441-09270-5*) Ace Bks.

— From Prussia with Love: A Castle Falkenstein Novel. 288p. 1995. mass mkt. 5.99 (*1-55958-772-5*) Prima Pub.

— Innerverse. 1996. pap. 5.99 (*0-614-98030-5*, Avon Bks); mass mkt. 5.99 (*0-380-78108-5*, Avon Bks) Morrow Avon.

— The Kruton Interface. 192p. (Orig.). 1993. pap. 4.50 (*0-441-14227-3*) Ace Bks.

— Living with Aliens. 192p. (Orig.). 1995. mass mkt. 4.99 (*0-441-00204-8*) Ace Bks.

— Magicnet. 1993. 18.00 (*0-688-12759-2*, Wm Morrow) Morrow Avon.

DeChancie, John. Magicnet. 240p. 1994. mass mkt. 4.99 (*0-380-77394-5*, Avon Bks) Morrow Avon.

— Magicnet. 2000. 18.00 (*0-380-97230-1*, Avon Bks) Morrow Avon.

DeChancie, John & Greenberg, Martin H., eds. Castle Fantastic. 320p. 1996. mass mkt. 5.99 (*0-88677-686-4*, Pub. by DAW Bks) Penguin Putnam.

DeChancie, John & Notkin, Debbie. Masterminds of Falkenstein: A Castle Falkenstein Novel. 312p. 1996. mass mkt., per. 5.99 (*0-7615-0484-2*) Prima Pub.

DeChancie, John, et al. Battle Magic. Greenberg, Martin H. & Segriff, Larry, eds. 1998. pap. 5.99 (*0-88677-820-4*, Pub. by DAW Bks) Penguin Putnam.

DeChant, Barry. The World's Funniest Clown Skits. LC 95-10589. 190p. 1995. pap. 15.00 (*0-941599-31-0*, Pub. by Piccadilly Bks) Empire Pub Srvs.

DeChant, Betsy. Women & Group Psychotherapy: Theory & Practice. LC 96-20155. 523p. 1996. lib. bdg. 55.00 (*1-57230-098-1*) Guilford Pubns.

DeChant, Carol. Momma's Enchanted Supper: And Other Stories for the Long Evenings of Advent. LC 98-56192. (Illus.). 224p. 1999. 17.95 (*0-8294-1272-7*, Wild Onion) Loyola Pr.

Dechant, Emerald. Understanding & Teaching Reading: An Interactive Model. 544p. 1991. pap. 45.00 (*0-8058-0839-6*); text 99.95 (*0-8058-0824-8*) L Erlbaum Assocs.

— Whole-Language Reading: A Comprehensive Teaching Guide. LC 93-60365. 225p. 1995. 39.95 (*1-56676-007-0*) Scarecrow.

Decharms, Christopher. Two Views of Mind: Abhidharma & Brain Science. LC 97-41162. 229p. 1997. pap. text 14.95 (*1-55939-081-6*) Snow Lion Pubns.

DeCharms, Richard. Enhancing Motivation: Change in the Classroom. enl. ed. 300p. 1988. text 29.50 (*0-8290-1248-6*); pap. text 16.95 (*0-8290-1249-4*) Irvington.

DeChellis, Anthony J., et al. A Guide to Tax Planning for Individuals, 3 vols. Incl. Vol. 1. 1997. ring bd. (*0-7646-0188-1*); Vol. 2. 1997. ring bd. (*0-7646-0189-X*); Vol. 3. 1997. ring bd. (*0-7646-0190-3*); 170.00 (*0-7646-0187-3*) Prctnrs Pub Co.

— Guide to Tax Planning for Individuals, 3 vols. Incl. Vol. 1. Guide to Tax Planning for Individuals. 1998. ring bd. 180.00 (*0-7646-0511-9*); Vol. 2. Guide to Tax Planning for Individuals. 1998. ring bd. 180.00 (*0-7646-0512-7*); Vol. 3. Guide to Tax Planning for Individuals. 1998. ring bd. (*0-7646-0513-5*); 168.00 (*1-56433-939-4*) Prctnrs Pub Co.

DeChellis, Anthony J., et al. Guide to Tax Planning for Individuals, 3 vols. Incl. Vol. 1. Guide to Tax Planning for Individuals. 1998. ring bd. 180.00 (*0-7646-0511-9*); Vol. 2. Guide to Tax Planning for Individuals. 1998. ring bd. 180.00 (*0-7646-0512-7*); Vol. 3. Guide to Tax Planning for Individuals. 1998. ring bd. (*0-7646-0513-5*); 180.00 (*0-7646-0510-0*) Prctnrs Pub Co.

— PPC's Tax Elections Deskbook. LC 98-114127. 1997. ring bd. 150.00 (*0-7646-0351-5*) Prctnrs Pub Co.

***DeChellis, Anthony J., et al.** PPC's Tax Elections Deskbook. 1998. ring bd. 150.00i (*0-7646-0654-9*) Prctnrs Pub Co.

— PPC's Tax Elections Deskbook. 1999. ring bd. 150.00i (*0-7646-0927-0*) Prctnrs Pub Co.

Dechema. Dechema Biotechnology Conferences, Vol. 5, Pts. A & B. 1663p. 1992. 165.00 (*3-527-28534-2*) Wiley.

Dechema, ed. Electrochemical Cell Design & Optimization Procedures. 431p. 1991. pap. 85.00 (*3-527-10217-5*) Wiley.

Dechema, ed. 4th International Workshop on Polymer Reaction Engineering. 537p. 1992. pap. 325.00 (*3-527-10221-3*) Wiley.

Dechend, Hertha Von, see De Santillana, Giorgio & Von Dechend, Hertha.

DeChene, Charlotte, ed. see Milanesi, Enza.

Dechene, Louise. Habitants & Merchants in Seventeenth-Century Montreal. Vardi, Liana, tr. (Illus.). 456p. 1993. 65.00 (*0-7735-0658-6*, Pub. by McG-Queens Univ Pr); pap. 24.95 (*0-7735-0951-8*, Pub. by McG-Queens Univ Pr) CUP Services.

Dechene, Louise & Depatie, Sylvie. Twenty Years Later: Reading the History of Seventeenth & Eighteenth-Century Canada. 1998. pap. 27.95 (*0-7735-1693-X*) McG-Queens Univ Pr.

Decher, Reiner. Direct Energy Conversion: Fundamentals of Electric Power Production. (Illus.). 272p. (C). 1996. text 59.95 (*0-19-509572-3*) OUP.

— Energy Conversion: Systems, Flow Physics & Engineering. (Illus.). 704p. (C). 1994. text 89.95 (*0-19-507959-0*) OUP.

Decherd, Joyce. Midwestern Tea Room Pleasures. 200p. 1994. pap. write for info. (*0-9642586-0-9*) J Decherd.

DeCherney, Alan H. Current Obstetric & Gynecologic Diagnosis & Treatment. 8th ed. 1230p. (C). 1996. pap. text 54.95 (*0-8385-1447-2*, A1447-0, Apple Lange Med) McGraw.

Decherney, Alan H. Current Obstetric & Gynecologic Diagnosis & Treatment. 9th ed. (Illus.). 1230p. (C). 1999. 45.00 (*0-8385-1401-4*) Appleton & Lange.

DeCherney, Alan H., ed. Reproductive Failure. LC 86-2654. (Illus.). 320p. reprint ed. pap. 99.20 (*0-7837-6253-4*, 204596500010) Bks Demand.

DeCherney, Alan H., et al. Complications of Laparoscopy & Hysteroscopy. Corfman, R. S. & Diamond, M., eds. (Illus.). 288p. 1992. 85.00 (*0-86542-201-X*) Blackwell Sci.

DeCherney, Nancy, et al. The Fiddlehead Cookbook: Recipes from Alaska's Most Celebrated Restaurant & Bakery. (Illus.). 256p. 1993. pap. 15.95 (*0-312-09806-5*) St Martin.

Dechert, Hans & Raupach, Manfred, eds. Psycholinguistic Models of Production. LC 87-17575. 320p. 1987. text 73.25 (*0-89391-211-5*) Ablx Pub.

Dechert, Hans W., et al, compiled by. Transfer & Interference in Language: A Selected Bibliography. LC 84-16830. (Library & Information Sources in Linguistics: 14). xiv, 488p. 1984. 91.00 (*90-272-3735-2*) J Benjamins Pubng Co.

Dechert, Hans W., ed. Current Trends in European Second Language Acquisition Research. 200p. 1989. 89.00 (*1-85359-024-X*, Pub. by Multilingual Matters); pap. 36.00 (*1-85359-023-1*, Pub. by Multilingual Matters) Taylor & Francis.

Dechert, Hans W. & Raupach, Manfred. Temporal Variables in Speech: Studies in Honour of Frieda Golman-Eisler. (Janua Linguarum, Series Major: No. 86). 370p. 1980. 69.25 (*90-279-7946-4*) Mouton.

Dechert, Hans W. & Raupach, Manfred, eds. Transfer in Language Production. LC 88-3377. 296p. (C). 1989. text 73.25 (*0-89391-399-5*) Ablx Pub.

Dechert, Hans W., jt. ed. see Appel, Gabriela.

Dechert, Peter. Canon SLR Cameras, 1959-1991. (Illus.). 100p. 1992. 19.95 (*1-879561-04-2*) Hist Camera Pubns.

— The Contax S Camera Family. (Illus.). 40p. 1991. 12.95 (*1-879561-10-7*) Hist Camera Pubns.

— The Contax S Family Camera. (Illus.). 50p. 1991. pap. 14.00 (*1-879561-01-8*) Hist Camera Pubns.

Dechert, W. Davis, ed. Chaos Theory in Economics: Methods, Models & Evidence. LC 96-5317. (International Library of Critical Writings in Economics: No. 66). 624p. 1996. 255.00 (*1-85898-216-2*) E Elgar.

Dechevrens, Antoine. Composition Musicale et Composition Litteraire a Propos du Chant Gregorrien. viii, 366p. 1981. reprint ed. lib. bdg. 54.60 incl. 3.5 hd (*3-487-06974-1*) G Olms Pubs.

DeChiaro, John Giovanni. Treasures of the Spanish Guitar. 72p. 1996. pap. 19.95 incl. audio compact disk (*0-7866-2738-7*, 95379BCD) Mel Bay.

***Dechochorn, Leila L.** In This Web. 28p. 1999. write for info. (*1-885206-71-2*) Cader Pubng.

Dechochran, Lela M. Heart & Voice. (C). 1990. pap. 5.90 (*0-9627574-0-3*) L M Dechochran.

Dechow, Frederick J. Separation & Purification Techniques in Biotechnology. LC 88-34502. (Illus.). 490p. 1989. 129.00 (*0-8155-1197-3*) Noyes.

***Dechtiarenko, Luba & Peacock, Donna.** Abortion: The World's Greatest Killer. 16p. 2000. pap. write for info. (*1-56773-006-X*) Slavic Gospel.

Deci, E. L. & Ryan, R. M. Intrinsic Motivation & Self-Determination in Human Behavior. LC 85-12413. (Perspectives in Social Psychology Ser.). (Illus.). 388p. (C). 1985. 44.50 (*0-306-42022-8*, Plenum Trade) Perseus Pubng.

Deci, Edward & Flaste, Richard. Why We Do What We Do: Understanding Self-Motivation. 240p. 1996. pap. 12.95 (*0-14-025526-5*, Penguin Bks) Viking Penguin.

DeCiani, Gina, jt. auth. see Morrison, Laura L.

DeCicco, John & Delucchi, Mark, eds. Transportation, Energy & Environment: How Far Can Technology Take Us? LC 97-36757. 278p. (C). 1997. pap. 33.00 (*0-918249-28-7*) Am Coun Energy.

DeCicco, John & Thomas, Martin. Green Guide to Cars & Trucks: Model Year 1998. (Illus.). 108p. 1998. pap. 8.95 (*0-918249-33-3*) Am Coun Energy.

DeCicco, John, et al. Audubon Policy Report No. 1: CO2 Diet for a Greenhouse Planet: A Citizen's Guide for Slowing Global Warming. LC 90-61726. 75p. 1990. pap. 5.95 (*0-930698-33-9*) Natl Audubon.

— Improving Energy Efficiency in Apartment Buildings. (Illus.). 300p. (Orig.). (C). 1996. pap. 31.00 (*0-918249-23-6*) Am Coun Energy.

DeCicco, John, ed. see ACEEE Staff.

DeCicco, John M. Green Guide to Cars & Trucks: Model Year 1999. (Illus.). 128p. 1999. pap. 8.95 (*0-918249-36-8*, Pub. by Am Coun Energy) Chelsea Green Pub.

DeCicco, Linda. SLF Album: An Informal History of Notre Dame's Sophomore Literary Festival 1967-1996. LC 96-27137. 200p. (Orig.). 1997. pap. text 12.95 (*0-268-01481-7*) U of Notre Dame Pr.

DeCicco, Lynne M. Women & Lawyers in the Mid-Nineteenth Century English Novel: Uneasy Alliances & Narrative Misrepresentation. LC 96-17583. (Studies in British Literature: Vol. 25). 328p. 1996. text 99.95 (*0-7734-8756-5*) E Mellen.

***DeCicco, Paul R.** The Behavior of Glass & Other Materials Exposed to Fire. LC 00-41428. (Applied Fire Science in Transition Ser.). 2000. pap. write for info. (*0-89503-221-X*) Baywood Pub.

— Computer Applications in Fire Protection Engineering. LC 00-41430. (Applied Fire Science in Transition Ser.). 2000. pap. write for info. (*0-89503-224-4*) Baywood Pub.

— Evacuation from Fires. LC 00-41429. (Applied Fire Science in Transition Ser.). 2000. pap. write for info. (*0-89503-222-8*) Baywood Pub.

— Special Problems in Fire Protection Engineering. LC 00-41431. (Applied Fire Science in Transition Ser.). 2000. pap. write for info. (*0-89503-223-6*) Baywood Pub.

Decima, Jay P. Fixin' Ugly Houses for Money: How Small-Time Real Estate Investors Can Earn $1,000,000 & Lots More. LC 97-75993. 480p. 1998. 24.95 (*0-9621023-1-8*) KJAY Pub.

— Fixing Rundown Houses & Small Apartments: Change Careers - Start New One. (Illus.). 375p. (Orig.). 1988. reprint ed. write for info. (*0-9621023-0-X*) KJAY Pub.

Decipher Inc. Staff. Roman Ruins. (How to Host a Murder Ser.). 1996. pap. 16.00 (*1-878875-91-4*) Decipher Inc.

Deck, Allan. Francisco Javier Alagre: A Study in Mexican Literary Criticism, Vol. 13. 112p. 1976. 18.00 (*88-7041-513-9*) Jesuit Hist.

Deck, Allan F. The Second Wave: Hispanic Ministry & the Evangelization of Cultures. 1989. pap. 14.95 (*0-8091-3042-4*) Paulist Pr.

Deck, Allan F., ed. Frontiers of Hispanic Theology in the United States. LC 92-14036. 225p. (Orig.). 1992. pap. 18.00 (*0-88344-826-2*) Orbis Bks.

Deck, Allan F., jt. ed. see Dolan, Jay P.

Deck, John, III. American Admiralty Bureau's Interim Recommendations for Tow Powering & Configuration for Western Rivers Push Tows. 32p. (C). 1996. pap. 21.75 (*1-879778-62-9*, BK-0693) Marine Educ.

***Deck, John & Tsui, Mary.** Aerial Imagery Guidelines. Ashley, Peter, ed. (Quick Study Ser.: Vol. 2). (Illus.). 19p. 1999. pap. 19.00 (*0-916848-11-6*) Urban & Regional Information Systems.

Deck, John N. Nature, Contemplation, & the One: A Study in the Philosophy of Plotinus. 2nd ed. 152p. 1991. reprint ed. pap. 14.95 (*0-943914-54-X*) Larson Pubns.

Deck, Michele. Instant Teaching Tools for Health Care Educators. LC 94-48054. (Illus.). 288p. (C). (gr. 13). 1995. pap. text 38.95 (*0-8151-2379-5*, 25191) Mosby Inc.

Deck, Michele, jt. auth. see Backer, Lori.

Deck, Michele L. More Instant Teaching Tools for Health Care Educators. LC 99-178835. 272p. 1998. pap. text 36.95 (*0-323-00085-1*) Mosby Inc.

Deck, Steven A., jt. auth. see Nevaer, Louis E.

Deck, Sylvia C. Ministry of Hospitality. LC 97-148973. (Pastoral Ministry Ser.). 70p. (Orig.). 1996. pap. 8.95 (*1-55612-951-3*, LL951) Sheed & Ward WI.

***Deck, Tom.** Orvis Streamside Guide to Fly Casting. LC 99-47874. 2000. 16.95 (*1-55821-987-0*) Lyons Pr.

Deckard, Bill, ed. see Graham, Billy.

Deckard, Bill, ed. & compiled by see Graham, Billy.

Deckard, Loren D. Minor Prophets: Blueprints for 28 Messages Built upon God's Word. (Sermon Starters Ser.). 64p. 1999. 5.99 (*0-7847-0934-3*, 23012) Standard Pub.

Deckard, Steve. Home Schooling Laws & Resources. 1996. pap. 22.00 (*1-884213-11-1*) Vision Christ.

***Decke-Cornill, Helene & Reichart-Wallrabenstein, Maike.** Sprache und Fremdverstehen. 241p. 1999. 37.95 (*3-631-34636-0*) P Lang Pubng.

Deckelbaum, Richard J., jt. ed. see Bendich, Adrianne.

Deckelbaum, Richard J., ed. see Nestle Company Staff.

Deckelman, Carolyn M. Ticket to the Future. LC 85-72041. 240p. (Orig.). 1985. pap. 1.95 (*0-9615639-0-7*) Callwyn.

Deckelmann, ed. Demetrii Cydonii. (GRE.). 1987. reprint ed. 15.95 (*3-322-00356-6*, T1251, Pub. by B G Teubner) U of Mich Pr.

Decker. Illinois Criminal Law, 2 vols., Issue 2. 500p. 1998. lib. bdg. write for info. (*0-327-00925-X*, 8108512) LEXIS Pub.

— Introduction to Programing Using Java. 2nd ed. LC 99-38991. (Computer Science Ser.). 617p. 1999. 58.95 (*0-534-37109-4*) Brooks-Cole.

— Lab Manual to Accompany Programming-Java. 11th ed. (Miscellaneous/Catalogs Ser.). 1997. pap. 17.95 (*0-534-95597-5*) Wadsworth Pub.

— Literature Express Level 3: Assessment. 2002. pap. 32.50 (*0-8384-0156-2*) Thomson Learn.

— Literature Express Level 3: Text. (C). 2002. pap. text 30.00 (*0-8384-0151-1*) Heinle & Heinle.

— Literature Express Level 3: Workbook. 2002. pap. 9.50 (*0-8384-0155-4*) Thomson Learn.

— Multivariable Calculus. (C). 2000. pap. text, student ed. 22.67 (*0-13-269440-9*) P-H.

— The Object Concept. (Computer Science Ser.). 1995. mass mkt., lab manual ed. 16.95 (*0-534-20500-3*) PWS Pubs.

— The Object Concept. 2nd ed. (Computer Science Ser.). (C). 2000. mass mkt. 52.95 (*0-534-95087-6*) PWS Pubs.

Decker & Berolzheimer. Policy Evolution. 388p. (C). 1997. 62.00 (*0-13-673716-1*) P-H.

Decker, jt. auth. see Ottley.

Decker, jt. auth. see Rhodes, Ron D.

Decker, tr. see Rossi, Cristina P.

***Decker, Alvin.** Born in the Illinois Cornfields. LC 00-25124. 2000. write for info. (*0-9641423-3-3*) Tales Pr.

Decker, Angel A. Medical Research of Women's Health: Index & Reference Book of New Information. 150p. 1996. 47.50 (*0-7883-0900-5*); pap. 44.50 (*0-7883-0901-3*) ABBE Pubs Assn.

Decker, Anne C. Songs of the Soul. LC 96-60622. 138p. (Orig.). 1996. pap. 14.95 (*0-9652504-0-7*) Veritas Pr Ltd.

Decker, Annegret. Pronounce It Perfectly in German, 2 cassettes. LC 93-49850. (Pronounce It Perfectly Ser.). (ENG & GER.). 140p. 1994. pap. 39.95 incl. audio (*0-8120-8034-3*) Barron.

Decker, Barbara. Proverbs for Parenting: A Topical Guide for Child Raising from the Book of Proverbs King James Version. 2nd ed. LC 87-50633. 320p. 1989. 15.95 (*0-9618608-3-9*) Lynns Bookshelf.

— Proverbs for Parenting: A Topical Guide for Child Raising from the Book of Proverbs New International Version. LC 87-50633. 336p. 1991. 15.95 (*0-9618608-5-5*) Lynns Bookshelf.

Decker, Barbara, ed. A Coloring Book of Bible Proverbs: NIV. (Illus.). 32p. (Orig.). (J). (ps-8). 1991. ring bd. 2.50 (*0-9618608-6-3*) Lynns Bookshelf.

Decker, Barbara & Decker, Robert. Mount St. Helens National Volcanic Monument. (Pocket Portfolio Ser.: Vol. 3). (Illus.). 32p. (Orig.). 1997. pap. 5.95 (*0-939365-54-5*); pap. 6.95 (*0-939365-80-4*); pap. 6.95 (*0-939365-79-0*); pap. 6.95 (*0-939365-77-4*); pap. 6.95 (*0-939365-78-2*) Panorama Intl.

— Road Guide to Death Valley. (Illus.). 48p. (Orig.). 1989. pap. 4.50 (*0-9621019-3-1*) Double Mariposa.

— Road Guide to Hawaii Volcanoes National Park. (Illus.). 48p. 1986. pap. 4.50 (*0-9621019-0-7*) Double Mariposa.

— Road Guide to Hawaii Volcanoes National Park. 2nd rev. ed. (Illus.). 48p. 1987. reprint ed. pap. 4.50 (*0-9621019-1-5*) Double Mariposa.

— Road Guide to Volcanoes National Park. (Illus.). pap. 5.95 (*0-9621019-5-8*) Double Mariposa.

Decker, Barbara, jt. auth. see Decker, Robert.

Decker, Barbara, jt. auth. see Decker, Robert W.

Decker, Bernard H. Gewalt und Zartlichkeit: Einfuhrung in die Militarbelletristik der DDR 1956-1986. Brown, Peter D., ed. LC 89-37821. (Studies in Modern German Literature: Vol. 35). (GER.). 275p. 1990. text 47.50 (*0-8204-1164-7*) P Lang Pubng.

Decker, Bert. The Art of Communicating: Achieving Interpersonal Impact in Business. rev. ed. Crisp, Michael J., ed. LC 96-85519. (Fifty-Minute Ser.). 100p. (Orig.). 1996. pap. 10.95 (*1-56052-409-X*) Crisp Pubns.

— You've Got to Be Believed to Be Heard. (Illus.). 320p. 1993. pap. 14.95 (*0-312-09949-5*) St Martin.

— You've Got to Be Believed to Be Heard, unabridged ed. 1992. pap. 15.95 incl. audio (*1-55927-192-2*) Audio Renaissance.

***Decker, Bert & York, Hershael W.** Speaking with Bold Assurance. 2001. pap. 16.99 (*0-8054-2210-2*) Broadman.

Decker, Bert, jt. auth. see Decker Communications Staff.

Decker, Celia A. Children: The Early Years. LC 98-53654. 544p. 2000. 46.60 (*1-56637-559-2*) Goodheart.

Decker, Celia A. & Decker, John R. Planning & Administering Early Childhood. 6th ed. 459p. (C). 1996. pap. text 48.00 (*0-02-327991-5*, Macmillan Coll) P-H.

— Planning & Administering Early Childhood Programs. 6th ed. 1997. pap. 48.00 (*0-13-027991-9*) P-H.

— Planning & Administering Early Childhood Programs. 7th ed. 476p. 2000. pap. 48.00 (*0-13-027168-3*) P-H.

Decker, Charles L. Winning the P&G 99: 99 Principles & Practices of Procter & Gamble's Success. LC 99-168701. 288p. 1998. 22.00 (*0-671-01739-X*) PB.

— Winning with the P&G 99: 99 Principles & Practices of Procter & Gamble's Success. 237p. 1999. pap. 14.00 (*0-671-01740-3*, PB Trade Paper) PB.

Decker, Christopher, ed. see Fitzgerald, Edward.

Decker, Clarence R. The Victorian Conscience. LC 77-8021. 213p. 1977. reprint ed. lib. bdg. 38.50 (*0-8371-9684-1*, DEVC, Greenwood Pr) Greenwood.

Decker Communications Staff & Decker, Bert. Creating Messages That Motivate. (Success Guide Ser.: No. 1). (Illus.). 90p. (Orig.). 1996. wbk. ed. 24.95 (*0-9655397-0-9*) Decker Communs.

D

An Asterisk (*) at the beginning of an entry indicates that the title is appearing for the first time.

Decker, Condax, jt. auth. see Delano, Kate.

Decker, Craig, tr. see Henisch, Peter.

Decker, Cynthia, ed. see Landrey, Dave & Landrey, Martha.

Decker, D. J., et al. Wildlife & Timber from Private Lands: A Landowner's Guide to Planning. 2nd rev. ed. (Information Bulletin Ser.). (Illus.). 56p. (Orig.). 1990. pap. 5.95 (*1-57753-031-4*, 1471B193) Corn Coop Ext.

Decker, Dale S., ed. see ASTM Committee D-4 on Road & Paving Materials.

Decker, Dale S., jt. ed. see Huber, Gerald A.

***Decker, Dan.** Anatomy of a Screenplay: Writing the American Screenplay from Character Structure to Convergence. (Illus.). 201p. 1998. pap. 19.95 (*0-9665732-0-X*) Screenwriters Grp.

Decker, Daniel J. Wildlife Notebook: Sketches of Selected Wildlife in New York State. (Information Bulletin Ser.). (Illus.). 80p. (Orig.). 1988. pap. 5.95 (*1-57753-030-6*, 1471B210) Corn Coop Ext.

Decker, Daniel J. & Kelley, John W. Enhancement of Wildlife Habitat on Private Lands. rev. ed. (Illus.). 42p. 1998. pap. 7.95 (*1-57753-223-6*, 1471B181) Corn Coop Ext.

Decker, Daniel J., et al. Guide to Freshwater Fishes of New York. 4th rev. ed. (Illus.). 140p. 1996. pap. 4.75 (*1-57753-000-4*, 147S108) Corn Coop Ext.

Decker, Daniel J., et al. Let's Go Fishing: A Fish & Fishing Project. (Four-H Ser.). (Illus.). 36p. (YA). (gr. 7-11). 1993. pap. 3.00 (*1-57753-205-8*, 147L-5-6) Corn Coop Ext.

— Wildlife Habitat Enhancement. (Four-H Ser.). (Illus.). 24p. (YA). (gr. 7-12). 1984. pap. 3.25 (*1-57753-207-4*, 147L-5-16) Corn Coop Ext.

Decker, Daniel J., jt. auth. see Howard, Ronald A., Jr.

Decker, David, jt. ed. see Lin, Phylis L.

Decker, David J. Stopping the Violence: A Group Model to Change Men's Abusive Attitudes & Behaviors. LC 98-51556. (Illus.). 456p. (C). 1999. lib. bdg. 39.95 (*0-7890-0169-1*) Haworth Pr.

— Stopping the Violence: A Group Model to Change Men's Abusive Attitudes & Behaviors: The Client Workbook. LC 98-33185. (Illus.). 324p. (C). 1999. pap. text, wbk. ed. 24.95 (*0-7890-0709-6*, Hawrth Medical) Haworth Pr.

Decker, David R. The Political, Economic, & Labor Climate in Argentina. LC 83-81084. (Multinational Industrial Relations Ser.: No. 4). (Illus.). 148p. 1983. reprint ed. pap. 45.90 (*0-608-04367-2*, 206514800001) Bks Demand.

Decker, David R. & Duran, Ignacio. The Political, Economic, & Labor Climate in Colombia. LC 82-82996. (Multinational Industrial Relations Ser.: No. 4). (Illus.). 146p. 1982. reprint ed. pap. 45.30 (*0-608-04366-4*, 206514700001) Bks Demand.

Decker, Diana P., tr. see Rossi, Cristina P.

Decker, Donald M. Luis Durand. LC 79-120022. (Twayne's World Authors Ser.). 1971. lib. bdg. 20.95 (*0-8057-2276-9*) Irvington.

Decker, Donald M. & Decker, Mary L. Laguna Niguel: The Legacy & the Promise. LC 90-63225. (Illus.). 120p. 1990. pap. 4.95 (*0-918329-19-1*) Royal Lit.

— Reflections on Elegance: Pasadena's Huntington Hotel since 1906. rev. ed. (Illus.). 80p. (Orig.). 1991. pap. 4.95 (*0-918329-24-8*) Royal Lit.

Decker, Donald M., ed. see Seti, D. Nathan.

***Decker, Donna.** Under the Influence of Paradise: Voices of Key West. 120p. 1999. pap. 10.00 (*0-9673407-0-5*) Head & a Half Pr.

Decker, Donna, jt. ed. see Ryals, Mary J.

Decker, Douglas A. & Berolzheimer, Alan R. Policy Evolution: Energy Conservation to Energy Efficiency: A Series of Speeches from the Energy Efficiency Forums. LC 97-12267. 365p. 1997. 62.00 (*0-88173-274-5*) Fairmont Pr.

***Decker, Drew.** Gis Data Sources. LC 00-33562. 2000. write for info. (*0-471-35505-4*) Wiley.

Decker, Dru S. Abundant Time: Using a Prayer Box to Focus, Balance & Simplify. 1998. 12.95 (*0-9660527-5-7*); pap. 12.95 (*0-9660527-7-3*) Bridgecross Pr.

— Abundant Time: Using a Prayer Box to Pray, Focus & Simplify a Busy Life. 1998. 12.95 (*0-9660527-2-2*); pap. 12.95 (*0-9660527-3-0*) Bridgecross Pr.

— The Prayer Box: Time Management for Your Prayer Life. 1998. 12.95 (*0-9660527-4-9*) Bridgecross Pr.

— Prayer Box Gift: Answers from God - Questions Busy People Ask about Guidance & Prayer. 1998. write for info. (*0-9660527-0-6*); pap. write for info. (*0-9660527-1-4*) Bridgecross Pr.

— Prayer Box Gift Time Management for Your Spiritual Life. 1998. write for info. (*0-9660527-9-X*) Bridgecross Pr.

Decker, Dwight & Wood, Teri S. Rhudiprrt Collection. (Illus.). 160p. 1996. pap. 13.95 (*1-883847-21-4*) MU Press.

Decker, Dwight F. Physics: Mastery Learning Approach to Laboratory Exercises. 287p. (C). 1993. spiral bd. 25.95 (*0-8403-9109-9*) Kendall-Hunt.

Decker, Dwight R., tr. see Leturgie, Jean & Luguy, Phillipe.

Decker, Dwight R., tr. see Peyo.

Decker, Dwight R., tr. see Wijn, Piet & Roep, Thom.

Decker, Ed. The Dark Side of Freemasonry. LC 94-77033. 224p. 1994. pap. 10.99 (*1-56384-061-8*) Huntington Hse.

— The Question of Freemasonry. LC 91-78414. (Salt Ser.). 48p. 1992. pap. 3.49 (*1-56384-020-0*) Huntington Hse.

Decker, Ed & Carlson, Ron. Fast Facts on False Teachings. LC 93-43729. 1994. pap. 9.99 (*1-56507-168-9*) Harvest Hse.

Decker, Ed & Hunt, Dave. Los Fabricantes de Dioses. Powell, Adriana, tr. from ENG.Tr. of Godmakers. (SPA.). 240p. 1987. pap. 8.95 (*0-88113-088-5*) Caribe Betania.

— The Godmakers. expanded rev. ed. LC 97-2665. 1997. pap. 10.99 (*1-56507-717-2*) Harvest Hse.

Decker, Ed, jt. auth. see Carbone, Linda.

Decker, Edith. Paik Video. Iselin, Marie-Genvieve et al, trs. from GER. LC 97-42066. (Illus.). 242p. (Orig.). 1996. pap. 18.95 (*1-886449-35-X*, P935X) Barrytown Ltd.

Decker, Eric & Faustman, Cameron. Antioxidants in Muscle Foods. LC 99-22777. 512p. 2000. text 110.00 (*0-471-31454-4*, Wiley-Interscience) Wiley.

Decker, Fred W. Weather Map Study. rev. ed. (C). 1999. pap. 1.25 (*0-931778-02-6*) Weather Wkbk.

— The Weather Workbook. rev. ed. (C). 1981. pap. 8.00 (*0-931778-03-4*) Weather Wkbk.

Decker, George & Williams, John P., eds. American Novelists: Fenimore Cooper. (Critical Heritage Ser.). 318p. (C). 1997. 125.00 (*0-415-15928-8*) Routledge.

Decker, Georgia L. Forever Alone. LC 99-93917. 226p. (Orig.). 1999. pap. 10.00 (*0-7392-0240-5*, PO3287) Morris Pubng.

***Decker, Georgia Lee.** Dixie Dreamin' 248p. 1999. pap. 10.00 (*0-7392-0430-0*, PO3710) Morris Pubng.

***Decker, Georgia M., ed.** An Introduction to Complementary & Alternative Therapies. (Illus.). 272p. 1999. pap. text 35.00 (*1-890504-14-9*) Oncology Nursing.

Decker, H. & Bernhard, F. Modern French Intermediate. (ENG & FRE.). 292p. 1967. lib. bdg. 9.95 (*0-8288-6972-3*, M10448) Fr & Eur.

Decker, Hannah. Freud in Germany: Revolution & Reaction in Science, 1893-1907. LC 77-20062. (Psychological Issues Monographs: No. 41). 360p. (Orig.). 1977. 52.50 (*0-8236-2023-9*); pap. 42.50 (*0-8236-2022-0*) Intl Univs Pr.

Decker, Hannah S. Freud, Dora & Vienna, 1900. 1990. 29.95 (*0-02-907830-X*) Free Pr.

Decker, Hannah S. Freud, Dora & Vienna, 1900. 320p. 1992. pap. 14.95 (*0-02-907212-3*) Free Pr.

Decker, Harold A. & Herford, Julius. Choral Conducting Symposium. 2nd ed. 320p. (C). 1987. text 48.00 (*0-13-133372-0*) P-H.

Decker, Harold A. & Kirk, Colleen J. Choral Conducting: Focus on Communication. (Illus.). 374p. (C). 1995. reprint ed. pap. text 37.95 (*0-88133-876-1*) Waveland Pr.

Decker, Henry & Decker, Jane. The Turfgrass Management Handbook: A Guide to Professional Lawn Care. (Illus.). 304p. 1988. text 20.00 (*0-13-933128-X*) P-H.

Decker, Jack. TRS-80 ROM Routines Documented. 126p. 1983. pap. text 19.95 (*0-915363-01-1*) Alter Source.

***Decker, James.** The Formless Sexist: Reassing Henry Miller. (Illus.). 56p. (C). 1999. pap. 20.00 (*1-893918-02-5*) R Jackson.

Decker, Jane, jt. auth. see Blackwell Science Inc., Publishing Staff.

Decker, Jane, jt. auth. see Decker, Henry.

Decker, Jeffrey L. Made in America: Self-Styled Success from Horatio Alger to Oprah Winfrey. LC 97-19568. 1997. pap. 17.95 (*0-8166-3021-6*); text 44.95 (*0-8166-3020-8*) U of Minn Pr.

Decker, Jennifer E. & Brown, Nicholas, eds. Recent Developments in Optical Gauge Block Metrology, Vol. 3477. LC 99-170349. 1998. 80.00 (*0-8194-2932-5*) SPIE.

Decker, Joachim, ed. see Nikephoros.

Decker, Joanne A. Making the Moments Count: Leisure Activities for Caregiving Relationships. LC 97-12488. xii, 192 p. 1997. pap. 14.95 (*0-8018-5700-7*); text 29.95 (*0-8018-5699-X*) Johns Hopkins.

Decker, John A. Labor Problems in the Pacific Mandates. LC 75-30053. (Institute of Pacific Relations Ser.). reprint ed. 47.50 (*0-404-59517-0*) AMS Pr.

Decker, John C., tr. see Von Gerstner, Franz A.

Decker, John F. Illinois Criminal Law: A Survey of Crimes & Defenses. 1994. pap., student ed. 45.00 (*0-250-40743-4*, MICHIE) LEXIS Pub.

— Illinois Criminal Law: A Survey of Crimes & Defenses, 2 vols. 2nd ed. 1993. ring bd. 170.00 (*0-327-01033-9*, 81081, MICHIE) LEXIS Pub.

— Illinois Criminal Law: A Survey of Crimes & Defenses, 2 vols., Set. 2nd ed. 1240p. 1993. spiral bd. 170.00 (*1-56257-679-8*, 81081-10, MICHIE) LEXIS Pub.

— Prostitution: Regulation & Control. (N. Y. U. Criminal Law Education & Research Center Publications: Vol. 13). xxvi, 572p. 1979. reprint ed. 65.00 (*0-8377-0507-X*, Rothman) W S Hein.

Decker, John L. The Reliable Healthcare Companions: Understanding & Managing Asthma. Kaliner, Michael A., ed. 192p. 1988. mass mkt. 6.95 (*0-380-75427-4*, Avon Bks) Morrow Avon.

Decker, John L., ed. The Reliable Healthcare Companions: Understanding & Managing Arthritis. 192p. (Orig.). 1987. mass mkt. 6.95 (*0-380-75011-2*, Avon Bks) Morrow Avon.

— The Reliable Healthcare Companions: Understanding & Managing Osteoporosis. 176p. 1988. mass mkt. 6.95 (*0-380-75429-0*, Avon Bks) Morrow Avon.

Decker, John L. & Gorden, Phillip, eds. The Reliable Healthcare Companions: Understanding & Managing Diabetes. 192p. 1987. mass mkt. 6.95 (*0-380-75247-6*, Avon Bks) Morrow Avon.

Decker, John L. & Keiser, Harry R. The Reliable Healthcare Companions: Understanding & Managing Hypertension. 224p. 1987. mass mkt. 6.95 (*0-380-75248-4*, Avon Bks) Morrow Avon.

Decker, John L. & Maton, Paul N. The Reliable Healthcare Companions: Understanding & Managing Ulcers. 1988. mass mkt. 6.95 (*0-380-75428-2*, Avon Bks) Morrow Avon.

Decker, John R., jt. auth. see Decker, Celia A.

Decker, Julie. Ice Breakers: Alaska's Most Innovative Artists. LC 98-93364. (Illus.). 255p. 1999. 55.00 (*0-9670709-0-2*) Decker Art.

Decker, K., ed. Cytokines & the Liver. (Falk Symposium Ser.). 256p. (C). 1995. text 102.50 (*0-7923-8878-X*) Kluwer Academic.

Decker, K. M. & Rehmann, R. M., eds. Programming Environments for Massively Parallel Distributed Systems: Working Conference of the IFIP WG10.3, April 25-29, 1994. LC 94-30359. (Monte Verita Ser.). 400p. 1994. 89.50 (*0-8176-5090-3*) Birkhauser.

Decker, Kurt H. Covenants Not to Compete, 2, Vol. 2. 2nd ed. (Employment Law Library). 880p. 1997. boxed set 265.00 (*0-471-58257-3*) Wiley.

— Drafting & Revising Employment Policies & Handbooks, 2, Vol. 2. 2nd ed. (Human Resources Library). 916p. 1994. boxed set 255.00 (*0-471-04663-9*) Wiley.

— Hiring Legally: A Guide for Employees & Employers. LC 99-17822. (Employment Rights Ser.). 230p. 1999. 28.95 (*0-89503-197-3*) Baywood Pub.

— The Individual Employment Rights Primer. 240p. 1991. pap. text 29.95 (*0-89503-089-6*) Baywood Pub.

— A Manager's Guide to Employee Privacy: Laws, Policies, & Procedures. 288p. 1989. 74.95 (*0-471-50909-5*) Wiley.

— Privacy in the Workplace: Rights, Procedures & Policies. LC 94-12177. 540p. 1994. ring bd. 62.50 (*0-318-72686-6*) LRP Pubns.

Decker, Kurt H., jt. auth. see Convington, Robert N.

Decker, Larry E. & Boo, Mary R. Community Schools: Serving Children, Families & Communities. (Illus.). 32p. (Orig.). 1998. pap. 2.95 (*0-930388-12-7*) Comm Collaborators.

Decker, Larry E. & Decker, Virginia A. Grantseeking: How to Find a Funder & Write a Winning Proposal. 96p. (Orig.). 1993. pap. 14.95 (*0-930388-08-9*) Comm Collaborators.

Decker, Larry E. & Romney, Valerie A. Educational Restructuring & the Community Education Process. 144p. 1992. pap. 9.95 (*0-614-12690-8*) Comm Collaborators.

Decker, Larry E., et al. Getting Parents Involved in Their Children's Education. 82p. 1994. 19.15 (*0-87652-212-6*, 021-0476) Am Assn Sch Admin.

— Home-School-Community Relations Manual. 152p. (Orig.). 1994. pap. text 19.95 (*0-930388-09-7*) Comm Collaborators.

— Teacher's Manual for Parent & Community Involvement. 96p. (Orig.). 1996. pap. text, teacher ed. 17.95 (*0-930388-13-5*) Comm Collaborators.

Decker, Larry E., jt. auth. see Ringers, Joseph, Jr.

Decker, Larry R. Out from the Inside: The Use of Creativity in Relationships. LC 84-90461. 1985. 10.95 (*0-87212-186-0*) Libra.

Decker, Lawrence A. A Change of Heart. LC 97-32524. 148p. 1998. 19.95 (*1-56072-526-5*, Nova Kroshka Bks) Nova Sci Pubs.

Decker, Lewis G. Gloversville. LC 98-86555. (Images of America Ser.). (Illus.). 128p. 1998. pap. 16.99 (*0-7524-1299-X*) Arcadia Publng.

***Decker, Lewis G.** Johnstown. (Images of America Ser.). 128p. 1999. pap. 18.99 (*0-7385-0174-3*) Arcadia Publng.

Decker, Malcolm. Brink of Revolution: New York in Crisis, 1765-1776. (Illus.). 1964. 15.00 (*0-87266-005-2*) Argosy.

— Ten Days of Infamy. LC 68-20204. (Illus.). 1969. reprint ed. 19.95 (*0-405-00053-7*) Ayer.

Decker, Malcolm, ed. Eyewitness Accounts of the American Revolution, 34 bks., Set, Ser. 1. (Illus.). 1968. reprint ed. 1947.50 (*0-405-01100-8*) Ayer.

— Eyewitness Accounts of the American Revolution, 42 bks., Set, Ser. 2. (Illus.). 1969. reprint ed. 702.00 (*0-405-01101-6*) Ayer.

— Eyewitness Accounts of the American Revolution, 35 bks., Set, Ser. 3. (Illus.). 1971. reprint ed. 526.00 (*0-405-01187-3*) Ayer.

Decker, Margaret S. Lark & Sky. 112p. 1972. pap. 3.00 (*0-913976-04-0*) Discovery Bks.

Decker, Marjorie. Christian Mother Goose: Little Tommy Tucker. (Christian Mother Goose Board Bks.). (J). (ps). 1989. 3.99 (*0-529-06685-8*) World Publng.

— Christian Mother Goose Big Book. LC 92-60502. (Illus.). 304p. (J). (ps-4). 1992. 17.99 (*0-529-07315-3*, CMG4) World Publng.

— Christian Mother Goose Humpty Dumpty. (Christian Mother Goose Board Bks.). (J). (ps). 1989. 3.99 (*0-529-06683-1*) World Publng.

— Christian Mother Goose Little Bo Peep. (Christian Mother Goose Board Bks.). (J). (ps). 1989. 3.99 (*0-529-06687-4*) World Publng.

— Christian Mother Goose Piano Book. (J). (gr. k-4). 1989. 8.99 (*0-529-06692-0*) World Publng.

— Christian Mother Goose Pop-Up Bedtime Rhymes. (Christian Mother Goose Pop-Up Bks.). (J). (ps). 1989. 6.99 (*0-529-06688-2*) World Publng.

— Christian Mother Goose Pop-Up Favorite Rhymes. (Christian Mother Goose Pop-Up Bks.). (J). (ps). 1989. 6.99 (*0-529-06691-2*) World Publng.

— Rock a Bye Christmas (Christian Mother Goose) 1991. 5.99 (*0-529-07082-0*, RD3) World Publng.

— Rock-a-Bye Prayers (Christian Mother Goose) (J). 1990. kivar 7.99 (*0-529-06843-5*, RDZ) World Publng.

— Rock-a-Bye Stories of Jesus (Christian Mother Goose) (J). (ps-3). 1993. 5.99 (*0-529-10003-7*, RD6) World Publng.

Decker, Marjorie A. Rock-A-Bye Christmas, 3 cass. (Christian Mother Goose Ser.). 14.99 incl. audio (*0-529-07467-2*, RD5) World Publng.

Decker, Mary L., jt. auth. see Decker, Donald M.

Decker, Matthew. An Essay on the Causes of the Decline of the Foreign Trade. 7th ed. LC 67-29502. vi, 186p. 1973. reprint ed. 35.00 (*0-678-00864-7*) Kelley.

Decker, Micahel W., jt. ed. see Brioni, Jorge D.

Decker, Michael, jt. auth. see Herwaldt, Loreen.

Decker, Nan. The Caption Workbook. (Caption Kit Ser.). (Illus.). 27p. (J). (gr. 5-8). 1984. pap. text 1.95 (*0-913072-61-3*) Natl Assn Deaf.

Decker, Nancy M., jt. auth. see Sedwick, Frank.

Decker, Norman, jt. auth. see Roessler, Robert.

Decker, P. L. Style & Mechanics of Liquefaction-Related Deformation, Lower Absaroka Volcanic Supergroup (Eocene), Wyoming. (Special Papers: No. 240). (Illus.). 80p. 1990. pap. 15.00 (*0-8137-2240-3*) Geol Soc.

Decker, Paul T. Education & the Economy: An Indicators Report. LC 97-188701. 134p. 1997. pap. 15.00 (*0-16-049036-7*) USGPO.

— Findings from Education & the Economy, an Indicators Report. 25p. 1997. pap. 4.25 (*0-16-049035-9*) USGPO.

Decker, Peter. A Descriptive Check List: Together with Short Title Index Describing Almost 7500 Items of Western Americana. 521p. 1997. reprint ed. 75.00 (*1-57898-039-9*) Martino Pubng.

— Peter Decker's Catalogues of Rare Americana, 1944-1963, 3 vols. 1980. 145.00 (*0-318-37954-6*, PA2-31-7179) Jenkins.

Decker, Peter, ed. see Barker, John.

Decker, Peter, ed. see Carroll, Charles H.

Decker, Peter, ed. see De Rosenthal, Gustavus.

Decker, Peter, ed. see Drayton, John.

Decker, Peter, ed. see Feltman, William.

Decker, Peter, ed. see Graydon, Alexander.

Decker, Peter, ed. see Laurens, John.

Decker, Peter, ed. see Lee, Henry.

Decker, Peter, jt. ed. see Moore, Frank.

Decker, Peter, ed. see Morris, Margaret.

Decker, Peter, ed. see Roberts, Lemuel.

Decker, Peter, ed. see Robin, Abbe.

Decker, Peter, ed. see Smith, Joshua H.

Decker, Peter, ed. see Smith, William, Jr.

Decker, Peter, ed. see Stedman, Charles.

Decker, Peter, ed. see Thacher, James.

Decker, Peter R. Fortunes & Failures: White-Collar Mobility in Nineteenth Century San Francisco. LC 77-12557. (Harvard Studies in Urban History). 351p. reprint ed. pap. 108.90 (*0-7837-2248-6*, 205733600004) Bks Demand.

— Old Fences, New Neighbors. LC 98-8925. 175p. 1998. 40.00 (*0-8165-1771-1*); pap. 19.95 (*0-8165-1905-6*) U of Ariz Pr.

Decker, Phillip J. & Decker, T. Newell. Renovating Brick Houses: For Yourself or for Investment. Watson, Ben, ed. LC 89-46019. (Illus.). 248p. (Orig.). 1990. 27.95 (*0-88266-593-6*, Garden Way Pub) Storey Bks.

Decker, Phillip J. & Nathan, Barry R. Behavior Modeling Training: Principles & Applications. LC 84-18155. 256p. 1985. 55.00 (*0-275-90084-3*, C0084, Praeger Pubs) Greenwood.

Decker, Phillip J. & Sullivan, Eleanor J. Nursing Administration: Micro Macro Approach. (Illus.). 704p. (C). 1992. pap. text 59.95 (*0-8385-7073-9*, A7073-8) Appleton & Lange.

Decker, Phillip J., jt. auth. see Sullivan, Eleanor J.

Decker, R. S. & Sherard, James L., eds. Dispersive Clays, Related Pipings & Erosion in Geotechnical Projects - STP 623. 479p. 1977. 40.75 (*0-8031-0192-9*, STP623) ASTM.

Decker, Randall E. & Schwegler, Robert A. Decker's Patterns of Exposition 15. 15th ed. LC 97-2028. 607p. (C). 1997. pap. text 42.00 (*0-321-01218-6*) Addson-Wesley Educ.

Decker, Randy. FJ & G Railroad. LC 98-87872. (Images of America Ser.). (Illus.). 128p. 1998. pap. 18.99 (*0-7524-1300-7*) Arcadia Publng.

***Decker, Randy, et al.** The Sacandaga Valley. LC 99-69485. (Images of America Ser.). (Illus.). 128p. 2000. pap. 18.99 (*0-7385-0404-1*) Arcadia Publng.

Decker, Raymond A. Our Conscious Universe: And the Mysteries Thereof. LC 98-65015. 165p. 1998. pap. 9.95 (*0-9660847-0-5*) OCU Bks.

Decker, Richard & Hirshfield, Stuart. The Analytical Engine: An Introduction to Computer Science Using HyperCard. 160p. (C). 1990. pap. 45.95 incl. disk (*0-534-12540-9*) PWS Pubs.

— The Analytical Engine: An Introduction to Computer Science Using ToolBook. 380p. (C). 1991. pap. 50.50 (*0-534-14046-7*) PWS Pubs.

Decker, Rick. Programming-Java: Beta Edition. LC 97-29138. (Miscellaneous/Catalogs Ser.). (C). 1997. mass mkt. 36.95 (*0-534-95588-6*) Wadsworth Pub.

Decker, Rick & Hirshfield, Stuart. The Analytical Engine: An Introduction to Computer Science Using the Internet. LC 97-46811. (C). 1998. mass mkt. 78.95 (*0-534-95365-4*) PWS Pubs.

— The Object Concept: An Introduction to Computer Programming Using C. LC 94-14279. 1994. pap. 36.95 (*0-534-20499-6*) PWS Pubs.

— The Object Concept: An Introduction to Computer Programming Using C++. LC 94-41156. 454p. 1995. 74.95 (*0-534-20496-1*) PWS Pubs.

— Working Classes: A Second Course in C++ Programming with Data Structures. LC 94-43941. 495p. (C). 1995. mass mkt. 81.95 (*0-534-94566-X*) PWS Pubs.

Decker, Robert & Decker, Barbara. Road Guide to Crater Lake National Park. (Illus.). 48p. (Orig.). 1988. pap. 4.50 (*0-9621019-2-3*) Double Mariposa.

— Road Guide to Haleakala & the Hana Highway. (Illus.). 48p. (Orig.). 1990. pap. 4.50 (*0-9621019-4-X*) Double Mariposa.

— Volcano Watching. 5th rev. ed. (Illus.). 84p. 1997. reprint ed. pap. text 9.95 (*0-940295-16-4*) HI Natural Hist.

D

— Volcanoes, Vol. 1. LC 97-17746. 1997. pap. text 19.95 (*0-7167-2440-5*) St Martin.

Decker, Robert & Marquez, Esther T. The Proud Mexicans. (Illus.). 250p. (gr. 7-12). 1976. pap. 5.95 (*0-88345-254-5*, 18450) Prentice ESL.

Decker, Robert & Varberg, Dale E. Calculus Preliminary Edition. 651p. 1996. pap. text 47.00 (*0-13-287640-X*) P-H.

Decker, Robert, jt. auth. see Decker, Barbara.

Decker, Robert H. When a Crisis Hits: Will Your School Be Ready? LC 97-4896. (Illus.). 184p. 1997. 69.95 (*0-8039-6615-6*); pap. 32.95 (*0-8039-6304-1*) Corwin Pr.

Decker, Robert J. Effective Psychotherapy: The Silent Dialogue. 177p. 1988. 78.95 (*0-89116-679-3*) Hemisp Pub.

Decker, Robert O. The Whaling City: A History of New London. LC 74-30794. (Illus.). 413p. 1976. 15.00 (*0-87106-053-1*) New London County.

Decker, Robert O. & Harris, Margaret A. Cromwell Connecticut, 1650-1990: The History of a River Port Town. LC 91-6465. (Illus.). 560p. 1991. 35.00 (*0-914659-51-0*) Phoenix Pub.

Decker, Robert W. & Decker, Barbara. Volcanoes. 3rd ed. LC 97-17746. 320p. 1997. pap. text 33.95 (*0-7167-3174-6*) W H Freeman.

Decker, Ronald Ray. Bomb Threat Management & Policy. LC 98-34863. 128p. 1998. pap. 29.95 (*0-7506-7112-2*, Newnes) Buttrwrth-Heinemann.

Decker, Sam, ed. see Inc. Magazine Editors.

Decker, Scott, tr. see Uchimaru, Kiyoshi, et al.

Decker, Scott H., ed. Juvenile Justice Policy: Analyzing Trends & Outcomes. LC 83-21187. (Perspectives in Criminal Justice Ser.: No. 7). (Illus.). 168p. reprint ed. pap. 52.10 (*0-8357-8454-1*, 203471800091) Bks Demand.

Decker, Scott H., jt. auth. see Curry, G. David.

Decker, Scott H., jt. auth. see Wright, Richard T.

***Decker, Sharon.** Critical Care Nursing. (C). 2002. pap. 18.75 (*0-7668-1386-X*) Delmar.

Decker, Sharon. Critical Care Nursing. (C). 2002. pap. 49.50 (*0-7668-1384-3*) Thomson Learn.

***Decker, Sharon, et al.** Critical Care Nursing: Clinical Companion. (C). 2002. pap. 20.25 (*0-7668-1387-8*) Thomson Learn.

Decker, Sid & Sigs Books Staff. Re-Engineering Business Solutions with Object-Oriented Development. (C). 1999. pap. text 28.00 (*0-13-443003-4*) P-H.

Decker, Steve & Van Winkle, Barrik. Life in the Gang: Family, Friends, & Violence. (Criminology Ser.). (Illus.). 314p. (C). 1996. text 59.95 (*0-521-56292-9*); pap. text 19.95 (*0-521-56566-9*) Cambridge U Pr.

Decker, Steven, tr. see Hahnemann, Samuel.

Decker, Susan & Traver, Karen. Elementary Through Intermediate Algebra. 314p. (C). 1997. pap. text 42.97 (*1-56226-354-4*); pap. text, teacher ed. write for info. (*1-56226-355-2*) CAT Pub.

Decker, T. N. Computers As Assistants: A New Generation of Support Systems. Hoschka, Peter, ed. (Computers, Cognition, & Work Ser.). 230p. 1996. pap. text 24.50 (*0-8058-2186-4*) L Erlbaum Assocs.

Decker, T. Newell, jt. auth. see Decker, Phillip J.

Decker, Therese & Walsh, Martin, eds. Mariken van Nieumeghen. (Medvl Ser.). viii, 144p. 1994. 55.00 (*1-879751-20-8*) Camden Hse.

Decker, Tom W. Didymus. LC 95-68666. (Illus.). 280p. (Orig.). 1995. pap. 9.95 (*1-887097-13-9*) Dayspring Pr.

Decker, Virginia A., jt. auth. see Decker, Larry E.

Decker-Voigt, Hans-Helmut. Lexikon der Musiktherapie. (GER.). 400p. 1992. 150.00 (*0-7859-8481-X*, 3801706362) Fr & Eur.

Decker-Walters, Deena, jt. auth. see Robinson, R. W.

Decker, Warren, jt. auth. see Lont, Cynthia.

Decker, William M. Epistolary Practices: Letter Writing in America Before Telecommunications. LC 98-5270. 1998. pap. 19.95 (*0-8078-4743-7*); lib. bdg. 49.95 (*0-8078-2438-0*) U of NC Pr.

— The Literary Vocation of Henry Adams. LC 89-36157. xii, 324p. (C). 1990. 45.00 (*0-8078-1874-7*) U of NC Pr.

Decker, Wolfgang. Werner Koerbs: Vom Sinn der Leibesubungen Zur Zeit der Italienischen Renaissance. (GER.). iv, 161p. 1988. 49.80 (*3-615-00037-4*, Pub. by Weidmann) Lubrecht & Cramer.

Decker, Wolfgang, et al. Nikephoros, Zeitschrift fur Sport und Kultur im Altertum. (GER., Illus.). 288p. 1996. 98.00 (*3-615-00191-5*) G Olms Pubs.

Decker, Wolfgang, ed. see Nikephoros.

Deckers. Motivation & Emotion. 448p. (C). 2000. 72.00 (*0-205-27115-4*) Allyn.

Deckert, Barbara. Sewing for Plus Sizes: Design, Construction & Fit. LC 99-12287. 154p. 1999. 24.95 (*1-56158-284-0*) Taunton.

Deckert, Brigitte, jt. auth. see Jaros, Karl.

Deckert, Frank J., ed. see Rudig, Doug.

Deckert, Gordon. Rypins' Intensive Reviews: Psychiatry & Behavioral Medicine. LC 96-22473. 144p. 1996. pap. text 19.95 (*0-397-51554-5*) Lppncott W & W.

Deckert, H., jt. contrib. by see Anders, F.

Deckert, Robert, ed. see Thurston, Doris.

Deckert, Robert A., see Sanders, Sharon, pseud.

Deckert, Robert A., ed. see Sanders, Sharon, pseud.

Deckey, George. Analysis of a Hydrogen Peroxide Solution. Neidig, H. Anthony, ed. (Modular Laboratory Program in Chemistry Ser.). 12p. (C). 1987. pap. text 1.50 (*0-87540-335-2*, ANAL 335-2) Chem Educ Res.

Deckey, George & Marzzacco, Charles. Determining Molar Mass by Freezing Point Depression. Stanitski, C. L., ed. (Modular Laboratory Program in Chemistry Ser.). 12p. (C). 1998. pap. text 1.50 (*0-87540-500-2*, PROP 500) Chem Educ Res.

Deckhart, H. & Cox, Peter H., eds. Principles of Radiopharmacology. 1987. text 161.50 (*0-89838-774-4*) Kluwer Academic.

Deckker, P. De, see De Deckker, P., ed.

***Deckker, Thomas.** The Modern City Revisited. LC 00-30085. (Illus.). 2000. pap. write for info. (*0-419-25640-7*, E & FN Spon) Routledge.

***Deckker, Zilah Quesado.** Brazil Built: The Architecture of the Modern Movement in Brazil. LC 00-30082. (Illus.). 2000. pap. write for info. (*0-415-23178-7*) Routledge.

Decklon, Ellen S. More Adventures of the Black Hole Modulator. (Black Hole Modulator Trilogy Ser.: Vol. 2). (Illus.). 300p. 1998. 19.95 (*1-884939-39-2*); pap. 10.95 (*1-884939-40-6*) Antoine Versailles.

Deckman, Larry. The Constellations: Glow-in-the-Dark Map. 1993. pap. 9.99 (*0-945200-01-3*) Star Finders.

— Pocket Star Finder: Guide to the Northern Sky. (C). 1992. pap. 5.99 (*0-945200-00-5*) Star Finders.

— The Star Finder: Guide to the Northern Sky. 1995. pap. 11.99 (*0-945200-02-1*) Star Finders.

Deckwer, Wolf-Dieter. Bubble Column Reactions. LC 91-11879. 548p. 1991. 835.00 (*0-471-91811-3*) Wiley.

Declair, Edward G. Politics on the Fringe: The People, Policies, & Organization of the French National Front. LC 98-25265. (Illus.). 261p. 1999. 49.95 (*0-8223-2237-4*); pap. 17.95 (*0-8223-2139-4*) Duke.

DeClaire, Joan, jt. auth. see Gottman, John M.

Declan, Joyce, ed. A Saving Faith: A New Look at a Disciple's Finances. 120p. 1999. pap. 9.99 (*1-57782-077-0*) Discipleshp.

Declareuil, Joseph. Rome, the Law-Giver. Parker, Edward A., tr. LC 73-98752. 400p. 1970. reprint ed. lib. bdg. 45.00 (*0-8371-2796-3*, DERL, Greenwood Pr) Greenwood.

DeClaris, N., ed. Proceedings of the First International Conference on Advances in Communication & Control Systems. LC 88-27478. 224p. 1988. pap. text 98.00 (*0-911575-47-2*) Optimization Soft.

Declement, Barthe. Spoiled Rotten. 64p. (J). (gr. 3-4). 1997. lib. bdg. 14.49 (*0-7868-2317-8*, Pub. by Hyprn Child) Little.

DeClements, Barthe. The Bite of the Gold Bug: A Story of the Alaskan Gold Rush. (Once Upon America Ser.). (Illus.). 64p. (J). (gr. 2-6). 1994. pap. 4.99 (*0-14-036081-6*, PuffinBks) Peng Put Young Read.

DeClements, Barthe. The Bite of the Gold Bug: A Story of the Alaskan Gold Rush. (Once upon America Ser.). 1994. 10.19 (*0-606-06938-0*, Pub. by Turtleback) Demco.

DeClements, Barthe. Chiller Thriller. (J). (gr. 7 up). 1992. pap., boxed set 13.00 (*0-590-66250-3*) Scholastic Inc.

— Double Trouble. 1997. 9.60 (*0-606-12911-1*, Pub. by Turtleback) Demco.

Declements, Barthe. The Fourth Grade Wizards. (J). 1990. 9.09 (*0-606-03293-2*, Pub. by Turtleback) Demco.

— I Never Asked You to Understand Me. LC 85-40839. (Puffin Novels Ser.). 144p. (J). (gr. 7-12). 1998. pap. 4.99 (*0-14-130059-0*) Peng Put Young Read.

DeClements, Barthe. Liar, Liar. LC 97-17716. 144p. (YA). (gr. 3-7). 1998. lib. bdg. 14.95 (*0-7614-5021-1*) Marshall Cavendish.

DeClements, Barthe. Nothing's Fair in Fifth Grade. 137p. (J). (gr. 3-5). pap. 4.50 (*0-8072-1413-2*) Listening Lib.

DeClements, Barthe. Nothing's Fair in Fifth Grade. LC 80-54195. 144p. (J). (gr. 4-7). 1981. 15.99 (*0-670-51741-0*, Viking Child) Peng Put Young Read.

— Nothing's Fair in Fifth Grade. LC 89-48757. (Illus.). 137p. (J). (gr. 3-7). 1990. pap. 4.99 (*0-14-034443-8*, PuffinBks) Peng Put Young Read.

DeClements, Barthe. Nothing's Fair in Fifth Grade. (J). 1981. 9.09 (*0-606-04491-4*, Pub. by Turtleback) Demco.

DeClements, Barthe. Sixth Grade Can Really Kill You. (Illus.). 160p. (J). (gr. 3 up). 1995. pap. 4.99 (*0-14-037130-3*, PuffinBks) Peng Put Young Read.

— 6th Grade Can Really Kill You. (J). 1995. 9.09 (*0-606-08169-0*, Pub. by Turtleback) Demco.

— Spoiled Rotten. (Illus.). (J). (gr. 3-4). 1996. 13.95 (*0-7868-0275-8*, Pub. by Hyprn Child) Time Warner.

— Spoiled Rotten. LC 95-51097. (Illus.). 64p. (J). (gr. 1-3). 1996. pap. 3.95 (*0-7868-1145-5*, Pub. by Hyprn Ppbks) Little.

Declements, Barthe. Spoiled Rotten. (Hyperion Chapters Ser.). 1996. 9.15 (*0-606-09883-6*, Pub. by Turtleback) Demco.

— Tough Loser. LC 94-20290. 1996. 9.09 (*0-606-10957-9*, Pub. by Turtleback) Demco.

Declements, Barthe. Wake Me at Midnight. 1993. 9.09 (*0-606-06080-4*, Pub. by Turtleback) Demco.

Declerc, Michel, jt. auth. see Ballan, Hussein.

DeClerck, D. Dental Extractions & Compromised Hemostasis. No. 14. 136p. (Orig.). 1989. pap. 32.50 (*90-6186-324-4*, Pub. by Leuven Univ) Coronet Bks.

DeClerck, I. Modulation of the Ca(2 plus) Movements in Vascular Smooth Muscle Cells by the Co-Transmitters Noradrenaline & ATP. No. 36. 135p. (Orig.). 1991. pap. 44.00 (*90-6186-431-3*, Pub. by Leuven Univ) Coronet Bks.

Declerck, R. Studies on Copular Sentences, Clefts & Pseudo-Clefts. 270p. (Orig.). 1988. pap. 49.50 (*90-6186-289-2*, Pub. by Leuven Univ) Coronet Bks.

DeClerck, Renaat. Studies on Copular Sentences, Clefts & Pseudo-Clefts. (Orig.). (C). 1988. pap. 57.70 (*90-6765-124-9*) Mouton.

Declerck, Renaat H. When Clauses & Temporal Structure. (Routledge Studies in Germanic Linguistics Ser.: No. 2). (Illus.). 304p. (C). 1997. 100.00 (*0-415-15488-X*) Routledge.

Declercq, Dominik. Writing Against the State: Political Rhetorics in Third & Fourth Century China. LC 97-42284. (Sinica Leidensia Ser.). viii, 436p. 1998. 112.00 (*90-04-10376-7*) Brill Academic Pubs.

DeClercq, Erik D., ed. Antiretroviral Therapy. (Illus.). 480p. 2001. 79.95 (*1-55581-156-6*) ASM Pr.

DeClerq, Erik, ed. Clinical Use of Antiviral Drugs. (Developments in Medical Virology Ser.). 416p. 1988. text 190.00 (*0-89838-357-9*) Kluwer Academic.

DeCles, Jon, jt. auth. see Zimmer, Paul E.

Decleve. Heidegger und Kant. (Phaenomenologica Ser.: No. 40). 389p. 1971. lib. bdg. 135.00 (*90-247-5016-4*, Pub. by M Nijhoff) Kluwer Academic.

DeClouet, Fredric. Cooking with St. Clair. Jones, Will, ed. LC 78-74175. 1978. pap. 10.95 (*0-9602228-0-4*) Dectur Corp.

DeCloux, Tina. Tina's Science Adventures. Werges, Rosanne, ed. (Illus.). 80p. (J). (ps-3). 1992. spiral bd. 12.95 (*0-9615903-3-5*) Symbiosis Bks.

DeCloux, Tina & Werges, Rosanne. Tina's Science Notebook. (Illus.). 80p. (J). (gr. k-3). 1985. pap. 12.95 (*0-9615903-0-0*) Symbiosis Bks.

Declue, Michael W. Secrets of Love & Marriage. 200p. 2000. pap. 15.95 (*1-879899-21-3*) Newjoy Pr.

Decluzeau, Jean-Luc, jt. auth. see Buys, Alain.

Deco, G. & Obradovic, Dragon. An Information-Theoretic Approach to Neural Computing. (Illus.). 261p. 1997. text 54.95 (*0-387-94666-7*) Spr-Verlag.

Deco, Gustavo & Obradovic, Dragan. An Information-Theoretic Approach to Neural Networks. LC 95-48306. 1996. write for info. (*0-03-879466-7*) Spr-Verlag.

***Deco, Gustavo & Schhurmann, Bernd.** Information Dynamics: Foundations & Applications. LC 00-41907. 2000. write for info. (*0-387-95047-8*) Spr-Verlag.

Decock, Jean, tr. see Laude, Jean.

DeCock, Liliane, ed. Photo-Lab Index. 40th ed. LC 40-847. 1400p. (C). 1985. ring bd. 69.00 (*0-87100-051-2*, 2051) Morgan.

Decof, Leonard. Art of Advocacy: Opening Statement. (Art of Advocacy Ser.). 1982. ring bd. 160.00 (*0-8205-1035-1*) Bender.

DeConcini, Barbara. Narrative Remembering. LC 89-39653. 308p. (C). 1990. lib. bdg. 49.00 (*0-8191-7632-X*) U Pr of Amer.

DeConde, Alexander. The American Secretary of State. LC 75-27680. 182p. 1976. reprint ed. lib. bdg. 55.00 (*0-8371-8453-3*, DEAS, Greenwood Pr) Greenwood.

— Ethnicity, Race, & American Foreign Policy: A History. 288p. 1992. pap. text 18.95 (*1-55553-215-2*) NE U Pr.

— Ethnicity, Race, & American Foreign Policy: A History. 288p. 1992. text 45.00 (*1-55553-133-4*) NE U Pr.

— Presidential Machismo: Executive Authority, Military Intervention, & Foreign Relations. LC 99-30588. 380p. 1999. text 40.00 (*1-55553-403-1*) NE U Pr.

— This Affair of Louisiana. LC 76-12468. (Illus.). 347p. 1976. reprint ed. pap. 107.60 (*0-7837-9879-2*, 206060500006) Bks Demand.

DeConde, Alexander, ed. see Bailey, Thomas A.

Deconinck, F., ed. Information Processing in Medical Imaging. LC 84-1121. 1984. text 282.00 (*0-89838-677-2*) Kluwer Academic.

Deconinck, F., jt. auth. see Bossuyt, A.

Deconinck, F., jt. ed. see Jonckheer, M. H.

Deconinck, J., et al. Current Distribution & Electrode Shape Changes in Electrochemical Systems. Brebbia, Carlos A. & Orszag, S. A., eds. (Lecture Notes in Engineering Ser.: Vol. 75). (Illus.). 281p. 1992. 80.95 (*0-387-55104-2*) Spr-Verlag.

Decorative Artist's Workbook Editors, ed. Decorative Painting Sourcebook. LC 96-41200. (Illus.). 128p. 1997. pap. 24.99 (*0-89134-782-8*, North Lght Bks) F & W Pubns Inc.

DeCordova Museum & Sculpture Park Staff, jt. auth. see Lafo, Rachel Rosenfield.

DeCormier, Regina. Hoofbeats on the Door: Poems. 97p. (Orig.). 1993. pap. 9.95 (*0-9627460-3-7*) Helicon Nine Eds.

Decorse. Record of the Past. LC 99-34373. 253p. 1999. pap. 49.33 (*0-13-490335-8*) P-H.

Decorse, Christopher R., jt. auth. see Scupin, Raymond.

Decorte, R. Application of the Polymerase Chain Reaction to Forensic DNA Analysis in Belgium. No. 105. 138p. (Orig.). 1994. pap. 39.50 (*90-6186-661-8*, Pub. by Leuven Univ) Coronet Bks.

Decosse. Treasury of Country Heritage. LC 95-23500. (SPA., Illus.). 512p. 1995. 24.95 (*2-89429-591-X*) Creat Pub Intl.

DeCosse, Cy. Kids' Furnishings. LC 96-17655. (Portable Workshop Ser.). (Illus.). 96p. 1996. spiral bd. 14.95 (*0-86573-682-0*) Creat Pub Intl.

— A Portfolio of Kitchen Ideas. rev. ed. LC 90-33946. (Illus.). 96p. 1995. pap. 9.95 (*0-86573-970-6*) Creat Pub Intl.

Decosse, Cy, Inc., Staff & Singer Co. Staff. Sewing Essentials. rev. ed. LC 96-18129. (Illus.). 1996. 18.95 (*0-86573-307-4*) Creat Pub Intl.

— Sewing Essentials. rev. ed. LC 96-18129. (Illus.). 128p. 1998. pap. 16.95 (*0-86573-308-2*) Creat Pub Intl.

DeCosse, Cy, Incorporated Staff. Porch, Patio & Deck Furnishings. LC 95-49810. (Portable Workshop Ser.). (Illus.). 96p. 1996. spiral bd. 14.95 (*0-86573-690-1*) Creat Pub Intl.

— A Portfolio of Porch & Patio Ideas. LC 95-49809. (Illus.). 96p. 1996. pap. 9.95 (*0-86573-983-8*) Creat Pub Intl.

— Sewing for the Holidays. LC 94-679. (Singer Sewing Reference Library). (Illus.). 128p. 1994. 18.95 (*0-86573-295-7*); pap. 16.95 (*0-86573-296-5*) Creat Pub Intl.

— Traditional Christmas Cooking, Crafts & Gifts. LC 93-50059. (Illus.). 320p. 1994. 32.95 (*0-86573-939-0*) Creat Pub Intl.

— Wood Accents for the Home. LC 95-49811. (Portable Workshop Ser.). (Illus.). 96p. 1996. spiral bd. 14.95 (*0-86573-695-2*) Creat Pub Intl.

— Workshop Tips & Techniques, Vol. 8. LC 90-28783. (Black & Decker Home Improvement Library). (Illus.). 128p. 1991. 16.95 (*0-86573-716-9*); pap. 14.95 (*0-86573-717-7*) Creat Pub Intl.

DeCosse, Jerome, jt. ed. see Condon, Robert E.

DeCosse, Jerome J. & Sherlock, Paul, eds. Clinical Management of Gastrointestinal Cancer. (Cancer Treatment & Research Ser.). 386p. 1984. text 192.50 (*0-89838-601-2*) Kluwer Academic.

DeCosse, Jerome J., jt. ed. see Condon, Robert E.

DeCosse, Jerome J., ed. see Sherlock, Paul.

DeCosta, Joeseph & Shukla, A. R. Authentic English-Hindi Dictionary. (ENG & HIN.). 59.95 (*0-8288-7692-4*, M3647) Fr & Eur.

DeCosta, Miriam. Erotique Noire Black Erotica. (FRE.). 496p. 1992. pap. 9.99 (*0-385-40381-X*) Doubleday.

DeCosta-Willis, Miriam, ed. The Memphis Diary of Ida B. Wells. 240p. (C). 1996. pap. 15.00 (*0-8070-7065-3*) Beacon Pr.

Decosta-Willis, Miriam, et al, eds. Erotique Noire/Black Erotica. (FRE.). 496p. 1992. pap. 15.95 (*0-385-42309-8*) Doubleday.

Decoste, Denise C., jt. auth. see Glennen, Sharon L.

DeCoste, F. C. & MacPherson, Lillian. Law, Religion, Theology: A Selective Annotated Bibliography. LC 97-22609. (C). 1997. lib. bdg. 48.00 (*0-933951-75-2*) Locust Hill Pr.

DeCoste, F. C., et al. Feminist Legal Literature: An Annotated Bibliography. LC 91-9731. 514p. 1991. text 25.00 (*0-8240-7117-4*, SS671) Garland.

DeCoster, Cyrus. Juan Valera. LC 74-3058. (Twayne's World Authors Ser.). 186p. (C). 1974. lib. bdg. 17.95 (*0-8057-2919-4*) Irvington.

DeCoster, Lester A. The Legacy of Penn's Woods: A History of the Pennsylvania Bureau of Forestry. (Illus.). 70p. 1995. pap. 12.95 (*0-89271-066-7*, 0425) Pa Hist & Mus.

DeCoster, Lester A., jt. auth. see Sampson, R. Neil.

DeCoster, Miles. Iconomics: Money. 1984. pap. 9.95 (*0-932526-08-X*) Nexus Pr.

— Television. 1985. 20.00 (*0-932526-67-5*) Nexus Pr.

Decoteau, A. E. The Handbook of Amazon Parrots. (Illus.). 256p. 1980. 23.95 (*0-87666-892-9*, H-1025) TFH Pubns.

— Handbook of Cockatoos. (Illus.). 160p. 1989. 24.95 (*0-86622-798-9*, H-1030) TFH Pubns.

Decoteau, Al E., jt. auth. see Andleton, Bobbie.

***Decoteau, Dennis R.** Vegetable Crops. LC 99-45819. 464p. 1999. 94.00 (*0-13-956996-0*) P-H.

Decoteau, Glynn T., jt. auth. see Keller, Mary M.

DeCotiis, Sue. A Woman's Guide to Sexual Health. 304p. (Orig.). 1989. mass mkt. 5.50 (*0-671-66011-X*) PB.

DeCotis, Ruth, jt. auth. see Lambert, Stephen.

Decoto, Jean. Heart's Awakening. large type ed. 512p. 1984. 27.99 (*0-7089-1067-X*) Ulverscroft.

DeCou, Herbert F. Antiquities from Boscoreale in Field Museum of Natural History: With Catalogue of Iron Implements. LC 12-15551. (Field Museum of Natural History Anthropological Ser.: Vol. 7, No. 4). (Illus.). 167p. 1912. reprint ed. pap. 51.80 (*0-608-02723-5*, 206338800004) Bks Demand.

DeCourcy, Lynne H. The Good Child. Warren, Shirley, ed. 40p. 1990. pap. 6.00 (*1-877801-09-7*) Still Waters.

— A Progress of Miracles. Iddings, Kathleen, ed. LC 92-61244. 90p. (Orig.). 1993. per. 10.00 (*0-931289-11-4*) San Diego Poet Pr.

Decourcy, Mike. Inside Basketball: From the Playgrounds to the NBA. (Illus.). 176p. 1996. 19.98 (*1-56799-384-2*, MetroBooks) M Friedman Pub Grp Inc.

DeCourt, Ann. Forbidden Love. LC 98-90421. x, 250p. (Orig.). 1998. pap. 13.95 (*0-9664753-0-5*, 1-125) Wabokat Pubg.

— Never Forget: Greatest Love Story Ever Told. LC 98-90469. x, 208p. (Orig.). 1998. pap. 14.95 (*0-9664753-1-3*, 1-126) Wabokat Pubg.

DeCourten, Frank. Dinosaurs of Utah. LC 98-2747. 300p. 1998. 45.00 (*0-87480-556-2*) U of Utah Pr.

Decovny, Sheree. Swaps. 2nd ed. 224p. 1998. 57.00 (*0-13-694258-X*) P-H.

DeCoy, Robert H. Jack Johnson: Champion Heavyweight Boxer. 320p. 1991. mass mkt. 4.95 (*0-87067-581-8*) Holloway.

Decoy, Robert H. Nigger Bible. 304p. 1998. mass mkt. 6.99 (*0-87067-981-3*) Holloway.

Decoz, Hans & Monte, Tom. Numerology: Key to Your Inner Self. LC 93-30671. 276p. pap. 12.95 (*0-89529-566-0*, Avery) Penguin Putnam.

Decraemer, W. The Family Trichodoridae: Stubby Root & Virus Vector Nematodes. (Developments in Plant Pathology Ser.: Vol. 6). 376p. (C). 1995. text 154.50 (*0-7923-3773-5*) Kluwer Academic.

Decredico, Mary A. Mary Boykin Chestnut: A Confederate Woman's Life. LC 95-11155. (American Profiles Ser.). (Illus.). 212p. (C). 1996. pap. text 14.95 (*0-945612-47-8*) Madison Hse.

— Mary Boykin Chestnut: A Confederate Woman's Life. LC 95-11155. (American Profiles Ser.). (Illus.). 212p. (C). 1996. text 29.95 (*0-945612-46-X*) Madison Hse.

DeCredico, Mary A. Patriotism for Profit: Georgia's Urban Entrepreneurs & the Confederate War Effort. LC 89-39132. (Fred W. Morrison Series in Southern Studies). (Illus.). 233p. 1990. pap. 72.30 (*0-608-05206-X*, 206574300005) Bks Demand.

DeCremer, Shirley. Freddie the Frog. LC 92-53094. (Illus.). 16p. (J). (ps-2). 1995. 15.00 (*0-935343-03-2*) Peartree.

DeCrescenzo, Teresa, ed. Gay & Lesbian Professionals in the Closet: Who's in, Who's Out, & Why. LC 97-16111. 94p. 1997. 29.95 (*0-7890-0331-7*); pap. 14.95 (*1-56023-104-1*, Harrington Park) Haworth Pr.

— Helping Gay & Lesbian Youth: New Policies, New Programs, New Practice. LC 94-31968. (Journal of Gay

& Lesbian Social Services). 188p. 1994. pap. text 14.95 (*1-56023-057-6*, Harrington Park); lib. bdg. 54.95 (*1-56024-678-2*, Harrington Park) Haworth Pr.

Decreusefond, Laurent. Stochastic Analysis & Related Topics VI: The Geilo Workshop, 1996. LC 97-29125. (Progress in Probability Ser.). 1997. 125.00 (*0-8176-4018-5*) Birkhauser.

DeCristofano, Carolyn C. Leonardo's ABC: Sharing Leonardo da Vinci with Children. (Illus.). 29p. (J). (ps-2). 1997. 12.95 (*0-918866-00-6*) Museum of Science.

DeCristofaro, Michael. Building a Better Bookshelf. LC 75-733230. 1975. student ed. 7.00 (*0-8064-0259-8*, 701) Bergwall.

DeCristofaro, Michael, jt. auth. see Thyen, John D.

DeCristoforo, R. J. Complete Book of Wood Joinery. LC 97-207414. (Illus.). 320p. 1997. 17.95 (*0-8069-9950-0*) Sterling.

— Housebuilding: A Do-It-Yourself Guide. LC 87-10127. (Illus.). 656p. (Orig.). 1987. pap. 21.95 (*0-8069-6512-6*) Sterling.

Decristoforo, R. J. Jigsaw - Scroll Saw. 1991. 27.95 (*0-8306-5317-1*) McGraw-Hill Prof.

DeCristoforo, R. J. The Ultimate Woodshop Jig Book. LC 98-40932. (Illus.). 160p. 1999. pap. 22.99 (*1-55870-491-4*, 70421, Popular Woodwkng Bks) F & W Pubns Inc.

— Woodworking Mistakes & Solutions: Professional Secrets for the Home Craftsman. LC 96-24178. (Illus.). 256p. 1996. pap. 19.95 (*0-8069-3886-2*) Sterling.

DeCroce, Patricia. Learning Spanish with Enza B Bk. 2: Regular Verbs & the Present Tense. (Learning Language with Enza B. Ser.). (SPA.). 60p. (YA). (gr. 6-8). 1993. write for info. (*1-886332-03-7*) Forlang Foreign.

Decroocq, Daniel. Catalytic Cracking of Heavy Petroleum Fractions. (Illus.). 140p. (C). 1984. 300.00 (*2-7108-0455-7*, Pub. by Edits Technip) Enfield Pubs NH.

Decroux, Etienne. Words on Mime. Leabhart, Thomas, ed. Piper, Mark, tr. from FRE. (Mime Journal Ser.). (Illus.). 160p. 1985. pap. 12.00 (*0-9611066-5-4*) Mime Jour.

DeCrow, Roger. New Learning for Older Americans. 1975. 5.75 (*0-88379-011-4*) A A A C E.

Decrow, Suzanne, ed. Cooking with St. Francis by the Sea. (Illus.). 176p. (Orig.). 1996. pap. 15.00 (*0-9630061-1-8*) St Francis Sea.

Decrow, Suzanne, ed. see St. Francis by the Sea Staff.

Decsenyi, J., tr. see Szentpeteri, Istvan.

Decsi, Gyula. Woerterbuch der Rechtssprache und Wirtschaftssprache Vol. 1: German-Russian. (GER & RUS.). 564p. 1990. 225.00 (*0-7859-8331-7*, 3406090222) Fr & Eur.

— Woerterbuch der Rechtssprache und Wirtschaftssprache Vol. 2: Russian-German. (GER & RUS.). 725p. 1985. 225.00 (*0-7859-8332-5*, 3406090230) Fr & Eur.

Decsy, Gyula. The Indo-European Protolanguage: A Computational Reconstruction. (Bibliotheca Nostratica Ser.: Vol. 10). 240p. 1991. 41.00 (*0-931922-40-2*) Eurolingua.

— Sprachherkunftsforschung Vol. I: Einleitung & Phonogenese. (Bibliotheca Nostratica Ser.: Vol 2). 87p. 1977. 22.00 (*3-447-01861-5*) Eurolingua.

— Sprachherkunftsforschung Vol. II: Semogenese-Palaosemiotik. (Bibliotheca Nostratica Ser.: Vol. 2). 78p. 1981. 22.00 (*0-931922-06-2*) Eurolingua.

— Yurak Chrestomathy. LC 65-63391. (Uralic & Altaic Ser.: Vol. 50). (Orig.). 1966. pap. text 9.00 (*0-87750-004-5*) Res Inst Inner Asian Studies.

Decsy, Gyula, ed. Eurasian Studies Yearbook, 1995 No. 67. 259p. 1995. 82.00 (*0-931922-54-2*) Eurolingua.

— A Select Catalog of Language Universals. (Bibliotheca Nostratica Ser.: Vol. 8). 141p. 1988. pap. 26.00 (*0-931922-29-1*) Eurolingua.

— Statistical Report on the Languages of the World As of 1985 Pt. I. 2nd ed. (Bibliotheca Nostratica Ser.: Vol. 6: 1). 98p. 1990. 26.00 (*0-931922-41-0*) Eurolingua.

Decsy, Gyula & Bodrogligeti, A. J., eds. Eurasian Studies Yearbook, Vol. 65. 192p. 1993. 74.00 (*0-931922-48-8*) Eurolingua.

— Eurasian Studies Yearbook, Vol. 66. 221p. 1994. 74.00 (*0-931922-50-X*) Eurolingua.

— Ural-Altaische Jahrbucher, Vol. 64, 1992. 210p. 1991. 74.00 (*0-931922-44-5*) Eurolingua.

— Ural-Altaische Jahrbucher: Ural-Altaic Yearbook, Vol. 59. 172p. 1987. 48.00 (*0-931922-23-2*) Eurolingua.

— Ural-Altaische Jahrbucher: Ural-Altaic Yearbook, Vol. 61. 187p. 1989. 74.00 (*0-931922-34-8*) Eurolingua.

— Ural-Altaische Jahrbucher - Ural-Altaic Yearbook, 1988, Vol. 60. anniversary ed. 224p. 1988. 74.00 (*0-931922-30-5*) Eurolingua.

— Ural-Altaische Jahrbucher - Ural-Altaic Yearbook, 1990, Vol. 62. 188p. 1990. 74.00 (*0-931922-37-2*) Eurolingua.

— Ural-Altaische Jahrbucher - Ural-Altraic Yearbook, Vol. 58. 172p. 1986. 48.00 (*0-931922-22-4*) Eurolingua.

— Ural-Altaische Jahrbucher - Ural-Altraic Yearbook, Vol. 63, 1991. 248p. 1990. 74.00 (*0-931922-39-9*) Eurolingua.

— Ural-Altaische Jahrbucher - Ural-Altraic Yearbook, 1977, Vol. 49.Tr. of Ural-Altaic Yearbook. 177p. 1977. 48.00 (*3-447-01806-2*) Eurolingua.

— Ural-Altaische Jahrbucher - Ural-Altraic Yearbook, 1978, Vol. 50.Tr. of Ural-Altaic Yearbook. 207p. 1978. 48.00 (*3-447-01891-7*) Eurolingua.

— Ural-Altaische Jahrbucher - Ural-Altraic Yearbook, 1981, Vol. 53.Tr. of Ural-Altaic Yearbook. 172p. 1981. 48.00 (*0-931922-08-9*) Eurolingua.

— Ural-Altaische Jahrbucher - Ural-Altraic Yearbook, 1982, Vol. 54.Tr. of Ural-Altaic Yearbook. 172p. 1982. 48.00 (*0-931922-09-7*) Eurolingua.

— Ural-Altaische Jahrbucher - Ural-Altraic Yearbook, 1983, Vol. 55. 174p. 1983. 48.00 (*0-931922-14-3*) Eurolingua.

— Ural-Altaische Jahrbucher - Ural-Altraic Yearbook, 1985, Vol. 57. 180p. 1980. 48.00 (*0-931922-20-8*) Eurolingua.

Decsy, Gyula & Brodrogligeti, A. J., eds. Ural-Altaische Jahrbucher - Ural-Altraic Yearbook, 1979, Vol. 51.Tr. of Ural-Altaic Yearbook. 183p. 1979. 48.00 (*0-931922-00-3*) Eurolingua.

— Ural-Altaische Jahrbucher - Ural-Altraic Yearbook, 1980, Vol. 52.Tr. of Ural-Altaic Yearbook. 191p. 1980. 48.00 (*0-931922-05-4*) Eurolingua.

— Ural-Altaische Jahrbucher - Ural-Altraic Yearbook, 1984, Vol. 56. 187p. 1985. 48.00 (*0-931922-17-8*) Eurolingua.

Decsy, Gyula & Dimov-Bogoev, Christo, eds. Eurasia Nostratica: Festschrift fuer Karl Heinrich Menges, 2 vols. in 1. (Bibliotheca Nostratica Ser.: Vol. 1). 473p. 1977. 86.00 (*3-447-01834-8*) Eurolingua.

Decsy, Gyula, et al. Carleton T. Hodge Bibliography, 1944-1997. (Arcadie Bibliographia Vixorum Exuditorum Ser.: Vol. 16). 35p. 1997. 26.00 (*0-931922-61-5*) Eurolingua.

Decter, Ann. Honour. LC PR9199.3.D388H66 199. 240p. 1996. pap. 14.95 (*0-88974-057-7*, Pub. by Press Gang Pubs) LPC InBook.

— Katie's Alligator Goes to Day Care. (Illus.). 24p. (J). pap. 3.95 (*0-88961-116-5*, Pub. by Womens Pr) LPC InBook.

— Paper, Scissors, Rock. 192p. 1992. pap. 12.95 (*0-88974-040-2*, Pub. by Press Gang Pubs) LPC InBook.

Decter, Jacqueline. Nicholas Roerich: The Life & Art of a Russian Master. (Illus.). 224p. 1989. 39.95 (*0-89281-156-0*, Park St Pr) Inner Tradit.

***Decter, Michael B.** Four Strong Winds: Navigating the Global Challenges to Health Care. 256p. 2000. 32.95 (*0-7737-3224-1*) Stoddart Publ.

Decuir, L. J. Southeastern Flies: A Collection of Flies, Fly-Tying & Fly-Fishing Tips for Use on the Tailwaters, Streams, & Lakes of the Southeastern United States. LC 99-27801. (Illus.). 256p. 1999. pap. 12.95 (*0-89732-304-1*) Menasha Ridge.

***Decuir, L. J.** Using AutoCAD: An Introduction to Computer-Assisted Design for the Theatre. LC 99-33509. 272p. 2000. pap. 31.95 (*0-325-00122-7*, Pub. by Heinemann) Natl Bk Netwk.

— Using 3D Studio MAX, Painter, & Poser: An Introduction to Computer-Assisted Design for the Theatre. LC 99-36491. 368p. 2000. pap. 34.95 (*0-325-00222-3*, Pub. by Heinemann) Natl Bk Netwk.

***Decuire, Ed.** America Dearest: Reflections of America's Child. (Illus.). 395p. 1999. pap. 25.00 (*1-885001-13-4*) Via Press.

DeCurtins, Robert J., ed. Model Plumbing Codes: A Comparison Study. 1176p. 1997. 122.95 (*1-891255-02-9*) Am Soc Plumb Eng.

Decurtis, Anthony. Rocking My Life Away: Writing about Music & Other Matters. LC 97-9717. 312p. 1998. 24.95 (*0-8223-2184-X*) Duke.

DeCurtis, Anthony. Rocking My Life Away: Writing About Music & Other Matters. 368p. 1999. pap. text 16.95 (*0-8223-2419-9*) Duke.

Decurtis, Anthony. The Rolling Stone Illustrated History of Rock & Roll: The Definitive History of the Most. 3rd ed. 1992. pap. 29.95 (*0-679-73728-6*) Random.

DeCurtis, Anthony, ed. Present Tense: Rock & Roll & Culture. LC 92-1651. (Illus.). 332p. 1992. pap. 17.95 (*0-8223-1265-4*); text 49.95 (*0-8223-1261-1*) Duke.

DeCurtis, Anthony, et al, eds. The Rolling Stone Album Guide: Completely New Reviews: Every Essential Album, Every Essential Artist. LC 92-50156. 1992. pap. 20.00 (*0-679-73729-4*) Random.

DeCusa, Nicolas. Idiota de Mente. Miller, Clyde L., tr. LC 77-86244. (Janus Ser.).Tr. of Lay Man: About Mind. 122p. 1979. 25.00 (*0-913870-65-X*) Abaris Bks.

DeCusatis, Casimer, ed. Handbook of Applied Photometry. LC 96-35231. (Illus.). 478p. 1997. reprint ed. 90.00 (*1-56396-416-3*, AIP Pr) Spr-Verlag.

DeCusatis, Casimer, et al, eds. Handbook of Fiber Optic Data Communication. LC 97-29071. (Illus.). 854p. 1997. text 95.00 (*0-12-437162-0*) Acad Pr.

***DED Associates Staff.** Travel Sickness. 2000. pap. text 42.00 (*3-931126-38-2*) Die Gestalten.

Dedad, John A. Practical Guide to Applying Low-Voltage Fuses. 2nd rev. ed. Reichenstein, Hermann W., ed. (Practical Guide to Ser.). (Illus.). 113p. 1992. pap. 23.95 (*0-87288-479-1*) Intertec Pub.

DeDatta, S. K. & Patrick, W. H., eds. Nitrogen Economy of Flooded Rice Soils. (Developments in Plant & Soil Sciences Ser.). 1986. text 139.00 (*90-247-3361-8*) Kluwer Academic.

Deddens, Karel. Where Everything Points to Him. Plantinga, Theodore, tr. from DUT. & intro. by. LC 93-24061. 170p. (Orig.). 1993. pap. 11.90 (*0-921100-39-6*) Inhtce Pubns.

Deddo, Cathy, jt. auth. see Deddo, Gary.

Deddo, Gary & Deddo, Cathy. George MacDonald. (Devotional Library). 1996. 11.90 (*0-7152-0720-2*, Pub. by St Andrew) St Mut.

Deddo, Gary W. Karl Barth's Theology of Relations: Trinitarian, Christological & Human: Towards an Ethic of the Family. LC 97-48467. (Issues in Systematic Theology Ser.: Vol. 4). XX, 440p. (C). 1999. text 66.95 (*0-8204-3761-1*) P Lang Pubng.

Dede, Chris, ed. see Kosma, Robert, et al.

Dede, Vivian. Jesus' First Miracle: John 2:1-11. LC 59-1445. (Arch Bks.). (Illus.). 24p. (J). (ps-4). 1990. pap. 1.99 (*0-570-09022-9*, 59-1445) Concordia.

***Dedeaux, P. N.** Algiers Tomorrow. 2000. mass mkt. 7.95 (*1-56201-211-8*) Blue Moon Bks.

Dedeaux, P. N. Aunt Anna. 208p. 1999. mass mkt. 7.95 (*1-56201-131-6*) Blue Moon Bks.

— Nothing Things. 1998. mass mkt. 6.95 (*1-56333-653-7*) Masquerade.

— The Prussian Girls. 223p. 1989. reprint ed. mass mkt. 4.95 (*0-929654-15-3*, 44) Blue Moon Bks.

— The Territory Within. 1998. mass mkt. 6.95 (*1-56333-640-5*) Masquerade.

DeDecker, Mary. Mines of the Eastern Sierra. 1996. pap. 4.50 (*0-87505-411-0*) Borden.

DeDeiros, Norma H. C. Dramatizaciones Infantil para Dias Especiales.Tr. of Children's Dramas for Special Occasions. (SPA.). 96p. 1961. reprint ed. pap. 3.99 (*0-311-07606-8*) Casa Bautista.

Dedek, Jan. Basics of SCSI. 3rd ed. 50p. 1997. pap. text 9.95 (*0-9637439-4-5*) Ancot Corp.

— Fibre Channel, the Basics. 2nd rev. ed. 1997. 39.00 (*0-9637439-3-7*) Ancot Corp.

— What Is Fiber Channel? 3rd rev. ed. (Illus.). 1996. pap. 9.50 (*0-9637439-5-3*) Ancot Corp.

Dedek, Oldrich, ed. The Break-up of Czechoslovakia: An In-Depth Economic Analysis. 224p. 1996. 68.95 (*1-85972-276-8*, Pub. by Avebry) Ashgate Pub Co.

***Dedekam, Ivar.** Sail & Rig Tuning. (Illus.). 80p. 2000. pap. 19.95 (*1-898660-67-0*) Fernhurst Bks.

Dedekind, Richard. Essays on the Theory of Numbers. Beman, Wooster W., tr. 115p. (C). 1998. pap. 5.95 (*0-486-21010-3*) Dover.

— Theory of Algebraic Integers. (Cambridge Mathematical Library). 165p. (C). 1996. pap. text 24.95 (*0-521-56518-9*) Cambridge U Pr.

Dedekind, Richard, jt. auth. see Lejeune-Dirichlet, Peter G.

Dedel, Peter. Johannes Brahms: A Guide to His Autographs in Facsimile. (Music Library Association Index & Bibliography Ser.: No. 18). 86p. 1978. pap. 8.50 (*0-914954-12-1*) Scarecrow.

***Dedera, Don.** Arizona's Mogollon Rim: Travel Guide to Payson & Beyond. 1999. pap. text 10.95 (*0-916179-90-7*) Ariz Hwy.

Dedera, Don. In Search of Jesus Garcia. (Illus.). 120p. (Orig.). 1989. pap. 7.95 (*0-9624499-0-3*) Prickly AZ.

— Navajo Rugs: How to Find, Evaluate, Buy & Care for Them. 2nd rev. ed. LC 96-10365. (Illus.). 136p. (Orig.). 1996. pap. 14.95 (*0-87358-635-2*) Northland AZ.

— You Know You're an Arizona Native, When. (Illus.). 100p. (Orig.). 1993. pap. 9.95 (*0-9624499-2-X*) Prickly AZ.

Dederer, John M. Making Bricks Without Straw: Nathaniel Greene's Southern Campaign & Mao Tse-Tung's Mobile War. (Illus.). 98p. 1983. pap. text 12.00 (*0-89745-049-3*) Sunflower U Pr.

Dederichs, P. H., et al. Point Defect in Metal's II: Dynamical Properties & Diffusion Controlled Reactions. (Tracts in Modern Physics Ser.: Vol. 87). 1980. 49.00 (*0-387-09623-X*) Spr-Verlag.

Dedeyan, Charles, jt. auth. see Montaigne, Michel de.

Dedeyan, Rita-Carole. Dictionnaire Fiscal Bilingue: Francais-Anglais, Anglais-Francais. (ENG & FRE.). 90p. 1996. 49.95 (*0-7859-9765-2*) Fr & Eur.

Dedham Historical Society Staff, ed. Dedham Historical Register, 1890-1903. 1999. 239.00 (*0-8328-9869-4*); pap. write for info. (*0-8328-9870-8*) Higginson Bk Co.

***Dedhia, Dilip.** Learn Java by Association with C, Cobol, Fortran, Pascal, Visual Basic: A Practical Dictionary of Programming Languages. 208p. 2000. 33.95 (*0-9679469-0-5*) Engineering Mech.

Dedic-Aievoli, Eleanor, ed. see Bellissino, Charles A.

Dedic, Charles E. Dreams of Beaver Creek. (Illus.). 150p. 1999. 65.00 (*0-9671444-0-X*) Beaver Creek MI.

Dedieu, A., ed. Transition Metal Hydrides. 399p. 1991. 139.00 (*0-471-18768-2*, Wiley-VCH) Wiley.

Dedieu, Alain, ed. Transition Metal Hydrides. (Illus.). x, 400p. 1991. 95.00 (*0-89573-781-7*, Wiley-VCH) Wiley.

Dedieu, Maurice. Senegal: Narrative Paintings. Barry, Diana & Henry, Jacques, trs. (ENG & FRE., Illus.). 100p. (Orig.). 1986. pap. 15.00 (*0-936819-02-2*) USL Art Museum.

Dedieu, Theirry. Hunting for Fur: The Adventures of Panda & Koala. LC 97-53077. (Illus.). 32p. (J). (ps-5). 1998. pap. 8.95 (*0-385-32636-X*) Doubleday.

Dedieu, Thierry. Baby Clown: A Pull-the-Tab Book. large type ed. LC 94-79166. (Illus.). 16p. (J). (ps-1). 1995. 12.95 (*0-7868-0075-5*, Pub. by Hyprn Child) Little.

— Baby Ringmaster. (Pull-the-Tab Bks.). (Illus.). 16p. (J). Date not set. 12.95 (*0-7868-0110-7*, Pub. by Disney Pr) Time Warner.

— The Boy Who Ate Words. Harris, Julie & Frankel, Lory, trs. from FRE. LC 97-158264. (Illus.). 40p. 1997. 16.95 (*0-8109-1245-7*, Pub. by Abrams) Time Warner.

— Out for Good: The Adventures of Panda & Koala. LC 98-17234. (Illus.). 32p. (J). (ps-3). 1999. 8.95 (*0-385-32634-3*) Doubleday.

Dedijer, Vladimir. The Battle Stalin Lost: Memoirs of Yugoslavia 1948-1953. 341p. 1978. reprint ed. 47.50 (*0-85124-223-5*, Pub. by Spkesman) Coronet Bks.

— Tito. LC 72-4269. (World Affairs Ser.: National & International Viewpoints). 450p. 1980. reprint ed. 35.95 (*0-405-04565-4*) Ayer.

— The Yugoslav Auschwitz & the Vatican: The Croatian Massacre of the Serbs During WWII. Kendall, Harvey, tr. LC 91-43150. (Illus.). 444p. (C). 1992. 31.95 (*0-87975-752-3*) Prometheus Bks.

Dedina, Jiri & Tsalev, Dimiter L. Hydride Generation Atomic Absorption Spectrometry. (Chemical Analysis: A Series of Monographs on Analytical Chemistry & Its Applications). 544p. 1995. 350.00 (*0-471-95364-4*) Wiley.

***Dedina, Serge.** Saving the Gray Whale: People, Politics & Conservation in Baja, California. LC 99-6766. (Society, Environment & Place Ser.). 200p. 2000. pap. 17.95 (*0-8165-1846-7*) U of Ariz Pr.

— Saving the Gray Whale: People, Politics & Conservation in Baja, California. 200p. 2000. 37.50 (*0-8165-1845-9*) U of Ariz Pr.

Dedik, Jan & Stephens, Gary. What Is Fibre Channel? 4th rev. ed. (Illus.). 1997. pap. 9.50 (*0-9637439-9-6*) Ancot Corp.

Dedman, jt. auth. see Smith, Vana L.

Dedman, John R., jt. ed. see Smith, Vana L.

Dedman, Martin J. Origins & Development of the European Union. 160p. (C). 1996. pap. 17.99 (*0-415-11161-7*) Routledge.

Dedman, Robert H. & DeLoach, Debbie. King of Clubs: Grow Rich in More Than Money. 220p. 1998. 21.95 (*0-87833-202-2*) Taylor Pub.

Dedman, Stephen. The Art of Arrow Cutting. LC 96-53282. 320p. 1997. text 22.95 (*0-312-86320-9*) St Martin.

— The Art of Arrow Cutting. 1999. pap. 13.95 (*0-312-86832-4*) St Martin.

***Dedman, Stephen.** The Art of Arrow Cutting. 1998. mass mkt. write for info. (*0-8125-4534-6*) Tor Bks.

— Foreign Bodies. 2000. pap. 14.95 (*0-312-87259-3*) St Martin.

— Foreign Bodies. LC 99-55808. 288p. 1999. 23.95 (*0-312-86864-2*, Pub. by Tor Bks) St Martin.

***Dedmondt, Glenn.** The Flags of Civil War South Carolina. LC 00-20694. (Illus.). 160p. 2000. pap. 17.95 (*1-56554-696-2*) Pelican.

Dedmondt, Glenn. Southern Bronze: Capt. Garden's (S.C.) Artillery Co. During the War Between the States. (Illus.). 255p. 1993. 30.00 (*0-9623065-4-1*) Palmetto Bookworks.

DeDombal, F. T. Diagnosis of Acute Abdominal Pain, No. 2E. (Illus.). 274p. 1990. text 39.95 (*0-443-03487-7*) Church.

DeDomenicis, MaryLisa W. Almost All Red. 28p. (Orig.). 1997. pap. 6.00 (*1-877801-34-8*) Still Waters.

DeDominic, Leslie M. Rocky Mountain Gourmet Cookbook. LC 97-26441. (Illus.). 224p. 1997. 24.95 (*1-56044-559-9*) Falcon Pub Inc.

Dedopulos, Tim. Best Book of Insults & Putdowns Ever! 1999. pap. text 12.95 (*1-85868-489-7*, Pub. by Carlton Bks Ltd) Natl Bk Netwk.

— Magic: The Gathering: The Official Deckbuilders' Guide. (Illus.). 144p. 1998. pap. text 13.95 (*1-56025-156-5*, Thunders Mouth) Avalon NY.

Dedora, Brian. With W. K. in the Workshop: William Kurelek. (Illus.). 64p. pap. 9.95 (*0-920544-68-1*, Pub. by Mercury Bk) LPC InBook.

DeDourek, John, jt. auth. see Tremblay, Jean-Paul.

***DeDreuille, Mayeul.** A History of Monasticism. 137p. 1999. pap. 16.95 (*0-8245-1810-1*) Crossroad NY.

Dedrick, Colleen, jt. auth. see Dedrick, William.

Dedrick, Don. Naming the Rainbow: Colour Language, Colour Science, & Culture. LC 98-30408. (Synthese Library). 215p. 1998. 97.00 (*0-7923-5239-4*) Kluwer Academic.

Dedrick, Jason & Kraemer, Kenneth L. Asia's Computer Challenge: Threat or Opportunity for the U. S. & the World? LC 98-19114. (Illus.). 384p. 1998. 39.95 (*0-19-512201-1*) OUP.

Dedrick, Jeff. Rock Licks for Bass. 32p. 1996. 9.95 incl. audio compact disk (*0-7866-2690-9*, 96545BCD) Mel Bay.

— Rock Studies for Bass: The Bottom Line. 32p. 1996. 9.95 incl. audio compact disk (*0-7866-2691-7*, 94534BCD) Mel Bay.

***Dedrick, Jonh M.** Sonoran Yaqui Language Structures. 480p. 1999. 45.00 (*0-8165-1981-1*) U of Ariz Pr.

Dedrick, William & Dedrick, Colleen. The Little Book of Christian Character & Manners. 128p. 1997. pap. 8.99 (*1-888306-22-X*) Holly Hall.

Dee. From Fire to Flight. 74p. 1992. 13.00 (*0-86690-412-3*) Am Fed Astrologers.

Dee, Abbie & Scott, Annie. Betsy's Riddles. (Emergent Reader Ser.). 11p. (J). (ps-1). 1991. pap. text 21.00 (*1-56843-035-3*); pap. text 4.25 (*1-56843-083-3*) EMG Networks.

— Brittany the Brontosaurus. (Emergent Reader Ser.). 8p. (J). (ps-1). 1991. pap. text 4.25 (*1-56843-080-9*) EMG Networks.

— Brittany the Brontosaurus: Big Book. (Emergent Reader Ser.). 8p. (J). (ps-1). 1991. pap. text 21.00 (*1-56843-032-9*) EMG Networks.

— Four Seasons. (Emergent Reader Ser.). 9p. (J). (ps-1). 1991. pap. text 21.00 (*1-56843-026-4*); pap. text 4.25 (*1-56843-074-4*) EMG Networks.

— Nature Hike. (Emergent Reader Ser.). 18p. (J). (ps-1). 1991. pap. text 4.25 (*1-56843-076-0*) EMG Networks.

— Nature Hike: Big Book. (Emergent Reader Ser.). 18p. (J). (ps-1). 1991. pap. text 21.00 (*1-56843-028-0*) EMG Networks.

— Opposites at the Zoo. (Emergent Reader Ser.). 12p. (J). (ps-1). 1991. pap. text 4.25 (*1-56843-077-9*) EMG Networks.

— Opposites at the Zoo: Big Book. (Emergent Reader Ser.). 12p. (J). (ps-1). 1991. pap. text 21.00 (*1-56843-029-9*) EMG Networks.

— Pets on Parade. (Emergent Reader Ser.). 14p. (J). (ps-1). 1991. pap. text 4.25 (*1-56843-075-2*) EMG Networks.

— Pets on Parade: Big Book. (Emergent Reader Ser.). 14p. (J). (ps-1). 1991. pap. text 21.00 (*1-56843-027-2*) EMG Networks.

— Sea Horse, Sea Horse. (Emergent Reader Ser.). 10p. (J). (ps-1). 1991. pap. text 4.25 (*1-56843-079-5*) EMG Networks.

— Sea Horse, Sea Horse: Big Book. (Emergent Reader Ser.). 10p. (J). (ps-1). 1991. pap. text 21.00 (*1-56843-031-0*) EMG Networks.

Dee, Anne P. Roots Illustrated: How to Bring Your Family Tree to Life. 128p. 1993. pap. 12.50 (*0-937448-00-1*) Juneberry Pr.

Dee, Arthur, jt. auth. see Abraham, Lyndy.

D

Dee-Burnett, Rita, et al. Human Resource Development Report: User's Guide. LC 99-191850. (Illus.). 64p. (Orig.). 1997. pap. text 28.00 (*0-918296-28-5*) Inst Personality & Ability.

***Dee, Catherine.** The Girl's Book of Wisdom. (J). 1999. pap. 8.95 (*0-316-17972-8*, Pub. by Little) Time Warner.

Dee, Catherine. The Girl's Guide to Life. LC 96-27958. (Illus.). 160p. (J). 1997. pap. 14.95 (*0-316-17952-3*) Little.

— The Girl's Guide to Life: How You Can Make the World a Great Place for Girls. (YA). (gr. 5 up). 1997. 13.95 (*0-614-28845-2*) Little.

— Who Says Girls Can't? The Girl's Guide to Women's Issues. LC 96-27958. 1997. write for info. (*0-316-17979-5*) Little.

— Women's Political Action Guide, 1993: The Women's Political Action Group. 1993. pap. 5.95 (*1-879682-33-8*) Bathroom Reader.

Dee, Catherine, ed. The Girl's Book of Wisdom. LC 99-24741. (Illus.). 144p. (YA). (gr. 5-8). 1999. pap. 8.95 (*0-316-17956-6*) Little.

Dee, Davi, jt. ed. see Allen, Bill.

Dee, Denise. Sowkins. Palme, Cole, ed. (Illus.). 112p. (Orig.). 1993. pap. 8.00 (*0-944388-02-7*) TBS Pubns.

Dee, Dianna. This Planet Is Mine. LC 95-163328. (Illus.). (J). 1994. pap. 14.95 (*0-590-48794-9*) Scholastic Inc.

Dee, Ed. Bronx Angel. 384p. 1996. reprint ed. mass mkt. 6.50 (*0-446-60337-6*, Pub. by Warner Bks) Little.

— 14 Peck Slip. 336p. 1995. reprint ed. mass mkt. 5.99 (*0-446-60238-8*, Pub. by Warner Bks) Little.

— Little Boy Blue. large type ed. LC 97-15302. (Wheeler Large Print Book Ser.). 1997. pap. 22.95 (*1-56895-452-2*) Wheeler Pub.

— Little Boy Blue. 320p. 1998. reprint ed. mass mkt. 6.99 (*0-446-60522-0*, Pub. by Warner Bks) Little.

***Dee, Ed, et al.** CopTales, 2000. 219p. 1999. pap. 18.95 (*0-9675749-0-0*) Pointthirtyeight.

Dee, Edward. Nightbird. LC 99-14591. 304p. 1999. 23.95 (*0-446-52039-X*, Pub. by Warner Bks) Little.

***Dee, Edward.** Nightbird. 338p. 2000. mass mkt. 6.99 (*0-446-60913-7*) Warner Bks.

Dee, Elain E. & Walton, Guy. Versailles: The View from Sweden. Aakre, Nancy, ed. LC 87-73539. (Exhibition Catalogue Ser.). (Illus.). 112p. 1988. pap. text 17.95 (*0-910503-56-7*) Cooper-Hewitt Museum.

Dee, Elaine E. To Embrace the Universe: Drawings by Frederic Edwin Church. LC 88-120547. (Illus.). 125p. (Orig.). 1984. pap. 5.00 (*0-943651-09-3*) Hudson Riv.

— Under Changing Skies: Landscapes by Frederic E. Church, Oil Sketches & Drawings from the Cooper-Hewitt Museum. (Illus.). 80p. (Orig.). (C). 1992. pap. 16.95 (*0-8122-1413-7*) U of Pa Pr.

Dee, Emily. Souls on Board: Responses to the United 232 Tragedy. LC 90-34136. (Illus.). 173p. (Orig.). 1990. pap. 9.95 (*0-9626818-1-4*) Loess Hills Pr.

— War Against Silence after Trauma: Unmasking & Managing the Stress of Change. LC 92-75053. x, 246p. (Orig.). 1993. 16.95 (*0-9626818-2-2*); pap. 9.95 (*0-9626818-3-0*) Loess Hills Pr.

Dee, Eugene H. Van, see Van Dee, Eugene H.

Dee, James H. A Lexicon of Latin Derivatives in Italian, Spanish, French & English. (Alpha-Omega, Reihe A Ser.: Bd. CXC). (ENG, FRE, ITA & SPA.). lvi, 1083p. 1997. write for info. (*3-487-10557-8*) G Olms Pubs.

Dee, James JyhRen, tr. see Wang, RuNan & Zhu, BaoXun.

Dee, John. The Enochian Magick of Dr. John Dee: The Most Powerful System of Magick in Its Original, Unexpurgated Form. James, Geoffrey, ed. LC 94-38268. Orig. Title: The Enochian Evocation of Dr. John Dee. (Illus.). 240p. 1994. pap. 14.95 (*1-56718-367-0*) Llewellyn Pubns.

— General & Rare Memorials Pertaining to Perfecte Arte of Navigation. LC 68-54635. (English Experience Ser.: No. 62). 82p. 1968. reprint ed. 45.00 (*90-221-0062-6*) Walter J Johnson.

— The Hieroglyphic Monad. 1986. pap. 7.95 (*0-916411-54-0*, Sure Fire) Holmes Pub.

***Dee, John.** The Hieroglyphic Monad. (Illus.). 96p. 2000. pap. 12.95 (*1-57863-203-X*) Weiser.

— Mathematical Preface to the Elements of Geometry of Euclid of Megara. 60p. 1999. reprint ed. pap. 17.95 (*0-7661-0766-3*) Kessinger Pub.

Dee, John. Private Diary of Dr. John Dee & the Catalogue of His Library of Manuscripts. Halliwell, James O., ed. (Camden Society, London. Publications, First Ser.: No. 19). reprint ed. 35.00 (*0-404-50119-2*) AMS Pr.

***Dee, John & Casaubon, Meric, eds.** True & Faithful Relation of What Passed for Many Years Between Dr. John Dee & Some Spirits. 478p. 1999. reprint ed. pap. 49.95 (*0-7661-0812-0*) Kessinger Pub.

***Dee, Jonathan.** Book of Prophecies: Discover the Secrets of the Past, Present & Future. (Illus.). 2000. 24.95 (*1-85585-683-2*) Collins & Br.

Dee, Jonathan. Chronicles of Ancient Egypt. 1999. 24.95 (*1-85585-606-9*) Collins & Br.

— The Liberty Campaign. 288p. 1995. pap. 10.00 (*0-671-89085-9*, WSP) PB.

Dee, Kit. Arizona Renegade. 384p. 1998. mass mkt. 5.99 (*0-380-79206-0*, Avon Bks) Morrow Avon.

***Dee, Kit.** Brit's Lady. 384p. 2000. mass mkt. 5.99 (*0-380-80693-2*, Avon Bks) Morrow Avon.

Dee, Kit. Destiny's Warrior. 384p. 1997. mass mkt. 5.99 (*0-380-79205-2*, Avon Bks) Morrow Avon.

Dee, Loa. May You Live in Interesting Times. 964p. 1998. write for info. (*0-7541-0285-8*) Communs Plus.

Dee, M. M. The Adventures of Jason Jackrabbit. LC 89-2164. 48p. (J). (gr. k-4). 1990. 9.95 (*0-937460-60-5*) Hendrick-Long.

Dee, Miss. Health, Astrology & Spirituality. LC 83-71864. 160p. 1984. 16.50 (*0-86690-247-3*, D2366-014) Am Fed Astrologers.

— The Yod, Your Special Life Purpose. LC 83-70271. 72p. 1983. 13.00 (*0-86690-234-1*, D2287-014) Am Fed Astrologers.

Dee, Nerys. The Dreamer's Workbook: A Complete Guide to Interpreting & Understanding Dreams. (Workbook Ser.). (Illus.). 240p. 1989. pap. 14.95 (*0-85030-705-8*) Sterling.

Dee, Nerys. Understanding Dreams: How to Benefit from the Power of Your Dreams. 1995. mass mkt. 10.00 (*1-85538-086-2*) Harper SF.

— Your Dreams & What They Mean: The Classic Bestseller. 176p. 1998. pap. 12.00 (*0-7225-3218-0*) Thorsons PA.

Dee, Norbert, et al, eds. Detection, Control, & Renovation of Contaminated Ground Water. 226p. 1987. 5.00 (*0-87262-595-8*) Am Soc Civil Eng.

Dee, Roger, et al, eds. Principles of Orthopedic Practice. 2nd ed. LC 96-38647. (Illus.). 1344p. 1996. text 179.00 (*0-07-016356-1*) McGraw-Hill HPD.

Dee, Ron. Blood. Isaacson, Dana, ed. 320p. (Orig.). 1993. mass mkt. 4.99 (*0-671-79242-3*) PB.

— Succumb. 1994. mass mkt. 5.50 (*0-671-87110-2*) PB.

Dee, Ruby. My One Good Nerve. LC 98-25196. 178p. 1998. 16.95 (*0-471-31704-7*) Wiley.

— Tower to Heaven. LC 90-34131. (Illus.). 32p. (J). (ps-2). 1995. 14.95 (*0-8050-1460-8*, Bks Young Read) H Holt & Co.

— Two Ways to Count to Ten: A Liberian Folktale. LC 86-33513. (Illus.). 32p. (J). (ps-2). 1995. pap. 5.95 (*0-8050-1314-8*, Owlet BYR) H Holt & Co.

— Two Ways to Count to Ten: A Liberian Folktale. (J). 1988. 11.15 (*0-606-04570-8*, Pub. by Turtleback) Demco.

Dee, Ruby, ed. Glowchild & Other Poems. LC 72-77858. 112p. (YA). (gr. 7 up). 1972. 12.95 (*0-89388-040-X*) Okpaku Communications.

Dee, Ruby, intro. In Good Company: A Woman's Journal for Spiritual Reflection 1998. (Illus.). 344p. 1997. spiral bd. 16.95 (*0-8298-1174-5*) Pilgrim OH.

Dee, Ruby, jt. auth. see Davis, Ossie.

Dee, Tonya. The Definitive Manual for Topless Dancers: Hey Mister, Why Are You Sitting There with My Money in Your Pocket? 3rd rev. unabridged ed. (Illus.). 200p. 1996. spiral bd. 32.40 (*0-9669340-0-8*) T Dees Manual.

Deeb, M. Daniel. Failing Schools: The Cause & the Cure. 319p. (Orig.). 1989. pap. 9.90 (*0-9625508-1-7*) Solomon Bks.

Deeb, Marius K. & Deeb, Mary J. Libya since the Revolution: Aspects of Social & Political Development. LC 81-19985. 156p. 1982. 57.95 (*0-275-90780-5*, C0780, Praeger Pubs) Greenwood.

Deeb, Mary J., jt. auth. see Deeb, Marius K.

Deeb, Mary-Jane & King, Mary E. Hasib Sabbagh: From Palestinian Refugee to Citizen of the World. LC 96-22920. 1996. write for info. (*0-916808-43-2*) Mid East Inst.

Deeb, Richard G. Live to Be 100 Plus: Healthy Choices for Maximizing Your Life. LC 94-43940. 225p. 1995. 11.95 (*1-885003-07-2*) R D Reed Pubs.

— The Longevity Equation: How to Eat As Much As You Like & Still Live over 100 Years to Tell about It! 246p. 1992. pap. text 11.95 (*0-9634020-0-5*) Long Life Pr.

Deeba, E. & Gunawardena, A. Interactive Linear Algebra with Maple V, Vol. 5. (TIMS Ser.). 302p. 1999. 89.95 incl. cd-rom (*0-387-98829-7*) Spr-Verlag.

Deeba, Elias Y. & Gunawardena, Ananda D. Interactive Linear Algebra with Maple V. LC 97-26974. (Textbooks in Mathematical Sciences Ser.). 288p. 1997. pap. 59.00 (*0-387-98240-X*) Spr-Verlag.

***Deeble, Mark & Stone, Victoria.** The Crocodile Family Book. (Illus.). 56p. (J). (gr. 1-5). 2000. pap. 8.95 (*0-7358-1317-5*, Pub. by North-South Bks NYC) Chronicle Bks.

Deeck, William F. The Mystery Fancier: An Index to Volumes I-XIII, November 1976-Fall 1992. LC 93-341. (Brownstone Mystery Guides Ser.: Vol. 9). (Illus.). ix, 169p. 1993. pap. 21.00 (*0-941028-12-7*, 27642983); lib. bdg. 31.00 (*0-941028-11-9*, 27642983) Millefleurs.

Deecke, L. & Dal-Bianco, P. Age-Associated Neurological Diseases LC 91-5013. (Journal of Neural Transmission Ser.). viii, 165 p. 1991. write for info. (*0-387-82261-5*) Spr-Verlag.

Deecke, L. & Dal-Bianco, P., eds. Age-Associated Neurological Diseases. (Journal of Neural Transmission: Suppl. 33). (Illus.). 180p. 1991. pap. 59.00 (*3-211-82261-5*) Spr-Verlag.

Deecke, L. & Mountcastle, V. B., eds. From Neuron to Action: An Appraisal of Fundamental & Clinical Research. (Illus.). 688p. 1991. 118.00 (*0-387-52072-4*) Spr-Verlag.

Deedat, A. Is Bible God's Word? 1981. 3.00 (*0-933511-04-3*) Kazi Pubns.

— Was Jesus Crucified? 1995. pap. 3.00 (*0-933511-85-X*) Kazi Pubns.

— What the Bible Says about Muhammad? (Illus.). 1978. write for info. (*0-686-63917-0*) African Islam Miss Pubns.

Deedat, A. What the Bible Says about Muhammad? 1991. 3.00 (*0-933511-12-4*) Kazi Pubns.

Deedat, Ahmad. Was Jesus Crucified? 1983. pap. 2.50 (*0-933511-23-X*) Kazi Pubns.

Deedat, Ahmed. Al-Quran: The Ultimate Miracle. 75p. (Orig.). 1989. pap. 4.50 (*1-56744-368-0*) Kazi Pubns.

— Al Quran the Ultimate Miracle. 96p. 1970. pap. text 6.95 (*0-916157-75-X*) African Islam Miss Pubns.

— Is the Bible God's Word? Obaba, Al I., ed. (Illus.). 80p. 1990. pap. text 6.00 (*0-916157-73-3*) African Islam Miss Pubns.

— Quran: The Ultimate Miracle. 75p. 1996. pap. 3.50 (*0-614-21067-4*, 1046) Kazi Pubns.

— Was Jesus Crucified? Obaba, Al I., ed. 49p. (Orig.). (YA). 1991. pap. text 2.00 (*0-916157-72-5*) African Islam Miss Pubns.

— What Is His Name? Obaba, Al I., ed. (Illus.). 49p. (Orig.). (YA). 1991. pap. text 4.00 (*0-916157-74-1*) African Islam Miss Pubns.

— What the Bible Says about Muhammad? 49p. 1970. pap. 2.50 (*0-916157-71-7*) African Islam Miss Pubns.

Deede, Barbara. Gift Wishes. 1992. spiral bd. 7.95 (*0-9627619-1-5*) Deede Pr.

— My Favorite Recipe Register. (Illus.). 72p. 1990. pap. 9.95 (*0-9627619-0-7*) Deede Pr.

— My Favorite Recipe Register. (Illus.). 144p. reprint ed. spiral bd. 6.95 (*0-9622412-5-3*) Pickle Point.

— A Register of My Favorite Recipes. rev. ed. (Illus.). 144p. 1995. student ed., spiral bd. 8.95 (*0-9622412-4-5*) Pickle Point.

Deedes-Vincke, Patrick. Photographer's: Paris & U . K . Editions. 1992. write for info. (*0-316-88892-3*) Little.

***Deedrick, Tami.** Astronauts. LC 97-38177. (Community Helpers Ser.). 24p. (J). 1998. lib. bdg. 13.75 (*1-56065-727-8*, Bridgestone Bks) Capstone Pr.

Deedrick, Tami. Bakers. LC 97-38174. (Community Helpers Ser.). 24p. (J). 1998. lib. bdg. 13.75 (*1-56065-728-6*) Capstone Pr.

— Construction Workers. LC 97-35602. (Community Helpers Ser.). 24p. (J). 1998. lib. bdg. 13.75 (*1-56065-729-4*) Capstone Pr.

***Deedrick, Tami.** Earthquakes. LC 99-59091. (Nature on the Rampage Ser.). (Illus.). 32p. (J). 2000. lib. bdg. 22.03 (*0-7398-1795-7*) Raintree Steck-V.

— Fires. LC 99-58673. (Illus.). 32p. (J). 2000. lib. bdg. 22.03 (*0-7398-1798-1*) Raintree Steck-V.

— Floods. LC 99-58672. (Nature on the Rampage Ser.). (Illus.). 32p. (J). 2000. lib. bdg. 22.03 (*0-7398-1797-3*) Raintree Steck-V.

Deedrick, Tami. Garbage Collectors. LC 97-31544. (Community Helpers Ser.). 24p. (J). 1998. lib. bdg. 13.75 (*1-56065-730-8*) Capstone Pr.

— Garbage Collectors. large type ed. (Community Helpers Ser.). (Illus.). 24p. (J). (gr. k-3). 1998. lib. bdg. 14.00 (*0-516-21259-1*) Childrens.

— Teachers. LC 97-40282. (Community Helpers Ser.). 24p. (J). 1998. lib. bdg. 13.75 (*1-56065-731-6*) Capstone Pr.

— Zoo Keepers. LC 97-38106. (Community Helpers Ser.). 24p. (J). 1998. lib. bdg. 13.75 (*1-56065-732-4*) Capstone Pr.

— Zoo Keepers. large type ed. (Community Helpers Ser.). (Illus.). 24p. (J). (gr. k-3). 1998. 14.00 (*0-516-21257-5*) Childrens.

Deeds, Jean M. There Are Mountains to Climb. (Illus.). v, 200p. (Orig.). 1996. pap. 12.95 (*0-9651487-1-8*) Slvrwood Pr.

Deedwania, Prakash, jt. ed. see Kupersmith, Joel.

Deedwania, Prakash C., ed. Circadian Rhythms of Cardiovascular Disoders. LC 96-44295. (Illus.). 240p. 1996. 55.00 (*0-87993-632-0*) Futura Pub.

Deedy, Carmen. The Yellow Star: The Legend of King Christian X of Denmark. (Illus.). 32p. (J). (gr. k-5). 2000. 16.95 (*1-56145-208-4*) Peachtree Pubs.

Deedy, Carmen A. Agatha's Feather Bed: Not Just Another Wild Goose Story. (Illus.). 32p. (J). (ps-3). 1994. pap. 6.95 (*1-56145-096-0*) Peachtree Pubs.

— Agatha's Feather Bed: Not Just Another Wild Goose Story. (Illus.). 32p. (J). (ps-3). 1994. 14.95 (*1-56145-088-0*) Peachtree Pubs.

— La Cama de Plumas de Agata. Orig. Title: Agatha's Feather Bed. (J). Date not set. 15.95 (*1-56014-667-2*) Santillana.

— The Last Dance. LC 95-16377. (Illus.). 32p. (J). (gr. 2-6). 1995. 16.95 (*1-56145-109-6*) Peachtree Pubs.

— The Library Dragon. LC 94-14754. (Illus.). 32p. (J). (ps-3). 1994. 16.95 (*1-56145-091-X*) Peachtree Pubs.

— The Secret of Old Zeb. LC 97-12346. (Illus.). 36p. (J). (gr. 1-5). 1997. 16.95 (*1-56145-115-0*) Peachtree Pubs.

***Deedy, Carmen A.** Treeman. (Illus.). 32p. (J). (ps-2). 2000. pap. 6.95 (*1-56145-227-0*) Peachtree Pubs.

Deedy, Carmen Agra. Tree Man. LC 93-1667. (Illus.). 32p. (J). (gr. 2 up). 1993. 16.95 (*1-56145-077-4*) Peachtree Pubs.

Deedy, J. American Catholicism: And Now Where? LC 87-12765. (Illus.). 328p. (C). 1987. 20.95 (*0-306-42706-0*, Plenum Trade) Perseus Pubng.

Deedy, John. The Book of Catholic Anecdotes. LC 98-170210. 288p. (Orig.). (C). 1997. pap. 15.95 (*0-88347-309-7*) Res Christian Liv.

***Deedy, John, ed.** The Catholic Church in the Twentieth Century: Renewing & Reimaging the City of God. 256p. 2000. pap. 24.95 (*0-8146-5947-0*) Liturgical Pr.

Deeg, D. J. & Westendorp De Seriere, M., eds. Autonomy & Well-Being in the Aging Population 1: Report from the Longitudinal Aging Study Amsterdam 1992-1993. 96p. 1995. pap. 15.00 (*90-5383-336-6*, Pub. by VU Univ Pr) Paul & Co Pubs.

Deeg, H. J. A Guide to Blood & Marrow Transplantation. 3rd ed. LC 98-35569. 1998. pap. write for info. (*0-387-62540-2*) Spr-Verlag.

Deeg, H. J., et al. A Guide to Blood & Marrow Transplantation. 3rd enl. rev. ed. LC 98-35569. (Illus.). xii, 223p. 1999. 99.00 (*3-540-62540-2*) Spr-Verlag.

— A Guide to Bone Marrow Transplantation. (Illus.). 210p. 1988. 76.50 (*0-387-18802-9*) Spr-Verlag.

— A Guide to Bone Marrow Transplantation. 2nd enl. rev. ed. LC 92-49684. (Illus.). 200p. 1993. 136.00 (*0-387-54831-9*) Spr-Verlag.

Deeg, Richard. Finance Capitalism Unveiled: Banks & the German Political Economy. LC 98-25519. (Illus.). 328p. 1999. text 49.50 (*0-472-10936-7*, 10936) U of Mich Pr.

Deegan, Arthur X., 2nd. Coaching: A Management Skill for Improving Individual Performance. LC 79-619. 1979. pap. text 16.95 (*0-201-01266-9*) Addison-Wesley.

Deegan, Arthur X., II. Developing a Vibrant Parish Pastoral Council. LC 94-39971. 176p. (Orig.). 1995. pap. 11.95 (*0-8091-3556-6*) Paulist Pr.

***Deegan, Gregory G. & Toman, James A.** The Heart of Cleveland: Public Square 1900-2000. (Illus.). 144p. 1999. 28.50 (*0-936760-12-5*, Pub. by Cleveland Landmarks) Partners Bk Dist.

Deegan, Gregory G., jt. auth. see Toman, James A.

Deegan, Gregory G., ed. see Hays, Blaine S. & Toman, James A.

Deegan, Gregory G., ed. see Toman, James A., et al.

Deegan, Heather. The Middle East & Problems of Democracy. LC 93-4446. (Issues in Third World Politics Ser.). 160p. (C). 1994. pap. text 16.95 (*1-55587-455-X*) L Rienner.

— The Middle East & Problems of Democracy. Randall, Vicky, ed. (Issues in Third World Politics Ser.). 160p. 1993. 9.00 (*0-335-15687-8*); pap. 2.00 (*0-335-15686-X*) OpUniv Pr.

— South Africa Reborn: Building a Democracy. LC 99-168983. 248p. 1999. 75.00 (*1-85728-709-6*); pap. text 23.95 (*1-85728-710-X*) UCL Pr Ltd.

Deegan, James & Dineen, Donal. Tourism Policy & Performance. (Tourism & Hospitality Management Ser.). 290p. 1997. pap. 50.00 (*0-415-09315-5*) Thomson Learn.

Deegan, James C. Children's Friendships in Culturally Diverse Classrooms. LC 96-10989. (World of Childhood & Adolescence Ser.). 192p. 1996. 79.95 (*0-7507-0266-4*, Falmer Pr); pap. 24.95 (*0-7507-0267-2*, Falmer Pr) Taylor & Francis.

Deegan, James F. An Econometric Model of the Gulf Coast Oil & Gas Exploration Industry. Bruchey, Stuart, ed. LC 78-22672. (Energy in the American Economy Ser.). (Illus.). 1979. lib. bdg. 18.95 (*0-405-11975-5*) Ayer.

Deegan, Marilyn, ed. see Buchan, John.

Deegan, Mary J. Jane Addams & the Men of the Chicago School, 1892-1918. 385p. (Orig.). 1986. 44.95 (*0-88738-077-8*) Transaction Pubs.

— Jane Addams & the Men of the Chicago School, 1892-1918. 385p. (Orig.). (C). 1990. pap. 24.95 (*0-88738-830-2*) Transaction Pubs.

Deegan, Mary J., ed. Women in Sociology: A Bio-Bibliographical Sourcebook. LC 90-43376. 488p. 1991. lib. bdg. 85.00 (*0-313-26085-0*, DWY/, Greenwood Pr) Greenwood.

Deegan, Mary J. & Hill, Michael, eds. Women & Symbolic Interaction. 265p. (C). 1987. pap. text 16.95 (*0-04-497006-4*) Routledge.

Deegan, Mary J., ed. see Gilman, Charlotte Perkins.

Deegan, Mary Jo. American Ritual Dramas: Social Rules & Cultural Meanings, 76. LC 88-17772. (Contributions in Sociology Ser.: No. 76). 201p. 1989. 45.00 (*0-313-26337-X*, DAU, Greenwood Pr) Greenwood.

Deegan, Mary Jo, ed. The American Ritual Tapestry: Social Rules & Cultural Meanings, 122. LC 98-14232. (Contributions in Sociology Ser.: Vol. 122). 192p. 1998. 55.00 (*0-313-30465-3*, Greenwood Pr) Greenwood.

Deegan, Mary Jo & Brooks, Nancy A. Women & Disability: The Double Handicap. 180p. 1984. 34.95 (*0-87755-017-4*) Transaction Pubs.

Deegan, Mary Jo, ed. see Gilman, Charlotte Perkins.

Deegan, Mary Jo, ed. see Mead, George Herbert.

Deegan, Paul. Clarence Thomas. Italia, Bob, ed. LC 92-13717. (Supreme Court Justices Ser.). (J). 1992. lib. bdg. 14.98 (*1-56239-088-0*) ABDO Pub Co.

— Sandra Day O'Connor. Italia, Bob, ed. LC 92-13716. (Supreme Court Justices Ser.). (J). 1992. lib. bdg. 14.98 (*1-56239-089-9*) ABDO Pub Co.

— Supreme Court Book. Italia, Bob, ed. LC 92-13715. (Supreme Court Justices Ser.). (J). 1992. lib. bdg. 14.98 (*1-56239-097-X*) ABDO Pub Co.

Deegan, Paul, jt. auth. see Italia, Bob.

Deegan, Paul, ed. see Italia, Bob.

Deegan, Paul, ed. see Italia, Robert.

Deegan, Paul, ed. see Wheeler, Jill.

Deegan, Paul J. The Arab-Israeli Conflict. LC 91-73073. (War in the Gulf Ser.). 202p. (J). (gr. 4 up). 1991. lib. bdg. 13.99 (*1-56239-028-7*) ABDO Pub Co.

— George Bush. Wallner, Rosemary, ed. LC 91-73077. (War in the Gulf Ser.). (J). (gr. 4 up). 1991. lib. bdg. 13.99 (*1-56239-024-4*) ABDO Pub Co.

— Operation Desert Shield. LC 91-730. (J). (gr. 4 up). 1991. lib. bdg. 13.99 (*1-56239-022-8*) ABDO Pub Co.

— Operation Desert Storm. LC 91-73078. (War in the Gulf Ser.). (J). (gr. 4 up). 1991. lib. bdg. 13.99 (*1-56239-023-6*) ABDO Pub Co.

— Persian Gulf Nations. LC 91-73072. (War in the Gulf Ser.). (J). (gr. 4 up). 1991. lib. bdg. 13.99 (*1-56239-029-5*) ABDO Pub Co.

— Saddam Hussein. Wallner, Rosemary, ed. LC 91-73076. (War in the Gulf Ser.). (J). (gr. 4 up). 1991. lib. bdg. 13.99 (*1-56239-025-2*) ABDO Pub Co.

Deegan, Paul L. Stephen Breyer. LC 96-3859. (United States Supreme Court Library). (J). 1996. lib. bdg. 14.98 (*1-56239-464-9*) ABDO Pub Co.

Deegan, Peter, jt. auth. see Leonhard, Woody.

Deegan, William L. Managing Student Affairs Programs: Methods, Models, Muddles. (Illus.). 240p. 1981. 24.95 (*0-88280-083-3*) ETC Pubns.

Deegans, Judy, jt. auth. see Deegans, Skip.

Deegans, Skip & Deegans, Judy. Anderson's Campground & RV Park Directory. 458p. 1999. pap. 7.95 (*1-881774-00-7*) Meadow Bluff.

Deehr, C. S. & Holtet, Jan A., eds. Exploration of the Polar Upper Atmosphere. 1981. text 220.50 (*90-277-1225-5*) Kluwer Academic.

Deehr, Kate. Scripture, Teens, & Values: 10 Activity-Centered Lessons & Prayer Services. 80p. 1997. pap., teacher ed. 12.95 (*0-937997-41-2*, 3750) Hi-Time Pflaum.

D

Deeks, David & Lejk, Mark. Introduction to Systems Analysis. LC 97-13972. 464p. 1997. pap. 77.00 (*0-13-857764-1*, Pub. by P-H) S&S Trade.

Deeks, John. Business & Culture of the Enterprise Society. LC 92-34951. 272p. 1993. 62.95 (*0-89930-791-4*, DBU, Quorum Bks) Greenwood.

Deekshatulu, B. L., jt. ed. see Khoshoo, T. N.

Deel, Evelyn K. The Virgin Wife. LC 83-25816. 1987. 13.95 (*0-87949-246-5*) Ashley Bks.

Deel, Kathleen. Figural Planters: A Pictorial Guide with Values. LC 95-26286. 160p. 1996. pap. 19.95 (*0-88740-970-9*) Schiffer.

***Deel, Kathleen.** Napco. LC 99-61231. (Illus.). 176p. 1999. pap. 29.95 (*0-7643-0844-0*) Schiffer.

***Deel, Robert.** The Strategic Electronic Day Trader. LC 99-55629. 224p. 2000. text 34.95 (*0-471-25488-6*) Wiley.

Deel, Robert. Trading the Plan: Build Wealth, Manage Money & Control Risk. LC 97-8981. (Wiley Finance Editions Ser.). 240p. 1997. 59.95 (*0-471-16979-X*) Wiley.

Deeley, Martin. Advanced Gundog Training: Practical Fieldwork & Competition. (Illus.). 176p. 1994. 34.95 (*1-85223-771-6*, Pub. by Crolwood) Trafalgar.

— Working Gundogs: An Introduction to Training & Handling. (Illus.). 176p. 1994. 34.95 (*1-85223-764-3*, Pub. by Crolwood) Trafalgar.

Deeley, Patrick. Names for Love. (C). 1990. 23.00 (*0-948268-79-4*, Pub. by Dedalus); pap. 15.00 (*0-948268-78-6*, Pub. by Dedalus) St Mut.

— Turane: The Hidden Village. LC 95-154793. 96p. 1995. 18.95 (*1-873790-70-8*); pap. 11.95 (*1-873790-69-4*) Dufour.

Deelstra, H., et al, eds. Food Policy Trends in Europe. 248p. 1991. 153.00 (*1-85573-284-X*) Am Educ Systs.

Deely, J. N. The Tradition Via Heidegger: An Essay on the Meaning of Being in the Philosophy of Martin Heidegger. 222p. 1971. pap. text 71.50 (*90-247-5111-X*, Pub. by M Nijhoff) Kluwer Academic.

Deely, John. Basics of Semiotics. LC 89-45354. (Advances in Semiotics Ser.). 168p. 1990. pap. 14.95 (*0-253-20568-9*, MB-568) Ind U Pr.

— The Human Use of Signs: Or Elements of Anthroposemiosis. 256p. (C). 1993. lib. bdg. 65.00 (*0-8476-7803-2*) Rowman.

— New Beginnings: Early Modern Philosophy & Postmodern Thought. (Studies in Semiotics). 310p. 1994. text 50.00 (*0-8020-0624-8*); pap. text 19.95 (*0-8020-7583-5*) U of Toronto Pr.

— Semiotics, 1995: Proceedings of the Twentieth Annual Meeting of the Semiotic Society of America. XIII, 419p. (C). 1996. text 59.95 (*0-614-17854-1*) P Lang Pubng.

***Deely, John.** What Distinguishes Human Understanding? LC 00-8721. 176p. 2000. 25.00 (*1-890318-97-3*, Pub. by St Augustines Pr) U Ch Pr.

Deely, John, ed. Semiotics, 1987. LC 84-640162. 510p. (C). 1988. lib. bdg. 85.50 (*0-8191-7163-8*) U Pr of Amer.

— Semiotics, 1994. (Proceedings of the Semiotic Society of America, 20-23 Oct. '94). IX, 494p. (C). 1996. text 69.95 (*0-8204-2876-0*) P Lang Pubng.

— Semiotics, 1993. (Proceedings of the 18th Annual Meeting of the Semiotic Society of America Ser.). 624p. (C). 1995. 74.95 (*0-614-08642-6*) P Lang Pubng.

— Semiotics, 1984: Proceedings of the Ninth Annual Meeting of the Semiotic Society of America, 11-14 October 1984, Bloomington, Indiana. LC 84-640162. (Illus.). 754p. (Orig.). 1985. pap. text 55.50 (*0-8191-4880-6*); lib. bdg. 91.00 (*0-8191-4879-2*) U Pr of Amer.

Deely, John, et al, eds. Semiotics, 1989. LC 84-640162. (Proceedings of the 14th Annual Meeting of the Semiotic Society of America Staff Ser.). 454p. (C). 1990. lib. bdg. 65.00 (*0-8191-7840-3*) U Pr of Amer.

Deely, John & Evans, Jonathan, eds. Semiotics, 1986. LC 84-640162. (Sources in Semiotics Ser.). (Illus.). 472p. (C). 1988. lib. bdg. 72.50 (*0-8191-6672-3*) U Pr of Amer.

— Semiotics, 1982. (Sources in Semiotics Ser.). 682p. (C). 1987. lib. bdg. 98.50 (*0-8191-5107-6*) U Pr of Amer.

Deely, John & Prewitt, Terry J., eds. Semiotics, 1991: Proceedings of the Sixteenth Annual Meeting of the Semiotic Society of America. 404p. (C). lib. bdg. 85.00 (*0-8191-8870-0*) U Pr of Amer.

Deely, John, ed. see Baer, Eugen.

Deely, John, ed. see Cahalan, John C.

Deely, John, jt. ed. see Evans, Jonathan.

Deely, John, ed. see Poinsot, John.

Deely, John, ed. see Scheer, Steven C.

Deely, John, jt. ed. see Spinks, C. W.

Deely, John, ed. & tr. see Poinsot, John.

Deely, John N. Introducing Semiotic: Its History & Doctrine. LC 82-47782. (Advances in Semiotics Ser.). 264p. reprint ed. pap. 81.90 (*0-8357-3949-X*, 20570440004) Bks Demand.

Deely, John N., et al, eds. Frontiers in Semiotics. LC 85-45982. (Advances in Semiotics Ser.). (Illus.). 351p. reprint ed. pap. 108.90 (*0-608-09332-7*, 205407800002) Bks Demand.

Deely, Nicholas. Dr. Deely, You Do Great Things: The Medicine of Laughter. 100p. 1995. pap. text 12.95 (*0-9648669-0-0*) Denali Desgns.

— Tanana Valley Railroad: The Gold Dust Line - Alaska. 161p. 1996. pap. text 50.00 (*0-9648669-1-9*) Denali Desgns.

Deem. Health Care Exploration. (C). 1998. pap. text, teacher ed. 15.00 (*0-8273-8005-4*); pap. text, wbk. ed. 21.95 (*0-8273-8007-0*) Delmar.

— Health Care Exploration. LC 98-26921. 208p. (C). 1998. text 35.95 (*0-8273-8004-6*) Delmar.

— Study Skills. (C). Date not set. pap., teacher ed., suppl. ed. write for info. (*0-395-66016-5*) HM.

— Study Skills. (C). 1992. pap., teacher ed. 2.76 (*0-395-58812-X*); pap. text 28.36 (*0-395-58811-1*) HM.

Deem, Bill R. Electronics Math. 6th ed. LC 98-43517. (Illus.). 841p. 1999. 93.00 (*0-13-010077-3*) P-H.

— Electronics Math. 6th ed. 1999. pap. text, student ed. 21.30 (*0-13-010078-1*) P-H.

Deem, James M. Bodies from the Bog. LC 97-12010. 42p. (J). (gr. 5-8). 1998. 16.00 (*0-395-85784-8*) HM.

— Frog Eyes Loves Pigs. 1988. 2.25 (*0-373-98030-2*) S&S Trade.

— Ghost Hunters. (Illus.). 128p. (Orig.). (YA). 1992. pap. 3.50 (*0-380-76682-5*, Avon Bks) Morrow Avon.

— How to Catch a Flying Saucer. (Illus.). 192p. (J). 1993. reprint ed. pap. 3.50 (*0-380-71898-7*, Avon Bks) Morrow Avon.

— How to Find a Ghost. 144p. (J). 1990. reprint ed. pap. 3.25 (*0-380-70829-9*, Avon Bks) Morrow Avon.

— How to Hunt Buried Treasure. (Illus.). 192p. (J). (gr. 3-7). 1992. 16.95 (*0-395-58799-9*) HM.

— How to Hunt Buried Treasure. 192p. (J). 1994. pap. 3.99 (*0-380-72176-7*, Avon Bks) Morrow Avon.

— How to Make A Mummy Talk. LC 94-2186. (Illus.). 192p. (J). (gr. 5-9). 1995. 14.95 (*0-395-62427-4*) HM.

— How to Make A Mummy Talk. (J). 1997. 8.60 (*0-606-11485-8*, Pub. by Turtleback) Demco.

— How to Make a Mummy Talk. (Illus.). 192p. (J). (gr. 4-7). 1997. pap. 3.50 (*0-440-41316-8*) Dell.

— How to Read Your Mother's Mind. LC 92-41351. (Illus.). 192p. (J). 1994. 17.00 (*0-395-62426-6*) HM.

— How to Read Your Mother's Mind. LC 92-41351. 1996. 9.09 (*0-606-09440-7*, Pub. by Turtleback) Demco.

— How to Travel Through Time. 128p. (Orig.). (J). 1993. pap. 3.50 (*0-380-76681-7*, Avon Bks) Morrow Avon.

— Three NBs of Julian Drew. LC 93-39306. 224p. (J). 1994. 15.95 (*0-395-69453-1*) HM.

— 3 NBs of Julian Drew. 176p. (YA). 1996. mass mkt. 4.50 (*0-380-72587-8*, Avon Bks) Morrow Avon.

***Deem, James M.** 3 NBs of Julian Drew. LC 99-96392. 160p. (YA). (gr. 8 up). 2000. mass mkt. 6.95 (*0-380-81098-0*, Avon Bks) Morrow Avon.

Deem, James M. 3 NBs of Julian Drew. LC 93-39306. 1996. 9.60 (*0-606-08959-4*, Pub. by Turtleback) Demco.

— The Very Real Ghost Book of Christina Rose. 176p. (YA). 1998. pap. 3.99 (*0-440-41426-1*) Dell.

— The Very Real Ghost Book of Christina Rose. LC 95-34127. 176p. (J). (gr. 3-7). 1996. 15.00 (*0-395-76128-X*) HM.

Deem, Rosemary, et al. Active Citizenship & the Governing of Schools. LC 95-5848. 192p. 1995. 108.95 (*0-335-19184-3*); pap. 31.95 (*0-335-19183-5*) OpUniv Pr.

Deem, S. M. Principles & Practice of Database Systems. (Computer Science Ser.). (Illus.). 404p. (Orig.). (C). 1985. pap. text 35.00 (*0-333-37100-3*) Scholium Intl.

Deem, Saitofi Anne. Myrtle Teachable Moments Series, 16 vols. Incl. Myrtle Learns About Asthma. (Illus.). 8p. (J). (ps-3). 1998. pap. text 7.95 (*1-930694-00-8*); Myrtle Learns About Dangerous Situations. (Illus.). 8p. (J). (ps-3). 1998. pap. text 7.95 (*1-930694-03-2*); Myrtle Learns About Diabetes. (Illus.). 12p. (J). (ps-3). 1998. pap. text 7.95 (*1-930694-04-0*); Myrtle Learns About Hygiene. (Illus.). 8p. (J). (ps-3). 1998. pap. text 7.95 (*1-930694-09-1*); Myrtle Learns About Lice. (Illus.). 12p. (J). (ps-3). 1998. pap. text 7.95 (*1-930694-11-3*); Myrtle Learns About Medicine. (Illus.). 8p. (J). (ps-3). 1998. pap. text 7.95 (*1-930694-12-1*); Myrtle Learns About Safety. (Illus.). 8p. (J). (ps-3). 1998. pap. text 7.95 (*1-930694-13-X*); Myrtle Learns About Seizures. (Illus.). 8p. (J). (ps-3). 1998. pap. text 7.95 (*1-930694-14-8*); Myrtle Learns How You Catch an Illness. (Illus.). 8p. (J). (ps-3). 1998. pap. text 7.95 (*1-930694-10-5*); Myrtle Learns to Eat Well. (Illus.). 12p. (J). (ps-3). 1998. pap. text 7.95 (*1-930694-05-9*); Myrtle Learns to Get Along. (Illus.). 8p. (J). (ps-3). 1998. pap. text 7.95 (*1-930694-08-3*); Myrtle Learns to Make Friends. (Illus.). 8p. (J). (ps-3). 1998. pap. text 7.95 (*1-930694-07-5*); Myrtle Learns to Take Care of Boo Boos. (Illus.). 12p. (J). (ps-3). 1998. pap. text 7.95 (*1-930694-01-6*); Myrtle Learns Why Exercise is Important. (Illus.). 8p. (J). 1998. pap. text 7.95 (*1-930694-06-7*); Myrtle Makes a Choice. (Illus.). 8p. (J). (ps-3). 1998. pap. text 7.95 (*1-930694-02-4*); Myrtle's Friend is Very Sick. (Illus.). 8p. (J). (ps-3). 1998. pap. text 7.95 (*1-930694-15-6*); (Illus.). (J). Set pap. text 114.48 (*1-930694-16-4*) Myrtle Learns.

***Deemer, B. Harlan.** Having Words Together. LC 98-90488. 1999. pap. 13.50 (*0-533-12812-9*) Vantage.

Deemer, Beth. The Secret of Poplar Island. Kemnitz, Myrna, ed. (Illus.). 126p. (Orig.). (J). (gr. 5-7). 1996. pap. 9.99 (*0-88092-129-3*) Royal Fireworks.

Deemer, Betty, ed. see Cecil, Larry & Beckwith, Jack.

Deemer, Bill. Diana. (Orig.). 1966. pap. 1.00 (*0-940556-01-4*) Coyote.

— This Is Just to Say. Hyner, Stefan, tr. from ENG. (GER.). (Orig.). 1981. pap. 4.00 (*0-940556-03-0*) Coyote.

— Variations. 38p. 1999. pap. 10.00 (*1-929048-01-7*) Longhouse Pubs.

Deemer, Charles. The Internet Classroom: Internet Projects for the Creative Teacher. (Illus.). 240p. (Orig.). 1996. pap. 14.95 (*0-945264-22-4*) Resolution Busn Pr.

— Screenwrighting: The Craft of Screenwriting. LC 98-83104. 365p. 1999. 25.00 (*0-7388-0335-9*); pap. 15.00 (*0-7388-0336-7*) Xlibris Corp.

— Secrets of the Webmasters. (Illus.). 240p. 1996. pap. 18.95 (*0-945264-20-8*) Resolution Busn Pr.

Deeming, Denis C., ed. The Ostrich: Biology, Production & Health. LC 99-17680. (CABI Publishing Ser.). 368p. 1999. 100.00 (*0-85199-350-8*) OUP.

Deeming, Denis C. & Ferguson, Mark W., eds. Egg Incubation: Its Effects on Embryonic Development in Birds & Reptiles. (Illus.). 462p. (C). 1992. text 200.00 (*0-521-39071-0*) Cambridge U Pr.

Deeming, Terry, jt. auth. see Bowers, Richard.

Deems, Edward M., compiled by. Holy Days & Holidays: A Treasury of Historical Material, Sermons in Full & in Brief, Suggestive Thoughts, & Poetry, Relating to Holy Days & Holidays. LC 89-71091. 768p. 1993. reprint ed. lib. bdg. 40.00 (*1-55888-910-8*) Omnigraphics Inc.

Deems, Eugene F., Jr. & Pursley, Duane. North American Furbearers: A Contemporary Reference. (Illus.). 217p. 1983. text 14.00 (*0-932108-08-3*) IAFWA.

Deems, Nyal & Stevenson, Jennette, 3rd. Practical Guide to Winning: Land Use Approvals & Permits. 1989. ring bd. 170.00 (*0-8205-1847-6*) Bender.

Deems, Nyal D. & Tervo, James M. Michigan Real Estate Practice & Forms, 2 Vols. LC 89-80297. 974p. 1989. ring bd., suppl. ed. 155.00 (*0-685-22742-1*, 89-001) U MI Law CLE.

— Michigan Real Estate Practice & Forms, 2 Vols. LC 89-80297. 974p. 1992. suppl. ed. 75.00 incl. disk (*0-685-58360-0*, 91-027) U MI Law CLE.

Deems, Richard S. Career Development in Adult Basic Education Programs. 43p. 1983. 4.95 (*0-318-22057-1*, IN263) Ctr Educ Trng Employ.

— Hiring: How to Find & Keep the Best People. LC 98-48155. 128p. 1998. pap. 12.99 (*1-56414-394-5*) Career Pr Inc.

— How to Fire Your Friends: A Win - Win Approach to Effective Termination. LC 89-61627. 141p. (Orig.). 1989. pap. 14.95 (*0-939644-57-6*) Media Pub.

— I Have to Fire Someone! LC 94-70862. (AMI How-to Ser.). 104p. (Orig.). 1994. pap. 12.95 (*1-884926-21-5*, FIRE) Amer Media.

— Interviewing: More Than a Gut Feeling. LC 94-70864. (AMI How-to Ser.). 96p. (Orig.). 1994. pap. 12.95 (*1-884926-22-3*, FEEL) Amer Media.

— Making Change Work for You! Kirchner, Dave, ed. LC 95-75608. (AMI How-to Ser.). 108p. 1995. per. 12.95 (*1-884926-38-X*, CHANG) Amer Media.

Deems, Richard S. & Warner, K. C. Making Change Work for You in Health Care. Miller, Karen M., ed. LC 98-70378. (How-To Book Ser.). 93p. 1998. pap. 14.95 (*1-884926-85-1*, CHANH) Amer Media.

Deen, Braswell D., Jr. Deen's List: ABC's on AIR; a Handbook for Busy Professionals, Parties, Practitioners, Persons & Participants. 100p. (Orig.). (C). 1995. pap. text 29.95 (*1-883793-13-0*) Wolfe Pubng.

Deen, Edith. All of the Women of the Bible. LC 55-8521. 432p. 1988. pap. 19.00 (*0-06-061852-3*, Pub. by Harper SF) HarpC.

— All the Women of the Bible. 432p. 1995. 9.98 (*0-7858-0471-4*) Bk Sales Inc.

Deen, Hanifa. Caravanserai: Journeys among Australian Muslims. 208p. 1995. pap. 19.95 (*1-86373-855-7*) Paul & Co Pubs.

Deen, M. J., et al, eds. Silicon Nitride & Silicon Dioxide Thin Insulating Films: 4th International Symposium. LC 98-100823. (Proceedings Ser.: Vol. 97-10). 588p. 1997. 78.00 (*1-56677-137-4*) Electrochem Soc.

Deen, Miriam. Composition Basics: The Sentence, the Paragraph, the Essay. (Illus.). 185p. 1999. pap. text 15.00 (*0-9672742-0-6*) M Deen.

Deen, Patricia & Trujillo, Al. Laboratory & Field Exercises in Oceanography. 1996. spiral bd. 25.00 (*0-88252-204-3*) Paladin Hse.

Deen, Paula H. The Lady & Sons Savannah Country Cookbook. LC 97-41561. 208p. 1998. pap. 14.95 (*0-375-75111-4*) Random.

***Deen, Paula H.** The Lady & Sons, Too! A Whole New Batch of Recipes from Savannah. LC 00-41744. 2000. write for info. (*0-375-75605-1*) Random.

Deen, Robert. Opportunities in Business Communications. (Illus.). 160p. 1990. 14.95 (*0-8442-6154-8*, 61548, VGM Career) NTC Contemp Pub Co.

Deen, Robert L., ed. The Alternatives to Gridlock: Perspectives on Meeting California's Transportation Needs. LC 89-23987. (Environmental Studies). 128p. (Orig.). 1990. pap. 10.00 (*0-912102-91-8*) Cal Inst Public.

Deen, Rosemary. Naming the Light: Familiar Essays, a Week of Years. LC 96-4529. (Creative Nonfiction Ser.). (Illus.). 168p. 1996. 14.95 (*0-252-06572-7*) U of Ill Pr.

Deen, Rosemary, jt. auth. see Ponsot, Marie.

Deen, S. M. CKBS '90: Proceedings of the International Working Conference on Cooperating Knowledge Based Systems, University of Keele, U. K. 3-5 October 1990. xiv, 327p. 1991. 61.95 (*0-387-19649-8*) Spr-Verlag.

Deen, William M. Analysis of Transport Phenomena. (Topics in Chemical Engineering Ser.). (Illus.). 624p. (C). 1998. text 79.00 (*0-19-508494-2*) OUP.

Deena, Lal. Christian Missions & Colonialism. 1988. 21.00 (*0-8364-2552-9*, Pub. by Usha) S Asia.

Deenen, L. L. Van, see Neuberger, A.

Deenen, L. L. Van, see Neuberger, A. & Van Deenen, L. L.

Deenen, L. L. Van, see Neuberger, A., ed.

Deenen, L. L. Van, see Neuberger, A. & Van Deenen, L. L., eds.

Deener, D. R., jt. auth. see Howard, L. V.

Deener, David R. De Lege Pactorum: Essays in Honor of R. R. Wilson. LC 70-101129. 288p. reprint ed. pap. 89.30 (*0-8357-9101-7*, 201789800010) Bks Demand.

Deeny, A. A., jt. auth. see Roe, F. J.

Deep ac, Sam. Smart Moves. 2nd ed. LC 97-34864. 1997. pap. 15.00 (*0-201-32812-7*) Addison-Wesley.

Deep, Christine, ed. Candlewood Classics: Cooking with Distinction. 2nd ed. 284p. 1995. reprint ed. 17.95 (*0-9657884-0-7*) Community Srvc Club.

Deep, D. K. The Nepal Festivals. (C). 1992. 30.00 (*0-7855-0201-7*, Pub. by Ratna Pustak Bhandar) St Mut.

Deep, Dhruba K. The Nepal Festivals. 128p. (C). 1982. 40.50 (*0-89771-067-3*, Pub. by Ratna Pustak Bhandar) St Mut.

— The Nepal Festivals. 1992. 30.00 (*0-7855-0261-0*, Pub. by Ratna Pustak Bhandar) St Mut.

Deep, Dhurba K. Popular Deities, Emblems & Images of Nepal. x, 170p. 1993. 20.00 (*81-85693-25-0*, Pub. by Nirala Pubns) Nataraj Bks.

Deep Foundations Ins. Staff. Piling & Deep Foundations 4th Edition, Vol. 2. 1994. 155.00 (*90-6191-197-4*) Ashgate Pub Co.

***Deep, John.** Complete Windows Nt Training Course. 1998. pap., student ed. 66.67 (*0-13-083041-0*, Prentice Hall) P-H.

Deep, John. Designing Interactive Documents with Adobe Acrobat Pro. 411p. 1996. pap. 34.95 (*0-471-12789-2*) Wiley.

— Developing CGI Applications with PERL. LC 95-43058. 320p. 1996. pap. 29.95 (*0-471-14158-5*) Wiley.

Deep, John, jt. auth. see Kear, Ed.

***Deep, Johnny.** The Complete Geek: An Operating Manual. (Illus.). 214p. 1999. reprint ed. pap. text 10.00 (*0-7881-6478-3*) DIANE Pub.

Deep, Sam. Power Tools: Newbridge Edition. 1998. 22.95 (*0-201-36033-0*) Addison-Wesley.

— Power Tools: 50 Management Inventions You Can Use Today. LC 97-39809. 256p. 1998. pap. 15.00 (*0-201-77297-3*) Addison-Wesley.

— Smart Moves. 1990. pap. 11.00 (*0-201-51812-0*) Addison-Wesley.

— Smart Moves for Selling. 1999. pap. write for info. (*0-201-77298-1*) Addison-Wesley.

— What to Ask When You Don't Know What to Say: Seven Hundred Twenty Powerful Questions to Use for Getting Your... LC 93-9657. (C). 1993. pap. text 14.95 (*0-13-953985-9*) P-H.

***Deep, Sam & Sussman, Lyle.** Act on It: Solving 101 of the Toughest Management Challenges. 240p. 2000. pap. text 13.00 (*0-7382-0245-2*) Perseus Pubng.

Deep, Sam & Sussman, Lyle. Close the Deal: 120 Checklists to Help You Close the Very Best Deal. 336p. 1998. pap. text 13.00 (*0-7382-0038-7*) Perseus Pubng.

— Smart Moves for People in Charge: 130 Checklists to Help You Be a Better Leader. LC 95-9571. 304p. 1995. pap. 15.00 (*0-201-48328-9*) Addison-Wesley.

— What to Ask When You Don't Know What to Say. 336p. 1997. 8.98 (*1-56731-190-3*, MJF Bks) Fine Comms.

— What to Ask When You Don't Know What to Say: 555 Powerful Questions to Use for Getting Your Way at Work. LC 93-9657. 310p. (C). 1990. 29.95 (*0-13-953977-8*) P-H.

— What to Say to Get What You Want: Strong Words for 40 Types of Bosses, Employees, Coworkers & Customers. 256p. 1991. pap. 14.00 (*0-201-57712-7*) Addison-Wesley.

— Yes, You Can! LC 95-40695. 288p. 1996. pap. 13.00 (*0-201-47965-6*) Addison-Wesley.

— Yes, You Can: One Thousand One Hundred Five Empowering Ideas for Life, Work, & Happiness. 288p. 1993. pap. write for info. (*0-9638019-3-7*) Sem by Sam Deep.

Deep, Samuel D., jt. auth. see Sussman, Lyle.

Deepak, Adarsh, ed. Atmospheric Aerosols: Their Formation, Optical Properties, & Effects. LC 81-51934. (Illus.). 480p. (C). 1982. 66.00 (*0-937194-01-8*) A Deepak Pub.

Deepak, Adarsh, et al, eds. Advances in Remote Sensing Retrieval Methods. LC 86-2057. (Illus.). 737p. 1986. 71.00 (*0-937194-07-7*) A Deepak Pub.

— RSRM '87: Advances in Remote Sensing Retrieval Methods. LC 89-36947. (Illus.). 519p. 1989. 78.00 (*0-937194-13-1*) A Deepak Pub.

Deepak, Adarsh & Rao, K. R., eds. Applications of Remote Sensing for Rice Production. LC 85-1677. (Illus.). 449p. (C). 1985. 74.00 (*0-937194-03-4*) A Deepak Pub.

Deepak, Adarsh & Vali, Gabor, eds. The International Global Aerosol Program (IGAP) Plan. (Orig.). 1992. pap. 27.00 (*0-937194-29-8*) A Deepak Pub.

Deepak, Adarsh, jt. ed. see Gerber, Hermann E.

Deepak, Adarsh, jt. ed. see Ruhnke, Lothar H.

Deeping, Warwick. Fox Farm. 1976. lib. bdg. 17.75 (*0-89968-021-6*, Lghtyr Pr) Buccaneer Bks.

— Kitty. 1976. lib. bdg. 16.75 (*0-89968-020-8*, Lghtyr Pr) Buccaneer Bks.

— The Red Saint. 1976. lib. bdg. 16.75 (*0-89968-024-0*, Lghtyr Pr) Buccaneer Bks.

Deeprose, Donna. How to Recognize & Reward Employees. LC 94-25065. (WorkSmart Ser.). 120p. (Orig.). 1994. pap. 10.95 (*0-8144-7832-8*) AMACOM.

***Deeprose, Donna.** Recharge Your Team: Keep Them Going & Going. LC 98-8850. 1998. 12.95 (*0-8144-2366-3*) AMACOM.

Deeprose, Donna. The Team Coach: Vital New Skills for Supervisors & Managers in a Team Environment. LC 95-638. 176p. (Orig.). 1995. pap. 17.95 (*0-8144-7859-X*) AMACOM.

Deepwell, K. Women & Modernism. LC 99-183601. 206p. 1998. 79.95 (*0-7190-5081-2*, Pub. by Manchester Univ Pr); pap. 29.95 (*0-7190-5082-0*, Pub. by Manchester Univ Pr) St Martin.

Deepwell, Katy, ed. New Feminist Art Criticism: Critical Strategies. LC 94-5414. (Illus.). 201p. 1995. text 24.95 (*0-7190-4258-5*, Pub. by Manchester Univ Pr) St Martin.

Deer. Rock Forming Minerals, Vol. 1. 1986. text. write for info. (*0-582-46521-4*, Pub. by Addison-Wesley) Longman.

— Rock-Forming Minerals: Non Silicates, Vol. 5B. 2nd ed. 1995. 165.08 (*0-582-30093-2*, Pub. by Addison-Wesley) Longman.

Deer, ed. Understanding Popular Arts. (C). 2000. pap. text. write for info. (*0-321-01587-8*) Addison-Wesley.

D

Deer & Deer Hunting Editors. Deer Hunter's 1999 Almanac. LC 92-74255. (Illus.). 208p. 1998. pap. 6.95 (*0-87341-687-2*, HA99) Krause Pubns.

***Deer & Deer Hunting Magazine Editors.** 2000 Deer Hunters' Almanac. LC 92-74255. (Illus.). 200p. 1999. pap. 6.95 (*0-87341-868-9*) Krause Pubns.

Deer & Deer Hunting Magazine Staff. Advanced Whitetail Details. LC 92-74792. 24p. 1992. pap. 14.95 (*0-87341-229-X*, DW01) Krause Pubns.

Deer & Deer Hunting Staff. 301 Venison Recipes: The Ultimate Deer Hunter's Cookbook. rev. ed. LC 92-74074. 128p. 1994. pap. 10.95 (*0-87341-227-3*) Krause Pubns.

Deer, Archie Fire Lame, see Erdoes, Richard & Fire Lame Deer, Archie.

Deer, Christine, jt. auth. see Seddon, Terri.

Deer, Glenn. Postmodern Canadian Fiction & the Rhetoric of Authority. 160p. 1994. 49.95 (*0-7735-1159-8*, Pub. by McG-Queens Univ Pr) CUP Services.

Deer, Josef. The Dynastic Porphyry Tombs of the Norman Period in Sicily. LC 60-3574. (Dumbarton Oaks Studies: Vol. 5). (Illus.). 188p. 1959. 30.00 (*0-88402-005-3*) Dumbarton Oaks.

***Deer, Randolph H.** And the Winner Is... LC 98-90899. 350p. 1999. 22.95 (*0-533-12974-5*) Vantage.

Deer, Richard E. Indiana Corporation Law & Practice. 1992. ring bd. 126.00 (*0-13-109158-1*) Aspen Law.

— The Lawyer's Basic Corporate Practice Manual. 3rd ed. LC 84-72759. 320p. 1984. ring bd., suppl. ed. 19.00 (*0-8318-0468-8*, B468/B580) Am Law Inst.

— Lawyer's Basic Corporate Practice Manual Supplement. 37p. 1988. pap. text 5.43 (*0-8318-0580-3*, B580) Am Law Inst.

Deer, Richard E. & Riffle, Timothy J. Indiana Limited Liability Company Forms & Practice Manual. LC 96-1124. 544p. 1996. ring bd. 219.90 (*1-57400-022-5*) Data Trace Pubng.

Deer, W. A. Intro Rock Forming Minrl. 2nd ed. (C). 1992. pap. text 52.50 (*0-582-30094-0*, Pub. by Addison-Wesley) Longman.

Deer, W. A., et al, eds. Disilicates & Ring Silicates. (Rock-Forming Minerals Ser.: Vol. 1B). (Illus.). 630p. 1997. 125.00 (*1-897799-89-6*, Pub. by Geol Soc Pub Hse) AAPG.

— Double-Chain Silicates. (Rock-Forming Minerals Ser.: No. 2B). (Illus.). 784p. 1997. 165.00 (*1-897799-77-2*, Pub. by Geol Soc Pub Hse) AAPG.

— Orthosilicates. (Rock-Forming Minerals Ser.: No. 1A). (Illus.). 932p. 1997. 125.00 (*1-897799-88-8*, Pub. by Geol Soc Pub Hse) AAPG.

— Single-Chain Silicates. (Rock-Forming Minerals Ser.: No. 2A). (Illus.). 680p. 1997. 125.00 (*1-897799-85-3*, Pub. by Geol Soc Pub Hse) AAPG.

Deere & Company Staff. Managing Livestock Production. 237p. 1994. teacher ed. 40.95 (*0-86691-215-0*, FBM12501T); student ed. 18.95 (*0-86691-216-9*, FBM12601W) Deere & Co.

— Managing Livestock Production. (Farm Business Management Ser.). (Illus.). 396p. (C). 1994. pap. text 35.95 (*0-86691-235-5*, FBM12101NC) Deere & Co.

Deere & Company Staff, ed. Belts & Chains. 5th rev. ed. (Fundamentals of Service Ser.). (Illus.). 72p. 1994. pap. text 12.95 (*0-86691-199-5*, FOS5305NC) Deere & Co.

— Chemical Applications Management. 3rd rev. ed. (Farm Business Management Ser.). (Illus.). 292p. 1994. pap. text 32.95 (*0-86691-234-7*, FBM19103NC) Deere & Co.

— Combine Harvesting. (Fundamentals of Machine Operation Ser.). (Illus.). 92p. 1991. pap. text, student ed. 16.95 (*0-86691-162-6*, FMO15604W) Deere & Co.

— Combine Harvesting. rev. ed. (Fundamentals of Machine Operation Ser.). (Illus.). 92p. 1991. pap. text, teacher ed. 39.95 (*0-86691-161-8*, FMO15504T) Deere & Co.

— Compact Equipment - Electrical Systems. 2nd rev. ed. (Fundamentals of Service Compact Equipment Ser.). (Illus.). 312p. 1994. pap. text 29.95 (*0-86691-205-3*, FCP83102B) Deere & Co.

— Compact Equipment - Engines. (Fundamentals of Service Ser.). (Illus.). 84p. 1992. pap. text, student ed. 16.95 (*0-86691-176-6*, FCP80303W) Deere & Co.

— Compact Equipment - Engines. rev. ed. (Fundamentals of Service Ser.). (Illus.). 245p. 1992. sl. 245.95 (*0-685-01387-1*, FCP80203S) Deere & Co.

— Compact Equipment - Engines. 2nd rev. ed. (Fundamentals of Service Compact Equipment Ser.). (Illus.). 288p. 1992. pap. text 29.95 (*0-86691-146-4*, FCP80103B) Deere & Co.

— Compact Equipment - Engines, Instr.'s Kit. (Fundamentals of Service Ser.). (Illus.). 1992. pap. text, teacher ed., student ed. 69.95 (*0-86691-203-7*, FCP80103KIT) Deere & Co.

— Compact Equipment - Hydraulics. 2nd rev. ed. (Fundamentals of Service Compact Equipment Ser.). 193p. 1994. sl. 193.95 (*0-614-24184-7*, FCP82202S) Deere & Co.

— Compact Equipment - Hydraulics. 2nd rev. ed. (Fundamentals of Service Compact Equipment Ser.). (Illus.). 192p. 1994. pap. text 29.95 (*0-86691-189-8*, FCP82102B) Deere & Co.

— Compact Equipment - Power Trains. (Fundamentals of Service Compact Equipment Ser.). 150p. 1983. sl. 150.95 (*0-614-24182-0*, FCP81201S) Deere & Co.

— Compact Equipment - Power Trains. rev. ed. (Fundamentals of Service Ser.). (Illus.). 40p. (C). 1991. pap. text, student ed. 16.95 (*0-86691-156-1*, FCP81302W) Deere & Co.

— Compact Equipment - Power Trains. 2nd rev. ed. (Fundamentals of Service Compact Equipment Ser.). (Illus.). 188p. (C). 1991. pap. text 29.95 (*0-86691-136-7*, FCP81102B) Deere & Co.

— Compact Equipment - Power Trains, Instr.'s Kit. (Fundamentals of Service Ser.). (Illus.). (C). 1991. pap. text, teacher ed., student ed. 69.95 (*0-86691-204-5*, FCP81102KIT) Deere & Co.

— Compact Equipment-Electrical Systems. 2nd rev. ed. (Illus.). 74p. 1994. pap. text, student ed. 16.95 (*0-86691-209-6*, FCP83302W) Deere & Co.

— Compact Equipment-Electrical Systems, Instr.'s Kit. 2nd ed. (Fundamentals of Service Ser.). (Illus.). 1994. pap. text, teacher ed., student ed. 69.95 (*0-86691-201-0*, FCP83102KIT) Deere & Co.

— Compact Equipment-Hydraulics. 2nd ed. (Illus.). 42p. 1994. pap. text, student ed. 16.95 (*0-86691-197-9*, FCP82302W) Deere & Co.

— Compact Equipment-Hydraulics, Instr.'s Kit. 2nd rev. ed. (Fundamentals of Service Ser.). (Illus.). 1994. pap. text, teacher ed., student ed. 69.95 (*0-86691-202-9*, FCP82102KIT) Deere & Co.

— Electronic & Electrical Systems. 7th rev. ed. (Fundamentals of Service Ser.). 337p. 1993. pap. 99.95 incl. trans. (*0-614-24185-5*, FOS2007M) Deere & Co.

— Electronic & Electrical Systems. 7th rev. ed. (Illus.). 392p. 1993. pap. text 27.95 (*0-86691-240-1*, FOS2007NC); pap. text, teacher ed. 27.95 (*0-86691-194-4*, FOS2007T); pap. text, student ed. 23.95 (*0-86691-193-6*, FOS2007W) Deere & Co.

— Engines. 7th ed. (Fundamentals of Service Ser.). (Illus.). 128p. 1991. pap. text, teacher ed. 28.95 (*0-86691-152-9*, FOS3007T) Deere & Co.

— Engines. 7th rev. ed. (Fundamentals of Service Ser.). 204p. 1991. pap. 67.95 incl. trans. (*0-614-24187-1*, FOS3007M) Deere & Co.

— Engines. 7th rev. ed. (Fundamentals of Service Ser.). (Illus.). 320p. 1991. pap. text 33.95 (*0-86691-246-0*, FOS3007NC); pap. text, student ed. 18.95 (*0-86691-153-7*, FOS3007W) Deere & Co.

— Farm & Ranch Business Management. 3rd rev. ed. (Farm Business Management Ser.). 296p. 1992. pap. text 31.95 (*0-86691-232-0*, FBM10103NC); pap. text, teacher ed. 29.95 (*0-86691-167-7*, FBM10503T); pap. text, student ed. 19.95 (*0-86691-168-5*, FBM10603W) Deere & Co.

— Farm & Ranch Safety Management. 4th rev. ed. (Fundamentals of Machine Operation Ser.). (Illus.). 304p. 1994. pap. text, teacher ed. 75.95 incl. trans. (*0-86691-187-1*, FBM18504T); pap. text, student ed. 25.95 (*0-86691-188-X*, FBM18604W) Deere & Co.

— Fiberglass. 4th rev. ed. (Fundamentals of Service Ser.). 84p. 1993. 84.95 incl. sl. (*0-614-24192-8*, FOS5904S) Deere & Co.

— Fiberglass. 4th rev. ed. (Fundamentals of Service Ser.). (Illus.). 36p. 1993. pap. text 11.95 (*0-86691-177-4*, FOS5904NC) Deere & Co.

— Fuels, Lubricants, & Coolants. 7th rev. ed. (Fundamentals of Service Ser.). (Illus.). 80p. 1992. pap. text 12.95 (*0-86691-228-2*, FOS5807NC) Deere & Co.

— A Glossary of Technical Terms. rev. ed. (Fundamentals of Service Ser.). (Illus.). 80p. (C). 1992. pap. text 12.95 (*0-86691-225-8*, FOS6201NC) Deere & Co.

— Hay & Forage Harvesting. 4th rev. ed. (Illus.). 276p. 1993. pap. text 32.95 (*0-86691-172-3*, FMO14104B); pap. text, teacher ed. 49.95 incl. trans. (*0-86691-191-X*, FMO14504T); pap. text, student ed. 16.95 (*0-86691-192-8*, FMO14604W) Deere & Co.

— Hoses, Tubing & Connectors. (Fundamentals of Service Ser.). (Illus.). 40p. 1993. pap. text 11.95 (*0-86691-224-X*, FOS6301NC) Deere & Co.

— Hydraulics. 5th rev. ed. (Fundamentals of Service Ser.). 240p. 1992. 240.95 incl. sl. (*0-614-24196-0*, FOS1005S); pap. 67.95 incl. trans. (*0-614-24195-2*, FOS1005M); pap. text, teacher ed. 28.95 (*0-86691-165-0*, FOS1005T); pap. text, student ed. 18.95 (*0-86691-166-9*, FOS1005W) Deere & Co.

— Hydraulics. 5th rev. ed. (Fundamentals of Service Ser.). 224p. 1992. pap. text 30.95 (*0-86691-239-8*, FOS1005NC) Deere & Co.

— Identification of Parts Failure. 4th rev. ed. (Fundamentals of Service Ser.). (Illus.). 200p. 1991. pap. text 32.95 (*0-86691-134-0*, FOS6104NC) Deere & Co.

— Machinery Maintenance. 2nd rev. ed. (Fundamentals of Machine Operation Ser.). (Illus.). 101p. 1991. pap. text, teacher ed. 22.55 (*0-86691-158-8*, FMW10502T) Deere & Co.

— Machinery Maintenance. 3rd rev. ed. (Fundamentals of Machine Operation Ser.). (Illus.). 150p. 1991. pap. text 19.95 (*0-86691-130-8*, FMW10103NC) Deere & Co.

— Machinery Management. 4th rev. ed. (Farm Business Management Ser.). (Illus.). 182p. 1992. pap. text 35.95 (*0-86691-262-2*, FBM17105NC); pap. text, teacher ed. 40.95 (*0-86691-183-9*, FBM17504T); pap. text, student ed. 19.95 (*0-86691-184-7*, FBM17604W) Deere & Co.

— Mowers & Sprayers. 5th rev. ed. (Fundamentals of Service Ser.). (Illus.). 88p. 1993. pap. text 15.95 (*0-86691-179-0*, FOS5605NC) Deere & Co.

— Planting. 3rd ed. (Fundamentals of Machine Operation Ser.). (Illus.). 96p. 1992. pap. text, teacher ed. 33.95 incl. trans. (*0-86691-173-1*, FMO12503T) Deere & Co.

— Planting. 3rd rev. ed. (Fundamentals of Machine Operation Ser.). (Illus.). 224p. 1992. pap. text 29.95 (*0-86691-148-0*, FMO12103B); pap. text, student ed. 16.95 (*0-86691-174-X*, FMO12603W) Deere & Co.

— Plastics Repair. rev. ed. (Fundamentals of Service Ser.). (Illus.). 48p. 1994. pap. text 11.95 (*0-86691-223-1*, FOS6501NC) Deere & Co.

— Power Trains. 5th rev. ed. (Fundamentals of Service Ser.). 130p. 1991. pap. 57.95 incl. trans. (*0-614-24202-9*, FOS4005M) Deere & Co.

— Power Trains. 6th rev. ed. (Fundamentals of Service Ser.). (Illus.). 176p. 1991. pap. text 21.95 (*0-86691-241-X*, FOS4006NC); pap. text, teacher ed. 14.95 (*0-86691-163-4*, FOS4006T); pap. text, student ed. 17.95 (*0-86691-164-2*, FOS4006W) Deere & Co.

***Deere & Company Staff, ed.** The Precision Farming Guide for Agriculturists. 70p. 1999. pap., teacher ed. 20.95 (*0-86691-263-0*, FP401T); pap., student ed. 15.95 (*0-86691-264-9*, FP401W) Deere & Co.

Deere & Company Staff, ed. Preventive Maintenance. 4th rev. ed. (Fundamentals of Machine Operation Ser.). 240p. 1991. 240.95 incl. sl. (*0-614-24204-5*, FMO16204S) Deere & Co.

— Preventive Maintenance. 5th rev. ed. (Fundamentals of Machine Operation Ser.). (Illus.). 276p. 1992. pap. text 31.95 (*0-86691-171-5*, FMO16105NC); pap. text, teacher ed. 33.95 incl. trans. (*0-86691-064-6*, FMO16503T); pap. text, student ed. 16.95 (*0-86691-065-4*, FMO16603W) Deere & Co.

— Shop Tools. 5th rev. ed. (Fundamentals of Service Ser.). (Illus.). 56p. 1992. pap. text 11.95 (*0-86691-226-6*, FOS5105NC) Deere & Co.

— Soil Management. (Farm Business Management Ser.). 140p. (Orig.). (C). 1993. pap. text 25.95 (*0-86691-229-0*, FBM11101NC); pap. text, teacher ed. 27.95 (*0-86691-185-5*, FBM11501T); pap. text, student ed. 17.95 (*0-86691-186-3*, FBM11601W) Deere & Co.

— Tillage. rev. ed. (Fundamentals of Machine Operation Ser.). (Illus.). 118p. 1993. pap. text, student ed. 21.95 (*0-86691-196-0*, FMO11603W) Deere & Co.

— Tillage. 3rd ed. (Fundamentals of Machine Operation Ser.). (Illus.). 232p. 1993. pap. text, teacher ed. 79.95 incl. trans. (*0-86691-195-2*, FMO11503T) Deere & Co.

— Tillage. 3rd rev. ed. (Fundamentals of Machine Operation Ser.). (Illus.). 164p. 1993. pap. text 29.95 (*0-86691-180-4*, FMO11103NC) Deere & Co.

— Tires & Tracks. 7th rev. ed. (Fundamentals of Service Ser.). (Illus.). 92p. 1992. pap. text 13.95 (*0-86691-142-1*, FOS5507NC) Deere & Co.

— Tractors. 3rd rev. ed. (Fundamentals of Machine Operation Ser.). 92p. 1994. 92.95 incl. sl. (*0-614-24209-6*, FMO10203S) Deere & Co.

— Tractors. 3rd rev. ed. (Fundamentals of Machine Operation Ser.). (Illus.). 280p. 1994. pap. text 34.95 (*0-86691-212-6*, FMO10103NCX); pap. text, teacher ed. 33.95 incl. trans. (*0-86691-160-X*, FMO10503T); pap. text, student ed. 16.95 (*0-86691-159-6*, FMO10603W) Deere & Co.

— Welding. 7th rev. ed. (Fundamentals of Service Ser.). 147p. 1991. 147.95 incl. sl. (*0-614-24210-X*, FOS5207S) Deere & Co.

— Welding. 7th rev. ed. (Fundamentals of Service Ser.). (Illus.). 168p. 1991. pap. text 19.95 (*0-86691-220-7*, FOS5207NC) Deere & Co.

Deere, Carmen & De Leal, Magdalena L. Women in Andean Agriculture: Peasant Production & Rural Wage Employment in Colombia & Peru. 2nd ed. (Women, Work & Development Ser.: No. 4). xii, 172p. 1985. pap. 18.00 (*92-2-103106-3*) Intl Labour Office.

Deere, Carmen D. Household & Class Relations: The Peasant Economy of the Northern Peruvian Highlands, 1900-1980. 1990. 55.00 (*0-520-06675-8*, Pub. by U CA Pr) Cal Prin Full Svc.

***Deere, Dicey.** The Irish Cottage Murder: A Torrey Tunet Mystery. 304p. 1999. mass mkt. 5.99 (*0-312-97131-1*, Minotaur) St Martin.

— Irish Manor House Murder. 2000. text 23.95 (*0-312-20606-2*) St Martin.

— The Irish Manor House Murder. mass mkt. write for info. (*0-312-97645-3*) St Martin.

Deere, Ed D. Animal Transport by Sea-Conference Papers. 1983. 35.00 (*0-7855-1117-2*) St Mut.

Deere, J. Sorprendido por el Poder del Espiritu Santo.Tr. of Surprised by the Power of the Holy Spirit. (SPA.). 338p. pap. 10.99 (*1-56063-753-6*, 550073) Editorial Unilit.

***Deere, Jack.** The Beginner's Guide to the Gift of Prophecy. 2001. pap. 9.99 (*1-56955-204-5*) Servant.

Deere, Jack. Surprised by the Power of the Spirit. LC 93-22158. 256p. 1993. 19.99 (*0-310-58790-5*) Zondervan.

— Surprised by the Power of the Spirit. 304p. 1996. pap. 10.99 (*0-310-21127-1*) Zondervan.

— Surprised by the Voice of God. Date not set. pap. 12.99 (*0-8297-1681-5*) Vida Pubs.

— Surprised by the Voice of God: How God Speaks Today Through Prophecies, Dreams & Visions. 256p. 1996. 18.99 (*0-310-46200-2*) Zondervan.

— Surprised by the Voice of God: How God Speaks Today Through Prophecies, Dreams & Visions. 384p. 1998. pap. 12.99 (*0-310-22558-2*) Zondervan.

Deerfield Parish Guild Staff. The Pocumtuck Housewife: A Guide to Domestic Cookery. 55p. 1985. reprint ed. pap. 4.95 (*0-9612876-4-0*) Pocumtuck Valley Mem.

Deering, Anne & Murphy, Anne. The Difference Engine: Achieving Powerful & Sustainable Partnership. LC 98-9612. 200p. 1998. 69.95 (*0-566-08048-6*, Pub. by Gower) Ashgate Pub Co.

Deering, B., jt. auth. see West, B. J.

Deering, Charles. Deering. Genealogical Notes on Some of the Descendants of George Dearing from Co. Devon, England, & John Whipple, from Co. Essex, England. 464p. 1997. reprint ed. pap. 61.50 (*0-8328-8252-6*); reprint ed. lib. bdg. 71.50 (*0-8328-8251-8*) Higginson Bk Co.

Deering, Christopher J. & Smith, Steven S. Committees in Congress. 3rd ed. LC 97-2898. 254p. (YA). (gr. 11). 1997. pap. text 24.95 (*0-87187-818-6*) Congr Quarterly.

Deering, Hallie. Do-it-Yourself Power Tools. 91p. (Orig.). 1995. pap. 25.00 (*0-929385-63-2*) Light Tech Pubng.

— Light from the Angels. 229p. (Orig.). 1995. pap. 15.00 (*0-929385-72-1*) Light Tech Pubng.

Deering, John. Deering's State of Mind. LC 90-63519. 96p. 1990. per. 9.95 (*0-914546-90-2*) Rose Pub.

Deering, John J. God, Was She a Man, or Is He a Woman? (The Politics of Religion) LC 96-94514. (Illus.). 160p. (Orig.). 1996. pap. 14.95 (*0-9652684-3-8*) Green D Pub.

***Deering, Kathryn.** Gifted for Good: Every Woman's Guide to Her Spiritual Gifts. 2000. pap. 9.99 (*1-56955-089-1*, Vine Bks) Servant.

Deering, Michael. Java 3D API Specification. LC 97-39034. (Java Ser.). 512p. (C). 1997. pap. text 39.95 (*0-201-32576-4*) Addison-Wesley.

Deering, Randy. Sailor's Guide to Life. (Wisdom Ser.). 1999. pap. text 6.95 (*1-58334-001-7*) Walnut Gr Pr.

Deerr, Kathleen, jt. auth. see Feinberg, Sandra.

Deery. Labour Law & Industrial Relations in Asia. Date not set. pap. text. write for info. (*0-582-86902-1*, Pub. by Addison-Wesley) Longman.

Deery, Ruth. Earthquakes & Volcanoes. (Natural Disaster Ser.). (Illus.). 48p. (J). (gr. 4-8). 1985. student ed. 7.99 (*0-86653-272-2*, GA 630) Good Apple.

— Tornadoes & Hurricanes. (Natural Disaster Ser.). (Illus.). 48p. (J). (gr. 4-8). 1985. student ed. 7.99 (*0-86653-318-4*, GA 631) Good Apple.

***Deery, Stephen & Mitchell, Richard, eds.** Employment Relations: Individualisation & Union Exclusion - An International Study. 254p. 1999. pap. 45.00 (*1-86287-344-5*, Pub. by Federation Pr) Gaunt.

Dees & Dornan. Four in One: Thinking, Reading, Writing, Researching. 733p. 1998. pap. text 46.00 (*0-205-15280-5*) Allyn.

Dees, jt. auth. see Dornan.

Dees, Beth. Santa's Price Guide to Contemporary Christmas Collectibles. LC 97-73039. (Illus.). 232p. 1997. pap. 24.95 (*0-87341-528-0*, XMCL) Krause Pubns.

Dees, Colette J., tr. see Comiskey, James A.

Dees, Colette J., tr. see Kwatera, Michael.

Dees, Colette J., tr. see Potin, Jacques.

Dees, Colette J., tr. see Wallace, James A.

Dees, Colette Joly, tr. see Lazarev, Viktor Nikitich.

Dees, Collettee J., tr. see Gutierrez, Gustavo.

Dees, Dee. LifeNotes: Recording YOUR Memories - The Legacy of a Lifetime. (Illus.). 90p. 1998. spiral bd. 12.95 (*0-9667829-0-9*) Double D Desktop Pubg.

Dees, Mark L. The Miller Dynasty. deluxe rev. ed. 560p. 1993. write for info. (*0-9638084-1-9*) Hippodrome.

— The Miller Dynasty. 2nd rev. ed. (Illus.). 564p. 1993. 129.50 (*0-9638084-0-0*) Hippodrome.

Dees, Mary R. The Bluff Beckons: A Novel. LC 99-93386. 256p. 1999. pap. 14.95 (*0-9630600-3-1*, 0-9630600) Marmor.

— Caught up in Time: Arduous Treks of Pioneers Who Migrated to the Untamed West. LC 91-91368. 200p. (Orig.). 1991. pap. 9.95 (*0-9630600-0-7*) Marmor.

— Delayed Concessions. Canon, Lana, ed. LC 93-91716. 256p. (Orig.). 1994. pap. 10.95 (*0-9630600-2-3*) Marmor.

— Mar's Meanderings: Things You Thought You Didn't Know - A Compilation of Educational, Humorous, & Thought-Provoking Articles. 128p. (Orig.). 1993. pap. 7.95 (*0-9630600-1-5*) Marmor.

— Quanah Parker's Strange Encounters: A Biography. LC 97-93449. (Illus.). 252p. (Orig.). 1997. pap. 14.95 (*0-9630600-4-X*, 0-9630600) Marmor.

Dees, Morris & Corcoran, James. Gathering Storm: America's Militia Threat. (Illus.). 288p. 1997. pap. 13.00 (*0-06-092789-5*, Perennial) HarperTrade.

Dees-Morse, Jane L., ed. Off to College, 1997: A Guide for College Bound Students. 68p. 1997. pap. text 3.00 (*0-9654246-0-X*) Dees Comm.

Dees, Robert, jt. auth. see Barnwell, William Hazzard.

Dees, Robert, tr. see Riddell, John, ed.

Dees, Russell, ed. see Logstrup, Knud.

Dees, Timothy. Online Services for Law Enforcement. vii, 243p. 1996. 19.95 (*1-889373-00-1*) Prof Trning.

***Deese, Alma Wynelle.** St. Petersburg: Now & Then. (Postcard History Ser.). (Illus.). 128p. 1999. pap. 18.99 (*0-7385-0131-X*) Arcadia Publng.

Deese, David A. The New Politics of American Foreign Policy. 285p. 1993. pap. 31.95 (*0-312-09133-8*) St Martin.

Deese, E. K., jt. auth. see Deese, James E.

Deese, Helen & Axelrod, Steven G. Critical Essays on William Carlos Williams. (Critical Essays on American Literature Ser.). 1994. 48.00 (*0-7838-0015-0*, Twyne) Mac Lib Ref.

Deese, Helen, jt. ed. see Axelrod, Steven G.

Deese, Helen R. Jones Very: The Complete Poems. LC 92-9301. 952p. 1993. 70.00 (*0-8203-1481-1*) U of Ga Pr.

Deese, J. The Structure of Associations in Language & Thought. LC 65-26181. 232p. reprint ed. pap. 72.00 (*0-608-11300-X*, 200383900037) Bks Demand.

Deese, J., jt. auth. see Szalay, Lorand B.

Deese, James E. & Deese, E. K. How to Study. 4th ed. 256p. (C). 1994. pap. 10.95 (*0-07-016269-7*) McGraw.

***Deese-Roberts, Susan.** Library Instruction: A Peer Tutoring Model. 185p. 2000. 46.00 (*1-56308-652-2*) Libs Unl.

Deese, Wynelle. Lexington: Changes in the Twentieth Century. LC 98-86344. (Images of America Ser.). (Illus.). 128p. 1998. pap. 16.99 (*0-7524-1386-4*) Arcadia Publng.

***Deese, Wynelle Scott.** Musing Through Towns in Mississippi. (Postcard History Ser.). (Illus.). 128p. 1999. pap. 18.99 (*0-7385-0038-0*) Arcadia Publng.

Deeson, E. Physics Basic Facts. (Collins Gem Ser.). 1996. pap. 8.00 (*0-00-470908-X*) Collins.

Deeson, Eric. Technician Physics, Level 2. LC QC0021.2. (Longman Technician Series, Mathematics & Sciences). 284p. reprint ed. pap. 88.10 (*0-8357-2978-8*, 203924000011) Bks Demand.

Deesudyka, Tracee. Integrating Technology into the Language Arts Curriculum. 144p. (J). (gr. 3-5). 1997. pap. 14.95 (*1-57690-422-9*) Tchr Create Mat.

Deeter, Catherine. Seymour Bleu: A Space Odyssey. LC 96-8584. (Illus.). 40p. (J). (ps-3). 1998. per. 16.00 (*0-689-80137-8*) S&S Childrens.

An Asterisk (*) at the beginning of an entry indicates that the title is appearing for the first time.

Deeter, D. & Bland, C. E. Technology in Rural Transportation: Simple Solutions. (Illus.). 125p. (C). 1998. pap. text 25.00 (*0-7881-7240-9*) DIANE Pub.

***Deeter, David P.** Textbook of Military Medicine, Disease & the Environment: Occupational Health, the Soldier & the Industrial Base, Vol. 2. 643p. 2000. boxed set 59.00 (*0-16-059136-8*) USGPO.

***Deeter, David P. & Gaydos, Joel C., eds.** Occupational Health: The Soldier & the Industrial Base. (Illus.). 643p. (C). 1999. reprint ed. text 75.00 (*0-7881-8259-5*) DIANE Pub.

Deeter, Kirk D., jt. auth. see Voy, Robert O.

Deeter, William R. Working with the Press: How to Achieve a Competitive Advantage. (Illus.). 100p. (Orig.). 1995. pap. 14.95 (*0-945609-17-5*) Keel Pubns.

***Deetjen, Peter & Falkenbach, Albrecht.** Radon und Gesundheit: Radon & Health. 199p. 1999. 37.95 (*3-631-35532-7*) P Lang Pubng.

Deetlefs, Rene. The Song of Six Birds. LC 99-25587. (Illus.). 32p. (J). (gr. 1-3). 1999. 15.99 (*0-525-46314-3*, Dutton Child) Peng Put Young Read.

— Tabu & the Dancing Elephants. 1999. pap. write for info. (*0-14-037976-2*) Viking Penguin.

Deets, Blair B. & Geimer, Allan F. It's Your Future: Plan for Success. (Illus.). 154p. (Orig.). (YA). (gr. 8 up). 1994. pap. 12.95 (*1-886358-00-1*) Cellular Pub.

Deets, Blair B., jt. auth. see Geimer, Allan F.

Deetz, Charles H. & Adams, Oscar S. Elements of Map Projection with Applications to Map & Chart Construction. 5th ed. LC 77-89015. 226p. 1970. reprint ed. lib. bdg. 38.50 (*0-8371-2268-6*, DEMP, Greenwood Pr) Greenwood.

Deetz, James. Flowerdew Hundred: The Archaeology of a Virginia Plantation 1619-1864. (Illus.). 224p. (C). 1995. pap. 14.00 (*0-8139-1639-9*) U Pr of Va.

— In Small Things Forgotten: The Archaeology of Early American Life. expanded rev. ed. (Illus.). 304p. 1996. pap. 11.95 (*0-385-48399-6*, Anchor NY) Doubleday.

***Deetz, James & Deetz, Patricia Scott.** The Times of Their Lives: Life, Love & Death at Plymouth Colony. 2000. pap. text 24.95 (*0-7167-3830-9*) W H Freeman.

Deetz, Patricia Scott, jt. auth. see Deetz, James.

Deetz, Stanley A. Communication Yearbook, Vol. 16. (Illus.). 640p. (C). 1992. 75.00 (*0-8039-4601-5*) Sage.

— Democracy in an Age of Corporate Colonization: Developments in Communication & the Politics of Everyday Life. LC 90-26171. (SUNY Series in Communication Studies). 399p. (C). 1992. pap. text 24.95 (*0-7914-0864-7*) State U NY Pr.

— Transforming Communication, Transforming Business: Building Responsive & Responsible Workplaces. LC 94-44000. (Communication Series). 1995. text 45.00 (*1-57273-036-6*); pap. text 22.95 (*1-57273-037-4*) Hampton Pr NJ.

Deetz, Stanley A., ed. Communication Yearbook. (Communication Yearbook Ser.: Vol. 15). 696p. (C). 1992. text 75.00 (*0-8039-3529-3*) Sage.

— Communication Yearbook, Vol. 17. (Illus.). 640p. (C). 1993. text 85.00 (*0-8039-5433-6*) Sage.

***Deetz, Stanley A., et al.** Leading Organizations Through Transition: Communication & Cultural Change. LC 99-50466. 1999. write for info. (*0-7619-2097-8*) Sage.

Deev, jt. auth. see Ryabov, V. R.

Deever, Allen. Total Writing Concept: World's Fastest Creative Writing Technique. LC 99-159492. 1998. pap. 69.50 (*1-886804-02-8*) Lightspeed Bk Pubs.

DeEver, Allen & DeEver, Ellie. Earn a Accredited College Degree in 4 Separate Months...or Less! 3rd ed. 300p. 1998. pap. 49.95 (*1-886804-06-0*) Lightspeed Bk Pubs.

— Earn a Real Master's or Doctorate Degree in 4 Months...or Less! 2nd ed. 400p. 1997. pap. text 69.95 (*1-886804-08-7*) Lightspeed Bk Pubs.

— How to Write a Book on ANYTHING in Two Weeks...or Less! Total Writing Concept 2000. 3rd ed. 350p. (Orig.). 1998. pap. 49.95 (*1-886804-11-7*) Lightspeed Bk Pubs.

DeEver, Ellie, jt. auth. see DeEver, Allen.

Deevey, Brian, jt. auth. see Haley, Barbara A.

Deevey, Edward S., Jr. Limnologic Studies in Middle America, with a Chapter on Aztec Limnology. (Connecticut Academy of Arts & Sciences Ser., Trans.: Vol. 39). 1957. pap. 69.50 (*0-685-22895-9*) Elliots Bks.

Deevey, Edward S., Jr., ed. Growth by Intussusception: Ecological Essays in Honor of G. Evelyn Hutchinson. (Connecticut Academy of Arts & Sciences Ser., Trans.: Vol. 44). 1972. pap. 59.50 (*0-685-22885-1*) Elliots Bks.

Deevi, Seetharama C., et al. International Symposium on Nickel & Iron Aluminides: Processing, Properties & Applications. LC 97-70495. 395p. 1997. 124.00 (*0-87170-590-7*, 6490) ASM.

Deevoy, Jacqui. Love Games. 144p. (J). 1997. pap. 6.95 (*0-09-925142-6*, Pub. by Random) Trafalgar.

Deevy. Creating Resilient Organzation. 1999. pap. text 14.00 (*0-7352-0110-2*) PH Pr.

Deevy, Edward. Creating the Resilient Organization: A Rapid Response Management Program. 256p. (C). 1995. text 21.95 (*0-13-169624-6*) P-H.

DeFabio, Richard B. The Complete Reference Manual for Credit & Collection Executives. (Illus.). 321p. 1998. 135.00 (*0-9660821-0-9*) Delta Credit.

DeFabio, Roseanne Y. Outcomes in Process: Setting Standards for Language Use. LC 93-42432. 211p. (C). 1994. pap. text 20.00 (*0-86709-341-2*, 0341, Pub. by Boynton Cook Pubs) Heinemann.

DeFabis, Sue, ed. see Radke, Linda F.

DeFail, Anthony J., jt. auth. see Bittman, Barry B.

DeFalco, Joseph, ed. see Cranch, Christopher P.

DeFalco, Nancy A., ed. see Jandrow, Richard E.

***DeFalco, Robert A.** Handel Metal Overlays. Accardi, Art, ed. & photos by by. Stubblebine, Ray, photos by. (Illus.). 112p. 1999. 100.00 (*0-9648116-1-8*) Gall Fivethirtytwo.

DeFalco, Tom. Fantastic Four: Nobody Gets Out Alive. (Fantastic Four Ser.). (Illus.). 144p. 1994. pap. 15.95 (*0-7851-0063-6*) Marvel Entrprs.

— Greatest Villains of the Fantastic Four. (Illus.). 144p. 1995. pap. 15.95 (*0-7851-0079-2*) Marvel Entrprs.

Defalco, Tom. Onslaught: Comrades in Arms, Vol. 3. (Illus.). 96p. 1997. pap. text 9.95 (*0-7851-0282-5*) Marvel Entrprs.

DeFalco, Tom. Spider-Man's Future. (X-Men: Spider-Man Ser.). (Illus.). 1998. mass mkt. 6.99 (*0-425-16500-0*) Berkley Pub.

***Defalco, Tom.** X-Men: Spider-Man Past. (X-Men: Vol. 1). 288p. 1998. mass mkt. 6.99 (*0-425-16452-7*) Berkley Pub.

***Defalco, Tom & Castro, Adam-Troy.** Time's Arrow: The Present. (X-Men: Bk. II). 293p. 1998. mass mkt. 6.99 (*0-425-16415-2*) Berkley Pub.

DeFalco, Tom & Stern, Roger. Spider-Man: Origin of Hobgoblin. (Illus.). 160p. 1992. pap. 14.95 (*0-87135-917-0*) Marvel Entrprs.

DeFalco, Tom, et al. Spider-Man: Saga of the Alien Costume. (Illus.). 192p. 1988. pap. 9.95 (*0-87135-396-2*) Marvel Entrprs.

Defant, A. Physical Oceanography, 2 vols. 1961. 584.00 (*0-08-009453-8*, Pub. by Pergamon Repr) Franklin.

Defant, Albert, jt. auth. see Wust, Georg.

Defant, Andreas & Floret, Klaus. Tensor Norms & Operator Ideals. LC 92-36408. (Mathematics Studies: Vol. 176). (Illus.). xii,566p. 1992. 177.00 (*0-444-89091-2*, North Holland) Elsevier.

Defant, Marc J. Voyage of Discovery from the Big Bang to the Ice Age. LC 97-14907. 288p. 1998. 34.50 (*0-931541-61-3*) Mancorp Pub.

DeFantini, Beatriz C., tr. see Moran, Patrick R.

***Defatta Barattini, Kathryn.** The Relationship of Ethnic Self-Identification of Latter Generations of Louisiana's Sicilian-Americans to Their Use of Ethnic Colloquial Phrases. LC 99-88002. (Studies in Linguistics & Semiotics: Vol. 7). 104p. 2000. text 59.95 (*0-7734-7796-9*) E Mellen.

Defaux, G. Pantagruel & les Sophistes: Contribution a l'Histoire de l'Humanisme Chretien au XVIieme Siecle. (International Archives of the History of Ideas Ser.: No. 63). 258p. 1973. lib. bdg. 99.50 (*90-247-1566-0*) Kluwer Academic.

Defaux, Gerard. Moliere, ou les Metamorphoses du Comique: De la Comedie Morale au Triomphe de la Folie. LC 79-53401. (French Forum Monographs: No. 18). (FRE.). 370p. (Orig.). 1980. pap. 17.95 (*0-917058-17-8*) French Forum.

Defay, Raymond & Prigogine, I. Surface Tension & Adsorption with the Collaboration of A. Bellemans. LC 67-71787. 464p. reprint ed. pap. 143.90 (*0-608-10094-3*, 200363900038) Bks Demand.

Defaye, D., jt. auth. see Dussart, B.

Defaye, D., jt. auth. see Dussart, B. H.

DeFazio, Albert J., jt. auth. see Hemingway, Ernest.

***Defazio, Alex S.** Christine. Lampert, Jeri, tr. 90p. (C). 2000. pap. 15.99 (*0-9676282-2-9*) Elixir Prods.

— Mirror of Monsters: (The Christabel) deluxe ed. (Illus.). 200p. 1999. pap. 17.99 (*0-9676282-0-2*) Elixir Prods.

— The Nightmares Desire Kept for Me. (Illus.). 100p. (C). 1999. pap. 17.99 (*0-9676282-1-0*) Elixir Prods.

DeFazio, Christine, jt. text see Mezzatesta, Philip.

DeFazio, David. Change Your Luck, Live Your Dreams. (Illus.). 190p. (Orig.). 1996. reprint ed. pap. 14.95 (*1-887969-00-4*) Cathedral PA.

DeFazio, Marjorie. A Quiet Noise. 32p. 1972. write for info. (*0-318-64132-1*) Poets Pr.

Defechereaux, Philippe. Watkins Glen 1948-1952: The Definitive Illustrated History. 1998. 29.95 (*0-929758-17-X*) Beeman Jorgensen.

Defechereux, Philippe & Graton, Jean. James Dean: The Untold Story of a Passion for Speed. 52p. 21.95 (*0-9651380-3-8*) MediaVision.

Defechereux, Phillippe. James Dean: The Untold Story of a Passion for Speed. LC 97-153313. 52p. 1996. pap. text 14.95 (*0-9651380-4-6*) MediaVision.

DeFelice, Barbara, ed. Science & Engineering Conference Proceedings: A Guide to Sources for Identification & Verification. LC 96-139042. 84p. (C). 1995. pap. 16.50 (*0-8389-7790-1*) Assn Coll & Res Libs.

DeFelice, Barbara J., ed. Expanding Boundaries: Geoscience Information for Earth System Science. (Proceedings Ser.: Vol. 27). (Illus.). 135p. 1997. pap. 45.00 (*0-934485-28-3*) Geosci Info.

DeFelice, Cynthia. Casey in the Bath. LC 95-8399. (Illus.). 32p. (J). (gr. k-2). 1996. 14.00 (*0-374-31173-0*) FS&G.

— Clever Crow. LC 97-10697. (Illus.). 32p. (J). (gr. k-3). 1998. 16.00 (*0-689-80671-X*) Atheneum Yung Read.

— The Dancing Skeleton. (Illus.). 32p. (gr. k-3). 1996. per. 5.99 (*0-689-80453-9*) S&S Childrens.

DeFelice, Cynthia. Devil's Bridge. 96p. (YA). (gr. 5 up). 1994. mass mkt. 4.99 (*0-380-72117-1*, Avon Bks) Morrow Avon.

DeFelice, Cynthia. Devil's Bridge. LC 92-7497. 96p. (YA). (gr. 5 up). 1992. mass mkt. 14.00 (*0-02-726465-3*, Mac Bks Young Read) S&S Childrens.

DeFelice, Cynthia. Light on Hogback Hill. LC 93-3507. 128p. (J). (gr. 3-7). 1993. mass mkt. 14.00 (*0-02-726453-X*, Mac Bks Young Read) S&S Childrens.

DeFelice, Cynthia. Light on Hogback Hill. (J). 1995. 9.60 (*0-606-07788-X*) Turtleback.

— Light on Hogback Hill. 144p. (J). (gr. 3-7). 1995. reprint ed. mass mkt. 4.50 (*0-380-72395-6*, Avon Bks) Morrow Avon.

— Lostman's River. 160p. (J). (gr. 4-7). 1995. mass mkt. 4.50 (*0-380-72396-4*, Avon Bks) Morrow Avon.

— Lostman's River. (J). 1995. 9.60 (*0-606-07810-X*, Pub. by Turtleback) Demco.

— Nowhere to Call Home. LC 98-36602. 208p. (YA). (gr. 5 up). 1999. 16.00 (*0-374-35552-5*) FS&G.

— The Strange Night Writing of Jessamine Colter. LC 88-4325. 56p. (YA). (gr. 5 up). 1988. mass mkt. 13.95 (*0-02-726451-3*, Mac Bks Young Read) S&S Childrens.

— Weasel. 128p. (YA). (gr. 5 up). 1991. mass mkt. 4.99 (*0-380-71358-6*, Avon Bks) Morrow Avon.

DeFelice, Cynthia. Weasel. LC 89-37794. 112p. (YA). (gr. 4-7). 1990. mass mkt. 15.00 (*0-02-726457-2*, Mac Bks Young Read) S&S Childrens.

DeFelice, Cynthia. Weasel. large type ed. (J). 199_. pap. 34.00 (*0-614-09879-3*, L-04422-00) Am Printing Hse.

— Willy's Silly Grandma. LC 96-42287. (Illus.). 32p. (J). (ps-2). 1997. 15.95 (*0-531-30012-9*); lib. bdg. 16.99 (*0-531-33012-5*) Orchard Bks Watts.

DeFelice, Cynthia & DeMarsh, Mary. Three Perfect Peaches: A French Folktale. LC 94-24872. (Illus.). 32p. (J). (gr. k-3). 1995. 15.95 (*0-531-06872-2*) Orchard Bks Watts.

DeFelice, Cynthia, et al. Three Perfect Peaches: A French Folktale. LC 94-24872. (Illus.). 32p. (J). (gr. k-3). 1995. lib. bdg. 16.99 (*0-531-08722-0*) Orchard Bks Watts.

DeFelice, Cynthia C. The Apprenticeship of Lucas Whitaker. 160p. (J). 1998. mass mkt. 4.99 (*0-380-72920-2*, Avon Bks) Morrow Avon.

— The Apprenticeship of Lucas Whittaker. LC 95-26728. 160p. (YA). (gr. 4-7). 1996. 15.00 (*0-374-34659-0*) FS&G.

— The Apprenticeship of Lucas Whittaker. (J). 1998. 9.60 (*0-606-13078-0*, Pub. by Turtleback) Demco.

— Casey in the Bath. (Illus.). 32p. (J). (ps up). 1998. pap. 4.95 (*0-374-41049-6*) FS&G.

***DeFelice, Cynthia C.** Cold Feet. LC 00-21279. (Illus.). 32p. (ps-3). 2000. 15.95 (*0-7894-2636-6*) DK Pub Inc.

DeFelice, Cynthia C. The Dancing Skeleton. 1996. 11.19 (*0-606-11235-9*, Pub. by Turtleback) Demco.

Defelice, Cynthia C. Devil's Bridge. LC 92-7497. 1992. 9.60 (*0-606-06320-X*, Pub. by Turtleback) Demco.

DeFelice, Cynthia C. The Ghost of Fossil Glen. LC 97-33230. 176p. (J). (gr. 3-7). 1998. 16.00 (*0-374-31787-9*) FS&G.

***DeFelice, Cynthia C.** The Ghost of Fossil Glen. 160p. (J). (gr. 3-7). 1999. mass mkt. 4.95 (*0-380-73175-4*, Avon Bks) Morrow Avon.

— The Ghost of Fossil Glen. LC 00-42573. (Illus.). (J). 2000. write for info. (*0-7862-2768-0*) Thorndike Pr.

DeFelice, Cynthia C. Lostman's River. LC 93-40857. 160p. (YA). (gr. 7 up). 1994. lib. bdg. 15.00 (*0-02-726466-1*) Atheneum Yung Read.

***DeFelice, Cynthia C.** Nowhere to Call. 2001. pap. 4.95 (*0-380-73306-4*, Wm Morrow) Morrow Avon

Defelice, Cynthia C. Strange Night Writing of Jessamine Colter. 1996. 9.19 (*0-606-09906-9*, Pub. by Turtleback) Demco.

— The Strange Night Writing of Jessamine Colter. LC 88-4325. 64p. (J). (gr. 4-7). 1996. mass mkt. 3.99 (*0-380-72663-7*, Avon Bks) Morrow Avon.

— Weasel. (J). 1990. 9.60 (*0-606-00819-5*, Pub. by Turtleback) Demco.

DeFelice, James. Filmguide to Odd Man Out. LC 74-6519. (Indiana University Press Filmguide Ser.: No. 9). 95p. reprint ed. pap. 30.00 (*0-8357-9209-9*, 201761600007) Bks Demand.

***DeFelice, Jim.** Brother's Keeper. 400p. 2000. mass mkt. 5.99 (*0-8439-4740-3*, Leisure Bks) Dorchester Pub Co.

DeFelice, Jim. Golden Flask. 1996. pap. 5.99 (*0-312-95762-9*) St Martin.

— Havana Strike. 400p. (Orig.). 2000. mass mkt. 5.99 (*0-8439-4330-0*, Leisure Bks) Dorchester Pub Co.

— Iron Chain, Vol. 1. 1995. mass mkt. 5.99 (*0-312-95635-5*) St Martin.

— Kill Grandma for Me. LC 98-235161. 320p. 1998. pap. 5.99 (*0-7860-0542-4*, Pinncle Kensgtn) Kensgtn Pub Corp.

***DeFelice, Jim.** Kill Grandma for Me. 2000. mass mkt. 5.99 (*0-7860-1282-X*) Kensgtn Pub Corp.

DeFelice, Jim. The Sixth Sense, Vol. 1. 1999. mass mkt. 6.99 (*0-425-17388-7*) Berkley Pub.

— War Breaker. 400p. 1996. reprint ed. mass mkt 6.99 (*0-8439-4043-3*, Leisure Bks) Dorchester Pub Co.

***DeFelice, Jim.** War Breaker. 448p. 1999. reprint ed. mass mkt. 5.99 (*0-8439-4601-6*, Leisure Bks) Dorchester Pub Co.

DeFelice, Louis J. Electrical Properties of Cells: Patch Clamp for Biologists. LC 97-14313. (Illus.). 256p. (C). 1997. text 49.50 (*0-306-45345-2*, Kluwer Plenum) Kluwer Academic.

DeFelice, Louis J. Introduction to Membrane Noise. LC 80-16163. 516p. 1981. 75.00 (*0-306-40513-X*, Plenum Trade) Perseus Pubng.

DeFelice, Louise, jt. auth. see Tovey, Luanne.

DeFelice, Sandi, ed. see Humphries, Christy.

***DeFelice, Stephen L.** The Carnitine Defense: A Nutraceutical Formula to Prevent & Treat Heart Disease. (Illus.). 288p. 2000. pap. 14.95 (*1-57954-335-1*, Rodale Reach) Rodale Pr Inc.

DeFelice, Stephen L. From Oysters to Insulin: Nature & Medicine at Odds. 192p. 1986. 15.95 (*0-8065-0995-3*, Citadel Pr) Carol Pub Group.

DeFelice, Stephen L., ed. Nutraceuticals: Developing, Claiming, & Marketing Medical Foods. LC 97-31840. (Illus.). 128p. 1997. text 85.00 (*0-8247-0107-0*) Dekker.

***DeFelice, Stephen L. & Kohl, Helen.** The Carnitine Defense: An All-Natural Nutraceutical Formula to Prevent & Treat Heart Disease, the Nation's #1 Killer. LC 99-46985. (Illus.). 240p. 1999. 24.95 (*1-57954-133-X*) Rodale Pr Inc.

Defelice, Thomas P. An Introduction to Meteorological Instrumentation & Measurement. LC 97-42092. 225p. 1997. 77.00 (*0-13-243270-6*) P-H.

DeFelipe, Javier & Jones, Edward G., eds. Cajal's Degeneration & Regeneration of the Nervous System. May, Raoul M., tr. (History of Neuroscience Ser.: No. 5). (Illus.). 976p. 1991. text 79.50 (*0-19-506516-6*, 11153) OUP.

DeFelipe, Javier, ed. & tr. see Cajal, Santiago R. & FIDIA Research Foundation Staff.

DeFelitta, Frank. For Love of Audrey Rose. 464p. (Orig.). 1982. mass mkt. 3.95 (*0-446-30206-6*, Pub. by Warner Bks) Little.

Defenders of Wildlife Staff, jt. auth. see Vickerman, Sara.

***Defendi, Robert.** Spacemaster: Privateers. (Illus.). 222p. (YA). (gr. 7 up). 2000. pap. 30.00 (*1-55806-562-8*, 4500) Iron Crown Ent Inc.

Defendorf, Richard, ed. see Conrad, Barnaby, III.

Defendorf, Richard, ed. see Dobbins, Dick.

Defendorf, Virginia. Recipes for a Healthy Lifestyle: Low Fat, Low Cholesterol, Low Sodium. 128p. 1994. ring bd. 6.95 (*0-914846-95-7*) Golden West Pub.

Defense Acquisition University (U.S.) Staff, jt. auth. see Williams, Michael D.

Defense Department, Army, Center of Military Histo, contrib. by. American Military History. rev. ed. (Illus.). 775p. 1989. boxed set 46.00 (*0-16-001991-5*) USGPO.

— Terrain Factors in the Russian Campaign. (Center for Military History Publication German Report Series, DA Pam: No. 104-5). (Illus.). 67p. (Orig.). 1986. reprint ed. pap. 3.00 (*0-16-001946-X*, S/N 008-029-00144-6) USGPO.

Defense Department, Army Staff, contrib. by. Angola: A Country Study. 3rd ed. (Illus.). 346p. 1991. boxed set 21.00 (*0-16-030844-5*) USGPO.

— Libya: A Country Study. 4th ed. LC 88-600480. (Illus.). 379p. 1996. boxed set 25.00 (*0-16-001711-4*) USGPO.

Defense Department, Defense Systems Management Col, contrib. by. Acquisition Logistics Guide. 3rd ed. (Illus.). 372p. 1997. per. 29.00 (*0-16-054762-8*) USGPO.

Defense Department, Navy, Naval Observatory, Nauti, contrib. by. Air Almanac, 1998. (Illus.). 904p. 1997. pap. 59.00 (*0-16-049034-0*) USGPO.

— Astronomical Almanac for the Year 1998: Data for Astronomy, Space Sciences, Geodesy, Surveying, Navigation & Other Applications. (Illus.). 564p. 1997. boxed set 38.00 (*0-16-049072-3*) USGPO.

Defense Department, Office of the Secretary of Def, contrib. by. Defense Department Annual Report, 1997. (Illus.). 402p. 1997. per. 31.00 (*0-16-049045-6*) USGPO.

— Report of the Secretary of Defense to the President & the Congress, 1998. (Illus.). 356p. 1998. per. 28.00 (*0-16-049428-1*) USGPO.

Defense Department Staff, Navy, Naval History Divi, contrib. by. Dictionary of American Naval Fighting Ships, Vol. 1, Pt. A. LC 91-28049. (Illus.). 542p. 1991. boxed set 38.00 (*0-16-002055-7*) USGPO.

— Dictionary of American Naval Fighting Ships, Vol. 2, C-F. (Illus.). 615p. 1998. boxed set 43.00 (*0-16-002017-4*) USGPO.

— Dictionary of American Naval Fighting Ships, Vol. 4, L-M. LC 60-60198. 1969. boxed set 49.00 (*0-16-002019-0*) USGPO.

— Dictionary of American Naval Fighting Ships, Vol. 5, N-Q. LC 60-60198. (Illus.). 639p. 1996. boxed set 51.00 (*0-16-002028-X*) USGPO.

— Dictionary of American Naval Fighting Ships, Vol. 6, R-S. LC 60-60198. (Illus.). 751p. 1996. boxed set 25.00 (*0-16-002030-1*) USGPO.

— Dictionary of American Naval Fighting Ships, Vol. 7, T-V. LC 60-60198. (Illus.). 755p. 1996. boxed set 56.00 (*0-16-002038-7*) USGPO.

— Dictionary of American Naval Fighting Ships, Vol. 8, W-Z. LC 60-60198. (Illus.). 597p. 1996. boxed set 68.00 (*0-16-002039-5*) USGPO.

***Defense Language Institute Staff.** Thai Intensive Basic Course, 3 vols. rev. ed. (THA & ENG.). 1624p. 1998. pap. 183.00 (*1-881265-57-9*, 3141) Dunwoody Pr.

Defense Nationale Staff. Dictionnaire Naval Francais - Chinois. (CHI & FRE.). 994p. 1985. 95.00 (*0-8288-9538-4*) Fr & Eur.

Defense Team Staff, jt. auth. see Weinglass, Leonard.

DeFerie, Steph. Once upon a Wolf: Steph DeFerie. 48p. (Orig.). (J). 1997. pap. 4.00 (*0-87440-037-6*) Bakers Plays.

DeFerrari, Gabriella. A Cloud on Sand. Rosenman, Jane, ed. 336p. 1992. reprint ed. pap. 9.00 (*0-671-73463-6*) PB.

Deferrari, R. J. Lucian's Atticism: The Morphology of the Verb. 81p. 1916. reprint ed. lib. bdg. 25.00 (*0-685-13370-2*, Pub. by AM Hakkert) Coronet Bks.

Deferrari, R. J., tr. see Hugh of St. Victor.

Deferrari, Ray J., tr. see Orosius, Paulus.

Deferrari, Ray J., tr. see Pamphili, Eusebius.

Deferrari, Roy J., ed. Essays on Catholic Education in the United States. LC 71-90629. (Essay Index Reprint Ser.). 1977. 36.95 (*0-8369-1347-7*) Ayer.

— Essays on Catholic Education in the United States. LC 71-90629. (Essay Index Reprint Ser.). 566p. reprint ed. lib. bdg. 35.00 (*0-8290-0814-4*) Irvington.

Deferrari, Roy J., tr. Early Christian Biographies: Lives of St. Cyprian, St. Ambrose, St. Augustine, St. Anthony, St. Paul the first Hermit, St. Hilarion, Malchus, St. Epiphanius. LC 64-19949. (Fathers of the Church Ser.: Vol. 15). 407p. 1952. 36.95 (*0-8132-0015-6*) Cath U Pr.

— Letters, 4 Vols, 4. LC 65-18318. (Loeb Classical Library: No. 190, 215, 243, 270). 472p. 1934. 18.95 (*0-674-99298-9*) HUP.

Deferrari, Roy J. & Campbell, J. M. A Concordance of Prudentius. 833p. 1966. reprint ed. write for info. (*0-318-71107-9*) G Olms Pubs.

Deferrari, Roy J. & Campbell, James M. A Concordance of Prudentius. 833p. reprint ed. lib. bdg. 232.70 (*0-685-13865-8*, 05101185) G Olms Pubs.

D

Deferrari, Roy J. & Eagan, Clement. A Concordance of Statius. 926p. 1965. reprint ed. write for info. (*0-318-71108-7*) G Olms Pubs.

Deferrari, Roy J. & Egan, C. A Concordance of Statius. 926p. reprint ed. lib. bdg. 258.70 (*0-685-13866-6*, 05101138) G Olms Pubs.

Deferrari, Roy J., et al. A Concordance of Lucan. 609p. 1940. reprint ed. lib. bdg. 193.70 incl. 3.5 hd (*3-487-00996-X*) G Olms Pubs.

— A Concordance of Lucan. vii, 602p. 1965. reprint ed. write for info. incl. 3.5 hd (*0-318-71109-5*) G Olms Pubs.

— A Concordance of Ovid, 2 vols., Set. 1968. reprint ed. write for info. incl. 3.5 hd (*0-318-72009-4*) G Olms Pubs.

Deferrari, Roy J., tr. see Cyprian, St.

Deferrari, Rroy J. & Eagan, Clement. A Concordance of Statius. 926p. 1965. reprint ed. write for info. (*0-318-72011-6*) G Olms Pubs.

DeFeudis, F. V. Gingko Biloba Extract (EGb 761) Pharmacological Activities & Clinical Applications. 204p. pap. 57.00 (*2-906077-21-6*) Elsevier.

DeFeudis, Francis V., jt. ed. see Mandel, Paul.

DeFever, Carolyn L. Entertaining Magic: China, Crystal & Silver. LC 94-69227. (Illus.). 80p. (Orig.). pap. text 12.95 (*0-9626117-7-8*) Paisley TX.

Defever, Carolyn L. Window Covering Basic Training Manual. 1992. pap. 12.95 (*0-9626117-4-3*) Paisley TX.

DeFever, Carolyn L. Window Covering Basics: A Complete Guide to Creative Window Decorating. 6th ed. LC 97-67580. (Illus.). 112p. 1998. pap. 14.00 (*1-890788-00-7*) Paisley TX.

— Window Covering Basics: How to Achieve Custom Looks with Ready-Made Products. LC 94-69226. (Illus.). 96p. (Orig.). 1996. pap. text 9.95 (*0-9626117-8-6*) Paisley TX.

— Window Covering Basics: How to Achieve Custom Looks with Ready-Made Products. 3rd ed. LC 91-90553. (Illus.). 80p. (Orig.). 1992. pap. 9.95 (*0-9626117-3-5*) Paisley TX.

— Window Covering Basics: How to Achieve Custom Looks with Ready-Made Products. 4th ed. LC 92-85371. (Illus.). 80p. (Orig.). 1994. pap. 9.95 (*0-9626117-5-1*) Paisley TX.

DeFever, Carolyn S. Las Vegas Illusion. LC 93-83080. 256p. 1993. text 21.95 (*0-9626117-6-X*) Paisley TX.

***Defever, F.** Geometry & Topology of Submanifolds Ix. 1999. 75.00 (*981-02-3897-5*) WSC Inst MA Studies.

Defeyster, J. Watts. Gettysburg & After. 162p. 1987. reprint ed. 12.00 (*0-942211-04-9*) Olde Soldier Bks.

***Deffaa, Chip.** Blue Rhythms: Six Lives in Rhythm & Blues. LC 99-42569. 352p. 1999. pap. text 16.00 (*0-306-80919-2*, Pub. by Da Capo) HarpC.

Deffaa, Chip. Blue Rhythms: Six Lives in Rhythm & Blues. (Music in American Life Ser.). (Illus.). 304p. 1996. 29.95 (*0-252-02203-3*) U of Ill Pr.

— In the Mainstream: Eighteen Portraits in Jazz. LC 92-8173. (Studies in Jazz). (Illus.). 402p. 1992. 47.50 (*0-8108-2558-9*) Scarecrow.

— Jazz Veterans: A Portrait Gallery. LC 95-83082. (Illus.). 288p. 1996. 44.95 (*1-879384-28-0*) Cypress Hse.

— Swing Legacy. (Studies in Jazz: No. 9). (Illus.). 393p. 1989. 45.00 (*0-8108-2282-2*) Scarecrow.

— Traditionalists & Revivalists in Jazz. LC 93-1875. (Studies in Jazz: No. 16). (Illus.). 401p. 1993. 47.50 (*0-8108-2704-2*) Scarecrow.

— Voices of the Jazz Age: Profiles of Eight Vintage Jazzmen. (Music in American Life Ser.). (Illus.). 312p. 1990. 29.95 (*0-252-01681-5*) U of Ill Pr.

— Voices of the Jazz Age: Profiles of Eight Vintage Jazzmen. (Music in American Life Ser.). (Illus.). 312p. 1992. 14.95 (*0-252-06258-2*) U of Ill Pr.

Deffaa, Chip, jt. auth. see Cassidy, David.

Deffaa, Chip, ed. see Fitzgerald, F. Scott.

Deffenbaugh, James F., ed. The Resistance Welding Manual. 4th rev. ed. LC 89-63296. (Illus.). 1989. text 80.00 (*0-9624382-0-0*) Resistance Welder.

Deffenbaugh, Joe, ed. Practice Standards of ASHP, 1996-1997. rev. ed. 400p. 1996. pap. 38.00 (*1-879907-65-8*) Am Soc Hlth-Syst.

Deffenbaugh, Joseph H., ed. Best Practices for Health-System Pharmacy: Positions & Practice Standards of SHP, 1999-2000. (Illus.). 600p. 1999. pap. write for info. (*1-879907-99-2*) Am Soc Hlth-Syst.

Deffenbaugh, Terry. Testing the Wind. 75p. 1993. pap. 12.95 (*1-877871-49-4*, 8421) Ed Ministries.

— Which Apostle Are You Most Like? 1988. pap. 6.50 (*0-940754-53-3*, 8411) Ed Ministries.

Deffner, Donald. Prayers for People under Pressure. LC 92-60994. 120p. (Orig.). 1992. pap. 8.99 (*0-8100-0429-1*, 06N0692) Northwest Pub.

— Secret Admirer & Other Short Stories. 1995. pap. 5.50 (*0-570-09530-1*, 20-2621) Concordia.

Deffner, Donald L. At Life's End: Words of Comfort & Hope. LC 95-537. 48p. 1995. 3.00 (*0-570-03559-7*, 14-2109) Concordia.

— At the Death of a Child: Words of Comfort & Hope. LC 93-3739. 32p. 1993. pap. 3.00 (*0-570-04608-4*, 14-2029) Concordia.

— The Bright Red Sports Car. 1993. teacher ed. 5.50 (*0-570-09351-1*, 20-2416) Concordia.

— The Bright Red Sports Car. 1997. student ed. 5.50 (*0-570-09350-3*, 20-2415) Concordia.

— Perfect Couple. 1993. pap. text, teacher ed. 5.50 (*0-570-09349-X*, 20-2414); pap. text, student ed. 5.50 (*0-570-09348-1*, 20-2413) Concordia.

— Seasonal Illustrations for Preaching & Teaching. LC 92-20122. (Illus.). 208p. (Orig.). (C). 1992. pap. 11.95 (*0-89390-234-9*) Resource Pubns.

— Sermons for Church Year Festivals. LC 97-2350. 1997. 10.99 (*0-570-04975-X*, 12-3325) Concordia.

— Sermons for Special Days & Occasions. LC 97-2362. 1997. 10.99 (*0-570-04976-8*) Concordia.

— The Unlocked Door & Other Short Stories. 1995. pap. 5.50 (*0-570-09529-8*, 20-2620) Concordia.

— Windows into the Lectionary: Seasonal Anecdotes for Preaching & Teaching. LC 96-42166. 160p. (Orig.). 1996. pap. 14.95 (*0-89390-393-0*) Resource Pubns.

Deffris, David. Encyclopedia. (DK Pockets Ser.). (YA). (gr. 3 up). 1997. 14.95 (*0-614-28710-3*) DK Pub Inc.

DeFigueiredo, R. J., jt. ed. see Jain, K. C.

DeFigueiredo, Rui J. & Chen, Guanrong. Nonlinear Feedback Control Systems: An Operator Theory Approach. LC 93-19434. (Illus.). 220p. 1993. text 36.00 (*0-12-208630-9*) Acad Pr.

DeFigueiredo, T. G. A New Boundary Element Formulation in Engineering. (Lecture Notes in Engineering Ser.: Vol. 68). ix, 198p. 1991. 50.95 (*0-387-54030-X*) Spr-Verlag.

DeFilippi, Jim. Duck Alley. LC 98-34206. 235p. (YA). 1999. 24.00 (*1-57962-024-8*) Permanent Pr.

DeFilippi, Louis J., jt. auth. see Lewandowski, Gordon A.

Defilippi, Paola. Signal Transduction by Integrins. Gismondi, Angela, ed. LC 97-24582. (Molecular Biology Intelligence Unit Ser.). 198p. 1997. 99.00 (*1-57059-472-4*) Landes Bioscience.

Defilippis, Christopher. Quantum Leap: Foreknowledge. 1998. mass mkt. 6.99 (*0-425-16487-X*) Berkley Pub.

— Quantum Leap Foreknowledge. (Quantum Leap Ser.). 1998. mass mkt. 5.99 (*1-57297-343-9*) Blvd Books.

DeFilippis, Christopher, ed. Catholic Press Directory, 1997. 236p. 1998. per. 48.00 (*0-614-32393-2*) Cath Pr Assn.

DeFilippis, Christopher F., ed. Catholic Press Directory, 1999. 236p. 1999. per. 48.00 (*0-614-28382-5*) Cath Pr Assn.

DeFilippis, Kimberly A. Cook 'Til Done? Now You Too Can Prepare Authentic Italian Cuisine. (Illus.). 138p. 1997. pap., spiral bd. 19.95 (*0-9659187-0-X*) Southpaw Pub.

DeFilippo, Eduardo. Napoli Milionaria. Haring-Smith, Tori, tr. & adapted by by. 101p. 1996. pap. 5.95 (*0-87129-601-2*, N35) Dramatic Pub.

Defilippo, Judy. Grammar Plus: A Basic Skills Course Workbook 1. 2nd ed. 1994. pap. text, wbk. ed. 7.72 (*0-201-59935-X*) Addison-Wesley.

— Grammar Plus a Basic Skills Course: A Basic Skills Course 2. 2nd ed. 1994. pap. text, wbk. ed. 7.72 (*0-201-59936-8*) Addison-Wesley.

— Grammar Plus Student, Bk. A. 2nd ed. 192p. 1994. pap. text, student ed. 13.23 (*0-201-54854-2*) Addison-Wesley.

— Grammar Plus Student, Bk. B. 144p. 1994. pap. text, student ed. 13.23 (*0-201-54976-X*) Addison-Wesley.

— NHE Lifeskills Workbook I. 1981. pap. text 8.48 (*0-201-05048-X*) Addison-Wesley.

— NHE Lifeskills Workbook II. 1982. pap. text 9.75 (*0-201-05049-8*) Addison-Wesley.

— Skill Sharpeners, No. 1. 2nd ed. (Illus.). 128p. 1991. pap. text 11.30 (*0-201-51325-0*) Addison-Wesley.

— Skill Sharpeners, No. 2. 2nd ed. (Illus.). 128p. 1991. pap. text 11.30 (*0-201-51326-9*) Addison-Wesley.

— Skill Sharpeners, No. 3. 2nd ed. (Illus.). 128p. 1991. pap. text 11.30 (*0-201-51327-7*) Addison-Wesley.

— Skill Sharpeners, No. 4. 2nd ed. (Illus.). 128p. 1991. pap. text 11.30 (*0-201-51328-5*) Addison-Wesley.

— Skill Sharpeners Level 1. 1984. pap. text 11.52 (*0-201-15623-7*) Addison-Wesley.

Defilippo, Judy, jt. auth. see Webster, Megan.

***DeFilippo, Kathleen.** PhotoDraw 2000: Module 2. Savage, Stephanie & Millhollon, Mary, eds. 205p. (YA). 1999. pap. write for info. (*0-7423-0350-0*) ComputerPREP.

***DeFilippo, M. Kathleen.** Excel 2000: Module 3 - Database Management & Analysis. Savage, Stephanie et al, eds. (Illus.). 190p. (YA). 2000. pap. write for info. (*0-7423-0447-7*) ComputerPREP.

— Excel 2000: Module 4 - Customizing Excel & Using Macros. Amstutz, Irina et al, eds. (Illus.). (YA). 2000. pap. write for info. (*0-7423-0449-3*, EXCL2K004LG) ComputerPREP.

— Windows 2000: Module 2. Savage, Stephanie & Kozakis, Ken, eds. (Illus.). 205p. (YA). 2000. pap. write for info. (*0-7423-0468-X*, WNDW2K002LG) ComputerPREP.

DeFilipps, Robert A. Medicinal Plants of the Guianas. (Medicinal Plants of the World Ser.: No. 7). (Illus.). Date not set. write for info. (*0-917256-47-6*) Ref Pubns.

DeFilipps, Robert A., jt. auth. see Ayensu, Edward S.

DeFilipps, Robert A., jt. auth. see Jain, S. K.

DeFilipps, Robert A., ed. see Mors, Walter B., et al.

DeFillippo, J. & Mackey, Daphne. Grammar Plus. (ESL Ser.). (C). 1987. teacher ed. 6.95 (*0-317-59396-X*); student ed. 7.50 (*0-685-18380-7*) Addison-Wesley.

DeFillippo, J., jt. auth. see Mackey, Daphne.

DeFina, Anthony V. Bioscience: An Outline Approach. rev. ed. (Illus.). 268p. 1992. reprint ed. teacher ed. 20.00 (*0-916209-05-9*) Owlet Pubns.

— Bioscience: An Outline Approach. rev. ed. (Illus.). 268p. (YA). (gr. 9-10). 1992. reprint ed. pap., student ed. 15.00 (*0-916209-03-2*) Owlet Pubns.

— Bioscience II: An Advanced Biology Course Manual. rev. ed. (Illus.). 396p. 1993. teacher ed. 27.50 (*0-916209-10-5*) Owlet Pubns.

— Bioscience II: An Advanced Biology Course Manual. rev. ed. (Illus.). 396p. (C). 1993. student ed. 25.00 (*0-916209-11-3*) Owlet Pubns.

— Field Trips in Natural History: A New York City Guide. (Illus.). 159p. (YA). (gr. 9 up). 1991. pap., student ed. 15.00 (*0-916209-04-0*) Owlet Pubns.

— Human Physiology: A Course Manual. (Illus.). 287p. 1991. teacher ed. 25.00 (*0-916209-08-3*) Owlet Pubns.

— Human Physiology: A Course Manual. rev. ed. (Illus.). 287p. (YA). (gr. 11 up). 1991. reprint ed. pap., student ed. 20.00 (*0-916209-00-8*) Owlet Pubns.

— Zoology: A Course Manual. rev. ed. (Illus.). 333p. 1991. reprint ed. teacher ed. 25.00 (*0-916209-09-1*) Owlet Pubns.

— Zoology: A Course Manual. rev. ed. (Illus.). 333p. (YA). (gr. 11 up). 1991. reprint ed. pap., student ed. 20.00 (*0-916209-01-6*) Owlet Pubns.

Deflem, Mathieu & Rasmussen, David M., eds. Habermas, Modernity, & Law. LC 96-68909. (Philosophy & Social Criticism Ser.). 224p. 1996. 65.00 (*0-7619-5136-9*); pap. 26.95 (*0-7619-5137-7*) Sage.

Defleur. Mass Communication, 5 vols. (C). 1993. pap., teacher ed. 5.96 (*0-395-67405-0*) HM.

— Mass Communication, 5 vols. 5th ed. (C). 1995. pap. text 47.96 (*0-395-74681-7*) HM.

— Mass Communications, 6 vols. 6th ed. (C). Date not set. 54.76 (*0-395-89764-5*) HM.

DeFleur, Lois B. Delinquency in Argentina: A Study of Cordoba's Youth. LC 73-20744. (Illus.). 190p. reprint ed. pap. 58.90 (*0-8357-8091-0*, 203410700088) Bks Demand.

DeFleur, Lois B., jt. ed. see Winfield, Betty H.

DeFleur, Margaret H. Computer-Assisted Investigative Reporting. LC 96-51568. (LEA's Communication Ser.). 272p. 1997. text 59.95 (*0-8058-2162-7*); pap. text 27.50 (*0-8058-2163-5*) L Erlbaum Assocs.

Defleur, Melvin L. Mass Communication, 5 vols. 5th ed. LC 93-78692. (C). 1993. pap. text 46.76 (*0-395-67404-2*) HM.

DeFleur, Melvin L. & Ball-Rokeach, Sandra J. Theories of Mass Communication. 5th ed. LC 81-8215. (Illus.). 368p. (C). 1989. pap. text 62.00 (*0-582-99870-0*, 75295) Addison-Wesley.

DeFleur, Melvin L. & Dennis, Everette E. Understanding Mass Communication: A Liberal Arts Perspective, Updated 1996 Edition, 5 vols. (C). 1995. text, teacher ed. 11.96 (*0-395-76556-0*) HM.

Defleur, Melvin L., et al. Fundamentals of Human Communication. 2nd ed. LC 97-24805. xiv, 466p. 1997. pap. text 43.95 (*1-55934-670-1*, 1670) Mayfield Pub.

DeFleur, Melvin L., et al. Mastering Communication in Contemporary America: Theory, Research & Practice. LC 92-4797. xii, 536p. (C). 1993. pap. text 46.95 (*1-55934-097-5*, 1097) Mayfield Pub.

— Mastering Communication in Contemporary America, Instructor's Manual: Theory, Research & Practice. (C). 1993. pap. text, teacher ed. write for info. (*1-55934-319-2*, 1319) Mayfield Pub.

DeFleur, Melvin L., jt. auth. see Lowery, Shearon A.

Deflice, Stephen L. Memory Loss. 1987. pap. 7.95 (*0-8184-0445-0*) Carol Pub Group.

Defliese, Philip L., et al. Montgomery's Auditing: College Version. 3rd rev. ed. LC 90-33826. 912p. 1990. text 106.95 (*0-471-50706-7*) Wiley.

Defliese, Philip L., jt. see Chippindale, Warren.

DeFlippo, Kathleen, ed. see Davenhauer, Frank.

Deflorian, Flavio, jt. ed. see Bonora, Pier L.

Defoe, Daniel. The Adventures of Robinson Crusoe. Vogel, Malvina, ed. (Great Illustrated Classics Ser.: Vol. 17). (Illus.). 240p. (J). (gr. 3-6). 1990. 9.95 (*0-86611-968-X*) Playmore Inc.

— The Agreement of the Customs of the East Indians with Those of the Jews, & Other Ancient People: The First Essay of This Kind Towards the Explaining of Several Difficult Passages in Scripture, Etc. Toland, John, tr. LC 97-35902. (Augustan Reprints Ser.). 289p. 1997. 94.00 (*0-404-70271-6*) AMS Pr.

— Atalantis Major. LC 92-2368. (Augustan Reprints Ser.: No. 198). 1979. reprint ed. 14.50 (*0-404-70198-1*, DA496 1711.D39) AMS Pr.

***Defoe, Daniel.** Aventuras de Robinson Crusoe. (Juvenil Ser.: Vol. 73). (SPA., Illus.). (J). (gr. 4-7). 1999. pap. 11.95 (*84-239-9043-5*) Espasa Calpe.

Defoe, Daniel. Captain Singleton. 1976. 24.95 (*0-8488-0978-5*) Amereon Ltd.

— Captain Singleton. Kumar, Shiv K., ed. (World's Classics Ser.). 306p. 1990. pap. 8.95 (*0-19-282200-4*) OUP.

— Captain Singleton. large type ed. LC 99-330195. 1999. pap. 24.95 (*0-7838-8682-9*) Mac Lib Ref.

— Colonel Jack. 1976. 25.95 (*0-8488-0979-3*) Amereon Ltd.

— Due Preparations for the Plague, As Well for Soul As Body. LC 74-13434. (Illus.). reprint ed. write for info. (*0-404-07925-3*) AMS Pr.

Defoe, Daniel. The Family Instructor. LC 89-10776. 464p. 1989. 50.00 (*0-8201-1440-5*) Schol Facsimiles.

Defoe, Daniel. The Farther Adventures of Robinson Crusoe, Being the Second & Last Part of His Life. LC 74-13446. (Illus.). reprint ed. write for info. (*0-404-07912-1*) AMS Pr.

— The Fortunate Mistress, 2 vols., Set. LC 74-13447. (Illus.). reprint ed. write for info. (*0-404-07922-9*) AMS Pr.

Defoe, Daniel. The Fortunes & Misfortunes of the Famous Moll Flanders. 352p. pap. 3.99 (*0-8125-6701-3*, Pub. by Tor Bks) St Martin.

Defoe, Daniel. The Fortunes & Misfortunes of the Famous Moll Flanders, 2 vols., Set. LC 74-13449. (Illus.). reprint ed. write for info. (*0-404-07917-2*) AMS Pr.

***Defoe, Daniel.** A General History of the Pyrates. Schonhorn, Manuel, ed. & contrib. by by. LC 98-53669. 1999. pap. text 18.95 (*0-486-40488-9*) Dover.

— A General History of the Robberies & Murders of the Most Notorious Pirates. 512p. 1999. pap. 16.95 (*0-7867-0622-8*) Carroll & Graf.

Defoe, Daniel. The History & Remarkable Life of the Truly Honourable Colonel Jacque, 2 vols., Set. (Illus.). reprint ed. write for info. (*0-404-07920-2*) AMS Pr.

— The History of the Life & Adventures of Mr. Duncan Campbell. LC 74-13463. (Illus.). reprint ed. write for info. (*0-404-07914-8*) AMS Pr.

— Journal de l'Annee de Peste. (FRE.). 1982. pap. 11.95 (*0-7859-2221-0*, 207037372X) Fr & Eur.

— A Journal of the Plague Year. Backsheider, Paula, ed. (Critical Editions Ser.). 361p. (C). 1992. pap. text 12.50 (*0-393-96188-5*) Norton.

— A Journal of the Plague Year. Landa, Louis, ed. LC 99-186599. (Oxford World's Classics Ser.). (Illus.). 336p. 1999. pap. 7.95 (*0-19-283618-8*) OUP.

— A Journal of the Plague Year. Man, John, ed. 336p. 1994. 5.50 (*0-460-87462-4*, Everyman's Classic Lib) Tuttle Pubng.

— A Journal of the Plague Year. Burgess, Anthony & Bristow, Christopher, eds. (English Library). 256p. 1966. pap. 8.95 (*0-14-043015-6*) Viking Penguin.

— A Journal of the Plague Year. LC 74-13469. (Illus.). reprint ed. write for info. (*0-404-07919-9*) AMS Pr.

— The King of Pirates: Being an Account of the Famous Enterprises of Captain Avery. LC 74-13451. (Illus.). xix, 381p. 1974. reprint ed. write for info. (*0-404-07926-1*) AMS Pr.

— The Life, Adventures & Piracies of the Famous Captain Singleton. LC 74-13433. (Illus.). xviii, 316p. 1974. reprint ed. write for info. (*0-404-07916-4*) AMS Pr.

***Defoe, Daniel.** The Life & Adventures of Robinson Crusoe. Ross, Angus, ed. & intro. by. LC 90-46733. (English Library). 320p. (YA). (gr. 9 up). 1998. pap. 4.67 (*0-14-043007-5*) Addson-Wesley Educ.

Defoe, Daniel. The Life & Adventures of Robinson Crusoe. abr. ed. Marshall, Michael J., ed. (Core Classics Ser.: Vol. 2). (Illus.). 160p. (J). (gr. 4-6). 1997. pap. 5.95 (*1-890517-02-X*); lib. bdg. 10.95 (*1-890517-03-8*) Core Knowledge.

— The Life & Strange & Surprising Adventures of Robinson Crusoe, of York, Mariner. LC 74-13442. (Illus.). reprint ed. write for info. (*0-404-07911-3*) AMS Pr.

— The Life & Strange Surprising Adventures of Robinson Crusoe, of York, Mariner. Crowley, Joseph Donald, ed. & intro. by. (Oxford World's Classics Ser.). (Illus.). 346p. 1998. pap. 6.95 (*0-19-283382-0*) OUP.

— The Manufacturer: The British Merchant; The Weaver. Gosselink, Robert, ed. LC 78-11810. 1979. reprint ed. 75.00 (*0-8201-1324-7*) Schol Facsimiles.

— The Master Mercury. LC 92-23722. (Augustan Reprints Ser.: No. 184). 1977. reprint ed. 14.50 (*0-404-70184-1*, DA490) AMS Pr.

— Memoirs of a Cavalier. LC 74-13443. (Illus.). reprint ed. write for info. (*0-404-07915-6*) AMS Pr.

— Moll Flanders. 1976. 24.95 (*0-8488-0473-2*) Amereon Ltd.

— Moll Flanders. 272p. 1989. mass mkt. 4.95 (*0-553-21328-8*, Bantam Classics) Bantam.

— Moll Flanders. 1996. 15.95 (*0-614-97638-3*) Everymns Lib.

— Moll Flanders. 320p. 1996. 15.95 (*0-679-40548-8*) Everymns Lib.

— Moll Flanders. (FRE.). 1979. pap. 12.95 (*0-7859-1890-6*, 2070371093) Fr & Eur.

Defoe, Daniel. Moll Flanders, 001. Sutherland, James R., ed. LC 59-16265. 1972. pap. 13.96 (*0-395-05129-0*, 3-47665, RivEd) HM.

Defoe, Daniel. Moll Flanders. 240p. 1998. 7.95 (*3-89508-687-8*) Konemann.

— Moll Flanders. (C). 1950. text 6.50 (*0-07-553573-4*) McGraw.

— Moll Flanders. 1996. mass mkt. 4.95 (*0-451-52633-3*, Sig Classics) NAL.

— Moll Flanders. Kelly, Edward, ed. LC 72-13807. (Critical Editions Ser.). 500p. (C). 1973. pap. text 14.75 (*0-393-09412-X*) Norton.

— Moll Flanders. Starr, G. A., ed. & intro. by. LC PR3404.M6 1998. (Oxford World's Classics Ser.). 432p. 1998. pap. 7.95 (*0-19-283403-7*) OUP.

— Moll Flanders. (C). 1950. pap. text. write for info. (*0-318-57395-4*) Random.

— Moll Flanders. 384p. 1996. 15.95 (*0-676-51349-2*) Random.

— Moll Flanders. LC 96-227072. 1996. 15.50 (*0-679-60260-7*) Random.

— Moll Flanders. Blewett, David, ed. & intro. by. 464p. 1989. pap. 8.95 (*0-14-043313-9*, Penguin Classics) Viking Penguin.

Defoe, Daniel. Moll Flanders. (Classics Library). 352p. 1997. pap. 3.95 (*1-85326-073-8*, 0738WW, Pub. by Wrdsworth Edits) NTC Contemp Pub Co.

Defoe, Daniel. Moll Flanders. abr. ed. 1996. 16.95 (*1-85998-593-9*) Trafalgar.

— Moll Flanders. large type ed. (Isis Clear Type Classic Ser.). (Illus.). 380p. 1992. 22.95 (*1-85089-574-0*, Pub. by ISIS Lrg Prnt) Transaction Pubs.

— Moll Flanders. 451p. 1983. reprint ed. lib. bdg. 25.95 (*0-89966-313-3*) Buccaneer Bks.

***Defoe, Daniel.** Moll Flanders. (Twelve-Point Ser.). 380p. 2000. reprint ed. lib. bdg. 24.00 (*1-58287-124-8*) North Bks.

Defoe, Daniel. Moll Flanders. unabridged ed. (Thrift Editions Ser.). 256p. 1998. reprint ed. pap. text 2.00 (*0-486-29093-X*) Dover.

— Moll Flanders. 2nd ed. (Critical Editions Ser.). (C). 1999. pap. write for info. (*0-393-96793-X*, Norton Paperbks) Norton.

— Moll Flanders Companion, Vol. 1. 2000. pap. text 9.95 (*0-312-09117-6*) St Martin.

— A New Voyage Round the World, by a Course Never Sailed Before. LC 74-13444. (Illus.). reprint ed. write for info. (*0-404-07924-5*) AMS Pr.

— Novels & Miscellaneous Works of Daniel Defoe, 20 vols. LC 79-154120. reprint ed. write for info. (*0-404-09300-0*) AMS Pr.

— The Novels & Selected Writings of Daniel Defoe: Shakespeare Head Edition, 14 vols., Set. 300p. 1974. reprint ed. 417.50 (*0-87471-521-0*); reprint ed. 417.50 (*0-87471-500-8*) Rowman.

An Asterisk (*) at the beginning of an entry indicates that the title is appearing for the first time.

— Robinson Crusoe. (Classics Illustrated Study Guides Ser.). (Illus.). 1997. mass mkt. 4.99 (*1-57840-043-0*, Pub. by Acclaim Bks) Penguin Putnam.

— Robinson Crusoe. (York Notes Ser.). 1992. pap. text. write for info. (*0-582-78111-6*, Pub. by Addison-Wesley) Longman.

— Robinson Crusoe. LC 90-46733. 24.95 (*0-88411-594-1*) Amereon Ltd.

— Robinson Crusoe. LC 83-14022. Vol. 1. (Illus.). 368p. (J). (gr. 4-7). 1983. 27.00 (*0-684-17946-6*) Atheneum Yung Read.

— Robinson Crusoe. LC 98-23279. (Eyewitness Classics Ser.). (Illus.). 64p. (J). 1998. pap. 14.95 (*0-7894-3625-6*) DK Pub Inc.

— Robinson Crusoe. LC 90-46733. (SPA.). 9.95 (*84-241-5636-6*) E Torres & Sons.

— Robinson Crusoe. LC 90-46733. (J). (gr. 2 up). 1993. 13.95 (*0-679-42819-4*) Everymns Lib.

— Robinson Crusoe. LC 90-46733. (Children's Classics Ser.). (Illus.). (J). 1992. write for info. (*0-89434-126-X*) Ferguson.

— Robinson Crusoe. (Illus.). 1991. pap. 3.95 (*0-425-12664-1*) First Classics.

***Defoe, Daniel.** Robinson Crusoe. LC 99-461940. 318p. 1999. 13.50 (*0-19-210033-5*) OUP.

— Robinson Crusoe. (Prentice-Hall Literature). 1999. text. write for info. (*0-13-981432-9*) P-H.

Defoe, Daniel. Robinson Crusoe. Fago, John N., ed. LC 90-46733. (Now Age Illustrated IV Ser.). (Illus.). (J). (gr. 4-12). 1978. student ed. 1.25 (*0-88301-344-4*); pap. text 2.95 (*0-88301-320-7*) Pendulum Pr.

***Defoe, Daniel.** Robinson Crusoe. (SPA.). 1998. pap. 11.95 (*84-320-4866-6*) Planeta.

— Robinson Crusoe. (Unabridged Classics Ser.). 296p. (YA). 2000. pap. 5.98 (*0-7624-0551-1*, Courage) Running Pr.

Defoe, Daniel. Robinson Crusoe. LC 90-46733. 368p. (J). (gr. 7-9). 1990. pap. 4.50 (*0-590-43285-0*) Scholastic Inc.

— Robinson Crusoe. 352p. (YA). (gr. 4-7). 1989. pap. 2.50 (*0-8125-0482-8*, Pub. by Tor Bks) St Martin.

— Robinson Crusoe. 1981. 9.05 (*0-606-08465-7*, Pub. by Turtleback) Demco.

— Robinson Crusoe. Man, John, ed. LC 90-46733. 336p. 1994. pap. text 4.50 (*0-460-87439-X*, Everyman's Classic Lib) Tuttle Pubng.

— Robinson Crusoe. (ACE.). pap. 9.95 (*0-14-043597-2*) Viking Penguin.

— Robinson Crusoe. (Classics Library). 1997. pap. 3.95 (*1-85326-045-2*, 0452WW, Pub. by Wrdsworth Edits) NTC Contemp Pub Co.

— Robinson Crusoe. abr. ed. LC 95-36752. (Children's Thrift Classics Ser.). (Illus.). 96p. (J). 1998. pap. 1.00 (*0-486-28816-1*) Dover.

— Robinson Crusoe. abr. ed. LC 95-33695. (Classics for Young Readers Ser.). (Illus.). 288p. (J). (gr. 4-7). 1995. pap. 4.99 (*0-14-036722-5*, PuffinBks) Peng Put Young Read.

— Robinson Crusoe. large type ed. LC 90-46733. (Isis Clear Type Classic Ser.). 358p. 1992. 24.95 (*1-85089-459-0*, Pub. by ISIS Lrg Prnt) Transaction Pubs.

— Robinson Crusoe. LC 90-46733. 1982. reprint ed. lib. bdg. 25.95 (*0-89966-403-2*) Buccaneer Bks.

***Defoe, Daniel.** Robinson Crusoe. (Twelve-Point Ser.). 370p. 2000. reprint ed. lib. bdg. 24.00 (*1-58287-119-1*); reprint ed. lib. bdg. 24.00 (*0-939495-98-8*) North Bks.

Defoe, Daniel. Robinson Crusoe. Dolch, Edward W. et al, eds. LC 90-46733. 128p. (J). (gr. k-3). 1988. reprint ed. pap. 2.99 (*0-590-41841-6*) Scholastic Inc.

— Robinson Crusoe. rev. ed. LC 98-19069. 320p. 1998. mass mkt. 5.95 (*0-451-52701-1*, Sig Classics) NAL.

— Robinson Crusoe. unabridged ed. (Thrift Editions Ser.). 288p. 1998. pap. 2.00 (*0-486-40427-7*) Dover.

— Robinson Crusoe. 2nd ed. (Illus.). 94p. 1993. pap. text 5.95 (*0-19-585336-9*) OUP.

— Robinson Crusoe, Vol. I. (FRE.). 1996. pap. 7.95 (*2-87714-319-8*, Pub. by Bookking Intl) Distribks Inc.

— Robinson Crusoe, Vol. II. (FRE.). 1996. pap. 7.95 (*2-87714-320-1*, Pub. by Bookking Intl) Distribks Inc.

— Robinson Crusoe: An Authoritative Text, Backgrounds & Sources, Criticism. 2nd ed. Shinagel, Michael, ed. LC 93-12217. (Critical Editions Ser.). (C). 1993. pap. text 11.25 (*0-393-96452-3*) Norton.

— Robinson Crusoe: Movie Tie-In Art. 1996. mass mkt. 4.99 (*0-8125-5763-8*) Tor Bks.

***Defoe, Daniel.** Robinson Crusoe: The Life & Adventures of Robinson Crusoe. (Signature Classics Ser.). (Illus.). 512p. 1999. 24.95 (*1-58279-034-5*) Trident Pr Intl.

— Robinson Crusoe: The Life & Adventures of Robinson Crusoe. deluxe ed. (Signature Classics Ser.). (Illus.). 512p. 1999. 29.95 (*1-58279-046-9*) Trident Pr Intl.

Defoe, Daniel. Robinson Crusoe Level 4. 1999. pap. text 8.99 (*1-56179-743-X*) Focus Family.

Defoe, Daniel. Robinson Crusoe of York, Mariner. LC 97-3248. (Classic Collection). 1997. 14.99 (*1-56179-557-7*) Focus Family.

Defoe, Daniel. Robinson Crusoe Readalong. (Illustrated Classics Collection 4). 64p. 1994. pap. 14.95 incl. audio (*0-7854-0770-7*, 40517) Am Guidance.

— Romances & Narrative, 16 vols. Aitken, George, ed. (Illus.). reprint ed. write for info. (*0-404-07910-5*) AMS Pr.

— Romans: Moll Flanders, Mme. Veal, Memoires d'un Canalier, Vie du Capitaine Singleton, Etc., Vol. 2. 1760p. 1970. 105.00 (*0-686-56494-4*, F77001) Fr & Eur.

— Romans: Robinson Crusoe, Journal de l'Annee de la Peste, Jean Gow, Jean Sheppard, Etc., Vol. 1. 1376p. 85.00 (*0-686-56493-6*, F77000) Fr & Eur.

— Romans Vol. 1: Crusoe, Etc. (FRE.). 1939. 85.00 (*0-8288-3473-3*, F77000) Fr & Eur.

— Romans Vol. 2: Moll Flanders, Etc. (FRE.). 1970. 105.00 (*0-8288-3474-1*, F77001) Fr & Eur.

***Defoe, Daniel.** Roxana. 1999. pap. 7.95 (*0-460-87676-7*, Everyman's Classic Lib) Tuttle Pubng.

Defoe, Daniel. Roxana. Blewett, David, ed. 416p. 1982. pap. 11.95 (*0-14-043149-7*, Penguin Classics) Viking Penguin.

***Defoe, Daniel.** Roxana: The Fortunate Mistress. 2nd ed. Mullan, John, ed. (Oxford World's Classics Ser.). (Illus.). 392p. 1998. pap. 9.95 (*0-19-283459-2*) OUP.

— The Secrets of the Invisible World Disclosed: An Essay on the History & Reality of Apparitions. fac. ed. Pretes, Jeffry, ed. (Illus.). xviii, 395p. 1999. 49.95 (*0-9675228-0-3*) Svantovit.

Defoe, Daniel. Serious Reflections During the Life & Surprising Adventures of Robinson Crusoe, with His Vision of the Angelic World. LC 74-13445. (Illus.). reprint ed. write for info. (*0-404-07913-X*) AMS Pr.

— The Shakespeare Head Edition of the Novels & Selected Writings of Daniel Defoe, 14 vols. Incl. Captain Singleton. 335p. 1999. reprint ed. lib. bdg. 88.00 (*1-58201-053-6*); Journal of the Plague Year. 302p. 1999. reprint ed. lib. bdg. (*1-58201-058-7*); Memoirs of a Cavalier. 318p. 1999. reprint ed. lib. bdg. 88.00 (*1-58201-059-5*); Plan of the English Commerce. 277p. 1999. reprint ed. lib. bdg. 88.00 (*1-58201-062-5*); Shortest Way with the Dissenters. 262p. 1999. reprint ed. lib. bdg. 88.00 (*1-58201-066-8*); Pt. 1. Adventures of Robinson Crusoe. 250p. 1999. reprint ed. lib. bdg. 88.00 (*1-58201-063-3*); Pt. 1. Colonel Jack. 223p. 1999. reprint ed. lib. bdg. 88.00 (*1-58201-054-4*); Pt. 1. Fortunate Mistress: or A History of the Life. 1999. reprint ed. lib. bdg. 88.00 (*1-58201-056-0*); Pt. 1. Moll Flanders. 203p. 1999. reprint ed. lib. bdg. 88.00 (*1-58201-060-9*); Pt. 2. Adventures of Robinson Crusoe. 222p. 1999. reprint ed. lib. bdg. 88.00 (*1-58201-064-1*); Pt. 2. Colonel Jack. 275p. 1999. reprint ed. lib. bdg. 88.00 (*1-58201-055-2*); Pt. 2. Fortunate Mistress: or A History of the Life. 246p. 1999. reprint ed. lib. bdg. 88.00 (*1-58201-057-9*); Pt. 2. Moll Flanders. 287p. 1999. reprint ed. lib. bdg. 88.00 (*1-58201-061-7*); Pt. 3. Adventures of Robinson Crusoe. 1999. reprint ed. 88.00 (*1-58201-065-X*); (Shakespeare Head Edition of the Writings of Daniel Defoe Ser.). 1999. reprint ed. Set lib. bdg. 88.00 (*1-58201-052-8*) Classic Bks.

— The Shakespeare Head Edition of the Novels & Selected Writings of Daniel Defoe. 1983. reprint ed. 695.00 (*0-403-04268-2*) Somerset Pub.

— The Shakespeare Head Edition of the Novels & Selected Writings of Daniel Defoe, 14 vols., Set. (BCL1-PR English Literature Ser.). 1992. reprint ed. lib. bdg. 1050.00 (*0-7812-7341-2*) Rprt Serv.

— A Short Narrative of the Life & Actions of His Grace John, D. of Marlborough. LC 92-23651. (Augustan Reprints Ser.: No. 168). 1974. reprint ed. 14.50 (*0-404-70168-X*, DA462) AMS Pr.

— Tour Thro' London about the Year 1725. Beeton, Mayson M. & Chancellor, E. Beresford, eds. LC 68-56542. (Illus.). 144p. 1972. reprint ed. 33.95 (*0-405-08441-2*, Pub. by Blom Pubns) Ayer.

— A Tour Through the Whole Island of Great Britain. abr. ed. Furbank, P. N. et al, eds. LC 90-48710. (Illus.). 432p. (C). 1991. 50.00 (*0-300-04980-3*) Yale U Pr.

Defoe, Daniel & Chorpenning, Charlotte B. Robinson Crusoe. (J). (gr. 1-9). 1952. 6.00 (*0-87602-192-5*) Anchorage.

Defoe, Daniel & Conrad, Joseph. Robinson Crusoe. 288p. 1982. mass mkt. 4.95 (*0-553-21373-3*, Bantam Classics) Bantam.

Defoe, Daniel & Knill, Harry. Pirates. (Illus.). 64p. 1975. pap. 5.95 (*0-88388-027-X*) Bellerophon Bks.

Defoe, Daniel & Novak, Maximillian E. Conjugal Lewdness, or Matrimonial Whoredom. LC 67-10178. 426p. 1967. reprint ed. 50.00 (*0-8201-1013-2*) Schol Facsimiles.

Defoe, Daniel & Van Gool Studio Staff. Robinson Crusoe. (Classic Ser.). (Illus.). 64p. (J). (ps-1). 1995. 4.98 (*0-8317-1665-7*) Smithmark.

Defoe, Daniel, et al. Accounts of the Apparition of Mrs. Veal (1705-1766) LC 92-22890. (Augustan Reprints Ser.: No. 115). 1965. reprint ed. 14.50 (*0-404-70115-9*, BF1473) AMS Pr.

***Defoe, Daniel, et al.** The Consolidator. LC 00-26751. (Studies in the Eighteenth Century). 2000. write for info. (*0-404-63538-5*) AMS Pr.

Defoe, Daniel, et al. An Essay upon Projects. Borck, Jim S. & Peters, John G., eds. LC 97-31900. (Studies in the Eighteenth Century). 6p. 1998. write for info. (*0-404-63530-X*) AMS Pr.

— Robinson Crusoe. LC 90-46733. (Classics Illustrated Ser.). (Illus.). 52p. (YA). pap. 4.95 (*1-57209-021-9*) Classics Int Ent.

Defoe, Daniel, jt. auth. see Drury, Robert.

DeFoe, Don, et al, eds. Hiking Trails of the Smokies. (Natural History Handbook Ser.). (Illus.). 576p. (Orig.). 1994. pap. 16.95 (*0-937207-15-2*) GSMNH.

DeFoe, Don, ed. see Kemp, Steve.

DeFoe, Don, ed. see White, Peter, et al.

Defoe, Louis V., ed. see Belasco, David.

DeFoe, Mark. Air. 28p. 1998. pap. 6.50 (*1-887240-03-9*) GreenTower Pr.

— Palmate. 40p. (Orig.). 1988. pap. 5.95 (*0-9620863-0-4*) Pringle Tree Pr.

DeFoe, Martha, jt. ed. see George, B.

***DeFoe, Roger.** From Victim to Victor. 176p. 2000. pap. 8.99 (*1-58158-009-6*) McDougal Pubng.

DeFonblanque, Edward B. Political & Military Episodes in the Latter Half of the Eighteenth Century Derived from the Life & Correspondence of the Right Hon. John Burgoyne. LC 72-8667. (American Revolutionary Ser.). (Illus.). 516p. reprint ed. lib. bdg. 66.00 (*0-8398-0378-8*) Irvington.

Defonseca, Misha. Misha: A Memoire of the Holocaust Years. (Illus.). 265p. 1997. 24.95 (*0-9635257-7-8*) Mt Ivy Pr.

DeFontaine, F. G., ed. see Dickens, Charles.

DeFontnouvelle, Pierre, tr. see Bouyer, Louis.

DeFoor, J. Allison, II. Odet Philippe: Peninsular Pioneer. (Illus.). viii, 69p. 1998. 17.95 (*0-9659395-0-2*) Safety Harbor Mus.

DeFoore, Bill. Anger: Deal with It, Heal with It, Stop It from Killing You. 180p. (Orig.). 1991. pap. 8.95 (*1-55874-162-3*) Health Comm.

Defoore, Bill & Kenasch, John, eds. Rediscovering the Soul of Business: A Renaissance of Values. 379p. 1995. 35.00 (*0-9630390-6-7*) New Leaders.

***DeFoore, William Gray.** Anger among Angels: Shedding Light on the Darkness of the Human Soul. 160p. 2000. pap. 10.95 (*1-55874-830-X*) Health Comm.

Defoort, Carine. The Pheasant Cap Master (He Guan Zi) A Rhetorical Reading. LC 95-43325. (SUNY Series in Chinese Philosophy & Culture). (Illus.). 376p. (C). 1996. text 75.50 (*0-7914-3073-1*); pap. text 25.95 (*0-7914-3074-X*) State U NY Pr.

DeFord, C. S. A Reparation: Universal Gravitation, a Universal Fake. LC 92-28003. 1992. pap. 5.95 (*0-87770-512-7*) Ye Galleon.

DeFord, Deborah. Seeking a Simpler Spirit. LC 98-50304. (Illus.). 240p. 1998. 17.95 (*0-7621-0128-8*, Pub. by RD Assn) Penguin Putnam.

Deford, Deborah. The Simpler Life: An Inspirational Guide to Living Better with Less. LC 97-46151. (Simple Life Bks.). (Illus.). 240p. 1998. 17.95 (*0-7621-0061-3*, Pub. by RD Assn) Penguin Putnam.

DeFord, Deborah H. An Enemy among Them. 1987. 11.05 (*0-606-07190-3*, Pub. by Turtleback) Demco.

DeFord, Deborah H. & Stout, Harry S. An Enemy among Them. 208p. (J). 1994. pap. 5.95 (*0-395-70108-2*) HM.

DeFord, Diane E. The Day Miss Francie Got Skunked. LC 98-164282. (Illus.). (J). 1997. pap. write for info. (*0-7685-0009-5*) Dominie CA.

DeFord, Diane E., et al, eds. Bridges to Literacy: Learning from Reading Recovery. LC 91-6551. (Illus.). 234p. (Orig.). (C). 1991. pap. text 24.00 (*0-435-08575-1*, 08575) Heinemann.

Deford, Frank. Alex: The Life of a Child. LC 97-26497. (Illus.). 224p. 1997. pap. 9.95 (*1-55853-552-7*) Rutledge Hill Pr.

***DeFord, Frank.** The Best of Frank DeFord: I'm Just Getting Started. LC 00-27190. 356p. 2000. 24.95 (*1-57243-360-4*, Pub. by Triumph Bks) Login Pubs Consort.

Deford, Frank. Casey at the Bat. 1999. pap. 7.95 (*0-14-012100-5*, Viking) Viking Penguin.

— Got to Do Some Coachin' Nolan's Play. LC 88-63035. 43p. 1988. 4.95 (*0-914546-78-3*) Rose Pub.

— Love & Infamy. 576p. 1995. mass mkt. 5.99 (*0-8217-0122-3*, Zebra Kensgtn); mass mkt. 5.99 (*0-7860-0122-4*, Pinncle Kensgtn) Kensgtn Pub Corp.

— The World's Tallest Midget: The Best of Frank Deford. 1988. pap. 8.95 (*0-316-17946-9*) Little.

Deford, Frank, jt. auth. see Ashe, Arthur.

DeFord, Sara & Lott, Clarinda H. Forms of Verse: British & American. LC 77-94257. (Illus.). 393p. (Orig.). (C). 1971. 16.95 (*0-89197-169-6*) Irvington.

— Forms of Verse, British & American. LC 77-94257. 393p. (C). 1971. reprint ed. 19.95 (*0-390-26000-2*) Brick Hse Bks.

***DeForest, Anna.** Courtship, Vol. 1. (Zebra Splendor Historical Romances Ser.). 1999. mass mkt. 4.99 (*0-8217-6353-9*, Zebra Kensgtn) Kensgtn Pub Corp.

— Cowboy & the Heiress, Vol. 44. (Zebra Bouquet Ser.). 2000. mass mkt. 3.99 (*0-8217-6580-9*, Zebra Kensgtn) Kensgtn Pub Corp.

— Cowboy for Christmas. 352p. 2000. mass mkt. 5.99 (*0-8217-6756-9*, Zebra Kensgtn) Kensgtn Pub Corp.

DeForest, Anna. Golden Dreams. 320p. (Orig.). 1997. mass mkt. 4.99 (*0-8439-4179-0*) Dorchester Pub Co.

DeForest, Calvert. Cheap Advice. (Illus.). 128p. (Orig.). 1994. pap. 8.99 (*0-446-67082-0*) Warner Bks.

DeForest, Gerda D. Denniston. Record of the Descendants of Ezekial Denniston, Son of Chas. Denniston, the Emigrant Ancestor Who Came to America from Ireland & Settled about 1773, near Mariaville, New York. 112p. 1997. reprint ed. pap. 18.00 (*0-8328-8264-X*); reprint ed. lib. bdg. 28.00 (*0-8328-8263-1*) Higginson Bk Co.

DeForest, Heman P. & Bates, Edw. C. History of Westborough, Ma. Part I, Early History, Part II, Later History. (Illus.). 504p. 1995. reprint ed. lib. bdg. 52.00 (*0-8328-4469-1*) Higginson Bk Co.

DeForest, Holly & Steinberg, Mary. Challenging Change: Five Steps for Dealing Positively with Change. Scanlon, Kelly, ed. LC 96-67063. 107p. (Orig.). 1996. pap. 12.95 (*1-57294-049-2*, 12-0031) SkillPath Pubns.

DeForest, John W. Poems: Medley & Palestina. 1902. 100.00 (*0-685-89770-2*) Elliots Bks.

DeForest, Louis E. Ballard & Allied Families. (Illus.). 64p. 1997. reprint ed. pap. 13.00 (*0-8328-7355-1*); reprint ed. lib. bdg. 23.00 (*0-8328-7354-3*) Higginson Bk Co.

DeForest, Mary, ed. Woman's Power, Man's Game: Essays on Classical Antiquity in Honor of Joy K. King. LC 93-17713. 458p. 1993. pap. 35.00 (*0-86516-258-1*) Bolchazy-Carducci.

DeForest, Mary M. Apollonius' Argonautica: A Callimachean Epic. LC 94-35522. (Supplements to Mnemosyne Ser.: Vol. 142). 1994. 60.50 (*90-04-10017-2*) Brill Academic Pubs.

DeForest, P. R., et al. Forensic Science: An Introduction to Criminalistics. (McGraw-Hill Series in Criminology & Criminal Justice). (Illus.). 512p. (C). 1983. 72.50 (*0-07-016267-0*) McGraw.

DeForest, Robert W. & Veiller, Lawrence, eds. Tenement House Problem: Including the Report of the New York State Tenement House Commission of 1900, 2 vols. LC 75-112537. (Rise of Urban America Ser.). (Illus.). 1974. reprint ed. 65.95 (*0-405-02446-0*) Ayer.

DeForest, Thomas E. Inventor's Guide to Successful Patent Applications. 176p. 1988. pap. 19.95 (*0-07-157281-3*) McGraw.

— Inventor's Guide to Successful Patent Applications. (Illus.). 176p. 1988. pap. 15.95 (*0-8306-9335-1*, 3035) McGraw-Hill Prof.

***Deforge, Donald.** Atlas of Veterinary Dental Radiology. LC 99-49133. 356p. 2000. 114.95 (*0-8138-2997-6*) Iowa St U Pr.

***DeForge, Lauretta.** Stand & Deliver: A Public Speaking Program. (Illus.). 35p. (YA). 1999. 6.00 (*0-9677846-0-3*) DeForge Comm.

— Take a Hike in Lane County. ed. (Illus.). 44p. (YA). 2000. pap. 5.95 (*0-9677846-1-1*) DeForge Comm.

Deforges, Regine. La Bicyclette Bleue. text 8.95 (*0-88436-990-0*) EMC-Paradigm.

Deforges, Regine. The Devil Laughs Again. Mueller, Elizabeth F., tr. from FRE. 396p. 1988. 18.95 (*0-8184-0473-6*) Carol Pub Group.

— The Storm & Other Erotica. Lamont, Rosette, tr. from FRE. LC 99-19684. 112p. 1999. pap. 12.00 (*0-8021-3632-X*, Grove) Grove-Atltic.

DeForrest, Jean P. No Choice. 264p. (C). 1991. 17.95 (*0-9619272-1-6*) Stonegate Rancho.

DeForrest, Matthew M. Yeats & the Stylistic Arrangements of Experience. LC 98-40557. 186p. 1998. 74.95 (*1-57309-312-2*) Intl Scholars.

Defourneaux, M. Do You Speak Chemistry? (ENG & FRE.). 200p. 1984. pap. 85.00 (*0-7859-4859-7*) Fr & Eur.

— Do You Speak Science? Comment S'Exprimer En Anglais Scientifique. (ENG & FRE.). 176p. 1991. pap. write for info. (*0-7859-4854-6*) Fr & Eur.

Defourneaux, Marcelin. Daily Life in Spain in the Golden Age. Branch, Newton, tr. (Illus.). 256p. 1971. reprint ed. pap. 14.95 (*0-8047-1029-5*) Stanford U Pr.

Defourneaux, Rene J. The Winking Fox: Twenty-Two Tears in Military Intelligence. 389p. 1998. pap. 16.00 (*0-9666208-0-1*) IN Creative Arts.

Defouw, Hart & Svoboda, Robert. Light on Life: An Introduction to the Astrology of India. LC 96-904741. 480p. 1996. pap. 14.95 (*0-14-019507-6*, Penguin Bks) Viking Penguin.

Defoyd, Katherine W., jt. auth. see Eckhardt, Linda W.

DeFoyd, Katherine West, jt. auth. see Eckhardt, Linda West.

DeFoyer, Crispin. Christmas Games for Adults & Children. (Games & Pastimes Ser.: Vol. 7). (Illus.). 64p. 1982. 9.95 (*0-906672-08-2*); pap. 4.95 (*0-906672-09-0*) Oleander Pr.

DeFrain, John D., et al. Sudden Infant Death: Enduring the Loss. 2nd ed. 273p. 1991. 19.95 (*0-669-24544-5*) Lxngtn Bks.

Defrain, John D., jt. auth. see LeMasters, E. E.

DeFrain, John D., jt. auth. see Olson, David H.

DeFrain, Judith. Book of Wisdom. Arielweehawk et al, eds. (Illus.). 269p. (Orig.). (C). 1988. pap. text 150.00 (*0-9619008-3-0*) Eye Cat.

— Hermetic Supplies Catalog. (Illus.). 110p. (Orig.). 1988. pap. 10.00 (*0-9619008-1-4*) Eye Cat.

DeFrain, Judith, et al. Beginning Wicca. Johnson, Ken & Arielweehawk, eds. (Illus.). 100p. (Orig.). 1988. pap. text 13.00 (*0-9619008-4-9*) Eye Cat.

DeFrain, Judith, ed. see Jade.

***Defraites, Henry.** Little Henry & the Phantom Dream. (Illus.). 32p. (J). (gr. 1-7). 1999. 7.95 (*0-9676825-0-9*) Abound Inc.

DeFraites, Sydney G., III. Beauty of the Stars. (Stareagle Adventures Ser.: No. 2). 320p. (Orig.). 1994. pap. 5.95 (*0-9640160-1-X*) JK Books.

— The Stars Are for Eagles: The Original Adventure. (Stareagle Adventures Ser.: No. 1). 320p. (Orig.). 1992. pap. 5.95 (*0-9640160-0-1*) JK Books.

DeFrance, Steve. Ordinary Angers. 96p. 1993. pap. 12.50 (*0-9624205-4-9*) Inevitable Pr.

— Signals from the Land. 107p. 1996. pap. write for info. (*0-9624205-8-1*) Inevitable Pr.

Defranceschi, Annelisse, jt. auth. see Braides, Andrea.

Defranceschi, M., jt. ed. see Ellinger, Y.

Defranceschi, Mireille & Delhalle, Joseph. Numerical Determination of the Electronic Structure of Atoms, Diatomic & Polyatomic Molecules. (C). 1989. text 186.00 (*0-7923-0170-6*) Kluwer Academic.

DeFrancesco, John & Goodfriend, Gary. The Common Sense Guide to Publicity: Practical Advice on How to Use the Power of Publicity. 128p. (Orig.). 1996. pap. 14.95 (*0-9650398-0-3*) DeFrancesco Gdfrnd.

DeFrancis. Intermediate Chinese. (ENG & CHI.). 1964. pap. 30.00 (*0-300-00064-2*) Yale U Pr.

Defrancis, Beth. The Parents' Resource Almanac: Where to Write, Who to Call, What to Buy & How to Find Out Everything You Need to Know. LC 94-15476. 1994. pap. 15.00 (*1-55850-394-3*) Adams Media.

DeFrancis, John. Annotated Quotations from Chairman Mao. LC 74-20080. 326p. reprint ed. pap. 101.10 (*0-7837-3317-8*, 205772100007) Bks Demand.

Defrancis, John. Beginning Chinese. 2nd rev. ed. LC 76-5099. (Yale Linguistic Ser.). 566p. 1976. pap. 30.00 (*0-300-02058-9*) Yale U Pr.

DeFrancis, John. Beginning Chinese Reader, 2 pts., 2. 2nd ed. LC 76-5103. 1977. pap. 30.00 (*0-300-02061-9*) Yale U Pr.

— Beginning Chinese Reader, 2 pts., Pt. I. 2nd ed. LC 76-5103. 1012p. 1977. 57.50 (*0-300-02056-2*) Yale U Pr.

— Beginning Chinese Reader, 2 pts., Pt. II. 2nd ed. LC 76-5103. Vol. II. 1977. 57.50 (*0-300-02057-0*) Yale U Pr.

D

— Beginning Chinese Reader, 2 pts., Vol. I, Pts. I & II. 2nd ed. LC 76-5103. Vol. 11. 1012p. 1977. pap. 30.00 (*0-300-02060-0*) Yale U Pr.

Defrancis, John. Character Text for Beginning Chinese. 2nd ed. LC 76-5105. 519p. 1976. 57.50 (*0-300-02055-4*); pap. 30.00 (*0-300-02059-7*) Yale U Pr.

***DeFrancis, John.** Character Text for Intermediate Chinese. (Yale Linguistic Ser.: Vol. 7/C02). (Illus.). 436p. (C). 1999. reprint ed. pap. 40.00 (*0-87415-340-9*) Foreign Lang.

DeFrancis, John. The Chinese Language: Fact & Fantasy. LC 84-8546. 342p. 1986. pap. text 19.00 (*0-8248-1068-6*) UH Pr.

— In the Footsteps of Genghis Khan. LC 92-36542. (Illus.). 296p. (C). 1993. 26.25 (*0-8248-1493-2*, Kolowalu Bk) UH Pr.

— Visible Speech: The Diverse Oneness of Writing Systems. LC 89-4708. 336p. 1989. text 32.00 (*0-8248-1207-7*) UH Pr.

DeFrancis, John, ed. ABC Chinese-English Dictionary: Alphabetically Based Computerized. LC 95-43629. 920p. 1996. pap. text 28.00 (*0-8248-1744-3*) UH Pr.

— ABC Chinese-English Dictionary: Alphabetically Based Computerized. (ABC Chinese Dictionary Ser.). (CHI & ENG.). 920p. 2000. text 32.00 (*0-8248-2320-6*) UH Pr.

DeFrancis, John, ed. ABC Chinese-English, Pocket Edition: Alphabetically Based Computerized. 912p. (C). 1998. pap. text 18.00 (*0-8248-2154-8*) UH Pr.

***DeFrancis, John & Chia-yee, Teng.** Intermediate Chinese. (Yale Linguistic Ser.: Vol. 7/CO1). 545p. (C). 1999. reprint ed. pap. 40.00 (*0-87415-339-5*) Foreign Lang.

DeFrancis, John, ed. see Lindell, Kristina.

DeFrancisco, Victoria L. & Jensen, Marvin D., eds. Women's Voices in Our Time: Statements by American Leaders. LC 94-221011. (Illus.). 281p. (C). 1994. pap. text 16.95 (*0-88133-761-7*) Waveland Pr.

Defranco, Agnes L. & Noriega, Pender B. Cost Control in the Hospitality Industry. LC 98-55472. (Illus.). 382p. (C). 1999. 66.00 (*0-13-575325-2*, Macmillan Coll) P-H.

DeFranco, Buddy. Buddy DeFranco - Hand in Hand with Hanon. LC 96-97165. (Illus.). 215p. (Orig.). 1996. pap. text, student ed. 25.00 (*0-9654244-0-5*) B DeFranco Ent.

DeFranco, Francine M. & Ferullo, Donna L., eds. Human Service Organizations & Their Publications: A Directory of Selected Sources. 100p. 1996. pap. text 12.50 (*0-87293-048-3*) Coun Soc Wk Ed.

Defrank, Carol & Brzeczek, Marietta. Visions of the Valley. LC 96-26890. (Illus.). 256p. 1996. 39.00 (*1-885352-38-7*) Community Comm.

DeFranza, James, jt. auth. see Faires, J. Douglas.

Defrates, Joanna. What Do We Know about the Aztecs? LC 92-16997. (What Do We Know about...? Ser.). (Illus.). 48p. (YA). (gr. 4-7). 1993. lib. bdg. 18.95 (*0-87226-357-6*, 63576B, P Bedrick Books) NTC Contemp Pub Co.

— What Do We Know about the Egyptians? LC 91-25175. (What Do We Know about...? Ser.). (Illus.). 40p. (YA). (gr. 3 up). 1992. lib. bdg. 18.95 (*0-87226-353-3*, P Bedrick Books) NTC Contemp Pub Co.

DeFrees, Madeline. The Light Station on Tillamook Rock. Wheatcroft, John, ed. (Bucknell University Fine Editions: Series in Contemporary Poetry). (Illus.). 60p. 1990. 125.00 (*0-916375-11-0*) Press Alley.

— Magpie on the Gallows. 82p. 1982. 12.00 (*0-914742-66-3*) Copper Canyon.

— Magpie on the Gallows. 84p. 1982. pap. 6.00 (*0-914742-65-5*) Copper Canyon.

— Possible Sibyls. 80p. 1991. 16.95 (*0-89924-079-8*); pap. 8.50 (*0-89924-080-1*) Lynx Hse.

Defreest, Anne Marie. Recipes & Reflections: A Journey of Food & Friendship from the Inn at the Round Barn Farm. 1. LC 98-75219. 1999. 29.95 (*0-9665263-0-9*) Cook Hrt Barn.

DeFreest, Shane, jt. auth. see Carl, Jason.

***DeFreitas, Frank, et al.** Shoebox Holography: A Step-by-Step Guide to Making Holograms Using Inexpensive Semiconductor Diode Laser. (Illus.). 124p. (YA). 2000. pap. 16.95 (*0-89496-060-1*) Ross Bks.

DeFreitas, Gregory. Inequality at Work: Hispanics in the U. S. Labor Force. (Illus.). 304p. 1991. text 55.00 (*0-19-506421-6*) OUP.

DeFreitas, Michael. Adventures in Nature: Caribbean. LC 98-31655. (Adventures in Nature Ser.). (Illus.). 328p. 1999. pap. 18.95 (*1-56261-452-5*) Avalon Travel.

DeFreitas, Stan. Complete Guide to Florida Gardening. rev. ed. LC 87-5038. 368p. 1987. 21.95 (*0-87833-572-2*) Taylor Pub.

— Stan DeFreitas Garden Answer Book. LC 98-9964. 208p. 1998. pap. text 15.95 (*0-87833-984-1*) Taylor Pub.

Defremery, G., tr. see Batoutah, Ibn.

DeFremery, Kathi, ed. see Freeman, Zu.

Defresny. Amusements Serieux et Comiques. Dunkley, ed. (Exeter French Texts Ser.: No. 23). (FRE.). 122p. Date not set. pap. text 19.95 (*0-85989-091-0*, Pub. by Univ Exeter Pr) Northwestern U Pr.

Defries, Amelia D. Pioneers of Science. LC 74-117782. (Essay Index Reprint Ser.). 1977. 19.95 (*0-8369-1646-8*) Ayer.

DeFries, Eleanora, jt. ed. see Palaliko, Lee.

DeFries, Zira, et al, eds. Sexuality: New Perspectives, 6. LC 84-28991. (Contributions in Psychology Ser.: No. 6). (Illus.). 362p. 1985. 69.50 (*0-313-24207-0*, DFS/, Greenwood Pr) Greenwood.

DeFriese, Gordon H., jt. ed. see Ory, Marcia G.

DeFrietas, Michael, ed. see Vipond, Anne.

DeFronzo, James. Revolutions & Revolutionary Movements. 2nd ed. LC 96-8447. 384p. (C). 1996. pap. text 32.00 (*0-8133-2394-0*, Pub. by Westview) HarpC.

Defronzo, Ralph. Current Management of Diabetes. LC 98-208447. (Illus.). 288p. (C). (gr. 13). 1997. text 59.95 (*0-8151-2757-X*, 22758) Mosby Inc.

DeFronzo, Ralph A., jt. auth. see Arieff, Allen I.

DeFronzo, Ralph A., jt. ed. see Arieff, Allen I.

DeFronzo, Ralph A., ed. see Zimmet, Paul Z.

Deftos, L. J. Medullary Thyroid Carcinoma. (Beitraege Zur Onkologie, Contributions to Oncology Ser.: Vol. 17). (Illus.). x, 114p. 1983. pap. 72.25 (*3-8055-3703-4*) S Karger.

***Deftos, Leonard J.** Clinical Essentials of Calcium & Skeletal Disorders. 314p. 1998. pap. text 19.95 (*1-884735-39-8*) Prof Comms.

Defty, Jeff. Creative Fingerplays & Action Rhymes: An Index & Guide to Their Use. LC 92-9655. (Illus.). 264p. 1992. pap. 29.50 (*0-89774-709-7*) Oryx Pr.

Defur, Brett. Show Me Mountain Biking. (Show Me Missouri Ser.). (Illus.). 224p. 1998. pap. 14.95 (*1-891708-02-3*, MG3480) Pebble Pub.

Defur, Brett, jt. auth. see Beatte, Brian.

***DeFur, Peter L., et al, eds.** Endocrine Disruption in Invertebrates: Endocrinology, Testing & Assessment. LC 99-45687. (Illus.). 303p. 1999. pap. 98.00 (*1-880611-27-9*, SETAC Pr) SETAC.

DeFuria, Steve. The MIDI Book: Using MIDI & Related Interfaces. (Illus.). 104p. (J). 1986. per. 14.95 incl. VHS (*0-88188-514-2*, HLO 8418400) H Leonard.

DeFuria, Steve & Scacciaferro, Joe. The Art of Digital Drumming. (Ferro Technologies Ser.). (Illus.). 144p. (Orig.). 1989. pap. 19.95 incl. audio (*0-88188-869-9*, HL 00237455) H Leonard.

— The MIDI Implementation Book. (Ferro Technologies Ser.). 208p. (Orig.). 1987. pap. 19.95 (*0-88188-558-4*, HL 00605601) H Leonard.

— The MIDI Resource Book. (Ferro Technologies Ser.). 148p. (Orig.). 1987. pap. 17.95 (*0-88188-587-8*, HL 00605602) H Leonard.

— Synthesis with Style. (Ferro Technologies Ser.). (Illus.). 120p. (Orig.). 1989. audio 19.95 (*0-88188-868-0*, HL 00239057) H Leonard.

DeFuria, Steve, jt. auth. see Scacciaferro, Joe.

DeGaetano, Gloria, jt. auth. see Grossman, David.

DeGaetano, Gloria M. Television & the Lives of Our Children: A Manual for Teachers & Parents. (Illus.). 128p. 1993. pap. text 10.95 (*0-9638737-0-9*) Train Thought.

DeGaetano, Jean G. Artic Plus. 100p. 1987. pap. text 29.95 (*1-886143-00-5*) Grt Ideas Tching.

— Articulation Curriculum I. 120p. 1987. pap. text 29.95 (*1-886143-01-3*) Grt Ideas Tching.

— Articulation Curriculum II. 100p. 1987. pap. text 29.95 (*1-886143-02-1*) Grt Ideas Tching.

— Articulation Curriculum Super Pack. 139p. 1993. pap. text 29.95 (*1-886143-03-X*) Grt Ideas Tching.

— Articulation Screening Assessment. rev. ed. 15p. 1989. pap. text 18.95 (*1-886143-04-8*) Grt Ideas Tching.

— Asking Good Questions. 60p. 1990. pap. text 21.00 (*1-886143-05-6*) Grt Ideas Tching.

— Asking More Specific Questions. 60p. 1992. pap. text 21.00 (*1-886143-06-4*) Grt Ideas Tching.

— Attention, Good Listeners! 52p. 1986. pap. text 24.95 (*1-886143-07-2*) Grt Ideas Tching.

— Auditory & Verbal Sequencing. 75p. 1992. pap. text 22.00 (*1-886143-08-0*) Grt Ideas Tching.

— Auditory Processing in Dinosaur Land. 60p. 1994. pap. text 22.00 (*1-886143-09-9*) Grt Ideas Tching.

— Auditory Processing of "WH" Words. 62p. 1995. pap. text 22.00 (*1-886143-28-5*) Grt Ideas Tching.

— Auditory Processing Super Pack. 114p. 1992. pap. text 26.00 (*1-886143-10-2*) Grt Ideas Tching.

— Big Comprehension of Little Words. 84p. 1991. pap. text 22.00 (*1-886143-11-0*) Grt Ideas Tching.

— A Bridge to Carryover S-R-L. 49p. 1986. pap. text 21.00 (*1-886143-12-9*) Grt Ideas Tching.

— Building Auditory Direction Skills. (Illus.). 60p. (Orig.). 1997. pap. text 22.00 (*1-886143-36-6*, G840) Grt Ideas Tching.

— Comprehending "Conditional Directions" That Begin with "If" (Illus.). 49p. (Orig.). (J). (gr. k-4). 1996. pap. text 18.00 (*1-886143-34-X*, G834) Grt Ideas Tching.

— Comprehending Descriptive Language. (Illus.). 90p. (Orig.). (J). (gr. k-5). 1996. pap. text 23.00 (*1-886143-33-1*, G832) Grt Ideas Tching.

— Coordinating Auditory Information. 75p. 1994. pap. text 22.00 (*1-886143-13-7*) Grt Ideas Tching.

— Create a Curriculum. 139p. 1993. pap. text 22.00 (*1-886143-14-5*) Grt Ideas Tching.

— Developing Alert Listening Skills. 84p. 1995. pap. text 24.00 (*1-886143-29-3*) Grt Ideas Tching.

— Developing Awareness of Similarities & Differences. (Illus.). 120p. (Orig.). 1997. pap. text 26.00 (*1-886143-38-2*, G842) Grt Ideas Tching.

— Developing Comprehension in Non or Minimally Verbal Children. 78p. (J). (ps-2). 1998. pap. text 26.00 (*1-886143-40-4*) Grt Ideas Tching.

— Developing Receptive & Expressive Language Skills in Young Learners. 66p. (J). (ps-2). 1998. pap. text 24.00 (*1-886143-44-7*) Grt Ideas Tching.

— Facilitating Word Recall. 100p. 1995. pap. text 26.00 (*1-886143-30-7*) Grt Ideas Tching.

— Following Auditory Directions. 66p. 1994. pap. text 22.00 (*1-886143-15-3*) Grt Ideas Tching.

— Four Hundred Eighty Action-Packed "Talk-Abouts" 80p. (J). (gr. k-2). 1991. pap. text 22.00 (*1-886143-16-1*) Grt Ideas Tching.

— Holidays: Articulation-Language Stimulation. 158p. (J). (ps-6). 1989. pap. text 29.95 (*1-886143-17-X*) Grt Ideas Tching.

— Interactive Language Skills. (Illus.). 73p. (Orig.). (J). (ps-2). 1996. pap. text 22.00 (*1-886143-32-3*, G831) Grt Ideas Tching.

— Language Development Lessons for Early Childhood. 80p. (J). (gr. k-3). 1998. pap. text 26.00 (*1-886143-43-9*) Grt Ideas Tching.

— Language Picture Dictionary. 205p. (J). (ps-2). 1989. pap. text 34.95 (*1-886143-18-8*) Grt Ideas Tching.

— Language Stimulation Activities. (Illus.). 90p. (Orig.). (J). (ps-2). 1996. pap. text 23.00 (*1-886143-31-5*, G833) Grt Ideas Tching.

— Listening & Processing Auditory Directions. 66p. 1995. pap. text 23.00 (*1-886143-27-7*) Grt Ideas Tching.

— Listening & Remembering Specific Details. (Illus.). 58p. (Orig.). 1997. pap. text 22.00 (*1-886143-37-4*, G841) Grt Ideas Tching.

— Listening from the Beginning to the End. 60p. (J). (gr. k). 1998. pap. text 23.00 (*1-886143-42-0*) Grt Ideas Tching.

— Mastering Auditory Sequencing. 60p. (J). (gr. 2-4). 1993. pap. text 22.00 (*1-886143-19-6*) Grt Ideas Tching.

— Mastering Basic Concepts & Specific Words. 93p. (J). (gr. k-2). 1991. pap. text 26.00 (*1-886143-20-X*) Grt Ideas Tching.

— Multiple Auditory Skills Super Pack. 118p. 1993. pap. text 26.00 (*1-886143-21-8*) Grt Ideas Tching.

— Problem Solving Activities. (Illus.). 120p. (Orig.). (J). (gr. 1-6). 1996. pap. text 26.00 (*1-886143-35-8*, G830) Grt Ideas Tching.

— Processing Auditory Messages Exactly & Totally. 60p. 1994. pap. text 22.00 (*1-886143-22-6*) Grt Ideas Tching.

— Put on Your Thinking Cap in Following Directions-Understanding Sentences. 80p. 1986. pap. text 27.95 (*1-886143-23-4*) Grt Ideas Tching.

— Recognizing & Verbalizing Correct Grammar. (Illus.). 80p. (Orig.). 1997. pap. text 24.00 (*1-886143-39-0*, G843) Grt Ideas Tching.

— Sound Construction. 85p. 1988. pap. text 29.95 (*1-886143-25-0*) Grt Ideas Tching.

— Therapy Fun with S & Z. 72p. 1991. pap. text 26.00 (*1-886143-26-9*) Grt Ideas Tching.

— Verbal Reasoning Activities. 64p. (J). (ps-3). 1998. pap. text 24.00 (*1-886143-41-2*) Grt Ideas Tching.

DeGaetano, Jean G. & Rosone, Geraldine A. Smart Kids Solve Double Meanings. 43p. 1988. pap. text 16.95 (*1-886143-24-2*) Grt Ideas Tching.

***DeGalan, Julie.** Foreign Language Majors. 2nd ed. (Great Jobs for ... Majors Ser.). 2000. pap. 12.95 (*0-658-00453-0*, VGM Career) NTC Contemp Pub Co.

— Psychology Majors. 2nd ed. (Great Jobs for ... Majors Ser.). 2000. pap. 12.95 (*0-658-00452-2*, VGM Career) NTC Contemp Pub Co.

DeGalan, Julie & Lambert, Stephen E. Great Jobs for Foreign Language Majors. LC 93-40677. (Illus.). 256p. 1994. pap. 11.95 (*0-8442-4351-5*, 43515, VGM Career) NTC Contemp Pub Co.

DeGalan, Julie, jt. auth. see Lambert, Stephen E.

***Degalan, Julie A.** Great Jobs for English Majors. LC 99-55167. (Great Jobs Ser.). 192p. 2000. pap. 11.95 (*0-658-00221-X*, 00221X, VGM Career) NTC Contemp Pub Co.

Degalan, Julie A. & Lambert, Stephen. Great Jobs for History Majors. (Great Jobs Ser.). (Illus.). 272p. 1994. pap. 11.95 (*0-8442-4353-1*, 43531, VGM Career) NTC Contemp Pub Co.

— Great Jobs for Psychology Majors. LC 94-19534. (Great Jobs Ser.). (Illus.). 192p. 1995. pap. 11.95 (*0-8442-4352-3*, 43523, VGM Career) NTC Contemp Pub Co.

DeGale, Laurice. Down to Earth Jamaican Cooking. 192p. 1996. pap. write for info. (*1-896705-00-6*) Sister Vis Pr.

Degan, James. The Irony of Exile: Memory & the Experience of Childhood. LC 96-20043. (American University Studies: Series IV, Vol. 188). 1997. pap. write for info. (*0-8204-3383-7*) P Lang Pubng.

Degan, V. D. Sources of International Law, Vol. DIIL 27. LC 97-16417. 1997. 295.00 (*90-411-0421-6*) Kluwer Law Intl.

Deganawidah, ed. see Seals, David.

DeGanck, Roger. Beatrice of Nazareth in Her Context, Vol. 1. (Cistercian Studies: No. 121). 341p. 1991. 28.95 (*0-87907-421-3*); pap. 12.95 (*0-87907-721-2*) Cistercian Pubns.

— Beatrice of Nazareth in Her Context Vol. No. 2: Towards Unification with God. (Cistercian Studies: No. 122). 262p. 1991. 28.95 (*0-87907-422-1*); pap. 12.95 (*0-87907-622-4*) Cistercian Pubns.

DeGange, Anthony R. A Conservation Assessment for the Marbled Murrelet in Southeast Alaska. (Illus.). 72p. 1997. pap. text 25.00 (*0-7881-4700-5*) DIANE Pub.

— A Conservation Assessment for the Marbled Murrelet in Southeast Alaska. (Illus.). 84p. 1997. reprint ed. 16.00 (*0-89904-550-2*, Wildlife Resrch Grp); reprint ed. pap. 11.00 (*0-89904-551-0*, Wildlife Resrch Grp) Crumb Elbow Pub.

DeGange, Susan & Verniero, Joan, eds. Food & Beverage Market Research Report. 117p. (Orig.). 1984. pap. text 95.00 (*0-931634-39-3*) FIND-SVP.

DeGangi, G., jt. auth. see Poisson, S.

Degangi, Georgia A. Documenting Sensorimotor Progress: A Pediatric Therapist's Guide. 157p. 1998. pap. text 42.00 (*0-12-784554-2*) Acad Pr.

***Degangi, Georgia A.** Pediatric Disorders of Regulation in Affect & Behavior: A Therapist's Guide to Assessment & Treatment. 316p. 2000. pap. 54.95 (*0-12-208770-4*) Acad Pr.

Degani, ed. Hipponactis. (GRE.). 1991. 59.50 (*3-8154-1956-5*, T1956, Pub. by B G Teubner) U of Mich Pr.

Degani, Nissan. Exodus Calling. Orig. Title: Exodus Meshaderet. 333p. 1997. 28.50 (*0-930832-07-8*) Herzl Pr.

Degano, P., et al, eds. Automata, Languages & Programming: Proceedings 24th International Colloquium, ICALP'97, Bologna, Italy, July 7-11, 1997. (Lecture Notes in Computer Science Ser.: Vol. 1256). xvi, 862p. 1997. pap. 99.95 (*3-540-63165-8*) Spr-Verlag.

Degano, Pierpaolo, et al, eds. Theoretical Computer Science: Proceedings of the 6th Italian Conference Prato, Italy 9 - 11 November 1998. 396p. 84.00 (*981-02-3655-7*) World Scientific Pub.

DeGarmo, E. Paul. Materials & Processes in Manufacturing. 8th ed. 1272p. 1997. text 102.95 (*0-471-36679-X*) Wiley.

Degarmo, E. Paul & Black, J. Temple. Materials & Processes in Manufacturing. 8th ed. 1172p. (C). 1996. text 96.00 (*0-02-328621-0*, Macmillan Coll) P-H.

DeGarmo, John. The Road to Ballybunion. LC 97-71941. (Illus.). 160p. 1997. 29.95 (*1-56352-433-3*) Longstreet.

DeGarmo, Scott & Tartaglia, Louis. Heart to Heart: The Real Power of Network Marketing. LC 99-15073. (Illus.). 333p. 1999. pap. 15.00 (*0-7615-1759-6*) Prima Pub.

***Degas, Edgar.** Degas Drawings of Dancers. LC 99-38288. (Art Library Ser.). (Illus.). 48p. 1999. pap. text 5.95 (*0-486-40698-9*) Dover.

Degas, Edgar. Degas's Atelier at Auction: Paintings, Pastels & Drawings, Paris, 1918-1919, 2 vols., Set. rev. ed. (ENG & FRE., Illus.). 1989. 295.00 (*1-55660-025-9*) A Wofsy Fine Arts.

***Degas, Edgar, et al.** Edgar Degas: An Album of Pencil Sketches. LC 00-26464. (Illus.). 120p. 2000. 39.95 (*0-89236-610-9*, J P Getty Museum) J P Getty Trust.

Degas, Hilaire. Drawings of Degas. Longstreet, Stephen, ed. (Master Draughtsman Ser.). (Illus.). (Orig.). 1964. pap. 4.95 (*0-87505-158-8*) Borden.

Degas, Hilaire G. Drawings. (Illus.). 100p. 1973. pap. 8.95 (*0-486-21233-5*) Dover.

— My Friend Degas. Curtiss, Mina, ed. LC 64-22375. (Illus.). 138p. reprint ed. pap. 42.80 (*0-608-18588-4*, 200523600051) Bks Demand.

DeGategno, Paul J. James MacPherson. (English Authors Ser.: No. 467). 224p. 1989. text 26.95 (*0-8057-6975-7*, TEAS 467) Macmillan.

DeGaulle, Charles. The Complete War Memoirs of Charles deGaulle. Griffin, Jonathan & Howard, Richard, trs. LC 98-6935. (Illus.). 1056p. 1998. pap. 19.95 (*0-7867-0546-9*) Carroll & Graf.

Degauque, Pierre & Hamelin, Joel, eds. Electromagnetic Compatibility. LinguaFranca Language Services Staff, tr. (Illus.). 678p. 1993. text 98.00 (*0-19-856375-2*) OUP.

DeGaydou, Nelda B., tr. see Ford, LeRoy.

DeGaydou, Nelda B., tr. see Witty, Robert G.

DeGeer, Maria E. & Reynolds, Benn P. Defense of Freemasonry & Masonic Gems of Jewels of Thought. 220p. 1998. reprint ed. pap. 17.95 (*0-7661-0215-7*) Kessinger Pub.

DeGeer, Stanley L. Pikes Peak Is Unser Mountain: Race to the Clouds. LC 90-62413. (Illus.). 216p. (Orig.). 1990. pap. 24.95 (*0-9626278-0-1*) Peak Pub NM.

— Pikes Peak or Bust, 1916-1996: Eighty Years of Racing to the Clouds. (Illus.). 100p. (Orig.). 1996. pap. 7.95 (*0-9626278-2-8*) Peak Pub NM.

— The Pikes Peak Race, 1916-1990. (Illus.). 330p. 1991. pap. 14.95 (*0-9626278-1-X*) Peak Pub NM.

Degefa, Tamiru, jt. auth. see Tsegaye, Webayehu.

Degeigel, Alma S., jt. auth. see Handschuh, Jeanne.

Degen, A. Allan. Ecophysiology of Small Desert Mammals. LC 96-32227. (Adaptations of Desert Organisms Ser.). 242p. 1996. 149.50 (*3-540-59259-8*) Spr-Verlag.

Degen, Bernd. Bernd Degen Discus: A Reference Book. (Illus.). 128p. 1991. 35.95 (*0-86622-545-5*, TS-163) TFH Pubns.

— Degen Discus. (Illus.). 320p. 1989. 29.95 (*0-86622-086-0*, TS-134) TFH Pubns.

— Discus: How to Breed Them. Hirschhorn, Howard, tr. from GER. (Illus.). 128p. 1990. 29.95 (*0-86622-641-9*, TS-137) TFH Pubns.

— Discus Breeding. (Illus.). 1998. 29.95 (*0-7938-2088-X*, TS-263) TFH Pubns.

— Discus Catalogue/Atlas. (Illus.), 320p. 1997. 69.95 (*0-7938-1890-7*, TS-279) TFH Pubns.

— Discus in the Community Tank. (Illus.). 144p. 1994. 19.95 (*1-56465-121-5*, 16585) Tetra Pr.

— Proper Care of Discus. (Illus.). 256p. 1995. 16.95 (*0-86622-548-X*, TW130) TFH Pubns.

— Wild Caught Discus. (Illus.). 112p. 1995. 29.95 (*0-7938-0296-2*, TS244) TFH Pubns.

Degen, Bernd & Wattley, Jack. Discus Today. (Illus.). 64p. 1996. 19.95 (*0-7938-0100-1*, WW004) TFH Pubns.

Degen, Bruce. Daddy Is a Doodlebug. LC 98-49563. 40p. (J). (ps-1). Date not set. pap. 5.95 (*0-06-443578-4*); bds. 7.95 (*0-694-01352-8*) HarpC Child Bks.

— Daddy Is a Doodlebug. LC 98-49563. (Illus.). 40p. (J). (ps-1). 2000. 15.95 (*0-06-028415-3*); lib. bdg. 15.89 (*0-06-028416-1*) HarpC Child Bks.

Degen, Bruce. Degen Picture Book. 32p. (ps-1). 5.95 (*0-06-443579-2*) HarpC.

Degen, Bruce. Jamberry. (I Can Read Bks.). 32p. (J). (ps-3). 1983. lib. bdg. 15.89 (*0-06-021417-1*) HarpC Child Bks.

— Jamberry. LC 82-47708. (I Can Read Bks.). (Illus.). 32p. (J). (ps-3). 1983. 15.95 (*0-06-021416-3*) HarpC Child Bks.

— Jamberry. LC 82-47708. (I Can Read Bks.). (Illus.). 32p. (J). (ps-1). 1985. pap. 5.95 (*0-06-443068-5*) HarpC Child Bks.

— Jamberry. LC 82-47708. (I Can Read Bks.). (Illus.). 32p. (J). (ps-3). 1992. 19.95 (*0-06-443311-0*, HarpTrophy) HarpC Child Bks.

— Jamberry. (I Can Read Bks.). (J). (ps-3). 1983. 10.15 (*0-606-02850-1*, Pub. by Turtleback) Demco.

— Jamberry, Set. (I Can Read Bks.). (Illus.). (J). (ps-3). 1986. 24.95 incl. audio (*0-87499-028-9*); pap. 15.95 incl. audio (*0-87499-026-2*) Live Oak Media.

— Jamberry, 4 bks., Set. (Illus.). (J). (ps-3). 1986. pap., teacher ed. 33.95 incl. audio (*0-87499-027-0*) Live Oak Media.

D

An Asterisk (*) at the beginning of an entry indicates that the title is appearing for the first time.

— Jamberry Board Book. LC 82-47708. (Illus.). 32p. (J). (ps-k). 1994. 7.95 (*0-694-00651-3*, HarpFestival) HarpC Child Bks.

— Jamberry Board Book & Tape. (Share a Story Ser.). (J). (ps up). 1998. 9.95 incl. audio (*0-694-70096-7*) HarpC.

Degen, Bruce. Jamberry Book & Tape. (Tell Me a Story Book Ser.). (Illus.). 32p. (J). (ps-3). 1996. pap. 8.95 incl. audio (*0-694-70038-X*) HarpC.

Degen, Bruce. Sailaway Home. LC 95-15737. (Illus.). 32p. (J). (ps-3). 1996. 14.95 (*0-590-46443-4*) Scholastic Inc.

***Degen, Bruce.** Sailaway Home Board Book. 32p. (J). (ps-1). 2000. 7.95 (*0-694-01448-6*, HarpFestival) HarpC Child Bks.

Degen, Bruce. Teddy Bear Towers. LC 90-31937. (Illus.). 32p. (J). (ps-1). 1991. 14.00 (*0-06-021420-1*); lib. bdg. 13.89 (*0-06-021430-9*) HarpC Child Bks.

Degen, Bruce. The Magic School Bus & the Electric Field Trip. LC 97-2080. (Magic School Bus Ser.). 56p. (J). (gr. 1-4). 1997. 15.95 (*0-590-44682-7*); pap. 4.99 (*0-590-44683-5*) Scholastic Inc.

***Degen, Bruce.** The Magic School Bus & the Electric Field Trip. (Magic School Bus Ser.). (J). (gr. k-4). 1999. pap. text 39.92 (*0-439-04356-5*) Scholastic Inc.

Degen, Bruce. The Magic School Bus Gets Planted: A Book about Photosynthesis. (Magic School Bus Ser.). (J). (gr. k-2). 1997. pap. 2.99 (*0-614-29015-5*) Scholastic Inc.

— The Magic School Bus Gets Planted: A Book about Photosynthesis. (Magic School Bus Ser.). (J). (gr. k-2). 1997. mass mkt. 2.99 (*0-590-92246-7*) Scholastic Inc.

— The Magic School Bus in the Time of the Dinosaurs. (Magic School Bus Ser.). (FRE.). (J). (gr. 1-4). pap. 6.99 (*0-590-24641-0*) Scholastic Inc.

— The Magic School Bus in the Time of the Dinosaurs. LC 93-5753. (Magic School Bus Ser.). 56p. (J). (ps-3). 1994. 15.95 (*0-590-44688-6*) Scholastic Inc.

— The Magic School Bus in the Time of the Dinosaurs. (Magic School Bus Ser.). 56p. (J). (gr. 1-4). 1995. pap. 4.95 (*0-590-44689-4*) Scholastic Inc.

— The Magic School Bus in the Time of the Dinosaurs. (Magic School Bus Ser.). (J). (gr. 1-4). 1995. 9.90 (*0-606-07823-1*, Pub. by Turtleback) Demco.

— The Magic School Bus Inside a Hurricane. LC 94-34703. (Magic School Bus Ser.). 56p. (J). (ps-3). 1995. 14.95 (*0-590-44686-X*, Scholastic Hardcover) Scholastic Inc.

— Shirley's Wonderful Baby. LC 99-11751. 32p. (J). 2000. 14.95 (*0-06-028132-4*) HarpC.

Degen, Bruce, et al. My Teddy Bear Library, 1, Set. (Illus.). (J). (ps-2). 1999. 19.95 (*0-694-01252-1*) HarpC Child Bks.

Degen, Bruce, jt. auth. see Cole, Joanna.

Degen, Bruce, jt. creator see Cole, Joanna.

Degen, Clara, intro. Communicators' Guide to Marketing. 226p. 1989. reprint ed. text 39.95 (*0-88133-492-8*) Sheffield WI.

Degen, Clare. Understanding & Using Video: A Guide for the Organizational Communicator. 211p. 1985. 34.95 (*0-582-28469-4*) Intl Assn Busn Comm.

Degen, F. J. Versuch Einer Vollstandigen Literatur der Romer, 3 vols. 1344p. 1997. reprint ed. write for info. (*3-487-10189-0*) G Olms Pubs.

Degen, G. H., et al, eds. Toxicology in Transition: Proceedings of the 1994 EUROTOX Congress Meeting Held in Basel, Switzerland, August 21-24, 1994, No. 17. LC 94-43580. (Archives of Toxicology Ser.: Vol. 17). 1995. 136.00 (*3-540-58781-0*) Spr-Verlag.

Degen, H., et al, eds. Gas Enzymology. 1984. text 160.50 (*90-277-1900-4*) Kluwer Academic.

Degen, J. Wolfgang. Systeme der kumulativen Logik. (Analytica Ser.). (GER.). 265p. 1984. 92.00 (*3-88405-038-9*) Philosophia Pr.

Degen, Johann F. Literatur der Deutschen Ubersetzer der Griechen, 3 vols. write for info. (*0-318-71761-1*) G Olms Pubs.

— Literatur der Deutschen Ubersetzer der Griechen: Altenburg und Erlangen, 1797-1801, 3 vols. (GER.). lxxxii, 1435p. 1999. reprint ed. 475.00 (*3-487-10185-8*, Pub. by G Olms Verlag) Lubrecht & Cramer.

— Versuch Einer Vollstandigen Litteratur der Deutschen Ubersetzungen der Romer, 3 vols. reprint ed. write for info. (*0-318-71762-X*) G Olms Pubs.

Degen, Kathleen & Nasper, Ellen. Return from Madness: Psychotherapy with People Taking the New Antipsychotic Medications. LC 95-44617. 256p. 1996. 50.00 (*1-56821-625-4*) Aronson.

***Degen, Michael, ed.** Prospero's Magic: Active Learning Strategies for the Teaching of Literature. rev. ed. 120p. 2000. pap. 17.95 (*0-9665125-4-5*) Telemachos Pub.

Degen, Michael E. Crafting Expository Argument: Practical Approaches to the Writing Process for Students & Teachers. 2nd rev. ed. 175p. 1999. pap. 13.00 (*0-9665125-2-9*) Telemachos Pub.

Degen, Paula. The Johnstown Flood of 1889: Tragedy of the Conemaugh. 64p. 1984. pap. 3.95 (*0-915992-31-0*) Eastern National.

Degen, Paula, jt. auth. see Wescott, Lynanne.

Degen, Paula A., ed. see Shields, A. Randolph.

Degen, Peter, et al. Stadt Und Industriekultur, Industrie Und Stadtkultur: Internationaler Workshop, Vitra/Weil Am Rhein, 17.-20. April 1991: Am Beispiel der Beziehungen Zwischen Den Vitra Unternehmungen Und der der Stadt Weil Am Rhein LC 92-1384. (ENG.). 117 p. 1992. write for info. (*3-7643-2724-3*) Birkhauser.

Degen, Richard. Tao Te Ching for the West. LC 99-10148. 144p. 1999. pap. 9.95 (*0-934252-92-0*) Hohm Pr.

Degenaar, Marjolein. Molyneux's Problem: Three Centuries of Discussion on the Perception of Forms. (Archives Internationales d'Historie des Idees Ser.: Vol. 147). 160p. (C). 1996. lib. bdg. 110.50 (*0-7923-3934-7*) Kluwer Academic.

DeGenaro, Jennie J. Flip for Phonics: For Tutors, Mothers & Others. rev. ed. (Illus.). 36p. 1997. 14.50 (*0-87517-096-X*) Dietz.

DeGenaro, Katherine, jt. auth. see Garfin, Susan.

Degener, Theresia & Koster-Dreese, Yolan, eds. Human Rights & Disabled Persons: Essays & Relevant Human Rights Instruments. LC 94-43563. (International Studies in Human Rights: Vol. 40). 1994. lib. bdg. 238.00 (*0-7923-3298-9*) Kluwer Academic.

***DeGeneres, Betty.** Just a Mom. 188p. 2000. 21.95 (*1-55583-613-5*, Pub. by Alyson Pubns) Consort Bk Sales.

— Love, Ellen: A Mother/Daughter Journey. 384p. 2000. pap. 14.00 (*0-688-17688-7*, Quil) HarperTrade.

DeGeneres, Betty. Love, Ellen: A Mother/Daughter Journey. LC 98-50367. (Illus.). 366p. 1999. 24.00 (*0-688-16274-6*, Wm Morrow) Morrow Avon.

DeGeneres, Ellen. The First Book by Ellen DeGeneres. 1995. 19.95 (*0-614-15500-2*) Bantam.

— My Point . . . & I Do Have One. 211p. 1996. mass mkt. 6.50 (*0-553-57361-6*) Bantam.

— North Carolina Corporation Laws, Partnership Laws & Securities Act, 1993 Edition. 30.00 (*0-614-05927-5*, MICHIE) LEXIS Pub.

DeGeneste, Henry I. & Sullivan, John P. Policing Transportation Facilities. LC 94-26575. (Illus.). 172p. (C). 1994. text 41.95 (*0-398-05929-2*) C C Thomas.

DeGeneste, Henry I. & Sullivan, John P. Policing Transportation Facilities. LC 94-26575. (Illus.). 172p. (C). 1994. pap. text 28.95 (*0-398-05946-2*) C C Thomas.

DeGeneste, Henry T. & Sullivan, John P. Policing a Multicultural Community. LC 97-69036. 28p. 1997. pap. 6.50 (*1-878734-53-9*) Police Exec Res.

Degenhard, William. The Regulators. LC 80-54849. 598p. 1981. reprint ed. 24.95 (*0-933256-22-1*) Second Chance.

Degenhardt, Richard K. Belleek: The Complete Collector's Guide & Illustrated Reference. 2nd ed. LC 93-30049. (Illus.). 256p. 1993. 60.00 (*0-87069-698-X*, Wllce-Homestd) Krause Pubns.

Degenhardt, William G., et al. Amphibians & Reptiles of New Mexico. LC 95-41784. (Illus.). 487p. 1996. 35.00 (*0-8263-1695-6*) U of NM Pr.

Degenhart, Bernhard & Schmitt, Annegrit. Jacopo Bellini: The Louvre Album of Drawings. Mecklenburg, Frank, tr. from GER. LC 84-12355. (Illus.). 200p. 1984. 95.00 (*0-8076-1097-6*) Braziller.

Degenhart, Curt & Muehlbauer, Jen. AOL in a Nutshell: A Desktop Guide to America Online. (Illus.). 536p. 1998. pap. 19.95 (*1-56592-424-X*) OReilly & Assocs.

Degenhart, Karen. The Fourth Coyote: A Personal Search for the Hidden History of Earth. (Illus.). 183p. (Orig.). 1995. pap. 12.95 (*0-916337-04-9*) Thndbird Pubns.

— A Medicine Story: The Return to Native American Consciousness. (Illus.). 284p. (Orig.). 1996. reprint ed. pap. 15.95 (*0-916337-03-0*) Thndbird Pubns.

Degenkolb, Oris H. Concrete Box Girder Bridges. (Monograph: No. 10). 1977. 59.95 (*0-685-85763-8*, 10BOW6) ACI.

— Concrete Box Girder Bridges. LC 76-43388. (ACI Monograph: No. 10). (Illus.). 116p. reprint ed. pap. 36.00 (*0-608-00560-6*, 206144300008) Bks Demand.

***DeGennaro, Dori J.** Wishing on a Star. (Illus.). 16p. (J). (ps-k). 1999. pap. 5.95 (*1-891846-07-8*) Busn Word.

DeGennaro, Dorothy A., ed. Profile: The Architects Sourcebook. rev. ed. 2000p. 1997. pap. 149.00 (*0-9651113-3-4*) Construct Mkt Data.

— Profile: The Architects Sourcebook. 12th rev. ed. 2000p. 1997. 175.00 (*0-9651113-2-6*) Construct Mkt Data.

— Profile: The Architects Sourcebook. 13th rev. ed. (Illus.). 2000p. 1998. 175.00 (*0-9651113-5-0*); pap. 149.00 (*0-9651113-4-2*) Construct Mkt Data.

— ProFile: The Sourcebook of U. S. Architectural Design Firms. 11th rev. ed. 1800p. 1996. pap. 149.00 (*0-9651113-1-8*); boxed set 175.00 (*0-9651113-0-X*) Construct Mkt Data.

DeGennaro, Lorraine, ed. see Balliro, Lenore.

DeGennaro, Lorraine, ed. see Hudzik, Robert S.

DeGennaro, Lorraine, ed. see Lautermilch, Steven.

DeGennaro, Lorraine, ed. see Sherman, Alana.

DeGennaro, Lorraine, ed. see Vernon, William.

DeGennaro, Lorraine S. Stoney Point Poems. Sherman, Alana, ed. (Chapbooks Third Ser.). 16p. (Orig.). 1990. pap. 3.50 (*0-939689-08-1*) Alms Hse Pr.

DeGennaro, Lorraine S., ed. see Sharenov, Evelyn.

DeGennaro, Richard. Libraries, Technology & the Information Marketplace. (Professional Librarian Ser.). 410p. 1987. 40.00 (*0-8161-1855-8*, Hall Reference); 30.00 (*0-8161-1869-8*, Hall Reference) Macmillan.

DeGennes, J. L., ed. HMG Coa Reductase Inhibitors: New Horizons in the Management of Hypercholesterolemia - Journal: Cardiology, 1990, Vol. 77, Suppl. 4. (Illus.). iv, 72p. 1991. pap. 23.50 (*3-8055-5278-5*) S Karger.

DeGennes, P. E. & Prost, J. The Physics of Liquid Crystals. 2nd ed. (International Series of Monographs on Physics: No. 83). (Illus.). 614p. 1995. reprint ed. pap. text 55.00 (*0-19-851785-8*) OUP.

DeGenova, Mary K. Families in Cultural Context: Strengths & Challenges in Diversity. LC 96-34123. xx, 277p. (C). 1997. pap. text 39.95 (*1-55934-581-0*, 1581) Mayfield Pub.

Degens. Freya on the Wall. 1996. pap. 3.95 (*0-15-200209-X*) Harcourt.

Degens, E. T. Perspectives in Biogeochemistry. (Illus.). 495p. 1989. 85.95 (*0-387-50191-6*) Spr-Verlag.

Degens, Egon T., et al, eds. Biogeochemistry of Major World Rivers. LC 90-35020. (Scientific Committee on Problems of the Environment Ser.: No. 42). 382p. 1991. 395.00 (*0-471-92676-0*) Wiley.

Degens, T. Freya on the Wall. LC 95-45545. 288p. (J). 1997. 19.00 (*0-15-200210-3*) Harcourt.

DeGeorge. Business Ethics. 5th ed. LC 98-42973. 626p. (C). 1999. pap. text 49.00 (*0-13-079772-3*) P-H.

DeGeorge, Barry. Interpreting Crisis: A Retrospective Analysis of the American News Media & the Energy Crisis of 1973-74. 197p. (Orig.). 1987. pap. 47.50 (*91-22-00845-4*) Coronet Bks.

Degeorge, Cheryle, ed. Hart's Oil & Gas Finance Sourcebook. 9th rev. ed. 650p. 1998. pap. text 595.00 (*0-912553-77-4*) Hart Pubns.

DeGeorge, Gail. The Making of a Blockbuster: How Wayne Huizenga Built a Sports & Entertainment Empire from Trash, Grit, & Videotape. LC 95-41880. 354p. 1995. 24.95 (*0-471-12269-6*); pap. 5.99 (*0-471-19172-8*) Wiley.

Degeorge, Gail. The Making of a Blockbuster: How Wayne Huizenga Built a Sports & Entertainment Empire from Trash, Grit & Videotape. 354p. 1997. pap. 14.95 (*0-471-15903-4*) Wiley.

DeGeorge, Louis. Total Quality Selling. (Business Skills Express Ser.). 1995. pap. 10.00 (*0-7863-0324-7*, Irwn Prfssnl) McGraw-Hill Prof.

DeGeorge, Richard. Academic Freedom & Tenure: Ethical Issues. LC 96-39513. (Issues in Academic Ethics Ser.: No. 41). 248p. 1997. 66.00 (*0-8476-8331-1*); pap. 25.95 (*0-8476-8332-X*) Rowman.

DeGeorge, Richard T. Business Ethics Reader. 512p. (C). 2001. pap. 27.00 (*0-02-328001-8*, Macmillan Coll) P-H.

Deger, Joseph. Greenberg's Guide to American Flyer S Gauge Vol. 1: Motive Power. 5th ed. LC 97-14495. (Illus.). 240p. (Orig.). 1997. pap. 49.95 (*0-89778-420-0*, 10-8065, Greenberg Books) Kalmbach.

Deger, Karin, jt. ed. see Ziegler, Wolfram.

Deger, Saadet & Sen, Somnath. Military Expenditure: The Political Economy of International Security. (SIPRI Strategic Issue Papers). (Illus.). 198p. 1991. text 48.00 (*0-19-829141-8*) OUP.

Degerbald, Jan-Eric, jt. auth. see Hagglund, Sam.

Degerbol, Magnus. Zoology I: Mammals. LC 74-20244. (Thule Expedition, 5th, 1921-1924 Ser.: Vol. 2, Pts. 4-5). (Illus.). 1976. reprint ed. 72.50 (*0-404-58309-_*) AMS Pr.

Degering & Hamblock. English-German Environmental Dictionary. (ENG & GER.). 480p. 1996. 120.00 (*0-320-01346-4*) Fr & Eur.

— German-English Environmental Dictionary. 1996. 120.00 incl. disk (*0-320-01345-6*) Fr & Eur.

Degering, Etta B. My Friend Jesus. (J). 1993. reprint ed. pap. 5.99 (*0-8280-0755-1*) Review & Herald.

Degering, Hermann. Lettering: Modes of Writing in Western Europe. (Illus.). 1978. pap. 9.95 (*0-8008-4727-X*) Taplinger.

Degering, Klaus. Defoes Gesellschaftskonzeption. (Bochum Studies in English: No. 5). (GER., Illus.). x, 512p. (Orig.). 1977. pap. 37.00 (*90-6032-079-4*) J Benjamins Pubng Co.

Degeste, Beatrix Chanson. The Romance of the Chevelere Assigne. Aldenham, Lord, ed. (EETS, ES Ser.: No. 6). 1974. reprint ed. pap. 30.00 (*0-527-00221-6*) Periodicals Srv.

***DeGex, Jenny.** Asian Style Source Book: Creative Ideas for Enhancing Space. (Illus.). 144p. 2000. text 29.95 (*0-7893-0400-7*, Pub. by Universe) St Martin.

***DeGezelle, Terri.** The ABC Book. LC 99-50152. (Alphabet Bks.). (Illus.). 32p. (J). 1999. 21.00 (*0-7368-7040-7*) Capstone Pr.

— The ABC of Birds. LC 99-52403. (Alphabet Bks.). (Illus.). 32p. (J). 2000. 21.00 (*0-7368-7038-5*) Capstone Pr.

— The ABC of Bugs. LC 99-52407. (Alphabet Bks.). (Illus.). 32p. (J). 2000. 21.00 (*0-7368-7036-9*) Capstone Pr.

Degge, Eldon. Praying Daily with Paul. (Horizon Ser.). 1997. pap. 9.99 (*1-56570-016-3*) Meridian MI.

Degge, Rogena M., jt. auth. see McFee, June K.

***Deggs, Mary Bernard.** No Cross on Earth, No Crown in Heaven: The History of the Sisters of the Holy Family. 2000. 39.95 (*0-253-33630-9*) Ind U Pr.

Degh, Linda. American Folklore & the Mass Media. LC 93-7543. (Folklore Today Ser.). (Illus.). 224p. 1994. 39.95 (*0-253-31677-4*); pap. 17.95 (*0-253-20844-0*) Ind U Pr.

— Folktales & Society: Story-Telling in a Hungarian Peasant Community. Shossberger, Emily M., tr. from HUN. LC 88-46025. (Illus.). 480p. 1989. 40.00 (*0-253-31679-0*); pap. 7.25 (*0-253-20526-3*, MB-526) Ind U Pr.

— Folktales of Hungary. Halasz, Judit, tr. from HUN. LC 64-19846. (Folktales of the World Ser.). 427p. reprint ed. pap. 132.40 (*0-608-09446-3*, 205424600005) Bks Demand.

— Narrative in Society: A Performer-Centered Study of Narration. 372p. 1995. text 45.00 (*0-253-31683-9*) Ind U Pr.

— People in the Tobacco Belt: Four Lives. Dorson, Richard M., ed. LC 80-792. (Folklore of the World Ser.). (Illus.). 1981. reprint ed. lib. bdg. 31.95 (*0-405-13331-6*) Ayer.

Degh, Linda, compiled by. Hungarian Folktales: The Art of Zsuzsanna Palko. LC 96-28121. (World Folktale Library). 408p. 1996. pap. 20.00 (*0-87805-912-1*) U Pr of Miss.

Degh, Linda, ed. Hungarian Folktales: The Art of Zsuzsanna Palko. Kalm, Vera, tr. LC 95-30866. (World Folktale Library). (Illus.). 408p. 1995. text 61.00 (*0-8153-1337-3*, H1736) Garland.

— Indiana Folklore: A Reader. LC 79-2970. (Illus.). 320p. 1980. pap. 14.95 (*0-253-20239-6*, MB-239) Ind U Pr.

Degh, Linda, ed. see Goodman, Felicitas D.

Degheele, Danny, jt. ed. see Ishaaya, I.

DeGiacomo, F. P. Chiropractic Analysis Through Palpation. McDonnell, James, ed. (Illus.). 192p. (C). 1980. 20.00 (*0-938470-00-0*) NY Chiro Coll.

***DeGiacomo, Mark G.** Massachusetts Basic Practice Manual: Representing Clients in the United States Bankruptcy Court. (Massachusetts Basic Practice Ser.). 150p. 1999. pap. write for info. (*1-57589-164-6*) Mass CLE.

DeGiacomo, Mark G. Representing the Debtor in a Chapter 7 Bankruptcy, 1996 Edition. rev. ed. LC 95-81324. 92p. 1995. pap. text 59.00 (*1-57589-007-0*, 96-03.03-QC) Mass CLE.

— Representing the Debtor in a Chapter 13 Consumer Bankruptcy. LC 94-73531. 1996. pap. text 59.00 (*0-944490-83-2*) Mass CLE.

DeGidio, Sandra. Prayer Services for the Elderly. LC 95-61900. 112p. (Orig.). 1996. pap. 19.95 (*0-89622-685-9*) Twenty-Third.

— R. C. I. A: The Rites Revisited. 144p. (Orig.). 1984. 7.95 (*0-86683-837-6*, 8436) Harper SF.

— Sacraments Alive: Their History, Celebration, & Significance. LC 91-65381. 160p. (Orig.). 1991. pap. 9.95 (*0-89622-489-9*, C59) Twenty-Third.

Degiorgio, V. Nonlinear Optical Materials: Principles & Applications. LC 94-73355. 490p. (gr. 12). 1995. 155.00 (*90-5199-204-1*) IOS Press.

Degiorgio, V., ed. Trends in Colloid & Interface Science II. (Progress in Colloid & Polymer Science Ser.: Vol. 76). 320p. 1988. 129.00 (*0-387-91335-1*) Spr-Verlag.

Degiorgio, V., ed. see Workshop on Quasielastic Light Scattering Studies.

DeGiovanni, Frank F. Displacement Pressures in the Lower East Side. LC 88-211301. 57p. 1987. pap. text 6.00 (*0-88156-053-7*) Comm Serv Soc NY.

DeGirolalmi-Cheney, Liana, ed. The Symbolism of Vanitas in the Arts, Literature & Music: Comparative & Historical Studies. LC 89-13788. (Illus.). 288p. 1993. lib. bdg. 89.95 (*0-88946-399-9*) E Mellen.

DeGirolami, Umberto, jt. auth. see Richardson, Edward P., Jr.

D'Eglantine, P. Fabre. Le Philinte de Moliere. Proud, Judith K., ed. (Exeter French Texts Ser.: No. 97). (FRE.). 100p. 1996. pap. 19.95 (*0-85989-496-7*, Pub. by Univ Exeter Pr) Northwestern U Pr.

Deglas, Christian. The Classic Beers of Belgium. (Illus.). 275p. 1997. pap. 24.95 (*1-887167-01-3*) G W Kent.

Degler, Carl N. In Search of Human Nature: The Decline & Revival of Darwinism in American Social Thought. 416p. 1992. reprint ed. pap. 13.95 (*0-19-507707-5*) OUP.

— Neither Black nor White: Slavery & Race Relations in Brazil & the U. S. LC 86-40780. 328p. 1986. reprint ed. pap. text 17.95 (*0-299-10914-3*) U of Wis Pr.

— The Ordeal of Herbert Hoover. (Irvington Reprint Series in American History). (C). 1991. reprint ed. pap. text 1.90 (*0-8290-2606-1*, H-52) Irvington.

***Degler, Carl N.** The Other South: Southern Dissenters in the Nineteenth Century. 2000. reprint ed. pap. 19.95 (*0-8130-1830-7*) U Press Fla.

Degler, Carl N. Out of Our Past: The Forces That Shaped Modern America. 3rd ed. LC 83-48021. 672p. 1983. pap. 18.00 (*0-06-131985-6*, TB1985, Torch) HarpC.

— Place over Time: The Continuity of Southern Distinctiveness. LC 97-6955. 1997. pap. 16.00 (*0-8203-1942-2*) U of Ga Pr.

Degler, Carl N., et al. The Democratic Experience Vol. 2: An American History: Civil War to Present. 5th ed. LC 80-26038. 495p. 1981. reprint ed. pap. 153.50 (*0-7837-3950-8*, 204377900002) Bks Demand.

— The Democratic Experience, An American History Vol. 1: Colonial Era to 1877. 5th ed. LC 80-26038. (Illus.). 383p. 1981. pap. 118.80 (*0-7837-8250-0*, 204912900001) Bks Demand.

Degler, Carl N., ed. see Abrams, Richard M.

Degler, Lois. Man & God. LC 74-28943. (Illus.). 1975. pap. 3.00 (*0-930422-04-X*) Dennis-Landman.

Degler, Teri. Everything Your Kids Ever Wanted to Know about Dinosaurs & You Were Afraid They'd Ask. (Illus.). 128p. (Orig.). 1991. pap. 9.95 (*1-55972-096-4*, Birch Ln Pr) Carol Pub Group.

Degler, Teri, jt. auth. see Kason, Yvonne.

Degli Atti, C. Ciofi, et al, eds. Few-Body Problems in Physics: Proceedings of the XIIIth European Conference, Marciana Marina, Isola d'Elba, Italy, September 9-14, 1991. LC 92-2231. (Few-Body Systems Ser.: Suppl. 6). (Illus.). xv, 635p. 1992. 158.95 (*0-387-82343-3*) Spr-Verlag.

Degli Atti, Claudio Ciofi, see Boffi, Sigfrido.

Degli-Esposti, Cristina, ed. Postmodernism in the Cinema. LC 97-46857. 272p. 1998. 59.95 (*1-57181-105-2*); pap. 22.50 (*1-57181-106-0*) Berghahn Bks.

Degli-Esposti, Cristina, jt. ed. see Bondanella, Peter E.

Degli Esposti, Giovani. Lady X Lust's Captive. pap. 9.95 (*1-56097-337-4*, Pub. by Fantagraph Bks) Seven Hills Bk.

Deglin, Judith H. Nurse's Med Deck. 6th ed. 432p. 1998. ring bd. 28.95 (*0-8036-0367-3*) Davis Co.

Deglin, Judith H. & Vallerand, April H. Davis's Drug Guide for Nurses. 6th ed. (Illus.). 123p. (C). 1998. text 31.95 (*0-8036-0366-5*) Davis Co.

— Davis's Electronic Drug Guide for Nurses: Includes Davis's Drug Guide for Nurses. 1203p. (C). 1999. 49.95 incl. cd-rom (*0-8036-0495-5*) Davis Co.

— Nurse's Med Deck. 6th ed. (C). 1998. boxed set 33.95 (*0-8036-0368-1*) Davis Co.

Deglin, Judith H., jt. auth. see MacDermott, Barbara.

Deglin, Judith H., jt. auth. see Vallerand, April H.

***Deglin, Judith Hopfer.** Nurse's Med Deck. 7th ed. (Illus.). 2000. 33.95 (*0-8036-0587-0*); pap. 28.95 (*0-8036-0588-9*) Davis Co.

***Deglin, Judith Hopfer & Vallerand, April Hazard.** Davis' Drug Guide for Nurses. 7th ed. 1320p. 2000. 32.95 (*0-8036-0583-8*); pap. text 35.95 incl. disk (*0-8036-0582-X*) Davis Co.

D

Deglin, Judith Hopfer & Vallerand, April Hazard. Davis's Drug Guide for Nurses. 6th ed. LC 98-16214. (Illus.). 1203p. 1998. pap. 35.95 incl. disk (*0-8036-0365-7*) Davis Co.

DeGlopper, Donald R. Lukang: Commerce & Community in a Chinese City. LC 95-2525. (SUNY Series in Chinese Local Studies). 296p. (C). 1995. text 59.50 (*0-7914-2689-0*); pap. text 19.95 (*0-7914-2690-4*) State U NY Pr.

Degn, H., et al. Chaos in Biological Systems. LC 87-7203. (NATO ASI Ser.: Vol. 138). (Illus.). 336p. (C). 1987. text 105.00 (*0-306-42685-4*, Kluwer Plenum) Kluwer Academic.

Degn, Ralph G. Keep the Spirit! Running Life's Race with Power & Purpose. 128p. 1997. pap. 10.98 (*0-88290-625-9*, 1077) Horizon Utah.

***Degnan, Frances Ann.** Under the Arctic Sun: The Life & Times of Frank & Ada Degnan. LC 99-94636. (Illus.). 365p. 1999. pap. 19.98 (*0-9669650-0-0*) Cottonwd.

***Degnan, Frank.** Aerospace Testing: Promise of Closer NASA/DOD Cooperation Remains Largely Unfulfilled. (Illus.). 46p. 1999. text. write for info. (*0-7881-8081-9*) DIANE Pub.

Degnan, Frank. A Guide for Teaching Scuba to Divers with Special Needs. LC 97-75325. (Illus.). 220p. 1998. pap. 19.95 (*0-941332-64-0*, D968) Best Pub Co.

Degnan, Lawrence. Yosemite Yarns-Stagecoach Stories. (Illus.). 24p. (YA). (gr. 7 up). 1958. pap. 3.50 (*0-915266-04-0*) Awani Pr.

***Degnen, Lisa.** Christina Aguilera. LC 00-33226. (Illus.). 96p. 2000. 9.98 (*1-58663-036-9*) M Friedman Pub Grp Inc.

— Dawson's Creek. 1. LC 99-13867. 1999. 12.98 (*1-56799-845-3*) M Friedman Pub Grp Inc.

Degnen, Lisa. Elijah Wood: Hollywood's Hottest Rising Star. LC 99-60267. 96p. 1999. mass mkt. 9.99 (*0-446-67581-4*, Pub. by Warner Bks) Little.

— Prince William: Prince of Hearts. LC 98-86955. 96p. 1998. mass mkt. 9.99 (*0-446-67539-3*, Pub. by Warner Bks) Little.

***Degnen, Lisa & Law, Deborah.** Meet 98 Degrees. LC 99-54033. 2000. 9.98 (*1-56799-975-1*, Friedman-Fairfax) M Friedman Pub Grp Inc.

***Degner, David Martin.** The N-Particle Model. (Illus.). 144p. 2000. pap. text 100.00 (*0-9668628-0-5*) Degner Pr.

Degner, Helen. Quarter-Mile Link: History & Reflection of Shady Oaks & the Rock Valley Community. vii, 120p. (Orig.). 1996. pap. 20.00 (*0-9652976-0-8*) M Gift.

Degner, Lesley F. & Beaton, Janet I., eds. Life-Death Decisions in Health Care. (Death Education, Aging & Health Care Ser.). 159p. 1987. 63.95 (*0-89116-399-9*) Hemisp Pub.

Degner, Mark, jt. auth. see Cernick, Paul.

Degnon, Dom. Sails Full & By. (Illus.). 240p. 1995. 27.50 (*0-924486-75-9*) Sheridan.

Dego, Giuliano. Doctor Max: A Novel. LC 96-40079. 768p. 1997. pap. 24.95 (*0-88268-201-6*) Station Hill Pr.

Degobert, P. Automobile & Pollution. 1995. 570.00 (*2-7708-0676-9*, Pub. by Edits Technip) Enfield Pubs NH.

Degobert, Paul. Automobile & Pollution. LC 95-69809. (Illus.). 520p. (C). 1995. 595.00 (*2-7108-0676-2*, Pub. by Edits Technip) Enfield Pubs NH.

— Automobiles & Pollution. 485p. 1994. 89.00 (*1-56091-563-3*, R-150) Soc Auto Engineers.

Degoede, Daniel L. & Drews, Danae. Belief Therapy a Guide to Enhancing Everyday Life. LC 98-92615. 150p. (Orig.). 1998. pap. 12.50 (*0-9663745-0-9*) Everyday Life.

DeGolyer, Michael E., jt. auth. see McMillen, Donald H.

DeGonzalez, Fe Acosta & DeMatos, Isabel Freire. Matematicas Modernas en el Nivel Elemental: Guia Metodologica. (Illus.). 245p. 1971. 5.00 (*0-8477-2700-9*) U of PR Pr.

DeGood, Douglas Earl, et al. The Headache & Neck Pain Workbook: An Integrated Mind & Body Program. LC 97-66083. (Illus.). 184p. (Orig.). 1997. pap. 14.95 (*1-57224-086-5*) New Harbinger.

DeGooysr, Kemit, jt. auth. see Brown, Geoff.

Degos, L., ed. see European School of Oncology Staff.

Degos, Laurent. Textbook of Malignant Haematology. 944p. 1999. text 185.00 (*1-85317-322-3*, M Dunitz) Scovill Paterson.

Degotardi, Peter & International Business Machines Corporation Staff. Beyond DHCP: Work Your TCP/IP Internetwork with Dynamic LP LC 99-180784. xxviii, 471 p. 1998. write for info. (*0-7384-0098-X*) IBM Cary NC.

Degoulet, Patrice. Introduction to Medical Informatics. LC 96-18687. 242p. 1996. 45.00 (*0-387-94641-1*) Spr-Verlag.

DeGourville, Frank. Universal School of Street Fighting. (Illus.). 1984. pap. 7.95 (*0-931981-03-4*) Am Martial Arts Pub.

DeGowin, Richard L. DeGowin & DeGowin's Diagnostic Examination. 6th ed. LC 93-38286. 1994. text 37.00 (*0-07-016338-3*) McGraw-Hill HPD.

— DeGowin's Diagnostic Examination. 7th ed. LC 99-19800. (Illus.). 1050p. 1999. 39.95 (*0-07-016443-6*) McGraw-Hill HPD.

Degraaf. College Physics. (C). 2001. text 65.00 (*0-03-073991-8*) Harcourt Coll Pubs.

DeGraaf, Donald G., et al. Programming for Parks, Recreation, & Leisure Services: A Servant Leadership Approach. LC 98-88780. 340p. 1999. 37.95 (*0-910251-99-1*, No. DEG104) Venture Pub PA.

— Steps to Successful Programming: A Student Handbook to Accompany Programming for Parks, Recreation, & Leisure Services: A Servant Leadership Approach. vlii, 132p. 1999. ring bd., wbk. ed. 10.95 (*1-892132-04-4*, DEG104) Venture Pub PA.

DeGraaf, Kathy H. Programming Embedded Systems for Microsoft Windows CE. 1999. pap. text 49.99 (*0-7356-0548-3*) Microsoft.

***DeGraaf, Richard M.** New England Wildlife: Management of Forested Habitats. 273p. 1998. per. 28.00 (*0-16-060837-6*, Agriculture Dept) USGPO.

DeGraaf, Richard M. & Rappole, John H. Neotropical Migratory Birds: Natural History, Distribution, & Population Change. (Comstock Bk.). (Illus.). 560p. 1995. pap. text 29.95 (*0-8014-8265-8*) Cornell U Pr.

DeGraaf, Richard M. & Rudis, Deborah D. Amphibians & Reptiles of New England: Habitats & Natural History. LC 83-5125. (Illus.). 96p. 1983. pap. 13.95 (*0-87023-400-5*) U of Mass Pr.

***DeGraaf, Richard M. & Yamasaki, Mariko.** New England Wildlife: Habitat, Natural History & Distribution. LC 99-86702. (Illus.). 560p. 2000. pap. 35.00 (*0-87451-957-8*) U Pr of New Eng.

DeGraaff, Robert M. The Book of the Toad: A Natural & Magical History of Toad-Human Relations. (Illus.). 192p. 1991. pap. 19.95 (*0-89281-261-3*) Inner Tradit.

***DeGraaff, Robert M.** Guide to South Florida Off-Road Bicycling. (Illus.). 80p. 1999. pap. 10.00 (*0-9678385-0-9*) Guide to S Florida.

DeGrace, Betty. Sunny Seniors Through Aging Eyes. (Illus.). 78p. 1995. 12.95 (*0-9621266-4-0*) IPPD.

Degrace, Peter. Wicked Problems, Righteous Solutions: Modern Paradigms in Software Engineering. (C). 1990. pap. text 39.00 (*0-13-590126-X*) P-H.

Degrada, Francesco, ed. Proceedings of the International Symposium. (Pergolesi Studies: Vol. 1). (ENG & ITA.). 217p. 1987. lib. bdg. 54.00 (*0-918728-79-7*) Pendragon NY.

— Proceedings of the International Symposium on Pergolesi. (Pergolesi Studies: Vol. 2). (ENG & ITA.). 1989. pap. text 54.00 (*88-221-0443-9*) Pendragon NY.

DeGraeve, G. M. & Eddleman, Karen. Wet Testing Program: Evaluation of Practices & Implementation, Project 94-HHE-1, 1998. LC 98-84607. 1998. write for info. (*0-9662553-3-X*) Wtr Environ Res.

DeGraf, Anna. Pioneering on the Yukon, 1892-1917. Brown, Roger S., ed. LC 92-14808. (Illus.). ix, 128p. (C). 1992. lib. bdg. 19.50 (*0-208-02362-3*, Archon Bks) Shoe String.

DeGraff, Amy. The Tower & the Well: A Psychological Interpretation of the Fairy Tales of Madame D'Aulnoy. LC 83-50517. (ENG & FRE.). 136p. 1984. pap. 12.00 (*0-917786-03-3*) Summa Pubns.

Degraff, Arthur C., et al, eds. Annual Review of Medicine: Selected Topics in the Clinical Sciences, Vol. 14. LC 51-1659. 1963. text 40.00 (*0-8243-0514-0*) Annual Reviews.

— Annual Review of Medicine: Selected Topics in the Clinical Sciences, Vol. 15. LC 51-1659. 1964. text 40.00 (*0-8243-0515-9*) Annual Reviews.

— Annual Review of Medicine: Selected Topics in the Clinical Sciences, Vol. 17. LC 51-1659. 1966. text 40.00 (*0-8243-0517-5*) Annual Reviews.

DeGraff, Deborah A. The Body Owner's Manual: An Acupuncturist's Teachings on Health & Well-Being. LC 98-234794. 336p. 1998. pap. 13.00 (*0-425-16503-5*) Berkley Pub.

DeGraff, Jerome V., jt. auth. see Johnson, Robert B.

Degraffenried, Alan. Adventures in Coloring. (Illus.). (J). 1998. pap. text 4.98 (*1-57833-008-4*) Todd Commns.

DeGraffenried, Doug, jt. auth. see Durham, Ron.

DeGraffenried, T. P. DeGraffenried: History of the DeGraffenried Family, from 1191 to 1925. (Illus.). 282p. 1992. reprint ed. pap. 44.50 (*0-8328-1778-3*); reprint ed. lib. bdg. 54.50 (*0-8328-1777-5*) Higginson Bk Co.

Degraft-Johnson, J. C. African Glory. 210p. 1986. reprint ed. pap. text 14.95 (*0-933121-03-2*) Black Classic.

DeGrand, Alexander J. Fascist Italy & Nazi Germany: The 'Fascist' Style of Rule. LC 95-14063. (Historical Connections Ser.). 128p. (C). 1995. pap. 14.99 (*0-415-10598-6*) Routledge.

Degrand, Thomas A. & Toussaint, Doug. From Actions to Answers: Proceedings of the 1989 Theoretical Advanced Study Institute on Particle Physics. 760p. 1990. text 106.00 (*981-02-0063-3*, PH-BP971); pap. text 59.00 (*981-02-0064-1*, PH-BP971S) World Scientific Pub.

DeGrandis, Robert. Healing Through the Mass. 192p. 1992. pap. 8.95 (*1-878718-10-X*, Resurrection Pr) Catholic Bk Pub.

DeGrandpre, Charles. New Hampshire Practice Vol. 7: Wills, Trusts & Gifts, 1998 Cumulative Supplement. 250p. 1998. pap. write for info. (*0-327-00703-6*, 8440914) LEXIS Pub.

— New Hampshire Practice, 1997 Vol. 7: Wills & Trusts. 3rd ed. LC 97-81025. 875p. 1997. text 70.00 (*1-55834-834-4*, 82049-11, MICHIE) LEXIS Pub.

Degrandpre, Charles A. New Hampshire Practice: Probate Law & Procedure, 1998 Cumulative Supplement (Vols. 10-12) 150p. 1998. pap. 225.00 (*0-327-00571-8*, 8203513) LEXIS Pub.

DeGrandpre, Charles A. Probate Law & Procedure Vol. 10, 11 & 12. 2nd ed. 225.00 (*0-327-12471-7*) LEXIS Pub.

DeGrandpre, Charles A. Wills, Trusts, & Gifts. 2nd ed. LC 92-32062. (New Hampshire Practice Ser.: Vol. 7). 1993. suppl. ed. 30.00 (*0-685-70868-3*, MICHIE) LEXIS Pub.

— Wills, Trusts, & Gifts. 2nd ed. LC 92-32062. (New Hampshire Practice Ser.: Vol. 7). xxiv, 655 p. 1994. 70.00 (*1-56257-339-X*, MICHIE) LEXIS Pub.

DeGrandpre, Charles A. & Robinson, Kathleen M. Probate Law & Procedure. (New Hampshire Practice Ser.: Vols. 10-12). 1130p. 1994. 210.00 (*0-88063-484-7*, MICHIE) LEXIS Pub.

DeGrandpre, Richard. Ritalin Nation: Rapid-Fire Culture & the Transformation of Human Consciousness. LC 98-20687. 160p. 1999. 23.95 (*0-393-04685-0*) Norton.

***DeGrandpre, Richard.** Ritalin Nation: Rapid-Fire Culture & the Transformation of Human Consciousness. 288p. 2000. pap. text 13.95 (*0-393-32025-1*) Norton.

DeGrandpre, Richard J., jt. ed. see Bickel, Warren K.

DeGrane, Lloyd, photos by. Tuned In: Television in American Life. (Illus.). 96p. 1991. 24.95 (*0-252-01809-5*); 11.95 (*0-252-06222-1*) U of Ill Pr.

Degrange, Michel & Roulet, Jean-Francois. Minimally Invasive Restorations with Bonding. LC 96-37504. (Illus.). 280p. 1997. 98.00 (*0-86715-327-X*) Quintessence.

Degranville, J. J., jt. auth. see Kahn, F.

Degras, Jane, ed. Communist International: Documents, 3 vols., Vol. 2. 1971. 55.00 (*0-7146-1555-2*, Pub. by F Cass Pubs) Intl Spec Bk.

— Communist International: Documents, 3 vols., Vol. 3. 1971. 55.00 (*0-7146-1556-0*, Pub. by F Cass Pubs) Intl Spec Bk.

Degras, Jane, tr. see Monnerot, Jules.

***DeGrasse, Dennis.** The Gifts of the Holy Spirit: Tools for Ministry. 72p. 1999. pap. 6.95 (*1-886973-40-7*) Dove Chr Fel.

DeGrasse, Robert W. Military Expansion, Economic Decline: The Impact of Military Spending on U. S. Economic Performance. expanded ed. LC 83-12680. (Illus.). 256p. 1983. reprint ed. pap. 79.40 (*0-7837-9964-0*, 206069100006) Bks Demand.

DeGrasse, Robert W., Jr. Military Expansion, Economic Decline: The Impact of Military Spending on U. S. Economic Performance. rev. ed. LC 83-12360. 260p. (gr. 13). 1983. pap. text 39.95 (*0-87332-260-6*) M E Sharpe.

DeGrave, Kathleen. Swindler, Spy, Rebel: The Confidence Woman in Nineteenth-Century America. 286p. 1995. 37.50 (*0-8262-1005-8*) U of Mo Pr.

DeGravelles, Charles. The Well Governed Son. Cassin, Maxine, ed. LC 87-62144. (Journal Press Bks.: Louisiana Legacy). (Illus.). 80p. (Orig.). 1987. pap. text 12.00 (*0-938498-07-X*) New Orleans Poetry.

DeGraw, Imelda G. The Denver Art Museum: Quilts & Coverlets. LC 74-7687. (Illus.). 1974. pap. 6.50 (*0-914738-02-X*) Denver Art Mus.

DeGrazia, David. Taking Animals Seriously: Mental Life & Moral Status. 312p. (C). 1996. text 59.95 (*0-521-56140-X*); pap. text 20.95 (*0-521-56760-2*) Cambridge U Pr.

DeGrazia, David, jt. ed. see Mappes, Thomas A.

DeGrazia, Emilio, et al. Likely Stories: A Collection of Untraditional Fiction. McPherson, Bruce R., ed. LC 82-129270. 224p. 1981. 14.50 (*0-914232-42-8*); pap. 7.95 (*0-914232-41-X*) McPherson & Co.

DeGrazia, Emilio, jt. ed. see DeGrazia, Monica D.

***DeGrazia, John.** The Three Little Tigers & Their Birthday Party. (Three Little Tigers Ser.: Vol. 1). (Illus.). 20p. (J). (gr. 1-8). 1999. pap. 6.00 (*0-9670522-0-3*) Tiger TImes Two.

— The Three Little Tigers Go Fishing. (Three Little Tigers Ser.: Vol. 2). (Illus.). 15p. (J). (gr. 1-8). 1999. pap. 5.00 (*0-9670522-1-1*) Tiger TImes Two.

DeGrazia, John. The Three Little Tigers Go to College. (Three Little Tigers Ser.: Vol. 4). (Illus.). 25p. (J). (gr. 1-8). 1999. pap. 6.00 (*0-9670522-3-8*) Tiger TImes Two.

DeGrazia, Monica D. & DeGrazia, Emilio, eds. 26 Minnesota Writers. 367p. 1995. pap. 13.95 (*0-931714-67-2*, Pub. by Nodin Pr) Bookmen Inc.

Degre, Alain. Tippe of Africa. LC 97-222241. 1998. pap. 15.95 (*1-86872-083-7*, Pub. by New5 Holland) Sterling.

DeGre, Gerard. The Social Compulsions of Ideas: Toward a Sociological Analysis of Knowledge. Levitt, Cyril, ed. 264p. 1984. 44.95 (*0-88738-003-4*) Transaction Pubs.

— Society & Ideology: An Inquiry into the Sociology of Knowledge. Coser, Lewis A. & Powell, Walter W., eds. LC 79-6991. (Perennial Works in Sociology). 1980. reprint ed. lib. bdg. 18.95 (*0-405-12091-5*) Ayer.

Degre, S. G., ed. Myocardial Revascularization in Acute Conditions. (Bibliotheca Cardiologica Ser.: No. 39). (Illus.). vi, 146p. 1986. 100.00 (*3-8055-4142-2*) S Karger.

DeGree, Melvin, ed. see Hamilton, Said.

DeGregori, Thomas R. A Theory of Technology: Continuity & Change in Human Development. LC 85-11800. 278p. (Orig.). 1985. reprint ed. pap. 86.20 (*0-608-00027-2*, 206079300006) Bks Demand.

DeGregorio, Christine A. Networks of Champions: Leadership, Access & Advisory in the U. S. House of Representatives. LC 96-39404. 304p. (C). 1997. text 42.50 (*0-472-10762-3*, 10762) U of Mich Pr.

***DeGregorio, Christine A.** Networks of Champions: Leadership, Access & Advocacy in the U.S. House of Representative. 304p. (C). 1999. pap. text 19.95 (*0-472-08614-6*, 08614) U of Mich Pr.

DeGregorio, George. Joe DiMaggio: An Informal Biography. LC 90-30669. (Illus.). 288p. 1990. reprint ed. pap. 8.95 (*0-939219-06-9*) Townhouse Pub.

***Degregorio, Jorge.** My Head & My Heart: Sex, Love, Life & the Unconscious. 2000. 24.95 (*0-679-46297-X*) Random.

Degregorio, Michael E. Secret Spot. LC TXU-753-190. (Illus.). 160p. (Orig.). 1996. pap. 14.95 (*0-9649417-6-7*) Big Water.

— Thunder Bay. LC TXU-686-966. (Illus.). 327p. (Orig.). 1995. pap. 14.95 (*0-9649417-7-5*) Big Water.

DeGregorio, Michael W. Tamoxifen & Breast Cancer. 2nd ed. LC 99-35322. 142p. 1999. pap. text 12.95 (*0-300-07951-6*) Yale U Pr.

DeGregorio, Michael W. & Wiebe, Valerie J. Tamoxifen & Breast Cancer. LC 93-43148. (Illus.). 136p. (C). 1994. 30.00 (*0-300-05907-8*) Yale U Pr.

Degregorio, Paul S. Kingdom of Cambodia: Pre-Election Technical Assessment, August 1995. ii, 84p. 1995. pap. 10.00 (*1-879720-82-5*) Intl Fndt Elect.

Degregorio, Paul S. & Ross, Kimberley L. Albania: A Pre-Election Technical Assessment, March 20-28, 1996. LC 96-31133. vi, 88p. 1996. pap. text 11.00 (*1-879720-12-4*) Intl Fndt Elect.

Degregorio, Paul S., et al. Albania: IFES Observer Coordination to the OSCE Albanian Election Observation Mission, June - July 1997. ii, 240p. 1997. pap. text 26.00 (*1-879720-53-1*) Intl Fndt Elect.

DeGregorio, Richard J. Epitaph. 192p. (Orig.). 1992. pap. 6.25 (*0-9633746-0-5*) Small Busn Improve.

***DeGregorio, Steve.** Confessions of a Stalker. LC 99-64382. 1999. 25.00 (*0-7388-0450-9*); pap. 18.00 (*0-7388-0451-7*) Xlibris Corp.

DeGregorio, William A. The Complete Book of U. S. Presidents. 4th ed. LC 93-13441. 784p. pap. 21.00 (*0-942637-92-5*) Barricade Bks.

Degrell, I. Atlas of the Diseases of the Mammary Gland: Atlas der Brustdruesenerkrankungen. (Illus.). 186p. 1976. 121.75 (*3-8055-2219-3*) S Karger.

Degremont. Water Treatment Glossary: English/French-French/English. (ENG & FRE.). 336p. 1995. 175.00 (*0-7859-9273-1*) Fr & Eur.

Degrift, Craig T. Van, see Van Degrift, Craig T.

***DeGroat, Diane.** Jingle Bells, Homework Smells. LC 99-50291. 32p. (J). (ps-3). 2000. 14.95 (*0-688-17543-0*, Wm Morrow); lib. bdg. 14.89 (*0-688-17544-9*, Wm Morrow) Morrow Avon.

DeGroat, Diane. Roses Are Pink, Your Feet Really Stink. LC 94-43774. (Illus.). (J). 1996. lib. bdg. 14.93 (*0-688-13605-2*, Wm Morrow) Morrow Avon.

— Roses Are Pink, Your Feet Really Stink. LC 94-43774. (Illus.). 32p. (J). (gr. k-3). 1996. 15.00 (*0-688-13604-4*, Wm Morrow) Morrow Avon.

Degroat, Diane. Roses Are Pink, Your Feet Really Stink. LC 94-43774. (Illus.). 32p. (J). (gr. k-3). 1997. mass mkt. 4.95 (*0-688-15220-1*, Wm Morrow) Morrow Avon.

Degroat, Diane. Thanksgiving. 1924. write for info. (*0-688-17540-6*, Wm Morrow) Morrow Avon.

***DeGroat, Diane.** Trick or Treat, Smell My Feet. LC 97-32916. (Illus.). 32p. (J). (gr. k-3). 1998. 14.93 (*0-688-15767-X*, Wm Morrow) Morrow Avon.

DeGroat, Florence. Animal Stories. (Illus.). 88p. (J). (gr. 2-6). 1983. pap. 2.95 (*0-87516-509-5*) DeVorss.

— Resurrection, Vol. 2. LC 81-67782. (Universal Man Ser.: Vol. 2). (Illus.). 168p. (Orig.). 1981. pap. 6.50 (*0-87516-456-0*) DeVorss.

— Tales from Galilee. 96p. (Orig.). (J). (gr. 4 up). 1982. pap. 4.50 (*0-87516-485-4*) DeVorss.

— This Drama Called Life: An Introduction to Advanced Christianity. (Illus.). 49p. 1984. pap. 6.95 (*0-942494-89-X*) Coleman Pub.

— Universal Man, Vol. 1. LC 80-69413. 117p. 1981. reprint ed. pap. 6.50 (*0-87516-428-5*) DeVorss.

DeGroff, Dolores F., jt. auth. see Neelakanta, Perambur S.

DeGrood, David H. Consciousness in Social Life, Vol. 15. (Philosophical Currents Ser.). 112p. (Orig.). 1976. pap. 21.00 (*90-6032-067-0*, Pub. by B R Gruner) Humanities.

— Haeckel's Theory of the Unity of Nature. (Praxis Ser.: Vol. 8). iv, 98p. (Orig.). 1982. pap. 21.00 (*90-6032-216-9*, Pub. by B R Gruner) Humanities.

— Radical Currents in Contemporary Philosophy. LC 73-110806. 286p. 1971. 15.00 (*0-87527-029-8*) Green.

Degroodt, Mary P. A Handbook for the Recovering Alcoholic-Addict. Rayha, Bonnie J., ed. (Illus.). 85p. (Orig.). 1989. pap. text 9.95 (*0-9625297-0-2*) Dunbar Bks.

DeGroot, Barb, jt. auth. see El-Hai, Jack.

DeGroot, David J. Basic Bon Sai Design. 3rd ed. (Illus.). 92p. 1998. reprint ed. pap. 12.95 (*0-9658313-1-0*) Am Bonsai.

DeGroot, Gerard J. Blighty. 320p. (C). 1996. text 73.25 (*0-582-06138-5*, Pub. by Addison-Wesley) Longman.

— Blighty: British Society in the Era of the Great War. LC 95-45475. 320p. (C). 1996. pap. text 30.94 (*0-582-06137-7*, Pub. by Addison-Wesley) Longman.

***DeGroot, Gerard J.** A Soldier & a Woman: Women in the Military, Women & Men in History Series. 448p. 2000. pap. 24.00 (*0-582-41438-5*) Longman.

***DeGroot, Gerard J. & Peniston-Bird, C. M.** Women in the Military. 400p. 2001. 69.95 (*0-582-41439-3*) Longman.

DeGroot, Henry. The Comstock Papers. Dickerson, Donald, ed. LC 85-80913. 111p. 1985. pap. 1.50 (*0-913205-08-7*) Grace Dangberg.

DeGroot, J. & Van Vliet, J. The High Pressure Sodium Lamp. 329p. 1986. 135.00 (*90-201-1902-8*, PB-19-86) Illum Eng.

DeGroot, J. J. The Religious System of China, 6 vols. 1982. reprint ed. 195.00 (*0-89986-346-9*) Oriental Bk Store.

DeGroot, J. J. & Van Vliet, A. J., eds. The High Pressure Sodium Lamp. (Philips Technical Library). (Illus.). 338p. (C). 1986. text 145.00 (*0-333-43245-2*) Scholium Intl.

DeGroot, Leslie J., et al, eds. Endocrinology, 1. 3rd ed. LC 93-8208. 1994. write for info. (*0-7216-4263-2*, W B Saunders Co) Harcrt Hlth Sci Grp.

— Endocrinology, 2. 3rd ed. LC 93-8208. 1994. write for info. (*0-7216-4264-0*, W B Saunders Co) Harcrt Hlth Sci Grp.

— Endocrinology, 3. 3rd ed. LC 93-8208. 1994. write for info. (*0-7216-4265-9*, W B Saunders Co) Harcrt Hlth Sci Grp.

— Endocrinology, Set. 3rd ed. LC 93-8208. 1994. text 475.00 (*0-7216-4262-4*, W B Saunders Co) Harcrt Hlth Sci Grp.

Degroot, Leslie J. & Jameson, Larry. Endocrinology, 3 vols. 4th ed. 2925p. Date not set. text. write for info. (*0-7216-7840-8*, W B Saunders Co) Harcrt Hlth Sci Grp.

DeGroot, Leslie J., et al. The Thyroid & Its Diseases. 5th ed. LC 83-27411. 907p. (C). 1984. 82.00 (*0-471-88688-2*) Church.

D

***Dehne, F., et al, eds.** Algorithms & Data Structures: 6th International Workshop, WADS'99, Vancouver, Canada, August 11-14, 1999, Proceedings. LC 99-40622. (Lecture Notes in Computer Science Ser.: Vol. 1663). x, 367p. 1999. pap. 62.00 (*3-540-66279-0*) Spr-Verlag.

Dehne, Frank, et al, eds. Advances in Computing & Information - ICCI '91: International Conference on Computing & Information, Ottawa, Canada, May 27-29, 1991 Proceedings. (Lecture Notes in Computer Science Ser.: Vol. 497). viii, 745p. 1991. 79.95 (*0-387-54029-6*) Spr-Verlag.

— Algorithms & Data Structures. (Lecture Notes in Computer Science Ser.: Vol. 382). ix, 592p. 1989. 63.00 (*0-387-51542-9*, 3415) Spr-Verlag.

— Algorithms & Data Structures: Second Workshop, WADS '91, Ottawa, Canada, August 14-16, 1991 Proceedings. (Lecture Notes in Computer Science Ser.: Vol. 519). x, 495p. 1991. 53.95 (*0-387-54343-0*) Spr-Verlag.

Dehne, Frank, et al. Algorithms & Data Structures: Proceedings of the Third Workshop, WADS 93, Montreal, Canada, August 11-13, 1993. LC 93-28887. (Lecture Notes in Computer Science Ser.: Vol. 709). 1993. 87.95 (*0-387-57155-8*) Spr-Verlag.

Dehne, Frank, ed. see Third Workshop on Algorithms & Data Structures Sta.

Dehne, George C., et al. Marketing Higher Education: A Handbook for College Administrators. 126p. (Orig.). 1991. 18.00 (*1-879994-02-X*) Consortium Advan.

Dehne, H. W., jt. auth. see European Foundation for Plant Pathology Staff.

Dehnel, Carolyn. A Little Mexican Cookbook. (Traditional Little Cookbooks of the World Ser.). (Illus.). 60p. 1991. 7.95 (*0-87701-860-X*) Chronicle Bks.

— A Little Texas Cookbook. (Illus.). 60p. 1992. 7.95 (*0-8118-0114-4*) Chronicle Bks.

Dehner, Louis P., jt. ed. see Humphrey, G. Bennett.

Dehner, Mary. How to Move from College into a Secure Job. LC 93-4124. 192p. 1993. pap. 12.95 (*0-8442-4170-9*, VGM Career) NTC Contemp Pub Co.

Dehning, W. The Adaptation of Virtual Man-Computer Interfaces to User Requirements in Dialogs. (Lecture Notes in Computer Science Ser.: Vol. 110). 142p. 1981. 30.00 (*0-387-10826-2*) Spr-Verlag.

Dehoff. Atlas of Small Animal Surgery. 1999. text 75.00 (*0-7216-6787-2*, W B Saunders Co) Harcrt Hlth Sci Grp.

— Thermodynamic in Materials Science. 2nd ed. 2000. 69.74 (*0-07-229137-0*) McGraw.

DeHoff, R. T. Thermodynamics in Materials Science. LC 92-40109. (Series in Materials Science & Engineering). 576p. (C). 1993. 90.00 (*0-07-016313-8*) McGraw.

DeHoff, Robert T. & Rhines, Frederick N. Quantitative Microscopy. (Illus.). 432p. (C). 1991. reprint ed. 104.00 (*1-878907-31-X*) TechBooks.

DeHoog, Genevieve & DeHoog, Herman. Devotions for Choirs, Bk. 1. 64p. 1997. pap. 6.95 (*0-687-05248-3*) Abingdon.

DeHoog, Herman, jt. auth. see DeHoog, Genevieve.

DeHoog, Susan, jt. auth. see Grant, Anne.

DeHoogh, Eugenia, et al. The Real World of Engineering: Case History, No. 50. (SPA & ENG., Illus.). 64p. 3.50 (*0-614-05219-X*, CHN05005913.5M) ASFE.

— The Real World of Engineering: Case History, No. 51. (SPA & ENG., Illus.). 64p. 3.50 (*0-614-05220-3*, CHN05105913.5M) ASFE.

— The Real World of Engineering: Case History, No. 52. (SPA & ENG., Illus.). 64p. 3.50 (*0-614-05221-1*, CHN05205913.5M) ASFE.

DeHoop, Adrianus T., ed. Handbook of Radiation & Scattering of Waves. (Illus.). 1120p. 1995. text 209.00 (*0-12-208655-4*) Acad Pr.

Dehoop, Helen. Case Configuration & Noun Phrase Interpretation. Horn, Laurence, ed. LC 96-21117. (Linguistics Ser.). 250p. 1996. text 74.00 (*0-8153-2560-6*) Garland.

Dehority, Burk A. Laboratory Manual for Classification & Morphology of Rumen Ciliate Protozoa. 128p. 1993. lib. bdg. 59.95 (*0-8493-4875-7*, QL368) CRC Pr.

Dehousse. Europe: Impossible States. Morgan, Caroline, tr. LC 96-38021. 152p. 1997. text 59.95 (*0-312-17357-1*) St Martin.

— European Courts of Justice. LC 98-13874. 213p. 1998. text 55.00 (*0-312-21510-X*) St Martin.

DeHoyos, Art, tr. The Bluntschli Rituals of Craft Masonry As Worked in the Grand Lodge of the Sun Bayreuth, Germany. 58p. 1992. reprint ed. pap. 9.95 (*1-56459-269-3*) Kessinger Pub.

DeHoyos, Genevieve. Stewardship: The Divine Order. LC 81-82055. 200p. 1982. 13.98 (*0-88290-191-5*, 1065) Horizon Utah.

Dehue, Trudy. Changing the Rules: Psychology in the Netherlands, 1900-1985. (Cambridge Studies in the History of Psychology). (Illus.). 216p. (C). 1995. text 59.95 (*0-521-47522-8*) Cambridge U Pr.

Dei-Anang, Michael F. & Osadebay, Dennis C. Early West African Poetry & Drama, 3 vols. in 1. (B. E. Ser.: No. 66). 1952. 30.00 (*0-8115-3016-7*) Periodicals Srv.

Dei, Edwin, jt. auth. see Stafford, Walter W.

***Dei, Lhashipriya.** Development of Temple Architecture in India: With Reference to Orissa in the Golden Age. LC 98-901727. 1998. 26.00 (*81-86791-12-4*, Pub. by Punthi Pus) S Asia.

Dei, Santilata. Vaisnavism in Orissa. (C). 1988. 34.00 (*0-685-33355-8*, Pub. by Punthi Pus) S Asia.

Deiara, Adelina. Finale. 1988. reprint ed. lib. bdg. 49.00 (*0-7812-0754-1*) Rprt Serv.

Deibel, Karen. Creating Peaceful Meals: A Vegetarian Cookbook. 208p. 1998. reprint ed. spiral bd. 20.00 (*0-9664136-0-1*) K Deibel.

Deibel, Marge. Crostics: Puzzles Designed from Quotations. 35p. (Orig.). 1998. pap. 9.00 (*0-9672106-0-7*) Anaxtix Pubs.

Deibel, Terrence L. Pakistan in the Bush Years: Foreign Aid & Foreign Influence. (Pew Case Studies in International Affairs). 50p. (C). 1994. pap. text 3.50 (*1-56927-365-0*, GU Schl Foreign) Geo U Inst Dplmcy.

Deibel, Terry L. Presidents, Public Opinion & Power. LC 87-80536. (Headline Ser.: No. 280). (Orig.). 1986. pap. 5.95 (*0-87124-112-9*) Foreign Policy.

Deibel, Terry L. & Gaddis, John L., eds. Containment: Concept & Policy. 746p. (Orig.). (C). 1995. pap. text 40.00 (*0-7881-2156-1*) DIANE Pub.

Deibel, Terry L., jt. ed. see Gaddis, John L.

Deibert, Edward, jt. auth. see Koretz, Daniel T.

Deibert, Kenneth, ed. see Gernes, Phyllis.

Deibert, Richard I. Mark. (Interpretation Bible Studies). (Illus.). 144p. 1999. pap. 7.00 (*0-664-50078-1*) Geneva Press.

Deibert, Ronald J. Parchment, Printing, & Hypermedia: Communication & World Order Transformation. LC 97-15336. (New Directions in World Politics Ser.). (Illus.). 344p. 1997. pap. 19.50 (*0-231-10713-7*); lib. bdg. 52.00 (*0-231-10712-9*) Col U Pr.

Deibler, Barbara E. A Valuable Collection of Neat Books Well Chosen: The Pennsylvania Assembly Library. 64p. 1994. write for info. (*0-9643048-1-3*) Penn Capitol Presrv.

Deibler, Ellis W. A Semantic & Structural Analysis of Romans. LC 98-61142. 382p. 1998. pap. 25.00 (*1-55671-072-0*) S I L Intl.

Deich, Joy. Activity Fun: Activities for Ages 3-8. 80p. 1991. pap., teacher ed. 12.95 (*0-9629698-8-5*) Aaron Lake Pub.

— J. P.'s Pumpkin Patch: Too Many Pumpkins. 32p. (J). (gr. k-4). 1993. pap. 2.95 (*0-9629698-5-0*) Aaron Lake Pub.

Deicher, Susanne. Mondrian. (Illus.). 1994. pap. 9.99 (*3-8228-8885-0*) Taschen Amer.

— Mondrian. 1995. pap. 5.99 (*3-8228-9237-8*) Taschen Amer.

— Mondrian. (SPA.). 1996. pap. 9.99 (*3-8228-8831-1*) Taschen Amer.

Deichert, Jerome. Nebraska Population Projections, 1985-2020. (Nebraska Economic & Business Reports: No. 32). 1982. 17.50 (*0-318-02059-9*) Bur Busn Res U Nebr.

Deichert, Jerome A., et al. Migration Patterns of Young Adults in Nebraska. (Nebraska Economic & Business Reports: No. 25). 1978. 5.00 (*0-686-28413-5*) Bur Busn Res U Nebr.

Deichert, Jerome A., jt. auth. see Love, Douglas O.

Deichert, Jerome A., jt. auth. see Pursell, Donald E.

Deichert, Ulrich & Schlief, Reinhard, eds. Hysterosalpingo-Contrast Sonography: An Atlas & Textbook. LC 94-48294. 1995. write for info. (*0-7923-3335-7*) Kluwer Academic.

Deichgraber, Karl. Ausgewahlte Kleine Schriften. x, 414p. 1984. write for info. (*3-615-00002-1*) G Olms Pubs.

— Die Griechische Empirikerschule. (GER.). viii, 398p. 1965. write for info. (*3-296-12120-X*) G Olms Pubs.

Deichgraeber, Karl. Die Epidemien und das Corpus Hippocraticum: Voruntersuchung zu einer Geschichte der koischen Aerzteschule. (GER.). 187p. (C). 1971. reprint ed. 84.60 (*3-11-003635-5*) De Gruyter.

Deichman, Elizabeth & Kociecki, Regina, eds. Working with the Elderly: An Introduction. LC 89-10856. (Golden Age Books - Perspectives on Aging Ser.). 299p. 1989. 31.95 (*0-87975-520-2*); pap. 19.95 (*0-87975-534-2*) Prometheus Bks.

Deichmann, Hans. Ordinary Objects. Constantine, Peter & Glassgold, Peter, trs. LC 97-32567. 1997. 22.00 (*1-56886-048-X*) Marsilio Pubs.

Deichmann, Paul. German Air Force Operations in Support of the Army. LC 68-22550. (German Air Force in World War 2 Ser.). (Illus.). 1968. reprint ed. 19.95 (*0-405-00040-5*) Ayer.

— Luftwaffe Methods in the Selection of Offensive Weapons: Karlsruhe Study, Vol. 1. (USAF Historical Studies: No. 187). 102p. 1955. reprint ed. pap. text 28.95 (*0-89126-149-4*) MA-AH Pub.

***Deichmann, Paul.** Spearhead for Blitzkrieg: Luftwaffe Operations in Support of Army, 1939-1945. 1999. mass mkt. 6.99 (*0-8041-1695-4*) Ivy Books.

Deichmann, Paul. Spearhead for Blitzkrieg: Luftwaffe Operations in Support of the Army, 1939-1945. Price, Alfred, ed. & intro. by. 160p. 1996. 29.95 (*1-85367-241-6*, Pub. by Greenhill Bks) Stackpole.

Deichmann, Ute. Biologists under Hitler. Dunlap, Thomas, tr. from GER. LC 95-33338.Tr. of Biologen unter Hitler. (Illus.). 480p. 1996. 44.50 (*0-674-07404-1*) HUP.

— Biologists under Hitler.Tr. of Biologen unter Hitler. 1999. pap. text 18.95 (*0-674-07405-X*) HUP.

Deickler, Judith, jt. auth. see Lank, Edith.

Deida, David. Intimate Communion: Awakening Your Sexual Essence. 250p. 1995. pap. 11.95 (*1-55874-374-X*, 374X) Health Comm.

— It's a Guy Thing: An Owner's Manual for Women. LC 97-21703. 200p. 1997. pap. 11.95 (*1-55874-464-9*); pap. 11.95 (*0-614-27648-9*) Health Comm.

— The Way of the Superior Man: A Spiritual Guide to Mastering the Challenge of Women, Work & Sexual Desire. LC 96-72534. 256p. 1997. 23.95 (*1-889762-10-5*) Plexus.

Deidra, Carol A. Creepy Crawlies. (J). (gr. k-2). 1997. 11.95 (*1-55734-603-8*) Tchr Create Mat.

— The Earth. (J). (gr. k-2). 1997. 11.95 (*1-55734-613-5*) Tchr Create Mat.

Deidre, Davis. Fresh Look at Saucing Foods. 1994. pap. write for info. (*0-201-62696-9*) Addison-Wesley.

Deif, A. Sensitivity Analysis in Linear Systems. (Illus.). 260p. 1986. 123.95 (*0-387-16312-3*) Spr-Verlag.

Deif, David M. Price of a Rumour. 165p. Date not set. 15.95 (*0-7541-0035-9*) Communs Plus.

Deifer, David E., ed. see Sheppard, Leah.

***Deift, P. A.** Orthogonal Polynomials & Random Matrices: A Riemann-Hilbert Approach. LC 98-74666. (Lecture Notes in Mathematics Ser.). 273p. 1999. write for info. (*0-9658703-2-4*) NYU Courant.

Deift, Percy, et al, eds. Dynamical Systems & Probabilistic Methods in Partial Differential Equations: 1994 Summer Seminar on Dynamical Systems & Probabilistic Methods for Nonlinear Waves, MSRI, Berkeley, CA, June 20-July 1, 1994. LC 95-44661. (Lectures in Applied Mathematics: Vol. 31). 268p. 1995. pap. 29.00 (*0-8218-0368-9*, LAM/31) Am Math.

Deift, Percy & McLaughlin, K. T. A Continuum Limit of the Toda Lattice. LC 97-31680. (Memoirs of the American Mathematical Society Ser.). 216p. 1998. pap. 51.00 (*0-8218-0691-2*) Am Math.

Deift, Percy, et al. Loop Groups, Discrete Versions of Some Classical Integrable Systems, & Rank 2 Extensions. LC 92-28571. (Memoirs Ser.: No. 479). 101p. 1992. pap. 26.00 (*0-8218-2540-2*, MEMO/100/479) Am Math.

***Deig, Denise.** Positional Release Techniques. (Illus.). 208p. 2000. 65.00 (*0-7506-7225-0*) Buttrwrth-Heinemann.

Deigaard, R., jt. auth. see Fredsoe, J.

Deigert, Paula. Bed & Breakfasts of Montana, Wyoming, Idaho, South Dakota Directory, 1993-94. (Illus.). 34p. (Orig.). 1993. pap. text. write for info. (*0-9625887-3-3*) B & B Western Ad.

Deigh, John. The Sources of Moral Agency: Essays in Moral Psychology & Freudian Theory. 269p. (C). 1996. text 59.95 (*0-521-55418-7*); pap. text 20.95 (*0-521-55622-8*) Cambridge U Pr.

Deigh, John, ed. Ethics & Personality: Essays in Moral Psychology. 272p. 1992. pap. text 18.50 (*0-226-14128-4*); lib. bdg. 42.50 (*0-226-14127-6*) U Ch Pr.

Deighan, Maurice. County Court Practice & Procedure. 1980. 45.00 (*0-7855-7329-1*, Pub. by Fourmat Pub) St Mut.

— County Court Practice & Procedure. 152p. 1984. 88.00 (*0-906840-80-5*, Pub. by Fourmat Pub) St Mut.

Deighan, Mike, jt. auth. see James, Stu.

Deighton, Anne. The Impossible Peace: Britain, the Division of Germany, & the Origins of the Cold War. (Illus.). 296p. 1993. reprint ed. pap. text 24.95 (*0-19-827898-5*) OUP.

Deighton, Anne, ed. Building Postwar Europe: National Decision-Makers & European Institutions, 1948-1963. LC 94-43717. 1995. text 75.00 (*0-312-12580-1*) St Martin.

Deighton, H. Day in the Life of Ancient Athens. 1995. pap. 16.95 (*1-85399-137-6*, Pub. by Brist Class Pr) Focus Pub-R Pullins.

— A Day in the Life of Ancient Rome. 1992. pap. 16.95 (*1-85399-136-8*, Pub. by Brist Class Pr) Focus Pub-R Pullins.

Deighton, L. Violent Ward. 1994. mass mkt. 6.50 (*0-06-109342-4*) HarpC.

***Deighton, Len.** Basic French Cookery Course. (Illus.). 223p. 2000. reprint ed. pap. text 14.00 (*0-7881-9017-2*) DIANE Pub.

Deighton, Len. Battle of Britain. 1999. pap. text 12.99 (*1-84022-208-5*) Wrdsworth Edits.

— Billion-Dollar Brain. large type ed. 384p. 1983. 11.50 (*0-7089-0900-0*) Ulverscroft.

***Deighton, Len.** Blitzkrieg. (Illus.). 2000. 9.99 (*0-7858-1207-5*) Bk Sales Inc.

Deighton, Len. Blood, Tears & Folly. 1999. 12.99 (*0-7858-1114-1*) Bk Sales Inc.

***Deighton, Len.** Catch a Falling Spy. large type ed. 328p. 2000. lib. bdg. 27.95 (*1-58547-030-9*) Ctr Point Pubg.

Deighton, Len. Charity. large type ed. LC 97-2924. (Large Print Book Ser.). 1997. 26.95 (*1-56895-436-0*) Wheeler Pub.

— City of Gold. large type ed. 595p. 1993. pap. 15.95 (*1-56054-898-3*) Thorndike Pr.

— City of Gold. large type ed. 595p. 1992. reprint ed. lib. bdg. 21.95 (*1-56054-545-3*) Thorndike Pr.

— Esperanza. 1999. 29.95 (*84-08-02842-1*) Planeta Edit.

— Faith. large type ed. LC 94-42518. 522p. 1995. lib. bdg. 25.95 (*0-7862-0381-1*) Thorndike Pr.

— Faith. large type ed. LC 94-42518. 522p. 1996. pap. 19.95 (*0-7862-0382-X*) Thorndike Pr.

***Deighton, Len.** Fighter. 2000. 9.99 (*0-7858-1208-3*) Bk Sales Inc.

Deighton, Len. Hope. 1996. 24.00 (*0-614-15487-1*) HarpC.

— Hope. 320p. 1996. mass mkt. 6.99 (*0-06-109555-9*, HarperPrism) HarpC.

— Hope. large type ed. (Bernard Samson Ser.). 1996. 26.95 (*1-56895-315-1*) Wheeler Pub.

— Only When I Laugh. 256p. 1987. 16.45 (*0-89296-175-9*, Pub. by Mysterious Pr) Little.

— Spy Hook. large type ed. LC 89-4673. 454p. 1990. pap. 14.95 (*0-89621-943-7*) Thorndike Pr.

— Spy Line. large type ed. LC 90-10799. 446p. 1990. 21.95 (*0-89621-992-5*) Thorndike Pr.

— Spy Line. large type ed. 1990. reprint ed. pap. 15.95 (*0-89621-983-6*) Thorndike Pr.

— Spy Line. 336p. 1991. reprint ed. mass mkt. 5.99 (*0-345-37006-6*) Ballantine Pub Grp.

— Spy Sinker. 448p. 1991. mass mkt. 5.99 (*0-06-109928-7*, Harp PBks) HarpC.

— Spy Sinker. large type ed. LC 90-29907. 556p. 1991. pap. 16.95 (*1-56054-992-0*) Thorndike Pr.

— Spy Sinker. large type ed. LC 90-29907. 556p. 1991. reprint ed. lib. bdg. 22.95 (*1-56054-121-0*) Thorndike Pr.

— Winter. 1989. mass mkt. 5.95 (*0-345-35931-3*) Ballantine Pub Grp.

— Winter. 1988. write for info. (*0-318-62991-7*) Random.

Deighton-Smith, Rex & Jacobs, Scott H., eds. Regulatory Impact Analysis: Best Practices in OECD Countries. LC 98-133466. 296p. 1997. pap. 37.00 (*92-64-15603-8*, 42-97-08-1, Pub. by Org for Econ) OECD.

Deignan, Kathleen P. Christ Spirit: The Eschatology of Shaker Christianity. LC 91-40688. (American Theological Library Association Monograph: No. 29). 316p. 1992. 44.50 (*0-8108-2489-2*) Scarecrow.

Deihl. The Teddy Bear That Prowled at Night. (J). 1998. pap. 7.95 (*0-671-75188-3*) S&S Bks Yung.

Deihl, Edna G. The Teddy Bear That Prowled at Night. (Illus.). 24p. (J). (gr. k-3). 1991. reprint ed. pap. 7.95 (*0-88138-079-2*, Green Tiger S&S) S&S Childrens.

***Deijord, Nils K.** Human Instincts Explained. LC 99-93745. 2000. pap. 10.95 (*0-533-13127-8*) Vantage.

Deike, Marta, ed. see Drucker, Johanna.

***Deike, Ruth.** Stone Wall Secrets Teacher's Guide: Exploring Geology in the Classroom. (Illus.). 80p. 1998. pap., teacher ed. 9.95 (*0-88448-196-4*) Tilbury Hse.

Deikert, Volker & Rozenberg, Grzegorz, eds. The Book of Traces. LC 94-39387. 588p. 1995. text 119.00 (*981-02-2058-8*) World Scientific Pub.

Deikman, Arthur J. Evaluating Spiritual & Utopian Groups. 16p. 1988. pap. 7.00 (*0-904674-13-4*, Pub. by Octagon Pr) ISHK.

— The Observing Self: Mysticism & Psychotherapy. LC 81-70486. 208p. 1983. reprint ed. pap. 14.50 (*0-8070-2951-3*) Beacon Pr.

— The Wrong Way Home: Uncovering the Patterns of Cult Behavior in American Society. 208p. (C). 1994. pap. 12.95 (*0-8070-2915-7*) Beacon Pr.

Deilege, I., jt. ed. see McAdams, Stephen.

Deiler, J. Hanno. A History of the German Churches in Louisiana, 1823-1893. Condon, Marie S., ed. 155p. 1995. pap. 17.50 (*0-8063-4577-2*) Clearfield Co.

— The Settlement of the German Coast of Louisiana & Creoles: With a New Preface, Chronology & Index. LC 67-28597. (Illus.). 154p. 1998. reprint ed. pap. 20.00 (*0-8063-0092-2*) Clearfield Co.

Deilgat, Valerie, jt. auth. see Halvorson, Ron.

Deilgat, Valerie, jt. auth. see Hill, Sally.

Deimann, Sven & Dyssli, Bernard, eds. Environmental Rights: Law, Litigation & Access to Justice. (Environmental Law Ser.). 2200p. 1995. 88.00 (*1-874698-11-2*, Pub. by Federation Pr) Gaunt.

Deimel, L. E., et al, eds. Software Engineering Education: SEI Conference 1990, Pittsburgh, Pennsylvania, U. S. A., April 2-3, 1990 Proceedings. (Lecture Notes in Computer Science Ser.: Vol. 423). vi, 164p. 1990. 32.95 (*0-387-97274-9*) Spr-Verlag.

Deimling, Barbara. Botticelli. 1996. pap. 9.99 (*3-8228-9313-7*) Taschen Amer.

Deimling, H., ed. The Chester Plays, Vol. I. (EETS Extra Ser.: Vol. 62). 1968. reprint ed. 14.95 (*0-19-722557-8*) OUP.

Deimling, Klaus. Multivalued Differential Equations. LC 92-16953. (Series in Nonlinear Analysis & Applications: Vol. 1). xii, 260p. (C). 1992. 99.95 (*3-11-013212-5*) De Gruyter.

Dein, Simon, jt. auth. see Littlewood, Roland.

Deineko, N. V., tr. see Krishtalik, L. I.

Deiner. Resources for Educating Children with Diverse Abilities: Birth to Eight. 3rd ed. LC 98-75254. 1998. pap. text 53.00 (*0-15-505471-6*, Pub. by Harcourt Coll Pubs) Harcourt.

Deiner, Penny L. Infants & Toddlers: Development & Program Planning. LC 96-75659. 594p. (C). 1996. text 51.00 (*0-15-502064-1*, Pub. by Harcourt Coll Pubs) Harcourt.

— Resources for Teaching Young Children with Diverse Abilities: Birth Through Eight. 2nd ed. 544p. (C). 1993. pap. text 52.50 (*0-15-500094-2*) Harcourt Coll Pubs.

Deines, Bradley W. Flight Maneuvers for the Private & Commercial Pilot: Step by Step Procedures Plus Profiles. (Illus.). 122p. (Orig.). (C). 1993. pap. text 18.95 (*1-886474-00-1*) Aero Tech AZ.

— Instrument Pilot Flight Maneuvers: Step by Step Procedures Plus Profiles. (Illus.). 101p. (Orig.). (C). 1993. pap. text 18.95 (*1-886474-01-X*) Aero Tech AZ.

— Instrument Pilot Flight Maneuvers: Step by Step Procedures Plus Profiles. 2nd ed. (Illus.). 132p. (Orig.). (C). 1996. pap. 18.95 (*1-886474-03-6*) Aero Tech AZ.

Deines, Bradley W., jt. auth. see Malmquist, Lisa.

Deines, Brian, jt. auth. see Waboose, Jan Bourdeau.

Deines, Dan, jt. auth. see Ainsworth, Penne.

Deines-Jones, Courtney & Van Fleet, Connie. Preparing Staff to Serve Patrons with Disabilities: A-How-to-Do-It Manual for Librarians. (A How-to-do-it Manual Ser.: Vol. 57). (Illus.). 160p. (Orig.). 1995. pap. 45.00 (*1-55570-234-1*) Neal-Schuman.

Deinhard, Hanna. Meaning & Expression: Toward a Sociology of Art. LC 83-18526. (Illus.). 120p. 1984. reprint ed. lib. bdg. 49.50 (*0-313-24252-6*, DEMX, Greenwood Pr) Greenwood.

Deinhardt, Friedrich & Deinhardt, Jean, eds. Viral Hepatitis: Laboratory & Clinical Science. LC 82-23675. (Liver, Normal Function & Disease Ser.: Vol. 3). (Illus.). 599p. reprint ed. pap. 185.70 (*0-608-08927-3*, 206956200005) Bks Demand.

Deinhardt, Jean, jt. ed. see Deinhardt, Friedrich.

Deinhart, Gregg J., et al, eds. Coal Combustion Products: Innovative for a Sustainable Future. (Illus.). 92p. 1998. 75.00 (*0-9662912-0-4*) Am Coal Ash Assn.

Deininger, G. & Grosskinsky, A. Der Melier-Dialog. Taran, Leonardo, ed. (Ancient Greek Literature Ser.). 263p. 1987. lib. bdg. 15.00 (*0-8240-7754-7*) Garland.

Deininger, Klaus W. Technical Change, Human Capital, & Spillovers in United States Agriculture, 1949-1985. rev. ed. LC 95-31442. (Studies on Industrial Productivity). (Illus.). 172p. 1995. text 20.00 (*0-8153-2139-2*) Garland.

***Deininger, Rolf A., et al.** Security of Public Water Supplies. 264p. 1999. pap. 59.00 (*0-7923-6122-9*) Kluwer Academic.

An Asterisk (*) at the beginning of an entry indicates that the title is appearing for the first time.

Deinzer, Harvey T. Development of Accounting Thought: With Book Review by Carl Thomas Devine. LC 83-49107. (Accounting Ser.). 192p. 1984. text 15.00 (*0-8240-6321-X*) Garland.

Deir, Costa. The Accountable Leader. Deir, Ruth N. & Deir, Salim C., eds. LC 99-71805. 288p. 1999. pap. 11.95 (*1-889433-01-2*) Intl Ldrship Sem.

Deir, Costa S. The Exemplary Leader. Deir, Ruth N. & Deir, Salim C., eds. (Orig.). 1996. pap. 11.95 (*1-889433-00-4*) Intl Ldrship Sem.

Deir, Ruth N., ed. see Deir, Costa.

Deir, Ruth N., ed. see Deir, Costa S.

Deir, Salim C., ed. see Deir, Costa.

Deir, Salim C., ed. see Deir, Costa S.

Deirmendjian, D. Electromagnetic Scattering on Spherical Polydispersions. LC 68-28759. 312p. reprint ed. pap. 96.80 (*0-608-30928-1*, 200776100064) Bks Demand.

Deiro, Judith A. Teaching with Heart: Making Healthy Connections with Students. LC 95-50203. (Illus.). 248p. 1996. 61.95 (*0-8039-6344-0*); pap. 27.95 (*0-8039-6345-9*) Corwin Pr.

Deiros, Eufrasio. La Mejor Etapa de la Vida - Hacia una Vejez Feliz: The Best Years of Your Life - Growing Old Happily. (SPA.). 144p. (Orig.). 1991. pap. 7.50 (*0-311-46127-1*) Casa Bautista.

Deiros, P. A. Diccionario Hispano-Americano de la Mision.Tr. of Hispanic-American Dictionary of the Mission. 12.99 (*0-7899-0444-6*, 498660) Editorial Unilit.

Deiros, Pablo. La Accion del Espiritu Santo en la Historia (The Work of the Holy Spirit in History) (SPA.). 1997. 10.99 (*0-89922-395-8*, C085-3958) Caribe Betania.

— El Protestantismo en America Latina.Tr. of Protestantism in Latin America. (SPA.). 1997. 8.99 (*0-89922-295-1*, C085-2951) Caribe Betania.

Deiros, Pablo A. El Amor Es Cosa Seria: Love Is Serious Business. (SPA.). 64p. 1988. pap. 3.99 (*0-311-12339-2*) Casa Bautista.

Deiros, Pablo A. & Mraida, Carlos. Latinoamerica en Llamas.Tr. of Latin America Aflame. (SPA.). 288p. 1994. 9.99 (*0-89922-457-1*, C085-4571) Caribe Betania.

Deiros, Pablo A., jt. auth. see Wagner, C. Peter.

Deis, Elizabeth J., ed. George Meredith's 1895 Collection of Three Stories: Explorations of Gender & Power. LC 96-49503. (Studies in British Literature: Vol. 26). 316p. 1997. text 99.95 (*0-7734-8779-4*) E Mellen.

Deisch, F. J. Heckaman-Heckeman Family (1729-1990), Include the Johann Adam Swank (1800-1900) Families (with Related Families) (Illus.). 945p. 1998. reprint ed. pap. 134.50 (*0-8328-9078-2*); reprint ed. lib. bdg. 144.50 (*0-8328-9077-4*) Higginson Bk Co.

Deisch, Frank J. Deisch - Teusch Family (1560-1985)m. (Illus.). 644p. 1997. reprint ed. pap. 94.50 (*0-8328-8254-2*); reprint ed. lib. bdg. 104.50 (*0-8328-8253-4*) Higginson Bk Co.

***Deise, Martin, et al.** Executive's Guide to E-Commerce: From Tactics to Strategy. LC 99-42978. 256p. 2000. 39.95 (*0-471-37639-6*) Wiley.

Deisenhofer, Johann & Norris, James R. The Photosynthetic Reaction Center, 2 vols. (Illus.). 1993. text 199.00 (*0-12-208660-0*) Acad Pr.

— The Photosynthetic Reaction Center, Vol. 1. (Illus.). 490p. 1993. text 100.00 (*0-12-208661-9*) Acad Pr.

— The Photosynthetic Reaction Center, Vol. 2. (Illus.). 574p. 1993. text 100.00 (*0-12-208662-7*) Acad Pr.

***Deiser, George F., ed.** Year Books Of Richard II. (Ames Foundation Publications). xxx,219,239p. 1999. 75.00 (*1-893606-05-8*, 323430, Pub. by W S Hein) W S Hein.

Deiser, Rudolf. Natural Health Care for Your Cat. LC 97-15620. 128p. 1997. pap. text 8.95 (*0-7641-0123-4*) Barron.

***Deisher, Beth & Gibbs, William T., eds.** Coin World Almanac: Millennium Edition. 7th ed. 720p. 2000. pap. 20.00 (*0-944945-34-1*, Coin World) Amos Ohio.

Deisler, Guillermo. Everything I Do Is Poetry. (Chapbook Ser.). 28p. 1996. pap. 6.00 (*0-945112-22-X*) Generator Pr.

Deiss, Joseph J. Herculaneum: Italy's Buried Treasure. rev. ed. LC 84-48097. (Illus.). 222p. 1989. pap. 15.95 (*0-89236-164-6*, Pub. by J P Getty Trust) OUP.

— The Town of Hercules: A Buried Treasure Trove. expanded rev. ed. LC 94-41648. (Illus.). 192p. (J). (gr. k-6). 1995. 24.95 (*0-89236-222-7*, Pub. by J P Getty Trust) OUP.

Deiss, Joseph J., ed. see Thoreau, Henry David.

Deiss, Kathryn J., tr. see Frampton, Kenneth, et al.

Deiss, Lucien. Celebration of the Word. 151p. (Orig.). 1993. pap. 11.95 (*0-8146-2090-6*) Liturgical Pr.

***Deiss, Lucien.** A Garden of Prayers. 1999. pap. 17.95 (*0-937690-39-2*, 7760) Wrld Lib Pubns.

Deiss, Lucien. God's Word Is Our Joy, Vol. 8. 1999. pap. 5.00 (*0-937690-84-8*, 3062) Wrld Lib Pubns.

— God's Word Is Our Joy: Advent, Christmas, Lent & Easter, Cycle A. Date not set. pap. text 14.95 (*0-937690-27-9*) Wrld Lib Pubns.

— God's Word Is Our Joy: Advent, Christmas, Lent, Easter, Cycle B. Date not set. pap. text 14.95 (*0-937690-29-5*) Wrld Lib Pubns.

— God's Word Is Our Joy: Advent, Christmas, Lent, Easter, Cycle C. Date not set. pap. text 14.95 (*0-937690-31-7*) Wrld Lib Pubns.

— God's Word Is Our Joy: Feasts & Holy Days. LC 98-102032. 1998. pap. text 14.95 (*0-937690-33-3*) Wrld Lib Pubns.

— God's Word Is Our Joy: Sundays 2-34 of the Year, Cycle A. Date not set. pap. text 17.95 (*0-937690-28-7*) Wrld Lib Pubns.

— God's Word Is Our Joy: Sundays 2-34 of the Year, Cycle B. LC 98-102032. 1998. pap. text 17.95 (*0-937690-30-9*) Wrld Lib Pubns.

— God's Word Is Our Joy: Sundays 2-34 of the Year, Cycle C. Date not set. pap. text 17.95 (*0-937690-32-5*) Wrld Lib Pubns.

— Joseph, Mary, Jesus. Beaumont, Madeleine, tr. 168p. (Orig.). 1996. pap. 14.95 (*0-8146-2255-0*, Liturg Pr Bks) Liturgical Pr.

— The Mass. 110p. (Orig.). 1992. pap. 9.95 (*0-8146-2058-2*) Liturgical Pr.

— Springtime of the Liturgy. rev. ed. O'Connell, Matthew J., tr. from FRE. LC 79-15603. 307p. (C). 1979. pap. 19.95 (*0-8146-1023-4*) Liturgical Pr.

— Visions of Liturgy & Music for a New Century. LC 96-17693. 280p. (Orig.). 1996. pap. 24.95 (*0-8146-2298-4*) Liturgical Pr.

***Deiss, Lucien & Marchionda, James V.** Your Morn Shall Rise. 1999. pap. 9.00 (*1-58459-001-7*, 3372) Wrld Lib Pubns.

Deiss, William A., jt. ed. see Hoage, R. J.

Deissenberg, Christoph, jt. auth. see Aurifeille, Jacques-Marie.

Deisseroth & Arlinghaus, Ralph B. Chronic Myelogenous Leukemia: Molecular Approaches. (Hematology Ser.: Vol. 13). (Illus.). 504p. 1990. text 199.00 (*0-8247-8352-2*) Dekker.

Deissler, Robert G. Turbulent Fluid Motion. LC 98-16863. (Combustion: an International Ser.). 1998. 89.95 (*1-56032-753-7*, Pub. by Tay Francis Ltd) Taylor & Francis.

Deissman, Adolph. Paul: A Study in Social & Religious History. Wilson, William W., tr. 1958. 16.50 (*0-8446-1965-5*) Peter Smith.

Deissmann, Adolf. Light from the Ancient East. Strachan, Lionel, tr. 536p. 1995. reprint ed. 29.95 (*1-56563-155-2*) Hendrickson MA.

Deissmann, G. Adolf. Bible Studies. 400p. 1988. reprint ed. 19.95 (*0-943575-08-7*) Hendrickson MA.

Deist, Wilhelm. The Wehrmacht & German Rearmament. LC 81-178952. 165p. reprint ed. pap. 51.20 (*0-8357-8372-3*, 203401600088) Bks Demand.

Deist, Wilhelm, ed. The German Military in the Age of Total War. LC 84-73479. 362p. 1987. 19.95 (*0-907582-14-1*) Berg Pubs.

Deist, Wilhelm, et al. Germany & the Second World War Vol. I: The Build-up of German Aggression. Falla, P. S., ed. & tr. by Osers, Ewald et al, trs. (Illus.). 828p. 1991. text 145.00 (*0-19-822866-X*) OUP.

***Deistler, M., et al, eds.** Management, Global & Educational Issues, Vol. M. 458p. 1999. pap. 126.00 (*0-08-043224-7*) Elsevier.

Deistler, M., jt. auth. see Hannan, E. J.

***Deistler, Petra.** Tradition und Transformation - der Fiktionale Dialog Mit Dem Viktorianischen Zeitalter Im (Post)Modernen Historischen Roman in Groabritannien. (Neue Studien zur Anglistik und Amerikanistik). xi, 295p. 1999. 51.95 (*3-631-34843-6*) P Lang Pubng.

Deitch, David A., ed. Addiction Counseling Competencies: The Knowledge, Skills & Attitudes of Professional Practice. 132p. (C). 1999. pap. text 30.00 (*0-7881-7607-2*) DIANE Pub.

Deitch, Edwin A. Surgical Techniques: Tools of the Trade & Rules of the Road. LC 97-5053. (Illus.). 432p. 1997. pap. text 39.95 (*0-397-51393-3*) Lppncott W & W.

Deitch, Jeffrey. Everything That's Interesting Is New: The Dakis Joannou Collection. (Illus.). 350p. 1996. write for info. (*0-9648530-0-0*); pap. write for info. (*0-9648530-1-9*) J Deitch NY.

— Post Human. LC 92-90272. (Illus.). 160p. 1994. 35.00 (*0-9633037-0-8*, Pub. by Deste Found) Dist Art Pubs.

— Strange Abstraction: Robert Gober, Cady Noland, Philip Taaffe, Christopher Wool. (Illus.). 92p. 1992. pap. 19.95 (*1-56466-017-6*) Archer Fields.

Deitch, Jeffrey & Morgan, Stuart, contrib. by. Everything That's Interesting Is New: The Dakis Joannou Collection. (Illus.). 350p. 1996. 85.00 (*3-89322-816-0*, Pub. by Deste Found); pap. 45.00 (*3-89322-817-9*, Pub. by Deste Found) Dist Art Pubs.

Deitch, JoAnne W. An Educator's Guide to the Perspectives on History Series. (Illus.). 100p. (Orig.). 1996. ring bd. 25.00 (*1-878668-72-2*) Disc Enter Ltd.

— An Educator's Guide to the Perspectives on History Series - Using Primary Source Documents. (Perspectives on History Ser.: Pt. III). 1998. pap. 15.00 (*1-57960-043-3*) Disc Enter Ltd.

— The Lowell Mill Girls: Life in the Factory. (Perspectives on History Ser.: Pt. I). 52p. 1998. pap. 6.95 (*1-57960-041-7*) Disc Enter Ltd.

Deitch, Kenneth M. A Guide to Teaching about the Columbus Controversy. 1991. pap. 8.95 (*1-878668-14-5*) Disc Enter Ltd.

Deitch, Kenneth M., ed. The Manhattan Project. LC 94-71896. (Perspectives on History Ser.). (Illus.). 64p. (C). 1995. pap. 6.95 (*1-878668-41-2*) Disc Enter Ltd.

Deitch, Kenneth M. & Weisman, JoAnne B. Dwight D. Eisenhower: Man of Many Hats; With a Message from John S. D. Eisenhower. LC 90-82588. (Picture-Book Biography). (Illus.). 48p. (J). (gr. 5-12). 1990. lib. bdg. 14.95 (*1-878668-02-1*) Disc Enter Ltd.

Deitch, Kenneth M., jt. auth. see Beyer, Janet.

Deitch, Kenneth M., jt. auth. see Weisman, JoAnne B.

Deitch, Kim. All-Waldo Comics. 64p. 1992. pap., per. 7.95 (*1-56097-078-2*) Fantagraph Bks.

— A Shroud for Waldo. 64p. 1992. pap. 7.95 (*1-56097-081-2*) Fantagraph Bks.

— Tales from Beyond the Pale. Fiore, Robert, ed. (Illus.). 136p. (Orig.). 1989. pap. 14.95 (*0-930193-83-0*) Fantagraph Bks.

***Deitch, Robert.** The Modern Architectural Dictionary & Quick Reference Guide for Architects, Interior Designers & the Construction Trades. (Illus.). 279p. 1999. pap. 25.95 (*0-9675345-6-9*) Rhinoceros W Pr.

Deitch, Samuel L., jt. auth. see Singer, Jonathan M.

Deitcher, David. Burg. (Illus.). 180p. 1998. 29.99 (*3-8228-7881-2*) Taschen Amer.

***Deitchman, Seymour J.** On Being a Superpower: Scenarios for Security in the New Century & Not Knowing What to Do About It. LC 99-39624. 1999. 32.00 (*0-8133-6775-1*, Pub. by Westview) HarpC.

Deitel. The Complete Visual Basic 6 Training Course. (C). 1998. 99.99 incl. cd-rom (*0-13-082929-3*) P-H.

— Java How to Program. 2nd ed. 1998. 56.00 (*0-13-011464-2*) P-H.

***Deitel.** Java How to Program. 3rd ed. 1999. supp. ed. write for info. (*0-13-018829-8*) P-H.

— Java Interactive Training Course. 1999. 49.33 (*0-13-016736-3*) P-H.

Deitel. Java Multimedia Cyber User. 1998. pap. text. write for info. (*0-13-841966-3*) P-H.

Deitel. Network Version C & C++ Multi. 1997. pap. text 790.00 (*0-13-890062-0*) P-H.

Deitel. Visual Basic: How to Program D-CART, Vol. 6. 6th ed. 1998. 57.99 (*0-13-020661-X*) P-H.

Deitel & Deitel. Java Super Media Training Course. 1997. pap. 526.67 (*0-13-907130-X*, Prentice Hall) P-H.

Deitel, jt. auth. see Deitel.

***Deitel & Associates Staff.** The Complete C++ Training Course. 3rd ed. 2000. 109.99 (*0-13-089564-4*); student ed. 58.95 (*0-13-089563-6*) P-H.

— The Complete E-Commerce & E-Business Training Course. 2000. 109.99 (*0-13-089549-0*) P-H.

— Complete E-commerce & E-business Training Course, Student Edition, The. 2000. 58.95 (*0-13-089551-2*) P-H.

Deitel & Associates Staff. The Complete JAVA Training Course. 2nd ed. 1168p. 1997. pap. text 99.99 (*0-13-790569-6*) P-H.

***Deitel & Associates Staff.** Visual Basic 6 Interactive Training Course. (C). 1999. pap. 49.33 (*0-13-023131-2*, Prentice Hall) P-H.

Deitel, H. M. & Deitel, P. J. C: How to Program. 2nd ed. LC 93-33697. 926p. (C). 1994. pap. 68.00 (*0-13-226119-7*) P-H.

Deitel, Harvey. Java Multimedia Cyber Classroom. (C). 1996. pap. text 69.95 incl. cd-rom (*0-13-271974-6*) P-H.

***Deitel, Harvey & Deitel, Paul.** The Complete Java 2 Training Course: Student Edition. 3rd ed. (C). 1999. boxed set 78.00 (*0-13-085248-1*) P-H.

— The Complete Java 2 Training Course. 3rd ed. 1999. pap. text 109.99 (*0-13-085247-3*) P-H.

***Deitel, Harvey M.** C++ Introducing OOAD with the UML. 3rd ed. (How to Program Ser.). 1230p. 2000. pap. 68.00 (*0-13-089571-7*) P-H.

Deitel, Harvey M. C++ How To Program. 2nd ed. LC 97-47128. 1130p. 1997. pap. 68.00 (*0-13-528910-6*) P-H.

— The Design of OS/2. (C). 1993. pap. text. write for info. (*0-201-59465-X*) Addison-Wesley.

***Deitel, Harvey M.** Getting Started with Visual C++ 6: With an Introduction to MFC. 1999. pap. 29.99 (*0-13-016147-0*) P-H.

Deitel, Harvey M. An Introduction to Operating Systems. rev. ed. LC 83-7153. 704p. (C). 1984. text 44.25 (*0-201-14501-4*) Addison-Wesley.

— An Introduction to Operating Systems. 2nd ed. 880p. (C). 1990. pap. text. write for info. (*0-201-50939-3*) Addison-Wesley.

— An Introduction to Operating Systems. 2nd ed. (Illus.). 853p. (C). 1990. 75.00 (*0-201-18038-3*) Addison-Wesley.

***Deitel, Harvey M.** Java How to Program. 3rd ed. LC 99-37546. (Illus.). 1355p. 1999. pap. text 68.00 incl. audio compact disk (*0-13-012507-5*) P-H.

Deitel, Harvey M. Sistemas Operativos. 2nd ed. (SPA.). 976p. (C). 1995. pap. text 37.33 (*0-201-51860-0*) Addison-Wesley.

— Solaris(TM) & Sparc(TM) (Technical Perspective Ser.). (Illus.). 608p. (C). 1992. text. write for info. (*0-201-54310-9*) Addison-Wesley.

— Visual Basic 6: How to Program. (Illus.). 1015p. 1998. pap. text 53.99 (*0-13-456955-5*) P-H.

***Deitel, Harvey M. & Deitel, Paul.** The Complete Internet & World Wide Web Programming Training Course. (Complete Training Course Ser.). 2000. pap., boxed set 109.99 incl. cd-rom (*0-13-085611-8*) P-H.

***Deitel, Harvey M. & Deitel, Paul J.** Complete Internet & World Wide Web Programming Training Course. 1000p. 2000. student ed. 78.00 (*0-13-085609-6*) P-H.

— Complete Java Training Course, Java 1.1. 1998. pap., student ed. 71.93 (*0-13-082927-7*, Prentice Hall) P-H.

Deitel, Harvey M. & Deitel, Paul J. Computer C++ Training Course. 2nd ed. (C). 1998. pap. text 109.99 (*0-13-916305-0*) P-H.

***Deitel, Harvey M. & Deitel, Paul J.** How to Program. 3rd ed. 926p. 2000. pap. 65.00 (*0-13-089572-5*, Prentice Hall) P-H.

Deitel, Harvey M. & Deitel, Paul J. Microsoft IBM QuickBASIC: A Structured Approach. 288p. 1989. pap. 27.00 (*0-13-587064-X*) P-H.

Deitel, Harvey M. & Deitel, Paul M. Java: How to Program. 2nd ed. LC 97-26424. 1063p. 1997. pap. 68.00 (*0-13-899394-7*) P-H.

***Deitel, Harvey M., et al.** E-Business & E-Commerce How to Program. 1000p. 2000. pap. 65.00 (*0-13-028419-X*, Prentice Hall) P-H.

— Internet & World Wide Web: How to Program. (Illus.). 1156p. 1999. pap. 68.00 (*0-13-016143-8*) P-H.

Deitel, Harvey M., jt. auth. see Deitel, Paul J.

Deitel, Harvey M., jt. auth. see Lorin, Harold.

Deitel, Havey M. & Deitel, Paul J. The Complete C++ Video Course: For Beginners. 1998. pap. 149.99 incl. cd-rom (*0-13-083697-4*) P-H.

Deitel, P. J., jt. auth. see Deitel, H. M.

Deitel, Paul, jt. auth. see Deitel, Harvey.

Deitel, Paul, jt. auth. see Deitel, Harvey M.

Deitel, Paul J. & Deitel, Harvey M. Visual C++ How to Program. 900p. (C). 2001. pap. 39.00 (*0-13-437377-4*, Macmillan Coll) P-H.

Deitel, Paul J., jt. auth. see Deitel, Harvey M.

Deitel, Paul J., jt. auth. see Deitel, Havey M.

Deitel, Paul M., jt. auth. see Deitel, Harvey M.

Deitering-Ancell, Carolyn. Can the Saints Come out to Play! (Pueden Salir a Jugar los Santos) Vol. 1: A Saint Story for Everyday - September Saints. Meehan, Rosario, tr. 32p. (J). (gr. 1-8). 1999. 9.95 (*1-893757-03-X*, 03) E T Nedder.

***Deitering-Ancell, Carolyn.** Practical Ideas for Celebrating Liturgies with Children: A Seasonal Guide. Larkin, Jean, ed. (Illus.). 108p. 1999. pap. 19.95 (*0-937997-48-X*) Hi-Time Pflaum.

Deitmer, T. Physiology & Pathology of the Mucociliary System: Special Regards to Mucociliary Transport in Malignant Lesions of the Human Larynx. (Advances in OtoRhinoLaryngology Ser.: Vol. 43). (Illus.). x, 136p. 1989. 115.00 (*3-8055-4944-X*) S Karger.

Deitmeyer, Robert. A Mighty Fortress. 1.25 (*0-687-05823-6*) Abingdon.

Deitrich, Richard A., et al, eds. Pharmacological Effects of Ethanol on the Nervous System. LC 95-9425. (Pharmacology & Toxicology Ser.). 480p. 1995. boxed set 139.95 (*0-8493-8389-7*, 8389) CRC Pr.

Deitrick, Bernard E. A Basic Book List for Church Libraries. 5th rev. ed. LC 77-4093. 17p. 1995. pap. 7.50 (*0-915324-10-5*); pap. 7.50 (*0-915324-32-6*) CSLA.

Deitrick, Frances I. I'm Not Crazy: The True Story of Frances Deitrick's Flight from a Psychiatric Snake Pit to Freedom. LC 91-66896. 295p. 1992. 21.95 (*0-88282-103-2*) New Horizon NJ.

***Deits.** Recovering after Loss. 256p. 2000. 6.98 (*1-56731-391-4*, MJF Bks) Fine Comms.

Deits, Bob. Life after Loss: A Personal Guide Dealing with Death, Divorce, Job Change & Relocation. 3rd ed. LC 99-47461. 272p. 1999. pap. 12.95 (*1-55561-189-3*) Fisher Bks.

— Life after Loss: A Personal Guide to Dealing with Death, Divorce, Job Change & Relocation. rev. ed. LC 92-29593. 256p. (Orig.). 1992. reprint ed. pap. 12.95 (*1-55561-049-8*) Fisher Bks.

— Vivir Despues de la Perdida. LC 94-30395. (SPA.). 240p. 1994. pap. 12.95 (*1-55561-062-5*) Fisher Bks.

Deitsch, Clarence R. & Dilts, David A. The Arbitration of Rights Disputes in the Public Sector. LC 90-30016. 200p. 1990. 65.00 (*0-89930-415-X*, DLB/, Quorum Bks) Greenwood.

Deitsch, Cyrel, jt. ed. see Blau, Esther.

Deitsch, Marian, ed. Directory of U. S. & Canadian Marketing Surveys & Services: Supplements Through 1983. 4th ed. 1981. ring bd. 145.00 (*0-917148-75-4*) Kline.

Deitsch, Marian & Rauch, James, eds. Kline Guide to Energy. LC 81-81264. (Illus.). 525p. 1981. pap. 85.00 (*0-917148-20-7*) Kline.

Deitsch, Marian, jt. ed. see Kollonitsch, Valerie.

Deitsch, Marian, ed. see Rich, Susan.

Deitsch, Richard. (Quarter)backs-to-(Running)backs: The NFL's Finest Passers & Rushers. Wolf, Cathrine, ed. 32p. (J). (gr. 4-6). 1998. pap. 3.95 (*1-886749-45-0*) SI For Kids.

— Super Bowl Heroes: Read about the Super Bowl's Biggest Stars. Sieck, Margaret, ed. 32p. (J). (gr. 2-7). 1999. pap. 3.99 (*1-886749-53-1*) SI For Kids.

***Deitsch, Richard & Schwarz, Alan.** NFL Rising Stars: The 10 Best Young Players in the NFL. Holder, Sherie, ed. 32p. (J). (gr. 3-8). 2000. pap. 3.99 (*1-930623-03-8*) SI For Kids.

Deitsch, Sarah E., jt. auth. see Meyer, Robert G.

***Deitschmann, Craig, reader.** Giants of Political Thought. unabridged ed. 1998. audio 22.00 (*0-671-57997-5*) S&S Audio.

Deitschmann, Craig & Armstrong, Tom C. Poetry Peddlers: Two from Music City Country. 127p. (Orig.). 1984. pap. 7.95 (*0-939298-46-5*, 465) AD HOC Bks.

***Deitz.** Above the Lower Sky. 2000. 23.00 (*0-380-97244-1*) Morrow Avon.

Deitz. Brief Course in Business Math, Pt. 1-5. 12th ed. (Miscellaneous/Catalogs Ser.). (C). 1998. pap. 57.95 (*0-538-86883-X*) S-W Pub.

— Business Math for Colleges Brief Course. 10th ed. (MB - Business/Vocational Math Ser.). (C). 1991. mass mkt. 25.75 (*0-538-81188-9*) S-W Pub.

— Business Mathematics. 12th ed. LC 98-17393. (Miscellaneous/Catalogs Ser.). (C). 1998. pap. 76.95 (*0-538-86882-1*) S-W Pub.

— Business Mathematics for Colleges. 12th ed. 1998. pap. 2.00 (*0-538-86898-8*) Thomson Learn.

— Business Mathematics for Colleges: Brief Course, Pts. 1-5. 11th ed. (MB - Business/Vocational Math Ser.). (C). 1995. pap., suppl. ed. 41.95 (*0-538-84035-8*) S-W Pub.

***Deitz.** Dreamseeker's Road. 2000. 20.00 (*0-380-97254-9*) Morrow Avon.

Deitz. Little Spooner Who Wouldn't Spoon. 1994. pap. 6.95 (*0-938985-11-6*) Mntn Memories Bks.

— Lost Years & Other Stories. 1994. pap. 6.95 (*0-938985-12-4*) Mntn Memories Bks.

— Mountain Memories V. 1995. pap. 6.95 (*0-938985-07-8*) Mntn Memories Bks.

Deitz, Dennis. The Greenbrier Ghost: And Other Strange Stories. 9.95 (*0-938985-08-6*) Mntn Memories Bks.

— The Greenbrier Ghost No. 2: Other Strange Stories. 1997. pap. 9.95 (*0-938985-13-2*) Mntn Memories Bks.

— The Man Who Saved Forty-Two Lives in the Layland Mine Explosion. (Illus.). 18p. (C). 1992. pap. 4.00 (*0-938985-09-4*) Mntn Memories Bks.

Deitz, Dennis & Mowery, Carlene. Buffalo Creek - Valley of Death. pap. 20.00 (*0-938985-10-8*) Mntn Memories Bks.

Deitz, Dennis J. Mountain Memories III. 180p. reprint ed. pap. text 6.95 (0-938985-00-0) Mntn Memories Bks.

— Mountain Memories II. (Illus.). 144p. 1983. pap. 6.95 (0-934750-18-1) Mntn Memories Bks.

Deitz, George, ed. see Deitz, Luke D.W.

Deitz, J. Dennis. The Flood & the Blood. Hawkinberry, Louise, ed. (Illus.). 160p. 1987. 20.00 (0-938985-03-5) Mntn Memories Bks.

— Mountain Memories, No. 4. 3rd ed. Browning, Kathleen, ed. 170p. (C). reprint ed. pap. 6.95 (0-934750-37-8) Mntn Memories Bks.

— The Search for Emily. (Illus.). 188p. 1989. pap. 6.95 (0-938985-04-3) Mntn Memories Bks.

Deitz, James A. & Southam, James L. Business Mathematics for Colleges. 10th ed. 512p. (C). 1991. mass mkt. 53.25 (0-538-81187-0, MB76JB) S-W Pub.

Deitz, James E. Business Mathematics for Colleges. 11th ed. (MB - Business/Vocational Math Ser.). 576p. (C). 1995. pap. 59.95 (0-538-84034-X) S-W Pub.

Deitz, Jennifer. German Skills for You Cassette. 1988. pap. 35.00 (0-09-172875-4) Dufour.

Deitz, Kristine, ed. see Deitz, Luke D.W.

Deitz, Lawrence. Jimmy Coon Story Book, No. 1. (Illus.). 34p. (Orig.). (J). 1985. pap. 2.95 (0-934750-79-3) Mntn Memories Bks.

— Jimmy Coon Story Book, No. 2. (Illus.). 37p. (Orig.). (J). 1985. pap. 2.95 (0-934750-42-4) Mntn Memories Bks.

— Jimmy Coon Story Book, No. 3. 37p. (Orig.). (J). 1986. pap. 2.95 (0-934750-85-8) Mntn Memories Bks.

— Jimmy Coon Story Book, No. 4. (Illus.). 30p. (Orig.). (J). 1986. pap. 2.95 (0-934750-14-9) Mntn Memories Bks.

— Jimmy Coon Story Book, No. 5. (Illus.). 40p. (Orig.). (J). (ps up). 1986. pap. 2.95 (0-938985-02-7) Mntn Memories Bks.

Deitz, Luke D.W. Haunting in the Graveyard. Deitz, George & Deitz, Kristine, eds. (Illus.). 16p. (J). (gr. 1-4). 3.00 (0-938985-21-3) Mntn Memories Bks.

Deitz, Robert, jt. auth. see Hodel, Donald P.

Deitz, Robert, jt. auth. see Koon, Stacey C.

Deitz, Roger. The Folk Music Chronicles. Talanian, Nancy, ed. (Illus.). 44p. (Orig.). 1986. pap. 9.95 (0-937737-00-3) Rescan Assocs Inc.

Deitz, Samuel M. & Hummel, John H. Discipline in the Schools: A Guide to Reducing Misbehavior. LC 78-18269. (Illus.). 280p. 1978. pap. 27.95 (0-87778-128-1) Educ Tech Pubns.

Deitz, Sheila R. & Thoms, William E., eds. Pilots, Personality, & Performance: Human Behavior & Stress in the Skies. LC 91-11427. 232p. 1991. 62.95 (0-89930-577-6, DPB/, Quorum Bks) Greenwood.

***Deitz, Southam.** Contemporary Business Mathematics. 12th ed. (SWC-Finance Ser.). (C). 1999. text 36.00 (0-324-03314-1) Sth-Wstrn College.

Deitz, Tom. Above the Lower Sky. LC 94-17819. 1994. 23.00 (0-688-13716-4, Avon Bks) Morrow Avon.

— Above the Lower Sky. 1996. mass mkt. 5.99 (0-380-77483-6, Avon Bks) Morrow Avon.

— Bloodwinter. LC 98-39999. 512p. 1999. pap. 13.95 (0-553-37863-5) Bantam.

***Deitz, Tom.** Bloodwinter. 608p. 2000. reprint ed. mass mkt. 6.50 (0-553-57646-1) Bantam.

Deitz, Tom. Darkthunder's Way. 352p. 1989. pap. 3.95 (0-380-75508-4, Avon Bks) Morrow Avon.

— The Demons in the Green. 432p. (Orig.). 1996. mass mkt. 5.99 (0-380-78271-5, Avon Bks) Morrow Avon.

— Dreambuilder. 432p. (Orig.). 1992. mass mkt. 4.99 (0-380-76290-0, Avon Bks) Morrow Avon.

— Dreamseeker's Road. 368p. 1996. mass mkt. 5.99 (0-380-77484-4, Avon Bks) Morrow Avon.

— Fireshaper's Doom. 320p. 1987. pap. 3.95 (0-380-75329-4, Avon Bks) Morrow Avon.

— The Gryphon King. 480p. (Orig.). 1989. pap. 3.95 (0-380-75506-8, Avon Bks) Morrow Avon.

— Landslayer's Law. 304p. 1997. mass mkt. 5.99 (0-380-78649-4, Avon Bks) Morrow Avon.

— Soulsmith. 464p. (Orig.). 1991. mass mkt. 4.99 (0-380-76289-7, Avon Bks) Morrow Avon.

***Deitz, Tom.** Springwar. LC PS3554.E425S57 2000. 448p. 2000. pap. 13.95 (0-553-37864-3, Spectra) Bantam.

Deitz, Tom. Stoneskin's Revenge. 320p. 1991. pap. 3.95 (0-380-76063-0, Avon Bks) Morrow Avon.

— Sunshaker's War. 368p. 1990. pap. 3.95 (0-380-76062-2, Avon Bks) Morrow Avon.

— Warstalker's Track. 375p. 1999. mass mkt. 6.50 (0-380-78650-8, Eos) Morrow Avon.

— Windmaster's Bane. 288p. (Orig.). 1986. mass mkt. 4.99 (0-380-75029-5, Avon Bks) Morrow Avon.

— Wordwright. 400p. (Orig.). 1993. mass mkt. 4.99 (0-380-76291-9, Avon Bks) Morrow Avon.

Deitz, William C. Drifter's War. 240p. (Orig.). 1992. mass mkt. 4.99 (0-441-16815-9) Ace Bks.

Deiulis, Guy. The Human Body Owner's Manual for Optimal Performance: Lifestyle Strategies for Keeping Physically, Mentally, & Nutritionally Fit for the 21st Century. unabridged ed. Adler, Carol, ed. LC 97-61861. (Illus.). 260p. 1998. pap. 19.95 (1-890243-05-1) Trineurogenics.

Deixler, Lyle. Which Phone System Should I Buy? The Complete Guide to Buying & Installing a Business Telephone, 1. 10th ed. 202p. 1998. pap. 24.95 (1-57820-027-X) Telecom Bks.

Deixonne, B., jt. ed. see Baumel, H.

DeJager, A. & Wild, C. Farm Labour: A Guide to Basic Labour Law in the Agriculture Sector. 122p. 1993. write for info. (0-7021-3000-1, Pub. by Juta & Co) Gaunt.

DeJager, A. E. Plaasarbeid - 'n Handleiding van Basiese Arbeidsreg in die Landbousektor. 1993. pap. write for info. (0-7021-3001-X, Pub. by Juta & Co) Gaunt.

Dejana, Elisabetta & Corada, Monica. Adhesion Protein Protocols. (Methods in Molecular Biology Ser.: Vol. 96). (Illus.). 240p. 1999. 79.50 (0-89603-417-8) Humana.

***DeJarnett, Don Patrick.** I Cry But I Shed No Tears. 136p. 2000. pap. 17.95 (1-56167-587-3) Am Literary Pr.

DeJarnett, L. R., ed. Information Strategy: The Executive's Journal. 165.00 (0-685-69682-0, ZEOJ) Warren Gorham & Lamont.

DeJarnette, jt. auth. see Webb.

Dejasu, Lee. Occurences of Duke Snyder. 1979. 3.50 (0-614-18200-X) Visual Studies.

Dejauregui, Ruth. 100 Medical Milestones of World History. 1997. pap. text 7.95 (0-912517-31-X) Bluewood Bks.

Dejauregui, Ruth, ed. see Birkmeier, Rana.

Dejavu & Byrne, D. All Things Natural: The Dallas Edition. (Illus.). 160p. (Orig.). 1989. pap. text 11.95 (0-685-30390-X) Deja vu TX.

DeJaynes, R. L. Come Out from among Them: A Journey Out of the Evangelical Lutheran Church in America. 52p. 1996. pap. 5.00 (1-893118-09-6) J Gerhard Inst.

Dejean, Joan. Ancients Against Moderns: Culture Wars & the Making of a Fin de Siecle. LC 96-19011. (Illus.). 216p. 1996. pap. text 16.95 (0-226-14138-1); lib. bdg. 42.00 (0-226-14137-3) U Ch Pr.

DeJean, Joan. Fictions of Sappho, Fifteen Forty-Six to Nineteen Thirty-Seven. LC 89-31843. (Women in Culture & Society Ser.). (Illus.). 402p. 1989. pap. text 19.95 (0-226-14136-5); lib. bdg. 66.00 (0-226-14135-7) U Ch Pr.

— Literary Fortifications: Rousseau, Laclos, Sade. LC 84-42593. 368p. 1984. reprint ed. pap. 114.10 (0-7837-9329-4, 206007000004) Bks Demand.

— Tender Geographies: Women & the Origins of the Novel in France. 352p. 1991. text 46.00 (0-231-06230-3) Col U Pr.

Dejean, Joan. Tender Geographies: Women & the Origins of the Novel in France. 1993. pap. 20.50 (0-231-06231-1) Col U Pr.

DeJean, Joan & Miller, Nancy K., eds. Displacements: Women, Tradition, Literatures in French. LC 90-38542. (Parallax: Re-Visions of Culture & Society Ser.). 300p. 1990. text 48.50 (0-8018-4070-8) Johns Hopkins.

DeJean, Joan, ed. & intro. see De Duras, Claire.

Dejence, Alemneh, et al. Land Degradation in Tanzania: Perception from the Village. LC 97-18344. (Technical Paper Ser.: No. 370). 92p. 1997. pap. 22.00 (0-8213-3993-1, 13993) World Bank.

Dejene, Alemneh. Environment, Famine, & Politics in Ethiopia: A View from the Village. LC 90-8816. 168p. 1990. lib. bdg. 32.00 (1-55587-240-9) L Rienner.

Dejerine, Joseph J. & Gauckler, E. Psychoneuroses & Their Treatment by Psychotherapy. Jelliffe, Smith E., tr. LC 75-16697. (Classics in Psychiatry Ser.). 1976. reprint ed. 34.95 (0-405-07425-5) Ayer.

DeJesus, C. M. Child of Dark. 1963. mass mkt. 5.99 (0-451-62731-8) NAL.

DeJesus, Ed. Microsoft Quickbasic: Quick Reference Guide. 1993. pap. 12.00 (1-56243-089-0, Y-17) DDC Pub.

DeJesus, Edward. Helping Young Adults Help Themselves: The Adult's Guide to Working with Young Adults. (Orig.). 1997. pap. 10.95 (0-9659130-2-3) Youth D&R Fund.

— The Young Adult's Guide to "Making It" Successful Strategies for Getting & Keeping a Job, Completing or Returning to School, & Preparing for Success in the 21st Century. 128p. (Orig.). (YA). (gr. 6 up). 1997. pap. 10.95 (0-9659130-0-7) Youth D&R Fund.

Dejeuski, Nikolai, jt. auth. see Miner-Gulland, Robin.

Dejeux, Jean. Dictionnaire des Auteurs Maghrebins Se Langue Francaise. (FRE.). 400p. 1984. pap. 59.95 (0-7859-8144-6, 2865370852) Fr & Eur.

DeJidas, Lloyd P. & Destree, Thomas M. Sheetfed Offset Press Operating. 2nd ed. LC 94-76299. (Illus.). 400p. (C). 1995. text 75.00 (0-88362-171-1, 1530) GATFPress.

Dejin, Li & Meizhen, Cheng, compiled by. A Practical Chinese Grammar for Foreigners. 742p. 1988. 22.95 (0-8351-1917-3) China Bks.

Dejnozka, Edward L. Educational Administration Glossary. LC 83-5719. 247p. 1983. lib. bdg. 65.00 (0-313-23301-2, DEA/, Greenwood Pr) Greenwood.

Dejnozka, Edward L., et al. American Educators' Encyclopedia. rev. ed. LC 90-41510. 752p. 1991. lib. bdg. 115.00 (0-313-25269-6, DAY/, Greenwood Pr) Greenwood.

Dejnozka, Jan. Bertrand Russell on Modality & Logical Relevance. (Avebury Series in Philosophy). 252p. 1999. text 65.95 (1-84014-981-7) Ashgate Pub Co.

— The Ontology of the Analytic Tradition & Its Origins: Realism, Possibility, & Identity in Frege, Russell, Wittgenstein, & Quine. LC 95-39426. 1996. pap. text 26.95 (0-8226-3053-2) Littlefield.

— The Ontology of the Analytic Tradition & Its Origins: Realism, Possibility, & Identity in Frege, Russell, Wittgenstein, & Quine. LC 95-39426. 1996. lib. bdg. 69.50 (0-8226-3052-4) Littlefield.

Dejo, Niccola D. Doctors & Their Practice Patterns: Index of New Information. 1998. 47.50 (0-7883-1818-7); pap. 44.50 (0-7883-1819-5) ABBE Pubs Assn.

***DeJohn, George.** Three Minutes to a Strong Mind & a Fit Body: Change Your Mind, Change Your Life. deluxe ed. (Illus.). 180p. 2000. pap. 14.95 (0-9674620-0-2, Pub. by DeJohn Prod) ACCESS Pubs Network.

Dejoie & Paradice. Ethical Issues in Information Systems. 2nd ed. (DC - Introduction to Computing Ser.). 1996. pap. 18.95 (0-7895-0554-1) Course Tech.

Dejoie, Paula. My Hair Is Beautiful . . . Because It's Mine. 12p. (J). 1994. 5.95 (0-86316-219-3) Writers & Readers.

DeJoie, Paula. My Skin Is Brown. (Illus.). 12p. (J). (ps-1). 1996. bds. 5.95 (0-86316-239-8) Writers & Readers.

Dejonckere, P. H., et al, eds. Vibrato. LC 95-24542. 128p. 1995. pap. 35.00 (1-56593-146-7, 1242) Thomson Learn.

Dejong. Interviewing for Solutions. (Social Work Ser.). 1997. wbk. ed. 15.00 (0-534-35432-7) Brooks-Cole.

DeJong & Jakabcin. Personal Tax Strategies, 1991. 1990. pap. 4.95 (0-13-660960-0) P-H.

DeJong, Alexander. Alcoholismo y Codependencia: Hechos Contemporaneos.Tr. of Alcoholism & Codependency: Contemporary Issues. (SPA.). 174p. 1994. write for info. (1-56063-758-7) Editorial Unilit.

DeJong, Alexander & Doot, Martin C. Dying for a Drink: A Clergyman & a Physician Talk about Alcoholism. LC 98-49965. 64p. 1999. pap. 8.00 (0-8028-4622-X) Eerdmans.

DeJong, Andy. The Kingdom Equation: A Fresh Look at the Parables of Jesus. 102p. 1990. pap. text, teacher ed. 11.95 (0-930265-88-2) CRC Pubns.

DeJong, Cheryl, ed. see Kane, Thomas A., et al.

DeJong, Constance, et al. Five. 56p. (Orig.). 1986. pap. 6.00 (0-917061-23-3) Top Stories.

— Tourist Attractions. Turyn, Anne & Wallis, Brian, eds. 80p. (Orig.). 1987. pap. 6.00 (0-917061-25-X) Top Stories.

DeJong, David. J. K. Lasser Year Round Tax Strategies, 1995. 1994. pap. 13.00 (0-671-89879-5) P-H.

DeJong, David H. Promises of the Past: A History of Indian Education in the United States. LC 93-10469. 304p. 1993. 24.95 (1-55591-905-7) Fulcrum Pub.

***Dejong, David S.** J. K. Lasser's Year-Round Tax Strategies 2000. 384p. 1999. pap. 14.95 (0-02-863556-6) JKL Pub.

Dejong, David S. & Jakabcin, Ann G. J. K. Lasser's Year-Round Tax Strategies, 1996 Edition. 240p. 1995. 14.95 (0-02-860569-1) Macmillan.

***DeJong, David S. & Jakabcin, Ann Gray.** J. K. Lasser's Year Round Tax Strategies. 384p. 2000. pap. 16.95 (0-471-39349-5) Wiley.

— J. K. Lasser's Year-Round Tax Strategies 2000. 372p. 1999. pap. 14.95 (0-471-38835-1) Wiley.

DeJong, Dola. The Field. Perkins, Maxwell, ed. Van Duyn, A. V., tr. from DUT. LC 79-84437. 215p. 1979. reprint ed. 22.00 (0-933256-02-7); reprint ed. pap. 16.00 (0-933256-05-1) Second Chance.

— The Field. Van Duyn, A. V., tr. LC 79-84437. 215p. 1983. reprint ed. pap. 5.95 (0-933256-39-6) Second Chance.

DeJong, Gerald, ed. Investigating Explanation-Based Learning. (C). 1992. text 183.00 (0-7923-9125-X) Kluwer Academic.

***DeJong, Gordon.** Pennsylania's Brain Drain: Migration in the Mid-1990s. (Illus.). 14p. 1999. pap. 20.00 (1-58036-135-8) Penn State Data Ctr.

DeJong, H. W., jt. ed. see Jacquemin, Alexis P.

DeJong, Hans. How to Use the Silva Mind Control Method. Set. unabridged ed. 1989. pap. 16.95 incl. audio (1-55927-017-9) Audio Renaissance.

DeJong, James A. & Van Dyke, Louis Y., eds. Building the House: Essays on Christian Education. 153p. (Orig.). 1981. pap. 5.95 (0-932914-05-5) Dordt Coll Pr.

DeJong, John H. & Stevenson, Douglas K., eds. Individualizing the Assessment of Language Abilities. (Multilingual Matters Ser.: No. 59). 298p. 1990. 99.00 (1-85359-067-3, Pub. by Multilingual Matters); pap. 39.95 (1-85359-066-5, Pub. by Multilingual Matters) Taylor & Francis.

DeJong-Kramer, E. Classic Beaded Purse Patterns. Llowarch, Tina, tr. from DUT. Orig. Title: Kralenbeursjes. (Illus.). 56p. 1996. pap. 15.00 (0-916896-67-6, LA17) Lacis Pubns.

Dejong, Marja G., jt. auth. see Davis, Amy.

DeJong, Marvin L. Mathematica for Calculus-Based Physics. LC 98-53298. 257p. (C). 1999. pap. text 21.40 (0-201-60339-X) Addison-Wesley.

DeJong, Meindert. Along Came a Dog. LC 57-9265. (Trophy Bk.). (Illus.). 192p. (J). (gr. 4-7). 1980. pap. 4.95 (0-06-440114-6, HarpTrophy) HarpC Child Bks.

— The Easter Cat. LC 90-24407. (Illus.). 128p. (J). (gr. 3-7). 1991. reprint ed. mass mkt. 3.95 (0-689-71468-8) Aladdin.

— The House of Sixty Fathers. LC 56-8148. (Illus.). 208p. (J). (gr. 4-7). 1956. lib. bdg. 15.89 (0-06-021481-3) HarpC Child Bks.

— The House of Sixty Fathers. LC 56-8148. (Trophy Bk.). (Illus.). 208p. (J). (gr. 5-8). 1987. pap. 5.95 (0-06-440200-2, HarpTrophy) HarpC Child Bks.

— Hurry Home, Candy. LC 53-8536. (Illus.). 256p. (J). (gr. 4-7). 1953. lib. bdg. 15.89 (0-06-021486-4) HarpC Child Bks.

— Hurry Home, Candy. LC 53-8536. (Trophy Bk.). (Illus.). 256p. (J). (gr. 4-7). 1972. pap. 6.95 (0-06-440025-5, HarpTrophy) HarpC Child Bks.

DeJong, Meindert. Hurry Home, Candy. (Harper Trophy Book Ser.). 1972. 9.05 (0-606-12348-2, Pub. by Turtleback) Demco.

DeJong, Meindert. Una Rueda en el Tejado (The Wheel on the School) 1996. pap. text 7.95 (84-279-3217-0) Lectorum Pubns.

— Shadrach. LC 53-5250. (Trophy Bk.). (Illus.). 192p. (J). (gr. 4-7). 1980. pap. 4.95 (0-06-440115-4, HarpTrophy) HarpC Child Bks.

— The Tower by the Sea. (Illus.). 1990. 17.00 (0-8446-6246-1) Peter Smith.

— The Wheel on the School. LC 54-8945. (Illus.). 256p. (J). (gr. 4-7). 1954. lib. bdg. 15.89 (0-06-021586-0) HarpC Child Bks.

— The Wheel on the School. LC 54-8945. (Illus.). 256p. (J). (gr. 4-7). 1954. 15.95 (0-06-021585-2) HarpC Child Bks.

— The Wheel on the School. LC 54-8945. (Trophy Bk.). (Illus.). 320p. (J). (gr. 4-7). 1972. pap. 5.95 (0-06-440021-2, HarpTrophy) HarpC Child Bks.

Dejong, Peter. Interviewing for Solutions. LC 97-8713. (Social Work Ser.). 1997. mass mkt. 43.95 (0-534-23160-8) Brooks-Cole.

DeJong, Peter & Smit, William. Planning Your Family: How to Decide What's Best for You. 208p. 1987. pap. 7.95 (0-310-37961-X, 12500P) Zondervan.

DeJong, William. Preventing Alcohol-Related Problems on Campus: Impaired Driving, a Guide for Program Coordinators. 72p. 1995. pap. 4.25 (0-16-048439-1) USGPO.

DeJong, William. Preventing Interpersonal Violence among Youth: An Introduction to School, Community, & Mass Media Strategies. (Illus.). 70p. 1995. pap. text 20.00 (0-7881-2520-6) DIANE Pub.

***DeJong, William.** Setting & Improving Policies for Reducing Alcohol & Other Drug Problems on Campus: A Guide for Administrators. 127p. 1998. per. 10.00 (0-16-049566-0) USGPO.

DeJonge, Marinus. Christology in Context: The Earliest Christian Response to Jesus. LC 87-30878. 276p. 1988. pap. 22.95 (0-664-25010-6) Westminster John Knox.

Dejongh, Monique J., jt. auth. see Cato-Louis, Cassandra.

Dejonghe, Herwig, ed. Galactic Bulges: Proceedings of the 153rd Symposium of the International Astronomical Union Held in Ghent, Belgium, August 17-22, 1992. LC 93-27853. 488p. (C). 1993. lib. bdg. 166.50 (0-7923-2424-2) Kluwer Academic.

DeJournette, Daun T., jt. auth. see DeJournette, Richard F.

DeJournette, Richard F. & DeJournette, Daun T. One Hundred Years of Brown's Park & Diamond Mountain. Huber, Ray L. & Colovich, Dana M., eds. LC 96-92971. (Illus.). 450p. (Orig.). 1996. pap. 37.50 (0-9651933-0-6) DeJournette.

Dejours, P., ed. Adaptations to Extreme Environments. (Comparative Physiology of Environmental Adaptations Ser.: Vol. 2). (Illus.). viii, 224p. 1987. 155.00 (3-8055-4471-5) S Karger.

Dejours, Pierre J., et al, eds. Comparative Physiology: Life in Water & on Land. (FIDIA Research Ser.: Vol. 9). (Illus.). x, 558p. 1987. 147.00 (0-387-96515-7) Spr-Verlag.

Dejoux, C. & Iltis, A., eds. Lake Titicaca: A Synthesis of Limnological Knowledge. (Monographiae Biologicae). 584p. (C). 1992. text 374.00 (0-7923-1663-0) Kluwer Academic.

Dejowski, Edmund F., ed. Protecting Judgment-Impaired Adults: Issues, Interventions & Policies. LC 90-45236. (Journal of Elder Abuse & Neglect). 178p. 1990. text 39.95 (1-56024-054-7) Haworth Pr.

DeJoy, David M. & Wilson, Mark G. Critical Issues in Worksite Health Promotion. 320p. (C). 1994. pap. text 42.00 (0-02-328292-4, Macmillan Coll) P-H.

Deju, Raul, et al. The Environment & Its Resources. 340p. 1972. 115.00 (0-677-14120-3) Gordon & Breach.

***DeJulio, Beverly.** Handy Ma'am. (Illus.). 224p. 2000. pap. 19.95 (0-7931-4243-1) Dearborn.

— HandyMa'am. LC 98-52978. (Illus.). 220p. 1999. 19.95 (0-7931-3341-6) Dearborn.

DeJulio, Beverly. HandyMa'am: Home Improvement, Decorating & Maintenance Tips & Projects for You & Your Family. 1996. 23.00 (0-614-96833-X, Harper Ref); 23.00 (0-614-96957-3, Harper Ref) HarpC.

DeJulio, Maryann, tr. see Hocquard, Emmanuel.

Dejussieu-Pontcarral, Pierre. Encyclopedie De l'Electricite 1: Production et Distribution. (FRE.). 1700p. 1969. 99.50 (0-8288-6593-0, M-6190) Fr & Eur.

— Encyclopedie de l'Electricite 2: Application. (FRE.). 1024p. 1970. 99.50 (0-8288-6530-2, M-6106) Fr & Eur.

Deka, Meeta. Student Movements in Assam. LC 95-911168. (C). 1996. 28.00 (0-7069-9882-0, Pub. by Vikas) S Asia.

Dekade, Luther. Reformation in Hildesheim. (GER.). 112p. 1984. write for info. (3-487-07412-5) G Olms Pubs.

DeKalb College Staff. The Polishing Cloth. 5th ed. 272p. (C). 1996. pap. text, per. 15.95 (0-7872-2462-6) Kendall-Hunt.

— The Polishing Cloth. 6th ed. 200p. (C). 1997. per. 11.00 (0-7872-4402-3) Kendall-Hunt.

— The Polishing Cloth. 7th ed. 202p. (C). 1998. per. 11.95 (0-7872-5115-1, 41511501) Kendall-Hunt.

DeKalb Historical Society Staff. Vanishing DeKalb. (Illus.). 240p. 1985. 30.00 (0-9615459-0-9) Dekalb.

Dekanich, Steve. Coming Together: Mind, Body, Spirit. 72p. 1994. pap. 7.95 (1-57087-201-5) Prof Pr NC.

Dekanova, N. P. Energy Reviews: Techniques for Investigating Thermal Power Plants, Vol. 6. (Soviet Technology Reviews Ser.: Vol. 6, Pt. 3). 67p. 1993. pap. text 135.00 (3-7186-5446-6, Harwood Acad Pubs) Gordon & Breach.

Dekant, Wolfgang & Neumann, H. G., eds. Tissue Specific Toxicity: Biochemical Mechanisms. (Illus.). 263p. 1992. text 110.00 (0-12-208860-3) Acad Pr.

DeKanter, Adriana. A Compact for Learning: An Action Handbook for Family-School-Community Partnerships. (Illus.). 76p. 1999. pap. text 20.00 (0-7881-7768-0) DIANE Pub.

***DeKanter, Adriana.** Keeping Schools Open As Community Learning Centers: Extending Learning in a Safe, Drug-Free Environment Before & After School. 51p. (C). 1999. pap. text 20.00 (0-7881-4103-1) DIANE Pub.

Dekar, Paul R. For the Healing of the Nations: Baptist Peacemakers. LC 93-14910. 312p. 1993. pap. 19.00 (1-880837-16-1) Smyth & Helwys.

DeKay, Charles. Barye: Life & Works of Antoine Louis Barye. LC 73-163696. (BCL Ser. I). (Illus.). reprint ed. 57.50 (0-404-02068-2) AMS Pr.

DeKay, James E. Anniversary Address on the Progress of the Natural Sciences of the United States. LC 76-125737. (American Environmental Studies). 1977. reprint ed. 14.95 (0-405-02662-5) Ayer.

— New York Natural History Survey: Zoology of New York, 5 vols., Set. 1993. reprint ed. lib. bdg. 375.00 (0-7812-5142-7) Rprt Serv.

***DeKay, James T.** Chronicles of the Frigate Macedonian, 1809-1922. 336p. 2000. pap. text 15.95 (0-393-32024-3) Norton.

DeKay, James T. The Left-Hander's Handbook. 408p. 1997. 9.98 (1-56731-229-2) Fine Comms.

D

An Asterisk (*) at the beginning of an entry indicates that the title is appearing for the first time.

— Meet Martin Luther King, Jr. rev. ed. (Bullseye Biographies Ser.). (Illus.). 112p. (J). (gr. 3-5). 1993. pap. 3.99 (*0-679-85411-8*, Pub. by Random Bks Yng Read) Random.

— Monitor: The Story of the Legendary Civil War Ironclad & the Man Whose Invention Changed the Course of History. 1999. pap. 11.95 (*0-345-42635-5*) Ballantine Pub Grp.

— Monitor: The Story of the Revolutionary Ship & the Men Whose Invention Changed the Course of History. LC 97-17500. (Illus.). 240p. 1997. 21.00 (*0-8027-1330-0*) Walker & Co.

DeKay, William. Down Home: A Journey into Rural Canada. (Illus.). 192p. 1996. 32.00 (*1-55046-186-9*, Pub. by Boston Mills) Genl Dist Srvs.

— Down Home: A Journey into Rural Canada. LC 98-111681. (Illus.). 184p. 1997. 32.95 (*0-7737-3039-7*) Stoddart Publ.

DeKaye. Instructor's Manual for Patient Accounts Management Handbook. 1998. teacher ed. write for info. (*0-8342-1119-X*) Aspen Pub.

DeKaye, Allan P. The Patient Accounts Management Handbook. LC 97-19454. 480p. 1997. 69.00 (*0-8342-0843-1*, 20843) Aspen Pub.

Deke, Meyer. McKenzie River Journal. (River Journal Ser.: Vol. 3, No. 3). 1997. pap. text 15.95 (*1-57188-053-4*) F Amato Pubns.

DeKeijzer, arne J., et al. China Guidebook, 1985. (Illus.). 672p. (Orig.). 1985. pap. 14.95 (*0-932030-18-1*) Eurasia Pr NY.

DeKeijzer, Arne J., jt. auth. see Burstein, Daniel.

Dekel, Avishai & Ostriker, Jeremiah P., eds. Formation of Structure in the Universe. LC 97-43008. (Illus.). 530p. (C). 1999. 80.00 (*0-521-58422-1*); pap. 34.95 (*0-521-58632-1*) Cambridge U Pr.

Dekel, Sheila C., jt. auth. see Lagnado, Lucette M.

DeKernion, Jean B., ed. Immunotherapy of Urological Tumours. (Illus.). 384p. 1990. text 121.00 (*0-443-04262-4*) Church.

DeKernion, Jean B. & Paulson, David F. Genitourinary Cancer Management. LC 86-7318. 309p. reprint ed. pap. 95.80 (*0-7837-2699-6*, 204307800006) Bks Demand.

DeKernion, Jean B., jt. auth. see Pavone-Macaluso, Michele.

Dekeseredy. Contemporary Criminology. 2nd ed. (Criminal Justice). 2002. pap. 50.00 (*0-534-52300-5*) Wadsworth Pub.

Dekeseredy, Ellis Alvi. Contemporary Social Problems In North American Society, 352p. 1999. pap. 38.95 (*0-201-61392-1*) Addison-Wesley.

***DeKeseredy, Walter S.** Women, Crime & the Canadian Criminal Justice System. LC 99-42601. 181p. 1999. pap. 30.95 (*0-87084-894-1*) Anderson Pub Co.

DeKeseredy, Walter S. & Schwartz, Martin D. Contemporary Criminology. 554p. (C). 1995. pap. 78.95 (*0-534-19764-7*) Wadsworth Pub.

— Woman Abuse on Campus: Results from the Canadian National Survey. LC 97-21054. (Series on Violence Against Women: Vol. 5). 200p. 1997. 46.00 (*0-7619-0567-7*); pap. 19.95 (*0-7619-0566-9*) Sage.

DeKeseredy, Walter S., jt. auth. see Schwartz, Martin D.

***Deketelaere, Kurt & Faure, Michael, eds.** Environmental Law in the United Kingdom & Belgium from a Comparative Perspective. 328p. 1999. pap. 98.00 (*90-5095-082-5*, Pub. by Intersentia Uitgevers) Gaunt.

Deketh, H. J. Wear of Rock Cutting Tools: Laboratory Experiments on the Abrasivity of Rock. LC 99-227350. (Illus.). 202p. (C). 1995. 91.00 (*90-5410-620-4*, Pub. by A A Balkema) Ashgate Pub Co.

Deketh, Jan R. & Heilbron, Hans C., eds. Engineering Geology Japan Study Tour, 1995: Final Report. (Illus.). 152p. Date not set. 91.00 (*90-5410-632-8*, Pub. by A A Balkema) Ashgate Pub Co.

Dekeuwer-Defossez, Francoise. Droit des Femmes: Dictionnaire Juridique. (FRE.). 458p. 1985. pap. 65.00 (*0-7859-7842-9*, 2247005683) Fr & Eur.

DeKeyser, V., et al. Time & the Dynamic Control of Behavior. LC 98-72179. 416p. 1998. pap. 45.00 (*0-88937-196-2*) Hogrefe & Huber Pubs.

Dekeyser, W., et al, eds. Electron Emission Spectroscopy. LC 73-83559. 1973. text 255.50 (*90-277-0366-3*) Kluwer Academic.

Dekhuijzen, R. Effects of Glyocorticosteroids on Rat Diaphram: A Physiological & Histopathological Study. No. 98. 109p. (Orig.). 1994. pap. 32.50 (*90-6186-644-8*, Pub. by Leuven Univ) Coronet Bks.

Dekieffer, Donald. How Lawyers Screw Their Clients: Gross Billable Hours-Outrageous Overcharging & What You... LC 95-709. 208p. 1995. 22.00 (*1-56980-055-3*) Barricade Bks.

DeKieffer, Donald E. The Citizen's Guide to Lobbying Congress. LC 96-25644. 304p. 1997. pap. 17.95 (*1-55652-194-4*) Chicago Review.

Dekiere, L. Old Babylonian Real Estate Documents from Sippar in the British Museum: Documents from the Reign of Hammurabi. (Texts Ser.: Series 3, Vol. 2). ix, 343p. 1995. pap. 65.00 (*0-614-96328-1*, Pub. by Recherches et Pubns) Eisenbrauns.

— Old Babylonian Real Estate Documents from Sippar in the British Museum: Documents from the Reign of Hammurabi. (Texts Ser.: Series 3, Vol. 2, Bk. 2). ix, 343p. 1995. 90.00 (*0-614-96327-3*, Pub. by Recherches et Pubns) Eisenbrauns.

— Old Babylonian Real Estate Documents from Sippar in the British Museum: Documents from the Reign of Samsu-Iluna. (Texts Ser.: Series 3, Vol. 2, Bk. 3). x, 224p. 1995. 90.00 (*0-614-96329-X*, Pub. by Recherches et Pubns) Eisenbrauns.

— Old Babylonian Real Estate Documents from Sippar in the British Museum: Documents from the Reign of Samsu-Iluna. (Texts Ser.: Series 3, Vol. 3). x, 224p. 1995. pap. 65.00 (*0-614-96330-3*, Pub. by Recherches et Pubns) Eisenbrauns.

— Old Babylonian Real Estate Documents from Sippar in the British Museum: Post-Samsu-Iluna Documents. (Texts Ser.: Series 3, Vol. 2, Bk. 4). x, 153p. 1995. 90.00 (*0-614-96331-1*, Pub. by Recherches et Pubns) Eisenbrauns.

— Old Babylonian Real Estate Documents from Sippar in the British Museum: Post-Samsu-Iluna Documents. (Texts Ser.: Series 3, Vol. 4). x, 153p. 1995. pap. 65.00 (*0-614-96332-X*, Pub. by Recherches et Pubns) Eisenbrauns.

— Old Babylonian Real Estate Documents from Sippar in the British Museum: Pre-Hammurabi Documents. (Texts Ser.: Series 3, Vol. 1). ix, 293p. 1995. pap. 65.00 (*0-614-96326-5*, Pub. by Recherches et Pubns) Eisenbrauns.

— Old Babylonian Real Estate Documents from Sippar in the British Museum: Pre-Hammurabi Documents. (Texts Ser.: Series 3, Vol. 2, Bk. 1). ix, 293p. 1995. 90.00 (*0-614-96325-7*, Pub. by Recherches et Pubns) Eisenbrauns.

Dekimpe, Karel. Almost-Bieberbach Groups: Affine & Polynomial Groups. LC 96-39127. (Lecture Notes in Mathematics Ser.: Vol. 1639). 259p. 1996. 52.00 (*3-540-61899-6*) Spr-Verlag.

Dekkar, Gerard, et al, eds. Rethinking Secularization: Reformed Reactions to Modernity. LC 96-48812. (Calvin Center Ser.). 312p. 1997. 64.50 (*0-7618-0645-8*); pap. 34.50 (*0-7618-0646-6*) U Pr of Amer.

Dekker, et al. The Witch of Edmonton. 1998. pap. text. write for info. (*0-393-90087-8*) Norton.

Dekker, jt. auth. see Parker, Peter J.

Dekker, Arie, et al, eds. Conflicts in Urban Development: A Comparison Between East & West Europe. 182p. 1992. 75.95 (*1-85742-040-3*, Pub. by Avebry) Ashgate Pub Co.

Dekker, Arnold J. Den, see Den Dekker, Arnold J.

Dekker, Cornelis. The Origins of Old Germanic Studies in the Low Countries. LC 98-41715. (Studies in Intellectual History). xii, 484p. 1998. 141.50 (*90-04-11031-3*) Brill Academic Pubs.

Dekker, Dick. Bolt from the Blue Vol. 1: Wild Peregrines on the Hunt. Miller, Nancy, ed. (Illus.). 140p. 1999. pap. 18.95 (*0-88839-434-9*) Hancock House.

— Hawks: Hunters on the Wing. LC 95-38566. (Illus.). 144p. 1996. pap. 14.95 (*1-55971-538-3*, NorthWord Pr) Creat Pub Intl.

— Wolves of the Rocky Mountains from Jasper to Yellowstone. (Illus.). 208p. 1997. pap. 19.95 (*0-88839-416-0*) Hancock House.

Dekker, Eduard D., see Multatuli, pseud.

Dekker, Edward N. & Newcomber, Joseph M. Developing Windows NT Device Drivers Vol. 1: A Programmer's Handbook. LC 98-38017. (Illus.). 1280p. (C). 1999. 59.95 (*0-201-69590-1*) Addison-Wesley.

Dekker, Eef, jt. ed. see van Asselt, Willem J.

Dekker, Elly. Globes from the Western World. 1991. 95.00 (*0-302-00618-4*, Pub. by Zwemmer Bks) Intl Spec Bk.

Dekker, Elly, ed. Globes at Greenwich: A Catalogue of the Globes & Armillary Spheres in the National Maritime Musuem. (Illus.). 604p. 2000. text 160.00 (*0-19-856559-3*) OUP.

Dekker, Eskil. Interaction Between Algorithms & Architectures in Parallel Computation. 111p. (Orig.). 1995. pap. 59.50 (*90-407-1216-6*, Pub. by Delft U Pr) Coronet Bks.

Dekker, George. The American Historical Romance. (Cambridge Studies in American Literature & Culture: No. 23). 384p. 1987. text 69.95 (*0-521-33282-6*) Cambridge U Pr.

— The American Historical Romance. (Cambridge Studies in American Literature & Culture: No. 23). 384p. (C). 1990. pap. text 24.95 (*0-521-38937-2*) Cambridge U Pr.

Dekker, George, ed. Donald Davie & the Responsibilities of Literature. LC 83-61320. 154p. 1984. 18.95 (*0-915032-38-4*) Natl Poet Foun.

Dekker, George & McWilliams, John P., Jr., eds. Fenimore Cooper: The Critical Heritage. (Critical Heritage Ser.). 318p. 1973. 69.50 (*0-7100-7635-5*, Routledge Thoemms) Routledge.

Dekker, Ige F., ed. The Gulf War of 1980-1988: The Iran-Iraq War in International Legal Perspective. 336p. 1992. lib. bdg. 135.50 (*0-7923-1334-8*) Kluwer Academic.

Dekker, J., ed. see Pure Mathematics Symposium Staff.

Dekker, James C., tr. see Hanks, Thomas D.

Dekker, John. Torches of Joy: The Dynamic Story of a Stone Age Tribe's Encounter with the Gospel of Jesus Christ. 1993. pap. 7.99 (*0-927545-43-8*) YWAM Pub.

Dekker, L., et al, eds. Massively Parallel Processing Applications & Development: Proceedings of the 1994 EUROSIM Conference on Massively Parallel Processing Applications & Development, Delft, The Netherlands, 21-23 June 1994. LC 94-33562. 996p. 1994. 241.50 (*0-444-81784-0*) Elsevier.

Dekker, L., et al. HPCN Challenges in Telecomp & Telecomunications: Parallel Simulation of Complex Systems & Large-Scale Applications: Proceedings of the EUROSIM International Conference, 10-12 June 1996, Delft, The Netherlands. LC 96-43302. 652p. 1996. 278.50 (*0-444-82559-2*) Elsevier.

— Management of Toxic Materials in an International Setting: A Case Study of Cadmium in the North Sea. 130p. (C). 1987. text 91.00 (*90-6191-795-6*, Pub. by A A Balkema) Ashgate Pub Co.

Dekker, Rene W. & McGowan, Phillip, compiled by. Megapodes: An Action Plan for Their Conservation 1995-1999. (Illus.). 41p. (Orig.). (C). 1995. pap. text 16.00 (*2-8317-0223-2*, Pub. by IUCN) Island Pr.

***Dekker, Rudolf M.** Childhood, Memory & Autobiography in Holland; From The Golden Age to Romanticism. LC 99-22582. 1999. text 59.95 (*0-312-22507-5*) St Martin.

Dekker, Rudolf M. The Tradition of Female Transvestism in Early Modern Europe. 256p. 1997. pap. 17.95 (*0-312-17334-2*) St Martin.

***Dekker, Sidney & Hollnagel, Erik, eds.** Coping with Computers in the Cockpit. 258p. 1999. text 70.95 (*0-7546-1147-7*, Pub. by Ashgate Pub) Ashgate Pub Co.

***Dekker, Ted.** Heaven's Wager. (Martyr's Song Ser.). 304p. 2000. pap. 12.99 (*0-8499-4241-1*) Word Pub.

Dekker, Thomas. The Dramatic works of Thomas Dekker, Vol. 1. LC 53-13115. 487p. reprint ed. pap. 150.00 (*0-608-15713-9*, 2031641) Bks Demand.

— Gull's Hornbook. McKerrow, R. M., ed. LC 74-136374. reprint ed. 59.50 (*0-404-02069-0*) AMS Pr.

— The Gull's Hornbook. (BCL1-PR English Literature Ser.). 126p. 1992. reprint ed. lib. bdg. 69.00 (*0-7812-7199-1*) Rprt Serv.

***Dekker, Thomas.** Honest Whore. 1999. pap. 27.00 (*0-87830-097-X*) Routledge.

Dekker, Thomas. Noble Soldier. LC 74-133655. (Tudor Facsimile Texts. Old English Plays Ser.: No. 140). reprint ed. 49.50 (*0-404-53440-6*) AMS Pr.

— Plague Pamphlets. (BCL1-PR English Literature Ser.). 268p. 1992. reprint ed. lib. bdg. 79.00 (*0-7812-7200-9*) Rprt Serv.

— The Plague Pamphlets of Thomas Dekker. LC 73-161963. 268p. 1925. reprint ed. 39.00 (*0-403-01319-4*) Scholarly.

— The Seven Deadly Sinnes of London. (BCL1-PR English Literature Ser.). 72p. 1992. reprint ed. lib. bdg. 59.00 (*0-7812-7201-7*) Rprt Serv.

— The Shoemaker's Holiday. 1979. pap. 4.95 (*0-8120-0314-4*) Barron.

— The Shoemaker's Holiday. Smallwood, R. L. & Wells, Stanley, eds. LC 79-87579. (Revels Plays Ser.). 241p. reprint ed. pap. 74.80 (*0-7837-4270-3*, 20439€200012) Bks Demand.

— The Shoemaker's Holiday. 2nd ed. Parr, Anthony, ed. (New Mermaids Ser.). 102p. (C). 1990. pap. text 9.75 (*0-393-90062-2*) Norton.

Dekker, Thomas & Webster, John. Northward Ho. LC 75-133655. (Tudor Facsimile Texts. Old English Plays Ser.: No. 119). reprint ed. 59.50 (*0-404-53419-8*) AMS Pr.

— Sir Thomas Wyatt. LC 75-133655. (Tudor Facsimile Texts. Old English Plays Ser.: No. 122). reprint ed. 59.50 (*0-404-53422-8*) AMS Pr.

— Westward Ho. LC 79-133656. (Tudor Facsimile Texts. Old English Plays Ser.: No. 123). reprint ed. 59.50 (*0-404-53423-6*) AMS Pr.

Dekker, Thomas, jt. auth. see Middleton, Thomas.

Dekker, Virginia M. Guns & Firearms: Index of New Information with Social, Medical, Psychological & Legal Implications. (Illus.). 160p. 1995. 47.50 (*0-7883-0420-8*); pap. 44.50 (*0-7883-0421-6*) ABBE Pubs Assn.

Dekkers, Odin. J. M. Robertson: Rationalist & Literary Critic. LC 98-8820. (Nineteenth Century Ser.). 10p. 1999. text 76.95 (*1-84014-668-0*, Pub. by Ashgate Pub) Ashgate Pub Co.

***Dekkers, Dieuwerte.** Jozef Israels, 1824-1911. 2000. 90.00 (*90-400-9400-4*) U of Wash Pr.

Dekkers, J., et al, eds. Optimality Theory: Phonology, Syntax & Acquisition. 640p. 2000. pap. text 45.00 (*0-19-823844-4*) OUP.

***Dekkers, Midas.** Dearest Pet: On Beastiality. (Illus.). 208p. 2000. pap. 17.00 (*1-85984-310-7*, Pub. by Verso) Norton.

Dekkers, Midas. Dearest Pet: On Bestiality. 276p. (gr. 13). 1994. 30.00 (*0-86091-462-3*, Pub. by Verso) Norton.

***Dekkers, Midas.** The Way of All Flesh: The Romance of Ruins. (Illus.). 256p. 2000. 25.00 (*0-374-28682-5*) FS&G.

***Dekking, Michel, et al.** Fractals: Theory & Applications in Engineering. LC 99-29644. viii, 352p. 1999. 119.00 (*1-85233-163-1*) Spr-Verlag.

Dekle, Hal, jt. auth. see Beverly, Don.

Dekleva, Jose, jt. ed. see Simmie, James.

Deklon, Ellen S. The Black Hole Modulator. (Black Hole Modulator Trilogy Ser.: Vol. 1). (Illus.). 300p. 1998. 19.95 (*1-884939-37-6*); pap. 10.95 (*1-884939-38-4*) Antoine Versailles.

— The Black Hole Modulator Users Manual. (Black Hole Modulator Trilogy Ser.: Vol. 3). (Illus.). 300p. 1998. 19.95 (*1-884939-41-4*); pap. 10.95 (*1-884939-42-2*) Antoine Versailles.

DeKlyen, Chuck, jt. auth. see Schwiebert, Pat.

DeKlyne, Betty. The Adventures of Alexandr & His Ragtime Gran: The Scourge of the Sand (Spanish Vocabulary) unabridged ed. LC 97-92776. (Illus.). 40p. (Orig.). (J). (gr. 3-5). 1997. pap. 10.00 (*0-9651559-1-9*) Rising Eagle.

— Have Sale - Will Travel Vol. 1: Secrets of an Estate Sale Agent. unabridged ed. LC 96-92049. (Illus.). ii, 100p. (Orig.). 1996. pap. 14.95 (*0-9651559-0-0*) Rising Eagle.

Dekmejian, R. H., ed. Multicultural Societies in Conflict & Coexistence. 100p. (C). 1999. pap. 6.95 (*0-9643432-1-5*) Millenia Pubs.

Dekmejian, R. Hrair. Egypt under Nasir: A Study in Political Dynamics. LC 70-152520. (Illus.). 366p. reprint ed. 119.70 (*0-8357-9593-4*, 201095600072) Bks Demand.

— Islam in Revolution: Fundamentalism in the Arab World. 250p. 1996. pap. 16.95 (*0-614-21487-4*, 587) Kazi Pubns.

— Islam in Revolution: Fundamentalism in the Arab World. 2nd ed. LC 93-46777. (Contemporary Issues in the Middle East Ser.). 320p. (C). 1994. pap. text 19.95 (*0-8156-2635-5*) Syracuse U Pr.

— Patterns of Political Leadership: Egypt, Israel, Lebanon. LC 74-20940. (Illus.). 368p. (C). 1975. text 24.50 (*0-87395-291-X*) State U NY Pr.

DeKnop, Paul, et al, eds. Worldwide Trends in Youth Sport. LC 95-33994. (Illus.). 320p. 1996. text 39.00 (*0-87322-729-8*, BDEK0729) Human Kinetics.

Dekock, John B. Extending Family Practice Medical Services to 24 Hours in Rural Areas: Studies of a Demonstration Model. (Illus.). 1975. pap. 7.95 (*0-916552-05-5*) Acoma Bks.

DeKock, Leola, ed. see Bresell, Ronald & Ben-Zikri, Abdul.

Dekock, Roger L. & Gray, Harry B. Chemical Structure & Bonding. 2nd ed. (Illus.). 491p. (C). 1989. reprint ed. pap. text 36.50 (*0-935702-61-X*) Univ Sci Bks.

DeKom, A. K., et al. Engineering Management: People & Projects. LC 94-9155. 310p. 1995. 24.95 (*0-935470-71-9*) Battelle.

Dekorme, Jim. Psychedelic Shamanism: The Cultivation, Preparation & Shamanic Use of Psychotropic Plants. 1998. pap. text 19.95 (*0-9666932-5-6*) Breakout Prods Inc.

DeKorne, James B. The Hydroponic Hot House: Low-Cost, High Yield Greenhouse Gardening. 1999. pap. text 16.95 (*1-893626-26-1*) Breakout Prods Inc.

DeKornfeld, Thomas. Specialty Board Review: Anesthesiology (MEPC) 9th ed. 356p. (C). 1996. pap. text 42.95 (*0-8385-0256-3*, A0256-6, Apple Lange Med) McGraw.

DeKorte, John. Chemistry 154 Lab Manual. 1997. pap. text 5.05 (*1-56870-273-6*) RonJon Pub.

DeKoster, Katie. Endangered Species. LC 98-18261. (Opposing Viewpoints Digests Ser.). (Illus.). 144p. (YA). (gr. 8 up). 1998. lib. bdg. 17.96 (*1-56510-747-0*) Greenhaven.

— Endangered Species. LC 98-18261. (Opposing Viewpoints Digests Ser.). (Illus.). 144p. (YA). (gr. 8 up). 1998. pap. 11.96 (*1-56510-746-2*) Greenhaven.

DeKoster, Katie, ed. The Call of the Wild. LC 98-48970. (Literary Companion Ser.). 224p. (YA). (gr. 9-12). 1998. pap. 17.45 (*1-56510-830-2*) Greenhaven.

— F. Scott Fitzgerald. LC 96-44977. (Literary Companion Ser.). 1997. lib. bdg. 20.96 (*1-56510-461-7*) Greenhaven.

— F. Scott Fitzgerald. LC 96-44977. (Literary Companion Ser.). (YA). (gr. 9 up). 1997. pap. 13.96 (*1-56510-460-9*) Greenhaven.

— Tom Sawyer. LC 98-26113. (Literary Companion Ser.). (YA). (gr. 9-12). 1998. pap. 16.20 (*1-56510-844-2*); lib. bdg. 26.20 (*1-56510-845-0*) Greenhaven.

DeKoster, Katie & Leone, Bruno, eds. Poverty: Opposing Viewpoints. LC 93-22397. 288p. (YA). 1994. pap. 16.20 (*1-56510-065-4*) Greenhaven.

DeKoster, Katie & Swisher, Karin L., eds. Child Abuse: Opposing Viewpoints. LC 93-9240. 288p. (YA). 1994. pap. 16.20 (*1-56510-055-7*) Greenhaven.

DeKoster, Katie, ed. see London, Jack.

DeKoster, Katie, jt. ed. see Swisher, Karin L.

DeKoster, Lester, jt. auth. see Berghoef, Gerard.

DeKoster, Lester R. I Believe...Living the Apostles Creed. LC 95-83975. 174p. 1996. 14.95 (*0-934874-13-1*) Chr Lib Pr.

DeKoven, Bernard. Connected Executives: A Strategic Communications Plan. (Illus.). 210p. 1990. pap. text 34.95 (*0-9625834-0-5*) B DeKoven.

DeKoven, Marianne. A Different Language: Gertrude Stein's Experimental Writing. LC 82-70558. 203p. reprint ed. pap. 63.00 (*0-608-20422-6*, 207167500002) Bks Demand.

DeKovic, Gene, photos by. Mt. St.Helena & Robert Louis Stevenson State Park: A History & Guide. 3rd rev. ed. LC 93-79308. (Illus.). 256p. 1993. pap. 17.95 (*0-9661209-0-6*) Bonnie View Bks.

Dekovic, Gene, ed. see Emerson, Ralph Waldo.

Dekovic, Gene, ed. see Stanton, Ken.

DeKovner-Mayer, Barbara. Shattered Silence: Letters from Former Soviets Struggling with Freedom at Home. (Illus.). 160p. 1993. pap. 14.95 (*0-935047-13-1*) Americas Group.

DeKretser, D. M., jt. auth. see Spera, G.

Dekro, Jeffrey, jt. auth. see Bush, Lawrence.

Dekro, Jeffrey, jt. auth. see Tessler, Betsy.

Dekryger. Auto Mechanics: Theory & Service. (Automotive Technology Ser.). 1986. text 36.95 (*0-538-33090-2*) S-W Pub.

— Auto Mechanics: Theory & Service SVC. (Automotive Technology Ser.). 1986. 19.95 (*0-538-33091-0*) S-W Pub.

— Automotive Technology: Theory & Service. 2nd ed. (Automotive Technology Ser.). 1990. pap., teacher ed. 17.50 (*0-8273-3812-0*) Delmar.

Dekryger, William J. Automotive Technology: Theory & Service. 2nd ed. (Automotive Technology Ser.). 1990. mass mkt. 56.75 (*0-8273-3811-2*) Delmar.

Deku, Afrikadzata. A Toi le Paradis de Ma Langue: Or in Honor of You My Afrikan Heaven on Earth. LC 91-72682. (Afrikan-Centric Poetry in French Ser.). 100p. 2000. write for info. (*1-56454-026-X*) Cont Afrikan.

— Ablodesafui: or, Discover the Inner Key to the Heaven of Your Divine Kingdom Within You. LC 91-72670. (Ewe Poetry Ser.). 90p. 2000. write for info. (*1-56454-014-6*) Cont Afrikan.

— Afrikamawunya or the Holy Ancient Afrikan Bible. LC 91-72674. (Afrikan Divine Revelation Ser.). 400p. 1997. 30.00 (*1-56454-018-9*) Cont Afrikan.

— Afrikan Crisis in Perspective: The Afrikan-Centric Perspective of the Afrikan World Crisis: or, The Root Causes of the Afrikan World's Crisis They Don't Want Us to Know About. LC 91-72667. (Afrikan Centric Essay Ser.). 270p. 1994. 25.00 (*1-56454-004-9*) Cont Afrikan.

D

— The Afrikan Gospel of Total Happiness Now & Always: or, Discover the Inner-Based Happiness as Your Freedom from the Hell of Your Things-Based Happiness. LC 91-72662. (Afrikan-Centric Research Work Ser.). 250p. 1994. 25.00 (*1-56454-007-3*) Cont Afrikan.

— Agbedefu: or, Turning the Impossible into Possible is What We Are Here For. LC 91-72671. (Ewe Poetry Ser.). 90p. 2000. write for info. (*1-56454-015-4*) Cont Afrikan.

— Agbenoxevie Menye: or, Why Life's Problems Are Meant to be Overcome by Us: Rather Than Allow Them to Overcome Us. LC 91-72669. (Ewe Poetry Ser.). 100p. 2000. write for info. (*1-56454-013-8*) Cont Afrikan.

— The Amazing Facts about Continental Afrikan Power in Figures & Charts: Why We Can No Longer Prefer the Crumbs of Colonial States-Based Power to the Leaf of Our Continental Afrika-Based Power. LC 91-72663. (Continental Afrikan Power Ser.). 210p. 2000. 25.00 (*1-56454-012-X*) Cont Afrikan.

— Breaking the Bloody Sword of Apartheid: or, Why Azanians of the Azania Republic are Yet to Be Free from the Hell of "South African" Apartheid. LC 91-72666. (Afrikan-Centric Play Ser.). 90p. 1995. pap. 13.00 (*1-56454-010-3*) Cont Afrikan.

— Continental Afrikan History Recovered: Or Afrika: From Two Hundred Million Seasons to the Present. LC 91-72692. 74p. 1995. pap. 15.00 (*1-56454-030-8*) Cont Afrikan.

— The Continental Afrikan Manifesto: or, The Afrikan-Centric Strategy for the Salvation of All Continental Afrikans. LC 91-72668. (Continental Afrikan Awareness Ser.). 250p. 1999. 25.00 (*1-56454-006-5*) Cont Afrikan.

— Continental Afrikan Power Now: or, How to Achieve Total Afrikan-Centric Continental Afrikan Rebirth & Empowerment for All Continentals. LC 91-72692. (Africkan-Centric Research Work Ser.). 261p. 1994. 25.00 (*1-56454-003-0*) Cont Afrikan.

— Coups de Marteau: Or My Hammer Blows for Freedom for All. LC 91-72690. (Afrikan-Centric Poetry in French Ser.). 90p. 2000. write for info. (*1-56454-028-6*) Cont Afrikan.

— Courage, Mere Afrique: Or Worry Not, Mother Continental Afrika. LC 91-72689. (Afrikan-Centric Poetry in French Ser.). 80p. 2000. write for info. (*1-56454-027-8*) Cont Afrikan.

— Cris de Tonnerre: Or My Thunder Cry for Justice for All. LC 91-72691. (Afrikan-Centric Poetry in French Ser.). 100p. 2000. write for info. (*1-56454-029-4*) Cont Afrikan.

— Discover the Limitless Power of Positive Goal Achievement Technology: or, Why Positive Goal Achievement is Not the Same as Negative Goal-Achievement. LC 91-72698. (Afrikan-Centric Self-Empowerment Ser.). 300p. 1999. 25.00 (*1-56454-036-7*) Cont Afrikan.

— Discover the Limitless Power of Positive Planning Technology or Why Positive Planning is a Technology, a Science & Art for You to Discover, Master & Use for the Benefit of All. LC 91-72702. (Afrikan-Centric Motivational Ser.). 80p. 1999. write for info. (*1-56454-040-5*) Cont Afrikan.

— Discover the Limitless Power of Positive Problem-Solving Technology: or, How to Positively Solve All Your Problems in Life or How to Live a Problem-Free Life. LC 91-72703. (Afrikan Self-Empowerment Ser.). 165p. 1995. 25.00 (*1-56454-038-3*) Cont Afrikan.

— Discover the Limitless Power of Positive Team-Building Technology: or, All You Have Ever Wanted to Know about Positive Team Building as a Techonology to Master & Use for the Benefit of All. LC 91-72701. (Afrikan-Centric Self-Empowerment Ser.). 100p. 2000. write for info. (*1-56454-039-1*) Cont Afrikan.

— Discover the Power & Benefits of Total Unlimited Wealth Technology: Discover the Blessings of Inner-Based Riches as Freedom from the Curse of Things-Based Riches. LC 91-72699. (Afrikan-Centric Self-Empowerment Ser.). 200p. 1999. 25.00 (*1-56454-037-5*) Cont Afrikan.

— From Eagle to Chicken & How to Become Eagle Again: or, How Today's Afrikans Are Being De-Afrikanized or Turned into Non-Afrikans in Their Hell of Self-Ignorance. LC 91-72696. (Afrikan-Centric Fiction Ser.). 100p. 1995. pap. 13.00 (*1-56454-034-0*) Cont Afrikan.

— Gouvernement Continental Africain Vol. 1: Benefices du Gouvernement Continental Africain (The Why of a Continental Afrikan Government) LC 91-72676. (Afrikan-Centric Research Work Ser.). 300p. 1986. write for info. (*1-56454-020-0*) Cont Afrikan.

— Gouvernement Continental Africain Vol. 2: Obstacles au Gouvernement Continental Africain (Obstacles Against the Creation of a Continental Afrikan Government) LC 91-72677. (Afrikan-Centric Research Work Ser.). 300p. 1986. write for info. (*1-56454-021-9*) Cont Afrikan.

— Gouvernement Continental Africain Vol. 3: Strategie pour la Creation du Gouvernement Continental Africain (Strategy for the Creation of the Continental Afrikan Government) LC 91-72678. (Research Work Ser.). 300p. 1986. write for info. (*1-56454-022-7*) Cont Afrikan.

— Gouvernement Continental Africain Vols. 1-3: Benefices, le Pourquoi, Obstacles et Strategie pour la Creation du Gouvernement Continental Africain (The What, Why, How & When of Continental Afrikan Government) LC 91-72675. (These de Doctorat d'Etat (PhD) Ser.). 900p. 1986. write for info. (*1-56454-019-7*) Cont Afrikan.

— I Want to Tell You Why...: or, Why Most USA Black Male Celebrities Are Obsessed to Death with the White Woman. LC 91-72695. (Afrikan-Centric Fiction Ser.). 52p. 1995. pap. 13.00 (*1-56454-033-2*) Cont Afrikan.

— The Illusions of Black & White Color: or, Discover the Lies They Don't Want Us to Know about "Black & White" Relations in U. S. A., Afrika & Europe. LC 91-72704. (Continental Afrikan Awareness Ser.). 10p. 1997. pap. 3.00 (*1-56454-042-1*) Cont Afrikan.

— La Negritude Radicale Contre la Negritude Moderee: Radical vs. Moderate Negritude. LC 91-72681. (BA. Double Hons Dissertation Ser.). 45p. 2000. write for info. (*1-56454-025-1*) Cont Afrikan.

— No Where Is Heaven: or, The Tragedy of Fighting & Dying to Make Our Chains More & More Comfortable Rather Than Removing Them. LC 91-72665. (Afrikan-Centric Play Ser.). 90p. 2000. pap. write for info. (*1-56454-011-1*) Cont Afrikan.

— Positive Continental Afrikan Self-Knowledge Technology: or, To Know We Are Continental Afrikans, Is to Be Afrikans in Thoughts, Words & Deeds. LC 91-72697. (Afrikan-Centric Self-Empowerment Ser.). 130p. 1998. 25.00 (*1-56454-035-9*) Cont Afrikan.

— The Power & Benefits of Afrikan-Centricity: or, How to Live in the Heaven of Self-Knowledge As Freedom from the Hell of Self-Igorance. LC 91-72694. (Afrikan Centric Essay Ser.). 185p. 1995. 25.00 (*1-56454-032-4*) Cont Afrikan.

— The Power & Benefits of Continental Afrikan Culture: or, Why continental Afrikan Culture is the Mother of All Cultures on Earth. LC 91-72673. (Afrikan Centric Essay Ser.). 10p. 1995. pap. 5.00 (*1-56454-017-0*) Cont Afrikan.

— The Power to Be a Continental Afrikan Again: or, Why We Can No Longer Destroy Ourselves with the Poison of Our Present Day Colonial/Slave Identities. LC 91-72672. (Afrikan Centric Essay Ser.). 44p. 1966. pap. 13.00 (*1-56454-016-2*) Cont Afrikan.

— Le Rastafari: Or the Pan-Afrikan Dimension of the Rastafari Movement. LC 91-72680. (D. E. S. (M. Phil) Thesis Ser.). 98p. 2000. write for info. (*1-56454-024-3*) Cont Afrikan.

— Sacred Afrikan Spiritual Power from Within: Sacred Afrikan Spiritual Verses; The Ancient Afrikan Secret Formula for Achieving Total Oneness with our Creator Afrikamawu Within Us in Heaven on Earth. LC 91-72660. (Sacred Afrikan Spiritual Poetry Ser.). 50p. 1994. pap. 10.00 (*1-56454-002-2*) Cont Afrikan.

— Sacred Verses for My Afrikan Queens: or, Sacred Love Poems in Honor of the Authentic Afrikan Woman as the Mother of Humanity. LC 91-72661. (Sacred Afrikan Love Poetry Ser.). 73p. 1994. pap. 13.00 (*1-56454-000-6*) Cont Afrikan.

***Deku, Afrikadzata.** Still Slaves in the Land of the "Free" The Awakened Afrikan in African America. LC 91-72705. (Afrikan-Centric Awareness Ser.). 180p. 2000. pap. 15.00 (*1-56454-043-X*) Cont Afrikan.

Deku, Afrikadzata. We Are All Continental Afrikans: or, Sacred Hymns in Celebration of Our Oneness as Afrikan-Centric Continental Afrikans at Home & Abroad. LC 91-72659. (Afrikan-Centric Pan-Afrikan Poetry Ser.). 44p. 1994. pap. 10.00 (*1-56454-001-4*) Cont Afrikan.

— Why the World Bank & the International Monetary Fund Are a Curse Rather Than a Blessing to Our Suffering Continental African Masses. LC 91-72703. (Continental Afrikan Awareness Ser.). 40p. 1997. pap. 8.00 (*1-56454-041-3*) Cont Afrikan.

Deku, Afrikadzata, et al. Communist - Socialist Practices by Capitalist U. S. A. Governments - Past & Present: or, How U. S. Governments Use Socialist/Communist Ideas/Principles to Keep Their Capitalism Alive. LC 91-72664. (Afrikan-Centric Research Work Ser.). 200p. 2000. 25.00 (*1-56454-008-1*) Cont Afrikan.

— In Defence of Kwame Nkrumah's Call for a United States of Afrika: or, Why Continental Afrika Has No Choice but to Unite Now. LC 91-72679. (M.Sc. Thesis Ser.). 98p. 2000. write for info. (*1-56454-023-5*) Cont Afrikan.

DeKuyper, Mary H. Trustee Handbook: A Guide to Effective Governance for Independent School Boards. 7th rev. ed. 204p. 1998. pap. 32.00 (*0-934338-96-5*) NAIS.

Del. Mexican Americans. 1997. pap. 20.00 (*0-8057-4587-4*) Macmillan.

Del Aguila, F., et al, eds. Precision Tests of the Standard Model at High Energy Colliders. 516p. (C). 1991. text 115.00 (*981-02-0685-2*) World Scientific Pub.

— Supersymmetry, Supergravity & Related Topics: Proceedings of the XVth GIFT International Seminar on Theoretical Physics, Sant Feliu de Guixols, Girona, Spain, June 4-9, 1984. 550p. 1985. 98.00 (*9971-966-79-4*); pap. 46.00 (*9971-966-92-1*) World Scientific Pub.

Del Aguila, Juan M. Cuba: Dilemmas of a Revolution. 3rd ed. (C). 1994. pap. 24.00 (*0-8133-8665-9*, Pub. by Westview) HarpC.

Del Aguila, Walter, tr. see Sosa, Marcelino.

del Alamo, Elizabeth, see Valdez del Alamo, Elizabeth.

Del Alamo, Jesus A. Integrated Microelectronic Devices: Physics & Modeling. (C). 2000. write for info. (*0-13-141509-3*, Macmillan Coll) P-H.

Del Amor Lopez Jimeno, Maria. Las Tabellae Defisionis de la Sicilia Griega. (C & BM Ser.: No. 22). (SPA.). 269p. 1992. pap. 52.00 (*90-256-1002-1*, Pub. by AM Hakkert) BookLink Distributors.

Del Arco, Jose Nunez, jt. ed. see Emmerij, Louis.

Del Arco Torres, Miguel A. Diccionario Enciclopedico Quimica. deluxe ed. (SPA.). 736p. 1984. 150.00 (*0-7859-6051-1*, 8470162586) Fr & Eur.

— Precis de Cadres Militaires: German-French, French-German. deluxe ed. (SPA.). 768p. 1984. 150.00 (*0-7859-6052-X*, 8470162594) Fr & Eur.

Del Arroyo, Isabel Guiterrez, see Guiterrez Del Arroyo, Isabel.

Del Bagno, Daniel, jt. auth. see Adamson, Mark.

Del Bagno, Daniel M. & Spina, R. Promotional Test Questions. 420p. 1991. 25.95 (*0-87526-381-X*) Gould.

Del Bagno, Daniel R., jt. auth. see Adamson, Mark.

***Del Bianco, Roberta, et al.** Bristol Banner Books: Anthology of Poems 2000. LC 00-104573. 80p. 2000. pap. 24.99 (*1-879183-46-3*) Bristol Banner.

Del Bimbo, Alberto. Visual Information Retrieval. 300p. (C). 1999. pap. text 69.95 (*1-55860-624-6*, Pub. by Morgan Kaufmann) Harcourt.

Del Bimbo, Alberto, et al, eds. Image Analysis & Processing: Proceedings of the 9th International Confernece, ICIAP '97, Florence, Italy, September 17-19, 1997. LC 97-29296. (Lecture Notes in Computer Science Ser.: Vol. 1310). xxii, 722p. 1997. pap. 99.00 (*3-540-63507-6*) Spr-Verlag.

— Image Analysis & Processing: Proceedings of the 9th International Confernece, ICIAP '97, Florence, Italy, September 17-19, 1997. LC 97-29296. (Lecture Notes in Computer Science Ser.: Vol. 1311). xxii, 794p. 1997. pap. 89.00 (*3-540-63508-4*) Spr-Verlag.

Del Buono, Barbara. Acknowledged a Man: Survivor of Assault in the YMCA. LC 98-73610. (Illus.). 400p. 1999. 22.95 (*0-9605698-1-2*, 77982) Ellingsworth Pr.

Del Buono, Barbara, jt. auth. see Del Buono, John.

Del Buono, John & Del Buono, Barbara. When Two Become One: The Miracle in Marriage. 100p. 1976. 17.95 (*0-9605698-0-4*) Ellingsworth Pr.

Del Busto, Charles. Case Studies on Documentary Credits under UCP 500. LC 98-130901. 162p. 1995. pap. 39.95 (*92-842-1183-2*, 535) ICC Pub.

Del Busto, Charles. Guia Sobre las Operaciones de Credito Documentario. (International Banking Ser.). (SPA., Illus.). 1994. pap. 39.95 (*84-920019-0-9*, 515SP) ICC Pub.

Del Busto, Charles. ICC Guide to Documentary Credit Operations for the UCP 500: A Stage-by-Stage Presentation of the Documentary Credit Process. rev. ed. (Illus.). 120p. (C). 1994. pap. 39.95 (*92-842-1159-X*, 515) ICC Pub.

Del Busto, Charles, ed. UCP 500 & 400 Compared: An Article-by-Article Detailed Analysis of the New UCP 500 Compared with the UCP400. rev. ed. 135p. (C). 1993. pap. text 39.95 (*92-842-1157-3*, 511) ICC Pub.

Del Busto, Charles, ed. see International Chamber of Commerce Staff.

Del C. Cerezo, Maria. El Obsceno Pajaro de la Noche: Ejercicio de Creacion. LC 87-82100. (SPA.). 192p. (Orig.). 1988. pap. 19.00 (*0-89729-456-4*) Ediciones.

Del Calzo, Nick, et al. The Triumphant Spirit - Portraits & Stories of Holocaust Survivors...Their Messages of Hope & Compassion. LC 97-89975. (Illus.). 172p. 1997. 45.00 (*0-9655260-0-3*); pap. 29.95 (*0-9655260-1-1*) Triump Spirit.

Del Campo, Carlos P. Is Brazil Sliding Toward the Extreme Left? Notes on the Land Reform Program in South America's Largest & Most Populous Country. Publications Department of the American TFP Staff, ed. & tr. by. from POR. LC 86-71922. (Illus.). 163p. (Orig.). (C). 1986. pap. 20.00 (*1-877905-22-4*) Am Soc Defense TFP.

Del Campo, Juana M. Let's Eat Mexican at Home! (Let's Eat...at Home! Ser.). 160p. 1995. pap. 5.95 (*0-572-01729-4*, Pub. by Foulsham UK) Assoc Pubs Grp.

Del Campo, Salustiano. La Sociedad de Clases Medias. (Nueva Austral Ser.: Vol. 85). (SPA.). 1991. pap. text 24.95 (*84-239-1885-8*) Elliots Bks.

Del Canizo, Jose A. Una Vida de Pelicula (A Life of the Movies) (SPA., Illus.). (YA). 1993. pap. 6.99 (*968-16-4168-X*, Pub. by Fondo) Continental Bk.

Del Carmen. Criminal Procedure. 2nd ed. (Criminal Justice Ser.). 1991. text, teacher ed. write for info. (*0-534-15553-7*) Wadsworth Pub.

— Criminal Procedure: Law & Practices. 5th ed. (Criminal Justice Ser.). 2000. pap. text 53.25 (*0-534-51471-5*) Wadsworth Pub.

***Del Carmen.** Law & Practice: Companion-Criminal Procedure. 5th ed. 2000. pap. 15.00 (*0-534-51474-X*) Thomson Learn.

Del Carmen Baerga, Maria. Genero y Trabajo: La Industria de la Aguja en P. R. y el Caribe Hispanico. 1993. pap. 11.95 (*0-8477-0190-5*) U of PR Pr.

Del Carmen Blazquez, Maria, tr. see Gomez-Navarro, Maria J., et al, eds.

Del Carmen Boza, Maria. Scattering the Ashes. LC 98-5512. 362p. 1998. pap. 15.00 (*0-927534-75-4*) Biling Rev-Pr.

Del Carmen Boza, Maria, et al, eds. Nosotras: Latina Literature Today. LC 85-73396. (ENG & SPA.). 96p. 1986. pap. text 10.00 (*0-916950-63-8*) Biling Rev-Pr.

Del Carmen, Concepcion M., jt. auth. see Silva, Carlos.

Del Carmen Herrero Aisa, Maria, notes. Antologia de la Novela Realista. (SPA.). (C). 1998. pap. 9.95 (*84-294-4627-3*) Santillana.

Del Carmen, Rolando V. Criminal Procedure: Law & Practice. 2nd ed. LC 90-49935. 483p. (C). 1991. pap. 43.95 (*0-534-15552-9*) Wadsworth Pub.

— Criminal Procedure: Law & Practice. 3rd ed. LC 90-49935. 522p. 1994. mass mkt. 53.95 (*0-534-21558-0*) Wadsworth Pub.

— Criminal Procedure: Law & Practice. 4th ed. LC 97-4170. (Criminal Justice Ser.). (C). 1997. 47.25 (*0-534-52695-0*) Wadsworth Pub.

— Criminal Procedure for Law Enforcement Personnel. LC 86-26411. (Criminal Justice Ser.). 446p. (C). 1987. pap. 37.95 (*0-534-08028-6*) Brooks-Cole.

Del Carmen, Rolando V. & Walker, Jeffery T. Briefs of Leading Cases in Law Enforcement. 3rd ed. LC 97-70109. 290p. (C). 1997. pap. text 22.95 (*0-87084-188-2*) Anderson Pub Co.

***Del Carmen, Rolando V. & Walker, Jeffery T.** Briefs of Leading Cases in Law Enforcement. 4th ed. LC 99-41191. 1999. pap. 25.95 (*1-58360-507-X*) Anderson Pub Co.

Del Carmen, Rolando V., et al. Briefs of Leading Cases in Corrections. 2nd ed. LC 97-75146. 270p. (C). 1998. pap. 22.95 (*0-87084-116-5*) Anderson Pub Co.

— Briefs of Leading Cases in Juvenile Justice. LC 97-75149. 288p. (C). 1997. pap. 22.95 (*0-87084-120-3*) Anderson Pub Co.

Del Caro, Adrian. Early Poetry of Paul Celan: In the Beginning Was the Word. LC 97-16227. 256p. 1997. text 45.00 (*0-8071-2209-2*) La State U Pr.

— Holderlin, the Poetics of Being. LC 90-25927. 145p. reprint ed. pap. 45.00 (*0-608-10564-3*, 207118400009) Bks Demand.

— Hugo von Hofmannsthal: Poets & the Language of Life. LC 92-22939. 184p. 1993. text 35.00 (*0-8071-1786-2*) La State U Pr.

— Nietzsche Contra Nietzsche: Creativity & the Anti-Romantic. LC 88-37659. 336p. 1989. text 47.50 (*0-8071-1493-6*) La State U Pr.

***Del Caro, Adrian & Ward, Janet, eds.** German Studies in the Post-Holocaust Age: The Politics of Memory, Identity, & Ethnicity. 256p. 2000. 55.00 (*0-87081-561-X*) U of Okla Pr.

Del Caro, Adrian, jt. frwd. see Callaway, H. G.

Del Caro, Adrian, tr. see Szyszkowitz, Gerald.

Del Casal, Julian. The Poetry of Julian Del Casal: A Critical Edition, 2 vols., Vol. 1. Glickman, Robert J., ed. LC 76-22800. (SPA., Illus.). 304p. 1976. reprint ed. pap. 94.30 (*0-7837-4878-7*, 204478800001) Bks Demand.

— The Poetry of Julian Del Casal: A Critical Edition, 2 vols., Vol. 2. Glickman, Robert J., ed. LC 76-22800. (SPA & ENG., Illus.). 486p. 1978. reprint ed. pap. 150.70 (*0-7837-4879-5*, 204478800002) Bks Demand.

— The Poetry of Julian Del Casal: A Critical Edition, Vol. 3. Glickman, Robert J., ed. LC 76-22800. (SPA., Illus.). 509p. reprint ed. pap. 157.80 (*0-608-04453-9*, 204478800003) Bks Demand.

Del Castillo, Adelaida, ed. Between Borders: Essays on Mexicana - Chicana History. (Mujer Latina Ser.). (Illus.). 560p. (C). 1990. pap. 45.00 (*0-915745-14-3*) Floricanto Pr.

del Castillo, Amelia. Geminis Deshabitado. LC 94-71769. (Coleccion Espejo de Paciencia). (SPA.). 68p. (Orig.). 1994. pap. 9.95 (*0-89729-744-X*) Ediciones.

***del Castillo, Amelia.** El Hombre de la Espiga. (Coleccion Espejo de Paciencia). 84p. 2000. pap. 9.95 (*0-89729-918-3*) Ediciones.

Del Castillo, Ana Hernandez, see Hernandez del Castillo, Ana.

Del Castillo De Mayada, Maruja, jt. auth. see Ackerman, James D.

Del Castillo, Diego. The Legal Literature of Accounting: On Accounts by Diego del Castillo. Mills, Patti A., tr. from SPA. (Foundations of Accounting Ser.: No. 12).Tr. of Tratado de Cuentas. 120p. 1988. text 10.00 (*0-8240-6118-7*) Garland.

Del Castillo, Gustavo. U. S. - Mexican Trade Relations: From the Generalized System of Preferences to a Formal Bilateral Trade Treaty. (Research Reports: No. 14). 27p. (Orig.). (C). 1985. pap. 5.00 (*0-935391-13-4*) UCSD Ctr US-Mex.

Del Castillo, Janet & Schwartz, Lois. Backyard Racehorse: A Comprehensive Off Track Program for Owners & Trainers. 3rd ed. (Illus.). 300p. 1996. pap. text 24.95 (*1-884475-01-9*) Predict Pubns.

Del Castillo, Julio. Repair Manual for Marx O Electric Locomotives & Accessories. (Illus.). 200p. (Orig.). 1994. pap. 29.95 (*0-9645454-0-3*) Top Hat Hobbies.

Del Castillo, Luis F. El Fenomeno Magico de la Osmosis. (Ciencia para Todos Ser.). (SPA.). pap. 6.99 (*968-16-2461-0*, Pub. by Fondo) Continental Bk.

Del Castillo, Michel. La Morte d'un Poete. (FRE.). 367p. 1991. pap. 11.95 (*0-7859-2164-8*, 2070383784) Fr & Eur.

Del Castillo, Patricia, tr. see Wyndham, John H.

Del Castillo, Richard G. La Familia: Chicano Families in the Urban Southwest, 1848 to the Present. LC 84-40356. 224p. 1984. pap. text 13.00 (*0-268-01273-3*) U of Notre Dame Pr.

Del Cecchetti, Giovanni, tr. see Leopardi, Giacomo.

Del Cervo, Diane M., ed. Witchcraft in Europe & America: Guide to the Microfilm Collection. 112p. 1983. 100.00 (*0-89235-074-1*) Primary Srce Media.

Del Cervo, Diane M., jt. ed. see Research Publications, Inc. Staff.

Del Chamberlain, Von. When Stars Came down to Earth: Cosmology of the Skidi Pawnee Indians of North America. LC 82-16390. (Anthropological Papers: No. 26). (Illus.). 272p. 1982. pap. 17.95 (*0-87919-098-1*) Ballena Pr.

Del Chiaro, Mario A. Classical Art: Sculpture. LC 84-23651. (Illus.). 112p. (Orig.). 1984. pap. 18.00 (*0-89951-055-8*) Santa Barb Mus Art.

— The Genucillia Group: A Class of Etruscan Red-Figured Plates. LC 57-9900. (University of California Publications in Social Welfare: Vol. 3, No. 4). 140p. reprint ed. pap. 43.40 (*0-608-13951-3*, 202133200021) Bks Demand.

Del Col, Andrea. Domenico Scandella Known As Menocchio: His Trials Before the Inquisition (1583-1599) Tedeschi, John & Tedeschi, Anne C., trs. LC 94-46794. (Medieval & Renaissance Texts & Studies: Vol. 139).Tr. of Domenico Scandella detto Menocchio. 288p. 1997. reprint ed. 26.00 (*0-86698-148-9*, MR139) MRTS.

Del Colle, Ralph. Christ & the Spirit: Spirit-Christology in Trinitarian Perspectives. LC 92-47399. 256p. 1994. text 49.95 (*0-19-507776-8*) OUP.

***Del Conde, Teresa, ed.** Tamayo. Long, Andrew & Panichi, Louisa, trs. LC 99-66037. (Illus.). 252p. 2000. 100.00 (*0-8212-2651-7*, Pub. by Bulfinch Pr) Little.

D

An Asterisk (*) at the beginning of an entry indicates that the title is appearing for the first time.

Del Conde, Teresa & Lozano, Louis-Martin. Maria Izquierdo, 1902-1955. White, Colin & Velasco, Alejandro, trs. from SPA. LC 97-217454. (ENG & SPA., Illus.). 126p. 1997. pap. 29.95 (*1-889410-00-4*) Mexican Fine Arts.

Del Conte, Anna. Gli Antipasti: Antipasti & Other Appetizers. LC 93-13389. (Anna del Cotne's Italian Kitchen Ser.). (Illus.). 64p. 1994. 14.00 (*0-671-87029-7*) S&S Trade.

— The Classic Food of Northern Italy. (Illus.). 254p. 1997. pap. 24.95 (*1-85793-841-0*, Pub. by Pavilion Bks Ltd) Trafalgar.

***Del Conte, Anna.** The Classic Food of Northern Italy. 1999. pap. text 16.95 (*1-86205-218-2*, Pub. by Pavilion Bks Ltd) Trafalgar.

Del Conte, Anna. I Dolci: Sweet Things. LC 93-17493. (Anna del Cotne's Italian Kitchen Ser.). (Illus.). 64p. 1993. 14.00 (*0-671-87032-7*) S&S Trade.

— A Little Italian Cookbook. (Illus.). 60p. 1990. 7.95 (*0-87701-754-9*) Chronicle Bks.

— A Little Italian Cookbook. 60p. 1996. 7.95 (*0-8118-1287-1*) Chronicle Bks.

— Pasta Dishes: La Pastaciutta. LC 93-13291. (Anna del Cotne's Italian Kitchen Ser.). (Illus.). 64p. 1994. 14.00 (*0-671-87031-9*) S&S Trade.

— I Risotti: Risottos & Other Appetizers. LC 93-13330. (Illus.). 64p. 1993. 14.00 (*0-671-87030-0*) S&S Trade.

Del Conte, Anna, jt. auth. see Treuille, Eric.

Del, Core A., ed. Advances in Onboard System Technologies. (European Community-Aeronautics Research Ser.). 264p. 1996. 95.00 (*0-471-95148-X*) Wiley.

Del Corso, Dante, jt. ed. see Conte, Gianni.

Del-Debbio, Andy, jt. auth. see Roche, Julie A.

Del Deo, Giovanna, jt. auth. see Del Deo, Josephine C.

***Del Deo, Josephine C.** Beginnings - The History of the Fine Arts Work Center, 1964-1969. (Illus.). iii, 57p. 1999. spiral bd. 20.00 (*0-9673628-2-2*) Three Dunes.

— Compass Grass Anthology: A Collection of Provincetown Portraits. (Illus.). iv, 83p. 1984. pap. 5.00 (*0-9673628-0-6*, A1) Three Dunes.

Del Deo, Josephine C. & Del Deo, Giovanna. Passaggi. (Illus.). 95p. 1995. pap. 17.50 (*0-9673628-1-4*) Three Dunes.

Del Deo, Josephine C. & Moffett, Ross. Figures in a Landscape: The Life & Times of the American Painter, Ross Moffett, 1888-1971. LC 94-12371. 1994. write for info. (*0-89865-901-9*) Donning Co.

Del Dotto, Dave. How to Make Nothing But Money: Discovering Your Hidden Opportunities for Wealth. (Illus.). 271p. 1991. mass mkt. 11.99 (*0-446-39237-5*, Pub. by Warner Bks) Little.

Del Dotto, Jerel E., jt. auth. see Rourke, Byron P.

Del Duca, Louis F., et al. Annotations to the Model Procurement Code for State & Local Governments, with Analytical Summary or State Enactments. LC 96-19388. 1996. pap. write for info. (*1-57073-334-1*) Amer Bar Assn.

— Commercial Transactions Vol. 2: Problems & Materials on Sales under the Uniform Commercial Code, Supplement. 129p. (C). 1997. pap. text 10.00 (*0-87084-239-0*) Anderson Pub Co.

— Commercial Transactions, Vol. 1: Problems & Materials on Secured Transactions under the Uniform Commercial Code. LC 91-38769. 471p. 1992. pap. 39.95 (*0-87084-151-3*) Anderson Pub Co.

— Negotiable Instruments: Under the Uniform Commercial Code & the United Nations Convention on International Bills of Exchange & International Promissory Notes, 3. LC 93-4774. (Commercial Transactions Ser.: Vols. 2 & 3). 417p. 1993. pap. 45.95 (*0-87084-153-X*) Anderson Pub Co.

— Sales under the Uniform Commercial Code & the Convention on International Sale of Goods, 2. LC 92-46580. (Commercial Transactions Ser.: Vols. 1, 2 & 3). 544p. 1993. pap. 45.95 (*0-87084-152-1*) Anderson Pub Co.

Del Duca, Louis F., et al. Secured Transactions under the Uniform Commercial Code & International Commerce. write for info. (*1-58360-758-7*) Anderson Pub Co.

Del Duca, Patrick, tr. see Mengozzi, Paolo.

Del Favero, Dennis. Dennis Del Favero: Cross-Currents: ZKM Digital Arts. 2nd ed. 1999. spiral bd. 24.95 (*3-89322-448-3*) Dr Cantz sche Druckerei GmbH.

Del Frate, Anna A., jt. ed. see Zvekic, Ugljesa.

Del Frate, Anna Alvazzi, see Zvekic, Ugljesa & Alvazzi Del Frate, Anna, eds.

Del Fuego, Laura. Maravilla. (Mujer Latina Ser.). 233p. (Orig.). 1990. pap. 19.95 (*0-915745-15-1*) Floricanto Pr.

Del Gaizo, Edward R., et al. The Alligator Trap: How to Sell Without Being Turned into a Pair of Shoes. 156p. 1996. text 21.95 (*0-7863-0856-7*, Irwn Prfssnl) McGraw-Hill Prof.

Del Galdo, Elisa. International User Interfaces. LC 96-195519. 288p. 1996. 59.99 (*0-471-14965-9*) Wiley.

***Del Giacco, Maureen.** Lost Inside My Brain: A Discovery of a New Therapy for Brain Injury & the Hidden Problems of Recovery. Booth Associates Staff, ed. (Illus.). 100p. 2000. pap. 29.99 (*0-9701233-0-2*) Del Giaccos Art.

Del Giudice, Daniele. Takeoff: The Pilot's Lore. Farrell, Joseph, tr. LC 96-45987. 176p. 1997. 20.00 (*0-15-100269-X*) Harcourt.

Del Giudice, Luisa, ed. Italian Traditional Song: A Music & Text Anthology. 2nd rev. ed. (ENG & ITA., Illus.). 140p. (Orig.). (C). 1995. pap. 25.00 (*0-9644842-0-X*) IIDC.

Del Giudice, Luisa, ed. Studies in Italian American Folklore. LC 93-21459. (Publications of the American Folklore Society, Bibliographical & Special Ser.). (Illus.). 285p. (C). 1994. pap. text 19.95 (*0-87421-171-9*) Utah St U Pr.

Del Gludice, Daniele. Lines of Light. 208p. 1988. 19.95 (*0-15-152420-3*) Harcourt.

Del Granado, Don J. Ballads & Sonnets of Don Javier del Granado. Phenix, Bruce, tr. from SPA. & intro. by. 80p. (Orig.). 1991. pap. 2.99 (*0-9628779-1-3*) Invesco LTDA.

Del Grande, John, et al. Geometry & Spatial Sense. LC 93-9346. (Curriculum & Evaluation Standards for School Mathematics Addenda Ser.: Grades K-6). (Illus.). 56p. 1993. pap. 13.95 (*0-87353-317-8*) NCTM.

Del Greco, A. A. Giacomo Leopardi in Hispanic Literature. 1952. 12.50 (*0-913298-63-8*) S F Vanni.

Del Guercio, Louis. Multilingual Manual for Medical History-Taking. (FRE.). 178p. 1972. pap. 39.95 (*0-7859-9618-4*) Fr & Eur.

Del Guercio, P. & Cruse, J. M., eds. B Lymphocytes: Function & Regulation. (Contributions to Microbiology & Immunology Ser.: Vol. 11). (Illus.). 310p. 1989. 241.75 (*3-8055-4995-4*) S Karger.

***Del 'Homme, Melissa.** Number Recognition & Counting & Quantity Workbook. 2nd ed. (Tutor Bks.). (Illus.). 160p. (YA). (gr. k up). 2000. pap., wbk. ed. 12.95 (*0-7373-0454-5*, 04545W, Pub. by Lowell Hse Juvenile) NTC Contemp Pub Co.

Del La Mina, Don F. My Escape from the Auto de Fe. (Illus.). 112p. 1997. pap. 9.95 (*0-9643914-2-2*) Shiloh Med.

Del Litto, ed. see Stendhal, pseud.

Del Litto, Victor, ed. see Stendhal, pseud.

Del Litto, Vittorio, jt. auth. see Stendhal, pseud.

Del Litto, Vittorio, ed. see Stendhal, pseud.

Del Mar, Alexander. Barbara Villiers. 1973. 250.00 (*0-87968-705-3*) Gordon Pr.

— A History of Monetary Crimes. 1977. 250.00 (*0-8490-0337-7*) Gordon Pr.

— History of Money in America. 1973. 59.95 (*0-8490-0338-5*) Gordon Pr.

— A History of the Precious Metals from the Earliest Times to the Present. 2nd rev. ed. LC 68-18230. (Library of Money & Banking History). (Illus.). xxii, 477p. 1969. reprint ed. 57.50 (*0-678-00475-7*) Kelley.

— Roman & Moslem Moneys. 1972. 59.95 (*0-8490-0968-5*) Gordon Pr.

— The Science of Money. 1973. 59.95 (*0-8490-1002-0*) Gordon Pr.

Del Mar, David P. What Trouble I Have Seen: A History of Violence Against Wives. LC 95-46974. 240p. (C). 1996. text 39.95 (*0-674-95076-3*) HUP.

— What Trouble I Have Seen: A History of Violence Against Wives. 256p. 1998. pap. text 16.95 (*0-674-95078-X*) HUP.

Del Mar, Eugene. The Conquest of Disease: The Psychology of Mental & Spiritual Healing. 250p. 1997. reprint ed. pap. 24.95 (*0-7661-0025-1*) Kessinger Pub.

Del Mar, Lee. The Aerosol Solution. 330p. (Orig.). 1997. pap. 12.00 (*0-9659542-1-8*) Aa Press.

Del Mar Martinez Rodriquez, Maria & Rodriguez Bravo, Juan L., eds. Text & Concordance of Escorial Manuscript M.III 7: Viajes de John of Mandeville. (Dialect Ser.: No. 7). 8p. 1984. text 10.00 incl. fiche (*0-942260-46-5*) Hispanic Seminary.

Del Mar, Norman. Anatomy of the Orchestra. LC 81-11559. 512p. 1996. pap. 22.50 (*0-520-05062-2*, Pub. by U CA Pr) Cal Prin Full Svc.

— Conducting Beethoven: The Symphonies, Vol. 1. (Illus.). 234p. (C). 1992. text 55.00 (*0-19-816218-9*); pap. text 27.95 (*0-19-816219-7*) OUP.

— Conducting Berlioz. LC 97-12605. 240p. 1999. text 49.95 (*0-19-816552-8*); pap. text 19.95 (*0-19-816559-5*) OUP.

— Conducting Brahms. (Illus.). 240p. (C). 1993. text 55.00 (*0-19-816356-8*, 14622); pap. text 27.95 (*0-19-816357-6*) OUP.

— Conducting Elgar. LC 97-25755. (Illus.). 288p. 1999. text 49.95 (*0-19-816551-X*); pap. text 19.95 (*0-19-816557-9*) OUP.

— Conducting Favourite Concert Pieces. LC 97-25753. (Illus.). 272p. 1999. text 49.95 (*0-19-816553-6*); pap. text 19.95 (*0-19-816558-7*) OUP.

— Richard Strauss: A Critical Commentary on His Life & Works, II. LC 85-19033. (Illus.). 1986. pap. text 21.95 (*0-8014-9318-8*) Cornell U Pr.

— Richard Strauss: A Critical Commentary on His Life & Works, III. LC 85-19033. (Illus.). 1986. pap. text 21.95 (*0-8014-9319-6*) Cornell U Pr.

— Richard Strauss: A Critical Commentary on His Life & Works, Vol. I. LC 85-19033. (Illus.). 464p. 1986. text 52.50 (*0-8014-1780-5*) Cornell U Pr.

— Richard Strauss: A Critical Commentary on His Life & Works, Vol. II. LC 85-19033. (Illus.). 480p. 1986. text 52.50 (*0-8014-1781-3*) Cornell U Pr.

— Richard Strauss: A Critical Commentary on His Life & Works, Vol. III. LC 85-19033. (Illus.). 584p. 1986. text 52.50 (*0-8014-1782-1*) Cornell U Pr.

Del Mar, Norman R. Conducting Brahms. LC 93-22072. (Illus.). 160p. 1993. text 55.00 (*0-19-816358-4*, Clarendon Pr); pap. text 27.95 (*0-19-816359-2*, Clarendon Pr) OUP.

— Mahler's 6th Symphony: A Study. (Eulenburg Music Ser.). (Illus.). 153p. 1982. reprint ed. pap. 22.50 (*0-903873-29-X*) Da Capo.

Del Mar, Walter. The Gold Mines of Blackhawk Canyon. (Illus.). 64p. 1998. pap. 10.00 (*0-9668925-1-8*) W H Del Mar.

Del Mar, William A., jt. ed. see Pender, Harold.

Del Mastro, M. L., tr. The Revelation of Divine Love in Sixteen Showings: Made to Dame Julian of Norwich. LC 94-338. (A Liguori Classic Ser.). 224p. (Orig.). 1994. pap. 10.95 (*0-89243-638-7*, Liguori Triumph) Liguori Pubns.

Del Mastro, M. L., jt. tr. see Meisel, Anthony C.

Del Mastro, M. L., tr. & intro. see Julian of Norwich Staff.

Del Mazo, J., ed. Reproductive Toxicology: In Vitro Germ Cell Developmental Toxicology from Science to Social. (Advances in Experimental Medicine & Biology Ser.: 444). (Illus.). 236p. (C). 1998. text 130.00 (*0-306-46025-4*, Kluwer Plenum) Kluwer Academic.

Del Mazza, Valentino. Show Us Your Face Lord, & We Shall Work Wonders. LC 93-10461.Tr. of Mostraci, Signore, Il Tuo Volto - E Compiremo Meraviglie. 107p. 1993. reprint ed. pap. 4.95 (*0-8198-6959-7*) Pauline Bks.

del Molino, Conchita Peraire, tr. see Suzanne, Jamie.

Del Monte, Alfredo, ed. Recent Developments in the Theory of Industrial Organization. LC 91-40854. 336p. (C). 1992. text 75.00 (*0-472-10337-7*, 10337) U of Mich Pr.

Del Monte, Frank. Motorcycle Arizona! A Guide to Touring Arizona by Motorcycle. LC 94-38135. (Illus.). 160p. (Orig.). 1994. pap. 9.95 (*0-914846-99-X*) Golden West Pub.

Del Negro, Giovanna. Looking Through My Mother's Eyes: Life Stories of Nine Italian Immigrant Women in Canada. LC 95-81766. 133p. 1996. pap. 12.00 (*1-55071-043-5*) Guernica Editions.

Del Negro, J. M., jt. auth. see Stevenson, D.

Del Negro, Janice. Lucy Dove. LC 97-43607. (Illus.). (J). (gr. 3-6). 1998. 16.95 (*0-7894-2514-9*) DK Pub Inc.

Del Ninno, Carlo. Welfare & Poverty in Conakry: Assessment & Determinants. (Working Papers: No. 66). 60p. (C). 1994. pap. 7.00 (*1-56401-166-6*) Cornell Food.

Del Ninno, Carlo, jt. auth. see Sahn, David E.

Del Olmo Lete, Gregorio. Canaanite Religion According to the Liturgical Texts of Ugarit. Watson, Wilfred G., tr. from SPA. LC 98-42318. Orig. Title: La Religion Cananea Segun la Liturgia de Ugarit. 420p. 1998. 50.00 (*1-883053-46-3*) CDL Pr.

Del Olmo Ordonez, Manuel F. Cristobal Colon: Descubrimiento Jibaro Del Fortin de la Navidad. (SPA., Illus.). 152p. 1997. pap. 19.95 (*0-944551-22-X*) Sundance Pr TX.

Del Paso, Fernando. Palinuro of Mexico. Plaister, Elisabeth, tr. LC 95-53205. 557p. 1996. pap. 14.95 (*1-56478-095-3*) Dalkey Arch.

Del Pedro, M. & Pahud, P. Vibration Mechanics: Linear Discrete Systems. (C). 1991. text 175.00 (*0-7923-1427-1*) Kluwer Academic.

Del Piero, G. & Maceri, Franco, eds. Unilateral Problems in Structural Analysis 2. (CISM Ser.: Vol. 304) (Illus.). vi, 314p. 1988. 68.95 (*0-387-82036-1*) Spr-Verlag.

— Unilateral Problems in Structural Analysis 4: Proceedings of the Fourth Meeting on Unilateral Problems in Structural Analysis, Capri, June 14-16, 1989. (International Series of Numerical Mathematics: Vol. 101). 240p. 1991. 91.00 (*0-8176-2487-2*) Birkhauser.

Del Piero, Ulisse, et al, eds. The Heritage of Cullman County, Alabama. (Heritage of Alabama Ser.: No. 22). (Illus.). 316p. 1998. 55.00 (*1-891647-12-1*) Herit Pub Consult.

Del Pilar Arguelles, Maria. Morality & Power: The U. S. Colonial Experience in Puerto Rico from 1898 to 1948, Vol. XIX. (American Values Projected Abroad Ser.: Vol. 19). 256p. (C). 1995. pap. text 28.50 (*0-7618-0109-X*); lib. bdg. 57.50 (*0-7618-0108-1*) U Pr of Amer.

Del Pilar de Restrepo, Maria, tr. see White, Jan.

Del Pinal, Jorge H. & Garcia, Jesus M. Hispanic Americans Today: A Report from Census Data. (Illus.). 48p. (Orig.). (C). 1994. pap. text 25.00 (*0-7881-0390-3*) DIANE Pub.

Del Pino, G. & Rebolledo, R., eds. Lectures in Probability & Statistics. (Lecture Notes in Mathematics Ser.: Vol. 1215). (ENG & FRE.). v, 491p. 1986. 58.30 (*0-387-16822-2*) Spr-Verlag.

del Pino, Salvador Rodriguez, see Rodriguez del Pino, Salvador, ed.

Del Pizzo, Wilson, jt. ed. see Fox, James M.

Del Pobil, Angel P., et al, eds. Industrial & Engineering Applications of Artificial Intelligence & Expert System: 11th International Conference, IEA-AIE-98, Benicssim, Castelln, Spain, June 1-4, 1998. Proceedings, Vol. 141. LC 98-8209. (Lecture Notes in Computer Science Ser.: Vol. I, Vol. 1415). xxiv, 887p. 1998. pap. 100.00 (*3-540-64582-9*) Spr-Verlag.

— Industrial & Engineering Applications of Artificial Intelligence & Expert System: 11th International Conference, IEA-AIE-98, Benicssim, Castelln, Spain, June 1-4, 1998. Proceedings, Vol. 141. LC 98-8209. (Lecture Notes in Computer Science Ser.: Vol. II, Vol. 1416). xxiii, 943p. 1998. pap. 100.00 (*3-540-64574-8*) Spr-Verlag.

del Pomar, Felipe Cossio, see Cossio del Pomar, Felipe.

Del Porto, Heriberto. La Decadencia de la Familia Aristocrativa y Su Reflejo en la Novela Espanola Moderna. LC 81-69539. (SPA.). 150p. (Orig.). 1984. pap. 12.95 (*0-89729-302-9*) Ediciones.

Del Pozo, Emilio, ed. Somatostatin: Recent Advances in Basic Research & Clinical Applications. (Journal: Hormone Research Ser.: Vol. 29, No. 2-3). 88p. (Orig.). 1988. pap. 102.75 (*3-8055-4809-5*) S Karger.

Del Pozo, Maruja, tr. see John, Laurie.

Del Pozo, Maruja, tr. see Suzanne, Jamie.

Del Pozo, Maruja, tr. see William, Kate.

Del Prado, Dana. Really Weird News Stories. LC 95-38663. (Kidbacks Ser.). 1996. 11.09 (*0-606-10292-2*, Pub. by Turtleback) Demco.

Del Prado, Dana. Terror Below! True Shark Stories. LC 96-35807. (All Aboard Reading Ser.). (Illus.). 48p. (Orig.). (J). (gr. 2-4). 1997. pap. 3.95 (*0-448-41124-5*, G & D) Peng Put Young Read.

Del Prado, Dana. Terror Below!, True Shark Stories. LC 96-35807. (All Aboard Reading Ser.). (J). 1997. 9.15 (*0-606-11972-8*, Pub. by Turtleback) Demco.

Del Prado, Wilfredo. Cuba: Destiny As Choice. LC 85-81350. (Coleccion Cuba y sus Jueces). (Illus.). 191p. (Orig.). 1986. pap. 14.95 (*0-89729-383-5*) Ediciones.

Del Prete, Thomas. Thomas Merton & the Education of the Whole Person. LC 89-27775. 195p. (Orig.). 1990. pap. 19.95 (*0-89135-074-8*) Religious Educ.

Del Prete, Tony. Where in the World? Travels & Travails in Search of the Good Life. LC 97-9685. 196p. (Orig.). 1996. reprint ed. pap. 13.95 (*1-887969-02-0*) Cathedral PA.

Del Prete, Tony, ed. see Randall, Marga L.

Del Principe, David. Rebellion, Death & Aesthetics in Italy: The Demons of Scapigliatura. LC 95-49129. (Illus.). 184p. (C). 1996. 32.95 (*0-8386-3638-1*) Fairleigh Dickinson.

Del Puerto, Carlos & Vergara, Silvio. The True Cuban Bass.Tr. of Verdadero Bajo Cubano. (ENG & SPA.). 63p. (Orig.). 1994. pap. text 20.00 (*1-883217-01-6*) Sher Music.

Del Re, E., ed. Mobile & Personal Communications: Proceedings of the 2nd Joint COST 227-231 Workshop on Mobile & Personal Communications, Florence, Italy, 20-21 April 1995. 382p. 1995. text 190.00 (*0-444-82328-X*) Elsevier.

Del Re, Gerard & Del Re, Patricia. The Christmas Almanac. 1979. 10.95 (*0-385-13353-7*) Doubleday.

— The Only Book: A Compendium of One-of-a-Kind Facts. 256p. (Orig.). 1994. pap. 9.00 (*0-449-90908-5*, Columbine) Fawcett.

Del Re, Gianmarco. Italian Scene. (Illus.). 200p. (Orig.). 1997. pap. 12.95 (*0-85449-247-X*, Pub. by Gay Mens Pr) LPC InBook.

***Del Re, Giuseppe.** The Cosmic Dance. LC 99-38482. 400p. 1999. 24.95 (*1-890151-25-4*) Templeton Fnd.

Del Re, Michele C., jt. auth. see Palermo, George B.

Del Re, Patricia, jt. auth. see Del Re, Gerard.

Del Re, Robert & McKittrick, Harold V., eds. The Role of the Resident Engineer: Proceedings of a Specialty Conference Sponsored by the Committee on Contract Administration of the Construction Division. 197p. 1985. 18.00 (*0-87262-477-3*) Am Soc Civil Eng.

***Del Real Eduardo, Garcia.** Nueva Guia De Ginecologia. 1999. pap. text 18.95 (*84-7880-977-5*) Planeta.

Del Real Francia, Pedro J. Lexikon Manilianum. (Alpha-Omega, Reihe A Ser.). (GER.). xii, 584p. 1998. write for info. (*3-487-10640-X*) G Olms Pubs.

Del Real, Maria E. Como Conocer y Resolver los Problemas Emocionales De Sus Hijos. (SPA., Illus.). 240p. (Orig.). 1990. pap. 3.50 (*0-944499-47-3*) Editorial Amer.

Del Real, Maria E., ed. see Editorial America, S. A. Staff.

Del Refugio Robledo, Maria. The Answer: Valuing Youth in Schools & Families: A Report on Hispanic Dropouts in the Dallas Independent School District. (Illus.). 79p. (Orig.). 1989. pap. text 9.00 (*1-878550-26-8*) Inter Dev Res Assn.

Del Refugio Robledo, Maria, et al. Texas School Dropout Survey Project: A Summary of Findings. (Illus.). 81p. (Orig.). 1986. pap. text 7.00 (*1-878550-37-3*) Inter Dev Res Assn.

Del Regato, Juan A. Radiological Physicists. 188p. 1985. 25.00 (*0-88318-469-9*, Pub. by Am Inst Physics) Med Physics Pub.

Del Rey, Judy-Lynn, ed. see Heinlein, Robert A.

***Del, Rey Maria.** Nexus Sisterhood of the Institute. 2000. mass mkt. 6.95 (*0-352-33456-8*) London Bridges.

***Del Rey, Maria.** Pleasure Principle. 2000. mass mkt. 6.95 (*0-352-33482-7*) Nexus.

del Rio, A. Ingles Basico. (SPA., Illus.). 153p. 1997. pap. 4.98 (*968-15-0643-X*) Edit Diana.

Del Rio, Amelia A., jt. auth. see Del Rio, Angel.

Del Rio, Angel, ed. Responsible Freedom in the Americas. 1969. reprint ed. lib. bdg. 95.00 (*0-8371-0199-9*, RIFA, Greenwood Pr) Greenwood.

Del Rio, Angel & Del Rio, Amelia A. Antologia General de La Literatura Espanola. (SPA.). 1982. 29.95 (*0-86515-001-X*) Edit Mensaje.

Del Rio De, La Hoz Isabel. Cathedral & the City of Toledo, 1. 1999. pap. text 25.00 (*1-85759-212-3*) Scala Books.

Del Rio, Eduardo, jt. auth. see RIUS Staff.

Del Rio, Fernando. Cosas de la Ciencia. (Ciencia para Todos Ser.). (SPA.). pap. 6.99 (*968-16-2536-6*, Pub. by Fondo) Continental Bk.

Del Rio Garcia, Eduardo. Manual of a Perfect Atheist. Miller, Samuel, tr. from SPA. (Illus.). 156p. (Orig.). 1984. reprint ed. pap. 13.00 (*0-910309-71-X*, 5441) Am Atheist.

Del Rio, Ignacio. A Guide to the Archivo Franciscano of the National Library of Mexico. (Miscellaneous Ser.). (SPA.). 1975. 25.00 (*0-88382-257-1*) AAFH.

Del-Rio, Marcela. Perfil del Teatro de la Revolucion Mexicana. LC 93-27274. (American University Studies, XXII: Latin American Literature: Vol. 17). XIII, 278p. (C). 1994. text 44.95 (*0-8204-1992-3*) P Lang Pubng.

Del Rio, Pablo, et al, eds. Sociocultural Studies of Mind. (Learning in Doing: Social, Cognitive & Computational Perspectives Ser.). (Illus.). 264p. (C). 1995. text 59.95 (*0-521-47056-0*); pap. text 18.95 (*0-521-47643-7*) Cambridge U Pr.

***Del Rio-Sukan, Isabel.** The Cathedral & City of Toledo. (Illus.). 128p. 1999. pap. 25.00 (*1-85759-208-5*, Pub. by Scala Books) Antique Collect.

Del Rio-Sukan, Isabel. Getting by in Spanish: A Quick Beginner's Course for Tourists & Business People. LC 96-857. (Getting by in...Ser.). Orig. Title: Get by in Spanish. 1996. reprint ed. pap. 18.95 incl. audio (*0-8120-8445-4*) Barron.

***del Rosario, Carina A., ed.** A Different Battle: Stories of Asian Pacific American Veterans. (Illus.). 128p. 2000. pap. 18.95 (*0-295-97919-4*) U of Wash Pr.

Del Rosario, E. S. For Teaching Is Living: It's Liking What You Do That Matters. LC 98-85214. 112p. 1998. pap. 10.95 (*1-56167-383-8*, Five Star Spec Ed) Am Literary Pr.

***Del Rosario, Emmanuel G.** Light Aglowing. LC 99-64126. 96p. 2000. 7.95 (*1-57258-151-4*) Teach Servs.

Del Rosario Marquez, Nieves. Una Isla, la Mas Bella. LC 81-65414. (Coleccion Espejo de Paciencia). 62p. (Orig.). 1981. pap. 4.50 (*0-89729-288-X*) Ediciones.

— Raices y Alas (Poesias para Ninos y Jovenes) LC 81-65415. (Coleccion Espejo de Paciencia). (Illus.). (Orig.). (J). (gr. 6). 1981. pap. 5.00 (*0-89729-289-8*) Ediciones.

Del Roscio, Nicola, ed. see Sylvester, David.

Del Rossi, Robert. C Standard Library Handbook. Leventhal, Lance A., ed. (Lance A. Leventhal Microtrend Ser.). 500p. (Orig.). 1992. pap. 29.95 (*0-915391-50-3*) Slawson Comm.

Del Rosso, Joy. Investing in Nutrition with World Bank Assistance. (SPA.). 28p. 1993. pap. 22.00 (*0-8213-2707-0*, 12707) World Bank.

Del Rosso, Joy M. Investir dans la Nutrition avec l'Aide de la Banque Mondiale: Investing in Nutrition. (FRE.). 32p. 1993. pap. 22.00 (*0-8213-2706-2*, 12706) World Bank.

Del Rosso, Joy M. & Marek, Tonia. Class Action: Improving School Performance in the Developing World Through Better Health & Nutrition. LC 96-9495. (Directions in Development Ser.). 60p. 1996. pap. 22.00 (*0-8213-3672-X*, 13672) World Bank.

Del Rosso, Mario, tr. see Artacho-Kintziger, Zenaida, ed.

Del Ryals, Clyde. 1852: Uncollected Letters of Thomas & Jane Welsh Carlyle. 416p. 1999. 60.00 (*0-8223-2410-5*) Duke.

Del Sesto, Steven L. Science, Politics, & Controversy: Civilian Nuclear Power in the United States 1946-1974. (Special Studies in Science, Technology, & Public Policy). 260p. 1979. text 38.50 (*0-89158-566-4*) Westview.

Del Testa, David W., ed. Government Leaders, Military Rulers & Political Activists. (Lives & Legacies Ser.: Vol. 3). (Illus.). 256p. 2001. boxed set 69.95 (*1-57356-153-3*) Oryx Pr.

Del Todesco, Charles. The Havana Cigar: Cuba's Finest. O'Toole, John, tr. LC 96-47588. (Illus.). 228p. 1997. 65.00 (*0-7892-0327-8*) Abbeville Pr.

Del Togno-Armanasco, Virginia, et al. Collaborative Nursing Case Management: A Handbook for Development & Implementation. LC 93-14984. 200p. 1993. 29.95 (*0-8261-8110-4*, 93-14984) Springer Pub.

Del Toro, Antonio G. Un Aniversario de Larga Duracion & el "Long Playing" de Nuestra Historia. (Biblioteca de Autores de Puerto Rico Ser.). (SPA.). 92p. 1992. pap. text 5.00 (*1-56328-021-3*) Edit Plaza Mayor.

— Donde Reinan las Arpias. (Biblioteca de Autores de Puerto Rico Ser.). (SPA.). 62p. 1992. pap. 5.00 (*1-56328-020-5*) Edit Plaza Mayor.

Del Toro, Josefina. A Bibliography of the Collective Biography of Spanish America. 1976. lib. bdg. 59.95 (*0-87968-741-X*) Gordon Pr.

Del Toro, Vincent. Basic Electric Machines. 704p. (C). 1989. text 36.00 (*0-13-060146-2*) P-H.

Del Tredici, Peter. Early American Bonsai: The Larz Anderson Collection of the Arnold Arboretum. (Illus.). 40p. (Orig.). 1989. pap. 4.95 (*1-878297-00-7*) Arnold Arboretum.

— A Giant among the Dwarfs: The Mystery of Sargent's Weeping Hemlock. (Illus.). 109p. 1983. 15.00 (*0-913728-34-9*) Theophrastus.

Del Tufo, Alisa. Domestic Violence for Beginners. (Illus.). 176p. 1995. pap. 11.00 (*0-86316-173-1*) Writers & Readers.

Del Turco, M. Rosselli, jt. ed. see Gad, A.

Del Valle, Elena. Hip Replacements: What You Need to Know. LC 98-39491. 277p. 2000. pap. 18.95 (*1-56072-474-9*, Nova Kroshka Bks) Nova Sci Pubs.

Del Valle, Francisca Javiera, see Javiera del Valle, Francisca.

Del Valle-Inclan, Ramon. Autumn & Winter Sonatas. Costa, Margaret J., tr. from SPA. (Empire of the Senses Ser.). 176p. 1998. pap. 11.99 (*1-873982-83-6*, Pub. by Dedalus) Subterranean Co.

— Baza de Espadas. Fin de un Revolucionario. Garcia de la Torre, Jose M., ed. (Nueva Austral Ser.: Vol. 253). (SPA.). 1993. pap. text 24.95 (*84-239-7253-4*) Elliots Bks.

— La Corte de los Milagros. Garcia de la Torre, Jose M., ed. (Nueva Austral Ser.: Vol. 108). (SPA.). 1991. pap. text 24.95 (*84-239-1908-0*) Elliots Bks.

— The Lamp of Marvels: Aesthetic Meditations. Lima, Robert, tr. from SPA. LC 86-7172. 160p. 1986. pap. 8.95 (*0-940262-14-2*, Lindisfarne) Anthroposophic.

— Luces de Bohemia. Zamora Vicente, Alonso, ed. (Nueva Austral Ser.: Vol. 1). (SPA.). 1991. pap. text 24.95 (*84-239-1801-7*) Elliots Bks.

— La Marquesa Rosalinda, Farsa Sentimental y Grotesca. Oliva, Cesar, ed. (Nueva Austral Ser.: Vol. 113). (SPA.). 1991. pap. text 24.95 (*84-239-1913-7*) Elliots Bks.

— Martes de Carnaval. Rubio Jimenez, Jesus, ed. (Nueva Austral Ser.: Vol. 256). (SPA.). 1991. pap. text 24.95 (*84-239-7256-9*) Elliots Bks.

— Retablo de la Avaricia, la Lujuria y la Muerte. Domenech, Ricardo, ed. (Nueva Austral Ser.: Vol. 170). (SPA.). 1991. pap. text 24.95 (*84-239-1970-6*) Elliots Bks.

— Savage Acts: Four Plays (Ligazon, La Rosa De Papel, La Cabeza Del Bautista, Sacrilegio. Halsey, Martha T., ed. Lima, Robert, tr. from SPA. LC 92-75690. (Contemporary Spanish Plays Ser.: Vol. 3). xvi, 68p. 1993. pap. 6.00 (*0-9631212-2-7*) Estreno.

— Sonata de Otono; Sonata de Invierno. Schiavo, Leda, ed. (Nueva Austral Ser.: Vol. 61). (SPA.). pap. 13.25 (*84-239-1861-0*) Elliots Bks.

— Sonata de Otono; Sonata de Invierno. (SPA.). 9.95 (*0-8288-2582-3*) Fr & Eur.

— Sonata de Primavera: Sonata de Estio. (Nueva Austral Ser.: Vol. 37). (SPA.). pap. 13.25 (*84-239-1837-8*) Elliots Bks.

— Spring & Summer Sonatas. Costa, Margaret J., tr. from SPA. (Empire of the Senses Ser.). 176p. (Orig.). 1997. pap. 11.99 (*1-873982-03-8*, Pub. by Dedalus) Subterranean Co.

— Tablado de Marionetas para Educacion de Principes. Oliva, Cesar, ed. (Nueva Austral Ser.: Vol. 129). (SPA.). 1991. pap. text 17.95 (*84-239-1929-3*) Elliots Bks.

— Viva Mi Dueno. (Nueva Austral Ser.: Vol. 193). (SPA.). 1993. pap. text. write for info. (*84-239-1993-5*) Elliots Bks.

Del Valle, Teresa. The Importance of the Mariana Islands to Spain at the Beginning of the Nineteenth Century. Driver, Marjorie G., ed. (Educational Ser.: No. 11). 71p. (Orig.). (C). 1991. pap. 5.95 (*1-878453-06-8*) Univ Guam MAR Ctr.

— Korrika: Basque Ritual for Ethnic Identity. White, Linda, tr. from SPA. LC 93-19034. (Basque Ser.). (Illus.). 336p. 1993. text 44.95 (*0-87417-215-2*) U of Nev Pr.

del Vascello, Giacomo Medici, photos by. Moremi Africa Calling, 1. 1998. 75.00 (*88-422-0624-5*) Dist Art Pubs.

Del Vasto, Lanza. Definitions of Nonviolence. Sidgwick, Jean, tr. from FRE. 27p. (Orig.). 1972. pap. 1.50 (*0-934676-06-2*) Greenlf Bks.

Del Vecchio, Deborah & Johnson, Tom. Peter Cushing: The Gentle Man of Horror & His 91 Films. LC 92-50302. (Illus.). 485p. 1992. lib. bdg. 52.50 (*0-89950-654-2*) McFarland & Co.

Del Vecchio, Deborah, jt. auth. see Johnson, Tom.

Del Vecchio, Gene. Creating Ever-Cool: A Marketer's Guide to a Kid's Heart. LC 97-1660. 256p. 1997. 18.95 (*1-56554-256-8*) Pelican.

Del Vecchio, Giorgia. Formal Bases of Law. Lisle, John, tr. (Modern Legal Philosophy Ser.: Vol. 10). lvii, 412p. 1969. reprint ed. 42.50 (*0-8377-2700-6*, Rothman) W S Hein.

— General Principles of the Law. Forte, Felix, tr. from ITA. ix, 111p. 1986. reprint ed. 35.00 (*0-8377-2028-1*, Rothman) W S Hein.

— Justice: An Historical & Philosophical Essay. Campbell, A. H., ed. xxi, 236p. 1982. reprint ed. 39.95 (*0-8377-1231-9*, Rothman) W S Hein.

Del Vecchio, Giorgio. The Formal Bases of Law. Lisle, John, tr. LC 68-54757. (Modern Legal Philosophy Ser.: Vol. 10). lvii, 412p. 1969. 37.50 (*0-678-04521-6*) Kelley.

***Del Vecchio, Giorgio.** Formal Bases of Law. (Modern Legal Philosophy Ser.: Vol. 10). xix, 412p. 1998. reprint ed. 139.00 (*1-56169-389-8*) Gaunt.

Del Vecchio, Gloria Caleina, see Caleina Del Vecchio, Gloria.

Del Vecchio, John. Darkness Falls. LC 98-23886. 384p. 1998. text 24.95 (*0-312-19216-9*) St Martin.

***Del Vecchio, John.** Darkness Falls. 384p. 2000. pap. 14.95 (*0-312-26488-7*) St Martin.

Del Vecchio, John M. The 13th Valley. LC 98-50904. 640p. 1999. pap. 14.95 (*0-312-20081-1*) St Martin.

***Del Vecchio, Michael J.** Iron Horses: The Illustrated History of the Tracks & Trains of North America. 176p. 1999. 19.98 (*0-7624-0598-8*) Running Pr.

***Del Vecchio, Michael J. & Peterson, Henry W.** Lackawanna Railroad Trackside with Henry Peterson. LC 98-68500. (Illus.). 128p. 1999. 54.95 (*1-58248-015-X*) Morning NJ.

***Del Vecchio, Mike.** Pictorial History of America's Railroads. LC 99-52134. (Illus.). 224p. 1999. pap. 19.95 (*0-7603-0829-2*, 129614AP, Pub. by MBI Pubg) Motorbooks Intl.

Del Vecchio, Mike. Railroads Across America: A Celebration of 150 Years of Railroading. LC 98-51781. (Illus.). 224p. 1998. 24.95 (*0-7603-0642-7*) MBI Pubg.

***Del Vecchio, Peter.** The Art of Being Human: Channeled Writings & Commentaries of an American Spiritualist. 114p. 1999. pap. 12.95 (*0-9672589-0-1*) P Del Vecchio.

Del Vecchio, Peter & White & Case LLP Staff. Big Bang or Whimper? Essential Insight into Japan's Financial Deregulation. 120p. 1998. pap. 100.00 (*962-360-032-1*, Pub. by Asia Law & Practice) Am Educ Systs.

Del Vecchio, R. J. Understanding Design of Experiments. LC 97-36330. (Understanding Bks.). 1997. 34.95 (*1-56990-222-4*) Hanser-Gardner.

Del Vecchio, Robert J. Physiological Aspects of Flight. LC 77-82675. 1977. pap. 10.00 (*0-917428-05-6*, Dowling College) Global Pubns.

Del Vecchio, Stephen. CD-ROM Reference Materials for Children & Young Adults: A Critical Guide for School & Public Libraries. 275p. 1999. pap. 35.00 (*1-56308-711-1*) Libs Unl.

Del Villar, Fred, jt. auth. see Del Villar, Mary.

Del Villar, Mary & Del Villar, Fred. Where the Strange Roads Go Down. LC 91-16622. 244p. 1991. reprint ed. pap. 16.95 (*0-8165-1273-6*) U of Ariz Pr.

Del Vizo, Hortensia R. Paginas Cubanas I. LC 97-80043. (Coleccion Cuba y sus Jueces). (SPA.). 143p. 1998. pap. 12.00 (*0-89729-848-9*) Ediciones.

Dela Cruz, C. R., ed. Role of Fish in Enhancing Ricefield Ecology & in Integrated Pest Management. (ICLARM Conference Proceedings Ser.: No. 43). 50p. 1994. write for info. (*971-8709-51-7*, Pub. by ICLARM) Intl Spec Bk.

Dela Cruz, C. R., et al, eds. Rice-Fish Research & Development in Asia. (ICLARM Conference Proceedings Ser.: No. 24). 457p. 1992. per. write for info. (*971-10-2288-5*, Pub. by ICLARM) Intl Spec Bk.

Dela Cruz, Christine M. & Kato, Harubumi. Lung Cancer Handbook: Evaluation & Management. LC 92-1694. 189p. 1993. pap. text 35.00 (*3-7186-5294-3*) Gordon & Breach.

***Dela, Helena & Piatkus Books Staff.** The Count. 256p. 2000. mass mkt. 6.50 (*0-06-109884-1*) HarpC.

Dela Mirandola, Giovanni Pico. Oracion Acerca de la Dignidad del Hombre. 33p. 1992. pap. 1.50 (*0-8477-0712-1*) U of PR Pr.

DeLa Selva, Salomon, tr. see Dario, Ruben.

Delaage, M., ed. Molecular Recognition Mechanisms. 285p. 1991. 150.00 (*0-471-18785-2*, Wiley-VCH) Wiley.

Delaage, Michel, ed. Molecular Recognition Mechanisms. 285p. 1991. text 95.00 (*1-56081-041-6*, Wiley-VCH) Wiley.

Delaat, Adrian N. Microbiology for the Allied Health Professions. 2nd ed. LC 78-5731. (Illus.). 470p. reprint ed. pap. 145.70 (*0-8357-7644-1*, 205696900096) Bks Demand.

DeLaat, Jacqueline. Gender in the Workplace: A Case Study Approach. LC 98-58080. 102p. 1999. 45.00 (*0-7619-1478-1*) Sage.

***DeLaat, Jacqueline.** Gender in the Workplace: A Case Study Approach. LC 98-58080. 1999. write for info. (*0-7619-1479-X*) Sage.

***Delabar, Walter, et al.** Banalitat Mit Stil. 290p. 1999. 44.95 (*3-906762-18-1*) P Lang Pubng.

Delabastita, Dirk & D'Hulst, Lieven, eds. European Shakespeares: Translating Shakespeare in the Romantic Age. Selected Papers from the Conference on Shakespeare Translations in the Romantic Age, Antwerp, 1990. LC 92-34481. 256p. 1993. 59.00 (*1-55619-486-2*) J Benjamins Pubng Co.

Delacampagne, Christian. A History of Philosophy in the Twentieth Century. DeBevoise, M. B., tr. LC 99-11237. 336p. 1999. 42.50 (*0-8018-6016-4*) Johns Hopkins.

Delacato, Carl H. The Ultimate Stranger: The Autistic Child. rev. ed. 240p. 1984. reprint ed. pap. 10.00 (*0-87879-446-8*, 446-8) Acad Therapy.

Delacenserie, Emily & Blasi, Susan. IRA Fundamentals - Making the Rules Work for Your Client. 176p. 1997. text 49.00 (*0-8080-0146-9*, 05001101) CCH INC.

DeLacerda, Fred. Surviving Spins. LC 89-15527. (Illus.). 134p. 1989. 21.95 (*0-8138-0142-7*) Iowa St U Pr.

DeLaceroa, Fred G. See & Avoid. (Illus.). 86p. (Orig.). (C). 1989. pap. text 6.00 (*0-9623197-0-8*) Delta Aviation.

Delacey, Philip & Walker, Susan-Lee. Advances in Applied Developmental Psychology Vol. 16: Children of the Dispossessed: Far-West Preschoolers 30 Years On. LC 98-55755. 1999. 73.25 (*1-56750-420-5*); pap. 39.50 (*1-56750-421-3*) Ablx Pub.

Delaco, Enrico & Hornell, Erik. Technology & Investment: Crucial Issues for the 1990s. 1991. text 59.00 (*0-86187-170-7*) St Martin.

Delaconte, Michael. Culture Change along the Eastern Sierra Nevada/Cascade Front Vol. VII: Pah Rah Uplands. fac. ed. (Far Western Anthropological Research Group, Inc. Ser.). (Illus.). 195p. (C). 1997. reprint ed. pap. text 20.63 (*1-55567-719-3*) Coyote Press.

Delacorta. Alba. LC 89-357. 208p. 1990. pap. 7.95 (*0-87113-387-3*, Atlntc Mnthly) Grove-Atltic.

— The Rap Factor: Novel. Texier, Catherine, tr. from FRE. LC 92-35562. 208p. 1993. pap. 11.00 (*0-87113-617-1*, Atlntc Mnthly) Grove-Atltic.

— Vida. write for info. (*0-318-59581-8*) S&S Trade.

Delacorte, Michael. Culture Change along the Eastern Sierra Nevada/Cascade Front Vol. I: History of Investigations & Summary of Findings. fac. ed. (Far Western Anthropological Research Group, Inc. Ser.). (Illus.). 159p. (C). 1997. reprint ed. pap. text 17.50 (*1-55567-675-8*) Coyote Press.

— Culture Change along the Eastern Sierra Nevada/Cascade Front Vol. III: South Fork Valley & Madeline Plains. fac. ed. (Far Western Anthropological Research Group, Inc. Ser.). (Illus.). 356p. (C). 1997. reprint ed. pap. text 37.50 (*1-55567-723-1*) Coyote Press.

Delacorte, Peter. Time on My Hands. (Illus.). 400p. 1998. pap. 14.00 (*0-671-02324-1*, Pocket Books) PB.

— Time on My Hands: A Novel with Photographs. LC 96-53316. 1997. 23.00 (*0-684-82651-8*) Scribner.

Delacorte, Shawna. Cassie's Last Goodbye. (Desire Ser.). 1993. per. 2.99 (*0-373-05814-4*, 5-05814-4) Silhouette.

— Cowboy Dreaming. (Desire Ser.). 1996. per. 3.50 (*0-373-76020-5*, 1-76020-6) Silhouette.

— The Daddy Search. (Desire Ser.: No. 1253). 1999. mass mkt. 3.75 (*0-373-76253-4*, 1-76253-3) Silhouette.

***Delacorte, Shawna.** Encuentro con el Pasado: (Meeting with the Past) (Deseo Ser.: No. 152).Tr. of Meeting with the Past. (SPA.). 1999. per. 3.50 (*0-373-35282-4*) Harlequin Bks.

— Fortune's Secret Child. (Desire Ser.: Bk. 1324). 2000. mass mkt. 3.99 (*0-373-76324-7*, 1-76324-2) Silhouette.

Delacorte, Shawna. Lover Unknown. (Lawman Ser.). 1997. per. 3.75 (*0-373-22413-3*, 1-22413-8) Harlequin Bks.

— The Millionaire's Christmas Wish. (Desire Ser.: No. 1187). 1998. per. 3.75 (*0-373-76187-2*, 1-76187-3) Silhouette.

— Miracle Baby. (Desire Ser.). 1995. per. 2.99 (*0-373-05905-1*, 1-05905-4) Silhouette.

— Much Ado about Marriage. 1998. per. 3.50 (*0-373-52069-7*, 1-52069-1) Silhouette.

— La Respuesta a Sus Suenos: (The Answer To Her Dreams) (Deseo Ser.: No. 130).Tr. of Answer to Her Dreams. (SPA.). 1998. per. 3.50 (*0-373-35260-3*, 1-35260-8) Harlequin Bks.

— Secret Lover. (Intrigue Ser.: No. 520). 1999. per. 3.99 (*0-373-22520-2*, 1-22520-0, Harlequin) Harlequin Bks.

— Un Secreto Deseo. 1999. per. 3.50 (*0-373-35298-0*, 1352988) Harlequin Bks.

— The Tycoon's Son. (Desire Ser.). 1998. per. 3.75 (*0-373-76157-0*, 1-76157-6) Silhouette.

— Wyoming Wife? 1997. per. 3.50 (*0-373-76110-4*, 1-76110-5) Silhouette.

Delacoste, Frederique. Sex Work: Writings by Women in the Sex Industry. 2nd ed. 380p. (Orig.). 1998. pap. 19.95 (*1-57344-042-6*) Cleis Pr.

Delacote, G., ed. Physics Teaching in Schools. 404p. 1978. pap. 55.00 (*0-85066-136-6*) Taylor & Francis.

Delacour, J. The Memory System of the Brain. LC 93-41418. (Advanced Series in Neuroscience: No. 4). 892p. 1994. text 178.00 (*981-02-1021-3*) World Scientific Pub.

Delacour, Jean. Dictionnaire des Mots d'Esprit. (FRE.). 352p. 1976. pap. 16.95 (*0-8288-5644-3*, M6627) Fr & Eur.

— Pheasant Breeding & Care. (Illus.). 192p. 1978. 29.95 (*0-87666-969-0*, AP-6450) TFH Pubns.

Delacre, Georges. El Tiempo en Perspectiva. 171p. (C). 1975. pap. 4.00 (*0-8477-0505-6*) U of PR Pr.

Delacre, Lulu. Arozz Con Leche. (SPA., Illus.). (J). (gr. 1-3). 1992. audio 4.95 (*0-590-60035-4*, Blue Ribbon Bks) Scholastic Inc.

— Arroz con Leche. (SPA., Illus.). 32p. (J). (ps-3). 1992. pap. 4.95 (*0-590-41886-6*, Blue Ribbon Bks) Scholastic Inc.

— Arroz Con Leche: Popular Songs & Rhymes from Latin America. (Illus.). 32p. (J). (ps-3). 1989. pap. 15.95 (*0-590-41887-4*) Scholastic Inc.

— Arroz Con Leche: Popular Songs & Rhymes from Latin America. (Blue Ribbon Bks.). (J). 1989. 10.15 (*0-606-01779-8*, Pub. by Turtleback) Demco.

— De Oro y Esmeraldas: Mitos, Leyendas y Cuentos Populares De Latinoamerica. (J). (ps-3). 1996. 18.95 (*0-590-67683-0*) Scholastic Inc.

— De Oro y Esmeraldas: Mitos, Leyendas y Cuentos Populares de Latinoamerica. 1998. pap. text 6.99 (*0-590-67684-9*) Scholastic Inc.

— Golden Tales: Myths, Legends, & Folktales from Latin America. LC 94-36724. (Illus.). 80p. (J). (ps-3). 1996. 18.95 (*0-590-48186-X*) Scholastic Inc.

— Las Navidades. (Illus.). 32p. (J). (gr. k-6). 1992. 4.95 (*0-590-43549-3*, Blue Ribbon Bks) Scholastic Inc.

— Las Navidades: Popular Christmas Songs from Latin America. 1990. 10.19 (*0-606-01883-2*, Pub. by Turtleback) Demco.

— Peter Cottontail's Easter Book. 32p. (J). (ps-1). 1992. pap. 2.99 (*0-590-43337-7*) Scholastic Inc.

***Delacre, Lulu.** Salsa Stories. LC 99-25534. (Illus.). 144p. (J). (gr. 2-6). 2000. 15.95 (*0-590-63118-7*, Scholastic Ref) Scholastic Inc.

Delacre, Lulu. Time for School, Nathan! (Illus.). 32p. (J). (ps-2). 1991. pap. 2.50 (*0-590-45688-1*) Scholastic Inc.

Delacre, Lulu. The Bossy Gallito (El Gallo de Bodas) A Traditional Cuban Folktale. LC 93-15541. (ENG & SPA.). 32p. (J). (ps-2). 1994. 15.95 (*0-590-46843-X*) Scholastic Inc.

DeLacre, Lulu. Senor Cat's Romance. LC 95-34144. 48p. (J). (ps-2). 1997. 17.95 (*0-590-48537-7*) Scholastic Inc.

Delacre, Lulu. Las Navidades: Popular Christmas Songs from Latin America. 32p. (J). (ps up). 1990. 13.95 (*0-590-43548-5*, Scholastic Hardcover) Scholastic Inc.

Delacretaz, Guy P., et al, eds. Laser-Tissue Interaction, Tissue Optics & Laser Welding III. LC 98-145663. (Europto Ser.: Vol. 3195). 358p. 1998. 80.00 (*0-8194-2627-X*) SPIE.

***Delacroix, Claire.** The Countess. (Bride Quest: Vol. 4). 416p. 2000. mass mkt. 6.50 (*0-440-23634-7*) Bantam Dell.

Delacroix, Claire. The Damsel. (Bride Quest Ser.: No. 2). 1999. mass mkt. 6.50 (*0-440-22588-4*) Dell.

— Enchanted. 1997. per. 4.99 (*0-373-28966-9*, 1-28966-9) Harlequin Bks.

***Delacroix, Claire.** The Heiress. (Bride Quest Ser.: No. 3). 384p. 1999. mass mkt. 6.50 (*0-440-22589-2*) Dell.

Delacroix, Claire. Honeyed Lies. (Historical Ser.). 1994. per. 3.99 (*0-373-28809-3*, 1-28809-1) Harlequin Bks.

— The Magician's Quest. LC 96-345. (Historical Ser.). 299p. 1995. per. 4.50 (*0-373-28881-6*, 1-28881-0) Harlequin Bks.

— My Lady's Champion. (Harlequin Historical Ser.: No. 326). 1996. per. 4.99 (*0-373-28926-X*, 1-28926-3) Harlequin Bks.

— My Lady's Desire. (Historical Ser.). 1998. per. 4.99 (*0-373-29009-8*, 1-29009-7) Harlequin Bks.

— Pearl Beyond Price. LC 95-8361. (Historical Ser.). 299p. 1995. per. 4.50 (*0-373-28864-6*, 1-28864-6) Harlequin Bks.

— The Princess. (Bride Quest Ser.: Vol. 1). 416p. 1998. mass mkt. 5.99 (*0-440-22603-1*) Dell.

— Roarke's Folly. (Historical Ser.). 1994. per. 3.99 (*0-373-28850-6*, 1-28850-5) Harlequin Bks.

— The Sorceress. (Historical Ser.). 1994. per. 3.99 (*0-373-28835-2*, 1-28835-6) Harlequin Bks.

— Unicorn Bride. 1994. per. 3.99 (*0-373-28823-9*, 1-28823-2) Harlequin Bks.

— Unicorn Vengeance. LC 95-21579. 297p. 1995. per. 4.50 (*0-373-28893-X*) Harlequin Bks.

Delacroix, Eugene. Eugene Delacroix: Further Correspondence, 1817-1863. Johnson, Lee, ed. (Illus.). 210p. 1991. text 69.00 (*0-19-817395-4*) OUP.

— The Journal of Eugene Delacroix. rev. ed. Wellington, Hubert, ed. Norton, Lucy, tr. (Arts & Letters Ser.). (Illus.). 520p. (C). 1995. pap. 14.95 (*0-7148-3359-2*, Pub. by Phaidon Press) Phaidon Pr.

Delacroix, Eugene, et al. Delacroix: The Late Work. LC 98-26927. 1998. 65.00 (*0-87633-122-3*); pap. 48.00 (*0-87633-123-1*) Phila Mus Art.

Delacroix, Michel. Michel Delacroix. Cassanetti, Michelle L., ed. LC 86-83287. (Illus.). 200p. 1987. 150.00 (*0-941393-05-4*) Lublin Graph.

Delacroix, Robert. Nostradamus & the '90s: Prophecies of Nostradamus Pertaining to the 1990's. 150p. 1993. pap. 5.95 (*0-9635358-0-3*) ARS Historica.

Delacruz, Elizabeth M. Design for Inquiry: Instructional Theory, Research & Practice in Art Education. (Point of View). 94p. (Orig.). 1997. pap. text 18.00 (*0-937652-98-9*, 228) Natl Art Ed.

Delacy, Richard. Lonely Planet Hindi & Urdu. 2nd ed. (Illus.). 256p. 1998. pap. 6.95 (*0-86442-425-6*) Lonely Planet.

Delaet, Debra L. U.S. Immigration Policy in an Age of Rights. LC 99-15396. 168p. 2000. 59.95 (*0-275-96733-6*); pap. 22.95 (*0-275-96764-6*, Praeger Pubs) Greenwood.

Delaet, Debra L., jt. auth. see Kelson, Gregory A.

DeLaet, Dianne T. Giants & Heroes: A Daughter's Memories of Y. A. Tittle. LC 95-35474. (Illus.). 261p. 1995. 25.00 (*1-883642-13-2*) Steerforth Pr.

Delaey, J. D. & Hanssens, M. Vascular Tumors & Malfunctions of the Ocular Fundus. (Monographs in Ophthalmology). (C). 1990. text 201.00 (*0-7923-0750-X*) Kluwer Academic.

Delafield, E. M. Diary of a Provincial Lady. (Illus.). 388p. 1998. reprint ed. pap. 15.00 (*0-89733-053-6*) Academy Chi Pubs.

***Delafield, E. M.** Late & Soon. large type unabridged ed. 2000. 25.95 (*0-7531-6037-4*, 160374, Pub. by ISIS Lrg Prnt) ISIS Pub.

— The Provincial Lady in America. (Illus.). 245p. 2000. reprint ed. pap. 16.95 (*0-89733-110-9*) Academy Chi Pubs.

Delafield, E. M. The Provincial Lady in London. (Provincial Lady Ser.). (Illus.). 302p. 1999. pap. 15.00 (*0-89733-085-4*) Academy Chi Pubs.

— The Provincial Lady in Russia: I Visit the Soviets. (Illus.). 344p. 1998. reprint ed. pap. 15.00 (*0-89733-156-7*) Academy Chi Pubs.

Delafield, E. M. The Provincial Lady in Wartime. LC 86-22140. (Illus.). 349p. 1986. pap. 8.95 (*0-89733-210-5*) Academy Chi Pubs.

***Delafield, John.** An Inquiry into the Origin of the Antiquities of America. (LC History-America-E). 142p. 1999. reprint ed. lib. bdg. 69.00 (*0-7812-4321-1*) Rprt Serv.

Delafons, John. Politics & Preservation 1882-1996: Policy History of the Built Heritage. 192p. (C). (gr. 13). 1997. 85.00 (*0-419-22390-8*) Routledge.

Delaforce, D. Burgundy & Beavjolais on a Budget. (C). 1989. text 40.00 (*0-948032-82-0*, Pub. by Rosters Ltd) St Mut.

— Champagne on a Budget. (C). 1989. text 40.00 (*0-948032-87-1*, Pub. by Rosters Ltd) St Mut.

— French Riviera on a Budget. (C). 1989. text 40.00 (*0-948032-92-8*, Pub. by Rosters Ltd) St Mut.

— Gascony & Armagnac on a Budget. (C). 1989. text 29.95 (*0-948032-33-2*, Pub. by Rosters Ltd) St Mut.

Delaforce, D., ed. Dordogne on a Budget. (C). 1989. text 40.00 (*0-948032-83-9*, Pub. by Rosters Ltd) St Mut.

— Provence on a Budget. (C). 1989. text 29.95 (*0-948032-88-X*, Pub. by Rosters Ltd) St Mut.

Delaforce, Patrick. Churchill's Desert Rats: From Normandy to Berlin with the 7th Armoured Division. (Illus.). 224p. 1993. pap. 20.00 (*0-7509-0625-1*, Pub. by A Sutton) Motorbooks Intl.

— Churchill's Desert Rats: From Normandy to Berlin with the 7th Armoured Division. (Illus.). 224p. 1993. 26.95 (*0-7509-0529-8*, Pub. by Sutton Pub Ltd) Intl Pubs Mktg.

***Delaforce, Patrick.** Churchill's Secret Weapon: The Story of Hobart's Funnies. 256p. 1999. 35.00 (*0-7090-6237-0*, Pub. by R Hale Ltd) Seven Hills Bk.

Delaforce, Patrick. Family History Research. 224p. 1984. pap. 35.00 (*0-7212-0688-3*, Pub. by Regency Pr GBR) St Mut.

— The Grand Tour: Today's Guide to Twenty-Five Cities of Europe in the Footsteps of Famous Travellers of the Past. (Illus.). 224p. (Orig.). 1991. pap. 19.95 (*1-85365-162-1*, Pub. by McCarta) Seven Hills Bk.

— Marching to the Sound of Gunfire: North-West Europe, 1944-1945. LC 96-20728. (Illus.). 224p. 1996. 30.95 (*0-7509-0780-0*, Pub. by Sutton Pub Ltd) Intl Pubs Mktg.

Delaforce, Patrick. Monty's Highlanders: 51st Highland Division at War. 224p. 1997. pap. (*1-871085-42-X*) Donovan Pub.

Delaforce, Patrick. Monty's Iron Sides: From the Normandy Beaches to Bremen with the 3rd Division. (British Army Divisional History Ser.). (Illus.). 224p. 1996. pap. 19.95 (*0-7509-0781-9*, Pub. by Sutton Pub Ltd) Intl Pubs Mktg.

Delaforce, Patrick. Monty's Marauders: Black Rat & Red Fox: 4th & 8th Independent Armoured Brigades in WW2. 224p. 1997. pap. (*1-871085-41-1*) Donovan Pub.

Delaforce, Patrick. Nelson's First Love: Fanny's Story. 1987. 16.95 (*1-85219-006-X*, Pub. by Bishopsgte Pr) Intl Spec Bk.

— The Polar Bears: Monty's Left Flank: From Normandy to the Relief of Holland with the 49th Division. LC 96-212600. (British Army Divisional History Ser.). (Illus.). 240p. 1996. pap. 19.95 (*0-7509-1062-3*, Pub. by Sutton Pub Ltd) Intl Pubs Mktg.

Delafosse, Claude. Cars & Trucks & Other Vehicles. LC 95-23693. (First Discovery Book). (Illus.). 24p. (J). (ps-2). 1996. 11.95 (*0-590-62371-0*, Cartwheel) Scholastic Inc.

Delafosse, Claude. Construction. (First Discovery Book). (Illus.). 24p. (J). (ps-2). 1997. pap. 11.95 (*0-590-93783-9*) Scholastic Inc.

— Egyptian Tomb. LC 98-47119. (Illus.). 26p. (J). (ps-2). 1999. 12.95 (*0-439-06776-6*) Scholastic Inc.

Delafosse, Claude. Hidden World: Under the Ground. LC 98-28654. (First Discovery Book). (J). 1999. write for info. (*0-590-43812-3*) Scholastic Inc.

— Hidden World: Under the Sea. LC 98-28656. (First Discovery Book). (Illus.). 26p. (J). (ps-2). 1998. 12.95 (*0-590-10992-8*) Scholastic Inc.

— Landscapes. Nelson, Pamela, tr. LC 94-49714. (First Discovery Art Bk.).Tr. of Paysages. (ENG & FRE.). Illus.). 28p. (J). (ps-2). 1996. 11.95 (*0-590-50216-6*, Cartwheel) Scholastic Inc.

— Musical Instruments. LC 96-181854. (First Discovery Book). (Illus.). 24p. (J). (ps-2). 1994. 11.95 (*0-590-47729-3*, Cartwheel) Scholastic Inc.

***Delafosse, Claude & Jeunesse, Gallimard.** Caves Hidden World. LC 99-13211. (First Discovery/Hidden World Ser.). (Illus.). 24p. (J). (ps-3). 2000. 12.95 (*0-439-10680-X*, Scholastic Ref) Scholastic Inc.

Delafosse, Claude & Mettler, Rene. Atlas of Animals: A First Discovery Book. (First Discovery Book). 30p. (J). (ps-3). 1996. 11.95 (*0-590-58280-1*, Cartwheel) Scholastic Inc.

Delafosse, Claude & Prunier, James. Dinosaurs. LC 96-181856. (First Discovery Book). (Illus.). 24p. (J). (ps-3). 1993. 11.95 (*0-590-46358-6*) Scholastic Inc.

Delafosse, Claude & Sautai, Raoul. Bees. LC 96-18238. (First Discovery Book). 30p. (J). (ps-2). 1997. 11.95 (*0-590-93780-4*) Scholastic Inc.

Delafosse, Claude, et al. Atlas of Countries. LC 95-31141. (First Discovery Book). (Illus.). 24p. (J). (ps-3). 1996. 11.95 (*0-590-58282-8*, Cartwheel) Scholastic Inc.

— Atlas of People: A First Discovery Book. (First Discovery Book). 30p. (J). (ps-3). 1996. 11.95 (*0-590-58281-X*, Cartwheel) Scholastic Inc.

— Fish. Miller, Heather, tr. from ENG. LC 97-15427. (First Discovery Book). (Illus.). 24p. (J). (ps-2). 1998. 11.95 (*0-590-38155-5*) Scholastic Inc.

***Delafosse, Claude, et al.** Human Body. LC 99-14289. (First Discovery/Hidden World Ser.). (Illus.). 24p. (J). (ps-3). 2000. 12.95 (*0-439-10681-8*, Scholastic Ref) Scholastic Inc.

Delafosse, Claude, jt. auth. see Biard, Phillip.

Delafosse, Claude, jt. auth. see Gallimard Jeunesse Publishing Staff.

DeLafosse, Peter H., ed. Trailing the Pioneers: A Guide to Utah's Emigrant Trails, 1829-1869. LC 94-825. (Illus.). 126p. 1994. pap. 12.95 (*0-87421-172-7*) Utah St U Pr.

Delafosse, Peter H., jt. auth. see Kelly, Charles.

Delafoy, Marie-Aude. Saint-Louis. (Illus.). 88p. 1999. 24.95 (*2-911589-38-6*, Pub. by Editions dIndochine) BHB Intl.

Delafuente, Jeffrey C. & Stewart, Ronald B., eds. Therapeutics in the Elderly. 3rd rev. ed. 588p. 2000. pap. text. write for info. (*0-929375-22-X*) H W Bks.

Delage, Denys. Bitter Feast: Amerindians & Europeans in Northeastern North America, 1600-64. (Illus.). 414p. 1993. pap. 29.95 (*0-7748-0451-3*) U of Wash Pr.

Delage, Gisele. English - French Lexicon of Security & Stock Exchange. (ENG & FRE.). 95p. 1992. pap. 39.95 (*0-8288-9415-9*) Fr & Eur.

Delage, P., jt. auth. see Alonso, E. E.

Delage, P., jt. ed. see Alonso, E. E.

Delahanty, Guillermo. Genesis de la Nocion Del Dinero en el Nino (Genesis of the Child's Notion of Money) (Breviarios Ser.). (SPA.). 165p. 1989. pap. 5.99 (*968-16-3285-0*, Pub. by Fondo) Continental Bk.

Delahanty, Linda C., ed. Make Audits Pay: Leveraging the Audit into Consulting Services. (AICPA Practice Aid Series). 245p. 1999. pap. 50.00 (*0-87051-247-1*, 006704) Am Inst CPA.

Delahanty, Linda C., ed. see Ramos, Michael J.

Delahay, John N., jt. auth. see Wiesel, Sam W.

Delahay, Paul. Double Layer & Electrode Kinetics. LC 65-16404. 333p. reprint ed. pap. 103.30 (*0-608-10199-0*, 200903300072) Bks Demand.

Delahaye, Brian L., jt. auth. see Smith, Barry.

Delahaye, Ernest. Documents relatifs a Paul Verlaine: Lettres, dessins, pages inedites recueillis et decrits. LC 77-10258. reprint ed. 39.50 (*0-404-16313-0*) AMS Pr.

Delahaye, J. P. Sequence Transformations. (Computational Mathematics Ser.: Vol. 11). (Illus.). 250p. 1988. 127.95 (*0-387-15283-0*) Spr-Verlag.

Delahaye, Michael. Stalking-Horse. large type ed. 496p. 1988. 27.99 (*0-7089-1896-4*) Ulverscroft.

Delahey, John, jt. auth. see Wiesel, Sam W.

Delahoyd, Mary. A New Beginning, 1968-1978. (Illus.). 128p. (Orig.). 1985. pap. 5.00 (*0-943651-19-0*) Hudson Riv.

— New England-New Mexico: Artistic Encounters, 1910-1940. (Illus.). 12p. 1989. 6.00 (*0-915171-12-0*) Katonah Gal.

DeLahunta, Alexander. Veterinary Neuroanatomy & Clinical Neurology. 2nd ed. LC 76-4246. (Illus.). (C). 1983. text 75.00 (*0-7216-3029-4*, W B Saunders Co) Harcrt Hlth Sci Grp.

DeLahunta, Alexander, jt. auth. see Evans, Howard E.

Delahunty, Andrew & Weiner, Edmund S. The Little Oxford Guide to English Usage. 256p. 1995. 13.95 (*0-19-861301-6*) OUP.

Delahunty, Andrew, jt. auth. see Weiner, Edmund S.

Delahunty, Brendan, et al. Indonesia. 6th ed. (Illus.). 1136p. 1997. pap. 25.95 (*0-86442-454-X*) Lonely Planet.

Delahunty, Gerald P. & Garvey, James J. Communication, Language & Grammar: A Course for Teachers. LC 93-39640. 576p. (C). 1994. 50.31 (*0-07-022911-2*) McGraw.

Delahunty, James T., ed. see Nichols, Nancy A.

Delahunty, Millie. Classic New England Dishes from Your Microwave. LC 93-185878. 120p. 1991. spiral bd. 12.95 (*0-89272-280-0*) Down East.

— The Microwave Cuisine Adult Education Microwave Cooking Course: Intermediate Techniques. 41p. (Orig.). 1985. pap. text 12.95 (*0-932243-07-X*) Microwave Cuisine.

— Microwave Cuisine Cooks Appetizers. (Illus.). 32p. (Orig.). 1984. pap. 2.95 (*0-932243-06-1*) Microwave Cuisine.

— Microwave Cuisine Cooks Desserts. (Illus.). 32p. (Orig.). 1989. pap. 2.95 (*0-932243-11-8*) Microwave Cuisine.

— Microwave Cuisine Cooks Italian-Style. (Illus.). 32p. (Orig.). 1985. pap. 2.95 (*0-932243-08-8*) Microwave Cuisine.

— Microwave Cuisine Cooks Low-Sodium. (Illus.). 32p. (Orig.). 1985. pap. 2.95 (*0-932243-09-6*) Microwave Cuisine.

— Microwave Cuisine Cooks New England Style. (Illus.). 32p. (Orig.). 1986. pap. 2.95 (*0-932243-10-X*) Microwave Cuisine.

— Teaching Microwave Cooking: A Basic Technique Course Guide. (Illus.). 114p. (Orig.). 1989. pap. text 18.95 (*0-932243-12-6*) Microwave Cuisine.

Delahunty, R. J. Spinoza. (Arguments of the Philosophers Ser.). 352p. 1985. 49.95 (*0-7102-0375-6*, Routledge Thoemms) Routledge.

Delaigue, jt. auth. see Schneider.

***Delaine, J. & Johnston, D. E., eds.** Roman Baths & Bathing Part 1 & Part 2: Proceedings of the First International Conference on Roman Baths Held at Bath, England, 30 March - 4 April 1992. (Illus.). 317p. 2000. 99.50 (*1-887829-37-7*) Jour Roman Arch.

DeLaine, Janet. The Baths of Caracalla: A Study in the Design, Construction & Economics of Large-Scale Building Projects in Imperial Rome. (Journal of Roman Archaeology Supplementary Ser.: No. 25). (Illus.). 271p. 1997. 99.00 (*1-887829-25-3*) Jour Roman Arch.

Delaine, John. Asbestos Removal, Management & Control. 149p. 1988. text 74.95 (*0-566-09000-7*, Pub. by Gower) Ashgate Pub Co.

Delair, Denis. Accompaniment on Theorbo & Harpsichord: Denis Delair's Treatise of 1690. Mattax, Charlotte, tr. & comment by. LC 90-49917. (Publications of the Early Music Institute Ser.). (Illus.). 173p. Date not set. reprint ed. pap. 53.70 (*0-608-20560-5*, 205447400002) Bks Demand.

Delair, J. B., jt. auth. see Allan, D. S.

Delaisement, ed. see Maupassant, Guy de.

Delaitre, Bernard J., jt. ed. see Testas, Pierre.

Delalande. Ballet De la Jeunesse. 11th ed. (Fropse Ser.: No. 10). 1996. 92.00 (*0-945193-55-6*) Pendragon NY.

DeLallo, Stephen P. The Sword of Christendom: The Work of Catholic Action for the Reign of Christ the King. 312p. 1994. pap. 10.95 (*0-935952-51-9*) Angelus Pr.

Delamar, Gloria, ed. see Hamburg, Jeannine W.

Delamar, Gloria T. Children's Counting-Out Rhymes, Fingerplays, Jump Rope & Bounce-Ball Chants & Other Rhythms: A Comprehensive English-Language Reference. LC 82-24904. 224p. 1983. lib. bdg. 32.50 (*0-89950-064-1*) McFarland & Co.

***Delamar, Gloria T.** Wishing Handbook More Than 500 Ways to Make Your Wishes Come True. (Illus.). 128p. 1999. 12.95 (*0-7624-0540-6*) Running Pr.

Delamar, Penny. Complete Make-up Artist: Working in Film, Television & Theatre. 209p. 1995. pap. 29.95 (*0-8101-1258-2*) Northwestern U Pr.

Delamare. Dictionnaire Francais-Anglais et Anglais-Francais des Termes Techniques de Medecine. (ENG & FRE.). 95.00 (*0-685-36680-4*) Fr & Eur.

Delamare, jt. auth. see Cazes, J.

Delamare, jt. auth. see Garnier.

Delamare, David. Cinderella. LC 92-25126. (Illus.). 56p. (J). (ps-3). 1993. 15.00 (*0-671-76944-8*) S&S Bks Yung.

***Delamare, Francois & Guineau, Bernard.** Colors: The Story of Dyes & Pigments. LC 00-25231. (Discoveries Ser.). (Illus.). 160p. 2000. 12.95 (*0-8109-2872-8*, Pub. by Abrams) Time Warner.

Delamare, J. Dictionary for Nurses. Orig. Title: Dictionnaire de l'Infirmiere. 512p. 1996. pap. 36.00 (*2-224-02293-X*, Pub. by Maloine) IBD Ltd.

Delamare, J. & Delamare-Riche. French-English-French Dictionary of Medical Sciences. 3rd ed. (ENG & FRE.). 542p. 1992. 225.00 (*0-8288-0564-4*, M6107) Fr & Eur.

Delamare, Jacques. Dictionnaire Abrege des Termes de Medecine. (FRE.). 1990. write for info. (*0-7859-7822-4*, 2-224-01940-8) Fr & Eur.

Delamare-Riche, jt. auth. see Delamare, J.

Delamare, Valery & Garnier, M. Dictionary of Technical Medical Terms: Dictionnaire des Termes Techniques de Medecine. 21st ed. (ENG & FRE.). 880p. 1984. 95.00 (*0-8288-1806-1*) Fr & Eur.

Delamare, Valery, jt. auth. see Garnier, M.

Delamater, Jerome. Dance in the Hollywood Musical. Kirkpatrick, Diane, ed. LC 81-7513. (Studies in Cinema: No. 4). 323p. 1981. reprint ed. pap. 100.20 (*0-8357-1893-X*, 207070800004) Bks Demand.

Delamater, Jerome H. & Prigozy, Ruth, eds. The Detective in American Fiction, Film & Television, 63. LC 97-1690. (Contributions to the Study of Popular Culture: Vol. 63). 160p. 1998. 55.00 (*0-313-30463-7*, Greenwood Pr) Greenwood.

— Theory & Practice of Classic Detective Fiction, 62. LC 97-1691. (Contributions to the Study of Popular Culture: Vol. 62). 224p. 1997. 57.95 (*0-313-30462-9*, Greenwood Pr) Greenwood.

DeLamater, John & MacCorquodale, Patricia. Premarital Sexuality: Attitudes, Relationships, Behavior. LC 78-65019. 293p. reprint ed. pap. 90.90 (*0-608-20423-4*, 207176000002) Bks Demand.

Delamater, John, jt. auth. see Fidell, Linda S.

DeLamater, John D., jt. auth. see Michener, H. Andrew.

DeLambo, David, jt. auth. see Murnion, Philip J.

Delamer, John J. The Tarnished Shield. 208p. (Orig.). 1995. pap. 12.95 (*1-56474-156-7*) Fithian Pr.

Delamont, Sara. Appetites & Identities: An Introduction to Social Anthropology of Western Europe. LC 94-9581. 240p. (C). (gr. 13). 1994. 90.00 (*0-415-06253-5*, B3963) Routledge.

— Fieldwork in Educational Settings: Methods, Pitfalls & Perspectives. 224p. 1992. 89.95 (*1-85000-956-2*, Falmer Pr); pap. 32.95 (*1-85000-957-0*, Falmer Pr) Taylor & Francis.

— Interaction in the Classroom. 2nd ed. (Contemporary Sociology of the School Ser.). 128p. 1983. pap. 10.95 (*0-416-35880-2*, NO. 3956) Routledge.

— Knowledgeable Women: Structuralism & the Reproduction of Elites. 352p. 1989. 35.00 (*0-415-01599-5*) Routledge.

— Sociology of Women: An Introduction. 256p. (Orig.). 1980. text 29.95 (*0-04-301119-5*) Routledge.

— A Woman's Place in Education: Historical & Sociological Perspectives on Gender & Education. (Cardiff Papers in Qualitative Research: Vol. 6). 224p. 1996. 72.95 (*1-85628-583-9*, Pub. by Avebry) Ashgate Pub Co.

Delamont, Sara, ed. The Primary School Teacher. (Contemporary Analysis in Education Ser.). 225p. 1987. 69.95 (*1-85000-281-9*, Falmer Pr) Taylor & Francis.

Delamont, Sara & Atkinson, Paul. Fighting Familiarity: Essays on Education & Ethnography. LC 94-31401. 256p. 1995. text 55.00 (*1-881303-14-4*); pap. text 24.95 (*1-881303-15-2*) Hampton Pr NJ.

— Supervising the PhD: A Guide to Success. LC 97-569. 1997. 108.00 (*0-335-19517-2*) Taylor & Francis.

Delamont, Sara & Galton, Maurice. Inside the Secondary Classroom. 292p. 1987. lib. bdg. 35.00 (*0-7102-0933-9*, Routledge Thoemms) Routledge.

Delamont, Sara, et al. Survival & Success in Graduate School: Disciplines, Disciples & the Doctorate. 192p. 1999. 66.00 (*0-7507-0927-8*, Pub. by Falmer Pr UK) Taylor & Francis.

Delamont, Sara, jt. auth. see Davies, Brian.

Delamont, Sara, jt. ed. see Salisbury, Jane.

Delamont, Sarah & Carter, Keith, eds. Qualitative Research: The Emotional Dimension. LC 96-83716. (Cardiff Papers in Qualitative Research). 160p. 1996. 68.95 (*1-85972-263-6*, Pub. by Avebry) Ashgate Pub Co.

Delamonte, E. Supervising the PHD: A Guide to Success. LC 97-569. 1997. pap. 30.95 (*0-335-19516-4*) OpUniv Pr.

Delamore. Haemotological Effect of Systemic Diseases. 1990. text 133.00 (*0-7020-1408-7*, W B Saunders Co) Harcrt Hlth Sci Grp.

Delamore, I. W. Multiple Myeloma & Other Paraproteinaemias. LC 86-9666. (Illus.). 377p. 1987. text 92.00 (*0-443-03134-7*) Church.

Delamothe, Tony, ed. Outcomes into Clinical Practice. 169p. (Orig.). 1994. pap. text 35.00 (*0-7279-0888-X*, Pub. by BMJ Pub) Login Brothers Bk Co.

Delamotte, Eugenia, et al, eds. Women Imagine Change: A Global Anthology of Women's Resistance, 600 B. C. E. to Present. LC 97-18037. 480p. (C). 1997. pap. 30.99 (*0-415-91531-7*) Routledge.

Delamotte, Eugenia C. Places of Silence, Journeys of Freedom: The Fiction of Paule Marshall. LC 97-47580. (Studies in Contemporary American Fiction). 240p. 1998. 39.95 (*0-8122-3437-5*) U of Pa Pr.

DeLamotte, Eugenia C., et al, eds. Women Imagine Change: A Global Anthology of Women's Resistance, 600 B. C. E. to Present. LC 97-18037. 480p. (C). 1997. 80.00 (*0-415-91530-9*) Routledge.

Delamotte, Philip H. The Practice of Photography. 2nd ed. LC 72-9193. (Literature of Photography Ser.). 1973. reprint ed. 18.95 (*0-405-04903-X*) Ayer.

Delancey, Diney. For Love of Oliver. large type ed. (Linford Romance Large Print Ser.). 272p. 1997. pap. 16.99 (*0-7089-5009-4*, Linford) Ulverscroft.

Delancey, John O. L., jt. ed. see Nichols, David H.

DeLancey, Marci M. & Hannan, Denise R. International Guide to Workplace Substance-Abuse Prevention. 246p. (Orig.). 1994. pap. text 80.00 (*1-889437-09-3*) Inst Drug-Free Wrkpl.

Delancey, Marcy M. Does Drug Testing Work? 2nd ed. 116p. 1994. pap. write for info. (*1-889437-04-2*) Inst Drug-Free Wrkpl.

DeLancey, Mark, ed. Handbook of Political Science Research on Sub-Saharan Africa: Trends from the 1960s to the 1990s. LC 91-44049. 448p. 1992. lib. bdg. 85.00 (*0-313-27509-2*, DHS/, Greenwood Pr) Greenwood.

Delancey, Mark & Delancey, Virginia. A Bibliography of Cameroon. LC 75-1165. (African Bibliography Ser.: Vol. 4). 675p. 1975. 45.00 (*0-8419-0167-8*, Africana) Holmes & Meier.

DeLancey, Mark Dike, jt. auth. see DeLancey, Mark W.

DeLancey, Mark W. African International Relations: An Annotated Bibliography. 366p. 1980. pap. text 53.00 (*0-89158-680-6*) Westview.

DeLancey, Mark W., ed. Aspects of International Relations in Africa. (African Humanities Ser.). 253p. (Orig.). 1980. reprint ed. pap. 9.00 (*0-941934-28-4*) Indiana Africa.

***DeLancey, Mark W., ed.** Cameroon. 2nd rev. ed. (World Bibliographical Ser.: Vol. 63). 236p. 1999. lib. bdg. 67.00 (*1-85109-301-X*) ABC-CLIO.

***DeLancey, Mark W. & DeLancey, Mark Dike.** Historical Dictionary of the Republic of Cameroon. 3rd rev. expanded ed. (African Historical Dictionaries Ser.: No. 81). (Illus.). 392p. 2000. 75.00 (*0-8108-3775-7*) Scarecrow.

DeLancey, Mark W. & Mays, Terry M. Historical Dictionary of International Organizations in Sub-Saharan Africa. LC 93-23353. (International Organizations Ser.: No. 3). (Illus.). 579p. 1994. 73.00 (*0-8108-2751-4*) Scarecrow.

Delancey, Mark W. & Mbella, Mokeba H. Historical Dictionary of the Republic of Cameroon. 2nd ed. LC 90-48044. (African Historical Dictionaries Ser.: No. 48). (Illus.). 321p. 1990. 45.00 (*0-8108-2370-5*) Scarecrow.

DeLancey, Mark W. & Schraeder, Peter J. Cameroon. (World Bibliographical Ser.: No. 63). 202p. 1986. lib. bdg. 55.00 (*1-85109-006-1*) ABC-CLIO.

Delancey, Mark W., et al. African International Relations: An Annotated Bibliography. 2nd ed. LC 97-10413. 416p. (C). 1997. text 95.00 (*0-8133-8653-5*, Pub. by Westview) HarpC.

D

— Somalia. LC 90-154402. (World Bibliographical Ser.: No. 92). 222p. 1989. lib. bdg. 43.50 (*1-85109-038-X*) ABC-CLIO.

Delancey, Morgan. The Dave Matthews Band: Step into the Light. LC 98-150780. (Illus.). 264p. 1998. pap. 16.95 (*1-55022-342-9*, Pub. by ECW) LPC InBook.

Delancey, Virginia, jt. auth. see Delancey, Mark.

DeLancie, jt. auth. see Friedman, Michael J.

Deland, Charles E. The Aborigines of South Dakota. LC 76-43688. (South Dakota Historical Collections: 3). 1977. reprint ed. 30.00 (*0-404-15521-9*) AMS Pr.

Deland, E. C., jt. auth. see Lance, G. N.

Deland, Margaret W. The Awakening of Helena Richie. LC 78-96881. (Illus.). reprint ed. lib. bdg. 19.00 (*0-8398-0358-3*) Irvington.

— Doctor Lavendar's People. LC 75-113656. (Short Story Index Reprint Ser.). 1977. 21.95 (*0-8369-3385-0*) Ayer.

— Doctor Lavendar's People. LC 70-90102. (BCL Ser. II). (Illus.). 1969. reprint ed. 34.50 (*0-404-02074-7*) AMS Pr.

— Doctor Lavendar's People. (Illus.). 1972. reprint ed. 14.00 (*0-8422-8036-7*) Irvington.

— Doctor Lavendar's People. 1988. reprint ed. lib. bdg. 65.00 (*0-7812-0140-3*) Rprt Serv.

— Doctor Lavendar's People. LC 77-129345. (Illus.). 1971. reprint ed. 69.00 (*0-403-00478-0*) Scholarly.

— Dr. Lavendar's People. (BCL1-PS American Literature Ser.). 369p. 1992. reprint ed. lib. bdg. 89.00 (*0-7812-6703-X*) Rprt Serv.

— John Ward, Preacher. LC 67-29263. (Americans in Fiction Ser.). reprint ed. pap. text 14.95 (*0-8290-0134-4*); reprint ed. lib. bdg. 29.00 (*0-8398-0359-1*) Irvington.

— Mister Tommy Dove & Other Stories. LC 75-94716. (Short Story Index Reprint Ser.). 1977. 20.95 (*0-8369-3095-9*) Ayer.

— Old Chester Days. LC 79-113657. (Short Story Index Reprint Ser.). 1977. 23.95 (*0-8369-3386-9*) Ayer.

— Old Chester Tales. LC 70-97884. (BCL Ser. I). reprint ed. 32.50 (*0-404-02075-5*) AMS Pr.

— Old Chester Tales. 1972. reprint ed. lib. bdg. 20.00 (*0-8422-8037-5*) Irvington.

— Old Chester Tales. (C). 1986. reprint ed. pap. text 7.95 (*0-8290-1940-5*) Irvington.

— Wisdom of Fools. LC 72-98567. (Short Story Index Reprint Ser.). 1977. 19.95 (*0-8369-3141-6*) Ayer.

DeLanda, Manuel. War in the Age of Intelligent Machines. LC 89-27027. (Illus.). 272p. 1991. pap. 16.95 (*0-942299-75-2*) Zone Bks.

Delane, Jack. Puerto Rico Mio, Four Decades of Change, in Photographs by Jack Delano: Puerto Rico Mio, Cuatro Decadas de Cambio, en Fotografias de Jack Delano. LC 89-600274. (Illus.). 242p. (Orig.). 1990. pap. 34.95 (*0-87474-389-3*) Smithsonian.

***Delaney.** CPA Exam, 2 vols. 26th ed. (C). 1999. pap. 99.90 (*0-471-32882-0*) Wiley.

Delaney. CPA Exam, Vol. 1. 26th ed. 1230p. (C). 1999. pap. 49.95 (*0-471-32883-9*) Wiley.

— CPA Exam, Vol. 2. 26th ed. 1294p. (C). 1999. pap. 49.95 (*0-471-32884-7*) Wiley.

Delaney. Landleaguers: (trollope 1995) 1995. 38.00 (*1-870587-41-3*) Ashgate Pub Co.

— Power Play. mass mkt. 6.95 (*0-7472-5447-8*, Pub. by Headline Bk Pub) Trafalgar.

Delaney, A. The Gunnywolf. LC 87-29351. (Illus.). 32p. (J). (ps-3). 1988. 11.95 (*0-06-021594-1*) HarpC Child Bks.

Delaney, Anita J., jt. ed. see Mizio, Emelicia.

Delaney, Ann. Politics for Dummies. (For Dummies Ser.). 368p. 1995. pap. 19.99 (*1-56884-381-X*) IDG Bks.

Delaney, Anne M., et al. Report on Needs Assessment Methodology: Sources of Needs Assessments in Public Law. LC 79-102731. (American Foundation for the Blind Research Ser.). 223p. reprint ed. pap. 69.20 (*0-7837-0136-5*, 204042500016) Bks Demand.

Delaney, Antoinette. The Gunnywolf. LC 87-29351. (Trophy Picture Bk.). (Illus.). 32p. (J). (ps-3). 1992. pap. 5.95 (*0-06-443304-8*, HarpTrophy) HarpC Child Bks.

Delaney, Ben. The Market for Visual Simulation/Virtual Reality Systems: A Study Conducted by CyberEdge Information Services. (Illus.). 33p. (C). 1997. pap. 775.00 (*1-929696-00-0*) CyberEdge Info.

— The Market for Visual Simulation/Virtual Reality Systems: A Study Conducted by CyberEdge Information Services. 2nd ed. (Illus.). 118p. (C). 1999. pap. 1820.00 (*1-929696-02-7*) CyberEdge Info.

Delaney, C. F. Science, Knowledge, & Mind: A Study in the Philosophy of C. S. Peirce. LC 92-53743. (C). 1993. text 33.50 (*0-268-01748-4*) U of Notre Dame Pr.

Delaney, C. F., ed. The Liberalism-Communitarianism Debate. LC 93-573. 260p. (C). 1994. pap. text 23.95 (*0-8476-7864-4*); lib. bdg. 59.50 (*0-8476-7863-6*) Rowman.

Delaney, C. F. & Finch, E. C. Radiation Detectors: Physical Principles & Applications. (Illus.). 375p. 1992. text 105.00 (*0-19-853923-1*) OUP.

Delaney, C. F., et al. The Synoptic Vision: Essays on the Philosophy of Wilfrid Sellars. LC 76-22406. 1977. text 23.00 (*0-268-01596-1*) U of Notre Dame Pr.

Delaney, Caldwell. Deep South. (Illus.). 1981. reprint ed. 15.00 (*0-940882-00-0*) HB Pubns.

— A Mobile Sextet. (Illus.). 187p. 1981. 15.00 (*0-940882-15-9*) HB Pubns.

— The Phoenix Volunteer Fire Company of Mobile, 1838-1888. (Illus.). (Orig.). 1967. pap. 2.00 (*0-914334-00-X*) Museum Mobile.

— Remember Mobile. (Illus.). 242p. 1980. reprint ed. 20.00 (*0-940882-13-2*) HB Pubns.

— The Story of Mobile. rev. ed. (Illus.). 352p. 1981. reprint ed. 25.00 (*0-940882-14-0*) HB Pubns.

Delaney, Caldwell, ed. Raphael Semmes, Rear Admiral, Confederate States Navy, Brigadier General, Confederate States Army. (Illus.). 1978. 25.00 (*0-914334-05-0*); pap. 10.00 (*0-914334-06-9*) Museum Mobile.

***Delaney, Carol.** Abraham on Trial: The Social Legacy of Biblical Myth. (Illus.). 296p. 2000. pap. 18.95 (*0-691-07050-4*) Princeton U Pr.

Delaney, Carol. The Seed & the Soil: Gender & Cosmology in Turkish Village Society. LC 90-28545. (Comparative Studies on Muslim Societies: No. 11). (Illus.). 393p. 1991. 55.00 (*0-520-07314-2*, Pub. by U CA Pr); pap. 22.50 (*0-520-07550-1*, Pub. by U CA Pr) Cal Prin Full Svc.

Delaney, Carol, jt. ed. see Yanagisako, Sylvia.

Delaney, Carol L. Abraham on Trial: The Social Legacy of Biblical Myth. LC 98-12174. 296p. 1998. text 29.95 (*0-691-05985-3*, Pub. by Princeton U Pr) Cal Prin Full Svc.

***DeLaney, Chuck.** Photography Your Way: A Career Guide to Satisfaction & Success. (Illus.). 282p. 2000. pap. text 18.95 (*1-58115-024-5*) Allworth Pr.

DeLaney, Chuck. Wedding Photography & Video: The Bride & Groom's Guide. LC 93-71918. 160p. (Orig.). 1994. pap. 10.95 (*1-880559-10-2*) Allworth Pr.

Delaney, Connie. Spindle Spinning: From Novice to Expert. (Illus.). 80p. 1998. pap. 12.00 (*0-9660952-0-0*, 0556) Kokovoko Pr.

Delaney, Connie W., jt. auth. see Moorhead, Sue.

Delaney, Connie White & Lauer, A. R. Intravenous Therapy: A Guide to Quality Care. (Illus.). 348p. 1988. text 21.50 (*0-397-54617-3*, Lippnctt) Lppncott W & W.

***Delaney, D. Neil.** 1998. mass mkt. 6.95 (*0-7472-6066-4*, Pub. by Headline Bk Pub) Trafalgar.

Delaney, Dan. Charity in the Workplace 1997. 36p. 1997. pap. 15.00 (*1-891465-10-4*) Natl Comm Philan.

Delaney, David. Race, Place, & the Law, 1836-1948. LC 97-36989. 248p. (C). 1998. 35.00 (*0-292-71596-X*, DELRAC); pap. 17.95 (*0-292-71597-8*, DELRAP) U of Tex Pr.

Delaney, Del. The Lord, the Lion & Mutu. (Literature Crusade Ser.). pap. 0.95 (*0-89985-379-X*) Christ for the Nations.

— The Lord, the Lion & Mutu. 1974. pap. 1.95 (*0-89985-995-X*) Christ for the Nations.

***Delaney, Edward L.** Drowning & Other Stories. (Series in Short Fiction). 1999. pap. 15.95 (*0-88748-314-3*) Carnegie-Mellon.

Delaney, Edward L., et al. Thinking about American Higher Education: 1990s & Beyond. Gilley, J. Wade & Vaughan, George B., eds. (ACE-Oryx Series on Higher Education). 224p. 1991. 27.95 (*0-02-897162-0*, ACE-Oryx) Oryx Pr.

Delaney, Emmett, et al. Integrating Unix & NT Technology: The Definitive Guide. LC 99-6338. (Illus.). 361p. 1999. pap. 59.95 (*1-882419-84-7*) News Four-Hund.

Delaney, F. M. Low Cost Rural Health Care & Health Manpower Training: An Annotated Bibliography with Special Emphasis on Developing Countries, Vol. 3. 187p. 1977. write for info. (*0-88936-138-X*) IDRC Bks.

— Low Cost Rural Health Care & Health Manpower Training: An Annotated Bibliography with Special Emphasis on Developing Countries, Vol. 4. 186p. 1979. write for info. (*0-88936-201-7*) IDRC Bks.

Delaney, F. M., jt. ed. see Rast, N.

Delaney, Frank. Walk to the Western Isles. 1994. 30.00 (*0-246-13745-2*) Granada Publ.

Delaney, Frank, ed. Silver Apples, Golden Apples: Best Loved Irish Verse. LC 87-24296. 157p. 1987. pap. 14.95 (*0-685-25871-8*, Pub. by Blackstaff Pr) Dufour.

— Silver Apples, Golden Apples: Best Loved Irish Verse. LC 87-24296. 157p. 1987. pap. 14.95 (*0-85640-391-1*) Dufour.

Delaney, Gayle. Breakthrough Dreaming: How to Tap the Power of Your 24-Hour Mind. 1996. 16.00 incl. audio (*0-671-53682-6*) S&S Trade.

— Living Your Dreams: The Classic Bestseller on Becoming Your Own Dream Expert. LC 96-14653. 400p. 1996. pap. 15.00 (*0-06-251446-6*, Pub. by Harper SF) HarpC.

— Sensual Dreaming: How to Understand & Interpret the Erotic Content of Your Dreams. 288p. 1995. pap. 12.00 (*0-449-90974-3*) Fawcett.

Delaney, Gayle, ed. New Directions in Dream Interpretation. LC 92-33941. (SUNY Series in Dream Studies). 308p. (C). 1993. text 59.50 (*0-7914-1605-4*); pap. text 24.95 (*0-7914-1606-2*) State U NY Pr.

Delaney, Gayle M. All About Dreams: Everything You Need To Know About* Why* What They Mean* anHow To Put Them To Work for You. LC 97-45891. 320p. 1998. pap. 15.00 (*0-06-251411-3*) HarpC.

— In Your Dreams: Falling, Flying, & Other Dream Themes: A New Kind of Dream Dictionary. LC 96-36862. 304p. 1997. pap. 13.00 (*0-06-251412-1*, Pub. by Harper SF) HarpC.

Delaney, Granger H. Muscle Contraction: Subject, Reference & Research Guidebook. LC 87-47640. 160p. 1987. 47.50 (*0-88164-584-2*); pap. 44.50 (*0-88164-585-0*) ABBE Pubs Assn.

Delaney, H. M. & Jason, R. Abdominal Trauma: Surgical & Radiologic Diagnosis. (Illus.). 224p. 1981. 142.00 (*0-387-90502-2*) Spr-Verlag.

Delaney, Harold D., jt. auth. see Maxwell, Scott E.

Delaney, Hearther. Having Our Say. 1995. mass mkt. 8.99 (*0-440-91089-7*) Dell.

Delaney, J. P. Glyn Philpot: His Life & Art. LC 98-53022. (Illus.). 250p. 1999. text 69.95 (*1-85928-355-1*) Ashgate Pub Co.

Delaney, Janice, et al. The Curse: A Cultural History of Menstruation. rev. ed. LC 87-5943. 352p. 1988. pap. text 15.95 (*0-252-01452-9*) U of Ill Pr.

Delaney, John. The Blitzkrieg Campaigns: Germany's Lightning War Strategy in Action. LC 97-136245. (Illus.). 176p. 1997. 29.95 (*1-85409-348-7*, Pub. by Arms & Armour) Sterling.

— Fighting the Desert Fox. LC 98-232712. (Illus.). 160p. 1998. 29.95 (*1-85409-407-6*, Pub. by Arms & Armour) Sterling.

***Delaney, John.** Fighting the Desert Fox: Rommel's Campaigns in North Africa April 1941 to August 1942. 160p. 1999. pap. text 19.95 (*0-304-35297-7*) Continuum.

Delaney, John. How to Do Your Best on Law School Exams. 2nd rev. ed. (Illus.). 235p. 1988. pap. text 14.95 (*0-9608514-5-3*) J Delaney Pubns.

— Learning Legal Reasoning: Briefing, Analysis & Theory. (Delaney Ser.). Orig. Title: How to Brief a Case, An Introduction to Jurisprudence. (Illus.). (C). 1987. pap. text 13.95 (*0-9608514-4-5*) J Delaney Pubns.

Delaney, John, compiled by. From Circle to Sphere: Historic Maps since Columbus: A Catalog of an Exhibition. (Illus.). 112p. 1992. pap. 5.00 (*0-87811-035-6*) Princeton Lib.

Delaney, John, ed. The Journal of Real Estate Taxation. 175.00 (*0-685-69564-6*, JRET) Warren Gorham & Lamont.

Delaney, John, tr. The Practice of the Presence of God. 144p. 1996. pap. 6.00 (*0-385-48240-X*) Doubleday.

Delaney, John & Boyd, Ron. How to Draw DC Comics Super Heroes. (DC Comics Ser.). 40p. (J). (gr. 3 up). 1998. pap. 7.95 (*1-56010-329-9*, CB04) W Foster Pub.

— How to Draw Wonder Woman. (DC Comics Ser.). 40p. 1998. pap. 7.95 (*1-56010-328-0*, CB03) W Foster Pub.

Delaney, John J. Pocket Dictionary of Saints. LC 82-45479. 528p. 1983. pap. 10.95 (*0-385-18274-0*, Image Bks) Doubleday.

Delaney, John J., ed. A Woman Clothed with the Sun. LC 60-5922. 272p. 1990. pap. 9.95 (*0-385-08019-0*, Image Bks) Doubleday.

— A Woman Clothed with the Sun: Eight Great Apparitions of Our Lady. large type ed. 320p. 1996. pap. 16.95 (*0-8027-2699-2*) Walker & Co.

Delaney, John J., et al. Land Use Practice & Forms: Handling the Land Use Case. 2nd ed. LC 96-38796. 1996. write for info. (*0-8366-1088-1*) West Group.

Delaney, John P. The Blue Devils in Italy: A History of the 88th Infantry Division in World War II. (Divisional Ser.). (Illus.). 359p. 1988. reprint ed. 49.95 (*0-89839-107-5*) Battery Pr.

Delaney, Joyce, jt. ed. see Mckinley, Catherine E.

***Delaney, Kalen.** Inside Microsoft SQL Server 2000. 2000. 59.99 (*0-7356-0998-5*) Microsoft.

Delaney, Kalen, jt. auth. see Soukup, Ron.

Delaney, Kathy, jt. auth. see Squillace, Marie R.

Delaney, Kevin J. Strategic Bankruptcy: How Corporations & Creditors Use Chapter 11 to Their Advantage. 224p. 1992. 45.00 (*0-520-07358-4*, Pub. by U CA Pr) Cal Prin Full Svc.

— Strategic Bankruptcy: How Corporations & Creditors Use Chapter 11 to Their Advantage. 224p. 1999. pap. 16.95 (*0-520-07359-2*, Pub. by U CA Pr) Cal Prin Full Svc.

Delaney, Laurel J. Start & Run a Profitable Exporting Business. xvi, 231p. 1998. 13.95 (*1-55180-139-6*) Self-Counsel Pr.

***Delaney, Leslie.** Saint Simon's Island Cooks. 92p. 1999. 19.95 (*0-9671690-0-3*, Pub. by St Simons Island) Wimmer Bks.

***Delaney, Leslie & McKim, David.** The Southern Plantations Cook. 126p. 1999. 24.95 (*0-9671690-1-1*, Pub. by St Simons Island) Wimmer Bks.

Delaney, Marfe Ferguson. Sea Otters. (Animal Safari Ser.). (Illus.). 10p. (J). (ps-k). 1999. per. 5.95 (*0-7922-7108-4*, Pub. by Natl Geog) Publishers Group.

Delaney, Marianne. Ireland. (Places & History Ser.). (Illus.). 136p. 1997. 24.95 (*1-55670-546-8*) Stewart Tabori & Chang.

Delaney, Mark. Growler's Horn. LC 99-86977. (Misfits, Inc. Ser.: No. 3). 192p. (YA). (gr. 6-10). 2000. pap. 5.95 (*1-56145-206-8*) Peachtree Pubs.

***Delaney, Mark.** Growler's Horn. (Illus.). (J). 2000. 11.30 (*0-606-18339-6*) Turtleback.

— The Kingfisher's Tale. (Misfits, Inc. Ser.: No. 4). 192p. (YA). 2000. pap. 5.95 (*1-56145-226-2*) Peachtree Pubs.

Delaney, Mark. Of Heroes & Villians. LC 98-36466. (Misfits, Inc. Ser.: No. 2). 207p. (YA). (gr. 7-11). 1999. pap. 5.95 (*1-56145-178-9*, 51789) Peachtree Pubs.

— The Vanishing Chip. LC 98-7209. (Misfits, Inc. Ser.: No. 1). 192p. (YA). (gr. 7-11). 1998. pap. 5.95 (*1-56145-176-2*, Peachtree) Peachtree Pubs.

Delaney, Martin. Biography of a Plague. 300p. Date not set. pap. write for info. (*0-465-00652-3*) Basic.

Delaney, Martin R. The Condition, Elevation, Emigration, & Destiny of the Colored People of the United States of America. 215p. 1994. reprint ed. pap. 11.95 (*0-933121-42-3*) Black Classic.

***Delaney, Mary.** The Art of Recovery: Thoughts & Meditations for the Recovering Artist. Jarrell, Robin, ed. (Illus.). xiv, 146p. 1999. pap. 7.95 (*0-9674781-0-3*) Ultimate Purpose Pub.

Delaney, Mary B., et al. Let's Be Better Friends: The Peer Intergration Program. (Illus.). 1997. spiral bd. 34.95 (*1-890265-01-2*, 0950) Janelle Pubns.

Delaney-McLoughlin, Katharine, jt. auth. see Rice-Licare, Jennifer.

Delaney, Michael. Deep Doo-Doo. (Puffin Novels Ser.). (J). (gr. 3-7). 1998. pap. 4.99 (*0-14-038747-1*) Peng Put Young Read.

***Delaney, Michael.** Walk a Mile in My Shoes. 540p. 2000. mass mkt. 9.99 (*1-55279-001-0*) Picasso Publ.

Delaney, Mike. With a Smile upon His Face: An Inspirational Tale from the Heartland. LC 95-83062. 256p. 1996. pap. 10.95 (*0-9644007-4-X*) Filibuster Pr.

Delaney, Ned. Cosmic Chickens. LC 86-19398. (Illus.). 48p. (J). (ps-3). 1988. 12.95 (*0-06-021583-6*) HarpC Child Bks.

— Two Strikes, Four Eyes. (J). Date not set. pap. write for info. (*0-679-84172-5*); lib. bdg. write for info. (*0-679-94172-X*) Random Bks Yng Read.

Delaney, Patrick R. The Wiley CPA Examination Review, 4 vols. 2860p. 1999. pap. text 153.80 (*0-471-29593-0*) Wiley.

— Wiley CPA Examination Review 2000, 4 vols. Incl. Accounting & Reporting: Taxation, Managerial, Governmental & Not-for-Profit Organizations., 4 Vols. Set 626p. 1999. pap. 39.95 (*0-471-35112-1*); Auditing 2000. 640p. 1999. pap. 39.95 (*0-471-35116-4*); Business Law & Professional Responsibilities 2000. 509p. 1999. pap. 39.95 (*0-471-35150-4*); Financial Accounting & Reporting: Business Enterprises., 4 Vols. Set 790p. 1999. pap. 41.95 (*0-471-35114-8*); 1999. Set pap. 161.80 (*0-471-35149-0*) Wiley.

***Delaney, Patrick R.** Wiley CPA Examination Review 2000-2001, 2 vols. 27th ed. 2560p. 2000. pap. 104.00 (*0-471-36085-6*) Wiley.

— Wiley CPA Examination Review 2000-2001: Problems & Solutions, Vol. 2. 27th ed. 1312p. 2000. pap. text 52.00 (*0-471-36056-2*) Wiley.

— Wiley CPA Examination Review 2000-2001 Vol. 1: Outlines & Study Guides. 27th ed. 1248p. 2000. pap. text 52.00 (*0-471-36055-4*) Wiley.

— Wiley Gaap: Interpretation & Application of Generally Accepted Accounting Principles 2000. 2000th ed. 1128p. 1999. pap. 64.00 (*0-471-35115-6*) Wiley.

— Wiley GAAP: Interpretation & Appreciation of Generally Accepted Accounting Principles 2001. (Illus.). 1128p. 2000. pap. 66.00 (*0-471-39069-0*) Wiley.

***Delaney, Paul, ed.** Brian Friel in Conversation. LC 99-6947. (Theater--Theory/Text/Performance Ser.). 312p. 2000. pap. 18.95 (*0-472-06710-9*, 06710); text 49.50 (*0-472-09710-5*, 09710) U of Mich Pr.

Delaney, Paul, ed. see Stoppard, Tom.

Delaney, Phyllis, ed. Report, Vol. 36. 1996. 27.00 (*0-935057-81-1*) OH Genealogical.

Delaney, R. W. Your Life in Your Words: Your Story As Only You Can Write It. 90p. 1995. pap. 19.95 (*0-9645363-0-7*) Flagship Pr.

Delaney, Richard J. Fostering Changes: Treating Attachment-Disordered Foster Children & Adopted. 2nd ed. 105p. 1997. pap. 15.95 (*1-885473-19-2*) Wood N Barnes.

— Healing Power of the Family: An Illustrated Overview of Life with the Disturbed Foster or Adopted Child. (Illus.). 123p. 1997. pap. 17.95 (*1-885473-16-8*) Wood N Barnes.

— The Long Journey Home: A Story of Separation & the Search for Love. (Illus.). 48p. (J). (gr. 3-7). 1997. pap. 10.95 (*1-885473-14-1*) Wood N Barnes.

***Delaney, Richard J.** Permutations of Permanency: Making Sensible Placement Decisions. 32p. 1999. spiral bd. 4.95 (*1-885473-30-3*) Wood N Barnes.

Delaney, Richard J. Raising Cain: Caring for Troubled Youngsters/Repairing Our Troubled System. (Illus.). 136p. 1998. pap. 17.95 (*1-885473-17-6*) Wood N Barnes.

***Delaney, Richard J.** Safe Passage: A Summary of the "Parent 2 Parent" Mentoring Program. 114p. 1999. pap. 16.95 (*1-885473-32-X*) Wood N Barnes.

Delaney, Richard J. & Kunstal, Frank R. Troubled Transplants: Unconventional Strategies for Helping Disturbed Foster & Adopted Children. 2nd ed. (Illus.). 180p. 1997. pap. 16.95 (*1-885473-18-4*) Wood N Barnes.

Delaney, Robert. Llamados a Peregrinar. (Vivamos las Sagradas Escrituras Ser.). (SPA., Illus.). 64p. 1992. pap. text 2.50 (*1-55944-030-9*) Franciscan Comns.

Delaney, Robert F. The Literature of Communism in America: A Selected Reference Guide. LC 62-6923. 447p. reprint ed. pap. 138.60 (*0-608-11183-X*, 200537800053) Bks Demand.

Delaney, Shelagh. A Taste of Honey. LC 59-8206. 96p. 1989. pap. 10.00 (*0-8021-3185-9*, Grove) Grove-Atltic.

Delaney, Sue. Mutu Finds the Way to Heaven. (Literature Crusade Ser.). pap. 0.95 (*0-89985-378-1*) Christ for the Nations.

— Mutu Finds the Way to Heaven. 1974. pap. 1.95 (*0-89985-996-8*) Christ for the Nations.

Delaney, Sue F. Women Smokers Can Quit: A Different Approach. 64p. (Orig.). 1989. pap. 6.95 (*0-9626223-1-1*) Womens Hlthcare Pr.

***Delaney, Susan.** A Star to Sail By. LC 00-25702. (Core Ser.). (Illus.). 2000. 28.95 (*0-7838-9011-7*, G K Hall Lrg Type) Mac Lib Ref.

— A Star to Sail By. 1999. mass mkt. 6.99 (*0-451-40899-3*, Onyx) NAL.

Delaney, Susan, tr. see Mache, Francois-Bernard.

Delaney, Thomas, jt. ed. see Lurie, Jaon B.

Delaney, Thomas J., jt. auth. see Indick, Murray A.

Delaney, William & Vaccari, Erminia. Dynamic Models & Discrete Event Simulation. (Electrical Engineering & Electronics Ser.: Vol. 53). (Illus.). 672p. 1988. text 190.00 (*0-8247-7654-2*) Dekker.

Delaney, William A. Micromanagement: How to Solve the Problems of Growing Companies. LC 80-69691. 174p. reprint ed. pap. 54.00 (*0-608-12161-4*, 202391400034) Bks Demand.

— The Thirty Most Common Problems in Management & How to Solve Them. LC 81-69375. 192p. reprint ed. pap. 59.60 (*0-608-11911-3*, 202356900033) Bks Demand.

— Why Small Businesses Fail: Don't Make the Same Mistake Once. 204p. 1984. 16.95 (*0-13-959016-1*, Busn); pap. 9.95 (*0-13-959008-0*, Busn) P-H.

Delange. Touch the Water, Touch the Wind. (C). 1993. pap. write for info. (*0-15-680722-X*) Harcourt Coll Pubs.

DeLange, Deon. Beaded Treasure Purses: Tubular Brick Stitch Designs. Knight, Denise, ed. & illus. by. LC 96-85685. 88p. (Orig.). 1997. pap., per. 10.95 (*0-943604-53-2*, BOO/42) Eagles View.

DeLange, Deon. More Techniques of Beading Earrings. Smith, Monte, ed. LC 83-82121. (Illus.). 68p. 1985. pap., per. 9.95 (*0-943604-12-5*, BOO/04) Eagles View.

DeLange, Deon. Techniques of Beading Earrings. Smith, Monte, ed. LC 83-82121. (Illus.). 76p. (Orig.). 1984. per. 9.95 (*0-943604-03-6*, BOO/03) Eagles View.

— Techniques of Fashion Earrings. Knight, Denise, ed. LC 94-72283. (Illus.). 64p. (Orig.). 1995. per. 9.95 (*0-943604-44-3*, BOO/37) Eagles View.

Delange, F. Endemic Goitre & Thyroid Function in Central Africa. Falkner, Frank et al, eds. (Monographs in Pediatrics: Vol. 2). (Illus.). xvi, 160p. 1974. 64.50 (*3-8055-1687-8*) S Karger.

Delange, F., et al, eds. Pediatric Thyroidology. (Pediatric & Adolescent Endocrinology Ser.: Vol. 14). (Illus.). x, 412p. 1985. 239.25 (*3-8055-3968-1*) S Karger.

Delange, F., et al, eds. Research in Congenital Hypothyroidism. (NATO ASI Series A, Life Sciences: Vol. 161). (Illus.). 380p. 1989. 105.00 (*0-306-43141-6*, Plenum Trade) Perseus Pubng.

Delange, F., et al. Iodine Deficiency in Europe: A Continuing Concern. (NATO ASI Ser.: Vol. 241). (Illus.). 510p. (C). 1993. text 139.50 (*0-306-44410-0*, Kluwer Plenum) Kluwer Academic.

DeLange, Jan, jt. auth. see Reynolds, John.

DeLange, Nicholas, tr. see Oz, Amos.

DeLange, Nicholas, tr. see Yehoshua, Abraham B.

DeLanghe, E. A. & Persley, Gabrielle J., eds. Banana & Plantain Breeding Strategies. 188p. (Orig.). 1987. pap. 99.00 (*0-949511-36-6*) St Mut.

Delanglez, Jean. The French Jesuits in Lower Louisiana, (1700-1763) LC 73-3576. (Catholic University of America. Studies in Romance Languages & Literatures: No. 21). reprint ed. 55.00 (*0-404-57771-7*) AMS Pr.

Delannay, Francis, ed. Characterization of Heterogeneous Catalysts. LC 83-26256. (Chemical Industries Ser.: No. 15). (Illus.). 423p. 1984. reprint ed. pap. 131.20 (*0-608-07898-0*, 206787900010) Bks Demand.

Delannoy, Claude. Turbo Pascal Programming. Stewart, M. J., tr. from FRE. (Computer Science Ser.). (Illus.). 273p. (C). 1989. pap. text 35.00 (*0-333-48426-6*) Scholium Intl.

Delannoy, Luc. Pres: The Story of Lester Young. Odio, Elena B., tr. from FRE. LC 92-22003. (Illus.). 280p. 1993. pap. 18.00 (*1-55728-264-1*); text 30.00 (*1-55728-263-3*) U of Ark Pr.

Delano, Alonzo. Life on the Plains & among the Diggings, Being Scenes & Adventures of an Overland Journey to California. LC 72-9440. (Far Western Frontier Ser.). (Illus.). 396p. 1973. reprint ed. 26.95 (*0-405-04970-6*) Ayer.

Delano, Amasa. Delano's Voyages of Commerce & Discovery: Amasa Delano in China, the Pacific Islands, Australia & South America, 1789-1807. abr. ed. Seagraves, Eleanor Roosevelt, ed. LC 94-9423. (American Classics Ser.). (Illus.). 464p. 1994. pap. 14.95 (*0-936399-56-2*) Berkshire Hse.

Delano, Frank. The Omnipowerful Brand. LC 98-20739. xvi, 256p. 1999. 35.95 (*0-8144-0459-6*) AMACOM.

Delano, Irene, jt. auth. see Delano, Jack.

Delano, Isaac O. The Soul of Nigeria. (B. E. Ser.: No. 140). 1937. 35.00 (*0-8115-3063-9*) Periodicals Srv.

— The Soul of Nigeria. LC 74-15026. (Illus.). reprint ed. 45.00 (*0-404-12024-5*) AMS Pr.

Delano, Jack. De San Juan a Ponce En el Tren. LC 90-46114. (SPA.). 123p. 1991. pap. 19.95 (*0-8477-2117-5*) U of PR Pr.

— Photographic Memories: The Autobiography of Jack Delano. LC 96-44181. 240p. 1997. 29.95 (*1-56098-741-3*) Smithsonian.

— That's Life: Cartoons by "Joaquin" (ENG & SPA., Illus.). 194p. 1996. pap. 11.95 (*0-8477-0247-2*) U of PR Pr.

Delano, Jack & Delano, Irene. En Busca del Maestro Rafael Cordero: In Search of Maestro Rafael Cordero. LC 94-6187. (ENG & SPA., Illus.). 1994. write for info. (*0-8477-0080-1*) U of PR Pr.

Delano, Jamie. Hellblazer: Original Sins. Kahan, Bob, ed. (Illus.). 256p. 1997. mass mkt. 19.95 (*1-56389-052-6*, Pub. by DC Comics) Time Warner.

— Vertigo Verite: Hell Eternal. Berger, Karen, ed. LC 98-207753. (Illus.). 64p. 1998. pap. 6.95 (*1-56389-448-3*) DC Comics.

Delano, Jamie, et al. John Constantine Hellblazer. (Original Sins Ser.). (Illus.). 256p. (Orig.). 1993. mass mkt. 14.99 (*0-446-39429-7*, Pub. by Warner Bks) Little.

Delano, JMamie. Batman: Man-Bat. (Illus.). 160p. 1997. pap. 14.95 (*1-56389-320-7*, Pub. by DC Comics) Time Warner.

Delano, June. The Supervisor's Log (A Professional's Graffiti) A Handbook for Supervision. 176p. (C). 1993. pap. text 18.95 (*0-8077-3292-3*) Tchrs Coll.

Delano, Kate & Decker, Condax. Riding: A Guide for New Riders. (Illus.). 192p. 1995. 24.95 (*1-55821-381-3*) Lyons Pr.

Delano, Marfe F. Sky. LC 97-28564. (National Geographic Nature Library). (J). 1998. write for info. (*0-7922-7047-9*) Natl Geog.

— Tigers. (Animal Safari Ser.). (Illus.). 10p. (J). (ps-k). 1999. bds. 5.95 (*0-7922-7107-6*, Pub. by Natl Geog) Publishers Group.

***Delano, Marfe Ferguson.** Deserts. LC 99-44331. (Nature Library). (Illus.). (J). 1999. write for info. (*0-7922-7544-6*) Natl Geog.

— Kangaroos. 10p. (J). 2000. bds. 5.95 (*0-7922-7125-4*) Natl Geog.

— Tree Frogs. 6p. (J). 2000. per. 5.95 (*0-7922-7127-0*) Natl Geog.

Delano, Pablo. Faces of America: Photographs by Pablo Delano. LC 92-4298. (Illus.). 144p. (Orig.). 1992. pap. 24.95 (*1-56098-179-2*) Smithsonian.

***DeLano, Patti.** Arkansas: Off the Beaten Path: A Guide to Unique Places. 4th ed. LC 99-48432. (Illus.). 256p. 2000. pap. 12.95 (*0-7627-0531-0*) Globe Pequot.

DeLano, Patti. Kansas: Off the Beaten Path: A Guide to Unique Places. 4th ed. LC 99-24580. (Off the Beaten Path Ser.). 225p. 1999. pap. text 12.95 (*0-7627-0457-8*) Globe Pequot.

***DeLano, Patti.** Missouri - Off the Beaten Path: A Guide to Unique Places. 5th ed. (Off the Beaten Path Ser.). (Illus.). 2000. pap. 12.95 (*0-7627-0777-1*) Globe Pequot.

Delano, Patti Ann & Johnson, Cathy. Missouri: Off the Beaten Path: A Guide to Unique Places. 4th ed. LC 98-8063. (Off the Beaten Path Ser.). (Illus.). 256p. 1998. pap. 12.95 (*0-7627-0192-7*) Globe Pequot.

***Delano, Poli & Ramirez, Rafael.** Cuento Chileno Contemporaneo. 358p. 1998. pap. 15.99 (*956-7083-94-0*) Fondo CA.

Delano, Sterling F. The Harbinger & New England Transcendentalism: A Portrait of Associationism in America. 224p. 1983. 35.00 (*0-8386-3138-X*) Fairleigh Dickinson.

Delanoe, Pierre. Great French Songs: La Vie en Rose & Other Hits. LC 97-15237. (Illus.). 112p. 1997. text 29.95 incl. audio compact disk (*0-86565-993-1*, 1997) Vendome.

Delanoy, Deborah L., jt. ed. see Cook, Emily W.

***Delanty, Gerard.** Citizenship in a Global Age: Society, Culture, Politics. LC 00-22511. (Issues in Society Ser.). 2000. pap. write for info. (*0-335-20489-9*, Pub. by OpUniv Pr) Taylor & Francis.

Delanty, Gerard. Inventing Europe: Idea, Identity, Reality. LC 95-3142. 200p. 1995. pap. 21.95 (*0-312-12569-0*); text 59.95 (*0-312-12568-2*) St Martin.

— Social Science. LC 97-33615. (Concepts in Social Thought Ser.). x, 159p. 1998. pap. 14.95 (*0-8166-3127-1*) U of Minn Pr.

— Social Science. LC 97-33615. (Concepts in Social Thought Ser.). 1998. text 37.95 (*0-8166-3126-3*) U of Minn Pr.

Delanty, Gerard. Social Theory in a Changing World: Conceptions of Modernity. LC 99-11068. 1999. pap. 26.95 (*0-7456-1918-5*) Blackwell Pubs.

***Delanty, Gerard.** Social Theory in a Changing World: Conceptions of Modernity. LC 99-11068. 1999. 59.95 (*0-7456-1917-7*) Blackwell Pubs.

Delanty, Greg. American Wake. LC 95-225430. 70p. 1996. pap. 12.95 (*0-85640-549-3*, Pub. by Blackstaff Pr) Dufour.

— Cast in the Fire. 56p. 1986. pap. 10.95 (*0-85105-455-2*, Pub. by Smyth) Dufour.

— The Hellbox. 56p. 1998. pap. 12.95 (*0-19-288088-8*) OUP.

— Southward. LC 91-27438. 64p. 1992. pap. 7.95 (*0-8071-1734-X*); text 15.95 (*0-8071-1733-1*) La State U Pr.

Delanty, Greg, ed. Selected Poems of Patrick Galvin. 128p. 1996. 40.00 (*1-85918-079-5*, Pub. by Cork Univ); pap. 19.95 (*1-85918-091-4*, Pub. by Cork Univ) Intl Spec Bk.

Delanty, Greg & Dhomhnaill, Nuala Ni. Jumping off Shadows. 270p. 1995. pap. 24.00 (*0-902561-91-X*, Pub. by Cork Univ) Stylus Pub VA.

Delanty, Greg, et al. Aristophanes Vol. 3: The New Class, Clouds, Birds. LC 98-8446. (Penn Greek Drama Ser.). 1999. pap. 16.95 (*0-8122-1698-9*) U of Pa Pr.

***Delanty, Norman, ed.** Seizures. 350p. 2000. 79.50 (*0-89603-827-0*) Humana.

Delany, A. Elizabeth, jt. auth. see Delany, Sarah L.

Delany, Alfonso T. Let Us Pray. (Illus.). 52p. 1999. pap. 9.95 (*0-7392-0189-1*, PO3161) Morris Pubng.

Delany, Ben, et al, eds. Simulation in Synthetic Environments '96: 1996 Simulation for Emergency Management. 74p. 1996. pap. 60.00 (*1-56555-094-3*, SS-28-4) Soc Computer Sim.

Delany, Delany & Hearth/Gaines Staff, jt. auth. see Center for Learning Network Staff.

Delany, Dudley. The Edgar Cayce Way of Overcoming Multiple Sclerosis - Vibratory Medicine. 4th large type rev. ed. LC 97-93411. (Illus.). 120p. 1998. pap. 10.95 (*0-9657903-3-9*, A04) Meridian VA.

***Delany, Dudley.** The Edgar Cayce Way of Overcoming Multiple Sclerosis - Vibratory Medicine. 5th large type rev. ed. LC 99-70273. (Illus.). 120p. 1999. pap. 10.95 (*0-9657903-4-7*) Meridian VA.

Delany, F. M., jt. auth. see Gupta, H. K.

Delany, Jim. Security for Costs. xvii, 215p. 1989. 45.50 (*0-455-20780-1*, Pub. by LawBk Co) Gaunt.

Delany, John J., III, et al. Toxic Tort Law & Science Manual. (Illus.). 712p. 1996. ring bd. 185.00 (*0-9657810-0-3*) Mealey Pubns.

Delany, M. J. & Happold, D. C. Ecology of African Mammals. LC 77-5611. (Tropical Ecology Ser.). (Illus.). 442p. reprint ed. pap. 137.10 (*0-608-18748-8*, 203035500068) Bks Demand.

Delany, Martin R. Blake: or The Huts of America. Miller, Floyd J., ed. LC 79-119677. 352p. 1971. reprint ed. pap. 16.50 (*0-8070-6419-X*) Beacon Pr.

— Condition, Elevation, Emigration & Destiny of the Colored People of the U. S. Politically Considered. LC 68-28993. (American Negro: His History & Literature. Series 1). 1968. reprint ed. 27.95 (*0-405-01812-6*) Ayer.

— Origin of Races & Color: With an Archeological Compendium of Ethiopian & Egyptian Civilization. LC 90-82685. 100p. 1991. reprint ed. 19.95 (*0-933121-51-2*); reprint ed. pap. 8.95 (*0-933121-50-4*) Black Classic.

Delany, Mary. Autobiography & Correspondence of Mary Granville, Mrs. Delany, 6 vols. Lady Llanover, ed. LC 75-163683. reprint ed. 300.00 (*0-404-02080-1*) AMS Pr.

***Delany, Mary M.** Of Irish Ways. 368p. (J). (gr. k-3). 2005. pap. 14.00 (*0-06-092421-7*, Perennial) HarperTrade.

Delany, Paul, ed. Hypermedia & Literary Studies. (Technical Communications Ser.). 345p. 1991. 52.50 (*0-262-04119-7*) MIT Pr.

— Hypermedia & Literary Studies. (Technical Communications Ser.). (Illus.). 356p. 1994. pap. text 24.00 (*0-262-54073-8*) MIT Pr.

Delany, Paul, intro. In the Year of Jubilee. 288p. 1994. 7.95 (*0-460-87533-7*, Everyman's Classic Lib) Tuttle Pubng.

Delany, Paul & Landow, George P., eds. The Digital Word: Text-Based Computing in the Humanities. LC 92-33742. (Technical Communication & Information Systems Ser.). (Illus.). 374p. 1993. 47.50 (*0-262-12176-X*) MIT Pr.

Delany, Ruth. The Grand Canal of Ireland. LC 96-163281. 280p. 1995. pap. 21.00 (*1-874675-65-1*) Dufour.

— Ireland's Royal Canal, 1798-1992. 1996. 31.95 (*0-946640-92-0*, Pub. by Lilliput Pr) Irish Bks Media.

Delany, Ruth, ed. Shell Guide to the River Shannon. (Illus.). 1996. pap. 125.00 (*1-873489-90-0*, Pub. by Laurie Norie & Wilson Ltd) St Mut.

Delany, Samuel R. The American Shore. 1978. 45.00 (*0-911499-00-8*) Ultramarine Pub.

— The American Shore. limited ed. 1978. 75.00 (*0-911499-01-6*) Ultramarine Pub.

— Atlantis: Three Tales. LC 94-48726. 224p. 1995. pap. 14.95 (*0-8195-6312-9*, Wesleyan Univ Pr); text 29.95 (*0-8195-5283-6*, Wesleyan Univ Pr) U Pr of New Eng.

— Bread & Wine: An Erotic Tale of New York. LC 98-17359. (Illus.). 80p. 1999. pap. 16.99 (*1-890451-02-9*, Pub. by Juno Bks) Consort Bk Sales.

— Dhalgren. aut. rev. ed. LC 95-42557. 817p. 1996. reprint ed. boxed set 125.00 (*0-8195-5305-0*, Wesleyan Univ Pr) U Pr of New Eng.

— Dhalgren. rev. ed. LC 95-42557. 817p. 1996. reprint ed. pap. 24.95 (*0-8195-6299-8*, Wesleyan Univ Pr) U Pr of New Eng.

— Einstein Intersection. rev. ed. LC 97-44598. 149p. 1998. reprint ed. pap. 12.95 (*0-8195-6336-6*, Wesleyan Univ Pr) U Pr of New Eng.

— Flight from Neveryon. LC 93-35916. (Return to Neveryon Ser.: Bk. 3). 378p. 1994. reprint ed. pap. 14.95 (*0-8195-6277-7*, Wesleyan Univ Pr) U Pr of New Eng.

— Heavenly Breakfast, an Essay on the Winter of Love. 116p. 1997. reprint ed. pap. 12.50 (*0-917453-33-6*) Bamberger.

— Longer Views: Extended Essays. LC 96-1237. 384p. 1996. pap. 22.00 (*0-8195-6293-9*, Wesleyan Univ Pr); text 50.00 (*0-8195-5281-X*, Wesleyan Univ Pr) U Pr of New Eng.

— The Mad Man. (Orig.). 1994. 23.95 (*1-56333-193-4*, R Kasak Bks) Masquerade.

— The Mad Man. (Orig.). 1996. mass mkt. 8.95 (*1-56333-408-9*, Rhinoceros) Masquerade.

— The Motion of Light in Water: Sex & Science Fiction Writing in the East Village, 1960-1965. 1993. reprint ed. pap. 12.95 (*1-56333-133-0*, R Kasak Bks) Masquerade.

— Neveryona: or The Tale of Signs & Cities Part 4: Some Informal Remarks Towards the Modular Calculus. LC 93-17847. (Return to Neveryon Ser.: Bk. 2). 402p. 1993. pap. 14.95 (*0-8195-6271-8*, Wesleyan Univ Pr) U Pr of New Eng.

***Delany, Samuel R.** 1984: Selected Letters. 384p. 2000. pap. 17.95 (*0-9665998-1-0*) Voyant Pubg.

Delany, Samuel R. Return to Neveryon. LC 93-31051. (Return to Neveryon Ser.: Bk. 4). 293p. 1994. reprint ed. pap. 14.95 (*0-8195-6278-5*, Wesleyan Univ Pr) U Pr of New Eng.

— Shorter Views: Queer Thoughts & the Politics of the Paraliterary. LC 99-16781. (Illus.). 352p. 1999. pap. 22.00 (*0-8195-6369-2*, Wesleyan Univ Pr); text 50.00 (*0-8195-6368-4*, Wesleyan Univ Pr) U Pr of New Eng.

— Silent Interviews: On Language, Race, Sex, Science Fiction & Some Comics. LC 93-35913. (Illus.). 334p. 1994. pap. 19.95 (*0-8195-6280-7*, Wesleyan Univ Pr) U Pr of New Eng.

— The Straits of Messina. 170p. 1989. 19.95 (*0-934933-02-2*) Serconia Pr.

— Tales of Neveryon. LC 93-17848. (Return to Neveryon Ser.: Bk. 1). 264p. 1993. reprint ed. pap. 14.95 (*0-8195-6270-X*, Wesleyan Univ Pr) U Pr of New Eng.

— They Fly at Ciron. 150p. 1992. 25.00 (*0-9633637-0-0*) Incunabula WA.

— They Fly at Ciron. mass mkt. write for info. (*0-614-08668-X*) Tor Bks.

— They Fly at Ciron. 204p. 1996. pap., mass mkt. 6.99 (*0-8125-4317-3*, Pub. by Tor Bks) St Martin.

— They Fly at Ciron. limited ed. 150p. 1992. write for info. (*0-9633637-1-9*) Incunabula WA.

— Times Square Red, Times Square Blue. LC 99-6130. 1999. 19.95 (*0-8147-1919-8*) NYU Pr.

— Trouble on Triton: An Ambiguous Heterotopia. rev. ed. LC 95-46796. 326p. 1996. reprint ed. pap. 14.95 (*0-8195-6298-X*, Wesleyan Univ Pr) U Pr of New Eng.

Delany, Sarah L. Having Our Say: The Delany Sisters' First 100 Years. 1993. 12.09 (*0-606-07151-2*, Pub. by Turtleback) Demco.

Delany, Sarah L. & Delany, A. Elizabeth. The Delany Sisters' Book of Everyday Wisdom. 1997. 3.99 (*0-681-07783-2*) Waldenbooks Co Inc.

— Having Our Say: The Delany Sisters' First 100 Years. 320p. 1994. mass mkt. 6.99 (*0-440-22042-4*) Dell.

— Having Our Say: The Delany Sisters' First 100 Years. large type ed. LC 93-24264. 1993. lib. bdg. 24.95 (*0-8161-5830-4*, G K Hall Lrg Type) Mac Lib Ref.

— Having Our Say: The Delany Sisters' First 100 Years. large type ed. LC 93-24264. 1994. 18.95 (*0-8161-5831-2*, G K Hall Lrg Type) Mac Lib Ref.

Delany, Sarah L. & Hearth, Amy H. On My Own at 107: Reflections on Life Without Bessie. large type ed. 176p. 1998. pap. 14.00 (*0-06-251486-5*) HarpC.

Delany, Sarah L., et al. The Delany Sisters' Book of Everyday Wisdom. De Angelis, Paul, ed. (Illus.). 144p. 1994. 15.00 (*1-56836-042-8*) Kodansha.

— The Delany Sisters' Book of Everyday Wisdom. Turner, Philip, ed. LC 94-34144. (Illus.). 144p. 1996. pap. 8.95 (*1-56836-166-1*) Kodansha.

— The Delany Sisters' Book of Everyday Wisdom. large type ed. LC 94-43787. 133p. 1995. lib. bdg. 21.95 (*0-7838-1198-5*, G K Hall Lrg Type) Mac Lib Ref.

— Having Our Say: The Delany Sisters' First 100 Years. 256p. 1997. pap. 11.95 (*0-385-31252-0*, Delta Trade) Dell.

— Having Our Say: The Delany Sisters' First 100 Years. 1996. pap. 5.25 (*0-8222-1502-0*) Dramatists Play.

— Having Our Say: The Delany Sisters' First 100 Years. De Angelis, Paul, ed. LC 93-23890. (Illus.). 224p. 1993. 20.00 (*1-56836-010-X*) Kodansha.

Delany, Selden P. Married Saints. LC 69-17573. (Essay Index Reprint Ser.). 1977. 20.95 (*0-8369-0071-5*) Ayer.

Delany, Sheila. Chaucer's House of Fame: The Poetics of Skeptical Fideism. LC 72-84406. 144p. (C). 1992. lib. bdg. 12.00 (*0-226-14181-0*) U Ch Pr.

— Chaucer's House of Fame: The Poetics of Skeptical Fideism. 152p. (C). 1994. pap. 19.95 (*0-8130-1259-7*) U Press Fla.

— Impolitic Bodies: Poetry, Saints, & Society in Fifteenth-Century: The Work of Osbern Bokenham. LC 97-40311. (Illus.). 256p. 1998. 45.00 (*0-19-510988-0*); pap. 19.95 (*0-19-510989-9*) OUP.

— A Legend of Holy Women: A Translation of Osbern Bokenham's Legends of Holy Women. LC 91-51117. (Notre Dame Texts in Medieval Culture Ser.: Vol. 1). (C). 1992. text 34.50 (*0-268-01294-6*); pap. text 17.50 (*0-268-01295-4*) U of Notre Dame Pr.

— The Naked Text: Chaucer's Legend of Good Women. LC 92-21191. 1994. 50.00 (*0-520-08119-6*, Pub. by U CA Pr) Cal Prin Full Svc.

Delap, Shirley. I Never Wore the Collar. LC 96-61779. (Illus.). 125p. 1996. 19.95 (*1-882194-25-X*) TN Valley Pub.

***Delapa, Gina.** 401(k) Success Stories... Discover How People Invest the Easy Way. Jacobs, Julyette & Guerriero, Anne, eds. (Illus.). 100p. 2001. pap. 9.95 (*0-9659638-7-X*) Fin Literacy.

DeLapa, Judith A. High-Impact Business Strategies. LC 93-80028. 300p. 1994. pap. 19.95 (*0-9638432-0-6*) High-Impact.

DeLapa, Judith A., ed. The McCormick-DeLapa Family Cookbook: A Collection of Receipes form Four Generations. 275p. 1997. 19.95 (*0-9638432-1-4*) High-Impact.

Delaplain, Laura. Cutting a New Path: Helping Survivors of Childhood Domestic Trauma. LC 97-33602. 136p. (Orig.). 1997. pap. 12.95 (*0-8298-1203-2*) Pilgrim OH.

Delaplaine, Ika T. Cotton - in Health, Work & Industry: Index of New Information & Research Bible. rev. ed. 177p. 1997. 47.50 (*0-7883-1498-X*); pap. 44.50 (*0-7883-1499-8*) ABBE Pubs Assn.

Delaplaine, Renee. The Sexually Tuned Body: Exercises Every Woman Should Do for a Better Sex Life. LC 96-90218. (Illus.). 96p. (Orig.). 1997. pap. 19.95 (*0-9651927-3-3*) Winning Tch.

Delaplane, Anne, jt. auth. see Delaplane, David.

Delaplane, David & Delaplane, Anne. Victims of Child Abuse, Domestic Abuse, Elderly Abuse, Rape, Robbery, Assault & Violent Death: A Manual for Clergy & Congregations. 4th ed. (Illus.). 189p. (C). 1996. pap. text 30.00 (*0-7881-3150-8*) DIANE Pub.

Delaplane, Stanton, et al. How to Choose a Cruise. 1986. pap. 9.95 (*0-934813-00-0*) Pic Postcard.

Delaporte. The Devil: Does He Exist & What Does He Do? LC 82-50598. 212p. 1992. reprint ed. pap. 6.00 (*0-89555-173-X*) TAN Bks Pubs.

Delaporte, Francois & Goldhammer, Arthur. The History of Yellow Fever: An Essay on the Birth of Tropical Medicine. (Illus.). 216p. 1991. 25.00 (*0-262-04112-X*) MIT Pr.

Delaporte, Francois, ed. see Canguilhem, Georges.

Delaporte, R. Elementary Breton-English Dictionary: Geriadurig Brezhoneg-Saozneg. 1992. pap. text 12.00 (*0-902561-16-2*) Intl Spec Bk.

Delaporte, Raymond. Elementary English-Breton Dictionary. 1990. pap. 12.00 (*0-902561-93-6*, Pub. by Cork Univ) Stylus Pub VA.

***DeLappi, Joseph J.** Wopaho. 230p. 1999. pap. 12.95 (*0-7392-0344-4*) Morris Pubng.

Delara, Adelina. Finale. LC 78-181138. 222p. 1955. reprint ed. 25.00 (*0-403-01539-1*) Scholarly.

Delargy, Marlaine, tr. see Schoultz, Solveig Von.

***Delaria, Lea & Cassella, Maggie.** Lea's Book of Rules for the World. 304p. 2000. pap. 12.95 (*0-440-50854-1*, Dell Trade Pbks) Dell.

DeLario, Karen, jt. auth. see Mundell, Susan.

Delaroche, Robert. Secret Life of Cats: Mini-Edition. 48p. 1997. 5.95 (*0-7641-5034-0*) Barron.

Delarue & Teneze. Essais sur la Peinture. (FRE.). 394p. 1976. 33.95 (*0-7859-1192-8*, 2706806346) Fr & Eur.

Delarue-Mardrus, Lucie. The Angels & the Perverts. Livia, Anna, tr. (The Cutting Edge: Lesbian Life & Literature Ser.).Tr. of Ange et les Pervers. (FRE.). 184p. (C). 1995. text 45.00 (*0-8147-5080-X*); pap. text 16.00 (*0-8147-5098-2*) NYU Pr.

Delarue, Norman C. & Eschapasse, Henri. International Trends in General Thoracic Surgery Vol. 1: Lung Cancer, Vol. 1. (Illus.). 315p. 1985. text 98.00 (*0-7216-1349-7*, W B Saunders Co) Harcrt Hlth Sci Grp.

Delarue, Paul. The Borzoi Book of French Folk Tales. Dorson, Richard M., ed. LC 80-743. (Folklore of the World Ser.). (Illus.). 1981. reprint ed. lib. bdg. 49.95 (*0-405-13309-X*) Ayer.

D

An Asterisk (*) at the beginning of an entry indicates that the title is appearing for the first time.

Delarue, Simone. What Price Vaccination? 1995. pap. 15.00 (0-916508-22-6) Happiness Pr.

Delasa, Hugo I., ed. Chemical Reactor Design & Technology: Overview of the New Developments of Energy & Petrochemical Reactor. (Technologies Projections for the 90's). 1986. text 345.50 (90-247-3315-4) Kluwer Academic.

***Delasara, Jan.** PopLit, PopCult & the X-Files: A Critical Explanation. 253p. 2000. lib. bdg. 39.95 (0-7864-0789-1) McFarland & Co.

***Delasfosse, Claude & Jeunesse, Gallimard.** Houses. LC 97-15434. (First Discovery Book). (Illus.). 24p. (J). (ps-2). 1998. 11.95 (0-590-38152-0) Scholastic Inc.

DeLashmitt, Eleanor. Checklist of State Bar Publications. (Legal Bibliography Ser.: No. 28). 82p. (Orig.). 1985. pap. 30.00 (0-935630-11-2) U of Tex Tarlton Law Lib.

DeLashmitt, Eleanor, compiled by. Annuals & Surveys Appearing in Legal Periodicals: An Annotated Listing. 1987. ring bd. write for info. (0-8377-2033-8, Rothman) W S Hein.

DeLashmutt, Gary. Loving God's Way: A Fresh Look at the One Another Passages. LC 95-37015. 144p. 1996. pap. 9.99 (0-8254-2454-2) Kregel.

Delaska, S. X. The Polish Viewpoint: Poland's Entry into the Second World War. 1991. lib. bdg. 67.95 (0-8490-4417-0) Gordon Pr.

DeLaTorre, Jose, jt. ed. see Goldstucker, Jac L.

Delatorre, Julio. The Completion of Samuel Taylor Coleridge's Kubla Khan: or A Vision in a Dream. (Illus.). 80p. 1997. 14.99 (0-9656819-0-4) Nova Classics.

Delatour, H. Downfall of Danielle. mass mkt. 6.95 (0-7472-4231-3, Pub. by Headline Bk Pub) Trafalgar.

DeLatte, Carolyn E. Lucy Audubon: A Biography. LC 82-15205. (Southern Biography Ser.). 264p. 1982. pap. 81.90 (0-7837-8449-X, 204925400010) Bks Demand.

Delatte, Louis, ed. see Aristotle.

Delatte, Louis, ed. see Seneca, Lucius Annaeus.

Delattre, Andre, ed. see Voltaire.

Delattre, Edwin J. Character & Cops: Ethics in Policing. 3rd rev. expanded ed. 350p. 1996. pap. 12.95 (0-8447-3973-1, AEI Pr) Am Enterprise.

— Education & the Public Trust: The Imperative for Common Purpose. 240p. (Orig.). 1993. pap. 14.95 (0-89633-115-6) Ethics & Public Policy.

— Education & the Public Trust: The Imperative for Common Purposes. LC 87-31170. 234p. (Orig.). (C). 1988. lib. bdg. 22.75 (0-89633-114-8) Ethics & Public Policy.

Delattre, J. & DeVernisy, G. Vocabulaire Barometre dans le Langage Economique. 3rd ed. (ENG & FRE.). 155p. 1978. pap. 29.95 (0-8288-6695-3, M-6109) Fr & Eur.

Delattre, J., et al. The Economy Through Boom & Slump: A Short French-English Dictionary. 2nd ed. 144p. 1980. pap. 29.95 (0-8288-0082-0, M12669) Fr & Eur.

— The Economy Through Boom & Slump: A Short French-English (Only) Dictionary. 2nd ed. 144p. 1980. pap. 22.50 (2-8257-0076-2) IBD Ltd.

Delattre, Pierre. Advanced Training in French Pronunciation. 1949. lp 9.95 (0-910408-04-1) Coll Store.

— Les Difficultes Phonetiques du Francais. (FRE.). 1948. pap. 4.95 (0-910408-02-5) Coll Store.

— Episodes. LC 92-39957. (Memoir Ser.). 192p. 1993. 11.00 (1-55597-180-6) Graywolf.

— Principes de Phonetique Francaise a l' Usage des Etudiants Anglo-Americains. (FRE.). 1951. pap. 4.95 (0-910408-01-7) Coll Store.

— Studies in French & Comparative Phonetics. (Janua Linguarum, Series Major: No. 18). (ENG & FRE.). 1966. text 80.00 (90-279-0610-6) Mouton.

— Tales of a Dalai Lama. LC 98-36973. xv, 159p. 1998. write for info. (0-89924-099-2) Lynx Hse.

Delattre, Pierre. Tales of a Dalai Lama. LC 98-36973. 1999. pap. 14.95 (0-89924-098-4) Lynx Hse.

***DeLattre, Pierre.** Tales of a Dalai Lama. 1998. pap. 14.95 (0-9668612-6-4) Lost Horse.

Delattre, Roland A. Beauty & Sensibility in the Thought of Jonathan Edwards: An Essay in Aesthetics & Theological Ethics. LC 68-13902. 254p. reprint ed. pap. 78.80 (0-8357-8701-X, 203370500087) Bks Demand.

Delattre, Susan & O'Halloran, Susan. The Woman Who Found Her Voice: A Tale of Transforming. LC 95-48125. 160p. 1997. pap. 12.95 (1-880913-18-6) Innisfree Pr.

Delattre, Susan, jt. auth. see O'Halloran, Susan.

DeLaubenfels, Ralph. Existence Families, Functional Calculi, & Evolution Equations. LC 93-47576. (Lecture Notes in Mathematics Ser.: Vol. 1570). 249p. 1994. 41.95 (0-387-57703-3) Spr-Verlag.

Delaud, Martine & Sword, Jacqueline. Vocabulary Trainer: French. 56p. 1997. 8.95 (0-7641-7123-2) Barron.

DeLauder, William B., jt. ed. see Watkins, Nellouise D.

DeLauer, Marjel Jean. The Mystery of the Phantom Billionaire. Young, Billie, ed. LC 72-83301. 1972. 22.95 (0-87949-005-5) Ashley Bks.

Delaughter. Marketing Operations. 1998. 23.50 (0-07-230286-0) McGraw.

***DeLaughter, Bobby.** Never Too Late: The Prosecutor's Story of Justice in the Medgar Evers Case. LC 00-30106. 2001. pap. 27.50 (0-684-86503-3) Scribner.

Delaughter, Jerry. Mountain Roads & Quiet Places: A Complete Guide to the Roads of Great Smoky Mountains National Park. (Illus.). 96p. (Orig.). 1986. pap. 8.95 (0-937207-00-4) GSMNH.

Delaughter, Thomas J. Malachi: Messenger of Divine Love. LC 75-40410. 160p. (Orig.). 1976. 6.00 (0-914520-08-3); pap. text 6.00 (0-914520-07-5) Insight Pr.

Delaunay, Charles. Django Reinhardt. 300p. 1987. pap. 14.95 (0-9506224-6-X, HL 00183208, Pub. by Ashley Mark Pub) H Leonard.

— Django Reinhardt. 300p. 1993. pap. 29.50 (0-9506224-5-1, 00183208, Pub. by Ashley Mark Pub) H Leonard.

— Django Reinhardt. James, Michael, tr. from FRE. (Quality Paperbacks Ser.). (Illus.). 247p. 1982. reprint ed. pap. 13.95 (0-306-80171-X) Da Capo.

— Django Reinhardt (Jazz) LC 80-27575. (Roots of Jazz Ser.). 247p. 1981. 27.50 (0-306-76057-6) Da Capo.

— New Hot Discography. 1948. 24.95 (0-910468-04-4) Criterion Mus.

Delaunay, Edward. Laura. LC 99-192598. 224p. 1996. mass mkt. 5.95 (1-56201-009-3, 112) Blue Moon Bks.

— Tangerine. 1993. pap. 5.95 (1-56201-008-5, 115) Blue Moon Bks.

Delaunay, Sonia. Sonia Delaunay: Art into Fashion. 104p. 1986. pap. 17.95 (0-8076-1166-2) Braziller.

— Sonia Delaunay: Patterns & Designs in Full Color. (Illus.). 64p. 1989. pap. 11.95 (0-486-25975-7) Dover.

— Sonia Delaunay's Alphabet. LC 72-172414. (Illus.). (J). (ps-3). 1972. 12.95 (0-690-75258-X) HarpC Child Bks.

Delaune. Fundamentals of Nursing - Standards & Practice Classroom Manager. 208p. 1998. text 250.00 (0-8273-9091-2) Delmar.

— Fundamentals of Nursing Standards & Practice: Student Study Guide. 192p. 1998. student ed. 18.95 (0-8273-9093-9) Delmar.

Delaune & Campbell. Fundamentals of Nursing & Practice Skills Checklist. (C). 1998. pap. 9.00 (0-7668-0899-8) Delmar.

Delaune, Sue C., ed. Fundamentals of Nursing. LC 97-22117. (Nursing Education Ser.). (C). 1997. mass mkt. 73.95 (0-8273-6378-8) Delmar.

Delaune, Sue C., et al. Fundamentals of Nursing: Standards & Practice Annotated Instructors Edition. annot. ed. LC 97-52692. 1364p. 1998. text, teacher ed. 250.00 (0-8273-9096-3) Delmar.

***Delauney, Edward.** The Calamities of Jane. 160p. 1999. reprint ed. mass mkt. 7.95 (1-56201-141-3, Pub. by Blue Moon Bks) Publishers Group.

Delauney, Jean-Claude. Services in Economic Thought: Three Centuries of Debate. (International Studies in the Service Economy). 144p. (C). 1992. lib. bdg. 113.00 (0-7923-9230-2) Kluwer Academic.

Delaunois, A. L., ed. Biostatistics in Pharmacology. LC 78-40220. (International Encyclopedia of Pharmacology & Therapeutics Ser.). 1979. 617.00 (0-08-023168-3, Pub. by Pergamon Repr) Franklin.

— Biostatistics in Pharmacology, Set, Vols. 1 & 2. 1128p. (C). 1973. 492.00 (0-08-016556-7, Pub. by Pergamon Repr) Franklin.

DeLaura, David J., ed. Victorian Prose: A Guide to Research. LC 73-80586. (Reviews of Research Ser.: No. 1). xvi, 560p. 1973. pap. 25.00 (0-87352-251-6, Z4200) Modern Lang.

DeLaurence, L. W. India's Hood Unveiled. (South India Mysteries Ser.: Bk. 1). 204p. 1994. reprint ed. spiral bd. 16.00 (0-7873-1187-1) Hlth Research.

— India's Hood Unveiled: South India Mysteries: Astral & Spirit Sight, 1910. 204p. 1996. reprint ed. pap. 17.95 (1-56459-926-4) Kessinger Pub.

— The Mystic Test Book of "The Hindu Occult Chambers" Magic & Occultism of India Hindu & Egyptian Crystal Gazing, the Hindu Magic Mirror. 1996. spiral bd. 16.50 (0-7873-0988-5) Hlth Research.

— The Mystic Test Book of "The Hindu Occult Chambers" The Magic & Occultism of India Hindu & Egyptian Crystal Gazing the Hindu Magic Mirror, 1909. 180p. 1996. reprint ed. pap. 15.50 (1-56459-920-5) Kessinger Pub.

DeLaurence, L. W., ed. Greater Key of Solomon. 128p. 1998. reprint ed. pap. 18.50 (0-7873-1103-0) Hlth Research.

DeLaurence, Lauron W. Master Key. 21.95 (0-685-22037-0) Wehman.

DeLaurier, Art, Jr., ed. see Hill, Gene.

DeLaurier, Art, Jr., ed. see Huggler, Tom.

DeLaurier, Art, Jr., ed. see Lundrigan, Ted N.

DeLaurier, Art, Jr., ed. see Mulak, Steven J.

DeLaurier, Art, Jr., ed. see Waterman, Charles F.

DeLauter, Roger. Eighteenth Virginia Cavalry. (Virginia Regimental Histories Ser.). (Illus.). 105p. 1985. 19.95 (0-930919-18-1) H E Howard.

Delauter, Roger U. McNeill's Rangers. (Illus.). 130p. 1986. 19.95 (0-930919-34-3) H E Howard.

— Sixty-Second Virginia Infantry. (Illus.). 121p. 1988. 19.95 (0-930919-53-X) H E Howard.

Delauter, Roger U., Jr. Winchester in the Civil War. (Virginia Civil War Battles & Leaders Ser.). (Illus.). 174p. 1992. 19.95 (1-56190-033-8) H E Howard.

***Delavan, Edith B. & Serling, Carolyn K.** Grace in the Afternoon: A Cayuga Lake Love Story. (Illus.). 104p. 1999. write for info. (0-9673820-0-9) Seneca Museum.

***Delavega.** Avanzando: Gramatica Espanola y Lectura. 4th ed. (SPA.). 176p. 1998. pap., wbk. ed. 37.95 (0-471-16589-1) Wiley.

— Cuaderno A: Ejercicios Para Los Estudiantes de Habla Inglesa-Avanzando Gramatica Espanola y Lectura 4th ed. 160p. 1998. pap. 37.95 (0-471-16577-8) Wiley.

Delavega, tr. see NASA Public Affairs Staff.

***Delavigne, Kenneth T.** The Spyderco Story: The New Shape of Sharp. (Illus.). 312p. 2000. 69.95 (1-58160-060-7) Paladin Pr.

Delavigne, Kenneth T. & Robertson, J. Daniel. Deming's Profound Changes: When Will the Sleeping Giant Wake Up? LC 93-42352. 300p. (C). 1994. 18.80 (0-13-292690-3) P-H.

Delavignette, Robert L. Freedom & Authority in French West Africa. LC 51-3505. 160p. reprint ed. pap. 49.60 (0-8357-3026-3, 205711300011) Bks Demand.

Delaware Art Museum Staff, et al. Wondrous Strange: The Wyeth Tradition. Bush, Janet & Pyle, Howard, eds. LC 98-10910. (Illus.). 167p. 1998. pap. 35.00 (0-8212-2536-7) Little.

Delaware Four-H Staff. Delaware Favorites. LC 93-73022. 1993. write for info. (0-87197-389-8) Favorite Recipes.

Delaware General Assembly Staff. Duke of York Record, 1646-1679: Original Land Titles in Delaware... Being an Authorized Transcript from the Official Archives of the State of Delaware, & Comprising Letters Patent, Commissions, Surveys, Plats & Confirmations by The Duke of York & Other High Officials, from 1646 to 1679. 199p. 1997. reprint ed. pap. 20.00 (0-8063-4697-3) Clearfield Co.

Delaware Public Archives Commission. Delaware Public Archives, 5 vols. reprint ed. lib. bdg. 382.50 (0-404-07170-8) AMS Pr.

***Delaware Technical & Comm.** Writing Skills Teaching Students. 4th ed. LC 99-31006. 394p. 1999. pap. text 39.80 (0-13-458860-6) P-H.

Delaware University Staff. Delaware Notes, Twenty-First Series. LC 74-38399. (Biography Index Reprint Ser.). 1977. reprint ed. 15.95 (0-8369-8120-0) Ayer.

Delay, Florence. Le Aie Aie de la Corne de Brume. (FRE.). 1984. pap. 11.95 (0-7859-1994-5, 2070375544) Fr & Eur.

— Riche et Legere. (FRE.). 252p. 1990. pap. 11.95 (0-7859-2143-5, 2070382575) Fr & Eur.

DeLay, Glen C. Atom One: Atomic Structure of the Atoms. (Illus.). 680p. 1996. pap. 38.00 (0-9654177-0-0) DeLays Printing.

***Delay, Nelly.** The Art & Culture of Japan. LC 99-24627. (Discoveries Ser.). 160p. 1999. pap. 12.95 (0-8109-2862-0, Pub. by Abrams) Time Warner.

DeLay, Peggy, jt. auth. see Sinotte, Barbara.

DeLay, Virginia, et al. NALS-The Career Legal Secretary: Instructor's Manual for Use with Student Study Guide & Work Projects. 4th ed. 360p. (C). 1997. pap. text, teacher ed., suppl. ed. write for info. (0-314-22787-3) West Pub.

— NALS-The Career Legal Secretary: Student Study Guide & Work Projects. 4th ed. (Practice Ser.). 260p. 1997. pap. text, student ed., suppl. ed. write for info. (0-314-22642-7) West Pub.

DeLazzari, JoAnn. Scoundrel's Captive. 416p. (Orig.). 1991. mass mkt. 4.50 (0-380-76420-2, Avon Bks) Morrow Avon.

— Scoundrel's Desire. 384p. (Orig.). 1993. mass mkt. 4.50 (0-380-76421-0, Avon Bks) Morrow Avon.

DelBagno, D. & Spina, R. Crime Investigation Quizzer. 230p. 1994. pap. 21.95 (0-87526-407-7) Gould.

DelBagno, Daniel, jt. auth. see Adamson, Mark.

Delbanco, Nicholas, ed. see Malamud, Bernard.

Delbanco, Andrew. The Death of Satan: How Americans Have Lost the Sense of Evil. LC 95-10007. (Illus.). 320p. 1995. 23.00 (0-374-13566-5) FS&G.

— The Death of Satan: How Americans Have Lost the Sense of Evil. 288p. 1996. pap. 13.00 (0-374-52486-6, Noonday) FS&G.

— The Puritan Ordeal. LC 88-11218. 306p. 1989. 42.00 (0-674-74055-6) HUP.

— The Puritan Ordeal. 320p. 1991. pap. 18.95 (0-674-74056-4, DELPUX) HUP.

— The Real American Dream: A Meditation on Hope. LC 99-21179. (History of American Civilization Ser.: Vol. 1998). 143p. 1999. 19.95 (0-674-74925-1) HUP.

***Delbanco, Andrew.** The Real American Dream: A Meditation on Hope. 160p. 2000. pap. 14.00 (0-674-00383-7) HUP.

Delbanco, Andrew. Required Reading: Why Our American Classics Matter Now. LC 97-11229. 256p. 1997. 24.00 (0-374-23007-2) FS&G.

— Required Reading: Why Our American Classics Matter Now. 240p. 1998. pap. 12.00 (0-374-52559-5) FS&G.

— William Ellery Channing: An Essay on the Liberal Spirit in America. LC 80-19304. 223p. (C). 1981. 33.95 (0-674-95335-5) HUP.

Delbanco, Andrew, intro. The Portable Abraham Lincoln. 384p. 1993. pap. 13.95 (0-14-017031-6, Penguin Bks) Viking Penguin.

***Delbanco, Nicholas.** The Countess of Stalein Restored: A History of the Paganini Stradivarius Cello of 1707. 120p. 2000. 19.00 (1-85984-761-7, Pub. by Verso) Norton.

Delbanco, Nicholas. In the Name of Mercy. 320p. 1998. mass mkt. 12.99 (0-446-67364-1, Pub. by Warner Bks) Little.

***Delbanco, Nicholas.** The Lost Suitcase: Reflections on the Literary Life. 227p. 2000. 24.95 (0-231-11542-3) Col U Pr.

— Old Scores. 2000. reprint ed. pap. 13.95 (0-446-67450-8) Warner Bks.

Delbanco, Nicholas. Running in Place: Scenes from the South of France. LC 88-27031. 1990. pap. 9.95 (0-87113-362-8, Atlntc Mnthly) Grove-Atltic.

***Delbanco, Nicholas.** What You Carry. 208p. 2000. 24.95 (0-446-52416-6) Warner Bks.

— The Writing Life Vol. IV: The Hopwood Lectures. 144p. 2000. pap. 15.95 (0-472-06717-6, 06717); text 44.50 (0-472-09717-2, 09717) U of Mich Pr.

Delbanco, Nicholas, ed. Speaking of Writing: Selected Hopwood Lectures. 404p. (C). 1990. reprint ed. pap. text 17.95 (0-472-06422-3, 06422) U of Mich Pr.

Delbanco, Nicholas, jt. ed. see Heimert, Alan.

Delbanco, Thomas L., jt. auth. see Aronson, Mark D.

Delbar, T., ed. Radioactive Nuclear Beams, 1991: Proceedings of the 2nd International Conference on Radioactive Nuclear Beams, Louvain-la-Neuve, Belgium, August 19-21, 1991. (Illus.). 464p. 1992. 210.00 (0-7503-0207-0) IOP Pub.

Delbard, Henri. Diary of a Rose Lover. LC 96-84215. (Illus.). 72p. 1996. 19.95 (0-8109-3786-7, Pub. by Abrams) Time Warner.

Delbarre, P. J., jt. auth. see Chassant, Louis-Alphonse.

Delbecq, Andre L. Sustaining Innovation As an American Competitive Advantage. (Urban Studies: No. 7). 46p. (Orig.). 1989. pap. 6.00 (0-913749-09-5) U MD Urban Stud.

Delbecq, Andre L., et al. Group Techniques for Program Planning: A Guide to Nominal Group & Delphi Processes. LC 86-80355. 174p. 1986. pap. 20.00 (0-9614511-1-4) Green Briar Pr.

***Delbee, Anne.** Camille Claudel: Une Femme. (Illus.). 380p. 2000. pap. 16.95 (1-56279-123-0) Mercury Hse Inc.

D'Elbee, Jean. I Believe in Love. 157p. (Orig.). 1983. pap. 9.95 (0-932506-25-9) St Bedes Pubns.

D'Elbee, Jean De Jesus, see De Jesus D'Elbee, Jean.

Delbeek, J. Charles & Sprung, Julian. The Reef Aquarium: A Comprehensive Guide to the Identification & Care of Tropical Marine Invertebrates. (Illus.). 560p. (C). 1994. 84.95 (1-883693-12-8) Ricordea Pubng.

Delbeek, J. Charles, jt. auth. see Sprung, Julian.

Delbene. When I'm Alone. 1988. pap. 3.95 (0-687-61316-7) Abingdon.

— When Your Son or Daughter Is Baptized. 1993. pap. 2.95 (0-687-61198-9) Abingdon.

Delbene, Ron. Alone with God. 13.35 (0-687-60016-2) Abingdon.

— Breath of Life. 1992. write for info. (0-687-60113-4) Abingdon.

— Breath of Life Series: A Simple Way to Pray. 1992. pap. 25.00 (0-8358-0669-3) Upper Room Bks.

— Christmas Remembered. 1991. write for info. (0-687-60163-0) Abingdon.

— Near Life's End. 1988. 5.95 (0-687-60804-X) Abingdon.

— A Time to Mourn. 1988. pap. 3.95 (0-687-61196-2) Abingdon.

— When You Are Living. 1992. pap. 2.95 (0-687-61187-3) Abingdon.

— When You Have a Decision to Make. 1992. pap. 2.95 (0-687-61189-X) Abingdon.

— When You Want Your Wish. 1993. pap. 2.95 (0-687-61195-4) Abingdon.

DelBene, Ron. When Your Son or Daughter Divorces. pap. 3.00 (0-8358-0678-2) Upper Room Bks.

DelBene, Ron, et al. Alone with God: A Guide for Personal Retreats. LC 92-80944. 128p. 1992. pap. 9.00 (0-8358-0668-5) Upper Room Bks.

— Alone with God: A Guide for Personal Retreats. Collett, Rita, ed. LC 97-167795. 144p. 1997. pap., wbk. ed. 10.00 (0-8358-0799-1, UR799) Upper Room Bks.

— The Breath of Life: A Simple Way to Pray - The Workbook. 160p. 1996. pap. 10.00 (0-8358-0766-5) Upper Room Bks.

— The Hunger of the Heart: A Call to Spiritual Growth. LC 92-80945. 112p. 1992. pap. 9.00 (0-8358-0667-7) Upper Room Bks.

— The Hunger of the Heart: A Workbook. LC 92-80945. 160p. 1995. pap. text, wbk. ed. 10.00 (0-8358-0738-X) Upper Room Bks.

— Into the Light. LC 87-51428. 144p. 1988. pap. 9.00 (0-8358-0576-X) Upper Room Bks.

— Into the Light Study Guide. 80p. 1989. pap. 5.00 (0-8358-0601-4) Upper Room Bks.

— Near Life's End: What Family & Friends Can Do. 24p. 1988. pap. 4.00 (0-8358-0578-6) Upper Room Bks.

— A Time to Mourn: Recovering from the Death of a Loved One. 24p. 1988. pap. 4.00 (0-8358-0577-8) Upper Room Bks.

— When an Aging Loved One Needs Care. (Times of Change, Times of Challenge Ser.). 32p. 1991. pap. 3.00 (0-8358-0636-7) Upper Room Bks.

— When I'm Alone. 24p. 1988. pap. 4.00 (0-8358-0579-4) Upper Room Bks.

— When You Are Facing Surgery. (Times of Change, Times of Challenge Ser.). 31p. 1991. pap. 3.00 (0-8358-0639-1) Upper Room Bks.

— When You Are Getting Married. (Times of Change, Times of Challenge Ser.). 32p. 1991. pap. 3.00 (0-8358-0637-5) Upper Room Bks.

— When You Are Living with an Illness That Is Not Your Own. (Times of Change, Times of Challenge Ser.). 32p. 1992. pap. 3.00 (0-8358-0653-7) Upper Room Bks.

— When You Have a Decision to Make. (Times of Change, Times of Challenge Ser.). 32p. 1992. pap. 3.00 (0-8358-0652-9) Upper Room Bks.

— When You Want Your Wishes Known. (Times of Change, Times of Challenge Ser.). 32p. 1993. pap. 3.00 (0-8358-0679-0) Upper Room Bks.

— When Your Child Is Baptized. (Times of Change, Times of Challenge Ser.). 32p. 1991. pap. 3.00 (0-8358-0638-3) Upper Room Bks.

Delbert & Philpott, Donna, eds. Hands Across the Elbe. LC 94-61947. 160p. 1995. 19.95 (1-56311-172-1) Turner Pub KY.

***Delbianco, Sue A.** Bridgeport. (Images of America Ser.). 128p. 1999. pap. 18.99 (0-7385-0253-7) Arcadia Publng.

Delbo, Charlotte. Auschwitz & After. Lamont, Rosette C., tr.Tr. of Auschwitz et Apres. 382p. 1997. pap. 17.00 (0-300-07057-8) Yale U Pr.

— Convoy to Auschwitz: Women of the French Resistance. Cosman, Carol, tr. LC 96-37825. 224p. 1997. text 28.95 (1-55553-313-2) NE U Pr.

— Days & Memory. LC 89-63596. 140p. (Orig.). 1990. pap. 12.95 (0-910395-55-1) Marlboro Pr.

Delbol, Barbara, jt. auth. see Reames, Richard.

Delbono, F., comment. Oswald Von Wolkenstein - Handschrift A. fac. ed. (Codices Selecti B Ser.: Vol. LIX). (GER., Illus.). 122p. 1977. 254.00 (3-201-00995-4, Pub. by Akademische Druck-und) Balogh.

D

An Asterisk (*) at the beginning of an entry indicates that the title is appearing for the first time.

Delbos, Victor. Le Probleme Moral dans la Philosophie de Spinoza et dans l'Histoire du Spinozisme. xii, 570p. 1988. reprint ed. write for info. (*3-487-07999-2*) G Olms Pubs.

Delbosco, Judith J. Effective Teaching Practices: An Instructional Handbook for Teachers & Supervisors. LC 86-72227. 128p. 1986. pap. 14.95 (*0-9617438-0-8*) Diamond Designs.

Delbourgo, R. & Fox, J., eds. TeV Physics & Beyond: Proceedings of the 8th & Nuclear Particle Physics Summer School. 324p. (C). 1987. pap. 79.00 (*9971-5-0304-2*); text 144.00 (*9971-5-0301-8*) World Scientific Pub.

Delboy, W. J., jt. auth. see AIChE Ammonia Plant Safety Committee Staff.

***Delbrel, Madeleine.** We, the Ordinary People of the Streets. LC 00-35428. (Ressourcement Ser.). 2000. pap. 24.00 (*0-8028-4696-3*) Eerdmans.

Delbridge, Joyce. Ferry Tales from Puget Sound & Georgia Strait: Collection of Stories, Poems & Anecdotes. (Illus.). 128p. (Orig.). 1990. pap. 9.95 (*0-88839-251-6*) Hancock House.

— Northwest Ferry Tales: Collection of Stories, Poems & Anecdotes from Washington, British Columbia & Alaska. (Illus.). 128p. 1990. reprint ed. pap. 9.95 (*0-88839-250-8*) Hancock House.

Delbridge, Joyce, et al, eds. Ferry Tales from Puget Sound: A Collection of Stories, Poems & Anecdotes. LC 86-50007. (Illus.). 104p. (Orig.). 1986. pap. 8.95 (*0-9616103-0-1*) Vashon Pt Prod.

— Northwest Ferry Tales: Stories, Poems & Anecdotes from Washington, British Columbia & Alaska. LC 88-50264. (Illus.). 128p. (Orig.). (YA). (gr. 5 up). 1989. pap. 8.95 (*0-9616103-8-7*) Vashon Pt Prod.

Delbridge, Linda, ed. see Estes, Simon & Swanson, Mary.

Delbridge, Pauline N., jt. auth. see Boyle, Elisabeth L.

***Delbridge, Rick.** Life on the Line in Contemporary Manufacturing: The Workplace Experience of Lean Production & the "Japanese" Model. LC 99-86545. 256p. 2000. pap. 24.95 (*0-19-924043-4*) OUP.

Delbridge, Rick & Lowe, James. Manufacturing in Transition. LC 97-51636. 288p. (C). 1998. 95.00 (*0-415-18271-9*); pap. 29.99 (*0-415-18272-7*) Routledge.

Delbruck, Hans. The Barbarian Invasions: History of the Art of War, Vol. II. Renfroe, Walter J., Jr., tr. LC 89-24980. (Illus.). 505p. 1990. pap. 26.00 (*0-8032-9200-7*, Bison Books) U of Nebr Pr.

— The Dawn of Modern Warfare: History of the Art of War, Vol. IV. Renfroe, Walter J., Jr., tr. LC 89-24980. (Illus.). xii, 487p. 1990. pap. 26.00 (*0-8032-6586-7*, Bison Books) U of Nebr Pr.

— Delbruck's Modern Military History. Bucholz, Arden, ed. & tr. by. LC 96-50000. (Illus.). xix, 244p. 1997. text 50.00 (*0-8032-1698-X*) U of Nebr Pr.

— History of the Art of War Within the Framework of Political History: Antiquity, 9. Renfroe, Walter J., Jr., tr. from GER. LC 72-792. (Contributions in Military History Ser.: No. 9). (Illus.). 604p. 1975. 95.00 (*0-8371-6365-X*, DEB/) Greenwood.

— History of the Art of War Within the Framework of Political History: The Middle Ages, 26. Renfroe, Walter J., Jr., tr. from GER. LC 72-792. (Contributions in Military History Ser.: No. 26). 711p. 1982. 105.00 (*0-8371-8164-X*, DED/) Greenwood.

— History of the Art of War Within the Framework of Political History: The Modern Era, 39. Renfroe, Walter J., Jr., tr. LC 72-792. (Contributions in Military History Ser.: No. 39). (GER.). 487p. 1985. 95.00 (*0-8371-8165-8*, DEE/) Greenwood.

— History of the Art of War Within the Framework of Political History Vol. II: The Germans, 20. Renfroe, Walter J., Jr., tr. from GER. LC 72-792. (Contributions in Military History Ser.: No. 20). (Illus.). 505p. 1980. 79.50 (*0-8371-8163-1*, DEC/) Greenwood.

— Medieval Warfare: History of the Art of War, Vol. III. Renfroe, Walter J., Jr., tr. LC 89-24980. (Illus.). 712p. 1990. reprint ed. pap. 25.00 (*0-8032-6585-9*, Bison Books) U of Nebr Pr.

— Das Mittelalter. LC 80-2677. reprint ed. 63.50 (*0-404-18559-2*) AMS Pr.

— Warfare in Antiquity: History of the Art of War, Vol. I. Renfroe, Walter J., Jr., tr. LC 89-24980. (Illus.). 604p. 1990. pap. 24.00 (*0-8032-9199-X*, Bison Books) U of Nebr Pr.

Delbruck, Max. A Physicist Looks at Biology: Sesquicentennial Celebration Proceedings, Pt. II. (Connecticut Academy of Arts & Sciences Ser., Trans.: Vol. 38). 1949. pap. 29.50 (*0-685-22900-9*) Elliots Bks.

Delbrueck, Berthold. Introduction to the Study of Language: A Critical Survey of the History & Methods of Comparative Philology of Indo-European Languages. 2nd rev. ed. LC 74-84633. (Amsterdam Classics in Linguistics Ser.: No. 8). xxvi, 148p. 1989. 39.00 (*90-272-0879-4*) J Benjamins Pubng Co.

Delbrueck, Berthold, jt. auth. see Brugmann, Karl.

Delbrueck, Richard. Spaetantike Kaiserportraits. (Studien zur Spaetantiken Kunstgeschichte: Vol. 8). (Illus.). xx, 252p. (C). 1978. reprint ed. 365.40 (*3-11-005700-X*) De Gruyter.

Delbrugge, Laura, ed. see De Li, Andres.

Delcampo. Sources:marriage & Family. 1998. pap., student ed. 20.94 (*0-07-303234-4*) McGraw.

DelCampo, Diana S. & DelCampo, Robert L. Clashing Views on Controversial Issues in Childhood & Society. 2nd ed. (Taking Sides Ser.). (Illus.). 384p. 1998. pap. text 13.00 (*0-697-39104-3*, Dshkn McG-Hill) McGrw-H Hghr Educ.

DelCampo, Diana S., jt. ed. see DelCampo, Robert L.

DelCampo, Robert L. & DelCampo, Diana S., eds. Taking Sides: Clashing Views on Controversial Issues in Childhood & Society. LC 95-121. 416p. (C). 1995. per. 13.95 (*1-56134-333-1*, Dshkn McG-Hill) McGrw-H Hghr Educ.

DelCampo, Robert L., jt. auth. see DelCampo, Diana S.

Delcanho, Martin, see Wells, Awesome, pseud.

Delcarmen. Criminal Justice. 2000. pap. text 11.97 (*0-395-97319-8*) HM.

Delchambre, A., ed. CAD Method for Industrial Assembly: Concurrent Design of Products, Equipments, & Control Systems. LC 95-48842. 306p. 1997. 90.00 (*0-471-96261-9*) Wiley.

Delchamps, D. F. State Space & Input-Output Linear Systems. (Illus.). 425p. 1987. 72.00 (*0-387-96659-5*) Spr-Verlag.

Delchar, T. A., jt. auth. see Woodruff, D. P.

Delchaye, Hippolyte. Synaxaires Byzantins, Menologes, Typica. (Collected Studies: No. CS66). 322p. (C). 1977. reprint ed. lib. bdg. 124.95 (*0-86078-010-4*, Pub. by Variorum) Ashgate Pub Co.

Delcher, A. L., ed. Waterfield's Guide to Computer Terms. LC 94-61448. (Waterfields Computer Guide Ser.). 160p. 1995. pap. 12.95 (*1-886271-00-3*) Waterflds Pr.

Delcher, Arthur L., ed. Waterfield's Guide to Computer Software: (Word Processing, Spreadsheet, Database Operating System, & More) (Waterfields Computer Guide Ser.). (Illus.). 700p. (Orig.). 1999. pap. 19.95 (*1-886271-05-4*) Waterflds Pr.

Delcor, Mathias. Environnement et Tradit de l'Ancien Testament. (Alter Orient und Altes Testament Ser.: Vol. 228). (FRE.). vii, 458p. 1990. text 62.50 (*3-7887-1339-9*) NeukirchenerV.

Delcourt, H. R., jt. auth. see Delcourt, P. A.

Delcourt, P. A. & Delcourt, H. R. Long-Term Forest Dynamics of the Temperate Zone. (Ecological Studies: Vol. 63). (Illus.). 450p. 1987. 152.00 (*0-387-96495-9*) Spr-Verlag.

Delden, Maarten Van, see Van Delden, Maarten.

D'Elden, Stephanie C. Van, see Van D'Elden, Stephanie C., ed.

D'Elden, Stephanie C. Van, see Akehurst, F. R. & Van D'Elden, Stephanie C.

Delderfield, Eric. Eric Delderfield's Bumper Book of Animal Stories. large type ed. 224p. (J). 1993. 24.95 (*1-85695-036-0*, Pub. by ISIS Lrg Prnt) Transaction Pubs.

— Kings & Queens of England & Great Britain. rev. ed. LC 98-203217. (Illus.). 192p. 1998. 24.95 (*0-7153-0812-2*, Pub. by D & C Pub) Sterling.

Delderfield, Eric R. Kings & Queens of England. 18.95 (*0-89190-587-1*) Amereon Ltd.

— Kings & Queens of England. LC 81-48535. 172p. 1995. pap. 14.95 (*0-8128-6161-2*, Scrbrough Hse) Madison Bks UPA.

— Kings & Queens of England & Great Britain. LC 89-25905. (Illus.). 192p. reprint ed. pap. 59.60 (*0-7837-6695-5*, 204631200011) Bks Demand.

Delderfield, R. D. Come Home Charlie & Face Them. large type ed. 1993. 39.95 (*0-7066-1022-9*, Pub. by Remploy Pr) St Mut.

Delderfield, R. F. For My Own Amusement. LC 77-356918. 255p. 1968. write for info. (*0-340-04392-X*) St Martin.

— God Is an Englishman. LC 98-6959. 704p. 1998. pap. 15.95 (*0-7867-0528-0*) Carroll & Graf.

— Imperial Sunset. LC 79-31696. (Illus.). 320p. 1980. pap. 9.95 (*0-8128-6056-X*, Scrbrough Hse) Madison Bks UPA.

— Overture for Beginners. LC 74-553890. (Illus.). 224 p. 1970. write for info. (*0-340-10628-X*) St Martin.

— Theirs Was the Kingdom. 800p. 1999. pap. 15.95 (*0-7867-0637-6*) Carroll & Graf.

— To Serve Them All My Days. 640p. 1998. pap. 15.95 (*0-7867-0595-7*) Carroll & Graf.

Delderfield, Ronald F. All over the Town. large type ed. 1979. 12.00 (*0-7089-0297-9*) Ulverscroft.

— Too Few for Drums. large type ed. 368p. 1988. 27.99 (*0-7089-1756-9*) Ulverscroft.

Delduca, Darla D. The Creative Teacher: An Instructor's Guide for Milady's Standard. 112p. 1992. pap. 18.00 (*1-56253-015-1*) Milady Pub.

DelDuca, Louis F., et al. State & Local Government Procurement: Developments in Legislation & Litigation. LC 87-108173. 67p. 1986. pap. 8.95 (*0-89707-253-7*, 533-0025) Amer Bar Assn.

Deleage, Andre. La Capitation Du Bas-Empire. LC 75-7313. (Roman History Ser.). (FRE., Illus.). 1975. reprint ed. 25.95 (*0-405-07195-7*) Ayer.

Deledalle, Gerard. Charles S. Peirce, 1839-1914: An Intellectual Biography. Petrilli, Susan, tr. LC 89-35843. xxxii, 92p. 1990. 41.00 (*1-55619-082-4*) J Benjamins Pubng Co.

— Charles S. Peirce, Phenomenologue et Semioticien. LC 86-3333. (Foundations of Semiotics Ser.: Vol. 14). ix, 114p. 1986. 35.00 (*90-272-3285-7*) J Benjamins Pubng Co.

***Deledalle, Gerard.** Charles S. Peirce's Philosophy of Signs: Essays in Comparative Semiotics. LC 00-24320. (Illus.). 2000. write for info. (*0-253-33736-4*) Ind U Pr.

Deledalle, Gerard, ed. Semiotics & Pragmatics: Proceedings of the Perpignan Symposium, 1983. LC 89-229. (Foundations of Semiotics Ser.: No. 18). xii, 476p. 1989. 133.00 (*90-272-3290-3*) J Benjamins Pubng Co.

Deledda. L'Edera: C Level. text 8.95 (*0-88436-884-X*) EMC-Paradigm.

Deledda, Grazia. After the Divorce. Ashe, Susan, tr. from ITA. LC 95-12351. (European Classics Ser.). 174p. 1995. pap. 13.95 (*0-8101-1249-3*); text 39.95 (*0-8101-1248-5*) Northwestern U Pr.

— Cosima. LC 87-45355. 153p. (Orig.). 1988. pap. 12.50 (*0-934977-06-2*) Italica Pr.

— Elias Portolu. King, Martha, tr. from ITA. LC 95-12332. (European Classics Ser.). 194p. 1995. pap. 13.95 (*0-8101-1251-5*); text 39.95 (*0-8101-1250-7*) Northwestern U Pr.

— La Madre: The Woman & the Priest. 2nd ed. Lawrence, D. M. & Lane, Eric, eds. Steegman, M. G., tr. from ITA. (European Classics). 224p. 1999. reprint ed. pap. 9.99 (*0-946626-20-0*, Pub. by Dedalus) Hippocrene Bks.

— Reeds in the Wind. King, Martha, tr. from ITA. LC 97-32515. (Italian Fiction in Translation Ser.). 224p. 1999. pap. 15.00 (*0-934977-63-1*) Italica Pr.

Delee. Orthopedic Sports Medicine, 3 Vols. 1993. text 320.00 (*0-7216-5602-1*) Harcourt.

— Orthopedic Sports Medicine, 3 Vols. 1993. text 350.00 (*0-7216-4194-6*, W B Saunders Co) Harcrt Hlth Sci Grp.

DeLee, Jesse C., Jr. & Drez, David, eds. Orthopaedic Sports Medicine, 2 vols., Set. (Illus.). 1888p. 1993. text 280.00 (*0-7216-2836-2*, W B Saunders Co) Harcrt Hlth Sci Grp.

Deleeck, Herman. Poverty & the Adequacy of Social Security in the EC: A Comparative Analysis. 221p. 1992. 65.95 (*1-85628-395-X*) Ashgate Pub Co

DeLeener, M., jt. auth. see Resibois, Pierre.

Deleenheer, et al, eds. Modern Chromatographic Analysis of Vitamins. 2nd ed. (Chromatographic Science Ser.: Vol. 60). (Illus.). 592p. 1992. text 225.00 (*0-8247-8626-2*) Dekker.

DeLeeuw, Brenda S. Hilda & Friends: Trail Side Poetry. LC 98-233659. (Illus.). 112p. 1998. pap. 12.95 (*1-888106-78-6*) Agreka Bks.

Delegation Generale. Dictionaire de Termes Officiels. (FRE.). 334p. 1993. 69.95 (*0-7859-5610-7*, 2110734299) Fr & Eur.

Delegorgue, Adulphe. Adulphe Delegorgue's Travels in Southern Africa, Vol. 1. Alexander, Stephanie & Webb, Colin D., eds. Webb, Fleur, tr. (Illus.). 400p. 1990. pap. 29.95 (*0-86980-727-7*, Pub. by Univ Natal Pr) Intl Spec Bk.

Delehanty, Elizabeth. With Generosity & Silence: Recollections of a Victorian Rebel. (Illus.). 104p. (Orig.). 1993. pap. 10.00 (*0-9632687-1-6*) Per Rose Pub.

Delehanty, Randolph. Art in the American South: Works from the Ogden Collection. LC 96-9373. (Illus.). 360p. 1996. 59.95 (*0-8071-2100-2*) La State U Pr.

— In the Victorian Style. (Illus.). 192p. 1991. 35.00 (*0-87701-750-6*) Chronicle Bks.

— In the Victorian Style. 1997. 40.00 (*0-8118-1789-X*); pap. 24.95 (*0-8118-1796-2*) Chronicle Bks.

— New Orleans: The Ultimate Guide. LC 97-26742. 496p. 1998. pap. 16.95 (*0-8118-0870-X*) Chronicle Bks.

— San Francisco: The Ultimate Guide. rev. ed. LC 94-17964. (Illus.). 496p. 1995. pap. 16.95 (*0-8118-0443-7*) Chronicle Bks.

***Delehanty, Randolph.** Victorians: San Francisco. LC 99-59474. (Illus.). 144p. 2000. 14.95 (*0-8118-2771-2*) Chronicle Bks.

Delehanty, Randolph & Martin, Van J. Classic Natchez: History, Homes, & Gardens. LC 95-81714. (Illus.). 164p. (C). 1996. 39.95 (*0-8203-1806-X*) Golden Coast.

Delehanty, Suzanne. Paul Thek - Processions. LC 77-92423. 1977. pap. 12.00 (*0-88454-023-5*) U of Pa Contemp Art.

Delehanty, Suzanne & Ashton, Dore. Eight Abstract Painters. (Illus.). 1978. pap. 4.00 (*0-88454-024-3*) U of Pa Contemp Art.

Delehaye, Hippolyte. Les Legendes Grecques des Saints Militaires. LC 75-7314. (Roman History Ser.). (FRE.). 1975. reprint ed. 30.95 (*0-405-07196-5*) Ayer.

— The Legends of the Saints. Attwater, Donald, tr. LC 61-18761. 272p. reprint ed. pap. 84.40 (*0-7837-0442-9*, 204076500018) Bks Demand.

— The Legends of the Saints. 288p. 1998. reprint ed. pap. 39.95 (*1-85182-370-0*, Pub. by Four Cts Pr) Intl Spec Bk.

— Les Origines du Culte des Martyrs. 2nd rev. ed. LC 78-63459. (Crusades & Military Orders Ser.: Second Series). reprint ed. 52.50 (*0-404-16518-4*) AMS Pr.

***Delelis, Philippe.** The Last Cantata. 2000. write for info. (*1-902881-30-3*, Pub. by Toby Pr Ltd); pap. 15.95 (*1-902881-31-1*, Pub. by Toby Pr Ltd) Toby Pr.

DeLellis. Tumors of the Parathyroid Gland. (AFIP Atlas of Tumor Pathology Ser.: Vol. 6). (Illus.). 102p. 1993. pap. text 32.00 (*1-881041-06-9*) Am Registry Path.

DeLellis, Leatrice, ed. & intro. see Portilla, Lorraine.

DeLellis, Ronald A., jt. ed. see LiVolsi, Virginia A.

Delendi, M., jt. ed. see Riboli, E.

Delendick, Thomas J. A Survey of Foliar Flavonoids in the Aceraceae. LC 89-29446. (Memoirs Ser.: No. 54). (Illus.). 136p. 1990. pap. 33.50 (*0-89327-343-0*) NY Botanical.

Delener, Nejdet. Strategic Planning & Multinational Trading Blocs. LC 99-18645. 224p. 1999. 65.00 (*1-56720-274-8*, Quorum Bks) Greenwood.

Delener, Nejdet, ed. Ethical Issues in International Marketing. LC 95-14390. (Journal of Euromarketing: Vol. 4, No. 2). 97p. 1995. 39.95 (*1-56024-735-5*, Intl Busn Pr) Haworth Pr.

Deleo, jt. auth. see Marks, James C.

Deleo, Sharon. Gracie. . .Iron Range Cooking with an Italian Mother...Pasta to Potica, Vol. 1. (Illus.). 124p. 1997. spiral bd. 10.95 (*0-9661858-0-3*) Carousel Sales.

Deleon. Multicultural Assessment. 1997. pap. text 24.95 (*0-205-26154-X*) Allyn.

DeLeon, Angelo & Weddle, Gary, eds. A Summary of U. S. Supreme Court Decisions for Correctional Services. 2nd ed. 240p. 2000. ring bd. 29.95 (*1-889031-21-6*) Looseleaf Law.

— A Summary of U. S. Supreme Court Decisions for the Criminal Justice Community with Database. 3rd ed. LC 99-171647. 240p. 1999. ring bd. 29.95 (*1-889031-10-0*) Looseleaf Law.

deLeon, Antonio C. Cardiac Auscultation. 29p. 9.75 (*1-886128-00-6*) Laennec Pub.

***DeLeon, Clark.** America's First Zoostory & Other Philadelphia Stories. LC 99-24040. 1999. write for info. (*1-57864-069-5*) Donning Co.

DeLeon, David. The American As Anarchist: Reflections on Indigenous Radicalism. LC 78-58290. (Illus.). 256p. reprint ed. pap. 79.40 (*0-8357-7885-1*, 203630300002) Bks Demand.

DeLeon, David, ed. Leaders from the 1960s: A Biographical Sourcebook of American Activism. LC 93-31603. 632p. 1994. 75.00 (*0-313-27414-2*, Greenwood Pr) Greenwood.

DeLeon, Delia. The Ocean of Love: My Life with Meher Baba. (Illus.). 240p. (Orig.). 1991. pap. 10.00 (*0-913078-68-9*) Sheriar Pr.

DeLeon, George & Ziegenfuss, James T., Jr. Therapeutic Communities for Addictions: Readings in Theory, Research & Practice. (Illus.). 282p. 1986. pap. 35.95 (*0-398-06087-8*) C C Thomas.

— Therapeutic Communities for Addictions: Readings in Theory, Research & Practice. (Illus.). 282p. (C). 1986. 51.95 (*0-398-05206-9*) C C Thomas.

DeLeon-Granados, William. Travels Through Crime & Place: Community-Building As Crime Control. LC 99-33755. 192p. 1999. text 50.00 (*1-55553-420-1*) NE U Pr.

— Travels Through Crime & Place: Community-Building As Crime Control. LC 99-33755. 192p. 2000. pap. text 20.00 (*1-55553-419-8*) NE U Pr.

DeLeon, Jean, jt. ed. see Hess, Robert E.

Deleon-Jones, Karen S. Giordano Bruno & the Kabbalah: Prophets, Magicians & Rabbis. LC 96-51858. (Yale Studies in Hermeneutics). 288p. 1997. 40.00 (*0-300-06807-7*) Yale U Pr.

DeLeon, Lon. Beyond Love & Loving: or Next Time I'd Rather Marry a Rhinoceros. (Illus.). 228p. (Orig.). 1993. pap. 12.95 (*0-9637320-0-5*, 524 577) Relation Inst Pr.

DeLeon, Peter. Advice & Consent: The Development of the Policy Sciences. LC 88-32140. 141p. 1989. 19.95 (*0-87154-215-3*) Russell Sage.

— Democracy & the Policy Sciences. LC 96-52831. (SUNY Series in Public Policy). 160p. (C). 1997. text 57.50 (*0-7914-3547-4*); pap. text 18.95 (*0-7914-3548-2*) State U NY Pr.

— Thinking about Political Corruption. LC 93-4026. 256p. (gr. 13). 1993. text 62.95 (*0-87332-838-8*); pap. text 29.95 (*0-87332-839-6*) M E Sharpe.

DeLeon, Peter, ed. The Evidentiary Basis of Policy Analysis: Empiricist vs. Postpositive Positions. (Policy Studies Journal: Vol. 26:1). 216p. 1998. pap. write for info. (*0-944285-55-4*) Pol Studies.

DeLeon, Ray G. Low Rider Hydraulics Basic Installation Manual. large type ed. (Illus.). 108p. (Orig.). 1995. pap. 49.95 (*0-9650586-0-3*) D C D T.

DeLeon, Richard E. Left Coast City: Progressive Politics in San Francisco, 1975-1991. LC 92-14119. (Studies in Government & Public Policy). (Illus.). xii, 244p. 1992. 35.00 (*0-7006-0554-1*); pap. 14.95 (*0-7006-0555-X*) U Pr of KS.

DeLeon, Richard E., jt. auth. see Anagnoson, J. Theodore.

DeLeon, Roderico, jt. auth. see Coombs, Ted.

***DeLeonibus, Gaetano.** Charles Maurras's Classicising Aesthetics: An Aestheticization of Politics. LC 99-19407. (Currents in Comparative Romance Languages & Literatures Ser.: No. 66). 184p. 2000. text 44.95 (*0-8204-3878-2*) P Lang Pubng.

Delepiere, Octave. A Sketch of the History of Flemish Literature from the Twelfth Century Down to the Present Time. LC 72-3215. (Studies in European Literature: No. 56). 1972. reprint ed. lib. bdg. 75.00 (*0-8383-1521-6*) M S G Haskell Hse.

Delepine, D., jt. auth. see Hotyat, Fernand.

Deleplace, Ghislain, et al. Private Money & Public Currencies: The 16th Century Challenge. Azodi, Azizeh, tr. LC 93-45467. (ENG & FRE.). 247p. (C). (gr. 13). 1994. text 85.95 (*0-87332-604-0*) M E Sharpe.

***Delerm, Philippe.** We Could Almost Eat Outside: An Appreciation of Life's Small Pleasures. LC 99-25536. 96p. 1999. text 14.00 (*0-312-20364-0*) St Martin.

Delery, Clayton J., ed. see Burney, Fanny.

Delery, John. U. S. Open 1895 to Today. LC 98-32004. 1999. text 17.98 (*1-56799-782-1*) M Friedman Pub Grp Inc.

***Delery, John & Garber, Greg.** 100 Years of the U. S. Open. LC 99-85983. (Illus.). 168p. 2000. 14.98 (*1-56799-957-3*, Friedman-Fairfax) M Friedman Pub Grp Inc.

Delery, Linda, ed. Four World's Fair 1984: The Official Guidebook. 160p. 1984. 10.95 (*0-317-12232-0*) Picayune Pr.

— 1984 World's Fair: The Official Guidebook. (Illus.). 160p. 1984. pap. 6.25 (*0-685-08335-7*) Picayune Pr.

— Official World's Fair Preview & Vacation Planner. (Illus.). 112p. (C). 1983. pap. 3.75 (*0-685-07793-4*) Picayune Pr.

***Delessert, Etienne.** The Cat Collection. LC 98-44383. 64p. 1998. 19.95 (*1-56846-160-7*, Creative Eds) Creative Co.

— Dance! (Illus.). 32p. (J). (gr. 2 up). 1994. 22.60 (*1-56846-088-0*, Creat Educ) Creative Co.

Delessert, Etienne. Yok-Yok, 10 bks. Incl. At Home. LC 93-27456. (Illus.). 32p. (J). (gr. 1-3). 1993. lib. bdg. 14.60 (*0-88682-646-2*, 97934-098, Creat Educ); Best Friends. LC 93-27461. (Illus.). 32p. (J). (gr. 1). 1993. lib. bdg. 14.60 (*0-88682-639-X*, 97927-098, Creat Educ); For the Birds. LC 93-27462. (Illus.). 32p. (J). (gr. 1-3). 1993. lib. bdg. 14.60 (*0-88682-638-1*, 97926-098, Creat Educ); Moonlight. LC 93-27458. (Illus.). 32p. (J). (gr. 1-3). 1993. lib. bdg. 14.60 (*0-88682-648-9*, 97936-098, Creat Educ); Nonsense. LC 93-27464. (Illus.). 32p. (J). (gr. 1-3). 1993. lib. bdg. 14.60 (*0-88682-641-1*, 97929-098, Creat Educ); Nuts! LC 93-27454. (Illus.). 32p. (J). (gr. 1-3). 1993. lib. bdg.

D

14.60 (*0-88682-644-6*, 97932-098, Creat Educ); Surprises. LC 93-27453. (Illus.). 32p. (J). (gr. 1-3). 1993. lib. bdg. 14.60 (*0-88682-643-8*, 97931-098, Creat Educ); Weird? LC 93-27455. (Illus.). 32p. (J). (gr. 1-3). 1993. lib. bdg. 14.60 (*0-88682-645-4*, 97933-098, Creat Educ); What a Circus! LC 93-27463. (Illus.). 32p. (J). (gr. 1-3). 1993. lib. bdg. 14.95 (*0-88682-640-3*, 97928-098, Creat Educ); (J). Set lib. bdg. 146.00 (*0-88682-637-3*, Creat Educ) Creative Co.

Deletant. Communist Terror in Romania: Gheorghiu-Dej & the Police State, 1948-1965. LC 99-13905. 380p. 2000. text 55.00 (*0-312-21904-0*) St Martin.

Deletant, A. & Walker, B., trs. An Anthology of Contemporary Romanian Poetry. LC 84-81308. 99p. 1990. reprint ed. pap. 16.95 (*0-9509487-4-8*, Pub. by Forest Bks) Dufour.

— Exile on a Peppercorn: The Poetry of Mircea Dinescu. LC 85-80387. (Illus.). 82p. 1990. reprint ed. pap. 18.95 (*0-948259-00-0*, Pub. by Forest Bks) Dufour.

— Silent Voices: An Anthology of Contemporary Romanian Women Poets. LC 85-80386. 161p. 1989. reprint ed. pap. 21.00 (*0-948259-03-5*, Pub. by Forest Bks) Dufour.

Deletant, A., tr. see Cassian, Nina.

Deletant, A., tr. see Sorescu, Marin.

Deletant, A., tr. see Stoica, Ion, ed.

Deletant, Andrea & Deletant, Dennis. Romania. (World Bibliographical Ser.: No. 59). 236p. 1987. lib. bdg. 38.00 (*1-85109-002-9*, Pub. by Clio Pr) ABC-CLIO.

Deletant, Andrea, tr. see Sorescu, Marin.

Deletant, Denis & Alexandrescu, Yvonne. Teach Yourself Romanian. (Teach Yourself Ser.). 1992. 19.95 (*0-8288-8383-1*); 45.00 incl. audio (*0-8288-8384-X*) Fr & Eur.

Deletant, Dennis. Ceausescu & the Securitate: Coercion & Dissent in Romania, 1965-1989. LC 95-30768. (Illus.). 456p. (C). (gr. 13). 1996. text 76.95 (*1-56324-633-3*) M E Sharpe.

— Colloquial Romanian. (Colloquials Ser.). (Orig.). 1983. pap. 15.95 (*0-7100-0834-1*) Routledge.

— Colloquial Romanian: A Complete Language Course. 2nd ed. LC 95-17121. 336p. (gr. 13). 1995. 39.99 incl. audio (*0-415-12900-1*) Routledge.

— Colloquial Romanian: A Complete Language Course. 2nd ed. LC 95-17121. (Colloquials Ser.). (Illus.). 338p. (C). 1995. pap. 19.99 (*0-415-12898-6*) Routledge.

— Colloquial Russian: A Complete Language Course. 2nd ed. (RUS.). 288p. 1995. 39.99 incl. cd-rom (*0-415-12684-3*) Routledge.

— Romania under Communist Rule. 200p. 1999. 45.00 (*973-98392-8-2*) Intl Spec Bk.

Deletant, Dennis & Alexandrescu, Yvonne. Romanian. 2nd ed. (Teach Yourself Ser.). (RUM., Illus.). 288p. 1998. pap. 16.95 (*0-8442-0039-5*, 00395, Teach Yrslf) NTC Contemp Pub Co.

— Teach Yourself Romanian: A Complete Course for Beginners, 2 cass. 2nd rev. ed. (Teach Yourself Ser.). (ENG & RUM.). 288p. 1998. pap. 27.95 incl. audio (*0-8442-0284-3*, 02843, Teach Yrslf) NTC Contemp Pub Co.

Deletant, Dennis & Alexandrescu, Yvonnne. Romanian: A Complete Course for Beginners. (Teach Yourself Ser.). (ROM.). 428p. pap. 27.95 incl. audio (*0-8442-3870-8*, Teach Yrslf) NTC Contemp Pub Co.

Deletant, Dennis, jt. auth. see Deletant, Andrea.

Deletant, Dennis, tr. see Sorescu, Marin.

Deleuze, Gilles. Bergsonism. Tomlinson, Hugh & Habberjam, Barbara, trs. from FRE. LC 87-34051. 131p. 1988. 24.95 (*0-942299-06-X*); pap. 12.95 (*0-942299-07-8*) Zone Bks.

— Cinema 1: The Movement-Image. Tomlinson, Hugh & Habberjam, Barbara, trs. from FRE. LC 85-28898. 263p. 1986. text 39.95 (*0-8166-1399-0*) U of Minn Pr.

Deleuze, Gilles. Cinema 1: The Movement-Image. Tomlinson, Hugh & Habberjam, Barbara, trs. from FRE. LC 85-28898. 263p. 1989. pap. 18.95 (*0-8166-1400-8*) U of Minn Pr.

Deleuze, Gilles. Cinema 2: The Time-Image. Tomlinson, Hugh & Galeta, Robert, trs. 362p. 1989. pap. 18.95 (*0-8166-1677-9*) U of Minn Pr.

***Deleuze, Gilles.** Deleuze & Guattari's Anti-Oedipus: Introduction to Schizoanalysis. LC 98-46665. 1999. write for info. (*0-415-11318-0*) Routledge.

Deleuze, Gilles. The Deleuze Reader. Boundas, Constantin V., ed. 416p. 1993. text 57.50 (*0-231-07268-6*) Col U Pr.

— Difference & Repetition. Patton, Paul, tr. from FRE. 400p. (C). 1994. 57.50 (*0-231-08158-8*) Col U Pr.

— Difference & Repetition. Patton, Paul, tr. 372p. 1995. pap. 18.50 (*0-231-08159-6*) Col U Pr.

— Essays Critical & Clinical. 1997. pap. text 14.00 (*0-86091-614-6*) Norton.

— Essays Critical & Clinical. 1997. 40.00 (*0-86091-464-X*) Norton.

— Essays Critical & Clinical. Smith, Daniel W. & Greco, Michael A., trs. LC 97-13300. 1997. write for info. (*0-8166-2568-9*); pap. write for info. (*0-8166-2569-7*) U of Minn Pr.

— Expressionism in Philosophy: Spinoza. Joughin, Martin, tr. from FRE. LC 88-20607. 445p. 1990. 28.95 (*0-942299-50-7*); pap. 16.95 (*0-942299-51-5*) Zone Bks.

— The Fold: Leibniz & the Baroque. Conley, Tom, tr. from FRE. & frwd. by. LC 92-14153. 192p. (C). 1992. pap. 15.95 (*0-8166-1601-9*); text 39.95 (*0-8166-1598-5*) U of Minn Pr.

— Foucault. Hand, Sean, tr. from FRE. LC 87-31668. 175p. 1988. pap. 14.95 (*0-8166-1675-2*) U of Minn Pr.

— Kant's Critical Philosophy. Tomlinson, Hugh & Habberjam, Barbara, trs. from FRE. LC 84-7548. 96p. 1985. pap. 12.95 (*0-8166-1436-9*) U of Minn Pr.

— The Logic of Sense. Lester, Mark & Stivale, Charles, trs. from FRE. (European Perspectives Ser.). 393p. (C). 1990. text 57.50 (*0-231-05982-5*) Col U Pr.

— The Logic of Sense. Lester, Mark & Stivale, Charles, trs. from FRE. (European Perspectives Ser.). 393p. (C). 1993. pap. 19.00 (*0-231-05983-3*) Col U Pr.

— Negotiations, 1972-1990.Tr. of Pourparlers, 1972-1990. 221p. 1997. pap. 17.50 (*0-231-07581-2*) Col U Pr.

— Nietzsche & Philosophy. Tomlinson, Hugh, tr. from FRE. LC 82-17676. (European Perspectives Ser.). 275p. 1985. pap. text 19.00 (*0-231-05669-9*) Col U Pr.

— Nietzsche & Philosophy. Tomlinson, Hugh, tr. LC 82-17676. (European Perspectives Ser.). 237p. reprint ed. pap. 73.50 (*0-7837-0428-3*, 204075100018) Bks Demand.

***Deleuze, Gilles.** Proust & Signs. LC 99-50616. (Theory Out of Bounds Ser.). 2000. write for info. (*0-8166-3258-8*) U of Minn Pr.

Deleuze, Gilles. Spinoza: Practical Philosophy. Hurley, Robert, tr. from FRE. 160p. (Orig.). 1988. pap. 10.95 (*0-87286-218-6*) City Lights.

***Deleuze, Gilles & Foucault, Michel.** Photogenic Painting: Gerard Fromanger. 160p. 1999. pap. 29.95 (*1-901033-56-2*, Pub. by Black Dog Pubg) RAM Publications.

Deleuze, Gilles & Guattari, Felix. Anti-Oedipus: Capitalism & Schizophrenia. Hurley, Robert et al, trs. from FRE. LC 83-14748. 424p. 1983. reprint ed. pap. 18.95 (*0-8166-1225-0*) U of Minn Pr.

— Kafka: Toward a Minor Literature. Polan, Dana B., tr. from FRE. LC 85-31822. (Theory & History of Literature Ser.: Vol. 30). 104p. (Orig.). 1986. pap. 11.95 (*0-8166-1515-2*) U of Minn Pr.

— Nomadology. 147p. Date not set. 7.00 (*0-936756-09-8*) Autonomedia.

— On the Line. 114p. Date not set. 7.00 (*0-936756-01-2*) Autonomedia.

— A Thousand Plateaus: Capitalism & Schizophrenia. LC 87-18623. 629p. 1987. pap. 19.95 (*0-8166-1402-4*); text 49.95 (*0-8166-1401-6*) U of Minn Pr.

— What Is Philosophy? 256p. 1996. pap. 18.00 (*0-231-07989-3*) Col U Pr.

Deleuze, Gilles & Parnet, Claire. Dialogues. Tomlinson, Hugh & Habberjam, Barbara, trs. from FRE. (European Perspectives Ser.). 200p. 1989. pap. text 17.50 (*0-231-06601-5*) Col U Pr.

Deleuze, Gilles & Von Sacher-Masoch, Leopold. Masochism: Coldness & Cruelty; Venus in Furs. McNeil, Jean, tr. from FRE. LC 88-20823. 293p. 1989. reprint ed. 25.95 (*0-942299-54-X*); reprint ed. pap. 13.50 (*0-942299-55-8*) Zone Bks.

Delevan, Sybil M., jt. auth. see Martinez-Brawley, Emilia E.

Deleveau, John. Smart Pool! The Mind Game. Campbell, Robert, ed. LC 98-65345. 1998. pap. 15.95 (*0-9660794-1-8*) Merrimack Pub.

Deleyto, Celestino, jt. ed. see Evans, Peter W.

Delf, Brian. Bible: The Really Interesting Bits. (J). (gr. 3-8). 1999. 16.99 (*0-8423-3161-1*) Tyndale Hse.

Delf, Brian. Picture Atlas of the World. LC 92-37056. (J). 1992. 19.95 (*0-528-83564-5*) Rand McNally.

— Rand McNally Picture Atlas of the World, 1995. rev. ed. LC 95-19966. 80p. (J). 1995. text 19.95 (*0-528-83756-7*) Rand McNally.

Delf, Brian & Platt, Richard. Great Events That Changed the World. LC 97-19925. (J). 1997. write for info. (*0-7894-2030-9*) DK Pub Inc.

Delf, George. Jomo Kenyatta: Towards Truth about "The Light of Kenya" LC 75-17469. 215p. 1975. reprint ed. lib. bdg. 55.00 (*0-8371-8307-3*, DEJK, Greenwood Pr) Greenwood.

DelFattore, Joan. What Johnny Shouldn't Read: Textbook Censorship in America. LC 92-3585. 224p. (C). 1992. 35.00 (*0-300-05709-1*) Yale U Pr.

— What Johnny Shouldn't Read: Textbook Censorship in America. 218p. 1994. pap. 15.00 (*0-300-06050-5*) Yale U Pr.

Delfavero, Carl. Well-Kept Marine Aquarium: Maintenance & Troubleshooting: A Workbook with Aquarist's Log. 1998. pap. 19.95 (*1-890087-49-1*) Microcosm Ltd.

Delffs, D. J. The Judas Tree. LC 99-6402. (Father Grif Mysteries Ser.). 320p. 1999. pap. text 9.99 (*0-7642-2087-X*) Bethany Hse.

Delffs, Dudley. Seeking God's Will. LC 99-173680. 96p. 1998. pap. 6.50 (*1-57683-086-1*) NavPress.

Delffs, Dudley J. Improving Your Relationships. (Thinking Through Discipleship Ser.). 80p. (Orig.). 1993. pap. 5.00 (*0-89109-738-4*) NavPress.

— Martyr's Chapel. 32p. 1998. pap. 9.99 (*0-7642-2086-1*) Bethany Hse.

— Martyr's Chapel. LC 98-53617. 1999. 22.95 (*0-7862-1808-8*) Thorndike Pr.

— Mastering Money. LC 99-180919. 96p. 1998. pap. 6.50 (*1-57683-085-3*) NavPress.

— The Prayer Centered Life: Living in Conversation with the Father. LC 96-50346. 191p. (Orig.). 1997. pap. 9.00 (*0-89109-997-2*) NavPress.

Delffs, Dudley J. A Repentant Heart. 150p. (Orig.). 1995. pap., per. 9.00 (*0-89109-877-1*) NavPress.

Delfin, Giovanni, et al. Italian-English - English-Italian Encyclopedic Dictionary of Biological Sciences & Medicine. (ENG & ITA.). 1726p. 195.00 (*0-8288-9421-3*, M4783) Fr & Eur.

Delfinado, Mercedes. Culicine Mosquitoes of the Philippines. (Memoir Ser.: No. 7). (Illus.). 252p. 1966. 45.00 (*1-56665-005-4*) Assoc Pubs FL.

Delfiner, Henry. The Vienna Broadcasts to Slovakia, 1938-1939: A Case Study in Subversion. (East European Monographs: No. 7). 142p. 1974. text 64.00 (*0-914710-00-1*, Pub. by East Eur Monographs) Col U Pr.

Delfiner, Pierre, jt. auth. see Chiles, Jean-Paul.

Delfino, G. Medical & Biological Dictionary Italian-English - English-Italian. (ENG & ITA.). 2144p. 1996. 125.00 (*88-08-08854-5*, Pub. by Zanichelli) IBD Ltd.

Delforge, P. Orchids. (Illus.). 480p. 1995. 29.95 (*0-00-220024-4*, Pub. by HarpC) Trafalgar.

Delfose, E. S. & Scott, R. R., eds. Biological Control of Weeds. (Illus.). 760p. (Orig.). 1996. pap. 89.95 (*0-643-05812-5*, Pub. by CSIRO) Accents Pubns.

***Delfosse, Pierre.** A Lie for the Truth. LC 00-190104. 2000. 25.00 (*0-7388-1544-6*); 18.00 (*0-7388-1545-4*) Xlibris Corp.

Delfosse, E. S. Pests of Pastures: Weed, Invertebrate & Disease Pests of Australian Sheep Pastures. (Illus.). 600p. 1992. pap. 75.00 (*0-643-05140-6*, Pub. by CSIRO) Accents Pubns.

Delfosse, Renee. Hospice & Home Health Agency Characteristics: United States, 1991. LC 95-1092. (Vital & Health Statistics: Series 13: Data from the National Health Survey Ser.: No. 120). 1995. write for info. (*0-8406-0505-6*) Natl Ctr Health Stats.

Delfour, Michel C. Boundaries, Interfaces, & Transitions. LC 97-52240. (CRM Proceedings & Lecture Notes Ser.). 343p. 1998. pap. 95.00 (*0-8218-0505-3*) Am Math.

Delfour, Michel C. & Sabidussi, Gert, eds. Shape Optimization & Free Boundaries. LC 92-18173. (NATO Advanced Study Institutes Series C, Mathematical & Physical Sciences: Vol. 380). 480p. 1992. text 241.50 (*0-7923-1944-3*) Kluwer Academic.

DelFranco, Randy & Flynn, Colin T. The Guide to America's Microbrewed Beers. LC 94-224123. 144p. (Orig.). 1994. pap. 9.95 (*0-9640948-0-0*) Rosehill Ent.

Delfs, H. Homology of Locally Semialgebraic Spaces. Dold, A. et al, eds. (Lecture Notes in Mathematics Ser.: Vol. 1484). ix, 136p. 1991. pap. 24.00 (*0-387-54615-4*) Spr-Verlag.

Delfs, H. & Knebusch, M. Locally Semialgebraic Spaces. (Lecture Notes in Mathematics Ser.: Vol. 1173). xvi, 329p. 1986. 46.95 (*0-387-16060-4*) Spr-Verlag.

Delft. European Simulation Symposium: Proceedings of 1993. 900p. 1993. pap. 140.00 (*1-56555-063-3*, ESS-93) Soc Computer Sim.

Delft, A. Van, see Van Delft, A.

Delft, Louis Van, see Van Delft, Louis.

Delft, Ron Van, see Van Delft, Ron.

Delft University of Technology Staff. The Architectural Annual: Delft University of Technology. (Illus.). 175p. (Orig.). 1996. pap. 19.95 (*90-6868-136-2*, Pub. by Thoth Pubs) Bks Nippan.

Delft University Staff, ed. Advances in Computer-Aided Engineering. 286p. (Orig.). 1994. pap. 67.50 (*90-407-1017-1*, Pub. by Delft U Pr) Coronet Bks.

***Delgadeo, Margarita & Martin, Teresa Castro.** Fertility & Family Surveys in Countries of the ECE Region: Standard Country Report: Spain. (Economic Studies of the UN - ECE: No. 10i). 104p. 1999. pap. 25.00 (*92-1-116702-7*) UN.

Delgadilli. Food for Thought. 1988. pap. text 14.62 (*0-673-19402-7*) Addison-Wesley.

Delgadillo. Let's Talk Turkey. 1989. text 14.62 (*0-673-19448-5*) Addison-Wesley.

— Let's Talk Turkey: Answer Key. 1997. text 15.66 (*0-673-19449-3*) Addison-Wesley.

Delgadillo, Claudio M., et al. LATMOSS, a Catalogue of Neotropical Mosses. 191p. 1995. 24.00 (*0-915279-35-5*, MSB-56) Miss Botan.

Delgadillo, Leon C. Coleccion Salud Tomo: La Dieta Feliz - Impireno en la Tierra, I. Camps, Janett & Ghezi, Maggie, eds. 200p. (Orig.). pap. text. write for info. (*0-9641506-3-8*) Edit Interamerica.

Delgadillo, Willivaldo, tr. see Crosthwaite, Luis H.

Delgado. Tips De Belleza Naturales. pap. 12.95 (*1-57954-179-8*) Rodale Pr Inc.

Delgado, et al. Groups & Graphs. (DMV Seminar Ser.: No. 6). 244p. 1985. 28.50 (*0-8176-1736-1*) Birkhauser.

Delgado, A. J., jt. ed. see Alfaro, E. J.

***Delgado, Abel.** Amor, Romance Intimidad. (Guides to Improve Your Health Ser.). 2000. pap. text 12.95 (*1-57954-204-2*) Rodale Pr Inc.

— El Boutiquin Natural. 2000. pap. 12.95 (*1-57954-206-9*) Rodale Pr Inc.

— Las Emociones, la Saludy y la Mujer de Hoy. LC 99-52074. (Guides to Improve Your Health Ser.). (SPA.). 192p. 2000. pap. 12.95 (*1-57954-203-4*) Rodale Pr Inc.

— La Familia Saludable. 2000. pap. 12.95 (*1-57954-205-0*) Rodale Pr Inc.

Delgado, Abel & Prevention Health Books Editors, eds. Los Mejores Remedios Caseros (The Best Home Remedies) 220 Consejos Practicos para Vencer Problemas Comunes de la Salud (220 Practical Tips to Conquer Common Health Conditions) (SPA.). 192p. 1998. pap. 12.95 (*1-57954-030-9*) Rodale Pr Inc.

Delgado, Abel & Prevention Magazine Staff, eds. Curas Para el Colesterol Alto: 40 Maneras de Cuidar su Corazon y Prevenir Enfermedades.Tr. of Cures for High Cholesterol. (SPA.). 192p. 1999. pap. 12.95 (*1-57954-180-1*) Rodale Pr Inc.

Delgado, Abel, ed. see Prevention Health Books Editors.

Delgado, Ana M. The Room In-Between. Miller, Yvette E., ed. Lipp, Sylvia E., tr. from SPA. LC 95-9455. (Discoveries Ser.). 92p. 1995. pap. 12.95 (*0-935480-76-5*) Lat Am Lit Rev Pr.

Delgado-Barrio, G., ed. Dynamical Processes in Molecular Physics: Lectures from the First EPS Southern European School of Physics, Avila, September 1991. (Illus.). 328p. 1993. 147.00 (*0-7503-0205-4*) IOP Pub.

Delgado, C. C. Lab Manual for General Biology. 3rd ed. 148p. (C). 1999. pap. text, lab manual ed. 19.95 (*0-7872-5684-6*, 41568401) Kendall-Hunt.

Delgado, Celeste F. & Munoz, Jose E., eds. Everynight Life: Culture & Dance in Latino America. LC 96-43796. (Latin America Otherwise Ser.). (Illus.). 368p. 1997. lib. bdg. 54.95 (*0-8223-1926-8*) Duke.

— Everynight Life: Culture & Dance in Latino America. LC 96-43796. (Latin America Otherwise Ser.). (Illus.). x,366p. 1997. pap. text 18.95 (*0-8223-1919-5*) Duke.

Delgado, Christina, jt. ed. see Francis, G. E.

Delgado, Christopher L. & International Food Policy Research Institute Staff. Agricultural Growth Linkages in Sub-saharan Africa. LC 98-52778. 1998. write for info. (*0-89629-110-3*) Intl Food Policy.

Delgado, Christopher L. & Jammeh, Sidi, eds. The Political Economy of Senegal under Structural Adjustment. LC 90-40946. 232p. 1991. 59.95 (*0-275-93525-6*, C3525, Praeger Pubs) Greenwood.

Delgado, Christopher L., jt. ed. see Abdulai, Awudu.

Delgado, Christopher L., jt. ed. see Zartman, I. William.

Delgado, Cindee, ed. see Ghostwolf, Robert.

Delgado, Conchita, tr. see Cummins, D. Duane.

Delgado, Domingo J. Legalidad y Derechos Humanos En Cuba. (SPA.). 164p. (Orig.). 1991. pap. 10.00 (*0-917049-51-9*) Saeta.

Delgado, Enrique, jt. ed. see Cline, William R.

Delgado-Escueta, Antonio V., et al, eds. Basic Mechanisms of the Epilepsies: Molecular & Cellular Approaches. LC 85-25800. (Advances in Neurology Ser.: Vol. 44). 1120p. 1986. reprint ed. pap. 200.00 (*0-608-04691-4*, 206541200004) Bks Demand.

— Status Epilepticus: Mechanisms of Brain Damage & Treatment. LC 80-6214. (Advances in Neurology Ser.: No. 34). (Illus.). 579p. 1983. reprint ed. pap. 179.50 (*0-608-00604-1*, 206119100007) Bks Demand.

Delgado-Escueta, Antonio V., et al. Jasper's Basic Mechanisms of the Epilepsies, Vol. 79. 3rd ed. 1,104p. text 159.00 (*0-7817-1438-9*) Lppncott W & W.

Delgado, Fernando. Escrito Por Luzbel, 1. LC 98-180669. (Autores Espanoles E Iberoamericanos Ser.). 1998. 24.95 (*84-08-02504-X*) Planeta.

Delgado-Figueroa, J. Mr. Doppler Is Survived by Those Who Loved Him. LC 94-73721.Tr. of Sus Desconsolados Deudos, al Comunicar la Sensible Perdida de Quien en Vida Fuera Frederick Doppler. (SPA.). 133p. 1995. pap. 7.95 (*0-9643486-1-6*) Hispanic Caribbean.

— The Rhetoric of Change: Metaphor & Politics in the Commonwealth of Puerto Rico. LC 94-96402. (Illus.). xvii, 354p. 1994. pap. 17.95 (*0-9643486-0-8*) Hispanic Caribbean.

***Delgado-Figueroa, J.** 'Twas the Season. LC 99-96477. 248p. 1999. pap. 8.95 (*0-9643486-3-2*) Hispanic Caribbean.

***Delgado-Figueroa, J., et al, eds.** Telecommunications & IT Convergence Towards Service Evolution: 7th International Conference on Intelligence in Services & Networks, IS&N 2000, Athens, Greece, February 23-25, 2000 Proceedings. (Lecture Notes In Computer Science: 1774). xiii, 350p. 2000. pap. text (*3-540-67152-8*) Spr-Verlag.

Delgado-Frias, J. G. & Moore, W. R. VLSI for Neural Networks & Artificial Intelligence. (Illus.). 330p. (C). 1994. 95.00 (*0-306-44722-3*, Plenum Trade) Perseus Pubng.

Delgado-Frias, Jose G. & Moore, W. R., eds. VLSI for Artificial Intelligence & Neural Networks. (Illus.). 432p. (C). 1991. 150.00 (*0-306-44029-6*, Plenum Trade) Perseus Pubng.

Delgado-Frias, Jose G. & Moore, Will R., eds. VLSI for Artificial Intelligence. (C). 1989. text 104.50 (*0-7923-9000-8*) Kluwer Academic.

Delgado, Gabriel. A Love Story. 64p. (Orig.). 1975. pap. 1.25 (*0-89228-046-8*) Impact Christian.

Delgado-Gaitan, Concha & Trueba, Henry T. Crossing Cultural Borders: Education for Immigrant Families in America. 224p. 1991. pap. 29.95 (*1-85000-886-8*, Falmer Pr) Taylor & Francis.

Delgado-Gaitan, Concha, jt. ed. see Trueba, Henry T.

Delgado, Gary. Beyond the Politics of Place: New Directions in Community Organizing. 84p. 1997. reprint ed. pap. 15.00 (*1-890759-00-7*) Chardon Pr.

— Beyond the Politics of Place: New Directions in Community Organizing in the 1990s. 99p. (Orig.). 1994. pap. 16.00 (*0-9636725-1-7*) Appl Res Ctr.

Delgado, Gary, intro. Reversing the Flow: A Practical Guide to Bay Area Corporate Giving Programs. rev. ed. 132p. (Orig.). 1993. pap. 49.95 (*0-9636725-0-9*) Appl Res Ctr.

Delgado, George. El Hotel Durascamas y Otras Historietas, No. 1.Tr. of Hardbed Hotel & Other Stories. (ENG & SPA., Illus.). 120p. 1985. pap. 4.25 (*0-940038-02-1*) Andante Pub.

Delgado, Gilbert L., ed. The Hispanic Deaf: Issues & Challenges for Bilingual Special Education. LC 84-8130. 223p. reprint ed. pap. 69.20 (*0-7837-1852-7*, 204205200001) Bks Demand.

Delgado, Gilbert L., jt. auth. see Christensen, Kathee M.

Delgado-Gomez, Angel, jt. auth. see Newbury, Susan L.

Delgado Gonzalez, Carlos. Diccionario de Gastronomia. 3rd ed. (SPA.). 240p. 1991. pap. 12.95 (*0-7859-5716-2*, 8420600997) Fr & Eur.

Delgado, Guillermo, jt. tr. see Hillman, Grady L.

Delgado, Guillermo, tr. see Schuler, Margaret, ed.

Delgado, Hector L. New Immigrants, Old Unions: Organizing Undocumented Workers in Los Angeles. LC 92-36423. 200p. (C). 1994. pap. 22.95 (*1-56639-205-5*) Temple U Pr.

Delgado, J., ed. see Sixpack, Jack.

Delgado, J. L., ed. see Menendez Pidal, Ramon.

***Delgado, J. S.** Libro Siembre Neuvo. (SPA.). 1999. 9.99 (*0-8297-0430-2*) Vida Pubs.

Delgado, Jaime N. & Remers, William A. Wilson & Gisvold's Textbook of Organic Medicinal & Pharmaceutical Chemistry. 9th ed. LC 65-10424. (Illus.). 860p. 1991. text 69.50 (*0-397-50877-8*, Lippncott) Lppncott W & W.

— Wilson & Gisvold's Textbook of Organic Medicinal & Pharmaceutical Chemistry. 10th ed. LC 98-22502. 1083p. 1998. text 69.50 (*0-397-51583-9*) Lppncott W & W.

Delgado, James & Haller, Stephen. Shipwrecks at the Golden Gate. (Illus.). 192p. (Orig.). 1989. 25.95 (*0-938530-50-X*); pap. 15.95 (*0-938530-49-6*) Lexikos.

Delgado, James P. Across the Top of the World: The Quest for the Northwest Passage. LC 99-33408. (Illus.). 228p. (YA). (gr. 7-12). 1999. 35.00 (*0-8160-4124-5*, Checkmark) Facts on File.

— Alcatraz: Island of Change. (Illus.). 48p. (Orig.). 1992. pap. 7.95 (*0-9625206-6-7*) Gldn Gate Natl Parks Assoc.

— Alcatraz: The Story Behind the Scenery. LC 85-80214. (Illus.). 48p. (Orig.). 1985. pap. 7.95 (*0-88714-001-7*) KC Pubns.

— Alcatraz: The Story Behind the Scenery. Sommer, Sigrid, tr. (GER., Illus.). 48p. (Orig.). 1996. pap. 8.95 (*0-88714-700-3*) KC Pubns.

— Ghost Fleet: The Sunken Ships of Bikini Atoll. (Illus.). 216p. 1996. 31.95 (*0-8248-1864-4*); pap. 21.95 (*0-8248-1868-7*) UH Pr.

— Native American Shipwrecks LC 99-25886. (Watts Library Ser.). 2000. 24.00 (*0-531-20379-4*) Watts.

***Delgado, James P.** Native American Shipwrecks. (Shipwrecks Library). (Illus.). (YA). 2000. pap. 8.95 (*0-531-16473-X*) Watts.

Delgado, James P. Shipwrecks from the Westward Movement. LC 99-25425. (Watts Library). 2000. 24.00 (*0-531-20380-8*) Watts.

***Delgado, James P.** Shipwrecks from the Westward Movement. (Shipwrecks Library). (Illus.). (YA). 2000. pap. 8.95 (*0-531-16484-5*) Watts.

Delgado, James P. To California by Sea: A Maritime History of the California Gold Rush. LC 89-39117. (Illus.). 251p. 1996. pap. 14.95 (*1-57003-153-3*) U of SC Pr.

— Wrecks of American Warships LC 99-25426. (Watts Library Ser.). 2000. 24.00 (*0-531-20376-X*) Watts.

***Delgado, James P.** Wrecks of American Warships. (Shipwrecks Library). (Illus.). (YA). 2000. pap. 8.95 (*0-531-16486-1*) Watts.

Delgado, James P., ed. Encyclopedia of Underwater & Maritime Archaeology. LC 97-61536. (Illus.). 496p. 1998. 55.00 (*0-300-07427-1*) Yale U Pr.

Delgado, James P. & Clifford, J. Candace. Great American Ships. LC 95-46318. (Great American Places Ser.). (Illus.). 312p. (Orig.). 1995. pap. 19.95 (*0-471-14384-7*) Wiley.

Delgado, Jane L. Salud! A Latina's Guide to Total Health - Body, Mind, & Spirit. (Illus.). 384p. 1998. pap. text 20.00 (*0-7881-5796-5*) DIANE Pub.

— Salud! A Latina's Guide to Total Health, Body, Mind & Spirit. LC 97-19202. 400p. 1997. pap. 20.00 (*0-06-095187-7*, Perennial) HarperTrade.

Delgado, Jane L., jt. auth. see National Hispanic Women's Health Initiative Staff.

Delgado, Jeanne H., ed. Advice to Farm Women. (Wisconsin Stories Ser.). 27p. pap. 1.25 (*0-87020-186-7*) State Hist Soc Wis.

Delgado-Jenkins, Humberto. Cuentos de Tierra, Agua, Aire y Mar. (SPA.). 1995. pap. 9.95 (*0-89729-769-5*) Ediciones.

Delgado, Joao Pinto. The Poem of Queen Esther. Slavitt, David R., tr. from SPA. LC 98-19437. 112p. 1999. 19.95 (*0-19-512374-3*) OUP.

***Delgado, Jose.** La Felicidad. 1999. pap. 18.95 (*84-7880-964-3*) Planeta.

Delgado, Jose, jt. auth. see Clemens, Peter.

Delgado, Jose M. Physical Control of the Mind: Toward a Psychocivilized Society. Anshen, Ruth N., ed. (Illus.). 280p. (C). 1971. 29.50 (*0-8290-0574-9*); pap. text 12.95 (*0-8290-1765-8*) Irvington.

Delgado, Joseph. Storms of a Soul. 40p. (Orig.). 1995. pap. 5.49 (*0-9646866-0-0*) Enchanted Quill Pr.

Delgado, Josie. El Arte de Ir Envejeciendo. (SPA.). 112p. 1993. pap. write for info. (*0-929441-54-0*) Pubns Puertorriquenas.

Delgado, Juan. El Campo: Poems & Paintings. LC 97-46495. (Illus.). 66p. 1998. pap. 22.95 (*0-88496-428-0*) Capra Pr.

— Green Web: Poems by Juan Delgado. LC 94-7789. (Contemporary Poetry Ser.). 64p. 1994. pap. 14.95 (*0-8203-1677-6*) U of Ga Pr.

Delgado, Linda C., jt. ed. see Matos-Rodriguez, Felix V.

Delgado, Linda C., jt. ed. see Matos-Rodriguez, Felix V.

Delgado, M., et al, eds. Fuzzy Optimization: Recent Advances. (Studies in Fuzziness: Vol. 2). xii, 459p. 1994. 122.95 (*0-387-91489-7*) Spr-Verlag.

Delgado, Maria, ed. Spanish Theatre, 1920-1995: Strategies in Protest & Imagination 1, Vol. 7, Pt 2. 88p. 1998. pap. text 14.00 (*90-5702-099-8*, Harwood Acad Pubs) Gordon & Breach.

— Spanish Theatre, 1920-1995: Strategies in Protest & Imagination 2, Vol. 7, Pt. 3. 88p. 1998. pap. text 14.00 (*90-5702-115-3*, Harwood Acad Pubs) Gordon & Breach.

— Spanish Theatre, 1920-1995: Strategies in Protest & Imagination 3, Vol. 7, Pt. 4. 88p. 1998. pap. text 14.00 (*90-5702-116-1*, Harwood Acad Pubs) Gordon & Breach.

Delgado, Maria I. Chave's Memories: Los Recuerdos de Chave. LC 95-47732. 32p. 1996. 14.95 (*1-55885-084-8*, Pinata Bks) Arte Publico.

Delgado, Maria J. Las Comedias de Ana Caro: Valor, Agravio y Mujer y El Conde Partinuples, Vol. 34. (Wor(l)ds of Change Ser.). 258p. (C). 1998. text 48.95 (*0-8204-3783-2*) P Lang Pubng.

Delgado, Maria M. In Contact with the Gods. LC 97-143897. (Illus.). 288p. 1997. pap. 22.95 (*0-7190-4763-3*, Pub. by Manchester Univ Pr) St Martin.

***Delgado, Maria M. & Svich, Caridad, eds.** Conducting a Life: Reflections on the Theatre of Maria Irene Fornes. LC 99-48899. 352p. 1999. pap. 19.95 (*1-57525-204-X*) Smith & Kraus.

Delgado, Melvin. Community Social Work Practice in an Urban Context: The Potential of a Capacity Enhancement Perspective. LC 98-49973. (Illus.). 288p. (C). 1999. text 45.00 (*0-19-512546-0*); pap. text 21.95 (*0-19-512547-9*) OUP.

***Delgado, Melvin.** New Arenas for Community Social Work Practice with Urban Youth: Use of the Arts, Humanities & Sports. LC 99-86564. (Illus.). 2000. 49.50 (*0-231-11462-1*); pap. 21.50 (*0-231-11463-X*) Col U Pr.

Delgado, Melvin. Social Services in Latino Communities: Research & Strategies. LC 97-28881. (Illus.). 153p. 1998. 29.95 (*0-7890-0428-3*); pap. 19.95 (*0-7890-0429-1*) Haworth Pr.

— Social Work Practice in Nontraditional Urban Settings. (Illus.). 272p. (C). 1999. text 48.00 (*0-19-511247-4*); pap. text 22.95 (*0-19-511248-2*) OUP.

Delgado, Melvin, ed. Alcohol Use - Abuse among Latinos: Issues & Examples of Culturally Competent Services. LC 97-46407. (Alcohol Treatment Quarterly Monograph Ser.: Vol. 16, Nos. 1-2). 208p. 1998. 49.95 (*0-7890-0392-9*); pap. 24.95 (*0-7890-0500-X*) Haworth Pr.

— Latino Elders & the Twenty-First Century: Issues & Challenges for Culturally Competent Research & Practice. LC 98-51288. 251p. 1998. 49.95 (*0-7890-0657-X*) Haworth Pr.

Delgado, Nick. Healthy Aging Breakthrough: Amazing Supplements for Ideal Weight & Disease Prevention. Kendell, Shawna, ed. LC 98-94176. (Illus.). 288p. 1999. pap. 15.95 (*1-879084-05-8*, Health Wellness Studios) Delgado.

— Mastering the Powers of Your Inner Health. 150p. (Orig.). 1992. pap. 19.95 (*1-879084-03-1*) Delgado.

***Delgado, Nick & Kendell, Shawna.** Grow Young & Slim: Overcome Obesity & Poor Health with a Startling New Concept. LC 99-97640. (Illus.). 352p. 2000. pap. 19.95 (*1-879084-06-6*, Health Wellness Studios) Delgado.

Delgado, Nick R. How to Look Great & Feel Sexy! Vol. 5: Revitalize Your Energy in 9 Days. 2nd rev. ed. Kendall, Shawna, ed. LC 97-178904. (Illus.). 400p. 1997. pap. text 21.95 (*1-879084-04-X*) Delgado.

Delgado, Osiris. Historical Synopsis of the Plastic Arts in Puerto Rico. (Puerto Rico Ser.). 1979. lib. bdg. 59.95 (*0-8490-2933-3*) Gordon Pr.

Delgado, Pat. Drivers Ed Is Dead. (Illus.). 20p. (Orig.). 1996. teacher ed., spiral bd. 5.00 (*0-943864-81-X*) Davenport.

— Drivers Ed Is Dead. LC 95-83548. (Illus.). 170p. (Orig.). (YA). (gr. 7-12). 1996. pap. text 8.95 (*0-943864-76-3*) Davenport.

Delgado, Pat & Andrews, Colin. Circular Evidence: A Detailed Investigation of the Flattened Swirled Crops Phenomenon. LC 91-381. (Illus.). 191p. 1991. pap. 16.95 (*0-933999-95-X*) Phanes Pr.

Delgado, Ramon. The Best Short Plays of 1988-89. (Best Short Plays Ser.). 536p. (C). 1989. 24.95 (*1-55783-187-4*) Applause Theatre Bk Pubs.

Delgado, Ramon, ed. The Best Short Plays: 1983. LC 38-8006. (Best Short Plays Ser.). 251p. 1983. 20.00 (*0-8019-7296-5*) Empire Pub Srvs.

— Best Short Plays: 1984. LC 38-8006. (Best Short Plays Ser.). 251p. 1984. 20.00 (*0-8019-7411-9*) Empire Pub Srvs.

— The Best Short Plays: 1985. LC 38-8006. (Best Short Plays Ser.). 243p. 1985. 20.00 (*0-8019-7541-7*) Empire Pub Srvs.

— The Best Short Plays of 1988. (Best Short Plays Ser.). 320p. 1988. pap. 10.95 (*1-55783-026-6*) Applause Theatre Bk Pubs.

— The Best Short Plays of 1989. (Best American Short Plays Ser.). 272p. 1989. text 23.95 (*1-55783-045-2*) Applause Theatre Bk Pubs.

— The Best Short Plays of 1986. 256p. 1986. pap. 10.95 (*0-936839-13-9*) Applause Theatre Bk Pubs.

— The Best Short Plays of 1987. (Best Short Plays Ser.). 288p. 1987. pap. 10.95 (*0-936839-94-5*) Applause Theatre Bk Pubs.

Delgado, Ricardo. Age of Reptiles: The Hunt. 1997. pap. text 17.95 (*1-56971-199-2*) Dark Horse Comics.

— Age of Reptiles: Tribal Warfare. (Illus.). 128p. 1996. pap. 14.95 (*1-56971-101-1*) Dark Horse Comics.

Delgado, Richard. The Coming Race War? And Other Apocalyptic Tales of America after Affirmative Action & Welfare. LC 96-7801. 280p. (C). 1996. text 30.00 (*0-8147-1877-9*) NYU Pr.

***Delgado, Richard.** Must We Defend Nazis? Hate Speech, Pornography & the New First Amendment. 1999. pap. text 20.00 (*0-8147-1923-6*) NYU Pr.

Delgado, Richard. The Rodrigo Chronicles: Conversations about America & Race. 275p. (C). 1995. text 40.00 (*0-8147-1863-9*) NYU Pr.

— The Rodrigo Chronicles: Conversations about America & Race. 275p. (C). 1996. pap. text 19.50 (*0-8147-1882-5*) NYU Pr.

— When Equality Ends: Stories about Race & Resistance. LC E185.615.D453 1999. 272p. 1999. 25.00 (*0-8133-3578-7*, Pub. by Westview) HarpC.

Delgado, Richard, ed. Critical Race Theory: The Cutting Edge. 664p. (C). 1995. pap. text 29.95 (*1-56639-348-5*); lib. bdg. 79.95 (*1-56639-347-7*) Temple U Pr.

Delgado, Richard & Stefancic, Jean. Critical White Studies: Looking Behind the Mirror. LC 96-46408. 592p. (C). 1997. 59.95 (*1-56639-531-3*); pap. text 29.95 (*1-56639-532-1*) Temple U Pr.

— Must We Defend Nazis? Hate Speech, Pornography, & the New First Amendment. 280p. (C). 1997. text 45.00 (*0-8147-1858-2*) NYU Pr.

Delgado, Richard & Stefancic, Jean, eds. Critical Race Theory: The Cutting Edge. 2nd ed. LC 99-20536. 704p. 2000. pap. 29.95 (*1-56639-714-6*) Temple U Pr.

***Delgado, Richard & Stefancic, Jean, eds.** Critical Race Theory: The Cutting Edge. 2nd ed. LC 99-20536. 704p. 2000. 79.50 (*1-56639-713-8*) Temple U Pr.

Delgado, Richard & Stefancic, Jean, eds. The Latinola Condition: A Critical Reader. LC 98-13514. 672p. 1998. text 75.00 (*0-8147-1894-9*); pap. text 25.00 (*0-8147-1895-7*) NYU Pr.

Delgado, Richard, jt. auth. see Stefaneic, Jean.

Delgado, Ruben. Music of Mexico Acoustic Guitar, Vol. 1. 56p. 1996. 19.95 incl. audio compact disk (*0-7866-2718-2*, 94863BCD) Mel Bay.

***Delgado, Ruben.** Music of Mexico for Acoustic Guitar, Vol. 2. 48p. 1998. pap. 19.95 incl. audio compact disk (*0-7866-4504-0*, 95347BCD) Mel Bay.

— Music of Mexico for Acoustic Guitar, Vol. 3. 40p. 1997. pap. 17.95 incl. audio compact disk (*0-7866-2566-6*, 96517BCD) Mel Bay.

Delgado-Sanchez, Joaquin. El Rumbo. LC 85-81208. (Coleccion Caniqui). (SPA.). 118p. (Orig.). 1986. pap. 9.95 (*0-89729-381-9*) Ediciones.

DelGaldo, Elisa M., jt. illus. see Prabhu, Girish V.

Delgatto, John, ed. see Griffin, Sid.

DelGaudio, Richard, jt. auth. see Lambers, Vincent.

Delgaudio, Richard A. Peril in Panama. (Illus.). 128p. 1998. write for info. (*0-9658348-1-6*) Nat Sec Ctr.

DelGaudio, Sybil. Dressing the Part: Sternberg, Dietrich, & Costume. LC 91-58953. (Illus.). 200p. 1993. 38.50 (*0-8386-3471-0*) Fairleigh Dickinson.

D'Elgin, Tershia. The Everything Bird Book. LC 98-7491. (Illus.). 304p. 1998. pap. 12.00 (*1-58062-061-2*) Adams Media.

Delgrado, David K. Health - How Americans Behave to Improve, Ignore or Ruin Their Best Planet Connection: Index of New Information with Authors, Subjects & References. (Illus.). 150p. 1996. 47.50 (*0-7883-1338-X*); pap. 44.50 (*0-7883-1339-8*) ABBE Pubs Assn.

Delgrossi, Luca. Design of Reservation Protocols for Multimedia Communication. LC 95-45773. 312p. (C). 1996. text 127.00 (*0-7923-9669-3*) Kluwer Academic.

Delguerra, Ronaldo. Diccionari Catala-Italia, Italia-Catala. (CAT & ITA.). 288p. 1990. pap. 11.95 (*0-7859-6471-1*) Fr & Eur.

Delhaes, P. & Drillon, M., eds. Organic & Inorganic Low-Dimensional Crystalline Materials. LC 87-28561. (NATO ASI Series B, Physics: Vol. 168). (Illus.). 496p. 1988. 125.00 (*0-306-42783-4*, Plenum Trade) Perseus Pubng.

Delhaes, P. & Kuzmany, H., eds. Fullerenes & Carbon Based Materials: Proceedings of Symposium A; Fullerenes & Carbon Based Materials, Strasbourg, France, June 1997. LC 99-183421. 376p. 1998. 278.50 (*0-444-20512-8*) Elsevier.

Delhaise, Philippe. Asia in Crisis: The Implosion of the Banking & Finance Systems LC 98-42024. 1998. write for info. (*0-471-83450-5*) Wiley.

— Asia in Crisis: What Went Wrong & Why. LC 98-42024. 292p. 1998. 34.95 (*0-471-83193-X*) Wiley.

Delhalle, Joseph, jt. auth. see Defranceschi, Mireille.

Delhaye, Jean-Marc, et al, eds. Multiphase Science & Technology, Vol. 2. (International Centre for Heat & Mass Transfer Ser.). (Illus.). 479p. 1986. 115.00 (*0-89116-282-8*) Hemisp Pub.

Delherbe, Nicole. Thesaurus du Cemagref, 3 vols. Incl. Vol. 1. Liste Alphabetique Globale. 242p. 1992. pap. 75.00 (*0-7859-5654-9*, 2853623149); Vol. 2. Liste Thematique. 205p. 1992. pap. 75.00 (*0-7859-5655-7*, 2853623157); Vol. 3. Index Permute. 345p. 1992. pap. 75.00 (*0-7859-5656-5*, 2853623165); 792p. 1992. Set pap. 225.00 (*0-7859-5653-0*, 2853623130) Fr & Eur.

Delheure, Jean. Dictionnaire Mozabite-Francais. (FRE.). 1984. 125.00 (*0-7859-8080-6*, 2-85297-166-6) Fr & Eur.

Delhey, Norbert. Apollinaris Sidonius, Carm. 22: Burgus Pontii Leontii: Einleitung, Text und Kommentar. (Untersuchungen zur Antiken Literatur und Geschichte Ser.: Vol. 40). (GER.). x, 225p. 1993. lib. bdg. 90.80 (*3-11-013631-7*) De Gruyter.

Delhez, R. & Mittemeijer, E. J., eds. EPDIC 1 - European Powder Diffraction. 960p. 1992. text 350.00 (*0-87849-634-3*, Pub. by Trans T Pub) Enfield Pubs NH.

— European Powder Diffraction, 2 vols., Set. 5th ed. (Materials Science Forum Ser.: Vol. 278-281). (Illus.). 1008p. 350.00 (*0-87849-807-9*, Pub. by Trans T Pub) Enfield Pubs NH.

— European Powder Diffraction: EPDIC 3, 2 Vols. (Materials Science Forum Ser.: Vol. 166-169). (Illus.). 866p. (C). 1994. 350.00 (*0-87849-682-3*, Pub. by Trans T Pub) Enfield Pubs NH.

***Delhez, R. & Mittemeijer, E. J., eds.** European Powder Diffraction: EPDIC 6, 2 vols. (Materials Science Forum Ser.: Vols. 321-324). (Illus.). 1232p. (C). 2000. text 350.00 (*0-87849-847-8*, Pub. by Trans T Pub) Enfield Pubs NH.

Delhez, R. & Mittermeijer, E. J., eds. European Powder Diffraction EPDIC2. 1110p. 1993. 350.00 (*0-87849-661-0*, Pub. by Trans T Pub) Enfield Pubs NH.

Del'Homme, Melissa. Counting & Quantity Workbook. (Tutor Bks.). (Illus.). 80p. (YA). (gr. k up). 1999. pap., wbk. ed. 8.95 (*1-56565-847-7*, 08477W, Pub. by Lowell Hse Juvenile) NTC Contemp Pub Co.

Delhomme, Melissa. Letter Recognition Workbook: Lowercase Letters. (Tutor Bks.). (Illus.). 96p. (YA). (gr. k up). 1997. pap. 8.95 (*1-56565-760-8*, 07608W, Pub. by Lowell Hse) NTC Contemp Pub Co.

***Del'Homme, Melissa.** Letter Recognition Workbook: Uppercase & Lowercase Letters. (Tutor Bks.). (Illus.). 160p. (YA). (ps up). 2000. pap. 12.95 (*0-7373-0455-3*, 04553W, Pub. by Lowell Hse Juvenile) NTC Contemp Pub Co.

Del'Homme, Melissa. Number Recognition Workbook. (Tutor Bks.). (Illus.). 80p. (YA). (gr. k up). 1998. pap., wbk. ed. 8.95 (*1-56565-849-3*, 08493W, Pub. by Lowell Hse Juvenile) NTC Contemp Pub Co.

Delhougne, Henri, ed. see Sartore, Domenico & Triacca, Achille M.

Delhoyd, Mary. Alternatives in Retrospect: An Historical Overview 1969-1975. LC 81-81185. (Illus.). 52p. (Orig.). 1996. pap. 4.00 (*0-614-18079-1*) New Mus Contemp Art.

D'Elia, Anthony A., Jr. By Choice: The Right School for Your Child! LC 84-91015. 70p. (Orig.). 1984. pap. 6.00 (*0-9613749-1-8*) Personal Assocs.

D'Elia, Anthony N. The Adirondack Rebellion. (Illus.). 1979. text 10.00 (*0-686-25749-9*) Onchiota Bks.

Delia, Diana. Alexandrian Citizenship During the Roman Principate. (American Philological Association, American Classical Studies). 222p. (C). 1991. pap. 19.95 (*1-55540-526-6*, 400423) OUP.

D'Elia, Donald. The Spirits of '76: A Catholic Inquiry. 182p. (Orig.). 1983. pap. 4.95 (*0-931888-10-7*) Christendom Pr.

D'Elia, Donald J. & Krason, Stephen M., eds. We Hold These Truths, & More: Further Catholic Reflections on the American Proposition: Essays on the Political Philosophy of Father John Courtney Murray, S. J. LC 92-40082. 263p. 1993. pap. 11.98 (*0-940535-48-3*, UP148) Franciscan U Pr.

D'Elia, George. Outsourcing in Metropolitan Libraries. Urban Libraries Council Staff, ed. & illus. by. (Frequent Fast Facts Survey Ser.). 304p. 1999. pap. 45.00 (*1-885251-22-X*) Urban Libraries.

D'Elia, George & Rodger, Eleanor J. The Roles of the Public Library in Society: The Results of a National Survey (Final Report) 1993. pap. 29.50 (*0-614-29740-0*) Urban Libraries.

— The Roles of the Public Library in Society: The Results of a National Survey (Technical Appendix) 1993. pap. 10.00 (*0-614-29741-9*) Urban Libraries.

Delia, Oliva. Aprendiendo Guitarra a Traves de la Canciones. (SPA.). 1997. pap. text 12.98 (*968-15-0428-3*) Ed Mex.

Delia, Thomas J., ed. Fused Pyrimidines: Miscellaneous Fused Pyrimidines, Vol. 24, Vol. 24, Pt. 4, Miscellaneous Fused Pyrimidines. (Chemistry of Heterocyclic Compounds, a Series of Monographs: Vol. 24, Pt. 4). 336p. 1991. 425.00 (*0-471-80462-2*) Wiley.

***DeLia, Tony, et al.** The Essential Guide to PeopleSoft. (Illus.). 1100p. 2000. pap. 64.95 (*1-884777-92-9*, Pub. by Manning Pubns) IPG Chicago.

Deliasement, ed. see Maupassant, Guy de.

Delibes, Miguel. El Camino. (SPA.). pap. 14.95 (*84-233-1035-3*, Pub. by Destino) Continental Bk.

— Five Hours with Mario. Lopez-Morillas, Frances M., tr. from SPA. (Twentieth-Century Continental Fiction Ser.). 224p. 1988. text 41.00 (*0-231-06828-X*) Col U Pr.

— The Hedge. Lopez-Morillas, Frances M., tr. from SPA. LC 83-7567. (Twentieth-Century Continental Fiction Ser.). 160p. 1983. text 57.50 (*0-231-05460-2*) Col U Pr.

— The Hedge. Lopez-Morillas, Frances M., tr. from SPA. LC 83-7567. (Twentieth-Century Continental Fiction Ser.). 160p. 1987. pap. text 17.50 (*0-231-05461-0*) Col U Pr.

— Los Santos Inocentes. 1997. pap. text 8.00 (*84-08-02047-1*) Planeta Editorial.

***Delibes, Miguel.** Los Ninos. 1999. pap. 9.95 (*84-08-02902-9*) Planeta Edit.

Delibes, Miguel. Los Santos Inocentes. (SPA.). 176p. 1993. pap. 14.95 (*0-7859-0509-X*, 8408000187) Fr & Eur.

Delic, George & Wheeler, Mary F., eds. Next Generation Environmental Models & Computational Methods. LC 96-71103. (Proceedings in Applied Mathematics Ser.: No. 87). (Illus.). xii, 375p. 1997. pap. 69.50 (*0-89871-378-1*, PR87) Soc Indus-Appl Math.

Delicado, Francisco. La Lozana Andaluza. (Nueva Austral Ser.: Vol. 38). (SPA.). 1991. pap. text 24.95 (*84-239-1838-6*) Elliots Bks.

— Portrait of Lozana: The Lusty Andalusian Woman. Damiani, Bruno M., tr. 1987. 45.50 (*0-916379-41-8*) Scripta.

***Delich, Dave.** Reflections of God. LC 99-16892. 110p. 1999. 12.95 (*1-58051-066-3*) Sheed & Ward WI.

Delicio, Roland. Merda! The Real Italian You Were Never Taught at School. LC 93-7731. (Illus.). 96p. 1993. pap. 10.95 (*0-452-27039-1*, Plume) Dutton Plume.

Delicostopoulos. English-Greek & Greek-English Dictionary of Law, Economic, Business & Management Terms. 2nd ed. (ENG & GRE.). 245p. 1989. 150.00 (*0-7859-9049-6*) Fr & Eur.

— Multilingual Dictionary of Banking-Commercial & Financial Terms: Greek, English, German, French, Italian. (ENG, FRE, GER, GRE & ITA.). 300p. 1991. vinyl bd. 95.00 (*0-7859-9048-8*) Fr & Eur.

Deliege, Irene & Sloboda, John A., eds. Musical Beginnings: Origins & Development of Musical Competence. (Illus.). 238p. 1996. pap. text 29.95 (*0-19-852332-7*) OUP.

— Perception & Cognition of Music. LC 97-202027. (Illus.). xvii, 461p. 1997. write for info. (*0-86377-452-0*, Pub. by Psychol Pr) Taylor & Francis.

Deliege, Robert. The Untouchables of India. Scott, Nora, tr. from FRE. 288p. 1999. 65.00 (*1-85973-209-7*, Pub. by Berg Pubs); pap. 19.50 (*1-85973-214-3*, Pub. by Berg Pubs) NYU Pr.

DeLien, Horace P. Cry of the Goosed: The Sacred & Profane Memories of a Public Servant. DeLien, Luz, ed. (Illus.). 164p. 1996. pap. 14.95 (*1-880470-43-8*) Creative Des.

DeLien, Luz, ed. see DeLien, Horace P.

Deligdisch, L., jt. auth. see Altcheck, A.

Deligdisch, Liane, et al. Atlas of Ovarian Tumors. LC 93-27160. (Illus.). 192p. 1994. 95.00 (*0-89640-240-1*) Igaku-Shoin.

Deligiorgis, Stavros, tr. see Valtinos, Thanases.

D

Deligiorgis, Stavros, tr. see Valtinos, Thanassis.

Deligne, P., et al. Hodge Cycles, Motives, & Shimura Varieties. (Lecture Notes in Mathematics Ser.: Vol. 900). 414p. 1989. pap. 55.95 (*0-387-11174-3*) Spr-Verlag.

Deligne, P., ed. see International Summer School, University of Antwerp.

Deligne, Pierre. Quantum Fields & Strings: A Course for Mathematicians. LC 99-20755. 1999. write for info. (*0-8218-1988-7*) Am Math.

Deligne, Pierre & Mostow, G. Daniel. Commensurabilities among Lattices in PU (1,n) (Annals of Mathematics Studies: No. 132). 176p. 1993. text 69.50 (*0-691-03385-4*, Pub. by Princeton U Pr); pap. text 35.00 (*0-691-00096-4*, Pub. by Princeton U Pr) Cal Prin Full Svc.

Deligny, Annick. Resins for Surface Coatings. 295.00 (*0-471-97897-3*) Wiley.

Deligny, Annick, tr. see Brown, Christopher.

Delijska, B. & Manoilov, P. Dictionary of Communications: In English, German, French & Russian. LC 97-31148. (ENG, FRE, GER & RUS., Illus.). 1054p. 230.00 (*0-444-82439-1*) Elsevier.

Delijska, B., jt. compiled by see Peeva, K.

Delilah. Love Someone Today: Stories of Encouragement & Inspiration for the Times of Our Lives. Date not set. write for info. (*0-7432-1078-6*) S&S Trade.

Delile, M. Fragments D'une Flore de L'Arabie Petree, 1833. 1987. 195.00 (*0-7855-2030-9*, Pub. by Scientific) St Mut.

Delille, Edward. Some French Writers. LC 78-37526. (Essay Index Reprint Ser.). 1977. reprint ed. 20.95 (*0-8369-2543-2*) Ayer.

***Delillo.** Advanced Java. 2002. pap. 38.00 (*0-534-37784-X*) Thomson Learn.

DeLillo, Don. Americana. 388p. 1989. pap. 13.95 (*0-14-011948-5*, Penguin Bks) Viking Penguin.

***DeLillo, Don.** The Body Artist. 2001. 22.00 (*0-7432-0395-X*) Scribner.

DeLillo, Don. The Day Room: A Play. 1988. pap. 5.25 (*0-8222-0278-6*) Dramatists Play.

— The Day Room: A Play. 112p. 1989. pap. 8.95 (*0-14-048229-6*) Viking Penguin.

— End Zone. (Contemporary American Fiction Ser.). 256p. 1986. pap. 12.95 (*0-14-008568-8*, Penguin Bks) Viking Penguin.

— Great Jones Street. 1983. pap. 7.95 (*0-394-71718-X*) Random.

DeLillo, Don. Great Jones Street. 1989. pap. 13.00 (*0-679-72303-X*) Random.

DeLillo, Don. Great Jones Street. 272p. 1994. pap. 10.95 (*0-14-017917-8*) Random.

— Libra. (Contemporary American Fiction Ser.). 464p. 1991. pap. 13.95 (*0-14-015604-6*, Penguin Bks) Viking Penguin.

— Mao II. 256p. 1992. pap. 12.95 (*0-14-015274-1*, Penguin Bks) Viking Penguin.

DeLillo, Don. The Names. (Vintage Contemporaries Ser.). 1989. pap. 13.00 (*0-679-72295-5*) Vin Bks.

DeLillo, Don. Players. (Vintage Contemporaries Ser.). 1989. pap. 12.00 (*0-679-72293-9*) Random.

— Ratner's Star. (Vintage Contemporaries Ser.). 1989. pap. 15.00 (*0-679-72292-0*) Random.

— Running Dog. (Vintage Contemporaries Ser.). 1989. pap. 14.00 (*0-679-72294-7*) Vin Bks.

— Underworld. LC 97-13825. 832p. 1997. 27.50 (*0-684-84269-6*) S&S Trade.

— Underworld. LC 97-13825. 832p. 1998. pap. 16.00 (*0-684-84815-5*) S&S Trade.

***DeLillo, Don.** Valparaiso: A Play. 112p. 2000. pap. 10.00 (*0-684-86568-8*, Touchstone) S&S Trade Pap.

DeLillo, Don. Valparaiso: A Play. LC 99-10488. 96p. 1999. 18.00 (*0-684-86421-5*) Scribner.

— White Noise. LC 85-12097. (Contemporay American Fiction Ser.). 326p. 1986. pap. 12.95 (*0-14-007702-2*) Viking Penguin.

— White Noise. 336p. (C). 2000. pap. 13.95 (*0-14-028330-7*) Viking Penguin.

— White Noise: Text & Critism. Osteen, Mark, ed. LC 98-28815. 544p. 1998. pap. 16.95 (*0-14-027498-7*) Viking Penguin.

DeLillo, Nicholas J., jt. auth. see Mallozzi, John S.

DeLima, Clara R. Tomorrow Will Always Come. 1965. 12.95 (*0-8392-1141-4*) Astor-Honor.

DeLima, Frank. Frank DeLima's Joke Book. (Illus.). 112p. 1991. pap. 9.95 (*0-935848-97-5*) Bess Pr.

Delin, Kevin A., jt. auth. see Orlando, Terry P.

Delin, Marilyn, ed. see Castleman, Vivian Rochelle Grant.

Delince, Guy. The Ecology of the Fish Pond Ecosystem with Special Reference to Africa. 248p. (C). 1992. text 236.00 (*0-7923-1628-2*) Kluwer Academic.

***Delind, Rahomme.** Lasonya: A Vestige of Western Intrusions. LC 99-91081. 324p. 1999. 25.00 (*0-7388-0598-X*); pap. 18.00 (*0-7388-0599-8*) Xlibris Corp.

Delinksy, Barbara. Sweet Ember. 240p. 1997. mass mkt. 5.99 (*0-06-101098-7*, Harp PBks) HarpC.

Delinois, Georgette, tr. see Fuller, Louisia.

***Delinsky, Barbara.** Ambicion Sin Limites. (SPA.). 512p. 2000. pap. 9.50 (*0-553-06127-5*) Bantam.

Delinsky, Barbara. Barbara Delinsky: Three Complete Novels. LC 93-10982. 848p. 1993. 10.99 (*0-517-09383-9*) Random Hse Value.

— Bronze Mystique. 1992. mass mkt. 4.50 (*0-373-83252-4*, 1-83252-6) Harlequin Bks.

— Bronze Mystique. (Mira Bks.). 1997. per. 5.50 (*1-55166-423-2*, 1-66423-4, Mira Bks) Harlequin Bks.

***Delinsky, Barbara.** Bronze Mystique. LC 00-39682. 2000. pap. write for info. (*0-7838-9047-8*, G K Hall & Co) Mac Lib Ref.

Delinsky, Barbara. Cardinal Rules. LC 96-547. (Mira Bks.). 249p. 1995. per. 4.99 (*1-55166-068-7*, 1-66068-7, Mira Bks) Harlequin Bks.

— The Carpenter's Lady. 304p. 1993. mass mkt. 6.99 (*0-06-104231-5*, Harp PBks) HarpC.

— The Carpenter's Lady. large type ed. LC 95-23554. (Large Print Bks.). 1995. pap. 21.95 (*1-56895-244-9*) Wheeler Pub.

***Delinsky, Barbara.** Carpenter's Lady, The, NEW EDITION. 336p. 1999. mass mkt. 6.99 (*0-06-103024-4*) HarpC.

Delinsky, Barbara. Chances Are. 1992. per. 4.50 (*0-373-83250-8*, 1-83250-0) Harlequin Bks.

— Chances Are. (Mira Bks.). 1998. per. 5.50 (*1-55166-447-X*, 1-66447-3, Mira Bks) Harlequin Bks.

***Delinsky, Barbara.** Chances Are. large type ed. LC 00-23439. (Famous Authors Ser.). 307p. Date not set. 27.95 (*0-7862-2593-9*, MML06400-172150) Thorndike Pr.

Delinsky, Barbara. Coast Road. Date not set. pap. 6.99 (*0-671-02604-6*) S&S Trade.

***Delinsky, Barbara.** Coast Road. LC 98-24113. 365p. 1998. write for info. (*0-684-85575-5*) S&S Trade.

Delinsky, Barbara. Coast Road. LC 98-24113. 368p. (YA). (gr. 10 up). 1998. 23.50 (*0-684-84576-8*) S&S Trade.

***Delinsky, Barbara.** Coast Road. large type ed. LC 98-39412. (Large Print Book Ser.). 1998. 26.95 (*1-56895-666-5*) Wheeler Pub.

Delinsky, Barbara. Coast Road. 480p. 1999. reprint ed. per. 7.50 (*0-671-02766-2*, Pocket Star Bks) PB.

— Commitments. 384p. 1988. mass mkt. 5.50 (*0-445-20600-4*, Pub. by Warner Bks) Little.

— Commitments. 384p. 1995. mass mkt. 7.50 (*0-446-60215-9*, Pub. by Warner Bks) Little.

***Delinsky, Barbara.** Commitments. 336p. 2001. 16.95 (*0-446-52725-4*) Warner Bks.

Delinsky, Barbara. Commitments. large type ed. LC 95-50391. (Large Print Ser.). 472p. 1995. lib. bdg. 23.95 (*1-57490-032-3*, Beeler LP Bks) T T Beeler.

— The Dream. (Temptation Ser.: No. 417). 1990. per. 2.65 (*0-373-25417-2*) Harlequin Bks.

— The Dream. LC 96-7350. (Mira Bks.). 250p. 1996. per. 5.50 (*1-55166-061-X*, Mira Bks) Harlequin Bks.

— The Dream Comes True. 1997. per. 5.50 (*1-55166-175-6*, 1-66175-0, Mira Bks) Harlequin Bks.

— The Dream Unfolds. 1996. per. 5.50 (*1-55166-161-6*, 1-66161-0, Mira Bks) Harlequin Bks.

— Dreams. 448p. 1999. pap. 12.95 (*1-55166-627-8*, Mira Bks) Harlequin Bks.

— Facets. 400p. 1990. mass mkt. 7.50 (*0-446-35945-9*, Pub. by Warner Bks) Little.

Delinsky, Barbara. Facets. large type ed. LC 96-29788. 1997. lib. bdg. 25.95 (*1-57490-115-X*, Beeler LP Bks) T T Beeler.

Delinsky, Barbara. Fast Courting. 272p. 1995. mass mkt. 5.99 (*0-06-100875-3*, Harp PBks) HarpC.

— Fast Courting. large type ed. LC 96-32965. (Star-Romance Ser.). 201p. 1997. 23.95 (*0-7862-0849-X*) Five Star.

— Fast Courting. large type ed. 316p. 1997. 26.95 (*0-7862-1111-3*) Thorndike Pr.

— Finger Prints. LC 96-29250. 421p. 1997. lib. bdg. 25.95 (*0-7862-0847-3*) Five Star.

— Finger Prints. 384p. 1988. spiral bd. 4.50 (*0-373-97087-0*) Harlequin Bks.

— Finger Prints. 496p. 1992. mass mkt. 6.99 (*0-06-104180-7*, Harp PBks) HarpC.

— First, Best, & Only. (Best of the Best Ser.). 1993. per. 4.50 (*0-373-83264-8*, 1-83264-1) Harlequin Bks.

— First Things First. 1992. mass mkt. 4.50 (*0-373-83249-4*, 1-83249-2) Harlequin Bks.

— For My Daughters. LC 94-2233. 416p. 1995. mass mkt. 6.99 (*0-06-109280-0*, Harp PBks) HarpC.

***Delinsky, Barbara.** Forever Yours. 1999. per. 12.95 (*0-373-83442-X*) Harlequin Bks.

Delinsky, Barbara. Fulfillment. 251p. 1995. per. 4.99 (*1-55166-026-1*, 1-66026-5, Mira Bks) Harlequin Bks.

— Gemstone. 288p. 1993. mass mkt. 5.50 (*0-06-104233-1*, Harp PBks) HarpC.

— Gemstone. large type ed. LC 95-38623. 254p. 1996. lib. bdg. 24.95 (*0-7838-1499-2*, G K Hall Lrg Type) Mac Lib Ref.

— Having Faith. (Temptation Ser.: No. 297). 1990. pap. 2.65 (*0-373-25397-4*) Harlequin Bks.

— Having Faith. 1997. per. 5.50 (*1-55166-271-X*, 1-66271-7, Mira Bks) Harlequin Bks.

— The Heart of the Night. 400p. 1989. mass mkt. 6.99 (*0-446-35477-5*, Pub. by Warner Bks) Little.

— The Heart of the Night. large type ed. LC 96-29611. 1996. lib. bdg. 24.95 (*1-57490-073-0*, Beeler LP Bks) T T Beeler.

— Heat Wave. (Best of the Best Ser.). (C). 1993. mass mkt. 4.50 (*0-373-83263-X*, 1-83263-3) Harlequin Bks.

— An Irresistible Impulse. 256p. 1995. mass mkt. 5.99 (*0-06-100876-1*, Harp PBks) HarpC.

— Lake News. 384p. 1999. 23.50 (*0-684-86432-0*) S&S Trade.

Delinsky, Barbara. Lake News. large type ed. LC 99-31498. 1950. 30.00 (*0-7838-8660-8*, G K Hall Lrg Type) Mac Lib Ref.

— Lake News. large type ed. LC 99-31498. 581p. 1999. 30.00 (*0-7838-8659-4*, G K Hall Lrg Type) Mac Lib Ref.

— Lake News. 544p. 2000. reprint ed. mass mkt. 7.99 (*0-671-03619-X*, Pocket Star Bks) PB.

Delinsky, Barbara. Moment to Moment. 352p. 1998. mass mkt. 6.99 (*0-06-101099-5*, Harp PBks) HarpC.

***Delinsky, Barbara.** Moment to Moment. 336p. 1999. 26.00 (*0-7278-2280-2*, Pub. by Severn Hse) Chivers N Amer.

Delinsky, Barbara. Moment to Moment. large type ed. LC 98-22070. (Large Print Book Ser.). 1998. 25.95 (*1-56895-580-4*) Wheeler Pub.

***Delinsky, Barbara.** Moment to Moment: Smith-Cameron,&J., Set. abr. ed. 1998. audio 18.00 (*0-694-51952-9*, CPN2736, Pub. by HarperAudio) Lndmrk Audiobks.

Delinsky, Barbara. Montana Man. LC 95-22355. 248p. 1995. per. 4.99 (*1-55166-077-6*, 1-66077-8, Mira Bks) Harlequin Bks.

— More Than Friends. 496p. 1993. mass mkt. 6.99 (*0-06-104199-8*, Harp PBks) HarpC.

— The Outsider. 1997. per. 5.50 (*1-55166-287-6*, 1-66287-3, Mira Bks) Harlequin Bks.

***Delinsky, Barbara.** The Outsider. LC 00-30291. 2000. write for info. (*0-7862-2617-X*) Thorndike Pr.

Delinsky, Barbara. Passion & Illusion. 256p. 1994. mass mkt. 5.99 (*0-06-104232-3*, Harp PBks) HarpC.

— Passion & Illusion. large type ed. LC 95-47629. (Large Print Bks.). 1996. 23.95 (*1-56895-278-3*) Wheeler Pub.

— The Passions of Chelsea Kane. 576p. 1992. mass mkt. 6.99 (*0-06-104093-2*, Harp PBks) HarpC.

— The Real Thing. 1994. mass mkt. 4.50 (*0-373-83277-X*, 1-83277-3) Harlequin Bks.

***Delinsky, Barbara.** The Real Thing. (Mira Bks.). 1998. per. 5.50 (*1-55166-438-0*, 1-66438-2, Mira Bks) Harlequin Bks.

Delinsky, Barbara. Rekindled. 400p. 1998. mass mkt. 6.99 (*0-06-101097-9*, Harp PBks) HarpC.

— Rekindled. LC 99-19125. 1999. 26.95 (*1-56895-707-6*) Wheeler Pub.

— Search for a New Dawn. LC 96-86055. (Five Star Romances Ser.). 1996. lib. bdg. 23.95 (*0-7862-0850-3*) Five Star.

— Search for a New Dawn. 1983. pap. 2.25 (*0-373-47449-0*, Harlequin) Harlequin Bks.

— Search for a New Dawn. 240p. 1995. mass mkt. 5.50 (*0-06-100874-5*, Harp PBks) HarpC.

— Secret of the Stone. 1992. per. 4.50 (*0-373-83251-6*, 1-83251-8) Harlequin Bks.

— Secret of the Stone. 256p. 1999. per. 5.99 (*1-55166-489-5*, Mira Bks) Harlequin Bks.

— Sensuous Burgundy. 272p. 1996. mass mkt. 5.99 (*0-06-101101-0*, Harp PBks) HarpC.

— Sensuous Burgundy. large type ed. LC 96-45009. 1996. pap. 22.95 (*1-56895-393-3*) Wheeler Pub.

— Shades of Grace. 464p. 1997. mass mkt. 6.99 (*0-06-109282-7*, Harp PBks) HarpC.

Delinsky, Barbara. A Single Rose. LC 97-10613. 249p. 1994. per. 4.50 (*0-373-83293-1*, 1-83293-0) Harlequin Bks.

Delinsky, Barbara. The Stud. (Temptation Ser.: No. 357). 1991. per. 2.95 (*0-373-25457-1*) Harlequin Bks.

***Delinsky, Barbara.** The Stud. 1999. per. 5.99 (*1-55166-518-2*, 1-66518-1, Mira Bks) Harlequin Bks.

Delinsky, Barbara. Suddenly. 480p. 1994. mass mkt. 6.99 (*0-06-104200-5*, Harp PBks) HarpC.

— Suddenly. large type ed. LC 94-13166. 567p. 1994. lib. bdg. 23.95 (*0-8161-7467-9*, G K Hall Lrg Type) Mac Lib Ref.

***Delinsky, Barbara.** Sweet Ember. 1999. 25.00 (*0-7278-5437-2*, Pub. by Severn Hse) Chivers N Amer.

Delinsky, Barbara. Sweet Ember. large type ed. LC 97-34581. (Large Print Bks.). 1997. pap. 23.95 (*1-56895-503-0*) Wheeler Pub.

— T. L. C. 256p. 1994. per. 4.99 (*1-55166-010-5*, 1-66010-9, Mira Bks) Harlequin Bks.

— Threats & Promises. (Best of the Best Ser.). 1993. per. 4.50 (*0-373-83262-1*, 1-83262-5) Harlequin Bks.

— Three Wishes: A Novel. 304p. 2000. per. 6.99 (*0-671-01665-2*) PB.

— Three Wishes: A Novel. LC 97-15217. 304p. 1997. 23.00 (*0-684-84507-5*) S&S Trade.

— Three Wishes: A Novel. large type ed. LC 97-36290. (Core Ser.). 1999. pap. 26.95 (*0-7838-8316-1*, G K Hall & Co) Mac Lib Ref.

— Through My Eyes. 248p. 1995. per. 4.99 (*1-55166-039-3*, 1-66039-8, Mira Bks) Harlequin Bks.

— A Time to Love. 256p. 1996. mass mkt. 5.99 (*0-06-101100-2*, Harp PBks) HarpC.

— A Time to Love. large type ed. LC 97-9212. (Large Print Book Ser.). 1997. pap. 22.95 (*1-56895-433-6*) Wheeler Pub.

— Together Alone. 512p. 1996. mass mkt. 6.99 (*0-06-109281-9*) HarpC.

— Twelve Across. 1994. per. 4.50 (*0-373-83290-7*, 1-83290-6) Harlequin Bks.

— Twelve Across. 2000. per. 6.99 (*1-55166-579-4*) Harlequin Bks.

— Twilight Whispers. 416p. 1989. mass mkt. 5.50 (*0-445-20968-2*, Pub. by Warner Bks) Little.

— Twilight Whispers. 416p. 1994. mass mkt. 7.50 (*0-446-60079-2*, Pub. by Warner Bks) Little.

— Twilight Whispers. 416p. 1998. mass mkt. 3.99 (*0-446-60686-3*, Pub. by Warner Bks) Little.

***Delinsky, Barbara.** Twilight Whispers. 2001. write for info. (*0-446-52702-5*) Warner Bks.

Delinsky, Barbara. Twilight Whispers. large type ed. LC 96-2653. 496p. 1996. lib. bdg. 24.95 (*1-57490-061-7*, Beeler LP Bks) T T Beeler.

— Variation on a Theme. 304p. 1994. mass mkt. 5.50 (*0-06-104234-X*, Harp PBks) HarpC.

Delinsky, Barbara. Variation on a Theme. 288p. 26.00 (*0-7278-5513-1*) Severn Hse.

Delinsky, Barbara. Variation on a Theme. large type ed. LC 96-11050. 1996. 24.95 (*1-56895-316-X*) Wheeler Pub.

***Delinsky, Barbara.** The Vineyard: A Novel. 592p. 2000. 24.50 (*0-7432-0426-3*) S&S Trade.

— The Vineyard: A Novel. LC 00-37311. 368p. 2000. 25.00 (*0-684-86484-3*) Simon & Schuster.

Delinsky, Barbara. Within Reach. LC 96-29251. (Star-Romance Ser.). 386p. 1997. 23.95 (*0-7862-0848-1*) Five Star.

— Within Reach. 400p. 1986. mass mkt. 3.95 (*0-373-97018-8*) Harlequin Bks.

— Within Reach. 528p. 1992. mass mkt. 6.99 (*0-06-104174-2*, Harp PBks) HarpC.

— A Woman Betrayed. 480p. 1991. mass mkt. 6.99 (*0-06-104034-7*, Harp PBks) HarpC.

— A Woman's Place. 416p. 1998. mass mkt. 7.50 (*0-06-109505-2*, Harp PBks) HarpC.

— A Woman's Place. large type ed. LC 97-15358. (Wheeler Large Print Book Ser.). 1997. 25.95 (*1-56895-446-8*) Wheeler Pub.

Delinsky, Barbara. Woman's Place, A Canadian edition. 1997. write for info. (*0-00-224564-7*) HarpC.

***Delinsky, Barbara & Roberts, Kelsey.** Father of the Bride, Handsome as Sin, 2 bks. 2000. mass mkt. 4.99 (*0-373-83453-5*, 1834530) Harlequin Bks.

Delinsky, Barbara & Stevens, Amanda. Harlequin 50th Anniversary Collection, 2 bks. in 1, No. 3. 1999. per. 6.99 (*0-373-83411-X*, 1-83411-8, Harlequin) Harlequin Bks.

Delinsky, Barbara, et al. Expecting! 1996. per. 5.99 (*0-373-20125-7*, 1-20125-0) Harlequin Bks.

***Delinsky, Barbara, et al.** Forever Yours: Threats & Promises; The Aristocrat; Loving Evangeline, 3 bks. 2001. pap. 12.95 (*0-373-83460-8*, 1-83460-5) Harlequin Bks.

Delinsky, Barbara, et al. Forever Yours: Threats & Promises; The Aristocrat; MacKenzie's Mountain, 3 bks. (Harlequin Promotion Ser.). 1997. per. 9.99 (*0-373-83353-9*, 1-8353-2) Harlequin Bks.

— Heart & Soul. (Promo Ser.). 1998. per. 9.99 (*0-373-83401-2*, 1-83401-9) Harlequin Bks.

***Delinsky, Barbara, et al.** Impulse. 1999. per. 9.99 (*0-373-83432-2*) Harlequin Bks.

***Delio, Ilia.** The Burning Love of the Crucified: Bonaventure's Mysticism of the Crucified Christ. 268p. 1998. pap. 15.95 (*0-8199-0988-2*) Franciscan Pr.

Delio, Sherry A. & Hein, George. The Making of an Efficient Physician. 110p. 1987. 7.00 (*0-89970-042-X*, OP653895WE) AMA.

— The Making of an Efficient Physician. 100p. 1995. 52.50 (*1-56829-042-X*, 4694) Med Group Mgmt.

DeLio, Thomas. Circumscribing the Open Universe: Essays on John Cage, Morton Feldman, Christian Wolff, Robert Ashley, Alvin Lucier. 120p. (Orig.). (C). 1984. pap. text 15.00 (*0-8191-3748-0*) U Pr of Amer.

— The Music of Morton Feldman, 36. LC 95-24022. (Contributions to the Study of Music & Dance Ser.: Vol. 36). 260p. 1996. 65.00 (*0-313-29803-3*, Greenwood Pr) Greenwood.

Delire, Marcel. Immunoglobulins: Rationale for the Clinical Use of Polyvalent Intravenous Immunoglobulins. LC 95-4162. 1995. 40.00 (*1-871816-29-7*, Pub. by Wrightson Biomed) Taylor & Francis.

Delis-Abrams, Alexandra. ABC Feelings: A Learning/Color Book/Audio Tape/Full Color Poster 22x28. 5th rev. ed. Follendore, Joan, ed. (Illus.). 64p. (J). (ps-5). 1993. pap. 21.95 (*1-879889-21-8*) Adage Pubns.

Delis-Abrams, Alexandra. ABC Feelings: A Learning Coloring Book/Audio Tape - 354 Word Feelings Awareness Chart. 5th rev. ed. Follendore, Joan, ed. (Illus.). 64p. (J). (ps-5). 1993. pap. 19.95 (*1-879889-15-3*) Adage Pubns.

— ABC Feelings: A Learning/Coloring Book. rev. ed. Follendore, Joan, ed. (Illus.). 64p. (J). (ps-4). 1991. reprint ed. pap. text 7.95 (*1-879889-00-5*) Adage Pubns.

— ABC Feelings: A Learning/Coloring Book & Companion 60 Minute Audio Tape. 5th rev. ed. Follendore, Joan, ed. (Illus.). 64p. (J). (ps-5). 1989. pap. 16.95 (*1-879889-04-8*) Adage Pubns.

— The Feelings Dictionary. 64p. 1999. pap. 7.95 (*1-879889-26-9*, ABC Feelings Inc) Adage Pubns.

— The Feelings Dictionary & Journal. 160p. 1999. pap. 14.95 (*1-879889-28-5*, ABC Feelings Inc) Adage Pubns.

— The Feelings Story Book: 26 Illustrated Feelings Stories. (Illus.). 32p. (J). (ps-k). 1998. pap. 9.95 (*1-879889-23-4*) Adage Pubns.

***Delis-Abrams, Alexandra.** Feelings Storybook, Vol. 1. 1998. pap. 14.95 (*1-879889-24-2*) Adage Bks.

Delisa, G., jt. auth. see Winsor, Phil.

DeLisa, James. Financial Accounting Flipper 1. 49p. 1990. 6.95 (*1-878383-25-6*) C Lee Pubns.

— Financial Accounting Flipper 2. 49p. (YA). (gr. 11 up). 1994. 6.95 (*1-878383-26-4*) C Lee Pubns.

— Managerial Accounting. 49p. (YA). (gr. 11 up). 1994. 6.95 (*1-878383-27-2*) C Lee Pubns.

DeLisa, Jeanette, ed. LeAnn Rimes - Blue. 52p. (Orig.). (YA). 1996. pap. text 16.95 (*1-57623-641-2*, PF9642) Wrner Bros.

DeLisa, Jeanette & Tucker, Dale, eds. Selections from Immortal Beloved. 44p. (Orig.). (YA). 1995. pap. text 17.95 (*0-89724-666-7*, PF9517) Wrner Bros.

DeLisa, Jeannette. Secada. (Illus.). 56p. (Orig.). (YA). 1997. pap. text 19.95 (*1-57623-986-1*, PF9717) Wrner Bros.

DeLisa, Jeanette, ed. Aaron Tippin: Lookin' Back at Myself. 44p. (Orig.). 1995. pap. text 14.95 (*0-89724-568-7*, PF9511) Wrner Bros.

— Alan Jackson: The Greatest Hits Collection. 88p. (Orig.). (YA). 1996. pap. text 19.95 (*1-57623-264-6*, PF9554); pap. text 24.95 (*1-57623-265-4*, PG9553) Wrner Bros.

— Albita: Dicen Que. (Illus.). 80p. (Orig.). 1997. pap. text 19.95 (*1-57623-890-3*, PF9651) Wrner Bros.

— Batman & Robin. 52p. (Orig.). (C). 1997. pap. text 16.95 (*0-7692-0163-6*, PF9725) Wrner Bros.

Delisa, Jeanette, ed. The Beach Boys: Made Easy for Piano. 52p. (Orig.). (C). 1989. pap. text 12.95 (*0-7692-0221-7*, P0825P2X) Wrner Bros.

An Asterisk (*) at the beginning of an entry indicates that the title is appearing for the first time.

DeLisa, Jeannette, ed. The Best of Tejano Music. 56p. (Orig.). (YA). 1996. pap. text 14.95 (*1-57623-434-7*, FB9601) Wrner Bros.

— The Best of the Samples. (Illus.). 168p. (Orig.). 1995. pap. text 24.95 (*0-89724-758-2*, PG9508) Wrner Bros.

— Bob Carlisle: Butterfly Kisses. 68p. (Orig.). 1997. pap. write for info. (*0-7692-0174-1*, PF9726) Wrner Bros.

— Bruce Springsteen: The Ghost of Tom Joad. 76p. 1996. pap. 19.95 (*1-57623-387-1*, PF9609) Wrner Bros.

— Bruce Springsteen Greatest Hits. 108p. (Orig.). (YA). 1996. pap. text 19.95 (*1-57623-275-1*, PF9541) Wrner Bros.

— Cachao: Master Sessions, Vol. 1. 88p. (YA). 1995. pap. text 24.95 (*0-89724-913-5*, PG9517) Wrner Bros.

— Country 'til I Die: John Anderson. 44p. (Orig.). (YA). 1995. pap. text 16.95 (*0-89724-537-7*, PF9502) Wrner Bros.

— Def Leppard - Hysteria. 128p. (Orig.). (YA). 1994. reprint ed. pap. text 18.95 (*0-89898-768-7*, P1062GTX) Wrner Bros.

Delisa, Jeannette, ed. Drum Techniques of Phil Collins. 76p. (Orig.). (C). 1986. pap. text 9.95 (*0-7692-0271-3*, DF0014) Wrner Bros.

DeLisa, Jeannette, ed. Everclear: Sparkes & Fade. (Illus.). 132p. (Orig.). 1996. pap. text 22.95 (*1-57623-499-1*, PG9624) Wrner Bros.

— Extreme/Waiting for the Punchline. (Illus.). 140p. (Orig.). (YA). 1995. pap. 21.95 (*0-89724-662-4*, PG9515) Wrner Bros.

— Garbage. 76p. (Orig.). (YA). 1996. pap. text 19.95 (*1-57623-476-2*, PG9626) Wrner Bros.

— Gill Vince: High Lonesome Sound. 44p. (Orig.). 1996. pap. 18.95 (*1-57623-530-0*, PF9626) Wrner Bros.

— Gill Vince: Souvenirs. 72p. (Orig.). (YA). 1996. pap. 18.95 (*1-57623-353-7*, PF9611) Wrner Bros.

— Gloria Estefan: Abriendo Puertas. 76p. (YA). 1995. pap. text 18.95 (*0-89724-977-1*, PF9537) Wrner Bros.

— Gloria Estefan: Destiny. 72p. (Orig.). 1996. pap. text 19.95 (*1-57623-523-8*, PF9623) Wrner Bros.

— Gloria Estefan: Mi Tierra. (Illus.). 96p. (Orig.). 1993. pap. 18.95 (*0-7692-0132-6*) Wrner Bros.

— Hanson/Middle of Nowhere. 68p. (Orig.). (C). 1997. pap. text 16.95 (*0-7692-0128-8*, 0095B) Wrner Bros.

— Jewel: Pieces of You. 60p. (Orig.). (YA). 1996. pap. text 19.95 (*1-57623-744-3*, PG9654) Wrner Bros.

— Jim Brickman: By Heart. (Illus.). 72p. (Orig.). 1996. pap. text 19.95 (*0-89724-802-3*, PF9542) Wrner Bros.

— Jim Brickman: Christmas Themes for Solo Piano. 24p. (Orig.). (YA). 1996. pap. text 9.95 (*1-57623-559-9*, PF9630) Wrner Bros.

— Jim Brickman: No Words. 80p. (YA). 1996. pap. text 19.95 (*1-57623-567-X*, PF9631) Wrner Bros.

— Jim Brickman: Picture This. (Illus.). 72p. (Orig.). (YA). 1997. pap. text 19.95 (*1-57623-884-9*, PF9704) Wrner Bros.

— John Anderson: Christmas Time. 32p. (Orig.). (YA). 1994. pap. text 14.95 (*0-7604-0071-7*, P1074SMX) Wrner Bros.

— John P. Kee: Colorblind. 76p. (Orig.). (YA). 1994. pap. text 14.95 (*0-7604-0015-6*) Wrner Bros.

— Jon Secada: Amor. (Illus.). 72p. (Orig.). 1996. pap. text 18.95 (*0-89724-926-7*, PF9543) Wrner Bros.

— Jon Secada: Heart, Soul & a Voice. 64p. (Orig.). (YA). (gr. 9-12). 1994. pap. text 14.95 (*0-89898-922-1*, P1071SMX) Wrner Bros.

— Jon Secada: Secada. 56p. 1997. pap. 19.95 (*0-7692-0122-9*, 0094B) Wrner Bros.

— Jon Secada: Si Te Vas. 56p. (Orig.). (YA). 1994. pap. text 14.95 (*0-910957-81-9*, P1083SMX) Wrner Bros.

— Juliana Hatfield: Only Everything. (Illus.). 68p. (Orig.). (YA). 1995. pap. text 18.95 (*0-89724-614-4*, PG9525) Wrner Bros.

— The Juliana Hatfield Three: Become What You Are. 56p. (Orig.). (YA). 1994. pap. text 17.95 (*0-89898-822-5*, P1033GTX) Wrner Bros.

Delisa, Jeannette, ed. Led Zeppelin. (Drum Superstar Ser.). 36p. (Orig.). (C). 1989. pap. text 12.95 (*0-7692-0696-4*, DF0028) Wrner Bros.

DeLisa, Jeannette, ed. Madonna: Bedtime Stories. (Illus.). 60p. (Orig.). 1995. pap. text 18.95 (*0-89724-505-9*, PF9507) Wrner Bros.

— Mark Knopfler - Guitar Styles, Vol. II. 104p. (Orig.). (YA). 1994. reprint ed. pap. text 19.95 (*0-89898-767-9*, P1065GTX) Wrner Bros.

— Melissa Etheridge. (Guitar Anthology Ser.). 128p. (YA). 1995. pap. text 22.95 (*0-89724-855-4*, PG9532) Wrner Bros.

— Melissa Etheridge: Your Little Secret. (Illus.). 80p. (Orig.). 1996. pap. text 19.95 (*0-89724-667-5*, PG9552) Wrner Bros.

— Nanci Griffith: Flyer. 96p. (Orig.). (YA). 1994. pap. text 16.95 (*0-89724-462-1*, P1086GTX) Wrner Bros.

— The New Best of Stevie Wonder. 96p. (Orig.). (YA). 1996. pap. text 12.95 (*1-57623-614-5*, PF9646) Wrner Bros.

— The New Life Community Choir Featuring John P. Kee: Show Up! 88p. (YA). 1995. pap. text 16.95 (*0-89724-923-2*, PF9531) Wrner Bros.

Delisa, Jeannette, ed. Nunsense Country Western Jamboree. 92p. (Orig.). (C). 1996. pap. text 16.95 (*1-57623-605-6*, PF9632) Wrner Bros.

DeLisa, Jeannette, ed. Paul Jefferson. 44p. (Orig.). (YA). 1996. pap. text 17.95 (*1-57623-574-2*, PF9636) Wrner Bros.

— The Rembrandts LP. (Illus.). 88p. (Orig.). 1995. pap. text 18.95 (*0-89724-768-X*, PF9518) Wrner Bros.

— Richard Marx: Paid Vacation. 60p. (Orig.). 1994. pap. 14.95 (*0-89898-915-9*, P1066SMX) Wrner Bros.

— Shania Twain: The Woman in Me. 56p. (Orig.). (YA). 1996. pap. text 18.95 (*1-57623-257-3*, PF9544) Wrner Bros.

— Sheryl Crow: Guitar. (Illus.). 124p. (Orig.). 1997. pap. text 22.95 (*1-57623-882-2*, 4847A) Wrner Bros.

— Sheryl Crow: Piano - Vocal - Chords. (Illus.). 72p. (Orig.). 1997. pap. text 19.95 (*1-57623-924-1*, 4846A) Wrner Bros.

Delisa, Jeannette, ed. The Songs of Berry Gordy: The Music, the Magic, the Memories of Motown. 236p. (Orig.). 1995. pap. 29.95 (*0-89724-721-3*, PF9510) Wrner Bros.

DeLisa, Jeannette, ed. Space Jam. 60p. (Orig.). (YA). 1996. pap. text 16.95 (*1-57623-695-1*, PF9657) Wrner Bros.

— Space Jam: Easy Piano Edition. 36p. (Orig.). (J). 1996. pap. text 12.95 (*1-57623-728-1*, AF96101) Wrner Bros.

— Stand! Victory in Praise Music & Arts Seminar Mass Choir. 52p. (Orig.). (YA). 1996. pap. text 16.95 (*1-57623-537-8*, PF9625) Wrner Bros.

— Stevie Wonder/Conversation Peace: Conversation Peace. 104p. (YA). 1995. pap. 19.95 (*0-89724-831-7*, PF9523) Wrner Bros.

— The Wallflowers/Bringing down the Horse. 72p. (YA). 1997. pap. 18.95 (*0-7692-0258-6*, 0133B) Wrner Bros.

— The Winans: All Out. 64p. (Orig.). (YA). 1994. pap. text 14.95 (*0-89898-784-9*, P1044SMX) Wrner Bros.

— The Winans: Heart & Soul. 88p. (Orig.). (YA). 1996. pap. text 18.95 (*1-57623-435-5*, PF9614) Wrner Bros.

Delisa, Jeannette, ed. The Wind Beneath My Wings Plus More Top of the Charts: Alto Sax. 24p. (Orig.). 1994. pap. 8.95 (*0-89724-188-6*, IF0428) Wrner Bros.

DeLisa, Jeannette, ed. Yesterday, Today, Tomorrow: The Greatest Hits of Kenny Loggins. 108p. (Orig.). (C). 1997. pap. text 14.95 (*0-7692-0076-1*, PF9721) Wrner Bros.

Delisa, Jeannette & Bryan, Colgan, eds. Blues Traveler: Four. 168p. (Orig.). (YA). 1995. pap. text 24.95 (*0-89724-584-9*, PG9506) Wrner Bros.

DeLisa, Jeannette & Bryan, Colgan, eds. Bruce Springsteen Greatest Hits. 124p. (Orig.). (YA). 1996. pap. text 24.95 (*1-57623-301-4*, PG9547) Wrner Bros.

DeLisa, Jeannette & Feldman, Sy. The Bridges of Madison County. 40p. (Orig.). 1995. pap. text 16.95 (*0-89724-887-2*, PF9540) Wrner Bros.

DeLisa, Jeannette & Feldman, Sy, eds. Batman & Robin: Souvenir Collector's Edition. 36p. (Orig.). 1997. pap. text 9.95 (*0-7692-0045-1*) Wrner Bros.

— Selections from Romeo & Juliet. (Illus.). 60p. (Orig.). 1997. pap. text 18.95 (*0-7692-0019-2*) Wrner Bros.

— Twister: Music from the Motion Picture Soundtrack. 52p. (Orig.). (YA). 1996. pap. text 16.95 (*1-57623-494-0*, PF9628) Wrner Bros.

DeLisa, Jeannette & Stang, Aaron, eds. Bruce Springsteen. (Guitar Anthology Ser.). 100p. (Orig.). (YA). 1996. pap. text 22.95 (*1-57623-601-3*, PG9621) Wrner Bros.

— Eels: Beautiful Freak. 64p. 1997. pap. text 19.95 (*1-57623-613-7*, PG9662) Wrner Bros.

— Poison. (Guitar Anthology Ser.). 116p. (Orig.). (YA). 1995. pap. text 19.95 (*0-89898-913-2*, P1054GTX) Wrner Bros.

— Testament: Low. 156p. (Orig.). (YA). 1995. pap. text 24.95 (*0-89724-461-3*, P1090GTX) Wrner Bros.

DeLisa, Jeannette, jt. ed. see Perez, Zobeida.

DeLisa, Jennette. The Wallflowers: Bringing down the House. 72p. (Orig.). 1997. pap. text 21.95 (*1-57623-934-9*, 0019B) Wrner Bros.

DeLisa, Jennette, ed. Me & You & the Hits of Kenny Chesney. (Illus.). 44p. (Orig.). 1997. pap. text 16.95 (*1-57623-972-1*, PF9714) Wrner Bros.

DeLisa, Jennette & Stang, Aaron, eds. Shawn Colvin: A Few Small Repairs. (Illus.). 100p. (Orig.). 1997. pap. text 19.95 (*1-57623-956-X*, PG9702) Wrner Bros.

***DeLisa, Joel A., ed.** Gait Analysis in the Science of Rehabilitation. (Illus.). 112p. (C). 2000. reprint ed. pap. text 25.00 (*0-7567-0021-3*) DIANE Pub.

DeLisa, Joel A., et al, eds. Rehabilitation Medicine: Principles & Practice. 2nd ed. LC 92-49401. 1,264p. 1993. text 129.00 (*0-397-51262-7*) Lppncott W & W.

Delisa, Joel A. & Gans, Bruce M. Rehabilitation Medicine: Principles & Practice. 3rd ed. LC 97-49687. 1822p. 1998. text 149.00 (*0-7817-1015-4*) Lppncott W & W.

DeLisa, Joel A., et al. Manual of Nerve Conduction Velocity & Clinical Neurophysiology. 3rd ed. LC 93-21370. 512p. 1994. spiral bd. 49.95 (*0-7817-0138-4*) Lppncott W & W.

— Manual of Nerve Conduction Velocity & Somatosensory Evoked Potentials. 2nd fac. ed. LC 85-43145. 288p. pap. 89.30 (*0-7837-7272-6*, 204703300005) Bks Demand.

Delisa, Joel A., jt. auth. see Lee, Hang J.

DeLisa, Sue. Just the Two of Us. (Aesop's Fables Running Start Ser.). (Illus.). 32p. (J). (ps-2). 1997. pap. 4.95 (*1-890570-11-7*) Huckleberry CT.

— Something Special. LC 97-61033. (Aesop's Fables Running Start Ser.). (Illus.). 32p. (J). (gr. 2-4). 1997. pap. 4.95 (*1-890570-09-5*) Huckleberry CT.

— Who Cares? LC 97-61035. (Aesop's Fables Running Start Ser.). (Illus.). 32p. (J). (ps-2). 1997. pap. 4.95 (*1-890570-13-3*) Huckleberry CT.

Delise, Frank. 3D Studio Max 2 Effects Magic. LC 98-84784. 1998. pap. 49.99 (*1-56205-883-5*) New Riders Pub.

Delisi, Charles & Hiernaux, Jacques R., eds. Regulation of Immune Response Dynamics, 2 vols., Vol. I. 176p. 1982. 104.00 (*0-8493-6632-1*, QR186) Franklin.

— Regulation of Immune Response Dynamics, 2 vols., Vol. II. 184p. 1982. 107.00 (*0-8493-6633-X*) Franklin.

***Delisi, Elizabeth.** Fatal Fortune. 1998. 5.50 (*1-892745-10-0*) Petals of Life.

Delisi, Elizabeth. Fatal Fortune. (Illus.). 150p. 1998. pap. 10.95 (*1-892745-09-7*) Petals of Life.

***Delisi, Elizabeth.** Since All Is Passing. 220p. 1999. mass mkt. 5.50 (*1-929613-24-5*) Avid MI.

Delisi-Holmes, Lesa, ed. see Cowdrey, Mike.

DeLisi, Lynn E. Depression in Schizophrenia. LC 89-15170. (Progress in Psychiatry Ser.: No. 18). (Illus.). 76p. 1990. reprint ed. pap. 54.60 (*0-608-06653-2*, 206685000009) Bks Demand.

Delisle. Gifted Child Education: In Their Own Words. LC 98-88540. (C). 1999. pap. 40.50 (*0-15-503192-9*, Pub. by Harcourt Coll Pubs) Harcourt.

— Microbiology Apps. Hyperclinic. 1997. 40.00 (*0-697-38672-4*, WCB McGr Hill) McGrw-H Hghr Educ.

Delisle, Deb, jt. auth. see Delisle, Jim.

Delisle, Francoise, tr. see Scheikevitch, Marie.

Delisle, James, et al. The Muffs Peer Identification Instrument for Grades 2-5. 1984. pap., student ed. 15.00 (*0-89824-124-3*) Trillium Pr.

Delisle, Jean & Woodsworth, Judith, eds. Translators Through History. LC 95-49054. (Benjamins Translation Library: Vol. 13). xvi, 346p. 1995. pap. 31.95 (*1-55619-697-0*); lib. bdg. 85.00 (*1-55619-694-6*) J Benjamins Pubng Co.

***Delisle, Jean, et al.** Terminologie de la Traduction: Translation Terminology. LC 99-34507. (FIT Monograph Ser.: Vol. 1). (ENG, GER & SPA.). vi, 433p. 1999. 37.95 (*1-55619-212-6*) J Benjamins Pubng.

Delisle, Jim. Kidstories: Biographies of 20 Young People You'd Like to Know. LC 91-18363. (Self-Help for Kids Ser.). (Illus.). 176p. (J). (gr. 3 up). 1991. pap. 9.95 (*0-915793-34-2*) Free Spirit Pub.

Delisle, Jim & Delisle, Deb. Growing Good Kids: 28 Activities to Enhance Self-Awareness, Compassion, & Leadership. Lisovskis, Marjorie, ed. LC 96-32528. (Free Spirited Classroom Ser.). (Illus.). 168p. (Orig.). 1996. pap. 21.95 (*1-57542-009-0*) Free Spirit Pub.

Delisle, Jim, jt. auth. see Galbraith, Judy.

DeLisle, Lee J., jt. auth. see Shivers, Jay S.

Delisle, Leopold V. Le Cabinet Des Manuscrits De la Bibliotheque Imperiale. lvi, 1654p. 1978. reprint ed. write for info. (*3-487-06485-5*) G Olms Pubs.

— Inventaire des Manuscrits Latins Conserves a la Bibliotheque Nationale sous les Numeros 8823-18613. (Et Faisant Suite a la Serie Dont le Catalogue A Ete Publie en 1744 Ser.). xliii, 520p. 1974. reprint ed. write for info. (*3-487-05210-5*) G Olms Pubs.

— Inventaire General et Methodique des Manuscrits Francais de la Bibliotheque Nationale, 2 vols., Set. clix, 556p. 1974. reprint ed. write for info. (*3-487-05300-4*) G Olms Pubs.

***Delisle, Paul-Claude.** French & Belgian Immigrants to Northern Rhode Island. iii, 156p. 1999. spiral bd. 15.00 (*1-929920-09-1*) American French.

Delisle, Robert & Association for Supervision & Curriculum Developme. How to Use Problem-Based Learning in the Classroom. LC 97-43045. 107p. 1997. pap. 12.95 (*0-87120-291-3*, 197166) ASCD.

Delisle, Steve. The Equipment of New France Militia, 1740-1760. LC 99-72059. (Illus.). iii, 56p. 1999. pap. 14.95 (*0-9671085-0-0*) Kebeca Liber.

Delissen, Astrid J., ed. Humanitarian Law of Armed Conflict: Challenges Ahead. (C). 1991. lib. bdg. 204.00 (*0-7923-1335-6*) Kluwer Academic.

DeLisser, Peter. Be Your Own Executive Coach: Master High Impact Communications Skills. 154p. 1999. pap. 16.95 (*1-886284-44-X*, Pub. by Chandler Hse) Natl Bk Netwk.

Delisser, Richard Lionel. Picturesque Ulster. (Illus.). 300p. 1998. reprint ed. pap. 35.00 (*0-910746-01-X*, PU01) Hope Farm.

Delissio, Joseph. The River Cafe Wine Primer. LC 99-35577. (Illus.). 288p. 2000. 25.95 (*0-316-18592-2*) Little.

Delitala, Giuseppe, et al, eds. Opioid Modulation of Endocrine Function. LC 83-43121. (Frontiers in Neuroscience Ser.). (Illus.). 296p. 1984. reprint ed. pap. 91.80 (*0-608-00623-8*, 206121000007) Bks Demand.

Delitala Y Castelvi, Jose. Las Tres Ultimas Musas Castellanas. Saraceno, Louis, ed. LC 96-9607. (Currents in Comparative Romance Languages & Literatures Ser.: Vol. 39). (SPA., Illus.). LXVIII, 323p. (C). 1997. text 58.95 (*0-8204-3392-6*) P Lang Pubng.

Delittle, Cathy. Blue Sharks in My Bathtub. LC 98-93051. (Illus.). 10p. (J). (ps-1). 1998. spiral bd. 7.95 (*1-892633-02-7*, GOCD210) Delittle Story.

— I'd Like to Have a Worm. LC 98-93045. (Illus.). 10p. (J). (ps-1). 1998. spiral bd. 7.95 (*1-892633-08-6*, OOCD206) Delittle Story.

— If You See Some Elephants. LC 98-93043. (Illus.). 8p. (J). (ps-1). 1998. spiral bd. 7.95 (*1-892633-01-9*, OOCD202) Delittle Story.

— It's My Potty . . . I'll Cry If I Want To. LC 98-93046. (Illus.). 10p. (J). (ps-1). 1998. spiral bd. 7.95 (*1-892633-09-4*, OOCD208) Delittle Story.

— Jungle Parade. LC 98-93050. (Illus.). 11p. (J). (ps-1). 1998. spiral bd. 7.95 (*1-892633-03-5*, OOCD201) Delittle Story.

— Peanut Butter Bob. LC 98-93049. (Illus.). 9p. (J). (ps-1). 1998. spiral bd. 7.95 (*1-892633-00-0*, OOCD203) Delittle Story.

— Sleepytime Train. LC 98-93048. (Illus.). 12p. (J). (ps-1). 1998. spiral bd. 7.95 (*1-892633-04-3*, OOCD204) Delittle Story.

— The Squirrel Who Loved Picnics. LC 98-93047. (Illus.). 9p. (J). (ps-1). 1998. spiral bd. 7.95 (*1-892633-05-1*, OOCD209) Delittle Story.

— There's a Skunk in My Diaper. LC 98-93039. (Illus.). 10p. (J). (ps-1). 1998. spiral bd. 7.95 (*1-892633-06-X*, OOCD207) Delittle Story.

— What Do You See When You Sleep? Book-in-a-Bag. LC 98-93044. (Illus.). 16p. (J). (ps-1). 1998. spiral bd. 9.95 (*1-892633-07-8*, OOCD205) Delittle Story.

Delitto, A. Low Back Pain. (Monograph Ser.). 1998. pap. write for info. (*1-887759-62-X*) Am Phys Therapy Assn.

Delitzsch, F., jt. auth. see Keil, C. F.

Delitzsch, Franz. Messianic Prophecies in Historic Succession. 232p. 1997. pap. 20.00 (*1-57910-077-5*) Wipf & Stock.

Delius, Barbara, ed. The Practical Decorator & Ornamentalist. (ENG, FRE & GER.). 260p. 2000. 39.95 (*3-89508-228-7*) Konemann.

Delius, Frederick. Brigg Fair & Other Orchestral. 1997. 13.95 (*0-486-29851-5*, 741694Q) Dover.

Delius, Harald. Self-Awareness: A Semantical Inquiry. 276p. 1987. 87.00 (*3-406-07945-8*) Philosophia Pr.

Delius, Nikolaus. Die Tieck'sche Shakespeare-Kritik Beleuchtet. 41st ed. (GER.). xvi, 182p. 1981. write for info. (*3-487-07043-X*) G Olms Pubs.

Delius, Peter. A Lion Amongst the Cattle: Reconstruction & Resistance in the Northern Transvaal. LC 96-41888. (Heinemann Social History of Africa Ser.). 1997. 60.00 (*0-435-07416-4*); pap. 24.95 (*0-435-07415-6*) Heinemann.

Delius, Peter & Sommer, Ulrike, eds. The Story of Architecture. (Compact Knowledge Ser.). (Illus.). 120p. 1998. pap. 7.95 (*3-89508-204-X*, 520159) Konemann.

— The Story of Painting. (Compact Knowledge Ser.). (Illus.). 128p. 1998. pap. 7.95 (*3-89508-083-7*, 520039) Konemann.

— World Religions. (Compact Knowledge Ser.). (Illus.). 120p. 1998. pap. 7.95 (*3-89508-854-4*, 520303) Konemann.

Delius, Ramon E., tr. see De Aldama, Antonio M.

Deliusin, Lev. The Cultural Revolution in China. 1976. lib. bdg. 59.95 (*0-8490-1693-2*) Gordon Pr.

Delivanis, Demetre J. & Cleveland, William C. Greek Monetary Developments, 1939-1948: A Case Study of the Consequences of World War II for the Monetary System of a Small Nation. LC 49-47294. (Indiana University, Indiana University Publications, Social Science: No. 6). 196p. reprint ed. pap. 60.80 (*0-608-13657-3*, 205520600011) Bks Demand.

Deliyannis, T. & Haritantis, I. Continuous Time Active Filter Design. (Electronic Engineering Systems Ser.). 1999. 75.00 (*0-8493-7893-1*) CRC Pr.

Deliyannis, T., et al. Active Filter Design Continuous Time. LC 98-44774. (Electronic Engineering Systems Ser.). 464p. 1998. boxed set 94.95 (*0-8493-2573-0*, 2573) CRC Pr.

Deliz, Monserrate. Hymn of Puerto Rico: Critical Studies of "La Borinquena" (Puerto Rico Ser.). 1979. lib. bdg. 59.95 (*0-8490-2942-2*) Gordon Pr.

— Songs & Folklore of Puerto Rico. (Puerto Rico Ser.). 1979. lib. bdg. 59.95 (*0-8490-3007-2*) Gordon Pr.

Deliz, Osdila O., ed. see Ronnholm, Ursala O.

Deliz, Wenceslao S. Adios Falcon. LC 85-1116. (Ninos y Letras Ser.). (SPA., Illus.). 15p. (J). (ps-3). 1985. pap. 2.00 (*0-8477-3530-3*) U of PR Pr.

Deliz, Wenceslao S., jt. ed. see Ramirez, Rafael L.

Delizia. Ramba. 3rd ed. (Love & Rockets Ser: Vol. 29). pap. 13.95 (*1-56097-235-1*) Seven Hills Bk.

Delizia, et al. Ramba, Bk. 1. (Eros Graphic Novel Ser.: No. 15). 120p. 1995. pap. 16.95 (*1-56097-213-0*) Fantagraph Bks.

DeLizia, James & American Society of Association Executives Staff. National Chapter Partnership: A Guide for the Chapter Relations Professional. 335p. 1992. pap. text 85.95 (*0-88034-058-4*) Am Soc Assn Execs.

Delizsch, Franz, ed. see Wright, Charles H.

Delizy, Bernadette. For the Sake of the Kingdom: Vocation, Community & Mission in Religious Life. 112p. (C). 1996. pap. 39.95 (*0-85439-406-0*, Pub. by St Paul Pubns) St Mut.

Delk, Cheryl L. Discovering American Culture. LC 96-60160. 152p. (Orig.). 1997. pap. text 16.95 (*0-472-08359-7*, 08359); pap. text, teacher ed. 14.95 (*0-472-08378-3*, 08378) U of Mich Pr.

Delk, Cheryl L. Discovering American Culture. LC 96-60160. (Illus.). 152p. (Orig.). (C). 1997. audio 15.00 (*0-472-00258-9*, 00258) U of Mich Pr.

Delk, James D. The Fighting Fortieth: In War & Peace. LC 97-41814. (Illus.). xii, 436p. 1998. 29.95 (*0-88280-140-6*) ETC Pubns.

— Fires & Furies - The Los Angeles Riots of 1992: The Los Angeles Riots of 1992. LC 94-13804. (Illus.). xiv, 376p. 1995. 28.95 (*0-88280-123-6*) ETC Pubns.

Delk, Marcus, jt. auth. see Schein, Jerome.

Delk, Patsy. Enchanted Color of the S. W. (Illus.). 1998. pap. 10.50 (*1-56770-441-7*) S Scheewe Pubns.

Delkeskamp-Hayes, Corinna & Cutter, Mary A., eds. Science, Technology, & the Art of Medicine: European-American Dialogues. Moskop, Ruth W. & Engelhardt, S. G., trs. LC 92-18579. (Philosophy & Medicine Ser.: Vol. 44). 346p. (C). 1993. lib. bdg. 160.50 (*0-7923-1869-2*, Pub. by Kluwer Academic) Kluwer Academic.

***Dell.** Architectural Visualization Using Autocad. (Student Material TV Ser.). (C). 2001. pap. 45.00 (*0-7668-1106-9*) Delmar.

Dell. AutoCAD Management: Guide to Maximizing Efficiency. (CAD/CAM Ser.). (C). 2000. pap. text 36.75 (*0-7668-1108-5*) Delmar.

***Dell.** The Complete IIS Training Course. (C). 1999. text, student ed. 99.95 incl. disk (*0-13-087414-0*) P-H.

— Lis Interactive Training Course. (C). 1999. pap. 49.33 (*0-13-017619-2*) P-H.

Dell, Alan, jt. auth. see Gibson, J. S. W.

Dell, B., et al, eds. The Jarrah Forest: A Complex Mediterranean Ecosystem. (Geobotany Ser.). (C). 1988. text 354.00 (*90-6193-658-6*) Kluwer Academic.

Dell, B. International Symposium on Boron in Soils, et al. Boron in Soils & Plants: Reviews: Invited Review Papers for Boron97, the International Symposium on "Boron in Soils & Plants" Held at Chiang Mai, Thailand, 7-11 September, 1997. LC 97-33654. (Developments in Plants & Soil Sciences Ser.). 232p. 1997. text 140.50 (*0-7923-4729-3*) Kluwer Academic.

D

Dell, Carl W., Jr. Treating the School Age Stutterer: A Guide for Clinicians, No. 14. LC 79-67284. 110p. (Orig.). 1997. pap. 2.00 (*0-933388-11-X*) Stuttering Fnd Am.

Dell, Cecily. Primer for Movement Description Using Effort/Shape. 2nd rev. ed. LC 78-111086. 123p. 1970. pap. text 17.95 (*0-932582-03-6*) Dance Notation.

Dell, Cecily, et al. Space Harmony. rev. ed. (Illus.). 24p. (C). 1972. reprint ed. pap. text 6.95 (*0-932582-12-5*, Pub. by Dance Notation) Princeton Bk Co.

Dell, Charles E. & Schwartz, Wayne E. The Modern Schuetzen Rifle. (Illus.). xxix, 358p. 1996. 45.00 (*0-9653702-0-8*) Chuckan Indust.

***Dell, Charles E. & Schwartz, Wayne E.** Modern Schuetzen Rifle. 2nd rev. ed. 410p. 2000. 60.00 (*0-9653702-1-6*) Chuckan Indust.

Dell, Diana L., jt. auth. see Judelson, Debra R.

Dell, Edmund. A Hard Pounding: Politics & Economic Crisis, 1974-1976. 320p. 1991. text 39.95 (*0-19-828394-6*) OUP.

— The Schuman Plan & the British Abdication of Leadership in Europe. 338p. 1995. text 59.00 (*0-19-828967-7*) OUP.

Dell, Edmund, ed. see Hill, Christopher.

Dell, Edward T., Jr. Of Mockingbirds & Other Irrelevancies. LC 93-79273. 100p. 1993. 9.95 (*0-8338-0208-9*) Audio Amateur.

***Dell, Elizabeth.** Burma: Frontier Photographs. 2000. 50.00 (*1-85894-103-2*) Merrell Holberton.

Dell, Elizabeth. Evocations of the Child: Fertility Figures of the Southern African Region. LC 98-215131. 1999. 35.00 (*0-7981-3830-0*) Human & Rousseau.

Dell, Ethel M. The Bars of Iron. 1976. 27.95 (*0-8488-0259-4*) Amereon Ltd.

— House of Happiness: And Other Stories. LC 72-5866. (Short Story Index Reprint Ser.). 1977. reprint ed. 23.95 (*0-8369-4209-4*) Ayer.

— Hundredth Chance. 1976. 24.95 (*0-8488-0260-8*) Amereon Ltd.

— The Knave of Diamonds. 1975. lib. bdg. 21.50 (*0-89966-069-X*) Buccaneer Bks.

— Lamp in the Desert. 1976. 25.95 (*0-8488-0261-6*) Amereon Ltd.

— The Passerby: And Other Stories. LC 72-5867. (Short Story Index Reprint Ser.). 1977. reprint ed. 23.95 (*0-8369-4210-8*) Ayer.

— The Reason Why. 402p. reprint ed. lib. bdg. 27.95 (*0-88411-293-4*) Amereon Ltd.

— Rosa Mundi, & Other Stories. LC 79-121535. (Short Story Index Reprint Ser.). 1977. 24.95 (*0-8369-3491-1*) Ayer.

— Swindler & Other Stories. LC 72-140329. (Short Story Index Reprint Ser.). 1977. 23.95 (*0-8369-3721-X*) Ayer.

— The Way of an Eagle. 398p. reprint ed. lib. bdg. 27.95 (*0-88411-294-2*) Amereon Ltd.

Dell, Felder, ed. Competency Based Teacher Education: Professionalizing Social Studies Teaching. LC 78-58629. (National Council for the Social Studies Bulletin: 56). 128p. reprint ed. pap. 39.70 (*0-608-15114-9*, 202319100032) Bks Demand.

Dell, Floyd. Diana Stair. LC 74-26100. reprint ed. 49.50 (*0-404-58419-5*) AMS Pr.

— Floyd Dell: Essays from "The Friday Literary Review," 1909-13. Sautter, R. Craig, ed. LC 94-69575. 228p. 1995. pap. 25.00 (*0-913204-32-3*) December Pr.

— Intellectual Vagabondage. 276p. 1990. reprint ed. pap. text 9.95 (*0-929587-42-1*, Elephant Paperbacks) I R Dee.

— King Arthur's Socks & Other Village Plays. LC 77-70353. (One-Act Plays in Reprint Ser.). 1977. reprint ed. 20.00 (*0-8486-2014-3*) Roth Pub Inc.

— Love in Greenwich Village. LC 73-128730. (Short Story Index Reprint Ser.). 1977. 20.95 (*0-8369-3621-3*) Ayer.

— Upton Sinclair: A Study in Social Protest. LC 73-133826. reprint ed. 24.50 (*0-404-02076-3*) AMS Pr.

Dell, George. The Earth Abideth. LC 86-2494. 314p. 1999. pap. 17.00 (*0-8142-5014-9*) Ohio St U Pr.

Dell, Gina V. After the Garden of Eden. 1998. pap. write for info. (*1-58235-001-9*) Watermrk Pr.

Dell Hobbs, Barbara. Conquering Obstacles. 1998. pap. write for info. (*1-57553-822-9*) Watermrk Pr.

Dell, John D. Southern Arizona Trails Resource Guide: A Reference for Hikers, Mountain Bicyclists, Equestrian, & OHV Enthusiasts. 1998. pap. 9.95 (*0-9665003-0-X*) J D Dell.

Dell, Katharine, jt. ed. see Attfield, Robin.

Dell, Katharine J. The Book of Job As Sceptical Literature. (Beiheft zur Zeitschrift fuer die Alttestamentliche Wissenschaft Ser.: Vol. 197). (GER.). x, 259p. (C). 1991. lib. bdg. 80.00 (*3-11-012554-4*) De Gruyter.

***Dell, Katharine J.** Get Wisdom, Get Insight: An Introduction to Israel's Wisdom Literature. LC 99-53152. 192p. Date not set. 20.00 (*1-57312-315-3*) Smyth & Helwys.

Dell, Katharine J. Shaking a Fist at God: Struggling with the Mystery of Undeserved Suffering. LC 96-26517. 128p. (Orig.). 1997. pap. 9.00 (*0-7648-0030-2*, Liguori Triumph) Liguori Pubns.

Dell Magazine Editors, ed. The Dell Book of Logic Problems, No. 5. 176p. (Orig.). 1992. pap. 11.99 (*0-440-50298-5*, Dell Trade Pbks) Dell.

Dell Magazines Staff. Isaac Asimov's Moons: Seven Tales of Lunar Adventure. 236p. 1997. mass mkt. 5.99 (*0-441-00453-9*) Ace Bks.

Dell, Mary, jt. auth. see Boynton, Marilyn I.

***Dell, Michael.** Direct from Dell: Strategies That Revolutionized an Industry. 288p. 2000. 15.00 (*0-88730-915-1*, Hrpr Busn) HarpCollins.

— Direct From Dell: Strategies That Revolutionized an IndustryDell,&Michael, Set. abr. ed. 1999. audio 18.00 (*0-694-52023-3*, 394587, Pub. by HarperAudio) Lndmrk Audiobks.

Dell, Michael & Fredman, Catherine. Direct from Dell: Strategies That Revolutionized an Industry. LC 98-53437. (Illus.). 256p. 1999. 26.00 (*0-88730-914-3*, HarpBusn) HarpInfo.

***Dell Orto, Arthur E. & Power, Paul W.** Brain Injury & the Family: A Life & Living Perspective. 2nd ed. LC 99-89634. 256p. 2000. per. 44.95 (*0-8493-1325-2*) CRC Pr.

Dell Orto, Arthur E. & Power, Paul W. Head Injury & the Family: A Life & Living Perspective. LC 93-85847. 256p. 1994. per. 39.95 (*1-878205-61-7*) St Lucie Pr.

Dell Orto, Arthur E., jt. ed. see Marinelli, Robert P.

Dell, Owen E. How to Start a Home-Based Landscaping Business. 3rd ed. LC 99-41693. (How to Start a Home-Based Business Ser.). 336p. 2000. pap. text 17.95 (*0-7627-0516-7*) Globe Pequot.

***Dell, Patricia.** Zander. (Illus.). 12p. (J). (gr. k-6). 2000. pap. 10.00 (*0-9702221-0-6*) Zanderbooks.

***Dell, Peter M.** Laboratory Safety & Chemical Hygiene Compliance. 2nd rev. ed. 176p. 2000. ring bd. 199.00 incl. disk (*0-86587-691-6*, 691) Gov Insts.

Dell Publishers Staff, ed. Best of Dell Crossword Puzzles. 224p. 1990. pap. 10.99 (*0-440-50277-2*) Dell.

Dell Publishing Staff. American Heritage Dictionary. 3rd ed. 960p. 1994. mass mkt. 5.99 (*0-440-21861-6*) Dell.

Dell Puzzle Magazine Staff. Instant Reference, 3 vols., Set. 1991. boxed set 14.85 (*0-440-36035-8*) Dell.

Dell, Robert W. Presence & Power. (Covenant Bible Studies). 40p. (Orig.). 1991. pap. 4.95 (*0-87178-720-2*, 8202) Brethren.

Dell, Robert W. & Mundey, Paul E. Including & Involving New People. LC 92-71476. (Evangelism Study Ser.: No. 3). 94p. 1992. reprint ed. pap. 30.00 (*0-608-04182-3*, 206491700011) Bks Demand.

Dell, Sidney. The Inter-American Development Bank: A Study in Development Financing. LC 70-185778. (Special Studies in International Economics & Development). 1972. 32.75 (*0-275-28606-1*) Irvington.

— International Development Policies: Perspectives for Industrial Countries. LC 90-38618. 390p. 1991. text 62.95 (*0-8223-1079-1*); pap. text 24.95 (*0-8223-1097-X*) Duke.

— The United Nations & International Business. LC 89-27999. 204p. (C). 1990. text 29.95 (*0-8223-0957-2*) UN.

Dell, Susanne & Robertson, Graham. Sentenced to Hospital: Offenders at Broadmoor. (Maudsley Monographs: No. 32). 180p. (C). 1988. 55.00 (*0-19-712156-X*) OUP.

Dell, Thomas R. Appleshare IPS. LC 97-31939. (Illus.). 630p. 1997. pap., pap. text 39.95 incl. cd-rom (*0-12-208866-2*) Morgan Kaufmann.

— Claris EMiler Companion. LC 97-14007. (Claris Press Ser.). (Illus.). 293p. 1997. pap. text 27.95 (*0-12-208865-4*) Morgan Kaufmann.

***Dell, Thomas R.** Core MCSE. LC 99-222908. 800p. 1998. 79.99 incl. cd-rom (*0-13-082861-0*) P-H.

— Core MCSE: Windows 2000 Edition. 920p. 2000. 79.99 (*0-13-083458-0*, Prentice Hall) P-H.

— Core MCSE Training Course: Student Edition. (C). 1999. student ed., boxed set 71.93 (*0-13-085394-1*, Prentice Hall) P-H.

— MSCE: Implementing & Supporting Internet Explorer 5. (Microsoft Technology Ser.). 2002. 49.99 (*0-13-014268-9*) P-H.

***Dell, Thomas R. & Leroux, Marine.** The Complete IIS Training Course. (Illus.). 361p. 1999. pap. text 99.99 (*0-13-026308-7*) P-H.

***Dell, Tom.** Implementing & Supporting Microsoft Exchange Server 5.5. 361p. 1999. text 49.99 incl. audio compact disk (*0-13-011392-1*) P-H.

Dell, Tom. Object Request Brokers for Webmasters. 350p. (C). 1999. pap. 39.95 (*0-12-209069-1*) Morgan Kaufmann.

***Dell, Tom & Leroux, Marine.** The Complete Core MCSE Training Course. 1999. boxed set 129.99 incl. cd-rom (*0-13-085256-2*) P-H.

Dell, Twyla. Call of the Rainbow Warrior: An Environmental Fable. 96p. 1990. 12.95 (*0-9626197-0-1*) Foresight Inst.

— Corporate Environmental Leader: Five Steps to a New Ethic. Keppler, Kay, ed. LC 93-72978. 163p. (Orig.). 1995. pap. 13.95 (*1-56052-253-4*) Crisp Pubns.

— Motivating at Work: Empowering Employees to Give Their Best. rev. ed. Crisp, Michael G., ed. LC 87-72484. (Fifty-Minute Ser.). (Illus.). 80p. (Orig.). 1993. pap. 10.95 (*1-56052-201-1*) Crisp Pubns.

***Della-Bescat, Gabrielle.** Love Lost & Other Poems. LC 99-90828. 1999. pap. 8.95 (*1-56167-556-3*, Five Star Spec Ed) Am Literary Pr.

Della Britta, Albert J., jt. auth. see Loudon, David L.

Della Casa, Giovanni. Galateo: A Treatise of the Manners & Behaviours. Peterson, Robert, tr. LC 73-26476. (English Experience Ser.: No. 120). 122p. 1969. reprint ed. 45.00 (*90-221-0120-7*) Walter J Johnson.

Della Casa, Giovanni & Van Sickle, John. Giovanni Della Casa's Poem Book: Ionnis [i.e. Jonnis] Casae Carminum Liber. LC 99-19158. (Medieval & Renaissance Texts & Studies: Vol. 194). 168p. 1999. 20.00 (*0-86698-236-1*) MRTS.

Della Coletta, Cristina. Plotting the Past: Metamorphoses of Historical Narrative in Modern Italian Fiction. LC 96-31663. (Studies in Romance Literatures: Vol. 12). 232p. 1996. pap. 38.95 (*1-55753-091-2*) Purdue U Pr.

Della Croce, Julia. Antipasti: The Little Dishes of Italy. LeBlond, Bill, ed. LC 92-34462. (Illus.). 152p. 1993. pap. 18.95 (*0-8118-0218-3*) Chronicle Bks.

— Antipasti: The Little Dishes of Italy. LeBlond, Bill, ed. LC 92-34462. (Illus.). 152p. 1994. 29.95 (*0-8118-0697-9*) Chronicle Bks.

***Della Croce, Julia.** Antipasti: The Little Dishes of Italy. (Illus.). 142p. 2000. reprint ed. 30.00 (*0-7881-9283-3*) DIANE Pub.

Della Croce, Julia. Pasta Book: Recipes in the Italian Tradition. 1997. 9.95 (*0-8118-1745-8*) Chronicle Bks.

— Pasta Classica: The Art of Italian Pasta Cooking. LC 87-13515. (Illus.). 160p. 1996. pap. 21.95 (*0-8118-0248-5*) Chronicle Bks.

— Salse Di Pomodoro: Over 60 Recipes for Italy's Great Tomato Sauces. (Illus.). 132p. 1996. pap. 14.95 (*0-8118-0930-7*) Chronicle Bks.

— Ultimate Pasta. LC 97-16375. 168p. 1997. 24.95 (*0-7894-2086-4*) DK Pub Inc.

— The Vegetarian Table: Italy. LeBlond, Bill, ed. (Illus.). 168p. 1994. 22.95 (*0-8118-0458-5*) Chronicle Bks.

Della Croce, Maria Laura. The World's Great Treasures. LC 98-17170. 336p. 1998. 60.00 (*1-55670-832-7*) Stewart Tabori & Chang.

Della Fazia, Alba, ed. see Anouilh, Jean.

della Fazia Amoia, Alba, see Amoia, Alba della Fazia.

Della Fontana, Jacopo, intro. Dubosc & Landowski: An Environmental Architecture. LC 98-196037. (I Talenti Ser.). (FRE, ITA & KOR., Illus.). 100p. 1998. pap. 35.00 (*88-7838-034-2*) Rockport Pubs.

Della-Giustina, Daniel. The Fire Safety Management Handbook. 2nd rev. ed. LC 99-12090. 189p. 1999. 34.95 (*1-885581-23-8*, 4373) ASSE.

***Della-Giustina, Daniel.** Key Elements in Developing a Safety & Health Program. LC 99-51555. 1999. write for info. (*1-56670-518-5*) Lewis Pubs.

Della-Giustina, Daniel & Yost, Charles P. Teaching Safety in the Elementary School. (Illus.). (Orig.). 1991. pap. text 5.00 (*0-88314-519-7*) AAHPERD.

Della-Giustina, Daniel E. Safety & Environmental Management. (Industrial Health & Safety Ser.). 306p. 1996. 76.95 (*0-471-28721-0*, VNR) Wiley.

Della-Giustina, Daniel E. Safety & Environmental Management. LC 96-19451. 306p. (C). 1996. text 62.95 (*0-442-02117-8*, VNR) Wiley.

Della Mirandola, Pico. Of Being & Unity. 1993. pap. 7.95 (*1-55818-206-3*, Sure Fire) Holmes Pub.

— On the Dignity of Man. Miller, Paul J. et al, trs. LC 97-51631. (Classics Ser.). 208p. (C). 1998. reprint ed. pap. text 8.95 (*0-87220-396-4*); reprint ed. lib. bdg. 29.95 (*0-87220-397-2*) Hackett Pub.

— A Platonic Discourse on Love. 1994. pap. 7.95 (*1-55818-279-9*) Holmes Pub.

Della Penna, Craig. Holyoke. LC 97-211070. (Images of America Ser.). 1997. pap. 16.99 (*0-7524-0582-9*) Arcadia Publng.

***Della Penna, Craig P.** 24 Great Rail-Trails of New Jersey: The Essential Outdoor Guide to the Garden State's Best Multi-Use Recreational Trails Built on Abandoned Railroad Grades. Vaughan, Valerie, ed. LC 98-89056. (Illus.). 212p. 1999. pap. 16.95 (*1-889787-04-3*) NE Cartographics.

Della Porta, Agostino, tr. see Gardner, Lilly B.

Della Porta, Donatella. Social Movements, Political Violence, & the State: A Comparative Analysis of Italy & Germany. (Cambridge Studies in Comparative Politics). (Illus.). 288p. (C). 1995. text 59.95 (*0-521-47396-9*) Cambridge U Pr.

Della Porta, Donatella & Diani, Mario. Social Movements: An Introduction. LC 98-28669. 320p. 1999. 59.95 (*0-631-19212-3*); pap. 24.95 (*0-631-19213-1*) Blackwell Pubs.

Della Porta, Donatella & Reiter, Herbert. Policing Protest: The Control of Mass Demonstrations in Western Democracies. LC 97-48500. (Social Movements, Protest, & Contention Ser.). 1998. pap. 22.95 (*0-8166-3064-X*) U of Minn Pr.

— Policing Protest: The Control of Mass Demonstrations in Western Democracies. LC 97-48500. (Social Movements, Protest & Contention Ser.). 1998. 57.95 (*0-8166-3063-1*) U of Minn Pr.

Della Porta, Donatella & Vannucci, Alberto. Corrupt Exchanges: Actors, Resources & Mechanisms of Political Corruption. LC 98-39625. (Social Problems & Social Issues Ser.). 328p. 1999. pap. text 25.95 (*0-202-30600-3*) Aldine de Gruyter.

— Corrupt Exchanges: Actors, Resources & Mechanisms of Political Corruption. LC 98-39625. (Social Problems & Social Issues Ser.). 328p. 1999. lib. bdg. 51.95 (*0-202-30574-0*) Aldine de Gruyter.

Della Riccia, G., et al, eds. Mathematical & Statistical Methods in Artificial Intelligence: Proceedings of the ISSEK94 Workshop. (International Centre for Mechanical Sciences Ser.: No.363). 256p. 1995. 86.95 (*3-211-82713-7*) Spr-Verlag.

Della Rocca & Maher. Ophthalmic Plastic Surgery. (C). 1999. text 130.00 (*0-8385-7427-0*) P-H.

Della Rocca, Michael. Representation & the Mind-Body Problem in Spinoza. 240p. 1996. text 45.00 (*0-19-509562-6*) OUP.

Della Rocca, Robert C., jt. auth. see Lemke, Bradley N.

Della Rochetta, Mario Incisa, see Incisa della Rochetta, Mario.

della Rovere, G. Querci, jt. auth. see Warren, R.

Della Sala, Sergio. Mind Myths: Exploring Popular Assumptions about the Mind & Brain. LC 98-38574. 310p. 1999. pap. 38.95 (*0-471-98303-9*) Wiley.

Della Selva, Patricia C. Intensive Short-Term Dynamic Psychotherapy: Theory & Technique. LC 95-38658. 272p. 1996. 67.50 (*0-471-04717-1*) Wiley.

Della Seta, Fabio. The Tiber Afire. Frenaye, Frances, tr. from ITA. LC 90-60882. 192p. 1992. pap. 10.95 (*0-910395-72-1*) Marlboro Pr.

Della Seta, Fabrizio, ed. see Verdi, Giuseppe.

Della Torre, Edward. Magnetic Hysteresis. LC 98-46940. 224p. 1999. 59.95 (*0-7803-4719-6*) IEEE Standards.

Della Valle, Joan. Teacher Career Starter. LC 98-23941. (Career Starters Ser.). 1998. pap. 14.95 (*1-57685-138-9*) LrningExprss.

Della Valle, Paula & Peterson, Lennie. Welcome to Your Midlife Crisis: Ways to Survive the Ultimate Rite of Passage. Carle, Cliff, ed. (Illus.). 96p. 1996. pap. 5.95 (*1-57644-000-1*) CCC Pubns.

Della Volpe, Angela, ed. see Andersen, Henning, et al.

Della Volpe, Galvano. Critique of Taste. Caesar, Michael, tr. from ITA. LC 91-39852. (Verso Modern Classics Ser.). 272p. (C). 1991. pap. 20.00 (*0-86091-565-4*, A6421, Pub. by Verso) Norton.

Dellabough, Grant. An Arch Dilemma. 221p. (Orig.). 1997. pap., per. 17.95 (*0-9656673-0-8*) Attic Salt Ent.

Dellabough, Robin. One-Hundred One Ways to Get Straight A's. LC 94-28851. (Illus.). 96p. (J). (gr. 3-8). 1997. pap. 2.95 (*0-8167-3565-4*) Troll Communs.

Dellabough, Robin, jt. auth. see Beardstown Ladies' Investment Club.

Dellabough, Robin, jt. auth. see Kirshbaum, Roberta.

Dellacamera, Robert J. Space Logistics. 1999. write for info. (*0-89464-052-6*) Krieger.

DellaCava, Frances A. & Engel, Madeline H. Female Detectives in American Novels: A Bibliography & Analysis of Serialized Female Sleuths. LC 93-30644. 176p. 1993. text 15.00 (*0-8153-1264-4*, H1685) Garland.

Dellacorte, Betty. Shelter from the Storm. 306p. 1985. pap. 9.95 (*0-933843-00-3*) Villa Pr AZ.

Dell'Acqua, Alexa A. & Mazzaferro, John F. Wireless Data Communications. 106p. 1995. pap. 100.00 (*0-9648176-0-8*) Pink Hse.

Dellaert, N. P. Production to Order. (Lecture Notes in Economics & Mathematical Systems Ser.: Vol. 333). vii, 158p. 1989. 30.10 (*0-387-51309-4*) Spr-Verlag.

Dell'Amico, Mauro, et al. Annotated Bibliographies in Combinatorial Optimization. 512p. 1997. 155.00 (*0-471-96574-X*) Wiley.

Dellamora. Victorian Sexual Dissidence. LC 98-44262. 1999. pap. text 20.00 (*0-226-14227-2*); lib. bdg. 50.00 (*0-226-14226-4*) U Ch Pr.

Dellamora, Richard. Apocalyptic Overtures: Sexual Politics & the Sense of An Ending. LC 93-27242. (Illus.). 240p. (C). 1994. text 48.00 (*0-8135-2056-8*); pap. text 20.00 (*0-8135-2057-6*) Rutgers U Pr.

— Masculine Desire: The Sexual Politics of Victorian Aestheticism. LC 89-16748. xii, 276p. (C). 1990. 45.00 (*0-8078-1882-8*); pap. 19.95 (*0-8078-4267-2*) U of NC Pr.

— Postmodern Apocalypse: Theory & Cultural Practice at the End. LC 96-32542. (New Cultural Studies). (Illus.). 288p. 1995. text 39.95 (*0-8122-3320-4*); pap. text 16.95 (*0-8122-1558-3*) U of Pa Pr.

Dellamora, Richard & Fischlin, Daniel, eds. The Work of Opera: Genre, Nationhood, & Sexual Difference. LC 98-12495. (Illus.). xi, 350p. 1997. write for info. (*0-231-10944-X*); pap. write for info. (*0-231-10945-8*) Columbia Univ Schl of Library.

DellaNeva, JoAnn. Song & Counter-Song: Sceve's Delie & Petrarch's Rime. LC 83-81597. (French Forum Monographs: No. 49). 128p. (Orig.). 1983. pap. 10.95 (*0-917058-49-6*) French Forum.

Dell'Antonio, Andrew, ed. Cesario Gussago: Sonate a Quattro, sei, et Otto, con Alcuni Concerti a Otto, Venice, 1608. LC 93-41237. (Italian Instrumental Music of the Sixteenth & Early Seventeenth Centuries Ser.: Vol. 20). 440p. 1994. text 138.00 (*0-8240-4519-X*) Garland.

— Lorenzo Allegri: Il Primo Libro delle Musiche (Venice, 1618) LC 95-7387. (Italian Instrumental Music of the Sixteenth & Seventeenth Centuries Ser.: No. 27). 120p. 1995. text 77.00 (*0-8240-4526-2*) Garland.

Dell'Antonio, G., jt. auth. see Dalmaso, G.

Dell'Antonio, G., ed. see Fabes, Eugene, et al.

Dell'Antonio, G., jt. ed. see Maso, G. Dal.

Dell'Antonio, G. F. & D'Onofrio, B., eds. Recent Advances in Hamiltonian Systems: Proceedings of the International Conference, L'Aquila, June 10-13, 1986. 256p. 1987. text 74.00 (*9971-5-0246-1*) World Scientific Pub.

Dell'Antonio, G. F., jt. ed. see Ambrosetti, Antonio.

***Dellapenna, Joseph W.** Suing Foreign Governments & Their Corporations. 2nd rev. ed. 550p. 2000. 115.00 (*1-57105-131-7*) Transnatl Pubs.

Dellapenna, Joseph W., ed. The Regulated Riparian Model Water Code: Final Report of the Water Laws Committee of the Water Resources Planning & Management Division of the American Society of Civil Engineers. LC 97-158. 376p. 1997. 32.00 (*0-7844-0226-4*) Am Soc Civil Eng.

***Dellapenna, Joseph W., et al.** China & Hong Kong in Transition: The Report of an Ilex Briefing Trip to Beijing & Hong Kong, May 6-13, 1998. LC 99-51548. (Illus.). 1999. write for info. (*1-57073-754-1*) Amer Bar Assn.

DellaPergola, Sergio, jt. ed. see Himmelfarb, Harold S.

DellaPorta, Donatella & Meny, Yves. Democracy & Corruption in Europe. (Social Change in Western Europe Ser.). 208p. (C). 1997. pap. 27.50 (*1-85567-367-3*) Bks Intl VA.

Dellar, Fred. Frank Sinatra: His Life & Times. (Illus.). 160p. (Orig.). 1995. pap. 19.95 (*0-7119-4978-6*, OP 47772) Omnibus NY.

Dellar, Pamela. Plays Without Theatres. (C). 1989. text 35.00 (*0-948929-27-8*) St Mut.

Dellar, Robert, ed. Gobbing Pogoing & Gratuitous Bad Language: An Anthology of Punk Short Stories. 153p. 1996. pap. 14.95 (*0-9525744-5-4*, Pub. by Spare Change) AK Pr Dist.

Dellarco, Maurizio F. De Chirico & America. LC 97-220685. (Illus.). 240p. 1997. 55.00 (*88-422-0682-2*) Antique Collect.

Dell'Arco, Maurizio F., jt. auth. see Sonino, Annalisa S.

An Asterisk (*) at the beginning of an entry indicates that the title is appearing for the first time.

Dellarco, Michael, et al, eds. Total Exposure & Assessment Methodology (TEAM) Toxic Substances & Chemicals, an International Symposium, Pt. II. (Journal of Exposure Analysis & Environmental Epidemiology Ser.: Vol. 1, No. 2). (Illus.). 1991. pap. text 60.00 (*0-911131-73-6*) Specialist Journals.

Dellarco, Michael J., jt. ed. see Breen, Joseph J.

Dellarco, Vicki L., et al, eds. Aneuploidy: Etiology & Mechanisms. LC 85-25696. (Basic Life Sciences Ser.: Vol. 36). 576p. 1985. 110.00 (*0-306-42118-6*, Plenum Trade) Perseus Pubng.

***Dellavecchio, M.** Unofficial Guide to Adopting a Child. (Unofficial Guides Ser.). 400p. 2000. pap. text 15.95 (*0-02-863494-2*) Macmillan Gen Ref.

Delle, James A. An Archaeology of Social Space: Analyzing Coffee Plantations in Jamaica's Blue Mountains. LC 98-17692. (Contributions to Global Historical Archaeology Ser.). (Illus.). 268p. (C). 1998. 39.50 (*0-306-45850-0*, Plenum Trade) Perseus Pubng.

***Delle, James A., et al, eds.** Lines That Divide: Historical Archaeologies of Race, Class & Gender. LC 99-50986. (Illus.). 368p. (C). 2000. text 52.00 (*1-57233-086-4*, Pub. by U of Tenn Pr) U Ch Pr.

Dellen, Robert J. Van, see Van Dellen, Robert J.

Dellenbaugh, David. Sports Illustrated Sailing. 1990. pap. 10.95 (*1-56800-029-4*, Pub. by Sports Illus Bks) Natl Bk Netwk.

Dellenbaugh, Frederick Samuel. A Canyon Voyage: The Narrative of the Second Powell Expedition down the Colorado River from Wyoming, & the Explorations on Land, in the Years 1871 & 1872. LC 84-8648. (Illus.). 277p. 1984. reprint ed. pap. 16.95 (*0-8165-0880-1*) U of Ariz Pr.

— The North-Americans of Yesterday: A Comparative Study of North-American Indian Life, Customs, & Products, on the Theory of the Ethnic Unity of Race. LC 74-7950. (Illus.). reprint ed. 49.50 (*0-404-11837-2*) AMS Pr.

— The Romance of the Colorado River. LC 98-35346. (Illus.). 399p. 1998. pap. 14.95 (*0-486-40439-0*) Dover.

Dellenbrant, Jan Ake. Soviet Regional Dilemma: Planning, People & Natural Resources. LC 86-13049.Tr. of Sovjetunionens Regionala Dilemma. 230p. (C). (gr. 13). 1986. text 85.95 (*0-87332-384-X*) M E Sharpe.

Dellepiane, Angela B., jt. auth. see Szmuk, Szilvia E.

Deller, Anthony W. & Lipscomb, Ernest B., 3rd. Patent Claims, 3 vols. annuals 2nd rev. ed. LC 76-112643. (IP Ser.). 1971. suppl. ed. 375.00 (*0-685-59813-6*) West Group.

Deller, D. Brian & Ellis, Christopher J. Thedford Two: A Paleo-Indian Site in the Ausable River Watershed of Southwestern Ontario. LC 91-25892. (Memoirs Ser.: No. 24). (Illus.). xii, 158p. (Orig.). (C). 1992. pap. 20.00 (*0-915703-25-4*) U Mich Mus Anthro.

Deller, John R., jt. auth. see Grover, Dale.

Deller, Sheelagh. Lessons From Learner. (Pilgrims Resource Bks.). 79p. 1990. pap. text 17.95 (*0-582-07004-X*, 78671) Longman.

***dell'Erba, D. N.** Thermoelastic Fracture Mechanics Using Boundary Elements. (Topics in Engineering Ser.). 200p. 2000. 109.00 (*1-85312-849-X*, Pub. by WIT Pr) Computational Mech MA.

Delles, Roger. Assessment of Effectiveness Measures for Local Government Recreation Agencies in Oregon. 99p. 1974. pap. 4.00 (*0-943272-09-2*) Inst Recreation Res.

Delleur, J. W. The Handbook of Groundwater Engineering. LC 97-46941. 992p. 1998. boxed set 104.95 (*0-8493-2698-2*) CRC Pr.

Delleur, J. W., et al. Applied Modeling of Hydrologic Time Series. LC 80-53334. 1981. reprint ed. pap. 45.00 (*0-918334-37-3*) WRP.

Delli-Carpini, John. Prayer & Piety in the Poems of Gerard Manley Hopkins: The Landscape of a Soul. LC 98-17419. (Studies in British Literature). 1998. 79.95 (*0-7734-8380-2*) E Mellen.

Delli Carpini, Michael X., et al, eds. Research in Micropolitics, Vol. 4: New Directions in Political Psychology. 243p. 1994. 73.25 (*1-55938-197-3*) Jai Pr.

— Research in Micropolitics, Vol. 6. Date not set. 78.50 (*0-7623-0227-5*) Jai Pr.

— Research in Micropolitics Vol. 3: Public Opinion. 247p. 1990. 78.50 (*0-89232-791-X*) Jai Pr.

— Voting Behavior II. (Research in Micropolitics Ser.: Vol. II). 304p. 1987. 78.50 (*0-89232-562-3*) Jai Pr.

Delli Carpini, Michael X. & Keeter, Scott. What Americans Know about Politics & Why It Matters. LC 95-24248. 386p. 1996. 42.00 (*0-300-06256-7*) Yale U Pr.

***Delli, Larry.** A Vapor in Time. (Illus.). vi, 206p. 1999. pap. 9.99 (*0-9676238-0-4*) Delli Pubs.

Dellin, Genell. After the Thunder. 384p. 1998. mass mkt. 5.99 (*0-380-78603-6*, Avon Bks) Morrow Avon.

— Cherokee Dawn. 368p. 1990. mass mkt. 4.50 (*0-380-76013-4*, Avon Bks) Morrow Avon.

— Cherokee Nights. 352p. 1991. mass mkt. 4.50 (*0-380-76014-2*, Avon Bks) Morrow Avon.

— Cherokee Sundown. 384p. (Orig.). 1992. mass mkt. 4.50 (*0-380-76716-3*, Avon Bks) Morrow Avon.

***Dellin, Genell.** Cole. (Renegades Ser.). 376p. 1999. mass mkt. 5.99 (*0-380-80352-6*, Avon Bks) Morrow Avon.

Dellin, Genell. Comanche Flame. 368p. (Orig.). 1994. mass mkt. 4.99 (*0-380-77524-7*, Avon Bks) Morrow Avon.

— Comanche Rain. 384p. (Orig.). 1995. mass mkt. 4.99 (*0-380-77525-5*, Avon Bks) Morrow Avon.

— Comanche Wind. 400p. (Orig.). 1993. mass mkt. 4.50 (*0-380-76717-1*, Avon Bks) Morrow Avon.

***Dellin, Genell.** Nick. (Renegades Ser.: Vol. 2). 384p. 2000. mass mkt. 5.99 (*0-380-80353-4*, Avon Bks) Morrow Avon.

Dellin, Genell. Red Sky Warrior. 336p. (Orig.). 1996. mass mkt. 5.50 (*0-380-77526-3*, Avon Bks) Morrow Avon.

— Silver Moon Song. 336p. (Orig.). 1996. mass mkt. 5.99 (*0-380-78602-8*, Avon Bks) Morrow Avon.

Dellin, Genell, ed. see Hager, Jean.

Delling, Manfred. Engagement fur ein neues Medium: Ausgewahlte Fernsehkritiken von 1964-1993. Kreuzer, Helmut & Riha, Karl, eds. (Trouvaillen - Editionen zur Literatur- und Kulturgeschichte Ser.: Bd. 13). (GER.). 267p. 1995. 46.95 (*3-631-48446-1*) P Lang Pubng.

Dellinger. Current Topics in Intensive Care, Vol. 3. 3rd ed. (C). 1996. pap. text 65.00 (*0-7020-2111-3*) Harcourt.

— Health: 1993 Supplement. 1993. 52.50 (*0-316-18060-2*) Little.

***Dellinger.** Sendas Literarias levels 1-2. (C). 1999. text 23.00 (*0-8384-0200-3*) Heinle & Heinle.

Dellinger, et al. Critical Care Medicine: A Concise Review. 283p. 1995. pap. 65.00 (*0-916609-06-5*) Am Chest Phys.

Dellinger, Ann M. Health Care Facilities Law. 1991. 110.00 (*0-316-18040-8*, Aspen Law & Bus) Aspen Pub.

Dellinger, Ann M., ed. Health Care Facilities Law: Management & Medical Aspects of Hospitals, HMOs, & Extended Care Facilities. 1989. write for info. (*0-318-65448-2*, Aspen Law & Bus) Aspen Pub.

Dellinger, Anne M. Hospital Law in North Carolina, Chpts. 1-14. LC 85-622120. (C). 1985. ring bd. 72.00 (*1-56011-072-4*) Institute Government.

***Dellinger, Anne M.** Legal Issues in Health Care for Prenant Adolescents: A Guide for North Carolina Providers. (C). 2000. pap. write for info. (*1-56011-378-2*) Institute Government.

Dellinger, Anne M. Medical Records. (Hospital Law in North Carolina Ser.: Chap. 8). 67p. (C). 1987. ring bd. 10.50 (*1-56011-080-5*, 85.03H) Institute Government.

Dellinger, Anne M. & Brannon, Joan G. The Law of Health Records in North Carolina. 86p. (Orig.). (C). 1987. pap. text 12.00 (*1-56011-093-7*, 87.04) Institute Government.

Dellinger, Annetta. The Jesus Tree. (Illus.). 32p. (J). (ps-2). 1991. 8.99 (*0-570-04191-0*, 56-1650) Concordia.

Dellinger, Annetta E. Adopted & Loved Forever. (Illus.). 24p. (J). (ps-2). 1987. 5.99 (*0-570-04167-8*, 56-1624) Concordia.

— Angels Are My Friends. LC 85-7858. 32p. (J). (gr. k-3). 1985. 6.99 (*0-570-04120-1*, 56-1531) Concordia.

Dellinger, Bill & Freeman, Bill. Competitive Runners Training Book. 160p. 1984. pap. 7.95 (*0-02-028340-7*) Macmillan.

Dellinger, David. From Yale to Jail: The Life Story of a Moral Dissenter. 508p. 1996. reprint ed. pap. 19.50 (*0-9636224-3-9*) Rose Hill Bks.

Dellinger, David, jt. ed. see Albert, Michael.

Dellinger, Edward A., et al. Essence of Engineering. LC 96-93024. 311p. (Orig.). 1996. 39.95 (*0-9656573-1-0*) E A Dellinger.

Dellinger, Edward A., jt. auth. see Billet, Donald F.

Dellinger, John. Homecoming to Murder. 176p. (Orig.). 1996. pap. 9.95 (*0-937693-05-7*) Lone Wolf.

— Quigly's Dilemma. 128p. (Orig.). 1986. pap. 6.95 (*0-937693-00-6*) Lone Wolf.

***Dellinger, Kip & Dellinger, Royal.** Offer in Compromise Process: Insights & Strategies. 344p. 1999. pap. text 45.00 (*0-8080-0417-4*) CCH INC.

Dellinger, Margaret, et al. Die AT&T Strategie Total Quality. 2nd rev. ed. (AT&T Quality Library). (Illus.). 20p. (Orig.). 1992. reprint ed. pap. 7.50 (*0-932764-41-X*) AT&T Customer Info.

— AT&T's Total Quality Approach. (AT&T Quality Library). (Illus.). 20p. (Orig.). 1992. pap. 7.50 (*0-932764-38-X*) AT&T Customer Info.

— Enfoque de Calidad Total de AT&T. 2nd rev. ed. (AT&T Quality Library). (Illus.). 20p. (Orig.). 1992. reprint ed. pap. 7.50 (*0-932764-40-1*) AT&T Customer Info.

Dellinger, Margaret, jt. auth. see Donnell, Augustus.

Dellinger, Phillip & Taylor, Robert, eds. Self Assessment in Multidisciplinary Critical Care: A Comprehensive Review. LC 86-60806. 1986. write for info. (*0-936145-25-0*) SCCM Fullerton.

Dellinger, R. P., et al, eds. Current Topics in Intensive Care, No. 4. 300p. 1997. pap. write for info. (*0-7020-2248-9*, Pub. by W B Saunders) Saunders.

Dellinger, R. Phillip, et al, eds. Society of Critical Care Medicine--Self-Assessment in Multidisciplinary Critical Care, Vol. 2: A Comprehensive Review. 500p. (Orig.). 1989. pap. 47.00 (*0-936145-29-3*) SCCM Fullerton.

Dellinger, Royal, jt. auth. see Dellinger, Kip.

Dellinger, Susan E. Communicating Beyond Our Differences: Introducing the Psycho-Geometrics System. rev. ed. (Illus.). 204p. 1996. reprint ed. pap. 14.95 (*1-892762-00-5*) Jade Ink.

Dellino, Clive V. J. Cold & Chilled Storage Technology. 1990. mass mkt. 134.95 (*0-442-20673-9*) Chapman & Hall.

Dellio, Phil & Woods, Scott. I Wanna Be Sedated: Pop Music in the Seventies. (Illus.). 192p. 1993. pap. 14.95 (*0-920151-16-7*, Pub. by Sound & Vision) Firefly Bks Ltd.

Dell'Isola, Alphonse, jt. auth. see Parker, Donald E.

Dell'Isola, Frank. Thomas Merton: A Bibliography. enl. rev. ed. LC 74-79148. (Serif Series: Bibliographies & Checklists: No. 31). 238p. reprint ed. pap. 73.80 (*0-8357-5570-3*, 203519700093) Bks Demand.

Dellmann, H. Dieter & Carithers, Jeanine A. Cytology & Microscopic Anatomy. LC 95-14964. (National Veterinary Medical Series for Independent Study). (Illus.). 420p. 1996. 29.95 (*0-683-01467-6*) Lppncott W & W.

Dellmann, Horst-Dieter. Textbook of Veterinary Histology. 4th ed. (Illus.). 351p. 1992. text 55.00 (*0-8121-1553-8*) Lppncott W & W.

— Veterinary Histology: An Outline Text-Atlas. LC 78-146030. 316p. reprint ed. pap. 90.10 (*0-608-17758-X*, 2056506) Bks Demand.

— Veterinary Histology: An Outline Text-Atlas. LC 78-146030. 317p. 1971. reprint ed. pap. 98.30 (*0-608-10386-1*, 205650600069) Bks Demand.

Dellmann, Horst-Dieter & Eurell, Jo Ann C. Textbook of Veterinary Histology. 5th ed. LC 98-4762. 380p. 1998. 62.00 (*0-683-30168-3*) Lppncott W & W.

Dello Joio. Sonata for Trumpet & Piano. 28p. 1986. pap. 11.95 (*0-7935-3720-7*) H Leonard.

Dello Joio, N. A Jubilant Song. 28p. 1986. pap. 1.75 (*0-7935-5492-6*, 50302650) H Leonard.

— Lyric Pieces for the Young: For Piano. 16p. 1984. pap. 3.95 (*0-7935-2053-3*, 00009283) H Leonard.

Dellock, Jean & Rice, Philip A. Mount Carmel Cemetery: Mt. Carmel, Northumberland Co., Pa. 145p. 1989. per. 16.00 (*1-55856-034-3*, 059) Closson Pr.

Dellock, Jean & Rice, Phillip A. St. Joseph - St. Mauritus Cemetery at Ashland, Schuylkill County, Pa. 65p. 1989. per. 8.50 (*1-55856-018-1*, 035) Closson Pr.

— Zion's Evangelical German Lutheran Church of Girardville, Schuylkill Co., Pa. 74p. 1989. per. 8.50 (*1-55856-017-3*, 399) Closson Pr.

Dellock, Jean, jt. auth. see Rice, Phillip A.

Dellock, Jean A. Schuylkill County, Pennsylvania Archives, Vol. 3. 573p. 1996. per. 39.95 (*1-55856-220-6* 013) Closson Pr.

Dellock, Jean A. & Rice, Phillip A. Bern Church Record: Bern Twp., Berks Co., Pa. Schuylkill Roots Staff, ed. 39p. 1989. per. 5.00 (*1-55856-032-7*, 036) Closson Pr.

— Cemeteries of Centralia. 78p. 1990. per. 9.50 (*1-55856-047-5*, 389) Closson Pr.

— Charles Baber Cemetery at Pottsville. 218p. 1990. per. 23.50 (*1-55856-050-5*, 107) Closson Pr.

— Early & Later Records of the Church of the Holy Apostles (Episcopal) at Saint Clair. 168p. 1990. per. 18.50 (*1-55856-071-8*, 050) Closson Pr.

— Early History of St. Paul's (Summer Hill) Lutheran & Reformed Church. 56p. 1989. per. 7.50 (*1-55856-033-5*, 396) Closson Pr.

— Early Records of Christ Protestant Episcopal Church. 63p. 1990. per. 7.50 (*1-55856-045-9*, 054) Closson Pr.

— Early Records of St. Paul's Episcopal Church at Minersville. 120p. 1990. per. 13.50 (*1-55856-042-4*, 184) Closson Pr.

— Early Records of the Memorial Church of St. John (Episcopal) at Ashland Branch Twp. 151p. 1990. per. 16.50 (*1-55856-048-3*, 127) Closson Pr.

— St. Paul or "White" Church at Ringtown, Union Township. 135p. 1990. per. 15.00 (*1-55856-056-4*, 400) Closson Pr.

— St. Peter's (Fetterhoff's) Evangelical Lutheran & German Reformed (Now United Church of Christ) Church Record. 112p. 1990. per. 12.75 (*1-55856-049-1*, 125) Closson Pr.

— Schwarzwald Church Register, Exeter Township, Berks Co., PA, Pts. 1 & 2. LC 96-85602. 445p. 1997. per. 39.95 (*1-55856-240-0*, 281) Closson Pr.

— Trinity Lutheran Church of Reading Pt. 3: Marriages, 1754-1812. 72p. 1990. per. 8.50 (*1-55856-038-6*, 394) Closson Pr.

Dellock, Jean A. & Rice, Phillip A., compiled by. Schuylkill County, Pennsylvania Archives, Vol. 2. 577p. 1996. per. 39.95 (*1-55856-219-2*, 012) Closson Pr.

Dellock, Jean A., jt. auth. see Rice, Phillip A.

Dellock, Jean A., jt. compiled by see Rice, Phillip A.

Dellock, Jean A., jt. ed. see Rice, Phillip A.

Dellock, Stephen J. Schuylkill County Death Records, Vol. 2. LC 96-85586. 195p. 1996. per. 19.95 (*1-55856-236-2*, 261) Closson Pr.

— Schuylkill County Death Records, 1893-1895. 201p. 1995. per. 19.95 (*1-55856-183-8*, 260) Closson Pr.

Delloff, Linda M., ed. see Sittler, Joseph A.

Dell'Oro, Regina, tr. see Rosty, Pal.

Dell'Oro, Regina O. From Existence to the Ideal: Continuity & Development in Kant's Theology. LC 92-27285. (AUS VII: Vol. 149). VI, 183p. (C). 1995. text 34.95 (*0-8204-2106-5*) P Lang Pubng.

Dell'Oro, Roberto, jt. ed. see Viafora, Corrado.

Dell'Oro, Roberto, tr. see Demmer, Klaus.

Dell'Oro, Suzanne P. Argentina. LC 97-41568. (Globe-Trotters Club Ser.). (Illus.). 48p. (J). (gr. 2-5). 1998. lib. bdg. 22.60 (*1-57505-114-1*, Carolrhoda) Lerner Pub.

Dell'Oro, Suzanne P. & Varela-Paul, Andres. Sneaky Salamanders. LC 98-5198. (Pull Ahead Bks.). (Illus.). 32p. (J). 1998. pap. 6.95 (*0-8225-3618-8*, Lerner Publctns) Lerner Pub.

— Sneaky Salamanders. LC 98-5198. (Pull Ahead Bks.). (Illus.). 32p. (J). (gr. k-2). 1999. 21.27 (*0-8225-3612-9*, Lerner Publctns) Lerner Pub.

Delloro, Suzanne Paul. Hiding Toads. LC 98-49380. (Pull Ahead Bks.). 32p. (J). (gr. k-2). 1999. pap. 5.95 (*0-8225-3630-7*, Lerner Publctns) Lerner Pub.

***Delloro, Suzanne Paul.** Hiding Toads. LC 98-49380. (Pull Ahead Bks.). 32p. (J). (gr. k-2). 1999. 21.27 (*0-8225-3626-9*, Lerner Publctns) Lerner Pub.

— Tunneling Earthworms. LC 00-8006. (Pull Ahead Ser.). (Illus.). 32p. (J). (gr. 4-7). 2000. 21.27 (*0-8225-3762-1*, Lerner Publctns); pap. 6.95 (*0-8225-3768-0*, Lerner Publctns) Lerner Pub.

Dellosa, Janet, jt. auth. see Carson, Patti.

***Dell'Osso, Monica, et al.** Funding a Revocable Trust - Action Guide - Fall 1999. Tom, Janette, ed. 100p. 1999. ring bd. 58.00 (*0-7626-0364-X*, ES-11614) Cont Ed Bar-CA.

***Dellums, Ronald V. & Halterman, H. Lee.** Lying Down with the Lions: A Public Life from the Streets of Oakland to the Halls of Power. LC 99-32097. (Illus.). 240p. 2000. 25.00 (*0-8070-4318-4*) Beacon Pr.

— Lying down with the Lions: A Public Life from the Streets of Oakland to the Halls of Power. 2001. pap. 14.00 (*0-8070-4319-2*) Beacon Pr.

Dellums, Ronald V., et al. Nuclear California: An Investigative Report. Kaplan, David E., ed. LC 82-1213. (Illus.). 144p. (Orig.). 1982. pap. 5.95 (*0-9607166-0-2*) Greenpeace-Ctr Invest Re.

Dellutri, S. El Mundo al Que Predicamos.Tr. of World We Preach To. (SPA.). 9.99 (*0-7899-0619-8*, 491070) Editorial Unilit.

Dellwo, Lisa, jt. auth. see Philyaw, Jessica.

Delly, John G. Teaching Microscopy, Vol. 52. (Illus.). 1994. 45.00 (*0-904962-14-8*) Microscope Pubns.

Delma, Adriana, ed. see Montfort, Matthew C.

Delman, Abner J., jt. auth. see Stein, Emanuel.

Delman, B., et al, eds. Preparation of Catalysts VII. 1006p. 1998. 431.00 (*0-444-50031-6*, Excerpta Medica) Elsevier.

Delman, David. The Last Gambit. large type ed. (Lythway Ser.). 236p. 1992. 15.95 (*0-7451-1616-7*, G K Hall Lrg Type) Mac Lib Ref.

Delman, Elisa, jt. auth. see Delman, Steven.

Delman, Jack Nye. The War for Brooklyn's Indy Pendance. 286p. mass mkt. 4.99 (*1-55197-079-1*) Picasso Publ.

***Delman, Joel.** Smart Cookies. 1999. 69.50 (*1-86204-521-6*, Pub. by Element MA) Penguin Putnam.

Delman, Joel. Smart Cookies: Wit & Wisdom from Fortune Cookies Around the World. LC 98-37624. 128p. 1999. pap. 5.95 (*1-86204-494-5*, Pub. by Element MA) Penguin Putnam.

Delman, Jorgen, et al, eds. Remaking Peasant China: Problems of Rural Development & Institutions at the Start of the 1990s. 226p. (Orig.). (C). 1991. 27.00 (*87-7288-294-8*, Pub. by Aarhus Univ Pr) David Brown.

Delman, Scott. How to Mean Business: A Pocket Guide to More Success at Work. LC 95-92023. 120p. (Orig.). 1995. pap. 8.95 (*0-9645063-9-4*) ClientKeep.

Delman, Steven & Delman, Elisa. The Boy Scout Council Shoulder Patch Guide: A Tour of Councils Through Their Patches. LC 97-91679. (Illus.). 100p. 1997. pap. 15.00 (*0-9657239-0-9*) S & E Pub.

Delman, Steven & Delman, Elisa. The Boy Scout Council Shoulder Patch Guide: A Tour of Councils Through Their Patches. (Illus.). 104p. 1998. pap. 16.00 (*0-9657239-1-7*) S & E Pub.

***Delman, Steven & Delman, Elisa.** The Boy Scout Council Shoulder Patch Guide: A Tour of Councils Through Their Patches. (Illus.). 103p. 1999. pap. 15.00 (*0-9657239-2-5*) S & E Pub.

Delman, Steven & Delman, Elisa. The Boy Scout Council Shoulder Patch Guide: 1997 National Jamboree Edition. (Illus.). 112p. (J). 1999. pap. 20.00 (*0-9657239-3-3*, Pub. by S & E Pub) Amazon Com.

***Delmar.** Automotive Dictionary. (C). 1999. text 8.00 (*0-7668-1445-9*) Delmar.

— Care of Patient with CVA. LC 99-26841. (Home Care Aide Ser.). (C). 1999. mass mkt. 20.95 (*0-7668-0209-4*) Delmar.

Delmar. Delmar's Travel & Tourism Pocket Pal. (C). 2001. pap. text 18.75 (*0-7668-1566-8*) Delmar.

***Delmar.** Delmars Veterinary Guide: Small Animal Care. (C). 2000. pap. 35.25 (*0-7668-1422-X*) Thomson Learn.

Delmar. Exploring Agriscience. 2nd ed. (C). 2001. pap. text, lab manual ed. 18.75 (*0-7668-1676-1*) Delmar.

— Firefighter's Handbook: Essential Firefighting & Emergency Response. LC 99-28643. (Fire Science Ser.). 916p. 2000. pap. 64.95 (*0-7668-0581-6*) Delmar.

— Introduction to Quality Control. (West Engineering Ser.). 1988. pap., student ed. 8.00 (*0-534-93873-6*); text 72.95 (*0-534-93814-0*) PWS Pubs.

Delmar & Altman, Gaylene. Delmar's Fundamental & Advanced Nursing Skills. LC 99-32852. 1416p. (C). 1999. pap. text 65.95 (*0-7668-0715-0*) Delmar.

Delmar & Meade. Foundations of Electronics Instructors Teaching System. 2nd rev. abr. ed. 1999. pap. text 200.00 (*0-7668-1028-3*) Delmar.

Delmar, Charles O. The Essential Cook: A Practical Guide to Foods & Cooking. Bergez, John, ed. LC 88-82339. (Illus.). 530p. 1989. 24.95 (*0-929694-00-7*); pap. 15.95 (*0-929694-01-5*) Hill Hse GA.

DelMar Communication International Staff, tr. see Joyce, Jacqueline.

DelMar Communication Int'l. Staff, tr. see Joyce, Jacqueline.

DelMar Communications International Staff, tr. see Joyce, Jacqueline.

DelMar Communications Int'l. Staff, tr. see Joyce, Jacqueline.

Delmar, Diana. The Guilt-Free Dog Owner's Guide: Caring for a Dog When You're Short on Time & Space. Watson, Ben, ed. LC 89-61788. (Illus.). 180p. (Orig.). 1990. pap. 10.95 (*0-88266-575-8*, Storey Pub) Storey Bks.

— Help! My Puppy Is Driving Me Crazy: A Guide to Solving Common Puppy Problems. LC 97-11740. 1997. pap. 12.95 (*0-88266-992-3*, Storey Pub) Storey Bks.

— Taking up Riding As an Adult. LC 98-25940. (Horse-Wise Guide Ser.). (Illus.). 160p. 1998. pap. 19.95 (*1-58017-081-1*) Storey Bks.

Delmar, Inc., Staff. Legal Terminology Flash. (Paralegal Ser.). 1996. 15.95 (*0-8273-7816-5*) Delmar.

Delmar Inc. Staff. Understanding Child Development. 4th ed. (Early Childhood Education Ser.). 1996. 15.00 (*0-8273-7335-X*) Delmar.

***Delmar, Michael.** Symbols of Astrology. 128p. 2000. 45.00 (*2-84323-185-X*) Assouline.

***Delmar Publishers Staff.** Delmar's Pharmacy Technician Exam Review. LC 99-25102. (Allied Health Ser.). 192p. (C). 1999. pap. 20.00 (*0-7668-0743-6*) Delmar.

— Medium/Heavy Duty Truck (T8) Preventative Maintenance. (ASE Test Prep Ser.). 1999. pap. 18.95 (*0-7668-0566-2*) Delmar.

— Medium/Heavy Duty Truck (T4) Brakes. (ASE Test Prep Ser.). 1999. pap. 18.95 (*0-7668-0562-X*) Delmar.

D

— Medium/Heavy Duty Truck (T7) Heating, Ventilation & Air Conditioning. (ASE Test Prep Ser.). 1999. pap. 18.95 (*0-7668-0565-4*) Delmar.

— Medium/Heavy Duty Truck (T6) Electrical & Electronic Systems. (ASE Test Prep Ser.). 1999. pap. 18.95 (*0-7668-0564-6*) Delmar.

Delmar Publishers Staff, ed. English to Spanish, Spanish to English Automotive Dictionary. LC 98-11945. (ENG & SPA.). 1998. write for info. (*0-7668-0544-1*) Delmar.

Delmar Publishers Staff & Summerlin, Kip. AccuNet: Dosage Calculations System CD (3) 1195.95 (*0-7668-0722-3*, Pub. by Delmar) Thomson Learn.

Delmar Publishers Staff, et al. Nurse's Research Library. 48p. pap. 48.95 (*0-7668-0587-5*, Pub. by Delmar) Thomson Learn.

Delmar Publishing Staff. Auto Heating & Air Conditioning. (Automotive Technology Test Prep Ser.). 1998. pap. 18.95 (*0-7668-0555-7*) Delmar.

***Delmar Publishing Staff.** Care of Patient with AIDS. LC 99-14434. (Home Care Aide Ser.). 224p. (C). 1999. mass mkt. 20.95 (*0-7668-0210-8*) Delmar.

Delmar Publishing Staff. Hotel, Restaurant & Food Service Pocket Pal. (Food & Hospitality). (C). 2000. pap. 18.75 (*0-7668-1213-8*) Thomson Learn.

— 1999 Veterinary Drug Guide. (C). 1999. mass mkt. 22.50 (*0-7668-0754-1*) Delmar.

***Delmar Publishing Staff, ed.** Creative Resources: Early Childhood Classroom. 3rd ed. LC 99-14792. (Illus.). 624p. (C). 1999. 47.95 (*0-7668-0543-3*) Delmar.

— Introductory Horticulture. 6th ed. 2000. 18.75 (*0-7668-1570-6*) Delmar.

Delmar, Rosalind, tr. see Aleramo, Sibilla.

Delmar Staff. Anatomy & Physiology. (C). 1997. pap. 20.00 (*0-8273-7937-4*) Delmar.

— ASE Test Prep Series - Auto Engine Repair (A1) (Test Prep Ser.). 144p. 1998. text 18.95 (*0-7668-0549-2*) Delmar.

***Delmar Staff.** ASE Test Prep Series Auto Adv Eng Performance (L1) 144p. 1998. pap. text 18.95 (*0-7668-0557-3*) Delmar.

Delmar Staff. ASE Test Prep Series Auto Elec/Elec (A6) (Automotive Technology Test Prep Ser.). 128p. 1998. pap. text 18.95 (*0-7668-0554-9*) Delmar.

— ASE Test Prep Series Auto Engine Performance (A8) (Automotive Technology Test Prep Ser.). 128p. 1998. text 18.95 (*0-7668-0556-5*) Delmar.

— ASE Test Prep Series, Auto Manual Drive Trains - Axle, No. A3. 128p. 1998. text 18.95 (*0-7668-0551-4*) Delmar.

— ASE Test Prep Series, Auto Parts Specialist, No. P2. 176p. 1998. text 18.95 (*0-7668-0558-1*) Delmar.

— ASE Test Prep Series Auto Susp/Steer (A4) (Automotive Technology Test Prep Ser.). 128p. 1998. pap. text 18.95 (*0-7668-0552-2*) Delmar.

— ASE Test Prep Series, Auto Transmission - Transaxle, No. A2. (Test Prep Ser.). 128p. 1998. text 18.95 (*0-7668-0550-6*) Delmar.

— ASE Test Prep Seriesm, Auto Brakes, No. A5. (Automotive Technology Test Ser.). 136p. 1998. text 18.95 (*0-7668-0553-0*) Delmar.

— ATC Challenge 2.1. 2nd ed. 1998. text 324.95 (*0-7668-0051-2*) Delmar.

— Delmar Education Catalog, 1996. (Career Education Ser.). 1996. pap. write for info. (*0-8273-7813-0*) Delmar.

— Delmar General Catalog, 1996. (Career Education Ser.). 1996. pap. write for info. (*0-8273-7811-4*) Delmar.

— Delmar's Agriscience Dictionary w/Searchable CD-ROM. LC 98-45647. (Student Material TV Ser.). 740p. (C). 1998. text 34.95 incl. cd-rom (*0-7668-1146-8*) Delmar.

— Delmar's Medical Terminology Challenge Software. (Medical Terminology Ser.). (C). 1995. pap. 18.00 (*0-8273-6675-2*) Delmar.

— Delmars Test Prep B2-coll Repr:paint/refinishing. (Automotive Technology). 128p. 1998. 20.95 (*0-7668-0567-0*) Delmar.

— Delmars Test Prep B3-coll Repr:non Struc Analysis. (Automotive Technology). 128p. 1998. text 20.95 (*0-7668-0568-9*) Delmar.

— Delmars Test Prep B4-coll Repr Struc Analysis/damage Repair. (Automotive Technology). 128p. 1998. text 20.95 (*0-7668-0569-7*) Delmar.

— Delmars Test Prep B5-coll Repr Mech/elect Components. (Automotive Technology). 128p. 1998. text 20.95 (*0-7668-0570-0*) Delmar.

— Delmars Test Prep B6-coll Repr Damage Anlys/estimating. (Automotive Technology). 128p. 1998. text 20.95 (*0-7668-0571-9*) Delmar.

— Delmar's Test Preparation, Series A1-P2, Automotive Test Set. (Automotive Technology Ser.). 1998. pap. 90.00 (*0-7668-0572-7*) Delmar.

— Delmar's Test Preparation, Test 1-Medium to Heavy Truck Gas Engines. (Automotive Technology Ser.). 1999. pap. 18.95 (*0-7668-0559-X*) Delmar.

— Delmar's Test Preparation, Test 2-Medium to Heavy Truck Diesel Engines. (Automotive Technology Ser.). 1999. pap. 18.95 (*0-7668-0560-3*) Delmar.

— Delmar's Test Preparation, Test 3-Medium to Heavy Truck Drive Trains. (Automotive Technology Ser.). 1999. pap. 18.95 (*0-7668-0561-1*) Delmar.

— Delmar's Test Preparation, Test 5-Medium to Heavy Truck Suspension & Steering. (Automotive Technology Ser.). 1999. pap. 18.95 (*0-7668-0563-8*) Delmar.

— Delmar's Veterinary Technology Pocket Dictionary. 2000. pap. 22.50 (*0-7668-1421-1*) Delmar.

— Firefighter's Handbook. (Fire Science Ser.). 2000. pap., wbk. ed. 18.75 (*0-7668-0582-4*) Delmar.

— Fluke Training Program. 126p. 1997. pap., teacher ed. write for info. (*0-8273-8290-1*) Delmar.

— Instant Nursing Assessment: Mental Health. (Nursing Education Ser.). 224p. (C). 1995. mass mkt. 31.95 (*0-8273-7104-7*) Delmar.

— Med-Heavy Truck Set: Med-Heavy Truck, Nos. T1-T8. (ASE Test Prep Ser.). 1998. 90.00 (*0-7668-0574-3*) Delmar.

— 97 Auto Scopemeter. 126p. 1996. pap., student ed., wbk. ed. 15.75 (*0-8273-8289-8*) Delmar.

— Nurse Assisting Challenge. (Home Care Aide Ser.). 1996. 16.95 (*0-8273-7870-X*) Delmar.

— Paralegal CTB, 1995. (Paralegal Ser.). 1996. 49.95 (*0-8273-7134-9*) Delmar.

***Delmar Staff.** St. Anthony Physician ICD-9-CM. 1998. 32.00 (*0-7668-0968-4*) Delmar.

Delmar Staff, creator. Delmar's Nurses Drug Reference 96. (Professional Reference - Nursing Ser.). 1440p. (C). 1996. pap. 26.95 (*0-8273-7540-9*) Delmar.

Delmar Staff & Bauman, Mark B. Respiratory Nursing. (Rapid Nursing Interventions Ser.). 224p. (C). 1995. pap. 31.95 (*0-8273-7095-4*) Delmar.

Delmar Staff & Beuman, Monika E. Pediatric Nursing. rev. ed. LC 95-20855. (Rapid Nursing Interventions Ser.). 224p. (C). 1995. mass mkt. 31.95 (*0-8273-7097-0*) Delmar.

Delmar Staff & Billings, Patricia C. Instant Nursing Assessment: Pediatric. LC 95-21008. (Nursing Education Ser.). 224p. (C). 1995. pap. 21.50 (*0-8273-7098-9*) Delmar.

Delmar Staff & Korolishin, Theresa M. Instant Nursing Assessment: Cardiovascular System. LC 95-21007. (Nursing Education Ser.). 256p. (C). 1995. pap. 31.95 (*0-8273-7102-0*) Delmar.

Delmar Staff & Mauro, Judith A. Instant Nursing Assessment: Neurologic. (Nursing Education Ser.). 224p. (C). 1995. mass mkt. 21.50 (*0-8273-7103-9*) Delmar.

Delmar Staff & Scheutz, Nancy. Mental Health Nursing. (Rapid Nursing Interventions Ser.). 224p. (C). 1995. pap. 31.95 (*0-8273-7096-2*) Delmar.

Delmar Staff & Summerlin, Kip. Delmar's Institutional Network Version: Nursing Skills. 1200.00 (*0-7668-0721-5*, Pub. by Delmar) Thomson Learn.

Delmar Staff & Wade, Carol R. Cardiovascular Nursing. (Nursing Education Ser.). 224p. (C). 1996. pap. 31.95 (*0-8273-7105-5*) Delmar.

Delmar Staff & Watanabe, Suzan J. Rapid Nursing Intervention. rev. ed. (Rapid Nursing Interventions Ser.). 224p. (C). 1995. mass mkt. 21.50 (*0-8273-7092-X*) Delmar.

Delmar Staff, et al. Gerontologic Nursing. LC 95-21869. (Rapid Nursing Interventions Ser.). 224p. (C). 1996. pap. 31.95 (*0-8273-7094-6*) Delmar.

Delmar Staff, jt. auth. see Vec Staff.

***Delmarcel, Guy.** Flemish Tapestry. (Illus.). 368p. 2000. 95.00 (*0-8109-3345-4*, Pub. by Abrams) Time Warner.

Delmarcel, Guy, jt. auth. see Brown, Clifford M.

DelMargo, Lynn D., ed. see Lifshin, Lyn.

Delmas-Harrap. Dictionnaire des Affaires Francais-Anglais, Anglais-Francais. (ENG & FRE.). 508p. 1981. 75.00 (*0-8288-9544-9*, M9452) Fr & Eur.

Delmas, Jean, ed. see Corvisier, Andre.

Delmas-Marty, Mireille, ed. The Criminal Process & Human Rights: Toward a European Consciousness. Summers, Mark A., tr. from FRE. LC 94-19838. 220p. (C). 1995. lib. bdg. 86.00 (*0-7923-2944-9*, Pub. by M Nijhoff) Kluwer Academic.

— The European Convention for the Protection of Human Rights International Protection vs. National Restrictions. (International Studies in Human Rights: No. 19). 364p. 1992. lib. bdg. 148.50 (*0-7923-1283-X*) Kluwer Academic.

Delmas-Marty, Mireille, et al. What Kind of Criminal Policy for Europe? LC 96-41628. 1996. 225.00 (*90-411-0310-4*) Kluwer Law Intl.

Delmas, Philippe. Rosy Future of War. LC 97-4177. 1997. 23.50 (*0-684-83370-0*) Free Pr.

Delmas, Robert J., ed. Ice Core Studies of Global Biogeochemical Cycles. LC 95-15268. (NATO ASI Ser.: Series I, Global Environmental Change: Vol. 30). 496p. 1995. 260.95 (*3-540-59274-1*) Spr-Verlag.

***Delmastro, Paolo.** Translin: Transmission Analysis Software & User's Manual. 70p. 1999. pap. 215.00 (*1-58053-039-7*) Artech Hse.

***Delmater, Rhonda & Hancock, Monte.** Data Mining Explained: A Manager's Guide to Customer-Centric Business Intelligence. (Illus.). 352p. 2000. pap. 39.95 (*1-55558-231-1*, Digital DEC) Buttrwrth-Heinemann.

***Delmon, B. & Froment, G. F., eds.** Catalyst Deactivation 1999. (Studies in Surface Science & Catalysis Ser.). 512p. 1999. 241.00 (*0-444-50213-0*) Elsevier.

Delmon, B. & Froment, G. F., eds. Catalyst Deactivation 1994: Proceedings of the Sixth International Symposium, Ostend, Belgium, October 3-5, 1994. (Studies in Surface Science & Catalysis: Vol. 88). 692p. 1994. 297.50 (*0-444-81682-8*) Elsevier.

Delmon, B., jt. ed. see Grange, P.

***Delmon, Bernard, et al.** Hydrotreatment & Hydrocracking of Oil Fractions: Proceedings of the 2nd International Symposium, 7th European Workshop, Antwerpen, Belgium, November 14-17, 1999. LC 99-51445. (Studies in Surface Science & Catalysis). 1999. write for info. (*0-444-50214-9*) Elsevier.

Delmonico, Rod. Baseball Defensive Drills. LC 96-52747. (Illus.). 160p. (Orig.). 1997. pap. 14.95 (*1-57028-110-6*, 81106H, Mstrs Pr) NTC Contemp Pub Co.

— Defensive Baseball. (Illus.). 160p. (Orig.). 1995. pap. 16.95 (*1-57028-029-0*, 80290H, Mstrs Pr) NTC Contemp Pub Co.

— Hit & Run Baseball. LC 91-43935. 184p. 1992. pap. 15.95 (*0-88011-327-8*, PDEL0327) Human Kinetics.

— Illinois Probate Laws Annotated, 1993 Edition. 152p. 22.50 (*0-614-05846-5*, MICHIE) LEXIS Pub.

— Offensive Baseball Drills. LC 95-42628. (Illus.). 184p. (Orig.). 1996. pap. 14.95 (*0-87322-865-0*, PDEL0865) Human Kinetics.

Delmont, J., ed. Milk Intolerances & Rejection. (Illus.). x, 170p. 1983. pap. 121.75 (*3-8055-3546-5*) S Karger.

Delmont, J. & Harris, A. G., eds. Cancer of the Exocrine Pancreas: From Oncogenes to Unresectable Tumors. (Frontiers of Gastrointestinal Research Ser.: Vol. 12). (Illus.). x, 306p. 1986. 216.75 (*3-8055-4329-8*) S Karger.

Delmont, J., ed. see Gastroenterological Symposium Staff.

Delmont, J., ed. see Hepato-Gastroenterology Symposium Staff.

Delmonte, Diana. Dynamics in the Arts. 1974. 6.00 (*0-8315-0144-8*) Speller.

Delmonte, John. Technology of Carbon & Graphite Fiber Composites. LC 86-20820. 464p. 1987. reprint ed. lib. bdg. 49.50 (*0-89874-981-6*) Krieger.

Delmonteque, Bob & Hays, Scott. Lifelong Fitness: How to Look Great at Any Age. 192p. (Orig.). 1993. mass mkt. 14.99 (*0-446-39488-2*) Warner Bks.

Delmore, Alton. Truth Is Stranger Than Publicity. Wolfe, Charles K., ed. LC 95-69025. (Illus.). 333p. 1995. reprint ed. pap. 14.95 (*0-915608-15-4*) Country Music Found.

***Delmore Staff.** Maine Map & Guide 2000. 2000. pap. 2.95 (*0-89933-082-7*) DeLorme Map.

Delmore Staff. Texas Atlas & Gazetteer. 2nd ed. LC 99-464941. (Atlas & Gazetteer Ser.). (Illus.). 1998. pap. text 24.95 (*0-89933-260-9*) DeLorme Map.

Delmore, T. A. Eclipsing F: Crow Poems in Three Parts. 65p. (Orig.). 1996. pap. 12.00 (*1-883957-05-2*, Robin Hood) R Hood Little.

Delmut, Kerl, jt. auth. see Ackerman, A. Bernard.

Delnick, F. M., ed. Electrochemical Capacitors, No. II. LC 97-137468. (Proceedings Ser.: Vol. 96-25). (Illus.). 338p. 1997. 56.00 (*1-56677-125-0*) Electrochem Soc.

Delnick, F. M. & Tomkiewicz, M., eds. Electrochemical Capacitors. LC 95-61602. (Proceedings Ser.: Vol. 95-29). (Illus.). 310p. 1996. 55.00 (*1-56677-150-1*) Electrochem Soc.

Delo, David M. Peddlers & Post Traders: The Army Sutler on the Frontier. rev. ed. (Illus.). 304p. 1998. pap. 24.00 (*0-9662218-1-8*) Kingfisher Bks.

***Delo, David M.** The Right Touch. Olsen, Erica S., ed. (The Touch Touchstone Action-Mystery Ser.). (Illus.). 304p. 2000. pap. 14.00 (*0-9662218-3-4*, Pub. by Kingfisher Bks) Partners-West.

Delo, David M. The Yellowstone, Forever! Olsen, Erica S., ed. LC 97-92846. (Illus.). 448p. (Orig.). 1998. pap. 15.00 (*0-9662218-0-X*) Kingfisher Bks.

Delo, David Marion. The Last Rites Never Came: Memoirs of a University Presidency, 1958-1971. LC 92-46302. 1993. 19.95 (*1-879852-50-0*) Univ Tampa.

DeLoach, et al, eds. Red Blood Cells As Carriers for Drugs. (Current Studies in Hematology & Blood Transfusion: No. 51). (Illus.). viii, 162p. 1985. 90.50 (*3-8055-3940-1*) S Karger.

Deloach & Ambrosio. Troubleshooting Digital Systems: Lab Ma. 6th ed. 1994. pap. text, lab manual ed. 44.00 (*0-13-303777-0*) P-H.

DeLoach & Way. Carrier & Bioreactor Red Blood Cells for Drug Delivery & Targeting. (Advances in the Biosciences Ser.: No. 92). (Illus.). 210p. 1994. 165.00 (*0-08-042496-1*, Pergamon Pr) Elsevier.

Deloach, Adrien, ed. see Gayles, Yolanda.

Deloach, Alan. Digital Systems. 7th ed. 1997. pap. text, lab manual ed. 39.60 (*0-13-727694-X*) P-H.

***DeLoach, Carolyn.** Shadow Chasers: The Woolfolk Tragedy Revisited. rev. ed. LC 00-132394. (Illus.). 400p. 2000. 24.95 (*0-9700656-0-4*) Eagles Pubng GA.

— Shadow Chasers: The Woolfolk Tragedy Revisited. 2nd ed. LC 00-132304. (Illus.). 400p. 2000. pap. 16.95 (*0-9700656-1-2*) Eagles Pubng GA.

DeLoach, Cartha D. Hoover's FBI: The Inside Story by Hoover's Trusted Lieutenant. (Illus.). 432p. 1995. 27.50 (*0-89526-479-X*) Regnery Pub.

DeLoach, Charles. The Angels' War Against GOD. LC 96-92979. 256p. (Orig.). 1997. pap., per. 16.95 (*0-9655956-5-X*) Suwannee Valley.

— Giants: A Reference Guide from History, the Bible, & Recorded Legend. LC 94-41625. (Illus.). 326p. 1995. 41.50 (*0-8108-2971-1*) Scarecrow.

Deloach, Charles. The Quotable Shakespeare: A Topical Dictionary. LC 87-46384. 568p. 1998. pap. 25.00 (*0-7864-0571-6*) McFarland & Co.

DeLoach, Debbie, jt. auth. see Dedman, Robert H.

DeLoach, J. R., jt. auth. see Magnani, M.

Deloach, J. R., jt. ed. see Green, R.

DeLoach, Marva L., jt. ed. see Josey, E. J.

DeLoach, Ned. Diving Guide to Underwater Florida. 9th ed. (Illus.). 325p. 1996. pap. 18.95 (*1-878348-13-2*) New World FL.

***DeLoach, Ned.** Reef Fish Behavior: Florida Caribbean Bahamas. (Illus.). 360p. 1999. spiral bd. 39.95 (*1-878348-28-0*) New World FL.

Deloach, Ned, jt. auth. see Humann, Paul.

DeLoach, Ned, ed. see Humann, Paul.

DeLoach, Ned, ed. & photos by see Humann, Paul.

***DeLoach, Nora.** Mama Pursues Murderous Shadows. 192p. 2000. mass mkt. 5.99 (*0-553-57722-0*) Bantam.

Deloach, Nora. Mama Rocks the Empty Cradle. 208p. 1999. mass mkt. 5.99 (*0-553-57720-4*) Bantam.

DeLoach, Nora. Mama Saves a Victim. (Mama Mystery Ser.: No. 4). 156p. (YA). (gr. 9 up). 1998. pap. 10.95 (*0-87067-874-4*) Holloway.

— Mama Stalks the Past. LC 97-10117. 208p. 1997. 21.95 (*0-553-10662-7*) Bantam.

— Mama Stalks the Past. 272p. 1998. mass mkt. 5.99 (*0-553-57721-2*) Bantam.

— Mama Stands Accused. (Mama Mystery Ser.: No. 3). 156p. 1998. pap. 10.95 (*0-87067-873-6*, BH 873-6) Holloway.

— Mama Traps a Killer. (Mama Mystery Ser.: No. 2). 192p. 1995. mass mkt. 4.95 (*0-87067-747-0*) Holloway.

— Silas: The Power of Evil. 160p. 1993. mass mkt. 3.95 (*0-87067-383-1*) Holloway.

Deloach, Nora L. Mama Solves a Murder. (Mama Mystery Ser.: No. 1). 192p. 1994. mass mkt. 4.95 (*0-87067-969-4*) Holloway.

DeLoach, Nuke. Do-It-Yourself Vinyl Siding. 40p. 1994. pap. 14.95 (*0-9640586-0-X*) Pick-Up Pubns.

DeLoach, P. F., et al, eds. Frontiers of Shrimp Research. (Developments in Aquaculture & Fisheries Science Ser.: No. 22). viii,294p. 1991. 131.50 (*0-444-88346-0*) Elsevier.

DeLoach, Sylvia. Girls in Action Guide. McClain, Cindy, ed. 42p. (Orig.). 1995. pap. text 3.95 (*1-56309-127-5*, W957111) Womans Mission Union.

***DeLoach, Sylvia & Massey, Barbara.** A is for Aleeya. (Child Like Me). (Illus.). 30p. (J). (gr. 4-6). 1999. 10.99 (*1-56309-366-9*, New Hope) Womans Mission Union.

DeLoach, Sylvia & Massey, Barbara. A Country for Katie. LC 98-212249. (Child Like Me Ser.). 32p. (J). (gr. 4-6). 1998. pap. text 6.99 (*1-56309-259-X*, N987106, New Hope) Womans Mission Union.

— Partners in Peru. LC 98-212787. (Child Like Me Ser.). 32p. (J). (gr. 1-6). 1998. per. 6.99 (*1-56309-258-1*, N987105, New Hope) Womans Mission Union.

DeLoach, Sylvia, jt. auth. see Massey, Barbara.

DeLoache, jt. auth. see Siegler.

DeLoache, Judy S. Current Readings in Child Development. 3rd ed. LC 99-165401. 256p. 1998. pap. text 31.00 (*0-205-27955-4*, T7955-2) Allyn.

***DeLoache, Judy S. & Gottlieb, Alma, eds.** A World of Babies: Imagined Childcare Guides for Seven Societies. LC GN482.W67 2000. (Illus.). 224p. 2000. 49.95 (*0-521-66264-8*); pap. 16.95 (*0-521-66475-6*) Cambridge U Pr.

Deloatch, Kimberly H., jt. auth. see Lindley, Celeste M.

Delobeau, F. The Environment of the Earth. LC 71-170338. (Astrophysics & Space Science Library: No. 28). 113p. 1971. text 118.50 (*90-277-0208-X*) Kluwer Academic.

Delobel, A. & Tran, M. Les Coleopteres des Denrees Alimentaires Entreposees dans les Regions Chaudes (Beetles in Stored Foodstuffs in Hot Regions) (Faune Tropicale Ser.: Vol. XXXII).Tr. of Beetles in Stored Foodstuffs in Hot Regions. (FRE., Illus.). 426p. 1993. pap. 28.00 (*2-7099-1130-2*, Pub. by LInstitut Francais) Balogh.

Delobel, Claude, et al. Databases: From Relational to Object-Oriented Systems. 480p. 1995. mass mkt. 38.95 (*1-85032-124-8*) ITCP.

Deloch-Hughes, Edye. I Like Gym Shoe Soup. (Illus.). 16p. (J). (gr. k-3). 1991. 10.75 (*0-941484-11-4*) Urban Res Pr.

Deloche, G. & Seron, X., eds. Mathematical Disabilities: A Cognitive Neuropsychological Perspective. (Harry Whitaker's Neuropsychology & Neurolinguistics Ser.). 304p. 1987. text 59.95 (*0-89859-891-5*) L Erlbaum Assocs.

Deloche, G., jt. ed. see Seron, X.

Deloche, Jean. Transport & Communications in India Prior to Steam Locomotion, Vol. I: Land Transport. (French Studies on South Asian Culture & Society: Vol. VIII). 360p. 1994. 35.00 (*0-19-563141-2*) OUP.

Deloche, Jen. Transport & Communication in India Prior to Steam Locomotion Vol. 2: Water Transport. Walker, James, tr. from FRE. (French Studies on South Asian Culture & Society; Oxford India Paperbacks: Vol. VIII). 306p. 1995. 32.00 (*0-19-563243-5*) OUP.

Deloe, Jesse B. Sweeter Than Honey. pap. 5.99 (*0-88469-105-5*) BMH Bks.

Deloffre, ed. see Prevost, Abbe.

Deloffre, Frederic, ed. see Voltaire.

Delogu, Nancy N., jt. auth. see De Bernardo, Mark A.

Delogu, Orlando E. Federal Environmental Regulation. 1100p. 1994. ring bd. 175.00 (*0-614-05818-X*, MICHIE) LEXIS Pub.

— Maine Land Use & Zoning Control: Case Law Perspectives on Planning & Growth. 870p. 1992. pap. 75.00 (*0-88063-324-7*, MICHIE) LEXIS Pub.

— Maineland Use Control Law: Cases, Notes, Comments. 2nd ed. LC 97-13537. 972p. (C). 1997. lib. bdg. 85.00 (*1-881758-34-6*) Tower Pub ME.

Delogu, Orlando E. & Davidson, John H., Jr. Federal Environmental Regulation, 1990, 2 vols. 1100p. 1994. pap., suppl. ed. 37.50 (*0-250-40707-8*, MICHIE) LEXIS Pub.

Deloitte. Business Asset. LC 95-81936. 1995. 125.00 (*0-316-18131-5*) Little.

— Executives Abroad. 1994. pap. text 109.00 (*90-6544-791-1*) Kluwer Academic.

Deloitte, et al. The TrueBlood Professors' Seminar: Accounting & Auditing Case Studies, 2 vols. 91p. 1988. student ed. 5.00 (*0-86539-046-0*); teacher ed. 5.00 (*0-86539-045-2*) Am Accounting.

Deloitte & Touche Consulting Group Staff. Corporate Kinetics. LC 98-16469. 256p. 1998. 24.50 (*0-684-83221-6*) S&S Trade.

Deloitte & Touche Staff. Abingdon Clergy Income Tax Guide 1998: For 1997 Returns. 112p. 1997. pap. 12.95 (*0-687-07039-2*) Abingdon.

Deloitte & Touche Staff, rev. Abingdon Clergy Income Tax Guide 1997: For 1996 Returns. 1996. pap. 24.95 (*0-687-05598-9*); mac hd 24.95 (*0-687-05595-4*) Abingdon.

— Abingdon Clergy Income Tax Guide 1997: For 1996 Returns. rev. ed. 112p. 1996. pap. 12.95 (*0-687-05594-6*) Abingdon.

Deloitte & Touche Staff, jt. auth. see ATA National Accounting & Finance Council Staff.

An Asterisk (*) at the beginning of an entry indicates that the title is appearing for the first time.

Deloitte, Haskins & Sells Staff. Summary Reporting of Financial Information, 2 vols., Set. LC 83-81991. 169p. 1983. 35.00 (0-910586-52-7, 054-83) Finan Exec.

Deloitz Touche Tohmatsu International Staff, et al. Coming Clean: Corporate Environmental Reporting Opening up for Sustainable Development. (Illus.). 64p. (C). 1993. 25.00 (0-942640-03-9) Touche Co.

Delol, J. Aeronautics Abbreviations Glossary: French-English Glossaire des Abrev. Orig. Title: Glossaire des Abreviations Aeronautiques. (ENG & FRE.). 129p. 1996. pap. 38.00 (2-85608-083-9, Pub. by La Maison Du Dict) IBD Ltd.

DeLolme, J. L. The Constitution of England: or An Account of the English Government; in Which It Is Compared Both with the Republican Form of Government & the Other Monarchies in Europe. LC 98-83245. (Preservation Ser.). xxiv, 404p. 1999. reprint ed. 85.00 (1-57588-500-X, 323010) W S Hein.

Delone, Boris N. & Faddeev, D. K. The Theory of Irrationalities of the Third Degree. Lehmer, Emna & Walker, Sue A., trs. from RUS. LC 63-21548. (Translations of Mathematical Monographs: Vol. 10). 531p. reprint ed. pap. 164.70 (0-7837-1634-6, 204192700024) Bks Demand.

*Delone, N. B. & Krainov, V. P. Multiphoton Processes in Atoms. 2nd enl. ed. LC 99-39037. (Series in Atoms, Molecular, Optical & Plasma Physics: Vol. 13). (Illus.). xii, 350p. 2000. 118.00 (3-540-64615-9) Spr-Verlag.

Delone, N. B. & Krainov, Vladimir P. Atoms in Strong Light Fields. (Chemical Physics Ser.: Vol. 28). (Illus.). 350p. 1985. 108.95 (0-387-12412-8) Spr-Verlag.

— Multiphoton Processes in Atoms. LC 93-25345. (Atoms & Plasmas Ser.: Vol. 13). 1993. 136.95 (0-387-56845-X) Spr-Verlag.

Delone, Nikolai B. & Krainov, Vladimir P. Fundamentals of Nonlinear Optics of Atomic Gases. LC 87-14775. (Pure & Applied Optics Ser.). 221p. 1988. 135.00 (0-471-89391-9) Wiley.

Delone, Richard, jt. auth. see Thomson, William.

DeLone, Richard H. Education, Employment, & the At-Risk Youth. 15p. 1985. pap. 5.95 (1-56602-006-9) Research Better.

Deloney, Thomas. The Novels of Thomas Deloney. Lawlis, Merritt E., ed. LC 77-18010. (Illus.). 462p. 1978. reprint ed. lib. bdg. 79.50 (0-313-20105-6, DENO, Greenwood Pr) Greenwood.

— The Works of Thomas Deloney. (BCL1-PR English Literature Ser.). 600p. 1992. reprint ed. lib. bdg. 99.00 (0-7812-7202-5) Rprt Serv.

Delong. Historic American Buildings: California, 4 vols. Incl. Texas., 2 vols. 1979. 1979. Set lib. bdg. 40.00 (0-318-59369-6) Garland.

— Macroeconomics. 2001. 60.25 (0-07-232848-7) McGraw.

DeLong, Amy S., jt. auth. see Sample, Tex.

Delong, Barbara M. Cosmic Deck of Initiation. 1997. 25.00 (0-88079-514-X) US Games Syst.

DeLong, Brad. Electronic Companion to Intermediate Macroeconomics. Boykin, John, ed. (Electronic Companion Ser.). (Illus.). 300p. (C). 1998. pap. text, wbk. ed. 34.95 (1-58032-008-2); pap. text, wbk. ed. 29.95 incl. cd-rom (1-58032-009-0) Cogito Lrning.

— An Electronic Companion to Principles of Macroeconomics. Boykin, John, ed. (Electronic Companion Ser.). (Illus.). 300p. (C). 1999. pap. text, wbk. ed. 34.95 (1-888902-93-0) Cogito Lrning.

— An Electronic Companion to Principles of Macroeconomics. Boykin, John, ed. (Electronic Companion Ser.). (Illus.). 300p. (C). 2000. pap. text, wbk. ed. 29.95 incl. cd-rom (1-888902-94-9) Cogito Lrning.

— 4-Wheel Freedom: The Art of Off-Road Driving. LC 96-204008. (Illus.). 152p. 1996. pap. 25.00 (0-87364-891-9) Paladin Pr.

DeLong, Charles E. The Murder of Julia Bulette: Virginia City, Nevada, 1867 - With the Life & Confession of John Millian, Convicted Murderer. Jones, William R., ed. 16p. 1978. pap. 2.00 (0-89646-044-4) Vistabooks.

DeLong, David G., jt. auth. see Brownlee, David B.

*DeLong, Deanna. Drink Water for Live: Your Journey to Better Health. (Illus.). 36p. 1998. pap. 25.00 (1-892972-00-X) Creative Market.

Delong, Deanna. How to Dry Foods. rev. ed. (Illus.). 160p. 1992. pap. 15.95 (1-55788-050-6, HP Books) Berkley Pub.

*DeLong, Douglas. Ancient Teachings for Beginners: A Course in Psychic & Spiritual Development. 2000. pap. 12.95 (1-56718-214-3) Llewellyn Pubns.

Delong, Dwight M. & Freytag, Paul H. Four Genera of World Gyponinae: Gypona, Gyponana, Rugosana & Reticana. (Bulletin New Ser.: Vol. 2, No. 3). 1964. pap. text 6.00 (0-86727-050-0) Ohio Bio Survey.

DeLong, G. R., et al, eds. Iodine & the Brain. (Illus.). 380p. 1989. 105.00 (0-306-43103-3, Plenum Trade) Perseus Pubng.

DeLong, Gail, jt. auth. see Gore, Carlyn.

DeLong, George. Awakening to Your Dreams: A Dreamers Handbook. 190p. (Orig.). 1991. pap. 12.95 (0-9628316-0-3) New World CA.

DeLong, George W. Her Long Black Hair: Poetic Thoughts & Love Stories. LC 81-90306. (Illus.). 128p. (Orig.). 1981. pap. 5.00 (0-9603414-1-2) DeLong & Assocs.

Delong, Howard. A Refutation of Arrow's Theorem. 102p. (C). 1991. lib. bdg. 37.00 (0-8191-8250-8) U Pr of Amer.

DeLong, I. H. Parker: Lineage of Malcolm Metzger Parker from Johannes DeLang. (Illus.). 62p. 1994. reprint ed. pap. 13.00 (0-8328-4230-3) Higginson Bk Co.

DeLong, James V. The New "Criminal" Classes: Legal Sanctions & Business Managers LC 99-165616. 47p. 1997. pap. write for info. (0-937299-58-8) Natl Legal Ctr Pub Interest.

— Property Matters. LC 96-48280. 352p. 1997. 27.00 (0-684-87437-7) S & S Enterprises.

*DeLong, Janice & Schwedt, Rachel. Contemporary Christian Authors. LC 99-41563. (Illus.). 1999. text 45.00 (0-8108-3688-2) Scarecrow.

DeLong, Kent. Mogadishu! Heroism & Tragedy. Tuckey, Steven, ed. LC 94-31744. 144p. 1994. 24.95 (0-275-94925-7, DT407, Praeger Pubs) Greenwood.

— War Heroes: Stories of Congressional Medal of Honor Recipients. LC 92-39283. 224p. 1993. 22.95 (0-275-94309-7, C4309, Praeger Pubs) Greenwood.

DeLong, Lea. Nature's Forms, Nature's Forces: The Work of Alexandre Hogue. LC 84-60404. (Illus.). 216p. (Orig.). 1984. pap. 25.00 (0-86659-005-6) Philbrook Mus Art.

DeLong, Lea R. Nature's Forms, Nature's Forces: The Art of Alexandre Hogue. LC 84-60404. (Illus.). 221p. 1984. pap. 22.95 (0-8061-1917-9) U of Okla Pr.

*DeLong, Lea Rosson. Christian Petersen, Sculptor. (Illus.). 200p. 2000. 44.95 (0-8138-2946-1) Iowa St U Pr.

— Shifting Vision. 72p. 1998. pap. 25.00 (1-879003-22-8) Edmundson.

Delong, Marilyn F. Medical Acronyms, Eponyms, & Abbreviations. 3rd ed. Swanson, Kathryn, ed. LC 94-40393. 400p. (C). 1995. pap. 15.95 (1-57066-007-7, ME063) Practice Mgmt Info.

DeLong, Marilyn F. Medical Acronyms, Eponyms, & Abbreviations. 3rd rev. ed. LC 96-78925. 332p. 1997. pap. 12.95 (1-885987-05-6, ME077, Health Info Pr) Practice Mgmt Info.

*DeLong, Marilyn R. The Way We Look: Dress & Aesthetics. 2nd ed. (Illus.). 96p. 1998. pap., teacher ed. write for info. (1-56367-148-4) Fairchild.

DeLong, Marilyn R. The Way We Look: Dress & Aesthetics. 2nd rev. ed. LC 97-77480. (Illus.). 350p. (C). 1998. pap. 54.00 (1-56367-071-2) Fairchild.

DeLong, Marilyn R. & Fiore, Ann M. Aesthetics of Textiles & Clothing: Advancing Multi-Disciplinary Perspectives, 7. LC 95-111053. (ITAA Special Publications: No. 7). (C). 1994. pap. text 35.00 (1-885715-03-X) Intl Textile.

DeLong, Mark R. & Howell, Webb C., eds. Full Potential: A Guide for Parents of Bright Teens. rev. ed. (Illus.). 200p. 1995. pap. 14.95 (0-9637364-8-5) Journalistic.

DeLong, Sylvia. Charting Presidential Elections. LC 82-70713. 160p. 1982. 17.00 (0-86690-030-6, D2456-0114) Am Fed Astrologers.

Delong, Sylvia. Guideposts to Mystical & Mundane Interpretations. 152p. 1985. 16.00 (0-86690-066-7, D1061-014) Am Fed Astrologers.

Delong, Ted. Barter Concepts That Work: Trade Anything. (Illus.). 96p. 1998. pap. 19.95 (1-885661-14-2) Estate Protection.

DeLong, Ted. A Business Trust. 86p. 1998. 45.00 (1-885661-08-8) Estate Protection.

— Estate Planning Forms. 90p. 1997. 14.95 (1-885661-05-3) Estate Protection.

— A Insurance Trust. 50p. 1998. 45.00 (1-885661-10-X) Estate Protection.

Delong, Ted. Keys to Riches in Estate Planning. LC 94-96336. (Illus.). 240p. 1996. pap. 59.90 incl. audio (1-885661-00-2) Estate Protection.

DeLong, Ted. A Limited Partnership. 90p. 1997. 49.00 (1-885661-07-X) Estate Protection.

— Personality Test. 40p. 1995. pap. text 15.00 (1-885661-04-5) Estate Protection.

— A Trustee's Manual. 86p. 1997. pap. text 35.00 (1-885661-03-7) Estate Protection.

DeLong, Thomas A. DeLong. The DeLongs of New York & Brooklyn: A Huguenot Family Portrait. 203p. 1996. reprint ed. pap. 29.50 (0-8328-5386-0); reprint ed. lib. bdg. 39.50 (0-8328-5385-2) Higginson Bk Co.

*DeLong, Thomas A. John Davis Lodge: A Life in Three Acts: Actor, Politician, Diplomat. LC 99-49123. (Illus.). xvi, 432p. 1999. 29.95 (1-888112-03-4) Sacred Hrt Univ.

Delong, Thomas A. Pops: Paul Whiteman, King of Jazz. LC 83-19291. (Illus.). 352p. 1983. 17.95 (0-8329-0264-0) New Win Pub.

DeLong, Thomas A. Quiz Craze: America's Infatuation with the Radio & Television Game Shows. LC 91-10573. 328p. 1991. 35.00 (0-275-94042-X, C4042, Praeger Pubs) Greenwood.

— Radio Stars: An Illustrated Biographical Dictionary of over 953 Performers, 1920 Through 1960. LC 96-24424. (Illus.). 316p. 1996. lib. bdg. 65.00 (0-7864-0149-4) McFarland & Co.

*DeLong, Thomas A. Stars in Our Eyes. 1999. 35.00 (0-912980-00-1) Sasco.

DeLong, Thomas A. & Steiner, Rodney. Frank Munn: A Biodiscography of the Golden Voice of Radio. LC 93-84355. (Illus.). 145p. (Orig.). 1993. pap. 12.50 (0-912980-11-7) Sasco.

DeLong, William R., intro. Organ Transplantation in Religious, Ethical & Social Context: No Room for Death. LC 93-29164. (Journal of Health Care Chaplaincy: Vol. 5, Nos. 1/2). (Illus.). 175p. 1993. lib. bdg. 39.95 (1-56024-470-4) Haworth Pr.

Delony, Eric. Landmark American Bridges, Vol. 1. (Illus.). 152p. 1993. 40.00 (0-8212-2036-5, Pub. by Bulfinch Pr) Little.

DeLony, Eric, ed. Landmark American Bridges. LC 92-24530. 160p. 1993. 43.00 (0-87262-857-4) Am Soc Civil Eng.

Delooz, H., jt. auth. see Berlot, G.

Delooze, Laurence, ed. & tr. see Froissart, Jean.

Delopez, Awilda Palau. Esbozo de la Historia Legal de las Instituciones y Tribunales de Menores en Puerto Rico. (SPA.). 119p. 1975. 3.00 (0-8477-2417-4) U of PR Pr.

DeLorean, John. DeLorean. 304p. 1985. 9.95 (0-310-37940-7, 12800) Zondervan.

DeLorenzo. Status Epilepticus. 1999. write for info. (0-7506-9413-0) Buttrwrth-Heinemann.

Delorenzo & Porter. Tactical Emergency Care: Military & Operational Out - of - Hospital Medicine. LC 98-52453. 400p. 1999. pap. text 47.00 (0-8359-5325-4) P-H.

Delorenzo & Porter. Weapons of Mass Destruction. 1999. pap. 21.00 (0-13-013923-8) S&S Trade.

DeLorenzo, Lori. HIV - AIDS: A 2 Hour Overview. 2nd ed. (Illus.). 78p. 1998. pap. 19.95 (1-57801-026-8) Western Schls.

— HIV - AIDS: An 1 Hour Overview. 2nd ed. Johnson, Kathy, tr. (Illus.). 61p. 1998. pap. 12.95 (1-57801-027-6) Western Schls.

*DeLorenzo, Lori. Nursing Care of the HIV Positive Patient. 3rd ed. (Illus.). 238p. 1999. pap. write for info (1-57801-043-8) Western Schls.

DeLorenzo, Lori A. Nursing Care of the HIV Positive Patient. 2nd rev. ed. Halliburton, Barbara, ed. 199p. 1997. pap. 59.95 (1-57801-014-4) Western Schls.

*DeLorenzo, Matt. Modern Chrysler Concept Cars: The Designs That Saved the Company. (Illus.). 128p. 2000. pap. 17.95 (0-7603-0848-9, 130021AP, Pub. by MBI Pubg) Motorbooks Intl.

DeLorenzo, Matt. The New VW Beetle. LC 98-30034. 1998. pap. 13.95 (0-7603-0644-3) MBI Pubg.

Delorenzo, Ronald. Problem Solving in General Chemistry. 2nd ed. 416p. (C). 1992. text. write for info. (0-697-16411-X) Brown & Benchmark.

DeLorenzo, William E., jt. auth. see Kennedy, Dora F.

DeLorenzo, Yusuf G., tr. see Alwani, Taha J.

DeLorenzo, Yusuf T., tr. see AbuSulayman, AbdulHamid.

Delorenzo, Yusuf T., tr. see Bukhari, Muhammad.

DeLorenzo, Yusuf T., tr. see Rida, Muhammad R.

Delorey, Alan. A Birder's Guide to New Hampshire. Baicich, Paul J., ed. LC 95-81410. (ABA-Lane Birdfinding Guide Ser.). (Illus.). 222p. (Orig.). 1996. pap. 18.95 (1-878788-11-6, 267) Amer Birding Assn.

*DeLorey, Christine. Life Cycles: Your Emotional Journey to Freedom & Happiness. LC 99-90582. 352p. 2000. pap. 18.99 (0-9673130-9-0, Pub. by Osmos Bks) New Leaf Dist.

DeLorey, Thomas K., jt. illus. see Alexander, David T.

Deloria, Barbara, ed. see Deloria, Vine, Jr.

Deloria, Ella. Dakota Texts. LC 73-3550. (American Ethnological Society Publications: No. 14). reprint ed. 45.00 (0-404-58164-1) AMS Pr.

Deloria, Ella, contrib. by. Speaking of Indians. LC 98-19607. xxiv, 163p. 1998. pap. 9.95 (0-8032-6614-6, Bison Books) U of Nebr Pr.

Deloria, Ella, jt. auth. see Boas, Franz.

Deloria, Ella C. Waterlily. LC 87-21462. xii, 244p. 1988. pap. 10.95 (0-8032-6579-4, Bison Books) U of Nebr Pr.

*Deloria, Philip J. Playing Indian. LC 97-30936. (Yale Historical Publications). (Illus.). 264p. 1998. 30.00 (0-300-07111-6) Yale U Pr.

Deloria, Philip Joseph. Playing Indian. (Illus.). 264p. 1999. pap. 13.95 (0-300-08067-0) Yale U Pr.

Deloria, Vine, Jr. Behind the Trail of Broken Treaties: An Indian Declaration of Independence. 310p. 1985. reprint ed. pap. 14.95 (0-292-70754-1) U of Tex Pr.

— Custer Died for Your Sins: An Indian Manifesto. LC 87-40561. 278p. 1988. pap. 14.95 (0-8061-2129-7) U of Okla Pr.

— Documents of American Indian Diplomacy: Treaties, Agreements, & Conventions, 1775-1979, 2 Vols. LC 98-45365. (Legal History of North America Ser.: Vol. 4). 1536p. 1999. 95.00 (0-8061-3118-7) U of Okla Pr.

— God Is Red. 1993. reprint ed. lib. bdg. 24.95 (1-56849-180-8) Buccaneer Bks.

— God Is Red: A Native View of Religion. 2nd ed. 320p. 1994. pap. 16.95 (1-55591-176-5) Fulcrum Pub.

Deloria, Vine. The Indian Affair. LC 74-13387. 95p. 1974. pap. 30.00 (0-7837-8498-8, 204930500010) Bks Demand.

Deloria, Vine, Jr. Indian Education in America: Eight Essays by Vine Deloria, Jr. 70p. (Orig.). 1991. pap. 10.95 (0-9630317-0-8) Am Indian Sci.

DeLoria, Vine, Jr. Red Earth, White Lies: Native Americans & the Myth of Scientific Fact. LC 97-21689. 288p. 1997. reprint ed. pap. 16.95 (1-55591-388-1) Fulcrum Pub.

*Deloria, Vine, Jr. Singing for a Spirit. LC 99-25080. (Illus.). 232p. 2000. pap. 14.95 (1-57416-048-6) Clear Light.

DeLoria, Vine, Jr. Singing for a Spirit: A Portrait of the Dakota Sioux. LC 99-25080. (Illus.). 232p. 2000. pap. 14.95 (1-57416-025-7) Clear Light.

Deloria, Vine, Jr. Spirit & Reason: A Vine Deloria, Jr. Reader. Deloria, Barbara et al, eds. LC 99-30110. 400p. 1999. pap. text 17.95 (1-55591-430-6) Fulcrum Pub.

Deloria, Vine, Jr., ed. American Indian Policy in the Twentieth Century. LC 85-1057. 272p. 1985. 24.95 (0-8061-1897-0) U of Okla Pr.

— American Indian Policy in the Twentieth Century. LC 85-1057. 272p. 1992. pap. 15.95 (0-8061-2424-5) U of Okla Pr.

— Frank Waters: Man & Mystic. 200p. (C). 1993. pap. 15.95 (0-8040-0979-1); text 29.95 (0-8040-0978-3) Swallow.

Deloria, Vine, Jr. & Lytle, Clifford M. American Indians, American Justice. 278p. (C). 1983. pap. 14.95 (0-292-73834-X) U of Tex Pr.

— The Nations Within: The Past & Future of American Indian Sovereignty. rev. ed. LC 97-33718. 296p. 1998. pap. 12.95 (0-292-71598-6, DELNAP) U of Tex Pr.

Deloria, Vine, Jr. & Treat, James. For This Land: Writings of Religion in America. LC 98-15500. 312p. 1999. pap. 19.99 (0-415-92115-5) Routledge.

Deloria, Vine & Treat, James. For This Land: Writings on Religion in America. LC 98-15500. 320p. (C). 1998. 75.00 (0-415-92114-7) Routledge.

*Deloria, Vine & Wilkins, David E. Tribes, Treaties & Constitutional Tribulations. LC 99-26402. 222p. 1999. 30.00 (0-292-71607-9); pap. 14.95 (0-292-71608-7) U of Tex Pr.

DeLoriea, Renee. Portal in Pensacola: The Real Thing Hits Brownsville. LC 97-149646. 182p. 1997. pap. 10.99 (1-56043-189-X, Revival Pr) Destiny Image.

Delorit, Richard, et al. Crop Production. 4th ed. 1973. text 31.52 (0-13-194761-3) P-H.

Delorit, Richard J. & Gunn, Charles R. Seeds of Continental United States Legumes (Fabaceae) (Illus.). 140p. (C). 1986. 32.00 (0-9616847-0-4); pap. 28.00 (0-9616847-1-2) Agronomy Pubns.

*DeLorme. Allagash/st. John Map & Guide. 1999. 4.95 (0-89933-157-2) DeLorme Map.

— Arizona Atlas & Gazetteer. 3rd ed. (Illus.). 76p. 1999. pap. 16.95 (0-89933-266-8) DeLorme Map.

DeLorme. Louisiana Atlas & Gazetteer. LC 99-462943. 1998. pap. 16.95 (0-89933-217-X) DeLorme Map.

— Minnesota Atlas & Gazetteer. 2nd ed. LC 94-675209. (Atlas & Gazetteer Ser.). (Illus.). 96p. (Orig.). 1997. pap. 16.95 (0-89933-222-6, AA-000017-000) DeLorme Map.

*DeLorme. Tennessee Atlas & Gazetteer. 5th ed. LC 99-464308. 1999. pap. 16.95 (0-89933-272-2) DeLorme Map.

*Delorme, David. Mississippi Atlas & Gazetteer. LC 99-462941. 1998. pap. text 16.95 (0-89933-223-4) DeLorme Map.

Delorme, David. Nebraska Atlas & Gazetteer. LC 99-462944. (Illus.). 1996. pap. 16.95 (0-89933-256-0, AA-000019-000) DeLorme Map.

— Nevada Atlas & Gazetteer. LC 96-675303. (Illus.). 1996. pap. 16.95 (0-89933-228-5, AA-000020-000) DeLorme Map.

— Vermont Atlas & Gazetteer. 9th ed. LC 96-675731. (Illus.). 1996. pap. 16.95 (0-89933-016-9, AA-000031-000) DeLorme Map.

Delorme, Eleanor P. Garden Pavilions & the 18th Century French Court: And the 18th Century Court. LC 96-154429. (Illus.). 250p. 1996. 59.50 (1-85149-189-9) Antique Collect.

Delorme, G., jt. ed. see Baert, A. L.

DeLorme, Harry H., Jr. & King, Pamela D. Looking Back: Art in Savannah, 1900-1960. LC 96-61004. (Illus.). 120p. (Orig.). 1996. pap. 25.00 (0-933075-02-2) Telfair Mus.

Delorme, Jean-Claude. Architects' Dream Houses: "Maisons D'Exception" (Illus.). 124p. 1996. 35.00 (0-7892-0127-5); pap. 27.50 (0-7892-0126-7) Abbeville Pr.

Delorme, M. & Mazoyer, J. Cellular Automata: A Parallel Model. LC 98-48550. (Mathematics & Its Applications Ser.). 1998. 177.00 (0-7923-5493-1) Kluwer Academic.

*DeLorme Mapping Co. Staff. Alabama Atlas & Gazetteer: GPS Grids, Topo Maps of the Entire State, Back Roads, Outdoor Recreation. (Illus.). 1998. pap. 16.95 (0-89933-200-5) DeLorme Map.

— Alabama Atlas & Gazetteer: GPS Grids, Topo Maps of the of the Entire State, Back Roads, Outdoor Recreation. (Illus.). 1998. pap. text 19.95 (0-89933-274-9) DeLorme Map.

— Boston Street Atlas 2000. (Illus.). 112p. 2000. pap. 14.95 (0-89933-401-6) DeLorme Map.

— Colorado Atlas & Gazetteer. 4th ed. 2000. pap. 19.95 (0-89933-273-0) DeLorme Map.

DeLorme Mapping Co. Staff. Idaho Atlas & Gazetteer. 2nd ed. LC 93-675064. (Atlas & Gazetteer Ser.). (Illus.). 64p. (Orig.). 1995. pap. 16.95 (0-89933-212-9, AAA-000010-000) DeLorme Map.

*DeLorme Mapping Co. Staff. Maine Atlas & Gazetteer. 23rd ed. (Illus.). 2000. pap. 19.95 (0-89933-282-X) DeLorme Map.

— Massachusetts Atlas & Gazetteer: Topo Maps of the Entire State. LC 99-462942. (Illus.). 1998. pap. text. write for info. (0-89933-220-X) DeLorme Map.

— New York Atlas. 5th ed. (Illus.). 2000. pap. 19.95 (0-89933-275-7) DeLorme Map.

— Ohio Atlas & Gazetteer. 5th ed. (Illus.). (Orig.). 2000. pap. 19.95 (0-89933-281-1) DeLorme Map.

— Ohio Atlas & Gazetteer: Detailed Maps of the Entire State: Back Roads, Outdoor Recreation. 5th ed. (Illus.). 1999. pap. 16.95 (0-89933-270-6) DeLorme Map.

— Oklahoma Atlas. (Illus.). 2000. pap. 19.95 (0-89933-283-8) DeLorme Map.

— Pennsylvania Atlas. 6th ed. (Illus.). 2000. pap. 19.95 (0-89933-280-3) DeLorme Map.

— Pennsylvania Atlas & Gazetteer: Topographic Maps of the Entire State, Back Roads, Outdoor Recreation. 5th ed. (Illus.). 1999. pap. write for info. (0-89933-269-2) DeLorme Map.

— Utah Atlas. 2nd ed. (Illus.). 2000. pap. 19.95 (0-89933-255-2) DeLorme Map.

DeLorme Mapping Company Staff. Illinois Atlas & Gazetteer. LC 93-675063. (Atlas & Gazetteer Ser.). (Illus.). 96p. (Orig.). 1996. pap. 16.95 (0-89933-213-7, AA-000011-000) DeLorme Map.

— Montana Atlas & Gazetteer. 3rd ed. LC 99-462933. (Orig.). 1999. pap. 16.95 (0-89933-226-9) DeLorme Map.

DeLorme Mapping Company Staff. Pennsylvania Atlas & Gazetteer. 4th ed. (Atlas & Gazetteer Ser.). (Illus.). 96p. (Orig.). 1996. pap. 16.95 (0-89933-236-6, AA-000026-000) DeLorme Map.

*DeLorme Mapping Company Staff. U. S. A. Street Atlas 7.0. (Illus.). 1999. pap. 44.95 (0-89933-912-3) DeLorme Map.

*DeLorme Mapping Company Staff, ed. Hawaii Atlas & Gazetteer: Topo Maps of the Entire State, Guide to Outdoor Recreation. LC 99-465703. (Illus.). 1999. pap. 16.95 (0-89933-208-0) DeLorme Map.

D

— Wisconsin Atlas & Gazetteer. 6th ed. 1999. pap. 19.95 (0-89933-252-8) DeLorme Map.

***DeLorme Mapping Staff.** New Hampshire Atlas & Gazetteer. 12th ed. (Illus.). 1999. pap. 19.95 (0-89933-242-0) DeLorme Map.

— Washington Atlas & Gazetteer: Detailed Topographic Maps, Back Roads, Outdoor Recreation. 2nd ed. LC 99-463853. (Illus.). 1998. pap. 16.95 (0-89933-263-3) DeLorme Map.

***DeLorme Mapping Staff, ed.** Maryland/Delaware Atlas. 2nd ed. (Illus.). 2000. pap. 19.95 (0-89933-279-X) DeLorme Map.

— Michigan Atlas & Gazetteer. 7th ed. (Illus.). 2000. pap. 19.95 (0-89933-278-1) DeLorme Map.

— North Carolina Atlas 2000. 4th ed. (Illus.). 2000. pap. 19.95 (0-89933-277-3) DeLorme Map.

— Southern California Atlas & Gazetteer. 2000th ed. (Illus.). 2000. pap. 19.95 (0-89933-285-4) DeLorme Map.

— Street Atlas: North of Boston & Merrimack Valley. (Illus.). 80p. 2000. 9.95 (0-89933-404-0) DeLorme Map.

Delorme, Mary. Alexis. large type ed. (General Fiction Ser.). 304p. 1992. 27.99 (0-7089-2659-2) Ulverscroft.

— Wandering Minstrels. large type ed. 1990. 27.99 (0-7089-2296-1) Ulverscroft.

Delorme Pub. Co. Staff. Indiana Atlas & Gazetteer. LC 98-675309. (Illus.). 1998. pap. 16.95 (0-89933-211-0) DeLorme Map.

***Delorme Publishing Company Staff.** Eartha Travelog. 2nd ed. 2000. pap. 19.95 (0-89933-323-0) DeLorme Map.

Delorme Publishing Company Staff. Iowa Atlas & Gazetteer. LC 98-675316. 1998. pap. text 16.95 (0-89933-214-5) DeLorme Map.

***Delorme Publishing Company Staff.** New Mexico Atlas. 2nd ed. (Illus.). 2000. pap. 19.95 (0-89933-317-6) DeLorme Map.

— Northern California Atlas. 5th ed. (Illus.). 2000. pap. 19.95 (0-89933-287-0) DeLorme Map.

Delorme Publishing Company Staff. Oklahoma Atlas & Gazetteer. (Illus.). 1998. pap. 19.95 (0-89933-234-X) DeLorme Map.

***DeLorme Publishing Company Staff.** Street Atlas: Portland Maine & Vicinity. LC 99-464933. (Illus.). 80p. 1999. pap. 9.95 (0-89933-400-8) DeLorme Map.

Delorme Publishing Staff. Alaska Atlas & Gazetteer. 2nd ed. (Illus.), 156p. 1998. pap. 19.95 (0-89933-259-5) DeLorme Map.

— EARTHA World Travelog. LC 99-464907. (Illus.). 168p. 1998. pap. 19.95 (0-89933-264-1) DeLorme Map.

***DeLorme Publishing Staff.** Florida Atlas & Gazetteer. 4th ed. (Illus.). 2000. pap. 19.95 (0-89933-276-5) DeLorme Map.

DeLorme Publishing Staff. Georgia Atlas & Gazetteer. (Illus.). 1998. pap. 16.95 (0-89933-210-2) DeLorme Map.

— New Mexico Atlas & Gazetteer. LC 99-464319. (Illus.). 1998. pap. 16.95 (0-89933-229-3) DeLorme Map.

Delorme Publishing Staff. Oregon Atlas & Gazetteer. 3rd ed. LC 99-464314. 88p. 1998. pap. 16.95 (0-89933-258-7) DeLorme Map.

— Wyoming Atlas & Gazetteer. 2nd ed. LC 99-463859. (Atlas & Gazetteer Ser.). (Illus.). 1998. pap. 16.95 (0-89933-261-7) DeLorme Map.

***DeLorme Publishing Staff, ed.** South Carolina Atlas & Gazetteer. (Illus.). 64p. 2000. pap. 19.95 (0-89933-237-4) DeLorme Map.

Delorme, Robert & Dopfer, Kurt, eds. The Political Economy of Diversity: Evolutionary Perspectives on Economic Order & Disorder. LC 94-6264. (European Association for Evolutionary Political Economy Ser.). 328p. 1994. 95.00 (1-85278-874-7) E Elgar.

Delorme, Robert L., compiled by. Latin America, 1983-1987: A Social Science Bibliography, Vol. 14. LC 88-25081. (Bibliographies & Indexes in Sociology Ser.: No. 14). 407p. 1988. lib. bdg. 85.00 (0-313-26406-6, DLA/, Greenwood Pr) Greenwood.

DeLorme Staff. Arkansas Atlas & Gazetteer. LC 98-675237. (Illus.). 64p. 1997. pap. 16.95 (0-89933-203-X, AA-001248-000) DeLorme Map.

— Kentucky Atlas & Gazetteer. (Illus.). 88p. 1997. pap. 16.95 (0-89933-216-1, AA-000013-000) DeLorme Map.

Delorme Staff. Missouri Atlas & Gazetteer. LC 98-675234. (Map Ser.). (Illus.). 1998. pap. 16.95 (0-89933-224-2, AA-001247-000) DeLorme Map.

DeLorme Staff. South Dakota Atlas & Gazetteer. LC 99-464317. (Illus.). 72p. 1997. pap. 16.95 (0-89933-239-0, AA-001249-000) DeLorme Map.

— Tennessee Atlas & Gazetteer. 3rd ed. LC 95-675214. (Illus.). 72p. (Orig.). 1997. pap. 16.95 (0-89933-240-4, AA-000028-000) DeLorme Map.

— Upstate New York: City Street Maps. LC 91-675034. 40p. 1990. pap. 9.95 (0-89933-300-1) DeLorme Map.

— Utah Atlas & Gazetteer. (Illus.). 64p. 1995. pap. 16.95 (0-89933-243-9, AA-000030-000) DeLorme Map.

***DeLorme US Staff.** Connecticut Rhode Island Atlas & Gazetteer. LC 99-462945. (Illus.). 80p. 1999. 16.95 (0-89933-207-2) DeLorme Map.

DeLorme US Staff. Kansas Atlas & Gazetteer: Topographic Maps of the Entire State. LC 00-555211. (Illus.). 80p. 1997. pap. 16.95 (0-89933-215-3, AA-000012-000) DeLorme Map.

***DeLorme US Staff.** Morrimac Valley & Vicinity Street Atlas: Area Includes Strafford, Nottingham, & Raymond Through Concord, Hooksett, Manchester & Nashua. (Illus.). 64p. 1999. 9.95 (0-89933-403-2) DeLorme Map.

— New Jersey Atlas & Gazetteer: Topo Maps of the Entire State. LC 99-464320. 88p. 1999. 16.95 (0-89933-227-7) DeLorme Map.

— Northern California Atlas & Gazetteer. 4th ed. (Illus.). 128p. 1998. reprint ed. 16.95 (0-89933-267-6) DeLorme Map.

— Portland Street Map. 2000. pap. 4.95 (0-89933-305-2) DeLorme Map.

— Virginia Atlas & Gazetteer: Detailed Maps of the Entire State. 3rd ed. LC 99-464309. 80p. 1999. reprint ed. 16.95 (0-89933-271-4) DeLorme Map.

DeLorme US Staff. West Virginia Atlas & Gazetteer: Topographic Maps of the Entire State, Back Roads, Outdoor Recreation. LC 99-464318. (Illus.). 1997. pap. 16.95 (0-89933-246-3, AA-000034-000) DeLorme Map.

Delors, Jacques, frwd. Multilingualism in Europe & the U. S.: A Communications Challenge for Transatlantic Relations & Global Business: Conclusions from an International Round Table Seminar. 38p. (Orig.). 1993. pap. 7.00 (0-9628287-4-2) European Inst.

Delort, Jean-Marc. F.B.I. Transformation: Second Microlocalization & Semilinear Caustics. Dold, A. et al, eds. LC 92-25539. (Lecture Notes in Mathematics Ser.: Vol. 1522). vii, 101p. 1992. 35.95 (0-387-55764-4) Spr-Verlag.

Delort, Robert. The Life & Lore of the Elephant. (Discoveries Ser.). (Illus.). 192p. 1992. pap. 12.95 (0-8109-2848-5, Pub. by Abrams) Time Warner.

Delos, Gilbert. Vodkas of the World. 1998. 17.99 (0-7858-1018-8) Bk Sales Inc.

— Wines of Bordeaux. 1998. 19.99 (0-7858-0951-1) Bk Sales Inc.

— World of Cognac. 1999. 19.99 (0-7858-1041-2) Bk Sales Inc.

Delos, Kate, jt. auth. see Rosenwasser, Rena.

Delost, Maria D. Introduction to Diagnostic Microbiology: A Text & Workbook. (Illus.). 592p. (C). (gr. 13). 1996. pap. text 48.00 (0-8016-7853-6, 07853) Mosby Inc.

Delouche, Frederic, ed. Illustrated History of Europe: A Unique Portrait of Europe's Common History. (Illus.). 384p. 1995. pap. 19.95 (0-8050-4235-0) H Holt & Co.

— The Illustrated History of Europe: A Unique Portrait of Europe's Common History. (Illus.). 384p. 1995. 35.00 (0-8050-2707-6) H Holt & Co.

Delougaz, P., jt. auth. see Kantor, Helene.

Delougaz, Pinhas. Pottery From Diyala Region. 1973. lib. bdg. 21.00 (0-226-14233-7) U Ch Pr.

— Pre-Sargonid Temples in Diyala. 1992. lib. bdg. 8.00 (0-226-14232-9) U Ch Pr.

— Temple Oval at Khafajah. 1972. lib. bdg. 7.50 (0-226-14234-5) U Ch Pr.

Deloughery, Grace L. Issues & Trends in Nursing. 3rd ed. LC 98-222026. (Illus.). 504p. (C). (gr. 13). 1997. pap. text 28.00 (0-8151-2608-5, 31078) Mosby Inc.

Deloughery, Paul. Pipe Music of the Great Plains: Highland Bagpipe Music by Midwestern & Canadian Composers. 64p. (Orig.). 1992. pap. 9.95 (1-880954-01-X) Kalevala Bks.

DeLoughery, Thomas G. Hemostasis & Thrombosis. LC 99-11152. (Vademecum Ser.). 212p. 1999. spiral bd. 45.00 (1-57059-558-5) Landes Bioscience.

Deloughry. DSP Systems. 1995. text 49.00 (0-07-707814-4) McGraw.

DeLoura, Mark, ed. Game Programming Gems. (Illus.). 600p. Date not set. 69.95 (1-58450-049-2) Chrles River Media.

DeLozier, Carolyn, ed. see Findley, K. C.

Delozier, Eric P., jt. ed. see Wood, M. Sandra.

DeLozier, Judith, jt. auth. see Grinder, John.

DeLozier, Judith A., jt. auth. see Dilts, Robert B.

DeLozier, Loretta. Collector's Encyclopedia of Lefton China. 144p. 1995. 19.95 (0-89145-640-6, 3962) Collector Bks.

— Collector's Encyclopedia of Lefton China, No. 3. 176p. 1999. pap. 24.95 (1-57432-145-5) Collector Bks.

— Collector's Encyclopedia of Lefton China Bk. II: Identification & Values. (Collector's Encyclopedia Ser.). (Illus.). 176p. 1997. 19.95 (0-89145-767-4, 4855) Collector Bks.

— Lefton China Price Guide. LC 99-208408. 96p. 1999. 9.95 (1-57432-113-7) Collector Bks.

Delp. Easy Rules: Punctuation. (EC - HS Communication/ English Ser.). 1993. pap. 2.95 (0-538-62796-4); mass mkt., wbk. ed. 15.95 (0-538-61500-1) S-W Pub.

— Easy Rules: The Comma. (EC - HS Communication/ English Ser.). 1989. mass mkt. 9.95 (0-538-60287-2) S-W Pub.

Delp, Charles J., ed. Fungicide Resistance in North America. LC 88-82917. (Illus.). 133p. 1988. 34.00 (0-89054-095-0) Am Phytopathol Soc.

Delp, Debra. Packing for Heaven. Zoglio, Suzanne W., ed. (Illus.). 32p. (Orig.). (J). (ps-k). 1991. pap. text 8.95 (0-941668-03-7) Tower Hill Pr.

Delp, Edward J., jt. ed. see Biemond, Jan.

Delp, Edward J., jt. ed. see Buda, Andrew J.

Delp, Edward J., jt. ed. see Wong, Ping W.

Delp, Frank. Aircraft Governors. LC 92-24618. (Aviation Technician Training Ser.). 50p. (Orig.). 1982. pap. text 10.35 (0-89100-156-5, JS312652) Jeppesen Sanderson.

— Aircraft Propellers & Controls. LC 92-24615. (Aviation Technician Training Ser.). (Illus.). 156p. 1979. pap. text 13.45 (0-89100-097-6, JS312651) Jeppesen Sanderson.

Delp, Frank, et al. Aircraft Maintenance & Repair. 5th ed. 576p. 1987. text 42.95 (0-07-004798-7) McGraw.

Delp, John. East Is West: Travels in Asia & the Pacific. (Illus.). 192p. (Orig.). 1996. pap. 14.95 (0-8048-2061-9) Tuttle Pubng.

Delp, Kathleen J. & Minnick, Molly A. Support Group Manual: A Training Manual for Conducting Support Programs for Parents Who Have Interrupted Pregnancies Secondary to Fetal Anomalies. (Illus.). 56p. (Orig.). 1995. pap. 14.95 (1-878526-41-3) Pineapple MI.

Delp, Michael. The Coast of Nowhere: Mediations on Rivers, Lakes, & Streams. LC 97-20632. (Great Lakes Book Ser.). 88p. (Orig.). 1997. pap. 14.95 (0-8143-2711-7, Great Lks Bks) Wayne St U Pr.

— Over the Graves of Horses. LC 88-11963. (Great Lakes Bks.). 86p. 1989. 21.95 (0-8143-2044-9); pap. 11.95 (0-8143-2045-7) Wayne St U Pr.

— Under the Influence of Water: Poems, Essays, & Stories. LC 92-10989. (Great Lakes Bks.). (Illus.). 98p. 1992. pap. 14.95 (0-8143-2391-X) Wayne St U Pr.

***Delp, Michael, et al, eds.** New Poems from the Third Coast: Contemporary Michigan Poetry. 480p. 1999. 44.95 (0-8143-2796-6); pap. 24.95 (0-8143-2797-4) Wayne St U Pr.

Delp, Peter. Systems Tools for Project Planning. LC 77-7588. 1976. pap. text 15.00 (0-89249-021-7) Intl Development.

Delp, Robert. Digital Electronics Through Experimentation. 2nd ed. (Illus.). 98p. 1984. pap. text 7.50 (0-911908-11-0) Tech Ed Pr.

Delp, Ron. How to Care for & Maintain Your Airplane. (Illus.). 176p. 1992. pap. 17.95 (0-87938-552-9) MBI Pubg.

Delp, S., et al, eds. Medical Image Computing & Computer-Assisted Intervention-MICCAI'98: First International Conference, Cambridge, MA, U. S. A., October 11-13, 1998, Proceedings. LC 98-45053. (Lecture Notes in Computer Science Ser.: Vol. 1496). xxii, 1256p. 1998. pap. 120.00 (3-540-65136-5) Spr-Verlag.

Delpal, Jacques-Louis. Paris Gourmet Guide. LC 95-15364. (Illus.). 142p. 1995. text 29.95 (0-86565-959-1) Vendome.

Delpar, Helen. The Enormous Vogue of Things Mexican: Cultural Relations Between the United States & Mexico, 1920-1935. LC 92-6125. (Illus.). 288p. (C). 1995. pap. text 19.95 (0-8173-0811-3) U of Ala Pr.

— Red Against Blue: The Liberal Party in Colombian Politics, 1863-1899. LC 79-19081. 278p. 1981. pap. 86.20 (0-7837-8368-X, 205917800009) Bks Demand.

Delpech, Henri M. La Tactique aux XIII Siecle, 2 vols., Set. LC 78-63493. reprint ed. 110.00 (0-404-17140-0) AMS Pr.

Delpech, Jean-Francois & Holder, Kate, eds. The Best of the Tocqueville Connection: A U. S.-Crest Publication. 33p. (Orig.). 1997. pap. 10.95 (0-9629930-7-7) US CREST.

Delpech, R., et al. Typological Vocabulary of Forestry Stations: Vocabulaire Typologie Des Stations Forestieres. (FRE.). 246p. 1986. 39.95 (0-8288-1430-9, M15565) Fr & Eur.

Delperier, L., jt. auth. see Shann, S.

Delph, Edward W. The Silent Community: Public Homosexual Encounters. LC 78-629. (Sociological Observations Ser.: No. 3). 186p. reprint ed. pap. 57.70 (0-608-09949-X, 202188600026) Bks Demand.

Delph, John. Firearms & Tackle Memorabilia. LC 91-65651. (Illus.). 124p. 1991. 39.95 (0-88740-332-8) Schiffer.

Delph, John & Delph, Shirley. Factory Decoys of Mason, Stevens, Dodge & Peterson. LC 80-52025. (Illus.). 168p. 1980. 35.00 (0-916838-33-1) Schiffer.

Delph, John, jt. auth. see Delph, Shirley.

Delph, Shirley & Delph, John. New England Decoys. LC 81-51445. (Illus.). 159p. 1981. 35.00 (0-916838-54-4) Schiffer.

Delph, Shirley, jt. auth. see Delph, John.

Delphi. Comprehensive Compound Interest Tables. rev. ed. 176p. 1986. pap. 5.95 (0-8092-4875-1) NTC Contemp Pub Co.

Delphi Consulting Group Staff. Delphi Insight Series on Document Management. 800p. 1997. pap., boxed set. write for info. (1-884277-10-1) Delphi Grp.

— Delphi Insight Series on Text Retrieval. 800p. 1997. pap., boxed set. write for info. (1-884277-11-X) Delphi Grp.

— Delphi Insight Series on Workflow. 800p. 1997. pap., boxed set. write for info. (1-884277-12-8) Delphi Grp.

Delphi Group Staff. The Delphi Intranet Report. 200p. 1997. pap., boxed set. write for info. (1-884277-09-8) Delphi Grp.

Delphi Internet Services Corp. Staff. Delphi: The Official Guide. 4th rev. ed. pap. text 19.95 (0-9625623-2-7) Genl Videotex.

Delphina. Dining with Delphina. 657p. 1991. pap. 19.95 (0-9630835-0-3) Whitefield Bks.

Delphinas. The Book of Lambspring. Waite, A. E., tr. from LAT. 1985. reprint ed. pap. 6.95 (0-916411-92-3) Holmes Pub.

Delphos Canal Commission, ed. see Ebbeskotte, Bob.

Delphos, William A. Asian Pocket Guide for International Environmental Executives. Beard, Alan J. et al, eds. 64p. 1994. write for info. (1-883917-04-2) Venture Pub NA.

— Capitol - Capital: Government Resources for High-Technology Companies. Beard, Alan J. et al, eds. 228p. 1994. pap. 49.95 (1-883917-01-8) Venture Pub NA.

— Environment Asia - Pacific: The Executive's Guide to Government Resources. Beard, Alan J. et al, eds. 262p. 1994. pap. write for info. (1-883917-03-4) Venture Pub NA.

— Inside the World Bank Group: The Practical Guide for International Business Executives. LC 98-206648. (A World Bank Publication). (Illus.). 246p. 1998. 50.00 (1-883917-10-7, 31629) OUP.

— Inside Washington: Government Resources for International Business. 5th rev. ed. Beard, Alan J. et al, eds. LC 98-228463. (Inside Washington Ser.). Orig. Title: Washington's Best Kept Secrets. (Illus.). 1998. mass mkt. 49.95 (1-883917-11-5) Venture Pub NA.

— Inside Washington: The International Business Executive's Guide to Government Resources. Johnson, W. Todd & Andrzejewski, Susan E., eds. 1991. pap. 24.95 (0-9628513-3-7) Venture Pub NA.

— Inside Washington & Spain: A Business Guide to U. S. & Spanish Government Assistance. Beard, Alan J. et al, eds. 154p. 1993. pap. 24.95 (0-9628513-7-X) Venture Pub NA.

— Inside Washington & Tokyo: A Business Guide to U.S. & Japanese Government Assistance. Beard, Alan J. et al, eds. 155p. 1993. pap. 24.95 (0-9628513-6-1) Venture Pub NA.

— Power Money: The International Business Executive's Guide to Government Resources. Beard, Alan J. et al, eds. 211p. 1994. 35.00 (1-883917-05-0) Venture Pub NA.

Delphos, William A., ed. Direct Marketing Guide to Canada. 180p. (Orig.). (C). 1995. pap. text 45.00 (0-7881-2361-0) DIANE Pub.

— Inside Washington: The International Business Executive's Guide to Government Resources. rev. ed. LC 88-1591. 310p. 1988. lib. bdg. 55.00 (0-8191-6934-X) Madison Bks UPA.

— International Direct Marketing Guide: Regional Markets & Selected Countries. (Illus.). 284p. 1996. reprint ed. pap. 50.00 (0-614-18672-2) DIANE Pub.

Delphy, Christine & Leonard, Diana. Familiar Exploitation: A New Analysis of Marriage in Contemporary Western Societies. LC 92-11058. (Feminist Perspectives Ser.). 1991. 58.95 (0-7456-0858-2); pap. 31.95 (0-7456-0985-6) Blackwell Pubs.

DelPico, Wayne. Basics for Builders: Plan Reading & Material Takeoff. Foley, Kevin & Greene, Mary, eds. (Illus.). 200p. 1994. pap. 35.95 (0-87629-348-8, 67307) R S Means.

Delpierre, Madeleine. Dress in France in the Eighteenth Century. LC 97-26412. 208p. 1997. 25.00 (0-300-07128-0) Yale U Pr.

DelPino, Jerome F. The Call to Preach. 56p. (Orig.). 1996. pap. 5.95 (1-885118-03-1) Prof World Peace.

Delpit, Lisa. Other People's Children: Cultural Conflict in the Classroom. 224p. 1995. 21.00 (1-56584-179-4, Pub. by New Press NY) Norton.

— Other People's Children: Cultural Conflict in the Classroom. 224p. 1996. pap. 14.95 (1-56584-180-8, Pub. by New Press NY) Norton.

Delpit, Lisa, jt. ed. see Perry, Theresa.

Delplanque, J. P., jt. ed. see Gritzo, L. A.

DelPopolo, Anthony J., Sr. Our Lady of Guadalupe Vol. 1: Blessed Mother of the Americas. (Illus.). 350p. (Orig.). 1996. pap. 18.95 (0-9619531-0-1) Cavalier Pub Hse.

Delport, H. J. South African Property Practice & the Law. 1987. ring bd. 129.00 (0-7021-1899-0, 15618, Pub. by Juta & Co) Gaunt.

Delport, H. J. & Olivier, N. J. Sakereg Vonnisbundel. 752p. 1985. pap. write for info. (0-7021-1559-2, Pub. by Juta & Co) Gaunt.

Delport, H. J. & Pretorius, J. T. Inleiding tot die Wet op Beslote Korporasies. 184p. 1990. pap. write for info. (0-7021-2389-7, Pub. by Juta & Co) Gaunt.

— Introduction to the Close Corporations Act. 175p. 1989. pap. 15.00 (0-7021-2307-2, Pub. by Juta & Co) Gaunt.

DelPorto, David & Steinfeld, Carol. The Composting Toilet System Book: A Practical Guide to Choosing, Planning & Maintaining Composting Toilet Systems, a Water-Saving, Pollution-Preventing Alternative. LC 98-88826. (Illus.). 192p. 1999. pap. 29.95 (0-9666783-0-3, 98001, Pub. by Ctr for Eco) Chelsea Green Pub.

Delprato, Dennis J., jt. ed. see Ruben, Douglas H.

Delprete, Piero G. Rondeletieae (Rubiaceae) Pt. 1: Rustia, Trasanthera, Condaminea, Picardaeo, Pogonopus, Chimarrhis, Dioicodendron, Molopanthera, Dolichedelphys & Parachimarrkis. (Flora Neotropica Monograph Ser.: Vol. 77). 1998. 48.00 (0-89327-429-1, FLN76) NY Botanical.

Delpuech, Jean-Jacques, ed. Dynamics of Solutions & Fluid Mixtures by NMR. 600p. 1995. 280.00 (0-471-95411-X) Wiley.

Delpy, David T., jt. auth. see Eke, Andras.

Delpy, David T., jt. ed. see Harrison, David K.

Delpy, Karl-Herbert. Lovebirds Today. (Illus.). 64p. 1996. 12.95 (0-7938-0118-4, WW021) TFH Pubns.

— The Proper Care of Cockatiels. (Illus.). 256p. 1992. text 16.95 (0-86622-189-1, TW105) TFH Pubns.

***Delre, Philip.** The Master Evangelist: How to Present the Gospel the Way Jesus Did. 112p. 2000. pap. text 10.00 (0-9677520-0-0) Voice Pubg IL.

***Delrey, Lester.** The Best of Lester Del Rey. 352p. 2000. pap. 12.00 (0-345-43949-X, Del Rey) Ballantine Pub Grp.

Delrio, G. & Brachet, J., eds. Steroids & Their Mechanism of Action in Nonmammalian Vertebrates. fac. ed. LC 79-5399. (Illus.). 251p. pap. 77.90 (0-7837-7531-8, 204697300005) Bks Demand.

Delrio, Martin. Global Terror. (Spider-Man Super-Thriller Ser.: No. 3). 1997. mass mkt. 4.99 (0-671-00799-8, Pocket Books) PB.

— Mortal Kombat. 1995. pap. 3.99 (0-8125-4453-6, Pub. by Tor Bks); pap., mass mkt. 5.99 (0-8125-4452-8, Pub. by Tor Bks) St Martin.

— Prince Valiant. LC 96-95128. 246p. (gr. 4-7). 1998. mass mkt. 5.99 (0-380-79405-5, Avon Bks) Morrow Avon.

***Delrio, Martin.** Prince Valiant. 1999. mass mkt. 3.99 (0-380-79404-7, Avon Bks) Morrow Avon.

Delrio, Martin. Spider Man: Eye of the Storm. 1996. mass mkt. 4.99 (0-671-56851-5, PB Trade Paper) PB.

DelRossi, A. J., jt. auth. see Cernaianu, A. C.

DelRossi, Anthony J., jt. ed. see Cernaianu, Aurel C.

Delsanto, Pier P. & Saenz, Albert W. New Perspectives on Problems in Classical & Quantum Physics, Vol. 1. 404p. 1998. text 51.00 (90-5699-548-0) Gordon & Breach.

— New Perspectives on Problems in Classical & Quantum Physics: A Festschrift in Honor of Herbert Uberall, vols. 2, Set. 743p. 1998. text 96.00 (90-5699-550-2) Gordon & Breach.

— New Perspectives on Problems in Classical & Quantum Physics: A Festschrift in Honor of Herbert

D

An Asterisk (*) at the beginning of an entry indicates that the title is appearing for the first time.

Uberall:Acoustic Propagation & Scattering, Electromagnetic Scattering, Vol. 2, Pt. 2. 440p. 1998. text 55.00 (*90-5699-549-9*) Gordon & Breach.

***Delsemme, Armand H.** Our Cosmic Origins: From the Big Bang to the Emergence of Life & Intelligence. (Illus.). 342p. 2001. pap. 14.95 (*0-521-79480-3*) Cambridge U Pr.

Delsemme, Armand H. Our Cosmic Origins: From the Big Bang to the Emergence of Life & Intelligence. rev. ed. LC 97-33010. (Illus.). 320p. (C). 1998. 24.95 (*0-521-62038-4*) Cambridge U Pr.

Delsen, Lei & De Jong, Eelke D., eds. The German & Dutch Economies: Who Follows Whom? LC 97-51874. (Contributions to Economics Ser.). (Illus.). xii, 188p. 1998. pap. 63.00 (*3-7908-1064-9*) Spr-Verlag.

Delsen, Lei & Reday-Mulvey, Genevieve, eds. Gradual Retirement in the OECD Countries: Macro & Micro Issues & Policies. (Illus.). 224p. 1996. text 73.95 (*1-85521-708-2*, Pub. by Dartmth Pub) Ashgate Pub Co.

***Delsohn, Steve.** Oral History LA Dodgers. 2001. write for info. (*0-380-97755-9*) Morrow Avon.

Delsohn, Steve. Talking Irish: The Oral History of Notre Dame. 1999. pap. 13.50 (*0-380-79253-2*, Avon Bks) Morrow Avon.

***Delsohn, Steve.** Talking Irish: The Oral History of Notre Dame Football. LC 98-18859. 384p. 1999. 24.00 (*0-380-97504-1*, Avon Bks) Morrow Avon.

Delsohn, Steve, jt. auth. see Smith, Emmitt.

Delsol, Paula. Chinese Astrology. rev. ed. 1986. mass mkt. 5.99 (*0-446-34300-5*, Pub. by Warner Bks) Little.

Delson, Donn & Hurst, Walter E. Delson's Dictionary of Radio & Record Industry Terms. Posner, Neil, ed. LC 80-24486. (Entertainment Communication Ser.: Vol. 2). 112p. (Orig.). (C). 1981. pap. 6.95 (*0-9603574-2-4*) Bradson.

Delson, Donn & Jacob, Stuart. Delson's Dictionary of Motion Picture Marketing Terms. rev. ed. (Entertainment Communication Ser.). 104p. 1990. pap. 9.95 (*0-9603574-7-5*, A-2B) Bradson.

Delson, Donn & Michalove, Ed. Delson's Dictionary of Cable, Video & Satellite Terms. Posner, Neil, ed. LC 82-17767. (Entertainment Communication Ser.: Vol. 3). (Orig.). 1982. pap. 4.95 (*0-9603574-3-2*, A-4) Bradson.

Delson, Eric, et al, eds. Encyclopedia of Human Evolution & Prehistory. LC 99-45824. (Illus.). 630p. 1998. 155.00 (*0-8153-1696-8*, H1845) Garland.

— Paleoanthropology Annual, 1990, Vol. 1. LC 10-594124. 304p. 1992. text 20.00 (*0-8153-0069-7*, H1428) Garland.

Delson, Eric, jt. auth. see Szalay, Frederick S.

Delson, Erwin B., ed. The Bar Coding Systems Industry: Rapid Growth in a Six Hundred Million Dollar Market. 268p. 1986. 995.00 (*0-931634-64-4*) FIND-SVP.

Delson, Roberta M. New Towns for Colonial Brazil: Spatial & Social Planning of the 18th Century. Robinson, David J., ed. LC 79-9347. (Dellplain Latin American Studies: No. 2). 228p. 1979. reprint ed. pap. 70.70 (*0-8357-0439-4*, 202259600028) Bks Demand.

— Readings in Caribbean History & Economics: An Introduction to the Region. (Caribbean Studies). xxii, 336p. 1981. text 251.00 (*0-677-05280-4*) Gordon & Breach.

DelSorbo, Anthony. QuickC for Windows. LC 93-39893. 1993. 49.95 (*0-07-016331-6*, Windcrest); pap. 34.95 (*0-07-016332-4*, Windcrest) TAB Bks.

Delta Delta Delta National Fraternity Staff. Pass It On: A Treasury of Tastes & Traditions. 288p. 1994. 17.95 (*0-9639957-0-7*) Delta Delta Delta.

Delta, George B. & Matsuura, Jeffrey H. Law of the Internet. LC 97-46405. 1997. ring bd. 160.00 (*1-56706-654-2*) Aspen Law.

Delta Kappa Gamma Staff. Key Issues. 528p. (C). 1995. 24.95 (*0-7872-0807-8*) Kendall-Hunt.

Delta Rice Promotions Staff. Between the Levees: A Collection of Mississippi Delta Rice Recipes. 237p. 1994. 12.00 (*0-9642126-0-9*) Delta Rice Promot.

Delta Soc. Staff. Standards of Practice for Animal-Assisted Activities & Animal Assisted Therapy. (Illus.). 92p. 1996. pap. text 20.00 (*1-889785-01-6*) Delta Soc.

Delta Society Staff. Delta Society Pet Partners Introductory Animal Handler Skills Course. (Illus.). 1995. 29.00 (*0-9627802-4-3*) Delta Soc.

— Pet Partners Volunteer Workshop Instructor Guide. (Illus.). Date not set. text. write for info. (*0-9627802-7-8*) Delta Soc.

Delta Society Working Group Staff. Learning in Dogs: The Principles of Canine Behavior & Learning Implications for Training. 1995. pap. 9.00 (*0-9627802-3-5*) Delta Soc.

Delta Staff. Atlas of Chinese Therapeutic Motion for Treatment & Health: A Guide to Traditional Chinese Massage & Exercise Therapy. (Illus.). 173p. 1995. 25.00 (*983-9808-31-1*, Pub. by Delta Edits) Weatherhill.

— Folk Tales from the East: Famous Stories from China. (Illus.). 32p. (J). 1995. pap. 3.50 (*983-9808-81-8*, Pub. by Delta Edits) Weatherhill.

— The Location of Acupoints. (Illus.). 184p. 1995. 25.00 (*983-9808-32-X*, Pub. by Delta Edits) Weatherhill.

***Delta Staff.** Practical Guide to Sales & Use Tax Book. 99th ed. 1999. pap. text 159.00 (*0-15-606631-9*) Harcourt.

Deltapoint Corporation Staff. Five S: Creating the Productive Workplace. (Illus.). 176p. 1998. pap. 59.95 (*0-9663133-0-5*) Deltapoint Corp.

Delteil, Gerard. N'Oubliez Pas l'Artiste. (FRE.). 248p. 1991. pap. 12.95 (*0-7859-2159-1*, 2070383393) Fr & Eur.

Delteil, Loys. Daumier's Complete Lithographs, 10 vols. (FRE., Illus.). 2500p. 1969. reprint ed. 2500.00 (*1-55660-030-5*) A Wofsy Fine Arts.

— Daumier's Lithographs, 1830-37: Catalogue Raisonne. (ENG & FRE., Illus.). 352p. 1999. reprint ed. 150.00 (*1-55660-250-2*) A Wofsy Fine Arts.

— Delacroix - The Graphic Work: Catalogue Raisonne. rev. ed. Strauber, Susan E., tr. & rev. by. (Illus.). 256p. 1997. 150.00 (*1-55660-252-9*) A Wofsy Fine Arts.

— Ensor, de Braekeleer & Leys: Catalogue Raisonne of Their Graphic Work. (FRE., Illus.). 276p. 1969. reprint ed. 75.00 (*1-55660-035-6*) A Wofsy Fine Arts.

— Frelaut (Jean) Catalogue Raisonne of the Graphic Work. (FRE., Illus.). 320p. 1969. reprint ed. 95.00 (*1-55660-038-0*) A Wofsy Fine Arts.

— Gericault, the Graphic Work: Catalogue Raisonne. (FRE., Illus.). 176p. 1999. reprint ed. 150.00 (*1-55660-094-1*) A Wofsy Fine Arts.

— Huet (Paul) Catalogue Raisonne of the Graphic Work. (FRE., Illus.). 128p. 1969. reprint ed. 75.00 (*1-55660-039-9*) A Wofsy Fine Arts.

— Leheutre (Gustave) Catalogue Raisonne of the Graphic Work. (FRE., Illus.). 192p. 1969. reprint ed. 95.00 (*1-55660-037-2*) A Wofsy Fine Arts.

— Pierre-Auguste Renoir: The Etchings & Lithographs. rev. ed. (ENG & FRE., Illus.). 132p. 1999. 175.00 (*1-55660-293-6*) A Wofsy Fine Arts.

Delteil, Loys & Cailac, Jean. Camille Pissarro-Peintre-Graveur: The Etchings & Lithographs. rev. ed. (ENG & FRE., Illus.). 403p. 1999. 225.00 (*1-55660-292-8*) A Wofsy Fine Arts.

Delteil, Loys & Wright, Harold J. Meryon's Etchings: A Catalogue Raisonne. rev. ed. 224p. 1989. 95.00 (*1-55660-021-6*) A Wofsy Fine Arts.

Deltenre, Chantal & Dauber, Maximilien. Russia. (Tintin's Travel Diaries). (Illus.). 76p. (YA). (gr. 5 up). 1995. 11.95 (*0-8120-6491-7*) Barron.

— Russia. (Illus.). 76p. (YA). (gr. 5 up). 1995. pap. 6.95 (*0-8120-9162-0*) Barron.

Deltenre, Chantal & Noblet, Martine. Peru & the Andean Countries. LC 94-25171. (Tintin's Travel Diaries). (Illus.). 76p. (J). (gr. 5 up). 1995. pap. 7.95 (*0-8120-9161-2*) Barron.

— Peru & the Andean Countries. Walker, Maureen, tr. from FRE. LC 94-25171. (Tintin's Travel Diaries). (Illus.). 76p. (J). (gr. 5 up). 1995. 11.95 (*0-8120-6490-9*) Barron.

— The United States. LC 94-10996. (Tintin's Travel Diaries). (Illus.). 76p. (J). (gr. 4-7). 1994. pap. 6.95 (*0-8120-1867-2*) Barron.

— The United States. (Tintin's Travel Diaries). (Illus.). 76p. (YA). (gr. 5 up). 1994. 11.95 (*0-8120-6428-3*) Barron.

Deltete, Robert John, jt. auth. see Dombrowski, Daniel A.

Deltoff, Marshall N. & Kogon, Peter L. The Portable Skeletal X-Ray Library: An Atlas of Correlative Radiology. LC 97-3246. (Illus.). 384p. (gr. 13). 1997. text 67.95 (*0-8151-2244-6*, 24846) Mosby Inc.

Delton, J. Angel in Charge. 160p. (J). (gr. 2-5). 1999. pap. 4.95 (*0-395-96061-4*) HM.

Delton, Judy. All Dads on Deck. (Pee Wee Scouts Ser.). 1994. 9.19 (*0-606-06173-8*, Pub. by Turtleback) Demco.

— Angel Bites the Bullet. (Illus.). (J). 2000. pap. 15.00 (*0-618-04085-4*) HM.

Delton, Judy. Angel in Charge, 001. LC 84-27862. (Illus.). 152p. (J). (gr. 2-5). 1985. 16.00 (*0-395-37488-X*) HM.

***Delton, Judy.** Angel in Charge. (Illus.). (J). 1999. 10.30 (*0-606-18206-3*) Turtleback.

Delton, Judy. Angel Spreads Her Wings. LC 98-30237. (Illus.). 160p. (J). (gr. 2-5). 1999. 15.00 (*0-395-91006-4*) HM.

— Angel's Mother's Baby. LC 89-7544. (Illus.). 144p. (J). (gr. 4-7). 1989. 16.00 (*0-395-50926-2*) HM.

— Angel's Mother's Boyfriend, 001. LC 82-27054. (Illus.). 176p. (J). (gr. 2-5). 1986. 16.00 (*0-395-39968-8*) HM.

***Delton, Judy.** Angel's Mother's Boyfriend. (Illus.). 176p. (J). (gr. 2-5). 1999. pap. 4.95 (*0-395-97913-7*, Chapters Bks) HM.

Delton, Judy. Angel's Mother's Wedding. 128p. (J). (gr. 3-7). 1987. 16.00 (*0-395-44470-5*) HM.

— Back Yard Angel, 001. (Illus.). 112p. (J). (gr. 2-5). 1983. 16.00 (*0-395-33883-2*) HM.

Delton, Judy. Back Yard Angel. (Illus.). (J). 1983. 10.30 (*0-606-18208-X*) Turtleback.

— Backyard Angel. (Illus.). 128p. (J). (gr. 2-5). 1999. pap. 4.95 (*0-395-96060-6*, Sandpiper) HM.

Delton, Judy. Bad, Bad Bunnies. (Pee Wee Scouts Ser.: No. 12). 80p. (J). (gr. k-6). 1990. pap. 3.99 (*0-440-40278-6*, YB BDD) BDD Bks Young Read.

— Bad, Bad Bunnies. (Pee Wee Scouts Ser.). (J). 1990. 9.19 (*0-606-03042-5*, Pub. by Turtleback) Demco.

***Delton, Judy.** A Big Box of Memories. (Pee Wee Scouts Ser.: Vol. 40). (Illus.). 112p. (J). 2000. pap. 3.99 (*0-440-41528-4*, YB BDD) BDD Bks Young Read.

Delton, Judy. Blue Skies, French Fries. (Pee Wee Scouts Ser.: No. 4). 96p. (J). (gr. k-6). 1988. pap. 3.99 (*0-440-40064-3*, YB BDD) BDD Bks Young Read.

— Blue Skies French Fries. 1988. 8.94 (*0-606-04050-1*, Pub. by Turtleback) Demco.

— Bookworm Buddies. (Pee Wee Scouts Ser.: No. 30). (Illus.). 112p. (J). 1996. pap. 3.99 (*0-440-40981-0*) Dell.

— Bookworm Buddies. (Pee Wee Scouts Ser.). (J). 1996. 9.09 (*0-606-10902-1*, Pub. by Turtleback) Demco.

— Cabin Surprise. (Lottery Luck Ser.: Bk. 8). (Illus.). 96p. (Orig.). (J). (gr. 2-5). 1995. pap. 3.95 (*0-7868-1025-4*, Pub. by Hyprn Ppbks) Little.

— Camp Ghost-Away. (Pee Wee Scouts Ser.: No. 2). 80p. (J). (gr. k-6). 1988. pap. 3.99 (*0-440-40062-7*, YB BDD) BDD Bks Young Read.

— Camp Ghost-Away. (Pee Wee Scouts Ser.). 1988. 9.19 (*0-606-06900-3*, Pub. by Turtleback) Demco.

***Delton, Judy.** Computer Clues. (Pee Wee Scouts Ser.: No. 36). 128p. (J). 1998. pap. 3.99 (*0-440-41339-7*) BDD Bks Young Read.

Delton, Judy. Cookies & Crutches. (Pee Wee Scouts Ser.: No. 1). 80p. (J). (gr. k-6). 1988. pap. 3.99 (*0-440-40010-4*, YB BDD) BDD Bks Young Read.

— Cookies & Crutches. (Pee Wee Scouts Ser.). (J). 1988. 9.44 (*0-606-07999-8*) Turtleback.

— Eggs with Legs. (Pee Wee Scouts Ser.: 28). (Illus.). 96p. (J). (gr. 1-4). 1996. pap. 3.99 (*0-440-40979-9*) Dell.

— Eggs with Legs. (Pee Wee Scouts Ser.). (J). 1996. 9.09 (*0-606-09738-4*, Pub. by Turtleback) Demco.

— Fishy Wishes. (Pee Wee Scouts Ser.). (J). 1993. 9.09 (*0-606-05291-7*, Pub. by Turtleback) Demco.

— Greedy Groundhogs. (Pee Wee Scouts Ser.: No. 22). 96p. (J). (ps-3). 1994. pap. 3.99 (*0-440-40931-4*) Dell.

— Greedy Groundhogs. (Pee Wee Scouts Ser.). (J). 1994. 9.09 (*0-606-05851-6*, Pub. by Turtleback) Demco.

— Grumpy Pumpkins. (Pee Wee Scouts Ser.: No. 5). 80p. (J). (gr. k-6). 1988. pap. 3.99 (*0-440-40065-1*, YB BDD) BDD Bks Young Read.

— Grumpy Pumpkins. (Pee Wee Scouts Ser.). (J). 1988. 9.19 (*0-606-04051-X*, Pub. by Turtleback) Demco.

— Halloween Helpers. (Pee Wee Scouts Ser.: No. 33). (Illus.). 128p. (Orig.). (J). (gr. 2-4). 1997. pap. 3.99 (*0-440-41330-3*) BDD Bks Young Read.

— Halloween Helpers. (Pee Wee Scouts Ser.). (Orig.). 1997. 9.09 (*0-606-13698-3*, Pub. by Turtleback) Demco.

— Kitty from the Start. LC 86-21481. 160p. (J). (gr. 3-5). 1987. 16.00 (*0-395-42847-5*) HM.

— Lights, Action, Land-Ho! (Pee Wee Scouts Ser.: No. 18). (Illus.). 112p. (J). (gr. 1-4). 1992. pap. 3.99 (*0-440-40732-X*, YB BDD) BDD Bks Young Read.

— Lights, Action, Land-Ho! (Pee Wee Scouts Ser.). (J). 1992. 9.09 (*0-606-05428-6*, Pub. by Turtleback) Demco.

— Lucky Dog Days. (Pee Wee Scouts Ser.: No. 3). 80p. (J). (gr. k-3). 1988. pap. 3.99 (*0-440-40063-5*, YB BDD) BDD Bks Young Read.

— Lucky Dog Days. (Pee Wee Scouts Ser.). (J). 1988. 9.44 (*0-606-08003-1*) Turtleback.

— Moans & Groans & Dinosaur Bones. (Pee Wee Scouts Ser.: No. 31). (Illus.). 112p. (J). 1997. pap. 3.99 (*0-440-40982-9*, YB BDD) BDD Bks Young Read.

— Moans & Groans & Dinosaur Bones. (Pee Wee Scouts Ser.). 1997. 9.09 (*0-606-11726-1*, Pub. by Turtleback) Demco.

***Delton, Judy.** Molly for Mayor. LC 98-53926. 128p. 1999. pap. 3.99 (*0-440-41525-X*) Bantam.

Delton, Judy. Moving Up. LC 94-43308. (Lottery Luck Ser.: Bk. 4). (Illus.). 96p. (J). (gr. 2-5). 1995. pap. 3.95 (*0-7868-1021-1*, Pub. by Hyprn Ppbks) Little.

— My Mom Made Me Go to Camp. (J). 1993. pap. 2.99 (*0-440-40838-5*) Dell.

— Next Stop, the White House! LC 95-11602. (Lottery Luck Ser.: No. 6). (Illus.). 96p. (J). (gr. 2-5). 1995. pap. 3.95 (*0-7868-1023-8*, Pub. by Hyprn Ppbks) Little.

— Peanut Butter Pilgrims. (Pee Wee Scouts Ser.: No. 6). 80p. (Orig.). (J). (gr. k-6). 1988. pap. 3.99 (*0-440-40066-X*, YB BDD) BDD Bks Young Read.

Delton, Judy. Peanut-Butter Pilgrims. (Pee Wee Scouts Ser.). (J). 1988. 9.19 (*0-606-04053-6*, Pub. by Turtleback) Demco.

Delton, Judy. Pedal Power. (Illus.). 96p. (J). (gr. 4-8). 1998. pap. 3.99 (*0-440-41336-2*) BDD Bks Young Read.

— Pedal Power, 35. (Pee Wee Scouts Ser.). 1998. 9.09 (*0-606-13700-9*, Pub. by Turtleback) Demco.

— A Pee Wee Christmas. (Pee Wee Scouts Ser.: No. 7). 96p. (Orig.). (J). (gr. k-6). 1988. pap. 3.99 (*0-440-40067-8*, YB BDD) BDD Bks Young Read.

Delton, Judy. Pee Wee Christmas. (Pee Wee Scouts Ser.). (J). 1988. 9.09 (*0-606-04054-4*, Pub. by Turtleback) Demco.

Delton, Judy. The Pee Wee Jubilee. 96p. (J). (gr. k-6). 1989. pap. 3.99 (*0-440-40226-3*, YB BDD) BDD Bks Young Read.

Delton, Judy. Pee Wee Jubilee. (Pee Wee Scouts Ser.). (J). 1989. 9.19 (*0-606-04296-2*, Pub. by Turtleback) Demco.

Delton, Judy. Pee Wee Pool Party. (Pee Wee Scouts Ser.: No. 29). (Illus.). 96p. (J). (gr. 1-4). 1996. pap. 3.99 (*0-440-40980-2*, YB BDD) BDD Bks Young Read.

— Pee Wee Pool Party. (Pee Wee Scouts Ser.). (J). 1996. 9.19 (*0-606-09739-2*, Pub. by Turtleback) Demco.

— Pee Wee Scouts, No. 24. 96p. (J). 1994. pap. 3.99 (*0-440-40976-4*) Dell.

— Pee Wees on First. LC 95-208324. (Pee Wee Scouts Ser.: No. 25). 96p. (J). 1995. pap. 3.99 (*0-440-40977-2*) Dell.

— Pee Wees on First. (Pee Wee Scouts Ser.). (J). 1995. 9.44 (*0-606-08000-7*) Turtleback.

— Pee Wees on Parade. (Pee Wee Scouts Ser.: No. 17). (Illus.). 96p. (J). (ps-3). 1992. pap. 3.99 (*0-440-40700-1*, YB BDD) BDD Bks Young Read.

— Pee Wees on Parade. (Pee Wee Scouts Ser.). 1992. 9.19 (*0-606-00958-2*, Pub. by Turtleback) Demco.

— Pee Wee's on Skis. 96p. (J). 1993. pap. 3.99 (*0-440-40885-7*) Dell.

— Pee Wees on Skis. (Pee Wee Scouts Ser.). (J). 1993. 9.19 (*0-606-05532-0*, Pub. by Turtleback) Demco.

— The Perfect Christmas Gift. LC 91-6549. (Illus.). 32p. (J). (gr. k-3). 1992. lib. bdg. 13.95 (*0-02-728471-9*, Mac Bks Young Read) S&S Childrens.

— Piles of Pets. (Pee Wee Scouts Ser.: No. 19). 96p. (J). (ps-3). 1993. pap. 3.99 (*0-440-40792-3*) Dell.

— Piles of Pets. (Pee Wee Scouts Ser.). (J). 1993. 9.19 (*0-606-05544-4*, Pub. by Turtleback) Demco.

— Planet Pee Wee, 34. (Pee Wee Scouts Ser.). 1998. 9.09 (*0-606-13699-1*, Pub. by Turtleback) Demco.

— The Pooped Troop. (Pee Wee Scouts Ser.: No. 10). (Illus.). 96p. (J). (ps-3). 1989. pap. 3.99 (*0-440-40184-4*, YB BDD) BDD Bks Young Read.

Delton, Judy. Pooped Troop. (Pee Wee Scouts Ser.). (J). 1989. 9.19 (*0-606-04302-0*, Pub. by Turtleback) Demco.

Delton, Judy. Prize-Winning Private Eyes. LC 94-40329. (Lottery Luck Ser.: Bk. 2). (Illus.). 96p. (J). (gr. 2-5). 1995. pap. 3.95 (*0-7868-1019-X*, Pub. by Hyprn Ppbks) Little.

— Rosy Noses, Freezing Toes. (Pee Wee Scouts Ser.: No. 13). (Illus.). 96p. (J). 1990. pap. 3.99 (*0-440-40384-7*, YB BDD) BDD Bks Young Read.

Delton, Judy. Rosy Noses, Freezing Toes. (Pee Wee Scouts Ser.). (J). 1990. 9.19 (*0-606-04786-7*, Pub. by Turtleback) Demco.

Delton, Judy. Royal Escapade. LC 95-18359. (Lottery Luck Ser.: Bk. 7). (Illus.). 96p. (J). (gr. 2-5). 1996. pap. 5.95 (*0-7868-1024-6*, Pub. by Hyprn Ppbks) Little.

— Send in the Clowns. (Pee Wee Scouts Ser.: No. 38). 112p. (J). 1999. pap. 3.99 (*0-440-41522-5*) BDD Bks Young Read.

— Ship Ahoy! LC 95-3285. (Lottery Luck Ser.: Bk. 5). (Illus.). 96p. (J). (gr. 2-5). 1995. pap. 3.95 (*0-7868-1022-X*, Pub. by Hyprn Ppbks) Little.

— Sky Babies. (Pee Wee Scouts Ser.: No. 15). 96p. (J). (ps-3). 1991. pap. 3.99 (*0-440-40530-0*, YB BDD) BDD Bks Young Read.

— Sky Babies. (Pee Wee Scouts Ser.). (J). 1991. 9.19 (*0-606-00753-9*, Pub. by Turtleback) Demco.

— Sonny's Secret. (Pee Wee Scouts Ser.). (J). 1991. 9.09 (*0-606-05018-3*, Pub. by Turtleback) Demco.

— Spring Sprouts. (Pee Wee Scouts Ser.: No. 9). (Illus.). 80p. (J). (gr. k-6). 1989. pap. 3.99 (*0-440-40160-7*, YB BDD) BDD Bks Young Read.

— Spring Sprouts. (Pee Wee Scouts Ser.). (J). 1989. 9.19 (*0-606-02534-0*, Pub. by Turtleback) Demco.

— Stage Frightened, 32. (Pee Wee Scouts Ser.). 1997. 9.09 (*0-606-11727-X*, Pub. by Turtleback) Demco.

— Super Duper Pee Wee! (Pee Wee Scouts Ser.). (J). 1995. 9.34 (*0-606-08001-5*) Turtleback.

— Super Duper Pee Wee: Pee Wee Scouts. 144p. (J). 1995. pap. 3.99 (*0-440-40992-6*) Dell.

— Teeny Weeny Zucchinis. (Pee Wee Scouts Ser.). (J). 1995. 9.19 (*0-606-08002-3*) Turtleback.

— Ten's a Crowd! LC 94-37179. (Lottery Luck Ser.: Bk. 3). (Illus.). 96p. (J). (gr. 2-5). 1995. pap. 3.95 (*0-7868-1020-3*, Pub. by Hyprn Ppbks) Little.

— That Mushy Stuff. (Pee Wee Scouts Ser.: No. 8). 80p. (J). (gr. k-6). 1989. pap. 3.99 (*0-440-40176-3*, YB BDD) BDD Bks Young Read.

— That Mushy Stuff. (J). 1990. pap. 4.99 (*0-440-80206-7*) Dell.

Delton, Judy. That Mushy Stuff. (Pee Wee Scouts Ser.). (J). 1989. 9.19 (*0-606-04056-0*, Pub. by Turtleback) Demco.

Delton, Judy. Trash Bash. (Pee Wee Scouts Ser.). 1992. 8.45 (*0-606-00949-3*, Pub. by Turtleback) Demco.

Delton, Judy. Tricks & Treats. (Pee Wee Scouts Ser.). (J). 1994. 9.09 (*0-606-07123-7*, Pub. by Turtleback) Demco.

Delton, Judy. Wild Wild West. (Pee Wee Scouts Ser.: No. 37). 112p. (J). (gr. 1-4). 1999. pap. 3.99 (*0-440-41342-7*) BDD Bks Young Read.

— Winnie the Pooh's Book of Manners. 176p. (J). (gr. 3-7). 2000. 13.99 (*0-7868-3206-1*, Pub. by Disney Pr) Time Warner.

— Winnie the Pooh's Book of Manners. (Illus.). 48p. 2000. lib. bdg. 13.49 (*0-7868-5083-3*, Pub. by Disney Pr) Little.

— Winning Ticket! (Lottery Luck Ser.: Bk. 1). (Illus.). 96p. (J). (gr. 2-5). 1995. pap. 3.95 (*0-7868-1018-1*, Pub. by Hyprn Ppbks) Little.

Delton, Judy & McCue, Noelle B. Mom Made Me Go to School. (J). 1993. pap. 2.99 (*0-440-40841-5*) Dell.

Delton, Julie. My Uncle Nikos. LC 81-43317. (Illus.). 32p. (J). (gr. 1-4). 1983. lib. bdg. 11.89 (*0-690-04165-9*) HarpC Child Bks.

Deluc, Yves & Ruck. Prisunic. 4.25 (*0-88436-905-6*) EMC-Paradigm.

DeLuca, Anthony, jt. auth. see Quinlan, Paul.

***DeLuca, Anthony R.** Gandhi, Mao, Mandela, & Gorbachev. LC 99-46619. 200p. 2000. write for info. (*0-275-95969-4*, Praeger Pubs) Greenwood.

Deluca, Anthony R. Great Power Rivalry at the Turkish Straits: The Montreux Conference & Convention of 1936. (East European Monographs: No. 77). 216p. 1981. text 52.50 (*0-914710-71-0*, Pub. by East Eur Monographs) Col U Pr.

— Politics, Diplomacy & the Media: Gorbachev's Legacy in the West. LC 98-4931. 176p. 1998. 55.00 (*0-275-95968-6*, Praeger Pubs) Greenwood.

DeLuca, Arnold A. Advertising Salesmanship. (Illus.). 500p. (C). 1990. text 49.50 (*1-878666-01-0*) Dynamo Intl.

— Advertising Salesmanship. (Illus.). 500p. 1992. 49.50 (*0-685-49849-2*) Dynamo Intl.

— Advertising Salesmanship Student Work Book. 83p. (C). 1992. pap. text, wbk. ed. 10.00 (*1-878666-02-9*) Dynamo Intl.

— The Idea Machine. LC 75-24150. (Illus.). 252p. 1975. 29.50 (*1-878666-06-1*) Dynamo Inc.

— Special Sections & Promotions. (Illus.). 48p. 1981. pap. 5.00 (*1-878666-08-8*) Dynamo Inc.

— Telemarketing Course & Workbook. (Illus.). 138p. 1985. pap. 34.50 (*1-878666-09-6*) Dynamo Inc.

DeLuca, Carlo J., jt. auth. see Basmajian, John V.

DeLuca, Christopher, ed. see Roe, Clifford A., Jr.

Deluca, Chuck. Firehouse Memorabilia: A Collectors Reference. LC 89-92765. (Illus.). 110p. (Orig.). 1990. pap. 19.95 (*0-9625218-0-9*) Maritime Antique.

***DeLuca, Fred & Hayes, John P.** Start Small, Finish Big: 15 Key Lessons to Start - And Run - Your Own Successful Business. 368p. 2000. 25.95 (*0-446-52402-6*, Pub. by Warner Bks) Little.

DeLuca, George. GMAT TestBuster. 250p. 2000. pap. 19.95 (*0-87891-142-1*) Res & Educ.

DeLuca, H. F. & Suttie, J. W., eds. The Fat-Soluble Vitamins. LC 70-106038. 549p. 1970. reprint ed. pap. 170.20 (*0-608-01957-7*, 206261200003) Bks Demand.

Deluca, J. English-French Dictionary of Telecommunications. (ENG & FRE.). 125.00 (*0-8288-7694-0*, M972) Fr & Eur.

DeLuca, Joanne, jt. auth. see Lopiano-Misdom, Janine.

DeLuca, Joel M. Political Savvy: Systematic Approaches to Leadership Behind-the-Scenes. LC 91-33528. (Illus.). 250p. 1992. 32.50 (*0-934753-60-1*) LRP Pubns.

D

DeLuca, Joel M., jt. auth. see Stumpf, Stephen A.

DeLuca, Joel R. Political Savvy: Systematic Approaches to Leadership Behind-the-Scenes. 2nd ed. (Illus.). 1999. 28.50 *(0-9667636-0-2)* Evergreen Bus Grp.

DeLuca, Joseph J. The Loneliness of Being Human. Date not set. write for info. *(0-9678892-0-0)* Ind Pubs Soc.

DeLuca, Joseph M. & Cagan, Rebecca E. The CEO's Guide to Health Care Information Systems. LC 96-16758. 128p. 1996. pap. 40.00 *(1-55648-158-6,* 093105) AHPI.

— Investing for Business Value: How to Maximize the Strategic Benefits of Health Care Information Technology. LC 96-42116. 196p. (Orig.). 1996. pap. 45.00 *(1-55648-170-5,* 093107) AHPI.

***DeLuca, Kevin Michael.** Image Politics: The New Rhetoric of Environmental Activism. LC 99-19839. (Revisioning Rhetoric Ser.). 205p. 1999. lib. bdg. 30.00 *(1-57230-461-8,* C0461) Guilford Pubns.

DeLuca, L. & Summerfield, M., eds. Nonsteady Burning & Combustion Stability of Solid Propellants. (PAAS Ser.: Vol. 143). 875p. 1992. 109.95 *(1-56347-014-4,* V-143) AIAA.

DeLuca, Lois H. How Big Am I? 24p. (J). (ps-2). 1994. pap. text 8.95 *(0-9643813-0-3)* L H Deluca.

DeLuca, Matthew J. Handbook of Compensation Management. LC 93-13378. 400p. (C). 1993. text 89.95 *(0-13-159658-6)* Prntice Hall Bks.

— How to Get a Job in 90 Days or Less: A Realistic Action Plan for Finding the Right Job Fast. LC 94-32878. 283p. 1994. pap. 14.95 *(0-07-016354-5)* McGraw.

— Nonprofit Personnel Forms & Guidelines: Compliance with Human Resource Law & Regulation, Suppl. No. 3. LC 93-49655. ring bd. 149.00 *(0-8342-0422-3,* S150) Aspen Pub.

— Best Answers to the 201 Most Frequently Asked Interview Questions. LC 99-165787. (Illus.). 208p. 1996. pap. 11.95 *(0-07-016357-X)* McGraw.

DeLuca, Matthew J. & DeLuca, Nanette. Get a Job in 30 Days or Less. LC 99-34291. 315p. 1999. pap. 12.95 *(0-07-016439-8)* McGraw.

DeLuca, Matthew J. & DeLuca, Nanette F. Wow! Resumes for Creative Careers. LC 97-9589. 168p. 1997. pap. 10.95 *(0-07-016381-2)* McGraw.

DeLuca, Matthew J. & Persons, Mark D. Personnel Record Keeper, 1991. 302p. 1990. text 86.00 *(0-916592-95-2)* Panel Pubs.

DeLuca, Michael. Kitchen & Bathroom Lighting . . . Made Easy. (Illus.). 217p. 1997. pap. 50.00 *(1-887127-06-2,* 5309) Natl Kit Bath.

DeLuca, Michael & Richardson, Mark. DreamLearning. Ridington, Richard, ed. 1996. pap. text, wbk. ed. 12.95 *(1-888864-02-8,* DLJ-1) InnrQuest.

— DreamLearning, Set. Ridington, Richard, ed. 1996. pap. 89.95 incl. audio *(1-888864-00-1,* DL) InnrQuest.

DeLuca, Nanette, jt. auth. see DeLuca, Matthew J.

DeLuca, Nanette F., jt. auth. see DeLuca, Matthew J.

DeLuca, Richard. We, the People! Bay Area Activism in the 1960s: Three Case Studies. LC 93-16623. (Great Issues of the Day Ser.: No. 7). (Illus.). 144p. 1994. pap. 19.00 *(0-89370-254-4)* Millefleurs.

Deluca, Steve, jt. auth. see Ga, Marcilina S.

DeLuca, Stuart M., jt. auth. see Stone, Alfred R.

DeLuca, Thomas S., Jr., jt. auth. see Buell, John.

DeLuca, Tom. The Two Faces of Political Apathy. 288p. (Orig.). (C). 1995. text 69.95 *(1-56639-314-0)*; pap. text 22.95 *(1-56639-315-9)* Temple U Pr.

DeLucca, Donald R., jt. auth. see Burch, William R.

DeLucca, John. Reason & Experience: Dialogues in Modern Philosophy. LC 72-91229. 448p. (C). 1973. 38.75 *(0-87735-517-7)* Jones & Bartlett.

***DeLucca, Maria L.** Through Rex's Eyes. 178p. 2000. pap. 10.95 *(0-9676447-0-4)* M L Delucca.

Delucchi, Christopher J. AutoCAD Cookbook for the IBM (for MS & PC DOS) 2nd ed. LC 88-17220. 446p. 1989. pap. 29.95 *(0-471-60837-8)* Wiley.

Delucchi, Mark, jt. ed. see DeCicco, John.

Delucchi, Vittorio L., ed. Studies in Biological Control. LC 75-16867. (International Biological Programme Ser.: No. 9). 320p. reprint ed. pap. 91.20 *(0-608-14083-X,* 2024479) Bks Demand.

DeLuce, Judith, jt. ed. see Falkner, Thomas M.

Deluce, Robert. Horary Astrology. 4th ed. (Illus.). 2000. reprint ed. pap. 12.95 *(0-88231-035-6)* ASI Pubs Inc.

***DeLucenayLeon, George.** Explorers of the Americas Before Columbus. (Illus.). 64p. (J). (gr. 5-7). 1999. text 17.00 *(0-7881-6846-0)* DIANE Pub.

***DeLucia, Al & DeLucia, Jackie.** Recipes for Project Success. LC 99-18505. 155p. 1999. pap. 32.95 *(1-880410-58-3)* Proj Mgmt Inst.

DeLucia, Alan A. Compact Atlas of Idaho. (Illus.). 117p. (Orig.). 1983. pap. 20.95 *(0-940982-02-1)* U ID Ctr Busn.

DeLucia, Jackie, jt. auth. see DeLucia, Al.

***DeLucia, John.** Sandcastles. 2000. write for info. *(1-58235-533-9)* Watermrk Pr.

DeLucia, Robert, ed. Transition: An Introduction to Urban College Student Life. 488p. (C). 1992. pap. text 43.00 *(0-536-58155-X)* Pearson Custom.

Delucia, Robert C. Urban Learners: Serious about College Success. 2nd ed. LC 98-22649. 352p. (C). 1998. pap. text 30.80 *(0-13-959693-3)* P-H.

Delucia, Robert C. & Doyle, Thomas J. Career Planning in Criminal Justice. 3rd ed. LC 98-22531. 226p. 1998. pap. 21.95 *(0-87084-209-9)* Anderson Pub Co.

DeLucia, Russell J., et al. Energy Planning for Developing Countries: A Study of Bangladesh. LC 81-20726. (Johns Hopkins Studies in Development). (Illus.). 320p. 1982. reprint ed. pap. 99.20 *(0-608-04062-2,* 206479800011) Bks Demand.

Delue, Norman. A Class Act: A Creative Drama Guide for Teachers. (Illus.). 80p. 1994. 10.99 *(0-86653-783-X,* GA1477) Good Apple.

Delue, Norman & Hayward, Thomas B. Stage Write: Playwriting Curriculum for Kids & Teachers. 64p. teacher ed. 8.99 *(1-56417-870-6,* GA1563) Good Apple.

DeLue, Steven M. Political Obligation in a Liberal State. LC 88-39159. (SUNY Series in Political Theory: Contemporary Issues). 179p. (C). 1989. pap. text 21.95 *(0-7914-0093-X)* State U NY Pr.

— Political Thinking, Political Theory, & Civil Society. LC 95-50511. 368p. (C). 1996. pap. text 43.00 *(0-205-16487-0)* Allyn.

DeLuise, Dom. Charlie the Caterpillar. LC 90-31557. (Illus.). 40p. (J). (ps-1). 1990. 15.00 *(0-671-69358-1)* S&S Bks Yung.

— Charlie the Caterpillar. LC 90-31557. (Illus.). 40p. (J). (ps-1). 1993. pap. 5.95 *(0-671-79607-0)* S&S Bks Yung.

— Dom Deluise's the Nightingale. LC 97-23473. Orig. Title: Nattergalen. (Illus.). 40p. (J). (gr. k-3). 1998. per. 15.00 *(0-689-81749-5)* S&S Bks Yung.

— Eat This Too! LC 97-69715. 1997. 24.00 *(0-671-00431-X,* PB Hardcover) PB.

— Eat This Too! It'll Also Make You Feel Better. (Illus.). 256p. 1998. per. 16.00 *(0-671-00432-8)* S&S Trade.

— Eat This...It'll Make You Feel Better. 1991. per. 16.00 *(0-671-74584-0)* PB.

— Goldilocks. (Illus.). 40p. (J). (ps-3). 1997. mass mkt. 5.99 *(0-689-81674-X)* Aladdin.

— Goldilocks. LC 91-2021. (Illus.). 40p. (J). (ps-1). 1992. pap. 16.00 *(0-671-74690-1)* S&S Bks Yung.

— Hansel & Gretel. LC 96-35047. (Illus.). 40p. (J). (ps-3). 1997. per. 15.00 *(0-689-81202-7)* S&S Childrens.

— King Bob's New Clothes. (Illus.). 40p. (J). 1999. per. 5.99 *(0-689-83050-5)* Aladdin.

DeLuise, Dom. King Bob's New Clothes. LC 94-19112. (Illus.). (J). 14.00 *(0-671-89727-6)* S&S Bks Yung.

— King Bob's New Clothes. (Illus.). 40p. (J). (ps-3). 1996. 15.00 *(0-689-80520-9)* S&S Childrens.

Delumeau, Jean. History of Paradise: The Garden of Eden in Myth & Tradition. 288p. 1994. 60.00 *(0-86012-249-2,* Pub. by Srch Pr) St Mut.

***Delumeau, Jean.** History of Paradise: The Garden of Eden in Myth & Tradition. LC 99-49451. 2000. pap. 14.95 *(0-252-06880-7)* U of Ill Pr.

Delumyea, R. Del, jt. auth. see Boehnke, D. Neal.

DeLuna, Anna, jt. auth. see Scott, Bradley.

DeLuna, Carmen, ed. & tr. see Esparza, June F.

Delunas, Eve. Survival Games Personalities Play. LC 92-64111. 304p. (Orig.). (C). 1992. pap. 15.00 *(0-931104-35-1)* SunInk Pubn.

DeLupis, Ingrid D. International Law & the Independent State. 286p. 1987. text 68.95 *(0-566-05140-0,* Pub. by Dartmth Pub) Ashgate Pub Co.

Delurgio, Stephen & Aczel, Amir D. Forecasting: Theory & Applications. LC 97-15142. 992p. (C). 1997. text 71.50 *(0-256-13433-2,* Irwn McGrw-H) McGrw-H Hghr Educ.

DeLurgio, Stephen A. Forecasting Principles & Applications. 1997. 74.38 *(0-07-561120-1,* Irwn McGrw-H) McGrw-H Hghr Educ.

Delury, George E. But What If She Wants to Die? A Husband's Diary. LC 97-7461. 256p. 1997. 21.95 *(1-55972-411-0,* Birch Ln Pr) Carol Pub Group.

Delux. American Heritage Linclon & Civil War. 1997. 39.95 *(0-671-57658-5)* PB.

Deluy, Henri. Carnal Love. Bennett, Guy, tr. from FRE. (Sun & Moon Classics Ser.: No. 121). 442p. (Orig.). 1996. pap. 11.95 *(1-55713-272-0)* Sun & Moon CA.

Deluz, Ariane, jt. ed. see Heald, Suzette.

***Delva, Jorge.** Substance Abuse Issues among Families in Diverse Populations. LC 00-31968. 2000. write for info. *(0-7890-1195-6)* Haworth Pr.

Delvac, William F., et al. Affordable Housing Through Historic Preservation: A Case Study Guide to Combining the Tax Credits. (Illus.). 74p. (Orig.). (C). 1995. pap. text 25.00 *(0-7881-2465-X)* DIANE Pub.

Delvaille, Jules. Essai Sur l'Histoire de l'Idee Du Progres Jusqu'a la Fin Du Thirteenth Siecle. (FRE.). xii, 761p. 1977. reprint ed. write for info. *(3-487-06409-X)* G Olms Pubs.

Delval, Marie-Helene. The Apple-Tree Canoe. (I Love to Read Collection). (Illus.). 48p. (J). (ps-3). 1992. lib. bdg. 12.79 *(0-89565-805-4)* Childs World.

Delvare, G. & Boucek, Z. On the New World Chalcididae (Hymenoptera) (Memoirs of the American Entomological Institute Ser.: No. 53). (Illus.). iv, 470p. 1992. 60.00 *(1-56665-053-4)* Assoc Pubs FL.

Delvau, Alfred. Dictionnaire Erotique. (FRE.). 288p. 1990. 95.00 *(0-7859-7946-8,* 2714443370) Fr & Eur.

***Delve.** Short Sunderland. (Illus.). 192p. 2000. 44.95 *(1-86126-355-4,* Pub. by Crolwood) Motorbooks Intl.

***Delve, Ken.** Avro Lancaster. (Illus.). 192p. 2000. 44.95 *(1-86126-222-1,* 129778AE, Pub. by Crolwood) Motorbooks Intl.

— Mustang Story. (Illus.). 2000. 34.95 *(1-85409-259-6)* Arms & Armour.

DelVecchio, et al. Sevenoaks Journal: Poetry for the Contemporary Ear. Collins, Denise A., ed. (Quarterly Newsletter Ser.). (Illus.). 16p. 1996. pap. 3.00 *(1-887213-05-8)* Blck Oak Pr.

DelVecchio, Douglas A., jt. ed. see Benson, John.

DelVecchio, Doreen, ed. see Shakespeare, William.

DelVecchio, Ellen, jt. auth. see Maestro, Betsy C.

***Delvecchio, Michael J.** Iron Horses: An Illustrated Tour of North America's Great Steam Railways. (Illus.). 2000. 19.98 *(0-7624-0880-4)* Running Pr.

DelVecchio, Valentine. Beginner's Guide to Model Photography: Techniques for the Photographer & Tips for the Aspiring Model. (Illus.). 128p. 1993. pap. 29.95 *(0-9625749-2-9)* Ref Desk Bks.

Delvecchio, Valentine. Beneath the Dome of PMC: The Story of Pennsylvania Military College, 1821-1972. (Illus.). 566p. 1996. 40.00 *(0-9625749-4-5)* Ref Desk Bks.

— Cadet Gray: Your Guide to Military Schools, Military Colleges & Cadet Programs. 2nd ed. (Illus.). 200p. 1997. pap. 25.00 *(0-9625749-5-3)* Ref Desk Bks.

DelVecchio, Valentine. Cadet Gray: Your Guidebook to Military Schools, Military Colleges, & Cadet Programs. (Illus.). 212p. (Orig.). (YA). (gr. 7-12). 1990. pap. 14.95 *(0-9625749-0-2)* Ref Desk Bks.

— Media Production for Business or Education. (Illus.). 96p. 1994. 28.50 *(0-9625749-3-7)* Ref Desk Bks.

Delvers, Ed, jt. auth. see Brouws, Jeffrey T.

Delves. Encyclopedia of Immunology, Vol. 4. 2nd ed. 1998. text 250.00 *(0-12-226769-9)* Harcourt.

Delves, John, jt. auth. see Laughlin, Terry.

Delves, L. M. & Walsh, J., eds. Numerical Solution of Integral Equations. (Illus.). 1974. 45.00 *(0-19-853342-X)* OUP.

Delves, P. J., ed. Cellular Immunology Labfax. (Labfax Ser.). (Illus.). 288p. (C). 1994. pap. 39.95 *(0-12-208885-9)* Acad Pr.

Delves, Peter, ed. Antibody Production: Essential Techniques. LC 97-1089. (Essential Techniques Ser.). 160p. 1997. pap. 49.95 *(0-471-97010-7)* Wiley.

Delves, Peter J. Antibody Applications: Essential Techniques. 164p. 1995. pap. 49.95 *(0-471-95698-8)* Wiley.

Delves, Peter J. & Roitt, Ivan M. Encyclopedia of Immunology. 2nd ed. LC 96-39910. (C). 1998. text 250.00 *(0-12-226766-4)*; text 250.00 *(0-12-226767-2)*; text 250.00 *(0-12-226768-0)* Acad Pr.

— Essential Immunology Review. 256p. 1995. pap. 19.95 *(0-86542-458-6)* Blackwell Sci.

Delves, Peter J. & Roitt, Ivan M., eds. Encyclopedia of Immunology, 4 vols. 2nd ed. LC 96-39910. (Illus.). 2516p. (C). 1998. text 925.00 *(0-12-226765-6)* Morgan Kaufmann.

Delville, Michel. The American Prose Poem: Poetic Form & the Boundaries of Genre. LC 97-43641. 368p. 1998. 39.95 *(0-8130-1591-X)* U Press Fla.

Delville, Philippe L., jt. auth. see Raynaut, Claude.

Delvin, David. Coping with a Hernia. LC 99-494989. (Overcoming Common Problems Ser.). 112p. 1998. pap. 9.95 *(0-85969-783-5,* Pub. by Sheldon Pr) Intl Pubs Mktg.

Delvin, Edgard. Vocabulary of Enzyme Engineering. (Terminology Bulletin Ser.: No. 217). (FRE.). 529p. (Orig.). 1993. pap. 38.95 *(0-660-58874-9,* Pub. by Canadian Govt Pub) Accents Pubns.

Delvin, Joseph. Dictionary of Synonyms & Antonyms: With 5000 Words Most Often Mispronounced. 1961. 10.60 *(0-606-00562-5,* Pub. by Turtleback) Demco.

Delvin, S. A History of Winchmore Hill. 112p. (C). 1988. 35.00 *(0-7212-0800-2,* Pub. by Regency Pr GBR) St Mut.

Delvoye, Francoise N., ed. Confluence of Cultures: French Contributions to Indo-Persian Studies. (C). 1994. text 28.00 *(81-7304-092-3,* Pub. by Manohar) S Asia.

Delwiche, Lora D. & Slaughter, Susan J. The Little SAS Book: A Primer. 240p. (C). 1998. pap. 24.95 *(1-55544-215-3,* BR55200) SAS Publ.

***Delwiche, Lora D. & Slaughter, Susan J.** The Little SAS Book: A Primer. 2nd ed. 300p. 1999. pap. 27.95 *(1-58025-239-7)* SAS Publ.

Delwiche, Reg. The Power of Prism: A Rigging & Jigging Breakthrough for the 90's. (Illus.). 44p. (Orig.). 1989. pap. 2.95 *(0-9624936-0-0)* Prog Fisherman.

Delworth, Ursula, et al, eds. Student Services: A Handbook for the Profession. LC 80-8008. (Jossey-Bass Series in Higher Education). 527p. reprint ed. pap. 163.40 *(0-8357-4877-4,* 203780900009) Bks Demand.

Delynn, Jane. Bad Sex Is Good. LC 97-43660. 1998. pap. text 12.00 *(1-891305-00-X)* Painted Leaf.

DeLynn, Jane, ed. New York Sex: Stories. LC 98-34182. 204p. 1998. pap. 12.00 *(1-891305-03-4)* Painted Leaf.

DeLyre, Wolf. Essentials of Dental Radiography for Dental Assistants & Hygienists. 5th ed. (C). 1994. pap. text 43.95 *(0-8385-2025-1,* A2025-3) Appleton & Lange.

Delys, Claudia. A Treasury of American Superstitions. LC 96-47411. 512p. 1997. 9.99 *(0-517-18130-4)* Random Hse Value.

DeLys, Edith & Volan, Leon. Jean de Reszke Teaches Singing to Edith de Lys: A True Copy of the Lesson Notebooks of Edith De Lys, Includes 41 Lessons, 23 Vocal Exercises, 230 Notations. (Illus.). 83p. (Orig.). 1979. pap., teacher ed. 20.00 *(1-881858-04-9)* J B Muns.

Delz, ed. Sili Italici. (LAT.). 1987. 105.00 *(3-519-01804-7,* T1804, Pub. by B G Teubner) U of Mich Pr.

— Taciti, P. Corneli Tom. II, Fascicule 3: Agricola. (Annales Ser.). (LAT.). 1983. pap. 19.95 *(3-519-01839-X,* T1839, Pub. by B G Teubner) U of Mich Pr.

Delza, Sophia. T'ai Chi Ch'uan: Body & Mind in Harmony (Integration of Meaning & Method) LC 84-23916. 244p. (C). 1985. pap. text 24.95 *(0-88706-030-7)* State U NY Pr.

— The T'ai-chi Ch'uan Experience: Reflections & Perceptions on Body-Mind Harmony. Neville, Robert C., ed. & intro. by. LC 96-3633. 330p. (C). 1996. text 59.50 *(0-7914-2897-4)*; pap. text 19.95 *(0-7914-2898-2)* State U NY Pr.

Delzell, Charles F. Mussolini's Enemies: The Italian Anti-Fascist Resistance. LC 61-7406. 641p. reprint ed. pap. 198.80 *(0-608-09164-2,* 200056200030) Bks Demand.

Delzell, Charles F., ed. The Unification of Italy, Eighteen Fifty-Nine to Eighteen Sixty-One. LC 76-15352. (European Problem Studies). 126p. 1976. reprint ed. pap. text 10.50 *(0-88275-658-3)* Krieger.

***Delzell, Charles N. & Madden, James J., eds.** Real Algebraic Geometry & Ordered Structures. LC 99-44086. (Contemporary Mathematics Ser.: Vol. 253). 287p. 2000. 75.00 *(0-8218-0804-4)* Am Math.

Delzell, Robert F., jt. ed. see Allen, Walter C.

Delzio, Suzanne & Ribarich, Cindy. Felinestein: Pampering the Genius in Your Cat. LC 98-43767. (Illus.). 176p. 1999. pap. 9.95 *(0-06-273630-2)* HarpC.

Delzio, Suzanne, jt. auth. see Fisher, Betty.

DelZoppo, Patrick M., ed. Mourning: The Journey from Grief to Healing. LC 95-15288. 46p. (Orig.). 1995. pap. 3.95 *(0-8189-0737-1)* Alba.

Dem, Tidiane. Masseni: A Novel. Frenaye, Frances, tr. from FRE. LC 82-36. xvii, 174p. 1982. 16.95 *(0-8071-1011-6)* La State U Pr.

***Demaagd, Kurt.** Sams Teach Yourself Code Fusion in 21 Days. (Teach Yourself... in 21 Days Ser.). (Illus.). 600p. 2000. pap. text 34.99 *(0-672-31908-X,* Waite Grp Pr) Sams.

Demac, Donna A. Liberty Denied: The Current Rise of Censorship in America. rev. ed. 180p. (Orig.). 1990. pap. 12.95 *(0-8135-1545-9)* Rutgers U Pr.

Demachy, C. Puyo, jt. auth. see Demacy, Robert.

Demacy, Robert & Demachy, C. Puyo. Les Procedes d'Art en Photographie. Sobieszek, Robert A. & Bunnell, Peter C., eds. LC 76-24673. (Sources of Modern Photography Ser.). (FRE., Illus.). 1979. reprint ed. lib. bdg. 19.95 *(0-405-09649-6)* Ayer.

Demaerel, Philippe. Clinical Applications of Localized 1H-NMR Spectroscopy in Intracranial Tumours. (Acta Biomedica Lovaniensia Ser.: Vol. 112). (Illus.). xi, 180p. (Orig.). 1995. pap. 29.50 *(90-6186-685-5,* Pub. by Leuven Univ) Coronet Bks.

DeMaeseneer, J. & Beolchi, L. Telematics in Primary Care. LC 94-73421. (Studies in Health Technology & Informatics: Vol. 20). 250p. (gr. 12). 1995. 70.00 *(90-5199-209-2)* IOS Press.

DeMaeyer, Catherine, tr. see Beyda, Vivian, et al.

DeMaeyer, E. & Dallman, P. Preventing & Controlling Iron Deficiency Anaemia through Primary Health Care: A Guide for Health Administrators & Programme Managers. 58p. 1989. 11.00 *(92-4-154249-7)* World Health.

DeMaeyer, Edouard M., ed. see Baker, Selwyn J. & Ramachandran, K.

DeMaeyer, Edouard M., ed. see Bothwell, Thomas H., et al.

DeMaggio, Paul. In Search of Andy: A Child's Love Lives On. 48p. 1995. pap. 5.95 *(1-880047-30-6)* Creative Des.

DeMaggio, S., jt. ed. see Diamond, R. A.

Demaid, A. & de Wit, J. H., eds. Case Studies in Manufacturing with Advanced Materials, Vol. 2. 340p. 1995. 205.00 *(0-444-88934-5,* North Holland) Elsevier.

DeMaille, Raymond J. Treaties for the Eighteen Sixties with the Southern Cheyenne & Arapaho. 15.00 *(0-944253-58-X)* Inst Dev Indian Law.

Demailly, Jean-Pierre, et al. Transcendental Methods in Algebraic Geometry: Lectures Given at the 3rd Session of the Centro Internazionale Matematico Estivo (C. I. M. E.) Held in Cetraro, Italy, July 4-12, 1994. Vol. 164. LC 96-49601. (Lecture Notes in Mathematics Ser.). 1996. pap. 52.00 *(3-540-62038-9)* Spr-Verlag.

Demain, A. L. & Solomon, Nadine A., eds. Antibiotics Containing the Beta-Lactam Structure One. (Handbook of Experimental Pharmacology Ser.: Vol. 67-I). (Illus.). 362p. 1983. 248.00 *(0-387-12107-2)* Spr-Verlag.

— Antibiotics Containing the Beta-Lactam Structure Two. (Handbook of Experimental Pharmacology Ser.: Vol. 67, II). (Illus.). 500p. 1983. 312.00 *(0-387-12131-5)* Spr-Verlag.

Demain, Arnold L. & Davies, Julian E., eds. Manual of Industrial Microbiology & Biotechnology. 2nd rev. ed. LC 98-44884. (Illus.). 600p. 1999. 93.95 *(1-55581-128-0)* ASM Pr.

Demaine, A. G., et al, eds. The Molecular Biology of Autoimmune Disease. (NATO ASI Series H: Vol. 38). (Illus.). 420p. 1990. 158.95 *(0-387-51771-5)* Spr-Verlag.

Demaine, Jack & Entwistle, Harold. Beyond Communitarianism: Citizenship, Politics & Education. LC 96-18827. 256p. 1997. text 59.95 *(0-312-16351-7)* St Martin.

***DeMaine, Mary R. & Taylor, Rabun M.** Life of the Average Roman: A Symposium. (Illus.). 137p. 1999. pap. 30.00 *(0-9673471-0-6)* PZA Pubng.

Demaine, Phyllis. The Chrysalis. large type ed. (Linford Romance Library). 272p. 1992. pap. 16.99 *(0-7089-7274-8)* Ulverscroft.

Demaine, Phyllis. Divided Loyalties. large type ed. 272p. pap. 18.99 *(0-7089-5449-9)* Ulverscroft.

— No Place for Tears. large type ed. 288p. 2000. pap. 18.99 *(0-7089-5649-1,* Linford) Ulverscroft.

Demaine, Phyllis. Shadows over Their Love. large type ed. 184p. 1992. 15.95 *(0-7451-1564-0,* G K Hall Lrg Type) Mac Lib Ref.

DeMaio, Daniel N. Registry Review for Computed Tomography. Biello, Lisa, ed. LC 95-49210. 240p. 1996. pap. text 26.00 *(0-7216-6285-4,* W B Saunders Co) Harcrt Hlth Sci Grp.

Demaio, Joe, et al. The New Darkroom Handbook: A Complete Guide to the Best Design, Construction & Equipment. 2nd ed. LC 97-24670. (Illus.). 188p. 1997. pap. 29.95 *(0-240-80260-8,* Focal) Buttrwrth-Heinemann.

Demaison, Gerard & Murris, Roelef J., eds. Petroleum Geochemistry & Basin Evaluation. LC 84-70675. (AAPG Memoir Ser.: No. 35). (Illus.). 436p. reprint ed. pap. 135.20 *(0-7837-5231-8,* 204496400005) Bks Demand.

DeMaison, H. Technical Dictionary of Aeronautics. (ENG, FRE & SPA.). 671p. 1978. 77.50 *(2-85608-007-3)* IBD Ltd.

Demaison, Henri. Complete Multilingual Dictionary of Aviation & Aeronautical Terminology. (ENG, FRE & SPA.). 680p. 1983. 75.00 (*0-8288-3915-8*, F20670) Fr & Eur.

***Demaison, J., et al.** Molecular Constants Mostly from Microwave, Molecular Beam, & Sub-Doppler Laser Spectroscopy Pt. B: Rotational, Centrifugal Distortion & Related Constants of Diamagnetic Assymmetric Top Molecules. Martienssen, W. & Huettner, W., eds. (Landolt-Boernstein Numerical Data & Functional Relationships in Science & Technology - New Series: Vol. 24). (Illus.). viii, 501p. 1999. 3388.00 (*3-540-65345-7*) Spr-Verlag.

DeMaistre, Joseph. Against Rousseau: On the State of Nature & on the Sovereignty of the People. Lebrun, Richard A., ed. & tr. by. from FRE. LC 97-158177. 248p. 1996. 70.00 (*0-7735-1415-5*, Pub. by McG-Queens Univ Pr) CUP Services.

Demaitre, Luke E. Doctor Bernard de Gordon: Professor & Practitioner. xii, 236p. pap. text 24.00 (*0-88844-051-0*) Brill Academic Pubs.

Demakis, J. Mount Athos: A Guide for Pilgrims. 1991. pap. 7.95 (*0-937032-78-6*) Light&Life Pub Co MN.

***Demakopoulos, Steve.** Do You Speak Greek? 192p. 2000. pap. 12.95 (*1-885778-51-1*, DSG500) Seaburn.

DeMaleissye-Melun, Judith, ed. The Fall of Detente: Soviet-American Relations During the Carter Years. LC 99-179652. 367p. (C). 1997. text 41.00 (*82-00-37671-0*) Scandnvan Univ Pr.

DeMaleissye-Melun, Judith & Chapman, D. L. Miracle of the Mind. 1986. pap. write for info. (*1-893310-03-5*) Science of Understand.

***DeMaleissye-Melun, Judith & Cloutier, Kenny.** God Is Good: Bedtime Morals for Children, 5 vols., Set. (J). (gr. k-12). 1999. pap. 44.75 (*1-893551-00-8*) Seabird Pubg.

DeMaleissye-Melun, Judith & Vetlesen, Arne J., eds. Closeness: An Ethics. 250p. (C). 1997. text 37.00 (*82-00-22563-1*) Scandnvan Univ Pr.

DeMaleissye-Melun, Judith & Ystad, Vigdis, eds. Contemporary Approaches to Ibsen, Vol. 9. 235p. (C). 1997. text 39.00 (*82-00-22697-2*) Scandnvan Univ Pr.

DeMaleissye-Melun, Judith, ed. see American Schools of Oriental Research Staff.

DeMalle, R. J. The Jerome Agreement Between the Kiowa, Comanche & Apache Tribes & the U. S. (Treaty Manuscripts Ser.: No. 27). 38p. 11.00 (*0-317-57464-7*) Inst Dev Indian Law.

DeMallie, R. J. Comanche Treaties: Historical Background. (Treaty Manuscripts Ser.: No. 14). 20p. 7.50 (*0-944253-36-9*) Inst Dev Indian Law.

— Comanche Treaties During the Civil War. (Treaty Manuscripts Ser.: No. 19). 30p. 10.00 (*0-944253-41-5*) Inst Dev Indian Law.

— Comanche Treaties of Eighteen Fifty, Eighteen Fifty-One, & Eighteen Fifty-Three with the U. S. (Treaty Manuscripts Ser.). 60p. 12.50 (*0-944253-40-7*) Inst Dev Indian Law.

— Comanche Treaties with the Republic of Texas. (Treaty Manuscripts Ser.: No. 15). 21p. 7.50 (*0-944253-38-5*) Inst Dev Indian Law.

— Comanche Treaty of Eighteen Forty-Six with the U. S. (Treaty Manuscripts Ser.: No. 17). 16p. 6.50 (*0-944253-37-7*) Inst Dev Indian Law.

— Comanche Treaty of Eighteen Thirty-Five with the United States. (Treaty Manuscripts Ser.: No. 15). 19p. 7.00 (*0-317-57440-X*) Inst Dev Indian Law.

— Historical Background of the Gila River Reservation. (Treaty Manuscripts Ser.: No. 11). 66p. 14.00 (*0-944253-33-4*) Inst Dev Indian Law.

— The Jerome Agreement of 1892 Between the Comanche & the U. S. (Treaty Manuscripts Ser.: No. 21). 51p. 12.50 (*0-944253-43-1*) Inst Dev Indian Law.

— The Kiowa Treaty of 1853. (Treaty Manuscripts Ser.: No. 23). 60p. 12.50 (*0-944253-78-4*) Inst Dev Indian Law.

— The Unratified Treaty Between the Kiowas, Comanches & Apaches & the United States of 1863. (Treaty Manuscripts Ser.: No. 24). 8p. 5.00 (*0-944253-46-6*) Inst Dev Indian Law.

DeMallie, R. J. & Kickingbird, Lynn. The Treaty of Medicine Lodge, 1867, Between the United States & the Kiowa, Comanche & Apache Indians. (Treaty Manuscripts Ser.: No. 26). 65p. 15.00 (*0-944253-48-2*) Inst Dev Indian Law.

— The Treaty on the Little Arkansas River, 1865. (Treaty Manuscripts Ser.: No. 25). 55p. 12.50 (*0-944253-47-4*) Inst Dev Indian Law.

DeMallie, Raymond J. Early Treaties with the Southern Cheyenne & Arapaho. 10.00 (*0-944253-57-1*) Inst Dev Indian Law.

DeMallie, Raymond J., ed. The Sixth Grandfather: Black Elk's Teachings Given to John G. Neihardt. LC 83-14452. (Illus.). xxix, 462p. 1984. pap. 15.00 (*0-8032-6564-6*, Bison Books) U of Nebr Pr.

DeMallie, Raymond J. & Ortiz, Alfonso, eds. North American Indian Anthropology: Essays on Society & Culture. LC 94-20618. (Illus.). 448p. 1996. pap. 18.95 (*0-8061-2808-9*) U of Okla Pr.

DeMallie, Raymond J. & Parks, Douglas R., eds. Sioux Indian Religion: Tradition & Innovation. LC 86-40527. (Illus.). 240p. 1989. pap. 14.95 (*0-8061-2166-1*) U of Okla Pr.

DeMallie, Raymond J., ed. see Walker, James R.

***Deman, Corinne.** Eleven Stories High: Growing up in Stuyvesant Town, 1948-1968. LC 00-22443. (C). 2001. pap. text 14.95 (*0-7914-4630-1*) State U NY Pr.

DeMan, Elaine, ed. see Barbour, Nancy.

Deman, Henry. The Psychology of Socialism. LC 73-14152. (Perspectives in Social Inquiry Ser.). 514p. 1974. reprint ed. 33.95 (*0-405-05498-X*) Ayer.

Deman, Paul. Allegories of Reading. LC 79-64075. 1982. pap. 18.00 (*0-300-02845-8*) Yale U Pr.

Demana. College Algebra & Trigonometry: Value Edition. 2nd ed. (C). 1996. text 51.00 (*0-201-40194-0*) Addison-Wesley.

— Demana Interim ALG/CH 7 Bndl. 1994. text 67.50 (*0-201-84630-6*) Addison-Wesley.

— Precalculus Functions & Graph Value Edition. 2nd ed. (C). 1996. text 40.00 (*0-201-40196-7*) Addison-Wesley.

— Precalculus Functions & Graph Value Edition. 3rd ed. (C). 1996. student ed. 90.00 (*0-201-85751-0*) Addison-Wesley.

Demana, Frank. Intermediate Algebra with Graphing Calculator Resource Manual. (C). 1995. 67.00 (*0-201-82086-2*) Addison-Wesley.

— Precalculus: Functions & Graphs with Lab Manual. 2nd ed. (C). 1993. 66.00 (*0-201-52910-6*) Addison-Wesley.

Demana, Frank & Waits, Bert K. Ans Bk Restrc Trig. (Illus.). (C). 1991. pap. text, teacher ed. 12.66 (*0-201-19575-5*) Addison-Wesley.

— College Algebra. (Illus.). (C). 1990. write for info. (*0-201-12193-X*); pap. text, teacher ed. 9.50 (*0-201-18659-4*); disk 9.50 (*0-201-18660-8*) Addison-Wesley.

— College Algebra. (Illus.). 64p. (C). 1998. pap. text, teacher ed. 8.82 (*0-201-18658-6*) Addison-Wesley.

— Computerized Testing. (Illus.). (C). 1990. student ed. 12.66 (*0-201-19577-1*) Addison-Wesley.

— Precalculus: Functions & Graphs. (Illus.). 718p. (C). 1990. text 36.76 (*0-201-52780-4*); pap. text, student ed. 21.50 (*0-201-52783-9*) Addison-Wesley.

— Precalculus Component. (Illus.). 718p. (C). 1990. text 38.25 (*0-201-52781-2*) Addison-Wesley.

— Precalculus Mathematics Vol. II: A Graphing Approach. (Illus.). 786p. (C). 1988. pap. text 10.75 (*0-201-19288-8*) Addison-Wesley.

— Printed Tests. (Illus.). (C). 1989. student ed. 12.66 (*0-201-19576-3*) Addison-Wesley.

— Trigonometry. 482p. 1990. 90.00 (*0-201-19572-0*) Addison-Wesley.

Demana, Frank & Waits, Bert K. Trigonometry. (Illus.). (C). 1990. pap. text, teacher ed. 19.00 (*0-201-19574-7*) Addison-Wesley.

Demana, Franklin. Beginning Algebra. (C). 1995. pap. text, lab manual ed. write for info. (*0-201-63123-7*); pap. text, lab manual ed. write for info. (*0-201-63127-X*) Addison-Wesley.

— Beginning Algebra. 2nd ed. (C). 1995. text. write for info. (*0-201-65013-4*) Addison-Wesley.

— College Algebra. 3rd ed. (C). 1997. text. write for info. (*0-201-54326-5*) Addison-Wesley.

— College Algebra: A Graphing Approach. 2nd ed. (C). 1993. pap. text, student ed. 26.00 (*0-201-55743-6*) Addison-Wesley.

— College Algebra & Trigonometry. 3rd ed. (C). 1997. text. write for info. (*0-201-54325-7*) Addison-Wesley.

— College Algebra & Trigonometry: Student Solutions Manual. 2nd ed. (C). 1993. pap. text 21.00 (*0-201-55733-9*) Addison-Wesley.

— College Algebra & Trigonometry with Graphing Calculator & Computer Graphing. 2nd ed. (C). 1992. lab manual ed. 88.00 (*0-201-56851-9*) Addison-Wesley.

— College Algebra with Graphing Calculator & Computer Graphing. 2nd ed. (C). 1992. lab manual ed. 80.00 (*0-201-56853-5*) Addison-Wesley.

— Graphing Calculator & Computer Graphing to Accompany College Algebra & Trigonometry. 2nd ed. 224p. (C). 1991. pap. text, lab manual ed. 18.00 (*0-201-56852-7*) Addison-Wesley.

— Graphing Calculator & Computer Lab Manual Supplement to Accompany Graphing Calculator & Computer Graphing Laboratory Manual. 3rd ed. 1995. ring bd. 12.00 (*0-201-58849-8*) Addison-Wesley.

— Graphing Calculator Resource Manual: Precalculus, a Graphing Approach. 4th ed. LC 96-233043. 224p. (C). 1996. pap. text, suppl. ed. 11.00 (*0-201-43200-5*) Addison-Wesley.

— Intermediate Algebra. 336p. (C). 1994. pap. text 24.00 (*0-201-59055-7*) Addison-Wesley.

— Intermediate Algebra & Beginning Algebra: A Combined Text. (C). 1995. text. write for info. (*0-201-80840-4*) Addison-Wesley.

— Precalculus: A Graphing Approach. 4th ed. 992p. (C). 1996. student ed. 81.00 (*0-201-87012-6*) Addison-Wesley.

— Precalculus: Functions & Graphs. 2nd ed. 192p. (C). 1993. pap. text 26.00 (*0-201-56734-2*) Addison-Wesley.

— Precalculus, Functions & Graphs. 4th ed. 1056p. (C). 1996. teacher ed. 72.00 (*0-201-87011-8*) Addison-Wesley.

— Precalculus Math, High School Version with Graphing Calculator & Computer Graphing. 2nd ed. (C). 1992. 68.00 (*0-201-56855-1*) Addison-Wesley.

— Proceedings of the Conference on Technology in Collegiate Mathematics: The Twilight of the... 1990. pap. text 22.75 (*0-201-50049-3*) Addison-Wesley.

Demana, Franklin, et al. Intermediate Algebra: A Graphing Approach. LC 94-19203. (C). 1994. text 62.81 (*0-201-80841-2*) Addison-Wesley.

— Intermediate Algebra: A Graphing Approach. LC 94-19063. (C). 1994. pap. text 28.50 (*0-201-58821-8*) Addison-Wesley.

Demana, Franklin, et al. Precalculus, Functions & Graphs. 3rd ed. LC 96-11383. 848p. (C). 1996. 86.00 (*0-201-82297-0*) Addison-Wesley.

Demana, Franklin D. Precalculus: OmniTest Mac Version & Functions & Graphs. 3rd ed. (C). 1996. 67.00 incl. disk (*0-201-44090-3*) Addison-Wesley.

Demana, Franklin D., et al, eds. College Algebra: A Graphing Approach. 2nd ed. (Illus.). 600p. (C). 1992. 67.00 (*0-201-57267-2*) Addison-Wesley.

— Precalculus Mathematics: A Graphing Approach. 2nd ed. (Illus.). 736p. (C). 1992. text 60.00 (*0-201-52626-3*) Addison-Wesley.

Demana, Franklin D., et al. College Algebra & Trigonometry: A Graphing Approach. 2nd ed. (Illus.). 736p. (C). 1992. text 84.00 (*0-201-56294-4*) Addison-Wesley.

— Intermediate Algebra: A Graphing Approach. (Illus.). 550p. (C). 1994. 84.00 (*0-201-65001-0*) Addison-Wesley.

— Precalculus: Functions & Graphs. 2nd ed. (Illus.). 784p. (C). 1992. text 65.00 (*0-201-56731-8*) Addison-Wesley.

— Precalculus Mathematics: A Graphing Approach. 3rd annot. ed. LC 92-44754. 1994. teacher ed. 88.00 (*0-201-52905-X*) Addison-Wesley.

— Precalculus Mathematics - A Graphing Approach: High School Version. 3rd ed. (Illus.). 800p. 1993. 87.00 (*0-201-52900-9*) Addison-Wesley.

— Transition to College Mathematics. (Illus.). 592p. 1984. text. write for info. (*0-201-11153-5*); pap. text, teacher ed. 5.50 (*0-201-11154-3*) Addison-Wesley.

Demand. Airplanes of the Second World War Coloring Book. (Illus.). (J). pap. 2.95 (*0-486-24107-6*) Dover.

— Airplanes of World War I Coloring Book. (Illus.). 181p. (J). pap. 2.95 (*0-486-23807-5*) Dover.

Demand, Nancy. Birth, Death, & Motherhood in Classical Greece. LC 93-39828. 276p. 1994. text 39.95 (*0-8018-4762-1*) Johns Hopkins.

— A History of Ancient Greece. 397p. (C). 1996. pap. 30.63 (*0-07-016207-6*) McGraw.

Demand, Nancy H. Urban Relocation in Archaic & Classical Greece: Flight & Consolidation. LC 89-40737. (Oklahoma Series in Classical Culture: Vol. 6). (Illus.). 256p. 1990. 45.00 (*0-8061-2278-1*) U of Okla Pr.

Demandt, Alexander. History That Never Happened: A Treatise on the Question, What Would Have Happened If? 3rd rev. ed. Thomson, Colin D., tr. from GER. LC 91-50952. (Illus.). 192p. 1993. lib. bdg. 32.50 (*0-89950-702-6*) McFarland & Co.

Demandt, Alexander, jt. ed. see Calder, William M., III.

Demandt, Sabine. Kleine Lexikon der Computerbegriffe. (GER.). 1993. 39.95 (*0-7859-8572-7*, 392945*7*024) Fr & Eur.

***DeMane, Erica.** Pasta Improvvisata: How to Improvise in Classic Italian Style. LC 99-21363. (Illus.). 320p. 1999. 24.50 (*0-684-82972-X*) Scribner.

***DeMann, Morgen Schick.** Your Makeover: Simple Ways for Any Woman to Look Her Best. (Illus.). 160p. 2000. 24.95 (*0-7893-0394-9*, Pub. by Universe) St Martin.

***Demant, C., et al.** Industrial Image Processing: Visual Quality Control in Manufacturing. Strick, M. & Schmidt, G., trs. from GER. (Illus.). 375p. 1999. 99.95 incl. cd-rom (*3-540-66410-6*) Spr-Verlag.

DeMar, Clarence. Marathon. LC 81-83460. (Illus.). 156p. 1981. reprint ed. 9.95 (*0-933050-09-7*) New Eng Pr VT.

— Marathon: The Clarence DeMar Story. 92p. 1991. reprint ed. pap. 12.95 (*0-915297-09-4*, CDM) Cedarwinds.

DeMar, Gary. America's Christian History: The Untold Story. 2nd rev. ed. (Illus.). 254p. 1993. pap. 10.95 (*0-915815-16-8*) American Vision.

— God & Government Vol. 1: A Biblical & Historical Study, 3 vols. 2nd ed. (Illus.). 222p. 1993. pap. 12.95 (*0-915815-09-5*) American Vision.

— God & Government Vol. 2: Issues in Biblical Perspective, 3 vols. (Illus.). 247p. 1990. reprint ed. pap. 12.95 (*0-915815-13-3*) American Vision.

— God & Government Vol. 3: The Restoration of the Republic. (Illus.). 324p. 1990. pap. 12.95 (*0-915815-14-1*) American Vision.

***DeMar, Gary.** Is Jesus Coming Soon? (Bible Prophecy Ser.: Vol. 1). 47p. 1999. pap. 3.95 (*0-915815-36-2*) American Vision.

— Last Days Madness: Obsession of the Modern Church. 4th rev. ed. 443p. 1999. pap. 19.95 (*0-915815-35-4*) American Vision.

DeMar, Gary & Leithart, Peter. The Reduction of Christianity: A Biblical Response to Dave Hunt. LC 87-73071. 403p. (Orig.). 1990. pap. 8.95 (*0-930462-63-7*) Inst Christian.

DeMar, Gary & Leithart, Peter J. The Legacy of Hatred Continues: A Response to Hal Lindsey's "The Road to Holocaust" 68p. 1989. pap. 3.95 (*0-930464-29-X*) Inst Christian.

DeMar, Gary & North, Gary. Christian Reconstruction: What It Is, What It Isn't. LC 90-22956. 219p. 1991. 25.00 (*0-930464-52-4*); pap. 8.95 (*0-930464-53-2*) Inst Christian.

DeMar, Gary & Young, Fred D. To Pledge Allegiance: A New World in View. Scott, Jane M., ed. (Illus.). 164p. 1996. reprint ed. pap. text 16.95 (*0-915815-19-2*) American Vision.

DeMar, Gary, et al. Theonomy: An Informed Response. LC 91-33321. 395p. 1991. 16.95 (*0-930464-59-1*) Inst Christian.

— To Pledge Allegiance: Reformation to Colonization. Scott, Jane M., ed. (Illus.). 320p. 1997. pap. text 22.95 (*0-915815-29-X*) American Vision.

Demarais Studio Press, Inc. Staff. Erotic Photography, an Exhibition. LC 81-70902. (Illus.). 102p. (Orig.). 1981. pap. 12.95 (*0-9607462-1-8*) Demarais Studio.

Demaray, C. E. Search the Scriptures, Old Testament Vol. 10: Ezra, Nehemiah, Esther. 1967. pap. 1.99 (*0-8341-0037-1*) Beacon Hill.

Demaray, Carolyn F. & Smith, Josette J. Triangle: Manuel de l'Etudiant: Applications Pratiques de la Langue Francaise. 3rd ed. (FRE., Illus.). 197p. (YA). (gr. 11-12). 1998. pap. text 18.60 (*1-877653-54-3*) Wayside Pub.

— Triangle: Manuel du Professeur. 3rd ed. (FRE.). 46p. (YA). (gr. 11-12). 1998. pap. text, teacher ed. 10.67 (*1-877653-61-6*) Wayside Pub.

***Demaray, Donald.** Experiencing Healing & Wholeness: A Journey in Faith. LC 99-214306. 312p. 1999. pap. 14.99 (*0-89367-233-5*) Light & Life Comm.

Demaray, Donald. How Are You Praying? 176p. (Orig.). 1985. pap. 7.70 (*0-310-23841-2*, 6801P) Zondervan.

Demaray, Donald, ed. see Wesley, John.

Demaray, Donald E. Basic Beliefs: An Introduction to Christian Theology. 144p. 1996. reprint ed. pap. 8.95 (*0-89367-178-9*) Light & Life Comm.

— The Innovation of John Newton, 1725-1807: Synergism of Word & Music in Eighteenth Century Evangelism. LC 87-30775. (Texts & Studies in Religion: Vol. 36). (Illus.). 392p. 1988. lib. bdg. 109.95 (*0-88946-824-9*) E Mellen.

— Introduccion a la Biblia.Tr. of Layman's Guide to Our Bible. (SPA.). Date not set. 11.99 (*0-7899-0250-8*, 491042) Editorial Unilit.

— Introduction to Homiletics. 2nd ed. (Illus.). 224p. (C). 1996. pap. text 11.99 (*0-89367-204-1*) Light & Life Comm.

— Laughter, Joy & Healing. 2nd rev. ed. (Illus.). 152p. 1995. reprint ed. pap. 9.99 (*0-89367-197-5*) Light & Life Comm.

— The Little Flowers of St. Francis: A Paraphrase. LC 91-42793. 170p. (Orig.). 1992. pap. 8.95 (*0-8189-0618-9*) Alba.

Demaray, Donald E., ed. Wesley's Daily Prayers. 1998. pap. 14.95 (*1-885224-19-2*) Bristol Hse.

Demaray, Donald E., ed. The Daily Roberts. 344p. (Orig.). 1996. pap. 13.95 (*0-89367-206-8*) Light & Life Comm.

Demaray, Donald E., ed. see Lawrence.

Demaray, Donald E., ed. see Thomas, a Kempis.

Demaray, John G. Cosmos & Epic Representation: Dante, Spenser, Milton & the Transformation of Renaissance Heroic Poetry. LC 90-21022. (Duquesne Studies: Language & Literature Ser.: Vol. 11). (Illus.). 284p. 1991. text 48.00 (*0-8207-0231-5*) Duquesne.

— Dante & the Book of the Cosmos. LC 86-72887. (Transactions Ser.: Vol. 77, Pt. 5). (Illus.). 115p. (Orig.). (C). 1987. pap. 18.00 (*0-87169-775-0*, T775-DEJ) Am Philos.

— The Invention of Dante's 'Commedia' LC 73-86888. 211p. reprint ed. pap. 65.50 (*0-8357-8733-8*, 203370600087) Bks Demand.

— Milton & the Masque Tradition: The Early Poems, Arcades & Comus. LC 68-14254. 212p. reprint ed. pap. 65.80 (*0-7837-2250-8*, 205733800004) Bks Demand.

— Milton's Theatrical Epic: The Invention & Design of Paradise Lost. LC 79-23139. (Illus.). 179p. 1980. 23.50 (*0-674-57615-2*) HUP.

— Shakespeare & the Spectacles of Strangeness: The Tempest & the Transformation of Renaissance Theatrical Forms. LC 97-33771. (Medieval & Renaissance Literary Studies). (Illus.). 200p. (C). 1998. text 48.00 (*0-8207-0284-6*) Duquesne.

Demaray, Kathleen. Instruye Al Nino. Orig. Title: Train up a Child. (SPA., Illus.). 24p. 1982. spiral bd. 5.75 (*0-89367-085-5*) Light & Life Comm.

— Train up a Child. (Illus.). 24p. 1974. spiral bd. 7.95 (*0-89367-059-6*) Light & Life Comm.

— Train Up a Child. 1993. pap. 6.95 (*0-89367-180-0*) Light & Life Comm.

Demaray, Sally. Way in the Wilderness. 1997. pap. text 89.95 (*1-888445-03-3*) Sonstar Pubns.

DeMarce, Virginia E. Mercenary Troops from Anhalt-Zerbst, Germany, During the American Revolution, 2 pts., Set. (German-American Genealogical Research Monographs: No. 19). (Orig.). 1984. pap. 40.00 (*0-915162-21-0*) Westland Pubns.

***Demarchalier, Patrick.** Patrick Demarchelier. 2000. pap. text 19.95 (*3-570-19240-7*) V C Bertelsman.

Demarchalier, Patrick. Patrick Demarchelier: Forms. 1998. 75.00 (*0-8478-2160-9*, Pub. by Rizzoli Intl) St Martin.

Demarchalier, Patrick, photos by. Patrick Demarchalier. (Illus.). 160p. 1998. 39.95 (*1-891475-11-8*, 810141) T Shafrazi.

DeMarche, Deborah, jt. ed. see Brigham, Steven.

Demarchelier, Patrick. Patrick Demarchelier: Photographs. (Illus.). 144p. 1995. 65.00 (*0-8212-2169-8*, Pub. by Bulfinch Pr) Little.

Demarchelier, Patrick, photos by. P. Demarchelier. (Illus.). 144p. 1998. pap. 35.00 (*0-8212-2514-6*, Pub. by Bulfinch Pr) Little.

Demarco. U. S. A. Divided Nation. LC 95-189467. 1994. pap. text. write for info. (*0-582-22674-0*, Pub. by Addison-Wesley) Longman.

***DeMarco, Tony.** Ed McCaffrey: Catching a Star. (SuperStar Series: Vol. 1). 96p. (J). 1999. pap. 4.95 (*1-58261-170-X*, Pub. by Sprts Pubng) Partners-West.

DeMarco, Tony. Ivan Rodriguez. LC 99-53058. (Latinos in Baseball Ser.). (Illus.). 64p. (YA). (gr. 5-10). 2000. lib. bdg. 18.95 (*1-58415-006-8*) M Lane Pubs.

— Vinny Castilla. (Latinos in Baseball Ser.). (Illus.). 64p. (YA). (gr. 5-10). 2000. lib. bdg. 18.95 (*1-58415-008-4*) M Lane Pubs.

***Demarco, Allison & Fairgrieve, Lindsay.** Dark Storms, Golden Journey: A Remarkable Spiritual Search for Inner Peace. 1999. pap. text 22.95 (*1-84018-151-6*, Pub. by Mainstream Pubng) Trafalgar.

DeMarco, Barbara, ed. see Naughton, Sean.

DeMarco, Carl. Pharmacy & the Law. 2nd ed. LC 84-2991. 464p. 1984. 93.00 (*0-89443-591-4*) Aspen Pub.

DeMarco, Donald. Abortion, in Perspective. 1982. pap. 5.95 (*0-910728-07-0*) Hayes.

— The Anesthetic Society. 182p. (Orig.). 1982. pap. 4.95 (*0-931888-09-3*) Christendom Pr.

Demarco, Donald. Character in a Time of Crisis. 120p. (Orig.). 1997. pap. 10.00 (*1-887567-06-2*) CBCCU Amer.

D

An Asterisk (*) at the beginning of an entry indicates that the title is appearing for the first time.

DeMarco, Donald. The Heart of Virtue: Lessons from Life & Literature Illustrating the Beauty & Moral Value of Character. LC 95-79949. (Orig.). Date not set. pap. 12.95 (*0-89870-568-1*) Ignatius Pr.

— The Incarnation in a Divided World. 208p. (Orig.). 1988. pap. 8.95 (*0-931888-27-1*) Christendom Pr.

***DeMarco, Donald.** New Perspectives in Contraception. 128p. 1999. pap. 12.00 (*0-9669777-1-8*) One More Soul.

— Timely Thoughts for Timeless Catholics. 183p. 2000. pap. 10.00 (*1-887567-13-5*) CBCCU Amer.

DeMarco, Frank. Messenger: A Sequel to Lost Horizon. LC 95-136277. 240p. (Orig.). 1994. pap. 9.95 (*1-57174-013-9*) Hampton Roads Pub Co.

DeMarco, Gordon. Elvis in Aspic. LC 93-61107. 224p. 1994. pap. 9.00 (*1-883303-11-7*, Pub. by Blue Heron OR) Consort Bk Sales.

— Frisco Blues. rev. ed. LC 95-24430. 160p. 1995. pap. 8.00 (*1-883303-18-4*, Pub. by Blue Heron OR) Consort Bk Sales.

— Murder at the Fringe. LC 87-63291. 190p. 1988. pap. 9.95 (*0-948275-41-3*) Dufour.

***Demarco, Guy.** Ships in Bottles. 2nd rev. ed. (Illus.). 64p. 2000. pap. 14.95 (*0-7643-0999-4*) Schiffer.

***Demarco, Guy & Demarco, Patricia.** Building Architectural Modals. LC 99-56130. (Illus.). 64p. 2000. pap. 14.95 (*0-7643-1071-2*) Schiffer.

DeMarco, John. Peer Helping Skills: A Program for Training Peer Helpers & Peer Tutors for Middle & High School, Peer Helper Handbook. LC 93-44890. 90p. 1993. pap. 32.95 (*1-56246-090-0*, 3104, HazeldenJohnson Inst); pap. 7.75 (*1-56246-089-7*, 3106, HazeldenJohnson Inst) Hazelden.

— Peer Mediation Skills: A Handbook for Peer Mediators. 43p. (YA). (gr. 7-12). 1998. pap. 9.95 (*1-56246-143-5*, 3074, HazeldenJohnson Inst) Hazelden.

— Peer Mediation Skills: Leader's Guide for Training Peer Mediators. 76p. 1998. pap. 35.00 (*1-56246-144-3*, 3075, HazeldenJohnson Inst) Hazelden.

Demarco, Joseph P. Moral Theory. (Philosophy). (C). 1995. 37.95 (*0-534-54247-6*) Wadsworth Pub.

DeMarco, Joseph P. & Fox, Richard M., eds. New Directions in Ethics: The Challenge of Applied Ethics. 320p. (C). 1986. text 47.50 (*0-7102-0639-9*, Routledge Thoemms) Routledge.

DeMarco, Joseph P., jt. auth. see Fox, Richard M.

Demarco, Patricia, jt. auth. see Demarco, Guy.

Demarco, Ric. The River & I: A Journey for Those of Us Who Occasionally Struggle with Confusion. Prow, Cameron, ed. (Illus.). 128p. 1998. pap. 11.95 (*0-9665689-0-7*) River Rider.

DeMarco, Tom. Controlling Software Projects: Management Measurement & Estimation. (Illus.). 284p. (C). 1986. pap. 49.60 (*0-13-171711-1*, Yourdon) P-H.

Demarco, Tom. The Deadline: A Novel about Project Management. LC 97-24716. 320p. 1997. pap. 24.95 (*0-932633-39-0*) Dorset Hse Pub Co.

DeMarco, Tom. Structured Analysis & System Specification. 352p. 1979. 55.60 (*0-13-854380-1*) P-H.

— Why Does Software Cost So Much? And Other Puzzles of the Information Age. LC 95-35656. 248p. 1995. pap. 29.95 (*0-932633-34-X*, QA76.754) Dorset Hse Pub Co.

DeMarco, Tom & Lister, Timothy R. Peopleware: Productive Projects & Teams. 2nd ed. LC 99-11525. 264p. 1999. pap. 33.95 (*0-932633-43-9*) Dorset Hse Pub Co.

DeMarco, Tom & Lister, Timothy R., eds. Software State-of-the-Art: Selected Papers. LC 89-83372. (Illus.). 584p. 1990. 45.95 (*0-932633-14-5*) Dorset Hse Pub Co.

DeMarco, Tony. Larry Walker: Colorado Hit Man! Rains, Rob, ed. (Super Star Ser.). 96p. (J). 1999. pap. 4.95 (*1-58261-052-5*) Sprts Pubng.

DeMarco, William J. Advanced IPA Management: Direct Contracting. LC 99-19184. 1999. write for info. (*0-07-134320-2*) McGraw.

DeMarco, William J. & Garvey, Thomas J. Going Prepaid: A Strategic Planning Decision. 121p. (Orig.). 1986. pap. text 24.00 (*0-933948-87-5*, 1468) Ctr Res Ambulatory.

DeMare, Patrick, et al. Koinonia: From Hate Through Dialogue to Culture in the Large Group. 256p. 1990. pap. text 30.00 (*0-946439-82-6*, Pub. by H Karnac Bks Ltd) Other Pr LLC.

DeMaree & McKinnon Fegan Staff. Idaho Supplement to "Fundamentals of Real Estate" & "Real Estate Principles & Practice" 8th ed. 1981. pap. 5.95 (*0-13-765917-2*) P-H.

Demaree, Albert L. The American Agricultural Press, 1819-1860. abr. ed. LC 73-16296. (Perspectives in American History Ser.: No. 4). (Illus.). xix, 430p. 1974. lib. bdg. 49.50 (*0-87991-331-2*) Porcupine Pr.

Demaree, Eric. Be Smart, Be Beautiful: How Your Conscience Creates Joy & Beauty. LC 98-93383. 120p. 1998. pap. 12.95 (*0-9619367-2-X*) Fellowship Bks.

— The Simplicity & Reality of the Bible: A Revolutionary Bible Handbook. LC 87-91608. (Illus.). 97p. (Orig.). 1988. pap. 6.00 (*0-9619367-0-3*) Fellowship Bks.

Demaree, Eric S. The Joy of Spirituality: How Overcoming Life's Obstacles with Wisdom Brings Extreme Happiness. 2nd rev. ed. LC 97-90311. 95p. (Orig.). 1997. pap. 12.95 (*0-9619367-1-1*) Fellowship Bks.

Demaree, George T. Termite Repair: How to: Make Repairs, Use Chemicals, Save Money. 2nd rev. ed. (Illus.). 128p. (Orig.). 1987. pap. 18.95 (*0-935831-00-2*) Tradesman Pub.

— Wood Rot: Repair & Prevention. (Orig.). pap. 15.95 (*0-935831-37-1*) Tradesman Pub.

Demaree, Robert W., Jr. & Moses, Don V. The Complete Conductor: A Comprehensive Resource for the Professional Conductor of the Twenty-First Century. LC 93-48392. 491p. 1994. 83.00 (*0-13-173014-2*) P-H.

Demaree, Scott & Steele, Eric. Marathoning 101: How to Finish Your First Marathon! (Illus.). 112p. 1999. pap. 14.95 (*0-9665512-1-4*) Stone Mason Inc.

Demaree, Tom, ed. Greater Chicago: The Best 200 Restaurants. (Menu Ser.). (Illus.). 448p. (Orig.). 1993. pap. 12.95 (*0-9628274-3-6*) D Thomas Pub.

— Los Angeles & Vicinity: The Best 200 Restaurants. (Menu Ser.). (Illus.). 448p. (Orig.). 1993. pap. 12.95 (*0-9628274-5-2*) D Thomas Pub.

— New York City & Vicinity: The Best 200 Restaurants. (Menu Ser.). (Illus.). 448p. (Orig.). 1993. pap. 12.95 (*0-9628274-4-4*) D Thomas Pub.

— San Francisco Bay Area: The Best 200 Restaurants. 2nd ed. (Menu Ser.). (Illus.). 448p. (Orig.). 1993. pap. 12.95 (*0-9628274-6-0*) D Thomas Pub.

Demarest. Engineer Electromagnet. 1997. pap. text, student ed. write for info. (*0-02-328522-2*) P-H.

— Seasons Board Book: Set of 4. 1997. pap. 19.80 (*0-15-201833-6*) Harcourt.

Demarest, Amy B. This Lake Alive! An Interdisciplinary Handbook for Teaching & Learning about the Lake Champlain Basin. (Illus.). 502p. 1999. pap., teacher ed. 29.95 (*0-9642163-1-0*, Pub. by Shelburne Farms) Chelsea Green Pub.

***Demarest, Anne.** Moonbeams on Water. 1999. mass mkt. 2.50 (*0-7390-0306-2*, 18540) Alfred Pub.

Demarest, Arthur. The Archaeology of Santa Leticia & the Rise of Maya Civilization. LC 84-62189. (Publications: No. 52). 272p. 1986. 40.00 (*0-939238-81-0*) Tulane MARI.

Demarest, Arthur A. Viracocha: The Nature & Antiquity of the Andean High God. LC 81-80344. (Peabody Museum Monographs: No. 6). (Illus.). 88p. 1981. reprint ed. pap. 8.00 (*0-87365-906-6*) Peabody Harvard.

Demarest, Arthur A. & Conrad, Geoffrey W., eds. Ideology & Pre-Columbian Civilizations. (Advanced Seminar Ser.). (Illus.). 280p. 1992. 24.95 (*0-933452-82-9*) Schol Am Res.

Demarest, Arthur A. & Houston, Stephen D. El Proyecto Arqueologico Regional Petexbatun: Primera Temporada - 1989. (Informe Preliminar Ser.: No. 1). (Illus.). 248p. 1989. spiral bd. 20.00 (*1-892940-00-0*) Vanderbilt Institute.

— Proyecto Arqueologico Regional Petexbatun: Segunda Temporada - 1990. (Informe Preliminar Ser.: No. 2). (Illus.). 643p. 1990. spiral bd. 50.00 (*1-892940-01-9*) Vanderbilt Institute.

Demarest, Arthur A., et al. Proyecto Arqueologico Cancuen: Primera Temporada - 1999. (Informe Preliminar Ser.: No. 1). (SPA., Illus.). 250p. 1999. spiral bd. 25.00 (*1-892940-07-8*) Vanderbilt Institute.

— Proyecto Arqueologico Cancuen: Segunda Temporada - 2000. (Informe Preliminar Ser.: No. 2). (SPA., Illus.). 450p. 2000. spiral bd. 35.00 (*1-892940-08-6*) Vanderbilt Institute.

— Proyecto Arqueologico Punta de Chimino, 1996-97. (Informe Preliminar Ser.). (SPA., Illus.). 210p. 1997. spiral bd. 20.00 (*1-892940-06-X*) Vanderbilt Institute.

— Proyecto Arqueologico Regional Petexbatun: Cuarta Temporada - 1992. (Informe Preliminar Ser.: No. 4). (SPA., Illus.). 393p. 1992. spiral bd. 30.00 (*1-892940-03-5*) Vanderbilt Institute.

— Proyecto Arqueologico Regional Petexbatun: Sexta Temporada - 1994. (Informe Preliminar Ser.: No. 6). (SPA.). 766p. 1995. spiral bd. 45.00 (*1-892940-05-1*) Vanderbilt Institute.

— Proyecto Arqueologico Regional Petexbatun: Tercera Temporada - 1991. (Informe Preliminar Ser.: No. 3). (Illus.). 952p. 1991. spiral bd. 70.00 (*1-892940-02-7*) Vanderbilt Institute.

Demarest, Arthur A., jt. auth. see Conrad, Geoffrey W.

Demarest, Bruce. The Cross & Salvation: The Doctrine of Salvation. LC 96-47760. (Foundations of Evangelical Theology Ser.). 576p. 1997. pap. 25.00 (*0-89107-937-8*) Crossway Bks.

— A History of Interpretation of Hebrews 7, 1-10 from the Reformation to the Present. 154p. 1976. pap. text 55.00 (*3-16-138531-4*, Pub. by JCB Mohr) Coronet Bks.

— Satisfy Your Soul. LC 99-19379. 1999. pap. 15.00 (*1-57683-130-2*) NavPress.

Demarest, Bruce A. General Revelation: Historical Views & Contemporary Issues. 320p. 1982. 11.95 (*0-310-44550-7*, 12706) Zondervan.

— Who Is Jesus? Chen, Ruth T., tr. (Basic Doctrine Ser.: Bk. 1). 1985. pap. write for info. (*0-941598-26-8*) Living Spring Pubns.

Demarest, Bruce A., jt. auth. see Lewis, Gordon R.

Demarest, Chris. All Aboard! (J). 1997. bds. write for info. (*0-614-29231-X*, Red Wagon Bks) Harcourt.

— Fall. LC 95-80921. (Illus.). 16p. (J). (ps). 1996. pap. 4.95 (*0-15-201026-2*) Harcourt.

— Winter. LC 95-80920. (Illus.). 16p. (J). (ps). 1996. pap. 4.95 (*0-15-201027-0*) Harcourt.

— Zookeeper Sue: A Lift-the-Flap Book. LC 98-85088. (Illus.). 16p. (J). 1999. 10.95 (*0-15-202017-9*) Harcourt.

Demarest, Chris L. All Aboard! LC 96-78054. (Illus.). 8p. (J). (ps). 1997. pap. 7.95 (*0-15-201413-6*) Harcourt.

— Bus. LC 95-6623. (J). (ps). 1996. pap. 4.95 (*0-15-200810-1*, Red Wagon Bks) Harcourt.

— The Cowboy ABC. LC 97-52630. (Illus.). 32p. (J). (ps-3). 1999. 15.95 (*0-7894-2509-2*, D K Ink) DK Pub Inc.

— Farmer Nat. LC 97-71671. (Illus.). 16p. (J). (ps). 1998. 10.95 (*0-15-200113-1*, Harcourt Child Bks) Harcourt.

— Honk! LC 97-77733. (Illus.). 16p. (J). (ps-1). 1998. 9.95 (*1-56397-221-2*) Boyds Mills Pr.

— Let's Go! Soft Cube with Rattle. (J). (ps-k). 1997. bds. 8.95 (*0-614-28821-5*, Red Wagon Bks) Harcourt.

— My Blue Boat. LC 94-10924. (Illus.). 32p. (J). 1998. pap. 6.00 (*0-15-201701-1*, Harcourt Child Bks) Harcourt.

***Demarest, Chris L.** My Blue Boat. 1998. 11.20 (*0-606-13629-0*, Pub. by Turtleback) Demco.

Demarest, Chris L. Ship. LC 94-74412. (Illus.). 16p. (J). (ps). 1995. pap. 4.95 (*0-15-200267-7*, Red Wagon Bks) Harcourt.

— Spring. LC 96-5255. (Illus.). 16p. 1997. pap. 4.95 (*0-15-201390-3*) Harcourt.

— Summer. LC 96-5257. (Illus.). 16p. 1997. pap. 4.95 (*0-15-201391-1*) Harcourt.

— Train. LC 95-6637. (Illus.). 16p. (J). (ps). 1996. pap. 4.95 (*0-15-200809-8*, Red Wagon Bks) Harcourt.

Demarest, Chris L., jt. illus. see Olaleye, Isaac.

Demarest, Dave, Jr., ed. The River Ran Red: Homestead, Eighteen Ninety-Two. LC 91-50935. (Illus.). 244p. 1992. pap. 19.95 (*0-8229-5478-8*); text 49.95 (*0-8229-3710-7*) U of Pittsburgh Pr.

Demarest, Donald. Fabulous Ancestor. (Humanities Ser.). 276p. 1992. pap. text. write for info. (*1-881383-00-8*) F Levy Endowment.

Demarest, Elizabeth J., et al. Review of Research on Achieving the Nation's Readiness Goal. (Illus.). 82p. (C). 1999. reprint ed. pap. text 25.00 (*0-7881-7669-2*) DIANE Pub.

Demarest, Gary. I, II Thessalonians; I, II Timothy & Titus. (Communicator's Commentary Ser.: Vol. 9). 333p. 22.99 (*0-8499-0162-6*); pap. 14.99 (*0-8499-3325-0*) Word Pub.

— Leviticus. (Communicator's Commentary Ser.: Vol. 3). 286p. 1990. 22.99 (*0-8499-0408-0*) Word Pub.

Demarest, Gary W. Leviticus. (Mastering the Old & New Testament Ser.: Vol. 3). pap. 14.99 (*0-8499-3542-3*) Word Pub.

Demarest, Geoff. Geoproperty: Foreign Affairs, National Security & Property Rights. LC 98-11815. 271p. 1998. 59.50 (*0-7146-4854-X*, Pub. by F Cass Pubs); pap. 24.50 (*0-7146-4475-7*, Pub. by F Cass Pubs) Intl Spec Bk.

Demarest, J., jt. auth. see Bosiljevac, Tim L.

Demarest, Jaki, jt. auth. see Fortschen, William R.

Demarest, Kenneth R. Engineering Electromagnetic. LC 97-26067. 672p. (C). 1997. 100.00 (*0-02-328521-4*) P-H.

Demarest, Larry. Looking at Type in the Workplace. 68p. 1997. pap. 7.00 (*0-935652-32-9*) Ctr Applications Psych.

Demarest, Larry, jt. auth. see Orem, Sara.

Demarest, Robert J., ed. History of the Association of Medical Illustrators. 50th anniversary ed. (Illus.). 256p. 1995. pap. text 20.00 (*1-883486-03-3*) Assn Med Illus.

Demarest, Robert J. & Charon, Rita. Illustrated Guide to Human Reproduction & Fertility Control. LC 95-23415. (Illus.). 96p. 1996. text 35.00 (*1-85070-697-2*) Prthnon Pub.

Demarest, Robert J., jt. auth. see Fink, B. Raymond.

Demarest, Robert J., jt. auth. see Kratzer, Guy L.

Demarest, Victoria B. God, Woman & Ministry. rev. ed. LC 76-42915. (Illus.). 1978. 12.95 (*0-912760-61-3*) Valkyrie Pub Hse.

— Sex & Spirit: God, Woman, & the Ministry. LC 76-42915. (Illus.). 146p. 1977. 15.00 (*0-912760-38-9*); pap. 10.00 (*0-912760-29-X*) Valkyrie Pub Hse.

— A Violin, a Lily & You. LC 76-42917. 56p. 1976. pap. 9.50 (*0-912760-28-1*) Valkyrie Pub Hse.

Demaret, F. Flore Generale de Belgique - Bryophytes, 3 vols. 1993. 109.00 (*1-878762-90-7*) Balogh.

Demaret, Paul. Patents, Territorial Restrictions, & EEC Law: A Legal & Economic Analysis. (IIC Studies Ser.: Vol. 2). 133p. 1978. pap. 44.00 (*3-527-25696-2*, Wiley-VCH) Wiley.

Demaria. College Handbook of Creative Writing. 3rd ed. LC 97-71997. 464p. (C). 1997. pap. text 28.50 (*0-15-505301-9*, Pub. by Harcourt Coll Pubs) Harcourt.

DeMaria, Alfred. Supervisor's Handbook on Maintaining Non-Union Status. rev. ed. 1986. pap. 9.95 (*0-88057-509-3*) Exec Ent Pubns.

— Supervisor's Handbook on Maintaining Non-Union Status. rev. ed. 80p. 1994. pap. 43.95 (*0-471-11286-0*) Wiley.

DeMaria, Alfred, jt. auth. see Hughes, Charles L.

***DeMaria, Alfred T.** Combating the Resurgence of Organized Labor: A Modern Guide to Union Prevention. (Illus.). 542p. 1998. pap. 125.00 (*1-929152-00-0*) Commns Train Inst.

DeMaria, Anthony J., ed. Lasers, Vol. 3. LC 66-11288. (Illus.). reprint ed. pap. 109.20 (*0-608-31015-8*) Bks Demand.

DeMaria, Anthony J., jt. ed. see Levine, Albert K.

DeMaria, Eric J., jt. auth. see Sugerman, Harvey J.

***DeMaria, Kristine.** The Packaging Development Process: A Guide for Engineers & Project Managers. LC 99-67777. 112p. 1999. pap. text 59.95 (*1-56676-801-2*) Technomic.

DeMaria, Michael. Horns & Halos: Towards the Blessing of Darkness. LC 91-37962. (Reshaping of Psychoanalysis: From Sigmund Freud to Ernest Becker Ser.: Vol. 2). 180p. (C). 1992. text 29.95 (*0-8204-1737-8*) P Lang Pubng.

DeMaria, Richard. Communal Love at Oneida: A Perfectionist Vision of Authority, Property & Sexual Order. LC 78-60958. (Texts & Studies in Religion: Vol. 2). 248p. 1983. 89.95 (*0-88946-988-1*) E Mellen.

Demaria, Rita. Focused Genograms: Intergenerational Assessment of Individuals, Couples, & Families. LC 98-51083. 1999. pap. 24.95 (*0-87630-881-7*) Brunner-Mazel.

DeMaria, Robert. Blowout. Date not set. 22.95 (*0-8488-2422-9*) Amereon Ltd.

DeMaria, Robert, Jr. British Literature, 1640-1789: A Critical Reader. LC 98-33639. 375p. 1999. 64.95 (*0-631-19739-7*); pap. 34.95 (*0-631-19741-9*) Blackwell Pubs.

DeMaria, Robert. Carnival of Angels. 233p. Date not set. 21.95 (*0-8488-2247-1*) Amereon Ltd.

— Clodia. 354p. Date not set. 25.95 (*0-8488-2250-1*) Amereon Ltd.

— Decline & Fall of America. 382p. Date not set. 26.95 (*0-8488-2243-9*) Amereon Ltd.

— Don Juan in Lourdes. 320p. Date not set. 24.95 (*0-8488-2246-3*) Amereon Ltd.

— The Empress. Date not set. 22.95 (*0-8488-2424-5*) Amereon Ltd.

— Extreme Remedies. 384p. Date not set. 26.95 (*0-8488-2245-5*) Amereon Ltd.

DeMaria, Robert, Jr. Johnson's Dictionary & the Language of Learning. LC 86-4285. xiv, 303p. 1986. 49.95 (*0-8078-1713-9*) U of NC Pr.

DeMaria, Robert. Outbreak. Date not set. 22.95 (*0-8488-2423-7*) Amereon Ltd.

— A Passion for Power. Date not set. 22.95 (*0-8488-2425-3*) Amereon Ltd.

DeMaria, Robert, Jr. Samuel Johnson & the Life of Reading. LC 96-38636. (Illus.). 256p. 1997. text 39.95 (*0-8018-5479-2*) Johns Hopkins.

DeMaria, Robert. The Satyr. 176p. Date not set. 19.95 (*0-8488-2249-8*) Amereon Ltd.

— The Satyr. LC 91-39571. 176p. 1992. 22.00 (*0-933256-78-7*) Second Chance.

— Secret Places. Date not set. 23.95 (*0-8488-2189-0*) Amereon Ltd.

— Sons & Brothers. 704p. Date not set. 37.95 (*0-8488-2248-X*) Amereon Ltd.

— Stone of Destiny. Date not set. 22.95 (*0-8488-2452-0*) Amereon Ltd.

— To Be a King. 368p. Date not set. 26.95 (*0-8488-2244-7*) Amereon Ltd.

***DeMaria, Robert.** The White Road. 304p. 2000. 25.00 (*1-57962-073-6*) Permanent Pr.

DeMaria, Robert, Jr., ed. British Literature, 1640-1789: An Anthology. LC 96-6257. (Blackwell Anthologies Ser.). 1996. 68.95 (*0-631-19527-0*); pap. 36.95 (*0-631-19528-9*) Blackwell Pubs.

DeMaria, Robert & Meyer, Ellen H., eds. A Contemporary Reader for Creative Writing. 320p. (Orig.). (C). 1993. pap. text 32.50 (*0-15-500727-0*, Pub. by Harcourt Coll Pubs) Harcourt.

***DeMaria, Rusel.** Asherton's Call: Official Strategies & Secrets. 256p. 1999. pap. 19.99 (*0-7821-2654-5*) Sybex.

Demaria, Rusel. Breath of Fire Authorized Game Secrets Vol. 1. LC 94-68165. (Illus.). 176p. 1994. pap. 14.95 (*1-55958-613-3*) Prima Pub.

— Dragon Lore: Official Strategy Guide. 1995. pap. 19.95 (*1-55958-672-9*) Prima Pub.

Demaria, Rusel. Dragon Lore 2: The Official Strategy. pap. 19.99 (*0-7615-0364-1*) Prima Pub.

DeMaria, Rusel. In the First Degree: The Official Strategy Guide. LC 95-69172. 1995. pap. 19.95 (*0-7615-0223-8*) Prima Pub.

— Klik & Play 1.0 Official Game Designers Guide. 1995. pap. text 19.95 (*0-7615-0153-3*) Prima Pub.

Demaria, Rusel. Mega Man X: Official Game Secrets. 1994. pap. 14.95 (*1-55958-787-3*) Prima Pub.

DeMaria, Rusel. Nintendo Secrets: The Power User's Guide. (Secrets of the Games Ser.). 368p. (Orig.). 1990. pap. 9.95 (*1-55958-062-3*) Prima Pub.

— Oddworld: Abe's Odyssee: The Official Strategy Guide. LC 97-69033. 144p. 1997. per. 12.99 (*0-7615-1086-9*) Prima Pub.

— Prince of Persia: The Official Strategy Guide. LC 93-9695. (Illus.). 272p. (Orig.). 1993. pap. 19.95 (*1-55958-373-8*) Prima Pub.

— Secret of Mana Official Game Secrets. (Illus.). 176p. 1993. pap. 15.99 (*1-55958-465-3*) Prima Pub.

— Sega Genesis Secrets, Vol. 6. 384p. (Orig.). 1994. pap. 12.95 (*1-55958-453-X*) Prima Pub.

— Sega Genesis Secrets: The Power User's Guide. (Secrets of the Games Ser.). 272p. (Orig.). 1990. pap. 9.95 (*1-55958-063-1*) Prima Pub.

— 7th Guest: The Official Strategy Guide. 368p. 1993. pap. 19.95 (*1-55958-468-8*) Prima Pub.

— SimEarth: The Official Strategy Guide. (Illus.). 336p. (Orig.). 1991. pap. 18.95 (*1-55958-103-4*) Prima Pub.

— Super Empire Strikes Back Official Game Secrets. 272p. 1993. pap. 12.95 (*1-55958-452-1*) Prima Pub.

— Super Metroid: Unauthorized Game Secrets. LC 94-67385. (Illus.). 192p. 1994. pap. 14.95 (*1-55958-610-9*) Prima Pub.

— Super Star Wars Official Game Secrets. (Illus.). 224p. (Orig.). 1993. pap. 12.95 (*1-55958-405-X*) Prima Pub.

Demaria, Rusel. Tie Fighter: Defender of the Empire: Official Secrets & Solutions. 112p. 1995. pap. text 12.95 (*0-7615-0142-8*) Prima Pub.

— TIE Fighter Collector's CD-ROM: The Official Strategy Guide. LC 95-70659. 528p. 1996. pap. 19.99 (*0-7615-0276-9*) Prima Pub.

— Working with Claris CAD. (Computer Graphics Technology & Management Ser.). (Illus.). 320p. 1991. pap. 19.95 (*0-8306-3545-9*) McGraw-Hill Prof.

DeMaria, Rusel. X-Wing: The Official Strategy Guide. LC 93-22788. (Illus.). 432p. (Orig.). 1993. pap. 19.95 (*1-55958-375-4*) Prima Pub.

Demaria, Rusel. X-Wing Collector's CD-ROM: The Official Strategy Guide. 1995. pap. text 19.95 (*1-55958-785-7*) Prima Pub.

DeMaria, Rusel & Barrera, Jeronimo. Sega Genesis & Sega CD Secrets, Vol. 5. (Illus.). 416p. (Orig.). 1993. pap. 12.95 (*1-55958-379-7*) Prima Pub.

DeMaria, Rusel & Eddy, Andy. TurboGrafx Secrets: The Power User's Guide. (Secrets of the Games Ser.). 272p. (Orig.). 1990. pap. 9.95 (*1-55958-064-X*) Prima Pub.

DeMaria, Rusel & Fontaine, George. Working with dBASE MAC: A User's Guide & Reference. 400p. (Orig.). (C). 1988. pap. 19.95 (*0-685-19366-7*) P-H.

DeMaria, Rusel & Meston, Zach. Nintendo Games Secrets, Vol. 2. (Secrets of the Games Ser.). (Illus.). 336p. 1991. pap. 11.95 (*1-55958-105-0*) Prima Pub.

— Nintendo Games Secrets, Vol. 4. (Secrets of the Games Ser.). (Illus.). 272p. 1992. pap. 9.99 (*1-55958-252-9*) Prima Pub.

— Sega Genesis Games Secrets, Vol. 2. (Secrets of the Games Ser.). (Illus.). 288p. (Orig.). 1991. pap. 9.95 (*1-55958-125-5*) Prima Pub.

— Sega Genesis Secrets. (Secrets of the Games Ser.: Vol. 3). (Illus.). 304p. (Orig.). 1992. pap. 9.99 (*1-55958-189-1*) Prima Pub.

— Super Mario World Secrets: Super Mario Bros. 4 for the Super Nintendo Entertainment System. (Secrets of the Games Ser.). (Illus.). 288p. 1991. pap. 12.95 (*1-55958-156-5*) Prima Pub.

— Super NES Games Secrets, Vol. 2. rev. ed. (Illus.). 268p. (Orig.). 1992. pap. 9.95 (*1-55958-193-X*) Prima Pub.

— Super NES Games Secrets, Vol. 3. (Secrets of the Games Ser.). (Illus.). 304p. (Orig.). 1992. pap. 11.95 (*1-55958-249-9*) Prima Pub.

DeMaria, Rusel & Spector, Caroline. Ultima: The Avatar Adventures. (Secrets of the Games Ser.). (Illus.). 416p. (Orig.). 1992. pap. 18.95 (*1-55958-130-1*) Prima Pub.

DeMaria, Rusel & Uttermann, Alex. 11th Hour: The Sequel to the Seventh Guest: The Official Strategy Guide. (Illus.). 320p. 1995. pap. 19.95 (*1-55958-528-5*) Prima Pub.

DeMaria, Rusel, jt. auth. see Barba, Rick.

DeMarinis, Paul, et al. Jim Pomeroy: A Retrospective. (Illus.). 72p. 1999. pap. 25.00 (*0-9627010-2-5*) New Langton Arts.

***DeMarinis, Rick.** Art & Craft of the Short Story. 240p. 2000. 18.99 (*1-884910-45-9*, Story Press) F & W Pubns Inc.

DeMarinis, Rick. Borrowed Hearts: New & Selected Stories. LC 98-55233. 336p. 1999. text 24.00 (*1-888363-98-3*, Pub. by Seven Stories) Publishers Group.

***DeMarinis, Rick.** Borrowed Hearts: New & Selected Stories. 336p. 2000. pap. 16.95 (*1-58322-040-2*, Pub. by Seven Stories) Publishers Group.

DeMarinis, Rick. The Coming Triumph of the Free World. 1991. pap. 7.95 (*0-393-30746-8*) Norton.

— Under the Wheat. LC 86-7007. (Drue Heinz Literature Prize Ser.). 168p. 1986. text 22.50 (*0-8229-3544-9*) U of Pittsburgh Pr.

— The Year of the Zinc Penny. 1999. pap. 18.95 (*0-670-82575-1*) Viking Penguin.

DeMarinis, Valerie, jt. ed. see Aune, Michael B.

DeMarinis, Valerie M. Critical Caring: A Feminist Model for Pastoral Psychology. 208p. 1993. text 23.00 (*0-664-22041-X*) Westminster John Knox.

Demarios & Mcgowen. Applying Algebraic Thinking to Data: Concepts & Processes for the Intermediate Algebra Student. alternate ed. 272p. (C). 1997. pap., student ed. 22.00 (*0-06-502379-X*) Addson-Wesley Educ.

DeMarios & McGowen. Mathematical Investigations: An Introduction to Algebraic Thinking. alternate ed. 144p. (C). 1997. pap., student ed. 25.00 (*0-06-502383-8*) Addson-Wesley Educ.

***Demaris.** Big Game Management in North America. LC 99-40881. (Illus.). 778p. 1999. 100.00 (*0-13-717422-5*) P-H.

DeMaris, Alfred. Logit Modeling: Practical Applications. LC 92-9657. (Quantitative Applications in the Social Sciences Ser.: Vol. 86). 96p. (C). 1992. pap. text 10.95 (*0-8039-4377-6*) Sage.

Demaris, Ovid. The Last Mafioso. 1980. mass mkt. write for info. (*0-394-59540-8*) Random.

Demaris, Ovid, jt. auth. see Reid, Ed.

Demaris, Ovid, jt. auth. see Wills, Garry.

DeMaris, Richard E. The Colossian Controversy: Wisdom in Dispute at Colossae. LC 94-212262. (JSNT Supplement Ser.: Vol. 96). 170p. 1994. 52.50 (*1-85075-473-X*, Pub. by Sheffield Acad) CUP Services.

DeMark, Dick Van, see Van DeMark, Dick.

DeMark, Thomas R. New Market Timing Techniques: Innovative Studies in Markets Rhythm & Price Exhaustion. LC 97-19962. (Trading Advantage Ser.). 368p. 1997. 69.95 (*0-471-14978-0*) Wiley.

— The New Science of Technical Analysis. (Wiley Finance Editions Ser.). 264p. 1994. 59.95 (*0-471-03548-3*) Wiley.

DeMark, Tom & Demark, Tom J., Jr. DeMark on Day Trading Options. LC 99-21299. 358p. 1999. 39.95 (*0-07-135059-4*) McGraw.

Demark, Tom J., Jr., jt. auth. see DeMark, Tom.

DeMarle, David J., jt. auth. see Shillito, M. Larry.

DeMarly, Diana. Fashion for Men: An Illustrated History. (Illus.). 166p. 1985. pap. 29.95 (*0-8419-1240-8*) Holmes & Meier.

Demarois. Applying Algebraic Thinking. (C). 1997. pap. text 21.00 (*0-201-30478-3*) Addison-Wesley.

Demarois, ed. Intermediate Algebra: Solution Manual. 752p. (C). 1998. pap. text, teacher ed. write for info. (*0-321-40030-5*) Addson-Wesley Educ.

***Demarois & Mcgowen.** Graphing Calculator Manual. 2nd ed. 2000. pap. 21.00 (*0-321-08351-2*) Addison-Wesley.

DeMarois, Phil. College Algebra Laboratories Using Derive. 120p. (Orig.). (C). 1992. pap. text 16.95 (*0-9623629-1-3*) MathWare.

— T183 or T182 Mini Labs: Algebraic Investigations. 200p. (Orig.). (C). 1996. pap. text 16.95 (*0-9623629-9-9*) MathWare.

***DeMarois, Phil, et al.** Applying Algebraic Thinking to Data. 2nd ed. LC 00-23160. 2000. pap. write for info. (*0-321-06934-X*) Addson-Wesley Educ.

DeMarois, Phil, et al. Applying Algebraic Thinking to Data: Concepts & Processes for the Intermediate Algebra Student. alternate ed. LC 95-15389. (Illus.). 544p. (C). 1997. pap. 48.00 (*0-06-501254-2*) Addson-Wesley Educ.

Demarois, Phil, et al. Introductory Algebra. LC 97-13156. (Illus.). 656p. (C). 1997. pap. 75.00 (*0-321-01049-3*) Addson-Wesley Educ.

***DeMarois, Phil, et al.** Mathematical Investigations: An Introduction to Algebraic Thinking. 2nd ed. LC 00-21999. 624p. 2000. pap. text 75.00 (*0-321-06931-5*) Addson-Wesley Educ.

Demarquez, Suzanne. Manuel de Falla. LC 82-23640. (Music Reprint Ser.). viii, 253p. 1983. reprint ed. lib. bdg. 32.50 (*0-306-76204-8*) Da Capo.

DeMarr, Mary J. Colleen McCullough: A Critical Companion. LC 95-50452. (Critical Companions to Popular Contemporary Writers Ser.). 208p. 1996. 29.95 (*0-313-29499-2*, Greenwood Pr) Greenwood.

— In the Beginning: First Novels in Mystery Series. LC 94-23676. 227p. 1995. 35.95 (*0-87972-673-3*); pap. 17.95 (*0-87972-674-1*) Bowling Green Univ Popular Press.

DeMarr, Mary Jean. Barbara Kingsolver: A Critical Companion. LC 98-55347. (Critical Companions to Popular Contemporary Writers Ser.). 176p. 1999. 29.95 (*0-313-30638-9*, GR0638, Greenwood Pr) Greenwood.

Demarrais. Understanding Children & Adolescence. 134p. (C). 1998. pap. text 14.50 (*0-536-01544-9*) S&S Trade.

***Demarrais.** The Way Schools Work. 3rd ed. 1998. 56.25 (*0-201-66656-1*) Addison-Wesley.

Demarrais, Kathleen. The Way Schools Work. 3rd ed. LC 98-20920. 384p. (C). 1998. pap. 60.00 (*0-8013-1956-0*) Longman.

DeMarrais, Kathleen B., ed. Inside Stories: Qualitative Research Reflections. LC 97-30928. 208p. 1997. pap. text. write for info. (*0-8058-8038-0*) L Erlbaum Assocs.

DeMarre, Dean A., et al. Applied Biomedical Electronics for Technicians. LC 79-4459. (Biomedical Engineering & Instrumentation Ser.: No. 5). 350p. reprint ed. pap. 108.50 (*0-7837-3373-9*, 204333100008) Bks Demand.

Demars & Chaney, eds. Geotechnical Properties, Behavior & Performance of Calcareous Soils - STP 777. 414p. 1982. 39.00 (*0-8031-0787-0*, STP777) ASTM.

DeMars, Douglas, ed. Nightsun, Vol. 15. 60p. (Orig.). 1995. 6.50 (*1-878306-07-3*) Nightsun Frostburg.

— Nightsun. 60p. (Orig.). 1993. pap. 5.00 (*1-878306-05-7*) Nightsun Frostburg.

— Nightsun, Vol. 16. 64p. (Orig.). (C). 1996. pap. 6.50 (*1-878306-08-1*) Nightsun Frostburg.

DeMars, Douglas & Wilson, Barbara, eds. Nightsun. 52p. (Orig.). 1991. pap. text 5.00 (*1-878306-02-2*) Nightsun Frostburg.

DeMars, Frances M. Rich: Joel Rich Ancestors & Descendants, from Dover, NH, Cape Cod & Gorham, ME to Jackson Plantation, Waldo County, 1677-1993. (Illus.). 175p. 1993. pap. 29.50 (*0-8328-3624-9*); lib. bdg. 39.50 (*0-8328-3623-0*) Higginson Bk Co.

DeMars, Jeanne, compiled by. Rhubarb Recipes. 3rd ed. 120p. (Orig.). 1997. 10.95 (*0-9627766-4-5*) Apple Blossom.

DeMars, Jo, jt. auth. see Norrgard, Lee E.

Demars, Kenneth R., et al, eds. Dredging, Remediation, & Containment of Contaminated Sediments. LC 95-37452. (STP, Special Technical Publication Ser.: No. 1293). (Illus.). 350p. 1995. text 95.00 (*0-8031-2028-1*, STP1230) ASTM.

Demars, Kenneth R. & Chaney, Ronald C., eds. Geotechnical Engineering of Ocean Waste Disposal. LC 90-644. (Special Technical Publication (STP) Ser.: No. 1087). (Illus.). 322p. 1990. text 79.00 (*0-8031-1390-0*, STP1087) ASTM.

Demars, Kenneth R., jt. ed. see Chaney, Ronald C.

DeMars, Mitch, jt. ed. see Proft, R. J.

DeMars, Nan. You Want Me to Do What? When, Where & How to Draw the Line. Thompson, Brad, ed. LC 97-66113. 320p. (Orig.). 1997. pap. 19.95 (*0-918351-04-9*) Thompson Co Inc.

Demars, Nan. You Want Me to Do What? When, Where & How to Draw the Line at Work. LC 98-11385. 336p. 1998. per. 12.00 (*0-684-85046-X*, Fireside) S&S Trade Pap.

DeMars, Wilson, ed. Nightsun. LC 89-63279. 50p. (Orig.). 1989. pap. 5.00 (*1-878306-00-6*) Nightsun Frostburg.

DeMarsche, Michael. The French Legacy: The American & European Collections of the Lauren Rogers Museum of Art. (Illus.). 32p. 1998. pap. 12.95 (*0-935903-03-8*) Lauren Rogers.

***DeMarse, Michael.** 37 Sexy Makeover Secrets for Success. (Illus.). 108p. 2000. pap. 19.95 (*1-887918-35-3*) Brockton Pubng.

DeMarsh, Mary, jt. auth. see DeFelice, Cynthia.

Demartini, John. Count Your Blessings! The Healing Power of Gratitude & Love. LC 96-35846. 1997. pap. 14.95 (*1-86204-021-4*, Pub. by Element MA) Penguin Putnam.

DeMartino, C. Practical Dictionary of Journalism - Dizionario Pratico Di Giornalismo. 1991. 75.00 (*0-8288-8434-X*) Fr & Eur.

***DeMartino, George.** Global Economy, Global Justice: Theoretical & Policy Alternatives to Neoliberalism. 280p. 2000. pap. 32.99 (*0-415-22401-2*); text 100.00 (*0-415-12427-1*) Routledge.

DeMartino, Manfred, ed. Human Autoerotic Practices. LC 78-8766. 378p. 1979. 43.95 (*0-87705-373-1*, Kluwer Acad Hman Sci); pap. 24.95 (*0-87705-403-7*, Kluwer Acad Hman Sci) Kluwer Academic.

***Demas, Corinne.** Eleven Stories High: Growing up in Stuyvesant Town, 1948-1968. LC 00-22443. 187p. 2000. 18.50 (*0-7914-4629-8*) State U NY Pr.

— If Ever I Return Again. LC 99-40586. (Illus.). 208p. (YA). (gr. 4-7). 2000. lib. bdg. 15.89 (*0-06-028718-7*) HarpC Child Bks.

— Middle Grade Novel. 196p. (gr. 3-7). 15.95 (*0-06-028725-X*) HarpC.

— Middle Grade Novel. 196p. (J). (gr. 3-7). 4.95 (*0-06-440845-0*) HarpC Child Bks.

— Nina's Waltz. LC 99-54152. (Illus.). 32p. (J). (gr. k-4). 2000. 16.95 (*0-531-30281-4*); 17.99 (*0-531-33281-0*) Orchard Bks Watts.

— The Perfect Pony. LC 99-46813. (Step into Reading Ser.: A Step 3 Book). (Illus.). 48p. (J). (gr. k-3). 2000. lib. bdg. 11.99 (*0-679-99199-9*, Pub. by Random Bks Yng Read) Random.

Demas, Corinne, jt. auth. see Bliss.

Demas, Corrine. If Ever I Return Again. LC 99-40586. 196p. (J). (gr. 5 up). Date not set. pap. 4.95 (*0-06-440844-2*) HarpC Child Bks.

— If Ever I Return Again. LC 99-40586. 208p. (YA). (gr. 4-7). 2000. 15.95 (*0-06-028717-9*) HarpC Child Bks.

Demas, Sophia. Sophia's Anthology of Poetry. 1998. pap. write for info. (*1-58235-013-2*) Watermrk Pr.

Demasio, Antonio. Choices: The Neurological Basis of Decision Making. 1994. write for info. (*0-201-56792-X*) Addison-Wesley.

Demassa. Electrical & Electronic Design. (West Engineering Ser.). 1989. pap., student ed. 8.00 (*0-534-93874-4*) PWS Pubs.

DeMassa, Thomas A. & Ciccone, Zack. Digital Integrated Circuits. LC 95-312. 700p. 1995. text 96.95 (*0-471-10805-7*) Wiley.

Demaster, D. J., jt. ed. see Nittrouer, C. A.

Demastes, William, jt. ed. see Schrank, Bernice W.

Demastes, William W. Beyond Naturalism: A New Realism in American Theatre, 27. LC 88-17787. (Contributions in Drama & Theatre Studies: No. 27). 182p. 1988. 47.95 (*0-313-26320-5*, DBN/, Greenwood Pr) Greenwood.

Demastes, William W. British Playwrights, 1956-1995: A Research & Production Sourcebook. LC 95-25609. 512p. 1996. lib. bdg. 99.50 (*0-313-28759-7*, Greenwood Pr) Greenwood.

Demastes, William W. Clifford Odets: A Research & Production Sourcebook, 1. LC 91-3757. (Modern Dramatists Research & Production Sourcebooks Ser.: No. 1). 224p. 1991. lib. bdg. 55.00 (*0-313-26294-2*, DCO, Greenwood Pr) Greenwood.

— Theatre of Chaos: Beyond Absurdism, into Orderly Disorder. LC 97-11055. (Illus.). 208p. (C). 1998. text 59.95 (*0-521-58245-8*) Cambridge U Pr.

Demastes, William W., ed. American Playwrights, 1880-1945: A Research & Production Sourcebook. LC 94-13690. 512p. 1994. lib. bdg. 89.50 (*0-313-28638-8*, Greenwood Pr) Greenwood.

Demastes, William W., ed. Realism & the American Dramatic Tradition. 312p. (Orig.). (C). 1996. pap. text 29.95 (*0-8173-0837-7*) U of Ala Pr.

Demastes, William W. & Kelly, Katherine E., eds. British Playwrights, 1880-1956: A Research & Production Sourcebook. LC 95-53105. 472p. 1996. lib. bdg. 95.00 (*0-313-28758-9*, Greenwood Pr) Greenwood.

Dematons, Charlotte. Looking for Cinderella. Sauerwein, Leigh, tr. & adapted by by. LC 96-11515. (Illus.). 40p. (J). 1996. 15.95 (*1-886910-13-8*) Front Str.

DeMatos, Isabel Freire, jt. auth. see DeGonzalez, Fe Acosta.

DeMatteis, Bob. From Patent to Profit. LC 97-94336. (Illus.). xiv, 285p. 1997. pap. 29.95 (*0-9660455-0-5*, B104) Inventions Co.

— From Patent to Profit. (Illus.). 320p. 1999. pap. text 29.95 (*0-89529-879-1*, Avery) Penguin Putnam.

— Inventors Journal. 95p. 1997. pap. 9.95 (*0-9660455-3-X*) Inventions Co.

DeMatteis, Bob & Antonucci, Mark. From Patent to Profit Resource Guide. (Illus.). 274p. 1997. pap. 8.95 (*0-9660455-2-1*) Inventions Co.

Dematteis, J. M. Batman/Spider-Man. LC 98-197942. (Illus.). 48p. 1997. pap. 4.95 (*1-56389-308-8*) DC Comics.

DeMatteis, J. M. Captain America: Deathlok Lives. 64p. 1993. 4.95 (*0-7851-0019-9*) Marvel Entrprs.

— Mercy. Berger, Karen, ed. (Illus.). 64p. 1993. pap. 5.95 (*1-56389-091-7*) DC Comics.

— Moonshadow, No. 18. deluxe limited ed. Clark, Margaret, ed. (Illus.). 396p. 1989. 39.95 (*0-936211-16-4*) Graphitti Designs.

Dematteis, J. M. Spider-Man: The Lost Years. (Illus.). 96p. 1996. pap. text 9.95 (*0-7851-0202-7*) Marvel Entrprs.

Dematteis, J. M. & Barreto, Eduardo. Superman: Speeding Bullets. (Illus.). 48p. (J). 1993. pap. 5.95 (*1-56389-117-4*, Pub. by DC Comics) Time Warner.

DeMatteis, J. M. & Giffen, Keith. Justice League: A New Beginning. Wald, Mark & Bruning, Richard, eds. (Illus.). 192p. 1989. pap. 12.95 (*0-930289-40-4*) DC Comics.

DeMatteis, J. M. & Muth, Jon. The Compleat Moonshadow. Kahan, Bob, ed. LC 98-207831. (Illus.). 464p. 1998. pap. text 39.95 (*1-56389-343-6*, Pub. by DC Comics) Time Warner.

DeMatteis, J.M. Batman: Two-Face - Crime & Punishment. Peterson, Scott, ed. LC 96-159044. (Illus.). 48p. 1995. pap. 4.95 (*1-56389-197-2*) DC Comics.

Dematteis, Lou. A Portrait of Vietnam. (Illus.). 128p. 1996. 35.00 (*0-393-03948-X*); pap. 22.50 (*0-393-31429-4*) Norton.

Dematteis, Phillip. Max Stirner Versus Karl Marx: Individuality & the Social Organism. 1975. lib. bdg. 250.00 (*0-87700-239-8*) Revisionist Pr.

Demattos, Frank, jt. auth. see Robinson, Charles.

DeMattos, Jack. Garrett & Roosevelt. LC 87-36530. 151p. 1988. 21.95 (*0-932702-42-2*) Creative Texas.

— Masterson & Roosevelt. LC 84-17591. (Early West Ser.). (Illus.). 151p. 1984. 21.95 (*0-932702-31-7*) Creative Texas.

— Mysterious Gunfighter: The Story of Dave Mather. LC 92-4022. (Illus.). 200p. 1992. 21.95 (*0-932702-95-3*) Creative Texas.

DeMattos, Jack, ed. The Earp Decision. limited ed. LC 89-23952. (Illus.). 208p. 1989. 21.95 (*0-932702-47-3*) Creative Texas.

Demattwis, J. M., et al. Spider-Man: Kraven's Last Hunt. (Illus.). 160p. 1990. pap. 15.95 (*0-87135-691-0*) Marvel Entrprs.

DeMauro, Thomas. Firebird Decoding Quick,1967-1981: Number Crunching for Trans Ams & Firebirds. (Illus.). 196p. (Orig.). 1997. pap. 12.95 (*1-57913-004-6*) CSK Pub.

DeMauro, Thomas, et al. Pontiac Power. (Illus.). 162p. (Orig.). 1994. pap. 19.95 (*1-57913-002-X*) CSK Pub.

Demaus, A. B. Motor Sports in the Twenties. 120p. 1989. 24.95 (*0-86299-599-X*, 3-AQ-0063) Auto Quarterly.

Demaus, R. The Life of Latimer: The Christian Martyr, Born 1485, Burned at the Stake 1555. reprint ed. pap. 40.00 (*0-943698-33-2*) Papyrus Letterbox.

DeMause, Alan. Complete Fingerstyle Jazz Guitar Book. 184p. 1996. pap. 37.95 incl. audio compact disk (*0-7866-1333-5*, 95434CDP) Mel Bay.

— How to Play Seven-String Guitar. 40p. 1999. pap. 17.95 incl. audio compact disk (*0-7866-4115-0*, 97113BCD) Mel Bay.

— Jazz Guitar Handbook. 40p. 1997. pap. 9.95 incl. audio compact disk (*0-7866-2702-6*, 94170BCD) Mel Bay.

DeMause, Lloyd. Foundations of Psychohistory. LC 81-90307. (Illus.). 350p. (C). 1982. 34.95 (*0-940508-00-1*); pap. 14.95 (*0-940508-01-X*) Creative Roots.

— Reagan's America. LC 82-73581. 200p. 1984. 23.95 (*0-940508-02-8*) Creative Roots.

DeMause, Lloyd, ed. The History of Childhood. 462p. 1995. pap. 60.00 (*1-56821-551-7*) Aronson.

DeMaw, Doug. Ferromagnetic-Core Design Manual. 2nd ed. (Illus.). 256p. 1996. reprint ed. pap. 19.95 (*1-891237-01-2*, MFJ-3506) MFJ Ent.

— First Steps in Radio. 1986. pap. 6.00 (*0-87259-228-6*) Am Radio.

— Practical RF Design Manual. 2nd ed. (Illus.). 246p. 1997. reprint ed. pap. 19.95 (*1-891237-00-4*, MFJ-3507) MFJ Ent.

— WIFB's QRP Notebook. 1991. pap. 10.00 (*0-87259-365-7*) Am Radio.

DeMay, Dennis L. Don't Hire a Crook: How to Avoid Common Hiring (and Firing) Mistakes. LC 99-179455. (Illus.). 480p. 1999. pap. 25.95 (*1-889150-09-6*, Pub. by Facts on Demand) Natl Bk Netwk.

Demay, G., ed. Inventaire des Sceaux de la Flandre, 2 vols., Set. 1990. reprint ed. 210.00 (*3-262-00238-0*) Periodicals Srv.

Demay, J. German Crowns - Multiples (1486-1599) (Illus.). 1975. lib. bdg. 50.00 (*0-932106-15-3*) S J Durst.

DeMay, Jessica H., ed. The Civil War Diary of Berea M. Willsey: The Intimate Daily Observations of a Massachusetts Volunteer in the Union Army, 1862-64. 196p. (Orig.). 1995. pap. text 17.50 (*0-7884-0168-8*) Heritage Bk.

DeMay, John A. Discovery & Settlement: How to Win Your Case Without Trial. 2nd ed. LC 92-16404. (C). 1992. text 59.95 (*0-13-224882-4*) P-H.

DeMay, Richard. The Art & Science of Cytopathology, 2 vols. 1280p. 1996. 295.00 (*0-89189-322-9*) Am Soc Clinical.

DeMay, Richard M. Practical Principles of Cytopathology. LC 98-32155. 1999. 150.00 (*0-89189-437-3*) Am Soc Clinical.

Demay, Sally. Almost Famous. Costa, Gwen, ed. LC 91-32394. 254p. 1992. 29.95 (*0-87949-365-8*) Ashley Bks.

Demazeau, Yves, jt. ed. see Werner, Eric.

Demazet. Aeronautique, Astronautique, Aerodynamique: Anglais Technique. (FRE.). 268p. 1976. pap. 59.95 (*0-8288-5573-0*, M6000) Fr & Eur.

— Construction Automobile: Anglais Technique. (ENG & FRE.). 216p. 1976. pap. 59.95 (*0-8288-5576-5*, M6086) Fr & Eur.

Demaziere, Christophe & Wilson, Patricia A., eds. Local Economic Development in Europe & the Americas. LC 95-18499. 256p. 1995. 110.00 (*0-7201-2269-4*) Continuum.

Demazure, M. Lectures on P-Divisible Groups. LC 72-94595. (Lecture Notes in Mathematics Ser.: Vol. 302). 98p. 1986. 31.95 (*0-387-06092-8*) Spr-Verlag.

Demazure, Michel. Bifurcations & Catastrophes: Geometry of Solutions to Nonlinear Problems. Chillingworth, D., tr. (Universitext Ser.). (Illus.). viii, 296p. 2000. pap. text 49.95 (*3-540-52118-6*) Spr-Verlag.

Demb, Ada & Neubauer, Franz-Friedrich. The Corporate Board: Confronting the Paradoxes. (Illus.). 232p. (C). 1992. text 45.00 (*0-19-507039-9*) OUP.

Dembe, Allard E. Occupation & Disease: How Social Factors Affect the Conception of Work-Related Disorders. LC 95-39781. 344p. 1996. 40.00 (*0-300-06436-5*) Yale U Pr.

Dembeck, Len, jt. auth. see Reeves, Ralph.

Dembeck, Mary G. Moonsnacks & Assorted Nuts. LC 94-75986. (Illus.). 40p. 1994. 15.95 (*1-880851-11-3*) Greene Bark Pr.

Dember, W. N., ed. Spontaneous Alternation Behavior. (Illus.). 175p. 1989. 78.95 (*0-387-96963-2*) Spr-Verlag.

Dembigh, Philip. System Analysis & Signal Processing: Solutions Manual. (C). 1998. pap. text. write for info. (*0-201-34289-8*) Addison-Wesley.

Dembinska, Maria & Weaver, William W. Food & Drink in Medieval Poland: Rediscovering a Cuisine of the Past. LC 99-12275. (Illus.). 200p. 1999. 29.95 (*0-8122-3224-0*) U of Pa Pr.

Dembinski, Ludwik. The Modern Law of Diplomacy. (C). 1988. lib. bdg. 74.00 (*90-247-3585-8*) Kluwer Academic.

Dembinski, Ludwik, ed. International Geneva Yearbook, 1988. 1988. lib. bdg. 77.50 (*90-247-3648-X*) Kluwer Academic.

D

Dembinski, Pawe. The Logic of Planned Economy: The Seeds of the Collapse. Cook, Kevin, tr. 264p. 1991. 75.00 (*0-19-828686-4*) OUP.

Dembitz, Lewis N. Jewish Services in Synagogue & Home. LC 74-27977. (Modern Jewish Experience Ser.). 1975. reprint ed. 44.95 (*0-405-06706-2*) Ayer.

Dembkowski, Harry E. The Union of Lublin: Polish Federalism in the Golden Age. (East European Monographs: No. 116). 380p. 1982. text 77.50 (*0-88033-009-0*, Pub. by East Eur Monographs) Col U Pr.

Dembling, Paul G. & Mason, Malcolm S. Essentials of Grant Law Practice. LC 91-70261. 254p. 1991. text 33.00 (*0-8318-0539-0*, B539) Am Law Inst.

Dembo. Keyboarding/Information Processing Supplement. (TA - Typing/Keyboarding Ser.). 1992. mass mkt. 17.25 (*0-538-61366-1*) S-W Pub.

Dembo, Amir & Zeitouni, Ofer. Large Deviations Techniques & Applications. 2nd ed. Balakrishnan, A. V. et al, eds. LC 97-45236. (Applications of Mathematics Ser.: Vol. 38). (Illus.). 416p. 1998. text 59.95 (*0-387-98406-2*) Spr-Verlag.

Dembo, D., et al. The International Context of Rural Poverty in the Third World: Issues for Research & Action by Grassroots Organizations & Legal Activists. 210p. (Orig.). 1986. pap. 20.00 (*0-936876-40-9*) Intl Ctr Law.

Dembo, David, et al, eds. Nothing to Lose but Our Lives: Enpowerment to Oppose Industrial Hazards in a Transitional World. 208p. (Orig.). (C). 1988. pap. 13.50 (*0-936876-38-7*) LRIS.

***Dembo, David & Morehouse, Ward.** The Underbelly of the U. S. Economy: Joblessness & Pauperization of Work in America. 8th rev. ed. (Illus.). 44p. 2000. pap. 5.00 (*1-891843-00-1*) Apex Pr.

Dembo, David, et al. Abuse of Power: Social Performance of Large Corporations: The Case of Union Carbide. LC 90-31342. (Illus.). 169p. (Orig.). 1990. pap. 13.50 (*0-945257-25-2*) Apex Pr.

Dembo, Jonathan, ed. see Littell, Norman M.

Dembo, L. S. Detotalized Totalities: Synthesis & Disintegration in Naturalist, Existential, & Socialist Fiction. LC 88-40429. 249p. 1989. reprint ed. pap. 77.20 (*0-608-01949-6*, 206260400003) Bks Demand.

— The Mongolian Jew: A Literary Study. LC 87-40517. 208p. reprint ed. pap. 64.50 (*0-608-09904-X*, 206924200003) Bks Demand.

Dembo, L. S., ed. Criticism: Speculative & Analytical Essays. LC 68-9830. 160p. 1968. reprint ed. pap. 49.60 (*0-608-01942-9*, 206259700003) Bks Demand.

— Interviews with Contemporary Writers: Second Series, 1972-1982. LC 82-51092. 391p. 1983. reprint ed. pap. 121.30 (*0-608-01940-2*, 206259500003) Bks Demand.

Dembo, L. S. & Pondrom, Cyrena N., eds. The Contemporary Writer: Interviews with Sixteen Novelists & Poets. LC 71-176410. 318p. 1972. reprint ed. pap. 98.60 (*0-608-01950-X*, 206260500003) Bks Demand.

Dembo, L. S. & Pratt, Annis, eds. Doris Lessing: Critical Essays. LC 74-5909. 184p. reprint ed. pap. 57.10 (*0-8357-9774-0*, 201018800068) Bks Demand.

Dembo, L. S., jt. ed. see Krieger, Murray.

Dembo, Margot B., tr. see Ehrhardt, Jana U.

Dembo, Margot B., tr. see Elias, Ruth.

Dembo, Margot B., tr. see Hermand, Jost.

Dembo, Margot B., tr. see Klein, Olaf G.

Dembo, Margot B., tr. see Perel, Solomon.

Dembo, Myron. Applying Educational Psychology Study Guide. 5th ed. (C). 1994. pap. text, student ed. 23.44 (*0-8013-1068-7*) Addison-Wesley.

Dembo, Myron H. Applying Educational Psychology. 5th ed. LC 93-13375. 720p. (C). 1994. pap. text 87.00 (*0-8013-1398-8*) Addison-Wesley.

Dembo, Myron H. Applying Educational Psychology. 5th ed. 720p. 1994. pap. write for info. (*0-8013-1308-2*) Longman.

Dembo, Myron H. Applying Educational Psychology in the Classroom. 5th ed. LC 93-13375. 704p. (C). 1994. teacher ed. write for info. (*0-8013-1067-9*, 79474) Longman.

***Dembo, Myron H.** Motivation & Learning Strategies for College Success. LC 99-48735. (C). 2000. pap. write for info. (*0-8058-3214-9*) L Erlbaum Assocs.

Dembo, Ron S. & Freeman, Andrew. Seeing Tomorrow: Rewriting the Rules of Risk. LC 97-49920. 260p. 1998. 27.95 (*0-471-24736-7*) Wiley.

Dembo, Shirley & Belis, Cynthia. Learning to Type with Microsoft Word 97. LC 98-194783. xv, 493p. 1997. 27.00 (*1-56243-551-5*, Z-24) DDC Pub.

Dembo, Shirley, ed. see Blanc, Iris.

Dembofsky, Tom. Test Preparation for Dental Assisting. (C). 1995. 24.00 (*0-13-034711-6*, Macmillan Coll) P-H.

— Test Preparation for Medical Assisting. (C). 1995. 24.00 (*0-13-034729-9*, Macmillan Coll) P-H.

— Test Preparation for Radiologic Technology. (C). 1995. 24.00 (*0-13-034752-3*, Macmillan Coll) P-H.

Dembofsky, Tom & Ford, Pamela T. Review Manual for Dental Assisting. (C). 1995. 24.00 (*0-13-034679-9*, Macmillan Coll) P-H.

Dembofsky, Tom & Johnston, Kris. Review Manual for Radiologic Technology. (C). 1995. 24.00 (*0-13-034695-0*, Macmillan Coll) P-H.

Demboski, Julie. Bread for Beginners. LC 97-185322. (Illus.). 104p. (Orig.). 1997. pap. 18.95 (*0-9658369-0-8*) Dog & Sunflower.

***Dembour, Marie-Benedicte.** Recalling the Belgian Congo: Conversations & Introspection. LC 98-50670. (New Directions in Anthropology Ser.: Vol. 9). (Illus.). 256p. 2000. 69.95 (*1-57181-945-2*); pap. write for info. (*1-57181-756-5*) Berghahn Bks.

***Dembowski, Hans.** Taking the State to Court: Public Interest Litigation & the Public Sphere in India. (Law in India Ser.). 227p. 2000. text 24.95 (*0-19-565309-2*) OUP.

Dembowski, Peter. Finite Geometries. LC 96-40096. (Classics in Mathematics Ser.). 375p. 1997. pap. 35.00 (*3-540-61786-8*) Spr-Verlag.

Dembowski, Peter F. Jean Froissart & His Meliador: Context, Craft & Sense. LC 82-84728. (Edward C. Armstrong Monographs on Medieval Literature: No. 2). 196p. (Orig.). 1983. pap. 14.95 (*0-917058-44-5*) French Forum.

Dembroski, S. A., jt. auth. see Siegman, A. W.

Dembroski, T. M., et al, eds. Coronary Prone Behavior. LC 78-9947. (Illus.). 1978. 52.00 (*0-387-08876-8*) Spr-Verlag.

Dembrowsky, Constance H. Mastering Anger - Resolving Conflict: Creating Peace & Harmony in Ourselves, Our Relationships & Our Communities, 3 vols. Incl. Mastering Anger - Resolving Conflict: Teacher Manual. (Illus.). 402p. 1999. teacher ed., ring bd. 200.00 (*0-924609-23-0*); Mastering Anger - Resolving Conflict: Transparencies. (Illus.). 101p. 1999. ring bd. 425.00 (*0-924609-25-7*); Mastering Anger Resolving Conflicting: Blackline Master. (Illus.). 186p. 1999. ring bd. 699.00 (*0-924609-24-9*); (Illus.). 689p. (YA). (gr. 6-8). Set ring bd. 945.00 (*0-924609-26-5*) Inst Affect Skill.

— Mastering Anger - Resolving Conflicts: Creating Peace & Harmony in Ourselves, Our Relationships & Our Communities. (Illus.). 700p. (YA). (gr. 7-12). 1999. ring bd. 945.00 (*0-924609-21-4*) Life Mission.

Dembrowsky, Constance H. Personal & Social Responsibility: Complete Set. Complete Set. rev. ed. (YA). (gr. 9-12). 1992. spiral bd. 299.00 (*0-924609-11-7*) Inst Affect Skill.

— Personal & Social Responsibility: Drug Prevention Component. rev. ed. 8p. 1992. spiral bd. write for info. (*0-924609-10-9*) Inst Affect Skill.

— Personal & Social Responsibility: Parent Activity Book. rev. ed. 65p. 1992. spiral bd. 7.95 (*0-924609-07-9*) Inst Affect Skill.

— Personal & Social Responsibility: Parent Leader Manual. rev. ed. 144p. 1992. spiral bd. 59.95 (*0-924609-06-0*) Inst Affect Skill.

— Personal & Social Responsibility: Student Activity Book. rev. ed. 400p. 1992. spiral bd. 16.95 (*0-924609-05-2*) Inst Affect Skill.

— Personal & Social Responsibility: Teacher Manual. rev. ed. 539p. 1992. spiral bd. 199.00 (*0-924609-04-4*) Inst Affect Skill.

— Self-Esteem: Appendix. 177p. 1989. pap. 99.00 (*0-924609-08-7*) Inst Affect Skill.

— Self-Esteem: Complete Set, 5 Vols., Set. rev. ed. (J). (gr. 6-8). 1989. spiral bd. 229.00 (*0-924609-18-4*) Inst Affect Skill.

— Self Esteem: Parent Activity Book. 79p. 1989. spiral bd. 6.95 (*0-924609-03-6*) Inst Affect Skill.

— Self-Esteem: Parent Leader Manual. 150p. 1989. spiral bd. 59.95 (*0-924609-02-8*) Inst Affect Skill.

— Self Esteem: Student Activity Book. 242p. 1989. spiral bd. 11.95 (*0-924609-01-X*) Inst Affect Skill.

— Self Esteem: Teacher Manual. 370p. 1989. spiral bd. 99.00 (*0-924609-00-1*) Inst Affect Skill.

— Wind Trails Vol. 1: Thoughts to Ponder. 1991. spiral bd. 10.00 (*0-924609-12-5*) Inst Affect Skill.

Dembski, Stephen & Straus, Joseph N., eds. Milton Babbitt: Words about Music. LC 86-40455. (Illus.). 208p. 1987. text 27.95 (*0-299-10790-6*) U of Wis Pr.

Dembski, William, ed. see Cole, Deborah D. & Duran, Maureen Gallagher.

Dembski, William A. The Design Inference: Eliminating Chance Through Small Probabilities. LC 98-3020. (Cambridge Studies in Probability, Induction & Decision Theory). 262p. (C). 1998. text 54.95 (*0-521-62387-1*) Cambridge U Pr.

***Dembski, William A.** Intelligent Design: The Bridge Between Science & Theology. LC 99-37141. 312p. 1999. 19.99 (*0-8308-1581-3*) InterVarsity.

Dembski, William A., ed. Mere Creation: Science, Faith & Intelligent Design. LC 98-20999. 475p. 1998. pap. 24.99 (*0-8308-1515-5*, 1515) InterVarsity.

Demby, B., ed. see Ryan, Michael W.

Demby, William. Beetlecreek. 2nd ed. LC 98-33592. 232p. 1998. reprint ed. pap. 17.00 (*1-57806-106-7*) U Pr of Miss.

Demby, William & Scott, Nathan A., Jr. The Catacombs. (Northeastern Library of Black Literature). 256p. 1991. reprint ed. pap. text 16.95 (*1-55553-099-0*) NE U Pr.

Demchak, Chris C. Military Organizations, Complex Machines: Modernization in the U. S. Armed Services. LC 90-55731. (Cornell Studies in Security Affairs). 224p. 1991. text 39.95 (*0-8014-2468-2*) Cornell U Pr.

Demchak, Chris C., jt. auth. see Rochlin, Gene I.

Demchak, Maryann & American Association on Mental Retardation Staff. Teaching Students with Severe Disabilities in Inclusive Settings. LC 97-36030. (Innovations Ser.). 1997. 21.95 (*0-940898-49-7*) Am Assn Mental.

Demchak, MaryAnn & Bossert, Karen W. Assessing Problem Behaviors. Browder, Diane M., ed. (Innovations Ser.). (Illus.). 44p. 1996. pap. 21.95 (*0-940898-39-X*) Am Assn Mental.

Demchenko, A. P. Ultraviolet Spectroscopy of Proteins. (Illus.). 340p. 1986. 139.00 (*0-387-16013-2*) Spr-Verlag.

***Demchinsky, Bryan & Naves, Elaine Kalman.** Storied Streets: Montreal in the Literary Imagination. (Illus.). 240p. 2000. 35.95 (*1-55199-044-X*) MW&R.

Demcho-Wagor, Marie, ed. see Lewis, Samuel L. & Douglas-Klotz, Neil.

Demco, Inc. Staff & De Broux, Jane. Little Wolf's Birthday. (Little Wolf Ser.). 20p. (J). (gr. k-2). 1994. student ed. 1.99 (*1-885360-02-9*) Demco WI.

— Little Wolf's School Day. (Little Wolf Ser.). 20p. (J). (gr. k-2). 1994. student ed. 1.99 (*1-885360-00-2*) Demco WI.

— Little Wolf's Seasons. (Little Wolf Ser.). 20p. (J). (gr. k-2). 1994. student ed. 1.99 (*1-885360-01-0*) Demco WI.

Demco Staff, jt. auth. see Jess, Denise.

Demco Staff, ed. see Bryant, Bonnie.

Demczyk, B. G., et al, eds. Evolution of Thin-Film & Surface Structure & Morphology. (MRS Symposium Proceedings Ser.: Vol. 355). 668p. 1995. 87.00 (*1-55899-256-1*) Materials Res.

Deme, Laszlo. The Radical Left in the Hungarian Revolution of 1848. (East European Monographs: No. 19). 162p. 1976. text 55.50 (*0-914710-12-5*, Pub. by East Eur Monographs) Col U Pr.

De'Medici, Lorenza. The De'Medici Kitchen. (Illus.). 128p. 1998. pap. text 17.00 (*0-7881-5890-2*) DIANE Pub.

— Italy: The Beautiful Cookbook. (Illus.). 256p. 1989. 50.00 (*0-00-215446-3*) Collins SF.

DeMedici, Lorenza. Lorenza's Antipasti. LC 98-4414. (Illus.). 176p. 1998. 40.00 (*0-609-60151-2*) C Potter.

***De'Medici, Lorenza.** Lorenza's Pasta: 200 Recipes for Family & Friends. 2000. reprint ed. pap. 24.95 (*1-86205-039-2*, Pub. by Pavilion Bks Ltd) Trafalgar.

De'Medici, Lorenza. Pasta. Lertz, Laurie, ed. LC 92-10314. (Williams-Sonoma Kitchen Library). (Illus.). 108p. 1992. lib. bdg. write for info. (*0-7835-0213-3*) Time-Life.

— Pasta. Lertz, Laurie, ed. LC 92-10314. (Williams-Sonoma Kitchen Library). (Illus.). 108p. (J). (gr. 11). 1999. 18.95 (*0-7835-0212-5*) Time-Life.

— The Renaissance of Italian Cooking. 176p. 1998. pap. 16.95 (*1-86205-186-0*, Pub. by Pavilion Bks Ltd) Trafalgar.

— Tuscany: The Beautiful Cookbook. LC 91-42832. (Illus.). 256p. 1992. 50.00 (*0-00-255032-6*) Collins SF.

— The Villa Table. 192p. 1998. pap. 16.95 (*1-86205-181-X*, Pub. by Pavilion Bks Ltd) Trafalgar.

DeMeester, Conrad, ed. see Brother Lawrence.

Demeester, Piet. Low Dimensional Structures Prepared by Epitaxial Growth or Regrowth on Patterned Subtrates: Proceedings of the NATO Advanced Research Workshop, Ringberg in Rottach Egern, Germany, February 20-24, 1995. Eberl, Karl & Petroff, Pierre M., eds. LC 95-34347. (NATO Advanced Science Institutes Ser.: Series E, Vol. 289). 400p. (C). 1995. text 206.00 (*0-7923-3679-8*) Kluwer Academic.

DeMeester, Tom R. & Levin, Bernard, eds. Cancer of the Esophagus. 320p. 1985. text 99.00 (*0-8089-1665-3*, 791023, Grune & Strat) Harcrt Hlth Sci Grp.

DeMeester, Tom R. & Skinner, David B., eds. Esophageal Disorders: Pathophysiology & Therapy. LC 84-22329. 687p. 1985. reprint ed. pap. 200.00 (*0-608-03402-9*, 206409900008) Bks Demand.

DeMeester, Tom R., jt. ed. see Peters, Jeffrey H.

DeMeij, Sjaak, jt. auth. see Abraham, Werner.

***DeMejo, Lawrence P., et al, eds.** Fundamentals of Adhesion & Interfaces. 327p. 1999. text 85.00 (*90-5699-682-7*, G & B Science) Gordon & Breach.

Demek, J., ed. see International Geographical Union Staff.

Demekas, Dimitrios & Khan, Mohsin S. The Romanian Economic Reform Program. LC 91-4066. (Occasional Paper Ser.: No. 89). v, 36p. 1991. 15.00 (*1-55775-190-0*) Intl Monetary.

***Demel, Bernhard.** Der Deutsche Orden Einst und Jetzt: Aufsatze Zu Seiner Mehr Als 800jahrigen Geschichte. (Europaische Hochschulschriften Geschichte und Ihre Hilfswissenschaften Ser.). 387p. 1999. 63.95 (*3-631-34999-8*) P Lang Pubng.

Demel, Marjorie. Facetas: Lectura. (Bridging the Gap Ser.). (C). 1993. mass mkt., student ed. 36.95 (*0-8384-4654-X*) Heinle & Heinle.

***Demel, Mark.** An Attractive Deal. 1998. pap. 15.00 (*0-310-67765-3*) Zondervan.

Demel, Mark. Sunday Morning Live Vol. 9: A Collection of 6 Drama Sketches. Pederson, Steve, ed. 64p. 1998. pap. 19.99 (*0-310-22158-7*) Zondervan.

— The Void. 1998. pap. 15.00 (*0-310-67766-1*) Zondervan.

Demelendez-Ostertag. Teaching Children in Multicultural Classrooms. (Early Childhood Education Ser.). 64p. 1996. pap., teacher ed. 10.00 (*0-8273-7276-0*) Delmar.

***Demelendez-Ostertag.** Teaching Social Studies in Early Education. LC 99-49327. (Early Childhood Education Ser.). (C). 2000. text 39.95 (*0-7668-0288-4*) Delmar.

Demell, Reinhardt & Maier, Hermann N. Das Wasser und Seine Bewohner: Ausgenommen die Fische, 3 vols. (GER., Illus.). xxvi, 479p. 1924. 50.00 (*3-510-41038-6*, Pub. by E Schweizerbartsche) Balogh.

DeMello. Anesthesiology Pearls of Wisdom. (Pearls of Wisdom Ser.). 1999. pap. 88.00 (*1-890369-08-X*) Boston Medical.

DeMello, ed. Cell Intercommunication. 184p. 1989. boxed set 160.95 (*0-8493-6257-1*, QH604) CRC Pr.

DeMello, Anthony. Heart of the Enlightened: A Book of Story Meditations. 192p. 1997. pap. 11.95 (*0-385-42128-1*) Doubleday.

— Sadhana: A Way to God, Christian Exercises in Eastern Form. LC 84-6735. 144p. 1984. pap. 10.95 (*0-385-19614-8*, Image Bks) Doubleday.

— Song of the Bird. LC 84-10105. (Illus.). 192p. 1984. pap. 10.95 (*0-385-19615-6*, Image Bks) Doubleday.

— Wellsprings: A Book of Spiritual Exercises. LC 86-4478. 240p. 1986. pap. 11.00 (*0-385-19617-2*, Image Bks) Doubleday.

DeMello, Ed. At the Expense of Victory: A Desert Storm Diary of News Media Coverage. LC 94-77217. (Illus.). 336p. (Orig.). 1994. pap. 18.95 (*0-9640530-0-4*) Kenobi Prods.

***DeMello, George.** Espanol Contemporaneo. LC 99-41915. (ITA, POR & SPA.). 608p. (C). 1999. pap. 47.50 (*0-7618-1506-6*) U Pr of Amer.

***DeMello, Margo.** Bodies of Inscription: A Cultural History of the Modern Tattoo Community. LC 99-29368. (Illus.). 248p. 2000. 49.95 (*0-8223-2432-6*); pap. text 16.95 (*0-8223-2467-9*) Duke.

DeMello, Vianna F. The Pocket Dictionary. large type ed. 392p. (YA). (gr. 10 up). 1985. reprint ed. 102.89 (*0-317-01921-X*, 4-21900-00) Am Printing Hse.

***DeMello, Victor Bandeira.** State of Public Elementary & Secondary Education, 1996-97. 501p. 2000. per. 47.00 (*0-16-050247-0*) USGPO.

DeMelo, Joseph. Threnodies to a Beloved Departed Wife from a Lovelorn Husband. 1997. pap. write for info. (*1-57553-584-X*) Watermrk Pr.

Demende, Hugues. Morocco. 1998. 19.99 (*3-8228-7757-3*) Taschen Amer.

Demengeot, J., et al, eds. Artificial Intelligence & Cognitive Sciences. LC 88-13210. (Proceedings in Nonlinear Science Ser.). 432p. 1988. text 110.00 (*0-7190-2679-2*, Pub. by Manchester Univ Pr) St Martin.

DeMenil. Economic Policy, No. 20. Date not set. pap. text 34.95 (*0-631-19857-1*) Blackwell Pubs.

DeMenil, Susan, jt. ed. see Lacy, Bill.

Demensions for Living Staff. Simple Pleasures for Teens. LC 98-168228. (Illus.). 64p. 1997. pap. 5.00 (*0-687-11139-0*) Abingdon.

Dement, L. R. Infinity: A Journey into the Light. LC 95-95194. 120p. (Orig.). 1995. pap. 12.00 (*0-9649251-0-9*) Infinity Arts.

Dement, William. Sleep. 1999. text 22.95 (*0-670-85367-4*) Viking Penguin.

Dement, William C. The Sleepwatcher's. 234p. (Orig.). (C). 1996. pap. text 16.95 (*0-9649338-0-2*) Nychthemeron Pr.

Dement, William C. & Vaughan, Christopher. The Promise of Sleep: A Pioneer in Sleep Medicine Explores the Vital Connection Between Health, Happiness, & a Good Nights Sleep. LC 98-23527. 540p. 1999. 24.95 (*0-385-32008-6*) Delacorte.

***Dement, William C. & Vaughan, Christopher.** The Promise of Sleep: A Pioneer in Sleep Medicine Explores the Vital Connection Between Health Happiness & a Good Nights Sleep. 560p. 2000. pap. 14.95 (*0-440-50901-7*, Dell Trade Pbks) Dell.

Demente, Boye L. NTC's Dictionary of China's Cultural Code Words. LC 95-42218. (BBC Phrase Bks.). (CHI., Illus.). 488p. 1995. 17.95 (*0-8442-8480-7*, 84807, Passprt Bks) NTC Contemp Pub Co.

Dementi, Elisabeth, ed. see Dementi, Wayne.

***Dementi, Wayne.** Celebrate Richmond. Dementi, Elisabeth, ed. (Illus.). 175p. 1999. write for info. (*0-87517-109-5*) Dietz.

Dementia. Bondage Obsession, , Vol. 2. (Illus.). 96p. 1997. 34.95 (*1-56097-244-0*, Eros Comics) Fantagraph Bks.

Dementia. Buffy. 1997. pap. text 14.95 (*1-56097-247-5*) Fantagraph Bks.

Demeny. Population & Develop Reader. LC 98-13495. 1998. pap. 26.95 (*0-312-21517-7*) St Martin.

— Population & Devlope Reader. LC 98-13495. 363p. 1998. text 65.00 (*0-312-21516-9*) St Martin.

Demeo. Passe Partout. 2nd ed. (C). 1996. pap. text 33.02 (*0-201-89211-1*) Addison-Wesley.

DeMeo, J. N. & DeMeo, John F. California Deposition & Discovery Practice, 4 vols. 1958. ring bd. 560.00 (*0-8205-1250-8*, 250) Bender.

DeMeo, James. The Orgone Accumulator Handbook: Construction Plans, Experimental Use & Protection Against Toxic Energy. 155p. 1989. pap. 12.95 (*0-9621855-0-7*) Natural Energy.

— Saharasia: The 4000 B. C. Origins of Child-Abuse, Sex-Repression, Warfare & Social Violence in the Deserts of the Old World. LC 98-91255. (Illus.). 420p. (C). 1998. 90.00 (*0-9621855-6-6*); pap. 34.00 (*0-9621855-5-8*) Natural Energy.

DeMeo, James, ed. Bibliography on Orgone Biophysics. 57p. (C). 1986. pap. text 10.00 (*0-9621855-1-5*) Natural Energy.

DeMeo, James, ed. see Reich, Wilhelm, et al.

DeMeo, John F., jt. auth. see DeMeo, J. N.

Demeo, Patricia. Situations: Textes Divers du Monde Francophone. 3rd ed. 304p. (Orig.). 1999. pap. 36.95 (*0-201-61435-9*) Addison-Wesley.

DeMeo, Terry A., jt. auth. see Kundell, James E.

DeMeo, Tony. 101 Ways to Run the Option. LC 98-89621. 138p. 1999. 16.95 (*1-57167-368-7*) Sagamore Pub.

DeMer, Madeline. Journey to Joy: A Guide to Enjoying Your Emotions. (Illus.). 225p. (Orig.). 1992. pap. 14.95 (*1-880916-00-2*) Vesper Pubns.

Demerast, Kathy K., ed. see Miller, William J., Jr.

Demerath, N. J., III & Williams, Rhys H. A Bridging of Faiths: Religion & Politics in a New England City. 368p. 1992. text 42.50 (*0-691-07413-5*, Pub. by Princeton U Pr) Cal Prin Full Svc.

Demerath, N. J., et al. Dynamics of Idealism: White Activists in a Black Movement. LC 75-148656. (Jossey-Bass Science Ser.). 252p. reprint ed. 78.20 (*0-8357-9317-6*, 201391800088) Bks Demand.

Demerath, N. J., III, ed. see Schmitt, Terry.

Demerath, Nicholas J., III. A Tottering Transcendance: Civil vs. Cultic Aspects of the Sacred. LC 73-10476. (Studies in Sociology). 39p. (C). 1973. pap. text. write for info. (*0-672-61175-9*, Bobbs) Macmillan.

Demerath, Nicholas J., jt. ed. see Vance, Rupert B.

Demerc, M. & Kaufmann, B. P. Drosophila Guide: Introduction to the Genetics & Cytology of Drosophila Melanogaster. 10th ed. (Illus.). 50p. 1996. reprint ed. pap. 2.50 (*0-87279-950-6*) Carnegie Inst.

***DeMercurio, David.** Hard-Core Collections: Brutal but Effective Techniques for Getting the Money. 128p. 1999. pap. 15.00 (*1-58160-028-3*) Paladin Pr.

D

An Asterisk (*) at the beginning of an entry indicates that the title is appearing for the first time.

Demerec, Milislav, ed. Biology of Drosophila. 632p. (C). 1995. reprint ed. text 39.00 (0-87969-441-6) Cold Spring Harbor.

Demerey, Ramona. Let There Be Limericks. pap. 6.95 (1-55517-399-3) CFI Dist.

***Demeri, M. Y. & Ghosh, A., eds.** Sheet Metal Forming Technology. LC 98-68630. (Illus.). 22p. 1999. 64.00 (0-87339-426-7, 4267) Minerals Metals.

Demeri, M. Y., ed. see Minerals, Metals & Materials Society Staff.

Demeri, Mahmoud Y., ed. Computer Applications in Shaping & Forming of Materials: Proceedings of a Symposium by the Shaping & Forming Committee, Held at the Annual Meeting of the Minerals, Metals & Materials Society (TMS) in Devener, CO, February 21-25, 1993. LC 94-222539. (Illus.). 321p. 1993. pap. 99.60 (0-608-04978-6, 206559500004) Bks Demand.

Demeritt, Dwight B., Jr. Maine Made Guns & Their Makers. rev. ed. LC 96-78221. (Illus.). 438p. 1997. 55.00 (0-913764-30-2) Maine St Mus.

Demeritt, Linda C. German Grammar. LC 93-36134. (Outline Ser.). 368p. 1994. pap. 15.00 (0-06-467159-3) HarpC.

Demeritt, Linda C., tr. see Reichart, Elisabeth.

Demerle, L. Jazz Rock Fusion, Vol. 1. rev. ed. 60p. 1988. pap. 9.95 (0-7935-2867-4, 06620609) H Leonard.

***Demerouti, Evangelia.** Burnout: Eine Folge Konkreter Arbeitsbedingungen Bei Dienstleistungs - Und Produktionstatigkeiten. (Studien zur Arbeits - und Organisationspsychologie. Bd. 17 Ser.). X, 186p. 1999. 35.95 (3-631-35306-5) P Lang Pubng.

Demers, Andre, tr. see Martinez, Patrick & Klotz, Alain.

Demers, Armand H., tr. see Tanguays, Cyprien.

***Demers, Barbara.** Willa's New World. (Fiction Ser.). 192p. (YA). (gr. 6-12). 2000. pap. 6.95 (1-55050-150-X, Pub. by Coteau) Genl Dist Srvs.

Demers, D. A., tr. see Chacel, Rosa.

Demers, David. Global Media: Menace or Messiah? LC 99-38555. (Mass Communication & Journalism Ser.). 224p. 1999. text 45.00 (1-57273-293-8); pap. text 19.95 (1-57273-294-6) Hampton Pr NJ.

Demers, David P. Breaking Your Child's TV Addiction: A Guide for Parents. LC 88-62927. (Orig.). 1989. pap. 14.95 (0-922993-00-9) Marquette Bks.

— The Menace of the Corporate Newspaper: Fact or Fiction. LC 95-41462. 350p. 1995. text 41.95 (0-8138-2269-6) Iowa St U Pr.

***Demers, David P. & Viswanath, K.** Mass Media, Social Control & Social Change: A Macrosocial Perspective. LC 98-26143. 468p. 1999. text 59.95 (0-8138-2682-9) Iowa St U Pr.

Demers, Dominique. Un Hiver de Tourmente. (Novels in the Roman Plus Ser.). (FRE.). 160p. (YA). (gr. 8 up). 1996. pap. 7.95 (2-89021-171-1, Pub. by Les Editions) Firefly Bks Ltd.

— Valentine Picotee. (Novels in the Premier Roman Ser.). (FRE.). 64p. (J). (gr. 2-5). 1996. pap. 7.95 (2-89021-164-9, Pub. by Les Editions) Firefly Bks Ltd.

Demers, James W. Children of Winter: On the Betrayal of Children by Catholic Educators. 217p. 1993. 14.95 (0-9639032-0-9) Sarto Hse.

DeMers, John. Caribbean Cooking. 1997. pap. 14.00 (0-614-28095-8, Perigee Bks) Berkley Pub.

— Caribbean Cooking. LC 96-49349. 240p. 1997. pap. 14.00 (1-55788-271-1, HP Books) Berkley Pub.

Demers, John. The Food of Jamaica: Authentic Recipes from the Jewel of the Caribbean. LC 97-40523. (Illus.). 144p. 1998. 16.95 (962-593-228-3, Periplus Eds) Tuttle Pubng.

— The Food of New Orleans: Authentic Recipes from the Big Easy. LC 97-69546. (Illus.). 144p. 1998. 16.95 (962-593-227-5, Periplus Eds) Tuttle Pubng.

DeMers, John. Great Chefs - Great Cities, Vol. I. Miller, Carolyn, ed. LC 95-78445. (Great Chefs - Creat Cities Ser.). (Illus.). 274p. (Orig.). 1996. 29.95 (0-929714-31-8); pap. 24.95 (0-929714-32-6) Great Chefs TV.

DeMers, John & Benghiat, Norma. The Food of Jamaica: Authentic Recipes from the Jewel of the Caribbean. LC 97-40523. 132 p. 1998. write for info. (962-593-101-5) Periplus.

DeMers, John & Jaeger, Andrew. Oysters. 96p. 1999. pap. 5.95 (0-89087-869-2) Celestial Arts.

DeMers, John, jt. auth. see Jaeger, Andrew.

Demers, Linda M. Work Hardening: A Practical Guide. (Illus.). 160p. 1992. pap. text 55.00 (1-56372-022-1) Buttrwrth-Heinemann.

DeMers, Michael N. Fundamentals of Geographic Information Systems. 2nd ed. LC 99-39851. 512p. 1999. text 88.95 (0-471-31423-4) Wiley.

DeMers, Michael N. & Environmental Systems Research Institute Staff. Fundamentals of Geographic Information Systems & Understanding GIS: The ARC/INFO Method, Version 7.1. 1106p. 1999. text 135.90 (0-471-34512-1) Wiley.

Demers, Michelle. Eggplants at the Edge of the Kalahari. (Illus.). (Orig.). 1994. 5.00 (0-9619744-1-9) Blue Light Pr.

Demers, Patricia. Heaven upon Earth: The Form of Moral & Religious Children's Literature, to 1850. LC 92-30408. (Illus.). 200p. (C). 1993. text 24.00 (0-87049-786-3) U of Tenn Pr.

— P. L. Travers. (Twayne's English Authors Ser.). 160p. 1991. 22.95 (0-8057-7005-4, TEAS 483, Twyne) Mac Lib Ref.

— A Seasonal Romance: Louis Hemon's Maria Chapdelaine. (Canadian Fiction Studies: No. 18). (C). 1993. pap. text 14.95 (1-55022-111-6, Pub. by ECW) Genl Dist Srvs.

— The World of Hannah More. LC 96-11179. (Illus.). 192p. 1996. text 32.95 (0-8131-1978-2) U Pr of Ky.

Demers, R. A. & Moyles, R. G., eds. From Instruction to Delight: An Anthology of Children's Literature to 1850. (Illus.). 312p. 1982. pap. text 25.95 (0-19-540384-3) OUP.

Demers, Richard A., jt. auth. see Farmer, Ann K.

Demers, S., ed. Particle Analysis in Oceanography. (NATO ASI Series G: Ecological Sciences: Vol. 27). (Illus.). 416p. 1991. 288.95 (0-387-51763-4) Spr-Verlag.

Demertzis, Strati. The Power of Modern Greek: Basic Course I in the Modern Greek Language. 2nd ed. 221p. (C). 1992. pap. text 22.22 (0-685-72071-3) Expressway Pubs.

— The Power of Modern Greek: Basic Course II in the Modern Greek Language. 2nd ed. 231p. (C). 1993. pap. text 24.44 (0-685-72072-1) Expressway Pubs.

— The Power of Modern Greek: Intermediate Modern Greek, Level III & IV. 217p. (Orig.). (C). 1992. pap. text 27.77 (0-9618466-2-3) Expressway Pubs.

***Demery, Angela & Muzikowski, Joseph.** Baldrige-Based Self-Assessments. Elliott, Susan, ed. (Illus.). 88p. 1999. spiral bd. 395.00 (1-928593-14-3) Am Prodtv Qual.

Demery, Curry J., ed. see Hughes, Detrick O.

Demery, David, et al. Macroeconomics. LC 83-710. (Surveys in Economics Ser.). 288p. reprint ed. pap. 89.30 (0-7837-1589-7, 204188100024) Bks Demand.

Demery, Lionel, et al, eds. Understanding the Social Effects of Policy Reform. LC 93-3805. 228p. 1993. pap. 22.00 (0-8213-2425-X, 12425) World Bank.

Demery, Lionel & Addison, Tony. Alleviation of Poverty under Structural Adjustment. 52p. 1987. pap. 22.00 (0-8213-0956-0, 10956) World Bank.

Demessieux, Jeanne. Twelve Choral Preludes on Gregorian. 32p. 1995. pap. text 6.95 (0-87487-603-6) Summy-Birchard.

DeMesy, Joe, jt. auth. see Ehrhardt, Roy.

Demeter, Richard. Irish America: The Historical Travel Guide, Vol. 1. expanded rev. ed. LC 97-94450. (Illus.). 632p. (Orig.). 1998. pap. write for info. (0-9648253-3-3) Cranfrd Pr.

— Irish America: The Historical Travel Guide, 2 vols., Vol. 2. LC 95-92465. (Illus.). 648p. (Orig.). 1996. pap. 20.95 (0-9648253-1-7) Cranfrd Pr.

***Demeter, Richard, ed.** Irish Americans: A Versified Company. 600p. 2000. pap. 20.95 (0-9648253-4-1) Cranfrd Pr.

Demeter, Stephen L., et al, eds. Disability Evaluation. LC 95-25683. (Illus.). 656p. (C). (gr. 13). 1996. text 79.95 (0-8151-2400-7, 23962) Mosby Inc.

Demetillo, Ricaredo. First & Last Fruit. 83p. (Orig.). (C). 1989. pap. 8.75 (971-10-0273-6, Pub. by New Day Pub) Cellar.

— Major & Minor Keys: Critical Essays on Philippine Fiction & Poetry. 180p. (Orig.). 1987. pap. 15.00 (971-10-0287-6, Pub. by New Day Pub) Cellar.

Demetracopoulou, Dorothy, jt. auth. see Dubois, Cora.

Demetracopoulou, E., jt. ed. see Arnakis, G. G.

Demetracopulou, E., jt. ed. see Arnakis, G. G.

Demetrakopoulos, Stephanie, jt. auth. see Holloway, Karla F.

Demetrakopulos, Andronicus. Bibliotheca Ecclesiastica Continens Graecorum Theologorum Opera. xliv, 415p. 1965. reprint ed. write for info. (0-318-70907-4) G Olms Pubs.

Demetrakopulos, Andronicus, ed. Bibliotheca Ecclesiastica Continens Graecorum Theologorum Opera. xliv, 415p. 1965. reprint ed. 60.00 (0-318-71763-8) G Olms Pubs.

Demetral, Ruth C. Buried Treasure. 86p. 1998. pap. 8.95 (1-57502-698-8, PO1975) Morris Pubng.

Demetre, James D., ed. An Introductory Reader in Developmental Psychology. LC 97-189286. 596p. (C). 1996. pap. 39.00 (1-874529-36-1, Pub. by Greenwich Univ Pr) NYU Pr.

Demetri, George D., jt. auth. see Wingard, John R.

Demetrician, Robert. Label & Package Graphic Design. LC 96-47088. (Illus.). 228p. 1996. 92.00 (1-885067-02-X) Jelmar Pub.

Demetrick, Mary R. First Pressing, Vol. 1. LC 94-96378. 64p. (Orig.). 1994. pap., per. 9.00 (0-9643477-0-9) Hale Mary Pr.

Demetrick, Mary R. & Fama, Maria. Italian Notebook: Poetry. 28p. (Orig.). 1995. pap. 6.00 (0-9643477-1-7) Hale Mary Pr.

Demetrion, James T. The Etchings of Jaques Bellange. LC 75-27177. (Illus.). 86p. 1975. pap. 14.00 (0-87846-094-2) Edmundson.

— The Nathan Emory Coffin Collection. LC 81-6726. (Illus.). 20p. 1977. pap. 10.95 (0-614-31044-X) Edmundson.

— Native American Art, Selections from the Torrence Collection. LC 84-70388. (Illus.). 47p. 1984. pap. 10.00 (0-614-31045-8) Edmundson.

Demetrion, James T. & Noun, Louise R. Des Moines Art Center, Selected Paintings, Sculptures & Works on Paper. LC 84-72620. (Illus.). 220p. (Orig.). 1985. pap. 15.00 (0-9614615-0-0) Edmundson.

Demetrion, James T. & Teuber, Marianne L. Paul Klee: The Bauhaus Years, 1921-1931. LC 73-86308. (Illus.). 144p. 1973. pap. 15.00 (0-614-06998-X) Edmundson.

Demetrion, James T., et al. Francis Bacon. (Illus.). 184p. (Orig.). (C). 1989. pap. write for info. (0-9623203-0-7) Hirshhorn.

— The Hirshhorn Collects: Recent Acquisitions 1992-1996. LC 97-18500. (Illus.). 112p. 1997. pap. write for info. (0-9623203-7-4) Hirshhorn.

— Hirshhorn Museum & Sculpture Garden: 150 Works of Art. (Illus.). 166p. 1997. 60.00 (0-8109-3436-1, Pub. by Abrams); pap. 16.40 (0-8109-2656-3) Abrams.

Demetrion, James T., jt. auth. see Alloway, Lawrence.

Demetrion, James T., jt. auth. see Kozloff, Max.

Demetrios, George. When Greek Meets Greek. LC 76-116949. (Short Story Index Reprint Ser.). (Illus.). 1977. 20.95 (0-8369-3452-0) Ayer.

***Demetriou, Achilles A.** Support of the Acutely Failing Liver. 2nd ed. (Tissue Engineering Intelligence Unit Ser.). 156p. 2000. 89.00 (1-57059-585-2) Landes Bioscience.

***Demetriou, Achilles A. & Watanabe, Frederick D.** Support of the Acutely Failing Liver. (Tissue Engineering Intelligence Unit Ser.). 156p. 2000. 99.00 (1-58706-001-9, Pub. by Eurekah) Landes Bioscience.

Demetriou, Andreas. Cypro-Aegean Relations in the Early Iron Age. (Studies in Mediterranean Archaeology: Vol. LXXXIII). (Illus.). 140p. (Orig.). 1989. pap. 79.50 (91-86098-75-6, Pub. by P Astroms) Coronet Bks.

Demetriou, Andreas, et al, eds. The Neo-Piagetian Theories of Cognitive Development: Implications & Applications for Education. LC 94-9764. (Illus.). 320p. (C). 1994. pap. 27.99 (0-415-11749-6, B4748) Routledge.

Demetriou, Andreas & Efklides, Anastasia, eds. Intelligence, Mind & Reasoning: Structure & Development. LC 94-4456. (Advances in Psychology Ser.: Vol. 106). 250p. 1994. 130.00 (0-444-89714-3, North Holland) Elsevier.

Demetriou, Andreas, et al. The Architecture & Dynamics of Developing Mind: Experiential Structuralism As a Frame for Unifying Cognitive Developmental Theories. (Monographs of the Society for Research in Child Development). 216p. 1993. pap. text 19.50 (0-226-14247-7) U Ch Pr.

Demetriou, Andrew J. & Dutton, Thomas E. Health Care Integration: Structural & Legal Issues. (BNA's Health Law & Business Ser.: No. 1300). 1996. 125.00 (1-55871-338-7) BNA.

Demetriou, George & Topp, Bill. Smart Baseball Umpiring Vol. 1: How to Get Better Every Game. 96p. 1999. pap. 12.95 (1-58208-007-0, Referee Books) Ref Enterps.

***Demetriou, Kyriacos N.** George Grote on Plato & Athenian Democracy: A Study in Classical Reception. (Koinon). (Illus.). XV, 310p. 1999. pap. 48.95 (3-631-32739-0) P Lang Pubng.

— George Grote on Plato & Athenian Democracy A Study in Classical Reception. LC 99-46616. (Koinon Ser.: Vol. 2). xv, 310p. (C). 1999. pap. 48.95 (0-8204-3554-6) P Lang Pubng.

Demetriou, Richard. Making Money Last: Financial Clarity for the Surviving Spouse. limited ed. 316p. 1996. pap. text 22.95 (0-7872-2322-0) Kendall-Hunt.

Demetrious, Andreas, et al. Life-Span Developmental Psychology: A European Perspective. LC 97-23240. 536p. 1998. pap. 54.00 (0-471-97078-6) Wiley.

Demetrius. On Style. (Loeb Classical Library). write for info. (0-318-53146-1) HUP.

Demetrius, C. Demetrius on Style. Connor, W. R., ed. LC 78-18597. (Greek Texts & Commentaries Ser.). (ENG & GRE.). 1979. reprint ed. lib. bdg. 28.95 (0-405-11438-9) Ayer.

Demetrius, F. Joseph. Brazil's National Alcohol Program: Technology & Development in an Authoritarian Regime. LC 89-16243. 181p. 1990. 52.95 (0-275-93183-8, C3183, Praeger Pubs) Greenwood.

Demetrius, Jo-Ellen. Reading People: How You See the World & How the World Sees You. LC 98-4934. 256p. 1998. 23.95 (0-375-50146-0) Random.

Demetrovics, J., et al. Computer-Aided Specification Techniques. (Computer Science Ser.: Vol. 1). 128p. 1986. text 55.00 (9971-978-53-9); pap. text 26.00 (9971-5-0095-7) World Scientific Pub.

Demetz, Peter. After the Fires: Recent Writing in the Germanies, Austria & Switzerland. 454p. 1992. pap. 16.95 (0-15-602892-1, Harvest Bks) Harcourt.

— Postwar German Literature: A Critical Introduction. LC 73-114169. 264p. 1970. 29.75 (0-8290-0198-0); pap. text 9.95 (0-8290-1889-1) Irvington.

— Prague in Black & Gold: Scenes from the Life of a European City. LC 96-52216. 1997. 27.50 (0-8090-7843-0) Hill & Wang.

— Prague in Black & Gold: Scenes from the Life of a European City. (Illus.). 432p. 1998. pap. text 15.00 (0-8090-1609-5) Hill & Wang.

Demetz, Peter, ed. Nathan the Wise, Minna Von Barnhelm & Other Plays & Writings: Gotthold Ephraim Lessing. LC 77-3139. (German Library: Vol. 12). 324p. 1991. 39.50 (0-8264-0706-4); pap. 19.95 (0-8264-0707-2) Continuum.

Demetz, Peter, ed. see Benjamin, Walter.

Demetz, Peter, ed. see Fontane, Theodor.

Demeude, Hugues. Animated Alphabet. LC 96-60951. 1997. pap. 24.95 (0-500-27908-X, Pub. by Thames Hudson) Norton.

— Portugal. (Illus.). 160p. 1999. 19.99 (3-8228-7065-X) Taschen Amer.

DeMeulemeester, Katie. Math Projects: Organization, Implementation, & Assessment. Gideon, Joan, ed. (Illus.). 73p. 1995. teacher ed. 12.95 (0-86651-836-3, 21340) Seymour Pubns.

Demeulenaere, B., jt. auth. see Storme, M.

Demeuse, Rick. Flying Rabbit: When You Dream Where Do Your Dreams Take You. 200p. 2000. 10.95 (0-9665796-1-5) Insiders Guide.

DeMey, Dennis L. Workers Compensation: The Dilemma & Practical Remedies. 22p. 1997. pap. 24.95 (0-9642774-8-4) BSP.

DeMey, G., jt. auth. see Kos, A.

DeMeyer, F., et al. Quadratic Forms over Q & Galois Extensions of Commutative Rings. LC 88-8167. (Memoirs Ser.: No. 77/394). 63p. 1989. pap 16.00 (0-8218-2457-0, MEMO/77/394) Am Math.

DeMeyer, Patricia. Little Horsey Little Lessons: A Young Girl & Her Special Horse Help Teach Skills for Life. LC 98-86663. (Illus.). 40p. (J). (gr. 1-6). 1998. pap. 9.95 (0-9666433-0-5) Saddle Tree.

Demeyer, Serge, jt. ed. see Bosch, Jan.

Demeyer, Serge, ed. see ECOOP '99 Staff.

DeMeyer, William. Technique of the Neurologic Examination: A Programmed Text. 4th ed. LC 93-25996. (Illus.). 553p. 1993. text 42.00 (0-07-016353-7) McGraw-Hill HPD.

Demeyere, Roland. Critical Evaluation of Strategies for a Successful Termination of Cardiopulmonary Bypass During Cardiac Surgery: Role of Pharmacologic Myocardial Protection; Appropriate Pharmacologic Support for the Postischemic Myocardium. (Acta Biomedica Lovaniensia Ser.). (Illus.). 150p. 1998. pap. 39.50 (90-6186-892-0, Pub. by Leuven Univ) Coronet Bks.

Demhardt, Imre J. Deutsche Kolonialgrenzen in Afrika. (Historische Texte und Studien Ser.: Bd. 16). (GER.). 608p. 1997. write for info. (3-487-10506-3) G Olms Pubs.

Demi. Buddha Stories. LC 96-31253. 32p. (J). (gr. 1-4). 1997. 16.95 (0-8050-4886-3) H Holt & Co.

Demi. Cuddly Chick. LC 87-71449. (Soft & Furry Board Bks.). (Illus.). 12p. (J). (ps-4). 1988. bds. 7.95 (0-448-19154-7, G & D) Peng Put Young Read.

— Dalai Lama: A Biography of the Tibetan Spiritual & Political Leader, Vol. 1. LC 97-30654. (J). (gr. 2-5). 1998. 16.95 (0-8050-5443-X) H Holt & Co.

— The Donkey & the Rock. LC 98-14743. (Illus.). 32p. (J). (ps-2). 1999. 16.95 (0-8050-5959-8) H Holt & Co.

— Dragon Kites & Dragonflies: A Collection of Chinese Nursery Rhymes. LC 86-7637. (Illus.). 32p. (J). (ps-3). 1986. 14.95 (0-15-224199-X, Harcourt Child Bks) Harcourt.

***Demi.** The Emperor's New Clothes: A Tale Set in China. LC 99-24883. 32p. 2000. 19.95 (0-689-83068-8) McElderry Bks.

Demi. Empty Pot. 1996. 12.15 (0-606-10801-7, Pub. by Turtleback) Demco.

— Fleecy Lamb. LC 86-80288. (Soft & Furry Board Bks.). (Illus.). 12p. (J). (ps-4). 1987. bds. 7.95 (0-448-19152-0, G & D) Peng Put Young Read.

***Demi.** Gandhi. 2000. text 16.95 (0-8050-6182-7) St Martin.

— The Greatest Treasure. LC 97-10825. (Illus.). 32p. (J). (gr. k-3). 1998. 16.95 (0-590-31339-8, Pub. by Scholastic) Scholastic Inc.

— Happy New Year! Kung_HSI Fa-ts'ai! (Illus.). 40p. (gr. k-3). 1999. pap. 6.99 (0-517-88592-1, Pub. by Crown Bks Yng Read) Random.

— Happy New Year Kung-Hsi! LC 97-11692. (Illus.). (ps-3). 1997. lib. bdg. 17.99 (0-517-70958-9) Crown Pub Group.

Demi. King Midas: The Golden Touch. (Illus.). (J). (gr. 4-6). 2001. pap. 19.00 (0-689-83297-4) S&S Trade.

***Demi.** Kites: Magic Wishes That Fly up to the Sky. (Illus.). (J). 2000. pap. 6.99 (0-375-81008-0, Pub. by Knopf Bks Yng Read) Random.

— Kung-Hsi Fa-Ts'Ai! LC 97-11692. (Illus.). 40p. (J). (gr. k-3). 1997. 16.00 (0-517-70957-0, Pub. by Crown Bks Yng Read) Random.

Demi. Liang & the Magic Paintbrush. LC 80-11351. (Illus.). 32p. (J). (ps-3). 1995. pap. 5.95 (0-8050-0801-2, Bks Young Read) H Holt & Co.

Demi. Little Bitty Bunny. LC 90-85828. (Mini Soft & Furry Board Bks.). (Illus.). 12p. (J). (ps-3). 1992. bds. 4.95 (0-448-41089-3, G & D) Peng Put Young Read.

— Little Chick Chick. LC 90-85829. (Mini Soft & Furry Board Bks.). (Illus.). 12p. (J). (ps-3). 1992. bds. 4.95 (0-448-41090-7, G & D) Peng Put Young Read.

— Little Lucky Ducky. LC 91-77464. (Mini Soft & Furry Board Bks.). (Illus.). 12p. (J). (ps-k). 1993. bds. 4.95 (0-448-40581-4, G & D) Peng Put Young Read.

Demi. One Grain of Rice: A Mathematical Folktale. LC 96-7002. (J). 1997. pap. write for info. (0-614-13399-8) Scholastic Inc.

Demi. One Grain of Rice: A Mathematical Folktale. LC 96-7002. (Illus.). 40p. (YA). (gr. 1-4). 1997. 19.95 (0-590-93998-X) Scholastic Inc.

Demi. Peek-a-Boo ABC. LC 82-60108. (Peek-a-Boo Board Bks.). (Illus.). (J). (ps-k). 1982. 5.95 (0-394-85418-7, Pub. by Random Bks Yng Read) Random.

Demi. Fluffy Bunny. (Soft & Furry Board Bks.). 12p. (J). (ps-4). 1987. 7.95 (0-448-19151-2, G & D) Peng Put Young Read.

Demi, Hitz. Buddha. LC 95-16906. (Illus.). 48p. (J). (gr. 2-5). 1995. 18.95 (0-8050-4203-2) H Holt & Co.

— Chingis Khan. LC 90-28807. (Illus.). 64p. (J). (gr. 3-5). 1995. 19.95 (0-8050-1708-9, Bks Young Read) H Holt & Co.

— Demi's Dragons & Fantastic Creatures. (Illus.). 88p. (J). (ps-2). 1995. 19.95 (0-8050-2564-2, Bks Young Read) H Holt & Co.

— The Dragon's Tale & Other Animal Fables of the Chinese Zodiac: And Other Animal Fables of the Chinese Zodiac. LC 95-44932. (Illus.). 32p. (J). (ps-2). 1995. 16.95 (0-8050-3446-3, B Martin BYR) H Holt & Co.

— The Empty Pot. LC 89-39062. (Illus.). 32p. (J). (ps-2). 1995. 15.95 (0-8050-1217-6, Bks Young Read) H Holt & Co.

— The Empty Pot. LC 89-39062. (Illus.). 32p. 1996. pap. 6.95 (0-8050-4900-2, B Martin BYR) H Holt & Co.

— The Firebird. 88p. (J). 1995. 16.95 (0-8050-3244-4) H Holt & Co.

— Liang & the Magic Paintbrush. 123p. (J). 1980. 11.15 (0-606-03845-0, Pub. by Turtleback) Demco.

— Santa's Furry Friends. (J). 1995. 9.95 (0-8050-2202-3) H Holt & Co.

Demi, Hitz. A Chinese Zoo: Fables & Proverbs. LC 86-33562. 32p. (J). (ps-3). 1987. 14.95 (0-15-217510-5, Harcourt Child Bks) Harcourt.

Demi, Hitz. Demi's Secret Garden. LC 92-27204. 50p. (J). (ps-2). 1995. 19.95 (0-8050-2553-7, Bks Young Read) H Holt & Co.

D

Demi, Hitz. The Magic Tapestry: A Chinese Folktale. LC 93-11426. (J). 1995. 17.95 (*0-8050-2810-2*) H Holt & Co.

Demi, Hitz & Huang, T. In the Eyes of the Cat: Japanese Poetry for All Seasons. LC 91-27728. 80p. (J). (ps-3). 1992. pap. 5.95 (*0-8050-3383-1*) H Holt & Co.

Demianczuk, Ioannes. Supplementum Comicum. 158p. 1967. reprint ed. write for info. (*0-318-70908-2*) G Olms Pubs.

Demianov, V. F. Quasidifferentiability & Nonsmooth Modelling in Mechanics, Engineering & Economics. LC 96-21725. 1996. lib. bdg. 169.00 (*0-7923-4093-0*, D Reidel) Kluwer Academic.

Demicco, Robert V. & Hardie, Lawrence A. Sedimentary Structures & Early Diagenetic Features of Shallow Marine Carbonate Deposits. (SEPM Atlas Ser.: No. 1). (Illus.). 272p. 1995. text 93.00 (*1-56576-013-1*) SEPM.

Demichael, Tom. Tasmanian Devil. (Look & Find Ser.). (Illus.). 24p. (J). (gr. k-6). 1996. lib. bdg. 14.95 (*1-56674-126-2*, HTS Bks) Forest Hse.

***DeMichele, Douglas.** 21st Century Dad: A New Father's Game Plan To Child Rearing. (Illus.). 120p. 2000. pap. 12.95 (*0-9673677-0-0*) J C P D.

DeMichele, Lynne B., ed. Treasure in Clay Jars: Personal Stories of Faith from Indiana United Methodists Told in Their Own Words. LC 98-65828. 160p. 1998. pap. 9.95 (*1-57736-101-6*) Providence Hse.

DeMichele, Michael D. The Italian Experience in America: A Pictorial History. LC 81-71921. (Illus.). 144p. 15.00 (*0-9607870-0-3*) U Scranton Ethnic.

DeMichele, William. The Illustrated Woman: Photographs by William DeMichele. (Illus.). 128p. 1992. 65.00 (*0-9631708-0-5*) Proteus NY.

–The Illustrated Woman: Photographs by William DeMichele. (Illus.). 128p. 1992. pap. 34.95 (*0-9631708-1-3*) Proteus NY.
The Illustrated Woman is in stock & available direct from the publisher.. This 11"x13" book is a unique collection of fine photographs of tattooed women. Photographer William DeMichele traveled the US & Europe for five years, photographing women who share a passion for individuality & a commitment to self expression. This book is a valuable addition to anyone who buys fine photographic books. In the tattoo community it has become a collectors item. This book surprises everyone who picks it up. They are shocked by the honesty & beauty of the over 130 color photographs, they praise the color printing & expert binding. Text includes a preface by tattooist Shotsie Gorman & an introduction by William DeMichele. Photograph William DeMichele continues to photograph the world of tattooing. After a recent exhibit at The American Museum of Natural History, his collection of photographs are considered one of the largest & finest documentation of this modern subculture. "After perusing The Illustrated Woman one could feel one's preconceptions about ... tattooing take a dive into a mire if primordial goo....we are given photographs of bold clarity that bridges art & documentation." Mark Moffett, Metroland Magazine. Available from the publisher: Proteus Press, PO Box 10124, Albany, New York 12201. Tel: 518-436-4927, Fax: 519-432-1963 *Publisher Paid Annotation.*

Demichele, William, ed. see Tuttle, Lyle.

Demichelis, F., ed. Physics & Applications of Amorphous Semiconductors: Proceedings of the 1st International Symposium Workshop, Torino, Villa Gualino, Italy. 424p. (C). 1988. text 99.00 (*9971-5-0550-9*) World Scientific Pub.

Demichelis, F., et al, eds. Physics & Applications of Amorphous Semiconductors: 2nd International Workshop, 1988. 252p. (C). 1989. text 92.00 (*9971-5-0879-6*) World Scientific Pub.

Demichev, A. P., jt. auth. see Chaichian, M.

DeMichiell, Robert L., jt. auth. see Wysocki, Robert K.

Demick, J. & Wapner, Seymour, eds. Field Dependence-Independence: Bio-Psycho-Social Factors Across the Life Span. 448p. (C). 1991. text 89.95 (*0-8058-0950-3*) L Erlbaum Assocs.

Demick, Jack, et al, eds. Parental Development. 296p. 1993. text 59.95 (*0-8058-1192-3*) L Erlbaum Assocs.

Demick, Jack & Miller, Patrice M., eds. Development in the Workplace. 264p. 1993. text 49.95 (*0-8058-1191-5*) L Erlbaum Assocs.

Demidenko, Serge, jt. ed. see Courtois, Bernard.

Demidov, Andrey A., jt. auth. see Andrews, David L.

Demidov, Audrey A., jt. ed. see Andrews, David L.

Demidov, Sergei S., et al. Amphora: Festschrift fur Hans Wussing Zu Seinem 65. Geburtstag - Festschrift for Hans Wussing on the Occasion of His 65th Birthday. LC 92-30657. (ENG, FRE, GER & ITA.). xi, 782p. 1992. 165.50 (*0-8176-2815-0*) Birkhauser.

Demikhov, Vladimir P. Experimental Transplantation of Vital Organs. Haigh, Basil, tr. from RUS. LC 61-17721. (Illus.). 300p. reprint ed. pap. 93.00 (*0-608-30515-4*, 202064800018) Bks Demand.

D'Emilio. Out of Line. 1997. 24.95 (*0-02-907355-3*) Free Pr.

Demilio. Out of Line. 2001. 24.95 (*0-684-82780-8*) Free Pr.

— Sexual Politics. 2nd ed. LC 98-24148. 269p. 1998. pap. 14.00 (*0-226-14267-1*) U Ch Pr.

D'Emilio, John. The Civil Rights Struggle: Leaders in Profile. LC 79-18006. 201p. reprint ed. pap. 62.40 (*0-608-18300-8*, 203155600075) Bks Demand.

— Sexual Politics, Sexual Communities: The Making of a Homosexual Minority in the United States, 1940-1970. LC 82-16000. 268p. (C). 1998. reprint ed. pap. 11.95 (*0-226-14266-3*) U Ch Pr.

Demilio, John. What Our Families Need: Toward a Policy Agenda for Lesbian & Gay Families. 1997. pap. text 10.00 (*0-9652779-3-3*) Natl Gay & Lesbian.

D'Emilio, John & Freedman, B. Estelle. Intimate Matters. 2nd ed. LC 97-25238. xxv, 438p. 1997. pap. text 15.00 (*0-226-14264-7*) U Ch Pr.

DeMille, Leslie B. Painting with Pastels. (Artist's Library). (Illus.). 64p. (Orig.). 1989. pap. 7.95 (*0-929261-08-9*, AL08) W Foster Pub.

DeMille, Nelson. By the Rivers of Babylon. large type ed. LC 98-24624. 1998. 30.00 (*0-7862-1560-7*) Thorndike Pr.

— By the Rivers of Babylon. large type ed. 624p. 1983. 27.99 (*0-7089-8091-0*, Charnwood) Ulverscroft.

— By the Rivers of Babylon. 432p. 1990. reprint ed. mass mkt. 7.99 (*0-446-35859-2*, Pub. by Warner Bks) Little.

***DeMille, Nelson.** Cathedral. large type ed. LC 99-29280. 1999. 29.95 (*0-7862-2030-9*) Thorndike Pr.

DeMille, Nelson. Cathedral. large type ed. 720p. 1982. 27.99 (*0-7089-8079-1*, Charnwood) Ulverscroft.

— Cathedral. 576p. 1990. reprint ed. mass mkt. 7.99 (*0-446-35857-6*, Pub. by Warner Bks) Little.

— The Charm School. 640p. 1989. reprint ed. mass mkt. 7.99 (*0-446-35320-5*, Pub. by Warner Bks) Little.

— The Charm School. 816p. 1999. reprint ed. mass mkt. 14.99 (*0-446-67509-1*, Pub. by Warner Bks) Little.

— The General's Daughter, 1 vol. 1999. mass mkt. 7.50 (*0-446-78656-X*) Warner Bks.

— The General's Daughter. large type ed. LC 92-44891. (Americana Series). 647p. 1993. reprint ed. lib. bdg. 23.95 (*1-56054-644-1*) Thorndike Pr.

— The General's Daughter. large type ed. LC 92-44891. (Americana Series). 647p. 1994. reprint ed. pap. 16.95 (*1-56054-884-3*) Thorndike Pr.

— The General's Daughter. 512p. 1993. reprint ed. mass mkt. 7.50 (*0-446-36480-0*, Pub. by Warner Bks) Little.

— The Gold Coast. 640p. 1991. reprint ed. mass mkt. 7.99 (*0-446-36085-6*, Pub. by Warner Bks) Little.

— The Gold Coast. 736p. 1997. reprint ed. mass mkt. 12.99 (*0-446-67321-8*, Pub. by Warner Bks) Little.

— The Lion's Game. LC 99-52476. 528p. 2000. 26.95 (*0-446-52065-9*, Pub. by Warner Bks) Little.

***DeMille, Nelson.** The Lion's Game. 2001. mass mkt. 7.99 (*0-446-60826-2*, Warner Vision) Warner Bks.

— The Lion's Game. large type ed. LC 99-88731. 1950. pap. 29.95 (*0-7862-2020-1*) Mac Lib Ref.

— The Lion's Game. large type ed. LC 99-88731. (Basic Ser.). 2000. 31.95 (*0-7862-2019-8*) Thorndike Pr.

— Mayday. LC 98-33102. 1999. 29.95 (*0-7862-1792-8*) Thorndike Pr.

DeMille, Nelson. Plum Island. 1998. mass mkt. 287.64 (*0-446-16544-1*) Warner Bks.

— Plum Island. large type ed. LC 97-11760. 1997. 28.95 (*0-7862-0979-8*) Thorndike Pr.

— Plum Island. large type ed. LC 97-11760. 821p. 1999. pap. 26.95 (*0-7862-0980-1*) Thorndike Pr.

— Plum Island. 592p. 1998. reprint ed. mass mkt. 7.99 (*0-446-60540-9*, Pub. by Warner Bks) Little.

— Spencerville. large type ed. LC 94-31286. 755p. 1995. pap. 20.95 (*0-7862-0341-2*) Thorndike Pr.

— Spencerville. 656p. 1995. reprint ed. mass mkt. 7.99 (*0-446-60245-0*, Pub. by Warner Bks) Little.

***DeMille, Nelson.** The Talbot Odyssey. LC 00-30296. 2000. write for info. (*0-7862-2668-4*) Thorndike Pr.

DeMille, Nelson. The Talbot Odyssey. 544p. 1991. reprint ed. mass mkt. 7.99 (*0-446-35858-4*, Pub. by Warner Bks) Little.

— Three Complete Novels. 1040p. 1992. 13.99 (*0-517-08237-3*) Random Hse Value.

— Word of Honor. 752p. 1987. reprint ed. mass mkt. 7.50 (*0-446-30158-2*, Pub. by Warner Bks) Little.

— Word of Honor. 880p. 1998. reprint ed. mass mkt. 14.00 (*0-446-67482-6*, Pub. by Warner Bks) Little.

DeMille, Nelson & Block, Thomas. Mayday. LC 98-33102. 621p. 1999. write for info. (*0-7540-2194-7*) Chivers N Amer.

DeMille, Nelson & Block, Thomas H. Mayday. 480p. 1998. reprint ed. mass mkt. 6.99 (*0-446-60476-3*, Pub. by Warner Bks) Little.

Demille, Richard. Put Your Mother on the Ceiling. 1976. pap. 8.95 (*0-14-004379-9*, Penguin Bks) Viking Penguin.

DeMille, William C. Strongheart. Meserve, Walter J. & Meserve, Mollie A., eds. (When Conscience Trod the Stage Ser.). 1998. pap., spiral bd. 4.95 (*0-937657-44-1*) Feedbk Theabks & Prospero.

Demiller, Anna. Linguistics: A Guide to the Reference Literature. 2nd ed. LC 99-16318. (Humanities Ser.). 400p. 1999. 65.00 (*1-56308-619-0*) Libs Unl.

DeMillion, Barry J. & Yoshitake, Yumiko. Kana Cards. (ENG & JPN., Illus.). 100p. 1993. ring bd. 11.95 (*1-889950-00-9*) Lang Express.

— Visual French Adjectives & Adverbs. (FRE., Illus.). 100p. 1997. ring bd. 11.95 (*1-889950-09-2*) Lang Express.

— Visual French Verbs. (FRE., Illus.). 100p. 1997. ring bd. 11.95 (*1-889950-08-4*) Lang Express.

— Visual French Vocabulary Connections. (FRE., Illus.). 100p. 1997. ring bd. 11.95 (*1-889950-10-6*) Lang Express.

— Visual German Adjectives & Adverbs. (GER., Illus.). 100p. 1997. ring bd. 11.95 (*1-889950-15-7*) Lang Express.

— Visual German Verbs. (GER., Illus.). 100p. 1997. ring bd. 11.95 (*1-889950-14-9*) Lang Express.

— Visual German Vocabulary Connections. (GER., Illus.). 100p. 1997. ring bd. 11.95 (*1-889950-03-3*) Lang Express.

— Visual Italian Adjectives & Adverbs. (ITA., Illus.). 100p. 1997. ring bd. 11.95 (*1-889950-12-2*) Lang Express.

— Visual Italian Verbs. (ITA., Illus.). 100p. 1997. ring bd. 11.95 (*1-889950-11-4*) Lang Express.

— Visual Italian Vocabulary Connections. (ITA., Illus.). 100p. 1997. ring bd. 11.95 (*1-889950-13-0*) Lang Express.

— Visual Japanese Adjectives & Adverbs. (ENG, JPN & LAT., Illus.). 100p. 1994. ring bd. 11.95 (*1-889950-02-5*) Lang Express.

— Visual Japanese Verbs. (ENG, JPN & LAT., Illus.). 100p. 1993. ring bd. 11.95 (*1-889950-01-7*) Lang Express.

— Visual Japanese Vocabulary Connections. (ENG & JPN., Illus.). 1997. ring bd. 11.95 (*1-889950-04-1*) Lang Express.

— Visual Spanish Adjectives & Adverbs. (SPA., Illus.). 100p. 1996. ring bd. 11.95 (*1-889950-06-8*) Lang Express.

— Visual Spanish Verbs. (SPA., Illus.). 100p. 1996. ring bd. 11.95 (*1-889950-05-X*) Lang Express.

— Visual Spanish Vocabulary Connections. (SPA., Illus.). 100p. 1996. ring bd. 11.95 (*1-889950-07-6*) Lang Express.

D'Emillo, John. Making Trouble: Essays on Gay History, Politics, & the University. LC 92-10049. 336p. (C). 1992. pap. 23.99 (*0-415-90510-9*, A6487) Routledge.

DeMillo, R. A., jt. auth. see Rice, J.

DeMillo, Richard, et al, eds. Applied Cryptology, Cryptographic Protocols, & Computer Security Models. LC 83-15548. (Proceedings of Symposia in Applied Mathematics Ser.: Vol. 29). 192p. 1983. reprint ed. pap. 34.00 (*0-8218-0041-8*, PSAPM/29) Am Math.

DeMillo, Rob. How Weather Works. LC 94-231832. (How It Works Ser.). (Illus.). 255p. (Orig.). 1994. pap. 19.95 (*1-56276-228-1*, Ziff-Davis Pr) Que.

Deming. Astronomy. (Astronomy Ser.). 2000. 48.50 (*0-534-55629-9*) Wadsworth Pub.

Deming, Alhambra G. Who is Tapping at My Window? (Picture Puffin Ser.). 1994. 10.19 (*0-606-06096-0*, Pub. by Turtleback) Demco.

Deming, Alison H. The Edges of the Civilized World. 256p. 1999. pap. 13.00 (*0-312-20406-X*) St Martin.

— Monarchs: A Poem Sequence. 88p. 1997. pap. 12.95 (*0-8071-2231-9*); text 19.95 (*0-8071-2230-0*) La State U Pr.

— Poetry of the American West. 328p. 1999. pap. text 18.95 (*0-231-10387-5*) Col U Pr.

— Science & Other Poems. LC 93-39187. 96p. 1994. pap. 14.95 (*0-8071-1915-6*); text 17.95 (*0-8071-1914-8*) La State U Pr.

— Temporary Homelands. LC 93-41676. 224p. 1994. 18.00 (*1-56279-062-5*) Mercury Hse Inc.

Deming, Alison H., ed. The Edges of the Civilized World: A Journey in Nature & Culture. LC 98-18714. 272p. 1998. text 23.00 (*0-312-19543-5*) St Martin.

— Poetry of the American West. (Illus.). 392p. 1996. 28.50 (*0-231-10386-7*) Col U Pr.

***Deming, Alison Hawthorne.** Writing the Sacred into the Real. (Credo Ser.). 176p. 2000. 20.00 (*1-57131-248-X*); pap. 12.00 (*1-57131-249-8*) Milkweed Ed.

Deming, Barbara. Prisons That Could Not Hold. Vanderlinde, Sky, ed. LC 94-49159. 248p. (Orig.). 1995. pap. 14.95 (*0-8203-1737-3*) U of Ga Pr.

Deming, Basil S. Evaluating Job-Related Training Programs. 144p. (C). 1983. text 33.00 (*0-13-292292-4*) P-H.

Deming, Brian. Jackson: An Illustrated History. 1984. 19.95 (*0-89781-113-5*, 5116) Am Historical Pr.

Deming, David. The SCSI Tutor: An In-Depth Exploration of SCSI. LC 91-17070. (ENDL SCSI Ser.). 390p. 1996. mass mkt., student ed. 395.00 (*1-879936-08-9*) ENDL Pubns.

Deming, Diane & Faberman, Hilarie. The Art of Collaborative Printmaking: Smith Andersen Editions. High, Steven S., ed. LC 98-67114. 62p. 1998. pap. 15.00 (*0-9658115-1-4*) NV Museum Art.

***Deming, Diane & Starrs, Paul F.** Edward Borein: On the Range. High, Steven S., ed. (Illus.). 80p. 1999. 15.00 (*0-9658115-3-0*) NV Museum Art.

Deming, Dianne E. A Time with Our Children: Stories for Use in Worship Year. rev. ed. LC 92-31638. (Illus.). 200p. (Orig.). 1993. pap. 9.95 (*0-8298-0953-8*) Pilgrim OH.

— A Time with Our Children: Stories for Use in Worship Year A. LC 92-31638. 208p. (Orig.). 1992. pap. 9.95 (*0-8298-0941-4*) Pilgrim OH.

— A Time with Our Children: Stories for Use in Worship, Year B. LC 92-31638. (Illus.). 200p. (Orig.). 1993. pap. 9.95 (*0-8298-0952-X*) Pilgrim OH.

Deming, J. Genealogy of the Descendants of John Deming of Wethersfield, Conn., with Historical Notes. (Illus.). 702p. 1989. reprint ed. pap. 99.00 (*0-8328-0469-X*); reprint ed. lib. bdg. write for info. (*0-8328-0468-1*) Higginson Bk Co.

Deming, James C. Religion & Identity in Modern France: The Modernization of the Protestant Community in Languedoc - 1815-1848. LC 99-20611. 2p. 1999. 43.00 (*0-7618-1382-9*) U Pr of Amer.

Deming, Lynn H., jt. ed. see Allen, O. Jane.

Deming, Lynne, ed. see Lownes, Millicent G.

Deming, Lynne M. Basic Bible Commentary Vol. 3: Numbers & Deuteronomy. LC 94-10965. 160p. (Orig.). 1994. pap. 5.95 (*0-687-02622-9*) Abingdon.

— Basic Bible Commentary Vol. 12: Isaiah. LC 94-10965. 160p. (Orig.). 1994. pap. 5.95 (*0-687-02631-8*) Abingdon.

— A User's Guide to the Bible. LC 99-32551. (Insights Ser.). 64p. 1999. pap. 6.95 (*0-8298-1335-7*) Pilgrim OH.

Deming, Lynne M., ed. Basic Bible Commentary New Testament Set. (Orig.). 1994. pap. 63.95 (*0-687-00682-1*) Abingdon.

— Basic Bible Commentary Old Testament Set. (Orig.). 1994. pap. 88.95 (*0-687-00816-6*) Abingdon.

— The Feminine Mystic: Readings from Early Spiritual Writers. LC 97-12040. 176p. (Orig.). 1997. pap. 14.95 (*0-8298-1167-2*) Pilgrim OH.

Deming, Lynne M., jt. ed. see Ackley, Kathleen C.

Deming, Lynne M., ed. see Blair, Edward P.

Deming, Lynne M., ed. see Conn, Robert H.

Deming, Lynne M., ed. see Hinton, Linda B.

Deming, Lynne M., ed. see Hutchinson, Orion N., Jr.

Deming, Lynne M., ed. see Jewett, Robert B.

Deming, Lynne M., ed. see Johnson, Earl S., Jr.

Deming, Lynne M., ed. see Johnson, Frank.

Deming, Lynne M., ed. see Luccock, Robert E.

Deming, Lynne M., ed. see Madsen, Norman P.

Deming, Lynne M., ed. see Mobberley, David G.

Deming, Lynne M., ed. see Perguson, Barbara P.

Deming, Lynne M., ed. see Sargent, James E.

Deming, Lynne M., ed. see Schoville, Keith N.

Deming, Lynne M., ed. see Weaver, Walter P.

Deming, Lynne M., ed. see Weeks, Gregory M.

Deming, Lynne M., ed. see Whitehead, Brady N., Jr.

Deming, Lynne M., ed. see Wolcott, Leonard T.

Deming, Margaret. Pen on the Wing. (Orig.). 1995. pap. write for info. (*1-56167-276-9*) Watermrk Pr.

— Under the Juniper Tree. (Orig.). 1995. pap. write for info. (*1-57553-086-4*) Watermrk Pr.

Deming, Margaret C. Hope on the Horizon. 1997. pap. 56.95 (*1-57553-645-5*) Watermrk Pr.

— Of Brevity & Wit. 1997. pap. write for info. (*1-57553-548-3*) Watermrk Pr.

Deming, Margaret Collins, see Collins Deming, Margaret.

Deming, Margaret E. Lighthouse by the Freeway. (Orig.). 1996. pap. write for info. (*1-57553-244-1*) Watermrk Pr.

Deming, Mary P., jt. auth. see Elifson, Joan M.

Deming, Mary P., jt. auth. see Valeri-Gold, Maria.

Deming, Philander. Adirondack Stories. 1972. reprint ed. 39.50 (*0-8422-8038-3*) Irvington.

— The Best Adirondack Stories of Philander Deming. LC 96-43635. (Ne York Classics Ser.). (Illus.). 221p. 1997. 24.95 (*0-8156-0442-4*) Syracuse U Pr.

— Story of a Pathfinder. LC 77-128731. (Short Story Index Reprint Ser.). 1977. 19.95 (*0-8369-3622-1*) Ayer.

— Tompkins & Other Folks: Stories of the Hudson & the Adirondacks. 1972. reprint ed. lib. bdg. 29.50 (*0-8422-8039-1*) Irvington.

Deming, Robert H. Ceremony & Art: Robert Herrick's Poetry. (De Proprietatibus Litterarum, Ser. Practica: No. 64). 1974. pap. text 64.65 (*90-279-2621-2*) Mouton.

Deming, Robert H., ed. James Joyce: The Critical Heritage, 2 vols., 1. 1987. write for info. (*0-318-55556-5*, Routledge Thoemms) Routledge.

— James Joyce: The Critical Heritage, 2 vols., Set. (Critical Heritage Ser.). 1987. 95.00 (*0-7100-6747-X*, Routledge Thoemms) Routledge.

— James Joyce: The Critical Heritage, 2 vols., Vol. 2, 1928-1941. 1987. write for info. (*0-318-55557-3*, Routledge Thoemms) Routledge.

Deming, Stanley N. & Morgan, Stephen L. Experimental Design: A Chemometric Approach. 2nd rev. ed. LC 92-38312. (Data Handling in Science & Technology Ser.: Vol. 3). 454p. 1993. 210.50 (*0-444-89111-0*) Elsevier.

— Experimental Design No. 11: A Chemometric Approach. 1993. write for info. (*0-318-70028-X*) Elsevier.

Deming, Vasudha K., jt. auth. see Caraw, Peggy.

Deming, Vasudha Kathleen, jt. auth. see Carlaw, Peggy.

***Deming, W. Edwards.** The New Economics: For Industry, Government, Education. 2nd ed. (Illus.). (C). 2000. pap. 19.95 (*0-262-54116-5*) MIT Pr.

Deming, W. Edwards. The New Economics for Industry, Government, Education. 2nd ed. (Illus.). 247p. (Orig.). (C). 1995. pap. 19.50 (*0-911379-07-X*) MIT Ctr Adv Educ.

— On Errors in Surveys. (Reprint Series in Social Sciences). (C). 1993. reprint ed. pap. text 5.00 (*0-8290-3430-7*, S-373) Irvington.

— Out of the Crisis. (Illus.). 507p. (C). 1986. 29.50 (*0-911379-01-0*) MIT Ctr Adv Educ.

***Deming, W. Edwards.** Out of the Crisis. (Illus.). 507p. (C). 2000. pap. 22.95 (*0-262-54115-7*) MIT Pr.

Deming, W. Edwards. Quotations of Dr. Deming: The Little Blue Book. 72p. 1996. 10.00 (*1-57074-237-5*) Greyden Pr.

Deming, W. Edwards. Sample Design in Business Research. (Classics Library). 544p. 1990. pap. 79.95 (*0-471-52370-4*) Wiley.

Deming, Wilbur S. Ramdas & the Ramdasis. 1990. reprint ed. 24.00 (*81-85326-22-3*, Pub. by Vintage) S Asia.

Deming, Will. Paul on Marriage & Celibacy: The Hellenistic Background of First Corinthians 7. (Society for New Testament Studies Monographs: No. 83). 279p. (C). 1995. text 69.95 (*0-521-47284-9*) Cambridge U Pr.

Deming, William E. Some Theory of Sampling. xvii, 602p. 1984. reprint ed. pap. 16.95 (*0-486-64684-X*) Dover.

— Statistical Adjustment of Data. 271p. 1984. reprint ed. pap. 9.95 (*0-486-64685-8*) Dover.

Demings, Patricia, ed. see Baker, Doris.

Demings, Patricia, ed. see Jones, Luther.

Demings, Patricia, ed. see Peters, Charles & Dillon, Kenneth.

Demir, Alper & Sangiovanni-Vincentelli, Alberto. Analysis & Simulation of Noise in Nonlinear Electronic Circuits & Systems. LC 97-37141. (The Kluwer International Series in Engineering & Computer Science). 288p. 1997. text 115.00 (*0-7923-8037-1*) Kluwer Academic.

Demir, Andre, tr. see Chaliand, Gerard.

Demir, G., jt. auth. see Attila, J.

Demir, Soliman. Arab Development Funds in the Middle East. LC 79-503. (Policy Studies). 1979. 74.00 (*0-08-022489-X*, Pergamon Pr) Elsevier.

— The Kuwait Fund & the Political Economy of Arab Regional Development. LC 75-45305. (Special Studies). (Illus.). 138p. 1976. 55.00 (*0-275-90247-1*, C0247, Praeger Pubs) Greenwood.

Demirag, Istemi. Corporate Governance, Accountability, & Pressures to Perform: An International Study. LC 98-36008. (Studies in Managerial & Financial Accounting: Vol. 8). 1998. 78.50 (*0-7623-0420-0*) Jai Pr.

Demirag, Istemi & Goddard, Scott. Financial Management for International Business. LC 94-14167. 1994. 19.95 (*0-07-707869-1*) McGraw.

Demiral, Sezai. Pollution Control & the Patterns of Trade. LC 90-3683. (Environment: Problems & Solutions Ser.). 214p. 1990. text 15.00 (*0-8240-0463-9*) Garland.

Demirbilek, Zeki, ed. Tension Leg Platform: A State of the Art Review. 342p. 1989. 36.00 (*0-87262-683-0*) Am Soc Civil Eng.

Demirdamar, R., jt. ed. see Jenner, P.

Demirel, Halim & Ersayin, Salih, eds. Progress in Mineral Processing Technology: Proceedings of the 5th International Mineral Processing Symposium, Cappadocia, Turkey, 6-8 September 1994. (Illus.). 596p. (C). 1994. text 142.00 (*90-5410-513-5*, Pub. by A A Balkema) Ashgate Pub Co.

***Demiris, John & Birk, Andreas, eds.** Robot Learning: An Interdisciplinary Approach. (Robotics & Intelligent Systems Ser.). 250p. 2000. 56.00 (*981-02-4320-0*) World Scientific Pub.

Demirjian, Annie, jt. auth. see Wicks, Ben.

DeMirjian, Arto, Jr. & Nelson, Eve, eds. Front Page History of the World Wars: As Reported by the New York Times. LC 76-7428. (Illus.). 1976. 7.98 (*0-405-06674-0*) Ayer.

Demirjian, David C., jt. ed. see Saha, Badal C.

Demirjian, Richard N. Armenian - American-Canadian Who's Who of Outstanding Athletes, Coaches & Sports Personalities. (Illus.). 520p. 1990. 49.95 (*0-9622945-0-0*) Ararat Heritage.

— Triumph & Glory: Armenian World War II Heroes. Demirjian, Satenig & Garabedian, Evelyn, eds. 480p. 1996. write for info. (*0-9622945-1-9*) Ararat Heritage.

Demirjian, Satenig, ed. see Demirjian, Richard N.

***Demirsar, Metin.** Insight Pocket Guide Istanbul with Map. 3rd rev. ed. (Illus.). 125p. 2000. pap. 12.95 (*1-58573-013-0*, Insight Guides) Langenscheidt.

Demis, D. Joseph. Clinical Dermatology, 3 vols. (C). 1993. ring bd. 495.00 (*0-685-74583-X*) Lppncott W & W.

Demis, D. Joseph, ed. see Loose Leaf Reference Services Staff.

Demisch, Edwin, jt. auth. see Schodorf, Konrad.

Demisco, Brandy K., ed. see Nystom, Fred & Nystrom, Mardi M.

Demise, Phil. What I Don't Know for Sure: Poems. deluxe ed. (Burning Deck Poetry Chapbooks Ser.). 1978. pap. 15.00 (*0-930900-55-3*) Burning Deck.

Demise, Phil & Smith, Phil. Periods: Selected Writings, 1972-1987, No. 23. (Illus.). 472p. (Orig.). 1988. pap. 15.00 (*0-943783-00-3*) Gegenschein.

Demise, Phil, jt. auth. see Smith, Phil.

Demissie, M., jt. ed. see Stout, G. E.

Demitchell, Lisa A., ed. see Bondy, Valerie Moore.

DeMitchell, Todd A. & Fossey, Richard. The Limits of Law-Based School Reform: Vain Hopes & False Promises. LC 96-61338. 210p. 1997. 39.95 (*1-56676-482-3*, 764823) Scarecrow.

DeMitchell, Todd A., jt. auth. see Streshly, William A.

Demitrack, Mark A. & Abbey, Susan E. Chronic Fatigue Syndrome: An Integrative Approach to Evaluation & Treatment. LC 95-26739. 317p. 1996. lib. bdg. 38.95 (*1-57230-038-8*, 0038) Guilford Pubns.

Demitrack, Mark A. & Abbey, Susan E., eds. Chronic Fatigue Syndrome: An Integrative Approach to Evaluation & Treatment. LC 95-26739, 317p. 1999. pap. text 20.00 (*1-57230-499-5*) Guilford Pubns.

Demitrion, James T. Abastenia St. Leger Eberle. LC 80-66884. (Illus.). 59p. 1980. pap. 8.00 (*0-614-06996-3*) Edmundson.

— Abastenia St. Leger Eberle. LC 80-66884. (Illus.). 59p. 1980. pap. 8.00 (*0-614-31043-1*) Edmundson.

***Demitropulos, Libertad.** River of Sorrows. Berg, Mary G., tr. from SPA. (Secret Weavers Ser.: Vol. 14). 196p. 2000. pap. 14.00 (*1-877727-88-1*, Pub. by White Pine) Consort Bk Sales.

Demitsas, Margarites. Sylloge Inscriptionum Graecarum et Latinarum Macedoniae, 2 vols. 1046p. 1980. 140.00 (*0-89005-324-3*) Ares.

***Dem'kilanov, V. F. & Rubinov, Aleksandr Moiseevich.** Quasidifferentiability & Related Topics. LC 00-38938. (Nonconvex Optimization & Its Applications Ser.). 2000. write for info. (*0-7923-6284-5*, Kluwer Plenum) Kluwer Academic.

Demko, George & Boe, Eugene. Why in the World? Adventures in Geography. 416p. 1992. pap. 14.95 (*0-385-26629-4*, Anchor NY) Doubleday.

Demko, George J. Russian Colonization of Kazakhstan, 1896-1916. LC 67-66166. (Uralic & Altaic Ser.: Vol. 99). 271p. 1969. pap. text. write for info. (*0-87750-082-7*) Curzon Pr Ltd.

Demko, George J., et al, eds. Population under Duress: The Geodemography of Post-Soviet Russia. LC 98-54405. 304p. (C). 1999. pap. 69.00 (*0-8133-8939-9*, Pub. by Westview) HarpC.

Demko, George J. & Wood, William B., eds. Reordering the World: Geopolitical Perspectives on the 21st Century. 2nd ed. LC 98-39355. 352p. 1998. 35.00 (*0-8133-3405-5*, Pub. by Westview) HarpC.

Demkov, Yu N. & Ostrovskii, V. N. Zero-Range Potentials & Their Applications in Atomic Physics. (Physics of Atoms & Molecules Ser.). (Illus.). 296p. (C). 1988. text 105.00 (*0-306-42779-6*, Kluwer Plenum) Kluwer Academic.

Demkowicz, Leszek F., jt. auth. see Oden, J. Tinsley.

Demler, Michael J. High-Speed Analog-to-Digital Conversion. (Illus.). 182p. 1991. text 59.00 (*0-12-209048-9*) Acad Pr.

Demling, L. & Fruhmorgen, P., eds. Non-Neoplastic Diseases of the Anorectum: Proceedings of the 64th Falk Symposium, Held in Titisee - Black Forest, Germany, October 11-13, 1991. LC 92-15602. 400p. (C). 1992. text 191.50 (*0-7923-8979-4*) Kluwer Academic.

Demling, L., jt. ed. see Lutz, H.

Demm, Eberhard, et al, eds. Independence of the Baltic States: Origins, Causes & Consequences: A Comparison of the Crucial Years 1918/1919 & 1990/1991. unabridged ed. LC 96-80315. 260p. 1996. pap. 24.95 (*0-929700-16-3*) Lith Res & Studies.

Demmel, James W. Applied Numerical Linear Algebra, Vol. OT56. LC 97-17290. (Miscellaneous Bks.). (Illus.). xi, 419p. 1997. pap. text 48.00 (*0-89871-389-7*) Soc Indus-Appl Math.

***Demmel, Roland.** Fiscal Policy, Public Debt & the Term Structure of Interest Rates. LC 99-36949. (Lecture Notes in Economics & Mathematical Systems Ser.: Vol. 476). (Illus.). x, 279p. 1999. pap. 67.00 (*3-540-66243-X*) Spr-Verlag.

Demmelmeyer, Helmut, jt. auth. see Westerkamp, Christian.

Demmer, John. Nutley. LC 97-191449. (Images of America Ser.). 1999. pap. 16.99 (*0-7524-0835-6*) Arcadia Publng.

***Demmer, Klaus.** Shaping the Moral Life: An Approach to Moral Theology. Keenan, James F., ed. Dell'Oro, Roberto, tr. from ITA. LC 00-27255. (Moral Traditions & Moral Arguments Ser.). Orig. Title: Introduzione alla Teologia Morale. 96p. 2000. text 35.00 (*0-87840-790-1*); pap. text 12.95 (*0-87840-791-X*) Georgetown U Pr.

Demmer, Klaus & Brenninkmeijer-Werhohn, Aldegonde, eds. Christian Marriage Today. LC 96-28093. 89p. 1997. text 23.95 (*0-8132-0876-9*); pap. text 13.95 (*0-8132-0877-7*) Cath U Pr.

Demmert. Economics. 2nd ed. (C). 1996. pap. text. write for info. (*0-03-097627-8*) Harcourt Coll Pubs.

Demmin, Peter E. Multiple Choice Questions in Preparation for the AP Chemistry Examination. 3rd ed. 1996. pap. 16.95 (*1-878621-39-4*) D & S Mktg Syst.

— Student's Solutions Manual to Accompany Multiple Choice Questions in Preparation for the AP Chemistry Exam. 3rd ed. 1996. pap., student ed. 13.95 (*1-878621-40-8*) D & S Mktg Syst.

Demming, Michael. Mechanic Accents: Dime Novels & Working Class Culture of America. 2nd ed. (Haymarket Ser.). 288p. 1998. pap. 18.00 (*1-85984-250-X*) Routledge.

Demmitt, Kevin. Marriage & Family: An Introduction Using ExplorIt. 2nd ed. (C). 1999. pap. text 18.00 (*0-922914-35-4*) Thomson Learn.

Demmon, Amy, ed. see Dennett, Preston E.

Demmon, Amy O., ed. see Bryant, Alice & Seebach, Linda.

Demmon, Amy O., ed. see Emmons, Charles.

Demmon, Amy O., ed. see Fowler, Raymond E.

Demnitz. Read English!, Bk. 3. (Speak English Ser.). (Illus.). 72p. (Orig.). (C). 1991. pap. text 7.95 (*0-8325-0512-9*, Natl Textbk Co) NTC Contemp Pub Co.

Demo, David H., et al, eds. Handbook of Family Diversity. LC 99-15341. (Illus.). 480p. (C). 1999. text 59.95 (*0-19-512038-8*) OUP.

***Demo, David H., et al, eds.** Handbook of Family Diversity. LC 99-15341. (Illus.). 480p. (C). 1999. pap. text 32.95 (*0-19-512039-6*) OUP.

Demo, David H., et al, eds. Parents & Adolescents in Changing Families. (Families in Focus Ser.: Vol. 3). 280p. (Orig.). (C). 1995. pap. text 36.95 (*0-916174-51-4*) Natl Coun Family.

Demo, David H., jt. auth. see Acock, Alan C.

Demo, David H., jt. ed. see Edwards, John N.

Demo, J. J. Structure, Constitution, & General Characteristics of Wrought Ferritic Stainless Steels-STP 619. 72p. 1977. 7.50 (*0-8031-0793-5*, STP619) ASTM.

Demodaran, A. Demodaran on Valuation: Security Analysis for Investment & Corporate Finance. 646p. 1994. text, student ed. 189.95 incl. disk (*0-471-11304-2*) Wiley.

DeModroff, Sonia S., tr. see Sisemore, John T.

DeMohan, Elias. The Harmonics of Sound, Color & Vibration. (Illus.). 160p. (Orig.). 1980. pap. 10.95 (*0-87516-411-0*) DeVorss.

DeMoivre, Abraham. The Doctrine of Chances: A Method of Calculating the Probabilities of Events in Play, Including Treatise on Annuities. 3rd ed. 1967. reprint ed. pap. 7.50 (*0-89197-736-8*); reprint ed. lib. bdg. 43.00 (*0-697-00052-4*) Irvington.

Demokan, M. S. Mode-Locking in Solid-State & Semiconductor Lasers. LC 82-8610. (Electronic & Electrical Engineering Research Ser.: No. 1). (Illus.). 239p. reprint ed. pap. 74.10 (*0-8357-6217-3*, 203422100089) Bks Demand.

Demola, David. Dominion & Authority. 62p. 1987. pap. 3.25 (*0-88144-098-1*) Christian Pub.

Demola, David T. Dominio y Autoridad: Para Gobernar y Reinar. 64p. 1990. pap. 3.95 (*0-88144-144-9*) Christian Pub.

— Tough Times, Tough People, & a Good God. 230p. 1994. pap. 9.99 (*0-88270-716-7*) Bridge-Logos.

— The Truth Shall Make You Free. 24p. 1987. pap. 1.50 (*0-88144-092-2*) Christian Pub.

— La Verdad Os Hara Libres. 21p. 1987. pap. 2.95 (*0-88144-145-7*) Christian Pub.

DeMola, Yolanda, tr. see Viola, Roberto.

DeMolen, Richard L. Richard Mulcaster (c. 1531-1611) & Educational Reform in the Renaissance. (Bibliotheca Humanistica & Reformatorica Ser.: No. XLIX). 242p. 1992. 72.50 (*90-6004-415-0*, Pub. by B De Graaf) Coronet Bks.

— The Spirituality of Erasmus of Rotterdam. (Bibliotheca Humanistica & Reformatorica Ser.: No. 40). 242p. 1987. lib. bdg. 77.50 (*90-6004-392-8*, Pub. by B De Graaf) Coronet Bks.

DeMolen, Richard L., ed. Erasmus of Rotterdam: A Quincentennial Symposium. LC 76-125264. 151p. 1971. text 32.00 (*0-8290-0170-0*) Irvington.

— Essays on the Works of Erasmus. LC 78-3481. 288p. reprint ed. pap. 89.30 (*0-8357-8715-X*, 203370700087) Bks Demand.

— Religious Orders of the Catholic Reformation. LC 93-23762. xix, 290p. (C). 1994. 35.00 (*0-8232-1512-1*) Fordham.

Demolins, Edmond. Anglo-Saxon Superiority. (Select Bibliographies Reprint Ser.). 1977. reprint ed. 24.95 (*0-8369-6875-1*) Ayer.

Demoll, Reinhard & Maier, Hermann N. Handbuch der Binnenfischerei Mitteleuropas. (GER.). 1967. 67.00 (*3-510-41000-9*, Pub. by E Schweizerbartsche) Balogh.

Demolombe, R. & Imielinski, Tomasz. Nonstandard Queries & Nonstandard Answers. (Illus.). 292p. 1994. text 79.00 (*0-19-853852-9*) OUP.

DeMond, C. W. Price, Waterhouse & Company in America: A History of a Public Accounting Firm. Brief, Richard P., ed. LC 80-1485. (Dimensions of a Accounting Firm Ser.). 1980. reprint ed. lib. bdg. 44.95 (*0-405-13515-7*) Ayer.

DeMond, Robert O. The Loyalists in North Carolina During the Revolution. LC 78-65828. 286p. 1979. reprint ed. pap. 28.50 (*0-8063-0839-7*) Clearfield Co.

Demone, Harold, Jr. & Gibelman, Margaret, eds. Services for Sale: Purchasing Health & Human Services. LC 88-18443. 500p. (C). 1989. pap. text 20.00 (*0-8135-1362-6*) Rutgers U Pr.

Demone, Harold W., Jr., jt. auth. see Gibelman, Margaret.

Demone, Harold W., Jr., jt. ed. see Gibelman, Margaret.

Demoney, Jerry & Meyer, Susan E. Pasteups & Mechanicals: A Step-by-Step Guide to Preparing Art for Reproduction. (Illus.). 176p. 1982. 24.95 (*0-8230-3924-2*) Watsn-Guptill.

Demongeot, J. & Sousa-Pereira, A., eds. ISCAMI: Integrated Systems for the Management & Manipulation of Medical Images. 120p. 1991. 69.95 (*0-387-59557-0*) Spr-Verlag.

DeMont, Billie C. & DeMont, Roger A. Accountability: An Action Model for the Public Schools. (Illus.) 1975. 19.95 (*0-88280-023-X*) ETC Pubns.

***DeMont, Philip.** Turning Point: Moving Beyond Neoconservation. 1999. 20.95 (*0-7737-3222-5*) Stoddart Publ.

***DeMont, Philip & Lang, Gene.** Turning Point: Moving Beyond Neoconservatism. 224p. (Orig.). 1999. pap. 15.95 (*0-7737-6061-X*, Pub. by Stoddart Pub) Genl Dist Srvs.

DeMont, Roger A., jt. auth. see DeMont, Billie C.

***DeMonte, Claudia.** Women of the World: A Global Collection of Art. (Illus.). 192p. 2000. pap. 35.00 (*0-7649-1334-4*, A540) Pomegranate Calif.

DeMontmollin, Richard H. The Scoja Story: Jobbers Working Together. LC 86-62676. (Illus.). 203p. 1986. 30.00 (*0-9617613-0-X*) SC Oil Job Assn.

Demontravel, Peter R. A Hero to His Fighting Men: Nelson A. Miles, 1839-1925. LC 97-35947. 455p. 1998. 45.00 (*0-87338-594-2*) Kent St U Pr.

DeMoor, Henry. Welcome to Our Church: A Three-Minute Tour. 1999. mass mkt. 0.75 (*1-56212-399-8*, 1920-0107) CRC Pubns.

DeMoor, Robert. Quest of Faith: Understanding What You Confess. 149p. (Orig.). (YA). (gr. 9 up). 1989. pap. text 7.50 (*0-930265-74-2*) CRC Pubns.

— Speaking of God . . . A User's Guide to Our Contemporary Testimony. 103p. (Orig.). 1995. pap. 5.95 (*1-56212-221-5*, 1344-2075) CRC Pubns.

— Straight Talk: A Fresh Look at 1 Timothy. (Fresh Look Ser.). 80p. (Orig.). 1996. pap., teacher ed. 11.95 (*1-56212-180-4*) CRC Pubns.

DeMooy, Wanda L. Addis Family History: Edward Addis of Preble, Ohio, 1843, His Wife Alice Reynolds. 1999. 28.00 (*0-8328-9782-5*) Higginson Bk Co.

— Addis Family History: Edward Addis of Preble, Ohio, 1843, His Wife Alice Reynols. 1999. pap. 18.00 (*0-8328-9783-3*) Higginson Bk Co.

Demopoulos, William. Frege's Philosophy of Mathematics. 480p. 1997. pap. text 24.95 (*0-674-31943-5*) HUP.

Demopoulos, William, ed. Frege's Philosophy of Mathematics. LC 94-34381. 480p. 1995. text 56.00 (*0-674-31942-7*, DEMFRE) HUP.

Demopoulos, William, et al, eds. Language Learning & Concept Acquisition: Foundational Issues. LC 85-13455. (Theoretical Issues in Cognitive Science Ser.: Vol. 1). 224p. (C). 1986. text 78.50 (*0-89391-316-2*) Ablx Pub.

Demopoulos, William, jt. ed. see Matthews, Robert J.

Demopoulos, William, jt. ed. see Pylyshyn, Zenon W.

DeMore, Louise. Painting Oils. LC 96-247. (First Steps Ser.). (Illus.). 128p. 1996. pap. 18.99 (*0-89134-676-7*, North Lght Bks) F & W Pubns Inc.

Demore, Paula M., jt. auth. see Cohen, Ronald J.

Demore, Sue, jt. auth. see Shub, Noreen.

DeMore, William B., jt. auth. see Yung, Yuk L.

Demorest, Margaret. Name in the Window, No. 1. LC 96-9725. (Illus.). x, 200p. 1996. 37.50 (*0-9655491-0-0*) M Demorest.

— Name in the Window, No. 2. LC 96-9725. (Illus.). x, 200p. 1996. pap. 18.95 (*0-9655491-1-9*) M Demorest.

Demorex, J. Vionnet. (Fashion Memoir Ser.). (Illus.). 1996. 24.00 (*0-500-01722-0*) Thames Hudson.

DeMorgan, J. Manuel de Numismatique Orientale de l'Antiquite et du Moyen Age. (FRE., Illus.). 1979. reprint ed. 30.00 (*0-916710-44-0*) Obol Intl.

DeMori, Renato, jt. ed. see Suen, Ching Y.

***Demornex, Jacqueline, et al.** Beauty: The Twentieth Century. (Illus.). 400p. 2000. pap. 29.95 (*0-7893-0512-7*) Universe.

Demornex, Jacqueline, jt. auth. see Universe Publishing Incorporated Staff.

Demoro, Harre & Harder, John. Light Rail Transit on the West Coast. 1989. pap. 13.95 (*0-915276-49-6*) Quadrant Pr.

Demoro, Harre & Sappers, Vernon. Rails to San Francisco Bay. 1992. pap. 15.95 (*0-915276-51-8*) Quadrant Pr.

Demory, Richard S., jt. auth. see Megill, Donald D.

Demos, Dietrich, et al, eds. Handbook of Liquid Crystals: Fundamentals, Vol. 1, Fundamentals. 950p. 1998. 498.00 (*3-527-29270-5*) Wiley.

Demos, E. Virginia, ed. Exploring Affect: The Selected Writings of Silvan S. Tomkins. (Studies in Emotion & Social Interaction). (Illus.). 539p. (C). 1995. text 69.95 (*0-521-44371-7*); pap. text 26.95 (*0-521-44832-8*) Cambridge U Pr.

Demos, George D., jt. ed. see Gallagher, Philip J.

Demos, George T., ed. see Bogdanos, Theodore.

Demos, Jean, tr. see Tsatsos, Ioanna.

Demos, Jean, tr. see Tsatsos, Jeanne.

Demos, John. A Little Commonwealth: Family Life in Plymouth Colony. 2nd ed. LC 99-12551. (Illus.). 240p. 1999. pap. 11.95 (*0-19-512890-7*) OUP.

— The Tried & the True: Native American Women Confronting Colonization, Vol. 1. (Young Oxford History of Women in the United States Ser.). (Illus.). 112p. (J). 1998. reprint ed. pap. 10.95 (*0-19-512399-9*) OUP.

— The Unredeemed Captive: A Family Story from Early America. 1995. pap. 13.00 (*0-679-75961-1*) Vin Bks.

Demos, John P. Entertaining Satan: Witchcraft & the Culture of Early New England. LC 81-22463. 560p. 1982. 40.00 (*0-19-503131-8*) OUP.

— Entertaining Satan: Witchcraft & the Culture of Early New England. LC 81-22463. (Illus.). 560p. 1983. pap. text 17.95 (*0-19-503378-7*) OUP.

— A Little Commonwealth: Family Life in Plymouth Colony. 1988. 24.00 (*0-8446-6308-5*) Peter Smith.

Demos, John P., ed. Remarkable Providences: Readings on Early American History. rev. ed. 455p. 1991. pap. text 20.00 (*1-55553-098-2*) NE U Pr.

Demos, Marian. Lyric Quotation in Plato. LC 98-36861. (Greek Studies: Vol. 38). 112p. 1999. 53.00 (*0-8476-8908-5*); pap. 21.95 (*0-8476-8909-3*) Rowman.

Demos, Peter G., Jr. Casino Supervision: A Basic Guide. LC 83-72779. (Illus.). 160p. (Orig.). 1983. pap. 24.95 (*0-913421-00-6*) CSI Pr.

Demos, Vasilikie, et al, eds. Advances in Gender Research, Vol. 1. 1996. 73.25 (*0-614-96753-8*) Jai Pr.

Demos, Vasilikie & Segal, Marcia. Advances in Gender Research, Vol. 3. 1998. 73.25 (*0-7623-0457-X*) Jai Pr.

Demos, Vasilikie & Segal, Marcia T. Ethnic Women: A Multiple Status Reality. LC 94-75857. 294p. (Orig.). 1994. text 39.95 (*1-882289-24-2*); pap. text 24.95 (*1-882289-23-4*) Gen Hall.

Demos, Vasilikie & Segall, Marcia T., eds. Advances in Gender Research, Vol. 2. 1997. 73.25 (*0-7623-0267-4*) Jai Pr.

Demoss, Daniel, jt. auth. see Cole, Deborah.

***DeMoss, Michael C.** Bible Briefs of the Old & New Testaments: The Bible Made Easy. LC 99-71849. 1999. pap. 9.95 (*1-880971-46-1*) Light&Life Pub Co MN.

***DeMoss, Nancy.** Place of Quiet Rest: Finding Intimacy with God Through Daily Devotional Life. 2000. 14.99 (*0-8024-7596-5*) Moody.

DeMoss, Nancy L. Singled Out for Him: Embracing the Gift, the Blessings, & the Challenges of Singleness. Hawkins, Sandra, ed. 76p. 1998. pap. 4.95 (*0-9667124-0-4*) Life Action Inc.

DeMoss, R. T. Brain Waves through Time: 12 Principles for Understanding the Evolution of the Human Brain & Man's Behav. LC QP376.D46 1999. (Illus.). 270p. (C). 1999. 26.95 (*0-306-46010-6*, Kluwer Plenum) Kluwer Academic.

DeMoss, Robert G., Jr. Better Family Entertainment. Benson, Dan, ed. LC 97-34174. (Twenty One Day Plan Ser.). 144p. 1998. pap. 6.99 (*0-310-21746-6*) Zondervan.

DeMoss, Virginia. Runner's World Vitamin Book. 204p. 1982. spiral bd. 11.95 (*0-89037-146-6*) Anderson World.

— Runner's World Vitamin Book. (Instructional Bks.: No. 9). (Illus.). 204p. 1983. reprint ed. pap. 9.95 (*0-89037-271-3*) Anderson World.

Demoss, Virginia. Your Baby Food Book. 1984. pap. 8.95 (*0-02-499930-X*, Macmillan Coll) P-H.

Demosthenes. All the Orations of Demosthenes. 2nd ed. Leland, Thomas, tr. LC 76-161787. (Augustan Translators Ser.). reprint ed. 59.00 (*0-404-54113-5*) AMS Pr.

— Ausgewahlte Reden. xxii, 690p. 1973. reprint ed. write for info. (*3-487-04823-X*) G Olms Pubs.

— Demosthenes Volumina 8 et 9: Scholia Graeca ex Codicibus Aucta et Emendata, ex Recensione Gulielmi Dindorfiu, 2 vols., Set. LC 72-7888. (Greek History Ser.). (GRE & LAT.). 1973. reprint ed. 59.95 (*0-405-04782-7*) Ayer.

— Demosthenes Volumina 8 et 9: Scholia Graeca ex Codicibus Aucta et Emendata, ex Recensione Gulielmi Dindorfiu, 2 vols., Vol. 8. LC 72-7888. (Greek History Ser.). (GRE & LAT.). 1973. reprint ed. 33.95 (*0-405-04783-5*) Ayer.

— Demosthenes Volumina 8 et 9: Scholia Graeca ex

D

Codicibus Aucta et Emendata, ex Recensione Gulielmi Dindorfiu, 2 vols., Vol. 9. LC 72-7888. (Greek History Ser.). (GRE & LAT.). 1973. reprint ed. 30.95 (*0-405-04784-3*) Ayer.
— Demosthenes Against Androtion & Against Timocrates. 2nd ed. Vlastos, Gregory, ed. LC 78-14602. (Morals & Law in Ancient Greece Ser.). (ENG & GRE.). 1979. reprint ed. lib. bdg. 25.95 (*0-405-11581-4*) Ayer.
— Demosthenes on the Crown. Vlastos, Gregory, ed. LC 78-19354. (Morals & Law in Ancient Greece Ser.). (ENG & GRE.). 1979. reprint ed. lib. bdg. 30.95 (*0-405-11547-4*) Ayer.
— The First Philippic & the Olynthiacs of Demosthenes. Connor, W. R., ed. LC 78-18599. (Greek Texts & Commentaries Ser.). (ENG & GRE., Illus.). 1979. reprint ed. lib. bdg. 36.95 (*0-405-11440-0*) Ayer.
— Funeral Speech, Vol. VII. Warmington, E. H., ed. (Loeb Classical Library: No. 374). (ENG & GRE.). 15.50 (*0-674-99412-4*) HUP.
— Les Harangues de Demosthene. lxviii, 484p. 1975. reprint ed. write for info. (*3-487-04486-2*) G Olms Pubs.
— On the Crown. 377p. 1973. reprint ed. lib. bdg. 77.50 (*3-487-05013-7*) G Olms Pubs.
***Demosthenes.** On the False Embassy (Oration 19) Edited with Introduction & Commentary. MacDowell, Douglas M., ed. 600p. 2000. text 130.00 (*0-19-815303-1*) OUP.
Demosthenes. On the Peace: Second Philippic on Chersonesus & Third Philippic. Connor, W. R., ed. LC 78-18602. (Greek Texts & Commentaries Ser.). 1979. reprint ed. lib. bdg. 36.95 (*0-405-11443-5*) Ayer.
— Orations of Demosthenes, 2 vols., Set. Kennedy, C. R., ed. 1977. lib. bdg. 250.00 (*0-8490-2378-5*) Gordon Pr.
— Les Plaidoyers Politiques de Demosthene, 2 vols. in 1. xiii, 935p. 1974. reprint ed. write for info. (*3-487-05053-6*) G Olms Pubs.
— Private Orations, Vol. VI: Nos. 50-58. (Loeb Classical Library: No. 318, 346, 351). 464p. 1939. 19.95 (*0-674-99386-1*) HUP.
— Private Orations, Vols. IV-VI. No. 318, 346, 351. write for info. (*0-318-53148-8*) HUP.
— Select Private Orations of Demosthenes, 2 vols., Pts. I & II. Connor, W. R., ed. LC 78-18601. (Greek Texts & Commentaries Ser.). (Illus.). 1979. reprint ed. lib. bdg. 61.95 (*0-405-11442-7*) Ayer.
— Selected Private Speeches. Carey, Christopher & Reid, R. A., eds. (Cambridge Greek & Latin Classics Ser.). 256p. 1985. pap. text 24.95 (*0-521-28373-6*) Cambridge U Pr.
— The Speech of Demosthenes Against the Law of Leptines. Sandys, John E., ed. LC 78-18605. (Greek Texts & Commentaries Ser.). (Illus.). 1979. reprint ed. lib. bdg. 22.95 (*0-405-11445-1*) Ayer.
— The Three Orations in Favour of the Olynthians with Fower Orations Against King Philip. Wilson, Thomas, tr. LC 68-54637. (English Experience Ser.: No. 54). 200p. 1968. reprint ed. 27.50 (*90-221-0054-5*) Walter J Johnson.
DeMot, Rene, jt. auth. see Verachtert, Hubert.
Demott. Ship Stability for Masters & Mates. 4th ed. 392p. 1990. 59.95 (*0-7506-0380-1*) Buttrwrth-Heinemann.
DeMott, Barbara. Dogon Masks: A Structural Study of Form & Meaning. Seidel, Linda, ed. LC 81-16308. (Studies in the Fine Arts: Iconography: No. 4). (Illus.). 220p. 1982. reprint ed. pap. 68.20 (*0-8357-1274-5*, 207003500063) Bks Demand.
DeMott, Benjamin. The Business Self: The Recovery of Public Esteem. (Philip Morris Lectures on Business & Society Ser.). 54p. 1993. pap. write for info. (*1-884663-01-X*) Baruch Coll Cty U.
— The Imperial Middle: Why Americans Can't Think Straight about Class. 264p. (C). 1992. reprint ed. pap. 19.00 (*0-300-05482-3*) Yale U Pr.
***DeMott, Benjamin.** Killer Woman Blues: Why Americans Can't Think Straight about Gender & Power. 256p. 2000. 25.00 (*0-395-84366-9*) HM.
DeMott, Benjamin. The Trouble with Friendship: Why Americans Can't Think Straight about Race. LC 97-50279. 224p. 1998. pap. 14.00 (*0-300-07394-1*) Yale U Pr.
Demott, Bobby. The History of Freemasonary in Tennessee. LC 94-61617. 500p. 1995. text. write for info. (*1-882194-12-8*) TN Valley Pub.
DeMott, Deborah A. Fiduciary Obligation, Agency & Partnership: Duties in Ongoing Business Relationships. (American Casebook Ser.). 740p. (C). 1991. 57.50 (*0-314-83000-6*) West Pub.
— Fiduciary Obligation, Agency & Partnership: Duties in Ongoing Business Relationships, Teacher's Manual to Accompnay. (American Casebook Ser.). 116p. 1991. reprint ed. pap. text. write for info. (*0-314-87665-0*) West Pub.
— Shareholder Derivative Actions: Law & Practice. LC 86-31029. 1990. 140.00 (*0-685-17693-2*) West Group.
— Shareholder Derivative Actions: Law & Practice. annuals 1990. suppl. ed. write for info. (*0-318-61654-8*) West Group.
DeMott, Dianne K., jt. auth. see Wood, Leland F.
DeMott, Donald W. Each Teach Two. (Illus.). 100p. 1987. pap. 2.50 (*0-9617217-1-5*) High Falls Pubns.
DeMott, Harold. Beacon Small-Group Bible Studies, Daniel: Daring to Live by Faith. Wolf, Earl C., ed. 76p. (Orig.). 1985. pap. 4.99 (*0-8341-0962-X*) Beacon Hill.
DeMott, Mary. Are We There Yet? LC 98-17567. 128p. (Orig.). 1998. 10.99 (*0-8280-1286-5*) Review & Herald.
Demott, Mary L. The Adventure of Lisa & the Drainpipe Prayer. LC 97-37233. (Orig.). (J). (gr. 1-3). 1998. pap. 7.99 (*0-8280-1266-0*) Review & Herald.
DeMott, Robert. Steinbeck's Typewriter: Essays on His Art. LC 93-60806. xxvi, 353p. 1996. 45.00 (*0-87875-446-6*) Whitston Pub.
DeMott, Robert, ed. see Steinbeck, John.
DeMott, Robert J. & Marovitz, Sanford E., eds. Artful Thunder: Versions of the Romantic Tradition in American Literature in Honor of Howard P. Vincent. LC 74-21886. (Illus.). 326p. reprint ed. pap. 101.10 (*0-7837-0508-5*, 204083200018) Bks Demand.
DeMott, Steve. Rodeo Rhymes & Sagebrush Satire: Cowboy Prose & Poetry. LC 97-90036. (Illus.). 96p. (Orig.). 1997. pap. 7.95 (*0-9656669-0-5*) Three Lazy D.
DeMott, Wes. Vapors. LC 98-74460. 340p. 1999. 24.00 (*0-9659602-7-7*, 744961-98) Admiral Hse.
— Walking K. LC 97-74742. 295p. 1998. 23.95 (*0-9659602-6-9*) Admiral Hse.
DeMotte, Charles. The Inner Side of History. LC 96-47298. 1998. pap. 19.95 (*0-9635766-1-5*) Source.
DeMotte, Charles & Sundgren, Katherine W. Restaurant Guide to the Finger Lakes. LC 88-2792. (Illus.). 184p. 1991. pap. 8.95 (*0-935526-18-8*) McBooks Pr.
Demotte, John B. Secret of Character Building (1894) 130p. 1998. reprint ed. pap. 14.95 (*0-7661-0488-5*) Kessinger Pub.
Demou, Doris B. A Part of Myself: I Give to You. 2nd rev. ed. Meredith, Mary, ed. (More to Give Ser.). (Illus.). (YA). (gr. 6 up). 1990. pap. text 6.00 (*0-9604794-0-6*) Doris Demou.
Demou, Doris B., ed. & pref. see Beck, Dorothy S.
Demouchette, Roy, intro. Putting the Brakes on Crime: A Modest Proposal. 144p. Date not set. pap. 19.95 (*0-89896-404-0*, Better Life Bks) Larksdale.
Demouchette, Roy, jt. auth. see Cherryholmes, J. Edward.
Demougin, Jacques. Dictionnaire de la Litterature Francaise et Francophone, 3 vols., Set. (FRE.). 1987. lib. bdg. 99.95 (*0-7859-5550-X*) Fr & Eur.
— Dictionnaire de la Litterature Francaise et Francophone, Vol. 1. (FRE.). 504p. 1987. pap. 26.95 (*0-7859-5602-6*, 2037200218) Fr & Eur.
— Dictionnaire de la Litterature Francaise et Francophone, Vol. 2. (FRE.). 506p. 1987. pap. 26.95 (*0-7859-5603-4*, 2037200226) Fr & Eur.
— Dictionnaire de la Litterature Francaise et Francophone, Vol. 3. (FRE.). 527p. 1987. pap. 26.95 (*0-7859-5604-2*, 2037200234) Fr & Eur.
— Dictionnaire des Litteratures Francaise et Etrangeres. (FRE.). 1861p. 1992. pap. 250.00 (*0-7859-7667-1*, 2035083044) Fr & Eur.
— Larousse Dictionnaire Historique, Thematique et Technique des Litteratures, 2 vols. (FRE.). 1985. 395.00 (*0-7859-7665-5*, 2035083001) Fr & Eur.
Demougin, Jacques, ed. Dictionnaire Historique, Thematique et Technique des Littera. (FRE.). 1986. 395.00 (*0-7859-7666-3*, 2035083028) Fr & Eur.
— Dictionnaire Historique, Thematique et Technique des Litteratures A-K, 2 vols. (FRE.). 1985. 450.00 (*0-7859-8608-1*, 203508301X) Fr & Eur.
Demoulin, Charles. Firebirds! Flying the Typhoon in Action. LC 87-600396. (Illus.). 296p. 1988. 34.00 (*0-87474-366-4*) Smithsonian.
Demoulin, Hubert. Epimenide de Crete. Vlastos, Gregory, ed. LC 78-19344. (Morals & Law in Ancient Greece Ser.). (FRE & GRE.). 1979. reprint ed. lib. bdg. 15.95 (*0-405-11539-3*) Ayer.
***DeMoura, Denise.** Heart-Beat of Healing. 2000. pap. 3.75 (*1-896647-27-8*) Genl Dist Srvs.
Demouy, Jane, et al, eds. The Pima Indians: Pathfinders for Health. (Illus.). 37p. 1998. pap. text 15.00 (*0-7881-7358-8*) DIANE Pub.
Demovek, Mary. Letters to Parents of Preschool Children. 39p. 1989. 3.00 (*1-55833-012-7*) Natl Cath Educ.
Dempcy, Mary H. & Tihista, Rene. Dear Job Stressed: Answers for the Overworked, Overwrought, & Overwhelmed. LC 96-21542. 176p. 1996. pap. 15.95 (*0-89106-089-8*, 7885, Davies-Black Pub) Consulting Psychol.
— Stress Personalities: A Look Inside Our Selves. 2nd ed. (Illus.). 232p. 1991. reprint ed. pap. 15.00 (*0-9631277-4-8*) Focal Pt Pr.
Dempf, Alois. Christliche Staatsphilosophie in Spanien. Mayer, J. P., ed. LC 78-67344. (European Political Thought Ser.). (GER.). 1979. reprint ed. lib. bdg. 15.95 (*0-405-11691-8*) Ayer.
Dempsey. Policing. Date not set. pap. text, teacher ed. write for info. (*0-314-03337-8*) West Pub.
***Dempsey, William.** Uniforms, a Love Story (1941-1967) 414p. 2000. 10.00 (*0-9679895-0-7*) W Dempsey.
***Dempsey, A.** Ballykissangel Cookbook. 1999. text 29.95 (*0-7472-2107-3*, Pub. by Headline Bk Pub) Trafalgar.
Dempsey, Al. Cattle. 18.95 (*0-312-93166-2*) Forge NYC.
— Oil. 1996. write for info. (*0-312-93167-0*) Tor Bks.
— Path of the Sun. 320p. 1994. mass mkt. 4.99 (*0-8125-8193-8*) Tor Bks.
— Pika Don. 384p. (Orig.). 1993. mass mkt. 4.99 (*0-8125-0939-0*) Tor Bks.
— Six States Super Centennial Celebration Book. 1989. pap. 1.95 (*0-8125-0015-6*, Pub. by Tor Bks) St Martin.
— What Law There Was. 1992. mass mkt. 3.99 (*0-8125-8184-9*) Tor Bks.
Dempsey, Al, jt. auth. see Moore, Robin.
Dempsey, Amy. Brad Pitt. LC 97-26961. (Superstars of Film Ser.). (Illus.). 48p. (YA). (gr. 5 up). 1999. lib. bdg. 15.95 (*0-7910-4649-4*) Chelsea Hse.
Dempsey, Anne, jt. auth. see Leahy, Alice.
Dempsey, Arthur D., jt. auth. see Dempsey, Patricia A.
Dempsey, Arthur D., jt. auth. see Dempsey, Patricia Ann.
Dempsey, B., jt. auth. see Perrin, D. D.
Dempsey, Bert J. & Jones, Paul, eds. Internet Issues & Applications, 1997-1998. LC 97-37152. (Illus.). 175p. 1998. 32.50 (*0-8108-3430-8*) Scarecrow.
Dempsey, Bruce H. & Kirby, Elizabeth, eds. Andrew Wyeth: Southeastern Collections: Jacksonville Art Museum, January 19, 1992-April 19, 1992. LC 92-70238. (Illus.). 100p. 1992. 50.00 (*0-916235-02-5*); pap. 20.00 (*0-916235-01-7*) Jacksonville Art.
Dempsey, Carla H. & Petty, James D. Laboratory Accreditation & Data Certification: A Guide for Successful Laboratories. 256p. 1991. lib. bdg. 119.00 (*0-87371-291-9*, L291) Lewis Pubs.
Dempsey, Carol J. All Creation is Groaning: An Interdisciplinary Vision for Life in a Sacred Universe. LC 99-29113. 1999. pap. text 27.95 (*0-8146-5932-2*) Liturgical Pr.
***Dempsey, Carol J.** Hope Amid the Ruins: The Ethics of Israel's Prophets. 2000. pap. 19.99 (*0-8272-1439-1*) Chalice Pr.
— Prophets: A Liberation-Critical Reading. LC 99-58914. 2000. pap. text 20.00 (*0-8006-3116-1*) Augsburg Fortress.
Dempsey, Charles. Annibale Carracci: The Farnese Palace, Rome. LC 95-3961. (Great Fresco Cyles of the Renaissance Ser.). (Illus.). 96p. 1995. 25.00 (*0-8076-1316-9*) Braziller.
— Annibale Carracci & the Beginnings of Baroque Style. 1977. 38.00 (*0-686-92334-0*) J J Augustin.
— Portrayal of Love: Botticelli's Primavera & Humanist Culture at the Time of Lorenzo the Magnificent. 187p. 1992. pap. text 29.95 (*0-691-01573-2*, Pub. by Princeton U Pr) Cal Prin Full Svc.
Dempsey, Charles, ed. Quattrocento Adriatico: Fifteenth-Century Art of the Adriatic Rim. (Villa Spelman Colloquium Ser.: Vol. 5). 348p. (C). 1996. text 49.95 (*88-7779-052-0*) Johns Hopkins.
Dempsey, Charles, jt. auth. see Cropper, Elizabeth.
***Dempsey, Chris.** Winter Horses. 32p. 2000. pap. 15.00 (*0-931659-58-2*) Limberlost Pr.
— Winter Horses. limited aut. ed. 32p. 2000. 55.00 (*0-931659-59-0*) Limberlost Pr.
Dempsey, Claire W. Building Hardwick: Community Histories in Landscape & Architecture. (Illus.). viii, 64p. (Orig.). 1991. pap. 10.00 (*0-9631184-0-4*) Hardwick Hist.
Dempsey, Clyde R., jt. ed. see Bridges, James S.
Dempsey, Corinne G. Kerala Christian Sainthood: Collisions of Cultures & Worldview in South Indian Christianity. LC 99-15339. (Illus.). 272p. 2000. text 45.00 (*0-19-513028-6*) OUP.
Dempsey, David, et al. Death, the Press & the Public: Presentations to, for & by the Media & Other Professionals. 17.95 (*0-405-14023-1*) Ayer.
Dempsey, Deborah D. & Foster, Joanne. The Captain's a Woman: Tales of a Merchant Mariner. LC 97-35201. (Illus.). 304p. 1997. 29.95 (*1-55750-164-5*) Naval Inst Pr.
Dempsey, Elbert, Jr. Untangling Our Faith. LC 93-28843. 1993. pap. 15.00 (*0-8309-0640-1*) Herald Pub Hse.
Dempsey, Elbert A. Power of the Prophetic. 1988. pap. 5.00 (*0-8309-0512-X*) Herald Pub Hse.
Dempsey, Eric & O'Clery, Michael. Pocket Guide to the Common Birds of Ireland. (Illus.). 249p. (Orig.). 1995. pap. 17.95 (*0-7171-2296-4*, Pub. by Gill & MacMill) Irish Bks Media.
Dempsey, Francine, ed. see Lomasney, Eileen.
Dempsey, Greg. The Perfect Cocktail: Hints, Tips, & Recipes from a Master Bartender. (Illus.). 208p. 1995. pap. 10.95 (*0-385-47914-X*, Main St Bks) Doubleday.
Dempsey, Guy C. Napoleon's Army, 1807-1814: As Depicted in the Prints of Aaron Martinet. LC 98-113836. (Illus.). 192p. 1997. 34.95 (*1-85409-347-9*, Pub. by Arms & Armour) Sterling.
Dempsey, Helen H. Hasler Families & Where They Came From. (Illus.). 382p. 1997. reprint ed. pap. 57.50 (*0-8328-9034-0*); reprint ed. lib. bdg. 67.50 (*0-8328-9033-2*) Higginson Bk Co.
Dempsey, Hugh Aylmer. The Amazing Death of Calf Shirt & Other Blackfoot Stories: Three Hundred Years of Blackfoot History. LC 95-38302. (Illus.). 256p. 1996. pap. 13.95 (*0-8061-2821-6*) U of Okla Pr.
— Charcoal's World. LC 79-14920. (Illus.). x, 178p. 1979. pap. 3.95 (*0-8032-6552-2*, Bison Books) U of Nebr Pr.
— Crowfoot. 226p. 1972. mass mkt. 5.95 (*0-88780-155-2*, Pub. by Formac Publ Co) Formac Dist Ltd.
— Crowfoot: Chief of the Blackfeet. LC 72-865. (Civilization of the American Indian Ser.: Vol. 122). (Illus.). 248p. 1989. pap. 13.95 (*0-8061-1596-3*) U of Okla Pr.
— The Golden Age of the Canadian Cowboy: An Illustrated History. 176p. 1999. pap. text 14.95 (*1-895618-76-2*) Fifth Hse Publ.
Dempsey, Hugh Aylmer & Moir, Lindsay. Bibliography of the Blackfoot. LC 89-6444. (Native American Bibliography Ser.: No. 13). 255p. 1989. 35.00 (*0-8108-2211-3*) Scarecrow.
***Dempsey, Hugh Aylmer & Taylor, Colin.** With Eagle Tail. LC 98-75009. (Illus.). 128p. 1999. 12.98 (*0-7651-1059-8*) Smithmark.
Dempsey, J. P., et al, eds. Ice Mechanics 1993. LC 93-71577. (AMD Ser.: Vol. 163). 281p. 1993. pap. 55.00 (*0-7918-1142-5*, G00786) ASME.
Dempsey, J. P. & Rajapakse, Y. D., eds. Ice Mechanics - 1995. (1995 Joint ASME Applied Mechanics & Materials Summer Meeting Ser.: Vol. 207). 284p. 1995. 112.00 (*0-7918-1322-3*, H00954) ASME.
Dempsey, Jack. Network Management Basics. LC 97-73097. 120p. (Orig.). 1997. pap. 29.95 (*0-87288-648-4*) Intertec IL.
— Transmission & Signaling Basics. LC 97-72592. 135p. (Orig.). 1997. pap. 29.95 (*0-87288-649-2*) Intertec IL.
Dempsey, Jack L. Telecom Basics. LC 87-83662. 104p. 1988. 19.95 (*0-917845-07-2*) Intertec IL.
— Transmission Basics. LC 89-45512. (Illus.). 83p. 1989. 29.95 (*0-917845-09-9*) Intertec IL.
Dempsey, James X. & Cole, David. Terrorism & the Constitution: Sacrificing Civil Liberties in the Name of National Security. LC 99-62055. (Illus.). 200p. (Orig.). 1999. mass mkt. 10.00 (*0-9627705-2-3*) Frst Amendment.
Dempsey, Janet. Cornwall Revisted: A Hudson River Community. LC 97-16916. 93p. 1997. pap. 25.00 (*0-912526-79-3*) Lib Res.
— Washington's Last Cantonment: High Time for a Peace. LC 86-10691. (Illus.). 250p. 1990. 24.95 (*0-912526-39-4*) Lib Res.
Dempsey, Janet, et al. Cornwall, New York: Images from the Past, 1788-1920. rev. ed. LC 94-35515. (Illus.). 142p. 1994. 25.00 (*0-912526-73-4*) Lib Res.
Dempsey, Jerome A. & Pack, Allan I., eds. Regulation of Breathing. 2nd expanded rev. ed. (Lung Biology in Health & Disease Ser.: Vol. 79). (Illus.). 1250p. 1994. text 215.00 (*0-8247-9227-0*) Dekker.
Dempsey, Jerome A. & Reed, Charles E., eds. Muscular Exercise & the Lung: Proceedings of a Symposium Held at the University of Wisconsin-Madison, 1976, with Support from Syntex Laboratories, Inc., & Boehringer Ingleheim Ltd. LC 76-16666. 415p. 1977. reprint ed. pap. 128.70 (*0-608-01954-2*, 206260900003) Bks Demand.
Dempsey, John A. Basic Digital Electronics with MSI Applications. LC 75-9009. 320p. (C). 1976. text. write for info. (*0-201-01478-5*) Addison-Wesley.
— Experimentation with Digital Electronics. 1977. pap. write for info. (*0-201-01479-3*) Addison-Wesley.
Dempsey, John Mark, ed. see Causey, Max.
Dempsey, John S. Introduction to Policing. 2nd ed. LC 98-28391. (Criminal Justice Ser.). 1998. 66.95 (*0-534-54675-7*) Wadsworth Pub.
— An Introduction to Public & Private Investigations. LC 98-38525. 450p. (C). 1996. pap. 79.95 (*0-314-06765-5*) West Pub.
— Policing: An Introduction to Law Enforcement. Baxter, ed. LC 93-21287. 400p. (C). 1994. pap. 36.25 (*0-314-02774-2*) West Pub.
Dempsey, John V. & Sales, Gregory C., eds. Interactive Instruction & Feedback. LC 92-47430. (Illus.). 385p. 1993. 49.95 (*0-87778-260-1*) Educ Tech Pubns.
Dempsey, K. Ann & Lagunoff, Susan. College Writing: A Survival Guide. 400p. (C). 1990. teacher ed. write for info. (*0-03-007204-2*); teacher ed. write for info. (*0-03-007203-4*); pap. text 36.50 (*0-03-007207-7*, Pub. by Harcourt Coll Pubs) Harcourt.
***Dempsey, Ken.** Inequalities in Marriage: Australia & Beyond. 264p. 1998. pap. text (*0-19-553373-9*) OUP.
Dempsey, Ken. A Man's Town: Inequality Between Women & Men in Rural Australia. 336p. (C). 1993. pap. text 29.95 (*0-19-554997-X*) OUP.
Dempsey, Kenneth R. Classroom Discipline Made Easy: A System That Works for the Inner City or Any City. LC 96-86501. 100p. (Orig.). 1996. pap. 12.95 (*0-9654015-0-2*) Deck Pubng.
Dempsey, Laura, ed. see Stewart, D. L.
Dempsey, Lorcam, et al. Networking & the Future of Libraries No. 2: Managing & Intellectual Record. LC 97-186374. 256p. 1995. pap. text 75.00 (*1-85604-158-1*, LAP1581, Pub. by Library Association) Bernan Associates.
Dempsey, Lorcan, ed. Bibliographic Access in Europe: First International Conference. (Illus.). 315p. 1990. text 83.95 (*0-566-03644-4*, Pub. by Gower) Ashgate Pub Co.
Dempsey-Lyle, Susan, jt. auth. see Hoffman, Therese L.
***Dempsey, Mark.** Robbing You Blind: Protecting Your Money from Wall Street's Hidden Costs & Half-Truths. LC 99-47463. 304p. 2000. 25.00 (*0-688-17034-X*, Wm Morrow) Morrow Avon.
Dempsey, Mark. Tricks of the Trade: An Insider's Guide to Using a Stockbroker. LC 97-38143. 224p. (Orig.). 1997. pap. 14.95 (*1-57112-084-X*) Park Ave.
Dempsey, Michael. Biennial Flight Review Guide: Official FAA Flight Training Reference for Private Pilot Recertification. (Illus.). 112p. 1993. pap. 12.95 (*1-880365-77-4*) Prof Pr NC.
— Professional Instrument Flight Review Guide. 112p. pap. write for info. (*1-57087-067-5*) Prof Pr NC.
— Student Atlas. Miles, John C. & Novis, Constance, eds. LC 90-675152. (Illus.). 128p. (J). (gr. 3-7). 1996. pap. 9.95 (*0-8167-2254-4*) Troll Communs.
Dempsey, Michael, ed. Growing up with Science: The Illustrated Encyclopedia of Invention, 28 vols., Set. rev. ed. LC 82-63047. (Illus.). (J). (gr. 5-10). 1987. 279.44 (*0-87475-841-6*) Websters Unified.
Dempsey, Michael W. Children's First Geography Encyclopedia. (J). 1985. 6.98 (*0-671-07746-5*) S&S Trade.
— Children's First Science Encyclopedia. (J). 1987. 6.98 (*0-671-07745-7*) S&S Trade.
Dempsey, Michael W. & Lye, Keith. Student Encyclopedia. LC 90-11116. (Illus.). 128p. (J). (gr. 3-7). 1991. lib. bdg. 20.65 (*0-8167-2257-9*) Troll Communs.
— Student Encyclopedia. LC 90-11116. (Illus.). 128p. (J). (gr. 3-7). 1996. pap. 9.95 (*0-8167-2258-7*) Troll Communs.
Dempsey, P. E., ed. see American Society of Mechanical Engineers Staff.
Dempsey, P. S., et al. Denver International Airport: Lessons Learned. LC 96-48396. (Illus.). 555p. 1997. 44.95 (*0-07-158184-7*) McGraw.
Dempsey, Patricia A. & Dempsey, Arthur D. Nursing Research: Text & Workbook. 4th ed. LC 95-40104. 250p. 1996. pap. text 29.95 (*0-316-18188-9*) Lppncott W & W.
— The Research Process in Nursing. 2nd ed. (Nursing-Health Science Ser.). 320p. (C). 1986. pap. 32.50 (*0-86720-350-1*) Jones & Bartlett.
Dempsey, Patricia Ann. The Research Process in Nursing. 3rd ed. (Nursing-Health Science Ser.). 336p. (C). 1992. 42.50 (*0-86720-449-4*) Jones & Bartlett.
Dempsey, Patricia Ann & Dempsey, Arthur D. Using Nursing Research: Process, Critical Evaluation & Utilization. 5th ed. LC 99-16519. 384p. 1999. pap. text 29.95 (*0-7817-1790-6*) Lppncott W & W.

An Asterisk (*) at the beginning of an entry indicates that the title is appearing for the first time.

Dempsey, Patrick. Chip's Favorite Season. LC PZ8.3.D159Ch 1998. (Disney First Reader Ser.). (Illus.). 24p. (J). (gr. k-1). 1998. pap. 2.95 (*0-7868-4172-9*, Pub. by Disney Pr) Time Warner.

Dempsey, Paul. How to Repair Briggs & Stratton Engines. 2nd ed. (Illus.). 192p. 1984. pap. 9.95 (*0-8306-1687-X*) McGraw-Hill Prof.

— How to Repair Briggs & Stratton Engines. 3rd ed. 222p. 1994. pap. 14.95 (*0-07-016347-2*) McGraw.

— How to Repair Diesel Engines. 2nd ed. 368p. 1990. 25.95 (*0-07-157414-X*) McGraw.

— How to Repair Diesel Engines. 2nd ed. (Illus.). 304p. 1990. 25.95 (*0-8306-6167-0*, 2167); pap. 16.95 (*0-8306-8167-1*) McGraw-Hill Prof.

— How to Repair Tecumseh Engines. (Illus.). 304p. 1990. 24.95 (*0-8306-8357-7*, 3357); pap. 14.95 (*0-8306-3357-X*) McGraw-Hill Prof.

— How to Troubleshoot & Repair Any Small Gas Engine. (Illus.). 272p. (Orig.). 1985. pap. 11.95 (*0-8306-1967-4*) McGraw-Hill Prof.

— How to Troubleshoot & Repair Any Small Gas Engine. 2nd ed. LC 92-12875. (Orig.). 1993. 24.95 (*0-8306-4141-6*); pap. 11.95 (*0-8306-4142-4*) McGraw-Hill Prof.

— Small Gas Engine Repair. 2nd ed. (Illus.). 240p. 1993. pap. 14.95 (*0-07-016342-1*) McGraw.

— Troubleshooting & Repairing Diesel Engines. 3rd ed. 1994. pap. 24.95 (*0-07-016348-0*) McGraw.

— Weekend Mechanic's Guide to Engine Rebuilding. (Weekend Mechanic Ser.). (Illus.). 256p. (Orig.). 1989. pap. 12.95 (*0-8306-3180-1*) McGraw-Hill Prof.

Dempsey, Paul & Reilly, Kevan. Big Money, Beautiful Game: Saving Football (Soccer) from Itself. (Illus.). 250p. 1998. 25.00 (*1-85788-215-6*) Nicholas Brealey.

Dempsey, Paul S. Flying Blind: The Failure of Airline Deregulation. LC 90-80866. 99p. 1990. 12.00 (*0-944826-23-7*) Economic Policy Inst.

— The Social & Economic Consequences of Deregulation: The Transportation Industry in Transition. LC 89-3168. 293p. 1989. 65.00 (*0-89930-380-3*, DYE, Quorum Bks) Greenwood.

Dempsey, Paul S. & Gesell, Laurence E. Air Transportation: Foundations for the 21st Century. LC 97-68504. 616p. (C). 1997. text 49.00 (*0-9606874-5-9*) Coast Aire.

— Airline Management, Strategies for the 21st Century. LC 97-69396. 550p. (C). 1997. text 49.00 (*0-9606874-9-1*) Coast Aire.

Dempsey, Paul S. & Goetz, Andrew R. Airline Deregulation & Laissez Faire Mythology. LC 91-35688. 392p. 1992. 65.00 (*0-89930-693-4*, DAK/, Quorum Bks) Greenwood.

Dempsey, Paul S. & Thoms, William E. Law & Economic Regulation in Transportation. LC 85-9593. (Illus.). 360p. 1986. 77.50 (*0-89930-138-X*, DLE/, Quorum Bks) Greenwood.

Dempsey, Paul S., et al. Aviation Law & Regulations. 570p. 1993. pap., student ed. 40.00 (*0-685-74656-9*, MICHIE) LEXIS Pub.

Dempsey, Richard A. & Traverso, Henry P. Scheduling the Secondary School. fac. ed. LC 83-215584. (Illus.). 88p. (Orig.). 1983. reprint ed. pap. 30.00 (*0-7837-7836-8*, 204759600007) Bks Demand.

Dempsey, Rob & Bruce, Glen. Security Distributed Computing: The Challenge of Security in Distributed Computing. 464p. (C). 1996. pap. 56.00 (*0-13-182908-4*) P-H.

— Security for Distributed Computing. 1996. 38.00 (*0-614-20317-1*) P-H.

Dempsey, Roberta, ed. see Bartok, Mira & Ronan, Christine.

Dempsey, Roberta, ed. see Ronan, Christine.

Dempsey, Ron D. Faith Outside the Walls: Why People Don't Come & Why the Church Must Listen. LC 97-8095. 144p. 1997. 15.00 (*1-57312-096-0*) Smyth & Helwys.

Dempsey, T. Delphic Oracle: Its Early History, Influence & Fall. LC 69-13234. 1972. reprint ed. 18.95 (*0-405-08442-0*) Ayer.

Dempsey, Terrence, jt. auth. see Ashton, Dore.

Dempsey, Tom. Classic Jazz Guitar Styles. 1997. pap. 14.95 incl. audio compact disk (*0-88284-852-6*) Alfred Pub.

— Contemporary Patrol Tactics: A Practical Guide for Patrol Officers. 304p. (C). 1992. text 48.80 (*0-13-175191-3*) P-H.

— The TRS-80 Beginner's Guide to Games & Graphics. 1984. 16.95 (*0-317-06048-1*); pap. 16.95 (*0-936200-10-3*) Blue Cat.

Dempsey, Travis J. Racism: Revolves Like a Merry Go Round. large type ed. LC 97-61980. (Illus.). 215p. 1998. 23.75 (*0-941484-27-0*) Urban Res Pr.

Dempsey, Van O., jt. auth. see Noblit, George W.

Dempsey, Walter. Children's First Encyclopedia. (J). 1985. 6.98 (*0-671-07744-9*) S&S Trade.

Dempsi, jt. auth. see Killion.

Dempster, Andrew. The Grahams: A Guide to Scotland's 2,000 Foot Peaks. (Illus.). 192p. 1998. 35.00 (*1-85158-847-7*, Pub. by Mainstream Pubng) Trafalgar.

— The Munro Phenomenon. (Illus.). 192p. 1996. 35.00 (*1-85158-698-9*, Pub. by Mainstream Pubng) Trafalgar.

Dempster, Barry. Ascension of Jesse Rapture. 256p. 1994. pap. 11.95 (*1-55082-083-4*, Pub. by Quarry Pr) LPC InBook.

— David & the Daydreams, Vol. 1. 144p. pap. 5.00 (*0-919349-49-8*) Guernica Editions.

Dempster, Barry. Fables for Isolated Men, Vol. 1. (Essential Poets Ser.: No. 12). 82p. 1982. pap. 5.00 (*0-919349-19-6*) Guernica Editions.

Dempster, Barry. Globe Doubts. 64p. 1983. pap. 12.95 (*0-919627-08-0*, Pub. by Quarry Pr) LPC InBook.

— Letters from a Long Illness with the World: The D. H. Lawrence Poems. 64p. 1993. pap. 11.95 (*0-919626-64-5*, Pub. by Brick Bks) Genl Dist Srvs.

— Positions to Pray In. 96p. 1989. pap. 8.00 (*0-920717-08-X*) Guernica Editions.

— Tributaries: An Anthology of Poems: Writer to Writer. 112p. 1991. pap. 8.95 (*0-88962-089-X*) Mosaic.

— The Unavoidable Man. 80p. 1990. pap. 12.95 (*0-919627-97-8*, Pub. by Quarry Pr) LPC InBook.

Dempster, Dan, jt. auth. see Barton, Peter.

Dempster, David W., et al, eds. Estrogens & Anti-Estrogens: Basic & Clinical Aspects. (Illus.). 450p. 1997. text 99.00 (*0-397-51719-X*) Lppncott W & W.

Dempster, Frank N. & Brainerd, Charles J., eds. Interference & Inhibition in Cognition. (Illus.). 423p. 1995. text 69.95 (*0-12-208930-8*) Acad Pr.

Dempster, J. A. The T&T Clark Story. 352p. (C). 1989. text 50.00 (*1-872795-09-9*, Pub. by Pentland Pr) St Mut.

***Dempster, Jack & McLean, Ian, eds.** Insect Populations: In Theory & in Practice. 1998. write for info. (*0-412-83260-7*) Kluwer Academic.

Dempster, John. The Computer Analysis of Electrophysiological Signals. (Biological Techniques Ser.). (Illus.). 228p. 1993. 73.00 (*0-12-208940-5*) Acad Pr.

Dempster, L. T. & Jepson, Willis L. Flora of California: Vol. 4, Pt. 2, Rubiaceae. (Illus.). 47p. 1979. pap. 3.00 (*0-935628-08-8*) Jepson Herbarium.

Dempster, L. T., jt. auth. see Andersson, L.

Dempster, M. A., ed. Stochastic Programming. LC 77-92826. (Institute of Mathematics & Its Applications Conference Series, New Ser.). 1980. text 289.00 (*0-12-208250-8*) Acad Pr.

Dempster, M. A., et al, eds. Deterministic & Stochastic Scheduling. 1982. text 197.50 (*90-277-1397-9*) Kluwer Academic.

Dempster, M. A. & Pliska, Stanley R., eds. Mathematics of Derivative Securities. LC 97-3027. (Publications of the Newton Institute: No. 15). 600p. 1997. text 85.00 (*0-521-58424-8*) Cambridge U Pr.

Dempster, Murray W., et al, eds. Called & Empowered: Global Mission in Pentecostal Perspective. LC 91-32846. 321p. 1991. pap. 16.95 (*0-943575-47-8*) Hendrickson MA.

***Dempster, Murray W., et al, eds.** The Globalization of Pentecostalism: A Religion Made to Travel. 406p. 1999. reprint ed. pap. 25.00 (*1-870345-29-0*, Pub. by Regnum Bks) OM Literature.

Dempster, Nigel. Heiress: Story of Christina Onassis. large type ed. (Illus.). 1990. 27.99 (*0-7089-8557-2*) Ulverscroft.

Dempster, Stuart. The Modern Trombone: A Definition of Its Idioms. 1994. 29.50 (*0-918194-27-X*) Accura.

Dempster, Thomas. Thomae Dempsteri Historia Ecclesiastica Gentis Scotorum: Sive, de Scriptoribus Scotis, 2 vols. Irving, David, ed. LC 72-163685. (Bannatyne Club, Edinburgh. Publications: No. 21). reprint ed. 125.00 (*0-404-52725-6*) AMS Pr.

Demrow, Carl. Complete Guide to Trail Building & Maintenance. 3rd ed. LC 98-9799. 1998. pap. text 14.95 (*1-878239-54-6*) AMC Books.

Demsetz. Supreme Court Economic Review, Vol. 6. Vol. 6. 280p. 1998. lib. bdg. 45.00 (*0-226-14287-6*) U Ch Pr.

Demsetz, Harold. The Economics of the Business Firm: Seven Critical Commentaries. (Illus.). 191p. (C). 1995. text 44.95 (*0-521-48119-8*) Cambridge U Pr.

— The Economics of the Business Firm: Seven Critical Commentaries. 191p. 1996. pap. text 16.95 (*0-521-58865-0*) Cambridge U Pr.

— The Emerging Theory of the Firm. (Studia Oeconomiae Negotiorum: No. 33). 55p. (Orig.). 1992. pap. 32.50 (*91-554-2949-1*) Coronet Bks.

Demsetz, Harold, et al, eds. The Supreme Court Economic Review, Vol. 5. 1997. lib. bdg. 45.00 (*0-226-28687-8*) U Ch Pr.

Demsetz, Harold & Gellhorn, Ernest, eds. Supreme Court Economic Review. 288p. 1995. lib. bdg. 60.00 (*0-913969-68-0*) U Pr of Amer.

— The Supreme Court Economic Review, Vol. 4. 216p. 1995. lib. bdg. 45.00 (*0-226-28685-1*) U Ch Pr.

Demsetz, Laura, ed. see Conference on Robotics for Challenging Environment & American Society of Civil Engineers Staff.

Demsetz, Laura A. & Klarer, Paul R., eds. Robotics for Challenging Environments: Proceedings of the ASCE Specialty Conference. LC 93-50192. 496p. 1994. 7.00 (*0-87262-913-9*) Am Soc Civil Eng.

Demsetz, Laura A., et al. Robotics '98: Proceedings of the 3rd ASCE Specialty Conference on Robotics for Challenging Environments, Albuquerque, New Mexico, April 26-30, 1998. LC 98-4521. 360p. 1998. 59.00 (*0-7844-0337-6*) Am Soc Civil Eng.

***Demsey.** Airport Project Development Handbook: A Global Survey. LC 99-30202. 589p. 1999. 79.95 (*0-07-134316-4*) McGraw.

Demsey, David & Prather, Ronald E. Alec Wilder: A Bio-Bibliography, 45. LC 92-38455. (Bio-Bibliographies in Music Ser.: No. 45). 320p. 1993. lib. bdg. 65.00 (*0-313-27820-2*, PAW/) Greenwood.

Demske, James M. Being, Man, & Death: A Key to Heidegger. LC 70-94065. 242p. reprint ed. pap. 75.10 (*0-8357-9783-X*, 201125200074) Bks Demand.

Demske, James M., tr. see Rahner, Karl.

Demske, R. J. Instant Home Repair. LC 72-91408. (Illus.). 320p. 1973. 6.95 (*0-911744-13-4*) Career Pub IL.

Demski, Joel. Managerial Uses of Accounting Information. 672p. (C). 1996. pap. text 69.95 (*0-7923-9847-5*) Kluwer Academic.

Demski, Joel S. Information Analysis. 2nd ed. LC 80-15971. (A-W Paperback Series in Accounting). 200p. 1980. pap. text 16.76 (*0-201-01231-6*) Addison-Wesley.

— Managerial Uses of Accounting Information. LC 93-34340. 672p. (C). 1993. lib. bdg. 105.50 (*0-7923-9406-2*) Kluwer Academic.

Demski, Joel S. & Feltham, Gerald A. Cost Determination: A Conceptual Approach. LC 76-14421. (Illus.). 282p. 1976. reprint ed. pap. 87.50 (*0-608-00170-8*, 206095200006) Bks Demand.

Demski, Leo S., ed. The Reproduction & Development of Sharks, Skates, Rays & Ratfishes. LC 93-30134. (Developments in Environmental Biology of Fishes Ser.: No. 14). 320p. (C). 1993. text 267.50 (*0-7923-2509-5*) Kluwer Academic.

Demsky, Andrew. Dark Refuge: A Story of Cults & Their Seductive Appeal. LC 94-35484. 1995. pap. 7.97 (*0-8163-1241-9*) Pacific Pr Pub Assn.

Demsky, Terri, jt. auth. see Haddad, Wadi D.

Demsrki, Aharon, et al. These Are the Names: Studies in Jewish Onomastics. LC 98-121471. 158p. 1997. write for info. (*965-226-192-0*) Bar Ilan U Pr.

Demster, Stanley J. & Chen, Steve. Variable Air Volume Systems for Environmental Quality. LC 95-22732. 373p. 1995. 55.00 (*0-07-011085-9*) McGraw.

Demster, Stanley M. Access Floor Technology Design Guide. (Illus.). 480p. 1998. 69.95 (*0-07-016336-3*) McGraw.

Demtroder, W. & Inguscio, M. Applied Laser Spectroscopy. LC 90-23596. (NATO ASI Ser.: Vol. 241). (Illus.). 512p. (C). 1991. text 145.00 (*0-306-43717-1*, Kluwer Plenum) Kluwer Academic.

Demtroder, Wolfgang. Laser Spectroscopy: Basic Concepts & Instrumentation. 2nd rev. ed. LC 94-11901 (Illus.). 941p. 1996. 69.00 (*0-387-57171-X*) Spr-Verlag.

Demtroeder, W. Laser Spectroscopy: Basic Concepts & Instrumentation. (Chemical Physics Ser.: Vol. 5). (Illus.). 694p. 1988. 42.00 (*0-387-10343-0*) Spr-Verlag.

DeMunn, Michael. Places of Power. LC 98-127246. (Illus.). 36p. (YA). (gr. k up). 1997. 16.95 (*1-883220-64-5*); pap. 7.95 (*1-883220-65-3*) Dawn CA.

Demura, Fumio. Bo: Karate Weapon of Self Defense. Johnson, Gil & Adachi, Geraldine, eds. LC 75-13757. (Weapons Ser.). (Illus.). 1976. pap. text 11.95 (*0-89750-019-9*, 124) Ohara Pubns.

— Bo: Karate Weapon of Self-Defense. 1999. pap. text 36.95 (*1-58133-145-2*) Black Belt Mag.

***Demura, Fumio.** Karate. 1999. pap. text 37.95 (*1-58133-135-5*) Black Belt Mag.

Demura, Fumio. Karate Shito-Ryu. LC 74-169720. (Japanese Arts Ser.). (Illus.). 96p. (YA). 1971. reprint ed. pap. 12.95 (*0-89750-005-9*, 110) Ohara Pubns.

— Nunchaku: Karate Weapon of Self-Defense. 1999. pap. text 35.95 (*1-58133-143-6*) Black Belt Mag.

— Nunchaku Karate Weapon of Self-Defense. LC 78-183341. (Weapons Ser.). (Illus.). 1971. pap. text 10.95 (*0-89750-006-7*, 111) Ohara Pubns.

— Sai: Karate Weapon of Self-Defense. 1999. pap. text 35.95 (*1-58133-144-4*) Black Belt Mag.

— Sai Karate Weapon of Self-Defense. LC 74-83597. (Weapons Ser.). (Illus.). 1974. pap. text 10.95 (*0-89750-010-5*, 115) Ohara Pubns.

— Tonfa: Karate Weapon of Self-Defense. Lee, Greglon, ed. LC 82-81557. (Weapons Ser.). (Illus.). 144p. (Orig.). 1982. pap. 13.95 (*0-89750-080-6*, 417) Ohara Pubns.

Demura, Fumio & Ivan, Dan. Advanced Nunchaku. Johnson, Gilbert & Adachi, Geraldine, eds. LC 76-40816. (Weapons Ser.). (Illus.). 1976. pap. text 14.95 (*0-89750-021-0*, 126) Ohara Pubns.

DeMuro, Paul, et al. Reforming the CYA: How to End Crowding, Diversify Treatment & Protect the Public Without Spending More Money. 129p. 1988. pap. 5.95 (*0-943004-04-7*) Common Knowledge.

DeMuro, Paul R. Financial Manager's Guide to Managed Care & Integrated Delivery Systems: Strategies for Contracting & Reimbursement. 94th ed. 200p. (C). 1995. text 45.00 (*1-55738-623-4*, Irwn Prfssnl) McGraw-Hill Prof.

DeMuro, Paul R. & Unruh, Marilee C. Health Care Mergers & Acquisitions: The Transactional Perspective. (BNA's Health Law & Business Ser.: No. 2100). 1996. 125.00 (*1-55871-344-1*) BNA.

Demus, Dietrich. Physical Properties of Liquid Crystals. LC 99-202912. 524p. 1999. 135.00 (*3-527-29747-2*) Wiley.

Demus, Dietrich, et al, eds. Handbook of Liquid Crystals, 4 Vols. 2400p. 1998. 1795.00 (*3-527-29502-X*) Wiley.

— Handbook of Liquid Crystals: High Molecular Weight Liquid Crystals, Vol. 3, High Molecular Weight Liquide Crystals. 650p. 1998. 498.00 (*3-527-29272-1*) Wiley.

— Handbook of Liquid Crystals: Low Molecular Weight Liquid Crystals I, 2A. 530p. 1998. 498.00 (*3-527-29271-3*) Wiley.

— Handbook of Liquid Crystals: Low Molecular Weight Liquid Crystals II, Vol. 2B, Low Molecular Weight Liquid Crystals II. 540p. 1998. 498.00 (*3-527-29491-0*) Wiley.

Demus, Otto. Byzantine Mosaic Decoration: Aspects of Monumental Art in Byzantium. (Illus.). 162p. (C). 1993. lib. bdg. 40.00 (*0-89241-018-3*) Caratzas.

— The Mosaic Decoration of San Marco, Venice. Kessler, Herbert L., ed. (Illus.). 278p. 1988. 72.00 (*0-226-14291-4*); pap. 30.00 (*0-226-14292-2*) U Ch Pr.

— The Mosaics of Norman Sicily. LC 86-81973. (Illus.). xx, 478p. 1988. reprint ed. lib. bdg. 95.00 (*0-87817-310-2*) Hacker.

— The Mosaics of San Marco in Venice: Part I: Eleventh & Twelfth Centuries; Part II: The Thirteenth Century, 4 vols. LC 82-2787. (Illus.). 360p. 1984. lib. bdg. 420.00 (*0-226-14289-2*) U Ch Pr.

— The Mosaics of San Marco in Venice: Part I: Eleventh & Twelfth Centuries; Part II: The Thirteenth Century, 4 vols. LC 82-2787. (Illus.). 80p. 1986. lib. bdg. 600.00 (*0-226-68975-1*) U Ch Pr.

***Demusz, Kerry.** Listening to the Displaced: Action Research to the Conflict Zones of Sri Lanka. (Working Papers). 80p. 2000. pap. 18.95 (*0-85598-437-6*, Pub. by Oxfam Pub) Stylus Pub VA.

DeMuth & Kristol. The Neoconservative Imagination: Essays in Honor of Irving Kristol. 150p. 1995. 24.95 (*0-8447-3898-0*) Am Enterprise.

Demuth, jt. auth. see Beale.

Demuth, Carol M., jt. auth. see Demuth, Dennis M.

Demuth, Christopher C., jt. auth. see Kristol, William.

Demuth, Dennis M. & Demuth, Carol M. Christian School Administration: Management Guide LC 98-156949. 191 p. 1995. write for info. (*1-880705-04-4*) Demuth Enter.

— Recruiting Strategies for Christian Schools: How to Recruit & Retain Students. 240p. 1991. pap. text 22.95 (*1-880705-00-1*) Demuth Enter.

Demuth, Howard B., et al. Neurall Network Design. 736p. 1995. mass mkt. 109.95 (*0-534-94332-2*) Wadsworth Pub.

***DeMuth, James E.** Basic Statistics & Pharmaceutical Statistical Applications. LC 99-30733. (Biostatistics Ser.). (Illus.). 624p. 1999. text 79.75 (*0-8247-1967-0*) Dekker.

Demuth, Katherine, jt. ed. see Morgan, James L.

Demuth, M., ed. Mathematical Results in Quantum Mathematics: International Conference in Blossin, Germany,May 17-21, 1993. LC 94-4710. (Operator Theory, Advances & Applications Ser.). 1994. 111.00 (*0-8176-5025-3*) Birkhauser.

Demuth, M., et al, eds. Operator Calculus & Spectral Theory: Symposium on Operator Calculus & Spectral Theory, Lambrecht, Germany, December, 1991. LC 92-27729. (Operator Theory, Advances & Applications Ser.: Vol. 57). xi, 359p. 1992. 122.00 (*0-8176-2792-8*, Pub. by Birkhauser) Princeton Arch.

— Schrodinger Operators, Markov Semigroups, Wavelet Analysis, Operator Algebras. 408p. 1996. 145.00 (*3-527-40085-0*) Wiley.

Demuth, M. & Schrohe, E., eds. Pseudo-Differential Calculus & Mathematical Physics: Advances in Partial Differential Equations. LC 94-28611. (Mathematical Topics Ser.). 392p. 1994. 102.90 (*3-05-501625-4*) Wiley.

— Schrodinger Operators, Markov Semigroups, Wavelet Analysis, Operator Algebras. 408p. 1996. 89.20 (*3-05-501710-2*) Wiley.

***Demuth, M., et al.** Spectral Theory, Microlocal Analysis, Singular Manifolds: Advances in Partial Differential Equations. Schrohe, Elmar, ed. 368p. 1998. 149.95 (*3-527-40120-2*) Wiley.

Demuth, Michael, et al, eds. Boundary Value Problems, Schroginger Operators, Deformation Quantization: Advances in Partial Differential Equations. (Mathematical Topics Ser.: Vol. 18). (Illus.). 400p. 1995. text 135.00 (*3-05-501699-8*, Pub. by Akademie Verlag) Wiley.

— Evolution Equations, Feshbach Resonances, Singular Hodge Theory: Advances in Partial Differential Equations. LC 99-212793. 434p. 1999. 155.00 (*3-527-40233-0*) Wiley.

Demuth, Michael & Schulze, Bert-Wolfgang, eds. Partial Differential Operators & Mathematical Physics: International Conference in Holzhau, Germany, July 3-9, 1994. LC 95-10776. (Operator Theory, Advances & Applications Ser.: Vol. 78). 1995. write for info. (*3-7643-5208-6*) Birkhauser.

— Partial Differential Operators & Mathematical Physics: International Conference in Holzhau, Germany, July 3-9, 1994. LC 95-10776. (Operator Theory, Advances & Applications Ser.: Vol. 78). 429p. 1995. 142.00 (*0-8176-5208-6*) Birkhauser.

Demuth, Norman. Albert Roussel, a Study: Music Book Index. 150p. 1993. reprint ed. lib. bdg. 69.00 (*0-7812-9617-X*) Rprt Serv.

— An Anthology of Musical Criticism. LC 72-138219. 397p. 1971. reprint ed. lib. bdg. 69.50 (*0-8371-5576-2*, DEMC, Greenwood Pr) Greenwood.

— An Anthology of Musical Criticism: Music Book Index. 397p. 1993. reprint ed. lib. bdg. 89.00 (*0-7812-9656-0*) Rprt Serv.

— Cesar Franck. (Music Book Index Ser.). 228p. 1993. reprint ed. lib. bdg. 79.00 (*0-7812-9598-X*) Rprt Serv.

— French Opera: Its Development to the Revolution. LC 77-27486. (Music Reprint Ser.: 1978). (Illus.). 1978. reprint ed. lib. bdg. 39.50 (*0-306-77576-X*) Da Capo.

— Musical Trends in the Twentieth Century. LC 73-6258. (Illus.). 359p. 1975. reprint ed. lib. bdg. 59.75 (*0-8371-6896-1*, DEMT, Greenwood Pr) Greenwood.

— Ravel: Music Book Index. 214p. 1993. reprint ed. lib. bdg. 79.00 (*0-7812-9615-3*) Rprt Serv.

Demuth, Patricia. Gorillas. LC 93-39844. (All Aboard Reading Ser.: Level 2). (Illus.). 32p. (J). (gr. 1-3). 1994. pap. 3.95 (*0-448-40217-3*, G & D) Peng Put Young Read.

Demuth, Patricia. Gorillas. (All Aboard Reading Ser.). 1994. 9.15 (*0-606-06420-6*, Pub. by Turtleback) Demco.

Demuth, Patricia. Johnny Appleseed. LC 96-4015. (All Aboard Reading Ser.: Level 1). (Illus.). 32p. (Orig.). (J). (ps-1). 1996. lib. bdg. 13.89 (*0-448-41131-8*, G & D) Peng Put Young Read.

— Johnny Appleseed; Level 1. (All Aboard Reading Ser.). 1996. 9.15 (*0-606-11521-8*, Pub. by Turtleback) Demco.

***Demuth, Patricia.** Mars: The Red Planet. LC 98-13996. (All Aboard Reading Ser.). (Illus.). 48p. (J). (gr. 2-4). 1998. pap. 3.99 (*0-448-41843-6*, G & D) Peng Put Young Read.

Demuth, Patricia. Mars: The Red Planet, Level 3. LC 98-13996. (All Aboard Reading Ser.). (Illus.). 32p. (J). (gr. 2-3). 1998. lib. bdg. 13.89 (*0-448-41888-6*, G & D) Peng Put Young Read.

— Snakes. LC 92-24466. (All Aboard Reading Ser.: Level 2). (Illus.). 48p. (J). (gr. 1-3). 1993. pap. 3.95 (*0-448-40513-X*, G & D) Peng Put Young Read.

D

An Asterisk (*) at the beginning of an entry indicates that the title is appearing for the first time.

— Snakes. (All Aboard Reading Ser.). (J). 1993. 9.15 (*0-606-05609-2*, Pub. by Turtleback) Demco.
— Way down Deep: Strange Ocean Creatures. (All Aboard Reading Ser.: Level 2). (Illus.). 48p. (J). (gr. 1-3). 1995. pap. 3.99 (*0-448-40851-1*, G & D) Peng Put Young Read.
— Way Down Deep, Strange Ocean Creatures. LC 94-39040. (All Aboard Reading Ser.). 1995. 9.15 (*0-606-10023-7*, Pub. by Turtleback) Demco.
Demuth, Patricia & Montgomery, Michael. Johnny Appleseed. LC 96-4015. (All Aboard Reading Ser.: Level 1). (Illus.). 32p. (Orig.). (J). (ps-1). 1996. pap. 3.99 (*0-448-41130-X*, G & D) Peng Put Young Read.
Demuth, Patricia B. Achoo! All about Colds. (All Aboard Reading Ser.: Level 1). (Illus.). 32p. (J). (ps-1). 1997. 13.99 (*0-448-41348-5*, G & D); pap. 3.95 (*0-448-41347-7*, G & D) Peng Put Young Read.
— Achoo! All about Colds. 1997. 9.15 (*0-606-11023-2*, Pub. by Turtleback) Demco.
— Cradles in the Trees: The Story of Bird Nests. LC 93-9114. (Illus.). 32p. (J). (ps-3). 1994. lib. bdg. 14.95 (*0-02-728466-2*, Mac Bks Young Read) S&S Childrens.
— Pick up Your Ears, Henry. LC 91-27162. (Illus.). 32p. (J). (ps-1). 1992. lib. bdg. 13.95 (*0-02-728465-4*, Mac Bks Young Read) S&S Childrens.
— Those Amazing Ants. LC 93-1769. (Illus.). 32p. (J). (ps-3). 1994. mass mkt. 14.95 (*0-02-728467-0*, Mac Bks Young Read) S&S Childrens.
***DeMuth, Suzanne.** Herbs & Herb Gardening: An Annotated Bibliography & Resource Guide (1996) 94p. (C). 1999. reprint ed. pap. text 20.00 (*0-7881-8369-9*) DIANE Pub.
DeMuth, Suzanne. Sustainable Agriculture in Print: Current Periodicals. 130p. (C). 1996. reprint ed. pap. text 35.00 (*0-7881-3382-9*) DIANE Pub.
Demutskii, V. P., jt. auth. see Polovin, R. V.
Demuynck, M., et al, eds. Biogas Plants in Europe: A Practical Handbook. (Solar Energy in the European Community Ser.: No. E, Vol. 6). 1984. lib. bdg. 139.50 (*90-277-1780-X*) Kluwer Academic.
Demy, Tim, jt. auth. see Ice, Thomas.
Demy, Timothy, jt. auth. see Ice, Thomas.
***Demy, Timothy J.** Politics & Public Policy: A Christian Response; Crucial Considerations for Governing Life. 2000. 19.99 (*0-8254-2362-7*) Kregel.
Demy, Timothy J. & Stewart, Gary. Suicide: A Christian Response : Five Crucial Considerations for Choosing Life. LC 97-36028. 496p. 1997. pap. 24.99 (*0-8254-2355-4*) Kregel.
Demy, Timothy J. & Stewart, Gary P. The Marriage Marathon: How to Go the Distance As Husband & Wife. LC 98-15295. 208p. 1998. pap. text 10.99 (*0-8254-2356-2*) Kregel.
Demy, Timothy J. & Stewart, Gary P., eds. Genetic Engineering - A Christian Response: Crucial Considerations in Shaping Life. LC 98-45988. (Christian Response Ser.: Bk. 2). 320p. 1999. 20.99 (*0-8254-2357-0*) Kregel.
Demy, Timothy J., jt. auth. see Ice, Thomas.
Demyanov, V. F. Introduction to Minimax. 320p. 1998. pap. 8.95 (*0-486-66423-6*) Dover.
Dem'yanov, V. F. & Rubinov, A. M. Quasidifferential Calculus. Balakrishnan, A. V., ed. LC 86-5422. (Translations Series in Mathematics & Engineering). 301p. (Orig.). 1986. text 92.00 (*0-911575-35-9*) Optimization Soft.
Dem'Yanov, V. F. & Vasil'ev, L. V. Nondifferentiable Optimization. (Translation Series in Mathematics & Engineering). xvii, 452p. 1985. 146.95 (*0-387-90951-6*) Spr-Verlag.
Dem'yanov, V. F. & Vasil'ev, L. V. Nondifferentiable Optimization. Balakrishnan, A. V., ed. Sasagawa, Tetsushi, tr. LC 85-18736. (Translations Series in Mathematics & Engineering). 472p. 1985. text 96.00 (*0-911575-09-X*) Optimization Soft.
Demyanov, Vladimir F. & Rubinov, Alexander M. Constructive Nonsmooth Analysis. LC 95-6876. (Approximation & Optimization Ser.: Vol. 7). 416p. 1995. pap. 57.95 (*3-631-46270-0*) P Lang Pubng.
Demyanyuk, F. & Blunn, O. Technological Principles Flow Line & Automated Production, 2 vols., Set. LC 61-9176. 1963. 405.00 (*0-08-009902-5*, Pub. by Pergamon Repr) Franklin.
DeMyer, W. NMS Neuroanatomy. (National Medical Ser.). 380p. 1990. 26.00 (*0-683-06236-0*) Lppncott W & W.
DeMyer, William. Neuroanatomy. 2nd ed. LC 97-18904. (National Medical Series for Independent Study). (Illus.). 380p. 1997. pap. 27.00 (*0-683-30075-X*) Lppncott W & W.
Den Abbeele, Georges Van, see Van Den Abbeele, Georges.
Den, B. van, see Van Den, B.
den Beld, A. Van, see Van den Beld, A.
Den Berg, A. J. Van, see Van Den Berg, A. J.
Den Berg, Albert J, Van, see Van Den Berg, Albert J., ed.
den Berg, Albert Jan van, see van den Berg, Albert Jan, ed.
Den Berg, Leo Van, see Van Den Berg, Leo.
Den Berg, Oona Van, see Van Den Berg, Oona.
Den Berg, Sjef Van, see Watt, James H. & Van Den Berg, Sjef.
Den Bergh, Nan Van, see Van Den Bergh, Nan, ed.
Den Bergh, Roger Van, see Van Den Bergh, Roger.
Den Bergh, Roger Van, see Faure, Michael.
Den Bergh, Roger Van, see Deketelaere, Kurt & Faure, Michael, eds.
Den Berghe, L. Van, see Van Den Berghe, L.
Den Berghe, Pierre L. Van, see Van Den Berghe, Pierre L.
Den Bleyker, Merle. Hechos de los Apostoles-C-Alumno, Pt. A. (SPA.). 1989. pap. 1.75 (*1-55955-004-X*) CRC Wrld Lit.
— Hechos de los Apostoles-C-Maestro, Pt. A. (SPA.). 1989. pap. 2.00 (*1-55955-005-8*) CRC Wrld Lit.
Den Boeft, J. Calcidius on Fate: His Doctrine & Sources. 1970. pap. 25.00 (*90-04-01730-5*, PHA, 18) Brill Academic Pubs.
Den Boeft, J., et al. Cognito Gestorum: The Historiographic Art of Ammianus Marcellinus. (Verhandelingen der Koninklijke Nederlandse Akademie van Wetenschappen, Afd. Letterkunde, Nieuwe Reeks Ser.: No. 148). 130p. 1992. pap. 35.00 (*0-444-85752-4*) Elsevier.
Den Boer & Sitsen, J. M., eds. Handbook of Depression & Anxiety: A Biological Approach. (Medical Psychiatry Ser.: Vol. 1). (Illus.). 712p. 1994. text 175.00 (*0-8247-8858-3*) Dekker.
Den Boer, J. A., et al, eds. Advances in the Neurobiology of Schizophrenia. LC 94-22397. 482p. 1995. 255.00 (*0-471-95287-7*) Wiley.
Den Boer, James. Lost in Blue Canyon. (Orig.). 1979. pap. 5.00 (*0-87922-108-9*) Christophers Bks.
Den Boer, James, jt. auth. see Olson, Charles.
Den Boer, Jaques A., jt. auth. see Vlaardingerbroek, Marinus T.
Den-Boer, Johan A., jt. auth. see Montgomery, S. A.
Den Boer, Johan A., ed. Clinical Management of Anxiety. LC 96-36584. (Medical Psychiatry Ser.: Vol. 5). (Illus.). 448p. 1996. text 165.00 (*0-8247-9777-9*) Dekker.
Den Boer, Liesbeth, et al. Website Graphics Now: The Best of Global Site Design. LC 98-75077. (Illus.). 160p. 1999. pap. 34.95 (*0-500-28119-X*, Pub. by Thames Hudson) Norton.
den Boer, Maria E. The Finish Line: Preparing on Index. (Author's Assistant Ser.: Vol. 6). (Illus.). 8p. 1999. 3.95 (*1-928929-05-2*) Blue Thunder.
— Get Ready! Preparing a Manuscript. (Author's Assistant Ser.: Vol. 1). (Illus.). 16p. 1999. 3.95 (*1-928929-00-1*) Blue Thunder.
— Get Set! Understanding Design - Typesetting. (Author's Assistant Ser.: Vol. 7). (Illus.). 8p. 1999. 3.95 (*1-928929-06-0*) Blue Thunder.
— The Home Stretch: Preparing Notes & Bibliographies - References. (Author's Assistant Ser.: Vol. 5). (Illus.). 16p. 1999. 3.95 (*1-928929-04-4*) Blue Thunder.
— In the Know: A Publishing Glossary. (Author's Assistant Ser.: Vol. 11). (Illus.). 24p. 1999. 3.95 (*1-928929-10-9*) Blue Thunder.
— On the Mark: A Manual on Proofreading Marks. (Author's Assistant Ser.: Vol. 4). (Illus.). 24p. 1999. 3.95 (*1-928929-03-6*) Blue Thunder.
— On the Town: A Marketing Preview. (Author's Assistant Ser.: Vol. 10). (Illus.). 10p. 1999. 3.95 (*1-928929-09-5*) Blue Thunder.
— Press On! An Overview of Printing - Binding. (Author's Assistant Ser.: Vol. 8). (Illus.). 10p. 1999. 3.95 (*1-928929-07-9*) Blue Thunder.
***den Boer, Maria E.** Register Now! A Guide to Copyrighting, ISBNs & CIP Data. (Author's Assistant Ser.: Vol. 12). 16p. 2000. pap. 3.95 (*1-928929-12-5*) Blue Thunder.
den Boer, Maria E. Right On! Obtaining Permissions. (Author's Assistant Ser.: Vol. 2). (Illus.). 8p. 1999. 3.95 (*1-928929-01-X*) Blue Thunder.
— Shaping Up: A Guide to Copyediting & Proofreading Basics. (Author's Assistant Ser.: Vol. 3). (Illus.). 8p. 1999. 3.95 (*1-928929-02-8*) Blue Thunder.
— Wrapping It Up: A Look at Cover - Jacket Design. (Author's Assistant Ser.: Vol. 9). (Illus.). 10p. 1999. 3.95 (*1-928929-08-7*) Blue Thunder.
Den Boer, Monica, jt. auth. see Anderson, Malcolm.
Den Boer, P. J. & Reddingius, Joannes. Regulation & Stabilization: Paradigms in Population Ecology. LC 96-84233. (Illus.). 416p. 1996. 167.95 (*0-412-57540-X*) Kluwer Academic.
Den Boer, Pim & Frijhoff, Willem, eds. Lieux de Memoire & Identites Nationales: La France & las Pays-Bas, Vol. 1. (FRE.). 284p. (Orig.). (C). 1993. pap. 34.95 (*90-5356-022-X*, Pub. by Amsterdam U Pr) U of Mich Pr.
Den Boer, W. Private Morality in Greece & Rome. 1979. pap. 41.00 (*90-04-05976-8*, MNS, 57) Brill Academic Pubs.
— Progress in the Greece of Thucydides. (Mededelingen der Koninklijke Nederlandse Akademie van Wetenschappen, Afd. Letterkunde Ser.: No. 40(2)). 82p. 1977. pap. text 22.00 (*0-7204-8455-3*) Elsevier.
Den Boer, W., see Boer, W. Den.
den Boogert, Bob Van, see Van den Boogert, Bob.
Den Bosch, F. A. Van, see Van Den Bosch, F. A.
Den Bout, David E. Van, see Van Den Bout, David E.
den Branden Abner, Monica Van, see Faragasso, Laura B.
Den Braven, K. R., et al, eds. Heat Pump & Refrigeration Systems Design, Analysis, & Applications. 149p. pap. 47.50 (*0-7918-1036-4*) ASME.
Den Braven, K. R. & Mei, V., eds. Heat Pump & Refrigeration Systems Design, Analysis, & Applications 1994: Proceedings: International Mechanical Engineering Congress & Exposition (1994: Chicago, IL) LC 94-78970. (Advanced Energy Systems Ser.: Vol. 32). 77p. 1995. pap. 40.00 (*0-7918-1398-3*, G00893) ASME Pr.
den Brink-Budgen, Roy Van, see Van den Brink-Budgen, Roy.
den Brink, W. J. Van, see Kuiper, J. & Van den Brink, W. J., eds.
den Brink, W. Van, see Van den Brink, W.
***Den Brinker, B., et al, eds.** Cognitive Ergonomics, Clinical Assessment & Computer-Assisted Learning. LC 99-32860. (Computers in Psychology Ser.: Vol. 6). (Illus.). 304p. 1999. 79.00 (*90-265-1553-7*) Swets.
Den Broeder, Frederick. The Academy of Europe: Rome in the Eighteenth Century. (Illus.). 168p. 1973. 7.50 (*0-918386-11-X*) W Benton Mus.
— Hendrik Goltzius & the Printmakers of Haarlem. (Illus.). 100p. 1972. 3.00 (*0-918386-06-3*) W Benton Mus.
den Broeke, P. W. Van, see Van den Broeke, P. W.
Den Bruck, Arthur Moeller Van, see Moeller Van Den Bruck, Arthur.
Den Bulcke, D. Van & Halsberghe, E. Employment Decision-Making in Multinational Enterprises: Survey Results from Belgium. (Multinational Enterprises Programme Working Papers: No. 32). (Illus.). v, 102p. 1984. pap. 13.50 (*92-2-103832-7*) Intl Labour Office.
***Den Butter, F. A. G. & Morgan, Mary S.** Empirical Models & Policy Making: Interaction & Institutions. LC 00-24810. 2000. write for info. (*0-415-23217-1*) Routledge.
den Butter, F.A.G., jt. auth. see Fase, M. M. G.
Den Dekker, Arnold J. Model-Based Resolution. (Illus.). 157p. 1997. pap. 45.00 (*90-407-1548-3*, Pub. by Delft U Pr) Coronet Bks.
den Doel, Theo van, see Houweling, Henk & Siccama, Jan G.
Den Dooven, K. C. Monument Valley: The Story Behind the Scenery. LC 92-70430. (Illus.). 48p. (Orig.). 1992. pap. 7.95 (*0-88714-062-9*) KC Pubns.
— Monument Valley: The Story Behind the Scenery. Morales, Brigitte, tr. (GER., Illus.). 48p. (Orig.). 1992. pap. 8.95 (*0-88714-737-2*) KC Pubns.
— Monument Valley: The Story Behind the Scenery. Le Bras, Yvon, tr. (FRE., Illus.). 48p. (Orig.). 1992. pap. 8.95 (*0-88714-738-0*) KC Pubns.
— Monument Valley: The Story Behind the Scenery. Petzinger, Saori, tr. (JPN., Illus.). 48p. (Orig.). 1993. pap. 8.95 (*0-88714-739-9*) KC Pubns.
Den Dungen, Peter Van, see Van Den Dungen, Peter, compiled by.
Den Dungen, Peter Van, see Grunewald, Guido & Van Den Dungen, Peter, eds.
Den Dungen, Peter Van, see Chatfield, Charles & Van Den Dungen, Peter, eds.
Den Dunnen, Emile. Instruments of Money Market & Foreign Exchange Market Policy in the Netherlands. 1985. pap. text 51.50 (*90-247-3206-9*) Kluwer Academic.
Den-Duyts, F. Anciennes Monnaies (Belgium, Flanders, Brubant Hainaut) (Illus.). 1972. pap. 20.00 (*0-932106-16-1*) S J Durst.
Den Elzen, Michel. Global Environmental Change: An Integrated Modelling Approach. 263p. (Orig.). 1994. pap. 65.00 (*90-6224-987-6*, Pub. by Uitgeverij Arkel) LPC InBook.
Den Ende, J. Van, see Van Den Ende, J.
den Exter, Andre & Hermans, Herbert E. The Right to Health Care in Several European Countries: Expert Meeting, Held in Rotterdam, The Netherlands, April 27-28, 1998. LC 98-39191. (Studies in Social Policy). 208p. 1999. 66.00 (*90-411-1087-9*) Kluwer Law Intl.
Den Haan, E., et al, eds. Advances in Understanding & Modelling the Behaviour of Past: Proceedings of the International Workshop, Delft, Netherlands, June 1993. (Illus.). 440p. (C). 1994. 136.00 (*90-5410-366-3*, Pub. by A A Balkema) Ashgate Pub Co.
Den Haan, E. J. Vertical Compressions of Soils. 96p. 1994. pap. 57.50 (*90-407-1062-7*, Pub. by Delft U Pr) Coronet Bks.
Den Hartog, A. P., et al. Manual for Social Surveys on Food Habits & Consumption in Developing Countries. 153p. 1995. pap. 16.00 (*3-8236-1237-9*, Pub. by Backhuys Pubs) Balogh.
Den Hartog, J. P. Advanced Strength of Materials. 388p. 1987. reprint ed. pap. text 10.95 (*0-486-65407-9*) Dover.
Den Hartog, Jacob P. Mechanics. 462p. 1961. pap. 11.95 (*0-486-60754-2*) Dover.
— Strength of Materials. 323p. 1961. pap. 9.95 (*0-486-60755-0*) Dover.
Den Hartog, Jacob P., ed. see Prandtl, Ludwig & Tietjens, O. G.
den Heever, Louw W. Van, see Van den Heever, Louw W.
Den Hertog, D. Interior Point Approach to Linear, Quadratic, & Convex Programming: Algorithms & Complexity. LC 94-2748. (Mathematics & Its Applications Ser.: Vol. 277). 224p. (C). 1994. text 145.50 (*0-7923-2734-9*) Kluwer Academic.
Den Hertog, Judy, tr. see Balkenende, William P.
Den Heuvel, Edward P. Van, see Van Den Heuvel, Edward P., ed.
Den Heuvel, Edward P. Van, see P. S. Associates Staff & Van Den Heuvel, Edward P.
Den Heuvel, Jacques Van, see Van Den Heuvel, Jacques.
den Heuvel, W. J. van, see Van den Heuvel, W. J.
***Den Heyer, C. J.** Jesus & the Doctrine of the Atonement. LC 98-33525. 140p. 1998. pap. 16.00 (*1-56338-245-8*) TPI PA.
— Jesus Matters: 150 Years of Research. LC 96-42948.Tr. of Opnieuw: Wie Is Jesus? Balans van 150 Jaar Onderzoek naar Jesus. 208p. (Orig.). 1997. pap. 16.00 (*1-56338-195-8*) TPI PA.
— Paul: A Man of Two Worlds. 320p. Date not set. pap. 29.00 (*1-56338-301-2*) TPI PA.
Den Hoedt, G. Geotextiles Geomembranes & Related Products, Vol. 2. 1990. 104.00 (*90-6191-121-4*) Ashgate Pub Co.
Den Hoedt, G., ed. Geotextiles, Geomembranes & Related Products: Proceedings of the 4th International Congress, the Hague, 28 May - 1 June 1990, 3 vols., Set. (Illus.). 1282p. (C). 1990. text 291.00 (*90-6191-119-2*, Pub. by A A Balkema) Ashgate Pub Co.
Den Hoek, A. W. Van, see Van Den Hoek, A. W.
***den Hollander, Frank.** Large Deviations. LC 99-58913. (FIM Ser.: Vol. 14). 143p. 2000. 49.00 (*0-8218-1989-5*) Am Math.
Den Hoven, Adrian Van, see Van Den Hoven, Adrian.
Den Kamp, J. A. Op, see Op Den Kamp, J. A., ed.
Den Nijs, Loes, jt. ed. see Booij, C. J.
Den Otter, A. A. The Philosophy of Railways: The Transcontinental Railway Idea in British North America. LC 97-185154. (Illus.). 292p. 1997. text 34.95 (*0-8020-4161-2*, HE2810) U of Toronto Pr.
Den Ouden, Bernard & Moen, Marcia, eds. The Presence of Feeling in Thought. LC 91-3822. (Revisioning Philosophy Ser.: Vol. 7). 243p. 1992. 44.95 (*0-8204-1503-0*) P Lang Pubng.
Den Ouden, Bernard D. Language & Creativity: An Interdisciplinary Essay in Chomskyan Humanism. vi, 107p. (Orig.). (C). 1975. pap. text 23.10 (*3-11-013329-6*) Mouton.
Den Ouden, C., ed. Thermal Storage of Solar Energy. 378p. 1981. text 182.50 (*90-247-2492-9*) Kluwer Academic.
Den Ouden, C. & Steemers, Theo C., eds. Building Two Thousand, 2 vols. (C). 1992. lib. bdg. 180.50 (*0-7923-1501-4*); lib. bdg. 180.50 (*0-7923-1502-2*) Kluwer Academic.
— Building Two Thousand, 2 vols., Set. (C). 1992. text 225.00 (*0-7923-1503-0*) Kluwer Academic.
Den Ouden, C., jt. ed. see Steemers, Theo C.
Den Pol, Rick Van, see Paulson, Lucy H. & Van Den Pol, Rick.
Den Putte, M. J. Van, see Van Den Putte, M. J.
***Den Tandt, Catherine M.** Virgins & Fleurs de Lys. LC 99-36457. 2000. write for info. (*0-8477-0389-4*) U of PR Pr.
Den Tandt, Christopher. The Urban Sublime in American Literary Naturalism. LC 97-45409. 320p. 1998. text 49.95 (*0-252-02402-8*); text 18.95 (*0-252-06704-5*) U of Ill Pr.
Den, Uyl. The Fountainhead. LC 98-49012. 1998. 32.00 (*0-8057-7932-9*, Twyne); per. write for info. (*0-8057-7931-0*, Twyne) Mac Lib Ref.
Den Uyl, Douglas, jt. auth. see Rasmussen, Douglas.
Den Uyl, Douglas J. The Virtue of Prudence. LC 90-25008. (Studies in Moral Philosophy: Vol. 5). (Illus.). 350p. (C). 1991. text 61.95 (*0-8204-1504-9*) P Lang Pubng.
Den Uyl, Douglas J. & Rasmussen, Douglas B., intros. The Philosophic Thought of Ayn Rand. LC 83-5844. 248p. 1984. text 24.95 (*0-252-01033-7*); pap. text 14.95 (*0-252-01407-3*) U of Ill Pr.
Den Uyl, Douglas J., jt. auth. see Rasmussen, Douglas B.
Den Uyl, Marion. Invisible Barriers: Gender, Caste & Kinship in a Southern Indian Village. LC 95-218621. 304p. (Orig.). 1995. pap. 39.95 (*90-6224-985-X*, Pub. by Uitgeverij Arkel) LPC InBook.
Den Velde, W. Op, see De Loos, W. S. & Op den Velde, W., eds.
den Wyngaert, Christine Van, see Dugard, John & Van den Wyngaert, Christine, eds.
Dena, Anael. Little Mouse's Learn-&-Play, 4 bks. Incl. Colors. LC 97-20901. (Illus.). 48p. (J). (ps up). 1997. lib. bdg. 22.60 (*0-8368-1984-5*); Letters. LC 97-14783. (Illus.). 48p. (J). (ps up). 1997. lib. bdg. 22.60 (*0-8368-1985-3*); Numbers. Neis, Janet, tr. from FRE. LC 97-20904. (Illus.). 48p. (J). (ps up). 1997. lib. bdg. 22.60 (*0-8368-1986-1*); Opposites. LC 97-14784. (Illus.). 48p. (J). (ps up). 1997. lib. bdg. 22.60 (*0-8368-1987-X*); (Illus.). (J). 1997. Set lib. bdg. 90.40 (*0-8368-1983-7*) Gareth Stevens Inc.
Denady, Alex. A Little Book of Hangover Cures. (Illus.). 60p. 1998. 9.95 (*0-86281-631-9*, Pub. by Appletree Pr) Irish Bks Media.
Denale, R., ed. Welding & Weld Automation in Shipbuilding. (Illus.). 257p. 1996. 20.00 (*0-87339-322-8*) Minerals Metals.
***Denardo.** Models for Decision Making. (C). 2000. pap. text, student ed. write for info. (*0-471-33281-X*) Wiley.
Denardo, G., et al, eds. Group Theoretical Methods in Physics: Proceedings of the XIIth International Colloquium, Held at the International Centre for Theoretical Physics, Trieste, Italy, Sept. 5-11, 1983. (Lecture Notes in Physics Ser.: Vol. 201). xxvii, 518p. 1984. 45.95 (*0-387-13335-6*) Spr-Verlag.
DeNardo, G. & Doebner, H. D., eds. Conference on Differential Geometric Methods in Theoretical Physics: Proceedings of June 30-July 3, 1981 Conference, Trieste, Italy. 300p. 1983. 52.00 (*9971-950-58-8*) World Scientific Pub.
Denardo, G., jt. auth. see Eissa, E.
DeNardo, James. The Amateur Strategist: Intuitive Deterrence Theories & the Politics of the Nuclear Arms Race. (Cambridge Studies in Political Psychology & Public Opinion). (Illus.). 329p. (C). 1995. text 59.95 (*0-521-48121-X*); pap. text 21.95 (*0-521-48446-4*) Cambridge U Pr.
DeNardo, Louise T. The Sacred Letter. (Illus.). 56p. 1998. pap. 8.00 (*0-8059-4393-5*) Dorrance.
Denari, Neil. Gyroscopic Horizons. LC 99-17886. (Illus.). 224p. 1999. pap. 40.00 (*1-878271-13-X*) Princeton Arch.
***Denari, Neil M.** Wet vs. Dry: The Chess/Go Project at La Beaute Avignon 2000. (Illus.). 80p. 2000. 45.00 (*3-907078-21-7*, Pub. by Lars Muller) Princeton Arch.
Denaro, Ronald C. Negative Cutting, 16mm: Includes Reversal Cutting. 106p. (C). 1991. pap. text 14.95 (*0-9630524-3-8*) Split-Reel.
Denaro, V. Stenosis of the Cervical Spine: Causes, Diagnosis, & Treatment. (Illus.). 225p. 1991. 225.00 (*0-387-53328-1*) Spr-Verlag.
Denarski, Diane T. Ozark Story Poems. LC 93-9915. 84p. 1993. pap. 7.95 (*0-935304-30-4*) August Hse.
DeNatale, Andrew, et al. Creditors' Committee Manual. 1992. ring bd. 165.00 (*0-685-69637-5*, CRCM) Warren Gorham & Lamont.
DeNatale, Douglas. Between the Branches. 1985. pap. 6.95 (*0-9622903-4-3*) DCHA.
DeNatale, Douglas, et al, eds. New Ways for Old Jugs: Tradition & Innovation at the Jugtown Pottery. LC 94-11701. 1994. pap. write for info. (*0-938983-11-3*) McKissick.

An Asterisk (*) at the beginning of an entry indicates that the title is appearing for the first time.

***DeNatale, F. & Pupolin, S., eds.** Multimedia Communications. LC 98-53818. (Illus.). 592p. 1999. pap. 119.00 (*1-85233-135-6*, Pub. by Spr-Verlag) Spr-Verlag.
DeNault, Cindy, ed. see Frissell-Deppe, Tammy.
DeNault, Cindy, ed. see Peterson, Kathrine P. & Palmer, Fannie R.
Denault, Gerard F., tr. see Houzeau, Jean-Charles.
Denavit-Saubie, M., jt. ed. see Bianchi, A. L.
***DeNayer, Lyn & Carpenter, Deb.** The Heart's Compass: Journey of Faith. (Illus.). 44p. 1999. spiral bd. 25.00 (*0-9625085-2-7*) PLAN Pubs.
Denbaars, S., et al, eds. Wide-Bandgap Semiconductors for High Power, High Frequency & High Temperature Vol. 512: Proceedings Materials Research Society Symposium. LC 98-28360. 565p. 1998. text 81.00 (*1-55899-418-1*) Materials Res.
Denbeaux, Mark P., et al. New Jersey Evidentiary Foundations. LC 95-75584. 364p. 1995. 85.00 (*1-55834-222-2*, 61180-10, MICHIE) LEXIS Pub.
Denber, H. C., jt. auth. see Rinkle, Max.
Denber, Herman C. Cardiac Surgery: Biological & Psychological Implications. LC 94-29707. 272p. 1994. 35.00 (*0-87993-599-5*) Futura Pub.
Denber, Herman C., ed. see International Symposium on Psychopharmacology Staff.
Denber, Herman C., ed. see Symposium on Psychopharmacologic Treatment in Psyc.
Denberg, Ken. Driving with One Light Out. 28p. 1993. pap. 5.00 (*1-889806-06-4*) Devils Millhopper.
Denbigh, K. G. The Principles of Chemical Equilibrium. 4th ed. (Illus.). 516p. 1981. pap. text 47.95 (*0-521-28150-4*) Cambridge U Pr.
Denbigh, Kenneth G. Three Concepts of Time. 160p. 1981. 50.95 (*0-387-10757-6*) Spr-Verlag.
Denbigh, Kenneth G. & Turner, J.C. Chemical Reactor Theory: An Introduction. LC 76-123661. 236p. reprint ed. pap. 67.30 (*0-608-18597-3*, 2013219) Bks Demand.
Denbigh, Philip. Continuous & Discrete Time Signal Processing. LC 97-40611. 576p. (C). 1998. pap. 81.95 (*0-201-17860-5*) Addison-Wesley.
DenBleyker, Merle. Hechos de los Apostoles, Parte B C-Alumno. (SPA.). 1992. pap. 1.75 (*1-55955-032-5*) CRC Wrld Lit.
— Hechos de los Apostoles, Parte B C-Maestro. (SPA.). 1992. pap. 2.00 (*1-55955-033-3*) CRC Wrld Lit.
Denbo, Bruce F., ed. see Wharton, Mary E. & Bowen, Edward L.
DenBoer, Gordon, ed. The Documentary History of the First Federal Elections, 1788-1790, Vol. IV. LC 74-5903. 408p. (C). 1989. text 34.95 (*0-299-12120-8*) U of Wis Pr.
DenBoer, Gordon, et al, eds. The Documentary History of the First Federal Elections, 1788-1790, Vol. III. LC 74-5903. (Documentary History of the First Federal Elections Ser.). 640p. 1986. text 34.95 (*0-299-10650-0*) U of Wis Pr.
DenBoer, Gordon, et al. The Documentary History of the First Federal Elections, 1788-1790, Vol. II. LC 74-5903. 544p. 1984. text 34.95 (*0-299-09510-X*) U of Wis Pr.
DenBoer, Gordon, jt. ed. see Long, John H.
***Denboer, Helen.** Pieter's & Anna's Trek. LC 98-35694. (Immigrants Chronicles Ser.). (J). 1999. 5.99 (*0-7814-3083-6*) Chariot Victor.
Denboer, Tony. Successful Technologies Review, 1998. rev. ed. (Illus.). 200p. 1998. ring bd. 1980.00 (*1-877750-66-2*) Integrated Circuit.
Denborough, M. The Role of Calcium Ions in Drug Action. (International Encyclopedia of Pharmacology & Therapeutics Ser.: No. 124). (Illus.). 200p. 1987. 192.50 (*0-08-034193-4*, Pergamon Pr) Elsevier.
Denbow, Claude. Denbow: Income Tax Law in the Commonwealth Caribbean. 1997. pap. write for info. (*0-406-99934-1*, DITL, MICHIE) LEXIS Pub.
Denbow, Claude H. Life Insurance Law in the Commonwealth Caribbean. 1984. 50.00 (*0-406-07630-8*, U.K., MICHIE) LEXIS Pub.
— Life Insurance Law in the Commonwealth Caribbean. (C). 1984. 175.00 (*0-7855-6046-7*, Pub. by Witherby & Co) St Mut.
Denburg, Eric J. Van, see Choca, James P.
Denburg, Eric J. Van, see Choca, James P. & Van Denburg, Eric J.
Denburg, Eric J. Van, see Choca, James P.
Denburg, Eric J. Van, see Choca, James P. & Van Denburg, Eric J.
Denburg, Ina, jt. auth. see Denburg, Ron.
Denburg, Joseph K. Van, see Van Denburg, Joseph K.
Denburg, Judah A. Allergy & Allergic Diseases: The New Mechanisms & Therapeutics. LC 98-17728. (Illus.). 608p. 1998. 145.00 (*0-89603-404-6*) Humana.
***Denburg, Ron & Denburg, Ina.** The Diamond Diet: A Multifaceted Path to Weight-Loss, Health & Wellness. (Illus.). 600p. 2000. 26.00 (*0-9677452-3-3*); pap. 18.00 (*0-9677452-0-9*) FourU Bayou.
Denby, B. & Perret-Gallix, D., eds. Artificial Intelligence in High Energy & Nuclear Physics: Proceedings of the Fourth International Workshop on Software Engineering, Artificial Intelligence, & Expert Systems in High Energy & Nuclear Physics, April 3-8, 1995, Pisa, Italy. 800p. 1995. 138.00 (*981-02-2436-2*) World Scientific Pub.
Denby, Charles. Indignant Heart: A Black Worker's Journal. 295p. write for info. (*0-919618-93-6*); pap. write for info. (*0-919618-67-7*) Black Rose.
— Indignant Heart: A Black Worker's Journal. LC 88-37883. (African American Life Ser.). 328p. (C). 1989. reprint ed. 35.00 (*0-8143-2219-0*); reprint ed. pap. 17.95 (*0-8143-2220-4*) Wayne St U Pr.
Denby, David. Great Books: My Adventures with Homer, Rousseau, Woolf & Other Indestructible Writers of the Western World. LC 96-18634. 492p. 1996. 30.00 (*0-684-80975-3*) S&S Trade.
— Great Books: My Adventures with Homer, Rousseau, Woolf & Other Indestructible Writers of the Western World. 496p. 1997. per. 15.00 (*0-684-83533-9*) S&S Trade Pap.
Denby, David, ed. Film Seventy-Two to Seventy-Three: An Anthology by the National Association of Film Critics. LC 73-1746. 304p. 1973. 7.95 (*0-685-32270-X*, Bobbs); pap. 3.95 (*0-672-51871-6*, Bobbs) Macmillan.
Denby, David J. Sentimental Narrative & the Social Order in France, 1760-1820. (Cambridge Studies in French: No. 47). (Illus.). 296p. (C). 1994. text 69.95 (*0-521-43086-0*) Cambridge U Pr.
Denby, Edwin. Dance Writings & Poetry. Cornfeld, Robert, ed. LC 98-2517. 336p. 1998. 40.00 (*0-300-07617-7*); pap. 18.00 (*0-300-06985-5*) Yale U Pr.
Denby, Elaine. Grand Hotels: Reality & Illusion. (Illus.). 304p. 1998. 65.00 (*1-86189-010-9*, Pub. by Reaktion Bks) Consort Bk Sales.
D'Encarnacao, Patricia W., jt. auth. see D'Encarnacao, Paul S.
D'Encarnacao, Paul S. & D'Encarnacao, Patricia W. The Joy of Journaling. (Illus.). 110p. 1991. pap. 11.95 (*0-940829-05-3*) Eagle Wing Bks.
D'Encausse, Helene C. Big Brother: The Soviet Union & Soviet Europe. Holoch, George, tr. from FRE. LC 86-31885. 380p. (C). 1987. 45.00 (*0-8419-1042-1*); pap. 26.95 (*0-8419-1043-X*) Holmes & Meier.
— The Great Challenge: Nationalities & the Bolshevik State, 1917-1930. Festinger, Nancy, tr. from FRE. LC 91-11293. 288p. 1992. 37.95 (*0-8419-1285-8*) Holmes & Meier.
— The Russian Syndrome: One Thousand Years of Political Murder. Higgitt, Caroline, tr. from FRE. LC 91-3752. 475p. (C). 1993. 34.95 (*0-8419-1293-9*) Holmes & Meier.
— Stalin: Man of History. Ionescu, Valence, tr. from FRE. 279p. (C). 1982. pap. text 17.95 (*0-582-29559-9*, 71797) Longman.
***d'Encausse, Helene Carrere.** Lenin. Holoch, George, tr. 512p. 2001. 45.00 (*0-8419-1412-5*) Holmes & Meier.
Dence, C. W., et al, eds. Methods in Lignin Chemistry. (Wood Science Ser.). (Illus.). 620p. 1992. 368.95 (*0-387-50295-5*) Spr-Verlag.
Dence, Carlton W. & Reeve, Douglas W., eds. Pulp Bleaching: Principles & Practice. LC 96-4084. 868p. 1996. 150.00 (*0-89852-063-0*, 0102B061) TAPPI.
Dence, Joseph B. Steroids & Peptides: Selected Chemical Aspects for Biology, Biochemistry & Medicine. LC 79-21236. (Illus.). 430p. reprint ed. pap. 133.30 (*0-7837-3522-7*, 205785700008) Bks Demand.
Dence, Joseph B. & Dence, Thomas P. A First Course of Collegiate Mathematics. LC 91-18208. 376p. (Orig.). (C). 1994. lib. bdg. 49.95 (*0-89464-592-7*) Krieger.
Dence, Joseph B. & Diestler, Dennis J. Intermediate Physical Chemistry: Stationary Properties of Chemical Systems. 358p. (C). 1987. reprint ed. text 46.50 (*0-471-81243-9*) Krieger.
Dence, Joseph B., jt. auth. see Dence, Thomas P.
Dence, Michael, jt. ed. see Davidson, Alex.
Dence, Thomas P. & Dence, Joseph B. Elements of the Theory of Numbers. LC 98-19868. 517p. (C). 1999. 64.95 (*0-12-209130-2*) Acad Pr.
Dence, Thomas P., jt. auth. see Dence, Joseph B.
Dench. Introduction to C Plus Plus. (ITCP-UK Computer Science Ser.). 1994. pap. 31.95 (*1-85032-256-2*) Thomson Learn.
Dench, et al, eds. Young at Eighty: The Prolific Public Life of Michael Young. 256p. (Orig.). 1996. 35.00 (*1-85754-243-6*, Pub. by Carcanet Pr) Paul & Co Pubs.
Dench, D. & Prior, B. Introduction to C++ 256p. (C). 1994. mass mkt. 27.50 (*0-412-55290-6*) Chapman & Hall.
Dench, Emma. From Barbarians to New Men: Greek, Roman, & Modern Perceptions of Peoples from the Central Apennines. (Oxford Classical Monographs). (Illus.). 268p. 1995. text 55.00 (*0-19-815021-0*) OUP.
Dench, Geoff. Transforming Men: Changing Patterns of Dependency & Dominance in Gender Relations. 275p. 1995. pap. 21.95 (*0-7658-0450-6*) Transaction Pubs.
— Transforming Men: Changing Patterns of Dependency & Dominance in Gender Relations. 275p. (C). 1996. text 34.95 (*1-56000-232-8*) Transaction Pubs.
Dench, Geoff, ed. Rewriting the Sexual Contract. LC 98-28945. 310p. 1999. pap. 24.95 (*0-7658-0466-2*) Transaction Pubs.
Dencher, Ted. An Alarming Situation for J. W.'s. (Vital Ser.). 1997. pap. 0.75 (*0-87508-500-8*) Chr Lit.
Denchfield, Nick. Charlie the Chicken. LC 96-9594. (Illus.). (J). 1997. pap. 12.95 (*0-15-201451-9*) Harcourt.
— Desmond the Dog. LC 96-9593. (Illus.). (J). (ps). 1998. pap. 12.95 (*0-15-201340-7*) Harcourt.
— Desmond the Dog. LC 99-215514. (Illus.). 24p. (J). 1997. write for info. (*0-333-67954-7*, Pub. by Macmillan Pr) Kelley.
Denck, H., ed. see Paquet, K. J., et al.
Denck, Hans. Selected Writings of Hans Denck, 1500-1527. Furcha, Edward J., tr. LC 89-28426. (Texts & Studies in Religion: Vol. 14). 563p. 1989. lib. bdg. 119.95 (*0-88946-833-8*) E Mellen.
Dencke, Christian F., tr. see St. John the Evangelist.
Dencker-Koenig, Karla. Problems Solving Strategies: Grades 2-3. Mufoletto, Mary L., ed. (Illus.). 64p. (Orig.). 1996. pap., teacher ed. 6.95 (*1-889369-00-4*, TI0003) Teaching Ink.
— Test Taking: Grades 1-3. Muffoletto, Mary L., ed. (Illus.). 64p. 1996. pap., teacher ed. 6.95 (*1-889369-09-8*, TI0020) Teaching Ink.
***Dencker-Koenig, Karla.** Test Taking: Grades 4-5. (Illus.). 64p. 1998. pap., teacher ed. 6.95 (*1-889369-24-1*, TI0021) Teaching Ink.
Denckla, Tanya. Gardening at a Glance: The Organic Gardener's Handbook on Vegetables, Fruits, Nuts & Herbs. LC 89-52156. (Illus.). 1991. pap. 22.95 (*0-9627331-0-5*) Wooden Angel.
— The Organic Gardener's Home Reference: A Plant-by-Plant Guide to Growing Fresh, Healthy Food. LC 93-22835. Orig. Title: Gardening at a Glance. (Illus.). 304p. 1994. reprint ed. 29.95 (*0-88266-840-4*, Garden Way Pub); reprint ed. pap. 21.95 (*0-88266-839-0*, Garden Way Pub) Storey Bks.
Dendegem, Jean P. Van, see Batens, Diderik & Van Dendegem, Jean P., eds.
Dendel, Esther W. Beauty & the Human Spirit: The Legacy of Harriet & Vetta Goldstein. (Illus.). 68p. (Orig.). pap. 10.00 (*0-939719-06-1*) UMN Goldstein Gall.
— You Cannot Unsneeze a Sneeze & Other Tales from Liberia. (Illus.). 144p. 1995. pap. 17.50 (*0-87081-415-X*) Univ Pr Colo.
Dendle, Brian J. Galdos: The Early Historical Novels. LC 86-6940. 192p. 1986. text 27.50 (*0-8262-0615-8*) U of Mo Pr.
— Galdos: The Mature Thought. LC 80-51013. 2[illegible]3p. reprint ed. pap. 66.10 (*0-7837-5795-6*, 204546100006) Bks Demand.
— Spain's Forgotten Novelist: Armando Palacio Valdes, 1853-1938. LC 94-28808. 1995. 34.50 (*0-8387-5294-2*) Bucknell U Pr.
Dendle, Brian J., ed. see Galdos, Benito Perez.
DenDooven, Nancy J. Portland's Best by Bus: A Public Transit Guide to Portland's 30 Most Interesting Places. LC 98-72104. (Illus.). 144p. 1998. pap. 10.95 (*0-9661854-1-2*) Around Town.
Dendrinos, D. S. & Sonis, M. Chaos & Socio-Spatial Dynamics. John, F. et al, eds. (Applied Mathematical Sciences Ser.: Vol. 86). (Illus.). xvii, 184p. 1990. 65.95 (*0-387-97283-8*) Spr-Verlag.
Dendrinou Kolias, Helen, ed. Readings in Modern Greek Literature: For Intermediate & Advanced Students in Modern Greek. 384p. 1998. text 45.00 (*0-89241-595-9*); pap. text 30.00 (*0-89241-589-4*) Caratzas.
***D'Endrody, A. L.** Give Your Horse a Chance. 576p. 1999. 75.00 (*0-85131-741-3*, Pub. by J A Allen) St Mut.
D'Endrody, Agoston. Give Your Horse a Chance. (Illus.). 1988. 39.95 (*0-85131-901-7*) Trafalgar.
***d'Endrody, Agoston L.** Give Your Horse a Chance: A Classic Work on the Training of Horse & Rider. LC 98-87637. (Classics Ser.). (Illus.). 544p. 1999. 34.95 (*1-57076-146-9*) Trafalgar.
Dendy & Brockway. Cereals & Cereal Products. (Illus.). 416p. 1999. pap. 45.95 (*0-412-63320-5*, Chap & Hall NY) Chapman & Hall.
Dendy, Arthur, ed. Problems of Modern Science: A Series of Lectures Delivered at King's College (University of London) LC 72-314. (Essay Index Reprint Ser.). 1977. reprint ed. 20.95 (*0-8369-2789-3*) Ayer.
Dendy, Chris A. Teenagers with ADD: A Parents' Guide. LC 95-524. (Special Needs Collection Ser.). (Illus.). 370p. (Orig.). 1995. pap. 18.95 (*0-933149-69-7*) Woodbine House.
***Dendy, Chris Zeigler.** Teaching Teenagers with ADD: A Quick Reference Guide for Educators & Parents. (Illus.). 225p. 2000. pap. 16.95 (*1-890627-20-8*) Woodbine House.
Dendy, David A., ed. Sorghum & Millets: Chemistry & Technology. LC 94-72775. (Monograph Ser.). (Illus.). 407p. 1995. 159.00 (*0-913250-84-8*, BEF 6255) Am Assn Cereal Chem.
Dendy, Leslie A. Tracks, Scats & Signs. LC 95-6207. (Take-Along Guide Ser.). 48p. 1995. pap. text 6.95 (*1-55971-599-5*, NorthWord Pr) Creat Pub Intl.
***Dendy, P. P.** Physics for Diagnostic Radiology. LC 99-24542. 1999. 160.00 (*0-7503-0590-8*) IOP Pub.
— Physics for Diagnostic Radiology. 2nd ed. LC 99-24542. 1999. pap. text 49.00 (*0-7503-0591-6*) IOP Pub.
Dendy, Philip P., ed. Technical Advances in Biomedical Physics. 1984. text 236.00 (*90-247-2934-3*) Kluwer Academic.
Dendy, R. O. Plasma Dynamics. (Illus.). 172p. 1990. text 65.00 (*0-19-851991-5*); pap. text 29.95 (*0-19-852041-7*) OUP.
Dendy, William. Lost Toronto. (Illus.). 1979. 25.00 (*0-19-540294-4*) OUP.
DeNeal, Gary. A Knight of Another Sort: Prohibition & Charlie Birger. 2nd rev. ed. LC 98-12837. (Illus.). 304p. 1998. 35.00 (*0-8093-2216-1*); pap. 16.95 (*0-8093-2217-X*) S Ill U Pr.
Deneberg. The True Story of J. Edgar Hoover & the F. B. I. (J). 1995. pap. 5.99 (*0-590-44157-4*) Scholastic Inc.
Deneberg, J., et al. Environmental Claims & Property Insurance Coverage. LC 89-46281. 364p. 1989. pap. 47.95 (*0-89707-503-X*, 519-0096) Amer Bar Assn.
Denecke, Edward J. Earth Science Power Pack: Let's Review: Earth Science & Barron's Regents Exams & Answers. 1995. pap., student ed. 15.95 (*0-8120-8013-0*) Barron.
— Let's Review: Earth Science. 1995. pap., student ed. 12.95 (*0-8120-1568-1*) Barron.
Denecke, H. J. & Meyer, R. Corrective & Reconstructive Rhinoplasty. Oxtoby, L., tr. (Plastic Surgery of Head & Neck Ser.: Vol. 1). (Illus.). 1967. 424.00 (*0-387-03757-8*) Spr-Verlag.
***Denecke, K. & Wismath, S. L.** Hyperidentities & Clones, Vol. 14. 264p. 2000. 75.00 (*90-5699-235-X*, G & B Science) Gordon & Breach.
Denecke, Karl H. Der Burger im Spannungsfeld von Sittlichkeit und Selbstbestimmung: Studien zur Franklin-Rezeption im Deutschland des 19. Jahrhunderts. Von Bardeleben, Renate & Herget, Winfried, eds. (Mainzer Studien zur Amerikanistik: Bd. 33). (GER.). 182p. 1996. 42.95 (*3-631-48857-2*) P Lang Pubng.
DeNee, JoAnne & Hand, Julia. Exploring the Secrets of the Meadow-Thicket. (Illus.). 248p. (Orig.). (J). (gr. 1-4). 1993. pap. 18.95 (*1-884430-02-3*) Food Works.
DeNeef, A. Leigh. Traherne in Dialogue: Heidegger, Lacan, & Derrida. LC 87-31952. ix, 312p. (C). 1988. text 54.95 (*0-8223-0832-0*) Duke.
DeNeef, A. Leigh & Goodwin, Craufurd D., eds. The Academic's Handbook. 2nd ed. LC 95-16775. 360p. 1995. text 54.95 (*0-8223-1661-7*); pap. text 18.95 (*0-8223-1673-0*) Duke.
Deneef, A. Leigh, ed. see Southeastern Renaissance Conference Staff.
Deneen, Lawrence J. & Corson, Norman E. The Enhanced Edition: Of the Technical Assistance Manual on the Employment Provision of the Americans with Disabilities Act. 148p. 1992. ring bd. 25.00 (*0-9614877-3-9*) Rehab Pubns.
Deneen, Lawrence J. & Hessellund, Thorvald A. Counseling the Able Disabled: Rehabilitation Consulting in Disability Compensation Systems. LC 86-61254. 344p. (Orig.). 1986. 34.95 (*0-9614877-1-2*) Rehab Pubns.
Deneen, Lawrence J., jt. auth. see Pastore, Mary.
***Deneen, Patrick.** Odyssey of Political Theory: The Politics of Departure & Return. 288p. 2000. 35.00 (*0-8476-9622-7*) Rowman.
Deneen, Robert N. Stock Investing for Beginners. Lindsay, Verna D., ed. LC 98-90068. (Illus.). 125p. (YA). (gr. 8 up). 1998. pap. 20.00 (*0-9663142-0-4*) SoloProse Pub.
Deneen, Sally. Foghorn Outdoors: Florida Camping. 2nd ed. 670p. 2000. pap. 20.95 (*1-57354-079-X*) Avalon Travel.
Deneen, Sally & McClure, Robert. Florida Dog Lover's Companion: The Inside Scoop on Where to Take Your Dog. 2nd ed. (Illus.). 580p. 1998. pap. text 20.95 (*1-57354-042-0*) Avalon Travel.
Deneen, Sally, et al. Foghorn Outdoors: Florida Camping: The Complete Fuide to More Tahn 110,000 Campsites for RV's, Car Campers & Tenters. 670p. 1998. pap. text 20.95 (*1-57354-018-8*, Foghorn Outdoors) Avalon Travel.
Deneen, Sally, ed. see Knight-Ridder Corporation Staff.
DeNeff, Steve. Whatever Became of Holiness? The Urgency of Holiness in the Post-Modern Age Student Book. Drury, Keith et al, eds. 150p. 1996. pap., student ed. 9.95 (*0-89827-156-8*, BK978) Wesleyan Pub Hse.
DeNeff, Steve, et al. Whatever Became of Holiness? The Urgency of Holiness in the Post Modern Age. 158p. 1996. spiral bd. 14.95 (*0-89827-163-0*) Wesleyan Pub Hse.
***Denegar, Craig R.** Therapeutic Modalities for Athletic Training. LC 99-57433. (Athletic Training Education Ser.). (Illus.). 200p. 2000. 32.00 (*0-88011-838-5*) Human Kinetics.
Denegre, J. Thematic Mapping from Satellite Imagery: A Guidebook. LC 94-19073. (International Catalog of Sources for History of Physics & Allied Sciences Ser.). (ENG & FRE.). 200p. 1994. 126.50 (*0-08-042351-5*, Pergamon Pr) Elsevier.
Denegre, J., ed. Thematic Mapping from Satellite Imagery: An International Report. (Illus.). 214p. 1988. 123.00 (*1-85166-217-0*) Elsevier.
Denehy, Janice Ann, jt. auth. see Craft-Rosenberg, Martha.
Deneke, Frederick J., jt. auth. see Grey, Gene W.
***Denemark, Robert A.** World System History: The Social Science of Long-Term Change. LC 99-87145. 2000. pap. 32.99 (*0-415-23277-5*) Routledge.
— World System History: The Social Science of Long-Term Change. LC 99-87145. (Illus.). 2000. 100.00 (*0-415-23276-7*) Routledge.
Denemark, Robert A., jt. auth. see Burch, Kurt.
Denemark, Robert A., jt. auth. see Miller, Mark J.
Denemark, Robert A., jt. ed. see Chew, Sing C.
Denenberg. Logic for Computer Science. (C). 1990. 91.00 (*0-673-39970-2*) Addison-Wesley.
Denenberg, Barry. An American Hero: The True Story of Charles A. Lindbergh. LC 95-24628. 288p. (YA). (gr. 5 up). 1996. 16.95 (*0-590-46923-1*) Scholastic Inc.
— An American Hero: The True Story of Charles A. Lindbergh. (J). 1998. pap. 5.99 (*0-590-46955-X*) Scholastic Inc.
— An American Hero: The True Story of Charles A. Lindbergh. (J). 1998. 11.09 (*0-606-13123-X*, Pub. by Turtleback) Demco.
— The Journal of Ben Uchida: Citizen 13559, Mirror Lake Internment Camp, California, 1942. LC 98-40956. (My Name Is America Ser.). (Illus.). 156p. (J). (gr. 4-9). 1999. 10.95 (*0-590-48531-8*, Pub. by Scholastic Inc) Penguin Putnam.
— The Journal of William Thomas Emerson: A Revolutionary War Patriot: Boston, Massachusetts, 1774. LC 97-52938. (My Name Is America Ser.). (Illus.). 156p. (J). (gr. 4-9). 1998. 9.95 (*0-590-31350-9*, Pub. by Scholastic Inc) Penguin Putnam.
— Nelson Mandela: "No Easy Walk to Freedom" LC 90-8496. 176p. (J). (gr. 4-7). 1991. pap. 3.50 (*0-590-44154-X*) Scholastic Inc.
***Denenberg, Barry.** One Eye Laughing, the Other Weeping: The Diary of Julie Weiss. LC 00-21920. (Dear America Ser.). (Illus.). 256p. (YA). (gr. 4-9). 2000. 12.95 (*0-439-09518-2*) Scholastic Inc.
Denenberg, Barry. So Far from Home: The Diary of Mary Driscoll, an Irish Mill Girl, Lowell, Massachusetts, 1847. LC 97-5846. (Dear America Ser.). 166p. (J). (gr. 4-9). 1997. 9.95 (*0-590-92667-5*) Scholastic Inc.
— Stealing Home: The Story of Jackie Robinson. 50th ed. 128p. (J). (gr. 4-7). 1997. pap. 3.99 (*0-590-42560-9*) Scholastic Inc.

— Stealing Home, the Story of Jackie Robinson. (Scholastic Biography Ser.). (J). 1990. 9.09 (*0-606-11909-4*, Pub. by Turtleback) Demco.

— Story of Jackie Robinson. (Stealing Home Ser.). 1997. pap. 3.99 (*0-590-04553-9*) Scholastic Inc.

— Voices from Vietnam. LC 93-44886. 272p. (J). (gr. 7-9). 1995. 16.95 (*0-590-44267-8*) Scholastic Inc.

— Voices from Vietnam. LC 93-44886. 272p. (J). (gr. 3-9). 1997. mass mkt. 4.99 (*0-590-43530-2*) Scholastic Inc.

— Voices from Vietnam. 1997. 10.09 (*0-606-12040-8*, Pub. by Turtleback) Demco.

— When Will This Cruel War Be Over? The Civil War Diary of Emma Simpson, Gordonsville, Virginia, 1864. LC 95-25540. (Dear America Ser.). (Illus.). 156p. (J). (gr. 4-7). 1996. 9.95 (*0-590-22862-5*) Scholastic Inc.

Denenberg, Dennis. Toward a Human Curriculum. 1990. pap. 9.99 (*0-89824-612-1*) Trillium Pr.

***Denenberg, Dennis & Roscoe, Lorraine.** 50 American Heroes Every Kid Should Meet. LC 00-20301. (Illus.). (J). 2000. lib. bdg. write for info. (*0-7613-1612-4*) Millbrook Pr.

Denenberg, Dennis & Roscoe, Lorraine. Hooray for Heroes! Books & Activities Kids Want to Share with Their Parents & Teachers. LC 93-48983. (Illus.). 255p. 1994. 29.00 (*0-8108-2846-4*) Scarecrow.

Denenberg, Herbert S., jt. auth. see Kimball, Spencer L.

Denenberg, Larry, jt. auth. see Lewis.

Denenberg, R. V., jt. auth. see Denenberg, Tia S.

Denenberg, Richard V. & Braverman, Mark. The Violence-Prone Workplace: A New Approach to Dealing with Hostile, Threatening & Uncivil Behavior. LC 99-40898. 1999. 32.50 (*0-8014-3396-7*) Cornell U Pr.

Denenberg, Risa. Gynecological Care Manual for HIV Positive Women. 173p. (Orig.). 1993. pap. 12.95 (*0-929240-58-8*) EMIS.

Denenberg, Tia S. & Denenberg, R. V. Attorney's Guide to Drugs in the Workplace. LC 97-215678. x, 52 p. 1996. write for info. (*1-57073-267-1*) Amer Bar Assn.

Denenberg, Tia S. & Dennenberg, R. V. Alcohol & Drugs: Issues in the Workplace. LC 83-7560. (Illus.). 219p. 1983. reprint ed. pap. 67.90 (*0-608-04260-9*, 206501500012) Bks Demand.

Denend, G. Van, see Van Denend, G.

Denes, Agnes. Book of Dust: The Beginning & the End of Time & Thereafter. LC 88-51541. (Illus.). 120p. 1989. 75.00 (*0-89822-057-2*) Visual Studies.

Denes, J. & Keedwell, A. D. Latin Squares: New Developments in the Theory & Applications. (Annals of Discrete Mathematics Ser.: No. 46). 454p. 1991. 169.50 (*0-444-88899-3*, North Holland) Elsevier.

Denes, Magda. Castles Burning: A Child's Life in War. LC 96-16311. 384p. 1997. 24.00 (*0-393-03966-8*) Norton.

— Castles Burning: A Child's Life in War. LC 97-41199. 384p. 1998. per. 13.00 (*0-684-84688-8*) S&S Trade.

Denes, Thomas A. The Waterproof Coach: The Waterproof Workout Book for Fitness Swimmers & Triathletes. LC 97-93074. (Illus.). 54p. 1997. pap. 29.95 (*0-9656230-0-9*) Ancnt Mariner.

Denes, Tibor. Fak, Tavak, Tengerek. LC 66-29554.Tr. of Trees, Lakes & Seas Short Stories. 1967. pap. 5.00 (*0-911050-29-9*) Occidental.

DeNeui, Don. America's Fighting Railroads: A World War II Pictorial History. LC 96-68879. (Illus.). 144p. (Orig.). 1996. pap. 12.95 (*1-57510-001-0*) Pictorial Hist.

Deneulin, Luc, et al, trs. from FRE. Four Plays of Paul Willems: Dreams & Reflections. LC 92-23402. (World Literature in Translation Ser.: Vol. 23). 484p. 1992. text 25.00 (*0-8240-0035-8*) Garland.

Denevan, W. M. & Padoch, Christine, eds. Swidden Fallow Agroforestry in the Peruvian Amazon. LC 87-30785. (Advances in Economic Botany Ser.: Vol. 5). (Illus.). 108p. (C). 1988. pap. 22.25 (*0-89327-325-2*) NY Botanical.

Denevan, William, tr. see Garcia, Ramiro.

Denevan, William, tr. see Silvers, Stephen Mark.

***Denevan, William M.** Cultivated Landscapes of Native Amazonia & the Andes: Triumph over the Soil. (Oxford Geographical & Environmental Studies). (Illus.). 400p. 2001. text 95.00 (*0-19-823407-4*) OUP.

Denevan, William M., ed. The Native Population of the Americas in 1492. 2nd ed. LC 91-40042. (Illus.). 398p. (C). 1992. reprint ed. pap. 19.95 (*0-299-13434-2*) U of Wis Pr.

Deneve, Carmen, tr. see Condon, John C.

DeNevers, Noel. Fluid Mechanics. LC 78-91144. (Engineering Ser.). (C). 1970. text. write for info. (*0-201-01497-1*) Addison-Wesley.

DeNevi, Angela. A Year in My Garden. (Illus.). 185p. 1989. pap. 7.50 (*0-930830-12-1*) Great Basin.

DeNevi, Don. Great West Train Robberies. 202p. 1976. pap. 12.95 (*0-88839-287-7*) Hancock House.

— Riddle of the Rock: The Only Successful Escape from Alcatraz. LC 90-26764. (Illus.). 245p. (C). 1991. 29.95 (*0-87975-647-0*) Prometheus Bks.

— U. S. Military Railway Service: America's Soldier-Railroaders in WW II. (Illus.). 160p. 28.00 (*1-55046-021-8*) Boston Mills.

DeNevi, Don & Moulin, Thomas. Gabriel Moulin's San Francisco Peninsula. Bonnett, Wayne, ed. LC 85-20236. (Illus.). 184p. 1985. 45.00 (*0-915269-01-5*) Windgate Pr.

DeNevi, Donald P., jt. auth. see Green, Aaron G.

Denevi, Marco. Rosaura a las Diez. Yates, Donald A., ed. (SPA., Illus.). 219p. (C). 1964. pap. text 21.00 (*0-13-783234-6*) P-H.

DeNevi, Mary K. Moving for Relief from the Automatic Stay in Bankruptcy. LC 92-60919. 114p. 1992. pap. text 45.00 (*0-944490-87-5*) Mass CLE.

Denez, Deeva. Uncaged. Bliss, Lee, ed. LC 97-78029. (Illus.). 257p. 1997. mass mkt. 14.95 (*0-9661625-5-2*) Advantage Pub.

Denez, Per. Dictionnaire du Breton Parle a Douarnenez Vol. 3: Geriadur Brehoneg Douarnenez, Ar Sevel-Bagou, Lien, Gwerniou. (BRE & FRE.). 136p. 1984. pap. 19.95 (*0-7859-8158-6*, 2868630006) Fr & Eur.

— Dictionnaire du Breton Parle a Douarnenez Vol. 4: Geriadur Brehoneg Douarnenez, Ar Beskerezh, No. 4. (BRE & FRE.). 152p. 1985. pap. 24.95 (*0-7859-8161-6*, 2868630103) Fr & Eur.

Deneze, Donna. The Lovers Voice. 50p. 1997. pap. text 10.00 (*1-886706-21-2*) Hickory Hse.

Denfeld, D. Colt. Hold the Marianas: The Japanese Defense of the Islands. LC 97-8219. (Illus.). 250p. 1997. 29.95 (*1-57249-014-4*) White Mane Pub.

Denfeld, Duane. A Guide to World War Two Museums, Relics & Sites in Europe. 222p. 1979. pap. text 36.95 (*0-89126-079-X*) MA-AH Pub.

Denfeld, Rene. The New Victorians: A Young Woman's Challenge to the Old Feminist Order. 352p. 1995. 21.95 (*0-446-51752-6*) Warner Bks.

Denffer, Ahmad Von. Ulum Al-Quran: An Introduction to the Sciences of the Quran. 1996. pap. text 10.50 (*0-86037-132-8*) Kazi Pubns.

Denffer, Ahmad Von, see Von Denffer, Ahmad.

Denfield, Duane. Streetwise Criminology. 1986. 15.95 (*0-87073-663-9*) Schenkman Bks Inc.

Deng, Dean Y. & Ballin, Enid. Qigong - a Legacy in Chinese Healing: The Eight Treasures. LC 97-67808. (Illus.). 160p. 1997. pap. 18.50 (*0-9657560-8-4*) Qigong Intl.

Deng, Francis. Security Problems: An African Predicament. LC 81-71701. (Hans Wolff Memorial Lectures). 1982. pap. text 5.00 (*0-941934-36-5*) Indiana Africa.

Deng, Francis M. Cry of the Owl. 340p. 1989. text 18.95 (*0-936508-25-6*) Barber Pr.

— Dinka Folktales: African Stories from the Sudan. LC 73-82901. (Illus.). 200p. 1974. 39.50 (*0-8419-0138-4*, Africana) Holmes & Meier.

— The Dinka of the Sudan. (Illus.). 174p. (C). 1984. reprint ed. pap. text 11.95 (*0-88133-082-5*) Waveland Pr.

— Protecting the Dispossessed: A Challenge for the International Community. 175p. (C). 1993. 34.95 (*0-8157-1826-8*); pap. 14.95 (*0-8157-1825-X*) Brookings.

— War of Visions: Conflicts of Identities in the Sudan. 577p. (C). 1995. 52.95 (*0-8157-1794-6*); pap. 24.95 (*0-8157-1793-8*) Brookings.

Deng, Francis M. & Gifford, Prosser. The Search for Peace & Unity in the Sudan. LC 87-50714. (Illus.). 208p. (Orig.). (C). 1987. pap. text 17.50 (*0-943875-00-5*); lib. bdg. 32.75 (*0-943875-01-3*) W Wilson Ctr Pr.

Deng, Francis M. & Lyons, Terrence, eds. African Reckoning: A Quest for Good Governance. LC 98-25409. 300p. 1998. pap. text 19.95 (*0-8157-1783-0*) Brookings.

— African Reckoning: A Quest for Good Governance. LC 98-25409. 300p. 1998. text 49.95 (*0-8157-1784-9*) Brookings.

Deng, Francis M. & Minear, Larry. The Challenges of Famine Relief: Emergency Operations in the Sudan. 165p. (C). 1992. 32.95 (*0-8157-1792-X*); pap. 12.95 (*0-8157-1791-1*) Brookings.

Deng, Francis M. & Zartman, I. William, eds. Conflict Resolution in Africa. 410p. 1991. 44.95 (*0-8157-1798-9*); pap. 19.95 (*0-8157-1797-0*) Brookings.

Deng, Francis M., et al. Sovereignty As Responsibility: Conflict Management in Africa. 275p. 1996. 42.95 (*0-8157-1828-4*); pap. 18.95 (*0-8157-1827-6*) Brookings.

Deng, Francis M., jt. auth. see Cohen, Roberta.

Deng, Francis M., jt. auth. see Daly, Martin W.

Deng, Francis M, jt. ed. see An-Na'im, Abdullahi A.

Deng, Francis M., jt. ed. see Cohen, Roberta.

Deng, Gang. Chinese Maritime Activities & Socioeconomic Development, c 2100 B.C.- 1900 A.D., 188. LC 96-53028. (Contributions in Economics & Economic History Ser.: Vol. 188). 248p. 1997. 65.00 (*0-313-29212-4*, Greenwood Pr) Greenwood.

— Development Versus Stagnation: Technological Continuity & Agricultural Progress in Pre-modern China, 141. LC 92-19427. (Contributions in Economics & Economic History Ser.: No. 141). 288p. 1993. 62.95 (*0-313-28646-9*, DDV, Greenwood Pr) Greenwood.

— Maritime Sector, Institutions & Sea Power of Premodern China, 212. LC 99-11267. (Contributions in Economics & Economic History Ser.: Vol. 212). 312p. 1999. 69.50 (*0-313-30712-1*) Greenwood.

***Deng, Gang.** The Premodern Chinese Economy: Structural Equilibrium & Capitalist Sterility. LC 98-25901. 5p. 1999. write for info. (*0-415-16239-4*) Routledge.

Deng, J. T., jt. ed. see Li, B. H.

Deng, Lual, et al, eds. Democratization & Structural Adjustment in Africa in the 1990s. 215p. (Orig.). 1991. pap. 15.00 (*0-942615-12-3*) U Wis African Stud.

Deng, Lual A. Rethinking African Development: Toward a Framework for Social Integration & Ecological Harmony. LC 97-36477. 193p. 1997. 79.95 (*0-86543-607-X*); pap. 21.95 (*0-86543-608-8*) Africa World.

Deng, M. & Dodson, C. T. J. Paper: An Engineered Stochastic Structure. LC 94-17554. 308p. 1994. 69.00 (*0-89852-283-8*, 0101R238) TAPPI.

Deng, Peng. China's Crisis & Revolution Through American Lenses, 1944-1949. LC 93-36355. (C). 1994. 34.50 (*0-8191-9313-5*) U Pr of Amer.

— Private Education in Modern China. LC 97-5584. 200p. 1997. 55.00 (*0-275-95639-3*, Praeger Pubs) Greenwood.

Deng, Peng, jt. auth. see Chen, Jie.

Deng, Shu-Sen & Wang, S. C., eds. Laser Processing of Materials & Industrial Applications, Vol. 2888. 438p. 1996. 102.00 (*0-8194-2289-4*) SPIE.

— Laser Processing of Materials & Industrial Applications II. (Proceedings of SPIE Ser.: Vol. 3550). 538p. 1998. 124.00 (*0-8194-3011-0*) SPIE.

Deng, Song-Jiu, ed. Heat Transfer Enhancement & Energy Conservation. 1000p. 1990. 295.00 (*0-89116-861-3*) Hemisp Pub.

Deng Xiaoping. Speeches & Writings. (Leaders of the World Ser.). (Illus.). 115p. 1984. 19.25 (*0-08-028165-6*, Pergamon Pr); pap. 9.75 (*0-08-028166-4*, Pergamon Pr) Elsevier.

Deng, Yong. Promoting Asia-Pacific Economic Cooperation: Perspectives from East Asia. LC 97-7476. 176p. 1997. text 65.00 (*0-312-17510-8*) St Martin.

Deng, Z., et al, eds. Differential Equations & Control Theory: Proceedings, International Conference on Differential Equations & Control Theory, Wuhan-Shih, China, 1994. LC 95-40842. (Lecture Notes in Pure & Applied Mathematics Ser.: Vol. 176). (Illus.). 544p. 1995. pap. text 180.00 (*0-8247-9658-6*, QA370) Dekker.

Dengel, A., jt. auth. see Spitz, Lewis.

***DENGELEGI, PAUL.** Liberator. 1999. mass mkt. 5.99 (*0-515-12689-6*, Jove) Berkley Pub.

Denger, Michael L. & American Bar Association Staff. State Antitrust Practice & Statutes , 3 vols. LC 90-85322. 1990. write for info. (*0-89707-637-0*, ABA4) ABA Prof Educ Pubns.

Dengerink, H. A. & Cross, H. J., eds. Training Professionals for Rural Mental Health. LC 81-16288. 143p. reprint ed. pap. 44.40 (*0-8357-3797-7*, 203652400003) Bks Demand.

Dengevin, K. The Idea of Justice in Christian Perspective. 1978. pap. 2.95 (*0-88906-102-5*) Shiloh Pubns.

Denglen, Amy. Between Leap & Landing. (Chapbook Ser.). 40p. 1999. pap. 8.95 (*0-9649463-9-4*) Folly Cove.

Dengler, et al. Lawrence. (Images of America Ser.). 1995. pap. 16.99 (*0-7524-0229-3*) Arcadia Publng.

Dengler, Marianna. Fiddlin' Sam. LC 99-19711. 32p. (J). (gr. 1-4). 1999. write for info. (*0-87358-742-1*, Rising Moon Bks) Northland AZ.

— The Worry Stone. LC 96-33837. (Illus.). 40p. (J). (gr. 1-3). 1996. lib. bdg. 14.95 (*0-87358-642-5*, Rising Moon Bks) Northland AZ.

Dengler, Sandra. Code of Honor. LC 88-18729. 256p. (Orig.). 1988. pap. 8.99 (*0-87123-994-9*) Bethany Hse.

***Dengler, Sandy.** Code of Honor. LC 00-34752. 2000. write for info. (*0-7862-2710-9*) Five Star.

Dengler, Sandy. D. L. Moody: God's Salesman. (Preteen Biography Ser.). (J). (gr. 2-7). mass mkt. 4.99 (*0-8024-1786-8*, 600) Moody.

— East of Outback. (Australian Destiny Ser.: Vol. 4). 336p. (Orig.). 1990. pap. 8.99 (*1-55661-117-X*) Bethany Hse.

— Gila Monster. LC 93-38158. (Mirage Mysteries Ser.: No. 4). 276p. (Orig.). 1994. pap. 9.99 (*1-56476-238-6*, 6-3238, Victor Bks) Chariot Victor.

— Hyaenas. LC 98-85605. 356p. 1998. 24.99 (*0-9661879-1-1*, SKP98-42) St Kitts.

— John Bunyan: Writer of Pilgrim's Progress. (Preteen Biography Ser.). (J). (gr. 2-7). mass mkt. 4.99 (*0-8024-4352-4*, 603) Moody.

— The Last Dinosaur. LC 93-36488. (Mirage Mysteries Ser.). 276p. (Orig.). 1994. pap. 9.99 (*1-56476-235-1*, 6-3235, Victor Bks) Chariot Victor.

— Opal Fire. (Serenade Saga Ser.: No. 27). 1986. pap. 1.49 (*0-310-47412-4*, 15587P) Zondervan.

— Power of Pinjarra. LC 88-32756. (Australian Destiny Ser.: No. 2). 272p. (Orig.). 1989. pap. 8.99 (*1-55661-057-2*) Bethany Hse.

— The Quick & the Dead. large type ed. LC 98-39768. 1998. 22.95 (*0-7862-1647-6*) Thorndike Pr.

— Song of the Nereids. (Serenade Saga Ser.: No. 5). 192p. 1984. pap. 1.49 (*0-310-46472-2*, 15507P) Zondervan.

— Summer Snow. (Serenade Saga Ser.: No. 1). 192p. 1984. pap. 1.49 (*0-310-46432-3*, 15503P) Zondervan.

— Susanna Wesley: Servant of God. (YA). (gr. 5 up). mass mkt. 5.99 (*0-8024-8414-X*, 295) Moody.

— Taste of Victory. LC 89-18075. (Australian Destiny Ser.: Vol. 3). 272p. (Orig.). 1989. pap. 8.99 (*1-55661-085-8*) Bethany Hse.

— This Rolling Land. (Serenade Saga Ser.: No. 30). 1986. pap. 1.49 (*0-310-46872-8*, 15546P) Zondervan.

— Winterspring, No. 12. (Serenade Saga Ser.). 1985. pap. 1.49 (*0-310-46632-6*, 15522P) Zondervan.

Dengler, Sandy, et al. Ageless Love Vol. 2: Juliana of Clover Hill; The Song of the Nereids; Yankee Bride, Vol. 2. 450p. 1996. 19.99 (*0-310-20956-0*) Zondervan.

Dengler, Sandy, jt. auth. see Jones, Robin L.

Dengler, Sandy, jt. auth. see Minirth, Frank.

Dengler, William. In Pictures Mount Rainier: The Continuing Story. LC 91-60039. (Illus.). 48p. (Orig.). 1992. pap. 7.95 (*0-88714-054-8*) KC Pubns.

— In Pictures Mount Rainier: The Continuing Story. Morales, Brigitte, tr. (GER., Illus.). 48p. (Orig.). 1992. pap. 8.95 (*0-88714-740-2*) KC Pubns.

— In Pictures Mount Rainier: The Continuing Story. Petzinger, Saori, tr. (JPN., Illus.). 48p. (Orig.). 1992. pap. 8.95 (*0-88714-742-9*) KC Pubns.

Dengler, William & Le Bras, Yvon. In Pictures Mount Rainier: The Continuing Story. (FRE., Illus.). 48p. (Orig.). 1992. pap. 8.95 (*0-88714-741-0*) KC Pubns.

Dengo, G. & Case, J., eds. The Caribbean Region. (DNAG, Geology of North America Ser.: Vol. H). (Illus.). 538p. 1990. 40.00 (*0-8137-5212-4*) Geol Soc.

Denham. Perspectives on the Third World. 1999. text 49.95 (*0-312-15881-5*) St Martin.

Denham, et al. Narrative of Travels & Discoveries in Northern & Central Africa, Vol. 1. 432p. 1985. 250.00 (*1-85077-057-3*, Pub. by Darf Pubs Ltd) St Mut.

— Narrative of Travels & Discoveries in Northern & Central Africa, Vol. 2. 432p. 1985. 250.00 (*1-85077-058-1*, Pub. by Darf Pubs Ltd) St Mut.

— Narrative of Travels & Discoveries in Northern & Central Africa, Vols. 1 & 2. 1985. write for info. (*0-7855-2568-8*, Pub. by Darf Pubs Ltd) St Mut.

Denham & Naylor Staff. Thirty Training Sessions for Effective Presentation. 348p. 1995. ring bd. 271.95 (*0-566-07517-2*) Ashgate Pub Co.

Denham, Alice. The Ghost & Mrs. Muir. 132p. reprint ed. lib. bdg. 18.95 (*0-88411-826-6*) Amereon Ltd.

***Denham, Alison.** Metaphor & Moral Experience. (Oxford Philosophical Monographs). 376p. 2000. text 65.00 (*0-19-824010-4*) OUP.

Denham, Andrew. British Think Tanks & the Climate of Opinion. LC 99-162570. 222p. 1998. 79.95 (*1-85728-496-8*); pap. 24.95 (*1-85728-497-6*) Taylor & Francis.

— Think-Tanks of the New Right. LC 96-24901. (Illus.). 240p. 1996. text 77.95 (*1-85521-868-2*, Pub. by Dartmth Pub) Ashgate Pub Co.

***Denham, C. Barry.** My Brothers Keeper. (Orig.). 2000. pap. 14.95 (*1-891929-61-5*) Four Seasons.

Denham, Dale H. Denham Threads: The Descendants of Hezekiah Stout Denham (1802-1886) & His Wife Winney Littell (1803-1863), 1802-1991. LC 90-85748. (Illus.). 302p. 1992. 35.00 (*0-9628552-0-0*) Denham Bks.

Denham, Diana. Gypsies in Social Space. LC 80-51689. 120p. 1981. per. 10.00 (*0-918660-14-9*) Ragusan Pr.

Denham, H. M. Southern Turkey, the Levant & Cyprus: A Sea-Guide to the Coasts & Islands. (Illus.). 1976. 19.95 (*0-393-03198-5*) Norton.

Denham, H. R., ed. A Catalogue of Printed Books in the Wellcome Historical Medical Library Vol. III: Books Printed from 1641-1850, F-L. 565p. 1976. 100.00 (*1-57898-250-2*) Martino Pubng.

Denham, H. R., jt. ed. see Symons, H. J. M.

Denham, Henry. Inside the Nazi Ring. LC 84-25295. (Illus.). 274p. 1985. 32.00 (*0-8419-1024-3*) Holmes & Meier.

***Denham, James M.** Cracker Times & Pioneer Lives: The Florida Reminiscences of George Gillett Keen & Sarah Pame. 272p. 2000. 39.95 (*1-57003-346-3*) U of SC Pr.

Denham, James M. A Rogue's Paradise: Crime & Punishment in Antebellum Florida, 1821-1861. LC 96-24837. 336p. 1997. text 39.95 (*0-8173-0847-4*) U of Ala Pr.

Denham, Jean. Enhancing Teaching & Learning: A Leadership Guide for School Library Media Specialists. LC 98-18950. xiii, 259p. 1998. pap. 45.00 (*1-55570-328-3*) Neal-Schuman.

Denham, John. Poetical Works. (BCL1-PR English Literature Ser.). 362p. 1992. reprint ed. lib. bdg. 89.00 (*0-7812-7344-7*) Rprt Serv.

Denham, Joyce. A Child's Book of Celtic Prayers. (Illus.). 26p. (J). (ps up). 1998. 14.95 (*0-8294-1077-5*) Loyola Pr.

Denham, M. J. Care of the Long-Stay Elderly Patient. 3rd ed. (Illus.). 320p. 1997. pap. 49.95 (*1-56593-445-8*, 1118) Singular Publishing.

Denham, M. J., ed. Infections in the Elderly. (Modern Geriatric Medicine Ser.). 1986. text 155.50 (*0-85200-800-7*) Kluwer Academic.

Denham, M. J. & Laub, A. J., eds. Advanced Computing Concepts & Techniques in Control Engineering. (NATO Asi Series F: Vol. 47). (Illus.). vi, 518p. 1988. 135.95 (*0-387-50037-5*) Spr-Verlag.

Denham, Mark E. & Lombardi, Mark O., eds. Perspectives on Third-World Sovereignty. LC 95-26835. (International Political Economy Ser.). 240p. 1996. text 59.95 (*0-312-16039-9*) St Martin.

Denham, Mark E., jt. ed. see Slawner, Karen.

Denham, Michael A. The Denham Tracts Vol. I-II: A Collection of Folk-Lore. Hardy, James, ed. (Folk-Lore Society, London Monographs: Vols. 29 & 35). 1972. reprint ed. pap. 78.00 (*0-8115-0513-8*) Periodicals Srv.

Denham, Paul. Dorothy Livesay & Her Works. (Canadian Author Studies). 47p. (C). 1987. pap. text 9.95 (*0-920763-22-7*, Pub. by ECW) Genl Dist Srvs.

Denham, Reginald. Suspect. 1944. pap. 5.25 (*0-8222-1103-3*) Dramatists Play.

Denham, Reginald, jt. auth. see Orr, Mary.

Denham, Reginald, jt. auth. see Percy, Edward.

Denham, Robert, jt. auth. see Strathmeyer, Jeffrey A.

Denham, Robert, ed. see Dennis-Strathmeyer, Jeffrey A.

Denham, Robert D. Northrop Frye: An Annotated Bibliography of Primary & Secondary Sources. 1987. text 60.00 (*0-8020-2630-3*) U of Toronto Pr.

Denham, Robert D. & Willard, Thomas. The World in a Grain of Sand: Twenty-Two Interviews with Northrop Frye. LC 90-15518. 359p. (C). 1991. text 59.95 (*0-8204-1215-5*) P Lang Pubng.

Denham, Robert D. & Willard, Thomas, eds. Visionary Poetics: Essays on Northrop Frye's Criticism. IX, 164p. 1991. 37.95 (*0-8204-1216-3*) P Lang Pubng.

Denham, Robert D., ed. see Frye, Northrop.

Denham, Robert D., ed. see Frye, Northrop & Kemp, Helen.

Denham, Robert D., jt. ed. see Lee, Alvin A.

Denham, Scott D. Visions of War: Ideologies & Images of War in German Literature Before & After the Great War. LC 92-13305. (Germanic Studies in America: Vol. 64). 197p. 1992. 34.00 (*3-261-04503-5*) P Lang Pubng.

Denham, Scott D., et al, eds. A User's Guide to German Cultural Studies. LC 97-4768. (Social History, Popular Culture, & Politics in Germany Ser.). 576p. (C). 1997. pap. text 24.95 (*0-472-06656-0*, 06656) U of Mich Pr.

— A User's Guide to German Cultural Studies. LC 97-4768. (Social History, Popular Culture, & Politics in Germany Ser.). 576p. (C). 1997. text 59.50 (*0-472-09656-7*, 09656) U of Mich Pr.

An Asterisk (*) at the beginning of an entry indicates that the title is appearing for the first time.

Denham, Susanne A. Emotional Development in Young Children. LC 98-24230. (Series on Social & Emotional Development). 260p. 1998. lib. bdg. 39.95 (*1-57230-352-2*) Guilford Pubns.
— Emotional Development in Young Children. LC 98-24230. (Series on Social & Emotional Development). 260p. (C). 1998. pap. text 21.00 (*1-57230-360-3*) Guilford Pubns.
Denham, T. World Directory of Airliner Crashes. LC 96-75173. (Illus.). 320p. 1996. 29.95 (*1-85260-554-5*, Pub. by P Stephens) Motorbooks Intl.
Denham, Veronica. Love & Charity. large type ed. (Linford Romance Large Print Ser.). 256p. 1998. pap. 17.99 (*0-7089-5239-9*, Linford) Ulverscroft.
Denham, W. W. West Indian Green Monkeys: Problems in Historical Biogeography. (Contributions to Primatology Ser.: Vol. 24). (Illus.). viii, 80p. 1987. 41.75 (*3-8055-4518-5*) S Karger.
Denham, Wendy & Sansom, Elizabeth. Presentation Skills Training: 30 High-Involvement Training Designs. 330p. 1997. pap. 89.95 (*0-07-016393-6*) McGraw.
Denhamer, Janet. Taxation in Canada: 1995-1996 Edition. 2nd ed. 560p. (C). 1995. per. 44.95 (*0-256-17503-9*, Irwn McGrw-H) McGrw-H Hghr Educ.
Denhard, Janet. Scent Sense: An Essential Introduction to Aromatherapy for Kids. LC 98-36444. (Cosmic Kits Ser.). (Illus.). 96p. (YA). (gr. 5 up). 1998. pap. 19.95 (*1-901881-56-3*, Pub. by Element MA) Penguin Putnam.
Denhard, Jennifer, tr. see Casajuana, Carles.
Denhardt, Bob. Public Administration: An Action Orientation. 3rd ed. LC 98-71721. 320p. (C). 1998. text 69.50 (*0-15-505524-0*) Harcourt Coll Pubs.
Denhardt, David T., et al, eds. Osteopontin: Role in Cell Signalling & Adhesion. LC 95-11516. (Annals Ser.: Vol. 760). 1995. pap. 110.00 (*0-89766-940-1*) NY Acad Sci.
— The Single-Stranded DNA Phages. LC 78-60445. (Cold Spring Harbor Monographs). 730p. reprint ed. pap. 200.00 (*0-7837-5840-5*, 204555900006) Bks Demand.
Denhardt, J. G., Jr. Complete Guide to Estate Accounting & Taxes. 2nd ed. 1978. 39.95 (*0-13-160242-X*) P-H.
Denhardt, J. G., Jr. & Grider, John D. Complete Guide to Estate Accounting & Taxes. 4th ed. 280p. 1988. text 59.95 (*0-13-159872-4*, Busn) P-H.
Denhardt, Kathryn G. The Ethics of Public Service: Resolving Moral Dilemmas in Public Organizations, 195. LC 87-15060. (Contributions in Political Science Ser.: No. 195). 207p. 1988. 59.95 (*0-313-25517-2*, DQU/, Greenwood Pr) Greenwood.
Denhardt, Robert B. In the Shadow of Organization. LC 89-16498. (Studies in Government & Public Policy). viii, 160p. 1989. reprint ed. pap. 12.95 (*0-7006-0451-0*) U Pr of KS.
— Public Administration: An Action Orientation. 2nd ed. 450p. (C). 1981. text 62.00 (*0-534-24738-5*) Harcourt.
***Denhardt, Robert B.** The Pursuit of Significance: Strategies for Managerial Success in Public Organizations. 300p. (C). 2000. pap. 19.95 (*1-57766-114-1*) Waveland Pr.
Denhardt, Robert B. & Hammond, Barry R. Public Administration in Action: Readings, Profiles & Cases. LC 91-25592. 413p. (C). 1980. pap. text 43.00 (*0-534-15960-5*) Harcourt.
Denhardt, Robert B. & Stewart, William H., eds. Executive Leadership in the Public Service. LC 91-32950. 191p. reprint ed. pap. 59.30 (*0-608-09222-3*, 205272600005) Bks Demand.
Denhardt, Robert M. Foundation Dams of the American Quarter Horse. LC 82-40323. 240p. 1995. pap. 15.95 (*0-8061-2748-1*) U of Okla Pr.
— Foundation Sires of the American Quarter Horse. LC 75-40956. 1976. 39.95 (*0-8061-1337-5*) U of Okla Pr.
— Foundation Sires of the American Quarter Horse. LC 75-40956. (Illus.). 280p. 1997. pap. 15.95 (*0-8061-2947-6*) U of Okla Pr.
— The King Ranch Quarter Horses: And Something of the Ranch & the Men That Breed Them. LC 73-123340. (Illus.). 312p. 1995. pap. 19.95 (*0-8061-2771-6*, 2771) U of Okla Pr.
— Quarter Horses: A Story of Two Centuries. LC 67-15580. (Illus.). 1991. pap. 15.95 (*0-8061-2285-4*) U of Okla Pr.
Denhart, Jeffrey. Just Bones. 1997. mass mkt. 5.95 (*1-885173-45-8*) Write Way.
Denhart, Jeffrey, jt. auth. see Tilles, Stanley.
Denhiere, G. & Rossi, J. P. Text & Text Processing. (Advances in Psychology Ser.: Vol. 79). xii,414p. 1991. 169.50 (*0-444-88484-X*, North Holland) Elsevier.
Denhoff, Eric & Feldman, Steven A. Developmental Disabilities: Management Through Diet & Medication. LC 81-15138. (Pediatric Habilitation Ser.: No. 2). (Illus.). 277p. reprint ed. pap. 85.90 (*0-7837-0913-7*, 204121800019) Bks Demand.
Denholm. Elementary Algebra Part 2. rev. ed. 1987. text, teacher ed. 78.04 (*0-395-43444-0*) HM.
***Denholm, Ian, et al.** Insecticide Resistance: From Mechanisms to Management. LC 99-17258. 136p. 1999. text 65.00 (*0-85199-367-2*) OUP.
Denholm, Richard A. Basic Mathematics with Applications. LC QA0107.D393. 482p. reprint ed. pap. 149.50 (*0-7837-4052-2*, 204388200011) Bks Demand.
— Elementary Algebra Part 1: New Edition. 1987. text, teacher ed. 72.00 (*0-395-43441-6*) HM.
Denholtz. Galaxy 3000: Read-Along. (Illus.). 32p. (J). (gr. 3-6). 1983. pap. 9.95 (*0-87386-297-X*) Jan Prods.
— The Gift That Wasn't Perfect: Read-Along. (Illus.). 32p. (J). (ps-2). 1985. pap. 9.95 (*0-87386-262-7*) Jan Prods.
— Jenny Gets Glasses. (Illus.). 32p. (J). (ps-2). 1985. pap. 9.95 (*0-87386-258-9*) Jan Prods.
— Mystery at the Gym: Read-Along. (Illus.). 32p. (J). (gr. 3-6). 1984. pap. 9.95 (*0-87386-308-9*) Jan Prods.
— Mystery of the Jelly Bean Trail: Read-Along. (Illus.). 32p. (J). (gr. 3-6). 1983. pap. 9.95 (*0-87386-288-0*) Jan Prods.
— The Spirit in the Theater: Read-Along. (Illus.). 32p. (J). (gr. 3-6). 1984. pap. 9.95 (*0-87386-294-5*) Jan Prods.
***Denholtz, Elaine.** Balancing Work & Love: Jewish Women Facing the Family-Career Challenge. LC 00-9416. 2000. write for info. (*1-58465-001-X*) U Pr of New Eng.
— Having It Both Ways: A Report on Married Women with Lovers. 244p. 2000. pap. 15.95 (*0-595-09237-3*) iUniversecom.
Denholtz, Elaine. Playing for High Stakes: The Men, Money & Power of Corporate Wives. LC 86-2020. 210p. 1985. 16.95 (*0-88191-030-9*) Freundlich.
***Denholtz, Elaine Grudin.** Balancing Work & Love: Jewish Women Facing the Family-Career Challenge. 2000. 24.95 (*1-58465-000-1*) U Pr of New Eng.
Denholtz, Roni S. The Day the T. V. Broke. LC 86-81371. (January Bks.). (Illus.). 32p. (J). (gr. k-2). 1986. pap. 2.95 (*0-87386-012-8*) Jan Prods.
— The Day the TV Broke. unabridged ed. LC 86-81371. (Friends & Neighbors Ser.). (Illus.). 32p. (J). (gr. k-2). 1986. lib. bdg. 16.99 incl. audio (*0-87386-016-0*) Jan Prods.
— The Ghost in the New House. LC 86-81369. (January Bks.). (Illus.). 32p. (J). (gr. k-2). 1986. pap. 2.95 (*0-87386-013-6*) Jan Prods.
— The Ghost in the New House. unabridged ed. LC 86-81369. (Friends & Neighbors Ser.). (Illus.). 32p. (J). (gr. k-2). 1986. lib. bdg. 16.99 incl. audio (*0-87386-017-9*) Jan Prods.
DeNicola, Alejandro F., jt. auth. see Brown.
DeNicola, Deborah. Where Divinity Begins. LC 94-5067. 80p. (Orig.). 1994. pap. 9.95 (*1-882295-02-1*) Alice James Bks.
DeNicola, Deborah, ed. Orpheus & Company: Contemporary Poems on Greek Mythology. LC 98-49534. 354p. 1999. pap. 19.95 (*0-87451-918-7*); text 50.00 (*0-87451-917-9*) U Pr of New Eng.
Denicola, Robert C., jt. auth. see Brown, Ralph S.
Denies, Mark, jt. auth. see Meyers, Thomas.
Denig, E., ed. A Geography of Public Relations Trends. 1985. lib. bdg. 152.00 (*90-247-3207-7*) Kluwer Academic.
Denig, Edwin T. Five Indian Tribes of the Upper Missouri: Sioux, Arickaras, Assiniboines, Crees & Crows. Ewers, John C., ed. LC 61-9005. (Civilization of the American Indian Ser.: No. 59). (Illus.). 1975. pap. 16.95 (*0-8061-1308-1*) U of Okla Pr.
— Of the Crow Nation. Ewers, John C., ed. LC 76-43690. (BAE. Bulletin Ser.: 151). reprint ed. 27.50 (*0-404-15532-4*) AMS Pr.
***Denig, Edwin Thompson.** Assiniboine. (Illus.). 304p. 2000. pap. text 14.95 (*0-8061-3235-3*) U of Okla Pr.
Denig, Joseph. Small Sawmill Handbook: Doing It Right & Making Money. (Illus.). 192p. (Orig.). 1993. pap. 37.00 (*0-87930-286-0*) Miller Freeman.
Deniker, Joseph. The Races of Man: Outline of Anthropology & Ethnography. (Select Bibliographies Reprint Ser.). 1977. reprint ed. 49.95 (*0-8369-5932-9*) Ayer.
Deniker, P., ed. Collegium Internationale Neuro-Psychopharmacologicum, 10th Congress: Proceedings, 2 vols., Set. 1978. 777.00 (*0-08-021506-8*, Pub. by Pergamon Repr) Franklin.
Denikin, Anton. The White Army. 1973. lib. bdg. 59.95 (*0-8490-1290-2*) Gordon Pr.
Denikin, Anton I. The Career of a Tsarist Officer: Memoirs, 1872-1916. Patoski, Margaret, tr. from RUS. LC 75-14625. (Illus.). 363p. reprint ed. pap. 112.60 (*0-608-15951-4*, 203321500084) Bks Demand.
Denilson, E., ed. see Csoma, Sandor K.
Denim, Sioux. The Ghost of Teec Nos Pos. (Pseudonymous Ser.). (Illus.). 666p. 2000. 24.00 (*0-915090-08-2*) Firefall.
Denim, Sue. The Dumb Bunnies. LC 93-2255. (Dumb Bunnies Ser.). (Illus.). 32p. (J). (ps-3). 1994. 12.95 (*0-590-47708-0*, Blue Sky Press) Scholastic Inc.
— The Dumb Bunnies. (Dumb Bunnies Ser.). (Illus.). 32p. (J). (ps-3). 1997. pap. 19.95 (*0-590-99718-1*) Scholastic Inc.
— The Dumb Bunnies. (Dumb Bunnies Ser.). (Illus.). (J). (ps-3). 1998. pap. 4.99 (*0-590-47709-9*) Scholastic Inc.
— The Dumb Bunnies' Easter. LC 94-15050. (Dumb Bunnies Ser.). (Illus.). 32p. (J). (ps-3). 1995. 12.95 (*0-590-20241-3*, Blue Sky Press) Scholastic Inc.
— The Dumb Bunnies' Easter. (Dumb Bunnies Ser.). (Illus.). (J). (ps-3). 1998. pap. 4.99 (*0-590-20242-1*) Scholastic Inc.
— The Dumb Bunnies Go to the Zoo. LC 96-19984. (Dumb Bunnies Ser.). (Illus.). 32p. (J). (ps-3). 1997. 13.95 (*0-590-84735-X*) Scholastic Inc.
— The Dumb Bunnies Go to the Zoo. (Dumb Bunnies Ser.). (Illus.). (J). (ps-3). 1997. pap. write for info. (*0-590-10259-1*) Scholastic Inc.
— The Dumb Bunnies Go to the Zoo. (Dumb Bunnies Ser.). (Illus.). 32p. (J). (ps-3). 1998. pap. 4.99 (*0-590-84743-0*) Scholastic Inc.
— Make Way for Dumb Bunnies. LC 95-15311. (Dumb Bunnies Ser.). (Illus.). 32p. (J). (ps-3). 1996. 12.95 (*0-590-58286-0*, Blue Sky Press) Scholastic Inc.
— Make Way for Dumb Bunnies. (Illus.). 32p. (J). (ps-3). 1998. pap. 4.99 (*0-590-58288-7*) Scholastic Inc.
Denim, Sue, jt. auth. see Pilkey, Dav.
Dening, Greg. The Death of William Gooch: A History's Anthropology. Orig. Title: A History's Anthropology: The Death of William Gooch. 192p. 1995. pap. 39.95 (*0-522-84692-0*, Pub. by Melbourne Univ Pr) Paul & Co Pubs.
— The Death of William Gooch: A History's Anthropology. LC 95-7563. Orig. Title: A History's Anthropology: The Death of William Gooch. (Illus.). 256p. (C). 1995. pap. text 20.00 (*0-8248-1754-0*) UH Pr.
— Mr. Bligh's Bad Language: Passion, Power & Theater on the "Bounty. (Illus.). 459p. (C). 1992. text 54.95 (*0-521-38370-6*) Cambridge U Pr.
— Mr. Bligh's Bad Language: Passion, Power & Theatre on the "Bounty" (Canto Book Ser.). (Illus.). 459p. (C). 1994. pap. 11.95 (*0-521-46718-7*) Cambridge U Pr.
— Performances. LC 96-5031. (Illus.). 324p. 1996. pap. 21.00 (*0-226-14298-1*); lib. bdg. 45.00 (*0-226-14297-3*) U Ch Pr.
***Dening, Greg.** Readings/Writings. LC 98-226583. ix, 235 p. 1999. 29.95 (*0-522-84841-9*, Pub. by Melbourne Univ Pr) Paul & Co Pubs.
Dening, Jim. Readymade Business Letters. 173p. 1993. pap. 14.95 (*0-87243-192-4*) Templegate.
Dening, Sarah. Everyday I Ching. LC 96-47906. 224p. 1997. pap. 12.95 (*0-312-15122-5*) St Martin.
— The Mythology of Sex. (Illus.). 224p. 1996. 27.50 (*0-02-861207-8*) Macmillan.
— The Mythology of Sex: An Illustrated Exploration of Sexual Customs & Practices from Ancient Times to the Present. (Illus.). 224p. 1998. text 28.00 (*0-7881-5536-9*) DIANE Pub.
Dening, Walter. Life of Toyotomi Hideyoshi. 3rd ed. LC 79-136391. (BCL Ser. II). reprint ed. 34.50 (*0-404-02078-X*) AMS Pr.
Denington, Brian. A Little Book of Campfire Songs. 60p. 1995. 7.95 (*0-8118-0821-1*) Chronicle Bks.
***DeNinno, Joanne P. & Gill, Kim A.** "Can Do" Around the Home Word Retrieval: Fun & Games. (Illus.). 119p. (J). (ps-6). 1999. spiral bd., wbk. ed. 25.95 (*1-58650-073-2*, BK-271) Super Duper.
— "Can Do" Oral Motor Fun & Games. (Illus.). 98p. (J). (ps-2). 1997. spiral bd., wbk. ed. 25.95 (*1-58650-059-7*, BK-256) Super Duper.
Denio, F. B. & Denio, H. W. Denio: A Genealogy of Aaron Denion of Deerfield, Mass., 1704-1925. 345p. 1991. reprint ed. pap. 53.00 (*0-8328-2137-3*); reprint ed. lib. bdg. 63.00 (*0-8328-2136-5*) Higginson Bk Co
Denio, H. W., jt. auth. see Denio, F. B.
DeNiro, Alan. Black Hare: A Sequence. (Illus.). 28p. 1998. pap. 3.00 (*1-888431-17-2*) ASGP.
DeNiro, Elaine, photos by see Martin, Clarece.
Denis. Le Tresor. pap. text 3.95 (*0-88436-910-2*) EMC-Paradigm.
Denis, Alberta J. Spanish Alta California. 1992. reprint ed. lib. bdg. 75.00 (*0-7812-5024-2*) Rprt Serv.
Denis, Brigitte, ed. Control Technology in Elementary Education. LC 93-31096. (NATO ASI Series F: Computer & Systems Sciences, Special Programme AET: Vol. 116). ix, 312p. 1993. 78.95 (*0-387-56710-0*) Spr-Verlag.
Denis, Christopher & Denis, Michael. Favorite Families of American TV: A Celebration of Nearly Fifty Years of Television Families. (Illus.). 256p. (Orig.). 1991. pap. 15.95 (*0-8065-1255-5*, Citadel Pr) Carol Pub Group.
Denis, Claude. We Are Not You: First Nations & Canadian Modernity. LC 98-143829. 208p. (C). 1997. pap. 16.95 (*1-55111-118-7*) Broadview Pr.
Denis, Delphine. Grammaire du Francais. 1994. pap. 19.95 (*0-7859-9175-1*) Fr & Eur.
Denis, Ernest. La Boheme Depuis la Montagne-Blanche, 2 vols. 1981. reprint ed. lib. bdg. 59.00 (*0-686-71907-7*) Scholarly.
— Boheme Depuis la Montagne-Blanche, 2 vols. LC 70-144973. (FRE.). reprint ed. 59.00 (*0-403-00941-3*) Scholarly.
— Fin de l'Independance Boheme, 2 vols., Set. LC 76-151601. (BCL Ser. I). reprint ed. 125.00 (*0-404-02087-9*) AMS Pr.
— Huss et les guerres hussites. LC 77-8424. reprint ed. 59.50 (*0-404-16126-X*) AMS Pr.
Denis, Francois, jt. auth. see Carpenter, Scott.
Denis, Francoise. Barons et Chevaliers dans Raoul de Cambrai: Autopsie d'un Phenomene de Glissement. (American University Studies: Romance Languages & Literature: Ser. II, Vol. 114). 267p. (C). 1989. text 39.95 (*0-8204-1087-X*) P Lang Pubng.
Denis, Gabriel. Reign of Jesus Thru Mary. 1949. .0.00 (*0-910984-03-4*) Montfort Pubns.
Denis, George, tr. see Tertz, Abram, pseud & Sinyavsky, Andrei.
Denis-Huot, Christine. The Zebra: Striped Horse. LC 98-6149. (Animal Close-Ups Ser.). 32p. (J). (gr. k-3). 1999. pap. 6.95 (*0-88106-882-9*) Charlesbridge Pub.
Denis-Huot, Christine & Denis-Huot, Michel. The Elephant: Peaceful Giant. LC 92-72905. (Animal Close-Ups Ser.). (Illus.). 28p. (J). (ps-3). 1992. pap. 6.95 (*0-88106-427-0*) Charlesbridge Pub.
— The Giraffe: A Living Tower. LC 90-80286. (Animal Close-Ups Ser.). (Illus.). 28p. (J). (ps-3). 1993. pap. 6.95 (*0-88106-431-9*, A327) Charlesbridge Pub.
— The Hippopotamus: River Horse. LC 94-1631. (Animal Close-ups Ser.). (Illus.). 28p. (J). (ps-3). 1994. pap. 6.95 (*0-88106-433-5*) Charlesbridge Pub.
***Denis-Huot, Christine & Denis-Huot, Michel.** The Lion, King of the Beasts. LC 99-48027. (Animal Close-Ups Ser.). (Illus.). (J). 2000. pap. 6.95 (*1-57091-426-5*) Charlesbridge Pub.
Denis-Huot, Michel, jt. auth. see Denis-Huot, Christine.
Denis, I., ed. The Medical Management of Prostate Cancer, No. II. (ESO Monographs). (Illus.). 112p. 1991. 64.95 (*0-387-53443-1*) Spr-Verlag.
Denis, Jean. Traite de l'Accord de L'Espinette. 2nd ed. LC 68-16229. (Music Ser.). 1969. reprint ed. 21.50 (*0-306-70950-3*) Da Capo.
Denis, L., ed. Prostate Cancer 2000. LC 94-30517. (Monographs European School of Oncology). 1994. write for info. (*3-540-58296-7*) Spr-Verlag.
— Prostate Cancer 2000. LC 94-30517. (Monographs of the European School of Oncology). 1994. 86.95 (*0-387-58296-7*) Spr-Verlag.
Denis, L. & Veronesi, U., eds. Antiandrogens in Prostate Cancer. LC 95-45831. (ESO Monographs). (Illus.). 120p. 1996. 95.00 (*3-540-60599-1*) Spr-Verlag.
Denis, L. J., jt. ed. see Altwein, J. E.
Denis, Livia P. Pensamiento Geometrico. (SPA.). 134p. 1996. pap. write for info. (*0-929441-59-1*) Pubns Puertorriquenas.
Denis, Louis, ed. Urinary Tract Cancer: State of the Art: EORTC Data Center, Brussels, November 1995. (Journal Ser.: Vol. 31, Supplement 1, 1997). (Illus.). vi, 82p. 1997. pap. 69.75 (*3-8055-6466-X*) S Karger.
Denis, Louis, et al, eds. Controlled Clinical Trials in Urologic Oncology. LC 83-23102. (Monograph Series of the European Organization for Research on Treatment of Cancer: No. 13). (Illus.). 349p. 1984. reprint ed. pap. 108.20 (*0-608-00656-4*, 206124400007) Bks Demand.
Denis, M., jt. auth. see Logie, Robert H.
Denis, Michael, jt. auth. see Denis, Christopher.
Denis, Michael J. Genealogical Researching in Eastern Canada: An Address Guide. (Genealogical Researching Address Guides Ser.). 39p. (Orig.). 1981. pap. 4.50 (*0-935207-09-0*) Danbury Hse Bks.
— Genealogical Researching in Ontario: An Address Guide. (Genealogical Researching Address Guides Ser.). 11p. (Orig.). 1984. pap. 2.50 (*0-935207-98-8*) Danbury Hse Bks.
— Machias, Maine, Marriages, 1767-1827. 20p. 1984. pap. 3.00 (*0-935207-14-7*) Danbury Hse Bks.
— Maine Towns & Counties. (New England Towns & Counties Ser.). 73p. (Orig.). 1981. pap. 8.50 (*0-935207-02-3*) Danbury Hse Bks.
— Massachusetts Towns & Counties. (New England Towns & Counties Ser.). 46p. 1984. pap. 6.00 (*0-935207-03-1*) Danbury Hse Bks.
— New Hampshire Towns & Counties. (New England Towns & Counties Ser.). 27p. (Orig.). 1982. pap. 4.00 (*0-935207-04-X*) Danbury Hse Bks.
— Rhode Island Towns & Counties. (New England Towns & Counties Ser.). 8p. (Orig.). 1983. pap. 2.00 (*0-935207-05-8*) Danbury Hse Bks.
— Scarboro, Maine, Marriages of the Second Congregational Church. 21p. 1983. pap. 3.50 (*0-935207-12-0*) Danbury Hse Bks.
— Vermont Towns & Counties. (New England Towns & Counties Ser.). 35p. 1983. pap. 4.50 (*0-935207-06-6*) Danbury Hse Bks.
— York, Maine, Marriages, 1697-1760. 25p. 1985. pap. 4.00 (*0-935207-15-5*) Danbury Hse Bks.
Denis, Michael J., ed. Connecticut Towns & Counties. (New England Towns & Counties Ser.). 45p. (Orig.). 1985. pap. 7.00 (*0-935207-01-5*) Danbury Hse Bks.
— Machias, Maine, Families, 1767-1827. 24p. (Orig.). 1985. pap. 3.50 (*0-935207-99-6*) Danbury Hse Bks.
Denis, Michel, et al, eds. Cognitive & Neurological Approaches to Mental Imagery. 1988. text 211.50 (*90-247-3659-5*) Kluwer Academic.
Denis-Papin, Maurice. Dictionnaire Analogique et de Synonymes pour la Resolution des Problemes des Mots Croises. 6th ed.Tr. of Dictionary of Analogies & Synonyms for Resolving the Problems of Crossword Puzzle. (FRE.). 1989. reprint ed. pap. 29.95 (*0-7859-5119-9*) Fr & Eur.
Denis, Paul. Opportunities in Dance. (Opportunities In . . . Ser.). (Illus.). 160p. pap. 12.95 (*0-8442-6658-2*, 2970ID, VGM Career) NTC Contemp Pub Co.
— Opportunities in Dance. (Illus.). 160p. 1989. 13.95 (*0-8442-6657-4*, VGM Career) NTC Contemp Pub Co.
Denis, Philippe. The Dominican Friars in Southern Africa: A Social History, 1577-1990. LC 98-23784. (Studies in Christian Mission). xiv, 338p. 1998. 105.50 (*90-04-11144-1*) Brill Academic Pubs.
— Notebook of Shadows: Selected Poems, 1974-1980. Irwin, Mark, tr. from FRE. LC 82-82907. (Contemporary European Poetry Ser.). Orig. Title: Cahier d'ombres. 68p. (Orig.). 1982. pap. 5.00 (*0-910321-00-0*) Globe Pr.
Denis, Philippe, ed. Clinical Implications of Irritable Bowel Syndrome. 56p. 1997. pap. 38.70 (*3-11-015860-4*) De Gruyter.
Denis, Pierre. The Argentine Republic, Its Development & the Progress. McCabe, Joseph, tr. LC 75-41073. reprint ed. 41.50 (*0-404-14530-2*) AMS Pr.
Denis, R. G. Gambling Times Guide to Thoroughbred Racing. (Illus.). (Orig.). 1984. pap. 5.95 (*0-89746-005-7*) Gambling Times.
***Denis, Rafael Cardoso.** Art Academy in the Nineteeth Century. 2000. text. write for info. (*0-7190-5495-8*, Pub. by Manchester Univ Pr) St Martin.
— Art & the Academy in the 19th Century. 2000. pap. write for info. (*0-7190-5496-6*, Pub. by Manchester Univ Pr) St Martin.
***Denis, Rafael Cardoso & Trodd, Colin, eds.** Art & the Academy in the Nineteenth Century. LC 99-44154. (Illus.). 288p. 2000. pap. 26.00 (*0-8135-2795-3*); text 58.00 (*0-8135-2794-5*) Rutgers U Pr.
Denis, Renee R. To Live in Paradise. LC 96-42545. 368p. 1996. pap. 15.95 (*1-882897-07-2*) Lost Coast.
Denis, Serge, et al. Le Dictionnaire Espagnol-Francais et Francais-Espagnol. (FRE & SPA.). 904p. 1976. 85.00 (*0-8288-5650-8*, S33062) Fr & Eur.
Denis, Terri. A Daycare Mother's Manual: How to Start & Operate a Childcare Service in Your Home. LC 85-82160. 1986. pap. 7.00 (*0-936733-02-0*) Fred Robot Factory.
Denise, et al. Great Traditions in Ethics. 9th ed. LC 98-23647. (Philosophy Ser.). 1998. pap. 52.95 (*0-534-55139-4*) Wadsworth Pub.
***Denise, et al.** Great Traditions in Ethics. 10th ed. (Philosophy Ser.). (C). 2001. text 37.50 (*0-534-56091-1*) Wadsworth Pub.
Denise, Christopher, jt. illus. see Cohen, Caron Lee.

D

Denise, J. Paul & Pas, Harold. Combined Production & Storage System Compass Latest Developments in System Design. 1989. 150.00 (*90-6314-560-8*, Pub. by Lorne & MacLean Marine) St Mut.

Denise, Paul S. & Harris, Ian M., eds. Experiential Education for Community Development, 31. LC 88-25092. (Contributions to the Study of Education Ser.: No. 31). 307p. 1989. 65.00 (*0-313-26405-8*, DEX/, Greenwood Pr) Greenwood.

Denise, Robert P. Hiking the Colorado Trail: A Guide to Short & Long Hiking Trips along the Colorado Trail. LC 93-91387. (Illus.). 316p. (Orig.). 1993. pap. 14.95 (*0-9636416-0-3*) Lothlorien Pr.

Denise, Theodore C. & Peterfreund, Sheldon P. Great Traditions in Ethics. 7th ed. 438p. (C). 1991. mass mkt. 31.95 (*0-534-16494-3*) Wadsworth Pub.

Denise, Theodore C., et al. Great Traditions in Ethics. 8th ed. LC 95-7796. 452p. 1995. pap. 33.25 (*0-534-25512-4*) Wadsworth Pub.

Denish, D. William. The Big Twin High-Performance Guide, Vol. 1. LC 95-168827. (Illus.). 238p. 1994. per. 27.95 (*0-9640115-2-2*) Crystal Publns AZ.

— The V-Twin Tuner's Handbook, Vol. 1. 160p. 1994. per. 23.95 (*0-9640115-3-0*) Crystal Publns AZ.

***Denish, D. William.** The V-Twin Tuner's Handbook: How to Design & Tune Your Harley for Maximum Performance, Vol. 2. (Performance Pro Ser.). 272p. 2000. per. 31.95 (*0-9640115-5-7*) Crystal Publns AZ.

DeNisi, Angelo S. A Cognitive Approach to Performance Appraisal: A Program of Research. LC 96-353. (People & Organizations Ser.). (Illus.). 240p. (C). 1997. 75.00 (*0-415-11251-6*) Routledge.

Denisiv, E., jt. auth. see Berezin, I.

Denisoff, Dennis. Dog Years. per. 9.95 (*0-88978-234-2*, Pub. by Arsenal Pulp) LPC InBook.

— Queeries: Anthology of Gay Male Prose. 217p. 1993. per. 14.95 (*0-88978-271-7*, Pub. by Arsenal Pulp) LPC InBook.

— Tender Agencies. LC 95-109986. 132p. 1995. per. 12.95 (*1-55152-012-5*, Pub. by Arsenal Pulp) LPC InBook.

Denisoff, R. Serge. Great Day Coming: Folk Music & the American Left. LC 74-155498. (Music in American Life Ser). (Illus.). 232p. reprint ed. 72.00 (*0-8357-9680-9*, 201904200010) Bks Demand.

— Inside MTV. 373p. (C). 1990. pap. 29.95 (*0-88738-864-7*) Transaction Pubs.

— Solid Gold: The Popular Record Industry. LC 74-20194. 504p. 1995. pap. 29.95 (*0-87855-586-2*) Transaction Pubs.

— Tarnished Gold: The Record Industry Revisited. 350p. 1986. 29.95 (*0-88738-618-0*) Transaction Pubs.

— Waylon: A Biography. LC 82-24786. 389p. reprint ed. 120.60 (*0-608-16800-9*, 202755600055) Bks Demand.

Denisoff, R. Serge & Plasketes, George. The True Disbelievers: Is Elvis Really Alive? (Illus.). 319p. (C). 1995. 39.95 (*1-56000-186-0*) Transaction Pubs.

Denisoff, R. Serge, jt. ed. see Mcquarie, Donald.

Denison, Cara D. Fantasy & Reality: Drawings from the Sunny Crawford von Bulow Collection. LC 95-431. (Illus.). 109p. (Orig.). 1995. pap. 27.50 incl. Apple II (*0-87598-114-3*) Pierpont Morgan.

Denison, Cara D., et al. Exploring Rome in the Eighteenth Century: Piranesi & His Contemporaries. (Illus.). 296p. 1993. pap. 39.95 (*0-87598-097-X*) Pierpont Morgan.

— The Master's Hand: Drawings & Manuscripts from the Morgan Library, New York. LC 98-36210. 1998. 29.95 (*0-87598-126-7*) Pierpont Morgan.

Denison, Cara Dufour, et al, texts. The Master's Hand: Drawings & Manuscripts from the Pierpont Morgan Library, New York. (Illus.). 304p. 1999. 65.00 (*3-7757-0785-9*, Pub. by Gerd Hatje) Dist Art Pubs.

Denison, Daniel R. Corporate Culture & Organizational Effectiveness. 2nd ed. 267p. 1997. reprint ed. pap. write for info. (*0-9658612-0-1*) Aviat.

Denison, Daniel R. & Hart, Stuart L. Revival in the Rust Belt: Tracking the Evolution of an Urban Industrial Region. LC 87-26264. 224p. (Orig.). reprint ed. pap. 69.50 (*0-7837-5246-6*, 204498100005) Bks Demand.

Denison, E. Glenn & Bolton, Harry E. Denison Genealogy: Record of the Ancestors & Descendants of James Post Denison, Revolutionary War Soldier Who Moved from Saybrook, Connecticut, to Burlington, Otsego County, New York, in 1796. (Illus.). 130p. 1997. reprint ed. pap. 22.00 (*0-8328-8260-7*); reprint ed. lib. bdg. 32.00 (*0-8328-8259-3*) Higginson Bk Co.

Denison, Edward. Packaging Prototypes. 1999. pap. 35.00 (*2-88046-389-0*, Rotovision) Watsn-Guptill.

Denison, Edward F. Accounting for Slower Economic Growth: The United States in the 1970s. LC 79-20341. 212p. 1979. 44.95 (*0-8157-1802-0*); pap. 19.95 (*0-8157-1801-2*) Brookings.

— Accounting for United States Economic Growth: 1929-1969. LC 74-278. 355p. 1974. pap. 22.95 (*0-8157-1803-9*) Brookings.

— Estimates of Productivity Change by Industry: An Evaluation & an Alternative. 78p. 1989. 22.95 (*0-8157-1800-4*) Brookings.

— Trends in American Economic Growth, 1929-1982. LC 85-17413. 141p. 1985. pap. 16.95 (*0-8157-1809-8*) Brookings.

— Why Growth Rates Differ: Postwar Experience in Nine Western Countries. LC 67-27682. 1967. pap. 16.95 (*0-8157-1805-5*) Brookings.

Denison, Edward F. & Chung, William K. How Japan's Economy Grew So Fast: The Sources of Postwar Expansion. LC 76-10836. 285p. reprint ed. pap. 88.40 (*0-608-14559-9*, 202496300040) Bks Demand.

Denison, Edward F. & Poullier, Jean-Pierre. Why Growth Rates Differ: Postwar Experience in Nine Western Countries. LC 67-27682. 516p. 1967. reprint ed. pap. 160.00 (*0-608-01998-4*, 206265400003) Bks Demand.

Denison, George B. Denison. Record of the Descendants of Samuel Denison, Late of Floyd, Oneida County, New York, with Notices of Its Ancestry, Commencing with William Denison, Who Came to America in 1631 & Settled in Roxbury, Massachusetts. (Illus.). 72p. 1997. reprint ed. pap. 14.50 (*0-8328-8262-3*); reprint ed. lib. bdg. 24.50 (*0-8328-8261-5*) Higginson Bk Co.

Denison, Herbert. A Treatise on Photogravure. Lyons, Nathan, ed. (Reprint & Research Ser.). (Illus.). 142p. 1974. reprint ed. 11.95 (*0-87992-004-1*); reprint ed. pap. 6.50 (*0-685-05260-5*) Visual Studies.

Denison, J. Guest Book Muskoka Chairs. 96p. 1996. 16.00 (*1-55046-189-3*, Pub. by Boston Mills) Genl Dist Srvs.

Denison, James C. Life on the Brick Pile: Answers to Suffering from the Letters of Revelation. LC 97-36158. 1997. 20.00 (*0-86554-595-2*) Mercer Univ Pr.

***Denison, Janelle.** Aimer n'Est Pas Jouer. (FRE.). 2000. mass mkt. 3.99 (*0-373-34816-9*) Harlequin Bks.

— Baby Surprise, Vol. 460. large type ed. (Large Print Ser.). 2000. mass mkt. 3.50 (*0-373-15860-2*) Harlequin Bks.

— The Baby Surprise: Baby Boom. 2000. mass mkt. 3.50 (*0-373-03614-0*) Harlequin Bks.

Denison, Janelle. Bride Included: Back to the Ranch. 1999. per. 3.50 (*0-373-15811-4*, 1-15811-2) Harlequin Bks.

— Bride Included: Back to the Ranch. 1999. per. 3.50 (*0-373-03565-9*, 1-03565-8) Harlequin Bks.

***Denison, Janelle.** Christmas Fantasy. (Harlequin Temptation Ser.). 1999. mass mkt. 3.75 (*0-373-25859-3*, Harlequin) Harlequin Bks.

Denison, Janelle. A Dad for Daniel. (Back to the Ranch Ser.: No. 3546). 1999. per. 3.50 (*0-373-03546-2*, 1-03546-8) Harlequin Bks.

— A Dad for Daniel. large type ed. (Back to the Ranch Ser.: No. 392). 1999. mass mkt. 3.50 (*0-373-15792-4*, 1-15792-4) Harlequin Bks.

***Denison, Janelle.** Un Enfant a Aimer. (Azur Ser.: No. 787). (FRE.). 1999. mass mkt. 3.99 (*0-373-34787-1*, 1-34787-1) Harlequin Bks.

Denison, Janelle. Forbidden: Blaze. (Temptation Ser.: No. 732). 1999. per. 3.75 (*0-373-25832-1*, 1-25832-6) Harlequin Bks.

— Nick of Time. 1999. mass mkt. 4.50 (*0-373-82597-8*, 1-82597-5) Harlequin Bks.

— Private Fantasies. (Temptation Ser.). 1998. per. 3.75 (*0-373-25782-1*, 1-25782-3) Harlequin Bks.

— Private Pleasures. (Temptation Ser.: Vol. 679). 1998. per. 3.75 (*0-373-25779-1*, 1-25779-9) Harlequin Bks.

— Ready-Made Bride: (Whirlwind Weddings) (Romance Ser.: No. 3531). 1998. per. 3.50 (*0-373-03531-4*, 0-03531-1) Harlequin Bks.

— Ready-Made Bride: (Whirlwind Weddings) large type ed. (Larger Print Ser.: No. 377). 1998. per. 3.50 (*0-373-15777-0*, 1-15777-5) Harlequin Bks.

***Denison, Janelle.** Seduced. (Temptation Ser.). 2000. mass mkt. 3.99 (*0-373-25911-5*, 1259118) Harlequin Bks.

— Substitute Father. (Romance Ser.: Vol. 359). 2000. per. 3.50 (*0-373-03597-7*) Harlequin Bks.

— Tempted. (Temptation Ser.: Vol. 799). 2000. mass mkt. 3.99 (*0-373-25899-2*, 1-25899-5) Harlequin Bks.

— Vuelta A Casa. (Bianca Ser.).Tr. of Return to Home. (SPA.). 2000. mass mkt. 3.50 (*0-373-33567-9*, 1-33567-8) Harlequin Bks.

Denison, John. Micklethwaite's Muskoka. (Illus.). 192p. 1995. 48.00 (*1-55046-069-2*, Pub. by Boston Mills) Genl Dist Srvs.

Denison, John, ed. Casa Loma & the Man Who Made It. (Illus.). 48p. (Orig.). pap. 5.99 (*0-919822-48-7*, Pub. by Boston Mills) Genl Dist Srvs.

Denison, John H., Jr., jt. auth. see Ruppert, Karl.

***Denison, Karen.** Fly Patterns of Northern New Mexico. LC SH451.D448 2000. (Illus.). 2000. pap. 14.95 (*0-8263-2030-9*) U of NM Pr.

Denison, Katherine. I Wish I Could Fly Like a Bird. LC 96-61166. (Illus.). 24p. (Orig.). (J). (ps-4). 1996. pap. 17.95 (*0-9654351-5-6*) Wldwood Creat Ent.

Denison, Laurie. Step Back in Time, No.1. (Illus.). 48p. 1999. pap. 10.95 (*1-57377-060-4*) Easl Pubns.

***Denison, Laurie.** Step Back in Time, Vol. 2. 46p. 2000. 10.95 (*1-57377-095-7*, 0-19884-02328) Easl Pubns.

Denison, Lyn. Dream Lover. LC 97-10805. 240p. (Orig.). 1997. pap. 11.95 (*1-56280-173-2*) Naiad Pr.

— Gold Fever. LC 97-52748. 224p. (Orig.). 1998. pap. 11.95 (*1-56280-201-1*) Naiad Pr.

— Silver Threads. LC 98-44747. 224p. 1999. pap. 11.95 (*1-56280-231-3*) Naiad Pr.

***Denison, Lyn.** Wild One. 2000. pap. 11.95 (*0-9677753-4-5*) Bella Bks.

Denison, Mary A. Out of Prison. LC 74-164558. (American Fiction Reprint Ser.). 1977. reprint ed. 29.95 (*0-8369-7034-9*) Ayer.

Denison, Michael S. & Helferich, William. Receptor Interactions: Modulation of Signal Transduction & Gene Expression. LC 97-49036. (Target Organ Toxicology Ser.). 243p. 1998. 145.00 (*1-56032-633-6*) Taylor & Francis.

Denison Newspaper, Inc. Staff. History of Crawford County Iowa. (Illus.). 621p. 1987. 62.50 (*0-88107-084-X*) Curtis Media.

Denison, Patricia D., ed. John Osborne: A Casebook. LC 96-11610. (Casebooks on Modern Dramatists Ser.: Vol. 16). (Illus.). 238p. 1997. text 60.00 (*0-8240-7442-4*) Garland.

Denison, Richard & Ruston, John. Recycling & Incineration: Evaluating the Choices. LC 90-37971. 320p. 1990. text 40.00 (*1-55963-055-8*); pap. text 24.95 (*1-55963-054-X*) Island Pr.

Denison, Robert. Acanthodii. Kuhn, O. & Schultze, H. P., eds. (Handbook of Paleoichthyology: Vol. 5). (Illus.). 62p. 1979. text 70.00 (*3-437-30291-4*) Lubrecht & Cramer.

— Placodermi. Kuhn, O. & Schultz, H. P., eds. (Handbook of Paleoichthyology: Vol. 2). (Illus.). 128p. 1978. text 90.00 (*3-437-30265-5*) Lubrecht & Cramer.

Denison, Robert H. Early Devonian Lungfishes from Wyoming, Utah, & Idaho. LC 68-26373. (Field Museum of Natural History, Publication 1044, Anthropological Ser.: Vol. 17, No. 4). 62p. (Orig.). reprint ed. pap. 30.00 (*0-608-03777-X*, 206462000009) Bks Demand.

— A Review of the Habitat of the Earliest Vertebrates. LC 56-14639. (Chicago Natural History Museum, Publication 800, Fieldiana, Geology Ser.: Vol. 11, No. 8). 100p. reprint ed. pap. 31.00 (*0-608-03774-5*, 206461600009) Bks Demand.

Denison, Stephen. The Monument or Tombe-Stone: A Sermon Preached at the Funeral of Mrs. Elizabeth Juxon (1620) LC 96-21877. (History of Psychology Ser.). 96p. 1996. 50.00 (*0-8201-1498-7*) Schol Facsimiles.

Denison, Susie. The Dog Lover's Guide to Lake Tahoe. LC 98-96270. 125p. 1998. write for info. (*0-9664908-0-0*) Timbercreek Pubg.

Denison, T. S. Friday Afternoon Dialogues. LC 79-139763. (Granger Index Reprint Ser.). 1977. 19.95 (*0-8369-6217-6*) Ayer.

— A Mexican-Aryan Comparative Vocabulary. (SPA.). 1976. lib. bdg. 59.95 (*0-8490-0613-9*) Gordon Pr.

Denison, Tom, et al. Electronic Sources for Information: For Businesses in Australia & New Zealand, 1998-1999. 200p. 1999. pap. 49.95 (*1-877133-63-9*) Univ Otago Pr.

***Denisov, A. M.** Elements of the Theory of Inverse Problems. (Inverse & Ill-Posed Problems Ser.). 280p. 1999. 185.00 (*90-6764-303-3*, Pub. by VSP) Coronet Bks.

Denisov, E. Sonate: Guitar Solo. 1987. 35.00 (*0-7935-5550-7*, 50541010) H Leonard.

***Denisov, E. T. & Denisova, Taissa G.** Handbook of Antioxidants: Bond Dissociation Energies, Rate Constants, Activation Energies & Enthalpies of Reactions. 2nd ed. LC 99-40087. 289p. 1999. boxed set 99.95 (*0-8493-9004-4*) CRC Pr.

Denisov, Evgenii T. Handbook of Antioxidants: Bond Dissociation Energies, Rate Constants, Activation Energies, & Enthalpies of Reactions. 192p. 1995. boxed set 169.95 (*0-8493-9426-0*, 9426) CRC Pr.

— Liquid-Phase Reaction Rate Constants. LC 73-79419. 797p. reprint ed. pap. 200.00 (*0-608-16624-3*, 202630300049) Bks Demand.

Denisov, P. N. Principles of Constructing Linguistic Models. LC 72-88205. (Janua Linguarum, Ser. Minor: No. 91). 173p. (Orig.). 1973. pap. text 52.35 (*90-279-2376-0*) Mouton.

Denisova, L. N. Rural Russia: Economic, Social, & Moral Crisis. (Illus.). 207p. (C). 1995. 115.00 (*1-56072-212-6*) Nova Sci Pubs.

Denisova, L. V., jt. auth. see Belousova, L. S.

Denisova, P. N. & Morkovkina, V. V. Student Dictionary of Compound Words of the Russian Language. 688p. (C). 1978. 25.95 (*0-8285-5190-1*) Firebird NY.

Denisova, Taissa G., jt. auth. see Denisov, E. T.

Denissen, H. Atlas of Porcelain Restorations. (Illus.). 94p. 1990. write for info. (*88-299-0831-2*, Pub. by Piccin Nuova) Gordon & Breach.

Denissen, H., et al. Atlas of Porcelain Restorations. 94p. 1990. text 50.00 (*1-57235-012-1*) Piccin Nuova.

— Hydroxylapatite Implants. (Illus.). 168p. 1985. write for info. (*88-299-0293-4*, Pub. by Piccin Nuova) Gordon & Breach.

Denisson, C. Navarre: or Researches after the Descendants of Robert Navarre. (Illus.). 418p. 1990. reprint ed. pap. 63.00 (*0-8328-1615-9*); reprint ed. lib. bdg. 71.00 (*0-8328-1614-0*) Higginson Bk Co.

Denissov, A. I., ed. see Voronine, V. V.

Deniston, Keith & Miller, Phil. From the Temperate Zone. 142p. 1995. pap. 12.00 (*1-884754-24-4*) Potpourri Pubns.

Denitch. Socialist Debate: Beyond Red & Green. 256p. 49.95 (*0-7453-0381-1*, Pub. by Pluto GBR) Stylus Pub VA.

— Socialist Debate: Beyond Red & Green. (C). pap. 18.95 (*0-7453-0382-X*, Pub. by Pluto GBR) Stylus Pub VA.

Denitch, Bogdan. Ethnic Nationalism: The Tragic Death of Yugoslavia. 2nd rev. ed. LC 96-202073. 224p. (C). 1996. pap. 17.95 (*0-8166-2947-1*) U of Minn Pr.

Denitch, Bogdan D. The Legitimation of a Revolution: The Yugoslav Case. LC 75-18170. 272p. 1976. 42.50 (*0-300-01906-8*) Yale U Pr.

Denitz Smith, Jane & Johnson, Stephen. Mary by Myself. LC 93-47457. (Illus.). 160p. (YA). (gr. 3-7). 1999. pap. 4.95 (*0-06-440568-0*) HarpC Child Bks.

***Deniz, Gerardo.** Poems/Poems: Poems by Gerardo Deniz. 2000. 12.00 (*0-918786-51-7*) Lost Roads.

Deniz, Tuncer. Marathon: The Official Strategy Guide. 1995. pap. 19.95 (*0-7615-0084-7*) Prima Pub.

— Power Pete Official Secrets & Solutions. 1995. pap. text 12.95 (*0-7615-0293-9*) Prima Pub.

Denizeau, Claude. Dictionnaire des Parlers Arabes de Syrie, Liban et Palestine. (ARA & FRE.). 581p. 1961. pap. 105.00 (*0-7859-4893-7*) Fr & Eur.

Denizeau, Gerard. Jean Lurcat: Monograph & Catalogue Raisonne, 1910-1965. 1998. 295.00 (*2-940033-22-6*, Pub. by Acatos Edit) Antique Collect.

Denizen, Early, ed. see American Society of Mechanical Engineers Staff.

Denjong, Meindert. The Wheel on the School. 82p. pap. 5.95 (*0-8072-1539-2*) Listening Lib.

Denk, James, ed. see Moreno, Nancy & Tharp, Barbara.

Denkberg, Nathan. Hotel-Casino Job Title Descriptions. Wittemann, Ad, ed. 178p. (Orig.). (C). 1987. pap. 75.00 (*0-938481-47-9*) Camelot Consult.

Denke, Debbie. The Aspiring Jazz Pianist: A Jazz Piano Method for Both the Solo & Combo Pianist with Play along Tape, Beginning through Intermediate. LC 91-90969. 156p. (Orig.). (C). 1991. pap. text 31.95 (*0-9629465-4-0*) Wingspan Pubns.

Denke, Debbie. The Aspiring Jazz Pianist - Piano Method. 160p. 1996. pap. 24.95 (*0-7935-6722-X*) H Leonard.

Denke, Nancy J., et al. Rashes of Childhood Diseases. (Illus.). 92p. 1999. ring bd. 55.00 (*0-935890-47-5*) Emerg Nurses IL.

Denkel, Arda. The Natural Background of Meaning. LC 98-42961. (Boston Studies in the Philosophy of Science). 1p. 1998. write for info. (*0-7923-5331-5*) Kluwer Academic.

— Object & Property. (Studies in Philosophy). 274p. (C). 1996. text 54.95 (*0-521-55010-6*) Cambridge U Pr.

Denkels, Rochel & Silberman, Miriam. Shlamo Homelich & the Ashmedai. write for info. (*0-9614920-0-7*) Shain F.

***Denker, Alfred.** Historical Dictionary of Heidegger's Philosophy, No. 30. (Religions, Philosophies & Movements Ser.). 416p. 2000. 69.50 (*0-8108-3737-4*) Scarecrow.

Denker, Arnold & Parr, Larry. The Bobby Fischer I Knew & Other Stories. (Great Chess Literature Ser.). (Illus.). 400p. (Orig.). 1995. pap. 19.95 (*1-886040-18-4*) Hypermodern Pr.

Denker, Bert, ed. The Substance of Style: Perspectives on the American Arts & Crafts Movement. (Illus.). 448p. 1996. 40.00 (*0-912724-33-1*) Winterthur.

Denker, Ellen P. Lenox China: Celebrating a Century of Quality. (Illus.). 92p. (Orig.). 1990. pap. 22.95 (*0-8122-1327-0*) NJ State Mus.

Denker, Ellen P., jt. auth. see Atterbury, Paul.

Denker, Eric. In Pursuit of the Butterfly: Portraits of James McNeill Whistler. LC 95-931. (Illus.). 176p. (C). 1995. pap. 24.95 (*0-295-97463-X*) U of Wash Pr.

Denker, H. W. & Aplin, J. D., eds. Trophoblast Research Vol. 4: Trophoblast Invasion & Endometerial Receptivity, Novel Aspects of the Cell Biology of Embryo Implantation. LC 90-7197. (Illus.). 463p. (C). 1990. text 180.00 (*0-306-43520-9*, Kluwer Plenum) Kluwer Academic.

Denker, Henry. Doctor on Trial. large type ed. 604p. 1993. reprint ed. lib. bdg. 18.95 (*1-56054-603-4*) Thorndike Pr.

— A Place for Kathy: A Novel. LC 96-7259. 320p. 1997. 24.00 (*0-688-14963-4*, Wm Morrow) Morrow Avon.

— A Place for Kathy Cameron. large type ed. (Charnwood Large Print Ser.). 448p. 1998. 29.99 (*0-7089-9008-8*, Charnwood) Ulverscroft.

— This Child Is Mine. large type ed. (Charnwood Large Print Ser.). 464p. 1997. 27.99 (*0-7089-8929-2*, Charnwood) Ulverscroft.

— To Marcy with Love. large type ed. (Charnwood Large Print Ser.). 448p. 1997. 27.99 (*0-7089-8973-X*) Ulverscroft.

Denker, Joel, jt. auth. see Bhaerman, Steve.

Denker, John S. Neural Networks for Computing. LC 86-72481. (AIP Conference Proceedings Ser.: No. 151). 464p. 1986. lib. bdg. 70.00 (*0-88318-351-X*) Am Inst Physics.

— See How It Flies: Perceptions, Procedures, & Principles of Flight. (Illus.). 400p. 1995. pap. text 34.95 (*0-07-016405-3*) McGraw.

Denker, Julie, ed. see Rainey, Dennis & Rainey, Barbara.

Denker, M., et al. Introductory Statistics & Random Phenomena: Uncertainty, Complexity, & Chaotic Behavior in Engineering & Science. Balakrishnan, N., ed. LC 98-4735. (Statistics for Industry & Technology Ser.). 509p. 1998. 55.00 (*0-8176-4031-2*) Birkhauser.

Denker, M., jt. ed. see Brunner, E.

Denker, Manfred, et al. Introductory Statistics & Random Phenomena: Uncertainty, Complexity, & Chaotic Behavior in Engineering & Science. LC 98-4735. (Statistics for Industry & Technology Ser.). 1998. write for info. (*3-7643-4031-2*) Birkhauser.

Denker, Manfred, jt. auth. see Bhattacharya, Rabi N.

Denker, Patrick R., ed. see Gazit, Shlomo.

***Denkin, Edythe.** Why Can't You Catch Me Being Good? LC 00-23819. 224p. 2000. pap. 10.95 (*1-58062-273-9*) Adams Media.

Denkler, Keith, jt. auth. see Sagebiel, Richard W.

Denkmayr, Helga. The Theme of Music in Peter Russell's Work. 70p. 1996. pap. 12.95 (*3-7052-0980-9*, Pub. by Poetry Salzburg) Intl Spec Bk.

Denley, Ian, et al. Designing User Interfaces for Broadband Services. LC 97-196508. 105p. 1996. text 49.95 (*1-85728-615-4*, Pub. by UCL Pr Ltd) Taylor & Francis.

Denley, Nick, jt. auth. see Arnold, Helen S.

***Denley, Peter.** History of Universities. (History of Universities). (Illus.). 380p. 2000. text 85.00 (*0-19-820533-3*) OUP.

Denley, Peter, ed. History of Universities: 1995-1996, Vol. XIV. (History of Universites Ser.). (Illus.). 372p. 1998. text 95.00 (*0-19-820532-5*) OUP.

Denley, Peter, ed. History of Universities 1994 Vol. XIII. (History of Universities Ser.: No. 13). (Illus.). 402p. 1995. text 89.00 (*0-19-820531-7*) OUP.

Denligher, Ken. For the Glory: College Football Dreams & Realities Inside Paterno's Program. (Illus.). 320p. 1995. pap. 12.95 (*0-312-13496-7*, Thomas Dunne) St Martin.

Denlinger. Elementary Real Analysis. (Mathematics Ser.). 2001. mass mkt. 62.95 (*0-534-34687-1*) Brooks-Cole.

Denlinger, A. Martha. Real People: Amish & Mennonites in Lancaster County, Pennsylvania. 4th rev. ed. LC 92-26887. (Illus.). 96p. 1993. pap. 4.99 (*0-8361-3616-0*) Herald Pr.

Denlinger, Charles G., jt. auth. see Kolman, Bernard.

Denlinger, Dean E. & Greenberg, Gary L. Employment Law Desk Book for Ohio Employers. 366p. 1997. ring bd. 127.00 (*0-925773-32-8*) M Lee Smith.

An Asterisk (*) at the beginning of an entry indicates that the title is appearing for the first time.

***Denlinger, Dean E. & Greenberg, Gary L.** Employment Law Desk Book for Ohio Employers. 2nd ed. LC 98-230013. 1998. write for info. (*0-925773-45-X*) M Lee Smith.

Denlinger, Donald M., jt. auth. see Warner, James A.

Denlinger, Jere. Flora Springs. LC 98-85307. 192p. 1999. pap. 11.95 (*1-56315-190-1*, Pub. by SterlingHse) Natl Bk Netwk.

Denlinger, Ken, jt. auth. see MacKenzie, Marlin M.

Denlinger, Sutherland & Gary, Charles B. War in the Pacific: A Study of Navies, Peoples, & Battle Problems. LC 77-111752. (American Imperialism: Viewpoints of United States Foreign Policy, 1898-1941 Ser.). 1977. reprint ed. 23.95 (*0-405-02011-2*) Ayer.

Denlinger, Teri E., jt. auth. see Emshoff, James R.

Denlinger, William W., ed. see Dean, Bob.

Denlinger, William W., ed. see Grossman, Alvin.

Denlinger, William W., ed. see Walkowicz, Chris.

***Denman, Barbara R.** In Contact. 2nd ed. LC 99-33872. 1999. 15.67 (*0-201-57979-0*) Addison-Wesley.

Denman, Cherry. Make Your Own Adventure Story. 24p. (J). (gr. k-3). 1999. pap. 9.95 (*0-316-85563-4*) Little.

— Make Your Own Space Story. (Illus.). 24p. (J). (gr. 2-5). 1998. pap. 8.95 (*0-316-85561-8*) Little.

— Make Your Own Spooky Story. 24p. (J). (gr. k-3). 1998. pap. 8.95 (*0-316-85562-6*) Little.

Denman, Clarence P. The Secession Movement in Alabama. LC 79-170695. (Black Heritage Library Collection). 1977. reprint ed. 22.95 (*0-8369-8885-X*) Ayer.

Denman, D. R. A Half & Half Affair: Chronicles of a Hybrid Don. (Illus.). 1995. boxed set 55.00 (*0-902782-28-2*, Pub. by Church Pr) St Mut.

Denman, Eric E. The Anatomy of the Human Skeleton: A Question & Answer Tutorial Text. (Illus.). 240p. (Orig.). 1991. pap. text 31.00 (*0-443-04498-8*) Church.

Denman, Eugene D., jt. auth. see Adams, Roy N.

Denman, G. L., ed. see American Institute of Physics.

Denman, Gregory A. Sit Tight, & I'll Swing You a Tail: Using & Writing Stories with Young People. LC 91-271. (Illus.). 184p. (Orig.). (C). (gr. 1). 1991. pap. text 22.00 (*0-435-08548-4*, 08548) Heinemann.

— When You've Made It Your Own . . . Teaching Poetry to Young People. LC 88-2989. 201p. (Orig.). (C). 1988. pap. text 23.00 (*0-435-08462-3*, 08462) Heinemann.

Denman, Harry H., et al. Angular Scattering Functions for Spheres. LC 66-14228. 315p. reprint ed. pap. 97.70 (*0-8357-5485-5*, 202765600055) Bks Demand.

***Denman, Julia.** Air Force Depot Maintenance: Management Changes Would Improve Implementation of Reform Initiatives. 56p. (C). 2000. pap. text 20.00 (*0-7881-8884-4*) DIANE Pub.

Denman, Peter. Samuel Ferguson: The Literary Achievement. 220p. (C). 1990. text 59.50 (*0-389-20927-9*) B&N Imports.

Denman, Peter, tr. see Tuama, Sean O.

Denman, R. P., jt. auth. see Dunlop, Jocelyn.

Denman, Terence. Ireland's Unknown Soldiers: The 16th (Irish) Division in the Great War. (Illus.). 208p. (C). 1992. 37.50 (*0-7165-2495-3*, Pub. by Irish Acad Pr) Intl Spec Bk.

— A Lonely Grave: The Life & Death of William Redmond. (Illus.). 208p. 1995. 29.50 (*0-7165-2561-5*, Pub. by Irish Acad Pr) Intl Spec Bk.

Denman-West, Margaret W. Children's Literature: A Guide to Information Sources. LC 98-10177. 300p. 1998. lib. bdg. 38.50 (*1-56308-448-1*) Libs Unl.

Denmark. The Classic Readings in Psychology of Women. 608p. (C). 2001. 23.00 (*0-02-328443-9*, Macmillan Coll) P-H.

***Denmark, Scott E.** Handbook of Reagents for Organic Synthesis, Reagents, Auxillaries & Catalysts for C-c Bond Formation. Coates, R.M., ed. LC 98-53088. 764p. 1999. 115.00 (*0-471-97924-4*) Wiley.

Denmark, Scott E. Topics in Stereochemistry, Vol. 22. 336p. 1999. 95.00 (*0-471-25316-2*) Wiley.

Denmark, Edward. Not for Queen & Country: A No-Holds Barred Account of Life As a British Soldier. 1998. pap. text 9.95 (*1-901442-08-X*, Pub. by Pharaoh Pr) Seven Hills Bk.

Denmark, F. L., jt. auth. see Sherman, J. A.

Denmark, Florence, ed. Who Discriminates Against Women? LC 74-78560. (Sage Contemporary Social Science Issues Ser.: No. 15). (Illus.). 144p. reprint ed. pap. 44.70 (*0-608-10099-4*, 202188700026) Bks Demand.

Denmark, Florence, et al. Engendering Psychology: Bringing Women into Focus. LC 99-19908. 527p. 1999. pap. text 50.00 (*0-205-14685-6*) Allyn.

Denmark, Florence, jt. auth. see Nadien, Margot B.

Denmark, Florence L., et al, eds. Women: A PDI Reference Work, Vol. 1. LC 75-5161. 626p. 1977. 39.95 (*0-88437-001-1*) Psych Dimensions.

Denmark, Florence L. & Paludi, Michele A., eds. Psychology of Women: A Handbook of Issues & Theories. LC 92-8642. 784p. 1993. lib. bdg. 135.00 (*0-313-26295-0*, DEH/, Greenwood Pr) Greenwood.

Denmark, Florence L., jt. auth. see Unger, Rhoda K.

Denmark, Herbert W. High Heels & Jeans: Poetry for the Foxy Teen. 3rd rev. ed. (Illus.). 39p. (YA). (gr. 7-12). 1997. mass mkt. 4.00 (*1-891511-02-5*) H W Denmark.

— The Medal of Honor & Two Dollars Will Buy You a Beer: Conflicts in the World of Black Men. 72p. 1997. mass mkt. 5.00 (*1-891511-01-7*) H W Denmark.

— The Prize: Conflicts in Love Matters. 118p. 1997. mass mkt. 6.00 (*1-891511-00-9*) H W Denmark.

— Second Finger, Left Hand: Love Conflicts for the Spiritual Woman. 161p. 1998. mass mkt. 8.00 (*1-891511-03-3*) H W Denmark.

Denmark, John C. Deafness & Mental Health. LC 94-181829. 160p. 1993. pap. 24.95 (*1-85302-212-8*) Taylor & Francis.

Denmark, Larry, jt. auth. see Keller, Mark.

Denmark, Vicki M., jt. auth. see Podsen, India.

Denmead, O. T., jt. ed. see Steffen, W. L.

Denmei Shudo. Japanese Classical Acupuncture: Introduction to Meridian Therapy. Brown, Stephen, tr. from JPN. LC 90-82526. (Illus.). 251p. (C). 1990. text 38.00 (*0-939616-11-4*) Eastland.

Denn, James, jt. ed. see Kane, Ilene W.

Denn, Morton M. Process Fluid Mechanics. 1979. text 67.60 (*0-13-723163-6*) P-H.

Denn, Robert, ed. see Anderson-Redick, Stacey.

Denn, Robert, ed. see Farquhar, David L.

Denn, Robert, ed. see Foster, Gerald.

Denn, Robert, ed. see Hunt, Craig & Thompson, Robert B.

Denn, Robert, ed. see Lowe-Norris, Alistair G.

Denn, Robert, ed. see McDowell, Steve.

Denn, Robert, ed. see Meggitt, Ashley J. & Lavy, Matthew M.

Denn, Robert, ed. see Neilson, Gregory G.

Denn, Robert, ed. see Robichaux, Paul.

Denn, Robert, ed. see Robinson, Andrew & Hammond, Mark.

Denn, Robert, ed. see Thompson, Robert B.

Denn, Robert, ed. see Thompson, Robert Bruce & Thompson, Barbara Frichtman.

Denn, Robert, ed. see Tulloch, Mitch.

Denn, Robert, ed. see Zacker, Craig.

Denn, Robert J., ed. see Laurie, Ben & Laurie, Peter.

Denn, Robert J., ed. see Meggitt, Ashley & Ritchey, Timothy D.

Denn, Robert J., ed. see Pearce, Eric.

Dennard, Deborah. Coyote at Pinon Place. LC 99-19242. (Smithsonian's Backyard Ser.: No. 18). (Illus.). 32p. (J). (ps-2). 1999. 15.95 (*1-56899-767-1*); 19.95 incl. audio (*1-56899-766-3*, BC5018) Soundprints.

— Coyote at Pinon Place, Includes toy. (Smithsonian's Backyard Ser.: Vol. 18). (Illus.). 32p. (J). (ps-2). 1999. 32.95 (*1-56899-764-7*); 12.95 (*1-56899-765-5*) Soundprints.

— Coyote at Pinon Place: Micro Edition. LC 99-19242. (Smithsonian's Backyard Ser.: Vol. 18). (Illus.). 32p. (J). (ps-2). 1999. 4.95 (*1-56899-763-9*) Soundprints.

— Daring Deborah's down under Safari Vol. 3: Animals of Australia. (Daring Deborah's Safaris Ser.). (Illus.). (J). (gr. k-5). 1998. 59.95 incl. cd-rom (*1-889081-05-1*); cd-rom 49.95 (*1-889081-03-5*) Electro Bks Kids.

— Daring Deborah's First Safari: Jungles & Plains. (Illus.). (J). (gr. k-6). 1996. ring bd. 59.95 (*1-889081-02-7*); cd-rom 49.95 (*1-889081-00-0*) Electro Bks Kids.

— Daring Deborah's Icky Slimy Creature Safari Vol. 2: Reptiles, Amphibians, Bugs & More. (Daring Deborah's Safaris Ser.). (Illus.). (J). (gr. k-5). 1997. 59.95 incl. cd-rom (*1-889081-08-6*); cd-rom 49.95 (*1-889081-06-X*) Electro Bks Kids.

— Do Cats Have Nine Lives? The Strange Things People Say about Animals Around the House. LC 92-10353. (Question of Science Ser.). (Illus.). (J). (gr. k-3). 1993. lib. bdg. 19.93 (*0-87614-720-1*, Carolrhoda) Lerner Pub.

— How Wise Is an Owl? The Strange Things People Say about Animals in the Woods. LC 92-10354. (Question of Science Book). (Illus.). (J). (gr. k-3). 1992. lib. bdg. 19.95 (*0-87614-721-X*, Carolrhoda) Lerner Pub.

***Dennard, Deborah.** Koala: A Story of an Australian Eucalyptus Forest. (Habitat Ser.: Vol. 17). (Illus.). 36p. (J). (gr. 1-4). 2000. pap. 16.95 (*1-56899-892-9*) Soundprints.

— Koala Country: A Story of an Australian Eucalyptus Forest. (Habitat Ser.: Vol. 17). (Illus.). 36p. (J). (gr. 1-4). 2000. 15.95 (*1-56899-887-2*); 26.95 (*1-56899-891-0*); pap. 5.95 (*1-56899-888-0*) Soundprints.

Dennard, Deborah & Stewart, Don. Coyote at Pidnon Place. LC 99-19242. (Smithsonian's Backyard Ser.). 1999. write for info. (*1-56899-748-5*) Soundprints.

Dennard, Giji M. Feasts Fit for a King: Food for the Body & Soul. Stephenson, Michelle & Sparks, Marita, eds. (Illus.). 150p. (Orig.). 1996. pap. 15.00 (*0-9655845-1-8*) Kingdom creationS.

Dennard, H. Lane, Jr. NLRB Remedies for Unfair Labor Practices, 1986-97 Supplement. rev. ed. (Labor Relations & Public Policy Ser.: Vol. 12). 158p. 1998. pap. 22.50 (*1-891496-02-6*) J M Olin.

Dennard, Linda F., jt. ed. see Morcol, Goktug.

Dennard, Tom. Buzzards Roost. 272p. (Orig.). 1996. pap. 14.95 (*0-9656138-0-1*) T Dennard.

— Discovering Life's Trails: Adventures in Living. LC 93-2903. (Illus.). 330p. (Orig.). 1993. pap. 14.95 (*0-935834-97-4*) Rainbow Bks.

Denne, W. Magnetic Compass Deviation & Correction. (C). 1987. 100.00 (*0-85174-332-3*) St Mut.

Dennee, JoAnne. Exploring the Forest with Grandforest Tree. (Illus.). 260p. (Orig.). (J). (gr. 1-4). 1993. pap. 18.95 (*1-884430-03-1*) Food Works.

— In the Three Sisters Garden. 376p. (J). (gr. 1-2). 1994. pap. 24.95 (*1-884430-01-5*) Food Works.

Denneerll. Medical Terminology Made Easy. 64p. 1997. text, teacher ed. 14.00 (*0-8273-8137-9*) Delmar.

Dennehy, Cad, jt. auth. see Alters, Sandra M.

Dennehy, R. & Grisez, G. Bioethical Issues. Lescoe, F. & Liptak, D., eds. (Pope John Paul II Lecture Series in Bioethics: Vol. II). 60p. (C). 1986. pap. 4.50 (*0-910919-04-6*) Mariel Pubns.

Dennehy, Robert P., jt. ed. see Sims, Ronald R.

***Denneler, Iris.** Die Formel und das Unverwechselbare: Interdisziplinare Beitrage Zu Topik, Rhetorik und Individualitat. (Illus.). 194p. 1999. 35.95 (*3-631-35240-9*) P Lang Pubng.

Dennen, Barry. My Life with Barbra: A Love Story. LC 97-24796. (Illus.). 281p. 1997. 24.95 (*1-57392-160-2*) Prometheus Bks.

***Dennen, Sue.** Make Your Own Calendar 2001. (Illus.). 24p. (J). (gr. 1-5). 2000. 6.95 (*0-316-19210-4*) Little.

Dennen, Sue. Who Says I Dont Have a Life. 24p. 1998. 11.95 (*0-316-37059-2*) Little Brown Yemanja Sings.

— Who Says I Don't Have a Life? A Make Your Own Calendar for 2000. 24p. 1999. write for info. (*0-316-18944-8*) Little Brown Yemanja Sings.

***Dennen, Sue, ed.** Make Your Own Calendar 2000. (Illus.). 24p. 1999. pap. 6.95 (*0-316-18888-3*) Little.

Dennen, Sue. The Baby Chronicles: A Make-Your-Own Record for New Moms & Moms-to-Be. 36p. 1999. 10.95 (*0-316-18581-7*) Little.

— Make Your Own Calendar 1997, Vol. 1. 24p. 1996. 6.95 (*0-316-18107-2*) Little.

Dennen, Vanessa, ed. see Thayer, Yvonne V. & Shortt, Thomas L.

Dennen, W. H. Mineral Resources. (Illus.). 380p. (C). 1989. 85.00 (*0-8448-1569-1*) Taylor & Francis.

Dennen, William H., jt. auth. see Blackburn, William H.

Dennenberg, R. V., jt. auth. see Denenberg, Tia S.

***Denner.** Student Motivation. 112p. 1998. pap. text 13.60 (*0-536-01596-1*) Pearson Custom.

Denner, Arthur, tr. see Heng, Cheng.

Denner, Arthur, tr. see Poizat, Michel.

Denner, Arthur, tr. see Todorov, Tzvetan.

Denner, Arthur, tr. see Valensi, Lucette.

Denner, Leonard, photos by. 50 Ways to Master Your Sewing Machine. (Illus.). 1996. pap. 18.00 (*0-517-88360-0*) Crown Pub Group.

Denner, Patricia. Language Through Play. LC 72-84851. (Illus.). (J). (ps-1). 1969. reprint ed. pap. 11.95 (*0-405-00118-5*) Ayer.

Denner, Richard E. California Family Law Trial Guide, 5 vols. Rothschild, Frances & Johnson, Earl, Jr. eds. LC 92-17407. 1992. 500.00 (*0-8205-1223-0*) Bender.

***Dennerlein, Norbert.** Die Bedeutung Jerusalems in Den Chronikbuchern. (Beitrage Zur Erforschung des Alten Testaments und Antiken Judentums Ser.). ix , 268p. 1999. 45.95 (*3-631-34632-8*) P Lang Pubng.

Dennerline, Jerry. The Chia-Ting Loyalists: Confucian Leadership & Social Change in Seventeenth-Century China. LC 80-21417. (Historical Publications, Miscellany Ser.: No. 126). (Illus.). 416p. 1981. 60.00 (*0-300-02548-3*) Yale U Pr.

Dennerll. Medical Terminology Made Easy. 2nd ed. (C). 1997. 28.00 incl. audio (*0-8273-8139-5*) Delmar.

— Medical Terms Made Easy. 1993. 25.95 incl. audio (*0-8273-5907-1*); text 36.95 incl. audio (*0-8273-5918-7*) Delmar.

Dennerll, Jean T. Instructor's Manual to Accompany Medical Terminology Made Easy. 44p. 1993. text, teacher ed. 14.00 (*0-8273-5909-8*) Delmar.

— Medical Terminology Made Easy. LC 92-48740. 296p. 1993. text 24.95 (*0-8273-5278-6*) Delmar.

Dennerll, Jean T. & Smith, Genevieve L. Medical Terminology Made Easy. 2nd ed. LC 97-21616. 384p. (C). 1997. mass mkt. 37.95 (*0-8273-8136-0*) Delmar.

Dennerstein, Lorraine & Shelly, Julia. A Woman's Guide to Menopause & Hormone Replacement Theory. LC 98-10653. 160p. 1998. 22.95 (*0-88048-782-8*, 8782) Am Psychiatric.

Dennerstein, Lorraine, et al. Hysterectomy: New Options & Advances. 2nd ed. (Illus.). 204p. 1999. pap. 22.95 (*0-19-551033-X*) OUP.

D'Ennery, Adolphe, jt. auth. see Verne, Jules.

Dennery, Philippe & Krzywicki, Andre. Mathematics for Physicists. unabridged ed. LC 96-10774. (Illus.). 400p. 1996. reprint ed. pap. text 12.95 (*0-486-69193-4*) Dover.

Dennes, William R. Some Dilemmas of Naturalism. (Select Bibliographies Reprint Ser.). 1977. 18.95 (*0-8369-5551-X*) Ayer.

Denness, Bruce, ed. Seabed Mechanics. 296p. 1985. lib. bdg. 163.00 (*0-86010-504-0*) G & T Inc.

Dennett. Fire Investigation. 1980. pap. text 7.75 (*0-08-025457-8*, Pergamon Pr) Elsevier.

Dennett, Andrea Stulman. Weird & Wonderful. LC 97-4880. 1997. pap. text 17.00 (*0-8147-1886-8*) NYU Pr.

— Weird & Wonderful. LC 97-4880. 1997. text 45.00 (*0-8147-1885-X*) NYU Pr.

Dennett, Daniel Clement. Brainchildren: Essays on Designing Minds. LC 97-9440. (Representation & Mind Ser.). (Illus.). 424p. 1998. 42.50 (*0-262-04166-9*, Bradford Bks) MIT Pr.

— Brainchildren: Essays on Designing Minds. LC 97-9440. (Representation & Mind Ser.). (Illus.). 424p. 1998. pap. text 20.00 (*0-262-54090-8*, Bradford Bks) MIT Pr.

— Brainstorms: Philosophical Essays on Mind & Psychology. LC 78-13723. (Bradford Bks.). 353p. 1981. pap. text 19.00 (*0-262-54037-1*) MIT Pr.

— Consciousness Explained. 511p. 1992. pap. 17.00 (*0-316-18066-1*) Little.

— Content & Consciousness. (International Library of Philosophy). 208p. (C). 1986. pap. 24.99 (*0-415-10431-9*, 08464) Routledge.

— Content & Consciousness. 2nd ed. (International Library of Philosophy). 208p. (C). 1986. pap. text 13.95 (*0-7102-0846-4*, Routledge Thoemms) Routledge.

— Darwin's Dangerous Idea: Evolution & the Meanings of Life. LC 94-49158. (Illus.). 586p. 1995. 30.00 (*0-684-80290-2*) S&S Trade.

— Darwin's Dangerous Idea: Evolution & the Meanings of Life. 592p. 1996. per. 16.00 (*0-684-82471-X*) S&S Trade Pap.

— Dennett Quartet: Brainstorms, Elbow Room, the Intentional Stance & Brainchildren. 1998. pap., boxed set 60.00 (*0-262-54091-6*) MIT Pr.

— Elbow Room: The Varieties of Free Will Worth Wanting. 256p. 1984. pap. text 14.95 (*0-262-54042-8*, Bradford Bks) MIT Pr.

— The Intentional Stance. LC 87-3018. 380p. 1987. 40.00 (*0-262-04093-X*, Bradford Bks) MIT Pr.

— The Intentional Stance. LC 87-3018. 380p. 1989. pap. text 20.00 (*0-262-54053-3*, Bradford Bks) MIT Pr.

— Kinds of Minds. (Science Masters Ser.). 176p. 1997. pap. 10.00 (*0-465-07351-4*, Pub. by Basic) HarpC.

Dennett, Daniel Clement, et al. The Robot's Dilemma Revisited. Ford, Kenneth & Pylyshyn, Zenon W., eds. (Illus.). 141p. 1996. pap. 39.50 (*1-56750-143-5*); text 78.50 (*1-56750-142-7*) Ablx Pub.

Dennett, Daniel Clement, jt. auth. see Dawkins, Richard.

Dennett, Diana J. Tell Me More Ancestor Stories, Grandma!, Vol. 1. rev. ed. Hamilton, Patricia A., ed. (Illus.). 176p. 1997. pap. 24.95 (*1-877809-79-9*) Park Pl Pubns.

Dennett, E. The Step I Have Taken. Daniel, R. P., ed. 53p. pap. 3.95 (*0-88172-140-9*) Believers Bkshelf.

Dennett, Edward. Recovered Truths. 52p. 1997. pap. text 2.50 (*0-9640037-6-7*) Pres Truth.

Dennett, John R. South As It Is, 1865-1866. Christman, Henry M., ed. 370p. 1995. pap. 15.95 (*0-8071-1998-9*) La State U Pr.

Dennett, M. F. Fire Investigation. (C). 1980. 80.00 (*0-7855-4167-5*, Pub. by Witherby & Co) St Mut.

Dennett, Mick. Profitable Free Range Egg Production. (Illus.). 128p. 1995. 22.95 (*1-85223-835-6*, Pub. by Crolwood) Trafalgar.

Dennett, Nolan. Place of Shelter. LC 94-28963. (New American Fiction Ser.: No. 30). 224p. 1994. 19.95 (*1-55713-130-9*) Sun & Moon CA.

Dennett, Preston. One in Forty - The UFO Epidemic: True Accounts of Close Encounters with UFO's. LC 95-46546. 227p. 1996. 25.00 (*1-56072-270-3*, Nova Kroshka Bks) Nova Sci Pubs.

***Dennett, Preston.** UFOs over Topanga Canyon: Eyewitness Accounts of the California Sightings. LC 99-17974. (Illus.). 384p. (Orig.). 1999. pap. 12.95 (*1-56718-221-6*) Llewellyn Pubns.

Dennett, Preston E. UFO Healings: True Accounts of People Healed by Extraterrestrials. Demmon, Amy, ed. LC 96-31331. (Illus.). 188p. 1997. per. 12.00 (*0-926524-33-X*) Granite Pub.

Dennett, Richard E. Notes on the Folklore of the Fjort. LC 78-67705. (Folktale Ser.). reprint ed. 29.50 (*0-404-16078-6*) AMS Pr.

Denney, Ardeth Elling. Land Lottery 1901: The Diary of Miss Minnie Johnson. LC 98-93736. (Illus.). 340p. 1998. pap. 16.95 (*0-9667576-0-2*) Blue Beaver.

Denney, Colleen. At the Temple of Art: The Grosvenor Gallery, 1877-1890. LC 98-56091. (Illus.). 264p. 2000. 59.50 (*0-8386-3850-3*) Fairleigh Dickinson.

Denney, Colleen, jt. ed. see Casteras, Susan P.

Denney, David. Racism & Anti-Racism in Probation. LC 92-2795. 224p. (C). 1993. pap. 27.99 (*0-415-06157-1*, A7064) Routledge.

— Social Policy & Social Work. 282p. 1998. pap. text (*0-19-878149-0*) OUP.

— Social Policy & Social Work. 282p. 1998. text 75.00 (*0-19-878150-4*) OUP.

Denney, David & Ely, Peter. Social Work in a Multiracial Society. 144p. 1987. text 82.95 (*0-566-00939-0*, Pub. by Avebry) Ashgate Pub Co.

Denney, Dick, jt. auth. see Peterson, David.

Denney, Donald B., ed. Techniques & Methods of Organic & Organometallic Chemistry, Vol. 1. LC 69-20008. 242p. 1969. reprint ed. pap. 75.10 (*0-608-08462-X*, 202712300001) Bks Demand.

Denney, James. The Christian Doctrine of Reconciliation. (Biblical Classics Library: Vol. 35). 339p. 1998. reprint ed. pap. 5.99 (*0-85364-859-X*, Pub. by Paternoster Pub) OM Literature.

— The Death of Christ. (Biblical Classics Library: Vol. 30). 207p. 1997. reprint ed. mass mkt. 5.99 (*0-85364-788-7*, Pub. by Paternoster Pub) OM Literature.

Denney, James B. When Duty Called: The Journal of an Enlisted Man, British Isles to Northwest France-April 1944-June 1945. (Illus.). 180p. 1994. pap. text 19.95 (*0-89745-176-7*) Sunflower U Pr.

Denney, James D., jt. auth. see Alexis, Kim.

Denney, James D., jt. auth. see Williams, Pat.

***Denney, Jim.** Answers to Satisfy the Soul: Clear, Straight Answers to Life's 20 Most Important Questions. 192p. 2000. 18.95 (*1-884956-20-3*) Quill Driver.

Denney, Jim, jt. auth. see Ford, Leighton.

Denney, Jim, jt. auth. see Whitney, Grace L.

Denney, John M. My Best Poems. (Illus.). 40p. 1996. pap. 4.95 (*0-9654698-1-6*) Denney Literary.

— The Sailor. Denney, Rose M., ed. (Illus.). 24p. (Orig.). (YA). (gr. 9-12). 1996. pap. 4.95 (*0-9654698-3-2*) Denney Literary.

— The Secret Fraternity. Denney, Rose M., ed. 24p. 1997. pap. 4.95 (*0-9654698-4-0*) Denney Literary.

— Self-Publishing Your Book (on a Budget) (Illus.). 52p. (Orig.). 1996. pap. 7.95 (*0-9654698-2-4*) Denney Literary.

Denney, Martha. Going Home: A Workbook for Reentry & Professional Integration. 147p. (Orig.). 1987. 15.00 (*0-912207-32-9*) NAFSA Washington.

Denney, Martha J., ed. Canada Nursing Job Guide, 1989. 166p. 1989. pap. 50.00 (*0-932834-06-X*) Prime Natl Pub.

***Denney, Nancy Hunter.** Life by Design: A Do-It-Yourself Approach to Achieving Happiness. (Illus.). 224p. 2000. pap. 14.95 (*1-930463-00-6*) Victory Inc.

Denney, Patrick. Colchester Past. unabridged ed. (Illus.). 64p. (Orig.). 1988. pap. 15.00 (*0-86025-421-6*, Pub. by I Henry Pubns) Empire Pub Srvs.

— Life in Edwardian Colchester. (Illus.). 112p. (Orig.). 1991. pap. 15.00 (*0-86025-429-1*, Pub. by I Henry Pubns) Empire Pub Srvs.

D

Denney, R. The Portfolio of Benjamin Latrobe. (QRL Poetry Bks.: Vol. XXV). 300p. 1984. 20.00 (*0-614-06408-2*) Quarterly Rev.

Denney, Reuel. Connecticut River & Other Poems. LC 79-144745. (Yale Series of Younger Poets: No. 38). reprint ed. 18.00 (*0-404-53838-X*) AMS Pr.

— Conrad Aiken. LC 64-64445. (University of Minnesota Pamphlets on American Writers Ser.: No. 38). 48p. (Orig.). reprint ed. pap. 30.00 (*0-7837-2891-3*, 205756400006) Bks Demand.

Denney, Reuel, ed. see Quagliano, Tony.

Denney, Robert E. Civil War Medicine: Care & Comfort of the Wounded. (Illus.). 422p. (Orig.). 1995. pap. 19.95 (*0-8069-0880-7*) Sterling.

— Civil War Prisons & Escapes: A Day by Day Chronicle. LC 93-23889. (Illus.). 424p. 1993. 27.95 (*0-8069-0414-3*) Sterling.

***Denney, Robert E.** The Civil War Years. LC 98-21562. 624p. 1998. 9.99 (*0-517-18945-3*) Random Hse Value.

***Denney, Rose M.** Contemporary Southern Poets of 1998: The Works of 20 Southern Poets of the United States of America. (Illus.). 48p. 1999. pap. 4.95 (*0-9654698-8-3*) Denney Literary.

Denney, Rose M. Poems for My Grandchildren, 1996: Collected from the Family. 32p. (Orig.). (J). (gr. k-6). 1996. pap. 4.95 (*0-9654698-5-9*) Denney Literary.

Denney, Rose M., ed. Contemporary Poems for Children - 1997. 48p. (J). (gr. k-12). 1997. pap. 4.95 (*0-9654698-6-7*) Denney Literary.

— Contemporary Southern Poets of 1997. 48p. 1997. pap. 4.95 (*0-9654698-7-5*) Denney Literary.

Denney, Rose M., ed. see Denney, John M.

Denney, Rosemary, ed. Contemporary Southern Poets of 1996. 51p. (Orig.). 1996. pap. 4.95 (*0-9654698-0-8*) Denney Literary.

Dennie, Janice L. The Lion of Judah. 250p. 1997. pap. 6.99 (*0-9643349-0-9*) Kente Pubns.

— Moon Goddess: The Queen of Sheba. (Romance Ser.). 245p. 1999. pap. 7.99 (*0-9643349-1-7*) Kente Pubns.

Dennie, Joseph. Collected Works. 1990. reprint ed. lib. bdg. 75.00 (*0-7812-2626-0*, 1506) Rprt Serv.

— Farrago. LC 85-18417. 104p. 1985. 50.00 (*0-8201-1406-5*) Schol Facsimiles.

— The Lay Preacher. (Notable American Authors Ser.). 1992. reprint ed. lib. bdg. 75.00 (*0-685-49851-4*) Rprt Serv.

— The Lay Preacher. (BCL1-PS American Literature Ser.). 184p. 1993. reprint ed. lib. bdg. 69.00 (*0-7812-6956-3*) Rprt Serv.

— The Lay Preacher. LC 43-9749. 196p. 1979. reprint ed. lib. bdg. 50.00 (*0-8201-1204-6*) Schol Facsimiles.

Dennie, Joseph C. & Weathers, Joseph. Smarty's New Friend. Bonnette, Charlotte A., ed. LC 93-39652. (Illus.). 20p. (Orig.). (J). (gr. 1-4). 1994. pap. 7.95 incl. audio (*1-877971-11-1*) Mid Atl Reg Pr.

Dennie, Ronald W., jt. auth. see Price, Craig G.

Dennie, Steve & Suggs, Rob. Murphy Goes to Church. LC 93-18096. (Illus.). 108p. (Orig.). 1993. pap. 6.99 (*0-8308-1837-5*, 1837) InterVarsity.

— Murphy's Laws of Marriage. LC 96-4165. (Illus.). 104p. (Orig.). 1996. pap. 6.99 (*0-8308-1674-7*, 1674) InterVarsity.

— Murphy's Laws of Parenting. LC 93-41358. (Illus.). 104p. (Orig.). 1994. pap. 6.99 (*0-8308-1839-1*, 1839) InterVarsity.

Dennin, Cheryl A. Poetry Highway. 1999. pap. 6.95 (*0-533-12923-0*) Vantage.

Dennin, Joseph F., ed. Law & Practice of the World Trade Organization: Commentary, Dispute Resolution & Treaties, 5 vols., Set. 1995. ring bd. 600.00 (*0-379-21358-3*) Oceana.

Denning. Computer under Attack. (C). 1994. pap. text. write for info. (*0-201-55688-X*) Addison-Wesley.

— Desarrolle Sus Poderes Psiquicos. LC 99-51875. (SPA.). 264p. 1999. pap. 9.95 (*1-56718-216-X*) Llewellyn Pubns.

— Women's I Ching. 1999. text 19.95 (*0-312-19189-8*) St Martin.

Denning & Phillips. Proyeccion Astral: Experiences Fuera del Cuerpo Fisico. 2nd ed. (SPA., Illus.). 260p. 1999. mass mkt. 8.95 (*1-56718-202-X*) Llewellyn Pubns.

Denning, jt. compiled by see Mitchell.

Denning, Adam. ActiveX Controls Inside Out. 2nd ed. LC 96-37066. 1997. pap. text 39.95 incl. cd-rom (*1-57231-350-1*) Microsoft.

Denning, Alfred. Changing Law. (Legal Reprint Ser.). viii, 122p. 1986. reprint ed. 32.50 (*0-8377-2029-X*, Rothman); reprint ed. 22.50 (*0-421-37580-9*) W S Hein.

— Road to Justice. (Legal Reprint Ser.). viii, 118p. 1988. reprint ed. 32.50 (*0-8377-2034-6*, Rothman); reprint ed. 22.50 (*0-421-40200-8*) W S Hein.

Denning, Anthony. Woodcarving, 2 bks. in 1. LC 98-47128. 1999. pap. 19.95 (*0-8069-2057-2*) Sterling.

Denning, Basil W., ed. Making Strategic Planning Work in Practice. LC 89-8826. (Best of Long Range Planning Ser.: Vol. 3). 130p. 1989. 72.00 (*0-08-037121-3*, 2905, Pub. by Pergamon Repr) Franklin.

Denning, Basil W., et al. Corporate Long Range Planning: Industry's Problems & National Policies: Papers Presented at A National Conference in London, February 1969. LC 76-472690. 214 p. 1969. write for info. (*0-582-44012-2*) Addison-Wesley.

Denning-Bolle, Sara J. & Gerow, Edwin, eds. The Persistence of Religions: Essays in Honor of Kees W. Bolle. LC 96-60545. (Other Realities Ser.: Vol. 9). xxii, 444p. (C). 1996. pap. 45.00 (*0-89003-500-8*) Undena Pubns.

Denning, Catherine, ed. Gifts & Exchanges: Problems, Frustrations... And Triumphs, No. 22. LC 99-27775. (Acquisitions Librarian Ser.: Vol. 11). 199p. (C). 1999. 49.95 (*0-7890-0678-2*) Haworth Pr.

Denning, Charles H., Jr. First Aid for Horses. 1981. pap. 7.00 (*0-87980-189-1*) Wilshire.

Denning, D. W., ed. Trends in the Management of Systemic Fungal Infections. (Journal: Chemotherapy: Vol. 38, Suppl. 1, 1992). (Illus.). iv, 96p. 1992. pap. 30.50 (*3-8055-5627-6*) S Karger.

Denning, Dorothy E. Information Warfare & Security. LC 98-31096. 544p. (C). 1998. pap. text 34.95 (*0-201-43303-6*) Addison-Wesley.

— Rights & Responsibilities of Participants in Networked Communities. Lin, Herbert S., ed. 172p. (Orig.). (C). 1994. pap. text 25.00 (*0-309-05090-1*) Natl Acad Pr.

Denning, Elizabeth, jt. auth. see Lowe, Terry C.

Denning, Hazel M. Life Without Guilt: Healing Through Past Life Regression. LC 98-13884. 240p. (Orig.). 1999. pap. 12.95 (*1-56718-219-4*) Llewellyn Pubns.

— True Hauntings: Spirits with a Purpose. LC 96-24923. (Illus.). 240p. (Orig.). 1999. pap. 12.95 (*1-56718-218-6*) Llewellyn Pubns.

Denning, Jenna. My Dad Drives an AFV (Alternative Fuel Vehicle) McCrea, Steve, ed. (Illus.). 28p. (J). 1995. pap. text 7.00 (*1-57074-245-6*) Greyden Pr.

Denning, Keith & Kemmer, Suzanne, eds. On Language: Selected Writings of Joseph H. Greenberg. LC 89-26199. 761p. 1990. 79.50 (*0-8047-1613-7*) Stanford U Pr.

Denning, Keith & Leben, William R. English Vocabulary Elements. (Illus.). 272p. (C). 1995. pap. text 22.95 (*0-19-506609-X*) OUP.

Denning, Lord. The Closing Chapter. 1983. pap. 28.00 (*0-406-17612-4*, UK, MICHIE) LEXIS Pub.

— Denning: What Next in the Law. 1982. 40.00 (*0-406-17601-9*, MICHIE); pap. 28.00 (*0-406-17602-7*, MICHIE) LEXIS Pub.

— The Discipline of Law. 1979. pap. 28.00 (*0-406-17605-1*, UK, MICHIE) LEXIS Pub.

— The Due Process of Law. 1980. 28.00 (*0-406-17608-6*, U.K., MICHIE) LEXIS Pub.

— The Influence of Religion on Law. LC 18-963630. 57p. 1997. pap. 10.00 (*1-896363-08-3*) CN Inst for Law.

— Landmarks in the Law. 1984. 40.00 (*0-406-17603-5*, UK, MICHIE); pap. 28.00 (*0-406-17614-0*, U.K., MICHIE) LEXIS Pub.

— Leaves from My Library. 1986. 40.00 (*0-406-17615-9*, U.K., MICHIE) LEXIS Pub.

— Legal Portraits. pap. text 14.00 (*0-406-03250-5*, UK, MICHIE) LEXIS Pub.

***Denning, Melita.** Foundations of High Magick: The Magical Philosophy. 2000. 9.99 (*0-7858-1193-1*) Bk Sales Inc.

Denning, Melita & Phillips, Osborne. Creative Visualization. 2nd ed. LC 83-80168. (Practical Guide to Personal Power Ser.), (Illus.). 294p. pap. 7.95 (*0-87542-183-0*) Llewellyn Pubns.

— The Llewellyn Practical Guide to Astral Projection: The Out-of-Body Experience. 2nd ed. LC 79-88141. (Practical Guide to Personal Power Ser.). (Illus.). 252p. 1979. reprint ed. pap. 9.95 (*0-87542-181-4*) Llewellyn Pubns.

— The Llewellyn Practical Guide to Psychic Self-Defense & Well-Being. 2nd enl. ed. LC 83-80169. (Practical Guide to Personal Power Ser.). (Illus.). 308p. 1999. pap. 9.95 (*0-87542-190-3*) Llewellyn Pubns.

— The Llewellyn Practical Guide to the Development of Psychic Powers. 3rd ed. LC 86-20856. (Illus.). 272p. 2000. pap. 9.95 (*0-87542-191-1*) Llewellyn Pubns.

— The Llewellyn Practical Guide to the Magick of Sex: The Book of Creative Loving. 312p. 1982. 6.95 (*0-87542-192-X*) Llewellyn Pubns.

— Planetary Magick: A Complete System for Knowledge & Attainment. LC 82-83316. (Aurum Solis Ser.). (Illus.). 456p. (Orig.). 1989. pap. 15.00 (*0-87542-193-8*) Llewellyn Pubns.

Denning, Michael. Cover Stories: Narrative & Ideology in the British Spy Thriller. LC 86-21968. 168p. 1987. pap. 11.95 (*0-7100-9642-9*, Routledge Thoemms) Routledge.

— The Cultural Front: The Laboring of American Culture in the Twentieth Century. LC 96-45602. 1997. 65.00 (*1-85984-815-X*, Pub. by Verso) Norton.

— The Cultural Front: The Laboring of American Culture in the Twentieth Century. 578p. 1998. pap. 22.00 (*1-85984-170-8*, Pub. by Verso) Norton.

Denning, P., ed. Talking Back to the Machine: Computers & Human Aspiration. (Illus.). 228p. 1998. 26.00 (*0-387-98413-5*) Spr-Verlag.

***Denning, Patt.** Practicing Harm Reduction Psychotherapy: An Alternative Approach to Addictions. 270p. 2000. lib. bdg. 35.00 (*1-57230-555-X*, C0555) Guilford Pubns.

Denning, Patt, jt. auth. see Zweben, Joan E.

Denning, Peter. Networks under Attack. LC 97-27279. 560p. (C). 1997. pap. text 34.95 (*0-201-30820-7*) Addison-Wesley.

Denning, Peter J., ed. Computers under Attack: Intruders, Worms & Viruses. (ACM Press Ser.). (Illus.). 492p. (C). 1990. pap. text 32.95 (*0-201-53067-8*) Addison-Wesley.

Denning, Peter J. & Metcalfe, B. Beyond Calculation: The Next Fifty Years of Computing. (Illus.). 320p. 1998. pap. 15.00 (*0-387-98588-3*) Spr-Verlag.

Denning, Peter J. & Metcalfe, Robert M. Beyond Calculation: The Next Fifty Years of Computing. LC 96-37790. (Copernicus Ser.). (Illus.). 350p. 1997. 27.00 (*0-387-94932-1*) Spr-Verlag.

Denning, R. Murray. My Search for Radionic Truths. LC 88-70943. (Illus.). 118p. (Orig.). 1988. pap. 9.95 (*0-945685-01-7*) Borderland Sciences.

Denning, Robert, ed. James Joyce, 1907-1927, Vol. 1. (Critical Heritage Ser.). 400p. (C). 1997. 140.00 (*0-415-15918-0*) Routledge.

— James Joyce, 1928-1941, Vol. 2. (Critical Heritage Ser.). 448p. (C). 1997. 140.00 (*0-415-15919-9*) Routledge.

***Denning, S. Lance.** Finding Virtue's Place: Examining America's Civic Life. LC 99-34440. 184p. 1999. 57.95 (*0-275-96459-0*) Greenwood.

Denning, S. Lance. The Practice of Workplace Participation: Management-Employee Relations at Three Participatory Firms. LC 97-32990. 192p. 1998. 55.00 (*1-56720-195-4*, Quorum Bks) Greenwood.

***Denning, Sarah.** Dreams Made Easy: An Introduction to the Basics of the Ancient Art of Dream Interpretation. LC 99-20770. 64p. 1999. pap. text 7.95 (*0-8069-9853-9*) Sterling.

Denning, Sarah. Women's I Ching. (Illus.). 224p. 1999. 19.95 (*0-312-24252-2*, Thomas Dunne) St Martin.

***Denning, Stephen.** The Springboard: How Storytelling Ignites Action in Knowledge-Era Organization. 192p. 2000. pap. 18.95 (*0-7506-7355-9*) Buttrwrth-Heinemann.

Denning, Teresa. Giving It Back: On Trauma & Recovery. 64p. 1998. pap. 8.95 (*0-9632861-2-9*) Dakota Bks.

Denning, Trevor. The Playing-Cards of Spain: A Guide for Historians & Collectors. LC 96-42278. (Illus.). 180p. 1996. 49.50 (*0-8386-3747-7*) Fairleigh Dickinson.

Denning, Troy. Beyond the High Road. 1999. pap. 5.99 (*0-7869-1436-X*) TSR Inc.

— Crucible: The Trial of Cyric the Mad. (Forgotten Realms Novel Ser.). 1998. pap. 5.99 (*0-7869-0724-X*, Pub. by TSR Inc) Random.

— Faces of Deception. 1998. pap. 5.99 (*0-7869-1183-2*, Pub. by TSR Inc) Random.

— Oath of Stonekeep, 1 vol. 264p. 1999. mass mkt. 6.99 (*0-425-17065-9*) Blvd Books.

— Pages of Pain. 1998. pap. 5.99 (*0-7869-0825-4*) TSR Inc.

Denning, Troy, jt. auth. see Greenwood, Ed.

***Denning, William.** Let Your Artist Out. 64p. 1999. 22.00 (*1-85608-185-0*, Pub. by Hunt GBR) St Mut.

Dennis. Apple Pascal: A Problem Solving Approach. 1985. 38.00 (*0-314-92881-2*) West Pub.

***Dennis.** Credit & Collection Hand Book. LC 99-48409. 1999. 69.95 (*0-13-082783-5*) P-H.

Dennis. Hilltops & Rivers, Vol. 1. 1999. text. write for info. (*0-312-16863-2*) St Martin.

— International Affairs since 1939. 4th ed. 1993. pap. text. write for info. (*0-582-71198-3*, Pub. by Addison-Wesley) Longman.

— International Financial Flows. 1984. lib. bdg. 123.00 (*0-86010-478-8*) Kluwer Academic.

— Lithographic Technology. 96p. 1996. teacher ed. 12.00 (*0-8273-8132-8*) Delmar.

— Nationalism & Desire in Early Historical Fiction. 210p. 1997. text 49.95 (*0-312-17244-3*) St Martin.

— PPM for Graphic Communications. 2nd ed. 32p. (C). 1998. pap. text, teacher ed. 12.00 (*0-8273-7947-1*); mass mkt. 22.95 (*0-8273-7946-3*) Delmar.

— Screen Printing Technology. (Graphic Communications Ser.). 1990. pap. 28.95 (*0-8273-3772-8*); pap., teacher ed. 12.00 (*0-8273-3773-6*) Delmar.

***Dennis.** Systems Analysis Design (SAD) 516p. 2000. text 91.75 (*0-471-24100-8*) Wiley.

Dennis, ed. Pselli, Michaelis: Orationes Panegyricae. (GRE.). 1994. 75.00 (*3-8154-1666-3*, T1666, Pub. by B G Teubner) U of Mich Pr.

Dennis, A. J., jt. auth. see Cooke, M.

***Dennis, Alan & Wixom, Barbara Haley.** Systems Analysis & Design: Additional Cases. 2000. pap. 14.95 (*0-471-36224-7*) Wiley.

Dennis, Alan, jt. auth. see FitzGerald, Jerry.

Dennis, Alfred P. The Romance of World Trade. 1977. lib. bdg. 59.95 (*0-8490-2538-9*) Gordon Pr.

Dennis, Allen. James Blackwood Memories. LC 96-6611. 1997. write for info. (*0-937552-79-8*) Quail Ridge.

Dennis, Anita. Creating a Virtual Office: Ten Case Studies for CPA Firms. LC 97-21467. 100p. 1997. pap. 41.00 (*0-87051-188-2*, 090426) Am Inst CPA.

Dennis, Anita, jt. auth. see Giudice, Maria.

Dennis, Anne. Taming the Diabetes Dragon. Mitchell, Barb, ed. LC 98-65127. (Illus.). 24p. (J). (gr. 3-7). 1998. pap. 14.95 (*1-891383-03-5*) JayJo Bks.

Dennis, Anne T. Marshall Yesterday: An Adventure Back in Time for Children & Adults. 36p. (J). (gr. 4 up). 1991. pap. 5.00 (*1-879703-00-9*) Marshall Regnl Arts.

Dennis, Anthony J. The Rise of the Islamic Empire & the Threat to the West. (Illus.). 180p. (C). 1996. text 40.00 (*1-55605-268-5*); pap. text 20.00 (*1-55605-267-7*) Wyndham Hall.

Dennis, Anthony J., jt. auth. see Cooke, Marcus.

Dennis, Anthony J., jt. ed. see Bjorseth, Alf.

Dennis, Anthony J., jt. ed. see Cooke, Marcus.

Dennis, Barbara. Charlotte Yonge, Novelist of the Oxford Movement, 1823-1901: A Literature of Victorian Culture & Society. LC 92-12773. (Illus.). 188p. 1992. lib. bdg. 79.95 (*0-7734-9544-4*) E Mellen.

— Elizabeth Barrett Browning: The Hope End Years. (Illus.). 148p. 1996. 29.95 (*1-85411-099-3*, Pub. by Seren Bks); pap. 16.95 (*1-85411-091-8*, Pub. by Seren Bks) Dufour.

***Dennis, Barbara.** The Victorian Novel. (Contexts in Literature Ser.). 128p. 2000. pap. write for info. (*0-521-77595-7*) Cambridge U Pr.

Dennis, Barbara & Skittoa, David. Reform & Intellectual Debate in Victorian England, 1830-1880. Armstrong, Isobel, ed. (World & Word Ser.). 240p. 1987. 67.50 (*0-685-19165-6*, Pub. by C Helm); pap. text 16.95 (*0-7099-5428-X*, Pub. by C Helm) Routldge.

Dennis, Barbara, ed. see Trollope, Anthony.

Dennis, Barbara, ed. & intro. see Yonge, Charlotte M.

Dennis, Barbara A., ed. see Dennis, Bobby.

Dennis, Barbara D., ed. see National Academy of Arbitrators, Meeting (31st: 19.

Dennis, Barbara D., ed. see National Academy of Arbitrators, Meeting (32nd: 1979: Dearborn, MI) Staff.

Dennis, Barbara D., ed. see National Academy of Arbitrators, Meeting (33rd, 1980, Los Angeles, CA) Staff.

Dennis, Barbara D., ed. see National Academy of Arbitrators, Meeting (36th: 1983: Quebec) Staff.

***Dennis, Barbara H., et al, eds.** Well-Controlled Diet Studies in Humans: A Practical Guide to Design & Management. LC 98-48694. 418p. 1999. pap. 57.00 (*0-88091-158-1*, QP143) Am Dietetic Assn.

Dennis, Beatrice. Health Care Conversions & Philanthropy: Important Issues for Practice & Research. (Nonprofit Sector Research Fund Ser.). 50p. pap. write for info. (*0-89843-267-7*) The Aspen Inst.

Dennis, Bobby. The Write Stuff: A Calligraphy Skills Manual. Dennis, Barbara A., ed. (Illus.). 41p. (Orig.). 1989. pap. text 14.95 (*0-944516-03-3*) Fidget Pubns.

Dennis, Brian. Winning at the Frontline. 168p. (Orig.). 1996. pap. 15.95 (*1-886094-37-3*) Chicago Spectrum.

***Dennis, C. J.** A Sentimental Bloke. (Illus.). 1999. pap. 14.95 (*1-875892-35-4*, Pub. by Edtns T Thompson) Intl Spec Bk.

***Dennis, Carl.** Poetry As Persuasion. LC 00-44728. 2001. pap. write for info. (*0-8203-2248-2*) U of Ga Pr.

Dennis, Carl. Ranking Wishes. LC 96-44352. 96p. 1997. pap. 14.95 (*0-14-058779-9*) Viking Penguin.

Dennis, Carol L. Dragon's Queen. 256p. 1991. mass mkt. 4.99 (*0-446-36152-6*, Aspect) Warner Bks.

Dennis, Caryl. Colorology: The Study of the Science of Color. (Illus.). 128p. (Orig.). 1990. pap. 14.00 (*0-9627845-0-8*) Rainbows Unltd.

Dennis, Caryl. Millennium Children: Tales of the Shift. Whitman, Parker, ed. (Orig.). 1997. pap. 18.00 (*0-9627845-1-6*) Rainbows Unltd.

Dennis, Charles, jt. auth. see Barrett, Margaret.

Dennis, Charles H. Eugene Field's Creative Years. (BCL1-PS American Literature Ser.). 339p. 1992. reprint ed. lib. bdg. 89.00 (*0-7812-6712-9*) Rprt Serv.

— Eugene Field's Creative Years. LC 72-144971. 339p. 1972. reprint ed. 24.00 (*0-403-00939-1*) Scholarly.

Dennis, Christopher J. Adorno's Philosophy of Modern Music. LC 97-9714. (Studies in the History & Interpretation of Music: Vol. 58). 144p. 1997. text 69.95 (*0-7734-8434-5*) E Mellen.

Dennis, Cindy & Neal, Linda. A Beginner's Guide to the TI-82 with Emphasis on Pre-Calculus Mathematics. (C). 1994. pap. text 7.25 (*0-07-016401-0*) McGraw.

Dennis, Clue T. & Miller, Luke. If You Like My Apples: A Simple Guide to Biodynamic Gardening. LC 96-46976. 144p. 1997. pap. 12.95 (*0-89529-760-4*, Avery) Penguin Putnam.

***Dennis, Colin & Stringer, Michael.** Chilled Foods: A Comprehensive Guide. 2nd ed. 480p. 2000. text 179.00 (*1-85573-499-0*, Pub. by Woodhead Pubng) Am Educ Systs.

Dennis, Colin, jt. ed. see Arthey, David.

Dennis, Connie M. Self Care Deficit Nursing Theory: In Practice. (Illus.). 176p. (C). (gr. 13). 1996. pap. text 28.00 (*0-8151-2426-0*, 28191) Mosby Inc.

***Dennis, Craig & Quinn, Eric.** CCNP CMTD/BCRAN Exam Cram. LC 99-51357. (Illus.). 400p. 1999. write for info. (*1-57610-437-0*) Coriolis Grp.

Dennis, Cynthia A. & Eisenberg, Ronald L. Applied Radiographic Calculations. (Illus.). 190p. 1993. pap. write for info. (*0-7216-4885-1*, W B Saunders Co) Harcrt Hlth Sci Grp.

— Applied Radiographic Calculations. LC 92-28280. (Illus.). 192p. 1993. pap. text 35.95 (*0-7216-6596-9*, W B Saunders Co) Harcrt Hlth Sci Grp.

Dennis, Cynthia A., et al. Radiographic Positioning Pocket Manual. LC 95-10054. 288p. 1995. spiral bd. 28.95 (*0-316-18096-3*) Lppncott W & W.

Dennis, Cynthia A., jt. auth. see Eisenberg, Ronald L.

Dennis, D., jt. auth. see Arensberg, S.

Dennis, D. J. One Day at a Time: A Vietnam Diary. (Orig.). 1992. pap. 16.95 (*0-7022-2442-1*, Pub. by Univ Queensland Pr) Intl Spec Bk.

Dennis, D. T. Biochemistry of Energy Utilization in Plants. (Tertiary Level Biology Ser.). (Illus.). 200p. 1987. text 55.00 (*0-412-00981-1*, 9438, Chap & Hall NY) Chapman & Hall.

— Biochemistry of Energy Utilization in Plants. (Tertiary Level Biology Ser.). (Illus.). 200p. 1987. mass mkt. 34.50 (*0-412-00991-9*, 9439, Chap & Hall NY) Chapman & Hall.

Dennis, Dale J. The Fifth Generation. 199p. (YA). 1995. 16.98 (*0-88290-571-6*, 1963) Horizon Utah.

Dennis, Daniel J., Jr. Gems: A Lively Guide for the Casual Collector. LC 99-11425. 192p. 1999. 29.95 (*0-8109-4126-0*, Pub. by Abrams) Time Warner.

Dennis, David. Plant Metabolism. 2nd ed. (C). 1996. pap. text 59.06 (*0-582-25906-1*, Pub. by Addison-Wesley) Longman.

Dennis, David B. Beethoven in German Politics, 1870-1989. LC 95-20936. 251p. 1996. 37.00 (*0-300-06399-7*) Yale U Pr.

Dennis, Deborah L. & Monahan, John, eds. Coercion & Aggressive Community Treatment: A New Frontier in Mental Health Law. (Plenum Series in Social-Clinical Psychology). (Illus.). 236p. (C). 1996. 47.00 (*0-306-45167-0*, Plenum Trade) Perseus Pubng.

Dennis, Delmar D. To Stand Alone: Inside the KKK for the FBI. 208p. (Orig.). 1991. pap. 14.95 (*0-925591-05-X*) Covenant Hse Bks.

Dennis, Denise & Willmarth, Susan. Black History for Beginners. 4th ed. 1990. pap. 21.00 (*0-7855-7029-2*, Pub. by Northcote House) St Mut.

— Black History for Beginners. 4th ed. (Illus.). 192p. 1984. 19.95 (*0-86316-069-7*); pap. 9.95 (*0-86316-068-9*) Writers & Readers.

An Asterisk (*) at the beginning of an entry indicates that the title is appearing for the first time.

Dennis, Don & Stevens, Shirley. From the Cell to the Cross. 2nd rev. ed. LC 98-66962. Orig. Title: Breaking Crime's Vicious Cycle. (Illus.). 240p. 1998. pap. 12.99 (*0-9657561-5-7*) Reflection TX.

Dennis, Don, ed. see Barrett, Kevin & Forbeck, Matt.

Dennis, Don, ed. see Dewey, Erik A.

Dennis, Donald G., ed. see Dewey, Erik A.

Dennis, Donald G., ed. see Dufault, Richard.

Dennis, Donald G., ed. see Forbeck, Matt & Barrett, Kevin.

Dennis, Donald G., ed. see Greaves, Sheldon.

Dennis, Donald G., ed. see Hopler, John.

Dennis, Donald G., ed. see Sigler, Scott.

Dennis, Dz. International Tectonics Dictionary: Introductory Part. (RUS.). 142p. 1982. 14.95 (*0-8288-1471-6*, M15266) Fr & Eur.

Dennis, E. A., jt. ed. see Wong, P. Y.

Dennis, E. S. & Llewellyn, D. J., eds. Molecular Approaches to Crop Improvement. (Plant Gene Research Ser.). (Illus.). ix, 166p. 1991. 90.95 (*0-387-82230-5*) Spr-Verlag.

Dennis, E. S., jt. ed. see Hohn, R. B.

Dennis, Earle S. & Smith, Jane E. Marriage Bonds of Bedford County, Virginia, 1755-1800: (Reprinted with) Bedford County, Virginia: Index of Wills, from 1754 to 1830. LC 75-4010. 99p. 1989. reprint ed. pap. 7.00 (*0-8063-0669-6*) Genealog Pub.

Dennis, Elsie F. Indian Slavery in Pacific Northwest, Pts. I, II & III. fac. ed. (Oregon Historical Quarterly, Articles Ser.: No. XXXI). 38p. (C). 1930. reprint ed. pap. text 4.38 (*1-55567-850-5*) Coyote Press.

Dennis, Emma, ed. see Schoenberg, Wilfred P.

Dennis, Erline. I Heard You, Lord. LC 97-90443. 1997. pap. 8.95 (*0-533-12400-X*) Vantage.

Dennis, Ervin A. Applied Photography. LC 84-23047. 512p. (C). 1985. text 37.95 (*0-8273-2292-5*) Delmar.

— Applied Photography. LC 84-23047. 512p. (C). 1985. student ed. 15.95 (*0-8273-2293-3*) Delmar.

— Applied Photography. 2nd ed. 353p. 1992. text 32.95 (*0-8273-4911-4*) Delmar.

— Applied Photography Instructors Guide. 1992. 10.95 (*0-8273-4912-2*) Delmar.

— Applied Photography Student Manual. 2nd ed. 1992. 14.95 (*0-8273-4910-6*) Delmar.

— Lithographic Technology. LC 96-210. (Graphic Communications Ser.). 640p. (C). 1996. mass mkt. 68.95 (*0-8273-6124-6*) Delmar.

— Lithographic Technology. LC 79-16756. 1980. write for info. (*0-672-97164-X*); teacher ed. write for info. (*0-672-97165-8*); student ed. write for info. (*0-672-97166-6*) Macmillan.

Dennis, Ervin A. & Jenkins, John D. Comprehensive Graphic Arts. LC 72-92620. 1974. 24.95 (*0-672-97607-2*, Bobbs) Macmillan.

— Comprehensive Graphic Arts. LC 72-92620. 1975. teacher ed. 6.67 (*0-672-97609-9*, Bobbs) Macmillan.

— Comprehensive Graphic Arts. LC 72-92620. 1976. student ed. 11.50 (*0-672-97608-0*, Bobbs) Macmillan.

— Comprehensive Graphic Arts. 2nd ed. (Illus.). 576p. (C). 1983. teacher ed. write for info. (*0-672-97682-X*); student ed. write for info. (*0-672-98447-4*); text. write for info. (*0-672-97681-1*) Macmillan.

Dennis-Escoffier, jt. auth. see Fortin.

Dennis-Escoffier, jt. ed. see Fortin.

Dennis, Everette. Of Media & People. 160p. (C). 1992. 42.00 (*0-8039-4746-1*); pap. 19.95 (*0-8039-4747-X*) Sage.

Dennis, Everette, ed. The Media in Black & White. 182p. 1996. pap. text 21.95 (*1-56000-873-3*) Transaction Pubs.

Dennis, Everette E. Of Media & People. LC 92-28903. 195p. 1992. reprint ed. pap. 60.50 (*0-608-04306-0*, 206508500012) Bks Demand.

— Reshaping the Media: Mass Communication in an Information Age. (Illus.). 300p. (C). 1989. text 49.95 (*0-8039-3660-5*); pap. text 24.00 (*0-8039-3661-3*) Sage.

— Reshaping the Media: Mass Communication in an Information Age. LC 89-10509. (Illus.). 208p. reprint ed. pap. 64.50 (*0-608-09800-0*, 206996900007) Bks Demand.

Dennis, Everette E., ed. Children & the Media. LC 95-46958. 224p. 1996. pap. text 24.95 (*1-56000-872-5*) Transaction Pubs.

Dennis, Everette E., et al, eds. Beyond the Cold War: Soviet & American Media Images. LC 90-23413. 180p. reprint ed. pap. 55.80 (*0-608-09772-1*, 206994600007) Bks Demand.

— Justice Hugo Black & the First Amendment: "No Law Means No Law" LC 78-685. 212p. 1978. reprint ed. pap. 65.80 (*0-608-06872-1*, 206707900009) Bks Demand.

— Media Freedom & Accountability, 14. LC 89-2148. (Contributions to the Study of Mass Media & Communications Ser.: No. 14). 220p. 1989. 45.00 (*0-313-26727-8*, DMF/, Greenwood Pr) Greenwood.

Dennis, Everette E. & LaMay, Craig L., eds. America's Schools & the Mass Media. 155p. (C). 1992. pap. 21.95 (*1-56000-652-8*) Transaction Pubs.

— The Culture of Crime. LC 95-7674. 1995. 24.95 (*1-56000-826-1*) Transaction Pubs.

— Higher Education in the Information Age. 181p. (C). 1992. pap. 24.95 (*1-56000-651-X*) Transaction Pubs.

***Dennis, Everette E. & Merrill, John C.** Media Debates: Issues in Mass Communication. 3rd ed. (Mass Communication Ser.). 2001. pap. 28.00 (*0-534-57933-7*) Wadsworth Pub.

Dennis, Everette E. & Pease, Edward, eds. Radio As the Forgotten Medium. 204p. (C). 1994. pap. 21.95 (*1-56000-798-2*) Transaction Pubs.

Dennis, Everette E. & Snyder, Robert W. Covering Congress. LC 97-5091. 150p. 1997. pap. text 21.95 (*1-56000-946-2*) Transaction Pubs.

— Media & Democracy. LC 97-23126. (Media Studies). 202p. 1997. pap. write for info. (*0-7658-0408-5*) Transaction Pubs.

Dennis, Everette E & Wartella, Ellen, eds. American Communication Research: The Remembered History. (LEA's Communication Ser.). 224p. 1996. pap. 24.50 (*0-8058-1744-1*); text 39.95 (*0-8058-1743-3*) L Erlbaum Assocs.

Dennis, Everette E., et al. Beyond the Cold War. (Illus.). 264p. 1991. 46.00 (*0-8039-3900-0*); pap. 21.95 (*0-8039-3901-9*) Sage.

Dennis, Everette E., jt. auth. see DeFleur, Melvin L.

Dennis, Everette E., jt. ed. see Pavlik, John V.

Dennis, Everette E., jt. ed. see Snyder, Robert W.

Dennis, Faith. Three Centuries of French Domestic Silver: Its Makers & Its Marks: The Metropolitan Museum of Art, 2 vols. (Illus.). 1993. reprint ed. 295.00 (*1-55660-175-1*) A Wofsy Fine Arts.

***Dennis, Ferdinand.** The Last Blues Dance. 256p. 1998. mass mkt. 10.95 (*0-00-649783-7*, Pub. by HarpC) Trafalgar.

***Dennis, Ferdinand & Khan, Naseem, eds.** Voices of the Crossing. 2000. pap. 17.00 (*1-85242-583-0*) Serpents Tail.

Dennis, Frank A., compiled by. Index to the Journal of Mississippi History, Vols. XXI-XL, 1959-1978. 569p. 1993. lib. bdg. 50.00 (*0-938896-61-X*) Mississippi Archives.

Dennis, Frank A., ed. The Journal of Mississippi History: Index to Volumes I-XX. 1984. text 40.00 (*0-938896-37-7*) Mississippi Archives.

Dennis, Franklin, ed. see Cheever, John.

Dennis, Frederick W. Here Today - Guam Tomorrow. 226p. 1994. 29.95 (*0-9644098-0-1*) Dennis PC Cnslting.

Dennis, Gartie, jt. auth. see Cardo, Ras.

Dennis, Geoffrey E. Monetary Economics. LC 80-40095. (Modern Economics Ser.). 328p. reprint ed. pap. 101.70 (*0-7837-1591-9*, 204188300024) Bks Demand.

Dennis, George. The Cities & Cemeteries of Etruria. abr. ed. Hemphill, Pamela, ed. LC 84-8431. (Illus.). 458p. pap. 142.00 (*0-7837-6495-2*, 204658500003) Bks Demand.

Dennis, Ginger, ed. see Turner, Kevin Lane.

Dennis, Gregory. Mission Critical Java Management: Business Strategies, Applications, & Development. LC 98-8514. 272p. (C). 1998. pap. text 34.95 (*0-201-32573-X*) Addison-Wesley.

Dennis, Helen M. A New Approach to the Poetry of Ezra Pound: Through the Medieval Provencal Aspect. LC 95-18360. 516p. 1996. text 119.95 (*0-7734-9010-8*) E Mellen.

Dennis, Helen M., ed. Willa Cather & European Cultural Influences. LC 95-43271. (Studies in American Literature: Vol. 16). 1996. write for info. (*0-7734-8858-8*) E Mellen.

***Dennis, Helen T.** 101 Questions Your Dog Would Ask: What's Bothering Your Dog & How to Solve It's Problems. (Illus.). 112p. 1999. pap. 12.95 (*0-7641-0886-7*) Barron.

Dennis, Ian. Prince of Stars in the Cavern of Time. 430p. 1989. 22.50 (*0-87951-298-9*, Pub. by Overlook Pr) Penguin Putnam.

Dennis, Ian & Tapsfield, Patrick, eds. Human Abilities: Their Nature & Measurement. 250p. 1996. 45.00 (*0-8058-1800-6*) L Erlbaum Assocs.

Dennis, J. E., Jr. & Schnabel, Robert B. Numerical Methods for Unconstrained Optimization & Nonlinear Equations. LC 95-51776. (Classics in Applied Mathematics Ser.: Vol. 16). xvi, 378p. 1996. pap. 37.00 (*0-89871-364-1*) Soc Indus-Appl Math.

Dennis, J. G., et al, eds. International Tectonic Lexicon: A Prodrome. (International Tectonic Lexicon Ser.: Vol. 1). vi, 153p. 1979. pap. text 29.00 (*3-510-65092-1*, Pub. by E Schweizerbartsche) Balogh.

Dennis, J. G. & Murawski, H., eds. International Tectonic Lexicon, Vol. 2. viii, 119p. 1988. pap. 32.00 (*3-510-65134-0*, Pub. by E Schweizerbartsche) Balogh.

Dennis J., Hutchinson, et al, eds. The Supreme Court Review, 1993. 456p. 1994. lib. bdg. 45.00 (*0-226-36248-5*) U Ch Pr.

Dennis, J. K. & Such, T. E. Nickel & Chromium Plating. 3rd ed. 464p. 1993. 170.00 (*1-85573-081-2*, 6337, Pub. by Woodhead Pubng) Am Educ Systs.

Dennis, Jack. Tying Flies with Jack Dennis. 1993. spiral bd. 29.95 (*0-937556-01-7*) Snake River Bk.

— Western Trout Fly Tying Manual I. 2nd ed. 1991. spiral bd. 24.95 (*0-937556-02-5*) Snake River Bk.

— Western Trout Fly Tying Manual II, Vol. 2. rev. ed. 1995. spiral bd. 34.95 (*0-937556-00-9*) Snake River Bk.

Dennis, Jack, jt. auth. see Easton, David.

Dennis, James M. Renegade Regionalists: The Modern Independence of Grant Wood, Thomas Hart Benton, & John Steuart Curry. LC 97-9184. (Illus.). 296p. 1998. pap. 21.95 (*0-299-15584-6*) U of Wis Pr.

***Dennis, Jeanne Gowen.** Homeschooling High School: Planning Ahead for College Admission. 280p. 2000. pap. 14.99 (*1-883002-69-9*) Emerald WA.

Dennis, Jeff. When the Sandman Meets the Reaper: 12 Tales of Magic & Terror. (Illus.). 260p. (Orig.). 1996. pap. 13.00 (*0-9655522-0-9*) Wordcraft Res.

Dennis, Jerome, ed. 1997 International Laser Safety Conference Proceedings, Vol. 3. (Illus.). 649p. 1997. pap. text 109.00 (*0-912035-13-7*, 215) Laser Inst.

Dennis, Jerry. Canadian Bicycle Tours: Twelve Breathtaking Tours Through Quebec, Ontario, Newfoundland, Nova Scotia, New Brunswick, & Prince Edward Island. (Illus.). 240p. 1995. pap. 14.95 (*0-8050-1492-6*, Owl) H Holt & Co.

— Canoeing Michigan Rivers. (Illus.). 152p. (Orig.). 1986. pap. 12.95 (*0-9608588-4-9*) Friede Pubns.

***Dennis, Jerry.** From a Wooden Canoe: Reflections on Canoeing, Camping & Classic Equipment. (Illus.). 224p. 2000. pap. 12.95 (*0-312-26738-X*) St Martin.

Dennis, Jerry. From a Wooden Canoe: Reflections on Canoeing, Camping & Classic Equipment. 2nd ed. LC 98-33238. (Illus.). 204p. 1999. text 21.95 (*0-312-19979-1*) St Martin.

— It's Raining Frogs & Fishes: Four Seasons of Natural Phenomena & Oddities of the Sky. LC 92-52603. (Illus.). 336p. 1993. reprint ed. pap. 14.00 (*0-06-092195-1*, Perennial) HarperTrade.

— Place on Water. (Illus.). 240p. 1996. pap. 10.95 (*0-312-14127-0*) St Martin.

— River Home. LC 98-11958. 240p. 1998. text 22.95 (*0-312-18594-4*) St Martin.

***Dennis, Jerry.** River Home: An Angler's Explorations. LC 98-11958. (Illus.). 240p. 2000. pap. 12.95 (*0-312-25415-6*) St Martin.

***Dennis, Jill C.** Privacy & Confidentiality of Health Information. LC 00-9556. 2000. 39.95 (*0-7879-5278-8*) Jossey-Bass.

Dennis, John. The Age of Pope. (Select Bibliographies Reprint Ser.). 1977. reprint ed. 20.95 (*0-8369-5765-2*) Ayer.

— The Critical Works of John Dennis, Vol. 1. Hooker, Edward N., ed. LC 39-5971. 549p. reprint ed. pap. 170.20 (*0-608-08153-1*, 202053700001) Bks Demand.

— The Critical Works of John Dennis, Vol. 2. Hooker, Edward N., ed. LC 39-5971. 731p. reprint ed. pap. 200.00 (*0-608-08154-X*, 202053700002) Bks Demand.

— Experiences. 224p. (J). 1987. mass mkt. 22.95 (*0-8384-2819-3*, Newbury) Heinle & Heinle.

Dennis, John & Griffin, Suzanne. Reflections. 2nd ed. LC 93-47459. 224p. (J). 1994. mass mkt. 21.95 (*0-8384-4846-1*) Heinle & Heinle.

Dennis, John, jt. auth. see Griffin, Suzanne M.

Dennis, John V. Beyond the Bird Feeder: The Habits & Behavior of Feeding Station Birds When They Are Not at Your Feeder. LC 81-47491. (Illus.). 224p. 1981. 25.00 (*0-394-50890-4*) Knopf.

— A Complete Guide to Bird Feeding. 1994. pap. 18.00 (*0-679-75052-5*) Knopf.

— Great Cypress Swamps. LC 88-19119. (Illus.). 142p. 1988. 29.95 (*0-8071-1501-0*) La State U Pr.

— A Guide to Western Bird Feeding. (Illus.). 1991. 9.95 (*1-880241-00-5*) Bird Watchers.

— Summer Bird Feeding: Audubon Workshop Guide to Feeding Wild Birds in Summer. (Illus.). 130p. 1989. pap. 9.95 (*0-9620001-0-8*) Audubon Workshop.

Dennis, John V., jt. auth. see Gunn, Charles R.

Dennis, Judith, jt. auth. see Adrian, Ann.

Dennis, Kenneth G. Rationality in Economics: Alternative Perspectives. LC 97-46442. (Recent Economic Thought Ser.). 149p. 1998. lib. bdg. 95.00 (*0-7923-8114-9*) Kluwer Academic.

Dennis, Kevin A. & Jenkins, John D. Comprehensive Graphic Arts. 3rd ed. (Illus.). 633p. (YA). (gr. 6-12). 1999. student ed. 45.35 (*0-02-681251-7*); student ed., wbk. ed. 10.37 (*0-02-681253-3*) Glencoe.

— Comprehensive Graphic Arts: Instructor's Guide. 3rd ed. 250p. 1999. teacher ed. 21.75 (*0-02-681252-5*) Glencoe.

Dennis, L. The Coming American Fascism. (Studies in Right Wing Ideology). 1994. lib. bdg. write for info. (*0-8490-8945-X*) Gordon Pr.

Dennis, La Rea J., et al. Plants of the Oregon Coastal Dunes. LC 98-49879. (Illus.). 128p. (Orig.). 1999. pap. 12.95 (*0-87071-457-0*) Oreg St U Pr.

Dennis, Landt. Santa Fe & Taos: Under a Coyote Moon. LC 95-30891. (Illus.). 144p. 1996. pap. 19.95 (*0-8118-0896-3*) Chronicle Bks.

Dennis, Landt & Dennis, Lisl. Behind Adobe Walls: Hidden Homes & Gardens of Santa Fe & Taos. LC 96-28036. 144p. 1997. pap. 22.95 (*0-8118-1164-6*) Chronicle Bks.

Dennis, Larry. A Beginner's Guide to Golf: How to Get Started... & Have Fun Doing It. rev. ed. LC 93-85975. 107p. 1998. pap. 14.95 (*0-9638647-0-X*, 99BG001) Natl Golf.

— Eighty-Eighth U. S. Open. Norwood, Bev, ed. (Illus.). 64p. 1987. 15.00 (*0-9615344-2-7*) Intl Merc OH.

— Eighty-Eighth U. S. Open. Norwood, Bev, ed. (Illus.). 64p. 1988. 15.00 (*0-9615344-3-5*) Intl Merc OH.

Dennis, Larry, jt. auth. see Floyd, Ray.

Dennis, Larry, jt. auth. see Kostis, Peter.

Dennis, Larry, jt. auth. see McLean, Jim.

Dennis, Larry, jt. auth. see Nelson, Byron.

Dennis, Larry, ed. see Toski, Bob & Flick, Jim.

Dennis, Larry W. Empowering Leadership. pap. 12.95 (*0-9631766-1-7*) Rising Tide Pub.

— How to Turbo Charge You: Six Steps to Top Your True Potential. 208p. 1994. pap. write for info. (*0-9631766-2-5*) Rising Tide Pub.

— In Information: How to Gain the 71Advantage. 1997. pap. 19.95 (*0-9631766-3-3*) Rising Tide Pub.

— Repeat Business. 1993. pap. 12.95 (*0-9631766-0-9*) Rising Tide Pub.

Dennis, Laurie B., jt. auth. see Dennis, Terry L.

Dennis, Lawrence. The Coming American Fascism: The Crisis of Capitalism. 330p. 1993. reprint ed. pap. text 13.98 (*0-939482-43-6*, 0197, Noontide Pr) Legion Survival.

— The Dynamics of War & Revolution: A Study of the Hidden Economic Origins of Conflict. 259p. 1993. reprint ed. pap. text 12.00 (*0-939482-41-X*, 0196, Noontide Pr) Legion Survival.

— The Dynamics of War & Revolutions. 1973. 250.00 (*0-87700-151-0*) Revisionist Pr.

— Operational Thinking for Survival. LC 73-85338. 1969. 5.95 (*0-87926-003-3*) R Myles.

— A Trial on Trial. 1978. lib. bdg. 75.00 (*0-87700-292-4*) Revisionist Pr.

Dennis, Lawrence & St. George, Maximillian. A Trial on Trial. 502p. 1984. pap. 9.98 (*0-939484-20-X*, 0616, Inst Hist Rev) Legion Survival.

Dennis, Lawrence E. & Jacobs, Renata M., eds. The Arts in Higher Education. LC 68-57442. (Jossey-Bass Higher Education Ser.). 176p. reprint ed. pap. 54.60 (*0-8357-5779-X*, 201394100087) Bks Demand.

Dennis, Lawrence J. From Prayer to Pragmatism: A Biography of John L. Childs. LC 91-23926. 240p. (C). 1992. 31.95 (*0-8093-1777-X*) S Ill U Pr.

Dennis, Lawrence J., ed. George S. Counts & Charles A. Beard: Collaborators for Change. LC 88-20153. (SUNY Series, the Philosophy of Education). 192p. (C). 1989. text 19.50 (*0-88706-992-4*) State U NY Pr.

Dennis, Leah H., et al. Word Lists from the South. (Publications of the American Dialect Society: No. 2). 72p. 1944. pap. text 7.20 (*0-8173-0602-1*) U of Ala Pr.

Dennis, Linda L., ed. see Weightman, R. T., et al.

Dennis, Lisl. Morocco: Casablanca to Marrakesh. LC 98-43875. 1999. pap. 25.00 (*0-609-80465-0*) Crown Pub Group.

Dennis, Lisl, photos by. Martha's Vineyard: Houses & Gardens. (Illus.). 240p. 1992. 50.00 (*0-316-18083-1*) Little.

Dennis, Lisl, jt. auth. see Dennis, Landt.

Dennis, Lloyd B., ed. Practical Public affairs in an Era of Change: A Cutting-Edge Communications Guide for Government, Business, & College. 450p. (C). 1995. pap. text 29.50 (*0-7618-0086-7*); lib. bdg. 62.50 (*0-7618-0085-9*) U Pr of Amer.

Dennis, Lorraine B. & Hassol, Joan. Introduction to Human Development & Health Issues. (Illus.). 320p. 1983. pap. text 39.00 (*0-7216-3030-8*, W B Saunders Co) Harcrt Hlth Sci Grp.

Dennis, Lynn. Garden for Life: Horticulture for People with Special Needs. (Illus.). 112p. 1997. pap. 15.95 (*0-88880-313-3*) Lone Pine.

Dennis, Maire, et al. St. Francis & the Foolishness of God. LC 93-28727. 175p. (Orig.). 1993. pap. 14.00 (*0-88344-899-8*) Orbis Bks.

Dennis, Marguerite J. Complete College Financing Guide. 4th ed. 288p. 1997. pap. text 14.95 (*0-8120-9523-5*) Barron.

— An Insider's Guide for International Students on Selecting a College or University in the United States. (Illus.). 12p. (Orig.). 1995. pap. 4.00 (*1-884241-52-2*, INSIDER3) Energeia Pub.

— An Insiders Guide to Selecting a College or University. (Illus.). 12p. 1994. pap. 3.00 (*1-884241-50-6*, INSIDER2) Energeia Pub.

— An Insiders' Guide to Surviving Freshman Year. (Illus.). 12p. 1994. pap. 3.00 (*1-884241-51-4*, INSIDER1) Energeia Pub.

— Keys to Financing a College Education. 2nd ed. LC 93-22320. (Barron's Business Keys Ser.). 160p. 1993. pap. 4.95 (*0-8120-1634-3*) Barron.

— A Practical Guide to Enrollment & Retention Management in Higher Education. LC 98-9532. 160p. 1998. 55.00 (*0-89789-591-6*, Bergin & Garvey) Greenwood.

Dennis, Marie. A Retreat with Oscar Romero & Dorothy Day: Walking with the Poor. Hutchinson, Gloria, ed. LC 98-101320. 112p. 1997. pap. 7.95 (*0-86716-261-9*, B2619) St Anthony Mess Pr.

***Dennis, Marie, et al.** Oscar Romero: Reflections on His Life & Writings. LC 99-52262. (Modern Spiritual Masters Ser.). 144p. 2000. pap. 13.00 (*1-57075-309-1*) Orbis Bks.

Dennis, Mark, jt. auth. see Burnett, Charles J.

Dennis, Marshall W. & Robertson, Michael J. Residential Mortgage Lending. 4th ed. LC 94-28986. (Illus.). 384p. 1994. 68.00 (*0-13-183815-6*) P-H.

Dennis, Martha, jt. ed. see Colowick, Sidney P.

Dennis, Martin, ed. see Warlow, Charles P., et al.

Dennis, Mary, jt. auth. see Kirchhoefer, Maureen.

Dennis, Mary, jt. auth. see Millin, Kathleen.

Dennis, Mary A. Melanie - And the Story of La Salette. (Illus.). 136p. 1995. pap. 9.00 (*0-89555-522-0*) TAN Bks Pubs.

***Dennis, Mary Alice S.** Betsy's Story. LC 99-97761. 2000. pap. 10.95 (*0-533-13475-7*) Vantage.

***Dennis, Mary L.** Brave New World. 40p. (YA). 1999. 11.95 (*1-56137-446-6*) Novel Units.

— Careers in Cosmetology. (Success Without College Ser.). 144p. 2000. pap. write for info. (*0-7641-1523-5*, Pub. by Barron) Prodn Assocs.

— A Christmas Carol. 28p. 1999. 9.95 (*1-56137-617-5*) Novel Units.

— Fahrenheit 451. 36p. (YA). 1999. 11.95 (*1-56137-302-8*) Novel Units.

— The Pearl. 28p. 1999. 9.95 (*1-56137-325-7*) Novel Units.

***Dennis, Mary L. & Kirchhoefer, Maureen.** Death of a Salesman. 36p. (YA). 1999. 11.95 (*1-56137-385-0*) Novel Units.

***Dennis, Mary L. & Millin, Kathleen.** Brave New World. 32p. 1999. 9.95 (*1-56137-445-8*) Novel Units.

— A Day No Pigs Would Die. 36p. (YA). 1998. 11.95 (*1-56137-394-X*, NU394XSP) Novel Units.

***Dennis, Mary L. & Millin, Kathleen.** A Day No Pigs Would Die. 28p. 1999. 9.95 (*1-56137-393-1*) Novel Units.

Dennis, Mary L., jt. auth. see Kirchhoefer, Maureen.

Dennis, Mary L., jt. auth. see Miller, Deborah.

Dennis, Matt. Introduction to the Blues: Keyboard Piano. 72p. 1976. pap. 8.95 (*0-87166-828-9*, 93397) Mel Bay.

— Midnight Piano Moods. pap. 12.95 (*0-943748-29-1*) Ekay Music.

— Pop Piano Studio. 1996. pap. 19.95 incl. cd-rom (*0-943748-75-5*) Ekay Music.

— You Can Teach Yourself Piano. 124p. 1989. pap. 9.95 (*0-87166-263-9*, 94302) Mel Bay.

D

An Asterisk (*) at the beginning of an entry indicates that the title is appearing for the first time.

— You Can Teach Yourself Piano. 1990. audio compact disk 15.98 (0-7866-0349-6, 94302CD) Mel Bay.

— You Can Teach Yourself Piano. 1995. VHS 29.95 (0-7866-0436-0, 94302VX) Mel Bay.

— You Can Teach Yourself Piano. (SPA.). 124p. 1996. pap. 11.95 (1-56222-431-X, 94302SP) Mel Bay.

***Dennis, Matt.** You Can Teach Yourself Piano. 124p. 1998. pap. 17.95 incl. audio compact disk (0-7866-4401-X, 94302BCD) Mel Bay.

Dennis, Matthew. Cultivating a Landscape of Peace: Iroquois-European Encounters in Seventeenth-Century America. LC 92-56771. (Illus.). 296p. 1993. text 47.50 (0-8014-2171-3) Cornell U Pr.

— Cultivating a Landscape of Peace: Iroquois-European Encounters in Seventeenth-Century America. (Illus.). 336p. 1995. pap. text 16.95 (0-8014-8301-8) Cornell U Pr.

Dennis-McCully, Annette, jt. auth. see Kinsella, John.

Dennis, Michael. Court & Garden: From the French Hotel to the City of Modern Architecture. (Graham Foundation Architecture Ser.). 412p. (Orig.). 1988. pap. text 31.50 (0-262-54051-7) MIT Pr.

— Dark Lover. 60p. 1997. pap. text 10.00 (1-887778-01-2) Free Mind Free Spirit.

— The German Democratic Republic: Politics, Economics & Society. 200p. 1992. pap. 49.00 (0-86187-413-7, Pub. by P P Pubs) Cassell & Continuum.

***Dennis, Michael.** Lessons in Progress: State Universities & Progressivism in the New South, 1880-1920. LC 00-9308. 2001. write for info. (0-252-02617-9) U of Ill Pr.

Dennis, Michael. On the Eighth Day Entered Satan. 60p. 1997. pap. text 10.00 (1-887778-02-0) Free Mind Free Spirit.

Dennis, Michael, jt. auth. see Horn, Jack.

Dennis, Michael Aaron, jt. auth. see Dyer, Davis.

Dennis, Mike. Social & Economic Modernization in Eastern Germany: From Honecker to Kohl. LC 93-8747. 252p. 1993. 45.00 (0-86187-166-9) St Martin.

Dennis, Nigel. Jose Benjamin: A Critical Introduction, 1920-1936. 272p. 1986. text 35.00 (0-8020-2561-7) U of Toronto Pr.

Dennis, Nigel. Kalahari: Survival in a Thirstland Wilderness. LC 98-103263. (Illus.). 168p. 1997. write for info. (1-86872-019-5) Struik Pubs.

***Dennis, Nigel, photos by.** The Ultimate African Wildlife. (Illus.). 160p. 2000. 50.00 (1-57805-045-6) Sierra.

Dennis, Nigel F. Dramatic Essays. LC 77-28431. 184p. 1978. reprint ed. lib. bdg. 49.75 (0-313-20244-3, DEDR, Greenwood Pr) Greenwood.

Dennis, Norman. The Invention of Permanent Poverty. LC 99-169609. (Choice in Welfare Ser.: No. 34). 212p. 1997. pap. 27.50 (0-255-36392-3, Pub. by Inst Economic Affairs) Coronet Bks.

— Rising Crime & the Dismembered Family: How Conformist Intellectuals Have Campaigned Common Sense. (Choice in Welfare Ser.: No. 18). 93p. 1993. pap. 16.95 (0-255-36350-8, Pub. by Inst Economic Affairs) Coronet Bks.

Dennis, Norman & Halsey, Albert H. English Ethical Socialism: Thomas More to R. H. Tawney. (Illus.). 298p. 1988. 65.00 (0-19-827284-7) OUP.

Dennis, P. F., jt. ed. see Freer, R.

Dennis, P. N. Photodetectors. (Updates in Applied Physics & Electrical Technology Ser.). (Illus.). 200p. (C). 1986. text 95.00 (0-306-42217-4, Kluwer Plenum) Kluwer Academic.

Dennis, Pascal. Quality, Safety, & Environment: Synergy in the 21st Century. LC 96-39878. 213p. 1997. 38.00 (0-87389-379-4, H0959) ASQ Qual Pr.

Dennis, Patrick. Around the World with Auntie Mame. 1976. 23.95 (0-8488-1287-5) Amereon Ltd.

— Around the World with Auntie Mame. large type ed. LC 95-12743. 416 p. 1995. 22.95 (0-7838-1378-3, G K Hall Lrg Type) Mac Lib Ref.

— Around the World with Auntie Mame. 1992. reprint ed. lib. bdg. 31.95 (0-89966-939-5) Buccaneer Bks.

— Auntie Mame. 1976. 23.95 (0-8488-0475-9) Amereon Ltd.

— Auntie Mame. 304p. 1994. mass mkt. 5.99 (0-345-37650-1) Ballantine Pub Grp.

— Auntie Mame. 275p. 1990. reprint ed. lib. bdg. 28.95 (0-89966-726-0) Buccaneer Bks.

— Auntie Mame: An Irreverent Escapade. large type ed. LC 94-15275. 446p. 1994. lib. bdg. 20.95 (0-8161-5987-4, G K Hall Lrg Type) Mac Lib Ref.

— A Joyous Season. 1992. reprint ed. lib. bdg. 29.95 (0-89966-940-9) Buccaneer Bks.

— Little Me. 1993. reprint ed. lib. bdg. 29.95 (1-56849-103-4) Buccaneer Bks.

***Dennis, Peter.** Handwriting Analysis: An Adventure in Self-Discovery. 2nd ed. 1999. pap. 12.95 (0-9698926-3-2) CN15.

Dennis, Peter. The Territorial Army, 1906-1940. (Royal Historical Society: Studies in History: No. 51). 282p. 1987. 75.00 (0-86193-208-0) Boydell & Brewer.

— Troubled Days of Peace: Mountbatten & South East Asia Command, 1945-46. (War, Armed Forces & Society Ser.). 1991. 37.50 (0-685-61135-3, Pub. by Manchester Univ Pr); pap. 22.95 (0-685-61136-1, Pub. by Manchester Univ Pr) St Martin.

Dennis, Peter, et al, eds. The Oxford Companion to Australian Military History. (Illus.). 714p. 1996. 75.00 (0-19-553227-9) OUP.

Dennis, Peter & Grey, Jeffrey. Emergency & Confrontation: Australian Military Operations in Malaya & Borneo 1950-66. (Illus.). 400p. 1996. 59.95 (1-86373-302-7, Pub. by Allen & Unwin Pty) Paul & Co Pubs.

Dennis, Philip A. Inter-Village Conflict in Oaxaca. 220p. 1987. text 35.00 (0-8135-1178-X) Rutgers U Pr.

Dennis, Philip A. & Aycock, Wendell M., eds. Literature & Anthropology. LC 89-4279. (Studies in Comparative Literature: No. 20). x, 227p. (C). 1989. 24.95 (0-89672-166-3) Tex Tech Univ Pr.

Dennis, Philip A., tr. see Bonfil Batalla, Guillermo.

Dennis, Phillip A. & Aycock, Wendell M., eds. Literature & Anthropology. LC 89-4279. (Comparative Literature Ser.: No. 20). 238p. (C). 1998. reprint ed. pap. 12.95 (0-89672-167-1) Tex Tech Univ Pr.

Dennis, R. Fungus Flora of Venezuela & Adjacent Countries. 1970. 75.00 (3-7682-0692-0) Lubrecht & Cramer.

Dennis, R. A. Making Wheels: A Technical Manual on Wheel Manufacture. (Illus.). 160p. 1992. pap. 29.50 (1-85339-141-7, Pub. by Intermed Tech) Stylus Pub VA.

Dennis, R. E. Methods of Teaching CAD. 128p. 1986. write for info. (0-07-018220-5) McGraw.

Dennis, R. K., jt. ed. see Stein, M. R.

Dennis, R. Keith, et al. Algebraic K-Theory, Commutative Algebra, & Algebraic Geometry. LC 91-45311. 230p. 1992. pap. 59.00 (0-8218-5130-6, CONM/126) Am Math.

Dennis, R. Keith, jt. auth. see Farb, Benson.

Dennis, R. W. British Ascomycetes. 3rd enl. rev. ed. (Illus.). 1981. 130.00 (3-7682-0552-5) Lubrecht & Cramer.

— Fungi of Southeast England. vi, 295p. 1995. pap. 35.00 (0-947643-80-X, Pub. by Royal Botnic Grdns) Balogh.

— Fungi of the Hebrides. (Illus.). 383p. 1986. pap. 20.00 (0-947643-02-8, Pub. by Royal Botnic Grdns) Balogh.

Dennis, Randall, jt. auth. see Henley, Karyn.

Dennis, Ray & White, Debra. Management for Opticians. 2nd ed. LC 98-27915. 295p. 1998. pap. text 45.00 (0-7506-9756-3) Buttrwrth-Heinemann.

Dennis, Regen. Amazing Airplanes Book & Kit. (Illus.). 36p. (J). 1995. pap. 18.00 (0-8362-4241-6) Andrews & McMeel.

— Tarot for Cats. 64p. 1996. 14.95 (0-02-860828-3) Macmillan.

Dennis, Richard. Doulton Pottery from the Lambeth & Burslem Studios 1873-1939, Pt. II. (Illus.). 165p. 1989. pap. 25.00 (0-903685-05-1, Pub. by R Dennis) Antique Collect.

— The Strangest Nutritional Secret! 104p. 1997. pap. 10.00 (0-9662441-0-9) RDMC Inc.

Dennis, Richard, ed. see ERDA Technical Information Center Staff.

Dennis, Robert G. & Hahn, John B. Total Strength: A Comprehensive Guide to Increasing Your Health Through Scientifically Founded Weightlifting. LC 95-69718. 160p. 1995. pap. 15.95 (1-886783-02-0) Prometheus OH.

Dennis, Robert L., jt. auth. see Doyle, Jean M.

Dennis, Rodney, ed. The Marks in the Field: Essays on the Uses of Manuscripts by Friends of the Houghton Library. (Illus.). 176p. 1992. pap. 25.00 (0-914630-07-5) Houghton Lib.

Dennis, Rodney G. Carolyn. 20p. 1997. pap. 5.00 (1-885141-07-6) Harlequin Ink.

Dennis, Roger D., jt. auth. see Robinson, Francis T.

Dennis, Roger L., ed. The Ecology of Butterflies in Britain. LC 92-11406. (Illus.). 368p. (C). 1992. text 95.00 (0-19-854025-6) OUP.

Dennis, Ron. The Ex-Gay Reality. 32p. 1997. pap. write for info. (0-939614-50-2) Day Star NV.

— The Ex-Gay Reality. 32p. 1997. pap. write for info. incl. disk (0-939614-51-0) Day Star NV.

— Guidelines for Design, Production & Testing of Animal-Drawn Carts. (Illus.). 160p. 1996. pap. 29.50 (1-85339-338-X, Pub. by Intermed Tech) Stylus Pub VA.

Dennis, Ron & Smith, Alan. Low-Cost Load-Carrying Devices: The Design & Manufacture of Some Basic Means of Transport. 192p. 1995. pap. 29.50 (1-85339-265-0, Pub. by Intermed Tech) Stylus Pub VA.

Dennis, Ronald, ed. Prophet of the Jubilee, Vol. 10. LC 96-71245. 1997. 28.95 (1-57008-296-0) Bookcraft Inc.

Dennis, Ronald A., ed. see Jones, William C.

Dennis, Ronald C. The Call of Zion: The Story of the First Welsh Mormon Emigration. (Specialized Monographs: Vol. 2). 1987. 10.95 (0-88494-628-2) Bookcraft Inc.

Dennis, Ronald D. Welsh Mormon Writings from 1844 to 1862: A Historical Bibliography. (Specialized Monographs: Vol. 4). 1988. 11.95 (0-88494-656-8) Bookcraft Inc.

Dennis, Rosemary. Path of the Lonely Ones. LC 79-89516. (Illus.). 1979. 4.50 (0-918482-02-X) Ageless Bks.

Dennis, Roy. Golden Eagles. (Illus.). 96p. (Orig.). (YA). 1997. pap. 24.95 (1-900455-40-4, Pub. by Colin Baxter Ltd) Voyageur Pr.

— The Loch: A Year in the Life of a Scottish Loch. (Illus.). 192p. 1995. 28.95 (0-563-36940-X, BBC-Parkwest) Parkwest Pubns.

— Loons. (WorldLife Library). (Illus.). 72p. (Orig.). (YA). 1993. pap. 16.95 (0-89658-224-8) Voyageur Pr.

— Ospreys. (Illus.). 48p. 1994. pap. 11.95 (0-948661-19-4, Pub. by Colin Baxter Ltd) Voyageur Pr.

— Puffins. (Illus.). 48p. (Orig.). 1994. pap. 11.95 (0-948661-16-X, Pub. by Colin Baxter Ltd) Voyageur Pr.

Dennis, Roy, jt. auth. see Campbell, Laurie.

Dennis, Rutledge, ed. Research in Race & Ethnic Relations, Vol. 3. 154p. 1982. 78.50 (0-89232-224-1) Jai Pr.

— Research in Race & Ethnic Relations, Vol. 4. 191p. 1985. 78.50 (0-89232-361-2) Jai Pr.

— Research in Race & Ethnic Relations, Vol. 5. 267p. 1989. 78.50 (0-89232-614-X) Jai Pr.

— Research in Race & Ethnic Relations, Vol. 6. 182p. Date not set. 78.50 (1-55938-045-4) Jai Pr.

— Research in Race & Ethnic Relations, Vol. 7. 319p. 1994. 78.50 (1-55938-570-7) Jai Pr.

— Research in Race & Ethnic Relations, Vol. 8. 243p. 1995. 78.50 (1-55938-889-7) Jai Pr.

— Research in Race & Ethnic Relations, Vol. 9. 1996. 78.50 (0-7623-0045-0) Jai Pr.

Dennis, Rutledge, et al, eds. Research in Race & Ethnic Relations, Vol. 1. 199p. 1979. 78.50 (0-89232-064-8) Jai Pr.

— Research in Race & Ethnic Relations, Vol. 2. 163p. 1980. 78.50 (0-89232-141-5) Jai Pr.

Dennis, Rutledge M., jt. auth. see Moeser, John V.

Dennis, Rutledge M., jt. auth. see Stanfield, John H., II.

Dennis, Sam J. An African-American Exodus & White Migration 1950 to 1970: A Comparative Analysis of Populations' Movements & Their Relations Labor. (Studies in Historical Demography). 368p. 1989. reprint ed. text 35.00 (0-8240-3351-5) Garland.

Dennis, Sandra. The Embrace of the Daimon: Sensuality, Vision & the Goddess of the Night. LC 99-38545. 192p. 1999. pap. 18.50 (0-88214-381-6) Spring Pubns.

Dennis, Sandy. Sandy Dennis: A Personal Memoir. LC 96-30607. (Illus.). 112p. 1997. 14.95 (1-57601-001-5) Taylor.

Dennis, Scott T., jt. auth. see Palazotto, Anthony N.

Dennis, Stacey. Remember Love. 512p. 1992. mass mkt. 4.50 (0-8217-3993-X, Zebra Kensgtn) Kensgtn Pub Corp.

Dennis, Stephen N. Historic Houses of the Sewickley Valley. Giles, Cindy, ed. (Illus.). 196p. 1996. 65.00 (0-9653015-1-6) Edgewrth Presvtn.

***Dennis-Strathmen, Jeffrey A.** California Will Drafting: April 2000 Update, 3 vols. 3rd ed. LC 92-70205. 516p. 2000. 80.00 (0-7626-0420-4) Cont Ed Bar-CA.

***Dennis-Strathmeyer, Jeffrey A.** Drafting California Irrevocable Trusts: January 2000 Update, 2 vols. 3rd ed. Denham, Robert, ed. LC 97-66099. 1378p. 2000. 119.00 (0-7626-0390-9, ES-32713) Cont Ed Bar-CA.

Dennis, Sue R. Homestead Girlhoods: Growing up on the Northwest Frontier. 92p. (Orig.). 1992. pap. 9.95 (0-918484-10-3) Smugglers.

Dennis, T. L., ed. Engineering Societies in the Life of a Country. 174p. 1968. 13.25 (0-901948-02-0) Am Soc Civil Eng.

Dennis, Terry L. Apple Pascal: A Problem-Solving Approach. (Illus.). 456p. 1985. pap. text 40.50 (0-314-85228-X); pap. text, teacher ed. write for info. (0-314-87191-8) West Pub.

Dennis, Terry L. & Dennis, Laurie B. Microcomputer Modules for Management Decision Making. 3rd ed. Fenton, ed. 350p. (C). 1993. pap. text 38.25 incl. disk (0-314-01252-4) West Pub.

Dennis, Tony. LANtastic: Running a Low-Cost Network. LC 94-2117. (Data Communications & Networks Ser.). 256p. 1994. 30.00 (0-201-63180-6) Addison-Wesley.

Dennis, Trevor. Sarah Laughed: Women's Voices in the Old Testament. LC 93-34719. 208p. (Orig.). 1994. pap. 16.95 (0-687-01371-2) Abingdon.

Dennis, Vernelle T. The Murray Resource Directory & Career Guide to Historically Black Colleges & Universities Black College & Career Guide Third Edition. 3rd ed. (Illus.). 342p. (YA). (gr. 9-12). 59.00 (1-885674-01-5) LED Pubng.

Dennis, W. M., ed. see ASTM Committee D-19 on Water.

Dennis, Warren L. & Zismar, Barry S. Banks & Thrifts: Introduction to FDIC-RTC Receivership Law. (Commercial Law & Practice Ser.). 585p. 1992. pap. text 70.00 (0-685-56877-6, A4-4373) PLI.

Dennis, Wayne. The Hopi Child. LC 75-169380. (Family in America Ser.). (Illus.). 232p. 1974. reprint ed. 18.95 (0-405-03857-7) Ayer.

Dennis, Wayne, ed. Readings in General Psychology. LC 71-167334. (Essay Index Reprint Ser.). 1977. reprint ed. 34.95 (0-8369-2493-2) Ayer.

Dennis, Welsey. The Ice Bird. 32p. (J). (gr. 1 up). 1981. reprint ed. pap. 4.50 (0-941402-01-0) Devon Pub.

Dennis, Wendy. Hot & Bothered. 1999. pap. write for info. (0-14-014725-X, Viking) Viking Penguin.

Dennis, William J., Jr. Small Business Problems & Priorities. 117p. (Orig.). 1986. pap. 6.00 (0-940791-02-1) NFIB Found.

Dennise. Lithographic Technology. 1986. pap. 9.32 (0-02-681700-4) Macmillan.

Dennison. Water Pollution Control Handbook. (Industrial Health & Safety Ser.). 1995. text 59.95 (0-442-02037-6, VNR) Wiley.

Dennison, ed. Paleozoic Sea-Level Changes in the Appalachian Basin, No. T354. (IGC Field Trip Guidebooks Ser.). 64p. 1989. 28.00 (0-87590-672-9) Am Geophysical.

Dennison, Cathee, jt. ed. see Giovanni, Nikki.

Dennison, Charles G. & Gamble, Richard C., eds. Pressing Toward the Mark: Essays Commemorating Fifty Years of the Orthodox Presbyterian Church (1936-1986) 489p. 1986. pap. 11.95 (0-934688-36-2) Comm Hist Orthodox.

Dennison, Clive. A Guide to Protein Isolation. LC 99-24639. 186p. 1999. write for info. (0-7923-5751-5) Kluwer Academic.

Dennison, Gail, jt. auth. see Dennison, Paul.

Dennison, Gail E., et al. Brain Gym for Business: Instant Brain Boosters for On-the-Job Success. (Illus.). 52p. (Orig.). 1994. pap. 12.95 (0-942143-03-5) Edu-Kinesthetics.

Dennison, Gail E., jt. auth. see Dennison, Paul E.

Dennison, Gail E., jt. auth. see Freeman, Cecilia K.

Dennison, George. The Lives of Children. 1990. pap. 10.95 (0-685-47600-6) Addison-Wesley.

— The Lives of Children: The Story of the First Street School. LC 99-218648. 320p. 1999. pap. text 15.95 (0-86709-483-4) Heinemann.

— Luisa Domic & Shawno. LC 94-6469. 213p. 1994. reprint ed. pap. 12.00 (1-883642-49-3) Steerforth Pr.

— Temple. LC 94-10060. 194p. 1994. 19.50 (1-883642-22-1) Steerforth Pr.

Dennison, George M. The Dorr War: Republicanism on Trial, 1831-1861. LC 75-3543. 264p. reprint ed. pap. 81.90 (0-7837-2419-5, 204256500005) Bks Demand.

Dennison, J. M. & Ettensohn, F. R., eds. Tectonic & Eustatic Controls on Sedimentary Cycles. LC 95-141016. (Concepts in Sedimentology & Paleontology Ser.: No. 4). (Illus.). 264p. 1994. pap. text 49.00 (1-56576-017-4) SEPM.

***Dennison, Jack.** City Reaching: On the Road to Community Transformation. LC 99-46764. 277p. 1999. pap. 14.99 (0-87808-777-X) William Carey Lib.

Dennison, James T., Jr., ed. see Turretin, Francis.

Dennison, John, tr. see Parkinson, Richard.

Dennison, John M. Analysis of Geologic Structures. (Illus.). (C). 1968. pap. text 22.25 (0-393-09801-X) Norton.

Dennison, Lisa. Angles of Vision: French Art Today, 1986 Exxon International Exhibition. (Illus.). 156p. 1986. 15.00 (0-89207-058-7) S R Guggenheim.

***Dennison, Lisa.** Clemente: A Retrospective. (Illus.). 400p. 1999. 75.00 (0-8109-6917-3, Pub. by Abrams) Time Warner.

Dennison, Lisa. Living with Art: The Collection of Ellyn & Saul Dennison. LC 93-79003. 96p. 1993. 9.00 (0-9613046-3-4) Morris Mus.

— New Horizons in American Art: 1985 Exxon National Exhibition. (Illus.). 120p. (Orig.). 1985. pap. 15.00 (0-89207-050-1) S R Guggenheim.

Dennison, Lisa, et al. Ross Bleckner. (Illus.). 250p. 1995. 85.00 (0-8109-6880-0) Abrams.

Dennison, Lisa, jt. auth. see Waldman, Diane.

Dennison, Margaret. All about MSM: Frequently Asked Questions. (FAQs All about Health Ser.). 1999. mass mkt. 2.99 (0-89529-970-4, Avery) Penguin Putnam.

Dennison, Mark. Environmental Record Keeping & Inspections. 272p. 1994. 69.95 (0-685-75063-9, VNR) Wiley.

Dennison, Mark A. Preparing for the Greatest Two Years of Your Life. pap. 3.95 (0-89036-128-2) Liahona Pub Trust.

Dennison, Mark S. Brownfields Redevelopment: Programs & Strategies for Rehabilitating Contaminated Real Estate. 407p. 1997. text 79.00 (0-86587-579-0, 579) Gov Insts.

— Environmental Reporting, Recordkeeping, & Inspections: A Compliance Guide for Business & Industry. (Industrial Health & Safety Ser.). 282p. 1995. 110.00 (0-471-29074-2, VNR) Wiley.

— Hazardous Waste Regulation Handbook: A Practical Guide to RCRA & Superfund. 538p. 1994. pap. 275.00 (0-471-11252-6) Wiley.

Dennison, Mark S. OSHA & EPA Process Safety Management Requirements: A Practical Guide for Compliance. (Industrial Health & Safety Ser.). 416p. 1994. 98.95 (0-471-28641-9, VNR) Wiley.

Dennison, Mark S. OSHA & EPA Process Safety Management Requirements: A Practical Guide to Compliance. LC 94-12507. 416p. 1994. text 76.95 (0-442-01876-2, VNR) Wiley.

— Pollution Prevention Strategies & Technologies. 463p. 1996. text 79.00 (0-86587-480-8) Gov Insts.

— RCRA Regulatory Compliance Guide. LC 92-32509. (Illus.). 354p. 1993. 79.00 (0-8155-1321-6) Noyes.

— Storm Water Discharges: Regulatory Compliance & Best. 464p. 1995. lib. bdg. 69.95 (1-56670-198-8, L1198) Lewis Pubs.

— Understanding Solid & Hazardous Waste Identification & Classification: A Practical Guide to the Waste Generator. 374p. 1994. pap. 275.00 (0-471-11264-X) Wiley.

Dennison, Mark S. & Berry, James F. Wetlands: Guide to Science, Law, & Technology. LC 93-5636. (Illus.). 439p. 1993. 109.00 (0-8155-1333-X) Noyes.

Dennison, Mark S. & Schmid, James A. Wetland Mitigation: Mitigation Banking & Other Strategies for Development & Compliance. LC 96-30343. 305p. 1997. pap. text 75.00 (0-86587-534-0) Gov Insts.

Dennison, Mark S., et al. Environmental Due Diligence for Lenders: Practical Guidance on Implementing & Maintaining an Environmental Risk Management Program. 400p. 1995. 165.00 (0-7913-2551-2) Warren Gorham & Lamont.

Dennison, Paul. Switching On. 1981. pap. 12.95 (0-942143-06-X) Edu-Kinesthetics.

Dennison, Paul & Dennison, Gail. Edu-Kinesthetics In-Depth: Advanced Workshop Manual. 29.95 (0-942143-08-6, 6) Edu-Kinesthetics.

Dennison, Paul E. & Dennison, Gail E. Brain Gym: Simple Activities for Whole Brain Learning. (Illus.). 40p. (Orig.). 1986. pap. 9.00 (0-942143-05-1) Edu-Kinesthetics.

— Brain Gym Teacher's Edition. (Illus.). 45p. (Orig.). 1994. pap., teacher ed. 16.95 (0-942143-02-7) Edu-Kinesthetics.

— Edu-K for Kids. rev. ed. (Illus.). 82p. 1987. pap. text 12.00 (0-942143-01-9) Edu-Kinesthetics.

— Personalized Whole Brain Integration: The Basic II Manual on Educational Kinesiology. (Illus.). 98p. (Orig.). 1985. pap. 15.95 (0-942143-07-8) Edu-Kinesthetics.

Dennison, Riffe. Schaum's College Physics. (C). 1996. pap. text 39.95 incl. disk (0-07-844268-0) McGraw.

Dennison, Robin D. Pass CCRN! (Illus.). 752p. (C). (gr. 13). 1996. pap. text 37.95 (0-8016-0128-2, 00128) Mosby Inc.

***Dennison, Robin D.** Pass CCRN! A Comprehensive Critical Care Review. 2nd ed. 750p. 2000. pap. text 44.95 (0-323-00999-9) Mosby Inc.

Dennison, S. Three Centuries of American Music, 12 vol. Set. 1993. 1000.00 (0-8161-0484-0, G K Hall & Co) Mac Lib Ref.

D

An Asterisk (*) at the beginning of an entry indicates that the title is appearing for the first time.

Dennison, S. R. & MacDonagh, Oliver. Guinness, 1886-1939: From Incorporation to the Second World War. LC 98-188954. 320p. 2000. 65.00 (*1-85918-175-9*, Pub. by Cork Univ) Stylus Pub VA.

Dennison, Sally. Alternative Literary Publishing: Five Modern Histories. LC 84-8700. 248p. (Orig.). reprint ed. pap. 76.90 (*0-7837-1620-6*, 204191300024) Bks Demand.

Dennison, Sam. Three Centuries of American Music: A Collection of Sacred & Secular Music: Orchestra, Vol. 9. 1992. 105.00 (*0-8161-0550-2*, G K Hall & Co) Mac Lib Ref.

— Three Centuries of American Music: A Collection of Sacred & Secular Music: Orchestra, Vol. 11. 1992. 105.00 (*0-8161-0551-0*, G K Hall & Co); 105.00 (*0-8161-0552-9*, G K Hall & Co) Mac Lib Ref.

Dennison, Sam, et al, eds. Three Centuries of American Music: A Collection of Sacred & Secular Music: Keyboard Music Through 1865, Vol. 3. 425p. 1990. 105.00 (*0-8161-0544-8*, G K Hall & Co) Mac Lib Ref.

— Three Centuries of American Music: A Collection of Sacred & Secular Music: Keyboard Music 1866 Through 1910, Vol. 4. 425p. 1990. 105.00 (*0-8161-0545-6*, G K Hall & Co) Mac Lib Ref.

Dennison, Scott, ed. see Bowman, Thomas L.

Dennison, Scott, ed. see Hawkins, Charles E. & Niewahner, James H.

Dennison, Susan. Creating Positive Support Group Curriculums for Children at Risk: Ten Complete Curriculums for the Most Common Problems among Elementary Students (Grades 1-8) Remkus, Susan, ed. LC 93-27101. 384p. (Orig.). 1996. pap. 41.95 (*1-880396-26-2*, JP9626-2) Jalmar Pr.

Dennison, Susan T. Activities for Adolescents in Therapy: A Handbook of Facilitating Guidelines & Planning Ideas for Group Therapy with Troubled Adolescents. 2nd ed. LC 97-25317. 264p. 1997. pap., spiral bd. 39.95 (*0-398-06807-0*) C C Thomas.

— Twelve Counseling Programs for Children at Risk. (Illus.). 430p. 1989. pap. 52.95 (*0-398-06090-8*) C C Thomas.

— Twelve Counseling Programs for Children at Risk. (Illus.). 430p. (C). 1989. text 83.95 (*0-398-05626-9*) C C Thomas.

Dennison, Susan T. & Knight, Connie M. Activities for Children in Therapy: A Guide for Planning & Facilitating Therapy with Troubled Children. 2nd ed. LC 99-18405. (Illus.). 290p. 1998. spiral bd. 45.95 (*0-398-06971-9*) C C Thomas.

Dennison, T. E., ed. see Bowman, Thomas.

Dennison, T. E., ed. see Finck, Joseph E.

Dennison, T. E., ed. see Wiggins, Arthur W.

Dennison-Tansey, Amy, jt. auth. see Britsch, Barbara M.

Dennison, Tim, ed. see Hicks, Vernon.

Dennison, W. F. & Shenton, Ken. Challenges in Educational Management: Principles into Practice. (Educational Management Ser.). 256p. 1987. 42.50 (*0-7099-0892-X*, Pub. by C Helm); lib. bdg. 42.50 (*0-685-19162-1*, Pub. by C Helm) Routldge.

Dennison, William D. Paul's Two-Age Construction & Apologetics. LC 85-20272. 144p. (Orig.). (C). 1985. pap. text 17.00 (*0-8191-5012-6*) U Pr of Amer.

— Paul's Two-Age Construction & Apologetics. LC 85-20272. 144p. (Orig.). (C). 1986. lib. bdg. 37.00 (*0-8191-5011-8*) U Pr of Amer.

Dennissen, H., et al. Hydroxylapatite Implants. 168p. 1985. text 64.00 (*1-57235-076-8*) Piccin Nuova.

Denniston. Churchill's Secret War, 1922 to 1944. LC 97-155547. (Illus.). 224p. 1997. text 39.95 (*0-312-16582-X*) St Martin.

Denniston, Denie. Older Workers: What Voc Ed Can Do. 48p. 1983. 4.95 (*0-318-22162-4*, IN256) Ctr Educ Trng Employ.

Denniston, Dorothy H. The Fiction of Paule Marshall: Reconstructions of History, Culture, & Gender. LC 94-18767. 216p. (C). 1995. pap. text 16.00 (*0-87049-839-8*); lib. bdg. 32.00 (*0-87049-838-X*) U of Tenn Pr.

Denniston, E. L. Stukey: Genealogy of the Stukey, Ream, Grove, Clem & Denniston Families. (Illus.). 591p. 1991. reprint ed. pap. 89.50 (*0-8328-1879-8*); reprint ed. lib. bdg. 99.50 (*0-8328-1878-X*) Higginson Bk Co.

***Denniston, George C., et al, eds.** Male & Female Circumcision: Medical, Legal & Ethical Considerations in Pediatric Practice. LC 99-37490. 547p. (C). 1999. text 155.00 (*0-306-46131-5*, Kluwer Plenum) Kluwer Academic.

Denniston, George C. & Milos, Marilyn F., eds. Sexual Mutilations: A Human Tragedy. LC 97-9243. 252p. (C). 1997. 79.50 (*0-306-45589-7*, Plenum Trade) Perseus Pubng.

Denniston, George C., jt. auth. see Ritter, Thomas J.

Denniston, J. D. The Greek Particles. 2nd ed. Dover, K. J., ed. LC 96-78782. 742p. 1996. reprint ed. lib. bdg. 60.00 (*0-87220-299-2*) Hackett Pub.

Denniston, J. D., ed. Cicero: Philippics I & II. (Bristol Latin Texts Ser.). (LAT.). 220p. 1978. reprint ed. 20.95 (*0-906515-08-4*, Pub. by Brist Class Pr) Focus Pub-R Pullins.

Denniston, John D. Greek Literary Criticism. (Library of Greek Thought: No. 1). reprint ed. 37.50 (*0-404-07801-X*) AMS Pr.

— Greek Prose Style. LC 78-31880. 139p. 1979. reprint ed. lib. bdg. 39.75 (*0-313-20960-X*, DEGP, Greenwood Pr) Greenwood.

Denniston, John D., jt. auth. see Euripides.

Denniston, Karol K. International Distressed Debt Trading. 1999. pap. text 200.00 (*1-85564-469-X*, Pub. by Euromoney) Am Educ Systs.

***Denniston, Katherine J., et al.** General, Organic & Biochemistry. 3rd ed. 880p. (C). 2000. 83.13 (*0-07-231784-1*) McGrw-H Hghr Educ.

— General, Organic & Biochemistry: Solutions Manual. 3rd ed. 578p. (C). 2000. pap., student ed. 25.31 (*0-07-231786-8*) McGrw-H Hghr Educ.

Denniston, Keith. Christmas 1956: A Poem. 6p. (Orig.). 1995. pap. 2.50 (*1-884235-09-3*) Helicon Nine Eds.

— Jazz Moods. (Illus.). 48p. 1987. pap. 3.00 (*0-939391-09-0*) B Woodley Pr.

Denniston, Keith, ed. see Miller, Philip.

Denniston, Lyle W. The Reporter & the Law: Techniques of Covering the Courts. LC 92-15053. 300p. 1992. pap. 19.50 (*0-231-08031-X*); text 46.00 (*0-231-08030-1*) Col U Pr.

Denniston, Philip L. Physicians Genrix, 1995: The Complete Drug Reference of FDA Prescribing Information &... 1995. 77.00 (*1-880891-07-7*) Work-Loss Data.

Denniston, Philip L., ed. Offical Disability Guidelines, on CD-Rom, 1999. 200p. 1999. pap. 165.00 (*1-880891-27-1*) Work-Loss Data.

— Offical Disability Guidelines, Top 200 Conditions, 1999. rev. ed. 200p. 1998. pap. 165.00 (*1-880891-26-3*) Work-Loss Data.

— Official Disability Guidelines: Length of Disability Data by ICD-9-CM from CDC & OSHA Plus NHDS Hospital Length of Stay. (Orig.). 1995. pap. 150.00 (*1-880891-21-2*) Work-Loss Data.

Denniston, Robin. Trevor Huddleston: A Life. LC 99-31545. (Illus.). 321p. 2000. text 35.00 (*0-312-22709-4*) St Martin.

Dennistoun, James, ed. Cartularium Comitatus de Levanax ab Initio Seculi Decimi Tertii Usque Ad Annum 1398. LC 72-1044. (Maitland Club, Glasgow. Publications: No. 24). reprint ed. 32.50 (*0-404-52969-0*) AMS Pr.

— Coltness Collections. LC 72-1031. (Maitland Club, Glasgow. Publications: No. 58). reprint ed. 65.00 (*0-404-53047-8*) AMS Pr.

Dennistoun, James, ed. see Cochrane, Andrew.

Dennistoun, Robert T. The Role of the Association President: The Role of the Association President, No. 23. rev. ed. (GAP Reports: Vol. 23). 20p. (C). 1996. pap. 17.50 (*0-944715-24-9*) CAI.

— The Role of the Association President No. 23: GAP Reports. 2nd ed. 36p. 1995. pap. 17.50 (*0-944715-41-9*) CAI.

Denno, Deborah W. Biology & Violence: From Birth to Adulthood. (Illus.). 232p. (C). 1990. text 49.95 (*0-521-36219-9*) Cambridge U Pr.

Denno, Deborah W. & Schwarz, Ruth M., eds. Biological, Psychological, & Environmental Factors in Delinquency & Mental Disorder: An Interdisciplinary Bibliography, 4. LC 85-5620. (Bibliographies & Indexes in Sociology Ser.: No. 4). 222p. 1985. lib. bdg. 62.95 (*0-313-24939-3*, DBP/) Greenwood.

Denno, K. Engineering Economics of Alternative Energy Sources. LC 90-1513. 366p. 1990. 203.00 (*0-8493-6641-0*, TJ808, CRC Reprint) Franklin.

Denno, Khalil. Power System Design Applications for Alternative Energy Sources. 272p. (C). 1988. text 50.20 (*0-13-688004-5*) P-H.

Denno, Khalil, ed. High Voltage Engineering in Power Systems. 416p. 1991. lib. bdg. 99.95 (*0-8493-4289-9*, TK3144) CRC Pr.

Denno, R. F. & Dingle, H., eds. Insect Life History Patterns: Habitat & Geographic Variation. (Proceedings in Life Sciences Ser.). (Illus.). 225p. 1981. 124.00 (*0-387-90591-X*) Spr-Verlag.

Denno, Sally A. American Carousel, The. LC 90-64384. (Illus.). 54p. 1991. pap. text 8.95 (*0-916809-48-X*) Scott Pubns MI.

— Collectible Steins. 40p. 1992. pap. text 9.95 (*0-916809-55-2*) Scott Pubns MI.

— Mystical Creations. 48p. 1996. pap. 11.95 (*1-879825-27-9*) Jones Publish.

— Native American Reflections. LC 93-83036. 52p. 1993. pap. 9.95 (*0-916809-60-9*) Scott Pubns MI.

— Wet Brushing. LC 98-137144. 44p. 1998. pap. text 12.95 (*0-916809-95-1*) Scott Pubns MI.

Dennon, Jerry. The Other Side Speaks: Survival Manual for Mankind. 86p. (Orig.). 1992. pap. 10.00 (*0-9633049-0-9*) Burdette Bks.

Dennu, Bobby. How to Make Money the "Write" Way. 2nd rev. ed. Date not set. pap. 10.95 (*0-944516-04-1*) Fidget Pubns.

Denny. Babies. 1995. pap. text 12.95 (*0-9641492-7-3*) Buffalo Hse.

Denny. Call of the Wild: Literature Unit. (Literature Units Ser.). (Illus.). 48p. (J). (gr. 5-8). 1995. pap. text, wbk. ed. 7.95 (*1-55734-446-9*) Tchr Create Mat.

— The Cay: Literature Unit. (Literature Units Ser.). (Illus.). 48p. (J). (gr. 5-8). 1995. pap. text, wbk. ed. 7.95 (*1-55734-447-7*) Tchr Create Mat.

Denny. Island Child: Kids & Kisses. 1994. per. 2.99 (*0-373-15566-2*) Harlequin Bks.

Denny, Alma. Blinkies: Funny Poems to Read in a Blink. LC 91-90241. (Illus.). 64p. (Orig.). 1991. pap. 6.95 (*1-879865-01-7*) Lamb & Lion.

Denny, Alvis S. Without Arms. LC 96-69568. 112p. (YA). 1996. 16.95 (*1-56167-322-6*) Noble Hse MD.

Denny, Arthur A. Pioneer Days on Puget Sound. rev. ed. 101p. 1980. 19.95 (*0-87770-226-8*) Ye Galleon.

***Denny, Arthur Armstrong.** Pioneer Days on Puget Sound. (Illus.). 101p. 1999. pap. 14.95 (*0-87770-674-3*) Ye Galleon.

Denny, Bill. Denny Family History: The Hugh & Susan Denny Family of Jefferson Co., NY, 1850. (Illus.). 300p. 1997. reprint ed. pap. 45.00 (*0-8328-8272-0*); reprint ed. lib. bdg. 55.00 (*0-8328-8271-2*) Higginson Bk Co.

Denny, Bill & Bruce, Howard C. Bruce Family, 1788 to 1992 (Descendants of John & Clarissa Bruce) (Illus.). 95p. (Orig.). 1996. reprint ed. pap. 17.00 (*0-8328-5390-9*); reprint ed. lib. bdg. 27.00 (*0-8328-5389-5*) Higginson Bk Co.

Denny, Bob, et al. CGI Programming for Windows: Developing Web Applications with Win-CGI. (Illus.). 400p. 1997. pap. 32.95 (*1-56592-215-8*) Thomson Learn.

Denny, Brewster C. Seeing American Foreign Policy Whole. LC 84-16390. 208p. 1985. text 19.95 (*0-252-01181-3*) U of Ill Pr.

Denny-Brown, D., ed. see Sherrington, Charles.

Denny-Brown, Derek, et al. Handbook of Neurological Examination & Case Recording. 3rd ed. LC 81-13315. (Illus.). 104p. 1982. pap. 18.00 (*0-674-37101-1*) HUP.

***Denny, C. M.** Mesh Friction in Gearing. (Technical Papers: Vol. 98FTM2). 11p. 1998. pap. 30.00 (*1-55589-720-7*) AGMA.

Denny, Cathy, jt. auth. see Black, Linda.

Denny, Charlotte, jt. auth. see McGregor, Fiona.

Denny, D. Michael. How to Get a Cat to Sit in Your Lap: Confessions of an Unconventional Cat Person. LC 95-94275. (Illus.). 72p. (Orig.). 1995. pap. 14.95 (*0-9645799-0-1*) Andiron Pr.

Denny, D. Roy. Steps along an Unknown Journey. 150p. 1998. pap. 10.00 (*1-57502-855-7*, PO2138) Morris Pubng.

Denny, Dallas. Current Concepts in Transgender Identity. LC 97-25972. (Gay & Lesbian Studies: Vol. 11). (Illus.). 452p. 1997. text 88.00 (*0-8153-1793-X*) Garland.

— Gender Dysphoria: A Guide to Research. LC 93-7266. (Gay & Lesbian Studies: Vol. 10). 704p. 1994. text 30.00 (*0-8153-0840-X*) Garland.

— Identity Management in Transsexualism: A Practical Guide to Managing Identity on Paper. 84p. 1994. pap. 15.00 (*1-880715-07-4*) Creat Des Srvs.

***Denny, Ebenezer.** Denny's Vocabulary of Delaware. LC 99-27831. (American Language Reprints Ser.: No. 12). (DEL & ENG.). 40p. 1999. lib. bdg. 16.95 (*1-889758-10-8*) Evol Pubng & Manuf.

— Denny's Vocabulary of Shawnee. LC 99-27830. (American Language Reprints Ser.: No. 14). 45p. 1999. lib. bdg. 16.00 (*1-889758-12-4*) Evol Pubng & Manuf.

Denny, Ebenezer. Military Journal of Major Ebenezer Denny: An Officer in the Revolutionary & Indian Wars. LC 70-140860. (Eyewitness Accounts of the American Revolution Ser.). 1971. reprint ed. 25.95 (*0-405-01214-4*) Ayer.

— Military Journal of Major Ebenezer Denny: An Officer in the Revolutionary & Indian Wars, with an Introductory Memoir. (American Biography Ser.). 288p. 1991. reprint ed. lib. bdg. 69.00 (*0-7812-8105-9*) Rprt Serv

***Denny, F.** Muslims in America. (Illus.). 2000. pap. 0.00 (*0-19-510919-8*) OUP.

Denny, Floyd W., Jr., ed. From Infancy to Maturity: The History of the Department of Pediatrics, the University of North Carolina at Chapel Hill, 1952-1995. (Illus.). 500p. 1996. write for info. (*0-9650394-0-4*) Univ NC Dept Ped.

Denny Fox, Roz. Having It All: Family Man. 1998. per. 4.25 (*0-373-70800-9*) Harlequin Bks.

— Mad about the Major: In Uniform. (In Uniform Ser.: No. 821). 1998. per. 4.25 (*0-373-70821-1*, 1-70821-3) Harlequin Bks.

Denny, Frederick, ed. see Asani, Ali S. & Abdel-Malek, Kamal.

Denny, Frederick, ed. see Hoffman, Valerie J.

Denny, Frederick, ed. see Kostarelos, Frances.

Denny, Frederick, ed. see Lawrence, Bruce B.

Denny, Frederick, jt. ed. see Wessinger, Catherine.

Denny, Frederick M. An Introduction to Islam. 432p. 1996. pap. 31.95 (*0-614-21414-9*, 508) Kazi Pubns.

— An Introduction to Islam. 2nd ed. LC 92-39701. 432p. (C). 1993. pap. text 51.00 (*0-02-328519-2*, Macmillan Coll) P-H.

— Islam. (Religious Traditions of the World Ser.). 136p. 1996. pap. 10.00 (*0-614-21464-5*, 1350) Kazi Pubns.

— Islam: The Muslim Community. 160p. (C). 1988. pap. 12.00 (*0-06-061875-2*, Pub. by Harper SF) HarpC.

— Islam & the Muslim Community. 138p. 1996. pap. 10.00 (*0-614-21462-9*, 557) Kazi Pubns.

— Islam & the Muslim Community. (Illus.). 137p. (C). 1998. reprint ed. pap. text 10.95 (*1-57766-007-2*) Waveland Pr.

Denny, Frederick M. & Taylor, Rodney L., eds. The Holy Book in Comparative Perspective. LC 95-8473. (Studies in Comparative Religion). 260p. (C). 1993. pap. text 18.95 (*0-87249-966-9*) U of SC Pr.

Denny, Frederick M., ed. see Hammond, Phillip E.

Denny, Frederick M., jt. ed. see Sheridan, Sybil.

Denny, Frederick M., ed. see Strenski, Ivan.

Denny, Frederick M., ed. see Thomas, Linda E.

Denny, George. The Dread Fishwish. (Illus.). 1974. 8.95 (*0-88395-024-3*) Freshet Pr.

***Denny, Hamish & Butterworth, Stephen J.** A Guide to Canine & Feline Orthopaedic Surgery. 4th ed. LC 99-25905. 640p. 2000. pap. text 89.95 (*0-632-05103-5*, Pub. by Blckwell Science) Iowa St U Pr.

Denny, Harold N. Dollars for Bullets: The Story of American Rule in Nicaragua. LC 79-25688. (Illus.). 411p. 1980. reprint ed. lib. bdg. 75.00 (*0-313-22269-X*, DEDB, Greenwood Pr) Greenwood.

— Dollars for Bullets: The Story of American Rule in Nicaragua. (BCL1 - U. S. History Ser.). 411p. 1991. reprint ed. lib. bdg. 99.00 (*0-7812-6048-5*) Rprt Serv.

Denny, Hugh W. Grounding for the Control of EMI. Price, Edward R., ed. LC 82-63066. 1983. text 65.00 (*0-932263-17-8*) emf-emi Control.

Denny-Hughes, Julie, jt. ed. see Engel, J. Ronald.

Denny, J. O., jt. auth. see Armstrong, Leroy.

Denny, James. Jesus & the Gospel. 1977. lib. bdg. 59.95 (*0-8490-2095-6*) Gordon Pr.

Denny, Jim. The Birds of Kaua'i. LC 98-39232. (Illus.). 128p. 1999. pap. 19.95 (*0-8248-2097-5*, Latitude Twenty) UH Pr.

Denny, Kevin M. A Teenager's Guide How to Manipulate Your Way to Happiness: Thirty-Seven Easy Steps in the Care & Feeding of Your Parents. 2nd ed. LC 92-81556. (Illus.). 240p. (Orig.). (YA). (gr. 8-12). 1995. pap. 12.95 (*0-9633108-0-1*) Warthog Pub.

Denny, Lesley. Morning Is Breaking. large type ed. 1990. 27.99 (*0-7089-2297-X*) Ulverscroft.

— Shadows of Darkness. large type ed. 1991. 27.99 (*0-7089-2498-0*) Ulverscroft.

— Water from the Moon. large type ed. 592p. 1988. 27.99 (*0-7089-1863-8*) Ulverscroft.

Denny, Ludwell. We Fight for Oil. 1979. lib. bdg. 59.95 (*0-8490-3014-5*) Gordon Pr.

Denny, M. Ray, ed. Fear, Avoidance & Phobias: A Fundamental Analysis. 456p. 1991. pap. 49.95 (*0-8058-0317-3*); text 89.95 (*0-8058-0316-5*) L Erlbaum Assocs.

Denny, Margaret M., ed. American Writers & the European Tradition. LC 68-24936. 1970. reprint ed. lib. bdg. 75.00 (*0-8383-0934-8*) M S G Haskell Hse.

Denny, Mark W. Air & Water: The Biology & Physics of Life's Media. LC 92-20969. (Illus.). 360p. (C). 1993. text 60.00 (*0-691-08734-2*, Pub. by Princeton U Pr); pap. text 27.95 (*0-691-02518-5*, Pub. by Princeton U Pr) Cal Prin Full Svc.

— Biology & the Mechanics of the Wave-Swept Environment. (Illus.). 400p. 1988. pap. text 37.50 (*0-691-08487-4*, Pub. by Princeton U Pr) Cal Prin Full Svc.

***Denny, Mark W. & Gaines, Steven.** Chance in Biology: Using Probability to Explore Nature. LC 00-36687. (Illus.). 424p. 2000. 39.50 (*0-691-00521-4*) Princeton U Pr.

Denny, Mary, et al. Pre End Stage Renal Disease: A Guide for the Professional Nutritionist. 218p. (C). pap. text 22.50 (*1-883146-52-6*) Coun Renal Nutrit.

Denny, Mary, jt. auth. see Patel, Chhaya.

Denny, Maurice. Freight Insurance: A Commentary. 237p. (C). 1986. 125.00 (*0-900886-41-2*, Pub. by Witherby & Co) St Mut.

— Freight Insurance-A Commentary: The Insurance of Shipowners Interest in Freight for the Carriage of Goods. (C). 1987. 125.00 (*0-7855-4165-9*, Pub. by Witherby & Co) St Mut.

Denny, Maurice, jt. auth. see Witherby & Co. Ltd. Staff.

Denny, Michael K. The MIA. LC 94-76850. 214p. 1994. pap. 8.95 (*0-9641492-9-X*) Buffalo Hse.

Denny, Norman, tr. see Renoir, Jean.

Denny, Norman, tr. see Tournier, Michel.

Denny, Norman, tr. & intro. see Hugo, Victor.

Denny, Patrick, ed. The Ecology & Management of African Wetland Vegetation. (Geobotany Ser.). 1985. text 306.50 (*90-6193-509-1*) Kluwer Academic.

Denny, Philip. The Indian in the Cupboard: A Literature Unit. Goldfluss, Karen J., ed. (Illus.). 48p. (J). (gr. 4-7). 1992. student ed. 7.95 (*1-55734-415-9*) Tchr Create Mat.

— Island of the Blue Dolphins: A Literature Unit. (Literature Units Ser.). (Illus.). 48p. (Orig.). (gr. 3-5). 1992. student ed. 7.95 (*1-55734-412-4*) Tchr Create Mat.

— Julie of the Wolves: A Literature Unit. (Literature Units Ser.). (Illus.). 48p. 1993. student ed. 7.95 (*1-55734-418-3*) Tchr Create Mat.

— The Pearl: A Literature Unit. Levin, Ina M., ed. (Literature Units Ser.). (Illus.). 48p. (Orig.). 1992. pap., student ed. 7.95 (*1-55734-407-8*) Tchr Create Mat.

Denny, Phyllis. An Affair of the Heart. LC 87-1092. 1988. 17.95 (*0-87949-278-3*) Ashley Bks.

Denny, Randal E. Alive & Well: A Study of the Church - First John. 192p. (Orig.). 1993. pap. 11.99 (*0-8341-1453-4*) Beacon Hill.

— Epidemic of Joy: A Study of Acts 13-16. 120p. (Orig.). 1988. pap. 8.99 (*0-8341-1238-8*) Beacon Hill.

— In Jesus' Strong Hands: Victors Instead of Victims (Acts 17-23) 132p. 1989. pap. 8.99 (*0-8341-1294-9*) Beacon Hill.

— In the Shadow of the Cross. 144p. 1995. pap. 9.99 (*0-8341-1535-2*) Beacon Hill.

— Intimacy with God. (Christian Living Ser.). 40p. (Orig.). 1987. pap. 3.50 (*0-8341-1186-1*) Beacon Hill.

— The Kingdom, the Power, the Glory: Embracing the Mystery of the Lord's Prayer. LC 96-39976. 160p. (Orig.). 1996. 15.99 (*0-8341-1596-4*) Beacon Hill.

— Where the Action Is. 128p. 1981. pap. 7.99 (*0-8341-0723-6*) Beacon Hill.

Denny, Randal Earl. Growing into Your Crown: A Study in 1 Thessalonians. 104p. pap. 10.99 (*0-8341-1780-0*) Beacon Hill.

Denny, Reuel. The Astonished Muse. 300p. 1989. pap. 24.95 (*0-88738-762-4*) Transaction Pubs.

Denny, Roz. Beans. LC 97-44108. (Food in Focus Ser.). (Illus.). 32p. 1998. 14.95 (*1-57572-653-X*) Heinemann Lib.

— The Cinderella Coach. large type ed. 328p. 1992. reprint ed. lib. bdg. 13.95 (*1-56054-408-2*) Thorndike Pr.

***Denny, Roz.** Cooking for Your Vegetarian Kids. 2000. 16.95 (*1-85967-964-1*, Lorenz Bks) Anness Pub.

— Gordon Ramsay's Passion for Seafood. (Illus.). 224p. 2000. 45.00 (*1-85029-993-5*, Pub. by Conran Octopus) Antique Collect.

Denny, Roz. Island Child. (Romance Ser.). 1994. per. 2.99 (*0-373-03320-6*, 1-03320-8) Harlequin Bks.

— Rice. LC 97-44109. (Food in Focus Ser.). (Illus.). 32p. (J). 1998. write for info. (*1-57572-658-0*) Heinemann.

***Denny, Roz.** Rice & Risottos. 96p. 2000. pap. 12.95 (*0-7548-0303-1*) Anness Pub.

Denny, Roz. Some Like It Hotter. 1994. per. 2.99 (*0-373-03336-2*, 1-03336-4) Harlequin Bks.

— Stubborn As a Mule Back to the Ranch. (Romance Ser.). 1993. per. 2.99 (*0-373-03276-5*, 1-03276-2) Harlequin Bks.

D

— A Taste of Britain: Culinary Tours Teach Children about a Country's History, Social Customs, Festivals & Much More. (Illus.). 48p. (J). 1997. 22.83 (*0-8172-4852-8*) Raintree Steck-V.

— A Taste of China: Culinary Tours Teach Children about a Country's History, Social Customs, Festivals & Much More. (J). 1997. 22.83 (*0-8172-4850-1*) Raintree Steck-V.

— A Taste of France: Culinary Tours Teach Children about a Country's History, Social Customs, Festivals & Much More. 48p. (J). 1997. 22.83 (*0-8172-4895-1*) Raintree Steck-V.

— A Taste of India. (Food Around the World Ser.). 1994. 22.83 (*0-8172-4855-2*) Raintree Steck-V.

— A Taste of India. LC 93-37197. (Food Around the World Ser.). (Illus.). 48p. (J). (gr. 3-6). 1994. lib. bdg. 22.83 (*1-56847-164-5*) Raintree Steck-V.

— Thirty-Six Strange Little Animals Waiting to Eat: With Simple Little Recipes to Make. LC 92-358. (Illus.). 32p. (J). 1992. 6.50 (*1-55670-272-8*) Stewart Tabori & Chang.

***Denny, Roz.** The Ultimate Vegetarian Cookbook: Over 200 Mouthwatering Recipes Shown Step-by-Step on 800 Photographs. rev. ed. (Ultimate Cookbook Ser.). (Illus.). 256p. 1998. 19.98 (*0-7651-0856-9*) Smithmark.

Denny, Roz & Watt, Fiona. Cooking for Beginners. (Cooking School Ser.). (Illus.). 48p. (YA). (gr. 4-7). 1998. pap. 7.95 (*0-7460-3036-5*, Usborne); lib. bdg. 15.95 (*1-58086-128-8*, Usborne) EDC.

Denny, Sidney G., et al. The Ancient Splendor of Prehistoric Cahokia. 2nd ed. LC 96-32662. 1997. write for info. (*1-56763-271-8*); pap. write for info. (*1-56763-272-6*) Ozark Pub.

Denny, Steven. Dandelion Crumbs: Growing up Catholic. Mackenzie, David, ed. LC 94-76785. (Illus.). 189p. 1994. pap. 12.95 (*0-9640652-0-7*) Innovate Pub.

Denny, W. W. Kendall - Gelette Family History. The Kendall, Gelette & Ellis Families of Minnesota, from 1860. (Illus.). 112p. 1996. reprint ed. pap. 19.00 (*0-8328-5388-7*); reprint ed. lib. bdg. 29.00 (*0-8328-5387-9*) Higginson Bk Co.

Denny, Walter B. The Image & the Word: Islamic Painting & Calligraphy. (Illus.). 55p. 1976. 3.00 (*0-916746-01-1*) Springfield Lib & Mus.

Denny, Walter B., et al, eds. Oriental Carpet & Textile Studies, Vol. 6. 1986. 49.95 (*1-889666-04-1*, 04) Phila Eighth ICOC.

Denny, Walter B. & Walker, Daniel. The Markarian Album: The Richard R. Markarian Collection of Oriental Rugs. Anderson, Jon M. & Fling, Russell S., eds. (Illus.). 432p. 1989. 195.00 (*0-9621115-0-3*) Markarian Found.

Denny, Walter B., et al. Court & Conquest: Ottoman Origins & the Design for Handel's "Tamerlano" at the Glimmerglass Opera. LC 99-490006. (Illus.). 96p. 1998. pap. 24.95 (*0-9668318-0-2*) Kent State Mus.

— Oriental & Islamic Art in the Isabella Stewart Gardner Museum. LC 75-22427. (Illus.). 136p. (Orig.). 1975. pap. 5.00 (*0-914660-01-2*) I S Gardner Mus.

Dennys, Nicholas B. The Folk-Lore of China: And Its Affinities with That of the Aryan & Semitic Races. LC 72-84000. 1972. reprint ed. 23.95 (*0-405-08443-9*, Pub. by Blom Pubns) Ayer.

Deno, Norm & Wise, Naomi. All about Seeds. Smith, Mike, ed. (Illus.). 96p. (Orig.). 1997. pap. 9.95 (*0-89721-337-8*, Ortho Bks) Meredith Bks.

Deno, Stanley, jt. auth. see Maruyama, Geoffrey.

Deno, Stanley, jt. ed. see Espin, Christine A.

Denobriga, Kathie, jt. ed. see Anderson, Valetta.

Denoeu, Francois. French Idioms. 2nd ed. LC 95-80221. 1996. pap. text 6.95 (*0-8120-9026-8*) Barron.

Denoeu, Francois & Hall, R. A., Jr. Spoken French, Units 1-12. LC 74-152740. (Spoken Language Ser.). 230p. 1973. pap. 15.00 (*0-87950-080-8*) Spoken Lang Serv.

Denoeu, Francois & Sices, Frances. 2001 French & English Idioms: Idiotismes Francais et Anglais 2001. 2nd ed. (ENG & FRE.). 1996. pap. text 13.95 (*0-8120-9024-1*) Barron.

Denoeu, Francois, et al. Spoken French. LC 74-152740. (Spoken Language Ser.). 230p. 1973. pap. 90.00 incl. audio (*0-87950-086-7*) Spoken Lang Serv.

Denoeu, Francois, et al. Spoken French. LC 74-152740. (Spoken Language Ser.). 230p. 1973. audio 75.00 (*0-87950-085-9*) Spoken Lang Serv.

Denoeux, Guilain. Urban Unrest in the Middle East: A Comparative Study of Informal Networks in Egypt, Iran, & Lebanon. LC 92-25353. (SUNY Series in the Social & Economic History of the Middle East). 310p. (C). 1993. text 64.50 (*0-7914-1523-6*); pap. text 21.95 (*0-7914-1524-4*) State U NY Pr.

***Denoix, Jean-Marie.** The Equine Distal Limb: An Atlas of Clinical Anatomy & Comparative Imaging. 400p. 2000. 154.95 (*0-8138-0249-0*) Iowa St U Pr.

Denolin, H., ed. Psychological Problems Before & after Myocardial Infarction. (Advances in Cardiology Ser.: Vol. 29). viii, 156p. 1982. 85.25 (*3-8055-3424-8*) S Karger.

Denolin, H., et al, eds. Neural Control of the Cardiovascular System & Orthostatic Regulation: Proceedings Basel, 1975. (Cardiology Ser.: Vol. 61, Suppl. 1). (Illus.). 250p. 1976. 61.00 (*3-8055-2260-6*) S Karger.

Denolin, H., ed. see International Congress on Cardiac Rehabilitation S.

***Denomme, Greg, et al.** Molecular Protocols in Transfusion Medicine. 200p. 2000. 99.95 (*0-12-209370-4*) Acad Pr.

Denomme, Jean-Marc. Recherches sur la Langue et le Style d'Isee. xiii, 395p. 1974. write for info. (*3-487-05085-4*) G Olms Pubs.

Denomme, Jean-Marc, ed. Isaeus - Index Isaeus. 148p. 1968. write for info. (*0-318-70656-3*); write for info. (*0-318-71971-1*) G Olms Pubs.

Denomme, Robert T. & Simon, Roland H. Unfinished Revolutions: Legacies of Upheaval in Modern French Culture. LC 97-49174. 178p. 1998. 40.00 (*0-271-01785-6*); pap. 16.95 (*0-271-01786-4*) Pa St U Pr.

***Denomme, Thomas J., et al, eds.** DOD's Mobility Requirements: Value of Intratheater Lift Analyses Can Be Enhanced. 46p. (C). 1999. pap. text 20.00 (*0-7881-8384-2*) DIANE Pub.

Denomme, Thomas J., et al. Military Airlift: Options Exist for Meeting Requirements While Acquiring Fewer C-17's. 62p. (C). 1999. reprint ed. pap. text 20.00 (*0-7881-4375-1*) DIANE Pub.

Denomy, Alexander J., ed. see Oresme, Nicole.

Denon, V. Travels in Egypt, Vol. 1. 346p. 1986. 180.00 (*1-85077-098-0*, Pub. by Darf Pubs Ltd) St Mut.

— Travels in Egypt, Vol. 2. 332p. 1986. 180.00 (*1-85077-099-9*, Pub. by Darf Pubs Ltd) St Mut.

— Travels in Egypt, Vols. 1 & 2. 1986. write for info. (*0-7855-2570-X*, Pub. by Darf Pubs Ltd) St Mut.

Denon, Vivant. Travels in Upper & Lower Egypt, 3 vols. LC 73-6275. (Middle East Ser.). 1973. reprint ed. 94.95 (*0-405-05331-2*) Ayer.

Denoncourt, Don. Java Application Strategies for the AS/400. (Illus.). 423p. 1999. pap. 79.00 (*1-883884-61-6*) Midrange Comput.

Denonn, Lester E., ed. The Bertrand Russell Dictionary of Mind, Morals, & Matter. LC 92-39508. 1993. reprint ed. 9.95 (*0-8065-1400-0*, Citadel Pr) Carol Pub Group.

***DeNonno, Sheryle.** Poetry & Style. 1999. pap. write for info. (*1-57553-860-1*) Watermrk Pr.

DeNoon, Chris. Posters of WPA. (Illus.). 176p. 1987. 39.95 (*0-295-96543-4*) U of Wash Pr.

DeNoon, Daniel J. & Henderson, Charles W. AIDS Therapies: 1992 Edition. 350p. 1992. reprint ed. student ed. 899.00 (*0-9631698-0-7*) C W Henderson.

Denoon, David B. Devaluation under Pressure: India, Indonesia, & Ghana. 240p. 1986. 32.50 (*0-262-04083-2*) MIT Pr.

— Real Reciprocity: Balancing U. S. Economic & Security Policies in the Pacific Basin. LC 93-12622. 100p. 1993. 14.95 (*0-87609-144-3*) Coun Foreign.

***Denoon, Donald.** Getting under the Skin: The Bougainville Copper Agreement & the Creation of the Panguna Mine. 250p. 2000. 39.95 (*0-522-84877-X*, Pub. by Melbourne Univ Pr) Paul & Co Pubs.

Denoon, Donald, ed. The Cambridge History of the Pacific Islanders. (Illus.). 540p. (C). 1997. text 80.00 (*0-521-44195-1*) Cambridge U Pr.

Denoon, Donald, et al, eds. Multicultural Japan: Palaeolithic to Postmodern. 304p. 1996. text 59.95 (*0-521-55067-X*) Cambridge U Pr.

Denoon, Donald & Nyeko, Balam. Southern Africa Since 1800. 2nd ed. 246p. (C). 1989. pap. text 33.75 (*0-582-72707-3*, 74744) Addison-Wesley.

Denooz, Joseph, ed. Seneca, Lucius Annaeus: Tragoediae, Index Verborum, Releves Lexicaux et Grammaticaux. (Alpha-Omega, Reihe A Ser.: Bd. XL). xiv, 628p. 1980. write for info. (*3-487-06962-8*) G Olms Pubs.

Denooz, Laurence. Platus, Asinaria: Index Verborum, Lexiques Inverses, Releves Lexicaux et Grammaticaux. Maniet, Albert, ed. (Alpha-Omega, Reihe A: Vol. XXVI). (GER.). ix, 211p. 1992. write for info. (*3-487-09465-7*) G Olms Pubs.

— Platus, Epidicus: Index Verborum, Lexiques Inverses, Releves Lexicaux et Grammaticaux. (Alpha-Omega, Reihe A Ser.: Vol. CLXXXVIII). vi, 222p. 1997. write for info. (*3-487-10313-3*) G Olms Pubs.

DeNora, Tia. Beethoven & the Construction of Genius: Musical Politics in Vienna, 1792-1803. LC 94-32544. 252p. 1996. 40.00 (*0-520-08892-1*, Pub. by U CA Pr) Cal Prin Full Svc.

Denora, Tia. Beethoven & the Construction of Genius: Musical Politics in Vienna, 1792-1803. 252p. 1997. pap. 16.95 (*0-520-21158-8*, Pub. by U CA Pr) Cal Prin Full Svc.

***DeNora, Tia.** Music's Social Powers: Soundtrack, Self & Embodiment in Everyday Life. LC 99-52606. 2000. write for info. (*0-521-62206-9*); write for info. (*0-521-62732-X*) Cambridge U Pr.

DeNoter, R. & Vuillermoz, P. Dictionnaire des Synonymes. (FRE.). 284p. 1969. 19.95 (*0-8288-6590-6*, M-6113) Fr & Eur.

***DeNoux, Deb, ed.** Erotic New Orleans. (Illus.). 378p. 1999. 24.95 (*1-891643-24-X*, Autumn Bks) Pontalba Pr.

Denoux, Jean-Marie & Pailloux, Jean-Pierre. Physical Therapy & Massage for the Horse: A Comprehensive Approach to Equine Kinesiology. LC 94-61970. (Illus.). 200p. 1996. 29.95 (*1-57076-021-7*, Trafalgar Sq Pub) Trafalgar.

***DeNoux, O'Neil.** La Stanza: New Orleans Police Stories. unabridged ed. 326p. 1999. 19.95 (*1-891643-73-8*, Autumn Bks) Pontalba Pr.

Denova, Charles C. Establishing a Training Function: A Guide for Management. LC 72-122813. 160p. 1971. 32.95 (*0-87778-005-6*) Educ Tech Pubns.

Denova, Rebecca I. The Things Accomplished among Us: Prophetic Tradition in the Structural Pattern of Luke - Acts. LC 97-202318. (JSNTS Ser.: Vol. 141). 264p. 1997. 75.00 (*1-85075-656-2*, Pub. by Sheffield Acad) CUP Services.

DeNovo, John A. American Interests & Policies in the Middle East, 1900-1939. LC 63-21129. 459p. reprint ed. pap. 142.30 (*0-8357-8795-8*, 203321600085) Bks Demand.

Denoya, Laila. How to Create Successful Academic Summer Programs. LC 98-65080. (Fastback Ser.: No. 432). 43p. 1998. pap. 3.00 (*0-87367-632-7*, FB#432) Phi Delta Kappa.

DeNoyelles, Griffith, Jr., jt. auth. see Chernofsky, Charles B.

***Denoyer, Marie.** Dictionary Des Themes Sanitaires: Sociaux. (FRE.). 1999. 49.95 (*0-320-01768-0*) Fr & Eur.

Dens, Jean-Pierre. L' Honnete Homme et la Critique du Gout: Esthetique et Societe au XVIIe Siecle. LC 81-68005. (French Forum Monographs: No. 28). 157p. (Orig.). 1981. pap. 9.95 (*0-917058-27-5*) French Forum.

Densch, Geoff. Minorities in the Open Society: Prisoners of Ambivalence & Containment. (Reports of the Institute of Community Studies). 256p. 1986. text 37.50 (*0-7102-0898-7*, 08987, Routledge Thoemms) Routledge.

Denscombe, Martyn. The Good Research Guide: For Small-Scale Social Research Projects. LC 98-12010. 247p. 1998. 75.00 (*0-335-19806-6*); pap. 22.95 (*0-335-19805-8*) OpUniv Pr.

Densehikoff, Chris. Web Management with Microsoft Visual SourceSafe. LC 97-67034. 247p. 1997. 39.99 (*0-7897-1233-4*) Que.

Denser, J. L. AIDS & the Heterosexual. LC 91-92002. 128p. (Orig.). 1991. pap. 7.95 (*0-9629513-0-7*) J L Denser.

Densham, H. A. Scammell & Densham's Law of Agricultural Holdings. 7th ed. 1989. 190.00 (*0-406-36813-9*, U.K., MICHIE) LEXIS Pub.

Densham, Jennifer. Deafness, Children & the Family: A Guide to Professional Practice. 224p. 1995. 64.95 (*1-85742-221-X*, Pub. by Arena) Ashgate Pub Co.

Denshi Jeoheo Tseushin Gakkai (Japan) Staff, jt. auth. see Asia & South Pacific Design Automation Conference Staff.

Denshuick, Lisa A., ed. Packaging Sourcebook 2000. 5th ed. 1999. pap. 349.00 (*1-888576-58-8*) North Am Pub Co.

— Printing Industry Goldbook, 2000. 1999. pap. 389.00 (*1-888576-62-6*) North Am Pub Co.

Denski, Stan, jt. auth. see Scholle, David.

Densley, Barbara. The ABCs of Home Food Dehydration. LC 75-23565. 112p. (Orig.). 1975. reprint ed. pap. 8.98 (*0-88290-051-X*) Horizon Utah.

— New Concepts in Dehydrated Food Cookery: Hundreds of New Ideas & Tested Recipes for Enjoying Home Dehydrated Foods. LC 79-89357. 191p. 1979. pap. 13.98 (*0-88290-126-5*) Horizon Utah.

Densley, Barbara & Flack, Dora D. Food Preservation Set: Fun with Fruit Preservation, ABC's of Home Food Dehydration, New Concepts in Dehydrated Food Cookery, 3 bks., Set. 1994. pap. 28.98 (*0-88290-495-7*) Horizon Utah.

Densley, Glenn. Sparta Gold, Vol. 1. (Illus.). Date not set. pap. write for info. (*0-9623748-1-4*) Snake Riv Secrets.

Densley, Lillian C. Saints, Sinners & Snake River Secrets: From Memories Recorded in Jessie's Journals. (Illus.). 136p. (Orig.). 1988. pap. 14.95 (*0-9623748-0-6*) Snake Riv Secrets.

Denslow, David, et al. The Economic Impact of Local Government Comprehensive Plans. (BEBR Monographs: Issue No. 8). 144p. (Orig.). 1994. pap. 17.00 (*0-930885-12-0*) Bur Econ & Bus Res.

Denslow, David A. & Badger-Dole, Carol. Principles of Macroeconomics: Outline & Notes. 208p. (C). 1993. spiral bd. 20.95 (*0-8403-9034-3*) Kendall-Hunt.

Denslow, Julie S. & Padoch, Christine, eds. People of the Tropical Rain Forest: In Association with Smithsonian Institution Traveling Exhibition Service. (Illus.). 240p. 1988. pap. 34.95 (*0-520-06351-1*, Pub. by U CA Pr) Cal Prin Full Svc.

Denslow, Orriene F. Daniel & Mary (Lee) Johnson & Their Descendants in Canada & Michigan: Daniel & Mary (Lee) Johnson Ancestry. 710p. 1994. 50.00 (*0-9636672-0-3*) O F Denslow.

Denslow, Ray V. Territorial Masonry: The Story of Freemasonry & the Louisiana Purchase, 1804-1821. 300p. 1996. reprint ed. pap. 19.95 (*1-56459-551-X*) Kessinger Pub.

Denslow, Sharon P. Big Wolf & Little Wolf. LC 99-11712. (Illus.). 32p. (J). (ps-3). 2000. 15.95 (*0-688-16174-X*, Grenwillow Bks); 15.89 (*0-688-16175-8*, Grenwillow Bks) HarpC Child Bks.

— Bus Riders. LC 92-14109. (Illus.). 32p. (J). (ps-2). 1993. text, lib. bdg. 14.95 (*0-02-728682-7*, Four Winds Pr) S&S Childrens.

— Hazel's Circle. LC 91-18182. (Illus.). 32p. (J). (ps-2). 1992. text 14.95 (*0-02-728683-5*, Mac Bks Young Read) S&S Childrens.

— Night Owls. LC 89-33937. (Illus.). 32p. (J). (ps-2). 1990. lib. bdg. 13.95 (*0-02-728681-9*, Bradbury S&S) S&S Childrens.

Denslow, Sharon P. On the Trail with Miss Pace. LC 94-38206. (Illus.). 40p. (J). (ps-3). 1995. pap. 15.00 (*0-02-728688-6*, Four Winds Pr) S&S Childrens.

Denslow, Van B. Modern Thinkers: Principally upon Social Science; What They Think & Why. LC 72-38744. (Essay Index Reprint Ser.). 1977. reprint ed. 28.95 (*0-8369-2646-3*) Ayer.

Denslow, W. W., jt. auth. see Baum, L. Frank.

Denslow, W. W., ed. see Baum, L. Frank.

Denslow, William R. Centennial History of Grundy County, Missouri, 1839-1939. (Illus.). 402p. 1997. reprint ed. lib. bdg. 45.00 (*0-8328-7135-4*) Higginson Bk Co.

Densmore, Brad. A Funny Thing Happened on My Way Through the Bible. 256p. 1998. mass mkt. 2.49 (*1-57748-215-8*) Barbour Pub.

Densmore, Brad, contrib. by. Amazing Bible Trivia, Bk. 1. 544p. 1999. pap. 9.99 (*0-7852-4259-7*) Nelson.

Densmore, C. Dana. A-Boat: Six Oceanographic Cruises in the World's Biggest Ketch. (Illus.). 195p. (Orig.). 1995. pap. 17.00 (*0-9645207-0-2*) C D Densmore.

***Densmore, C. Dana.** An Irregular Sort of Life. (Illus.). 308p. 2000. pap. write for info. (*0-9645207-1-0*) C D Densmore.

Densmore, Christopher. Red Jacket: Iroquois Diplomat & Orator. LC 98-29828. 1998. 39.95 (*0-8156-2785-8*); pap. 17.95 (*0-8156-0548-X*) Syracuse U Pr.

Densmore, D., tr. see Tchernia, P. & Swallow, J.

Densmore, Dana. Newton's Principia: The Central Argument. Donahue, William H., tr. from LAT. & illus. by. 473p. 1995. pap. 26.95 (*1-888009-00-4*) Grn Lion Pr.

Densmore, Dana, ed. Syllabus Sourcebook on Media & Women. 48p. 1980. 5.50 (*0-930470-06-0*) Womens Inst Free Press.

Densmore, Dana, ed. see Apollonius of Perga.

Densmore, Emmet. How Nature Cures. 413p. 1996. reprint ed. spiral bd. 23.50 (*0-7873-0280-5*) Hlth Research.

Densmore, Frances. Cheyenne & Arapaho Music. 111p. 1964. reprint ed. pap. 5.00 (*0-916561-12-7*) Southwest Mus.

— Chippewa Customs. (Bureau of American Ethnology Bulletins Ser.). 204p. 1995. lib. bdg. write for info. (*0-7812-4086-7*) Rprt Serv.

— Chippewa Customs. LC 79-15400. (Illus.). xxiv, 204p. 1979. reprint ed. pap. 12.95 (*0-87351-142-5*, Borealis Book) Minn Hist.

— Chippewa Customs. 1988. reprint ed. lib. bdg. 75.00 (*0-7812-0221-3*) Rprt Serv.

— Chippewa Customs. reprint ed. 49.00 (*0-403-03556-2*) Scholarly.

— Chippewa Music. (Bureau of American Ethnology Bulletins Ser.). 216p. 1995. lib. bdg. 89.00 (*0-7812-4045-X*); lib. bdg. 99.00 (*0-7812-4053-0*) Rprt Serv.

Densmore, Frances. Chippewa Music, Bulletin 45. (Smithsonian Institution, Bureau of American Ethnology Ser.). (Illus.). 245p. 1910. pap. text 26.25 (*1-55567-710-X*) Coyote Press.

Densmore, Frances. Choctaw Music. LC 72-1883. (Music Ser.). (Illus.). 110p. 1972. reprint ed. lib. bdg. 22.50 (*0-306-70511-7*) Da Capo.

— Choctaw Music. LC 90-44635. (Illus.). 100p. 1990. reprint ed. pap. 15.00 (*1-878592-21-1*); reprint ed. lib. bdg. 29.00 (*1-878592-22-X*) Native Amer Bk Pubs.

— Handbook of the Collection of Musical Instruments in the United States National Museum. LC 79-155231. (Music Ser.). 1971. reprint ed. lib. bdg. 32.50 (*0-306-70167-7*) Da Capo.

— How Indians Use Wild Plants for Food, Medicine & Crafts. (Illus.). 155p. 1974. reprint ed. pap. 6.95 (*0-486-23019-8*) Dover.

— Mandan & Hidatsa Music. (Bureau of American Ethnology Bulletins Ser.). 192p. 1995. lib. bdg. 79.00 (*0-7812-4080-8*) Rprt Serv.

— Mandan & Hidatsa Music. LC 72-1886. (Music Ser.). (Illus.). 236p. 1972. reprint ed. lib. bdg. 27.50 (*0-306-70514-1*) Da Capo.

— Menominee Music. (Bureau of American Ethnology Bulletins Ser.). 230p. 1995. lib. bdg. 89.00 (*0-7812-4102-2*) Rprt Serv.

— Menominee Music. LC 72-1882. (Music Ser.). (Illus.). 286p. 1972. reprint ed. lib. bdg. 29.50 (*0-306-70510-9*) Da Capo.

— Menominee Music. 1988. reprint ed. lib. bdg. 75.00 (*0-317-90154-0*) Rprt Serv.

— Music of Acoma, Isleta, Cochiti, & Zuni Pueblos. (Bureau of American Ethnology Bulletins Ser.). 117p. 1995. lib. bdg. 79.00 (*0-7812-4165-0*) Rprt Serv.

— Music of Acoma, Isleta, Cochiti, & Zuni Pueblos. LC 72-1877. (Music Ser.). (Illus.). 142p. 1972. reprint ed. lib. bdg. 22.50 (*0-306-70505-2*) Da Capo.

— Music of Santo Domingo Pueblo, New Mexico. 186p. 1938. pap. 5.00 (*0-916561-53-4*) Southwest Mus.

— Music of the Indians of British Columbia. LC 72-1879. (Music Ser.). (Illus.). 118p. 1972. reprint ed. lib. bdg. 21.50 (*0-306-70507-9*) Da Capo.

— Nootka & Quileute Music. (Bureau of American Ethnology Bulletins Ser.). 358p. 1995. lib. bdg. 99.00 (*0-7812-4124-3*) Rprt Serv.

— Nootka & Quileute Music. LC 72-1885. (Music Ser.). (Illus.). 416p. 1972. reprint ed. lib. bdg. 42.50 (*0-306-70513-3*) Da Capo.

— Northern Ute Music. (Bureau of American Ethnology Bulletins Ser.). 213p. 1995. lib. bdg. 89.00 (*0-7812-4075-1*) Rprt Serv.

— Northern Ute Music. LC 72-1887. (Music Ser.). (Illus.). 236p. 1972. reprint ed. lib. bdg. 27.50 (*0-306-70515-X*) Da Capo.

— Papago Music. (Bureau of American Ethnology Bulletins Ser.). 229p. 1995. lib. bdg. 89.00 (*0-7812-4090-5*) Rprt Serv.

— Papago Music. LC 72-1881. (Music Ser.). (Illus.). 276p. 1972. reprint ed. lib. bdg. 27.50 (*0-306-70509-5*) Da Capo.

— Pawnee Music. LC 72-1880. (Music Ser.). 160p. 1972. reprint ed. lib. bdg. 21.50 (*0-306-70508-7*) Da Capo.

— Pawnee Music: Bureau of American Ethnology Bulletins. (Bureau of American Ethnology Bulletins Ser.). 129p. 1995. lib. bdg. 79.00 (*0-7812-4093-X*) Rprt Serv.

— Seminole Music. (Bureau of American Ethnology Bulletins Ser.). 223p. 1995. lib. bdg. 89.00 (*0-7812-4161-8*) Rprt Serv.

— Teton Sioux Music. (Bureau of American Ethnology Bulletins Ser.). 561p. 1995. lib. bdg. 119.00 (*0-7812-4061-1*) Rprt Serv.

— Teton Sioux Music. 1988. reprint ed. lib. bdg. 75.00 (*0-7812-0222-1*) Rprt Serv.

— Teton Sioux Music & Culture. LC 92-16223. (Illus.). xviii, 644p. 1992. pap. 19.95 (*0-8032-6593-X*, Bison Books) U of Nebr Pr.

— Yuman & Yaqui Music. (Bureau of American Ethnology Bulletins Ser.). 216p. 1995. lib. bdg. 89.00 (*0-7812-4110-3*) Rprt Serv.

Densmore, Frances. Yuman & Yaqui Music. fac. ed. (Smithsonian Institution, Bureau of American Ethnology, Bulletins Ser.: No. 110). (Illus.). 263p. (C). 1932. reprint ed. pap. text 27.50 (*1-55567-807-6*) Coyote Press.

D

An Asterisk (*) at the beginning of an entry indicates that the title is appearing for the first time.

Densmore, Frances. Yuman & Yaqui Music. LC 72-1884. (Music Ser.). (Illus.). 272p. 1972. reprint ed. lib. bdg. 27.50 (*0-306-70512-5*) Da Capo.

Densmore, Frances, jt. auth. see Rhodes, Willard.

Densmore, Francis. Chippewa Music. reprint ed. 49.00 (*0-403-03557-0*) Scholarly.

Densmore, John. Riders on the Storm: My Life with Jim Morrison & the Doors. 336p. 1991. pap. 14.95 (*0-385-30447-1*, Delta Trade) Dell.

— Time Was Fleeting. Date not set. mass mkt. 5.99 (*0-06-105788-6*) HarpC.

Densmore, L. W. Hartwell Family: Account of the Descendants of William Hartwell of Concord, Mass., 1636-1895. 80p. 1993. reprint ed. pap. 16.00 (*0-8328-3585-4*); reprint ed. lib. bdg. 26.00 (*0-8328-3584-6*) Higginson Bk Co.

Densmore, Lisa Feinberg. Ski Faster: Lisa Feinberg Densmore's Guide to High Performance Skiing & Racing. LC 99-30599. 224p. 1999. pap. 19.95 (*0-07-134381-4*) McGraw.

Denson, Al. I Gotta Know! Answers to Tough Questions Students Ask. LC 98-48045. 1999. pap. text 9.99 (*0-8423-3859-4*) Tyndale Hse.

— Take Me to the Cross Devotional. LC 97-216171. 232p. (J). 1997. pap. 8.99 (*0-8423-7003-X*) Tyndale Hse.

Denson, Jo. Whispers & Wonders. LC 96-13451. 184p. 1996. 14.95 (*1-56554-143-X*) Pelican.

Denson, John V., ed. The Costs of War: America's Pyrrhic Victories. 2nd expanded ed. LC 98-8759. 450p. 1998. pap. 29.95 (*0-7658-0487-5*) Transaction Pubs.

Denson, Judy M. & Smallwood, Beverly. Kid Spirational Keepsakes: The Journal. (Illus.). 104p. (Orig.). (J). 1997. 12.95 (*0-937552-87-9*) Quail Ridge.

— KidSpiration: Out of the Mouths of Babes. LC 97-2935. (Illus.). 208p. (Orig.). 1997. pap. 9.95 (*0-937552-86-0*) Quail Ridge.

— KidSpiration Out of the Mouths of Babes & KidSpirational Keepsakes: The Journal Combination Set. 1997. pap. 19.95 (*0-937552-90-9*) Quail Ridge.

Denson, Wil. Artie. (Illus.). 32p. (YA). (gr. 7-12). 1988. pap. 4.00 (*0-88680-292-X*) I E Clark.

— A Friend Like Artie: One-Act Version of "Artie" 16p. 1988. pap. 3.00 (*0-88680-330-6*) I E Clark.

— Hucklebee & the Rhyming Mountain. 1992. pap. 3.50 (*0-87129-164-9*, H61) Dramatic Pub.

— Tinker Autumn. 1987. pap. 3.50 (*0-87129-008-1*, T78) Dramatic Pub.

— Welcome to Carnie: A 2-Act Play. (Illus.). (YA). (gr. 7-12). 1989. pap. 4.00 (*0-88680-315-2*) I E Clark.

Denson, Wil & Cunningham, Michael. Aladdin McFaddin: A Musical Comedy. (Illus.). 44p. (J). (gr. 2 up). 1977. pap. 4.00 (*0-88680-004-8*) I E Clark.

Denstbier, Richard A., jt. ed. see Melbon, Gary B.

***Denston, Richard O.** Listening for the Night Bird Collection V: The Poetry of Richard Otis Denston. LC 99-94752. (Illus.). iv, 29p. 1999. pap. 5.00 (*1-890770-00-0*, Swann Pubns) F Swann Pubns.

Dent. Cartography. 5th ed. LC 98-25683. 1998. 55.74 (*0-697-38495-0*) McGraw.

— A Guide to Unix. (Networking Ser.). (C). 1999. 53.95 (*0-7600-1096-X*) Course Tech.

— Zulu-English - English-Zulu Compact Dictionary. 5th ed. (ENG & ZUL.). 150p. 1990. pap. 9.50 (*0-7960-0265-7*, Pub. by Shuter & Shooter) IBD Ltd.

— Zulu-English, English-Zulu Dictionary. (ENG & ZUL.). 150p. 1990. pap. 9.95 (*0-7859-7484-9*) Fr & Eur.

Dent, Alan, ed. see Shaw, George Bernard.

Dent, Alastair, jt. auth. see Aslam, Mo.

Dent, Andrew. Who Killed Kurt? The Cobain Dossier. (Illus.). 144p. 1995. per. 19.95 (*0-85965-225-4*, Pub. by Plexus) Publishers Group.

Dent, Aneilla, ed. Ecology & Faith: The Writings of Pope John Paul II. 48p. 1997. pap. 5.95 (*0-85305-410-X*, 6333, Pub. by Arthur James) Morehouse Pub.

Dent, Anthony. Cleveland Bay Horses. 87p. 1990. pap. 21.00 (*0-85131-283-7*, Pub. by J A Allen) St Mut.

— The Horse Through Fifty Centuries of Civilisation. 288p. (C). 1990. 65.00 (*0-85131-291-8*, Pub. by J A Allen) St Mut.

Dent, Anthony, intro. The Reign of the Horse: The Horse in Print, 1500-1715. (Illus.). 64p. (Orig.). 1991. pap. 4.95 (*0-9629254-0-3*) Folger.

Dent, Anthony & Goodall, Daphne M. A History of British Native Ponies. Orig. Title: Foals of Epona. 305p. 1990. reprint ed. 62.00 (*0-85131-436-8*, Pub. by J A Allen) St Mut.

Dent, Arthur. The Plain Man's Pathway to Heaven. 332p. 1993. reprint ed. 24.95 (*1-877611-69-7*) Soli Deo Gloria.

— The Plaine Mans Path-Way to Heaven. LC 74-80173. (English Experience Ser.: No. 652). 430p. 1974. reprint ed. 45.00 (*90-221-0652-7*) Walter J Johnson.

Dent, Barbara J., ed. see Walton, John R.

Dent, Bob. Blue Guide Hungary. 2nd ed. (Illus.). 384p. 1998. pap. 26.95 (*0-393-31800-1*) Norton.

— Blue Guide to Budapest. (Illus.). 224p. 1996. pap. 19.95 (*0-393-31422-7*) Norton.

Dent, Borden D. Cartography: Thematic Map Design. 4th ed. 464p. (C). 1996. text 79.06 (*0-697-22970-X*, WCB McGr Hill) McGrw-H Hghr Educ.

— Principles of Thematic Design. (Geography Ser.). (Illus.). 400p. 1985. write for info. (*0-201-11334-1*) Addison-Wesley.

***Dent-Brockelhurst, Mollie, ed.** Jenny Saville: Territories. (Illus.). 50p. 1999. pap. 40.00 (*1-880154-35-8*) Gagosian Gallery.

Dent-Brocklehurst, Mollie, ed. see Chapman, Jake.

Dent-Brocklehurst, Mollie, ed. see Fenton, James.

Dent Brocklehurst, Mollie, ed. see Kuspit, Donald & Spender, Matthew.

Dent, C. M. Protestant Reformers in Elizabethan England. (Oxford Theological Monographs). 272p. (C). 1983. text 49.95 (*0-19-826723-1*) OUP.

Dent, Christopher M. The European Economy: The Global Context. LC 96-19787. 480p. (C). 1997. 110.00 (*0-415-13487-0*); pap. 29.99 (*0-415-13488-9*) Routledge.

Dent, Christopher M. European Union & East Asia: Economic Relationship. LC 98-55762. 1999. pap. write for info. (*0-415-17200-4*) Routledge.

***Dent, Christopher M.** European Union & East Asia: Economic Relationship. LC 98-55762. 352p. (C). 1999. text. write for info. (*0-415-17199-7*) Routledge.

Dent, Colin. Construction Cost Appraisal: DCF Techniques in the Construction Industry. LC 75-322708. 182p. reprint ed. pap. 56.50 (*0-608-13230-6*, 202526600043) Bks Demand.

Dent, Craig. Broken Drought. (C). 1990. 30.00 (*0-89771-039-8*, Pub. by Pascoe Pub) St Mut.

***Dent, D.** Insect Pest Management. 2nd ed. LC 99-87126. (CABI Publishing Ser.). 550p. 1999. text 110.00 (*0-85199-340-0*); pap. text 55.00 (*0-85199-341-9*) OUP.

Dent, D., ed. Acid Sulphate Soil: A Baseline for Research & Development. (C). 1991. text 460.00 (*0-89771-593-4*, Pub. by Intl Bk Distr) St Mut.

Dent, D., jt. auth. see Harris, J.

Dent, D. R. & Walton, M. P. Methods in Ecological & Agricultural Entomology. LC 96-48888. (A CAB International Publication). (Illus.). 400p. (C). 1997. pap. text 45.00 (*0-85199-132-7*) OUP.

Dent, D. R. & Walton, M. P., eds. Methods in Ecological & Agricultural Entomology. LC 96-48888. (A CAB International Publication). 400p. (C). 1997. text 100.00 (*0-85199-131-9*) OUP.

Dent, David. Insect Pest Management. 604p. 1991. pap. text 50.00 (*0-85198-667-6*) OUP.

Dent, David, jt. auth. see Dalal-Clayton, Barry.

Dent, David J. In Search of Black America: Discovering the African American Dream. LC 99-59843. 416p. 2000. 25.00 (*0-684-81072-7*) S&S Trade.

***Dent, David J.** In Search of Black America: Discovering the African American Dream. 2001. pap. 14.00 (*0-7432-0305-4*, Touchstone) S&S Trade Pap.

Dent, David W. Monroe's Ghosts. LC 98-15326. 432p. 1999. 59.95 (*0-313-30109-3*, Greenwood Pr) Greenwood.

— U. S. Latin American Policymaking: A Reference Handbook. LC 94-27947. 592p. 1995. lib. bdg. 110.00 (*0-313-27951-9*, Greenwood Pr) Greenwood.

Dent, David W., ed. Handbook of Political Science Research on Latin America: Trends from the 1960s to the 1990s. LC 90-36626. 464p. 1990. lib. bdg. 99.50 (*0-313-26446-5*, DPS, Greenwood Pr) Greenwood.

Dent, David W., jt. auth. see Wilson, Larman C.

Dent, Dorothy. The Joy of Country Painting. (Illus.). 68p. (Orig.). 1989. pap. 11.95 (*0-924639-00-8*) Bob Ross Inc.

Dent, Edward, tr. see Mozart, Wolfgang Amadeus.

Dent, Edward E. Betrayal: Employee Relations at DuPont: 1981-1994. LC 95-14896. (Illus.). 198p. (Orig.). 1995. pap. 18.00 (*1-55618-152-3*) Brunswick Pub.

Dent, Edward J. Alessandro Scarlatti: His Life & Works. 1988. reprint ed. lib. bdg. 59.00 (*0-7812-0141-1*) Rprt Serv.

— Alessandro Scarlatti: His Life & Works. LC 76-181140. 252p. 1960. reprint ed. 49.00 (*0-403-01541-3*) Scholarly.

— Foundations of English Opera. 2nd ed. LC 65-18501. (Music Ser.). 1965. reprint ed. lib. bdg. 32.50 (*0-306-70905-8*) Da Capo.

— Handel: Music Book Index. 140p. 1993. reprint ed. lib. bdg. 69.00 (*0-7812-9599-8*) Rprt Serv.

— Mozart's Operas: A Critical Study. 276p. reprint ed. lib. bdg. 59.00 (*0-685-14896-3*) Rprt Serv.

— Mozart's Operas: A Critical Study. 2nd ed. LC 83-45429. reprint ed. 32.50 (*0-404-20077-X*) AMS Pr.

— Notes on Fugue for Beginners. (Music Book Index Ser.). 47p. 1992. reprint ed. lib. bdg. 59.00 (*0-7812-9504-1*) Rprt Serv.

Dent, Edward J., tr. see Rossini, Gioachino.

Dent, G., jt. auth. see Chalmers, J. M.

Dent, G. R. Scholar's Zulu Dictionary (English-Zulu - Zulu-English) 4th ed. 519p. 1993. pap. 39.95 (*0-7859-8719-3*) Fr & Eur.

Dent, Gene. The Truth about Helping: Strategies & Tactics for Helping Injured, Ill, & Disabled Persons Get Better & Go Back to Work & Life. (Practical Management Ser.). 175p. 1995. pap. write for info. (*1-878403-05-2*) Martin-Dennison Pr.

Dent, Gene L. Absenteeism Checklist. (Practical Management Ser.). 20p. (Orig.). 1990. pap. text 4.00 (*1-878403-02-8*) Martin-Dennison Pr.

— Disability Helper's Guide to Mastering Resistance & Motivating Change. (Practical Management Ser.). (C). 1991. pap. write for info. (*1-878403-04-4*) Martin-Dennison Pr.

— Return to Work by Design: "Managing the Human & Financial Costs of Disability" (Practical Management Ser.). 111p. (Orig.). 1990. pap. text 24.00 (*1-878403-00-1*) Martin-Dennison Pr.

Dent, George, jt. auth. see Sim, Albert E.

Dent, George, jt. auth. see Sims, Albert E.

Dent, Gina, ed. see Wallace, Michele.

Dent, Gregory L. & Johnson, Jeffrey E. Tax Planning & Preparation Made Easy for the Self-Employed. LC 96-148007. 205p. 1995. pap. 15.95 (*0-471-11493-6*) Wiley.

Dent, Harry S., Jr. The Great Boom Ahead: Your Comprehensive Guide to Personal & Business Profit in the New Era of Prosperity. 288p. (J). 1993. 19.45 (*1-56282-943-2*, Pub. by Hyperion) Time Warner.

— The Great Boom Ahead: Your Comprehensive Guide to Personal Business Profit in the New Era of Prosperity. LC 93-39181. (Illus.). 272p. (YA). 1993. pap. 10.45 (*1-56282-758-8*, Pub. by Hyperion) Time Warner.

— Job Shock: Four New Principles Transforming Our Work & Business. (Illus.). 295p. 1999. reprint ed. text 23.00 (*0-7881-6166-0*) DIANE Pub.

— Job Shock: How You Can Prosper During the Work Revolution Ahead. 1995. 22.95 (*0-312-11835-X*) St Martin.

— Our Power to Predict: Revolutionary New Tools for Predicting Our Economy & the Future of Business. LC 90-1572. 128p. (Orig.). 1990. pap. write for info. (*0-938545-06-X*) Jennings & Keefe.

— The Roaring 2000's: Building the Wealth & Lifestyle You Desire in the Greatest Boom in History. LC 93-9943. 288p. 1998. 25.00 (*0-684-83818-4*) S&S Trade.

— The Roaring 2000's: Building the Wealth & Lifestyle You Desire in the Greatest Boom in History. LC 93-9943. 320p. 1999. per. 13.00 (*0-684-85310-8*, Touchstone) S&S Trade Pap.

***Dent, Harry S., Jr.** The Roaring 2000s Investor: Strategies for the Life You Want. LC 99-43185. (Illus.). 288p. 1999. 24.50 (*0-684-86232-8*) S&S Trade Pap.

***Dent, Harry S.** The Roaring 2000s Investor: Strategies for the Life You Want. 2000. pap. 14.00 (*0-684-85231-X*, Touchstone) S&S Trade Pap.

Dent, Harry S., Jr. Teaching Jack & Jill Right vs. Wrong in the Homes & Schools, Vol. 1. 150p. (Orig.). 1996. pap. write for info. (*0-9652786-0-3*) Laity Alive.

Dent, Helen, ed. Clinical Psychology: Research & Developments. 368p. 1987. lib. bdg. 59.50 (*0-7099-4544-2*, Pub. by C Helm) Routldge.

Dent, Huntley. The Feast of Santa Fe. pap. 13.00 (*0-671-89302-5*, Fireside) S&S Trade Pap.

— The Feast of Santa Fe: Cooking of the American Southwest. 400p. 1993. pap. 14.00 (*0-671-87302-4*, Fireside) S&S Trade Pap.

Dent, J. & Yeomans, N. D., eds. Acid-Related Diseases: Improving the Treatment Options - Journal: Digestion, Vol. 51, Suppl. 1, 1992. (Illus.). vi, 126p. 1992. pap. 41.00 (*3-8055-5685-3*) S Karger.

Dent, J. B. & McGregor, M. J., eds. Rural & Farming Systems Analysis: European Perspectives. (Illus.). 384p. 1994. text 105.00 (*0-85198-914-4*) OUP.

Dent, J. B., jt. ed. see Blackie, Malcolm J.

Dent, Jennifer. Crystal Clear: A Guide to Quartz Crystal. 1994. pap. 17.95 (*1-898307-30-X*) Holmes Pub.

— Healing Homes. (Illus.). (Orig.). 1995. pap. 19.95 (*1-898307-46-6*, Pub. by Capall Bann Pubng) Holmes Pub.

Dent, Jenny. A Quiet Mind Companion: A Personal Journey Through White Eagle's Teaching. 158p. (Orig.). 1993. pap. (*0-85487-091-1*) White Eagle.

***Dent, Jim.** The Junction Boys: How Ten Days in Hell with Bear Bryant Forged a Championship Team at Texas A & M. (Illus.). 304p. 2000. reprint ed. pap. 13.95 (*0-312-26755-X*, Thomas Dunne) St Martin.

Dent, Jim. The Junction Boys: How Ten Days in Hell with Bear Bryant Forged a Championship Team at Texas A & M. 2nd ed. LC 99-22179. (Illus.). 336p. 1999 text 24.95 (*0-312-19293-2*) St Martin.

Dent, Jim, jt. auth. see Merrill, Durwood.

Dent, Jim, ed. see Merrill, Durwood.

Dent, John. David & Marianne Long ORG3. 1997. pap. text 7.35 (*0-582-27395-1*) Addison-Wesley.

Dent, John A. Surgery: A Core Text with Self-Assessment Covering Orthopaedics, Ear, Nose & Throat, Vol. 2. 1997. pap. text 19.95 (*0-443-05171-2*) Church.

Dent, John A., jt. auth. see Rowley, D. I.

Dent, John C. The Story of the Upper Canadian Rebellion: Largely Derived from Original Sources & Documents Upper Canadian Rebellion. 1977. 57.95 (*0-8369-7157-4*, 7989) Ayer.

Dent, Joseph B., et al. Fundamentals of Engineering Graphics. 4th ed. 410p. (C). 1987. pap. text 62.20 (*0-02-328690-3*, Macmillan Coll) P-H.

Dent, Julianne. College for Kids. 48p. (J). (gr. 3-8). 1993. pap. text 7.50 (*1-881986-07-1*) Demibach Eds.

Dent, Julianne & Bauer, Kathleen. Duet Edition. Vol. 3. 35p. 1993. pap. text 8.00 (*1-881986-12-8*) Demibach Eds.

— Supplementary Pieces for Volume 2, Vol. 2. 23p. (J). (gr. k-3). 1993. suppl. ed. 8.00 (*1-881986-05-5*) Demibach Eds.

— Young Beginner Workbook for Volume 1, Vol. 1. 57p. (J). (gr. k-3). 1992. wbk. ed. 8.00 (*1-881986-00-4*) Demibach Eds.

— Young Beginner Workbook for Volume 3, Vol. 3. 57p. (J). (gr. k-3). 1992. wbk. ed. 8.00 (*1-881986-02-0*) Demibach Eds.

— Young Beginner Workbook for Volume 2, Vol. 2. 57p. (J). (gr. k-3). 1992. wbk. ed. 8.00 (*1-881986-01-2*) Demibach Eds.

Dent, Julianne, et al. Supplementary Pieces for Volume 1, Vol. 1. 23p. (J). (gr. k-3). 1992. suppl. ed. 8.00 (*1-881986-04-7*) Demibach Eds.

Dent, Julianne, jt. auth. see Bauer, Kathleen.

Dent, Karen. The Soaps: Scene Stealing Scenes for Actors. Zapel, Arthur L., ed. LC 89-37760. 128p. (Orig.). (YA). (gr. 9 up). 1989. pap. 9.95 (*0-916260-60-7*, B123) Meriwether Pub.

Dent, Lester. The Sinister Ray. (Illus.). 175p. (Orig.). 1987. pap. 9.95 (*0-936071-04-4*) Gryphon Pubns.

***Dent, Martin & Peters, Bill.** The Crisis of Poverty & Debt in the Third World. 290p. 1999. text 72.95 (*0-7546-1027-6*, Pub. by Ashgate Pub) Ashgate Pub Co.

Dent, Mike. Professions, Information Technology & Management in Hospitals. LC 96-84597. xii, 212 p. 1996. pap. 63.95 (*1-85628-869-2*, Pub. by Avebry) Ashgate Pub Co.

Dent, Nicola. Little Book of Collectible Teddy Bears. 1995. 4.98 (*0-7858-0237-1*) Bk Sales Inc.

— Little Book of Creative Cocktails. 1995. 4.98 (*0-7858-0344-0*) Bk Sales Inc.

Dent, Nigel. Good Research Practices: A Practical Guide to the Implementation of the GXPs. LC 96-44739. (Illus.). 552p. 1997. text 115.00 (*0-7506-2266-0*) Buttrwrth-Heinemann.

Dent, Nigel J., ed. Implementing International Good Practices: GAPs, GCPs, GLPs, & GMPs. (Illus.). 273p. 1993. 169.00 (*0-935184-44-9*) Interpharm.

Dent, Nigel J., et al. International Good Clinical Practice: The GCP Compliance Handbook. (Illus.). 380p. 1995. ring bd. 249.00 (*0-935184-83-X*) Interpharm.

Dent, Peter. Breaking Shadows. (Chickadee Ser.: Vol. 12). 20p. 1999. pap. 6.00 (*1-55780-179-7*) Juniper Pr ME.

Dent, R. J., Jr. Chesapeake Prehistory: Old Traditions, New Directions. (Interdisciplinary Contributions to Archaeology Ser.). (Illus.). 334p. (C). 1995. 59.00 (*0-306-45028-3*, Kluwer Plenum) Kluwer Academic.

Dent, R. W. Colloquial Language in Ulysses: A Reference Tool. (Illus.). 296p. 1995. 38.50 (*0-87413-546-X*) U Delaware Pr.

Dent, Raymond D. & Ball, Martin J., eds. The Handbook of Voice Quality Measurement. LC 99-19664. (Illus.). 475p. 1999. pap. 65.00 (*1-56593-991-3*, 1960) Thomson Learn.

Dent-Read, Cathy & Zukow-Goldring, Patricia, eds. Evolving Explanations of Development: Ecological Approaches to Organism-Environment Systems. LC 96-46275. (Illus.). 601p. 1997. text 49.95 (*1-55798-382-8*) Am Psychol.

Dent, Rik. Reality: How It Works & Why It Mostly Doesn't. (Orig.). 1997. pap. 22.95 (*1-86163-018-2*, Pub. by Capall Bann Pubng) Holmes Pub.

Dent, Robert. The International Multi-Lingual Field Manual for Public Safety Professionals. World Trade Center School of Languages Staff, tr. from FRE. 208p. (Orig.). 1995. pap., spiral bd. 39.95 (*1-883339-01-4*) Constable Grp.

***Dent, Robert & Morris, Alan.** Silent Universal Signals for Public Safety & Education Professionals: A Guide to Saving Lives Through Silent Communication. (Illus.). 200p. 2000. 29.99 (*1-883339-08-1*) Constable Grp.

Dent, Robert L. The Complete Spanish Field Reference Manual for Public Safety Professionals. 6th rev. ed. O'Hearn, Frank, tr. from ENG. 200p. 1998. 35.00 (*1-883339-04-9*) Constable Grp.

Dent, Stephen M. Partnering Intelligence: Creating Value for Your Business by Building Strong Alliances. LC 99-22739. 256p. 1999. 29.95 (*0-89106-132-0*, Pub. by Consulting Psychol) Consulting Psychol.

Dent, Thomas L., ed. Surgical Endoscopy. LC 85-5298. (Illus.). 560p. reprint ed. pap. 173.60 (*0-8357-7611-5*, 205693400096) Bks Demand.

Dent, Tory. HIV, Mon Amour: Poems. LC 99-46988. 142p. 1999. pap. 19.95 (*1-878818-81-3*, Pub. by Sheep Meadow) U Pr of New Eng.

— What Silence Equals: Poems. LC 93-3466. 80p. (Orig.). 1993. pap. 9.95 (*0-89255-196-8*) Persea Bks.

Dent-Walton, Barbara J., ed. see Hinono, John Walton.

Dent-Young, Alex, jt. auth. see Dent-Young, John.

Dent-Young, Alex, tr. see Shi Nai'an & Lo Kuan-Chung.

Dent-Young, Esther, tr. see Loo, Andre.

Dent-Young, John. The Language of English Studies: A Handbook for Advanced Students of English. LC 97-195177. 338p. (Orig.). (C). 1997. pap. text 17.95 (*962-201-648-0*, Pub. by Chinese Univ) U of Mich Pr.

Dent-Young, John & Dent-Young, Alex. The Broken Seals Pt. 1: The Marshes of Mount Liang. 1997. pap. text 32.50 (*962-201-602-2*, Pub. by Chinese Univ) U of Mich Pr.

Dent-Yuong, John, tr. see Shi Nai'an & Lo Kuan-Chung.

Dentali, Stephen. The Natural Pharmacist: Ginko & Memory. LC 98-50708. (Illus.). 164p. 2000. pap. 6.99 (*0-7615-1552-6*) Prima Pub.

Dentan, Robert C. Holy Scriptures: A Survey. (Orig.). 1984. 5.95 (*0-8164-2031-9*, SP1) Harper SF.

Dentan, Robert C., ed. The Idea of History in the Ancient Near East. (American Oriental Ser.: Vol. 38). 376p. 1955. pap. 12.95 (*0-940490-38-2*) Am Orient Soc.

Dentan, Robert K. A Dream of Senoi. (Council on International Studies & Programs Special Studies: No. 150). 61p. 1985. pap. text 10.00 (*0-924197-01-3*, 150) SUNYB Coun Intl Studies.

Dentan, Robert K., et al. Malaysia & the "Original People" A Case Study of the Impact of Development on Indigenous Peoples. LC 98-122138. 175p. 1996. pap. text 20.00 (*0-205-19817-1*) Allyn.

Dentato & Progris. How to Play Jazz Flute. 1990. 15.95 (*0-685-32128-2*, K296) Hansen Ed Mus.

Dentato, J. Jazz Flute for Christmas. 1990. 5.95 (*0-685-32133-9*, 77123) Hansen Ed Mus.

Dente, Anita, jt. auth. see Arnaldo, D.

Dente, Bruno, ed. Environmental Policy in Search of New Instruments. LC 94-21240. (Environment, Science & Society Ser.: Vol. 3). 240p. (C). 1995. lib. bdg. 151.00 (*0-7923-2949-X*) Kluwer Academic.

Dente, Bruno & Kjellberg, Francesco, eds. The Dynamics of Institutional Change: Local Government Reorganization in Western Democracies. (Modern Politics Ser.: Vol. 19). 224p. (C). 1988. text 39.95 (*0-8039-8043-4*) Sage.

Dente, Bruno, et al. The Creation of Waste Facilities: Success Stories in Six European Countries. LC 98-14449. (Environment & Management Ser.). 223p. 1998. write for info. (*0-7923-5028-6*) Kluwer Academic.

Dente-Cassidy, Marie, jt. auth. see Lester, Robert.

Dente, Gregory A. Poetic Tranquility. 1998. pap. 8.95 (*0-533-12679-7*) Vantage.

Dente, James M. Basic Law Text: Torts. (Winning in Law School Ser.: Bk. 6). 199p. (Orig.). 1986. pap. text 12.95 (*0-915667-11-8*) Spectra Pub Co.

D

An Asterisk (*) at the beginning of an entry indicates that the title is appearing for the first time.

Dente, Leonard A. Veblen's Theory of Social Change. Bruchey, Stuart, ed. LC 76-39826. (Nineteen Seventy-Seven Disserataions Ser.). (Illus.). 1980. lib. bdg. 31.95 (*0-405-09906-1*) Ayer.

Dentel, Steven K., et al. Guidance Manual for Polymer Selection in Wastewater Treatment Plants: Guidance Manual. 212p. 1993. pap. 75.00 (*1-881369-54-4*) Water Environ.

Dentemaro, Christine & Kranz, Rachel. Straight Talk about Anger. LC 94-34591. 160p. (YA). (gr. 6-12). 1995. 19.95 (*0-8160-3079-0*) Facts on File.

— Straight Talk about Anger. (Straight Talk Ser.). 160p. (YA). (gr. 6-12). 1996. pap. 9.95 (*0-8160-3551-2*) Facts on File.

— Straight Talk about Student Life. LC 92-31488. 144p. (YA). (gr. 6-12). 1993. 19.95 (*0-8160-2735-8*) Facts on File.

Denters, Erik. Law & Policy of IMF Conditionality. LC 96-2484. (Legal Aspects of International Organization Ser.: Vol. 27). 1996. write for info. (*90-411-0211-6*) Kluwer Law Intl.

Denters, Erik M. & Schrijver, Nico, eds. Reflections on International Law from the Low Countries in Honour of Paul de Waart. LC 97-49294. 528p. 1998. text 128.00 (*90-411-0503-4*) Kluwer Law Intl.

***Denti, A. Ballarin, et al.** Chemistry, Man & Environment: The Seveso Accident 20 Years On: Monitoring, Epidemiology & Remediation: Proceedings of the Meeting Promoted by the Fondazione Lombardia per l'Ambiente, Milan, Italy, 21-22 October 1996. LC 99-29614. 217p. 1999. 92.00 (*0-08-043644-7*, Pub. by Elsevier) Elsevier.

Denti, R. Italian-English - English-Italian Technical Dictionary. 11th ed. (ENG & ITA.). 2023p. 1985. lib. bdg. 150.00 (*0-8288-3364-8*, M8445) Fr & Eur.

— Italian-English - English-Italian Technical Dictionary. 11th ed. 2023p. 1981. 110.00 (*88-203-1465-7*) IBD Ltd.

— Italian-French - French-Italian Technical Dictionary: Dizionario Tecnico Italiano-Francese: Francese-Italiano. 5th ed. (FRE & ITA.). 1304p. 1988. lib. bdg. 125.00 (*0-8288-3363-X*, M8444) Fr & Eur.

Denti, Renzo. Dizionario Tecnico Italiano-Inglese, Inglese-Italiano. 11th rev. ed. (ENG & ITA.). 2010p. (C). 1991. 100.00 (*88-203-1052-X*) S F Vanni.

Dentinger, Jane. Murder on Cue. 224p. 1992. reprint ed. pap. 5.95 (*0-14-015841-3*, Penguin Bks) Viking Penguin.

— The Queen Is Dead. 288p. 1995. pap. 5.95 (*0-14-015835-9*, Penguin Bks) Viking Penguin.

— Who Dropped Peter Pan? A Jocelyn O'Roarke Mystery. 288p. 1996. pap. 5.95 (*0-14-024554-5*, Penguin Bks) Viking Penguin.

Dentinger, Ron. Down Time. 192p. 1996. pap. text, per. 15.95 (*0-8403-9364-4*) Kendall-Hunt.

Dentith, Simon. Bakhtinian Thought: An Introductory Reader. LC 94-16524. 256p. (C). 1994. pap. 25.99 (*0-415-11899-9*, B4523) Routledge.

***Dentith, Simon.** Parody. LC 99-88778. 200p. 2000. pap. 14.99 (*0-415-18221-2*) Routledge.

— Parody. LC 99-88778. (New Critical Idiom Ser.). 200p. 2000. 50.00 (*0-415-18220-4*) Routledge.

Dentith, Simon. Society & Cultural Forms in Nineteenth Century England. LC 98-18587. (Social History in Perspective Ser.). 224p. 1999. text 55.00 (*0-312-21631-9*) St Martin.

Dentler, Larry M. Inviting & Welcoming New People. LC 91-34232. (Evangelism Study Ser.: No. 2). 95p. 1992. reprint ed. pap. 30.00 (*0-608-04170-X*, 206490400011) Bks Demand.

Dentler, Robert & Hafner, Anne. Hosting Newcomers: Structuring Educational Opportunities for Immigrant Children. LC 96-50969. (Sociology of Education Ser.). 192p. (C). 1997. text 46.00 (*0-8077-3613-9*); pap. text 21.95 (*0-8077-3612-0*) Tchrs Coll.

Dentler, Robert A., et al. University on Trial: The Case of the University of North Carolina. 212p. 1984. reprint ed. lib. bdg. 58.50 (*0-8191-4083-X*) U Pr of Amer.

Dentler, Robert A., jt. auth. see Rossi, Peter H.

Denton. A Marriage Worth Keeping. large type ed. 1997. per. 3.25 (*0-373-15728-2*, Harlequin) Harlequin Bks.

Denton, A. S. North Midland Trains in the Thirties. 64p. (C). 1985. 39.00 (*0-85361-267-6*) St Mut.

Denton, Barry. Only in Heaven: The Life & Campaigns of Sir Arthur Hesilrige, 1601-1661. (Illus.). 248p. 1997. 27.00 (*1-85075-645-7*, Pub. by Sheffield Acad) CUP Services.

Denton, Betty. Acrylics Light. (Illus.). 32p. (Orig.). (C). 1995. pap. 8.95 (*0-9628339-4-0*) Giftways-B Denton.

— Acrylics Light Too. (Illus.). 32p. (Orig.). (C). 1995. pap. 8.95 (*0-9628339-5-9*) Giftways-B Denton.

— Beyond the Garden of Watercolors. (Illus.). (Orig.). 1992. pap. 11.95 (*0-9628339-1-6*) Giftways-B Denton.

— Delicate Touches in Watercolors. (Illus.). (Orig.). 1994. pap. 12.95 (*0-9628339-3-2*) Giftways-B Denton.

— Floral Soft Strokes. Brubaker, Jean & Cohen, Mary, eds. (Martin F. Weber Fine Arts Library). (Illus.). 32p. 1987. pap. 6.95 (*0-917121-17-1*, 50-103) M F Weber Co.

— A Garden of Watercolors. (Illus.). (Orig.). 1990. pap. 11.95 (*0-9628339-0-8*) Giftways-B Denton.

— Watercolor Naturals. (Illus.). 28p. (Orig.). (C). 1993. pap. 7.95 (*0-9628339-2-4*) Giftways-B Denton.

Denton, Bob C. & Nasby, David P. Finite Mathematics: Preliminary Edition. (C). 1993. mass mkt. 47.25 (*0-534-17370-5*) PWS Pubs.

Denton, Bradley. Blackburn: A Novel. LC 95-5218. 304p. 1995. pap. 12.00 (*0-312-13029-5*) St Martin.

— Buddy Holly Is Alive & Well on Ganymede. 304p. 1992. mass mkt. 4.50 (*0-380-71876-6*, Avon Bks) Morrow Avon.

— One Day Closer to Death: Eight Stabs at Immortality. LC 97-38440. 352p. 1997. text 23.95 (*0-312-18150-7*) St Martin.

Denton, Brian, ed. Southern Survey. 48p. (C). 1987. pap. 30.00 (*0-7855-2236-0*, Pub. by Picton) St Mut.

Denton, Carolyn S., jt. auth. see Yater, George H.

Denton, Clara J. Entertainments for All the Year. LC 72-5524. (Granger Index Reprint Ser.). 1977. reprint ed. 18.95 (*0-8369-6370-9*) Ayer.

— Little People's Dialogues. LC 70-98080. (Granger Index Reprint Ser.). 1977. 15.95 (*0-8369-6075-0*) Ayer.

Denton, Craig. People of the West Desert: Finding Common Ground. LC 98-58065. (Illus.). 208p. 1999. 44.95 (*0-87421-263-4*); pap. 24.95 (*0-87421-262-6*) Utah St U Pr.

— River Returns. LC 93-72956. 64p. (Orig.). 1993. pap. 7.98 (*0-9638655-0-1*) Footfalls Pr.

***Denton, Craig.** University of Utah: 150 Years of Excellence. LC 99-86073. (Illus.). 211p. 2000. 34.95 (*0-87480-657-7*) U of Utah Pr.

Denton, D. Keith. Horizontal Management: Beyond Total Customer Satisfaction. 211p. 1991. 25.95 (*0-669-26936-0*) Lxngtn Bks.

— Recruitment, Retention, & Employee Relations: Field-Tested Strategies for the '90s. LC 92-162. 232p. 1992. 55.00 (*0-89930-661-6*, DRB/, Quorum Bks) Greenwood.

Denton, D. Keith & Boyd, Charles D. Employee Complaint Handling: Tested Techniques for Human Resource Managers. LC 89-24371. 208p. 1990. 59.95 (*0-89930-433-8*, DEL/, Quorum Bks) Greenwood.

Denton, D. Keith & Denton, Rebecca A. The Toolbox for the Mind: Finding & Implementing Creative Solutions in the Workplace. LC 99-18724. (Illus.). 235p. 1999. 33.00 (*0-87389-448-0*) ASQ Qual Pr.

Denton, David E., ed. Existentialism & Phenomenology in Education: Collected Essays. LC 73-85246. 231p. 1974. pap. 71.70 (*0-7837-7448-6*, 204904000010) Bks Demand.

Denton, Donald D., Jr. Religious Diagnosis in a Secular Society: A Staff for the Journey. 158p. (C). 1997. pap. 26.50 (*0-7618-0965-1*) U Pr of Amer.

Denton, Dottie. Musings with God. (Illus.). 90p. (Orig.). 1987. reprint ed. 7.00 (*0-9625420-0-8*); reprint ed. pap. 5.00 (*0-9625420-1-6*) Dottie May Pub.

Denton, E. N., jt. auth. see Glanvill, A. B.

Denton, Elizabeth. Kneeling on Rice: Stories. 184p. (C). 1994. pap. 17.95 (*0-8262-0968-8*) U of Mo Pr.

Denton, Elizabeth A., jt. auth. see Mitroff, Ian I.

Denton, F. T., et al. Unemployment & Labour Force Behaviour in Young People: Evidence from Canada & Ontario. (Ontario Economic Council Research Studies). 232p. 1980. pap. text 7.95 (*0-8020-3379-2*) U of Toronto Pr.

Denton, Frank & Kurtz, Howard. Reinventing the Newspaper: Essays. LC 93-9255. (Perspectives on the News Ser.: Vol. 3). (Orig.). 1993. pap. 9.95 (*0-87078-350-5*) Century Foundation.

Denton, Gail L. Brainlash: Maximize Your Recovery from Mild Brain Injury. Fagan & Gerard, eds. LC 95-94718. (Illus.). 383p. 1996. pap. 39.95 (*0-9646653-5-2*) Attention Span Bks.

— Brainlash: Maximize Your Recovery from Mild Brain Injury. 2nd ed. (Illus.). 256p. 1999. pap. 24.95 (*1-888799-37-4*) Demos Medical.

Denton, Geoffrey. A New Transatlantic Partnership: Report by the Trans-Europe Policy Studies Association. 77p. 1999. pap. 20.00 (*0-901573-87-6*, Kogan Pg Educ) Stylus Pub VA.

Denton-Hatten, JimmieLee. The African-American Family Reunion. 100p. 1991. 16.25 (*0-9638137-0-6*) AA Family.

Denton, Ivan. The Art of I. Denton. LC 88-1162. (Illus.). 104p. (Orig.). 1988. 34.00 (*1-55728-009-6*); pap. 18.00 (*1-55728-010-X*) U of Ark Pr.

Denton, J., jt. auth. see Freemont, A. J.

Denton, J. C. Energy Use Management. 1983. pap. 45.00 (*0-08-030533-4*, Pergamon Pr) Elsevier.

Denton, J. H. Philip the Fair & the Ecclesiastical Assemblies of 1294-95. LC 90-56108. (Transactions Ser.: Vol. 81, Pt. 1). 83p. (Orig.). (C). 1991. pap. 18.00 (*0-87169-811-0*, T811-DEJ) Am Philos.

Denton, James. Circuit Hikes in Shenandoah National Park. 13th ed. LC 96-67649. 106p. 1994. pap. 6.00 (*0-915746-76-X*) Potomac Appalach.

— Guide to Massanutten Mountain. LC 87-63260. 74p. 1993. 6.00 (*0-915746-47-6*, PC-160) Potomac Appalach.

Denton, James A. Rocky Mountain Radical: M. W. Reed, Christian Socialist. LC 97-4846. 208p. 1997. 45.00 (*0-8263-1814-2*) U of NM Pr.

Denton, James S. & Moynihan, Daniel P., eds. Welfare Reform: Consensus or Conflict? (Illus.). 136p. (Orig.). (C). 1988. pap. text 15.00 (*0-8191-6903-X*); lib. bdg. 37.00 (*0-8191-6902-1*) U Pr of Amer.

***Denton, Jamie.** Breaking the Rules. (Temptation Ser.: Vol. 797). 2000. mass mkt. 3.99 (*0-373-25897-6*, 1-25897-9) Harlequin Bks.

Denton, Jamie. Flirting with Danger: Blaze. 1998. mass mkt. 3.75 (*0-373-25808-9*, 1-25808-6) Harlequin Bks.

***Denton, Jamie.** Gracias Al Destino. (Deseo Ser.: Bk. 208).Tr. of Thanks to the Destiny. (SPA.). 2000. per. 3.50 (*0-373-35338-3*, 1-35338-2) Harlequin Bks.

— Rules of Engagement. (Temptation Ser.). 2000. mass mkt. 3.99 (*0-373-25893-3*, 1-258938) Harlequin Bks.

Denton, Jamie. The Seduction of Sydney. (Temptation Ser.). 1999. per. 3.75 (*0-373-25848-8*, 1-25848-2) Harlequin Bks.

***Denton, Jamie.** Valentine Fantsay: (Fantasy For Hire) (Temptation Ser.: No. 767). 2000. per. 3.99 (*0-373-25867-4*, 1-25867-2, Harlequin) Harlequin Bks.

Denton, Jamie A. The Secret Child. LC 96-515. 297p. 1995. per. 3.75 (*0-373-70663-4*, 1-70663-9) Harlequin Bks.

Denton, Jeannette M., et al, eds. Parasession on the Cycle in Linguistic Theory, Vol. 2. 315p. 1992. pap. 16.00 (*0-914203-40-1*) Chicago Ling.

Denton, Jeffrey, ed. Hierarchies & Orders in Late Medieval & Early Renaissance Europe. 256p. 1999. text 50.00 (*0-8020-4483-2*) U of Toronto Pr.

— Hierarchies & Orders in Late Medieval & Renaissance Europe. 206p. 1999. pap. 19.95 (*0-8020-8264-5*) U of Toronto Pr.

Denton, Jeffrey H. & Dooley, John P. Representatives of the Lower Clergy in Parliament, 1295-1340. (Royal Historical Society: Studies in History: No. 50). 150p. 1987. 75.00 (*0-86193-207-2*) Boydell & Brewer.

Denton, Jeremiah A. When Hell Was in Session. 1998. 29.95 (*0-9660597-0-0*); pap. 14.95 (*0-9660597-2-7*) Morley Bks.

Denton, John. Organisational Learning & Effectiveness. (Illus.). 224p. (C). (gr. 13). 1998. 85.00 (*0-415-19214-5*, D6249); pap. 27.99 (*0-415-19215-3*, D6253) Routledge.

***Denton, John, ed.** Developments in Turbomachinery Design. 205p. 1999. 150.00 (*1-86058-237-0*) Prof Eng Pubng.

Denton, John, tr. see Poma, Andrea.

Denton, John A. Society & the Official World: A Reintroduction to Sociology. LC 89-80376. (Illus.). 200p. (Orig.). 1990. text 35.95 (*0-930390-95-4*); pap. text 22.95 (*0-930390-94-6*) Gen Hall.

Denton, Jorge L. Reflexiones para el Enfermo y Su Familia. 130p. 1991. pap. 6.50 (*0-9630759-4-2*) J L H Denton.

Denton, K. Safety Management. 416p. (C). 1982. 101.56 (*0-07-016410-X*) McGraw.

Denton, K. MacDonald. Til All the Stars Have Fallen: Canadian Poems for Children. 96p. (J). 1989. 16.95 (*0-921103-90-5*) Kids Can Pr.

Denton, Kady M. Christmas Boot. (J). (ps). 1990. 12.95 (*0-316-18091-2*) Little.

— Would They Love a Lion? LC 94-28576. (Illus.). 32p. (J). (ps-k). 1995. 16.95 (*1-85697-546-0*) LKC.

— Would They Love a Lion? (J). (ps-2). 1998. pap. 8.95 (*0-7534-5018-6*) LKC.

Denton, Kady M. A Child's Treasury of Nursery Rhymes. LC 97-41369. 91p. (J). (ps-4). 1998. 18.95 (*0-7534-5109-3*, Kingfisher) LKC.

Denton, Kady M., jt. auth. see Gibson, Betty.

Denton, Kate. The Bachelor Bid. (Romance Ser.: No. 403). 1998. pap. 3.50 (*0-373-17403-9*, 1-17403-6) Harlequin Bks.

— Cross Purposes. 1994. per. 2.99 (*0-373-03332-X*, 1-03332-3) Harlequin Bks.

— The Daddy Dilemma: Daddy Boom. 1999. per. 3.50 (*0-373-15812-2*, 1-15812-0) Harlequin Bks.

— The Daddy Dilemma: Daddy Boom. 1999. per. 3.50 (*0-373-03566-7*, 1-03566-6) Harlequin Bks.

— Mail-Order Mother. (Romance Ser.). 1998. per. 3.50 (*0-373-03510-1*, 1-03510-4) Harlequin Bks.

— Mail-Order Mother. large type ed. (Larger Print Ser.). 1998. per. 3.50 (*0-373-15756-8*, 1-15756-9) Harlequin Bks.

— A Marriage Worth Keeping. 1997. per. 3.25 (*0-373-03482-2*, 1-03482-6) Harlequin Bks.

— No Objections. (Romance Ser.). 1993. per. 2.99 (*0-373-03281-1*, 1-03281-2) Harlequin Bks.

— Valentine, Texas. LC 95-22563. (Romance Ser.). 186p. 1996. per. 3.25 (*0-373-03398-2*, 1-03398-4) Harlequin Bks.

— The Wedding Escapade. 1997. per. 3.25 (*0-373-03452-0*, 1-03452-9) Harlequin Bks.

— The Wedding Escapade. large type ed. 1997. per. 3.25 (*0-373-15698-7*, 1-15698-3) Harlequin Bks.

Denton, Kirk A. The Problematic of Self in Modern Chinese Literature: Hu Feng & Lu Ling. LC 97-41689. 344p. 1998. 49.50 (*0-8047-3128-4*) Stanford U Pr.

Denton, Kirk A., ed. Modern Chinese Literary Thought: Writings on Literature, 1893-1945. LC 95-1269. 564p. 1995. 75.00 (*0-8047-2558-6*); pap. 24.95 (*0-8047-2559-4*) Stanford U Pr.

Denton, Lawrence M. A Southern Star for Maryland: Maryland & the Secession Crisis. (Illus.). 256p. 1999. pap. 20.00 (*0-9635159-4-2*) Pub Concepts.

— A Southern Star for Maryland: Maryland & the Secession Crisis, 1860-1861. LC 95-74770. 256p. 1995. 23.95 (*0-9635159-3-4*) Pub Concepts.

Denton, Leo F., Sr. From Grandy with Love, Vol. 1. LC 97-92387. (Illus.). 54p. 1997. pap. 5.95 (*0-9661198-0-0*) Rainbw Pubns.

Denton, Lynn. Designing, Writing, & Producing Computer Documentation. 1993. pap. 24.95 (*0-07-016417-7*) McGraw.

Denton, Martin. The New York Theatre Experience Book of the Year 1998. ii, 322p. 1999. pap. 29.50 (*0-9670234-0-8*) NY Theatre Exp.

Denton, Martin, ed. see Bromley, Kirk Wood, et al.

Denton, Max W. Veterinarians' New Research Bible: Index of New Information. LC 95-19209. 1995. write for info. (*0-7883-0494-1*); pap. write for info. (*0-7883-0495-X*) ABBE Pubs Assn.

— Veterinary Medicine: Subject, Reference & Research Guide. LC 87-47614. 160p. 1987. 44.50 (*0-88164-532-X*); pap. 39.50 (*0-88164-533-8*) ABBE Pubs Assn.

— Veterinarians' New Research Bible & Index of New Information. 150p. 1994. 47.50 (*0-7883-0060-1*); pap. 44.50 (*0-7883-0061-X*) ABBE Pubs Assn.

Denton, Michael. Evolution: A Theory in Crisis. (Illus.). 368p. 1997. pap. 19.95 (*0-917561-52-X*) Adler & Adler.

— Nature's Destiny: How the Laws of Biology Reveal Purpose in the Universe. LC 98-3295. (Illus.). 480p. 1998. 27.00 (*0-684-84509-1*) S&S Trade.

Denton, Molly T. Wildflowers of the Potomac Appalachians: A Hiker's Guide. LC 63-85307. 58p. 1979. 2.50 (*0-915746-11-5*) Potomac Appalach.

Denton, Nancy A., jt. auth. see Massey, Douglas S.

Denton, Oliver. Budgies for Those Who Care: Parakeets as Pets. (Illus.). 32p. 1994. pap. 4.95 (*0-7938-1386-7*, B108) TFH Pubns.

— Lovebirds As a New Pet. (Illus.). 64p. (Orig.). 1990. pap. 6.95 (*0-86622-617-6*, TU-009) TFH Pubns.

***Denton, Paula & Kriete, Roxann.** The First Six Weeks of School. (Strategies for Teachers Ser.: Vol. 2). (Illus.). 228p. 2000. pap. 16.95 (*1-892989-04-2*) NE Found Child.

Denton, Pedro. Boats of Alaska: An Artist's Guide to Commercial Fishing Boats. LC 98-84548. (Illus.). 80p. 1998. pap. 24.95 (*1-888125-28-4*) Publ Consult.

Denton, Peggy. Psychiatric Occupational Therapy: A Workbook of Practical Skills. 208p. (Orig.). 1986. pap. text 38.00 (*0-316-18088-2*) Lppncott W & W.

Denton, Peter. The World Wildlife Fund. (Organizations That Help the World Ser.). (Illus.). 64p. (YA). (gr. 6 up). 1995. pap. 7.95 (*0-382-24983-6*) Silver Burdett Pr.

— The World Wildlife Fund. LC 94-7491. (Organizations That Help the World Ser.). 64p. (J). 1995. lib. bdg. 13.95 (*0-02-726334-7*, New Dscvry Bks) Silver Burdett Pr.

Denton, Rebecca A., jt. auth. see Denton, D. Keith.

Denton, Robert & Keshavan, M. K., eds. Wear & Friction of Elastomers. LC 92-17236. (Special Technical Publication Ser.: No. 1145). (Illus.). 135p. 1992. text 40.00 (*0-8031-1467-2*, STP1145) ASTM.

***Denton, Robert E., Jr.** Political Communication Ethics: An Oxymoron? LC 99-55872. (Praeger Series in Political Communication). 288p. 2000. 69.50 (*0-275-96482-5*, Praeger Pubs) Greenwood.

Denton, Robert E., Jr. The Primetime Presidency of Ronald Reagan: The Era of the Television Presidency. LC 88-5910. 128p. 1988. 47.95 (*0-275-92603-6*, C2603, Praeger Pubs) Greenwood.

Denton, Robert E., Jr., ed. Ethical Dimensions of Political Communication. LC 91-3552. (Praeger Series in Political Communication). 264p. 1991. 65.00 (*0-275-93550-7*, C3550, Praeger Pubs); pap. 18.95 (*0-275-93551-5*, B3551, Praeger Pubs) Greenwood.

— The Media & the Persian Gulf War. LC 92-36554. (Series in Political Communication). 344p. 1993. 65.00 (*0-275-94232-5*, C4232, Praeger Pubs) Greenwood.

— The 1996 Presidential Campaign: A Communication Perspective. LC 97-33709. (Praeger Series in Political Communication). 320p. 1998. 65.00 (*0-275-95681-4*, Auburn Hse); pap. 24.95 (*0-275-96152-4*, Praeger Pubs) Greenwood.

Denton, Robert E., ed. The 1992 Presidential Campaign: A Communication Perspective. LC 93-50064. (Series in Political Communication). 288p. 1994. 75.00 (*0-275-94559-6*, Praeger Pubs); pap. 20.95 (*0-275-94560-X*, Praeger Pubs) Greenwood.

***Denton, Robert E., Jr., ed.** Political Communication Ethics: An Oxymoron? LC 99-55872. 288p. 2000. 19.95 (*0-275-96483-3*, Praeger Pubs) Greenwood.

Denton, Robert E., Jr. & Hahn, Dan F. Presidential Communication: Description & Analysis. LC 86-9294. 356p. 1986. pap. 21.95 (*0-275-92176-X*, B2176, Praeger Pubs) Greenwood.

— Presidential Communication: Description & Analysis. LC 86-9294. 356p. 1986. 59.95 (*0-275-92175-1*, C2175, Praeger Pubs) Greenwood.

Denton, Robert E., Jr. & Holloway, Rachel L., eds. The Clinton Presidency: Images, & Communication Strategies. LC 95-37650. (Praeger Series in Political Communication). 288p. 1996. 65.00 (*0-275-95109-X*, C5109, Praeger Pubs); pap. 21.95 (*0-275-95110-3*, Praeger Pubs) Greenwood.

Denton, Robert E. & Woodward, Gary C. Mass Media & Politics. 432p. (C). 1997. 22.00 (*0-02-328721-7*, Macmillan Coll) P-H.

Denton, Robert E., Jr. & Woodward, Gary C. Political Communication in America. 3rd ed. LC 98-24557. 328p. 1998. 65.00 (*0-275-95782-9*, Praeger Pubs); pap. 22.95 (*0-275-95783-7*, Praeger Pubs) Greenwood.

Denton, Robert E., jt. auth. see Woodward, Gary C.

Denton, Rocky, jt. auth. see Denton, Terry.

Denton, Roger M. Louisiana Civil Practice Forms 2d. LC 84-52338. 1985. 135.00 (*0-318-04535-4*) West Group.

Denton, S. Breast Cancer Nursing. (Illus.). 256p. 1995. pap. text 57.50 (*1-56593-033-9*, 0281) Thomson Learn.

Denton, Sally. The Bluegrass Conspiracy. 408p. 1991. reprint ed. mass mkt. 5.99 (*0-380-71441-8*, Avon Bks) Morrow Avon.

***Denton, Sally & Morris, Robert.** Falls the Shadow: The Rise & Reign of Las Vegas. 2001. 30.00 (*0-375-40130-X*) Knopf.

Denton, Terry. Gasp! LC 96-7103. (Illus.). 32p. (J). (gr. 1-5). 1996. pap. 4.95 (*1-57255-223-9*) Mondo Pubng.

Denton, Terry & Denton, Rocky. Never Say "Hi Jack" in an Airport: And 101 Other Life-Saving Travel Tips. LC 93-51042. 128p. (Orig.). 1994. pap. 8.95 (*1-56530-104-8*) Summit TX.

Denton, Timothy & Matloff, Jack. Coronary Bypass Surgery: A Guide for Patients. Rapaport, Elliot, ed. (Cardiology Ser.). (Illus.). 32p. (Orig.). 1996. pap. 2.95 (*1-885274-33-5*) Health InfoNet Inc.

Denton, Tom. Automobile Electrical & Electronic Systems. 304p. 1995. 39.00 (*1-56091-735-0*, R-164) Soc Auto Engineers.

***Denton, Tom.** Automobile Electrical & Electronic Systems. 2nd ed. 480p. 2000. 45.00 (*0-7680-0271-0*, R-240) Soc Auto Engineers.

Denton, Virginia L. Booker T. Washington & the Adult Education Movement. LC 92-27094. (Illus.). 280p. 1993. 49.95 (*0-8130-1182-5*) U Press Fla.

Denton, W., ed. see Mijatovic, Elodie L.

D

An Asterisk (*) at the beginning of an entry indicates that the title is appearing for the first time.

Denton, Wallace. Marriage & Family Enrichment. LC 86-308. (Journal of Psychotherapy & the Family: Vol. 2, No. 1). 125p. 1986. text 39.95 (*0-86656-495-0*) Haworth Pr.

Denton, William. Montenegro: Its People & Their History. LC 77-87162. x, 292p. 1977. reprint ed. 54.00 (*0-404-16896-5*) AMS Pr.

D'Entreves, Alexander P. Natural Law: An Introduction to Legal Philosophy. LC 92-37171. 226p. (C). 1994. pap. text 24.95 (*1-56000-673-0*) Transaction Pubs.

D'Entreves, Maurizio P. The Political Philosophy of Hannah Arendt. LC 93-18492. 224p. (C). (gr. 13). 1993. pap. 23.99 (*0-415-08791-0*, B2462) Routledge.

D'Entreves, Maurizio P. & Benhabib, Seyla, eds. Habermas & the Unfinished Project of Modernity: Critical Essays on the Philosophical Discourse of Modernity. (Studies in Contemporary German Social Thought). 320p. 1997. 36.00 (*0-262-04156-1*); pap. text 18.00 (*0-262-54080-0*) MIT Pr.

***Dentz, H. Russell.** Green Normandy Apples. Watry, Charles, ed. LC 99-93131. 275p. 1999. pap. 19.95 (*1-929121-25-3*) Pacific Shore.

Dentzer, Jean-Marie, jt. auth. see Auge, Christian.

DeNucci, Peter. Captain's Discretions: Taking Command of Your Life in the Confusion of a Balanced World. 128p. (Orig.). 1996. pap. 14.95 (*1-889013-00-5*, 101) Apollo Publng.

DeNure, Dennis. The Age of the Video Athlete. (Games with Video Games Ser.). (Illus.). (J). 1984. write for info. (*0-915659-00-X*) Video Athlete.

— Common Sense III: Growlin' for Peace, Moewing for Love. 140p. (Orig.). 1986. 15.00 (*0-915659-05-0*) Video Athlete.

— How to Play a ValGame. (Illus.). 110p. 1984. write for info. (*0-915659-02-6*) Video Athlete.

— The Joystick of Thought. (Illus.). 125p. (Orig.). 1985. reprint ed. 9.95 (*0-915659-03-4*) Video Athlete.

— The New Peace Sign. (Illus.). 125p. (Orig.). 1985. 4.95 (*0-915659-04-2*) Video Athlete.

— Star Scorers of AVAA. (Illus.). 125p. 1984. 19.95 (*0-915659-01-8*) Video Athlete.

Denuziere, Jacqueline & Denuziere, Maurice. Les Annees Louisiane. (FRE.). 442p. 1989. pap. 12.95 (*0-7859-2127-3*, 2070381897) Fr & Eur.

Denuziere, Maurice. L' Adieu au Sud. (FRE.). 653p. 1989. pap. 11.95 (*0-7859-2092-7*, 2070380408) Fr & Eur.

— L' Amour Flou. (FRE.). 338p. 1991. pap. 10.95 (*0-7859-2163-X*, 2070383725) Fr & Eur.

— Les Trois-Chenes. (FRE.). 945p. 1989. pap. 13.95 (*0-7859-2126-5*, 2070381846) Fr & Eur.

Denuziere, Maurice, jt. auth. see Denuziere, Jacqueline.

Denver, Bob. Gilligan, Maynard, & Me. LC 92-37556. (Illus.). 1993. pap. 12.95 (*0-8065-1413-2*) Carol Pub Group.

Denver Broncos Staff. Denver Broncos. CWC Sports Inc., ed. (NFL Team Yearbooks Ser.). (J). (gr. 1-12). 1998. pap. 9.99 (*1-891613-07-3*) Everett Sports.

Denver Business Journal Staff. The Denver Business Journal Book of Lists, 1990-1991: Top 25. 1991. pap. text 15.95 (*0-685-51036-0*) Denver Busn Media.

— The Denver Business Journal Book of Lists, 1991-1992: Top 25. 1992. pap. 19.95 (*0-685-63138-9*) Denver Busn Media.

Denver Catholic Biblical School Staff. Old & New Testaments Concluded: Word in the Hellenistic World, Year 4. (Denver Catholic Biblical School Program Ser.). 224p. (Orig.). 1997. pap., teacher ed. 29.95 (*0-8091-9426-0*, 9426-0); pap., student ed., wbk. ed. 19.95 (*0-8091-9425-2*, 9425-2) Paulist Pr.

Denver Dance Net Staff. Dancing in Denver. (Illus.). 173p. (Orig.). 1996. pap., spiral bd. 19.95 (*0-9652647-0-X*) Stones & Bones.

Denver, David, et al, eds. British Elections & Parties Review Vol. 8: The General Election of 1997. 292p. 1998. 65.00 (*0-7146-4909-0*, Pub. by F Cass Pubs); pap. 32.50 (*0-7146-4466-8*, Pub. by F Cass Pubs) Intl Spec Bk.

***Denver, David, et al.** Scotland Decides: The Devolution Issue & the 1997 Referendum. LC 99-88817. (Illus.). 256p. 2000. 59.50 (*0-7146-5053-6*, Pub. by F Cass Pubs); pap. 26.50 (*0-7146-8104-0*, Pub. by F Cass Pubs) Intl Spec Bk.

Denver, David T. & Hands, Gordon. Modern Constituency Electioneering: Local Campaigning in the 1992 General Election. LC 97-19213. 368p. 1997. 55.00 (*0-7146-4789-6*, Pub. by F Cass Pubs); pap. 25.00 (*0-7146-4345-9*, Pub. by F Cass Pubs) Intl Spec Bk.

Denver, John. Earth Songs (Piano - Vocal) Okun, Milton, ed. (Illus.). 71p. (Orig.). pap. text 14.95 (*0-89524-589-2*) Cherry Lane.

— John Denver - All Aboard! (Illus.). 80p. 1998. pap. 16.95 (*1-57560-098-6*, HL2502226, Pub. by Cherry Lane) H Leonard.

— John Denver - Seasons of the Heart (Piano - Vocal) Okun, Milton, ed. (Illus.). 66p. (Orig.). (YA). 1982. pap. text 9.95 (*0-89524-159-5*) Cherry Lane.

Denver Museum of Natural History Staff. Explore Colorado: A Naturalist's Notebook. (Illus.). 128p. 1995. pap. 19.95 (*1-56579-124-X*) Westcliffe Pubs.

— Prehistoric Coloring Book. (Illus.). 32p. 1998. pap. text 4.95 (*1-57098-216-3*) Roberts Rinehart.

Denver Parent, Inc. Staff & Padgett, Barbara. The Colorado Parent's Directory: 1992 Edition. 2nd ed. Sheldon, Edith, ed. 126p. 1992. pap. 4.95 (*0-9634804-0-5*) Denver Parent.

Denver Public Library Staff. Catalog of the Conservation Library, 6 vols, Set. 1974. 655.00 (*0-8161-1113-8*, G K Hall & Co) Mac Lib Ref.

Denver Research Institute Hypervelocity Symposium. Advances in Hypervelocity Techniques: Prodeedings of the Second Symposium on Hypervelocity Techniques, Sponsored by University of Denver, Denver Research Institute, 20 & 21 March, 1962. Krill, Arthur M., ed. LC 62-3095. 807p. reprint ed. 200.00 (*0-8357-5167-8*, 201938600011) Bks Demand.

Denver Research Institute Staff. Viscosity & Density of Liquid Copper & Copper Alloys. 86p. 1974. 13.35 (*0-317-34555-9*, 176) Intl Copper.

***Denver University Staff.** The Business Environment. 1999. write for info. (*0-07-239242-8*) McGraw.

Denver University Staff. W99-global Management. 1999. 35.10 (*0-07-233126-7*) McGraw.

Denver, Walt. Blood Wager. 1989. mass mkt. 2.95 (*0-8217-2798-2*, Zebra Kensgtn) Kensgtn Pub Corp.

— Pistolero. 1984. mass mkt. 2.25 (*0-8217-1331-0*, Zebra Kensgtn) Kensgtn Pub Corp.

— Tombstone Showdown. 1990. mass mkt. 2.95 (*0-8217-2873-3*, Zebra Kensgtn) Kensgtn Pub Corp.

Denver Water, American Staff & Water Works Assn. Staff, eds. Xeriscape Color Guide. LC 97-38109. (Illus.). 64p. 1998. pap. 14.95 (*1-55591-391-1*) Fulcrum Pub.

***Denvir, Bernard.** The Chronicle of Impressionism: An Intimate Diary of the Lives & World of the Great Artists. 2nd ed. LC 99-69563. (Illus.). 288p. 2000. reprint ed. pap. 24.95 (*0-500-28214-5*, Pub. by Thames Hudson) Norton.

— Impressionism: The Painters & Paintings. (Illus.). 424p. 2000. 94.95 (*0-9684749-4-2*, Pub. by NDE Pub) IPG Chicago.

Denvir, Bernard. The Impressionists at First Hand. LC 86-51261. (World of Art Ser.). (Illus.). 296p. 1987. pap. 14.95 (*0-500-20209-5*, Pub. by Thames Hudson) Norton.

— Post-Impressionism. LC 91-65995. (World of Art Ser.). (Illus.). 216p. 1992. pap. 14.95 (*0-500-20255-9*, Pub. by Thames Hudson) Norton.

— The Thames & Hudson Encyclopedia of Impressionism. (World of Art Ser.). (Illus.). 1990. pap. 14.95 (*0-500-20239-7*, Pub. by Thames Hudson) Norton.

— Toulouse-Lautrec. LC 90-71451. (World of Art Ser.). (Illus.). 216p. (Orig.). 1991. pap. 14.95 (*0-500-20250-8*, Pub. by Thames Hudson) Norton.

Denvir, John, ed. Legal Reelism: Movies As Legal Texts. LC 95-32511. (Illus.). 336p. 1996. text 39.95 (*0-252-02231-9*); pap. text 19.95 (*0-252-06535-2*) U of Ill Pr.

***Denvir, Paul.** Managing Key Clients. 2000. pap. text 31.95 (*0-8264-4710-4*) Continuum.

Denvir, Tim, et al, eds. Formal Aspects of Measurement: Proceedings of the BCS-FACS Workshop on Formal Aspects of Measurement, South Bank University, London, 5 May 1991. LC 92-29927. (Workshops in Computing Ser.). viii, 260p. 1992. 59.00 (*0-387-19788-5*) Spr-Verlag.

Denwit, B. T., et al, eds. The Analysis of Concurrent Systems. (Lecture Notes in Computer Science Ser.: Vol. 207). vii, 398p. 1985. 42.00 (*0-387-16047-7*) Spr-Verlag.

***Denwood, Philip.** Tibetan. LC 99-22267. (London Oriental & African Language Library: Vol. 3). xxii, 374p. 1999. 99.00 (*1-55619-727-6*) J Benjamins Pubng Co.

Denwood, Philip, jt. auth. see Singer, Jane C.

Deny, Maurice. Introduction to General Average. 58p. 1986. 100.00 (*0-948691-10-7*, Pub. by Witherby & Co) St Mut.

Denyer, Bob, jt. auth. see Mueller, Gene.

Denyer, C. P., tr. see Halley, Henry H.

Denyer, Carlos. Concordancia de las Sagradas Escrituras. LC 74-21722. (SPA.). 936p. 1978. 32.99 (*0-89922-004-5*) Caribe Betania.

Denyer, Frank & Landy, Leigh, eds. Leaving the Twentieth Century: Ideas & Visions of New Musics. (Contemporary Music Review Ser.). 165p. 1997. pap. text 28.00 (*90-5702-104-8*, Harwood Acad Pubs) Gordon & Breach.

Denyer-Green, Barry. Wildlife & Countryside Act, 1981. 265p. (C). 1983. text 110.00 (*0-85406-187-8*, Pub. by Surveyors Pubns) St Mut.

***Denyer, Margaret.** The Freewood Years: My Son, His Animals & Me. large type unabridged ed. 1999. 25.95 (*0-7531-5703-9*, 157039, Pub. by ISIS Lrg Prnt) ISIS Pub.

***Denyer, Mary.** The Freewood Years: My Son, His Animals & Me. (Illus.). 144p. 1999. 22.95 (*1-85479-389-6*, Pub. by M OMara) Trafalgar.

Denyer, Paulene, jt. auth. see Miles, George.

Denyer, Peter B., jt. auth. see Smith, Stewart G.

Denyer, Ralph. The Guitar Handbook. rev. ed. LC 92-53164. (Illus.). 256p. 1992. pap. 25.00 (*0-679-74275-1*) Knopf.

Denyer, S. & Hugo, W. B. Mechanisms of Action of Chemical Biocides. 1990. 95.00 (*0-632-02928-5*) Blackwell Sci.

Denyer, S. P., et al, eds. Microbial Biofilms: Formation & Control. LC 93-17040. (Society for Applied Bacteriology Technical Ser.: No. 30). 1993. 65.00 (*0-632-03753-9*) Blackwell Sci.

Denyer, Stephen, ed. Privatisation in Central & Eastern Europe. 2nd ed. 1995. pap. write for info. (*0-406-05049-X*, BPCE2, MICHIE) LEXIS Pub.

***Denyer, Susan.** At Home with Beatrix Potter: The Creator of Peter Rabbit. LC 99-44929. 144p. (J). 2000. 24.95 (*0-8109-4112-0*, Pub. by Abrams) Time Warner.

Denyes, Jim, ed. see Mogensen, Allan H. & Rausa, Rosario.

Denys, Nicolas. Description: Natural History of the Coasts of North America, Vol. 2. Ganong, William F., ed. LC 68-28597. 625p. 1968. reprint ed. lib. bdg. 85.00 (*0-8371-3873-6*, DEDH, Greenwood Pr) Greenwood.

***Denys, Patti, et al.** Animal Magnetism: At Home with Celebrities & Their Animal Companions. LC 97-62147. (Illus.). 160p. 1998. 19.98 (*0-7651-9051-6*) Smithmark.

Denys, R., ed. Pipeline Technology: Proceedings of the 2nd International Pipeline Technology Conference, Ostend (Belgium), September 11-14, 1995, Set. LC 95-23454. (Illus.). 1376p. 1995. text 406.50 (*0-444-82197-X*) Elsevier.

Denz, O. Natuerliche Habichtskraut-Traubeneichenwaelder. (Dissertationes Botanicae Ser.: Band 229). (Illus.). 160p. 1994. pap. 56.00 (*3-443-64143-1*, Pub. by Gebruder Borntraeger) Balogh.

Denza, Eileen. Diplomatic Law: A Commentary on the Vienna Convention on Diplomatic Relations. 2nd ed. 472p. 1998. 170.00 (*0-19-826582-4*) OUP.

Denzel, Justin. Boy of the Painted Cave. 160p. (J). (gr. 3-7). 1988. 14.95 (*0-399-21559-X*, Philomel) Peng Put Young Read.

— Boy of the Painted Cave. LC 87-36609. (Illus.). 160p. (J). (gr. 3-7). 1996. pap. 4.99 (*0-698-11377-2*, PapStar) Peng Put Young Read.

Denzel, Justin F. Boy of the Painted Cave. LC 87-36609. 1996. 10.05 (*0-606-09099-1*, Pub. by Turtleback) Demco.

***Denzer, Kiko.** Build Your Own Earth Oven: A Low Cost Wood-Fired Mud Oven - Simple Sourdough Bread - Perfect Loaves. 2nd rev. ed. (Illus.). 128p. 2000. pap. 14.95 (*0-9679846-0-2*) Hand Print.

***Denzer, Ralf, et al.** Environmental Software Systems - Environmental Information And Decision Support. 280p. 2000. 145.00 (*0-7923-7832-6*) Kluwer Academic.

Denzi, Riccardo De, see De Denzi, Riccardo, ed.

Denzin, Norman. The Cinematic Society. (Theory, Culture & Society Ser.: Vol. 34). 224p. 1995. text 65.00 (*0-8039-8657-2*); pap. text 22.95 (*0-8039-8658-0*) Sage.

— Cultural Studies, Vol. 3. 1998. 78.50 (*0-7623-0419-7*) Jai Pr.

Denzin, Norman, jt. auth. see Hendricks, Katy.

Denzin, Norman K. The Alcoholic Society: Addiction & Recovery of the Self. LC 92-35675. 355p. (C). 1993. pap. text 29.95 (*1-56000-669-2*) Transaction Pubs.

— Childhood Socialization: Studies in the Development of Language, Social Behavior, & Identity. LC 77-82914. (Jossey-Bass Social & Behavioral Science Ser.). 249p. reprint ed. pap. 77.20 (*0-608-17044-5*, 202775000056) Bks Demand.

— Hollywood Shot by Shot: Alcoholism in American Cinema. (Communication & Social Order Ser.). 309p. (C). 1991. pap. text 29.95 (*0-202-30345-4*); lib. bdg. 49.95 (*0-202-30344-6*) Aldine de Gruyter.

— Images of Postmodernism Society: Social Theory & Contemporary Cinema. (Theory, Culture & Society Ser.: Vol. 11). 192p. (C). 1991. text 59.95 (*0-8039-8515-0*); pap. text 22.95 (*0-8039-8516-9*) Sage.

— Interpretive Biography. (Qualitative Research Methods Ser.: Vol. 17). 96p. (C). 1989. text 24.00 (*0-8039-3358-4*); pap. text 10.50 (*0-8039-3359-2*) Sage.

— Interpretive Ethnography: Ethnographic Practices for the 21st Century. LC 96-25245. 320p. 1996. 56.00 (*0-8039-7298-9*); pap. 26.95 (*0-8039-7299-7*) Sage.

— Interpretive Interactionism. (Applied Social Research Methods Ser.: Vol. 16). 160p. (C). 1989. text 42.00 (*0-8039-3002-X*); pap. text 18.95 (*0-8039-3003-8*) Sage.

— On Understanding Emotion. LC 83-23853. (Jossey-Bass Social & Behavioral Science Ser.). 335p. reprint ed. pap. 103.90 (*0-7837-2518-3*, 204267700006) Bks Demand.

— Studies in Symbolic Interaction: An Annual Compilation of Research, Vol. 1. 1978. lib. bdg. 73.25 (*0-89232-065-6*) Jai Pr.

— Symbolic Interactionism & Cultural Studies: The Politics of Interpretation. Lemert, Charles, ed. (Twentieth-Century Social Theory Ser.). 224p. 1992. pap. text 27.95 (*1-55786-291-5*) Blackwell Pubs.

— Treating Alcoholism: An Alcoholics Anonymous Approach. LC 87-4846. (Sage Human Services Guides Ser.: No. 46). 149p. 1987. reprint ed. pap. 46.20 (*0-608-04307-9*, 206508600012) Bks Demand.

Denzin, Norman K., ed. Children & Their Caretakers. LC 72-91470. 252p. 1973. pap. text 19.95 (*0-87855-559-5*) Transaction Pubs.

— Cultural Studies, Vol. 2. 1997. 78.50 (*0-7623-0241-0*) Jai Pr.

— Studies in Symbolic Interaction, Vol. 2. 456p. 1979. 73.25 (*0-89232-105-9*) Jai Pr.

— Studies in Symbolic Interaction, Vol. 3. 304p. 1981. 73.25 (*0-89232-153-9*) Jai Pr.

— Studies in Symbolic Interaction, Vol. 4. 269p. 1982. 73.25 (*0-89232-232-2*) Jai Pr.

— Studies in Symbolic Interaction, Vol. 5. 289p. 1984. 73.25 (*0-89232-362-0*) Jai Pr.

— Studies in Symbolic Interaction, Vol. 6. 432p. 1986. 73.25 (*0-89232-625-5*) Jai Pr.

— Studies in Symbolic Interaction, 2 pts., Vol. 7. 521p. 1987. 5.25 hd 146.50 (*0-89232-743-X*) Jai Pr.

— Studies in Symbolic Interaction, Vol. 8. 233p. 1988. 73.25 (*0-89232-719-7*) Jai Pr.

— Studies in Symbolic Interaction, Vol. 9. 243p. 1988. 73.25 (*0-89232-934-3*) Jai Pr.

— Studies in Symbolic Interaction, 2 pts., Vol. 10. 544p. 1990. 146.50 (*0-89232-974-2*) Jai Pr.

— Studies in Symbolic Interaction, Vol. 11. 439p. 1990. 73.25 (*1-55938-100-0*) Jai Pr.

— Studies in Symbolic Interaction, Vol. 12. 299p. 1991. 73.25 (*1-55938-395-X*) Jai Pr.

— Studies in Symbolic Interaction, Vol. 13. 303p. 1992. 73.25 (*1-55938-479-4*) Jai Pr.

— Studies in Symbolic Interaction, Vol. 14. 288p. 1993. 73.25 (*1-55938-579-0*) Jai Pr.

— Studies in Symbolic Interaction, Vol. 15. 289p. 1994. 73.25 (*1-55938-764-5*) Jai Pr.

— Studies in Symbolic Interaction, Vol. 16. 1994. 73.25 (*1-55938-862-5*) Jai Pr.

— Studies in Symbolic Interaction, Vol. 17. 1995. 73.25 (*1-55938-863-3*) Jai Pr.

— Studies in Symbolic Interaction, Vol. 18. 282p. 1995. 73.25 (*1-55938-977-X*) Jai Pr.

— Studies in Symbolic Interaction, Vol. 20. 238p. 1996. 73.25 (*0-7623-0224-0*) Jai Pr.

— Studies in Symbolic Interaction: Original Essays in Symbolic Interaction, Supp. 1: Foundations of Interpretive Sociology: Or. (Studies in Symbolic Interaction: Suppl. 1). 357p. 1985. 73.25 (*0-89232-550-X*) Jai Pr.

— Studies in Symbolic Interaction: The Iowa School, Supp. 2. 484p. 1986. 146.50 (*0-89232-552-6*) Jai Pr.

— The Values of Social Science. rev. ed. LC 72-94545. 194p. 1973. reprint ed. pap. 18.95 (*0-87855-547-1*) Transaction Pubs.

— The Values of Social Science. 2nd rev. ed. LC 72-94545. 194p. 1973. reprint ed. 32.95 (*0-87855-054-2*) Transaction Pubs.

Denzin, Norman K. & Lincoln, Yvonna S. The Landscape of Qualitative Research: Theories & Issues. LC 98-8869. 1998. pap. 28.95 (*0-7619-1433-1*) Sage.

— Strategies of Qualitative Inquiry. LC 98-8894. 1998. pap. write for info. (*0-7619-1435-8*) Sage.

Denzin, Norman K. & Lincoln, Yvonna S., eds. Collecting & Interpreting Qualitative Materials. LC 98-8868. 1998. pap. 28.95 (*0-7619-1434-X*) Sage.

— Handbook of Qualitative Research. (C). 1993. text 99.95 (*0-8039-4679-1*) Sage.

***Denzin, Norman K. & Lincoln, Yvonna S., eds.** The Handbook of Qualitative Research. 2nd ed. LC 00-8104. 1065p. 2000. 109.95 (*0-7619-1512-5*) Sage.

Denzinger, Carol, jt. auth. see Thomas, Stephen B.

***Denzinger, Enrique.** El Magisterio Symbolorium. (SPA.). 1998. pap. 24.95 (*0-8245-2154-4*) Crossroad NY.

Denzler, David, jt. auth. see Melnyk, Steven A.

Denzler, Georg, jt. auth. see Andresen, Carl.

Deo, Madhav G. Tropical Molecular Medicine. LC 99-937586. (Illus.). 208p. 1999. text 36.50 (*0-19-564630-4*) OUP.

Deo, Narsingh. System Simulation with Digital Computer. (Illus.). 224p. (C). 1983. 38.00 (*0-13-881789-8*) P-H.

Deo, Pramod, et al. Decentralised Energy Planning. (C). 1991. text 17.50 (*81-204-0629-X*, Pub. by Oxford IBH) S Asia.

Deo, Ravi & Saff, Charles R., eds. Composite Materials: Testing & Design, Vol. 12. (STP Ser.: No. 1274). (Illus.). 428p. 1996. 129.00 (*0-8031-2404-X*, STP1274) ASTM.

Deo, S. G., jt. auth. see Lakshmikantham, V.

Deo, Som. Multinational Corporations & the Third World. 1986. 27.50 (*81-7024-051-4*, Pub. by Ashish Pub Hse) S Asia.

Deodene, Frank & French, William. Black American Poetry since Nineteen Forty-Four: A Preliminary Checklist. 41p. 1971. pap. 7.00 (*0-911860-07-X*) Chatham Bkseller.

Deodhar, B. R. Pillars of Hindustani Music. 1993. 23.00 (*81-7154-555-6*, Pub. by Popular Prakashan) S Asia.

Deodhar, P. S. The Third Parent: Growth & Development of Indian Electronics Media. 123p. 1991. text 18.95 (*0-7069-5801-2*) Advent Bks Div.

Deodhar, Vinay. Kazhdan-Lusztig Theory & Related Topics: (Proceedings of an AMS Special Session Held May 19-20, 1989 at the University of Chicago, Lake Shore Campus, Chicago, Illinois) LC 92-27738. (Contemporary Mathematics Ser.: Vol. 139). 277p. 1992. pap. 46.00 (*0-8218-5150-0*, CONM/139) Am Math.

Deodikar, Sanjay G. Upanishads & Early Buddhism. xi, 223p. 1992. 22.00 (*0-685-62637-7*, Pub. by Eastern Bk Linkers) Nataraj Bks.

Deofleurs, Ramona, tr. see De La Baume, Cecile.

Deogaonkar, S. G. The Banjara. (C). 1992. 17.00 (*81-7022-443-8*, Pub. by Concept) S Asia.

Deogaonkar, S. G. & Deogaonkar, S. S. Korku Tribals. (Castes & Tribes of India Ser.: No. 1). (C). 1990. text 20.00 (*81-7022-297-4*, Pub. by Concept) S Asia.

Deogaonkar, S. S., jt. auth. see Deogaonkar, S. G.

Deok Ryong Yoon. Die Deutsch-Deutsch Wahrungsunion und ihre Implikationen fur den Fall einer Koreanischen Wiedervereinigung. (Europaische Hochschulschriften: Reihe 5: Bd. 1851). (GER., Illus.). 214p. 1996. pap. 42.95 (*3-631-49891-8*) P Lang Pubng.

Deol, D. Charisma & Commitment: The Mind & Political Thinking of Indira Gandhi. 136p. 1981. 14.95 (*0-940500-56-6*, Pub. by Sterling) Asia Bk Corp.

Deol, Daler, jt. auth. see Deol, Surinder.

Deol, Surinder & Deol, Daler. Japji: The Path of Devotional Meditation. LC 97-92703. (Illus.). 176p. (Orig.). 1998. pap. 15.00 (*0-9661027-0-3*) Mount Meru Bks.

DeOld, Alan R., et al. Space Travel: A Technological Frontier. (Illus.). 144p. (J). (gr. 7-12). 1990. pap. 14.95 (*0-87192-206-1*) Thomson Learn.

— Transportation: Technology of Moving People & Goods. LC 86-70174. (Illus.). 534p. (J). 1986. pap., student ed. 11.68 (*0-87192-127-8*) Thomson Learn.

***DeOliveira, Betty Pontes & Bral, Eddy.** My Midnight. LC 99-91945. 2000. 25.00 (*0-7388-1444-X*); pap. 18.00 (*0-7388-1445-8*) Xlibris Corp.

Deoll, Rajendra Kumar, see Kumar Deoll, Rajendra.

Deollos. Cv:soc 100:departmental Reader Spring 97. (C). 1996. pap. text 29.50 (*0-15-505772-3*) Harcourt Coll Pubs.

— Sociology Reader. 1998. 24.00 (*0-07-228708-X*) McGraw.

DeOllos, Ione Y. On Becoming Homeless: The Shelterization Process for Homeless Families. LC 97-13285. 272p. (C). 1997. 56.00 (*0-7618-0839-6*); pap. 34.50 (*0-7618-0838-8*) U Pr of Amer.

D'Eon, Marcel, jt. auth. see Haylock, Derek.

Deon, Michel. Bagages Pour Vancouver. (Mes Arches De Noe Ser.: Vol. II). (FRE.). 249p. 1987. pap. 11.95 (*0-7859-2075-7*, 2070378861) Fr & Eur.

— Le Balcon de Spetsai. (FRE.). 256p. 1984. pap. 11.95 (*0-7859-1984-8*, 2070375242) Fr & Eur.

D

An Asterisk (*) at the beginning of an entry indicates that the title is appearing for the first time.

— La Carotte et le Baton. (FRE.). 384p. 1983. pap. 12.95 (*0-7859-1975-9*, 2070374718) Fr & Eur.

— La Corrida. (FRE.). 1982. pap. 10.95 (*0-7859-1948-1*, 2070373509) Fr & Eur.

— Les Gens de la Nuit. (FRE.). 224p. 1974. pap. 10.95 (*0-7859-1781-0*, 2070365573) Fr & Eur.

— Je Ne Veux Jamais l'Oublier. (FRE.). 376p. 1990. pap. 16.95 (*0-7859-2140-0*, 2070382478) Fr & Eur.

— Je Vous Ecrit d'Italie. (FRE.). 411p. 1986. pap. 11.95 (*0-7859-2028-5*, 2070377202) Fr & Eur.

— Le Jeune Homme Vert. (FRE.). 512p. 1980. pap. 11.95 (*0-7859-1926-0*, 2070372448) Fr & Eur.

— Louis the Fourteenth. (FRE.). 1991. pap. 15.95 (*0-7859-2174-5*, 2070384195) Fr & Eur.

— La Montee du Soir. (FRE.). 151p. 1989. pap. 10.95 (*0-7859-2115-X*, 2070381269) Fr & Eur.

— Un Parfum de Jasmin. (FRE.). 243p. 1978. pap. 10.95 (*0-7859-1878-7*, 2070370550) Fr & Eur.

— Les Poneys Sauvages. (FRE.). 1972. pap. 11.95 (*0-7859-1692-X*, 2070360717) Fr & Eur.

— Le Rendez-Vous de Patmos. (FRE.). 306p. 1977. pap. 10.95 (*0-7859-1859-0*, 2070369692) Fr & Eur.

— Un Taxi Mauve. (FRE.). 160p. 1992. pap. 11.95 (*0-7859-2183-4*, 2070385108) Fr & Eur.

— Tout l'Amour du Monde. (FRE.). 1978. pap. 11.95 (*0-7859-2215-6*, 207037016X) Fr & Eur.

— Les Trompeuses Esperances. (FRE.). 1972. pap. 10.95 (*0-7859-1720-9*, 2070362795) Fr & Eur.

— Les Vingt Ans du Jeune Homme Vert. (FRE.). 608p. 1981. pap. 12.95 (*0-7859-1938-4*, 2070373010) Fr & Eur.

Deon-Solek, Baba U. IKO - Meditation Technique - Guidebook: "How Not to Lose Yourself While Finding Yourself!" (Illus.). 48p. 1998. pap. 10.95 (*0-939366-06-1*) AKU Pr.

***Deonandan, Raywat.** Sweet Like Saltwater. 113p. 1999. pap. 15.95 (*0-920661-77-7*, Pub. by TSAR Pubns) SPD-Small Pr Dist.

Deonier, D. L. A Manual of the Common North American Species of the Aquatic Leafmining Genus Hydrellia (Diptera: Ephydridae) Gupta, Virendra K., ed. LC 98-19928. (Memoirs on Entomology, International Ser.: Vol. 12). (Illus.). 368p. 1998. 65.00 (*1-56665-069-0*) Assoc Pubs FL.

Deonna, Laurence. On Persian Roads: Glimpses of Revolutionary Iran, 1985-1998. Snow, Christopher, tr. from FRE. LC 98-52712. Orig. Title: Persianeries: Rapportage dans l'Iran des Mollahs, 1995-1998. (Illus.). 180p. 1998. pap. 16.00 (*1-57889-088-8*) Passeggiata.

— Syrians: A Travelogue 1992-1994. Snow, Christopher, tr. from FRE. Orig. Title: Syriens, Syriennes. (Illus.). 160p. 1997. 24.00 (*1-57889-041-1*); pap. 14.00 (*1-57889-040-3*) Passeggiata.

— The War with Two Voices.Tr. of La/Guerre a Deux Voix. (Illus.). 240p. 1989. pap. 12.00 (*1-57889-005-5*) Passeggiata.

— The War with Two Voices: Journalism.Tr. of La/Guerre a Deux Voix. (Illus.). 258p. 1989. 24.00 (*1-57889-006-3*) Passeggiata.

— Yemen. Borel, Corinne, tr. (Illus.). 201p. 1991. 20.00 (*0-89410-710-0*, Three Contnts); pap. 10.00 (*0-89410-711-9*, Three Contnts) L Rienner.

Deora, M. S. Akali Agitation to Operation Bluestar, 2 vols. (C). 1991. 94.00 (*81-7041-450-4*, Pub. by Anmol) S Asia.

— Documents on Kashmir Problem Vols. 16-19: World Opinion, Set. (C). 1992. 150.00 (*81-7141-155-X*) S Asia.

Deora, M. S., ed. Aftermath of Operation Bluestar, 2 vols., Set. (Political Developments in Punjab Ser.: No. 2). (C). 1992. text 78.50 (*81-7041-645-0*, Pub. by Anmol) S Asia.

Deoras, P. J. Snakes of India. (Illus.). 152p. 1990. 11.95 (*0-318-36997-4*) Asia Bk Corp.

De'Orville, Hans. The Impact of Europe in Nineteen Ninety-Two on West Africa. Obasanjo, Olusegun, ed. 120p. (C). 1990. text 75.00 (*0-8448-1672-8*, Crane Russak) Taylor & Francis.

DEP, Bureau of Mining & Reclamation Staff. 1997 Annual Report on Mining Activities in the Commonwealth of PA, DEP. 410p. 1998. 13.38 (*0-8182-0233-5*) Commonweal PA.

DePace, jt. auth. see Pratt.

DePalma, Angelo, jt. auth. see Bratman, Steven.

DePalma, Brenda. I Am Italian American. LC 96-54019. (Our American Family Ser.: Set 2). (J). (gr. k-4). 1997. lib. bdg. 15.93 (*0-8239-5015-8*, PowerKids) Rosen Group.

DePalma, David J. & Foley, Jeanne M. Moral Development: Current Theory & Research. LC 75-14211. (Child Psychology Ser.). 206p. 1975. text 39.95 (*0-89859-116-3*) L Erlbaum Assocs.

DePalma, M. E., jt. auth. see Haehle, Robert G.

Depalma, Robert & Depalma, Roxanne. Mastering the Floral Classic. (Illus.). 50p. 1999. 19.95 (*0-9673044-0-7*) H I S C.

Depalma, Roxanne, jt. auth. see Depalma, Robert.

DePalo, William A., Jr. The Mexican National Army, 1822-1852. LC 96-51447. (Military History Ser.: Vol. 52). (Illus.). 272p. (C). 1997. text 39.95 (*0-89096-744-X*) Tex A&M Univ Pr.

DePamphilis, Melvin L., ed. Concepts in Eukaryotic DNA Replication. LC 98-73326. (Illus.). 520p. (C). 1998. pap. text 57.00 (*0-87969-557-9*) Cold Spring Harbor.

— DNA Replication in Eukaryotic Cells. (Monographs: Vol. 31). (Illus.). 650p. (C). 1996. text 129.00 (*0-87969-459-9*) Cold Spring Harbor.

DePanfilis, Diane. Literature Review of Sexual Abuse. Salus, Marsha K., ed. 48p. 1986. write for info. (*0-318-61650-5*) US HHS.

DePanfilis, Diane & Salus, Marsha K. Child Protective Services: A Guide for Caseworkers. 98p. (Orig.). (C). 1995. pap. text 25.00 (*0-7881-1948-6*) DIANE Pub.

— A Coordinated Response to Child Abuse & Neglect: A Basic Manual. 64p. (Orig.). (C). 1994. pap. text 25.00 (*0-7881-0646-5*) DIANE Pub.

DePanfilis, Diane, jt. auth. see Dubowitz, Howard.

***DePaola, Richard K., Sr.** The Mystery of Playland Park. LC 99-91123. (J). 1999. 25.00 (*0-7388-0628-5*); pap. 18.00 (*0-7388-0629-3*) Xlibris Corp.

— The Rembrandt's of Junior High. LC 99-91624. 187p. 1999. 25.00 (*0-7388-0632-3*); pap. 18.00 (*0-7388-0633-1*) Xlibris Corp.

DePaola, Richard K. Samantha & the Christmas Spirit. LC 98-89503. 375p. 1998. text 25.00 (*0-7388-0233-6*); pap. text 15.00 (*0-7388-0234-4*) Xlibris Corp.

DePaolis, Mark. Are You a Real Doctor? More Humorous Second Opinions for Everyday Life. LC 96-29732. 224p. (Orig.). 1997. pap. 12.95 (*1-57749-028-2*) Fairview Press.

— Get Well Sooner: A Dose of Laughter from the Humor Doctor. LC 96-29720. 128p. 1997. pap. 7.95 (*1-57749-029-0*) Fairview Press.

— Trust Me, I'm a Doctor: Humorous Second Opinions for Everyday Life. LC 95-3180. 240p. 1995. pap. 10.95 (*0-925190-39-X*) Fairview Press.

***DePaolo, Audrey F.** Rebel Nun. 260p. 2000. pap. 13.95 (*1-891929-34-8*) Four Seasons.

DePaolo, D. J. Neodymium Isotope Geochemistry. (Minerals & Rocks Ser.: Vol. 20). (Illus.). 200p. 1988. 79.95 (*0-387-18648-4*) Spr-Verlag.

DePaolo, Robert. Society Reconsidered: A Debate on the Issues of Modern Times. 306p. (Orig.). 1996. pap. 12.95 (*0-9654686-0-7*) Ecclectic Bks.

Depardon, Raymond. Depardon - Voyages: Raymond Depardon - Journeys & Homecomings. (ENG & FRE., Illus.). 605p. 1998. pap. 55.00 (*2-85025-642-0*) Gingko Press.

***Depardon, Raymond.** The Desert. LC 00-100982. (Illus.). 208p. 2000. 45.00 (*0-500-97491-8*, Pub. by Thames Hudson) Norton.

Depardon, Raymond. Return to Vietnam. 160p. (gr. 13). 1994. pap. 20.00 (*0-86091-643-X*, Pub. by Verso) Norton.

DeParis, Richard. Neighborhood Team Policing: Organizational Opportunities & Obstacles. LC 97-69038. 60p. 1997. pap. 6.50 (*1-878734-51-2*) Police Exec Res.

DeParle, Nancy-Ann M., ed. Medicare & You 1999: Original Medicare Plan & Other Medicare Health Plan Choices. rev. ed. 35p. 1999. pap. text 15.00 (*0-7881-7978-0*) DIANE Pub.

DeParrie, Paul. Dark Cures: Have Doctors Lost their Ethics? LC 95-77223. 224p. 1998. pap. 11.99 (*1-56384-099-5*) Huntington Hse.

DeParrie, Paul & Pride, Mary. Ancient Empires of the New Age. LC 89-50335. 228p. 1989. pap. 10.99 (*0-89107-530-5*) Crossway Bks.

Departamento De Ciencias Fisicas. Ciencias Fisicas. 9th ed. (C). 1995. 6.50 (*0-8477-2340-2*) U of PR Pr.

Departamento De Espanol, Facultad De Estudios Gene. Manual de Nociones y Ejercicios Gramaticales: Unidad de Composicion y Otras Destrezas Linguisticas. enl. rev. ed. LC 76-4501. (SPA.). 148p. (C). 1989. pap. text 5.95 (*0-8477-3164-2*) U of PR Pr.

Departamento Espanol Comercial UPR Staff. Comunicacion Comercial en Espanol. (SPA.). 218p. 1993. pap. write for info. (*0-929441-02-8*) Pubns Puertorriquenas.

Department for Economic & Social Affairs Statistics Division Staff. Industrial Commodity Statistics Yearbook 1996: Production Statistics, 1987-1996. 908p. 1998. 115.00 (*92-1-061176-4*, Pub. by UN) Bernan Associates.

— Statistical Yearbook, 1995. 42nd ed. 923p. 120.00 (*92-1-061174-8*) UN.

Department for Economic & Social Information & Pol. Demographic Yearbook, Vol. 47. (ENG & FRE.). 1087p. 1997. 125.00 (*92-1-051086-0*, B.97.XIII.1) UN.

— Energy Balances & Electricity Profiles. 490p. 75.00 (*92-1-061158-6*) UN.

— Energy Balances & Electricity Profiles, 1994. 472p. 1996. pap. 75.00 (*0-614-27165-7*, HD2321) UN.

— Industrial Commodity Statistics Yearbook: Production & Consumption Statistics. 996p. 110.00 (*92-1-061165-9*) UN.

— Levels & Trends of Contraceptive Use As Assessed in 1994. LC 97-114933. (Population Studies: No. 146). 171p. pap. 17.50 (*92-1-151310-3*, RG133) UN.

— Review & Appraisal of the World Population Plan of Action: 1994 Report. (Population Studies: No. 152). 160p. pap. 10.00 (*92-1-151299-9*, 68803) UN.

Department for Economic & Social Information & Policy Analysis, Population Division Staff. Global Population Policy: Database, 1997. (United Nations Publications, Databases & Software on Population). 205p. 1998. pap. 35.00 (*92-1-151323-5*) UN.

— World Urbanization Prospects; The 1996 Revision; Estimates & Projections of Urban & Rural Populations & of Urban Agglomerations. (United Nations Publications, Databases & Software on Population). 191p. 1998. pap. 37.50 (*92-1-151317-0*) UN.

Department for Economic and Social Information and Policy Analysis Staff. Glossary of Environment Statistics. LC 97-168765. (Studies in Methods: No. 67). 83p. 1996. pap. 25.00 (*92-1-161386-8*) UN.

— Sustaining Social Security. LC 97-168764. 1997. 20.00 (*92-1-130185-8*) UN.

Department for Economic Staff. International Trade Statistics Yearbook, 2 vols. 1696p. 135.00 (*92-1-061164-0*) UN.

Department for Policy Coordination & Sustainable D. Consolidated List of Products Whose Consumption and/or Sale Have Been Banned, Withdrawn, Severely Restricted or Not Approved by Governments. 5th ed. 935p. 100.00 (*92-1-130160-2*) UN.

Department for the Aging, City of New York. Older Women in the City. Kastenbaum, Robert J., ed. LC 78-73649. (Aging & Old Age Ser.). 1979. lib. bdg. 19.95 (*0-405-11839-2*) Ayer.

Department of Agriculture Staff, U. S. Home Canning of Fruits & Vegetables. (Shorey Lost Arts Ser.). (Illus.). 31p. reprint ed. 10.00 (*0-8466-6050-4*) Shoreys Bkstore.

Department of Army Publication Staff. Achievements of the Signal Security Agency in World War II. (Cryptographic Ser.: Vol. 70). 82p. 1995. reprint ed. pap. 16.80 (*0-89412-250-9*, C-70) Aegean Park Pr.

Department of Aviation Education Staff. Flight Maneuvers: Complete Programmed Course. 2nd ed. LC 67-8780. (Illus.). 332p. 1969. pap. 14.95 (*0-685-62816-7*) Aero Products.

Department of Commerce, ed. Inventory of Research Units in Pennsylvania. 464p. (Orig.). (C). 1983. pap. 11.70 (*0-8182-0016-2*) Commonweal PA.

Department of Defense Staff. Defense FAR Supplement. 1991. ring bd. 258.00 (*1-56726-073-X*) Mgmt Concepts.

Department of Economic & Social Affairs Division f. Aspects of World Employment Strategy. LC 98-105658. 87p. 1997. pap. 12.50 (*92-1-130189-0*, HD6971) UN.

— Family-Building & Family Planning Evaluation. LC 98-111056. 112p. 1997. pap. 19.95 (*92-1-151314-6*, HQ766) UN.

— World Population Monitoring, 1997: International Migration & Development. 204p. pap. 45.00 (*92-1-151315-4*) UN.

Department of Economic & Social Affairs Division f, jt. auth. see Division of Public Administration & Development Management Staff.

***Department of Economic & Social Affairs, Statistics Division Staff, ed.** Handbook of Input-Output Table Compilation & Analysis. (Studies in Methods of National Accounting: No. 74). 266p. 1999. 30.00 (*92-1-161416-3*) UN.

Department of Economic & Social Information & Poli. Handbook for Producing National Statistical Reports on Women & Men. LC 98-147349. (Social Statistics & Indicators Ser.: 14). 315p. 1997. pap. 24.95 (*92-1-161394-9*) UN.

Department of Economic & Social Information & Poli, jt. auth. see U. N. Statistical Division Staff.

Department of Economic and Social Affairs, Population Division Staff. Population Distribution & Migration: Proceedings: United Nations Expert Group Meeting on Population Distribution & Migration (1993: Santa Cruz, Bolivia) LC 99-176675. 400p. 1998. pap. 45.00 (*92-1-151324-3*) UN.

— User's Guide to the Population, Resources, Environment & Development Databank (PRED Bank, Version 2.1) LC 98-190483. vi, 59p. 1998. pap. write for info. (*92-1-151321-9*) UN.

Department of Economic and Social Information Statistics Division Staff. Geographic Information Systems & Population Statistics. LC 97-227986. 1997. 25.00 (*92-1-161389-2*) UN.

Department of Education-Arts Staff. Pathways of Language Development. (C). 1990. 90.00 (*0-86431-066-8*, Pub. by Aust Council Educ Res) St Mut.

Department of Education New Zealand Staff. Reading in Junior Classes. 160p. (Orig.). (C). 1985. pap. text 25.00 (*0-913461-77-6*, 15) R Owen Pubs.

Department of Energy Staff. Department of Energy Acquisition Regulation. 1997. ring bd. 125.00 (*1-56726-077-2*) Mgmt Concepts.

Department of Environment, BDOR Ltd. Staff & Newcastle Architecture Cooperative Staff. Community Involvement in Planning & Development Processes. LC 96-208991. viii, 71p. 1995. pap. text 34.00 (*0-11-753007-7*, HM30077, Pub. by Statnry Office) Balogh.

Department of Environmental Resources Geological S, ed. see Commonwealth of Pennsylvania Staff.

Department of Environmental Resources Staff, et al. Groundwater Resources of the Berwick-Bloomsburg-Danville Area, East Central PA. (Water Resource Reports: No. 61). (Illus.). 76p. (Orig.). 1987. pap. text 10.65 (*0-8182-0084-7*) Commonweal PA.

***Department of Foreign Affairs & Trade DFAT Staff.** Australia & Indonesia's Incorporation of Portuguese Timor, 1974-76. 450p. 2000. 59.95 (*0-522-84928-8*, Pub. by Melbourne Univ Pr) Paul & Co Pubs.

Department of Geography, Lerner Publications. Egypt in Pictures. rev. ed. (Visual Geography Ser.). (Illus.). 64p. (YA). (gr. 5 up). 1992. lib. bdg. 19.93 (*0-8225-1840-6*, Lerner Publctns) Lerner Pub.

— Ethiopia in Pictures. rev. ed. (Visual Geography Ser.). (Illus.). 64p. (YA). (gr. 5 up). 1994. lib. bdg. 19.93 (*0-8225-1836-8*, Lerner Publctns) Lerner Pub.

Department of Geography, Lerner Publications. Israel in Pictures. (Visual Geography Ser.). (Illus.). 64p. (YA). (gr. 5 up). 1992. lib. bdg. 19.93 (*0-8225-1833-3*, Lerner Publctns) Lerner Pub.

Department of Geography, Lerner Publications. Jordan in Pictures. rev. ed. (Visual Geography Ser.). (Illus.). 64p. (YA). (gr. 5 up). 1992. lib. bdg. 19.93 (*0-8225-1834-1*, Lerner Publctns) Lerner Pub.

— Liberia in Pictures. rev. ed. (Visual Geography Ser.). (Illus.). 64p. (YA). (gr. 5 up). 1988. lib. bdg. 19.93 (*0-8225-1837-6*, Lerner Publctns) Lerner Pub.

— Madagascar in Pictures. rev. ed. (Visual Geography Ser.). (Illus.). 64p. (YA). (gr. 5 up). 1988. lib. bdg. 19.93 (*0-8225-1841-4*, Lerner Publctns) Lerner Pub.

— Malawi in Pictures. (Visual Geography Ser.). (Illus.). 64p. (YA). (gr. 6-9). 1989. lib. bdg. 19.93 (*0-8225-1842-2*, Lerner Publctns) Lerner Pub.

— Mexico in Pictures. (Visual Geography Ser.). (Illus.). 64p. (YA). (gr. 6-9). 1994. lib. bdg. 19.93 (*0-8225-1801-5*, Lerner Publctns) Lerner Pub.

— Nigeria in Pictures. (Visual Geography Ser.). (Illus.). 64p. (YA). (gr. 5 up). 1988. lib. bdg. 19.95 (*0-8225-1826-0*, Lerner Publctns) Lerner Pub.

— Senegal in Pictures. (Visual Geography Ser.). (Illus.). 64p. (YA). (gr. 5 up). 1988. lib. bdg. 19.95 (*0-8225-1827-9*, Lerner Publctns) Lerner Pub.

— South Africa in Pictures. (Visual Geography Ser.). (Illus.). 64p. (YA). (gr. 5 up). 1988. lib. bdg. 19.95 (*0-8225-1835-X*, Lerner Publctns) Lerner Pub.

— Sudan in Pictures. (Visual Geography Ser.). (Illus.). 64p. (YA). (gr. 5 up). 1988. lib. bdg. 19.95 (*0-8225-1839-2*, Lerner Publctns) Lerner Pub.

Department of Geography, Lerner Publications. Tanzania in Pictures. (Visual Geography Ser.). (Illus.). 64p. (YA). (gr. 5 up). 1988. lib. bdg. 19.95 (*0-8225-1838-4*, Lerner Publctns) Lerner Pub.

Department of Geography, Lerner Publications. Turkey in Pictures. (Visual Geography Ser.). (Illus.). 64p. (YA). (gr. 5 up). 1989. lib. bdg. 19.95 (*0-8225-1831-7*, Lerner Publctns) Lerner Pub.

— Zimbabwe in Pictures. (Visual Geography Ser.). (Illus.). 64p. (YA). (gr. 5 up). 1988. lib. bdg. 19.95 (*0-8225-1825-2*, Lerner Publctns) Lerner Pub.

Department of Health & Human Services, Food & Drug Administration Staff. FDA Investigations Operations Manual. 541p. 1994. pap. text 85.00 (*0-86587-416-6*) Gov Insts.

***Department of Health Staff.** Assessing Children in Need & Their Families: Practice Guidance. (Illus.). xii, 129p. 2000. 21.00 (*0-11-322418-4*, Pub. by Statnry Office) Balogh.

Department of Health Staff. Capital Investment Manual. 294p. 1994. 70.00 (*0-11-321776-5*, HM17765, Pub. by Statnry Office) Bernan Associates.

***Department of Health Staff.** Caring for Children Away from Home: Messages from Research. LC HV887.G7C37 1998. 118p. 1998. pap. 48.50 (*0-471-98475-2*) Wiley.

Department of Health Staff. Mental Illness: Key Area Handbook. 180p. 1994. pap. 30.00 (*0-11-321829-X*, HM1829X, Pub. by Statnry Office) Bernan Associates.

— UK's First Report to the UN Committee on the Rights of the Child. 136p. 1994. pap. 25.00 (*0-11-321715-3*, HM17153, Pub. by Statnry Office) Bernan Associates.

***Department of Health Staff.** Working Together to Safeguard Children. viii, 120p. 1999. 20.00 (*0-11-322309-9*, Pub. by Statnry Office) Balogh.

Department of History & Archives Staff, ed. A Commemorative List of the Departed Servants of Orthodoxy in North America. LC 92-90727. 88p. 1992. pap. 6.00 (*0-86642-051-7*, C11) Ortho Church Am.

Department of Humanitarian Affairs Staff. Humanitarian Report, 1997. 109p. 1997. pap. 45.00 (*92-1-100745-3*, HV553) UN.

Department of Industrial Accidents, Reviewing Boar & Gargano, Paul A. Massachusetts Workers' Compensation Reports. annuals 300p. 1990. boxed set 95.00 (*0-88063-401-4*, 81512-10, MICHIE) LEXIS Pub.

Department of Interior, National Park Service, Off. National Parks: Index 1997-1999, Revised to Include the Actions of the 104th Congress Ending December 31, 1996. (Illus.). 128p. 1997. per. 6.50 (*0-16-054883-7*) USGPO.

Department of International Economic and Social Affairs Staff. Consumer Protection for Asia & the Pacific: Proceedings: Report of the International Conference on Consumer Protection: Consumers in the Global Age (1997: New Dehli) LC 99-159911. 123p. 1998. pap. 25.00 (*92-1-104481-2*) UN.

— Poverty Reduction Strategies: A Review. LC 99-172462. vii, 58p. 1998. write for info. (*92-1-104484-7*) UN.

***Department of Labor Staff.** Career Guide to Industries, 2000. 2000. pap. text 16.95 (*1-56370-804-3*) JIST Works.

Department of Labor Staff, jt. auth. see JIST Staff.

Department of Management. Business Strategy & Policy. 1999. 45.00 (*0-07-234447-4*) McGraw.

Department of Nutrition & Dietetics Staff. Thomas Jefferson University Hospital Nutrition Manual. LC 93-2824. 650p. 1993. ring bd. 196.00 (*0-8342-0335-9*) Aspen Pub.

Department of Policy Coordination & Sustainable De. Critical Trends: Global Change & Sustainable Development. LC 97-93071. 76p. 1997. pap. 25.00 (*92-1-106311-6*) UN.

Department of Public Information, UN, ed. Yearbook of the United Nations, Vol. 40. 1333p. lib. bdg. 95.00 (*0-7923-1076-4*) UN.

Department of Public Information United Nations, S, ed. Yearbook of the United Nations, Vol. 45. 1124p. (C). lib. bdg. 115.00 (*0-7923-1970-2*) UN.

Department of Public Information United Nations, S, ed. Yearbook of the United Nations, 1985, Vol. 39. (C). 1990. lib. bdg. 146.00 (*0-7923-0503-5*) Kluwer Academic.

Department of Social Security Staff. Incapacity Benefit & Severe Disablement Allowance Quarterly Summary of Statistics. LC 98-220962. 26p. 1998. write for info. (*1-85197-859-3*) Dept of Social Security.

Department of Sociology Murray Knuttila Staff. Introducing Sociology: A Critical Perspective. 2nd rev. ed. LC 96-221661. 308p. (Orig.). 1996. pap. text 29.95 (*0-19-541207-9*) OUP.

Department of Special Collections Staff, ed. ABHB - Annual Bibliography of the History of the Printed Books & Libraries Vol. 20: Publications of 1989 & Additions from the Preceding Years. 436p. (C). 1991. lib. bdg. 278.50 (*0-7923-1362-3*) Kluwer Academic.

Department of State Staff. Documentary History of the Constitution of the United States of America, 1786-1870: Derived from the Records, Manuscripts &

D

An Asterisk (*) at the beginning of an entry indicates that the title is appearing for the first time.

Rolls Deposited in the Bureau of Rolls & Library of the Department of State, 3 vols. LC 98-25017. 2232p. 1998. reprint ed. 625.00 (*0-8377-2045-1*, Rothman) W S Hein.

Department of Statistics International Monetary Fu. The IMF's Statistical Systems in the Context of Revision of the United Nations' "System of National Accounts" Galbis, Vicente, ed. LC 91-2489. xxvii, 599p. (Orig.). (C). 1991. pap. 35.00 (*1-55775-159-5*) Intl Monetary.

Department of the Army. First Aid for Soldiers: An Army Field Manual. 1982. lib. bdg. 250.00 (*0-87700-402-1*) Revisionist Pr.

— Guerrilla Warfare. 1982. lib. bdg. 250.00 (*0-87700-400-5*) Revisionist Pr.

— Ranger Training & Operations. 1982. lib. bdg. 250.00 (*0-87700-376-9*) Revisionist Pr.

Department of the Army Publication Staff. Basic Cryptanalysis, Field Manual 34-40-2. 360p. 1997. pap. 28.80 (*0-89412-272-X*) Aegean Park Pr.

Department of the Army Staff. Major Automotive Items & Combinations, WW II: ORD 3 SNL G-1. (Illus.). 168p. 1988. reprint ed. pap. 20.00 (*0-910667-15-2*) Victory WW Two.

— U. S. Army Field Manual 100-5: Fighting Future Wars. (Association of the U. S. Army Book Ser.). 172p. 1994. pap. 21.95 (*0-02-881103-8*) Brasseys.

Department of the Army Staff, ed. Hand-to-Hand Combat. 1982. lib. bdg. 250.00 (*0-87700-405-6*) Revisionist Pr.

Department of the Environment for Northern Ireland Staff. Fermanagh: Its Special Landscapes, a Study of the Fermanagh Countryside & Its Heritage. (Illus.). 91p. 1991. pap. 15.00 (*0-337-08276-5*) Statnry Office.

Department of the Environment Staff. The Impact of Environmental Improvements on Urban Regeneration. LC 96-141461. xii, 117p. 1995. pap. 42.00 (*0-11-753110-3*, HM31103, Pub. by Statnry Office) Balogh.

— Landfill Design, Construction & Operational Practice. (Waste Management Paper Ser.: No. 26B). 299p. 1995. 50.00 (*0-11-753185-5*, Pub. by Statnry Office) Balogh.

Department of the Environment Staff. Restoration of Damaged Peatlands, 1995. (Illus.). 252p. 1995. pap. 75.00 (*0-11-752978-8*, Pub. by Statnry Office) Balogh.

— Sustainable Development: The U. K. Strategy, Cm. 2426. LC 95-194740. (Command Papers: No. 2426). 268p. 1994. pap. 45.00 (*0-10-124262-X*, HM4262X, Pub. by Statnry Office) Bernan Associates.

***Department of the Environment Staff.** Transport Trends: 1998 Edition. 82p. 1998. pap. (*0-11-551987-4*, Pub. by Statnry Office) Balogh.

Department of the Environment Staff & Price Waterhouse Staff. Evaluation of Urban Development Grant, Urban Regeneration Grant & City Grant. (Inner Cities Research Programme Ser.). iii, 76p. 1993. pap. 29.00 (*0-11-752879-X*, HM2879X, Pub. by Statnry Office) Balogh.

Department of the Environment Staff, tr. see Mattheck, Claus, et al.

***Department of the Environment, Transport & the Regions Staff.** Focus on Freight: 1998 Edition. (Focus On Ser.). 40p. 1998. 59.00 (*0-11-552054-6*, Pub. by Statnry Office) Balogh.

— Focus on Personal Travel: 1998 Edition. (Focus On Ser.). 83p. 1998. 59.00 (*0-11-552055-4*, Pub. by Statnry Office) Balogh.

— Focus on Public Transport: 1998 Edition. (Focus On Ser.). 86p. 1999. 59.00 (*0-11-552083-X*, Pub. by Statnry Office) Balogh.

— Focus on Roads: 1998 Edition. LC 98-208021. (Focus On Ser.). 45p. 1998. 59.00 (*0-11-552056-2*, Pub. by Statnry Office) Balogh.

— Transport Statistics Report: Maritime Statistics 1998. 160p. 1999. 62.00 (*0-11-552162-3*, Pub. by Statnry Office) Balogh.

Department of the Interior, U. S. Geological Surve & Osborn, Henry F. The Titanotheres of Ancient Wyoming, Dakota & Nebraska. Gould, Stephen Jay, ed. LC 79-83341. (History of Paleontology Ser.: 2 vols.). (Illus.). 1980. reprint ed. lib. bdg. 246.95 (*0-405-12729-4*) Ayer.

— The Titanotheres of Ancient Wyoming, Dakota & Nebraska, 1. Gould, Stephen Jay, ed. LC 79-83341. (History of Paleontology Ser.: 2 vols.). (Illus.). 1980. reprint ed. lib. bdg. 123.95 (*0-405-12730-8*) Ayer.

— The Titanotheres of Ancient Wyoming, Dakota & Nebraska, Vol. 2. Gould, Stephen Jay, ed. LC 79-83341. (History of Paleontology Ser.: 2 vols.). (Illus.). 1980. reprint ed. lib. bdg. 123.95 (*0-405-12731-6*) Ayer.

Department of the Interior's Bureau of Reclamation Staff, contrib. by. Construction of Hoover Dam. LC 77-79677. (Illus.). 48p. 1976. reprint ed. pap. 1.50 (*0-916122-51-4*) KC Pubns.

Department of Tourism, Philippines Staff, jt. contrib. by see World Tourism Organization Staff.

Department of Trade & Industry Staff. The Energy Report, 1998 Vol. 1: Transforming Markets. LC 99-201399. (Illus.). x, 300p. 1998. pap. 76.00 (*0-11-515446-9*, Pub. by Statnry Office) Balogh.

Department of Transport Staff. Survey of Fire Protection Arrangements in Merchant Ships: Instructions for the Guidance of Surveyors. xxiv, 423p. 1993. ring bd. 90.00 (*0-11-550949-6*, Pub. by Statnry Office) Balogh.

Department of Transportation, Federal Aviation Adm. Aircraft Inspection, Repair & Alterations AC43.13B: Acceptable Methods, Techniques & Practices. 2nd rev. ed. (Illus.). 768p. 1998. pap. 18.95 (*1-56027-331-3*) ASA Inc.

Department of Transportation Staff. The Highway Code. (Illus.). 94p. 1997. pap. 2.95 (*0-11-551843-6*, Pub. by Statnry Office) Seven Hills Bk.

Department of Transportation Staff. International Comparisons of Transport Statistics, 1970-1994. 108p. 1997. 50.00 (*0-11-551932-7*, Pub. by Statnry Office) Balogh.

Department of Transportation Staff, contrib. by. Highway Laws of Virginia, 1998 Edition. LC 99-160556. 470p. 1998. pap. 95.00 (*0-327-06512-5*, 3551112) LEXIS Pub.

Department 56, Inc., Staff. The Original Snow Village Collector's Album: 1990 Edition. 116p. 1990. 24.95 (*0-9622603-3-9*) Dept Fifty Six.

Depas, Albert. Metamorphosis of Joy. LC 96-94500. (Illus.). 64p. (Orig.). 1996. pap. 8.95 (*0-9651473-0-4*) Mega Pr.

DePasquale, Dan & Peterson, Larry. Red Wing Collectibles. (Illus.). 160p. 1995. pap. 9.95 (*0-89145-313-X*, 1670) Collector Bks.

DePasquale, Dan, et al. Red Wing Stoneware. (Illus.). 160p. 1995. pap. 9.95 (*0-89145-234-6*, 1440) Collector Bks.

DePasquale, David. Get on Track Fitness & Nutrition Training Log. (Illus.). 55p. (Orig.). 1993. reprint ed. pap. text, spiral bd. 12.95 (*0-9640918-0-1*) D DiPasquale.

DePasquale, Iris H., ed. see DePasquale, Louis A., et al.

DePasquale, Louis A. National Firefighters Coloring Book. (Illus.). 26p. (J). 1997. pap. write for info. (*0-9635356-1-7*) All Hands.

DePasquale, Louis A., et al. National Firefighters Recipe Book. 3rd ed. DePasquale, Iris H., ed. LC 93-71381. (Illus.). 270p. 1993. reprint ed. spiral bd. 15.00 (*0-9635356-0-9*) All Hands.

DePasquale, Nicholas, jt. auth. see Burch, George E.

DePasquale, Paula, jt. auth. see Dickson, Carolyn.

DePasquale, Peter. The Boxer's Workout. LC 90-82757. (Illus.), 176p. 1990. reprint ed. pap. 14.95 (*0-9627050-0-4*) Fighting Fit.
Boxing workout for whole-body conditioning, aerobic fitness & fun. Presents the non-contact workout program that boxers use to get into shape. Starts with the basics: pre-conditioning, roadwork, when & where to train, diet, & equipment. Over eighty photo illustrations on warm-up, movement, shadow boxing, heavy bag, speed bag, punches, circuit, developing your own boxing style & more. Assumes no prior knowledge of boxing. Suitable for men, women, teens & seniors. Available from the Publisher: Fighting Fit, 47 Hicks Street, Brooklyn, NY 11201. 718-855-2450, FAX: 718-858-2474. e-mail: FFI42@AOL.COM. Also available through: Baker & Taylor & Brodart.
Publisher Paid Annotation.

DePastino, Valerie S. Endtime Commissions - Endtime Anointings. 80p. 1988. pap. 3.95 (*0-88144-130-9*) Christian Pub.

— Identification of Intercession. 1988. pap. 3.95 (*0-88144-123-6*) Christian Pub.

— Trusting God in Times & Seasons of Change. 128p. 1989. pap. 5.95 (*0-88144-138-4*) Christian Pub.

Depatie, Sylvie, et al, eds. Twenty Years Later: Reading the History of Seventeenth & Eighteenth-Century Canada. (Illus.). 312p. 1998. text 60.00 (*0-7735-1692-1*, Pub. by McG-Queens Univ Pr) CUP Services.

Depatie, Sylvie, jt. auth. see Dechene, Louise.

***DePaul, Amy.** What to Expect Your First Year of Teaching. 48p. 1998. pap. 7.00 (*0-16-049719-1*) USGPO.

DePaul, F. Thomas & Crowder, Jerry W. Control of Emissions from Municipal Solid Waste Incinerators. LC 89-8688. (Pollution Technology Review Ser.: No. 169). (Illus.). 275p. 1990. 39.00 (*0-8155-1209-0*) Noyes.

Depaul, Kim, ed. Children of Cambodia's Killing Fields: Memoirs by Survivors. (Illus.). 224p. 1999. pap. 14.95 (*0-300-07873-0*) Yale U Pr.

Depaul, Kim, jt. auth. see Dith, Pran.

DePaul, Michael R. & Ramsey, William, eds. Rethinking Intuition: The Psychology of Intuition & Its Role in Philosophical Inquiry. LC 98-23794. (Studies in Epistemology & Cognitive Theory). 288p. 1998. 68.00 (*0-8476-8795-3*); pap. 23.95 (*0-8476-8796-1*) Rowman.

Depaul University English Dept Staff. Writing for Business Professionals. 210p. 1995. pap. text 34.20 (*0-536-59113-X*) Pearson Custom.

DePaula, C., ed. Brazilian Product Guide. 350p. 2000. pap. 95.00 (*0-915344-65-3*) Todd Pubns.

— Latin American Product Guide. 450p. 1994. pap. 125.00 (*0-915344-42-4*) Todd Pubns.

— Mexican Product Guide. 350p. 2000. pap. 95.00 (*0-915344-87-4*) Todd Pubns.

— Taiwan Product Guide. 350p. 1997. pap. 100.00 (*0-915344-72-6*) Todd Pubns.

— Thailand Product Guide. 350p. 1992. pap. 75.00 (*0-915344-47-5*) Todd Pubns.

— U. S. Importers Product Guide. 500p. 1998. pap. 195.00 (*0-915344-77-7*) Todd Pubns.

DePaula, Ramon P. & Berthold, John W., eds. Fiber Optic & Laser Sensors XIV, Vol. 2839. 444p. 1996. 85.00 (*0-8194-2227-4*) SPIE.

DePauli-Schimanovich, Werner, ed. The Foundational Debate: Complexity & Constructivity in Mathematics & Physics. (Vienna Circle Institute Yearbook VCIY Ser.: Vol. 3). 368p. (C). 1995. text 144.00 (*0-7923-3737-9*) Kluwer Academic.

Depaulis, A. & Bandler, Richard, eds. The Midbrain Periaqueductal Gray Matter: Functional, Anatomical & Neurochemical Organization. (NATO ASI Ser.: Vol. 213). (Illus.). 490p. (C). 1991. text 186.00 (*0-306-44033-4*, Kluwer Plenum) Kluwer Academic.

DePaulo, J. Raymond & Ablow, Keith Russell. How to Cope with Depression: A Complete Guide for You & Your Family. 240p. 1989. text 19.95 (*0-07-016409-6*) McGraw.

Depauw. Ethics, Leadership & Business. (C). 1995. pap. text 70.25 (*0-07-016423-1*) McGraw.

DePauw. In the Rainforest. (Illus.). 48p. (J). (gr. 1-3). 1993. pap., teacher ed. 9.95 (*1-55799-255-X*, 274) Evan-Moor Edu Pubs.

DePauw, Carl & Luijten, Ger, eds. Anthony van Dyck: As a Printmaker. (Illus.). 400p. 1999. 75.00 (*0-8478-2235-4*, Pub. by Rizzoli Intl) St Martin.

DePauw, Debbie. Tropical Rainforests. (Illus.). 48p. (J). (gr. 3-6). 1994. pap. text 5.95 (*1-55799-276-2*, EMC 283) Evan-Moor Edu Pubs.

DePauw, John W. U. S.-Chinese Trade Negotiations. LC 80-272. 252p. 1981. 59.95 (*0-275-90603-5*, C0603, Praeger Pubs) Greenwood.

DePauw, Karen P. & Gavron, Susan J. Disability & Sport. LC 94-25215. (Illus.). 312p. 1995. text 38.00 (*0-87322-848-0*, BDEP0848) Human Kinetics.

DePauw, Linda G. Founding Mothers: Women of American in the Revolutionary Era. 228p. (J). (gr. 4-7). 1994. pap. 5.95 (*0-395-70109-0*) HM.

Depel, Jim. The Baseball Handbook for Coaches & Players. (Illus.). 96p. 1991. reprint ed. pap. 9.95 (*0-02-042861-8*) Macmillan.

Depender, William & Ikeda-Chandler, Wanda. Clinical Ethics: An Invitation to Healing Professionals. LC 89-16224. 152p. 1990. 49.95 (*0-275-93437-3*, C3437, Praeger Pubs) Greenwood.

Deperet, Charles. The Transformations of the Animal World: Being the Authorized Translation of "Les Transformations Du Monde Animal. Gould, Stephen Jay, ed. LC 79-8330. (History of Paleontology Ser.). 1980. reprint ed. lib. bdg. 35.95 (*0-405-12711-1*) Ayer.

DePersia, A. Trent, et al, eds. Surveillance & Assessment Technologies for Law Enforcement, Vol. 2935. LC 96-69885. 196p. 1997. 56.00 (*0-8194-2337-8*) SPIE.

Depestre, Rene. Alleluia pour une Femme-Jardin. (FRE.). 215p. 1986. pap. 10.95 (*0-7859-2230-X*, 2070377I3X) Fr & Eur.

— Alleluia pour une Femme-Jardin. (Folio Ser.: No. 1713). (FRE.). 215p. 1986. pap. 8.95 (*2-07-037713-X*) Schoenhof.

— The Festival of the Greasy Pole. Arnold, A. J. & Drame, K., eds. Coates, Carrol F., tr. from FRE. & intro. by. (CARAF Bks.). 142p. 1990. text 28.50 (*0-8139-1281-4*) U Pr of Va.

— Hadriana Dans Tous Mes Reves. (FRE.). 214p. 1990. pap. 10.95 (*0-7859-2147-8*, 2070382729) Fr & Eur.

— Hadriana Dans Tous Mes Reves. (Folio Ser.: No. 2182). (FRE.). 1990. pap. 8.95 (*2-07-038272-9*) Schoenhof.

Depestre, Rene, et al. Haitian Revolutionary Poets. (B. E. Ser.: No. 55). 1969. 60.00 (*0-8115-3006-X*) Periodicals Srv.

DePetrillo, Paolo B. & McDonough, Mark K. Alcohol Withdrawal Treatment Manual. (Alcohol & Drug Abuse Treatment Ser.: No. 1). 215p. 1999. 75.00 (*0-9661673-0-9*) Focused Treat.

DePew, Alfred. The Melancholy of Departure: Stories by Alfred DePew. LC 91-24281. (Flannery O'Connor Award for Short Fiction Ser.). 144p. 1992. 19.95 (*0-8203-1405-6*) U of Ga Pr.

Depew, Chauncey M. My Memories of Eighty Years. (American Biography Ser.). 417p. 1991. reprint ed. lib. bdg. 89.00 (*0-7812-8106-7*) Rprt Serv.

Depew, David, jt. ed. see Hollinger, Robert.

Depew, David J., ed. The Greeks & the Good Life. 305p. 1980. pap. text 8.95 (*0-937622-01-X*); lib. bdg. 25.00 (*0-937622-00-1*) CSU Fullerton.

Depew, David J. & Weber, Bruce H. Darwinism Evolving: Systems Dynamics & the Genealogy of Natural Selection. LC 94-16590. 1994. 49.95 (*0-262-04145-6*, Bradford Bks) MIT Pr.

— Darwinism Evolving: Systems Dynamics & the Genealogy of Natural Selection. (Illus.). 608p. 1996. pap. text 27.50 (*0-262-54083-5*, Bradford Bks) MIT Pr.

Depew, David J. & Weber, Bruce H., eds. Evolution at a Crossroads: The New Biology & the New Philosophy of Science. 288p. 1985. 32.50 (*0-262-04079-4*, Bradford Bks) MIT Pr.

— Evolution at a Crossroads: The New Biology & the New Philosophy of Science. 288p. 1989. pap. text 17.50 (*0-262-54052-5*, Bradford Bks) MIT Pr.

DePew, Dawn. Now That Mom's Not Around Cookbook. 2nd rev. ed. 343p. 1998. pap. 16.95 (*0-9628409-1-2*) D DePew.

Depew, Edward. House Inspection: A Home Buyer's/Homeowner's Guide. LC 97-73258. (Illus.). 210p. 1991. pap. 11.95 (*0-9614876-4-X*) Golden Hl Pr NY.

DePew, John N. A Library, Media & Archival Preservation Glossary. 200p. 1992. lib. bdg. 59.00 (*0-87436-576-7*) ABC-CLIO.

— A Library, Media & Archival Preservation Handbook. LC 91-16501. 550p. 1991. lib. bdg. 51.50 (*0-87436-543-0*) ABC-CLIO.

***Depew, Mary.** Matrices of Genre: Authors, Canons & Society. 352p. 2000. 50.00 (*0-674-00338-1*) HUP.

Depew, R. Ray. HP-48 Graphics. 304p. 1991. 9.95 (*0-931011-33-7*) Grapevine Pubns.

Depew, Ray. Graphics on the HP48G - GX. 330p. 1993. pap. 19.95 (*0-931011-42-6*) Grapevine Pubns.

Depew, Wally. The Equalizer. LC 98-88478. 325p. 1998. 25.00 (*0-7388-0171-2*); pap. 15.00 (*0-7388-0172-0*) Xlibris Corp.

— Nine Essays on Concrete Poems. (Illus.). 68p. (Orig.). 1974. pap. 5.95 (*0-914974-00-9*) Holmgangers.

DePiano, Frank A., et al, eds. Clinical Applications of Hypnosis. LC 85-13492. (Developments in Clinical Psychology Ser.). 272p. 1986. text 73.25 (*0-89391-297-2*) Ablx Pub.

DePietro, Anne C. The Paintings of Eduard Steichen. Shoenfeld, Alayne, ed. LC 85-80519. (Illus.). 48p. (Orig.). 1985. pap. text 8.95 (*1-879195-00-3*) Heckscher Mus.

DePietro, Anne C. & Rehm, Mary T. Arthur Dove & Helen Torr: The Huntington Years. Jones, Penny, ed. LC 89-80260. (Illus.). 100p. (Orig.). 1989. pap. text 16.95 (*1-879195-03-8*) Heckscher Mus.

DePietro, Anne Cohen. Shaping a Generation: The Art & Artists of Betty Parsons. Welker, Janie M., ed. 76p. 1999. pap. text 21.95 (*1-879195-08-9*) Heckscher Mus.

Depin, Daniel. Conflicts of Interest. unabridged ed. Morales, Alessandra, ed. 279p. 1998. pap. 12.99 (*0-9666391-0-3*) D Depin Pubg.

DePina Araujo, A. De Pina's Technical Dictionary Vol. 1: English-Portuguese. (ENG & POR.). 616p. 1975. 125.00 (*0-7859-7138-6*) Fr & Eur.

— De Pina's Technical Dictionary Vol. 2: Portuguese-English. (ENG & POR.). 495p. 1975. 125.00 (*0-7859-7139-4*) Fr & Eur.

DePinto, Joseph V. Transport & Transformation of Contaminants Near the Sediment-Water Interface. 368p. 1993. lib. bdg. 95.00 (*0-87371-887-9*, L887) Lewis Pubs.

D'Epiro, Desmond, et al. The Seven Wonders of the World? And 100 Other Great Cultural Lists-Fully Explicated. LC 98-23377. (Illus.). 536p. 1998. pap. 14.95 (*0-385-49062-3*) Doubleday.

D'Epiro, Peter. A Touch of Rhetoric: Ezra Pound's Malatesta Cantos. LC 83-5729. (Studies in Modern Literature: No. 2). (Illus.). 182p. reprint ed. pap. 56.50 (*0-8357-1404-7*, 207052900097) Bks Demand.

***Depken, Christian.** Neue Entwicklungen Bei der Bilanziellen Behandlung Von Schadstoffelasteten Vermogensgegenstanden. 176p. 1998. 39.95 (*3-631-34055-9*) P Lang Pubng.

Deplanne, Veronique. Legacies of a French Empire in North America. LC 98-44502. 1998. write for info. (*1-57864-075-X*) Donning Co.

Depledge, P., et al, eds. Software Engineering for Microprocessor Systems. (Computing Ser.). 273p. 1984. boxed set 53.00 (*0-86341-087-1*, CM002) INSPEC Inc.

Deply, Karl-Herbert & American Society for the Prevention of Cruelty to. Lovebirds Today: A Complete & Up-to-Date Guide. LC 97-3626. (Basic Domestic Pet Library). 76p. (J). (gr. 3 up). 1997. 19.95 (*0-7910-4614-1*) Chelsea Hse.

Depner, Charlene E. & Bray, James H., eds. Nonresidential Parenting: New Vistas in Family Living. (Focus Editions Ser.: Vol. 155). (Illus.). 240p. (C). 1993. text 59.95 (*0-8039-5050-0*); pap. text 26.00 (*0-8039-5051-9*) Sage.

Depner, D. A. Prescribing Hemodialysis: A Guide to Urea Modeling, No. 29. (Developments in Nephrology Ser.). (C). 1990. text 152.00 (*0-7923-0833-6*) Kluwer Academic.

Depoe, Stephen P. Arthur M. Schlesinger, Jr., & the Ideological History of American Liberalism. LC 93-5806. (Studies in Rhetoric & Communication). 216p. 1994. text 34.95 (*0-8173-0718-4*) U of Ala Pr.

DePoint, Beth. Enhancing Your Public Relations: A Guide for Designing Effective Communication Strategies for Community-Based Vocational Rehabilitation Programs. (Illus.). 82p. (Orig.). (C). 1989. pap. write for info. (*0-916671-93-3*) TRR.

Depoitetto, James. Practical Kitten Care. LC 96-24293. (Illus.). 192p. 1996. 12.95 (*0-87605-763-6*) Howell Bks.

***DePol, John.** Five Decades of the Burin: The Wood Engravings of John DePol. 2000. pap. 16.95 (*1-56792-162-0*) Godine.

DePollo, Daryl, ed. see McCants, Glynis.

***Depolo, Radoslav.** Latin American Antitrust Law. 600p. 1999. ring bd. 195.00 (*1-57823-067-5*) Juris Pubng.

Depolo, Zora, tr. see Krleza, Miroslav.

DePompei, Roberta, jt. auth. see Blosser, Jean L.

DePompei, Roberta, jt. auth. see Kilpatrick, Kathryn.

deProncins, Leon. Freemasonry & the Vatican. unabridged ed. 224p. 1968. reprint ed. pap. 12.00 (*0-945001-31-2*) GSG & Assocs.

— Grand Orient: Freemasonry Unmasked. unabridged ed. 200p. 1967. reprint ed. pap. 12.00 (*0-945001-28-2*) GSG & Assocs.

— Judaism & the Vatican. unabridged ed. 199p. 1967. reprint ed. pap. 12.00 (*0-945001-36-3*) GSG & Assocs.

— The Secret Powers Behind Revolution: Freemasonry & Judaism. unabridged ed. 260p. 1929. reprint ed. pap. 12.00 (*0-945001-40-1*) GSG & Assocs.

— State Secrets. unabridged ed. 101p. 1975. reprint ed. pap. 12.00 (*0-945001-33-9*) GSG & Assocs.

DePoncins, Leon V. Freemasonry & the Vatican. 1973. 59.95 (*0-8490-0196-X*) Gordon Pr.

— Freemasonry & the Vatican. 1982. lib. bdg. 250.00 (*0-87700-351-3*) Revisionist Pr.

— Judaism & the Vatican. 1974. 59.95 (*0-8490-0466-7*) Gordon Pr.

— Secret Powers Behind the Revolution. 1973. 59.95 (*0-8490-1013-6*) Gordon Pr.

***Deponte, Paige.** Gaia 1: Journey into Vanishing Worlds. (Illus.). 168p. 2000. 65.00 (*1-891024-15-9*) Dist Art Pubs.

Depoortere, Kristiaan. A Different God. 1995. pap. text 25.00 (*0-8028-0559-0*) Eerdmans.

DePorte, A. France: The Challenges of Renewal. LC 87-82323. (Headlines Ser.: No. 282). 80p. 1987. pap. 5.95 (*0-87124-116-1*) Foreign Policy.

DePorte, Anton W. DeGaulle's Foreign Policy: 1944-1946. LC 67-29624. 340p. 1968. 42.00 (*0-674-19550-7*) HUP.

Deporte, Francois, tr. see Wright, Machaelle S.

DePorte, Michael V. Nightmares & Hobbyhorses: Swift, Sterne, & Augustan Ideas of Madness. LC 73-78048. (Illus.). 176p. reprint ed. pap. 54.60 (*0-7837-6679-3*, 204629500011) Bks Demand.

D

An Asterisk (*) at the beginning of an entry indicates that the title is appearing for the first time.

Deporter, Bobbi. Quantum Teaching: Orchestrating Student Success. LC 98-186080. 230p. 1998. pap. text 27.95 (*0-205-28664-X*) P-H.

Deporter, Bobbi & Hernacki, Mike. Quantum Learning: Unleashing the Genius in You. 368p. 1992. pap. 13.95 (*0-440-50427-9*, Dell Trade Pbks) Dell.

Depoy, jt. auth. see Gilson.

***DePoy, Philip.** Dancing Made Easy. (Flap Tucker Mystery Ser.). 304p. 1999. mass mkt. 5.99 (*0-440-22618-X*) Dell.

DePoy, Phillip. Angels - Musical. 1995. 5.95 (*0-87129-480-X*, A09) Dramatic Pub.

***Depoy, Phillip.** Dead Easy. 2000. mass mkt. 5.99 (*0-440-23643-6*) Dell.

Depoy, Phillip. Easy. (Flap Tucker Mystery Ser.). 288p. 1997. mass mkt. 5.99 (*0-440-22494-2*) Dell.

— Easy as 1-2-3. (Flap Tucker Mystery Ser.: Bk. 3). 1999. mass mkt. 5.99 (*0-440-22617-1*) Dell.

— Too Easy. 288p. 1998. mass mkt. 5.99 (*0-440-22495-0*) Dell.

Depp, Johnny, et al. Fear & Loathing: The Strange & Terrible Saga of Hunter S. Thompson. (Illus.). 288p. 13.95 (*1-56025-065-8*, Thunders Mouth) Avalon NY.

Deppa, James W. The Marriage That Did Succeed for Mary, Queen of Scots. LC 89-81233. (Illus.). 325p. 1990. 14.50 (*0-9623620-1-8*) Ironwood MD.

Deppa, Joan, et al. The Media & Disaster: Pam Am 103. 224p. 1993. pap. 34.00 (*1-85346-225-X*) St Martin.

— The Media & Disasters: Pan Am 103. LC 93-34893. (Disasters in the Press Ser.). (C). 1994. text 45.00 (*0-8147-1857-4*); pap. text 19.50 (*0-8147-1856-6*) NYU Pr.

Deppe, Carol. Breed Your Own Vegetable Varieties: The Gardener's & Farmer's Guide to Plant Breeding & Seed Saving. (Illus.). 400p. pap. 27.95 (*1-890132-72-1*) Chelsea Green Pub.

Deppe, Darla, jt. auth. see McRoberts, Greg.

Deppe, Dean B. The Sayings of Jesus in the Epistle of James. 1994. 29.95 (*0-317-05949-1*) Dove Bkslrs.

***Deppe, Gunter & Baker, Vicki, eds.** Gynecologic Oncology. LC 99-42910. (An Arnold Publication). (Illus.). 384p. 2000. text 59.50 (*0-340-74204-6*, Pub. by E A) OUP.

Deppe, Gunter, jt. auth. see Baker, Vicki V.

Deppe, Rupert M. Die Erbsunde in der Philosophischen Theologie Frederick Robert Tennants: Zur Ortung Eines Naturwissenschaftlich-Evolutiv-Psychologischen Ansatzes. (Theologie Im Ubergang Ser.: Bd. 11). (GER.). VIII, 348p. 1990. 63.80 (*3-631-42257-1*) P Lang Pubng.

Deppe, Theodore. Children of the Air. LC 89-24409. 72p. 1990. pap. 9.95 (*0-914086-91-X*) Alice James Bks.

— The Wanderer King. 80p. (Orig.). 1996. pap. 9.95 (*1-882295-08-0*) Alice James Bks.

Deppen, E. E. & Deppen, M. L. Deppen: Counting Kindred of Christian Deppen & History of Christian Ruchty & Other Collateral Lines; Also the Complete Genealogical Family Refist of Christian & Veronica (Ruchty) Deppen's Family, with Biographies of All Their Descendants from the Earliest Records. (Illus.). 625p. 1995. reprint ed. pap. 92.50 (*0-8328-4770-4*); reprint ed. lib. bdg. 102.50 (*0-8328-4769-0*) Higginson Bk Co.

Deppen, M. L., jt. auth. see Deppen, E. E.

Deppenschmidt, Kurt, jt. auth. see Barry, Amy J.

Depper, Estelle M. California Trust Administration: September 1992 Update. Archer, Carine, ed. LC 86-70263. 145p. 1992. ring bd. 45.00 (*0-88124-558-5*, ES-31701) Cont Ed Bar-CA.

Depper, Estelle M. & Bannon, Alexander L. California Trust Administration. rev. ed. Allison, Cherri N., ed. LC 86-70263. 326p. 1996. ring bd. 69.00 (*0-88124-948-3*, ES-31704) Cont Ed Bar-CA.

Depper, Estelle M., et al. California Trust Administration: January 1994 Update. rev. ed. Archer, Carine, ed. LC 86-70263. 224p. 1994. 59.00 (*0-88124-702-2*, ES-31702) Cont Ed Bar-CA.

Depper, Nancy. Bodies of Work. 20p. (Orig.). 1994. pap. 3.00 (*0-916397-34-3*) Manic D Pr.

Deppermann, Arnulf. Glaubwurdigkeit im Konflikt: Rhetorische Techniken in Streitgesprachen Prozesanalysen Von Schlichtungsgesprachen. (Europaische Hochschulschriften, Reihe 21 Ser.: No. 184). 415p. 1997. 63.95 (*3-631-31400-0*) P Lang Pubng.

Deppermann, Klaus. Melchior Hoffman: Social Unrest & Apocalyptic Visions in the Age of Reformation. Wren, Malcolm, tr. 440p. 69.95 (*0-567-09338-7*, Pub. by T & T Clark) Bks Intl VA.

Deppermann, Klaus. Melchior Hoffman: Social Unrest & Apocalyptic Visions in the Age of Reformation. 448p. pap. 44.95 (*0-567-08654-2*) T&T Clark Pubs.

Depperschmidt, Thomas O., jt. ed. see Ireland, Thomas R.

Deppert, Jochim. India & the West. 1984. 42.50 (*0-8364-1152-8*, Pub. by Manohar) S Asia.

Deppert, Wolfgang, et al, eds. Der Einflub der Unitarier Auf die Europaisch-Amerikanische Geistesgeschichte: Vortrage zur Ersten Deutschen Wissenschaftlichen Tagung zur Unitarismusforschung vom 13. - 14. Juni 1985 in Hamburg. (Unitarismusforschung Ser.: Bd. 1). (GER.). 170p. 1990. 34.80 (*3-631-41859-0*) P Lang Pubng.

Depraetere, Ilse. The Tense System in English Relative Clauses: A Corpus-Based Analysis. (Topics in English Linguistics Ser.: No. 16). xvi, 434p. (C). 1995. lib. bdg. 144.65 (*3-11-014685-1*) Mouton.

Depraz, Natalie & Zahavi, Dan. Alterity & Facticity: New Perspectives on Husserl, Vol. 148. LC 98-27158. (Phaenomenologica Ser.). 1998. 97.00 (*0-7923-5187-8*) Kluwer Academic.

Depre, C., et al. Atlas of Cardiac NMR with Anatomical Correlations. (Series in Radiology). (C). 1991. text 208.50 (*0-7923-0941-3*) Kluwer Academic.

Depre, M. Leukotrinenes: Development of Assay Methodology in Biologic Fluids & Evaluation of Antagonists In Vitro & In Vivo in Man. No. 91. 185p. (Orig.). 1994. pap. 44.50 (*90-6186-633-2*, Pub. by Leuven Univ) Coronet Bks.

DePree, Gladis. Festival! An Experiment in Living. 208p. 1986. 14.95 (*0-310-44110-2*, 9488) Zondervan.

DePree, John & Swartz, Charles. Introduction to Real Analysis. LC 87-34622. 368p. 1988. text 105.95 (*0-471-85391-7*) Wiley.

Depree, Max. Leadership Is an Art. 176p. 1990. pap. 14.95 (*0-440-50324-8*, Dell Trade Pbks) Dell.

— Leadership Jazz: The Art of Conducting Business Through Leadership, Followership, Teamwork, Voice, Touch. 240p. 1993. pap. 13.95 (*0-440-50518-6*, Dell Trade Pbks) Dell.

— Leading Without Power. LC 97-21017. 1997. mass mkt. 19.50 (*0-7879-1063-5*) Jossey-Bass.

DePreist, James. The Distant Siren. 64p. (Orig.). 1989. pap. 8.00 (*0-9623976-0-1*) Wllmtt U Pr.

Depres, Lisa & Vachier, Paul. DeBabelizer: The Authorized Edition. 384p. 1997. 45.00 (*1-56830-324-6*) Hayden.

Depres, Lise. Mastering Photoshop 5 for the Web. 704p. 1998. pap. text 49.99 (*0-7821-2230-2*) Sybex.

***Deprest, Jan A.** Endoscopic Feto-Placental Surgery: From Animal Experiments to Early Human Applications. (Acta Biomedica Lovaniensia Ser.: Vol. 198). (Illus.). 164p. 1999. pap. 49.50 (*90-6186-963-3*, Pub. by Leuven Univ) Coronet Bks.

Deprez, Johan & Harvey, John T. Foundations of International Economics: Post-Keynesian Perspectives. LC 98-38603. 1998. write for info. (*0-415-14650-X*); pap. 29.99 (*0-415-14651-8*) Routledge.

Deprez, K., ed. Sociolinguistics in the Low Countries. LC 84-24240. (Studies in the Sciences of Language: No. 5). viii, 359p. 1984. pap. 78.00 (*90-272-2321-1*) J Benjamins Pubng Co.

Deprez, Kas, ed. Language & Intergroup Relations in Flanders & in the Netherlands. (Topics in Sociolinguistics Ser.: No. 6). vi, 198p. 1989. pap. 52.35 (*90-6765-391-8*) Mouton.

Deprez, Kas & Vos, Louis. Nationalism in Belgium: Shifting Identities, 1780-1995. LC 97-38683. 281p. 1998. write for info. (*0-333-65737-3*) St Martin.

***Depriest, Derryl.** Collectible GI Joe: The Ultimate Guide to His Action-Packed World. 176p. 1999. 19.98 (*0-7624-0536-8*) Running Pr.

DePriest, Douglas J., jt. auth. see Wegman, Edward J.

DePriest, James. This Precipice Garden. 60p. 1987. reprint ed. 15.00 (*0-940869-00-4*); reprint ed. pap. 8.00 (*0-940869-01-2*) Univ Portland Pr.

Deprima, Jennifer, et al. Martha Odum: Watercolors. LC 96-52377. (Illus.). 80p. 1997. pap. 20.00 (*0-915977-32-X*) Georgia Museum of Art.

DePrince, Thessalonia. The Book of Forbidden Knowledge. 132p. 1986. pap. 4.95 (*0-935611-03-7*) United Spirit.

— DePrince Master Dream Book. 140p. (Orig.). 1985. pap. 4.95 (*0-318-18391-9*) United Spirit.

— The Mystical Key to the Psalms. LC 92-62658. (Illus.). 110p. (Orig.). 1994. pap. 7.95 (*0-935611-11-8*) United Spirit.

— Secrets of Attracting Good Luck. (Illus.). 113p. (Orig.). 1994. pap. 7.95 (*0-935611-12-6*) United Spirit.

— Six Lessons in Crystal Gazing. 122p. 1986. pap. 4.95 (*0-935611-04-5*) United Spirit.

DePrisco, Andrew & Johnson, James. Choosing a Dog for Life. LC 98-130482. (Illus.). 384p. 1996. 34.95 (*0-7938-2087-1*, TS257) TFH Pubns.

DePrisco, Andrew & Johnson, James B. The Most Complete Book Published Canine Lexicon. (Illus.). 896p. 1993. text 89.95 (*0-86622-198-0*, TS175) TFH Pubns.

DePrisco, Andrew, jt. auth. see Johnson, James.

DeProspero, Dan & DeProspero, Jackie. Illuminated Spirit: Conversations with a Kyudo Master. Floyd, E. et al, eds. LC 96-43498. (Illus.). 160p. 1997. 18.00 (*4-7700-1970-X*) Kodansha.

DeProspero, Jackie, jt. auth. see DeProspero, Dan.

DeProspo, Nancy. Affairs of the Heart: How to Start & Operate a Successful Special Event Planning Service. 144p. 1993. pap. 64.00 (*0-9638085-0-8*) N DeProspo.

DePrott, I. & Ziehen, L. Leges Graecorum Sacrae. (GER & GRE.). 372p. (Orig.). 1988. reprint ed. pap. 35.00 (*0-89005-478-9*) Ares.

DePryck, Koen. Knowledge, Evolution, & Paradox: The Ontology of Language. LC 92-26006. (SUNY Series, The Margins of Literature). 184p. (C). 1993. text 64.50 (*0-7914-1533-3*); pap. text 21.95 (*0-7914-1534-1*) State U NY Pr.

***Dept Of Hist Swtsu.** American Voices: Primary Documents American. 1999. pap. text 28.00 (*0-201-57605-8*) Addison-Wesley.

Dept. English & Historical & Cultural Studies, Gol, ed. see Desmarais, Jane H.

Dept. English, Osmania Univ. Staff. Critical Responses Vol. I: Commonwealth Literature. (C). 1993. write for info. (*81-207-1635-3*) Sterling Pubs.

Dept. for Economic & Social Information & Policy A. Industrial Commodity Statistics Yearbook: Production & Consumption Statistics. 1000p. 110.00 (*92-1-061162-4*) UN.

Dept. of Civil Engineering University of Roorkee,. Wind Loads on Structures: Proceedings of an International Symposium, New Delhi, 5-7. (Illus.). 325p. (C). 1991. text 136.00 (*90-6191-178-8*, Pub. by A A Balkema) Ashgate Pub Co.

Dept. of Defense Staff. Handbook for U.S. Forces in Vietnam. 169p. (YA). (gr. 9-12). 1996. pap. 15.00 (*0-88092-374-1*, 3741, Kav Bks) Royal Fireworks.

Dept. of East Asian Languages & Literatures, Unive, jt. rev. see Haig, John H.

Dept. of Economic & Social Affairs Statistics Division Staff. Handbook on Civil Registration & Vital Statistics Systems: Preparation of a Legal Framework. LC 99-172398. (Studies in Methods: No. 71). 215p. 1998. pap. 40.00 (*92-1-161401-5*) UN.

Dept. of Economic & Social Affairs Statistics Division Staff, jt. auth. see United Nations Staff.

Dept. of Economic & Social Information & Policy St. Challenge of Urbanization: World's Largest Cities. LC 96-128536. (Population Studies: No. 151). 290p. 29.00 (*92-1-151301-4*) UN.

Dept. of Economics & Social Affairs, Population Division Staff. Too Young to Die: Genes or Gender? LC 99-168875. 260p. 1998. pap. 25.00 (*92-1-151325-1*) UN.

Dept. of Educ. Staff, et al. California's Gold, 1993 ("400" Series) (Four Hundred Ser.). 114p. (Orig.). 1994. pap. text, teacher ed. 15.00 (*0-929722-77-9*) CA State Library Fndtn.

Dept. of Education, Office for Pastoral Care of Mi. Celebraudo la Presencia de Jesucristo: Celebrating the Presence of Christ Jesus. (SPA., Illus.). 48p. (Orig.). 1996. pap. text 3.95 (*1-57455-030-6*) US Catholic.

Dept. of Foreign Affairs & Trade Staff. Australia in Brief. 42nd rev. ed. (Illus.). 112p. 1996. pap. 16.00 (*0-644-46276-0*, Pub. by Aust Gov Pub) Accents Pubns.

Dept. of Mines & Energy Staff. South Australia's Opal. (C). 1989. pap. text 60.00 (*0-89771-036-3*, Pub. by Bob Mossel) St Mut.

Dept. of Public Libraries Staff. The Beach: A History of Virginia Beach, Virginia. rev. ed. (Illus.). 1996. 7.95 (*0-9653325-0-0*) VA Beach Pub Lib.

Dept. of Spec. Coll. of Koninklijke Bibliotheek St, ed. ABHB Annual Bibliography of the History of the Printed Book & Libraries, Vol. 23. 482p. (C). 1995. lib. bdg. 264.50 (*0-7923-3249-0*) Kluwer Academic.

Dept. of the Army Tech. Manual Staff. Japanese Explosive Ordnance. (Illus.). 282p. 1993. pap. 25.00 (*0-9623208-6-2*) F L Honeycutt Jr.

DEPT OF THE NAVY-AVY HISTORIAL CENTER, compiled by. Dictionary of American Naval Aviation Squadrons Vol. 1: The History of VA, VAH, VAK, VAL, VAP & VFA Squadrons. 1995. boxed set 46.00 (*0-16-045296-1*) USGPO.

Dept. of the Navy Staff. Navy Acquisition Procedures Supplement. 96p. 1992. ring bd. 125.00 (*1-56726-064-0*) Mgmt Concepts.

***Depta, Victor.** The Gate of Paradise. 255p. 2000. pap. 11.95 (*0-9666608-2-X*) Blair Mtn Pr.

Depta, Victor. The Silence of Blackberries. LC 98-74248. 72p. 1999. pap. 11.95 (*0-9666608-0-3*) Blair Mtn Pr.

Deptula. Preparation for the SAT. 12th ed. 1995. pap. 12.00 (*0-671-89962-7*) PB.

Deptula, Edward J. Arco Preparation for the SAT with Study Planning Software. 11th ed. 640p. 1994. 22.95 (*0-671-52028-8*, Arco) Macmillan Gen Ref.

— Sat & PSAT with Tests on Disk: 1999 Edition. 670p. 1998. pap. 29.95 incl. cd-rom (*0-02-862479-3*, Arco) Macmillan Gen Ref.

Deptula, Edward J., ed. Everything You Need to Score High on the SAT & PSAT. LC 97-81112. 672p. 1998. pap. text 12.95 (*0-02-862465-3*, Arco) Macmillan Gen Ref.

— Preparation for the SAT & PSAT. 12th ed. 640p. 1995. 12.95 (*0-02-860323-0*, Arco) Macmillan Gen Ref.

— Preparation for the SAT & PSAT. 12th ed. 640p. 1995. 22.95 incl. disk (*0-02-860324-9*, Arco) Macmillan Gen Ref.

— SAT 1998. (Illus.). 680p. 1997. 29.95 incl. cd-rom (*0-02-861932-3*) Macmillan.

***Deptula, Judy & Deptula, Lynne.** Painting Blooms & Blossoms. LC 99-16726. (Illus.). 128p. 2000. pap. 24.99 (*0-89134-989-8*, 31460, North Lght Bks) F & W Pubns Inc.

Deptula, Lynne, jt. auth. see Deptula, Judy.

***DePucchio, Ralph. Prophecy to Presidency. v, 46p. 2000. per. 7.99 (*0-9676558-0-3*) Deeds of Christ.**

God spake & I believe. I have created & have acted on what I believe God has called me to to. That is to give a declaration to a nation that has totally red lined the mandates that God has given to His creation. The book includes warnings to four specific groups, the church being one of them. Do not be deceived, God is not mocked. The sin that has become prevalent throughout this nation has reached its point of judgment. That is to say predominant, widely existing, generally practiced & accepted. Before this devasting judgment, enlighten your heart & come to know that God is God of order. That life is a gift. A precious gift that is given to us by God.

Publisher Paid Annotation.

Depue, Anne & Mayer, Becker J. I'd Rather Be Sailing: Photographs & Reflections. LC 96-86637. (I'd Rather Be Ser.). (Illus.). 96p. (Orig.). 1997. pap. 9.95 (*0-8362-2732-8*) Andrews & McMeel.

DePuey, E. Gordon, et al, eds. Cardiac SPECT Imaging. (Illus.). 304p. 1994. text 151.00 (*0-7817-0189-9*) Lppncott W & W.

DePuey, E. Gordon, et al. Cardiac Spect Imaging. 2nd ed. 304p. text 149.95 (*0-7817-2007-9*) Lppncott W & W.

***Deputte, B. L. & Hill, R., eds.** Scientific Meetings of la Societe Francophone de Primatologie & the Primate Society of Great Britain: Societe Francophone de Primatologie, 9th Annual Meeting, Lyon, October, 1997, 10th Annual Meeting, Rousset-sur-Arc. October, 1998; Primate Society of Great Britain, Spring Meeting, Liverpool April, 1999; Abstracts. (Folia Primatologica Ser.: Vol. 70, No. 4, (1999)). (Illus.). 50p. 1999. pap. 25.25 (*3-8055-6935-1*) S Karger.

***Deputy, Allison.** The Song of Enchantment: Poems by Allison Deputy. limited ed. (Illus.). 42p. 1999. pap. 10.00 (*0-9671838-3-9*) Moonwolf Pr.

Deputy, Erby C. Predicting First Grade Reading Achievement: A Study in Reading Readiness. LC 77-176705. (Columbia University. Teachers College. Contributions to Education Ser.: No. 426). reprint ed. 37.50 (*0-404-55426-1*) AMS Pr.

Depuydt, Leo. Conjunction, Contiguity, Contingency: On Relationships Between Events in the Egyptian & Coptic Verba. LC 92-29818. 304p. 1993. text 80.00 (*0-19-508092-0*) OUP.

DePuydt, Peter J., jt. auth. see Ahler, Steven R.

DePuydt, Rita E. Baking with Stevia: Recipes for the Sweet Leaf. LC 96-92989. (Illus.). vi, 100p. (Orig.). 1997. pap. 12.95 (*0-9656073-0-5*) Sun Coast Ent.

— Baking with Stevia II: More Recipes for the Sweet Leaf. 112p. 1998. pap. 12.95 (*0-9656073-1-3*) Sun Coast Ent.

DeQuaine, Lester. Razor Blade Banks: An Illustrated History & Price Guide. LC 98-92965. (Illus.). 59p. 1998. pap. 19.95 (*0-9664487-0-7*) L Dequaine.

***Dequasie, Andrew.** The Diamonds of Kronos. LC 00-190487. 202p. 2000. 25.00 (*0-7388-1780-5*); pap. 18.00 (*0-7388-1781-3*) Xlibris Corp.

Dequasie, Andrew. The Green Flame: Surviving Government Secrecy. LC 91-28935. (Illus.). 232p. 1991. 22.95 (*0-8412-1857-9*) Am Chemical.

***Dequasie, Andrew.** A Lifetime Nature Walk: Always a Babe in the Woods. LC 99-91803. 2000. 25.00 (*0-7388-1280-3*); pap. 18.00 (*0-7388-1281-1*) Xlibris Corp.

— The Spruce Valley Miracle. LC 99-90813. 1999. 25.00 (*0-7388-0536-X*); pap. 18.00 (*0-7388-0537-8*) Xlibris Corp.

— Thirsty. large type ed. LC 99-46552. 354p. 1999. 24.95 (*0-7838-8810-4*, G K Hall Lrg Type) Mac Lib Ref.

— Vermont Mosaic: Whizzers & Other Short Fictional Tales of Vermont. LC 00-190070. 239p. 2000. 25.00 (*0-7388-1470-9*); pap. 18.00 (*0-7388-1471-7*) Xlibris Corp.

Dequeker, J., et al, eds. Bone Mineral Measurements by Photon Absorptiometry: Methodological Problems. 491p. (Orig.). 1988. pap. 87.50 (*90-6186-275-2*, Pub. by Leuven Univ) Coronet Bks.

DeQuesada, A. M., Jr. The Men of Fort Foster: Enlisted Uniforms, Equipments & Artifacts of the United States Armed Forces 1835-1842. (Illus.). 96p. (Orig.). 1996. pap. 14.95 (*1-877704-25-3*) Pioneer Pr.

DeQuesada, A. M., Jr., jt. auth. see Hickox, Ron G.

DeQuesada, Alejandro M., Jr. & Luisi, Vincent. Pinellas County. LC 98-86768. (Images of America Ser.). (Illus.). 128p. 1998. pap. 16.99 (*0-7524-1236-1*) Arcadia Publng.

DeQuille, Dan. History of the Big Bonanza. 488p. 1983. pap. 27.95 (*0-913814-66-0*) Nevada Pubns.

DeQuoy, Alfred. The Irish Wolfhound Guide. 3rd rev. ed. LC 87-91493. (Illus.). 564p. 1987. lib. bdg. 45.00 (*0-9622015-1-0*) M deQuoy.

— The Irish Wolfhound in Competition. LC 80-70114. 287p. 1980. lib. bdg. 30.00 (*0-9622015-0-2*) M deQuoy.

— Irish Wolfhound Saga: Prehistory, Protohistory. Castillo, Glenna D. & Castillo, Edmund, eds. (Illus.). 461p. 1993. lib. bdg. 105.00 (*0-9622015-3-7*) M deQuoy.

Der Aalst, Wil Van, see Van Der Aalst, Wil.

Der Bagdasarian, Nicholas. The Austro-German Rapprochement, 1870-1879: From the Battle of Sedan to the Dual Alliance. LC 74-199. 334p. 1976. 28.50 (*0-8386-1527-9*) Fairleigh Dickinson.

Der Bedrosian, Robert, jt. ed. see Der Bedrosian, Zabel.

Der Bedrosian, Zabel & Der Bedrosian, Robert, eds. A Picture Book of Armenian Miniatures. LC 68-59356. (Illus.). 63p. (Orig.). 1968. pap. 4.95 (*0-935411-03-8*) Natl Assn Arm.

der Berg, Leo Van, see Van der Berg, Leo.

der Berlin, Herausgegeben von, see von der Berlin, Herausgegeben.

Der Bijl, Nicholas Van, see Van Der Bijl, Nicholas.

Der Borg, I. H. Van, see Van Der Borg, I. H.

Der Derian, James, ed. The Virilio Reader. (Reader Ser.). 288p. 1998. 59.95 (*1-55786-652-X*); pap. 24.95 (*1-55786-653-8*) Blackwell Pubs.

Der Derian, James & Shapiro, Michael J. International-Intertextual Relations: Postmodern Readings of World Politics. LC 88-45105. (Issues in World Politics Ser.). 353p. 1989. pap. 25.95 (*0-669-18955-3*) Lxngtn Bks.

der Dunk, Klaus Von, see Buff, Wolfram & Von der Dunk, Klaus.

Der Eijk, Cees Van, see Van Der Eijk, Cees.

Der, G. & Everitt, B. S. Handbook of Statistical Analysis Using SAS. 160p. 1996. per. 39.95 (*0-412-71050-1*, BR56378, Chap & Hall CRC) CRC Pr.

Der Heide, F. Meyer Auf, see Auf der Heide, F. Meyer.

Der Heide, Lisl Auf, see Auf der Heide, Lisl.

***der Heyde, Claudia Brinker-von & Largier, Niklaus, eds.** Homo Medietas: Aufsatze zu Religiostat, Literatur und Denkformen des Menschen Vom Mittelalter Bis in die Neuzeit Festschrift fur Alois Maria Haas Zum 65. Geburtstag. 670p. 1998. 96.95 (*3-906760-81-2*, Pub. by P Lang) P Lang Pubng.

der Hoek, Peter Van, see Van der Hoek, Peter, ed.

der Hoogt, Madelyn Van, see Van der Hoogt, Madelyn.

Der-Hovanessian, tr. see Banus, Maria.

***Der-Hovanessian, Diana.** Any Day Now. LC 98-51952. 96p. 1999. pap. 12.95 (*1-878818-75-9*, Pub. by Sheep Meadow) U Pr of New Eng.

Der-Hovanessian, Diana. The Circle Dancers. LC 96-30893. 112p. (Orig.). 1997. pap. 12.95 (*1-878818-55-4*, Pub. by Sheep Meadow) U Pr of New Eng.

Der Hovanessian, Diana. How to Choose Your Past. LC 78-67675. 1978. 6.95 (*0-933706-00-6*); pap. 3.95 (*0-933706-01-4*) Ararat Pr.

Der-Hovanessian, Diana. Selected Poems. LC 94-1260. 77p. (Orig.). 1994. pap. 12.95 (*1-878818-27-9*, Pub. by Sheep Meadow) U Pr of New Eng.

Der Hovanessian, Diana, pref. Gorbachev in Concert (& Other Poems) 60p. 1991. pap. 6.95 (*0-918680-75-1*) Griffon House.

Der Hucht, Karel A. Van, see Van Der Hucht, Karel A., ed.

der Hulst, Harry & Ritter, Nancy A., eds. The Syllable: Views & Facts. LC 99-26547. (Studies in Generative Grammar). 777p. 1999. 192.30 (*3-11-016274-1*) De Gruyter.

Der Kaloustian, V. M. & Kurban, A. K. Genetic Diseases of the Skin. LC 78-25740. (Illus.). 1979. 195.00 (*0-387-09151-3*) Spr-Verlag.

Der Kaloustian, Vazken M., jt. ed. see Tewik, Ted L.

der Kamp, Leo J. Van, see International Symposium on Educational Testing (3d.

der Kamp, Leo J. Van, see De Gruijter, D. N.

der Kamp, Leo J. Van, see De Gruijter, D. N. & Van der Kamp, Leo J.

Der Kamp, Leo Van, ed. see Mooijaart, Ab, et al.

Der Kooi, Cornelis Van, see Van Der Kooi, Cornelis, ed.

der Korst, M. van, see Van der Korst, M.

der Laan, Ray Van, see Van der Laan, Ray.

der Lecq, Fieke Van, see Van der Lecq, Fieke.

der Leeuw, Gerardus Van, see Van der Leeuw, Gerardus.

Der Linde, Ada Van, see Van Der Linde, Ada.

der Linden, Robert van, see Van der Linden, Robert.

Der Ling. Golden Phoenix. LC 70-101799. (Short Story Index Reprint Ser.). (Illus.). 1977. 20.95 (*0-8369-3187-4*) Ayer.

der Lippe, Anna L. von, see Skoe, Eva & Von Der Lippe, Anna L.

der Lube, Barbara von, see von der Luhe, Barbara.

Der Manuelian, Lucy & Eiland, Murray L. Weavers, Merchants, & Kings: The Inscribed Rugs of Armenia. LC 84-48115. (Illus.). 216p. (Orig.). 1984. 40.00 (*0-295-96548-7*) U of Wash Pr.

Der Manuelian, Peter. Hieroglyphs from A to Z. (gr. 4-7). 1996. pap. text 5.99 (*0-590-40008-8*) Scholastic Inc.

— Living in the Past: Studies in Archaism of the Egyptian Twenty-Sixth Dynasty. LC 92-26097. (Studies in Egyptology). (Illus.). 488p. 1994. 144.50 (*0-7103-0461-7*) Routledge.

Der Manuelian, Peter, ed. see Brovarski, Edward.

Der Marderosian, Ara H. & Liberti, Lawrence E. Natural Product Medicine: A Scientific Guide to Foods, Drugs, Cosmetics. LC 85-62568. (Illus.). 400p. 1988. reprint ed. pap. 124.00 (*0-608-05868-8*, 205983500007) Bks Demand.

der Marel, J. Van, see Van der Marel, J.

Der Maslburg, Christoph Von, see Eckmiller, Rolf & Von Der Maslburg, Christoph, eds.

der Meer, Cor Van, see Rees, Roy & Van der Meer, Cor.

Der Meer, J. W. Van, see Van Der Meer, J. W., ed.

der Meer, L. B. Van, see Van der Meer, L. B.

der Meer, Patrick Van, see Van der Meer, Patrick.

Der, Mehden, see Von Der Mehden, Fred R., pseud.

der Merwe, Dana va, see van der Merwe, Dana.

der Merwe, Derek van, see Bradfield, Graham & van der Merwe, Derek, eds.

Der Merwe, Hendrik W. Van, see Hund, John & Van Der Merwe, Hendrik W.

Der Merwe, Nan Van, see Van Der Merwe, Nan.

der Meulen, D. Van, see Van der Meulen, D.

Der Musikwelt, Jahrbuch. The Yearbook of the Music World. 696p. 1993. reprint ed. lib. bdg. 109.00 (*0-7812-9559-9*) Rprt Serv.

Der Nersessian, Sirarpie. Miniature Painting in the Armenian Kingdom of Cilicia from the Twelfth to the Fourteenth Century, 2 vols. LC 92-14829. (Dumbarton Oaks Studies: No. 31). (Illus.). 882p. 1993. 165.00 (*0-88402-202-1*, DEMP, Dumbarton Rsch Lib) Dumbarton Oaks.

Der Osten, Gert Von, see Von Der Osten, Gert.

der Plancke, Chantal van, see Van der Plancke, Chantal.

Der Poel, M. G. Van, see Van Der Poel, M. G.

der Pot, Johan Hendril Jacob van, see van der Pot, Johan Hendrik Jacob.

der Put, Marius van, see Van Der Put, Marius.

Der Reis, Leo Van, see Van Der Reis, Leo, ed.

Der Reis, Leo Van, see Williams, Erin & Van Der Reis, Leo.

Der Schaft, Arjan Van, see Van Der Schaft, Arjan.

Der Schulenburg, Fritz Von, see Vickers, Hugo.

Der Schulenburg, Fritz Von, see Benge, Sophie.

der Schulenburg, J. M. Graf Von, see Graf von der Schulenburg, J. M., ed.

Der Sijde, Peter Van, see Tomic, Welko & Van der Sijde, Peter.

Der Societat, Herausgegeben Von, see Von Der Societat, Herausgegeben.

Der Steeren, Paul Van, see Van Der Steeren, Paul.

der Toorn, Karel Van, see Van der Toorn, Karel.

der Toorn, Karel Van, see Platvoet, Jan & Van der Toorn, Karel, eds.

der Toorn, Karel Van, see Van der Toorn, Karel.

Der, Van, see Bergman, J. & Van Der.

der Vat, Dan Van, see Gardiner, Robin.

Der Veen, Alle-Jan Van, see Dewilde, P.

Der Veen, Alle-Jan Van, see Dewilde, P. & Van Der Veen, Alle-Jan.

Der Veen, Alle-Jan Van, see Dewilde, P., ed.

der Ven, Thea S. Van, see Colgin, Mary L.

der Ven, Thea S. Van, see Colgin, Mary L. & Van der Ven, Thea S.

der Vossen, Ham Van, see Van der Vossen, Ham.

der Waal, Cornelis Van, see Van der Waal, Cornelis.

der Wagen, Van, see Van der Wagen.

Der Wal, N. Van, see Van Der Wal, N., ed.

der Watt, J. G. Van, see Van der Watt, J. G.

Der-Wei Wang, David. Fictional Realism in Twentieth-Century China: Mao Dun, Lao She, Shem Congwen. 384p. 1992. text 57.50 (*0-231-07656-8*) Col U Pr.

Der Weijer, P. G. Van, see Van Der Weijer, P. G.

der Wissenschaften, Brandenburgischen Akademie, jt. auth. see von der Berlin, Herausgegeben.

Der Wolf, J. C. Van, see Letiche, H. K.

Der Zweerde, Evert Van, see Van Der Zweerde, Evert.

Dera, J. Marine Physics. (Oceanography Ser.: Vol. 53). 516p. 1991. 245.00 (*0-444-98716-9*) Elsevier.

DeRaad, Carolyn, jt. auth. see Lederman, Ed.

Derache, R., ed. see Commission of the European Communities.

DeRadwan, C. The Secret of Mind-Power & How to Use It. 1991. lib. bdg. 79.95 (*0-8490-4961-X*) Gordon Pr.

DeRaedt, Luc, jt. ed. see Bergadano, Francesco.

Derains. ICC Awards, 3 vols., Set. 1997. lib. bdg. 500.00 (*90-411-0495-X*) Kluwer Law Intl.

Derains, Yves & Arnaldez, Jean-Jacques, eds. Collection of ICC Arbitral Awards, 1986-1990: Recueil des Sentences Arbitrales de la CCI, 1986-1990. LC 93-30240. (ICC Publication Ser.: Vol. 514). 1993. 173.50 (*90-6544-670-2*) Kluwer Law Intl.

Derains, Yves & Schwartz, Eric A. A Guide to the New ICC Rules of Arbitration. LC 98-16779. (International Court of Arbitration Ser.). 480p. 1998. text 135.00 (*90-411-0595-6*, 946-A) ICC Pub.

Derakhshani, Ali-Akbar. The Memoirs of General Ali-Akbar Derakhshani. LC 94-94333. (PER., Illus.). 570p. (Orig.). 1994. pap. 19.95 (*0-936347-53-8*) IBEX.

Derakhshani, Mana. Voix Francophones: Le Monde Francophone en Textes. (Bridging the Gap Ser.). (FRE.). (C). 1994. text 36.95 (*0-8384-4626-4*) Heinle & Heinle.

D'Eramo, Nello. Neurological Symptoms in Blood Diseases. Iliffe, John, tr. LC 72-1871. 297p. reprint ed. pap. 92.10 (*0-608-12372-2*, 205206900033) Bks Demand.

DeRamus, Barnett. From Juby to Arras: Engagement in Saint-Exupery. 182p. (C). 1990. lib. bdg. 39.00 (*0-8191-7725-3*) U Pr of Amer.

DeRamus, Dorothy, jt. ed. see Brown, John.

Deran, Elisabeth. Low-Cost Marketing Strategies: Field-Tested Techniques for Tight Budgets. LC 86-30640. 160p. 1987. 47.95 (*0-275-92341-X*, C2341, Praeger Pubs) Greenwood.

Deranian, H. Martin, tr. & rev. see Deranian, Marderos.

Deranian, Marderos. Hussenig: The Origin, History & Destruction of an Armenian Town. rev. ed. Deranian, H. Martin, tr. from ARM. & rev. by. LC 94-35369. (Illus.). 1994. 24.95 (*0-935411-12-7*) Natl Assn Arm.

Deranja, Michael, jt. auth. see Cornell, Joseph.

Deransart, P., et al, eds. Attribute Grammars & Their Applications: International Workshop WAGA Paris, France, September 19-21, 1990 Proceedings. (Lecture Notes in Computer Science Ser.: Vol. 461). viii, 358p. 1990. 40.00 (*0-387-53101-7*) Spr-Verlag.

— Programming Language Implementation & Logic Programming: International Workshop PLILP '90 Linkoping, Sweden, August 20-22, 1990 Proceedings. (Lecture Notes in Computer Science Ser.: Vol. 456). viii, 401p. 1990. 43.00 (*0-387-53010-X*) Spr-Verlag.

— Programming Languages Implementation & Logic Programming. (Lecture Notes in Computer Science Ser.: Vol. 348). 299p. 1989. 44.95 (*0-387-50820-1*) Spr-Verlag.

Deransart, P., et al. Attribute Grammars. (Lecture Notes in Computer Science Ser.: Vol. 323). ix, 232p. 1988. 33.00 (*0-387-50056-1*) Spr-Verlag.

Deransart, Pierre, et al. Prolog: The Standard: Reference Manual. LC 96-15173. 300p. 1996. pap. text 44.95 (*3-540-59304-7*) Spr-Verlag.

Deransert, Pierre & Maluszynski, Jan. A Grammatical View of Logic Programming. 420p. 1993. 58.00 (*0-262-04140-5*) MIT Pr.

***D'Erasmo, Stacey.** Tea. LC 99-33337. 317p. 2000. 21.95 (*1-56512-243-7*, 72243) Algonquin Bks.

— Tea. 2001. pap. 13.95 (*0-684-87404-0*, WSP) PB.

D'Erasmo, Stacey, jt. auth. see Bingham, Robert.

Derato. Auto Brakes. 1988. 45.66 (*0-07-909010-9*) McGraw.

Derato, Frank C. Automotive Electrical & Electronic Systems. 320p. 1985. pap. text 59.50 (*0-07-079803-6*) McGraw.

— Automotive Electrical & Electronic Systems. 2nd ed. LC 93-35420. 1993. pap. text, student ed. write for info. (*0-02-800412-4*); pap. text, student ed. write for info. (*0-02-800402-7*) Glencoe.

— Victor W. Page: Automotive & Aviation Pioneer. LC 91-71257. (Illus.). 343p. (Orig.). 1991. pap. 24.95 (*0-9629323-0-2*) Cranbury Pubns.

Derber. Wilding, Money, Murder & the American Dream. 189p. 1995. pap. text 12.95 (*0-312-13290-5*) St Martin.

***Derber, Charles.** Corporation Nation: How Corporations are Taking Over Our Lives & What We Can Do About It. 384p. 2000. pap. 14.95 (*0-312-25461-X*) St Martin.

Derber, Charles. Corporation Nation: How Corporations Are Taking over Our Lives & Wht We Can Do about It. LC 98-23514. 384p. 1998. text 24.95 (*0-312-19288-6*) St Martin.

***Derber, Charles.** The Pursuit of Attention: Power & Ego in Everyday Life. 2nd ed. LC 99-56755. 160p. 2000. 25.00 (*0-19-513550-4*); 10.95 (*0-19-513549-0*) OUP.

Derber, Charles. The Pursuit of Attention: Power & Individualism in Everyday Life. 110p. 1979. pap. 21.95 (*0-87073-885-2*) Transaction Pubs.

— The Wilding of America: How Greed & Violence Are Eroding Our Nation's Character. LC 95-3630. (Contemporary Social Issues Ser.). 192p. 1995. text 22.95 (*0-312-14069-X*) St Martin.

Derber, Charles, et al. Power in the Highest Degree: Professionals, Capitalism, & the Rise of a New Mandarin Order. 287p. 1990. text 19.95 (*0-19-503778-2*) OUP.

— What's Left? Radical Politics in the Postcommunist Era. LC 94-36925. 240p. (C). 1995. 40.00 (*0-87023-953-8*); pap. 17.95 (*0-87023-954-6*) U of Mass Pr.

Derber, Milton. The American Idea of Industrial Democracy, 1865-1965. LC 70-100376. 569p. reprint ed. pap. 176.40 (*0-8357-5371-9*, 202021600016) Bks Demand.

— Changing Values in American Industrial Relations, 1933-1985. (Occasional Publications: No. 156). 54p. 1986. 3.00 (*0-318-21794-5*) U Hawaii.

— Competing Values in American Industrial Relations. (Occasional Publications: No. 160). 16p. 1987. 3.00 (*0-318-23505-6*) U Hawaii.

— Labor in Illinois: The Affluent Years, 1945-80. LC 88-1339. 472p. 1989. 47.50 (*0-252-01529-0*) U of Ill Pr.

Derbers, Milton & Stein, Leon, eds. The Aged & Society. LC 79-8665. (Growing Old Ser.). (Illus.). 1980. reprint ed. lib. bdg. 24.95 (*0-405-12783-9*) Ayer.

Derbes, Anne. Picturing the Passion in Late Medieval Italy: Narrative Painting, Franciscan Ideologies & the Levant. LC 95-10981. (Illus.). 286p. (C). 1996. text 80.00 (*0-521-47481-7*) Cambridge U Pr.

— Picturing the Passion in Late Medieval Italy: Narrative Painting, Franciscan Ideologies, & the Levant (Illus.). 286p. (C). 1998. reprint ed. pap. text 22.95 (*0-521-63926-3*) Cambridge U Pr.

Derbolav, Josef, jt. auth. see Ikeda, Daisaku.

Derby, B., jt. ed. see Lee, W. E.

Derby, Blanche C. My Wild Friends: Free Food from Field & Forest. LC 96-90924. (Illus.). 264p. (Orig.) 1997. pap., ring bd. 22.50 (*0-9626131-2-6*) White Star MA.

Derby, Charles E. Inspired by Dreams: Selections from the Derby Collection. (Illus.). 96p. (Orig.). 1995. pap. 25.00 (*0-9626131-1-8*) White Star MA.

***Derby, Chet E.** Rebel Flight. i, 250p. 1999. 12.95 (*0-9677072-0-X*) Derby Hill.

***Derby, Eddy A., et al, eds.** Optomechanical Engineering & Vibration Control. 1999. pap. text 111.00 (*0-8194-3272-5*) SPIE.

Derby, George H. Phoenixiana. 1992. reprint ed. lib. bdg. 75.00 (*0-7812-5025-0*) Rprt Serv.

— Phoenixiana: or Sketches & Burlesques. LC 72-174198. reprint ed. 42.50 (*0-404-05045-X*) AMS Pr.

Derby, George H., jt. auth. see Carson, James H.

Derby, Harry L. The Hand Cannons of Imperial Japan. LC 82-90099. (Illus.). 304p. 1981. 37.95 (*0-940424-00-2*) Derby Pub.

***Derby Historical Society Staff.** Derby. (Images of America Ser.). 128p. 1999. pap. 18.99 (*0-7385-0254-5*) Arcadia Publng.

Derby, Janice. Are You My Friend? LC 92-38779. (Illus.). 40p. (J). (ps-3). 1993. 11.99 (*0-8361-3609-8*) Herald Pr.

Derby, Jennifer, jt. auth. see Puterbaugh, Parke.

Derby, Jennifer, ed. see Puterbaugh, Parke.

Derby, Kathleen, jt. auth. see Machale, D. J.

Derby, Ken. Robert Falcon Scott. (YA). (gr. 5 up). Date not set. pap. 6.99 (*0-88092-552-3*) Royal Fireworks.

***Derby, Loyd P., et al.** Sales & Leases on California Commercial Law Practice - 7/99 Update, 2 vols. Peyerwold, David, ed. LC 93-70675. 444p. 1999. ring bd. 46.00 (*0-7626-0351-8*, BU-32074) Cont Ed Bar-CA.

Derby, Mary P., jt. auth. see Buckingham, Robert W.

Derby, Pat. Grams, Her Boyfriend, My Family & Me. LC 93-73169. 256p. (YA). (gr. 5 up). 1994. 16.00 (*0-374-38131-3*) FS&G.

— Grams, Her Boyfriend, My Family & Me. 208p. (YA). (gr. 5 up). 1997. pap. 5.95 (*0-374-42790-9*) FS&G.

Derby, Pat. Grams, Her Boyfriend, My Family, & Me. LC 93-73169. 1997. 11.05 (*0-606-11413-0*, Pub. by Turtleback) Demco.

— Visiting Miss Pierce. 144p. (J). (gr. 4-7). 1989. pap. 3.50 (*0-374-48156-3*) FS&G.

Derby, Patricia, et al. New York Legal Assistant Handbook. 772p. 1996. ring bd. 89.98 (*0-938065-96-3*) James Pub Santa Ana.

***Derby, Sally.** Bluebird in the Snow. 2001. text 16.95 (*0-8050-6420-6*) St Martin.

Derby, Sally. Jacob & the Stranger. LC 93-11022. (Illus.). 32p. (J). (ps-3). 1994. 11.95 (*0-395-66897-2*) Ticknor & Flds Bks Yng Read.

— King Kenrick's Splinter. LC 94-4360. (Illus.). 32p. (J). 1994. 14.95 (*0-8027-8322-8*); lib. bdg. 15.85 (*0-8027-8323-6*) Walker & Co.

— Mi Escalera. De la Vega, Eida, tr. LC 97-43713. (SPA., Illus.). 32p. (J). (ps-4). 1998. 15.95 (*1-880000-74-1*); pap. 6.95 (*1-880000-75-X*) Lee & Low Bks.

— The Mouse Who Owned the Sun. LC 91-40965. (Illus.). 32p. (J). (ps-3). 1993. lib. bdg. 14.95 (*0-02-766965-3*, Four Winds Pr) S&S Childrens.

— My Steps. LC 96-33847. (Illus.). 32p. (J). (ps-4). 1999. 14.95 (*1-880000-40-7*) Lee & Low Bks.

— My Steps. LC 96-33847. (Illus.). 32p. (J). (gr. 1-4). 1999. pap. 6.95 (*1-880000-84-9*, Pub. by Lee & Low Bks) Publishers Group.

***Derby, Sally.** Taiko on a Windy Night. LC 99-47549. 2001. text 15.95 (*0-8050-6401-X*) St Martin.

Derbyshire, A. Leslie. Mastering Management: Practical Procedures for Effective Business Control. LC 80-83028. 300p. 1981. 19.98 (*0-88290-159-1*, 2046) Horizon Utah.

Derbyshire, Desmond C. Hixkaryana. (Descriptive Grammars Ser.). 208p. 1979. pap. 72.50 (*0-7099-0877-6*, Pub. by C Helm) Routldge.

— Hixkaryana & Linguistic Typology. LC 85-50398. (Publications in Linguistics: No. 76). 265p. (Orig.). 1985. pap. 24.00 (*0-88312-082-8*) S I L Intl.

Derbyshire, Desmond C. & Pullman, Geoffrey K., eds. Handbook of Amazonian Languages, Vol. 1. (Illus.). xiv, 642p. 1986. lib. bdg. 152.35 (*0-89925-124-2*) Mouton.

— Handbook of Amazonian Languages, Vol. 2. (Illus.). x, 474p. 1990. lib. bdg. 144.65 (*0-89925-421-7*) Mouton.

Derbyshire, Desmond C. & Pullum, G. K., eds. Handbook of Amazonian Languages, Vol. 3. xii, 517p. (C). 1991. lib. bdg. 183.10 (*0-89925-813-1*) Mouton.

Derbyshire, E., jt. ed. see Singhvi, A. K.

Derbyshire, Edward D., ed. Genesis & Properties of Collapsible Soils: Proceedings of the NATA ARW, Loughborough, U. K. 11-14 April, 1994. (NATA Advanced Science Institutes Ser.: C). 424p. (C). 1995. text 217.50 (*0-7923-3587-2*) Kluwer Academic.

— Geomorphology & Climate. LC 75-4523. 525p. reprint ed. 162.80 (*0-8357-9899-2*, 201602600097) Bks Demand.

— Wind Blown Sediments in the Quaternary Record. (Quaternary Proceedings Ser.). 104p. 1995. pap. text 100.00 (*0-471-95860-3*, ES00) Wiley.

Derbyshire, Edward D., et al, eds. Landslides in the Thick Loess Terrain of Northwest China. LC 99-24962. 352p. 2000. 245.00 (*0-471-97349-1*) Wiley.

Derbyshire, Edward D. & Owen, L. A., eds. Quaternary of the Karakoram & Himalya. (Annals of Geomorphology Ser.: Suppl. 76). (Illus.). 255p. 1989. pap. text 107.50 (*3-443-21076-7*, Pub. by Gebruder Borntraeger) Balogh.

Derbyshire, Ian. The Hutchinson Dictionary of World History. 699p. 1994. lib. bdg. 49.50 (*0-87436-765-4*) ABC-CLIO.

Derbyshire, Ian, jt. auth. see Derbyshire, J. Denis.

Derbyshire, Ian D. India. 2nd rev. ed. LC 96-192289. (World Bibliographical Ser.). 390p. 1995. lib. bdg. 90.00 (*1-85109-200-5*) ABC-CLIO.

Derbyshire, J. Denis & Derbyshire, Ian. Political Systems of the World. 2nd ed. 698p. 1996. text 95.00 (*0-312-16172-7*) St Martin.

Derbyshire, J. Denis, et al. Encyclopedia of World Political Systems, 2 vols. LC 99-34093. 800p. 1999. text 185.00 (*0-7656-8025-4*, Sharpe Ref) M E Sharpe.

Derbyshire, John. Seeing Calvin Coolidge in a Dream: A Novel. 1997. pap. 11.95 (*0-312-15649-9*, St Martin Griffin) St Martin.

Derbyshire, Philip, ed. In Foucault's Wake: Essays on Power, Resistance & Subjectivity. 256p. (C). 1997. pap. 18.50 (*0-85315-801-0*, Pub. by Lawrence & Wishart) NYU Pr.

Derbyshire, Robert C. Medical Licensure & Discipline in the United States. LC 78-17712. 183p. 1978. reprint ed. lib. bdg. 59.50 (*0-313-20528-0*, DEML, Greenwood Pr) Greenwood.

Derbyshire, William W. A Basic Reference Grammar of Slovene. 154p. (Orig.). (C). 1993. pap. text 16.95 (*0-89357-236-5*) Slavica.

Derche. Etudes de Textes Francais, 6 tomes, Set. (FRE.). 47.90 (*0-8288-9545-7*, F140641) Fr & Eur.

Dercksen, J. G. Old Assyrian Copper Trade in Anatolia. LC 96-140142. x, 280p. (Orig.). 1996. pap. text 59.50 (*90-6258-076-9*, Pub. by Netherlands Inst) Eisenbrauns.

***Dercksen, J. G., ed.** Trade & Finance in Ancient Mesopotamia: Proceedings of the First MOS Symposium. (MOS Studies 1). 205p. 1999. pap. text 42.00 (*90-6258-085-8*, Pub. by Netherlands Inst) Eisenbrauns.

***Dercon, Chris.** Avery Preesman. 1999. pap. text 35.00 (*90-5662-119-X*) NAi Uitgevers.

Dercum, Edna S. It's Easy, Edna, It's Downhill All the Way. 2nd rev. ed. Bullard, Jean V., ed. (Illus.). 213p. reprint ed. pap. 16.95 (*0-9606460-0-0*) Sirpos Pr.

Dercy, Palat dit, jt. auth. see Le Sueur, Jean-Francois.

Derdak, Tom, ed. International Directory of Company Histories, Vol. 1. 758p. 1988. 161.00 (*0-912289-10-4*) St James Pr.

Derdarian, Mae M. & Meghrouni, Virginia. Vergeen: A Survivor of the Armenian Genocide. LC 97-158293. xiii, 270 p. 1996. write for info. (*1-888156-02-3*) Atmus Pr.

Derderian, Robert L. & Case, Deborah A., eds. Perceptions. LC 94-72201. (Illus.). 320p. 1995. text 45.00 (*1-885206-07-0*, Iliad Pr) Cader Pubng.

Derderian, Sharon. Reflections, Cader Publishing. 132p. 1991. 45.00 (*0-8187-0148-X*) Harlo Press.

Derderian, Tom. Boston Marathon: The First Century of the World's Premier Running Event. 2nd ed. LC 95-39944. (Illus.). 664p. 1995. pap. 21.95 (*0-88011-479-7*, PDER0479) Human Kinetics.

Derdzinski, A. Geometry of the Standard Model of Elementary Particles. Beiglbock, W. et al, eds. (Texts & Monographs in Physics). 212p. (C). 1992. 53.95 (*0-387-54356-2*) Spr-Verlag.

Dere, jt. auth. see Stults, Kenneth.

Dere, Nicole. The Naked Truth. 1998. pap. 9.95 (*1-897809-50-6*) Silver Moon.

***Dere, Nicole.** Naked Truth Ii: The Whip Hand. 1999. pap. text 9.99 (*1-897809-63-8*) Silver Moon.

Dere, Nicole. Voyage of Shame. 1998. pap. text 8.95 (*1-897809-40-9*) Silver Moon.

Derecskey, Susan. French Made Simple. rev. ed. LC 86-21803. (Illus.). 336p. 1990. pap. 12.95 (*0-385-26521-2*) Doubleday.

— The Hungarian Cookbook: With a Note on Wines by Charles G. Derecskey. 60th ed. LC 87-45135. (Illus.). 288p. 1987. pap. 17.00 (*0-06-091437-8*, PL/1437, Perennial) HarperTrade.

Deredita, John F., tr. see Maura, Juan F.

D

An Asterisk (*) at the beginning of an entry indicates that the title is appearing for the first time.

Derefeldt, Gunilla, et al. Colour Vision Deficiencies: Matching & Confusion of Computer Colours. (Illus.). 67p. (Orig.). (C). 1995. pap. text 30.00 (*0-7881-2176-6*) DIANE Pub.

DeRegniers, Beatrice, jt. auth. see Schenck.

Deregowski, J. B., et al, eds. Expiscations in Cross-Cultural Psychology. viii, 456p. 1983. pap. 60.75 (*90-265-0450-0*) Swets.

Derek, Edwin. Rowdy's Raiders. large type ed. (Linford Western Library Ser.). 272p. 1997. pap. 16.99 (*0-7089-5131-7*, Linford) Ulverscroft.

Derek, Kelly. A Layman's Introduction to Robotics. (Illus.). 220p. 1986. text 27.95 (*0-89433-265-1*) Petrocelli.

Derek Lovejoy Partnership Staff & Davis Langdon & Everest Staff. Spon's Landscape & External Works Price Book, 1997. 16th ed. 1996. mass mkt. 105.95 (*0-419-22220-0*, E & FN Spon) Routledge.

***Derelanko, Michael J.** Toxicologist's Pocket Handbook. 256p. 2000. per. 39.95 (*0-8493-0009-6*) CRC Pr.

Derelanko, Michael J. & Hollinger, Mannfred A., eds. Handbook of Toxicology. LC 95-8043. (Illus.). 976p. 1995. boxed set 159.95 (*0-8493-8668-3*, 8668) CRC Pr.

Deremer, Dale. Water Flying Concepts: An Advanced Text on Wilderness Water Flying. 2nd ed. LC 89-91576. (Illus.). 288p. 1997. pap. 19.95 (*0-9622159-1-0*) D De Remer.

DeRemer, Dale & Baj, Cesare. Seaplane Operations: Basic & Advanced Techniques for Floatplanes, Amphibians & Flying Boats from Around the World. (Illus.). 450p. (Orig.). (C). 1996. pap. write for info. (*0-9622159-4-5*) D De Remer.

DeRemer, Dale & McLean, Donald W. Global Navigation for Pilots: International Flight Techniques & Procedures. 2nd rev. ed. LC 94-210279. (Illus.). 370p. (Orig.). 1998. pap. text 29.95 (*1-56027-312-7*, ASA-GNP-2) ASA Inc.

DeRemer, Kathleen R. HealthMate Medical Planner: A Practical Guide for Taking Control of Your Health & Having Your Medical Records Always Available...Even When Your Doctor Isn't. LC 97-65096. 1997. ring bd. 29.95 (*0-9656350-5-8*) Six Ponies Pr.

Deremer, Susan. Atlanta - an Artist's Sketchbook. 94p. (Orig.). 1997. pap. 18.00 (*1-884824-11-0*, Timonier Bks) Tryon Pubng.

Deren, Barry J., et al. The Economics of Project Analysis: A Practitioner's Guide. (EDI Technical Materials Ser.). 336p. 1991. pap. 30.00 (*0-8213-1751-2*, 11751) World Bank.

Deren, Jane M., jt. ed. see Hayes, Christopher L.

Deren, Maya. Divine Horsemen: The Living Gods of Haiti. LC 83-16228. (Illus.). 350p. (C). 1984. reprint ed. pap. 16.00 (*0-914232-63-0*, Documentext) McPherson & Co.

***Deren, Maya.** Essential Deren: Complete Film Writings. 2000. pap. 18.00 (*0-929701-65-8*) McPherson & Co.

Deren, S. & Finkelstein, R. J., eds. Themes in Contemporary Physics II: Essays in Honor of Julian Schwinger's 70th Birthday. 104p. (C). 1989. text 54.00 (*9971-5-0961-X*) World Scientific Pub.

Derenbourg, Hartwig. Les Manuscrits Arabes de l'Escurial Decrits, Vol. 1. (Publications De 'Ecole Des Langues Orientales Vivantes Ser. No. 2: Vol. X). xliii, 525p. 1976. reprint ed. write for info. (*3-487-06091-4*) G Olms Pubs.

Derendorf, Hartmut, jt. auth. see Mutschler, Ernst.

Derendorf, Hartmut & Hochhaus, Gunther, eds. Handbook of Pharmacokinetic Pharmacodynamic Correlation. LC 94-22365. 496p. 1995. boxed set 179.95 (*0-8493-8303-X*) CRC Pr.

Dereniak, E. L. & Crowe, D. G. Optical Radiation Detectors. LC 84-7356. (Pure & Applied Optics Ser.: No. 1-349). 320p. 1984. 120.00 (*0-471-89797-3*) Wiley.

Dereniak, Eustace L. & Boreman, G. D. Infrared Detectors & Systems. LC 96-212. 592p. 1996. 89.95 (*0-471-12209-2*) Wiley.

Dereniak, Eustace L. & Sampson, Robert E., eds. Infrared Detectors & Focal Plane Arrays V, Vol. 3379. LC 98-226773. 642p. 1998. 107.00 (*0-8194-2828-0*) SPIE.

Derenne. Play Ball. 1993. mass mkt. 23.25 (*0-314-02575-8*) West Pub.

— Power Baseball. 1992. mass mkt. 20.00 (*0-314-01849-2*) West Pub.

Derenne, Eudore. Les Proces D'impiete Intentes Aux Philosophes a Athenes Au Vme & Au Ivme Siecles. LC 75-13260. (History of Ideas in Ancient Greece Ser.). (FRE.). 1976. reprint ed. 19.95 (*0-405-07302-X*) Ayer.

Derenne, Jackqueline, tr. see Ramond, Pierre.

Derenne, Jean-Philippe, et al, eds. Acute Respiratory Failure in Chronic Obstructive Pulmonary Disease. LC 96-2512. (Lung Biology in Health & Disease Ser.: No. 92). (Illus.). 952p. 1996. text 250.00 (*0-8247-9487-7*) Dekker.

Derensbourg, Edwin. Liberated Mind. 1997. pap. 8.99 (*1-56229-476-8*) Pneuma Life Pub.

DeRenzis, Roxanne & Feix Alberts, Emma, eds. Traveled Paths: An Anthology of Prose & Poetry. LC 98-67150. 135p. 1998. pap. 13.95 (*0-9638215-7-1*, KELLS-0612) Kells Media.

Derera, N. F., ed. Preharvest Field Sprouting in Cereals. LC 87-32553. 192p. 1989. 110.00 (*0-8493-6848-0*, SB189, CRC Reprint) Franklin.

DERERIAN & Drederian, Robert, eds. Crossroads. (Illus.). 236p. 1999. 49.95 (*1-885206-66-6*) Cader Pubng.

Dereshinsky, Ralph M., et al. The NLRB & Secondary Boycotts. rev. ed. LC 81-52616. (Labor Relations & Public Policy Ser.: No. 4). 349p. 1981. pap. 22.00 (*0-89546-027-0*) U PA Ctr Hum Res.

***Deresiewicz, William, et al, eds.** Perspecta 29: The Yale Architectural Journal "Into the Fire" (Illus.). 120p. 1998. pap. text 20.00 (*0-262-54092-4*) MIT Pr.

Dereske, Jo. Cut & Dry. 352p. 1997. mass mkt. 5.99 (*0-440-22222-2*) Dell.

— Final Notice: A Miss Zukas Mystery Bk 3. (Miss Zukas Mystery Ser.). 240p. 1998. mass mkt. 5.99 (*0-380-78245-6*, Avon Bks) Morrow Avon.

— Miss Zukas & Island Murd. 224p. 1995. mass mkt. 5.99 (*0-380-77031-8*, Avon Bks) Morrow Avon.

— Miss Zukas & Library M. 224p. 1994. mass mkt. 5.99 (*0-380-77030-X*, Avon Bks) Morrow Avon.

— Miss Zukas & Raven. LC 96-96492. 256p. 1996. mass mkt. 5.99 (*0-380-78243-X*, Avon Bks) Morrow Avon.

— Miss Zukas & Stroke of D. (Miss Zukas Ser.: No. 3). 224p. 1995. mass mkt. 5.99 (*0-380-77033-4*, Avon Bks) Morrow Avon.

***Dereske, Jo.** Miss Zukas in Death's Shadow. 224p. 1999. mass mkt. 5.99 (*0-380-80472-7*, Avon Bks) Morrow Avon.

— Miss Zukas Shelves the Evidence. 2000. mass mkt. 5.99 (*0-380-80474-3*) Morrow Avon.

Dereske, Jo. Out of Circulation: Miss. LC 97-93011. (Miss Zukas Ser.). 212p. 1997. mass mkt. 5.99 (*0-380-78244-8*, Avon Bks) Morrow Avon.

— Short Cut: A Ruby Crane Mystery. 336p. 1998. mass mkt. 5.99 (*0-440-22223-0*) Dell.

Dereske, Jo, et al. ULRO: Paintings by Adam. unabridged ed. Stoneking, Jason, ed. (Illus.). 24p. (Orig.). 1997. pap. 8.95 (*0-9658336-0-7*) Adam Studio.

Deresky, Helen. International Management. LC 93-1298. 656p. (C). 1997. pap. 78.00 (*0-06-500151-6*) Addison-Wesley Educ.

— International Management. 2nd ed. 1997. text. write for info. (*0-321-00984-3*) Addison-Wesley.

— International Management: Managing Across Borders & Cultures. 3rd ed. LC 99-23032. 614p. (C). 1999. 88.00 (*0-321-02829-5*, Prentice Hall) P-H.

DeReuck, K. M., et al. International Thermodynamic Tables of the Fluid States: Methanol, 12. (IUPAC Chemical Data Ser.). (Illus.). 320p. 1993. 85.00 (*0-632-02379-1*, UP2379) Blackwell Sci.

DeRevec, Jeff, ed. see DeBevec, Joseph J.

Derevianko, A. P., et al. The Paleolithic of Siberia: New Discoveries & Interpretations. Karucgeva, Inna P., tr. from ENG. LC 97-4703. 416p. 1998. text 59.95 (*0-252-02052-9*) U of Ill Pr.

Derevlany, John, jt. ed. see Barry, Joseph.

Derevzhantschenko, Ludmilla, et al. Stories from Today's Russia. (BBC Phrase Books for Teenagers). (Illus.). 80p. 1994. pap. 9.95 (*0-8442-4252-7*, 42527, Passprt Bks) NTC Contemp Pub Co.

Derewianka, Beverly. Exploring How Texts Work. 88p. (C). 1991. pap. text 18.50 (*0-909955-90-5*, 00687) Heinemann.

Derewicz, Kristine G., jt. auth. see Castagnera, James O.

***Derex, David.** Studio Portrait Photography in Black & White. (Illus.). 128p. 2000. pap. 29.95 (*1-58428-029-8*) Amherst Media.

Derezinski, Jan & Gerard, Christian. Scattering Theory of Classical & Quantum N-Particle Systems, Vol. XII. LC 96-46757. (Texts & Monographs in Physics). (Illus.). 456p. 1997. 89.95 (*3-540-62066-4*) Spr-Verlag.

Derfler. An Age of Conflict. 2nd ed. LC 96-76630. (C). 1996. pap. text 37.00 (*0-15-502329-2*) Harcourt.

Derfler & Rigney. TCP/IP: A Survival Guide. 1997. 24.95 (*0-8052-8564-4*, M&T Bks) IDG Bks.

Derfler, Frank. How Networks Work. 4th ed. LC 98-85230. 208p. 1998. 29.99 (*0-7897-1595-3*, Que New Media) MCP SW Interactive.

***Derfler, Frank.** How Networks Work: Millennium Edition. 256p. 2000. pap. 29.99 (*0-7897-2445-6*) Que.

Derfler, Frank. Using Networks. LC 98-84376. 1998. 29.99 (*0-7897-1596-1*, Que New Media) MCP SW Interactive.

Derfler, Frank & Freed, Les. Get a Grip on Network Cabling. (Illus.). 219p. 1993. pap. 29.95 (*1-56276-057-2*, Ziff-Davis Pr) Que.

— How Networks Work. (How It Works Ser.). (Illus.). 216p. 1993. pap. 24.95 (*1-56276-129-3*, Ziff-Davis Pr) Que.

Derfler, Frank, Jr. & Freed, Les. PC Magazine Guide to Windows for Workgroups. (Guide to...Ser.). (Illus.). 219p. (Orig.). 1992. pap. 22.95 (*1-56276-120-X*, Ziff-Davis Pr) Que.

Derfler, Frank, jt. auth. see Freed, Les.

Derfler, Frank J., Jr. PC Magazine Guide to Connectivity. 2nd ed. (Guide to...Ser.). (Illus.). 463p. 1992. pap. 39.95 incl. disk (*1-56276-047-5*, Ziff-Davis Pr) Que.

— PC Magazine Guide to Connectivity: Intermediate Level. (Guide to...Ser.). 448p. (Orig.). 1991. pap. 39.95 incl. disk (*1-56276-001-7*, Ziff-Davis Pr) Que.

Derfler, Frank J., Jr., jt. auth. see Freed, Les.

Derfler, Leslie. Paul Lafargue & the Flowering of French Socialism, 1882-1911. LC 97-42404. 384p. 1999. 45.00 (*0-674-65912-0*) HUP.

— Paul Lafargue & the Founding of French Marxism, 1842-1882. LC 90-36659. (Illus.). 304p. 1991. 51.95 (*0-674-65903-1*, DERPAU) HUP.

— President & Parliament: A Short History of the French Presidency. LC 82-16133. 296p. 1983. reprint ed. pap. 91.80 (*0-608-04487-3*, 206523200001) Bks Demand.

— The Third French Republic, 1870-1940. LC 82-177. (Anvil Ser.). 192p. (C). 1982. reprint ed. pap. text 11.50 (*0-89874-480-6*) Krieger.

Derfler, Leslie, ed. Alexandre Millerand: The Socialist Years. (Issues in Contemporary Politics Ser.: No. 4). 1977. text 50.80 (*3-11-000172-1*) Mouton.

Derfler, Steven. The Hellenistic Temple at Tel Beersheva. LC 93-24801. (Illus.). 328p. 1993. text 99.95 (*0-7734-9301-8*) E Mellen.

Derfler, Steven L. The Hasmonean Revolt: Rebellion or Revolution. LC 89-12698. (Ancient Near Eastern Texts & Studies: Vol. 5). (Illus.). 128p. 1990. lib. bdg. 69.95 (*0-88946-258-5*) E Mellen.

Derfner, Mary F. & Wolf, Arthur D. Court Awarded Attorney Fees, 3 vols. 1983. ring bd. 800.00 (*0-8205-1168-4*) Bender.

Dergarabedian, Martha. Descubre tu Biblia, Bk. 1.Tr. of Bible Book by Book. (SPA.). 1992. pap., teacher ed. 5.25 (*0-311-11055-X*) Casa Bautista.

Dergarabedian, Paul, jt. ed. see Forbes, Fred W.

Derges, Susan. Woman Thinking River: Susan Derges. (Illus.). 80p. 1999. write for info. (*1-881337-06-5*) Fraenkel Gal.

Derges, Tricia A. Greater Ozarks Antique Directory. (Illus.). 130p. 1990. pap. 6.95 (*0-9626095-0-1*) Derges.

Derham, Anthony, et al. The Collector's Eye: Japanese Art Lent by Friends of Japan Society Gallery. LC 89-84125. (Illus.). 25p. 1995. pap. 25.00 (*0-913304-27-1*, 271X) Japan Soc.

Derham, Paz. Sonic 3D Blast Survival Guide. 1996. pap. 12.95 (*1-884364-46-2*) Sandwich Islands.

Derham, Rory, ed. Set-Off. 2nd ed. 774p. 1996. text 175.00 (*0-19-825907-7*) OUP.

Derham, W., ed. see Hooke, Robert.

Derham, William. Astro-Theology: or a Demonstration of Being & Attributes of God, from a Survey of the Heavens. (Anglistica & Americana Ser.: No. 78). xxvi, 246p. 1976. reprint ed. 50.70 (*3-487-06132-5*) G Olms Pubs.

— Physico-Theology: A Demonstration of the Being & Attributes of God, from His Works of Creation. Egerton, Frank N., 3rd, ed. LC 77-74212. (History of Ecology Ser.). 1978. reprint ed. lib. bdg. 41.95 (*0-405-10383-2*) Ayer.

— Physico-Theology: or A Demonstration of the Being & Attributes of God, from His Works of Creation. (Anglistica & Americana Ser.: No. 162). xiv, 482p. 1976. reprint ed. 76.70 (*3-487-05924-X*) G Olms Pubs.

Derham, William, ed. see Ray, John.

DeRhodes, David, jt. auth. see Bosveld, Jennifer.

Deri, Susan K. Symbolization & Creativity. LC 83-26482. xii, 364p. 1984. 55.00 (*0-8236-6292-6*) Intl Univs Pr.

Deriabin, Peter. The Watchdogs of Terror. LC 84-11873. (Foreign Intelligence Book Ser.). 456p. 1984. lib. bdg. 65.00 (*0-313-27040-6*, U7040, Greenwood Pr) Greenwood.

***Deriabin, Peter S.** Inside Stalin's Kremlin: An Eyewitness Account of Brutality, Duplicity & Intrigue. 2000. pap. text 15.95 (*1-57488-235-X*) Brasseys.

Deriabin, Peter S. & Evans, Joseph C. Inside Stalin's Kremlin: An Eyewitness Account of Brutality, Duplicity, & Intrigue. LC 98-16578. (Illus.). 272p. 1998. 27.50 (*1-57488-174-4*) Brasseys.

Deriabin, Peter S., jt. auth. see Schecter, Jerrold L.

Deriada, Leoncio P. Night Mares & Other Stories of Fantasy & Horror. 129p. (Orig.). (C). 1988. pap. 10.75 (*971-10-0367-8*, Pub. by New Day Pub) Cellar.

— The Week of the Whales & Other Stories. 132p. (Orig.). 1994. pap. 11.00 (*971-10-0483-6*, Pub. by New Day Pub) Cellar.

Derian, James D., ed. International Theory: Critical Investigations. LC 94-7501. 328p. (C). 1994. text 55.00 (*0-8147-1861-2*); pap. text 18.50 (*0-8147-1862-0*) NYU Pr.

Derian, James Der, see Der Derian, James.

Derian, Jean-Claude. America's Struggle for Leadership in Technology. Schaeffer, Severen L., tr. (Illus.). 324p. 1992. pap. text 17.50 (*0-262-54070-3*) MIT Pr.

DeRicci, intro. Catalogue of a Collection of Ancient Rings Formed by the Late E. Guilhou. 2nd rev. ed. (Illus.). 194p. 1980. 100.00 (*0-930088-01-8*) Antique Classic.

De'Ricci, Catherine. St. Catherine de'Ricci: Selected Letters. Tugwell, Simon, ed. Petrie, Jennifer, tr. (Dominican Sources: New Editions in English Ser.). 71p. 1985. pap. 4.00 (*0-9511202-2-0*, Pub. by Dominican Sources) Parable.

Derick & Baker. FORTH Encyclopedia. 2nd ed. 256p. 1983. 30.00 (*0-914699-02-4*) Mntn View Pr.

— FORTH Encyclopedia: Pocket Guide. 10.00 (*0-318-01345-2*) Mntn View Pr.

Derick, Burton N. Cemetery Inscriptions of Dennis, Massachusetts. 567p. (Orig.). 1994. pap. 37.00 (*1-55613-901-2*) Heritage Bk.

Derick, Elbert O., ed. see Derick, Pauline W.

Derick, Elbert O., ed. see Derick, Pauline W., et al.

Derick, L., jt. auth. see Derick, M.

Derick, M. & Derick, L. MVP-FORTH Expert System Tutorial. Haydon, Glen B., ed. (MVP-Forth Bks.: Vol. 6). 80p. (Orig.). 1984. pap. 22.00 (*0-317-56527-3*) Mntn View Pr.

Derick, Pauline W. The Nickerson Family Vol. IV: The Descendants of William Nickerson. Derick, Elbert O., ed. LC 97-68761. (Illus.). 768p. 1997. 50.00 (*0-9659269-1-5*) Nickerson Fam.

Derick, Pauline W., et al. The Nickerson Family Vols. 1-3: The Descendants of William Nickerson. 2nd rev. ed. Derick, Elbert O., ed. LC 97-68760. (Illus.). 500p. 1997. 50.00 (*0-9659269-0-7*) Nickerson Fam.

Derickson, Alan. Black Lung: Anatomy of a Public Disaster. LC 98-13612. (Illus.). 244p. 1998. text 29.95 (*0-8014-3186-7*) Cornell U Pr.

— Black Lung: The Human Cost of Industrialization. LC 98-13612. 1998. pap. write for info. (*0-8014-8286-0*) Cornell U Pr.

— Workers' Health, Workers' Democracy: The Western Miners' Struggle, 1891-1925. LC 88-47722. 264p. 1988. text 37.50 (*0-8014-2060-1*) Cornell U Pr.

Derickson, Dennia, jt. auth. see Derickson, Dennis.

Derickson, Dennis & Derickson, Dennia. Fiber Optic Test & Measurement. LC 97-20323. 672p. (C). 1997. 85.00 (*0-13-534330-5*) P-H.

***Derico, Laura.** Jesus, God's Precious Gift. (Illus.). 10p. (J). 2000. 9.99 (*0-7847-1059-8*, 03536) Standard Pub.

— Noah & God's Promise. (Illus.). 10p. (J). 2000. 9.99 (*0-7847-1059-7*, 03535) Standard Pub.

Derico, Laura, ed. see Bennett, Marian.

Derico, Laura, ed. see Harrast, Tracy.

Derico, Laura, ed. see Head, Heno, Jr.

Derico, Laura, ed. see Mahany, Patricia Shely.

Derico, Laura, ed. see Stewart, Jennifer.

Derie, Kate, ed. The Deadly Directory, 1999: Your Complete Guide to the International Mystery, Crime & Detective Fiction Community. rev. ed. 192p. 1998. pap. 25.00 (*0-9667534-2-9*) Deadly Serious.

***Derie, Kate, ed.** The Deadly Directory 2000: Your Guide to the World of Mystery & Crime Fiction. rev. ed. 1999. pap. 25.00 (*0-9667534-3-7*) Deadly Serious.

Derieg, A., tr. see Probst, S. & Flaxa, R.

DeRiemer, W. E. DeReimer Family, A. D. 1640 to 1903. 47p. 1997. reprint ed. lib. bdg. 19.00 (*0-8328-8273-9*) Higginson Bk Co.

— DeReimer Family, A.D. 1640 to 1903. 47p. 1997. reprint ed. pap. 9.00 (*0-8328-8274-7*) Higginson Bk Co.

Derig, Betty. Roadside History of Idaho. LC 95-42565. 480p. 1995. 30.00 (*0-87842-327-3*) Mountain Pr.

— Roadside History of Idaho. LC 95-42565. (Illus.). 480p. 1995. pap. text 18.00 (*0-87842-328-1*) Mountain Pr.

Derigs, U., jt. auth. see Bachem, A.

Derigs, Ulrich, et al, eds. Operations Research Proceedings, 1994: Selected Papers of the International Conference on Operations Research, Berlin, August 30-September 2, 1994. LC 94-47366. 1995. 143.00 (*3-540-58793-4*) Spr-Verlag.

Dering, Edward. M. Derings Workes: More at Large Than Ever Hath Heer-to-Fore Been Printed, 3 pts. LC 74-38171. (English Experience Ser.: No. 448). 692p. 1972. reprint ed. 105.00 (*90-221-0448-6*) Walter J Johnson.

Dering, Richard. Eight Fantasias for Five Viols. Brookes, Virginia, ed. (Viol Consort Ser.: No. 19). ii, 64p. 1994. pap. text 25.00 (*1-56571-079-7*) PRB Prods.

— Six Fantasias for Six Viols (Two Trebles, Two Tenors, Two Basses) Brookes, Virginia, ed. (Viol Consort Ser.: No. 24). ii, 60p. 1994. pap. text 27.00 (*1-56571-117-3*) PRB Prods.

— Two in Nomines for Six Viols. Brookes, Virginia, ed. ii, 23p. 1992. pap. text 12.00 (*1-56571-051-7*, VC12) PRB Prods.

Dering, Sue. Nothing Sensible: Erotic Haiku. 12p. (Orig.). 1994. pap. 6.95 (*0-9644532-0-7*) S Dering Pub.

Deringil, Selim. Turkish Foreign Policy During the Second World War: An Active Neutrality. (London School of Economics Monographs in International Studies). (Illus.). 256p. 1989. text 69.95 (*0-521-34466-2*) Cambridge U Pr.

— The Well-Protected Domains: Ideology & the Legitimation of Power in the Ottoman Empire, 1876-1909. 256p. 1998. text 59.50 (*1-86064-307-8*, Pub. by I B T) St Martin.

***Deringil, Selim.** Well-protected Domains: Ideology & The Legitimation of Power in The Ottoman Empire, 1876-1909. 1999. pap. text 22.50 (*1-86064-472-4*, Pub. by I B T) St Martin.

Deringil, Selim, ed. Ottoman Almanacs of the Arab Provinces, 1888-1902, 7 vols. (ENG & TUR.). 1999. reprint ed. lib. bdg. 1495.00 (*1-85207-850-2*, Pub. by Archive Editions) N Ross.

DeRis, Margaret, tr. see Steiner, Rudolf.

DeRisi, William J. & Butz, George. Writing Behavioral Contracts: A Case Simulation Practice Manual. (Illus.). 94p. (Orig.). 1975. pap. text 9.95 (*0-87822-123-9*, 1239) Res Press.

Derisiotis. EDV-Fachenglisch. 3rd ed. (ENG & GER.). 203p. 1989. 95.00 (*0-7859-7540-3*, 3448020516) Fr & Eur.

Deriso, Richard B., jt. auth. see Quinn, Terrance J.

***DeRitis, Joseph.** HMS Revenge. 319p. 1999. pap. 17.95 (*0-7414-0150-9*) Buy Books.

DeRitter, Jones. The Embodiment of Characters: The Representation of Physical Experience on State & in Print, 1728-1749. LC 94-16539. (New Cultural Studies). 192p. (C). 1994. text 29.95 (*0-8122-3265-8*) U of Pa Pr.

Derivan, William J. & Silverstein, Natalie A. Prevention Education: A Guide to Research. LC 89-39996. (Bibliographies in Contemporary Education Ser.: Vol. 9). 302p. 1990. reprint ed. text 44.00 (*0-8240-3716-2*, SS524) Garland.

Derivatives Study Group. Global Derivatives Appendix I: Working Papers. 140p. (Orig.). 1993. pap. text 60.00 (*1-56708-091-X*) Grp of Thirty.

— Global Derivatives Appendix II: Legal Enforceability: A Survey of Nine Jurisdictions. 313p. (Orig.). 1993. pap. text 100.00 (*1-56708-092-8*) Grp of Thirty.

Derix, M. M. Neuropsychological Differentiation of Dementia Syndrome. LC 94-9130. 184p. 1994. 54.00 (*90-265-1312-7*) Swets.

Derjaguin, B. V. Theory of Stability of Colloids & Thin Films. (Illus.). 272p. (C). 1989. text 95.00 (*0-306-11022-9*, Kluwer Plenum) Kluwer Academic.

Derjaguin, B. V. & Fedoseev, D. V. Diamonds Wrought by Man. 142p. (C). 1985. 40.00 (*0-7855-5000-3*, Pub. by Collets) St Mut.

Derjaguin, B. V., et al. Surface Forces. Kitchener, J. A., tr. from RUS. LC 87-13599. (Illus.). 460p. (C). 1987. text 156.00 (*0-306-11011-3*, Kluwer Plenum) Kluwer Academic.

Derk, Donald R. On the Sawdust Trail: A Collection of Poems & Ballads. 60p. 1998. pap. 10.95 (*1-57502-992-8*, PO2704) Morris Pubng.

Derkacz, Melissa, ed. Chicago Special Events Sourcebook: The Comprehensive Guide to Great Locations in the City & Suburbs for Meetings, Parties, Weddings, & Other Special Occasions. LC 99-173818. (Illus.). 336p. 1998. pap. 20.00 (*1-55652-294-0*) Chicago Review.

Derkinderen, Frans G. & Crum, Roy L. Project Set Strategies. (Nijenrode Studies in Business: Vol. 4). 1979. lib. bdg. 73.50 (*0-89838-014-6*) Kluwer Academic.

— Readings in Strategy for Corporate Investment. 219p. 1986. text 19.95 (*0-273-01635-0*, HarpBusn) HarpInfo.

D

An Asterisk (*) at the beginning of an entry indicates that the title is appearing for the first time.

— Risk, Capital Costs & Project Financing Decisions. (Nijenrode Studies in Business: Vol. 6). 288p. 1980. lib. bdg. 111.00 (0-89838-046-4) Kluwer Academic.

Derkow-Disselbeck, Barbara, et al. Anna, Schmidt und Oskar. (GER.). 88p. (J). (gr. 2-6). 1996. 18.50 incl. audio (3-468-96850-7) Langenscheidt.

— Anna, Schmidt und Oskar, Set. (GER.). 88p. (J). (gr. 2-6). 1996. 14.95 incl. audio (3-468-96851-5) Langenscheidt.

— Anna, Schmidt und Oskar Level 1, Handbuch: A Video Language Course for Children. (GER.). 72p. (J). 1996. 14.95 (3-468-96852-3) Langenscheidt.

— Anna, Schmidt und Oskar Level 2: A Video Language Course for Children: Bilder und Ubungsbuch. (GER.). 112p. (J). 1996. 20.00 (3-468-96841-8) Langenscheidt.

Derks, J. P. Cold Fluid Driven Crack Propagation: Thermo-Mechanical Behavior of Rock Caverns. (Illus.). 208p. 1997. pap. 57.50 (90-407-1501-7, Pub. by Delft U Pr) Coronet Bks.

***Derks, Scott.** Working Americans, 1880-1999 Vol. II: The Middle Class. 2000. 125.00 (1-891482-72-6) Grey Hse Pub.

Derks, Scott, jt. auth. see Dorn, William J.

Derks, Scott, ed. see Grey House Publishing Staff.

Derks, Ton. Gods, Temples & Religious Practices. LC 98-197993. x, 325 p. (Orig.). 1998. pap. 39.50 (90-5356-254-0, Pub. by Amsterdam U Pr) U of Mich Pr.

***Derksen, Cori & Harder, Myra.** Town & Country: Houses & Buildings to Paper Piece. (Illus.). 112p. 2001. pap. 27.95 (1-56477-326-4) Martingale & Co.

Derksen, Dirk V., jt. auth. see Alaska Flyfishers Club Staff.

Derksen, J. J. L. Personality Disorders. 1995. pap. text 71.95 (0-471-95549-3) Wiley.

***Derksen, Jan, ed.** Treatment of Personality Disorders. LC 99-47601. 312p. 1999. 149.50 (0-306-46215-X, Kluwer Plenum) Kluwer Academic.

Derksen, Jeff. Down Time. 80p. 1990. pap. 9.95 (0-88922-278-9) SPD-Small Pr Dist.

Derksen, Jeff. Dwell. LC 94-172819. 112p. 1994. pap. 10.95 (0-88922-328-9) Genl Dist Srvs.

— Until. 1987. pap. 4.00 (0-921331-04-5, Pub. by Tsunami Edits) SPD-Small Pr Dist.

Derksen, Johannes T., jt. ed. see Knothe, Gerhard.

Derksen, L. D. Dialogues on Women: Images of Women in the History of Philosophy. LC 96-215664. 183p. pap. 22.50 (90-5383-460-5, Pub. by VU Univ Pr) Paul & Co Pubs.

***Derlath, Gunter, photos by.** Venice - Camera Obscura: Photographs with the Pinhole Camera. (Illus.). 2000. 70.00 (3-908163-21-8, Pub. by Edit Stemmle) Abbeville Pr.

Derlega, V. J. & Berg, J. H. Self-Disclosure: Theory, Research, & Therapy. LC 87-18654. (Perspectives in Social Psychology Ser.). (Illus.). 380p. (C). 1987. 70.00 (0-306-42635-8, Plenum Trade) Perseus Pubng.

Derlega, V. J. & Winstead, Barbara A., eds. Friendship & Social Interaction. (Social Psychology Ser.). (Illus.). 312p. 1986. 92.95 (0-387-96230-1) Spr-Verlag.

Derlega, Valerian J. & Barbee, Anita P. HIV & Social Interaction. LC 98-8900. 280p. 1998. pap. 14.99 (0-7619-0372-0) Sage.

— HIV & Social Interaction. LC 98-8900. 280p. 1998. 33.00 (0-7619-0371-2) Sage.

Derlega, Valerian J., et al. Personality: Contemporary Theory & Research. 2nd rev. ed. LC 98-14938. (Psychology). 450p. 1999. pap. text 49.95 (0-8304-1422-3) Thomson Learn.

— Psychotherapy As a Personal Relationship. LC 90-3997. 227p. 1991. lib. bdg. 31.50 (0-89862-554-8) Guilford Pubns.

— Self-Disclosure. (Series on Close Relationships: Vol. 5). (Illus.). 160p. (C). 1993. text 42.00 (0-8039-3954-X); pap. text 17.95 (0-8039-3955-8) Sage.

***Derleth.** The Original Text Solar Pons Omnibus. (August Derleth Library). 2000. 60.00 (1-55246-077-0) Battered Silicon.

Derleth, contrib. by. East European Comparative Politics. LC 99-24870. (Illus.). 338p. (C). 1999. pap. text 39.80 (0-13-756453-8, Macmillan Coll) P-H.

Derleth, August. The Angler's Companion. (August Derleth Library). pap. 17.00 (1-55246-015-0) Battered Silicon.

— The Angler's Companion. (August Derleth Library). 2000. 25.00 (1-55246-014-2) Battered Silicon.

Derleth, August. Aunt May Strikes Again! 53p. (Orig.). 1996. pap. 10.00 (1-896648-64-9) Battered Silicon.

— Bright Journey. 342p. 1997. 28.00 (1-55246-004-5); pap. 18.00 (1-55246-005-3) Battered Silicon.

— Bright Journey. 1993. reprint ed. lib. bdg. 21.95 (1-56849-123-9) Buccaneer Bks.

— Collected Poems, 1937-1967. 254p. 1995. text 25.00 (1-896032-70-2) Battered Silicon.

— Country Matters. LC 97-141027. 308p. 1996. text 25.00 (1-896648-29-0) Battered Silicon.

— Evening in Spring. 232p. 1997. 24.00 (1-55246-006-1); pap. 16.00 (1-55246-007-X) Battered Silicon.

— Evening in Spring. 1993. reprint ed. lib. bdg. 21.95 (1-56849-125-5) Buccaneer Bks.

***Derleth, August.** Father Marquette & the Great Rivers. LC 98-71258. 1998. write for info. (0-89870-664-5) Ignatius Pr.

— The Final Adventures of Solar Pons. (August Derleth Library). 240p. 1998. 28.00 (1-55246-012-6) Battered Silicon.

Derleth, August. Harrigan's File. LC 75-2522. 1975. 12.95 (0-87054-070-X) Arkham.

***Derleth, August.** The Hills Stand Watch. (August Derleth Library). 2000. 25.00 (1-55246-140-8); pap. 17.00 (1-55246-141-6) Battered Silicon.

Derleth, August. The Hills Stand Watch. 1993. reprint ed. lib. bdg. 21.95 (1-56849-124-7) Buccaneer Bks.

— The House on the Mound: The Wisconsin Saga. 250p. 1996. reprint ed. 25.00 (1-896648-26-6) Battered Silicon.

— In a Quiet Graveyard: Poems of the Sac Prarie People. LC 98-119372. (Illus.). 136p. 1997. pap. 10.00 (1-55246-002-9) Battered Silicon.

— The Mask of Cthulhu. 256p. 1996. mass mkt. 4.95 (0-7867-0337-7) Carroll & Graf.

***Derleth, August.** The Quest for Cthulhu. 448p. 2000. pap. 12.95 (0-7867-0752-6, Pub. by Carroll & Graf) Publishers Group.

Derleth, August. Return to Sac Prairie. LC 97-141034. 331p. 1996. 25.00 (1-896648-95-9); pap. 17.00 (1-896648-96-7) Battered Silicon.

***Derleth, August.** Shane's Girls: Lamplight for the Dark. (The August Derleth Library). 2000. 25.00 (1-55246-010-X); pap. 17.00 (1-55246-011-8) Battered Silicon.

Derleth, August. Someone in the Dark. 335p. 1980. reprint ed. lib. bdg. 15.50 (0-89968-213-8, Lghtyr Pr) Buccaneer Bks.

***Derleth, August.** St. Ignatius & the Company of Jesus. 1999. pap. text 9.95 (0-89870-722-6) Ignatius Pr.

Derleth, August. The Trail of Cthulhu. 256p. 1996. mass mkt. 4.95 (0-7867-0341-5) Carroll & Graf.

— Walden West. LC 92-50264. (North Coast Bks.). (Illus.). 278p. 1992. reprint ed. pap. 14.95 (0-299-13594-2); reprint ed. lib. bdg. 35.00 (0-299-13590-X) U of Wis Pr.

***Derleth, August.** The Wind in the Cedars: The Odyssey of Janna Mead. (The August Derleth Library). 2000. 25.00 (1-55246-008-8) Battered Silicon.

— The Wind in the Cedars: The Odyssey of Janna Meade. (August Derleth Library). 2000. pap. 17.00 (1-55246-009-6) Battered Silicon.

Derleth, August. The Wisconsin: River of a Thousand Isles. LC 85-40367. 368p. 1985. reprint ed. pap. 14.95 (0-299-10374-9) U of Wis Pr.

Derleth, August. Wisconsin Writers & Writing. pap. 16.00 (1-896648-98-3) Battered Silicon.

Derleth, August, ed. New Horizons: Yesterday's Portraits of Tomorrow. LC 98-49573. xv, 299p. 1999. 25.95 (0-87054-174-9) Arkham.

Derleth, August & Wrzos, Joseph P. In Lovecraft's Shadow: The Cthulhu Mythos. (August Derleth Library). 60.00 (1-55246-003-7) Battered Silicon.

Derleth, August, jt. auth. see Lovecraft, H. P.

Derleth, August, ed. see Lovecraft, H. P.

Derleth, August W. Writing Fiction. LC 72-141413. 201p. 1971. reprint ed. lib. bdg. 38.50 (0-8371-4694-1, DEWF, Greenwood Pr) Greenwood.

Derleth, August W., ed. Dark of the Moon. LC 73-80374. (Granger Index Reprint Ser.). 1977. 24.95 (0-8369-6056-4) Ayer.

— Fire & Sleet & Candlelight. LC 72-11987. (Granger Index Reprint Ser.). 1977. reprint ed. 20.95 (0-8369-6402-0) Ayer.

Derleth, August W., ed. see Lovecraft, H. P.

Derlin, Edward S., et al. Business Resumption Planning. 96th ed. 592p. (C). 1997. lib. bdg. 225.00 (0-7913-2127-4) Warren Gorham & Lamont.

Derloshon, Jerry, ed. Music U. S. A., 1995: Statistical Review of the Music Products Industry. (Illus.). 68p. (Orig.). 1995. pap. text 20.00 (0-9641677-1-9) Natl Music Merchants.

— Music U. S. A., 1996: Statistical Review of the Music Products Industry. 68p. 1996. pap. 20.00 (0-9641677-2-7) Natl Music Merchants.

***Derluguian, Georgi M. & Greer, Scott L., eds.** Dilemmas of Globalization: Political Projects in a Changing World-System, 216. LC 99-49047. (Contributions in Economics & Economic History Ser.: Vol. 216). 264p. 2000. 65.00 (0-313-31082-3, Greenwood Pr) Greenwood.

— Questioning Geopolitics: Political Projects in a Changing World-System. LC 99-49047. 264p. 2000. pap. 22.95 (0-275-96656-9, Praeger Pubs) Greenwood.

Derlycia, Zirka. Everyday Ukrainian, Set. unabridged ed. 342p. 1993. pap. text 195.00 incl. audio (0-88432-491-5, AFUK10) Audio-Forum.

Derlyn, Edita Van, see Van Derlyn, Edita.

Derman, Andrew B. Model Form International Operating Agreement: An Analysis & Interpretation of the 1995 Form. LC 97-70751. (Section of Natural Resources, Energy, & Environmental Law Monograph Ser.). ix, 146 p. 1997. write for info. (1-57073-430-5) Amer Bar Assn.

Derman, Bruce. We'd Have a Great Relationship if It Weren't for You. 1994. pap. text 12.95 (0-9663704-0-6) Mutual Connect.

Derman, Bruce & Hauge, Michael. We'd Have a Great Relationship If It Weren't for You: Regaining Love & Intimacy Through Mutuality. LC 94-23088. 335p. (Orig.). 1994. pap. 12.95 (1-55874-316-2, 3162) Health Comm.

Derman, Cyrus & Ross, Sheldon M. Statistical Aspects of Quality Control. LC 96-25651. (Statistical Modeling & Decision Science Ser.). (Illus.). 200p. 1996. text 59.95 (0-12-210010-7) Acad Pr.

Derman, Elizabeth, ed. see Moore, Eugenia.

Derman, Karen. The Magic Hole in the Sky. (Illus.). 48p. (Orig.). (J). 1995. pap. 14.95 (0-9630026-0-0); pap. 9.95 (0-9630026-1-9); pap. 24.95 incl. audio (0-9630026-2-7) Childlight Pr.

Derman, M. Ugur. Letters in Gold: Ottoman Calligrahy from the Sakip Sabanci Collection, Istanbul. LC 98-21945. (Illus.). 208p. 1998. 65.00 (0-8109-6526-7, Pub. by Abrams) Time Warner.

Derman, M. Ugur, et al. Letters in Gold: Ottoman Calligraphy from the Sak P. Sabanc Collection, Istanbul. LC 98-21945. 196p. 1998. 50.00 (0-87099-873-0); pap. 35.00 (0-87099-874-9) Metro Mus Art.

Derman, R. J., jt. ed. see Corson, S. L.

Derman-Sparks, Louise. Future Vision, Present Work: Learning from the Culturally Relevant Anti-Bias Leadership Project. LC 98-40490. 1998. 16.95 (1-884834-59-0) Redleaf Pr.

Derman-Sparks, Louise, jt. auth. see ABC Task Force Staff.

Derman-Sparks, Louise, jt. auth. see Phillips, Carol B.

Derman, Sylvia, ed. see Tarthang Tulku.

***Dermanis, Athanasios, et al.** Geomatic Methods for the Analysis of Data in the Earth Sciences. LC 00-41039. (Lecture Notes In Earth Sciences). 2000. pap. write for info. (3-540-67476-4) Spr-Verlag.

Dermarders. Guide to Pharmacologic Effects. 1998. text. write for info. (0-7216-6236-6, W B Saunders Co) Harcrt Hlth Sci Grp.

Dermek, Aurel. Boletes III. (Fungorum Rariorum Icones Coloratae Ser.: Pars XVI). (FRE., Illus.). 23p. 1987. pap. 27.00 (3-443-69002-5, Pub. by Gebruder Borntraeger) Balogh.

— Pleurot, Hohenbuehelia, Hypsizygus, Calocybe, Lepista, Armillar, Amanita, Pluteus, Phaeolepiota, Crepidotus, Lactar. (Fungorum Rariorum Icones Coloratae Ser.: Pars XVII). (FRE., Illus.). 23p. 1987. pap. 27.00 (3-443-69003-3, Pub. by Gebruder Borntraeger) Balogh.

Dermen, Elizabeth, ed. see Leiper, Esther M.

Dermenghem, Emile. Muhammad & the Islamic Tradition. Watt, Jean M., tr. from FRE. LC 81-47412. (Spiritual Masters Ser.). (Illus.). 192p. 1982. 18.95 (0-87951-130-3, Pub. by Overlook Pr) Penguin Putnam.

— Muhammad & the Islamic Tradition. Watt, Jean M., tr. from FRE. LC 81-47412. (Spiritual Masters Ser.). (Illus.). 192p. 1983. pap. 9.95 (0-87951-170-2, Pub. by Overlook Pr) Penguin Putnam.

Dermenjian, A. A., ed. Developments in Pressure Vessels & Piping: Proceedings of the Pressure Vessels & Piping Conference, Minneapolis, MN, 1994. LC 94-71746. (PVP Ser.: Vol. 278). 239p. 1994. pap. 65.00 (0-7918-1351-7) ASME.

— Piping, Supports, & Structural Dynamics. (PVP Ser.: Vol. 264). 184p. 1993. 45.00 (0-7918-0991-9, H00823) ASME.

— Pressure Vessels & Piping Design Analysis & Severe Accidents. 213p. 1996. pap. text 100.00 (0-7918-1778-4, TS283) ASME Pr.

Dermer, Charles D., et al, eds. Proceedings of the Fourth Compton Symposium Pt. 1: The Compton Observatory in Review. LC 97-77179. (Conference Proceedings Ser.: Vol. 410). (Illus.). xxviii, 534p. 1997. 120.00 (1-56396-772-3) Am Inst Physics.

Dermer, Charles S., et al, eds. Proceedings of the Fourth Compton Symposium. (AIP Conference Proceedings Ser.: Vol. 410). (Illus.). 1760p. 1998. 300.00 (1-56396-659-X) Am Inst Physics.

Dermer, Gerald B. The Immortal Cell: Why Cancer Research Fails. LC 93-26852. 224p. pap. 11.95 (0-89529-582-2, Avery) Penguin Putnam.

Dermer, Joseph. How to Write Successful Foundation Presentations. 80p. (Orig.). 1993. pap. text 25.00 (0-914977-10-5, 600021) Taft Group.

Dermer, Joseph, ed. A Treasury of Successful Appeal Letters. 176p. 1985. pap. 49.50 (0-914977-07-5, 600028) Fund Raising.

Dermer, Joseph & Wertheimer, Stephen, eds. The Complete Guide to Corporate Fund Raising. 1991. pap. 19.95 (0-914977-12-1, 600031) Fund Raising.

Dermietzel, Rolf, jt. auth. see Spray, David C.

Dermine, J. Pricing Policies of Financial Intermediaries. (Studies in Contemporary Economics: Vol. 5). 174p. 1984. pap. 29.00 (0-387-13080-2) Spr-Verlag.

Dermine, Jean, ed. European Banking in the Nineteen Nineties. 2nd ed. LC 92-26973. 1993. pap. 38.95 (0-631-18843-6) Blackwell Pubs.

Dermine, Jean & Hillion, Pierre, eds. European Capital Markets with a Single Currency. LC 99-214742. 376p. 1999. text 90.00 (0-19-829539-1) OUP.

Dermineur, Bernard, ed. Catalogue General des Ouvrages en Langue Francaise 1926-1929, 9 vols., Set. (FRE.). 7250p. 1986. lib. bdg. 1835.00 (3-598-30990-2) K G Saur Verlag.

— Catalogue General des Ouvrages en Langue Francaise 1926-1929: Auteurs, 3 vols. (FRE.). 7250p. 1986. lib. bdg. write for info. (3-598-30991-0) K G Saur Verlag.

— Catalogue General des Ouvrages en Langue Francaise 1926-1929: Matieres, 4 vols. (FRE.). 7250p. 1986. lib. bdg. write for info. (3-598-30995-3) K G Saur Verlag.

— Catalogue General des Ouvrages en Langue Francaise 1926-1929: Titres, 2 vols. (FRE.). 7250p. 1986. lib. bdg. write for info. (3-598-30992-9) K G Saur Verlag.

— Catalogue General des Ouvrages en Langue Francaise 1930-1933, 15 vols., Set. (FRE.). 7500p. 1992. lib. bdg. 4470.00 (3-598-32860-5) K G Saur Verlag.

Dermitzakis, M. D., jt. ed. see Theodorou, G. E.

Dermody, Kathleen. A Nation at Last: The Story of Federation. (Illus.). 1997. pap. 25.95 (0-644-47536-6, Pub. by Aust Gov Pub) Accents Pubns.

Dermody, Susan & Jacka, Elizabeth. The Screening of Australia: Anatomy of a National Cinema, 2 vols., Vol. 2. 290p. (C). 1988. pap. 24.95 (0-86819-187-6, Pub. by Currency Pr) Accents Pubns.

Dermond, Susan, ed. see Knox, Lorna Ann.

***Dermott, Brigit.** The Complete Professional. LC 00-42842. 2000. pap. write for info. (1-57685-344-6) LrnngExprss.

Dermott, S. F., ed. see NATO Advanced Study Institute on the Origin of the.

Dermott, Stanley F., jt. auth. see Murray, Carl D.

Dern, Daniel. Internet Business Handbook. 350p. 2000. pap. text 29.95 (0-13-185620-0) P-H.

Dern, Daniel, et al. Managing Employee Internet Access: A Guide for Creating & Administering Corporate Access Policy with Monitoring & Filtering Software. (Illus.). 54p. (C). 1998. pap. text 25.00 (0-7881-7070-8) DIANE Pub.

Dern, Daniel P. Dern's Internet Guide for New Users. 2nd ed. 700p. 1997. text 40.00 (0-07-016513-0) McGraw.

— Dern's Internet Guide for New Users. 2nd ed. (Illus.). 800p. 1997. pap. text 27.95 (0-07-016514-9) McGraw.

Dern, J. C., jt. ed. see Murthy, T. K.

***Dern, John A.** Martians, Monsters, & Madonna: Fiction & Form in the World of Martin Amis. LC 98-54323. (Studies in Twentieth-Century British Literature: No. 2). 28p. (C). 2000. pap. text 25.95 (0-8204-4457-X) P Lang Pubng.

Dern, John P. Genealogical Contribution Reprinted from the Albany Protocol: Wilhelm Christoph Berkenmeyer's Chronicle of Lutheran Affairs in New York Colony, 1731-1750. 1981. pap. 5.00 (0-910746-08-7) Hope Farm.

Dern, John P. & Waidner, M. Marjorie. Rauenzahner to Routson: A Family on the Move. 779p. 1997. 59.95 (0-89725-139-3, 1453) Picton Pr.

Dern, John P., jt. auth. see Tracey, Grace L.

Dern, John P., jt. ed. see Weiser, Frederick S.

Dern, Peggy. County Nurse. large type ed. (Linford Romance Library). 272p. 1993. pap. 16.99 (0-7089-7451-1) Ulverscroft.

— Nurse at Burford's Landing. large type ed. (Linford Romance Library). 304p. 1993. pap. 16.99 (0-7089-7335-3, Linford) Ulverscroft.

— Understand, My Love. large type ed. (Linford Romance Library). 320p. 1992. pap. 16.99 (0-7089-7240-3, Linford) Ulverscroft.

Dernay, Eugene. Longitudes & Latitudes in the U. S. 128p. 1945. 13.00 (0-86690-067-5, D1062-014) Am Fed Astrologers.

Dernbach, John C., et al. Practical Guide to Legal Writing & Legal Method. 2nd ed. LC 94-16472. xxiii, 399p. 1994. pap. 19.95 (0-8377-0561-4, Rothman) W S Hein.

Dernberger, Robert, ed. China's Development Experience in Comparative Perspective: A Social Science Research Council Study. LC 80-418. (East Asian Monographs: No. 93). 358p. 1980. 49.95 (0-674-11890-1) HUP.

Dernberger, Robert F., et al, eds. The Chinese: Adapting the Past, Facing the Future. 2nd ed. LC 91-19453. 802p. 1991. pap. text 35.00 (0-89264-100-2) Ctr Chinese Studies.

Dernberger, Robert F. & Eckaus, Richard S. Financing Asian Development No. 2: China & India. (Asian Agenda Reports: No. 8). (Illus.). 142p. (Orig.). (C). 1988. pap. text 15.00 (0-8191-6589-1); lib. bdg. 34.00 (0-8191-6588-3) U Pr of Amer.

Dernberger, Robert F., jt. ed. see Morrison, Charles E.

Dernburg, Judith D., jt. auth. see Dernburg, Thomas F.

Dernburg, Thomas F. Deficits, Debts, & the Economy: Getting Out of the Financial Maze. (Orig.). 1995. pap. 14.95 (0-9644810-0-6) T D Econ.

Dernburg, Thomas F. & Dernburg, Judith D. Macroeconomic Analysis: An Introduction to Comparative Statics & Dynamics. LC 75-76072. 302p. reprint ed. pap. 93.70 (0-608-15177-7, 205607900046) Bks Demand.

Derne, Steve. Culture in Action: Family Life, Emotion, & Male Dominance in Banaras, India. LC 94-18314. 232p. (C). 1995. text 54.50 (0-7914-2425-1); pap. text 19.95 (0-7914-2426-X) State U NY Pr.

Derner, Otis C., jt. auth. see Eubanks, I. Dwaine.

Derniame, J. C., ed. Software Process Technology: Proceedings of Second European Workshop, Trondheim, Norway, September 7-8, 1992. LC 92-28845. (Lecture Notes in Computer Science Ser.: Vol. 635). ix, 253p. 1992. 47.00 (0-387-55928-0); pap. 43.00 (3-540-55928-0) Spr-Verlag.

Derniame, J. C., et al, eds. Software Process: Principles, Methodology & Technology. LC 99-11670. (Lecture Notes in Computer Science Ser.: Vol. 1500). xiii, 307p. 1999. pap. 55.00 (3-540-65516-6) Spr-Verlag.

Dernie, David. Architecture Imagination & Matter. pap. text. write for info. (0-471-48951-4) Wiley.

Dernie, David. Victor Horta. LC 96-146342. (Illus.). 224p. 1995. 69.00 (1-85490-418-3, Pub. by Wiley) Wiley.

Dernie, David. The Villa d'Este at Tivoli. (Illus.). 128p. 1996. 50.00 (1-85490-447-7, Pub. by Wiley) Wiley.

Dernocoeur, Kate B. Streetsense: Communication, Safety & Control. 3rd rev. ed. LC 96-31540. (Illus.). 330p. 1996. pap. 22.95 (0-938106-21-X) Laing Res Servs.

Dernocoeur, Kate B., jt. auth. see Clawson, Jeff J.

Dernoga, Lenora. The Girl Who Loved Juice. (Illus.). 32p. (J). (ps-2). 1998. pap. 6.99 (1-891043-03-X) Perry Pubng.

Dernouchamps, J. P., et al, eds. Recent Advances in Uveitis. (Illus.). 632p. 1993. lib. bdg. 183.00 (90-6299-092-4) Kugler Pubns.

DeRobeck, Nesta. St. Clare of Assisi. 242p. (Orig.). 1980. reprint ed. pap. 7.95 (0-8199-0808-8, Frncscn Herld) Franciscan Pr.

DeRobertis, Eugene M. Phenomenological Psychology: A Text for Beginners. LC 96-33420. 88p. 1996. pap. text 17.50 (0-7618-0500-1) U Pr of Amer.

Derobertis, Samuel & Irwin, Joseph N. Texas Real Estate. 2nd ed. 448p. (C). 1996. pap. text 32.00 (0-13-777756-6) P-H.

Deroc, M. British Special Operations Explored: Yugoslavia in Turmoil, 1941-1943, & the British Response. 349p. 1988. text 71.00 (0-88033-139-9, Pub. by East Eur Monographs) Col U Pr.

Deroche. Introduction to Poetry. 6th ed. LC 99-71997. 2000. pap. text 20.07 (0-395-95824-5) HM.

— Principles of Accounting. 6th ed. 1995. pap. text, student ed., wbk. ed. 28.60 (0-13-442112-4) P-H.

D

An Asterisk (*) at the beginning of an entry indicates that the title is appearing for the first time.

Deroche, A. G. The Principles of Auto Body Repairing & Repainting. 6th ed. LC 95-18952. 664p. 1995. 92.00 (*0-13-440033-X*) P-H.

Deroche, Andre G. & Hildebrand, N. N. The Principles of Auto Body Repairing & Repainting. 4th ed. (Illus.). 752p. (C). 1986. text 43.00 (*0-13-708173-1*) P-H.

DeRoche, Edward F. The Newspaper: A Reference Book for Teachers & Librarians. LC 91-633. 170p. 1991. lib. bdg. 35.00 (*0-87436-584-8*) ABC-CLIO.

DeRoche, Edward F. & Williams, Mary M. Educating Hearts & Minds: A Comprehensive Character Education Framework. LC 97-21110. (Illus.). 216p. 1997. 55.95 (*0-8039-6514-1*); pap. 24.95 (*0-8039-6515-X*) Corwin Pr.

***DeRoche, Edward F. & Williams, Mary M.** Educating Hearts & Minds: A Comprehensive Character Education Framework. 2nd ed. LC 00-9508. 2000. pap. write for info. (*0-7619-7690-6*) Corwin Pr.

Deroche, Francois. The Abbasid Tradition: Qur'ans of the 8th to 10th Centuries. (Nassar D. Khalili Collection of Islamic Art: Vol. I). (Illus.). 192p. 1992. text 330.00 (*0-19-727600-8*) OUP.

DeRoche, Frederick W. & McDougall, Mary A. Now It's Your Move: A Guide for the Outplaced Employee. (Illus.). 224p. (C). 1984. pap. 16.95 (*0-13-625426-8*) P-H.

DeRoche, Joseph. The Heath Introduction to Poetry. 5th ed. LC 95-68035. 581p. (C). 1996. pap. text 23.96 (*0-669-35504-6*) HM Trade Div.

***Derocher, Andrew E.** Black, White & Chrome: The United States & Zimbabwe, 1953 to 1998 LC 99-31452. 1999. write for info. (*0-86543-792-0*) Africa World.

DeRoest, J. AIX for RS-6000: System & Administration Guide. (Ranade Workstation Ser.). 452p. 1994. pap. 44.95 (*0-07-036439-7*) McGraw.

DeRoest, James. AIX Version 4 System & Administration Guide. LC 97-6203. (Illus.). 591p. 1997. pap. 44.95 (*0-07-036688-8*) McGraw.

— Samba: UNIX & NT Internetworking. 1999. write for info. (*0-07-135105-1*) McGraw.

— Samba: UNIX & NT Internetworking. LC 99-41251. 304p. 2000. pap. 39.99 (*0-07-135104-3*) McGraw.

DeRoever, W. & Engelhardt, Kai. Data Refinement: Model-Oriented Proof Methods & Their Comparison. LC 98-24731. (Cambridge Tracts in Theoretical Computer Science Ser.: No. 47). (Illus.). 450p. (C). 1998. 59.95 (*0-521-64170-5*) Cambridge U Pr.

DeRogatis, Jim. Kaleidoscope Eyes: Psychedelic Rock from the '60s to the '90s. (Citadel Underground Ser.). (Illus.). 288p. 1996. pap. 16.95 (*0-8065-1788-3*, Citadel Pr) Carol Pub Group.

***DeRogatis, Jim.** Let It Blurt: The Life & Times of Lester Bangs, America's Greatest Rock Critic. (Illus.). 331p. 2000. pap. 15.95 (*0-7679-0509-1*) Broadway BDD.

Derogy, Jaques. Resistance & Revenge: The Armenian Assassination of the Turkish Leaders Responsible for the 1915 Massacres & Deportations. 180p. (C). 1990. 34.95 (*0-88738-338-6*) Transaction Pubs.

DeRohan, Ceanne. Right Use of Will: Healing & Evolving the Emotional Body. xi, 125p. 1984. 9.00 (*1-929113-00-5*, Pub. by Fr Winds Pubns) DeVorss.

DerOhannesian, Paul, II. Sexual Assault Trials. 1099p. 1994. 105.00 (*0-614-05964-X*, MICHIE); 125.00 (*1-55834-206-0*, 61175-10, MICHIE) LEXIS Pub.

— Sexual Assault Trials, 2 vols. Incl. Vol. 1. 2nd ed. LC 98-88609. 1998. (*0-327-00826-1*); Vol. 2. 2nd ed. LC 98-88609. 1998. (*0-327-00827-X*); LC 98-88609. 1500p. 1998. 125.00 (*0-327-00666-8*, 3117511) LEXIS Pub.

DeRolf, Shane. The Crayon Box That Talked. LC 97-19092. (J). 1997. 12.00 (*0-679-88611-7*, Pub. by Random Bks Yng Read) Random.

Derolf, Shane. The Little Box of Crayons. (J). 1998. pap. 16.99 (*0-679-85460-6*) Knopf Bks Yng Read.

Derolfe, Shane. The Crayon Box That Talked. (J). 1997. lib. bdg. 13.99 (*0-679-98611-1*, Pub. by Random Bks Yng Read) Random.

Derome, A. E. Modern NMR Techniques for Chemical Research. (Organic Chemistry Ser.). (Illus.). 295p. 1987. text 167.00 (*0-08-032514-9*, Pergamon Pr); pap. text 50.00 (*0-08-032513-0*, Pergamon Pr) Elsevier.

Derome, Pierre-Andre, jt. auth. see Gauthier, Gilles.

DeRomilly, Jacqueline. A Short History of Greek Literature. Doherty, Lillian, tr. from FRE. LC 84-16457. (Illus.). 304p. 1985. lib. bdg. 32.50 (*0-226-14311-2*) U Ch Pr.

— A Short History of Greek Literature. Doherty, Lillian, tr. from FRE. LC 84-16457. (Illus.). 310p. 1996. pap. text 12.00 (*0-226-14312-0*) U Ch Pr.

DeRonde, John A., Jr., jt. auth. see Coats, Susan S.

DeRoo, Deborah, jt. auth. see Tullman, Marcia.

DeRoo, John, ed. see James, Will.

Derooy, Jacob. Economic Literacy: What Everyone Needs to Know about Money & Markets. 448p. 1996. pap. 16.00 (*0-517-88683-9*) Crown Pub Group.

DeRopp, Robert S. Warrior's Way: The Challenging Life Games. 1984. 18.75 (*0-8446-6174-0*) Peter Smith.

DeRopp, Robert S., ed. Conversations with Madame Ouspensky: 1939-40 at Lyne. 22p. 1995. pap. 7.00 (*0-914480-00-6*) Far West Edns.

DeRosa, Carl, jt. auth. see Porterfield, James A.

***DeRosa, Christopher, ed.** Cancer Policy Framework. 57p. (C). 2000. reprint ed. pap. text 20.00 (*0-7881-8864-X*) DIANE Pub.

Derosa, David. Currency Derivatives: The Handbook of Instruments, Strategies, & Applications. 350p. text 70.00 (*1-55738-876-8*, Irwn Prfssnl) McGraw-Hill Prof.

***Derosa, David, ed.** Currency Derivatives: Pricing Theory, Exotic Options Hedging Applications. LC 98-5653. (Financial Engineering Ser.). 387p. 1998. 69.95 (*0-471-25267-0*) Wiley.

***DeRosa, David F.** In Defense of Free Capital Markets: The Case Against a New International Financial Architecture. 2000. 27.95 (*1-57660-036-X*) Bloomberg NJ.

Derosa, David F. Managing Foreign Exchange Risk: Advanced Strategies for Global Investors, Corporations. rev. ed. 304p. 1996. per. 65.00 (*1-55738-566-1*, Irwn Prfssnl) McGraw-Hill Prof.

— Managing Foreign Exchange Risk: Advanced Strategies for Global Investors, Corporations, & Financial Institutions. 2nd rev. ed. Fabozzi, Frank J., ed. LC 96-3753. 304p. 1996. 65.00 (*0-7863-1022-7*, Irwn Prfssnl) McGraw-Hill Prof.

DeRosa, David F. Options on Foreign Exchange. (Institutional Investor Publications). 250p. 1992. text 65.00 (*1-55738-249-2*, Irwn Prfssnl) McGraw-Hill Prof.

— Options on Foreign Exchange. 2nd rev. ed. LC 99-38491. (Series in Financial Engineering). 240p. 2000. 69.95 (*0-471-31641-5*) Wiley.

DeRosa, Dean A. Regional Trading Arrangements among Developing Countries: The ASEAN Example. LC 95-20612. (Research Reports - International Food Policy Research Institute Ser.: Vol. 103). 1995. write for info. (*0-89629-106-5*) Intl Food Policy.

Derosa, Gaetano. Italian GT Cars: Alfa Romeo, Lamborghini, Maserati & Other Makes. (Illus.). 93p. 1995. pap. 7.98 (*0-7603-0195-6*) MBI Pubg.

DeRosa, Laura. How to Cut Your Child's Hair at Home: A Step-by-Step Guide to Giving Your Child a Professional Looking Haircut at Home. LC 94-10817. (Illus.). 160p. pap. 9.95 (*0-89529-612-8*, Avery) Penguin Putnam.

DeRosa, Marshall L. The Confederate Constitution of 1861: An Inquiry into American Constitutionalism. 192p. (C). 1991. pap. 16.95 (*0-8262-0812-6*) U of Mo Pr.

— The Ninth Amendment & the Politics of Creative Jurisprudence: Disparaging the Fundamental Right of Popular Control. 148p. (C). 1996. text 39.95 (*1-56000-233-6*) Transaction Pubs.

DeRosa, Marshall L., ed. The Politics of Dissolution: The Quest for a National Identity & the American Civil War. LC 97-29445. 356p. 1997. text 39.95 (*1-56000-349-9*) Transaction Pubs.

DeRose, Paulette, ed. see Lindell, Colleen.

Derose, A. J., jt. auth. see Cowper, C. J.

DeRose, Chris. In Your Face: From Actor to Animal Activist. Tiger, Steve, ed. LC 96-86045. (Illus.). 303p. 1997. 21.00 (*0-9653219-0-8*) Duncan Pub.

***DeRose, Garry J.** Outsourcing Training & Education. LC 99-72435. 247p. 1999. pap. 27.95 (*1-56286-112-3*) Am Soc Train & Devel.

***DeRose, James F.** Unrestricted Warfare: Hoe a New Breed of Officers Led the Submarine Force to Victory in World War II. LC 00-24299. (Illus.). 320p. 2000. 27.95 (*0-471-38495-X*) Wiley.

DeRose, James F. The Wireless Data Handbook. 4th ed. LC 99-30369. 388p. 1999. 94.95 (*0-471-31651-2*) Wiley.

DeRose, Keith & Warfield, Ted A., eds. Skepticism: A Contemporary Reader. 320p. (C). 1999. text 47.00 (*0-19-511826-X*); pap. text 27.95 (*0-19-511827-8*) OUP.

Derose, Laurie F., et al. Who's Hungry? & How Do We Know? Food Shortage, Poverty, & Deprivation. LC 97-45294. (Illus.). 201p. 1998. pap. 19.95 (*92-808-0985-7*, Pub. by UN Univ Pr) Brookings.

DeRose, Richard. Retail to Hell: Why We Need to Fear the Information Highway, Super Stores & Super Powers! LC 97-94849. 144p. 1998. pap. 9.95 (*0-9662178-1-0*) Am at Risk.

Derose, Steven J. The SGML FAQ Book: Understanding the Foundation of HTML & XML. LC 97-20857. (Electronic Publishing Ser.). 1997. text 68.00 (*0-7923-9943-9*) Kluwer Academic.

DeRose, Steven J. & Durand, David G. Making Hypermedia Work: A User's Guide to HyTime. LC 94-16201. 408p. (C). 1994. text 95.50 (*0-7923-9432-1*) Kluwer Academic.

Derosia, Victoria R. Living Inside Prison Walls: Adjustment Behavior. LC 98-15659. 224p. 1998. 55.00 (*0-275-95895-7*, Praeger Pubs) Greenwood.

DeRosier, Arthur H., Jr. The Removal of the Choctaw Indians. (Illus.). 224p. 1970. pap. text 16.95 (*0-87049-329-9*) U of Tenn Pr.

***DeRosier, Linda S.** Creeker: A Woman's Journey. LC 98-32029. (Women in Southern Culture Ser.). 272p. 1999. 27.50 (*0-8131-2123-X*) U Pr of Ky.

***DeRosis, Helen.** Parent Power - Child Power: The Win-Win Way to Rasie Your Child. 2000. pap. 14.95 (*1-57826-043-4*, Pub. by Hatherleigh) Norton.

Derosis, Helen A. Women & Anxiety: A Step-by-Step Program for Managing Anxiety & Depression. rev. ed. LC 97-41355. (Hatherleigh Self-Help Classic Ser.). 304p. 1998. pap. 14.95 (*1-886330-99-9*, Pub. by Hatherleigh) Norton.

DeRossa, Julie, jt. auth. see Veveris, Mike.

DeRossi, D., et al. Polymer Gels: Fundamentals & Biomedical Applications. LC 91-2631. (Illus.). 354p. (C). 1991. text 110.00 (*0-306-43805-4*, Kluwer Plenum) Kluwer Academic.

Derossi, Flavia. The Technocratic Illusion: A Study of Managerial Power in Italy. LaBello, Susan, tr. LC 81-14341.Tr. of L'illusione Tecnocratica. (Illus.). 247p. reprint ed. pap. 76.60 (*0-608-18124-2*, 2032777000081) Bks Demand.

DeRosso, H. A. The Dark Brand. 224p. 1998. reprint ed. mass mkt. 4.50 (*0-8439-4412-9*, Leisure Bks) Dorchester Pub Co.

— .44. large type ed. LC 97-13074. (Nightingale Ser.). 248p. (Orig.). 1997. pap. 17.95 (*0-7838-8206-8*, G K Hall Lrg Type) Mac Lib Ref.

— .44. 208p. (Orig.). 1998. reprint ed. mass mkt. 4.50 (*0-8439-4357-2*, Leisure Bks) Dorchester Pub Co.

***DeRosso, H. A.** The Gun Trail. 1999. 19.00 (*0-7540-8072-2*, Gunsmoke) Chivers N Amer.

DeRosso, H. A. Riders of the Shadowlands: Western Stories. Date not set. 19.95 (*0-7862-1329-9*) Thorndike Pr.

***DeRosso, H. A.** Under the Burning Sun. 288p. 2000. mass mkt. 4.50 (*0-8439-4712-8*, Leisure Bks) Dorchester Pub Co.

DeRosso, H. A. Under the Burning Sun. Pronzini, Bill, ed. LC 96-43956. (Five Star Ser.). 263p. 1997. 17.95 (*0-7862-0737-X*) Five Star.

Derouane, E. G. & North Atlantic Treaty Organization Staff. Advances & Challenges in the Catalytic Activation & Functionalisation of Light Alkanes. LC 97-49074. (NATO ASI Series). 504p. 1998. 242.00 (*0-7923-4960-1*) Kluwer Academic.

***DeRouen, Karl R., Jr., ed.** Historical Encyclopedia of U.S. Presidential Use of Force, 1789-2000. LC 00-20467. 2000. lib. bdg. write for info. (*0-313-30732-6*) Greenwood.

DeRouge, J. & Feaurdent, F. The Coins of the Nomes & Prefecture of Roman Egypt. (FRE., Illus.). 1979. reprint ed. 20.00 (*0-916710-41-6*); reprint ed. pap. 20.00 (*0-685-95531-1*) Obol Intl.

***DeRouin, Ed.** Trackside in Chicago with Geo. Speir. (Illus.). 128p. 1999. 54.95 (*1-58248-026-5*) Morning NJ.

***Derouin, R. E.** San Juan Solution. LC 00-102172. 288p. 2000. pap. 14.95 (*1-890437-52-2*) Western Reflections.

***Derouin, Ray.** Time Trials: A Mountain Time Mystery. LC 99-61617. (Illus.). 223p. 1999. pap. 12.95 (*1-890437-27-1*) Western Reflections.

Derounian, Kathryn Z., ed. The Journal & Occasional Writings of Sarah Wister. LC 85-46012. (Illus.). 1987. 32.50 (*0-8386-3288-2*) Fairleigh Dickinson.

Derounian-Stodola, Kathryn Z., ed. Early American Literature & Culture: Essays Honoring Harrison T. Meserole. LC 90-50936. (Illus.). 264p. 1992. 39.50 (*0-87413-423-4*) U Delaware Pr.

Derounian-Stodola, Kathryn Zabelle. Women's Indian Captivity Narratives. LC 98-21291. (Penguin Classics Ser.). 432p. 1998. pap. 13.95 (*0-14-043671-5*) Viking Penguin.

DeRousseau, C. J. Osteoarthritis in Rhesus Monkeys & Gibbons: A Locomotor Model of Joint Degeneration. (Contributions to Primatology Ser.: Vol. 25). (Illus.). xiv, 146p. 1988. 83.50 (*3-8055-4700-5*) S Karger.

Derowitsch, Charles. Nile Journeys. LC 97-75987. (Illus.). 160p. 1998. 19.95 (*1-57197-106-8*) Pentland Pr.

Derowitz, Alan. Shouting Fire. 1995. write for info. (*0-316-18141-2*) Little.

DeRoy, Craig, jt. auth. see Polland, Barbara Kay.

Deroy, Louis. Dictionnaire des Noms de Lieux. (FRE.). 560p. 1992. 110.00 (*0-7859-9211-1*) Fr & Eur.

DerPriest, Paul D., jt. auth. see Van Nagell, John R.

***Derr.** Statistical Consulting: A Guide to Effective Communication. LC 99-54462. (Statistics Ser.). 200p. 1999. pap. text 79.95 (*0-534-36228-1*) Brooks-Cole.

Derr, C. Brooklyn, ed. Work, Family & the Career: New Frontiers in Theory & Research. LC 80-13598. 365p. 1980. 40.95 (*0-275-90469-5*, C0469, Praeger Pubs) Greenwood.

Derr, Clyde B. Managing the New Careerists: The Diverse Career Success Orientations of Today's Workers. LC 85-45901. (Joint Publication in the Jossey-Bass Management Series & the Jossey-Bass Social & Behavioral Science Ser.). 312p. reprint ed. pap. 96.80 (*0-7837-2515-9*, 204267400006) Bks Demand.

Derr, Don A. & Small, Leslie, eds. Property Rights in Transition. 243p. (C). 1977. text 32.50 (*0-8422-5252-5*); pap. text 11.95 (*0-8422-0554-3*) Irvington.

Derr, J. Russell. Employment Law Desk Book for Nebraska Employers. LC 97-121075. 300p. 1996. ring bd. 127.00 (*0-925773-34-4*) M Lee Smith.

Derr, Jill M., et al. Women of Covenant: The Story of Relief Society. LC 91-47981. (Illus.). 544p. 1992. 21.00 (*0-87579-593-5*) Deseret Bk.

Derr, Kurt W. Applying OMT: A Practical Step-by-Step Guide to Using the Object Modeling Technique. (Advances in Object Technology: No. 8). 557p. (Orig.). 1995. pap. 44.95 (*0-13-231390-1*) Cambridge U Pr.

Derr, Mark. Dog's Best Friend: Annals of the Dog-Human Relationship. LC 96-49795. 1995. 25.00 (*0-8050-4063-3*) H Holt & Co.

— Over Florida. Fraser, Jane & Jacobson, Ruth, eds. (Wings over America Ser.). (Illus.). 256p. 1995. reprint ed. pap. 35.00 (*1-887451-04-8*) Weldon Owen.

— Some Kind of Paradise: A Chronicle of Man & the Land in Florida. LC 98-8860. 448p. 1998. reprint ed. pap. 17.95 (*0-8130-1629-0*) U Press Fla.

Derr, Thomas S., et al. Environmental Ethics & Christian Humanism. LC 96-43923. (Abingdon Press Studies in Christian Ethics & Economic Life). 144p. 1997. pap. 17.95 (*0-687-00161-7*) Abingdon.

Derradji, Abder-Rahmane. The Algerian Guerrilla Campaign Strategy & Tactics. LC 97-19082. 348p. 1997. text 99.95 (*0-7734-2292-7*) E Mellen.

Derraugh, Lynn. Dottie Duck's Fluffy Feathers. (Touch 'n' Squeak Ser.). (Illus.). 14p. (J). (gr. k-3). 1998. bds. 7.99 (*1-57584-091-X*, Pub. by Rdrs Digest) Random.

— Puppy Dog's Special Friends. LC 98-224241. (Touch & Squeak Bks.). (Illus.). 14p. (J). (gr. k-3). 1998. bds. 7.99 (*1-57584-092-8*) Rdrs Digest.

Derraugh, Pat. Wedding Etiquette: The What, How & When of Weddings. 1998. pap. 7.95 (*0-572-02409-6*, Pub. by W Foulsham) Trans-Atl Phila.

Derrek, Kristen. Dancing with the Skeleton: Meditations for Suicide Survivors. Johnson, Joy, ed. (Illus.). 32p. (Orig.). 1996. pap. 3.95 (*1-56123-081-2*) Centering Corp.

Derrer, Douglas S. We Are All the Target: A Handbook of Terrorism Avoidance & Hostage Survival. LC 92-4415. 112p. 1992. pap. 16.95 (*1-55750-150-5*) Naval Inst Pr.

Derret, J. Duncan, tr. see Lingat, Robert.

Derrett, D. R. & Barrass, B. Ship Stability for Masters & Mates. 5th ed. LC 99-20870. 447p. 1999. write for info. (*0-7506-4101-0*) Buttrwrth-Heinemann.

Derrett, J. D., tr. see Lingat, Robert.

Derrett, J. Duncan. The Sea-Change of the Old Testament in the New. (Studies in the New Testament: Vol. 5). xii, 245p. 1989. 88.00 (*90-04-09110-6*) Brill Academic Pubs.

Derrett, J Duncan M. Religion, Law & the State in India. LC 99-933479. (Law in India Ser.). 616p. 1999. pap. text 23.95 (*0-19-564793-9*) OUP.

Derrey, Francois. The Earth Is Alive: Origins of the Earth & the Solar System. Roy, Gregor, tr. from FRE. 1968. 24.00 (*0-8464-0346-3*) Beekman Pubs.

Derrick, Christopher. The Delicate Creation. 144p. 1972. 9.95 (*0-8159-5304-6*) Devin.

— Escape from Scepticism: Liberal Education As If Truth Mattered. 1977. pap. 5.95 (*0-89385-002-0*) Sugden.

— Joy Without a Cause: Selected Essays of Christopher Derrick. 254p. 1979. pap. 6.95 (*0-89385-004-7*) Sugden.

— That Strange Divine Sea: Reflections on Being a Catholic. LC 83-80190. 189p. (Orig.). 1983. pap. 8.95 (*0-89870-029-9*) Ignatius Pr.

Derrick, Dan, jt. auth. see Derrick, Dennis.

Derrick, David. Identifying Knots. 80p. 1996. 7.98 (*0-7858-0575-3*) Bk Sales Inc.

Derrick, Dennis & Derrick, Dan. Master SimCity-SimEarth. 425p. 1991. 16.95 (*0-672-22787-8*) Sams.

Derrick, John. The Office Equipment Adviser. 3rd rev. ed. 500p. 1995. pap. text 24.95 (*1-882568-58-3*) What to Buy Busn.

Derrick, John, jt. ed. see Bowman, Howard.

Derrick, Jonathan M., jt. auth. see Austen, Ralph A.

Derrick, M., ed. Physics in Collision: Proceedings of the 6th International Conference, Chicago, Illinois, September, 3-5, 1986. 552p. 1987. pap. 47.00 (*9971-5-0282-8*); text 144.00 (*9971-5-0281-X*) World Scientific Pub.

Derrick, Michael. The Portugal of Salazar. (Select Bibliographies Reprint Ser.). 1977. reprint ed. 15.95 (*0-8369-9959-2*) Ayer.

***Derrick, Michele R., et al.** Infrared Spectroscopy in Conservation Science. LC 99-37860. (New in the Scientific Tools for Conservation Ser.). (Illus.). 320p. 1999. pap. 75.00 (*0-89236-469-6*, Pub. by J P Getty Trust) OUP.

Derrick, Neil, jt. auth. see Field, Edward.

Derrick, Paul. Men over Industry. 1980. lib. bdg. 59.95 (*0-8490-3079-X*) Gordon Pr.

***Derrick, Peter.** Tunneling to the Future: The Story of the Great Subway Expansion That Saved New York. 2001. 34.95 (*0-8147-1910-4*) NYU Pr.

Derrick, Peter & Hermalyn, Cary, eds. The Bronx Cookbook. LC 98-137533. (Illus.). 126p. 1998. 12.00 (*0-941980-37-5*) Bronx County.

***Derrick, Rachel Christmas.** Bahamas for Dummies. (For Dummies Ser.). 384p. 2000. pap. 16.99 (*0-7645-6203-7*) IDG Bks.

Derrick, Rachel Christmas. Hawaii Guide. 8th ed. 1999. pap. 18.95 (*1-892975-12-2*) Open Rd Pub.

Derrick, Samuel. The Dramatic Censor: Remarks upon the Tragedy of Venice Preserv'd; with Some Observations on the Performers from "The Dramatic Censor; Being Remarks upon the Conduct, Characters, & Catastrophe of Our Most Celebrated Plays by Several Hands" LC 92-22025. (Augustan Reprints Ser.: Nos. 233-234). reprint ed. 21.50 (*0-404-70233-3*) AMS Pr.

Derrick, Sara M., et al. Hospitalized Children Play & Play Activities. (Illus.). 106p. (Orig.). 1983. pap. write for info. (*0-89279-049-0*) S M Derrick.

Derrick, Scott S. Monumental Anxieties: Homoerotic Desire & Feminine Influence in 19th-Century U. S. Literature. LC 97-17699. (Illus.). 256p. 1997. 50.00 (*0-8135-2471-7*); pap. 20.00 (*0-8135-2472-5*) Rutgers U Pr.

Derrick, Thomas J. Understanding Shakespeare's Julius Caesar: A Student Casebook to Issues, Sources, & Historical Documents. LC 96-25005. (Literature in Context Ser.). 256p. 1998. 39.95 (*0-313-29638-3*) Greenwood.

Derrick, Tony. Hardy Houseplants. 128p. 1996. write for info. (*1-57215-170-6*) World Pubns.

Derrick, William R. & Grossman, Stanley I. Elemetary Differential Equation & Boundary. 4th rev. ed. LC 96-13215. 704p. (C). 1997. 103.00 (*0-673-98555-5*) Addison-Wesley.

Derrick, William R. & Grossman, Stanley I. Answer Book. 2nd ed. (Mathematics Ser.). (Illus.). 576p. (C). 1981. pap. text, teacher ed. 1.50 (*0-201-03166-3*) Addison-Wesley.

— Elem Diftl Equatn w/Appl. 2nd ed. (Mathematics Ser.). (Illus.). 576p. (C). 1981. text 21.95 (*0-201-03162-0*) Addison-Wesley.

— Elementary Differential Equations. 4th abr. ed. LC 96-16335. (C). 1996. 41.65 (*0-06-500789-1*) Addson-Wesley Educ.

— Elementary Differential Equations with Applications: A Short Course. 2nd ed. (Mathematics Ser.). (Illus.). 384p. (C). 1981. text 30.00 (*0-201-03164-7*) Addison-Wesley.

— Elementary Differential Equations with Boundary Value Problems. 4th rev. ed. LC 96-13215. Orig. Title: Introduction to Differential Equations with Boundary Value Problems. (C). 1997. write for info. (*0-06-500790-5*) Addson-Wesley Educ.

— Introduction to Differential Equations with Boundary Value Problems. LC 86-24641. (Illus.). 554p. (C). 1987. student ed. 16.25 (*0-685-17250-3*) West Pub.

— Introduction to Differential Equations with Boundary Value Problems. 3rd ed. LC 86-24641. (Illus.). 554p. (C). 1987. mass mkt. 56.75 (*0-314-26897-9*) West Pub.

Derricke, John. The Image of Irelande with a Discouerie of Woodkarne. LC 98-7328. (Facsimiles & Reprints Ser.: Vol. 511). 206p. 1998. 50.00 (*0-8201-1511-8*) Schol Facsimiles.

Derrickson, Carol M. Chinese for the Martial Arts. 90 min. cass. (CHI & ENG., Illus.). 48p. 1996. pap. 16.95 incl. audio (*0-8048-2044-9*) Tuttle Pubng.

D

Derrickson, Margaret, ed. The Literature of the Nonprofit Sector Vol. 1: A Bibliography with Abstracts. (Orig.). 1989. pap. text 55.00 (*0-87954-287-X*) Foundation Ctr.

Derrickson, Margaret, ed. see Foundation Center Staff.

Derrico, Karen. Unforgettable Mutts: Pure of Heart Not of Breed. LC 99-14107. (Illus.). 220p. 1999. pap. 14.95 (*0-939165-34-1*) NewSage Press.

Derricott, Betty A. Free to Lead: The Doctor's Guide to Profitable Leadership Performance. Khoury, Martha & Campbell, Ellen, eds. LC 93-74929. (Illus.). 200p. 1994. pap. 29.95 (*0-9640156-0-9*) Derricott Dental.

Derricott, R. & Chissick, Seymour S., eds. Energy Conservation & Thermal Insulation. LC 80-41587. (Properties of Materials Safety & Environmental Factors Ser.). (Illus.). 807p. reprint ed. pap. 200.00 (*0-8357-8635-8*, 203505900092) Bks Demand.

— Rebuild. LC 81-21942. (Properties of Materials Safety & Environmental Factors Ser.). (Illus.). 300p. reprint ed. pap. 93.00 (*0-608-17541-2*, 203051900069) Bks Demand.

Derricott, R., jt. ed. see Chissick, Seymour S.

Derricott, Ray, jt. auth. see Cogan, John.

Derricott, Ray, jt. ed. see Cogan, John.

Derricotte, Toi. The Black Notebooks: An Interior Journey. LC 97-5855. 160p. 1997. 21.95 (*0-393-04544-7*) Norton.

— The Black Notebooks: An Interior Journey. abr. ed. 205p. 1999. pap. 13.00 (*0-393-31901-6*) Norton.

— Captivity. LC 89-31840. (Poetry Ser.). 74p. 1989. pap. 10.95 (*0-8229-5422-2*) U of Pittsburgh Pr.

***Derricotte, Toi.** Natural Birth. 88p. 2000. pap. 10.95 (*1-56341-120-2*, Pub. by Firebrand Bks); lib. bdg. 22.95 (*1-56341-121-0*, Pub. by Firebrand Bks) LPC InBook.

Derricotte, Toi. Tender. LC 97-4602. (Poetry Ser.). 83p. 1997. pap. 12.95 (*0-8229-5640-3*); text 25.00 (*0-8229-3993-2*) U of Pittsburgh Pr.

Derricourt, Robin. An Author's Guide to Scholarly Publishing. LC 95-36849. 264p. 1996. pap. text 17.95 (*0-691-03709-4*, Pub. by Princeton U Pr) Cal Prin Full Svc.

— Man on the Kafue: The Archaeology & History of the Itezhitezhi Area of Zambia. LC 84-6293. (Illus.). 272p. 1985. text 37.50 (*0-936508-10-8*) Barber Pr.

Derrida, Jacques. Acts of Literature. Attridge, Derek, ed. 432p. (C). (gr. 13). 1991. pap. 19.99 (*0-415-90057-3*, A2414) Routledge.

***Derrida, Jacques.** Adieu to Emmanuel Levinas LC 99-21519. (Meridian, Crossing Aesthetics Ser.). 1999. 14.95 (*0-8047-3275-2*) Stanford U Pr.

— Adieu to Emmanuel Levinas. LC 99-21519. 162p. 1999. 39.50 (*0-8047-3267-1*) Stanford U Pr.

Derrida, Jacques. Aporias. Dutoit, Thomas, tr. from FRE. 104p. (C). 1994. 32.50 (*0-8047-2233-1*); pap. 12.95 (*0-8047-2252-8*) Stanford U Pr.

— The Archeology of the Frivolous: Reading Condillac. Leavey, John P., Jr., tr. from FRE. LC 86-25106. 143p. 1987. reprint ed. pap. 13.00 (*0-8032-6571-9*, Bison Books); reprint ed. text 40.00 (*0-8032-1678-5*) U of Nebr Pr.

— Archive Fever. 1998. pap. text 12.00 (*0-226-14367-8*) U Ch Pr.

— Archive Fever: A Freudian Impression. Prenowitz, Eric, tr. LC 96-18568. 144p. 1996. 17.95 (*0-226-14336-8*) U Ch Pr.

— The Derrida Reader: Writing Performances. Wolfreys, Julian, ed. & intro. by. LC 98-224252. 1998. text 70.00 (*0-8032-4788-5*); pap. text 27.50 (*0-8032-9807-2*) U of Nebr Pr.

— Dissemination. 1994. 27.50 (*0-8446-6737-4*) Peter Smith.

— Dissemination. Johnson, Barbara, tr. LC 81-3359. xxiv, 400p. (C). 1983. pap. text 17.95 (*0-226-14334-1*) U Ch Pr.

— The Ear of the Other: Otobiography, Transference, Translation. McDonald, Christie, ed. Kamuf, Peggy & Ronell, Avital, trs. from FRE. LC 88-14336. xii, 190p. 1988. reprint ed. pap. 12.00 (*0-8032-6575-1*, Bison Books) U of Nebr Pr.

— Edmund Husserl's "Origins of Geometry" An Introduction. Leavey, John P., Jr., tr. from FRE. LC 88-38638. vii, 205p. 1989. reprint ed. pap. 14.00 (*0-8032-6580-8*, Bison Books) U of Nebr Pr.

— Eperson: Les Styles de Nietzsche. (FRE.). 1991. pap. 12.95 (*0-7859-3004-3*) Fr & Eur.

— The Gift of Death. Wills, David, tr. LC 94-28893. (FRE.). 123p. 1995. 18.95 (*0-226-14305-8*) U Ch Pr.

— The Gift of Death. (Religion & Postmodernism Ser.). 124p. (C). 1996. reprint ed. pap. 11.00 (*0-226-14306-6*) U Ch Pr.

— Given Time: I. Counterfeit Money. Kamuf, Peggy, tr. 182p. 1994. pap. text 14.00 (*0-226-14314-7*) U Ch Pr.

— Glas. Leavey, John P., Jr. & Rand, Richard, trs. from FRE. LC 85-28877. v, 262p. 1986. reprint ed. pap. text 45.00 (*0-8032-6581-6*, Bison Books) U of Nebr Pr.

— Heidegger et la Question. (FRE.). 1990. pap. 19.95 (*0-7859-3005-1*) Fr & Eur.

— Limited Inc. Weber, Samuel & Mehlmann, Jeffrey, trs. from FRE. 160p. 1988. 29.95 (*0-8101-0787-2*); pap. 14.95 (*0-8101-0788-0*) Northwestern U Pr.

— Margins of Philosophy. Bass, Alan, tr. from FRE. LC 82-11137. 360p. (C). 1984. pap. text 16.95 (*0-226-14326-0*) U Ch Pr.

— Memoires for Paul de Man. Lindsay, Cecile et al, trs. LC 85-27999. 1986. text 44.00 (*0-231-06232-X*) Col U Pr.

— Memoires for Paul de Man. rev. ed. Lindsay, Cecile et al, trs. LC 85-27999. 153p. 1989. pap. text 20.00 (*0-231-06233-8*) Col U Pr.

— Memoirs of the Blind: The Self-Portrait & Other Ruins. Brault, Pascale-Anne & Naas, Michael, trs. LC 92-27027. (Illus.). 152p. (C). 1993. pap. 32.50 (*0-226-14308-2*); lib. bdg. 71.50 (*0-226-14307-4*) U Ch Pr.

— Monolingualism of the Other: or The Prosthesis of Origin. Mensah, Patrick, tr. (Cultural Memory in the Present Ser.). 108p. 1998. pap. 12.95 (*0-8047-3289-2*) Stanford U Pr.

— Monolingualism of the Other: or The Prosthesis of Origin. Mensah, Patrick, tr. from ENG. LC 98-4454. (Cultural Memory in the Present Ser.). 108p. 1998. 39.50 (*0-8047-3288-4*) Stanford U Pr.

— Of Grammatology. Spivak, Gayatri Chakravorty, tr. LC 76-17226. (Illus.). 446p. 1977. pap. 18.95 (*0-8018-1879-6*) Johns Hopkins.

— Of Grammatology. Spivak, Gayatri Chakravorty, tr. LC 76-17226. 450p. 1998. pap. text 19.95 (*0-8018-5830-5*) Johns Hopkins.

— Of Grammatology. (C). 1994. text 28.50 (*81-208-1187-9*, Pub. by Motilal Bnarsidass) S Asia.

— Of Spirit: Heidegger & the Question. Bennington, Geoffrey & Bowlby, Rachel, trs. LC 88-32212. 147p. 1989. 23.95 (*0-226-14317-1*) U Ch Pr.

— Of Spirit: Heidegger & the Question. LC 88-32212. 152p. 1991. pap. 12.00 (*0-226-14319-8*) U Ch Pr.

— On the Name. Dutoit, Thomas, ed. Wood, David et al, trs. from FRE. LC 94-42209. (Meridian: Crossing Aesthetics Ser.). 168p. 1995. 37.50 (*0-8047-2554-3*); pap. 14.95 (*0-8047-2555-1*) Stanford U Pr.

— Points: Interviews. Weber, Elisabeth, ed. Kamuf, Peggy, tr. from FRE. LC 94-26823. (Meridian: Crossing Aesthetics Ser.). Orig. Title: Points de Suspension. (ENG.). xiv , 502p. 1995. 57.50 (*0-8047-2395-8*); pap. 18.95 (*0-8047-2488-1*) Stanford U Pr.

— The Politics of Friendship. Collins, George, tr. LC 97-11930. 1997. pap. 20.00 (*1-85984-033-7*, Pub. by Verso) Norton.

***Derrida, Jacques.** Politics of Mourning. 1999. 22.00 (*0-226-14316-3*) U Ch Pr.

Derrida, Jacques. Positions. Bass, Alan, tr. from FRE. LC 80-17620. 1981. 11.95 (*0-226-14332-5*) U Ch Pr.

— Positions. Bass, Alan, tr. from FRE. LC 80-17620. 128p. 1982. pap. text 8.00 (*0-226-14331-7*) U Ch Pr.

— The Post Card: From Socrates to Freud & Beyond. Bass, Alan, tr. LC 86-27259. (Illus.). 552p. (C). 1987. pap. text 26.00 (*0-226-14322-8*) U Ch Pr.

— Le Problem Genese Husseri. 300p. 2000. lib. bdg. 34.95 (*0-226-14315-5*) U Ch Pr.

— Psyche: Invention of the Other. 1993. pap. text 25.95 (*0-226-14310-4*); lib. bdg. 95.95 (*0-226-14309-0*) U Ch Pr.

— Resistances of Psychoanalysis. LC 97-45151. (Meridian Crossing Aesthetics Ser.). 1998. 39.50 (*0-8047-3018-0*); pap. 14.95 (*0-8047-3019-9*) Stanford U Pr.

— Rights of Inspection. LC 98-35774. 144p. 1998. pap. 29.95 (*1-58093-018-2*, Pub. by Monacelli Pr) Penguin Putnam.

— Specters of Marx: The State of the Debt, the Work of Mourning, & the New International. Kamuf, Peggy, tr. from FRE. LC 94-20564.Tr. of Spectres de Marx. 256p. (gr. 13). 1994. pap. 19.99 (*0-415-91045-5*, B4396) Routledge.

— Specters of Marx: The State of the Debt, the Work of Mourning, & the New International. Kamuf, Peggy, tr. from FRE. LC 94-20564.Tr. of Spectres de Marx. 256p. (C). (gr. 13). 1994. 75.00 (*0-415-91044-7*, B4392) Routledge.

— Speech & Phenomena: And Other Essays on Husserl's Theory of Signs. Allison, David B., tr. from FRE. LC 72-80565. (Studies in Phenomenology & Existential Philosophy). 166p. (C). 1973. pap. 16.95 (*0-8101-0590-X*) Northwestern U Pr.

— Spurs: Nietzsche's Styles. Harlow, Barbara, tr. from FRE. LC 79-31. vi, 172p. (C). 1981. reprint ed. pap. text 10.00 (*0-226-14333-3*) U Ch Pr.

— The Truth in Painting. Bennington, Geoffrey & McLeod, Ian, trs. (Illus.). xvi, 408p. 1987. pap. text 24.00 (*0-226-14324-4*) U Ch Pr.

— The Truth in Painting. Bennington, Geoffrey & McLeod, Ian, trs. (Illus.). xvi, 386p. 1987. lib. bdg. 49.95 (*0-226-14323-6*) U Ch Pr.

— La Verite en Peinture. (FRE.). 1990. pap. 21.95 (*0-7859-3402-2*) Fr & Eur.

— Writing & Difference. 1994. 26.25 (*0-8446-6738-2*) Peter Smith.

— Writing & Difference. Bass, Alan, tr. from FRE. LC 77-25933. 362p. 1980. pap. text 15.00 (*0-226-14329-5*, P863) U Ch Pr.

Derrida, Jacques & Eisenman, Peter. Chora 1 Works. LC 96-41372. (Illus.). 208p. 1997. 40.00 (*1-885254-40-7*, Pub. by Monacelli Pr) Penguin Putnam.

Derrida, Jacques & Thevenin, Paule. The Secret Art of Antonin Artaud. LC 97-44637. (Illus.). 176p. 1998. 27.50 (*0-262-04165-0*) MIT Pr.

***Derrida, Jacques & Thevenin, Paule.** The Secret Life of Antonin Artaud. (Illus.). 176p. 2000. reprint ed. pap. 16.00 (*0-262-54108-4*) MIT Pr.

Derrida, Jacques & Vattimo, Gianni, eds. The Complete Works of Friedrich Nietzsche: Religion. Webb, David et al, trs. from FRE. LC 98-60374. (Cultural Memory in the Present Ser.). 224p. 1998. pap. 14.95 (*0-8047-3487-9*) Stanford U Pr.

— Religion. Webb, David et al, trs. from FRE. LC 98-60374. (Cultural Memory in the Present Ser.). 224p. 1998. 49.50 (*0-8047-3486-0*) Stanford U Pr.

Derrida, Jacques, et al. Suitcase Vol. 1: A Journal of Transcultural Traffic. annuals (Illus.). 354p. pap. 20.00 (*0-9659565-0-4*) Suitcase.

Derrida, Jacques, jt. auth. see Bennington, Geoffrey.

Derrida, Jacques, jt. auth. see Blanchot, Maurice.

Derrida, James. Given Time: Counterfeit Money, Pt. 1. Kamuf, Peggy, tr. LC 92-7091. 182p. 1992. lib. bdg. 26.00 (*0-226-14313-9*) U Ch Pr.

Derrien, J., jt. ed. see Vial, J. C.

Derriey, Charles. Borders, Frames & Decorative Motifs from the 1862 Derriey Typographic Catalog. (Pictorial Archive Ser.). 144p. 1987. reprint ed. pap. 9.95 (*0-486-25322-8*) Dover.

Derrig, Leslie A. & Westdyk, Roxanne H. Mommy in the Sky. LC 83-73248. (Working Mommy Ser.: Vol. 2). (Illus.). 32p. (Orig.). (J). (gr. k-5). 1983. pap. 6.95 (*0-915479-68-0*) Cottage Pub Co.

Derrig, R. A., jt. auth. see Cummins, J. David.

Derrig, Richard A., jt. ed. see Cummins, J. David.

Derringh, Edward. Computational Engineering Geology. LC 97-34433. 323p. (C). 1997. pap. text 32.00 (*0-13-834236-9*) P-H.

Derrington, Justice & Ashton, Ronald S. The Law of Liability Insurance. 880p. 1990. boxed set 154.00 (*0-409-49494-1*, Austral, MICHIE) LEXIS Pub.

***Derrington, Patricia.** Serpent of Good & Evil: A Reconciliation in the Life & Art of Miriam-Rose Ungunmeer-Baumann. 2000. 25.95 (*1-86447-070-4*) Hyland Hse.

Derroitte, Henri, jt. ed. see Pirotte, Jean.

Derry, Alice. Clearwater. 1997. pap. 11.00 (*0-911287-23-X*) Blue Begonia.

— Not As You Once Imagined. LC 93-60592. 25p. 1993. pap. 7.00 (*0-932264-00-X*) Trask Hse Bks.

— Stages of Twilight. LC 86-17554. 74p. 1987. 14.95 (*0-932576-38-9*); pap. 7.95 (*0-932576-39-7*) Breitenbush Bks.

Derry, Andrew & Pradhan, Mahmood. Tax Specific Term Structures of Interest Rates: Evidence from the United Kingdom Government Bond Market. LC HG4651.. (Bank of England, Working Paper Ser.: Vol. 11). 29p. 1993. reprint ed. pap. 30.00 (*0-608-05320-1*, 206585800001) Bks Demand.

Derry, Andrew, jt. auth. see Deacon, Mark.

Derry, Ellis L. Old & Historic Churches of New Jersey, Vol. 2. 372p. 1994. 29.95 (*0-937548-25-1*); pap. 19.95 (*0-937548-26-X*) Plexus Pub.

***Derry, Gregory N.** What Science Is & How It Works. LC 99-17186. (Illus.). 1999. 29.95 (*0-691-05877-6*) Princeton U Pr.

Derry Historical Research Committee. From Turnpike to Interstate: The 150 Years of Derry, N. H. LC 77-20952. (Illus.). 1977. 12.00 (*0-914016-47-4*) Phoenix Pub.

Derry, Joseph T. The Story of the Confederate States. 1995. 29.99 (*0-87377-169-9*) GAM Pubns.

— Story of the Confederate States: or History of the War for Southern Independence Embracing the Early Settlement of the Country, Trouble with the Indians, the French, Revolutionary & Mexican Wars. 1980. 42.95 (*0-405-12295-0*) Ayer.

Derry, Robert, jt. auth. see Sciacca, Jan.

***Derry, Roger.** PC Audio Editing. LC 99-89555. 240p. 2000. pap. 39.95 (*0-240-51596-X*, Focal) Buttrwrth-Heinemann.

Derry, Sharon, jt. auth. see Lajoie, Susanne.

Derry, T. K. The Campaign in Norway. (Official Ser.: No. 12). (Illus.). 368p. 1995. reprint ed. 49.95 (*0-89839-220-9*) Battery Pr.

— A History of Scandinavia: Norway, Sweden, Denmark, Finland, & Iceland. LC 78-14284. 459p. 1979. pap. 19.95 (*0-8166-0936-5*) U of Minn Pr.

Derry, T. K. & Williams, Trevor I. A Short History of Technology from Ancient Times to A. D. 1900. LC 92-46454. (Illus.). xviii, 782p. 1993. reprint ed. pap. 17.95 (*0-486-27472-1*) Dover.

Derry, Thomas K. A Short History of Norway. LC 79-10688. (Illus.). 281p. 1979. reprint ed. lib. bdg. 79.50 (*0-313-21467-0*, DESH, Greenwood Pr) Greenwood.

Derry, Warren, ed. see Burney, Fanny.

Derryberry, Bill. Trouble Shooting Irrigation Control Systems. 3rd ed. vii, 141p. 1982. spiral bd. 25.00 (*0-9674584-0-4*, 2000-20) B Derryberry.

Dersch, jt. auth. see Riposa.

Derse, Ed. Explosive Power. LC 93-79689. 141p. 1993. pap. 19.95 (*0-944831-28-1*) Health Life.

Derse, Edward, jt. ed. see Wilson, Wayne.

Dershaw, D. David, ed. Interventional Breast Procedures. LC 95-41719. 1995. text 78.00 (*0-443-07630-8*) Church.

Dershem, Herbert L. & Jipping, Michael J. Programming Languages: Structures & Models. 413p. (C). 1990. text 55.95 (*0-534-12900-5*) PWS Pubs.

Dershem, Larry D. California Legal Research Handbook. LC 96-24429. (Illus.). xiv, 594p. 1997. ring bd. 95.00 (*0-8377-9311-4*, Rothman) W S Hein.

— Library of Congress Classification: Class J, Political Science, Cumulative Schedule & Index. LC 86-51384. (LC Class Ser.: No. 1). 800p. 1987. 105.00 (*0-941235-00-9*) Time Saver Pubns.

— Library of Congress Classification: Class J Political Science Cumulative Schedule & Index. 1987. ring bd. 105.00 (*0-318-39895-8*) W S Hein.

***Dershem, Larry D.** Library of Congress Classification, Class KD Law of the United Kingdom & Ireland: Cumulative Schedule & Index. LC 98-52339. No. 57. 1999. lib. bdg. 67.50 (*0-8377-9333-5*, Rothman) W S Hein.

Dershem, Larry D., compiled by. Library of Congress Classification: Class H, Social Sciences: Cumulative Schedule & Index. 4th ed. LC 95-30738. (AALL Publications: No. 48). 1995. write for info. (*0-8377-9299-1*, Rothman) W S Hein.

— Library of Congress Classification: Class K Subclass K Law (General) Cumulative Schedule & Index. (AALL Publications Ser.: No. 24). 1985. ring bd. 60.00 (*0-8377-0122-8*, Rothman) W S Hein.

— Library of Congress Classification: Class K Subclass KD Law of the United Kingdom & Ireland Cumulative Schedule & Index. LC 85-25597. (AALL Publications Ser.: No. 25). xiv, 431p. 1985. ring bd. 75.00 (*0-8377-0124-4*, Rothman) W S Hein.

— Library of Congress Classification: Class K Subclass KE Law of Canada Cumulative Schedule & Index. (AALL Publications Ser.: No. 27). xiv, 460p. 1987. ring bd. 75.00 (*0-8377-0126-0*, 312090, Rothman) W S Hein.

— Library of Congress Classification: Class KDZ, KG-KH Law of the Americas, Latin America & the West Indies Cumulative Schedule & Index. (AALL Publications Ser.: No. 28). 1988. ring bd. 85.00 (*0-8377-0127-9*, Rothman) W S Hein.

— Library of Congress Classification: Class KJV-KJW Law of France Cumulative Schedule & Index. (AALL Publications Ser.: No. 30). 1999. ring bd. 85.00 (*0-8377-0131-7*, Rothman) W S Hein.

— Library of Congress Classification: Class KL-KWX, Law of Asia & Eurasia, Africa, Pacific Area, & Antarctica Cumulative Schedule, 2 vols., 1. 1992. write for info. (*0-318-69560-X*) W S Hein.

— Library of Congress Classification: Class KL-KWX, Law of Asia & Eurasia, Africa, Pacific Area, & Antarctica Cumulative Schedule, 2 vols., 2. LC 92-25906. 1992. write for info. (*0-8377-9285-1*, Rothman) W S Hein.

***Dershem, Larry D., compiled by.** Library of Congress Classification Class H, Social Sciences, Cumulative Schedule & Index: 1997 Edition. 1997th ed. LC 98-8003. (AALL Publications: No. 48). 1998. ring bd. 125.00 (*0-8377-9328-9*, Rothman) W S Hein.

— Library of Congress Classification Class J Political Science Cumulative Schedule & Index: 1997 Edition. 1997th ed. LC 98-8005. (AALL Publications: No. 54). 1998. ring bd. 110.00 (*0-8377-9329-7*, Rothman) W S Hein.

— Library of Congress Classification Class K: Law in General Comparative & Uniform Law Jurisprudence Cumulative Schedule & Index 1998. annuals LC 99-42658. (AALL Publications: No. 24). 1998. ring bd. 62.00 (*0-8377-9335-1*) W S Hein.

Dershem, Larry D., compiled by. Library of Congress Classification Class K Subclass KF Law of the United States Cumulative Schedule & Index. (AALL Publications Ser.: No. 18). vii, 326p. 1982. ring bd. 75.00 (*0-8377-0115-5*, Rothman) W S Hein.

— Library of Congress Classification Class K Subclass KF Law of the United States Cumulative Schedule & Index. (AALL Publications Ser.: No. 20). 1984. ring bd. 82.00 (*0-8377-0118-X*, Rothman) W S Hein.

— Library of Congress Classification Class KJ-KKZ Law of Europe Cumulative Schedule & Index. (AALL Publications Ser.: No. 37). 1988. ring bd. 95.00 (*0-8377-9259-2*, Rothman) W S Hein.

— Library of Congress Classification Class KK-KKC Law of Germany Cumulative Schedule & Index. (AALL Publications Ser.: No. 35). 1990. ring bd. 95.00 (*0-8377-9255-X*, Rothman) W S Hein.

— Library of Congress Classification Class KL-KWX Law of Asia & Eurasia, Africa, Pacific Area & Antarctica Cumulative Schedule & Index, 2 vols., Set. LC 92-25906. (AALL Publications Ser.: No. 43). 1992. ring bd. 130.00 (*0-8377-9283-5*, Rothman) W S Hein.

— Library of Congress Classification Class R, Medicine Cumulative Schedule & Index. LC 96-5206. (AALL Publications: No. 50). 916p. 1996. ring bd. 110.00 (*0-8377-9325-4*, Rothman) W S Hein.

— Library of Congress Classification Class Z Bibliography & Library Science Cumulative Schedule & Index. (AALL Publications Ser.: No. 40). 1996. ring bd. 110.00 (*0-8377-9261-4*, Rothman) W S Hein.

***Dershem, Larry D., compiled by.** Library of Congress Classification K Tables Forms Division Tables for Law. LC 99-51310. (AALL Publications Ser.: No. 59). 1999. ring bd. 35.00 (*0-8377-9336-X*, 323750, Rothman) W S Hein.

***Dershem, Larry D. & American Association of Law Libraries Staff.** Library of Congress Classification: 1999 Edition. LC 00-20491. (AALL Publication Ser.). 2000. ring bd. write for info. (*0-8377-9339-4*, Rothman) W S Hein.

***Dershem, Larry D., et al.** Library of Congress Classification 1999: Class KF, Law of the United States: Cumulative Schedule. LC 00-27726. 2000. ring bd. write for info. (*0-8377-9341-6*, Rothman) W S Hein.

Dershem, Larry D., jt. auth. see Library of Congress Staff.

Dershewitz, Robert A. Ambulatory Pediatric Care. 3rd ed. LC 98-35195. 1106p. 1998. text 67.50 (*0-7817-1014-6*) Lppncott W & W.

Dershewitz, Robert A., ed. Ambulatory Pediatric Care. 2nd ed. LC 92-13524. 864p. 1993. text 72.00 (*0-397-51196-5*) Lppncott W & W.

Dershowitz, Alan M. The Advocate's Devil. 384p. 1995. mass mkt. 6.50 (*0-446-60291-4*, Pub. by Warner Bks) Little.

— The Advocate's Devil. 352p. 1999. reprint ed. 35.95 (*0-7351-0066-7*) Replica Bks.

— The Best Defense. LC 82-40426. (Illus.). 464p. 1983. pap. 17.00 (*0-394-71380-X*) Vin Bks.

— Contrary to Popular Opinion. 416p. 1994. reprint ed. pap. 12.00 (*0-425-14147-0*) Berkley Pub.

***Dershowitz, Alan M.** The Genesis of Justice: Ten Stories of Biblical Injustice that Led to the Ten Commandments & Modern Law. 2001. reprint ed. pap. 14.95 (*0-446-67677-2*) Warner Bks.

— The Genesis of Justice: Ten Stories of Biblical Injustices That Led to the Ten Commandments & Modern Law. LC 99-50220. 288p. 2000. 25.95 (*0-446-52479-4*, Pub. by Warner Bks) Little.

Dershowitz, Alan M. Great Trials of the Centuries. 1998. write for info. (*0-446-52058-6*) Warner Bks.

***Dershowitz, Alan M.** Just Revenge. LC 99-25632. 352p. 1999. 24.95 (*0-446-51983-9*, Pub. by Warner Bks) Little.

— Just Revenge. 2000. mass mkt. 7.99 (*0-446-60871-8*) Warner Bks.

D

Dershowitz, Alan M. Reasonable Doubts. LC 97-156738. 272p. 1997. per. 13.00 (*0-684-83264-X*, Touchstone) S&S Trade Pap.

— Reasonable Doubts: The O. J. Simpson Case & the Criminal Justice System. LC 96-1688. 238p. 1996. 20.00 (*0-684-83021-3*) S&S Trade.

— Reversal of Fortune. Peters, Sally, ed. 360p. 1990. reprint ed. mass mkt. 4.99 (*0-671-70724-8*, Archway) PB.

***Dershowitz, Alan M.** Sexual Mccarthyism. 2000. pap. 16.00 (*0-465-01629-4*, Pub. by Basic) HarpC.

— Sexual McCarthyism: Clinton, Starr, & the Emerging Constitutional Crisis. LC E886.2.D49 1998. 256p. 1998. 23.00 (*0-465-01628-6*, Pub. by Basic) HarpC.

Dershowitz, Alan M. The Vanishing American Jew: In Search of Jewish Identity for the Next Century. 416p. 1998. pap. 14.00 (*0-684-84898-8*) S&S Trade.

— The Vanishing American Jews: Is There a Future for Us? 1997. 24.95 (*0-614-27525-3*) Little.

Dershowitz, Barbara. Advanced Practice Book for the Degrees of Reading Power Test, No. I. 121p. 1990. student ed. 5.25 (*1-56078-019-3*) Comp Pr.

— The Affluent Spirit: Lessons in Spiritual & Material Abundance. LC 95-78373. 125p. (Orig.). 1995. pap. 12.95 (*0-9647619-1-2*) BDCI.

Dershowitz, Barbara, jt. auth. see Kaminoff, Leslie.

Dershowitz, N., ed. Rewriting Techniques & Applications. (Lecture Notes in Computer Science Ser.: Vol. 355). vii, 579p. 1989. 61.00 (*0-387-51081-8*) Spr-Verlag.

Dershowitz, Nachum. Evolution of Programs. (Progress in Computer Science Ser.: Vol. 5). 1983. 35.75 (*3-7643-3156-9*); 32.50 (*0-8176-3171-2*) Birkhauser.

Dershowitz, Nachum & Lindenstrauss, Naomi, eds. Conditional & Typed Rewriting Systems: 4th International Workshop, CTRS-94, Jerusalem, Israel, July 1994: Proceedings. LC 95-39593. (Lecture Notes in Computer Science Ser.: No. 968). 375p. 1995. 62.00 (*3-540-60381-6*) Spr-Verlag.

Dershowitz, Nachum & Reingold, Edward M. Calendrical Calculations. LC 96-45964. 330p. (C). 1997. text 69.95 (*0-521-56413-1*); pap. text 23.95 (*0-521-56474-3*) Cambridge U Pr.

***Dershowitz, Nachum & Reingold, Edward M.** Calendrical Calculations: The Millennium Edition. 268p. (C). 2000. pap. 24.95 (*0-521-77752-6*) Cambridge U Pr.

— Calendrical Calculations: The Millennium Edition. rev. ed. 268p. (C). 2000. 64.95 (*0-521-77167-6*) Cambridge U Pr.

Dershowitz, Yosef, jt. auth. see Mindel, Nissan.

Dershwitz. Board Reverse Anesthes Organ. 5th ed. 1998. pap. text 22.00 (*0-8385-0830-8*) Appleton & Lange.

Dershwitz, Mark. The MGH Board Review of Anesthesiology. 4th rev. ed. (C). 1994. pap. text 47.95 (*0-8385-8611-2*, A8611-4) Appleton & Lange.

Dershwitz, Mark, et al. The MGH Board Review of Anesthesiology. 5th ed. LC 98-21937. (Illus.). 302p. (C). 1999. pap. 49.95 (*0-8385-6348-1*) McGraw.

— National Boards Examination Review Pt. I: Basic Science (MEPC) 3rd ed. 422p. 1995. pap. text 35.00 (*0-8385-6655-3*, A6655-3, Apple Lange Med) McGraw.

Dersom, Omer K., ed. see Tullock, John H.

Derson, Anne. Something in the Air. 1994. teacher ed., spiral bd. 5.00 (*0-943864-93-3*) Davenport.

— Something in the Air. LC 93-74951. 136p. (J). (gr. 4-6). 1994. pap. 6.95 (*0-943864-74-7*) Davenport.

Derstine, Jill B. & Drayton-Hargrove, Shirlee. Comprehensive Rehabilitation Nursing. LC 99-40815. (Illus.). 830p. 2000. text. write for info. (*0-7216-6977-8*, W B Saunders Co) Harcrt Hlth Sci Grp.

Derstine, Rosita B., jt. auth. see Smith, Alonna F.

Derthick, Mark. Formulation of Tradeoffs in Planning under Uncertainty. (Research Notes in Artificial Intelligence Ser.). 200p. 1990. pap. 38.95 (*1-55860-132-5*) Morgan Kaufmann.

Derthick, Martha. Agency under Stress: The Social Security Administration & American Government. 231p. 1990. 36.95 (*0-8157-1824-1*); pap. 15.95 (*0-8157-1823-3*) Brookings.

— Between State & Nation: Regional Organizations of the United States. LC 74-727. 242p. 1974. 32.95 (*0-8157-1812-8*); pap. 12.95 (*0-8157-1811-X*) Brookings.

— Influence of Federal Grants: Public Assistance in Massachusetts. LC 73-95919. (Joint Center for Urban Studies). 297p. 1970. 41.00 (*0-674-45425-1*) HUP.

— The National Guard in Politics. LC 65-11588. (Harvard Political Studies). 210p. reprint ed. pap. 65.10 (*0-7837-2251-6*, 205733900004) Bks Demand.

— Policymaking for Social Security. LC 78-24811. 446p. 1979. 36.95 (*0-8157-1816-0*); pap. 16.95 (*0-8157-1815-2*) Brookings.

— Uncontrollable Spending for Social Services Grants. LC 75-5155. 149p. reprint ed. pap. 46.20 (*0-8357-7063-X*, 203359200086) Bks Demand.

Derthick, Martha, ed. Dilemmas of Scale in America's Federal Democracy. (Woodrow Wilson Center Press Ser.). 384p. (C). 34.95 (*0-521-64039-3*) Cambridge U Pr.

Derthick, Martha & Quirk, Paul J. The Politics of Deregulation. LC 85-16602. 265p. 1985. 36.95 (*0-8157-1818-7*) Brookings.

Dertol, Joseph Van. Unlocking DCOM. 1997. 45.00 (*1-56205-758-8*) Macmillan.

***Dertouzos, James N. & Ebener, Patricia A.** A Profile of San Bernardino County, CalWORKs Caseload. ix, 47p. 2000. pap. 12.00 (*0-8330-2864-2*, DB-304) Rand Corp.

Dertouzos, James N., et al. The Economic Costs & Implications of High-Technology Hardware Theft. LC 99-202909. 78p. 1999. pap. 15.00 (*0-8330-2727-1*) Rand Corp.

— Facilitating Effective Reform in Army Acquisition. LC 99-168189. (Illus.). 50p. 1998. pap. text 6.00 (*0-8330-2590-2*, DB-233-A) Rand Corp.

Dertouzos, James N., jt. auth. see Asch, Beth J.

***Dertouzos, Michael L.** What Will Be: How the New World of Information Will Change Our Lives. 336p. 1998. text 25.00 (*0-7881-5965-8*) DIANE Pub.

Dertouzos, Michael L. What Will Be: How the New World of Information Will Change Our Lives. LC 96-37301. 352p. 1997. 25.00 (*0-06-251479-2*, Pub. by Harper SF) HarpC.

— What Will Be: How the New World of Information Will Change Our Lives. 384p. 1998. pap. 15.00 (*0-06-251540-3*, Pub. by Harper SF) HarpC.

Dertouzos, Michael L., et al. Made in America: Regaining the Productive Edge. 248p. 1989. 35.00 (*0-262-04100-6*) MIT Pr.

DeRubeis, Robert J., jt. ed. see Routh, Donald K.

DeRubertis, Barbara. Bitty Fish. LC 96-75013. (Let's Read Together Ser.). (Illus.). 32p. (J). (ps-2). 1996. pap. 4.95 (*1-57565-002-9*) Kane Pr.

— Bouncy Mouse. LC 97-44311. (Let's Read Together Ser.). (Illus.). 32p. (J). (ps-3). 1998. pap. 4.95 (*1-57565-043-6*) Kane Pr.

***DeRubertis, Barbara.** Collection for Kate. (Math Matters Ser.). (Illus.). (J). 1999. 10.40 (*0-606-18216-0*) Turtleback.

DeRubertis, Barbara. A Collection for Kate: Math Concept: Addition. LC 98-51116. (Math Matters Ser.). (Illus.). 32p. (J). (gr. k-2). 1999. pap. text 4.95 (*1-57565-089-4*) Kane Pr.

— Columbus Day: Let's Meet Christopher Columbus. (Holidays & Heroes Ser.). (Illus.). (Orig.). (J). (gr. 1-5). 1991. pap. 4.95 (*0-7915-1904-X*) Kane Pr.

— Columbus Day: Let's Meet Christopher Columbus. (Holidays & Heroes Ser.). (Illus.). 32p. (Orig.). (J). (gr. 1-5). 1996. pap. 7.95 incl. audio (*1-57565-011-8*) Kane Pr.

***DeRubertis, Barbara.** Count on Pablo. (Math Matters Ser.). (Illus.). (J). 1999. 10.40 (*0-606-18217-9*) Turtleback.

— Count on Pablo: Math Concept: Counting & Skip Counting. LC 98-51119. (Math Matters Ser.). (Illus.). 32p. (J). (gr. k-2). 1999. pap. text 4.95 (*1-57565-090-8*) Kane Pr.

— Deena's Lucky Penny. (Math Matters Ser.). (Illus.). (J). 1999. 10.40 (*0-606-18218-7*) Turtleback.

— Deena's Lucky Penny: Math Concept: Money. LC 98-51117. (Math Matters Ser.). 32p. (J). (ps-1). 1999. pap. text 4.95 (*1-57565-091-6*) Kane Pr.

DeRubertis, Barbara. Earth Day: Let's Meet the Earth Kids. (Holidays & Heroes Ser.). (Illus.). (Orig.). (J). (gr. 1-5). 1992. pap. 4.95 (*0-7915-1946-5*) Kane Pr.

— Earth Day: Let's Meet the Earth Kids. (Holidays & Heroes Ser.). (Illus.). 32p. (Orig.). (J). (gr. 1-5). 1996. pap. 7.95 incl. audio (*1-57565-013-4*) Kane Pr.

— Foxy Fox. LC 96-75014. (Let's Read Together Ser.). (Illus.). 32p. (J). (ps-2). 1996. pap. 4.95 (*1-57565-003-7*) Kane Pr.

— Holidays & Heroes Series, 5 vols., Set. (Orig.). (J). (gr. 1-5). 1993. pap. 24.75 (*0-7915-1961-9*) Kane Pr.

— Janey Crane. LC 96-52643. (Illus.). 32p. (J). (ps-2). 1997. pap. 4.95 (*1-57565-022-3*) Kane Pr.

— Joey Goat. LC 96-6564. (Illus.). 32p. (J). (ps-2). 1997. pap. 4.95 (*1-57565-025-8*) Kane Pr.

— Let's Read Together, 15 bks. (Illus.). 480p. (J). (ps-3). 1998. pap. 134.25 incl. audio (*1-57565-087-8*) Kane Pr.

— Let's Read Together: Long & Short Vowel Books, 10 vols., Set. (Illus.). (Orig.). (J). (ps-2). 1997. pap. 49.50 (*1-57565-020-7*) Kane Pr.

— Let's Read Together: Short Vowel Packages. (Let's Read Together Ser.: No. 3). (Illus.). 32p. (J). (ps-2). 1996. pap. 44.75 incl. audio (*1-57565-040-1*) Kane Pr.

— Let's Read Together Set 5: Vowel Team Books. (Illus.). 32p. (J). (ps-3). 1998. pap. 24.75 (*1-57565-079-7*) Kane Pr.

— Let's Read Together Set 6: Vowel Team Book & Tape Packages. (Illus.). 32p. (J). (ps-3). 1998. pap. 44.75 incl. audio (*1-57565-080-0*) Kane Pr.

— Let's Read Together Series: Long Vowel Book & Tape Packages. (Let's Read Together Ser.: No. 4). (Illus.). 32p. (J). (ps-1). 1997. pap. 44.75 incl. audio (*1-57565-041-X*) Kane Pr.

— Let's Read Together Series: Set 7 (5 Short Vowel, 5 Long Vowel, 5 Vowel Team Book Titles), 15 bks. (Illus.). 480p. (J). (ps-3). 1998. pap. 74.25 (*1-57565-086-X*) Kane Pr.

— Let's Read Together Series: Short & Long Vowel Book & Tape Packages. (Illus.). 32p. (J). (ps-2). 1997. pap. 89.50 incl. audio (*1-57565-039-8*) Kane Pr.

— Lucky Duck. LC 96-75015. (Let's Read Together Ser.). (Illus.). 32p. (J). (ps-2). 1996. pap. 4.95 (*1-57565-004-5*) Kane Pr.

***DeRubertis, Barbara.** Lulu's Lemonade. LC 99-42677. (Math Matters Ser.). (Illus.). 32p. (J). (gr. k-2). 2000. pap. 4.95 (*1-57565-093-2*) Kane Pr.

DeRubertis, Barbara. Martin Luther King Day: Let's Meet Martin Luther King, Jr. (Holidays & Heroes Ser.). (Illus.). (Orig.). (J). (gr. 1-5). 1992. pap. 4.95 (*0-7915-1932-5*) Kane Pr.

— Martin Luther King, Jr. Let's Meet Martin Luther King, Jr. (Holidays & Heroes Ser.). (Illus.). 32p. (Orig.). (J). (gr. 1-5). 1996. pap. 7.95 incl. audio (*1-57565-010-X*) Kane Pr.

***DeRubertis, Barbara.** Marty Aardvark. LC 97-44312. (Let's Read Together Ser.). (Illus.). 32p. (J). (ps-3). 1998. pap. 4.95 (*1-57565-042-8*) Kane Pr.

DeRubertis, Barbara. Patty Cat. LC 96-75011. (Let's Read Together Ser.). (Illus.). 32p. (J). (ps-2). 1996. pap. 4.95 (*1-57565-000-2*) Kane Pr.

— Penny Hen. LC 96-75012. (Let's Read Together Ser.). (Illus.). 32p. (J). (ps-2). 1996. pap. 4.95 (*1-57565-001-0*) Kane Pr.

— Perky Otter. LC 97-44314. (Let's Read Together Ser.). (Illus.). 32p. (J). (ps-3). 1998. pap. 4.95 (*1-57565-045-2*) Kane Pr.

— President's Day: Let's Meet George Washington & Abraham Lincoln. (Holidays & Heroes Ser.). (Illus.). (Orig.). (J). (gr. 1-5). 1991. pap. 4.95 (*0-7915-1918-X*) Kane Pr.

— President's Day: Let's Meet George Washington & Abraham Lincoln. (Holidays & Heroes Ser.). (Illus.). 32p. (Orig.). (J). (gr. 1-5). 1996. pap. 7.95 incl. audio (*1-57565-014-2*) Kane Pr.

— Rooney 'Roo. LC 97-44310. (Let's Read Together Ser.). (Illus.). 32p. (J). (ps-3). 1998. pap. 4.95 (*1-57565-044-4*) Kane Pr.

— Suzy Mule. LC 96-53889. (Illus.). 32p. (J). (ps-2). 1997. pap. 4.95 (*1-57565-026-6*) Kane Pr.

— Thanksgiving Day: Let's Meet the Wampanoags & the Pilgrims. (Holidays & Heroes Ser.). (Illus.). (Orig.). (J). (gr. 1-5). 1991. pap. 4.95 (*0-7915-1911-2*) Kane Pr.

— Thanksgiving Day: Let's Meet the Wampanoags & the Pilgrims. (Holidays & Heroes Ser.). (Illus.). 32p. (Orig.). (J). (gr. 1-5). 1996. pap. 7.95 incl. audio (*1-57565-012-6*) Kane Pr.

— Tiny Tiger. LC 96-53272. (Illus.). 32p. (J). (ps-2). 1997. pap. 4.95 (*1-57565-024-X*) Kane Pr.

— Wally Walrus. LC 97-44315. (Let's Read Together Ser.). (Illus.). 32p. (J). (ps-3). 1998. pap. 4.95 (*1-57565-046-0*) Kane Pr.

— Zeely Zebra. LC 96-52644. (Illus.). 32p. (J). (ps-2). 1997. pap. 4.95 (*1-57565-023-1*) Kane Pr.

Derucher. Durability. 450p. 90.00 (*0-471-15598-5*) Wiley.

Derucher, Kenneth N. & Heins. Bridge & Pier Protective Systems & Devices. (Civil Engineering Ser.: Vol. 1). (Illus.). 344p. 1979. text 175.00 (*0-8247-6895-7*) Dekker.

Derucher, Kenneth N. & Korfiatis, George. Materials for Civil & Highway Engineers. 4th ed. LC 98-187494. 470p. (C). 1998. 95.00 (*0-13-905043-4*) P-H.

Derucher, Kenneth N., jt. auth. see Heins, Conrad P., Jr.

Derugin, Vladimir, ed. see Chrysostomos, Archimandrite & Ambrosios, Hieromonk.

Deruguine, Tania, tr. see Dyadkin, Iosif G.

DeRuiter, Gerald L., jt. auth. see Allen, Pat.

Derum, John. More Than a Sentimental Bloke. (Illus.). 152p. 1990. pap. 19.95 (*0-86840-116-1*, Pub. by New South Wales Univ Pr) Intl Spec Bk.

Derungs, Kurt. Struktur des Zaubermarchens II Transformation und Narrative Formen. (Germanistische Texte und Studien: Vol. 47). (GER.). 314p. 1994. write for info. (*3-487-09898-9*) G Olms Pubs.

Derus, Richard M., ed. In Your Eyes: Quotations on Gay Love. 96p. 1996. text 11.00 (*0-312-14057-6*) St Martin.

DeRusso, Paul M., et al. State Variables for Engineers. Desrochers, Alan, tr. LC 97-35773. 592p. 1997. 79.95 (*0-471-57795-2*, Wiley-Interscience) Wiley.

DeRussy, W. Cary. Fishing Inshore Salt Water. 1991. pap. 4.95 (*0-917131-03-7*) FIM Pub.

— Pocket Guide to Fishing Lakes & Reservoirs. (Pocket Guide to Fishing Ser.). (Illus.). 96p. (Orig.). 1989. pap. 4.95 (*0-917131-01-0*) FIM Pub.

— Pocket Guide to Fishing Rivers & Streams. (Pocket Guide to Fishing Ser.). (Illus.). 96p. (Orig.). 1989. pap. 4.95 (*0-917131-02-9*) FIM Pub.

DeRuth, Jan. Painting Portraits, Nudes & Clothed Figures. (Illus.). 143p. 1999. reprint ed. text 22.00 (*0-7881-6383-3*) DIANE Pub.

Deruytter, Wouter. Knights of the Impossible. 1998. pap. text 35.00 (*90-74377-65-3*, Pub. by Stichting Kunst) Dist Art Pubs.

***Deruytter, Wouter, photos by.** Wouter Deruytter: Cowboy Code. (Illus.). 132p. 2000. 60.00 (*1-892041-34-0*) Arena Editions.

***Dervacs, Claudine.** The Travel & Tourism Student Workbook. 96p. (YA). 2000. pap. 7.95 (*0-933143-63-X*) Solitaire Pub.

Dervaes, Claudine. International Travel & Ticketing. rev. ed. (Travel Training Ser.). (Illus.). 200p. 1998. pap. 24.95 (*0-933143-57-5*) Solitaire Pub.

— Teaching Travel: A Handbook for the Educator. 356p. 1998. 42.95 (*0-933143-08-7*) Solitaire Pub.

— The Travel Dictionary. LC 98-60065. 384p. 1998. pap. 19.95 (*0-933143-58-3*) Solitaire Pub.

— The Travel Training Series, 7 vols., Set. rev. ed. (Illus.). 1300p. (C). 1998. pap. 129.95 (*0-933143-50-8*) Solitaire Pub.

— Travel Training Series: Domestic Travel & Ticketing. 1998. pap. 29.95 (*0-933143-56-7*) Solitaire Pub.

— The Travel Training Series: Sales & Marketing Techniques. rev. ed. (Travel Training Ser.). (Illus.). 252p. 1998. pap. 24.95 (*0-933143-55-9*) Solitaire Pub.

— The Travel Training Series: Selling Tours & Independent Travel. rev. ed. (Travel Training Ser.). (Illus.). 212p. 2000. pap. 15.95 (*0-933143-61-3*) Solitaire Pub.

— The Travel Training Series, 1999 Section 5: Cruises. (Travel Training Ser.). (Illus.). 150p. 1998. pap. 15.95 (*0-933143-23-0*) Solitaire Pub.

— The Travel Training Series, 2000: Travel Geography. rev. ed. (Travel Training Ser.). (Illus.). 352p. 2000. pap. 24.95 (*0-933143-52-4*) Solitaire Pub.

Dervaes, Claudine & Hunter, John. The U. K. to U. S. A. Dictionary. LC 94-92182. 112p. (Orig.). 1994. pap. 3.95 (*0-933143-18-4*) Solitaire Pub.

Dervakos, George A., jt. ed. see Webb, Colin.

Dervan, Cathal, jt. auth. see McGrath, Paul.

Dervan, Cathal, jt. auth. see Smith, Michelle.

Dervan, Peter A & DiGaetani, John L. Understanding Cancer: A Scientific & Clinical Guide for the Lay Person. LC 99-14626. (Illus.). 208p. 1999. pap. 29.50 (*0-7864-0628-3*) McFarland & Co.

Dervaux, B. Dictionnaire de Management et Controle du Gestion. (ENG & FRE.). 233p. 1986. 75.00 (*0-8288-7696-7*) Fr & Eur.

Derven, David, et al. HTML 3 How-To: The Definitive HTML Problem-Solver. (Illus.). 680p. 1996. pap. 39.99 (*1-57169-050-6*) Sams.

Dervieux, A. & Larrouturou, Bernard, eds. Numercial Combustion. (Lecture Notes in Physics Ser.: Vol. 351). vii, 481p. 1989. 70.95 (*0-387-51968-8*) Spr-Verlag.

Derville, Andre. Dictionnaire de Spiritualite.Tr. of Dictionary of Spirituality. (FRE.). 1993. pap. 325.00 (*0-7859-5633-6*, 2701012783) Fr & Eur.

Dervin, A. Daniel. Bernard Shaw: A Psychological Study. LC 73-8301. 350p. 1975. 36.50 (*0-8387-1418-8*) Bucknell U Pr.

Dervin, Brenda. Doing Research on Women's Communication: Perspectives on Theory & Method. Carter, Kathryn & Spitzack, Carole, eds. LC 89-14900. (Communication & Information Science Ser.). 304p. (C). 1989. pap. 39.50 (*0-89391-616-1*); text 73.25 (*0-89391-483-5*) Ablx Pub.

Dervin, Brenda, ed. Progress in Communication Sciences, Vol. 1. (Communication & Information Science Ser.). 208p. 1979. text 78.50 (*0-89391-010-4*) Ablx Pub.

— Progress in Communication Sciences, Vol. 3. (Communication & Information Science Ser.). 368p. (C). 1982. text 78.50 (*0-89391-081-3*) Ablx Pub.

— Progress in Communication Sciences, Vol. 4. (Communication & Information Science Ser.). 288p. 1984. text 78.50 (*0-89391-102-X*) Ablx Pub.

— Progress in Communication Sciences, Vol. 5. (Communication & Information Science Ser.). 336p. 1984. text 78.50 (*0-89391-141-0*) Ablx Pub.

— Progress in Communication Sciences, Vol. 6. (Progress in Communication Science Ser.). 336p. 1985. text, teacher ed. 78.50 (*0-89391-306-5*) Ablx Pub.

— Progress in Communication Sciences, Vol. 7. (Communication & Information Science Ser.). 288p. 1986. text 78.50 (*0-89391-325-1*) Ablx Pub.

— Progress in Communication Sciences, Vol. 8. (Communication & Information Science Ser.). 320p. 1986. text 78.50 (*0-89391-392-8*) Ablx Pub.

— Progress in Communication Sciences, Vol. 9. (Communication & Information Science Ser.). 320p. (C). 1989. text 78.50 (*0-89391-474-6*) Ablx Pub.

— Progress in Communication Sciences, Vol. 10. 336p. 1991. text 78.50 (*0-89391-645-5*) Ablx Pub.

— Progress in Communication Sciences, Vol. 11. 348p. (C). 1993. text 78.50 (*0-89391-723-0*) Ablx Pub.

Dervin, Brenda, et al, eds. Rethinking Communication Vol. 1: Paradigm Issues. LC 88-38979. 240p. 1989. pap. 74.40 (*0-7837-8961-0*, 204974200001) Bks Demand.

— Rethinking Communication Vol. 1: Paradigm Issues. 240p. (C). 1989. text 27.50 (*0-8039-3029-1*) Sage.

— Rethinking Communication Vol. 2: Paradigm Exemplars. LC 88-38979. 511p. 1989. reprint ed. pap. 158.50 (*0-608-01613-6*, 205959200002) Bks Demand.

— Rethinking Communication Vol. 2: Paradigm Exemplars, Vol. 2. 544p. (C). 1989. text 44.00 (*0-8039-3031-3*) Sage.

Dervin, Brenda, ed. see Abelman, Robert & Hoover, Stewart M.

Dervin, Brenda, ed. see Alexandre, Laurien.

Dervin, Brenda, ed. see Anderson, Rob, et al.

Dervin, Brenda, ed. see Arno, Andrew.

Dervin, Brenda, ed. see Carbaugh, Donal.

Dervin, Brenda, ed. see Casmir, Fred L.

Dervin, Brenda, ed. see Compaine, Benjamin.

Dervin, Brenda, jt. ed. see Conrad, Charles.

Dervin, Brenda, ed. see Ganley, Gladys D.

Dervin, Brenda, ed. see Ganley, Gladys & Ganley, Oswald.

Dervin, Brenda, ed. see Ganley, Oswald H. & Ganley, Gladys.

Dervin, Brenda, ed. see Gonzalez-Manet, Enrique.

Dervin, Brenda, ed. see Greenberg, Bradley S. & Gantz, Walter.

Dervin, Brenda, ed. see Gumpert, Gary & Fish, Sandra L.

Dervin, Brenda, ed. see Hackett, Robert A.

Dervin, Brenda, ed. see Hamelink, Cees J.

Dervin, Brenda, ed. see Haslett, Beth, et al.

Dervin, Brenda, ed. see Heeter, Carrie & Greenberg, Bradley S.

Dervin, Brenda, ed. see Jacobson, Robert.

Dervin, Brenda, ed. see Johnson, J. David.

Dervin, Brenda, jt. ed. see Kochen, Manfred.

Dervin, Brenda, jt. ed. see Lederman, Linda C.

Dervin, Brenda, jt. ed. see Lundstedt, Sven B.

Dervin, Brenda, ed. see Mandeville, Thomas.

Dervin, Brenda, ed. see Mosco, Vincent.

Dervin, Brenda, ed. see Nordenstreng, Kaarle & Schiller, Herbert I.

Dervin, Brenda, jt. ed. see Phillips, Gerald M.

Dervin, Brenda, ed. see Priest, Patricia J.

Dervin, Brenda, ed. see Rosengren, Karl E. & Windahl, Sven.

Dervin, Brenda, ed. see Rubin, Michael R.

Dervin, Brenda, ed. see Splichal, Slavko & Sparks, Colin.

Dervin, Brenda, ed. see Splichal, Slavko & Wasko, Janet.

Dervin, Brenda, jt. ed. see Tardy, Charles H.

Dervin, Brenda, ed. see Tehranian, Majid.

Dervin, Brenda, jt. ed. see Voigt, Melvin J.

Dervin, Brenda, ed. see Wasko, Janet, et al.

Dervin, Brenda, ed. see Wober, Mallory.

Dervin, Brenda, ed. see Wood, Julia T.

An Asterisk (*) at the beginning of an entry indicates that the title is appearing for the first time.

Dervin, Daniel. Creativity & Culture: A Psychoanalytic Study of the Creative Process in the Arts, Sciences & Culture. LC 88-46150. (Illus.). 408p. 1990. 55.00 (*0-8386-3366-8*) Fairleigh Dickinson.
— Enactments: American Modes & Psychohistorical Models. LC 95-40625. (Illus.). 360p. 1996. 49.50 (*0-8386-3591-1*) Fairleigh Dickinson.
— Matricentric Narratives: Recent British Women's Fiction in a Postmodern Mode. LC 97-14786. (Women's Studies: Vol. 16). 290p. 1997. text 89.95 (*0-7734-8644-5*) E Mellen.
— A "Strange Sapience" The Creative Imagination of D. H. Lawrence. LC 84-2681. (Illus.). 256p. 1984. lib. bdg. 30.00 (*0-87023-455-2*) U of Mass Pr.
— Through a Freudian Lens Deeply: A Psychoanalysis of Cinema. LC 85-1430. 256p. reprint ed. pap. 79.40 (*0-8357-2736-X*, 203984500013) Bks Demand.
Dervin, Rita, et al. Take Heart: Your Life after Coronary Artery Bypass. (Illus.). 64p. 1990. pap. text 3.50 (*0-916999-08-4*) HERC Inc.
Dervish, H. B. Journeys with a Sufi Master. Griffiths, A. L., ed. Tiryaqi, A. W., tr. 243p. 1982. pap. 16.00 (*0-86304-041-1*, Pub. by Octagon Pr) ISHK.
Dervishian, William A. White House on the Pamunkey & the Peninsula Campaign in Virginia, 1862, 6 vols., Set. LC 96-133837. 1659p. 1995. pap. text 119.70 (*1-887667-00-8*) Pamunkey River Pub.
— White House on the Pamunkey & the Peninsula Campaign in Virginia, 1862 Vol I: On to White House, 2nd Part. 260p. 1995. pap. text 19.95 (*1-887667-02-4*) Pamunkey River Pub.
— White House on the Pamunkey & the Peninsula Campaign in Virginia, 1862 Vol. I: On to Yorktown, 1st Part. 260p. 1995. pap. text 19.95 (*1-887667-01-6*) Pamunkey River Pub.
— White House on the Pamunkey & the Peninsula Campaign in Virginia, 1862 Vol. III: White House Depot, 3rd Part. 1995. pap. text 19.95 (*1-887667-03-2*) Pamunkey River Pub.
— White House on the Pamunkey & the Peninsula Campaign in Virginia, 1862 Vol. IV: On to Harrison's Landing, 4th Part. 275p. 1995. pap. text 19.95 (*1-887667-04-0*) Pamunkey River Pub.
— White House on the Pamunkey & the Peninsula Campaign in Virginia, 1862 Vol. V: On Back to Washington, D. C., 5th Part. 275p. 1995. pap. text 19.95 (*1-887667-05-9*) Pamunkey River Pub.
— White House on the Pamunkey & the Peninsula Campaign in Virginia, 1862 Vol. VI: Cumulative Supplement. 250p. 1995. pap. text 19.95 (*1-887667-06-7*) Pamunkey River Pub.
Derwald, Richard & Chiappone, Anthony. For Men Only: Secrets of a Successful Image. LC 94-24932. (Illus.). 244p. (C). 1995. 25.95 (*0-87975-910-0*) Prometheus Bks.
Derwent. Thesaurus of Agricultural Organisms, 2 vols. (Agriculture Ser.). 1991. text 424.95 (*0-442-30422-6*, VNR) Wiley.
Derwent & Parker. Fair Enough? Date not set. pap. text, student ed. write for info. (*0-582-87582-X*, Pub. by Addison-Wesley) Longman.
Derwent, jt. auth. see Parker.
Derwent, Lavinia. Tale of Greyfriar's Bobby. (Illus.). (J). (gr. 3-6). 1986. pap. 7.95 (*0-14-031181-5*, Pub. by Pnguin Bks Ltd) Trafalgar.
Derwent Publications Staff. Thesaurus Agricultural Organisims. 1990. ring bd. 595.00 (*0-412-37290-8*) Chapman & Hall.
Derwent, Richard. Financial Reporting & Auditing Newsletter. ring bd. 180.00 (*0-406-02171-6*, UK, MICHIE) LEXIS Pub.
Derwin, Susan. The Ambivalence of Form: Lukacs, Freud & the Novel. LC 92-6557. 224p. 1992. text 38.00 (*0-8018-4381-2*) Johns Hopkins.
Derwingson, Richard, jt. auth. see Emerson, Roger.
Dery, David. Computers in Welfare: The MIS-Match. LC 81-2240. (Managing Information Ser.: No. 3). 260p. reprint ed. pap. 80.60 (*0-8357-8455-X*, 203471900091) Bks Demand.
— Data & Policy Change. (C). 1989. lib. bdg. 80.00 (*0-7923-9057-1*, Pub. by Graham & Trotman) Kluwer Academic.
Dery, Luis C. From Ibalon to Sorsogon: A Historical Survey of Sorsogon Province to 1905. (Illus.). 327p. (Orig.). (C). 1992. pap. 17.50 (*971-10-1423-8*, Pub. by New Day Pub) Cellar.
Dery, Mark. Escape Velocity: Cyberculture at the End of the Century. 400p. 1997. pap. 15.00 (*0-8021-3520-X*, Grove) Grove-Atltic.
***Dery, Mark.** The Pyrotechnic Insanitarium: American Culture on the Brink of the Millennium. LC 98-40837. (Illus.). 304p. 1999. 25.00 (*0-8021-1640-X*, Grove) Grove-Atltic.
— The Pyrotechnic Insanitarium: American Culture on the Brink of the Millennium. 304p. 2000. pap. 14.00 (*0-8021-3670-2*, Grove) Grove-Atltic.
Dery, Mark, ed. Flame Wars: The Discourse of Cyberculture. LC 94-24517. (Illus.). 320p. 1994. text 49.95 (*0-8223-1531-9*); pap. text 15.95 (*0-8223-1540-8*) Duke.
Dery, Robert. Business Welsh: A User's Manual. LC 95-23374. 104p. (C). 1995. pap. 14.99 (*0-415-12998-2*) Routledge.
Dery, Tibor. Portuguese Princess. 1996. pap. 14.95 (*0-7145-0485-8*) Riverrun NY.
Deryagin, B. V., ed. see Konferentsiia Po Poverkhnostym Silam Staff.
Deryagin, Boris V., et al. Adhesion of Solids. Johnston, Robert K., tr. from RUS. LC 78-1843. (Studies in Societ Science). (Illus.). 473p. 1978. reprint ed. pap. 146.70 (*0-608-05497-6*, 206596600006) Bks Demand.
Derycke, Luc & Van De Veire, San, contrib. by. Belgian Fashion Design. (Illus.). 304p. 1999. pap. text 39.50 (*90-5544-244-5*) Ludion.
Derzack, Thomas A., et al, eds. Saint Michael the Archangel Roman Catholic Parish, Lansford, PA 1891-1991 - A Century of Faith & Heritage - "Viera a Dedicstvo" Storocna Pamatnica. LC 96-207454. (Illus.). 295p. 1995. 35.00 (*0-9643755-0-8*, TX 4-195-727) St Michael the Archangel.
Des Aulniers, Guy. Les Lois Electorales d'Afrique Francophone. International Foundation Election Systems Staff, ed. (FRE.). xi, 663p. 1998. pap. text 24.00 (*1-879720-51-5*) Intl Fndt Elect.
***Des Aulniers, Guy, et al.** Evaluation Technique Preelectorale au Gabon du 8 au 25 Octobre 1998. ii, 52p. 1999. pap. text 7.00 (*1-879720-33-7*) Intl Fndt Elect.
— Gabon Pre-Election Technical Assessment: October 8-25, 1998. ii, 48p. 1999. pap. text 7.00 (*1-879720-32-9*) Intl Fndt Elect.
Des Barres, Pamela. I'm with the Band. 1988. mass mkt. 4.99 (*0-515-09712-8*, Jove) Berkley Pub.
— Rock Bottom: Dark Moments in Music Babylon, Vol. 1. 1998. write for info. (*0-312-96633-4*) Tor Bks.
— Take Another Little Piece of My Heart. 1993. mass mkt. 5.50 (*0-425-13945-X*) Berkley Pub.
Des Bouvrie, Synnove. Women in Greek Tragedy: An Anthropological Approach. (Symbolae Osloenses Fasc. Supplement Ser.: No. XXVII). 394p. 1990. pap. 96.00 (*91-0-021125-7*) Coronet Bks.
Des Cars, Guy. Amour de Ma Vie. (FRE.). 320p. 1973. pap. 10.95 (*0-7859-4789-2*); pap. 6.95 (*0-686-55606-2*) Fr & Eur.
— L' Amour s'en va-t-en Guerre. (FRE.). 1978. pap. 6.95 (*0-8288-9548-1*, M4669) Fr & Eur.
— La Brute. 304p. 1951. 10.95 (*0-686-55610-0*) Fr & Eur.
— La Brute. (FRE.). 448p. 1960. pap. 6.95 (*0-8288-9552-X*, M5716) Fr & Eur.
— La Cathedrale de Haine. (FRE.). 280p. 1969. pap. 6.95 (*0-8288-9553-8*, M5717); pap. 3.95 (*0-686-55613-5*) Fr & Eur.
— Une Certaine Dame. 392p. 1971. 17.95 (*0-686-55614-3*) Fr & Eur.
— Une Certaine Dame. (FRE.). 1978. pap. 9.95 (*0-8288-9573-2*, M5718) Fr & Eur.
— Cette Etrange Tendresse. 336p. 1960. 9.95 (*0-686-55616-X*) Fr & Eur.
— Cette Etrange Tendresse. (FRE.). 320p. 1968. pap. 6.95 (*0-8288-9547-3*, M5719) Fr & Eur.
— Le Chateau de la Juive. 384p. 1958. 11.95 (*0-686-55618-6*) Fr & Eur.
— Le Chateau de la Juive. (FRE.). 378p. 1989. reprint ed. pap. 11.95 (*0-7859-4790-6*) Fr & Eur.
— Le Chateau du Clown. (FRE.). 380p. 1982. pap. 11.95 (*0-7859-4729-9*) Fr & Eur.
— La Corruptrice. 272p. 1952. 11.95 (*0-686-55621-6*) Fr & Eur.
— La Corruptrice. (FRE.). 384p. 1985. pap. 10.95 (*0-7859-4791-4*) Fr & Eur.
— La Dame Du Cirque. 256p. 1962. 9.95 (*0-686-55623-2*) Fr & Eur.
— La Dame Du Cirque. (FRE.). 320p. 1968. pap. 6.95 (*0-8288-9555-4*, M5722) Fr & Eur.
— La Demoiselle d'Opera. (FRE.). 384p. 1966. pap. write for info. (*0-7859-4792-2*) Fr & Eur.
— Le Donneur. (FRE.). 288p. 1978. pap. 10.95 (*0-7859-4784-1*) Fr & Eur.
— L' Envouteuse. (FRE.). 416p. 1975. 22.50 (*0-686-55632-1*) Fr & Eur.
— Un Faussaire. (FRE.). 448p. 1967. pap. 19.95 (*0-7859-4793-0*, M5728) Fr & Eur.
— Les Filles de Joie. (FRE.). 320p. 1985. pap. 10.95 (*0-7859-4794-9*) Fr & Eur.
— Geologie, 2 vols. (FRE.). 448p. 1970. pap. 4.95 (*0-686-55631-3*) Fr & Eur.
— Geologie, 2 vols., Set. (FRE.). 448p. 1970. pap. 10.95 (*0-7859-1214-2*, 227712639X) Fr & Eur.
— Le Grand Monde. (FRE.). 624p. 1961. 24.95 (*0-7859-1161-8*, 2080600184) Fr & Eur.
— Le Grand Monde Vol. 1: L'Alliee. (FRE.). 320p. 1972. 6.95 (*0-8288-9565-1*, M5736) Fr & Eur.
— Le Grand Monde Vol. 2: La Trahison. (FRE.). 320p. 1972. 6.95 (*0-8288-9566-X*, M5731) Fr & Eur.
— L' Habitude d'Amour. (FRE.). 320p. 1985. pap. 7.95 (*0-7859-4795-7*) Fr & Eur.
— L' Impure. (FRE.). 371p. 1963. pap. 11.95 (*0-7859-4796-5*) Fr & Eur.
— L' Insolence de sa Beaute. (FRE.). 240p. 1978. pap. 11.95 (*0-7859-5572-0*) Fr & Eur.
— J'ose. (FRE.). 192p. 1981. 6.95 (*0-7859-1187-1*, 2277212369) Fr & Eur.
— La Justiciere. 1981. pap. 7.95 (*0-7859-5251-9*) Fr & Eur.
— Louis II de Baviere du le Roi Foucroye. 9.95 (*0-686-55666-6*) Fr & Eur.
— Louis II de Baviere du le Roi Foucroye: Documents Hors Texte. 318p. 1975. 19.95 (*0-686-55647-X*) Fr & Eur.
— Le Mage: La Boule de Cristal, Vol. 1. (FRE.). 190p. 1974. 6.95 (*0-8288-9567-8*, M5736) Fr & Eur.
— Le Mage et les Signes de la Main. (FRE.). 240p. 1976. 13.95 (*0-7859-1166-9*, 2080608800) Fr & Eur.
— La Maudite. (FRE.). 320p. 1971. pap. 10.95 (*0-7859-4797-3*) Fr & Eur.
— L' Officier Sans Nom. (FRE.). 320p. 1985. pap. 7.95 (*0-7859-4787-6*) Fr & Eur.
— La Revoltee. (FRE.). 370p. 1985. pap. 11.95 (*0-7859-4798-1*) Fr & Eur.
— Robin des Bois. (FRE.). 304p. 1978. 6.95 (*0-686-55645-3*, 2277128589) Fr & Eur.
— Sang d'Afrique: L'Africain, Vol. 1. (FRE.). 1971. 6.95 (*0-8288-9570-8*, M5741) Fr & Eur.
— Sang d'Afrique: L'Amoureuse, Vol. 2. (FRE.). 1971. 6.95 (*0-8288-9571-6*, M5742) Fr & Eur.
— Les Sept Femmes. (FRE.). 384p. 1985. pap. 11.95 (*0-7859-4799-X*) Fr & Eur.
— La Tricheuse. (FRE.). 320p. 1989. pap. 10.95 (*0-7859-4800-7*) Fr & Eur.
— La Vie Secrete de Dorothee Gindt. (FRE.). 504p. 1987. 10.95 (*0-7859-1188-X*, 2277222917) Fr & Eur.
— La Vipere. (FRE.). 448p. 1955. pap. 11.95 (*0-7859-4801-5*) Fr & Eur.
Des Cars, Guy & Halbout, Dominique. Sang d'Afrique. (FRE & TUR.). 1992. 125.00 (*0-7859-1189-8*, 2700501667) Fr & Eur.
***Des Cars, Laurence.** The Pre-Raphaelites: Romance & Realism. LC 99-45854. (Discoveries Ser.). 128p. 2000. pap. 12.95 (*0-8109-2891-4*, Pub. by Abrams) Time Warner.
***Des Chene, Dennis.** Life's Forms: Late Aristotelian Conceptions of the Soul. 2000. write for info. (*0-8014-3763-6*) Cornell U Pr.
Des Chene, Dennis. Physiologia: Natural Philosophy in Late Aristotelian & Cartesian Thought. (Illus.). 456p. 1996. text 45.00 (*0-8014-3072-0*) Cornell U Pr.
***Des Chene, Dennis.** Physologia: Natural Philosophy in Late Aristotelian & Cartesian Thought. 2000. reprint ed. pap. 19.95 (*0-8014-8687-4*) Cornell U Pr.
Des Chenes. Authors & Artists for Young Adults. (Authors & Artists Ser.: Vol. 17). 250p. 1996. text 82.00 (*0-8103-9369-7*) Gale.
Des Chenes, Betz, contrib. by. Women's Reference Library Cumulative Index. LC 98-195261. 1998. 5.00 (*0-7876-1923-X*, UXL) Gale.
Des Chenes, E. A. Authors & Artists for Young Adults. (Authors & Artists Ser.: Vol. 16). 250p. 1995. text 82.00 (*0-8103-9368-9*) Gale.
— Authors & Artists for Young Adults. (Authors & Artists Ser.: Vol. 18). 250p. 1996. text 82.00 (*0-8103-9942-3*) Gale.
Des Cognets, Anna R. Garrard, Governor Garrard of Kentucky, His Descendants & Relatives. (Illus.). 134p. 1997. reprint ed. pap. 19.50 (*0-8328-8708-0*); reprint ed. lib. bdg. 29.50 (*0-8328-8707-2*) Higginson Bk Co.
Des Cognets, Anna R. & Des Cognets, Louis, Jr. Russell: William Russell & Descendants, & the Russell Family of Virginia. (Illus.). 319p. 1993. reprint ed. pap. 46.50 (*0-8328-2975-7*); reprint ed. lib. bdg. 56.50 (*0-8328-2974-9*) Higginson Bk Co.
Des Cognets, Louis, Jr., jt. auth. see Des Cognets, Anna R.
Des Cordes, J. Chalom, see Chalom Des Cordes, V. & Chalom Des Cordes, J.
Des Cordes, V. Chalom, see Chalom Des Cordes, V.
Des Dixon, R. G. Future Schools & How to Get There from Here: A Primer for Evolutionaries. 505p. (Orig.). 1993. pap. 16.95 (*1-55022-172-8*, Pub. by ECW) LPC InBook.
— Tell Me Who You Are. 234p. 1995. pap. 16.95 (*1-55022-231-7*) LPC InBook.
Des Forets, Louis R. Children's Room. Stewart, Jean, tr. from FRE. 240p. (Orig.). 1987. pap. 11.95 (*0-7145-0165-4*) Riverrun NY.
Des Forges, Roger, et al, eds. China: The Crisis of Nineteen Eighty-Nine: Origins & Implications, 2 vols., . (Council on International Studies & Programs Special Studies). 447p. 1990. pap. 10.00 (*0-924197-11-0*) SUNYB Coun Intl Studies.
— China: The Crisis of Nineteen Eighty-Nine: Origins & Implications, 2 vols., 2. (Council on International Studies & Programs Special Studies). 447p. 1990. pap. 10.00 (*0-685-74308-X*) SUNYB Coun Intl Studies.
Des Forges, Roger V. Hsi-Liang & the Chinese National Revolution. LC 73-77147. (Historical Publications, Miscellany Ser.: No. 99). (Illus.). 296p. reprint ed. 91.80 (*0-8357-9255-2*, 201109200074) Bks Demand.
Des Forges, Roger V., et al, eds. Chinese Democracy & the Crisis of 1989: Chinese & American Reflections. LC 91-45279. 371p. (C). 1992. pap. text 21.95 (*0-7914-1270-9*) State U NY Pr.
— Chinese Democracy & the Crisis of 1989: Chinese & American Reflections. LC 91-45279. 371p. (C). 1993. text 64.50 (*0-7914-1269-5*) State U NY Pr.
Des Glaubens, Wort, tr. see Copeland, Kenneth.
Des Groselliers, Marge, jt. auth. see Smilovitz, Robert.
Des Jardins, Joseph R. Environmental Ethics. 2nd ed. LC 96-33992. (Philosophy Ser.). 250p. 1996. 43.95 (*0-534-50508-2*) Wadsworth Pub.
Des Jardins, Terry. Cardiopulmonary Anatomy & Physiology: Essentials for Respiratory Care. 2nd ed. LC 92-14625. 454p. (C). 1993. pap. 45.95 (*0-8273-5007-4*) Delmar.
Des Jardins, Terry. Clinical Manifestations of Respiratory Disease. 3rd ed. (Illus.). 584p. (C). (gr. 13). 1995. pap. text 53.00 (*0-8016-7988-5*, 07988) Mosby Inc.
— Instructor's Guide to Accompany Cardiopulmonary Anatomy & Physiology Essentials for Respiratory Care. 2nd ed. 205p. 1993. pap., teacher ed. 16.00 (*0-8273-5008-2*) Delmar.
— Workbook to Accompany Cardiopulmonary Anatomy & Physiology Essentials for Respiratory Care. 2nd ed. 203p. (C). 1993. pap., wbk. ed. 14.95 (*0-8273-5006-6*) Delmar.
Des Jardins, Terry R. Cardiopulmonary Anatomy & Physiology: Essentials for Respiratory Care. 3rd ed. LC 97-8797. (C). 1997. pap. 49.95 (*0-8273-8256-1*) Delmar.
Des, K. Fundamentals of E. N. T. 45th ed. (C). 1990. 70.00 (*0-7855-4659-6*, Pub. by Current Dist) St Mut
Des Lauriers Cieri, Carol & Ctold, Donna. The Insiders' Guide to Maine's Mid Coast. 2nd ed. (Insiders' Guide Travel Ser.). 1998. pap. 15.95 (*1-57380-067-8*, The Insiders Guide) Falcon Pub Inc.
Des Lauriers, Don & Hinton, Mardene. Riverview Historic District, 1866-1935: Tales of Villas, Bungalows, Parks & Drives, Vol. 1500. (Illus.). 200p. 1997. 34.95 (*0-9663608-0-X*) Kankakee Cnty.
des Lauries Cieri, Carol & Gold, Donna. The Insiders' Guide to Maine's Mid-Coast. 3rd ed. (Insiders' Guide Travel Ser.). 1999. pap. 15.95 (*1-57380-114-3*, The Insiders Guide) Falcon Pub Inc.
Des Moines Register Staff & Iowa State University Press Staff. Iowa's Lost Summer: The Flood of '93. LC 93-30245. (Illus.). 120p. (Orig.). (C). 1993. pap. 19.95 (*0-8138-1809-5*) Iowa St U Pr.
***Des Ouches, Thierry.** France. (Illus.). 2000. 45.00 (*2-84576-019-1*) Vilo Intl.
Des Pres, Francois Turenne, see Turenne des Pres, Francois.
Des Pres, J. Guitar Fitness. 80p. 1992. otabind 9.95 (*0-7935-1697-8*, 00660328) H Leonard.
Des Pres, J. Muted Grooves Bass Builders. 64p. 1995. pap. 16.95 (*0-7935-3455-0*, 00696555) H Leonard.
***Des Pres, Josquin Turenne.** Daily Chop-Builders for Bass. 56p. 1999. pap. 17.95 incl. audio compact disk (*0-7866-4477-X*, 97774BCD) Mel Bay.
Des Pres, Terrence. The Survivor: An Anatomy of Life in the Death Camps. (Illus.). 230p. 1980. pap. text 13.95 (*0-19-502703-5*) OUP.
Des Pres, Terrence, jt. ed. see Gibbons, Reginald.
Des Prez, Josquin. Keyboard Intabulations of Music by Josquin Des Prez. Warburton, Thomas, ed. (Recent Researches in Music of the Renaissance Ser.: Vol. RRR34). (Illus.). xv, 96p. 1980. pap. 40.00 (*0-89579-125-0*, RRR34) A-R Eds.
Des Reaux, Tallemant. Historiettes, Vol. 1. (FRE.). 1960. lib. bdg. 110.00 (*0-8288-3542-X*, F122960) Fr & Eur.
— Historiettes, Vol. 2. (FRE.). 1961. lib. bdg. 99.50 (*0-8288-3543-8*, F124390) Fr & Eur.
Des Rivieres, Jim, jt. auth. see Kiczales, Gregor.
Des Roches, Brian. Your Boss Is Not Your Mother: Breaking Free from Emotional Politics to Achieve Independence & Success at Work. 240p. 1996. pap. 11.00 (*0-380-71924-X*, Avon Bks) Morrow Avon.
Des Rosieres, Alain. The Politics of Large Numbers: A History of Statistical Reasoning. Naish, Camille, tr. from FRE. LC 98-3199. 368p. 1998. 45.00 (*0-674-68932-1*) HUP.
Des Ruisseaux, P. Tresors Expressions Populaires - Litterature Quebecoise. (FRE.). 1998. 65.00 (*0-320-00217-9*) Fr & Eur.
***des Sagettes, Christiane.** The Key to Paradise. Poletti, Jacques, tr. from FRE. LC 98-90803. 2000. 12.95 (*0-533-12921-4*) Vantage.
Des Serres, Olivier. The Perfect Use of Silkworms. Geffe, N., tr. LC 72-232. (English Experience Ser.: No. 345). 100p. 1971. reprint ed. 30.00 (*90-221-0345-5*) Walter J Johnson.
Des Verney Sinnette, Elinor. Arthur Alfonso Schomburg: Black Bibliophile & Collector, a Biography. LC 88-29001. (African American Life Ser.). 276p. (C). 1989. pap. 18.95 (*0-8143-2157-7*) Wayne St U Pr.
DeSa, Catherine & Klein, Carol. Experiments for Principles of Inorganic Chemistry. (C). 1993. student ed. 13.70 (*1-56870-090-3*) RonJon Pub.
***DeSa, Douglas O. J.** Instrumentation for Process Control Fundamentals. LC 00-41189. 2000. write for info. (*1-56032-901-7*) Taylor & Francis.
DeSabbata, Venzo & Singh, T., eds. New Directions in Relativity & Cosmology. (Illus.). 250p. (C). 1998. pap. text 65.00 (*1-57485-030-X*) Hadronic Pr Inc.
Desachy, Jacky, ed. Image & Signal Processing for Remote Sensing III, Vol. 295. (Europto Ser.). 326p. 1996. 76.00 (*0-8194-2359-9*) SPIE.
***Desachy, Jacky & Tajbakhsh, Shahram, eds.** Image Processing, Signal Processing & Synthetic Aperture Radar for Remote Sensing, Vol. 3217. LC 98-143988. 466p. 1998. 89.00 (*0-8194-2649-0*) SPIE.
DeSade, Mark. Psychic Sexual Command. Templar, James, ed. LC 93-79465. 120p. (Orig.). 1993. pap. 25.00 (*1-883147-05-0*); pap. 25.00 (*1-883147-06-9*) Intern Guild ASRS.
— Psychic Warfare. Templar, Thorguard, ed. 87p. (Orig.). 1993. 65.00 (*1-883147-91-3*); 65.00 (*1-883147-92-1*) Intern Guild ASRS.
DeSade, Marquis. Selected Letters. 186p. 1992. pap. 18.95 (*0-7206-0860-0*, Pub. by P Owen Ltd) Dufour.
— Selected Letters of M. de Sade. St. Ives, L., tr. 306p. 1954. reprint ed. pap. 25.00 (*0-87556-698-7*) Saifer.
— Selected Writings of M. de Sade. Lely, Gilbert, ed. 185p. 1954. reprint ed. pap. 25.00 (*0-87556-045-8*) Saifer.
Desae, Jaikishan, jt. auth. see Sahn, David E.
Desaguliers, J. T., tr. see Mariotte, Edme.
***Desai.** Social Background of Indian Nationalism. 5th ed. 1998. reprint ed. pap. 15.00 (*81-7154-152-6*, Pub. by Popular Prakashan) S Asia.
***Desai, A. R.** Recent Trends in Indian Nationalism. 1998. pap. 12.00 (*81-7154-042-2*, Pub. by Popular Prakashan) S Asia.
Desai, A. R. Social Background of Indian Nationalism. 1986. reprint ed. 10.00 (*0-86132-086-7*, Pub. by Popular Prakashan) S Asia.
— Urban Family & Family Planning in India. 224p. 1980. reprint ed. 22.95 (*0-940500-70-1*) Asia Bk Corp.
Desai, A. R., ed. Agrarian Struggles in India after Independence. (Illus.). 653p. 1986. 42.00 (*0-19-561681-2*) OUP.
— Expanding Governmental Lawlessness & Organized Struggles: Violation of Democratic Rights of the Minorities, Women, Slum Dwellers, Press & Some Other Violations. (C). 1991. 30.00 (*81-7154-529-7*, Pub. by Popular Prakashan) S Asia.
— Repression & Resistance in India. 1990. 52.50 (*0-86132-225-8*, Pub. by Popular Prakashan) S Asia.

D

An Asterisk (*) at the beginning of an entry indicates that the title is appearing for the first time.

Desai, A. R. & D'Costa, Wilfred. State & Repressive Culture: A Case Study of Gujarat. (C). 1994. text 18.00 (*81-7154-702-8*, Pub. by Popular Prakashan) S Asia.

Desai, A. R., jt. auth. see Tagore, Rabindranath.

***Desai, Anil.** MCSE: Windows 2000 Directory Services Administration Exam Notes. 2000. pap. 24.99 (*0-7821-2762-2*) Sybex.

— SQL Server 7 Backup & Recovery. (Database Professional's Library). (Illus.). 2000. pap. 44.99 (*0-07-212410-5*) Osborne-McGraw.

Desai, Anil. Windows NT Administration Handbook. LC 98-89435. 447p. 1999. pap. 29.99 incl. cd-rom (*1-56205-946-7*) New Riders Pub.

***Desai, Anil.** Windows 2000 Directory Services Administration Study Guide. (MCSE Ser.). (Illus.). 2000. pap. text 49.99 (*0-7821-2756-8*, Network Pr) Sybex.

***Desai, Anita.** Baumgartner's Bombay. (Illus.). 240p. 2000. pap. 13.00 (*0-618-05680-7*) HM.

Desai, Anita. Clear Light of Day. 192p. 1989. pap. 11.95 (*0-14-010859-9*, Penguin Bks) Viking Penguin.

***Desai, Anita.** Clear Light of Day: A Novel. 192p. 2000. pap. 12.00 (*0-618-07451-1*, Mariner Bks) HM.

— Diamond Dust: Stories. LC 00-35082. 224p. 2000. pap. 12.00 (*0-618-04213-X*) HM.

— Fasting, Feasting. LC 99-488483. 227p. 1999. write for info. (*0-7011-6894-3*, Pub. by Chatto & Windus) Trafalgar.

— Fasting, Feasting. LC 99-58524. 240p. 2000. pap. 13.00 (*0-618-06582-2*, Mariner Bks) HM.

— Fasting, Feasting. large type ed. LC 00-37762. 316p. 2000. pap. 27.95 (*0-7862-2638-2*) Thorndike Pr.

Desai, Anita. Fire on the Mountain. 145p. 1977. 10.50 (*0-318-36954-0*) Asia Bk Corp.

— Fire on the Mountain. 1985. reprint ed. 7.50 (*0-8364-1455-1*, Pub. by Allied Pubs) S Asia.

— Journey to Ithaca. 336p. 1996. pap. 12.95 (*0-14-025818-3*) Viking Penguin.

Desai, Arvindrai N. Environment & Entrepreneur. (C). 1988. 34.00 (*81-7024-209-6*, Pub. by Ashish Pub Hse) S Asia.

— Helping the Handicapped: Problems & Prospects. 1990. 24.00 (*81-7024-261-4*, Pub. by Ashish Pub Hse) S Asia.

— Research Methodology in Management. 1990. 22.50 (*81-7024-290-8*, Pub. by Ashish Pub Hse) S Asia.

Desai, Ashok. Environmental Jurisprudence. LC 98-903627. 1998. 34.00 (*81-259-0512-X*, Pub. by Vikas) S Asia.

Desai, Ashok, ed. Energy Economics. (Energy Research Group Review Ser.). (C). 1990. 14.00 (*81-224-0203-8*) S Asia.

Desai, Ashok V. Energy in Latin America. (Energy Research Group Review Ser.). (C). 1990. 14.00 (*81-224-0290-9*) S Asia.

— My Economic Affair. (C). 1994. text 24.00 (*81-224-0582-7*) S Asia.

Desai, Ashok V., ed. Energy in Africa. (Energy Research Group Review Ser.). (C). 1990. 14.00 (*81-224-0199-6*) S Asia.

— Human Energy. (Energy Research Group Review Ser.). (C). 1990. 14.00 (*81-224-0209-7*) S Asia.

— Patterns of Energy Use in Developing Countries. (Energy Research Group Review Ser.). (C). 1990. 17.50 (*81-224-0201-1*) S Asia.

D

***Desai, B. B.** Handbook of Nutrition & Diet. LC 00-40479. (Food Science & Technology Ser.). (Illus.). 2000. write for info. (*0-8247-0375-8*) Dekker.

Desai, B. B., et al. Seeds Handbook: Biology, Production, Processing & Storage. LC 97-183191. (Books in Soils, Plants & the Environment: Vol. 55). (Illus.). 632p. 1997. text 185.00 (*0-8247-0042-2*) Dekker.

Desai, B. B., jt. auth. see Salunkhe, D. K.

Desai, B. G. Emerging Youth. 199p. 1967. 9.95 (*0-318-36939-7*) Asia Bk Corp.

Desai, B. M. Agricultural Development Paradigm for the Ninth Plan under New Economic Environment LC 97-906167. (CMA Monograph Ser.). xix, 1032 p. 1997. write for info. (*81-204-1177-3*, Pub. by Oxford & IBH Pubng) Science Pubs.

Desai, B. M., et al. Food Processing Industry in India. 1991. 18.00 (*81-204-0554-4*, Pub. by Oxford IBH) S Asia.

— Rural Financial Institutions. (C). 1989. 17.50 (*81-204-0389-4*, Pub. by Oxford IBH) S Asia.

Desai, B. N., ed. Oceanography of the Indian Ocean. (Illus.). 788p. (C). 1993. text 149.00 (*90-5410-228-4*, Pub. by A A Balkema) Ashgate Pub Co.

Desai, Bharat. Environmental Laws of India: Basic Documents. (C). 1994. 42.50 (*0-8364-2895-1*) S Asia.

Desai, Bhupat M. & Mellor, John W. Institutional Finance for Agricultural Development: An Analytical Survey of Some Critical Issues. LC 93-34703. (Literature Review Ser.: Vol. 1). 1993. write for info. (*0-89629-500-1*) Intl Food Policy.

Desai, Bipin C. Database Management Systems. Westby, ed. 820p. (C). 1990. mass mkt. 59.25 (*0-314-66771-7*) West Pub.

Desai, C. S. & Gallagher, R. H., eds. Mechanics of Engineering Materials. LC 83-12556. (Wiley Series in Numerical Methods in Engineering). 705p. reprint ed. pap. 200.00 (*0-7837-6370-0*, 204608200010) Bks Demand.

Desai, C. S. & Gioda, G. Numerical Methods & Constitutive Modelling in Geomechanics. (CISM Ser.: Vol. 311). (Illus.). v, 407p. 1990. 86.95 (*0-387-82215-1*) Spr-Verlag.

Desai, C. S., ed. see Symposium, Chicago, Illinois Staff.

Desai, Chintamani N. Shakespearean Comedy. LC 79-144595. reprint ed. 37.50 (*0-404-02099-2*) AMS Pr.

Desai, Chirag & Phillips, Fred Y. New Software Technologies: Future Directions & Market Implications. 116p. 1993. pap. 30.00 (*1-887406-00-X*) ICTwo Inst.

Desai, D. A., frwd. Law of Torts, a Very Exhaustive Standard Publication. (C). 1987. 200.00 (*0-7855-5113-1*) St Mut.

Desai, Devangana. Erotic Sculpture of India: A Socio-Cultural Study. (Illus.). 290p. 1984. text 55.00 (*0-685-13845-3*) Coronet Bks.

***Desai, Devangana.** Khajuraho. (Monumental Legacy Ser.). (Illus.). 96p. 2000. text 15.95 (*0-19-565391-2*) OUP.

Desai, Gunvant M., jt. ed. see Mellor, John W.

Desai, H. B. Current Issues in Indian Shipping. 1989. 16.50 (*81-7169-014-9*, Pub. by Commonwealth) S Asia.

Desai, I. D., ed. see Simopoulos, A. P.

Desai, I. P., jt. auth. see Shah, A. M.

Desai, Kiran. Hullabaloo in the Guava Orchard. LC 99-13507. 224p. 1999. pap. 12.95 (*0-385-49370-3*, Anchor NY) Doubleday.

— Hullabaloo in the Guava Orchard. LC 97-51148. 224p. (YA). (gr. 8 up). 1998. 22.00 (*0-87113-711-9*, Atlntc Mnthly) Grove-Atltic.

***Desai, Kiran.** Hullabaloo in the Guava Orchard. large type unabridged ed. 232p. 1999. 26.95 (*0-7531-5949-X*, 15949X, Pub. by ISIS Lrg Prnt) ISIS Pub.

Desai, Mahadev. Day to Day with Mahatma Gandhi: Secretary's Diary 1917-1927 & 1932, 10 Vols., Set. Dalal, C. B. & Parikh, Narahari D., eds. Nilkanth, H. G. & Desai, V. G., trs. 3800p. 1984. text 235.00 (*0-934676-64-X*) Greenlf Bks.

— The Story of Bardoli Satyagraha. 257p. 1983. pap. 5.00 (*0-934676-46-1*) Greenlf Bks.

Desai, Mahadev, tr. see Gandhi, Mohandas Karamchand.

Desai, Mahesh, ed. Construction Practices & Instrumentation in Geotechnical Engineering: Proceedings of the International Conference, Surat, India, 20-23 December 1982, 2 vols., Set. 559p. (C). 1984. text 252.00 (*90-6191-539-2*, Pub. by A A Balkema) Ashgate Pub Co.

Desai, Meghnad. The Collected Essays of Meghnad Desai, 2 Vols., Set. (Economists of the Twentieth Century Ser.). 336p. 1995. 90.00 (*1-85898-095-X*) E Elgar.

— Macroeconomics & Monetary Theory Vol. 1: The Selected Essays of Meghnad Desai. (Economists of the Twentieth Century Ser.). 336p. 1995. 95.00 (*1-85278-689-2*) E Elgar.

— Poverty, Famine & Economic Development: The Selected Essays of Meghnad Desai, 2 vols., Vol. II. (Economists of the Twentieth Century Ser.). 1995. 90.00 (*1-85278-690-6*) E Elgar.

Desai, Meghnad & London School of Economics & Political Science Dep. On Equality. LC 97-3858. 308p. 1997. pap. text 24.95 (*1-56000-979-9*) Transaction Pubs.

Desai, Meghnad & Redfern, Paul, eds. Global Governance: Ethics & Economics of the New World Order. LC 95-18013. 224p. 1995. 79.50 (*1-85567-332-0*) Bks Intl VA.

Desai, Meghnad, jt. ed. see Kumar, Dharma.

Desai, Mohamed A. Downstream Processing of Proteins: Methods & Protocols. LC 99-30429. (Methods in Biotechnology Ser.: Vol. 9). 240p. 2000. 99.50 (*0-89603-564-6*) Humana.

Desai, Morarji. The Story of My Life, 3 vols. LC 78-40613. 1979. 77.00 (*0-08-023566-2*, Pergamon Pr) Elsevier.

Desai, Narayan. Gandhi Through a Child's Eyes: An Intimate Memoir. (Peacewatch Editions Ser.). 96p. 1992. pap. 8.00 (*0-943734-23-1*) Ocean Tree Bks.

— A Nonviolent Revolutionary: Story of a Gandhian Educator. Hare, A. Paul, ed. LC 97-29282. (Illus.). 208p. 1997. 89.95 (*0-7734-8543-0*) E Mellen.

Desai, Neera. Women in Modern India. 334p. 1977. 12.95 (*0-318-37323-8*) Asia Bk Corp.

Desai, Neera & Krishnaraj, Maithreyi. Women & Society in India. 1987. 41.00 (*81-202-0188-4*, Pub. by Ajanta) S Asia.

Desai, Neera & Patel, V. Indian Women: Change & Challenge in the International Decade 1975-85. 1986. 15.00 (*0-86132-117-0*, Pub. by Popular Prakashan) S Asia.

Desai, P. B., jt. ed. see Bose, Ashish.

Desai, Padma, ed. Going Global: Transition from Plan to Market in the World Economy. LC 97-14607. (Illus.). 650p. 1997. 63.00 (*0-262-04161-8*) MIT Pr.

— Marxism, Central Planning & the Soviet Economy: Economic Essays in Honor of Alexander Erlich. (Illus.). 352p. 1983. 42.50 (*0-262-04071-9*) MIT Pr.

***Desai, Padma & Idson, Todd.** Work Without Wages: Russia's Nonpayment Crisis. (Illus.). 300p. (C). 2001. 29.95 (*0-262-04184-7*) MIT Pr.

Desai, Praful R. Principles of Law of Contract. (C). 1988. 80.00 (*0-7855-3720-1*) St Mut.

— The Sale of Goods Act, 1930. (C). 1990. 95.00 (*0-89771-233-1*) St Mut.

Desai, Pramod D., jt. auth. see Gilp, Brian F.

Desai, Pramod D., jt. auth. see Hultgren, Ralph.

Desai, Pramod D., jt. auth. see Payne, James E.

Desai, Pramod D., jt. ed. see Welsch, Gerhard.

Desai, R. W. Frailty, Thy Name Is Woman. (C). 1993. 24.00 (*81-241-0087-X*) S Asia.

Desai, Radhika. Intellectuals & Socialism: Social Democrats & the Labour Party. LC 94-200864. 256p. (C). 1994. pap. 35.00 (*0-85315-795-2*, Pub. by Lawrence & Wishart) NYU Pr.

Desai, Rajiv. Indian Business Culture: An Insider's Guide. LC 99-204215. 157p. 1999. pap. write for info. (*981-00-9327-6*, Pub. by AgBe Pub) Balogh.

Desai, Rupin W. Sir John Falstaff Knight. Westburg, John E., ed. LC 75-5210. (Comparative Literature Studies). (Illus.). 133p. 1975. pap. 10.00 (*0-87423-013-6*) Westburg.

Desai, S. T., ed. The Law of Partnership in India. (C). 1990. 120.00 (*0-89771-232-3*) St Mut.

Desai, Santosh N. & Ambree, A. Hinduism in Thai Life. 163p. 1980. 23.95 (*0-940500-66-3*) Asia Bk Corp.

Desai, Shantinath K., ed. Contemporary Indian Short Stories. (C). 1997. pap. 12.00 (*81-260-0137-2*, Pub. by Indian Pubs) S Asia.

Desai, Shulpa. Ophthalmology Resident Pocket Survival Guide. 100p. (C). 1999. pap. 9.95 (*1-883205-37-9*) Intl Med Pub.

Desai, Tripta. Women in India: A Brief Historical Survey. (C). 1992. 21.00 (*81-215-0532-1*, Pub. by M Manoharial) Coronet Bks.

Desai, Uday, ed. Comparative Environmental Politics & Policy. (Orig.). 1992. pap. 15.00 (*0-944285-31-7*) Pol Studies.

— Ecological Policy & Politics in Developing Countries: Economic Growth, Democracy, & Environment. LC 97-27167. (SUNY Series in International Environmental Policy & Theory). 327p. (C). 1998. text 83.50 (*0-7914-3779-5*) State U NY Pr.

— Ecological Policy & Politics in Developing Countries: Economic Growth, Democracy, & Environment. LC 97-27167. (SUNY Series in International Environmental Policy & Theory). (Illus.). 327p. (C). 1998. pap. text 27.95 (*0-7914-3780-9*) State U NY Pr.

— Federalism, Implementation & Surface Mining. (Orig.). 1989. pap. 15.00 (*0-944285-18-X*) Pol Studies.

— Moving the Earth: Cooperative Federalism & Implementation of the Surface Mining Act, 308. LC 92-25744. (Contributions in Political Science Ser.: No. 308). 272p. 1992. 55.00 (*0-313-28698-1*, DMV, Greenwood Pr) Greenwood.

Desai, Uday, et al, eds. The Politics of Policy. (Policy Studies Journal: Vol. 26:3). 232p. 1998. pap. write for info. (*0-944285-56-2*) Pol Studies.

Desai, Uday B. Modelling & Application of Stochastic Processes. 1986. text 127.00 (*0-89838-177-0*) Kluwer Academic.

Desai, Urmila, jt. auth. see Morningstar, Amadea.

Desai, Urmila, ed. see Morningstar, Amadea.

Desai, V. G., tr. see Desai, Mahadev.

Desai, V. G., tr. see Gandhi, M. K.

Desai, Vandana. Community Participation & Slum Housing: A Study of Bombay. LC 94-45235. (Illus.). 347p. 1995. 28.00 (*0-8039-9228-9*) Sage.

Desai, Visbakba, ed. Gods, Guardians & Lovers: Temple Sculptures of North India. (Illus.). 288p. 1997. 65.00 (*0-944142-92-3*) Grantha.

Desai, Vishakha N. & Leidy, Denise P. Faces of Asia: Portraits from the Permanent Collection. Jupe, Margaret, ed. LC 89-63303. (Illus.). 71p. 1989. pap. text 15.95 (*0-87846-314-3*) Mus Fine Arts Boston.

Desai, Vishakha N. & Mason, Darielle, eds. Gods, Guardians & Lovers: Temple Sculptures from North India A. D. 700-1200. (Illus.). 288p. 1993. 65.00 (*81-85822-10-7*, Pub. by Mapin Pubng) Antique Collect.

Desai, Yogi A., jt. auth. see Kripalvanandji, Shri.

***Desai, Z. A.** Arabic, Persian & Urdu Inscriptions of West India: A Topographical List. LC 99-932917. 1999. 102.00 (*81-7574-051-5*, Pub. by Sundeep Prak) S Asia.

DeSain, Carol. Documentation Basics that Support Good Manufacturing Practices. LC 92-31545. (Illus.). 88p. 1993. pap. 42.95 (*0-943330-41-6*) Advanstar Commns.

— Drug, Device & Diagnostic Manufacturing: The Ultimate Resource Handbook. 2nd ed. 429p. 1992. 149.00 (*0-935184-38-4*) Interpharm.

DeSain, Carol & Sutton, Charmaine V. Meeting GMP & ISO Expectations for Product Development. LC 98-148363. 183p. (Orig.). 1996. pap. 145.00 (*1-882615-31-X*) Parexel Intl.

Desain, Carol & Sutton, Charmaine V. Validation for Medical Device & Diagnostic Manufacturers. 2nd ed. LC 97-31031. 1997. 192.00 (*1-57491-063-9*) Interpharm.

DeSain, Carol & Vercimak, Charmaine. Documentation Practices: A Complete Guide to Document Development & Management of GMP & ISO 9000 Compliant Industries. LC 96-84474. 150p. 1996. 124.95 (*0-929870-39-5*) Advanstar Commns.

Desaint, A. Ideas in Stenciling. 1990. 12.98 (*1-55521-547-5*) Bk Sales Inc.

DeSaix, Deborah D. In the Back Seat. LC 92-54647. 32p. (J). (ps-3). 1993. 15.00 (*0-374-33639-3*) FS&G.

DeSaix, Deborah D., jt. illus. see George, Kristine O'Connel.

Desaix, Frank. Hilary & the Lions. LC 90-55162. 32p. (J). (ps-3). 1990. 15.00 (*0-374-33237-1*) FS&G.

— Hilary & the Lions. 1996. 11.15 (*0-606-10843-2*, Pub. by Turtleback) Demco.

DeSaix, Frank. Hilary & the Lions. (Illus.). 32p. (J). (gr. k-3). 1996. pap. 5.95 (*0-374-43065-9*) FS&G.

DeSales, Deroussy. Noel. 1994. pap. 13.99 (*0-8442-1008-0*) NTC Contemp Pub Co.

deSales, Francis. Introduction to the Devout Life. pap. 2.00 (*0-8358-0161-6*) Upper Room Bks.

DeSalle, Barb, jt. auth. see DeSalle, Don.

DeSalle, Don. Collector's Guide to Tonka Trucks 1947-1963. 2nd rev. ed. (Illus.). 126p. 1996. pap. 19.95 (*0-89538-055-2*) L-W Inc.

DeSalle, Don & DeSalle, Barb. The DeSalle Collection of Smith-Miller & Doepke Trucks. (Illus.). 88p. 1997. 19.95 (*0-89538-093-5*) L-W Inc.

DeSalle, R. & Schierwater, B., eds. Molecular Approaches to Ecology & Evolution. 300p. 1998. 69.50 (*3-7643-5725-8*) Spr-Verlag.

DeSalle, Rob. Epidemic! The World of Infectious Disease. LC 99-14127. (Illus.). 1999. pap. 19.95 (*1-56584-546-3*, Pub. by New Press NY) Norton.

DeSalle, Rob & Schierwater, B. Molecular Approaches to Ecology & Evolution. LC 98-15347. 1998. pap. write for info. (*0-8176-5725-8*) Birkhauser.

Desalmand, Fancoise, jt. ed. see Desbois, Michel.

DeSalvo, Antonino. References in Biology: A Selected Topical Bibliography. rev. ed. 287p. (YA). (gr. 9 up). 1994. reprint ed. student ed., ring bd. 25.00 (*0-916209-07-5*) Owlet Pubns.

DeSalvo, Donna & Caws, Mary A. Staging Surrealism: A Succession of Collections (2) (Succession of Collections: Vol. 2). (Illus.). 96p. 1997. pap. 18.95 (*1-881390-18-7*, 811002) OSU Wexner Ctr.

DeSalvo, Donna & Massie, Annetta. Apocalyptic Wallpaper. (Illus.). 64p. (C). 1997. pap. 17.95 (*1-881390-16-0*) OSU Wexner Ctr.

DeSalvo, Donna & Moos, David. Forces of the '50s: Selections from the Albright-Knox Art Gallery. (Succession of Collections: Vol. 1). (Illus.). 80p. 1996. pap. 16.95 (*1-881390-14-4*) OSU Wexner Ctr.

Desalvo, Jean-Luc. Le Topos du Mundus Inversus dans l'Oeuvre d'Antonine Maillet. (FRE.). 356p. 1999. 74.95 (*1-57309-266-5*) Intl Scholars.

DeSalvo, John A., ed. see Adams, Frank O.

***DeSalvo, Louise.** Adultery. LC 99-14814. 176p. 1999. 20.00 (*0-8070-6224-3*) Beacon Pr.

— Adultery. 2000. pap. 13.00 (*0-8070-6225-1*) Beacon Pr.

DeSalvo, Louise. Breathless: An Asthma Journal. LC 96-46405. 168p. 1998. pap. 12.00 (*0-8070-7097-1*) Beacon Pr.

— Conceived with Malice: Literature As Revenge. 437p. 1998. reprint ed. text 20.00 (*0-7881-5196-7*) DIANE Pub.

— Vertigo. 288p. 1997. pap. 11.95 (*0-452-27324-2*, Plume) Dutton Plume.

— Virginia Woolf: The Impact of Childhood Sexual Abuse on Her Life & Work. 400p. 1990. pap. 14.50 (*0-345-36639-5*) Ballantine Pub Grp.

DeSalvo, Louise, et al, eds. Short Fiction by Irish Women. rev. ed. LC 98-35268. 296p. 1999. reprint ed. pap. 15.00 (*0-8070-8341-0*) Beacon Pr.

DeSalvo, Louise A. Writing as a Way of Healing. LC 98-35064. xiii, 226 p. 2000. pap. 13.00 (*0-06-251520-9*) Harper SF.

***DeSalvo, Louise A.** Writing As a Way of Healing. 2000. pap. 14.00 (*0-8070-7243-5*) Beacon Pr.

DeSalvo, Louise A. Writing as a Way of Healing: How Telling Our Stories Transforms Our Lives. LC 98-35064. 224p. 1999. 22.00 (*0-06-251519-5*, Pub. by Harper SF) HarpC.

DeSalvo, Nancy. Beginning with Books: Library Programming for Infants, Toddlers, & Preschoolers. LC 92-14858. (Illus.). xiii, 186p. (C). 1993. pap. 27.50 (*0-208-02318-6*, Lib Prof Pubns) Shoe String.

DeSamper, Hugh. Welcome to the Williamsburg Inn. (Illus.). 112p. 1997. 24.95 (*1-890674-04-4*) Lickle Pubng.

Desamper, Hugh & Colonial Williamsburg Foundation Staff. Welcome to the Williamsburg Inn. LC 97-10002. (Illus.). 108p. 1997. 19.95 (*0-87935-169-1*) Colonial Williamsburg.

Desan, Philippe, ed. Montaigne Studies: An Interdisciplinary Forum. (Illus.). 187p. 1989. 11.95 (*1-878417-01-0*) Hestia Pr.

Desan, Philippe, et al, eds. Literature & Social Practice. 307p. 1989. pap. text 16.50 (*0-226-14342-2*) U Ch Pr.

— Literature & Social Practice. 202p. 1989. lib. bdg. 36.00 (*0-226-14341-4*) U Ch Pr.

Desan, Philippe & Wolff, Mark. Literary Objects: Flaubert. LC 96-86470. (Illus.). 64p. (Orig.). 1996. pap. 9.95 (*0-935573-17-8*) D & A Smart Museum.

Desan, Phillipe, ed. Humanism in Crisis: The Decline of the French Renaissance. (Studies in Medieval & Early Modern Civilization). 336p. (C). 1991. text 49.50 (*0-472-10239-7*, 10239) U of Mich Pr.

Desan, Suzanne. Reclaiming the Sacred: Lay Religion & Popular Politics in Revolutionary France. Laitin, David, ed. LC 90-55120. (Wilder House Series in Politics, History, & Culture). (Illus.). 272p. 1990. text 39.95 (*0-8014-2404-6*) Cornell U Pr.

Desan, Wilfrid. Let the Future Come: Perspectives for a Planetary Peace. LC 87-3. (Planetary Man Ser.: No. 3). 164p. reprint ed. pap. 50.90 (*0-7837-6316-6*, 204603100010) Bks Demand.

***DeSanctis, Gerardine & Fulk, Janet, eds.** Shaping Organizational Form: Communication, Connection & Community. LC 99-6233. (Organization Science Ser.). 523p. 1999. 89.95 (*0-7619-0494-8*) Sage.

DeSanctis, Gerardine, jt. auth. see Dickson, Gary W.

DeSanctis, Gerardine, jt. auth. see Fulk, Janet.

DeSanctis, Michael E. Renewing the City of God. Philippart, David, ed. (Meeting House Essays Ser.: Vol. 5). 55p. 1994. pap. 6.00 (*0-929650-69-7*, RENEW) Liturgy Tr Pubns.

DeSandies, Andre, jt. auth. see Wollman, Larry.

Desani, G. V. Hali, & Collected Stories. LC 90-46599. 224p. 1991. 20.00 (*0-929701-12-7*) McPherson & Co.

DeSante, David, jt. auth. see DeSante, Gilbert.

DeSante, Gilbert & DeSante, David. Exact Point Count: A System for Bidding Contract Bridge. LC 88-90521. viii, 176p. (Orig.). 1988. pap. 10.95 (*0-9618940-1-6*) Slate Creek Pr.

Desanti, Dominique. La Banquiere des Annees Folles: Marthe Hanau. (FRE.). 1980. pap. 11.95 (*0-7859-1915-5*, 2070371956) Fr & Eur.

DeSanti, Louis A. Columbus & the New World: Hero of the Millennium. (Orig.). 1991. pap. text 11.95 (*0-9631581-0-4*, TXU 418-851) Millennium VA.

DeSanti, Roger, jt. auth. see Pedigo, Patricia.

DeSanti, Roger, ed. see Drumm, Susan T.

DeSanti, Roger, ed. see Jacobi, Dawn T.

DeSanti, Roger, ed. see Notarianni, Barbara.

DeSanti, Roger, ed. see Roberson, Rae Anne.

DeSantis, Cari, jt. auth. see Billington, Mike.

DeSantis, Carl, jt. auth. see Platt, Donald M.

***Desantis, Christopher.** 15 Easy to Intermediate Christmas Favorites: Piano. 1998. pap. text 10.95 (*0-7692-6426-3*) Wrner Bros.

DeSantis, Deirdre, jt. auth. see Harr, Robert R.

Desantis, Diana O., tr. see Salaices, Jose.

DeSantis, Eric, ed. see Arcudi, John.

DeSantis, Gene, jt. auth. see Whitaker, Jerry.

DeSantis, Gennaro, jt. auth. see Mircos, Gus.

Desantis, John. New Untouchables: How America Sanctions Police Violence. LC 94-18643. 288p. 1994. 22.95 (*1-879360-31-4*) Noble Pr.

Desantis, Kenny. A Dentist's Tools. LC 89-8375. (Illus.). (J). 1997. 10.99 (*0-399-61231-9*) Putnam Pub Group.

***DeSantis, Ronald J.** An Art Show Without Paintings. 83p. 1999. 9.95 (*0-9668280-1-1*) Asphalt Warriors.

— Lawrence Police Department. (Images of America Ser.). 1999. pap. 18.99 (*0-7385-0153-0*) Arcadia Publng.

DeSantis, Vincent P. Republicans Face the Southern Question: The New Departure Years, 1877-1897. LC 78-64231. (Johns Hopkins University. Studies in the Social Sciences. Thirtieth Ser. 1912: 1). reprint ed. 13.00 (*0-404-61336-5*) AMS Pr.

DeSantis, Vincent P. The Shaping of Modern America, 1877-1920. 2nd ed. (Forum's American History Ser.). 14.95 (*0-88295-136-X*) Forum Pr IL.

— The Shaping of Modern America, 1877-1920. 3rd ed. LC 99-39792. 328p. (C). 2000. pap. text 16.95 (*0-88295-953-0*) Harlan Davidson.

DeSanto, J. A. Scalar Wave Theory: Green's Functions & Applications. Brekhovskikh, L. M. et al, eds. LC 92-15953. (Wave Phenomena Ser.: No. 12). (Illus.). xiii, 193p. 1992. 69.95 (*0-387-55263-4*) Spr-Verlag.

DeSanto, Jerry. Bitterroot Montana State Flower. LC QK85.3.M6D47. (Illus.). 120p. 1991. pap. 13.00 (*0-9637889-0-6*) Falcon Pub Inc.

— Logan Pass: Alpine Splendor in Glacier National Park. LC 95-9692. (Illus.). 64p. (Orig.). 1995. pap. 8.95 (*1-56044-158-5*) Falcon Pub Inc.

DeSanto, N. G., jt. ed. see Alon, Uri.

DeSanto, R. S., jt. ed. see Effler, Steven W.

DeSanto, R. S., ed. see Geipel, R.

DeSanto, R. S., ed. see Moore, J. W.

Desaran, Forrest A., ed. see Fossett, Mark A. & Siebert, M. Therese.

Desario, Daniel, et al. Blond's Contracts Essay Questions: Essay Questions. (Blond's Essay Ser.). 160p. (Orig.). 1992. pap. 21.99 (*0-945819-22-6*) Sulzburger & Graham Pub.

— Blond's Essays Questions for Torts. (Blond's Essay Ser.). 160p. (Orig.). (C). 1992. pap. 21.99 (*0-945819-21-8*) Sulzburger & Graham Pub.

DeSario, Jack & Langton, Stuart, eds. Citizen Participation & Public Policy. (Orig.). 1984. pap. 15.00 (*0-918592-65-8*) Pol Studies.

— Citizen Participation in Public Decision Making, 158. LC 86-7571. (Contributions in Political Science Ser.: No. 158). 249p. 1987. 59.95 (*0-313-25478-8*, DCZ/, Greenwood Pr) Greenwood.

Desario, Jack P. International Public Policy Sourcebook, Vol. 2. 1989. lib. bdg. 225.00 (*0-313-26779-0*, DEI/) Greenwood.

Desario, Jack P., ed. International Public Policy Sourcebook Vol. 1: Health & Social Welfare, Vol. 1. LC 88-16290. 358p. 1989. lib. bdg. 150.00 (*0-313-24907-5*, DEI/, Greenwood Pr) Greenwood.

DeSario, Jack P., et al. Local Government Information & Training Needs in the 21st Century. LC 93-30989. 160p. 1994. 52.95 (*0-89930-697-7*, Quorum Bks) Greenwood.

Desarmenien, J., ed. TEX for Scientific Documentation. (Lecture Notes in Computer Science Ser.: Vol. 236). vi, 204p. 1988. 33.00 (*0-387-16807-9*) Spr-Verlag.

Desarmes, Jean R. Love in Motion. 1998. pap. 8.95 (*0-533-12773-4*) Vantage.

DeSarno, James V., ed. Law Enforcement Officers Killed & Assaulted (1997) (Illus.). 93p. 1999. text 25.00 (*0-7881-7912-8*) DIANE Pub.

Desatnick, Robert L. & Detzel, Denis H. Managing to Keep the Customer: How to Achieve & Maintain Superior Customer Service Throughout the Organization. rev. ed. LC 93-6842. 235p. 1993. 28.50 (*1-55542-415-5*) Jossey-Bass.

deSaules, T., jt. auth. see BSRIA Staff.

Desauliers, F. L. Richer, la Genealogie des Familles Richer de la Fleche et Hamelin, avec Notes Historiques sur Sainte Anne de la Perade, les Grondines, Etc. (FRE., Illus.). 241p. 1998. reprint ed. pap. 37.50 (*0-8328-9579-2*); reprint ed. lib. bdg. 47.50 (*0-8328-9578-4*) Higginson Bk Co.

Desauliners, Mary. Carlyle & the Economics of Terror: A Study of Revisionary Gothicism in the French Revolution. 152p. 1995. 60.00 (*0-7735-1269-1*, Pub. by McG-Queens Univ Pr) CUP Services.

Desaulniers, Marcel. The Burger Meisters: America's Best Chefs Give Their Recipes for America's Best Burgers, Plus the Fixins. LC 93-13662. (Illus.). 144p. 1994. 20.00 (*0-671-86538-2*) S&S Trade.

— Death by Chocolate. 1993. 25.46 (*0-394-22352-7*) Beginner.

— Death by Chocolate: The Last Word on a Consuming Passion. LC 91-45878. (Illus.). 144p. 1993. 29.95 (*0-8478-1564-1*, Pub. by Rizzoli Intl) St Martin.

***Desaulniers, Marcel.** Death by Chocolate Cakes: An Astonishing Array of Chocolate Enchantments. (Illus.). 224p. 2000. 32.50 (*0-688-16297-5*, Wm Morrow) Morrow Avon.

Desaulniers, Marcel. Death by Chocolate Cookies. LC 96-54840. (Illus.). 144p. 1997. 29.50 (*0-684-83197-X*, Scribner Pap Fic) S&S Trade Pap.

— Desserts to Die For. LC 95-1152. (Illus.). 144p. 1995. 30.00 (*0-684-81139-1*) S&S Trade.

— Salad Days: Main-Course Salads for a First-Class Meal. LC 97-47083. 176p. 1998. 27.00 (*0-684-82261-X*) S&S Trade.

— The Trellis Cookbook. 368p. 1992. pap. 16.00 (*0-671-74842-4*, Fireside) S&S Trade Pap.

deSaussure, Charlton. Low Country Carolina Genealogies: Including the Following Families, DeSaussure, Huger, Horry, Laurens, Bishop Smith, Ford, Mitchel King, Boone. LC 97-67552. (Illus.). write for info. (*0-89308-395-X*) Southern Hist Pr.

DeSautel, Madeline, tr. see Mattina, Anthony, ed.

Desautels, Julianne. I Should Be Me! (Illus.). (J). 1996. pap. 4.95 (*0-9652527-0-1*) Make Me Believe.

Desautels, Paul E. The Jade Kingdom. (Illus.). 128p. (gr. 13). 1986. text 57.95 (*0-442-21797-8*) Chapman & Hall.

DesAutels, Peggy, et al. Praying for a Cure: When Medical & Religious Practices Conflict. LC 98-45358. (Point/Counterpoint Ser.). 160p. 1999. 57.00 (*0-8476-9262-0*); pap. 17.95 (*0-8476-9263-9*) Rowman.

Desbarats, Jacqueline. Prolific Survivors: Population Change in Cambodia, 1975-1993. LC 98-127600. (Illus.). 250p. (Orig.). 1995. pap. text 19.95 (*1-881044-13-0*) ASU Prog SE Asian.

Desbarats, Peter. Somalia Cover-Up: A Commissioner's Journal. LC 98-101406. 288p. 1998. 23.95 (*0-7710-2684-6*) McCland & Stewart.

Desbazielle, G., jt. auth. see Kaufmann, A.

Desberg. Teaching with Technology. 2nd ed. 1997. cd-rom 53.00 (*0-205-26405-0*) Allyn.

— Teaching With Technology. 3rd ed. 2000. cd-rom 46.00 (*0-205-31397-3*) Allyn.

Desberg & Colb. Interactive Cases in Teaching Education: Classroom Management. 1995. cd-rom 35.00 (*0-205-16289-4*) Allyn.

Desberg, Peter. No More Butterflies: Overcoming Stagefright, Shyness, Interview Anxiety & Fear of Public Speaking. LC 95-72226. 176p. 1996. pap. 13.95 (*1-57224-041-5*) New Harbinger.

Desberg, Peter & Fisher, Farah. Teaching with Technology. 2nd ed. 1998. text, teacher ed. write for info. (*0-205-26406-9*, T6406-7) Allyn.

Desberg, Peter, jt. auth. see Colbert, Joel.

Desbiens, Jean P. For Pity's Sake. LC 65-28218. (French Canadian Renaissance Ser.). 134p. reprint ed. pap. 41.60 (*0-608-13583-6*, 202229200026) Bks Demand.

— The Impertinences of Brother Anonymous. LC 62-14443. (French Canadian Renaissance Ser.: Vol. 2). 126p. reprint ed. pap. 39.10 (*0-608-13580-1*, 202229100026) Bks Demand.

Desbiens, Patrice. The Invisible Man (L'Homme Invisible) 64p. 1981. 7.95 (*0-920806-27-9*, Pub. by Penumbra Pr) U of Toronto Pr.

***Desbitt, John D.** Wild Rose of Ruby Canyon. 240p. 1999. mass mkt. 3.99 (*0-8439-4520-6*, Leisure Bks) Dorchester Pub Co.

***Desbois, Herve.** For the Love of Women. 2000. pap. 6.95 (*2-89523-024-2*, Pub. by Modus Viv) Genl Dist Srvs.

Desbois, Michel & Desalmand, Fancoise, eds. Global Precipitations & Global Change. LC 94-36781. (NATO ASI Ser.: Series I, Global Environmental Change: Vol. 26). 1994. 238.95 (*3-540-58439-0*) Spr-Verlag.

Desbonnes, R. A. Living Faith: A Study in the Book of James. 70p. (Orig.). 1996. pap. write for info. (*1-57502-155-2*) Morris Pubng.

***Desbonnet, Alan.** Aquidneck Island Open Space: An Economic Prospective. (Aquidneck Island Partnership Coastal Management Report Ser.: No. 3300). (Illus.). 1998. pap. write for info. (*1-885454-32-5*) Coastal Res.

— Pawcatuck Watershed - Water Resources: A Management Issues Profile. (Sustainable Coastal Communities Reports: Vol. 4400). (Illus.). 1999. write for info. (*1-885454-31-7*) Coastal Res.

***Desbonnet, Alan & Hale, Lynne Z.** Project Monitoring Plan: Results Framework, Results Indicators, Worksheets, Coastal Resources Management Project II. (Coastal Management Report Ser.: Vol. 2209). (Illus.). 1998. pap. write for info. (*1-885454-09-0*) Coastal Res.

Desbonnets, Theophile. From Intuition to Institution: The Franciscans. Duggan, Paul & Ducharme, Jerry, trs. from FRE. 165p. 1988. 12.00 (*0-8199-0913-0*, Frncscn Herld) Franciscan Pr.

Desbordes-Valmore, Marceline. Poesies. (Poesie Ser.). (FRE.). pap. 13.95 (*2-07-032243-2*) Schoenhof.

***Desborough, James & Mortimer, Steve.** Munchkin's Guide to Power Gaming. Masters, Phil, ed. 128p. 1999. pap. 19.95 (*1-55634-347-7*, Pub. by S Jackson Games) BookWorld.

Desborough, John. Cold Fusion: Intranet Application & Developemental. LC 97-23629. (ITCP - US Computer Science Ser.). 320p. 1997. pap. 39.99 (*1-85032-899-4*) ITCP.

Desborough, V. R. The Greek Dark Ages. LC 72-171997. 388p. 1972. write for info. (*0-510-03261-3*) A & C Blk.

Desboulmiers, Jean A. Histoire du Theatre de l'Opera Comique, 2 vols. 2nd ed. LC 76-43914. (Music & Theatre in France in the 17th & 18th Centuries Ser.). reprint ed. 97.50 (*0-404-60160-X*) AMS Pr.

Desbrandes, Robert. Encyclopedia of Well Logging: Design Guides for Offshore Structures. (Design Guides for Offshore Structures Ser.). 608p. 1985. 900.00 (*2-7108-0464-6*, Pub. by Edits Technip) Enfield Pubs NH.

DesBrisay, Mather B. History of the County of Lunenburg. (Illus.). 586p. 1996. reprint ed. lib. bdg. 62.00 (*0-8328-5153-1*) Higginson Bk Co.

Desbrueres, Michel, ed. see Lorrain, Jean.

Desbrueres, Michel, ed. see Loti, Pierre.

Desbrueres, Michel, ed. see Loti-Viaud, Pierre P.

Desbrueres, Michel, jt. ed. see Loti-Viaud, Pierre P.

Descamp, Meg. Slug Tossing: And Other Adventures of a Reluctant Gardener. 208p. 1998. pap. 16.95 (*1-57061-044-4*) Sasquatch Bks.

Descamps, Beatrix, tr. see Van Lipp-Biesterfeld, Irene.

Descamps, Jorge, jt. auth. see Louisell, Robert D.

Descamps-Lequime, Sophie. The Ancient Greeks: In the Land of the Gods. LaRose, Mary K., tr. (Peoples of the Past Ser.). (Illus.). 64p. (J). (gr. 4-6). 1996. 7.95 (*0-7613-0096-1*) Millbrook Pr.

Descamps-Lequime, Sophie. Ancient Greeks: In the Land of the Gods. LC 91-35941. (Peoples of the Past Ser.). 1992. 13.15 (*0-606-09001-0*, Pub. by Turtleback) Demco.

Descamps-Lequime, Sophie & Vernerey, Denise. The Ancient Greeks: In the Land of the Gods. LaRose, Mary K., tr. from FRE. LC 91-35941. (Peoples of the Past Ser.). (Illus.). 64p. (J). (gr. 4-6). 1992. lib. bdg. 22.40 (*1-56294-069-4*) Millbrook Pr.

Descamps, Rose-Marie. French & Russian Lexicon of Economic & Commercial Terms: Lexique de Termes Economiques et Commerciaux. 132p. 1986. pap. 35.00 (*0-8288-0827-9*, M2360) Fr & Eur.

Descarries, Laurent, jt. auth. see Jasper, Herbert H.

Descartes. Le Discours de la Methode. unabridged ed. (FRE.). pap. 5.95 (*2-87714-295-7*, Pub. by Booking Intl) Distribks Inc.

— Discourse on Method & the Meditations. (C). 1997. pap. text. write for info. (*0-321-02594-6*) Addson-Wesley Educ.

Descartes, Alligator. Java Native Methods. Ferguson, Paula, ed. 300p. 2000. pap. 29.95 (*1-56592-345-6*) OReilly & Assocs.

Descartes, Alligator & Bunce, Tim. Programming the Perl DBI: Database Programming for Perl & CGI. Mui, Linda, ed. (Illus.). 356p. 1999. pap. 34.95 (*1-56592-699-4*) OReilly & Assocs.

Descartes, Rene. Concordance to Descartes' Meditationes de Prima Philosophia. xii, 355p. 1995. write for info. (*3-487-09886-5*) G Olms Pubs.

— Correspondance avec Elisabeth, et Autres Lettres. Beysade, ed. (FRE.). 1989. pap. 12.95 (*0-7859-3400-6*) Fr & Eur.

— Descartes: The World: And Other Writings. Gaukroger, Stephen, ed. & tr. by. LC 98-14404. (Cambridge Texts in the History of Philosophy Ser.). (Illus.). 220p. (C). 1998. text 59.95 (*0-521-63158-0*); pap. text 18.95 (*0-521-63646-9*) Cambridge U Pr.

— Discours de la Methode. (FRE., Illus.). 1965. pap. 10.95 (*0-8288-9574-0*, 2253012181) Fr & Eur.

— Discours De la Methode. De Buzon, F., ed. (FRE.). 341p. 1991. pap. 11.95 (*0-7859-1674-1*, 2070326136) Fr & Eur.

— Discours de la Methode: Avec: Extraits de la Dioptrique, des Meteores, du Mond, de Homme, de Lettres et de la Vie de Descartes par Baillet. (FRE.). 254p. 1965. 9.95 (*0-7859-1169-3*, 2080701096) Fr & Eur.

— Discours de la Methode (Discourse on the Method) A Bilingual Edition with an Interpretive Essay. Heffernan, George, tr. LC 93-42435. (ENG & FRE.). (C). 1994. pap. text 9.50 (*0-268-00871-X*) U of Notre Dame Pr.

— Discourse on Method. 3rd ed. Cress, Donald, tr. from FRE. LC 98-30370. (HPS Classics Ser.). 58p. (C). 1998. pap. text 4.95 (*0-87220-422-7*) Hackett Pub.

— Discourse on Method & Meditations. Lafleur, Laurence J., tr. LC 60-13395. 1960. pap. write for info. (*0-672-60278-4*, LLA 89) Macmillan.

— Discourse on Method & Meditations on First Philosophy. 4th ed. Cress, Donald, tr. from FRE. LC 98-38149. (Classics Ser.). 120p. (C). 1998. pap. text 6.95 (*0-87220-420-0*); lib. bdg. 24.95 (*0-87220-421-9*) Hackett Pub.

***Descartes, Rene.** Discourse on Method & the Meditations. (Classics Ser.). 188p. (Orig.). 1998. pap. 5.33 (*0-14-044206-5*) Addson-Wesley Educ.

Descartes, Rene. Discourse on Method & the Meditations. Veitch, John, tr. LC 88-43455. (Great Books in Philosophy). 123p. (Orig.). 1989. pap. 6.95 (*0-87975-526-1*) Prometheus Bks.

— A Discourse on Method, Meditations & Principles. Lindsay, A. D., ed. 280p. 1994. 6.95 (*0-460-87411-X*, Everyman's Classic Lib) Tuttle Pubng.

— Discourse on the Method & Meditations on First Philosophy. Weissman, David, ed. LC 96-5885. (Rethinking the Western Tradition Ser.). (Illus.) 400p. 1996. 37.50 (*0-300-06772-0*) Yale U Pr.

— Discourse on the Method & Meditations on First Philosophy. Weissman, David, ed. LC 96-5885. (Rethinking the Western Tradition Ser.). (Illus.) 400p. 1997. pap. 17.00 (*0-300-06773-9*) Yale U Pr.

— Discurso del Metodo. Frondizi, Risieri, ed. Aranda, M., tr. (Biblioteca De Cultura Basica Ser.). (ENG & SPA.). 239p. 1994. 6.80 (*0-8477-0705-9*) U of PR Pr.

— Discurso del Metodo. Meditaciones Metafisicas. Garcia Morente, Manuel, ed. & tr. by. (Nueva Austral Ser.: Vol. 166). (SPA.). 1991. pap. text 24.95 (*84-239-1966-8*) Elliots Bks.

— The Geometry of Rene Descartes. Latham, Marcia L. & Smith, David E., trs. (ENG & FRE.). 244p. (C) 1954. pap. 8.95 (*0-486-60068-8*) Dover.

— Key Philosophical Writings. (Classics of World Literature Ser.). 1997. pap. 5.95 (*1-85326-470-9*, 4709WW, Pub. by Wrdsworth Edits) NTC Contemp Pub Co.

— Lettres a Regius et Remarques sur l'Explication de l'Esprit Humain. (FRE.). 216p. 1959. 20.95 (*0-8288-9575-9*, F36630) Fr & Eur.

***Descartes, Rene.** Meditations & Other Metaphysical Writings. (Penguin Classics Ser.). 256p. 1999. pap. 9.95 (*0-14-044701-6*, Penguin Classics) Viking Penguin.

Descartes, Rene. Meditations Metaphysiques. 7th ed. (FRE.). 320p. 1974. 13.95 (*0-8288-9576-7*, 2080703285) Fr & Eur.

— Meditations on First Philosophy. Heffernan, George, tr. from LAT. LC 91-50569. (C). 1992. pap. text 5.00 (*0-268-01397-7*) U of Notre Dame Pr.

— Meditations on First Philosophy. 2nd ed. Rubin, Ronald, tr. from LAT. 53p. (C). 1986. pap. text 4.95 (*0-941736-11-3*) Arete Pr.

— Meditations on First Philosophy: In Which the Existence of God & the Distinction of the Soul from the Body Are Demonstrated. 3rd ed. Cress, Donald A., tr. from LAT. LC 93-21653. (Hackett Classics Ser.).Tr. of Meditationes de Prima Philosophia. 72p. (C). 1993. pap. text 4.95 (*0-87220-192-9*) Hackett Pub.

— Meditations on First Philosophy-Meditationes de Prima Philosophia: A Bilingual Edition. Heffernan, George, ed. & tr. by. LC 89-40751. (ENG & LAT.). 208p. (C). 1990. pap. text 9.50 (*0-268-01381-0*) U of Notre Dame Pr.

— Le Monde. Mahoney, Michael S., tr. LC 77-86236. (Janus Ser.).Tr. of World. 224p. 1979. lib. bdg. 35.00 (*0-913870-35-8*) Abaris Bks.

— Musicae Compendium. fac. ed. (Monuments of Music & Music Literature in Facsimile Ser., Series II: Vol. 87). 1968. lib. bdg. 32.50 (*0-8450-2287-3*) Broude.

— Oeuvres. (FRE.). 1937. 99.50 (*0-8288-3425-3*, F36590) Fr & Eur.

— Oeuvres et Lettres. deluxe ed. (Pleiade Ser.). (FRE.). 1423p. 1983. 72.95 (*2-07-010166-5*) Schoenhof.

— Oeuvres et Lettres: Avec: Discours de la Methode. 1424p. 1937. 99.50 (*0-8288-9577-5*, F36590) Fr & Eur.

— Oeuvres Philosophiques, 3 vols. Alquie, Ferdinand, ed. Incl. Vol. 1. 1618-1637. 1963. 18.50 Vol. 2. 1638-1642. 1975. 22.50 Vol. 3. 1643-1650. 1973. 37.50 write for info. (*0-318-52181-4*) Fr & Eur.

— Les Passions de l'Ame. (Tel Ser.). (FRE.). 1970. pap. 16.95 (*2-07-071318-0*) Schoenhof.

— Passions of the Soul. Voss, Stephen H., tr. from FRE. LC 87-23818. (HPC Classics Ser.). 191p. (C). 1989. lib. bdg. 34.95 (*0-87220-036-1*) Hackett Pub.

Descartes, Rene. Passions of the Soul. Voss, Stephen H., tr. from FRE. LC 87-23818. (HPC Classics Ser.). 191p. (C). 1989. pap. text 11.95 (*0-87220-035-3*) Hackett Pub.

— Philosophical Essays & Correspondence. Ariew, Roger, ed. LC 99-49303. 320p. (C). 2000. pap. 14.95 (*0-87220-502-9*); lib. bdg. 37.95 (*0-87220-503-7*) Hackett Pub.

Descartes, Rene. Philosophical Writings Vol. 3: The Correspondence. Cottingham, John E. et al, eds. 430p. (C). 1991. text 69.95 (*0-521-40323-5*) Cambridge U Pr.

— Principes de la Philosophie, Vol. 1. 3rd ed. (FRE.). 158p. 1989. 13.95 (*0-7859-1194-4*, 2711601870) Fr & Eur.

— Principles of Philosophy. Reynolds, Blair, tr. LC 88-26640. (Studies in the History of Philosophy: Vol. 6). 250p. 1989. lib. bdg. 89.95 (*0-88946-308-5*) E Mellen.

— Qui Ne Souffre Pas. Sirvan, Jean, tr. from LAT. (FRE.). 152p. 1990. 13.95 (*0-7859-1215-0*, 271160182X) Fr & Eur.

— Regles Utiles et Claires pour la Direction de l'Esprit et la Recherche de la Verite. (Archives Internationales d'Histoire des Idees (International Archives of the History of Ideas) Ser.: No. 88). 364p. 1978. lib. bdg. 199.50 (*90-247-1907-0*, Pub. by M Nijhoff) Kluwer Academic.

— Regulae Ad Directionem Ingenii: Texte Critique Etabli Par G. Crapulli avec la Version Hollandaise du XVIIieme Siecle. (International Archives of the History of Ideas Ser.: No. 12). 278p. 1966. lib. bdg. 99.50 (*90-247-0188-0*, Pub. by M Nijhoff) Kluwer Academic.

— Rene Descartes: Meditation on First Philosophy, with Selections from the Objections & Replies. rev. ed. Cottingham, John, ed. (Cambridge Texts in the History of Philosophy Ser.). 167p. (C). 1996. pap. text 12.95 (*0-521-55818-2*) Cambridge U Pr.

— Rene Descartes: Principles of Philosophy. Miller, Valentine R. & Miller, Reese P., trs. (Synthese Historical Library: No. 4). 353p. 1982. lib. bdg. 158.50 (*90-277-1451-7*) Kluwer Academic.

— Selected Philosophical Writings. Cottingham, John et al, eds. 272p. 1993. pap. text 16.95 (*0-521-35812-4*) Cambridge U Pr.

— Trois Maitres. (FRE., Illus.). 91p. 1991. 34.95 (*0-7859-1203-7*, 2876470195) Fr & Eur.

Descartes, Rene & Adam, Charles. Comedies et Actes Divers: Comedie; Va-et-Vient; Cascando; Parole et Musique; Dis Joe; Acte Sans. 2nd ed. (FRE.). 160p. 1975. 13.95 (*0-7859-1195-2*, 2711601889) Fr & Eur.

***Descartes, Rene & Clarke, Desmond M.** Discourse on Method & Related Writings. 256p. 2000. pap. 7.95 (*0-14-044699-0*, Penguin Classics) Viking Penguin.

Descartes, Rene & Lewis, G. Meditationes de Prima Philosophia: Meditations Metaphysiques. (FRE & LAT.). 178p. 1967. 24.95 (*0-8288-9578-3*, 2711601854) Fr & Eur.

Descartes, Rene & Robinet, Andre. Cogito 75: Meditations Metaphysiques. (FRE.). 152p. 1976. 19.95 (*0-7859-1196-0*, 2711601897) Fr & Eur.

Descartes, Rene & Ross, G. R. The Philosophical Works of Descartes, Vol. 1. Haldane, Elizabeth S., ed. 460p. reprint ed. pap. 131.10 (*0-608-12050-2*, 2024470) Bks Demand.

Descartes, Rene, et al. The Philosophical Writings, 1. Cottingham, John G. & Murdoch, Dugald, trs. 432p. 1985. pap. text 29.95 (*0-521-28807-X*) Cambridge U Pr.

— The Philosophical Writings, 2. Cottingham, John G. & Murdoch, Dugald, trs. 448p. 1985. pap. text 24.95 (*0-521-28808-8*) Cambridge U Pr.

Descartes, S. L. Credit Institutions for Local Authorities in Latin America. LC 73-75403. 81p. 1973. pap. 1.50 (*0-913480-16-9*) Inter Am U Pr.

Descartes, Sol L. Puerto Rico: Trasfondo de su Economia. LC 73-84204. (SPA.). 50p. 1973. pap. 1.95 (*0-913480-14-2*) Inter Am U Pr.

Desch. Wireless. text. write for info. (*0-471-37397-4*) Wiley.

D

An Asterisk (*) at the beginning of an entry indicates that the title is appearing for the first time.

Desch, H. E. Timber: Structure, Properties, Conversion, & Use. 7th rev. ed. LC 95-49033. 1996. 59.95 (*1-56022-861-X*) Haworth Jrnl Co-Edits.

Desch, Larry W., jt. auth. see Nickel, Robert E.

***Desch, Michael C.** Civilian Control of the Military: The Changing Security Environment. LC 98-46418. 1999. 34.95 (*0-8018-6059-8*) Johns Hopkins.

Desch, Michael C. When the Third World Matters: Latin America & United States Grand Strategy. LC 92-36818. 224p. 1993. text 38.50 (*0-8018-4552-1*) Johns Hopkins.

Desch, Michael C., et al, eds. From Pirates to Drug Lords: The Post-Cold War Caribbean Security Environment. LC 97-23334. (SUNY Series in Global Politics). 160p. (C). 1998. text 59.50 (*0-7914-3749-3*); pap. text 19.95 (*0-7914-3750-7*) State U NY Pr.

Desch, Neal E. Marriage or Mistake: A Workbook for Couples Who Are Thinking about Marriage. 110p. 1993. write for info. (*0-9635884-0-0*) Life Improve Sem.

Desch, Samuel, tr. see Landa, L. N.

Desch, Samuel, tr. see Steiner, Rudolf.

Desch, W., et al, eds. Control & Estimation of Distributed Parameter Systems: Nonlinear Phenomena : International Conference in Vorau (Austria), July 18-24, 1993. LC 94-23455. (International Series in Numerical Mathematics: Vol. 118). 1994. 136.00 (*0-8176-5098-9*) Birkhauser.

— Control & Estimation of Distributed Parameter Systems: Nonlinear Phenomena:International Conference in Vorau (Austria), July 18-24, 1993. LC 94-23455. (International Series in Numerical Mathematics: 118). 1994. write for info. (*3-7643-5098-9*) Birkhauser.

— Estimation & Control of Distributed Parameter Systems. (International Series of Numerical Mathematics: Vol. 100). 389p. 1991. 52.00 (*3-7643-2676-X*) Birkhauser.

— Estimation & Control of Distributed Parameter Systems: Proceedings of an International Conference on Control & Estimation of Distributed Parameter Systems, Vorau, July 8-14, 1990. (International Series of Numerical Mathematics: Vol. 100). 402p. 1991. 128.50 (*0-8176-2676-X*) Birkhauser.

Desch, W., et al. Control & Estimation of Distributed Parameter Systems: International Conference in Vorau (Austria), July 14-20, 1996. LC 97-46761. (International Series of Numerical Mathematics). 1998. write for info. (*0-8176-5835-1*) Birkhauser.

— Control & Estimation of Distributed Parameter Systems: International Conference in Vorau (Austria), July 14-20, 1996. LC 97-46761. (International Series of Numerical Mathematics: Vol. 126). 320p. 1998. 98.00 (*3-7643-5835-1*, Pub. by Birkhauser) Spr-Verlag.

Deschaine, Scott. A Bug's Gift. (Illus.). 20p. (J). 1991. pap. 1.95 (*1-878181-01-7*) Discovery Comics.

— Funny. (Illus.). 36p. 1995. pap. 2.95 (*1-878181-09-2*) Discovery Comics.

— Monster Love. (Illus.). 36p. (J). 1993. pap. 2.50 (*1-878181-05-X*) Discovery Comics.

— Popcorn! (Illus.). 68p. (J). 1993. pap. 4.95 (*1-878181-06-8*) Discovery Comics.

— Screaming Eagle. (Illus.). 296p. 1999. 19.95 (*1-878181-04-1*) Discovery Comics.

Deschaine, Scott & Bonno, Chris. Head On. (Illus.). 36p. (J). 1990. pap. 2.00 (*1-878181-02-5*) Discovery Comics.

Deschaine, Scott, et al. Free Laughs. (Illus.). 68p. 1991. pap. 2.95 (*1-878181-00-9*) Discovery Comics.

Deschamps. Product Juggernauts. 1995. 29.95 (*0-07-103614-8*) McGraw.

Deschamps, jt. auth. see Brunel.

Deschamps-Adams, Helene. Spyglass: An Autobiography 19960316 [00ac]9. LC 94-39233. 89p. (YA). (gr. 7 up). 1995. 16.95 (*0-8050-3536-2*) H Holt & Co.

Deschamps, David, jt. auth. see Singer, Bennett L.

Deschamps, Francois. The Return of the Slapstick Papyrus. (Illus.). 132p. 1988. pap. 14.95 (*0-89822-051-3*) Visual Studies.

Deschamps, Francois & Mohns, Judith. Particle Theory. 1991. pap. 15.00 (*0-932526-35-7*) Nexus Pr.

***Deschamps, Henri & Franz, Erich.** Pablo Picasso: The Lithographs. (Illus.). 2000. 85.00 (*3-7757-0981-9*, A20411, Pub. by Gerd Hatje) Dist Art Pubs.

Deschamps, J. P. Prevention of Traffic Accidents in Childhood: Report on a WHO Study. (EURO Reports & Studies: No. 26). 54p. 1981. pap. text 4.00 (*92-9020-165-7*, 1330026) World Health.

Deschamps, Jean. Cours Abrege de la Philosophie Wolfienne en Forme des Lettres. rev. ed. (Christian Wolff, Gesammelte Werke, Materialien und Dokumente Ser.: No. 13). 1161p. 1991. write for info. incl. 3.5 hd (*3-487-09203-4*) G Olms Pubs.

Deschamps, Jean-Philippe & Nayak, P. Ranganath. Product Juggernauts: How Companies Mobilize to Generate a Stream of Market Winners. LC 94-39670. 480p. 1995. 29.95 (*0-87584-341-7*) Harvard Busn.

Deschamps, Judith, jt. ed. see Eagle, Selwyn.

Deschamps, Louis. The SDI & European Security Interests. (Atlantic Papers: No. 62). 80p. 1987. pap. 12.95 (*0-7099-4549-3*, Pub. by C Helm) Routldge.

Deschamps, Madeleine. Empire. LC 94-9021. (Illus.). 248p. 1994. 95.00 (*1-55859-032-3*) Abbeville Pr.

Deschamps, Pierre. Dictionnaire de Geographie Ancienne et Moderne. 2nd ed. (FRE.). 804p. 1990. 225.00 (*0-7859-5127-X*) Fr & Eur.

— Dictionnaire de Geographie Ancienne et Moderne a l'Usage Du Libraire et De l'Amateur Des Livres. (FRE.). 796p. 1965. reprint ed. write for info. (*0-318-71337-3*) G Olms Pubs.

Deschamps, Pierre C. Dictionnaire de Geographie Ancienne et Moderne. 1994. reprint ed. write for info. (*3-487-09859-8*) G Olms Pubs.

— Dictionnaire de Geographie Ancienne et Moderne a l'Usage Du Libraire et De l'Amateur Des Livres. (FRE.). 796p. 1965. reprint ed. write for info. (*0-318-70585-0*) G Olms Pubs.

— Dictionnaire de Geographie Ancienne et Moderne a l'Usage Du Libraire et de l'Amateur Des Livres. (FRE.). 796p. 1965. reprint ed. write for info. (*0-318-71764-6*) G Olms Pubs.

— Dictionnaire de G026327255 Ancienne et Moderne a l'Usage Du Libraire et De l'Amateur Des Livres. (FRE.). 796p. 1965. reprint ed. write for info. (*0-318-70735-7*) G Olms Pubs.

Descharnes, Robert. Dali. LC 74-4257. (Library of Great Painters). (Illus.). 176p. 1976. 49.50 (*0-8109-0222-2*) Abrams.

— Dali. (Masters of Art Ser.). (Illus.). 128p. 1985. 24.95 (*0-8109-0830-1*, Pub. by Abrams) Time Warner.

— Dali. 1994. pap. 19.99 (*3-8228-0298-0*) Taschen Amer.

— Dali. (SPA.). 1996. pap. 19.99 (*3-8228-0226-3*) Taschen Amer.

— Dali: The Work, the Man. (Illus.). 456p. 1997. reprint ed. pap. 59.98 (*0-8109-8162-9*, Pub. by Abrams) Time Warner.

— Salvador Dali. (Big Art Ser.). 1998. 19.99 (*3-8228-7205-9*) Taschen Amer.

Deschauer, Thomas. Illustrated Phytotherapy, Bk. Two. 120p. 1996. reprint ed. spiral bd. 12.50 (*0-7873-0281-3*) Hlth Research.

Deschenaux, Joanne. Bernan's Case Summary: Jury Instructions; Includes 1999 Supplement. LC 98-20631. (Case Summaries Ser.). 1998. 90.00 (*0-89059-095-8*, BPL0958) Bernan Associates.

Deschenaux, Joanne, jt. auth. see Eng, Vincent A.

DesChene, Helen. Reflections: Of Quiet Times. LC 96-70327. (Illus.). 64p. 1999. 12.95 (*0-8233-0513-9*) Golden Quill.

***DesChenes, Betz, ed.** Civil Rights in America Primary Source Material. LC 99-27167. 240p. (J). 1999. text 39.00 (*0-7876-3170-1*) Gale.

DesChenes, Betz, ed. see Nagel, Rob.

DesChenes, E. A., ed. Authors & Artists for Young Adults, Vol. 14. 250p. 1994. text 82.00 (*0-8103-5730-5*) Gale.

— Authors & Artists for Young Adults, Vol. 15. 250p. 1995. text 82.00 (*0-8103-5731-3*, 003495) Gale.

Deschenes, Jules, jt. auth. see Shetreet, Shimon.

DeSchepper, A. M., jt. auth. see Shamsi, Kohkan.

Deschepper, Christian, jt. auth. see Reudelhuber, Timothy L.

DeScherer, Mildred, ed. Directory of Natural Science Centers, 1984. (Illus.). 1985. pap., spiral bd. 15.00 (*0-317-20046-1*) Natural Sci Youth.

***Deschler, Jean-Paul.** Die Astrologie in Goethes Weltschau: Ein Beitrag zur Gottesfrage in Seinem Leben und Werk. 123p. 1999. 25.95 (*3-906764-20-6*, Pub. by P Lang) P Lang Pubng.

***Deschler, Lewis.** Deschler-Brown Precedents of the United States House of Representatives: Covering Precedents Through the 104th Congress, Vol. 12. 1131p. 1998. boxed set 74.00 (*0-16-063284-6*) USGPO.

Deschner, Donald. The Complete Films of Spencer Tracy. (Illus.). 272p. 1987. reprint ed. pap. 12.95 (*0-8065-1038-2*, Citadel Pr) Carol Pub Group.

— The Complete Films of W. C. Fields. (Illus.). 1989. pap. 14.95 (*0-8065-1136-2*, Citadel Pr) Carol Pub Group.

— The Films of Cary Grant. LC 73-84151. (Illus.). 288p. 1983. pap. 17.95 (*0-8065-0376-9*, Citadel Pr) Carol Pub Group.

— The Films of Spencer Tracy. 1972. pap. 16.95 (*0-8065-0272-X*, Citadel Pr) Carol Pub Group.

Deschner, Jeanne P. The Hitting Habit: Anger Control for Battering Couples. LC 83-48413. 240p. (C). 1986. pap. 14.95 (*0-02-908080-0*) Free Pr.

Deschner, John. Wesley's Christology: An Interpretation. 240p. 1988. 12.95 (*0-310-36861-8*, 17114P) Zondervan.

— Wesley's Christology: An Interpretation. LC 85-2274. 244p. 1985. reprint ed. pap. 12.95 (*0-87074-200-0*) SMU Press.

Deschner, Whit. Burning the Iceberg: The Alaskan Fisherman's Novel. 2nd ed. LC 90-71536. 260p. (Orig.). 1992. pap. 12.95 (*0-9605388-3-6*) Tern Pr.

— How to Be a Jerk in Bristol Bay: An Abusers Guide. (Illus.). 72p. 1992. pap. 9.95 (*0-9605388-4-4*) Tern Pr.

— Travels with a Kayak. LC 97-90587. (Illus.). 272p. 1997. pap. 19.95 (*0-9605388-6-0*) Tern Pr.

Deschouwer, Kris, jt. auth. see Luther, Kurt R.

Descles, Jean-Pierre, et al. Theoretical Aspects of Passivization in the Framework of Applicative Grammar. LC 85-26794. (Pragmatics & Beyond Ser.: VI:1). viii, 115p. 1985. pap. 41.00 (*0-915027-67-4*) J Benjamins Pubng Co.

Desclos, Jean. Values for Life: The Sources of Morality & Ethical Criteria. 176p. 1993. 35.00 (*0-85439-440-0*, Pub. by St Paul Pubns) St Mut.

Desclot, Bernardo. Chronicle of the Reign of King Pedro III of Aragon, 2 vols., Set. Critchlow, F. L., tr. from CAT. LC 79-8360. reprint ed. 75.00 (*0-404-18340-9*) AMS Pr.

Descoendres, Jean-Paul, ed. Greek Colonists & Native Populations. 768p. 1991. 195.00 (*0-19-814869-0*) OUP.

Descola, Jean. The Conquistadors. Barnes, Malcolm, tr. LC 72-122060. (Illus.). vi, 404p. 1970. reprint ed. lib. bdg. 49.50 (*0-678-03151-7*) Kelley.

Descola, Philippe. In the Society of Nature: A Native Ecology in Amazonia. (Cambridge Studies in Social & Cultural Anthropology: No. 93). (Illus.). 394p. (C). 1994. text 69.95 (*0-521-41103-3*) Cambridge U Pr.

— In the Society of Nature: A Native Ecology in Amazonia. (Cambridge Studies in Social & Cultural Anthropology: No. 93). 394p. 1996. pap. text 24.95 (*0-521-57467-6*) Cambridge U Pr.

— The Spears of Twilight: Life & Death in the Amazon Jungle. Lloyd, Janet, tr. from FRE. LC 96-12955. (Illus.). 400p. 1996. 25.00 (*1-56584-228-6*, Pub. by New Press NY) Norton.

— The Spears of Twilight: Life & Death in the Amazon Jungle. Lloyd, Janet, tr. from FRE. (Illus.). 480p. 1998. pap. 18.95 (*1-56584-438-6*, Pub. by New Press NY) Norton.

Descola, Philippe & Palsson, Gisli, eds. Nature & Society: Anthropological Perspectives. 320p. (C). 1996. 85.00 (*0-415-13215-0*); pap. 25.99 (*0-415-13216-9*) Routledge.

Descombes, Vincent. Modern French Philosophy. Scott-Fox, L. & Harding, J. M., trs. 208p. 1981. pap. text 23.95 (*0-521-29672-2*) Cambridge U Pr.

— Objects of All Sorts: A Philosophical Grammar. Scott-Fox, Lorna & Harding, Jeremy, trs. from FRE. LC 86-164.Tr. of Grammaire d'objets en tous genres. 272p. 1987. text 38.50 (*0-8018-2551-2*) Johns Hopkins.

— Objects of All Sorts: A Philosophical Grammar. LC 86-164.Tr. of Grammaire d'objets en tous genres. 239p. reprint ed. pap. 74.10 (*0-608-08802-1*, 206944100004) Bks Demand.

— Proust: Philosophy of the Novel. Macksey, Catherine C., tr. from FRE. 336p. (C). 1992. 42.50 (*0-8047-2000-2*) Stanford U Pr.

Descoteaux, Gerry. The Lawnchair Astronomer. LC 94-39694. 144p. 1995. pap. 10.95 (*0-440-50696-4*) Dell.

Descotes. Principles of Environmental Medicine. pap. text 45.00 (*0-471-97786-1*) Wiley.

Descotes, Franck, tr. see Jones, Thomas & Jones, Sheila, eds.

Descotes, G., ed. Carbohydrates as Organic Raw Materials II. (Carbohydrates As Raw Materials Ser.). 279p. 1993. 152.00 (*3-527-30007-4*) Wiley.

***Descotes, J., et al, eds.** Carbon Monoxide. (Indoor & Build Environment Ser.: Vol. 8, No. 3, 1999). (Illus.). 64p. 1999. pap. 25.25 (*3-8055-6994-7*) S Karger.

Descotes, Jacques. Human Toxicology. LC 96-26766. (Illus.). 858p. 1996. 255.50 (*0-444-81557-0*) Elsevier.

Descotes, Jacques & Bernard, Claude. An Introduction to Immunotoxicology. LC 99-181168. 250p. 1998. text 89.95 (*0-7484-0306-X*, Pub. by Tay Francis Ltd); pap. text 29.95 (*0-7484-0307-8*, Pub. by Tay Francis Ltd) Taylor & Francis.

***Descour, Michael R. & Shen, Sylvia S., eds.** Imaging Spectrometry V. 1999. pap. text 103.00 (*0-8194-3239-3*) SPIE.

Descour, Michael R., jt. ed. see Shen, Sylvia S.

Descour, Michael R. & Mooney, Jonathan M., eds. Imaging Spectrometry II, Vol. 2819. 366p. 1996. 85.00 (*0-8194-2207-X*) SPIE.

Descour, Michael R. & Shen, Sylvia S., eds. Imaging Spectrometry III, Vol. 3118. LC 98-122012. 404p. 1997. 89.00 (*0-8194-2540-0*) SPIE.

— Imaging Spectrometry IV, Vol. 3438. LC 99-170362. 1998. 69.00 (*0-8194-2893-0*) SPIE.

Descour, Michael R., jt. ed. see Shen, Sylvia S.

Descout, LeFant, ed. Applied Arabic Linguistics & Signal & Information Processing. LC 66-55815. 242p. 1987. 165.00 (*0-89116-421-9*) Hemisp Pub.

Descouvemont, Pierre. Therese of Lisieux & Marie of the Trinity: A Transformative Relationship. Plettenberg-Serban, Alexandra, tr. from FRE. LC 97-20167. Orig. Title: Une Novice de Sainte Therese. (Illus.). 188p. (Orig.). 1997. pap. 14.95 (*0-8189-0732-0*) Alba.

Descovich, G. C., jt. ed. see Lenzi, S.

Descovisch, G. & Lenzi, S., eds. Artherosclerosis: Clinical Evaluations & Therapy. (Illus.). 500p. 1982. text 179.50 (*0-85200-449-4*) Kluwer Academic.

Descovitch, G. C., ed. Atherosclerosis & Cardiovascular Disease: 7th International Meeting. (C). 1990. text 294.00 (*0-7923-8949-2*) Kluwer Academic.

Descreux, V., jt. compiled by see Jouin, E.

Descy, J. P., et al, eds. Phytoplankton in Turbid Environments - Rivers & Shallow Lakes: Proceedings of the 9th Workshop of the International Association of Phytoplankton Taxonomy & Ecology (IAP) Held in Mont Rigi (Belgium), 10-18 July 1993. LC 94-32312. (Developments in Hydrobiology Ser.: Vol. 100). 240p. (C). 1994. text 213.00 (*0-7923-3111-7*) Kluwer Academic.

DeSeife, Rudolphe, jt. auth. see Wilner, Gabriel M.

Desek, Shannon, jt. ed. see Platsky, Scott.

Desel, J., et al, eds. Application & Theory of Petri Nets, 1998: 19th International Conference, ICATPN '98, Lisbon, Portugal, June 22-26, 199. Proceedings. (Lecture Notes in Computer Science Ser.: Vol. 1420). viii,385p. 1998. pap. 59.00 (*3-540-64677-9*) Spr-Verlag.

Desel, Jorg, ed. Structures in Concurrency Theory: Proceedings of the International Workshop on Structures in Concurrency Theory (STRICT), Berlin, 11-13 May 1995. LC 95-32279. (Workshops in Computing Ser.). 364p. 1995. 74.00 (*3-540-19982-9*) Spr-Verlag.

Desel, Jorg & Esparza, Javier. Free Choice Petri Nets. (Cambridge Tracts in Theoretical Computer Science Ser.: No. 40). (Illus.). 252p. (C). 1995. text 47.95 (*0-521-46519-2*) Cambridge U Pr.

Deselm, Joel, jt. auth. see Fishel, Kent.

***DeSena, Bronwen & Zucker, Linda.** Babu's Babushka. LC 99-54790. (Publish-a-Book Ser.). (Illus.). 24p. (J). (ps-3). 2000. 5.95 (*0-7398-2368-X*) Raintree Steck-V.

DeSena, Carmine. The Comedy Market: A Writer's Guide to Making Money Being Funny. 224p. (Orig.). 1996. pap. 12.95 (*0-399-52215-8*, Perigee Bks) Berkley Pub.

— Lies: The Whole Truth. 128p. (Orig.). 1993. pap. 5.95 (*0-399-51820-7*, Perigee Bks) Berkley Pub.

DeSena, Carmine, jt. auth. see Alicea, Gil C.

DeSena, Jeannie M., ed. The Best of the Proverbs 31 Homemaker: Encouragement & Ideas for Wives & Mothers. LC 95-92751. 112p. (Orig.). 1996. pap. 8.95 (*0-9649507-8-2*) Proverbs Thirty-One.

***DeSena, Judith N.** People Power: Grass Roots Politics & Race Relations. LC 99-32759. 152p. 1999. 49.00 (*0-7618-1461-2*); pap. 28.50 (*0-7618-1462-0*) U Pr of Amer.

DeSena, Judith N. Protecting One's Turf: Social Strategies for Maintaining Urban Neighborhoods. 168p. (C). 1990. lib. bdg. 38.00 (*0-8191-7716-4*) U Pr of Amer.

Desenclos, J. C. Guide Clinique et Therapeutique. Pour les Programmes Curatifs des Hopitaux, des Dispensaires Ruraux et des Camps des Refugies. A l'Usagedes Medecins et Infirmier(e) s: Pour les Programmes Curatifs des Hopitaux, des Dispensaires Ruraux et des Camps des Refugies. A l'Usagedes Medecins et Infirmier(e)s. (Medecins Sans Frontieres - Hatier Ser.). (FRE.). 255p. 1991. pap. 26.95 (*2-218-01739-3*) Schoenhof.

Desenclos, J. C., ed. Clinical Guidelines: Diagnostic & Treatment Manual. 3rd ed. (Medecins Sans Frontieres - Hatier Ser.). 283p. 1993. vinyl bd. 27.95 (*2-218-03480-8*) Hatier Pub.

Desender, Konjev, et al, eds. Carabid Beetles: Ecology & Evolution. LC 93-31137. (Series Entomologica: Vol. 51). 492p. (C). 1994. text 369.50 (*0-7923-2464-1*) Kluwer Academic.

Desens, Marliss C. The Bed-Trick in English Renaissance Drama: Explorations in Gender, Sexuality, & Power. LC 92-50885. 1994. 32.50 (*0-87413-476-5*) U Delaware Pr.

DeSensi, Joy T. & Rosenberg, Danny. Ethics in Sport Management. LC 95-83627. 215p. (C). 1996. text 33.00 (*1-885693-04-4*) Fit Info Tech.

Deser, S., jt. ed. see Chretien, M.

Deseret Book Company Editors. Peace. LC 98-12794. 1998. write for info. (*1-57345-271-8*) Deseret Bk.

***Deseret Book Company Ser.** Sunshine for the Latter-Day Saint Mother's Soul. LC 99-86857. 2000. pap. write for info. (*1-57345-628-4*) Deseret Bk.

Deseret Book Company Staff. The Balm of Gilead: Women's Stories of Finding Peace. LC 97-5130. vii, 156p. 1997. 15.95 (*1-57345-248-3*) Deseret Bk.

— The Deseret Book Treasury of LDs Quotations: 20,000 Quotations from Prophets & Apostles of the Church of Jesus Christ of Latter-Day Saints. LC 98-35957. 1998. 39.95 (*1-57345-232-7*) Deseret Bk.

— I'll Be Home for Christmas: Heartwarming True Stories for the Season. LC 98-29419. 1998. 17.95 (*1-57345-437-0*) Deseret Bk.

— Missionary Reference Library. 2234p. pap. 20.95 (*0-87579-951-5*) Deseret Bk.

Deseret Book Company Staff, jt. auth. see Millet, Robert L.

Deseret Staff. Hymnbook Blue Chorister. x, 434p. 1985. spiral bd. 14.95 (*0-87579-042-9*) Deseret Bk.

— Hymnbook Orange Large. x, 434p. 1985. spiral bd. 15.95 (*0-87579-013-5*) Deseret Bk.

Deserno, Heinrich. The Analyst & the Working Alliance: The Reemergence of Convention in Psychoanalysis. Jenkins, Andrew, tr. from ENG. LC 98-10469. 167p. 1998. 30.00 (*0-8236-0134-X*, 00134) Intl Univs Pr.

Deserrano, Irma G. Manual para la Preparacion de Informes y Tesis. LC 76-11003. (C). 1992. pap. 8.25 (*0-8477-2312-7*) U of PR Pr.

***DeSersa, Esther Black Elk, et al.** Black Elk Lives: Conversations with the Black Elk Family. Neihardt, Hilda & Utecht, Lori, eds. LC 00-28665. (Illus.). 176p. 2000. 25.00 (*0-8032-3340-X*, Bison Books) U of Nebr Pr.

***Desert Botanical Garden Staff.** Desert Wildflowers: A Guide for Identifying, Locating, & Enjoying Arizona Wildflowers & Cactus Blossoms. rev. ed. (Illus.). 112p. 1999. pap. 10.95 (*1-893860-06-X*) Ariz Hwy.

Desert Fathers. Daily Readings with the Desert Fathers. Ward, Benedicta, ed. 96p. 1990. pap. 4.95 (*0-87243-185-1*) Templegate.

Desert First Works, Inc, ed. see Hallgren, Stephanie.

Desert, Gabriel. Une Societe Rurale Au XIX Siecle: Les Paysans Du Calvados, Eighteen Fifteen to Eighteen Ninty-Five. Bruchey, Stuart, ed. LC 77-77166. (Dissertations in European Economic History Ser.). (FRE., Illus.). 1978. lib. bdg. 77.95 (*0-405-10780-3*) Ayer.

***Desesquelles, Anne-Claire.** L'Expression Musicale. (Publications Universitaires Europeennes Ser.: Vol. 591). xv, 281p. 1999. 44.95 (*3-906763-26-9*, Pub. by P Lang) P Lang Pubng.

***Desetta, Al & Wolin, Sybil, eds.** The Struggle to Be Strong: True Stories by Teens about Overcoming Tough Times. LC 99-56600. (Illus.). 192p. (YA). (gr. 8 up). 2000. pap. 14.95 (*1-57542-079-1*) Free Spirit Pub.

***Desetta, Al, et al.** Leader's Guide to The Struggle to Be Strong: How to Foster Resilience in Teens. 176p. 2000. pap. 21.95 (*1-57542-080-5*) Free Spirit Pub.

Desetta, Al, ed. see Youth Communication Staff.

Desetta, Al, ed. & intro. see Youth Communication Staff.

Desetto, Lori-Ann. The Meaning of Love. 1999. pap. 7.95 (*0-533-12840-4*) Vantage.

DesFeuilles, Pierre. Dictionnaire Bordas des Rimes. (FRE.). 365p. 1993. 39.95 (*0-7859-0964-8*, 2040195130) Fr & Eur.

Desfontaines. La Voltairomanie. Waddicor, M. H., ed. (Exeter French Texts Ser.: No. 50). (FRE.). 127p. Date not set. pap. text 19.95 (*0-85989-149-6*, Pub. by Univ Exeter Pr) Northwestern U Pr.

Desfontaines, Pierre F., Jr. & Gulliver, Lemuel. Gulliveriana, No. 2: Travels of Mr. John Gulliver; Modern Gulliver's Travels: Lilliput. LC 72-162479. 680p. 1971. reprint ed. 90.00 (*0-8201-1098-1*) Schol Facsimiles.

An Asterisk (*) at the beginning of an entry indicates that the title is appearing for the first time.

Desforges, Charles, ed. Educational Attainment. (Essential Readings in Developmental Psychology Ser.). (Illus.). 256p. 1999. 59.95 (*0-631-21748-7*); pap. 24.95 (*0-631-21749-5*) Blackwell Pubs.

— An Introduction to Educational Psychology: Psychological Perspectives. (Illus.). 384p. (C). 1995. 68.95 (*0-631-18726-X*); pap. 29.95 (*0-631-18727-8*) Blackwell Pubs.

Desforges, Charles & Cockburn, Anne D. Understanding the Mathematics Teacher: A Study of Practice in First Schools. 180p. 1987. 65.00 (*1-85000-212-6*, Falmer Pr); pap. 29.95 (*1-85000-213-4*, Falmer Pr) Taylor & Francis.

Desforges, Regine. The Blue Bicycle. Schwartz, Ros, tr. from FRE. 384p. 1986. 17.95 (*0-8184-0402-7*) Carol Pub Group.

— Lea. Failey-Mueller, Elizabeth, tr. 384p. 1987. write for info. (*0-8184-0435-3*) Carol Pub Group.

Desfosses, Helen, jt. ed. see Baaklini, Abdo I.

Desfour, A. Dictionary Mots, Expressions Couleur 20e Siecle. (FRE.). 1998. 69.95 (*0-320-00236-5*) Fr & Eur.

Desgodetz, Antoine. The Ancient Buildings of Rome: Les Edifices Antiques de Rome, 1682. (Printed Sources of Western Art Ser.). (FRE., Illus.). 324p. 1981. reprint ed. pap. 150.00 (*0-915346-49-4*) A Wofsy Fine Arts.

Desgranges, ed. see Pascal, Blaise.

***Desgrippes, Annie.** African Style. 144p. 2000. 30.00 (*2-08-013681-X*, Pub. by Flammarion) Abbeville Pr.

Desguin, Lillian C. Unidentified Flying Objects: Fact or Fiction? (Illus.). 250p. (Orig.). 1992. pap. 12.80 (*0-89412-188-X*) Aegean Park Pr.

Desha, Gil. Laboratory Exercises for & Introduction to Biological Principles. 4th ed. 200p. (C). 1996. spiral bd. 21.95 (*0-8403-9190-0*) Kendall-Hunt.

Desha Lucas, Jo. 1998 Statute, Rule & Case Supplement for Use with Cases & Materials on Admirality. (University Casebook Ser.). 300p. 1998. pap. text. write for info. (*1-56662-690-0*) Foundation Pr.

Deshaies, Ken. How to Make Your Realtor Get You the Best Deal: Step-by-Step Guide Through the Real Estate Purchasing Process... from Choosing a Realtor to Negotiating the Best Deal for You! 120p. 1999. pap. 17.95 (*1-891689-77-0*) Gabriel Pubns.

DeShalit, Ehud. Iwasawa Theory of Elliptic Curves with Complex Multiplications-p-Adic L Functions. (Perspectives in Mathematics Ser.). 154p. 1987. text 53.00 (*0-12-210255-X*) Acad Pr.

Deshannon, Yolanda. Ten Weeks. 165p. (Orig.). (J). (gr. 7-10). 1997. pap. 5.00 (*1-884429-04-1*) Frst Choice.

Desharnais, Guylaine, jt. auth. see Mayall, Jan K.

Desharnais, R. A., jt. auth. see Costantino, R. F.

***Desharnais, Robert A.** Biology Labs On-line User's Manual: Mitochondrialab. 1999. pap. 7.40 (*0-8053-6533-8*) Benjamin-Cummings.

DeShay, Bernice A., jt. auth. see DeShay, Samuel L.

DeShay, Samuel L. & DeShay, Bernice A. Plus 15: Fifteen Days to Lower Blood Pressure & Cholesterol. rev. ed. (YA). (gr. 10). 1992. 14.95 (*0-945460-16-3*) Upward Way.

Deshazer, ed. Anthology of Women's Literature. 1696p. (C). 2000. pap. 49.33 (*0-321-01006-X*) Addson-Wesley Educ.

DeShazer, James A., jt. ed. see Meyer, George E.

DeShazer, James A., jt. ed. see Meyer, George E.

Deshazer, M. K. Inspiring Women: Reimagining the Muse. (Athene Ser.). 224p. 1987. text 37.50 (*0-08-034475-5*, Pergamon Pr); pap. text 16.95 (*0-08-034474-7*, Pergamon Pr) Elsevier.

DeShazer, Mary K. Inspiring Women: Reimagining the Muse. (Athene Ser.). 272p. (C). 1987. text 37.50 (*0-8077-6229-6*); pap. text 18.95 (*0-8077-6228-8*) Tchrs Coll.

— A Poetics of Resistance: Women Writing in El Salvador, South Africa, & the United States. LC 94-6207. 368p. (C). 1994. pap. text 18.95 (*0-472-06563-7*, 06563) U of Mich Pr.

DeShazo, Peter. Urban Workers & Labor Unions in Chile, 1902-1927. LC 82-70557. (Illus.). 384p. 1983. 35.00 (*0-299-09220-8*) U of Wis Pr.

— Urban Workers & Labor Unions in Chile, 1902-1927. LC 82-70557. (Illus.). 384p. reprint ed. pap. 119.10 (*0-608-09905-8*, 206924300003) Bks Demand.

Deshazo, Randy & Sutherlin, John W. Building Bridges: Diplomacy & Regime Formation in the Jordan River Valley. 190p. (Orig.). (C). 1996. lib. bdg. 29.50 (*0-7618-0272-X*) U Pr of Amer.

***Deshefy, Gregory S.** Houyhnhnms All: Selected Poems by G. Scott Deshefy. LC 98-93876. 82p. 1998. per. 7.00i (*0-9673139-1-0*, AP2679PGSD) Ahimsa Pr.

DeShell, Jeffrey. In Heaven Everything Is Fine. 108p. 1991. 18.95 (*0-932511-39-2*); pap. 8.95 (*0-932511-40-6*) Fiction Coll.

— The Peculiarity of Literature: An Allegorical Approach to Poe's Fiction. LC 96-29067. 176p. 1997. 32.50 (*0-8386-3666-7*) Fairleigh Dickinson.

Deshen, Shlomo. Blind People: The Private & Public Life of Sightless Israelis. LC 91-20397. (SUNY Series, The Body in Culture, History, & Religion). 197p. (C). 1992. pap. text 21.95 (*0-7914-1036-6*) State U NY Pr.

— The Mellah Society: Jewish Community Life in Sherifian Morocco. rev. ed. LC 88-27818. (Illus.). 184p. 1989. pap. text 14.95 (*0-226-14340-6*) U Ch Pr.

— The Mellah Society: Jewish Community Life in Sherifian Morocco. rev. ed. LC 88-27818. (Illus.). 184p. 1996. lib. bdg. 36.00 (*0-226-14339-2*) U Ch Pr.

Deshen, Shlomo, ed. Jews among Muslims. (C). 1996. pap. text 20.00 (*0-8147-9676-1*) NYU Pr.

Deshen, Shlomo & Zenner, Walter P., eds. Jews among Muslims: Communities in the Precolonial Middle East. 330p. (C). 1996. text 55.00 (*0-8147-9675-3*) NYU Pr.

Deshen, Solomon. Ethnic Boundaries & Cultural Paradigms: The Case of Southern Tunisian Immigrants in Israel. 35p. 1976. pap. 2.00 (*0-686-74366-0*) Adelantre.

DeSherer, Dorinda D., jt. auth. see Meyers, Terence M.

DeShields, James T. Border Wars of Texas. LC 93-15163. (Illus.). 412p. 1993. 29.95 (*0-938349-98-8*) State House Pr.

Deshimaru, Taisen. The Zen Way to the Martial Arts: A Japanese Master Reveals the Secrets of the Samurai. Amphoux, Nancy, tr. (Illus.). 128p. 1992. pap. 11.95 (*0-14-019344-8*, Arkana) Viking Penguin.

Deshler, Don. Teaching Every Adolescent Every Day: Learning in Diverse High School Classrooms. LC 99-11951. 1999. pap. 19.95 (*1-57129-060-5*) Brookline Bks.

Deshler, Donald D., et al. Teaching Adolescents with Learning Disabilities: Strategies & Methods. 2nd ed. LC 95-75399. 656p. 1995. 69.00 (*0-89108-241-7*) Love Pub Co.

Deshman, Robert. Anglo-Saxon & Anglo-Scandinavian Art: An Annotated Bibliography. (Reference Publications in Art History). 1984. 65.00 (*0-8161-8344-9*, Hall Reference) Macmillan.

— The Benedictional of Aethelwold. LC 94-36661. (Studies in Manuscript Illumination). (Illus.). 432p. 1995. text 110.00 (*0-691-04386-8*, Pub. by Princeton U Pr) Cal Prin Full Svc.

Deshmaru, Taisen. Sit: Zen Teachings of Master Taisen Deshimaru. Coupey, Philip, ed. LC 95-51033. (Illus.). 420p. (Orig.). 1996. pap. 19.95 (*0-934252-61-0*, Pub. by Hohm Pr) SCB Distributors.

Deshmukh, C. D., ed. see Baba, Meher.

Deshmukh, D. Chintaman & I. 121p. 1980. 14.95 (*0-318-37204-5*) Asia Bk Corp.

Deshmukh, Vinod D. The Last Leaf. (Illus.). 191p. 1993. pap. 7.50 (*0-615-11302-8*) S V Deshmukh.

Deshon, Denis, ed. see Ward, Kirby & Smith, Andy.

Deshon, George. Guide for Catholic Young Women. 1978. 26.95 (*0-405-10816-8*) Ayer.

***Deshong, H., et al.** Operational Field Assessments: An Analysis. LC 98-29716. (Illus.). 85p. 1999. pap. text 15.00 (*0-8330-2642-9*, MR-982-JS) Rand Corp.

Deshong, Howard, jt. auth. see Peters, John E.

DeShong, Molly, ed. see Shropshire, Renee & Haislip, Christina L.

***Deshpande.** A Comp. Review in Respiratory Care. 2nd ed. 2000. pap. text 39.95 (*0-8385-1498-7*) Appleton & Lange.

Deshpande. Objective Questions in Medical Physiology. 304p. 1995. pap. 14.95 (*0-07-462358-3*) McGraw.

Deshpande, Arvind M. John Briggs in Maharashtra: A Study of District Administration under Early British Rule. 1987. 19.00 (*0-8364-2250-3*, Pub. by Mittal Pubs Dist) S Asia.

Deshpande, B. G. World of Petroleum. (C). 1992. 36.00 (*81-224-0370-0*) S Asia.

Deshpande, C. D. India: A Regional Interpretation. (C). 1992. 33.00 (*81-7211-081-2*, Pub. by Northern Bk Ctr) S Asia.

Deshpande, Chris. Diwali. (J). pap. 4.95 (*0-7136-4082-0*, 93345) A & C Blk.

Deshpande, Chris & Macleod-Brudenell, Iain. Worldwide Crafts, 4 bks. Incl. Animal Crafts. LC 94-11434. (Illus.). 32p. (YA). (gr. 3 up). 1994. lib. bdg. 22.60 (*0-8368-1151-8*); Costume Crafts. LC 94-11432. (Illus.). 32p. (YA). (gr. 3 up). 1994. lib. bdg. 22.60 (*0-8368-1152-6*); Festival Crafts. LC 94-11431. (Illus.). 32p. (YA). (gr. 3 up). 1994. lib. bdg. 22.60 (*0-8368-1153-4*); Food Crafts. LC 94-11430. (Illus.). 32p. (YA). (gr. 3 up). 1994. lib. bdg. 22.60 (*0-8368-1154-2*); Set lib. bdg. 90.40 (*0-8368-1150-X*) Gareth Stevens Inc.

Deshpande, G. P. Chanakya Vishnugupta. LC 96-914266. (C). 1997. pap. 7.00 (*81-7046-133-2*, Pub. by Seagull Bks) S Asia.

— Man in Dark Times (Uddhivasta Dharmashala) (C). 1990. pap. 10.00 (*81-7046-036-0*, Pub. by Seagull Bks) S Asia.

— Political Plays for Children: The Grips Theater of Berlin. LC 98-901897. xxiv, 154p. 1998. write for info. (*81-7046-132-4*) Seagull Bks.

Deshpande, G. T. Abhinavagupta. (C). 1992. pap. 5.00 (*0-8364-2824-2*, Pub. by Indian Pubs) S Asia.

Deshpande, J. V. & Koul, Hira L., eds. Analysis of Censored Data. LC 95-81795. (Lecture Notes-Monographs Ser.: Vol. 27). (Illus.). 291p. 1995. 30.00 (*0-940600-39-0*) Inst Math.

Deshpande, J. V., et al. Statistical Analysis of Nonnormal Data. 240p. 1995. text 49.95 (*0-470-22057-0*) Halsted Pr.

Deshpande, Jayant K. & Tobias, Joseph D. The Pediatric Pain Handbook. (Illus.). 384p. (C). (gr. 13). 1995. pap. text 36.95 (*0-8151-2431-7*, 25783) Mosby Inc.

Deshpande, L. K. & Rodgers, Gerry, eds. Indian Labour Market & Economic Structural Change. (C). 1994. 20.00 (*81-7018-804-0*, Pub. by BR Pub) S Asia.

Deshpande, Madhav. Critical Studies in Indian Grammarians I, Theory of Homogeneity (Savarnya) LC 75-36896. (Michigan Papers in South & Southeast Asia: No. 2). xiv, 221p. (Orig.). 1975. pap. 10.00 (*0-89148-052-8*) Ctr S&SE Asian.

***Deshpande, Madhav M.** Samskrta-Subodhini: A Sanskrit Primer. 47. (Illus.). 504p. (C). 1999. text 46.00 (*0-89148-078-1*); pap. text 26.00 (*0-89148-079-X*) Ctr S&SE Asian.

Deshpande, Madhav M., ed. Saunakiya Caturadhyayika: A Pratisakhya of the Saunakiya Atharvaveda. (Harvard Oriental Ser.: Vol. 52). (Illus.). 821p. 1998. 75.00 (*0-674-78987-3*) HUP.

Deshpande, Madhav M. & Bhate, Saroja, eds. Paninian Studies: Professor S. D. Joshi Felicitation Volume. LC 90-86276. (Michigan Papers on South & Southeast Asia: No. 37). 331p. 1991. 31.95 (*0-89148-064-1*); pap. 15.95 (*0-89148-065-X*) Ctr S&SE Asian.

Deshpande, Madhav M. & Hook, Peter E., eds. Aryan & Non-Aryan in India. LC 78-60016. (Michigan Papers on South & Southeast Asia: No. 14). xii, 315p. 1979. 10.00 (*0-89148-045-5*); pap. 5.00 (*0-89148-014-5*) Ctr S&SE Asian.

Deshpande, N. A. Padma Purana, Pt. 8. (C). 1991. 26.00 (*81-208-0807-X*, Pub. by Motilal Bnarsidass) S Asia.

— Padma Purana Pt. 9: Ancient Indian Tradition & Mythology, Vol. 47. (C). 1991. 26.00 (*81-208-0881-9*, Pub. by Motilal Bnarsidass) S Asia.

Deshpande, N. A., ed. Padma Purana, Pt. III. (Ancient Puranas Ser.). 1990. 26.00 (*81-208-0624-7*, Pub. by Motilal Bnarsidass) S Asia.

Deshpande, N. A., ed. Padma Purana, Vol. 40, Pt. II. (Ancient Indian Tradition & Mythology Ser.). 1989. 26.00 (*81-208-0583-6*, Pub. by Motilal Bnarsidass) S Asia.

Deshpande, N. A., tr. Padma Purana (AITM 43) Vol. 5: Ancient Indian Tradition & Mythology. 1990. 26.00 (*81-208-0701-4*, Pub. by Motilal Bnarsidass) S Asia.

— Siva Purana, Pt. IV. (Ancient Indian Tradition & Mythology Ser.: Vol. 4). 1990. 26.00 (*0-685-35376-1*, Pub. by Motilal Bnarsidass) S Asia.

Deshpande, P. G. Concise English-Gujarati Dictionary. 468p. 1987. 16.95 (*0-19-561827-0*) OUP.

— A Modern English-Gujarati Dictionary. (ENG & GUJ.). 820p. 1983. 39.95 (*0-8288-1147-4*, M14254) Fr & Eur.

— A Modern English-Gujarati Dictionary. (ENG & GUJ.). 806p. 1983. text 45.00 (*0-19-561140-3*) OUP.

Deshpande, P. G., tr. Universal English-Gujarati Dictionary. (ENG & GUJ.). 966p. 1989. text 35.00 (*0-19-561828-9*) OUP.

Deshpande, Pradeep B. Distillation Dynamics & Control. LC 85-5110. (Illus.). 529p. 1985. reprint ed. pap. 164.00 (*0-7837-9047-3*, 204979800003) Bks Demand.

Deshpande, R. Y. The Ancient Tale of Savitri. 2nd ed. 49p. 1997. pap. 6.50 (*81-7058-429-9*, Pub. by SAA) E-W Cultural Ctr.

***Deshpande, Rohit.** Using Market Knowledge. LC 00-9186. 2000. write for info. (*0-7619-2198-2*) Sage.

Deshpande, Rohit & Marketing Science Institute Staff. Developing a Market Orientation. LC 98-40184. 1999. pap. 29.95 (*0-7619-1693-8*) Sage.

***Deshpande, Rohit & Marketing Science Institute Staff.** Developing a Market Orientation. LC 98-40184. 3p. 1999. 65.00 (*0-7619-1692-X*) Sage.

Deshpande, S. M., ed. see Fourteenth International Conference on Numerical M.

Deshpande, S. S. Enzyme Immunoassays: From Concept to Product Development. 464p. (C). (gr. 13). 1996. 115.00 (*0-412-05601-1*) Kluwer Academic.

Deshpande, Salil. CORBA & Distributed Applications. 300p. (C). 1999. text 45.00 (*0-13-349960-X*) P-H.

Deshpande, Shashi. A Matter of Time. LC 98-52896. 272p. 1999. 21.95 (*1-55861-214-9*, Pub. by Feminist Pr) Consort Bk Sales.

Deshpande, V. S. Women & the New Law. 1985. pap. text 9.50 (*0-8364-1368-7*, Pub. by Punjabi U) S Asia.

Deshpande, V. W. The Impact of Ancient Indian Thought on Christianity. xi, 359p. (C). 1996. 49.00 (*81-7024-712-8*, Pub. by Ashish Pub Hse) Nataraj Bks.

Deshpande, Vamanrao H. Between Two Tanpuras. (C). 1989. 32.50 (*0-86132-226-6*) S Asia.

Deshpande, Vijay M., et al. A Comprehensive Review in Respiratory Care. (Illus.). 398p. (C). 1988. pap. text 47.95 (*0-8385-1295-X*, A1295-3) Appleton & Lange.

Deshusses, Marc A., jt. auth. see Devinny, J.S.

Desi, Donna K., et al. Country-Style Painted Wood Projects. LC 96-3958. (Illus.). 128p. 1996. 27.95 (*0-8069-3150-7*, Chapelle) Sterling.

Desia, A. R. India's Path of Development: A Marxist Approach. 1985. 22.00 (*0-8364-1332-6*, Pub. by Popular Prakashan) S Asia.

Desia, Govind, jt. auth. see El Nazir, Osman.

DeSiano, Frank. Evangelization: A Parish Planning Workbook. (Follow Me! Ser.). 1998. pap. 9.95 (*1-881307-10-7*, B7107) Natl Pastoral LC.

DeSiano, Frank & Boyack, Kenneth. Creating the Evangelizing Parish. LC 93-14483. 208p. (Orig.). 1993. pap. 11.95 (*0-8091-3387-3*) Paulist Pr.

— Descubrir Mi Experiencia de Dios: Conciencia y Testimonio.Tr. of Discovering My Experience of God: Conscience & Testimony. (SPA.). 80p. Date not set. pap. 3.95 (*0-8091-3911-1*) Paulist Pr.

— Discovering My Experience of God: Awareness & Witness. 80p. 1992. pap. 5.95 (*0-8091-3300-8*) Paulist Pr.

DeSiano, Frank & Gerding, Susan B. Lay Ministers, Lay Disciples: Evangelizing Power in the Parish. LC 99-17006. 224p. 1999. pap. 14.95 (*0-8091-3895-4*) Paulist Pr.

***DeSiano, Frank P.** Catolicos Evangelizadores: Un Manual Practico para Extender la Fe.Tr. of Evangelizing Catholic. (SPA.). 160p. 2000. pap. 15.95 (*0-8091-3928-6*) Paulist Pr.

— The Evangelizing Catholic: A Practical Handbook for Reaching Out. LC 98-38276. 224p. 1998. pap. 11.95 (*0-8091-3836-0*) Paulist Pr.

DeSiano, Michael. Principles & Elements of Art & Design. 1992. pap. 9.99 (*0-685-24556-X*) Trillium Pr.

Desiatnik, Ronald. Building Licensing Laws NSW. 433p. 1996. pap. 50.00 (*0-455-21399-2*, Pub. by Cavendish Pubng) Gaunt.

Desiderati, Barbara M., et al, eds. A Pictorial History of Diving. 150p. 1988. 97.00 (*0-941332-09-8*, D270) Best Pub Co.

Desidereo, Dominic M., ed. Mass Spectrometry of Peptides. 440p. 1990. lib. bdg. 239.00 (*0-8493-6293-8*, QP551) CRC Pr.

Desideri, J. A. Experimentation, Modelling, Computation in Flow, Turbulence & Combustion, Vol. 1. Periaux, J. et al, eds. 372p. 1996. 210.00 (*0-471-94824-1*) Wiley.

Desideri, J. A., et al, eds. Eccomas '96 Vol. 1: Computational Fluid Dynamics '96, Vol. 1, Computational Fluid Dynamics '96. LC 96-217681. 1128p. 1996. 660.00 (*0-471-95851-4*) Wiley.

— Eccomas '96 Vol. 2: Numerical Methods in Engineering '96, Vol. 2. LC 96-217632. 1062p. 1996. 540.00 (*0-471-96692-4*) Wiley.

— ECCOMAS '96, Vol. 3, Computational Methods in Applied Sciences '96, Vol. 3, Computational Methods in Applied Sciences. LC 96-217659. 588p. 1996. 310.00 (*0-471-96226-0*) Wiley.

— Hypersonic Flows for Reentry Problems: Proceedings of a Workshop Held at Antibes, France, 22-25 January 1990, Vol. I: Survey Lectures & Test Cases for Analysis. (Illus.). x, 260p. 1992. 136.95 (*0-387-54428-3*) Spr-Verlag.

— Hypersonic Flows for Reentry Problems: Proceedings of a Workshop Held at Antibes, France, 22-25 January 1990, Vol. II: Test Cases - Experiments & Computations. (Illus.). 1240p. 1992. 258.95 (*0-387-53859-3*) Spr-Verlag.

Desiderio, D. M. Mass Spectrometry Vol. 1: Clinical & Biomedical Applications, Vol. 1. (Illus.). 368p. (C). 1993. text 79.50 (*0-306-44261-2*, Kluwer Plenum) Kluwer Academic.

Desiderio, Robert J., ed. see Shepard's Mcgraw-Hill Staff.

Design & Type Staff, ed. see Allen, Debbie.

Design Automation Conference Staff. Advances in Design Automation 1994: Proceedings of the Design Automation Conference, Minneapolis, MN, 2 vols. 1220p. 1994. pap. 200.00 (*0-7918-1283-9*) ASME.

Design Basic Staff. Homes of Distinction: Gold Seal Home Plans. 1997. pap. text 19.95 (*1-892150-06-9*) Design Basics.

— Homes of Elegance: Gold Seal Home Plans. 1997. pap. text 19.95 (*1-892150-08-5*) Design Basics.

— Homes of Grandeur: Gold Seal Home Plans. 1997. pap. text 19.95 (*1-892150-10-7*) Design Basics.

— Homes of Sophistication: Gold Seal Home Plans. 1997. pap. text 19.95 (*1-892150-07-7*) Design Basics.

Design Basics Staff. Easy Living: One Story Designs. rev. ed. 144p. pap. 7.95 (*1-892150-21-2*) Design Basics.

— Nostalgia Home Plans: 100 Time-Honored Designs Updated with Today's Features. 2000. pap. 14.95 (*1-881955-69-9*) Home Planners.

Design Conference Staff. Polymer Processing: Analysis & Innovation: Presented at the Design Conference of ASME, Washington, D. C., September 13-15, 1982. Suh, Nam P. et al, eds. LC 82-72702. (PED Ser.: Vol. 5). 169p. reprint ed. pap. 52.40 (*0-8357-8751-6*, 203364400087) Bks Demand.

Design Council Staff. Attaining Competence in Engineering Design (ACED) (C). 1991. pap. text 55.00 (*0-85072-296-9*) St Mut.

— Attitudes of Industrial Managers to Product Design. (C). 1988. pap. text 95.00 (*0-85072-232-2*) St Mut.

— The Benefits of Computer-Aided Design & Manufacture-Clothing & Textiles. (C). 1992. pap. text 130.00 (*0-85072-307-8*) St Mut.

— Design & Primary Education. 64p. (C). 1987. pap. text 30.00 (*0-85072-212-8*) St Mut.

— Design Courses, 1992-1993. 200p. (C). 1992. pap. text 39.00 (*0-85072-300-0*) St Mut.

— Design Courses, 1993-1994. 200p. (C). 1992. pap. text 70.00 (*0-85072-309-4*) St Mut.

— Design Expertise Nineteen Eighty-Six. 176p. 1986. 65.00 (*0-85072-139-3*) St Mut.

— Designing Against Vandalism. 108p. (C). 1979. pap. text 40.00 (*0-85072-092-3*) St Mut.

— Directory of Designers, 1993. 224p. (C). 1993. text 175.00 (*0-85072-295-0*) St Mut.

— From Spitfire to Microchip. 96p. (C). 1984. pap. text 60.00 (*0-85072-134-2*) St Mut.

— Information Technology & the Leisure Industry: The Textiles Industry & the Car Industry. 82p. 1987. pap. 20.00 (*0-85072-178-4*); pap. 115.00 (*0-85072-164-4*) St Mut.

Design Council Staff. Products for World Markets. 60p. 1994. pap. 78.95 (*0-566-07624-1*) Ashgate Pub Co.

Design Council Staff. Profit by Design. (C). 1989. pap. text 60.00 (*0-85072-261-6*) St Mut.

— Royal Designers on Design. 200p. 1987. 100.00 (*0-85072-167-9*) St Mut.

— Signs of Design: An Introduction. (C). 1990. pap. text 39.00 (*0-85072-268-3*) St Mut.

— Signs of Design: English. (C). 1991. pap. text 60.00 (*0-85072-271-3*) St Mut.

— Signs of Design: Mathematics. (C). 1990. pap. text 60.00 (*0-85072-269-1*) St Mut.

— Signs of Design: Science. (C). 1990. pap. text 60.00 (*0-85072-270-5*) St Mut.

— Signs of Design: The Early Years. (C). 1991. pap. text 60.00 (*0-85072-290-X*) St Mut.

— Stories As Starting Points for Design & Technology. (C). 1991. pap. text 50.00 (*0-85072-288-8*) St Mut.

Design Council Staff. UK Product Development: A Benchmarking Survey. 44p. 1994. pap. 78.95 (*0-566-07623-3*) Ashgate Pub Co.

Design Council Staff. William Morris & Kelmscott. 192p. 1987. pap. 50.00 (*0-85072-121-0*) St Mut.

Design Down Under Staff. Design down Under, Vol. 3. (Illus.). 256p. 1994. 55.00 (*0-646-17734-6*, Pub. by Design Down Under) Bks Nippan.

D

Design down Under Staff. Design down Under: Student's Edition. 1996. pap., student ed. 27.95 (*962-7561-25-8*, Pub. by Art Dist Centre) Bks Nippan.

Design Engineering Conference. New Design Standards for Flexible Couplings: Design Engineering Conference, Chicago, May 10, 1966. LC TJ0183.A7. 33p. reprint ed. pap. 30.00 (*0-608-11677-7*, 201132400077) Bks Demand.

Design Engineering Conference (1979: Chicago, IL). Fundamentals of the Design of Fluid Film Bearings: Presented at the Design Engineering Conference, May 7-10, 1979, Chicago, IL. Rohde, S. M. et al, eds. LC 79-50211. 199p. pap. 61.70 (*0-608-15563-2*, 205639200064) Bks Demand.

Design Engineering Technical Conference (1977: Chi. Passenger Vibration in Transportation Vehicles: Presented at the Design Engineering Technical Conference, Chicago, Illinois, September 26-28, 1977. Berman, Alex & Hannibal, Alan J., eds. LC 77-82212. (AMD Ser.: Vol. 24). 136p. reprint ed. pap. 42.20 (*0-608-13159-8*, 201539300093) Bks Demand.

Design Guide Staff. Selection & Use of Titanium. 50p. 1995. pap. 50.00 (*0-901716-97-9*) Institute of Management Consultants.

Design Information Technical Committee Staff. Design Representation Programming Interface: Electrical Connectivity, 4 vols., 1. 475p. 1993. pap. text 150.00 (*1-882750-01-2*) CAD Framewk.

— Design Representation Programming Interface: Electrical Connectivity, 4 vols., Set. 475p. 1993. pap. text. write for info. (*1-882750-00-4*) CAD Framewk.

Design Institute for Emergency Releif Systems User. Proceedings of the 2nd International Symposium on Runaway Reactions, Pressure Relief Design & Effluent Handling. Melhem, G. A. & Fisher, H. G., eds. (Illus.). 694p. 1998. 125.00 (*0-8169-0761-7*, P-90) Am Inst Chem Eng.

Design, Jennifer B. & Greenleigh, Stephanie. Baked from the Heart. LC 97-20706. (Illus.). 112p. 1997. 17.95 (*0-89815-938-5*) Ten Speed Pr.

Design, Jennifer B., jt. auth. see Johns, Pamela S.

Design of Computer Simulation Experiments Symposiu. The Design of Computer Simulation Experiments: (Papers) Naylor, Thomas H., ed. LC 79-100090. 429p. reprint ed. pap. 133.00 (*0-608-11983-0*, 202342500033) Bks Demand.

Design Online Staff, jt. auth. see Fraterdeus, Peter.

Design Schools Staff. Your Future in Art. (Illus.). 32p. (YA). (gr. 10-12). 1981. pap. text 1.25 (*0-9607016-0-5*) Design Schools.

— Your Future in Fashion. (Illus.). 32p. (YA). (gr. 10-12). 1983. pap. text 1.25 (*0-9607016-1-3*) Design Schools.

***Design Science Inc. Staff, ed.** MathType: The Mathematical Equation Editor: Version 3.5 for Windows. 150p. 1998. 150.00 incl. cd-rom (*3-540-14713-6*) Spr-Verlag.

Designers & Art Directors Assoc. Staff, ed. British Design & Art Direction 1996. (Illus.). 688p. 1997. 79.95 (*1-86154-025-6*) Gingko Press.

Designs for Learning, Inc. Staff. Joining Hands: A Resource Book on Integrating Experiential Learning into the School Curriculum. 114p. 1996. pap. text 25.00 (*0-7872-2885-0*) Kendall-Hunt.

Designs in Modern Learning Staff. Essential Functions for Public Safety Personnel: A Guide for Compliance with Title I of the Americans with Disabilities Act. (Public Safety Educational Technology Ser.). 44p. 1992. student ed. 35.00 (*1-885602-01-4*) Designs in Modern.

— Public Safety Background Investigation Sourcebook. (Public Safety Educational Technology Ser.). 196p. 1994. student ed. 35.00 (*1-885602-00-6*) Designs in Modern.

Designs, Lucy B. The Cottages of Thomas Kinkade. 34p. 1998. pap. 11.95 (*0-9638635-7-6*) Lightpost Pubng.

— A Father's Heart by Thomas Kinkade. 50p. 1998. pap. 12.95 (*0-9638635-9-2*) Lightpost Pubng.

— Messengers of Light by Thomas Kinkade. 44p. 1998. pap. 14.95 (*0-9638635-8-4*) Lightpost Pubng.

Desikachar, T. K. The Heart of Yoga: Developing a Personal Practice. (Illus.). 272p. 1995. pap. 19.95 (*0-89281-533-7*) Inner Tradit.

— The Heart of Yoga: Developing a Personal Practice. LC 99-462597. (Illus.). 272p. 1999. 19.95 (*0-89281-764-X*) Inner Tradit.

— Religiousness in Yoga: Lectures on Theory & Practice. Skelton, Mary L. & Carter, J. R., eds. LC 79-9643. (Illus.). 314p. 1980. pap. text 28.00 (*0-8191-0967-3*) U Pr of Amer.

Desikachar, T. K. & Cravens, R. H. Health, Healing & Beyond: The Living Tradition of Krishnamacharya. (Illus.). 256p. 1997. 53.00 (*0-89381-731-7*) Aperture.

Desikachari, Sri T. The South Indian Coins. (Illus.). 210p. 1986. 18.00 (*0-8364-1724-0*, Pub. by Chanakya) S Asia.

Desikachary, T. V. & Prima, P. Silicoflagellates (Dictyochophyceae) (Bibliotheca Phycologica Ser.: Vol. 100). (Illus.). 300p. 1996. pap. 112.00 (*3-443-60027-1*, Pub. by Gebruder Borntraeger) Balogh.

Desikachary, T. V. & Sreelatha, P. M. Oamaru Diatoms. (Bibliotheca Diatomologica Ser.: Vol. 19). (Illus.). 330p. 1989. pap. text 130.00 (*3-443-57010-0*, Pub. by Gebruder Borntraeger) Balogh.

DeSilva, Bruce, ed. see Hartford Courant Staff.

DeSilva, C. W., jt. ed. see Shoureshi, R.

***DeSilva, David A.** Bearing Christ's Reproach: The Challenge of Hebrews in an Honor Culture. 1999. pap. 13.95 (*0-941037-86-X*) D & F Scott.

Desilva, David A. The Credentials of an Apostle: Paul's Gospel in 2 Corinthians 1-7. LC 98-5595. (Bibal Monograph Ser.). 1998. 15.95 (*0-941037-55-X*, BIBAL Press) D & F Scott.

***DeSilva, David A.** Honor, Patronage, Kinship & Purity: Unlocking New Testament Culture. 375p. 2000. pap. 24.99 (*0-8308-1572-4*) InterVarsity.

— Perseverance in Gratitude: A Socio-Rhetorical Commentary on the Epistle "To the Hebrews" 560p. 2000. pap. 40.00 (*0-8028-4188-0*) Eerdmans.

DeSilva, David A. Untold Stories of the Bible. LC 99-193135. 256 p. 1998. write for info. (*0-7853-2945-5*) Pubns Intl Ltd.

Desilva, David Arthur. The Hope of Glory: Honor Discourse & New Testament Interpretation. LC 98-34346. 228p. 1999. pap. 22.95 (*0-8146-5823-7*) Liturgical Pr.

DeSilva, Derrick. Ask the Doctor: Herbs & Supplements for Better Health. LC 97-2748. (Illus.). 160p. 1997. pap. 12.95 (*1-883010-31-4*) Interweave.

DeSilva, Derrick M., Jr. Coping with Lyme Disease: A Practical Guide to Dealing with Diagnosis & Treatment. LC 93-16442. 88p. (Orig.). 1995. pap. 12.95 (*0-8050-2650-9*, Owl) H Holt & Co.

DeSilva, Raul. Making Money in Film & Video: A Freelancer's Handbook. 2nd ed. LC 92-13908. 192p. 1992. pap. 34.95 (*0-240-80144-X*, Focal) Buttrwrth-Heinemann.

DeSilva, Roland, et al, eds. The M&A Dictionary: Mergers & Acquisitions Definitions, Phrases & Examples. 360p. 1999. pap. 19.95 (*0-9670699-0-4*) Fulcurm Info Serv.

DeSilva, S. L. & Francis, Peter. Volcanoes of the Central Andes. (Illus.). viii, 216p. 1991. 135.95 (*0-387-53706-6*) Spr-Verlag.

Desimini, Lisa. Feelings. (J). Date not set. 15.95 (*0-8050-4577-5*) H Holt & Co.

— Moon Soup. LC 92-55041. (Illus.). 32p. (J). (ps-3). 1993. 14.95 (*1-56282-463-5*, Pub. by Hyprn Child); lib. bdg. 14.89 (*1-56282-464-3*, Pub. by Hyprn Child) Little.

— My House. (J). 1995. write for info. (*0-8050-3144-8*) H Holt & Co.

Desimini, Lisa. My House. 1997. 11.15 (*0-606-13634-7*, Pub. by Turtleback) Demco.

Desimini, Lisa. Sun & Moon: A Giant Love Story. LC 98-28836. (Illus.). 40p. (YA). (ps-3). 1999. 16.95 (*0-590-18720-1*, Blue Sky Press) Scholastic Inc.

Desimini, Lisa, et al. All Year Round: A Book to Benefit Children in Poverty. LC 96-29915. (Illus.). 32p. (J). (ps-1). 1997. 15.95 (*0-590-36097-3*) Scholastic Inc.

Desimini, Lisa, jt. illus. see Lewis, J. Patrick.

Desimone. Human Resource Development. 2nd ed. (C). 1997. pap. text, teacher ed. 40.00 (*0-03-024922-8*) Harcourt Coll Pubs.

— Human Resources Development. 2nd ed. LC 97-68510. (C). 1997. text 74.00 (*0-03-024612-1*) Harcourt Coll Pubs.

DeSimone, Anna. Reverse Mortgages: Financing Options for Senior Households. 123p. 1998. pap. 45.00 (*1-57599-052-0*, Real Est Fin Pr) Mortgage Bankers.

DeSimone, Cathleen. Death on Demand: Physician-Assisted Suicide in the United States a Legal Research Pathfinder. LC 95-33290. (Legal Research Guides Ser.: Vol. 26). ix, 57p. 1996. 42.00 (*0-89941-983-6*, 308910) W S Hein.

Desimone, Diane M. Transnational Marketing in the Information Age. rev. ed. LC 98-42965. (Transnational Business & Corporate Culture Ser.). (Illus.). 168p. 1998. 45.00 (*0-8153-3311-0*) Garland.

DeSimone, Elizabeth H. Out & about Portland with Kids: The Ultimate Guide for Fun & Learning. 240p. (Orig.). 1997. pap. 12.95 (*0-9614626-7-1*) NW Parent Pub.

DeSimone, Fred. Cold Sweat. 256p. 1999. pap. 17.00 (*0-8059-4644-6*) Dorrance.

DeSimone, James. The Official G. I. Joe Collectors Guide to Completing & Collating Your G. I. Joes & Accessories. (J). 1993. pap. 11.94 (*0-9635956-0-1*) GI Joe Collect.

Desimone, Livio D., et al. Eco-Efficiency: The Business Link to Sustainable Development. LC 96-49857. 292p. 1997. 27.50 (*0-262-04162-6*) MIT Pr.

***Desimone, Livio D., et al.** Eco-Efficiency: The Business Link to Sustainable Development. (Illus.). 306p. 2000. reprint ed. pap. 17.95 (*0-262-54109-2*) MIT Pr.

DeSimone, Patricia, ed. see Marchok, Janice M.

DeSimone, Paula. The Decorative Painter's Colour Shaper Book: A Creative Guide for the Decorative Artist. (Illus.). 108p. 1999. pap. 15.99 (*1-56496-539-2*, Quarry Bks) Rockport Pubs.

***DeSimone, Paula.** Painting Faux Finishes with the Color Shaper Wide: A Creative Guide for Faux Finish Painters, 2000. pap. text 29.99 (*1-56496-634-8*) Rockport Pubs.

— Painting Faux Finishes with the Color Shaper Wide: A Creative Guide for Faux Finish Painters, (Illus.). 96p. 2000. pap. text 16.99 (*1-56496-635-6*) Rockport Pubs.

— Painting Glass with the Color Shaper: A Creative Guide for Decorating Glass. (Illus.). 2000. pap. 17.00 (*1-56496-713-1*) Rockport Pubs.

DeSimone, Paula & Stewart, Pat. Brush, Sponge, Stamp: A Creative Guide to Painting Beautiful Patterns on Everyday Surfaces. LC 98-134645. (Illus.). 144p. 1998. pap. 24.99 (*1-56496-353-5*, Quarry Bks) Rockport Pubs.

DeSimone, Peter. Multinational Business in South Africa, 1996: Executive Summary. Lally, Rosemary & Voorhes, Meg, eds. 20p. (Orig.). 1996. pap. text 25.00 (*1-879775-38-7*) IRRC Inc DC.

— Multinational Business in South Africa, 1996 Vol. I: U. S. Companies. Lally, Rosemary & Voorhes, Meg, eds. 240p. (Orig.). 1996. pap. text 125.00 (*1-879775-39-5*) IRRC Inc DC.

— Multinational Business in South Africa, 1996 Vol. II: Non-U. S. Companies. Lally, Rosemary & Voorhes, Meg, eds. 220p. 1996. pap. text 125.00 (*1-879775-40-9*) IRRC Inc DC.

DeSimone, Peter, et al. U. S. Business in South Africa 1995. 11th rev. ed. Voorhes, Meg, ed. 224p. (Orig.). 1995. pap. 125.00 (*1-879775-24-7*) IRRC Inc DC.

DeSimone, r., et al. Atlas of Transesophageal Color Doppler Echocardiography & Intraoperative Imaging. LC 94-31740. 200p. 1994. 147.00 (*0-387-57938-9*) Spr-Verlag.

DeSimone, Rebecca & Haman, Edward A. How to File for Divorce in Pennsylvania. 2nd ed. LC 97-45619. (Legal Survival Guides Ser.). 224p. 1997. pap. 19.95 (*1-57071-177-1*) Sourcebks.

***DeSimone, Rebecca & Haman, Edward A.** How to File for Divorce in Pennsylvania. 2nd rev. ed. LC 00-29703. (Legal Survival Guides Ser.). 224p. 2000. pap. 19.95 (*1-57248-127-7*, Sphinx Pubng) Sourcebks.

Desimoni, Giovanni, et al, eds. Natural Products Synthesis through Pericyclic Reactions. LC 83-12303. (ACS Monograph: No. 180). 456p. 1983. text 110.00 (*0-8412-0757-7*, Pub. by Am Chemical) OUP.

Desind, Philip. Jewish & Russian Revolutionaries Exiled to Siberia, 1901-1917. LC 90-28796. (Jewish Studies: Vol. 6). (Illus.). 732p. 1991. lib. bdg. 139.95 (*0-7734-9762-5*) E Mellen.

Desing, Mike, ed. Chem Sources - International, Vol. 7. 7th ed. 1600p. 1998. 875.00 (*0-937020-30-3*) Chem Srcs Intl.

— Chem Sources - U. S. A., Vol. 39. 7th ed. 1445p. 1999. 395.00 (*0-937020-31-1*) Chem Srcs Intl.

***Desinger, Bernd.** Rock auf Deutsch Booklet: Die, Sterne Video Booklet. (Illus.). 1999. pap. 8.00 (*0-942017-64-1*, 4-6438B) Amer Assn Teach German.

DeSio, Dolores. Rescue of the Gem Children. (Illus.). 35p. (J). (gr. 3-6). 1998. pap. 10.00 (*0-9670347-0-1*) Desio Foundation.

DeSipio, Louis. Counting on the Latino Vote: Latinos As a New Electorate. (Race, Ethnicity, & Politics Ser.). 256p. (C). 1996. text 35.00 (*0-8139-1660-7*) U Pr of Va.

— Counting on the Latino Vote: Latinos as a New Electorate. (Race-Ethnicity, & Politics Ser.). 240p. 1998. reprint ed. pap. 16.00 (*0-8139-1829-4*) U Pr of Va.

Desipio, Louis & De La Garza, Rodolfo. Awash in the Mainstream: Latino Politics in the 1996 Election. 256p. 2000. pap. text 60.00 (*0-8133-6685-2*) Westview.

DeSipio, Louis & De la Garza, Rodolfo O. Making Americans, Remaking America: Immigration & Immigrant Policy. LC 98-10675. (Dilemmas in American Politics Ser.). 168p. (C). 1998. pap. 17.00 (*0-8133-1944-7*, Pub. by Westview) HarpC.

DeSipio, Louis & De La Garza, Rodolfo O., eds. Awash in the Mainstream: Latino Politics in the 1996 Election. LC 98-49320. 304p. 1999. 75.00 (*0-8133-6686-0*, Pub. by Westview) HarpC.

DeSipio, Louis, jt. auth. see De la Garza, Rodolfo O.

Desiraju, G. R. Crystal Engineering: The Design of Organic Solids. (Materials Science Monographs: No. 54). xiv,312p. 1989. 178.00 (*0-444-87457-7*) Elsevier.

Desiraju, Gautam R., ed. The Crystal as a Supramolecular Entity. (Perspectives in Supramolecular Chemistry Ser.: Vol. 2). 326p. 1996. 265.00 (*0-471-95015-7*) Wiley.

Desiraju, Gautam R. & Steiner, Thomas D. The Weak Hydrogen Bond: Applications to Structural Chemistry & Biology. LC 99-20408. 9. (Illus.). 528p. 1999. text 150.00 (*0-19-850252-4*) OUP.

DeSirey, Jan, jt. ed. see Dodge, Chris.

DeSisto, Pete, jt. auth. see Albert, Linda.

***Desjardien, Teresa.** Bartered Bridegroom. (Regency Romance Ser.). 2000. mass mkt. 4.99 (*0-451-19962-6*, Sig) NAL.

Desjardien, Teresa. Borrowed Kisses. 1995. mass mkt. 4.50 (*0-8217-5110-7*, Zebra Kensgtn) Kensgtn Pub Corp.

DesJardien, Teresa. The Reluctant Lord. 256p. 1997. mass mkt. 4.99 (*0-8217-5646-X*, Zebra Kensgtn) Kensgtn Pub Corp.

— A Scandalous Proposal. 320p. 1994. mass mkt. 3.99 (*0-8217-4504-2*, Zebra Kensgtn) Kensgtn Pub Corp.

Desjardien, Teresa. The Skeptical Heart. 256p. 1996. mass mkt. 4.50 (*0-8217-5355-X*, Zebra Kensgtn) Kensgtn Pub Corp.

DesJardien, Teresa. A Winsome Widow. 256p. 1994. mass mkt. 3.99 (*0-8217-4724-X*, Zebra Kensgtn) Kensgtn Pub Corp.

Desjardien, Teresa, et al. Bewitched by Love. 352p. 1996. mass mkt. 4.50 (*0-8217-5430-0*, Zebra Kensgtn) Kensgtn Pub Corp.

Desjardin, Dennis. Agaricales of California 7: Tricholomataceae: Marasmioid Genera. (Agaricales of California Ser.). (Illus.). 97p. (Orig.). 1987. pap. 38.95 (*0-916422-75-5*) Mad River.

DesJardin, Marie. For the Time Being. 436p. (Orig.). 1998. pap. 15.95 (*1-885173-46-6*) Write Way.

***Desjardin, Thomas A.** Joshua L. Chamberlain. (Illus.). 100p. 1999. pap. 9.95 (*1-892636-15-8*) Greystone Inc.

Desjardin, Thomas A. Stand Firm Ye Boys from Maine: The 20th Maine & the Gettysburg Campaign. LC 96-180330. (Illus.). 256p. (C). 1995. text 28.00 (*0-939631-89-X*) Thomas Publications.

— Stand Firm Ye Boys from Maine: The 20th Maine & the Gettysburg Campaign. 4th ed. (Illus.). 256p. 1998. pap. 15.00 (*1-57747-034-6*) Thomas Publications.

***Desjardins.** Cardiopulmonary Anatomy & Physiology. 4th ed. (C). 2001. pap. 38.25 (*0-7668-2533-7*) Delmar.

— Cardiopulmonary Anatomy & Physiology. 4th ed. (C). 2001. pap., wbk. ed. 16.75 (*0-7668-2535-3*) Delmar.

DesJardins. Cardiopulmonary Anatomy & Physiology: Essentials for Respiratory Care. 3rd ed. 240p. 1998. pap. text, teacher ed. 18.00 (*0-8273-8257-X*) Delmar.

Desjardins. Contemporary Issues in Business Ethics. 4th ed. LC 99-49166. (Philosophy Ser.). 1999. 60.95 (*0-534-50598-8*) Wadsworth Pub.

***Desjardins.** Environmental Ethics: An Introduction to Environmental Philosophy. 3rd ed. 2000. pap. 31.00 (*0-534-51966-0*) Wadsworth Pub.

DesJardins. Workbook for Cardiopulmonary Anatomy & Physiology: Essentials for Respiratory Care. 3rd ed. 224p. (C). 1997. pap., wbk. ed. 16.95 (*0-8273-8258-8*) Delmar.

Desjardins, Arnaud. The Jump into Life: Moving Beyond Fear. Kennedy, Kathleen, tr. from FRE. LC 93-80524. 216p. (Orig.). 1994. pap. 12.95 (*0-934252-42-4*, Pub. by Hohm Pr) SCB Distributors.

— Toward the Fullness of Life: The Fullness of Love. Kennedy, Kathleen, tr. from FRE. LC 89-29545. 182p. 1990. pap. 12.95 (*0-934252-55-6*, Pub. by Hohm Pr) SCB Distributors.

Desjardins, Claude, ed. Cellular & Molecular Regulation of Testicular Cells. LC 95-46670. (Illus.). 336p. 1996. 129.00 (*0-387-94648-9*) Spr-Verlag.

Desjardins, Claude & Ewing, Larry L., eds. Cell & Molecular Biology of the Testis. (Illus.). 512p. (C). 1993. text 125.00 (*0-19-506269-8*) OUP.

Desjardins, Joseph. Environmental Ethics: Concepts, Policy & Theory. LC 98-5946. 640p. 1998. pap. text 46.95 (*1-55934-986-7*) Mayfield Pub.

DesJardins, Joseph R. Environmental Ethics: An Introduction to Environmental Philosophy. 272p. (C). 1992. mass mkt., teacher ed. 24.25 (*0-534-20046-X*) Wadsworth Pub.

DesJardins, Joseph R. & McCall, John J. Contemporary Issues in Business Ethics. 3rd ed. (C). 1995. pap. 39.00 (*0-534-25542-6*) Wadsworth Pub.

DesJardins, Joseph R. & McCall, John J., eds. Contemporary Issues in Business Ethics. 510p. (C). 1984. pap. write for info. (*0-534-03693-7*) Wadsworth Pub.

— Contemporary Issues in Business Ethics. 2nd ed. 485p. (C). 1989. mass mkt. 33.75 (*0-534-12090-3*) Wadsworth Pub.

DesJardins, Marie & Ram, Ashwin, eds. Goal-Driven Learning: Papers from the 1994 Spring Symposium. (Technical Reports). (Illus.). 136p. (Orig.). 1994. spiral bd. 25.00 (*0-929280-58-X*) AAAI Pr.

Desjardins, Marie-France. Rethinking Confidence-Building Measures. (Adelphi Papers, No. 307; International Institute for Strategic Studies: No. 307). 72p. 1997. pap. text 28.00 (*0-19-829321-6*) OUP.

Desjardins, Michel. Peace, Violence & the New Testament. (Biblical Seminar Ser.: Vol. 46). 130p. 1997. pap. 17.95 (*1-85075-799-2*, Pub. by Sheffield Acad) CUP Services.

Desjardins, Michel, jt. ed. see Arnal, William E.

***Desjardins, Michel Robert, et al.** Text & Artifact in the Religions of Mediterranean Antiquity: Essays in Honour of Peter Richardson. LC 00-93095. (Studies in Christianity & Judaism: Vol. 9). (Illus.). 632p. 2000. 69.95 (*0-88920-356-3*) Wilfrid Laurier.

Desjardins, R. L., et al. Advances in Bioclimatology, Vol. 1. Stanhill, G. et al, eds. (Illus.). x, 157p. 1992. 103.95 (*0-387-53843-7*) Spr-Verlag.

Desjardins, Rosemary. The Rational Enterprise: Logos in Plato's Theaetetus. LC 88-20001. (SUNY Series in Ancient Greek Philosophy). 275p. (C). 1990. pap. text 19.95 (*0-88706-838-3*) State U NY Pr.

Desjardins, Terry R. Cardiopulmonary Anatomy & Physiology. (Respiratory Care Ser.). 1988. pap. 29.95 (*0-8273-2836-2*) Delmar.

Desjarlais. The House. LC 94-232323. (New Readers Ser.). 1993. pap. text. write for info. (*0-15-599355-0*) Harcourt Schl Pubs.

— Shuttle Mission. (New Readers Ser.). 1993. pap. text. write for info. (*0-15-599354-2*) Harcourt Schl Pubs.

— Treasure Dive. (New Readers Ser.). 1993. pap. text. write for info. (*0-15-599353-4*) Harcourt Schl Pubs.

Desjarlais, Robert, et al, eds. World Mental Health: Problems & Priorities in Low-Income Countries. (Illus.). 400p. 1996. reprint ed. pap. text 32.50 (*0-19-511311-X*) OUP.

— World Mental Health: Problems, Priorities & Responses in Low-Income Countries. (Illus.). 400p. 1995. text 49.50 (*0-19-509540-5*) OUP.

Desjarlais, Robert R. Body & Emotion: The Aesthetics of Illness & Healing in the Nepal Himalayas. (Orig.). 1994. pap. 54.00 (*0-7855-0429-X*, Pub. by Ratna Pustak Bhandar) St Mut.

— Body & Emotion: The Aesthetics of Illness & Healing in the Nepal Himalayas. LC 92-23545. (Contemporary Ethnography Ser.). (Illus.). 320p. (Orig.). (C). 1992. text 45.00 (*0-8122-3166-X*); pap. text 18.95 (*0-8122-1434-X*) U of Pa Pr.

Desjonqueres, M. C. Concepts in Surface Physics. 2nd ed. 624p. 1996. pap. 69.00 (*3-540-58622-9*) Spr-Verlag.

Desjonqueres, M. C. & Spanjaard, D. Concepts in Surface Physics. LC 93-18561. (Surface Sciences Ser.: Vol. 30). (Illus.). 624p. 1993. 98.00 (*0-387-56506-X*) Spr-Verlag.

Desk. Biography: Visionaries of the 20th Century. 112p. 1999. pap. 16.95 (*0-06-270241-6*) HarpC.

— Inner Reflections. 1999. 12.95 (*0-87612-342-6*) Self Realization.

— Mariner's Book of Days. 1999. 12.95 (*0-937822-52-3*) WoodenBoat Pubns.

— Thomas Kinkade Painter of Light. 1998. pap. 11.95 (*1-57624-272-2*) A M C A L.

— World Of Boating. 1999. 15.95 (*0-937822-53-1*) WoodenBoat Pubns.

Desk & Derrick Club Staff. Dilbert Drop It in the "To Do Basket" 1998. 9.99 (*0-8362-5523-2*) Andrews & McMeel.

Deskin, Gerald & Steckler, Greg. Parent's Answer Book: Over 100 Most-Asked Questions about Your Child's Emotional Well-Being. 224p. 1995. 22.95 (*0-925190-79-9*) Fairview Press.

— Parent's Answer Book: Over 100 Most-Asked Questions about Your Child's Emotional Well-Being. 224p. 1996. pap. 12.95 (*1-57749-005-3*) Fairview Press.

— When Nothing Makes Sense: Disaster, Crisis, & Their Effects on Children. 224p. 1996. 19.95 (*0-925190-95-0*) Fairview Press.

— When Nothing Makes Sense: Disaster, Crisis, & Their Effects on Children. 192p. 1997. reprint ed. pap. 12.95 (*1-57749-027-4*) Fairview Press.

***Deskin, Michael.** The Managed Pharmacy Benefit Market. 22p. 1998. spiral bd. 47.00 (*0-929156-49-8*) Atlantic Info Services Inc.

Deskins, Barbara, jt. auth. see Anderson, Jean.

Deskins, Donald R., Jr. Minority Recruitment Data: An Analysis of Baccalaureate Degree Production in the United States. LC 83-19159. 832p. (C). 1984. 95.50 (*0-86598-145-0*) Rowman.

Deskins, W. E. Linear Algebra. unabridged ed. LC 95-38346. (Illus.). 640p. 1996. reprint ed. pap. 15.95 (*0-486-68888-7*) Dover.

Deskis, Susan E. Beowulf & the Medieval Proverb Tradition. (Medieval & Renaissance Texts & Studies: Vol. 155). 192p. 1996. 22.00 (*0-86698-195-0*, MR155) MRTS.

Desko, Susan, ed. AIA/Los Angeles 1996 Design & Next LA Awards. LC 97-73418. (Illus.). 56p. (Orig.). 1997. pap. 19.50 (*0-940512-05-X*) Hennessey.

Desktop Publishing Inc. Staff, ed. see Provenzano, Steven A.

Deslandres, Maurice C. Histoire Constitutionnelle de la France de 1789 a 1870, Vol. 2. 1980. 53.95 (*0-405-11843-0*) Ayer.

— Histoire Constitutionnelle de la France de 1789 a 1970, 3 vols., Set. LC 78-67346. (European Political Thought Ser.). (FRE.). 1980. reprint ed. lib. bdg. 160.95 (*0-405-11692-6*) Ayer.

Deslauriers, Christine, ed. In the Presence of a Master: Yogi Amrit Desai. LC 92-72739. (Illus.). 231p. 1992. pap. 29.95 (*0-940258-26-9*) Kripalu Pubns.

Deslauriers, Gilles, jt. auth. see Dubuc, Serge.

***Deslippe, Dennis A.** Rights, Not Roses: Unions & the Rise of Working-Class Feminism, 1945-80. LC 99-6426. (Working Class in American History Ser.). 2000. 21.95 (*0-252-06834-3*) U of Ill Pr.

Desloge, Edward A. Classical Mechanics, Vol. 2. LC 88-12969. 514p. (C). 1989. reprint ed. lib. bdg. 68.50 (*0-89464-322-3*) Krieger.

Desloge, Joseph, Jr. Passport to Manhood. 150p. 1995. 15.00 (*0-9616369-1-2*) St Louis Human.

Desloge, Nora. Toulouse-Lautrec: The Baldwin M. Baldwin Collection, San Diego Museum of Art. 1989. pap. 29.95 (*0-937108-07-3*) San Diego Museum of Art.

Desloge, Nora, jt. auth. see San Diego Museum of Art Staff.

Deslongchamps, Pierre. Stereoelectronic Control in the Cleavage of Tetrahedral Intermediates in the Hydrolysis of Esters & Amides. Barton et al, eds. 1976. pap. 15.50 (*0-08-020480-5*, Pergamon Pr) Elsevier.

Desmaison, Christopher. Learn French the Lazy Way. 240p. 1999. pap. 12.95 (*0-02-863011-4*, Pub. by Macmillan) S&S Trade.

Desmaisons. Psychiatry in Russia & Spain: An Original Anthology. LC 75-16729. (Classics in Psychiatry Ser.). (FRE & GER.). 1976. 26.95 (*0-405-07452-2*) Ayer.

DesMaisons, Kathleen. Potatoes Not Prozac. LC 97-43174. 256p. 1998. 22.50 (*0-684-84953-4*) S&S Trade.

— Potatoes Not Prozac: A Natural Seven-Step Plan to: Control Your Cravings & Lose Weight, Recognize How Foods Affect the Way You Feel, Stabilize the Level of Sugar in Your Blood. (Illus.). 256p. 1999. per. 12.00 (*0-684-85014-1*) S&S Trade.

***DesMaisons, Kathleen.** Sugar Addict's Total Recovery. 2000. 22.95 (*0-345-44132-X*) Ballantine Pub Grp.

Desmand, Sean. A Touch of the Irish: Wit & Wisdom & a Bit o' Blarney. 1999. pap. 5.99 (*0-517-20653-6*) Random Hse Value.

Desmangles, Leslie G. The Faces of the Gods: Vodou & Roman Catholicism in Haiti. LC 92-53625. (Illus.). xx, 220p. (C). 1992. 39.95 (*0-8078-2059-8*); pap. 17.95 (*0-8078-4393-8*) U of NC Pr.

Desmarais, ed. see Mertin, Roger.

Desmarais, Chantal, ed. see Carlson, Daniel J.

Desmarais, Charles. Humongolous: Sculpture & Other Works by Tim Hawkinson. LC 96-9528. (Illus.). 64p. (Orig.). 1996. pap. 18.95 (*0-917562-69-0*) Contemp Arts.

***Desmarais, Charles.** Jim Dine Photographs. Stoddard, Leah, ed. 16p. 1999. pap. 14.95 (*0-917562-72-0*) Contemp Arts.

Desmarais, Charles, ed. Michael Bishop. LC 79-10942. (Illus.). 1979. pap. 5.00 (*0-932026-03-6*) Columbia College Chi.

Desmarais, Charles, ed. Proof: Los Angeles Art & the Photograph, 1960-1980. LC 92-72754. (Illus.). 144p. 1992. pap. 45.00 (*0-911291-20-2*, Pub. by Fellows Cont Art) RAM Publications.

Desmarais, Jane H. The Beardsley Industry: The Critical Reception in England & France from 1893 to 1914. Dept. English & Historical & Cultural Studies, Gol, ed. LC 98-29312. (Illus.). 165p. (C). 1998. text 84.95 (*1-84014-205-7*, NC242.B3D475, Pub. by Ashgate Pub) Ashgate Pub Co.

Desmarais, Louis. Introduction to Applied Electro Optics. LC 97-48448. 352p. (C). 1997. pap. text 62.99 (*0-13-802711-0*) P-H.

***DesMarais, Lynette Marie.** The Spiritual Life of Horses. Estes, Sara, ed. 106p. 2000. 21.95 (*0-9700446-0-7*) Barah Pr.

***Desmarais, Norman.** The ABCs of XML: The Librarian's Guide to the Extensible Markup Language. (Illus.). 2000. pap. 28.00 (*0-9675942-0-0*) New Tech.

Desmarais, Norman, tr. see Leo XIII, pseud.

Desmarais, Rene, et al. The Coumadin Cookbook: A Complete Guide to Healthy Meals When Taking Coumadin. 320p. 1998. pap. 16.95 (*0-9664308-0-8*) Marsh Pubng.

Desmarais, Roger. Roots & Wings - Poems to My Daughter. LC 95-26686. 64p. 1996. pap. 7.95 (*0-88396-423-6*) Blue Mtn Art.

***Desmarais, Charles.** Shapes Balkenhol. Padilla, Michelle, ed. 2000. pap. write for info. (*0-917562-73-9*) Contemp Arts.

Desmarets, Peter, jt. auth. see Neuner, Gerd.

Desmedt, J. E., ed. Attention, Voluntary Contraction & Event-Related Cerebral Potentials. (Progress in Clinical Neurophysiology Ser.: Vol. 1). 1977. 85.75 (*3-8055-2438-2*) S Karger.

— Auditory Evoked Potentials in Man: Psychopharmacology Correlates of EPS. (Progress in Clinical Neurophysiology Ser.: Vol. 2). 1977. 85.25 (*3-8055-2626-1*) S Karger.

— Cerebral Motor Control in Man: Cerebral Event-Related Potentials. (Progress in Clinical Neurophysiology Ser.: Vol. 4). (Illus.). 1978. 102.75 (*3-8055-2712-8*) S Karger.

— Cognitive Components in Cerebral Event Related Potentials & Selective Attention. (Progress in Clinical Neurophysiology Ser.: Vol. 6). (Illus.). 1979. 102.75 (*3-8055-2760-8*) S Karger.

— Computer-Aided Electromyography. (Progress in Clinical Neurophysiology Ser.: Vol. 10). (Illus.). x, 334p. 1983. 143.50 (*3-8055-3748-4*) S Karger.

— Language & Hemispheric Specialization in Man: Cerebral Event-Related Potentials. (Progress in Clinical Neurophysiology Ser.: Vol. 3). (Illus.). 1977. 85.25 (*3-8055-2629-6*) S Karger.

— Motor Unit Types, Recruitment & Plasticity in Health & Disease. (Progress in Clinical Neurophysiology Ser.: Vol. 9). (Illus.). x, 418p. 1981. 128.75 (*3-8055-1929-X*) S Karger.

— New Developments in Electromyography & Clinical Neurophysiology, Set. Incl. Vol. 1. Motor Unit, Neuromuscular Disorders, Electromyographic Kinesiology. (Illus.). x, 700p. 1973. 208.75 (*3-8055-1451-4*); Vol. 2. Pathological Conduction in Nerve Fibers, Electromyography of Sphincter Muscles, Automatic Analysis of Electrogram with Computers. (Illus.). x, 500p. 1973. 156.75 (*3-8055-1452-2*); Vol. 3. Human Reflexes, Pathophysiology of Motor Systems, Methodology of Human Reflexes. (Illus.). x, 850p. 1973. 252.25 (*3-8055-1453-0*); 1973. 521.75 (*3-8055-1409-3*) S Karger.

— Physiological Tremor, Pathological Tremor & Clonus. (Progress in Clinical Neurophysiology Ser.: Vol. 5). (Illus.). 1978. 85.25 (*3-8055-2713-6*) S Karger.

— Spinal & Supraspinal Mechanisms of Voluntary Motor Control & Locomotion. (Progress in Clinical Neurophysiology Ser.: Vol. 8). (Illus.). x, 374p. 1980. 120.00 (*3-8055-0022-X*) S Karger.

Desmedt, J. E., ed. see Quantitative Methods of Investigations in the Clin.

Desmedt, John E., ed. Clinical Uses of Cerebral, Brainstem & Spinal Somatosensory Evoked Potentials. (Progress in Clinical Neurophysiology Ser.: Vol. 7). (Illus.). 1979. 120.00 (*3-8055-2936-8*) S Karger.

Desmedt, Y. G., et al, eds. CRYPTO 1994: Advances in Cryptography. (Lecture Notes in Computer Science Ser.: Vol. 839). 439p. 1994. 62.00 (*0-387-58333-5*) Spr-Verlag.

Desmet, Christy. Reading Shakespeare's Characters: Rhetoric, Ethics, & Identity. LC 92-14742. (Massachusetts Studies in Early Modern Culture). 232p. 1992. 30.00 (*0-87023-807-8*) U of Mass Pr.

***Desmet, Christy & Sawyer, Robert.** Shakespeare & Appropriation. LC 99-31115. (Accents on Shakespeare Ser.). 256p. 1999. pap. 20.99 (*0-415-20726-6*) Routledge.

***Desmet, Christy & Sawyer, Robert, eds.** Shakespeare & Appropriation. LC 99-31115. 256p. (C). 1999. text 65.00 (*0-415-20725-8*) Routledge.

Desmet, G., et al. Freshwater & Estuarine Radioecology: Proceedings of an International Seminar, Lisbon, Portugal, 21-25 March 1994, Vol. 68. LC 97-20761. (Studies in Environmental Science Ser.). 524p. 1997. 258.50 (*0-444-82533-9*) Elsevier.

DeSmet, P. J. New Indian Sketches. 175p. reprint ed. pap. 10.00 (*0-8466-4049-X*, I49) Shoreys Bkstore.

DeSmet, Pierre-Jean. Indian Missions. 67p. 1985. 14.95 (*0-87770-359-0*) Ye Galleon.

Desmet, W. Restenosis after Percutaneous Transluminal Coronary Angioplasty: Detection, Assessment & Modes of Prevention. No. 88. 168p. (Orig.). 1994. pap. 39.50 (*90-6186-626-X*, Pub. by Leuven Univ) Coronet Bks.

Desmett, Don, jt. contrib. by see Hanhardt, John G.

Desmett, Don, jt. contrib. by see Lippard, Lucy R.

***DeSmith, David.** The Colombian Coffee Book. LC 99-23380. 1999. write for info. (*0-9665006-2-8*) Fort Rowley.

***Desmoinaux, Christel.** Mrs. Hen's Big Surprise. (Illus.). 32p. (ps-2). 2000. per. 12.95 (*0-689-83403-9*) S&S Childrens.

Desmond. Physical Evidence. LC 99-18914. 1994. pap. 20.00 (*0-226-14376-7*) U Ch Pr.

— Physical Evidence. LC 99-18914. 1999. 30.00 (*0-226-14375-9*) U Ch Pr.

***Desmond.** The Windows 2000 Professional Bible. LC 99-46678. (Bible Ser.). 900p. 2000. pap. 39.99 (*0-7645-3424-6*) IDG Bks.

Desmond, Adrian. Archetypes & Ancestors: Palaeontology in Victorian London 1850-1875. LC 83-18104. (Illus.). 288p. 1986. pap. text 11.95 (*0-226-14344-9*) U Ch Pr.

— Archetypes & Ancestors: Palaeontology in Victorian London 1850-1875. LC 83-18104. (Illus.). 288p. 1994. 22.50 (*0-226-14343-0*) U Ch Pr.

— Darwin: The Life of a Tormented Evolutionist. 1994. pap. 23.95 (*0-393-31150-3*) Norton.

— Huxley: From Devil's Disciple to Evolution's High Priest. LC 97-22480. 848p. 1997. 37.50 (*0-201-95987-9*) Addison-Wesley.

— Huxley: From Devil's Disciple to Evolution's High Priest. 848p. 1999. pap. text 22.50 (*0-7382-0140-5*, Pub. by Perseus Pubng) HarpC.

— The Politics of Evolution: Morphology, Medicine, & Reform in Radical London. (Science & Its Conceptual Foundations Ser.). (Illus.). 514p. 1990. 41.95 (*0-226-14346-5*) U Ch Pr.

— The Politics of Evolution: Morphology, Medicine, & Reform in Radical London. LC 89-5137. (Science & Its Conceptual Foundations Ser.). (Illus.). 514p. 1992. pap. text 22.95 (*0-226-14374-0*) U Ch Pr.

Desmond, Betty. Bull Terriers: A New Owner's Guide. LC 99-205931. 1998. 12.95 (*0-7938-2769-8*) TFH Pubns.

Desmond, Charles. Wooden Ship-Building. 2nd ed. 224p. 1984. reprint ed. pap. 24.95 (*0-911572-37-6*, Vestal Pr) Madison Bks UPA.

Desmond, Charles K. Stock Money: Raising Money to Start or Expand Your Business Through a SCOR (Small Corporate Offering Registration) Savio, Eileen, ed. 97p. 1998. spiral bd. 47.00 (*0-9660547-1-7*) Infoware.

Desmond, Charles S. Sharp Quillets of the Law. xx, 245p. 1949. lib. bdg. 37.50 (*0-89941-595-4*, 500310) W S Hein.

Desmond, Cheryl T. Shaping the Culture of Schooling: The Rise of Outcome-Based Education. LC 95-44256. (SUNY Series, Education & Culture). 181p. (C). 1996. text 49.50 (*0-7914-2955-5*); pap. text 17.95 (*0-7914-2956-3*) State U NY Pr.

Desmond, Dennis. Camouflage Uniforms of the Soviet Union & Russia: 1937-to the Present. LC 97-80200. (Illus.). 160p. 1998. 45.00 (*0-7643-0462-3*) Schiffer.

Desmond, Derry, jt. auth. see Keating, Paul.

Desmond, Glenn. Un-Risky Business: Your Ratings Guide to Choosing a Small Business That Makes Sense. Faulkner, Monica, ed. 300p. (Orig.). 1994. pap. 14.95 (*0-935853-01-4*) Camden Harbor Pub.

Desmond, Glenn & Faulkner, Monica. The Ideal Entrepreneurial Business for You. LC 95-13731. 261p. 1995. 34.95 (*0-471-11812-5*); pap. 12.95 (*0-471-11813-3*) Wiley.

Desmond, Glenn M. & Kelley, Richard E. Business Valuation Handbook. 322p. 1988. 58.95 (*0-930458-03-6*) Marshall & Swift.

— Handbook of Small Business Valuation Formulas & Rules of Thumb. 3rd ed. Storm, Sandra, ed. 391p. 1993. 79.95 (*0-930458-06-0*) Marshall & Swift.

Desmond, Glenn M., et al. Business Valuation Handbook. rev. ed. 322p. 1988. 65.50 (*0-930458-02-8*) Appraisal Inst.

Desmond, Humphrey. A. P. A. Movement: A Sketch. LC 69-18772. (American Immigration Collection: Series 1). 1969. reprint ed. 12.95 (*0-405-00519-9*) Ayer.

Desmond, Jane C. Meaning in Motion: New Cultural Studies of Dance. LC 96-43776. (Post-Contemporary Interventions Ser.). (Illus.). 392p. 1997. pap. 18.95 (*0-8223-1942-X*); lib. bdg. 54.95 (*0-8223-1936-5*) Duke.

***Desmond, Jean.** Look Back & Laugh. 407p. 2000. 25.00 (*0-7388-1738-4*); pap. 18.00 (*0-7388-1739-2*) Xlibris Corp.

Desmond, Jerry T. Chattanooga, Tennessee. (Images of America Ser.). (Illus.). 128p. 1996. pap. 16.99 (*0-7524-0516-0*) Arcadia Publng.

***Desmond, Joanne.** Communicating with Today's Patient: Essentials to Save Time, Decrease Risk & Increase Patient Compliance. 2000. pap. 34.95 (*0-7879-4797-0*) Jossey-Bass.

Desmond, John. Louisiana's Antebellum Architecture. 1970. 25.00 (*0-87511-023-1*) Claitors.

Desmond, John F. At the Crossroads: Ethical & Religious Themes in the Writings of Walker Percy. LC 96-60695. viii, 148p. 1997. 35.00 (*0-87875-480-6*) Whitston Pub.

Desmond, John F. Risen Sons: Flannery O'Connor's Vision of History. LC 86-30828. (Illus.). 144p. 1987. 24.00 (*0-8203-0945-1*) U of Ga Pr.

***Desmond, Jones.** Eye of the Storm: Storm, E Weather, Vol. 2, set. abr. ed. (YA). (gr. 7-12). 1999. 22.00 incl. audio pap. 30.00 incl. audio (*0-9669585-3-5*) Eye Storm.

— Eye of the Storm: Storm, E Weather, Vol. 2. set. 2nd abr. rev. ed. Golden Arts Photos & Graphics Staff, tr. 72p. (YA). (gr. 7-12). 1999. 22.00 incl. audio (*0-9669585-4-3*) Eye Storm.

***Desmond, Kevin.** Aviation Ghosts: South by Southeast 165 Degrees. (Illus.). 224p. 1998. 36.95 (*0-85052-620-5*, Pub. by Leo Cooper) Trans-Atl Phila.

Desmond, Lawrence G. & Messenger, Phyllis M. A Dream of Maya: Augustus & Alice Le Plongeon in Nineteenth-Century Yucatan. LC 87-19122. 159p. reprint ed. pap. 52.40 (*0-7837-5849-9*, 204556800005) Bks Demand.

Desmond, Leslie, jt. auth. see Dorrance, Bill.

Desmond, Margaret G. Modifying the Work Environment for the Physically Disabled: An Accessibility Checklist for Employers. LC 80-83500. (Illus.). 128p. 1981. 8.95 (*0-686-38822-4*) Human Res Ctr.

Desmond, Marilyn & State University of New York at Binghamton Staff. Christine De Pizan & the Categories of Difference. LC 97-44280. (Medieval Cultures Ser.). xix, 287p. 1998. pap. 22.95 (*0-8166-3081-X*) U of Minn Pr.

— Christine De Pizan & the Categories of Difference. LC 97-44280. (Medieval Cultures Ser.). 1998. 57.95 (*0-8166-3080-1*) U of Minn Pr.

Desmond, Marilynn. Reading Dido: Gender, Textuality, & Medieval Aeneid. LC 94-6447. (Medieval Cultures Ser.: Vol. 8). 1994. pap. 19.95 (*0-8166-2247-7*); text 49.95 (*0-8166-2246-9*) U of Minn Pr.

***Desmond, Michael.** Upgrading & Repairing Windows 98. (Illus.). 1999. pap. 49.99 (*0-7897-1872-3*) Que.

Desmond, Michael & Dixon, Christine. 1968. LC 95-61180. (Illus.). 112p. (Orig.). 1996. pap. 19.95 (*0-500-97433-0*, Pub. by Thames Hudson) Norton.

Desmond, Michael, jt. auth. see Norton, Peter.

Desmond, Murdina M. Newborn Medicine & Society: European Background & American Practice (1750-1975) LC 97-43737. 1998. 26.95 (*1-57168-219-8*, Eakin Pr) Sunbelt Media.

Desmond, Nancy, jt. ed. see House, Peggy.

Desmond, Paula A., jt. ed. see Hancock, Peter A.

Desmond, Ray. Bibliography of British & Irish Gardens. 326p. pap. 47.50 (*1-873040-41-5*) St Pauls Bibliog.

— The European Discovery of the Indian Flora. (Illus.). 400p. 1992. text 125.00 (*0-19-854684-X*) OUP.

Desmond, Ray. The India Museum, 1801-79. xvi, 216p. 1982. 25.00 (*0-11-580088-3*, Pub. by Statnry Office) Balogh.

Desmond, Ray. Kew: The History of the Royal Botanic Gardens. (Illus.). 448p. 1998. pap. 32.00 (*1-86046-529-3*, Pub. by Harvill Press) FS&G.

— Sir Joseph Dalton Hooker. (Illus.). 250p. 1999. 49.50 (*1-85149-305-0*) Antique Collect.

Desmond, Ray & Ellwood, Christine, eds. Dictionary of British & Irish Botanists & Horticulturalists: (Including Plant Collectors, Flower Painters, & Garden Designers) rev. ed. 900p. 1993. 250.00 (*0-85066-843-3*, Pub. by Tay Francis Ltd) Taylor & Francis.

Desmond, Robert G. Give Thanks to the Lord: Passing on the Faith Through Mealtime Prayer & Catholic Devotion. (Illus.). 216p. (Orig.). 1994. pap. 10.75 (*1-884713-01-7*) Kerygmatic Pubns.

Desmond, Robert W. The Information Process: World News Reporting to the Twentieth Century. LC 77-9491. (World News Reporting Ser.: Vol. 1). 445p. 1978. text 65.00 (*0-87745-070-6*) U of Iowa Pr.

— The Press & World Affairs. LC 72-4665. (International Propaganda & Communications Ser.). (Illus.). 449p. 1972. reprint ed. 27.95 (*0-405-04746-0*) Ayer.

— Tides of War: World News Reporting, 1931-1945. LC 84-2504. (World News Reporting Ser.: Vol. IV). 608p. 1984. text 75.00 (*0-87745-125-7*) U of Iowa Pr.

Desmond, S. The Soul of Denmark. 1977. lib. bdg. 59.95 (*0-8490-2632-6*) Gordon Pr.

***Desmond, Sean.** Adams Fall. 272p. 2000. 22.95 (*0-312-26254-X*, Thomas Dunne) St Martin.

Desmond, Theresa. Beavers. (Illus.). (J). 1995. pap. 4.95 (*0-590-47084-1*) Scholastic Inc.

Desmond, Theresa, jt. auth. see Almonte, Paul.

Desmond, William. Art & the Absolute: A Study of Hegel's Aesthetics. LC 85-9886. (SUNY Series in Hegelian Studies). 222p. (C). 1986. text 21.50 (*0-88706-150-8*) State U NY Pr.

— Being & the Between. LC 94-8840. (SUNY Series in Philosophy). 557p. (C). 1995. text 74.50 (*0-7914-2271-2*); pap. text 24.95 (*0-7914-2272-0*) State U NY Pr.

— Beyond Hegel & Dialectic: Speculation, Cult, & Comedy. LC 91-26541. (SUNY Series in Hegelian Studies). 377p. (C). 1992. pap. text 19.95 (*0-7914-1104-4*) State U NY Pr.

***Desmond, William.** Ethics & the Between. (C). 2001. pap. text 29.95 (*0-7914-4848-7*) State U NY Pr.

— Ethics & the Between. (C). 2001. text 86.50 (*0-7914-4847-9*) State U NY Pr.

Desmond, William. Perplexity & Ultimacy: Metaphysical Thoughts from the Middle. LC 94-17003. 263p. (C). 1995. text 59.50 (*0-7914-2387-5*); pap. text 19.95 (*0-7914-2388-3*) State U NY Pr.

— Philosophy & Its Others: Ways of Being & Mind. LC 89-37872. (SUNY Series in Systematic Philosophy). 396p. (C). 1990. text 59.50 (*0-7914-0307-6*); pap. text 21.95 (*0-7914-0308-4*) State U NY Pr.

Desmond, William, ed. Hegel & His Critics: Philosophy in the Aftermath of Hegel. LC 87-16185. (SUNY Series in Hegelian Studies). 242p. (C). 1988. text 21.50 (*0-88706-667-4*) State U NY Pr.

***Desmond, William & Grange, Joseph, eds.** Being & Dialectic: Metaphysics as a Cultural Presence. (C). 2000. text 59.50 (*0-7914-4625-5*); pap. text 19.95 (*0-7914-4626-3*) State U NY Pr.

Desmond, William, tr. see Heyde, Ludwig.

Desmons, Giles. Walking Paris. LC 93-86821. (Illus.). 208p. 1994. pap. 12.95 (*0-8442-9214-1*, Passprt Bks) NTC Contemp Pub Co.

Desmons, Gilles. Walking Paris: Thirty Original Walks in & Around Paris. 2nd ed. LC 98-67236. (Illus.). 192p. 1999. pap. 14.95 (*0-8442-0141-3*, 01413) NTC Contemp Pub Co.

Desmont, Mark, jt. ed. see Blaukopf, Kurt.

Desmoulins, Camille. Oeuvres, 2 vols. in 1. LC 72-164282. reprint ed. 72.50 (*0-404-07124-4*) AMS Pr.

DeSmoulins, Melanie. The Snake. 160p. 1998. reprint ed. pap. 12.95 (*1-871592-82-8*, Velvet Pub) Creation Books.

Desmoulisre, A., et al, eds. Tissue Repair & Fibrosis: The Role of the Myofibroblast. LC 99-19995. (Current Topics in Pathology Ser.: Vol. 93). (Illus.). 250p. 1999. 170.00 (*3-540-65244-2*) Spr-Verlag.

Desmurs, Jean-Roger, et al, eds. Advances in Organobromine Chemistry II: Proceedings of ORGABROM '93, Held in Jerusalem, June 28 - July 2, 1993. LC 94-39317. (Industrial Chemistry Library: Vol. 7). (Illus.). 440p. 1994. 285.50 (*0-444-82105-8*) Elsevier.

Desmurs, Jean-Roger & Ratton, Serge, eds. The Roots of Organic Development. LC 96-5960. (Industrial Chemistry Library: No. 8). 578p. 1996. text 301.50 (*0-444-82434-0*) Elsevier.

Desmyter, J., ed. see International Symposium on Basic Progress in Blood.

Desne, R., jt. auth. see Diderot, Denis.

Desner, Raymond P., jt. ed. see Martinez, Joe L., Jr.

Desnick, R. J., jt. auth. see Hirschhorn, K.

Desnick, R. J., jt. ed. see Bishop, D. F.

D

Desnick, Robert J., ed. Enzyme Therapy in Genetic Diseases: Part 2. LC 79-48026. (Alan R. Liss Ser.: Vol. 16, No. 1). 1980. 77.00 (0-686-29474-2) March of Dimes.

— Treatment of Genetic Diseases. (Illus.). 350p. 1991. text 99.00 (0-443-08773-3) Church.

Desnoes, et al. Literatures in Transition: The Many Voices of the Caribbean Area. Minc, Rose S., ed. LC 82-84104. (ENG & SPA.). 180p. 1983. pap. 13.00 (0-935318-10-0) Edins Hispamerica.

Desnoes, Edmundo. Memories of Underdevelopment & Inconsolable Memories. Chanan, Michael, ed. (Films in Print Ser.). (Illus.). 220p. (C). 1990. text 37.00 (0-8135-1536-X); pap. text 17.00 (0-8135-1537-8) Rutgers U Pr.

Desnoes, Edmundo & Luis, William. Los Dispositivos en la Flor: Cuba: Literatura Desde la Revolucion. (SPA.). 557p. 1981. 18.00 (0-910061-03-3, 1104) Ediciones Norte.

Desnos, Robert. Chantefables. Annen, Sharon, tr. from FRE. LC 84-61257. (Illus.). 60p. (J). (gr. 1-6). 1988. 17.95 (0-9613938-0-7) Penstemon Pr.

— Chantefables et Chantefleurs. (FRE., Illus.). 7.95 (0-8288-9579-1, F98094) Fr & Eur.

***Desnos, Robert.** The Circle & the Star. Sanders, Todd, tr. & afterword by by. (Illus.). 64p. 2000. 65.00 (0-9679429-0-X) Air & Nothing.

Desnos, Robert. Corps et Biens. (FRE.). 1968. pap. 11.95 (0-7859-2761-1) Fr & Eur.

— Corps et Biens. (Poesie Ser.). (FRE.). 192p. 1968. 9.95 (2-07-030085-4) Schoenhof.

— Destinee Arbitraire. Dumas, J., ed. (FRE.). 1975. pap. 11.95 (0-7859-2779-4) Fr & Eur.

— Fortunes. (FRE.). 1969. pap. 11.95 (0-7859-2762-X, 2070300862) Fr & Eur.

— Fortunes. (Poesie Ser.). (FRE.). 192p. 1969. 9.95 (2-07-030086-2) Schoenhof.

— La Liberte ou l'Amour. (FRE.). 168p. 1982. pap. 13.95 (0-7859-4723-X) Fr & Eur.

— Liberte ou l'Amour & Deuil pour Deuil. (Imaginaire Ser.). (FRE.). pap. 10.95 (2-07-027695-3) Schoenhof.

— Liberty or Love! Hale, Terry, tr. from FRE. 1994. reprint ed. pap. 12.99 (0-947757-66-X, Pub. by Atlas Pr) Serpents Tail.

— Le Vin Est Tire. (FRE.). 206p. 1992. 11.95 (0-7859-1159-6, 2070725502) Fr & Eur.

Desnos, Robert & Dumas, Marie-Claire. Destinee Arbitraire. (Poesie Ser.). (FRE.). 88p. 1975. 13.95 (2-07-032154-1) Schoenhof.

Desnos, Robert, et al. The Automatic Muse: Surrealist Novels. (Atlas Anti-Classics Ser.). 150p. 1995. reprint ed. pap. 14.99 (0-947757-79-1, Pub. by Atlas Pr) Serpents Tail.

Desnuelle, P., jt. auth. see Mathieu, Jean P.

Desoe, Carol. Activities for Reflect-It Hinged Mirror. (Illus.). 72p. 1994. pap. text 9.50 (0-938587-73-0) Cuisenaire.

Desoer, C. A., jt. auth. see Callier, F. M.

Desoer, C. A., jt. auth. see Gundes, A. N.

Desoer, Charles A., jt. auth. see Zadeh, Lofti A.

DeSola, Carla. PeaceRites. Kane, Thomas A., ed. (Illus.). 1993. spiral bd. 11.95 (1-56929-006-7, Pastoral Press) OR Catholic.

DeSola, R. Abbreviations Dictionary. 7th ed. 966p. 1991. 135.00 (0-8288-0001-4, M8229) Fr & Eur.

DeSola, Ralph. Abbreviations Dictionary. 8th ed. 1328p. 1992. 81.95 (0-8493-4247-3, PE1693) CRC Pr.

DeSole, Gloria & Hoffmann, Leonore, eds. Rocking the Boat: Academic Women & Academic Processes. LC 81-14030. 141p. (Orig.). 1981. pap. 43.80 (0-608-05578-6, 206603900006) Bks Demand.

DeSole, Gloria, jt. ed. see Hoffmann, Leonore.

DeSollar, R., jt. ed. see Baxter, L.

***DeSombre, Elizabeth R.** Domestic Sources of International Environmental Policy: Industry, Environmentalists & U. S. Power. LC 99-41745. (American & Comparative Environmental Policy Ser.). (Illus.). 314p. 2000. 60.00 (0-262-04179-0); pap. 22.00 (0-262-54107-6) MIT Pr.

Desombres, Benonit. The Wisdom of Ancient Rome. LC 96-17065. (Illus.). 56p. 1996. 8.95 (0-7892-0242-5) Abbeville Pr.

DeSomma, Vince. The Mission to Mars & Beyond. Goetzmann, William H., ed. (World Explorers Ser.). (Illus.). 120p. (YA). (gr. 5 up). 1992. lib. bdg. 19.95 (0-7910-1325-1) Chelsea Hse.

de'Sommi, Leone. A Comedy of Betrothal: Leone de Sommi Ebreo. Golding, Alfred S., tr. (Carleton Renaissance Plays in Translation Ser.: No. 9). 145p. 1988. pap. 8.00 (0-919473-79-2, Pub. by Dovehouse) Sterling.

DeSomogyi, J., tr. & rev. see Goldziher, Ignaz.

Desomogyi, Joseph. A Short History of Oriental Trade. 281p. 1968. write for info. (0-318-71499-X); lib. bdg. 37.70 (0-317-93808-8, 05101831) G Olms Pubs.

Desonie, Dana. Cosmic Collisions. LC 95-24460. (Scientific American Focus Bks.). 1995. 22.50 (0-8050-3843-4); pap. 9.95 (0-8050-3844-2) H Holt & Co.

DeSonne, Marcia. Telco-Video: Competitive Issues & Broadcast Industry Directions. 29p. 1989. 30.00 (0-89324-078-8) Natl Assn Broadcasters.

DeSonne, Marcia, ed. see Tondro, LaRene, et al.

DeSonne, Marcia L., ed. The Datacasting Business: Future Application, Business Development Strategiest International Market Developments. (Illus.). 100p. 1996. pap. 149.95 (0-89324-239-X, 3818) Natl Assn Broadcasters.

DeSonne, Marcia L., ed. see Chamberlain, David E., et al.

Desotelle, Joanne R., ed. Who's Who: American Law Students, Vol. 15. unabridged ed. 402p. 1996. write for info. (0-614-16496-6) Summa Pub Bur.

— Who's Who among American Law Students. 4th ed. LC 81-645742. 364p. 1984. 35.00 (0-317-19181-0) Summa Pub Bur.

— Who's Who among American Law Students. 5th ed. 366p. 1985. 35.00 (0-317-52484-4) Summa Pub Bur.

— Who's Who among American Law Students. 6th ed. 350p. 1986. 39.95 (0-04-396000-6) Summa Pub Bur.

— Who's Who among American Law Students, 1983. LC 81-645742. 160p. 1982. 30.00 (0-685-05964-2) Summa Pub Bur.

— Who's Who among American Law Students, 1984. 3rd ed. LC 81-645742. 321p. 1983. 35.00 (0-685-08313-6) Summa Pub Bur.

DeSoto, Clinton. Two Hundred Meters & Down. 1985. pap. 8.00 (0-87259-001-1) Am Radio.

DeSoto, Hermine G., ed. Culture & Contradiction: Dialectics of Wealth, Power & Symbol. LC 92-24002. 480p. 1992. pap. text 39.95 (0-7734-1938-1) E Mellen.

Desoto, J. Sex Files 3: Unnatural Blonde. 1997. mass mkt. 6.95 (0-7472-5730-2, Pub. by Headline Bk Pub) Trafalgar.

DeSoto, Richard J. & Bascom, Lionel. Bailout: The Bankrupting of America. Cronin, Christopher, ed. (Illus.). 200p. 1992. 19.95 (0-9634254-0-4) Futura Pr.

DeSourdis, Ron, jt. auth. see Henry, Marilyn.

DeSousa, A., ed. Women in Contemporary India & South Asia. 227p. 1980. 19.95 (0-318-37321-1) Asia Bk Corp.

DeSousa, Luis, et al. Common Medical Abbreviations. LC 94-26241. 288p. (C). 1994. mass mkt. 31.95 (0-8273-6643-4) Delmar.

Desoutter, Denny. The Boat-Owner's Practical Dictionary. (Practical Handbooks for the Yachtsman Ser.). (Illus.). 1978. 14.95 (0-370-30041-6) Transatl Arts.

Desoutter, Nicholas & Kennedy, Jena L. Intro to Life & Health Insurance: Instructor's Kit. (Step One Ser.). 77p. (C). teacher ed., ring bd. 55.00 (1-57974-001-4, Pub. by Life Office) PBD Inc.

Desoutter, Nicholas L. Guide d'Etude Pour le Cours 2: Course 290. (FRE.). 311p. pap., student ed. 22.00 (0-939921-49-9, Pub. by Life Office) PBD Inc.

— Intro to Annuities Instructor's Kit. (Step One Ser.). 57p. ring bd. 55.00 (0-939921-93-6, Pub. by Life Office) PBD Inc.

Desoutter, Nicholas L. & Huggins, Kenneth, eds. Loma's Glossary of Insurance Terms. 3rd ed. 190p. pap. text 16.00 (1-57974-004-9, Pub. by Life Office) PBD Inc.

Desoutter, Nicholas L. & Kennedy, Jena L. Intro to Life & Health Insurance. (Step One Ser.). 94p. spiral bd. 29.95 (1-57974-000-6, Pub. by Life Office) PBD Inc.

Desoutter, Nicholas L., et al. Instructor's Kit for FLMI 371. (FLMI Insurance Education Program Ser.). 184p. ring bd. 200.00 (0-939921-86-3, Pub. by Life Office) PBD Inc.

Desoutter, Nicholas L., ed. see Huggins, Kenneth & Land, Robert D.

Desouttes, Nicholas, et al. Gestion Enfonction de la Soluabilite et de la Rentabilite dans les Compagnies d'Assurances de Personnes. Conant, Susan & Basarich, Joel V., eds. (FLMI Insurance Education Progam Ser.). (FRE.). (C). pap. text 88.00 (0-939921-98-7, Pub. by Life Office) PBD Inc.

Desouza, A., ed. Children in India: Critical Issues in Human Development. 262p. 1979. 24.95 (0-318-36938-9) Asia Bk Corp.

DeSouza, Alfred, ed. The Indian City. 2nd ed. 1983. 16.00 (0-8364-0998-1, Pub. by Manohar) S Asia.

Desouza, Anthony R. & Stutz, Frederick P. Economic Geography. 3rd ed. LC 97-35050. 596p. (C). 1997. 84.00 (0-13-727769-5) P-H.

***DeSouza, Blaise.** Dr. Death. 160p. 2000. pap. 14.00 (0-8059-4789-2) Dorrance.

DeSouza, Patrick J., ed. Economic Strategy & National Security. LC 99-38483. 300p. 2000. 35.00 (0-8133-6834-0) HarpC.

Desowitz, Robert S. The Malaria Capers: Tales of Parasites & People. 288p. 1993. pap. 13.95 (0-393-31008-6) Norton.

— New Guinea Tapeworms & Jewish Grandmothers: Tales of Parasites & People. 224p. 1987. reprint ed. pap. 12.95 (0-393-30426-4) Norton.

***Desowitz, Robert S.** Tropical Diseases: From 50,000 BC to 2500 AD. 256p. 2000. reprint ed. text 30.00 (0-7881-9032-6) DIANE Pub.

Desowitz, Robert S. Who Gave Pinta to Santa Maria? LC 98-15031. 256p. (C). 1998. pap. 13.00 (0-15-600585-9, Harvest Bks) Harcourt.

— Who Gave Pinta to the Santa Maria? Tropical Diseases in a Temperate Climate. LC 96-44741. 256p. 1997. 25.00 (0-393-04084-4) Norton.

D'Espagnat, B. In Search of Reality. Ehlers, A., tr. (Illus.). 210p. 1983. 42.95 (0-387-11399-1) Spr-Verlag.

D'Espagnat, Bernard. Conceptual Foundations of Quantum Mechanics. 2nd ed. (Classics Ser.). (Illus.). 360p. (C). 1989. 43.00 (0-201-09388-X) Addison-Wesley.

— Conceptual Foundations of Quantum Mechanics. 2nd ed. LC 99-60031. 352p. 1999. pap. text 35.00 (0-7382-0104-9, Pub. by Perseus Pubng) HarpC.

— Reality & the Physicist: Knowledge, Duration & the Quantum World. (Illus.). 286p. (C). 1989. pap. text 31.95 (0-521-33846-8) Cambridge U Pr.

Despain, Donald, ed. Yellowstone Vegetation: Consequences of Environment & History in a Natural Setting. 254p. 1991. pap. 14.95 (0-911797-75-0) Roberts Rinehart.

***Despain, J. J.** Pieces from the Past. LC 00-26549. (Illus.). 224p. 2000. pap. 16.95 (1-58017-249-0) Storey Bks.

— A Writer's Guide to Getting Published in Magazines. LC 99-97215. 200p. 2000. pap. 19.95 (1-929129-01-7) Aletheia.

***Despain, Kellene.** A Certain Kind of Treasure. LC 00-90798. 220p. (YA). (gr. 5-9). 2000. 5.95 (0-9679046-0-9) Gray Hse Bks.

Despain, LaRene. Writing: A Workshop Approach. LC 91-33509. 365p. (C). 1992. pap. text 35.95 (0-87484-988-8, 988); pap. text, teacher ed. write for info. (1-55934-024-X, 1024) Mayfield Pub.

DeSpain, Pleasant. The Dancing Turtle: A Folktale from Brazil. LC 97-38866. (Illus.). 32p. (J). (ps-2). 1998. 15.95 (0-87483-502-X) August Hse.

Despain, Pleasant. Eleven Nature Tales: A Multicultural Journey. (Illus.). 1996. pap. text 4.50 (0-87483-458-9) August Hse.

DeSpain, Pleasant. Eleven Turtle Tales: Adventure Tales from Around the World. LC 94-23093. 1994. 12.95 (0-87483-388-4) August Hse.

— The Emerald Lizard: 15 Latin American Tales to Tell in English & Spanish. LC 99-10537. 192p. 1999. pap. 11.95 (0-87483-552-6) August Hse.

— Twenty-Two Splendid Tales, Vol. I. (Illus.). 128p. (J). 1993. pap. 11.95 (0-87483-340-X) August Hse.

— Twenty-Two Splendid Tales, Vol. II. (Illus.). 128p. (J). 1994. pap. 11.95 (0-87483-341-8) August Hse.

DeSpain, Pleasant, reader. Eleven Turtle Tales. (Illus.). (J). 1995. 12.00 incl. audio (0-87483-425-2) August Hse.

DeSpain, Pleasant, retold by. Textbook of Basic Life Support for Healthcare Providers. LC 98-203738. (Illus.). 116p. 1997. pap. text. write for info. (0-87493-615-2) Am Heart.

Despain, Sharon. Christmas Reflections: A True Story. 12p. 1996. pap. text 2.98 (1-57636-033-4) SunRise Pbl.

Despalatovic, Marijan, tr. see Gulyga, Arsenij.

Despande, S. D., tr. see Despande, Vamarao H.

Despande, Vamarao H. Indian Musical Traditions: An Aesthetic Study of the Gharanas in Hindustani Music. Despande, S. D., tr. 222p. (C). 1987. 26.50 (0-86132-144-8, Pub. by Popular Prakashan) S Asia.

Despard. Folk Art - North America. (Illus.). 80p. (J). (gr. 1-6). 1997. pap., teacher ed. 7.95 (1-55799-624-5, 724) Evan-Moor Edu Pubs.

Despard & Supancich. More Than a Report - Celebrations. (More Than a Report Ser.). (Illus.). 80p. (J). (gr. 3-6). 1996. pap., teacher ed. 9.95 (1-55799-574-5, 560) Evan-Moor Edu Pubs.

— More Than a Report - Science. (More Than a Report Ser.). (Illus.). 80p. (J). (gr. 3-6). 1996. pap., teacher ed. 9.95 (1-55799-573-7, 559) Evan-Moor Edu Pubs.

— More Than a Report - Social Studies. (More Than a Report Ser.). (Illus.). 80p. (J). (gr. 3-6). 1996. pap., teacher ed. 9.95 (1-55799-572-9, 558) Evan-Moor Edu Pubs.

Despard, Yvonne, ed. see White, Tekla.

Despautz, Joseph, ed. Automation & Validation of Information in Pharmaceutical Processing. LC 98-21356. (Drugs & the Pharmaceutical Sciences Ser.: 0). (Illus.). 464p. 1998. text 175.00 (0-8247-0119-4) Dekker.

Despax, M. & Rojot, J. Labour Law & Industrial Relations in France. 314p. 1987. pap. 55.00 (90-6544-343-6) Kluwer Law Intl.

DeSpelder, Lynne & Strickland, Albert L. Family Life Education: Resources for the Elementary Classroom. 339p. 1982. 34.95 (0-941816-06-0) ETR Assocs.

Despelder, Lynne A. & Strickland, Albert L. The Last Dance: Encountering Death & Dying. 5th ed. LC 98-3326. 672p. 1998. text 51.95 (0-7674-0217-0, 0217-0) Mayfield Pub.

DeSpelder, Lynne A. & Strickland, Albert L., eds. The Path Ahead: Readings in Death & Dying. 3rd ed. LC 94-30529. 396p. (C). 1995. pap. text 29.95 (1-55934-256-0, 1256) Mayfield Pub.

D'Esperance, E. Shadow Land: Light from the Other Side. 414p. 1996. reprint ed. spiral bd. 24.50 (0-7873-0236-8) Hlth Research.

DesPeres, Josquin. Classical Masterpieces for Bass. 48p. 1997. pap. 19.95 incl. audio compact disk (0-7866-2890-1, 96307BCD) Mel Bay.

— J. S. Bach for Bass. 48p. 1996. pap. 17.95 incl. audio compact disk (0-7866-2843-X, 95254BCD) Mel Bay.

Despierres, G. Alencon Lace. Morgan, Roberta, ed. Orig. Title: Histoire du Point d'Alecon. (Illus.). 180p. 1987. pap. 29.95 (0-08-034512-3, Pub. by Aberdeen U Pr) Macmillan.

DeSpinoza, Benedict. Ethics: Preceded by On the Improvement of Understanding. 336p. 1970. pap. 13.95 (0-02-852650-3) Hafner.

Despins, Cindy R., ed. see Kaopuiki, Stacey S.

Despland, Michael & Vallee, Gerard, eds. Religion in History (La Religion dans L'Histoire) The Word, the Idea, the Reality/Le Mot, l'Idee, la Realite. 336p. (C). 1992. pap. 19.95 (0-88920-211-7) W Laurier U Pr.

Despland, Michel. The Education of Desire: Plato & the Philosophy of Religion. 400p. 1985. pap. text 32.50 (0-8020-6524-4) U of Toronto Pr.

— Reading an Erased Code: Romantic Religion & Literary Aesthetics in France. (Romance Ser.). 223p. 1994. text 45.00 (0-8020-0578-0) U of Toronto Pr.

Desplanques, B., et al, eds. Few-Body Problems in Physics '98: Proceedings of the 16th European Conference on Few-Body Problems in Physics, Autrans, France, June 1-6, 1998. LC 99-22223. 570p. 1999. 139.00 (3-211-83280-7) Spr-Verlag.

Desplanques, B. & Goutte, D., eds. Hadronic Physics with Multi-Gev Electrons. 360p. 1991. text 195.00 (1-56072-008-5) Nova Sci Pubs.

Despommier, D. D. & Karapelou, W. Parasite Life Cycles. (Illus.). 210p. 1987. 79.00 (0-387-96486-X) Spr-Verlag.

Despommier, D. D., et al. Parasitic Diseases. 3rd ed. (Illus.). 348p. 1994. 55.95 (0-387-94223-8) Spr-Verlag.

Despontin, M., et al. Macro-Economic Planning with Conflicting Goals: Proceedings of a Workshop Held at the Vrije Universiteit of Brussels, Beligum, December 10, 1982. (Lecture Notes in Economics & Mathematical Systems Ser.: Vol. 230). vi, 297p. 1984. 41.00 (0-387-13367-4) Spr-Verlag.

Despopoulos, A. & Silbernagl, S. Color Atlas of Physiology. 4th rev. ed. Wieser, Joy, tr. (Flexibook Ser.). (Illus.). 369p. 1991. pap. 29.90 (0-86577-382-3) Thieme Med Pubs.

Desposito, James. The MT-80Z Microcomputer Explained: The First Steps. (Series 871). (Orig.). 1983. pap., student ed. 7.00 (0-8064-0357-8) Bergwall.

Desposito, Joe & Garabedian, Kevin. Complete VCR Troubleshooting & Repair Guide. LC 97-154381. (Illus.). 184p. 1997. pap. 34.95 (0-7906-1102-3) Prompt Publns.

— Computer Monitor Troubleshooting & Repair. LC 97-69163. (Illus.). 308p. (Orig.). 1997. pap. 34.95 (0-7906-1100-7, 61100) Prompt Publns.

— Howard W. Sams Camcorder Troubleshooting & Repair Guide. (Illus.). 240p. 1998. pap. 34.95 (0-7906-1105-8) Prompt Publns.

Desposito, Joseph. Computer Upgrades & Repair, Vol. II. 1995. pap. text 24.80 (0-929321-30-8) WEKA Pub.

— Computer Upgrades & Repairs, Vol. I. 1994. pap. text 24.80 (0-929321-17-0) WEKA Pub.

— Electronics Repair Manual. Williams, Gene B., ed. (Illus.). 900p. 1992. ring bd. 59.95 (0-929321-06-5) WEKA Pub.

— The Modern Electronics Manual: A Practical Reference Manual on Electronics Technology Today. Kanter, Elliott S., ed. (Illus.). 400p. 1988. ring bd. 59.95 (0-929321-02-2, 42000) WEKA Pub.

— Projection TV Troubleshooting & Repair. (Illus.). 336p. 1998. pap. 34.95 (0-7906-1134-1) Prompt Publns.

Despostio, James. Assembly Language with Z80. (Series 872). (Orig.). 1985. pap., student ed. 7.00 (0-8064-0359-4, 872) Bergwall.

Despot, Maggi, tr. see Matura, Thaddbee.

***D'Espouy, Hector, ed.** Greek & Roman Architecture in Classic Illustrations. LC 98-53668. (Illus.). 1999. pap. text 12.95 (0-486-40491-9) Dover.

***Despres, Charles & Chauvel, Daniel.** Future Vision in Knowledge Management. 256p. 2000. pap. 22.50 (0-7506-7247-1) Buttrwrth-Heinemann.

Despres, David, jt. auth. see Adair, John Eric.

Despres, David, jt. ed. see Adair, John Eric.

Despres, Denise. Bright Ideas. (Illus.). 192p. 1998. 35.00 (2-08-013656-9, Pub. by Flammarion) Abbeville Pr.

— Ghostly Sights: Visual Meditation in Late Medieval Literature. LC 89-38444. 165p. 1911. 29.95 (0-937664-81-2) Pilgrim Bks OK.

Despres, Denise L., jt. auth. see Kerby-Fulton, Kathryn.

Despres, Joseph, jt. auth. see Blumenthal, Richard.

Despres, Joseph A. Tech Decisions: The Hottest Tech Prep Careers. 1997. 20.00 (1-878172-48-4, 397TDB, Wintergreen-Orchard) Riverside Pub Co.

Despres, Leo A. Manaus: Social Life & Work in Brazil's Free Trade Zone. LC 90-35150. (SUNY Series in Anthropological Studies of Contemporary Issues). 322p. (C). 1991. pap. text 24.95 (0-7914-0537-0) State U NY Pr.

Despres, Leo A., ed. Ethnicity & Resource Competition in Plural Societies. (World Anthropology Ser.). xii, 222p. 1975. 26.95 (90-279-7539-6) Mouton.

D'Esprit, Jean, jt. auth. see Peniel, Jon.

***d'Esprit, Jurella.** Living with Spirit: Conversations on Life in the New Age. Sewalk, Kathleen M., ed. Blake, Catherine, tr. 96p. 1999. pap. 8.00 (0-941461-11-4) Tunnel Press.

Desproges, Pierre. Dictionnaire Superflu. (FRE.). 1985. 19.95 (0-7859-7624-8, 2020086581) Fr & Eur.

Desputeaux, Helene, jt. auth. see Chartrand, Micheline.

Desputeaux, Helene, jt. auth. see Tregebov, Rhea.

Desquiron, Lilas. Reflections of Loko Miwa. Bodkin, Robin O., tr. from FRE. LC 97-25472. (CARAF Bks.).Tr. of Les Chemins de Loco-Miroir. 232p. 1998. pap. 16.95 (0-8139-1753-0); text 55.00 (0-8139-1752-2) U Pr of Va.

Desramaut, Francis. Don Bosco & the Spiritual Life. Luna, Roger M., tr. from FRE. LC 79-52674. 361p. (Orig.). 1979. pap. 8.95 (0-89944-022-3) Salesiana Pubs.

Desrat, G. Dictionnaire de la Danse Historique, Theorique, Pratique et Bibliographique. (FRE.). vi, 484p. 1977. reprint ed. write for info. (3-487-06327-1) G Olms Pubs.

Desris, Joe. Batman Detective Comics Vol. II: Featuring the Complete Covers of the Second 25 Years. LC 93-22768. (Tiny Folios Ser.). (Illus.). 320p. 1994. pap. 11.95 (1-55859-837-5) Abbeville Pr.

Desris, Joe, intro. Batman in Detective Comics: Featuring the Complete Covers of the First 25 Years. LC 93-22768. (Tiny Folios Ser.). (Illus.). 320p. 1996. pap. 11.95 (1-55859-643-7) Abbeville Pr.

Desroche, Henri. Jacob & the Angel: An Essay in Sociologies of Religion. Savacool, John K., ed. & tr. by. from FRE. LC 72-77575. 196p. 1973. 27.50 (0-87023-109-X) U of Mass Pr.

Desrochers, Alan, tr. see DeRusso, Paul M., et al.

Desrochers, Alan A., ed. Intelligent Robotic Systems for Space Exploration. 368p. (C). 1992. text 139.50 (0-7923-9197-7) Kluwer Academic.

DesRochers, Diane. Walker Between the Worlds. LC 95-3286. (Psi-Fi Ser.). 448p. 1999. mass mkt. 6.99 (1-56718-224-0) Llewellyn Pubns.

Desrochers, M., et al, eds. Computer-Aided Transit Scheduling: Proceedings of the Fifth International Workshop on Computer-Aided Scheduling of Public Transport Held in Montreal, Canada, August 19-23, 1990. LC 92-20795. (Lecture Notes in Economics & Mathematical Systems Ser.: Vol. 386). (Illus.). xiv, 432p. 1992. 78.95 (0-387-55634-6) Spr-Verlag.

Desrochers, P., jt. ed. see Phillips, D.

DesRochers, Rick. Playing Director: A Handbook for the Beginning Director. LC 95-4974. 144p. 1995. pap. 13.95 (0-435-08668-5, 08668) Heinemann.

Desroches-Noblecourt, Christiane. Tutankhamen: Life & Death of a Pharaoh. 312p. 1990. pap. 19.95 (0-14-011665-6, Penguin Bks) Viking Penguin.

An Asterisk (*) at the beginning of an entry indicates that the title is appearing for the first time.

Desroschers, Alan A., jt. auth. see Al-Jaar, Robert Y.

Desrosier, Georges & Boulay, Jacques. Vocabulaire des Assurances Sociales. (FRE.). 21p. 1980. pap. 19.95 (0-8288-9393-4) Fr & Eur.

Desrosiers, G. & Boulay, Jacques. Vocabulaire des Assurances Sociales. (FRE.). 21p. 1971. pap. 9.95 (0-8288-6486-1, M-9231) Fr & Eur.

Desrosiers, J. A. Jacques. Monologue from a Doomed Fetus in Utero & Other Works. LC 97-90183. 69p. 1998. pap. 8.95 (0-533-12316-X) Vantage.

Desrosiers, R. C., jt. ed. see Letvin, N. L.

DesRosiers, Ronald, tr. see Laurentin, Rene.

Desrosiers, Sylvie. Les Cahiers d'Elisabeth. (Novels in the Roman Plus Ser.). (FRE.). 160p. (YA). (gr. 8 up). 1990. pap. 8.95 (2-89021-136-3, Pub. by La Courte Ech) Firefly Bks Ltd.

— Faut-Il Croire A la Magie? (Novels in the Roman Jeunesse Ser.). (FRE.). 96p. (J). (gr. 4-7). 1993. pap. 8.95 (2-89021-201-7, Pub. by La Courte Ech) Firefly Bks Ltd.

— Le Long Silence. (Novels in the Roman Plus Ser.). (FRE., Illus.). 160p. (YA). (gr. 8 up). 1996. pap. 8.95 (2-89021-256-4, Pub. by La Courte Ech) Firefly Bks Ltd.

— Mais Qui Va Trouver le Tresor? (Novels in the Roman Jeunesse Ser.). (FRE.). 96p. (J). (gr. 4-7). 1992. pap. 8.95 (2-89021-175-4, Pub. by La Courte Ech) Firefly Bks Ltd.

— Mefiez-Vous des Monstres Marins. (Novels in the Roman Jeunesse Ser.). (FRE.). 96p. (J). (gr. 4-7). 1991. pap. 8.95 (2-89021-146-0, Pub. by La Courte Ech) Firefly Bks Ltd.

— Le Mystere du Lac Carre. (Novels in the Roman Jeunesse Ser.). (FRE.). 96p. (J). (gr. 4-7). 1988. pap. 8.95 (2-89021-079-0, Pub. by La Courte Ech) Firefly Bks Ltd.

— Ou Sont Passes les Dinosaures? (Novels in the Roman Jeunesse Ser.). (FRE.). 96p. (J). (gr. 4-7). 1990. pap. 7.95 (2-89021-119-3, Pub. by La Courte Ech) Firefly Bks Ltd.

— La Patte Dans le Sac. (Novels in the Roman Jeunesse Ser.). (FRE.). 96p. (J). (gr. 4-7). 1987. pap. 8.95 (2-89021-063-4, Pub. by La Courte Ech) Firefly Bks Ltd.

— Les Princes Ne Sont Pas Tous Charmants. (Novels in the Roman Jeunesse Ser.). (FRE.). 96p. (J). (gr. 4-7). 1995. pap. 8.95 (2-89021-233-5, Pub. by La Courte Ech) Firefly Bks Ltd.

— Quatre Jours de Liberte. (Novels in the Roman Plus Ser.). (FRE., Illus.). 160p. (YA). (gr. 8 up). 1989. pap. 7.95 (2-89021-108-8, Pub. by La Courte Ech) Firefly Bks Ltd.

— Qui a Peur des Fantomes? (Novels in the Roman Jeunesse Ser.). (FRE.). 96p. (J). (gr. 4-7). 1988. pap. 8.95 (2-89021-073-1, Pub. by La Courte Ech) Firefly Bks Ltd.

Desruelle, Paul, jt. auth. see Steudel, Harold J.

Desrves. Explorations in Mathcad for Windows. pap. text 14.36 (0-201-42792-3) Addison-Wesley.

Dess, Gregory G. & Picken, Joseph C. Beyond Productivity: How Leading Companies Achieve Superior Performance by Leveraging Their Human Capital. LC 98-49319. (Illus.). 244p. 1999. 27.95 (0-8144-0435-9) AMACOM.

Dess, Gregory G., jt. auth. see Miller, Alex.

Dess, Gregory G., jt. auth. see Picken, Joseph C.

Dessaigne, Jacques, jt. auth. see Carrere, Jean.

Dessain, Charles S. John Henry Newman. 2nd ed. 189p. 1971. 29.50 (0-8047-0778-2) Stanford U Pr.

Dessain, Charles S., ed. see Newman, John Henry.

Dessaint, Alain Y. Minorities of Southwest China: An Introduction to the Yi (Lolo) & Related Peoples & an Annotated Bibliography. LC 80-80017. (Bibliographies Ser.). 381p. 1980. 25.00 (0-87536-250-8) HRAFP.

Dessaix, Robert. Night Letters: A Journey Through Switzerland & Italy. LC 97-17701. 276p. 1997. text 22.95 (0-312-16950-7, Wyatt Bk) St Martin.

— Night Letters: A Journey Through Switzerland & Italy. LC 98-49197. 276p. 1999. pap. 13.00 (0-312-19939-2, Picador USA) St Martin.

Dessaix, Robert, ed. Anthology of Australian Gay & Lesbian Writing. 392p. 1994. 45.00 (0-19-553457-3) OUP.

Dessaix, Robert, jt. auth. see Daniel, Helen.

Dessaix, Robert, tr. see Dostoyevsky, Fyodor.

Dessart, George, jt. auth. see Baker, William F.

Dessau, Adalbert. La Novela de la Revolucion Mexicana (Novel of the Mexican Revolution) 3rd ed. (SPA.). 478p. 1986. reprint ed. pap. 10.99 (968-16-0542-X, Pub. by Fondo) Continental Bk.

***Dessau, Bruce.** Bean There Done That: The Life & Times of Rowan Atkinson. (Illus.). 112p. 1999. pap. 17.95 (1-56649-068-5) Welcome Rain.

Dessau, Bruce. The Funny Side of Victoria Wood. (Illus.). 112p. 1998. 35.00 (0-7528-1015-4, Pub. by Orion Pubng Grp) Trafalgar.

***Dessau, Bruce.** Rowan Atkinson: A Biography. 278p. 2000. 24.95 (0-7528-0088-4, Pub. by Orion) Trafalgar.

Dessau, Hermann. Geschichte der Romischen Kaiserzeit, 2 vols., Set. LC 75-7316. (Roman History Ser.). 1975. reprint ed. 116.95 (0-405-07197-3) Ayer.

— Geschichte der Romischen Kaiserzeit, 2 vols., Vol. 1. LC 75-7316. (Roman History Ser.). 1975. reprint ed. 58.95 (0-405-07198-1) Ayer.

— Geschichte der Romischen Kaiserzeit, 2 vols., Vol. 2. LC 75-7316. (Roman History Ser.). 1975. reprint ed. 58.95 (0-405-07199-X) Ayer.

Dessau, Hermann, ed. Inscriptiones Latinae Selectae, Vol. I. 580p. 1997. 160.00 (3-296-13601-0) G Olms Pubs.

— Inscriptiones Latinae Selectae, Vol. II, Pars 1. 737p. 1974. 180.00 (3-296-13602-9) G Olms Pubs.

— Inscriptiones Latinae Selectae, Vol. II, Pars 2. 580p. 1974. 180.00 (3-296-13603-7) G Olms Pubs.

— Inscriptiones Latinae Selectae, Vol. III, Pars 1. 600p. 1997. 160.00 (3-296-13604-5) G Olms Pubs.

— Inscriptiones Latinae Selectae, Vol. III, Pars 2. cxcii, 954p. 1997. 140.00 (3-296-13605-3) G Olms Pubs.

***Dessau, Joanna.** Absolute Elizabeth. large type ed. 288p. 2000. 31.99 (0-7089-4166-4) Ulverscroft.

Dessau, Joanna. All or Nothing. large type ed. 320p. 1998. 29.99 (0-7089-3964-3) Ulverscroft.

— The Blacksmith's Daughter. large type ed. (General Ser.). 320p. 1993. 27.99 (0-7089-2908-7) Ulverscroft.

— The Constant Lover. large type ed. 272p. 1996. 27.99 (0-7089-3627-X) Ulverscroft.

— Crown of Sorrows. large type ed. 336p. 1995. 27.99 (0-7089-3362-9) Ulverscroft.

***Dessau, Joanna.** Gloriana. 288p. 2000. 31.99 (0-7089-4228-8) Ulverscroft.

Dessau, Joanna. The Grey Goose. large type ed. 288p. 1992. 27.99 (0-7089-2569-3) Ulverscroft.

— No Way Out. large type ed. 1996. 27.99 (0-7089-3458-7) Ulverscroft.

***Dessau, Joanna.** The Red-Haired Brat. large type ed. 336p. 1999. 31.99 (0-7089-4098-6, Linford) Ulverscroft.

Dessau, Joanna. Take Now, Pay Later. large type ed. (Ulverscroft Large Print Ser.). 272p. 1997. 27.99 (0-7089-3715-2) Ulverscroft.

Dessauce, Marc, ed. The Inflatable Moment: Pneumatics & Protest in '68. LC 98-46587. (Illus.). 144p. 1999. pap. 27.50 (1-56898-176-7) Princeton Arch.

Dessauer, Herbert C. & Hafner, Mark S., eds. Collections of Frozen Tissues: Value, Management, Field & Laboratory Procedures, & Directory of Existing Collections. (Illus.). 74p. (Orig.). 1984. pap. 7.00 (0-942924-10-X) Assn Syst Coll.

Dessauer, John P. Book Publishing: The Basic Introduction. 3rd ed. LC 96-48455. 1993. pap. 19.95 (0-8264-0621-1) Continuum.

Desseauve, jt. auth. see Bettane.

***Desseauve, Thierry.** Book of Wine. (Illus.). 216p. 2000. text 50.00 (2-08-013662-3, Pub. by Flammarion) Abbeville Pr.

Dessein, Bart, jt. auth. see Dharmatreata Staff.

Desselberger, U., ed. Medical Virology: A Practical Approach. (The Practical Approach Ser.: No. 147). (Illus.). 232p. 1995. pap. text 55.00 (0-19-963329-0); spiral bd. 115.00 (0-19-963330-4) OUP.

Desselberger, Ulrich, jt. ed. see Gray, James.

Dessem. Pretrial Litigation in a Nutshell. LC 97-225463. (Paralegal Ser.). (C). 1998. pap. 15.00 (0-314-22438-6) West Pub.

Dessem, Lawrence. Pretrial Litigation: Law Policy & Practice. 2nd ed. LC 95-25323. (Paralegal). 625p. (C). 1996. pap. text 38.50 (0-314-06775-2) West Pub.

— Pretrial Litigation in a Nutshell. LC 92-16019. (Nutshell Ser.). 382p. (C). 1992. pap. text 17.00 (0-314-00844-6) West Pub.

Dessem, R. Lawrence. Pre-Trial Litigation: Law, Policy & Practice. (American Casebook Ser.). 190p. (C). 1991. pap. text, teacher ed. write for info. (0-314-90908-7) West Pub.

— Pre-Trial Litigation: Law, Policy & Practice. (American Casebook Ser.). 608p. 1993. reprint ed. pap. text 35.50 (0-314-81932-0) West Pub.

Dessem, Ralph E. Twentieth Century Worship Services, Vol. III. 1991. pap. 10.75 (1-55673-402-6, 9215) CSS OH.

Dessem, Ralph E., jt. auth. see Tozer, Tom.

Dessemontet, F. Introduction to Swiss Law. LC 95-9327. 1995. lib. bdg. 121.00 (90-6544-858-6) Kluwer Academic.

Dessemontet, F. & Ansay, Tugrul, eds. Introduction to Swiss Law. 1995. write for info. (90-6544-856-X) Kluwer Law Intl.

***Dessemontet, Francois.** Intellctual Property Law in Switzerland. 212p. 2000. pap. 43.00 (90-411-1361-4) Kluwer Law Intl.

Dessemontet, Francois. Legal Protection of Know-How in the United States of America. 2nd ed. Clarke, H. W., tr. from FRE. (Studies in Researches of the Institute of Comparative Law, Faculty of Law of the University of Lausanne). 487p. 1976. reprint ed. pap. 30.00 (0-8377-0504-5, Rothman) W S Hein.

Dessen, Alan C. Jonson's Moral Comedy. LC 76-126900. 266p. (C). reprint ed. pap. 82.50 (0-8357-9461-X, 201477800093) Bks Demand.

— Recovering Shakespeare's Theatrical Vocabulary. 297p. (C). 1995. text 59.95 (0-521-47080-3) Cambridge U Pr.

— Shakespeare & the Late Moral Plays. LC 85-8625. 208p. 1986. reprint ed. pap. 64.50 (0-7837-9008-2, 204957100001) Bks Demand.

***Dessen, Alan C. & Thomson, Leslie.** A Dictionary of Stage Directions in English Drama, 1580-1642. LC 98-44871. 266p. (C). 1999. 69.95 (0-521-55250-8) Cambridge U Pr.

Dessen, Alan C., jt. ed. see Schoenbaum, S.

Dessen, Andrea & Zerio, John, trs. from POR. Nosso Lar - A Spiritual Home. pap. 10.00 (0-9649907-1-7) A Kardec Educ.

Dessen, C. The Satires of Persius. (Bristol Classical Paperbacks Ser.). 128p. (Orig.). 1996. pap. text 20.95 (1-85399-487-1, Pub. by Brist Class Pr) Focus Pub-R Pullins.

Dessen, Cynthia S. & Abricka, Maria V. Lexitect. (C). 1988. teacher ed. 32.50 incl. disk (0-15-550626-9, Pub. by Harcourt Coll Pubs) Harcourt.

***Dessen, Sarah.** Dreamland. LC 99-44102. (Illus.). 280p. (J). (gr. 7 up). 2000. 15.99 (0-670-89122-3, Viking Child) Peng Put Young Read.

— Keeping the Moon. (Illus.). 256p. (J). (gr. 7 up). 2000. pap. 4.99 (0-14-131007-3, PuffinBks) Peng Put Young Read.

Dessen, Sarah. Keeping the Moon. LC 99-19597. (Illus.). 224p. (J). (gr. 7-12). 1999. 15.99 (0-670-88549-5, Viking) Viking Penguin.

***Dessen, Sarah.** Someone Like You. (Illus.). 288p. (J). (gr. 7-12). 2000. pap. 4.99 (0-14-130269-0, PuffinBks) Peng Put Young Read.

Dessen, Sarah. Someone Like You. LC 97-36437. 272p. (J). (gr. 7-12). 1998. 16.99 (0-670-87778-6) Viking Penguin.

— That Summer. LC 96-7643. 208p. (YA). (gr. 7 up). 1996. 16.95 (0-531-09538-X); lib. bdg. 17.99 (0-531-08888-X) Orchard Bks Watts.

***Dessen, Sarah.** That Summer. LC 97-50534. (Illus.). 208p. (J). (gr. 5-9). 1998. pap. 4.99 (0-14-038688-2, PuffinBks) Peng Put Young Read.

Dessen, Sarah. That Summer. (J). 1998. 10.09 (0-606-13842-0, Pub. by Turtleback) Demco.

Dessent, Tony. Making the Ordinary Schools Special. 192p. 1987. pap. 34.95 (1-85000-236-3, Falmer Pr) Taylor & Francis.

Desser, David. Eros Plus Massacre: An Introduction to the Japanese New Wave Cinema. LC 87-45245. (Illus.). 250p. 1988. 42.00 (0-253-31961-7); pap. 5.25 (0-253-20469-0, MB-469) Ind U Pr.

— Eros Plus Massacre: An Introduction to the Japanese New Wave Cinema. LC 87-45245. (Midland Bks.). (Illus.). 247p. Date not set. reprint ed. pap. 76.60 (0-608-20537-0, 205445100002) Bks Demand

— The Samurai Films of Akira Kurosawa. LC 83-15563. (Studies in Cinema: No. 23). 172p. reprint ed. pap. 53.40 (0-8357-1495-0, 207063300011) Bks Demand.

Desser, David, ed. Ozu's "Tokyo Story" LC 96-46113. (Cambridge Film Handbooks Ser.). (Illus.). 208p. (C). 1997. text 49.95 (0-521-48204-6); pap. text 13.95 (0-521-48435-9) Cambridge U Pr.

Desser, David & Friedman, Lester D. American-Jewish Filmmakers: Traditions & Trends. LC 92-39669. 336p. (C). 1993. text 44.95 (0-252-01564-9); pap. text 16.95 (0-252-06301-5) U of Ill Pr.

***Desser, David & Jowett, Garth.** Hollywood Goes Shopping. LC 99-56290. (Commerce & Mass Culture Ser.). 2000. pap. 19.95 (0-8166-3513-7) U of Minn Pr.

Desser, David, jt. ed. see Ehrlich, Linda C.

Desser, David, jt. ed. see Fu, Poshek.

Desser, David, jt. ed. see Nolletti, Arthur, Jr.

Desser, David, jt. ed. see Studlar, Gaylyn.

Desser, Robin, ed. see De Bernieres, Louis.

Dessewffy, Gyula & Kovacs, Zoltan. Mi Sem Volunk Rosszabbak Masoknal Es Pillanatfelvetel a Mai Magyarorszagrol, 1985. LC 86-51435. 121p. (Orig.). pap. write for info. (0-935484-15-9) Universe Pub Co.

Dessing, Maryke. Support for Microenterprises: Lessons for Sub-Saharan Africa. (Technical Papers: No. 122). 84p. 1990. pap. 22.00 (0-8213-1553-6, 11553) World Bank.

Dessing, R. P., jt. auth. see Muller, N. F.

Dessinov, Lev V., jt. auth. see Lulla, Kamlesh.

Dessler. Essential Human Resource Management. LC 98-45633. 298p. 1998. pap. text 49.33 (0-13-080329-4) P-H.

— Management: Leading People & Organizations in the 21st Century D-CART. 1999. 76.00 (0-13-011086-8) P-H.

— Managing Organizations. LC 94-69149. (C). 1994. text 87.50 (0-03-096612-4) Harcourt Coll Pubs.

***Dessler & Starke.** Management: Leading & Organizing in the 21st Century. 2000. 113.27 (0-13-016348-1) Prntice Hall Bks.

Dessler, A. J., jt. ed. see Birmingham, T. J.

Dessler, E. E. Strive for the Truth Vol. 1: The World of Rav E. E. Dessler. Carmell, Aryeh, tr. from HEB. Tr. of Michtav M'Eliyahu. 1978. 18.95 (0-87306-139-X) Feldheim.

Dessler, Eliyahu. Strive for Truth, Vol. 2. 1985. 18.95 (0-87306-395-3) Feldheim.

***Dessler, Gary.** Essentials of Management. LC 98-54951. (Illus.). 1999. 50.67 (0-13-012770-1) P-H.

Dessler, Gary. Human Resource Management. 8th ed. LC 99-11243. 699p. 1999. 96.00 (0-13-014124-0) P-H.

— Management: Leading People & Organizations in the 21st Century. LC 97-32116. 703p. (C). 1997. 96.00 (0-13-862970-6) P-H.

***Dessler, Gary.** Management: Leading People & Organizations in the 21st Century. 2nd ed. 608p. 2000. 86.67 (0-13-017780-6, Prentice Hall) P-H.

Dessler, Gary. Organization & Management: A Contingency Approach. (Illus.). 1976. 22.95 (0-685-03884-X) P-H.

— Personnel Management. 4th ed. (Illus.). 704p. (C). 1988. text. write for info. (0-318-62356-0) P-H.

Dessler, N. W., contrib. by. Suggested Hebrew Studies Curriculum for the Day School. (HEB.). 1997. pap. 12.00 (0-914131-63-X, C010) Torah Umesorah.

Dessler, Rabbi E. Strive for Truth, Vol. 3. Carmel. Aryeh, tr. from HEB. 1989. 18.95 (0-87306-519-0) Feldheim.

Dessouki, Ali E., jt. ed. see Cudsi, Alexander S.

Dessouki, Ali E. Hillal. Islamic Resurgence in the Arab World. LC 81-12135. 274p. 1982. 42.95 (0-275-90781-3, C0781, Praeger Pubs) Greenwood.

Dessureault, Pierre. Travel Journals: Carnets de Voyage. 95p. 1995. 32.95 (0-88884-569-3) U Ch Pr.

Dessureault, Pierre, ed. Serge Tousignant: Phases Through Photography. (Illus.). 84p. (C). 1993. pap. 35.00 (0-88884-561-8, Pub. by CN Mus Contemporary Photo) U Ch Pr.

Dessy, Raymond E. The Electronic Laboratory: Tutorials & Case Histories in Laboratory Automation. LC 85-15111. (Illus.). 167p. reprint ed. pap. 51.80 (0-7837-1968-X, 205244600001) Bks Demand.

Dessy, Raymond E., et al, eds. Chemical Sensors & Microinstrumentation. LC 89-15149. (Symposium Ser.: No. 403). (Illus.). 395p. 1989. 89.95 (0-8412-1661-4) Am Chemical.

Dessy, Steve, jt. auth. see Sutton, Joe.

Dessypris, Emmanuel N. Pure Red Cell Aplasia. LC 87-27378. (Johns Hopkins Series in Contemporary Medicine & Public Health). (Illus.). 176p. 1988. reprint ed. pap. 54.60 (0-608-05949-8, 206628600008) Bks Demand.

Desta, Asayehgn. Environmentally Sustainable Economic Development. LC 99-31366. 256p. 1999. pap. 27.95 (0-275-96628-3, C5741, Praeger Pubs) Greenwood.

***Desta, Asayehgn.** Environmentally Sustainable Economic Development. LC 98-31366. 256p. 1999. 65.00 (0-275-95741-1, C5741, Praeger Pubs) Greenwood.

Desta, Ketema. Aleka. 144p. 10.95 (0-9642068-0-3) Nyala Pubng.

D'Estaing, Charles-Henri. Rozenie ou Les Moscovites. LC 93-73005. 154p. 1994. 25.50 (0-88033-280-8, 383, Pub. by East Eur Monographs) Col U Pr.

D'Estaing, Valery G., et al. East-West Relations. (Triangle Papers: Vol. 36). 1989. 6.00 (0-930503-06-6) Trilateral Comm.

Destang, Francoise, jt. auth. see Paschos, Jacqueline.

Destani, Beitullah, ed. Albania & Kosovo: Political & Ethnic Boundaries, 1867-1946, Documents & Maps, 2 vols. (Illus.). 650p. 1999. reprint ed. lib. bdg. 595.00 (1-85207-910-X, Pub. by Archive Editions) N Ross.

D'Este. Eisenhower: The War Years. Date not set. 35.00 (0-8050-5686-6); pap. 17.95 (0-8050-5687-4, Owl) H Holt & Co.

D'Este, Carlo. Decision in Normandy: Fiftieth Anniversary Edition. (Illus.). 576p. (Orig.). 1994. pap. 17.50 (0-06-092495-0, Perennial) HarperTrade.

— Patton: A Genius for War. 1996. 35.00 (0-614-12874-9) HarpC.

Deste, Carlo. Patton: A Genius for War. LC 95-38433. 1024p. 1996. pap. 20.00 (0-06-092762-3) HarpC.

D'Este, Carlo. World War II in the Mediterranean, 1942-1945. (Major Battles & Campaigns Ser.: Vol. II). 272p. 1990. 22.95 (0-945575-04-1) Algonquin Bks.

Destefano, Anthony. Gloria Estefan. 1999. pap. 22.95 (0-525-94377-3) NAL.

DeStefano, Josephine, ed. see D'Amato, James J.

DeStefano, Mike. Bada Bing Bada Buddha: Deep Thoughts from the Bronx. deluxe ed. Huston, River, ed. (Illus.). 150p. 1999. pap. 10.00 (0-9673038-0-X) Laugh & Learn Pubng.

***DeStefano, Paul.** Necessary Evil. 2000. 22.00 (0-8059-4982-8) Dorrance.

DeStefano, Sal. The Methuselah Gene: A Science Fiction Adventure Thriller. LC 99-34321. (New Millennium Writers Ser.). 340p. 2000. 24.95 (1-891696-10-6) BainBridgeBooks.

DeStefano, Susan. Chico Mendes: Fight for the Forest. (Earth Keepers Ser.). (Illus.). 76p. (J). (gr. 4-7). 1995. lib. bdg. 14.95 (0-8050-2887-0) TFC Bks NY.

Destefano, Susan. Theodore Roosevelt: Conservation, Vol. 1. (J). 1995. 14.98 (0-8050-2788-2) H Holt & Co.

Desteian, John. Coming Together - Coming Apart: The Union of Opposites in Love Relationships. 184p. 1989. pap. 14.95 (0-938434-44-6) Sigo Pr.

DeSteiguer, J. Edward. The Age of Enviornmentalism. (Illus.). 224p. (C). 1996. pap. 31.25 (0-07-060841-5) McGraw.

DeStephano, Mary, jt. auth. see Justice, Maria D.

Destexhe, Alain. Rwanda & Genocide in the Twentieth Century. Marschner, Alison, tr. 140p. (C). 1995. text 21.00 (0-8147-1873-6) NYU Pr.

Desti-Demanti, Zoe. Early American Women Dramatists, 1780-1860. LC 98-45560. 240p. 1998. 56.00 (0-8153-3304-8) Garland.

Desti, Mary. The Untold Story: The Life of Isadora Duncan, 1921-1927. LC 80-26739. (Series in Dance). (Illus.). 281p. 1981. reprint ed. lib. bdg. 35.00 (0-306-76044-4) Da Capo.

Destiny, David. Holistic Health Resource Directory of New Jersey & Pennsylvania. 7th ed. 160p. 1997. pap. 9.95 (0-9651767-1-1) Hlistic Hlth Assn.

Destiny Image Staff, ed. see Wilke, Lori.

Destiny Images Staff, jt. auth. see Arnott, John.

***Destiny, Vanessa.** I Love My Mummy & I Love My Daddy Too: A Child's Plead for Love & Protection (Listen to Your Baby) large type ed. LC 99-76490. 24p. (J). 1999. per. 5.99 (0-9665098-2-X) Universal Express.

— Let's Talk about Love, Marriage & Family Life. LC 99-93954. 106p. 1999. per. 10.00 (0-9665098-1-1) Universal Express.

Destiny, Vanessa. Why Do Men Look at Other Women & Fantasize about Sex? The Reality of Men & Women in Relationships. LC 98-90393. 96p. 1999. pap. 5.99 (0-9665098-0-3) Universal Express.

Destler, Chester M. American Radicalism, 1865-1901, Essays & Documents. (History - United States Ser.). 276p. 1993. reprint ed. lib. bdg. 79.00 (0-7812-4905-8) Rprt Serv.

— Roger Sherman & the Independent Oil Men. fac. ed. LC 67-13466. 317p. 1967. reprint ed. pap. 98.30 (0-608-01013-8, 206187100012) Bks Demand.

***Destler, I. M.** American Trade Politics & Supplement, 2 vols. Incl. American Trade Politics. 3rd ed. LC 94-44644. 337p. (C). 1995. pap. text 19.95 (0-88132-215-6); New Politics of U. S. Trade Policy. Balint, Peter J. LC 99-52383. 100p. 1999. pap. 15.95 (0-88132-269-5); 2000. Set pap. 25.00 (0-88132-292-X) Inst Intl Eco.

Destler, I. M. Making Foreign Economic Policy. LC 79-5119. 244p. 1980. 34.95 (0-8157-1822-5); pap. 14.95 (0-8157-1821-7) Brookings.

— National Economic Council: A Work in Progress. LC 96-46215. (Policy Analysis in International Economics Ser.: No. 46). (Illus.). 75p. 1996. pap. 11.95 (0-88132-239-3) Inst Intl Eco.

— Renewing Fast-Track Legislation. LC 97-39550. (Policy Analyses in International Economics Ser.: No. 50). 1997. pap. 11.95 (0-88132-252-0) Inst Intl Eco.

D

Destler, I. M. & Henning, C. Randall. Dollar Politics: Exchange Rate Policymaking in the U. S. LC 89-19972. (Illus.). 192p. 1989. pap. 59.60 (*0-7837-8347-7*, 204913600010) Bks Demand.

Destler, I. M. & Kull, Steven. Misreading the Public. LC 98-40102. 1998. 44.95 (*0-8157-1766-0*) Brookings.

— Misreading the Public. LC 98-40102. xiv, 312p. 1999. pap. 18.95 (*0-8157-1765-2*) Brookings.

Destler, I. M. & Schott, Jeffrey J. Restarting Fast Track. LC 98-3097. (Special Report Ser.: No. 11). 1998. 16.95 (*0-88132-259-8*) Inst Intl Eco.

Destler, I. M., et al. Managing an Alliance: The Politics of U. S. - Japanese Relations. LC 75-44501. 224p. 1976. 32.95 (*0-8157-1820-9*); pap. 12.95 (*0-8157-1819-5*) Brookings.

— Managing an Alliance: The Politics of U. S. - Japanese Relations. LC 75-44501. 219p. reprint ed. pap. 67.90 (*0-608-17499-8*, 203000600067) Bks Demand.

— The Textile Wrangle: Conflict in Japanese - American Relations, 1969-1971. LC 78-14429. 397p. reprint ed. pap. 123.10 (*0-608-08090-X*, 206904900002) Bks Demand.

Destler, I. M., jt. ed. see Yankelovich, Daniel.

Destler, Paul A., ed. Ethics & the Professions. LC 93-34564. (President's Symposium Ser.: Vol. 4). 1993. write for info. (*0-929900-08-1*) VPI St Univ Pr.

Destler, William W., et al. High Brightness Beams for Advanced Accelerator Applications. LC 92-52705. (AIP Conference Proceedings Particle & Fields Series 47: No. 253). (Illus.). 256p. 1992. lib. bdg. 90.00 (*0-88318-947-X*) Am Inst Physics.

Destouches, J. L., ed. see Beth Memorial Colloquium Staff.

Destrade, C., ed. Proceedings of 1st International Symposium on Ferroelectric Liquid Crystals. 900p. 1988. pap. text 1500.00 (*2-88124-304-5*) Gordon & Breach.

Destree, Sabine, tr. see Lhomeau, Franck & Coelho, Alain.

Destree, Thomas M., ed. Lithographers Manual. 9th rev. ed. LC 93-78999. (Illus.). 426p. (C). 1994. text 75.00 (*0-88362-169-X*, 1407) GATFPress.

Destree, Thomas M., jt. auth. see DeJidas, Lloyd P.

Destriau, M., jt. auth. see Borghi, R. P.

Destro, Robert A., jt. auth. see Ariens, Michael S.

Destroyer Escort Sailors Association Staff. Destroyer Escort Sailors Association: Trim but Deadly, Vol. I. LC 86-51635. 352p. 1987. 52.50 (*0-938021-10-9*) Turner Pub KY.

— Destroyer Escort Sailors Association: Trim but Deadly, Vol. II. LC 86-51635. 252p. 1989. 49.95 (*0-938021-49-4*) Turner Pub KY.

— Destroyer Escort Sailors Association: Trim but Deadly, Vol. III. LC 86-51635. (Illus.). 208p. 1992. 44.95 (*1-56311-052-0*) Turner Pub KY.

DeStrulle, Arlene & Johnson, Tora. Guide to Freshwater Animals Without Backbones. (Illus.). (Orig.). (J). (gr. 4-6). Date not set. pap. text 10.95 (*0-9616712-6-2*) Catskill Ctr.

Destuynder, P. & Salaun, M. Mathematical Analysis of Thin Plate Models, Vol. 24. Ghidaglia, Jean-Michel & Lascaux, P., eds. LC 96-201278. (Mathematics & Its Applications Ser.). viii, 238p. 1996. pap. 59.95 (*3-540-61167-3*) Spr-Verlag.

Desu, S. B., et al, eds. Ferroelectric Thin Films V. (MRS Symposium Proceedings Ser.: Vol. 433). 449p. 1996. 73.00 (*1-55899-336-3*, 433) Materials Res.

Desu, S. B., et al, eds. Metal-Organic Chemical Vapor Deposition of Electronic Ceramics Vol. 335: Materials Research Society Symposium Proceedings. LC 94-5807. 365p. 1994. text 30.00 (*1-55899-234-0*) Materials Res.

Desu, Seshu B., et al, eds. Metal-Organic Chemical Vapor Deposition of Electronic Ceramics II: Materials Research Society Symposium Proceedings. (MRS Symposium Proceedings Ser.: Vol. 415). 264p. 1996. 75.00 (*1-55899-318-5*) Materials Res.

DeSumichrast, F. C., tr. see Gautier, Theophile.

Desurvire, Emmanuel. Erbium-Doped Fiber Amplifiers: Principles & Applications. 800p. 1994. 165.00 (*0-471-58977-2*) Wiley.

Desutter, Paula A. Denial & Jeopardy: Deterring Iranian Use of NBC Weapons. LC 97-38081. 1997. write for info. (*1-57906-003-X*) Natl Defense.

Desveaux, James A. Designing Bureaucracies: Institutional Capacity & Large-Scale Problem Solving. LC 94-11685. xx, 252p. 1995. 35.00 (*0-8047-2281-1*) Stanford U Pr.

Desvergne, J. P., et al. Chemosensors of Ion & Molecule Recognition. LC 97-10635. (NATO ASI Series. Mathematical & Physical Sciences: Series C). 1997. text 130.50 (*0-7923-4555-X*) Kluwer Academic.

Desvergnes, Alain. Yoknapatawpha: The Land of William Faulkner. 1993. pap. text 21.95 (*2-86234-041-3*, Pub. by Marval) Dist Art Pubs.

Desvigne, Michel & Dalnoky, Christine. Desvigne & Dalnoky. (Illus.). 96p. 1997. pap. 29.95 (*0-8230-1348-0*, Whitney Lib) Watsn-Guptill.

Desvignes-Parent. Marivaux et l'Angleterre: Essai sur une Creation Dramatique Originale. 52.50 (*0-685-34043-0*) Fr & Eur.

DeSwaan, Constance, jt. auth. see Lauersen, Niels H.

Deswarte, Y., et al, eds. Computer Security - ESORICS '92: Second European Symposium on Research in Computer Security, Toulouse, France, November 23-25, 1992 Proceedings. (Lecture Notes in Computer Science Ser.: Vol. 648). xi, 451p. 1992. 69.95 (*0-387-56246-X*) Spr-Verlag.

Deswarte, Y., ed. see Quisquater, J. J.

Desy, Jeanne, et al. Assessing Learning Time at the Co-op Training Station. 58p. 1985. 6.25 (*0-318-17849-4*, SN 50) Ctr Educ Trng Employ.

— High School Vocational Education Experiences: In School & in the Labor Market. 64p. 1984. 7.95 (*0-318-22115-2*, RD244) Ctr Educ Trng Employ.

— The Long-Term Effects of Vocational Education: Earnings, Employment, Education, & Aspirations. 41p. 1984. 4.25 (*0-318-22146-2*, RD246) Ctr Educ Trng Employ.

Desy, Jeanne, jt. auth. see Halasz, Ida M.

Desy, Peter. Driving from Columbus: Poems. LC 91-34457. (Lewiston Poetry Ser.: Vol. 19). 68p. 1992. pap. 14.95 (*0-7734-9617-3*) E Mellen.

***Desypris, Yiannis.** 777 Greek Islands. (Illus.). 1999. pap. text 16.95 (*960-540-122-3*) M Toumpis.

Deszo, Laszlo. Contrastive Studies. 122p. 1982. 30.00 (*0-569-08714-7*, Pub. by Collets) St Mut.

***deTagle, Lillian Lorca.** Honorable Exiles: A Chilean Woman in the Twentieth Century. Billington, Joy & Lucas, Chris, eds. (Illus.). 232p. 2000. 35.00 (*0-292-71606-0*); pap. 16.95 (*0-292-71609-5*) U of Tex Pr.

Detaille, Edouard. L'Armee Francaise: An Illustrated History of the French Army 1790-1885. Reinertsen, Maureen C., tr. from FRE. LC 92-60331. (Illus.). 354p. 1992. reprint ed. 49.95 (*0-9632558-0-0*) Howell Pr VA.

Detaille, Edouard. L'Armee Francaise: An Illustrated History of the French Army, 1790-1885. Reinertsen, Maureen Carlson, tr. 354p. 1997. 160.00 (*1-86227-000-7*, Pub. by Spellmnt Pubs) St Mut.

Detaille, Georges. Les Ballets de Monte-Carlo. lib. bdg. 24.95 (*0-8288-2635-8*) Fr & Eur.

Detaille, Georges & Mulys. Les Ballets de Monte Carlo, 1911-44. (FRE., Illus.). 269p. 1954. lib. bdg. 24.95 (*0-8288-3935-2*) Fr & Eur.

Detambel, Daniel. Verkundigung Durch das Fernsehen. (Illus.). XVII, 306p. 1998. 51.95 (*3-631-32949-0*) P Lang Pubng.

DeTar, C., jt. ed. see Ball, J.

DeTar, Delos F., ed. Molecular Mechanics: A Symposium. LC 77-14614. 1978. pap. 40.00 (*0-08-022070-3*, Pergamon Pr) Elsevier.

Detay, Michel. Water Wells: Implementation, Maintenance & Restoration. 394p. 1997. pap. 75.00 (*0-471-96695-9*) Wiley.

Detchon, Jack. The Flat Back Four . . . And All That Stuff. Dunn, Bob, ed. (Illus.). (Orig.). 1996. pap. 9.95 (*1-896466-11-7*) World of Soccer.

***Detective Shadow.** Lateral Mindtrap Puzzles. 2000. pap. 6.95 (*0-8069-7135-5*) Sterling.

— Tricky Mindtrap Puzzles. 2000. pap. 6.95 (*0-8069-4488-9*) Sterling.

Detel, Wolfgang. Scientia Rerum Natura Occultarum Methodologische Studien Zur Physik Pierre Gassendis. (Quellen und Studien zur Philosophie: Vol. 14). (C). 1978. 100.00 (*3-11-007320-X*) De Gruyter.

***DeTellis, George.** A Leaf in the Wind: I Say, "Yes Lord" Even When I Want to Say, No." 150p. 2000. pap. write for info. (*0-9653234-3-9*) New Missions.

DeTellis, George, Jr. Mending & Washing Your Nets: Fishing Lessons from the Disciples. 124p. 1998. pap. 9.95 (*0-9653234-1-2*) New Missions.

DeTellis, Jeanne & Meloche, Renee. A Stubborn Hope: Without Disappointment. 244p. (Orig.). 1996. pap. write for info. (*0-9653234-0-4*) New Missions.

Detels, Claire. Music in the Western Tradition. LC 99-178818. 76p. 1997. pap. text 7.95 (*0-7674-0015-1*); pap. text 7.95 (*0-7674-0073-9*) Mayfield Pub.

— Soft Boundaries: Re-Visioning the Arts & Aesthetics in American Education. LC 99-14844. 200p. 1999. 57.95 (*0-89789-666-1*, H666, Bergin & Garvey) Greenwood.

Detels, P., ed. see Thomas, Deborah & Clauser, Suzanne S.

Detels, Pamela & Harris, Janet. Canoeing: Trips in Connecticut. (Illus.). 1977. pap. 3.95 (*0-931964-03-2*) Birch Run Pub.

— Inside the Breakwater: A Guide to Coastal Conn. 1979. pap. 6.95 (*0-931964-02-4*) Birch Run Pub.

Detemple, jt. auth. see Long.

Detemple, jt. auth. see Long, Calvin T.

DeTemple, Donald D. Three Robeson Township Cemeteries. LC 95-206844. 223p. 1995. per. 21.95 (*1-55856-188-9*, 057) Closson Pr.

DeTemple, Duane, jt. auth. see Long, Calvin T.

DeTemple, Duane W., jt. auth. see Long, Calvin T.

Deter, Arthur. Forty Years in the Land of Tomorrow, 1901-1940: American Autobiography. 207p. 1995. lib. bdg. 79.00 (*0-7812-8498-8*) Rprt Serv.

Deter, Dianalee, jt. auth. see Athan, Mattie S.

***DeTeran, Lisa St. Aubin.** The Palace. 2000. pap. 13.00 (*0-06-095653-4*, Ecco Press) HarperTrade.

Deterding, Curtis, jt. auth. see Bickel, Philip.

Deterding, David, tr. see Bo Yang.

Deterding, David, tr. see Yang, Bo.

Deterding, Henri. An International Oilman, As Told to Stanley Naylor. Wilkins, Mira, ed. LC 76-29771. (European Business Ser.). 1977. reprint ed. lib. bdg. 17.95 (*0-405-09784-2*) Ayer.

Deterding, Paul E. Echoes of Pauline Concepts in the Speech at Antioch. (Concordia Student Journal Monographs: No. 1). (Illus.). 50p. (Orig.). 1980. pap. 2.50 (*0-911770-51-8*) Concordia Seminary.

Detering, Georgia. Out of a Wilderness. 91p. 1989. reprint ed. pap. 10.00 (*0-685-30402-7*) Fernwood Pr.

Detering, Hermann. Paulusbriefe Ohne Paulus? Die Paulusbriefe in der Hollandischen Radikalkritik. (Kontexte Ser.: Bd. 10). (GER.). XVII, 535p. 1992. 81.80 (*3-631-44787-6*) P Lang Pubng.

Detering, Julia R. Bringing Out Baby: Seattle & the Eastside. LC 99-40753. 1999. pap. 12.95 (*1-881409-50-3*) Jhnstn Assocs.

Determined Productions. Pet Snoopy. (Illus.). (J). (ps). 1983. pap. 4.95 (*0-915696-72-X*) Determined Prods.

***Deters, Lisa.** Better Phonics for Reading in 5 Minutes a Day: Phonics Fun for Kids & Parents on the Run. (Five Minutes a Day Ser.). (Illus.). 144p. (J). 2000. pap. 9.99 (*0-7615-2428-2*) Prima Pub.

Deth, Jan W. Van, see Van Deth, Jan W., ed.

Deth, Ron Van, see Vandereycken, Walter & Van Deth, Ron.

Dethefsen, Thorwald. Healing Power of Illness: The Meaning of Symptoms & How to Interpret. 160p. 1997. pap. 15.95 (*1-86204-080-X*, Pub. by Element MA) Penguin Putnam.

Detheridge, Mike, jt. auth. see Detheridge, Tina.

Detheridge, Tina & Detheridge, Mike. Literacy Through Symbols: Improving Access for Children & Adults. LC 97-197225. 144p. 1997. pap. 24.95 (*1-85346-483-X*, Pub. by David Fulton) Taylor & Francis.

Dethero, J. H. Exporting Guide for California. 140p. 1993. pap. text 17.50 (*1-878630-44-X*) CA Chamber Commerce.

***Dethier, Bernard E. & Dethier, Merrily M.** Eagle Island. LC 99-97492. 2000. 21.50 (*0-533-13404-8*) Vantage.

***Dethier, Brock.** The Composition Instructor's Survival Guide. LC 99-15380. 1999. 16.00 (*0-86709-489-3*, Pub. by Boynton Cook Pubs) Heinemann.

Dethier, David P., jt. ed. see Colman, Steven M.

Dethier, Jean-Jacques, jt. ed. see Bokros, Lajos.

Dethier, Merrily M., jt. auth. see Dethier, Bernard E.

Dethier, V. G. The Ant Heap. LC 79-52701. (Illus.). 151p. 1979. 7.95 (*0-87850-034-0*) Darwin Pr.

Dethier, Vincent G. Crickets & Katydids, Concerts & Solos. (Illus.). 144p. 1992. text 18.95 (*0-674-17577-8*) HUP.

— The Hungry Fly: A Physiological Study of the Behavior Associated with Feeding. (Commonwealth Fund Publications). (Illus.). 512p. 1976. 55.50 (*0-674-42710-6*) HUP.

— Man's Plague? Insects & Agriculture. LC 75-15216. 245p. 1976. reprint ed. pap. 76.00 (*0-608-01041-3*, 205254700001) Bks Demand.

— To Know a Fly. (C). 1988. text 18.00 (*0-07-016574-2*) McGraw.

Dethier, Vincent G. The World of the Tent-Makers: A Natural History of the Eastern Tent Caterpillar. LC 80-11361. (Illus.). 160p. 1980. pap. 15.95 (*0-87023-301-7*) U of Mass Pr.

Dethlefsen, L. A., ed. Cell Cycle Effects of Drugs. (International Encyclopedia of Pharmacology & Therapeutics Ser.: Section 121). (Illus.). 351p. 1986. 228.50 (*0-08-032015-5*, Pub. by PPL) Elsevier.

Dethlefsen, Merle & Canfield, James D. Transition from Military to Civilian Life: How to Plan a Bright Future Now for You & Your Family. LC 84-10536. (Illus.). 256p. (Orig.). 1984. reprint ed. pap. 79.40 (*0-608-00472-3*, 206129100007) Bks Demand.

Dethlefsen, Thorwald. Enfermedad Como Camino. 1998. pap. 8.50 (*84-01-52028-2*) Lectorum Pubns.

Dethlefson, Ronald, ed. Edison Blue Amberol Recordings, 1915-1929. (Illus.). 512p. 1981. 175.00 (*0-937612-01-4*) A P M Pr.

— Edison Disc Records: Preliminary List - May, 1913. (Illus.). 16p. (Orig.). 1990. pap. 5.95 (*0-937612-11-1*) A P M Pr.

Dethloff, Diana, ed. Drawing: Masters & Methods: Raphael to Redon. (Illus.). 224p. 1992. 75.00 (*0-8109-3208-3*) Abrams.

Dethloff, Henry, ed. see Auernheimer, Leonardo.

Dethloff, Henry, ed. see Fraser, Donald R.

Dethloff, Henry, ed. see Greenhut, Melvin.

Dethloff, Henry, ed. see Greenhut, Melvin L.

Dethloff, Henry, ed. see Greenhut, Melvin & Smithson, Charles W.

Dethloff, Henry, ed. see Hamilton, Billy.

Dethloff, Henry, ed. see Maurice, S. Charles & Smithson, Charles W.

Dethloff, Henry, ed. see Moore, John H.

Dethloff, Henry, ed. see Pejovich, Steve.

Dethloff, Henry, ed. see Reynolds, Morgan O.

Dethloff, Henry, ed. see Saving, Thomas R.

Dethloff, Henry, ed. see Walker, Deborah.

Dethloff, Henry, ed. see Wiggins, Steven N.

Dethloff, Henry C. A Unit Operation: A History of Chemical Engineering at Texas A&M University. LC 98-21859. (Illus.). 168p. (C). 1998. 24.95 (*0-944091-07-5*) Intaglio Pr.

— A Bookmark: Texas A & M University Press LC 99-17968. (Joe & Betty Moore Texas Art Ser.). 1999. write for info. (*0-89096-878-0*) Tex A&M Univ Pr.

— Texas A & M University: A Pictorial History, 1876-1996. 2nd ed. LC 96-17320. (Centennial Series of the Association of Former Students: No. 63). (Illus.). 248p. 1996. 29.95 (*0-89096-704-0*) Tex A&M Univ Pr.

Dethloff, Henry C. & Bryant, Keith L., Jr. Entrepreneurship: A U. S. Perspective. Pejovich, Steve, ed. (Series on Public Issues: No. 5). 22p. (Orig.). 1983. pap. 2.00 (*0-86599-014-X*) PERC.

— A History of American Business. 2nd ed. 384p. (C). 1989. pap. text 36.80 (*0-13-389255-7*) P-H.

Dethloff, Henry C. & Dyal, Donald H. A Special Kind of Doctor: A History of Veterinary Medicine in Texas. LC 91-456. (Illus.). 232p. 1991. 29.50 (*0-89096-483-1*) Tex A&M Univ Pr.

Dethloff, Henry C. & May, Irvin M. Southwestern Agriculture: Pre-Columbian to Modern. LC 81-48381. 320p. 1982. 27.50 (*0-89096-121-2*) Tex A&M Univ Pr.

Dethloff, Henry C., et al. The United States & Global Economy since 1945. 208p. (C). 1996. pap. text 22.50 (*0-15-502854-5*, Pub. by Harcourt Coll Pubs) Harcourt.

Dethloff, Henry C., jt. auth. see Caddy, Douglas.

Dethloff, Henry C., jt. auth. see Cooper, Jerry C.

Dethman, Linda & King, Sally. Commercial & Industrial Energy Efficiency: Profiles of Northwest Electric Utility Programs (1992) 100p. (Orig.). (C). 1995. pap. text 40.00 (*0-7881-2119-7*) DIANE Pub.

DeThomas, Art. Financial Management Techniques for Small Business. Crawford, Scott, ed. (Successful Business Library). (Illus.). 250p. 1991. pap. 19.95 (*1-55571-124-3*, Oasis Pr) PSI Resch.

DeThomas, Art & Fredenberger, Bill. Writing a Convincing Business Plan. LC 95-7940. (Barron's Business Library). 249p. 1995. pap. 16.95 (*0-8120-9091-8*) Barron.

***DeThomas, Art & Grensing, Lin.** Writing a Convincing Business Plan. 2nd ed. LC 00-40403. (Business Library). 2001. write for info. (*0-7641-1399-2*) Barron.

DeThomas, Arthur R. Financing Your Small Business: Techniques for Planning, Acquiring, & Managing Debt. Reierson, Vickie, ed. LC 92-50147. (Successful Business Library). (Illus.). 206p. 1992. pap. 19.95 (*1-55571-160-X*, Oasis Pr) PSI Resch.

DeThomasis, Louis. Imagination: A Future for Religious Life. (Illus.). 129p. (Orig.). 1992. pap. 11.95 (*0-9631835-1-6*) Metanoia Grp.

DeThomasis, Louis, et al. The Transformal Organization: A Business Paradigm for the 1990s. (Illus.). vii, 171p. (Orig.). 1991. pap. 11.95 (*0-9631835-0-8*) Metanoia Grp.

Dethy, Ray C. Integrated Business Strategy & Policy Simulation. 2nd ed. 206p. (C). 1997. text 45.00 (*0-536-00194-4*) Pearson Custom.

Dethy, Ray C. & Miller, Daniel. Integrated Business Strategy & Policy Simulation. 296p. (C). 1994. text 42.00 (*0-536-58739-6*) Pearson Custom.

Detienne, C. Physical Development of Natural & Criminal Fires. (Illus.). 176p. (C). 1994. text 57.95 (*0-398-05902-0*) C C Thomas.

Detienne, Francoise & Rist, Robert, eds. Empirical Studies of Object-Oriented Design: A Special Issue of "Human-Computer Interaction", Vol. 10, Nos. 2 & 3, 1995. 224p. 1995. pap. 40.00 (*0-8058-9942-1*) L Erlbaum Assocs.

Detienne, M. G. Lotus 1-2-3 Version 4.0 (DOS) Basics & Beyond. 119p. 1995. pap. text 29.00 (*1-887580-00-X*) Tec Trek.

— Lotus 1-2-3 Version 2.4: Basics & Beyond. 112p. 1993. pap. text 29.00 (*1-887580-01-8*) Tec Trek.

— Microsoft Access 2.0: Introduction. 50p. 1994. pap. text 29.00 (*1-887580-02-6*) Tec Trek.

— Microsoft Word 6.0: Basics & Beyond. (Illus.). 118p. pap. text 29.00 (*1-887580-06-9*) Tec Trek.

— PageMaker 5.0: Basics & Beyond. (Illus.). 97p. pap. text 29.00 (*1-887580-05-0*) Tec Trek.

Detienne, M. G. & Marcotte, J. Microsoft Excel 5.0: Basics & Beyond. 116p. 1995. pap. text 29.00 (*1-887580-03-4*) Tec Trek.

— WordPerfect 5.1 Plus: Basics & Beyond. 105p. 1995. pap. text 29.00 (*1-887580-04-2*) Tec Trek.

Detienne, Marcel. The Creation of Mythology. Cook, Margaret, tr. LC 85-24658. 192p. 1996. pap. text 12.95 (*0-226-14348-1*) U Ch Pr.

***Detienne, Marcel.** Daily Life of The Greek Gods. LC 99-87856. 2000. pap. text 17.95 (*0-8047-3614-6*) Stanford U Pr.

Detienne, Marcel. Dionysos at Large. Goldhammer, Arthur, tr. from FRE. LC 88-21474. (Revealing Antiquity Ser.: No. 1). 90p. 1989. 22.00 (*0-674-20773-4*) HUP.

— Dionysos Slain. Muellner, Mireille & Muellner, Leonard, trs. LC 78-20518. (Illus.). 144p. reprint ed. pap. 44.70 (*0-608-17570-6*, 203057500069) Bks Demand.

— The Garden of Adonis: Spices in Greek Mythology. Lloyd, Janet, tr. LC 93-5590. (Mythos: The Princeton - Bollingen Series in World Mythology).Tr. of Jardins d'Adonis. (FRE.). 256p. 1994. reprint ed. pap. text 17.95 (*0-691-00104-9*, Pub. by Princeton U Pr) Cal Prin Full Svc.

— Jardins d'Adonis: La Mythologie des Aromates en Grece. (Gallimard Ser.). (FRE.). 248p. 1972. pap. 37.95 (*2-07-028112-4*) Schoenhof.

***Detienne, Marcel.** The Masters of Truth in Archaic Greece. 1999. pap. 16.00 (*0-942299-86-8*) Zone Bks.

Detienne, Marcel & Vernant, Jean-Pierre. The Cuisine of Sacrifice among the Greeks. Wissing, Paula, tr. LC 88-39143. (Illus.). 288p. 1989. lib. bdg. 48.00 (*0-226-14351-1*) U Ch Pr.

— The Cuisine of Sacrifice among the Greeks. Wissing, Paula, tr. LC 88-39143. (Illus.). 288p. 1998. pap. text 15.95 (*0-226-14353-8*) U Ch Pr.

— The Cuisine of Sacrifice among the Greeks. 2nd ed. Wissing, Paula, tr. from GRE. LC 88-39143. (Illus.). 284p. reprint ed. pap. 88.10 (*0-608-09447-1*, 205424700005) Bks Demand.

— Cunning Intelligence in Greek Culture & Society. Lloyd, Janet, tr. 344p. 1996. pap. text 18.95 (*0-226-14347-3*) U Ch Pr.

Detienne, Marcel & Vidal-Naquet, Pierre. The Masters of Truth in Archaic Greece. Lloyd, Janet, tr. from FRE. 232p. 1996. 24.00 (*0-942299-85-X*) Zone Bks.

Detienne, P., et al. Phanerogams Fascicle 16: Phanerogamae: Hippocrateaceae & Icacinaceae; Including Wood & Timber. Goerts-Van-Rijn, A. R., ed. (Flora of the Guianas Ser.: Series A, Fascicle 16). (Illus.). 157p. 1995. pap. 68.00 (*1-878762-63-X*, 056670, Pub. by Koeltz Sci Bks) Lubrecht & Cramer.

***DeTinguy, Anne.** U. S. - Soviet Relations During the Detente. 220p. 1999. 45.50 (*0-88033-424-X*, 536, Pub. by East Eur Monographs) Col U Pr.

DeTitta, Tom. I Think I'll Drop You Off in Deadwood: A Hitchhiker's Story. Selph, Alexa M., ed. LC 89-7368. 232p. 1994. 22.95 (*0-87797-167-6*) Cherokee.

— The Reach of Song. LC 90-14996. 96p. 1990. pap. 6.95 (*0-87797-199-4*) Cherokee.

— The Reach of Song: An Appalachian Drama. (Illus.). 96p. (Orig.). 1990. pap. 6.95 (*0-685-45899-7*) Larlin Corp.

D

Detje, Frank. Sprichwörter und Handeln: Eine Psychologische Untersuchung. (GER.). 1996. 40.95 (*3-906756-35-1*) P Lang Pubng.

Detjen. Don't Do-It-Yourself Course. 1999. pap. text. write for info. (*0-13-405522-5*) P-H.

— How to Don't Do-It-Yourself. 1999. text. write for info. (*0-13-405530-6*) P-H.

Detjen, David W. Licensing Technology & Trademarks in the United States: Lizenzierung von Technologie und Warenzeichen in den U. S. A. (ENG & GER.). 1997. 60.00 (*0-86640-068-0*) German Am Chamber.

Detjens, Wilma. Teresa y Los Otros: Voces Narrativas En la Novelistica De Hilda Perera. LC 92-74698. (SPA.). 83p. (Orig.). 1993. pap. 9.95 (*0-89729-661-3*) Ediciones.

Detjens, Wilma E. Home as Creation: The Influence of Early Childhood Experience in the Literary Creation of Gabriel Garcia Marquez, Agustin Yanez, & Juan Rolfo. LC 93-9538. (American University Studies: Latin American Literature: Ser. XXII, Vol. 18). 152p. (C). 1993. text 36.95 (*0-8204-2055-7*) P Lang Pubng.

Detlefs, Dale. 2000 Mercer Guide to Social Security & Medicare. 28th ed. 2000. pap. 12.95 (*1-880754-00-2*, Pub. by W M Mercer) IPG Chicago.

Detlefs, Dale & Myers, Robert J. 1998 Mercer Guide to Social Security & Medicare. 26th ed. (Illus.). 200p. 1997. pap. 9.95 (*1-880754-98-3*) W M Mercer.

— 1996 Mercer Guide to Social Security & Medicare. 24th ed. 200p. 1995. pap. 9.95 (*1-880754-96-7*) W M Mercer.

Detlefsen, Ellen G., jt. ed. see Epstein, Barbara A.

Detlefsen, Michael. Hilbert's Program: An Essay on Mathematical Instrumentalism. 182p. 1986. text 138.00 (*90-277-2151-3*, D Reidel) Kluwer Academic.

— Proof, Logic & Formalization. LC 91-17469. 272p. (C). 1992. 85.00 (*0-415-02335-1*, A6498) Routledge.

Detlefsen, Robert. Civil Rights under Reagan. 300p. (C). 1991. 24.95 (*1-55815-111-7*) ICS Pr.

Detlovs, V. K., et al. Nine Papers on Logic & Quantum Electrodynamics. LC 51-5559. (Translations Ser.: Series 2, Vol. 23). 335p. 1963. 38.00 (*0-8218-1723-X*, TRANS2/23) Am Math.

Detmer, Dick. A Practical Guide to Working in an Equipment Rental Business. 114p. 1986. pap. 45.00 (*0-685-19239-3*) Am Rent Assn.

Detmer, Martin. Gott in Jesus Christus Mit Den Menschen: Zum Offenbarungstheologischen Ansatz Bei Wilfried Joest. (Kontexte Ser.: Bd. 22). (GER.). 235p. 1997. 44.95 (*3-631-31547-3*) P Lang Pubng.

Detmer, Richard C. 80 x 86 Assembly Language: Introduction to Complete Architecture. (Computer Science Ser.). 544p. 1999. 60.00 (*0-7637-0678-7*) Jones & Bartlett.

Detmers, Fred, ed. American Cinematographer Manual. 6th ed. 396p. 1986. 34.95 (*0-935578-07-2*) ASC Holding.

Detmold, C. E., tr. see Machiavelli, Niccolo.

***DeTocqueville, Alexis.** Writings on Empire & Slavery. Pitts, Jennifer, ed. & tr. by. 296p. 2000. 42.50 (*0-8018-6509-3*) Johns Hopkins.

DeTommaso, Dianne. Units. (Illus.). 192p. (Orig.). 1994. spiral bd. 24.00 (*1-884135-03-X*) Mayer-Johnson.

Detorie, Rich. Crazy Classroom Dictionary. 64p. (Orig.). (YA). 1994. pap. 2.99 (*0-8125-9432-0*, Pub. by Tor Bks) St Martin.

Detorie, Rick. Land Animals. (Magic Answer Bks.). (J). 1990. pap. 1.95 (*0-8125-7321-8*, Pub. by Tor Bks) St Martin.

— None of This Fun Is My Fault. (One Big Happy Ser.). (Illus.). 128p. (J). 1998. pap. 9.95 (*1-56163-217-1*) NBM.

— Number Games. (Magic Answer Bks.). 1989. pap. 1.95 (*0-8125-7318-8*, Pub. by Tor Bks) St Martin.

— One Big Happy: Should I Spit on Him? (Illus.). 128p. 1997. pap. 9.95 (*1-56163-172-8*) NBM.

***Detorie, Rick.** One Big Happy Vol. 3: Nice Costs Extra! (Illus.). 128p. 1999. pap. 9.95 (*1-56163-239-2*) NBM.

Detorie, Rick. Reading Riddles. 1989. 1.95 (*0-8125-7313-7*, Pub. by Tor Bks) St Martin.

— Red-Headed Gooseberry Ghost. (Haunted House Storybks.). 24p. (J). (gr. k-3). 1997. pap. 2.25 (*0-8167-1458-4*) Troll Communs.

— Sea Animals. (Magic Answer Bks.). (J). 1990. pap. 1.95 (*0-8125-7319-6*, Pub. by Tor Bks) St Martin.

— Swamp Monster. (Magic Answer Bks.). (J). 1989. pap. 1.95 (*0-8125-7315-3*, Pub. by Tor Bks) St Martin.

— Word Games. (Magic Answer Bks.). 1989. pap. 1.95 (*0-8125-7323-4*, Pub. by Tor Bks) St Martin.

DeToro, Irving J. Doing It Right: Quality Through Employee Involvement. 168p. (Orig.). 1990. pap. 18.95 (*0-943456-38-X*) Bearly Ltd.

Detoro, Irving J. & Tenner, Arthur R. Process Redesign: The Implementation Guide for Managers. (Engineering Process Improvement Ser.). 352p. (C). 1996. 42.00 (*0-201-63391-4*) Addison-Wesley.

***Detournay, Christine & Hart, Roger, eds.** FLAC & Numerical Modelling in Geomechanics: Proceedings of the International FLAC Symposium, Minneapolis, Minnesota, 1-3 September 1999. (Illus.). 512p. 1999. text 105.00 (*90-5809-074-4*) A A Balkema.

***Detrain, C., et al, eds.** Information Processing in Social Insects. LC 99-25668. 432p. 1999. 130.00 (*3-7643-5792-4*, Pub. by Birkhauser) Spr-Verlag.

***Detrain, C., et al.** Information Processing Social Insects. LC 99-25668. 1999. write for info. (*0-8176-5792-4*) Birkhauser.

Detre, Charles, see Teder, pseud.

Detre, Roland. Old World Recollections: Writings & Pastels of a Denver Painter. LC 94-16300. (Documents of Colorado Art Ser.: Vol. 3). (Illus.). 1994. pap. 34.95 (*0-938075-44-6*) Ocean View Bks.

Detrekoi, A., jt. auth. see Joo, I.

Detrez, Raymond. Historical Dictionary of Bulgaria. LC 96-33921. (European Historical Dictionaries Ser.). 576p. 1997. 82.00 (*0-8108-3177-5*) Scarecrow.

Detrich, Richard L. & Steele, Nicola J. How to Recover from Grief. 2nd rev. ed. 184p. (Orig.). 1996. pap. 16.00 (*0-8170-1237-0*) Judson.

Detrick, Mia. Sushi. LC 81-12224. (Illus.). 96p. 1983. pap. 12.95 (*0-87701-238-5*) Chronicle Bks.

Detrick, R. Blaine. Favorite Children of the Bible: Ten Sermons on the Lives of Familiar Children of Scripture. LC 92-35096. 1992. pap. 9.95 (*1-55673-511-1*, 9303) CSS OH.

— Favorite Women of the Bible. Sherer, Michael L., ed. 1987. pap. 7.95 (*1-55673-028-4*, 8813) CSS OH.

***Detrick, Sharon.** A Commentary on the United Nations Convention on the Rights of the Child. LC 99-31245. 1999. 255.00 (*90-411-1229-4*) Kluwer Law Intl.

Detrick, Sharon, ed. The United Nations Convention on the Rights of the Child: A Guide to the "Travaux Preparatoires" 724p. (C). 1992. lib. bdg. 245.50 (*0-7923-1671-1*) Kluwer Academic.

Detrick, Sharon & Vlaardingerbroek, P. Globalization of Child Law: The Role of the Hague Conventions. LC 99-21284. 1999. 78.00 (*90-411-0511-5*) Kluwer Law Intl.

Detrie, Philippe. Techniques in Abdominal Surgery. Pryer, Richard R., tr. from FRE. LC 73-593870. 127p. reprint ed. pap. 39.40 (*0-608-12371-4*, 205207000033) Bks Demand.

Detriot News Press. Detroit Red Wing History. (Fan Series of Sports Bks.). 1997. 99.95 (*1-57028-177-7*, Mstrs Pr) NTC Contemp Pub Co.

Detro, Gene. The Honey Dwarf. 1974. 5.95 (*0-913218-23-5*); pap. 2.50 (*0-913218-24-3*) Dustbooks.

— The Mary Caper. LC 81-51876. (Sunburst Originals Ser.: No. 10). (Illus.). 130p. (Orig.). 1982. pap. 4.65 (*0-934648-09-3*) Sunburst Pr.

— Mary Militant. (Orig.). 1979. pap. 3.00 (*0-914974-24-6*) Holmgangers.

Detro, Gene. Moon Horns-Razor Door. LC 81-6493. 72p. 1981. pap. 7.95 (*0-914974-31-9*) Holmgangers.

Detro, Gene. When All the Wild Summer. (Kestrel Ser.: No. 7). 28p. 1983. pap. 3.00 (*0-914974-39-4*) Holmgangers.

Detro, Gene, ed. see Stock, Susan.

Detro, John. St. Joseph's Blues. 63p. Date not set. pap. 10.00 (*0-932662-86-2*) St Andrews NC.

Detro, Randall A., jt. ed. see Walker, H. Jesse.

Detroit Black Writers Guild Staff. Before I Wake...& Other Tales by Detroiters. LC 91-70953. (Illus.). 160p. 1991. pap. 7.95 (*0-9613078-7-0*) Detroit Black.

— Innervisions. LC 94-69087. 200p. 1995. pap. 15.00 (*0-9613078-8-9*) Detroit Black.

Detroit Black Writer's Guild Staff. Paradise Valley Days: A Photo Album Poetry Book. Metoyer, Herbert R. & Watson, Debraha, eds. LC 97-78432. (Illus.). 120p. 1998. 35.00 (*1-888754-02-8*) Detroit Black.

Detroit Black Writers Guild Staff. Through Ebony Eyes. 105p. 1987. pap. 6.00 (*0-9613078-6-2*) Detroit Black.

***Detroit Free Press Staff.** Corner to Copa. 2000. pap. text 12.95 (*1-57243-396-5*) Triumph Bks.

Detroit Free Press Staff, ed. Believe! 1998. pap. 12.95 (*0-937247-27-8*) Detroit Pr.

Detroit Free Press Staff, jt. auth. see Henry Ford Health System Staff.

Detroit Institute of Arts Staff. Images in Ivory: Precious Objects of the Gothic Age. Barnet, Peter, ed. LC 96-52331. (Illus.). 296p. 1997. text 80.00 (*0-691-01611-9*, Pub. by Princeton U Pr); pap. text 37.50 (*0-691-01610-0*, Pub. by Princeton U Pr) Cal Prin Full Svc.

Detroit Institute of Arts Staff, jt. auth. see Fike, Bonita.

Detroit Lions Staff. Detroit Lions. CWC Sports Inc., ed. (NFL Team Yearbooks Ser.). (J). (gr. 1-12). 1998. pap. 9.99 (*1-891613-08-1*) Everett Sports.

Detroit Marine Historical Society. Great Lakes Ships We Remember. rev. ed. Van der Linden, Peter J., ed. (Illus.). 415p. 1984. 35.00 (*0-912514-24-8*) Freshwater.

— Great Lakes Ships We Remember II. Van der Linden, Peter J., ed. (Illus.). 400p. 1984. 35.00 (*0-912514-25-6*) Freshwater.

Detroit Marine Historical Society Staff. Great Lakes Ships We Remember III. (Illus.). 400p. 1994. 35.00 (*0-912514-50-7*) Freshwater.

Detroit News Staff. Quest for the Cup. 1997. 24.95 (*1-57243-257-8*); pap. text 9.95 (*1-57243-258-6*) Triumph Bks.

***Detroit News Staff.** They Earned Their Stripes: The Detroit Tigers All-Time Team. (Illus.). 192p. 2000. 29.95 (*1-58382-061-2*) Sports Pub.

Detroit Public Library Staff. Automotive History Collection of the Detroit Public Library: Simplified Guide. 1970. 230.00 (*0-8161-1446-3*, G K Hall & Co) Mac Lib Ref.

Detroit Public Library Staff, jt. contrib. by see Gale Group.

Detsch, Richard. Georg Trakl & the Brenner Circle. LC 90-41226. (American University Studies: Germanic Languages & Literature: Ser. I, Vol. 41). 208p. (C). 1992. text 39.95 (*0-8204-1323-2*) P Lang Pubng.

— Georg Trakl's Poetry: Toward a Union of Opposites. LC 82-42780. (Studies in German Literature). 160p. 1983. 30.00 (*0-271-00343-X*) Pa St U Pr.

Detscher, Alan F., frwd. Masses with Children. (Liturgy Documentary Ser.: Vol. 12). 47p. (Orig.). 1996. pap. 5.95 (*1-57455-107-8*) US Catholic.

— Solemn Exposition of the Holy Eucharist. (Liturgy Documentary Ser.: Vol. 11). 37p. (Orig.). 1996. pap. 5.95 (*1-57455-106-X*) US Catholic.

— Sunday Celebrations in the Absence of a Priest. (Liturgy Documentary Ser.: Vol. 10). 57p. (Orig.). 1996. pap. 5.95 (*1-57455-105-1*) US Catholic.

Detsicas, A. The Cantiaci. (Peoples of Roman Britain Ser.). (Illus.). 230p. 1991. text 26.95 (*0-86299-117-X*, Pub. by Sutton Pub Ltd) Intl Pubs Mktg.

Dett, R. Nathaniel. The Collected Piano Works of R. Nathaniel Dett. rev. ed. (Illus.). 203p. 1973. pap. 16.50 (*0-87487-080-1*, 0080) Summy-Birchard.

— Juba. 5p. 1913. pap. text 2.95 (*0-87487-661-3*) Summy-Birchard.

Dett, Robert N., ed. Religious Folk Songs of the Negro. LC 72-1595. reprint ed. 29.50 (*0-404-09920-3*) AMS Pr.

Dette, Holger & Studden, William J. The Theory of Canonical Moments with Applications in Statistics, Probability & Analysis. LC 96-53188. (Wiley Series in Probability & Statistics Ser.). 324p. 1997. 89.95 (*0-471-10991-6*) Wiley.

Dettelbach, Cynthia G. In the Driver's Seat: The Automobile in American Literature & Popular Culture, 25. LC 75-35342. (Contributions in American Studies: No. 25). (Illus.). 140p. 1976. 49.95 (*0-8371-8593-9*, DDS/, Greenwood Pr) Greenwood.

Dettenmaier, Paul & Jahn, Bart. Offsite Construction. LC 96-40097. (Illus.). 452p. 1997. 49.95 (*0-07-016561-0*) McGraw.

Dettenmeier, Patricia. Pulmonary Nursing Care. (Illus.). 465p. (C). (gr. 13). 1991. pap. text 31.95 (*0-8016-5876-4*, 05876) Mosby Inc.

Dettenmeier, Patricia A. X-Ray Assessment for Nurses. (Illus.). 256p. (C). (gr. 13). 1994. pap. text 35.95 (*0-8016-7245-7*, 07245) Mosby Inc.

Detter. International Legal Order. 608p. 1994. pap. 59.95 (*1-85521-590-X*) Ashgate Pub Co.

Detter, Ingrid. The Concept of International Law. 2nd ed. 143p. (Orig.). 1993. pap. 87.50 (*91-38-50194-5*) Coronet Bks.

— The International Legal Order. 608p. 1994. 115.95 (*1-85521-580-2*, Pub. by Dartmth Pub) Ashgate Pub Co.

***Detter, Ingrid.** The Law of War. LC 99-86452. 384p. (C). 2000. text Price not set. (*0-521-78256-2*); pap. text Price not set. (*0-521-78775-0*) Cambridge U Pr.

Detter, Thomas. Nellie Brown: or The Jealous Wife, with Other Sketches. LC 96-1023. (Blacks in the American West Ser.). xxi, 122p. (C). 1996. text 30.00 (*0-8032-1704-8*) U of Nebr Pr.

***Detterbeck, Frank C., et al.** Diagnosis & Treatment of Lung Cancer. (Illus.). 670p. 2001. text. write for info. (*0-7216-9192-7*, W B Saunders Co) Harcrt Hlth Sci Grp.

Detterer, Gabriele. Art Recollection: Artists' Interviews & Statements in the Nineties. 272p. 1998. pap. 22.50 (*1-56466-058-3*) Archer Fields.

Detterman, Douglas. Current Topics in Human Intelligence: Research Methodology, Vol. 1. (Current Topics in Human Intelligence Ser.). 344p. 1985. text 78.50 (*0-89391-173-9*) Ablx Pub.

Detterman, Douglas K. Current Topics in Human Intelligence Vol. 2: Is Mind Modular or Unitary? 282p. (C). 1992. 78.50 (*0-89391-703-6*) Ablx Pub.

Detterman, Douglas K., ed. Current Topics in Human Intelligence Vol. 4: Theories in Intelligence. 432p. 1994. text 78.50 (*1-56750-103-6*) Ablx Pub.

Detterman, Douglas K. & Sternberg, Robert J. Transfer on Trial: Intelligence, Cognition, & Construction. 304p. (C). 1993. pap. 39.50 (*0-89391-826-1*) Ablx Pub.

Detterman, Douglas K. & Sternberg, Robert J., eds. How & How Much Can Intelligence Be Increased. LC 82-1787. 256p. 1982. text 73.25 (*0-89391-117-8*) Ablx Pub.

— Transfer on Trial: Intelligence, Cognition, & Construction. 304p. (C). 1993. text 78.50 (*0-89391-825-3*) Ablx Pub.

Detterman, Douglas K., jt. auth. see Sternberg, Robert J.

Detterman, Douglas K., ed. see Keating, Daniel P., et al.

Detterman, Douglas K., jt. ed. see Sternberg, Robert J.

Detterman, Paul. Worship Resources for Congregations. Hainer, Frank, ed. (Illus.). 32p. 1997. pap. 3.95 (*1-57895-050-3*) Curriculum Presbytrn KY.

Dettke, Barbara. Die Asiatische Hydra: Die Cholera von 1830-31 in Berlin und den Preussischen Provinzen Posen, Preussen und Schlesien. (Veroeffentlichungen der Historischen Kommission zu Berlin Ser.: Bd. 89). (GER.). xiii, 383p. (C). 1995. lib. bdg. 152.30 (*3-11-014493-X*) De Gruyter.

Dettke, Dieter, ed. The Challenge of Globalization for Germany's Social Democracy: A Policy Agenda for the 21st Century. (Illus.). 256p. 1998. 39.95 (*1-57181-180-X*) Berghahn Bks.

Dettke, Dieter, ed. see Amirahmadi, Hooshang, et al.

Dettlaff, T. A. & Vassetzky, S. G. Animal Species for Developmental Studies: Invertebrates, Vol. 1. (Illus.). 336p. (C). 1990. text 110.00 (*0-306-11031-8*, Kluwer Plenum) Kluwer Academic.

— Animal Species for Developmental Studies Vol. 2: Vertebrates, Vol. 2. (Illus.). 466p. (C). 1990. text 130.00 (*0-306-11032-6*, Kluwer Plenum) Kluwer Academic.

— Oocyte Growth & Maturation. LC 88-3966. (Illus.). 464p. (C). 1988. text 135.00 (*0-306-11013-X*, Kluwer Plenum) Kluwer Academic.

Dettlaff, T. A., et al. Sturgeon Fishes: Developmental Biology & Aquaculture. Gause, G. G. & Vassetzky, S. G., trs. from RUS. (Illus.). 312p. 1992. 238.95 (*0-387-54744-4*) Spr-Verlag.

Dettloff, Paul. How I See It. (Illus.). 172p. (Orig.). 1992. pap. 13.95 (*0-9632897-0-5*) Million Mile.

— Milking Machine Guide. (Illus.). 164p. 1998. spiral bd. 16.95 (*0-9632897-2-1*) Million Mile.

Dettloff, Paul W. Cream Separator Guide. (Illus.). 480p. 1993. 54.95 (*0-9632897-1-3*) Million Mile.

***Dettman, Alex, et al.** Russian Cryptology During World War II. IV, 51p. 1999. pap. 26.80 (*0-89412-279-7*, C-85) Aegean Park Pr.

Dettman, B., jt. auth. see Bedford, Michael.

Dettman, David L., jt. auth. see Helms, Philip W.

Dettman, John W. Applied Complex Variables. (Mathematics Ser.). 481p. 1984. reprint ed. pap. 12.95 (*0-486-64670-X*) Dover.

— Introduction to Linear Algebra & Differential Equations. 416p. 1986. reprint ed. pap. text 11.95 (*0-486-65191-6*) Dover.

— Mathematical Methods in Physics & Engineering. (Illus.). 448p. 1988. reprint ed. pap. text 10.95 (*0-486-65649-7*) Dover.

***Dettmar, Jorg.** Bedford Anthology of Poetry. 2000. pap. text. write for info. (*0-312-25600-0*) St Martin.

Dettmar, Jorg. Industrietypische Flora und Vegetation Im Ruhrgebiet. (Dissertationes Botanicae Ser.: Band 191). (GER., Illus.). ii, 397p. 1992. pap. 83.00 (*3-443-64103-2*, Pub. by Gebruder Borntraeger) Balogh.

Dettmar, Kevin J. The Illicit Joyce of Postmodernism: Reading Against the Grain. LC 96-1194. (Illus.). 292p. (Orig.). 1996. 50.00 (*0-299-15060-7*); pap. 22.95 (*0-299-15064-X*) U of Wis Pr.

— Rereading the New: A Backward Glance at Modernism. LC 92-27427. 400p. (C). 1993. text 47.50 (*0-472-10290-7*, 10290) U of Mich Pr.

***Dettmar, Kevin J. & Richey, William, eds.** Reading Rock & Roll: Authenticity, Appropriation & Aesthetics. LC 99-11659. 352p. 1999. 49.50 (*0-231-11398-6*) Col U Pr.

Dettmar, Kevin J. & Watt, Stephen, eds. Marketing Modernisms: Self-Promotion, Canonization, & Rereading. 384p. (Orig.). 1996. text 44.50 (*0-472-09641-9*, 09641); pap. text 19.95 (*0-472-06641-2*, 06641) U of Mich Pr.

***Dettmar, Kevin J. H. & Richey, William.** Reading Rock & Roll: Authenticity, Appropriation & Aesthetics. LC 99-11659. 352p. 1999. pap. 18.50 (*0-231-11399-4*) Col U Pr.

Dettmar, Ralf J., jt. ed. see Lesch, Harald.

Dettmer, Anne & Lloyd-Davies, Victoria. The Rice Cookbook. LC 93-32746. (Illus.). 96p. 1994. pap. 11.95 (*1-56440-360-2*) Globe Pequot.

Dettmer, Elke, tr. see Bausinger, Hermann.

Dettmer, H. William. Breaking the Constraints to World-Class Performance. LC 98-7622. 305p. 1998. 33.00 (*0-87389-437-5*, H1003) ASQ Qual Pr.

— Goldratt's Theory of Constraints: A Systems Approach to Continuous Improvement. LC 96-23664. (Illus.). 378p. 1997. text 54.00 (*0-87389-370-0*, H0935) ASQ Qual Pr.

Dettmer, Helena. Horace: A Study in Structure. (Altertumswissenschaftliche Texte und Studien: Vol. 12). (GER.). xxvii, 577p. 1984. 57.20 (*3-487-07455-9*) G Olms Pubs.

— Love by the Numbers: Form & Meaning in the Poetry of Catullus. LC 96-41571. (Lang Classical Studies: No. 10). XVIII, 366p. (C). 1997. text 58.95 (*0-8204-3663-1*) P Lang Pubng.

Dettmer, Helena & Lindgren, Marcia. Workbook of Donald M. Ayer's English Words from Latin & Greek Elements. 291p. 1986. student ed. 14.95 (*0-8165-0905-0*) U of Ariz Pr.

Dettmer, Peggy & Landrum, Mary, eds. Staff Development: The Key to Effective Gifted Education Programs. 125p. 1997. pap. 19.95 (*1-882664-41-8*) Prufrock Pr.

Dettmer, Peggy, et al. Consultation, Collaboration & Teamwork for Students with Special Needs. 3rd ed. LC 98-30852. 384p. 1998. pap. text 67.00 (*0-205-29065-5*) P-H.

***Dettmeyer, Reinhard.** Die Verfassungsrechtlichen Grenzen Fur die Gesetzliche Einfuhrung einer Verwaltungssektion Bei Medizinisch Unklaren Todesfallen. (Bochumer Schriften Zum Sozialrecht. Ser.: Bd. 3). 236p. 1999. 42.95 (*3-631-35404-5*) P Lang Pubng.

Dettmore, Diane, ed. see Brawer, Richard H.

Dettmore, Diane, ed. see Stephan, Audrey.

Dettner, H. Fachwoerterbuch Fuer der Metalloberflaechenveredelung. (ENG & GER.). 391p. 1969. 34.25 (*0-8288-6597-3*, M7939) Fr & Eur.

Dettner, K., et al, eds. Vertical Food Web Interactions: Evolutionary Patterns & Driving Forces. LC 97-6984. (Ecological Studies: No. 130). (Illus.). 390p. 1997. 129.00 (*3-540-62561-5*) Spr-Verlag.

Dettner, Konrad, jt. auth. see Vondel, Bernard J.

Dettoni, John M. Down from the Ivory Tower: Eight Sessions on the Roles of Men & Women. LC 93-50844. 144p. 1994. pap. 6.50 (*1-56476-323-4*, 6-3323, Victor Bks) Chariot Victor.

— Open to Closeness. (Groupbuilders Series for Adults). 144p. 1991. pap. 6.50 (*0-89693-881-6*, 6-1881, Victor Bks) Chariot Victor.

Dettoni, John M., jt. ed. see Wilhoit, James C.

***Dettore, Mariapaola.** Sicily. LC 98-52936. (Flavors of Italy Ser.). (Illus.). 120p. (YA). (gr. 11). 1999. 16.95 (*0-7370-0012-0*) T-L Custom Pub.

Dettre, Judith. One, Two, Three, Read! LC 79-52661. 1980. pap. 9.99 (*0-8224-5788-1*) Fearon Teacher Aids.

Dettwiler, Alma. Harvest of Tears. 1989. pap. 3.50 (*0-87813-530-8*) Christian Light.

Dettwyler, Katherine. Dancing Skeletons: Life & Death in West Africa. (Illus.). 172p. (C). 1994. pap. text 11.50 (*0-88133-748-X*) Waveland Pr.

Dettwyler, Katherine, jt. auth. see Stuart-Macadam, Patricia.

Detty, Michael R. & O'Regan, Marie B. Tellurium-Containing Heterocycles, Vol. 53, Vol. 53. (Chemistry of Heterocyclic Compounds, a Series of Monographs: Vol. 53). 511p. 1994. 315.00 (*0-471-63395-X*) Wiley.

DeTurck, D., ed. Nonlinear Problems in Geometry. LC 86-1151. (Contemporary Mathematics Ser.: Vol. 51). 130p. 1986. pap. 25.00 (*0-8218-5053-9*, CONM/51) Am Math.

D

DeTurck, Dennis M., ed. Nonlinear Problems in Geometry: Proceedings of an AMS Special Session Held May 3-4, 1985. LC 86-1151. (Contemporary Mathematics Ser.: No. 51). (Illus.). 140p. 1986. pap. 43.40 (*0-608-05567-0*, 205260400006) Bks Demand.

DeTurk, Eugene P. DeTurk: History & Genealogy of the DeTurk-DeTurck Family, Descendants of Isaac DeTurk & Maria DeHarcourt, with Supplement. (Illus.). 1997. reprint ed. pap. 57.50 (*0-8328-8278-X*); reprint ed. lib. bdg. 67.50 (*0-8328-8277-1*) Higginson Bk Co.

DeTurk, Philip, compiled by. Tutt: An Annotated Bibliography of Arthur Train's Tutt Short Stories. (Tarlton Law Library Legal Bibliography Ser.: No. 39). 33p. (C). 1994. 16.00 (*0-935630-44-9*) U of Tex Tarlton Law Lib.

Detweiler, Clinton. Ventriloquism in a Nutshell. (Illus.). 1974. pap. 5.00 (*0-686-20905-2*, 065) Maher Ventril Studio.

Detweiler, Gerri. The Ultimate Credit Handbook. rev. ed. LC 96-36209. 1997. pap. 12.95 (*0-452-27712-4*, Plume) Dutton Plume.

Detweiler, Gerri, et al. Slash Your Debt: Save Your Money & Secure Your Future. LC 98-76185. (Illus.). 100p. 1999. pap. 10.95 (*0-9659638-3-7*) Fin Literacy.

***Detweiler, Lowell.** The Hammer Rings Hope: Photos & Stories from Fifty Years of Mennonite Disaster Service. LC 99-87272. 186p. 2000. 19.99 (*0-8361-9110-2*) Herald Pr.

Detweiler, M. David. Evenings along the Stream. LC 90-9536. 144p. 1990. 16.95 (*0-8117-0746-6*) Stackpole.

— The Tree of Life: A Novel. LC 95-8864. (Fiction Bk.). 540p. 1995. 24.95 (*0-8117-1600-7*) Stackpole.

***Detweiler, Molly.** God Loves Me Baby Bible. 1999. 9.99 (*0-310-97950-1*) Zondervan.

Detweiler, Nancy B. A New Age Christian: My Spiritual Journey. LC 97-93620. (Illus.). 240p. (Orig.). (C). 1997. pap. 24.95 (*0-9658949-0-8*) Bridging Gap.

Detweiler, Richard C. Mennonite Statements on Peace. 80p. (Orig.). 1968. pap. 2.99 (*0-8361-1581-3*) Herald Pr.

Detweiler, Robert. Breaking the Fall: Religious Readings of Contemporary Fiction. 216p. 1996. pap. 22.95 (*0-664-25630-9*) Westminster John Knox.

— Four Spiritual Crises in Mid-Century American Fiction. LC 78-121461. (Essay Index Reprint Ser.). 1977. 15.95 (*0-8369-1799-5*) Ayer.

— Four Spiritual Crises in Mid-Century American Fiction. LC 64-63316. (University of Florida Humanities Monographs: No. 14). 60p. reprint ed. pap. 30.00 (*0-7837-4982-1*, 204464800004) Bks Demand.

— John Updike. rev. ed. (United States Authors Ser.: No. 481). 208p. (C). 1984. 28.95 (*0-8057-7422-X*) Macmillan.

— Uncivil Rites: American Fiction, Religion, & the Public Sphere. (Public Expressions of Religion in America Ser.). 250p. 1996. text 29.95 (*0-252-01932-6*) U of Ill Pr.

— Uncivil Rites: American Fiction, Religion & the Public Sphere. (Public Expressions of Religion in America Ser.). 250p. 1996. 17.95 (*0-252-06580-8*) U of Ill Pr.

Detweiler, Robert, ed. John Updike. LC 74-187611. (Twayne's United States Authors Ser.). 183p. (C). 1972. pap. text. write for info. (*0-672-61506-1*, Bobbs) Macmillan.

***Detweiler, Robert & Jasper, David, eds.** Religion & Literature: A Reader. LC 99-47561. 296p. 2000. pap. 29.95 (*0-664-25846-8*, Pub. by Westminster John Knox) Presbyterian Pub.

Detweiler, Robert & Meeter, Glenn, eds. Faith & Fiction: The Modern Short Story. LC 78-32082. 347p. reprint ed. pap. 107.60 (*0-608-11858-3*, 202321000032) Bks Demand.

Detweiler, Robert, jt. ed. see Starr, Raymond.

Detweiler, Steven, ed. Black Holes: Selected Reprints. 112p. 1982. per. 17.00 (*0-917853-70-9*, RB-35) Am Assn Physics.

Detweiler, Susan G. Washington's Chinaware. (Illus.). 244p. 1982. 40.00 (*0-8109-1779-3*, Pub. by Abrams) Time Warner.

***Detweiler, Tim.** Making Working Wooden Locks: Complete Plans for 5 Working Wooden Locks. (Illus.). 96p. 2000. pap. 21.95 (*0-941936-60-0*, Pub. by Linden Pub Fresno) IPG Chicago.

Detwiler, Bruce. Nietzsche & the Politics of Aristocratic Radicalism. LC 89-375. 252p. 1999. 29.95 (*0-226-14354-6*) U Ch Pr.

***Detwiler, Donald S.** Germany: A Short History. 3rd ed. LC 98-23290. 1999. pap. 19.95 (*0-8093-2231-5*) S Ill U Pr.

Detwiler, Donald S. & Detwiler, Ilse E. West Germany. LC 90-156464. (World Bibliographical Ser.: No. 72). 372p. 1988. lib. bdg. 70.00 (*1-85109-017-7*) ABC-CLIO.

Detwiler, Donald S., ed. see Schramm, Percy.

***Detwiler, Fritz.** Standing on the Premises of God: The Christian Right's Fight to Redefine America's Public School. LC 99-6790. 2000. text 30.00 (*0-8147-1914-7*) NYU Pr.

Detwiler, Ilse E., jt. auth. see Detwiler, Donald S.

Detwiler, Kurt B. Coasting Along: A Bicycling Guide to the New Jersey Shore, Pine Barrens, & Delaware Bay Region. LC 97-25540. 1997. pap. 14.95 (*1-889324-06-X*, EPM) Howell Pr VA.

— Shifting Gears: A Bicycling Guide to West Virginia. LC 95-39712. (Illus.). 160p. 1995. spiral bd. 14.95 (*0-939009-93-5*, EPM) Howell Pr VA.

Detwiler, Sam, jt. auth. see Clapp, Steve.

***Detwiler, Susan.** The Super Searchers on Health & Medicine: The Online Secrets of Top Health & Medical Researchers. Basch, Reva, ed. 260p. 2000. pap. 24.95 (*0-910965-44-7*, Pub. by Info Today Inc) IPG Chicago.

Detwiller, Dennis, et al. Delta Green: A Call of Cthulhu Sourcebook of Modern Horror & Conspiracy. (Illus.). 304p. (Orig.). 1997. pap. 27.95 (*1-887797-08-4*) Tynes Cowan.

Detz, Jim, jt. auth. see Carrell, Ross.

Detz, Joan. Can You Say a Few Words? 1991. pap. 12.95 (*0-312-05830-6*) St Martin.

— How to Write & Give a Speech: A Practical Guide for Executives, PR People, Managers, Fund-Raisers, Politicians, Educators, & Anyone Who Has to Make Every Word Count. 2nd rev. ed. 224p. 1992. pap. 9.95 (*0-312-08218-5*) St Martin.

***Detz, Joan.** It's Not What You Say, It's How You Say It: Ready-to-Use Advice for Presentations, Speeches & Other Speaking Occasions Large & Small. 192p. 2000. pap. 12.95 (*0-312-24305-7*) St Martin.

Detz, Joan. You Mean I Have to Stand Up & Say Something? LC 86-3611. (Illus.). 96p. (J). (gr. 5-9). 1986. lib. bdg. 13.95 (*0-689-31221-0*) Atheneum Yung Read.

Detzel, Denis H., jt. auth. see Desatnick, Robert L.

***Detzer.** Allegiance. 2001. write for info. (*0-15-100641-5*) Harcourt.

Detzer, Dorothy. Appointment on the Hill: American Autobiography. 262p. 1995. lib. bdg. 79.00 (*0-7812-8499-6*) Rprt Serv.

Detzler, Robert E. The Freedom Path: Your Mind Net to Clear Your Soul Records. rev. ed. Lange, Karen & Grobes, Elizabeth, eds. LC 96-67786. (Illus.). 150p. 1996. pap. 15.95 (*0-9640041-2-7*) S R C Pubng.

— Re-Nacer del Alma: Desarrollo de Su Potencial Cosmico. rev. ed. Loreto-Perez, Mariela, ed. Gimenez, Lolimar, tr.Tr. of Soul ReCreation - Developing Your Cosmic Potential. (SPA., Illus.). 150p. 1997. pap. 22.00 (*0-9640041-3-5*) S R C Pubng.

— Soul Re-Creation: Developing Your Cosmic Potential. LC 94-92009. (Illus.). 240p. 1994. pap. 15.95 (*0-9640041-1-9*) S R C Pubng.

— Soul Re-Creation: Developing Your Cosmic Potential. 2nd rev. ed. Hamilton, Kathryn & Grobes, Elizabeth, eds. LC 97-92398. (Illus.). 240p. 1999. pap. 15.95 (*0-9640041-4-3*) S R C Pubng.

— Spiritual Healing. Grobes, Elizabeth, ed. LC 97-61836. (Illus.). 210p. 1997. pap. 19.95 (*0-9640041-5-1*) S R C Pubng.

Detzler, Wayne. Living Words in First Corinthians. 1983. pap. 8.99 (*0-85234-177-6*, Pub. by Evangelical Pr) P & R Pubng.

— Living Words in First Peter. 1982. pap. 8.99 (*0-85234-165-2*, Pub. by Evangelical Pr) P & R Pubng.

— Living Words in Philippians. 1984. pap. 8.99 (*0-85234-183-0*, Pub. by Evangelical Pr) P & R Pubng.

Deuber, Carl G. Vegetative Propagation of Conifers. (CT Academy of Arts & Science Transactions Ser.: Vol. 34). 1940. pap. 49.50 (*0-686-51323-1*) Elliots Bks.

Deuber, W., et al, eds. Trends in Discrete Mathematics. LC 95-8188. (Topics in Discrete Mathematics Ser.: Vol. 9). 398p. 1995. 205.50 (*0-444-82192-9*) Elsevier.

Deubler, Christopher. Trout Fishing Wisconsin Spring Ponds. unabridged ed. LC 96-92605. (Illus.). viii, 128p. (Orig.). 1996. pap. 12.95 (*0-9654303-0-8*) Siskiwit Pr.

— Trout Ponds & Lakes in the Upper Peninsula of Michigan: An Angler's Guide. unabridged ed. LC 99-93585. (Illus.). 128p. 1999. pap. 12.95 (*0-9654303-2-4*) Siskiwit Pr.

Deubner, ed. Iamblichi: De Vita Pythagorica Liber. rev. ed. (GRE.). 1975. pap. 33.50 (*3-519-01445-9*, T1445, Pub. by B G Teubner) U of Mich Pr.

Deubner, Ludwig. Attiscshe Feste. 269p. 1969. reprint ed. write for info. (*0-318-70909-0*) G Olms Pubs.

***Deuby, Sean.** Windows 2000 Server. 400p. 1999. 40.00 (*1-57870-023-X*) Macmillan Tech.

Deuchar, Elizabeth M. Xenopus: The South African Clawed Frog. LC 73-18927. 256p. reprint ed. pap. 79.40 (*0-608-13827-4*, 202097200020) Bks Demand.

***Deuchar, Margaret & Quay, Suzanne.** Bilingual Acquisition: Theoretical Implications of a Case Study. LC 99-88863. (Illus.). 200p. 2000. text 70.00 (*0-19-823685-9*) OUP.

Deuchar, Stephen. Noble Exercise: The Sporting Ideal in Eighteenth-Century British Art. LC 82-50676. (Illus.). 48p. (Orig.). 1982. pap. 5.75 (*0-930606-41-8*) Yale Ctr Brit Art.

— Sporting Art & English Society. LC 88-165. 195p. (C). 1988. 55.00 (*0-300-04116-0*) Yale U Pr.

Deuchar, Stephen, et al. Nelson: The Immortal Memory. (Illus.). 176p. 1995. pap. 24.95 (*1-85669-061-X*, Pub. by Law King Ltd) Trafalgar.

Deuchler, Florens, comment. Ingeborg-Psalter (Chantilly, Musee Conde, Ms. 9 Olim 1695) fac. limited ed. (Codices Selecti A Ser.: Vol. LXXX). (FRE., Illus.). 400p. 1985. lthr. 3632.00 (*3-201-01274-2*, Pub. by Akademische Druck-und) Balogh.

Deuchler, Martina. The Confucian Transformation of Korea: A Study of Society & Ideology. LC 92-18507. (Harvard-Yenching Institute Monographs: No. 36). 439p. 1993. text 35.00 (*0-674-16088-6*) HUP.

— The Confucian Transformation of Korea: A Study of Society & Ideology. (Harvard-Yenching Institute Monographs: No. 36). (Illus.). 439p. 1995. pap. 19.00 (*0-674-16089-4*, DEUCOX) HUP.

Deuchler, Martina, jt. auth. see Haboush, Jahyun Kim.

Deudney, Daniel. Rivers of Energy: Harnessing the Hydropower Potential. 1981. pap. write for info. (*0-916468-43-7*) Worldwatch Inst.

— Whole-Earth Security: A Geopolitics of Peace. 1983. pap. write for info. (*0-916468-54-2*) Worldwatch Inst.

Deudney, Daniel H. & Matthew, Richard A., eds. Contested Grounds: Security & Conflict in the New Environmental Politics. LC 98-43907. (SUNY Series in International Environmental Policy & Theory). 320p. (C). 1999. text 62.50 (*0-7914-4115-6*) State U NY Pr.

— Contested Grounds: Security & Conflict in the New Environmental Politics. LC 98-43907. (SUNY Series in International Environmental Policy & Theory). (Illus.). 312p. (C). 1999. pap. text 20.95 (*0-7914-4116-4*) State U NY Pr.

Deudon, Eric H., tr. see Seignolle, Claude.

Deuel, Austin. Canon de los Artistas. Cross, Gail, ed. (SPA., Illus.). 106p. 1986. 35.00 (*0-9615217-1-6*) Desert Wind Pub.

— Vietnam. (Illus.). 160p. 1988. 28.95 (*0-9615217-3-2*) Desert Wind Pub.

Deuel, Douglas. Returning to God: Sermons for Lent/Easter. LC 96-52620. (First Lessons Ser.). 152p. 1997. pap. 16.25 (*0-7880-1029-8*) CSS OH.

Deuel, Harry. Chester's Paradise. LC 70-2567. (Orig.). 1976. pap. 3.00 (*0-912860-00-6*) Total Graphics.

Deuel, L. E. & Holliday, George H. Soil Remediation for the Petroleum Extraction Industry. 2nd ed. LC 98-15341. 1997. 84.95 (*0-87814-740-3*) PennWell Bks.

Deuel, Thorne. The Human Factor in the Behavior of Peoples. (Scientific Papers: Vol. XIII). (Illus.). 204p. 1971. pap. 5.75 (*0-89792-047-3*) Ill St Museum.

— Man's Venture in Culture. (Story of Illinois Ser.: No. 6). (Illus.). 40p. (J). (ps-12). 1955. pap. 1.00 (*0-89792-008-2*) Ill St Museum.

— Power Adaptations & Changing Cultures. (Scientific Papers: Vol. XV). (Illus.). 204p. 1976. pap. 4.00 (*0-89792-063-5*) Ill St Museum.

Deuel, Thorne, jt. auth. see Cole, Fay-Cooper.

Deufel, Thomas, jt. ed. see Harding, A. E.

Deufert, M., tr. see Brink, Charles O.

Deufert, Marcus. Pseudo-Lukrezisches im Lukrez: Die Unechten Verse in Lukrezens "De Rerum Natura" (Untersuchungen zur Antiken Literatur und Geschichte Ser.: Vol. 48). (GER.). ix, 343p. (C). 1996. lib. bdg. 161.50 (*3-11-015046-8*) De Gruyter.

Deuflhard, P. & Reich, S., eds. Computational Molecular Dynamics: Challenges, Methods, Ideas. LC 98-44483. 489p. 1999. pap. 89.00 (*3-540-63242-5*) Spr-Verlag.

Deuflhard, Peter & Engquist, B., eds. Large-Scale Scientific Computing. (Progress in Scientific Computing Ser.: No. 7). 408p. 1987. 115.00 (*0-8176-3355-3*) Birkhauser.

Deuflhard, Peter & Hohmann, Andreas. Numerical Analysis: A First Course in Scientific Computation. Potra, F. A. & Schulz, F., trs. from GER. LC 94-46993. (C). 1995. pap. text 42.95 (*3-11-013882-4*); lib. bdg. 69.95 (*3-11-014031-4*) De Gruyter.

D'Eugenio, D. B. Developmental Programming for Infants & Young Children, Vol. 5. 20p. 1981. pap. text 2.50 (*0-472-08145-4*, 08145) U of Mich Pr.

D'Eugenio, Diane B. & Moersch, Martha S., eds. Developmental Programming for Infants & Young Children. (Illus.). 80p. (C). 1981. pap. text. write for info. (*0-472-08144-6*, 08144) U of Mich Pr.

D'Eugenio, Diane B. & Moersch, Martha S., eds. Developmental Programming for Infants & Young Children, 2 vols., Vols. 4-5. LC 80-50630. 80p. (C). 1981. text 24.95 (*0-472-08150-0*, 08150) U of Mich Pr.

Deugo, Dwight, ed. Java Gems: Jewels from Java Report. (SIGS Reference Library: No. 10). 248p. 1998. pap. 29.95 (*0-521-64824-6*) Cambridge U Pr.

***Deugo, Dwight, ed.** More Java Gems. (SIGS Reference Library Ser.: No. 16). 450p. 2000. pap. 40.00 (*0-521-77477-2*) Cambridge U Pr.

Deuink, James. Management Principles for Christian Schools. 3rd rev. ed. 448p. 1996. pap. 21.95 (*0-89084-874-2*, 094441) Bob Jones Univ.

Deuink, James W. Christian Education: Its Mandate & Mission. Horton, Ronald A., ed. LC 92-22625. 283p. (C). 1992. pap. 10.95 (*0-89084-639-1*, 058586) Bob Jones Univ.

— Christian School Finance. (Illus.). 160p. 1985. pap. 8.50 (*0-89084-304-X*, 026005) Bob Jones Univ.

— A Fresh Look at Christian Education. 168p. (Orig.). 1988. pap. 5.95 (*0-89084-448-8*, 034397) Bob Jones Univ.

— The Ministry of the Christian School Guidance Counselor: Pupil Personnel Services in the Christian School. (Illus.). 175p. 1985. pap. 8.50 (*0-89084-273-6*, 023416) Bob Jones Univ.

— The Proper Use of Standardized Tests. (Illus.). 64p. (Orig.). 1986. pap. 4.95 (*0-89084-355-4*, 030858) Bob Jones Univ.

Deuink, James W., ed. Some Light on Christian Education. (Illus.). 195p. (Orig.). 1984. pap. 5.95 (*0-89084-262-0*, 022848) Bob Jones Univ.

Deuink, James W. & Herbster, Carl D. Effective Christian School Management. 2nd ed. (Illus.). 291p. 1986. pap. 10.95 (*0-89084-319-8*, 019278) Bob Jones Univ.

Deuker, Carl. Heart of a Champion. LC 92-37231. 176p. (YA). (gr. 7-12). 1994. mass mkt. 4.50 (*0-380-72269-0*, Avon Bks) Morrow Avon.

Deuker, Carl. Heart of a Champion. LC 92-37231. (YA). 1993. 9.60 (*0-606-06454-0*, Pub. by Turtleback) Demco.

— Night Hoops. LC 99-47882. (Illus.). 256p. (YA). (gr. 7-12). 2000. 15.00 (*0-395-97936-6*) HM.

— On the Devil's Court. 256p. (YA). 1991. mass mkt. 4.99 (*0-380-70879-5*, Avon Bks) Morrow Avon.

Deuker, Carl. On the Devil's Court. (YA). 1998. 19.25 (*0-8446-6969-5*) Peter Smith.

— On the Devil's Court. 1991. 9.60 (*0-606-04995-9*, Pub. by Turtleback) Demco.

— Painting the Black. LC 96-23763. 256p. (YA). (gr. 6 up). 1997. 14.95 (*0-395-82848-1*) HM.

— Painting the Black. 256p. (YA). (gr. 7 up). 1999. mass mkt. 4.50 (*0-380-73104-5*, Avon Bks) Morrow Avon.

Deuker, Carol. Painting the Black. (YA). (gr. 7 up). 1997. 14.95 (*0-614-28826-6*) HM.

***Deuling, Maria.** Qualifikationsanforderungen in den Kaufmannischen Berufen: Regionale Arbeitskraftebedarfsanalyse. (Arbeit - Technik - Organisation - Soziales Ser.). 306p. 1999. 48.95 (*3-631-32738-2*) P Lang Pubng.

Deumlich, Fritz. Surveying Instruments. 336p. (C). 1981. text 85.40 (*3-11-007765-5*) De Gruyter.

Deupi, Carlos. Un Dia . . . Tal Vez un Viernes: Una Novela No Muy Seria, Pero Eso Si, Romantica. LC 92-70486. (Coleccion Caniqui). (SPA.). 243p. (Orig.). 1992. pap. 19.00 (*0-89729-638-9*) Ediciones.

Deupree, Robert G. The Wholesale Marketing of Fruits & Vegetables in Baltimore. LC 78-64175. (Johns Hopkins University. Studies in the Social Sciences. Thirtieth Ser. 1912: 2). 128p. 1982. reprint ed. 39.50 (*0-404-61284-9*) AMS Pr.

Deur, John. William Tell, 1984. 72p. 1986. pap. 11.95 (*0-918805-33-3*) Pac Aero Pr.

Deur, Lynne. Nishnawbe: A Story of Indians in Michigan. 2nd ed. (Illus.). 54p. (J). (gr. 4-6). 1981. pap. 8.95 (*0-938682-01-6*) River Rd Pubns.

— Settling in Michigan & Other True Pioneer Stories. (Illus.). 80p. (Orig.). (J). (gr. 3-6). 1992. pap. 9.95 (*0-938682-22-9*) River Rd Pubns.

Deur, Lynne, jt. auth. see Shafer, Jean.

Deurbrouck, Jo, jt. auth. see Burns, Candace.

Deursen, A. Van, see Van Deursen, A.

Deus, J. Dias De, see Costa Ramos, S. & Dias de Deus, J., eds.

***Deuschl, G., et al.** Recommendations for the Practice of Clinical Neurophysiology: Guidelines of the International Federation of Clinical Neurophysiology. 2nd rev. ed. LC 99-37656. 320p. 1999. 99.00 (*0-444-50295-5*) Elsevier.

***Deuschle, C.** Stop the Bus: A Handbook for Assessing Critical Issues with Students. LC 99-57992. 128p. 2000. pap. 22.50 (*0-7618-1600-3*) U Pr of Amer.

Deusen, A. H. Van, see Van Deusen, A. H.

Deusen, Glenn C. Van, see Van Deusen, Glenn C.

Deusen, John G. Van, see Van Deusen, John G.

Deusen, Julia M. Van, see Van Deusen, Julia M.

Deusen, Julia Van, see Van Deusen, Julia.

Deusen, Kira Van, see Van Deusen, Kira.

Deusen, M. Van, see Van Deusen, M.

Deusen, Nancy Van, see Van Deusen, Nancy, ed.

Deusen, Nancy Van, see Grundler, Otto & Van Deusen, Nancy.

Deusen, Richard Van, see Van Deusen, Richard.

Deuser, Hermann. Gott - Geist & Natur: Theologische Konsequenzen Aus Charles S. Pierce' Religionsphilosophie. (Theologische Bibliothek Toepelmann Ser.: Vol. 56). (GER.). xii, 257p. 1993. lib. bdg. 106.15 (*3-11-013742-9*) De Gruyter.

Deuser, Hermann, jt. ed. see Cappelorn, Niels J.

Deuss, Jean. Banking in the U. S. An Annotated Bibliography. LC 90-9069. 174p. 1990. 26.50 (*0-8108-2348-9*) Scarecrow.

Deuss, Jean, ed. Banking & Finance Collections. LC 83-26466. (Special Collections: Vol. 2, No. 3). 164p. 1984. text 49.95 (*0-86656-252-4*) Haworth Pr.

Deussen, P., ed. Theoretical Computer Science: 5th Conference. (Lecture Notes in Computer Science Ser.: Vol. 104). 261p. 1981. 28.00 (*0-387-10576-X*) Spr-Verlag.

Deussen, Paul. My Indian Reminiscences. King, A., tr. 1995. 17.00 (*81-206-1054-7*, Pub. by Asian Educ Servs) S Asia.

***Deussen, Paul.** Philosophy of the Upanishads. 429p. 1999. pap. 120.00 (*81-208-1620-X*, Pub. by Motilal Bnarsidass) St Mut.

Deussen, Paul. Die Sutra's des Vedanta. (GER.). xxiv, 768p. 1982. reprint ed. write for info. (*3-487-01369-X*) G Olms Pubs.

— The System of the Vedanta. (C). 1990. reprint ed. 15.00 (*81-85395-88-8*, Pub. by Low Price) S Asia.

Deuster, Patricia A., et al. The Navy Seal Nutrition Guide. (Illus.). 208p. (Orig.). 1996. reprint ed. pap. text 30.00 (*0-7881-2990-2*) DIANE Pub.

***Deustua, Jose R.** The Bewitchment of Silver: The Social Economy of Mining in Nineteenth-Century Peru. LC 99-34816. (Monographs in International Studies, Latin America Ser.: Vol. 31). 280p. 1999. pap. text 28.00 (*0-89680-209-4*) Ohio U Pr.

Deutch, Howard E. High Profits Without Risk. (Illus.). 1977. 29.95 (*0-917244-01-X*) Jefren Pub.

— Proxy Statements: Strategy & Forms, 12 vols. 15,000p. 1985. ring bd. 975.00 (*0-917244-02-8*) Jefren Pub.

Deutch, Miriam. Primitivism in Modern Art: A Research Guide. (Art-Architect Reference Ser.). 300p. Date not set. text 45.00 (*0-8153-1942-8*) Garland.

Deutch, Yvonne, ed. Painting in Watercolours. (Illus.). 128p. pap. 22.50 (*0-85532-704-9*, 704-9, Pub. by Srch Pr) A Schwartz & Co.

Deutches Dokumentationszentrum fur Kuntsgeschichte, jt. ed. see Bildarchiv Foto Marburg Staff.

Deutchman, Donna E., jt. auth. see Birren, James E.

Deutchman, Jeremy, jt. auth. see Percelay, James.

Deutelbaum, Marshall, ed. Image on the Art & Evolution of Film: Photographs & Articles from the Magazine of the International Museum of Photography. LC 78-94843. (Illus.). 256p. 1979. pap. 10.95 (*0-486-23777-X*) Dover.

Deutelbaum, Marshall & Poague, Leland, eds. A Hitchcock Reader. LC 86-176. (Illus.). 356p. (Orig.). 1986. pap. text 24.95 (*0-8138-0892-8*) Iowa St U Pr.

Deutermann, Peter T. The Edge of Honor. 1995. mass mkt. 5.99 (*0-312-95396-8*) St Martin.

— Official Privilege. 1996. mass mkt. 6.50 (*0-312-95713-0*) St Martin.

— The Red Crown. 1999. pap. write for info. (*0-451-18304-5*, Sig) NAL.

D

An Asterisk (*) at the beginning of an entry indicates that the title is appearing for the first time.

— Scorpion in the Sea. 1999. pap. write for info. (*0-451-18303-7*) NAL.

— Scorpion in the Sea. 1994. mass mkt. 6.99 (*0-312-95179-5*) St Martin.

— Scorpion in the Sea: The Goldsborough Incident. LC 92-30827. 496p. 1992. 19.95 (*0-913969-49-4*) Univ Pub Assocs.

— Sweepers. LC 97-5772. 1997. text 23.95 (*0-312-15669-3*) St Martin.

— Sweepers. 1998. mass mkt. 6.99 (*0-312-96447-1*, St Martins Paperbacks) St Martin.

***Deutermann, Peter T.** Train Man. 1999. mass mkt. write for info. (*0-312-97370-5*) St Martin.

Deutermann, Peter T. Train Man. 2nd ed. LC 99-23846. 384p. 1999. text 25.95 (*0-312-20375-6*) St Martin.

— Zero Option. 1999. mass mkt. 6.99 (*0-312-97004-8*, St Martins Paperbacks) St Martin.

— Zero Option: A Novel of Suspense. LC 98-21117. 384p. 1998. text 25.95 (*0-312-19210-X*) St Martin.

Deutman, A. F. & Cruysberg, J. R., eds. Neurogenetics & Neuro-Ophthalmology. (Documenta Ophthalmologica Proceedings Ser.: No. 17). 1979. text 255.50 (*90-6193-159-2*) Kluwer Academic.

Deutsch. New History of American People. (History Ser.). 1919. pap., wbk. ed. 10.00 (*0-534-55019-3*) Wadsworth Pub.

Deutsch. New History of American People. (History Ser.). 1919. 24.00 (*0-534-55021-5*); 50.00 (*0-314-22556-0*) Wadsworth Pub.

— New History of American People, Vol. 1. (History Ser.). 1919. 30.00 (*0-534-55017-7*) Wadsworth Pub.

— New History of American People, Vol. 2. (History Ser.). 1919. 30.00 (*0-534-55018-5*) Wadsworth Pub.

— New History of the American People Map Workbook. (History Ser.). 1919. pap., wbk. ed. 10.00 (*0-534-55020-7*) Thomson Learn.

Deutsch, et al. Construction Industry Insurance Handbook. LC 91-15623. (Construction Law Library). 416p. 1991. boxed set 150.00 (*0-471-52714-9*) Wiley.

Deutsch, Albert. Our Rejected Children. LC 74-1680. (Children & Youth Ser.: Vol. 29). 316p. 1974. reprint ed. 25.95 (*0-405-05958-2*) Ayer.

— The Shame of the States. LC 73-2394. (Mental Illness & Social Policy; the American Experience Ser.). 1980. reprint ed. 19.95 (*0-405-05202-2*) Ayer.

Deutsch, Albert, jt. auth. see Schneider, David M.

Deutsch, Alina. Sanda Marin's Traditional Romanian Cooking: Translated & Enhanced by Alina Deutsch. Anzick, William, ed. & illus. by.Tr. of Carte de Bucate by Sanda Marin. 487p. 1996. 24.65 (*0-9671692-0-8*) Black Sea Pubns.

Deutsch, Andrew. MRI of the Musculoskeletal System: A Teaching File. 2nd ed. 864p. 1996. text 156.00 (*0-397-51672-X*) Lppncott W & W.

Deutsch, Andrew L., et al, eds. MRI of the Foot & Ankle. 400p. 1992. text 153.00 (*0-88167-899-6*) Lppncott W & W.

Deutsch, Axel & Dietrich, John. Twilight in Berlin. (Illus.). 222p. 1998. pap. 7.95 (*1-901388-03-4*, Pub. by Chimera Pub) Xclusiv Distrib.

Deutsch, Babette. Poetry Handbook: A Dictionary of Terms. 4th ed. 224p. 1982. reprint ed. pap. 14.00 (*0-06-463548-1*, EH 548) HarpC.

— Poetry in Our Time. LC 73-191121. 457p. 1975. reprint ed. lib. bdg. 35.00 (*0-8371-7309-4*, DEPT, Greenwood Pr) Greenwood.

Deutsch, Babette & Yarmolinsky, Avrahm, eds. Contemporary German Poetry. LC 77-76934. (Granger Index Reprint Ser.). 1977. 19.95 (*0-8369-6010-6*) Ayer.

Deutsch, Babette, tr. see Pushkin, Aleksandr.

Deutsch, Babette, tr. & intro. see Rilke, Rainer Maria.

Deutsch, Bob. The Real Estate Agent's Action Guide to Listing & Sales Success. 209p. 1993. pap. 23.95 (*0-7931-0714-8*, 19070701, Real Estate Ed) Dearborn.

Deutsch, Celia M. Hidden Wisdom & the Easy Yoke: Wisdom, Torah & Discipleship in Matthew 11-25-30. (JSNTS Ser.: Vol. 18). 1987. pap. 18.95 (*1-85075-057-2*, Pub. by Sheffield Acad) CUP Services.

— Lady Wisdom, Jesus & the Sages: Metaphor & Social Context in Matthew's Gospel. LC 96-32904. 240p. (Orig.). 1996. pap. 20.00 (*1-56338-163-X*) TPI PA.

Deutsch, Charles. Broken Bottles, Broken Dreams: Understanding & Helping the Children of Alcoholics. LC 81-5729. 232p. 1982. pap. text 18.95 (*0-8077-2663-X*) Tchrs Coll.

Deutsch, Clayton V. & Journel, Andre G. GSLIB: Geostatistical Software Library & User's Guide. 2nd ed. (Illus.). 384p. (C). 1997. text 62.95 (*0-19-510015-8*) OUP.

Deutsch, Dale G., ed. Analytical Aspects of Drug Testing. LC 88-17291. (Chemical Analysis Ser.). 304p. 1989. 205.00 (*0-471-85309-7*) Wiley.

Deutsch, David. The Fabric of Reality: The Science of Parallel Universes & Its Implications. LC 97-6171. 400p. 1998. pap. 14.95 (*0-14-027541-X*) Viking Penguin.

Deutsch, Diana. The Psychology of Music. 1984. pap. text 54.00 (*0-12-213562-8*) Acad Pr.

— The Psychology of Music. 2nd ed. LC 98-85210. (Illus.). 807p. (C). 1998. pap. text 69.95 (*0-12-213565-2*); boxed set 129.95 (*0-12-213564-4*) Acad Pr.

Deutsch, Diana, des. The Intelligent Ear. pap. text. write for info. (*0-7167-5063-5*) W H Freeman.

Deutsch, Didier. Rodgers & Hammerstein. (Illus.). 192p. 1998. pap. 29.95 (*0-7893-0231-4*, Pub. by Universe) St Martin.

Deutsch, Didier C. MusicHound Soundtracks: The Essential Album Guide to Film, Television & Stage Music. 2nd ed. LC 99-42807. (Illus.). 872p. 1999. pap. text 26.95 (*1-57859-101-5*) Visible Ink Pr.

Deutsch, E., et al, eds. Laboratoriumsdiagnostik: Normalbereich der Ergebnisse und Interpretation Abnormer Befunde. 3rd ed. (Illus.). x, 1168p. 1991. 71.50 (*3-8055-5487-7*) S Karger.

Deutsch, Eliot. Advaita Vedanta: A Philosophical Reconstruction. LC 69-19282. (C). 1980. pap. text 8.00 (*0-8248-0271-3*) UH Pr.

— Essays on the Nature of Art. LC 95-26407. (Illus.). 122p. (C). 1996. text 44.50 (*0-7914-3111-8*); pap. text 14.95 (*0-7914-3112-6*) State U NY Pr.

— Introduction to World Philosophies. LC 96-22934. 509p. 1996. pap. text 56.00 (*0-13-227505-8*) P-H.

— Religion & Spirituality. LC 94-33771. 151p. (C). 1995. text 39.50 (*0-7914-2457-X*); pap. text 12.95 (*0-7914-2458-8*) State U NY Pr.

Deutsch, Eliot, ed. Culture & Modernity: East - West Philosophic Perspectives. LC 91-19107. 664p. (C). 1991. text 39.25 (*0-8248-1370-7*) UH Pr.

Deutsch, Eliot & Bontekoe, Ron, eds. A Companion to World Philosophies. LC 96-36179. (Companions to Philosophy Ser.). 608p. (C). 1997. 99.95 (*0-631-19871-7*) Blackwell Pubs.

— A Companion to World Philosophies. (Blackwell Companions to Philosophy Ser.). 608p. 1999. reprint ed. pap. 34.95 (*0-631-21327-9*) Blackwell Pubs.

Deutsch, Eliot & Van Buitenen, J. A. A Source Book of Advaita Vedanta. LC 75-148944. 345p. reprint ed. pap. 98.40 (*0-608-11847-8*, 2017216) Bks Demand.

Deutsch, Eliot, jt. ed. see Larson, Gerald J.

Deutsch, Evelyn, jt. auth. see Drutman, Ave D.

***Deutsch, Ezra & Schwartz, Robert, eds.** Coronary Artery Restenosis. 375p. 2000. 125.00 (*0-89603-740-1*) Humana.

Deutsch, F., jt. ed. see Brosowski, F.

Deutsch, Felix, ed. On the Mysterious Leap from the Mind to the Body: A Workshop Study on the Theory of Conversion. LC 59-8411. 1969. reprint ed. pap. 24.95 (*0-8236-8174-2*, 023800) Intl Univs Pr.

Deutsch, Felix & Murphy, William F. The Clinical Interview Vol. 1: Diagnosis, Vol. 1. 613p. 1997. text 70.00 (*0-8236-0920-0*) Intl Univs Pr.

— The Clinical Interview Vol. 2: Therapy. LC 54-12140. 355p. 1967. text 52.50 (*0-8236-0940-5*) Intl Univs Pr.

Deutsch, Francine, jt. auth. see Hultsch, David F.

Deutsch, Francine M. Halving It All: How Equally Shared Parenting Works. LC 98-30738. 336p. 1999. 24.95 (*0-674-36800-2*) HUP.

***Deutsch, Francine M.** Halving It All: How Equally Shared Parenting Works. 2000. pap. 14.95 (*0-674-00209-1*) HUP.

Deutsch, Geog, jt. auth. see Springer, Sally P.

Deutsch, Gitta. The Red Thread. unabridged ed. (Studies in Austrian Literature, Culture, & Thought). Orig. Title: Bocklinstrassenelegie. (Illus.). 145p. 1996. 16.95 (*1-57241-019-1*) Ariadne CA.

Deutsch, Guy N. Iconographie de l'Illustration de Flavius Josephe au Temps de Jean Fouquet. (Arbeiten zur Literatur und Geschichte des Hellenistischen Judentums Ser.: Band 12). (FRE., Illus.). xi, 225p. 1986. 82.00 (*90-04-07121-0*) Brill Academic Pubs.

Deutsch, Harold C. The Conspiracy Against Hitler in the Twilight War. LC 68-22365. 406p. reprint ed. pap. 125.90 (*0-608-16705-3*, 205619900055) Bks Demand.

— Hitler & His Generals: The Hidden Crisis, January-June 1938. LC 73-86627. 488p. reprint ed. pap. 151.30 (*0-608-16695-2*, 205619400055) Bks Demand.

***Deutsch, Helen.** Case of Doctor Johnson. 1999. lib. bdg. 42.00 (*0-226-14382-1*) U Ch Pr.

— Case Of Dr. Johnson. 1999. pap. text 16.00 (*0-226-14384-8*) U Ch Pr.

Deutsch, Helen. Resemblance & Disgrace: Alexander Pope & the Deformation of Culture. (Illus.). 304p. 1996. 43.50 (*0-674-76489-7*) HUP.

***Deutsch, Helen & Nussbaum, Felicity, eds.** Defects: Engendering the Modern Body. LC 99-6767. (Illus.). 344p. 2000. text 57.50 (*0-472-09698-2*, 09698); pap. text 22.95 (*0-472-06698-6*, 06698) U of Mich Pr.

Deutsch, Helene. Neuroses & Character Types: Clinical Psychoanalytic Studies. LC 65-15288. xii, 388p. (Orig.). 1965. 57.50 (*0-8236-3560-0*) Intl Univs Pr.

— Psychoanalysis of the Sexual Functions of Women. Roazen, P., ed. 149p. 1991. pap. text 25.00 (*0-946439-95-8*, Pub. by H Karnac Bks Ltd) Other Pr LLC.

— Psychoanalytic Study of the Myth of Dionysus & Apollo: Two Variants of the Son-Mother Relationship. LC 70-85198. (New York Psychoanalytic Institute Freud Anniversary Lecture Ser.). 101p. 1969. 27.50 (*0-8236-4975-X*) Intl Univs Pr.

— The Psychology of Women, 2 vols. Incl. Vol. I. Girlhood. LC 44-5287. 413p. 1944. text 72.00 (*0-8089-0115-X*, 791031, W B Saunders Co); Vol. II. Motherhood. LC 44-5287. 505p. 1945. text 60.00 (*0-8089-0116-8*, 791032, W B Saunders Co); LC 44-5287. write for info. (*0-318-52863-0*, Grune & Strat) Harcrt Hlth Sci Grp.

— Selected Problems of Adolescence: With Emphasis on Group Formation. LC 67-28587. (Psychoanalytic Study of the Child Monographs: No. 3). 246p. (Orig.). 1967. 27.50 (*0-8236-6040-0*) Intl Univs Pr.

— The Therapeutic Process, the Self, & Female Psychology: Collected Psychoanalytic Papers. Roazen, Paul, ed. 376p. (C). 1991. text 44.95 (*0-88738-429-3*) Transaction Pubs.

Deutsch, Herbert A. Synthesis, An Introduction to the History, Theory & Practice of Electronic Music. rev. ed. LC 85-30824. (Illus.). 132p. 1976. pap. 15.95 (*0-88284-348-6*, 1439) Alfred Pub.

Deutsch, Herman J., ed. Surveying the Forty-Ninth Parallel, 1858-61. (Illus.). 17p. 1962. pap. 1.00 (*0-917048-24-5*) Wash St Hist Soc.

Deutsch, Hermann B. Brennan's New Orleans Cookbook. LC 60-53567. (Illus.). 256p. 1982. 17.95 (*0-88289-382-3*) Pelican.

Deutsch, Howard, jt. auth. see Collard, David.

Deutsch, Howard D. Employer's Complete Guide to Immigration: New Law, New Questions, New Answers. 300p. 1987. 35.00 (*0-13-274713-8*, Busn) P-H.

— Immigration the Easy Way: Including a Guide to Canadian Immigration. LC 92-27054. 320p. 1993. pap. 14.95 (*0-8120-4798-2*) Barron.

Deutsch, Howard M. & Kitzler, Kim M. Exploring Organic Chemistry. (C). 1997. text 20.00 (*0-13-281438-2*, Macmillan Coll) P-H.

Deutsch, J. Anthony. Structural Basis of Behavior. LC 60-12466. 1995. lib. bdg. 19.50 (*0-226-14345-7*) U Ch Pr.

— The Structural Basis of Behavior. LC 60-12466. (Illus.). 195p. reprint ed. pap. 60.50 (*0-608-09448-X*, 205424800005) Bks Demand.

Deutsch, Jan G. Selling the People's Cadillac: The Edsel & Corporate Responsibility. LC 75-37292. 300p. 1976. 57.50 (*0-300-01950-5*) Yale U Pr.

Deutsch, Karl W. The Growth of Nations: Some Recurrent Patterns of Political & Social Integration. (Reprint Series in Social Sciences). (C). 1993. reprint ed. pap. text 5.00 (*0-8290-3553-2*, PS-62) Irvington.

Deutsch, Karl W., et al. Comparative Government: Politics of Industrialized & Developing Nations. (Illus.). 494p. (C). 1981. teacher ed. 2.36 (*0-685-02286-2*) HM.

— Political Community & the North Atlantic Area: International Organization in the Light of Historical Experience. LC 69-13882. 228p. 1969. reprint ed. lib. bdg. 38.50 (*0-8371-1054-8*, DEPO, Greenwood Pr) Greenwood.

Deutsch, Kenneth L. & Murley, John A., eds. Leo Strauss: The Straussians & the Study of the American Regime. LC 99-22578. 472p. 1999. 70.00 (*0-8476-8691-4*); pap. 29.95 (*0-8476-8692-2*) Rowman.

Deutsch, Kenneth L. & Nicgorski, Walter, eds. Leo Strauss: Political Philosopher & Jewish Thinker. 406p. (C). 1993. lib. bdg. 64.50 (*0-8476-7837-7*) Rowman.

— Leo Strauss: Political Philosopher & Jewish Thinker. 406p. (C). 1994. pap. text 24.95 (*0-8476-7838-5*) Rowman.

Deutsch, Kenneth L. & Soffer, Walter, eds. The Crisis of Liberal Democracy: A Straussian Perspective. LC 86-5908. (SUNY Series in Political Theory). 304p. (C). 1987. text 24.50 (*0-88706-388-8*) State U NY Pr.

***Deutsch, Klaus-Gunter.** Politics of Freer Trade in Europe: Three-level Games in The Common Commercial Policy of The Eu. LC 99-12710. 1999. text 59.95 (*0-312-22347-1*) St Martin.

Deutsch, Lawrence J. & Richards. Elementary Hearing Science. 208p. 1991. pap. text 56.00 (*0-205-13558-7*) P-H.

Deutsch, Lenna A., ed. see Conant, Roger.

Deutsch, Marilyn W. Are You Tired Again? . . . I Understand: An Activities Workbook to Help Children Understand & Live with a Person Who Has a Chronic Illness or Disability. (Illus.). 42p. (YA). (ps-8). 1998. pap., wbk. ed. 14.95 (*0-87424-331-9*, W-331A) Manson Western Corp.

Deutsch, Melvin, ed. Management of Childhood Brain Tumors. (Foundations of Neurological Surgery Ser.). (C). 1990. text 303.50 (*0-7923-0669-4*) Kluwer Academic.

Deutsch, Michael S. & Willis, Ronald R. Software Quality Engineering: A Total Technical & Management Approach. (Illus.). 416p. (C). 1988. text 34.67 (*0-685-37792-X*) P-H.

— Software Quality Engineering: A Total Technical & Management Approach. LC 87-25712. (C). 1988. text 65.20 (*0-13-823204-0*) P-H.

Deutsch, Mina. Mina's Story: Memoir of the Holocaust. LC 96-145562. (Illus.). 184p. 1994. pap. 14.95 (*1-55022-212-0*, Pub. by ECW) Genl Dist Srvs.

Deutsch, Monroe E. Letter & the Spirit: A Selection from His Addresses. (Essay Index Reprint Ser.). 1977. 23.95 (*0-8369-0372-2*) Ayer.

Deutsch, Morton. Distributive Justice: A Social-Psychological Perspective. LC 84-19695. 321p. reprint ed. pap. 99.60 (*0-7837-4535-4*, 208025500004) Bks Demand.

— The Resolution of Conflict: Constructive & Destructive Processes. LC 73-80080. (Carl Hovland Memorial Lectures). (Illus.). 448p. 1977. pap. 25.00 (*0-300-02186-0*) Yale U Pr.

***Deutsch, Morton & Coleman, Peter, eds.** Handbook of Conflict Resolution: Theory & Practice. LC 99-50875. 608p. 2000. 59.95 (*0-7879-4822-5*, Pfffr & Co) Jossey-Bass.

Deutsch, N. Guardians of the Gate, Angelic Vice Regency in Late Antiquity. LC 98-45877. (Brill's Series in Jewish Studies). 1998. 63.50 (*90-04-10909-9*) Brill Academic Pubs.

Deutsch, Nathaniel. The Gnostic Imagination: Gnosticism, Mandaeism, & Merkabah Mysticism. LC 95-17253. (Jewish Studies: Vol. 13). x, 163p. 1995. 67.50 (*90-04-10264-7*) Brill Academic Pubs.

Deutsch, Nathaniel, jt. ed. see Chireau, Yvonne.

Deutsch, Nicholas, jt. ed. see Barnes, Noreen C.

Deutsch, Otto. Handel: A Documentary Biography. LC 74-3118. (Music Ser.). 942p. 1974. reprint ed. lib. bdg. 85.00 (*0-306-70624-5*) Da Capo.

Deutsch, Otto E. Mozart: A Documentary Biography. xii, 680p. 1966. 59.50 (*0-8047-0233-0*) Stanford U Pr.

— Schubert: A Documentary Biography. Blom, Eric, tr. LC 77-5499. (Music Reprint Ser.). (Illus.). 1977. reprint ed. lib. bdg. 125.00 (*0-306-77420-8*) Da Capo.

— The Schubert Reader: Music Book Index. 1039p. 1993. reprint ed. lib. bdg. 119.00 (*0-7812-9618-8*) Rprt Serv.

— The Schubert Thematic Catalogue. unabridged ed. LC 95-14500. Orig. Title: Schubert, Thematic Catalogue of All His Works in Chronological Order. 592p. 1995. reprint ed. pap. text 16.95 (*0-486-28685-1*) Dover.

Deutsch, Otto E., ed. Schubert: Memoirs by His Friends. (Illus.). 520p. 2000. pap. text 35.00 (*0-19-816436-X*) OUP.

Deutsch, Otto E., ed. see Schubert, Franz.

***Deutsch, Otto Erich.** Schubert: A Documentary Biography. 2000. reprint ed. lib. bdg. 169.00 (*0-7812-9724-9*) Rprt Serv.

Deutsch, Paul & Sawyer, Horace W. A Guide to Rehabilitation, 2 vols., Set. 3000p. 1985. text 180.00 (*1-887515-02-X*) AHAB Press.

Deutsch, Paul M. A Guide to Rehabilitation Testimony: The Expert's Role As an Educator. 135.00 (*1-878205-21-8*) St Lucie Pr.

— A Guide to Rehabilitation Testimony: The Expert's Role As an Educator. LC 90-93269. 512p. 1990. boxed set 62.95 (*1-878205-02-1*) St Lucie Pr.

— Life Care Planning for the Spinal Cord Injured: A Step-by-Step Guide. 88p. 1989. per. 26.95 (*0-945019-08-4*) St Lucie Pr.

Deutsch, R. & Heltzer, M. Forty New Ancient West Semitic Inscriptions. 100p. 1994. text 48.00 (*965-222-511-8*, Pub. by Archaeol Ctr) Eisenbrauns.

Deutsch, R. L., et al. Butterworths Australian Taxation Handbook, 1994. 1994. pap. 68.00 (*0-409-30838-2*, A.T., MICHIE) LEXIS Pub.

Deutsch, Richard. Passers & Receivers: The NFL's Top Touchdown Duos. Gramling, Scott & Northrop, Michael, eds. 32p. (J). (gr. 2-8). 1999. pap. 3.99 (*1-886749-67-1*) SI For Kids.

Deutsch, Robert. Messages from the Past: Hebrew Bullae from the Time of Isaiah through the Destruction of the First Temple-Shlomo Moussaieff Collection & an Updated Corpus. (HEB.). 172p. 1997. text 80.00 (*965090240-3-7*, Pub. by Archaeol Ctr) Eisenbrauns.

Deutsch, Robert. Messages from the Past: Hebrew Bullae from the Time of Isaiah through the Destruction of the First Temple-Shlomo Moussaieff Collection & an Updated Corpus. (HEB.). 172p. 1997. text 60.00 (*965-222-795-1*, Pub. by Archaeol Ctr) Eisenbrauns.

***Deutsch, Robert.** Messages from the Past: Hebrew Bullae from the Time of Isaiah through the Destruction of the First Temple-Shlomo Moussaieff Collection & an Updated Corpus. 206p. 1999. text 80.00 (*965-90240-5-3*, Pub. by Archaeol Ctr) Eisenbrauns.

Deutsch, Robert & Heltzer, Michael. New Epigraphic Evidence from the Biblical Period. (Illus.). 116p. 1995. text 48.00 (*965-222-612-2*, Pub. by Archaeol Ctr) Eisenbrauns.

***Deutsch, Robert & Heltzer, Michael.** West Semitic Epigraphic News of the 1st Millennium BCE. 96p. 1999. text 48.00 (*965-90240-4-5*, Pub. by Archaeol Ctr) Eisenbrauns.

Deutsch, Robert & Heltzer, Michael. Windows in the Past. 93p. 1997. text 48.00 (*965-222-839-7*, Pub. by Archaeol Ctr) Eisenbrauns.

Deutsch, Robert, jt. ed. see Avishur, Yitzhak.

Deutsch, Robert W. & Whitney, J. W. Physics. (Academic Program for Nuclear Power Plant Personnel Ser., BWR Version: Vol. II). (Illus.). 532p. 1972. teacher ed., ring bd. 195.00 (*0-87683-154-4*); teacher ed., ring bd. 35.00 (*0-87683-161-7*); teacher ed., ring bd. 25.00 (*0-87683-168-4*); ring bd. 39.50 (*0-87683-147-1*, A 373978) GP Courseware.

D

Deutsch, Robert W. & Whitney, J. W., eds. Academic Program for Nuclear Power Plant Personnel: BWR. (Illus.). 1754p. 1974. teacher ed. 595.00 (*0-87683-151-X*); ring bd. 129.50 (*0-87683-144-7*); 75.00 (*0-87683-158-7*); 95.00 (*0-87683-165-X*) GP Courseware.

— Academic Program for Nuclear Power Plant Personnel: PWR, 4 vols. (Illus.). 1762p. text 129.50 (*0-87683-145-5*); teacher ed. 595.00 (*0-87683-152-8*); 75.00 (*0-87683-159-5*); 195.00 (*0-87683-166-8*) GP Courseware.

— BWR Nuclear Power Plant Technology. (Academic Program for Nuclear Power Plant Personnel Ser., BWR Version: Vol. III). (Illus.). 396p. 1974. teacher ed. 195.00 (*0-87683-155-2*); student ed. 25.00 (*0-87683-162-5*); student ed. 35.00 (*0-87683-169-2*); ring bd. 39.50 (*0-87683-148-X*, A 373878) GP Courseware.

— Chemistry, Health Physics, & Nuclear Instrumentation. (Academic Program for Nuclear Power Plant Personnel Ser., BWR Version: Vol. IV). (Illus.). 454p. 1972. teacher ed. 195.00 (*0-87683-157-9*); student ed. 25.00 (*0-87683-164-1*); student ed. 35.00 (*0-87683-171-4*); ring bd. 39.50 (*0-87683-150-1*, A 373977) GP Courseware.

— Mathematics. (Academic Program for Nuclear Power Plant Personnel Ser., BWR Version: Vol. I). (Illus.). 372p. 1972. teacher ed. 195.00 (*0-87683-153-6*); ring bd. 39.95 (*0-87683-146-3*, A 326517); 25.00 (*0-87683-160-9*); 35.00 (*0-87683-167-6*) GP Courseware.

— PWR Nuclear Power Plant Technology. (Academic Program for Nuclear Power Plant Personnel Ser., BWR Version: Vol. III-CPWR Version). (Illus.). 404p. 1972. teacher ed., ring bd. 195.00 (*0-87683-156-0*); teacher ed., ring bd. 25.00 (*0-87683-163-3*); teacher ed., ring bd. 35.00 (*0-87683-170-6*); ring bd. 39.50 (*0-87683-149-8*, A 377747) GP Courseware.

Deutsch, Robert W., et al. Introduction to Boiling Water Reactor Nuclear Power Plants. (Illus.). 240p. 1976. ring bd. 95.00 (*0-87683-298-2*) GP Courseware.

— Practical Nuclear Power Plant Technology, 2 vols. (Illus.). 1973. ring bd. 175.00 (*0-87683-295-8*) GP Courseware.

Deutsch, Roger D. & Rivera, Rudy. Your Hidden Food Allergies Are Making You Fat: The ALCAT Food Sensitivities Weight Loss Breakthrough. LC 98-25791. 240p. 1998. per. 14.00 (*0-7615-1434-1*) Prima Pub.

Deutsch, Ronald M. & Morrill, Judi S. Realities of Nutrition. 2nd ed. 400p. 1993. pap. 24.95 (*0-923521-25-9*) Bull Pub.

Deutsch, Ronald M., jt. auth. see Bach, George R.

Deutsch, Ronald W. Inspirational Hollywood: Reflections on Life , Love & the Art of Filmmaking. LC 97-26510. 128p. Date not set. pap. 12.95 (*0-941188-63-9*, 32rls) M Wiese.

Deutsch, S. I., et al. Application of Basic Neuroscience to Child Psychiatry. LC 90-7203. (Illus.). 420p. (C). 1990. text 69.50 (*0-306-43357-5*, Kluwer Plenum) Kluwer Academic.

Deutsch, Sandra M. Counterrevolution in Argentina, 1900-1932: The Argentine Patriotic League. LC 85-16388. x, 319p. 1986. text 50.00 (*0-8032-1669-6*) U of Nebr Pr.

Deutsch, Sandra McGee. Las Derechas: The Extreme Right in Argentina, Brazil & Chile, 1890-1939. LC 99-19783. 1999. 60.00 (*0-8047-3208-6*) Stanford U Pr.

Deutsch, Sarah. No Separate Refuge: Culture, Class & Gender on an Anglo-Hispanic Frontier in the American Southwest, 1880-1940. 368p. (C). 1989. reprint ed. pap. text 23.95 (*0-19-506073-3*) OUP.

***Deutsch, Sarah.** Women & the City: Gender, Power & Space in Boston, 1870-1940. LC 99-34659. (Illus.). 402p. 2000. 35.00 (*0-19-505705-8*) OUP.

Deutsch, Sarah J. From Ballots to Breadlines: American Women 1920-1940, Vol. 8. (Young Oxford History of Women in the United States Ser.). (Illus.). 144p. (J). 1998. reprint ed. pap. 10.95 (*0-19-512406-5*) OUP.

Deutsch, Shaul S. Larger Than Life: The Life & Times of the Lubavitcher Rebbe Rabbi Menachem M. Schneerson, Vol. I. (Illus.). 277p. 1995. 25.00 (*0-9647243-0-8*) Chasidic Hist Prodns.

— Larger Than Life Vol. II: The Lubavitcher Rebbe's Years in Riga & Berlin. (Illus.). 1997. 25.00 (*0-9647243-1-6*) Chasidic Hist Prodns.

Deutsch, Sheryl, jt. ed. see Mobley, Christine.

Deutsch, Sheryl K., jt. auth. see Mobley, Christine S.

Deutsch, Sid. Return of the Ether: When Theory & Reality Collide. 13p. 1999. 24.95 (*1-891121-10-3*) SciTech Pub.

Deutsch-Skandinavisches Symposium, Kopenhagen, 197. Parenterale Ernaehrung (Forschung und Praxis) Zoellner, N., ed. (Beitraege zur Infusionstherapie und Klinische Ernaehrung Ser.: Band 1). (Illus.). 1978. pap. 15.00 (*3-8055-2963-5*) S Karger.

Deutsch Staff. Biometrisches Woerterbuch. 3rd ed. (CZE, ENG, FRE, GER & HUN.). 965p. 1988. write for info. (*0-614-00671-6*, 3817110529) Fr & Eur.

Deutsch, Stefanie. Barbie the First Thirty Years, 1959 Through 1989: An Identification & Value Guide. 288p. 1995. 24.95 (*0-89145-665-1*) Collector Bks.

Deutsch, Susan L., ed. Community-Based Teaching: A Guide to Developing & Implementing Education Programs for Medical Students & Residents in the Practitioner's Office. LC 97-6376. 100p. (Orig.). (C). 1997. pap. text 34.00 (*0-943126-59-2*) Amer Coll Phys.

Deutsch, Thomas A. & Feller, Daniel B. Paton & Goldberg's Management of Ocular Injuries. 2nd ed. (Illus.). 248p. 1985. text 82.00 (*0-7216-1173-7*, W B Saunders Co) Harcrt Hlth Sci Grp.

Deutsch, Tibor, et al. Dealing with Medical Knowledge: Computers in Clinical Decision Making. LC 94-24011. (Illus.). 310p. (C). 1994. text 79.50 (*0-306-44849-1*, Kluwer Plenum) Kluwer Academic.

Deutsch, Valerie W., jt. auth. see Sutherland, Laura.

Deutsch Verein Staff. Woerterbuch Soziale Arbeit: German-French, French-German. (FRE & GER.). 136p. 1988. 39.95 (*0-7859-7094-0*) Fr & Eur.

***Deutsch, Yosef.** Let My Nation Go. LC 99-220860. 404p. 1998. 21.95 (*0-87306-818-1*) Feldheim.

Deutschbein, Mary J. Maggie's Weaning. 27p. (J). 1994. pap. 6.95 (*1-885678-08-8*) Moon Gold.

— Maggie's Weaning. 2nd ed. LC 99-63807. (Illus.). 24p. (J). (ps-1). 1999. pap. 6.95 (*0-912500-58-1*) La Leche.

Deutsche Babcock-Werke Staff. Multilingual Dictionary of Steam Engineering Terms. (GER, ENG, SPA & FRE). (ENG, GER & SPA.). 1994. 225.00 (*0-7859-7040-1*) Fr & Eur.

Deutsche Bundesbank Staff, ed. Fifty Years of the Deutsche Mark: The Central Bank & the Currency since 1948. LC 99-214315. (Illus.). 864p. 1999. text 90.00 (*0-19-829254-6*) OUP.

Deutsche Forschungsgemeinschaft Staff. Boundary Element Topics: Proceedings of the Final Conference of the Priority Research Program. Boundary Element Methods 1989-1995 of the German Research Foundation, Stuttgart, October 2-4, 1995. Wendland, W. L., ed. LC 97-31134. (Illus.). xviii, 498p. 1997. 129.00 (*3-540-62850-9*) Spr-Verlag.

Deutsche Forschungsgemeinschaft Staff, ed. List of MAK & BAT Values 1997 Report No. 33: Maximum Concentrations & Biological Tolerance Values at the Workplace. 212p. 1997. pap. 84.95 (*3-527-27575-4*, Wiley-VCH) Wiley.

Deutsche Gesellschaft fur Klinishe Chemie Symposiu. Heparin: New Biochemical & Medical Aspects: Proceedings. Witt, Irene, ed. xvi, 372p. 1983. 119.25 (*3-11-008637-9*) De Gruyter.

Deutsche Gesellschaft Fur Luft und Raumfahrt. Utilization of Space Shuttle & Spacelab: Proceedings of an International Meeting Held in Bonn, 1976. (Illus.). 1976. pap. 30.00 (*3-88135-034-9*) Univelt Inc.

Deutsche, Rosalyn. Evictions: Art & Spatial Politics. LC 96-15527. (Graham Foundations/MIT Press Series in Contemporary Architecture Discourse). (Illus.). 400p. (C). 1996. 40.00 (*0-262-04158-8*) MIT Pr.

— Evictions: Art & Spatial Politics. 3rd ed. LC 96-15527. (Graham Foundations/MIT Press Series in Contemporary Architecture Discourse). (Illus.). 394p. 1998. pap. text 20.00 (*0-262-54097-5*) MIT Pr.

Deutsche, Rosalyn, et al. Krzysztof Wodiczko - New York City Tableaux: Tomkins Square: The Homeless Vehicle Project. Ingberman, Jeanette, ed. (Illus.). 48p. (Orig.). 1991. pap. 20.00 (*0-913263-29-X*) Exit Art.

Deutsche Schwestergemeinschaft Staff. Sprachfuehrer fuer die Krankenpflege. 253p. 1968. pap. 19.95 (*0-8288-6662-7*, M-7627) Fr & Eur.

Deutsche Verein Staff. Worterbuch Soziale Arbeit, in Zweites Bandes Vol. 1. (ENG & GER.). 120p. 1988. lib. bdg. 45.00 (*0-8288-3406-7*, F106530) Fr & Eur.

Deutschen Akademie der Wissenschaften Staff. Rudolfs von Ems Weltchronik. (Deutsche Texte des Mittelalters Ser.: Band XX). (GER.). xxxvii, 634p. 1967. write for info. (*3-296-17220-3*, Pub. by Weidmann) Lubrecht & Cramer.

Deutschen Akademie der Wissenschaften Staff & Heidlauf, Felix. Lucidarius. (Deutsche Texte des Mittelalters Ser.: Band XXVIII). (GER.). xviii, 98p. write for info. (*3-296-17228-9*, Pub. by Weidmann) Lubrecht & Cramer.

Deutschen Akademie der Wissenschaften Staff & Hubner, Alfred. Ulrich Von Turheim. (Deutsche Texte des Mittelalters Ser.: Band XXXIX). (GER.). li, 614p. 1966. write for info. (*3-296-17239-4*, Pub. by Weidmann) Lubrecht & Cramer.

Deutschen Akademie der Wissenschaften Staff & Kopp, Arthur. Volks-Und Gesellschaftslieder des 15. und 16. Jahrhunderts. (Deutsche Texte des Mittelalters Ser.: Band V). (GER.). xviii, 254p. 1970. write for info. (*3-296-17250-5*, Pub. by Weidmann) Lubrecht & Cramer.

Deutschen Akademie der Wissenschaften Staff & Mayer, A. L. Hans Folz. (Deutsche Texte des Mittelalters Ser.: Band XII). (GER.). xxii, 438p. 1970. write for info. (*3-296-17212-2*, Pub. by Weidmann) Lubrecht & Cramer.

Deutschen Akademie der Wissenschaften Staff & Papke, Max. Wernher der Schweizer. (Deutsche Texte des Mittelalters Ser.: Band XXVII). (GER.). xviii, 287p. 1967. write for info. (*3-296-17227-0*, Pub. by Weidmann) Lubrecht & Cramer.

Deutschen Akademie der Wissenschaften Staff & Pyritz, Hans. Die Minneburg. (Deutsche Texte des Mittelalters Ser.: Band XLIII). (GER.). lxxvi, 219p. 1991. reprint ed. 118.00 (*3-615-00068-4*, Pub. by Weidmann) Lubrecht & Cramer.

Deutschen Akademie der Wissenschaften Staff & Reissenberger, Karl. Das Vaterbuch. (Deutsche Texte des Mittelalters Ser.: Band XXII). (GER.). xxv, 634p. 1967. write for info. (*3-296-17222-X*, Pub. by Weidmann) Lubrecht & Cramer.

Deutschen Akademie der Wissenschaften Staff & Rosenhagen, Gustav. Kleinere Mittelhochdeutsche Erzahlungen, Fabeln und Lehrgedichte - III. (Deutsche Texte des Mittelalters Ser.: Band XVII). (GER.). xli, 251p. 1970. write for info. (*3-296-17217-3*, Pub. by Weidmann) Lubrecht & Cramer.

Deutschen Akademie der Wissenschaften Staff & Thiele, Gerhard. Mittelhochdeutsche Minnereden II. (Deutsche Texte des Mittelalters Ser.: Band XLI). (GER.). xxviii, 249p. 1967. write for info. (*3-296-17224-6*, Pub. by Weidmann) Lubrecht & Cramer.

Deutschen Akademie der Wissenschaften Staff & Vetter, Ferdinand. Tauler. (Deutsche Texte des Mittelalters Ser.: Band XI). (GER.). xx, 518p. 1968. write for info. (*3-296-17211-4*, Pub. by Weidmann) Lubrecht & Cramer.

Deutschen Akademie der Wissenschaften Staff & Von Orlens, Willehalm. Rudolf von Ems. (Deutsche Texte des Mittelalters Ser.: Band II). (GER.). xliii, 278p. 1967. write for info. (*3-296-17210-6*, Pub. by Weidmann) Lubrecht & Cramer.

Deutschen Akademie der Wissenschaften Staff, et al. Johann von Wurzburg. (Deutsche Texte des Mittelalters Ser.: Band III). (GER.). xxii, 334p. 1970. write for info. (*3-296-17230-0*, Pub. by Weidmann) Lubrecht & Cramer.

— Kleinere Mittelhochdeutsche Erzahlungen, Fabeln, Lehrgedichte. (Deutsche Texte des Mittelalters Ser.: Band IV). (GER.). xvi, 55p. 1970. write for info. (*3-296-17240-8*, Pub. by Weidmann) Lubrecht & Cramer.

Deutschen Archaeologischen Institut Staff, ed. Inschriften von Milet Teil 1: Ergebnisse der Ausgrabungen und Untersuchungen seit dem Jahre 1899. (Milet - Ergebnisse der Ausgrabungen und Untersuchungen seit dem Jahre 1899 Ser.: Vol. VI, Pt. 1). (GER., Illus.). ix, 231p. (C). 1996. lib. bdg. 214.00 (*3-11-014540-5*) De Gruyter.

— IX Bericht Ueber die Ausgrabungen in Olympia: Herbst, 1962 Bis Fruehjahr, 1966. (Bericht Ueber die Ausgrabungen in Olympia Ser.: No. 9). (GER.). vii, 229p. (C). 1995. lib. bdg. 176.95 (*3-11-014243-0*) De Gruyter.

Deutschen Archaeologischen Institut Staff, ed. see Hausmann, Ulrich.

Deutschen Archaeologischen Institut Staff, ed. see Hitzl, Konrad.

Deutschen Archaeologischen Institut Staff, ed. see Spieser, Jean-Michael.

Deutschen Archaeologisches Institut Staff, ed. see Schilbach, Jueregen.

Deutschen Historischen Institut in Rom Staff. Repertorium Germanicum Bd. I: Clemens VII. von Avignon, 1378-1394. (GER.). xvi, 182p. 1991. reprint ed. write for info. (*3-615-00063-3*, Pub. by Weidmann) Lubrecht & Cramer.

— Repertorium Germanicum Bd. II, Lieferung 1: Einleitung und Regesten. (GER.). iv, 578p. 1961. write for info. (*3-296-21002-4*, Pub. by Weidmann) Lubrecht & Cramer.

— Repertorium Germanicum Bd. II, Lieferung 2: Personenregister. (GER.). iv, 578p. 1961. write for info. (*3-296-21003-2*, Pub. by Weidmann) Lubrecht & Cramer.

— Repertorium Germanicum Bd. II, Lieferung 3: Ortsregister. (GER.). iv, 578p. 1961. write for info. (*3-296-21004-0*, Pub. by Weidmann) Lubrecht & Cramer.

— Repertorium Germanicum Bd. III: Alexander V., Johann XXIII., Konstanzer Konzil 1409-1417. (GER.). viii, 48p. 1991. reprint ed. write for info. (*3-615-00064-1*, Pub. by Weidmann) Lubrecht & Cramer.

— Repertorium Germanicum Bd. IV, Teilband 1: Martin V., 1417-1431. (GER.). x, 1492p. 1991. reprint ed. write for info. (*3-615-00065-X*, Pub. by Weidmann) Lubrecht & Cramer.

— Repertorium Germanicum Bd. IV, Teilband 2: (I, J, Y) (GER.). iv, 1493p. 1957. write for info. (*3-296-21007-5*, Pub. by Weidmann) Lubrecht & Cramer.

— Repertorium Germanicum Bd. IV, Teilband 3: (L-Z) (GER.). iv, 2569p. 1958. write for info. (*3-296-21008-3*, Pub. by Weidmann) Lubrecht & Cramer.

Deutschen Literaturarchiv Margach am Neckar Staff, ed. Deutsche Literartur Zeitschriften, 1880-1945: Ein Repertorium, 5 vols., Set. (GER.). 1623p. 1988. lib. bdg. 500.00 (*3-598-10645-9*) K G Saur Verlag.

Deutschen Tanzarchiv Koln Staff, ed. see Chadzis, Athina.

Deutschendorf, Harvey. Of Work & Men: How Men Can Become More Than Their Careers. 224p. 1996. 19.95 (*1-57749-013-4*) Fairview Press.

Deutscher Akademikerinnenbund, ed. Die Frauenfrage in Deutschland: Bibliographie Neue Folge, Vol. 3 1984. (GER.). 343p. 1987. lib. bdg. 45.00 (*3-598-20191-5*) K G Saur Verlag.

***Deutscher, B.** Tennis Course Vol. 2: Lessons & Training. (Illus.). 260p. 2000. pap. 18.95 (*0-7641-1486-7*) Barron.

***Deutscher, Guy.** Syntactic Change in Akkadian: The Evolution of Sentential Complementation. (Illus.). 224p. 2000. text 65.00 (*0-19-824136-4*) OUP.

Deutscher, Irwin. Making a Difference: The Practice of Sociology. LC 98-8590. 468p. 1998. text 49.95 (*1-56000-359-6*) Transaction Pubs.

Deutscher, Irwin, et al. Sentiments & Acts. LC 92-27887. (Communication & Social Order Ser.). 280p. 1993. pap. text 24.95 (*0-202-30445-0*); lib. bdg. 46.95 (*0-202-30444-2*) Aldine de Gruyter.

Deutscher, Isaac. The Prophet Outcast: Trotsky, 1929-1940. 559p. 1997. reprint ed. lib. bdg. 39.95 (*0-7351-0016-0*) Replica Bks.

— The Prophet Unarmed: Trotsky: 1921-1929. 504p. 1997. lib. bdg. 39.95 (*0-7351-0015-2*) Replica Bks.

***Deutscher, Max, ed.** Michele Le Doeuff: Operative Philosophy & Imaginary Practice. 316p. 2000. 65.95 (*1-57392-863-1*) Prometheus Bks.

Deutscher, Murray P., jt. ed. see Glasel, Jay A.

Deutscher, Penelope. Enigmas: Essays on Sarah Kofman. LC 98-39688. 288p. 1999. pap. text 14.95 (*0-8014-8141-4*) Cornell U Pr.

— Unstable Tendencies: Feminism, Deconstruction & the History of Philosophy. LC 97-7477. 232p. (C). 1997. 65.00 (*0-415-13944-9*); pap. 20.99 (*0-415-13945-7*) Routledge.

Deutscher, Penelope & Oliver, Kelly, eds. Enigmas: Essays on Sarah Kofman. LC 98-39688. 288p. 1999. 49.95 (*0-8014-2912-9*) Cornell U Pr.

***Deutscher, Tennis B.** Tennis Course Vol. 1: Techniques & Tactics. (Illus.). 180p. 2000. pap. 16.95 (*0-7641-1485-9*) Barron.

Deutscher Tennis Bund Staff. Step by Step Tennis. 144p. 1990. pap. 16.95 (*0-8120-4473-8*) Barron.

Deutscher, Thomas B., jt. ed. see Bietenholz, Peter G.

Deutscher, Thomas B., ed. see Erasmus, Desiderius.

Deutsches Archaeologisches Institut Staff, ed. see Ohnesorg, Aenne.

Deutsches Archalolgisches Institut Staff, ed. see Alfoldi, Andreas, et al.

Deutsches Architektur-Museum Staff, et al, eds. Dam: Architecture Annual, 1996. (Illus.). 192p. 1996. pap. 45.00 (*3-7913-1705-9*, Pub. by Prestel) te Neues.

Deutsches Institut fur Entwicklungspolitik Staff, jt. auth. see Meyer-Stamer, Jorg.

Deutsches Institut fur Wirtschaftsforschung Staff, jt. auth. see Greenpeace Staff.

Deutsches Institute Staff, jt. auth. see Messner, Dirk.

Deutsches Komitee fur Reprographie Staff. Dictionary of Reprography. 2nd ed. (ENG, FRE, GER & SPA.). 353p. 1982. 115.00 (*0-8288-0692-6*, M6961) Fr & Eur.

Deutsches Krebsforschungszentrum Staff, ed. Current Cancer Research, 1997. (Illus.). 280p. 1998. pap. 21.00 (*3-7985-1122-5*) Spr-Verlag.

Deutsches Literaturarchiv Marbach Am Neckar, ed. Deutsche Literarische Zeitschriften, 1945-1970: Ein Repertorium, 4 vols., Set. (GER.). 1304p. 1992. lib. bdg. 500.00 (*3-598-22000-6*) K G Saur Verlag.

Deutsches Museum Staff. Fur Geschichte, Literatur, Kunst- und Alterthumsforschung. (GER.). xiv, 682p. 1973. reprint ed. write for info. (*3-487-04647-4*) G Olms Pubs.

Deutschlander, Daniel M. Civil Government: God's Other Kingdom. LC 97-69965. (People's Bible Teachings Ser.). 215p. 1998. 10.99 (*0-8100-0763-0*, 15N0608) Northwest Pub.

***Deutschle, Phil.** Across Africa the HArd Way: Journeys of a Witch-Doctor's Son-in-Law. LC 99-67881. (Illus.). 333p. 2000. 24.95 (*0-931625-37-8*); pap. 19.95 (*0-931625-36-X*) DIMI Pr.

Deutschman, Aaron D., et al. Machine Design: Theory & Practice. (Illus.). 768p. (C). 1975. text 72.00 (*0-02-329000-5*, Macmillan Coll) P-H.

***Deutschman, Alan.** The Second Coming of Steve Jobs. LC 00-35796. 304p. 2000. 26.00 (*0-7679-0432-X*) Broadway BDD.

Deutschman, Alan. Winning Money for College. 4th ed. LC 97-209692. (Peterson's Guides Ser.). 208p. 1997. pap. text 12.95 (*1-56079-876-9*) Petersons.

— Winning Money for College: The High School Student's Guide to Scholarship Contests. 3rd ed. LC 92-21967. 207p. (Orig.). (YA). (gr. 10-12). 1992. pap. 10.95 (*1-56079-059-8*) Petersons.

Deutschman, Harold, compiled by. Urban Transportation Planning. 106p. 1968. pap. 3.00 (*0-87262-019-0*) Am Soc Civil Eng.

***Deutschman, Patricia.** Titanic Movie - Titanic Message. 140p. 1999. pap. 10.00 (*0-9673176-0-6*) L Publishing.

Deutschmann, ed. Images of Cuba. 2000. pap. 16.95 (*1-875284-60-5*, 92673) Ocean Pr NJ.

Deutschmann, David, ed. Changing the History of Africa: Angola & Namibia. (Illus.). 177p. 1993. pap. 12.95 (*1-875284-00-1*) Ocean Pr NJ.

— Che: A Memoir by Fidel Castro. LC 96-181102. (Illus.). 165p. 1994. pap. 13.95 (*1-875284-15-X*) Ocean Pr NJ.

***Deutschmann, David & Ratner, Michael, eds.** Washington on Trial: The People of Cuba Versus U.S. Government. 48p. 2000. pap. 4.95 (*1-876175-23-0*, Pub. by Ocean Pr NJ) LPC InBook.

Deutschmann, David, ed. see Castro, Fidel.

Deutschmann, David, ed. see Guevara, Ernesto.

Deutsh, Georg, jt. auth. see Springer, Sally P.

Deux, Les. Oral Sex for Dodos. (Illus.). 59p. 1999. pap. 9.95 (*1-892896-40-0*) Buy Books.

Dev Gaur, Keshav. Extent & Measurement of Poverty in India: A Case Study of Rajasthan. (C). 1988. 21.50 (*81-7099-054-8*, Pub. by Mittal Pubs Dist) S Asia.

Dev Jager, Rama & Ortiz, Rafael. In the Company of Giants: Candid Conversations with the Visionaries of Cyberspace. LC 97-1906. 256p. 1997. 24.95 (*0-07-032934-6*) McGraw.

— In the Company of Giants: Candid Conversations with the Visionaries of the Digital World. 256p. 1998. pap. 14.95 (*0-07-032965-6*) McGraw.

***Dev Jager, Rama & Ortiz, Rafael.** In the Company of Giants: Candid Conversations with the Visionaries of the Digital World. 232p. 2000. reprint ed. text 25.00 (*0-7881-9175-6*) DIANE Pub.

Dev, Rajiv. Math Smart for Businesses: Essentials of Managerial Finance. LC 97-208384. (Princeton Review Ser.). 1997. pap. 12.00 (*0-679-77356-8*) Villard Books.

Dev, S. Handbook of Terpenoids, 6 vols. 1632.00 (*0-8493-3603-1*, CRC Reprint) Franklin.

Dev, Sukh & Koul, Opender. Insecticides of Natural Origin. 352p. 1997. text 78.00 (*3-7186-5913-1*, Harwood Acad Pubs) Gordon & Breach.

Dev, Sukh & Misra, Renuka. Handbook of Terpenoids: Diterpenoids, Vol. I. 328p. 1985. lib. bdg. 279.95 (*0-8493-3604-X*, QD416, CRC Reprint) Franklin.

— Handbook of Terpenoids: Diterpenoids, Vol. II. 712p. 1985. lib. bdg. 279.95 (*0-8493-3605-8*, CRC Reprint) Franklin.

Dev, Sukh & Misra, Renuka, eds. Handbook of Terpenoids: Diterpenoids. 1986. 265.00 (*0-685-43138-X*, QD416, CRC Reprint) Franklin.

— Handbook of Terpenoids: Diterpenoids, Vol. III. 560p. 1986. lib. bdg. 279.95 (*0-8493-3606-6*, CRC Reprint) Franklin.

— Handbook of Terpenoids: Diterpenoids, Vol. VI. 592p. 1986. lib. bdg. 279.95 (*0-8493-3607-4*, CRC Reprint) Franklin.

Dev, Sukh, et al. Handbook of Terpenoids: Monoterpenoids, 2 vols., Set. 1982. 358.95 (*0-8493-3600-7*, QD416, CRC Reprint) Franklin.

— Handbook of Terpenoids: Monoterpenoids, 2 vols., Vol. I. 272p. 1982. 149.00 (*0-8493-3601-5*, CRC Reprint) Franklin.

— Handbook of Terpenoids: Monoterpenoids, 2 vols., Vol. II. 528p. 1982. 289.00 (*0-8493-3602-3*, CRC Reprint) Franklin.

Deva, Acharya D., tr. Rigveda, Vol. 4. (ENG, HIN & SAN.). 808p. 1986. 17.00 (*0-685-72921-4*, Pub. by Sarvadeshik Arya) Nataraj Bks.

Deva, Acharya D. & Saraswati, Swami D., trs. Hymns of the Samaveda Sanhita. 909p. 1989. 17.00 (*0-685-72924-9*, Pub. by Sarvadeshik Arya) Nataraj Bks.

Deva, Acharya D., tr. see Snatak, Brahma D. & Hindi, Surendra K., eds.

Deva, B. C. Indian Music. unabridged ed. (C). 1995. reprint ed. 28.00 (*81-224-0730-7*, Pub. by Wiley Estrn) Franklin.

Deva, B. Chaitanya. Musical Instruments. 108p. 1977. 8.95 (*0-318-36330-5*) Asia Bk Corp.

— Musical Instruments of India: Their History & Development. 1987. 32.00 (*81-215-0048-6*, Pub. by M Manoharial) Coronet Bks.

Deva, Chaitanya. Musical Instruments in Sculpture in Karnataka. 1989. 38.50 (*81-208-0641-7*, Pub. by Motilal Bnarsidass) S Asia.

Deva, Indra. Folk Culture & Peasant Society in India. (C). 1989. 44.00 (*81-7033-074-2*, Pub. by Rawat Pubns) S Asia.

Deva, Jeannie. The Contemporary Vocalist Improvement Course: The Deva Method, a Non-Classical Approach for Singers. Lieberman, Julie L., ed. LC 96-121968. (Illus.). 180p. 1994. pap. 49.95 incl. audio (*1-882224-10-8*) Voice Studio.

— The Voice Studio Manual: Introduction to the Deva Method. 8th ed. Scoglio, Joe, ed. (Illus.). 80p. 1996. pap. 12.95 (*1-882224-12-4*) Voice Studio.

Deva, Krishna. The Sculptural Art of Khajuraho. (Illus.). 160p. 1991. 39.00 (*81-7107-002-7*, Pub. by Bamboo Pub) Antique Collect.

— Temples of India, Set, Vols. 1 & 2. (C). 1995. text 195.00 (*81-7305-054-6*, Pub. by Aryan Bks Intl) S Asia.

D

An Asterisk (*) at the beginning of an entry indicates that the title is appearing for the first time.

Deva, Krishna & Trivedi, S. D. Stone Sculpture in the Allahabad Museum, Vol. 2. (C). 1996. 80.00 (*81-7304-140-7*, Pub. by Manohar) S Asia.

***Deva, Sri Harsha.** Buddhist Legend of Jimuatavahana: From the Kath-Sarita Sagara (the Ocean River Story) Dramatized in Naganada (the Joy of the World of Serpents) a Buddhist Drama. 1999. 18.00 (*0-8364-5677-7*) S Asia.

Devadas, Srinivas, et al. Logic Synthesis. LC 93-41524. 448p. 1993. 55.00 (*0-07-016500-9*) McGraw.

***Devadhar, C. R., ed.** Works of Kalidasa: Dramas, Vol. I. 312p. 1999. reprint ed. 250.00 (*81-208-0023-0*, Pub. by Motilal Bnarsidass) S Asia.

Devadhar, C. R., ed. Works of Kalidasa: Kavya, Vol. 11. 1093p. 1984. reprint ed. 42.00 (*0-317-60584-4*, Pub. by Motilal Bnarsidass) S Asia.

— Works of Kalidasa: Kayva, Vol. II. 1093p. 1984. reprint ed. 46.00 (*81-208-0024-9*, Pub. by Motilal Bnarsidass) S Asia.

Devadoss, S., et al. Macrolinkages Between the Farm & Nonfarm Sectors & the Impact of Monetary Policy Decisions, Vol. 87-M1. (Illus.). 110p. (Orig.). 1988. pap. text 15.00 (*0-936911-00-X*) Ctr Agri & Rural Dev.

Devahuti, D. Harsha: A Political Study. 3rd rev. ed. LC 98-915483. (Illus.). 390p. (Orig.). 1999. pap. text 26.95 (*0-19-564237-6*) OUP.

— The Unknown Hsuan-tsang. (Illus.). 192p. 2000. text 22.00 (*0-19-564372-0*) OUP.

Deval, Jacqueline. Reckless Appetites: A Culinary Romance. 208p. 1995. pap. 12.00 (*0-88001-412-1*) HarpC.

DeVale, Sue C., ed. Selected Reports in Ethnomusicology Vol. 8: Issues in Organology. 279p. 1990. 30.00 (*0-88287-024-6*) UCLA Dept Ethnom.

DeValeria, Dennis & Burke-DeValeria, Jeanne. Honus Wagner: A Bibliography. LC 97-45771. (Illus.). 334p. 1998. reprint ed. pap. 16.95 (*0-8229-5665-9*) U of Pittsburgh Pr.

***DeValk, J.** Ben Webster: His Life & Music. (Illus.). 2000. pap. 15.95 (*1-893163-17-2*) Berkeley Hills.

Devall, Bill, ed. Clearcut: The Tragedy of Industrial Forestry. LC 93-35989. (Illus.). 300p. 1994. 50.00 (*0-87156-494-7*, Pub. by Sierra) Random.

— Clearcut: The Tragedy of Industrial Forestry. LC 93-35989. 1995. pap. 30.00 (*0-87156-361-4*, Pub. by Sierra) Random.

Devall, Bill & Sessions, George. Deep Ecology: Living As If Nature Mattered. 266p. 1987. pap. 17.95 (*0-87905-247-3*) Gibbs Smith Pub.

Devall, Sandra. Desktop Publishing Style Guide. abr. rev. ed. LC 98-27400. 512p. (C). 1998. pap. 36.95 (*0-8273-7900-5*) Delmar.

DeValle, Susana. Discourses of Ethnicity: Culture & Protest in Jharkhand. LC 91-42550. (Illus.). 280p. (C). 1992. text 45.00 (*0-8039-9416-8*) Sage.

Devalls, Nathalie. Etiqueta Hoy. (SPA.). 368p. (Orig.). 1986. pap. 4.95 (*0-939193-08-6*) Edit Concepts.

— Etiqueta Hoy. (SPA.). (Orig.). 1990. pap. write for info. (*0-944499-84-8*) Editorial Amer.

Devamata. Days in an Indian Monastery. 3rd ed. 1975. pap. 5.95 (*0-911564-20-9*) Vedanta Ctr.

Devambez, Pierre. L' Art au Siecle de Pericles. (FRE., Illus.). 112p. 1955. lib. bdg. write for info. (*0-8288-3944-1*) Fr & Eur.

— Diccionario de la Civilizacion Griega: Dictionary of the Greek Civilization. (SPA.). 482p. 1972. 53.95 (*0-8288-6357-1*, S-50367) Fr & Eur.

— Histoire de l'Art: Le Monde non Chretien, Vol. 1. (Historique Ser.). 2236p. 48.95 (*0-686-56450-2*) Fr & Eur.

— Histoire de l'Art, Vol. 1: Le Monde Non Chretien. (FRE.). 2240p. 140.00 (*0-8288-7697-5*) Fr & Eur.

***Devan, Shoba.** Insight Pocket Guide Kuala Lumpur with Map. 5th rev. ed. (Illus.). 100p. 2000. pap. 12.95 (*1-58573-014-9*, Insight Guides) Langenscheidt.

DeVan, William, jt. ed. see Maxwell, Carolyn.

***Devanand.** Psych Symptoms & Their Treatment in Alzheimers Disease: Pocketbook Edition. 2000. 14.95 (*1-85317-918-3*, Pub. by Martin Dunitz) Blackwell Sci.

Devanand, Swami Guru & Maharaj, Saraswati J. Nacimos para Triunfar. (SPA., Illus.). 226p. 1993. pap. write for info. (*1-893261-02-6*) USA Dev Yoga.

— Las Sagradas Ensenanzas de Swami Guru Devanand. (SPA.). Date not set. pap. 15.00 (*1-893261-08-5*) USA Dev Yoga.

DeVananda, Angelo, ed. see Mother Teresa of Calcutta.

***Devananda, Vishnu.** Hatha Yoga Pradipika: Classic Guide for the Advanced Practice of Hatha Yoga. 230p. 1999. pap. 75.00 (*81-208-1614-5*, Pub. by Motilal Bnarsidass) St Mut.

— Meditation & Mantras: An Authoritative Text by Vishnu Devananda. 267p. 1999. pap. 75.00 (*81-208-1615-3*, Pub. by Motilal Bnarsidass) St Mut.

Devanathan, R. Intelligent Tuning & Adaptive Control: Selected Papers from the IFAC Symposium, Singapore, 15-17 January 1991. (IFAC Symposia Ser.: 9107). (Illus.). 433p. 1991. 193.00 (*0-08-040935-0*, Pergamon Pr) Elsevier.

Devander, Charles W. Van, see Van Devander, Charles W.

DeVane, Lindsay. Fundamentals of Monitoring Psychoactive Drug Therapy. (Illus.). 298p. 1989. 31.00 (*0-683-02452-3*) Lppncott W & W.

DeVane, M. P., ed. see Tennyson, Alfred Lord.

Devane, Richard S. The Failure of Individualism: A Documented Essay. LC 75-28664. (Illus.). 1977. reprint ed. lib. bdg. 75.00 (*0-8371-8484-3*, DEFI, Greenwood Pr) Greenwood.

Devane, Tom, jt. ed. see Holman, Peggy.

DeVane, William C. The American University in the Twentieth Century. LC 57-7496. (Davis Washington Mitchell Lectures, Tulane University). 84p. 1957. reprint ed. pap. 30.00 (*0-7837-9871-7*, 206059700006) Bks Demand.

— Browning's Parleyings: The Autobiography of a Mind. (BCL1-PR English Literature Ser.). 306p. 1992. reprint ed. lib. bdg. 89.00 (*0-7812-7462-1*) Rprt Serv.

— Higher Education in Twentieth-Century America. LC 65-13839. (Library of Congress Series in American Civilization). 221p. reprint ed. pap. 68.60 (*0-7837-2060-2*, 204233500004) Bks Demand.

DeVane, William C., ed. see Browning, Robert.

DeVane, William C., ed. see Tennyson, Alfred Lord.

Devaney, jt. auth. see Blanchard.

Devaney, D. M. & Eldredge, L. G., eds. Reef & Shore Fauna of Hawaii: Platyhelminthes Through Phoronida, & Sipuncula Through Annelida, Sections 2 & 3. (Illus.). 468p. 1987. 39.00 (*0-930897-11-0*, SP64) Bishop Mus.

— Reef & Shore Fauna of Hawaii: Protozoa Through Ctenophora. LC 77-89747. (Special Publications: No. 64 (1)). (Illus.). 290p. 1977. pap. 22.50 (*0-910240-22-1*) Bishop Mus.

Devaney, Dennis & Thieblot, Armand J., Jr. Union Violence: The Record & the Response of the Courts, Legislators & NLBR. rev. ed. (Labor Relations & Public Policy Ser.: Vol. 25). 300p. 1998. 45.00 (*1-891496-10-7*) J M Olin.

Devaney, F. John. Tracking the American Dream: 50 Years of Housing History from the Census Bureau: 1940-1990. (Illus.). 58p. 1998. pap. text 20.00 (*0-7881-7238-7*) DIANE Pub.

DeVaney, Janet S. Speech Stations: The One-Stop Speech Book. (Illus.). 205p. (J). (ps-5). 1987. 27.50 (*0-937857-03-3*, 1552) Speech Bin.

Devaney, John. America Fights the Tide, 1942. (World War II Ser.). 192p. (YA). (gr. 12 up). 1991. lib. bdg. 18.85 (*0-8027-6998-5*) Walker & Co.

Devaney, John. America Fights the Tide, 1942. (World War II Ser.). 192p. (YA). (gr. 12 up) 1991. 17.95 (*0-8027-6997-7*) Walker & Co.

Devaney, John. America Goes to War, 1941. (World War II Ser.). 192p. (YA). (gr. 7 up). 1991. lib. bdg. 17.85 (*0-8027-6980-2*) Walker & Co.

Devaney, John. America Goes to War, 1941. LC 90-41739. (World War II Ser.). 192p. (YA). (ps up). 1991. 16.95 (*0-8027-6979-9*) Walker & Co.

— America on the Attack, 1943. LC 92-8993. (World War II Ser.). (YA). 1992. lib. bdg. 18.85 (*0-8027-8195-0*) Walker & Co.

Devaney, John. America Storms the Beaches, 1944. LC 92-47057. (World War II Ser.). (Illus.). 176p. (YA). (gr. 7 up). 1993. lib. bdg. 18.85 (*0-8027-8245-0*) Walker & Co.

Devaney, John. America Storms the Beaches, 1944. LC 92-47057. (World War II Ser.). (Illus.). 176p. (YA). (gr. 7 up). 1993. 17.95 (*0-8027-8244-2*) Walker & Co.

— America Triumphs, 1945. LC 94-13255. (World War II Ser.). (Illus.). 224p. (J). 1995. 18.95 (*0-8027-8328-7*) Walker & Co.

Devaney, John. America Triumphs: 1945. (World War II Ser.). (YA). 1995. lib. bdg. 19.85 (*0-8027-8347-3*) Walker & Co.

— Bo Jackson: A Star for All Seasons. 132p. (YA). 1992. 14.95 (*0-8027-8178-0*); lib. bdg. 15.85 (*0-8027-8179-9*) Walker & Co.

— Franklin Delano Roosevelt, President. LC 86-46254. (Illus.). 76p. (J). (gr. 5-9). 1987. 12.95 (*0-8027-6713-3*) Walker & Co.

— Franklin Delano Roosevelt, President. LC 86-46254. (Illus.). 76p. (J). (gr. 7 up). 1987. lib. bdg. 13.85 (*0-8027-6714-1*) Walker & Co.

— Lyndon Baines Johnson, President. LC 85-31751. (Presidential Biography Ser.). 128p. (J). (gr. 5 up). 1986. 12.95 (*0-8027-6638-2*); lib. bdg. 13.85 (*0-8027-6639-0*) Walker & Co.

— Ronald Reagan. (Presidential Biography Ser.). (Illus.). (YA). (gr. 7 up). 1990. 13.95 (*0-8027-6931-4*); lib. bdg. 14.85 (*0-8027-6932-2*) Walker & Co.

— The Vietnam War. large type ed. (First Bks.). (Illus.). 64p. (J). (gr. 5-8). 1993. pap. 6.95 (*0-531-15658-3*) Watts.

— Winners of the Heisman Trophy. 2nd ed. (Illus.). (J). (gr. 5 up). 1990. 14.95 (*0-8027-6906-3*); lib. bdg. 15.85 (*0-8027-6907-1*) Walker & Co.

Devaney, John, jt. auth. see Ostroske, Walter.

Devaney, M. J. "Since at Least Plato" & Other Postmodern Myths. LC 97-7781. 220p. 1997. text 39.95 (*0-312-17511-6*) St Martin.

Devaney, R. & Keen, L. Chaos & Fractals: The Mathematics Behind the Computer Graphics. LC 89-7003. (PSAPM Ser.: Vol. 39). 148p. 1989. text 28.00 (*0-8218-0137-6*, PSAPM/39) Am Math.

Devaney, R. L. & Nitecki, Z. H. Classical Mechanics & Dynamical Systems. (Lecture Notes in Pure & Applied Mathematics Ser.: 70). (Illus.). 256p. 1981. pap. text 145.00 (*0-8247-1529-2*) Dekker.

Devaney, Robert L. Chaos, Fractals & Dynamics. 1990. pap. text 19.95 (*0-201-23288-X*) Addison-Wesley.

— Chaos, Fractals & Dynamics: Computer Experiments in Mathematics, incl. 2 videocassettes, Set. 181p. (Orig.). 1989. pap. 99.00 incl. VHS (*1-878310-34-8*) Science TV.

— A First Course in Dynamical Systems: Theory & Experiment. (Studies in Nonlinearity Ser.). (C). 1992. 51.00 (*0-201-55406-2*) Addison-Wesley.

— Introduction to Chaotic Dynamic of Systems. (Illus.). 320p. 1986. text 35.50 (*0-8053-1601-9*) Addison-Wesley.

— An Introduction to Chaotic Dynamical Systems. 2nd ed. (Studies in Nonlinearity Ser.). (Illus.). 360p. (C). 1989. 49.00 (*0-201-13046-7*) Addison-Wesley.

Devaney, Robert L., ed. Complex Dynamical Systems: The Mathematics Behind the Mandelbrot & Julia Sets. LC 94-24190. (Proceedings of Symposia in Applied Mathematics Ser.: Vol. 49). 209p. 1995. text 35.00 (*0-8218-0290-9*, PSAPM/49) Am Math.

***Devaney, Tom.** The American Pragmatist. (Illus.). 72p. 1999. pap. 10.00 (*1-928823-01-7*) Banshee Pr.

Devanna, Mary A. Male-Female Careers - The First Decade: A Study of MBA's. 1984. pap. 17.50 (*0-317-11513-8*) CU Ctr Career Res.

Devanna, Mary A., et al. Human Resource Management: Issues for the 1980's. 1983. pap. 15.00 (*0-317-11512-X*) CU Ctr Career Res.

Devanna, Mary A., jt. auth. see Collins, Eliza G.

Devanna, Mary A., jt. auth. see Tichy, Noel M.

Devanny, Jean. Point of Departure: The Autobiography of Jean Devanny. Ferrier, Carole, ed. LC 86-7068. (Illus.). 332p. 1987. text 44.95 (*0-7022-1979-7*, Pub. by Univ Queensland Pr) Intl Spec Bk.

Devany, Joe. Politics & Commentary. LC 96-60008. (Illus.). 212p. 1996. 19.95 (*0-9650890-0-2*) J A Devary.

Devaquet, A., et al. Triplet States 1. (Topics in Current Chemistry Ser.: Vol. 54). (Illus.). iv, 164p. 1975. 55.95 (*0-387-07107-5*) Spr-Verlag.

Devaraj, ed. see Osho.

***Devaraj, P., ed.** Monograph on Silver Oak (Grevillea Robusta) 167p. 1999. pap. 325.00 (*81-7089-257-8*, Pub. by Intl Bk Distr) St Mut.

Devaraj, Sambuddha S., ed. see Osho.

***Devaraj, T. L.** Ayurveda: The Complete Handbook. 2000. pap. 14.95 (*81-7476-287-6*, Pub. by UBS Pubs) S Asia.

Devaraj, T. L. Ayurveda for Health & Family Welfare. (Illus.). 312p. 1999. pap. 19.95 (*0-8464-4940-4*) Beekman Pubs.

***Devaraj, T. L.** Ayurveda for Health & Family Welfare. 1998. pap. 18.50 (*81-7476-186-1*, Pub. by UBS Pubs) S Asia.

Devaraj, T. L. Ayurveda for Healthy Living. 110p. 1999. pap. 9.95 (*0-8464-4939-0*) Beekman Pubs.

***Devaraj, T. L.** Panchakarma Treatment of Ayurveda. 1998. 36.00 (*81-7030-591-8*, Pub. by Sri Satguru Pubns) S Asia.

Devaraj, T. L. Speaking of Ayurvedic Remedies for Common Diseases. 145p. 1985. 17.95 (*0-318-36357-7*) Asia Bk Corp.

— Speaking of Ayurvedic Remedies for Common Diseases. (C). 1995. pap. write for info. (*81-207-1611-6*) Sterling Pubs.

Devarajan, G. Social Reform Movement in Kerala: An Annotated Bibliography of Source Materials. (C). 1990. 16.00 (*0-8364-2642-8*, Pub. by Indian Doc Serv) S Asia.

Devarajan, Shantayanan, jt. auth. see Eskeland, Gunnar S.

Devarennes, Fernand. Asia-Pacific Human Rights Documents & Resources. LC 98-12734. 1998. 81.00 (*90-411-0578-6*); write for info. (*90-411-0575-4*) Kluwer Law Intl.

Devargas, Mario. Total Quality Management Approach to IT Security. 224p. 1995. text 55.95 (*1-85554-352-4*) Blackwell Pubs.

Devarim. Linear Chumash. 1997. 16.95 (*0-87306-798-3*) Feldheim.

Devaris, Dionisios P., jt. ed. see Wain, Harold J.

Devars, G., jt. auth. see Bescherelle, Louis-Nicolas.

Devas, Nick. Managing Fast Growing Cities: New Approaches to Urban Planning. 1993. pap. 41.95 (*0-582-09304-X*, Pub. by Addison-Wesley) Longman.

Devas, Nick, et al. Financing Local Government in Indonesia. LC 89-32704. (Monographs in International Studies, Southeast Asia Ser.: No. 84). 360p. 1989. pap. text 20.00 (*0-89680-153-5*) Ohio U Pr.

Devash, Isaac, et al, eds. Vision: Harvard Students Look Ahead. 1993. pap. text 11.95 (*0-07-103454-4*) McGraw.

Devasia, Leelamma. Female Criminals & Female Victims: An Indian Perspective. (C). 1990. 150.00 (*0-89771-184-X*) St Mut.

— Girl Child in India. (C). 1991. 22.50 (*0-8364-2706-8*, Pub. by Ashish Pub Hse) S Asia.

— Women in India. (C). 1990. text 11.00 (*0-685-50086-1*, Pub. by Manohar) S Asia.

Devasia, Leelamma & Devasia, V. V. Empowering Women for Sustainable Development. xxiii, 209p. 1994. 25.00 (*81-7024-621-0*, Pub. by Ashish Pub Hse) Nataraj Bks.

— Girl Child in India. xxiv, 243p. 1992. 15.95 (*1-881338-13-4*) Nataraj Bks.

Devasia, Leelamma, jt. auth. see Devasia, V. V.

Devasia, V. V. & Devasia, Leelamma. Women, Social Justice & Human Rights. LC 98-908063. 1998. 54.00 (*81-7024-996-1*, Pub. by Ashish Pub Hse) S Asia.

Devasia, V. V., jt. auth. see Devasia, Leelamma.

Devasthali, G., ed. Glimpses of Veda & Vyakarana. 1985. 26.00 (*0-8364-1408-X*, Pub. by Popular Prakashan) S Asia.

DeVaughn, Melissa. Alaska: Off the Beaten Path: A Guide to Unique Places. 2nd ed. LC 99-33144. (Off the Beaten Path Ser.). (Illus.). 288p. 1999. pap. 12.95 (*0-7627-0261-3*) Globe Pequot.

DeVaughn, Tanya, jt. ed. see Rydesky, Mary.

DeVaul, R. A., ed. see Gildenberg, Philip L.

Devault, jt. auth. see Strong.

DeVault, Barbara D. Castle of Personality, Vol. P-1705. unabridged ed. (Illus.). 100p. (J). (gr. 1-6). 1997. pap. 12.99 incl. audio (*1-891536-02-8*, BD9197A) DeVault Ents.

— A Gentle Breed: The Story of Bathsheba, "A Town Without Men" 217p. 1997. pap. 6.99 (*1-891536-00-1*, BD9197C) DeVault Ents.

— Kittydid & Tad in "A Cat Such As I", Vol. P-1704. (Illus.). 89p. (J). (gr. 1 up). 1997. pap. 6.99 (*1-891536-01-X*, BD9197B) DeVault Ents.

— Poetry & Prose, Vol. de-1001. 55p. 1997. pap. 4.99 (*1-891536-03-6*, BD8197A) DeVault Ents.

— Short-Shorts & Short Stories, Vol. de-1000. 90p. 1997. pap. 5.95 (*1-891536-04-4*, BD8197B) DeVault Ents.

DeVault, Barbara D. & Waggoner, Joann. Visualization & Relaxation, Vol. de-1002. unabridged ed. 58p. 1997. pap. 12.95 incl. audio (*1-891536-05-2*, BDJW82397) DeVault Ents.

DeVault, Christine. Taking Chances with Sex. 1990. pap. 3.95 (*0-941816-77-X*) ETR Assocs.

DeVault, Christine, jt. auth. see Gonick, Larry.

DeVault, Christine, jt. auth. see Strong, Bryan.

DeVault, George, ed. Gardening for Profit: Peter Henderson Great-Grandfather of Truck Farming. (American Horticultural Ser.: No. 3). (Illus.). 400p. (Orig.). Date not set. reprint ed. pap. 19.95 (*0-929332-09-1*) Amer Botanist.

— Return to Pleasant Valley: Louis Bromfield's Best from Malabar Farm & His Other Country Classics. 317p. (Orig.). 1996. pap. 19.45 (*0-929332-06-7*) Amer Botanist.

DeVault, George, ed. see Sinclair, Ward.

DeVault, Ileen A. Sons & Daughters of Labor: Class & Clerical Work in Turn-of-the-Century Pittsburgh. (Illus.). 208p. 1995. pap. text 13.95 (*0-8014-8307-7*) Cornell U Pr.

DeVault, James M. The Efficiency of Antidumping Duties. LC 92-2465. (Government & the Economy: Outstanding Studies & Recent Dissertations). 160p. 1992. text 10.00 (*0-8153-1222-9*) Garland.

DeVault, M. Vere, jt. auth. see Cooper, James M.

Devault, Marjorie L. Feeding the Family: The Social Organization of Caring & Gendered Work. (Women in Culture & Society Ser.). (Illus.). 200p. 1994. 24.95 (*0-226-14359-7*) U Ch Pr.

DeVault, Marjorie L. Liberating Method: Feminism & Social Research. LC 98-31712. (Illus.). 256p. 1999. 59.50 (*1-56639-697-2*) Temple U Pr.

***DeVault, Marjorie L.** Liberating Method: Feminism & Social Research. LC 98-31712. (Illus.). 256p. 1999. pap. 19.95 (*1-56639-698-0*) Temple U Pr.

DeVault, Marjorie L. & Stimpson, Catharine R. Feeding the Family: The Social Organization of Caring as Gendered Work. (Women in Culture & Society Ser.). xiv, 284p. 1994. pap. text 12.95 (*0-226-14360-0*) U Ch Pr.

DeVault, Marjorie L., ed. see Paget, Marianne A.

DeVault, Mike, jt. auth. see Angel, Dan.

DeVault, Mike, jt. ed. see Angel, Dan.

DeVault, William F. Pantheon. Innes, Jan, ed. (Illus.). 64p. 1997. pap. 10.00 (*0-9659576-0-8*, 5561) PanteraPress.

***Devaux, Claudia & Wong, George B.** Bamboo Swaying in the Wind: A Survivor's Story of Faith & Imprisonment in Communist China. LC 00-27371. 2000. pap. 21.95 (*0-8294-1458-4*) Loyola Pr.

***DeVaux, Stephen A.** Total Project Control: A Manager's Guide to Integrated Project Planning, Measuring & Tracking. LC 98-54154. (Operations Management Series for Professionals). 352p. 1999. 58.95 (*0-471-32859-6*) Wiley.

Devavrata Basu Ray, tr. see Swami Vishwashrayananda.

Devay, James E., jt. auth. see Katan, Jaacov.

Deveau, Eleanor J., jt. ed. see Adams, David W.

Deveau, Linsley & Deveau, Patricia. Introduction to Hospitality & Tourism Management. (C). 2001. 48.00 (*0-13-228958-X*, Macmillan Coll) P-H.

DeVeau, Linsley T., et al. Front Office Management & Operations. 362p. 1995. 70.00 (*0-13-334145-3*) P-H.

Deveau, Patricia, jt. auth. see Deveau, Linsley.

***DeVeau, Russell L.** Fiber Optic Lighting: A Guide for Specifiers. 2nd ed. LC 00-33854. 2000. write for info. (*0-88173-325-3*) Fairmont Pr.

Deveaud, Benoit. Luminescence of Semiconductor Microstructures. 300p. 1998. text 53.00 (*981-02-2214-9*) World Scientific Pub.

DeVeaux, Scott. The Birth of Bebop: A Social & Musical History. LC 96-46887. (Illus.). 664p. 1997. 45.00 (*0-520-20579-0*, Pub. by U CA Pr) Cal Prin Full Svc.

DeVeaux, Scott K. Jazz in America: Who's Listening: Research Division Report. LC 95-4463. (National Endowment for the Arts Research Division Report Ser.: No. 31). 69p. 1996. pap. 10.95 (*0-929765-40-0*) Seven Locks Pr.

DeVebers, Gabrielle, jt. auth. see Andrew, Maureen.

Devecmon, William C. In Re Shakespeare's Legal Acquirements No. 12. LC 79-170139. (Shakespeare Society of N. Y. Ser.: Pub. No. 12). reprint ed. 27.50 (*0-404-54212-3*) AMS Pr.

Devegh, Imre. The Pound Sterling. Wilkins, Mira, ed. LC 78-3908. (International Finance Ser.). 1979. reprint ed. lib. bdg. 17.95 (*0-405-11213-0*) Ayer.

Develin, Dora H. Historic Lower Merion & Blockley. (Illus.). 131p. 1997. reprint ed. pap. 21.00 (*0-8328-5467-0*); reprint ed. lib. bdg. 31.00 (*0-8328-5468-9*) Higginson Bk Co.

Develin, L. Patrick, ed. Political Persuasion in Presidential Campaigns. 275p. (Orig.). 1986. 34.95 (*0-88738-078-6*) Transaction Pubs.

Devellis, Robert F. Scale Development: Theories & Applications. (Applied Social Research Methods Ser.: Vol. 26). (Illus.). 160p. 1991. text 42.00 (*0-8039-3775-X*); pap. text 18.95 (*0-8039-3776-8*) Sage.

Developemental Studies Center Staff. Reading for Real Teacher's Guide to "Petunia" Read Aloud Unit, Grade 1. (Reading for Real Ser.). 24p. 1996. pap., teacher ed. 13.95 (*1-57621-028-6*) Develop Studies.

***Developemental Studies Center Staff.** Reading for Real Teacher's Guide to "Summer Wheels" Partner Unit, Grade 3. (Reading for Real Ser.). 26p. 1998. teacher ed. 13.95 (*1-57621-181-9*, LPT315) Develop Studies.

D

Development Associates, Inc. Staff. Communication Manual for Drug Abuse Prevention Programs. 192p. 1991. pap. text 15.00 (*1-879839-00-8*) Develop Assocs.
— A Strategy for Promoting Sustainability in Narcotics Awareness & Education Projects. 43p. 1993. pap. 15.00 (*1-879839-04-0*) Develop Assocs.
— Survey on Drug Prevalence & Attitudes in the Dominican Republic. 115p. 1993. pap. text 15.00 (*1-879839-03-2*) Develop Assocs.
Development Education Centre Staff. The Barn Owl. (Natural History Ser.). (Illus.). 42p. (C). 1991. pap. 5.25 (*0-7478-0024-3*, Pub. by Shire Pubns) Parkwest Pubns.
Development Educational Centre Staff. Values, Cultures & Kids: Approaches & Resources for Teaching Child Development & about the Family. 80p. (C). 1989. 47.50 (*0-7487-0024-2*, Pub. by S Thornes Pubs) Trans-Atl Phila.
Development in Practice Staff. Priorities & Strategies for Education: A World Bank Review. LC 95-18770. 176p. 1995. pap. 22.00 (*0-8213-3311-9*, 13311) World Bank.
Development Prima. Combat Flight Simulator: Unauthorized Strategy Guide. 1998. pap. 19.99 (*0-7615-2000-7*) Prima Pub.
*__Development Staff.__ Lands of Lore III: Prima's Official Strategy Guide. LC 98-68559. 240p. 1999. pap. 19.99 (*0-7615-2015-5*, Prima Games) Prima Pub.
Development Staff. The U.S. & the Soviet Union: Choices for the Twenty-First Century. (Illus.). (C). 1990. per. 10.95 (*0-87967-899-2*, Dshkn McG-Hill) McGrw-H Hghr Educ.
— Warcraft II Platinum: Prima's Official Strategy Guide. 1999. pap. 14.99 (*0-7615-1944-0*, Prima Games) Prima Pub.
Development Studies Center Staff. Reading for Real Teacher's Guide to "Cat Running" Read Aloud Unit, Grade 5. (Reading for Real Ser.). 20p. (Orig.). 1996. pap., teacher ed. 13.95 (*1-57621-129-0*) Develop Studies.
*__Development Studies Center Staff.__ Reading for Real Teacher's Guide to "Jamaica Louise James" Read Aloud Unit, Grade K. (Reading for Real Ser.). 20p. 1999. teacher ed. 13.95 (*1-57621-180-0*, LRA018) Develop Studies.
— Reading for Real Teacher's Guide to "Somewhere in the Darkness" Partner Unit, Grade 8. (Reading for Real Ser.). 34p. 1999. teacher ed. 13.95 (*1-57621-213-0*, LPT814) Develop Studies.
Development Team. Career Quest Interest Inventory Form L. 12p. 1991. pap. text 1.00 (*1-55631-178-8*) Chron Guide.
— Career Quest Interest Inventory Form S. 8p. 1991. pap. text 1.00 (*1-55631-179-6*) Chron Guide.
— Career Quest Technical Manual. 1992. pap. text 15.00 (*1-55631-181-8*) Chron Guide.
Development Team Staff. Chronicle Career Quest Administrator's Guide. rev. ed. Downes, Paul, ed. 12p. 1992. pap. text 1.25 (*1-55631-182-6*) Chron Guide.
Developmental Immunology Workshop Staff. Ontogeny of Immunity. Smith, Richard R. et al, eds. LC 66-29457. (Illus.). 222p. reprint ed. pap. 68.90 (*0-7837-5003-X*, 204467000004) Bks Demand.
Developmental Research & Programs, Inc. Staff & Roberts, Fitzmahan & Associates Staff. Preparing for the Drug (Free) Years: A Family Activity Book. 2nd ed. 142p. (Orig.). 1988. pap. text 16.95 (*0-935529-03-9*) Comprehen Health Educ.
*__Developmental Studies Center Staff.__ Among Friends: Collegial Study Guide. 56p. 1999. pap., student ed. 9.95 (*1-57621-252-1*, AMG000) Develop Studies.
— Among Friends: Teacher Educator Guide. (Illus.). 68p. 1998. pap. write for info. (*1-57621-182-7*) Develop Studies.
Developmental Studies Center Staff. At Home in Our Schools: A Guide to Schoolwide Activities That Build Community. (Illus.). 136p. (Orig.). 1994. pap. 14.95 (*1-885603-00-2*) Develop Studies.
— At Home in Our Schools Collegial Study Guide. (Building Schoolwide Community Ser.). (Illus.). 48p. 1997. pap. 9.95 (*1-57621-139-8*) Develop Studies.
*__Developmental Studies Center Staff.__ Blueprints for a Collaborative Classroom: Collegial Study Guide. 56p. 1999. pap., student ed. 9.95 (*1-57621-251-3*, BCG000) Develop Studies.
— Blueprints for a Collaborative Classroom: Teacher Educator Guide. 64p. 1999. pap., teacher ed. 12.95 (*1-57621-215-7*, BCT000) Develop Studies.
Developmental Studies Center Staff. Blueprints for a Collaborative Classroom: 25 Designs for Partner & Group Work. (Illus.). 192p. 1997. pap. 16.95 (*1-57621-141-X*) Develop Studies.
— Choosing Community: Classroom Strategies for Learning & Caring. (Alfie Kohn Ser.: Vol. A). 1995. 150.00 incl. VHS (*1-885603-68-1*) Develop Studies.
— Choosing Community: Classroom Strategies for Learning & Caring. (Alfie Kohn Ser.: Vol. B). 1995. 150.00 incl. VHS (*1-885603-69-X*) Develop Studies.
— Choosing Community: Classroom Strategies for Learning & Caring. (Alfie Kohn Ser.: Vol. C). 1995. 150.00 incl. VHS (*1-885603-70-3*) Develop Studies.
— Choosing Community: Classroom Strategies for Learning & Caring. (Video Series by Alfie Kohn: Vol. D). 1995. 150.00 incl. VHS (*1-885603-71-1*) Develop Studies.
— Choosing Community: Classroom Strategies for Learning & Caring, 4 cass.; set. (An Alfie Kohn Ser.). 1995. 475.00 incl. VHS (*1-885603-67-3*) Develop Studies.
— Reading for Real Teacher's Guide to "8 + 1" Read Aloud Unit, Grade 8. (Reading for Real Ser.). 32p. (Orig.). 1996. pap., teacher ed. 13.95 (*1-57621-090-1*) Develop Studies.
— Homeside Activities Collegial Study Guide. (Building Schoolwide Community Ser.). (Illus.). 48p. 1997. pap. 9.95 (*1-57621-137-1*) Develop Studies.
— Homeside Activities, Grade K: Conversations & Activities That Bring Parents into Children's Schoolside Learning. (Homeside Activities Ser.). 128p. (Orig.). 1995. pap. 13.95 (*1-885603-59-2*) Develop Studies.
— Homeside Activities, Grade 1: Conversations & Activities That Bring Parents into Children's Schoolside Learning. (Homeside Activities Ser.). 128p. 1995. pap. 13.95 (*1-885603-60-6*) Develop Studies.
— Homeside Activities, Grade 2: Conversations & Activities That Bring Parents into Children's Schoolside Learning. (Homeside Activities Ser.). 128p. (Orig.). 1995. pap. 13.95 (*1-885603-61-4*) Develop Studies.
— Homeside Activities, Grade 3: Conversations & Activities That Bring Parents into Children's Schoolside Learning. (Homeside Activities Ser.). 128p. (Orig.). 1995. pap. 13.95 (*1-885603-62-2*) Develop Studies.
— Homeside Activities, Grade 4: Conversations & Activities That Bring Parents into Children's Schoolside Learning. (Homeside Activities Ser.). 128p. (Orig.). 1995. pap. 13.95 (*1-885603-63-0*) Develop Studies.
— Homeside Activities, Grade 5: Conversations & Activities That Bring Parents into Children's Schoolside Learning. (Homeside Activities Ser.). 128p. (Orig.). 1995. pap. 13.95 (*1-885603-64-9*) Develop Studies.
— Homeside Activities Grade 6: Conversations & Activities That Bring Parents into Children's Schoolside Learning. (Illus.). 128p. 1998. pap. 13.95 (*1-57621-149-5*) Develop Studies.
*__Developmental Studies Center Staff.__ Rading for Real Teacher's Guide to "The Watsons Go to Birmingham-1963" Read Aloud Unit, Grade 5. (Reading for Real Ser.). 28p. 1999. teacher ed. 13.95 (*1-57621-208-4*, LRA515) Develop Studies.
Developmental Studies Center Staff. Reading for Real 1997-98 Annotated Bibliography: Grades K-3. (Reading for Real Ser.). 42p. 1998. pap. 11.00 (*1-885603-57-6*) Develop Studies.
— Reading for Real, 1997-98 Edition, Annotated Bibliography: Grades 4-8. (Reading for Real Ser.). 64p. (Orig.). 1998. pap. 11.00 (*1-885603-56-8*) Develop Studies.
— Reading for Real Revised Program Manual: Grades K-3. (Reading for Real Ser.). 84p. 1998. pap. 19.00 (*1-885603-65-7*) Develop Studies.
— Reading for Real Revised Program Manual: Grades 4-8. 76p. (Orig.). 1998. pap. 19.00 (*1-885603-66-5*) Develop Studies.
— Reading for Real Teacher's Guide to "A Bargain for Frances" Partner Unit, Grade 2. (Reading for Real Ser.). 20p. 1996. pap. 13.95 (*1-885603-95-9*) Develop Studies.
— Reading for Real Teacher's Guide to "A Boy, a Dog & a Frog" Partner Unit, Grade K. (Reading for Real Ser.). 16p. 1996. pap. 13.95 (*1-885603-84-3*) Develop Studies.
— Reading for Real Teacher's Guide to "A Chair for My Mother" Partner Unit, Grade 2. (Reading for Real Ser.). 32p. 1996. pap. 13.95 (*1-885603-96-7*) Develop Studies.
— Reading for Real Teacher's Guide to "A Day No Pigs Would Die" Partner Unit, Grade 7. (Reading for Real Ser.). 28p. (Orig.). 1996. pap., teacher ed. 13.95 (*1-57621-091-X*) Develop Studies.
— Reading for Real Teacher's Guide to "A Fruit & Vegetable Man" Read Aloud Unit, Grade 2. (Reading for Real Ser.). 16p. 1996. pap., teacher ed. 13.95 (*1-57621-127-4*) Develop Studies.
— Reading for Real Teacher's Guide to "A Gathering of Days" Partner Unit, Grade 8. (Reading for Real Ser.). 32p. (Orig.). 1996. pap., teacher ed. 13.95 (*1-57621-134-7*) Develop Studies.
— Reading for Real Teacher's Guide to "A Gathering of Flowers" Read Aloud Unit, Grade 8. (Reading for Real Ser.). 28p. (Orig.). 1996. pap., teacher ed. 13.95 (*1-57621-092-8*) Develop Studies.
— Reading for Real Teacher's Guide to "A Gift for Mama" Partner Unit, Grade 4. (Reading for Real Ser.). 24p. (Orig.). 1996. pap., teacher ed. 13.95 (*1-57621-052-9*) Develop Studies.
*__Developmental Studies Center Staff.__ Reading for Real Teacher's Guide to "A Letter to Amy" Read Aloud Unit, Grade 1. (Reading for Real Ser.). 22p. 1998. teacher ed. 13.95 (*1-57621-178-9*, LRA120) Develop Studies.
Developmental Studies Center Staff. Reading for Real Teacher's Guide to "A Place for Grace" Read Aloud Unit, Grade 3. (Reading for Real Ser.). 20p. 1996. pap., teacher ed. 13.95 (*1-57621-130-4*) Develop Studies.
— Reading for Real Teacher's Guide to "A Raisin in the Sun" Partner Unit, Grade 8. (Reading for Real Ser.). 40p. (Orig.). 1996. pap., teacher ed. 13.95 (*1-57621-093-6*) Develop Studies.
— Reading for Real Teacher's Guide to "A Thief in the Village" Combined Units, Grade 7: Partner & Read Aloud. (Reading for Real Ser.). 16p. (Orig.). 1996. pap., teacher ed. 13.95 (*1-57621-094-4*); pap., teacher ed. 13.95 (*1-57621-095-2*) Develop Studies.
*__Developmental Studies Center Staff.__ Reading for Real Teacher's Guide to "A Weed Is a Flower" Read Aloud Unit, Grade 1. (Reading for Real Ser.). 26p. 2000. pap., teacher ed. 13.95 (*1-57621-256-4*, LRA122) Develop Studies.
Developmental Studies Center Staff. Reading for Real Teacher's Guide to "Adam & Eve & Pinch-Me" Partner Unit, Grade 8. (Reading for Real Ser.). 28p. (Orig.). 1996. pap., teacher ed. 13.95 (*1-57621-068-5*) Develop Studies.
— Reading for Real Teacher's Guide to "Alfie Gives a Hand" Read Aloud Unit, Grade K. (Reading for Real Ser.). 24p. 1996. pap., teacher ed. 13.95 (*1-57621-012-X*) Develop Studies.
— Reading for Real Teacher's Guide to "Aliens in the Family" Partner Unit, Grade 7. (Reading for Real Ser.). 24p. (Orig.). 1996. pap., teacher ed. 13.95 (*1-57621-067-7*) Develop Studies.
— Reading for Real Teacher's Guide to "All Joseph Wanted" Read Aloud Unit, Grade 6. (Reading for Real Ser.). 16p. (Orig.). 1996. pap. 13.95 (*1-885603-44-4*) Develop Studies.
— Reading for Real Teacher's Guide to "America Street" Partner Unit, Grade 6. (Reading for Real Ser.). 44p. (Orig.). 1996. pap. 13.95 (*1-885603-54-1*) Develop Studies.
— Reading for Real Teacher's Guide to "Amos & Boris" Read Aloud Unit, Grade 2. (Reading for Real Ser.). 16p. 1996. pap., teacher ed. 13.95 (*1-57621-030-8*) Develop Studies.
— Reading for Real Teacher's Guide to "Amy's Goose" Read Aloud Unit, Grade 1. (Reading for Real Ser.). 24p. 1996. pap., teacher ed. 13.95 (*1-57621-020-0*) Develop Studies.
*__Developmental Studies Center Staff.__ Reading for Real Teacher's Guide to "An Island Like You", Including "The One Who Watches", "Don Jose of La Mancha" Partner Unit, Grade 8. (Reading for Real Ser.). 60p. 1999. teacher ed. 13.95 (*1-57621-216-5*, LPT813) Develop Studies.
Developmental Studies Center Staff. Reading for Real Teacher's Guide to "And Now Miguel" Read Aloud Unit, Grade 6. (Reading for Real Ser.). 20p. (Orig.). 1996. pap., teacher ed. 13.95 (*1-885603-08-8*) Develop Studies.
— Reading for Real Teacher's Guide to "Annie John" Read Aloud Unit, Grade 8. (Reading for Real Ser.). 24p. (Orig.). 1996. pap., teacher ed. 13.95 (*1-57621-096-0*) Develop Studies.
— Reading for Real Teacher's Guide to "Arthur's Funny Money" Partner Unit, Grade 2. (Reading for Real Ser.). 20p. 1996. pap. 13.95 (*1-885603-94-0*) Develop Studies.
— Reading for Real Teacher's Guide to "Baseball in April (La Bamba)" Read Aloud Unit, Grade 6. (Reading for Real Ser.). 20p. (Orig.). 1996. pap., teacher ed. 13.95 (*1-885603-09-6*) Develop Studies.
— Reading for Real Teacher's Guide to "Baseball in April (Seventh Grade)" Read Aloud Unit, Grade 6. (Reading for Real Ser.). 20p. (Orig.). 1996. pap., teacher ed. 13.95 (*1-885603-10-X*) Develop Studies.
— Reading for Real Teacher's Guide to "Best Friends for Frances" Read Aloud Unit, Grade K. (Reading for Real Ser.). 16p. 1996. pap., teacher ed. 13.95 (*1-57621-013-8*) Develop Studies.
— Reading for Real Teacher's Guide to "Best Teacher in the World" Partner Unit, Grade 2. (Reading for Real Ser.). (Illus.). 20p. 1998. teacher ed. 13.95 (*1-57621-172-X*) Develop Studies.
— Reading for Real Teacher's Guide to "Bigmama's" Read Aloud Unit, Grade K. (Reading for Real Ser.). 20p. 1996. pap., teacher ed. 13.95 (*1-885603-01-0*) Develop Studies.
— Reading for Real Teacher's Guide to "Born in the Gravy" Read Aloud Unit, Grade K. (Reading for Real Ser.). 20p. 1996. pap. 13.95 (*1-885603-25-8*) Develop Studies.
— Reading for Real Teacher's Guide to "Brave Irene" Read Aloud Unit, Grade 2. (Reading for Real Ser.). 16p. 1996. pap., teacher ed. 13.95 (*1-57621-031-6*) Develop Studies.
— Reading for Real Teacher's Guide to "Bread & Jam for Frances" Read Aloud Unit, Grade K. (Reading for Real Ser.). 20p. 1996. pap., teacher ed. 13.95 (*1-57621-014-6*) Develop Studies.
— Reading for Real Teacher's Guide to "Bridge to Terabithia" Read Aloud Unit, Grade 5. (Reading for Real Ser.). 28p. (Orig.). 1996. pap., teacher ed. 13.95 (*1-57621-079-0*) Develop Studies.
— Reading for Real Teacher's Guide to "Bunkhouse Journal" Read Aloud Unit, Grade 7. (Reading for Real Ser.). 28p. (Orig.). 1996. pap., teacher ed. 13.95 (*1-57621-097-9*) Develop Studies.
— Reading for Real Teacher's Guide to "Bunny Cakes" Read-Aloud Unit for Grade K. (Reading for Real Ser.). 20p. 1998. teacher ed. 13.95 (*1-57621-171-1*) Develop Studies.
*__Developmental Studies Center Staff.__ Reading for Real Teacher's Guide to "Butterfly Boy" Read Aloud Unit, Grade 1. (Reading for Real Ser.). 18p. 1999. pap., teacher ed. 13.95 (*1-57621-218-1*, LRA119) Develop Studies.
Developmental Studies Center Staff. Reading for Real Teacher's Guide to "By the Dawn's Early Light" Read-Aloud Unit, Grade 2. (Reading for Real Ser.). 24p. 1998. teacher ed. 13.95 (*1-57621-173-8*) Develop Studies.
— Reading for Real Teacher's Guide to "C. O. L. A. R." Read Aloud Unit, Grade 5. (Reading for Real Ser.). 24p. (Orig.). 1996. pap., teacher ed. 13.95 (*1-57621-080-4*) Develop Studies.
*__Developmental Studies Center Staff.__ Reading for Real Teacher's Guide to "Chang's Paper Pony" Partner Unit, Grade 2. (Reading for Real Ser.). 28p. 1998. teacher ed. 13.95 (*1-57621-192-4*, LPT213) Develop Studies.
Developmental Studies Center Staff. Reading for Real Teacher's Guide to "Charlotte's Web" Read Aloud Unit, Grade 3. (Reading for Real Ser.). 20p. 1996. pap., teacher ed. 13.95 (*1-57621-042-1*) Develop Studies.
— Reading for Real Teacher's Guide to "Chicken Sunday" Read Aloud Unit, Grade 2. (Reading for Real Ser.). 24p. 1996. pap., teacher ed. 13.95 (*1-885603-02-9*) Develop Studies.
— Reading for Real Teacher's Guide to "Child of the Owl" Partner Unit, Grade 6. (Reading for Real Ser.). 28p. (Orig.). 1996. pap. 13.95 (*1-885603-17-7*) Develop Studies.
— Reading for Real Teacher's Guide to "Child of the Silent Night" Read Aloud Unit, Grade 4. (Reading for Real Ser.). 24p. (Orig.). 1996. pap., teacher ed. 13.95 (*1-57621-070-7*) Develop Studies.
— Reading for Real Teacher's Guide to "Children of the Dust Bowl" Read Aloud Unit, Grade 5. (Reading for Real Ser.). 32p. (Orig.). 1996. pap. 13.95 (*1-885603-42-8*) Develop Studies.
*__Developmental Studies Center Staff.__ Reading for Real Teacher's Guide to "Coco Grimes" Partner Unit, Grade 4. (Reading for Real Ser.). 30p. 1999. teacher ed. 13.95 (*1-57621-210-6*, LPT413) Develop Studies.
Developmental Studies Center Staff. Reading for Real Teacher's Guide to "Come Back, Salmon" Partner Unit, Grade 4. (Reading for Real Ser.). 24p. 1998. pap., teacher ed. 13.95 (*1-57621-154-1*) Develop Studies.
— Reading for Real Teacher's Guide to "Come Sing, Jimmy Jo" Read Aloud Unit, Grade 6. (Reading for Real Ser.). 28p. (Orig.). 1996. pap., teacher ed. 13.95 (*1-885603-11-8*) Develop Studies.
— Reading for Real Teacher's Guide to "Cousins" Read Aloud Unit, Grade 6. (Reading for Real Ser.). 20p. (Orig.). 1996. pap., teacher ed. 13.95 (*1-885603-12-6*) Develop Studies.
*__Developmental Studies Center Staff.__ Reading for Real Teacher's Guide to "Crash" Partner Unit, Grade 7. (Reading for Real Ser.). 28p. 1999. pap., teacher ed. 13.95 (*1-57621-222-X*, LPT715) Develop Studies.
Developmental Studies Center Staff. Reading for Real Teacher's Guide to "Crazy Lady!" Read Aloud, Grade 7. (Reading for Real Ser.). 24p. (Orig.). 1996. pap. 13.95 (*1-885603-47-9*) Develop Studies.
— Reading for Real Teacher's Guide to "Crow Boy" Partner Unit, Grade 2. (Reading for Real Ser.). 20p. 1996. pap., teacher ed. 13.95 (*1-885603-03-7*) Develop Studies.
— Reading for Real Teacher's Guide to "Crow Boy" Read Aloud Unit, Grade 6. (Reading for Real Ser.). 32p. (Orig.). 1996. pap., teacher ed. 13.95 (*1-885603-13-4*) Develop Studies.
— Reading for Real Teacher's Guide to "Daniel's Duck" Partner Unit, Grade 2. (Reading for Real Ser.). 20p. 1996. pap. 13.95 (*1-885603-97-5*) Develop Studies.
— Reading for Real Teacher's Guide to "Dear Mr. Henshaw" Partner Unit, Grade 4. (Reading for Real Ser.). 32p. (Orig.). 1996. pap., teacher ed. 13.95 (*1-57621-050-2*) Develop Studies.
— Reading for Real Teacher's Guide to "Digby" Partner Unit, Grade 1. (Reading for Real Ser.). 20p. 1998. teacher ed. 13.95 (*1-57621-170-3*) Develop Studies.
— Reading for Real Teacher's Guide to "Evan's Corner" Read Aloud Unit, Grade 2. (Reading for Real Ser.). 16p. 1996. pap., teacher ed. 13.95 (*1-57621-032-4*) Develop Studies.
— Reading for Real Teacher's Guide to "Fallen Angels" Partner Unit, Grade 8. (Reading for Real Ser.). 32p. (Orig.). 1996. pap., teacher ed. 13.95 (*1-57621-098-7*) Develop Studies.
— Reading for Real Teacher's Guide to "Family Pictures" Partner Unit, Grade 3. (Reading for Real Ser.). 28p. 1996. pap., teacher ed. 13.95 (*1-57621-006-5*) Develop Studies.
— Reading for Real Teacher's Guide to "Farewell to Manzanar" Partner Unit, Grade 8. (Reading for Real Ser.). 40p. (Orig.). 1996. pap., teacher ed. 13.95 (*1-57621-099-5*) Develop Studies.
— Reading for Real Teacher's Guide to "Farmer Schulz's Ducks" Read Aloud Unit, Grade 2. (Reading for Real Ser.). 24p. 1996. pap., teacher ed. 13.95 (*1-57621-033-2*) Develop Studies.
— Reading for Real Teacher's Guide to "Fast Sam, Cool Clyde & Stuff" Partner Unit, Grade 7. (Reading for Real Ser.). 24p. (Orig.). 1996. pap., teacher ed. 13.95 (*1-57621-100-2*) Develop Studies.
— Reading for Real Teacher's Guide to "Felita" Partner Unit, Grade 4. (Reading for Real Ser.). 36p. (Orig.). 1996. pap. 13.95 (*1-885603-40-1*) Develop Studies.
— Reading for Real Teacher's Guide to "First Grade Takes a Test" Read Aloud Unit, Grade 1. (Reading for Real Ser.). 16p. 1996. pap., teacher ed. 13.95 (*1-57621-021-9*) Develop Studies.
— Reading for Real Teacher's Guide to "Follow the Drinking Gourd" Partner Unit, Grade 3. (Reading for Real Ser.). 20p. 1996. pap. 13.95 (*1-885603-83-5*) Develop Studies.
— Reading for Real Teacher's Guide to "Freedom Train, The Story of Harriet Tubman" Read Aloud Unit, Grade 4. (Reading for Real Ser.). 24p. (Orig.). 1996. pap., teacher ed. 13.95 (*1-57621-072-3*) Develop Studies.
— Reading for Real Teacher's Guide to "Frog & Toad Are Friends" Partner Unit, Grade 1. (Reading for Real Ser.). 52p. 1996. pap. 13.95 (*1-885603-88-6*) Develop Studies.
*__Developmental Studies Center Staff.__ Reading for Real Teacher's Guide to "Ginger Brown: The Nobody Boy" Partner Unit, Grade 3. (Reading for Real Ser.). 26p. 1999. teacher ed. 13.95 (*1-57621-214-9*, LPT314) Develop Studies.
Developmental Studies Center Staff. Reading for Real Teacher's Guide to "Go Fish" Partner Unit, Grade 3. (Reading for Real Ser.). 28p. 1996. pap. 13.95 (*1-885603-37-1*) Develop Studies.
*__Developmental Studies Center Staff.__ Reading for Real Teacher's Guide to "Going Home" Read Aloud Unit, Grade 3. (Reading for Real Ser.). 22p. 1998. pap., teacher ed. 13.95 (*1-57621-221-1*, LRA315) Develop Studies.
— Reading for Real Teacher's Guide to "Going Home to Nicodemus" Read Aloud Unit, Grade 8. (Reading for Real Ser.). 26p. 1999. pap., teacher ed. 13.95 (*1-57621-223-8*, LRA812) Develop Studies.
Developmental Studies Center Staff. Reading for Real Teacher's Guide to "Grab Hands & Run" Read Aloud, Grade 7. (Reading for Real Ser.). 24p. (Orig.). 1996. pap. 13.95 (*1-885603-49-5*) Develop Studies.
— Reading for Real Teacher's Guide to "Grandfather's Dream" Read Aloud Unit, Grade 1. (Reading for Real Ser.). 28p. 1998. teacher ed. 13.95 (*1-57621-177-0*) Develop Studies.
— Reading for Real Teacher's Guide to "Grandfather's

An Asterisk (*) at the beginning of an entry indicates that the title is appearing for the first time.

Journey" Read Aloud Unit, Grade 8. (Reading for Real Ser.). 16p. (Orig.). 1996. pap., teacher ed. 13.95 (*1-57621-089-8*) Develop Studies.

— Reading for Real Teacher's Guide to "Gregory Cool" Read Aloud Unit, Grade 3. (Reading for Real Ser.). 20p. 1996. pap., teacher ed. 13.95 (*1-57621-131-2*) Develop Studies.

— Reading for Real Teacher's Guide to "Heartbeats & Other Stories" Read Aloud Unit, Grade 8. (Reading for Real Ser.). 24p. (Orig.). 1996. pap., teacher ed. 13.95 (*1-57621-101-0*) Develop Studies.

***Developmental Studies Center Staff.** Reading for Real Teacher's Guide to "Home to Medicine Mountain" Read Aloud Unit, Grade 3. (Reading for Real Ser.). 24p. 2000. pap., teacher ed. 13.95 (*1-57621-227-0*, LRA317) Develop Studies.

Developmental Studies Center Staff. Reading for Real Teacher's Guide to "Homecoming" Read Aloud Unit, Grade 6. (Reading for Real Ser.). 36p. (Orig.). 1996. pap., teacher ed. 13.95 (*1-885603-14-2*) Develop Studies.

— Reading for Real Teacher's Guide to "How My Parents Learned to Eat" Read Aloud Unit, Grade 2. (Reading for Real Ser.). 20p. 1996. pap., teacher ed. 13.95 (*1-57621-036-7*) Develop Studies.

— Reading for Real Teacher's Guide to "I Am an American - A True Story of Japanese Internment" Partner Unit, Grade 7. (Reading for Real Ser.). 24p. 1998. pap., teacher ed. 13.95 (*1-57621-157-6*) Develop Studies.

— Reading for Real Teacher's Guide to "I Heard the Owl Call My Name" Read Aloud Unit, Grade 8. (Reading for Real Ser.). 24p. (Orig.). 1996. pap., teacher ed. 13.95 (*1-57621-102-9*) Develop Studies.

— Reading for Real Teacher's Guide to "I Know a Lady" Partner Unit, Grade 1. (Reading for Real Ser.). 16p. 1996. pap. 13.95 (*1-885603-89-4*) Develop Studies.

— Reading for Real Teacher's Guide to "If You Give a Mouse a Cookie" Partner Unit, Grade 1. (Reading for Real Ser.). 16p. 1996. pap., teacher ed. 13.95 (*1-57621-002-2*) Develop Studies.

— Reading for Real Teacher's Guide to "In the Year of the Boar & Jackie Robinson" Read Aloud Unit, Grade 5. (Reading for Real Ser.). 24p. (Orig.). 1996. pap., teacher ed. 13.95 (*1-57621-081-2*) Develop Studies.

— Reading for Real Teacher's Guide to "Ira Sleeps Over" Partner Unit, Grade 1. (Reading for Real Ser.). 24p. 1996. pap. 13.95 (*1-885603-90-8*) Develop Studies.

— Reading for Real Teacher's Guide to "Is That You, Miss Blue?" Partner Unit, Grade 7. (Reading for Real Ser.). 28p. (Orig.). 1996. pap., teacher ed. 13.95 (*1-57621-103-7*) Develop Studies.

— Reading for Real Teacher's Guide to "Island of the Blue Dolphins" Partner Unit, Grade 6. (Reading for Real Ser.). 28p. (Orig.). 1996. pap. 13.95 (*1-885603-18-5*) Develop Studies.

— Reading for Real Teacher's Guide to "J. T." Partner Unit, Grade 4. (Reading for Real Ser.). 24p. (Orig.). 1996. pap., teacher ed. 13.95 (*1-57621-053-7*) Develop Studies.

— Reading for Real Teacher's Guide to "Jamaica's Find" Read Aloud Unit, Grade 1. (Reading for Real Ser.). 28p. 1996. pap., teacher ed. 13.95 (*1-57621-023-5*) Develop Studies.

— Reading for Real Teacher's Guide to "Jim's Dog Muffins" Partner Unit, Grade 1. (Reading for Real Ser.). 16p. 1996. pap. 13.95 (*1-885603-91-6*) Develop Studies.

— Reading for Real Teacher's Guide to "Journey for Peace - The Story of Rigoberta Menchu" Read Aloud, Grade 5. (Reading for Real Ser.). 24p. 1998. pap., teacher ed. 13.95 (*1-57621-155-X*) Develop Studies.

— Reading for Real Teacher's Guide to "Journey to Jo'Burg" Partner Unit, Grade 7. (Reading for Real Ser.). 24p. (Orig.). 1996. pap., teacher ed. 13.95 (*1-57621-104-5*) Develop Studies.

— Reading for Real Teacher's Guide to "Justin & the Best Biscuits in the World" Partner Unit, Grade 4. (Reading for Real Ser.). 24p. (Orig.). 1996. pap., teacher ed. 13.95 (*1-57621-054-5*) Develop Studies.

— Reading for Real Teacher's Guide to "Keep the Lights Burning, Abbie" Partner Unit, Grade 2. (Reading for Real Ser.). 20p. 1996. pap. 13.95 (*1-885603-99-1*) Develop Studies.

— Reading for Real Teacher's Guide to "Lincoln: A Photobiography" Read Aloud Unit, Grade 8. (Reading for Real Ser.). 28p. (Orig.). 1996. pap., teacher ed. 13.95 (*1-57621-105-3*) Develop Studies.

— Reading for Real Teacher's Guide to "Little Bear" Partner Unit, Grade 1. (Reading for Real Ser.). 40p. 1996. pap. 13.95 (*1-885603-92-4*) Develop Studies.

— Reading for Real Teacher's Guide to "Little Brother" Partner Unit, Grade 6. (Reading for Real Ser.). 24p. (Orig.). 1996. pap., teacher ed. 13.95 (*1-57621-066-9*) Develop Studies.

— Reading for Real Teacher's Guide to "Luka's Quilt" Read Aloud Unit, Grade 1. (Reading for Real Ser.). 20p. 1996. pap., teacher ed. 13.95 (*1-57621-125-8*) Develop Studies.

— Reading for Real Teacher's Guide to "Lyddie" Read Aloud, Grade 8. (Reading for Real Ser.). 20p. (Orig.). 1996. pap. 13.95 (*1-885603-52-5*) Develop Studies.

— Reading for Real Teacher's Guide to "Maebelle's Suitcase" Read Aloud Unit, Grade 1. (Reading for Real Ser.). 16p. 1996. pap., teacher ed. 13.95 (*1-57621-024-3*) Develop Studies.

— Reading for Real Teacher's Guide to "Maizon at Blue Hill" Read Aloud Unit, Grade 7. (Reading for Real Ser.). 24p. (Orig.). 1996. pap. 13.95 (*1-885603-50-9*) Develop Studies.

— Reading for Real Teacher's Guide to "Make Lemonade" Read Aloud, Grade 8. (Reading for Real Ser.). 20p. (Orig.). 1996. pap. 13.95 (*1-885603-53-3*) Develop Studies.

— Reading for Real Teacher's Guide to "Martin Luther King, Jr. - A Man Who Changed Things" Partner Unit, Grade 2. (Reading for Real Ser.). 20p. 1998. pap., teacher ed. 13.95 (*1-57621-153-3*) Develop Studies.

— Reading for Real Teacher's Guide to "Matthew & Tilly" Read-Aloud Unit for Grade K. (Reading for Real Ser.). 20p. 1998. teacher ed. 13.95 (*1-57621-174-6*) Develop Studies.

***Developmental Studies Center Staff.** Reading for Real Teacher's Guide to "Midwife's Apprentice" Partner Unit, Grade 7. (Reading for Real Ser.). 28p. 1999. teacher ed. 13.95 (*1-57621-209-2*, LPT716) Develop Studies.

Developmental Studies Center Staff. Reading for Real Teacher's Guide to "Mike Mulligan & His Steam Shovel" Read Aloud Unit, Grade 1. (Reading for Real Ser.). 16p. 1996. pap., teacher ed. 13.95 (*1-57621-025-1*) Develop Studies.

— Reading for Real Teacher's Guide to "Miss Maggie" Read Aloud Unit, Grade 3. (Reading for Real Ser.). 24p. 1996. pap., teacher ed. 13.95 (*1-57621-043-X*) Develop Studies.

— Reading for Real Teacher's Guide to "Missing May" Partner Unit, Grade 8. (Reading for Real Ser.). 24p. (Orig.). 1996. pap., teacher ed. 13.95 (*1-57621-069-3*) Develop Studies.

— Reading for Real Teacher's Guide to "Morning Girl" Read Aloud Unit, Grade 6. (Reading for Real Ser.). 20p. (Orig.). 1996. pap. 13.95 (*1-885603-45-2*) Develop Studies.

— Reading for Real Teacher's Guide to "Mrs. Fish, Ape & Me, the Dump Queen" Partner Unit, Grade 4. (Reading for Real Ser.). 24p. (Orig.). 1996. pap., teacher ed. 13.95 (*1-885603-05-3*) Develop Studies.

— Reading for Real Teacher's Guide to "Mrs. Frisby & the Rats of NIMH" Partner Unit, Grade 5. (Reading for Real Ser.). 36p. (Orig.). 1996. pap., teacher ed. 13.95 (*1-57621-060-X*) Develop Studies.

— Reading for Real Teacher's Guide to "Mrs. Tibbles & the Special Someone" Read Aloud Unit, Grade 1. (Reading for Real Ser.). 16p. 1996. pap., teacher ed. 13.95 (*1-57621-026-X*) Develop Studies.

***Developmental Studies Center Staff.** Reading for Real Teacher's Guide to "Ms. Davison, Our Librarian" Read Aloud Unit, Grade K. (Reading for Real Ser.). 22p. 2000. pap., teacher ed. 13.95 (*1-57621-254-8*, LRA019) Develop Studies.

Developmental Studies Center Staff. Reading for Real Teacher's Guide to "Mufaro's Beautiful Daughters" Read Aloud Unit, Grade 2. (Reading for Real Ser.). 16p. 1996. pap., teacher ed. 13.95 (*1-57621-037-5*) Develop Studies.

— Reading for Real Teacher's Guide to "My Brother Sam Is Dead" Partner Unit, Grade 5. (Reading for Real Ser.). 44p. (Orig.). 1996. pap., teacher ed. 13.95 (*1-57621-061-8*) Develop Studies.

***Developmental Studies Center Staff.** Reading for Real Teacher's Guide to "My Name Is Seepeetza" Read Aloud Unit, Grade 6. (Reading for Real Ser.). 24p. 1999. teacher ed. 13.95 (*1-57621-207-6*, LRA615) Develop Studies.

Developmental Studies Center Staff. Reading for Real Teacher's Guide to "Nadia the Willful" Read Aloud Unit, Grade 2. (Reading for Real Ser.). 24p. 1996. pap., teacher ed. 13.95 (*1-57621-038-3*) Develop Studies.

— Reading for Real Teacher's Guide to "Nathaniel Talking" Read Aloud Unit, Grade 3. (Reading for Real Ser.). 16p. 1996. pap., teacher ed. 13.95 (*1-57621-044-8*) Develop Studies.

***Developmental Studies Center Staff.** Reading for Real Teacher's Guide to "Neeny Coming, Neeny Going" Read Aloud Unit, Grade 4. (Reading for Real Ser.). 18p. 1998. teacher ed. 13.95 (*1-57621-193-2*, LRA413) Develop Studies.

Developmental Studies Center Staff. Reading for Real Teacher's Guide to "Nights of the Pufflings" Read Aloud Unit. (Reading for Real Ser.). 20p. (J). (gr. 1). 1998. pap., teacher ed. 13.95 (*1-57621-151-7*) Develop Studies.

— Reading for Real Teacher's Guide to "Niki's Little Donkey" Read Aloud Unit, Grade 1. (Reading for Real Ser.). 24p. 1996. pap., teacher ed. 13.95 (*1-57621-027-8*) Develop Studies.

— Reading for Real Teacher's Guide to "No Good in Art" Read Aloud Unit, Grade K. (Reading for Real Ser.). 20p. 1996. pap., teacher ed. 13.95 (*1-57621-016-2*) Develop Studies.

— Reading for Real Teacher's Guide to "Number the Stars" Read Aloud Unit, Grade 6. (Reading for Real Ser.). 24p. (Orig.). 1996. pap. 13.95 (*1-885603-15-0*) Develop Studies.

— Reading for Real Teacher's Guide to "Officer Buckle & Gloria" Read-Aloud Unit, Grade 1. (Reading for Real Ser.). 20p. 1998. teacher ed. 13.95 (*1-57621-176-2*) Develop Studies.

— Reading for Real Teacher's Guide to "Old Mother Witch" Partner Unit, Grade 3. (Reading for Real Ser.). 24p. 1996. pap., teacher ed. 13.95 (*1-57621-007-3*) Develop Studies.

— Reading for Real Teacher's Guide to "One-Eyed Cat" Partner Unit, Grade 6. (Reading for Real Ser.). 32p. (Orig.). 1996. pap. 13.95 (*1-885603-19-3*) Develop Studies.

— Reading for Real Teacher's Guide to "One Frog Too Many" Partner Unit, Grade K. (Reading for Real Ser.). 20p. 1996. pap. 13.95 (*1-885603-85-1*) Develop Studies.

— Reading for Real Teacher's Guide to "Orphan Train Rider - One Boy's True Story" Read Aloud, Grade 6. (Reading for Real Ser.). 24p. 1998. pap., teacher ed. 13.95 (*1-57621-156-8*) Develop Studies.

— Reading for Real Teacher's Guide to "Out of Nowhere" Read Aloud Unit, Grade 7. (Reading for Real Ser.). 24p. (Orig.). 1996. pap., teacher ed. 13.95 (*1-57621-087-1*) Develop Studies.

— Reading for Real Teacher's Guide to "Owen" Read Aloud Unit, Grade K. (Reading for Real Ser.). 20p. 1996. pap., teacher ed. 13.95 (*1-57621-124-X*) Develop Studies.

***Developmental Studies Center Staff.** Reading for Real Teacher's Guide to "Passage to Freedom: The Sugihara Story" Read Aloud Unit, Grade 6. (Reading for Real Ser.). 24p. 2000. pap., teacher ed. 13.95 (*1-57621-253-X*, LRA616) Develop Studies.

Developmental Studies Center Staff. Reading for Real Teacher's Guide to "Peter's Chair" Read Aloud Unit, Grade K. (Reading for Real Ser.). 16p. 1996. pap., teacher ed. 13.95 (*1-57621-017-0*) Develop Studies.

— Reading for Real Teacher's Guide to "Peter's Place" Read-Aloud Unit, Grade 2. (Reading for Real Ser.). 24p. 1998. teacher ed. 13.95 (*1-57621-175-4*) Develop Studies.

— Reading for Real Teacher's Guide to "Queenie Peavy" Partner Unit, Grade 5. (Reading for Real Ser.). 28p. (Orig.). 1996. pap., teacher ed. 13.95 (*1-57621-062-6*) Develop Studies.

— Reading for Real Teacher's Guide to "Rachel Carson - Pioneer of Ecology" Partner Unit, Grade 5. (Reading for Real Ser.). 28p. 1998. pap., teacher ed. 13.95 (*1-57621-159-2*) Develop Studies.

— Reading for Real Teacher's Guide to "Ramona Forever" Partner Unit, Grade 3. (Reading for Real Ser.). 44p. 1996. pap., teacher ed. 13.95 (*1-57621-008-1*) Develop Studies.

— Reading for Real Teacher's Guide to "Ramona the Pest" Partner Unit, Grade 3. (Reading for Real Ser.). 52p. 1996. pap., teacher ed. 13.95 (*1-57621-009-X*) Develop Studies.

— Reading for Real Teacher's Guide to "Rasmus & the Vagabond" Partner Unit, Grade 4. (Reading for Real Ser.). 24p. (Orig.). 1996. pap. 13.95 (*1-57621-135-5*) Develop Studies.

***Developmental Studies Center Staff.** Reading for Real Teacher's Guide to "'Raymond's Run' & 'Hamadi' in 'America Street'" Partner Unit, Grade 7. (Reading for Real Ser.). 48p. 1999. teacher ed. 13.95 (*1-57621-212-2*, LPT714) Develop Studies.

— Reading for Real Teacher's Guide to "Richard Wright & the Library Card" Read Aloud Unit, Grade 5. (Reading for Real Ser.). 22p. 2000. pap., teacher ed. 13.95 (*1-57621-258-0*, LRA516) Develop Studies.

Developmental Studies Center Staff. Reading for Real Teacher's Guide to "Roll of Thunder, Hear My Cry" Read Aloud Unit, Grade 7. (Reading for Real Ser.). 24p. (Orig.). 1996. pap., teacher ed. 13.95 (*1-57621-106-1*) Develop Studies.

— Reading for Real Teacher's Guide to "Rosalie" Read Aloud Unit, Grade 1. (Reading for Real Ser.). 24p. 1996. pap., teacher ed. 13.95 (*1-57621-029-4*) Develop Studies.

— Reading for Real Teacher's Guide to "Ruby the Copycat" Real Aloud Unit, Grade K. (Reading for Real Ser.). 36p. 1996. pap. 13.95 (*1-885603-27-4*) Develop Studies.

***Developmental Studies Center Staff.** Reading for Real Teacher's Guide to "Ruth Law Thrills a Nation" Read Aloud Unit, Grade 2. (Reading for Real Ser.). 24p. 2000. pap., teacher ed. 13.95 (*1-57621-230-0*, LRA218) Develop Studies.

Developmental Studies Center Staff. Reading for Real Teacher's Guide to "Sadako & the Thousand Paper Cranes" Read Aloud Unit, Grade 4. (Reading for Real Ser.). 20p. (Orig.). 1996. pap., teacher ed. 13.95 (*1-57621-077-4*) Develop Studies.

***Developmental Studies Center Staff.** Reading for Real Teacher's Guide to "Salmon Summer" Read Aloud Unit, Grade 2. (Reading for Real Ser.). 24p. 2000. pap., teacher ed. 13.95 (*1-57621-228-9*, LRA217) Develop Studies.

Developmental Studies Center Staff. Reading for Real Teacher's Guide to "Sam" Read Aloud Unit, Grade K. (Reading for Real Ser.). 20p. 1996. pap., teacher ed. 13.95 (*1-57621-018-9*) Develop Studies.

— Reading for Real Teacher's Guide to "Sam, Bangs & Moonshine" Read Aloud Unit, Grade 3. (Reading for Real Ser.). 24p. 1996. pap., teacher ed. 13.95 (*1-57621-045-6*) Develop Studies.

— Reading for Real Teacher's Guide to "Sami & the Time of the Troubles" Read Aloud Unit, Grade 5. (Reading for Real Ser.). 20p. (Orig.). 1996. pap. 13.95 (*1-885603-41-X*) Develop Studies.

— Reading for Real Teacher's Guide to "Sarah, Plain & Tall" Read Aloud Unit, Grade 5. (Reading for Real Ser.). 32p. (Orig.). 1996. pap., teacher ed. 13.95 (*1-57621-083-9*) Develop Studies.

— Reading for Real Teacher's Guide to "School" Partner Unit, Grade K. (Reading for Real Ser.). 20p. 1996. pap., teacher ed. 13.95 (*1-57621-121-5*) Develop Studies.

— Reading for Real Teacher's Guide to "Scorpions" Partner Unit, Grade 7. (Reading for Real Ser.). 32p. (Orig.). 1996. pap., teacher ed. 13.95 (*1-57621-107-X*) Develop Studies.

— Reading for Real Teacher's Guide to "See Ya, Simon" Read Aloud Unit, Grade 7. (Reading for Real Ser.). 24p. (Orig.). 1996. pap., teacher ed. 13.95 (*1-57621-088-X*) Develop Studies.

— Reading for Real Teacher's Guide to "Shadow of a Bull" Partner Unit, Grade 6. (Reading for Real Ser.). 32p. (Orig.). 1996. pap. 13.95 (*1-885603-21-5*) Develop Studies.

Developmental Studies Center Staff. Reading for Real Teacher's Guide to "She's Wearing a Dead Bird on Her Head!" Partner Unit, Grade 4. (Reading for Real Ser.). 28p. 1996. pap., teacher ed. 13.95 (*1-57621-224-6*, LPT414) Develop Studies.

Developmental Studies Center Staff. Reading for Real Teacher's Guide to "Shoeshine Girl" Partner Unit, Grade 3. (Reading for Real Ser.). 24p. 1996. pap., teacher ed. 13.95 (*1-57621-010-3*) Develop Studies.

— Reading for Real Teacher's Guide to "Six-Dinner Sid" Partner Unit, Grade 3. (Reading for Real Ser.). 20p. 1996. pap., teacher ed. 13.95 (*1-57621-123-1*) Develop Studies.

— Reading for Real Teacher's Guide to "Sixth Grade Can Really Kill You" Partner Unit, Grade 6. (Reading for Real Ser.). 28p. (Orig.). 1996. pap. 13.95 (*1-885603-22-3*) Develop Studies.

— Reading for Real Teacher's Guide to "Sky - A True Story of Resistance During World War II" Read Aloud, Grade 8. (Reading for Real Ser.). 28p. 1998. pap., teacher ed. 13.95 (*1-57621-158-4*) Develop Studies.

— Reading for Real Teacher's Guide to "Slake's Limbo" Partner Unit, Grade 6. (Reading for Real Ser.). 28p. (Orig.). 1996. pap. 13.95 (*1-885603-23-1*) Develop Studies.

— Reading for Real Teacher's Guide to "Somehow Tenderness Survives" Read Aloud Unit, Grade 8. (Reading for Real Ser.). 64p. (Orig.). 1996. pap., teacher ed. 13.95 (*1-57621-108-8*) Develop Studies.

— Reading for Real Teacher's Guide to "Song & Dance Man" Read Aloud Unit, Grade 3. (Reading for Real Ser.). 20p. 1996. pap., teacher ed. 13.95 (*1-57621-046-4*) Develop Studies.

— Reading for Real Teacher's Guide to "Sophie & Lou" Partner Unit, Grade 3. (Reading for Real Ser.). 24p. 1996. pap. 13.95 (*1-885603-36-3*) Develop Studies.

— Reading for Real Teacher's Guide to "Storm in the Night" Read Aloud Unit, Grade 3. (Reading for Real Ser.). 32p. 1996. pap., teacher ed. 13.95 (*1-57621-047-2*) Develop Studies.

— Reading for Real Teacher's Guide to "Story of Ferdinand" Partner Unit, Grade 1. (Reading for Real Ser.). 24p. 1996. pap. 13.95 (*1-885603-93-2*) Develop Studies.

***Developmental Studies Center Staff.** Reading for Real Teacher's Guide to "Story Painter: The Life of Jacob Lawrence" Read Aloud Unit, Grade 6. (Reading for Real Ser.). 30p. 2000. pap., teacher ed. 13.95 (*1-57621-226-2*, LRA617) Develop Studies.

Developmental Studies Center Staff. Reading for Real Teacher's Guide to "Sunshine" Partner Unit, Grade K. (Reading for Real Ser.). 16p. 1996. pap. 13.95 (*1-885603-86-X*) Develop Studies.

— Reading for Real Teacher's Guide to "Taking Care of Yoki" Partner Unit, Grade 4. (Reading for Real Ser.). 32p. (Orig.). 1996. pap., teacher ed. 13.95 (*1-57621-055-3*) Develop Studies.

— Reading for Real Teacher's Guide to "Talk about a Family" Read Aloud Unit, Grade 5. (Reading for Real Ser.). 20p. (Orig.). 1996. pap., teacher ed. 13.95 (*1-57621-084-7*) Develop Studies.

— Reading for Real Teacher's Guide to "Ten Top Stories" Partner Unit, Grade 8. (Reading for Real Ser.). 24p. 1996. pap., teacher ed. 13.95 (*1-57621-109-6*) Develop Studies.

— Reading for Real Teacher's Guide to "The Angel & the Soldier Boy" Partner Unit, Grade K. (Reading for Real Ser.). 24p. 1996. pap., teacher ed. 13.95 (*1-57621-000-6*) Develop Studies.

***Developmental Studies Center Staff.** Reading for Real Teacher's Guide to "The Ballad of Lucy Whipple" Partner Unit, Grade 6. (Reading for Real Ser.). 40p. 1999. teacher ed. 13.95 (*1-57621-206-8*, LPT613) Develop Studies.

— Reading for Real Teacher's Guide to "The Barn" Read Aloud Unit, Grade 4. (Reading for Real Ser.). 24p. 1999. pap., teacher ed. 13.95 (*1-57621-220-3*, LRA412) Develop Studies.

Developmental Studies Center Staff. Reading for Real Teacher's Guide to "The Best Bad Thing" Partner Unit, Grade 5. (Reading for Real Ser.). 32p. (Orig.). 1996. pap. 13.95 (*1-885603-43-6*) Develop Studies.

***Developmental Studies Center Staff.** Reading for Real Teacher's Guide to "The Birthday Swap" Read Aloud Unit, Grade K. (Reading for Real Ser.). 20p. 1998. pap., teacher ed. 13.95 (*1-57621-217-3*, LRA017) Develop Studies.

Developmental Studies Center Staff. Reading for Real Teacher's Guide to "The Book of Three" Read Aloud Unit, Grade 5. (Reading for Real Ser.). 20p. (Orig.). 1996. pap., teacher ed. 13.95 (*1-57621-078-2*) Develop Studies.

— Reading for Real Teacher's Guide to "The Bridge Dancers" Read Aloud Unit, Grade 4. (Reading for Real Ser.). 16p. (Orig.). 1996. pap. 13.95 (*1-885603-39-8*) Develop Studies.

— Reading for Real Teacher's Guide to "The Bully of Barkham Street" Partner Unit, Grade 5. (Reading for Real Ser.). 28p. (Orig.). 1996. pap., teacher ed. 13.95 (*1-57621-057-X*) Develop Studies.

— Reading for Real Teacher's Guide to "The Captive" Partner Unit, Grade 6. (Reading for Real Ser.). 32p. (Orig.). 1996. pap., teacher ed. 13.95 (*1-57621-065-0*) Develop Studies.

— Reading for Real Teacher's Guide to "The Carp in the Bathtub" Read Aloud Unit, Grade 3. (Reading for Real Ser.). 16p. 1996. pap., teacher ed. 13.95 (*1-57621-041-3*) Develop Studies.

***Developmental Studies Center Staff.** Reading for Real Teacher's Guide to "The Circuit" Read Aloud Unit, Grade 5. (Reading for Real Ser.). 24p. 1999. pap., teacher ed. 13.95 (*1-57621-225-4*, LRA614) Develop Studies.

Developmental Studies Center Staff. Reading for Real Teacher's Guide to "The Clay Marble" Partner Unit, Grade 7. (Reading for Real Ser.). 28p. (Orig.). 1996. pap. 13.95 (*1-885603-51-7*) Develop Studies.

D

— Reading for Real Teacher's Guide to "The Crying Christmas Tree" Read Aloud Unit, Grade 1. (Reading for Real Ser.). 20p. 1996. pap. 13.95 (*1-885603-28-2*) Develop Studies.

— Reading for Real Teacher's Guide to "The Day of Ahmed's Secret" Read Aloud Unit, Grade 1. (Reading for Real Ser.). 20p. 1996. pap. 13.95 (*1-885603-29-0*) Develop Studies.

— Reading for Real Teacher's Guide to "The Endless Steppe" Read Aloud Unit, Grade 7. (Reading for Real Ser.). 16p. (Orig.). 1996. pap., teacher ed. 13.95 (*1-57621-110-X*) Develop Studies.

— Reading for Real Teacher's Guide to "The First Strawberries" Read Aloud Unit, Grade 4. (Reading for Real Ser.). 16p. (Orig.). 1996. pap. 13.95 (*1-885603-38-X*) Develop Studies.

— Reading for Real Teacher's Guide to "The Flunking of Joshua T. Bates" Read Aloud Unit, Grade 4. (Reading for Real Ser.). 28p. (Orig.). 1996. pap., teacher ed. 13.95 (*1-57621-071-5*) Develop Studies.

— Reading for Real Teacher's Guide to "The Friends" Partner Unit, Grade 8. (Reading for Real Ser.). 36p. (Orig.). 1996. pap., teacher ed. 13.95 (*1-57621-111-8*) Develop Studies.

— Reading for Real Teacher's Guide to "The Friendship/The Gold Cadillac" Partner Unit, Grade 7. (Reading for Real Ser.). 32p. (Orig.). 1996. pap. 13.95 (*1-885603-58-4*) Develop Studies.

— Reading for Real Teacher's Guide to "The Gift-Giver" Partner Unit, Grade 5. (Reading for Real Ser.). 28p. (Orig.). 1996. pap., teacher ed. 13.95 (*1-57621-058-8*) Develop Studies.

— Reading for Real Teacher's Guide to "The Giver" Partner Unit, Grade 7. (Reading for Real Ser.). 28p. (Orig.). 1996. pap. 13.95 (*1-885603-48-7*) Develop Studies.

— Reading for Real Teacher's Guide to "The Goat in the Rug" Read Aloud Unit, Grade 2. (Reading for Real Ser.). 36p. 1996. pap., teacher ed. 13.95 (*1-57621-034-0*) Develop Studies.

— Reading for Real Teacher's Guide to "The Goats" Partner Unit, Grade 7. (Reading for Real Ser.). 36p. (Orig.). 1996. pap., teacher ed. 13.95 (*1-57621-112-6*) Develop Studies.

— Reading for Real Teacher's Guide to "The Great Brain" Read Aloud Unit, Grade 4. (Reading for Real Ser.). 20p. (Orig.). 1996. pap., teacher ed. 13.95 (*1-57621-073-1*) Develop Studies.

— Reading for Real Teacher's Guide to "The Great Gilly Hopkins" Partner Unit, Grade 5. (Reading for Real Ser.). 48p. (Orig.). 1996. pap., teacher ed. 13.95 (*1-57621-059-6*) Develop Studies.

— Reading for Real Teacher's Guide to "The Green Book" Read Aloud Unit, Grade 4. (Reading for Real Ser.). 24p. (Orig.). 1996. pap., teacher ed. 13.95 (*1-57621-074-X*) Develop Studies.

— Reading for Real Teacher's Guide to "The Half-Birthday Party" Read Aloud Unit, Grade 1. (Reading for Real Ser.). 24p. 1996. pap., teacher ed. 13.95 (*1-57621-022-7*) Develop Studies.

— Reading for Real Teacher's Guide to "The Hundred Dresses" Read Aloud Unit, Grade 4. (Reading for Real Ser.). 20p. (Orig.). 1996. pap., teacher ed. 13.95 (*1-57621-075-8*) Develop Studies.

— Reading for Real Teacher's Guide to "The Josefina Story Quilt" Partner Unit, Grade 2. (Reading for Real Ser.). 28p. 1996. pap. 13.95 (*1-885603-98-3*) Develop Studies.

— Reading for Real Teacher's Guide to "The Lion, the Witch & the Wardrobe" Read Aloud Unit, Grade 4. (Reading for Real Ser.). 24p. (Orig.). 1996. pap., teacher ed. 13.95 (*1-57621-076-6*) Develop Studies.

— Reading for Real Teacher's Guide to "The Little Painter of Sabana Grande" Read Aloud Unit, Grade 3. (Reading for Real Ser.). 20p. 1996. pap. 13.95 (*1-885603-33-9*) Develop Studies.

— Reading for Real Teacher's Guide to "The Lost Lake" Partner Unit, Grade 3. (Reading for Real Ser.). 24p. 1996. pap. 13.95 (*1-885603-35-5*) Develop Studies.

— Reading for Real Teacher's Guide to "The Mice Who Lived in a Shoe" Partner Unit, Grade 2. (Reading for Real Ser.). 24p. 1996. pap., teacher ed. 13.95 (*1-57621-003-0*) Develop Studies.

— Reading for Real Teacher's Guide to "The Miracle Worker" Partner Unit, Grade 8. (Reading for Real Ser.). 52p. (Orig.). 1996. pap., teacher ed. 13.95 (*1-885603-07-X*) Develop Studies.

— Reading for Real Teacher's Guide to "The Mother's Day Mice" Read Aloud Unit, Grade K. (Reading for Real Ser.). 16p. 1996. pap., teacher ed. 13.95 (*1-57621-015-4*) Develop Studies.

— Reading for Real Teacher's Guide to "The Outside Dog" Partner Unit, Grade 1. (Reading for Real Ser.). 24p. 1996. pap., teacher ed. 13.95 (*1-57621-122-3*) Develop Studies.

— Reading for Real Teacher's Guide to "The Outsiders" Partner Unit, Grade 7. (Reading for Real Ser.). 28p. (Orig.). 1996. pap., teacher ed. 13.95 (*1-57621-113-4*) Develop Studies.

— Reading for Real Teacher's Guide to "The Patchwork Quilt" Read Aloud Unit, Grade 2. (Reading for Real Ser.). 16p. 1996. pap., teacher ed. 13.95 (*1-57621-039-1*) Develop Studies.

— Reading for Real Teacher's Guide to "The Pearl" Partner Unit, Grade 8. (Reading for Real Ser.). 28p. (Orig.). 1996. pap., teacher ed. 13.95 (*1-57621-114-2*) Develop Studies.

— Reading for Real Teacher's Guide to "The Pinballs" Partner Unit, Grade 6. (Reading for Real Ser.). 28p. (Orig.). 1996. pap. 13.95 (*1-885603-20-7*) Develop Studies.

— Reading for Real Teacher's Guide to "The Quarreling Book" Partner Unit, Grade 1. (Reading for Real Ser.). 20p. 1996. pap. 13.95 (*1-885603-31-2*) Develop Studies.

— Reading for Real Teacher's Guide to "The Real Thief" Read Aloud Unit, Grade 5. (Reading for Real Ser.). 24p. (Orig.). 1996. pap., teacher ed. 13.95 (*1-57621-082-0*) Develop Studies.

— Reading for Real Teacher's Guide to "The Red Comb" Partner Unit, Grade 4. (Reading for Real Ser.). 28p. (Orig.). 1996. pap., teacher ed. 13.95 (*1-57621-132-0*) Develop Studies.

— Reading for Real Teacher's Guide to "The Sign of the Beaver" Partner Unit, Grade 5. (Reading for Real Ser.). 40p. (Orig.). 1996. pap., teacher ed. 13.95 (*1-57621-063-4*) Develop Studies.

— Reading for Real Teachers Guide to "The Sign of the Chrysanthemum" Partner Unit, Grade 8. (Reading for Real Ser.). 32p. (Orig.). 1996. pap. 13.95 (*1-885603-55-X*) Develop Studies.

— Reading for Real Teacher's Guide to "The Signmaker's Assistant" Read Aloud Unit, Grade 1. (Reading for Real Ser.). 20p. 1996. pap. 13.95 (*1-885603-30-4*) Develop Studies.

— Reading for Real Teacher's Guide to "The Stories Julian Tells" Partner Unit, Grade 3. (Reading for Real Ser.). 44p. 1996. pap., teacher ed. 13.95 (*1-57621-011-1*) Develop Studies.

*__Developmental Studies Center Staff.__ Reading for Real Teacher's Guide to "The Treasure Hunt" Partner Unit, Grade 2. (Reading for Real Ser.). 24p. 1999. teacher ed. 13.95 (*1-57621-190-8*, LPT215); teacher ed. 13.95 (*1-57621-191-6*, LPT214) Develop Studies.

— Reading for Real Teacher's Guide to "The True Adventure of Daniel Hall" Read Aloud Unit, Grade 5. (Reading for Real Ser.). 24p. 1999. teacher ed. 13.95 (*1-57621-205-X*, LRA514) Develop Studies.

Developmental Studies Center Staff. Reading for Real Teacher's Guide to "The Whipping Boy" Read Aloud Unit, Grade 5. (Reading for Real Ser.). 20p. (Orig.). 1996. pap., teacher ed. 13.95 (*1-57621-085-5*) Develop Studies.

*__Developmental Studies Center Staff.__ Reading for Real Teacher's Guide to "The Wild Boy" Read Aloud Unit, Grade 4. (Reading for Real Ser.). 20p. 2000. pap., teacher ed. 13.95 (*1-57621-229-7*, LRA414) Develop Studies.

Developmental Studies Center Staff. Reading for Real Teacher's Guide to "The Winter Camp" Read Aloud Unit, Grade 5. (Reading for Real Ser.). 24p. (Orig.). 1996. pap., teacher ed. 13.95 (*1-57621-133-9*) Develop Studies.

— Reading for Real Teacher's Guide to "The Winter Room" Read Aloud Unit, Grade 7. (Reading for Real Ser.). 24p. (Orig.). 1996. pap., teacher ed. 13.95 (*1-57621-115-0*) Develop Studies.

— Reading for Real Teacher's Guide to "The 18th Emergency" Partner Unit, Grade 4. (Reading for Real Ser.). 24p. (Orig.). 1996. pap., teacher ed. 13.95 (*1-57621-051-0*) Develop Studies.

— Reading for Real Teacher's Guide to "Theodor & Mr. Balbini" Read Aloud Unit, Grade 3. (Reading for Real Ser.). 24p. 1996. pap., teacher ed. 13.95 (*1-57621-048-0*) Develop Studies.

— Reading for Real Teacher's Guide to "Throwing Shadows - At the Home" Read Aloud Unit, Grade 7. (Reading for Real Ser.). 16p. (Orig.). 1996. pap., teacher ed. 13.95 (*1-57621-116-9*) Develop Studies.

— Reading for Real Teacher's Guide to "Throwing Shadows - In the Village of the Weavers" Read Aloud Unit, Grade 7. (Reading for Real Ser.). 32p. (Orig.). 1996. pap., teacher ed. 13.95 (*1-57621-117-7*) Develop Studies.

— Reading for Real Teacher's Guide to "Throwing Shadows - On Shark's Tooth Beach" Read Aloud Unit, Grade 7. (Reading for Real Ser.). 20p. (Orig.). 1996. pap. 13.95 (*1-57621-118-5*) Develop Studies.

*__Developmental Studies Center Staff.__ Reading for Real Teacher's Guide to "Throwing Shadows" Including "At the Home" & "On Shark's Tooth Beach" Read Aloud Unit, Grade 7. (Reading for Real Ser.). 32p. 2000. pap., teacher ed. 13.95 (*1-57621-250-5*, LRA705) Develop Studies.

Developmental Studies Center Staff. Reading for Real Teacher's Guide to "Thy Friend, Obadiah" Partner Unit, Grade 2. (Reading for Real Ser.). 20p. 1996. pap., teacher ed. 13.95 (*1-885603-04-5*) Develop Studies.

— Reading for Real Teacher's Guide to "To Hell with Dying" Read Aloud Unit, Grade 7. (Reading for Real Ser.). 20p. (Orig.). 1996. pap., teacher ed. 13.95 (*1-57621-119-3*) Develop Studies.

— Reading for Real Teacher's Guide to "Tuck Everlasting" Read Aloud Unit, Grade 6. (Reading for Real Ser.). 32p. (Orig.). 1996. pap. 13.95 (*1-885603-16-9*) Develop Studies.

— Reading for Real Teacher's Guide to "Twenty & Ten" Partner Unit, Grade 5. (Reading for Real Ser.). 24p. (Orig.). 1996. pap., teacher ed. 13.95 (*1-57621-064-2*) Develop Studies.

*__Developmental Studies Center Staff.__ Reading for Real Teacher's Guide to "Twins" Read Aloud Unit, Grade K. (Reading for Real Ser.). 20p. 2000. pap., teacher ed. 13.95 (*1-57621-255-6*, LRA020) Develop Studies.

Developmental Studies Center Staff. Reading for Real Teacher's Guide to "Uncle James" Read Aloud Unit, Grade 6. (Reading for Real Ser.). 16p. (Orig.). 1996. pap., teacher ed. 13.95 (*1-57621-086-3*) Develop Studies.

— Reading for Real Teacher's Guide to "Uncle Jed's Barbershop" Read Aloud Unit, Grade 3. (Reading for Real Ser.). 20p. 1996. pap. 13.95 (*1-885603-34-7*) Develop Studies.

— Reading for Real Teacher's Guide to "Very Last First Time" Read Aloud Unit, Grade 2. (Reading for Real Ser.). 24p. 1996. pap., teacher ed. 13.95 (*1-57621-040-5*) Develop Studies.

— Reading for Real Teacher's Guide to "Wagon Wheels" Partner Unit, Grade 2. (Reading for Real Ser.). 24p. 1996. pap., teacher ed. 13.95 (*1-57621-004-9*) Develop Studies.

— Reading for Real Teacher's Guide to "War Comes to Willy Freeman" Partner Unit, Grade 5. (Reading for Real Ser.). 28p. (Orig.). 1996. pap., teacher ed. 13.95 (*1-885603-06-1*) Develop Studies.

— Reading for Real Teacher's Guide to "Wednesday Surprise" Partner Unit, Grade 2. (Reading for Real Ser.). 20p. 1996. pap., teacher ed. 13.95 (*1-57621-005-7*) Develop Studies.

— Reading for Real Teacher's Guide to "Westmark" Partner Unit, Grade 8. (Reading for Real Ser.). 28p. (Orig.). 1996. pap., teacher ed. 13.95 (*1-57621-120-7*) Develop Studies.

*__Developmental Studies Center Staff.__ Reading for Real Teacher's Guide to "What Zeesie Saw on Delancy Street" Read Aloud Unit, Grade 3. (Reading for Real Ser.). 24p. 1999. teacher ed. 13.95 (*1-57621-211-4*, LRA316) Develop Studies.

Developmental Studies Center Staff. Reading for Real Teacher's Guide to "When the Monkeys Came Back" Read Aloud Unit, Grade 4. (Reading for Real Ser.). 16p. (Orig.). 1996. pap., teacher ed. 13.95 (*1-57621-128-2*) Develop Studies.

— Reading for Real Teacher's Guide to "When Will I Read?" Read Aloud Unit, Grade K. (Reading for Real Ser.). 20p. 1996. pap., teacher ed. 13.95 (*1-57621-019-7*) Develop Studies.

— Reading for Real Teacher's Guide to "Where Once There Was a Wood" Read Aloud Unit, Grade K. (Reading for Real Ser.). 20p. 1998. pap., teacher ed. 13.95 (*1-57621-150-9*) Develop Studies.

— Reading for Real Teacher's Guide to "Where the Lilies Bloom" Partner Unit, Grade 6. (Reading for Real Ser.). 28p. (Orig.). 1996. pap. 13.95 (*1-885603-24-X*) Develop Studies.

— Reading for Real Teacher's Guide to "Where's Al?" Partner Unit, Grade K. (Reading for Real Ser.). 16p. 1996. pap. 13.95 (*1-885603-87-8*) Develop Studies.

— Reading for Real Teacher's Guide to "Wild Fox - A True Story" Read Aloud Unit, Grade 3. (Reading for Real Ser.). 20p. 1998. pap., teacher ed. 13.95 (*1-57621-152-5*) Develop Studies.

— Reading for Real Teacher's Guide to "Will Gets a Haircut" Read Aloud Unit, Grade 1. (Reading for Real Ser.). 16p. 1996. pap., teacher ed. 13.95 (*1-57621-126-6*) Develop Studies.

— Reading for Real Teacher's Guide to "Words of Stone" Partner Unit, Grade 6. (Reading for Real Ser.). 24p. (Orig.). 1996. pap. 13.95 (*1-885603-46-0*) Develop Studies.

— Reading for Real Teacher's Guide to "Yang the Youngest & His Terrible Ear" Read Aloud Unit, Grade 3. (Reading for Real Ser.). 24p. 1996. pap., teacher ed. 13.95 (*1-57621-049-9*) Develop Studies.

*__Developmental Studies Center Staff.__ Reading for Real Teacher's Guide to "Yolanda's Genius" Partner Unit, Grade 5. (Reading for Real Ser.). 36p. 1999. pap., teacher ed. 13.95 (*1-57621-219-X*, LPT512) Develop Studies.

Developmental Studies Center Staff. Reading for Real Teacher's Guide to "Zeely" Partner Unit, Grade 4. (Reading, Thinking & Caring Ser.). 28p. (Orig.). 1996. pap., teacher ed. 13.95 (*1-57621-056-1*) Develop Studies.

— Reading for Real Teacher's Guide to "Zinnia & Dot" Read Aloud Unit, Grade K. (Reading for Real Ser.). 16p. 1996. pap. 13.95 (*1-885603-26-6*) Develop Studies.

*__Developmental Studies Center Staff.__ Reading for Real Teacher's Guide to "Zora Hurston & the Chinaberry Tree" Read Aloud Unit, Grade 1. (Reading for Real Ser.). 22p. 1998. teacher ed. 13.95 (*1-57621-179-7*, LRA121) Develop Studies.

Developmental Studies Center Staff. That's My Buddy! Friendship & Learning Across the Grades: Ideas from the Child Development Project. 144p. (Orig.). 1996. pap. 14.95 (*1-885603-81-9*) Develop Studies.

— That's My Buddy! Collegial Study Guide. (Building Schoolwide Community Ser.). (Illus.). 48p. 1997. pap. 9.95 (*1-57621-136-3*) Develop Studies.

— Ways We Want Our Class to Be: Class Meetings That Build Commitment to Kindness & Learning. LC 96-135339. 120p. (Orig.). 1996. pap. 14.95 (*1-885603-80-0*) Develop Studies.

— Ways We Want Our Class to Be: Collegial Study Guide. (Building Schoolwide Community Ser.). (Illus.). 48p. 1997. pap. 9.95 (*1-57621-140-1*) Develop Studies.

Developmental Stuides Center Staff. Reading for Real Teacher's Guide to "Moonlight" Partner Unit, Grade K. (Reading for Real Ser.). 24p. 1996. pap., teacher ed. 13.95 (*1-57621-001-4*) Develop Studies.

Developments in Industrial Microbiology Staff. Developments in Industrial Microbiology Vol. 2: Proceedings of the Seventeenth General Meeting of the Society for Industrial Microbiology, Held at Stillwater, OK, August 28-September 1, 1960. LC 60-13953. 320p. reprint ed. pap. 99.20 (*0-608-05474-7*, 206594300002) Bks Demand.

D'Evelyn, C., ed. The Latin Text of the Ancrene Riwle from Merton College MS 44 & British Museum MS Cotton Vitellius E.vii. (EETS Original Ser.: Vol. 216). 1963. reprint ed. 30.00 (*0-19-722216-1*, Pub. by EETS) Boydell & Brewer.

— The South English Legendary Vol. III: Introduction & Glossary, Vol. III, Intro. & Glossary. (EETS Original Ser.: Vol. 244). 1963. reprint ed. 30.00 (*0-19-722244-7*, Pub. by EETS) Boydell & Brewer.

D'Evelyn, C. & Mill, Anna J., eds. The South English Legendary: Corpus Christi College Cambridge, MS 145 & British Museum MS Harley 2277 with Variants, Vol. I. (EETS Original Ser.: Vol. 235). 1967. reprint ed. 30.00 (*0-19-722235-8*, Pub. by EETS) Boydell & Brewer.

— The South English Legendary Vol. II: Text, Vol. II. (EETS Original Ser.: Vol. 236). 1967. reprint ed. text 30.00 (*0-19-722236-6*, Pub. by EETS) Boydell & Brewer.

D'Evelyn, David S. Educational Clinics: Rescue Plan for Dropouts. (Issue Papers: No. 3-87). 13p. 1987. pap. text 8.00 (*1-57655-006-0*) Independ Inst.

— Lotto's Losing Numbers: Fifteen Reasons Why Colorado Can't Afford a Bigger Lottery. 6p. 1998. pap. text 8.00 (*1-57655-024-9*) Independ Inst.

— School Choice: Not Yet Real in Colorado's Biggest District. 14p. 1989. pap. text 8.00 (*1-57655-121-0*) Independ Inst.

D'Evelyn, David S. & Spakoski, Marsha L. Colorado Sourcebook on Equal Opportunity. (Issue Papers: No. 6-86). 100p. 1986. pap. text 8.00 (*1-57655-001-X*) Independ Inst.

Deven, F., jt. auth. see de Beer, Joop.

Devencenzi, Jayne & Pendergast, Susan. Belonging: Self & Social Discovery for Children of All Ages. (Illus.). 265p. (Orig.). 1988. 24.95 (*0-9623822-0-5*) Belonging.

Devender, Thomas R. Van, see McClaran, Mitchel P. & Van Devender, Thomas R., eds.

Devendorf, John F. Great Lakes Bulk Carriers, 1869-1985. (Illus.). 244p. 1996. pap. 30.00 (*1-889043-03-6*) Frost Lke Pr.

Devendra, C. Sustainable Animal Production from Small Farm Systems in South-East Asia. (Animal Production & Health Papers: No. 106). 152p. 1993. pap. 17.00 (*92-5-103168-1*, F31681, Pub. by FAO) Bernan Associates.

Devendra, C. & Burns, M. Goat Production in the Tropics. 183p. 1983. 45.00 (*0-85198-519-X*) OUP.

Devendra, C., jt. ed. see D'Mello, J. P.

Devendra, Kiran. Changing Status of Women in India. 3rd rev. ed. 1996. reprint ed. pap. 10.00 (*0-7069-7982-6*, Pub. by Vikas) S Asia.

Devendra, Kiran. Changing the Status of Women in India. 3rd ed. (C). 1994. text 28.50 (*0-7069-7618-5*, Pub. by Vikas) S Asia.

Devendra, Tissa. Sri Lanka: The Emerald Island. Clarke, Arthur C., tr. & frwd. by. 96p. 1996. 19.95 (*81-7437-066-8*, Pub. by Roli Bks) Heian Intl.

Deveney, John P. Astral Projection or Liberation of the Double & the Work of the Early Theosophical Society. unabridged ed. (Theosophical History Occasional Papers: Vol. VI). iii, 84p. 1997. pap. 22.00 (*1-883279-06-2*) J Santucci.

— Paschal Beverly Randolph: A Nineteenth-Century Black American Spiritualist, Rosicrucian, & Sex Magician. LC 95-52244. (SUNY Series in Western Esoteric Traditions). (Illus.). 607p. (C). 1996. text 86.50 (*0-7914-3119-3*); pap. text 29.95 (*0-7914-3120-7*) State U NY Pr.

Deveney, Thomas G. Cain on Screen: Contemporary Spanish Cinema. LC 99-26229. (Illus.). 352p. 1999. pap. 32.50 (*0-8108-3618-1*) Scarecrow.

*__Devenish, Colin.__ Limp Bizkit. LC 00-39061. 192p. 2000. pap. 12.95 (*0-312-26349-X*, St Martin Griffin) St Martin.

Devenish, G. E. A Commentary on the South African Constitution. LC 98-189382. xix, 390 p. 1998. write for info. (*0-409-02181-4*) Buttrwrth-Heinemann.

— The Interpretation of Statutes. 350p. 1992. 60.00 (*0-7021-2754-X*, Pub. by Juta & Co); pap. 41.50 (*0-7021-3445-7*, 15623, Pub. by Juta & Co) Gaunt.

Devenish, Philip E. & Goodwin, George L., eds. Witness & Existence: Essays in Honor of Schubert M. Ogden. LC 89-30283. (Illus.). 256p. 1989. pap. text 24.00 (*0-226-14358-9*) U Ch Pr.

— Witness & Existence: Essays in Honor of Schubert M. Ogden. LC 89-30283. (Illus.). 257p. 1998. lib. bdg. 54.00 (*0-226-14357-0*) U Ch Pr.

Devenish, Philip E., tr. & intro. see Marxsen, Willi.

Devenish, R. Into Life. 1981. pap. 3.99 (*0-9505476-5-4*, Pub. by Evangelical Pr) P & R Pubng.

Devenish, Robert J. & McLaughlin, Charles H. Devenish: Historical & Genealogical Records of the Devenish Families of England & Ireland. (Illus.). 409p. 1993. reprint ed. pap. 62.50 (*0-8328-3101-8*); reprint ed. lib. bdg. 72.50 (*0-8328-3100-X*) Higginson Bk Co.

Devenish, Ross, jt. auth. see Fugard, Athol.

Devenney, Christopher, jt. ed. see Sussman, Henry.

DeVenney, David P. American Choral Music since 1920: An Annotated Guide. LC 93-21428. (Fallen Leaf Reference Books in Music: No. 27). xviii, 279p. 1994. 49.50 (*0-914913-28-X*, Fallen Lef Pr) Scarecrow.

— American Masses & Requiems: A Descriptive Guide. LC 90-48578. (Reference Books in Music: No. 15). xvii, 210p. 1991. 33.00 (*0-914913-14-X*, Fallen Lef Pr) Scarecrow.

— The Broadway Song Companion: An Annotated Guide to Musical Theater Literature by Voice Type & Song Style. LC 97-42486. 272p. 1998. 35.00 (*0-8108-3373-5*) Scarecrow.

— Nineteenth Century American Choral Music. LC 87-80918. (Reference Books in Music: No. 8). xxi, 182p. (Orig.). 1987. pap. 19.95 (*0-914913-08-5*, Fallen Lef Pr) Scarecrow.

— Varied Carols: A Survey of American Choral Literature. LC 99-13706. 328p. 1999. lib. bdg. 89.50 (*0-313-31051-3*, Greenwood Pr) Greenwood.

DeVenney, David P. & Johnson, Craig R. The Chorus in Opera: A Guide to the Repertory. LC 92-33252. 220p. 1992. 32.00 (*0-8108-2620-8*) Scarecrow.

Devenny, Darlynne, jt. ed. see Turkewitz, Gerald.

Devenport, Emily. Godheads. 1998. mass mkt. 5.99 (*0-451-45680-7*, ROC) NAL.

D

An Asterisk (*) at the beginning of an entry indicates that the title is appearing for the first time.

Devenport, Mark, jt. auth. see Sharrock, Daviod.

Devenport, William R. Experiments for Industrial Electronics. 4th ed. 294p. 1993. mass mkt., student ed. 40.95 (*0-8273-5969-1*) Delmar.

Devens, Carol. Countering Colonization: Native American Women & Great Lakes Missions, 1630-1900. (C). 1992. 45.00 (*0-520-07557-9*, Pub. by U CA Pr) Cal Prin Full Svc.

Devens, Richard & Sandler, Norman. Martial Arts for Kids: The Road to Inner Strength, Self-Awareness & a Peaceful World. LC 97-28591. 1997. pap. write for info. (*0-8348-0401-8*) Weatherhill.

Deventer, Cyrus C. Nan, see Nan Deventer, Cyrus C.

Deventer, Donald R. Van, see Van Deventer, Donald R.

Deventer, Donald R. Van, see Uyemura, Dennis G. & Van Deventer, Donald R.

Deventer, M. J. Van, see Baca, Elmo.

Deventer, M. J. Van, see Baca, Elmo & Van Deventer, M. J.

Deventer, M. J. Van, see Baca, Elmo.

Deventer, M. J. Van, see Van Deventer, M. J.

Deventer, M. Oskar Van, see Van Deventer, M. Oskar.

Deveny, Thomas G. Cain on Screen: Contemporary Spanish Cinema. LC 93-39695. (ENG & SPA., Illus.). 352p. 1993. 45.00 (*0-8108-2707-7*) Scarecrow.

— Contemporary Spanish Film from Fiction: Literary Tales on Screen. LC 99-11960. (Illus.). 496p. 1999. 55.00 (*0-8108-3635-1*) Scarecrow.

Devenyi, Jutka. Metonymy & Drama: Essays on Language & Dramatic Strategy. LC 96-697. 120p. 1996. 27.50 (*0-8387-5313-2*) Bucknell U Pr.

Devenyi, Kinga, ed. & tr. see Goldziher, Ignaz.

DeVenzio, Dick. Rip-Off U: The Annual Theft & Exploitation of Major College Revenue Producing Student-Athletes. 256p. 1986. 15.95 (*0-910305-01-3*) Fool Court.

— Smart Moves: How to Succeed in School, Sports, Career & Life. LC 89-10541. (Young Readers Ser.). 293p. (YA). (gr. 6-12). 1989. pap. 16.95 (*0-87975-546-6*) Prometheus Bks.

— Stuff! Good Players Should Know. (Illus.). 320p. 1983. 19.95 (*0-910305-00-5*) Fool Court.

— There's Only One Way to Win: Modern Success Principles, & the Colorful Style of an Old-Fashioned Coach. 224p. 1992. 17.95 (*0-910305-02-1*) Fool Court.

— Think Like a Champion: A Guide to Championship Performance for Athletes in All Sports. 416p. 1997. 24.95 (*0-614-29694-3*) Fool Court.

Dever, Aileen, jt. auth. see Dever, Maria.

Dever, Barbara. AIDS - Answers to Questions Kids Ask. Clark, Kimberley, ed. LC 96-180952. (Illus.). 64p. (J). 1996. pap. 7.95 (*0-88160-286-8*, LW356) Learning Wks.

— AIDS - What Teens Need to Know. Clark, Kimberly, ed. (Illus.). 80p. (Orig.). (YA). (gr. 9-12). 1996. pap. 9.95 (*0-88160-233-7*, LW328) Learning Wks.

Dever, Barbara, ed. see Schwartz, Linda.

Dever-Boaz, Carie & Rains, Sally T. Softball Pitching Fundamentals & Techniques. LC 97-67169. (Art & Science of Coaching Ser.). (Illus.). 100p. 1998. pap. 16.95 (*1-57167-142-0*) Coaches Choice.

Dever, Carolyn. Death & the Mother from Dickens to Freud: Victorian Fiction & the Anxiety of Origins. LC 97-27250. (Studies in Nineteenth-Century Literature & Culture: No. 17). 251p. (C). 1998. text 52.95 (*0-521-62280-8*) Cambridge U Pr.

Dever, Carolyn, jt. ed. see Taylor, Marvin J.

Dever, G. E. Epidemiology in Health Services Management. 350p. (C). 1984. pap. 72.00 (*0-89443-850-6*) Aspen Pub.

— Improving Outcomes in Public Health Practice: Strategy & Methods. LC 96-45614. 375p. 59.00 (*0-8342-0637-4*, 20637) Aspen Pub.

Dever, G. E.Alan. Community Health Analysis: A Global Awareness at the Local Level. 2nd rev. ed. (Health Care Administration Ser.). (Illus.). 416p. (C). 1991. 54.00 (*0-8342-0191-7*) Aspen Pub.

Dever, Joe. Lone Wolf: Wolf's Bane, No. 19. 224p. (Orig.). 1995. mass mkt. 4.50 (*0-425-14976-5*) Berkley Pub.

— Lone Wolf No. 12: The Masters of Darkness. (Lone Wolf Ser.: No. 12). 1989. mass mkt. 4.50 (*0-425-11718-9*) Berkley Pub.

— Lone Wolf No. 18: Dawn of the Dragons. 208p. (Orig.). 1995. pap. text 3.99 (*0-425-14568-9*) Berkley Pub.

Dever, Joe & Chalk, Gary. Lone Wolf No. 1: Flight from the Dark. 192p. 1985. mass mkt. 4.50 (*0-425-08436-1*) Berkley Pub.

— Lone Wolf No. 10: The Dungeons of Torgar. 1988. mass mkt. 4.50 (*0-425-10930-5*) Berkley Pub.

Dever, Maria & Dever, Aileen. Relative Origins: Famous Foster & Adopted People. 201p. 1992. pap. 15.95 (*0-89420-286-3*, 402020) Natl Book.

Dever, Mark. 9 Marks of a Healthy Church. 29p. 1997. pap. 4.00 (*0-9654955-4-X*) Founders Pr.

***Dever, Mark.** Nine Marks of a Healthy Church. rev. expanded ed. LC 00-9045. 304p. 2000. pap. 15.99 (*1-58134-163-6*) Crossway Bks.

***Dever, Mark E.** Richard Sibbes: Puritanism & Calvinism in Late Elizabethan & Early Stuart England. 208p. 2000. pap. 19.95 (*0-86554-657-6*) Mercer Univ Pr.

Dever, Mary F. My Heritage. LC 96-90827. 1997. 12.95 (*0-533-12182-5*) Vantage.

Dever, Maryanne, ed. Australia & Asia: Cultural Transactions. LC 96-49250. (ConsumAsiaN Ser.). (Illus.). 240p. 1997. text 40.00 (*0-8248-1953-5*) UH Pr.

Dever, Pat & Arthur, Margy. Discover the CSU: A Subjective Guide to the California State University. LC 94-79125. 208p. (Orig.). 1994. pap. 10.00 (*0-9643053-0-5*) Coll Campus.

Dever, Richard B. & Knapczyk, Dennis R. Teaching Persons with Mental Retardation: A Model for Curriculum Development & Teaching. LC 96-83803. 496p. (C). 1996. text. write for info. (*0-697-20559-2*) Brown & Benchmark.

Dever, S. M. & Pederson, A. If... A Book of Thought Provoking Questions for People with Way Too Much Time on Their Hands. 150p. 1999. pap. 7.99 (*0-9658180-4-7*) Fox Bks.

Dever, Sean. So Others May Live. 250p. 1999. pap. 10.99 (*0-9658180-2-0*) Fox Bks.

***Dever, Sean M.** The Adventures of Parsley Dumpling. (J). 1999. pap. 4.99 (*0-9658180-5-5*) Fox Bks.

Dever, Sean M. Blind Pass. Martin, Laura A., ed. & photos by. by. (Illus.). 250p. (Orig.). 1997. pap. 8.99 (*0-9658180-0-4*, 9701, Duchess Pubns) Fox Bks.

***Dever, Sean M.** Every Day's a Holiday: A Holiday for Every Day of the Year. 1999. pap. 7.99 (*0-9658180-3-9*) Fox Bks.

— Parsley Dumpling & the Peppermint Caribou. (J). 1999. pap. 4.99 (*0-9658180-6-3*) Fox Bks.

Dever, Will. Recent Archaeological Discoveries. (Illus.). 200p. (C). 1993. pap. 14.95 (*0-295-97261-0*) U of Wash Pr.

Dever, William G., ed. Gezer IV: The Nineteen Sixty-Nine to Seventy-One Seasons in Field VI, the "Acropolis", 2 pts. (Illus.). x, 277p. 1986. text 65.00 (*0-87820-304-4*) Hebrew Union Coll Pr.

— Sardis, Bir Umm Fawakhir, Tell el-Umeiri, the Combined Caesarea Expeditions & Tell Dothan. LC 95-6929. (Annual of the American Schools of Oriental Research Ser.: Vol. 52). (Illus.). 194p. (C). 1994. reprint ed. 51.00 (*0-7885-0099-6*, 850202, Pub. by Am Sch Orient Res) David Brown.

— Sardis, Paphos, Caesarea Maritima, Shiqmim, Ain Ghazal. LC 93-40735. (Annual of the American Schools of Oriental Research Ser.: Vol. 51). (Illus.). 132p. 1993. reprint ed. 42.00 (*1-55540-926-1*, 850201, Pub. by Am Sch Orient Res) David Brown.

Dever, William G., et al, eds. Gezer II: Report of the, 1967-70 Seasons in Fields I & II. (Illus.). ix, 138p. 1974. text 25.00 (*0-87820-302-8*) Hebrew Union Coll Pr.

Dever, William G. & Lance, H. Darrell, eds. A Manual of Field Excavation: Handbook for Field Archaeologists. iv, 240p. 1978. pap. text 20.00 (*0-87820-303-6*) Hebrew Union Coll Pr.

Dever, William G., et al. Gezer I: Preliminary Report of the 1964-1966 Seasons. (Illus.). viii, 109p. 1970. text 20.00 (*0-87820-300-1*) Hebrew Union Coll Pr.

Dever, William G., ed. see American Schools of Oriental Research Staff.

Dever, William G., jt. ed. see Gitin, Seymour.

Deveraux, Jude. An Angel for Emily. 1998. per. 7.50 (*0-671-00359-3*) PB.

— An Angel for Emily. large type ed. LC 98-17697. 318p. 1998. 20.00 (*0-7838-0185-8*, G K Hall Lrg Type); 20.00 (*0-7838-0186-6*, G K Hall Lrg Type) Mac Lib Ref.

— The Awakening. 352p. 1991. mass mkt. 6.99 (*0-671-74378-3*) PB.

— The Black Lyon. LC 96-54264. (Star-Romance Ser.). 339p. 1997. 23.95 (*0-7862-0951-8*) Five Star.

— The Black Lyon. LC 80-67437. 288p. 1980. mass mkt. 6.99 (*0-380-75911-X*, Avon Bks) Morrow Avon.

***Deveraux, Jude.** The Black Lyon. LC 99-95445. 352p. 2000. pap. 12.50 (*0-380-81206-1*, Avon Bks) Morrow Avon.

Deveraux, Jude. The Blessing. LC 99-216686. 288p. 1998. 22.00 (*0-671-89108-1*, PB Hardcover) PB.

— The Blessing. 327p. 1999. mass mkt. 6.99 (*0-671-89109-X*, Pocket Star Bks) PB.

***Deveraux, Jude.** The Blessing. LC 98-46993. 1999. 26.95 (*1-56895-629-0*, Wheeler) Wheeler Pub.

Deveraux, Jude. The Conquest. Marrow, Linda, ed. 320p. 1991. mass mkt. 6.99 (*0-671-64447-5*, Pocket Star Bks) PB.

— The Conquest. large type ed. LC 91-22528. (General Ser.). 408p. 1991. lib. bdg. 20.95 (*0-8161-5231-4*, G K Hall Lrg Type) Mac Lib Ref.

— Counterfeit Lady. Marrow, Linda, ed. 1991. mass mkt. 6.99 (*0-671-73976-X*) PB.

— The Duchess. Marrow, Linda, ed. 368p. 1992. mass mkt. 6.99 (*0-671-68972-X*) PB.

— The Duchess. 1999. pap. 9.98 (*0-671-04415-X*) PB.

— The Enchanted Land. LC 96-54897. 484p. 1997. lib. bdg. 25.95 (*0-7862-0952-6*) Five Star.

— Enchanted Land. 448p. 1978. mass mkt. 6.99 (*0-380-40063-4*, Avon Bks) Morrow Avon.

— Eternity. Marrow, Linda, ed. 352p. 1992. per. 6.99 (*0-671-74457-7*) PB.

— The Heiress. 384p. 1995. mass mkt. 6.99 (*0-671-74462-3*) PB.

— The Heiress. large type ed. LC 95-52064. 1996. 26.95 (*1-56895-290-2*, Compass) Wheeler Pub.

***Deveraux, Jude.** La Heredera. (SPA.). 304p. 2000. pap. 9.50 (*0-553-06130-5*) Bantam.

— High Tide. 311p. 1999. 24.00 (*0-671-01416-1*, PB Hardcover) PB.

— High Tide. 352p. 2000. mass mkt. 7.99 (*0-671-01417-X*) S&S Trade.

— High Tide. abr. ed. 1999. audio 24.00 (*0-671-04623-3*) S&S Audio.

— High Tide. large type ed. LC 99-54333. 1999. 24.95 (*1-56895-800-5*) Wheeler Pub.

Deveraux, Jude. Highland Velvet. Marrow, Linda, ed. (Montgomery Annals Ser.: No. 3). 1991. mass mkt. 6.99 (*0-671-73972-7*) PB.

— Highland Velvet. 1997. mass mkt. 3.99 (*0-671-01134-0*) PB.

— The Invitation. Marrow, Linda, ed. 320p. 1994. mass mkt. 6.99 (*0-671-74458-5*) PB.

— A Knight in Shining Armor. 384p. 1990. mass mkt. 6.99 (*0-671-70509-1*) PB.

— A Knight in Shining Armor. 1996. mass mkt. 3.99 (*0-671-00759-9*) PB.

— Legend. LC 96-216382. 416p. 1996. 23.00 (*0-671-74461-5*, PB Hardcover) PB.

Deveraux, Jude. Legend. 1997. 23.00 (*0-671-00170-1*, Pocket Books) PB.

— Legend. ed. 1998. per. 23.00 (*0-671-03694-7*, Pocket Books) PB.

Deveraux, Jude. Legend. large type ed. LC 96-39756. (Large Print Bks.). 1997. 26.95 (*1-56895-395-X*) Wheeler Pub.

— Lost Lady. Marrow, Linda, ed. 1991. mass mkt 6.99 (*0-671-73977-8*) PB.

— The Maiden. 1991. mass mkt. 7.50 (*0-671-74379-1*) PB.

Deveraux, Jude. Mountain Laurel. abr. ed. 1990. 14.95 incl. audio (*0-671-70872-4*, Audioworks) S&S Trade.

Deveraux, Jude. Mountain Laurel. large type ed. (General Ser.). 405p. 1991. lib. bdg. 21.95 (*0-8161-5124-5*, G K Hall Lrg Type) Mac Lib Ref.

— Mountain Laurel. Marrow, Linda, ed. 320p. 1991. reprint ed. per. 6.99 (*0-671-68976-2*) PB.

— The Princess. 1991. per. 6.99 (*0-671-74380-5*) PB.

— The Raider. 1991. mass mkt. 6.99 (*0-671-74381-3*) PB.

— Remembrance. 1995. pap. 6.99 (*0-671-74460-7*, Pocket Books) PB.

— Remembrance. 1997. mass mkt. 6.99 (*0-671-02357-8*, Pocket Books) PB.

***Deveraux, Jude.** Remembrance. 1999. 9.98 (*0-671-04608-X*) S&S Trade.

Deveraux, Jude. Remembrance. large type ed. LC 94-42981. 601p. 1995. 25.95 (*0-7838-1171-3*, G K Hall Lrg Type); pap. 19.95 (*0-7838-1172-1*, G K Hall Lrg Type) Mac Lib Ref.

— River Lady. Marrow, Linda, ed. 1991. per. 7.50 (*0-671-73978-6*) PB.

— Sweet Liar. Marrow, Linda, ed. 1993. mass mkt. 6.99 (*0-671-68974-6*) PB.

***Deveraux, Jude.** Sweet Liar. 1999. pap. 9.98 (*0-671-04417-6*) PB.

Deveraux, Jude. Sweet Liar. abr. ed. Marrow, Linda, ed. 384p. 1992. pap. 17.00 incl. audio (*0-671-79190-7*, Audioworks) PB.

— Sweet Liar. large type ed. LC 92-38592. (General Ser.). 586p. 1993. pap. 18.95 (*0-8161-5623-9*, G K Hall Lrg Type) Mac Lib Ref.

— Sweetbriar. 1991. mass mkt. 6.99 (*0-671-74382-1*) PB.

— The Taming. Morrow, Linda, ed. 1991. mass mkt. 6.99 (*0-671-74383-X*) PB.

— The Taming. large type ed. (General Ser.). 382p. 1990. lib. bdg. 20.95 (*0-8161-4937-2*, G K Hall Lrg Type) Mac Lib Ref.

***Deveraux, Jude.** Temptation. 368p. 2000. 24.95 (*0-671-00203-1*) PB.

Deveraux, Jude. The Temptress. Morrow, Linda, ed. 1991. mass mkt. 6.99 (*0-671-74384-8*) PB.

— Twin of Fire. Marrow, Linda, ed. 1991. mass mkt. 6.99 (*0-671-73979-4*) PB.

— Twin of Fire. large type ed. 432p. 1992. pap. 17.95 (*0-8161-5340-X*, G K Hall Lrg Type) Mac Lib Ref.

— Twin of Fire & Ice. 1997. 12.00 (*0-671-01689-X*, PB Hardcover) PB.

— Twin of Ice. Marrow, Linda, ed. 1991. mass mkt. 6.99 (*0-671-73971-9*) PB.

— Twin of Ice. large type ed. (General Ser.). 406p. 1992. pap. 17.95 (*0-8161-5333-7*, G K Hall Lrg Type) Mac Lib Ref.

— Velvet Angel. Marrow, Linda, ed. 1991. mass mkt. 6.99 (*0-671-73973-5*) PB.

— The Velvet Promise. Marrow, Linda, ed. (Richard Gallen Bks.). 416p. 1991. pap. 5.50 (*0-685-47135-7*); per. 6.99 (*0-671-73974-3*) PB.

— Velvet Song. Marrow, Linda, ed. 1991. mass mkt. 6.99 (*0-671-73975-1*) PB.

— Wishes. 1991. mass mkt. 6.99 (*0-671-74385-6*, Pocket Books) PB.

***Deveraux, Jude, et al.** A Season in the Highlands. 2000. per. 6.99 (*0-7434-0341-X*) PB.

Deveraux, Jude, et al. Upon a Midnight Clear. 490p. 1997. 16.00 (*0-671-01374-2*) PB.

— Upon a Midnight Clear. 421p. 1998. mass mkt. 6.99 (*0-671-01988-0*) S&S Trade.

— Upon a Midnight Clear. large type ed. LC 98-27444. 1998. 30.00 (*0-7862-1568-2*) Thorndike Pr.

Deveraux, Lara L. & Hammerman, Ann J. Infertility & Identity: New Strategies for Treatment. LC 97-49290. 288p. 1998. 34.95 (*0-7879-3881-5*) Jossey-Bass.

Deverdun, A. The True Mexico: Tenochtitlan. 1976. lib. bdg. 59.95 (*0-8490-2773-X*) Gordon Pr.

Devere. Agriscience & Technology. 2nd ed. (Agriculture Ser.). 1997. teacher ed. 13.95 (*0-8273-6748-1*, VNR) Wiley.

Devere, Christian Van, see Van Devere, Christian.

Devere, Heather, jt. auth. see King, Preston T.

Devere, L., jt. auth. see Burton.

Devere, Louis. The Handbook of Practical Cutting on the Centre Point System, (1866) rev. ed. Shep, R. L., ed. & intro. by. LC 86-90526. (Illus.). 236p. 1986. reprint ed. pap. 17.95 (*0-914046-03-9*) R L Shep.

DeVere, Paul. I Golf, Therefore I Am: Frustrated, Humble...but Hopeful. Hammet, Lewis, ed. LC 95-73105. (Illus.). 64p. (Orig.). 1996. pap. 12.95 (*0-9650791-0-4*, 11013D) Saron Pr.

DeVere, Paul, jt. auth. see Sorrell, Charles.

DeVere, S., tr. see Spielhagen, Friedrich.

Devere-Summers, Anthony. War & the Royal Houses of Europe in the Twentieth Century. LC 97-129126. (Illus.). 176p. 1997. 27.95 (*1-85409-310-X*, Pub. by Arms & Armour) Sterling.

Devereaux, Charla. Nutrition & Diet Logic. 160p. (Orig.). 1995. pap. 7.95 (*0-572-01801-0*, Pub. by Foulsham UK) Assoc Pubs Grp.

Devereaux, Eve. Ultimate Card Trick Book. 128p. 1995. 19.95 (*0-7858-0323-8*) Bk Sales Inc.

***Devereaux, Grant.** Nevada Bluff. 288p. 2000. 19.95 (*0-9701466-0-4*); pap. 12.95 (*0-9701466-1-2*) Athenean.

Devereaux, Leslie & Hillman, Roger, eds. Fields of Vision: Essays in Visual Anthropology, Cinema & Photography. LC 94-646. 1995. 50.00 (*0-520-08522-1*, Pub. by U CA Pr); pap. 17.95 (*0-520-08524-8*, Pub. by U CA Pr) Cal Prin Full Svc.

Devereaux, Linda E. The Texas Navy: Freedom Fighters for the Republic of Texas. Ericson, Joe E., ed. LC 83-81716. (Illus.). 1983. pap. 14.50 (*0-911317-21-X*) Ericson Bks.

Devereaux Macy. How Do I Say Goodbye. Date not set. pap. write for info. (*1-886716-07-2*) Devereaux.

Devereaux Macy Staff. Endless Love. Date not set. pap. write for info. (*1-886716-08-0*) Devereaux.

— 100 Different Places for Sex. 1994. pap. write for info. (*1-886716-00-5*) Devereaux.

— 100 Ways for Romance. 1993. pap. write for info. (*1-886716-01-3*) Devereaux.

— 100 Ways to Erotic Sex. 1992. pap. write for info. (*1-886716-02-1*) Devereaux.

— 100 Ways to Passion. 1994. pap. write for info. (*1-886716-06-4*) Devereaux.

— 100 Ways to Say I Love You. 1993. pap. write for info. (*1-886716-05-6*) Devereaux.

— Love Has No Bonds. 1990. pap. write for info. (*1-886716-04-8*) Devereaux.

— To the One I Love. Date not set. pap. write for info. (*1-886716-09-9*) Devereaux.

***Devereaux, Margaret.** Ride the Restless Tide: A Story of Old Marblehead. LC 99-91619. 414p. 1999. 25.00 (*0-7388-1134-3*); pap. 18.00 (*0-7388-1135-1*) Xlibris Corp.

Devereaux, Robert. Santa Steps Out: A Fairy Tale for Grown-Ups. LC 98-213928. (Illus.). 252p. 1998. 39.95 (*0-9662629-0-5*) Dark Hwy.

Devereaux, Steve. Practical Drilling & Well Planning Manual. LC 97-47327. 1998. 89.95 (*0-87814-696-2*) PennWell Bks.

Deverell. West History of Nation. 2000. pap. text 32.95 (*0-312-19171-5*) St Martin.

— West History of Nation, Vol. 2. 2000. pap. text 32.95 (*0-312-19211-8*) St Martin.

Deverell, Catherine. Stradivari's Singing Violin. (J). (gr. 1-3). 1992. lib. bdg. 13.95 (*0-87614-732-5*, Carolrhoda) Lerner Pub.

— Stradivari's Singing Violin. (Illus.). (J). (gr. 1-3). 1992. pap. 5.95 (*0-87614-583-7*, Carolrhoda) Lerner Pub.

Deverell, Christine, jt. auth. see Deverell, Richard.

Deverell, Diana. Night on Fire. LC 99-14874. 304p. 1999. 23.00 (*0-380-97611-0*, Avon Bks) Morrow Avon.

— 12 Drummers Drumming. 1999. mass mkt. 6.99 (*0-380-79594-9*, Avon Bks) Morrow Avon.

***Deverell, Diana.** 12 DRUMMERS DRUMMING (H) LC 97-44188. 304p. 1998. 23.00 (*0-380-97610-2*, Avon Bks) Morrow Avon.

***Deverell, Dore.** Light Beyond the Darkness: How I Healed My Suicide Son after His Death. (Illus.). 144p. 2000. pap. 16.95 (*1-902636-19-8*, Pub. by Temple Lodge) Anthroposophic.

Deverell, Rex. Boiler Room Suite. 96p. 1978. pap. 10.95 (*0-88922-137-5*, Pub. by Talonbks) Genl Dist Srvs.

— Plays of Belonging: Three Plays. (Playwrights Canada Ser.). 1998. text 12.95 (*0-88754-531-9*) Theatre Comm.

Deverell, Rex. Uphill Revival; Shinbone General Store; Underground Lake: Three Plays. LC 77-378638. 102p. 1977. write for info. (*0-88754-053-8*, Pub. by Playwrights) Consort Bk Sales.

Deverell, Richard & Deverell, Christine. Abingdons Bible Handbook for Young Readers. (J). 1995. 9.95 (*0-687-00809-3*) Abingdon.

Deverell, William. Dance of Shiva. 456p. 1996. mass mkt. 6.95 (*0-7710-2664-1*) McCland & Stewart.

Deverell, William. Kill All the Lawyers. 356p. 1995. mass mkt. 7.99 (*0-345-39817-3*, Ballantine) Ballantine Pub Grp.

Deverell, William. Platinum Blues. 261p. 1996. mass mkt. 5.95 (*0-7710-2662-5*) McCland & Stewart.

— Railroad Crossing: Californians & the Railroad. LC 92-40128. (Illus.). 278p. (C). 1996. pap. 16.95 (*0-520-20505-7*, Pub. by U CA Pr) Cal Prin Full Svc.

— Railroad Crossing: Californians & the Railroad, 1850-1910. LC 92-40128. xiii, 278p. 1994. 45.00 (*0-520-08214-1*, Pub. by U CA Pr) Cal Prin Full Svc.

— Street Legal: The Betrayal. LC 96-140203. 356p. 1996. 22.95 (*0-7710-2669-2*) McCland & Stewart.

Deverell, William. Trial of Passion. LC 98-177002. 382p. 1997. write for info. (*0-7710-2673-0*) McCland & Stewart.

— Trial of Passion. 1999. mass mkt. 29.99 (*0-7704-2781-2*) McCland & Stewart.

Deverell, William & Sitton, Tom, eds. California Progressivism Revisited. LC 93-11110. 240p. 1994. 45.00 (*0-520-08469-1*, Pub. by U CA Pr); pap. 16.95 (*0-520-08470-5*, Pub. by U CA Pr) Cal Prin Full Svc.

***Deverell, William F. & Hise, Greg.** Eden by Design: The 1930 Olmsted-Bartholomew Regional Plan for Los Angeles. LC 99-45101. (Illus.). 248p. 2000. 17.95 (*0-520-22415-9*, Pub. by U CA Pr) Cal Prin Full Svc.

***Devereux.** GIS/GPS/CAD: An Integrated Approach. (Student Material TV Ser.). 2001. pap. 45.00 (*0-7668-1216-2*) Delmar.

Devereux, jt. auth. see Day.

Devereux, Anthony Q. Juan Ponce de Leon, King Ferdinand, & the Fountain of Youth. LC 92-45888. 1993. reprint ed. 25.00 (*0-87152-464-3*) Reprint.

D

Devereux, Carole. The Northwest Oregon Stable Guide: One Hundred Boarding, Breeding & Training Stables for Horses. LC 93-74828. 144p. 1993. pap. 15.95 (*1-884422-13-6*) Centaur Pubns.

— Spirit of the Horse. 242p. 1998. pap. 25.00 (*1-884422-24-1*) Centaur Pubns.

Devereux, Charla. The Aroma-Therapy Kit. 112p. 1993. boxed set 24.95 (*0-8048-1981-5*) Tuttle Pubng.

***Devereux, Charla & Stockel, Fran.** The Mediatation Kit: Everything You Need to Relax & Rejuvenate. (Illus.). 120p. 2000. reprint ed. pap. text 28.00 (*0-7881-6448-1*) DIANE Pub.

Devereux, Charla & Stockel, Fran. The Meditation Kit, Boxed Set: The Complete Pack for Meditation & Visualization. LC 97-16729. 128p. 1997. 27.95 incl. audio (*1-885203-48-9*) Jrny Editions.

Devereux, Charla, jt. auth. see Devereux, Paul.

Devereux, E. J. A Bibliography of John Rastell. LC 98-90112. (Illus.). 192p. 65.00 (*0-7735-1841-X*) McG-Queens Univ Pr.

Devereux, Edward C., Jr. Gambling & the Social Structure: A Sociological Study of Lotteries & Horse Racing in Contemporary America, 2 vols., Set. Zuckerman, Harriet & Merton, Robert K., eds. LC 79-8993. (Dissertations on Sociology Ser.). 1980. lib. bdg. 113.95 (*0-405-12964-5*) Ayer.

Devereux, Eve. Card Tricks: Projects for Beginners. 48p. 1996. 14.95 (*0-7858-0571-0*) Bk Sales Inc.

— Coddle Your Cat: How to Pamper Your Kitty in Style - Practical Projects to Prove You Care. (Illus.). 96p. 1998. pap. 11.95 (*1-85967-664-2*) Anness Pub.

Devereux, Frederick L., Jr. Famous American Horses. LC 75-13347. (Illus.). 128p. (YA). (gr. 8 up). 1975. 24.95 (*0-8159-5512-X*) Devin.

Devereux, George. Basic Problems of Enthnopsychiatry. Gulati, Basia M., tr. from FRE. LC 79-11104. 384p. 1980. reprint ed. lib. bdg. 37.50 (*0-226-14355-4*) U Ch Pr.

— Mohave Ethnopsychiatry & Suicide: Psychiatric Knowledge & the Psychic Disturbances of an Indian Tribe. (Bureau of American Ethnology Bulletins Ser.). 586p. 1995. lib. bdg. 119.00 (*0-7812-4175-8*) Rprt Serv.

— Mohave Ethnopsychiatry & Suicide: The Psychiatric Knowledge & the Psychic Disturbances of an Indian Tribe. reprint ed. 95.00 (*0-403-03650-X*) Scholarly.

— A Study of Abortion in Primitive Societies. rev. ed. LC 75-10572. 390p. 1976. 57.50 (*0-8236-6245-4*); pap. 24.95 (*0-8236-8311-7*, 26245) Intl Univs Pr.

Devereux, George, ed. Psychoanalysis & the Occult. 432p. 1970. pap. 24.95 (*0-8236-8240-4*, 25180) Intl Univs Pr.

Devereux, Godfrey. Dynamic Yoga: The Ultimate Workout That Chills Your Mind As It Changes Your Body. (Illus.). 256p. 1999. 18.00 (*0-7225-3657-7*) Thorsons PA.

— Elements of Yoga. LC 97-177825. (Elements of...Ser.). (Illus.). 144p. 1997. pap. 9.95 (*1-86204-074-5*, Pub. by Element MA) Penguin Putnam.

***Devereux, Godfrey.** 15 Minute Yoga: Yoga for a Busy World. (Illus.). 2000. pap. 12.00 (*0-7225-3966-5*, Pub. by Thorsons PA) HarpC.

Devereux, James. The Story of Wake Island. (Elite Unit Ser.: Vol. 33). (Illus.). 252p. 1997. reprint ed. 29.95 (*0-89839-264-0*) Battery Pr.

Devereux, James A., ed. The Moral Dimensions of the International Conduct: The Jesuit Community Lectures, 1982. LC 83-11660. 118p. reprint ed. pap. 36.60 (*0-7837-6317-4*, 204603200010) Bks Demand.

Devereux, John. Medical Law Text, Cases & Materials. LC 98-111617. xxv, 440p. 1997. pap. 62.00 (*1-876213-11-6*, Pub. by Cavendish Pubng) Gaunt.

Devereux, O. F., et al, eds. Corrosion Fatigue (NACE Reference Book 2) (Illus.). 762p. 1972. 92.00 (*0-915567-58-X*) NACE Intl.

Devereux, Owen F. Topics in Metallurgical Thermodynamics. LC 88-13172. 508p. (C). 1989. reprint ed. lib. bdg. 57.50 (*0-89464-329-0*) Krieger.

***Devereux, Paul.** Illustrated Encyclopedia of Ancient Earth Mysteries. (Illus.). 2000. 24.95 (*0-7137-2764-0*) Blandford Pr.

Devereux, Paul. The Long Trip: The Prehistory of Psychedelia. LC 96-53444. (Illus.). 224p. 1997. pap. 15.95 (*0-14-019540-8*) Viking Penguin.

— The Long Trip: The Prehistory of Psychedelia. 1999. pap. 12.95 (*0-14-025378-5*) Viking Penguin.

— Places of Power: Measuring the Secret Energy of Ancient Sites. (Illus.). 224p. 1999. pap. 16.95 (*0-7137-2765-9*, Pub. by Blandford Pr) Sterling.

— Shamanism & the Mystery Lines: Ley Lines, Spirit Paths, Shape-Shifting & Out-of-Body Travel. LC 92-35728. (Illus.). 240p. 1999. pap. 12.95 (*0-87542-189-X*) Llewellyn Pubns.

Devereux, Paul & Brookesmith, Peter. UFOs & Ufology: The First Fifty Years. LC 97-34486. (Illus.). 192p. 1998. 29.95 (*0-8160-3800-7*) Facts on File.

Devereux, Paul & Cornelius, Geoffrey. The Secret Language of the Stars & Planets: A Visual Key to the Heavens. LC 95-23316. 176p. 1996. 29.95 (*0-8118-1225-1*); pap. 19.95 (*0-8118-1200-6*) Chronicle Bks.

Devereux, Paul & Devereux, Charla. The Lucid Dreaming Kit: How to Awaken Within, Control & Use Your Dreams. LC 98-86146. (Illus.). 128p. 1998. pap. 22.95 (*1-885203-66-7*) Jrny Editions.

Devereux, Paul, et al. Earthmind: Communicating with the Living World of Gaia. 235p. 1992. pap. 12.95 (*0-89281-367-9*) Inner Tradit.

Devereux, Richard B. Mitral Valve Prolapse. 350p. 1996. text. write for info. (*0-7817-0199-6*) Lppncott W & W.

Devereux, Robert. The First Ottoman Constitutional Period: A Study of the Midhat Constitution & Parliament. LC 78-64239. (Johns Hopkins University. Studies in the Social Sciences. Thirtieth Ser. 1912: 1). reprint ed. 26.00 (*0-404-61344-6*) AMS Pr.

Devereux, Robert & Wingfield, Anthony. True Copie of a Discourse Written by a Gentleman, Employed in the Late Voyage of Spaine & Portingale. LC 78-38172. (English Experience Ser.: No. 449). 1972. reprint ed. 15.00 (*90-221-0449-4*) Walter J Johnson.

Devereux, Stephen. Theories of Famine. 288p. (C). 1994. pap. text 42.00 (*0-13-302217-X*) P-H.

Devereux, Stephen & Hoddinott, John, eds. Fieldwork in Developing Countries. LC 92-16847. 229p. 1992. pap. 19.95 (*1-55587-392-8*) L Rienner.

Devereux, Stephen, et al. Credit & Savings for Development: A Practical Guide. (Illus.). 80p. (C). 1990. 39.95 (*0-85598-159-8*, Pub. by Oxfam Pub); pap. 9.95 (*0-85598-160-1*, Pub. by Oxfam Pub) Stylus Pub VA.

***Devereux, Steve.** Drilling Technology in Nontechnical Language. LC 99-55192. 1999. write for info. (*0-87814-762-4*) PennWell Bks.

— Gun for Hire. 320p. 2000. 26.00 (*1-85782-367-2*) Blake Publng.

Devereux, Steve. No Fear. 1999. 26.00 (*1-85782-355-9*, Pub. by Blake Publng) Seven Hills Bk.

Devereux, Sue & Morrison, Liz. The Veterinary Care of the Horse. 245p. 1990. 90.00 (*0-85131-543-7*, Pub. by J A Allen) Trafalgar.

Devereux, Tony. Messenger Gods of Battle: The History of Electronic Warfare. 348p. 1990. 52.00 (*0-08-035829-2*, Pub. by Brasseys) Brasseys.

Devergnas, Meery, tr. see Ratushinskaya, Irina.

Devergne, O. Hybridization in Situ. (ENG & FRE.). 80p. 1991. 75.00 (*0-8288-7376-3*, 2855984726) Fr & Eur.

Deveria, Theodule. Catalogue des Manuscrits Egyptiens. (FRE.). iv, 272p. 1980. reprint ed. write for info. (*3-487-06908-3*) Lubrecht & Cramer.

Deverill, Helen. The Haflinger. (Allen Breed Ser.). (Illus.). 1996. 42.00 (*0-85131-644-1*, Pub. by J A Allen) Trafalgar.

DeVernisy, G., jt. auth. see Delattre, J.

Devers, Albany S. Crippled Pockets. 102p. 1994. 9.95 (*1-885110-00-6*) Devers Pubng.

Devers, Edie. After-Death Communications: Experiences with Departed Loved Ones. 162p. 22.95 (*0-7090-6152-8*, Pub. by R Hale Ltd) Seven Hills Bk.

Devers Eye Institute Staff, jt. auth. see Cioffi, George A.

***Devers, John C.** The Coal Cracker. LC 99-94060. v, 350p. 1999. pap. 16.95 (*0-9673902-0-6*) Layton Pubs.

Devers, William J., III & Cipielewski, James. Every Teacher's Thematic Booklist. 176p. (gr. 1-7). 1993. pap. 19.95 (*0-590-49170-9*) Scholastic Inc.

Devers, William J., III, et al. Every Teacher's Thematic Booklist. 210p. pap. 26.95 (*0-590-24385-3*) Scholastic Inc.

***Devesa, Susan S.** Atlas of Cancer Mortality in the U. S. 1950-1994. (Illus.). 360p. 2000. pap. text 35.00 (*0-7567-0049-3*) DIANE Pub.

DeVese, Sunny. But We Have to Kill the Blonde. 146p. 1995. 15.95 (*1-888180-52-8*) Clark Pubng.

— The Divorce Manual. Hughes, Madeleine, ed. LC 96-83796. 120p. 1996. pap. 18.95 (*1-888180-69-2*) Clark Pubng.

Deveson, Richard, tr. see Mommsen, Wolfgang J.

Deveson, Richard, tr. see Peuckert, Detley J.

Deveson, Richard, tr. see Peukert, Detlev J.

Devet, Donald, jt. auth. see Allison, Drew.

Devet, Rebecca M. Mrs. Houdini. LC 88-13884. (University of Central Florida Contemporary Poetry Ser.). 72p. 1989. 17.95 (*0-8130-0914-6*) U Press Fla.

Devet, Rebeccca M. Mother Tongue. LC 86-16100. (University of Central Florida Contemporary Poetry Ser.). 79p. 1987. 17.95 (*0-8130-0858-1*) U Press Fla.

***Devettere, Raymond J.** Practical Decision Making in Health Care Ethics: Cases & Concepts. 2nd rev. ed. LC 99-38611. 656p. 2000. pap. text 35.00 (*0-87840-763-4*) Georgetown U Pr.

***Devey, Andrew.** Jagdtiger: The Most Powerful Armoured Fighting Vehicle of World War II, 2 vols. LC 98-88850. (Military History Ser.). 1999. write for info. (*0-7643-0751-7*) Schiffer.

Devey, Louisa, jt. auth. see Bulwer Lytton, Edward.

***DeVeyrz, Alipio A.** Poetic Adventures of a Romantic Rogue. 68p. 1999. pap. write for info. (*0-7392-0267-7*, PO3348) Morris Pubng.

Devi. Fragrant Memories. 1993. 10.50 (*1-879649-04-7*) Osiris Pr.

***Devi, ed.** Caste System in India. 1999. 34.00 (*81-7132-192-5*, Pub. by Pointer Pubs) S Asia.

Devi, jt. ed. see Pruthi, Devi.

Devi, A. D. History of Andhra Country: 1000 AD-1500 AD. 1993. 44.00 (*81-212-0438-0*, Pub. by Gian Publng Hse) S Asia.

Devi, Alakananda. Pilgrimage to the Mother: A Woman's Journey to the Source of the Ganges. LC 97-66228. (Pathwork Mandala Ser.: Vol. 1). (Illus.). 360p. 1999. pap. 17.95 (*0-9657559-0-8*) Prema Pr.

— Return from the Source: Prophetic Encounters with the Dervish Path & Awakening the Feminine. (Patchwork Mandala Trilogy Ser.). (Illus.). 320p. 2000. pap. 17.95 (*0-9657559-1-6*) Prema Pr.

Devi, B. Nirmala. A Study of the Dialectic of Hegel. vi, 168p. 1995. 15.00 (*81-86339-17-5*, Pub. by Eastern Bk Linkers) Nataraj Bks.

Devi, Chand, tr. from SAN. The Samaveda: Sanskrit Text with English Translation. 304p. (C). 1981. 35.00 (*0-8364-2352-6*, Pub. by M Manoharial) S Asia.

Devi, Chitrita. Upanisads for All. (C). 1997. 44.00 (*81-7102-067-4*, Pub. by Firma KLM) S Asia.

Devi-Doolin, Daya. All There Is to Know...Is Inside. 50p. (Orig.). 1989. pap. text 8.00 (*1-877945-04-8*) Padaran Pubns.

— Dabney, Dormck & Wiggle's Slakadunan Adventure. (Illus.). 50p. (Orig.). (J). (gr. 4-8). 1989. pap. text 6.50 (*1-877945-02-1*) Padaran Pubns.

— Dormck. LC 89-8613. (Illus.). 10p. (Orig.). (J). (gr. 2-5). 1989. pap. 4.50 (*1-877945-01-3*) Padaran Pubns.

— Dormck & the Temple of the Healing Light. LC 89-63461. (Illus.). 50p. (Orig.). (J). (gr. 4-8). 1989. pap. text 6.50 incl. audio (*1-877945-05-6*) Padaran Pubns.

***Devi-Doolin, Daya.** Super Vita-Minds: How to Stop Saying I Hate You . . . To Yourself! 2nd rev. ed. Bandini, Lydia, ed. LC 97-69170. (Illus.). 224p. (Orig.). (C). 1998. mass mkt., per. 21.95 (*1-889131-23-7*, 150X) CasAnanda.

— Super Vita-Minds: How to Stop Saying I Hate You... To Yourself. LC 98-93137. (Illus.). 204p. 1997. pap. 21.95 (*1-877945-06-4*) Padaran Pubns.

Devi, Gauri. Hindu Deities in Thai Art. (C). 1996. 72.00 (*81-86471-10-3*, Pub. by Aditya Prakashan) S Asia.

Devi, Gayatri. One Life's Pilgrimage. 1977. pap. 7.95 (*0-911564-27-6*) Vedanta Ctr.

Devi, Gayatri, jt. auth. see Maurya, S. D.

Devi, Gourie, ed. Motor Neurone Disease. (C). 1987. 50.00 (*81-204-0195-6*, Pub. by Oxford IBH) S Asia.

Devi, H. Maheswari, et al, eds. Recent Advances in Developmental Morphology of Crop Plants: Proceedings of the Symposium Held at the Andhra University, India 1985. (Illus.). 405p. 1990. text 45.00 (*81-211-0040-2*, Pub. by Mahendra Pal Singh) Lubrecht & Cramer.

Devi, I. Yoga: The Technique of Health & Happiness. 76p. 1992. 6.95 (*0-318-37203-7*) Asia Bk Corp.

— Yoga for You. 184p. 1991. 9.95 (*0-318-37200-2*) Asia Bk Corp.

Devi, Laxmi. Encyclopaedia of Educational Development & Planning, 5 vols. 1996. 2500.00 (*81-7488-211-1*, Pub. by Print Hse) St Mut.

— Encyclopaedia of Rural Development, 5 vols. 1996. 2000.00 (*81-7488-204-9*, Pub. by Print Hse) St Mut.

Devi, Laxmi, ed. Child & Family Welfare. (Encyclopedia of Child & Family Welfare Ser.). 1998. 94.00 (*81-7488-931-0*) Anmol.

***Devi, Laxmi, ed.** Encyclopaedia of Sociology, 5 vols. 1920p. 1998. pap. 2750.00 (*81-7488-514-5*, Pub. by Print Hse) St Mut.

Devi, Lila. The Essential Flower Essence Handbook: Remedies for Inner Well-Being. 2nd ed. LC 97-41535. 368p. 1997. reprint ed. pap. 13.95 (*1-56170-511-X*, 874) Hay House.

***Devi, Lila.** Flower Essences for Animals: Remedies for Helping the Pets You Love. (Illus.). 2000. pap. 12.95 (*1-58270-039-7*) Beyond Words Pub.

Devi, Mahasweta. Imaginary Maps: Three Stories by Mahasweta Devi. Spivak, Gayatri Chakravorty, tr. LC 93-1284. 200p. (C). (gr. 13). 1994. pap. 20.99 (*0-415-90463-3*, A6255) Routledge.

Devi, Maitreyi. It Does Not Die: A Romance. LC 93-38599. 280p. 1994. 22.50 (*0-226-14363-5*) U Ch Pr.

— It Does Not Die: A Romance. 264p. 1995. pap. 14.95 (*0-226-14365-1*) U Ch Pr.

Devi, Maya S. In Love: A Conflict Resolution Workbook for Couples. (Illus.). 60p. (Orig.). 1992. pap. 15.95 (*0-9625744-3-0*) Dawn Rose Pr.

Devi, Maya S., et al. Regaining Consciousness in the Western World: Radical Essays on the Human Experience. (Illus.). 96p. 1990. 14.95 (*0-9625744-0-6*); teacher ed. write for info. (*0-318-66966-8*); pap. 9.95 (*0-318-50017-5*); lib. bdg. 14.95 (*0-318-50016-7*) Dawn Rose Pr.

Devi, Mondira. Women, Education, Employment: Family Living (A Study of Emerging Hindu Wives in Urban India) 224p. (C). 1987. 32.00 (*81-212-0104-7*, Pub. by Gian Publng Hse) S Asia.

***Devi, Nischala J.** The Healing Path of Yoga: Time-Honored Wisdom & Scientifically Proven Methods That Alleviate Stress, Open Your Heart & Enrich Your Life. LC 99-55314. (Illus.). 240p. 2000. pap. 17.00 (*0-609-80502-9*, HEA025000, Three Riv Pr) Crown Pub Group.

Devi, Ragini. Dance Dialects of India. (C). 1990. reprint ed. 75.00 (*81-208-0674-3*, Pub. by Motilal Bnarsidass) S Asia.

— Dances of India. LC 79-7751. (Dance Ser.). 1980. reprint ed. lib. bdg. 18.95 (*0-8369-9282-2*) Ayer.

***Devi, Ramashwari & Prakash, Ravi, eds.** Social Work & Social Welfare Administration: Methods & Practices, 2 vols. 1998. 96.00 (*81-7594-019-0*, Pub. by Mangal Deep) S Asia.

Devi, S. Uma. Women, Work, Development, & Ecology. (C). 1994. 14.00 (*81-241-0235-X*, Pub. by Har-Anand Pubns) S Asia.

Devi, Sarada. Teachings of Sri Sarada Devi: The Holy Mother. 175p. 1996. pap. 4.95 (*81-7120-624-7*, Pub. by Ramakrishna Math) Vedanta Pr.

Devi, Savitri. The Impeachment of Man. 200p. 1991. pap. 6.25 (*0-939482-33-9*, 0783, Noontide Pr) Legion Survival.

— Son of the Sun: The Life & Philosophy of Akhnaton, King of Egypt. 4th ed. LC 80-54808. (Illus.). 323p. 1946. reprint ed. pap. 15.95 (*0-912057-95-5*, 510686) GLELJ AMORC.

Devi, Shakuntala. Awaken the Genius in Your Child: A Practical Guide for Parents. LC 98-46433. 224p. 1999. pap. 12.95 (*1-86204-324-8*, Pub. by Element MA) Penguin Putnam.

Devi, T. Nirmala. Regional Economic Co-Operation in South Asia. 1989. 26.00 (*81-85076-83-9*) S Asia.

Devi, Usha R. Divorced Women: Socio-Psychological Problems. 1998. 30.00 (*81-7024-963-5*) Ashish Pub Hse.

***Devi, Vrnda.** Compassionate Cuisine: Gourmet Vegetarian Recipes & the Philosophy & Culture of Caring. 2000. 29.95 (*1-56833-168-1*, Pub. by Madison Bks UPA) Natl Bk Netwk.

Devi, Vrnda, jt. auth. see Giuliano, Geoffrey.

***Devi, Yamuna.** India. (Vegetarian Table Ser.). 2000. pap. 16.95 (*0-8118-3033-0*) Chronicle Bks.

Devi, Yamuna. Lord Krishna's Cuisine: The Art of Indian Vegetarian Cooking. (Illus.). 824p. (Orig.). 1987. 34.95 (*0-525-24564-2*, Dutt) Dutton Plume.

— The Vegetarian Table: India. LC 96-18697. 1997. 22.95 (*0-8118-1144-1*) Chronicle Bks.

Devichand, tr. Yajur Veda. 479p. 1992. 17.00 (*0-685-72923-0*, Pub. by Sarvadeshik Arya) Nataraj Bks.

***Devienne, Francois.** Francois Devienne's Nouvelle Methode Theorique et Pratique pour la Flute: Facsimile of the Original Treatise. fac. ed. Boehm, Thomas, ed. Bowers, Jane, tr. from FRE. LC 98-53895. (Illus.). 142p. 1999. text 78.95 (*1-84014-642-7*, Pub. by Ashgate Pub) Ashgate Pub Co.

Devienne, Francois. Les Visitandines: Comedie Melee D'Ariettes. Dudley, Sherwood, ed. LC 92-756190. (French Opera in the 17th & 18th Centuries Ser.: No. 9, Vol. LXXIIa). (Illus.). 1992. lib. bdg. 86.00 (*0-945193-22-X*) Pendragon NY.

Devigal, Andrew. Photoshop Glows & Shadows Magic. 1997. 39.99 (*1-56830-384-X*) Hayden.

— Photoshop Image Magic. Date not set. 39.99 (*1-56830-449-8*) Hayden.

Devigne, Robert. Recasting Conservatism: Michael Oakeshott, Leo Strauss, & Conservative Political Thought's Response to Postmodernism. LC 93-29941. 256p. 1994. 37.50 (*0-300-05594-3*) Yale U Pr.

— Recasting Conservatism: Oakeshott, Strauss & the Response to Postmodernism. 256p. 1996. pap. 18.00 (*0-300-06868-9*) Yale U Pr.

Devijver, H. The Equestrian Officers of the Roman Imperial Army. (Mavors Roman Army Researches Ser.: Vol. 6). xii, 474p. 1989. 127.00 (*90-5063-007-3*, Pub. by Gieben) J Benjamins Pubng Co.

Devijver, Pierre A. & Kittler, J., eds. Pattern Recognition Theory & Applications. (NATO Asi Series F: Vol. 30). xi, 543p. 1987. 136.95 (*0-387-17700-0*) Spr-Verlag.

DeVilbiss, Melvin L., et al. A Guide to Procurement of Trusted Systems: Language for RFP Specifications & Statements of Work - An Aid to Procurement Initiators. 60p. (C). 1998. reprint ed. pap. text 25.00 (*0-7881-7449-5*) DIANE Pub.

DeVillar, Robert A., et al, eds. Cultural Diversity in Schools: From Rhetoric to Practice. LC 93-24309. 401p. (C). 1994. text 74.50 (*0-7914-1673-9*); pap. text 24.95 (*0-7914-1674-7*) State U NY Pr.

DeVillar, Robert A., jt. intro. see Faltis, Christian J.

DeVille, Alice, et al, contrib. by. Llewellyn's 2000 Sun Sign Book: Horoscopes for Everyone. annuals (Illus.). 480p. 1999. pap. 6.95 (*1-56718-954-7*, K-954-7) Llewellyn Pubns.

Deville, Adrian & Harding, Ronnie. Applying the Precautionary Principle. 79p. 1997. pap. 24.00 (*1-86287-203-1*, Pub. by Federation Pr) Gaunt.

Deville, Nancy, jt. auth. see Schwarzbein, Diana.

DeVille, Paul. Universal Method for Saxophone. 320p. 1907. pap. 23.95 (*0-8258-0146-X*, 0532) Fischer Inc NY.

Deville, Yves, ed. Logic Program Synthesis & Transformation: Proceedings of International Workshop on Logic Program Synthesis & Transformation, Louvain-la-Neuve, Belgium, 7-9 July 1993. LC 93-45325. (Workshops in Computing Ser.). 1994. 71.95 (*0-387-19864-4*) Spr-Verlag.

Devillers, Charles & Chaline, Jean. Evolution: An Evolving Theory. Reimer, Thomas, tr. LC 93-8408. (Illus.). 264p. 1993. 79.95 (*0-387-54674-X*) Spr-Verlag.

***DeVillers, David.** The John Brown Slavery Revolt Trial: A Headline Court Case. LC 99-40386. (Headline Court Cases Ser.). (Illus.). 104p. (gr. 6 up). 2000. lib. bdg. 20.95 (*0-7660-1385-5*) Enslow Pubs.

DeVillers, David. Marbury vs. Madison: Powers of the Supreme Court. LC 97-24865. (Landmark Supreme Court Cases Ser.). (Illus.). 112p. (YA). (gr. 6 up). 1998. lib. bdg. 20.95 (*0-89490-967-3*) Enslow Pubs.

Devillers, J., ed. Ecotoxicity of Chemicals to Amphibians, Vol. 1. (Handbooks of Ecotoxicological Data Ser.). 351p. 1992. text 132.00 (*2-88124-872-1*) Gordon & Breach.

Devillers, J. & Exbrayat, J. M., eds. Ecotoxicity of Chemicals to Amphibians. LC 92-11413. (Handbooks of Ecotoxicological Data Ser.: Vol. 1). 122p. 1992. pap. text 191.00 (*2-88124-873-X*) Gordon & Breach.

Devillers, J. & Karcher, Walter, eds. Applied Multivariate Analysis in SAR & Environmental Studies. (C). 1991. text 237.50 (*0-7923-1290-2*) Kluwer Academic.

Devillers, J., jt. auth. see Kaiser, K. L.

Devillers, J., jt. ed. see Karcher, Walter.

Devillers, James. Comparative Qsar. LC 97-18160. 408p. 1997. 135.00 (*1-56032-716-2*) Hemisp Pub.

Devillers, James, ed. Genetic Algorithms in Molecular Modeling. (Principles of QSAR & Drug Design Ser.). (Illus.). 368p. (C). 1996. text 74.95 (*0-12-213810-4*) Acad Pr.

— Neural Networks in QSar & Drug Design. (Principles in QSAR & Drug Design Ser.). (Illus.). 304p. 1996. text 99.00 (*0-12-213815-5*) Acad Pr.

***Devillers, James & Balaban, Alexandru T., eds.** Topological Indices & Related Descriptors in QSAR & QSPAR. 824p. 2000. text 198.00 (*90-5699-239-2*, G & B Science) Gordon & Breach.

DeVillers, Julie, ed. see Meeks, Linda B. & Heit, Philip.

DeVillers, Julie, ed. see Meeks, Linda B., et al.

DeVillers, Julie, ed. see Meeks, Linda, et al.

DeVillers, Julie, ed. see Page, Randy, et al.

An Asterisk (*) at the beginning of an entry indicates that the title is appearing for the first time.

Devillers, Marceau. James Dean. Marks, Jonathan, tr. from FRE. (Illus.). 207p. 1998. pap. text 20.00 (*0-7881-5307-2*) DIANE Pub.
— James Dean on Location. 1993. 8.98 (*1-55521-943-8*) Bk Sales Inc.
Devillers, Philippe. Histoire de Viet-Nam de Dix-Neuf Cents Quarante & Dix-Neuf Cents Cinquante-Deux. LC 73-179189. (Illus.). reprint ed. 64.50 (*0-404-54819-9*) AMS Pr.
DeVillers, Sylvia. Lectionary-Based Catechesis for Children: A Catechist's Guide. LC 94-21261. 176p. 1994. pap. 10.95 (*0-8091-3505-1*) Paulist Pr.
DeVillers, Sylvia, jt. auth. see Finley, Kathy.
***DeVillers, Victor & Birch, Paul.** DeVillers & Taylor on Point & Finger Charting. (Traders Masterclass Ser.). (Illus.). 350p. 2000. 65.00 (*0-273-64975-2*, Pub. by F T P H) Trans-Atl Phila.
Devillez, Randy. Step by Step College Writing. 7th ed. 548p. (C). 1996. pap., per. 26.95 (*0-7872-2203-8*) Kendall-Hunt.
— Step by Step College Writing. 8th ed. 548p. 1998. per. 28.95 (*0-7872-4902-5*) Kendall-Hunt.
DeVilliers, ed. The Acquisition of English: The Crosslinguistic Study of Language Acquisition. (Crosslinguistic Study of Language Acquisition Ser.). 136p. 1986. pap. 14.95 (*0-89859-840-0*) L Erlbaum Assocs.
Devilliers De Knight, Silvia, tr. see Barnett, Charles R.
DeVilliers, Jill, jt. auth. see DeVilliers, Peter.
DeVilliers, Les. In Sight of Surrender: The U. S. Sanctions Campaign Against South Africa, 1946-1993. LC 94-29920. 248p. 1995. 59.95 (*0-275-94982-6*, Praeger Pubs) Greenwood.
Devilliers, Marq. Down Volga. 1999. pap. 9.00 (*0-14-017427-3*, Viking) Viking Penguin.
DeVilliers, Peter & DeVilliers, Jill. Early Language. LC 78-9862. (Developing Child Ser.). (Illus.). 160p. 1979. pap. text 14.00 (*0-674-22141-9*) HUP.
DeVilliers, Victor. The Point & Figure Method of Anticipating Stock Price. 82p. 1995. pap. 19.95 (*1-883272-16-5*) Traders Lib.
Devin-Adair Staff. Dogmatic Canons & Decrees of the Council of Trent, Vatican Council I, Plus the Decree on the Immaculate Conception & the Syllabus of Errors. LC 79-112469. 1977. reprint ed. pap. 9.50 (*0-89555-018-0*) TAN Bks Pubs.
Devin, Mary & Lockhart, Julie. Astrology & Relationships. LC 88-50300. (Illus.). 300p. 1988. pap. 19.95 (*0-914918-77-X*, Whitford) Schiffer.
Devin, Nancy Jensen & Simpson, Richard. Portsmouth. LC 97-158045. (Images of America Ser.). 1997. pap. 16.99 (*0-7524-0408-3*) Arcadia Publng.
— Tiverton & Little Compton. LC 98-102729. (Images of America Ser.). 1997. pap. 16.99 (*0-7524-0577-2*) Arcadia Publng.
— Tiverton & Little Compton, Vol. II. (Images of America Ser.). (Illus.). 128p. 1998. pap. 16.99 (*0-7524-1237-X*) Arcadia Publng.
Devin, Phillip D. & Robyn, Abby E. Evaluation of the NJROTC Multimedia Instructional System. LC 97-27816. 1997. pap. text 15.00 (*0-8330-2539-2*) Rand Corp.
Devin, Richard. Actor's Resumes: The Definitive Guidebook. LC 94-70807. 72p. 1994. pap. 11.00 (*0-9640253-7-X*, Pub. by Entertain Mktg) Empire Pub Srvs.
Devinat, Paul, Jr. International Labour Office Studies & Reports. Chandler, Alfred D., ed. LC 79-7540. (Scientific Management in Europe: Economic Conditions No. 17, History of Management Thought & Practice Ser.). 1980. reprint ed. lib. bdg. 28.95 (*0-405-12325-6*) Ayer.
Devinatz, A., jt. auth. see Ben-Artzi, M.
DEVINATZ, VICTOR G. High-Tech Betrayal: Open Your Life to God's Power & Provision. LC 98-52237. 1999. pap. text 22.95 (*0-87013-493-0*) Mich St U Pr.
***DeVincent-Hayes, Nan.** 22 Friar Street. LC 99-88652. 2000. write for info. (*1-886388-21-0*) Flower Valley Pr.
DeVincent-Hayes, Nan. 22 Friar Street. 2000. pap. 24.95 (*1-886388-17-2*) Flower Valley Pr.
***DeVincent-Hayes, Nan & Bennett, Bo.** Chincoteague & Assateague Islands. (Images of America Ser.). (Illus.). 128p. 2000. pap. 18.99 (*0-7385-0562-5*) Arcadia Publng.
***DeVincent-Hayes, Nan & Jacob, John E.** Ocean City, Vol. I. (Images of America Ser.). (Illus.). 128p. 1999. pap. 18.99 (*0-7385-0122-0*) Arcadia Publng.
— Ocean City, Vol. II. (Images of America Ser.). (Illus.). 128p. 1999. pap. 18.99 (*0-7385-0123-9*) Arcadia Publng.
DeVincentis-Hayes, Nan, jt. auth. see Wallenda, Delilah.
DeVincenzi, Patti & Curtis, Suzanne. Foreplay: The Art of Stretching for Golf. 50p. 1992. pap. 11.95 (*0-9631840-8-3*) Pica La Balle.
Devinck, Christopher. Songs of Innocence & Experience. 1999. pap. 9.95 (*0-14-023296-6*) Viking Penguin.
DeVinck, Richard. Albert Collins Vital Blues Guitar. (Illus.). 152p. (Orig.). 1994. pap. 19.95 (*1-56922-047-6*, 07-4041) Creat Cncpts.
— B. B. King Vital Blues Guitar. (Illus.). 176p. (Orig.). 1994. pap. 19.95 (*1-56922-026-3*, 07-4030) Creat Cncpts.
— Buddy Guy "Vital Blues Guitar" (Illus.). 168p. (Orig.). 1993. pap. 19.95 (*1-56922-022-0*, 07-4032) Creat Cncpts.
— Elmore James Vital Blues Guitar. (Illus.). 96p. (Orig.). 1996. pap. 19.95 (*1-56922-028-X*, 07-4029) Creat Cncpts.
— Johnny Winter "The Texas Blues Masters" (Illus.). 132p. (Orig.). 1994. pap. 29.95 incl. audio compact disk (*1-56922-057-3*, 07-4045) Creat Cncpts.
— Lightnin' Hopkins "The Ultimate Texas Bluesman" (Illus.). 128p. (Orig.). 1995. pap. 29.95 (*1-56922-068-9*, 07-4051) Creat Cncpts.
— Lonnie Mack Vital Blues Guitar. (Illus.). 216p. (Orig.). 1996. pap. 24.95 (*1-56922-009-3*, 07-4036) Creat Cncpts.
— T-Bone Walker Vital Blues Guitar. (Illus.). 128p. (Orig.). 1994. pap. 19.95 (*0-614-14365-9*, 07-4033) Creat Cncpts.
DeVinck, Richard, ed. see Hooker, John L.
Devine, et al. An Introduction to Industrial Economics. 1990. 528p. 1990. 200.00 (*81-7041-460-1*, Pub. by Scientific Pubs) St Mut.
***Devine, A. M., ed.** Aelian: Commentary on the Poliorceticus - Text, Translation & Commentary. (Ancient Greek & Latin Author Ser.). (ENG & GRE.). 200p. 2000. pap. write for info. (*0-89005-579-3*) Ares.
Devine, A. M. & Stephens, Laurence D. Discontinuous Syntax: Hyperbaton in Greek. LC 99-15285. (Illus.). 360p. 2000. text 45.00 (*0-19-513270-X*) OUP.
— The Prosody of Greek Speech. (Illus.). 584p. 1994. text 60.00 (*0-19-508546-9*) OUP.
Devine, Andrew M. The Latin Thematic Genitive Singular. 136p. (Orig.). 1972. reprint ed. pap. 56.50 (*0-915838-60-5*) Anma Libri.
Devine, Andrew M. & Stephens, Laurence D. Language & Metre: Resolution, Porson's Bridge, & Their Prosodic Basis. LC 84-1395. (American Philological Association, American Classical Studies). 147p. 1984. pap. 15.95 (*0-89130-735-4*, 40 04 12) OUP.
— Two Studies in Latin Phonology. (Studia Linguistica et Philological Ser.: No. 3). 1978. pap. 56.50 (*0-915838-42-7*) Anma Libri.
Devine, Angela. Cleopatra. 1999. pap. write for info. (*0-451-18314-2*, Sig) NAL.
— Crock of Gold. large type ed. 306p. 1993. 27.99 (*0-7505-0578-8*) Ulverscroft.
— Dark Pirate. large type ed. (Harlequin Ser.). 1996. 20.95 (*0-263-14413-5*) Thorndike Pr.
— Diamonds from Dr. Daly. large type ed. (Dales Large Print Ser.). 288p. 1998. pap. 19.99 (*1-85389-806-6*, Dales) Ulverscroft.
— Fiancailles par Procuration. (Azur Ser.: Vol. 706). 1998. mass mkt. 3.50 (*0-373-34706-5*, 1-34706-1) Harlequin Bks.
— El Hombre del Mar - Dark Pirate. (Bianca Ser.). (SPA.). 1997. per. 3.50 (*0-373-33394-3*, 1-33394-7) Harlequin Bks.
— Mistress for Hire. large type ed. 288p. 1996. 23.99 (*0-263-14508-5*, Pub. by Mills & Boon) Ulverscroft.
— Seed of the Fire Lily. (Presents Ser.). 1994. per. 2.99 (*0-373-11621-7*, 1-11621-9) Harlequin Bks.
— Seed of the Fire Lily. large type ed. (Harlequin Ser.). 1993. reprint ed. lib. bdg. 18.95 (*0-263-13273-0*) Mac Lib Ref.
— Southern Aurora. large type ed. (Linford Romance Library). 320p. 1992. pap. 16.99 (*0-7089-7192-X*, Linford) Ulverscroft.
— La Sustituta (The Substitute) (Bianca Ser.). (SPA.). 1998. per. 3.50 (*0-373-33446-X*, 1-33446-5) Harlequin Bks.
— Unwelcome Invader. large type ed. 288p. 1995. 23.99 (*0-263-14259-0*, Pub. by Mills & Boon) Ulverscroft.
— Wife for a Night. (Presents Ser.). 1993. per. 2.89 (*0-373-11538-5*, 1-11538-5) Harlequin Bks.
— Yesterday's Husband. large type ed. (Harlequin Romance Ser.). 286p. 1995. 19.95 (*0-263-14212-4*) Mac Lib Ref.
***Devine, Arlene P., et al.** Among Friends. (Illus.). 136p. 1999. pap. 12.95 (*1-928970-05-2*) GWR Pr.
Devine, Betsy, jt. auth. see Wilczek, Frank.
Devine, Bob. Historias de Animales para Toda la Familia. Orig. Title: Uncle Bob's Animal Stories. (SPA., Illus.). 128p. 1990. pap. 5.99 (*0-8254-1161-0*, Edit Portavoz) Kregel.
Devine, Bob & Schofield, Phil. Pacific Northwest, Oregon, Washington, & Alaska. LC 97-5864. (Driving Guides to America Ser.). 1997. 45.00 (*0-7922-3429-4*) Natl Geog.
Devine, Bob, et al. America's Wildlife Hideaways. deluxe ed. Furlow, Elaine, ed. LC 89-8290. (Illus.). 240p. 1989. 40.00 (*0-945051-12-3*, 19739) Natl Wildlife.
Devine, Carl T. Essays in Accounting Theory, 2 vols., Vol. 22. LC 85-70990, (Studies in Accounting Research). 892p. 1985. 80.00 (*0-86539-055-X*) Am Accounting.
— Essays in Accounting Theory, Vol. 22, No. 1. LC 85-70990. (Studies in Accounting Research). 172p. 1985. pap. 12.00 (*0-86539-050-9*) Am Accounting.
— Essays in Accounting Theory, Vol. 22, No. 2. LC 85-70990. (Studies in Accounting Research). 160p. 1985. pap. 12.00 (*0-86539-051-7*) Am Accounting.
— Essays in Accounting Theory, Vol. 22, No. 3. LC 85-70990. (Studies in Accounting Research). 144p. 1985. pap. 12.00 (*0-86539-052-5*) Am Accounting.
— Essays in Accounting Theory, Vol. 22, No. 4. LC 85-70990. (Studies in Accounting Research). 192p. 1985. pap. 12.00 (*0-86539-053-3*) Am Accounting.
— Essays in Accounting Theory, Vol. 22, No. 5. LC 85-70990. (Studies in Accounting Research). 224p. 1985. pap. 12.00 (*0-86539-054-1*) Am Accounting.
— Inventory Valuation & Periodic Income. Brief, Richard P., ed. LC 80-1486. (Dimensions of Accounting Theory & Practice Ser.). 1980. reprint ed. lib. bdg. 24.95 (*0-405-13516-5*) Ayer.
Devine, Carol. Beauty & the Beastmaster: Premiere. (Desire Ser.). 1993. mass mkt. 2.99 (*0-373-05816-0*, 5-05816-9) Silhouette.
— The Billionaire's Secret Baby. (Desire Ser.: No. 1218). 1999. per. 3.75 (*0-373-76218-6*, 1-76218-6) Silhouette.
— Un Extrano en Mi Corazon. (Deseo Ser.).Tr. of Stranger in My Heart. (SPA.). 1999. per. 3.50 (*0-373-35310-3*, 1-35310-1) Harlequin Bks.
— A Man of the Land. (Desire Ser.). 1995. per. 3.25 (*0-373-05909-4*, 1-05909-6) Silhouette.
***Devine, Carol.** Marriage for Sale. (Desire Ser.). 2000. per. 3.99 (*0-373-76284-4*) Silhouette.
Devine, Carol M., jt. auth. see Farrell, Tracy J.
Devine, Dan & Steele, Michael. Simply Devine (ND Cover) Memoirs of a Hall of Fame Coach. 200p. 2000. 22.95 (*1-58261-007-X*, Pub. by Sprts Pubng) Partners-West.
***Devine, Dan & Steele, Mike.** Simply Devine (Missouri Cover) Memoirs of a Hall of Fame Coach. (Illus.). 200p. 2000. 22.95 (*1-58261-204-8*, Pub. by Sprts Pubng) Partners-West.
Devine, Dominic. My Brother's Killer. large type ed. 388p. 1983. 27.99 (*0-7089-1026-2*) Ulverscroft.
Devine, Donald. Reagan's Terrible Swift Sword. 228p. 1991. 19.95 (*0-89803-163-X*) Jameson Bks.
— Restoring the 10th Amendment: The American Federalist Agenda. Gee, Charles G., ed. 350p. Date not set. text 25.00 (*0-9645786-3-8*) VYTIS Pub.
Devine, Donald F. Elementary Mathematics for Teachers. 2nd ed. LC 89-24816. 944p. 1991. text 86.95 (*0-471-85947-8*) Wiley.
Devine, Donald F. & Kaufman, Jerome E. Elementary Mathematics. LC 76-24805. 539p. reprint ed. pap. 167.10 (*0-608-16464-X*, 202675800052) Bks Demand.
Devine, Donald J. Does Freedom Work: Liberty & Justice in America. LC 77-15914. (Illus.). 192p. 1978. pap. 5.95 (*0-916054-56-X*) Jameson Bks.
— Reagan Electionomics: How Reagan Ambushed the Pollsters, 1976-1984. LC 84-108682. 105p. 1984. 14.95 (*0-89803-130-3*) Jameson Bks.
Devine, Edward, jt. auth. see Staudinger, Lenette.
Devine, Edward T. Misery & Its Causes. LC 70-137161. (Poverty U. S. A. Historical Record Ser.). 1973. reprint ed. 20.95 (*0-405-03100-9*) Ayer.
— Principles of Relief. LC 74-137162. (Poverty U. S. A. Historical Record Ser.). 1971. reprint ed. 27.95 (*0-405-03132-7*) Ayer.
— The Spirit of Social Work. LC 75-17216. (Social Problems & Social Policy Ser.). 1976. reprint ed. 21.95 (*0-405-07487-5*) Ayer.
Devine, Elizabeth. Travelers Guide to Asian Customs & Manners. rev. expanded ed. Braganti, Nancy L., ed. 352p. 1998. pap. 16.95 (*0-312-19531-1*) St Martin.
— Travellers' Guide to African Customs & Manners. 1995. pap. 14.95 (*0-312-11909-7*) St Martin.
Devine, Elizabeth, ed. Annual Obituary 1983. 83rd ed. 1984. 100.00 (*0-912289-07-4*) St James Pr.
Devine, Elizabeth & Held, Michael. Thinkers of the Twentieth Century. 635p. (C). 1987. 350.00 (*81-7002-026-3*, Pub. by Himalayan Bks) St Mut.
Devine, Elizabeth, jt. auth. see Braganti, Nancy L.
Devine, F. E. Commercial Bail Bonding: A Comparison of Common Law Alternatives. LC 91-8605. 232p. 1991. 62.95 (*0-275-93732-1*, C3732, Praeger Pubs) Greenwood.
DeVine, Fanny K. Fanny's Essays. 1996. 15.00 (*1-886796-03-3*) DEramo Pub.
— If I Were Clay. 77p. 1993. 11.95 (*1-886796-01-7*) DEramo Pub.
— Legend of the South Meadow: Stories for Readers of All Ages. LC 94-80120. 1996. 15.50 (*1-886796-02-5*) DEramo Pub.
— A Star on His Shoulder. 88p. 1962. 12.50 (*1-886796-00-9*) DEramo Pub.
Devine, Fiona. Affluent Workers Revisited: Privatism & the Working Class. (Edinburgh Education & Society Ser.). 336p. 1993. text 68.00 (*0-7486-0370-0*, Pub. by Edinburgh U Pr) Col U Pr.
Devine, Frank, ed. The Best of the Independent: A Selection of Australia's Finest Contemporary Journalism. 216p. 1992. pap. 90.00 (*0-949823-29-5*, Pub. by Deakin Univ) St Mut.
Devine, George. For Sale by Owner. 3rd ed. LC 97-14488. 256p. 1997. pap. 24.95 (*0-87337-394-4*) Nolo com.
— For Sale by Owner in California. 4th ed. Leonard, Robin, ed. LC 98-17306. (Nolo Press Self-Help Law Ser.). (Illus.). 272p. 1999. pap. 24.95 (*0-87337-474-6*) Nolo com.
***Devine, George.** For Sale by Owner in California. 5th ed. LC 99-53672. (California Edition Ser.). 2000. pap. 34.95 (*0-87337-570-X*) Nolo com.
Devine, George. Managing Your Employees. LC 96-39736. 224p. (C). 1997. pap. text 13.95 (*0-13-603341-5*) P-H.
— Responses to 101 Questions on Business Ethics. 144p. 1996. pap. 9.95 (*0-8091-3647-3*, 3647-3) Paulist Pr.
Devine, George, ed. A World More Human: A Church More Christian. 204p. 1984. reprint ed. pap. text 17.00 (*0-8191-3851-7*) U Pr of Amer.
Devine, George, jt. auth. see Warner, Ralph E.
Devine, Glenda. Deer Sightings: Poems from Thorn Creek. (Orig.). (YA). (gr. 8 up). 1995. pap. 5.00 (*0-9633569-2-5*) Home Imag.
***Devine, Hazel Uhlir.** The Changing Winds: One Family's Czech-American Experience. (Illus.). viii, 264p. 1999. pap. write for info. (*0-9676049-0-7*) H U Devine.
***Devine, J. T.** California Wine Winners 2000: The Best of the 1999 Judgings. 1999. pap. text 8.95 (*1-881796-06-X*) Varietal Fair.
***Devine, J. T., ed.** California Wine Winners, 2001: The Best of the 2000 Judgings. 18th ed. (Illus.). 224p. 2000. pap. 9.95 (*1-881796-07-8*, Pub. by Varietal Fair) Publishers Group.
Devine, J. T., ed. California Wine Winners, 1994: The Best of the 1993 Competitions. (Illus.). 160p. (Orig.). 1993. pap. 6.95 (*1-881796-00-0*) Varietal Fair.
Devine, J. T. & Ahlstrom, Trudy, eds. California Wine Winners, 1998: The Best of the 1997 Judgings. (Illus.). 184p. 1997. pap. 8.95 (*1-881796-04-3*) Varietal Fair.
Devine, J. T., jt. auth. see Ahlstrom, Trudy.
Devine, J. T., jt. auth. see Ahlstrom, Trudy H.
Devine, J. T., jt. ed. see Ahlstrom, Trudy.
Devine, James R. Non-Jury Case Files on Trial Advocacy. (American Casebook Ser.). 258p. (C). 1991. 22.50 (*0-314-87894-7*) West Pub.
Devine, James R. & Terry, Nicolas P. Insurance Law, Teacher's Manual to Accompany Problems In. (American Casebook Ser.). 205p. (C). 1989. pap. text. write for info. (*0-314-67665-1*) West Pub.
Devine, Jane A., ed. 100 Years of Architecture at Notre Dame: A History of the School of Architecture, 1898-1998. (Illus.). 120p. 1999. pap. 23.95 (*0-9670548-0-X*, Pub. by U Notre Dame Sch Arch) Hammes Notre Dame.
Devine, Jeremy. Vietnam at 24 Frames a Second: A Critical & Thematic Analysis of over 350 Films about the Vietnam War. LC 98-51732. 415p. 1999. pap. 19.95 (*0-292-71601-X*) U of Tex Pr.
Devine, Jeremy M. Vietnam at 24 Frames a Second: A Critical & Thematic Analysis of over 350 Films about the Vietnam War. LC 92-56639. (Illus.). 416p. 1994. lib. bdg. 42.50 (*0-89950-848-0*) McFarland & Co.
Devine, Jerry. Children of the Wind. 1974. pap. 5.25 (*0-8222-0204-2*) Dramatists Play.
Devine, Joe. Commas Are Our Friends: The Easy, Enjoyable Way to Master Grammar & Punctuation. Hayes, Rita, ed. (Illus.). 263p. (Orig.). 1989. pap. 11.95 (*1-882010-07-8*) Green Stone Pubns.
Devine, Joe, et al. Collectors Guide to Royal Copley, Vol. 1. (Illus.). 160p. 1999. pap. text 14.95 (*1-57432-123-4*) Collector Bks.
Devine, Joel A. & Wright, James D. The Greatest of Evils: Urban Poverty & the American Underclass. LC 93-6873. (Social Institutions & Social Change Ser.). 264p. 1993. pap. text 21.95 (*0-202-30474-4*); lib. bdg. 41.95 (*0-202-30473-6*) Aldine de Gruyter.
Devine, Joel A., jt. auth. see Wright, James D.
Devine, John. Maximum Security: The Culture of Violence in Inner-City Schools. LC 96-8910. (Illus.). 256p. 1996. pap. text 15.95 (*0-226-14387-2*) U Ch Pr.
— Maximum Security: The Culture of Violence in Inner-City Schools. LC 96-8910. (Illus.). 256p. 1997. lib. bdg. 40.00 (*0-226-14386-4*) U Ch Pr.
Devine, John, jt. auth. see Gillies, Cliff.
Devine, Judy. How to Quest for Camelot. (Warner Bros. How to Draw Ser.). (Illus.). 40p. 1998. pap. 7.95 (*1-56010-295-0*, WBO1) W Foster Pub.
Devine Jump, Harriet. Women's Writing of the Romantic Period, 1789-1836: An Anthology. LC 98-114009. 288p. 1997. pap. 25.00 (*0-7486-0915-6*, Pub. by Edinburgh U Pr) Col U Pr.
— Women's Writing of the Victorian Period, 1837-1901: An Anthology. LC 98-50772. 384p. 1999. pap. 21.95 (*0-312-22198-3*) St Martin.
Devine Jump, Harriet, ed. Women's Writing of the Victorian Period, 1837-1901: An Anthology. LC 98-50772. 384p. 1999. text 59.95 (*0-312-22197-5*) St Martin.
Devine, Kathleen, ed. Modern Irish Writers & the Wars. LC 98-189006. 328p. 1999. text 60.00 (*0-86140-353-3*) OUP.
Devine, Kathleen & Peacock, Alan J., eds. Louis MacNeice & His Influence. (A Colin Smythe Publication). 180p. (C). 1998. text 60.00 (*0-86140-391-6*) OUP.
***Devine, Laura.** Immigration in Employment Law: Practical Guide. 200p. 2000. pap. 87.00 (*1-902558-09-X*, Pub. by Palladian Law) Gaunt.
Devine, M. Baby Talk: The Art of Communicating with Infants & Toddlers. LC 90-28793. (Illus.). 290p. (C). 1991. 21.50 (*0-306-43762-7*, Plen Insight) Perseus Pubng.
Devine, Maria T., jt. auth. see Napolitano, Annamaria.
Devine, Marsha. Hantavirus Infection in the United States & California. 4p. 1993. pap. write for info. (*1-58703-014-4*) CA St Libry.
Devine, Mary A. Float Plan: Study Guide for Use with Takashi's Voyage. (Illus.). 84p. (J). (gr. 4-7). 1998. pap. 12.95 (*0-945582-52-8*) Down the Shore Pub.
Devine, Mary E. & Summerfield, Carol, eds. International Dictionary of University Histories. LC 98-163032. (Illus.). 1000p. 1998. lib. bdg. 125.00 (*1-884964-23-0*) Fitzroy Dearborn.
Devine, Maureen. Woman & Nature: Literary Reconceptualizations. LC 92-33985. 251p. 1992. 35.00 (*0-8108-2612-7*) Scarecrow.
Devine, Michael. Border Collies. LC 97-12565. (Barron's Complete Pet Owner's Manuals). (Illus.). 120p. 1997. pap. 6.95 (*0-8120-9801-3*) Barron.
Devine, Mike & Routh, David. Real Intimacy. 1991. pap. 5.95 (*0-9625096-0-4*) Starside Pub.
— Real Intimacy: Extended Lovemaking in the Committed Relationship. (Illus.). 74p. 1989. reprint ed. pap. 5.95 (*0-685-29990-2*) Starside Pub.
Devine, Monica. The Iditarod: The Greatest Win Ever LC 98-134170. (Cover-to-Cover Bks.). 56p. (J). 1997. write for info. (*0-7807-6108-1*, Covercraft) Perfection Learn.
Devine, Pat, et al, eds. Competitiveness, Subsidiarity & Industrial Policy. LC 95-31900. (Industrial Economic Strategies for Europe Ser.). 264p. (C). 1996. 90.00 (*0-415-13985-6*) Routledge.
Devine, Patricia G., et al, eds. Social Cognition: Impact on Social Psychology. (Illus.). 403p. 1994. text 69.95 (*0-12-213630-6*) Acad Pr.
DeVine, Patrick. Blood Brothers. 1987. 17.95 (*0-911349-01-4*) English Fact.
Devine, Patrick, compiled by. Insurance Intermediaries in the EEC: An Industry Report. 250p. 1992. pap. 250.00 (*1-85044-380-7*) LLP.
Devine, Patrick F. & White, Harry, eds. Irish Musical Studies: The Maynooth International Musicological Conference: Selected Proceedings, Vol. 4. 320p. 1996. 45.00 (*1-85182-260-7*, Pub. by Four Cts Pr) Intl Spec Bk.
— Irish Musical Studies: The Maynooth International

D

Musicological Conference: Selected Proceedings, Vol. 5. LC 97-162430. 320p. 1996. 45.00 (*1-85182-261-5*, Pub. by Four Cts Pr) Intl Spec Bk.

Devine, Pauline. Best Friends. 192p. 1994. pap. 8.95 (*0-947962-79-4*) Dufour.

***Devine, Pauline.** Best Friends Again. 128p. 2000. pap. 8.95 (*1-901737-14-4*, Pub. by Anvil Books Ltd) Dufour.

Devine, Pauline. Riders by the Grey Lake. LC 97-207220. 144p. 1997. pap. 8.95 (*0-947962-99-9*) Dufour.

Devine, Peter. Real Women Only Want One Thing! 140p. 1995. pap. write for info. (*0-9645804-1-1*) Devine Prod.

— Twenty Three Strategies to Build Your Empire. 40p. 1993. 5.95 (*0-9645804-0-3*) Devine Prod.

Devine, Peter, intro. Selected Paintings of Anthony Terenzio. LC 10-6949. (Illus.). 32p. Date not set. 3.00 (*0-614-10421-1*) W Benton Mus.

Devine, Philip E. Human Diversity & the Culture Wars: A Philosophical Perspective on Contemporary Cultural Conflict. LC 96-15319. 224p. 1996. 55.00 (*0-275-95205-3*, Praeger Pubs) Greenwood.

— Natural Law Ethics, 72. LC 99-25006. (Contributions in Philosophy Ser.: No. 72). 216p. 2000. 59.95 (*0-313-30702-4*, GM702, Greenwood Pr) Greenwood.

Devine, R. A., et al, eds. Amorphous Insulating Thin Films II: Proceedings of Symposium A of the 1994 E-MRS Spring Conference, Strasbourg, France, 24-27 May, 1994. LC 95-224311. (European Materials Research Society Symposia Proceedings Ser.: Vol. 46). 522p. 1995. 256.25 (*0-444-82161-9*) Elsevier.

Devine, R. A. B., ed. The Physics & Technology of Amorphous SiO2. LC 88-17464. (Illus.). 592p. 1988. 125.00 (*0-306-42929-2*, Plenum Trade) Perseus Pubng.

Devine, Richard J. Good Care, Painful Choices: Medical Ethics for Ordinary People. 256p. 1996. pap. 16.95 (*0-8091-3631-7*, 3631-7) Paulist Pr.

***Devine, Richard J.** Good Care, Painful Choices: Medical Ethics of Ordinary People. 2nd ed. LC 99-48585. 272p. 2000. pap. 17.95 (*0-8091-3924-3*) Paulist Pr.

Devine, Robert, ed. & pref. see New York State Bar Association Staff.

Devine, Robert C. Immigration Law & Procedure. LC 57-63886. 1000p. 1994. 105.00 (*0-614-10375-4*, MICHIE) LEXIS Pub.

Devine, Robert S. Alien Invasion: America's Battle with Non-Native Animals & Plants. LC 98-9730. 277p. 1998. 24.00 (*0-7922-7372-9*) Natl Geog.

— Alien Invasion: America's Battle with Non-Native Animals & Plants. 1999. pap. 15.00 (*0-7922-7449-0*) Natl Geog.

Devine, Susan E., jt. auth. see Sakheim, David K.

Devine, T. M. Celebrating Columba: Irish Scottish Connections, 597-1997. 198p. 1998. pap. 45.00 (*0-85976-493-1*, Pub. by J Donald) St Mut.

— Clanship to Crofter's War: The Social Transformation of the Scottish Highlands. LC 93-30886. 1994. text 29.95 (*0-7190-3482-5*, Pub. by Manchester Univ Pr) St Martin.

— Conflict & Stability in Scottish Society, 1700-1850. 200p. (C). 1997. text 50.00 (*0-85976-296-3*, Pub. by J Donald) St Mut.

— Farm Servants & Labour in Lowland Scotland, 1770-1914. 272p. 1996. pap. 48.00 (*0-85976-439-7*, Pub. by J Donald) St Mut.

— Irish Immigrants & Scottish Society, 1790-1990. 160p. (C). 1997. text 50.00 (*0-85976-318-8*, Pub. by J Donald) St Mut.

— St. Mary's, Hamilton: A Social History 1846-1996. 208p. 1996. pap. 30.00 (*0-85976-429-X*, Pub. by J Donald) St Mut.

***Devine, T. M.** Scottish Nation, 1700-2000. LC 99-38391. 608p. 1999. pap. 40.00 (*0-670-88811-7*, Viking) Viking Penguin.

Devine, T. M. The Transformation of Rural Scotland: Social Change & the Agrarian Economy, 1660-1815. LC 94-184650. 275p. 1994. 76.00 (*0-7486-0452-9*, Pub. by Edinburgh U Pr) Col U Pr.

Devine, T. M. & Banko, William, eds. Phacoemulsification Surgery. (Illus.). 144p. 1991. 125.00 (*0-08-036840-9*) McGraw.

Devine, T. M. & Finlay, Richard J., eds. Scotland in the Twentieth Century. LC 97-135232. 352p. Date not set. 68.00 (*0-7486-0751-X*, Pub. by Edinburgh U Pr) Col U Pr.

— Scotland in the Twentieth Century. LC 97-135232. 352p. 1996. pap. 25.00 (*0-7486-0839-7*, Pub. by Edinburgh U Pr) Col U Pr.

Devine, T. M. & Jackson, Gordon, eds. Glasgow Vol. 1: Beginnings to 1830, Vol. I. LC 93-47156. 435p. 1995. text 90.00 (*0-7190-3691-7*) Manchester Univ Pr.

Devine, T. M. & Mrrchison, R. People & Society in Scotland, 1760-1830: A Social History of Modern Scotland. (People & Society of Scotland Ser.). 316p. (Orig.). (C). 1998. pap. 48.00 (*0-85976-210-6*, Pub. by J Donald) St Mut.

Devine, T. M., jt. ed. see Cummings, A. J.

Devine, Thea. All I Desire, 1. (Zebra Splendor Historical Romances Ser.). 352p. 1999. mass mkt. 4.99 (*0-8217-6259-1*) Kensgtn Pub Corp.

— By Desire Bound. 352p. 1998. pap. 4.99 (*0-8217-5988-4*) Kensgtn Pub Corp.

— Desire Me Only. 416p. 1997. mass mkt. 4.99 (*0-8217-5666-4*, Zebra Kensgtn) Kensgtn Pub Corp.

***Devine, Thea.** Night Moves: Blaze. (Harlequin Temptation Ser.). 1999. mass mkt. 3.75 (*0-373-25860-7*, Harlequin) Harlequin Bks.

— Secret Pleasures. 2000. pap. 12.00 (*1-57566-583-2*, Knsington) Kensgtn Pub Corp.

Devine, Thea. Secret Pleasures. 1995. pap. 4.99 (*0-8217-4995-1*) NAL.

— Sinful Secrets. 480p. 1998. pap. 4.99 (*0-8217-5996-5*, Zebra Kensgtn) Kensgtn Pub Corp.

Devine, Theresa J. & Kiefer, Nicholas M. Empirical Labor Economics: The Search Approach. (Illus.). 360p. (C). 1991. text 67.95 (*0-19-505936-0*) OUP.

Devine, Thomas & Meagher, Linda D. The Reading Connection. 400p. (C). 1996. text 17.50 (*0-256-22036-0*, Irwn McGrw-H) McGrw-H Hghr Educ.

Devine, Thomas E. & Daley, Richard M. Eyewitness: The Amelia Earhart Incident. LC 87-4505. (Illus.). 300p. 1987. pap. 12.95 (*0-939650-48-7*) R H Pub.

Devine, Thomas G. & Meagher, Linda D. Mastering Study Skills: A Student Guide. (Illus.). 320p. 1988. pap. text 26.20 (*0-13-560021-9*) P-H.

Devine, Thomas G., jt. auth. see Meagher, Linda D.

Devine, Thomas M. Improvement & Enlightenment: Proceedings of the Scottish Historical Studies Seminar. (Illus.). 150p. (C). 1997. text 50.00 (*0-85976-258-0*, Pub. by J Donald) St Mut.

— The Tobacco Lords: A Study of the Tobacco Merchants of Glasgow & Their Trading Activities, 1740-1790. (Illus.). 222p. 1990. pap. 28.00 (*0-7486-0172-4*, Pub. by Edinburgh U Pr) Col U Pr.

Devine, Toni, jt. auth. see Taylor, Brian J.

Devine, Trudy, ed. see Sherman, Ed.

Devine, Virginia, jt. auth. see Misner, Ivan R.

Devine, William F., Jr. Soul Proprietor. 2001. 23.00 (*0-609-60328-0*) Crown Pub Group.

— Women, Men & Money: The Four Keys for Using Money to Nourish Your Relationship, Bankbook & Soul. 1999. pap. 14.00 (*0-609-80279-8*, Three Riv Pr) Crown Pub Group.

Devineni, Ram. Tango in the Square. (Lost City: Poetic Broadside Ser.: Vol. 1). (Illus.). 2p. 1998. pap. 2.00 (*1-892494-06-X*) Repossessed Head.

Devines, James R. & Terry, Nicholas P. Problems in Insurance Law. (American Casebook Ser.). 240p. (C). 1989. pap. 25.50 (*0-314-56417-9*) West Pub.

Deviney, David E. Outstanding Customer Service: The Key to Customer Loyalty. Miller, Karen Massetti, ed. LC 98-72664. (How-to Book Ser.). 103p. 1998. pap. 12.95 (*1-884926-95-9*) Amer Media.

Deviney, Marvin L. & Gland, John L., eds. Catalyst Characterization Science: Surface & Solid State Chemistry. LC 85-20081. (ACS Symposium Ser.: Vol. 288). 632p. reprint ed. pap. 196.00 (*0-608-03916-0*, 206436300009) Bks Demand.

Devinne, Paul. Day of Prosperity: A Vision of the Century to Come. LC 73-154439. (Utopian Literature Ser.). 1976. reprint ed. 23.95 (*0-405-03522-5*) Ayer.

Devinney, Margaret K. The Legends of Gertrud von Le Fort: Text & Audience. (Studies in Modern German Literature: Vol. 27). 223p. (C). 1989. text 34.00 (*0-8204-0719-4*) P Lang Pubng.

Devinney, Richard. The Wednesday Workout: Practical Techniques for Rehearsing the Church Choir Series & Series Editor. LC 93-8285. 96p. (Orig.). 1993. pap. 9.95 (*0-687-44312-1*) Abingdon.

DeVinney, Timothy. A Degree of Order. (Illus.). 199p. (Orig.). 1993. pap. 12.00 (*960-7459-03-2*, Pub. by Talos Pr) Bosphorus Bks.

Devinney, Timothy, jt. auth. see Davis, Jeremy.

DeVinney, Timothy, jt. auth. see Stavroulakis, Nicholas.

Devinny, Joseph S., jt. ed. see Pirbazari, Massoud.

Devinny, J.S. & Deshusses, Marc A. Biofiltration for Air Pollution Control. LC 98-35184. 1998. lib. bdg. 69.95 (*1-56670-289-5*) Lewis Pubs.

Devins, D. W., ed. see Momentum Wave Function Determination in Atomic, Mo.

Devins, Delbert W. Energy: Its Physical Impact on the Environment. LC 87-29764. 590p. (C). 1988. reprint ed. lib. bdg. 64.50 (*0-89464-271-5*) Krieger.

Devins, Neal. Shaping Constitutional Values: Elected Government, the Supreme Court, & the Abortion Debate. LC 95-39584. (Interpreting American Politics Ser.). 224p. (C). 1996. text 47.50 (*0-8018-5284-6*); pap. text 14.95 (*0-8018-5285-4*) Johns Hopkins.

Devins, Neal & Douglas, Davison M., eds. Redefining Equality. (Illus.). 256p. 1998. text 50.00 (*0-19-511664-X*); pap. text 19.95 (*0-19-511665-8*) OUP.

Devins, Neal & Fisher, Louis. Political Dynamics of Constitutional Law. 333p. (C). 1992. pap. text 21.00 (*0-314-00657-5*) West Pub.

Devins, Neal & Watson, Wendy L., eds. Executive Initiatives Pts. I-II: A Documentary History. LC 94-49562. (Federal Abortion Politics Ser.: Vol. 2). 747p. 1995. text 154.00 (*0-8153-1907-X*) Garland.

— Judicial Nominations. LC 94-49562. (Federal Abortion Politics Ser.: Vol. 3). 433p. 1995. text 94.00 (*0-8153-1908-8*) Garland.

Devins, Neal, jt. auth. see Fisher, Louis.

Devins, Neal, ed. see Barrett, Paul, et al.

***Devins, Susan.** Bakin' Brownies, Vol. 1. 1999. 12.99 (*0-525-46255-4*, Dutton Child) Peng Put Young Read.

Devins, Susan. Chew on This! (Illus.). 32p. (J). (gr. 1-5). 1998. pap. 9.99 (*1-58184-007-1*) Somerville Hse.

— Chew on This! Book & Kit. (Illus.). 32p. (J). (gr. 1-5). 1998. pap. 9.99 (*1-894042-23-9*) Somerville Hse.

— Makin' Muffins. (Illus.). (J). (gr. 1-5). 1998. pap. 12.99 (*0-525-46002-0*, Dutton Child) Peng Put Young Read.

— Makin' Muffins. (Illus.). 32p. (J). (gr. 1 up). 1998. pap. 12.99 (*1-894042-22-0*) Somerville Hse.

***Devinsky.** Epilepsy & Developmental Disabilities. 464p. 2001. 125.00 (*0-7506-7273-0*) Buttrwrth-Heinemann.

Devinsky, Orrin. Behavior Neurology. LC 92-49804. (One Hundred Maxims in Neurology Ser.). 1992. 35.95 (*0-8016-7280-5*) Mosby Inc.

— A Guide to Understanding & Living with Epilepsy. LC 94-10823. (Illus.). 345p. (C). 1994. pap. text 19.95 (*0-8036-2556-1*) Davis Co.

Devinsky, Orrin, et al, eds. Electrical & Magnetic Stimulation of the Brain & Spinal Cord. LC RC0321.A276. (Advances in Neurology Ser.: No. 63). (Illus.). 343p. 1993. reprint ed. pap. 106.40 (*0-608-05828-9*, 205979300007) Bks Demand.

Devinsky, Orrin & Feldmann, Edward. Examination of the Cranial & Peripheral Nerves. (Illus.). 118p. 1987. text 30.00 (*0-443-08562-5*) Church.

Devinsky, Orrin, et al. Neurologic Pearls. (Illus.). 286p. (C). 2000. pap. text 19.95 (*0-8036-0433-5*) Davis Co.

— The Resident's Neurology Book. LC 96-48408. (Illus.). 282p. (C). 1997. pap. text 24.95 (*0-8036-0186-7*) Davis Co.

Devinsky, Orrinere & Theodore, William H. Epilepsy & Behavior. LC 91-22881. (Frontiers of Clinical Neuroscience Ser.). 442p. 1991. 395.00 (*0-471-56163-0*, Wiley-Interscience) Wiley.

Devir, Adam D., et al, eds. Optics in Atmospheric Propagation, Adaptive Systems & Lidat Techniques for Remote Sensing. (Europto Ser.: Vol. 2956). 262p. 1997. 94.00 (*0-8194-2360-2*) SPIE.

Devir, Adam D., jt. ed. see Kohnle, Anton.

Devir, Ori. Off the Beaten Track in Israel. LC 85-128603.Tr. of Nekudat-Chen. (Illus.). 200p. 1985. 24.95 (*0-915361-28-0*) Lambda Pubs.

Devires. Sonderstab Musik. LC 96-207900. pap. 22.95 (*90-5356-181-1*, Pub. by Amsterdam U Pr) U of Mich Pr.

***DeVirgilio-Lam, Teresa.** Unbearably Good! Mochi Lovers' Cookbook. 97p. 1999. pap. 7.95 (*0-9673851-0-5*) T Devirgilio-Lam.

Devis, Arthur. Polite Society. (Illus.). 122p. 1983. pap. 8.95 (*0-9591141-2-2*) Antique Collect.

Devis, Ricardo. JavaBeans Handbook. (Advanced & Emerging Communications Technologies Ser.). 1999. 74.95 (*0-8493-9596-8*) CRC Pr.

Devisch, Rene. Weaving the Threads of Life: The Khita Gyn-Eco-Logical Healing Cult among the Yaka. LC 93-355. (ENG & FRE., Illus.). 352p. 1993. pap. text 19.95 (*0-226-14362-7*) U Ch Pr.

— Weaving the Threads of Life: The Khita Gyn-Eco-Logical Healing Cult among the Yaka. LC 93-355. (ENG & FRE., Illus.). 344p. 1993. lib. bdg. 53.95 (*0-226-14361-9*) U Ch Pr.

Devisch, Rene & Brodeur, Claude. Forces et Signes: Regards Croises d'un Anthropologue et d'un Psychanalyste Sur les Yaka. (FRE.). 422p. 1996. pap. text 63.00 (*90-5709-001-5*, edit archives) Gordon & Breach.

— The Law of the Lifegivers: The Domestication of Desire. 288p. 1999. pap. 27.00 (*90-5702-423-3*) Gordon & Breach.

— The Law of the Lifegivers: The Domestication of Desire. 292p. 1999. text 48.00 (*90-5702-422-5*, Harwood Acad Pubs) Gordon & Breach.

Devisser, John. Newfoundland Souvenir. 240p. 1997. pap. text 15.95 (*1-55046-203-2*, Pub. by Boston Mills) Genl Dist Srvs.

DeVisser, John, photos by. Hope College - Then & Now. (First Edition Ser.). (Illus.). 112p. 1991. 39.95 (*0-916509-82-6*) Harmony Hse Pub.

— St. Lawrence University. (Illus.). 112p. 1991. 39.00 (*0-916509-72-9*) Harmony Hse Pub.

DeVisser, John & De Visser, John, photos by. University of Guelph. (Illus.). 112p. 1990. 49.00 (*0-916509-58-3*) Harmony Hse Pub.

DeVisser, John & Fleming, Patsy. One Thousand Islands. (Illus.). 120p. 1990. 29.95 (*1-55046-044-7*, Pub. by Boston Mills) Genl Dist Srvs.

DeVisser, John & Ross, Judy. Georgian Bay. (Illus.). 120p. 1992. 45.00 (*1-55046-060-9*, Pub. by Boston Mills) Genl Dist Srvs.

DeVisser, John, jt. auth. see Credit Valley Conservation Foundation Staff.

DeVita, Gregg & Editing, Franks. Selling in the '90s: The Fundamentals of Selling Success. 240p. (C). 1991. pap. text 18.00 (*0-9628645-5-2*) PST Lrn Systs.

DeVita, James. Bambi, a Life in the Woods. (J). (gr. 4 up). 1995. pap. 7.00 (*0-87602-347-2*) Anchorage.

— The Christmas Angel. 70p. 1989. pap. 5.60 (*0-87129-888-0*, CA5) Dramatic Pub.

***DeVita, James.** Excavating Mom. Orig. Title: Dinosaur!. 48p. (YA). (gr. 7 up). 1998. pap. 5.50 (*0-87129-904-6*, E40) Dramatic Pub.

DeVita, Jim. Waiting for Vern. 30p. (Orig.). 1995. pap. 3.50 (*1-57514-105-1*, 1048) Encore Perform Pub.

Devita, Joe. Upgrading & Repairing PCS: Linux Ed. LC 99-62355. (Illus.). 1200p. 1999. pap. text 49.99 (*0-7897-2075-2*) Que.

DeVita, Philip R. The Humbled Anthropologist: Tales from the Pacific. 184p. (C). 1989. mass mkt. 20.00 (*0-534-12570-0*) Wadsworth Pub.

— The Naked Anthropologist: Tales from Around the World. 263p. (C). 1991. 20.00 (*0-534-16266-5*) Wadsworth Pub.

***DeVita, Philip R., ed.** Stumbling Toward Truth: Anthropologists at Work. 272p. (C). 2000. pap. 14.95 (*1-57766-125-7*) Waveland Pr.

DeVita, Philip R. & Armstrong, James D. Distant Mirrors: America As a Foreign Culture. 2nd ed. LC 97-23146. (Anthropology Ser.). 176p. (C). 1997. pap. 24.95 (*0-534-25734-8*) Wadsworth Pub.

DeVita, Philip R. & Armstrong, James D., eds. Distant Mirrors: America As a Forgien Culture. 3rd ed. 2000. pap. 1650.00 (*0-534-55648-5*) Thomson Learn.

***Devita, Sabina.** Electromagnetic Pollution: A Hidden Stress to Your System. 2nd ed. (Illus.). 80p. 2000. pap. 9.00 (*0-934426-94-5*) NAPSAC Reprods.

***DeVita, Sharon.** Marriage Promise. (Special Edition Ser.). 2000. per. 4.50 (*0-373-24313-8*) Silhouette.

Devita, Vincent, Jr. Important Advances In Oncology 1996, Vol. 199. 320p. 1996. text 94.00 (*0-397-51601-0*) Lppncott W & W.

DeVita, Vincent T., Jr., et al, eds. AIDS: Etiology, Diagnosis, Treatment & Prevention. 4th ed. LC 96-17611. 664p. 1996. text 95.00 (*0-397-51538-3*) Lppncott W & W.

— Biologic Therapy of Cancer. 2nd ed. LC 94-40512. (Illus.). 944p. 1994. text 157.00 (*0-397-51416-6*) Lppncott W & W.

— Cancer: Principles & Practice of Oncology. 5th ed. (Illus.). 3456p. 1996. 325.00 incl. cd-rom (*0-397-58425-3*); 355.00 incl. cd-rom (*0-397-58426-1*) Lppncott W & W.

— Cancer Updates: A Compilation of the Cancer Updates That Were Published Monthly in 1987 under Commercial Sponsorship. LC 90-170245. 168p. reprint ed. pap. 52.10 (*0-608-03403-7*, 206410000001) Bks Demand.

— Important Advances in Oncology, 1993. LC 85-642211. 224p. 1993. pap. 69.50 (*0-608-05597-2*, 206605700093) Bks Demand.

— Important Advances in Oncology, 1994. LC 85-642211. 264p. 1994. pap. 81.90 (*0-608-05598-0*, 206605700094) Bks Demand.

— Important Advances in Oncology, 1995. LC 85-642211. 271p. 1995. pap. 84.10 (*0-608-05599-9*, 206605700095) Bks Demand.

DeVita, Vincent T., Jr., et al. Cancer: Principles & Practice of Oncology. 5th ed. 3456p. 325.00 (*0-7817-2396-5*); 385.00 (*0-7817-2397-3*) Lppncott W & W.

DeVita, Vincent T., Jr., et al. Cancer: Principles & Practice of Oncology. 5th ed. (Illus.). 3312p. 1996. text 225.00 (*0-397-51573-1*) Lppncott W & W.

DeVita, Vincent T., Jr., et al. Cancer: Principles & Practice of Oncology. 6th ed. 3456p. write for info. (*0-7817-2387-6*); text 235.00 (*0-7817-2229-2*) Lppncott W & W.

Devita, Vincent T., jt. auth. see Golematis, Basil C.

DeVita, Vincent T., ed. see Important Advances on Oncology Staff.

DeVita, Vincent T., jt. ed. see Rosenberg, et al.

DeVitis, A. A. Graham Greene. rev. ed. (Twayne's English Authors Ser.: 3). 248p. 1986. 32.00 (*0-8057-6911-0*) Macmillan.

Devitis, Joseph L., et al, eds. To Serve & Learn: The Spirit of Community in Liberal Education. LC 96-38659. (Counterpoints Ser.: Vol. 37). IX, 181p. (C). 1998. pap. text 29.95 (*0-8204-3450-7*) P Lang Pubng.

DeVitis, Joseph L. & Rich, John M. Helping & Intervention: The Impossible Social Service Professions. (C). 1989. text 29.95 (*0-8290-2374-7*) Irvington.

— The Success Ethic, Education, & the American Dream. LC 96-3227. (SUNY Series, Education & Culture). 227p. (C). 1996. text 54.50 (*0-7914-2993-8*); pap. text 17.95 (*0-7914-2994-6*) State U NY Pr.

DeVitis, Joseph L. & Sola, Peter A., eds. Building Bridges for Educational Reform: New Approaches to Teacher Education. LC 88-37673. 248p. 1989. reprint ed. pap. 76.90 (*0-608-00134-1*, 206091500006) Bks Demand.

DeVitis, Joseph L., jt. auth. see Rich, John M.

DeVitis, Joseph L., jt. ed. see Vold, David J.

Devito. Basic Speech. (C). 1997. pap. text 19.69 (*0-201-30689-1*) Addison-Wesley.

DeVito. Human Communication. 8th ed. LC 99-19728. 460p. (C). 1999. pap. text 53.00 (*0-321-04420-7*) Addson-Wesley Educ.

Devito. Interpersonal Communication. 8th ed. (C). 1998. pap. text 55.00 (*0-201-32238-2*) Addison-Wesley.

***Devito.** The Interpersonal Communication Book. 8th ed. 1998. 55.93 (*0-321-03286-1*) Longman.

DeVito. Messages. 4th ed. 416p. (C). 1999. 49.00 (*0-321-05562-4*) Addison-Wesley.

Devito. Messages: Building Interpersonal Communication Skills. 4th ed. 416p. (C). 1998. pap. text, student ed. 24.00 (*0-321-04083-X*) Addson-Wesley Educ.

Devito, ed. Effective Oral Communication. 2nd ed. (C). 1997. text 37.00 (*0-673-99937-8*) Addison-Wesley.

DeVito, Albert. Chord Approach to Pop Piano Playing Complete. (Illus.). 1994. pap. 15.95 (*0-934286-68-X*) Kenyon.

— Dictionary of Music Terms & Chords. rev. ed. LC 95-79742. 112p. 1995. pap., per. 8.95 (*0-934286-69-8*) Kenyon.

— Secrets of Piano Technique & Tone. LC 96-94778. 80p. 1996. pap. 14.95 (*0-934286-70-1*) Kenyon.

Devito, Alfred. Geometry, Art & Science: A Union for Teachers & Children. (Illus.). 158p. 1993. pap. 25.99 (*0-942034-07-4*) Creat Ventures IN.

DeVito, Alfred. Mapping: Earth Science Translated. (Illus.). 130p. 1986. pap. 14.95 (*0-942034-05-8*) Creat Ventures IN.

Devito, Alfred. Recycling 35 mm Cannisters for the Teaching of Science. (Illus.). 40p. 1993. pap. 12.95 (*0-942034-08-2*) Creat Ventures IN.

— Recycling Two-Liter Containers for the Teaching of Science. (Illus.). 88p. 1995. pap. 14.95 (*0-942034-09-0*) Creat Ventures IN.

DeVito, Carlo. The Everything Beer Book: Everything You Need to Know to Buy & Enjoy the Best Beers - Or Even How to Brew Your Own. LC 97-48839. (Everything Ser.). (Illus.). 320p. 1998. pap. 12.95 (*1-55850-843-0*) Adams Media.

— Everything Dog Book. Adams Media Corporation Staff, ed. LC 98-51816. 1999. pap. 12.95 (*1-58062-144-9*) Adams Media.

***DeVito, Carlo & Skomal, Gregory.** Everything Tropical Fish B: Setting up & Maintaining Freshwater & Saltwater Aquariums. (Illus.). 304p. 2000. pap. 12.95 (*1-58062-343-3*) Adams Media.

DeVito, Carlo & Skomal, Gregory. The Goldfish: Owner's Guides to a Happy, Healthy Pet. (Owner's Guide to a Happy Healthy Pet Ser.). (Illus.). 128p. 1996. 12.95 (*0-87605-398-3*) Howell Bks.

D

An Asterisk (*) at the beginning of an entry indicates that the title is appearing for the first time.

*Devito, Don. Irrational Exuberance & the Illusion of Prosperity. 2000. 40.00 (0-8144-0609-2) AMACOM.

Devito, E. Elementary Public Speaking. 4th ed. (C). 1989. text, teacher ed. 11.00 (0-06-361695-5) HarpC.

DeVito, Frank & Serrano, Joseph. The Proper Care of Cocker Spaniels, AKC Rank No. 6. (Illus.). 256p. (J). (gr. 5). 1996. 16.95 (0-7938-1970-9, TW141) TFH Pubns.

DeVito, Jill & Markow, Joseph. Amphibians & Reptiles of the Connecticut College Arboretum. Dreyer, Glenn, ed. (Connecticut College Arboretum Bulletin Ser.: No. 36). (Illus.). 52p. 1998. pap. 5.00 (1-878899-07-4) CT Coll Arboretum.

DeVito, Joseph A. Elements of Public Speaking. 7th ed. LC 99-14865. 579p. (C). 1999. pap. text 52.00 incl. cd-rom (0-321-04422-3) Addson-Wesley Educ.

Devito, Joseph A. Essentials of Human Communication. 3rd ed. LC 98-10127. 448p. (C). 1998. pap. text 52.00 (0-321-01683-1) Addison-Wesley.

— Messages Building Interpersonal Communication Skills 416p. 2000. pap. 59.95 (0-201-61409-X) Addison-Wesley.

*Devito, Joseph A. Messages: Building Interpersonal Communication Skills. 4th ed. LC 98-29692. 448p. (C). 1998. pap. text 56.00 (0-321-02509-1) Addson-Wesley Educ.

DeVito, Joseph A. The Nonverbal Communication Workbook. (Illus.). 287p. (C). 1989. pap. text 19.95 (0-88133-393-X) Waveland Pr.

— Psycholinguistics. LC 73-183112. (Studies in Communicative Disorders). 36p. (C). 1971. pap. write for info. (0-672-61277-1, Bobbs) Macmillan.

Devito, Joseph A., ed. The Interpersonal Communication Book. 8th ed. LC 97-18770. 506p. (C). 1997. pap. 56.00 (0-321-01302-6) Addson-Wesley Educ.

— The Interpersonal Communication Book. 8th ed. (C). 1998. text. write for info. (0-321-01543-6) Addson-Wesley Educ.

DeVito, Joseph A., et al. Articulation & Voice: Effective Communication, No. 20. LC 74-14615. 127p. (C). 1975. pap. write for info. (0-672-61350-6, SC20, Bobbs) Macmillan.

DeVito, Michael C. Diary of a Trolley Road. (Illus.). 1975. 10.00 (0-910506-16-7) De Vito.

— East Windsor, Through the Years. (Illus.). 1968. 12.00 (0-910506-04-3) De Vito.

DeVito, Pam. Lydia & the Purple Paint. Weinberger, Jane, ed. LC 89-50681. (Illus.). 52p. (J). (ps-4). 1989. pap. 4.00 (0-932433-59-6) Windswept Hse.

DeVito, Pasquale J., ed. see National Research Council Staff.

DeVito, Richard A., ed. see Maloney, Robert M.

Devito, Stephen C. & Farris, Carol A. Premanufacture Notification: Chemistry Assistance for Submitters. LC 97-1034. 138p. 1997. 59.95 (0-471-19151-5) Wiley.

DeVito, Stephen C. & Garrett, Roger L., eds. Designing Safer Chemicals: Green Chemistry for Pollution Prevention. LC 96-24785. (ACS Symposium Ser.: No. 640). 264p. 1996. text 95.00 (0-8412-3443-4, Pub. by Am Chemical) OUP.

Devito, Vincent. Experiences Activity Manual. (C). 1990. pap. 15.00 (0-06-041605-X) HarperTrade.

Devitt, Amy J. Standardizing Written English: Diffusion in the Case of Scotland, 1520-1659. (Illus.). 136p. (C). 1989. text 52.95 (0-521-36446-9) Cambridge U Pr.

*Devitt, Don. Turnabout. 2000. pap. 9.95 (0-533-13462-5) Vantage.

Devitt, Don, jt. auth. see Prentice-Hall Staff.

*Devitt, Jack. Ohio Toolmakers & Their Tools. 400p. 2000. 30.00 (1-886855-39-0) Tavenner Pub.

Devitt, Michael. Coming to Our Senses: A Naturalistic Program for Semantic Localism. (Cambridge Studies in Philosophy). 350p. (C). 1995. text 64.95 (0-521-49543-1); pap. text 21.95 (0-521-49887-2) Cambridge U Pr.

— Realism & Truth. 2nd ed. LC 96-28286. 340p. 1997. pap. text 18.95 (0-691-01187-7, Pub. by Princeton U Pr) Cal Prin Full Svc.

*Devitt, Michael & Sterelny, Kim. Language & Reality: An Introduction to the Philosophy of Language. 2nd ed. LC 98-47178. 1999. 60.00 (0-262-04173-1) MIT Pr.

Devitt, Michael & Sterelny, Kim. Language & Reality: An Introduction to the Philosophy of Language. 2nd ed. LC 98-47178. (Illus.). 325p. 1999. pap. text 30.00 (0-262-54099-1, Bradford Bks) MIT Pr.

Devitt, Napier. More Memories of a Magistrate: Including Twenty-Five Years on the South African Bench. 263p. 1999. reprint ed. 80.00 (1-56169-302-2) Gaunt.

Devitt, Patrick J., jt. auth. see Tobin, L. Michael.

Devitt, Patrick M., jt. auth. see Moran, Gabrial.

Devitt, Peter & Barker, Juliet. Clinical Problems in General Medicine & Surgery: A Problem-Solving Approach to Medicine & Surgery. (Illus.). 533p. 1993. text 52.50 (0-7295-1409-9) Bailliere Tindall.

*Devitto, Darnella. Medical Practice, Defensive Medicine & Legal Issues: Index of New Information with Authors, Subjects, Research Categories & References. rev. ed. 160p. (Orig.). 1998. 47.50 (0-7883-2086-6); pap. 44.50 (0-7883-2087-4) ABBE Pubs Assn.

Devivier, Michel. Data Processing & Related Fields Dictionary. 280p. 1989. lib. bdg. 89.95 (0-8288-2608-0) Fr & Eur.

Devkin, V. D. German - Russian Dictionary of Spoken Vocabulary. (GER & RUS.). 768p. 1994. 59.95 (0-8285-5435-8) Firebird NY.

Devkota, L. P. Muna Madan: A Play in the Jhyaure Folk Tradition. 1995. pap. write for info. (0-7855-0414-1, Pub. by Ratna Pustak Bhandar) St Mut.

Devlin. Management of Abdominal Hernias. 2nd ed. 344p. 1999. text 135.00 (0-412-73820-1, Pub. by E A) OUP.

*Devlin. Math Gene. 2000. pap. 16.00 (0-465-01619-7, Pub. by Basic) HarpC.

Devlin. Numbers. 224p. (C). 1999. pap. 18.95 (0-471-32822-7) Wiley.

— Slavophies & Commissars. LC 98-50836. 1999. text 45.00 (0-312-22200-9) St Martin.

Devlin, Albert J., ed. Conversations with Tennessee Williams. LC 86-9180. (Literary Conversations Ser.). 370p. 1986. pap. 17.00 (0-87805-263-1); text 39.50 (0-87805-262-3) U Pr of Miss.

— Welty: A Life in Literature. LC 87-14267. (Illus.). 290p. 1987. text 37.50 (0-87805-315-8) U Pr of Miss.

Devlin, Angela. Invisible Women: What's Wrong with Women's Prisons? 397p. 1998. pap. 39.00 (1-872870-59-7, Pub. by Waterside Pr) Gaunt.

Devlin, Angela & Devlin, Tim. Anybody's Nightmare: The Sheila Bowler Story. LC 98-215918. 368p. 1998. pap. 30.00 (1-901470-04-0, Pub. by Taverner) Gaunt.

Devlin, Anne. After Easter. LC 99-462451. (Orig.). 1999. pap. 5.25 (0-8222-1671-X) Dramatists Play.

— Ourselves Alone. 1999. pap. 5.25 (0-8222-1672-8) Dramatists Play.

— Ourselves Alone. 2nd ed. 192p. 1986. pap. 9.95 (0-571-14457-8) Faber & Faber.

Devlin, Barry. Data Warehouse: From Architecture to Implementation. LC 96-27708. 448p. (C). 1996. 49.95 (0-201-96425-2) Addison-Wesley.

Devlin, Bernie. Intelligence & Success: Is It All in the Genes?: Scientists Respond to the Bell Curve. LC 97-9792. 1997. text. write for info. (0-387-98234-5); pap. text. write for info. (0-387-94986-0) Spr-Verlag.

Devlin, C. Greg. Think Neon. LC 95-71327. (Illus.). 36p. (J). (ps-3). 1996. pap. text 6.95 (1-887654-12-7) Premium Pr TN.

Devlin, Christopher. Hamlet's Divinity & Other Essays. (Essay Index Reprint Ser.). 1977. 18.95 (0-8369-1915-7) Ayer.

Devlin, D. Stargate: Penguin Readers Level 3. 1998. pap. 7.00 (0-14-081581-3) Viking Penguin.

Devlin, D. W. & Rusch, K. K. Arrival. (The Tenth Planet Ser.: Vol. 1). 1999. mass mkt. 5.99 (0-345-42140-X, Del Rey) Ballantine Pub Grp.

Devlin, Daniel H. The Right of Rights: The United States' Constitutional, Natural, Moral & Absolute Essential Right to Be. 264p. 1995. pap. 19.95 (1-886866-00-7) Postrty Pr.

Devlin, David. The Good Sex Guide: The Illustrated Guide to Enhance Your Lovemaking. (Illus.). 144p. 1993. pap. 17.95 (0-88184-862-X) Carroll & Graf.

— The Pocket Good Sex Guide. (Illus.). 96p. 1999. 10.95 (0-7867-0616-3) Carroll & Graf.

Devlin, Dean. Independence Day, #4 2000. mass mkt. 6.50 (0-06-105828-9) HarpC.

*Devlin, Dean. Independence Day: War in Desert, Vol. 3. 336p. 1999. mass mkt. 6.99 (0-06-105829-7) HarpC.

— Stargate. large type ed. LC 99-46179. (Science Fiction Ser). 1999. 30.00 (0-7838-8784-1) Mac Lib Ref.

Devlin, Denis. Collected Poems of Denis Devlin. Mays, J. C., ed. LC 89-51505. 365p. 1990. 29.95 (0-916390-37-3) Wake Forest.

Devlin, Denis & Little, Roger. Translations into English. 354p. 1992. pap. 19.95 (1-873790-18-X) Dufour.

Devlin, Dennis S. Muskegon's Jewish Community: A Centennial History, 1888-1988. (Illus.). 84p. (Orig.). 1988. pap. text 9.95 (0-9620751-0-8) Congr Bnai Israel.

Devlin, Diana. Mask & Scene: An Introduction to a World View of Theatre. LC 89-33471. (Illus.). 227p. 1989. 34.50 (0-8108-2234-2) Scarecrow.

Devlin, Edward, jt. ed. see Silny, Josef.

Devlin, Edward S. Business Resumption Planning 1999. 99th ed. 128p. 1998. ring bd. 95.00 (0-8493-9975-0) CRC Pr.

Devlin, Edward S., et al. Business Resumption Planning: 1998 Edition. 98th ed. 992p. 1997. ring bd. 225.00 (0-8493-9945-9, TK5102) CRC Pr.

Devlin, Gerard M. Paratrooper! The Saga of the U. S. Army & Marine Parachute & Glider Combat Troops During World War II. (Illus.). 736p. 1986. pap. 14.95 (0-312-59652-9) St Martin.

Devlin, Harry, jt. auth. see Devlin, Wende.

Devlin, Iseult. Winter Sports: A Woman's Guide. 144p. 2000. pap. 14.05 (0-07-158188-X) McGraw.

Devlin, J. Greg, et al. Think Neon. abr. ed. (Illus.). 24p. (J). (ps-7). 1995. mass mkt. 6.95 incl. audio (0-9649889-0-9, SK-1001) Skedaddle.

*Devlin, James E. Elmore Leonard. LC 99-42756. (Twayne's United States Authors Ser.). (J). 1999. write for info. (0-8057-1694-7, Twyne) Mac Lib Ref.

Devlin, Jean H. Sexual Dysfunction in Human Males & Females Including Analysis, Treatments, Methods & Devices: Index of New Information with References. 172p. 1997. 47.50 (0-7883-1562-5); pap. 44.50 (0-7883-1563-3) ABBE Pubs Assn.

Devlin, Jim. Leonard Cohen: Every Style of Passion. (Illus.). 392p. 1996. pap. 24.95 (0-7119-5496-8) Omnibus NY.

— Leonard Cohen: In His Own Words. (Illus.). 96p. 1998. pap. 15.95 (0-7119-6878-0, op 48 63) Omnibus NY.

Devlin, John P. High Throughput Screening: The Discovery of Bioactive Substances. LC 97-9333. (Illus.). 704p. 1997. text 225.00 (0-8247-0067-8) Dekker.

Devlin, John T., jt. ed. see Williams, Clyde.

Devlin, Joseph. A Dictionary of Synonyms & Antonyms. 384p. 1984. reprint ed. mass mkt. 5.99 (0-446-31310-6, Pub. by Warner Bks) Little.

Devlin, Joyce. Women's Scenes & Monologues. 244p. 1989. pap. text 8.95 (0-87440-007-4) Bakers Plays.

Devlin, Judith. The Rise of the Russian Democrats: The Causes & Consequences of the Elite Revolution. LC 94-48417. (Studies of Communism in Transition). 304p. 1995. 9500.00 (1-85898-251-0) E Elgar.

— Superstitious Mind: French Peasants & the Supernatural in the Nineteenth Century. LC 86-23341. 336p. 1987. 42.50 (0-300-03710-4) Yale U Pr.

Devlin, Judith & Fanning, Ronan. Religion & Rebellion. LC 97-163312. 232p. 1997. 59.95 (1-900621-03-7) Dufour.

Devlin, Julia, ed. Gulf Economics: Strategies for Growth in the 21st Century. (Illus.). 73p. 1997. pap. 9.95 (0-932568-50-5) GU Ctr CAS.

*Devlin, Keith. Infosense: Turning Information into Knowledge. 2001. pap. 14.95 (0-7167-4164-4) W H Freeman.

— The Language of Mathematics: Making the Invisible Visible. (Illus.). 352p. 2000. pap. text 14.95 (0-7167-3967-4) W H Freeman.

Devlin, Keith J. All the Math That's Fit to Print: Articles from the Manchester Guardian. LC 94-77346. (Spectrum Ser.). 345p. 1994. pap. 29.95 (0-88385-515-1, ATMA) Math Assn.

— Calculus I. Pritchard-Martinez, Carol, ed. (Electronic Companion Ser.). (Illus.). 300p. (Orig.). (C). 1997. pap. text, wbk. ed. write for info. (1-888902-52-3) Cogito Lrning.

— Constructibility. (Perspectives in Mathematical Logic Ser.). (Illus.). 425p. 1984. 169.95 (0-387-13258-9) Spr-Verlag.

— Goodbye, Descartes: The End of Logic & the Search for a New Cosmology of the Mind. LC 96-25493. 320p. 1996. 27.95 (0-471-14216-6) Wiley.

*Devlin, Keith J. Goodbye, Descartes: The End of Logic & the Search for a New Cosmology of the Mind. 320p. 1998. pap. 14.95 (0-471-25186-0) Wiley.

Devlin, Keith J. Infosense: Understanding Information to Survive in the Knowledge Society. 256p. 1999. pap. text 24.95 (0-7167-3484-2) W H Freeman.

— The Joy of Sets: Fundamentals of Contemporary Set Theory. 2nd ed. (Undergraduate Texts in Mathematics Ser.). (Illus.). 210p. 1993. write for info. (3-540-94094-4) Spr-Verlag.

— The Joy of Sets: Fundamentals of Contemporary Set Theory. 2nd ed. LC 93-4692. (Undergraduate Texts in Mathematics Ser.). (Illus.). 192p. 1997. 39.95 (0-387-94094-4) Spr-Verlag.

— Life by the Numbers. LC 97-41059. 214p. 1998. 29.95 (0-471-24044-3) Wiley.

— Logic & Information. 320p. (C). 1991. text 47.95 (0-521-41030-4) Cambridge U Pr.

— Logic & Information. 324p. (C). 1995. pap. text 21.95 (0-521-49971-2) Cambridge U Pr.

*Devlin, Keith J. The Math Gene: How Mathematical Thinking Evolved & Why Numbers Are Like Gossip. 2000. 25.00 (0-465-01618-9, Pub. by Basic) HarpC.

— Mathematics: The New Golden Age. LC 99-23438. 312p. 1999. 24.95 (0-231-11638-1) Col U Pr.

Devlin, Keith J. Mathematics - The Science of Patterns: The Search for Order in Life, Mind & the Universe. (Illus.). 224p. 1996. pap. text 19.95 (0-7167-6022-3) W H Freeman.

Devlin, Keith J. & Rosenberg, Duska. Language at Work: Analyzing Communication in the Workplace to Inform Systems Design. LC 96-24100. (Lecture Notes Ser.). 224p. 1996. 59.95 (1-57586-050-3); pap. 20.95 (1-57586-051-1) CSLI.

Devlin, Kieran, jt. auth. see Daly, Edward.

Devlin, Kieran, jt. ed. see Jefferies, Henry A.

Devlin, Kimberly, jt. ed. see Pinet, Celine.

Devlin, Kimberly J. Wandering & Return in "Finnegan's Wake" An Integrative Approach to Joyce's Fictions. LC 90-47136. 218p. 1991. reprint ed. pap. 67.60 (0-608-04586-1, 206535600003) Bks Demand.

Devlin, Kimberly J. & Reizbaum, Marilyn, eds. Ulysses - En-Gendered Perspectives: Eighteen New Essays on the Episodes. LC 98-40221. 384p. 55.00 (1-57003-287-4) U of SC Pr.

— Ulysses - En-Gendered Perspectives: Eighteen New Essays on the Episodes. LC 98-40221. (Cultural Frames, Framing Culture Ser.). 384p. 1999. pap. 29.95 (1-57003-288-2) U of SC Pr.

*Devlin, Lucinda, et al. Rooms. (Illus.). 136p. 2000. 35.00 (3-88375-368-8, Pub. by Walther Konig) Dist Art Pubs.

Devlin, Mary. Astrology & Past Lives. LC 86-62344. 287p. 1989. pap. 19.95 (0-914918-71-0, Whitford) Schiffer.

Devlin, Maureen. Primary Health Care & the Private Sector. LC 98-198177. (National Primary Care Research & Development Centre Ser.). 79 p. 1998. write for info. (1-85775-244-9) Scovill Paterson.

*Devlin, Michael. Etudes at Twilight. 2000. write for info. (1-58235-482-0) Watermrk Pr.

Devlin, Michael B. Appearance & Reality. 1998. pap. write for info. (1-57553-747-8) Watermrk Pr.

— Morning Glories & Sapphires. 1999. pap. write for info. (1-58235-045-0) Watermrk Pr.

— Through the Laughter & the Tears. 60p. (Orig.). Date not set. write for info. (0-614-08589-6) Watermrk Pr.

Devlin, Nancy. Arrows Swift & Far: Guiding Your Child Through School. 100p. (Orig.). 1993. pap. text 9.95 (0-9635217-0-5) Archr Pub NJ.

Devlin, Paddy. Straight Left: An Autobiography. 312p. 1994. pap. 17.95 (0-85640-514-0, Pub. by Blackstaff Pr) Dufour.

Devlin, Patricia. The Light of Love: My Angel Shall Go Before Thee. LC 95-68111. 382p. (Orig.). 1994. pap. 8.75 (1-882972-53-8, 3401) Queenship Pub.

Devlin, Patrick. The Judge. xiv, 208p. 1995. pap. text 8.50 (0-226-14356-2) U Ch Pr.

— Trial by Jury. (Legal Reprint Ser.). viii, 216p. 1988. reprint ed. 40.00 (0-8377-2035-4, Rothman) W S Hein.

— Trial by Jury: Trial by Jury. (Legal Reprint Ser.). viii, 216p. 1988. reprint ed. 24.00 (0-421-40210-5) W S Hein.

*Devlin, Robert. Business Resumption Planning. 128p. 1999. ring bd. 95.00 (0-8493-9835-5) CRC Pr.

Devlin, Robert. Debt & Crisis in Latin America: The Supply Side of the Story. 338p. 1989. pap. text 20.95 (0-691-00079-4, Pub. by Princeton U Pr) Cal Prin Full Svc.

— Debt & Crisis in Latin America: The Supply Side of the Story. (Illus.). 312p. (C). 1989. text 55.00 (0-691-07797-5, Pub. by Princeton U Pr) Cal Prin Full Svc.

Devlin, Robert, jt. ed. see Jackson, George.

*Devlin, Robert T. A Treatise on the Law of Negotiable Instruments, 3 vols. 2nd ed. LC 99-73239. xlviii, 2200p. 1999. reprint ed. 450.00 (1-56169-523-8) Gaunt.

Devlin, Robert T. Treaty Power under the Constitution of the United States: Commentaries on the Treaty Clauses of the Constitution, Construction of Treaties, Extent of Treaty-Making Power, Conflict Between Treaties & Acts of Congress, State Constitutions & Statutes, International Extradition, Acquisition of Territory, Ambassadors, Consuls & Foreign Judgments, Naturalization & Expatriation, Responsibility of Government for Mob Violence & Claims Against Governments. lxx, 864p. 1996. reprint ed. 125.00 (0-8377-2041-9, Rothman) W S Hein.

*Devlin, Rose Anne & Grafton, R. Quentin. Economic Rights & Environmental Wrongs: Property Rights for the Common Good. LC 97-33596. 208p. 2000. pap. 25.00 (1-84064-328-5) E Elgar.

Devlin, Sam. Devlin's Boatbuilding: How to Build Any Boat the Stitch & Glue Way. 1993. pap. text 22.95 (0-87742-256-7) Intl Marine.

— Devlin's Boatbuilding: How to Build Any Boat the Stitch & Glue Way. 198p. 1995. pap. 22.95 (0-07-157990-7) McGraw.

Devlin, Thomas M., ed. Textbook of Biochemistry: With Clinical Correlations. 4th ed. LC 97-1078. 1216p. 1997. 98.95 (0-471-15451-2) Wiley.

Devlin, Tim, jt. auth. see Devlin, Angela.

Devlin, Wende. Cranberry Christmas. 1991. 11.19 (0-606-04897-9, Pub. by Turtleback) Demco.

— Cranberry Easter. (J). 1993. 10.15 (0-606-02574-X, Pub. by Turtleback) Demco.

Devlin, Wende. Cranberry Halloween. (J). 1985. pap. 9.95 (0-590-07854-2) Scholastic Inc.

Devlin, Wende. Cranberry Halloween. (J). 1990. 10.15 (0-606-03170-7, Pub. by Turtleback) Demco.

— Cranberry Thanksgiving. (J). 1990. 11.19 (0-606-03171-5, Pub. by Turtleback) Demco.

Devlin, Wende. How Fletcher Was Hatched: 30th Anniversary Edition. anniversary ed. LC 98-86646. (Illus.). 48p. (J). (gr. 2-3). 1998. 14.00 (1-892657-00-7) Town Bk Pr.

— Kiss for a Warthog. LC 98-36370. (Illus.). 48p. (J). (gr. 1-3). 1999. 14.00 (1-892657-01-5) Town Bk Pr.

Devlin, Wende & Devlin, Harry. Cranberry Birthday. LC 92-23541. (Illus.). 40p. (J). (ps-3). 1993. reprint ed. pap. 4.95 (0-689-71697-4) Aladdin.

— Cranberry Christmas. LC 91-1988. (Illus.). 40p. (J). (gr. k-3). 1991. reprint ed. mass mkt. 5.99 (0-689-71510-2) Aladdin.

— Cranberry Christmas. LC 80-16971. (Illus.). 40p. (J). (ps-3). 1984. reprint ed. lib. bdg. 13.95 (0-02-729900-7, Four Winds Pr) S&S Childrens.

— Cranberry Easter. LC 88-21370. (Cranberryport Ser.). (Illus.). 40p. (J). (gr. k-3). 1990. lib. bdg. 15.00 (0-02-729935-X, Four Winds Pr) S&S Childrens.

— Cranberry Easter. LC 92-23537. (Illus.). 40p. (J). (ps-3). 1993. reprint ed. mass mkt. 4.95 (0-689-71698-2) Aladdin.

— Cranberry Halloween. LC 81-22134. (Illus.). 40p. (J). (gr. k-3). 1984. lib. bdg. 13.95 (0-02-729910-4, Four Winds Pr) S&S Childrens.

— Cranberry Halloween. LC 89-18666. (Cranberryport Ser.). (Illus.). 40p. (J). (gr. k-3). 1990. reprint ed. mass mkt. 4.95 (0-689-71428-9) Aladdin.

— Cranberry Thanksgiving. LC 89-18642. (Cranberryport Ser.). (Illus.). 40p. (J). (gr. k-3). 1990. reprint ed. mass mkt. 5.99 (0-689-71429-7) Aladdin.

— Cranberry Thanksgiving. LC 80-17070. (Illus.). 48p. (J). (ps-3). 1984. reprint ed. lib. bdg. 15.00 (0-02-729930-9, Four Winds Pr) S&S Childrens.

— Cranberry Valentine. LC 91-6915. (Illus.). 32p. (J). (gr. k-3). 1992. reprint ed. mass mkt. 5.99 (0-689-71509-9) Aladdin.

— Old Black Witch. LC 91-42133. (Illus.). 32p. (J). (gr. k-3). 1992. reprint ed. mass mkt. 3.95 (0-689-71636-2) Aladdin.

— Old Black Witch. 2nd ed. LC 92-19897. (Illus.). 32p. (J). (gr. k-3). 1992. text 13.95 (0-02-729185-5, Four Winds Pr) S&S Childrens.

*Devlin, Wende & Devlin, Harry. The Trouble with Henriette! (Illus.). 30p. (J). (ps-2). 1999. reprint ed. text 15.00 (0-7881-6637-9) DIANE Pub.

Devney, Darcy C. Organizing Special Events & Conferences: A Practical Guide for Busy Volunteers & Staff. LC 89-30179. 130p. 1990. pap. 18.95 (0-910923-63-9) Pineapple Pr.

— The Volunteer's Survival Manual: The Only Practical Guide to Giving Your Time & Money. (Illus.). 192p. (Orig.). 1992. pap. 15.95 (0-9630686-9-5) Prctcl Pr MA.

Devney, Dorothy M. Guide to Spanish Suffixes. (SPA., Illus.). 256p. 1994. pap. 13.95 (0-8442-7323-6, 73236, Natl Textbk Co) NTC Contemp Pub Co.

— Practice Makes Perfect: Spanish Verb Tenses. (Illus.). 320p. 1995. pap. 9.95 (0-8442-7334-1, 73341) NTC Contemp Pub Co.

Devo. Roots of True Faith. 1993. pap. 3.99 (0-946462-28-3, Pub. by Evangelical Pr) P & R Pubng.

D

Devoe, Charles D. Maine Workers' Compensation Act, 2 vols., Set. 4th rev. ed. 790p. 1992. ring bd. 135.00 (*1-56257-315-2*, MICHIE) LEXIS Pub.

Devoe, Charles D., ed. Maine Workers' Compensation Commission: Appellate Division Decisions, 1982-1992. 1994. ring bd. 475.00 (*0-614-05892-9*, MICHIE) LEXIS Pub.

— Maine Workers' Compensation Commission: Appellate Division Decisions, 1982-1993. 900p. 1994. suppl. ed. 120.00 (*0-685-74265-2*, MICHIE) LEXIS Pub.

— Maine Workers' Compensation Commission: Appellate Division Decisions, 1982-1993, Set. 900p. 1993. 475.00 (*0-685-46118-1*, MICHIE) LEXIS Pub.

Devoe, Howard. Thermodynamics & Chemistry. 416p. (C). 2000. 58.00 (*0-02-328741-1*) P-H.

DeVoe, James R., ed. Validation of the Measurement Process: A Symposium. LC 77-15555. (ACS Symposium Ser.: No. 63). (Illus.). 215p. 1977. reprint ed. pap. 66.70 (*0-608-04341-9*, 206512100001) Bks Demand.

DeVoe, M. Richard, ed. Introductions & Transfers of Marine Species: Achieving a Balance Between Economic Development & Resource Protection. LC 92-83774. (Illus.). 198p. 1992. 10.00 (*0-685-63259-8*) SC Sea Grant.

DeVoe, Pamela, ed. Selected Papers on Refugee Issues, 1992. LC 92-38436. 1992. write for info. (*0-913167-54-1*) Am Anthro Assn.

DeVoe, Shirley S. The Art of the Tinsmith: English & American. LC 81-85999. 222p. 1982. 27.50 (*0-916838-59-5*) Schiffer.

Devoe, T. F. Genealogy of the De Veaux Family. (Illus.). 302p. 1989. reprint ed. pap. 45.00 (*0-8328-0473-8*); reprint ed. lib. bdg. 53.00 (*0-8328-0472-X*) Higginson Bk Co.

DeVoe, Walter. Mystic Words of Mighty Power. 213p. 1971. reprint ed. spiral bd. 15.00 (*0-7873-0282-1*) Hlth Research.

— Mystic Words of Mighty Power: The Power of "I Am" 1991. lib. bdg. 79.95 (*0-8490-4994-6*) Gordon Pr.

— Mystic Words of Mighty Power, 1905. 214p. 1996. reprint ed. pap. 13.95 (*1-56459-941-8*) Kessinger Pub.

Devol, George H. Forty Years a Gambler on the Mississippi. LC 95-36846. (Illus.). 312p. 1996. reprint ed. pap. 12.95 (*1-55709-110-2*) Applewood.

DeVol, Karen R. Income Replacement for Long-Term Disability: The Role of Workers' Compensation & SSDI. (Illus.). 95p. 1986. 35.00 (*0-935149-04-X*, SP-86-2) Workers Comp Res Inst.

DeVol, Philip, jt. auth. see Christensen, Linda.

Devon, David. Over Forty & Fit: The Baby Boomer's Common Sense Guide for Staying Lean, Muscular, & Healthy. LC 94-96747. (Illus.). 120p. (Orig.). 1995. pap. 9.99 (*0-9644558-0-3*) Grunt.

Devon, Gary. Wedding Night. 1997. mass mkt. 5.99 (*0-380-72812-5*, Avon Bks) Morrow Avon.

— Wedding Night. 1995. 21.00 (*0-684-80183-3*) S&S Trade.

***Devon, Georgina.** Betrayal. large type ed. 320p. 2000. 25.99 (*0-263-16326-1*, Pub. by Mills & Boon) Ulverscroft.

Devon, Georgina. Scandals. 1996. per. 4.99 (*0-373-83322-9*, 1-83322-7) Harlequin Bks.

***Devon, Georgina.** Scandals. large type ed. 320p. 2000. 25.99 (*0-263-16324-5*, Pub. by Mills & Boon) Ulverscroft.

Devon, Georgina. Scarlet Lady. 352p. 1991. mass mkt. 3.95 (*0-8217-3400-8*, Zebra Kensgtn) Kensgtn Pub Corp.

— Untamed Heart. LC 97-10620. 395p. 1994. per. 4.99 (*0-373-31215-6*, 1-31215-6) Harlequin Bks.

***Devon, Georgina.** Untamed Heart. large type ed. 320p. 2000. 25.99 (*0-263-16273-7*, Pub. by Mills & Boon) Ulverscroft.

Devon, Jacques. Sun Spots. Johns, Rose, ed. (Illus.). 92p. (Orig.). 1988. pap. write for info. (*0-318-63128-8*) Prairie Rose Pub.

Devon, Marian. On the Way to Gretna Green. large type ed. LC 98-41392. 1998. 30.00 (*0-7838-0381-8*, G K Hall Lrg Type) Mac Lib Ref.

***Devon, Marjorie.** Tamarind: 40 Years. LC 99-6548. (Illus.). 216p. 2000. pap. 29.95 (*0-8263-2073-2*) U of NM Pr.

***Devon, Marjorie, ed.** Tamarind: Forty Years. 2000. 59.95 (*0-8263-2072-4*) U of NM Pr.

Devon, Marjorie & Walch, Peter, intros. Tamarind Lithography Workshop Inc. Catalog Raisonne, 1960-1970. (Illus.). 284p. (Orig.). 1989. pap. 45.00 (*0-944282-08-3*) UNM Art Mus.

Devon, Molly, jt. auth. see Miller, Philip.

Devon, Paddy. The Grumpy Shepherd. (Illus.). 32p. (J). (gr. 2-5). 1995. pap. 6.95 (*0-687-00129-3*) Abingdon.

Devon, Sarah. A Husband for Helen. large type ed. (Linford Romance Library). 320p. 1985. pap. 16.99 (*0-7089-6068-5*) Ulverscroft.

— Stranger in My Heart. large type ed. 1990. 27.99 (*0-7089-2168-X*) Ulverscroft.

Devon, Scott. The Lord's Prayer, a Devotional Meditation: And Ye Shall Find Rest unto Your Souls. LC 97-77064. 128p. 1998. 14.95 (*1-890394-16-5*) Rhodes & Easton.

DeVone, James M. A Beautiful Dreamer: Love & Inspirational Poetry. LC 90-93124. (Illus.). 50p. (Orig.). (C). 1990. pap. text 9.95 (*0-9625092-6-4*) Schl Univ Studies.

DeVone, James M., Sr. The Big Mother - Big Father Counseling Booklet for Big Mother - Big Father Trainers. LC 90-93012. (Illus.). 50p. (Orig.). (gr. 9-12). 1989. pap. text 9.95 (*0-9625092-2-1*) Schl Univ Studies.

DeVone, James M. Clyde McPhatter: Michael Jackson's U. S. A. Roots, Durham, NC (Unauthorized) LC 90-93013. (Illus.). (Orig.). 1990. pap. text 9.95 (*0-9625092-4-8*) Schl Univ Studies.

DeVone, James M., Sr. Clyde McPhetter: Michael Jackson's U. S. A. Roots, Durham, NC (Unauthorized) LC 90-93013. (Illus.). (Orig.). 1990. pap. text 9.95 (*0-685-35357-5*) Schl Univ Studies.

DeVone, James M. How to Avoid Immediate Eviction: A Survival Guide for Youths & Adults. LC 90-93121. 50p. (C). 1989. pap. text 9.95 (*0-9625092-5-6*) Schl Univ Studies.

— Simple Ways to Protect Your Inventions (Ideas) LC 90-91834. (Illus.). 50p. (Orig.). (C). 1990. pap. text 49.95 (*0-9625092-7-2*) Schl Univ Studies.

— Who Destroyed the Jews? Hitler: The Scapegoat? - The Final Solutions? LC 90-93013. (Illus.). 50p. (Orig.). (C). 1989. pap. text 9.95 (*0-9625092-0-5*) Schl Univ Studies.

DeVone, James M., Sr. & Akhenaton, Susu. Didn't It Rain? Will It Be Fire? Solutions for Global Air Warming. LC 89-92762. (Illus.). 50p. (C). 1989. pap. text 9.95 (*0-9625092-1-3*) Schl Univ Studies.

Devons, Ely. Essays in Economics. LC 79-17089. (Illus.). 203p. 1980. reprint ed. lib. bdg. 69.50 (*0-313-21296-1*, DEEE, Greenwood Pr) Greenwood.

Devons, Ely & Cairncross, Alec. Papers on Planning & Economic Management. LC 77-542200. vii, 278p. 1970. write for info. (*0-7190-0408-X*) Manchester Univ Pr.

Devor. Introduction to Manufacturing. 1999. lab manual ed. 79.00 (*0-07-016625-0*) McGraw.

***Devor.** Introduction to Manufacturing. 1999. 29.50 (*0-07-016626-9*) McGraw.

Devor, Eric J., ed. Molecular Applications in Biological Anthropology. (Studies in Biological Anthropology: No. 10). (Illus.). 272p. (C). 1993. text 74.95 (*0-521-39109-1*) Cambridge U Pr.

Devor, Holly. FTM: Female-to-Male Transsexuals in Society. LC 97-18640. (Illus.). 720p. 1999. pap. 27.50 (*0-253-21259-6*) Ind U Pr.

— Gender Blending: Confronting the Limits of Duality. LC 88-46041. (Illus.). 192p. 1989. 37.50 (*0-253-31637-5*); pap. 14.95 (*0-253-20533-6*, MB-533) Ind U Pr.

***Devor, Marshall, et al, eds.** Proceedings of the Ninth World Congress on Pain. (Progress in Pain Research & Management Ser.: No. 16). (Illus.). xxiv, 1154p. 2000. 80.00 (*0-931092-31-0*) Intl Assn Study Pain.

***Devor, Nina.** It Must Be Mary Margaret. (Mary Margaret Adventure Stories Ser.). (Illus.). (J). (ps-1). 2000. pap. 6.50 (*0-9676428-0-9*) N Devor.

Devor, R. E., et al. Statistical Methods for Quality Design & Control: Contemporary Concepts & Methods. (Illus.). 832p. (C). 1992. 99.00 (*0-02-329180-X*, Macmillan Coll) P-H.

DeVor, Richard E., intro. Transactions of the North American Manufacturing Research Institution of SME 1991 (NAMRC) (Illus.). 372p. 1991. 80.00 (*0-87263-404-3*) SME.

Devor, Richard E. & Chang, Tsong-How. Engineering Statistics. 944p. (C). 1994. 58.00 (*0-02-329140-0*, Macmillan Coll) P-H.

Devorak, Charles R. Smart Car Buying & Leasing 101. (Illus.). 166p. (Orig.). 1997. pap. 8.95 (*1-890172-00-6*) Vehicle Info.

Devore. Applied Engineering Statistics. LC 99-10841. (Statistics Ser.). 577p. 1999. pap. 85.95 (*0-534-35601-X*) Brooks-Cole.

***Devore.** Applied Engineering Statistics. (Statistics Ser). 1999. pap. 15.00 (*0-534-36140-4*) Brooks-Cole.

Devore. Applied Engineering Statistics. (Statistics Ser.). 1999. pap., student ed. 17.50 (*0-534-36139-0*) PWS Pubs.

— Introductory Statistics. 2nd ed. (ME - Statistics Ser.). 1994. pap., student ed. 19.25 (*0-314-03499-4*) West Pub.

— Matlab Companion Prob & Stats F/Eng & The Sci 5th ed. 2000. pap. text 14.00 (*0-534-37474-3*) Thomson Learn.

— PPM for Heating & Cooling Technicians. 3rd ed. LC 97-37160. 304p. (C). 1998. mass mkt. 18.95 (*0-8273-7948-X*) Delmar.

— PPM for Heating & Cooling Technicians - IML. 3rd ed. 32p. (C). 1998. teacher ed. 12.00 (*0-8273-7949-8*) Delmar.

— Probability & Statistics. 4th ed. 1995. 41.50 (*0-534-24266-9*) Thomson Learn.

— The Science of Probability & Statistics for Engineering. 5th ed. LC 99-46944. (Statistics Ser.). 775p. 1999. pap. text 83.95 (*0-534-37281-3*) PWS Pubs.

— Statistics. Date not set. pap. text, teacher ed. write for info. (*0-314-97130-0*) West Pub.

— Statistics: Exploration & Analysis. 3rd ed. (Statistics Ser.). 1997. pap., student ed. 19.95 (*0-534-22899-2*) Wadsworth Pub.

Devore & Peck. Statistics: Exploration & Analysis. 2nd ed. (Statistics Ser.). 1993. pap., student ed. 16.50 (*0-534-19616-0*) Wadsworth Pub.

— Statistics: The Exploration & Analysis of Data. 3rd ed. 1996. mass mkt. 44.25 (*0-534-22898-4*) Brooks-Cole.

***Devore, et al.** Graphing Calculator Versus Statistics: Exploration & Analysis of Data. (Statistics Ser.). 2000. pap. 53.00 (*0-534-37092-6*) Brooks-Cole.

Devore, Cynthia D. Breakfast for Dinner. LC 93-13066. (Children of Courage Ser.). 32p. (J). (gr. 5 up). 1993. lib. bdg. 14.98 (*1-56239-245-X*) ABDO Pub Co.

— Do Rainbows Last Forever? LC 93-7720. (Children of Courage Ser.). (YA). (gr. 5 up). 1993. lib. bdg. 14.98 (*1-56239-248-4*) ABDO Pub Co.

— Kids & Drugs. LC 94-17687. (Kids in Crisis Ser.). (Illus.). 48p. (J). (gr. 4 up). 1994. lib. bdg. 21.27 (*1-56239-322-7*, ABDO & Dghtrs) ABDO Pub Co.

— Kids & Gangs. LC 94-16821. (Kids in Crisis Ser.). (Illus.). 48p. (J). (gr. 4 up). 1994. lib. bdg. 21.27 (*1-56239-323-5*, ABDO & Dghtrs) ABDO Pub Co.

— Kids & Racism. LC 95-2214. (Kids in Crisis Ser.). (J). (gr. 4-6). 1995. lib. bdg. 15.98 (*1-56239-443-6*) ABDO Pub Co.

— Kids in Crisis: Kids & Media Influence. LC 94-25562. (Kids in Crisis Ser.). 40p. (J). (gr. 4 up). 1994. 15.98 (*1-56239-324-3*) ABDO Pub Co.

— A Week Past Forever. LC 93-7722. (Children of Courage Ser.). (J). 1993. lib. bdg. 14.98 (*1-56239-246-8*) ABDO Pub Co.

— The Wind Before It Blows. LC 93-7723. (Children of Courage Ser.). (Illus.). (J). 1993. lib. bdg. 14.98 (*1-56239-247-6*) ABDO Pub Co.

DeVore, Dixon, II. Mortimer: The Very Rich Mouse. 2nd rev. ed. (Illus.). 32p. (J). (gr. k-5). 1987. pap. Price not set. incl. audio (*0-9614998-1-8*, CP3109-A) Cricket Power.

DeVore, Horton & DeVore, Lawson. Creativity Design & Technology. 79p. (J). 1990. pap. 13.50 (*0-87192-217-7*) Thomson Learn.

***DeVore, Howard.** The Hugo, Nebula & World Fantasy Awards. vi, 332p. 1998. pap. 14.00 (*0-911682-32-5*) Advent.

DeVore, Irven, jt. ed. see Lee, Richard B.

Devore, Jay & Peck, Roxy L. Introductory Statistics. 2nd ed. Marshall, ed. LC 93-33055. 550p. (C). 1994. pap. 60.25 (*0-314-02766-1*) West Pub.

— Statistics: The Exploration & Analysis of Data. 3rd ed. LC 96-28744. (Statistics Ser.). (C). 1996. pap. 90.95 (*0-534-22896-8*) Wadsworth Pub.

Devore, Jay L. Probability & Statistics F/eng & The Sci. 2nd ed. LC 86-20731. (Statistics). 672p. (C). 1987. pap. 48.00 (*0-534-06828-6*) Brooks-Cole.

— Probability & Statistics F/eng & The Sci. 3rd ed. (Statistics). 704p. (C). 1990. pap. 59.25 (*0-534-14352-0*) Wadsworth Pub.

— Probability & Statistics for Engineering & Science. (Statistics). 1982. 7.50 (*0-534-01985-4*) Brooks-Cole.

***Devore, Jay L.** Probability & Statistics for Engineering & Science. 5th ed. 2000. pap., student ed. 20.00 (*0-534-37283-X*) Brooks-Cole.

Devore, Jay L. Probability & Statistics for Engineering & the Physical Sciences. LC 81-21744. (Statistics Ser.). (Illus.). 700p. (C). 1982. pap. 36.25 (*0-8185-0514-1*) Brooks-Cole.

— Probability & Statistics for Engineering & the Sciences. 4th ed. 743p. 1994. text, mass mkt. 82.95 incl. 3.5 hd (*0-534-24264-2*) Wadsworth Pub.

— Probability & Statistics for Engineers & Scientists. 4th ed. (Statistics Ser.). 1995. pap. 22.95 (*0-534-24265-0*) Wadsworth Pub.

DeVore, Lawson, jt. auth. see DeVore, Horton.

DeVore, Nicholas, III. Village Japan: The Four Seasons of Shimukappu. LC 93-29378. (Illus.). 160p. 1994. 29.95 (*0-8348-0312-7*) Weatherhill.

Devore, Paul. Exploring Construction. 1990. teacher ed. 13.95 (*0-87192-227-4*) Delmar.

DeVore, Paul, ed. see Pytlik, Edward C., et al.

Devore, Peck. Statistics: The Exploration & Analysis of Data. 4th ed. (Statistics Ser.). 2000. pap. text. write for info. (*0-534-35867-5*) Brooks-Cole.

DeVore, R. William, et al, eds. Proceedings - Fifth International Carnahan Conference on Security Technology: Electronic Crime Countermeasures. (Illus.). 255p. (Orig.). 1986. pap. 10.00 (*0-89779-066-9*, UKY BU141) OES Pubns.

DeVore, R. William & Graves, Donald H. Symposium on Mining, Hydrology, Sedimentology & Reclamation: Proceedings, 1986. LC 83-60966. (Illus.). 283p. (Orig.). 1986. pap. 10.00 (*0-89779-067-7*, UKY BU142) OES Pubns.

— Symposium on Surface Mining, Hydrology, Sedimentology & Reclamation, 1985: Proceedings. LC 83-60966. (Illus.). 439p. (Orig.). 1985. pap. 10.00 (*0-89779-064-2*, UKY BU139) OES Pubns.

DeVore, R. William & Graves, Donald H., eds. Proceedings, Symposium on Surface Mining, Hydrology, Sedimentology, & Reclamation, 1982. LC 82-51182. (Illus.). 728p. (Orig.). 1982. pap. 10.00 (*0-89779-054-5*, UKY BU129) OES Pubns.

— Symposium on Surface Mining, Hydrology, Sedimentology & Reclamation, 1984: Proceedings. LC 83-60966. (Illus.). 492p. (Orig.). 1984. pap. 10.00 (*0-89779-062-6*, UKY BU136) OES Pubns.

DeVore, R. William & Jackson, J. S., eds. Proceedings, 1984 Carnahan Conference on Security Technology. LC 82-64615. (Illus.). 218p. 1984. pap. 10.00 (*0-89779-059-6*, UKY BU134) OES Pubns.

DeVore, Ronald A. & Lorentz, George G. Constructive Approximation. (Grundlehren der Mathematischen Wissenschaften Ser.: Vol. 303). (Illus.). vii, 534p. 1993. write for info. (*3-540-50627-6*) Spr-Verlag.

— Constructive Approximation: Polynomials & Splines Approximation. LC 93-18420. (Grundlehren der Mathematischen Wissenschaften Ser.: Vol. 303). 1993. 142.95 (*0-387-50627-6*) Spr-Verlag.

DeVore, Ronald A. & Sharpley, Robert C. Maximal Functions Measuring Smoothness. LC 83-21494. (Memoirs Ser.: No. 47/293). 116p. 1984. pap. 18.00 (*0-8218-2293-4*, MEMO/47/293) Am Math.

DeVore, Sharyl, ed. see Hochgesang, Jim.

DeVore, Sheryl. Northern Flights: Tracking the Birds & Birders of Michigan's Upper Peninsula. LC 99-29655. (Illus.). 166p. 1999. pap. 12.00 (*0-87842-400-8*) Mountain Pr.

— Songs Running Deep: Notes from a Birder's Paradise. LC 97-64. (Illus.). 176p. 1997. 21.95 (*1-883755-12-3*, 5123) Lost Riv Pr.

DeVore, Sheryl, ed. see Hochgesang, Jim.

DeVore, Silver. Alpharetta Homes & Gardens, 1938. LC 97-77271. 136p. 1997. pap. 12.00 (*0-9634253-3-1*) Chattahoochee.

— Garden Talk, 1930s. LC 96-84369. (Orig.). 1996. pap. 5.00 (*0-9634253-2-3*) Chattahoochee.

Devore, Steve & Lagoon, Steve. Blood, Medicine & the Jehovah's Witnesses: A Century of a Cult in Chaos. 1995. pap. 11.95 (*1-883858-56-9*) Witness CA.

***DeVore, Trane.** Series - Mnemonic. 59p. 1999. pap. 10.00 (*1-880713-17-9*, Pub. by AVEC Bks) SPD-Small Pr Dist.

DeVore Williams, Susan, jt. auth. see Brother Andrew.

Devore, Wynetta & Schlesinger, Elfriede G. Ethnic-Sensitive Social Work Practice. 5th ed. LC 98-6774. 332p. (C). 1998. pap. text 37.00 (*0-205-28165-6*) Allyn.

Devoret, M. H., jt. auth. see Grabert, H.

Devorin, Ruth, jt. auth. see Kidwell, Kelly F.

DeVorkin, D. H. Science with a Vengeance: The Military Origins of the Space Sciences in the American V-2 Era. (Illus.). 376p. 1992. 69.00 (*0-387-97770-8*) Spr-Verlag.

DeVorkin, David H. The American Astronomical Society's First Century. LC 98-37594. 10p. 1999. 45.95 (*1-56396-683-2*) Am Inst Physics.

***DeVorkin, David H.** Henry Norris Russell: Dean of American Astronomers. LC 99-59472. (Illus.). 528p. 2000. text 49.50 (*0-691-04918-1*, Pub. by Princeton U Pr) Cal Prin Full Svc.

DeVorkin, David H. Science with a Vengeance: How the Military Created the U. S. Space Sciences after World War II. LC 93-30683. (Illus.). 432p. 1995. 43.95 (*0-387-94137-1*) Spr-Verlag.

DeVorsey, Louis, Jr. Columbus & the Age of Explorers: First American Encounters. 260p. 1992. student ed. 39.00 (*1-56696-009-6*) Jackdaw.

DeVorsey, Louis, et al. Columbus & the Land of Ayllon: The Exploration & Settlement of the Southeast. (Illus.). 145p. (Orig.). 1992. pap. 8.50 (*0-9632876-0-5*) Lower Altamana.

DeVorsey, Louis, Jr., jt. ed. see Dallmeyer, Dorinda G.

DeVorss, Pat, jt. auth. see Smith, Beverly B.

Devos, Anthony. The Pollution Reader: Based on the National Conference on "Pollution & Our Environment" Pearson, Norman H. et al, eds. LC 68-31597. (Harvest House Environment Ser.). (Illus.). 264p. reprint ed. pap. 81.90 (*0-608-30096-9*, 202229300026) Bks Demand.

DeVos, Dick. The Book of Values. 1997. 23.95 (*0-614-19855-0*) NAL.

— Rediscovering American Values: The Foundations of Our Freedom for the 21st Century. 320p. 1998. pap. 13.95 (*0-452-27758-2*, Plume) Dutton Plume.

DeVos, George, jt. ed. see Romanucci-Ross, Lola.

Devos, Merilyn. Boston Bean Pot Cookery. 4th large type ed. Zarrilli, Vincent F., ed. 89p. 1996. pap. 11.95 (*1-891827-00-6*) Pot Shop.

— Custard Cup Cookery. Zarrilli, Vincent F., ed. 60p. 1997. pap. 11.95 (*1-891827-02-2*) Pot Shop.

— High on Pie. Zarrilli, Vincent F., ed. 146p. 1997. pap. 15.95 (*1-891827-01-4*) Pot Shop.

— Olde Boston Soup Bowl Cookery. Zarrilli, Vincent F., ed. 84p. 1998. pap. 11.95 (*1-891827-03-0*) Pot Shop.

DeVos, Rich. Compassionate Capitalism: People Helping People Help Themselves. 352p. 1994. pap. 12.95 (*0-452-27051-0*, Plume) Dutton Plume.

Devos, Richard M. & Conn, Charles P. Believe. 160p. 1985. pap. 5.50 (*0-425-07456-0*) Berkley Pub.

DeVos, Ton. Multinational Corporations in Democratic Host Countries: U. S. Multinationals & the Vredeling Proposal. 288p. 1989. text 82.95 (*1-85521-048-7*, Pub. by Dartmth Pub) Ashgate Pub Co.

Devos, Ton. U. S. Multinationals & Worker Participation in Management: The American Experience in the European Community. LC 80-23597. 229p. 1981. 55.00 (*0-89930-004-9*, DUM/, Quorum Bks) Greenwood.

Devoss, David. Portrait of Thailand, 1. 1998. 17.98 (*1-57717-092-X*) Todtri Prods.

DeVoss, Vicki, jt. auth. see Pierson, Caryl K.

Devoto, Alejandra, tr. see Conable, Barbara & Conable, William.

DeVoto, Bernard. Mark Twain's America. LC 96-37754. (Illus.). xxiii, 351p. 1997. pap. 15.00 (*0-8032-6607-3*, Bison Books) U of Nebr Pr.

***Devoto, Bernard A.** Year of Decision 1846. (Illus.). 576p. 2000. pap. 15.95 (*0-312-26794-0*) St Martin.

Devoto, Daniel, ed. see De Berceo, Gonzalo.

Devoto, G. & Oli, G. C., eds. Dizionario della Lingua Italiano. (ITA.). 2712p. write for info. (*0-318-56661-3*, M-9196) Fr & Eur.

Devoto, Giacomo. The Languages of Italy. Katainen, V. Louise, tr. LC 78-3391. (History & Structure of Languages Ser.). 1978. lib. bdg. 30.00 (*0-226-14368-6*) U Ch Pr.

— Linguistics & Literary Criticism. Edgerton, M. F., Jr., tr. 1963. 20.00 (*0-913298-08-5*) S F Vanni.

DeVoto, James G., ed. Claudius Aelianus: Varia Historia. 1995. pap. 20.00 (*0-89005-548-3*) Ares.

— Philon & Heron: Artillery & Siegecraft in Antiquity. LC 96-209336. 1996. pap. 15.00 (*0-89005-561-0*) Ares.

Devoto, Pat Cunningham. My Last Days As Roy Rogers. LC 98-22788. 358p. 1999. 20.00 (*0-446-52388-7*, Pub. by Warner Bks) Little.

***Devoto, Pat Cunningham.** My Last Days As Roy Rogers. 368p. 2000. mass mkt. 12.95 (*0-446-67564-4*, Pub. by Warner Bks) Little.

Devoure, Cynthia D. Kids & Guns. LC 94-10003. (Kids in Crisis Ser.). (Illus.). 48p. (J). (gr. 4 up). 1994. lib. bdg. 21.27 (*1-56239-321-9*, ABDO & Dghtrs) ABDO Pub Co.

DeVours, Lanier. Trey-Beaux. Cowan, Linda, ed. (Illus.). 215p. (Orig.). 1990. pap. 4.95 (*0-9624545-0-8*) Lanier-DeVours.

Devoy, R. J., ed. Sea Surface Studies: A Global View. 650p. 1987. lib. bdg. 110.00 (*0-7099-0871-7*, Pub. by C Helm) Routldge.

DeVoy, Robert S., jt. auth. see Costonis, John J.

Devrais, Joanna, jt. auth. see Reno, Liz.

D

Devraj, Venkat S. & Balwada, Ravi. Oracle 24x7 Tips & Techniques. 1008p. 2000. pap. text 49.99 (*0-07-211999-3*) Osborne-McGraw.
Devreese, J. T., ed. Scientific Computing on Supercomputers 2. (Illus.). 260p. (C). 1990. text 114.00 (*0-306-43712-0*, Kluwer Plenum) Kluwer Academic.
Devreese, J. T. & Van Camp, P. E., eds. Scientific Computing on Supercomputers 3. (Illus.). 224p. (C). 1992. text 114.00 (*0-306-44118-7*, Kluwer Plenum) Kluwer Academic.
— Scientific Computing with Supercomputers. (Illus.). 292p. (C). 1989. text 114.00 (*0-306-43217-X*, Kluwer Plenum) Kluwer Academic.
Devreese, Josef T. & Van Camp, Piet, eds. Electronic Structure, Dynamics & Quantum Structural Properties of Condensed Matter. LC 84-26483. (NATO ASI Series B, Physics: Vol. 121). 604p. 1985. 135.00 (*0-306-41912-2*, Plenum Trade) Perseus Pubng.
Devreese, Jozef T. & Van Camp, P. E., eds. Supercomputers in Theoretical & Experimental Science. 238p. 1985. 89.50 (*0-306-42107-0*, Plenum Trade) Perseus Pubng.
Devresse, J. T. & Peeters, F. M., eds. The Physics of the 2-Dimensional Electron Gas. LC 87-13983. (NATO ASI Series B, Physics: Vol. 157). (Illus.). 452p. 1987. 105.00 (*0-306-42605-6*, Plenum Trade) Perseus Pubng.
Devriendt, Betty, et al, eds. Complex Structures: A Functionalist Perspective, Vol. 17. LC 95-24643. (Functional Grammer Ser.: No. 17). xxiv, 386p. (C). 1995. lib. bdg. 136.95 (*3-11-014385-2*) Mouton.
Devriendt, K. Molecular Characterization of the Human Pregancy Zone Protein. No. 52. 106p. (Orig.). 1992. pap. 32.00 (*90-6186-496-8*, Pub. by Leuven Univ) Coronet Bks.
Devries. Color Atlas of Brain Disorders in the Newborn. (Illus.). (C). (gr. 13). 1990. 105.00 (*0-8151-2964-5*, 20267) Mosby Inc.
DeVries. He's All the Hero I Need. 1996. pap. 6.95 (*0-7601-0641-X*) Brentwood Music.
Devries. My Tribute: The Songs of Andrae Crouch. 1995. pap. 6.95 (*0-7601-0163-9*) Brentwood Music.
DeVries, A. & Kochva, E., eds. Toxins of Animal & Plant Origin, 3 vols., Vol. 3. LC 71-130967. (Illus.). 1088p. 1973. text 849.00 (*0-677-14710-4*) Gordon & Breach.
Devries, Anik. Dictionnaire des Editeurs de Musique Francais Vol. 1: Origines a 1820. (FRE.). 770p. 1979. 495.00 (*0-7859-8045-8*, 2826604600) Fr & Eur.
— Dictionnaire des Editeurs de Musique Francais Vol. 2: 1820-1914. (FRE.). 512p. 1988. 550.00 (*0-7859-8046-6*, 2826604619) Fr & Eur.
DeVries, Ann. Microsoft PowerPoint 97 for Windows Quickstart. LC 97-160194. 1996. pap. text 29.99 incl. cd-rom (*1-56276-472-1*, Ziff-Davis Pr) Que.
DeVries, Arlene R., jt. auth. see Webb, James T.
***DeVries, Catherine.** My Very First Devotional Bible. (Illus.). (J). 2000. 14.99 (*0-310-93251-3*) Zondervan.
DeVries, David L. Executive Selection: A Look at What We Know & What We Need to Know. LC 93-73328. (Special Reports: No. 321G). 57p. (Orig.). 1993. pap. text 20.00 (*0-912879-74-2*) Ctr Creat Leader.
DeVries, David L., et al. Teams-Games-Tournament: The Team Learning Approach. Langdon, Danny G., ed. LC 79-26378. (Instructional Design Library). 104p. 1980. 27.95 (*0-87778-157-5*) Educ Tech Pubns.
DeVries, David L., jt. auth. see Rosen, Marvin J.
DeVries, Dawn. Jesus Christ in the Preaching of Calvin & Schleiermacher. (Columbia Series in Reformed Theology). 120p. 1996. 16.00 (*0-664-22067-3*) Westminster John Knox.
***DeVries, Debra.** Encyclopedic Dictionary of Style & Usage. (Illus.). (J). 1999. 12.34 (*0-606-18008-7*) Turtleback.
DeVries, Denise. Wheat. (Premier Ser.: Vol. 9). (Illus.). 25p. 1997. pap. 5.00 (*0-9654421-8-7*) Mica Press.
***DeVries, Dirk.** Changing the World: 32 Powerful Sessions on Real-Life for Teens. (Attitude Ser.: Vol. 3). 136p. (J). (gr. 8-13). 2000. pap. 14.95 (*1-889108-44-8*) Liv Good News.
DeVries, Dirk. Quick-Takes for Teens, Family Issues Vol. 1: Easy, On-the-Spot Resources for Youth Ministry, 4 vols. Mulhern, Kathy, ed. (Illus.). 48p. (Orig.). 1996. pap. 5.95 (*1-889108-05-7*) Liv Good News.
— Quick-Takes for Teens, Relationship Issues Vol. 4: Easy, On-the-Spot Resources for Youth Ministry, 4 vols. Mulhern, Kathy, ed. (Illus.). 48p. (Orig.). 1996. pap. 5.95 (*1-889108-08-1*) Liv Good News.
— Quick-Takes for Teens, Tough Emotions Vol. 2: Easy, On-the-Spot Resources for Youth Ministry, 4 vols. Mulhern, Kathy, ed. 48p. 1996. pap. 5.95 (*1-889108-06-5*) Liv Good News.
— Quick-Takes for Teens, World Problems Vol. 3: Easy, On-the-Spot Resources for Youth Ministry, 4 vols. Mulhern, Kathy, ed. (Illus.). 48p. (Orig.). 1996. pap. 5.95 (*1-889108-07-3*) Liv Good News.
***DeVries, Dirk.** Wholeness & Holiness: 32 Powerful Sessions on Real-Life Issues for Teens. (Attitude Ser.: Vol. 1). 136p. (J). (gr. 8-13). 2000. pap. 14.95 (*1-889108-42-1*) Liv Good News.
DeVries, Dirk & Gluckstern, Dina. Back in the Days of Jesus Series: Gospel Homilies for Children, 4 vols. Incl. Back in the Days of Jesus: John: Gospel Homilies for Children. (Illus.). 104p. (J). (ps-3). 1996. pap. 4.95 (*1-889108-01-4*); Back in the Days of Jesus: Luke: Gospel Homilies for Children. (Illus.). 103p. (J). (ps-3). 1996. pap. 4.95 (*1-889108-00-6*); Back in the Days of Jesus: Matthew: Gospel Homilies for Children. (Illus.). 102p. (J). (ps-3). 1996. pap. 4.95 (*0-8192-8010-0*); Vol. 2. Back in the Days of Jesus: Mark: Gospel Homilies for Children. (Illus.). 88p. (J). (ps-3). 1996. pap. 4.95 (*0-8192-8011-9*); 55.95 (*1-889108-04-9*) Liv Good News.
DeVries, Dirk, ed. see Morris, Thomas H. & Coffey, Kathy.
DeVries, Dirk, ed. see Piercy, Robert W. & Bross, Jean E.
DeVries, Dirk, ed. see Pike, Maggie, et al.
DeVries, Dirk, ed. see Taylor, Beverly.
DeVries, Douglas. Fevering for Gold: A Historical Novel about the 1900 Rush to Nome, Alaska. LC 99-64097. 192p. (YA). (gr. 7). 1999. pap. 12.00 (*1-877721-05-0*, Pub. by Jade Ram Pub) Publ Consult.
— Fevering for Gold: A Historical Novel about the 1900 Rush to Nome, Alaska. LC 99-64097. 192p. (YA). (gr. 7 up). 1999. 17.00 (*1-877721-06-9*, Pub. by Jade Ram Pub) Publ Consult.
— Gold Rush Runaway: A Historical Novel of Alaska Exploration & Adventure. LC 97-69457. 192p. (J). 1997. 17.00 (*1-877721-04-2*) Jade Ram Pub.
— Gold Rush Runaway: A Historical Novel of Alaska Exploration & Adventure. LC 97-69457. 192p. (J). 1997. pap. 10.00 (*1-877721-03-4*) Publ Consult.
— Muscles, Bull Moose from Alaska. LC 95-76041. (Illus.). 88p. (Orig.). (J). (gr. k-5). 1995. pap. text 12.00 (*1-877721-02-6*) Jade Ram Pub.
— Muscles, the Moose Calf. LC 89-84651. (Illus.). 32p. (Orig.). (J). (ps-3). 1989. pap. text 10.00 (*1-877721-00-X*) Jade Ram Pub.
— Muscles Visits Anchorage. LC 90-61154. (Illus.). 32p. (Orig.). (J). (ps-3). 1990. pap. text 10.00 (*1-877721-01-8*) Jade Ram Pub.
***DeVries, Duane.** General Studies of Charles Dickens & His Writings & Collected Editions of His Works: An Annotated Bibliography. LC 99-86395. (Studies in the Nineteenth Century). 2000. write for info. (*0-404-64452-X*) AMS Pr.
DeVries, Hent & Weber, Samuel. Violence, Identity & Self-Determination. LC 97-13450. 400p. 1997. 55.00 (*0-8047-2995-6*); pap. 18.95 (*0-8047-2996-4*) Stanford U Pr.
Devries, Herbert A. & Housh, Terry J. Physiology of Exercise for Physical Education, Athletics & Exercise Science. 5th ed. 112p. (C). 1995. text, student ed. 10.00 (*0-697-29080-8*) Brown & Benchmark.
DeVries, Herbert A. & Housh, Terry J. Physiology of Exercise for Physical Education, Athletics & Exercise Science. 5th ed. 640p. (C). 1993. text. write for info. (*0-697-10097-9*) Brown & Benchmark.
Devries, Herbert A., et al. Physiology of Exercise for Physical Education, Athletics & Excerise Science. (C). 1995. text, student ed. write for info. (*0-697-28495-6*) Brown & Benchmark.
Devries, Jeffrey. Unto Us a Child: Meditations for Advent. LC 96-24444. 111p. (Orig.). 1996. pap. 7.95 (*1-56212-191-X*, 1701-0670) CRC Pubns.
DeVries, Johannes J. & Woled, Jeff, eds. "Ground Water & Future Supply" Proceedings of the 21st Biennial Ground Water Conference. (Illus.). 1998. pap. text. write for info. (*1-887192-09-3*) U Cal CWWR.
— Making the Connections: Proceedings of the 20th Biennial Conference on Ground Water. 197p. 1996. pap. text. write for info. (*1-887192-03-4*) U Cal CWWR.
DeVries, John. Destroyed Foundations. LC 96-96552. 200p. (Orig.). 1996. pap. 10.90 (*0-9652944-0-4*) Five-Fold Fndtn.
DeVries, John A. & Phillips, Richard D. VIP's Directory of Giant Scale Plans, Vol. 1. (Illus.). 120p. 1987. pap. 11.95 (*0-934575-02-9*) Vip Pubs.
— VIP's Directory of Giant Scale Plans, Vol. 2. (Illus.). 120p. 1987. pap. 11.95 (*0-934575-06-1*) Vip Pubs.
— VIP's Directory of Giant Scale Plans, Vol. 3. (Illus.). 120p. 1987. pap. 11.95 (*0-934575-09-6*) Vip Pubs.
DeVries, Julian, ed. see Finnerty, Margaret & Blanc, Tara.
DeVries, Keith, ed. see Dyson, R. H., et al.
DeVries, Kelly. Infantry Warfare in the Early Fourteenth-Century: Discipline, Tactics, & Technology. (Warfare in History Ser.: Vol. 2). (Illus.). 224p. 1999. pap. 29.95 (*0-85115-571-5*, Boydell Pr) Boydell & Brewer.
***DeVries, Kelly.** Joan of Arc: A Military Leader. (Illus.). 224p. 2000. 27.95 (*0-7509-1805-5*, Pub. by Sutton Pub Ltd) Bks Intl VA.
DeVries, Kelly. Medieval Military Technology. 240p. 1991. pap. 22.95 (*0-921149-74-3*) Broadview Pr.
***DeVries, Kelly.** Military Campaigns of the 100 Years War. 2000. 39.95 (*0-7509-1804-7*, Pub. by Sutton Publng) Intl Pubs Mktg.
— The Norwegian Invasion of England in 1066. LC 99-37405. (Warfare in History Ser.). 352p. 1999. 60.00 (*0-85115-763-7*) Boydell & Brewer.
Devries, Kets, et al. Life & Death in the Executive Fast Lane: Essays on Irrational Organizations & Their Leaders. LC 95-4952. (Management Ser.). 274p. 1995. 29.95 (*0-7879-0112-1*) Jossey-Bass.
DeVries, LaMoine F. Cities of the Biblical World: An Introduction to the Archaeology, Geography, & History of Biblical Sites. LC 97-2235. 398p. 1997. 29.95 (*1-56563-145-5*) Hendrickson MA.
DeVries, Linda. Spiritual Nightlights: Meditations for the Middle of the Night. LC 96-39578. 144p. 1997. 14.99 (*0-87788-743-8*, H Shaw Pubs) Waterbrook Pr.
Devries, Linda K. Insomnia: Don't Lose Sleep Over It...Find the Help You Need. LC 97-50626. 168p. 1998. pap. text 11.99 (*0-87788-184-7*, H Shaw Pubs) Waterbrook Pr.
DeVries, Mark. Family-Based Youth Ministry: Reaching the Been-There, Done-That Generation. LC 94-28335. 240p. (Orig.). 1994. pap. 11.99 (*0-8308-1396-9*, 1396) InterVarsity.
Devries, Mark. True Love Waits. LC 97-8903. (YA). 1997. pap. 5.99 (*0-8054-6352-6*) Broadman.
Devries, Mark & Freeman, Kirk. John Calvin's Institutes of the Christian Religion. LC 98-21466. (Shepherd's Notes Ser.). 1999. 5.95 (*0-8054-9200-3*) Broadman.
— St. Augustine's Confessions. LC 98-21267. (Shepherd's Notes Ser.). 1999. 5.95 (*0-8054-9199-6*) Broadman.
DeVries, Marten, et al. The Use & Abuse of Medicine. LC 82-7563. 296p. 1982. 75.00 (*0-275-91362-7*, C1362, Praeger Pubs) Greenwood.
DeVries, Mary. Professional Secretary's Encyclopedic Dictionary. 5th ed. LC 94-28490. 608p. 1994. text 29.95 (*0-13-030453-0*) P-H.
DeVries, Mary A. The Business Writer's Book of Lists. 384p. 1998. pap. 14.00 (*0-425-16312-1*) Berkley Pub.
— The Encyclopedic Dictionary of Business Terms. LC 97-133597. 1997. mass mkt. 7.99 (*0-425-15612-5*) Berkley Pub.
— Encyclopedic Dictionary of Style & Usage. 1999. mass mkt. 6.99 (*0-425-16942-1*) Berkley Pub.
Devries, Mary A. How to Run a Meeting: A Step-by-Step Guide Based upon the New Robert's Rules of Order. 1999. pap. 2.99 (*0-451-17877-7*, Sig) NAL.
DeVries, Mary A. Internationally Yours: Writing & Communicating Successfully in Today's Global Marketplace. 352p. 1999. reprint ed. pap. text 11.00 (*0-7881-6172-5*) DIANE Pub.
***DeVries, Mary A.** New American Handbook of Letter Writing: Plus Other Forms of Correspondence. 2nd ed. 416p. 2000. mass mkt. 6.99 (*0-451-19931-6*) NAL.
Devries, Mary A. New Roberts Rules of Order: The Essential Reference. 2nd ed. 272p. 1998. mass mkt. 6.99 (*0-451-19517-5*, Sig) NAL.
DeVries, Mary A. Secretary's Standard Reference Manual & Guide. (Illus.). 1986. 19.95 (*0-13-797712-3*, Parker Publishing Co) P-H.
DeVries, Mary A., jt. auth. see Blake.
Devries, P. J. The Butterflies of Costa Rica & Their Natural History: Riodinidae, Vol. 2. 368p. 1997. text 90.00 (*0-691-02890-7*, Pub. by Princeton U Pr) Cal Prin Full Svc.
DeVries, Paul L. A First Course in Computational Physics. LC 93-15694. 440p. 1993. 78.95 incl. disk (*0-471-54869-3*) Wiley.
DeVries, Philip J. The Butterflies of Costa Rica & Other Natural History: Papilionidae, Pieridae, Nymphalidae. LC 85-28340. (Illus.). 390p. 1986. pap. 35.00 (*0-691-02403-0*, Pub. by Princeton U Pr); text 95.00 (*0-691-08420-3*, Pub. by Princeton U Pr) Cal Prin Full Svc.
Devries, Philip J. Riodinidae, Vol. 2. (Butterflies of Costa Rica Ser.). 368p. 1997. pap. text 29.95 (*0-691-02889-3*, Pub. by Princeton U Pr) Cal Prin Full Svc.
DeVries, Rachel G. How to Sing to a Dago. LC 94-74386. (Essential Poets Ser.: No. 69). 70p. 1996. pap. 10.00 (*1-55071-028-1*) Guernica Editions.
— Tender Warriors: A Novel. LC 86-4690. 192p. (Orig.). 1986. pap. 8.95 (*0-932379-14-1*); lib. bdg. 18.95 (*0-932379-15-X*) Firebrand Bks.
Devries, Raymond & Subedi, Janardan. Bioethics & Society: Constructing the Ethical Enterprise. LC 97-18359. 320p. (C). 1998. 33.40 (*0-13-531252-3*) P-H.
DeVries, Raymond G. Making Midwives Legal: Childbirth, Medicine, & the Law. LC 96-6312. (Women & Health Ser.). Orig. Title: Regulating Birth. 232p. 1996. reprint ed. pap. text 19.95 (*0-8142-0703-0*) Ohio St U Pr.
DeVries, Rheta & Kohlberg, Lawrence. Constructivist Early Education: Overview & Comparison with Other Programs. LC 90-60618. 423p. 1987. pap. text 10.00 (*0-935989-33-1*, NAEYC#235) Natl Assn Child Ed.
DeVries, Rheta & Zan, Betty. Moral Classrooms, Moral Children: Creating a Constructivist Atmosphere in Early Education. LC 93-44317. (Early Childhood Education Ser.). 320p. (C). 1994. text 48.00 (*0-8077-3342-3*); pap. text 21.95 (*0-8077-3341-5*) Tchrs Coll.
DeVries, Rheta, jt. auth. see Kamii, Constance.
DeVries, Simon J. Bible & Theology in the Netherlands. 2nd ed. (American University Studies: Theology & Religion: Ser. VII, Vol. 22). XI, 171p. (C). 1989. text 31.95 (*0-8204-1052-7*) P Lang Pubng.
— I Kings. (Biblical Commentary Ser.: Vol. 12). 29.99 (*0-8499-0211-8*) Word Pub.
DeVries, Steve. A & P Technician Oral & Practical Test Guide. LC 93-5671. (Illus.). 113p. 1993. pap. text 13.95 (*0-89100-428-9*, JS-332806) Jeppesen Sanderson.
DeVries, Thomas D. Discovering Our Gifts. 1992. pap. 2.50 (*0-8091-9328-0*) Paulist Pr.
DeVries, W. R. Analysis of Material Removal Processes. Ling, Frederick F., ed. (Texts in Mechanical Engineering Ser.). (Illus.). xvii, 254p. 1991. 69.95 (*0-387-97728-7*) Spr-Verlag.
DeVries, W. R., ed. see American Society of Mechanical Engineers Staff.
DeVries, Walter, jt. auth. see Bass, Jack.
DeVries, Warren R., jt. auth. see Ulsoy, A. Galip.
DeVries, Willem A. Hegel's Theory of Mental Activity. LC 88-47723. 248p. 1988. 37.50 (*0-8014-2133-C*) Cornell U Pr.
***DeVries, Willem A., et al.** Knowledge, Mind & the Given: Reading Wilfrid Sellars's Empiricism & the Philosophy of Mind, Including the Complete Text of Sellars' Essay. LC 00-32029. 2000. write for info. (*0-87220-550-9*) Hackett Pub.
DeVriese, Stephanie, jt. auth. see Christophe, Armand B.
Devroey, Jean-Pierre. Etudes Sur le Grand Domaine Carolingien. (Collected Studies: Vol. CS391). 336p. 1993. 117.95 (*0-86078-345-6*, Pub. by Variorum) Ashgate Pub Co.
Devroye, L. Non-Uniform Random Variate Generation. 865p. 1986. 107.95 (*0-387-96305-7*) Spr-Verlag.
Devroye, Luc. A Course in Density Estimation. (Progress in Probability & Statistics Ser.: No. 14). 208p. 1987. 45.00 (*0-8176-3365-0*) Birkhauser.
— Lecture Notes on Bucket Algorithms. (Progress in Computer Science Ser.: Vol. 6). 1986. 48.50 (*0-8176-3328-6*) Birkhauser.
Devroye, Luc, et al. Probabilistic Theory of Pattern Recognition. LC 95-44633. (Illus.). 672p. 1997. 69.95 (*0-387-94618-7*) Spr-Verlag.
Devry, jt. auth. see Wright.
***Devrye, Catherine.** Good Service Is Good Business. 1999. pap. 19.95 (*0-13-012953-4*) Prntice Hall Bks.
Devsetty, Bala N., ed. Pesticide Formulations & Application System (STP 1146), Vol. 12. 381p. 1993. 60.00 (*0-8031-1439-7*, STP1146) ASTM.
Devy, Elie. Dictionary of Physics: Dictionnaire de Physique. (ENG & FRE.). 904p. 1988. 195.00 (*0-8288-2234-4*, F65440) Fr & Eur.
Devy, G. N. "Of Many Heroes" An Indian Essay in Literary Historiography LC 98-905080. 213 p. 1998. write for info. (*81-250-1309-1*) Orient Longman Ltd.
Devyatykh, G. G. & Burkhanov, G. S. High-Purity Refractory & Rare Metals. 180p. (C). 1995. pap. 89.00 (*1-898326-05-3*, Pub. by CISP) Balogh.
Devyr, Ainge, jt. auth. see Davenport, Allen.
DeVyver, Frank T., jt. ed. see McKinney, John C.
Dew, Anthony. The Rocking-Horse Maker: Nine Easy-to-Follow Projects. (Illus.). 160p. 1997. pap. 19.95 (*0-7153-0554-9*) Sterling.
Dew, Charles B. Bond of Iron: Master & Slave at Buffalo Forge. (Illus.). 448p. 1995. pap. 14.00 (*0-393-31359-X*, Norton Paperbks) Norton.
Dew, Charles B., et al. Slavery in Ante-bellum Southern Industries. LC 91-33943. (Black Studies Research Sources). 1991. write for info. (*1-55655-282-3*) U Pubns Amer.
Dew, Edward. Politics in the Altiplano: The Dynamics of Change in Rural Peru. LC 77-79542. (University of Texas, Institute of Latin American Studies, Latin American Monographs: No. 15). 234p. reprint ed. pap. 72.60 (*0-608-16492-5*, 202732900055) Bks Demand.
Dew, Edward M. The Difficult Flowering of Surinam: Ethnicity & Politics in a Plural Society. LC 78-12295. x, 234p. 1978. write for info. (*90-247-2057-5*) M Nijhoff.
— The Trouble in Surinam, 1975-1993. LC 94-11301. 264p. 1994. 59.95 (*0-275-94834-X*, Praeger Pubs) Greenwood.
***Dew, Greg.** On the Trip & Around the Bend. Burns, Haggard, ed. 212p. 1999. pap. write for info. (*0-7392-0393-2*, PO3618) Morris Pubng.
Dew, Gregory. The Barefoot Fisherman - Guide to the Emerald Coast: From Gulf Shores, Alabama, to Apalachicola, Florida. LC 99-17166. (Illus.). 180p. 1998. pap. 10.95 (*1-57587-093-2*) Crane Hill AL.
Dew-Hughes, D. Applied Superconductivity 1995: Proceedings of the Second European Conference on Applied... LC 95-48886. (Conference Ser.: 148). 1750p. 1995. 651.00 (*0-7503-0348-4*) IOP Pub.
Dew-Hughes, D., ed. International Cryogenic Engineering Conference. 895p. 1998. 350.00 (*0-7503-0597-5*) IOP Pub.
Dew, James E., jt. auth. see Ling, Vivian.
Dew, John R. Empowerment & Democracy in the Workplace: Applying Adult Education Theory & Practice for Cultivating Empowerment. LC 96-17926. 208p. 1997. 57.95 (*1-56720-094-X*, Quorum Bks) Greenwood.
— Quality-Centered Strategic Planning: A Step-by-Step Guide. LC 97-505. 222p. 1997. 42.50 (*0-527-76308-X*) Productivity Inc.
Dew, John Robert. Managing in a Team Environment. LC 98-6018. 176p. 1998. 55.00 (*1-56720-228-4*, Quorum Bks) Greenwood.
Dew, Kevin, jt. ed. see Davis, Peter.
Dew, Lee A. Kentucky Home Place. LC 98-49552. (New Books for New Readers). (Illus.). 80p. (YA). (gr. 4 up). 1999. pap. 5.95 (*0-8131-0911-6*) U Pr of Ky.
Dew, Michelle L., ed. Rockhurst Review, 1990: A Fine Arts Journal, Vol. III. 72p. 1990. pap. 5.00 (*1-886761-02-7*) Rockhurst Col.
Dew, P. M., jt. ed. see Davy, J. R.
Dew, Peter M. & James, K. R. Introduction to Numerical Computation in Pascal. 304p. 1986. pap. 36.00 (*0-387-91216-9*) Spr-Verlag.
Dew, Richard A. Rachel's Cry: A Journey Through Grief. LC 96-60727. 73p. 1996. pap. 12.00 (*1-882194-19-5*) TN Valley Pub.
Dew, Robb Forman. Family Heart: A Memoir of When Our Son Came Out. 1994. 22.00 (*0-201-62450-8*) Addison-Wesley.
— The Family Heart: A Memoir of When Our Son Came out. 229p. 1995. pap. 11.00 (*0-345-39408-9*) Ballantine Pub Grp.
— A Southern Thanksgiving: Recipes & Musings for a Manageable Feast. LC 92-11561. (Illus.). 80p. 1992. 10.00 (*0-201-63215-2*) Addison-Wesley.
Dew, Sheri L. Go Forward with Faith: The Biography of Gordon B. Hinckley. LC 96-36014. xviii, 653p. 1996. 23.95 (*1-57345-165-7*) Deseret Bk.
Dew, Thomas R. Lectures on the Restrictive System. LC 68-55701. (Reprints of Economic Classics Ser.). viii, 195p. 1969. reprint ed. 35.00 (*0-678-00441-2*) Kelley.
Dew, Tina, et al. Bluebirds: Their Daily Lives & How to Attract & Raise Bluebirds. LC 86-70315. (Illus.). 224p. 1986. 14.95 (*0-912542-06-3*); pap. 10.95 (*0-685-13982-4*) Nature Bks Pubs.
DeWaal, Esther. The Way of Simplicity: The Cistercian Tradition. LC 98-18341. (Traditions of Christian Spirituality Ser.). 128p. 1998. pap. 14.00 (*1-57075-195-1*) Orbis Bks.
— Word & Spirit: The Spiritual Journey. (Word & Spirit Ser.: No. 15). 108p. 1993. pap. 8.00 (*1-879007-02-9*) St Bedes Pubns.
DeWaal, M. Medicines from the Bible. 1994. pap. 8.95 (*0-942272-37-4*) Original Pubns.
Dewaard, John. History of NASA: America's Voyage to the Stars. (J). 1984. 12.98 (*0-671-06983-7*) S&S Trade.
***Dewachter, Ilse.** Analysis of Amyloid Precursor Protein in Cells & Brain of Transgenic Mice as the Biochemical Correlat for their Phenotype. (Illus.). 164p. 1999. 49.50 (*90-5867-006-6*, Pub. by Leuven Univ) Coronet Bks.

D

DeWaele, M., et al. Self Management in Organizations: The Dynamics of Interaction. 236p. 1993. text 26.95 (*0-88937-079-6*) Hogrefe & Huber Pubs.

Dewald, Carolyn, ed. see Herodotus.

Dewald, Jonathan. Aristocratic Experience & the Origins of Modern Culture: France, 1570-1715. (C). 1993. 45.00 (*0-520-07837-3*, Pub. by U CA Pr) Cal Prin Full Svc.

— The European Nobility, 1400-1800. (New Approaches to European History Ser.: No. 9). (Illus.). 226p. (C). 1996. pap. text 16.95 (*0-521-42528-X*) Cambridge U Pr.

— The European Nobility, 1400-1800. (New Approaches to European History Ser.: No. 9). (Illus.). 226p. (C). 1996. text 54.95 (*0-521-41512-8*) Cambridge U Pr.

— The Formation of a Provincial Nobility: The Magistrates of the Parlement of Rouen, 1490-1610. LC 79-83986. (Illus.). 419p. reprint ed. pap. 129.90 (*0-8357-3846-9*, 203657900004) Bks Demand.

Dewald, Linus J. Prentice. History & Genealogy of the Prentice, Prentis & Prentiss Families in New England from 1631 to 1883 (Based on the 1883 Edition by C. J. F. Binney, Which Is Included) 551p. 1997. pap. 79.50 (*0-8328-9493-1*); lib. bdg. 89.50 (*0-8328-9492-3*) Higginson Bk Co.

Dewald, Linus J., Jr. Valentine Prentice, His Origins & the Descsendents of His Grandsons John, Jonathan, Stephan & Thomas, 2 vols. (Illus.). 620p. (Orig.). 1993. pap. 60.00 (*1-55613-696-X*) Heritage Bk.

Dewald, Louise. Arizona Highways Heritage Cookbook. Holden, Wesley & Dyer, Bob, eds. (Illus.). 176p. 1994. 13.95 (*0-916179-16-8*) Ariz Hwy.

— Chabela's Fiesta Memories & Recipes. (Illus.). 88p. (Orig.). 1995. pap. 15.95 (*1-885001-08-8*) Via Press.

DeWald, Louise. Outdoor Cooking: From Backyard to Backpack. 176p. 1991. 13.95 (*0-916179-32-X*) Ariz Hwy.

Dewald, Paul A. Learning Process in Psychoanalytic Supervision. 1987. 72.50 (*0-8236-2965-1*, BN#02965) Intl Univs Pr.

— The Psychoanalytic Process: A Case Illustration. LC 93-74370. 682p. 1994. pap. 50.00 (*1-56821-194-5*) Aronson.

— The Supportive & Active Psychotherapies: A Dynamic Approach. LC 93-74969. 354p. 1995. pap. 50.00 (*1-56821-221-6*) Aronson.

***DeWald, Sandi.** Gazing Forward, Glancing Back, Remembering Always: Memories Retold & Relived by the Community of Streeter, North Dakota. (Illus.). 100'p. 2000. pap. 20.00 (*1-891193-13-9*) ND State Univ.

DeWall, Carole S., et al. Electronic Prepress: Setting the Standards. (Illus.). 152p. (Orig.). 1997. pap. text. write for info. (*0-9659704-0-X*) Maple-Vail Bk.

DeWall, K. Motor-Operated Valve (MOV) Actuator Motor & Gearbox Testing. 52p. 1997. pap. 5.00 (*0-16-054688-5*) USGPO.

***DeWall, K. G.** Results of Pressure Locking & Thermal Binding Tests of Gate Valves. 71p. 1998. pap. 6.00 (*0-16-062923-3*) USGPO.

DeWall, Robb. Crazy Horse & Korczak: The Story of an Epic Mountain Carving. LC 82-72726. (Illus.). 154p. 1982. 15.95 (*0-318-18777-9*, AACR2); pap. 7.95 (*0-317-05568-2*) Crazy Horse.

— Korczak, Storyteller in Stone. LC 84-52404. (Illus.). 80p. 1984. pap. 3.25 (*0-318-18775-2*) Crazy Horse.

— The Saga of Sitting Bull's Bones: The Unusual Story Behind Sculptor Korczak Ziolkowski's Memorial to Chief Sitting Bull. LC 84-48122. (Illus.). 320p. 1984. 9.95 (*0-318-18779-5*) Crazy Horse.

DeWall, Skip, jt. auth. see Black, Charles A.

DeWalt, Billie R. Modernization in a Mexican Ejido: A Study in Economic Adaptation. LC 78-3412. (Cambridge Latin American Studies: Vol. 33). 319p. reprint ed. pap. 91.00 (*0-608-16885-8*, 2027247) Bks Demand.

DeWalt, Billie R., et al. End of Agrarian Reform in Mexico: Past Lessons, Future Prospects. (Transformation of Rural Mexico Ser.: No. 3). 76p. 1994. pap. 8.00 (*1-878367-21-8*, DP-03) UCSD Ctr US-Mex.

Dewalt, Bryan & National Museum of Science and Technology (Canada). Building a Digital Network: Data Communications & Digital Telephony, 1950-1990. LC 92-223319. (Transformation Ser.). 70 p. 1992. write for info. (*0-660-12018-6*) Natl Mus S&T.

DeWalt, G. Weston, jt. auth. see Boukreev, Anatoli.

Dewalt, Loretta. From the Heart. 50p. 1994. pap. text 8.95 (*0-9643594-0-5*) Aljen Pubng.

DeWalt, Suzanne. How to Start a Home-Based Interior Design Business. 2nd ed. LC 99-41694. (How to Start a Home-Based Business Ser.). 216p. 1999. pap. 17.95 (*0-7627-0513-2*) Globe Pequot.

DeWalt, Weston, jt. auth. see Boukreev, Anatoli.

Dewan, David M. Practical Obstetric Anesthesia. Hood, David D. & Day, Lesley, eds. 320p. 1996. text 58.00 (*0-7216-3658-6*, W B Saunders Co) Harcrt Hlth Sci Grp.

Dewan, Dick B. Education in the Darjeeling Hills. (C). 1991. 33.00 (*81-85182-60-4*, Pub. by Indus Pub) S Asia.

Dewan, Disha. My Color Is Skin Deep. LC 97-74758. (Illus.). 48p. (J). (ps-6). 1997. pap. 5.99 (*1-883477-18-2*) Lone Oak MN.

Dewan, John. The Scouting Notebook, 1998. 5th ed. Zminda, Don, ed. 720p. 1998. pap. 19.95 (*1-884064-47-7*) STATS.

— The Scouting Notebook, 1995. 1995. pap. 16.00 (*1-884064-12-4*) STATS.

— The Scouting Notebook 1997. 3rd ed. Zminda, Don, ed. 680p. 1997. pap. 18.95 (*1-884064-35-3*) STATS.

— Stats Baseball Scoreboard, 1995. 1995. pap. 15.00 (*1-884064-11-6*) STATS.

— Stats Basketball Scoreboard, 1994-95. 2nd ed. 307p. 1994. pap. 15.00 (*1-884064-06-X*) STATS.

Dewan, John & Zminda, Don. The Scouting Notebook, 1999. 10th ed. 709p. 1999. pap. 19.95 (*1-884064-59-0*) STATS.

— Stats, 1992 Baseball Scoreboard. (Illus.). 330p. (Orig.). (C). 1992. per. 12.95 (*0-9625581-4-1*) STATS.

Dewan, John, et al. The Scouting Notebook, 1994. (Illus.). 682p. (Orig.). 1994. pap. 16.00 (*0-06-273231-5*) STATS.

— STATS Baseball Scoreboard, 1993. (Illus.). 330p. (Orig.). 1993. pap. 12.95 (*0-06-273138-6*) STATS.

— Stats Baseball Scoreboard, 1991. (Illus.). 325p. (Orig.). 1991. pap. 12.95 (*0-9625581-2-5*) STATS.

— STATS Basketball Scoreboard, 1993-94. (Illus.). 279p. (Orig.). 1993. pap. 15.00 (*0-06-273035-5*) STATS.

Dewan, John, ed. see STATS, Inc. Staff.

Dewan, John, ed. see STATS, Inc. Staff & James, Bill.

Dewan, John G. & Spaulding, William B. The Organic Psychoses: A Guide to Diagnosis. LC RC0528.O7D49. (Illus.). 184p. reprint ed. pap. 57.10 (*0-608-30249-X*, 201418600096) Bks Demand.

Dewan, John T. Essentials of Modern Open-Hole Log-Interpretation. LC 83-4228. 374p. 1983. 84.95 (*0-87814-233-9*) PennWell Bks.

Dewan, M. L. People's Participation in Himalayan Ecosystem Development. (C). 1990. text 35.00 (*81-7022-298-2*, Pub. by Concept) S Asia.

***Dewan, Paddy & Mitchell, Michael E., eds.** Bladder Augmentation. (An Arnold Publication). 2000. text 120.00 (*0-340-75957-7*) E A.

Dewan, Shuby. India: Questions of Culture. LC 97-73233. 215p. 1997. pap. 16.85 (*0-9658946-0-6*) Amaron Pub.

***Dewan, Ted.** Crispin, the Pig Who Had It All. LC 00-24715. (Illus.). (J). 2000. 15.95 (*0-385-32540-1*) Doubleday.

Dewan, Ted. The Sorcerer's Apprentice. LC 97-12073. 32p. (J). (ps-3). 1998. reprint ed. 15.95 (*0-385-32537-1*, DD Bks Yng Read) BDD Bks Young Read.

— Three Billy Goats Gruff. 32p. (J). (ps-3). 1995. pap. 4.95 (*0-590-20515-3*) Scholastic Inc.

— Top Secret. 32p. (J). 1999. pap. 6.99 (*0-440-41616-7*) BDD Bks Young Read.

Dewan, Ted, jt. auth. see Parker, Steve.

Dewan, V. K. Cases & Materials on Indian Penal Code. (C). 1988. 110.00 (*0-685-25698-7*) St Mut.

— Law Relating to Terrorists. (C). 1990. 120.00 (*0-89771-183-1*) St Mut.

Dewan, Vijay K. Law Relating to Terrorists. 500p. (C). 1990. 120.00 (*0-7855-5240-5*, Pub. by Capital Law Hse) St Mut.

Dewanjee, Mrinal K. Radioiodination: Theory Practice & Biomedical Application. (Developments in Nuclear Medicine Ser.). 658p. (C). 1992. text 265.00 (*0-7923-1491-3*) Kluwer Academic.

Dewar. Computers from Beads to Bytes. 1991. pap. text. write for info. (*0-00-370281-2*) Addison-Wesley.

Dewar, jt. auth. see Baker.

Dewar, jt. auth. see Daniels.

Dewar, jt. auth. see Oxlade.

Dewar, Angela. The New Church Kneeler Book: A Step-by-Step Guide to Canvaswork Kneelers. 48p. 1997. pap. 11.95 (*0-85532-825-8*, 8258, Pub. by Srch Pr) A Schwartz & Co.

Dewar, Angela & Banbury, Gisela. How to Design & Make Banners for Sacred & Secular Festivals. (Illus.). 64p. 2000. pap. 20.00 (*0-85532-681-6*, Pub. by Srch Pr) Midpt Trade.

— How to Design & Make Church Kneelers. 32p. 1994. pap. 20.00 (*0-85532-594-1*, Pub. by Srch Pr) St Mut.

Dewar, Bob. Laughter Lines: Family Wit & Wisdom. 88p. (C). 1989. 25.00 (*0-903065-61-4*, Pub. by G Wright Pub) St Mut.

Dewar, D. Birds of the Indian Hills. 1986. 150.00 (*0-7855-6655-4*, Pub. by Intl Bk Distr) St Mut.

— The Transformist Illusion. 1996. pap. 25.95 (*0-614-21246-4*, 1253) Kazi Pubns.

Dewar, D., ed. Birds of the Indian Hills. 264p. (C). 1987. text 150.00 (*0-89771-594-2*, Pub. by Intl Bk Distr) St Mut.

Dewar, Donald L. Control Charts No. 1: Leader Manual & Instructional Guide. rev. ed. (Illus.). 43p. (Orig.). 1993. pap. 15.00 (*0-937670-20-0*) QCI Intl.

— Control Charts No. 2: Leader Manual & Instructional Guide. rev. ed. (Illus.). 43p. 1993. pap. 15.00 (*0-937670-21-9*) QCI Intl.

— The Employee Involvement Team: What You Should Know about It. (Illus.). 29p. 1993. pap. 2.95 (*0-937670-04-9*) QCI Intl.

— Employee Involvement Team Manual & Instructional Guide. 332p. 1992. pap. 25.95 (*0-937670-02-2*) QCI Intl.

— Employee Involvement Team Member Manual. (Illus.). 268p. (Orig.). 1991. pap. 17.95 (*0-937670-01-4*) QCI Intl.

— The Employee Involvement Teams: Answers to One Hundred Frequently Asked Questions. rev. ed. (Illus.). 43p. 1992. reprint ed. pap. 6.45 (*0-937670-00-6*) QCI Intl.

— The Facilitator Handbook. 700p. 1993. pap. 74.00 (*0-937670-03-0*) QCI Intl.

— Histograms: Leader Manual & Instructional Guide. rev. ed. (Illus.). 50p. (Orig.). 1993. pap. 15.00 (*0-937670-19-7*) QCI Intl.

— Scatter Diagrams: Leader Manual & Instructional Guide. rev. ed. (Illus.). 58p. 1993. pap. 15.00 (*0-937670-22-7*) QCI Intl.

— Stratification: Leader Manual & Instructional Guide. rev. ed. (Illus.). 42p. (Orig.). 1993. pap. 15.00 (*0-937670-18-9*) QCI Intl.

Dewar, Douglas. The Transformist Illusion. 2nd ed. Wetmore, James R., ed. (Illus.). 306p. 1995. reprint ed. pap. text 22.95 (*0-900588-18-7*) S Perennis.

***Dewar, Elaine.** Bones: Discovering the First Americans. (Illus.). 2000. write for info. (*0-679-31065-7*) Random.

Dewar, Elaine. Cloak of Green: The Links Between Key Environmental Groups, Government & Big Business. LC 95-192427. 497p. 35.00 (*1-55028-451-7*, Pub. by J Lorimer); pap. 22.95 (*1-55028-450-9*, Pub. by J Lorimer) Formac Dist Ltd.

Dewar, Isla. Keeping up with Magda. 256p. 1996. pap. 10.95 (*0-7472-5112-6*, Pub. by Headline Bk Pub) Trafalgar.

Dewar, J., jt. auth. see Willoughby, I.

Dewar, J. D. Computer Modelling of Concrete Mixtures. LC 98-55726. 1999. text. write for info. (*0-419-23020-3*) Routledge.

Dewar, J. D. & Anderson, R. Manual of Ready-Mixed Concrete. 2nd ed. (Illus.). 256p. 1992. text 70.50 (*0-7514-0079-3*, Pub. by B Acad & Prof) Routldge.

Dewar, Jacqueline, jt. auth. see Zill, Dennis G.

***Dewar, James A.** Expandability of the 21st Century Army. LC 00-35302. 2000. write for info. (*0-8330-2843-X*) Rand Corp.

Dewar, James A. & Builder, Carl H. Assumption-Based Planning: A Planning Tool for Very Uncertain Times. LC 93-7133. 96p. 1993. pap. text 15.00 (*0-8330-1341-6*, MR-114-A) Rand Corp.

Dewar, James A., et al. Assumption-Based Planning & Force XXI. 112p. 1997. pap. text 6.00 (*0-8330-2490-6*, DB-172-A) Rand Corp.

— Credible Uses of the Distributed Interactive Simulation (DIS) Environment. LC 95-36628. 95p. (Orig.). 1996. pap. text 15.00 (*0-8330-2303-9*, MR-607-A) Rand Corp.

Dewar, Jeff. How to Out-Participate Your Participative Manager & Never Say You're Sorry. (Illus.). 169p. 1986. pap. 15.00 (*0-937670-36-7*) QCI Intl.

Dewar, John, jt. ed. see Bright, Susan.

Dewar, John K. Law & the Family. 2nd ed. 546p. 1992. pap. 40.00 (*0-406-00133-2*, UK, MICHIE) LEXIS Pub.

Dewar, K. A Guide to Employment Law. 154p. 1991. pap. 43.00 (*0-409-02242-X*, SA, MICHIE) LEXIS Pub.

Dewar, Lindsay. Imagination & Religion. 167p. 1998. reprint ed. spiral bd. 13.00 (*1-885395-72-8*) Book Tree.

Dewar, M. D. Collisions at Sea - How? 917p. 1989. text 295.00 (*0-85174-561-X*) Sheridan.

Dewar, M. J., et al, eds. Physical Organic Chemistry. (Topics in Current Chemistry Ser.: Vol. 146). (Illus.). 270p. 1988. 128.95 (*0-387-18541-0*) Spr-Verlag.

— Radicals in Biochemistry. (Topics in Current Chemistry Ser.: Vol. 108). (Illus.). 140p. 1982. 61.95 (*0-387-11864-0*) Spr-Verlag.

— Synchrotron Radiation in Chemistry & Biology, Vol. I. (Topics in Current Chemistry Ser.: Vol. 145). (Illus.). 240p. 1988. 141.95 (*0-387-18385-X*) Spr-Verlag.

Dewar, M. J., ed. see Statius.

Dewar, Margaret E., ed. Industry Vitalization: Toward a National Industrial Policy. (Illus.). 230p. 1982. 64.00 (*0-08-028829-4*, Pergamon Pr) Elsevier.

Dewar, Michael, ed. & tr. see Claudian.

Dewar, Michael J. Michael J. S. Dewar: A Semiempirical Life. Seeman, Jeffrey I., ed. LC 90-911. (Profiles, Pathways, & Dreams Ser.). (Illus.). 216p. 1992. text 36.00 (*0-8412-1771-8*, Pub. by Am Chemical) OUP.

Dewar, R. L., et al, eds. Nonlinear Dynamics & Chaos. 450p. (C). 1992. text 99.00 (*981-02-0770-0*) World Scientific Pub.

Dewar, R. L., jt. auth. see Joshi, N.

Dewar, Ross L. & Griffiths, Ross W., eds. Two-Dimensional Turbulence in Plasmas & Fluids Research Workshop. (AIP Conference Proceedings Ser.: Vol. 414). (Illus.). 320p. 1998. 90.00 (*1-56396-764-2*) Am Inst Physics.

Dewar, Thadys J. & Daniels, H. Frances. Programmed Proofreading. 2nd ed. 208p. (C). 1987. mass mkt. 22.95 (*0-538-23020-7*, WO2) S-W Pub.

Dewar, Thomas, jt. auth. see Chestnutt, Mary.

Dewar, Tom & Scheie, David. Promoting Job Opportunities: Towards a Better Future for Low Income Children & Families. (Illus.). 98p. (Orig.). 1995. pap. write for info. (*0-9624428-9-5*) Rainbow Research.

Dewart, Hazel, jt. auth. see Groome, David.

Dewart, Janet, ed. The State of Black America, 1986. 235p. 1986. pap. text 24.00 (*0-914759-37-X*) Transaction Pubs.

— The State of Black America, 1989, Vol. 10. 325p. 1986. pap. 18.00 (*0-685-35028-2*) Natl Urban.

— The State of Black America, 1987, Vol. 11. 261p. 1988. pap. 24.00 (*0-914758-07-1*) Transaction Pubs.

— The State of Black America, 1988, Vol. 12. 239p. 1988. pap. 24.00 (*0-914758-08-X*) Transaction Pubs.

— The State of Black America, 1989, Vol. 13. 257p. 1989. pap. 24.00 (*0-914758-10-1*) Transaction Pubs.

— The State of Black America, 1990. 332p. 1990. pap. 24.00 (*0-914758-11-X*) Transaction Pubs.

Dewart, Leslie. Evolution & Consciousness: The Role of Speech in the Origin & Development of Human Nature. 411p. 1989. text 50.00 (*0-8020-2690-7*) U of Toronto Pr.

— Foundations of Belief. LC 69-17777. 1984. 12.95 (*0-8164-2549-3*) Harper SF.

Dewart, Rosamond R., ed. Health Information for International Travel (1996-97) (Illus.). 210p. (Orig.). 1997. pap. text 35.00 (*0-7881-4498-7*) DIANE Pub.

***Dewart, Rosamond R., ed.** Health Information for International Travel, 1999-2000. (Illus.). 225p. 1999. pap. text 40.00 (*0-7881-8395-8*) DIANE Pub.

Dewart, Tracey, jt. ed. see Collins, Carol C.

***Dewasar, Ahba.** MiniPlanner: A Novel. 250p. 2000. pap. 12.95 (*1-57344-115-5*, Pub. by Cleis Pr) Publishers Group.

DeWater, Charles. Electronic Communications Instructor's Guide. 2nd ed. 1992. teacher ed. 16.00 (*0-8273-5085-6*) Delmar.

***DeWaters, Holly, ed.** Nelson's Directory of Pension Fund Consultants, 1999. 600p. 1999. pap. 350.00 (*1-891851-04-7*) Nelson Info.

— Nelson's Directory of Plan Sponsors, 1999, 3 vols. 5000p. 1998. pap. 545.00 (*1-891851-01-2*) Nelson Info.

Dewatripoint, Mathias, et al, eds. Trade & Jobs in Europe: Much Ado about Nothing? (Illus.). 200p. 1999. text 45.00 (*0-19-829360-7*) OUP.

Dewatripont, Mathias & Ginsburgh, Victor, eds. European Economic Integration: A Challenge in a Changing World. LC 94-10008. (Contributions to Economic Analysis Ser.: Vol. 224). 348p. 1994. 123.50 (*0-444-89174-9*, North Holland) Elsevier.

Dewatripont, Mathias & Tirole, Jean. The Prudential Regulation of Banks. LC 94-30751. Vol. 1. (Illus.). 276p. 1994. 35.50 (*0-262-04146-4*) MIT Pr.

Dewazien, Karl. FUNdamental Soccer - Guide. Monson, Terri, ed. (Illus.). 128p. (Orig.). 1995. pap. 12.95 (*0-9619139-3-2*) Fun Soccer Ent.

— Fundamental Soccer Goalkeeping. Lavery, Vincent J., ed. (Illus.). 128p. (Orig.). (J). (gr. 6). 1986. pap. 12.95 (*0-9619139-1-6*) Fun Soccer Ent.

— Fundamental Soccer Practice. Lavery, Vincent J., ed. (Illus.). 128p. (Orig.). (J). (gr. 6). 1995. pap. 12.95 (*0-9619139-0-8*) Fun Soccer Ent.

— Fundamental Soccer Tactics. Lavery, Vincent J., ed. (Illus.). 128p. (Orig.). (J). (gr. 6). 1987. pap. 12.95 (*0-9619139-2-4*) Fun Soccer Ent.

— Totally - FUNdamental Soccer. Monson, Terri & Maher, Alan, eds. (Illus.). 64p. (Orig.). (J). (gr. k-6). 1996. 6.95 (*0-9619139-4-0*) Fun Soccer Ent.

***Dewberry, Donna.** Decorative Murals with Donna Dewberry. (Illus.). 144p. 1999. pap. 24.99 (*0-89134-988-X*, 31459, North Lght Bks) F & W Pubns Inc.

***Dewberry, Donna S.** Decorative Furniture with Donna Dewberry. LC 00-41862. (Illus.). 2000. write for info. (*1-58180-017-7*, North Lght Bks) F & W Pubns Inc.

Dewberry, Donna S. Donna Dewberry's Complete Book of One-Stroke Painting. LC 98-11489. (Illus.). 128p. 1998. pap. 23.99 (*0-89134-802-6*, North Lght Bks) F & W Pubns Inc.

— Donna Dewberry's One-Stroke Painting Course. LC 98-40843. 1999. 27.95 (*0-8069-1875-6*) Sterling.

Dewberry, Doris E., jt. auth. see Dewberry, Jimmie.

Dewberry, Elizabeth. Flesh & Blood. 64p. 1997. pap. 5.60 (*0-87129-738-8*, F60) Dramatic Pub.

***Dewberry, Harold R.** Vessel of Honor. 2000. pap. 7.99 (*0-88270-804-X*) Bridge-Logos.

Dewberry, Jimmie. Johnson County, Arkansas, Federal Census 1900. 440p. (Orig.). 1997. pap. 45.00 (*1-56546-107-X*) Arkansas Res.

Dewberry, Jimmie & Dewberry, Doris E. Johnson County, Arkansas, 1880 Federal Census. 305p. 1996. pap. 28.00 (*1-56546-072-3*) Arkansas Res.

— Johnson County, Arkansas, Marriages, 1908-1924. 132p. 1997. pap. 21.00 (*1-56546-121-5*) Arkansas Res.

Dewberry, S. Davis. The Land Development Handbook: Planning, Engineering, & Surveying. LC 95-37873. (Illus.). 1000p. 1995. 140.00 (*0-07-016644-7*) McGraw.

Dewberry, T. C. Can We Diagnose the Health of Ecosystems? 176p. (Orig.). 1996. pap. 19.95 (*0-9649534-0-4*) NW Sci & Photo.

Dewbury, Keith, et al, eds. Clinical Ultrasound: Abdominal & General Ultrasound: A Comprehensive Text, 2 vols. (Illus.). 2048p. 1993. text 320.00 (*0-443-04277-2*) Church.

— Clinical Ultrasound: Ultrasound in Obstetrics & Gynecology: A Comprehensive Text. (Illus.). 600p. 1993. text 188.00 (*0-443-04279-9*) Church.

Dewdeny, A. K. The Tinkertoy Computer & Other Machinations: Computer Recreations from the Pages of Scientific American & Algorithm. LC 93-10478. 1993. pap. text 23.95 (*0-7167-2489-8*); pap. text 15.95 (*0-7167-2491-X*) W H Freeman.

Dewdney, A. K. The Armchair Universe: An Exploration of Computer Worlds. LC 87-25046. 320p. 1987. pap. text 16.95 (*0-7167-1939-8*) W H Freeman.

— Dewdney, the Magic Machine: More Computer Recreations from Scientific American. LC 90-31250. 320p. 1990. pap. text 24.95 (*0-7167-2125-2*); pap. text 15.95 (*0-7167-2144-9*) W H Freeman.

— Hungry Hollow: The Story of a Natural Place. LC 97-48857. (Illus.). 200p. 1998. 23.00 (*0-387-98415-1*) Spr-Verlag.

— Introduction to Computer Science. 1996. pap. text, teacher ed. 16.00 (*0-7167-8299-5*) W H Freeman.

— Introduction to Computer Science: Bits of Theory, Bytes of Practice. 464p. (C). 1996. pap. text 41.95 (*0-7167-8286-3*) W H Freeman.

— A Mathematical Mystery Tour: Discovering the Truth & Beauty of the Cosmos. LC 98-36470. 218p. 1999. 22.95 (*0-471-23847-3*) Wiley.

— New Turing Omnibus: Sixty-Six Excursions in Computer Science. LC 93-17330. 458p. (C). 1993. pap. text 24.95 (*0-7167-8271-5*) W H Freeman.

***Dewdney, A. K.** The Planiverse: Computer Contact with a Two-Dimensional World. LC 99-42454. (Illus.). 272p. 1999. pap. 20.00 (*0-387-98916-1*) Spr-Verlag.

D

An Asterisk (*) at the beginning of an entry indicates that the title is appearing for the first time.

Dewdney, A. K. Solutions Manual Turing Omnibus. 1993. pap. text, student ed. 16.00 (*0-7167-8287-1*) W H Freeman.

— 200of Nothing: An Eye Opening Tour Through the Twists & Turns of Math Abuse & Innmumeracy. LC 92-42173. 192p. 1996. pap. 14.95 (*0-471-14574-2*) Wiley.

— Two Hundred Percent of Nothing: An Eye-Opening Tour Through the Twists & Turns of Math Abuse & Innumeracy. Ross, S., ed. LC 92-42173. 192p. 1993. 22.95 (*0-471-57776-6*) Wiley.

***Dewdney, A. K.** Yes, We Have No Neutrons: An Eye-Opening Tour Through the Twists & Turns of Bad Science. 192p. 1998. pap. 14.95 (*0-471-29586-8*) Wiley.

Dewdney, A. K. Yes, We Have No Neutrons: An Eye Opening Tour Through the Twists & Turns of Bad Science. LC 96-35312. 192p. 1997. 22.95 (*0-471-10806-5*) Wiley.

Dewdney, Andrew, et al. Down but Not Out. 144p. 1994. pap. 27.50 (*0-948080-57-4*, Trentham Bks) Stylus Pub VA.

Dewdney, Christopher. Concordat Proviso Ascendant. deluxe ed. 1991. per. 7.50 (*0-935724-42-7*) Figures.

— Last Flesh: Life in the Transhuman Era. LC 98-164826. 188p. 1998. pap. 20.00 (*0-00-638472-2*) Collins SF.

Dewdney, Christopher. The Secular Grail: Paradigms of Perception: A Patrick Crean Book. 208p. pap. 17.95 (*0-921051-92-1*) Somerville Hse.

— The Secular Grail: Paradigms of Perception: Collector's Edition. 208p. 35.00 (*0-921051-96-4*) Somerville Hse.

Dewdney, Christopher, ed. see De Kerckhove, Derrick.

Dewdney, John C. A Geography of the Soviet Union. 3rd ed. LC 78-40992. (Pergamon Oxford Geography Ser.). (Illus.). 1979. 85.00 (*0-08-023739-8*, Pub. by Pergamon Repr) Franklin.

Dewdney, Micheline, jt. auth. see Charlton, Ruth.

Dewdney, P. E., jt. ed. see Roger, R. S.

Dewdney, Patricia, jt. auth. see Harris, Roma M.

Dewdney, Patricia, jt. auth. see Ross, Catherine.

Dewdney, Selwyn. The Hungry Time. (Kids of Canada Ser.). (Illus.). 32p. (J). 1980. pap. 5.95 (*0-88862-262-7*, Pub. by J Lorimer); bds. 12.95 (*0-88862-261-9*, Pub. by J Lorimer) Formac Dist Ltd.

Dewdney, Selwyn & Kidd, Kenneth E. Indian Rock Paintings of the Great Lakes. LC 67-98487. (Quetico Foundation Ser.: 4). 201p. reprint ed. pap. 62.40 (*0-608-14678-1*, 205588180038) Bks Demand.

Dewdney, Selwyn H. The Sacred Scrolls of the Southern Ojibway. LC 73-90150. (Illus.). 211p. reprint ed. pap. 65.50 (*0-8357-3991-0*, 203669000005) Bks Demand.

Dewe, J. A. History of Economics: Or, Economics As a Factor in the Making of History. 1977. lib. bdg. 59.95 (*0-8490-1973-7*) Gordon Pr.

Dewe, Michael. Local Studies Collections, Vol. 1. 1987. text 96.95 (*0-566-03522-7*, Pub. by Gower) Ashgate Pub Co.

— Local Studies Collections Vol. 2: A Manual. 528p. 1991. text 96.95 (*0-566-03631-2*, Pub. by Gower) Ashgate Pub Co.

***Dewe, Philip, et al, eds.** Coping, Health & Organizations. LC 99-35798. (Issues in Occupational Health Ser.). 256p. 1999. pap. 39.95 (*0-7484-0823-1*) Taylor & Francis.

***Dewe, Pjilip, et al, eds.** Coping, Health & Organizations. LC 99-35798. (Issues in Occupational Health Ser.). 256p. 1999. 85.00 (*0-7484-0824-X*) Taylor & Francis.

DeWeerd, H. A., ed. see Marshall, George C.

Deweerd, Harvey A. Great Soldiers of the Two World Wars. LC 69-18926. (Essay Index Reprint Ser.). 1977. 26.95 (*0-8369-1032-X*) Ayer.

Deweerdt, Jacques. Vocabulaire Fondamental de Technologie: Fundamental Vocabulary of Technology. (FRE.). 272p. 1974. pap. 49.95 (*0-7859-0773-4*, M-4654) Fr & Eur.

DeWees, Aletha, tr. see Orizet, Jean.

Dewees, Christopher. The Printer's Catch: An Artist's Guide to Pacific Coast Edible Marine Animals. 2nd ed. LC 95-50354. (Illus.). 112p. 1996. reprint ed. pap. 22.50 (*1-883319-41-2*) Frog Ltd CA.

Dewees, Donald N. Controlling Asbestos in Buildings: An Economic Investigation. LC 86-42611. 106p. 1986. pap. 12.95 (*0-915707-27-6*) Resources Future.

Dewees, Donald N., et al. Economic Analysis of Environmental Policies. LC 75-38798. (Ontario Economic Council Research Studies: No. 1). 185p. reprint ed. pap. 57.40 (*0-8357-4022-6*, 203671400005) Bks Demand.

Dewees, Jacob. Great Future of America & Africa. LC 75-154075. (Black Heritage Library Collection). 1977. 22.95 (*0-8369-8786-1*) Ayer.

— Great Future of America & Africa. LC 72-92425. 1854. 12.00 (*0-403-00158-7*) Scholarly.

Dewees, Peter A. Trees, Land, & Labor. LC 93-43865. (Environment Papers: No. 4). 62p. 1994. pap. 22.00 (*0-8213-2733-X*, 12733) World Bank.

Dewees, Peter A., jt. ed. see Arnold, J. E.

Dewees, Peter E., jt. ed. see Arnold, J. E.

DeWeese. Matter & Energy. (Illus.). 32p. (J). (gr. 4-6). 1997. pap., teacher ed. 2.95 (*1-55799-521-4*, 4123) Evan-Moor Edu Pubs.

— Our Neighbors in Space. (Illus.). 32p. (J). (gr. 4-6). 1997. pap., teacher ed. 2.95 (*1-55799-519-2*, 4121) Evan-Moor Edu Pubs.

— The Peacekeepers. (Star Trek: The Next Generation Ser.: No. 2). 1990. mass mkt. 5.50 (*0-671-73653-1*) PB.

DeWeese & Fene. United States Geography. (Illus.). 32p. (J). (gr. 4-6). 1996. pap., teacher ed. 2.95 (*1-55799-542-7*, 4144) Evan-Moor Edu Pubs.

DeWeese & Law. Science Magic. (Illus.). 32p. (J). (gr. 4-6). 1996. pap., teacher ed. 2.95 (*1-55799-517-6*, 4119) Evan-Moor Edu Pubs.

DeWeese, Bob. Adding Without Carrying: Basic Mathematics Skills. Moore, Jo Ellen, ed. (Illus.). 30p. (J). (gr. 2-3). 1995. pap., wbk. ed. 2.50 (*1-58610-072-6*, Learn on the Go) Learn Horizon.

DeWeese, Bob. Addition W/O Carrying (Math) (Mathematics Ser.). (Illus.). 32p. (J). (gr. 2-3). 1996. pap., teacher ed. 2.95 (*1-55799-451-X*, 4053) Evan-Moor Edu Pubs.

DeWeese, Bob. Advanced Multiplication: Basic Mathematics Skills. Moore, Jo Ellen, ed. (Illus.). 30p. (J). (gr. 4-6). 1995. pap., wbk. ed. 2.50 (*1-58610-091-2*, Learn on the Go) Learn Horizon.

DeWeese, Bob. Advanced Multiplication (Math) (Mathematics Ser.). (Illus.). 32p. (J). (gr. 4-6). 1996. pap., teacher ed. 2.95 (*1-55799-470-6*, 4072) Evan-Moor Edu Pubs.

DeWeese, Bob. Beginning Subtraction: Basic Mathematics Skills. Moore, Jo Ellen, ed. (Illus.). 30p. (J). (gr. 1-2). 1995. pap., wbk. ed. 2.50 (*1-58610-069-6*, Learn on the Go) Learn Horizon.

DeWeese, Bob. Beginning Subtraction (Math) (Mathematics Ser.). (Illus.). 32p. (J). (gr. 1-2). 1996. pap., teacher ed. 2.95 (*1-55799-447-1*, 4049) Evan-Moor Edu Pubs.

DeWeese, Bob. Decimals & Percentages: Basic Mathematics Skills. Moore, Jo Ellen, ed. (Illus.). 30p. (J). (gr. 5-6). 1995. pap., wbk. ed. 2.50 (*1-58610-100-5*, Learn on the Go) Learn Horizon.

— Division - Basic Facts: Basic Mathematics Skills. Moore, Jo Ellen, ed. (Illus.). 30p. (J). (gr. 3-5). 1995. pap., wbk. ed. 2.50 (*1-58610-086-6*, Learn on the Go) Learn Horizon.

DeWeese, Bob. Division Basic Facts (Math) (Mathematics Ser.). (Illus.). 32p. (J). (gr. 3-5). 1996. pap., teacher ed. 2.95 (*1-55799-465-X*, 4067) Evan-Moor Edu Pubs.

— Math about Me. (Math Is Everywhere Ser.). (Illus.). 48p. (J). (gr. 2-3). 1994. pap. text, teacher ed. 6.45 (*1-55799-336-X*, EMC 088) Evan-Moor Edu Pubs.

— Math at the Mall. (Math Is Everywhere Ser.). (Illus.). 48p. (J). (gr. 2-3). 1994. pap. text, teacher ed. 6.45 (*1-55799-326-2*, EMC 098) Evan-Moor Edu Pubs.

— Math on a Trip. (Math Is Everywhere Ser.). (Illus.). 48p. (J). (gr. 4-6). 1994. pap. text, teacher ed. 6.45 (*1-55799-324-6*, EMC 096) Evan-Moor Edu Pubs.

— Math with Games. (Math Is Everywhere Ser.). (Illus.). 48p. (J). (gr. 2-3). 1994. pap. text, teacher ed. 6.45 (*1-55799-325-4*, EMC 097) Evan-Moor Edu Pubs.

— Multiplication Basic Facts. (Mathematics Ser.). (Illus.). 32p. (J). (gr. 3-5). 1996. pap., teacher ed. 2.95 (*1-55799-464-1*, 4066) Evan-Moor Edu Pubs.

DeWeese, Bob. Multiplication Basic Facts: Basic Multiplication Skills. Moore, Jo Ellen, ed. (Illus.). 30p. (J). (gr. 3-5). 1995. pap., wbk. ed. 2.50 (*1-58610-085-8*, Learn on the Go) Learn Horizon.

— Working with Fractions: Basic Mathematics Skills. Moore, Jo Ellen, ed. (Illus.). 30p. (J). (gr. 4-6). 1995. pap., wbk. ed. 2.50 (*1-58610-094-7*, Learn on the Go) Learn Horizon.

DeWeese, Bob, ed. see Camilli, Thomas.

DeWeese, Bob, ed. see Evans, Joy.

DeWeese, Bob, ed. see Moore, Jo Ellen.

Deweese, Charles. The Power of Freedom: First Baptist Church, Asheville, North Carolina, 1829-1997. LC 97-75413. (Illus.). 384p. 1997. 24.95 (*1-57736-076-1*) Providence Hse.

Deweese, Charles W. The Emerging Role of Deacons. LC 79-50337. 1979. pap. 4.99 (*0-8054-3512-3*, 4235-12) Broadman.

— Researching, Writing & Publishing Your Church's History. (Resource Kit for Your Church's History Ser.). 8p. 1984. pap. 0.60 (*0-939804-19-0*) Hist Comm S Baptist.

Deweese, Charles W., ed. Defining Baptist Convictions: Guidelines for the Twenty-First Century. 224p. (Orig.). 1996. pap. 15.95 (*1-881576-83-3*) Providence Hse.

Deweese, Charles W., ed. see Anderson, Fred.

Deweese, Charles W., ed. see Brown, Pat.

Deweese, Charles W., ed. see Hack, John.

Deweese, Charles W., ed. see May, Lynn E.

Deweese, Charles W., ed. see Owens, Loulie L.

Deweese, Charles W., ed. see Sumners, Bill.

Deweese, Charles W., ed. see Tonks, Ronald A.

DeWeese, Devin. Islamization & Native Religion in the Golden Horde: Baba Tukles & Conversion to Islam in Historical & Epic Tradition. 640p. 1996. pap. 24.95 (*0-614-21158-1*, 665) Kazi Pubns.

— Islamization & Native Religion in the Golden Horde: Baba Tukles & Conversion to Islam in Historical & Epic Tradition. LC 93-18488. (Hermeneutics, Studies in the History of Religions). (Illus.). 608p. (C). 1994. 90.00 (*0-271-01072-X*); pap. 30.00 (*0-271-01073-8*) Pa St U Pr.

DeWeese, Eldonna, ed. Southern Baptist Periodical Index, 1987. LC 72-625602. xv, 490p. (C). 1988. lib. bdg. 50.00 (*0-925359-01-7*) SBU Library.

— Southern Baptist Periodical Index, 1988. LC 72-625602. xvii, 563p. 1989. lib. bdg. 50.00 (*0-925359-02-5*) SBU Library.

— Southern Baptist Periodical Index, 1989. LC 72-625602. xix, 575p. 1990. lib. bdg. 50.00 (*0-925359-03-3*) SBU Library.

— Southern Baptist Periodical Index, 1990. LC 72-625602. xxii, 349p. 1991. lib. bdg. 95.00 (*0-925359-04-1*) SBU Library.

— Southern Baptist Periodical Index, 1992. LC 72-625602. xxii, 397p. 1993. lib. bdg. 95.00 (*0-925359-06-8*) SBU Library.

— Southern Baptist Periodical Index, 1993. LC 72-625602. xxii, 409p. 1995. lib. bdg. 95.00 (*0-925359-07-6*) SBU Library.

— Southern Baptist Periodical Index, 1991. LC 72-625602. xxii, 364p. 1992. lib. bdg. 95.00 (*0-925359-05-X*) SBU Library.

— Southern Baptist Periodical Index, 1997. Van Blair, Betty & Heifner, Betty, trs. LC 72-625602. xxiv, 476p. 1998. lib. bdg. 95.00 (*0-925359-11-4*) SBU Library.

DeWeese, Eldonna & Heifner, Betty, eds. Southern Baptist Periodical Index, 1985-1986. LC 72-625602. xx, 727p. 1994. lib. bdg. 150.00 (*0-925359-00-9*) SBU Library.

Deweese, Eldonna & Heifner, Betty, eds. Southern Baptist Periodical Index, 1995. LC 72-625602. 1997. lib. bdg. 95.00 (*0-925359-09-2*) SBU Library.

DeWeese, Eldonna & Heifner, Betty, eds. Southern Baptist Periodical Index, 1996. LC 72-625602. 1997. lib. bdg. 95.00 (*0-925359-10-6*) SBU Library.

— Southern Baptist Periodical Index, 1998. LC 72-625602. xxiv, 489p. 1999. lib. bdg. 95.00 (*0-925359-12-2*) SBU Library.

***DeWeese, Eldonna & Heifner, Betty, eds.** Southern Baptist Periodical Index 1999. 2000. lib. bdg. 100.00 (*0-925359-13-0*) SBU Library.

DeWeese, Eldonna & Heifner, Betty, eds. Southern Baptist Periodical Index, 1994. LC 72-625602. (C). 1996. lib. bdg. 95.00 (*0-925359-08-4*) SBU Library.

Deweese, Eugene. Lord of the Necropolis. (Ravenloft Ser.). 1997. pap. 5.99 (*0-7869-0660-X*, Pub. by TSR Inc) Random.

DeWeese, Gene. Chain of Attack. (Star Trek Ser.: No. 32). 1988. mass mkt. 5.50 (*0-671-66658-4*) PB.

***DeWeese, Gene.** Engines of Destiny. (Star Trek The Next Generation Ser.). 2000. mass mkt. 6.50 (*0-671-03702-1*, Star Trek) PB.

Deweese, Gene. Firestorm. LC 97-66111. (Dinotopia Ser.). (YA). (gr. 5-8). 1997. pap. 3.99 (*0-679-88619-2*, Pub. by Random Bks Yng Read) Random.

— Firestorm. (Dinotopia Ser.). (YA). (gr. 5-8). 1997. 9.09 (*0-606-11329-0*, Pub. by Turtleback) Demco.

— Into the Nebula. (Star Trek: The Next Generation Ser.: No. 36). 1995. mass mkt. 5.99 (*0-671-89455-6*) PB.

DeWeese, Gene. Lost in Space: The Vault. 320p. (Orig.). 1999. mass mkt. 5.99 (*0-06-105910-2*) HarpC.

— Renegade. Stern, Dave, ed. (Star Trek Ser.: No. 55). 288p. 1991. per. 4.95 (*0-671-65814-X*) PB.

DeWeese, James A., ed. see Dale, W. Andrew.

DeWeese, June L. & Humphreys, Jo A. Comparable Worth: An Annotated Bibliography. (CompuBibs Ser.: No. 12). 81p. 1985. pap. 15.00 (*0-914791-11-7*) Vantage Info.

DeWeese, Robert. Big Book of Geography Rhymes & Chants. (Illus.). 32p. (J). (gr. 1-5). 1994. pap. text 11.95 (*1-55799-268-1*, 384) Evan-Moor Edu Pubs.

DeWeese, Robert, ed. Big Book of Playground Rhymes & Chants. (Illus.). 32p. (J). (gr. k-3). 1994. pap. text 11.95 (*1-55799-266-5*, 382) Evan-Moor Edu Pubs.

DeWeese, Robert & Moore, Jo E. The Arctic & Antarctica. (Illus.). 48p. (J). (gr. 3-6). 1994. pap. text 5.95 (*1-55799-280-0*, EMC 285) Evan-Moor Edu Pubs.

— Big Book of Math Rhymes & Chants. (Illus.). 32p. (J). (gr. k-3). 1994. pap., teacher ed. 11.95 (*1-55799-267-3*, EMC 383) Evan-Moor Edu Pubs.

— Weather. (Illus.). 48p. (J). (gr. 3-6). 1994. pap text 5.95 (*1-55799-279-7*, EMC 284) Evan-Moor Edu Pubs.

DeWell, Charles S. Kawabunga's South Seas Adventure: Blue Water Cruising in a Twenty Foot Boat. LC 98-61208. 286p. 1999. 29.95 (*0-9666472-0-3*) South Seas Pubg.

Dewell, Michael, tr. see Garcia Lorca, Federico.

Dewell, P. Simple Noise Calculations. (Handbook Ser.: No. 6). (C). 1991. 51.00 (*0-948237-05-8*, Pub. by H&H Sci Cnslts) St Mut.

— Some Applications of Statistics in Occupational Hygiene. (Technical Handbook Ser.: No. 1). 75p. (C). 1989. 156.00 (*0-905927-18-4*, Pub. by H&H Sci Cnslts) St Mut.

Dewell, Peter. Concentrations of Cadmium in Air & Urine in an Alkaline Battery Works: A Case Study. 1994. 100.00 (*0-948237-20-1*, Pub. by H&H Sci Cnslts) St Mut.

DeWelt, Chris, ed. see DeWelt, Don.

DeWelt, Don. Happy on My Way to Heaven: Autobiography of Don DeWelt. LC 88-63242. (Illus.). 230p. (Orig.). 1989. pap. 5.99 (*0-89900-325-7*) College Pr Pub.

— If You Want to Preach. 8th ed. LC 56-13226. 168p. (C). 1957. reprint ed. pap. 13.99 (*0-89900-111-4*) College Pr Pub.

— Personal Worship, 7 vols., Vol. 2. LC 88-62771. (Orig.). 1989. pap. 9.99 (*0-89900-451-2*) College Pr Pub.

— Personal Worship, 7 vols., Vol. 3. LC 88-62771. (Orig.). 1989. pap. 9.99 (*0-89900-452-0*) College Pr Pub.

— Personal Worship, 7 vols., Vol. 5. LC 88-62771. (Orig.). 1989. pap. 9.99 (*0-89900-454-7*) College Pr Pub.

— Personal Worship, 7 vols., Vol. 6. LC 88-62771. (Orig.). 1989. pap. 9.99 (*0-89900-455-5*) College Pr Pub.

— Personal Worship, 7 vols., Vol. 7. LC 88-62771. (Orig.). 1989. pap. 9.99 (*0-89900-456-3*) College Pr Pub.

— Power of the Holy Spirit, Vol. 1. 8th ed. 150p. (Orig.). (C). 1963. pap. 5.99 incl. VHS (*0-89900-123-8*) College Pr Pub.

Dewelt, Don. The Power of the Holy Spirit, Vol. 3. 3rd ed. 256p. (C). 1972. pap. 5.99 incl. VHS (*0-89900-125-4*) College Pr Pub.

DeWelt, Don. Sweet Hour of Prayer. rev. ed. DeWelt, Chris, ed. (Small Group Studies). 64p. 1999. reprint ed. pap. 5.99 (*0-89900-716-3*) College Pr Pub.

DeWelt, Don, jt. auth. see Johnson, B. W.

DeWerth, D. W. Energy Consumption of Contemporary Nineteen Seventy-Three Gas Range Burners & Pilots Under Typical Cooking Loads. 53p. 1974. pap. 5.00 (*0-318-12607-9*, M50155) Am Gas Assn.

— A Study of Infra-Red Energy Generated by Radiant Gas Burners. 61p. 1962. 2.00 (*0-318-12707-5*, L71141) Am Gas Assn.

DeWerth-Pallmeyer, Dwight. The Audience in the News. (Communication Ser.). 200p. (C). 1996. text 32.50 (*0-8058-2110-4*); pap. text 17.50 (*0-8058-2111-2*) L Erlbaum Assocs.

Dewes, Simon. Marian: The Life of George Eliot. LC 74-28384. (English Literature Ser.: No. 33). 1974. lib. bdg. 75.00 (*0-8383-1745-6*) M S G Haskell Hse.

D'Ewes, Simonds, compiled by. A Compleat Journal of the Votes, Speeches & Debates Both of the House of Lords & House of Commons Throughout the Whole Reign of Queen Elizabeth, of Glorious Memory. LC 74-75952. 1974. reprint ed. 60.00 (*0-8420-1739-9*) Scholarly Res Inc.

DeWese, Harris. Now Get Out There & Sell Something. 272p. 34.00 (*0-614-25577-5*, 00SM44703) Print Indus Am.

Dewet, Andrew, jt. auth. see Merritts.

Dewey, A. M., et al. Life of Admiral George Dewey & the Dewey Family History. (Illus.). 1120p. 1989. reprint ed. pap. 159.00 (*0-8328-0475-4*); reprint ed. lib. bdg. 167.00 (*0-8328-0474-6*) Higginson Bk Co.

Dewey, Allen. Analysis & Design of Digital Systems with VHDL. LC 96-24465. 704p. 1996. mass mkt. 99.95 (*0-534-95410-3*) PWS Pubs.

Dewey, Allen M. Analysis & Design of Digital Systems. (C). 1995. text. write for info. (*0-201-54974-3*) Addison-Wesley.

Dewey, Allen M. & Director, Stephen W. Principles of VLSI System Planning: A Framework for Conceptual Design. (C). 1990. text 108.00 (*0-7923-9102-0*) Kluwer Academic.

Dewey, Ariane. Narrow Escapes Of Davy Crockett. 1993. 10.15 (*0-606-05503-7*, Pub. by Turtleback) Demco.

***Dewey, Ariane & Aruego, Jose.** Splash! LC 00-9723. (Green Light Readers Series). (Illus.). 2001. write for info. (*0-15-216262-3*) Harcourt.

Dewey, Ariane & Aruego, Jose. Five Little Ducks. LC 88-3752. (Raffi Songs to Read Ser.). 32p. (J). (ps-2). 1992. pap. 5.99 (*0-517-58360-7*, Pub. by Crown Bks Yng Read) Random.

Dewey, Ariane, jt. auth. see Aruego, Jose.

Dewey, Arthur J. Spirit & Letter in Paul. (Studies in the Bible & Early Christianity: Vol. 33). 256p. 1996. 89.95 (*0-7734-9703-X*) E Mellen.

Dewey, Arthur J., tr. see Cologne Mani Codex, English & Greek Staff.

Dewey, Barbara. As You Believe. LC 85-70370. (Illus.). 208p. 1989. pap. 14.95 (*0-933123-03-5*) Bartholomew Bks.

— Consciousness & Quantum Behavior. (Illus.). 104p. (Orig.). 1993. pap. 12.95 (*0-933123-04-3*) Bartholomew Bks.

— The Creating Cosmos. rev. ed. 110p. 1994. pap. 12.95 (*0-933123-05-1*) Bartholomew Bks.

Dewey, Barbara I., ed. Raising Money for Academic & Research Libraries: A How-to-Do-It Manual for Librarians. (How-to-Do-It Ser.). 160p. 1991. 45.00 (*1-55570-082-9*) Neal-Schuman.

Dewey, Barbara I. & Creth, Sheila D., eds. Team Power: Making Library Meetings Work. LC 93-1075. 130p. 1993. pap. text 25.00 (*0-8389-0616-8*) ALA.

Dewey, Charles R., see Uncle Hyggly, pseud.

Dewey, Clive. Anglo-Indian Attitudes: The Mind of the Indian Civil Service. LC 93-10710. 328p. 1993. 55.00 (*1-85285-097-3*) Hambledon Press.

— The Passing of Barchester. 236p. 1991. 45.00 (*1-85285-039-6*) Hambledon Press.

Dewey, Clive, ed. see Darling, Malcolm L.

Dewey, David. The Watercolor Book: Materials & Techniques for Today's Artist. (Illus.). 176p. 1995. 35.00 (*0-8230-5641-4*) Watsn-Guptill.

***Dewey, David.** The Watercolor Book: Materials & Techniques for Today's Artists. (Illus.). 176p. 2000. pap. 19.95 (*0-8230-5639-2*) Watsn-Guptill.

Dewey, Davis & Shugrue, Martin. Banking & Credit. Bruchey, Stuart, ed. LC 80-1144. (Rise of Commercial Banking Ser.). (Illus.). 1981. reprint ed. lib. bdg. 49.95 (*0-405-13646-3*) Ayer.

Dewey, Davis R., ed. see Walker, Francis A.

Dewey, Donald. The Antitrust Experiment: 1890-1990. 1990. text 60.00 (*0-231-06710-0*) Col U Pr.

— Marcello Mastorianni: An Intimate Biography. (Illus.). 288p. 1993. 21.95 (*1-55972-158-8*) Carol Pub Group.

***Dewey, Donald.** Marcello Mastroianni: His Life & Art. (Illus.). 312p. 2000. reprint ed. 22.00 (*0-7881-9393-7*) DIANE Pub.

Dewey, Donald. Modern Capital Theory. LC 65-22157. (Illus.). 238p. 1965. text 57.50 (*0-231-02831-8*) Col U Pr.

— Monopoly in Economics & Law. LC 76-5436. (Illus.). 328p. 1976. reprint ed. lib. bdg. 35.00 (*0-8371-8811-3*, DEME, Greenwood Pr) Greenwood.

Dewey, Donald, jt. auth. see Acocella, Nicholas.

Dewey, E., et al. Pulp Adventures (Genre Book) (Rolemaster Standard System Ser.). (Illus.). 144p. 1997. pap. 16.00 (*1-55806-311-0*, 5701) Iron Crown Ent Inc.

Dewey, Edward H. The No Breakfast Plan & the Fasting Cure. 2nd ed. 207p. 1998. reprint ed. pap. 20.00 (*0-7873-0283-X*) Hlth Research.

Dewey, Edward R. Cycles: Selected Writings. 810p. 1970. 65.00 (*1-879192-03-9*) Fndtn Study Cycles.

Dewey, Edward R. & Dakin, Edwin F. Cycles, the Science of Prediction. 255p. 1964. pap. 15.00 (*1-879192-01-2*) Fndtn Study Cycles.

Dewey, Edward R., et al. Cycle Synchronies. 90p. 1990. pap. 45.00 (*1-879192-06-3*) Fndtn Study Cycles.

— Cycles Classic Library Collection, 4 vols., Set. 1698p. 1987. 125.00 (*1-879192-08-X*) Fndtn Study Cycles.

Dewey, Erik A. Hostile Takeover: Silent Death Annex Book. Dennis, Donald G., ed. (Silent Death - The Next Millennium Ser.). (Illus.). 44p. (YA). (gr. 7 up). 1997. pap. 12.00 (*1-55806-347-1*, 7221) Iron Crown Ent Inc.

D

Dewey, Erik A. The Kashmere Commonwealth. Dennis, Don, ed. (Silent Death - The Next Millennium Ser.). (Illus.). 68p. 1997. pap. 14.00 (1-55806-310-2, 7217) Iron Crown Ent Inc.

— Space Junk: Silent Death Annex Book. (Silent Death - The Next Millennium Ser.). (Illus.). 66p. 1997. pap. 14.00 (1-55806-314-5, 7219) Iron Crown Ent Inc.

Dewey, Ethel L., ed. see Dewey, Richard.

Dewey, Evelyn. Behavior Development in Infants: A Survey of the Literature on Prenatal & Postnatal Activity 1920-1932. LC 72-343. (Body Movement Perspectives in Research Ser.). 334p. 1973. reprint ed. 24.95 (0-405-03142-4) Ayer.

Dewey, Frank L. Thomas Jefferson, Lawyer. LC 85-26571. 184p. 1986. text 29.50 (0-8139-1079-X) U Pr of Va.

Dewey, George. Autobiography. LC 74-108813. (BCL Ser. I). (Illus.). reprint ed. 39.50 (0-404-02121-2) AMS Pr.

— Autobiography of Admiral George Dewey. LC 86-23711. (Classics of Naval Literature Ser.). 297p. 1987. 32.95 (0-87021-028-9) Naval Inst Pr.

— Autobiography of George Dewey. (History - United States Ser.). 337p. 1992. reprint ed. lib. bdg. 79.00 (0-7812-6212-7) Rprt Serv.

— Autobiography of George Dewey: Admiral of the Navy. (American Biography Ser.). 337p. 1991. reprint ed. lib. bdg. 79.00 (0-7812-8107-5) Rprt Serv.

Dewey, Godfrey. English Spelling: Roadblock to Reading. LC 77-141240. 193p. reprint ed. pap. 59.90 (0-608-14944-6, 202600400048) Bks Demand.

— Relative Frequency of English Speech Sounds. rev. ed. (Studies in Education: No. 4). 199p. 1950. 15.00 (0-674-75450-6) HUP.

— Relative Frequency of English Spellings. LC 71-118887. 154p. reprint ed. pap. 47.80 (0-608-14941-1, 202600500048) Bks Demand.

Dewey, Horace W. Reading & Translating Contemporary Russian. (RUS & ENG.). 208p. 1995. pap. 17.95 (0-8442-4243-8, Natl Textbk Co) NTC Contemp Pub Co.

Dewey, J. F., et al, eds. Tectonics: A Selection of Papers. 150p. 1981. pap. 25.00 (0-08-028742-5, Pergamon Pr) Elsevier.

Dewey, J. H., jt. auth. see Dewey, M. D.

Dewey, Jack. Burned Out: A Teacher Speaks Out. LC 86-60763. (Illus.). 96p. (Orig.). 1986. pap. 6.95 (0-933050-37-2) New Eng Pr VT.

***Dewey, Jack E.** The Dead Salesman. Edwards, Tab, ed. 1999. pap. 12.00 (0-9700891-0-4) Kixx.

Dewey, James F., jt. auth. see Dewey, William T.

Dewey, Jeannette M. Say & Spell: The Bridge from Speaking to Spelling. LC 95-92563. 464p. (Orig.). 1995. pap. 10.95 (0-9648519-0-3) Seneca Pubng.

Dewey, Jennifer. Birds of Antarctica: The Adelie Penguin. (J). 1989. write for info. (0-316-88854-0) Little.

— Birds of Antarctica: The Wandering Albatros. (J). 1989. write for info. (0-316-88853-2) Little.

— Can You Find Me? A Book about Animal Camouflage. 40p. (J). (ps-3). 1994. pap. 3.95 (0-590-41553-0) Scholastic Inc.

— Family Ties: Raising Wild Babies. LC 98-5201. (J). (gr. 5-7). 1998. lib. bdg. 15.95 (0-7614-5037-8) Marshall Cavendish.

— Rattlesnake Dance. LC 96-84170. (Illus.). 48p. (J). (gr. 1 up). 1997. 17.95 (1-56397-247-6) Boyds Mills Pr.

Dewey, Jennifer O. Faces Only a Mother Could Love, Vol. 1. LC 95-76353. (Illus.). 32p. (J). (gr. 2-4). 1996. 14.95 (1-56397-046-5) Boyds Mills Pr.

— Mud Matters. LC 97-32929. (Illus.). 64p. (J). (gr. 2-5). 1998. lib. bdg. 15.95 (0-7614-5014-9) Marshall Cavendish.

— Navajo Summer. LC 97-72770. (Illus.). 136p. (J). (gr. 5-9). 1998. 14.95 (1-56397-248-4) Boyds Mills Pr.

— Wildlife Rescue: The Work of Dr. Kathleen Ramsay. LC 93-71478. (Illus.). 64p. (J). (gr. 3-7). 1999. pap. 9.95 (1-56397-762-1) Boyds Mills Pr.

***Dewey, Jennifer Owings.** The Antarctic Journal. LC 99-89065. 48p. (J). 2001. lib. bdg. 15.89 (0-06-028587-7) HarpC Child Bks.

— The Antarctic Journal. LC 99-89065. 64p. (J). (gr. 1 up). 2001. 15.95 (0-06-028586-9) HarpC Child Bks.

Dewey, Jennifer Owings. Bedbugs in Our House: True Tales of Insect, Bug & Spider Discovery. LC 97-12787. (Illus.). 64p. (J). (gr. 2-5). 1997. 14.95 (0-7614-5006-8) Marshall Cavendish.

***Dewey, Jennifer Owings.** Navajo Summer. LC 97-72770. (Illus.). 136p. (YA). (gr. 5 up). 2000. pap. 9.95 (1-56397-855-5) Boyds Mills Pr.

Dewey, Jennifer Owings. Poison Dart Frogs. LC 97-74194. (Illus.). 32p. (J). (gr. 2-4). 1998. 15.95 (1-56397-655-2) Boyds Mills Pr.

***Dewey, Jennifer Owings.** Rattlesnake Dance: True Tales, Mysteries & Rattlesnake Ceremonies. LC 96-84170. (Illus.). 48p. (J). (gr. 3-7). 2000. pap. write for info. (1-56397-877-6) Boyds Mills Pr.

Dewey, Joanna. Markan Public Debate: Literary Technique, Concentric Structure, & Theology in Mark 2: 1-3: 6. LC 79-17443. (Society of Biblical Literature. Dissertation Ser.: No. 48). 289p. reprint ed. pap. 89.60 (0-7837-5441-8, 20452060005) Bks Demand.

Dewey, John. The Antarctic Journal. LC 99-89065. 48p. (J). (gr. 1 up). pap. 6.95 (0-06-446225-0) HarpC Child Bks.

Dewey, John. The Child & the Curriculum & the School & Society. (Centennial Publication Ser.). (Illus.). 252p. 1990. pap. text 10.00 (0-226-14396-1) U Ch Pr.

— The Child & the Curriculum & the School & Society. (Centennial Publication Ser.). (Illus.). 252p. 1999. lib. bdg. 19.50 (0-226-14395-3) U Ch Pr.

— Child & the Curriculum & the School & Society. 2nd ed. LC 56-13578. 1997. pap. 6.95 (0-226-14392-9, P3); lib. bdg. 12.00 (0-226-14394-5, P3) U Ch Pr.

Dewey, John. The Collected Works of John Dewey, 1882-1953: (Macintosh) Boydston, Jo Ann & Hickman, Larry, eds. (Past Masters Ser.). (C). write for info. (1-57085-042-9) Intelex.

— The Collected Works of John Dewey, 1882-1953: (Windows) Boydston, Jo Ann & Hickman, Larry, eds. (Past Masters Ser.). (C). write for info. (1-57085-118-2) Intelex.

Dewey, John. Common Faith. LC 91-23976. (Terry Lectures Ser.). 1960. pap. 10.00 (0-300-00069-3, Y18) Yale U Pr.

— Democracy & Education. 384p. 1997. 16.95 (0-684-83631-9) Free Pr.

— Democracy & Education: An Introduction to the Philosophy of Education. 1966. pap. 15.95 (0-02-907370-7) Free Pr.

— Dewey & His Critics. Morgenbesser, Sidney, ed. LC 77-94488. 752p. (C). 1978. pap. text 19.95 (0-931206-01-4); lib. bdg. 37.95 (0-931206-00-6) Hackett Pub.

— Dictionary of Education. Winn, Ralph B., ed. LC 72-139129. 150p. 1972. reprint ed. lib. bdg. 45.00 (0-8371-5745-5, DEDE, Greenwood Pr) Greenwood.

— Education Today. Ratner, Joseph, ed. LC 74-95118. 373p. 1970. reprint ed. lib. bdg. 65.00 (0-8371-2550-2, DEED, Greenwood Pr) Greenwood.

— Educational Situation. LC 71-89173. (American Education: Its Men, Institutions, & Ideas. Series 1). 1978. reprint ed. 13.95 (0-405-01411-2) Ayer.

— Essays on China, Japan, & the War, 1918-1919, Vol. 11. abr. ed. Boydston, Jo Anne, ed. (Middle Works of John Dewey: 1899-1924). 448p. 1988. pap. text 16.95 (0-8093-1434-7) S Ill U Pr.

— Essays on Philosophy, Education, & the Orient, 1921-1922, Vol. 13. abr. ed. Boydston, Joanne, ed. (Middle Works of John Dewey: 1899-1924). 554p. 1988. pap. text 16.95 (0-8093-1436-3) S Ill U Pr.

— Experience & Education. 96p. 1963. pap. 5.50 (0-02-013660-9) Macmillan.

— Experience & Education. 1983. 22.00 (0-8446-5961-4) Peter Smith.

— Experience & Education. 1997. per. 7.00 (0-684-83828-1) S&S Trade.

— Experience & Education: The 60th Anniversary Edition. 60th anniversary ed. 194p. 1998. 26.00 (0-912099-34-8, 520); pap. 18.00 (0-912099-35-6, 521) Kappa Delta Pi.

— Experience & Nature. (Illus.). 443p. 1929. pap. 10.95 (0-486-20471-5) Dover.

— Experience & Nature. rev. ed. (Paul Carus Lectures). 380p. 1971. pap. 12.50 (0-87548-097-7) Open Court.

— Foxes. 1979. mass mkt. 1.95 (0-446-90156-3, Pub. by Warner Bks) Little.

— Freedom & Culture. LC 89-62323. (Great Books in Philosophy). 132p. 1989. reprint ed. pap. 10.95 (0-87975-560-1) Prometheus Bks.

— German Philosophy & Politics. (Select Bibliographies Reprint Ser.). 1977. 15.95 (0-8369-5552-8) Ayer.

— How We Think. (Great Books in Philosophy). 224p. 1991. pap. 10.95 (0-87975-701-9) Prometheus Bks.

— How We Think. unabridged ed. LC 97-26316. (Illus.). 224p. 1997. reprint ed. pap. 6.95 (0-486-29895-7) Dover.

— How We Think. rev. ed. LC 97-73886. (C). 1997. text 38.76 (0-395-89754-8) HM.

— How We Think: A Restatement of the Relation of Reflective Thinking to the Educative Process. 301p. (C). 1933. text 39.16 (0-669-20024-7) HM Trade Div.

— Human Nature & Conduct, 1922, Vol. 14. abr. ed. Boydston, Jo Anne, ed. (Middle Works of John Dewey: 1899-1924). 260p. 1988. pap. 14.95 (0-8093-1437-1) S Ill U Pr.

***Dewey, John.** Individualism Old & New. LC 99-10420. (Great Books in Philosophy). 110p. 1999. pap. 9.95 (1-57392-693-0) Prometheus Bks.

Dewey, John. Influence of Darwin on Philosophy & Other Essays. LC 97-4502. 309p. 1997. pap. 11.95 (1-57392-137-8) Prometheus Bks.

— John Dewey on Education. Archambault, Reginald D., ed. & intro. by. LC 64-18939. xxx, 470p. 1974. reprint ed. pap. text 18.95 (0-226-14390-2, P598) U Ch Pr.

— The Later Works of John Dewey, 1925-1953, 17 vols. Boydston, Jo Ann, ed. Incl. Vol. 2: 1925-1927: Essays, Reviews, Miscellany, & "The Public & Its Problems" Gouinlock, James, intro. LC 80-27285. 576p. 1984. 52.00 (0-8093-1131-3); Vol. 3: 1927-1928: Essays, Reviews, Miscellany, & "Impressions of Soviet Russia" Sidorsky, David, intro. LC 80-27285. 584p. 1984. 52.00 (0-8093-1132-1); 1925. Hook, Sidney, intro. LC 80-27285. 462p. 1981. 52.00 (0-8093-0986-6); 1925. Hook, Sidney, intro. LC 80-27285. 434p. 1988. pap. 14.95 (0-8093-1490-8); 1925-1927: Essays, Reviews, Miscellany, & "The Public & Its Problems" Gouinlock, James, intro. LC 80-27285. 488p. 1988. pap. 16.95 (0-8093-1491-6); 1927-1928: Essays, Reviews, Miscellany, & "Impressions of Soviet Russia" Sidorsky, David, intro. LC 80-27285. 482p. 1988. pap. 16.95 (0-8093-1492-4); 1929: "The Quest for Certainty" Toulmin, Stephen, intro. LC 80-27285. 296p. 1984. 52.00 (0-8093-1162-3); 1929: "The Quest for Certainty" Toulmin, Stephen, intro. LC 80-27285. 288p. 1988. pap. 14.95 (0-8093-1493-2); 1929-1930: Essays, "The Sources of a Science of Education," "Individualism," "Old & New," & "Construction of a Criticism" Kurtz, Paul, intro. LC 80-27285. 558p. 1984. 52.00 (0-8093-1163-1); 1929-1930: Essays, "The Sources of a Science of Education," "Individualism," "Old & New," & "Construction of a Criticism" Kurtz, Paul, intro. LC 80-27285. 480p. 1988. pap. 16.95 (0-8093-1494-0); 1931-1932: Essays, Reviews, & Miscellany. Ratner, Sidney, intro. LC 80-27285. 640p. 1985. 52.00 (0-8093-1199-2); 1931-1932: Essays, Reviews, & Miscellany. Ratner, Sidney, intro. LC 80-27285. 558p. 1989. pap. 16.95 (0-8093-1574-2); 1932: "Ethics" Flower, Elizabeth, ed. LC 80-27285. 574p. 1985. 52.00 (0-8093-1200-X); 1932: "Ethics" Flower, Elizabeth, ed. LC 80-27285. 548p. 1989. pap. 16.95 (0-8093-1575-0); 1933: Essays & "How We Think" rev. ed. Rorty, Richard McKay, intro. LC 80-27285. 435p. 1986. 52.00 (0-8093-1246-8); 1933: Essays & "How We Think" rev. ed. Rorty, Richard McKay, intro. LC 80-27285. 410p. 1989. pap. 16.95 (0-8093-1576-9); 1933-1934: Essays, Reviews, Miscellany, & "A Common Faith" Konvitz, Milton R., intro. LC 80-27285. 460p. 1987. 52.00 (0-8093-1266-2); 1925-1953: Art As Experience. Boydston, JoAnn & Simon, Harriet F., eds. LC 80-27285. 434p. 1989. pap. 14.95 (0-8093-1578-5); 1935-1937: Essays & "Liberalism & Social Action" McDermott, John J., intro. LC 80-27285. 786p. 1987. 52.00 (0-8093-1267-0); 1938. Ernest, Nagel, intro. LC 80-27285. 788p. 1986. 52.00 (0-8093-1268-9); 1938-1939: "Experience & Education," "Freedom & Culture," "Theory of Valuation," & Essays. Cahn, Steven M. LC 80-27285. 612p. 1988. 52.00 (0-8093-1425-8); 1939-1941. Sleeper, R. W. LC 80-27285. 612p. 1988. 52.00 (0-8093-1426-6); 1942-1948. LC 80-27285. 724p. 1989. 52.00 (0-8093-1535-1); 1949-1952. Lavine, T. Z., intro. LC 80-27285. 779p. 1990. 52.00 (0-8093-1537-8); 1985-1953. Hook, Sydney, intro. LC 80-27285. 820p. 1991. 52.00 (0-8093-1661-7); LC 80-27285. 1988. pap. write for info. (0-318-68540-X) S Ill U Pr.

— Lectures on Ethics, 1900-1901. Koch, Donald F., ed. LC 90-36858. 608p. (C). 1991. 57.00 (0-8093-1663-3) S Ill U Pr.

***Dewey, John.** Liberalism & Social Action. LC 99-39280. (Great Books in Philosophy Ser.). 100p. 1999. pap. 9.95 (1-57392-753-8) Prometheus Bks.

Dewey, John. Logic: Theory of Inquiry. 1982. reprint ed. 49.50 (0-89197-831-3) Irvington.

— Moral Principles in Education. LC 74-18472. (Arcturus Books Paperbacks). 79p. 1975. reprint ed. pap. 12.95 (0-8093-0715-4) S Ill U Pr.

— Outlines of a Critical Theory of Ethics. LC 71-92299. 253p. 1969. reprint ed. lib. bdg. 35.00 (0-8371-2707-6, DETE, Greenwood Pr) Greenwood.

— The Philosophy of John Dewey, 2 vols. McDermott, John J., ed. LC 80-39766. xiii, 768p. 1981. pap. text 25.00 (0-226-14401-1) U Ch Pr.

— The Poems of John Dewey. Boydston, Jo Ann, ed. LC 77-4718. 220p. 1977. 16.95 (0-8093-0800-2) S Ill U Pr.

— Political Writings. Shapiro, Ian, ed. LC 93-8944. (Hackett Classics Ser.). 288p. (Orig.). (C). 1993. pap. text 9.95 (0-87220-190-2); lib. bdg. 32.95 (0-87220-191-0) Hackett Pub.

— The Principles of Instrumental Logic: John Dewey's Lectures in Ethics & Political Ethics, 1895-1896. Koch, Donald F., ed. LC 97-48994. (Illus.). 272p. 1998. 39.95 (0-8093-2173-4) S Ill U Pr.

— Public & Its Problems. LC 76-178242. 236p. 1954. pap. text 11.95 (0-8040-0254-1) Swallow.

Dewey, John. Reconstruction in Philosophy. 1957. pap. 17.50 (0-8070-1585-7) Beacon Pr.

Dewey, John. The School & Society. LC 79-26919. (Arcturus Books Paperbacks). 124p. 1980. pap. 11.95 (0-8093-0967-X) S Ill U Pr.

— Studies in Logical Theory. LC 75-3128. reprint ed. 34.50 (0-404-59129-9) AMS Pr.

— Theory of the Moral Life. 1992. pap. 14.95 (0-8290-3150-2) Irvington.

— Theory of Valuation. Neurath, Otto, ed. (Foundations of the Unity of Science Ser.: Vol. 2, No. 4). 1994. pap. text 9.50 (0-226-57594-2) U Ch Pr.

— Understanding Chemistry. Date not set. pap. text, teacher ed. write for info. (0-314-03268-1) West Pub.

— Understanding Chemistry: Testbank. Date not set. pap. text, suppl. ed. write for info. (0-314-03266-5) West Pub.

— Way Out of Educational Confusion. LC 72-104267. 41p. 1971. reprint ed. lib. bdg. 49.50 (0-8371-3918-X, DEEC, Greenwood Pr) Greenwood.

— Wit & Wisdom of John Dewey. Johnson, A. H., ed. LC 69-13883. 111p. 1969. reprint ed. lib. bdg. 45.00 (0-8371-0380-0, DEWW, Greenwood Pr) Greenwood.

Dewey, John & Bentley, Arthur F. Knowing & the Known. LC 75-31432. 334p. 1976. reprint ed. lib. bdg. 47.50 (0-8371-8498-3, DEKK, Greenwood Pr) Greenwood.

Dewey, John & Kallen, Horace M. The Bertrand Russell Case. LC 78-37289. (Civil Liberties in American History Ser.). 228p. 1972. reprint ed. lib. bdg. 29.00 (0-306-70426-9) Da Capo.

Dewey, John & Sigler, Julius A. Science, Technology & Society. 2nd ed. LC 97-22237. (Lynchburg College Symposium Readings Ser.). 1997. pap. write for info. (0-7618-0835-3) U Pr of Amer.

Dewey, John, et al. Am I Getting an Education? LC 75-3114. (Philosophy America Ser.). reprint ed. 27.50 (0-404-59110-8) AMS Pr.

— Not Guilty: Report of the 1937-38 Commission of Inquiry into the Charges Made Against Leon Trotsky in the Moscow Trials. LC 72-87928. 422p. 1973. reprint ed. lib. bdg. 65.00 (0-913460-00-1) Pathfinder NY.

— Seminal Research Papers, 11. LC 77-72191. (Contributions to the History of Psychology Ser.: No. 11, Pt. A, Orientations). 454p. 1977. reprint ed. lib. bdg. 75.00 (0-313-26935-1, U6935, Greenwood Pr) Greenwood.

Dewey, Joseph. In a Dark Time: The Apocalyptic Temper in the American Novel of the Nuclear Age. LC 89-35864. 268p. 1990. 49.95 (1-55753-001-7) Purdue U Pr.

— Novels from Reagan's America: A New Realism. LC 99-36889. 1999. write for info. (0-8130-1714-9) U Press Fla.

***Dewey, Joseph & Horvath, Brooke.** The Finer Thread, the Tighter Weave: New Essays on the Short Fiction of Henry James. LC 00-8149. 2000. write for info. (1-55753-207-9) Purdue U Pr.

Dewey, Joseph J. The Immortal, Bks. I & II. unabridged ed. 365p. 1998. pap. 19.95 (0-9665053-0-1) Great AD-Vent.

***Dewey, Katherine.** Creating Life-Like Animals in Polymer Clay. LC 99-46378. (Illus.). 128p. (YA). 2000. pap. 22.99 (0-89134-955-3, North Lght Bks) F & W Pubns Inc.

Dewey, Kirk M. Stories: God's Hand in My Life. Heald, Jane D., ed. LC 89-91377. 208p. (Orig.). 1990. pap. 10.95 (0-9619558-2-1) Support Source.

Dewey, Laurel. The Humorous Herbalist. 2nd ed. 204p. 1996. reprint ed. pap. 14.95 (1-884820-23-9) SAFE GOODS.

***Dewey, Laurel.** Plant Power: The Humorous Herbalist's Guide to Finding, Growing, Gathering & Using 30 Great Medicinal Herbs. 422p. 1999. 19.95 (1-884820-37-9) SAFE GOODS.

***Dewey, Lisa.** Spank. (Illus.). 60p. 2000. pap. 15.00 (1-880855-07-0) Fifth Planet.

Dewey, M. D. & Dewey, J. H. The Way, the Truth & the Life: A Handbook of Christian Theosophy, Healing, Psychic Culture Based upon the Ideal & Method of the Christ. 424p. 1997. reprint ed. pap. 29.95 (0-7661-0031-6) Kessinger Pub.

Dewey, Margaret. Light from Within: Perspective on the Biblical Drama. 206p. 1994. pap. 9.95 (1-85311-072-8, 844, Pub. by Canterbury Press Norwich) Morehouse Pub.

Dewey, Melvil. Abridged Dewey Decimal Classification & Relative Index. 13th abr. ed. Mitchell, Joan S. et al, eds. LC 97-10791. 1023p. 1997. text 90.00 (0-910608-59-8) OCLC Forest Pr.

— A Classification & Subject Index for Cataloguing & Arranging the Books & Pamphlets of a Library. 1979. lib. bdg. 250.00 (0-8490-1637-1) Gordon Pr.

— Dewey Decimal Classification: 200 Religion Class. Mitchell, Joan S. et al, eds. LC 97-25487. 272p. 1997. reprint ed. pap. 20.00 (0-910608-60-1) OCLC Forest Pr.

— Dewey Decimal Classification & Relative Index. 10th abr. ed. LC 70-164427. 1971. 18.00 (0-910608-13-X) OCLC Forest Pr.

— Dewey Decimal Classification & Relative Index. 11th abr. ed. LC 78-12514. 1979. 35.00 (0-910608-22-9) OCLC Forest Pr.

— Dewey Decimal Classification & Relative Index, 3 vols. 19th ed. LC 77-27967. 1979. 120.00 (0-910608-23-7); 42.00 (0-910608-19-9); 42.00 (0-910608-20-2); 42.00 (0-910608-21-0) OCLC Forest Pr.

— Dewey Decimal Classification & Relative Index, 4 vols., Set. 20th ed. LC 88-24629. 1989. 275.00 (0-910608-37-7) OCLC Forest Pr.

— Sistema de Clasificacion Decimal Dewey, 4 vols., Set. 20th ed. Octavio, G. & Rojas, L., eds. De Heredia, Margarita A., tr. (SPA.). 3300p. 1995. text 180.00 (958-9121-03-9) OCLC Online Comp.

***Dewey, Melvil, et al.** Dewey: Table 2 Geographic Areas: Great Britain & Republic of South Africa. LC 99-18163. viii, 87 p. 1999. 20.00 (0-910608-66-0) OCLC Forest Pr.

Dewey, Mora & Rainbow, Amy. Aspects of the One: The 99 Names of God. (Illus.). iv, 102p. (Orig.). 1994. pap. 26.00 (0-9656984-4-0) Neti Neti Ent.

Dewey, Orville. Moral Views of Commerce, Society & Politics in 12 Discourses. LC 68-27851. (Reprints of Economic Classics Ser.). 300p. 1969. reprint ed. 45.00 (0-678-00527-3) Kelley.

Dewey, Patrick. One Hundred One Microcomputer Projects to Do in Your Library: Putting Your Micro to Work. 176p. 1990. pap. text 6.00 (0-8389-0518-8) ALA.

Dewey, Patrick R. The Essential Guide to Bulletin Board Systems. LC 97-30193. 165p. 1997. 39.50 (1-57387-035-8) Info Today Inc.

— Fan Club Directory: Over 2400 Fan Clubs & Fan-Mail Internet & EMail Addresses in the United States & Abroad. 2nd ed. LC 97-44308. 176p. 1998. pap. 29.95 (0-7864-0291-1) McFarland & Co.

***Dewey, Patrick R.** 101 Computer Projects for Libraries. LC 99-38371. 224p. 1999. pap. 42.00 (0-8389-0772-5) ALA.

Dewey, Patrick R. One Hundred One Desktop Publishing & Graphics Programs. LC 93-13642. (One Hundred One Micro Ser.). 225p. 1993. pap. text 30.00 (0-8389-0606-0) ALA.

— Public Access Microcomputers. 2nd ed. (Professional Librarian Ser.). 300p. (C). 1990. 40.00 (0-8161-1896-5, Hall Reference); 30.00 (0-8161-1897-3, Hall Reference) Macmillan.

— Three Hundred Three CD-ROMs to Use in Your Library: Descriptions, Evaluations, & Practical Advice. LC 95-23607. (One Hundred One Micro Ser.). 238p. (Orig.). 1995. pap. 30.00 (0-8389-0666-4, 0666-4-2045) ALA.

— 303 Software Programs to Use in Your Library: Descriptions, Evaluations, & Practical Advice. LC 97-18210. 240p. 1997. 36.00 (0-8389-0722-9) American Library Association National Library.

— Two Hundred Two Plus Microcomputer Software Packages to Use in Your Library: Descriptions, Evaluations & Practical Advice. LC 91-42688. (One Hundred One Micro Ser.). 190p. (C). 1992. pap. 6.00 (0-8389-0582-X) ALA.

Dewey, Peter. British Agriculture in the First World War. 242p. (C). 1989. lib. bdg. 59.95 (0-415-02637-7, A2525) Routledge.

— War & Progress: Britain, 1914-1945. LC 96-16228. (Economic & Social History of Britain Ser.). (C). 1997. text 61.95 (0-582-04587-8, Pub. by Addison-Wesley) Longman.

An Asterisk (*) at the beginning of an entry indicates that the title is appearing for the first time.

Dewey, R. E. The Philosophy of John Dewey: A Critical Exposition of His Method, Metaphysics & Theory of Knowledge. 188p. 1978. pap. text 112.00 (*90-247-1980-1*, Pub. by M Nijhoff) Kluwer Academic.

Dewey, Ralph G. Dewey's Amusing Rubber Antics. (Illus.). 16p. 1989. pap. 4.00 (*1-880215-09-8*) Deweys GNB.

— Dewey's Balloon & Clown Notebook. (Illus.). 52p. 1981. pap. 6.00 (*1-880215-00-4*) Deweys GNB.

— Dewey's Balloon Anomalies. (Illus.). 36p. (Orig.). 1996. pap. 5.00 (*1-880215-27-6*) Deweys GNB.

— Dewey's Basic Balloon Sculpturing Course. (Illus.). 12p. 1978. pap. 4.00 (*1-880215-10-1*) Deweys GNB.

— Dewey's Bubble Buddies. (Illus.). 48p. 1978. pap. 6.00 (*1-880215-07-1*) Deweys GNB.

— Dewey's Clown Clip Art, No. 1. (Illus.). 15p. 1996. pap. text 10.00 (*1-880215-24-1*) Deweys GNB.

— Dewey's Clown Gags & Giggles. (Illus.). 32p. 1990. pap. 5.00 (*1-880215-13-6*) Deweys GNB.

— Dewey's Easy Gospel Chalk Talks. (Illus.). 48p. 1983. pap. 6.00 (*1-880215-02-0*) Deweys GNB.

— Dewey's Extra Easy Balloons. (Illus.). 32p. 1987. pap. 4.50 (*1-880215-15-2*) Deweys GNB.

— Dewey's Gospel Balloon Routines, No. 1. (Illus.). 14p. 1977. pap. 4.00 (*1-880215-04-7*) Deweys GNB.

— Dewey's Gospel Balloon Routines, No. 2. (Illus.). 32p. 1985. pap. 4.50 (*1-880215-05-5*) Deweys GNB.

— Dewey's Gospel Balloon Routines, No. 3. (Illus.). 28p. 1988. pap. 4.50 (*1-880215-06-3*) Deweys GNB.

— Dewey's Gospel Cartoon Chalk Talks. (Illus.). 36p. 1979. pap. 5.50 (*1-880215-01-2*) Deweys GNB.

— Dewey's Gospel Cartoon Fun. (Illus.). 32p. 1989. pap. 5.50 (*1-880215-03-9*) Deweys GNB.

— Dewey's Gospel Clown Skits, No. 1. (Illus.). 30p. 1986. pap. 4.50 (*1-880215-18-7*) Deweys GNB.

— Dewey's Gospel Clown Skits, No. 2. (Illus.). 32p. 1992. pap. 4.50 (*1-880215-21-7*) Deweys GNB.

— Dewey's Gospel Juggling Skits. (Illus.). 16p. 1990. pap. 4.00 (*1-880215-12-8*) Deweys GNB.

— Dewey's Gospel Paper Tricks. (Illus.). 28p. 1991. pap. 4.50 (*1-880215-14-4*) Deweys GNB.

— Dewey's Klown Komedy. (Illus.). 36p. 1994. pap. text 5.00 (*1-880215-23-3*) Deweys GNB.

— Dewey's Mammoth Multiple Balloons. (Illus.). 28p. 1985. pap. 4.50 (*1-880215-08-X*) Deweys GNB.

— Dewey's New Balloon Animals. (Illus.). 46p. 1976. pap. 6.00 (*1-880215-11-X*) Deweys GNB.

— Dewey's Rubber Rascals. (Illus.). 44p. 1984. pap. 5.50 (*1-880215-16-0*) Deweys GNB.

— Dewey's Solo Clown Ministry. (Illus.). 32p. (Orig.). 1997. pap. 6.00 (*1-880215-28-4*) Deweys GNB.

— Dewey's Zany Balloons. (Illus.). 44p. 1991. pap. 5.00 (*1-880215-17-9*) Deweys GNB.

— Purdy's Instrument Handbook. 2nd ed. (Illus.). 104p. 1996. pap. 9.95 (*1-880215-26-8*, Glen Enterp) Deweys GNB.

Dewey, Ralph G., et al. Dewey's Gospel Balloon Routines, No. 4. (Illus.). 40p. 1998. pap. 7.00 (*1-880215-29-2*) Deweys GNB.

Dewey, Richard. Recollections of Richard Dewey: Pioneer in American Psychiatry. Dewey, Ethel L., ed. LC 73-2395. (Mental Illness & Social Policy; the American Experience Ser.). 1973. reprint ed. 23.95 (*0-405-05203-0*) Ayer.

Dewey, Richard L. John Lathrop: Arrival in America & Family Tree. 106p. 1988. pap. 16.95 (*0-9616024-4-9*) Paramount Bks.

— Rockwell: U. S. Marshal. 216p. 1987. 15.95 (*0-9616024-2-2*) Paramount Bks.

Dewey, Richard Lloyd. Porter Rockwell: A Biography. LC 65-63355. (Illus.). 612p. 1986. 22.95 (*0-9616024-0-6*) Paramount Bks.

***Dewey, Richard Lloyd.** The Porter Rockwell Chronicles, Vol. I. 490p. 1999. 21.95 (*0-9616024-6-5*) Paramount Bks.

Dewey, Richard S. Feudalism on Campus (An Insider's View) 109p. 1992. per. 7.40 (*1-880847-00-0*) DEWMAR Hse.

Dewey, Rob, ed. The One-Hundred Show: The Seventeenth Annual of the American Center for Design. (Illus.). 160p. 1995. pap. 30.00 (*0-941447-05-7*) Amer Ctr Design.

***Dewey, Scott Hamilton.** Don't Breathe the Air: Air Pollution & U. S. Environmental Politics, 1945-1970. LC 99-88267. (Environmental History Ser.: Vol. 16). 336p. (C). 2000. 39.95 (*0-89096-914-0*) Tex A&M Univ Pr.

Dewey, T. G. Biophysical & Biochemical Aspects of Fluorescence Spectroscopy. (Illus.). 312p. (C). 1990. text 95.00 (*0-306-43627-2*, Kluwer Plenum) Kluwer Academic.

Dewey, T. G., jt. ed. see Novak, M. M.

Dewey, T. Gregory. Fractals in Molecular Biophysics. LC 96-46067. (Topics in Physical Chemistry Ser.). (Illus.). 288p. 1998. text 65.00 (*0-19-508447-0*) OUP.

***Dewey, Thomas P.** Descendants of William Dewey. 116p. 2000. 29.50 (*0-7404-0614-0*) Higginson Bk Co.

Dewey, Thomas P. Dewey. Descendants of William Dewey. LC 99-215215. (Illus.). 115p. 1998. pap. 19.50 (*0-8328-9586-5*); lib. bdg. 29.50 (*0-8328-9585-7*) Higginson Bk Co.

Dewey, Veronica, tr. see Gorky, Maxim.

Dewey, W. A. Essentials of Homeopathic Therapeutics. 286p. 1993. spiral bd. 18.00 (*0-7873-0285-6*) Hlth Research.

Dewey, W. B., et al, photos by. Lotusland: A Photographic Odyssey. LC 95-14944. (Illus.). 144p. 1996. 65.00 (*0-9627297-5-2*) A A Knoll Pubs.

Dewey, William J. Sleeping Beauties: The Jerome L. Joss Collection of African Headrests at UCLA. LC 92-82945. (Illus.). 214p. 1993. 45.00 (*0-930741-27-7*); pap. 27.00 (*0-930741-28-5*) UCLA Fowler Mus.

Dewey, William T. Marriages in Montpelier, Vermont. 1984. reprint ed. pap. 6.00 (*0-912606-17-7*) Hunterdon Hse.

Dewey, William T. & Dewey, James F. Marriage Records of Barre & of Berlin, Washington County, Vermont. 64p. 1984. pap. 7.00 (*0-912606-24-X*) Hunterdon Hse.

Dewey, Willis, jt. auth. see Boericke, William.

Dewey, Willis A., jt. auth. see Boericke, William.

Dewhirst, Carin. The Nutcracker. LC 96-32661. (Life, Times, & Music Ser.). (Illus.). (J). 1996. write for info. (*1-56799-361-3*, Friedman-Fairfax) M Friedman Pub Grp Inc.

— Peter & The Wolf Level 4. (J). 1996. 16.98 incl. audio, cd-rom (*1-56799-303-6*) Friedman Pub.

— The Roads To Congress 1998. LC 99-38108. (Political Science). 1999. pap. 40.95 (*0-8304-1529-7*) Thomson Learn.

Dewhirst, Paul A. The Fall & Redemption of Man & the Will of God. LC 96-71762. 144p. 1997. 17.95 (*1-57197-046-0*) Pentland Pr.

Dewhirst, Robert E., jt. auth. see Ahuja, Sunil.

DeWhitt, Benjamin, jt. auth. see Wehmann, Howard H.

***DeWhitt, Benjamin L.** Records Relating to Personal Participation in World War 2: American Prisoners of War & Civilian Internees. 96p. 2000. per. 7.00 (*0-16-050200-4*) USGPO.

Dewhurst. Modern Circuit & System Design. (C). 2000. pap. text 50.00 (*0-13-267790-3*) P-H.

Dewhurst, C. J., jt. auth. see Chamberlain, Geoffrey V.P.

Dewhurst, C. Kurt. Grand Ledge Folk Pottery: Traditions at Work. Bronner, Simon J., ed. LC 86-11340. (American Material Culture & Folklife Ser.). 155p. reprint ed. 48.10 (*0-8357-1732-1*, 207045100093) Bks Demand.

Dewhurst, C. Kurt & Lockwood, Yvonne R., eds. Michigan Folklife Reader. LC 88-42622. (Illus.). 400p. (C). 1987. 17.00 (*0-87013-259-8*) Mich St U Pr.

Dewhurst, C. Kurt & McDowell, Marsha, eds. To Honor & Comfort: Native Quilting Traditions. LC 97-27063. (Illus.). 240p. 1997. 50.00 (*0-89013-316-6*); pap. 35.00 (*0-89013-317-4*) Museum NM Pr.

Dewhurst, Eileen. Alias the Enemy. 256p. 1997. 24.00 (*0-7278-5123-3*) Severn Hse.

— Death in Candie Gardens. large type ed. (Ulverscroft). 416p. 1994. 27.99 (*0-7089-3056-5*) Ulverscroft.

— Death of a Stranger. 224p. 1999. 25.00 (*0-7278-2282-9*, Pub. by Severn Hse) Chivers N Amer.

***Dewhurst, Eileen.** Death of a Stranger. large type ed. 368p. 2000. 31.99 (*0-7505-1489-2*, Pub. by Mgna Lrg Print) Ulverscroft.

— Double Act. 224p. 26.00 (*0-7278-5533-6*) Severn Hse.

Dewhurst, Eileen. A Nice Little Mystery. large type ed. (Mystery Ser.). 416p. 1992. 27.99 (*0-7089-2601-0*) Ulverscroft.

— Now You See Her. 256p. 1995. 20.00 (*0-7278-4733-3*) Severn Hse.

— Now You See Her. large type ed. (Large Print Ser.). 432p. 1996. 27.99 (*0-7089-3550-8*) Ulverscroft.

— Roundabout. LC 98-28865. 266 p. 1999. write for info. (*0-7540-3474-7*) Chivers N Amer.

— Roundabout. large type ed. LC 98-28865. 284p. 1999. 30.00 (*0-7862-1598-4*) Thorndike Pr.

— The Sleeper. large type ed. 1990. 27.99 (*0-7089-2188-4*) Ulverscroft.

Dewhurst, J. Frederic, jt. auth. see Bossard, James H.

Dewhurst, J. Frederic, jt. auth. see Stewart, Paul W.

Dewhurst, J. H., et al. Regional Input-Output Modelling: New Developments & Interpretations. 282p. 1991. text 79.95 (*1-85628-119-1*, Pub. by Avebry) Ashgate Pub Co.

Dewhurst, Jack. Attended with Miracles. (C). 1989. text 50.00 (*1-85821-013-5*, Pub. by Pentland Pr) St Mut.

Dewhurst, John. Migration: United Kingdom. 1986. 44.00 (*90-6544-196-4*) Kluwer Law Intl.

— Practical Pediatric & Adolescent Gynecology. LC 80-24015. (Reproductive Medicine Ser.: Vol. 1). (Illus.). 288p. reprint ed. pap. 89.30 (*0-608-08928-1*, 206956300005) Bks Demand.

Dewhurst, John, jt. auth. see Edmonds, Keith.

Dewhurst, Keith. Lark Rise to Candleford. 171p. 1990. pap. 15.95 (*0-7487-0375-6*) Dufour.

— War Plays. (Oberon Bks.). 264p. 1997. pap. 18.95 (*1-870259-63-7*) Theatre Comm.

Dewhurst, Keith, tr. see Sophocles.

Dewhurst, Kenneth, jt. auth. see Sydenham, Thomas.

Dewhurst-Maddock, Olivea. The Book of Sound Therapy: Heal Yourself with Music & Voice. LC 92-13804. 128p. 1993. pap. 14.00 (*0-671-78639-3*, Fireside) S&S Trade Pap.

Dewhurst, Stephen C. & Stark, Kathy T. Programming in C++ 2nd ed. LC 95-2776. 320p. (C). 1995. pap. 42.00 (*0-13-182718-9*) P-H.

Dewi, I. A., et al, eds. Pollution in Livestock Production Systems. (Illus.). 464p. 1994. text 130.00 (*0-85198-857-1*) OUP.

Dewick, Paul M. Medicinal Natural Products: A Biosynthetic Approach. LC 97-12100. 476p. 1997. pap. 72.95 (*0-471-97478-1*) Wiley.

— Medicinal Natural Products: A Biosynthetic Approach. LC 97-12100. 476p. 1997. 200.00 (*0-471-97477-3*) Wiley.

Dewick, S. A. Gustin: Ancestry of John S. Gustin & His Wife Susan McComb, Including an Account of John Hubbard, 2nd Husband of Elinor Shepherd. 136p. 1994. reprint ed. pap. 22.00 (*0-8328-4101-3*); reprint ed. lib. bdg. 32.00 (*0-8328-4100-5*) Higginson Bk Co.

Dewild, Patrick & Vandewalle, Joos, eds. Computer Systems & Software Engineering: State of the Art. LC 92-8523. 436p. (C). 1992. text 164.50 (*0-7923-1718-1*) Kluwer Academic.

DeWilde, John. Agriculture, Marketing & Pricing in Sub-Saharan Africa. 1984. pap. 18.50 (*0-918456-48-7*) African Studies Assn.

Dewilde, P., ed. Integrated Circuit Design Book: Papers on the VSLI Design Methodology from the ICD NELSIS Project. 960p. (Orig.). 1986. pap. text 110.00 (*90-6275-246-2*, Pub. by Delft U Pr) Coronet Bks.

Dewilde, P., et al, eds. Challenges of a Generalized System Theory: Proceedings of the Colloquium, Amsterdam, the Netherlands, June 1992. 252p. 1993. pap. 50.00 (*0-444-85769-9*, North Holland) Elsevier.

Dewilde, P. & Van Der Veen, Alle-Jan. Time-Varying Systems & Computations. LC 98-22287. 1998. 122.00 (*0-7923-8189-0*) Kluwer Academic.

Dewilde, Patrick & Ning, Zhen-Qiu. Models for Large Integrated Circuits. (C). 1990. text 103.50 (*0-7923-9115-2*) Kluwer Academic.

DeWilde, W. P., jt. ed. see Blain, W. R.

DeWind, Adrian W. & Woodhouse, John. Persecution of Defence Lawyers in South Korea: Report of a Mission to South Korea. LC KZ0372.. 72p. reprint ed. pap. 30.00 (*0-608-18111-0*, 203271000081) Bks Demand.

DeWindt, Anne R. & DeWindt, Edwin B. Royal Justice & the Medieval English Countryside: The Huntingdonshire Eyre of 1286, the Ramsey Abbey Banlieu Court of 1287, & the Assizes of 1287-88. xvi, viii, 766p. pap. 64.57 (*0-88844-057-X*) Brill Academic Pubs.

DeWindt, Edwin B. The Liber Gersumarum of Ramsey Abbey: A Calendar & Index. (Illus.). viii, 455p. pap. text 59.43 (*0-88844-356-0*) Brill Academic Pubs.

DeWindt, Edwin B., ed. The Salt of Common Life: Individuality & Choice in the Medieval Town, Countryside, & Church. LC 95-30224. (Studies in Medieval Culture: Vol. 36). 1995. pap. 20.00 (*1-879288-47-8*); boxed set 50.00 (*1-879288-46-X*) Medieval Inst.

DeWindt, Edwin B. & Consortium for the Teaching of the Middle Ages Sta. A Slice of Life: Selected Documents of Medieval English Peasant Experience. LC 96-45726. 1996. pap. 6.00 (*1-879288-73-7*) Medieval Inst.

DeWindt, Edwin B., jt. auth. see DeWindt, Anne R.

***DeWine, Mike, ed.** Airline Hubs: Fair Competition or Predatory Pricing?: Congressional Hearing. 82p. (C). 1999. reprint ed. pap. text 20.00 (*0-7881-8413-X*) DIANE Pub.

DeWine, Mike, ed. Improving the Well-Being of Abused & Neglected Children: Hearing Before the Committee on Labor & Human Resources, U. S. Senate. 61p. 1998. pap. text 25.00 (*0-7881-7112-7*) DIANE Pub.

***DeWine, Mike, ed.** Violent & Drug Trafficking Crimes: The Bailey Decision's Effect on Prosecutions under 9249(c): Congressional Hearing. 51p. 2000. reprint ed. pap. text 20.00 (*0-7881-8858-5*) DIANE Pub.

***DeWine, Sue.** Consultants Craft. 2nd ed. 2000. pap. text. write for info. (*0-312-24824-5*) St Martin.

DeWine, Sue. The Consultant's Craft: Improving Organizational Communication. 396p. 1993. pap. text 46.95 (*0-312-06151-X*) St Martin.

DeWine, Sue, et al. Exploring Human Communication. LC 98-19381. (Illus.). 400p. (C). 1999. pap. text. write for info. (*1-891487-10-8*) Roxbury Pub Co.

Dewing, Arthur S. Corporate Promotion & Reorganizations. LC 14-6465. (Business Enterprises Reprint Ser.). 1986. reprint ed. lib. bdg. 52.00 (*0-89941-444-3*, 303830) W S Hein.

Dewing, Douglass W. A Virginia Title Examiner's Manual. 2nd ed. 661p. 1992. 75.00 (*0-87473-998-5*, 61225-10, MICHIE) LEXIS Pub.

— A Virginia Title Examiners' Manual. 3rd ed. LC 98-87039. 707p. 1998. 90.00 (*0-327-00301-4*, 6122511) LEXIS Pub.

Dewing, Martha. Beyond TV: Activities for Using Video with Children. LC 91-40441. 140p. 1991. pap. text 45.00 (*0-87436-601-1*) ABC-CLIO.

— Home Video in Libraires: How Libraries Buy & Circulate Prerecorded Home Video. (Professional Librarian Ser.). 220p. 1989. 40.00 (*0-8161-1914-7*, Hall Reference) Macmillan.

Dewing, Rolland. Wounded Knee II. 230p. 1995. 21.95 (*0-9646780-0-4*); pap. 10.95 (*0-9646780-1-2*) Grt Plains Ntwrk.

Dewing, Thomas, jt. auth. see Musbach, Joan M.

DeWinte, Mike, ed. Assessing Problems in Monitoring & Enforcing Hearing Parole under the Interstate Compact Before the Committee on the Judiciary, U. S. Senate. (Illus.). 57p. (C). 1999. reprint ed. pap. text 20.00 (*0-7881-3497-3*) DIANE Pub.

***Dewire, Bob.** My Guide to America's Animals & Plants. (Illus.). 48p. (J). (gr. 1-2). 2000. 2.50 (*1-56762-126-0*) Modern Learn Pr.

— My Guide to America's Habitats. (Illus.). 72p. 2000. 2.95 (*1-56762-128-7*) Modern Learn Pr.

— My Guide to Our Habitat. (Illus.). 64p. (J). (gr. 2-3). 2000. 2.75 (*1-56762-127-9*) Modern Learn Pr.

***Dewire, Bob & Sullivan, Beth, contrib. by.** Introducing America's Habitats: Natural Science Information & Interdisciplinary Activities. (Illus.). 180p. (J). (gr. 1-4). 2000. teacher ed. 14.95 (*1-56762-125-2*) Modern Learn Pr.

Dewire, D. Travis. Second Generation Client - Server Computing. LC 96-35817. (Illus.). 448p. 1995. pap. 49.95 (*0-07-016736-2*) McGraw.

DeWire, Elinor. The Lighthouse Activity Book. (Illus.). 88p. (Orig.). (J). (gr. k-8). 1995. pap. 11.95 (*0-9657313-0-8*) Sentinel Pubns.

Dewire, Travis. Thin Clients: Web-Based Client/Server Architecture & Applications. LC 98-2839. (Illus.). 416p. 1998. pap. 49.95 (*0-07-016738-9*) McGraw.

Dewis, Malcolm. Tolley's Health & Safety at Work Handbook. 900p. 1995. pap. 180.00 (*1-86012-070-9*, Pub. by Tolley Pubng) St Mut.

— Tolley's Health & Safety at Work Handbook, 1994. 730p. 1993. 150.00 (*0-85459-745-X*, Pub. by Tolley Pubng) St Mut.

Dewis, Malcolm, jt. auth. see Stranks, Jeremy.

Dewit. Essentials of Nursing Care. 2001. text. write for info. (*0-7216-6923-9*, W B Saunders Co); pap. text, student ed. write for info. (*0-7216-6929-8*, W B Saunders Co) Harcrt Hlth Sci Grp.

DeWit, Augusta. Java: Facts & Fancies. (Illus.). 332p. 1988. pap. text 19.95 (*0-19-582609-4*) OUP.

DeWit, B. Q. & Smith, J. Field Theory in Particle Physics, Vol. 1. (North-Holland Personal Library). xii, 490p. 1986. 111.75 (*0-444-86996-4*, North Holland); pap. 65.75 (*0-444-86999-9*, North Holland) Elsevier.

DeWit, Susan C. Essentials of Medical-Surgical Nursing. 4th ed. Rader, Ilze, ed. (Illus.). 1088p. 1998. text 47.50 (*0-7216-6920-4*, W B Saunders Co) Harcrt Hlth Sci Grp.

— Keane's Essentials of Medical-Surgical Nursing. 3rd ed. (Illus.). 1992. teacher ed. write for info. (*0-7216-4508-9*, W B Saunders Co) Harcrt Hlth Sci Grp.

— Rambo's Nursing Skills for Clinical Practice. 4th rev. ed. LC 93-36409. (Illus.). 1200p. 1994. pap. text 37.00 (*0-7216-3642-X*, W B Saunders Co) Harcrt Hlth Sci Grp.

— Saunders Student Nurse Planner. LC 95-11490. 1995. pap. text 15.00 (*0-7216-5831-8*, W B Saunders Co) Harcrt Hlth Sci Grp.

— Saunders Student Nurse Planner. 2nd ed. LC 99-31884. (Illus.). 335p. 1999. pap. text 13.95 (*0-7216-8606-0*, W B Saunders Co) Harcrt Hlth Sci Grp.

DeWit, Susan C., ed. Essentials of Medical-Surgical Nursing. 4th ed. (Illus.). 1085p. 1998. student ed. write for info. (*0-7216-6922-0*, W B Saunders Co); pap., teacher ed. write for info. (*0-7216-6921-2*, W B Saunders Co) Harcrt Hlth Sci Grp.

— Rambo's Nursing Skills for Clinical Practice. 4th ed. (Illus.). 1994. pap., teacher ed. write for info. (*0-7216-4178-4*, W B Saunders Co) Harcrt Hlth Sci Grp.

— Rambo's Nursing Skills for Clinical Practice. 4th ed. (Illus.). 1994. pap. text, student ed. 18.00 (*0-7216-4324-8*, W B Saunders Co) Harcrt Hlth Sci Grp.

DeWitt. The Food of Santa Fe: Authentic Recipes from the American Southwest. LC 97-32182. (Illus.). 144p. 1998. 16.95 (*962-593-229-1*, Periplus Eds) Tuttle Pubng.

DeWitt, jt. auth. see Roberts.

DeWitt, jt. ed. see DeWitt, C.

***DeWitt, Abigail.** Lili. LC 00-8058. 307p. 2000. 26.95 (*0-8101-5100-6*, TriQuart) Northwestern U Pr.

DeWitt-Arar, Keren C., jt. ed. see Shapira, Amos.

DeWitt, Ben. Death of a Hummingbird. 256p. 1998. pap. 7.50 (*0-9665387-3-0*) Oso Pr.

— Graveyard Grove. 264p. 1999. pap. 10.00 (*0-9665387-4-9*) Oso Pr.

— No Other Way. 256p. 1999. pap. 10.00 (*0-9665387-0-6*) Oso Pr.

***DeWitt, Ben.** The Third Valley. 256p. 2000. 21.00 (*0-9665387-1-4*) Oso Pr.

DeWitt, Beverley J., ed. see Levy, Harold P.

DeWitt Bockstruck, Lloyd. Virginia's Colonial Soldiers. 443p. 1998. reprint ed. 30.00 (*0-8063-1219-X*, 490) Genealog Pub.

DeWitt, Bryce S. Dynamical Theory of Groups & Fields. xiv, 238p. 1965. text 274.00 (*0-677-00985-2*) Gordon & Breach.

DeWitt, Bryce S. & Graham, Neill, eds. The Many-Worlds Interpretation of Quantum Mechanics. LC 72-12116. (Princeton Series in Physics). (Illus.). 255p. reprint ed. pap. 79.10 (*0-7837-1942-6*, 204215700001) Bks Demand.

DeWitt, C., ed. Les Houches Lectures. Incl. Vol. 63. Relativity, Groups & Topology, 1963. DeWitt, B. S., ed. xvi, 930p. 1964. text 1096.00 (*0-677-10080-9*); Vol. 67. 1967, Many-Body Physics. Balian, R., ed. xviii, 426p. 1968. text 552.00 (*0-677-12700-6*); write for info. (*0-318-52701-4*) Gordon & Breach.

DeWitt, C. & DeWitt, eds. Les Houches Lectures: 1972, Black Holes, Vol. 72. xii, 552p. 1973. text 552.00 (*0-677-15610-3*) Gordon & Breach.

DeWitt, C. & Peyraud, J., eds. Les Houches Lectures: 1972, Plasma Physics, Vol. 72. xiv, 542p. 1975. text 552.00 (*0-677-15740-1*) Gordon & Breach.

Dewitt, Calvin B. Caring for Creation: Responsible Stewardship of God's Handiwork. LC 97-39356. 112p. 1998. pap. 11.99 (*0-8010-5802-3*) Baker Bks.

DeWitt, Calvin B. Earth Wise: A Biblical Response to Environmental Issues. LC 94-6513. (Issues in Christian Living Ser.). 1994. pap. 7.75 (*1-56212-057-3*) CRC Pubns.

DeWitt, Calvin B. & Prance, Ghillean T., eds. Missionary Earthkeeping. (C). 1992. lib. bdg. 30.00 (*0-86554-390-9*, H318) Mercer Univ Pr.

DeWitt County Historical Comm. The History of DeWitt County, TX. (Illus.). 859p. 1991. 70.00 (*0-88107-175-7*) Curtis Media.

DeWitt, D. J. & Boral, H., eds. Database Machines. (Illus.). viii, 376p. 1985. 63.95 (*0-387-96200-X*) Spr-Verlag.

DeWitt, D. P., jt. ed. see Richmond, J. C.

Dewitt, Dave. The Chile Pepper Encyclopedia: Everything You'll Ever Need to Know about Hot Peppers, with More Than 100 Recipes. LC 98-29314. (Illus.). 352p. 1999. pap. 19.95 (*0-688-15611-8*, Wm Morrow) Morrow Avon.

— Flavors of Africa: Spicy African Cooking. LC 97-26084. 272p. 1998. pap. 16.00 (*0-7615-0520-2*) Prima Pub.

DeWitt, Dave. Hot & Spicy Southeast Asian Dishes: The Best Fiery Food from the Pacific Rim. (Illus.). 336p. 1995. pap. 14.95 (*1-55958-577-3*) Prima Pub.

— Hot Spots: Spicy Recipes from America's Most Celebrated Fiery-Foods Restaurants. 300p. 1991. pap. 14.95 (*1-55958-109-3*) Prima Pub.

— Hot Spots: Spicy Recipes from the Most Celebrated Fiery Food. 2nd expanded rev. ed. 224p. 1995. pap. 14.95 (*1-55958-699-0*) Prima Pub.

Dewitt, Dave. Pepper Garden. LC 93-30508. (Illus.). 240p. 1993. pap. 15.95 (*0-89815-554-1*) Ten Speed Pr.

D

— Whole Chile Pepper Book. 373p. 1990. pap. 22.95 (*0-316-18223-0*) Little.

DeWitt, Dave & Bosland, Paul W. Peppers of the World: An Identification Guide. LC 96-15364. (Illus.). 219p. (Orig.). 1997. pap. 19.95 (*0-89815-840-0*) Ten Speed Pr.

DeWitt, Dave & Evans, Chuck. The Hot Sauce Bible. (Illus.). 384p. 1996. pap. text 20.00 (*0-89594-760-9*) Crossing Pr.

— The Pepper Pantry: Chiptles. LC 96-30488. (Pepper Pantry Ser.). (Illus.). 96p. 1997. pap. 5.95 (*0-89087-828-5*) Celestial Arts.

***DeWitt, Dave & Gerlach, Nancy.** Barbecue Inferno: Cooking with Chile Peppers on the Grill. LC 00-37793. (Illus.). 192p. 2001. pap. 16.95 (*1-58008-154-1*) Ten Speed Pr.

DeWitt, Dave & Gerlach, Nancy. Fiery Appetizers: Seventy Hot & Spicy Hors d'oeuvres. 2nd ed. (Chile Pepper Cookbook Ser.). 85p. 1993. pap. 6.95 (*0-9623865-2-9*) Out West Pub.

— Fiery Appetizers: 70 Spicy Hot Hors d'Oeuvres. LC 95-65. (Illus.). 96p. 1995. pap. 8.95 (*0-89594-785-4*) Crossing Pr.

— The Food of Santa Fe: Authentic Recipes from the American Southwest LC 97-32182. 144p. 1998. write for info. (*962-593-102-3*) Periplus.

— Habanero Cookbook. LC 94-13961. (Illus.). 176p. 1995. pap. 17.95 (*0-89815-638-6*) Ten Speed Pr.

— Just North of the Border: From the Editors of Chile Pepper Magazine, a Collection of Their Favorite Southwestern Dishes. (Illus.). 250p. (Orig.). 1992. pap. 14.95 (*1-55958-214-6*) Prima Pub.

— The Pepper Pantry: Habaneros. LC 96-31709. (Pepper Pantry Ser.). (Illus.). 96p. 1997. pap. 5.95 (*0-89087-827-7*) Celestial Arts.

DeWitt, Dave & Longacre, W. C. Great Bowls of Fire. LC 97-25881. (Illus.). 160p. (Orig.). 1997. pap. 16.95 (*0-89815-901-6*) Ten Speed Pr.

DeWitt, Dave & Stock, Melissa. Sweet Heat. (Illus.). 201p. (Orig.). 1996. pap. 16.95 (*0-89815-817-6*) Ten Speed Pr.

DeWitt, Dave & Wilan, Mary J. Pasta Exotica. LC 97-24694. (Illus.). 102p. 1997. pap. text 14.95 (*0-89815-905-9*) Ten Speed Pr.

DeWitt, Dave, et al. The Healing Power of Peppers: Chile Pepper Recipes & Folk Remedies. LC 97-45527. 192p. 1998. pap. 12.00 (*0-609-80002-7*) C Potter.

— Hot & Spicy & Meatless 2, Vol. 2. LC 96-29311. (Illus.). 304p. 1996. pap. 12.95 (*0-7615-0543-1*) Prima Pub.

— Hot & Spicy Caribbean: Over 150 of the Best & Most Flavorful Island Recipes. (Illus.). 336p. 1995. pap. 14.95 (*0-7615-0126-6*) Prima Pub.

DeWitt, Dave, jt. auth. see Longacre, W. C.

Dewitt, David, et al, eds. Building A New Global Order: Emerging Trends In International Security. (Illus.). 436p. (C). 1994. pap. text 24.95 (*0-19-540964-7*) OUP.

— Proceedings of the XII International Congress on Mathematical Physics, Vol. 12. (Series in Mathematical Physics: Vol. 12). (Illus.). 411p. 1998. 42.00 (*1-57146-055-1*, 1CMP12) Intl Pr Boston.

Dewitt, David B., jt. ed. see Gross-Stein, Janice.

Dewitt, David M. Assassination of Abraham Lincoln & Its Expiation. (Select Bibliographies Reprint Ser.). 1977. 19.95 (*0-8369-5574-9*) Ayer.

DeWitt, David M. Judicial Murder of Mary E. Surratt. LC 71-108472. 1970. reprint ed. 59.00 (*0-403-00423-3*) Scholarly.

DeWitt, David P. & Albright, Lyle F. Tube-Wall Temperature Measurement in Fired Process Heaters. LC TJ0320.D39. (MTI Publication Ser.: No. 24). 167p. 1986. reprint ed. pap. 51.80 (*0-608-06692-3*, 206688900009) Bks Demand.

DeWitt, David P., jt. auth. see Incropera, Frank P.

DeWitt, Dawn E., jt. auth. see Romaine, Deborah S.

DeWitt, Donald L. Articles Describing Archives & Manuscript Collections in the United States: An Annotated Bibliography, 11. LC 96-37042. (Bibliographies & Indexes in Library & Information Science: Vol. 11). 480p. 1997. lib. bdg. 95.00 (*0-313-29598-0*, Greenwood Pr) Greenwood.

— Guide to the Manuscript Collections, Western History Collections, University of Oklahoma. 318p. (Orig.). 1995. pap. text 24.00 (*0-7884-0117-3*) Heritage Bk.

DeWitt, Donald L., compiled by. Guides to Archives & Manuscript Collections in the United States: An Annotated Bibliography, 8. LC 93-37179. (Bibliographies & Indexes in Library I Information Science: No. 8). 496p. 1994. lib. bdg. 99.50 (*0-313-28499-7*, Greenwood Pr) Greenwood.

DeWitt, Donald L., ed. American Indian Resource Materials in the Western History Collection, University of Oklahoma. LC 90-50232. (Illus.). 288p. 1990. 39.95 (*0-8061-2289-7*) U of Okla Pr.

— Going Digital: Strategies for Access, Preservation, & Conversion of Collections to a Digital Format. LC 98-6626. 232p. 1998. 59.95 (*0-7890-0521-2*) Haworth Pr.

DeWitt, Donald L., jt. auth. see Lovett, John R., Jr.

DeWitt, Frances B., ed. see Institute for Enlightenment Founders.

***DeWitt, Gary, et al.** Client-Server Applications with Visual FoxPro & SQL Server. Charon, Chaim, ed. 400p. 2000. pap. 49.95 (*1-930919-01-8*) Hentzenwerke.

DeWitt, Gary, ed. see Strahl, Rick.

Dewitt, Georgeann. The Rescue from the Dark Side. 1984. pap. 5.95 (*0-88144-029-9*, CPS029) Christian Pub.

***DeWitt, Helen.** The Seventh Samurai: A Novel. 544p. 2000. 24.95 (*0-7868-6668-3*, Pub. by Talk Miramax Bks) Time Warner.

***DeWitt, Henry.** Breaking into Print: Early Stories & Insights into Getting Published; A Ploughshares Anthology. 304p. 2000. pap. 16.00 (*0-8070-6235-9*) Beacon Pr.

DeWitt Historical Society of Tompkins County, ed. see Vanas, Ellen.

DeWitt, Howard. The California Dream. 2nd ed. LC 97-73456. 400p. (C). 1997. per. 41.95 (*0-7872-3926-7*) Kendall-Hunt.

***DeWitt, Howard.** The California Dream. 2nd ed. LC 97-73. 396p. (C). 1999. per. 53.95 (*0-7872-5993-4*, 41599303) Kendall-Hunt.

DeWitt, Howard. The Fragmented Dream: Multicultural California. 274p. (C). 1996. pap. text, per. 32.74 (*0-7872-1978-9*) Kendall-Hunt.

***DeWitt, Howard.** The Fragmented Dream: Multicultural California. 294p. (C). 1999. per. 39.95 (*0-7872-6287-0*, 41628703) Kendall-Hunt.

DeWitt, Howard. Jose Rizal: Philippine Nationalist as Political Scientist. 2nd ed. LC 99-159310. 318p. (C). 1998. per. 54.95 (*0-7872-5457-6*, 41545701) Kendall-Hunt.

— Readings in California Civilization. 4th ed. LC 98-215364. 274p. (C). 1998. per. 32.95 (*0-7872-5093-7*, 41509301) Kendall-Hunt.

DeWitt, Howard, jt. auth. see Cotten, Lee.

DeWitt, Howard A. Beatle Poems. (Illus.). 60p. (Orig.). 1987. pap. 6.95 (*0-938840-06-1*) Horizon Bks CA.

***DeWitt, Howard A.** The Beatles: Untold Tales. 294p. (C). 2000. per. 37.95 (*0-7872-7282-5*) Kendall-Hunt.

DeWitt, Howard A. The Beatles: Untold Tales. (Illus.). 272p. 1994. reprint ed. pap. text 14.95 (*0-938840-03-7*) Horizon Bks CA.

— Paul McCartney: From Liverpool to Let It Be. (Illus.). 276p. (Orig.). 1992. pap. text 14.95 (*0-938840-04-5*) Horizon Bks CA.

— Van Morrison: The Mystic's Music. (Illus.). 114p. 1983. reprint ed. pap. text 14.95 (*0-938840-02-9*) Horizon Bks CA.

Dewitt, Hugh E., jt. ed. see Rogers, Forrest J.

DeWitt, Jamie & Klein, David J. Irwin the Sock. LC 87-16535. (Publish-a-Book Contest Ser.). (Illus.). 32p. (J). (gr. 1-6). 1987. lib. bdg. 22.83 incl. audio (*0-8172-3157-9*) Raintree Steck-V.

DeWitt, Jim. Cloud Reflections in My Soup. LC 83-90475. (Poetry for Schools Ser.). (Illus.). 64p. (Orig.). (J). (gr. 3-12). 1984. pap. text 5.95 (*0-915199-01-7*) Pen-Dec.

— The En-Dec System of Writing & Reading. (Illus.). 52p. (Orig.). (YA). (gr. 9-12). 1987. pap. 6.95 (*0-915199-74-2*) Pen-Dec.

— Fingernail Souffle. (Illus.). 136p. (Orig.). (J). (gr. 4-12). 1987. pap. 6.00 (*0-915199-03-3*) Pen-Dec.

Dewitt, Jim. Give All the Flowers Smiles. (Libraries-School Libraries). (Illus.). 64p. (Orig.). 1985. pap. 5.00 (*0-915199-15-7*) Pen-Dec.

— Glacial Blue Slippers on a Tear. (Libraries-School Libraries). (Illus.). 64p. 1985. pap. 5.00 (*0-915199-12-2*) Pen-Dec.

DeWitt, Jim. Glints from the Sphinx's Right Eye. (Illus.). 64p. (Orig.). 1980. pap. 3.95 (*0-915199-99-8*) Pen-Dec.

— Jammy Donuts a Season After. LC 83-90481. (Poetry for Schools Ser.). (Illus.). 64p. (Orig.). (J). (gr. 4-12). 1984. pap. text 5.95 (*0-915199-04-1*) Pen-Dec.

Dewitt, Jim. Lasers in a Closed Sparkle Spin. (Libraries-School Libraries). (Illus.). 64p. 1985. pap. 5.00 (*0-915199-14-9*) Pen-Dec.

DeWitt, Jim. Means Something Else--"Not Literally" Figures-of-Speech Writing Book. (Figurative Expressions (for Schools, Libraries, School Libraries) Ser.: Vol. 6). (Illus.). 64p. (Orig.). 1987. student ed. 6.00 (*0-915199-55-6*) Pen-Dec.

— Means Something Else--"The Doubles" Figures-of-Speech Writing Book. (Figurative Expressions (for Schools, Libraries, School Libraries) Ser.: Vol. 3). (Illus.). 64p. (Orig.). 1987. pap., student ed. 6.00 (*0-915199-52-1*) Pen-Dec.

— Means Something Else--"The Doubles" Figures-of-Speech Writing Book. (Figurative Expressions (for Schools, Libraries, School Libraries) Ser.: Vol. 4). (Illus.). 64p. (Orig.). 1987. pap., student ed. 6.00 (*0-915199-53-X*) Pen-Dec.

— Means Something Else--"The Doubles" Figures of Speech Writing Book, No. 2. (Figurative Expressions (for Schools, Libraries, School Libraries) Ser.). (Illus.). 64p. (Orig.). (YA). (gr. 6-12). 1987. student ed. 6.00 (*0-915199-51-3*) Pen-Dec.

Dewitt, Jim. Night Ballon Fever Rising. (Libraries-School Libraries). 64p. 1985. pap. 5.00 (*0-915199-10-6*) Pen-Dec.

DeWitt, Jim. People I've Known & Places I've Been. (Illus.). (Orig.). 1989. pap. 5.95 (*0-938991-49-3*) Colonial Pr AL.

— Quiet-Time Thoughts. LC 83-90474. (Poetry for Schools Ser.). (Illus.). 64p. (Orig.). (J). (gr. 3-10). 1984. pap. text 5.95 (*0-915199-00-9*) Pen-Dec.

— Sex: Hot, Love; Warm. (Illus.). 64p. (Orig.). 1978. pap. 3.95 (*0-915199-97-1*) Pen-Dec.

— Sharpshooting at Kinkajous. (Illus.). 136p. (J). (gr. 4-12). 1987. pap. 6.00 (*0-915199-06-8*) Pen-Dec.

Dewitt, Jim. Sprinting into Sun. (Illus.). 64p. (Orig.). 1979. pap. 3.95 (*0-915199-98-X*) Pen-Dec.

DeWitt, Jim. Twin Talk: Vocabulary Study Writing Book, Bk. 1. (Vocabulary Studies). (Illus.). 78p. (Orig.). (YA). (gr. 4-12). 1987. pap., student ed. 6.00 (*0-915199-25-4*) Pen-Dec.

DeWitt, Jim, see Dilemma, Diana, pseud.

DeWitt, Jim, see Freefoam, Juliet, pseud.

DeWitt, Jim, see Touchtome, Samantha, pseud.

Dewitt, John R. Amazing Love: The Parable of the Prodigal Son. 160p. 2000. pap. text 6.99 (*0-85151-328-X*) Banner of Truth.

DeWitt, John R. What Is the Reformed Faith? (Orig.). 1981. pap. text 2.50 (*0-85151-326-3*) Banner of Truth.

DeWitt, Leonard. Jehovah-Jireh Is His Name. 91p. 1990. pap. 5.99 (*0-934998-41-8*) Evangel Indiana.

DeWitt, Lisa F. Cue Cards: Famous Women of the Twentieth Century. Clark, Raymond C., ed. (Supplementary Materials Handbook Ser.: No. 8). (Illus.). 96p. (Orig.). 1993. pap. text 14.00 (*0-86647-077-8*) Pro Lingua.

— Nobel Prize Winners: Biographical Sketches for Listening & Reading. (Illus.). 142p. 1991. pap. text 12.50 (*0-86647-047-6*) Pro Lingua.

— Nobel Prize Winners: Biographical Sketches for Listening & Reading, 3 cass., Set. (Illus.). 142p. 1991. audio 27.00 (*0-86647-049-2*) Pro Lingua.

DeWitt, Lonnie F. In the Car. (Illus.). 211p. 1997. text 19.95 (*0-9657816-0-7*) RLD Ent.

Dewitt, Lynda. What Will the Weather Be? (Let's-Read-And-Find-Out Book Ser.). (J). 1993. 10.15 (*0-606-02979-6*, Pub. by Turtleback) Demco.

DeWitt, Lynda. What Will the Weather Be. LC 90-1446. (Trophy Let's Read-&-Find-Out Science Bk.: Stage 2). (Illus.). 32p. (J). (gr. k-4). 1993. pap. 4.95 (*0-06-445113-5*, HarpTrophy) HarpC Child Bks.

***DeWitt, M. Ross.** Beyond Equilibrium Theory: Theories of Social Action & Social Change Applied to a Study of Power Sharing in Transition. 368p. 2000. 67.00 (*0-7618-1738-7*); pap. 47.50 (*0-7618-1739-5*) U Pr of Amer.

DeWitt, Marguerite E., et al. Practical Methods in Choral Speaking. 1973. text 2.50 (*0-686-09411-5*) Expression.

Dewitt, Marie. Daniel's Deception. (Stolen Moments Ser.). 1993. pap. 1.99 (*0-373-83284-2*, 1-83284-9) Harlequin Bks.

Dewitt, Martin. Glenn C. Nelson: A Tribute Exhibition. (Illus.). 56p. (Orig.). 1992. pap. 10.00 (*1-889523-08-9*) Tweed Mus.

Dewitt, Martin, jt. auth. see Biddle, Mason.

Dewitt, Michelle. Competitive Intelligence, Competitive Advantage: Real Internet Tactics. 1997. pap. text 26.95 (*1-55755-324-6*) Abacus MI.

DeWitt-Morette, C., jt. auth. see Choquet-Bruhat, Y.

Dewitt-Morette, C., jt. auth. see Choquet-Bruhat, Yvonne.

DeWitt-Morette, Cecile, et al, eds. Functional Integration: Basics & Applications: Proceedings of a NATO ASI Held in Cargese, France, September 1-14, 1996. LC 97-22007. (NATO ASI Ser.: Vol. 361). 442p. (C). 1997. text 135.00 (*0-306-45617-6*, Kluwer Plenum) Kluwer Academic.

DeWitt-Morette, Cecile, et al. Quantum Field Theory: Perspective & Prospective. LC 99-13269. (NATO ASI Series, Series C, Mathematical & Physical Sciences). 14p. 1999. write for info. (*0-7923-5672-1*) Kluwer Academic.

DeWitt-Morette, Cecile, ed. see International Astronomical Union Staff.

Dewitt, Norman J., et al. College Latin. (C). 1954. 39.06 (*0-673-05105-6*) Addson-Wesley Educ.

DeWitt, Robert N., et al, eds. The Behavior of Systems in the Space Environment: Proceedings of the NATO Advanced Study Institute, Pitlochry, Scotland, July 7-19, 1991. LC 93-26845. (NATO Advanced Science Institutes Series C: Mathematical & Physical Sciences). 976p. (C). 1993. text 442.00 (*0-7923-2453-6*) Kluwer Academic.

DeWitt, Ross & Stevens Staff, et al. Wisconsin Environmental Law Handbook. 3rd ed. 399p. 1995. pap. text 89.00 (*0-86587-457-3*) Gov Insts.

Dewitt, Scott. Easiest Country Pedal Steel Guitar Book. 28p. 1994. pap. 3.95 (*0-7866-0086-1*, 95242) Mel Bay.

***Dewitt, Scott L. & Strasma, Kip, eds.** Contexts, Intertexts & Hypertexts. LC 99-22897. (Written Language Ser.). 336p. (C). 1999. 69.50 (*1-57273-214-8*); pap. 27.50 (*1-57273-215-6*) Hampton Pr NJ.

DeWitt, Sheila H., jt. ed. see Czarnik, Anthony W.

Dewitt, Sorena. String Figures from Around the World. Vol. 1. (Illus.). 32p. (J). (gr. 4-7). 1992. pap. 5.95 (*0-89346-356-6*) Heian Intl.

Dewitt-Wiley, Preston. Sounds for the Inner Ear. 100p. 1999. pap. 10.00 (*0-7392-0223-5*, PO3259) Morris Pubng.

DeWitt, William C. People's History of Kingston, Rondout & Vicinity: The First Capitol of N. Y. State (1820-1943) (Illus.). 445p. 1997. reprint ed. lib. bdg. 46.50 (*0-8328-6891-4*) Higginson Bk Co.

DeWitt, William H. Theory & Practice of Radiation Thermometry. LC 88-14272. 1152p. 1988. 275.00 (*0-471-61018-6*) Wiley.

Dewitte. Common Law of Europe. 1992. pap. text 114.00 (*90-6544-630-3*) Kluwer Academic.

Dewitz. Semantic Object Modeling. 1994. 23.00 (*0-07-911793-7*) McGraw.

— System Analysis Design Trans. OBJ. 1996. 102.25 (*0-07-847678-X*) McGraw.

***Dewitz, Jean.** De Franz Pruller a Ludwig Thoma. (Contacts Ser.: Vol. 20). xx, 537p. 1999. 62.95 (*3-906763-38-2*, Pub. by P Lang) P Lang Pubng.

Dewitz, Sandra. Systems Analysis, Design, & the Transition to Objects. LC 95-81167. 600p. (C). 1995. 84.38 (*0-07-016763-X*) McGraw.

Dewitz, Sandra D. Systems Analysis & Design & the Transition to Objects. 1996. pap. text, wbk. ed. 20.00 (*0-07-016768-0*) McGraw.

***Dewji, Fatemah H.** Where Have You Come From: By Nahal, the Bee. (Illus.). 28p. (J). (gr. 1-5). 2000. bds. 16.00 (*1-879402-68-8*) Tahrike Tarsile Quran.

Dewoff. Human Development. 2nd ed. (Psychology Ser.). 1999. pap., student ed. 21.25 (*0-534-36790-9*) Brooks-Cole.

Dewolf. Taylor Special Masterguide. 1997. 60.00 (*0-395-90684-9*) HM.

***DeWolf, David.** The Law of Torts. 660p. (C). 1999. ring bd. 78.00 (*1-879581-73-6*) Lupus Pubns.

***DeWolf, Francis C.** General Synopsis of Treaties of Arbitration, Conciliation, Judicial Settlement, Security & Disarmament, Actually in Force Between Countries Invited to the Disarmament Conference. LC 99-44896. 2000. write for info. (*1-57588-577-8*) W S Hein.

DeWolf, Gordon P., Jr. Taylor's Guide to Vegetables & Herbs. (Illus.). 480p. (Orig.). 1987. pap. 19.95 (*0-395-43092-5*) HM.

DeWolf, Gordon P., jt. auth. see Howard, Richard A.

DeWolf, Gordon P., Jr., ed. see Taylor, Norman.

DeWolf, John T. & Ricker, David T. Column Base Plates. 51p. 1990. 20.00 (*1-56424-032-0*, D801) Am Inst Steel Construct.

DeWolf, Rose, jt. auth. see Freeman, Arthur.

***Dewolfe, Adrienne.** Always Her Hero. 384p. 2000. mass mkt. 5.99 (*0-380-80528-6*, Avon Bks) Morrow Avon.

— Scoundrel for Hire. 384p. 1999. mass mkt. 5.99 (*0-380-80527-8*, Avon Bks) Morrow Avon.

DeWolfe, Barbara, ed. Discoveries of America: Personal Accounts of British Emigrants to North America During the Revolutionary Era. LC 96-21690. 250p. (C). 1997. text 54.95 (*0-521-38542-3*); pap. text 17.95 (*0-521-38694-2*) Cambridge U Pr.

DeWolfe, Fred. Heritage Lost: Two Great Portland Houses Through the Lens of Minor White. aut. deluxe limited ed. 1995. boxed set 450.00 (*0-87595-248-8*) Oregon Hist.

DeWolfe, Michele, jt. auth. see Peschko, Edward S.

DeWolff. Developmental Psychology Study Guide. 5th ed. 1993. pap. text, student ed. 15.00 (*0-13-205196-6*) P-H.

DeWolff, Frederick A., et al, eds. Therapeutic Relevance of Drug Assays. (Boerhaave Series for Postgraduate Medical Education: No. 14). 1979. text 112.50 (*90-6021-443-9*) Kluwer Academic.

Dewoody, Betty N., jt. auth. see Dewoody, Darrel W.

Dewoody, Darrel W. & Dewoody, Betty N. C. T. the Living Christmas Tree. (Illus.). (J). (gr. k-6). 1989. write for info. (*0-318-64917-9*) Old Amer Pr.

DeWoody, Madelyn. Adoption & Disclosure: A Review of the Law. 1993. pap. 12.95 (*0-87868-577-4*) Child Welfare.

— Confronting Homelessness among American Families: Federal Programs & Strategies. 1992. pap. 8.95 (*0-87868-526-X*, 5260) Child Welfare.

— Health Care Reform & Child Welfare: Meeting the Needs of Abused & Neglected Children. 1994. pap. 12.95 (*0-87868-507-3*) Child Welfare.

— Making Sense of Federal Dollars: A Funding Guide for Social Service Providers. LC 94-214548. (Orig.). 1994. pap. 9.95 (*0-87868-505-7*) Child Welfare.

— Medicaid & Supplemental Security Income: Options & Strategies for Child Welfare Agencies. 64p. 1991. pap. 9.95 (*0-87868-450-6*) Child Welfare.

DeWoody, Madelyn, et al. Independent Living Services for Youths in Out-of-Home Care. 1993. pap. 9.95 (*0-87868-582-0*) Child Welfare.

Deworken, Barbara J. & Gordon, Lori. Teenage Rider's Handbook: A Guide for Buying, Training, Showing & Selling Your Horse. LC 97-184734. 187p. (J). 1997. pap. 14.95 (*1-56315-046-8*) SterlingHse.

DeWoskin, Kenneth J. A Song for One or Two: Music & the Concept of Art in Early China. LC 81-19519. (Michigan Monographs in Chinese Studies: No. 42). (Illus.). 202p. (Orig.). (C). 1982. pap. text 15.00 (*0-89264-042-1*) Ctr Chinese Studies.

DeWoskin, Kenneth J. & Crump, James I., Jr., trs. from CHI. In Search of the Supernatural: The Written Record. LC 95-22091.Tr. of Sou Shen Chi. 328p. 1996. 39.50 (*0-8047-2506-3*) Stanford U Pr.

DeWoskin, Kenneth J., et al. Stories from China's Past: Han Dynasty Pictorial Tomb Reliefs & Archaeological Objects from Sichuan Province, PRC. (Illus.). 212p. 1987. 25.00 (*0-9609784-4-5*); pap. 15.00 (*0-9609784-3-7*) CCF San Francisco.

DeWoskin, Robert. Quality Assurance SOPs for GLP Compliance. 1994. ring bd. 247.00 (*0-935184-63-5*) Interpharm.

DeWoskin, Robert S. & Taulbee, Stephanie M., eds. International GLPs. 400p. 1993. ring bd. 219.00 (*0-935184-42-2*) Interpharm.

Dewran, Hasan. A Thousand Winds May Make a Storm: Poems & Aphorisms. Panthel, Hans W., tr. LC 90-6215. (Studies in Germanic Language & Literature: Vol. 4).Tr. of Tausend Winde - Ein Sturm. (ENG & GER.). 120p. 1990. lib. bdg. 59.95 (*0-88946-582-7*) E Mellen.

Dews, Bob, Jr. Largo. 140p. (Orig.). pap. 5.95 (*0-9618541-0-3*) Goldn Marsh Pubs.

Dews, C. L. & Law, Carolyn L., eds. This Fine Place So Far from Home: Voices of Academics from the Working Class. LC 94-28730. 384p. (Orig.). (C). 1995. pap. text 24.95 (*1-56639-291-8*); lib. bdg. 69.95 (*1-56639-290-X*) Temple U Pr.

Dews, C. L. Barney, jt. auth. see McCullers, Carson.

***Dews, Carlos L. & Law, Carolyn Leste, eds.** Out in the South. 256p. 2001. 69.50 (*1-56639-813-4*); pap. 22.95 (*1-56639-814-2*) Temple U Pr.

Dews, Cynthia, ed. see Ruchhoft, Robert H.

Dews, Jule N. Decision Structure of Organization. LC 78-53774. (Illus.). 120p. 1978. pap. 15.00 (*0-937300-00-4*) Stoneridge Inst.

— Humanagement. LC 85-62905. (Illus.). 73p. (Orig.). (C). 1985. pap. text 16.00 (*0-937300-01-2*) Stoneridge Inst.

— One World Government a Struggle Between Surrogate Elitism & Popular Will: Uncle Sam or Aunt Geneva? LC 96-67795. (Illus.). 57p. (Orig.). 1996. pap. 16.00 (*0-937300-04-7*) Stoneridge Inst.

— Windows of Confederate Finance: CSA Bearer Bonds. LC 89-62057. (Illus.). 58p. 1989. pap. 16.00 (*0-937300-02-0*) Stoneridge Inst.

— Wing-Smiths of Japan: A Story of Japan's World War II Aircraft. LC 93-85597. 61p. 1993. pap. 16.00 (*0-937300-03-9*) Stoneridge Inst.

Dews, Pat. Creative Discoveries in Watermedia. LC 98-9463. (Illus.). 128p. 1998. 27.99 (*0-89134-830-1*, North Lght Bks) F & W Pubns Inc.

An Asterisk (*) at the beginning of an entry indicates that the title is appearing for the first time.

Dews, Peola B. On Being a Woman: Psychopoetic Notes from a Sister Traveler. (Illus.). 115p. (Orig.). 1993. pap. 13.95 (*0-9639674-0-1*) DEWS HRD Assocs.

Dews, Peter. Habermas: A Critical Reader. LC 99-17545. 350p. 1999. 59.95 (*0-631-20134-3*); pap. 24.95 (*0-631-20135-1*) Blackwell Pubs.

— The Limits of Disenchantment: Essays on Psychoanalysis, Deconstruction & Critical Theory. 224p. (C). 1996. pap. 19.00 (*1-85984-022-1*, Pub. by Verso) Norton.

Dews, Peter, jt. ed. see Critchley, Simon.

Dews, Peter B., ed. Festschrift for B. F. Skinner. LC 76-133193. (Century Psychology Ser.). (Orig.). (C). 1977. reprint ed. 42.00 (*0-89197-497-0*) Irvington.

Dews, Philip. How to Take Advantage of Myanmar, Burma, Manufacturing Skills & Low Cost Labour: The Last Real Unexplored Country in the World. LC 93-18789. 54p. 1993. text 39.95 (*0-7734-9467-7*) E Mellen.

Dews, Robert P. Early Joel. 2nd ed. 194p. 1982. 6.00 (*0-940184-03-6*) R P Dews.

— Georgia-Florida League, Nineteen Thirty-Five to Nineteen Fifty-Eight: Extra Innings. (Illus.). 200p. 1985. pap. 6.00 (*0-940184-08-7*) R P Dews.

Dews, Shelly, jt. ed. see Kreuz, Roger J.

Dewsberry, Elise, jt. auth. see Ritchie, Carl.

***Dewsbury, Donald A.** Unification Through Division, 5. 250p. 2000. pap. 24.95 (*1-55798-683-5*) Am Psychol.

Dewsbury, Donald A., ed. Leaders in the Study of Animal Behavior. LC 83-46153. (Illus.). 512p. 1985. 65.00 (*0-8387-5052-4*) Bucknell U Pr.

— Studying Animal Behavior: Autobiographies of the Founders. (Illus.). 512p. 1989. reprint ed. pap. text 24.00 (*0-226-14410-0*) U Ch Pr.

***Dewsbury, Donald A., ed.** Unification Through Division: Histories of the Divisions of the American Psychological Association. Vol. 3. 208p. 1999. pap. 24.95 (*1-55798-540-5*) Am Psychol.

Dewsbury, Donald A., ed. Unification Through Division: Histories of the Divisions of the American Psychological Association, Vol. 2. LC 96-41480. 325p. 1997. pap. text 24.95 (*1-55798-430-1*) Am Psychol.

— Unification Through Division Vol. 1: Histories of the Divisions of the American Psychological Association, Vol. 1. LC 96-41480. 317p. 1996. pap. 24.95 (*1-55798-379-8*) Am Psychol.

***Dewsbury, Donald A., ed.** Unification Through Division Vol. 4: Histories of the Divisions of the American Psychological Association. 187p. 1999. pap. 24.95 (*1-55798-600-2*, 431-623A) Am Psychol.

Dewsnap, David C. The Severance Genealogy. (Illus.). 516p. (Orig.). 1995. pap. 36.00 (*0-7884-0357-5*, D187) Heritage Bk.

Dewsnap, Don. Desktop Publisher's Easy Type Guide: The 150 Most Important Typefaces. 176p. (Orig.). 1992. pap. 19.95 (*1-56496-007-2*, 30398) Rockport Pubs.

— Sign Design: Easy Type Guide. 160p. 1993. pap. 16.95 (*1-56496-035-8*, 30502) Rockport Pubs.

Dewsnap, Lois, jt. auth. see Mitchell, Grace.

Dewsnap, Terence. Monarch Notes on Wolfe's Look Homeward Angel, Of Time & the River & Other Writings. (Orig.). (C). 3.95 (*0-671-00702-5*, Arco) Macmillan Gen Ref.

Dewtherer, James, ed. see Uehli, Ernst.

Dewulf, G. P. R. M., jt. auth. see Vos, P. G. J. C.

***Dewulf, Jeroen.** Hugo Loetscher und die Portugiesischsprachige Welt: Werdegang eines Literarischen Mulatten. (Europaische Hochschulschriften Ser.). 275p. 1999. 44.95 (*3-906763-78-1*) P Lang Pubng.

Dewynne, Jeffrey N., jt. auth. see Hill, James M.

Dewyze, Jeannette, jt. auth. see Mallinger, Allan.

Dex, Shirley. Women's Attitudes Towards Work. LC 87-32365. 224p. 1988. text 45.00 (*0-312-01611-5*) St Martin.

Dexeus, Victoria C. Rafols-Casamada. (Illus.). 128p. 1989. 65.00 (*84-343-0563-1*) A Wofsy Fine Arts.

Dexheimer, R. Water Source Heat Pump Handbook. 180p. 1985. 18.75 (*1-56034-059-2*) Natl Grnd Water.

Dexheimer, William R. Beyond the Smoke & Mirrors: Turmoil in the PPM Industry. LC 98-53529. 1999. 27.95 (*1-57359-018-5*, Starrhill Press) Black Belt Communs.

Dexippus. On Aristotle's Categories. Dillon, John, tr. (Ancient Commentators on Aristotle Ser.). 1988. text 47.50 (*0-8014-2266-3*) Cornell U Pr.

Dexter. Around the World with My Recorder. 1990. 6.95 (*0-685-32161-4*, T072) Hansen Ed Mus.

Dexter, Alison. Grandma. LC 92-6473. (Willa Perlman Bks.). (Illus.). 32p. (J). (ps-2). 1993. 15.00 (*0-06-021143-1*) HarpC Child Bks.

Dexter, Amby. Target Tennis: Learning to Play Tennis Using Tennis Court Trainer. LC 92-70292. (Illus.). 94p. 1992. pap. 30.00 (*1-881123-01-4*) The Catacombs.

Dexter, Arthur L. Microcomputer Bus Structures & Bus Interface Design. (Electrical Engineering & Electronics Ser.: No. 32). (Illus.). 368p. 1986. text 155.00 (*0-8247-7435-3*) Dekker.

Dexter, Catherine. A Is for Apple. LC 95-33658. (Illus.). 160p. (J). (gr. 3-7). 1997. reprint ed. pap. 4.99 (*0-7636-0385-6*) Candlewick Pr.

— A Is for Apple, W Is for Witch. LC 95-33658. (Illus.). 160p. (J). (gr. 4-7). 1996. 14.99 (*1-56402-541-1*) Candlewick Pr.

Dexter, Catherine. Alien Game. LC 94-33240. (Illus.). 208p. (YA). (gr. 7 up). 1995. 15.00 (*0-688-11332-X*, Wm Morrow) Morrow Avon.

Dexter, Catherine. Alien Game. LC 94-33240. 208p. (YA). 1997. pap. 4.95 (*0-688-15290-2*, Wm Morrow) Morrow Avon.

— The Doll Who Knew the Future. Cohn, Amy, ed. LC 94-82. (YA). 1994. 10.05 (*0-606-06331-5*, Pub. by Turtleback) Demco.

— The Doll Who Knew the Future. Cohn, Amy, ed. LC 94-82. 208p. (YA). (gr. 5 up). 1994. reprint ed. mass mkt. 4.95 (*0-688-13117-4*, Wm Morrow) Morrow Avon.

***Dexter, Catherine.** Driving Lessons. LC 00-20925. (Illus.). 160p. (YA). (gr. 7 up). 2000. 16.99 (*0-7636-0515-8*) Candlewick Pr.

Dexter, Catherine. Gertie's Green Thumb. (J). 1995. 10.05 (*0-606-07559-3*) Turtleback.

— I Dream of Murder. LC 96-29346. (Illus.). 160p. (YA). (gr. 5 up). 1997. 15.00 (*0-688-13182-4*, Wm Morrow) Morrow Avon.

— I Dream of Murder. 160p. (YA). 1999. mass mkt. 5.95 (*0-688-16668-7*, Wm Morrow) Morrow Avon.

— Safe Return. LC 96-7737. 96p. (J). (gr. 4-7). 1996. 15.99 (*0-7636-0005-9*) Candlewick Pr.

— Safe Return. LC 96-7737. 96p. (J). (gr. 8-10). 1998. pap. 4.99 (*0-7636-0486-0*) Candlewick Pr.

Dexter, Colin. The Daughters of Cain. 1996. mass mkt. 5.99 (*0-8041-1364-5*) Ivy Press.

— The Daughters of Cain. large type ed. (Charnwood Large Print Ser.). 448p. 1995. 27.99 (*0-7089-8869-5*, Charnwood) Ulverscroft.

— The Dead of Jericho. 1997. mass mkt. 5.99 (*0-8041-1486-2*) Ivy Books.

— The Dead of Jericho, Set. (Inspector Morse Mystery Ser.). 1998. audio 29.95 (*0-7540-7519-2*) Chivers N Amer.

— Death is Now My Neighbor: An Inspector Morse Novel. 1998. mass mkt. 6.99 (*0-8041-1572-9*) Ivy Books.

— The Jewel That Was Ours: An Inspector Morse Mystery. 1993. mass mkt. 5.99 (*0-8041-0981-8*) Ivy Books.

— Last Bus to Woodstock. 1996. mass mkt. 5.99 (*0-8041-1490-0*) Ivy Books.

Dexter, Colin. Last Seen Wearing: An Inspector Morse Mystery. 272p. 1988. mass mkt. 5.99 (*0-553-28003-1*) Bantam.

Dexter, Colin. Last Seen Wearing: An Inspector Morse Mystery. 1997. mass mkt. 5.99 (*0-8041-1491-9*) Ivy Books.

— Morse's Greatest Mystery & Other Stories. 1996. mass mkt. 5.99 (*0-8041-1309-2*) Ivy Books.

***Dexter, Colin.** The Remorseful Day. LC 00-39860. 2000. write for info. (*1-56895-883-8*) Wheeler Pub.

— The Remorseful Day: Signed Edition. aut. ed. 374p. 2000. 24.00 (*0-609-50295-6*, Crown) Crown Pub Group.

— The Remorseful Day: The Final Inspector Morse Novel. LC 99-59840. 320p. 2000. 24.00 (*0-609-60622-0*, Crown) Crown Pub Group.

Dexter, Colin. The Riddle of the Third Mile. 224p. 1988. mass mkt. 5.99 (*0-553-27363-9*) Bantam.

— The Riddle of the Third Mile. 1997. mass mkt. 5.99 (*0-8041-1488-9*) Ivy Books.

***Dexter, Colin.** The Secret of Annexe 3. large type ed. LC 00-37749. 349p. 2000. pap. 26.95 (*0-7862-2676-5*) Thorndike Pr.

— The Secret of Annexe 3. 224p. 1988. reprint ed. mass mkt. 5.99 (*0-553-27549-6*) Bantam.

Dexter, Colin. The Secret of Annexe 3, Vol. 3. LC 97-97032. 285p. 1998. mass mkt. 5.99 (*0-8041-1489-7*) Ivy Books.

— Service of All the Dead. 1996. mass mkt. 5.99 (*0-8041-1485-4*) Ivy Books.

Dexter, Colin. The Silent World of Nicholas Quinn. 224p. 1988. mass mkt. 5.99 (*0-553-27238-1*) Bantam.

Dexter, Colin. The Silent World of Nicholas Quinn. 1997. mass mkt. 5.99 (*0-8041-1487-0*) Ivy Books.

— The Way Through the Woods: An Inspector Morse Mystery. 1994. mass mkt. 5.99 (*0-8041-1142-1*) Ivy Books.

— The Way Through the Woods: An Inspector Morse Mystery. large type ed. LC 93-13448. 1993. lib. bdg. 21.95 (*1-56054-764-2*) Thorndike Pr.

— The Wench is Dead. 208p. 1991. mass mkt. 5.99 (*0-553-29120-3*) Bantam.

— The Wench is Dead. (Inspector Morse Novel Ser.). 290p. 1999. mass mkt. 6.99 (*0-8041-1889-2*) Ivy Books.

Dexter, Daniel L., jt. ed. see Leith, John T.

Dexter, Dave, Jr. Jazz Cavalcade. LC 77-8035. (Roots of Jazz Ser.). (Illus.). 1977. reprint ed. lib. bdg. 29.50 (*0-306-77431-3*) Da Capo.

Dexter, David S. The ANU Campus. LC 92-235597. xii, 470p. 1991. (*0-7315-1216-2*) ANU Res Sch.

Dexter, David S., ed. see American Institute of Certified Public Accountants.

Dexter, Elisha. Narrative of the Wreck & Loss of the Whaling Brig William & Joseph. 56p. 1987. 14.95 (*0-87770-418-X*); pap. 9.95 (*0-87770-417-1*) Ye Galleon.

Dexter, Franklin B. Ohio Country Missionary: The Diary of David McClure, 1748-1820. LC 96-69206. 245p. 1996. reprint ed. pap. 19.00 (*0-89725-272-1*, 1766) Picton Pr.

Dexter, Franklin B., ed. Documentary History of Yale University. LC 75-89174. (American Education: Its Men, Institutions, & Ideas. Series 1). 1978. reprint ed. 19.95 (*0-405-01412-0*) Ayer.

Dexter, G. & Wash, David B. Psychiatric Nursing Skills. 2nd ed. (Illus.). 336p. 1994. pap. text 45.95 (*1-56593-098-3*, 0431) Singular Publishing.

***Dexter, Gary.** A Tourist's Guide to Europe. (Modern Anthropologist Ser.). (Illus.). 64p. 2000. mass mkt. 5.99 (*1-903222-05-2*, Pub. by Wimbledon Publishing Co) Anthem.

— A Tourist's Guide to the U. S. A. (Modern Anthropologist Ser.). (Illus.). 64p. 2000. mass mkt. 5.99 (*1-903222-04-4*, Pub. by Wimbledon Publishing Co) Anthem.

Dexter, Gerry L. Shortwave Clandestine Confidential. (Illus.). 86p. (Orig.). 1984. pap. 8.95 (*0-916661-02-4*, 203) Universal Elect.

Dexter, Graham & Wash, Michael. Psychiatric Nursing Skills: A Patient-Centered Approach. LC 85-13252. 320p. (C). 1985. pap. 19.95 (*0-7099-3617-6*, Pub. by C Helm) Routldge.

— Psychiatric Nursing Skills: A Patient-Centered Approach. 2nd ed. LC 94-68797. 318p. 1995. pap. 41.50 (*0-412-55320-1*) Chapman & Hall.

Dexter, Helen. It's Never Too Late with God! Vol. 1: Tales of a Late-Life Journey in India. LC 98-91324. (Illus.). xii, 180p. 1998. pap. 14.95 (*1-892121-01-8*, The Lakeside Pr) Lion Media.

Dexter, James R., jt. auth. see Wilkins, Robert L.

Dexter, James R., jt. ed. see Wilkins, Robert L.

Dexter, John. Honourable Beast. LC 93-244183. (Illus.). 320p. (C). 1993. 45.00 (*0-87830-035-X*, Thtre Arts Bks) Routledge.

Dexter, John H., et al. John Haven Dexter's Memoranda of the Town of Boston in the 18th & 19th Centuries. LC 97-35258. 1998. 60.00 (*0-88082-068-3*) New Eng Hist.

Dexter, Lewis A. How Organizations Are Represented in Washington: Toward a Broader Understanding of the Seeking of Influence & of Patterns of Representation. LC 87-18953. (Constitutional Government in Theory & Practice Ser.). (Illus.). 180p. (C). 1987. reprint ed. pap. text 21.00 (*0-8191-6053-9*) U Pr of Amer.

— Representation Versus Direct Democracy in Fighting about Taxes. 155p. 1982. pap. 21.95 (*0-87073-426-1*) Transaction Pubs.

Dexter, Lewis Anthony. How Organizations Are Represented in Washington. LC 69-15729. 1969. pap. 5.95 (*0-672-60748-4*, Bobbs) Macmillan.

Dexter, Lincoln A., ed. The Contested Coast: Europe's Westward Quest. LC 94-68171. (Illus.). 401p. (Orig.). 1995. pap. 30.00 (*0-9601210-5-6*) L A Dexter.

Dexter, Lincoln A., ed. see Apes, William.

Dexter, Miriam R. Whence the Goddesses: A Source Book. (Athene Ser.). 384p. 1990. text 47.50 (*0-08-037279-1*, Pergamon Pr); pap. text 18.95 (*0-08-037281-3*, Pergamon Pr) Elsevier.

— Whence the Goddesses: A Source Book. (Athene Ser.). 304p. (C). 1990. pap. text 20.95 (*0-8077-6234-2*) Tchrs Coll.

Dexter, Miriam R., jt. auth. see Gimbutas, Marija.

Dexter, Miriam R., ed. see Barber, E. J., et al.

Dexter, Miriam R., ed. see Gimbutas, Marija.

Dexter, Pat E. Children, Imagination & Prayer: Creative Techniques for Middle Grade Students. LC 93-60437. 80p. (Orig.). 1993. pap. 7.95 (*0-89622-565-8*) Twenty-Third.

— 25 Guided Prayer Services for Middle Graders. LC 95-62342. 88p. (Orig.). 1996. pap., teacher ed. 12.95 (*0-89622-688-3*) Twenty-Third.

Dexter, Pat Egan. Coping as Caregivers: When a Loved One is Ill. LC 98-60128. 111p. 1999. pap. 9.95 (*0-89622-925-4*) Twenty-Third.

Dexter, Pete. Brotherly Love. (Contemporary American Fiction Ser.). 288p. 1992. reprint ed. pap. 12.95 (*0-14-016773-0*, Penguin Bks) Viking Penguin.

— Deadwood. 1989. pap. 13.95 (*0-14-012729-1*, Penguin Bks) Viking Penguin.

— Deadwood. large type ed. (Niagara Large Print Ser.). 584p. 1997. pap. 29.50 (*0-7089-5862-1*, Linford) Ulverscroft.

— God's Pocket. 288p. 1988. mass mkt. 4.95 (*0-446-35781-2*, Pub. by Warner Bks) Little.

— God's Pocket. 288p. 1990. mass mkt. 8.95 (*0-446-39140-9*, Pub. by Warner Bks) Little.

— The Paperboy. 336p. 1996. pap. 12.95 (*0-385-31572-4*) Dell.

— The Paperboy. large type ed. LC 95-15715. (Large Print Bks.). 1995. pap. 22.95 (*1-56895-217-1*) Wheeler Pub.

— Paris Trout. 320p. 1989. pap. 12.95 (*0-14-012206-0*, Penguin Bks) Viking Penguin.

Dexter, Planet. Planet Ant. LC 96-210795. (Illus.). 48p. 1996. pap. 14.99 (*0-201-48985-6*) Addison-Wesley.

Dexter, R. L., jt. auth. see Warden, W. A.

Dexter, Robin. Estrellas: Cercanas y Lejanas. enl. ed. (SPA.). (J). 1999. pap. text 16.95 (*0-8167-3983-8*) Troll Communs.

— Estrellas: Cercanos y Lejanos. (SPA.). 1999. pap. text 2.50 (*0-8167-4053-4*) Troll Communs.

— Frogs. LC 95-22524. (First-Start Science Ser.). (Illus.). 32p. (J). (gr. k-2). 1995. lib. bdg. 13.05 (*0-8167-3860-2*) Troll Communs.

— Frogs. LC 95-22524. (First-Start Science Ser.). (Illus.). 32p. (J). (gr. k-2). 1996. pap. 2.95 (*0-8167-3861-0*) Troll Communs.

— Frogs, Big Book ed. 1999. pap. text 16.95 (*0-8167-3958-7*) Troll Communs.

— Stars. LC 95-4869. (First Start Science Ser.). (Illus.). 32p. (J). (gr. k-3). 1995. lib. bdg. 13.05 (*0-8167-3858-0*) Troll Communs.

— Stars. (First Start Science Ser.). (Illus.). 32p. (J). (gr. k-3). 1996. pap. 2.95 (*0-8167-3859-9*) Troll Communs.

— Young Arthur Ashe: Brave Champion. LC 95-10021. (Troll First-Start Biography Ser.). 1996. 8.70 (*0-606-10100-4*, Pub. by Turtleback) Demco.

Dexter, Robin, comment. Stars, Big Book 1999. pap. text 16.95 (*0-8167-3960-9*) Troll Communs.

Dexter, Robin, ed. Young Arthur Ashe: Brave Champion. LC 95-10021. (First-Start Biography Ser.). (Illus.). 32p. (J). (ps-2). 1996. pap. 3.50 (*0-8167-3773-8*) Troll Communs.

— Young Arthur Ashe: Brave Champion. LC 95-10021. (First-Start Biography Ser.). (Illus.). 32p. (J). (gr. k-2). 1997. lib. bdg. 17.25 (*0-8167-3772-X*) Troll Communs.

***Dexter, Rosalyn.** Chinese Whispers Feng Shui: Techniques for Transforming Life, Work, & Home. (Illus.). 160p. 2000. text 45.00 (*0-8478-2265-6*) Rizzoli Intl.

Dexter, Sandi. Joyful Play with Toddlers: Recipes for Fun with Odds & Ends. (Tools for Everyday Parenting Ser.). (Illus.). 128p. (Orig.). 1995. pap. 9.95 (*1-884734-00-6*); lib. bdg. 18.95 (*1-884734-01-4*) Parenting Pr.

Dexter, Seymour. Seymour Dexter, Union Army: Journal & Letters of Civil War Service in Company K, 23rd New York Volunteer Regiment of Elmira; with Illustrations. Morrell, Carl A., ed. LC 96-33265. (Illus.). 168p. 1996. lib. bdg. 28.50 (*0-7864-0197-4*) McFarland & Co.

Dexter-Smith, R., ed. Civil Engineering in the Nuclear Industry. 372p. 1991. text 97.00 (*0-7277-1643-3*, Pub. by T Telford) RCH.

Dexter, Susan. The Ring of Allaire. 1981. mass mkt. 2.50 (*0-345-29273-1*) Ballantine Pub Grp.

Dexter, Susan. The Ring of Allaire. 224p. 1983. mass mkt. 4.99 (*0-345-31121-3*, Ballantine) Ballantine Pub Grp.

— The Wind Witch. 1994. mass mkt. 5.99 (*0-345-38770-8*, Del Rey) Ballantine Pub Grp.

Dexter, T. F. Fire Worship in Britain. (Illus.). 1995. pap. 8.95 (*1-55818-314-0*, Sure Fire) Holmes Pub.

***Dexter, Troy.** 50s Rockabilly Guitar. 152p. 1998. otabind 14.95 incl. VHS (*0-7935-9490-1*, 00320118) H Leonard.

Dexter, W. Some Rogues & Vagabonds of Dickens. 1972. 59.95 (*0-8490-1080-2*) Gordon Pr.

Dexter, W., ed. see Dickens, Charles.

Dexter, Walter. Days in Dickensland. LC 72-3610. (Studies in Dickens: No. 52). (Illus.). 1972. reprint ed. lib. bdg. 75.00 (*0-8383-1559-3*) M S G Haskell Hse.

— Kent of Dickens. LC 72-2105. (Studies in Dickens: No. 52). 1972. reprint ed. lib. bdg. 75.00 (*0-8383-1482-1*) M S G Haskell Hse.

— Mr. Pickwick's Pilgrimages. LC 72-3637. (Studies in Dickens: No. 52). 1972. reprint ed. lib. bdg. 75.00 (*0-8383-1587-9*) M S G Haskell Hse.

Dexter, Walter, ed. see Dickens, Charles.

Dexter, Warren W. Ogam Consaine & Tifinag Alphabets - Ancient Uses. LC 84-70953. (Illus.). 72p. (Orig.). 1984. pap. text 8.50 (*0-914960-44-X*) Academy Bks.

Dexter, Warren W. & Hanson, Barbara C. Vermont: Wilderness to Statehood, 1748-1791. LC 89-80734. (Illus.). 180p. (Orig.). 1989. pap. 8.95 (*0-914960-71-7*) Academy Bks.

Dextreit, Raymond. Earth Cures: A Handbook of Natural Medicine for Today. Abehsera, Michel, ed. & tr. by. LC 97-15454. (Illus.). 216p. 1997. pap. 16.95 (*0-8065-1888-X*, Citadel Pr) Carol Pub Group.

— Our Earth, Our Cure: A Handbook of Natural Medicine for Today. Abehsera, Michel, ed. & tr. by. from FRE. (Illus.). 210p. 1993. reprint ed. pap. 15.95 (*0-8065-1013-7*, Citadel Pr) Carol Pub Group.

Dey, A. N., ed. Lithium Batteries: Proceedings of the Symposium, San Diego, CA, 1986. LC 87-80472. (Electrochemical Society Proceedings Ser.: No. 87-1). 568p. reprint ed. pap. 176.10 (*0-7837-1454-8*, 205243000022) Bks Demand.

Dey, A. N., ed. see Symposium on Lithium Batteries Staff.

***Dey, Aloke & Mukerjee, Rahul.** Fractional Factorial Plans. LC 98-45208. (Series in Probability & Statistics). 232p. 1999. 94.95 (*0-471-29414-4*) Wiley.

***Dey, B. P.** Microbiological Laboratory Guidebook: Nineteen Ninety Eight, 2, V. 1&2. 620p. 1998. boxed set 63.00 (*0-16-060823-6*, Agriculture Dept) USGPO.

Dey-Bergmoser, Olga & Majumder, Khaletum. Many Faces - Many Spaces: Artists of Ontario. (Illus.). 128p. 1993. 29.95 (*0-88962-350-3*) Mosaic.

Dey-Bergmoser, Olga, jt. auth. see Coulter, Elizabeth.

Dey, Carol, jt. auth. see Thieman, LeAnn.

Dey, Charmaine. The Magic Candle. 62p. 1982. pap. 4.95 (*0-942272-00-5*) Original Pubns.

Dey, Dena & Layne, Leah. How to Save Money Doing Home Improvements & How to Get Financing in Texas. 56p. (Orig.). 1992. pap. 24.95 (*1-881879-24-0*) HKM Grp.

Dey, Denny. Harnessing Motivation: 10 Steps to Overcoming Obstacles in Your Life. 236p. 1997. pap. 9.95 (*0-9646898-7-1*) Leathers Pub.

***Dey, Dipak, et al.** Generalized Linear Models: A Bayesian Perspective. LC 00-24055. (Biostatistics Ser.). 2000. write for info. (*0-8247-9034-0*) Dekker.

Dey, Dipak, et al. Practical Nonparametric & Semiparametric Bayesian Statistics, Vol. 133. LC 98-16460. (Lecture Notes in Statistics). 1998. pap. 49.95 (*0-387-98517-4*) Spr-Verlag.

Dey, E. L., et al. The American College Teacher: National Norms for the 1992-93 HERI Faculty Survey. 109p. (Orig.). 1993. pap. 20.00 (*1-878477-13-7*) UCLA Higher Educ Rsch Inst.

— The American Freshman: National Norms for Fall, 1992. (Illus.). 162p. (Orig.). pap. 20.00 (*1-878477-12-9*) UCLA Higher Educ Rsch Inst.

Dey, Eric, ed. Sumatra. 288p. 1993. 37.50 (*0-945971-24-9*) Periplus.

Dey, Frederic V. Magic Story. 1928. pap. 4.50 (*0-87516-020-4*) DeVorss.

Dey, Frederic Van Rensselaer, see Van Rensselaer Dey, Frederic.

***Dey, Ian.** Grounding Grounded Theory. LC 98-83122. 296p. 1999. 44.95 (*0-12-214640-9*) Acad Pr.

Dey, Ian. Qualitative Data Analysis: A User-Friendly Guide. LC 92-26082. (Illus.). 304p. (C). 1993. pap. 24.99 (*0-415-05852-X*, B0240) Routledge.

Dey, J., jt. auth. see Dey, Mira.

Dey, J. N. Problems of Accountancy. 1985. 69.00 (*0-7855-0748-5*, Pub. by Current Dist) St Mut.

Dey, J. N., tr. see Jnanatmananda, Swami.

Dey, J. N., tr. see Saradeshananda, Swami.

Dey, K. L. The Indigenous Drugs of India. 187p. (C). 1984. 85.00 (*81-7089-900-1*, Pub. by Intl Bk Distr); 350.00 (*0-7855-6887-5*, Pub. by Intl Bk Distr) St Mut.

— The Indigenous Drugs of India. 387p. 1984. reprint ed. pap. 475.00 (*81-7089-017-9*, Pub. by Intl Bk Distr) St Mut.

Dey, K. L., ed. The Indigenous Drugs of India. (C). 1984. text 350.00 (*0-89771-595-0*, Pub. by Intl Bk Distr) St Mut.

D

Dey, K. L. & Raioahadur, R. The Indigenous Drugs of India: Short Descriptive Notices of the Principal Medicinal Products Met with in British India. 2nd ed. (C). 1984. 60.00 (*0-7855-3300-1*, Pub. by Scientific) St Mut.

Dey, Lala K. The Intermediary World & Patterns of Perfection in Philo & Hebrews. LC 75-22457. (Society of Biblical Literature. Dissertation Ser.: No.25). 251p. reprint ed. pap. 77.90 (*0-608-11838-9*, 201752400007) Bks Demand.

***Dey, M.** International Collaborative Project to Evaluate Fire Models for Nuclear Power Plant Applications: Planning Meeting, at University of Maryland, October 25-26, 1999. 172p. 2000. per. 17.00 (*0-16-059220-8*) USGPO.

Dey, M., tr. see De Musset, Alfred.

Dey, Martha J., jt. auth. see Beusse, William E.

Dey, Mira & Day, Jishnu. Nuclear & Particle Physics: The Changing Interface. LC 93-14273. (Series in Nuclear & Particle Physics). 1994. 86.95 (*0-387-56790-9*) Spr-Verlag.

Dey, Mira & Dey, J. Nuclear & Particle Physics: The Changing Interface. (Series in Nuclear & Particle Physics). (Illus.). 120p. 1993. write for info. (*3-540-56790-9*) Spr-Verlag.

Dey, N. C. Medical Parasitology. rev. ed. (C). 1984. 57.00 (*0-7855-4660-X*, Pub. by Current Dist) St Mut.

— Textbook of Pathology. (C). 1988. 200.00 (*0-7855-4661-8*, Pub. by Current Dist) St Mut.

Dey, N. C., ed. Medical Bacteriology. 14th ed. (C). 1988. 155.00 (*0-7210-0123-8*, Pub. by Current Dist) St Mut.

— Practical Pathology & Microbiology. 11th ed. (C). 1982. 55.00 (*0-7855-4662-6*, Pub. by Current Dist) St Mut.

Dey, Niranjan, ed. Management of Business Enterprises. 352p. 1990. 140.00 (*81-7041-251-X*, Pub. by Scientific Pubs) St Mut.

Dey, P. M., ed. Methods in Plant Biochemistry Vol. 2: Carbohydrates. 657p. 1990. text 104.00 (*0-12-461012-9*) Acad Pr.

Dey, P. M., et al, eds. Methods in Plant Biochemistry Vol. 8: Tropane Alkaloids. (Illus.). 605p. 1993. text 104.00 (*0-12-461018-8*) Acad Pr.

Dey, P. M. & Harborne, Jeffrey B. Plant Biochemistry. (Illus.). 576p. 1997. text 74.95 (*0-12-214674-3*) Acad Pr.

Dey, S. C. Fragrant Flowers for Homes & Gardens. 1996. 22.00 (*81-7017-335-3*, Pub. by Abhinav) S Asia.

Dey, S. K. Molecular & Cellular Aspects of Periimplanation Processes. LC 95-21136. (Serono Symposia Ser.). (Illus.). 384p. 1995. 142.00 (*0-387-94569-5*) Spr-Verlag.

Dey, Suresh C. Industrial Security Management. 1987. 35.00 (*81-7024-088-3*, Pub. by Ashish Pub Hse) S Asia.

— Quest for Music Divine. 1990. 38.00 (*81-7024-301-7*, Pub. by Ashish Pub Hse) S Asia.

Deye, Gladys, ed. Glady's Apron Strings: Twenty Five Years of the Best Recipes from the Pages of the Lutheran Journal. 160p. 1998. pap. 12.95 (*1-886158-17-7*) Macalester.

Deyell, John S. Living Without Silver: The Monetary History of Early Medieval North India. (Illus.). 392p. 1990. text 35.00 (*0-19-562216-2*) OUP.

Deyermond, et al, eds. Medieval & Renaissance Spanish Literature: Selected Essays of Keith Whinnom. (Illus.). 320p. 1994. text 50.00 (*0-85989-219-0*, Pub. by Univ Exeter Pr) Northwestern U Pr.

Deyermond, A. D. Epic Poetry & the Clergy: Studies on the "Mocedades de Rodrigo" (Monografias A Ser.: Vol. V). 312p. (Orig.). (C). 1968. pap. 51.00 (*0-900411-08-2*, Pub. by Tamesis Bks Ltd) Boydell & Brewer.

Deyermond, A. D., ed. Medieval Hispanic Studies Presented to Rita Hamilton. (Monagrafias A Ser.: Vol. XLII). (ENG & SPA., Illus.). 281p. (Orig.). (C). 1976. pap. 46.00 (*0-900411-98-8*, Pub. by Tamesis Bks Ltd) Boydell & Brewer.

— Mio Cid Studies. (Monagrafias A Ser.: No. 59). (SPA.). 210p. (C). 1977. 51.00 (*0-7293-0023-4*, Pub. by Tamesis Bks Ltd) Boydell & Brewer.

Deyermond, Alan, jt. ed. see Vaquero, Mercedes.

Deyhim, Mehrbanoo Nasser, tr. see Sayyah, Muhammad 'Ali.

Deyl, Z. TrAC Directory of Hypenated Techniques, Suppl. 2. LC 95-128124. 178p. 1994. pap. 84.50 (*0-444-82126-0*) Elsevier.

Deyl, Z., ed. Quality Control in Pharmaceutical Analysis: Separation Methods. 252p. 1997. 187.00 (*0-444-82876-1*) Elsevier.

Deyl, Z., et al, eds. Advanced Chromatographic & Electromigration Methods in BioSciences. LC 99-164248. (Journal of Chromatography Library: Vol. 60). 1998. write for info. (*0-444-82594-0*) Elsevier.

Deyl, Z. & Adam, M. Collagen in Aging & Disease Studie CSAV, 1982, Pt. 11. 198p. 1982. 97.00 (*0-7855-2038-4*) St Mut.

Deyl, Zdenek & Zicha, Joseph, eds. Methods in Animal Physiology. 448p. 1988. lib. bdg. 295.00 (*0-8493-6965-7*, QP43) CRC Pr.

Deyle, Robert E. Hazardous Waste Management in Small Businesses: Regulating & Assisting the Smaller Generator. LC 89-32859. 182p. 1989. 59.95 (*0-89930-349-8*, DYR, Quorum Bks) Greenwood.

DeYmaz, Linda. Mommy, Please Don't Cry. (Illus.). 1996. 11.99 (*1-885305-45-1*) Multnomah Pubs.

***Deymeer, F. S., ed.** Neuromuscular Disease. (Monographs in Clinical Neuroscience: Vol. 18). (Illus.). viii, 200p. 2000. 174.00 (*3-8055-7056-2*) S Karger.

Deyn. Guanidino Comp in Biol & Med, No. II. 450p. 1997. 105.00 (*0-86196-543-4*, Pub. by J Libbey Med) Bks Intl VA.

Deyn. Guanidino Compounds in Biology & Medicine. 450p. 80.00 (*0-86196-330-X*, Pub. by J Libbey Med) Bks Intl VA.

Deyn, De, see De Deyn.

Deyneka, N. V., tr. see Dnestrovskii, Y. N. & Kostomarov, D. P.

***Deyneka, Peter.** Much Prayer - Much Power: Change Your World Through the Power of Prayer. 2nd ed. 96p. 1999. pap. write for info. (*1-56773-003-5*) Slavic Gospel.

Deynoux, M., et al, eds. Earth's Glacial Record. LC 93-29826. (World & Regional Geology Ser.). (Illus.). 284p. (C). 1994. text 110.00 (*0-521-42022-9*) Cambridge U Pr.

Deyo, David D., Jr., ed. All the Devils Are Here. (Illus.). x, 118p. 1986. pap. 8.50 (*0-934227-02-0*) Unnameable Pr.

Deyo, Frederic C., ed. Competition, Power, & Industrial Flexibility: Social Reconstructions of the World Automobile Industry. LC 95-36937. (International Political Economy Ser.). 250p. 1996. pap. 24.95 (*0-312-12737-5*); text 59.95 (*0-312-12736-7*) St Martin.

— The Political Economy of the New Asian Industrialism. LC 86-29103. (Cornell Studies in Political Economy). (Illus.). 254p. (C). 1987. pap. text 16.95 (*0-8014-9449-4*) Cornell U Pr.

Deyo, Frederick C. Beneath the Economic Miracle: Labor Subordination in the New Asian Industrialism. (C). 1993. pap. 16.95 (*0-520-08262-1*, Pub. by U CA Pr) Cal Prin Full Svc.

Deyo, James. Parent & Child: Understanding the Generation Gap. (Illus.). (Orig.). 1994. pap. 4.00 (*0-9642851-0-X*) Deyo Prods.

Deyo, R. C., jt. ed. see Haug, Edward J.

Deyo, S. L., jt. ed. see Kingsbury, Henry D.

Deyo, Simeon, ed. History of Barnstable County, Mass., 1620-1890. (Illus.). 1010p. 1996. reprint ed. lib. bdg. 99.00 (*0-8328-5205-8*) Higginson Bk Co.

Deyo, Simeon L., jt. ed. see Kingsbury, Henry D.

***DeYoreo, J., et al, eds.** Morphology & Dynamics of Crystal Surfaces in Complex Molecular Systems: Materials Research Society Symposium Proceedings, Vol. 620. 2000. text 77.00 (*1-55899-528-5*) Materials Res.

DeYoung, Alan J. Economics & American Education: A Historical & Critical Overview of the Impact of Economic Theories on Schooling in the United States. 176p. 1989. pap. text 20.95 (*0-8013-0064-9*, 75728) Longman.

— The Life & Death of a Rural American High School: Farewell, Little Kanawha. LC 94-22298. (Illus.). 360p. 1995. text 61.00 (*0-8153-0744-6*) Garland.

DeYoung, Curtiss Paul. Coming Together: The Bible's Message in an Age of Diversity. LC 94-41664. (Christianity & Justice Ser.). 240p. 1995. pap. 15.00 (*0-8170-1226-5*) Judson.

— Reconciliation: Our Greatest Challenge - Our Only Hope. LC 96-49543. 144p. (Orig.). 1997. pap. 15.00 (*0-8170-1256-7*) Judson.

DeYoung, Curtiss Paul, jt. auth. see Hines, Samuel George.

DeYoung, Don B. Physical Science & Creation: An Introduction. Goette, Robert L., ed. (Reader Ser.: Vol. 2). (Illus.). 81p. 1997. pap. 5.00 (*0-940384-19-1*) Creation Research.

DeYoung, Donald B. Astronomy & the Bible: Questions & Answers. LC 89-39. (Illus.). 150p. (YA). (gr. 11). 1989. pap. 8.99 (*0-8010-2991-0*) Baker Bks.

***DeYoung, Donald B.** Astronomy & the Bible: Questions & Answers. 2nd ed. 176p. 2000. pap. 9.99 (*0-8010-6225-X*) Baker Bks.

— Dinosaurs & Creation. 144p. (gr. 13 up). 2000. pap. 9.99 (*0-8010-6306-X*) Baker Bks.

DeYoung, Donald B. Science & the Bible: 30 Scientific Demonstrations Illustrating Scriptural Truths. LC 93-21085. (Illus.). 112p. (Orig.). (J). (gr. 10). 1994. pap. 8.99 (*0-8010-3023-4*) Baker Bks.

— Science & the Bible Vol. 2: 30 Scientific Demonstrations Illustrating Scriptural Truths. LC 93-21085. (Illus.). 112p. 1997. pap. 8.99 (*0-8010-5773-6*) Baker Bks.

***DeYoung, Donald B.** 365 Fascinating Facts from the World of Discovery. (Illus.). 2000. pap. 10.99 (*0-89221-500-3*) New Leaf.

DeYoung, Donald B. Weather & the Bible: 100 Questions & Answers. LC 92-6248. (Illus.). 162p. (YA). (gr. 10). 1992. pap. 8.99 (*0-8010-3013-7*) Baker Bks.

DeYoung, Donald B., jt. auth. see Whitcomb, John C.

DeYoung, Garry. The De Young Rare Book & Nursery Catalog. (Illus.). 90p. 1997. pap. 10.00 (*0-936128-80-1*) De Young Pr.

— The Dynamics of Discrimination: Systemic Discrimination, Generic Racism, Administrative Lynching. 1989. 20.95 (*0-936128-38-0*) De Young Pr.

***DeYoung, L.** Conrail Color Guide to Freight Equipment, Vol. 1. (Illus.). 128p. 1999. 54.95 (*1-58248-034-6*) Morning NJ.

DeYoung, Larry. EL Color Guide to Freight & Passenger Equipment. (Illus.). 128p. 1995. 49.95 (*1-878887-51-3*) Morning NJ.

— Erie Lackawanna in Color Vol. 1: The West End. LC 91-60917. (Illus.). 128p. 1991. 45.00 (*1-878887-05-X*) Morning NJ.

— Erie Lackawanna in Color Vol. 2: New York State. LC 91-60917. (Illus.). 128p. 1992. 45.00 (*1-878887-12-2*) Morning NJ.

— Erie Lackawanna In Color Vol. 3: The East End. LC 91-60917. (Illus.). 128p. 1993. 49.95 (*1-878887-21-1*) Morning NJ.

— Erie Lackawanna in Color Vol. 4: The Early Years. (Illus.). 128p. 1996. 49.95 (*1-878887-79-3*) Morning NJ.

— ERIE Railroad Trackside with Robert F. Collins. LC 97-75968. (Illus.). 128p. 1998. 49.95 (*1-878887-91-2*) Morning NJ.

DeYoung, Lorie. Addition & Subtraction 2. 2nd ed. Hoffman, Joan, ed. (I Know It! Book Ser.). (Illus.). 32p. (J). (ps-3). 1993. student ed. 2.49 (*0-938256-32-7*, 02032) Sch Zone Pub Co.

— Time, Money & Fractions. Hoffman, Joan, ed. (I Know It! Book Ser.). (Illus.). 32p. (J). (ps-3). 1993. student ed. 2.49 (*0-938256-44-0*, 02044) Sch Zone Pub Co.

DeYoung, Lorie, ed. see Gregorich, B.

DeYoung, Marie E. This Woman's Army: The Dynamics of Sex & Violence in the Military. LC 99-47438. 392p. 1999. pap. text 16.95 (*1-55571-507-9*) PSI Resch.

DeYoung, Mary, intro. Call to Reason: An Introduction to Atheism. 2nd ed. 1979. reprint ed. 12.50 (*0-936128-01-1*) De Young Pr.

DeYoung, Sandra. Teaching Nursing. Hunter, Debra, ed. 258p. (C). 1990. pap. text 45.00 (*0-201-09265-4*) Addison-Wesley.

DeYoung, Terri. Placing the Poet: Badr Shakir Al-Sayyab & Postcolonial Iraq. LC 97-23836. 320p. (C). 1998. text 74.50 (*0-7914-3731-0*); pap. text 24.95 (*0-7914-3732-9*) State U NY Pr.

DeYoung, Terri, jt. ed. see Boullata, Issa J.

DeYoung, Thomas I., tr. see Wiseman, Nigel, ed.

Deyrup, Mark. Florida's Fabulous Insects, Vol. I. (Florida's Fabulous Ser.). (Illus.). 166p. 2000. pap. 16.95 (*0-911977-14-7*) Wrld Tampa.

Deyrup, Mark & Franz, Richard, eds. Rare & Endangered Biota of Florida No. IV: Invertebrates. (Illus.). 828p. 1995. 75.00 (*0-8130-1322-4*); pap. 39.95 (*0-8130-1323-2*) U Press Fla.

Deysine, Anne. Dictionnaire de l'Anglais Economique et Juridique - English-French/French-English. (ENG & FRE.). 490p. 1996. 39.95 (*0-7859-9354-1*) Fr & Eur.

Deyuan, Li & Feng, Da-Hsuan, eds. Computational Physics. 516p. (C). 1989. text 130.00 (*9971-5-0711-0*) World Scientific Pub.

Deyuan, Xu & Wei Jiang, eds. Hua Mulan: China's Sweetest Magnolia. Jian, Wang, tr. (Illus.). 126p. 1996. 12.95 (*981-3029-91-9*, Pub. by Asiapac) China Bks.

Deyvi, S., ed. see Tukarama.

Deza, M., et al. Combinatorics & Computer Science: 8th Franco-Japanese & 4th Franco-Chinese Conference, Brest, France, July 1995: Selected Papers. LC 96-32852. (Lecture Notes in Computer Science Ser.: Vol. 1120). 415p. 1996. 68.00 (*3-540-61576-8*) Spr-Verlag.

Deza, M. M., et al, eds. Algebraic, Extremal & Metric Combinatorics 1986. (London Mathematical Society Lecture Note Ser.: No. 131). 256p. 1988. pap. text 57.95 (*0-521-35923-6*) Cambridge U Pr.

Deza, M. M. & Laurent, M. Geometry of Cuts & Metrics. LC 97-15140. (Algorithms & Combinatorics Ser.: Vol. 15). 600p. 1997. 129.00 (*3-540-61611-X*) Spr-Verlag.

Dezago, Todd. Spider-Man: Revelations. (Illus.). 112p. 1997. pap. text 14.95 (*0-7851-0560-3*) Marvel Entrprs.

Dezago, Todd, et al. Spider-Man: Identity Crisis. (Marvel's Finest' Collection). 208p. 1998. 19.95 (*0-7851-0663-4*) Marvel Entrprs.

Dezalay, Yves & Garth, Bryant G. Dealing in Virtue: International Commercial Arbitration & the Construction of a Transnational Legal Order. (Illus.). 360p. 1996. 35.00 (*0-226-14422-4*) U Ch Pr.

— Dealing in Virtue: International Commerical Arbitration & the Construction of a Transnational Legal Order. (Language & Legal Discourse Ser.). (Illus.). 344p. 1998. pap. text 17.00 (*0-226-14423-2*) U Ch Pr.

Dezalay, Yves & Sugarman, David, eds. Professional Competition & Professional Power. LC 94-28910. 304p. (C). 1995. 85.00 (*0-415-09362-7*, C0444) Routledge.

Dezan, Nancy. Barbers, Cars, & Cigars: Activity Programming for Older Men. 52p. (Orig.). 1992. pap. 8.95 (*1-879633-12-4*) Eldersong.

— Yesterdays: A Collection of Short Stories, Nostalgic Photographs, & Related Programming Materials for Older Adults. 106p. (Orig.). 1995. pap. 30.95 (*1-879633-23-X*, P211) Eldersong.

— You Be the Judge: True Stories to Jump-Start Lively Discussions. 43p. 1996. pap. text 7.95 (*1-879633-27-2*, P213) Eldersong.

***Dezan, Nancy.** You Be the Judge Vol. 2: More True Stories to Jump-Start Lively Discussions. 39p. 1998. pap. text 7.95 (*1-879633-36-1*, P221) Eldersong.

Dezani-Ciancaglini, Mariangiola & Plotkin, Gordon, eds. Typed Lambda Calculi & Applications: Second International Conference on Typed Lambda Calculi & Applications, TLCA '95, Edinburgh, United Kingdom, April 1995: Proceedings. LC 95-5969. (Lecture Notes in Computer Science Ser.: No. 902). 443p. 1995. pap. 68.00 (*0-387-59048-X*) Spr-Verlag.

DeZardain, Paul F., tr. see Potter, Beatrix.

DeZardain, Paul F., tr. see Potter, Beatrix & Pomaska, Anna.

Dezeeuw, P.J. Augustine: The Farmer's Boy of Tagaste. LC 98-37869. (Illus.). 93p. (Orig.). (YA). 1988. pap. 6.90 (*0-921100-05-1*) Inhtce Pubns.

***Dezell, Maureen.** Irish America: Coming into Clover. 2001. 24.95 (*0-385-49595-1*) Doubleday.

Dezenhall, Eric. Nail 'Em: Confronting High-Profile Attacks on Celebrities & Businesses. LC 99-26828. 250p. 1999. 27.95 (*1-57392-719-8*) Prometheus Bks.

Dezettel, Louis M. Masons & Builders Libary 1972. 17.95 (*0-672-23185-9*) Sams.

Dezettel, Louis M. & Philbin, Tom. Masons & Builders Library, 2 vols, Set. 2nd ed. LC 83-22352. (Illus.). 1984. text 29.95 (*0-672-23401-7*) Macmillan.

DeZevallos, Felipe O. The Peruvian Puzzle: A Twentieth Century Fund Paper. 85p. 1989. 18.95 (*0-87078-233-9*); pap. 8.95 (*0-87078-232-0*) Century Foundation.

Dezhnev, Nikolai. Concert Performance. Szporluk, Mary A., tr. from RUS. LC 99-20438. 288p. 1999. 23.95 (*0-385-49326-6*) Doubleday.

Dezi, Wang, et al, eds. Mesozoic Volcanic-Intrusive Complexes & Their Metallogenic Relations in East China. (Illus.). 174p. 1996. 95.00 (*90-6764-227-4*, Pub. by VSP) Coronet Bks.

***Deziel.** Applied Digital Signal Processing. LC 99-58865. 400p. 2000. 86.00 (*0-13-775768-9*) P-H.

Deziel, Daniel J., et al. Rush University Review of Surgery. 3rd ed. LC 99-23140. (Illus.). 575p. (C). 1999. pap. text 47.95 (*0-7216-7581-6*, W B Saunders Co) Harcrt Hlth Sci Grp.

Dezilwa & Mansour. Mathematics for Consumers. 2nd ed. 1990. pap. text. write for info. (*0-582-86900-5*, Pub. by Addison-Wesley) Longman.

Dezin, A. A. Partial Differential Equations. LC 87-9421. (Soviet Mathematics Ser.). 180p. 1987. 159.95 (*0-387-16699-8*) Spr-Verlag.

Dezin, Aleksei A. Multidimensional Analysis & Discrete Models. Aleksanova, Irene, tr. from RUS. LC 95-16807. 256p. 1995. boxed set 134.95 (*0-8493-9425-2*, 9425) CRC Pr.

Dezolt, Denise M., jt. auth. see Nastasi, Bonnie K.

Dezsenyi-Szemzo, P. & Mezey, L. Armarium. (ENG, FRE & GER., Illus.). 382p. (C). 1976. pap. 72.00 (*963-05-1016-2*, Pub. by Akade Kiado) St Mut.

Dezso, Douglas M., et al. Collector's Guide to Candy Containers. LC 98-140093. (Illus.). 160p. 1997. pap. 19.95 (*1-57432-009-2*, 4936) Collector Bks.

Dezso, L. & Hajdu, P., eds. Theoretical Problems of Typology & the Northern Eurasian Languages. 184p. 1970. 38.00 (*90-6032-062-X*) J Benjamins Pubng Co.

Dezso, L. & Nemser, W., eds. Studies in English & Hungarian Contrastive Linguistics. 589p. (C). 1980. 170.00 (*963-05-1376-5*, Pub. by Akade Kiado) St Mut.

Dezsoe, Laslo. Studies on Syntactic Topology & Contrastive Grammar. (Janua Linguarum, Series Major). 307p. 1982. pap. text 64.65 (*90-279-3108-9*) Mouton.

Dezsone, S., jt. auth. see Rudolf, C.

DeZur, Mary A. Auntie Mame's Wedding Foo-Foo's: Favor Ideas for Weddings, Parties, Holidays. (Illus.). 32p. 1997. mass mkt. 3.95 (*0-9660497-0-5*) Auntie Mames Wed.

***DeZure, Deborah, ed.** Learning from Change: Landmarks in Teaching & Learning in Higher Education from Change Magazine, 1969-1999. 256p. 2000. 49.95 (*1-57922-001-0*); pap. 27.50 (*1-57922-002-9*) Stylus Pub VA.

DFG Staff, jt. ed. see Kettrup, A.

DGE Acquisition Workshop Staff. Advances in Knowledge Acquisition: Proceedings of the 9th European Knowledge Acquisition Workshop, Ekaw '96, Nottingham, United Kingdom, May 14-17, 1996. O'Hara, Kieron & Schreiber, Guus, eds. LC 96-15539. (Lecture Notes in Artificial Intelligence Ser.: Vol. 107). 371p. 1996. pap. 62.00 (*3-540-61273-4*) Spr-Verlag.

DGM Consulting Inc. Staff. Clincial Practice with Adolescents. 2001. 39.00 (*0-534-52382-X*) Wadsworth Pub.

DGM Continuous Casting Division Staff, ed. A Technical & Economical Comparison of Conventional & Continuous Casting & Rolling Methods for the Production of Cold-Rolled Aluminum Strip: Information Sheets Issued by the DGM Casting Division, Committee on Continuous Casting with Moving Molds. 48p. (Orig.). 1992. ring bd. 35.00 (*3-88355-175-9*, Pub. by DGM Metallurgy Info) IR Pubns.

DGM Materials Science Information Staff, compiled by. Atlas der Kaltformgebungseigenschaften - Atlas of Cold Working Properties, 3 Vols., Vol. 1: Aluminum Materials. (ENG & GER., Illus.). 157p. 1987. ring bd. 140.00 (*3-88355-114-7*, Pub. by DGM Metallurgy Info) IR Pubns.

— Atlas der Kaltformgebungseigenschaften - Atlas of Cold Working Properties, 3 Vols., Vol. 2: Copper Materials. (ENG & GER., Illus.). 287p. 1987. ring bd. 160.00 (*3-88355-115-5*, Pub. by DGM Metallurgy Info) IR Pubns.

— Atlas der Kaltformgebungseigenschaften - Atlas of Cold Working Properties, 3 Vols., Vol. 3: Precious Metals. (ENG & GER., Illus.). 280p. 1987. ring bd. 155.00 (*3-88355-116-3*, Pub. by DGM Metallurgy Info) IR Pubns.

— Atlas of Cold Working Properties of Non-Ferrous Metals, 3 vols., Set. 1987. ring bd. 200.00 (*0-614-11675-9*, Pub. by DGM Metallurgy Info) IR Pubns.

DGW Staff. Dixie Gun Works: Book of Southern Recipes. 1994. 14.95 (*1-877704-14-8*) Pioneer Pr.

Dhada, Mustafah. Warriors at Work: How Guinea Was Really Set Free. (Illus.). 352p. 1993. 34.95 (*0-87081-287-4*) Univ Pr Colo.

D'Haem, Jeanne. The Last Camel: Stories about Somalia. LC 97-8108. 1997. 59.95 (*1-56902-040-X*); pap. 16.95 (*1-56902-041-8*) Red Sea Pr.

D'Haen, Theo. Text to Reader: A Communicative Approach to Fowles, Barth, Cortazar & Boon. (Utrecht Publications in General & Comparative Literature: Vol. 16). x, 162p. 1983. 59.00 (*90-272-2191-X*); pap. 32.95 (*90-272-2201-0*) J Benjamins Pubng Co.

D'Haen, Theo, et al, eds. Convention & Innovation in Literature. LC 89-355. (Utrecht Publications in General & Comparative Literature: No. 24). xxii, 434p. 1989. 106.00 (*90-272-2209-6*) J Benjamins Pubng Co.

D'Haen, Theo & Bertens, Hans, eds. Writing Nation & Writing Region in America. LC 98-139661. 300p. 1996. pap. 40.00 (*90-5383-422-2*, Pub. by VU Univ Pr) Paul & Co Pubs.

D'Haen, Theo, jt. ed. see Bertens, Hans.

D'Haene, Elise. Licking Our Wounds. 1998. mass mkt. 7.95 (*1-56333-605-7*, Hard Candy) Masquerade.

— Licking Our Wounds. 1997. 24.00 (*0-614-20642-1*) Perm Pr FL.

— Licking Our Wounds. LC 96-19008. 208p. 1997. 24.00 (*1-877946-81-8*) Permanent Pr.

Dhaene, G. Encompassing Vol. X: Formulation, Properties & Testing. LC 96-36816. (Lecture Notes in Economics & Mathematical Systems Ser.: Vol. 446). (Illus.). 160p. 1997. pap. 49.00 (*3-540-61890-2*) Spr-Verlag.

D'haeseleer, W. D., et al. Flux Coordinates & Magnetic Field Structure: A Guide to Fundamental Tool of Plasma Theory. Glowinski, Roland et al, eds. (Computational Physics Ser.). (Illus.). 240p. 1991. 115.95 (*0-387-52419-3*) Spr-Verlag.

Dhagamwar, Vasudha. Criminal Justice or Chaos? LC 97-906389. (C). 1997. 30.00 (*81-241-0418-2*, Pub. by Har-Anand Pubns) S Asia.

— Law, Power, & Justice: Protection of Personal Rights under the Indian Penal Code. 2nd ed. LC 92-20728. 400p. (C). 1992. text 38.95 (*0-8039-9441-9*) Sage.

— Towards a Uniform Civil Code. (C). 1990. 50.00 (*0-89771-246-3*) St Mut.

Dhainaut. Septic Shock. (Illus.). 300p. 2000. text 120.00 (*0-7020-1773-6*, W B Saunders Co) Harcrt Hlth Sci Grp.

Dhainaut, Jean-Francois A., jt. auth. see Pinsky, Michael R.

Dhakal, D. N. & Strawn, Christopher. Bhutan: A Movement in Exile. xxviii, 631p. 1994. 39.00 (*81-85693-41-2*, Pub. by Nirala Pubns) Nataraj Bks.

Dhake, Arvind M. Television Engineering. (Illus.). 440p. 1986. pap. text 27.50 (*0-07-096389-4*) McGraw.

Dhaki, M. A. Stones of Sanctity: Art & Architecture of the Jain Temples. (Illus.). 192p. 1996. 65.00 (*0-944142-65-6*, Pub. by Mapin Pubng) Antique Collect.

Dhal, P. C. A Textbook of Cooperative Management. 120p. 1990. text 7.95 (*81-220-0158-0*, Pub. by Konark Pubs Pvt Ltd) Advent Bks Div.

Dhal, Upendra N. Goddess Lakshmi: Origin & Development. xvi, 229p. (C). 1995. 20.00 (*81-86339-07-8*, Pub. by Eastern Bk Linkers) Nataraj Bks.

— Mahisasura in Art & Thought. (Illus.). 95p. (C). 1991. 24.00 (*81-85133-47-6*, Pub. by Eastern Bk Linkers) Nataraj Bks.

Dhaleine, L. N. Hawthorne, Sa Vie et Son Oeuvre. LC 77-164828. (BCL Ser. I). reprint ed. 45.00 (*0-404-02122-0*) AMS Pr.

Dhaleine, L. N. Hawthorne, Sa Vie et Son Oeuvre. (BCL1-PS American Literature Ser.). 510p. 1992. reprint ed. lib. bdg. 129.00 (*0-7812-6724-2*) Rprt Serv.

Dhaliwal, Sarindar, et al. Of Mudlarkers & Measurers. LC 98-171464. 23 p. 1997. pap. write for info. (*0-88911-742-X*) Queens U Inst Intergov.

Dhall, Manjusri. British Rule: Missionary Activities in Orissa, 1822-1947. LC 97-904397. (C). 1997. 48.00 (*81-241-0385-2*, Pub. by Har-Anand Pubns) S Asia.

Dhall, S. K., jt. auth. see Lakshmivarahan, S.

Dhalla, M. N. Zoroastrian Civilization from the Earliest Times to the Downfall of the Last Zoroastrian Empire, 651 A.D. 1976. lib. bdg. 59.95 (*0-8490-2857-4*) Gordon Pr.

Dhalla, Maneckji N. History of Zoroastrianism. LC 74-21256. reprint ed. 45.00 (*0-404-12806-8*) AMS Pr.

— Our Perfecting World: Zarathushtra's Way of Life. LC 74-21257. reprint ed. 55.00 (*0-404-12807-6*) AMS Pr.

— Zoroastrian Civilization: From the Earliest Times to the Downfall of the Last Zoroastrian Empire, 651 A.D. LC 74-21258. reprint ed. 45.00 (*0-404-12808-4*) AMS Pr.

— Zoroastrian Theology from the Earliest Times to the Present Day. LC 70-131038. reprint ed. 42.50 (*0-404-02123-9*) AMS Pr.

Dhalla, Maneckji N., ed. The Nyaishes, or Zoroastrian Litanies. LC 70-164829. (Columbia University. Indo-Iranian Ser.: No. 6). reprint ed. 37.50 (*0-404-50476-0*) AMS Pr.

Dhalla, N. S., ed. Methods in Studying Cardiac Membranes, Vol. II. 344p. 1984. 189.00 (*0-8493-5996-1*, QP114, CRC Reprint) Franklin.

Dhalla, Naranjan S. Angiotensin II Receptor Blockade: Physiological & Clinical Implications. LC 98-15948. (Progress in Experimental Cardiology Ser.). 1998. write for info. (*0-7923-8147-5*) Kluwer Academic.

Dhalla, Naranjan S., et al, eds. The Failing Heart. LC 95-19810. (Illus.). 512p. 1995. text 99.00 (*0-7817-0311-5*) Lppncott W & W.

— Heart Function & Metabolism. (Developments in Cardiovascular Medicine Ser.). 1987. text 186.00 (*0-89838-865-1*) Kluwer Academic.

— Heart Hypertrophy & Failure, Vol. 169. LC 95-23370. (Developments in Cardiovascular Medicine Ser.). 560p. (C). 1996. text 284.50 (*0-7923-3572-4*) Kluwer Academic.

— Myocardial Ischemia. (Developments in Cardiovascular Medicine Ser.). 1987. text 161.50 (*0-89838-866-X*) Kluwer Academic.

— Pathophysiology of Heart Failure. (Developments in Cardiovascular Medicine Ser.: No. DICM 168). 624p. (C). 1996. text 272.50 (*0-7923-3571-6*) Kluwer Academic.

— Pharmacological Aspects of Heart Disease. (Developments in Cardiovascular Medicine Ser.). 1987. text 176.50 (*0-89838-867-8*) Kluwer Academic.

Dhalla, Naranjan S., jt. ed. see Korecky, Borivoj.

Dhalla, Naranjan S., jt. ed. see Nagano, Makoto.

Dhalla, Naranjan S., jt. ed. see Ostadal, Bohuslav.

Dhalle, Katherine, ed. see Osborn, Thomas W.

Dhama, K. P. & Dhama, Suman. Homeopathy: The Complete Handbook. 1998. reprint ed. pap. 16.00 (*81-86112-59-6*, Pub. by UBS Pubs) S Asia.

Dhama, Suman, jt. auth. see Dhama, K. P.

Dhamala, Ranuu R. Problems & Strategies of Development in the Eastern Himalayas. (C). 1993. text 21.00 (*81-212-0450-X*, Pub. by Gian Publng Hse) S Asia.

Dhameja, Sandeep. Electric Vehicle Battery Systems. 256p. 2000. text 64.95 (*0-7506-9916-7*, Newnes) Buttrwrth-Heinemann.

***Dhami, Narinder.** Annie's Game. 192p. (J). 2001. 14.99 (*0-7868-0616-8*, Pub. by Hyperion); lib. bdg. 15.49 (*0-7868-2528-6*, Pub. by Hyperion) Little.

Dhami, Sadhu S. Maluka: A Novel , 2 pts. LC 98-908045. 345p. 1997. write for info. (*81-7380-402-8*, Pub. by Pubn Bureau) S Asia.

Dhamiasiri, Gunapala. Fundamentals of Buddhist Ethics. 189p. 1989. pap. 11.95 (*0-942353-02-1*) Gldn Leaves Pub.

Dhamija, J. N. A Quest for the Eternal. 224p. 1998. pap. 14.95 (*1-86204-360-4*, Pub. by Element MA) Penguin Putnam.

Dhamija, P. V. The Encounter: A Novel. 1993. text 8.95 (*81-85218-68-4*, Pub. by Prestige) Advent Bks Div.

Dhamija, S. C., tr. see Bocharov, A. P., ed.

Dhamma-Kitti. A Manual of Buddhist Historical Traditions - Saddhamma - Sangaha. Law, Bimala Churn, tr. LC 78-72418. reprint ed. 21.50 (*0-404-17279-2*) AMS Pr.

Dhamma, Rewata. The First Discourse of the Buddha. LC 96-9912. 128p. 1997. pap. 14.95 (*0-86171-104-1*) Wisdom MA.

Dhammadinna, ed. The FWBO Puja Book. 5th ed. (Illus.). 40p. 1996. pap. 6.95 (*0-904766-40-3*) Windhorse Pubns.

Dhammakitti, et al. A Manual of Buddhist Historical Traditions (Saddhammma-sangaha) LC 99-932500. vi, 140 p. 1999. write for info. (*81-206-1386-4*, Pub. by Asian Educ Servs) S Asia.

Dhammapada. The Buddha's Path of Virtue. 2nd ed. Woodward, F. L., tr. LC 78-72419. reprint ed. 21.50 (*0-404-17283-0*) AMS Pr.

— Texts from the Buddhist Canon. Beal, Samuel, tr. from CHI. LC 78-72420. reprint ed. 22.50 (*0-404-17284-9*) AMS Pr.

Dhammapadatthakatha. Buddhist Legends, 3 vols., Set. Burlingame, Eugene W., tr. from PLI. LC 78-72421. reprint ed. 105.00 (*0-404-17610-0*) AMS Pr.

— The Commentary on the Dhammapada, 5 vols. in 4. Norman, H. C., ed. LC 78-72423. reprint ed. 155.00 (*0-404-17620-8*) AMS Pr.

Dhammapala. The Udana Commentary, Vol. I. Masefield, Peter, tr. from PLI. 582p. (C). 1994. 50.00 (*0-86013-316-8*) Wisdom MA.

Dhammapala, Achariya. A Treatise on the Paramis. 80p. 1996. 4.50 (*955-24-0146-1*, Pub. by Buddhist Pub Soc) Vipassana Res Pubns.

Dhammika, S. Gemstones of the Good Dhamma. 82p. 1987. 3.75 (*955-24-0001-5*, Pub. by Buddhist Pub Soc) Vipassana Res Pubns.

— Middle Land, Middle Way: A Pilgrim's Guide to the Buddha's India. 208p. 1992. 12.00 (*955-24-0095-3*, Pub. by Buddhist Pub Soc) Vipassana Res Pubns.

Dhammika, S., intro. Encounters with Buddhism. 2nd ed. 60p. 1991. reprint ed. pap. 9.95 (*9971-4-9270-9*) Heian Intl.

Dhammika, S., tr The Edicts of King Asoka. 40p. 1993. 3.00 (*955-24-0104-6*, Pub. by Buddhist Pub Soc) Vipassana Res Pubns.

— Matrceta's Hymn to the Buddha. 48p. 1989. 3.00 (*955-24-0050-3*, Pub. by Buddhist Pub Soc) Vipassana Res Pubns.

Dhamotharan, Dhamo, ed. see American Water Resources Association Staff.

Dhanagare, D. N. Peasant Movements in India, 1920 to 1950. 1983. 34.50 (*0-19-561390-2*) OUP.

— Themes & Perspectives in Indian Sociology. (C). 1993. 18.50 (*81-7033-198-6*, Pub. by Rawat Pubns) S Asia.

Dhanamjaya. Dasarupa: A Treatise on Hindu Dramaturgy. Haas, George C., tr. LC 75-164830. (Columbia University. Indo-Iranian Ser.: No. 7). reprint ed. 35.00 (*0-404-50477-9*) AMS Pr.

Dhanani, Alnoor. The Physical Theory of Kalam: Atoms, Space & Void in Basrian Mutazili Cosmology. LC 93-35729. (Islamic Philosophy, Theology & Science, Studies & Texts Ser.: Vol. 14). 1993. 72.00 (*90-04-09831-3*) Brill Academic Pubs.

Dhananjay, L. Shah, jt. auth. see Shroff, Arvind. V.

***Dhanapala, Jayantha.** Small Arms Control: Old Weapons, New Issues. Donowaki, Mitsuro et al, eds. (UNIDIR Ser.). 322p. 1999. text 74.95 (*0-7546-2076-X*, Pub. by Ashgate Pub) Ashgate Pub Co.

Dhanapala, Jayantha, ed. Regional Approaches to Disarmament, Security, & Stability: Security & Stability. LC 93-21137. (U. N. Institute for Disarmament Research (UNIDIR) Ser.). 256p. 1993. 72.95 (*1-85521-363-X*, Pub. by Dartmth Pub) Ashgate Pub Co.

D'Hancarville. The Private Lives of the Twelve Caesars. Niemoeller, A. F., tr. 54p. 1983. reprint ed. 7.50 (*0-914937-03-0*) Ind Pubns.

D'Hancarville, Pierre. Recherches sur l'Origine, l'Esprit et la Progres des Arts de la Grece. LC 78-60885. (Myth & Romanticism Ser.: Vol. 12). 1203p. 1984. text 25.00 (*0-8240-3561-5*) Garland.

Dhanda, Amita. Legal Order & Mental Disorder. LC 99-17486. 1999. write for info. (*0-7619-9324-X*) Sage.

***Dhanda, Amita & Parashar, Archana, eds.** Engendering Law: Essays in Honour of Lotika Sarkas. 1999. pap. 100.00 (*81-7012-666-5*, Pub. by Eastern Book) St Mut.

Dhanda, Kanwalroop K., et al, contrib. by. Environmental Networks: A Framework for Economic Decision-Making & Policy Analysis. LC 98-48847. 432p. 1999. 100.00 (*1-84064-041-3*) E Elgar.

Dhanjal, Beryl. Amritsar. LC 93-31445. (Holy Cities Ser.). (Illus.). 48p. (YA). (gr. 5 up). 1994. lib. bdg. 21.00 (*0-87518-571-1*, Dillon Silver Burdett) Silver Burdett Pr.

— What Do We Know about Sikhism? LC 96-32619. (What Do We Know about...? Ser.). (Illus.). 40p. (YA). (gr. 3 up). 1996. lib. bdg. 18.95 (*0-87226-387-8*, 63878B, P Bedrick Books) NTC Contemp Pub Co.

Dhankhar, D. Hand Book for Bank Managers. (C). 1988. 85.00 (*0-7855-6033-5*) St Mut.

***Dhar.** Artisan of the Paradise a Study of Art & Artisans of Kashmir: From Ancient to Modern Times. 1999. 110.00 (*81-86505-25-3*, Pub. by Deep & Deep Pubns) S Asia.

Dhar, B. B. & Sexena, N. C., eds. Socio-Economic Impacts of Environment. (Illus.). x, 296p. 1994. 30.00 (*81-7024-603-2*, Pub. by Ashish Pub Hse) Nataraj Bks.

Dhar, Bharat B. Environmental Management of Mining Operations. 1990. 46.00 (*81-7024-273-8*, Pub. by Ashish Pub Hse) S Asia.

Dhar, Bharat B. & Bhowmick, B. C., eds. Mine Safety (Select Papers) Proceedings of the 27th International Conference on Safety in Mines Research Institute, New Delhi, 20-22 February 1997. (Illus.). 624p. (C). 1997. text 162.00 (*90-5410-738-3*, Pub. by A A Balkema) Ashgate Pub Co.

Dhar, Bharat B. & Thakur, D. N., eds. Mining Environment: Proceedings of the First World Mining Environment Congress. LC 99-227031. (Illus.). 416p. (C). 1996. text 91.00 (*90-5410-715-4*, Pub. by A A Balkema) Ashgate Pub Co.

Dhar, Bharat B., jt. ed. see Singh, T. N.

Dhar, Niranjan. Aurobindo, Gandhi & Roy: A Yogi, a Mahatma & a Rationalist. 1986. 13.50 (*0-8364-1578-7*, Pub. by Minerva) S Asia.

***Dhar, P. N.** Indira Gandhi, the 'emergency' & Indian Democracy. (Illus.). 375p. 2000. text 26.95 (*0-19-564899-4*) OUP.

***Dhar, Pannalal.** Ethnic Unrest in India & Her Neighbours: Also Includes Europe, West Asia, the Balkans & Africa. 1998. 88.00 (*81-7100-818-6*) Deep & Deep Pubns.

Dhar, Pannalal. India & Her Domestic Problems. (Religion State & Secularism Ser.). (C). 1993. text 48.00 (*81-85094-68-3*, Pub. by Punthi Pus) S Asia.

— India, Her Neighbours & Foreign Policy. (C). 1991. 21.50 (*81-7100-309-5*, Pub. by Deep & Deep Pubns) S Asia.

***Dhar, Sanjiv.** Indian Cooking Light & Easy. 52p. 1999. pap. 11.95 (*0-9673402-0-9*) India Hse Inc.

Dhar, Satchidananda. Transformation & Trend of Buddhism in the 20th Century. 189p. 1991. 22.00 (*0-8364-1951-0*) S Asia.

Dhar, Sheila. Here's Someone I'd Like You to Meet: Tales of Innocents, Musicians & Bureaucrats. LC 96-219785. 260p. 1996. text 19.95 (*0-19-563627-9*) OUP.

— "Here's Someone I'd Like You to Meet" Tales of Innocents, Musicians & Bureaucrats. (Illus.). 260p. 1997. pap. 10.95 (*0-19-564054-3*) OUP.

Dhar, Somnath. Jammu & Kashmir. rev. ed. LC 99-932698. (India, the Land & the People Ser.). 226p. 1999. write for info. (*81-237-2533-7*, Pub. by Natl Bk Trust) S Asia.

Dhar, Sunita. Senia Gharana: Its Contribution to Indian Classical Music. (C). 1989. 23.50 (*0-685-33358-2*, Pub. by Reliance Pub Hse) S Asia.

***Dhar, T. N.** History-Fiction Interface in Indian English Novel: Mulk Raj Anand, Nayantara Sahgal, Salman Rushdie, Shashi Tharoor, O. V. Vijayan. LC 99-932411. 271 p. 1999. write for info. (*81-7551-059-5*, Pub. by Prestige) Advent Bks Div.

Dhar, U. & Kachroo, P. Alpine Flora of Kashmir Himalaya. 280p. 1983. 210.00 (*81-85046-08-5*, Pub. by Scientific) St Mut.

Dhar, Vasant & Stein, Roger. Intelligent Decision Support Methods: The Science of Knowledge Work. LC 96-44084. 244p. (C). 1996. 54.00 (*0-13-519925-2*) P-H.

— Seven Methods for Transforming Corporate Data into Business Intelligence. LC 96-37191. 269p. (C). 1996. pap. text 29.95 (*0-13-282006-4*) P-H.

Dharamdasani, D. Democratic Nepal. (C). 1992. 60.00 (*0-7855-0175-4*, Pub. by Ratna Pustak Bhandar) St Mut.

Dharamdasani, M. Political Economy of Foreign Aid in the Third World. 1984. pap. 32.00 (*0-7855-7476-X*, Pub. by Ratna Pustak Bhandar) St Mut.

Dharamdasani, M. D. Nepal in Transition. 1997. pap. 67.00 (*0-7855-7443-3*, Pub. by Ratna Pustak Bhandar) St Mut.

Dharan, Bala G., jt. auth. see Ziff, Stephen A.

Dharan, Bala G., jt. ed. see Zeff, Stephen A.

Dharanjit, Singh. Secrets of the Universe. 1998. pap. 14.95 (*1-889534-13-7*) Jay St Pubs.

D'Harcourt, Claire, jt. auth. see Fontanel, Beatrice.

Dhargyey, Geshe, jt. auth. see Rabten, Geshe.

Dharhyey, G. L. Kalacakra Tantra: A Commentary. Kelsang, G. P., tr. 1994. reprint ed. pap. 15.00 (*81-85102-41-4*, Pub. by Lib Tibetan W&A) S Asia.

Dharker, Imtiaz. Postcards from God. LC 97-223654. 160p. 1997. pap. 19.95 (*1-85224-407-0*, Pub. by Bloodaxe Bks) Dufour.

Dharker, Rani. The Virgin Syndrome. LC 97-913982. 1997. write for info. (*0-14-027021-3*) Penguin Books.

***Dharma, Krishna.** Mahabharata: The Condensed Version of the World's Greatest Epic. abr. ed. (Illus.). 283p. 2000. 19.95 (*1-887089-25-X*, Pub. by Torchlght Pub) Natl Bk Netwk.

Dharma, Krishna. Mahabharata: The Greatest Spiritual Epic of All Time. LC 98-50280. (Illus.). 960p. 1999. 39.95 (*1-887089-17-9*) Torchlght Pub.

Dharma Publishing Staff. Jataka Teachers' Resource Guide. 120p. 1995. ring bd. 15.95 (*0-89800-249-4*) Dharma Pub.

— Secret of the Healing Treasures. LC 96-48214. (King Gesar Ser.). (Illus.). 1996. write for info. (*0-89800-217-6*) Dharma Pub.

Dharma Publishing Staff, tr. The Fortunate Aeon, 4 vols., Set. LC 87-578. (Tibetan Translation Ser.: Vol. 13).Tr. of Bhadrakalpika-Sutra. (ENG & TIB.). 1873p. 1987. 180.00 (*0-89800-136-6*) Dharma Pub.

Dharma Publishing Staff & Tulko, Tarthang, eds. Footsteps on the Diamond Path, 3 vols. in 1. enl. rev. ed. LC 92-21924. (Crystal Mirror Ser.: Vols. 1-3). (Illus.). 577p. (Orig.). 1992. pap. 18.95 (*0-89800-243-5*) Dharma Pub.

Dharma Publishing Staff, ed. & tr. see Buddha Sakyamuni.

***Dharma Realm Buddhist Association Members.** In Memory of the First Anniversary of the Nirvana of Venerable Master Hsuan Hua (Shuan Hua Lao Ho Shang Chi Chou Nien) Shr, Heng-Yin, ed. (CHI & ENG., Illus.). 447p. 1999. 30.00 (*0-88139-557-9*) Buddhist Text.

Dharma Realm Buddhist Association Members. In Memory of the Venerable Master Hsuan Hua, Vol. 1. Buddhist Text Translation Society Staff, ed. & tr. by. Heng Yin, ed. (CHI & ENG., Illus.). 249p. 1995. 25.00 (*0-88139-554-4*) Buddhist Text.

— In Memory of the Venerable Master Hsuan Hua Vol. 1. Buddhist Text Translation Society Staff, ed. & tr. by. Heng Yin, ed. (CHI & ENG., Illus.). 249p. 1995. pap. 25.00 (*0-88139-551-X*) Buddhist Text.

— In Memory of the Venerable Master Hsuan Hua Vol. 2. Buddhist Text Translation Society Staff, ed. & tr. by. Heng-Yin, ed. (CHI & ENG., Illus.). 506p. 1996. 35.00 (*0-88139-553-6*) Buddhist Text.

Dharma Realm Buddhist University Faculty. Human Roots Vol. 2: Buddhist Stories for Young Readers. (Illus.). 140p. (J). (gr. 3 up). 1984. pap. 5.00 (*0-88139-017-8*) Buddhist Text.

Dharma Realm Buddhist University Faculty, compiled by. Human Roots Vol. 1: Buddhist Stories for Young Readers. (Illus.). 89p. (Orig.). (J). (gr. 3 up). 1982. pap. 5.00 (*0-88139-500-5*) Buddhist Text.

Dharmadasa, K. N. Language, Religion, & Ethnic Assertiveness: The Growth of Sinhalese Nationalism in Sri Lanka. 384p. (C). 1993. text 65.00 (*0-472-10288-5*, 10288) U of Mich Pr.

Dharmadasa, K. N. & Samarasinghe, S. W. The Vanishing Aborigines. 1990. text 27.95 (*0-7069-5298-7*, Pub. by Vikas) S Asia.

Dharmadhikari, Sudhakar & Joag-dev, Kumar, eds. Unimodality, Convexity & Applications. (Probability & Mathematical Statistics Ser.: Vol. 27). 278p. 1988. text 122.00 (*0-12-214690-5*) Acad Pr.

Dharmajog, Anita, jt. auth. see Singh, Jogendra P.

Dharmakumarsinhji, R. S. Reminiscences of Indian Wildlife. LC 98-902942. (Illus.). 128p. 1998. 22.95 (*0-19-564255-4*) OUP.

***Dharmakumsinhji, R. S.** Reminiscences of Indian Wildlife. (Illus.). 128p. 2000. pap. text 13.95 (*0-19-565167-7*) OUP.

Dharmananda, Subhuti, ed. see Santillo, Humbart.

Dharmap, Ala, jt. auth. see Keenan, John P.

Dharmaraj, Ramola. Invisible Season. Galvin, Martin, ed. LC 98-12279. 1998. pap. 12.00 (*0-931846-51-X*) Wash Writers Pub.

Dharmarajan, S. & Seth, Rabindra. Tourism in India: Trends & Issues. (C). 1994. 28.00 (*81-241-0204-X*, Pub. by Har-Anand Pubns) S Asia.

***Dharmarajan, Shivani.** NGO Development Initiative & Public Policy. LC 98-908067. 1998. 36.00 (*81-7391-265-3*, Pub. by Kaniska Pubs Dist) S Asia.

Dharmasadza, Drikung B. The Jewel Treasury of Advice: A Hundred Teachings from the Heart. Finney, Rick, ed. Gyaltshen, Khenpo K., tr. from TIB. 100p. (Orig.). 1997. pap. 9.95 (*0-9655988-0-2*) Vajra Pubns.

Dharmatreata Staff & Dessein, Bart. Sarmyukteabhidharmahrdaya = Pt. 1, 2, 3: Heart of Scholasticism with Miscellaneous Additions. LC 98-915925. (ENG & SAN.). 779, 568, 583p. 1998. pap. 1000.00 (*81-208-1583-1*, Pub. by Motilal Bnarsidass) St Mut.

Dharmdasani, M. D. Nepal Political Economy of Foreign Aid. 1994. pap. 60.00 (*0-7855-0470-2*, Pub. by Ratna Pustak Bhandar) St Mut.

Dharmendra. Leprosy, Vol. 2. (Illus.). 900p. 1985. 52.95 (*0-318-36371-2*) Asia Bk Corp.

D'Harnoncourt, Anne & McShine, Kynaston, eds. Marcel Duchamp. (Illus.). 360p. 1989. 65.00 (*3-7913-1018-6*, Pub. by Prestel) te Neues.

D'Harnoncourt, Rene, jt. auth. see Bennett, Wendell C.

D'Harnoncourt, Rene, jt. auth. see Douglas, Frederic H.

***Dharwadker, Vinay.** Cosmopolitan Geographies: New Locations in Literature & Culture. 224p. 2000. 75.00 (*0-415-92506-1*); pap. 19.99 (*0-415-92507-X*) Routledge.

Dharwadker, Vinay & Ramanujan, A. K., eds. The Oxford Anthology of Modern Indian Poetry. 286p. 1995. text 19.95 (*0-19-562865-9*) OUP.

— The Oxford Anthology of Modern Indian Poetry. 286p. 1998. pap. 12.95 (*0-19-563917-0*) OUP.

Dharwadker, Vinay, jt. auth. see Bien, Gloria.

Dharwadker, Vinay, ed. see Ramanujan, A. K.

Dhatwalia, H. R. Familial Relationships in Jane Austen's Novels. 166p. 1988. text 25.00 (*81-85135-26-6*, Pub. by Natl Bk Orgn) Advent Bks Div.

Dhaubhadel, M. N., et al, eds. Advances in Finite Element Analysis in Fluid Dynamics, 1992. (FED Ser.: Vol. 137). 124p. 1992. 37.50 (*0-7918-1066-6*, G00710) ASME.

— Advances in Finite Element Analysis in Fluid Dynamics, 1993. LC 93-73724. 125p. 1993. pap. text 40.00 (*0-7918-1015-1*) ASME.

D

— Numerical Developments in CFD - 1995. LC 95-78824. (1995 ASME/JSME Fluids Engineering Conference Ser.: FED-Vol. 215). 120p. 1995. 76.00 (*0-7918-1470-X*, G00965) ASME.

Dhavale, Dileep. Management Accounting Issues in Cellular Manufacturing & Focused-Factory Systems. Barth, Claire, ed. (Illus.). 268p. (Orig.). 1995. pap. 60.00 (*0-86641-247-6*, 96310) Inst Mgmt Account.

Dhavalikar, M. K. Cultural Imperialism: Indus Civilization in Western India. LC 95-900047. (C). 1995. 54.00 (*81-85016-42-9*, Pub. by Bks & Bks) S Asia.

Dhavalikar, M. K. Indian Protohistory. LC 97-902622. 1997. 98.00 (*81-85016-52-6*, Pub. by Bks & Bks) S Asia.

***Dhavalikar, Madhukar K.** Historical Archaeology of India. LC 99-933501. xi, 274 p. 1999. write for info. (*81-85016-55-0*, Pub. by Bks & Bks) S Asia.

Dhavamony, Mariasusai. Christian Theology of Religions: A Systematic Reflection on the Christian Understanding of World Religions. LC 98-13519. (Studies in the Intercultural History of Christianity: Vol. 108). 242p. (C). 1998. pap. text 40.95 (*0-8204-3436-1*) P Lang Pubng.

— Christian Theology of Religions: A Systematic Reflection on the Christian Understanding of World Religions, Vol. 108. Friedli, Richard et al, eds. 242p. 1998. pap. 40.95 (*3-906760-07-3*) P Lang Pubng.

Dhavan, R., et al, eds. Access to Legal Education & the Legal Professions. 1989. pap. 68.00 (*0-406-70065-6*, UK, MICHIE) LEXIS Pub.

Dhavan, Rajeev. Only the Good News: On the Law of the Press in India. 514p. (C). 1987. 47.50 (*81-85054-38-X*, Pub. by Manohar) S Asia.

Dhawan, B. D. Indian Water Resource Development for Irrigation: Issues, Critiques, Reviews. (C). 1993. 28.00 (*81-7169-259-1*, Commonwealth) S Asia.

— Irrigation in India's Agricultural Development: Productivity, Stability, & Equity. 196p. (C). 1988. text 26.00 (*0-8039-9544-X*) Sage.

— Irrigation in India's Agricultural Development: Productivity, Stability, Equity. (C). 1994. text 30.00 (*81-7169-275-3*, Pub. by Commonwealth) S Asia.

— Mysticism & Symbolism. 1988. 24.95 (*81-212-0094-6*) Asia Bk Corp.

— Studies in Irrigation & Water Management. 1989. 38.00 (*81-7169-027-0*, Pub. by Commonwealth) S Asia.

— Studies in Minor Irrigation with Special Reference to Ground Water. 1990. 29.00 (*81-7169-061-0*, Commonwealth) S Asia.

Dhawan, B. D., ed. Big Dams: Claims, Counter Claims. 1990. 34.50 (*81-7169-063-7*, Commonwealth) S Asia.

Dhawan, B. N., ed. Pharmacology for Health in Asia: Proceedings of Asian Congress of Pharmacology. (C). 1988. 55.00 (*0-8364-2336-4*, Pub. by Allied Pubs) S Asia.

Dhawan, B. N., ed. see International Congress of Pharmacology Staff.

Dhawan, Chander. Enabling Remote Network Access with PSTN, ISDN & Internet. LC 97-41018. (Computer Communications Ser.). (Illus.). 384p. 1997. pap. 49.95 (*0-07-016774-5*) McGraw.

Dhawan, Chandler. Mobile Computing: A Systems Integrator's Handbook. LC 96-33611. (s). (Illus.). 452p. 1996. pap. 60.00 (*0-07-016769-9*) McGraw.

Dhawan, I. K. & Kapoor, V. K. Carcinoma of the Breast. (C). 1987. 170.00 (*81-85017-37-9*, Pub. by Interprint) St Mut.

Dhawan, J., jt. auth. see Saldhana, Cecil J.

Dhawan, R. K. Arundhati Roy, the Novelist Extraordinary LC 99-932399. 422 p. 1999. write for info. (*81-7551-060-9*) Advent Bks Div.

***Dhawan, R. K.** The Novels of Amitav Ghosh. LC 98-915589. 296p. 1999. write for info. (*81-7551-011-0*, Pub. by Prestige) Advent Bks Div.

Dhawan, R. K. The Novels of Joseph Conrad. 224p. 1992. text 27.50 (*81-85218-07-2*, Pub. by Prestige) Advent Bks Div.

Dhawan, R. K., ed. Development of Tubewell Irrigation in India. 256p. 1982. 29.95 (*0-318-36788-2*) Asia Bk Corp.

— Explorations in Modern Indo-English Fiction. 256p. 1982. 17.95 (*0-318-36948-6*) Asia Bk Corp.

— Indian Women Novelists, 5 vols., Set II, Vols. 6-10. 1992. text 150.00 (*81-85218-39-0*) Advent Bks Div.

— Indian Women Novelists, 5 vols., Set, Vols. 1-5. 1400p. 1991. text 150.00 (*81-85218-18-8*, Pub. by Prestige) Advent Bks Div.

— The Novels of Arun Joshi. 288p. 1992. 32.50 (*81-85218-62-5*, Pub. by Prestige) Advent Bks Div.

— The Novels of Mulk Raj Anand. 288p. (C). 1992. 27.50 (*81-85218-63-3*, Pub. by Prestige) Advent Bks Div.

Dhawan, R. K., et al, eds. Recent Commonwealth Literature, 2 vols. 300p. 1989. text 50.00 (*81-85218-09-9*, Pub. by Prestige) Advent Bks Div.

Dhawan, R. K. & Indian Association for English Studies Staff. 50 Years of Indian Writing: A Commemorative Volume Highlighting the Achievement of Post-Independence Indian Writing in English & Literature in Translation. LC 99-932068. 160p. 1999. write for info. (*81-7551-067-6*, Pub. by Prestige) Advent Bks Div.

Dhawan, R. K. & Kerr, David, eds. Australian Literature Today. 256p. (C). 1992. 35.00 (*81-85218-70-6*, Pub. by Prestige) Advent Bks Div.

Dhawan, R. K. & Taneja, G. R., eds. The Novels of Salman Rushdie. 225p. 1991. text 30.00 (*81-85218-33-1*, Pub. by Prestige) Advent Bks Div.

Dhawan, R. K. & Tonett, Walter, eds. New Zealand Literature Today. 192p. (C). 1992. 30.00 (*81-85218-69-2*, Pub. by Prestige) Advent Bks Div.

Dhawan, Sanjay. Networking Device Drivers. (B & F - Computer Science Ser.). 398p. 1994. pap. 48.95 (*0-442-01943-2*, VNR) Wiley.

— Networking Device Drivers. (VNR Communications Library). 416p. 1995. pap. 59.95 (*0-471-28671-0*, VNR) Wiley.

Dhawan, Savitri. Mother Goddesses in Early Indian Religion. LC 97-901637. 1997. 30.00 (*81-86803-07-6*, Pub. by Natl Pub Hse) S Asia.

Dhawan, V., ed. Applications of Biotechnology in Forestry & Horticulture. (Illus.). 398p. 1989. 115.00 (*0-306-43375-3*, Plenum Trade) Perseus Pubng.

Dheensaw, Cleve & Binder, Deanna. Celebrate the Spirit: The Olympic Games. (Illus.). 80p. (J). 1996. pap. text 9.95 (*1-55143-066-5*) Orca Bk Pubs.

***Dheer, Sudarshan.** Symbols, Logos, & Trademarks: 1500 Outstanding Designs from India. LC 97-46751. 1998. pap. 12.95 (*0-486-40039-5*) Dover.

— The World of Symbols/Logos & Trademarks India 2. 200p. 2000. 39.95 (*0-88108-212-0*) Art Dir.

Dheere, R.F.B.M. Universal Computer Interfaces. (European Patent Office Ser.: No. 11). 394p. 1988. 228.50 (*0-08-036610-4*, Pergamon Pr) Elsevier.

Dheilly, Joseph. Dictionnaire Biblique. (FRE.). 1284p. 1964. 29.95 (*0-8288-6761-5*, M-6114) Fr & Eur.

Dhein, Stefan. Cardiac Gap Junctions: Physiology, Regulation, Pathophysiology & Pharmacology. LC 97-48990. (Illus.). xii, 148p. 1998. 112.25 (*3-8055-6567-4*) S Karger.

D'Hendecourt, L., et al, eds. Solid Interstellar Matter: The ISO Revolution: Les Houche's Workshop, February 2-6, 1998. xx, 340p. 1999. pap. 82.00 (*3-540-65809-2*) Spr-Verlag.

D'Herbemont, Olivier & Cesar, Bruno. Managing Sensitive Projects: Lateral Approach. LC 98-20625. 232p. (C). (gr. 13). 1998. 29.95 (*0-415-92166-X*) Routledge.

D'Herelle, Felix. Felix d'Herelle & the Origins of Molecular Biology. LC 98-44302. (Illus.). 224p. 1999. 30.00 (*0-300-07127-2*) Yale U Pr.

Dheri, V., jt. auth. see Basha, Y.

Dhesi, S S, jt. auth. see Barrett, S. D.

D'Heylli, Georges, pseud. Dictionnaire Des Pseudonymes. iii, 559p. 1977. reprint ed. write for info. (*3-487-06339-5*) G Olms Pubs.

Dhez, P., jt. ed. see Weisbuch, Claude.

DHHS Staff, jt. auth. see CDC Staff.

Dhiarmada, Briona N., jt. ed. see Annrachain, Maire N.

Dhillion, Harinder J. Thirty Two Basic Steps into Panjabi Vocabulary: A Vocabulary Workbook. (PAN., Illus.). 143p. (Orig.). 1986. pap. 15.00 (*0-9617188-1-1*); audio 14.95 (*0-317-54405-5*) H J Dhillon.

Dhillion, K. S., tr. see Mardzhanishvili, M. A.

Dhillon. Quality Control, Reliability, & Engineering Design. (Industrial Engineering Ser.: Vol. 10). (Illus.). 312p. 1985. text 135.00 (*0-8247-7278-4*) Dekker.

Dhillon, B. S. Engineering Design: A Modern Approach. LC 95-37446. 448p. (C). 1995. text 29.95 (*0-256-18312-0*, Irwn McGrw-H) McGrw-H Hghr Educ.

— Engineering Maintainability: How to Design for Reliability & Easy Maintenance. LC 99-18585. 350p. 1999. 75.00 (*0-88415-257-X*) Gulf Pub.

— Engineering Management: Concepts, Procedures & Models. LC 87-71933. 373p. 1987. 24.95 (*0-87762-532-8*) Technomic.

— Life Cycle Costing: Techniques, Models & Applications. xviii, 354p. 1989. text 101.00 (*2-88124-302-9*) Gordon & Breach.

— Mechanical Reliability. (Educ Ser.). 330p. 1988. 57.95 (*0-930403-38-X*, 38-X) AIAA.

— Robot Reliability & Safety. (Illus.). 280p. 1991. 109.95 (*0-387-97535-7*) Spr-Verlag.

Dhillon, B. S. & Raouf, A. Safety Assessment: A Quantitative Approach. 208p. 1993. lib. bdg. 85.00 (*0-87371-675-2*, L675) Lewis Pubs.

***Dhillon, Balbir S.** Medical Device Reliability & Associated Areas. 264p. 2000. 99.95 (*0-8493-0312-5*) CRC Pr.

Dhillon, Balhir. Systems Reliability, Maintainability & Management. (Illus.). 376p. 1983. text 32.50 (*0-89433-195-7*) Petrocelli.

Dhillon, Baljean & Millar, Geoffrey T. The Child's Eye. LC 92-48410. (Oxford Medical Publications). 144p. 1995. 85.00 (*0-19-262303-6*) OUP.

— The Child's Eye. LC 92-48410. (Oxford Medical Publications). (Illus.). 142p. 1995. pap. text 46.00 (*0-19-262302-8*) OUP.

Dhillon, B.S. Advanced Design Concepts for Engineers. LC 98-60043. 250p. 1998. 74.95 (*1-56676-626-5*) Technomic.

***Dhillon, B.S.** Design Reliability: Fundamentals & Applications. LC 99-28211. 416p. 1999. boxed set 79.95 (*0-8493-1465-8*) CRC Pr.

Dhillon, Gurpreet. Managing Information System Security. (Illus.). 210p. (C). 1997. pap. text 35.00 (*0-333-69260-8*, Pub. by Macmillan Ed) Scholium Intl.

Dhillon, H. J. Some Key-Points of Hindi, Panjabi (Gurmukhi), Panjabi (Persian) or Urdu Grammar. (PER.). 85p. (Orig.). (C). 1990. pap. text. write for info. (*0-9617188-9-7*); pap. text, student ed. 10.00 (*0-9617188-7-0*); write for info. (*0-9617188-8-9*) H J Dhillon.

Dhillon, H. S. & Philip, L. Health Promotion & Community Action for Health in Developing Countries. LC 95-129771. (ENG, FRE & SPA.). vii, 122p. 1994. pap. text 25.00 (*92-4-156167-X*, 1150411) World Health.

Dhillon, Harinder J. ABC of Hindi, Panjabi, Urdu. (HIN, PAN & URD.). 164p. (Orig.). 1988. student ed. 16.00 (*0-9617188-6-2*) H J Dhillon.

— Thirty-Two Basic Steps into Hindi Vocabulary: A Vocabulary Workbook. (HIN., Illus.). 143p. (Orig.). 1986. 15.00 (*0-9617188-0-3*); audio 14.95 (*0-685-14680-4*) H J Dhillon.

— Thirty-Two Basic Steps into Panjabi Vocabulary: A Vocabulary Workbook. (PAN., Illus.). 143p. (Orig.). 1986. pap. 15.00 (*0-9617188-2-X*); audio 14.95 (*0-685-37382-7*) H J Dhillon.

— Thirty Two Basic Steps into Urdu Vocabulary: A Vocabulary Workbook. (URD., Illus.). 143p. (Orig.). 1986. pap. 15.00 (*0-9617188-3-8*); audio 14.95 (*0-317-54404-7*) H J Dhillon.

***Dhillon, Harish.** Lives & Teachings of the Sikh Gurus. 1998. pap. 16.00 (*81-7476-173-X*, Pub. by UBS Pubs) S Asia.

Dhillon, K., tr. see Mardzhanishvilli, M. A. & Mardzhanishvilli, L.

***Dhillon, K. S.** Defenders of the Establishment: Ruler-Supportive Police Forces of South Asia LC 98-903599. 289 p. 1998. write for info. (*81-85952-52-3*) Indian Inst.

Dhillon, K. S., tr. see Khachatryan, K. A., ed.

Dhillon, K. S., tr. see Mardzhanishvili, M. A.

***Dhillon, Kris.** The Curry Secret: Indian Restaurant Cookery at Home. 3rd ed. (Illus.). 128p. 2001. pap. 6.95 (*0-7160-2054-8*, Pub. by Elliot RW Bks) Midpt Trade.

Dhillon, Paramjeet K. Psycho-Social Aspects of Aging in India. (C). 1992. text 36.00 (*81-7022-426-8*, Pub. by Concept) S Asia.

***Dhillon, Polly.** Kijabe: An African Historical Saga. LC 00-28574. 320p. 2000. 10.95 (*1-885288-21-2*, 914-017, Pub. by PREP Pubng) BookWorld.

Dhillon, R. S. & East, C. A. Ear, Nose, & Throat, & Head & Neck Surgery: An Illustrated Colour Text. 2nd ed. LC 99-11695. 1999. write for info. (*0-443-05955-1*) Church.

— Ear, Nose & Throat, Head & Neck Surgery. (Illus.). 128p. 1994. pap. text 33.00 (*0-443-04299-3*) Church.

Dhillon, R. S., et al. MCQS in Otolaryngology. 2nd ed. 257p. 1999. pap. text 32.50 (*0-7506-2165-6*) Buttrwrth-Heinemann.

Dhillon, Sukhraj. Genetic Engineering: Technolgoy & Its Applications. 73p. (YA). (gr. 7-12). 1990. pap. 6.95 (*1-57515-000-X*) PPI Pubng.

Dhillon, Sukhraj S. Cigarette Smoking: What Its Doing to Smokers & Nonsmokers. 64p. (YA). (gr. 7-12). 1993. pap. 6.95 (*1-57515-037-9*) PPI Pubng.

— Industrial Leaks & Air Pollution. 59p. (YA). (gr. 7-12). 1993. pap. 6.95 (*1-57515-034-4*) PPI Pubng.

— A New Look at Vegetarianism. 60p. (YA). (gr. 7-12). 1993. pap. 6.95 (*1-57515-029-8*) PPI Pubng.

Dhilorm, Gurubkshasirmh. From My Bones: Memoirs of Col. Gurbaksh Singh Dhillon of the Indian National Army, Including 1945 Red Fort Trial. LC 98-908714. xviii, 598p. 1998. write for info. (*81-7305-148-8*) Aryan Bks Intl.

Dhindsa, Dharam S. & Bahl, Om P., eds. Molecular & Cellular Aspects of Reproduction. LC 86-20533. (Advances in Experimental Medicine & Biology Ser.: Vol. 205). 392p. 1986. 85.00 (*0-306-42403-7*, Plenum Trade) Perseus Pubng.

Dhindsa, K. S. Indian Immigrants in United Kingdom: A Socio-economic Analysis. LC 98-915424. 70p. 1998. write for info. (*81-7022-728-3*) Concept.

Dhingra, Amrit, jt. auth. see Kapoor, M. M.

Dhingra, Ashok K. & Fishman, Steven G., eds. Interfaces in Metal-Matrix Composites: Proceedings of a Symposium. LC 86-20106. (Illus.). 265p. reprint ed. pap. 82.20 (*0-608-16017-2*, 203311100084) Bks Demand.

Dhingra, Onkar D. & Sinclair, James B. Basic Plant Pathology Methods. 376p. 1985. 205.00 (*0-8493-5921-X*, SB732, CRC Reprint) Franklin.

— Basic Plant Pathology Methods. 2nd ed. 448p. 1995. lib. bdg. 69.95 (*0-87371-638-8*, L638) Lewis Pubs.

Dhir, K. K. Current Research in Plant Sciences. Prof. S. C. Verma Commemorative Volume. 1997. pap. 50.00 (*81-7089-225-2*, Pub. by Intl Bk Distr) St Mut.

— Ferns of the Northwestern Himalayas. (Bibliotheca Pteridologica Ser.: Bd. 1). (Illus.). 1979. pap. text 40.00 (*3-7682-1222-X*) Lubrecht & Cramer.

Dhir, K. K. & Sood, A. Fern Flora of Mussoorie Hills. (Bibliotheca Pteridologica Ser.: Bd. 2). (Illus.). 1981. pap. text 40.00 (*3-7682-1232-7*) Lubrecht & Cramer.

Dhir, K. K., et al. New Trends in Plant Physiology. Dua, I. S. & Chark, K. S., eds. (Illus.). 300p. 1991. 69.00 (*1-55528-217-2*, Pub. by Today Tomorrow) Scholarly Pubns.

Dhir, R. Euro-Cements: Impact of ENV 197 on Concrete. (Illus.). 256p. (C). 1994. 125.00 (*0-419-19980-2*, E & FN Spon) Routledge.

Dhir, R. & Green, J., eds. Protection of Concrete: Proceedings of the International Conference, University of Dundee, September 1990. (Illus.). 1136p. (C). 1990. 250.00 (*0-419-15490-6*, E & FN Spon) Routledge.

Dhir, R. & Jones Staff, eds. Concrete 2000: Economic & Durable Concrete Through Excellence. (Illus.). 2000p. (C). 1994. 535.00 (*0-419-18120-2*, E & FN Spon) Routledge.

Dhir, R. K., jt. ed. see Jackson, N.

Dhir, Ravindra, ed. Concrete in the Service of Mankind: Appropriate Concrete Technology. LC 96-69825. 641p. (C). 1996. 200.00 (*0-419-21470-4*) Routledge.

— Concrete in the Service of Mankind: Concrete for Environment Protection & Enhancement. LC 96-69824. 712p. (C). 1996. 200.00 (*0-419-21450-X*) Routledge.

— Concrete in the Service of Mankind: Concrete for Infrastructure & Utilities. LC 96-69826. 623p. (C). 1996. 200.00 (*0-419-21460-7*) Routledge.

— Concrete in the Service of Mankind: Concrete Repair Rehabilitation & Protection. LC 96-69828. 630p. (C). 1996. 200.00 (*0-419-21490-9*) Routledge.

Dhir, Ravindra, ed. Concrete in the Service of Mankind: Proceedings of the International Congress Dundeejanuary 1996, 5 vols., Set. (Illus.). 3816p. (C). (gr. 13). 1996. 910.00 (*0-419-21500-X*) Routledge.

Dhir, Ravindra, ed. Concrete in the Service of Mankind: Radical Concrete Technology. LC 96-69827. 641p. (C). 1996. 200.00 (*0-419-21480-1*) Routledge.

Dhir, Sunita. Styles of Theater Acting. 1991. text 17.50 (*81-212-0393-7*, Pub. by Gian Publng Hse) S Asia.

Dhir, V. K., ed. Proceedings of the 1995 National Heat Transfer Conference: August 6-9, 1995, Portland, Oregon, Vol. 6. 156p. 1995. 88.00 (*0-7918-1707-5*, H00989) ASME.

Dhir, V. K., ed. see National Heat Transfer Conference Staff.

Dhirananda, Swami. Glimpses of Light. 150p. 1994. reprint ed. pap. 23.95 (*0-937134-19-8*) Amrita Found.

Dhirananda, Swami, jt. auth. see Yogananda, Paramhansa.

Dhiravamsa. The Dynamic Way of Meditation. 1985. pap. 9.95 (*1-85274-045-0*, Pub. by Crucible Pr) Cavendish Bks.

— The Middle Path of a Life: Talks on the Practice of Insight Meditation. LC 88-38455. 96p. (Orig.). 1989. pap. 9.95 (*0-931892-22-8*) B Dolphin Pub.

— The Way of Non-Attachment. 1989. 12.00 (*1-85274-044-2*, Pub. by Crucible Pr) Cavendish Bks.

Dhiravamsa, V. Turning to the Source: An Eastern View of Western Mind - Using Insight Meditation & Psychotherapy for Personal Growth, Health & Wholeness. LC 90-47087. 256p. (Orig.). 1990. pap. 19.95 (*0-931892-20-1*) B Dolphin Pub.

Dhiravegin, Likhit. Demi-Democracy: The Evolution of the Thai Political System. 256p. 1992. pap. 25.00 (*981-210-018-0*, Pub. by Times Academic) Intl Spec Bk.

Dhlen, Morten & Tveito, Aslak. Numerical Methods & Software Tools in Industrial Mathematics. LC 97-185. 416p. 1997. write for info. (*3-7643-3973-X*) Birkhauser.

Dhody, Chandan L. The Japu Ji Sahib (The Chant Sublime) (C). 1991. 12.00 (*81-7000-125-0*, Pub. by Manohar) S Asia.

Dhody, Chandan Lal, see Lal Dhody, Chandan, tr.

Dhofier, Zamakhsyari. The Pesantren Tradition: The Role of the Kyai in the Maintenance of Traditional Islam in Java. (Illus.). xxxii, 254p. 1999. pap. 19.95 (*1-881044-19-X*) ASU Prog SE Asian.

Dhokalia, R. P. & Pathak, R. S., eds. International Law in Transition: Essays in Memory of Judge Nagendra Singh. LC 92-8465. 350p. (C). 1992. lib. bdg. 124.00 (*0-7923-1715-7*) Kluwer Academic.

Dholakia, Ajay. Introduction to Convolutional Codes with Applications. LC 94-16299. (International Series in Engineering & Computer Science, VLSI, Computer Architecture, & Digital Screen Processing: SECS 275). 264p. (C). 1994. text 100.50 (*0-7923-9467-4*) Kluwer Academic.

Dholakia, Nikhilesh, jt. auth. see Firat, A. Fuat.

Dholakia, Ruby R., et al, eds. New Infotainment Technologies in the Home: Demand-Side Perspectives. (LEA's Communication Ser.). 296p. 1996. text 59.95 (*0-8058-1626-7*) L Erlbaum Assocs.

D'Holbach, Baron P. Ecce Homo! An Eighteenth Century Life of Jesus. Hunwick, Andrew, ed. Houston, George, tr. LC 95-16826. (History of Religions in Translation Ser.: No. 1). (FRE.). xiii, 343p. (C). 1995. lib. bdg. 90.75 (*3-11-014521-9*) Mouton.

d'Holbach, Baron P. Ecce Homo! An Eighteenth Century Life of Jesus. Hunwick, Andrew, ed. (History of Religions in Translation Ser.: No. 1). xiii, 343p. (C). 1995. pap. text 43.35 (*3-11-014520-0*) Mouton.

***d'Holbach, Baron P.** The System of Nature, Vol. 1. Diderot, Denis, ed. Robinson, H. D., tr. 296p. 2000. pap. 35.00 (*1-903083-02-8*, Pub. by Clinamen Pr) Paul & Co Pubs.

D'Holbach, Paul H. Le Bon Sens Du Cure Meslier Suivi De Son Testament. 388p. 1970. reprint ed. 70.00 (*0-318-71352-7*) G Olms Pubs.

— Christianity Unveiled. 1973. 250.00 (*0-87968-068-7*) Gordon Pr.

— Ecce Home Leucippe. 1973. 250.00 (*0-87968-077-6*) Gordon Pr.

— L' Ethocratie. viii, 293p. 1973. reprint ed. 65.00 (*3-487-04649-0*) G Olms Pubs.

— Nature & Her Laws. 1972. 59.95 (*0-8490-0714-3*) Gordon Pr.

— La Politique Naturelle, 2 vols. in 1. viii, 512p. 1971. reprint ed. 120.00 (*3-487-04191-X*) G Olms Pubs.

— Systeme de la Nature ou des Lois du Monde Physique et Du Monde Moral, 2 vols., Set. xl, 1009p. 1974. reprint ed. 225.00 (*3-487-05377-2*) G Olms Pubs.

— Systeme Social, 3 vols. in 1. viii, 558p. 1969. reprint ed. 130.00 (*0-318-71353-5*) G Olms Pubs.

— Theologie Portative ou Dictionnaire Abrege de la Religion Chretienne. rev. ed. 229p. 1977. 55.00 (*3-487-06411-1*) G Olms Pubs.

D'Holbach, Paul H. & Meslier, Jean. Superstition in All Ages. 1973. 250.00 (*0-87968-108-X*) Gordon Pr.

D'Holbach, Paul-Henri T. Systeme Social Oder Naturliche Principien der Moral und der Politik. xi, 552p. 1969. reprint ed. 130.00 (*0-318-71461-2*) G Olms Pubs.

Dhole, Heeralal. The Mystery of Being: or Oriental Teachings vs. Occidental Theories. 69p. 1997. pap. 6.00 (*0-89540-262-9*, SB-262) Sun Pub.

Dhole, Heeralal, ed. Mystery of Being or Oriental Teachings vs. Occidental Theories (1907) 74p. 1998. reprint ed. pap. 5.50 (*0-7661-0486-9*) Kessinger Pub.

D'Hollander, E. Parallel Computing: Fundamentals, Applications, & New Directions. LC 98-20528. (Advances in Parallel Computing Ser.). 748p. 1998. 258.50 (*0-444-82882-6*) Elsevier.

D'Hollander, E., ed. see Joubert, G. R., et al.

***D'Hollander, E. H., et al, eds.** Parallel Computing: Fundamentals & Applications. 850p. 2000. 138.00 (*1-86094-235-0*, Pub. by Imperial College) World Scientific Pub.

Dhombres, J., jt. auth. see Aczel, J.

Dhomhnaill, Nuala N. Pharaoh's Daughter. rev. ed. LC 92-51046. 160p. 1993. pap. 10.95 (*0-916390-53-5*) Wake Forest.

Dhomhnaill, Nuala Ni, jt. auth. see Delanty, Greg.

Dhomhnaill, Nwala Ni, see Ni Dhomhnaill, Nwala.

Dhondt, Steven, et al. Indicators of Working Conditions in the European Union. LC 98-197564. xv, 100p. 1997. 13.00 (*92-828-1887-X*, Pub. by Comm Europ Commun) Bernan Associates.

D'Hondt, Jacques & Roland, Nelson. Hegel in His Time. Burbidge, John W. et al, trs. from GER. 224p. 1988. 29.95 (*0-921149-13-1*) Broadview Pr.

Dhondt, Jean-Louis, jt. ed. see Farriaux, Jean-Pierre.

D'Hondt, John. The Bunny Book. (Illus.). 276p. (Orig.). 1991. pap. 11.95 (*1-879194-05-8*) GLB Pubs.

***Dhondt, Mildred.** Family Poems of Christian Thoughts. 1999. pap. write for info. (*1-58235-297-6*) Watermrk Pr.

Dhongde, Ramesh V. Oxford English-Marathi Dictionary. 823p. (C). 1998. text 9.95 (*0-19-564244-9*) OUP.

Dhont, Jan K. An Introduction to Dynamics of Colloids. LC 96-12846. (Studies in Interface Science: Vol. 2). 660p. 1996. 293.25 (*0-444-82009-4*) Elsevier.

Dhont, Rene-Charles. Clare among Her Sisters. (Franciscan Pathways Ser.). 174p. 1987. pap. 12.00 (*1-57659-068-2*) Franciscan Inst.

***D'Hooge, Jan.** Interaction of Ultrasonic Waves & Tissues: Modeling, Simulations & Applications. (Illus.). 260p. 1999. 53.50 (*90-6186-990-0*, Pub. by Leuven Univ) Coronet Bks.

***Dhooghe, Alain.** Great Pyramids of Giza. (Illus.). 2000. 45.00 (*2-84576-008-6*) Vilo Intl.

Dhooper, Surjit S. Social Work & Transplantation of Human Organs. LC 93-14136. 256p. 1993. 62.95 (*0-275-94338-0*, C4338, Praeger Pubs) Greenwood.

— Social Work in Health Care in the 21st Century. LC 96-45777. (Sourcebooks for the Human Serives Ser.). 416p. 1997. 56.00 (*0-8039-5932-X*); pap. 26.00 (*0-8039-5933-8*) Sage.

***Dhooper, Surjit Singh & Moore, Sharon E.** Social Work with Culturally Diverse People. LC 00-9185. 2000. write for info. (*0-7619-1297-5*) Sage.

Dhopeshwarkar, A. D. J. Krishnamurthi & Awareness in Action. (Orig.). (C). 1993. text 7.00 (*81-7154-759-1*, Pub. by Popular Prakashan) S Asia.

Dhopeshwarkar, Govind A. Nutrition & Brain Development. LC 83-8139. (Illus.). 210p. 1983. 55.00 (*0-306-41060-5*, Plenum Trade) Perseus Pubng.

Dhority, Lynn. The ACT Approach: The Artful Use of Suggestion for Integrative Learning. 2nd ed. LC 92-15712. 231p. 1992. text 59.00 (*2-88124-553-6*); pap. text 29.00 (*2-88124-556-0*) Gordon & Breach.

***Dhority, Lynn & Jensen, Eric.** Joyful Fluency. LC 99-176073. xi, 148 p. 1998. write for info. (*1-890460-01-X*) Brain Store.

***Dhornyei, Zoltan.** Teaching & Researching Motivation. LC 00-33121. (Applied Linguistics in Action Ser.). 2000. write for info. (*0-582-38238-6*) Longman.

***D'Hose, Olivier.** Microsoft Exchange Server Connectivity: Bridging the Gap to Lotus Messaging Systems. 304p. 1999. pap. text 34.95 (*1-55558-223-0*) Buttrwrth-Heinemann.

Dhote, A. K., tr. from RUS. Systematics, Breeding & Seed Production of Potatoes. 219p. (C). 1986. text 97.00 (*90-6191-452-3*, Pub. by A A Balkema) Ashgate Pub Co.

Dhote, A. K., tr. see Berezina, N. M. & Kaushankii, D. A.

Dhote, A. K., tr. see Fadeev, Iu. N. & Novoshilov, K. V., eds.

Dhote, A. K., tr. see Ivanov, A. I.

Dhote, A. K., tr. see Metlitskii, L. V., et al, eds.

Dhote, R. K., tr. see Moshkin, V. A., ed.

Dhotel, Andre. Les Chemins du Long Voyage. (FRE.). 1984. pap. 11.95 (*0-7859-1991-0*, 2070375404) Fr & Eur.

— Le Village Pathetique. (FRE.). 320p. 1974. pap. 10.95 (*0-7859-1766-1*, 2070365824) Fr & Eur.

D'Houtaud, A. Cultural Images of Health: A Neglected Dimension. 177p. 1995. lib. bdg. 95.00 (*1-56072-228-2*) Nova Sci Pubs.

Dhruvarajan, Vanaja. Hindu Women & the Power of Ideology. LC 88-28692. 176p. 1988. 45.00 (*0-89789-145-7*, Bergin & Garvey) Greenwood.

Dhruvarajan, Vanaja, ed. Women & Well-Being. (ENG & FRE.). 260p. (C). 1990. text 65.00 (*0-7735-0734-5*, Pub. by McG-Queens Univ Pr); pap. text 24.95 (*0-7735-0762-0*, Pub. by McG-Queens Univ Pr) CUP Services.

Dhrymes, D. J. Topics in Advanced Econometrics. xii, 379p. 1989. 54.95 (*0-387-97178-5*) Spr-Verlag.

Dhrymes, P. J. Econometrics: Statistical Foundations & Applications. rev. ed. LC 74-10898. xvi, 592p. 1984. 76.95 (*0-387-90095-0*) Spr-Verlag.

— Introductory Econometrics. LC 78-18907. (Illus.). 1985. 84.95 (*0-387-90317-8*) Spr-Verlag.

— Mathematics for Econometrics. 2nd ed. 150p. 1990. 48.95 (*0-387-90988-5*) Spr-Verlag.

— Topics in Advance Econometrics: Linear & Nonlinear Simultaneous Equations, Vol. 2. 408p. 1994. 65.95 (*0-387-94156-8*) Spr-Verlag.

Dhrymes, Phoebus. Time Series, Unit Rotos, & Cointegration. LC 97-80318. (Illus.). 524p. 1997. text 89.95 (*0-12-214695-6*) Morgan Kaufmann.

***Dhrymes, Phoebus J.** Mathematics for Econometrics. 3rd ed. LC 00-30761. (Illus.). 264p. 2000. pap. 44.95 (*0-387-98995-1*) Spr-Verlag.

Dhrymes, Phoebus J. Theoretical & Applied Econometrics: The Selected Papers of Phoebus J. Dhrymes. LC 94-48416. (Economists of the Twentieth Century Ser.). 672p. 1995. 120.00 (*1-85898-092-5*) E Elgar.

Dhudshia, Vallabh H. Hi-Tech Equipment Reliability: A Practical Guide for Engineers & the Engineering Manager. LC 95-80604. 140p. 1995. 26.95 (*1-57321-003-X*) Lanchester Pr.

Dhuibhne, Eilis N. Hugo & the Sunshine Girl. (Illus.). 129p. (Orig.). (J). (gr. 5-9). 1991. pap. 7.95 (*1-85371-160-8*, Pub. by Poolbeg Pr) Dufour.

***Dhuibhne, Eilis Ni.** The Dancers Dancing. LC 99-488013. 242p. 2000. pap. 18.95 (*0-85640-650-3*, Pub. by Blackstaff Pr) Dufour.

Dhuicq, B. Bilingual Lexique of Legal English: French/English/French. (ENG & FRE.). 1996. pap. 24.95 (*0-320-00528-3*) Fr & Eur.

D'Hulst, Annick. Linear Carbohydrates As Chiral Selectors in Capillary Electrophoresis. (Acta Biomedica Lovaniensia Ser.: No. 135). (Illus.). 141p. (Orig.). 1996. pap. 42.50 (*90-6186-760-6*, Pub. by Leuven Univ) Coronet Bks.

D'Hulst, Lieven, jt. ed. see Delabastita, Dirk.

D'Hulst, R. A. Jacob Jordaens. LC 82-70747. (Illus.). 374p. 1982. text 135.00 (*0-8014-1519-5*) Cornell U Pr.

D'Humieres, Jean B., et al. The Suez Canal Company. Hartmann, Leonard H., ed. LC 85-90306. (Private Ship Letter Stamps of the World Ser.: Pt. 3). (Illus.). 288p. 1985. 45.00 (*0-917528-07-7*) L H Hartmann.

Dhungel, jt. auth. see Rana.

***Dhungel, D. & Adhikari, A.** Commentary on the Nepalese Constitutions. 1998. pap. 168.00 (*0-7855-7529-4*) St Mut.

Dhuoda. Handbook for William: A Carolingian Woman's Counsel for Her Son. Neel, Carol, tr. & intro. by. LC 90-43359. (Regents Studies in Medieval Culture). 181p. 1991. reprint ed. pap. 56.20 (*0-608-02685-9*, 206333800004) Bks Demand.

— Handbook for William: A Carolingian Women's Counsel for Her Son. Neel, Carol, tr. from LAT. LC 98-45770. (Medieval Texts in Translation Ser.). 192p. 1999. pap. 14.95 (*0-8132-0938-2*) Cath U Pr.

Dhurandhar, Sanjeev & Padmanabhan, T. Gravitation & Cosmology Vol. 211: Proceedings of the ICGC-95 Conference, Pune, India, 1995. LC 97-3535. (Astrophysics & Space Science Library). 303p. 1997. text 147.00 (*0-7923-4478-2*) Kluwer Academic.

Dhurjati, P. S. & Cauvin, Sylvie, eds. On-Line Fault Detection & Supervision in the Chemical Process Industries, 1998: Proceedings of the 3rd IFAC Workshop, IFP, Solaize (Lyon), France, 4-5 June 1998. LC 98-31476. 416p. 1998. pap. 96.50 (*0-08-043233-6*, Pergamon Pr) Elsevier.

Dhurjati, P. S. & Stephanopoulos, George, eds. On-Line Fault Detection & Supervision in the Chemical Process Industries: Selected Papers from the IFAC Symposium, Newark, Delaware, U. S. A., 22-24 April 1992. LC 92-44353. (IFAC Symposia Ser.: 9301). 328p. 1993. 167.00 (*0-08-041896-1*, Pergamon Pr) Elsevier.

Dhwan, R. K., jt. auth. see Kerr, David.

Dhyana, Isana M. More Than Me: Confessions, Perceptions & Inspirations of a Modern-Day Mystic. LC 92-97500. 151p. (Orig.). 1993. pap. 10.95 (*0-9635218-0-2*) Dhyana Pr.

Dhyani, S. N. Wildlife Management. (C). 1995. 32.00 (*81-7033-242-7*, Pub. by Rawat Pubns) S Asia.

Di. Schaum's Statistics. 2nd ed. 519p. (C). 1996. pap. text 39.95 incl. disk (*0-07-843990-6*) McGraw.

Di Bacco, M., et al. Statistical Tools in Human Biology: Proceedings of the 17th Course of the Internatioanl School of Mathematics. (Science & Culture Series, Mathematics). 350p. 1994. text 99.00 (*981-02-1782-X*) World Scientific Pub.

Di Bari, G. A., jt. ed. see Harding, W. B.

Di Bartolo, B. Nonlinear Spectroscopy of Solids: Advances & Applications. (NATO ASI Series B: Vol. 339). (Illus.). 668p. (C). 1995. 159.50 (*0-306-44916-1*) Plenum.

— Optical Properties of Excited States in Solids. LC 92-30374. (NATO ASI Ser.: Vol. 301). (Illus.). 766p. (C). 1993. text 165.00 (*0-306-44316-3*, Kluwer Plenum) Kluwer Academic.

Di Bartolo, Baldassare, ed. Advances in Nonradiative Processes in Solids. (NATO ASI Ser.: Vol. 249). (Illus.). 678p. (C). 1991. text 186.00 (*0-306-43838-0*, Kluwer Plenum) Kluwer Academic.

— Spectroscopy of Solid-State Laser-Type Materials. LC 87-15271. (Ettore Majorana International Science Series, Life Sciences: Vol. 30). (Illus.). 618p. 1987. 135.00 (*0-306-42617-X*, Plenum Trade) Perseus Pubng.

— Ultrafast Dynamics of Quantum Systems: Physical Processes & Spectroscopic Techniques. (NATO ASI Series B: 372). (Illus.). 725p. (C). 1999. text 140.00 (*0-306-45929-9*) Plenum.

Di Bartolo, Baldassare & Powell, Richard C. Phonons & Resonances in Solids. LC 75-35691. (Illus.). 533p. reprint ed. pap. 165.30 (*0-608-10320-9*, 201243000081) Bks Demand.

Di Bartolo, Baldassare, ed. see North Atlantic Treaty Organization Staff.

Di Bartolo, Joel. Serious Electric Bass: The Bass Player's Complete Guide to Scales & Chords. Stang, Aaron, ed. (Contemporary Bass Ser.). 280p. 1997. pap. text 24.95 (*1-57623-883-0*, EL9710) Wrner Bros.

Di-Bella, Jose M., et al, eds. Literatura de Frontera Mexico, Estados Unidos: Mexican & American Border Writing. 212p. 1987. text 10.00 (*0-614-25814-6*) SDSU Inst Reg Studies.

Di Bella, Jose M., et al, eds. U. S. - Mexican Border Literature: Short Stories. (Binational Press Ser.: No. 2). (ENG & SPA.). 144p. 1989. pap. 10.00 (*0-916304-97-3*) SDSU Press.

Di-Bella, Jose M., jt. ed. see Polkinhorn, Harry.

***di Bella, M. Pia, ed.** Vols et Sanctions en Mediterranee. (Ordres Sociaux Ser.). (FRE.). 276p. 1998. pap. text 42.00 (*90-5709-009-0*) Gordon & Breach.

Di Benedetti, Charles, jt. auth. see Starr, Jerold M.

Di Benedetto, Angelo. How the Donkeys Came to Haiti & Other Folk Tales. 124p. (J). (gr. 4-9). 12.95 (*0-8159-5706-8*) Devin.

***Di Benedetto, Anthony & Kamins, Michael A.** NYT Sales & Marketing: 25 Keys to Selling Your Products. Redburn, Tom, ed. LC 99-27702. 104p. 1999. pap. 12.95 (*0-86730-773-0*) Lebhar Friedman.

Di Benedetto, Antonio. Animal World (Mundo Animal) Francis, H. E., tr. LC 96-24824. (Xenos Dual-Language Book Ser.). (ENG & SPA.). 138p. 1997. pap. 13.00 (*1-879378-17-5*) Xenos Riverside.

Di Benedetto, C. Anthony, ed. Successful Industrial Product Innovation: An Integrative Literature Review, 11. LC 90-41840. (Bibliographies & Indexes in Economics & Economic History Ser.). 184p. 1990. lib. bdg. 59.95 (*0-313-27571-8*, CIK/, Greenwood Pr) Greenwood.

Di Benedetto, H. & Francken, L., eds. Mechanical Tests for Bituminous Materials/Essais Mecaniques pour les Materiaux Bitumineux: Proceedings of the Fifth International RILEM Symposium/Actes du Cinquieme Symposium RILEM, Lyon, 14-16 May 1997. (ENG & FRE., Illus.). 644p. (C). 1997. text 142.00 (*90-5410-876-2*, Pub. by A A Balkema) Ashgate Pub Co.

Di Benedetto, U. Spanish-English (New Comprehensive) Dictionary. 1500p. 1983. 100.00 (*84-7166-383-X*) IBD Ltd.

Di Berardino, Angelo. Dictionnaire Encyclopedique du Christianisme Ancien Vol. 2: J-Z. Vial, Francois, ed. (FRE.). 1990. write for info. (*0-7859-7764-3*, 2204041823) Fr & Eur.

Di Berardino, Angelo, jt. auth. see Studer, Basil.

Di Bernado, Dominic, tr. see Bove, Emmanuel.

Di Bernardi, Dominic, jt. auth. see Hyvernaud, Georges.

Di Bernardi, Dominic, jt. auth. see Roubaud, Jacques.

Di Bernardi, Dominic, tr. see Bove, Emmanuel.

Di Bernardi, Dominic, tr. see Butor, Michel.

Di Bernardi, Dominic, tr. see Celine, Louis-Ferdinand.

Di Bernardi, Dominic, tr. see Cerf, Muriel.

Di Bernardi, Dominic, tr. see Cholodenko, Marc.

Di Bernardi, Dominic, tr. see Grainville, Patrick.

Di Bernardi, Dominic, tr. see Hyvernaud, Georges.

Di Bernardi, Dominic, tr. see Hyvernaud, Georges, et al.

Di Bernardi, Dominic, tr. see Navarre, Yves.

Di Bernardi, Dominic, tr. see Ollier, Claude.

Di Bernardi, Dominic, tr. see Roubaud, Jacques.

Di Bernardi, Dominic, tr. & afterword by see Ollier, Claude.

Di Biase, F. Maximal Functions & Approach Regions in Theorems of Fatou Type. Bass, H. et al, eds. LC 97-30694. (Progress in Mathematics Ser.). 160p. 1997. 38.50 (*0-8176-3976-4*) Birkhauser.

Di Biase, Fausto. FATOU Type Theorems: Maximal Functions & Approach Regions. LC 97-30694. (Progress in Mathematics Ser.). 1997. write for info. (*3-7643-3976-4*) Birkhauser.

Di Biasio, Rodolfo. Wayfarers Four. Vitiello, Justin, tr. from ITA. LC 98-14540. (Crossings Ser.: No. 1). 121p. (C). 1998. pap. 11.00 (*1-884419-17-8*) Bordighera.

Di Bisceglie, A. M., jt. ed. see Bacon, B. R.

Di Blasi, Debra. Drought & Say What You Like. LC 96-24621. 96p. (Orig.). 1997. pap. 10.95 (*0-8112-1332-3*, NDP836, Pub. by New Directions) Norton.

— Prayers of an Accidental Nature. LC 98-56287. 224p. 1999. pap. 13.95 (*1-56689-083-7*, Pub. by Coffee Hse) Consort Bk Sales.

Di Blasi, Maria, tr. see Trape, Agostino.

di Borhamaie, H. L. Rabino, see Rabino di Borhamaie, H. L.

Di Bosco Koken, Veronica M. Winds of Change. 1997. pap. 56.95 (*1-57553-648-X*) Watermrk Pr.

Di Brino, Nicholas. The History of the Morris Park Racecourse & the Morris Family. (Illus.). 48p. 1977. pap. 12.00 (*0-941980-27-8*) Bronx County.

di caccia di Stupinigi, Reale Palazzina. The Triumph of the Baroque: Architecture in Europe, 1600-1750. Millon, Henry A., ed. LC 99-14173. (Illus.). 704p. 1999. 85.00 (*0-8478-2219-2*, Pub. by Rizzoli Intl) St Martin.

Di Cagno. Regulation & Bank Behavior Towards Risk. 1990. 72.95 (*1-85521-081-9*) Ashgate Pub Co.

Di Cagno, Gabriella. Michelangelo. LC 97-118074. (Masters of Art Ser.). (Illus.). 64p. (J). (gr. 5). 1996. lib. bdg. 22.50 (*0-87226-319-3*, 63193B, P Bedrick Books) NTC Contemp Pub Co.

***Di Cagno, Gabriella, et al.** Michelangelo. 2nd ed. LC 00-39747. (Masters of Art Ser.). (Illus.). 2000. write for info. (*0-87226-641-9*, P Bedrick Books) NTC Contemp Pub Co.

***Di Camillo, Kevin.** Occasionally Yours (& Others' The Occasional Verse of Kevin Di Camillo, 1990-99. (Illus.). 32p. 1999. pap. 20.00 (*0-930126-58-0*) Typographeum.

Di Camillo, Kevin. Why I Drive Alfa Romeos & Other Excuses: Poems. LC 97-199194. (Illus.). 72p. 1997. 50.00 (*0-930126-54-8*) Typographeum.

di Camillo, Kevin T. Patrick, see Patrick di Camillo, Kevin T.

Di Canio, Judy. Beloved Warrior, 1 vol. (Perfect Heroes Ser.). 368p. 1999. mass mkt. 5.50 (*0-505-52325-6*) Dorchester Pub Co.

Di Canzio, Albert. Galileo: His Science & His Significance for the Future of Man. LC 97-119302. (Illus.). 415p. 1997. 54.00 (*0-9641295-6-6*) ADASI Pubng.

Di Carcaci, Diana, tr. see Cardella, Lara.

Di Carlo, Frederick J., ed. Drug Metabolism Reviews Vol. 3: 1975. LC 72-76719. (Illus.). 367p. reprint ed. pap. 113.80 (*0-7837-0784-3*, 204109800003) Bks Demand.

Di Castri, F., jt. ed. see Groves, R. H.

Di Castri, F., jt. ed. see Hansen, A. J.

Di Castri, Francesco & Younes, Talal, eds. Biodiversity, Science & Development: Towards a New Partnership. (A CAB International Publication). (Illus.). 668p. 1996. text 130.00 (*0-85198-973-X*) OUP.

Di Ceglie, Domenico, jt. ed. see Freedman, D.

Di Cera, Enrico. Thermodynamic Theory of Site-Specific Binding Processes in Biological Macromolecules. (Illus.). 312p. (C). 1996. text 85.00 (*0-521-41659-0*) Cambridge U Pr.

***Di Cera, Enrico, ed.** Thermodynamics in Biology. LC 99-86282. (Illus.). 240p. 2000. text 59.95 (*0-19-512327-1*) OUP.

Di Cesare, Mario A., ed. Milton in Italy: Contexts, Images, Contradictions. (Medieval & Renaissance Texts & Studies: Vol. 90). 616p. 1991. 40.00 (*0-86698-103-9*, MR90) MRTS.

Di Cesare, Mario A., ed. Reconsidering the Renaissance: Papers of the 21st Annual Conference of CEMERS. LC 92-17281. (Medieval & Renaissance Texts & Studies: Vol. 93). (Illus.). 544p. 1992. 40.00 (*0-86698-107-1*, MR93) MRTS.

Di Cesare, Mario A., ed. see Herbert, George.

Di Cesare, Mario A., ed. see Jonson, Ben.

Di, Chatrio. Morgantina, No. 3. 264p. (C). 1991. text 80.00 (*0-691-04014-1*, Pub. by Princeton U Pr) Cal Prin Full Svc.

Di Chiara, A. & Russo, M. Tunneling Phenomena in High & Low Tc Superconductors. 300p. 1993. text 91.00 (*981-02-1030-2*) World Scientific Pub.

Di Chiara, Robert. Deal with the Devil. 1996. mass mkt. 6.99 (*0-614-20504-2*) Forge NYC.

Di Cicco, Pier G. Les Amours Difficiles. (FRE.). 96p. 1989. pap. 7.00 (*2-89135-027-8*) Guernica Editions.

— Post-Sixties Nocturne. 49p. 1985. pap. 5.95 (*0-86492-050-4*, Pub. by Goose Ln Edits) Genl Dist Srvs.

— The Tough Romance. 102p. 1990. pap. 8.00 (*0-920717-03-9*) Guernica Editions.

Di Cocco, G., jt. ed. see Bassani, L.

Di Conversino da Ravenna, Giovanni. Dragmalogia de Eligibili Vitae Genere (1404) Kohl, Benjamin G. & Eaker, Helen L., eds. (Renaissance Text Ser.: No. 7). 1980. 24.50 (*0-318-11900-5*) Renaiss Society Am.

Di Coppo, Giovanni. Legend of the Holy Fina, Virgin of Santo Gemignano. Mansfield, M., tr. LC 66-25699. (Medieval Library). (ENG & ITA., Illus.). reprint ed. 42.00 (*0-8154-0054-3*) Cooper Sq.

Di Cortona, Pietro Grilli, see Grilli Di Cortona, Pietro.

***Di Cosmo, Nicola & Bao, Dalizhabu.** Manchu-Mongol Relations on the Eve of the Qing Conquest: A Documentary History. (Illus.). 170p. 2000. 62.00 (*90-04-11777-6*) Brill Academic Pubs.

Di Cosmo, Roberto. Isomorphisms of Types: From Lambda-Calculus to Information Retrival & Language Design. LC 94-36650. (Progress in Theoretical Computer Science Ser.). (Illus.). viii, 235p. 1994. 54.50 (*0-8176-3763-X*) Birkhauser.

Di Crescenzo, Casimiro. Alberto Giacometti: Early Works in Paris (1922 - 1930) Hayes, Craig S., ed. Rudolph, Camilla B. et al, trs. (Illus.). 148p. (Orig.). 1994. pap. 25.55 (*0-9626731-7-X*) Yoshii Gallery.

— Matisse & Teriade: Collaborative Works by the Artist & Art Publisher. Riley, Charles A., 2nd, ed. Fournier, Christian, tr. from ITA. (FRE.). 141p. 1997. 35.00 (*1-887054-02-2*) Yoshii Gallery.

di Cristina, George R. A Simplified Guide to Custom Stairbuilding & Tangent Handrailing. rev. ed. LC 94-7753. (Illus.). 278p. 1994. 34.95 (*0-941936-27-9*, Pub. by Linden Pub Fresno) IPG Chicago.

— A Simplified Guide to Custom Stairbuilding & Tangent Handrailing. 2nd rev. ed. (Illus.). 278p. 2000. pap. 28.95 (*0-941936-63-5*, Pub. by Linden Pub Fresno) IPG Chicago.

Di Cristo, Albert, jt. ed. see Hirst, Daniel.

Di Curcio, Robert A. Art on Nantucket: The History of Painting on Nantucket Island. Kelsey, Susan et al, eds. LC 81-83847. (Illus.). xvi, 272p. 1982. 250.00 (*0-9607340-0-7*) Nantucket Hist Assn.

— A Nantucket Skeptic Reads the New Testament: Robert A. di Curcio's Companion Reader to the Gospels. 105p. 1998. pap. 18.00 (*0-917358-12-0*) Aeternium Pubng Co.

Di Domenico, Ruth L. & Ziegler, Wilma Z. Practical Rehabilitation Techniques for Geriatric Aides. 2nd ed. LC 93-39450. (Illus.). 220p. 1994. 88.00 (*0-8342-0548-3*) Aspen Pub.

Di Donato. The Metabolic Encephalopathies. 216p. 68.00 (*0-86196-489-6*, Pub. by J Libbey Med) Bks Intl VA.

Di Donato, Lisa, ed. see Davis, Carolyn O.

Di Donato, Pietro. Christ in Concrete. LC 39-10762. 320p. 1975. 8.95 (*0-672-52161-X*, Bobbs); pap. 5.95 (*0-672-52187-3*, Bobbs) Macmillan.

— Christ in Concrete: A Novel. LC 92-39372. 1993. mass mkt. 5.95 (*0-451-52575-2*, Sig Classics) NAL.

Di Donato, Robert & Clyde, Monica. Deutsch, Na Klar! An Introductory German Course. 3rd ed. LC 98-12953. 1998. 53.25 (*0-07-013705-6*) McGraw.

Di Donato, Robert, et al. Deutsch: Na klar! 2nd ed. (C). 1995. pap., lab manual ed. 24.69 (*0-07-016972-1*) McGraw.

— Deutsch, Na Klar! An Introductory German Course. 2nd ed. LC 94-40903. 576p. (C). 1995. student ed. 71.88 (*0-07-016969-1*); text, teacher ed. 68.12 (*0-07-016970-5*) McGraw.

***Di Donato, Robert, et al.** Deutsch, Na Klar! An Introductory German Course. 3rd ed. LC 98-12953. 1998. write for info. (*0-07-013706-4*) McGraw-Hill Sch.

— Na Klar! An Introductory German Course. 3rd ed. 560p. (C). 1998. pap., student ed. 68.13 incl. audio compact disk (*0-07-230561-4*) McGrw-H Hghr Educ.

D

Di Fabio, ed. Balance. (Monograph Ser.). (Illus.). 261p. 1997. pap. 25.00 (*1-887759-17-4*, P-146) Am Phys Therapy Assn.

Di Fabio, Anthony. The Art of Getting Well. LC 87-62790. (Illus.). 141p. 1997. pap. 7.00 (*0-9615437-1-X*) Arthritis Trust.

— Arthritis: Little Known Treatments. LC 93-83495. (Orig.). 1995. pap. 7.00 (*0-9615437-2-8*) Arthritis Trust.

— How to Spot & Handle Suppression in Medicine: Identical Medical & Religious Patterns of Suppression in the Late Twentieth Century. LC 93-90267. 126p. 1997. pap. 12.00 (*0-9658941-0-X*) Confront Pubns.

Di Fabio, Anthony & Jaconello, Paul. Soft Tissue Arthritis: Bursitis, Fibromyalgia, Fibromyositis, Fibrositis, Rheumatism. LC 97-71310. 104p. 1998. pap. 10.00 (*0-9615437-4-4*) Arthritis Trust.

Di Fabio, Anthony & Prosch, Gus J., Jr. Arthritis: Osteoarthritis & Rheumatoid Disease Including Rheumatoid Arthritis. LC 97-71310. (Illus.). 360p. (Orig.). 1997. pap. 10.00 (*0-9615437-3-6*) Arthritis Trust.

Di Fate, Vincent. Infinite Worlds: The Fantastic Visions of Science Fiction Art. LC 98-108729. 288p. 1997. 45.00 (*0-670-87252-0*) Viking Penguin.

Di Filippo, Paul. Ciphers: A Post-Shannon Rock 'N' Roll Mystery. unabridged ed. LC 95-75546. (Illus.). 540p. 1997. pap. 16.95 (*1-882633-30-X*) Permeable.

— Fractal Paisleys. LC 97-11712. 320p. 1997. 20.00 (*1-56858-032-0*) FWEW.

— Lost Pages. LC 98-8394. 304p. 1998. pap. 15.95 (*1-56858-099-1*) FWEW.

— Ribofunk. LC 96-6902. 304p. 1996. 20.00 (*1-56858-062-2*) FWEW.

— The Steampunk Trilogy. LC 94-42282. 354p. 1995. 20.00 (*1-56858-028-2*) FWEW.

— The Steampunk Trilogy. LC 94-42282. 354p. 1997. pap. 14.95 (*1-56858-102-5*) FWEW.

Di Fiore, Frank R. It's Stunning Kid. LC 78-65136. 1978. 7.95 (*0-932896-00-6*) Westcliff Pubns.

— You Can Conquer Your Headaches. (Illus.). 66p. (Orig.). 1980. pap. 10.00 (*0-932896-03-0*) Westcliff Pubns.

Di Fiore, Frank R., ed. see Goodwon, Katcha.

***Di Fiori, Judy.** The Pregnancy Exercise Book: A Step-by-Step Program for Achieving Optimal Fitness Throughout the Trimesters. LC 99-39669. (Illus.). 96p. 2000. pap. 19.95 (*0-06-273734-1*, HarpRes) HarpInfo.

***Di Fiori, Russell & Jarrell, Paul.** Physiology Laboratory Book. 94p. (C). 1999. spiral bd., lab manual ed. 28.95 (*0-7872-6523-3*) Kendall-Hunt.

Di Francesca, Sal. Straight A's: How to Help Your Child Improve School Grades. Solano, Ric, ed. LC 84-82154. (Illus.). 150p. 1985. 24.95 (*0-931657-00-8*) Learning Proc Ctr.

Di Francesco, Philippe & Mathieu, Pierre. Conformal Field Theories. LC 96-23155. (Graduate Texts in Contemporary Physics Ser.). 890p. 1996. 89.00 (*0-387-94785-X*) Spr-Verlag.

Di Franco, J. Philip. American Indians. LC 95-1245. 120p. (YA). (gr. 5 up). 1995. pap. 9.95 (*0-7910-3377-5*) Chelsea Hse.

Di Franco, J. Phillip. The Italian Americans. rev. ed. LC 94-40430. (Immigrant Experience Ser.). 120p. (YA). (gr. 5 up). 1995. pap. 9.95 (*0-7910-3375-9*) Chelsea Hse.

— The Italian Americans. rev. ed. LC 94-40430. (Immigrant Experience Ser.). (Illus.). (J). (gr. 5). 1995. lib. bdg. 19.95 (*0-7910-3353-8*) Chelsea Hse.

Di Gammateo, F., jt. ed. see Lacalamita, M.

Di Gangi, Mario, jt. tr. see McClelland, Joseph C.

Di Gesu, V., et al, eds. Data Analysis in Astronomy, Vol. 2. LC 86-25456. (Ettore Majorana International Science Series, Life Sciences: Vol. 27). (Illus.). 412p. 1986. 95.00 (*0-306-42473-8*, Plenum Trade) Perseus Pubng.

Di Gesu, V., et al, eds. Data Analysis in Astronomy: Proceedings of the 5th Workshop Ettore Majorana Center for Scientific Culture, Erice, Italy, 27 October-3 November 1996. LC 98-131558. (Science & Culture Ser.). 440p. 1998. 86.00 (*981-02-3171-7*) World Scientific Pub.

— Data Analysis in Astronomy 4. (Ettore Majorana International Science Ser., Life Sciences: Vol. 59). (Illus.). 376p. (C). 1992. text 138.00 (*0-306-44106-3*, Kluwer Plenum) Kluwer Academic.

Di Gesu, V., et al. Data Analysis in Astronomy, Vol. 3. (Ettore Majorana International Science Series, Life Sciences: Vol. 40). (Illus.). 428p. 1989. 105.00 (*0-306-43158-0*, Plenum Trade) Perseus Pubng.

Di Giacomantonio, Antonio, tr. see Corsi, Pietro.

Di Giacomo, A. & Diakonov, D., eds. Selected Topics in Non-Perturbative QCD. LC 96-78119. (International School of Physics Enrico Fermi Ser.: Vol. 130). 504p. (gr. 12). 1997. 170.00 (*90-5199-293-9*, 293-9) IOS Press.

Di Giacomo, Giulio. Reliability of Electronic Packages & Semiconductor Devices. LC 96-29181. (Illus.). 410p. 1996. 65.00 (*0-07-017024-X*) McGraw.

Di Giacomo, Salvatore. Love Poems: Selected Poems, Bilingual Edition. Palescandolo, Frank, tr. from ITA. (Essential Poets Ser.: Vol. 79). 151p. 1999. pap. 15.00 (*1-55071-060-5*) Guernica Editions.

— I Quattro Antichi Conservatorii Musicali di Napoli, 2 vols., Nos. MDXLIII-MDCCC. (Illus.). 616p. reprint ed. write for info. (*0-318-71585-6*) G Olms Pubs.

Di Giammarco, Rodolfo. Stage & Set Design. (Illus.). 24p. 5.00 (*0-930209-04-4*) Otis Gallery.

Di Giandomenico, Robert, jt. auth. see Carlson, Reinhold A.

Di Giovanni, Carmelo. Light from Behind the Bars. 158p. (C). 1990. 39.00 (*0-85439-271-8*, Pub. by St Paul Pubns) St Mut.

Di Giovanni, George, ed. Essays on Hegel's Logic. LC 89-29183. 218p. (C). 1990. pap. text 21.95 (*0-7914-0292-4*) State U NY Pr.

***Di Giovanni, George & Harris, H. S., eds.** Between Kant & Hegel: Texts in the Development of Post-Kantian Idealism. LC 99-48592. 456p. (C). 2000. pap. 18.95 (*0-87220-504-5*); lib. bdg. 45.00 (*0-87220-505-3*) Hackett Pub.

Di Giovanni, George, ed. & tr. see Jacobi, Friedrich H.

Di Giovanni, George, tr. see Kant, Immanuel.

Di Giovanni, Janine. The Quick & the Dead. 1995. mass mkt. 13.95 (*1-85799-333-0*, Pub. by Orion Pubng Grp) Trafalgar.

Di Giovanni, Norman, tr. see Garcia Lorca, Federico.

Di Giovanni, Norman T., tr. from SPA. Colombia: A New Vision. LC 92-43127. (Illus.). 160p. 1993. 19.98 (*1-55859-498-1*) Abbeville Pr.

Di Giovanni, Norman T., ed. see Borges, Jorge Luis.

Di Giovanni, Norman T., tr. see Bonet, Pilar.

Di Giovanni, Norman T., tr. see Quesada, Maria S.

Di Girolamo, Costanzo. A Critical Theory of Literature. LC 80-52289. 123p. reprint ed. pap. 38.20 (*0-608-01952-6*, 206260700003) Bks Demand.

Di Giulio, Richard & Tillitt, Donald, eds. Reproductive & Developmental Effects of Contaminants in Oviparous Vertebrates. LC 98-56080. (Illus.). 447p. 1999. 98.00 (*1-880611-37-6*) SETAC.

Di Grappa, Carol, ed. Landscape: Theory. LC 80-81182. (Illus.). 176p. 1982. 35.00 (*0-912810-27-0*); pap. 19.95 (*0-912810-32-7*) Lustrum Pr.

Di Grappa, Carol, et al, eds. Fashion: Theory. LC 80-81181. (Illus.). 176p. 1982. 35.00 (*0-912810-28-9*); pap. 19.95 (*0-912810-29-7*) Lustrum Pr.

Di Grassi, Giacomo, et al. Three Elizabethan Fencing Manuals: True Arte of Defence; His Practice; Paradoxes of Defence. Jackson, James L., ed. LC 72-6321. 640p. 1972. reprint ed. 75.00 (*0-8201-1107-4*) Schol Facsimiles.

Di Gregorio, Mario A., ed. see Darwin, Charles.

Di Gregorio, Silvana, ed. Social Gerontology: New Directions. 300p. 1987. lib. bdg. 49.95 (*0-7099-3894-2*, Pub. by C Helm) Routldge.

Di, Hua & Australian National University Press Staff. Recent Developments in China's Domestic & Foreign Affairs. LC 93-195313. (Working Paper / Australian National University, Strategic & Defence Studies Centre). 24p. 1992. write for info. (*0-7315-1379-7*) Aust Nat Univ.

Di Ianni, Marisa, ed. see Rose, Linda M.

Di Iorio, Frank & Hardy, Kenneth C. Quick Start to Data Analysis with SAS. LC 95-18388. 301p. (C). 1995. mass mkt. 38.95 (*0-534-23760-6*, BR55550) PWS Pubs.

Di Kelly, ed. Researching Industrial Relations. 2nd ed. 201p. 1999. pap. 29.00 (*1-86287-313-5*, Pub. by Federation Pr) Gaunt.

Di Lasso, Orlando. Orlando Di Lasso: The Complete Motets I: Il Primo Libro de Mottetti a Cinque et a Sei Voici (Antwerp, 1556) Erb, James, ed. (Recent Researches in Music of the Renaissance Ser.: No. RRR114). (Illus.). xxxv, 116p. 1998. pap. 55.00 (*0-89579-415-2*) A-R Eds.

— Orlando di Lasso: The Complete Motets 10: The Four-Language Print for Four & Eight Voices (Munich, 1573) Bergquist, Peter, ed. (Recent Researches in Music of the Renaissance Ser.: Vol. RRR102). (Illus.). xxiv, 125p. 1995. pap. 50.00 (*0-89579-323-7*) A-R Eds.

— Orlando Di Lasso: The Complete Motets 14. Crook, David & Bergquist, Peter, eds. (Recent Researches in Music of the Renaissance Ser.: Vol. RRR111). (Illus.). xxiii, 120p. 1997. pap. 50.00 (*0-89579-392-X*) A-R Eds.

— Orlando di Lasso: The Complete Motets 7. Bergquist, Peter, ed. (Recent Researches in Music of the Renaissance Ser.: Vol. RRR112). (Illus.). xxxii, 219p. 1998. pap. 85.00 (*0-89579-410-1*) A-R Eds.

***Di Lasso, Orlando.** Orlando di Lasso: The Complete Motets 9, Patrocinium Musices Prima Parts (Munich 1573) Bergquist, Peter, ed. (Recent Researches in the Music of the Renaissance Ser.: Vol. R120). (Illus.). xxviii, 189p. 2000. pap. 55.00 (*0-89579-455-1*) A-R Eds.

Di Lasso, Orlando. Orlando Di Lasso: The Seven Penitential Psalms & Laudate Dominum de Caelis. Bergquist, Peter, ed. (Recent Researches in Music of the Renaissance Ser.: Vols. RRR86-87). (Illus.). xxviii, 200p. 1990. pap. 70.00 (*0-89579-247-8*) A-R Eds.

— Orlando Di Lasso: Two Motet Cycles for Matins for the Dead. Bergquist, Peter, ed. (Recent Researches in Music of the Renaissance Ser.: No. RRR55). (Illus.). 110, xxip. 1983. pap. 45.00 (*0-89579-164-1*) A-R Eds.

***Di Lasso, Orlando.** Orlando di Lasso - The Complete Motets 8: Moduli Quinis Vocibus Nunquam Hactenus Editi (Paris, 1571) Bergquist, Peter, ed. (Recent Researches in Music of the Renaissance Ser.: Vol. RRR118). (Illus.). xxiv, 140p. 1999. pap. 55.00 (*0-89579-442-X*) A-R Eds.

— Orlando di Lasso - The Complete Motets 15: Cantica Sacra Sex et Octo Vocibus (Munich, 1585) Crook, David, ed. (Recent Researches in the Music of the Renaissance Ser.: Vol. RRR117). (Illus.). xxii, 138p. 1999. pap. 55.00 (*0-89579-440-3*) A-R Eds.

Di Lasso, Orlando. Orlando di Lasso - The Complete Motets 11: Liber Motte Tarum Trium Vocum (Munich, 1575); Novae Aliquot, Ad Duas Voces Cantiones (Munich, 1577) Bergquist, Peter et al, eds. (Recent Reserches in Music of the Renaissance Ser.: Vol. RRR103). (Illus.). xx, 119p. 1995. pap. 50.00 (*0-89579-327-X*) A-R Eds.

— Orlando di Lasso - The Complete Motets 5: Motets for Quinque et Sex Vocibus Peromatae Sacrae Cantiones (Venice, 1565); Motets for Five to Eight Voices from Sacrae Cantiones, Liber Secundus, Tertius, Quartus (Venice, 1566) Bergquist, Peter et al, eds. (Recent Researches in Music of the Renaissance Ser.: Vol. RRR109). (Illus.). xxix, 306p. 1997. pap. 105.00 (*0-89579-385-7*) A-R Eds.

— Orlando di Lasso - The Complete Motets 6: Motets for Four to Eight Voices from Selectissimae Cantiones (Nuremberg, 1568) Bergquist, Peter et al, eds. (Recent Researches in Music of the Renaissance Ser.: Vol. RRR110). (Illus.). xxxvii, 206p. 1997. pap. 80.00 (*0-89579-389-X*) A-R Eds.

— Orlando di Lasso: The Complete Motets 4: Motets for Six Voices from Primus Liber Concentuum Sacrorum (Paris, 1564); Motets for Four to Ten Voices from Modulorum Secundum Volumen (Paris, 1565) Bergquist, Peter et al, eds. (Recent Researches in Music of the Renaissance Ser.: Vol. RRR105). (Illus.). xxiv, 224p. 1996. pap. 75.00 (*0-89579-335-0*) A-R Eds.

Di Lasso, Orlando, et al. Orlando di Lasso & Others: Canzoni Villanesche & Villanelle. Jackson, Donna C., ed. (Recent Researches in Music of the Renaissance Ser.: Vol. RRR82-83). (Illus.). lviii, 149p. 1991. pap. 65.00 (*0-89579-245-1*, RRR82-83) A-R Eds.

Di Lella, Alexander. Daniel: A Book for Troubling Times. LC 96-46248. (Spiritual Commentaries on the Old Testament Ser.). 232p. (Orig.). 1997. pap. 11.95 (*1-56548-087-2*) New City.

Di Lella, Alexander A., jt. auth. see Hartman, Louis F.

Di Lella, Alexander A., jt. auth. see Sehan, Patrick W.

Di Lello, Richard. The Longest Cocktail Party: An Insider's Diary of the Beatles. LC 72-85965. (Rock & Roll Remembrances Ser.: No. 2). (Illus.). 352p. 1983. 40.00 (*1-56075-044-8*) Popular Culture.

***Di Leo, G.** Altering Extending & Converting Houses: Owner's Guide to Procedure. 70p. (C). (gr. 13). 1998. pap. text 29.99 (*1-85032-043-8*) ITCP.

Di Leo, Joseph H. Physical Factors in Growth & Development: A Manual for Educators, Nurses, & Social Workers. LC 75-106235. (TC Series in Special Education). 64p. reprint ed. pap. 30.00 (*0-608-17725-3*, 203014700067) Bks Demand.

Di Leonardo. Exotics at Home. 2000. pap. text 18.00 (*0-226-47264-7*) U Ch Pr.

Di Leonardo, Micaela. Exotics at Home. LC 97-48475. (Illus.). 445p. 1998. 35.00 (*0-226-47263-9*) U Ch Pr.

— Exotics at Home: Anthropologies, Others, American Modernity. (Illus.). 265p. 1998. 30.00 (*0-226-14910-2*) U Ch Pr.

— The Varieties of Ethnic Experience: Kinship, Class, & Gender among California Italian-Americans. LC 83-45929. (Anthropology of Contemporary Issues Ser.). (Illus.). 263p. reprint ed. pap. 81.60 (*0-608-20089-1*, 207136100011) Bks Demand.

Di Leonardo, Micaela, intro. Gender at the Crossroads of Knowledge: Feminist Anthropology in the Postmodern Era. LC 90-11297. (Illus.). 423p. 1991. 55.00 (*0-520-07092-5*, Pub. by U CA Pr); pap. 19.95 (*0-520-07093-3*, Pub. by U CA Pr) Cal Prin Full Svc.

Di Leonardo, Micaela, jt. ed. see Lancaster, Roger.

Di Lima, Sara N., et al, eds. Spinal Cord Injury Patient Education Resource Manual. LC 96-11459. 1996. 169.00 (*0-8342-0772-9*) Aspen Pub.

— Women's Health Care Administration: Forms, Checklists, & Guidelines. 1997. 175.00 (*0-8342-0773-7*) Aspen Pub.

Di Lima, Sara N. & Johns, Lisa T., eds. Nonprofit Organization Management: Forms, Checklists & Guidelines. LC 95-51518. 1996. 149.00 (*0-8342-0710-9*, S191) Aspen Pub.

Di Lima, Sara N. & Niemeyer, Suzanne, eds. Medical Laboratory Management: Forms, Checklists & Guidelines. LC 94-34047. ring bd. 190.00 (*0-8342-0667-6*) Aspen Pub.

Di Lima, Sara N., et al. Correctional Health Care: Forms, Checklists & Guidelines. LC 98-55498. 1999. write for info. (*0-8342-1134-3*) Aspen Pub.

— Infectious Disease Resource Manual. LC 98-43499. 1999. write for info. (*0-8342-1051-7*) Aspen Pub.

— A Practical Introduction to Health Information Management. LC 98-34764. 1998. write for info. (*0-8342-1231-5*) Aspen Pub.

— Private School Administration Forms, Checklists & Guidelines. LC 97-37187. 1998. write for info. (*0-8342-0992-6*) Aspen Pub.

Di Lima, Sara N., jt. auth. see Aspen Reference Group Staff.

Di Lima, Sara N., jt. auth. see Beard, Shawn.

Di Lima, Sara N., jt. auth. see Johns, Lisa T.

Di Lima, Sara N., ed. see Aspen Reference Group Staff.

Di Lima, Sara N., ed. see Aspen Reference Group Staff & Lawrence, Kenneth E.

Di Liscia, Daniel A., et al. Method & Order in Renaissance Philosophy of Nature: The Aristotle Commentary Tradition. LC 97-77049. 450p. 1998. 96.95 (*0-86078-666-8*, Pub. by Ashgate Pub) Ashgate Pub Co.

di Lodovico Buonarroti Simoni, Michelangelo. Art Mini-Michelangelo. (Illus.). 96p. 2000. pap. text 4.95 (*3-8290-2931-4*) Konemann.

— The Complete Poems of Michelangelo. Tusiani, Joseph, tr. from ITA. LC 86-71314. 217p. 1986. 32.00 (*0-7206-6616-3*, Pub. by P Owen Ltd) Dufour.

***di Lodovico Buonarroti Simoni, Michelangelo.** The Complete Poems of Michelangelo. Nims, John Frederick, tr. 186p. 2000. pap. 14.00 (*0-226-08030-7*) U Ch Pr.

di Lodovico Buonarroti Simoni, Michelangelo. Drawings of Michelangelo. Stone, Irving, ed. (Master Draughtsman Ser.). (Illus.). (Orig.). 1962. pap. 4.95 (*0-87505-176-6*) Borden.

— Life, Letters & Poetry. (Oxford World Classics Ser.). 206p. 1999. pap. 9.95 (*0-19-283770-2*) OUP.

— Love Sonnets & Madrigals to Tommaso de'Cavalieri. Sullivan, Michael, tr. from ITA. LC 98-111568. (Illus.). 128p. 1998. 32.00 (*0-7206-1040-0*, Pub. by P Owen Ltd) Dufour.

***di Lodovico Buonarroti Simoni, Michelangelo.** Michelangelo. (Illus.). 2000. pap. 1.00 (*0-486-41077-3*) Dover.

di Lodovico Buonarroti Simoni, Michelangelo, jt. auth. see Beck, James H.

Di Lorenzo, Enrico & Giordano, Fausto, contrib. by. Bucolica Latina: Bucolicorum Latinorum Poetarum Lexicon. (Alpha-Omega, Reihe A Ser.: Bd. CLXVIII). (LAT.). 442p. 1996. write for info. (*3-487-10129-7*) G Olms Pubs.

Di Lorenzo, Marjorie, jt. auth. see Strasinger, Susan K.

Di Lorenzo, Marjorie A., jt. auth. see Strasinger, Susan K.

Di Lorenzo, Vincent M. New York Condominium & Cooperative Law. LC 84-82172. 1991. suppl. ed. 55.00 (*0-317-03257-7*) West Group.

— New York Condominium & Cooperative Law. 2nd ed. LC 84-82172. 1984. 135.00 (*0-318-04263-0*) West Group.

Di Luzio, Aldo, jt. ed. see Auer, Peter.

Di Luzio, N. R., ed. see International Symposium on Atherosclerosis Staff.

***Di Maggio, Joyce.** Out on a Farm. (Illus.). 24p. (J). (ps-1). 1999. pap. 5.00 (*1-928970-10-9*) GWR Pr.

— There's a Frog up Top My Head. (Illus.). 64p. (J). (ps-5). 1999. pap. 7.95 (*1-928970-04-4*) GWR Pr.

Di Maio, Dominic J. Forensic Pathology. (Practical Aspects of Criminal & Forensic Investigation Ser.). 528p. 1992. boxed set 94.95 (*0-8493-9503-8*) CRC Pr.

Di Maio, Vincent J. Gunshot Wounds: Practical Aspects of Firearms, Ballistics, & Forensic Techniques. LC 93-13497. 352p. 1992. reprint ed. boxed set 78.95 (*0-8493-9504-6*, RA1121) CRC Pr.

— Gunshot Wounds: Practical Aspects of Firearms, Ballistics, & Forensic Techniques. 2nd ed. LC 99-187476. (Practical Aspects Of Criminal & Forensic Investigation Ser.). 424p. 1998. boxed set 84.95 (*0-8493-8163-0*) CRC Pr.

— Gunshot Wounds: Practical Aspects of Firearms, Ballistics, Evidence & Forensic Techniques. (Series in Practical Aspects of Criminal & Forensic Investigations: Vol. 3). 454p. 1985. 43.00 (*0-444-00928-0*) CRC Pr.

Di Maio, Vincent J. & Dana, Suzanna E. Forensic Pathology. LC 98-4300. 176p. 1998. spiral bd. 45.00 (*1-57059-495-3*) Landes Bioscience.

Di Marco, Susan, ed. see Ivankovich, Michael.

Di Maria, Audrey E., ed. Art Therapy: A Bridge Between Worlds. (Conference Proceedings Ser.). 121p. (Orig.). 1981. pap. 7.00 (*1-882147-11-1*) Am Art Therapy.

— Art Therapy: Still Growing. (Conference Proceedings Ser.). 171p. (Orig.). 1982. pap. 14.00 (*1-882147-06-5*) Am Art Therapy.

Di Maria, Salvatore, jt. auth. see Rodini, Robert J.

***Di Mario, F.** Gallstone Disease in the Elderly. (Advances in Gastroenterology Ser.: Vol. 9). (Illus.). 150p. 1999. 35.00 (*88-299-1272-7*, Pub. by Piccin Nuova) Gordon & Breach.

Di Mario, F., et al. Chronic Atrophic Gastritis. (Advances in Gastroenterology Ser.: No. 4). 132p. 1991. text 32.00 (*1-57235-020-2*) Piccin Nuova.

Di Mario, F., et al. Chronic Atrophic Gastritis. (Advances in Gastroenterology Ser.: Vol. 4). (Illus.). 132p. 1991. text 36.00 (*88-299-0997-1*, Pub. by Piccin Nuova) Gordon & Breach.

— Gallbladder Wall Lesions. (Advances in Gastroenterology Ser.: Vol. 10). (Illus.). 100p. 1999. text 35.00 (*88-299-0247-0*, Pub. by Piccin Nuova) Gordon & Breach.

— Gastric Secretion. (Advances in Gastroenterology Ser.: Vol. 5). (Illus.). 160p. 1992. text 36.00 (*88-299-1097-X*, Pub. by Piccin Nuova) Gordon & Breach.

— Gastric Ulcer. (Advances in Gastroenterology Ser.: Vol. 7). (Illus.). 120p. 1994. text 39.00 (*88-299-1179-8*, Pub. by Piccin Nuova) Gordon & Breach.

Di Mario, F., et al. Made-to-Person Therapy for Ulcer Disease. (Advances in Gastroenterology Ser.: No. 6). 216p. 1993. text 32.00 (*1-57235-022-9*) Piccin Nuova.

Di Mario, F., et al. Made-to-Person Therapy for Ulcer Disease. (Advances in Gastroenterology Ser.: Vol. 6). (Illus.). 216p. 1993. text 36.00 (*88-299-1124-0*, Pub. by Piccin Nuova) Gordon & Breach.

Di Mario, F., et al. New Trends in Ulcer Disease. 314p. 1988. text 40.00 (*1-57235-018-0*) Piccin Nuova.

Di Mario, F., et al. New Trends in Ulcer Disease. (Advances in Gastroenterology Ser.: Vol. 2). (Illus.). 314p. 1988. text 44.00 (*88-299-0633-6*, Pub. by Piccin Nuova) Gordon & Breach.

Di Mario, F., et al. Non-Ulcer Dyspepsia. (Advances in Gastroenterology Ser.: No. 3). 130p. 1991. text 32.00 (*1-57235-019-9*) Piccin Nuova.

Di Mario, F., et al. Non-Ulcer Dyspepsia. (Advances in Gastroenterology Ser.: Vol. 3). (Illus.). 130p. 1991. text 36.00 (*88-299-0970-X*, Pub. by Piccin Nuova) Gordon & Breach.

Di Mario, F., et al. Peptic Secretion. (Advances in Gastroenterology Ser.: No. 1). 116p. text 32.00 (*1-57235-017-2*) Piccin Nuova.

Di Mario, F., et al. Peptic Secretion. (Advances in Gastroenterology Ser.: Vol. 1). (Illus.). 116p. 1985. text 36.00 (*88-299-0408-2*, Pub. by Piccin Nuova) Gordon & Breach.

— Ulcer Disease in the Elderly. (Advances in Gastroenterology Ser.: Vol. 8). (Illus.). 188p. 1996. 35.00 (*88-299-1180-1*, Pub. by Piccin Nuova) Gordon & Breach.

Di Mario, F., jt. auth. see Plebani, M.

Di Martin, L., et al, eds. Groups & Geometries. LC 98-4851. (Trends in Mathematics Ser.). 280p. 1998. 98.00 (*3-7643-5881-5*) Birkhauser.

Di Martino, Lino. Groups & Geometries: Siena Conference, September 1996. LC 98-4851. (Trends in Mathematics Ser.). 1998. write for info. (*0-8176-5881-5*) Birkhauser.
Di Martino, Lino, jt. ed. see Kantor, William M.
Di Martino, Luis A. Japanese Engineers in the Early Nineties: Tendencies in Personnel Management & Working Conditions. (Illus.). 234p. 1998. text 79.95 (*0-9664654-0-7*) Index Intl.
Di Martino, V. & Corlett, N., eds. Work Organization & Ergonomics. LC 98-220558. 1998. pap. 23.00 (*92-2-109518-5*) Intl Labour Office.
***Di Martino, Vittorio.** The High Road to Teleworking. 208p. 2000. pap. 18.95 (*92-2-110843-0*, Pub. by ILO) ILO Pubns Ctr.
Di Martino, Vittorio, jt. auth. see Chappell, Duncan.
Di Martino, Vittorio, jt. ed. see Yoxen, Edward.
Di Marzo, Luigi. Component Units of Federal States & International Agreement. LC 80-83265. 272p. 1981. lib. bdg. 90.00 (*90-286-0330-1*) Kluwer Academic.
Di Masi, G. B., et al, eds. Modeling, Estimation & Control of Systems with Uncertainty: Proceedings of a Conference Held in Sopron, Hungary, September 1990. (Progress in Systems & Control Theory Ser.: Vol. 10). ix, 467p. 1991. 127.50 (*0-8176-3580-7*) Birkhauser.
Di Masso, Gerardo. The Shadow by the Door. Jacques, Richard, tr. LC 87-73441. 96p. 1988. pap. 8.95 (*0-915306-76-X*) Curbstone.
Di Matteo, M., et al, eds. Technological & Social Factors in Long Term Fluctuations. (Lecture Notes in Economics & Mathematical Systems Ser.: Vol. 321). ix, 442p. 1989. 61.95 (*0-387-50663-2*) Spr-Verlag.
Di Mauro, Laurie, ed. Twentieth-Century Literary Criticism, Vol. 5. 500p. 1993. text 150.00 (*0-8103-8914-2*) Gale.
— Twentieth-Century Literary Criticism, 2 Vols., Vol. 47. 500p. 1993. text 150.00 (*0-8103-8912-6*, 001767) Gale.
— Twentieth Century Literary Criticism: Excerpts from Criticism of the Works of Novelists, Poets, Playwrights, Short Story Writers, & Other Creative Writers Who Died Between 1900 & 1960, Vol. 43. 492p. 1992. text 150.00 (*0-8103-8910-X*, 001763) Gale.
Di Meana, Gabriella Ripa. Figures of Lightness: Anorexia, Bulimia & Psychoanalysis. LC 99-193562. 1998. pap. text 34.95 (*1-85302-617-4*) Jessica Kingsley.
Di Megilo, Lora, et al. Wisconsin's Early Home Remedies. (Illus.). 172p. (Orig.). 1991. pap. text 9.95 (*1-878488-55-4*) Quixote Pr IA.
Di Meola, Al. Al Di Meola: A Guide to Chords, Scales & Arpeggios. 112p. 1987. per. 14.95 (*0-7935-2677-9*, 00604042) H Leonard.
— Al Di Meola's Picking Techniques. 32p. 1987. pap. 8.95 (*0-7935-1018-X*, 00604044) H Leonard.
— Friday Night in San Francisco. (Piano-Guitar Ser.). 96p. 1992. per. 14.95 (*0-7935-1246-8*, 00660115) H Leonard.
***Di Michele, A.** Black Market Pneuma. (Illus.). 24p. 1999. pap. 4.00 (*0-9663846-5-2*) Lavender Ink.
Di, Michele M. Under My Skin. LC 94-159060. 1994. pap. 12.95 (*1-55082-099-0*, Pub. by Quarry Pr) LPC InBook.
Di Michele, Mary. Stranger in You. 92p. 1995. pap. (*0-19-541158-7*) OUP.
Di Michele, Mary, ed. Anything Is Possible: A Selection of 11 Women Poets. 190p. 1994. pap. 12.95 (*0-88962-251-5*) Mosaic.
Di Napoli, Carlo. How They Owned a Boat & Didn't Spend Any Money. rev. ed. (Illus.). 188p. 1994. pap. 9.95 (*1-883213-00-2*) Hawk FL.
Di Napoli, Peter J. Homework in New York City Elementary Schools. LC 77-176721. (Columbia University. Teachers College. Contributions to Education Ser.: No. 719). reprint ed. 37.50 (*0-404-55719-8*) AMS Pr.
***Di Nardo, Anthony.** Rogue Pawn. 240p. 1998. 19.00 (*0-8059-4454-0*) Dorrance.
Di Nardo, Paolo, jt. ed. see Claycomb, William C.
Di Nicola, Vincenzo. Stranger in the Family: Culture, Families & Therapy. LC 96-40310. 384p. 1997. 45.00 (*0-393-70228-6*) Norton.
Di Nino, Carmen. How to Survive Bad Bosses. 1996. pap. 8.95 (*1-880092-38-7*) Bright Bks TX.
Di Niscemi, Maita. Manor Houses & Castles of Sweden: A Voyage Through Five Centuries. LC 87-60276. (Illus.). 216p. 1994. 55.00 (*0-935748-73-3*) Antique Collect.
Di Nola, Alfonso, ed. Prayers of Man. 1960. 27.95 (*0-8392-1152-X*) Astor-Honor.
Di Nola, Antonio, et al. Fuzzy Relation Equations & Their Applications to Knowledge Engineering. (C). 1989. text 175.00 (*0-7923-0307-5*) Kluwer Academic.
Di Nolfo, Ennio, ed. The Atlantic Pact Forty Years Later: A Historical Reappraisal. viii, 268p. (C). 1991. lib. bdg. 106.15 (*3-11-012738-5*, 168-91) De Gruyter.
— Power in Europe? II: Great Britain, France, Germany & Italy & the History of the EEC, 1952-1957. viii, 598p. (C). 1992. lib. bdg. 183.10 (*3-11-012158-1*) De Gruyter.
Di Norcia, Vincent. Hard Like Water: Ethical Frameworks in Business. 320p. 1998. pap. text 29.95 (*0-19-541210-9*) OUP.
Di Notto, Elisabetta & Fuggetta, Alfonso, eds. Process Technology. LC 97-39191. 140p. 1998. text 127.50 (*0-7923-8090-8*) Kluwer Academic.
Di Nunzio, Mario R. American Democracy & the Authoritarian Tradition of the West. 192p. (Orig.). (C). 1987. pap. text 21.50 (*0-8191-6113-6*) U Pr of Amer.
Di Palma, Giuseppe. To Craft Democracies: An Essay on Democratic Transitions. 214p. 1990. 40.00 (*0-520-07213-8*, Pub. by U CA Pr); pap. 17.95 (*0-520-07214-6*, Pub. by U CA Pr) Cal Prin Full Svc.
Di Palma, Ray. The Jukebox of Memnon. 110p. (Orig.). (C). 1988. pap. 8.50 (*0-937013-24-2*) Potes Poets.
— Letters. (Littoral Bks.). 63p. 1998. pap. 10.95 (*1-55713-374-3*) Sun & Moon CA.
Di Paolo, Franco. Networks & Devices Using Planar Transmission Lines. 1999. 129.00 (*0-8493-1835-1*, 1835) CRC Pr.
***Di Pasquale, Emanuel P.** The Silver Lake Love Poems. LC 99-50002. 34p. 2000. pap. 5.00 (*1-884419-32-1*) Bordighera.
Di Pasquale, Emanuel P., tr. see Salerno, Joe.
Di Pasquale, Giuseppe & Pinelli, Giuseppe, eds. Heart-Brain Interactions. LC 92-2301. (Illus.). xiii, 228p. 1992. write for info. (*3-540-54052-0*) Spr-Verlag.
Di Pasquale, Mauro G. Amino Acids & Proteins for the Athlete: The Anabolic Edge. LC 97-4307. (Nutrition in Exercise & Sport Ser.). 272p. 1997. boxed set 74.95 (*0-8493-8193-2*) CRC Pr.
— High Performance Nutrition Diets & Supplements for the Competitive Athlete. (Nutrition in Exercise & Sport Ser.). 1999. 89.95 (*0-8493-8195-9*, 8195) CRC Pr.
Di Pasquale, Remo, tr. see Giussani, Angela & Giussani, Luciana.
Di Pasquale, Robert. Men Like Trees Walking. LC 97-68993. 192p. 1998. 23.50 (*0-88739-149-4*); pap. 13.95 (*0-88739-167-2*) Creat Arts Bk.
Di Perna, Paula. The Discoveries of Mrs. Christopher Columbus. LC 93-27525. 287p. 1994. 24.00 (*1-877946-48-6*) Permanent Pr.
Di Piero, W. S. The Dog Star. LC 89-20273. 64p. (C). 1990. pap. 9.95 (*0-87023-704-7*); lib. bdg. 17.50 (*0-87023-703-9*) U of Mass Pr.
— Memory & Enthusiasm: Essays, 1975-1985. LC 88-17939. 269p. 1989. reprint ed. pap. 83.40 (*0-608-02527-5*, 206317100004) Bks Demand.
— Out of Eden: Essays on Modern Art. LC 90-48336. (Illus.). 269p. 1991. 45.00 (*0-520-07065-8*, Pub. by U CA Pr); pap. 16.95 (*0-520-08432-2*, Pub. by U CA Pr) Cal Prin Full Svc.
— The Restorers. LC 91-29065. (Phoenix Poets Ser.). 86p. 1992. pap. 9.95 (*0-226-15347-9*) U Ch Pr.
— The Restorers. LC 91-29065. (Phoenix Poets Ser.). 86p. 1992. lib. bdg. 23.00 (*0-226-15346-0*) U Ch Pr.
— Shooting the Works: On Poetry & Pictures. LC 95-51559. 216p. 1996. pap. 14.95 (*0-8101-5052-2*); text 29.95 (*0-8101-5051-4*) Northwestern U Pr.
Di Piero, W. S. & Wilken, Karen, texts. Paul Resika. (Illus.). 18p. 1993. pap. 20.00 (*1-58821-061-8*) Salander OReilly.
Di Piero, W. S., tr. see Leopardi, Giacomo.
Di Pillo, G. & Giannessi, F. Nonlinear Optimization & Applications: Proceedings of the International School of Mathematics "G Stampacchia" 21st Workshop Held in Erice, Italy, June 13-21, 1995. LC 96-21924. (Illus.). 380p. (C). 1996. 132.00 (*0-306-45316-9*, Kluwer Plenum) Kluwer Academic.
***Di Pillo, G. & Giannessi, F.** Nonlinear Optimization & Related Topics. LC 99-56953. (Applied Optimization Ser.). (C). 1999. text. write for info. (*0-7923-6109-1*) Kluwer Academic.
Di Plan Carpini, Giovanni. Story of the Mongols Whom We Call the Tartars. Caso, Adolph, ed. Hildinger, Erik, tr. 1996. pap. text 14.95 (*0-8283-2017-9*) Branden Bks.
Di Porzio, Umberto, ed. Development of Dopaminergic Neurons. LC 98-52676. (Neuroscience Intelligence Unit Ser.: No. 4). 192p. 1999. 99.00 (*1-57059-565-8*) Landes Bioscience.
Di Prampero, P. E. & Poortmans, J. R., eds. Physiological Chemistry of Exercise & Training. (Medicine & Sport Science Ser.: Vol. 13). (Illus.). viii, 216p. 1981. 85.25 (*3-8055-2028-X*) S Karger.
Di Prampero, Pietro, jt. ed. see Tavazzi, Luigi.
Di Prima, Diana. Loba. LC 97-41144. 325p. 1998. pap. 14.95 (*0-14-058752-7*) NAL.
Di Prima, Diane. Dinners & Nightmares. 3rd ed. 159p. Date not set. pap. 14.95 (*0-86719-395-6*) Last Gasp.
— Memoirs of a Beatnik. LC 99-158607. 194p. 1998. pap. 12.95 (*0-14-023539-6*) Viking Penguin.
— Seminary Poems. 48p. (Orig.). 1991. pap. 6.00 (*0-912449-34-9*) Floating Island.
Di Prima, Diane & Jones, LeRoi, eds. The Floating Bear: A Newsletter, Nos. 1-37, 1961-1969. LC 72-79790. 1973. pap. 20.00 (*0-910938-54-7*); lib. bdg. 30.00 (*0-910938-29-6*) McGilvery.
Di Prisco, C. A., ed. Methods in Mathematical Logic. (Lecture Notes in Mathematics Ser.: Vol. 1130). vii, 407p. 1985. 54.95 (*0-387-15236-9*) Spr-Verlag.
Di Prisco, Carlos A., et al, eds. Set Theory: Techniques & Applications: Cura Cao, 1995 & Barcelona, 1996 Conferences. LC 97-46592. 228p. 1998. text 117.50 (*0-7923-4905-9*) Kluwer Academic.
Di Prisco, G., ed. Life under Extreme Conditions: Biochemical Adaptation. (Illus.). 160p. 1991. 78.95 (*0-387-53108-4*) Spr-Verlag.
Di Prisco, G., et al, eds. Biology of Antarctic Fish. (Illus.). 288p. 1991. 140.00 (*0-387-53350-8*) Spr-Verlag.
***Di Prisco, G., et al, eds.** Fishes of Antarctica: A Biological Overview. LC 98-25736. xi, 363p. 1998. 139.00 (*88-470-0028-9*, Pub. by Spr-Verlag) Spr-Verlag.
***Di Prisco, Guido, et al.** Hemoglobin Function in Vertebrates. LC 00-30756. 2000. write for info. (*88-470-0107-2*, Pub. by Spr-Verlag) Spr-Verlag.
Di Prisco, Joseph, jt. auth. see Riera, Michael.
Di Raimondo, P. Domenico, tr. see Hart, Corinne.
Di Raimondo, P. Domenico, tr. see Shannon, Ellen & Hart, Corinne.
Di Renzo, Anthony. American Gargoyles: Flannery O'Connor & the Medieval Grotesque. LC 95-11478. (Illus.). 272p. (C). 1995. reprint ed. pap. 16.95 (*0-8093-2030-4*) S Ill U Pr.
Di Renzo, Anthony, ed. see Lewis, Sinclair.
Di Renzo, G. C., et al, eds. Recent Advances in Perinatal Medicine. LC 93-12026. (Ettore Majorana International Life Sciences Ser.: Vol. 10). 350p. 1994. text 85.00 (*3-7186-5348-6*) Gordon & Breach.
Di Renzo, G. C., jt. ed. see Cosmi, E. V.
di Renzo, Olivia, jt. auth. see Houle, Paul.
Di Rienzo, M., ed. Frontiers of Blood Pressure & Heart Rate Analysis. LC 96-79143. (Studies in Health Technology & Informatics: Vol. 35). 280p. (YA). (gr. 12). Date not set. 105.00 (*90-5199-312-9*, 312-9) IOS Press.
Di Rienzo, M., et al. Computer Analysis of Cardiovascular Signals. LC 94-75419. (Studies in Health Technology & Informatics: Vol. 13). 350p. (gr. 12). 1995. 104.00 (*90-5199-158-4*) IOS Press.
Di Robbio, Armando, et al. Let Us Sing unto the Lord. (Illus.). 92p. (Orig.). 1997. spiral bd. 30.00 (*0-9661540-0-2*) Far Memory.
Di Rocco, C. The Treatment of Infantile Hydrocephalus, Vol. 1. LC 86-24451. 1987. 96.00 (*0-8493-5721-7*, RJ496, CRC Reprint) Franklin.
Di Rocco, Concezio. The Treatment of Infantile Hydrocephalus, 2 vols. LC 86-24451. 1987. 205.00 (*0-8493-5720-9*, RJ469, CRC Reprint) Franklin
— The Treatment of Infantile Hydrocephalus, 2 vols., Vol. I. 160p. 1987. write for info. (*0-318-62350-1*) CRC Pr.
— The Treatment of Infantile Hydrocephalus, 2 vols., Vol. II. 160p. 1987. write for info. (*0-318-62351-X*) CRC Pr.
— The Treatment of Infantile Hydrocephalus, Vol. 2. LC 86-24451. 184p. 1987. reprint ed. 109.00 (*0-8493-5722-5*, CRC Reprint) Franklin.
Di Rosa, Rene. Local Color: The di Rosa Collection of Contemporary California Art. LC 98-38931. (Illus.). 190p. 1999. 60.00 (*0-8118-2376-8*); pap. 35.00 (*0-8118-2377-6*) Chronicle Bks.
Di Sabatino, David. The Jesus People Movement, 49. LC 98-39931. (Bibliographies & Indexes in Religious Studies: Vol. 49). 280p. 1999. lib. bdg. 69.50 (*0-313-30268-5*, Greenwood Pr) Greenwood.
Di Sabato, Giovanni, ed. Immunochemical Techniques Pt. L: Chemotoxins & Inflammation. (Methods in Enzymology Ser.: Vol. 162). 717p. 1988. text 146.00 (*0-12-182063-7*) Acad Pr.
Di Sabato, Giovanni, et al, eds. Immunochemical Techniques Vol. 108, Pt. G: Separation & Characterization of Lymphoid Cells. (Methods in Enzymology Ser.). 1984. text 179.00 (*0-12-182008-4*) Acad Pr.
Di Salvatore, Bryan. A Clever Base-Ballist: The Life & Times of John Montgomery Ward. LC 98-54189. 448p. 1999. 27.50 (*0-679-44234-0*) Pantheon.
Di Salvo, Angelo. Cervantes & the Augustinian Religious Tradition. LC 88-62645. 260p. 1989. 25.00 (*0-938972-15-4*) Spanish Lit Pubns.
***Di Salvo, Angelo J.** The Spiritual Literature of Recollection in Spain (1500-1620) The Reform of the Inner Person. LC 99-47829. (Texts & Studies in Religion: Vol. 84). 240p. 1999. text 89.95 (*0-7734-7874-4*) E Mellen.
Di Salvo, Joe & DiGeronimo, Theresa. College Admissions for the High School Athlete. LC 93-16811. 176p. 1993. pap. 9.95 (*0-8160-2816-8*) Facts on File.
Di Salvo, Vincent S. & Monroe, Craig. The Competent Communicator at Work: A Humanistic Perspective. 416p. 1995. per. 32.95 (*0-7872-8435-1*) Kendall-Hunt.
Di San Filippo, Pietro A. Biografia Dei Viaggiatori Italiani: Colla Bibliografia Delle Loro Opere. (ITA., Illus.). 1152p. 1996. reprint ed. 125.00 (*1-888262-20-6*) Martino Pubng.
Di Sante, Carmine. Jewish Prayer: The Origins of Christian Liturgy. O'Connell, Matthew, tr. 1992. pap. 14.95 (*0-8091-3207-9*) Paulist Pr.
Di Scala, Spencer. Italy: From Revolution to Republic, 1700 to the Present. 2nd ed. LC 98-121339. 464p. (C) 1998. pap. text 30.00 (*0-8133-3469-1*, Pub. by Westview) HarpC.
Di Scala, Spencer M., ed. Italian Socialism: Between Politics & History. LC 95-38480. 256p. 1996. text 35.00 (*1-55849-012-4*) U of Mass Pr.
Di Scala, Spencer M. & Mastellone, Salvo. European Political Thought, 1815-1989. LC 97-31708. 272p. (C). 1998. pap. text 26.00 (*0-8133-1739-8*, Pub. by Westview) HarpC.
Di Sciullo, Anna-Maria, ed. Projections & Interface Conditions: Essays on Modularity. (Illus.). 272p. 1997. text 65.00 (*0-19-510414-5*) OUP.
Di Sciullo, Anne-Marie, ed. Configurations: Essays on Structure & Interpretation. LC 96-8926. 1996. pap. 23.95 (*1-57473-006-1*) Cascadilla Pr.
— Configurations: Essays on Structure & Interpretation. (Illus.). vii, 352p. (C). 1996. lib. bdg. 53.95 (*1-57473-106-8*) Cascadilla Pr.
Di Sessa, A. A., et al, eds. Computers & Exploratory Learning. rev. ed. (NATO ASI Ser.: Series F, Computer & Systems Sciences: Vol. 146). 482p. 1995. 149.00 (*3-540-59202-4*) Spr-Verlag.
Di Siena, Doug, jt. auth. see Schuller, Robert A.
Di Siena, Douglas, jt. auth. see Schuller, Robert A.
Di Silverio, F., ed. Markers in Urology: Journal: European Urology, Vol. 21, Suppl. 1, 1992. (Illus.). iv, 116p. 1992. pap. 36.75 (*3-8055-5612-8*) S Karger.
— Markers in Urology, Abstracts Vol. 19, Suppl. 2: Journal: European Urology, Vol. 19, Suppl. 1. xvi, 44p. 1991. pap. 18.50 (*3-8055-5453-2*) S Karger.
Di Silverio, F., jt. ed. see Jardin, A.
Di Silvestro, Frank. Americans Are Singing about Lady Liberty. (Illus.). 74p. 1986. pap. 10.95 (*0-934591-01-6*) Songs & Stories.
— Boy Jesus & His Dog. (Illus.). 127p. (YA). (gr. 4-11). 1998. pap. 24.95 (*0-934591-03-2*) Songs & Stories.
Di Silvestro, G. 9th International Conference on the Chemistry of the Organic Solid State, Set, Pts. 1 & 2. 642p. 1990. text 1917.00 (*2-88124-463-7*) Gordon & Breach.
Di Stefano, Christine. Configurations of Masculinity: A Feminist Perspective on Modern Political Theory. LC 90-55730. 256p. 1991. pap. text 15.95 (*0-8014-9765-5*) Cornell U Pr.
Di Stefano, Giuseppe. Dictionnaire des Locutions en Moyen Francais. (FRE.). 930p. 1992. 375.00 (*0-7859-8595-6*, 0919089550) Fr & Eur.
***di Stefano, Ted.** You Can Buy a Business: How to Become Happily Self-Employed. Rosen, Laurie, ed. 106p. 1999. 9.95 (*0-9675969-1-2*) acquisitionsol.
Di Suvero, Victor. Naked Heart. 32p. 1996. pap. 12.00 (*0-938631-28-4*) Pennywhistle Pr.
Di Suvero, Victor, jt. ed. see Williams, Jeanie C.
Di Suvero, Victor, ed. & intro. see Addonizio, Kim, et al.
Di Tella, Torcuato S. Latin American Politics: A Theoretical Framework. (Translations from Latin America Ser.). 348p. 1989. text 27.50 (*0-292-74661-X*) U of Tex Pr.
— National Popular Politics in Early Independent Mexico, 1820-1847. 384p. 1996. 55.00 (*0-8263-1673-5*) U of NM Pr.
***Di Terlizzi, Maurizio.** Fiat G.55 Centauro. Napoleone, Angelo, ed. Richards, Stephen, tr. (Aviolibri Ser.: Vol. 3). (Illus.). 64p. 1998. pap. 14.95 (*88-86815-35-2*, Pub. by Istituto Bibliograf) Pacific Coast Mod.
— Hughes 500 Family. Napoleone, Angelo, ed. Richards, Stephen, tr. 64p. 1998. pap. 14.95 (*88-86815-31-X*, Pub. by Istituto Bibliograf) Pacific Coast Mod.
— Macchi MC.205 "Veltro" 2nd rev. ed. Napoleone, Angelo, ed. Charlesworth, Kay, tr. (Aviolibri Ser.: Vol. 1). (Illus.). 64p. 1997. pap. 14.95 (*88-86815-55-7*, Pub. by Istituto Bibliograf) Pacific Coast Mod.
— Macchi MC.202 Folgore, Pt. 1. Napoleone, Angelo, ed. Richards, Stephen, tr. (Aviolibri Special Ser.: Vol. 1). (ITA & ENG., Illus.). 64p. 1999. pap. 21.95 (*88-86815-42-5*, Pub. by Istituto Bibliograf) Pacific Coast Mod.
— Reggiane RE 2005 Sagittario. Napoleone, Angelo, ed. Richards, Stephen, tr. (Aviolibri Ser.: Vol. 4). (Illus.). 64p. 1999. pap. 14.95 (*88-86815-38-7*, Pub. by Istituto Bibliograf) Pacific Coast Mod.
Di Tommaso, Andrea, ed. Amorum Libri: The Lyric Poems of Matteo Maria Boiardo. (Medieval & Renaissance Texts & Studies: Vol. 101). 320p. 1993. 25.00 (*0-86698-117-9*, MR101) MRTS.
Di Toro, Dominic M. Sediment Flux Modeling. LC 99-51839. (Environmental Science & Technology). 448p. 2000. text 64.95 (*0-471-13535-6*) Wiley.
Di Toro, M., et al, eds. Phase Space Approach to Nuclear Dynamics: Proceedings to the Topical Meeting on Phase Space Approach to Nuclear Dynamics, Sept. 3-Oct. 4, 1985, Trieste, Italy. 812p. 1986. text 175.00 (*9971-5-0015-9*) World Scientific Pub.
Di Toro, R., ed. Infantile Nutrition - an Update. (Beitraege zur Infusionstherapie und Klinische Ernaehrung Ser.: Vol. 27). (Illus.). viii, 170p. 1991. 68.75 (*3-8055-5343-9*) S Karger.
— Nutrition in Preventive Pediatrics. (Contributions to Infusion Therapy Ser.: Vol. 22). (Illus.). vi, 168p. 1989. 65.25 (*3-8055-4852-4*) S Karger.
— Nutritional Support for Sick Children. (Contributions to Infusion Therapy Ser.: Vol. 19). (Illus.). vi, 150p. 1988. 51.50 (*3-8055-4705-6*) S Karger.
Di Valmarana, Mario, ed. Building by the Book, Vol. 2. LC 84-2249. (Palladian Studies in America: Vol. 1). 160p. 1990. reprint ed. pap. 49.60 (*0-608-03809-1*, 206466000002) Bks Demand.
— Building by the Book, Vol. 3. LC 84-2249. (Palladian Studies in America: Vol. 1). 138p. 1990. reprint ed. pap. 42.80 (*0-608-03810-5*, 206466000003) Bks Demand.
Di Vecchia, P. & Petersen, J. L., eds. Perspectives in String Theory: Proceedings of the Niels Bohr Institute-Nordita Meeting, Copenhagen, Denmark. 524p. (C). 1988. pap. 61.00 (*9971-5-0534-7*); text 123.00 (*9971-5-0526-6*) World Scientific Pub.
Di Vincenzo, D., jt. ed. see Steinhardt, P.
Di Vinenzo, Janet, ed. see National Security Archive Staff & Chadwyck-Healey Staff.
Di Vita, Antonino & Bacchielli, Lidiano. Libya: Lost Sites of the Roman Empire. (Illus.). 160p. 1999. 29.95 (*3-89508-844-7*, 520509) Konemann.
***Di, Xve, et al.** Poems from the Heron Clan. 144p. 1999. pap. 11.95 (*0-9673855-0-4*) K James Bks.
Di, Zhou, ed. Oceanology of China Seas, Vol. 2. 240p. (C). 1994. lib. bdg. 111.50 (*0-7923-2617-2*) Kluwer Academic.
Di, Zhou & Cheng-Kui, Zeng, eds. Oceanology of China Seas. LC 93-39781. 360p. (C). 1994. lib. bdg. 194.00 (*0-7923-2618-0*); lib. bdg. 155.50 (*0-7923-2616-4*) Kluwer Academic.
Dia, Mamadou. The African Nations & World Solidarity. LC 86-25734. Orig. Title: Nations Africaines et Solidarite Mondiale. 157p. 1987. reprint ed. lib. bdg. 59.50 (*0-313-24569-X*, DIAN, Greenwood Pr) Greenwood.
— Africa's Management in the 1990s & Beyond: Reconciling Indigenous & Transplanted Institutions. LC 95-49805. 306p. 1996. pap. 22.00 (*0-8213-3431-X*, 13431) World Bank.
— A Governance Approach to Civil Service Reform in Sub-Saharan Africa. LC 93-23486. (Technical Papers: No. 225). 61p. 1993. pap. 22.00 (*0-8213-2630-9*, 12630) World Bank.
Diab, Hassan. Beirut: Reviving Lebanon's Past. LC 98-33611. 144p. 1999. 55.00 (*0-275-96210-5*, Praeger Pubs) Greenwood.
Diab, Hassan B. Design & Implementation of a Flight Simulation System. (Illus.). 152p. (Orig.). (C). 1993. pap. text 19.95 (*0-8156-6088-X*) Syracuse U Pr.
Diab, Lutfy N., jt. auth. see Prothro, Edwin T.
***Diab, Mohammad.** Lexicon of Orthopaedic Etymology. 460p. 1999. text 92.00 (*90-5702-597-3*, Harwood Acad Pubs) Gordon & Breach.
Diab, Robert. Probate Reform in New Jersey. 205p. 1990. ring bd. 30.00 (*0-685-14667-7*) NJ Inst CLE.
Diabelli, Anton, et al. The Diabelli Variations: Variations on a Theme by Fifty Composers & Virtuosos. pap. 25.00 (*0-912028-09-2*) Music Treasure.

D

Diabetes Care & Education Dietetic Practice Group. Jewish Food Practices, Customs, & Holidays. (Ethnic & Regional Food Practices Ser.). 1990. ring bd. 5.75 (0-88091-049-6, 0866) Am Dietetic Assn.

— Mexican American Food Practices, Customs, & Holidays. (Ethnic & Regional Food Practices Ser.). 1989. ring bd. 10.00 (0-88091-048-8, 0865) Am Dietetic Assn.

Diabetes Care & Education Dietetic Practice Group & Leistner, Colette G. Cajun & Creole Food Practices, Customs, & Holidays. LC 95-15006. (Ethnic & Regional Food Practices - A Ser.). 1996. 10.00 (0-88091-145-X) Am Dietetic Assn.

Diabetes Care & Education Dietetic Practice Group, jt. auth. see Ikeda, Joanne P.

Diabetes Care & Education Dietetic Practice Group Staff, jt. auth. see Halderson, Karen.

Diabetes Trust Fund Staff. For Goodness Sake. LC 93-74179. 1993. pap. 12.95 (0-87197-395-2) Favorite Recipes.

D'Iachenko, G., ed. Complete Church - Slavonic Dictionary. 2nd ed. (RUS.). 1120p. 1993. reprint ed. 49.95 (0-8285-5374-2) Firebird NY.

Diachenko, Gregory. Dukhovnija Posjevi.Tr. of Spiritual Sowing. (Illus.). 475p. 1977. reprint ed. 20.00 (0-317-30414-3); reprint ed. pap. 15.00 (0-317-30415-1) Holy Trinity.

Diachok, O., et al, eds. Full Field Inversion Methods in Ocean & Seismo-Acoustics. LC 95-11663. (Modern Approaches in Geophysics Ser.: Vol. 12). 1995. text 206.00 (0-7923-3459-0) Kluwer Academic.

Diack, Hunter. Reading & the Psychology of Perception. LC 77-138220. (Illus.). 155p. 1971. reprint ed. lib. bdg. 69.50 (0-8371-5577-0, DIRP, Greenwood Pr) Greenwood.

Diacogiannis, George P. Financial Management: A Modelling Approach Using Spreadsheets. LC 93-983. 1993. 19.95 (0-07-707730-X) McGraw.

Diacon, Diane. Deterioration of the Public Sector Housing Stock. 280p. 1991. text 82.95 (1-85628-110-8, Pub. by Avebry) Ashgate Pub Co.

Diacon, S. R. C. I. I. Economic Organisation, No. 820. (C). 1981. 230.00 (0-7855-4298-1, Pub. by Witherby & Co) St Mut.

— C. I. I. Economics, No. 030. (C). 1981. suppl. ed. 230.00 (0-7855-4297-3, Pub. by Witherby & Co) St Mut.

Diacon, S. R., jt. auth. see Carter, R. L.

Diacon, Todd A. Millenarian Vision, Capitalist Reality: Brazil's Contestado Rebellion, 1912-1916. LC 91-521. 215p. 1991. pap. text 19.95 (0-8223-1167-4); lib. bdg. 45.50 (0-8223-1157-7) Duke.

Diaconescu, Razvan & Futatsugi, Kokichi. CafeOBJ Report: The Language, Proof Techniques & Methodologies for Object-Oriented Algebraic Specification. (AMAST Series in Computing: Vol. 6). 196p. 1998. 26.00 (981-02-3513-5) World Scientific Pub.

Diaconics, P., et al, eds. Ecole d'Ete de Probabilites de Saint-Flour, 1985-87, Nos. XV-XVII. (Lecture Notes in Mathematics Ser.: Vol. 1362). 450p. 1989. 68.95 (0-387-50549-0) Spr-Verlag.

Diaconis, John S. Reinsurance Law & Practice: New Legal & Business Developments in a Changing Global Environment 1998. LC 98-223147. (Commercial Law & Practice Course Handbook Ser.). 248 p. 1998. 129.00 (0-87224-513-6) PLI.

Diaconis, Pamela. Scandinavian Country. LC 98-43516. (Architecture & Design Library Ser.). (Illus.). 96p. 1999. text 17.95 (1-56799-721-X) M Friedman Pub Grp Inc.

Diaconis, Persi W. Group Representations in Probability & Statistics. (IMS Lecture Notes - Monographs: Vol. 11). vi, 198p. 1988. pap. 30.00 (0-940600-14-5) Inst Math.

Diacono, Mario. Vito Acconci: Dal Testo-Azione Al Corpo Come Testo. LC 75-22995.Tr. of The/Work of Vito Acconci As a Form of Writing. (ITA., Illus.). 245p. 1975. 9.95 (0-915570-03-3) Oolp Pr.

Diacono, Mario & Dickhoff, Wilfred. Rosemarie Trockel: Herde, Catalogue Raisonnee. (Illus.). 88p. (C). 1997. 70.00 (3-932189-00-0) Dist Art Pubs.

Diacono, Mario, ed. see Katz, Vincent.

Diacono, Mario, tr. see Ricard, Rene.

***Diaconu, Madalina.** Blickumkehr: Mit Martin Heidegger zu einer relationalen Asthetik. 2000. 47.95 (3-631-35420-7) P Lang Pubng.

***Diacu, Florin.** Celestial Encounters: The Origins of Chaos & Stability. 1999. pap. text 14.95 (0-691-00545-1, Pub. by Princeton U Pr) Cal Prin Full Svc.

— Order & Chaos: An Introduction to Differential Equations. 2000. pap. text. write for info. (0-7167-3296-3) W H Freeman.

Diacu, Florin & Holmes, Philip. Celestial Encounters: The Origins of Chaos & Stability. LC 96-108. 280p. 1996. text 24.95 (0-691-02743-9, Pub. by Princeton U Pr) Cal Prin Full Svc.

Diadochus, Proclus. Commentarius in Platonis Parmenidem. Cousin, Victor, ed. 1314p. 1980. reprint ed. write for info. incl. 3.5 hd (3-487-00166-7) G Olms Pubs.

— In Primum Euclidis Elementorum Librum Commentarii. viii, 507p. 1992. reprint ed. write for info. (3-487-01465-3) G Olms Pubs.

Diaferia, Michele G. Li Proverbes au Conte de Bretaigne: A Critical Study. LC 90-5985. (Currents in Romance Languages & Literature Ser.: Vol. 3). (FRE., Illus.). XIV, 166p. (C). 1990. text 40.95 (0-8204-1231-7) P Lang Pubng.

Diafora. Diafora Dictionary of the Spanish Language: Diccionario Esencial Diafora de al Lengua Espanola. (SPA.). 592p. 1983. 29.95 (0-8288-2013-9, S40511) Fr & Eur.

Diage, Katherine & Wortz, Melinda. Diversity & Presence: Women Faculty Artists of the University of California. Henger, Sue, ed. LC 87-50967. (Illus.). 72p. (Orig.). (C). 1987. pap. 12.00 (0-932173-03-9) Sweeney Art Gallery.

Diagger, jt. ed. see Grady.

Diagne, Ahmadou M., et al. Early Writings from Francophone Africa, 3 vols. in 1. (B. E. Ser.: No. 104). 1964. 30.00 (0-8115-3035-3) Periodicals Srv.

Diagram Group. Human Body on File: Physiology. (Illus.). 288p. 1996. ring bd. 165.00 (0-8160-3415-X) Facts on File.

— The Little Giant Encyclopedia of Fortune Telling. LC 98-47995. (Little Giant Ser.). 510 p. 1999. pap. 9.95 (0-8069-4823-X) Sterling.

***Diagram Group Ltd. Staff.** The Facts on File Handbook of Chemistry. LC 99-48563. (Illus.). 224p. 2000. 29.95 (0-8160-4080-X) Facts on File.

— The Facts on File Handbook of Earth Science. (Illus.). 224p. 2000. 29.95 (0-8160-4081-8) Facts on File.

— The Facts on File Handbook of Physics. LC 99-48564. (Illus.). 224p. 2000. 29.95 (0-8160-4082-6) Facts on File.

Diagram Group Staff. African History on File. LC 93-10078. (Illus.). 288p. 1993. ring bd. 165.00 (0-8160-2910-5) Facts on File.

***Diagram Group Staff.** Ancient & Medieval World--From the Beginnings to A. D. 1500, 1. (Timelines on File Ser.). 249p. 2000. 125.00 (0-8160-4304-3) Facts on File.

Diagram Group Staff. Animal Anatomy on File: An Internal & External Guide. (Illus.). 288p. 1990. ring bd. 165.00 (0-8160-2244-5) Facts on File.

— Animal Anatomy on File: An Internal & External Guide. rev. ed. LC 98-55740. (Illus.). 316p. 1999. ring bd. 165.00 (0-8160-3875-9, Checkmark) Facts on File.

— Business Forms on File: 1998 Edition. 252p. 1998. ring bd. 125.00 (0-8160-3820-1) Facts on File.

— Charts on File. (On File Ser.). (Illus.). 300p. 1988. ring bd. 165.00 (0-8160-1727-1) Facts on File.

***Diagram Group Staff.** Chemistry Experiments on File. (On File Ser.). (Illus.). 288p. 2000. 165.00 (0-8160-4425-2) Facts on File.

Diagram Group Staff. Comparapedia. 1999. text. write for info. (0-312-13244-1) St Martin.

***Diagram Group Staff.** Comparative Religions on File. (Illus.). 288p. 2000. ring bd. write for info. (0-8160-4254-3) Facts on File.

Diagram Group Staff. Comparisons. (Illus.). 240p. 1982. pap. 9.95 (0-312-15485-2) St Martin.

— Design on File. (On File Ser.). 345p. 1984. ring bd. 155.00 (0-87196-270-5) Facts on File.

— The Dinosaur Data Book. 320p. (Orig.). 1990. pap. 12.95 (0-380-75896-2, Avon Bks) Morrow Avon.

— Earth Science on File. rev. ed. LC 98-55739. (Illus.). 314p. 1999. ring bd. 165.00 (0-8160-3873-2, Checkmark) Facts on File.

— Earth Sciences on File. (Illus.). 300p. 1988. ring bd. 165.00 (0-8160-1625-9) Facts on File.

— Environment on File. (Illus.). 288p. 1991. 165.00 (0-8160-2695-5) Facts on File.

— Europe on File, 2 vols. 384p. 1997. ring bd. 185.00 (0-8160-3508-3) Facts on File.

— European History on File. 288p. 1997. ring bd. 165.00 (0-8160-3480-X) Facts on File.

***Diagram Group Staff.** Expanding World, 1500-1900: The Arts, 2. (Timelines on File Ser.). 249p. 2000. ring bd. 125.00 (0-8160-4305-1) Facts on File.

Diagram Group Staff. Family Fun & Games. LC 92-21169. (Illus.). 800p. 1994. pap. 19.95 (0-8069-8777-4) Sterling.

— A Field Guide to Dinosaurs: The First Complete Guide to Every Dinosaur Now Known. (Illus.). 256p. 1983. pap. 9.95 (0-380-83519-3, Avon Bks) Morrow Avon.

— Forms on File: 1998 Edition, 2 vols. 628p. 1998. ring bd. 195.00 (0-8160-3822-8) Facts on File.

— Funky, Freaky Facts Most People Don't Know. LC 98-136851. (Illus.). 192p. (J). 1998. 6.95 (0-8069-4288-6) Sterling.

— Genetics & Cellular Biology on File. LC 97-26287. 288p. 1997. ring bd. 165.00 (0-8160-3572-5) Facts on File.

— Historical Inventions on File. (On File Ser.). (Illus.). 288p. (J). (gr. 4-12). 1994. ring bd. 165.00 (0-8160-2911-3) Facts on File.

— Historical Science Experiments on File: Experiments, Demonstrations, & Projects for the School & Home. LC 92-37877. (Illus.). 288p. (J). (gr. 4-12). 1993. ring bd. 165.00 (0-8160-2806-0) Facts on File.

— Human Body on File: Anatomy. (Illus.). 300p. 1996. ring bd. 165.00 (0-8160-3527-X) Facts on File.

— Junior Science Experiments on File. LC 93-33381. (Illus.). 288p. (J). (gr. k-6). 1993. ring bd. 165.00 (0-8160-2921-0) Facts on File.

— Junior Science on File. (Illus.). 288p. (J). (gr. 4-6). 1991. ring bd. 165.00 (0-8160-2706-4) Facts on File.

— Lettering & Calligraphy Workbook. LC 98-3576. (Illus.). 288p. 1998. 14.95 (0-8069-4273-8) Sterling.

— Life Sciences on File. (Illus.). 304p. 1986. ring bd. 165.00 (0-8160-1284-9) Facts on File.

— Life Sciences on File. rev. ed. LC 98-55738. (Illus.). 302p. 1999. ring bd. 165.00 (0-8160-3872-4, Checkmark) Facts on File.

— The Little Giant Encyclopedia of Card & Magic Tricks. LC 96-25432. (Illus.). 512p. 1996. pap. 9.95 (0-8069-9347-2) Sterling.

— The Little Giant Encyclopedia of Card Games. LC 94-45496. (Illus.). 512p. 1995. pap. 9.95 (0-8069-1330-4) Sterling.

— The Little Giant Encyclopedia of Card Games Gift Set. 1995. pap. text 19.95 (0-8069-3815-3) Sterling.

— The Little Giant Encyclopedia of Gambling Games. LC 96-24655. (Illus.). 512p. 1996. pap. 9.95 (0-8069-8128-8) Sterling.

— Little Giant Encyclopedia of Games for One or Two. LC 98-14805. (Illus.). 512p. 1998. 9.95 (0-8069-0981-1) Sterling.

— The Little Giant Encyclopedia of Mazes. 1995. pap. text. write for info. (0-8069-3808-0) Sterling.

— The Little Giant Encyclopedia of Mazes. LC 98-141286. (Illus.). 512p. (J). 1997. 9.95 (0-8069-9724-9) Sterling.

— The Little Giant Encyclopedia of Natural Healing. LC 99-21691. (Little Giant Ser.). 512p. 1999. pap. 9.95 (0-8069-3948-6) Sterling.

— The Little Giant Encyclopedia of Puzzles. LC 95-43151. (Illus.). 512p. 1996. 9.95 (0-8069-4258-4) Sterling.

***Diagram Group Staff.** The Little Giant Encyclopedia of Spells & Magic. LC 99-36257. (Little Giant Ser.). 512p. 1999. pap. 9.95 (0-8069-1833-0) Sterling.

Diagram Group Staff. The Little Giant Encyclopedia of Superstitions. LC 99-22531. (Little Giant Ser.). 1999. pap. 9.95 (0-8069-6913-X) Sterling.

— The Little Giant Encyclopedia of the Zodiac. LC 96-48341. (Illus.). 512p. 1997. 9.95 (0-8069-9529-7) Sterling.

— The Little Giant Encyclopedia of Toasts & Quotes. (Illus.). 512p. 1998. pap. 9.95 (0-8069-6337-9) Sterling.

— The Little Giant Encyclopedia of Travel & Holiday Games. LC 96-48345. (Illus.). 512p. 1997. 9.95 (0-8069-9531-9) Sterling.

— The Macmillan Visual Desk Reference. (Illus.). 608p. 1993. 29.95 (0-02-531310-X) Macmillan.

— The Macmillan Visual Dictionary. (Illus.). 864p. 1992. 45.00 (0-02-528160-7) Macmillan.

***Diagram Group Staff.** Man's Body: An Owner's Manual, 1. rev. ed. LC 99-11777. 480p. 1999. pap. 16.95 (0-8092-2619-7, 261970, Contemporary Bks) NTC Contemp Pub Co.

Diagram Group Staff. Maps on File: 1998 Edition, 2 vols. (Illus.). 592p. 1998. ring bd. 195.00 (0-8160-3816-3) Facts on File.

— Maps on File Updates: 1998 Update. (Illus.). 1998. ring bd. 45.00 (0-8160-3817-1) Facts on File.

***Diagram Group Staff.** Marine Science on File. (On File Ser.). (Illus.). 288p. 2000. 165.00 (0-8160-4251-9) Facts on File.

Diagram Group Staff. Math on File. (Illus.). 288p. 1995. ring bd. 165.00 (0-8160-2936-9) Facts on File.

***Diagram Group Staff.** Nations & States, set of 4, 4. (Timelines on File Ser.). 249p. 2000. 125.00 (0-8160-4307-8) Facts on File.

Diagram Group Staff. Nations of Africa. LC 96-38734. (Peoples of Africa Ser.). (Illus.). 112p. (YA). (gr. 6-12). 1997. 19.95 (0-8160-3488-5) Facts on File.

— Nature Projects on File. (Illus.). 288p. (J). (gr. 4-12). 1992. ring bd. 165.00 (0-8160-2705-6) Facts on File.

— 1002 Ways to Waste Your Working Time. (Illus.). 256p. 1996. pap. 9.95 (0-312-14534-9) St Martin.

— Peoples of Africa Series, 6 vols. (Illus.). 672p. (YA). (gr. 6-12). 1997. 119.70 (0-8160-3482-6) Facts on File.

— Peoples of Central Africa. LC 96-38733. (Peoples of Africa Ser.). (Illus.). 112p. (YA). (gr. 8 up). 1997. 19.95 (0-8160-3486-9) Facts on File.

— Peoples of East Africa. LC 96-38735. (Peoples of Africa Ser.). (Illus.). (YA). (gr. 6-12). 1997. 19.95 (0-8160-3484-2) Facts on File.

— Peoples of Northern Africa. LC 96-41273. (Peoples of Africa Ser.). (Illus.). 112p. (YA). (gr. 8 up). 1997. 19.95 (0-8160-3483-4) Facts on File.

— Peoples of Southern Africa. LC 96-38736. (Peoples of Africa Ser.). (Illus.). (YA). (gr. 6-12). 1997. 19.95 (0-8160-3487-7) Facts on File.

— Peoples of West Africa. LC 96-38737. (Peoples of Africa Ser.). (Illus.). (YA). (gr. 6-12). 1997. 19.95 (0-8160-3485-0) Facts on File.

— Personal Forms on File: 1998 Edition. 314p. 1998. ring bd. 125.00 (0-8160-3818-X) Facts on File.

— Personal Forms on File: 1998 Update. 1998. ring bd. 45.00 (0-8160-3819-8) Facts on File.

— Physical Sciences on File. (Illus.). 300p. 1989. ring bd. 165.00 (0-8160-2068-X) Facts on File.

— Predicting Your Future. 128p. 1985. pap. 10.00 (0-345-33579-1) Ballantine Pub Grp.

— Religions on File. (Illus.). 200p. 1990. ring bd. 165.00 (0-8160-2224-0) Facts on File.

***Diagram Group Staff.** Rule Book. 1999. pap. 23.70 (0-8335-3794-6) Econo-Clad Bks.

Diagram Group Staff. Rules of the Game: The Complete Illustrated Encyclopedia of all the Sports of the World. 3rd ed. 1994. pap. 17.95 (0-312-11940-2) St Martin.

— Running Press Cyclopedia: The Portable Visual Encyclopedia. 2nd ed. (Illus.). 640p. 1995. pap. 9.95 (1-56138-661-8) Running Pr.

— Sex: A User's Manual. 352p. 1985. reprint ed. mass mkt. 6.99 (0-425-08972-X) Berkley Pub.

***Diagram Group Staff.** Sports Rules on File. LC 00-37137. (Illus.). 288p. 2000. ring bd. write for info. (0-8160-4117-2, Checkmark) Facts on File.

Diagram Group Staff. Timelines on File. 300p. 1988. ring bd. 165.00 (0-8160-1897-9) Facts on File.

***Diagram Group Staff.** Twentieth Century. (Timelines on File Ser.). 2000. 125.00 (0-8160-4306-X, Checkmark) Facts on File.

Diagram Group Staff. Weapons: An International Encyclopedia from 5000 B.C. to 2000 A.D. 6th ed. (Illus.). 336p. (Orig.). 1991. pap. 21.95 (0-312-03950-6) St Martin.

***Diagram Group Staff.** Weather & Climate on File. (On File Ser.). (Illus.). 2000. 165.00 (0-8160-4396-5) Facts on File.

— Woman's Body: An Owner's Manual, 1. rev. ed. LC 99-12092. 480p. 1999. pap. text 16.95 (0-8092-2618-9, 261890) NTC Contemp Pub Co.

Diagram Group Staff & Riches, Catherine. Physical Sciences on File. rev. ed. LC 98-55737. (Illus.). 318p. 1999. ring bd. 165.00 (0-8160-3874-0, Checkmark) Facts on File.

Diagram Group Staff, jt. auth. see Lambert, David.

Diagram Group Staff, jt. auth. see Sterling Publishing Staff.

***Diagram Staff.** Body Language. (Collins Gem Ser.). (Illus.). 256p. 2000. pap. 7.95 (0-00-472307-4, Pub. by HarpC) Trafalgar.

— Card Games. rev. ed. (Collins Gem Ser.). (Illus.). 256p. 2000. pap. 7.95 (0-00-472317-1, Pub. by HarpC) Trafalgar.

— Collins Gem Weddings. (Illus.). 1999. 7.95 (0-00-472336-8, Pub. by HarpC) Trafalgar.

***Diagram Visual Information Ltd. Staff.** Encyclopedia of African Peoples. LC 99-55125. (Illus.). 400p. 2000. 55.00 (0-8160-4099-0) Facts on File.

Diakhate, Ousmane, et al, eds. World Encyclopedia of Contemporary Theatre Vol. 3: Africa. (Illus.). 448p. (C). 1997. 160.00 (0-415-05931-3, B0384) Routledge.

Diakite, Baba W. The Hunterman & the Crocodile: A West African Folktale. (J). (gr. 4-7). 1997. 15.95 (0-614-25385-3) Scholastic Inc.

— The Hunterman & the Crocodile: A West African Folktale. LC 95-25975. (Illus.). 32p. (J). (ps-2). 1997. 15.95 (0-590-89828-0) Scholastic Inc.

Diakite, Baba W. Crocodile Tears. Date not set. write for info. (0-614-10316-9) Scholastic Inc.

— The Hatseller & the Monkeys. LC 98-16250. 32p. (J). (ps-2). 1999. 15.95 (0-590-96069-5) Scholastic Inc.

Diakite, Madubuko. Film, Culture, & the Black Filmmaker. Jowett, Garth S., ed. LC 79-6679. (Dissertations on Film, 1980 Ser.). 1980. lib. bdg. 24.95 (0-405-12907-6) Ayer.

Diakite, Soumaila, tr. see Conrad, David C., ed.

Diakonoff, I. M., ed. Early Antiquity. Kirjanov, Alexander, tr. (Illus.). 486p. 1991. 57.00 (0-226-14465-8) U Ch Pr.

Diakonoff, Igor M. The Paths of History. LC 98-30994. 400p. 1999. pap. 19.95 (0-521-64398-8) Cambridge U Pr.

***Diakonoff, Igor M.** The Paths of History. LC 98-30994. 400p. 1999. 54.95 (0-521-64348-1) Cambridge U Pr.

Diakonov, D., jt. ed. see Di Giacomo, A.

Diakonov, I. M. & Neroznak, V. P. Phrygian. LC 85-453. (Anatolian & Caucasian Studies). 176p. 1986. 50.00 (0-88206-042-2) Caravan Bks.

Diakonov, Sergei, jt. auth. see Harris, Godfrey.

D'Iakov, Vladimir A., jt. ed. see Bromlei, Iulian V.

Diakun, Nadia O., ed. Ucrainica at the University of Toronto Library: A Catalogue of Holdings, 2 vols. 1845p. 1985. text 90.00 (0-8020-3430-6) U of Toronto Pr.

Dial. Guide to College Writing. 3rd ed. (Illus.). 1999. text 12.25 (0-07-236901-9) McGraw.

Dial-a-Fax Directories Corp. Staff. Dial-a-Fax Directory: The Fax Phone Book. LC 87-656600. (Illus.). 1500p. 1991. reprint ed. pap. 94.00 (0-945622-00-7) Dial-A-Fax.

Dial, Adolph L. & Eliades, David K. The Only Land I Know: A History of the Lumbee Indians. (Illus.). 188p. (Orig.). 1995. pap. 17.95 (0-8156-0360-6) Syracuse U Pr.

Dial, Esther F., ed. see Fuller, Gerald R.

Dial, Lanyard K. & American Academy of Family Physicians Staff. Conditions of Aging in the Academy Collection: Quick Reference Guides for Family Physicians. LC 98-22643. (Academy Collection). 179p. 1998. pap. 29.95 (0-683-30421-6) Lppncott W & W.

Dial, Micah, jt. ed. see Stevens, Carla J.

Dial, Scott D. Silver Insights. (Illus.). 105p. (Orig.). 1982. reprint ed. pap. 25.00 (0-912497-00-9) Silver D Invest Inc.

Dial, Sharon. Just Four Ingredients: Cookbook. (Illus.). 254p. 1998. 14.95 (0-9664509-0-6) Four Color Graphics.

Dialdin, Ali M., ed. see Pledge, Thomas A.

Diallo, Abdoulaye. Probleme und Chancen der Integration Westafrikas: Analyse und Evaluierung der Integrationsansatze Westafrikas von der Vorkolonialzeit bis zur Gegenwart. (Europaische Hochschulschriften: Reihe 5: Bd. 2038). (GER., Illus.). 311p. 1996. pap. 57.95 (3-631-31096-X) P Lang Pubng.

***Diallo, Abdourahmane.** Grammaire descriptive du pular du Fuuta Jaloo, Guinee. 2000. 47.95 (3-631-34701-4) P Lang Pubng.

Diallo, Garba. Mauritania - The Other Apartheid? (Current African Issues Ser.: No. 16). 57p. 1993. 4.95 (91-7106-339-0, Pub. by Nordic Africa) Transaction Pubs.

Diallo, Ibrahima K. My Father's Assassins. 1997. pap. 10.95 (0-533-12369-0) Vantage.

Diallo, Yaya & Hall, Mitchell. The Healing Drum: African Wisdom Teachings. 222p. 1989. pap. 14.95 (0-89281-256-7, Destiny Bks) Inner Tradit.

Dialogos International Staff, ed. see Lozoff, Bo.

Diaman, N. A. Castro Street Memories. LC 88-2503. 206p. (Orig.). 1988. pap. 14.95 (0-931906-05-9, Persona Pr) Persona Prod.

— Ed Dean Is Queer. 2nd ed. LC 78-57153. (Illus.). 175p. 1981. pap. 7.95 (0-931906-02-4, Persona Pr) Persona Prod.

— Private Nation. LC 97-114803. 128p. (Orig.). 1997. pap. 10.95 (0-931906-08-3, Persona Pr) Persona Prod.

— Reunion. LC 83-4051. (Illus.). 164p. (Orig.). 1983. pap. 8.95 (0-931906-04-0, Persona Pr) Persona Prod.

— Second Crossing. LC 82-7564. (Illus.). 240p. (Orig.). 1982. pap. 9.95 (0-931906-03-2, Persona Pr) Persona Prod.

Diamand, Salim. Dottore... Internment in Italy, 1940-1945. (Illus.). 140p. 1995. pap. 12.95 (0-88962-369-4) Mosaic.

Diamandis, Eleftherios P. & Christopoulos, Theodore K., eds. Immunoassay. LC 97-1262. (Illus.). 579p. 1996. pap. text 69.95 (0-12-214730-8) Acad Pr.

D

An Asterisk (*) at the beginning of an entry indicates that the title is appearing for the first time.

***Diamandouros, Nikiforos P. & Gunther, Richard.** Parties, Politics & Democracy in the New Southern Europe. Social Science Research Council Staff & American Council of Learned Societies, eds. LC 00-8848. 2001. pap. write for info. (*0-8018-6518-2*) Johns Hopkins.

***Diamant.** The New Jewish Wedding. 2001. write for info. (*0-7432-0255-4*) S&S Trade.

Diamant, Alfred. Austrian Catholics & the First Republic: Democracy, Capitalism, & the Social Order, 1918-1934. LC 60-5745. 337p. reprint ed. pap. 104.50 (*0-8357-5896-6*, 201522600095) Bks Demand.

— Austrian Catholics & the Social Question, 1918-1933. LC 59-62692. (University of Florida Monographs: Social Sciences: No. 2). 88p. reprint ed. pap. 30.00 (*0-7837-4992-9*, 204465900004) Bks Demand.

Diamant, Anita. Bible Baby Names: Spiritual Choices from Judeo-Christian Tradition. LC 96-25012. 144p. (Orig.). 1996. pap. 9.95 (*1-879045-62-1*) Jewish Lights.

— Choosing a Jewish Life. 1998. pap. 14.00 (*0-8052-1095-4*) Schocken.

— The New Jewish Baby Book: Names, Ceremonies & Customs - A Guide for Today's Families. LC 93-25870. 336p. (Orig.). 1994. pap. 16.95 (*1-879045-28-1*) Jewish Lights.

— The New Jewish Wedding. (Illus.). 272p. 1986. per. 12.00 (*0-671-62882-8*) S&S Trade Pap.

***Diamant, Anita.** The Red Tent. LC 00-30727. 2000. write for info. (*1-56895-897-8*) Wheeler Pub.

Diamant, Anita. The Red Tent. 5th ed. LC 98-30122. 321p. 1998. pap. 14.00 (*0-312-19551-6*, Picador USA) St Martin.

— Saying Kaddish: How to Comfort the Dying, Bury the Dead. LC 98-16646. 288p. 1998. 23.00 (*0-8052-4149-3*) Schocken.

***Diamant, Anita.** Saying Kaddish: How to Comfort the Dying, Bury the Dead & Mourn as a Jew. 288p. 1999. pap. 13.00 (*0-8052-1088-1*) Schocken.

Diamant, Anita & Cooper, Howard. Living a Jewish Life: Jewish Traditions, Customs & Values for Today's Families. LC 96-18370. 352p. 1996. pap. 15.00 (*0-06-273443-1*) HarpC.

***Diamant, Anita & Kushner, Karen.** How to Be a Jewish Parent: A Practical Handbook for Family Life. LC 00-26574. 352p. 2000. 26.00 (*0-8052-4170-1*); pap. 15.00 (*0-8052-1116-0*) Schocken.

Diamant, B., ed. see Collegium Internationale Allergologicum Symposium.

Diamant, E., et al, eds. Surveys of Research in Transportation Technology: Presented at the Winter Annual Meeting of the ASME, November 11-15, 1973. LC 73-90322. (American Society of Mechanical Engineers, Applied Mechanics Division Ser.: Vol. 5). (Illus.). 182p. reprint ed. pap. 56.50 (*0-608-11112-0*, 201680800005) Bks Demand.

Diamant, Lincoln. Bernard Romans: Forgotten Patriot of the American Revolution, Military Engineer & Cartographer of West Point & the Hudson Valley. LC 85-5421. (Illus.). 160p. 1985. 9.95 (*0-916346-56-0*) Harbor Hill Bks.

— Broadcast Communications Dictionary. 3rd ed. (Illus.). 256p. 1994. pap. 27.95 (*0-8442-3325-0*, Natl Textbk Co) NTC Contemp Pub Co.

— Chaining the Hudson: The Fight for the River in the American Revolution. 1989. 21.95 (*0-8184-0502-3*) Carol Pub Group.

— Yankee Doodle Days: Exploring the American Revolution. LC 96-17054. 179p. 1996. 25.00 (*0-935796-73-8*) Purple Mnt Pr.

Diamant, Lincoln, ed. The Broadcast Communications Dictionary. 3rd rev. ed. LC 88-25093. 266p. 1989. lib. bdg. 57.95 (*0-313-26502-X*, DBD/, Greenwood Pr) Greenwood.

— Revolutionary Women in the War for American Independence: A One-Volume Revised Edition of Elizabeth Ellet's 1848 Landmark Series. rev. ed. LC 98-5391. 240p. 1998. 35.00 (*0-275-96263-6*, Praeger Pubs) Greenwood.

Diamant, Lincoln, jt. auth. see Davidson, Charles.

Diamant, Lincoln, jt. auth. see Davidson, Charles S.

Diamant, Louis. Homosexual Issues in the Workplace. 1993. 44.95 (*1-56032-038-9*) Hemisp Pub.

— Male & Female Homosexuality: Psychological Approaches. (Clinical & Community Psychology Ser.). 292p. 1987. 63.95 (*0-89116-449-9*) Hemisp Pub.

— Mind-Body Maturity: Psychological Approaches to Sports, Exercise, & Fitness. 304p. 1991. 79.95 (*0-89116-892-3*) Hemisp Pub.

— Psychology of Sports, Exercise, & Fitness: Social & Adjustmental Issues. 256p. 1991. 79.95 (*1-56032-170-9*) Hemisp Pub.

Diamant, Louis & McAnulty, Richard D., eds. The Psychology of Sexual Orientation, Behavior, & Identity: A Handbook. LC 95-7512. 544p. 1995. lib. bdg. 119.50 (*0-313-28501-2*, Greenwood Pr) Greenwood.

Diamant, Neil Jeffrey. Revolutionizing the Family: Politics, Love & Divorce in Urban & Rural China, 1949-1968. LC 99-32304. 502p. 2000. 55.00 (*0-520-21720-9*, Pub. by U CA Pr) Cal Prin Full Svc.

Diamant, R. M. Total Energy. 1970. 190.00 (*0-08-006918-5*, Pub. by Pergamon Repr) Franklin.

Diamant, Rolf, et al. A Citizen's Guide to River Conservation. LC 84-7799. (Illus.). 125p. (Orig.). reprint ed. pap. 38.80 (*0-7837-1210-3*, 204174200023) Bks Demand.

Diamant, Zuzana, jt. ed. see Yeadon, Michael.

Diamantaras, Kostas. Principal Component Neural Networks: Theory & Applications. LC 95-242. (Adaptive & Learning Systems for Signal Processing, Communications & Control Ser.). 272p. 1996. 84.95 (*0-471-05436-4*) Wiley.

Diamantes. Fire Prevention: Inspection & Code Enforcement. 104p. 1997. pap. text, teacher ed. 15.95 (*0-8273-8413-0*) Delmar.

Diamantes, David. Fire Prevention: Inspection & Code Enforcement. LC 97-26378. 304p. 1997. mass mkt. 42.95 (*0-8273-8412-2*) Delmar.

Diamantes, Kitty. Favorite Tales from Grimm. 96p. (J). (gr. 3 up). 1988. 9.95 (*0-02-689060-7*) Checkerboard.

Diamanti, J., tr. see Lebovici, Serge & Widlocher, K., eds.

Diamanti, Joyce, tr. see Chauvin, Remy.

Diamanti, Joyce, tr. see Decarie, Therese G., et al.

Diamanti, Joyce, tr. see Droz, R. & Rahmy, M.

Diamantopolous, Costas, jt. auth. see Baxter, G. David.

Diamantopoulos. Taking the Fear Out of Data Analysis. 1998. pap. 18.99 (*1-86152-430-7*) Thomson Learn.

Diamantopoulos, A. Managing Pricing Decisions: Study of Managerial Practices. 168p. 1994. mass mkt. 47.00 (*0-412-49240-7*, Chap & Hall NY) Chapman & Hall.

DiAMAR Staff, jt. auth. see Peterson, Bryan.

Diambrini-Palazzi, G. Phenomenology of Unification from Present to Future. (High Energy Physics Conference Proceedings Ser.). 1998. 78.00 (*981-02-3591-7*) World Scientific Pub.

Diambrini-Palazzi, G., jt. auth. see Cosmelli, C.

Diament. Dynamic Electromagnetics. LC 99-55286. 1999. text 68.25 (*0-02-328760-8*) P-H.

Diament, Carol. Zionism: The Sequel. LC 98-35844. 1998. write for info. (*1-889525-06-5*) WZO.

Diament, Carol, ed. Jewish Women Living the Challenge: A Hadassah Compendium. LC 98-101606. 280p. (Orig.). 1997. pap. 20.00 (*1-889525-04-9*) WZO.

***Diament, Carol, ed.** Moonbeams: A Hadassah Rosh Hodesh Guide. 2000. pap. 20.00 (*1-58023-099-7*) Jewish Lights.

Diament, Carol, ed. Zionism: The Sequel. LC 98-35844. 504p. 1998. pap. 25.00 (*1-889525-05-7*) WZO.

Diament, Carol & Rattok, Lily, eds. Ribcage: Israeli Women's Fiction. xxxiv, 281p. (Orig.). 1994. pap. 15.00 (*1-889525-01-4*) WZO.

Diament, Carol, ed. see Furstenberg, Rochelle.

Diament, Carol, ed. see Rothenberg, Naftali, et al.

Diament, Carol, ed. see Tanenbaum, Leora, et al.

Diament, Nic. Dictionnaire des Ecrivains Francais pour la Jeunesse 1914-1991. (FRE.). 783p. 1993. 325.00 (*0-7859-7767-8*, 2211071252) Fr & Eur.

Diamon, Irving L., ed. see Nordenskiold, Gustaf E.

Diamond. Fashion Advertising & Promotion. (Fashion Merchandising Ser.). 32p. 1996. teacher ed. 10.00 (*0-8273-5627-7*, VNR) Wiley.

— Financial Accounting. 4th ed. (AM - Financial Accounting Ser.). 1995. mass mkt., student ed. 25.95 (*0-538-85408-1*) S-W Pub.

— Financial Accounting - Working Papers. 3rd ed. (AB - Accounting Principles Ser.). (C). 1993. mass mkt., wbk. ed. 22.50 (*0-538-82269-4*) S-W Pub.

— Financial Accounting Study Guide. 3rd ed. (AB - Accounting Principles Ser.). (C). 1993. mass mkt., student ed. 18.75 (*0-538-82268-6*) S-W Pub.

— Financial Accounting, Working Papers. 4th ed. (AB - Accounting Principles Ser.). (C). 1995. mass mkt. 26.95 (*0-538-84074-9*) S-W Pub.

***Diamond.** Headache Relief. 240p. 2000. 7.98 (*1-56731-388-4*, MJF Bks) Fine Comms.

Diamond. MCQ Tutor for Principles & Practice of Surgery. 1996. pap. text 21.00 (*0-443-05192-5*) Harcourt.

— Prefrontal Cortex. 220p. 1997. pap. text 15.00 (*0-226-14477-1*) U Ch Pr.

— Retail Buying. 5th ed. 1997. pap. text, teacher ed. write for info. (*0-13-659939-7*) P-H.

Diamond. Retailing. 6th ed. 1996. text 100.00 (*0-13-448838-5*) P-H.

Diamond. Twenty-Four Hour Trading: Network of Futures & Options Markets. LC 88-29980. 304p. 1989. 29.95 (*0-471-60072-5*) Wiley.

***Diamond & Blatt, eds.** Attachment Research & Psychoanalysis Pt. I: Theoretical Considerations. (Psychoanalytic Inquiry Ser.: Vol. 19, No. 4). 1999. pap. 20.00 (*0-88163-923-0*) Analytic Pr.

— Attachment Research & Psychoanalysis Pt. 2: Clinical Implications. (Psychoanalytic Inquiry Ser.: Vol. 19, No. 5). 1999. pap. 20.00 (*0-88163-922-2*) Analytic Pr.

Diamond & Flamholtz & Flamholtz. Financial Accounting Working Papers. 2nd ed. (Swc-Accounting). 1992. mass mkt. 22.50 (*0-538-82320-8*) S-W Pub.

— Financial Accounting, '89 Toys R Us Annual Report. 2nd ed. (Swc-Accounting). Date not set. 11.75 (*0-538-82326-7*) S-W Pub.

Diamond & Stice, James D. Financial Accounting. 5th ed. LC 98-43554. (SWC-Accounting). 1999. pap. 101.95 (*0-538-87301-9*) S-W Pub.

***Diamond, et al.** Literacies: Reading, Writing, Interpretation. 2nd ed. LC 99-48832. 2000. pap. text 26.00 (*0-393-97537-1*) Norton.

Diamond, jt. ed. see Applebaum.

Diamond & Diamond Staff. The World of Fashion. 61p. 1997. teacher ed. 3.50 (*1-56367-076-3*) Fairchild.

Diamond, A. J. & Donald Schmitt & Company Staff. Works: The Architecture of A. J. Diamond, Donald Schmitt & Company, 1968-1995. Carter, Brian, ed. (Documents in Canadian Architecture Ser.). (Illus.). 148p. 1996. pap. 26.95 (*0-929112-31-8*, Pub. by Tuns Pr) Baker & Taylor.

Diamond, A. L. Commercial & Consumer Credit - An Introduction. 1982. pap. 42.00 (*0-406-57405-7*, UK, MICHIE) LEXIS Pub.

Diamond, A. R. Pete. The Confessions of Jeremiah in Context: Scenes of Prophetic Drama. (JSOT Supplement Ser.: No. 45). 308p. 1987. 85.00 (*1-85075-032-7*, Pub. by Sheffield Acad); pap. 28.50 (*1-85075-033-5*, Pub. by Sheffield Acad) CUP Services.

***Diamond, A. R. Pete, et al, eds.** Troubling Jeremiah. LC 99-488648. (Journal for the Study of the Old Testament Supplement Ser.: No. 260). 464p. 1999. 85.00 (*1-85075-910-3*, Pub. by Sheffield Acad) CUP Services.

Diamond, A. S. Primitive Law. x, 451p. 1998. reprint ed. 135.00 (*1-56169-410-X*, 15576) Gaunt.

Diamond, A. W. & Filion, F. L., eds. The Value of Birds. 280p. 1987. pap. 27.95 (*1-56098-432-5*) Smithsonian.

Diamond, A. W., jt. auth. see Coniam, S. W.

***Diamond Aircraft Industries Staff.** Katana DA20-C1 Flight Manual: Diamond Aircraft Industries, Flight Information Manual. (Illus.). 180p. 1999. spiral bd. 19.95 (*1-56027-383-6*) ASA Inc.

Diamond Aircraft Staff. Katana DA20-A1 Information Manual: #ASA-DA20A-FIM. (Illus.). 100p. 1998. reprint ed. spiral bd. 19.95 (*1-56027-322-4*, ASA-DA20A-FIM) ASA Inc.

Diamond, Andrew & Coniam, Stephen. The Management of Chronic Pain. 2nd ed. LC 96-30136. (Illus.). 190p. (C). 1997. text 59.50 (*0-19-262695-7*) OUP.

Diamond, Ann. Evil Eye. Leith, Linda, ed. 132p. 1994. pap. 12.95 (*1-55065-043-2*, Pub. by Vehicule Pr) Genl Dist Srvs.

Diamond, Anna. The Temari Book: Techniques & Patterns for Making Japanese Thread Balls. LaFerla, Jane, ed. LC 99-21155. (Illus.). 128p. 1999. 21.95 (*1-57990-024-0*) Lark Books.

Diamond, Arlyn & Edwards, Lee R., eds. The Authority of Experience: Essays in Feminist Criticism. LC 88-1071. 320p. (C). 1988. pap. 18.95 (*0-87023-622-9*) U of Mass Pr.

Diamond, Arthur. Alcoholism. LC 92-23601. (Overview Ser.). (Illus.). 112p. (J). (gr. 5-8). 1992. lib. bdg. 22.45 (*1-56006-136-7*) Lucent Bks.

— Charlie Chaplin. LC 94-23272. (Importance of...Ser.). 112p. (J). 1995. lib. bdg. 22.45 (*1-56006-064-6*) Lucent Bks.

— Egypt: Gift of the Nile. LC 91-43105. (Discovering Our Heritage Ser.). (Illus.). 128p. (J). (gr. 4 up). 1992. text 14.95 (*0-87518-511-8*, Dillon Silver Burdett) Silver Burdett Pr.

— Prince Hall: Social Reformer. Huggins, Nathan I., ed. (Black Americans of Achievement Ser.). (Illus.). 124p. (YA). (gr. 5 up). 1992. lib. bdg. 19.95 (*1-55546-588-9*) Chelsea Hse.

Diamond, Arthur S. The Evolution of Law & Order. LC 72-9372. 342p. 1973. reprint ed. lib. bdg. 69.50 (*0-8371-6580-6*, DIEL, Greenwood Pr) Greenwood.

Diamond, Arthur S., ed. Handbook of Imaging Materials. (Illus.). 648p. 1991. text 255.00 (*0-8247-8451-0*) Dekker.

Diamond, Barbara J. Multicultural Literacy. 2nd ed. (C). 1998. pap. text. write for info. (*0-8013-1862-9*) Addison-Wesley.

Diamond, Barbara J. & Moore, Margaret A. Multicultural Literacy: Mirroring the New Reality of the Classroom. 380p. (C). 1994. pap. 60.00 (*0-8013-1141-1*) Longman.

— Multicultural Literacy: Mirroring the Reality of the Classroom. 2nd ed. LC 94-27767. (C). 1995. write for info. (*0-8013-1411-9*) Longman.

Diamond, Bernard. Odyssey of Revenge. 204p. 1983. pap. 10.95 (*0-914366-21-1*) Columbia Pub.

Diamond, Beverley, et al. Visions of Sound: Musical Instruments of First Nations Communities in Northeastern America. (Illus.). 1994. cd-rom 60.00 (*0-88920-246-X*) W Laurier U Pr.

Diamond, Beverley, jt. auth. see Moisala, Pirkko.

Diamond, Beverly, et al. Visions of Sound: Musical Instruments of First Nations Communities in Northeastern America. LC 94-10337. (Chicago Studies in Ethnomusicology). (Illus.). 240p. 1995. pap. 19.95 (*0-226-14476-3*); lib. bdg. 47.50 (*0-226-14475-5*) U Ch Pr.

Diamond, C. T., jt. ed. see Mullen, Carol A.

Diamond, Carlin J. Love It, Don't Label It: A Practical Guide for Using Spiritual Principles in Everyday Life. Peterson, Kim, ed. (Illus.). 200p. (Orig.). 1986. pap. 10.00 (*0-911761-03-9*) Fifth Wave Pr.

Diamond, Christine & Moriarty, Andrea. Kids Take New York. 2nd ed. LC 98-149359. (Illus.). 260p. 1999. pap. 15.95 (*0-9660893-1-6*, Pub. by Book Happy Bks) IPG Chicago.

Diamond, Christine, jt. auth. see Moriarty, Andrea.

Diamond, Cora. Realistic Spirit: Wittgenstein, Philosophy & the Mind. 1995. pap. text 20.00 (*0-262-54074-6*, Bradford Bks) MIT Pr.

Diamond, Cora, ed. see Wittgenstein, Ludwig Josef Johann.

Diamond, D. Kaddish Violin Cello & Orchestra Piano Reduction. 24p. 1992. pap. 14.95 (*0-7935-1385-5*) H Leonard.

Diamond, D. R., jt. auth. see Sasson, Helen.

***Diamond, Dan.** Hockey Rules! The Official, Illustrated Kids' Guide to NHL Rules & Fundamentals. (Illus.). (J). 2000. pap. 6.99 (*1-58184-101-9*) Somerville Hse.

Diamond, Dan. NHL Official Guide & Record Book: 1999-2000 Edition. 544p. 1999. 21.95 (*1-892129-11-6*) Total Sprts.

— The Official NHL Rule Book, 1994-95. 1994. pap. 9.95 (*0-7710-2820-2*) McCland & Stewart.

***Diamond, Dan.** Total Stanley Cup: An Official Publication of the National Hockey League. (Illus.). 2000. pap. 12.95 (*1-892129-07-8*) Total Sprts.

Diamond, Dan, ed. The Official NHL 1980s Quiz Book. (Illus.). 128p. (Orig.). 1993. pap. 9.95 (*0-7710-0067-7*) McCland & Stewart.

— The Official NHL 1970s Quiz Book. 128p. 1994. pap. 9.95 (*0-7710-2812-1*) McCland & Stewart.

— The Official NHL Philadelphia Flyers Quiz Book. 112p. 1994. pap. 9.95 (*0-7710-2811-3*) McCland & Stewart.

— The Official NHL Toronto Maple Leafs Quiz Book. (Illus.). 128p. 1993. pap. 9.95 (*0-7710-0166-5*) McCland & Stewart.

— The Spirit of the Game: Exceptional Photographs from the Hockey Hall of Fame. (Illus.). 240p. 1996. 34.95 (*1-57243-096-6*) Triumph Bks.

— Years of Glory, 1942-1967: The National Hockey League's Official Book of the Six-Team Era. (Illus.). 256p. 1994. text 40.00 (*0-7710-2817-2*) McCland & Stewart.

***Diamond, Dan, et al, eds.** Total Hockey: The Official Encyclopedia of the National Hockey League. 2nd ed. LC 00-101619. (Illus.). 1800p. 2000. 54.95 (*1-892129-85-X*) Total Sprts.

***Diamond, Dan.** NHL Official Guide & Record Book, 2001: New & Revised for the 2000-01 Season. 608p. 2000. pap. 23.95 (*1-892129-46-9*) Total Sprts.

Diamond, Dan, ed. see Duplacey, James.

Diamond, Dan, ed. see Gretzky, Wayne & Davidson, John.

Diamond, Dan, ed. see Smith, Beverley.

Diamond, Dan, ed. see Smith, Beverly.

Diamond, Daniel E., ed. Contemporary Challenges: American Business in a Global Economy. LC 94-44880. (Joseph I. Lubin Memorial Lectures: Vol. 7). (Illus.). 152p. (C). 1995. text 18.00 (*0-8147-1868-X*) NYU Pr.

Diamond, David, rev. The Bulfinch Pocket Dictionary of Art Terms. 3rd rev. ed. (Illus.). 144p. 1992. pap. 10.95 (*0-8212-1905-7*, Pub. by Bulfinch Pr) Little.

Diamond, David & Berliner, Terry. The Stage Director's Handbook. LC 98-16284. 200p. 1998. pap. 16.95 (*1-55936-150-6*) Theatre Comm.

Diamond, Denise. The Complete Book of Flowers. 2nd ed. LC 90-32744. (Illus.). 312p. 1990. pap. 16.95 (*1-55643-079-5*) North Atlantic.

Diamond, Dermot, ed. Principles of Chemical & Biological Sensors. LC 97-31765. (Chemical Analysis). 368p. 1998. 98.95 (*0-471-54619-4*, Wiley-Interscience) Wiley.

Diamond, Dermot & Hanratty, Venita C. Spreadsheet Applications in Chemistry Using Microsoft Excel. LC 96-26223. 256p. 1997. pap. text 44.95 incl. disk (*0-471-14087-2*, Wiley-Interscience) Wiley.

***Diamond, Diana.** The Trophy Wife. 261p. 2000. 23.95 (*0-312-20600-3*) St Martin.

***Diamond, Diana & Wrye, Harriet K., eds.** Projections of Psychic Reality: A Centennial of Film & Psychoanalysis. (Psychoanalytic Inquiry Ser.: Vol. 18, No. 2). 1998. pap. 20.00 (*0-88163-931-1*) Analytic Pr.

Diamond, Diana, jt. auth. see Doane, Jeri A.

Diamond, Dickson. Don't Complain, You Picked Him! Boucke, Laurie & Carlson, Linda, eds. LC 97-2095. 1997. pap. 12.50 (*1-888580-03-8*) White-Boucke.

Diamond, Donald R., ed. Progress in Planning, Vol. 20. (Illus.). 260p. 1984. 66.00 (*0-08-031490-2*, Pergamon Pr) Elsevier.

— Progress in Planning, Vol. 23. (Illus.). 260p. 1985. 66.00 (*0-08-033213-7*, Pub. by PPL) Elsevier.

Diamond, Donald R. & McLoughlin, J. B. Progress in Planning, Vol. 13, (complete) (Illus.). 174p. 1981. 68.00 (*0-08-028398-5*, Pergamon Pr) Elsevier.

Diamond, Donald R. & McLoughlin, J. B., eds. Progress in Planning, Vol. 9. 300p. 1979. 61.00 (*0-08-025221-4*, Pergamon Pr) Elsevier.

— Progress in Planning, Vol. 10. (Illus.). 247p. 1980. 61.00 (*0-08-025788-7*, Pergamon Pr) Elsevier.

— Progress in Planning, Vol. 11. (Illus.). 280p. 1980. 61.00 (*0-08-025802-6*, Pergamon Pr) Elsevier.

— Progress in Planning, Vol. 12. 224p. 1980. 61.00 (*0-08-026100-0*, Pergamon Pr) Elsevier.

— Progress in Planning, Vol. 17. 268p. 1982. 68.00 (*0-08-029701-3*, Pergamon Pr) Elsevier.

— Progress in Planning, Vol. 18. (Illus.). 384p. 1983. 66.00 (*0-08-030415-X*, Pergamon Pr) Elsevier.

— Progress in Planning, Vol. 19. (Illus.). 280p. 1983. 66.00 (*0-08-031035-4*, Pergamon Pr) Elsevier.

— Progress in Planning, Vol. 21. (Illus.). 230p. 1985. 66.00 (*0-08-032325-1*, Pergamon Pr) Elsevier.

— Progress in Planning, Vol. 22. LC 73-66. (Illus.). 266p. 1985. 66.00 (*0-08-033206-4*, Pub. by PPL) Elsevier.

— Progress in Planning, Vol. 24. (Illus.). 250p. 1986. 60.00 (*0-08-034144-6*, Pub. by PPL) Elsevier.

Diamond, Dorothy B., jt. auth. see Diamond, Walter H.

Diamond, Drew C. "QRP Projects from Down Under" Radio Projects for the Amateur. 2nd ed. (Illus.). 136p. 1998. reprint ed. pap. 19.95 (*1-891237-22-5*, MFJ-3510) MFJ Ent.

Diamond, Edwin. Behind the Times: Inside the New "New York Times" vi, 450p. 1995. pap. 16.95 (*0-226-14472-0*) U Ch Pr.

— Good News, Bad News. 1978. 25.00 (*0-262-04057-3*) MIT Pr.

— Good News, Bad News. 1980. pap. text 6.95 (*0-262-54035-5*) MIT Pr.

— The Media Show: The Changing Face of the News, 1985-1990. (Illus.). 244p. 1991. 27.50 (*0-262-04125-1*) MIT Pr.

— Sign off: The Last Days of Television. 288p. 1982. 27.50 (*0-262-04069-7*) MIT Pr.

— Sign off: The Last Days of Television. 288p. 1983. pap. text 9.95 (*0-262-54039-8*) MIT Pr.

Diamond, Edwin & Bates, Stephen. The Spot: The Rise of Political Advertising on Television. 3rd ed. (Illus.). 432p. 1992. pap. text 18.50 (*0-262-54065-7*) MIT Pr.

— The Spot: The Rise of Political Advertising on Television. 3rd ed. (Illus.). 432p. 1992. 37.00 (*0-262-04130-8*) MIT Pr.

Diamond, Edwin & Silverman, Robert A. White House to Your House: Media & Politics in Virtual America. (Illus.). 202p. 1997. reprint ed. pap. text 14.00 (*0-262-54086-X*) MIT Pr.

Diamond, Elin. Pinter's Comic Play. LC 84-45230. (Illus.). 248p. 1985. 37.50 (*0-8387-5068-0*) Bucknell U Pr.

D

— Unmaking Mimesis: Essays on Feminism & Theater. LC 96-8881. 256p. (C). 1997. pap. 24.99 (*0-415-01229-5*) Routledge.
— Unmaking Mimesis: Essays on Feminism & Theater. LC 96-8881. 256p. (C). 1997. 85.00 (*0-415-01228-7*) Routledge.
Diamond, Elin, ed. Performance & Cultural Politics. LC 95-20972. 304p. (C). 1996. 90.00 (*0-415-12767-X*) Routledge.
Diamond, Ellen. Fashion Retailing. LC 92-20912. 431p. (C). 1992. mass mkt. 51.95 (*0-8273-5621-8*) Delmar.
— Fashion Retailing. 48p. 1993. teacher ed. 13.00 (*0-8273-5622-6*) Delmar.
Diamond, Ellen, jt. auth. see Diamond, Jay.
Diamond, Erin. Performance & Cultural Politics. LC 95-20972. 304p. (C). 1996. pap. 27.99 (*0-415-12768-8*) Routledge.
***Diamond, Etan.** And I Will Dwell in Their Midst: Orthodox Jews in Suburbia. 256p. 2000. pap. 18.95 (*0-8078-4889-1*) U of NC Pr.
— And I Will Dwell in Their Midst: Orthodox Jews in Suburbia. LC 00-29880. (Illus.). 256p. 2000. lib. bdg. 39.95 (*0-8078-2576-X*) U of NC Pr.
***Diamond, Ethel.** Aristotle Would Have Liked Oprah: And Other Philosophic Musings. LC 99-37667. 220p. 1999. pap. 10.95 (*1-55874-720-6*) Health Comm.
Diamond, Eugene. The Large Family: A Blessing & a Challenge. LC 95-79946. 167p. (Orig.). 1996. pap. 9.95 (*0-89870-571-1*) Ignatius Pr.
Diamond, Eugene F. & Griese, Orville N. The AIDS Crisis & the Contraceptive Mentality. 69p. 1988. pap. 3.95 (*0-935372-22-9*) NCBC.
Diamond-Falk, Judi, jt. auth. see Diamond, Seymour.
Diamond Farm Book Publishers Staff. Principles of Dairy Farming. (Illus.). 1991. 38.95 (*0-85236-147-5*) Farming Pr.
Diamond, G. E. The Secret of Long Life: or How to Live in Three Centuries. 1991. lib. bdg. 79.95 (*0-87700-952-X*) Revisionist Pr.
Diamond, Gila. Full Circle. LC 94-22920. 1994. 15.95 (*0-87306-690-1*); pap. 12.95 (*0-87306-691-X*) Feldheim.
Diamond, Glenn S. Little Love Notes: A Poet's Heart Beat. Ewing, Jeanne B., ed. 155p. (Orig.). 1995. pap. 24.95 (*1-884690-09-2*) Owl Press.
Diamond, Goddard E. The Secret of Long Life: or How to Live in Three Centuries. 90p. 1996. reprint ed. spiral bd. 11.00 (*0-7873-0287-2*) Hlth Research.
Diamond, Graham. Forest Wars. 416p. 1995. 21.95 (*0-9641740-4-9*) Lion Press.
Diamond, H. G., ed. see Pure Mathematics Symposium Staff.
***Diamond, Hanna.** Women & the Second World War in France 1939-1948: Choices & Constraints. LC 99-25044. (Women & Men in History Ser.). 231p. 1999. pap. 25.66 (*0-582-29909-8*) Longman.
— Women & the Second World War in France 1939-1948: Choices & Constraints. LC 99-25044. (Women & Men in History Ser.). 240p. (C). 1999. 65.95 (*0-582-29910-1*) Longman.
Diamond, Harold G., jt. auth. see Pollard, Harry.
Diamond, Harold J. Music Analyses: An Annotated Guide to the Literature. 716p. 1991. 43.00 (*0-02-870110-0*, Schirmer Books) Mac Lib Ref.
Diamond, Harriet. Writing the Easy Way. 2nd ed. 1991. pap. 12.95 (*0-8120-4615-3*) Barron.
Diamond, Harriet & Dutwin, Phyllis. English the Easy Way. 3rd ed. LC 95-21206. (Barron's Easy Way Ser.). 352p. 1996. pap. 12.95 (*0-8120-9142-6*) Barron.
— Grammar in Plain English. 3rd ed. LC 96-41601. 1997. pap. 12.95 (*0-8120-9648-7*) Barron.
Diamond, Harriet, et al. Executive Writing: A Style Manual for the Business World. LC 96-41426. 176p. 1997. pap. text 24.80 (*0-13-304650-8*) P-H.
Diamond, Harvey. Fit for Life II: Living Healthy. (Illus.). 490p. 1989. mass mkt. 7.50 (*0-446-35875-4*, Pub. by Warner Bks) Little.
***Diamond, Harvey.** Fit for Life 2000. 208p. 2000. 24.00 (*1-57566-569-7*) Kensgtn Pub Corp.
Diamond, Harvey. You Can Prevent Breast Cancer. (Illus.). 273p. (Orig.). 1995. pap. 12.95 (*1-57901-011-3*) Intl Promotions.
Diamond, Harvey & Diamond, Marilyn. Fit for Life. 352p. 1987. mass mkt. 7.50 (*0-446-30015-2*, Pub. by Warner Bks) Little.
Diamond, Harvey, jt. auth. see Graci, Sam.
Diamond, Henry L. & Noonan, Patrick F. Land Use in America. LC 95-47012. 368p. (Orig.). (C). 1996. pap. text 29.95 (*1-55963-464-2*) Island Pr.
Diamond, Herbert S., jt. ed. see Greenwald, Robert A.
Diamond, Howard H. The One-Hundred Hour War. (Pew Case Studies in International Affairs). 50p. (C). 1996. pap. text 3.50 (*1-56927-469-X*, GU Schl Foreign) Geo U Inst Dplmcy.
Diamond, I. A., jt. auth. see Wilder, Billy.
Diamond, I. T., jt. ed. see Jones, E. G.
Diamond, Irene. Fertile Ground: Women, Earth & the Limits of Control. LC 93-39064. 224p. 1997. pap. 14.00 (*0-8070-6773-3*) Beacon Pr.
Diamond, Irene & Orenstein, Gloria F. Reweaving the World: The Emergence of Ecofeminism. LC 89-29295. (Illus.). 324p. 1990. 25.00 (*0-87156-694-X*, Pub. by Sierra); pap. 16.00 (*0-87156-623-0*, Pub. by Sierra) Random.
Diamond, Irene & Quinby, Lee, eds. Feminism & Foucault: Reflections on Resistance. 246p. 1988. pap. text 17.95 (*1-55553-033-8*) NE U Pr.
Diamond, J., jt. auth. see Gruber, D.
Diamond, Jack, jt. auth. see Heller, Peter.
Diamond, Jacqueline. And the Bride Vanishes. 1997. per. 3.75 (*0-373-22435-4*, 1-22435-1) Harlequin Bks.

D

— Assignment: Groom! (American Romance Ser.). 1999. per. 3.99 (*0-373-16791-1*, 1-16791-5) Harlequin Bks.
***Diamond, Jacqueline.** Captured by a Sheikh. (Intrigue Ser.: No. 550). 2000. per. 4.25 (*0-373-22550-4*, 1-22550-7, Harlequin) Harlequin Bks.
Diamond, Jacqueline. The Cowboy & the Heiress. (American Romance Ser.). 1996. per. 3.75 (*0-373-16631-1*, 1-16631-3) Harlequin Bks.
— The Cowboy & the Shotgun Bride: The Brides of Brazer's Corner. (American Romance Ser.: Vol. 734). 1998. per. 3.99 (*0-373-16734-2*, 1-16734-5) Harlequin Bks.
***Diamond, Jacqueline.** Daddy, M. D. (American Romance Ser.). 2000. mass mkt. 4.25 (*0-373-16855-1*, 1168558) Harlequin Bks.
Diamond, Jacqueline. Daddy Warlock. (American Romance Ser.: No. 687). 1997. per. 3.75 (*0-373-16687-7*, 1-16687-5) Harlequin Bks.
— Dear Lonely in L. A. ... (American Romance Ser.). 1996. per. 3.75 (*0-373-16645-1*, 1-16645-3) Harlequin Bks.
— The Forgetful Lady. 192p. 1986. mass mkt. 3.95 (*0-446-32795-6*, Pub. by Warner Bks) Little.
***Diamond, Jacqueline.** His Secret Son. 1999. per. 3.99 (*0-373-22512-1*, 1-22512-7, Harlequin) Harlequin Bks.
— I Do! I Do! Maitland Maternity, Vol. 833. (American Romance Ser.). 2000. mass mkt. 4.25 (*0-373-16833-0*, 1-16833-5) Harlequin Bks.
Diamond, Jacqueline. Kidnapped?/I Got You, Babe, 2. Vol. 2. 1999. per. 5.99 (*0-373-44068-5*) Harlequin Bks.
— Let's Make a Baby. 1999. per. 3.99 (*0-373-16763-6*, Harlequin) Harlequin Bks.
— Million-Dollar Mommy. 1997. per. 3.75 (*0-373-16674-5*, 1-16674-3) Harlequin Bks.
***Diamond, Jacqueline.** Mistletoe Daddy: Sex Single Dads. (American Romance Ser.: Vol. 804). 1999. mass mkt. 3.99 (*0-373-16804-7*) Harlequin Bks.
Diamond, Jacqueline. One Husband Too Many. (American Romance Ser.). 1996. per. 3.75 (*0-373-16642-7*, 1-16642-0) Harlequin Bks.
— Punchline. 1997. per. 3.50 (*0-373-44011-1*, 1-44011-4) Silhouette.
— A Real-Live Sheikh. (American Romance Ser.: No. 716). 1998. per. 3.99 (*0-373-16716-4*, 1-16716-2) Harlequin Bks.
— The Runaway Bride: (In Name Only) LC 95-8352. (American Romance Ser.). 248p. 1995. per. 3.50 (*0-373-16583-8*, 1-16583-6) Harlequin Bks.
— Sandra & the Scoundrel, Vol. 32. LC 97-13813. (Love & Laughter Ser.). 187p. 1997. per. 3.50 (*0-373-44032-4*) Harlequin Bks.
— Yours, Mine & Ours. LC 96-3410. (American Romance Ser.). 248p. 1996. per. 3.50 (*0-373-16615-X*, 1-16615-6) Harlequin Bks.
— Yours, Mine & Ours. (Promo Ser.). 1999. per. 4.50 (*0-373-21990-3*, 1-21990-6) Harlequin Bks.
***Diamond, Jacqueline & Maclay, Charlotte.** Designer Genes & Two for One! (Duets Ser.: No. 37). 2000. mass mkt. 4.99 (*0-373-44103-7*, 1-44103-9) Harlequin Bks.
Diamond, Jacqueline & South, Tracy. The Bride Wore Gym Shoes: Maddie's Millionaire. 1999. per. 5.99 (*0-373-44074-X*, 1-44074-2) Harlequin Bks.
Diamond, James. The Art of Starter Barter. large type ed. (Illus.). 315p. 1996. 75.00 (*0-9650221-0-2*) The Word.
Diamond, James S. Homeland or Holy Land? The "Canaanite" Critique of Israel. LC 85-45671. (Illus.). 192p. 1986. 11.95 (*0-253-13823-X*) Ind U Pr.
Diamond, Jane A. Friendship Note Paper (TM) The Fundraiser that Builds a Community of Learners. (Illus.). 96p. (Orig.). 1996. pap. text 15.95 (*0-9652229-0-X*) Great Eye-deas.
Diamond, Jaqueline. A Dangerous Guy. (American Romance Ser.). 1993. per. 3.50 (*0-373-16491-2*, 1-16491-2) Harlequin Bks.
Diamond, Jared M. Avifauna of the Eastern Highlands of New Guinea. (Publications of the Nuttall Ornithological Club: No. 12). (Illus.). 438p. (C). 1972. 15.00 (*1-877973-22-X*) Nuttall Ornith.
— Guns, Germs & Steel: The Fates of Human Societies. LC 96-37068. (Illus.). 480p. 1997. 27.50 (*0-393-03891-2*) Norton.
— Guns, Germs & Steel: The Fates of Human Societies. (Illus.). 480p. 1999. pap. 15.95 (*0-393-31755-2*) Norton.
— The Third Chimpanzee: The Evolution & Future of the Human Animal. LC 91-50455. (Illus.). 416p. 1992. pap. 14.00 (*0-06-098403-1*, Perennial) HarperTrade.
— Why Sex Is Fun? The Evolution of Human Sexuality. 1998. pap. 11.00 (*0-465-03126-9*, Pub. by Basic) HarpC.
Diamond, Jared M., jt. ed. see Cody, Martin L.
***Diamond, Jason, et al.** Professional Java Server Programming. 2nd ed. 1200p. 2000. pap. 59.99 (*1-86100-465-6*) Wrox Pr Inc.
Diamond, Jay. World of Fashion. 2nd ed. 508p. 1997. 63.00 (*1-56367-075-5*) Fairchild.
Diamond, Jay & Diamond, Ellen. Contemporary Visual Merchandising. 2nd ed. LC 98-4441. 248p. 1998. pap. text 34.00 (*0-13-741794-2*) P-H.
— Fashion Apparel & Accessories. 28p. 1993. teacher ed. 13.00 (*0-8273-5625-0*) Delmar.
— Fashion Apparel & Accessories. LC 93-31762. 421p. (C). 1994. pap. 61.95 (*0-8273-5624-2*) Delmar.
Diamond, Jay & Pintel, Gerald. Introduction to Contemporary Business. 1975. 25.75 (*0-13-487991-0*) P-H.
— Mathematics for Business. 4th ed. (C). 1990. pap. text, wbk. ed. 19.20 (*0-13-563081-9*) P-H.
— Mathematics of Business. 4th ed. 368p. (C). 1990. text 45.80 (*0-13-563057-6*) P-H.
— Principles of Marketing. 4th ed. 496p. (C). 1990. text 55.60 (*0-13-714668-X*) P-H.
— Retail Buying. 5th ed. LC 96-24452. 350p. 1996. 68.00 (*0-13-496464-0*) P-H.

***Diamond, Jay & Pintel, Gerald.** Retail Buying. 6th ed. LC 00-25977. 384p. 2000. pap. 46.67 (*0-13-025432-0*) P-H.
Diamond, Jed. Inside Out: Becoming My Own Man. LC 83-90225. (Orig.). 1983. pap. 10.00 (*0-911761-35-7*) Fifth Wave Pr.
— Looking for Love in All the Wrong Places: Overcoming Romantic & Sexual Addictions. 256p. 1989. reprint ed. mass mkt. 4.99 (*0-380-70774-8*, Avon Bks) Morrow Avon.
— Male Menopause. LC 97-26509. 384p. 1997. 22.95 (*1-57071-143-7*) Sourcebks.
— Male Menopause. 432p. 1998. reprint ed. pap. 14.95 (*1-57071-397-9*) Sourcebks.
***Diamond, Jed.** Surviving Male Menopause. 2000. pap. 16.95 (*1-57071-433-9*) Sourcebks.
Diamond, Jed. The Warrior's Journey Home: Healing Men, Healing the Planet. LC 93-86801. 268p. (Orig.). 1994. pap. 13.95 (*1-879237-60-1*) New Harbinger.
***Diamond, Jill & Kirkpatrick, Peter.** Literary Sydney: A Walking Guide. 2000. pap. 19.95 (*0-7022-3150-9*, Pub. by Univ Queensland Pr) Intl Spec Bk.
Diamond, Joel, jt. auth. see Wugnet.
Diamond, John. Because Cowards Get Cancer Too: A Hypochondriac Confronts His Nemesis. LC 99-20686. 240p. 1999. pap. 20.00 (*0-8129-3177-7*, Times Bks) Crown Pub Group.
— The Healer: Heart & Hearth. Orig. Title: A Prayer on Entering: The Healer's Hearth a Sanctuary. (Illus.). 112p. 2000. pap. 13.95 (*1-890995-00-2*, Enhancement Bks) Vital Health.
***Diamond, John.** Healer: Heart & Hearth. 2000. pap. 13.95 (*1-890995-22-3*, Creativiity Pubg) Vital Health.
Diamond, John. Life Energy: Using the Meridians to Unlock the Hidden Power of Your Emotions. (Illus.). 252p. 1990. reprint ed. pap. 12.95 (*1-55778-281-4*) Paragon Hse.
— Life Enhancement Through Music. 150p. (Orig.). 1999. pap. 14.95 (*1-890995-01-0*, 0011, Enhancement Bks) Vital Health.
***Diamond, John.** The Veneration of Life: Through the Disease to the Soul. 80p. 2000. pap. 9.95 (*1-890995-14-2*, Enhancement Bks) Vital Health.
Diamond, John. The Way of the Pulse: Drumming with Spirit. 116p. 1999. pap. 13.95 (*1-890995-02-9*, Enhancement Bks) Vital Health.
— The Wellspring. (Wellspring: Vol. 1). 87p. 1998. write for info. (*1-890995-04-5*, Enhancement Bks) Vital Health.
— The Wellspring. (Wellspring: Vol. 2). 1998. write for info. (*1-890995-05-3*, Enhancement Bks) Vital Health.
— Your Body Doesn't Lie. 208p. 1989. mass mkt. 5.99 (*0-446-35847-9*, Pub. by Warner Bks) Little.
Diamond, John, ed. The Healing Power of Blake: A Distillation. 180p. 1998. pap. 14.95 (*1-890995-03-7*, CP0100, Enhancement Bks) Vital Health.
Diamond, John C., ed. see Rooks, Charles S.
Diamond, John L., et al. Understanding Torts. LC 96-21224. (Legal Text Ser.). 1996. pap. 30.00 (*0-8205-2486-7*) Bender.
***Diamond, Jonathan.** Narrative Means to Sober Ends: Treating Addiction & Its Aftermath. (Guilford Family Therapy Ser.). 344p. 2000. lib. bdg. 37.95 (*1-57230-566-5*, C0566) Guilford Pubns.
Diamond, Joseph A. A Tradition of Three Tropes. (Wissenschaftliche Abhandlungen-Musicological Studies: Vol. 54). (ENG.). 127p. 1991. 46.00 (*0-931902-67-3*) Inst Mediaeval Mus.
Diamond, Judith. Solomon Islands. LC 95-2691. (Enchantment of the World Ser.). 172p. (J). (gr. 6-9). 1995. lib. bdg. 32.00 (*0-516-02637-2*) Childrens.
***Diamond, Judy.** Practical Evaluation Guide: Tools for Museums & Other Informal Educational Settings. LC 98-40238. (American Association for State & Local History Book Ser.). 200p. 1999. 59.00 (*0-7619-8939-0*); pap. 21.95 (*0-7619-8940-4*) AltaMira Pr.
Diamond, Judy & Bond, Alan B. Kea, Bird of Paradox: The Evolution & Behavior of a New Zealand Parrot. LC 98-19180. (Illus.). 244p. 1999. 29.95 (*0-520-21339-4*, Pub. by U CA Pr) Cal Prin Full Svc.
Diamond, Julie. Status & Power in Verbal Interaction: A Study of Discourse in a Close-Knit Social Network. LC 96-4154. (Pragmatics & Beyond New Ser.: Vol. 40). viii, 184p. 1996. lib. bdg. 55.00 (*1-55619-801-9*) J Benjamins Pubng Co.
Diamond, Kathleen. Motherhood after Miscarriage. 252p. 1991. pap. 10.95 (*1-55850-043-X*) Adams Media.
Diamond, Kathy, ed. see Page, Patrick & Goshman, Albert.
Diamond, L. Frog & Toad Together: A Study Guide. Friedland, J. & Kessler, R., eds. (Novel-Ties Ser.). (J). (gr. k-2). 1997. pap. text 15.95 (*0-7675-0144-6*) Lrn Links.
— Keeping Basements Dry. 1983. pap. 2.95 (*0-88266-200-7*, Storey Pub) Storey Bks.
Diamond, Larry. Class, Ethnicity, & Democracy in Nigeria: The Failure of the First Republic. (Illus.). 416p. (C). 1988. text 45.00 (*0-8156-2422-0*) Syracuse U Pr.
— Developing Democracy: Toward Consolidation: Toward Consolidation. LC 98-42981. 1999. pap. text 17.95 (*0-8018-6156-X*) Johns Hopkins.
— Prospects for Democratic Development in Africa. LC 96-6718. (Essays in Public Policy Ser.: No. 74). 1996. pap. 5.00 (*0-8179-5792-8*) Hoover Inst Pr.
Diamond, Larry, ed. Political Culture & Democracy in Developing Countries: Textbook Edition. LC 94-2568. 266p. (C). 1994. pap. text 19.95 (*1-55587-515-7*) L Rienner.
Diamond, Larry, et al, eds. Consolidating the Third Wave Democracies. (Journal of Democracy Bks.). (Illus.). 728p. 1997. text 45.00 (*0-8018-5793-7*) Johns Hopkins.

— Consolidating the Third Wave Democracies: Regional Challenges. (Journal of Democracy Bks.). (Illus.). 384p. 1997. pap. text 14.95 (*0-8018-5795-3*) Johns Hopkins.
— Democracy in Developing Countries: Latin America. 2nd ed. LC 99-24155. 640p. 1999. pap. 24.50 (*1-55587-798-2*) L Rienner.
— Transition Without End: Nigerian Politics & Civil Society under Babangida. LC 97-13579. 516p. 1997. 59.95 (*1-55587-591-2*) L Rienner.
Diamond, Larry, intro. The Democratic Revolution: Struggles for Freedom & Pluralism in the Developing World. LC 91-20648. 220p. (C). 1991. 24.95 (*0-932088-69-4*); pap. 12.95 (*0-932088-68-6*) Freedom Hse.
***Diamond, Larry & Kim, Byung-Kook, eds.** Consolidating Democracy in South Korea. LC 99-89664. 254p. 2000. lib. bdg. 52.00 (*1-55587-848-2*) L Rienner.
Diamond, Larry & Plattner, Marc F., eds. Capitalism, Socialism, & Democracy Revisited. LC 93-4362. (Journal of Democracy Bks.). 152p. (C). 1993. text 38.50 (*0-8018-4746-X*); pap. text 14.95 (*0-8018-4747-8*) Johns Hopkins.
— Civil-Military Relations & Democracy. LC 96-23229. (Journal of Democracy Bks.). 152p. 1996. text 38.50 (*0-8018-5535-7*); pap. text 14.95 (*0-8018-5536-5*) Johns Hopkins.
— Democracy in East Asia. LC 95-16415. (Journal of Democracy Bks.). (Illus.). 272p. 1996. text 38.50 (*0-8018-5963-8*); pap. text 14.95 (*0-8018-5964-6*) Johns Hopkins.
— Economic Reform & Democracy. (Journal of Democracy Bks.). 152p. 1995. text 40.00 (*0-8018-5256-0*); pap. text 14.95 (*0-8018-5257-9*) Johns Hopkins.
— The Global Resurgence of Democracy. LC 92-26344. 368p. 1993. text 50.00 (*0-8018-4564-5*) Johns Hopkins.
— The Global Resurgence of Democracy. 2nd ed. LC 96-16415. (Journal of Democracy Bks.). 432p. 1996. text 55.00 (*0-8018-5304-4*); pap. text 15.95 (*0-8018-5305-2*) Johns Hopkins.
Diamond, Larry, et al. Democracy in Developing Countries Vol. 2: Africa. LC 87-23457. 275p. (C). 1987. pap. text 19.95 (*1-55587-040-6*) L Rienner.
Diamond, Larry, jt. auth. see Marks, Gary.
Diamond, Larry J. Developing Democracy: Toward Consolidation. LC 98-42981. 1999. 49.95 (*0-8018-6014-8*) Johns Hopkins.
Diamond, Larry J., et al, eds. Consolidating the Third Wave Democracies. LC 97-72775. (Journal of Democracy Book Ser.). 414p. reprint ed. pap. 128.40 (*0-608-08808-0*, 206944700004) Bks Demand.
***Diamond, Larry J. & Plattner, Marc F., eds.** Democratization in Africa. LC 99-20503. 288p. 1999. 42.00 (*0-8018-6272-8*) Johns Hopkins.
Diamond, Larry Jay. Democratization in Africa. LC 99-20503. (Journal of Democracy Bks.). 288p. 1999. pap. 15.95 (*0-8018-6273-6*) Johns Hopkins.
Diamond, Laurie. Anastasia Krupnik: A Study Guide. Friedland, Joyce & Kessler, Rikki, eds. (Novel-Ties Ser.). 26p. (J). (gr. 3-6). 1990. pap. text 15.95 (*0-88122-402-2*) Lrn Links.
— Arthur's Camp-Out: A Study Guide. Friedland, J. & Kessler, R., eds. (Novel-Ties Ser.). (J). (gr. 1-2). 1996. pap. text 15.95 (*1-56982-591-2*) Lrn Links.
— A Bargain for Frances: A Study Guide. Friedland, J. & Kessler, R., eds. (Novel-Ties Ser.). (J). (gr. 1-3). 1994. pap. text, student ed. 15.95 (*1-56982-050-3*) Lrn Links.
— Cam Jansen & the Mystery of the Gold Coins: A Study Guide. Friedland, J. & Kessler, R., eds. (Novel-Ties Ser.). (J). (gr. 1-3). 1992. pap. text, student ed. 15.95 (*0-88122-720-X*) Lrn Links.
— The Chalk Box Kid: A Study Guide. Friedland, Joyce & Kessler, Rikki, eds. (Novel-Ties Ser.). 23p. (YA). (gr. 9-12). 1990. pap. text 15.95 (*0-88122-398-0*) Lrn Links.
— Chang's Paper Pony: A Study Guide. Friedland, J. & Kessler, R., eds. (Novel-Ties Ser.). (J). (gr. 1-3). 1995. pap. text, student ed. 15.95 (*1-56982-263-8*) Lrn Links.
— Grandmas at Bat: A Study Guide. Friedland, J. & Kessler, R., eds. (Novel-Ties Ser.). (gr. k-2). 1998. pap. text, student ed. 15.95 (*0-7675-0302-3*) Lrn Links.
— Henry & Mudge: A Study Guide. Friedland, J. & Kessler, R., eds. (Novel-Ties Ser.). (J). (gr. 1-3). 1993. pap. text, student ed. 15.95 (*0-88122-880-X*) Lrn Links.
— Here Comes the Strikeout: A Study Guide. Friedland, J. & Kessler, R., eds. (Novel-Ties Ser.). (J). (gr. k-2). 1996. pap. text 15.95 (*1-56982-592-0*) Lrn Links.
— The Hundred Dresses: A Study Guide. Friedland, Joyce & Kessler, Rikki, eds. (Novel-Ties Ser.). 21p. (J). (gr. 2-4). 1990. pap. text 15.95 (*0-88122-404-9*) Lrn Links.
— Jacob Two-Two Meets the Hooded Fang: A Study Guide. Friedland, Joyce & Kessler, Rikki, eds. (Novel-Ties Ser.). (J). (gr. 4-6). 1991. pap. text 15.95 (*0-88122-568-1*) Lrn Links.
— The Josefina Story Quilt: A Study Guide. Friedland, J. & Kessler, R., eds. (Novel-Ties Ser.). (J). (gr. 1-3). 1995. pap. text, student ed. 15.95 (*1-56982-265-4*) Lrn Links.
— Julian's Glorious Summer: A Study Guide. (Novel-Ties Ser.). (J). (gr. 1-3). 1989. pap. text, teacher ed., student ed. 15.95 (*0-88122-040-X*) Lrn Links.
— Little Soup's Hayride: A Study Guide. Friedland, J. & Kessler, R., eds. (Novel-Ties Ser.). 20p. (J). (gr. 2-4). 1992. pap. text 15.95 (*0-88122-699-8*) Lrn Links.
— The Monster in the Third Dresser Drawer: A Study Guide. (Novel-Ties Ser.). (J). (gr. 1-3). 1989. pap. text, teacher ed., student ed. 15.95 (*0-88122-041-8*) Lrn Links.
— The Most Beautiful Place in the World: A Study Guide. Friedland, J. & Kessler, R., eds. (Novel-Ties Ser.). (J). (gr. 2-4). 1994. pap. text, student ed. 15.95 (*1-56982-056-2*) Lrn Links.
— Mouse Tales: A Study Guide. Friedland, J. & Kessler, R., eds. (Novel-Ties Ser.). (J). (gr. k-2). 1998. pap. text, student ed. 15.95 (*0-7675-0311-2*) Lrn Links.

An Asterisk (*) at the beginning of an entry indicates that the title is appearing for the first time.

— Nate the Great & the Musical Note: A Study Guide. Friedland, J. & Kessler, R., eds. (Novel-Ties Ser.). (J). (gr. 1-3). 1992. pap. text, student ed. 15.95 (*0-88122-726-9*) Lrn Links.

— Next Spring an Oriole. Friedland, Joyce & Kessler, Rikki, eds. (Novel-Ties Ser.). (J). (gr. 1-3). 1991. pap. text, student ed. 15.95 (*0-88122-565-7*) Lrn Links.

— O'Diddy: A Study Guide. Friedland, Joyce & Kessler, Rikki, eds. (Novel-Ties Ser.). (J). (gr. 2-4). 1991. pap. text 15.95 (*0-88122-570-3*) Lrn Links.

— The One in the Middle Is the Green Kangaroo: A Study Guide. Friedland, Joyce & Kessler, Rikki, eds. (Novel-Ties Ser.). 16p. (J). (gr. 1-3). 1990. pap. text 15.95 (*0-88122-408-1*) Lrn Links.

— Rip-Roaring Russell: A Study Guide. Friedland, Joyce & Kessler, Rikki, eds. (Novel-Ties Ser.). 20p. (J). (gr. 1-3). 1990. pap. text 15.95 (*0-88122-405-7*) Lrn Links.

— The Smallest Cow: A Study Guide. Friedland, J. & Kessler, R., eds. (Novel-Ties Ser.). (J). (gr. k-2). 1995. pap. text, student ed. 15.95 (*1-56982-254-9*) Lrn Links.

— Tales of Oliver Pig: A Study Guide. Friedland, J. & Kessler, R., eds. (Novel-Ties Ser.). (J). (gr. k-2). 1996. pap. text 15.95 (*1-56982-593-9*) Lrn Links.

Diamond, Lawrence A. Take the Mystery Out of Boat Maintenance. (Illus.). 1989. 22.50 (*0-393-03335-X*) Norton.

Diamond, Lawrence W., jt. auth. see Nguyen, Doyen T.

Diamond, Leonard. How to Handle Your Child Custody Case: A Manual for Parents, Psychologists, & Attorneys. LC 89-34701. 171p. 1989. 29.95 (*0-87975-543-1*); pap. 18.95 (*0-87975-570-9*) Prometheus Bks.

— The Total Success Book: A Guide to Personal Fulfillment. LC 94-4483. 192p. (C). 1994. pap. 15.95 (*0-87975-871-6*) Prometheus Bks.

***Diamond Library Staff.** Rotisserie League Baseball: The Official Rule Book & Draft Day Guide, 2000 Ed. 1999. pap. 14.95 (*1-880876-86-8*) Diamond Lib.

Diamond, Linda, ed. see Klein, Irving J.

***Diamond, Louise.** The Courage for Peace: Creating Harmony in Ourselves & the World. LC 99-42068. 256p. 2000. pap. 15.95 (*1-57324-165-2*) Conari Press.

Diamond, Louise & McDonald, John. Multi-Track Diplomacy: A Systems Approach to Peace. 3rd ed. LC 95-42452. (Books for a World That Works). (Illus.). 192p. 1996. pap. 19.95 (*1-56549-057-6*) Kumarian Pr.

Diamond, Lynell. Let's Discover Bryce & Zion National Parks. (Children's Activity Bks. for Ages 6-11). (Illus.). 32p. (J). (gr. 1-6). 1990. pap. 4.95 (*0-89886-253-1*) Mountaineers.

Diamond, Lynn & Roberts, Stephanie. Effective Videoconferencing: Techniques for Better Business Meetings. Keppler, Kay, ed. LC 95-68747. (Fifty-Minute Ser.). (Illus.). 101p. (Orig.). 1996. pap. 10.95 (*1-56052-354-9*) Crisp Pubns.

Diamond, Lynnell. Let's Discover Capitol Reef, Arches, & Canyonlands National Parks: A Children's Activity Book for Ages 6-11. (Let's Discover Ser.). (Illus.). 32p. (J). (gr. 1-6). 1991. pap. 4.95 (*0-89886-285-X*) Mountaineers.

— Lets Discover Petrified Forest: A Children's Activity Book for Ages 6-11. (Let's Discover Ser.). (Illus.). 32p. (J). (gr. 1-6). 1991. pap. 4.95 (*0-89886-286-8*) Mountaineers.

— Let's Discover the Grand Canyon. 32p. (J). (gr. 1-6). 1990. pap. 4.95 (*0-89886-252-3*) Mountaineers.

— New Mexico for Kids: A Learning - Activity Guidebook for Young People. (America for Kids Ser.). (Illus.). 48p. (YA). (gr. 3-6). 1997. pap. 7.95 (*0-9651853-0-3*) Otter Be Reading Bks.

Diamond, Lynnell & Mueller, Marge. Let's Discover the San Juan Islands. (Illus.). 32p. (Orig.). (J). 1989. pap. 4.95 (*0-89886-220-5*) Mountaineers.

Diamond, M., ed. see DeCherney, Alan H., et al.

Diamond, M. J. Women & Revolution: Global Expressions. LC 98-27173. 1998. 150.00 (*0-7923-5182-7*) Kluwer Academic.

Diamond, Malcolm L. & Litzenburg, Thomas V., Jr. The Logic of God: Theology & Verification. LC 74-32235. 562p. 1975. 17.95 (*0-672-60792-1*, Bobbs) Macmillan.

Diamond, Marian. Magic Trees of the Mind: How to Nurture Your Child's Intelligence, Creativity, & Healthy Emotions from Birth through Adolescence. LC 97-36971. 1998. 26.95 (*0-525-94308-0*) NAL.

— Magic Trees of the Mind: How to Nurture Your Child's Intelligence, Creativity & Healthy Emotions from Birth Through Adolescence. 480p. 1999. pap. 13.95 (*0-452-27830-9*, Plume) Dutton Plume.

Diamond, Marian C., et al. The Human Brain Coloring Book. (Illus.). 320p. (Orig.). 1986. pap. 18.00 (*0-06-460306-7*, CO 306, Harper Ref) HarpC.

Diamond, Marie. Crossings. LC 86-83204. 160p. (Orig.). 1987. pap. 6.00 (*0-9605008-6-3*) Hermes Hse Pr.

Diamond, Marilyn. The American Vegetarian Cookbook from the Fit for Life Kitchen. 422p. 1990. 28.00 (*0-446-51561-2*, Pub. by Warner Bks) Little.

— Fitonics for Life. 448p. 1998. mass mkt. 6.99 (*0-380-78967-1*, Avon Bks) Morrow Avon.

— A New Way of Eating: The Proper Foods, Combinations, & Recipes to Start You on the Road to Good Health. 176p. (Orig.). 1987. mass mkt. 8.99 (*0-446-38404-6*, Pub. by Warner Bks) Little.

— A New Way of Eating from the Fit for Life Kitchen. 176p. 1993. mass mkt. 5.99 (*0-446-36488-6*, Pub. by Warner Bks) Little.

Diamond, Marilyn & Neuwirth, Lisa. Recipes for Life: From the Fitonics Kitchen. LC 97-44150. 384p. 1998. mass mkt. 25.00 (*0-380-97487-8*, Avon Bks) Morrow Avon.

Diamond, Marilyn & Schnell, Donald B. Fitonics for Life. LC 96-22815. 1996. 24.00 (*0-380-97437-1*, Avon Bks) Morrow Avon.

Diamond, Marilyn, jt. auth. see Diamond, Harvey.

Diamond, Marion. Ben Boyd of Boydtown. LC 95-160096. 280p. 1995. 39.95 (*0-522-84673-4*, Pub. by Melbourne Univ Pr) Paul & Co Pubs.

— Emigration & Empire: The Life of Maria S. Rye. LC 98-39991. (Literature & Society in Victorian Britain Ser.: No. 6). 324p. 1999. 60.00 (*0-8153-2528-2*, H2035) Garland.

Diamond, Martin. The Founding of the Democratic Republic. LC 80-84210. 190p. (C). 1981. pap. text 27.50 (*0-87581-271-6*, FDR) F E Peacock Pubs.

Diamond, Maxine & Hemmings, Harriet. Matt Damon: A Biography. LC 99-195303. (J). 1998. per. 4.99 (*0-671-02649-6*) S&S Childrens.

Diamond, Melvin. Notes in Verse. Norton, Donna, ed. & illus. by. LC 96-4627. 1996. pap. 6.95 (*0-910733-03-1*) ICTL Pubns.

Diamond, Merle L. & Solomon, Glen D. Diamond & Dalessio's the Practicing Physician's Approach to Headache. 6th ed. Kersey, Ray, ed. LC 98-7039. (Illus.). 270p. 1999. text 45.00 (*0-7216-6999-9*, W B Saunders Co) Harcrt Hlth Sci Grp.

Diamond, Michael. If You Can Keep It: A Constitutional Roadmap to Environmental Security. LC 96-83905. ix, 148p. (Orig.). 1996. pap. 15.00 (*0-9651309-0-8*, 961) Brass Ring NJ.

— Managing & Operating a Closely-Held Corporation. LC 90-24802. 243p. 1991. 135.00 (*0-471-52107-8*) Wiley.

Diamond, Michael, et al, eds. Hysterectomy. (Illus.). 208p. 1994. 85.00 (*0-86542-355-5*) Blackwell Sci.

Diamond, Michael A. Financial Accounting. 3rd ed. LC 92-28587. (C). 1992. mass mkt. 83.00 (*0-538-82267-8*) S-W Pub.

— Financial Accounting. 4th ed. LC 95-11388. (C). 1995. mass mkt. 75.95 (*0-538-84073-0*) S-W Pub.

— The Unconscious Life of Organizations: Interpreting Organizational Identity. LC 93-6766. 272p. 1993. 65.00 (*0-89930-833-3*, Q833, Quorum Bks) Greenwood.

Diamond, Michael A., et al. Accounting Principles. (C). 1994. text. write for info. (*0-538-81676-7*, AB68AA) S-W Pub.

Diamond, Michael A., jt. auth. see Allcorn, Seth.

Diamond, Michael A., jt. auth. see Arnold, Jerry L.

Diamond, Michael B. How to Incorporate. 3rd ed. 320p. 1996. pap. 19.95 (*0-471-13913-0*) Wiley.

Diamond, Michael P. & Osteen, Kevin G. Endometrium & Endometriosis. LC 97-12678. (Illus.). 704p. 1997. pap. 145.00 (*0-86542-502-7*) Blackwell Sci.

Diamond, Michael P., et al. A Manual of Clinical Laparoscopy. LC 97-18021. (Illus.). 120p. 1998. 72.00 (*1-85070-640-9*) Prthnon Pub.

Diamond, Michael P., jt. ed. see Sutton, Chris.

Diamond, Michael R. How to Incorporate: A Handbook for Entrepreneurs & Professionals. 3rd ed. 310p. 1996. 49.95 (*0-471-13912-2*) Wiley.

— Real Estate Law. LC 97-21662. (Paralegal). 512p. (C). 1998. 66.95 (*0-314-12615-5*) Delmar.

— Real Estate Law Study Guide. abr. rev. ed. (Paralegal Ser.). 128p. (C). 1998. text, student ed. 14.95 (*0-314-13020-9*) Delmar.

***Diamond, Michael R. & Williams, Julie L.** How to Incorporate. 4th ed. 340p. 2000. pap. 24.95 (*0-471-39257-X*) Wiley.

Diamond, Milton, jt. auth. see Steinhoff, Patricia G.

Diamond, Milton, ed. see Beach, Frank A.

Diamond, Nancy, jt. auth. see Graham, Hugh D.

Diamond, Neil. Tennessee Moon. 104p. 1996. per. 15.95 (*0-7935-6362-3*) H Leonard.

Diamond, Nikki & Cheshire, Carolyn. Body Dynamics: The Ultimate Women's Workout Book. (Illus.). 208p. 1997. pap. 14.95 (*0-7063-7537-8*, Pub. by WrLock) Sterling.

***Diamond, Nina L.** Voices of Truth: Conversations with Scientists, Thinkers & Healers. 450p. 2000. pap. 24.95 (*0-914955-82-9*) Lotus Pr.

Diamond, Norma. K'un Shen: A Taiwan Village. Spindler, Louise S. & Spindler, George D., eds. (Case Studies in Cultural Anthropology). 128p. 1982. reprint ed. pap. text 16.95 (*0-8290-0280-4*) Irvington.

Diamond, Norman. A Practice Almost Perfect: The Early Days at Arnold, Fortas & Porter. LC 96-47284. 376p. 1997. text 29.95 (*0-7618-0627-X*) U Pr of Amer.

Diamond, Norman & Bigelow, William. The Power in Our Hands: A Curriculum on the History of Work & Workers in the United States. 256p. (Orig.). 1988. pap., teacher ed. 18.00 (*0-85345-753-0*, Pub. by Monthly Rev); pap., student ed. 10.00 (*0-85345-754-9*, Pub. by Monthly Rev) NYU Pr.

Diamond, Olivia. Land of the Four Quarters. Olmsted, Robert, ed. LC 94-66927. (Illus.). 104p. (Orig.). 1994. pap. 8.95 (*0-89002-322-0*) Northwoods Pr.

Diamond, Pamela M., et al. Community Mental Health Centers under Managed Care: Authority Or Provider? LC 97-75770. (Policy Research Project Report Ser.). 184p. 1998. pap. 17.00 (*0-89940-741-2*) LBJ Sch Pub Aff.

Diamond, Paul S. Federal Grand Jury Practice & Procedure. 525p. 1995. ring bd. 146.00 (*1-56706-159-1*) Aspen Law.

— Federal Grand Jury Practice & Procedure. 2nd ed. 650p. 1993. ring bd. 126.00 (*0-13-288911-0*) Aspen Law.

Diamond, Paula M., ed. see Mitchell, William A., Jr.

Diamond, Peter. Growth-Productivity-Unemployment. 254p. 1990. 37.50 (*0-262-04110-3*) MIT Pr.

— On Time. (Churchill Lectures in Economics). (Illus.). 134p. (C). 1994. text 30.95 (*0-521-46289-4*) Cambridge U Pr.

Diamond, Peter, et al, eds. Social Security: What Role for the Future? LC 95-41812. 1996. write for info. (*0-8157-1836-5*) Natl Acad.

Diamond, Peter, ed. see Seigel, Lenny, et al.

Diamond, Peter A. A Search-Equilibrium Approach to the Micro Foundations of Macroeconomics. (Illus.). 88p. 1984. 15.00 (*0-262-04076-X*) MIT Pr.

Diamond, Peter A., et al, eds. Social Security: What Role for the Future? LC 95-41812. 233p. 1996. pap. 19.95 (*0-8157-1835-7*) Brookings.

Diamond, Peter A., jt. auth. see National Academy of Social Insurance (U.S.) Staff.

Diamond, Peter J. Common Sense & Improvement: Thomas Reid As Social Theorist. Drescher, Horst W., ed. (Scottish Studies International: Vol. 24). 406p. 1998. 56.95 (*3-631-33552-0*) P Lang Pubng.

— Common Sense & Improvement Vol. 24: Thomas Reid as Social Theorist, No.24. LC 98-48844. (Scottish Studies International). 406p. 1998. pap. 56.95 (*0-8204-3607-0*) P Lang Pubng.

Diamond, Phil. Metric Spaces of Fuzzy Sets: Theory & Applications. 188p. 1994. text 48.00 (*981-02-1731-5*) World Scientific Pub.

Diamond, R., et al, eds. Molecular Structures in Biology. LC 92-28936. (Illus.). 352p. 1993. text 79.00 (*0-19-854771-4*) OUP.

***Diamond, R. A. & DeMaggio, S., eds.** In Living Color: Protocols in Flow Cytometry & Cell Sorting. (Springer Lab Manuals Ser.). (Illus.). 825p. 2000. 165.00 (*3-540-65149-7*) Spr-Verlag.

Diamond, R. B., et al. Etude Sur Les Engrais en Afrique de L'Ouest, 7 vols. (West African Fertilizer Study Ser.). (FRE., Illus.). 293p. (Orig.). 1982. pap. 35.00 (*0-88090-002-4*) Intl Fertilizer.

— Etude Sur Les Engrais en Afrique de L'Ouest: Volume 1 - Apercu Regional. (Technical Bulletin Ser.: No. TF-3). (FRE., Illus.). 84p. (Orig.). 1977. pap. 4.00 (*0-88090-038-5*) Intl Fertilizer.

— Etude Sur les Engrais en Afrique de L'Ouest Vol. 2: Senegal. (Technical Bulletin Ser.: No. TF-4). (FRE., Illus.). 70p. (Orig.). 1977. pap. 4.00 (*0-88090-032-6*) Intl Fertilizer.

— Etude Sur les Engrais en Afrique de L'Ouest Vol. 3: Mali. (Technical Bulletin Ser.: No. TF-5). (FRE., Illus.). 73p. (Orig.). 1976. pap. 4.00 (*0-88090-033-4*) Intl Fertilizer.

— Etude Sur les Engrais en Afrique de L'Ouest Vol. 4: Haute Volta. (Technical Bulletin Ser.: No. TF-6). (FRE., Illus.). 65p. (Orig.). 1977. pap. 4.00 (*0-88090-034-2*) Intl Fertilizer.

— Etude Sur les Engrais en Afrique de L'Ouest Vol. 5: Niger. (Technical Bulletin Ser.: No. TF-7). (FRE., Illus.). 51p. (Orig.). 1978. pap. 4.00 (*0-88090-035-0*) Intl Fertilizer.

— Etude Sur les Engrais en Afrique de L'Ouest Vol. 6: Tchad. (Technical Bulletin Ser.: No. TF-8). (FRE., Illus.). 63p. (Orig.). 1977. pap. 4.00 (*0-88090-036-9*) Intl Fertilizer.

— Etude Sur les Engrais en Afrique de L'Ouest Vol. 7: Mauritanie. (Technical Bulletin Ser.: No. TF-9). (FRE., Illus.). 42p. (Orig.). 1978. pap. 4.00 (*0-88090-037-7*) Intl Fertilizer.

— West Africa Fertilizer Study: Chad, Vol. VI. (Technical Bulletin Ser.: No. T-8). (Illus.). 55p. (Orig.). 1977. pap. 4.00 (*0-88090-007-5*) Intl Fertilizer.

— West Africa Fertilizer Study: Mauritania, Vol. VII. (Technical Bulletin Ser.: No. T-9). (Illus.). 39p. (Orig.). 1978. pap. 4.00 (*0-88090-008-3*) Intl Fertilizer.

— West Africa Fertilizer Study: Niger, Vol. V. (Technical Bulletin Ser.: No. T-7). (Illus.). 47p. (Orig.). 1978. pap. 4.00 (*0-88090-006-7*) Intl Fertilizer.

— West Africa Fertilizer Study: Regional Overview, Vol. I. (Technical Bulletin Ser.: No. T-3). 79p. (Orig.). 1977. pap. 4.00 (*0-88090-039-3*) Intl Fertilizer.

— West Africa Fertilizer Study: Upper Volta, Vol. IV. (Technical Bulletin Ser.: No. T-6). (Illus.). 60p. (Orig.). 1977. pap. 4.00 (*0-88090-005-9*) Intl Fertilizer.

— West Africa Fertilizer Study Vol. II: Senegal. (Technical Bulletin Ser.: No. T-4). (Illus.). 64p. (Orig.). 1977. pap. 4.00 (*0-88090-003-2*) Intl Fertilizer.

***Diamond, Richard.** Dental First Aid for Families. LC 99-40278. 2000. pap. 10.00 (*1-882883-39-X*) Idyll Arbor.

Diamond, Rickey G. Second Sight: A Novel. LC 98-42115. 272p. 1999. 24.00 (*0-06-019203-8*) HarpC.

***Diamond, Rickey Gard.** Second Sight. 272p. 2000. pap. 13.00 (*0-06-092940-5*, Cliff Street) HarperTrade.

Diamond, Robert E. Old English: Grammar & Reader. LC 89-5763. (Waynebooks Ser.: No. 38). 304p. (C). 1970. pap. text 17.95 (*0-8143-1510-0*) Wayne St U Pr.

***Diamond, Robert M.** Aligning Faculty Rewards with Institutional Mission: Statements, Policies & Guidelines. 200p. 1999. 34.95 (*1-882982-26-6*) Anker Pub.

Diamond, Robert M. Designing & Assessing Courses & Curricula: A Practical Guide. 2nd ed. LC 97-17599. 1997. pap. 34.95 (*0-7879-1030-9*) Jossey-Bass.

— Preparing for Promotion & Tenure Review: A Faculty Guide. 80p. (C). 1995. pap. text 9.50 (*1-882982-07-X*) Anker Pub.

— Serving on Promotion & Tenure Committees: A Faculty Guide. LC 94-220158. 64p. (C). 1994. pap. text 7.50 (*1-882982-02-9*) Anker Pub.

Diamond, Robert M. & Adam, Bronwyn E., eds. The Disciplines Speak: Rewarding the Scholarly, Professional & Creative Work of Faculty. 175p. 1995. pap. 12.00 (*1-56377-034-2*, FR9502) Am Assn Higher Ed.

Diamond, Robert M. & Adam, Bronwyn E., eds. The Disciplines Speak Vol. II: More Statements on Rewarding the Scholarly Professional. Date not set. pap. 12.00 (*1-56377-047-4*) Am Assn Higher Ed.

Diamond, Robert M. & Adam, Bronwyn E., eds. Recognizing Faculty Work: Reward Systems for the Year 2000. LC 85-644752. (New Directions for Higher Education Ser.: No. HE 81). 125p. (Orig.). 1993. pap. 22.00 (*1-55542-691-3*) Jossey-Bass.

Diamond, Robert M., et al. Instructional Development for Individualized Learning in Higher Education. LC 74-18398. 208p. 1975. pap. 34.95 (*0-87778-077-3*) Educ Tech Pubns.

Diamond, Ron, jt. auth. see Rubin, Michael.

Diamond, Ronald J. Instant Psychopharmacology: A Guide for the Non-Medical Mental Health Professional. LC 98-9703. 120p. 1998. pap. 17.00 (*0-393-70269-3*) Norton.

Diamond, Ronny, et al. Couple Therapy for Infertility. LC 99-16283. (Family Therapy Ser.). 234p. 1999. lib. bdg. 31.00 (*1-57230-511-8*, CO511) Guilford Pubns.

***Diamond, Sander A.** The German Table. rev. ed. 261p. 1999. pap. 15.95 (*1-58444-100-3*) DiscUs Bks.

Diamond, Sandra F., ed. see Richards, Ralph.

***Diamond, Sandy.** The Hunchback. 2000. pap. 15.00 (*0-88739-288-1*) Creat Arts Bk.

Diamond, Sandy. Miss Coffin & Mrs. Blood: Poems of Art & Madness. LC 94-70717. (Illus.). 80p. (Orig.). (C). 1994. pap. 15.00 (*0-88739-104-4*) Creat Arts Bk.

Diamond, Sara. Facing the Wrath: Confronting the Right in Dangerous Times. 300p. (Orig.). 1996. pap. 16.95 (*1-56751-078-7*); lib. bdg. 29.95 (*1-56751-079-5*) Common Courage.

***Diamond, Sara.** Not by Politics Alone: The Enduring Influence of the Christian Right. LC 98-24502. 280p. 1998. lib. bdg. 29.95 (*1-57230-385-9*) Guilford Pubns.

— Not by Politics Alone: The Enduring Influence of the Christian Right. 280p. 2000. pap. text 17.95 (*1-57230-494-4*, C0494) Guilford Pubns.

Diamond, Sara. Roads to Dominion: Right-Wing Movements & Political Power in the United States. LC 95-12887. (Critical Perspectives Ser.). 445p. 1995. pap. text 19.95 (*0-89862-864-4*); lib. bdg. 44.00 (*0-89862-862-8*) Guilford Pubns.

— Spiritual Warfare: The Politics of the Christian Right. 304p. write for info. (*0-921689-65-9*); pap. write for info. (*0-921689-64-0*) Black Rose.

— Spiritual Warfare: The Politics of the Christian Right. LC 89-6121. 292p. 1989. 30.00 (*0-89608-362-4*); pap. 18.00 (*0-89608-361-6*) South End Pr.

Diamond, Seymour. Contemporary Diagnosis & Management of Headache & Migraine. LC 98-70181. (Illus.). 145p. (Orig.). (C). 1998. pap. text 29.95 (*1-884065-28-7*) Assocs in Med.

— Coping with Your Headaches. 12th ed. 1988. pap. 15.95 (*0-8236-1083-7*) Intl Univs Pr.

— Diagnosis & Management of Headaches. 2nd ed. 192p. 1998. pap. text 19.95 (*1-884735-27-4*) Prof Comms.

— Migraine Headache Prevention & Management. (Illus.). 256p. 1990. text 125.00 (*0-8247-8212-7*) Dekker.

— A Pain Specialist's Approach to the Headache Patient. LC 93-13888. 162p. 1993. 27.50 (*0-8236-3930-4*) Intl Univs Pr.

Diamond, Seymour & Dalessio, Donald J. The Practicing Physician's Approach to Headache. 5th ed. 320p. 1991. 49.00 (*0-683-02506-6*) Lppncott W & W.

Diamond, Seymour & Diamond-Falk, Judi. Advice from the Diamond Headache Clinic. LC 82-8973. ix, 194p. 1982. 30.00 (*0-8236-0119-6*) Intl Univs Pr.

Diamond, Seymour & Maliszewski, Michael, eds. Sexual Aspects of Headaches. LC 91-46626. 520p. (C). 1992. 75.00 (*0-8236-6071-0*) Intl Univs Pr.

Diamond, Seymour & Vye, Amy D. Hope for Your Headache Problem, 2nd rev. ed. Orig. Title: More than Two Aspirin. 300p. 1988. 42.50 (*0-8236-2350-5*, BN 02350) Intl Univs Pr.

Diamond, Seymour, et al. Headache & Diet: Tyramine-Free Recipes. LC 89-26854. 280p. 1990. spiral bd. 27.50 (*0-8236-2315-7*) Intl Univs Pr.

— The Hormone Headache: New Ways to Prevent, Manage, & Treat Migraines & Other Headaches. LC 95-1478. (Illus.). 240p. 1995. per. 11.95 (*0-02-008315-7*) Macmillan.

Diamond, Sigmund. The Reputation of the American Businessman. 1990. 18.50 (*0-8446-0581-6*) Peter Smith.

Diamond, Sigmund & Gutman, Herbert G. Main Problems in American History Vol. 2: The Impact of Industrialization on American Society Labor's Response to Modern Industrialism. abr. ed. (PaperBook Series in History). (Illus.). 128p. (C). 1996. pap. text 2.25 (*1-877891-33-9*) Paperbook Pr Inc.

Diamond, Sigmund, ed. & tr. see De Rothschild, Salomon.

Diamond, Stanley. Going West. LC 86-80689. 80p. (Orig.). 1986. pap. 5.50 (*0-9605008-5-5*) Hermes Hse Pr.

— In Search of the Primitive: A Critique of Civilization. 387p. 1987. pap. 24.95 (*0-87855-582-X*) Transaction Pubs.

— Totems. 96p. 1983. pap. 13.00 (*0-940170-02-7*) Open Bk Pubns.

Diamond, Stanley, ed. Theory & Practice: Essays Presented to Gene Weltfish. (Studies in Anthropology). 1979. text 67.70 (*90-279-7958-8*) Mouton.

— Toward a Marxist Anthropology: Problems & Perspectives. (World Anthropology Ser.). 492p. 1979. text 69.25 (*90-279-7780-1*) Mouton.

Diamond, Stephen A. Anger, Madness, & the Daimonic: The Psychological Genesis of Violence, Evil, & Creativity. LC 96-27865. (SUNY Series in the Philosophy of Psychology). 402p. (C). 1999. pap. text 19.95 (*0-7914-3076-6*) State U NY Pr.

Diamond, Stephen C. Leveraged Buyouts. LC 84-73255. 1985. 70.00 (*0-87094-579-3*, Irwn Prfssnl) McGraw-Hill Prof.

Diamond, Stephen F., jt. ed. see Compa, Lance A.

***Diamond, Steve.** WWW.Wild, Wicked Web. LC 00-190635. 524p. 2000. 25.00 (*0-7388-1878-X*); pap. 18.00 (*0-7388-1879-8*) Xlibris Corp.

***Diamond, Stice.** Financial Accounting: Reporting & Analysis. 5th ed. (SWC-Accounting Ser.). (C). 1999. text 26.00 (*0-324-03307-9*) Sth-Wstrn College.

D

An Asterisk (*) at the beginning of an entry indicates that the title is appearing for the first time.

***Diamond, Susan.** Little Love Notes. 2000. 4.99 (*1-56245-405-6*) Great Quotations.
— Mother, with Love. 2000. 4.99 (*1-56245-401-3*) Great Quotations.

Diamond, Susan L. Hard Labor. 1998. pap. 17.95 (*0-312-85308-4*, Pub. by Forge NYC) St Martin.
— Hard Labor: Reflections of an Obstetrical Nurse. LC 96-1555. 384p. 1996. 25.95 (*0-312-85682-2*, Pub. by Tor Bks) St Martin.

Diamond, Susan Z. Records Management: A Practical Guide. LC 82-18477. 192p. reprint ed. pap. 59.60 (*0-7837-4242-8*, 204393100012) Bks Demand.
— Records Management: A Practical Guide. 3rd ed. LC 95-4604. 272p. 1995. 29.95 (*0-8144-0295-X*) AMACOM.

Diamond, Sylvia. Calligraphy with Class. (Illus.). 105p. 1988. pap. 14.95 (*0-932906-23-0*) Pan-Am Publishing Co.

Diamond, T., et al. Qbase Surgery No. 1: Mcq Companion to 'Fundamentals of Surgical Practice' 208p. 2000. pap. text 47.50 (*1-84110-005-6*) OUP.

Diamond, Timothy. Making Gray Gold: Narratives of Nursing Home Care. 296p. 1995. pap. text 13.95 (*0-226-14474-7*) U Ch Pr.
— Making Gray Gold: Narratives of Nursing Home Care. LC 91-45755. (Women in Culture & Society Ser.). 296p. 1998. 24.95 (*0-226-14473-9*) U Ch Pr.

Diamond, Troy. Nose Smoking, How to Help Children Avoid the Addiction of Nicotine, Rings, Spings & Thingamajigs: Old Hound Dog's Story. LC 90-61384. (Illus.). 100p. (J). 1990. pap. 17.95 (*0-945437-08-0*) MacDonald-Sward.

Diamond, W. John, et al. An Alternative Medicine Definitive Guide to Cancer. LC 96-6580. (Alternative Medicine Definitive Guide to...Ser.). (Illus.). 1116p. 1997. 49.95 (*1-887299-01-7*) AlternMed Bks.

***Diamond, W. John, et al.** Cancer Diagnosis: What To Do Next. (Illus.). 400p. 2000. pap. 14.95 (*1-887299-40-8*) AlternMed Bks.

Diamond, Walter H. Foreign Tax & Trade Briefs, 2 vols., Set. 1951. ring bd. 470.00 (*0-8205-1290-7*) Bender.
— International Withholding Tax Treaty Guide. 1974. ring bd. 245.00 (*0-8205-1292-3*) Bender.

Diamond, Walter H. & Diamond, Dorothy B. Capital Formatic & Investment Incentives Around the World, 2 vols. 1981. ring bd. 830.00 (*0-8205-1195-1*) Bender.
— Tax Havens of the World, 3 vols. 1974. ring bd. 390.00 (*0-8205-1722-4*) Bender.

Diamond, Walter H., et al. International Trust Laws & Analysis, Set, Vols. 1 & 2. 1995. 345.00 (*0-7913-2458-3*) Warren Gorham & Lamont.
— International Trust Laws & Analysis, Vol. 1. 1995. write for info. (*0-7913-2456-7*) Warren Gorham & Lamont.
— International Trust Laws & Analysis, Vol. 2. 1995. write for info. (*0-7913-2457-5*) Warren Gorham & Lamont.

Diamond, Wendy. All Star Feast Cookbook: Recipes from over 100 of the World's Best Athletes. Parella, Elizabeth et al, eds. LC 97-93426. (Illus.). 128p. 1997. 19.95 (*0-9647316-1-4*) Global Liaisons.
— A Musical Feast: Recipes from over 100 of the World's Top Musical Artist: Proceeds Help the Homeless. Narlock, Lori et al, eds. LC 95-78322. (Illus.). 117p. 1995. 19.95 (*0-9647316-0-6*) Global Liaisons.

Diamond, Wendy, ed. A Musical Feast: Recipes from over 100 of the World's Most Famous Musical Artists. (Illus.). 113p. 1999. text 22.00 (*0-7881-6014-1*) DIANE Pub.

Diamond, William. The Economic Thought of Woodrow Wilson. LC 78-64192. (Johns Hopkins University. Studies in the Social Sciences. Thirtieth Ser. 1912). 216p. 1982. reprint ed. 37.50 (*0-404-61299-7*) AMS Pr.

Diamond, William, ed. Development Finance Companies: Aspects of Policy & Operation. LC 81-21252. 368p. reprint ed. pap. 114.10 (*0-608-08665-7*, 206918800003) Bks Demand.

Diamond, William J. Practical Experiment Designs. 2nd ed. 1989. text 60.95 (*0-442-31849-9*, VNR) Wiley.

Diamond, William J. Practical Experiment Designs for Engineers & Scientists. 2nd ed. (Competitive Manufacturing Ser.). 408p. 1989. 75.00 (*0-471-28971-X*, VNR) Wiley.

Diamondis, Peter J. Underwater Photography Now. LC 83-136151. (Illus.). 154p. 1983. 6.00 (*0-9612110-0-8*) P J Diamondis.

Diamondston, B. L., jt. auth. see Carter, G. C.

Diamondstone, J. Designing, Leading & Evaluating Workshops for Teachers & Parents. 44p. 1980. 10.95 (*0-931114-81-0*, F1007) High-Scope.

Diamondstone, Judy & Barnhardt, Ray. Curriculum Resources for the Alaskan Environment. (Illus.). 130p. (Orig.). (C). 1980. pap. 10.00 (*1-877962-12-0*) Univ AK Ctr CCS.

Diamonstein, Barbaralee. Handmade in America: Conversations with Fourteen Craftmasters. (Illus.). 232p. 1995. pap. 24.95 (*0-8109-2618-0*, Pub. by Abrams) Time Warner.
— The Landmarks of New York, Vol. III. LC 97-23865. (Illus.). 544p. 1998. 49.50 (*0-8109-3594-5*, Pub. by Abrams) Time Warner.
— Singular Voices: Conversations with Americans Who Make a Difference. LC 96-35204. (Illus.). 224p. 1997. 19.95 (*0-8109-2698-9*, Pub. by Abrams) Time Warner.

Diamonstein, Barbaralee, jt. auth. see Arnason, H. Horvard.

Diamonstein, Barbaralee, jt. auth. see Monroe, Michael W.

Diamont, Lincoln. Chaining the Hudson: The Fight for the River in the American Revolution. LC 94-20044. (Illus.). 320p. 1994. pap. 16.95 (*0-8065-1535-X*, Citadel Pr) Carol Pub Group.

Diamonti, Joyce, tr. see Sow, I.

Diamos, Kerson D. The First Letters in Love: Stories of Nogales, Sonora, & the Guaymas, Sonora, Mexico Areas. (ENG & SPA.). 152p. (Orig.). 1986. pap. 15.00 (*0-9614985-3-6*) El Siglo Bks.
— How to Speak Spanish, Pronto. 120p. (Orig.). 1985. pap. 15.00 (*0-9614985-2-8*) El Siglo Bks.
— Ojos del Griego (Greek's Springs) Ranch. 184p. (Orig.). 1985. pap. 7.95 (*0-9614985-0-1*) El Siglo Bks.
— Remembrance of Tucson's Past: Century Ago & More, & Less in Tucson Arizona. 150p. (Orig.). 1985. pap. 14.00 (*0-9614985-1-X*) El Siglo Bks.

Dian, Guy S. Codice de Xicotepec (Codex of Xicotepec) deluxe ed. (SPA.). 1995. pap. text 119.99 (*968-16-4761-0*, Pub. by Fondo) Continental Bk.

Dian, Janet. In Search of Yourself: Finding the Balance. (Self-Healing Through Self-Awareness Ser.: Bk. 3). (Illus.). 200p. (Orig.). 1993. pap. 15.00 (*0-9626446-2-5*) Expan Pub Co.
— In Search of Yourself: Moving Forward. LC 91-71002. (Self-Healing Through Self-Awareness Ser.: Bk. 2). (Illus.). 200p. (Orig.). 1991. pap. 15.00 (*0-9626446-1-7*) Expan Pub Co.
— In Search of Yourself: The Beginning. LC 90-81726. (Self-Healing Through Self-Awareness Ser.: Bk. 1). (Illus.). 179p. (Orig.). 1990. pap. 15.00 (*0-9626446-0-9*) Expan Pub Co.

Diana, J. N., ed. Tobacco Smoking & Atherosclerosis: Pathogenesis & Cellular Mechanisms. LC 90-7922. (Advances in Experimental Medicine & Biology Ser.: Vol. 273). (Illus.). 404p. (C). 1990. text 156.00 (*0-306-43668-X*, Kluwer Plenum) Kluwer Academic.

Diana, James S. Biology & Ecology of Fishes. (Illus.). 440p. (Orig.). (C). 1995. pap. text 45.00 (*1-884125-24-7*) Cooper Pubng.

Diana, Joan, jt. auth. see Fitzsimmons, Richard P.

Diana, Joan P., ed. Pro-Choice-Pro-Life: An Annotated, Selected Bibliography (1972-1989). 20. LC 91-12625. (Bibliographies & Indexes in Sociology Ser.: No. 20). 264p. 1991. lib. bdg. 59.95 (*0-313-27579-3*, FPJ, Greenwood Pr) Greenwood.

Diana, John. The Left-Handers Guide & Reference Manual. LC 92-70141. (Illus.). 126p. 1992. 12.95 (*1-880896-00-1*) Left-Handed Sol.

Diana, John N. & Pryor, William A., eds. Tobacco Smoking & Nutrition: Influence of Nutrition on Tobacco-Associated Health Risks. LC 93-10409. (Annals Ser.: Vol. 686). 366p. 1993. pap. 90.00 (*0-89766-808-1*) NY Acad Sci.

Diana Princess of Wales, frwd. Heart of Britain: The People's Photographs Capture. (Illus.). 256p. 1997. 32.95 (*1-898718-52-0*, Pub. by Bookman Pubs) Seven Hills Bk.

Diana Staff. Commercial Dictionary in Six Languages: Diccionario Comercial en Seis Idiomas. (ENG, FRE, GER, ITA & POR.). 636p. 1982. pap. 39.95 (*0-8288-0140-1*, S20108) Fr & Eur.
— Enciclopedia Universal Diana. (SPA.). 65.00 (*0-7859-0426-3*, S25236) Fr & Eur.

Diandra. A New Day Is Dawning: A Powerful New Message from Jesus for Your Life Today & the Future of Our Planet. LC 95-82254. 188p. Date not set. pap. text 12.95 (*1-888473-87-8*) Inward Jrney.

Diane August, ed. see Institute of Medicine Staff.

***Diane, de Grazia, ed.** Master Drawings from the Cleveland Museum of Art. (Illus.). 288p. 2000. 75.00 (*0-8478-2296-6*) Rizzoli Intl.

Diane Publication Staff. Communities at Work: Addressing the Urban Challenge. (Illus.). 123p. 1998. pap. text 30.00 (*0-7881-4789-7*) DIANE Pub.
— Establishment & Discontinuance Criteria for Airport Traffic Control Towers. (Illus.). 44p. (C). 1998. pap. text 25.00 (*0-7881-4790-0*) DIANE Pub.

DIANE Publishing Company. Consumer's Guide to Intelligence. 50p. 1994. pap. text 25.00 (*1-57979-247-2*) DIANE Pub.
— A Consumer's Guide to Intelligence (Government) (Illus.). 43p. (Orig.). (C). 1995. pap. text 25.00 (*0-7881-1640-1*) DIANE Pub.

Diane Publishing Staff. America's Commitment: Federal Programs Benefiting Women & New Initiatives As Follow-Up to the U. N. Fourth World Conference on Women. (Illus.). 199p. 1998. pap. text 30.00 (*0-7881-4910-5*) DIANE Pub.
— Asian Development Bank: Questions & Answers. Leonard, Barry, ed. 66p. (C). 2000. pap. text 20.00 (*0-7881-7129-1*) DIANE Pub.
— Clinical Research: Hearing Before the Committee on Appropriations, United States Senate. 59p. 1998. pap. text 25.00 (*0-7881-4882-6*) DIANE Pub.
— Ecotourism Marshaling Resources to Promote New Jersey's Ecotourism Treasures: Public Hearing Before Senate Natural Resources & Economic Development Committee. (Illus.). 251p. 1998. pap. text 45.00 (*0-7881-4891-5*) DIANE Pub.
— Federal Nutrition Programs: Hearing Before the Committee on Agriculture, Nutrition, & Forestry U. S. Senate. 162p. (C). 1998. pap. text 35.00 (*0-7881-4916-4*) DIANE Pub.
— General Explanation of Tax Legislation Enacted in the 104th Congress. (Illus.). 419p. (C). 1998. pap. text 50.00 (*0-7881-4884-2*) DIANE Pub.
— The Growing Threat of Internationalized Crime: Hearing Before the Committee on the Judiciary, U. S. House of Representatives. 128p. (C). 1998. pap. text 35.00 (*0-7881-4918-0*) DIANE Pub.
— Idaho Elementary School Teachers' 1991 "Innovation Inventory" A Resource Book of Ideas by & for the Teacher of Idaho. 85p. 1998. pap. text 30.00 (*0-7881-2806-X*) DIANE Pub.
— Lead Based Paint in Housing. (Illus.). 47p. 1998. pap. text 20.00 (*0-7881-4895-8*) DIANE Pub.
— Marijuana Use in America: Hearing Before the Committee on the Judiciary, U. S. House of Representatives. (Illus.). 191p. (C). 1998. pap. text 35.00 (*0-7881-4921-0*) DIANE Pub.
— National Truck Equipment Association, 1997 Membership Roster & Product Directory. 180p. 1998. pap. text 40.00 (*0-7881-4493-6*) DIANE Pub.
— Native American Housing Assistance: Joint Hearing Before the Committee on Indian Affairs & the Committee on Banking. (Illus.). 246p. (C). 1998. pap. text 45.00 (*0-7881-4917-2*) DIANE Pub.
— Origins & Scope of Roe vs. Wade: Hearing Before the Committee on the Judiciary, U. S. House of Representatives. 125p. (C). 1998. pap. text 35.00 (*0-7881-4919-9*) DIANE Pub.
— Professional Sports: The Challenges Facing the Future of the Industry: Hearing Before the Committee on the Judiciary U. S. Senate. 154p. (C). 1998. pap. text 35.00 (*0-7881-4920-2*) DIANE Pub.
— U. S. Space Launch Strategy: Hearing Before the Committee on Science, U. S. House of Representatives. 226p. (C). 1998. pap. text 45.00 (*0-7881-4915-6*) DIANE Pub.

Diane Publishing Staff, ed. Bosnia: Country Handbook. (Illus.). 530p. 1998. pap. text 30.00 (*0-7881-4798-6*) DIANE Pub.
— Crime in the United States, 1996. (Illus.). 410p. 1998. pap. text 50.00 (*0-7881-4342-5*) DIANE Pub.
— Federal Libraries & Information Centers in the United States, 1994. (Illus.). 67p. (C). 1998. reprint ed. pap. text 20.00 (*0-7881-4450-2*) DIANE Pub.
— Peacekeeping: A Selected Bibliography. 47p. 1998. pap. text 20.00 (*0-7881-4326-3*) DIANE Pub.
— Report on Minnesota Government Use of Copyright & Intellectual Property. (Illus.). 174p. (C). 1998. pap. text 35.00 (*0-7881-4808-7*) DIANE Pub.
— Rural Credit: Hearing Before the Subcommittee on Capital Markets, Securities, & Government Sponsored Enterprises. 77p. 1998. pap. text 30.00 (*0-7881-4539-8*) DIANE Pub.
— Sustainable Energy Strategy: Clean & Secure Energy for a Competitive Economy. (Illus.). 73p. (C). 1998. pap. text 25.00 (*0-7881-4807-9*) DIANE Pub.

Diani, Marco & Ingraham, Catherine A., eds. Restructuring Architectural Theory. (Studies in Phenomenology & Existential Philosophy). (Illus.). 128p. (Orig.). 1989. 32.95 (*0-8101-0834-8*); pap. 16.95 (*0-8101-0835-6*) Northwestern U Pr.

Diani, Marco, jt. ed. see Clark, Jon.

Diani, Mario. Green Networks: A Structural Analysis of the Italian Environmental Movement. (Environment, Politics, & Society Ser.). 300p. 1994. 85.00 (*0-7486-0500-2*, Pub. by Edinburgh U Pr) Col U Pr.

Diani, Mario & Eyerman, Ron, eds. Studying Collective Action. (Modern Politics Ser.: Vol. 30). 272p. (C). 1992. 55.00 (*0-8039-8524-X*) Sage.

Diani, Mario, jt. auth. see Della Porta, Donatella.

Dianich, Severino. A Short Introduction to the Catholic Church. 110p. 1994. pap. 11.50 (*0-85439-490-7*, Pub. by St Paul Pubns) St Mut.

Dianin, Sergei A. Borodin. Lord, Robert, tr. from RUS. LC 80-16820. (Illus.). 356p. 1980. reprint ed. lib. bdg. 69.50 (*0-313-22529-X*, DIBO, Greenwood Pr) Greenwood.

Dianov, E. M., et al. Nonlinear Effects in Optical Fibers. (Laser Science & Technology Ser.: Vol. 2). viii, 60p. 1989. pap. text 74.00 (*3-7186-4889-X*) Gordon & Breach.

Dianov, Y. M., ed. Fiber Optics: Research & Development. Peabody, Al, tr. (Proceedings of the Institute of General Physics of the Academy of Sciences of the U. S. S. R. Ser.: Vols. 15 & 203). 278p. (C). 1992. 175.00 (*1-56072-070-0*) Nova Sci Pubs.

Dianov, Ye. M., ed. Fiber Optics. (Proceedings of the Institute of General Physics of the Academy of Sciences of the U. S. S. R. Ser.: Vol. 5). 221p. (C). 1988. text 165.00 (*0-941743-16-0*) Nova Sci Pubs.

Dianthus. Angel Stories. LC 91-92941. (Illus.). 48p. 1991. pap. 8.75 (*0-9622160-1-1*) Dianthus.
— Aquarius: A Coming of Age. LC 88-90502. 128p. 1990. pap. 8.75 (*0-9622160-0-3*) Dianthus.
— Stonehenge: A Doorway of Recall. LC 93-90485. (Illus.). 160p. (Orig.). 1994. pap. 12.95 (*0-9622160-2-X*) Dianthus.

***Di'Antonio, Bob.** Greater Philadelphia: An Atlas of Delaware Valley's Greatest Off-Road Bicycle Rides. (Mountain Bike America Guidebks.). (Illus.). 256p. 2000. pap. 17.95 (*0-7627-0698-8*) Globe Pequot.

DiAntonio, Robert & Glickman, Nora, eds. Tradition & Innovation: Reflections on Latin American Jewish Writing. LC 92-25845. (SUNY Series in Modern Jewish Literature & Culture). 225p. (C). 1993. text 64.50 (*0-7914-1509-0*); pap. text 21.95 (*0-7914-1510-4*) State U NY Pr.

Dianu, Tiberio. Non-Custodial Sanctions: Alternative Models for Post-Communist Societies. LC 98-123981. 163p. 1998. 65.00 (*1-56072-509-5*) Nova Sci Pubs.

Dianzani, M. U. & Gentilini, Paolo, eds. Chronic Liver Disease. (Frontiers of Gastrointestinal Research Ser.: Vol. 9). (Illus.). x, 282p. 1986. 170.50 (*3-8055-4205-4*) S Karger.

Dianzani, M. U., jt. ed. see Gentilini, Paolo.

Dianzani, Mario U., ed. see Italian National Programme on Liver Cirrhosis & Vi.

Diao, Eva. My Years in Communist China. 1993. 13.95 (*0-533-10480-7*) Vantage.

Diao, Tahirou. Trilingual Vocabulary of the Environment: English/French/German. (ENG, FRE & GER.). 342p. 1996. 175.00 (*0-7859-9292-8*) Fr & Eur.

Diaper, D., et al, eds. Human-Computer Interaction-Interact 1990: Proceedings of the IFIP TC13 International Conference, Third, Cambridge, UK, 27-31 Aug., 1990. xl,1078p. 1990. 206.50 (*0-444-88817-9*, North Holland) Elsevier.
— People & Computers VII. (British Computer Society Conference Ser.). (Illus.). 544p. (C). 1992. pap. text 95.00 (*0-521-44591-4*) Cambridge U Pr.

Diaper, D. & Hammond, Nicholas G., eds. People & Computers VI. (British Computer Society Conference Ser.). (Illus.). 464p. (C). 1991. text 95.00 (*0-521-41694-9*) Cambridge U Pr.

Diaper, D. & Winder, Russell, eds. People & Computers III. (British Computer Society Conference Ser.). 492p. 1988. text 105.00 (*0-521-35197-9*) Cambridge U Pr.

Diaper, Dan. Task Analysis for Human-Computer Interaction. 1990. text 61.95 (*0-470-21606-9*) P-H.

Diaper, Dan & Sanger, Colston, eds. CSCW in Practice: An Introduction & Case Studies. LC 92-39255. (Computer Supported Cooperative Work Ser.). 1993. 59.00 (*0-387-19784-2*) Spr-Verlag.

Diaper, Dan E., ed. Knowledge Elicitation: Principles, Techniques & Applications. 1989. text 52.95 (*0-470-21410-4*) P-H.

Diarra, Nyamaton, et al. The Artfulness of M'Fa Jigi: An Interview with Nyamaton Diarra. LC 96-51143. (BAM.). 1996. write for info. (*0-942615-31-X*) U Wis African Stud.

Dias, Antonio. Designer & Client: Eight Boat Design Commissions from Kayak to Cruiser. (Illus.). 160p. 1998. pap. 22.95 (*0-937822-51-5*) WoodenBoat Pubns.

Dias, C. J., et al, eds. Studies of Law in Social Change & Development: Lawyers in the Third World-Comparative & Developmental Perspectives. 1981. 25.00 (*91-7106-179-7*); pap. 12.00 (*91-7106-176-2*) Intl Ctr Law.

Dias, Danielle & Le Barz, Patrick. Configuration Spaces over Hilbert Schemes & Applications, Vol. VII. LC 96-51088. (Lecture Notes in Mathematics Ser.: Vol. 1647). 143p. 1997. pap. 29.00 (*3-540-62050-8*) Spr-Verlag.

Dias de Deus, J., jt. ed. see Costa Ramos, S.

Dias, Dexter. Error of Judgment. 400p. 1997. pap. 6.50 (*0-446-40527-2*, Mysterious Paperbk) Warner Bks.
— Error of Judgment. large type ed. LC 97-28003. (Myst-Hall Ser.). 512p. 1997. lib. bdg. 26.95 (*0-7838-8282-3*, G K Hall Lrg Type) Mac Lib Ref.

Dias, Eduardo, jt. auth. see Lathrop, Thomas.

Dias, Eduardo, jt. auth. see Lathrop, Thomas A.

Dias, Eduardo M. O Meu Portugal Antigo e Distante: Textos. unabridged ed. Peregrinacao Publications Staff, ed. (Prosa Ser.: No. 4). (POR.). 128p. 1997. 12.00 (*1-889358-09-6*, 07) Peregrinacao.

***Dias, Eduardo M.** Portugal's Secret Jews, the End of an Era: Essays. unabridged ed. Peregrinacao Publications Staff, ed. (English Books, Essays Ser.: No. 2). (POR.). 112p. 1999. 12.00 (*1-889358-16-9*, 13) Peregrinacao.

Dias, Eduardo M., jt. auth. see Lathrop, Thomas A.

Dias, Eduardo Mayone. Criptojudeus Portugueses, O Fim de Uma Era (Portugal's Secret Jews, the End of an Era) Ensaios. unabridged ed. (English Books, Essays Ser.: Vol. 1). (POR & ENG.). 208p. 1999. boxed set 18.00 (*1-889358-18-5*, 12) Peregrinacao.

***Dias, Eduardo Mayone.** A Presenca Portuguesa Na California. Peregrinacao Publications Staff, ed. (Documentos Ser.). (POR.). 128p. 2000. boxed set 13.95 (*1-889358-23-1*, 24) Peregrinacao.

***Dias, Eduardo Mayone, ed.** Portugueses Na America Do Norte: Ensaios/Essays. unabridged ed. (Documentos Ser.: Vol. 1). (POR & ENG.). 192p. 1999. boxed set 18.00 (*1-889358-08-8*, 16) Peregrinacao.

Dias, Eduardo Mayone, jt. ed. see Cabral, Adalino.

Dias, F. & Ghidaglia, Jean-Michel. Mathematical Problems in the Theory of Water Waves: A Workshop on the Problems in the Theory of Nonlinear Hydrodynamic Waves, May 15-19, 1995, Luminy, France, Vol. 197. LC 96-22083. (Contemporary Mathematics Ser.: Vol. 200). 235p. 1996. pap. 55.00 (*0-8218-0510-X*, CONM/200) Am Math.

Dias, J. R. Handbook of Polycyclic Hydrocarbons: Benzenoid Hydrocarbons, Pt. A. 388p. 1987. 224.50 (*0-444-42802-X*) Elsevier.

Dias, Jerry R. Molecular Orbital Calculations Using Chemical Graph Theory. LC 92-44419. 1993. 103.95 (*0-387-56134-X*) Spr-Verlag.

Dias, Joao C. The Mother of Good Counsel of Genazzano. LC 91-68343. (Illus.). 244p. (Orig.). 1992. 23.95 (*0-685-70864-0*); pap. 19.95 (*1-881008-03-7*) Am Soc Defense TFP.

Dias, L. Alver & Coble, Richard, eds. Implementation of Safety & Health on Construction Sites: Proceedings of the First International Conference, Lison, 4-7 September 1996. (Illus.). 550p. (C). 1996. 149.00 (*90-5410-847-9*, Pub. by A A Balkema) Ashgate Pub Co.

Dias, Maria O. Power & Everyday Life: The Lives of Working Women in Nineteenth-Century Brazil. Frost, Ann, tr. (Illus.). 240p. 1995. text 45.00 (*0-8135-2204-8*) Rutgers U Pr.
— Power & Everyday Life: The Lives of Working Women in Nineteenth-Century Brazil. Frost, Ann, tr. LC 94-47497. (Illus.). 240p. (C). 1995. pap. text 15.95 (*0-8135-2205-6*) Rutgers U Pr.

Dias-Mas, Paloma. Sephardim: The Jews from Spain. Zucker, George K., ed. & tr. by. LC 92-15523. 250p. 1992. 32.50 (*0-226-14483-6*) U Ch Pr.

Dias, Oscar, jt. auth. see Andrea, Mario.

Dias, Patrick. Reading & Responding to Poetry: Patterns in the Process. LC 95-43115. 124p. 1995. pap. text 22.00 (*0-86709-372-2*, 0372, Pub. by Boynton Cook Pubs) Heinemann.

D

An Asterisk (*) at the beginning of an entry indicates that the title is appearing for the first time.

***Dias, Patrick & Parbe, Anthony.** Transitions: Writing in Academic & Workplace Settings. LC 00-25935. (Written Language Ser.). 2000. pap. write for info. (*1-57273-270-9*) Hampton Pr NJ.

Dias, Patrick, et al. Worlds Apart: Acting & Writing in Academic & Workplace Contexts. LC 98-49931. (Rhetoric, Society, & Knowledge Ser.). 296p. 1999. 59.95 (*0-8058-2147-3*); pap. 29.95 (*0-8058-2148-1*) L Erlbaum Assocs.

Dias, Robert Vas, see Vas Dias, Robert.

Dias, Ron. Disney's the Little Mermaid. LC 92-74259. (Illustrated Classics Ser.). 96p. (J). 1993. 14.95 (*1-56282-429-5*, Pub. by Disney Pr) Little.

— Disney's the Little Mermaid. LC 92-74260. (Junior Novelization Ser.). 64p. (J). (gr. 2-6). 1993. pap. 2.95 (*1-56282-436-8*, Pub. by Disney Pr) Little.

Dias, Zwinglio M. & Hill, Joyce. Brazil: A Gracious People in a Heartless System. LC 96-40060. 1997. 8.95 (*0-377-00315-8*) Friendship Pr.

Diasio, Robert B. & Sommadossi, Jean-Pierre. Advances in Chemotherapy of AIDS. (Illus.). 160p. 1990. 44.00 (*0-08-040315-8*) McGraw.

Diaspro, Alberto. Focusing on Modern Microscopy: An Introduction from General Principles to Bioimaging. 352p. 2000. 79.95 (*0-7803-3414-0*, PC5687-QOE) Inst Electrical.

Diavies, Nicholas. Deadly Kind of Love. 1996. mass mkt. 4.99 (*1-85782-101-7*, Pub. by Blake Publng) Seven Hills Bk.

Diawara, Manthia. African Cinema: Politics & Culture. LC 91-24579. (Blacks in the Diaspora Ser.). (Illus.). 208p. 1992. text 35.00 (*0-253-31704-5*); pap. text 14.95 (*0-253-20707-X*, MB-707) Ind U Pr.

Diawara, Manthia. In Search of Africa. LC 98-17149. 288p. 1998. 27.95 (*0-674-44611-9*) HUP.

***Diawara, Manthia.** In Search of Africa. 288p. 2000. pap. 16.95 (*0-674-00408-6*) HUP.

Diawara, Manthia, ed. Black American Cinema: Aesthetics & Spectatorship. LC 92-32907. (AFI Film Readers Ser.). 256p. (gr. 13). 1993. pap. 19.99 (*0-415-90397-1*, A5303) Routledge.

— Black American Cinema: Aesthetics & Spectatorship. LC 92-32907. (AFI Film Readers Ser.). (Illus.). 256p. (C). (gr. 13). 1993. 75.00 (*0-415-90396-3*, A5299) Routledge.

Diawara, Manthia, et al, eds. Black British Cultural Studies: A Reader. LC 95-42672. (Black Literature & Culture Ser.). 384p. (C). 1996. pap. text 16.95 (*0-226-14482-8*) U Ch Pr.

Diaz. Abriendo Paso. (Secondary Spanish Ser.). (SPA.). 1995. pap., wbk. ed. 42.95 (*0-8384-4944-1*) Heinle & Heinle.

— Abriendo Paso. (Secondary Spanish Ser.). (SPA.). 1996. pap., suppl. ed. 36.95 (*0-8384-4946-8*) Heinle & Heinle.

— Abriendo Paso: Grammatica. (Secondary Spanish Ser.). 1995. pap. 25.95 (*0-8384-6737-7*) Heinle & Heinle.

— Abriendo Paso: Lectura. (Secondary Spanish Ser.). 1995. pap. 49.95 (*0-8384-4943-3*) Heinle & Heinle.

***Diaz.** Abriendo Paso Gramatica. 1999. 30.00 (*0-8384-2624-7*) Heinle & Heinle.

Diaz. Abriendo Paso Lectura-lesson Plans+script+ak. 2nd ed. (Secondary Spanish). 1999. pap. 32.50 (*0-8384-4949-2*) Heinle & Heinle.

— Manual of Perinatal Anesthesia & Critical Care. (Illus.). 416p. 1991. pap. text 64.00 (*0-7216-1874-X*, W B Saunders Co) Harcrt Hlth Sci Grp.

— Myth Maker: J. R. R. Tolkien. LC 96-50032. 1998. write for info. (*0-15-200835-7*) Harcourt.

— The Rebellious Alphabet. 1996. pap. 6.95 (*0-8050-4901-0*, Bks Young Read) H Holt & Co.

— Untitled John Henry. Date not set. 15.95 (*0-15-200403-3*) Harcourt.

***Diaz & Collins.** Abriendo Paso Gramatica. 1999. 34.25 (*0-8384-0096-5*) Heinle & Heinle.

Diaz, et al. Global Perspectives for Educators. LC 98-20918. 227p. 1998. pap. text 26.00 (*0-205-26366-6*) P-H.

***Diaz, A. A.** Evaluation of Ultrasonic Inspection Techniques for Coarse-Grained Materials. 178p. 1998. per. 26.00 (*0-16-062963-2*) USGPO.

Diaz, Adriana. Freeing the Creative Spirit: Drawing on the Power of Art to Tap the Magic & Wisdom Within. LC 90-55771. (Illus.). 240p. 1992. pap. 20.00 (*0-06-250182-8*, Pub. by Harper SF) HarpC.

***Diaz Agen, Manzani & Perez de Ayala, Juan, eds.** Manuel de Falla: His Life & Works. Abril, Chi Qui, tr. (Illus.). 303p. 1999. pap. text 34.95 (*0-7119-6909-4*, OP48U71) Omnibus NY.

Diaz, Albert. The Airport Book: The Passenger's Guide to Major Airports in the United States & Canada. (Illus.). 1979. pap. 3.95 (*0-935866-00-0*) Airport Bk Pr.

Diaz Alejandro, Carlos F. Colombia. LC 75-24035. (Foreign Trade Regimes & Economic Development Ser.: No. 9). (Illus.). 309p. reprint ed. pap. 95.80 (*0-8357-7567-4*, 205688800096) Bks Demand.

Diaz-Alejandro, Carlos F. Colombia. (Special Conference Series on Foreign Trade Regimes & Economic Development: No. 9). 309p. 1976. reprint ed. 80.40 (*0-87014-509-6*) Natl Bur Econ Res.

Diaz Alejandro, Carlos F. Essays on the Economic History of the Argentine Republic. LC 70-118727. (Publication of the Economic Growth Center, Yale University Ser.). 569p. reprint ed. pap. 176.40 (*0-8357-8714-1*, 203371000087) Bks Demand.

Diaz Alejandro, Carlos F., jt. auth. see Bacha, Edmar L.

Diaz, Alejandro H. The Cuban Mile. Cluster, Dick, tr. from SPA. LC 98-5433. (Discoveries Ser.). 120p. 1998. pap. 13.95 (*0-935480-94-3*) Lat Am Lit Rev Pr.

Diaz, Alvaro, jt. auth. see Martinez, Javier.

Diaz-Andreu, Magarita & Sorensen, Marie L., eds. Excavating Women: History of Women in European Archaeology. LC 98-149911. (Illus.). 336p. (C). 1998. 85.00 (*0-415-15760-9*) Routledge.

Diaz-Andreu, Margarita & Keay, Simon, eds. The Archaeology of Iberia: The Dynamics of Change. LC 96-7550. (Illus.). 336p. (C). 1997. 75.00 (*0-415-12012-8*) Routledge.

Diaz-Andreu, Margarita, ed. see Champion, Timothy C.

***Diaz, Anthony Case.** Best Restaurants in New York. 2000. pap. 9.95 (*0-9701338-0-4*, Pub. by Best Restrnts) Seven Hills Bk.

Diaz, Aura S., jt. auth. see De Beauport, Elaine.

Diaz Ayala, Cristobal. Cuando Sali de la Habana, 1898-1997: Cien Anos de Musica Cubana por el Mundo. (SPA., Illus.). 240p. 1998. pap. 30.00 incl. audio compact disk (*1-56328-217-8*) Edit Plaza Mayor.

— Cuba Canta y Baila Vol. II: Discografia de la Musica Cubana, 1925 to Present. (SPA.). Date not set. pap. write for info. (*0-89729-751-2*) Ediciones.

— The Roots of Salsa: A History of Cuban Music. LC 95-24021. (Contributions to the Study of Music & Dance Ser.: Vol. 37). 296p. 1996. text 59.95 (*0-313-29804-1*, Greenwood Pr) Greenwood.

Diaz Balsera, Viviana. Calderon y las Quimeras de la Culpa: Alegoria, Seduccion y Resistencia en Cinco Autos Sacramentales. LC 96-53347. (Purdue Studies in Romance Literatures: Vol. 13). (SPA.). 288p. 1997. 38.95 (*1-55753-098-X*) Purdue U Pr.

Diaz, Bernal. The Conquest of New Spain. Cohen, J. M., tr. 416p. (Orig.). (YA). (gr. 9 up). 1963. pap. 11.95 (*0-14-044123-9*, Penguin Classics) Viking Penguin.

Diaz-Bobillo, Ignacio J., jt. auth. see Dahleh, Munther A.

Diaz-Briquets, Sergio. The Health Revolution in Cuba. LC 82-10865. (Institute of Latin American Studies Special Publication). 245p. 1983. text 19.95 (*0-292-75071-4*) U of Tex Pr.

Diaz-Briquets, Sergio, ed. Cuban Internationalism in Sub-Saharan Africa. LC 89-16974. 250p. 1989. pap. text 18.95 (*0-8207-0226-9*) Duquesne.

***Diaz-Briquets, Sergio & Perez-Lopez, Jorge.** Conquering Nature: The Environmental Legacy of Socialism in Cuba. LC 99-50680. 416p. 2000. pap. 22.95 (*0-8229-5721-3*); text 50.00 (*0-8229-4118-X*) U of Pittsburgh Pr.

Diaz, C., et al, eds. Smelting, Technology Development, Process Modeling & Fundamentals. (Illus.). 643p. write for info. (*0-87339-440-2*) Minerals Metals.

Diaz, Carlos, ed. Multicultural Education for the Twenty-First Century. 208p. 1992. pap. 18.95 (*0-8106-1849-4*) NEA.

Diaz, Carlos A. Balada Gregoriana. LC 87-81810. (Coleccion Caniqui). (SPA.). 119p. (Orig.). 1988. pap. 9.95 (*0-89729-442-4*) Ediciones.

Diaz, Carlos A. Toro, see Toro Diaz, Carlos A.

Diaz, Carlos H., et al. Modeling of Electrical Overstress in Integrated Circuits. LC 94-31195. (International Series in Engineering & Computer Science, Natural Language Processing & Machine Translation). 176p. (C). 1994. text 113.00 (*0-7923-9505-0*) Kluwer Academic.

Diaz Castanon, Carmen, ed. see Casona, Alejandro.

Diaz, Cervantes. El Adgua de Tlacote. (SPA.). 1997. pap. text 4.98 (*968-409-695-X*) Edamex.

Diaz-Cobo, Oscar. Silencing Sentries. LC 88-45738. 104p. 1988. pap. text 14.95 (*0-915179-84-9*) Loompanics.

***Diaz-Cobo, Oscar, et al, eds.** Urban Transport & Environment.Tr. of Trasport Urbain et Environnement. 1100p. (C). 2000. text 99.00 (*90-5809-128-7*, Pub. by A A Balkema) Ashgate Pub Co.

Diaz, Collin. Abriendo Paso Lectura: Text. 2nd ed. 1999. pap. text 39.25 (*0-8384-0934-2*) Heinle & Heinle.

Diaz-Cotto, Juanita. Gender, Ethnicity & the State: Latina & Latino Prison Politics. LC 95-16255. (SUNY Series in New Directions in Crime & Justice Studies). 480p. (C). 1996. text 74.50 (*0-7914-2815-X*); pap. text 24.95 (*0-7914-2816-8*) State U NY Pr.

Diaz, David. Be Not Far from Me: The Oldest Love Story: Legends from the Bible. LC 97-24543. 256p. (J). (gr. 4 up). 1998. 25.00 (*0-689-81088-1*) S&S Bks Yung.

Diaz, David J., ed. Quantitative Microscopy & Image Analysis: ASM 1993 Charleston, SC International Conference Proceedings. 135p. 1994. 49.00 (*0-87170-511-7*, 6399) ASM.

Diaz De Bustamente, Jose M. Instrumentum Emblematicum, 2 vols., Set. (Alpha-Omega, Reihe B Ser.: Bd. V). (GER.). 1388p. 1991. write for info. (*3-487-09510-6*) G Olms Pubs.

Diaz De Gamez. The Unconquered Knight: A Chronicle of the Deeds of Don Pero Nino. Evans, Joan, tr. LC 78-63494. reprint ed. 34.50 (*0-404-17143-5*) AMS Pr.

Diaz De Grana, Lydia. Los Objetivos Educacionales: Criterios Basicos para la Evaluacion del Aprendizaje. LC 76-8191. (SPA.). 94p. (Orig.). (C). 1983. pap. 4.50 (*0-8477-2721-1*) U of PR Pr.

Diaz De Ilarraza Sanchez, Arantza & Fernandez De Castro, I., eds. Computer Aided Learning & Instruction in Science & Engineering: Proceedings of the International Conference, CALISCE '96, San Sebastian, Spain, held July 29-31, 1996. Vol. 110. LC 96-29061. (Lecture Notes in Computer Science Ser.). 480p. 1996. pap. 75.00 (*3-540-61491-5*) Spr-Verlag.

Diaz de la Rubia, Thomas, et al, eds. Multiscale Modelling of Materials Vol. 538: Materials Research Society Symposium Proceedings. LC 99-13247. (Symposium Proceedings Ser.). 591p. 1999. 89.00 (*1-55899-444-0*) Materials Res.

Diaz de la Rubia, Tomas, et al, eds. Defects & Diffusion in Silicon Processing: Symposium Held in San Francisco, California, April 1-4, 1997. LC 97-36151. (Materials Research Society Symposium Proceedings Ser.: Vol. 469). (Illus.). 559p. reprint ed. pap. 173.30 (*0-608-07979-0*, 206700500001) Bks Demand.

Diaz de Leon, M. A. Legal Dictionary of the Penal System: Diccionario de Derecho Procesal Penal y Terminos Usuales En el Proceso Penal, 2 vols. (SPA.). 2249p. 1986. 175.00 (*0-8288-1529-1*, S608) Fr & Eur.

Diaz Del Castillo, Bernal. The Discovery & Conquest of Mexico. Garcia, Genaro, ed. Maudslay, A. P., tr. from SPA. LC 95-45871. (Illus.). 512p. 1996. reprint ed. pap. 16.95 (*0-306-80697-5*) Da Capo.

Diaz-Diocaretez, M. & Zavala, Iris M. Breve Historia Feminista II. 144p. 1995. pap. write for info. (*0-614-16495-8*) U of PR Pr.

Diaz-Diocaretz, Myriam. Translating Poetic Discourse: Questions of Feminist Strategies in Adrienne Rich. LC 84-28245. (Critical Theory Ser.: No. 2). vii, 167p. 1985. 55.00 (*0-915027-52-6*); pap. 29.00 (*0-915027-53-4*) J Benjamins Pubng Co.

Diaz-Diocaretz, Myriam & Zavala, Iris M. Breve Historia Feminista de la Literatura Espanola: En Lengua Castellana, Tomo I. 143p. 1993. pap. 10.50 (*84-7658-403-2*) U of PR Pr.

Diaz-Diocaretz, Myriam & Zavala, Iris M., eds. Women, Feminist Identity & Society in the 1980's: Selected Papers. LC 84-28286. (Critical Theory Ser.: No. 1). x, 138p. 1985. 52.00 (*0-915027-50-X*); pap. 26.00 (*0-915027-51-8*) J Benjamins Pubng Co.

Diaz, Emilio G. La Politica de los Empresarios Puertorriquenos. (SPA.). 124p. 1991. pap. 6.50 (*0-929157-13-3*) Ediciones Huracan.

Diaz-Gilbert, Miriam. Communicating Effectively with Hispanic Patients: The Complete Guide to Key Vocabulary Words & Essential & Functional Phrases in Spanish for Direct Patient Contact, 4 cass., Set unabridged ed. (ENG & SPA.). 96p. (Orig.). 1991. pap., pap. text 175.00 incl. audio (*0-9628364-0-0*) ICPC.

Diaz, Gisele & Rodgers, Alan. The Codex Borgia: A Full-Color Restoration of the Ancient Mexican Manuscript. LC 93-6714. (Illus.). 96p. 1998. reprint ed. pap. 15.95 (*0-486-27569-8*) Dover.

Diaz, Gloria C. El Sol de los Venados (The Sun of the Deer) (J). (gr. 7). 1996. pap. 6.95 (*84-348-3976-8*) Lectorum Pubns.

Diaz-Granados, Carol. Petrography & Pictographs of Missouri. 341p. 2000. pap. text 29.95 (*0-8173-0988-8*) U of Ala Pr.

Diaz-Guerrero, R. & Szalay, L. B. Understanding Mexicans & Americans: Cultural Perspectives in Conflict. (Cognition & Language). (Illus.). 308p. (C). 1991. pap. 70.00 (*0-306-43817-8*, Kluwer Plenum) Kluwer Academic.

Diaz-Guerrero, Rogelio. Psychology of the Mexican: Culture & Personality. LC 74-23309. (Texas Pan American Ser.). 193p. 1975. pap. 7.95 (*0-292-76430-8*) U of Tex Pr.

Diaz-Guerrero, Rogelio, jt. auth. see Marino, Carlos.

Diaz-Guerrero, Rogelio, jt. ed. see Spielberger, Charles D.

***Diaz, Gwedolyn M.** Adventures of Mighty Mom: Here She Comes to Save the Day... If Only She Can Find the Keys! 228p. 2000. pap. 12.99 (*1-56292-773-6*) Honor Bks OK.

***Diaz, Henry F. & Markgraf, Vera, eds.** El Nino & the Southern Oscillation: Multiscale Variability & Global & Regional Impacts. (Illus.). 480p. (C). 2000. 90.00 (*0-521-62138-0*) Cambridge U Pr.

Diaz, Henry F. & Pulwarty, Roger S. Hurricanes: Climate & Socioeconomic Impacts. LC 96-29974. 304p. 1997. 78.00 (*3-540-62078-8*) Spr-Verlag.

Diaz-Herrera, Jorge L., ed. see Seventh SEI Conference on Software Engineering Edu.

Diaz, Ivan. On the Nature of the Puerto Rican Universe: De Rerum Natura Puertorriquena. 286p. (Orig.). 1997. pap. 12.00 (*0-9655929-0-1*) Domino Pr.

Diaz, J. El Espanol Sin Problemas. (Spanish K-12 Ser.). (SPA., Illus.). 364p. 1989. pap. text 40.25 (*0-685-33277-2*) Addison-Wesley.

Diaz, J. & Ramos, I., eds. Formalization of Programming Concepts: Proceedings. (Lecture Notes in Computer Science Ser.: Vol. 107). 478p. 1981. 38.00 (*0-387-10699-5*) Spr-Verlag.

Diaz, J. & Serna, Maria. Algorithms - ESA '96: Fourth Annual European Symposium, Barcelona, Spain, September 25-27, 1996: Proceedings. LC 96-30961. (Lecture Notes in Computer Science Ser.: Vol. 1136). 566p. 1996. pap. 87.00 (*3-540-61680-2*) Spr-Verlag.

Diaz, J., et al. Gamma Rays & Particle Production in Intermediate Energy Heavy Ion Reactions. 800p. 1994. text 213.00 (*981-02-1775-7*) World Scientific Pub.

— Paradigms for Fast Parallel Approximability. LC 96-51778. (Cambridge International Series in Parallel Computation). 166p. 1997. text 44.95 (*0-521-43170-0*) Cambridge U Pr.

Diaz, J., jt. auth. see Orejas, Fernando.

Diaz, J. C. Mathematics for Large Scale Computing. (Lecture Notes in Pure & Applied Mathematics Ser.: Vol. 120). (Illus.). 368p. 1989. pap. text 155.00 (*0-8247-8122-8*) Dekker.

Diaz, J. I. & North Atlantic Treaty Organization Staff. The Mathematics of Models for Climatology & Environment. LC 96-46904. (NATO ASI Ser.: Vol. 48). 478p. 1996. 239.00 (*3-540-61879-1*) Spr-Verlag.

Diaz, Jaime. Hallowed Ground: Golf's Greatest Places. LC 99-35011. (Illus.). 156p. 1999. 45.00 (*0-86713-057-1*) Greenwich Wrkshop.

— How Drugs Influence Behavior: A Neurobehavioral Approach. LC 96-35333. 285p. (C). 1996. pap. text 57.00 (*0-02-328764-0*, Macmillan Coll) P-H.

Diaz, James, jt. auth. see Floyd, Raymond.

***Diaz, James W.** Blue: A Touchy Feely First Words Color Book. (Touchy Feely First Words Bks.). (Illus.). 10p. (J). 2000. 5.95 (*1-58117-071-8*, Piggy Toes Pr) Intervisual Bks.

— Green: A Touchy Feely First Words Book. (Touchy Feely First Words Bks.: Vol. 2). (Illus.). 10p. (J). 2000. 5.95 (*1-58117-072-6*, Piggy Toes Pr) Intervisual Bks.

— Red: A Touchy Feely First Words Book. (Touchy Feely First Words Bks.: Vol. 3). (Illus.). 10p. (J). 2000. 5.95 (*1-58117-070-X*, Piggy Toes Pr) Intervisual Bks.

— Yellow: A Touchy Feely First Words Book. (Touchy Feely First Words Bks.: Vol. 4). (Illus.). 10p. (J). 2000. 5.95 (*1-58117-069-6*, Piggy Toes Pr) Intervisual Bks.

Diaz, Jamie, Studios Staff. Batman Vol. 19: Look & Find. large type ed. (Look & Find Ser.). 24p. (J). (gr. k-6). 1998. lib. bdg. 14.95 (*1-56674-230-7*, HTS Bks) Forest Hse.

— Disney's Beauty & the Beast. (Look & Find Ser.). 24p. (J). (gr. k-6). 1996. lib. bdg. 14.95 (*1-56674-093-2*, HTS Bks) Forest Hse.

— Pooh. (Look & Find Ser.). 24p. (J). 1996. lib. bdg. 14.95 (*1-56674-168-8*) Forest Hse.

— The Puzzle Place. (Look & Find Ser.). 24p. (J). 1996. lib. bdg. 14.95 (*1-56674-210-2*, HTS Bks) Forest Hse.

— Shari Lewis' Lamp Chops & Friends. (Look & Find Ser.). (J). (gr. k-6). 1996. lib. bdg. 14.95 (*1-56674-167-X*, HTS Bks) Forest Hse.

— Space Jam. (Look & Find Ser.). 24p. (J). (gr. k-6). 1996. lib. bdg. 14.95 (*1-56674-209-9*, HTS Bks) Forest Hse.

Diaz, Janet W. Ana Maria Matute. LC 70-125268. (Twayne's World Authors Ser.). 165p. 1971. lib. bdg. 17.95 (*0-8290-1753-4*) Irvington.

— Miguel Delibes. (Twayne's World Authors Ser.). 1971. lib. bdg. 17.95 (*0-8290-0119-0*) Irvington.

Diaz, Jim. Colors Flip-Pop Fun. 10p. 1999. pap. text 9.95 (*1-58117-067-X*) Intervisual Bks.

— Counting Flip-Pop Fun. 10p. (YA). (gr. k up). 1999. 9.95 (*1-58117-068-8*) Intervisual Bks.

Diaz, Joaquin & Diaz Viana, Luis. Romances Tradicionales de Castilla y Leon. (Spanish Ser.: No. 7). iv, 160p. 1982. 12.50 (*0-942260-22-8*) Hispanic Seminary.

Diaz, Jorge. The Rebellious Alphabet. Fox, Geoffrey, tr. LC 93-12697. (Edge Graphics Ser.). (Illus.). 88p. (YA). (gr. 7 up). 1995. 14.95 (*0-8050-2765-3*, Bks Young Read) H Holt & Co.

Diaz, Jorge A. Pablo Recuerda: La Fiesta del Dia de los Muertos (Pablo Remembers) (SPA.). 48p. (YA). (gr. 4-7). 1993. 16.00 (*0-688-12894-7*) Lothrop.

Diaz, Jorge E., tr. see Ford, LeRoy.

Diaz, Jose, et al. AP Spanish: A Guide for the Language Course. 1989. teacher ed. 11.95 (*0-8013-0168-8*, 78002); pap. text 18.45 (*0-8013-0167-X*, 78001) Longman.

— AP Spanish: A Guide for the Language Course, Set. 1989. audio 39.95 (*0-8013-0169-6*, 78003) Longman.

Diaz, Jose L. El Abaco, la Lira y la Rosa. (Ciencia Para Todos Ser.). (SPA.). pap. 6.99 (*968-16-5127-8*, Pub. by Fondo) Continental Bk.

Diaz, Jose M. & Nadel, Maria. Let's Review: Spanish with Compact Disk. (Let's Review Ser.). (ENG & SPA.). 500p. 1998. pap. 11.95 (*0-7641-0133-1*, 835991Q) Barron.

Diaz, Jose M. & Nadel, Maria F. Let's Review: Spanish Power Pack, 2 vols. (ENG & SPA.). 1998. pap. 19.95 (*0-7641-7161-5*) Barron.

— Let's Review: Spanish with Compact Disk. (Let's Review Ser.). 500p. 1998. pap. 16.95 incl. audio compact disk (*0-7641-7216-6*) Barron.

Diaz, Jose M., et al. AP Spanish: Preparing for the Language Examination. 2nd ed. 1995. pap. text. write for info. (*0-8013-1531-X*) Addison-Wesley.

— AP Spanish 2: Preparing for the Language Examination. 2nd ed. 1995. pap. text, teacher ed. write for info. (*0-8013-1532-8*) Addison-Wesley.

Diaz, Jose Simon & Prades, Juana de Jose. Ensayo de Una Bibliografia de las Obras y Articulos sobre la Vida y Escritos de Lope de Vega Carpio. (SPA.). 325p. 1968. pap. 100.00 (*0-614-00129-3*) Elliots Bks.

Diaz, Junot. Drown. 224p. 1997. reprint ed. pap. 12.00 (*1-57322-606-8*, Riverhd Trade) Berkley Pub.

— Negocios (Spanish-Language Edition of Drown) (SPA.). 1997. pap. 11.00 (*0-679-77657-5*) Vin Bks.

Diaz, Karen R., ed. Reference Sources on the Internet: Off the Shelf & onto the Web. LC 97-28052. 266p. 1997. 49.95 (*0-7890-0358-9*) Haworth Pr.

Diaz, Katacha. Fiesta! Trumbauer, Lisa, ed. (Multicultural Big Bks.). (Illus.). 16p. (J). (ps-2). 1994. pap. 16.95 (*1-56784-502-9*) Newbridge Educ.

Diaz Larios, Luis F., ed. see De Larra, Mariano J.

***Diaz-Lefebvre.** Coloring Outside the Lines. 1999. pap. text 22.00 (*0-471-48043-6*) Wiley.

Diaz, Leo & Milligan, Thomas A. Antenna Engineering Using Physical Optics: Practical Cad Techniques & Software. LC 96-28233. 306p. 1996. 105.00 incl. cd-rom (*0-89006-732-5*) Artech Hse.

Diaz, Lidia, tr. see Swamp, Jake.

Diaz, Lilita B., tr. see Woodbury, Michael A., ed.

Diaz-Limaco, Jane H. De, see De Diaz-Limaco, Jane H.

Diaz, Lorena Martinez, ed. see McLaughlin, Karen A. & Brilliant, Kelly J.

Diaz, Luis F. Composting & Recycling Municipal Solid Waste. 320p. 1993. lib. bdg. 85.00 (*0-87371-563-2*, L563) Lewis Pubs.

— Ironia e Ideologia en "La Regenta" de Leopoldo Alas. LC 92-20558. (American University Studies: Romance Languages & Literature: Ser. II, Vol. 186). 277p. (C). 1992. text 48.95 (*0-8204-1734-3*) P Lang Pubng.

Diaz, Luis F. & Golueke, Clarence G. Resource Recovery from Municipal Solid Wastes, 2 vols. Incl. Vol. I. Primary Processing. 176p. 1982. 112.00 (*0-8493-5613-X*); Vol. II. Final Processing. 192p. 1982. 111.00 (*0-8493-5614-8*, CRC Reprint); 1982. write for info. (*0-318-56976-0*, TD794) CRC Pr.

Diaz, M. C., ed. see Menendez Pidal, Ramon.

Diaz, M. Richard. Topics in the Logic of Relevance. (Analytica Ser.). 144p. 1981. lib. bdg. 52.00 (*3-88405-003-6*) Philosophia Pr.

Diaz, Manuel C. El Ano del Ras de Mar. LC 93-72253. (Coleccion Caniqui). (SPA.). 79p. (Orig.). 1993. pap. 9.95 (*0-89729-699-0*) Ediciones.

D

— Un Paraiso Bajo las Estrellas. LC 95-61239. (Coleccion Caniqui). (SPA.). 91p. (Orig.). 1995. pap. 9.95 (*0-89729-783-0*) Ediciones.

Diaz, Manuel G. Neoclassicals in Puerto Rico. (Puerto Rico Ser.). 1979. lib. bdg. 59.95 (*0-8490-2975-9*) Gordon Pr.

Diaz, Manuel S. Rice for the Moon & Other Stories. 117p. (Orig.). (C). 1986. pap. 7.50 (*971-10-0247-7*, Pub. by New Day Pub) Cellar.

Diaz, Manuel S., jt. ed. see Alcantara, Pelagio.

***Diaz, Maria Elena.** The Virgin, the King & the Royal Slaves of el Cobre: Negotiating Freedom in Colonial Cuba, 1670-1780. LC 00-32197. (Illus.). 2000. write for info. (*0-8047-3718-5*) Stanford U Pr.

Diaz, Marino. Easy Steps to Building Your Own Computer: Easy Illustrated Step by Step Instructions to Build Your Own Computer. Pieper, Vicki, ed. (Illus.). x, 105p. 1999. pap. 17.95 (*0-9669939-0-X*) M Diaz.

***Diaz, Marino A.** Easy Steps to Building Your Own Computer: Easy Illustrated Step by Step Instructions to Build Your Own Computer. 2nd ed. (Illus.). 128p. 2000. pap. 15.95 (*0-9669939-1-8*) M Diaz.

Diaz, Mary K. Case Studies in Contemporary Marriage. 133p. (C). 1998. pap. text 16.00 (*1-891877-00-3*) Sheron Ent.

***Diaz, Michel, et al, eds.** Interactive Distributed Multimedia Systems & Telecommunication Services: Proceedings of the 6th International Workshop, IDMS'99, Toulouse, France, October 12-15, 1999. LC 99-49616. (Lecture Notes In Computer Science: Vol. 1718). xi, 386p. 1999. pap. 62.00 (*3-540-66595-1*) Spr-Verlag.

Diaz, Miguel H., jt. ed. see Espin, Orlando O.

Diaz, Miguel M. Persistent Peasants: Smallholders, State Agencies & Involuntary Migration in Western Venezuela. (Stockholm Studies in Social Anthropology: No. 35). (Illus.). 291p. (Orig.). 1996. pap. 67.50 (*91-7153-523-3*) Coronet Bks.

Diaz, Mildred, ed. see Allred, Jeannette A.

Diaz, Modesto, tr. see Keirsey, David West.

Diaz, Nadel. En Marcha Lectura. 2001. pap. 39.00 (*0-8384-0295-X*) Heinle & Heinle.

Diaz, Nancy G. The Radical Self: Metamorphosis to Animal Form in Modern Latin American Narrative. LC 88-10000. 136p. 1989. text 23.00 (*0-8262-0692-1*) U of Mo Pr.

Diaz Navarro, Epiteto, tr. see Zavala, Iris M.

Diaz, Nidia. I Was Never Alone: A Prison Diary From El Salvador. 1999. pap. 16.95 (*1-876175-17-6*) Ocean Pr NJ.

— I Was Never Alone: A Prison Diary from El Salvador. (Illus.). 220p. 1992. 34.95 (*1-875284-14-1*); pap. 12.95 (*1-875284-13-3*) Ocean Pr NJ.

Diaz, Olimpia, tr. see St. Roman, Philip.

Diaz, Olimpia, tr. see Una Publicacion Pastoral Redentorista Staff.

Diaz, Pietro P. Glosario de Terminos Mineros. (SPA.). 1995. 32.00 (*0-7859-9733-4*) Fr & Eur.

Diaz Plaja, Fernando. La Sociedad Espanola: Desde 1500 Hasta Nuestros Dias. (C). pap. 3.00 (*0-8477-3117-0*) U of PR Pr.

Diaz-Plaja, Fernando & Cressey, William W. La Espana Que Sobrevive. LC 96-26244. (SPA.). 224p. 1997. pap. 22.95 (*0-87840-631-X*) Georgetown U Pr.

Diaz Plaja, Guillermo, ed. see Mosquera, Cristobal.

Diaz Polanco, Hector. Indigenous Peoples in Latin America: The Quest for Self-Determination. Rayas, Lucia, tr. LC 96-39371. (Latin American Perspectives Ser.). 176p. (C). 1997. pap. 24.00 (*0-8133-8699-3*, Pub. by Westview) HarpC.

Diaz Portillo, J. Aspectos Basicos de Bioquimica Clinica. (SPA.). 293p. 1997. pap. 37.50 (*84-7978-282-X*, Pub. by Ediciones Diaz) IBD Ltd.

Diaz, Prieto P. Mining Dictionary (Glosario de Terminos Mineros) (ENG & SPA.). 291p. 1995. pap. 39.00 (*84-7719-506-4*) IBD Ltd.

Diaz, R. J., jt. ed. see Brinkhurst, R. O.

Diaz, R. Moreno, jt. ed. see Pichler, Franz R.

Diaz, R. Moreno, jt. ed. see Pichler, Franz.

Diaz, R. Moreno, jt. ed. see Picler, F.

Diaz, Rafael G. Diccionario Tecnico: Ingles-Espanol, Espanol-Ingles. 2nd ed. (ENG & SPA.). 836p. 1996. 95.00 (*0-7859-9466-1*) Fr & Eur.

Diaz, Rafael M. Latino Gay Men & HIV: Culture, Sexuality & Risk Behavior. LC 97-23167. 208p. (C). 1997. pap. 18.99 (*0-415-91388-8*) Routledge.

— Latino Gay Men & HIV: Culture, Sexuality & Risk Behavior. LC 97-23167. 208p. (C). 1997. 75.00 (*0-415-91387-X*) Routledge.

Diaz, Rafael M. & Berk, Laura E., eds. Private Speech: From Social Interaction to Self-Regulation. 312p. 1992. pap. 32.50 (*0-8058-0887-6*); text 59.95 (*0-8058-0886-8*) L Erlbaum Assocs.

Diaz, Ralph. The Complete Folding Kayaker. (Illus.). 144p. 1994. 16.95 (*0-07-016734-6*, Ragged Mntain) McGraw-Hill Prof.

Diaz, Ricardo & Muniak, Sasha. Mangia Cookbook. 1999. write for info. (*0-316-18464-0*) Little.

Diaz-Rico, Lynne T. & Weed, Kathryn Z. The Crosscultural, Language, & Academic Development Handbook. 352p. (C). 1994. pap. text 56.95 (*0-205-16555-9*, Longwood Div); pap. text 44.00 (*0-205-15048-9*, Longwood Div) Allyn.

Diaz-Rivera, Maria. Refranes Mas Usados en Puerto Rico. (SPA.). 174p. 1994. pap. 3.00 (*0-8477-0064-X*) U of PR Pr.

Diaz-Rivera, Tulio. Hacia Donde Vamos? Radiografia del Presente Cuban. LC 84-73320. (Coleccion Cuba y sus Jueces). (SPA.). 144p. (Orig.). 1985. pap. 5.00 (*0-89729-367-3*) Ediciones.

Diaz-Rodriguez, Ernesto. Sea of My Infancy. Male, Belkis C., ed. Klee, Ildara, tr. from SPA. Orig. Title: Mar de Mi Infancia. (Illus.). 96p. (Orig.). (C). 1991. pap. 10.00 (*0-913827-04-5*) Linden Ln Pr.

Diaz, Rogelio D., tr. see Francen, Mike.

Diaz, Ruben. Florida Should I Come? The Do's & Don'ts of Moving to Florida. (Illus.). 88p. (Orig.). 1989. pap. 12.95 (*0-317-93399-X*) Green Leaf FL.

Diaz, S. Exceptional Weierstrass Points & the Divisor on Moduli Space That They Define. LC 85-9207. (Memoirs of the AMS Ser.: No. 56/327). 69p. 1985. pap. 18.00 (*0-8218-2328-0*, MEMO/56/327) Am Math.

Diaz, Sam. "Is, This Your Life"???, Pt. I. LC 87-51505. 268p. (Orig.). 1987. pap. 14.95 (*0-9619776-0-4*) Zorro Pub.

Diaz Soler, Luis M. Puerto Rico desde Sus Origenes Hasta el Cese de la Dominacion e Panola. 1995. pap. 12.95 (*0-8477-0177-8*) U of PR Pr.

Diaz-Stevens, Ana M. Oxcart Catholicism on Fifth Avenue: The Impact of the Puerto Rican Migration upon the Archdiocese of New York. LC 92-53747. (Studies in American Catholicism: Vol. 12). (C). 1993. text 40.50 (*0-268-01509-0*) U of Notre Dame Pr.

— Oxcart Catholicism on Fifth Avenue: The Impact of the Puerto Rican Migration upon the Archdiocese of New York. LC 92-53747. (Notre Dame Studies in American Catholicism: Vol. 12). (C). 1995. reprint ed. pap. text 15.00 (*0-268-01510-4*) U of Notre Dame Pr.

Diaz-Stevens, Ana M. & Stevens-Arroyo, Anthony M. Recognizing the Latino Resurgence in U. S. Religion: The Emmaus Paradigm. LC 97-35173. (Explorations Ser.). 296p. (C). 1997. pap. 27.00 (*0-8133-2510-2*, Pub. by Westview) HarpC.

Diaz-Stevens, Ana M., jt. ed. see Stevens-Arroyo, Anthony M.

Diaz, Tom. Making a Killing: The Business of Guns in America. LC 98-34227. 256p. 1999. 25.00 (*1-56584-470-X*, Pub. by New Press NY) Norton.

***Diaz, Tom.** Making a Killing: The Business of Guns in America. 2000. pap. 14.95 (*1-56584-567-6*, Pub. by New Press NY) Norton.

Diaz, Tony. The Aztec Love God. LC 98-17585. 150p. 1998. pap. 12.95 (*1-57366-036-1*) Fiction Coll.

— Latino Heretics. 213p. 1999. pap. 12.95 (*1-57366-077-9*, Pub. by Fiction Coll) SPD-Small Pr Dist.

Diaz Valcarcel, Emilio. Hot Soles in Harlem. Miller, Yvette E., ed. Fayen, Tanya T., tr. from SPA. LC 92-21226. (Discoveries Ser.). 175p. 1993. pap. 16.95 (*0-935480-61-7*) Lat Am Lit Rev Pr.

— Schemes in the Month of March. Sebastiani, Nancy A., tr. from SPA. LC 76-45296. Orig. Title: Figuraciones en el mes de marzo. 1979. pap. text 17.00 (*0-916950-05-0*); lib. bdg. 27.00 (*0-916950-06-9*) Biling Rev-Pr.

Diaz-Valcarcel, Emilio. La Vision del Mundo en la Novela: Tiempo de silencio, de Luis Martin-Santos. (SPA.). 98p. (Orig.). (C). 1982. pap. 5.00 (*0-8477-3506-0*) U of PR Pr.

Diaz-Veizades, Jeannette, jt. auth. see Chang, Edward.

Diaz Velasquez, Mariano. Diccionario Basico de Matematicas. 5th ed. (SPA.). 224p. 1990. pap. 22.95 (*0-7859-5733-2*, 8420714348) Fr & Eur.

Diaz Viana, Luis, jt. auth. see Diaz, Joaquin.

Diaz, Victoria, tr. see Hagee, John.

Diaz-Vilar, Juan, ed. see Cervantes, Carmen M.

Diaz y Diaz, Manuel C. Vie Chretienne et Culture dans l'Espagne de VII au Xe Siecles. (Collected Studies: Vol. CS377). 304p. 1992. 109.95 (*0-86078-331-6*, Pub. by Variorum) Ashgate Pub Co.

Diaz y Diaz, Manuel C., et al. Historia de Espana Vol. 3: Espana Visigoda, V. 1 las Invasiones, las Sociedades, la Iglesia. (SPA.). 596p. 1992. 189.50 (*84-239-4995-8*) Elliots Bks.

Diaz Zayas, Carmen E. Practicas de Oficina, Vol. 89. (SPA.). (C). 1997. pap. 11.66 (*0-673-19283-0*) HEPC Inc.

Diaz Zayas, Carmen E., tr. see Bowdoin, Ruth.

Diazaki, Suzie K. Nihmmachi: A Story of San Francisco's Japantown. (Illus.). 135p. (Orig.). 1985. pap. text 25.00 (*0-9615546-0-6*) SKO Studios.

Dib, Albert. Forms & Agreements for Architects, Engineers & Contractors, 4 vols. LC 75-37971. (Real Property - Zoning Ser.). (C). 1976. ring bd. 495.00 (*0-87632-215-1*) West Group.

Dib, Mohammed. Omneros. Lettieri, Carol & Vangelisti, Paul, trs. 1978. pap. 3.00 (*0-88031-050-2*) Invisible-Red Hill.

***Dib, Mohammed.** The Savage Night. Dickson, C., tr. 256p. 2001. text 50.00 (*0-8032-1713-7*) U of Nebr Pr.

Dib, Mohammed & Bordas, Philippe. Tlemcen Ou les Lieux de L'Ecriture. (Illus.). 160p. 1996. 29.95 (*2-909571-05-X*, 610601, Pub. by Revue Noire) Dist Art Pubs.

Dib, Pierre. Guide to Owning a Poodle: AKC Rank #6. LC 99-15128. (Illus.). 64p. (gr. 4-7). 1999. 19.95 (*0-7910-5474-8*) Chelsea Hse.

— Guide to Owning a Poodle: AKC Rank #6. (Guide to Owning Ser.). (Illus.). 64p. 1995. pap. 6.95 (*0-7938-1863-X*, RE-313) TFH Pubns.

Diba, Layla S., et al. Royal Persian Paintings: The Qajar Epoch, 1779-1924. LC 98-18387. 1998. pap. 65.00 (*1-86064-256-X*, Pub. by I B T) St Martin.

DiBacco. History Lesson Plan User Guide. 1990. pap. write for info. (*0-395-54403-3*) HM.

Dibacco. History of the United States. (C). 1992. pap., wbk. ed. 9.52 (*0-395-63657-4*) HM.

— History of the U.S. 1992. text, teacher ed. 98.88 (*0-395-62768-0*); text, student ed. 72.64 (*0-395-62767-2*) HM.

— History of the U.S. LC 94-227215. 1994. text, teacher ed. 101.84 (*0-395-68885-X*) HM.

DiBacco. History of the U.S., 2. 1991. text, teacher ed. 93.36 (*0-395-58292-X*) HM.

— History of the U.S., 2. 1991. text, teacher ed. 102.16 (*0-395-58297-0*) HM.

Dibacco. History of the U.S., vol. 1. 1991. text, teacher ed. 93.36 (*0-395-56765-3*); text, student ed. 71.28 (*0-395-56764-5*) HM.

— History of the U.S., vol. 2. 1991. text, teacher ed. 102.16 (*0-395-58291-1*); text, student ed. 72.20 (*0-395-58290-3*); text, student ed. 72.20 (*0-395-58296-2*) HM.

— History of the U.S., vol. 2. 1993. text 72.20 (*0-395-58369-1*) HM.

— History of the U.S., vol. 2. 1994. text, student ed. 68.04 (*0-395-68863-9*) HM.

— History of the U.S., vol. 2. 1994. text, teacher ed. 101.84 (*0-395-68864-7*) HM.

— The History of U.S. Geography. 1990. 87.36 (*0-395-54393-2*) HM.

— United States History. (C). 1990. pap., student ed. 57.80 (*0-395-48751-X*) HM.

Dibadj, Seyed Musa. The Authenticity of the Text in Hermeneutics No. 4. LC 98-6099. (Cultural Heritage & Contemporary Change. Series IIA, Islam: Vol. 4). 1998. pap. 17.50 (*1-56518-117-4*) Coun Res Values.

Dibango, Manu & Rouard, Danielle. Three Kilos of Coffee: An Autobiography. Raps, Beth G., tr. LC 93-44597. 158p. 1994. pap. 13.95 (*0-226-14490-9*); lib. bdg. 32.00 (*0-226-14491-7*) U Ch Pr.

DiBartola, Stephen P. Fluid Therapy in Small Animal Practice. (Illus.). 736p. (C). 1992. text 89.00 (*0-7216-3182-7*, W B Saunders Co) Harcrt Hlth Sci Grp.

— Fluid Therapy in Small Animal Practice. 2nd ed. LC 99-46857. (C). 1999. text. write for info. (*0-7216-7739-8*, W B Saunders Co) Harcrt Hlth Sci Grp.

DiBartola, Stephen P., jt. auth. see Chew, Dennis J.

DiBartolo, Anne S. The Measure of My Days. 1998. pap. write for info. (*1-57553-863-6*) Watermrk Pr.

***Dibartolomeis, Michael J., Jr., ed.** Toward the 21st Century: Planning for the Protection of California's Environment: Summary Report. (Illus.). 54p. (C). 2000. reprint ed. pap. text 20.00 (*0-7881-8599-3*) DIANE Pub.

Dibattista, G., ed. Graph Drawing: Proceedings, 5th International Symposium, GD '97, Rome, Italy, September 18-20, 1997. LC 97-48778. (Lecture Notes in Computer Science Ser.: Vol. 1353). xii, 448p. 1997. pap. 69.00 (*3-540-63938-1*) Spr-Verlag.

DiBattista, Maria. First Love: The Affections of Modern Fiction. LC 90-46356. 294p. 1991. 28.95 (*0-226-14498-4*) U Ch Pr.

DiBattista, Maria & McDiarmid, Lucy, eds. High & Low Moderns: Literature & Culture, 1839-1939. (Illus.). 272p. 1996. text 60.00 (*0-19-508266-4*) OUP.

Dibb. Marketing: Concepts & Strategies, 3 vols. 3rd ed. (C). 1995. pap. text 47.16 (*0-395-79005-0*) HM.

***Dibb & Simkin.** Marketing Casebook: Cases & Concepts. 2nd ed. 2000. pap. write for info. (*1-86152-624-5*, Pub. by ITBP) Thomson Learn.

— Marketing Casebook: Keynote Cases. 1993. pap. write for info. (*1-86152-471-4*, Pub. by ITBP) Thomson Learn.

— Marketing Planning. 1996. pap., wbk. ed. 19.99 (*1-86152-349-1*, Pub. by ITBP) Thomson Learn.

Dibb, Paul. The Soviet Union: The Incomplete Superpower. 2nd ed. 320p. (Orig.). 1988. pap. text 12.95 (*0-252-06017-2*) U of Ill Pr.

— Towards a New Balance of Power in Asia. (Illus.). 93p. 1995. pap. text 23.00 (*0-19-828069-6*) OUP.

Dibb, Paul, jt. ed. see Blackwill, Robert D.

Dibb, Sally & Simkin, Lyndon. The Market Segmentation Workbook: Target Marketing for Marketing Managers. LC 95-35968. (Marketing Workbooks Ser.). 240p. (C). 1996. pap. 19.99 (*0-415-11892-1*) Thomson Learn.

— The Marketing Casebook. 150p. (C). 1993. pap., teacher ed. 62.95 (*0-415-10513-7*) Thomson Learn.

— The Marketing Casebook: Cases & Concepts. LC 93-9645. 336p. (C). 1993. pap. 29.95 (*0-415-08950-6*) Thomson Learn.

Dibb, Sally, et al. The Marketing Planning Workbook: Effective Marketing for Marketing Managers. LC 95-30550. (Marketing Workbooks Ser.). 256p. (C). 1996. pap. 29.95 (*0-415-11891-3*) Thomson Learn.

Dibbell, Julian. My Tiny Life: Crime & Passion in a Virtual World. LC 98-13636. 324p. 1999. 14.95 (*0-8050-3626-1*, Owl) H Holt & Co.

Dibben-Young, Arleone. Windshopping Maui: A Serious Sailor's Guide to the Valley Isle. (Illus.). 176p. (Orig.). 1987. pap. 12.95 (*0-9617864-0-X*) A Dibben-Young.

Dibbert, Michael T., et al. Growth Groups: A Key to Christian Fellowship & Spiritual Maturity in the Church. 160p. (Orig.). 1985. pap. 9.99 (*0-310-23121-3*, 11673P) Zondervan.

Dibble, Anne & Odell, John. Brazilian Informatics & the United States: Defending Infant Industry vs. Opening Foreign Markets. (Pew Case Studies in International Affairs). 50p. (C). 1992. pap. text 3.50 (*1-56927-128-3*) Geo U Inst Dplmcy.

Dibble, Brian, et al, eds. Celebrations: A Bicentennial Anthology of Fifty Years of Western Australian Poetry & Prose. 1994. 12.95 (*0-85564-297-1*, Pub. by Univ of West Aust Pr); pap. 4.95 (*0-85564-293-9*, Pub. by Univ of West Aust Pr) Intl Spec Bk.

Dibble, C., et al. A Reprint of the Archaeology & Ethmology Papers, No. 1-8. fac. ed. Jennings, Jesse, ed. (University of Utah, Museum of Anthropology, Anthropological Papers). (Illus.). 113p. 1950. reprint ed. pap. text 12.50 (*1-55567-861-0*) Coyote Press.

Dibble, Carl M. Student's Guide to American Government. 96p. 1993. spiral bd. 12.95 (*0-8403-8973-6*) Kendall-Hunt.

***Dibble, Carole H. & Lee, Kathy.** 101 Easy, Wacky, Crazy Activities for Young Children. LC 00-24165. (Illus.). 144p. 2000. pap. 12.95 (*0-87659-207-8*) Gryphon Hse.

Dibble, Carole H. & Lee, Kathy H. Get Real Get Messy: Ideas for Real Teachers. (Illus.). 208p. 1999. pap. 12.95 (*0-9670187-0-6*, Pub. by Early Childhd) Gryphon Hse.

Dibble, Charles E. Codex en Cruz, 2 vols. LC 80-21241. 148p. 1981. 45.00 (*0-87480-124-9*) U of Utah Pr.

Dibble, Charles E., tr. see Sahagun, Bernardino de.

Dibble, Charles F., tr. see De Sahagun, Bernardino.

Dibble, David S. & Kent, C. Day. A Preliminary Survey of the Fontenelle Reservoir, Wyoming. (Upper Colorado Ser.: No. 7). reprint ed. 18.00 (*0-404-60658-X*) AMS Pr.

Dibble, Harold L. & Lenoir, Michel, eds. The Middle Paleolithic Site of Combe-Capelle Bas (France) LC 95-35093. (Illus.). xxi, 365p. 1995. 40.00 (*0-924171-38-3*) U Museum Pubns.

Dibble, Harold L. & Mellars, Paul, eds. The Middle Paleolithic: Adaptation, Behavior & Variability. (University Museum Monographs: University Museum Symposium Ser.: Nos. 78 & IV). (Illus.). 217p. (C). 1992. text 50.00 (*0-924171-07-3*) U Museum Pubns.

Dibble, Harold L. & Monte-White, Anta, eds. Upper Pleistocene Prehistory of Western Eurasia. (University Museum Monographs: University Museum Symposium Ser.: No. 54/I). xxii, 462p. 1988. text 50.00 (*0-934718-53-9*) U Museum Pubns.

Dibble, Harold L., jt. auth. see Debenath, Andre.

Dibble, Harold L., jt. ed. see Olszewski, Deborah I.

Dibble, Jeremy. C. Hubert H. Parry: His Life & Music. (Illus.). 570p. 1998. reprint ed. pap. text 29.95 (*0-19-816702-4*) OUP.

Dibble, Jerry A. The Pythia's Drunken Song. (International Archives of the History of Ideas Ser.: No. 19). 87p. 1978. pap. text 57.00 (*90-247-2011-7*, Pub. by M Nijhoff) Kluwer Academic.

Dibble, Jerry A. & Langford, T. E. Communication Skills & Strategies: Guidelines for Managers at Work. (C). 1994. mass mkt. 22.95 (*0-538-83520-6*, EH63AA) S-W Pub.

Dibble, L. Grace. More Return Tickets. 373p. (C). 1991. 35.00 (*0-7223-1320-9*, Pub. by A H S Ltd) St Mut.

— Return Tickets to Scandinavia. 160p. (C). 1991. 35.00 (*0-7223-1681-X*, Pub. by A H S Ltd) St Mut.

— Return Tickets to Southern Europe. 1981. 35.00 (*0-7223-1423-X*, Pub. by A H S Ltd) St Mut.

— Return Tickets to Yugoslavia. 249p. (C). 1991. pap. 35.00 (*0-7223-1809-X*, Pub. by A H S Ltd) St Mut.

Dibble, Lisa. Food & Farming. LC 93-19073. (Picturepedia Ser.). (J). (gr. 4 up). 1993. write for info. (*1-56458-387-2*) DK Pub Inc.

***Dibble, Peter.** Real-time Programming with the Java Platform. 2001. pap. 49.99 (*0-13-028261-8*) P-H.

Dibble, Peter, jt. auth. see Puckett, Dale.

Dibble, Peter C. OS-9 Insights: An Advanced Programmers Guide to OS-9. Beck, Eileen et al, eds. 645p. (C). 1994. write for info. (*0-918035-05-8*, INS68TE68MO) Microware Systs.

— OS-9 Insights: An Advanced Programmers Guide to OS-9. 2nd ed. Davis, David F., ed. 542p. (C). 1992. write for info. (*0-918035-03-1*, INS68SE68MO) Microware Systs.

***Dibble, Suzanne.** Keeping Your Valuable Employees: Retention Strategies for Your Organization's Most Valuable Resource. LC 99-20330. 284p. 1999. 34.95 (*0-471-32053-6*) Wiley.

Dibble, Terry J. Scarlet Letter Notes. (Cliffs Notes Ser.). 96p. 1960. pap. 4.95 (*0-8220-1165-4*, Cliff) IDG Bks.

Dibble, Vernon K. The Legacy of Albion Small. LC 74-16686. (Heritage of Sociology Ser.). x, 288p. 1996. lib. bdg. 24.00 (*0-226-14520-4*) U Ch Pr.

Dibbley, Dale C. From Achilles' Heel to Zeus' Shield. 176p. (Orig.). 1993. pap. 8.00 (*0-449-90735-X*, Columbine) Fawcett.

Dibblin, Jane. Day of Two Suns: U. S. Nuclear Testing & the Pacific Islanders. LC 90-39780. 299p. 1989. pap. 12.95 (*0-941533-83-2*, NAB) I R Dee.

Dibbs, John & Holmes, Tony. Spitfire: The Fighter Legend. (Illus.). 192p. 1996. 34.95 (*1-85532-594-2*, Pub. by Ospry) Motorbooks Intl.

Dibbs, John M. Flying Legends: A Photographic Study of the Great Piston Combat Aircraft of WW II. LC 98-24689. 243p. 1998. reprint ed. pap. 39.95 (*0-7603-0563-3*) MBI Pubg.

— RAF Frontline: The Royal Air Force Defending the Realm. (Illus.). 144p. 1999. 29.95 (*1-85310-884-7*, Pub. by Airlife) Motorbooks Intl.

***Dibbs, John M.** Warbird Legends. (Illus.). 244p. 2000. reprint ed. pap. 24.95 (*0-7603-0967-1*, 130741AP, Pub. by MBI Pubg) Motorbooks Intl.

Dibbs, Owen & Pereira, Patricia. Promoting Sales: A Systematic Approach to Benefit Selling: An ILO Programmed Book. ix, 248p. 1976. 13.50 (*92-2-101393-6*) Intl Labour Office.

Dibdin, Charles. The Professional Life of Mr. Dibdin, Written by Himself, 4 vols. in 2. LC 80-2272. reprint ed. 150.00 (*0-404-18835-4*) AMS Pr.

***Dibdin, Michael.** Blood Rain. LC 99-46938. (Aurelio Zen Mystery Ser.). 256p. 2000. 23.00 (*0-375-40915-7*) Pantheon.

— Cabal. 256p. 2000. pap. 12.00 (*0-375-70770-0*) Vin Bks.

Dibdin, Michael. Cosi Fan Tutti. LC 96-45387. 256p. 1997. 4.99 (*0-679-44272-3*) Pantheon.

— Cosi Fan Tutti. 256p. 1998. pap. 12.00 (*0-679-77911-6*) Vin Bks.

— Cosi Fan Tutti: An Aurelio Zen Mystery. large type ed. LC 97-36864. (CD Ser.). 423p. 1997. 23.95 (*0-7862-1244-6*) Thorndike Pr.

— Dark Specter: A Novel. 352p. 1996. 4.99 (*0-679-44221-9*) Pantheon.

— Dark Spectre. 1998. pap. 13.00 (*0-679-76723-1*) Random.

An Asterisk (*) at the beginning of an entry indicates that the title is appearing for the first time.

— Dead Lagoon: An Aurelio Zen Mystery. 320p. 1996. pap. 12.00 (*0-679-75311-7*) Random.

— Dirty Tricks. 1997. pap. write for info. (*0-375-70009-9*) Vin Bks.

— Dirty Tricks. Chelius, Jane, ed. 256p. 1992. reprint ed. mass mkt. 4.99 (*0-671-69546-0*) PB.

— The Dying of the Light: A Mystery. 1995. pap. 10.00 (*0-679-75310-9*) Vin Bks.

— The Last Sherlock Holmes Story. 192p. 1996. pap. 10.00 (*0-679-76658-8*) Random.

— A Long Finish: An Aurelio Zen Mystery. LC 98-15764. 272p. 1998. 24.00 (*0-375-40429-5*) Pantheon.

— A Long Finish: An Aurelio Zen Mystery. 2000. pap. 12.00 (*0-375-70401-9*) Vin Bks.

***Dibdin, Michael.** A Long Finish: An Aurelio Zen Mystery. large type ed. LC 98-46980. 1999. 26.95 (*0-7862-1762-6*) Thorndike Pr.

Dibdin, Michael. Ratking. (Portway Ser.). 376p. 1991. 21.95 (*0-7451-7247-4*, G K Hall Lrg Type) Mac Lib Ref.

— Ratking. LC 96-45600. 1997. pap. 12.00 (*0-679-76854-8*) Vin Bks.

— A Rich Full Death. 1997. pap. write for info. (*0-375-70010-2*) Vin Bks.

— A Rich Full Death. LC 98-53060. 288p. 1999. pap. 12.00 (*0-375-70614-3*) Vin Bks.

— Vendetta. LC 96-46856. 272p. 1999. pap. 12.00 (*0-679-76853-X*) Vin Bks.

Dibdin, Michael, ed. The Vintage Book of Classic Crime. LC 96-9620. (Black Lizard Ser.). 1997. pap. 14.00 (*0-679-76855-6*) Vin Bks.

Dibdin, Thomas F. Bibliographical, Antiquarian, & Picturesque Tour in France & Germany, 3 vols. 2nd ed. LC 76-111768. reprint ed. 195.00 (*0-404-02130-1*) AMS Pr.

— Horace Bibliographicae Cantabrigienses: A Facsimile of Dibdin's Cambridge, Notebook, 1823. LC 89-3236. (Illus.). 80p. 1989. 185.00 (*0-938768-15-8*) Oak Knoll.

— An Introduction to the Knowledge of Rare & Valuable Editions of the Greek & Latin Classics, 2 vols. in 1. xviii, 1121p. 1977. reprint ed. 226.20 (*3-487-06243-7*) G Olms Pubs.

Dibdin, Thomas J. Reminiscences of Thomas Dibdin, 2 vols. LC 70-111769. reprint ed. 74.50 (*0-404-02124-7*) AMS Pr.

Dibeh. Persistence of Fluctuation in Capitalist Economies. 55.95 (*1-85972-088-9*) Ashgate Pub Co.

***Dibelius, Martin.** Studies in the Acts of the Apostles. 240p. 1999. reprint ed. pap. 20.00 (*1-888961-10-4*) Sigler Pr.

Dibelius, Martin & Conzelmann, Hans. The Pastoral Epistles. Koester, Helmut, ed. Buttolph, Philip & Yarbro, Adela, trs. from GER. LC 71-157549. (Hermeneia: A Critical & Historical Commentary on the Bible Ser.). 176p. 1972. 38.00 (*0-8006-6002-1*, 1-6002, Fortress Pr) Augsburg Fortress.

Dibelius, Martin & Greeven, Heinrich. James. Koester, Helmut, ed. Williams, Michael A., tr. LC 74-80428. (Hermeneia: A Critical & Historical Commentary on the Bible Ser.). 288p. 1975. 48.00 (*0-8006-6006-4*, 1-6006, Fortress Pr) Augsburg Fortress.

Dibell, Ansen. Plot. (Elements of Fiction Writing Ser.). 176p. 1988. 15.99 (*0-89879-303-3*, Wrtrs Digest Bks) F & W Pubns Inc.

— Plot. (Elements of Fiction Writing Ser.). 176p. 1999. pap. 12.00 (*0-89879-946-5*, 10644, Wrtrs Digest Bks) F & W Pubns Inc.

Dibella, Anthony. How Organizations Learn: An Integrated Approach to Building Learning Capability. LC 97-21112. 300p. 1997. 32.95 (*0-7879-1107-0*) Jossey-Bass.

***Dibella, Anthony.** Learning Practices: Assessment & Action for Organizational Improvement. 250p. 2000. pap. 42.67 (*0-13-017380-0*, Prentice Hall) P-H.

DiBella, John D. Hello, It's Me. LC 97-194940. (Illus.). 100p. 1997. 12.95 (*0-9658920-0-X*) Fore Angels.

DiBello, P., jt. auth. see Amery, H.

DiBenedetto, Barbara. Vocabulary Builder Game Pack Levels 8-11: Short Vowel II Sequence. (Linguistic Pattern Ser.). 49p. (Orig.). 1993. 20.00 (*1-56775-051-6*) ISM Teach Systs.

— Vocabulary Builder Game Pack Levels 12-15: Long Vowel Sequence. (Linguistic Pattern Ser.). 71p. (Orig.). 1993. 20.00 (*1-56775-052-4*) ISM Teach Systs.

DiBenedetto, Barbara, jt. auth. see Richardson, Ellis.

DiBenedetto, Barbara D. Sentence Maker for Levels A-D: Beginner Sequence. (Linguistic Pattern Ser.). 10p. (Orig.). 1993. 10.00 (*1-56775-048-6*) ISM Teach Systs.

— Vocabulary Builder Game Pack Levels 1-3: Introductory Sequence. (Linguistic Pattern Ser.). 21p. (Orig.). 1993. 15.00 (*1-56775-049-4*) ISM Teach Systs.

— Vocabulary Builder Game Pack Levels 4-7: Short Vowel I Sequence. (Linguistic Pattern Ser.). 29p. (Orig.). 1993. 15.00 (*1-56775-050-8*) ISM Teach Systs.

DiBenedetto, Deborah V., et al. Oem Occupational Health & Safety Manual. 2nd ed. LC 98-180607. 1996. 495.00 (*1-883595-09-6*, OEM Pr) OEM Health.

DiBenedetto, Emmanuele. Degenerate Parabolic Equations. LC 93-285. (Illus.). 387p. 1993. 47.95 (*0-387-94020-0*) Spr-Verlag.

— Partial Differential Equations. LC 94-42625. 416p. 1994. 49.00 (*0-8176-3708-7*); write for info. (*3-7643-3708-7*) Birkhauser.

DiBenedetto, Michele & Shapiro, Mark. GRE TestBuster. 250p. 2000. pap. 19.95 (*0-87891-143-X*) Res & Educ.

Diberardinis, Louis J. Handbook of Occupational Safety & Health. 2nd ed. LC 97-49069. 1224p. 1998. 149.00 (*0-471-16017-2*) Wiley.

Diberardinis, Louis J., ed. ANSI - AIHA Z9.5 Standard for Laboratory Ventilation. (C). 1993. pap. 30.00 (*0-932627-50-1*, 143-EQ-93) Am Indus Hygiene.

Diberardinis, Louis J., et al. Guidelines for Laboratory Design: Health & Safety Considerations. 2nd ed. LC 92-16785. 528p. 1992. 89.95 (*0-471-55463-4*) Wiley.

DiBerardino, M. A. & Etkin, L. D. Adaptability in Somatic Cell Specialization, Vol. 6. LC 85-3406. (Developmental Biology Ser.). (Illus.). 256p. (C). 1989. text 85.00 (*0-306-43177-7*, Kluwer Plenum) Kluwer Academic.

DiBerardino, Marie A. Genomic Potential of Differentiated Cells. LC 96-33173. 1997. 68.50 (*0-231-06986-3*) Col U Pr.

DiBerardo, Robert J., ed. see Hubbard, L. Ron.

DiBernard, Barbara. Alchemy & Finnegans Wake. LC 79-22809. 163p. (C). 1980. text 64.50 (*0-87395-388-6*); pap. text 21.95 (*0-87395-429-7*) State U NY Pr.

Dibernardo, Cathy, et al. Ophthalmic Ultrasound: A Diagnostic Atlas. LC 98-14389. 1998. 69.00 (*0-86577-765-9*) Thieme Med Pubs.

Dibiase, Ted. Every Man Has His Price: The True Story of Wrestling's Million Dollar Man. LC 97-14403. 180p. 1997. pap. 10.99 (*1-57673-175-8*, Multnomah Bks) Multnomah Pubs.

Dibie, Robert A. The Military-Bureaucracy Relationship in Nigeria: Public Policy Making & Implementation. LC 98-38257. 256p. 2000. 69.95 (*0-275-96447-7*, Praeger Pubs) Greenwood.

— Understanding Public Policy In Nigeria: A Twenty-First Century Approach. LC 99-14382. 288p. 2000. 65.00 (*0-275-96616-X*) Greenwood.

Dibinga, Said K. Mfecane: Scattering of the People. LC 95-67261. (Illus.). 24p. (Orig.). (J). 1994. pap. 4.95 (*0-943324-58-0*) Omenana.

Dibinga wa Said. The Unification Church Policy on South Africa. (Christian Churches Policies on South Africa Ser.). 14p. (Orig.). 1986. pap. write for info. (*0-943324-26-2*) Omenana.

Dibirov, M. P., jt. auth. see Portnoi, L. M.

DiBlase, Antonietta, jt. auth. see Marchisio, Sergio.

DiBlasi, Joan, et al, eds. Pursuing Excellence in a Time of Declining Resources - The Role of Automated Information Systems: Proceedings, Ninth Annual MSIS National Users Group Conference. (Orig.). 1986. pap. 20.00 (*0-936934-05-0*) N S Kline Inst.

***DiBlasi, Joseph P. & Warda, Mark.** How to Form a Corporation in Massachusetts. (Legal Survival Guides Ser.). 272p. 2000. pap. 19.95 (*1-57248-115-3*, Sphinx Pubng) Sourcebks.

DiBlasi, Joseph P. & Warda, Mark. How to Make a Massachusetts Will. 2nd ed. LC 99-31258. (Legal Survival Guides Ser.). 120p. 1999. pap. 12.95 (*1-57248-108-0*, Sphinx Pubng) Sourcebks.

— Landlord's Rights & Duties in Massachusetts. 2nd ed. LC 99-33638. (Legal Survival Guides Ser.). 224p. 1999. pap. 19.95 (*1-57248-107-2*, Sphinx Pubng) Sourcebks.

DiBlasio, Paola, jt. auth. see Cirillo, Stefano.

Dible, Henry. Pathology of Limb Ischaema. LC 67-27239. (Illus.). 110p. 1967. 9.00 (*0-87527-030-1*) Green.

Dibner, Andrew S., intro. Personal Response Systems: An International Report of a New Home Care Service. LC 92-25580. (Home Health Care Services Quarterly Ser.: Vol. 13, Nos. 3 & 4, 1992). (Illus.). 280p. 1993. lib. bdg. 49.95 (*1-56024-272-8*) Haworth Pr.

Dibner, Bern. Heralds of Science. rev. ed. LC 80-25340. (Illus.). 96p. 1981. reprint ed. 14.95 (*0-88202-191-5*); reprint ed. pap. 8.95 (*0-88202-192-3*) Watson Pub Intl.

Dibner, David R., ed. see National Research Council Staff.

Dibner, Ellen J. & Gustafson, Ronald. Book Finders for Kids: The "Easy to Use" Subject Guide to Finding Non-fiction Books in a Library. LC 88-61646. (Illus.). 16p. (Orig.). (J). (gr. 2-8). 1998. pap. 3.95 (*0-9620888-0-3*) Point Publications.

***Dibner, Ellen J., et al.** Sand to Settlement: Story of Long Beach Barrier Island: From Discovery to 1931. (Illus.). 40p. 1999. pap. 12.00 (*0-9677925-0-9*) Long Beach Cty.

Dibner, Mark D. Biotechnology Guide U. S. A. Companies, Data & Analysis. 4th ed. 616p. 1997. pap. 249.00 (*1-886041-11-3*) Inst Biotech Info.

Dibner, Martin, jt. auth. see Sobol, Judith.

Dibner, Robin & Colman, Carol. The Lupus Handbook for Women: Up-to-Date Information on Understanding & Managing the Disease Which Affects One in Five Hundred Women. LC 94-17984. 176p. 1994. per. 11.00 (*0-671-79031-5*) S&S Trade.

Dibon, P. Inventaire de la Correspondance d'Andre Rivet, 1595-1650. (International Archives of the History of Ideas Ser.: No. 43). 429p. 1971. lib. bdg. 191.50 (*90-247-5112-8*) Kluwer Academic.

Dibon-Smith, Richard. Starlist Two Thousand: A Quick Reference Star Catalog for Astronomers. LC 92-2907. 416p. 1992. pap. 29.95 (*0-471-55895-8*) Wiley.

***DiBona, Chris & Ockman, Sam.** Open Sources: Voices from the Open Source Revolution. Stone, Mark, ed. (Illus.). 250p. 1999. pap. 27.95 (*1-56592-582-3*) OReilly & Assocs.

DiBona, G. F., ed. Renal Nerves: Journal: Mineral & Electrolyte Metabolism, Vol. 15, Nos. 1 & 2. (Illus.). 96p. 1989. pap. 73.25 (*3-8055-4887-7*) S Karger.

DiBona, Leslie, jt. auth. see Collins, John W., III.

***Dibra, Bash & Crenshaw, Mary Ann.** Dogspeak: How to Learn It, Speak It, Use It to Have a Happy, Healthy, Well-Behaved Dog. LC 99-30194. (Illus.). 288p. 1999. 22.50 (*0-684-82417-5*) Simon & Schuster.

Dibra, Bash & Randolph, Elizabeth. Simple Solutions to the Most Common Dog Problems. Orig. Title: Teach Your Dog to Behave. (Orig.). Date not set. reprint ed. pap. write for info. (*0-9655908-1-X*) Petlab.

Dibra, Bashkim & Randolph, Elizabeth. Dog Training by Bash: The Tried & True Techniques of the Dog Trainer to the Stars. 368p. 1992. mass mkt. 6.99 (*0-451-17166-7*, Sig) NAL.

— Teach Your Dog to Behave: Simple Solutions to over 300 Common Dog Behavior Problems from A to Z. 400p. 1994. mass mkt. 6.99 (*0-451-17926-9*, Sig) NAL.

Dibrova, Volodymyr, et al. Peltse: And Pentameron. LC 96-27239. (Writings from an Unbound Europe). 236p. 1996. 39.95 (*0-8101-1219-1*); pap. 14.95 (*0-8101-1237-X*) Northwestern U Pr.

***Dicaire, David L.** Blues Singers: Biographies of 50 Legendary Artists of the Early 20th Century. LC 99-16594. (Illus.). 300p. 1999. pap. 29.95 (*0-7864-0606-2*) McFarland & Co.

***DiCamillo, Kate.** Because of Winn-Dixie. LC 99-34260. 184p. (J). (gr. 3-7). 2000. 15.99 (*0-7636-0776-2*) Candlewick Pr.

DiCandia, Thomas A. Car Washing for Car Lovers: A Guidebook to Proper Car Washing, Waxing, & Other Maintenance Procedures to Keep Your Car Beautiful. Goldstein, Ann R. & Berne, Doreen S., eds. (Illus.). 96p. 1990. pap., per. 13.95 (*0-9626744-0-0*) CA Bound Bks.

DiCandilo, Elizabeth, ed. see Kent, Shawn.

Dicanio, Margaret. Encyclopedia of American Activism, 1960 to the Present. LC 98-39933. 336p. 1998. lib. bdg. 75.00 (*0-87436-899-5*) ABC-CLIO.

DiCanio, Margaret. Encyclopedia of Violence: Origins, Attitudes, Consequences. 416p. 1993. lib. bdg. 45.00 (*0-8160-2332-8*) Facts on File.

DiCanio, Margaret, ed. The Facts on File Scientific Yearbook, 1988. LC 85-642413. (Illus.). 224p. reprint ed. pap. 69.50 (*0-7837-1569-2*, 204186100024) Bks Demand.

— The Facts on File Scientific Yearbook, 1990. LC 85-642413. 224p. pap. 69.50 (*0-7837-1367-3*, 204151600021) Bks Demand.

***DiCanio, Margaret B.** Doing Well Is Doing Good: Portrait of an Armenian Heritage. 196p. 2000. pap. 17.95 (*0-9653718-8-3*) Mayreni Pubng.

Dicarco, Lawrence, ed. see Cutler, Jody.

Dicarlo. Experiments & Demonstrations in Physical Therapy: An Inquiry Approach to Learning. LC 98-41442. 144p. (C). 1998. pap. text 24.80 (*0-13-095686-4*, Macmillan Coll) P-H.

Dicarlo, Lawrence. Jane Wilson. LC 97-61545. (Illus.). 48p. (Orig.). 1997. pap. write for info. (*0-9626097-9-X*) Fischbach Gal.

Dicarlo, Lawrence, ed. Glen Hansen: The Paris Series. LC 97-60585. (Illus.). 38p. (Orig.). 1997. pap. 10.00 (*0-9626097-8-1*) Fischbach Gal.

— Jane Wilson. (Illus.). 48p. (Orig.). 1995. 15.00 (*0-9626097-7-3*) Fischbach Gal.

DiCarlo, Russell, jt. auth. see Tolle, Eckhart.

DiCarlo, Russell E. Towards a New World View Vol. I: Conversation at the Leading Edge. unabridged ed. 377p. (Orig.). 1996. pap. text 16.95 (*1-886718-00-8*) Epic Publ.

Dicarlo, Stephen E. Experiments & Demonstration in Physiology. 110p. (C). 1997. pap. text 14.60 (*0-13-636457-8*) P-H.

DiCastri, F., et al, eds. Biological Invasions in Europe & the Mediterranean Basin. (Monographiae Biologicae). (C). 1990. text 336.00 (*0-7923-0411-X*) Kluwer Academic.

DiCataldo, Andrew, jt. auth. see Rodriguez, Douglas.

Dicato, M., ed. Mechanisms & Management of Nausea & Emesis Associated with Cancer Therapy. (Journal Ser.: Vol. 53, Suppl. 1, 1996). (Illus.). iv, 110p. 1996. 49.75 (*3-8055-6335-3*) S Karger.

***Dicato, Mario.** Colorectal Cancer - Questions & Answers. (Questions & Answers Ser.). (Illus.). 2000. pap. text 17.95 (*1-873413-18-1*) Merit Pub Intl.

***Dice, J. Fred.** Lysomal Pathways of Protein Degradation. LC 99-27040. (Molecular Biology Intelligence Ser.). 2000. write for info. (*1-57059-568-2*) Landes Bioscience.

— Lysosomal Pathways of Protein Degradation. (Molecular Biology Intelligence Unit Ser.). 144p. 2000. 99.00 (*1-58706-003-5*, Pub. by Eurekah) Landes Bioscience.

***Dice, Kathy.** Personal Devotion: Taking God's Word to Heart. (Bible 101 Ser.). 64p. 2000. pap. 4.99 (*0-8308-2068-X*) InterVarsity.

— Study Methods: Unlocking the Power of God's Word. (Bible 101 Ser.). 64p. 2000. pap. 4.99 (*0-8308-2064-7*) InterVarsity.

Dice, Lee R. & Clark, Philip J. Variation in Measures of Behavior among Three Races of Peromyscus. LC QH0431.A1M5. (University of Michigan, Contributions from the Laboratory of Vertebrate Biology Ser.: No. 76). 28p. reprint ed. pap. 30.00 (*0-608-07031-9*, 206723800009) Bks Demand.

Dice, Marvin L. Intervention Strategies for Children with Emotional or Behavioral Disorders. LC 93-22671. (Illus.). 276p. (Orig.). (C). 1993. pap. text 39.95 (*1-56593-166-1*, 0474) Thomson Learn.

Dice, Peg, ed. Chocolate Arts: A Collection of Recipes with Chocolate. 256p. 1995. 17.95 (*0-9648821-0-8*) Chocolate Church.

DiCecco, Doroothea V. A Lab Guide to Plants. 201p. 1993. pap. text 27.95 (*0-88725-198-6*) Hunter Textbks.

DiCenso, James. Hermeneutics & the Disclosure of Truth: A Study in the Work of Heidegger, Gadamer, & Ricoeur. LC 89-37909. (Studies in Religion & Culture). 202p. 1990. reprint ed. pap. 62.70 (*0-7837-9996-9*, 206072300006) Bks Demand.

— The Other Freud: Religion, Culture & Psychoanalysis. LC 98-23772. 192p. (C). 1999. pap. 24.99 (*0-415-19659-0*, D6256) Routledge.

— The Other Freud: Religion, Culture & Psychoanalysis. LC 98-23772. 192p. (C). (gr. 13). 1999. 75.00 (*0-415-19658-2*, D6252) Routledge.

DiCenzo, Maria. The Politics of Alternative Theatre in Britain, 1968-1990: The Case of 7:84 (Scotland) LC 97-5359. (Studies in Modern Theatre). (Illus.). 261p. (C). 1996. text 59.95 (*0-521-55456-X*) Cambridge U Pr.

DiCesare, Frank, jt. auth. see Zhou, Mengchu.

Dicesare, Mario. George Herbert. 2nd ed. (Critical Editions Ser.). (C). Date not set. pap. write for info. (*0-393-96283-0*, Norton Paperbks) Norton.

DiCesare, Mario, ed. George Herbert & the Seventeenth Century Religious Poets. LC 77-28074. (Critical Editions Ser.). 401p. (C). 1978. pap. text 20.25 (*0-393-09254-2*) Norton.

Dicesare, Michele, jt. auth. see Pereni, Angelo.

Dicey, A. V. Introduction to the Study of the Law of the Constitution. 8th ed. 682p. 1996. reprint ed. 165.00 (*1-56169-220-4*) Gaunt.

— Lectures on the Relation Between Law & Public Opinion in England: During the Nineteenth Century. 524p. 1996. reprint ed. 125.00 (*1-56169-227-1*) Gaunt.

Dicey, Albert V. Introduction to the Study of the Law of the Constitution. LC 81-82778. 586p. 1982. 20.00 (*0-86597-002-5*); pap. 8.50 (*0-86597-003-3*) Liberty Fund.

— Lectures on the Relation Between Law & Public Opinion in England: During the Nineteenth Century. 2nd ed. LC 75-41074. reprint ed. 49.50 (*0-404-14532-9*) AMS Pr.

***Dicey, Albert V.** Lectures on the Relation Between Law & Public Opinion in England: During the Nineteenth Century. 2nd ed. xciv, 506p. 1999. reprint ed. 180.00 (*1-56169-488-6*) Gaunt.

Dicey, Albert V. & Cosgrove, Richard A. Lectures on the Relation Between Law & Public Opinion in England: During the Nineteenth Century. LC 81-2391. (Social Science Classics Ser.). 506p. 1981. pap. 24.95 (*0-87855-869-1*) Transaction Pubs.

Dicey, E. England & Egypt. 432p. 1986. 350.00 (*1-85077-134-0*, Pub. by Darf Pubs Ltd) St Mut.

— England & Egypt. 320p. (C). 1989. 100.00 (*1-85077-139-1*, Pub. by Darf Pubs Ltd) St Mut.

Dicey, E. M., tr. see Boutmy, Emile.

Dicey, Edward. Six Months in the Federal States. 1977. text 29.95 (*0-8369-9221-0*, 9075) Ayer.

Dichaira. Take Note. 24p. 2000. pap. text 32.00 (*0-13-022209-7*) S&S Trade.

Dichanz, Horst & Zahorik, John A. Changing Traditions in Germany's Public Schools. LC 97-76529. 93p. 1998. pap. 9.50 (*0-87367-396-4*, CTGPS) Phi Delta Kappa.

Dicharry, Warren. Human Authors of the New Testament: Mark, Matthew, & Luke, Vol. 1. (Illus.). 224p. (C). 1990. pap. 9.95 (*0-8146-1956-8*) Liturgical Pr.

DiCharry, Warren. Human Authors of the New Testament: Paul & John. 256p. 1992. pap. text 12.95 (*0-8146-2099-X*) Liturgical Pr.

Dicharry, Warren. Human Authors of the New Testament Vol. 1: Mark, Matthew & Luke. 222p. (C). 1996. pap. 39.95 (*0-85439-372-2*, Pub. by St Paul Pubns) St Mut.

— Human Authors of the New Testament, Vol. 2: Paul & John. 254p. (Orig.). (C). 1996. pap. 39.95 (*0-85439-412-5*, Pub. by St Paul Pubns) St Mut.

— A Personal Year of Grace: Spiritual Growth Through the Liturgical Year. LC 95-13676. 104p. (Orig.). 1996. pap. 8.95 (*0-8146-2221-6*, Liturg Pr Bks) Liturgical Pr.

Dicharry, Warren F. Praying the Rosary: The Joyful, Fruitful, Sorrowful & Glorious Mysteries. LC 97-34281. 1998. pap. 4.95 (*0-8146-2484-7*) Liturgical Pr.

Dichele, Ernest M., et al. Massachusetts Corporate Tax Manual, 2 vols. 3rd ed. 800p. 1993. suppl. ed. 60.00 (*0-685-74464-7*, MICHIE) LEXIS Pub.

— Massachusetts Corporate Tax Manual, 2 vols., Set. 3rd ed. 800p. 1993. ring bd. 160.00 (*0-88063-817-6*, MICHIE) LEXIS Pub.

D

Dichgans, J., et al, eds. Cerebellar Functions. (Proceedings in Life Sciences Ser.). (Illus.). 350p. 1984. 127.95 (*0-387-13728-9*) Spr-Verlag.

Dichiara, Robert. Dick & the Devil. 1990. mass mkt. 4.95 (*0-8125-1698-2*, Pub. by Tor Bks) St Martin.

Dichmann, Kurt. Operations East Africa. Brown, Bill, ed. Bk. I. (Illus.). 96p. (Orig.). (YA). (gr. 9-12). 1989. pap. write for info. (*0-318-65532-2*) Ceise Corp.

DiChristina, Samuel J., ed. see Erbes, Cynthia.

Dichter, C. Art Brut Lexicon, German to English. (ENG & GER.). 160p. 1997. 105.00 (*0-320-00453-8*) Fr & Eur.

Dichter, H. Handbook of American Sheet Music, 2 vols. (Illus.). 1953. pap. 20.00 (*0-87556-077-6*) Saifer.

Dichter, Harry. Handbook of American Sheet Music: First Annual Issue. 100p. 1993. reprint ed. lib. bdg. 69.00 (*0-7812-9697-8*) Rprt Serv.

Dichter, Harry. Handbook of American Sheet Music from the Authors' Collection. (Illus.). 1953. pap. 20.00 (*0-87556-591-3*) Saifer.

— Handbook of American Sheet Music from the Authors' Collection. Vol. 2. (Illus.). 1953. pap. 20.00 (*0-87556-592-1*) Saifer.

Dichter, M. A., ed. Mechanisms of Epileptogenesis: The Transition to Seizure. LC 88-25274. (Illus.). 298p. 1988. 79.50 (*0-306-43010-X*, Plenum Trade) Perseus Pubng.

Dicianni, Ron. Beyond Words: A Treasury of Paintings & Devotional Writings. LC 98-17526. 96p. 1998. 24.95 (*0-8423-0176-3*) Tyndale Hse.

DiCianni, Ron. Beyond Words: A Treasury of Paintings & Devotional Writings. LC 98-17526. xii, 84p. 1998. write for info. (*0-8423-0191-7*) Tyndale Hse.

***Dicianni, Ron.** For This Child I Pray: A Father's Prayer Journal. 1999. 14.99 (*1-57051-397-X*) Brownlow Pub Co.

— For This Child I Pray: A Mother's Prayer Journal. 1999. 14.99 (*1-57051-398-8*) Brownlow Pub Co.

— A Mother's Love: A Treasury of Love & Inspiration. 2000. 12.99 (*0-8054-2370-2*) Broadman.

***DiCianni, Ron.** Travels of the Messenger. 2000. 16.99 (*0-8423-3614-1*) Tyndale Hse.

DiCiccio, Carmen. Coal & Coke in Pennsylvania. LC 97-141385. (Illus.). 224p. 1996. pap. 16.95 (*0-89271-072-1*, 1006) Pa Hist & Mus.

DiCicco Digital Arts Staff. Let's Count. LC 98-208280. 1998. write for info. (*0-7853-2705-3*) Pubns Intl Ltd.

DiCicco Digital Arts Staff. Baby's First Getting Dressed Songs. LC 97-216212. (Baby Looney Tunes Song Bks.). 8p. (J). (ps). 1997. pap. 7.98 (*0-7853-2323-6*, PI23) Pubns Intl Ltd.

— Baby's First Scrub-a-Dub Songs. LC 97-216129. (Baby Looney Tunes Song Bks.). 8p. (J). (ps). 1997. 7.98 (*0-7853-2322-8*, PI22) Pubns Intl Ltd.

— On the Go Songs LC 98-162776. (Disney Babies Ser.). 6p. (J). 1998. write for info. (*0-7853-2339-2*) Pubns Intl Ltd.

Dicicco, Gil. Walt Disney's One Hundred One Dalmatians. LC 90-85425. (Junior Novelization Ser.). 72p. (J). (gr. 2-6). 1991. pap. 2.95 (*1-56282-013-3*, Pub. by Disney Pr) Little.

DiCicco, Gil. Walt Disney's Three Little Pigs. LC 92-53443. 32p. (J). 1993. 12.95 (*1-56282-381-7*, Pub. by Disney Pr) Time Warner.

***Dicicco, Joe.** The Li'l Mac Baseball Book: Stories for Future Baseball Players, Vol. 1. large type ed. Jimenez, Ruben D., tr. (ENG & SPA., Illus.). iii, 17p. (J). (ps). 1999. 7.95 (*1-929528-00-0*) Booker Lane.

— The Li'l Mac Baseball Book: Stories for Future Baseball Players, Vol. 2. large type ed. Jimenez, Ruben D., tr. (ENG & SPA., Illus.). iii, 16p. (J). (ps-3). 1999. 7.95 (*1-929528-01-9*) Booker Lane.

— The Li'l Mac Baseball Book: Stories for Future Baseball Players, Vol. 3. large type ed. Jimenez, Ruben D., tr. (ENG & SPA., Illus.). iii, 17p. (J). (ps-3). 1999. 7.95 (*1-929528-02-7*) Booker Lane.

— The Li'l Mac Baseball Book: Stories for Future Baseball Players, Vol. 4. large type ed. Jimenez, Ruben D., tr. (ENG & SPA., Illus.). iii, 14p. (J). (ps-3). 1999. 7.95 (*1-929528-03-5*) Booker Lane.

DiCicco, Mario M. Paul's Use of Ethos, Pathos, & Logos in Second Corinthians 10-13. LC 94-31547. (Biblical Press Ser.: Vol. 31). 316p. 1995. 99.95 (*0-7734-2369-9*) E Mellen.

Dicillo, Tom. Box of Moonlight & Notes from Overboard: A Film-Maker's Diary. 128p. 1997. pap. 14.95 (*0-571-19169-X*) Faber & Faber.

Dick. Anatomy of Film. LC 97-66542. 1997. pap. text 32.95 (*0-312-15399-6*) St Martin.

— Calculus of a Single Variable. 2nd ed. (Mathematics Ser.). 1998. text 65.95 (*0-534-95544-4*) PWS Pubs.

— Calculus of Several Variables. 2nd ed. (Mathematics Ser.). 1998. text 65.95 (*0-534-95550-9*) PWS Pubs.

Dick & Preaux, eds. Martiani Capellae: De Nuptiis Mercurii et Philologiae. rev. ed. (LAT.). 1978. reprint ed. 69.50 (*3-519-01532-3*, T1532, Pub. by B G Teubner) U of Mich Pr.

Dick, ed. see Howd, Richard N.

Dick, Alexandra, tr. see Lagerkvist, Par.

Dick, Andrew. Industrial Policy & Semiconductors: Missing the Target. 200p. 1995. 29.95 (*0-8447-7055-8*, AEI Pr); pap. 9.75 (*0-8447-7043-4*, AEI Pr) Am Enterprise.

Dick, Anne R. The Search for Philip K. Dick, 1928-1982: A Memoir. LC 95-8690. (Illus.). 396p. 1996. text 99.95 (*0-7734-9137-6*) E Mellen.

***Dick, Arthur.** Absolute Beginners Guitar: The Complete Picture Guide to Playing the Guitar. (Illus.). 48p. 1999. pap. text 11.95 (*0-7119-7428-4*, AM92615) Music Sales.

— Absolute Beginners Guitar: The Complete Picture Guide to Playing the Guitar. (Illus.). 48p. 2000. pap. text 11.95 (*0-7119-8059-4*, AM962820) Music Sales.

Dick, Arthur. The Complete Guitar Player: Blues Songbook. (Illus.). 48p. 1992. pap. 12.95 (*0-7119-2620-4*, AM84484) Music Sales.

— The Complete Guitar Player: Cat Stevens Songbook. (Illus.). 48p. 1989. pap. 15.95 (*0-7119-1836-8*, AM74741) Music Sales.

— The Complete Guitar Player: Paul Simon Songbook Two. (Illus.). 48p. 1992. pap. 12.95 (*0-7119-2655-7*, PS11220) Music Sales.

Dick, Arthur, contrib. by. The Complete Guitar Player: Chord Encyclopedia CD Chordfinder. LC 97-125370. (Illus.). 1996. 15.95 (*0-7119-3196-8*, AM 90134) Omnibus NY.

Dick, Arthur, selected by. The Complete Guitar Player: Paul Simon Songbook. (Illus.). 48p. 1988. pap. 12.95 (*0-7119-1156-8*, PS10875) Music Sales.

Dick, Arthur, jt. auth. see Jones, Andy.

Dick, Arthur, jt. auth. see Music Sales Corporation Staff.

Dick, Auguste. Emmy Noether, 1882-1935. 192p. 1980. 32.00 (*0-8176-0519-3*) Birkhauser.

***Dick, B. & Schwenn, O.** Viscoelastics in Ophthalmic Surgery. LC 00-39482. 2000. write for info. (*3-540-67330-X*) Spr-Verlag.

Dick, Bernard F. City of Dreams: The Making & Remaking of Universal Pictures. LC 96-40094. (Illus.). 344p. 1997. 29.95 (*0-8131-2016-0*) U Pr of Ky.

— Hellman in Hollywood. LC 81-72044. (Illus.). 220p. 1983. 29.50 (*0-8386-3140-1*) Fairleigh Dickinson.

— The Merchant Prince of Poverty Row: Harry Cohn of Columbia Pictures. LC 93-3348. 248p. 1993. 29.95 (*0-8131-1841-7*) U Pr of Ky.

— Radical Innocence: A Critical Study of the Hollywood Ten. LC 88-17366. 280p. 1988. 29.95 (*0-8131-1660-0*) U Pr of Ky.

— The Star-Spangled Screen: The American World War II Film. LC 85-9205. 304p. 1996. 32.00 (*0-8131-1531-0*) U Pr of Ky.

— The Star-Spangled Screen: The American World War II Film. (Illus.). 304p. 1996. pap. 18.00 (*0-8131-0885-3*) U Pr of Ky.

Dick, Bernard F., ed. Columbia Pictures: Portrait of a Studio. LC 91-13459. (Illus.). 320p. 1992. 29.95 (*0-8131-1769-0*) U Pr of Ky.

— Dark Victory. LC 81-50822. (Warner Bros. Screenplay Ser.). (Illus.). 216p. (Orig.). 1981. 14.95 (*0-299-08760-3*) U of Wis Pr.

Dick, Bruce & Singh, Amritjit, eds. Conversations with Ishmael Reed. LC 95-20381. (Literary Conversations Ser.). 272p. 1995. pap. 15.95 (*0-87805-815-X*); text 39.50 (*0-87805-814-1*) U Pr of Miss.

Dick, Bruce, ed. see Anaya, Rudolfo A.

Dick, Bruce Allen, ed. The Critical Response to Ishmael Reed, 31. LC 98-31018. (Critical Responses in Arts & Letters Ser.: Vol. 31). 304p. 1999. lib. bdg. 65.00 (*0-313-30025-9*, Greenwood Pr) Greenwood.

Dick, Carson, jt. ed. see Goodacre, J.

Dick, Dan. Quest: A Journey Toward a New Kind of Church. LC 98-88788. 96p. 1999. pap. write for info. (*0-88177-261-5*, DR261, Pub. by Discipleship Res) P B D Inc.

Dick, Dan R. Choices & Challenges: Stewardship Strategies for Youth. LC 94-72155. 72p. (J). 1994. pap. 9.95 (*0-88177-135-X*, DR135) Discipleship Res.

— Devotions for Dieters: A Guide to a Lighter You. (Value Book Ser.). 1997. pap. text 0.99 (*1-55748-953-X*) Barbour Pub.

Dick, Dan R. Devotions for Dieters: A 365-Day Guide to a Lighter You. 384p. 1997. 7.97 (*1-57748-092-9*) Barbour Pub.

Dick, Dan R. Revolutionizing Christian Stewardship: Lessons from Copernicus. LC 96-72437. 112p. 1997. pap. 15.95 (*0-88177-212-7*, DR212) Discipleship Res.

— Wisdom from the Psalms. (Inspirational Library Ser.). 336p. 1989. im. lthr. 4.97 (*1-55748-026-5*) Barbour Pub.

— Wisdom from the Psalms. 1997. pap. 4.97 (*1-57748-021-X*) Barbour Pub.

Dick, Dan R. & Dick, Nancy. Wisdom from the Proverbs: Daily Thoughts from the Proverbs. 368p. 1998. pap. 4.97 (*0-916441-75-X*) Barbour Pub.

Dick, David. All Modern Slavery Indefensible: Intended for All Places Where Slavery Does Exist. LC 72-6533. (Black Heritage Library Collection). 1977. reprint ed. 30.95 (*0-8369-9165-6*) Ayer.

— Capital Walks in Edinburgh: The New Town. (Illus.). 224p. 1996. pap. 11.95 (*1-897784-20-1*, Pub. by N Wilson Pubng) Interlink Pub.

— The Scourges of Heaven. LC 98-29012. 288p. 1998. 25.00 (*0-8131-2074-8*) U Pr of Ky.

Dick, David B. A Conversation with Peter P. Pence. LC 95-92250. (Illus.). 128p. 1995. 15.95 (*0-9632886-3-6*) Plum Lick Pub.

— Peace at the Center. LC 94-92164. (Illus.). 242p. 1994. 17.95 (*0-9632886-2-8*) Plum Lick Pub.

— The Quiet Kentuckians. LC 96-68559. (Illus.). 256p. 1996. 16.95 (*0-9632886-4-4*) Plum Lick Pub.

— The View from Plum Lick. (Illus.). 248p. (Orig.). 1992. pap. 14.95 (*0-9632886-0-1*) Plum Lick Pub.

— The View from Plum Lick. LC 97-91895. (Illus.). 256p. (Orig.). 1997. 17.95 (*0-9632886-6-0*) Plum Lick Pub.

Dick, David B., jt. auth. see Dick, Eulalie C.

***Dick, David J.** A Practical Guide to Peripheral Nerve & Neuromuscular Disorders. (Illus.). 320p. 2002. pap. 67.50 (*0-7506-4895-3*) Buttrwrth-Heinemann.

***Dick, E., et al, eds.** Multigrid Methods VI: Proceedings of the Sixth Multigrid Conference Held in Gent, Belgium, September 27-30, 1999. (Lecture Notes in Computational Science & Engineering Ser.: Vol. 14). ix, 293p. 2000. pap. 82.00 (*3-540-67157-9*) Spr-Verlag.

Dick, E. A., jt. auth. see Snell, W. H.

Dick, Eddie, ed. From Limelight to Satellite: A Scottish Film Book. (Distributed for the British Film Institute Ser.). (Illus.). 256p. 1991. 13.50 (*0-85170-281-3*, Pub. by British Film Inst); pap. 23.95 (*0-85170-282-1*, Pub. by British Film Inst) Ind U Pr.

Dick, Eddie, et al, eds. Bill Douglas: A Lanternist's Account. (Illus.). 240p. (C). 1993. 49.95 (*0-85170-347-X*, Pub. by British Film Inst); pap. 19.95 (*0-85170-348-8*, Pub. by British Film Inst) Ind U Pr.

Dick, Ernst S., jt. ed. see Jankowsky, Kurt R.

Dick, Esther A., jt. auth. see Snell, Walter.

Dick, Eulalie C. & Dick, David B. Home Sweet Kentucky. (Illus.). 258p. 1999. 17.95 (*0-9632886-7-9*) Plum Lick Pub.

Dick, Everett. Conquering the Great American Desert: Nebraska. LC 74-17591. (Nebraska State Historical Publications: Vol. 27). 456p. 1975. 5.00 (*0-933307-06-3*) Nebraska Hist.

— The Dixie Frontier: A Social History of the Southern Frontier from the First Transmontaine Beginnings to the Civil War. LC 92-54144. 1993. pap. 16.95 (*0-8061-2385-0*) U of Okla Pr.

— Sod-House Frontier. 550p. 12.95 (*0-934904-38-3*) J & L Lee.

— Tales of the Frontier: From Lewis & Clark to the Last Roundup. LC 62-14664. (Illus.). x, 390p. 1963. pap. 15.95 (*0-8032-5744-9*, Bison Books) U of Nebr Pr.

Dick, Everett N. The Lure of the Land: A Social History of the Public Lands from the Articles of Confederation to the New Deal. LC 66-13015. (Illus.). 460p. 1970. pap. 142.60 (*0-608-05113-6*, 206567200005) Bks Demand.

— The Sod-House Frontier, 1854-1890: A Social History of the Northern Plains from the Creation of Kansas & Nebraska to the Admission of the Dakotas. LC 78-24204. (Illus.). 634p. reprint ed. pap. 196.60 (*0-8357-6601-2*, 203523100094) Bks Demand.

— Vanguards of the Frontier: A Social History of the Northern Plains & Rocky Mountains from the Fur Traders to the Sod Busters. LC 41-6157. 594p. reprint ed. pap. 184.20 (*0-7837-4659-8*, 204438300002) Bks Demand.

— William Miller & the Advent Crisis: 1831-1844. Land, Gary, ed. LC 94-72521. (Illus.). 250p. 1994. pap. 16.99 (*1-883925-02-9*) Andrews Univ Pr.

Dick, Frank. Sports Training Principles. 3rd rev. ed. 320p. 1997. pap. write for info. (*0-7136-4149-5*, Pub. by A & C Blk) Midpt Trade.

Dick, Frederick, jt. ed. see Riehl, Dan.

Dick, G. Practical Immunisation. 1986. text 82.00 (*0-85200-525-9*) Kluwer Academic.

Dick, Harold G. & Robinson, Douglas H. The Golden Age of the Great Passenger Airships: Graf Zeppelin & Hindenburg. LC 84-600298. (Illus.). 226p. 1992. pap. 29.95 (*1-56098-219-5*) Smithsonian.

Dick, Harold M., et al, eds. Dying & Disabled Children: Dealing with Loss & Grief. LC 88-15364. (Loss, Grief & Care Ser.: Vol. 2, Nos. 3 & 4). (Illus.). 153p. 1989. text 39.95 (*0-86656-759-3*) Haworth Pr.

Dick, Hermann, jt. auth. see Cathie, John.

Dick, Howard, et al, eds. Balanced Development: East Java in the New Order. (South-East Asian Social Science Monographs). (Illus.). 398p. 1993. text 75.00 (*0-19-588597-X*) OUP.

Dick, J. W. The Small Business Legal Kit & Disk. (Adams Expert Advice for Small Business Ser.). 435p. 1997. pap. 19.95 incl. disk (*1-55850-701-9*) Adams Media.

Dick, James C., ed. see Burns, Robert.

Dick, Jane. Conceptions. 48p. 1992. pap. 6.00 (*0-920717-49-7*) Guernica Editions.

Dick, Jill. Freelance Writing for Newspapers. 2nd ed. 1998. pap. 19.95 (*0-7136-4737-X*, Pub. by A & C Blk) Midpt Trade.

— Writing for Magazines. 2nd ed. pap. 18.95 (*0-7136-4485-0*, Pub. by A & C Blk) Midpt Trade.

Dick, Joab J. & Monk, Lee H. 101 Reasons I'm Glad I Quit. 136p. 1999. 8.95 (*0-9669802-0-4*, 1996-1) Dick & Monk.

Dick, John. Raeburn. (Illus.). 176p. 1997. 70.00 (*0-903598-76-0*, Pub. by Natl Galleries) Antique Collect.

Dick, John, ed. American Admiralty Bureau's Preview of a Tow Configuration & Power Guide. 20p. (Orig.). 1995. pap. text 21.75 (*1-879778-36-X*, BK-0436) Marine Educ.

Dick, John A. & Richardson, Anne, eds. William Tyndale & the Law. LC 94-5589. (Sixteenth Century Essays & Studies: Vol. 25). 135p. 1993. 40.00 (*0-940474-26-3*, SCJP) Truman St Univ.

Dick, John H. Other Edens: The Sketchbook of an Artist Naturalist. LC 79-67270. (Illus.). 1979. 19.95 (*0-8159-6412-9*) Devin.

***Dick, Judy.** The Seder Activity Book. (Illus.). (J). 2000. 6.95 (*0-8074-0728-3*) UAHC.

Dick, Judy, jt. auth. see Wengrov, Charles.

Dick, Jutta & Schoeps, Julius H. Salomon Ludwig Steinheim - Johanna Steinheim: Briefe. (GER.). 446p. 1996. write for info. (*3-487-10158-0*) G Olms Pubs.

Dick, Karen L., ed. The Whole Costumer's Catalogue. 14th ed. 224p. 1998. pap. 17.00 (*1-888288-02-7*) CBTB Pr.

***Dick, Kevin.** XML: A Manager's Guide. LC 99-41252. 208p. 1999. pap. text 29.95 (*0-201-43335-4*) Addison-Wesley.

Dick-Larkham, Richard. Cutting Energy Costs. 1977. pap. 24.95 (*0-8464-0309-9*) Beekman Pubs.

Dick, Lennox, et al. The Art & Science of Fly Fishing. (Illus.). 132p. 1993. pap. 19.95 (*1-878175-41-6*) F Amato Pubns.

Dick, Lenox. The Art & Science of Fly Fishing. (Illus.). 1977. pap. 7.95 (*0-8065-0587-7*, Citadel Pr) Carol Pub Group.

— Experience the World of Shad Fishing. 1996. pap. 7.95 (*1-57188-062-3*) F Amato Pubns.

Dick, Lenox, jt. auth. see Iman, Ed.

Dick, Leslie. Kicking. 256p. (Orig.). 1993. pap. 10.95 (*0-87286-282-8*) City Lights.

— The Skull of Charlotte Corday & Other Stories. LC 97-2204. 240p. 1997. 22.50 (*0-684-83439-1*, Scribner Pap Fic) S&S Trade Pap.

— Without Falling. 160p. (Orig.). 1988. pap. 6.95 (*0-87286-224-0*) City Lights.

Dick Lister John C. The Country Music Cookbook. LC 99-31922. 1999. 8.99 (*0-517-20616-1*) Random Hse Value.

Dick, Lois H. Amy Carmichael: Let the Little Children Come. mass mkt. 4.99 (*0-8024-0433-2*, 78) Moody.

— Isobel Kuhn. LC 87-71603. (Women of Faith Ser.). 16p. (Orig.). 1987. mass mkt. 4.99 (*0-87123-976-0*) Bethany Hse.

Dick, Lois Hoadley. False Coin, True Coin. LC 92-39280. (YA). 1993. pap. 6.49 (*0-89084-664-2*, 063701) Bob Jones Univ.

Dick, Lorraine. First Steps for Kids: Lessons to Help Children Grow More As Christians. 48p. (Orig.). (J). (gr. 2-5). 1995. pap., teacher ed. 5.95 (*0-921788-19-3*); pap., student ed. 2.95 (*0-921788-20-7*) Kindred Prods.

Dick, Louise, ed. see Olson, Marie.

Dick, Louise L. Old College Reflections: A Family Story. 148p. 1999. 21.95 (*0-9668657-3-1*) Ark Pubg.

Dick, Louise L., ed. Clips from Tom M. Olson: Nuggets from the Writings of Tom M. Olson Provide the Only-Way to View Events. LC 86-90141. (LeTourneau One-Way Ser.: Vol. 10). 251p. (Orig.). 1986. pap. 15.95 (*0-935899-06-5*) LeTourneau Pr.

Dick, Louise L. & LeTourneau, Richard H., eds. R. G. Talks About: Nuggets from the Writings of R. G. LeTourneau Provide the Only Way to Live. LC 86-91106. (LeTourneau One-Way Ser.: Vol. 9). 317p. (Orig.). 1986. pap. 15.95 (*0-935899-05-7*) LeTourneau Pr.

Dick, M. Half of Glasgow's Gone. (C). 1987. 110.00 (*0-85174-509-1*) St Mut.

Dick, Manfred, ed. see Wentzlaff-Eggebert, Friedrich-Wilhelm.

Dick, Marrissa R. Cousins. Date not set. pap. 14.95 (*1-893979-01-6*) Nubian Romance.

— Deja Vu Desires. Date not set. pap. 14.95 (*1-893979-00-8*) Nubian Romance.

— Letters. Date not set. pap. 14.95 (*1-893979-02-4*) Nubian Romance.

— Them's Eve's Daughter's. Date not set. pap. 14.95 (*1-893979-03-2*) Nubian Romance.

Dick, Martin. Wirtschaft und Umwelt Cortaillod- und Horgenzeitlicher Seeufersiedlungen In Zurich (Schweiz) Ergebnisse Samenanalytischer Untersuchungen Aus der Praehistorischen Station 'Mozartstrasse' (Dissertationes Botanicae Ser.: Band 132). (ENG & GER., Illus.). 144p. 1989. pap. 36.00 (*3-443-64044-3*, Pub. by Gebruder Borntraeger) Balogh.

Dick, Martin S. The Out of Control Room: A Hilarious Look at TV Production. LC 87-90747. 103p. (Orig.). 1988. pap. 9.24 (*0-9618502-0-5*) Sugma Press.

Dick, Mathew H. & Ross, June R. Intertidal Bryozoa (Cheilostomata) of the Kodiak Vicinity, Alaska. (Occasional Papers: Vol. 23). 1989. pap. write for info. (*1-882008-00-6*) WWU CPNS.

Dick, Michael B., ed. Born in Heaven, Made on Earth: The Creation of the Cult Image in the Ancient Near East. LC 99-12840. xii, 243p. 1999. text 35.00 (*1-57506-024-8*) Eisenbrauns.

Dick, Michael J. High-Tech Creativity. (IEEE Engineers Guide to Business Ser.: Vol. 3). 1992. 19.95 (*0-7803-0351-2*, EG103) Inst Electrical.

Dick, Molly. The San Francisco Survival Guide: A Complete Resource Guide. 125p. 1993. pap. 11.95 (*0-9635622-0-7*) CrossRds Calif.

Dick, Nancy, jt. auth. see Dick, Dan R.

Dick, Oliver L., ed. see Aubrey, John.

Dick, Pastor. Heavenly Groundwork. 196p. (Orig.). 1985. 3.95 (*0-934109-00-1*) Banquet Hse.

Dick, Patrick, jt. auth. see Dobb, Linda S.

Dick, Paul. ASNT Level II Study Guide: Magnetic Particle Testing Method. (Illus.). 56p. (C). 1996. pap. 29.95 (*1-57117-016-2*, 6100) Am Soc Nondestructive.

***Dick-Peddie, William A.** New Mexico Vegetation: Past, Present & Future. (Illus.). 2000. pap. 24.95 (*0-8263-2164-X*) U of NM Pr.

Dick-Peddie, William A. New Mexico Vegetation: Past, Present, & Future. LC 92-3138. (Illus.). 276p. 1993. reprint ed. pap. 85.60 (*0-608-07284-2*, 206751200009) Bks Demand.

Dick, Philip K. Blade Runner. 224p. 1987. mass mkt. 5.99 (*0-345-35047-2*, Del Rey) Ballantine Pub Grp.

— Clans of the Alphane Moon. 269p. 1988. mass mkt. 4.95 (*0-88184-436-5*) Carroll & Graf.

— The Collected Stories of Philip K. Dick Vol. 5: The Eye of the Sibyl. 408p. 1992. pap. 12.95 (*0-8065-1328-4*, Citadel Pr) Carol Pub Group.

— Confessions of a Crap Artist. LC 91-45313. 1992. pap. 11.00 (*0-679-74114-3*) Vin Bks.

— Dark-Haired Girl. 1988. 19.95 (*0-929480-03-1*) Mark Ziesing.

— The Divine Invasion. LC 90-55677. 240p. 1991. pap. 11.00 (*0-679-73445-7*) Vin Bks.

— Do Androids Dream of Electric Sheep? 256p. (YA). (gr. 9). 1996. pap. 12.00 (*0-345-40447-5*, Del Rey) Ballantine Pub Grp.

— Dr. Bloodmoney. 320p. 1988. mass mkt. 3.95 (*0-88184-389-X*) Carroll & Graf.

— Flow My Tears, the Policeman Said. LC 92-50649. 1993. pap. 11.00 (*0-679-74066-X*) Vin Bks.

— Galactic Pot-Healer. LC 93-42195. 1994. pap. 12.00 (*0-679-75297-8*) Random.

— The Game-Players of Titan. 1992. pap. 12.00 (*0-679-74065-1*) Vin Bks.

— I Hope I Shall Arrive Soon. 1987. pap. 3.50 (*0-317-64192-1*) St Martin.

— The Man in the High Castle. 1992. pap. 12.00 (*0-679-74067-8*) Vin Bks.

— Martian Time-Slip. LC 94-42802. 1995. pap. 11.00 (*0-679-76167-5*) Vin Bks.

— A Maze of Death. LC 93-42196. 1994. pap. 11.00 (*0-679-75298-6*) Random.

***Dick, Philip K.** Minority Report. 1999. pap. text 14.95 (*0-8065-2168-6*, Citadel Pr) Carol Pub Group.

Dick, Philip K. Now Wait for Last Year. LC 92-50645. 1993. pap. 12.00 (*0-679-74220-4*) Vin Bks.

— The Penultimate Truth. 201p. 1989. mass mkt. 3.95 (*0-88184-493-4*) Carroll & Graf.

— The Philip K. Dick Reader. LC 96-52695. 410p. 1997. pap. 14.95 (*0-8065-1856-1*, Citadel Pr) Carol Pub Group.

— Puttering about in a Small Land. 290p. 1985. reprint ed. pap. 11.95 (*0-89733-384-5*) Academy Chi Pubs.

— Radio Free Albemuth. 224p. 1987. mass mkt. 4.99 (*0-380-70288-6*, Avon Bks) Morrow Avon.

— Radio Free Albemuth. LC 85-11171. 214p. 1985. 25.00 (*0-89366-172-4*) Ultramarine Pub.

— Radio Free Albemuth. LC 98-160902. 1998. pap. 11.00 (*0-679-78137-4*) Vin Bks.

— A Scanner Darkly. LC 91-50090. 256p. 1991. pap. 11.00 (*0-679-73665-4*) Vin Bks.

— The Selected Letters of Philip K. Dick - 1974. deluxe limited ed. 310p. 1991. boxed set 60.00 (*0-88733-105-X*) Underwood Bks.

— The Selected Letters of Philip K. Dick - 1974, 1974. 310p. 1991. 39.95 (*0-88733-104-1*) Underwood Bks.

— The Selected Letters of Philip K. Dick, 1938-1971, 1. 350p. 1994. 39.95 (*1-887424-20-2*) Underwood Bks.

— The Selected Letters of Philip K. Dick, 1972-1973, Vol. 2. 360p. 1993. 39.95 (*0-88733-161-0*) Underwood Bks.

— The Selected Letters of Philip K. Dick, 1977-1979, 6 vols., Vol. 5. 296p. 1992. 39.95 (*0-88733-120-3*) Underwood Bks.

— The Selected Letters of Philip K. Dick, 1938-1971, Vol. 5. 350p. 1994. 39.95 (*0-88733-169-6*) Underwood Bks.

— The Selected Letters of Philip K. Dick, 1977-1979, 6 vols., Vol. 5. deluxe limited ed. 296p. 1992. boxed set 60.00 (*0-88733-121-1*) Underwood Bks.

— The Selected Letters of Philip K. Dick, 1975-1976, 6 vols., Vol. 4. 384p. 1992. 39.95 (*0-88733-111-4*) Underwood Bks.

D

An Asterisk (*) at the beginning of an entry indicates that the title is appearing for the first time.

— The Selected Letters of Philip K. Dick, 1975-1976, 6 vols., Vol. 4. deluxe limited ed. 384p. 1992. boxed set 60.00 (0-88733-112-2) Underwood Bks.

— The Shifting Realities of Philip K. Dick: Selected Writings. Sutin, Lawrence, ed. LC 94-27812. 1995. 27.50 (0-679-42644-2) Pantheon.

— Short Happy Life of the Brown Oxford. 1990. pap. 12.95 (0-8065-1153-2, Citadel Pr) Carol Pub Group.

— The Three Stigmata of Palmer Eldritch. LC 91-50091. 208p. 1991. pap. 11.00 (0-679-73666-2) Vin Bks.

— Time Out of Joint. 263p. 1987. reprint ed. pap. 4.95 (0-88184-352-0) Carroll & Graf.

— The Transmigration of Timothy Archer. LC 90-55675. 256p. 1991. pap. 12.00 (0-679-73444-9) Random.

— Ubik. LC 91-50097. 224p. 1991. pap. 11.00 (0-679-73664-6) Vin Bks.

— Valis. LC 90-55676. 240p. 1991. pap. 11.00 (0-679-73446-5) Vin Bks.

— We Can Build You. LC 93-43977. 1994. pap. 11.00 (0-679-75296-X) Random.

— Welcome to Reality: The Nightmares of Philip K. Dick. Anton, Uwe, ed. Young, Jim, tr. 208p. 1991. reprint ed. 55.00 (0-9623824-4-2); reprint ed. pap. 12.95 (0-9623824-5-0) Broken Mirrors Pr.

— The World Jones Made. LC 92-50644. 1993. pap. 11.00 (0-679-74219-0) Vin Bks.

— The Zap Gun. 258p. 1989. mass mkt. 3.95 (0-88184-553-1) Carroll & Graf.

Dick, R. A. The Ghost & Mrs. Muir. 1993. reprint ed. lib. bdg. 27.95 (0-89968-395-9, Lghtyr Pr) Buccaneer Bks.

Dick-Read, Grantly. Childbirth Without Fear. 1979. mass mkt. 3.95 (0-06-080490-4, Perennial) HarperTrade.

Dick, Remi Van, see Van Dick, Remi.

Dick, Richard S., et al, eds. The Computer-Based Patient Record: An Essential Technology for Health Care. rev. ed. LC 97-31030. 270p. 1997. 34.95 (0-309-05532-6) Natl Acad Pr.

Dick, Robert. Circular Breathing for the Flutist. LC 87-60128. (Illus.). 53p. (Orig.). 1987. pap. 16.95 (0-939407-01-9) Multiple Breath Music.

— I Was Not Alone. 184p. 1998. pap. 30.00 (1-84017-006-9) St Mut.

— The Other Flute: A Performance Manual of Contemporary Techniques with 33.3 RPM Mono Record. 2nd ed. LC 88-92275. 144p. 1989. spiral bd. 39.95 (0-939407-02-7) Multiple Breath Music.

— Tone Development Through Extented Techniques. rev. ed. LC 86-61675. 60p. (Orig.). 1986. pap. 19.95 (0-939407-00-0) Multiple Breath Music.

Dick, Robert C. Black Protest: Issues & Tactics, 14. LC 72-794. 338p. 1974. 75.00 (0-8371-6366-8, DNAPB, Greenwood Pr) Greenwood.

Dick-Rombauer, Marjorie. Legal Problem Solving: Analysis, Research & Writing. 5th ed. LC 83-9860. (American Casebook Ser.). 524p. (C). 1991. pap. 45.50 (0-314-84243-8) West Pub.

Dick, Ron. American Eagles: A History of the United States Air Force. LC 97-1502. (Illus.). 464p. 1997. 65.00 (1-57427-065-6) Howell Pr VA.

— Reach & Power: The Heritage of the United States Air Force in Pictures & Artifacts. LC 97-26252. (Illus.). 564p. 1998. 78.00 (0-16-049271-8) AFH & MP.

— Spitfire: RAF Fighter. LC 97-75156. (Living History Ser.: Vol. 6). (Illus.). 64p. 1997. pap. 15.95 (1-57427-071-0) Howell Pr VA.

Dick, Ron, jt. ed. see Patterson, Dan.

Dick, Samuel, et al. Mathematica in the Laboratory. (Illus.). 338p. 1997. text 74.95 (0-521-58137-0); pap. text 30.95 (0-521-49906-2) Cambridge U Pr.

Dick, Steve. The Working Folding Knife. 1998. pap. 21.95 (0-88317-210-0) Stoeger Pub Co.

Dick, Steven J. The Biological Universe: The Twentieth Century Extraterrestrial Life Debate & the Limits of Science. (Illus.). 525p. (C). 1996. text 54.95 (0-521-34326-7) Cambridge U Pr.

***Dick, Steven J.** The Biological Universe: The Twentieth Century Extraterrestrial Life Debate & the Limits of Science. 540p. 1999. pap. 21.95 (0-521-66361-X) Cambridge U Pr.

Dick, Steven J. Life on Other Worlds: The Twentieth Century Extraterrestrial Life Debate. LC 98-20465. (Illus.). 304p. (C). 1998. 24.95 (0-521-62012-0) Cambridge U Pr.

***Dick, Steven J.** Many Worlds: The New Universe & Its Theological Implications. LC 00-20804. 256p. 2000. 22.95 (1-890151-37-8) Templeton Fnd.

— Many Worlds: The New Universe & Its Theological Implications. LC 00-20804. 256p. 2000. pap. 14.95 (1-890151-42-4) Templeton Fnd.

Dick, Susan. Virginia Woolf. 128p. 1989. pap. text 9.95 (0-7131-6561-8, A3521, Pub. by E A) Routldge.

— Virginia Woolf LC 88-34069. (Modern Fiction Ser.). xiv, 97 p. 1989. write for info. (0-7131-6560-X) Arnld Pub.

Dick, Susan, et al, eds. Essays for Richard Ellmann: Omnium Gatherum. 496p. 1989. 65.00 (0-7735-0707-8, Pub. by McG-Queens Univ Pr) CUP Services.

Dick, Susan, ed. see Woolf, Virginia.

Dick, Thom. Street Talk: Stories from a Rescuer. Howell, Valla & Williams, Gary R., eds. LC 88-80335. (Illus.). 192p. 1988. text 15.95 (0-936174-05-6) Jems Comm.

Dick, Trevor J. An Economic Theory of Technological Change: The Case of Patents & United States Railroads, 1871-1950. LC 77-14769. (Dissertations in American Economic History Ser.). 1978. 18.95 (0-405-11031-6) Ayer.

Dick, Trevor J., ed. Business Cycles since 1820: New International Perspectives from Historical Evidence. LC 97-38474. 320p. 1998. 95.00 (1-85898-350-9) E Elgar.

Dick, Trevor J. & Floyd, John E. Canada & the Gold Standard: Balance of Payments Adjustment under Fixed Exchange Rates, 1871-1913. (Studies in Monetary & Financial History). (Illus.). 252p. (C). 1992. text 80.00 (0-521-40408-8) Cambridge U Pr.

Dick, W. Carson, jt. ed. see Calabro, John J.

Dick, Walter & Carey, Lou M. The Systematic Design of Instruction. 4th ed. LC 95-34392. (Illus.). 384p. (C). 1997. pap. text 73.00 (0-673-99084-2) Addson-Wesley Educ.

Dick, Walter & Reiser, Robert A. Instructional Planning: A Guide for Teachers. 2nd rev. ed. LC 95-17021. 192p. 1995. pap. text 40.00 (0-205-16614-8) Allyn.

Dick, Warren A. Soil Biochemistry. 1999. 55.00 (0-87371-549-7) CRC Pr.

Dick, William. Byron & His Poetry. LC 76-52949. (Studies in Byron: No. 5). 1977. lib. bdg. 75.00 (0-8383-2142-9) M S G Haskell Hse.

Dick, William B. Dick's One Hundred Amusements. LC 67-16293. (Illus.). 184p. 1967. reprint ed. pap. 7.50 (0-89366-051-5) Ultramarine Pub.

Dick, William B., compiled by. Dick's Festival Reciter: Containing Appropriate Pieces & Programs, Original & Selected for Washington's Birthday, Memorial Day... LC 78-39484. (Granger Index Reprint Ser.). 1977. reprint ed. 17.95 (0-8369-6340-7) Ayer.

Dickas, Albert B., ed. Lake Superior Basin Segment of the Midcontinent Rift System. (IGC Field Trip Guidebooks Ser.). 72p. 1989. 13.00 (0-87590-557-9, T344) Am Geophysical.

Dickas, Albert B., ed. see International Conference on Basement Tectonics Sta.

***Dickason.** Enfermeria Maternoinfantil. 3rd ed. (C). 1999. text 51.57 (84-8174-360-7) Harcourt.

Dickason. Sheet Metal Drawing. 1990. pap. text. write for info. (0-582-99482-9, Pub. by Addison-Wesley) Longman.

Dickason, C. Fred. Angels Elect & Evil. LC 96-203372. pap. 12.99 (0-8024-0734-X, 79) Moody.

— Demon Possession & the Christian: A New Perspective. LC 88-63692. 355p. 1989. pap. 14.99 (0-89107-521-6) Crossway Bks.

— Names of Angels. (Names of Ser.). 160p. 1997. mass mkt. 4.99 (0-8024-6181-6, 15) Moody.

***Dickason, C. Fred.** Los Nombres de los Angeles. (SPA.). 160p. 1999. pap. 5.99 (0-8254-1165-3, Edit Portavoz) Kregel.

— La Posesion Demoniaca y el Cristiano (Demon Possession & the Christian) (SPA & ENG.). 368p. 1999. 12.99 (0-88113-511-9) Caribe Betania.

Dickason, David G., jt. ed. see Ziring, Lawrence.

Dickason, David H. The Daring Young Men: The Story of the American Pre-Raphaelites. LC 69-13235. (Illus.). 330p. 1972. 24.95 (0-405-08444-7, Pub. by Blom Pubns) Ayer.

Dickason, Elizabeth J. Maternal & Infant Nursing Care. 3rd ed. LC 97-10756. (Illus.). 928p. (C). (gr. 13). 1997. text 55.00 (0-8151-2517-8, 29925) Mosby Inc.

— Maternal & Infant Nursing Care. 3rd ed. (Illus.). 128p. (C). (gr. 13). 1997. pap. text, student ed. 14.95 (0-8151-2518-6, 29926) Mosby Inc.

— Maternal-Infant Nursing Care Pocket Handbook. 3rd ed. (Illus.). 400p. (C). (gr. 13). 1998. pap. text 14.95 (0-8151-2519-4, 29927) Mosby Inc.

Dickason, Elizabeth J. & Schultz, Martha O. Maternal-Infant Nursing Care, Includes Testbank. 3rd ed. (Illus.). 1998. teacher ed. write for info. (0-8151-2563-1) Mosby Inc.

***Dickason, Elizabeth J., et al.** Maternal-Infant Nursing Care: Text, Student Learning Guide Package, Set. 3rd ed. (Illus.). (C). 1998. text, student ed. write for info. (0-8151-2521-6) Mosby Inc.

Dickason, Fred. Los Angeles: Escogidos y Malignos. (SPA.). 232p. 1995. pap. 8.99 (0-8254-1164-5, Edit Portavoz) Kregel.

Dickason, Kathleen S. Garden Styles. LC 95-72543. 192 p. 1996. write for info. (0-7853-1685-X) Pubns Intl Ltd.

Dickason, Olive Patricia. Canada's First Nations: A History of Founding Peoples from Earliest Times. LC 91-50884. (Civilization of the American Indian Ser.: Vol. 208). (Illus.). 624p. 1992. 45.00 (0-8061-2438-5) U of Okla Pr.

— Canada's First Nations: A History of Founding Peoples from Earliest Times. LC 91-50884. (Civilization of the American Indian Ser.: Vol. 208). (Illus.). 624p. (C). 1992. pap. 19.95 (0-8061-2439-3) U of Okla Pr.

— The Native Imprint: The Contribution of First Peoples to Canada's Character. LC 97-200355. 1996. write for info. (0-919737-30-7) Athabasca Univ Pr.

Dickason, Vance. The Loudspeaker Design Cookbook. 5th ed. (Illus.). 165p. 1995. pap. text 34.95 (1-882580-10-9) Audio Amateur.

— Loudspeaker Recipes: Four Two-Way Designs, Bk. 1. LC 94-71764. (Illus.). 144p. (Orig.). 1994. pap. 24.95 (1-882580-04-4) Audio Amateur.

Dicke, Karel A. & Keating, Armand, eds. Autologous Blood & Marrow Transplantation: Proceedings of the 9th International Symposium. (Illus.). 1999. pap. text 95.00 (1-891524-04-6) Carden Jennings.

— Autologous Marrow & Blood Transplantation: Proceedings of the 8th International Symposium. (Illus.). 744p. 1997. pap. text 65.00 (1-891524-02-X) Carden Jennings.

***Dicke, Melissa.** Upon a Star Come Nighttime. 1999. write for info. (1-58235-497-9) Watermrk Pr.

Dicke, Robert, Jr., jt. auth. see Martin, Lance.

Dicke, Robert H. Theoretical Significance of Experimental Relativity. (Documents on Modern Physics Ser.). xii, 154p. (C). 1965. text 237.00 (0-677-00220-3) Gordon & Breach.

Dicke, Robert H. & Wittke, J. P. Introduction to Quantum Mechanics. 1960. write for info. (0-201-01510-2) Addison-Wesley.

Dicke, Thomas S. Franchising in America: The Development of a Business Method, 1840-1980. LC 91-43618. (Illus.). xii, 204p. (C). 1992. pap. 18.95 (0-8078-4378-4) U of NC Pr.

— Franchising in America: The Development of a Business Method, 1840-1980. LC 91-43618. (Illus.). 216p. 1992. reprint ed. pap. 67.00 (0-608-08014-4, 2067979(0001) Bks Demand.

Dickel, Karl E., ed. see Rowe, Alan J. & Mason, Richard O.

Dickelmann, Nancy L. & Rather, Marsha L., eds. Transforming RN Education: Dialogue & Debate. (Illus.). 416p. (C). 1993. pap. text 29.95 (0-88737-573-1, 14-2511) Natl League Nurse.

Dicken, Bruce & Semon, James. Nickel Plate Color Photography of Willis McCaleb Vol. 1: Buffalo-Bellevue. LC 95-79970. (Illus.). 128p. 1995. 49.95 (1-878887-52-1) Morning NJ.

Dicken, Bruce & Semon, Jim. Baltimore & Ohio Trackside with Willis McCaleb. LC 97-75969. (Illus.). 128p. 1998. 49.95 (1-878887-90-4) Morning NJ.

— Nickel Plate Color Photography of Willis McCaleb Vol. 2: Bellevue-Chicago-Wheeling District. (Illus.). 1996. 49.95 (1-878887-66-1) Morning NJ.

Dicken, Emily F., jt. auth. see Dicken, Samuel N.

Dicken-Garcia, Hazel. Journalistic Standards in Nineteenth-Century America. LC 89-40252. 352p. (C). 1989. pap. text 17.95 (0-299-12174-7) U of Wis Pr.

— To Western Woods: The Breckinridge Family Moves to Kentucky in 1793. LC 89-46408. 1991. 39.50 (0-8386-3342-0) Fairleigh Dickinson.

Dicken, Howard. Asic Outlook, 1998: An Application Specific IC Report & Directory. Griffith, Mike, ed. (Illus.). 400p. 1997. reprint ed. ring bd. 835.00 (1-877750-63-8) Integrated Circuit.

Dicken, Howard K. Physics of Semiconductor Failures. 4th rev. ed. (Illus.). 270p. 1998. ring bd. 395.00 (1-878266-00-4) DM Data.

— The Semiconductor Picture Dictionary. 2nd ed. 1996. cd-rom 195.00 (0-614-30074-6) DM Data.

Dicken, Howard K., ed. How to Analyze Failures of Semiconductor Parts. (Illus.). 96p. (Orig.). 1987. student ed. 195.00 (1-878266-01-2) DM Data.

— The Semiconductor Picture Dictionary. 2nd ed. (Illus.). 186p. 1996. student ed., ring bd. 295.00 (1-878266-03-9) DM Data.

***Dicken, Peter.** Global Shift: Transforming the World Economy. 3rd ed. LC 98-9582. 496p. 1998. pap. text 40.00 (1-57230-303-4, C0303) Guilford Pubns.

Dicken, Peter & Lloyd, Peter E. Location in Space: Theoretical Perspectives in Economic Geography. 3rd ed. 431p. (C). 1997. 115.00 (0-06-041677-7) Addison-Wesley Educ.

— Modern Western Society: A Geographical Perspective on Work, Home & Well-Being. 408p. (C). 1981. 44.00 (0-06-318048-0, Pub. by P Chapman) St Mut.

Dicken, Samuel N. & Dicken, Emily F. Making of Oregon: A Study in Historical Geography. LC 79-89087. (Two Centuries of Oregon Geography Ser.: Vol. 1). (Illus.). 222p. 17.95 (0-87595-081-7) Oregon Hist.

— Oregon Divided: A Regional Geography. LC 80-84480. (Two Centuries of Oregon Geography Ser.: Vol. 2). (Illus.). 192p. 1982. 17.95 (0-87595-082-5); pap. 10.95 (0-87595-064-7) Oregon Hist.

***Dickens.** Hard Times. 2001. text. write for info. (0-312-22760-4) St Martin.

Dickens, jt. auth. see McKee.

Dickens, A. G. The Counter-Reformation. (Library of World Civilization Ser.). (Illus.). (C). 1979. pap. text 11.25 (0-393-95086-7) Norton.

— The English Reformation. 2nd ed. 462p. 1991. pap. 22.50 (0-271-00798-2) Pa St U Pr.

— Late Monasticism & the Reformation. LC 94-1587. 224p. 1994. 55.00 (1-85285-091-4) Hambledon Press.

— Lollards & Protestants in the Diocese of York. 280p. (C). 1983. 50.00 (0-907628-05-2); pap. 18.00 (0-907628-06-0) Hambledon Press.

— Reformation Studies. 624p. (C). 1983. 75.00 (0-907628-04-4) Hambledon Press.

Dickens, A. G. & Jones, Whitney R. D. Erasmus the Reformer. Date not set. pap. 12.99 (0-7493-2103-2) Heinemann.

Dickens, A. G., et al. The Reformation in Historical Thought. 456p. 1985. 45.00 (0-674-75311-9) HUP.

Dickens, A. S. & Ebert, H. 100 Classics of the Chessboard. (Illus.). 217p. 1998. pap. text 17.00 (0-7881-5631-9) DIANE Pub.

Dickens, Al. Uncle Yah Yah: 21st Century Man of Wisdom. 209p. 1998. reprint ed. pap. 12.95 (1-56411-170-9) Untd Bros & Sis.

Dickens, Albert, jt. ed. see Andrews, Earl.

Dickens, B., jt. auth. see Cook, R.

Dickens, Benjamin F., jt. auth. see Phillips, Terry M.

Dickens, Bernard M., ed. Medicine & the Law. LC 93-16964. (C). 1993. lib. bdg. 150.00 (0-8147-1846-9) NYU Pr.

Dickens, Cedric. Drinking with Dickens. (Illus.). 127p. (C). 1988. pap. 11.95 (0-941533-34-4, NAB) I R Dee.

Dickens, Charles. American Notes. (Green Integer Bks.: No. 27). 200p. 1999. pap. text 13.95 (1-892295-17-2, Pub. by Green Integer) Consort Bk Sales.

— American Notes. 378p. 1996. 15.50 (0-679-60185-6) Random.

— American Notes. 92p. 1993. reprint ed. lib. bdg. 89.00 (0-7812-5121-4); reprint ed. lib. bdg. 89.00 (0-7812-5356-X) Rprt Serv.

— American Notes & Pictures from Italy. 448p. 1993. pap. 8.95 (0-460-87685-6, Everyman's Classic Lib) Tuttle Pubng.

Dickens, Charles. American Notes for General Circulation. Whitley, John S. & Goldman, Arnold, eds. (Classics Ser.). 368p. 1974. pap. 10.95 (0-14-043077-6, Penguin Classics) Viking Penguin.

Dickens, Charles. L' Ami Commun: Le Mystere d'Edwin Drood. Monod, Sylvere, ed. (FRE.). 1991. lib. bdg. 135.00 (0-7859-3891-5) Fr & Eur.

— Les Aventures d'Olivier Twist. (FRE.). 1973. pap. 11.95 (0-7859-1745-4, 2070363864) Fr & Eur.

— Barnaby Rudge. Spence, G. W., ed. LC 74-177047. (English Library). 768p. 1974. pap. 9.95 (0-14-043090-3, Penguin Classics) Viking Penguin.

— Barnaby Rudge. rev. ed. Hawes, Donald, ed. (Everyman Paperback Classics Ser.). (Illus.). 600p. 1996. pap. 8.95 (0-460-87715-1, Everyman's Classic Lib) Tuttle Pubng.

— The Baron of Grogzwig. Greenway, Shirley, ed. LC 93-18627. (Illus.). 32p. (J). (gr. k-5). 1993. 14.95 (1-879085-81-X, Whispering Coyote) Charlesbridge Pub.

— The Bible Promise Book. deluxe ed. 173p. 1992. pap. 3.97 (0-916441-87-3) Barbour Pub.

— Bleak House. LC 84-25543. 848p. 1992. mass mkt. 6.95 (0-553-21223-0, Bantam Classics) Bantam.

— Bleak House. 832p. 1991. 23.00 (0-679-40568-2) Everymns Lib.

Dickens, Charles. Bleak House, 001. Zabel, Morton D., ed. LC 84-25543. (YA). (gr. 9 up). 1956. pap. 13.96 (0-395-05104-5, RivEd) HM.

Dickens, Charles. Bleak House. 1964. mass mkt. 6.95 (0-451-52402-0, CE1739, Sig Classics) NAL.

— Bleak House. Ford, George & Monod, Sylvere, eds. LC 77-7783. (Critical Editions Ser.). (Illus.). 986p. (C). 1977. pap. text 21.75 (0-393-09332-8) Norton.

— Bleak House. Gill, Stephen, ed. & intro. by. (Oxford World's Classics Ser.). (Illus.). 966p. 1998. pap. 9.95 (0-19-283401-0) OUP.

— Bleak House. (Bantam Classics Ser.). 1983. 11.05 (0-606-03733-0, Pub. by Turtleback) Demco.

— Bleak House. 512p. 1994. 5.95 (0-460-87423-3, Everyman's Classic Lib) Tuttle Pubng.

— Bleak House. Bradbury, Nicola, ed. & intro. by. LC 97-109166. 1997. pap. 10.95 (0-14-043496-8) Viking Penguin.

— Bleak House. (Classics Library). 725p. 1997. pap. 3.95 (1-85326-082-7, 0827WW, Pub. by Wrdsworth Edits) NTC Contemp Pub Co.

— Character Portraits from Dickens. Welsh, Charles, ed. LC 72-3628. (Studies in Dickens: No. 52). 1972. reprint ed. lib. bdg. 75.00 (0-8383-1552-6) M S G Haskell Hse.

— Charles Dickens. 114p. 1993. 12.99 (0-517-09339-1) Random Hse Value.

— Charles Dickens: The Writer & His Work. Floyd, M. & Floyd, P., eds. LC 74-920. (Biography Index Reprint Ser.). 1977. 11.95 (0-8369-8196-0) Ayer.

— Charles Dickens: Three Great Novels: Hard Times - A Tale of Two Cities - Great Expectations. 836p. 1994. pap. 15.95 (0-19-282332-9) OUP.

— Charles Dickens' A Christmas Carol. Richardson, I. M., ed. LC 87-11270. (Illus.). 32p. (J). (gr. 2-6). 1988. lib. bdg. 10.50 (0-8167-1053-8) Troll Communs.

— Charles Dickens' A Christmas Carol. Richardson, I. M., ed. LC 87-11270. (Illus.). 32p. (J). (gr. 2-6). 1997. pap. 3.95 (0-8167-1054-6) Troll Communs.

— Charles Dickens' A Christmas Carol: With 45 Lost Gustave Dore Engravings (1861) & 100 Other Victorian Illustrations. LC 96-2766. (Illus.). 176p. 1996. 19.95 (1-888957-00-X) MCE Publ Co.

— Charles Dickens as Editor. Lehmann, R., ed. LC 73-38842. (Studies in Dickens: No. 52). 403p. 1972. reprint ed. lib. bdg. 75.00 (0-8383-1393-0) M S G Haskell Hse.

— Charles Dicken's Best Stories. 669p. Date not set. 36.95 (0-8488-2251-X) Amereon Ltd.

— Charles Dickens' Book of Memoranda. Kaplan, Fred, ed. LC 81-18872. (Harcourt Brace Jovanovich Fund Ser.: No. 2). (Illus.). 118p. (C). 1981. 20.00 (0-87104-279-7) NY Pub Lib.

— The Chimes. (Illus.). 1993. pap. 20.00 (0-87556-788-6) Saifer.

— The Christmas Books. Stater, Michael, ed. (English Library). 366p. 1971. pap. 9.95 (0-14-043069-5, Penguin Classics) Viking Penguin.

— Christmas Books. 1999. pap. 7.50 (0-460-87952-9) Tuttle Pubng.

Dickens, Charles. Christmas Books. (Classics Library). pap. 3.95 (1-85326-268-4, 2684WW, Pub. by Wrdsworth Edits) NTC Contemp Pub Co.

Dickens, Charles. The Christmas Books, 1. Stater, Michael, ed. (English Library). 266p. 1971. pap. 7.95 (0-14-043068-7, Penguin Classics) Viking Penguin.

— A Christmas Carol. Date not set. pap. text. write for info. (0-17-557046-9) Addison-Wesley.

— A Christmas Carol. 1994. pap. text. write for info. (0-582-23664-9, Pub. by Addison-Wesley) Longman.

— A Christmas Carol. (YA). (gr. 7 up). 1963. mass mkt. 2.95 (0-8049-0026-4, CL-26) Airmont.

— A Christmas Carol. (Illustrated Classics Collection 4). 64p. 1994. pap. 4.95 (0-7854-0747-2, 40494) Am Guidance.

— A Christmas Carol. 144p. (J). 1997. pap. 3.99 (0-440-41421-0) BDD Bks Young Read.

— A Christmas Carol. LC 93-54577. (Illus.). 48p. (J). (ps-3). 1993. 15.95 (1-56402-204-8) Candlewick Pr.

— A Christmas Carol. (Classics Illustrated Ser.). (Illus.). 52p. (YA). 1990. pap. 4.95 (1-57209-016-2) First Classics.

— A Christmas Carol. (Illus.). 118p. 1989. 100.00 (0-933861-07-9) H Berliner.

— A Christmas Carol. LC 95-9990. (Illus.). 32p. (J). 1995. 14.95 (1-57102-047-0, Ideals Child) Hambleton-Hill.

D

— A Christmas Carol. LC 96-18967. (Illus.). 24p. (J). (gr. k-4). 1996. 6.95 (*1-57102-097-7*, Ideals Child); pap. 2.49 (*1-57102-074-8*, Ideals Child) Hambleton-Hill.

— A Christmas Carol. 1995. pap. 20.00 (*0-15-200952-3*) Harcourt.

— A Christmas Carol. LC 85-15815. (Illus.). 128p. (J). (gr. 4-6). 1983. 18.95 (*0-8234-0486-2*) Holiday.

— A Christmas Carol. 1997. text 8.25 (*0-03-051492-4*) Holt R&W.

— A Christmas Carol. LC 94-48346. (Illus.). 144p. (J). 1995. mass mkt. 19.95 (*0-689-80213-7*) McElderry Bks.

— A Christmas Carol. LC 95-35453. (Books of Wonder). (Illus.). 64p. (J). 1996. 18.00 (*0-688-13606-0*, Wm Morrow) Morrow Avon.

— A Christmas Carol. 128p. 1997. pap. 2.95 (*0-89375-356-4*) NAL.

— A Christmas Carol. LC 85-15815. (Illus.). 240p. 1983. mass mkt. 3.99 (*0-671-47369-7*, WSP) PB.

— A Christmas Carol. 224p. 1997. per. 3.99 (*0-671-52078-4*) PB.

— A Christmas Carol. LC 90-39341. (Illus.). 48p. (J). (gr. 7-12). 1990. 14.95 (*0-88289-812-4*) Pelican.

— A Christmas Carol. Fagan, Tom, ed. (Now Age Illustrated IV Ser.). (Illus.). (J). (gr. 4-12). 1978. student ed. 1.25 (*0-88301-337-1*); pap. text 2.95 (*0-88301-313-4*) Pendulum Pr.

— A Christmas Carol. (Puffin Classics Ser.). (Illus.). 144p. (YA). (gr. 5 up). 1995. pap. 3.99 (*0-14-036723-3*, PuffinBks) Peng Put Young Read.

— A Christmas Carol. (Classics Ser.). (Illus.). 52p. (J). 1994. text 3.50 (*0-7214-1729-9*, Ladybrd) Penguin Putnam.

— A Christmas Carol. (Illus.). 208p. 1994. 13.95 (*0-679-43639-1*) Random.

— A Christmas Carol. Green, Frank, ed. (Thornes Classic Novels Ser.). (Illus.). 221p. 1995. pap. 14.95 (*0-7487-1832-X*, Pub. by S Thornes Pubs) Trans-Atl Phila.

— A Christmas Carol. LC 88-15161. (Illus.). 68p. (J). (ps up). 1995. 19.95 (*0-88708-069-3*, Picture Book Studio) S&S Childrens.

— A Christmas Carol. (Illus.). 128p. (J). (gr. 4-7). 1987. pap. 3.50 (*0-590-43527-2*, Apple Classics) Scholastic Inc.

— A Christmas Carol. 128p. (J). 1990. pap. 2.50 (*0-8125-0434-8*, Pub. by Tor Bks) St Martin.

— A Christmas Carol. 128p. (J). 1996. pap. 2.95 (*0-8167-2883-6*) Troll Communs.

— A Christmas Carol. 1997. 9.09 (*0-606-13273-2*, Pub. by Turtleback) Demco.

— A Christmas Carol. (Illus.). 112p. 1990. pap. 7.95 (*0-14-007120-2*, Penguin Bks) Viking Penguin.

— A Christmas Carol. 1999. audio 10.95 (*0-14-086224-2*) Viking Penguin.

— A Christmas Carol. (Children's Library). 1998. pap. 3.95 (*1-85326-121-1*, 1211WW, Pub. by Wrdsworth Edits) NTC Contemp Pub Co.

— The Christmas Carol. 1931. pap. 3.50 (*0-87129-314-5*, C23) Dramatic Pub.

— A Christmas Carol. Barbour Publishing, Inc. Editors, ed. 99p. 1997. pap. text 0.99 (*1-55748-963-7*) Barbour Pub.

***Dickens, Charles.** Christmas Carol. (Focus on the Family Great Stories). 1999. pap. text 7.99 (*1-56179-746-4*) Focus Family.

— A Christmas Carol. (Illus.). 72p. (ps up). 2000. 19.95 (*0-7358-1259-4*) North-South Bks NYC.

— A Christmas Carol. (Illus.). 144p. (J). 2000. pap. 2.99 (*0-439-10133-6*) Scholastic Inc.

— Christmas Carol. (Illus.). 112p. (J). (gr. 7 up). 2000. 25.99 (*0-670-88878-8*, Viking Child); pap. 17.99 (*0-670-88879-6*, Viking Child) Peng Put Young Read.

— A Christmas Carol. large type ed. (Large Print Heritage Ser.). 140p. (YA). (gr. 7-12). 1999. lib. bdg. 24.95 (*1-58118-041-1*, 22510) LRS.

Dickens, Charles. A Christmas Carol. limited ed. (Illus.). 116p. 1993. 685.00 (*0-910457-28-X*) Arion Pr.

— A Christmas Carol. (Bantam Classics Ser.). 112p. 1986. reprint ed. mass mkt. 3.95 (*0-553-21244-3*, Bantam Classics) Bantam.

— A Christmas Carol. LC 85-15815. 150p. (J). 1980. reprint ed. lib. bdg. 15.95 (*0-89967-017-2*, Harmony Rain) Buccaneer Bks.

— A Christmas Carol. LC 85-15815. 191p. (YA). 1981. reprint ed. lib. bdg. 15.95 (*0-89966-344-3*) Buccaneer Bks.

— A Christmas Carol. LC 92-54577. (Illus.). 48p. (J). (gr. 3-7). 1996. reprint ed. pap. 6.99 (*1-56402-977-8*) Candlewick Pr.

— A Christmas Carol. LC 85-73687. (Illus.). 104p. 1986. reprint ed. 15.95 (*0-936695-26-9*) Carrington Hse Ltd.

— A Christmas Carol. (Thrift Editions Ser.). 80p. 1991. reprint ed. pap. 1.00 (*0-486-26865-9*) Dover.

— A Christmas Carol. 2nd ed. (Illus.). 78p. 1993. pap. text 5.95 (*0-19-585258-3*) OUP.

— A Christmas Carol. 2nd ed. (Illustrated Classic Book Ser.: Vol. III). (Illus.). 61p. (J). 1998. reprint ed. pap. text 4.95 (*1-56767-241-8*) Educ Insights.

— A Christmas Carol: A Facsimile Edition of the Autograph Manuscript in the Pierpont Morgan Library. (Illus.). 139p. 1993. write for info. (*0-87598-098-8*) Pierpont Morgan.

— A Christmas Carol: A Musical. 39p. (Orig.). 1995. pap. 4.50 (*1-57514-243-0*, 0036) Encore Perform Pub.

***Dickens, Charles.** A Christmas Carol: A Young Reader's Edition of the Classic Holiday Tale. (Illus.). (J). 2000. 9.98 (*0-7624-0848-0*) Running Pr.

Dickens, Charles. A Christmas Carol: Adapted for Theater. LC 93-14679. (Illus.). 48p. 1993. 14.95 (*0-8362-4507-5*) Andrews & McMeel.

— A Christmas Carol: By Charles Dickens. (Illus.). 78p. (YA). (gr. 1 up). 1990. text 46.65 (*0-88682-327-7*, 97200-098, Creative Eds) Creative Co.

Dickens, Charles. A Christmas Carol: Charles Dickens' Tale. LC 97-16460. (Eyewitness Classics Ser.). (Illus.). 64p. (J). (gr. 3 up). 1997. 14.95 (*0-7894-2070-8*) DK Pub Inc.

Dickens, Charles. A Christmas Carol: In Prose, Being a Ghost Story of Christmas. LC 97-11632. (Illus.). 159p. 1997. 19.95 (*1-55670-648-0*) Stewart Tabori & Chang.

— A Christmas Carol: The Ghost Story of Christmas. 37p. (Orig.). 1993. pap. 4.00 (*1-57514-211-2*, 1150) Encore Perform Pub.

— A Christmas Carol: The Original Manuscript. (Illus.). 144p. 1971. reprint ed. pap. 8.95 (*0-486-20980-6*) Dover.

— A Christmas Carol: The Public Reading Version. Collins, Philip, ed. (Illus.). 232p. 1971. 20.00 (*0-87104-228-2*) NY Pub Lib.

— A Christmas Carol & Other Christmas Stories. 224p. (YA). 1984. mass mkt. 3.95 (*0-451-52283-4*, Sig Classics) NAL.

Dickens, Charles. A Christmas Carol & Other Christmas Stories. (Signet Classics). 1984. 9.05 (*0-606-04893-6*, Pub. by Turtleback) Demco.

Dickens, Charles. A Christmas Carol & Other Stories. LC 95-21257. 266p. 1995. 14.50 (*0-679-60179-1*) Modern Lib NY.

— A Christmas Carol & Other Xmas Stories. 1976. 21.95 (*0-8488-0796-0*) Amereon Ltd.

***Dickens, Charles.** A Christmas Carol Coloring Book. (Illus.). 48p. (J). 1999. pap. 2.95 (*0-486-40563-X*) Dover.

Dickens, Charles. A Christmas Carol in Prose: A Ghost Story of Christmas. LC 97-14293. (Classic Collection). 1997. 12.99 (*1-56179-556-9*) Focus Family.

— A Christmas Carol Readalong. (Illustrated Classics Collection 4). 64p. (Orig.). 1994. pap. 14.95 incl. audio (*0-7854-0763-4*, 40496) Am Guidance.

— A Christmas Carol, Story Book Set & Advent Calendar. (Illus.). 4p. 1995. bds. 17.95 (*0-7611-0036-9*, 10036) Workman Pub.

— Christmas Stories. Glancy, Ruth, ed. 432p. 1996. pap. 6.95 (*0-460-87712-7*, Everyman's Classic Lib) Tuttle Pubng.

— Christmas Stories: Mini Edition. 1996. pap. 1.99 (*0-679-77516-1*) Modern Lib NY.

— Christmas Tales from Charles Dickens. 1994. 9.98 (*0-7858-0205-3*) Bk Sales Inc.

— Collected Classics. 1997. 19.95 (*1-57840-116-X*, Pub. by Acclaim Bks) Penguin Putnam.

— Collected Classics: Dickens. (Classics Illustrated Collections). 1997. pap. text 12.95 (*1-57840-117-8*, Pub. by Acclaim Bks) Penguin Putnam.

— Un Conte De Deux Villes. (FRE.). 416p. 1989. pap. 16.95 (*0-7859-2128-1*, 2070381951) Fr & Eur.

— The Cricket on the Hearth. large type ed. (Large Print Heritage Ser.). 150p. 1997. lib. bdg. 25.95 (*1-58118-017-9*, 21492) LRS.

— The Cricket on the Hearth. (BCL1-PR English Literature Ser.). 171p. 1992. reprint ed. lib. bdg. 69.00 (*0-7812-7510-5*) Rprt Serv.

— Cricket on the Hearth. 62p. 1957. reprint ed. pap. 3.50 (*0-87129-048-0*, C75) Dramatic Pub.

— The Cricket on the Hearth & Other Christmas Stories. 128p. (Orig.). 1994. pap. 1.00 (*0-486-28039-X*) Dover.

— The D. Case: Or the Truth about the Mystery of Edwin Drood. 608p. 1993. pap. 12.95 (*0-15-623600-1*) Harcourt.

— David Copperfield. (Classics Illustrated Study Guides Ser.). (Illus.). 1997. mass mkt. 4.99 (*1-57840-039-2*, Pub. by Acclaim Bks) Penguin Putnam.

— David Copperfield. Date not set. pap. text. write for info. (*0-17-557022-1*) Addison-Wesley.

— David Copperfield. 832p. (YA). (gr. 7 up). 1981. mass mkt. 4.95 (*0-553-21189-7*, Bantam Classics) Bantam.

— David Copperfield. (Barron's Book Notes Ser.). 1985. pap. 3.95 (*0-8120-3509-7*) Barron.

— David Copperfield. LC 91-52995. (Everyman's Library: Vol. 31). 912p. 1991. 23.00 (*0-679-40571-2*) Everymns Lib.

— David Copperfield. LC 98-21424. 1998. 22.95 (*0-679-60320-4*) Modern Lib NY.

— David Copperfield. 880p. (J). (gr. 7). 1962. mass mkt. 5.95 (*0-451-52292-3*, Sig Classics) NAL.

— David Copperfield. Buckley, Jerome H., ed. (Critical Editions Ser.). (Illus.). 854p. (C). 1989. pap. text 18.75 (*0-393-95828-0*) Norton.

— David Copperfield. Burgis, Nina, ed. (Clarendom Dickens Ser.). (Illus.). 858p. 1981. text 160.00 (*0-19-812492-9*) OUP.

***Dickens, Charles.** David Copperfield. (Oxford World Classics Ser.). (Illus.). 932p. 1999. pap. 6.95 (*0-19-283578-5*) OUP.

— David Copperfield. (Oxford World's Classics Hardcovers Ser.). 1008p. 2000. 18.00 (*0-19-210043-2*) OUP.

— David Copperfield. (Illus.). 2000. pap. 8.00 (*0-14-029738-3*) Penguin Putnam.

Dickens, Charles. David Copperfield. Vogel, Malvina, ed. (Great Illustrated Classics Ser.: Vol. 23). (Illus.). 240p. (J). (gr. 3-6). 1992. 9.95 (*0-86611-974-4*) Playmore Inc.

— David Copperfield. 880p. 1993. pap. 6.95 (*0-460-87236-2*, Everyman's Classic Lib) Tuttle Pubng.

— David Copperfield. LC 97-224922. (Illus.). 912p. 1997. pap. 7.95 (*0-14-043494-1*) Viking Penguin.

— David Copperfield. (Classics Library). 752p. 1997. pap. 3.95 (*1-85326-024-X*, 024XWW, Pub. by Wrdsworth Edits) NTC Contemp Pub Co.

***Dickens, Charles.** David Copperfield. (Norton Critical Editions Ser.). (C). 1999. pap. text 37.00 (*0-393-98913-5*) Norton.

Dickens, Charles. David Copperfield. 1982. reprint ed. lib. bdg. 45.95 (*0-89966-370-2*) Buccaneer Bks.

***Dickens, Charles.** David Copperfield, Pt. 1, set. unabridged ed. 1999. 77.95 incl. audio (*1-55685-565-6*) Audio Bk Con.

Dickens, Charles. David Copperfield, Vol. I. (FRE.). 1996. pap. 7.95 (*2-87714-325-2*, Pub. by Bookking Intl) Distribks Inc.

— David Copperfield, Vol. 1. 1998. mass mkt. 4.99 (*0-8125-4404-8*, Pub. by Tor Bks) St Martin.

— David Copperfield, Vol. II. (FRE.). 1996. pap. 7.95 (*2-87714-326-0*, Pub. by Bookking Intl) Distribks Inc.

— David Copperfield: Grandes Esperances. (FRE.). 105.00 (*0-8288-3432-6*, M5090) Fr & Eur.

— Dickens' Christmas. (Illus.). 128p. 1997. pap. 17.95 (*0-7509-1502-1*, Pub. by Sutton Pub Ltd) Intl Pubs Mktg.

— A Dickens Christmas Collection. 176p. 1995. 14.99 (*0-87788-170-7*, H Shaw Pubs) Waterbrook Pr.

Dickens, Charles. Dickens Journalism "Sketches by Boz" & Other Early Papers, 1833-40. pap. 11.95 (*0-460-87188-9*, Everyman's Classic Lib) Tuttle Pubng.

Dickens, Charles. Dickens' Journalism Vol. 2: Sketches by Boz & Other Early Papers, 1833-39, 3 vols. Slater, Michael, ed. LC 93-36399. 580p. (C). 1994. text 50.00 (*0-8142-0629-8*) Ohio St U Pr.

— Dickens Journalism, 'Gone Astray' & Other Papers from Household Words, 1851-59, Vol. III. Slater, Michael, ed. LC 98-41994. 1999. text 50.00 (*0-8142-0820-7*) Ohio St U Pr.

— Dickens to His Oldest Friend: Letters to Thomas Beard. Dexter, W., ed. LC 72-6506. (Studies in Dickens: No. 52). 315p. 1972. reprint ed. lib. bdg. 75.00 (*0-8383-1620-4*) M S G Haskell Hse.

— Dickens vs. Barrabas. LC 72-3173. (Studies in Dickens: No. 52). 1972. reprint ed. lib. bdg. 49.00 (*0-8383-1523-2*) M S G Haskell Hse.

— Dickens' Working Notes for His Novels. Stone, Harry, ed. LC 84-23918. (Illus.). 432p. 1987. 89.95 (*0-226-14590-5*) U Ch Pr.

— Dombey & Son. LC 94-4778. (Everyman's Library of Children's Classics). 960p. 1994. 23.00 (*0-679-43591-3*) Knopf.

— Dombey & Son. Horsman, Alan, ed. & intro. by. (Oxford World's Classics Ser.). (Illus.). 782p. 1999. pap. 7.95 (*0-19-283632-3*) OUP.

— Dombey & Son. Purton, Valerie, ed. (Everyman Paperback Classics). 600p. 1997. pap. 6.95 (*0-460-87684-8*, Everyman's Classic Lib) Tuttle Pubng.

— Dombey & Son. Fairclough, Peter, ed. (English Library). 992p. 1970. pap. 8.95 (*0-14-043048-2*, Penguin Classics) Viking Penguin.

Dickens, Charles. Dombey & Son. (Classics Library). pap. 3.95 (*1-85326-257-9*, 2579WW, Pub. by Wrdsworth Edits) NTC Contemp Pub Co.

Dickens, Charles. Dombey et Fils: Temps Difficiles. (FRE.). 1956. 95.00 (*0-8288-3426-1*, F77002) Fr & Eur.

— Esquisses de Boz: Martin Chuzzlewit. (FRE.). 1986. 150.00 (*0-8288-3427-X*, F79720) Fr & Eur.

— Everything in Dickens: Ideas & Subjects Discussed by Charles Dickens in His Complete Works. Newlin, George, ed. LC 96-6347. 1168p. 1996. lib. bdg. 145.00 (*0-313-29874-2*, Greenwood Pr) Greenwood.

— Fireside Dickens. DeFontaine, F. G., ed. LC 77-148773. (Illus.). reprint ed. 45.00 (*0-404-08746-9*) AMS Pr.

— Ghost Stories. (Wordsworth Classics). 288p. 1998. pap. 3.95 (*1-85326-734-1*, Pub. by Wrdsworth Edits) NTC Contemp Pub Co.

— The Ghostlight Theatre Company's "A Christmas Carol" 53p. (Orig.). 1992. pap. 4.00 (*1-57514-210-4*, 1001) Encore Perform Pub.

***Dickens, Charles.** Great Expectations. 544p. 1998. pap. 4.67 (*0-14-043489-5*) Addson-Wesley Educ.

Dickens, Charles. Great Expectations. (Illustrated Classic Collection 5). 64p. 1994. pap. 4.95 (*0-7854-0777-4*, 40550) Am Guidance.

— Great Expectations. 334p. Date not set. 25.95 (*0-8488-2527-6*) Amereon Ltd.

— Great Expectations. (Cyber Classics Ser.). 1997. pap. text 14.95 (*1-55701-196-6*) BNI Pubns.

— Great Expectations. 496p. 1982. mass mkt. 4.95 (*0-553-21342-3*, Bantam Classics) Bantam.

***Dickens, Charles.** Great Expectations. (Literature Made Easy Ser.). 96p. (YA). 1999. pap. 4.95 (*0-7641-0823-9*) Barron.

— Great Expectations. Law, Graham & Pinnington, Adrian, eds. (Literary Texts Ser.). 654p. 1998. pap. 8.95 (*1-55111-174-8*) Broadview Pr.

Dickens, Charles. Great Expectations. Seward, Tim, ed. LC 96-147566. (Literature Ser.). (Illus.). 512p. (YA). (gr. 9 up). 1996. pap. 11.95 (*0-521-48472-3*) Cambridge U Pr.

— Great Expectations. (Classics Illustrated Ser.). (Illus.). 52p. (YA). pap. 4.95 (*1-57209-001-4*) Classics Int Ent.

— Great Expectations. 127p. (YA). (gr. 10 up). 1994. pap. 5.50 (*0-87129-355-2*, G56) Dramatic Pub.

— Great Expectations. (Illus.). 52p. 1990. pap. 3.75 (*0-425-12021-X*) First Classics.

— Great Expectations. 1997. text 8.25 (*0-03-051493-2*) Holt R&W.

***Dickens, Charles.** Great Expectations. (Cloth Bound Pocket Ser.). 1999. 7.95 (*3-8290-2968-3*) Konemann.

Dickens, Charles. Great Expectations. Pearce, Tim, ed. (Study Texts Ser.). 1988. pap. text 5.95 (*0-582-33088-2*, 72040) Longman.

— Great Expectations. McMaster, R. D., ed. (Odyssey Ser.). 512p. 1965. pap. text 5.50 (*0-672-63042-7*, Bobbs) Macmillan.

— Great Expectations. 1992. 20.00 (*0-679-40579-8*) McKay.

— Great Expectations. (Signet Classics Ser.). 494p. 1998. mass mkt. 4.95 (*0-451-52671-6*, Sig Classics) NAL.

— Great Expectations. Rosenberg, Edgar, ed. LC 91-43432. (Critical Editions Ser.). (C). 1999. pap. 16.75 (*0-393-96069-2*, Norton Paperbks) Norton.

— Great Expectations. (Illus.). 486p. 1987. 16.95 (*0-19-254511-6*) OUP.

— Great Expectations. Cardwell, Margaret, ed. (Clarendon Dickens Ser.). (Illus.). 584p. (C). 1993. text 110.00 (*0-19-818591-X*, 10961) OUP.

— Great Expectations. Cardwell, Margaret, ed. & notes by. (Oxford World's Classics Ser.). (Illus.). 530p. 1998. pap. 6.95 (*0-19-283359-6*) OUP.

— Great Expectations. LC 99-461939. (Oxford World's Classics Hardcovers Ser.). 530p. 1999. 16.00 (*0-19-210034-3*) OUP.

— Great Expectations. (Now Age Illustrated V Ser.). (Illus.). 64p. (J). (gr. 4-12). 1979. 1.25 (*0-88301-412-2*); pap. text 2.95 (*0-88301-388-6*) Pendulum Pr.

— Great Expectations. Vogel, Malvina, ed. (Great Illustrated Classics Ser.: Vol. 21). (Illus.). 240p. (J). (gr. 3-6). 1992. 9.95 (*0-86611-972-8*) Playmore Inc.

— Great Expectations. Carlisle, Janice, ed. 641p. 1995. pap. 11.95 (*0-312-08082-4*) St Martin.

— Great Expectations. 528p. 1998. mass mkt. 3.99 (*0-8125-6311-5*, Pub. by Tor Bks) St Martin.

***Dickens, Charles.** Great Expectations. (Signature Classics Ser.). 456p. 1999. 24.95 (*1-58279-036-1*) Trident Pr Intl.

Dickens, Charles. Great Expectations. pap. 2.95 (*0-89375-785-3*) Troll Communs.

— Great Expectations. 1963. 10.05 (*0-606-00191-3*, Pub. by Turtleback) Demco.

Dickens, Charles. Great Expectations. 1981. 10.05 (*0-606-13450-6*, Pub. by Turtleback) Demco.

Dickens, Charles. Great Expectations. 1999. audio 10.95 (*0-14-086417-2*) Viking Penguin.

— Great Expectations. (Classics Library). 395p. 1997. pap. 3.95 (*1-85326-004-5*, 0045WW, Pub. by Wrdsworth Edits) NTC Contemp Pub Co.

***Dickens, Charles.** Great Expectations. (Illus.). 504p. 2000. mass mkt. 4.99 (*0-7434-0636-2*, WSP) PB.

Dickens, Charles. Great Expectations. abr. ed. (Classics for Young Readers Ser.). (Illus.). 432p. (YA). (gr. 5 up). 1995. pap. 4.99 (*0-14-036681-4*, PuffinBks) Peng Put Young Read.

— Great Expectations. abr. ed. (Classics on Audio Ser.). 1994. pap. 16.95 incl. audio (*0-14-086041-X*, Png AudioBks) Viking Penguin.

***Dickens, Charles.** Great Expectations. deluxe ed. (Signature Classics Ser.). 456p. 1999. 29.95 (*1-58279-048-5*) Trident Pr Intl.

Dickens, Charles. Great Expectations. large type ed. 1997. pap. 21.95 (*1-55701-212-1*) BNI Pubns.

— Great Expectations. 528p. 1986. reprint ed. lib. bdg. 28.95 (*0-89966-518-7*) Buccaneer Bks.

***Dickens, Charles.** Great Expectations. (Twelve-Point Ser.). 600p. 2000. reprint ed. lib. bdg. 25.00 (*1-58287-127-2*) North Bks.

Dickens, Charles. Great Expectations. rev. ed. Klischer, Beth, ed. (Literature for Christian Schools Ser.). (Illus.). 610p. (YA). (gr. 10 up). 1989. pap. 11.06 (*0-89084-504-2*, 046516) Bob Jones Univ.

— Great Expectations. unabridged ed. (Classics Ser.). (YA). (gr. 9 up). 1963. mass mkt. 3.95 (*0-8049-0068-X*, CL-68) Airmont.

— Great Expectations Readalong. (Illustrated Classics Collection 5). 64p. 1994. pap. 14.95 (*0-7854-0793-6*, 40552) Am Guidance.

— Great Writers: Charles Dickens. (Illus.). 64p. 1995. 9.95 (*1-85410-261-3*, Pub. by Aurum Pr) London Brdge.

— Hard Times. 1995. pap. text. write for info. (*0-582-25407-8*, Pub. by Addison-Wesley) Longman.

— Hard Times. 304p. (YA). (gr. 9-12). 1981. mass mkt. 4.95 (*0-553-21016-5*, Bantam Classics) Bantam.

— Hard Times. (Barron's Book Notes Ser.). 1985. pap. 2.50 (*0-8120-3518-6*) Barron.

— Hard Times. Jose, Gwen, ed. (Cambridge Literature Ser.). 336p. (C). 1996. pap. 11.95 (*0-521-56089-6*) Cambridge U Pr.

— Hard Times. 1992. 17.00 (*0-679-41323-5*) Everymns Lib.

— Hard Times. (Cloth Bound Pocket Ser.). 240p. 1998. 7.95 (*3-89508-229-5*) Konemann.

— Hard Times. Adams, Richard, ed. (Study Texts Ser.). (YA). (gr. 7 up). 1988. pap. text 5.72 (*0-582-24396-3*, 78095) Longman.

Dickens, Charles. Hard Times. 1966. pap. 2.50 (*0-393-99774-X*) Norton.

Dickens, Charles. Hard Times. Schlicke, Paul, ed. & intro. by. (Oxford World's Classics Ser.). 462p. 1998. pap. 5.95 (*0-19-283367-7*) OUP.

— Hard Times. Krishnan, S. V., ed. (Sangam Abridged Texts Ser.). xii, 107p. 1983. pap. text 4.95 (*0-86131-176-0*, Pub. by Orient Longman Ltd) Apt Bks.

— Hard Times. (J). 1997. pap. 2.95 (*0-8167-1463-0*) Troll Communs.

— Hard Times. 1997. mass mkt. 4.95 (*0-451-52672-4*, Penguin Classics) Viking Penguin.

— Hard Times. (Classics Library). 562p. pap. 3.95 (*1-85326-232-3*, 2323WW, Pub. by Wrdsworth Edits) NTC Contemp Pub Co.

— Hard Times. anniversary ed. LC 97-91580. (Illus.). 234p. 1995. pap. 4.95 (*0-12-345678-9*) Dell.

— Hard Times. 288p. 1986. reprint ed. lib. bdg. 25.95 (*0-89966-519-5*) Buccaneer Bks.

— Hard Times. 2nd ed. Ford, George H. & Monod, Sylvere, eds. LC 89-16394. (Critical Editions Ser.). 434p. (C). 1990. pap. text 11.25 (*0-393-95900-7*) Norton.

— Hard Times: For These Times. Law, Graham, ed. 464p. 1996. pap. 7.95 (*1-55111-075-X*) Broadview Pr.

— Hard Times for These Times. (Signet Modern Classic). 1961. 10.05 (*0-606-03526-5*, Pub. by Turtleback) Demco.

— Hard Times for these Times. Flint, Kate, ed. & intro. by. 384p. 1998. pap. text 4.00 (*0-14-043398-8*) Addson-Wesley Educ.

D

— Hunted Down: The Detective Stories of Charles Dickens. Haining, Peter, ed. & intro. by. LC 96-173950. 224p. 1996. 32.00 (*0-7206-0994-1*, Pub. by P Owen Ltd) Dufour.
— The Letters of Charles Dickens: The Pilgrim Edition, Vol. 1, 1820-1839. House, Madeline & Story, Graham, eds. 796p. (C). 1982. reprint ed. text 140.00 (*0-19-811447-8*) OUP.
— The Letters of Charles Dickens: The Pilgrim Edition, Vol. 2, 1840-1841. House, Madeline & Storey, Graham, eds. (Illus.). 570p. 1969. text 110.00 (*0-19-811478-8*) OUP.
— The Letters of Charles Dickens: The Pilgrim Edition, Vol. 3, 1842-1843. House, Madeline et al, eds. (Illus.). 720p. (C). 1974. text 120.00 (*0-19-812474-0*) OUP.
— The Letters of Charles Dickens: The Pilgrim Edition, Vol. 5, 1847-1849. Storey, Graham & Fielding, Kenneth J., eds. (Illus.). 778p. (C). 1981. 150.00 (*0-19-812514-3*) OUP.
— The Letters of Charles Dickens: The Pilgrim Edition, Vol. 6, 1850-1852. Burgis, Nina & Storey, Graham, eds. (Illus.). 928p. 1988. text 175.00 (*0-19-812617-4*) OUP.
— The Letters of Charles Dickens: 1862-1864, Vol. 10. Storey, Graham & Brown, Margaret, eds. (Illus.). 530p. 1998. text 130.00 (*0-19-812294-2*) OUP.
— The Letters of Charles Dickens: 1865-1867; The Pilgrim Edition, Vol. 11. Storey, Graham et al, eds. (British Academy Ser.). (Illus.). 602p. 2000. text 120.00 (*0-19-812295-0*) OUP.
— The Letters of Charles Dickens Vol. 4: The Pilgrim Edition, 1844-1846. Tillotson, Kathleen & Burgis, Nina, eds. (Illus.). 798p. 1978. text 140.00 (*0-19-812475-9*) OUP.
— The Letters of Charles Dickens Vol. 8: The Pilgrim Edition, 1856-1858. Storey, Graham & Tillotson, Kathleen, eds. (Illus.). 834p. 1995. text 170.00 (*0-19-812662-X*) OUP.
— The Letters of Charles Dickens: The Pilgrim Edition Vol. 9: 1859-1861. Storey, Graham & Brown, Margaret, eds. (British Academy Ser.). (Illus.). 634p. 1998. text 140.00 (*0-19-812293-4*) OUP.
— Letters of Charles Dickens to Willkie Collins. LC 73-20382. (Studies in Dickens: No. 52). 1974. lib. bdg. 75.00 (*0-8383-1823-1*) M S G Haskell Hse.
— The Life & Adventures of Nicholas Nickleby, Vol. 1. adapted ed. 1982. pap. 5.25 (*0-8222-0817-2*) Dramatists Play.
— The Life & Adventures of Nicholas Nickleby, Vol. 2. adapted ed. 1982. pap. 5.25 (*0-8222-0818-0*) Dramatists Play.
— The Life of Our Lord. LC 99-48913. 128p. 1999. 14.95 (*0-684-86537-8*) S&S Trade.
— The Life of Our Lord. LC 86-28079. (Illus.). 128p. 1981. reprint ed. pap. 19.95 (*0-664-25680-5*) Westminster John Knox.
— Listen & Read Charles Dickens' a Christmas Carol. 96p. (J). 1996. pap. 5.95 incl. audio (*0-486-29103-0*) Dover.
— Little Dorrit. LC 92-52919. 1992. 20.00 (*0-679-41725-7*) Everymns Lib.
— Little Dorrit. Sucksmith, Harvey Peter, ed. (Oxford World's Classics Ser.). (Illus.). 750p. 1999. pap. 7.95 (*0-19-283566-1*) OUP.
— Little Dorrit. LC 99-462630. 752p. 1998. pap. 8.95 (*0-14-043492-5*) Viking Penguin.
Dickens, Charles. Little Dorrit. (Classics Library). Date not set. pap. 3.95 (*1-85326-182-3*, 1823WW, Pub. by Wrdsworth Edits) NTC Contemp Pub Co.
Dickens, Charles. Little Dorrit. (J). (ps-8). 1990. reprint ed. lib. bdg. 39.95 (*0-89966-680-9*) Buccaneer Bks.
— Magasin D'Antiquites: Barnabe Rudge. (FRE.). 1962. 99.50 (*0-8288-3428-8*, F77005) Fr & Eur.
— The Magic Fishbone. LC 96-53972. (Illus.). (J). 2000. 17.00 (*0-15-201080-7*, Harcourt Child Bks) Harcourt.
— La Maison apres Vent: Recits Noels. (FRE.). 1979. 110.00 (*0-8288-3429-6*, F77240) Fr & Eur.
***Dickens, Charles.** Martin Chuzzelwit. (Penguin Classics Ser.). 912p. 2000. pap. 10.95 (*0-14-043614-6*, Penguin Classics) Viking Penguin.
Dickens, Charles. Martin Chuzzlewit. 1995. 20.00 (*0-679-43884-X*) Everymns Lib.
— Martin Chuzzlewit. Cardwell, Margaret, ed. (Clarendon Dickens Ser.). (Illus.). 940p. 1983. text 145.00 (*0-19-812488-0*) OUP.
— Martin Chuzzlewit. Monod, Sylvere & Rawson, Claude, eds. (Unwin Critical Library). 192p. 1985. text 55.00 (*0-04-800028-0*) Routledge.
— Martin Chuzzlewit. Furbank, P. N., ed. (English Library). 1968. pap. 10.95 (*0-14-043031-8*, Penguin Classics) Viking Penguin.
— Martin Chuzzlewit. (Classics Library). 765p. 1998. pap. 3.95 (*1-85326-205-6*, 2056WW, Pub. by Wrdsworth Edits) NTC Contemp Pub Co.
— Martin Chuzzlewit. Cardwell, Margaret, ed. & intro. by. (Oxford World's Classics Ser.). (Illus.). 766p. 1998. reprint ed. pap. 9.95 (*0-19-283461-4*) OUP.
— The Memorable Trial of Bardell Against Pickwick. (Extract from Pickwick Papers). (Illus.). 71p. 1989. 75.00 (*0-933861-10-9*) H Berliner.
— Merry Christmas. Exley, Helen, ed. (So-Much-More-Than-a-Card Ser.). (Illus.). 28p. (Orig.). 1995. pap. 2.99 (*1-85015-652-2*) Exley Giftbooks.
— Mr. & Mrs. Charles Dickens: His Letters to Her. Dexter, Walter, ed. LC 72-1331. (Studies in Dickens: No. 52). 1972. reprint ed. lib. bdg. 75.00 (*0-8383-1429-5*) M S G Haskell Hse.
— Mr. Pickwick's Promise. Landes, William-Alan, ed. & frwd. by. LC 97-27757. 55p. 1997. pap. 6.00 (*0-88734-709-6*) Players Pr.
— Monarch Quick & Easy Notes: "David Copperfield" by Charles Dickens. write for info. (*0-318-58792-0*) S&S Trade.
— Monarch Quick & Easy Notes: "Great Expectations" by Charles Dickens. write for info. (*0-318-58793-9*) S&S Trade.
— Ms. Scrooge. 1985. 3.50 (*0-87129-444-3*, M63) Dramatic Pub.
Dickens, Charles. My Early Life. LC 98-215834. (Illus.). 224p. 1997. 24.95 (*1-85410-518-3*, Pub. by Aurum Pr) London Brdge.
Dickens, Charles. The Mystery of Edwin Drood. 22.95 (*0-88411-276-4*) Amereon Ltd.
— The Mystery of Edwin Drood. LC 75-42303. (Studies in Dickens: No. 52). 1974. lib. bdg. 75.00 (*0-8383-1962-9*) M S G Haskell Hse.
***Dickens, Charles.** The Mystery of Edwin Drood. (Oxford World's Classics Ser.). (Illus.). 266p. 1999. pap. 6.95 (*0-19-283660-9*) OUP.
Dickens, Charles. The Mystery of Edwin Drood. Connor, Steven, ed. 352p. 1996. pap. 6.95 (*0-460-87663-5*, Everyman's Classic Lib) Tuttle Pubng.
— The Mystery of Edwin Drood. Cox, A., ed. (English Library). 320p. 1974. pap. 7.95 (*0-14-043092-X*, Penguin Classics) Viking Penguin.
— The Mystery of Edwin Drood. (Classics Library). 1998. pap. 3.95 (*1-85326-729-5*, 7295WW, Pub. by Wrdsworth Edits) NTC Contemp Pub Co.
— The Mystery of Edwin Drood. large type ed. (Isis Clear Type Classic Ser.). 323p. 1991. 24.95 (*1-85089-399-3*, Pub. by ISIS Lrg Prnt) Transaction Pubs.
— Nicholas Nickleby. LC 93-1856. 1993. 20.00 (*0-679-42307-9*) Everymns Lib.
— Nicholas Nickleby. 926p. 1998. pap. 6.95 (*0-19-283623-4*) OUP.
— Nicholas Nickleby. 992p. 1998. mass mkt. 5.99 (*0-8125-6584-3*, Pub. by Tor Bks) St Martin.
— Nicholas Nickleby. 864p. 1999. pap. 7.95 (*0-14-043512-3*, Penguin Classics) Viking Penguin.
Dickens, Charles. Nicholas Nickleby. (Classics Library). (YA). (gr. 7 up). Date not set. pap. 3.95 (*1-85326-264-1*, 2641WW, Pub. by Wrdsworth Edits) NTC Contemp Pub Co.
Dickens, Charles. Nicholas Nickleby. 1990. reprint ed. lib. bdg. 49.95 (*0-89966-681-7*) Buccaneer Bks.
— Nicholas Nickleby - Full. 1981. 5.50 (*0-87129-416-8*, N27) Dramatic Pub.
— Nicolas Nickleby & Livres de Noel. (FRE.). 1966. 99.50 (*0-8288-3433-4*, F77430) Fr & Eur.
Dickens, Charles. The Old Curiosity Shop. 1995. 23.00 (*0-679-44373-8*) Knopf.
Dickens, Charles. The Old Curiosity Shop. Brennan, Elizabeth M., ed. LC 97-6474. (Clarendon Dickens Ser.). (Illus.). 742p. 1998. 175.00 incl. cd-rom (*0-19-812493-7*) OUP.
— The Old Curiosity Shop. Brennan, Elizabeth M., ed. & intro. by. (Oxford World's Classics Ser.). (Illus.). 658p. 1998. pap. 7.95 (*0-19-282924-6*) OUP.
— The Old Curiosity Shop. Schlicke, Paul, ed. 512p. 1995. pap. 6.95 (*0-460-87600-7*, Everyman's Classic Lib) Tuttle Pubng.
— The Old Curiosity Shop. Easson, Angus, ed. (English Library). 720p. 1972. pap. 8.95 (*0-14-043075-X*, Penguin Classics) Viking Penguin.
— The Old Curiosity Shop. (Classics Library). 350p. pap. 3.95 (*1-85326-244-7*, 2447WW, Pub. by Wrdsworth Edits) NTC Contemp Pub Co.
— The Old Curiosity Shop. 1990. reprint ed. lib. bdg. 21.95 (*0-89966-682-5*) Buccaneer Bks.
— Oliver Twist. 478p. Date not set. 30.95 (*0-8488-2536-5*) Amereon Ltd.
— Oliver Twist. 448p. (YA). (gr. 7-12). 1982. mass mkt. 4.95 (*0-553-21102-1*, Bantam Classics) Bantam.
— Oliver Twist. (Barron's Book Notes Ser.). 1985. pap. 2.95 (*0-8120-3532-1*) Barron.
— Oliver Twist. LC 98-44179. (Eyewitness Classics Ser.). (J). 1999. 14.95 (*0-7894-3959-X*) DK Pub Inc.
***Dickens, Charles.** Oliver Twist. LC 99-50014. (Read & Listen Ser.). (Illus.). 64p. (J). (gr. 4-7). 2000. pap. text 7.95 (*0-7894-5463-7*, D K Ink) DK Pub Inc.
Dickens, Charles. Oliver Twist. LC 92-52899. 1992. 20.00 (*0-679-41724-9*) Everymns Lib.
***Dickens, Charles.** Oliver Twist. (Illus.). 1999. 7.95 (*3-8290-3004-5*) Konemann.
Dickens, Charles. Oliver Twist. Adams, Richard, ed. (Study Texts Ser.). 1988. pap. text 5.95 (*0-582-33150-1*, 72056) Longman.
— Oliver Twist. (English As a Second Language Bk.). 1988. pap. text 4.46 (*0-582-53496-8*) Longman.
— Oliver Twist. LC 93-36278. (Books of Wonder). (Illus.). 464p. (gr. 4-7). 1994. 20.00 (*0-688-12911-0*, Wm Morrow) Morrow Avon.
— Oliver Twist. 496p. (J). (gr. 7). 1961. mass mkt. 4.95 (*0-451-52351-2*, Sig Classics) NAL.
— Oliver Twist. Kaplan, Fred, ed. LC 92-34792. (Critical Editions Ser.). 611p. (C). 1992. pap. text 20.25 (*0-393-96292-X*) Norton.
— Oliver Twist. (Now Age Illustrated V Ser.). (Illus.). 64p. (gr. 4-12). 1979. student ed. 1.25 (*0-88301-418-1*); pap. text 2.95 (*0-88301-394-0*) Pendulum Pr.
— Oliver Twist. Vogel, Malvina, ed. (Great Illustrated Classics Ser.: Vol. 5). (Illus.). 240p. (J). (gr. 3-6). 1989. 9.95 (*0-86611-956-6*) Playmore Inc.
— Oliver Twist. 1998. mass mkt. 3.99 (*0-8125-8003-6*, Pub. by Tor Bks) St Martin.
— Oliver Twist. 1993. pap. 2.95 (*0-89375-784-5*) Troll Communs.
— Oliver Twist. (Signet Classics). 1961. 10.05 (*0-606-00928-0*, Pub. by Turtleback) Demco.
— Oliver Twist. Fairclough, Peter, ed. (English Library). 496p. 1966. pap. 6.95 (*0-14-043017-2*, Penguin Classics) Viking Penguin.
— Oliver Twist. (Classics Library). 355p. 1997. pap. 3.95 (*1-85326-012-6*, 0126WW, Pub. by Wrdsworth Edits) NTC Contemp Pub Co.
— Oliver Twist. LC 89-24279. (Step into Classics Ser.). (Illus.). 96p. (J). (gr. 2-6). 1990. pap. 3.99 (*0-679-80391-2*, Pub. by Random Bks Yng Read) Random.
— Oliver Twist. abr. ed. (Classics for Young Readers Ser.). (Illus.). 448p. (YA). (gr. 5 up). 1994. pap. 4.99 (*0-14-036814-0*, PuffinBks) Peng Put Young Read.
***Dickens, Charles.** Oliver Twist. deluxe ed. (Signature Classics Ser.). 464p. 1999. 29.95 (*1-58279-049-3*) Trident Pr Intl.
Dickens, Charles. Oliver Twist. large type ed. 560p. 1998. lib. bdg. 24.00 (*0-939495-52-X*) North Bks.
— Oliver Twist. large type ed. (Classics Ser.). 13.95 (*0-7089-8019-8*, Charnwood) Ulverscroft.
— Oliver Twist. 1982. reprint ed. lib. bdg. 28.95 (*0-89966-372-9*) Buccaneer Bks.
***Dickens, Charles.** Oliver Twist. 482p. 1998. reprint ed. lib. bdg. 24.00 (*1-58287-054-3*) North Bks.
Dickens, Charles. Oliver Twist. unabridged ed. (Classics Ser.). (YA). (gr. 9 up). 1963. mass mkt. 3.50 (*0-8049-0009-4*, CL-9) Airmont.
***Dickens, Charles.** Oliver Twist. 2nd ed. Tillotson, Kathleen, ed. (Oxford World's Classics Ser.). (Illus.). 538p. 1999. pap. 5.95 (*0-19-283339-1*) OUP.
Dickens, Charles. Oliver Twist: In Arabic. 1982. pap. 14.95 (*0-86685-138-0*) Intl Bk Ctr.
***Dickens, Charles.** Oliver Twist: The Adventures of Oliver Twist. (Signature Classics Ser.). 464p. 1999. 24.95 (*1-58279-037-X*) Trident Pr Intl.
Dickens, Charles. Our Mutual Friend. 1994. mass mkt. 6.95 (*0-553-85016-4*) Bantam.
— Our Mutual Friend. 1994. 20.00 (*0-679-42028-2*) Everymns Lib.
— Our Mutual Friend. LC 92-50212. 824p. 1992. 19.00 (*0-679-60022-1*) Modern Lib NY.
— Our Mutual Friend. Poole, Adrian, ed. & intro. by. 928p. 1998. pap. 10.95 (*0-14-043497-6*) Viking Penguin.
***Dickens, Charles.** Our Mutual Friend. (Classics Library). 1998. pap. 3.95 (*1-85326-194-7*, 1947WW, Pub. by Wrdsworth Edits) NTC Contemp Pub Co.
Dickens, Charles. Our Mutual Friend. 900p. 1990. reprint ed. lib. bdg. 49.95 (*0-89966-683-3*) Buccaneer Bks.
— Our Mutual Friend. Cotsell, Michael, ed. & intro. by. (Oxford World's Classics Ser.). 878p. 1998. reprint ed. pap. 9.95 (*0-19-283523-8*) OUP.
— Papiers du Pickwick: Oliver Twist. (Pleiade Ser.). (FRE.). 1958. 99.50 (*0-8288-3430-X*, F79856) Fr & Eur.
— Personal History, Adventures, Experience & Observation of David Copperfield. (Signet Classics). 1962. 10.05 (*0-606-00529-3*, Pub. by Turtleback) Demco.
***Dickens, Charles.** The Personal History of David Copperfield. LC 99-25972. (Focus on the Family Great Stories Ser.). 1999. pap. 14.99 (*1-56179-761-8*) Tyndale Hse.
Dickens, Charles. Petite Dorrit: Conte de Deux Villes. (FRE.). 1970. 99.50 (*0-8288-3431-8*, F77450) Fr & Eur.
— The Pickwick Papers. 784p. 1983. mass mkt. 5.95 (*0-553-21123-4*, Bantam Classics) Bantam.
— The Pickwick Papers. 1964. mass mkt. 6.95 (*0-451-51756-3*, CE1756, Sig Classics) NAL.
— The Pickwick Papers. Kinsley, James, ed. (Clarendon Dickens Ser.). (Illus.). 600p. 1986. 149.00 (*0-19-812631-X*) OUP.
— The Pickwick Papers. Kinsley, James, ed. & intro. by. (Oxford World's Classics Ser.). (Illus.). 772p. 1998. pap. 8.95 (*0-19-283457-6*) OUP.
— The Pickwick Papers. 960p. (YA). (gr. 7 up). 1998. mass mkt. 5.99 (*0-8125-6719-6*, Pub. by Tor Bks) St Martin.
— The Pickwick Papers. 1964. 11.05 (*0-606-00941-8*, Pub. by Turtleback) Demco.
— The Pickwick Papers. Andrews, Malcolm, ed. (Everyman Paperback Classics). (Illus.). 960p. 1997. pap. 5.95 (*0-460-87664-3*, Everyman's Classic Lib) Tuttle Pubng.
— The Pickwick Papers. Patten, Robert L., ed. LC 73-154771. (English Library). (Illus.). 960p. 1973. pap. 9.95 (*0-14-043078-4*, Penguin Classics) Viking Penguin.
— The Pickwick Papers. (Classics Library). 720p. pap. 3.95 (*1-85326-052-5*, 0525WW, Pub. by Wrdsworth Edits) NTC Contemp Pub Co.
Dickens, Charles. Pickwick Papers. abr. ed. LC 66-1746. 1972. audio 14.00 (*0-694-50091-7*, SWC 1121, Caedmon) HarperAudio.
Dickens, Charles. The Pickwick Papers. 495p. 1983. reprint ed. lib. bdg. 49.95 (*0-89966-314-1*) Buccaneer Bks.
— The Pickwick Papers, Vol. 1. large type ed. (Isis Clear Type Classic Ser.). 450p. 1991. 24.95 (*1-85089-464-7*, Pub. by ISIS Lrg Prnt) Transaction Pubs.
— The Pickwick Papers, Vol. 2. large type ed. (Isis Clear Type Classic Ser.). 540p. 1991. 24.95 (*1-85089-514-7*, Pub. by ISIS Lrg Prnt) Transaction Pubs.
— Pictures from Italy. Flint, Kate, ed. & intro. by. LC 98-164810. xxxvii, 220p. 1998. pap. 11.95 (*0-14-043431-3*) Viking Penguin.
— The Posthumous Papers of the Pickwick Club. LC 99-214739. 1999. 23.00 (*0-375-40548-8*) Everymns Lib.
***Dickens, Charles.** The Posthumous Papers of the Pickwick Club. (Penguin Classics Ser.). (Illus.). 960p. 2000. pap. 9.95 (*0-14-043611-1*, Penguin Classics) Viking Penguin.
Dickens, Charles. The Religious Sentiments of Charles Dickens: Collected from His Writings. McKenzie, C., ed. LC 73-7504. (Studies in Dickens: No. 52). 1973. reprint ed. lib. bdg. 75.00 (*0-8383-1697-2*) M S G Haskell Hse.
— Reminiscences of My Father. LC 72-6292. (Studies in Dickens: No. 52). (Illus.). 1972. reprint ed. lib. bdg. 75.00 (*0-8383-1626-3*) M S G Haskell Hse.
— Scrooge. adapted ed. 1959. pap. 5.25 (*0-8222-1001-0*) Dramatists Play.
— Selected Journalism, 1850-1870. Pascoe, David, ed. & notes by. LC 98-131576. (Penguin Classics Ser.). 672p. 1998. pap. 15.95 (*0-14-043580-8*, Penguin Bks) Viking Penguin.
— Selected Short Fiction. Thomas, Deborah A., ed. LC 76-368436. (English Library). 368p. 1976. pap. 8.95 (*0-14-043103-9*, Penguin Classics) Viking Penguin.
— Senor Scrooge: Charles Dickens' A Christmas Carol adapted for the Bilingual Stage. Alderete, Betty, tr. (Illus.). 32p. (Orig.). 1995. pap. 3.25 (*0-88680-404-3*, 404-3) I E Clark.
— The Signalman. (Classic Frights Ser.). (Illus.). 64p. (YA). (gr. 5 up). 1998. pap. 5.95 (*0-929605-85-3*, Classic Frights) Books of Wonder.
***Dickens, Charles.** The Signalman. (Short Stories Ser.). 22p. 2000. pap. 3.95 (*1-86092-038-1*, Pub. by Travelman Pub) IPG Chicago.
Dickens, Charles. The Signalman & Other Ghost Stories. 152p. 1985. pap. 6.00 (*0-89733-107-1*) Academy Chi Pubs.
— The Signalman & Other Ghost Stories. (Pocket Classics Ser.). 272p. 1996. pap. 10.95 (*0-86299-858-1*, Pub. by Sutton Pub Ltd) Intl Pubs Mktg.
— Sketches by Boz. Walder, Dennis, ed. & intro. by. LC 96-164047. (Illus.). 635p. 1995. pap. 13.95 (*0-14-043345-7*) Viking Penguin.
— Steel Specialty Tubular Products. 118p. 1980. 8.00 (*0-614-05636-5*) Iron & Steel.
***Dickens, Charles.** Stories for Christmas. 802p. 1999. 29.95 (*1-879582-41-4*) Platinum Pr.
Dickens, Charles. A Tale of Two Cities. 96p. 1998. pap. text 7.00 (*0-14-081505-8*) Addison-Wesley.
— A Tale of Two Cities. (Illustrated Classics Collection 2). 64p. 1994. pap. 4.95 (*0-7854-0724-3*, 40418) Am Guidance.
— A Tale of Two Cities. LC 95-77835. (Classroom Reading Plays Ser.). 32p. (YA). (gr. 6-12). 1995. pap. 3.95 (*0-7854-1119-4*, 40207) Am Guidance.
— A Tale of Two Cities. 27.95 (*0-8488-0076-1*) Amereon Ltd.
— A Tale of Two Cities. (Cyber Classics Ser.). 1997. pap. text 14.95 (*1-55701-205-9*) BNI Pubns.
— A Tale of Two Cities. 384p. (gr. 9-12). 1984. mass mkt. 4.95 (*0-553-21176-5*, Bantam Classics) Bantam.
— A Tale of Two Cities. 368p. (YA). (gr. 9-12). 1989. teacher ed. write for info. (*0-318-51005-7*, Bantam Classics) Bantam.
— A Tale of Two Cities. LC 92-73542. 1993. 20.00 (*0-679-42073-8*) Everymns Lib.
***Dickens, Charles.** A Tale of Two Cities. (Cloth Bound Pocket Ser.). 1998. 7.95 (*3-8290-0880-5*, 520656) Konemann.
Dickens, Charles. A Tale of Two Cities. 384p. 1997. mass mkt. 4.95 (*0-451-52656-2*, Sig Classics) NAL.
— A Tale of Two Cities. (Illus.). 380p. 1987. 15.95 (*0-19-254504-3*) OUP.
— A Tale of Two Cities. Sanders, Andrew, ed. & intro. by. (Oxford World's Classics Ser.). 554p. 1998. pap. 5.95 (*0-19-283390-1*) OUP.
— A Tale of Two Cities. Shefter, Harry et al, eds. 528p. 1989. mass mkt. 4.99 (*0-671-69583-5*, WSP) PB.
— A Tale of Two Cities. 528p. 1996. per. 5.99 (*0-671-00274-0*) PB.
— A Tale of Two Cities. LC 95-77835. (Illus.). 384p. (YA). (gr. 5 up). 1996. pap. 3.99 (*0-14-037336-5*, PuffinBks) Peng Put Young Read.
— A Tale of Two Cities. Vogel, Malvina, ed. (Great Illustrated Classics Ser.: Vol. 26). (Illus.). 240p. (J). (gr. 3-6). 1993. 9.95 (*0-86611-977-9*) Playmore Inc.
— A Tale of Two Cities. 1998. pap. 6.95 (*0-8114-6840-2*) Raintree Steck-V.
— A Tale of Two Cities. 1996. 18.50 (*0-679-60208-9*) Random.
Dickens, Charles. A Tale of Two Cities. (Literary Classics Ser.). 272p. 1992. 5.98 (*0-7624-0554-6*) Running Pr.
Dickens, Charles. A Tale of Two Cities. write for info. (*0-318-58796-3*) S&S Trade.
— A Tale of Two Cities. 384p. (YA). 1989. pap. 2.50 (*0-8125-0506-9*, Pub. by Tor Bks) St Martin.
— A Tale of Two Cities. 1997. pap. 2.95 (*0-89375-783-7*) Troll Communs.
— A Tale of Two Cities. 1996. 11.09 (*0-606-13049-7*, Pub. by Turtleback) Demco.
— A Tale of Two Cities. 1997. 10.05 (*0-606-00203-0*, Pub. by Turtleback) Demco.
— A Tale of Two Cities. Page, Norman, ed. 1994. pap. text 4.95 (*0-460-87451-9*, Everyman's Classic Lib) Tuttle Pubng.
— A Tale of Two Cities. Woodcock, George, ed. (Penguin English Library Ser.). (Illus.). 410p. 1970. pap. 6.99 (*0-14-043054-7*, Penguin Classics) Viking Penguin.
***Dickens, Charles.** A Tale of Two Cities. (Penguin Classics Ser.). 528p. 2000. pap. 6.95 (*0-14-043730-4*, Penguin Classics) Viking Penguin.
Dickens, Charles. A Tale of Two Cities. (Vintage Classics Ser.). 384p. 1990. pap. 10.00 (*0-679-72965-8*) Vin Bks.
— A Tale of Two Cities. (Classics Library). 310p. 1997. pap. 3.95 (*1-85326-039-8*, 0398WW, Pub. by Wrdsworth Edits) NTC Contemp Pub Co.
— A Tale of Two Cities. large type ed. 1997. pap. 21.95 (*1-55701-213-X*) BNI Pubns.
— A Tale of Two Cities. large type ed. (Clear Type Classics Ser.). 485p. 1992. 23.95 (*1-85695-315-7*, Pub. by ISIS Lrg Prnt) Transaction Pubs.
***Dickens, Charles.** A Tale Of Two Cities. large type ed. 544p. 1999. pap. 22.00 (*0-06-093323-2*) HarpC.
Dickens, Charles. A Tale of Two Cities. large type ed. 515p. 1996. reprint ed. lib. bdg. 24.00 (*0-939495-00-7*) North Bks.
— A Tale of Two Cities. 1982. reprint ed. lib. bdg. 20.95 (*0-89966-371-0*) Buccaneer Bks.

***Dickens, Charles.** A Tale of Two Cities. 422p. 1998. reprint ed. lib. bdg. 24.00 (*1-58287-073-X*) North Bks.

— A Tale of Two Cities. unabridged ed. LC 98-52971. 304p. 1999. pap. text 2.00 (*0-486-40651-2*) Dover.

Dickens, Charles. A Tale of Two Cities. 2nd ed. (Illus.). 94p. 1993. pap. text 5.95 (*0-19-585452-7*) OUP.

— Tale of Two Cities: Longman Fiction-Intermd. (Longman Fiction Ser.). 1996. pap. text 7.86 (*0-582-27500-8*, Pub. by Addison-Wesley) Longman.

Dickens, Charles. A Tale of Two Cities: Mason,&James, Set. abr. ed. 1992. audio 17.00 (*1-55994-635-0*, DCN 2079) HarperAudio.

Dickens, Charles. A Tale of Two Cities - Straight. 1995. 5.50 (*0-87129-503-2*, T31) Dramatic Pub.

— A Tale of Two Cities Readalong. (Illustrated Classics Collection 2). 64p. 1994. pap. 14.95 incl. audio (*0-7854-0690-5*, 40420) Am Guidance.

— Tales of Mystery & Suspense. 1997. 8.99 (*0-517-18304-8*) Random Hse Value.

— Temps Difficile. (FRE.). 435p. 1985. pap. 16.95 (*0-7859-2011-0*, 2070376478) Fr & Eur.

***Dickens, Charles.** Unabridged Charles Dickens. 1248p. 1999. 18.98 (*0-7624-0672-0*) Running Pr.

Dickens, Charles. Unpublished Letters of Charles Dickens: To Mark Lemon. Dexter, Walter, ed. LC 76-155146. (Studies in Dickens: No. 52). 1971. reprint ed. lib. bdg. 75.00 (*0-8383-1281-0*) M S G Haskell Hse.

Dickens, Charles. Wishbone Classic: Oliver Twist, No. 5. LC 97-160190. (Wishbone Ser.: No. 5). 128p. 1996. mass mkt. 3.99 (*0-06-106419-X*, Harp PBks) HarpC.

Dickens, Charles. The Works of Charles Dickens. 797p. 1995. pap. write for info. (*1-57215-128-5*) World Pubns.

— The Works of Charles Dickens. deluxe ed. 864p. 1990. 19.99 (*0-517-05360-8*) Random Hse Value.

***Dickens, Charles, contrib. by.** A Thanksgiving Carol. adapted ed. (Adventures in Odyssey Ser.). 2-16p.p. (J). (gr. 2 up). 1999. pap., boxed set 8.99 incl. audio (*1-56179-803-7*) Focus Family.

Dickens, Charles & Chiel, Deborah. Great Expectations, Vol. 1. 1998. mass mkt. 5.99 (*0-312-96303-3*) St Martin.

Dickens, Charles & Haining, Peter. Hunted Down: The Detective Stories of Charles Dickens. 224p. 1997. pap. 23.95 (*0-7206-1045-1*, Pub. by P Owen Ltd) Dufour.

Dickens, Charles & Jakes, John. A Christmas Carol - A Play with Music. 90p. 1998. pap. 5.95 (*0-87129-813-9*, CA4) Dramatic Pub.

Dickens, Charles & Rizvi, S. N. Oliver Twist. 122p. 1997. pap. 20.00 (*81-209-0071-5*, Pub. by Pitambar Pub) St Mut.

Dickens, Charles & Saxena, Paresh. David Copperfield. 154p. 1997. pap. 24.00 (*81-209-0026-X*, Pub. by Pitambar Pub) St Mut.

Dickens, Charles & Schor, Hilary M. Hard Times: A Cultural Edition. pap. 11.95 (*0-312-13261-1*) St Martin.

Dickens, Charles & Sharma, V. A. Great Expectations. 144p. 1996. pap. 20.00 (*81-209-0070-7*, Pub. by Pitambar Pub) St Mut.

Dickens, Charles & Skarmeas, Nancy J. A Christmas Carol in Prose: Being a Ghost Story of Christmas. LC 98-7137. (Illus.). (J). (gr. 1-5). 1998. 14.00 (*0-8249-4096-2*, Candy Cane Pr) Ideals.

***Dickens, Charles & Wheatcroft, Andrew.** A Christmas Carol. LC 99-86030. (Read & Listen Ser.). (J). 2000. pap. write for info. incl. cd-rom (*0-7894-6363-6*) DK Pub Inc.

Dickens, Charles, et al. Christmas with Dickens: The Dickens' Family's 150th Anniversary Gift of A Christmas Carol for Modern-Day Families at Yuletide. LC 93-39711. 1993. 12.95 (*0-911057-02-1*) Belvedere Pr.

— The Letters of Charles Dickens. 1977. 52.95 (*0-8369-7100-0*, 7934) Ayer.

— Mr. Scrooge - Mus. 72p. 1963. pap. 5.95 (*0-87129-605-5*, M01) Dramatic Pub.

— A Treasury of Christmas Classics. 168p. 1994. 14.99 (*0-87788-819-1*, H Shaw Pubs) Waterbrook Pr.

Dickens, Charles, jt. auth. see Center for Learning Network Staff.

Dickens, Charles, jt. auth. see Cox, Don R.

Dickens, Charles, jt. auth. see Kulling, Monica.

Dickens, Charles, jt. auth. see Linney, Romulus.

Dickens, Charles, jt. auth. see Moore, Mavor.

Dickens, Charles, jt. auth. see Oppenlander, Ella Ann.

Dickens, Charles, jt. auth. see Random House Value Publishing Staff.

Dickens, Charles, jt. auth. see Smath, Jerry.

Dickens, David B. Negative Spring: Crisis Imagery in the Works of Brentano, Lenau, Rilke & T. S. Eliot. (Studies in Modern German Literature: Vol. 24). XII, 242p. (C). 1988. text 36.50 (*0-8204-0735-6*) P Lang Pubng.

Dickens, David R. & Fontana, Andrea, eds. Postmodernism & Social Inquiry. LC 93-50860. (Critical Perspectives Ser.). 259p. 1994. pap. 21.95 (*0-89862-422-3*, 2422); lib. bdg. 40.00 (*0-89862-415-0*, C2415) Guilford Pubns.

Dickens, Deborah S., ed. see Dickens, Nathaniel A.

Dickens, Edwin L. Texas Politics. 160p. (C). 1996. pap. text 12.36 (*0-669-41706-8*) HM Trade Div.

Dickens, Estelle & Sellon, Jeffrey. Cuisenaire Roddles: Games & Puzzles to Measure Thinking Skills. (Illus.). 28p. (J). (gr. 3-12). 1981. pap. text 11.50 (*0-914040-90-1*) Cuisenaire.

Dickens, Floyd, Jr. & Dickens, Jacqueline B. The Black Manager: Making It in the Corporate World. rev. ed. 335p. 1991. pap. 22.95 (*0-8144-7770-4*) AMACOM.

Dickens, Frank. Albert Herbert Hawkins: The Naughtiest Boy in the World. LC 72-149044. (Illus.). 32p. (J). (ps-3). 12.95 (*0-87592-000-4*) Scroll Pr.

Dickens, Henry F. Memories of My Father. LC 72-3169. (Studies in Dickens: No. 52). 1972. reprint ed. lib. bdg. 75.00 (*0-8383-1509-7*) M S G Haskell Hse.

Dickens, Homer. The Complete Films of James Cagney. (Citadel Film Ser.). (Illus.). 1989. pap. 14.95 (*0-8065-1152-4*, Citadel Pr) Carol Pub Group.

— The Complete Films of Marlene Dietrich. rev. ed. LC 92-17767. (Illus.). 256p. 1992. pap. 16.95 (*0-8065-1354-3*, Citadel Pr) Carol Pub Group.

— The Films of Katharine Hepburn. rev. ed. Quirk, Lawrence J., ed. (Illus.). 286p. 1990. pap. 14.95 (*0-8065-1175-3*, Citadel Pr) Carol Pub Group.

Dickens, Jacqueline B., jt. auth. see Dickens, Floyd, Jr.

Dickens, Jane D. A Touch of the Master's Hand: Messages of Inspiration. 40p. 1997. spiral bd. write for info. (*0-9663660-0-X*) Touch Mstrs Handi.

Dickens, Joy, ed. Family Outing: A Guide for Parents of Gays, Lesbians & Bisexuals. 128p. 1996. pap. 19.95 (*0-7206-0961-5*, Pub. by P Owen Ltd) Dufour.

Dickens, M. My Father As I Recall Him. LC 73-21523. (Studies in Dickens: No. 52). 1974. lib. bdg. 75.00 (*0-8383-1814-2*) M S G Haskell Hse.

Dickens, Mary. Charles Dickens. LC 76-52967. (Studies in Dickens: No. 52). 1977. lib. bdg. 75.00 (*0-8383-2174-7*) M S G Haskell Hse.

Dickens, Milton. Speech: Dynamic Communication. 3rd ed. 400p. (C). 1974. pap. text 42.00 (*0-15-583193-3*) Harcourt Coll Pubs.

Dickens, Milton & McBath, James H. Guidebook for Speech Communication. 183p. (C). 1973. pap. text 32.00 (*0-15-530006-7*, Pub. by Harcourt Coll Pubs) Harcourt.

Dickens, Monica. Befriending: The American Samaritans. Jackson, Carlton, ed. & epil. by. LC 96-10815. 141p. 1996. 35.95 (*0-87972-699-7*); pap. 19.95 (*0-87972-700-4*) Bowling Green Univ Popular Press.

— One Pair of Hands. 310p. Date not set. 24.95 (*0-8488-2667-1*) Amereon Ltd.

— One Pair of Hands. large type ed. LC 94-21544. 361p. 1994. lib. bdg. 17.95 (*0-7862-0249-1*) Thorndike Pr.

— One Pair of Hands. 220p. 1998. reprint ed. pap. 14.00 (*0-89733-304-7*) Academy Chi Pubs.

— An Open Book. LC 79-313102. xi, 210 p. 1978. write for info. (*0-434-19225-2*) Buttrwrth-Heinemann.

— Scarred. large type ed. 288p. 1992. 27.99 (*0-7089-8655-2*) Ulverscroft.

Dickens, Nathaniel A. Get Paid. (Orig.). 1990. pap. write for info. (*0-916191-04-4*) Dickens Pubns.

— The Gospel Singer. Dickens, Deborah S., ed. LC 84-90448. (Orig.). 1985. pap. write for info. (*0-916191-01-X*) Dickens Pubns.

— The Lottery: America's Latest Financial Security. (Orig.). 1985. pap. write for info. (*0-916191-02-8*) Dickens Pubns.

— Mumps. (Orig.). 1990. pap. write for info. (*0-916191-05-2*) Dickens Pubns.

— Murder on a Black College Campus. (Orig.). 1990. pap. write for info. (*0-916191-06-0*) Dickens Pubns.

— The Official District of Columbia Book of Numbers. Lipkowitz, Brenda, ed. LC 83-90486. (Illus.). 90p. (Orig.). 1984. pap. 4.00 (*0-916191-00-1*) Dickens Pubns.

— William Manson Seabron: A Triumph in Time. Dickens, Deborah S., ed. (Illus.). 1995. 10.00 (*0-916191-07-9*) Dickens Pubns.

Dickens, Paul. Quality & Excellence in Human Services. LC 93-36190. (Clinical Psychology Ser.). 220p. 1994. pap. 89.95 (*0-471-94054-2*) Wiley.

Dickens, Peter. Narvik: Battles in the Fjords. LC 96-23431. (Classics of Naval Literature Ser.). (Illus.). 240p. 1996. 32.95 (*1-55750-744-9*) Naval Inst Pr.

— Reconstructing Nature: Alienation, Emancipation, & the Division of Labour. LC 95-26748. 240p. (C). 1996. 80.00 (*0-415-08921-2*); pap. 24.99 (*0-415-08922-0*) Routledge.

— Sas: Secret War in South-East Asia. 1997. pap. 12.00 (*0-449-00140-7*) Fawcett.

— Sas: Secret War in Southeast Asia. 1992. mass mkt. 5.99 (*0-8041-0833-1*) Ivy Books.

***Dickens, Peter.** Social Darwinism: Linking Evolutionary Thought to Social Theory. LC 99-56450. (Concepts in the Social Sciences Ser.). 2000. 19.95 (*0-335-20218-7*) OpUniv Pr.

Dickens, Peter. Society & Nature. (C). 1992. 59.95 (*0-87722-968-6*); pap. 19.95 (*0-87722-969-4*) Temple U Pr.

Dickens, R. R. International Comparison of Asset Market Volatility: A Further Application of the ARCH Model. LC HG1581.D57. (Bank of England Technical Ser.: Vol. 15). 56p. 1987. reprint ed. pap. 30.00 (*0-608-07952-9*, 206792500012) Bks Demand.

Dickens, Rex M., jt. auth. see Marsh, Diane T.

Dickens, Ross N. Contestable Markets Theory, Competition, & the United States Commercial Banking Industry. rev. ed. LC 95-52164. (Financial Sector of the American Economy Ser.). 256p. 1996. text 77.00 (*0-8153-2390-5*) Garland.

Dickens, Roy S., Jr., ed. Archaeology of Urban America: The Search for Pattern & Process. (Studies in Historical Archaeology). 1982. text 79.95 (*0-12-214980-7*) Acad Pr.

Dickens, Roy S., Jr. & Ward, H. Trawick, eds. Structure & Process in Southeastern Archaeology. LC 84-23. (A Dan Josselyn Memorial Publication). (Illus.). 365p. 1985. pap. 113.20 (*0-7837-8369-8*, 205917900009) Bks Demand.

Dickens, Susan. The Art of Tassel Making. (Illus.). 128p. 1995. 29.95 (*1-86373-618-2*) IPG Chicago.

— Art of Tassel Making. (Illus.). 152p. 1996. pap. 24.95 (*1-86448-122-6*) IPG Chicago.

***Dickens, Susan.** Tassels. (Illus.). 144p. 2000. 29.95 (*1-86508-081-0*, Pub. by Allen & Unwin Pty) IPG Chicago.

Dickens, Thomas L. & Crumbley, D. Larry. Keys to Understanding Social Security Benefits. (Retirement Keys Ser.). 160p. 1992. pap. 5.95 (*0-8120-4466-5*) Barron.

Dickens, William T. Employment Effects of European Economic Integration. 141p. (Orig.). (C). 1995. pap. text 35.00 (*0-7881-2096-4*) DIANE Pub.

Dickens, William T., et al. Does the Bell Curve Ring True? 200p. (C). 1997. pap. 15.95 (*0-8157-7763-9*) Brookings.

Dickens, William T., jt. ed. see Ferguson, Ronald F.

Dickens, William T., jt. ed. see Weaver, R. Kent.

Dickensheet, Jan. I'll Never Ask Why. Spears-Stewart, Reta, ed. 144p. 1998. pap. 9.95 (*1-892477-04-1*) Barnabs Pub.

***Dickenson.** Britain & the American Revolution. LC 98-36815. 284p. (C). 1998. pap. 31.20 (*0-582-31839-4*) Longman.

Dickenson, ed. Valves, Piping & Pipelines Handbook. 3rd ed. LC 99-26575. 650p. 1999. text 215.00 (*1-85617-252-X*) Elsevier.

Dickenson, A., jt. auth. see Bunker, D.

Dickenson, A., jt. auth. see Fenimore, C.

Dickenson, A. H., et al, eds. The Pharmacology of Pain. LC 97-23531. (Handbook of Experimental Pharmacology Ser.: No. 130). (Illus.). 450p. 1997. 325.00 (*3-540-62785-5*) Spr-Verlag.

Dickenson, A. H., jt. auth. see Dale, M. M.

Dickenson, C. Reginald. Chang. (Illus.). 264p. 1995. pap. 12.50 (*0-8059-3719-6*) Dorrance.

Dickenson, C. Reginald & Dickenson, John. The Brotherhood. 144p. 1997. pap. 15.00 (*0-8059-4268-8*) Dorrance.

Dickenson, Christopher. Pumping Manual. 9th ed. LC 95-127127. 1995. 190.25 (*1-85617-215-5*, R101, Pub. by Elsvr Adv Tech) Elsevier.

Dickenson, Donna. Property, Women & Politics: Subjects or Objects? LC 97-21504. 210p. 1997. 48.00 (*0-8135-2457-1*); pap. 18.00 (*0-8135-2458-X*) Rutgers U Pr.

Dickenson, Donna & Johnson, Malcolm, eds. Death, Dying & Bereavement. (Illus.). 252p. (C). 1993. text 65.00 (*0-8039-8796-X*); pap. text 21.95 (*0-8039-8797-8*) Sage.

Dickenson, Emily. Poems of Emily Dickinson, 3 vols. 1998. 156.00 (*0-674-67601-7*) HUP.

Dickenson, Fred. Drink & Drugs at Work: The Consuming Problem. 90p. (C). 1988. 65.00 (*0-85292-410-0*) St Mut.

Dickenson, George-Therese. Transducing. LC 85-62145. (Segue Bks.). 150p. (Orig.). 1985. pap. text 7.50 (*0-937804-17-7*) Segue NYC.

Dickenson, Gill. Children's Costume. 96p. (J). 1993. 12.98 (*1-55521-919-5*) Bk Sales Inc.

— Children's Costumes. (Crafts for Children Ser.). (Illus.). 32p. (YA). (gr. 3 up). 1997. pap. 4.95 (*1-56010-214-4*, CC04) W Foster Pub.

— Face Painting: Art for Children. 96p. (J). 1993. 12.98 (*1-55521-918-7*) Bk Sales Inc.

Dickenson, J. P., et al. A Geography of the Third World. LC 83-7927. 1983. pap. 14.95 (*0-416-74170-3*, NO. 3909) Routledge.

Dickenson, James R. Home on the Range: A Century on the High Plains. LC 94-26800. 272p. 1995. write for info. (*0-689-12194-6*) Glencoe.

— Home on the Range: A Century on the High Plains. (Illus.). 304p. 1996. pap. 14.95 (*0-7006-0758-7*) U Pr of KS.

Dickenson, John, jt. auth. see Dickenson, C. Reginald.

Dickenson, John P. Brazil, Vol. 57. 2nd rev. ed. (World Bibliographical Ser.). 274p. 1997. lib. bdg. 73.00 (*1-85109-259-5*) ABC-CLIO.

Dickenson, John P., ed. The Geography of the Third World. 2nd ed. LC 95-37939. (Illus.). 368p. (C). 1996. 85.00 (*0-415-10672-9*); pap. 24.99 (*0-415-10673-7*) Routledge.

Dickenson, Joy. Haunted City: An Unauthorized Guide to the Magical, Magnificent New Orleans of Anne Rice. (Illus.). 256p. 1995. pap. 14.95 (*0-8065-1696-8*, Citadel Pr) Carol Pub Group.

— Scarlett Slept Here: A Book Lover's Guide to the South. LC 99-39097. (Illus.). 208p. 1999. pap. 14.95 (*0-8065-2092-2*, Citadel Pr) Carol Pub Group.

Dickenson, Lee. The Keepers of the Keys. LC 99-13912. 128p. 1999. pap. 14.95 (*1-882897-32-3*) Lost Coast.

— The Sounding Tree: Voices along the Razor Wire. LC 98-18684. 176p. 1998. pap. 14.95 (*1-882897-24-2*) Lost Coast.

Dickenson, Luella. Reminiscences of a Trip Across the Plains in 1846 & Early Days in California. 48p. 1977. 14.95 (*0-87770-180-6*) Ye Galleon.

Dickenson, Margaret. Basic Dental Anatomy. 175p. (C). 1994. 26.79 (*1-56870-147-0*) RonJon Pub.

— Biomedical Sciences. 165p. (C). 1994. 24.22 (*1-56870-146-2*) RonJon Pub.

— Clinical Sciences I. 183p. (C). 1994. 25.07 (*1-56870-142-X*) RonJon Pub.

— Clinical Sciences II. 173p. (C). 1994. 23.09 (*1-56870-141-1*) RonJon Pub.

— Clinical Sciences III. 192p. (C). 1994. 28.21 (*1-56870-143-8*) RonJon Pub.

— Clinical Sciences IV. 152p. (C). 1994. 22.80 (*1-56870-144-6*) RonJon Pub.

— Dental Sciences. 89p. (C). 1994. 19.36 (*1-56870-145-4*) RonJon Pub.

Dickenson, Peter. Shadow of a Hero. 1995. 20.95 (*0-385-30976-7*) Doubleday.

Dickenson, Reginald. African Ambit. x, 313p. 1992. boxed set 19.50 (*1-85821-244-8*, Pub. by Pentland Pr) St Mut.

Dickenson, S. E., jt. auth. see Schroeder, W. L.

Dickenson, Stephen E., ed. see American Society of Civil Engineers, Committee on.

Dickenson, T. Christopher. Filters & Filtration Handbook. 4th ed. LC 97-37600. 1094p. 1997. 243.00 (*1-85617-322-4*) Elsevier.

Dickenson, Victoria. Drawn from Life: Science & Art in the Portrayal of the New World. LC 99-176068. (Illus.). 320p. 1998. text 75.00 (*0-8020-4225-2*); pap. text 24.95 (*0-8020-8073-1*) U of Toronto Pr.

Dicker, A. Dicker: Taxation of U. K. Corporate Investment in the U. S. 2nd ed. 1995. write for info. (*0-406-05044-9*, DTCI2, MICHIE) LEXIS Pub.

— Taxation of U. K. Corporate Investment in the U. S. Burke, W., ed. 1988. 120.00 (*0-406-50173-4*, UK, MICHIE) LEXIS Pub.

Dicker, Eva B., jt. auth. see Barash, Harvey L.

Dicker, Eva B., jt. auth. see Greene, Laura.

Dicker, Georges. Descartes: An Analytical & Historical Introduction. (Illus.). 272p. (C). 1993. pap. text 25.95 (*0-19-507590-0*) OUP.

— Hume's Epistemology & Metaphysics: An Introduction. LC 97-34891. (Illus.). 232p. (C). 1998. 75.00 (*0-415-16318-8*); pap. 24.99 (*0-415-16319-6*) Routledge.

— Perceptual Knowledge. (Philosophical Studies: No. 22). 235p. 1980. text 96.00 (*90-277-1130-5*, D Reidel) Kluwer Academic.

Dicker, Herman. Creativity, Holocaust, Reconstruction: Jewish Life in Wuertemberg, Past & Present. (Illus.). 1984. 18.50 (*0-87203-118-7*) Hermon.

— The Mayer Sulzberger - Alexander Marx Correspondence, 1904-1923. x, 206p. (Orig.). 1990. 29.50 (*0-87203-133-0*) Hermon.

— Of Learning & Libraries: The Seminary Library at One Hundred. 1988. 22.50 (*0-87334-045-0*) Ktav.

Dicker, Herman & Wiesel, Elie. Piety & Perseverance: Jews from the Carpathian Mountains. LC 80-54595. (Illus.). 252p. 1981. pap. 10.00 (*0-87203-098-9*) Hermon.

Dicker, Sue. Personal Expressions: Writing Your Way into English. rev. ed. 72p. (C). 1987. pap. text 4.00 (*0-317-93602-6*) D Blot Pubns.

Dicker, Susan J. Languages in America: A Pluralist View. LC 96-21874. (Bilingual Education & Bilingualism Ser.). 250p. 1996. 69.00 (*1-85359-337-0*, Pub. by Multilingual Matters); pap. 19.95 (*1-85359-336-2*, Pub. by Multilingual Matters) Taylor & Francis.

Dicker, Todd J., jt. ed. see Lynch, Thomas D.

***Dicker, Wilson.** Biblical Equality & Secular Education. 181p. 1999. pap. 19.95 (*1-929342-06-3*) Olde Ridge Bk.

— The Church Which Jesus Built. 82p. 2000. pap. write for info. (*1-929342-12-8*) Olde Ridge Bk.

— The Secular Divorce. 45p. 2000. pap. write for info. (*1-929342-13-6*) Olde Ridge Bk.

— The Silent Divorce. 47p. 1999. pap. 12.95 (*1-929342-07-1*) Olde Ridge Bk.

Dickerman, Alexandra. Exploring Biodiversity Indicators & Targets under the Convention on Biological Diversity: A Synthesis Report of the Sixth Session of the Global Biodiversity Forum : U. N. Headquarters, New York, 3-4 April 1997. 1998. text 5.74 (*0-07-229414-0*) McGraw.

— Following Your Path: A Self Discovery Adventure Journal Using Myths, Symbols & Images. (Illus.). 338p. (Orig.). 1990. pap. 19.95 (*0-9624170-7-6*) New Dimensions.

— Organisms & Populations. 1998. text 5.25 (*0-07-229413-2*) McGraw.

Dickerman, Alexandra C. Following Your Path: Using Myths, Symbols, & Images to Explore Your Inner Life. LC 92-6000. (Illus.). 330p. (Orig.). 1992. pap. 16.95 (*0-87477-687-2*, Tarcher Putnam) Putnam Pub Group.

Dickerman, Carol. Urban Housing & Land Markets: Bujumbura, Burundi. (Research Paper Ser.: Vol. 97). (Illus.). 32p. (C). 1988. pap. 4.00 (*0-934519-07-2*, RP97) U of Wis Land.

Dickerman, Carol, jt. auth. see Riddell, James.

Dickerman, Carol W. & Bloch, Peter C. Land Tenure & Agricultural Productivity in Malawi. (LTC Paper Ser.: Vol. 143). vii, 56p. (C). 1991. pap. 7.00 (*0-934519-61-7*, LTC143) U of Wis Land.

Dickerman, Carol W., et al. Security of Tenure & Land Registration in Africa: Literature Review & Synthesis. (LTC Papers: No. 137). 316p. 1989. 16.00 (*0-934519-53-6*, LTC 137) U of Wis Land.

Dickerman, Edmund H. Bellievre & Villeroy: Power in France under Henry III & Henry IV. LC 70-127365. 212p. reprint ed. 65.80 (*0-8357-7124-5*, 202750200055) Bks Demand.

Dickerman, G. S. Plant: The House of Plant of Macon, Ga. (Illus.). 259p. 1990. reprint ed. pap. 39.50 (*0-8328-1519-5*); reprint ed. lib. bdg. 47.50 (*0-8328-1518-7*) Higginson Bk Co.

Dickerman, J. Colonial History of the Parish of Mount Carmel, Ct. As Read in Its Geologic Formations, Records & Traditions. 109p. 1994. reprint ed. pap. 17.50 (*0-8328-4410-1*) Higginson Bk Co.

***Dickerman, John.** Investigating Biological Concepts: A Laboratory Manual. (Illus.). 296p. (C). 2000. pap. text 29.95 (*0-89582-508-2*) Morton Pub.

Dickerman, Joseph D. & Lucey, Jerold F. Smith's the Critically Ill Child: Diagnosis & Medical Management. 3rd ed. (Illus.). 352p. 1985. text 85.00 (*0-7216-8386-X*, W B Saunders Co) Harcrt Hlth Sci Grp.

Dickerman, Kenneth N. Hospital Space Programming: Guidelines for Departmental Space Requirements, Set. 257p. 1992. ring bd. 350.00 (*1-881556-00-X*) Hlth Facility.

— Hospital Space Programming: Guidelines for Departmental Space Requirements, Vol. 1. 149p. 1992. write for info. (*1-881556-01-8*) Hlth Facility.

— Hospital Space Programming: Guidelines for Departmental Space Requirements, Vol. 2. 108p. 1992. write for info. (*1-881556-02-6*) Hlth Facility.

Dickerman, Kenneth N., et al. Florida Project Development Manual: A Guide to Planning, Design & Construction of Healthcare Facilities in the State of Florida. (Illus.). 216p. 1994. pap. 39.95 (*1-881556-03-4*) Hlth Facility.

An Asterisk (*) at the beginning of an entry indicates that the title is appearing for the first time.

Dickerman, Leah, ed. Building the Collective: Soviet Graphic Design, 1917-1937. (Illus.). 128p. 1996. pap. 24.95 (*1-56898-074-4*) Princeton Arch.

Dickerman, Leah, ed. see Branch, Melville C.

***Dickerman, Mike.** Along the Beaten Path: Collected Writings from a White Mountain Tramper. LC 00-190511. (Illus.). 224p. 2000. pap. 14.95 (*0-9657475-9-X*) Bondcliff Bks.

Dickerman, Mike. Why I'll Never Hike the Appalachian Trail: More Collected Writings from a White Mountain Tramper. LC 97-74688. (Illus.). 224p. 1997. pap. 14.95 (*0-9657475-1-4*) Bondcliff Bks.

***Dickerman, Mike, ed.** The White Mountain Reader. LC 00-190959. (Illus.). 336p. 2000. pap. 21.95 (*0-9657475-8-1*) Bondcliff Bks.

Dickerman, Mike, et al. A Guide to Crawford Notch. LC 97-71040. (Illus.). 160p. (Orig.). 1997. pap. 12.95 (*0-9657475-0-6*) Bondcliff Bks.

Dickerman, Pat. Farm, Ranch & Country Vacations. (Illus.). 1989. pap. 10.95 (*0-913214-00-0*) Farm Ranch Ctry Vac.

Dickerman, Pat. Farm, Ranch & Country Vacations: In America. 45th anniversary ed. (Illus.). 248p. 1995. pap., per. 19.95 (*0-913216-02-X*) Adven Guides.

Dickerman, Pat, ed. Adventure Travel North America. 9th ed. (Illus.). 288p. 1993. per. 16.95 (*0-913216-01-1*) Adven Guides.

Dickerman, Philip J., ed. see Optical Spectrometric Measurements of High Tempera.

Dickerman, Robert W., et al. The Era of Allan R. Phillips: A Festschrift. (Illus.). 264p. 1997. text 37.50 (*0-913945-58-7*) Horizon Comms.

Dickersin, Richard. Diagnostic Electron Microscopy: A Text-Atlas. LC 87-30997. (Illus.). 640p. 1988. 110.00 (*0-89640-137-5*) Igaku-Shoin.

***Dickersin, Richard.** Diagnostic Electron Microscopy: A Text-Atlas. 2nd ed. LC 99-32439. (Illus.). 556p. 1999. 275.00 (*0-387-98388-0*) Spr-Verlag.

Dickerson. The Forgotten Filly. 192p. 1998. mass mkt. 4.50 (*0-06-106486-6*, Harp PBks) HarpC.

— Introduction to Financial Management. 4th ed. (C). 1994. pap. text, student ed. 30.50 (*0-03-098077-1*) Harcourt Coll Pubs.

Dickerson, A. Darby. Advice & Consent - The Selection of United States Supreme Court Justices: Proceedings of a Symposium. (Institute & Seminar Proceedings Ser.). 94p. 1994. pap. 9.50 (*0-89940-106-6*) LBJ Sch Pub Aff.

***Dickerson, Alice.** I'm Going to High School: A Guide to the Private High School Admissions Process. (Illus.). 100p. (YA). (gr. 5-7). 1999. wbk. ed. 20.00 (*0-9670338-0-2*) N B I.

Dickerson, Ann. Family System Fallout. LC 97-62446. 256p. 1998. pap. 14.99 (*1-57921-081-3*) WinePress Pub.

Dickerson, Anne, tr. see Bouvier, Nicolas.

Dickerson, Bette J. African American Single Mothers. (Sage Series on Race & Ethnic Relations: Vol. 10). 272p. 1995. 52.00 (*0-8039-4911-1*); pap. text 24.00 (*0-8039-4912-X*) Sage.

Dickerson, Beverly, jt. auth. see Short, J. Rodney.

Dickerson, Bodil, et al. Introduction to Financial Management. 4th ed. LC 93-46765. 928p. (C). 1994. text 94.00 (*0-03-097602-2*) Dryden Pr.

— Introduction to Financial Management. 4th ed. 518p. (C). 1994. pap. text, teacher ed. 82.25 incl. trans. (*0-03-098076-3*) Dryden Pr.

— Introduction to Financial Management, Test bank. 4th ed. 614p. (C). 1994. pap. text 43.50 (*0-03-098078-X*) Dryden Pr.

Dickerson, Brent C. The Old Rose Adventurer: The Once-Blooming Old European Roses & More. LC 98-19092. (Illus.). 680p. 1999. 69.95 (*0-88192-466-0*) Timber.

Dickerson, Charles S. The Credit Department: Its Role in Training. 2nd ed. LC 84-2009. 48p. (Orig.). 1984. pap. text 10.00 (*0-936742-15-1*) Robt Morris Assocs.

— Current Approaches to Grading Commercial Loans. Behr, Joan H., ed. LC 87-18458. (Illus.). 44p. 1987. pap. text 39.00 (*0-936742-43-7*) Robt Morris Assocs.

***Dickerson, Charlyne.** The Misssing Link. 2000. pap. 8.95 (*1-58571-037-7*, 909-110, Pub. by Genesis Press) BookWorld.

Dickerson, Claire M. Partnership Law Adviser. 540p. 1991. 95.00 (*0-685-69470-4*) PLI.

***Dickerson, Darby & Association of Legal Writing Directors Staff.** ALWD Citation Manual: A Professional System of Citation. LC 99-462165. 2000. pap. 20.95 (*0-7355-1193-4*) Panel Pubs.

Dickerson, Debra. Can't Keep My Mouth Shut. 272p. 1999. write for info. (*0-316-32074-9*) Little.

***Dickerson, Debra J.** An American Story. LC 00-29862. 288p. 2000. 24.00 (*0-375-42069-X*) Pantheon.

Dickerson, Dennis C. Militant Mediator: Whitney M. Young, Jr. LC 97-43456. (Illus.). 416p. 1998. 32.50 (*0-8131-2058-6*) U Pr of Ky.

— Out of the Crucible: Black Steel Workers in Western Pennsylvania, 1875-1980. LC 85-30450. (SUNY Series in Afro-American Studies). 323p. (C). 1986. text 21.50 (*0-88706-305-5*); pap. text 21.50 (*0-88706-306-3*) State U NY Pr.

Dickerson, Donald, ed. see DeGroot, Henry.

Dickerson, Donna L. Florida Media Law. 2nd ed. 280p. 1991. 39.95 (*0-8130-1039-X*); pap. 19.95 (*0-8130-1035-7*) U Press Fla.

— Freedom of Press in Nineteenth-Century America, 24. LC 90-38525. (Contributions to the Study of Mass Media & Communications Ser.: No. 24). 272p. 1990. 59.95 (*0-313-27534-3*, DFP/, Greenwood Pr) Greenwood.

Dickerson, Donna L., jt. auth. see Trager, Robert.

***Dickerson, Donya, ed.** Guide to Literary Agents. 368p. 2001. pap. 21.99 (*1-58297-011-4*) F & W Pubns Inc.

— 2000 Guide to Literary Agents: 500+ Agents Who Sell What You Write. (Illus.). 368p. 2000. pap. 21.99 (*0-89879-936-8*, 10627, Wrtrs Digest Bks) F & W Pubns Inc.

Dickerson, Doug. Doing My Duty: The Life Story of Douglas "Curly" Dickerson. Washburn, Bruce, ed. & told to by. LC 98-88342. (Illus.). 152p. 1998. pap. 14.00 (*0-923687-50-5*) Celo Valley Bks.

***Dickerson, Eric & Walsh, Richard G.** E Dickersons Secrets of Pro Power P. rev. ed. (Illus.). 224p. 1999. reprint ed. pap. 9.95 (*1-56743-018-X*, Amistad) HarperTrade.

Dickerson, Fay, jt. ed. see Stevenson, Katherine.

Dickerson, Frank. I Saw the Wind. 32p. 1999. pap. 6.95 (*0-9657398-2-1*) Pamet River.

— Lifesavers & Other Poems. (Illus.). 48p. (Orig.). 1997. pap. 6.95 (*0-9657398-1-3*) Pamet River.

— Le Menage a Trois. (Illus.). 32p. 1996. pap. 6.00 (*0-9657398-0-5*) Pamet River.

Dickerson, Frank W. Dearest Father: The Civil War Letters of Lt. Frank Dickerson, a Son of Belfast, Maine. Hunt, H. Draper, ed. LC 92-28299. (Illus.). 216p. (Orig.). 1992. pap. 14.95 (*0-945980-36-1*) Nrth Country Pr.

***Dickerson, George.** Selected Poems, 1959-1999. LC 99-69792. (Illus.). 160p. 2000. 24.93 (*1-892494-19-1*); pap. 14.95 (*1-892494-17-5*) Repossessed Head.

Dickerson, George, et al, eds. Rattapallax, No. 2. LC 98-97633. (Illus.). 128p. 1999. pap. 7.95 (*1-892494-14-0*) Repossessed Head.

***Dickerson, George, et al, eds.** Rattapallax, No. 3. LC 98-87633. (Illus.). 160p. 2000. pap. 7.95 (*1-892494-15-9*, Pub. by Repossessed Head) Bernhard DeBoer Inc.

Dickerson, George, et al. Rattapallax. LC 98-87633. (Illus.). 128p. 1999. per. 7.95 (*1-892494-05-1*) Repossessed Head.

Dickerson, Georgie. The Haunting & Healing of Anna. 160p. 1997. per. 8.95 (*0-9660147-0-7*) Wrtrs Blck.

Dickerson, Gloria D. A Guide to Black Children's Books. (Illus.). 28p. 1990. pap. text 10.00 (*0-9629968-0-7*) Maral Ent.

Dickerson, Gregory W., tr. see Sophocles.

Dickerson, Horace G. Onward Two Thousand & Beyond: Concepts for Changes. (Energy, Transportation, Environment Ser.). 168p. 1991. 27.95 (*0-9631966-1-8*); pap. 22.95 (*0-9631966-4-2*); text 25.95 (*0-9631966-3-4*); pap. text 17.95 (*0-9631966-5-0*); lib. bdg. 37.95 (*0-9631966-2-6*) Univ Pr.

Dickerson, James. Country Music's Most Embarrassing Moments. rev. ed. LC 96-46449. (Illus.). 112p. (Orig.). 1996. pap. 7.95 (*1-888952-33-4*) Cumberland Hse.

— Dixie's Dirty Secret: The True Story of How the Government, the Media & the Mob Conspired to Combat Integration & the Vietnam Antiwar Movement. LC 98-3165. (Illus.). 270p. (C). (gr. 13). 1998. text 26.95 (*0-7656-0340-3*) M E Sharpe.

***Dickerson, James.** Goin' Back to Memphis: A Century of Blues, Rock 'n Roll & Glorious Soul. 2000. pap. write for info. (*0-8154-1049-2*) Cooper Sq.

Dickerson, James. North to Canada: Men & Women Against the Vietnam War. LC 98-23568. 232p. 1999. 35.00 (*0-275-96211-3*, Praeger Pubs) Greenwood.

— The Secret Life of Colonel Tom Parker: The Carny Who Managed the King. (Illus.). 288p. 1999. 24.95 (*0-8230-8421-3*) Watsn-Guptill.

— Women on Top: The Quiet Revolution That's Rocking the American Music Industry. LC 98-19826. (Illus.). 256p. 1998. 21.95 (*0-8230-8489-2*) Watsn-Guptill.

Dickerson, James, jt. auth. see Moore, Scotty.

Dickerson, James L. Country Music's Most Embarrassing Moments. 88p. (Orig.). 1996. pap. 5.95 (*1-55793-059-7*) Guild Bindery Pr.

***Dickerson, James L.** Dixie Chicks: Down-Home & Backstage. 2000. pap. 16.95 (*0-87833-189-1*) Taylor Pub.

— I'm So Sorry: The Stories Behind 101 Very Public Apologies. 208p. 2000. pap. 12.95 (*0-86730-814-1*) Lebhar Friedman.

Dickerson, James L. Last Suppers: If the World Ended Tomorrow, What Would Be Your Last Meal? LC 98-55744. (Illus.). 208p. 1999. 24.95 (*0-86730-758-7*, Pub. by Lebhar Friedman) Natl Bk Netwk.

Dickerson, Joe, jt. auth. see Lepp, George.

Dickerson, John, jt. auth. see Davies, Jill.

Dickerson, John W. T. & McGurk, Harry, eds. Brain & Behavioural Development: Interdisciplinary Perspectives on Structure & Function. (Illus.). 266p. 1982. 69.95 (*0-903384-27-2*) Trans-Atl Phila.

Dickerson, Julie G. The Broken Butterfly: A Story to Help Children Understand Responsibility & Forgiveness. (Helping Children Understand Ser.). (Illus.). 32p. (J). (gr. k-6). 1997. pap. 11.95 (*0-9646576-8-6*) Cherubic Pr.

— Grandpa's Berries: A Story to Help Children Understand Grief & Loss. (Helping Children Understand Ser.). 32p. (J). (gr. k-6). 1995. pap. 11.95 (*0-9646576-9-4*) Cherubic Pr.

— Helping Children Understand Series. (Illus.). 96p. (Orig.). (J). (gr. k-6). 1998. pap. 21.95 (*0-9646576-0-0*) Cherubic Pr.

***Dickerson, Julie G.** Patrick Loves Peaches: A Story to Help Children Understand Peer Pressure & Loyalty. (Helping Children Understand Ser.). (Illus.). 32p. (Orig.). (J). (gr. k-6). 1998. pap. 11.95 (*0-9646576-7-8*) Cherubic Pr.

Dickerson, Kitty G. Textiles & Apparel in the Global Economy. 3rd ed. LC 98-13493. (Illus.). 606p. (C). 1998. 77.00 (*0-13-647280-X*, Merrill Coll) P-H.

Dickerson, Kitty G., jt. auth. see Jarnow, Jeannette A.

Dickerson, Lonna & Dow, Dianne, eds. Handbook for Christian EFL Teachers: Christian Teacher-Preparation Programs, Overseas Teaching Opportunities Instructional Materials & Resources. LC 98-143065. 71p. (Orig.). 1996. pap. text. write for info. (*0-9635856-1-4*) Berry Pub Srv.

Dickerson, Lonna J., ed. Helping the Missionary Langauge Learner Succeed: Proceedings from the First International Congress on Missionary Language Learning. 263p. (Orig.). (C). 1995. pap. text. write for info. (*0-942726-02-2*) Mission Trng.

Dickerson, Lonna J. & Dow, Dianne F. Handbook for Christian EFL Teachers: Christian Teacher-Preparation Programs, Overseas Teaching Opportunities, Instructional Materials & Resources. LC 98-143065. (Monograph Ser.). 96p. 1997. pap. 9.00 (*1-879089-25-4*) B Graham Ctr.

Dickerson, Lonna J., jt. auth. see Dickerson, Wayne B.

Dickerson, Martha U. Our Four Boys: Foster Parenting Retarded Teenagers. LC 78-5642. 246p. reprint ed. pap. 76.30 (*0-8357-3976-7*, 203667400005) Bks Demand.

Dickerson, Mary C. Frog Book. (Illus.). 1969. reprint ed. pap. 12.95 (*0-486-21973-9*) Dover.

Dickerson, Mary D. Grow Your Goal$, Vol. 1. LC 97-92833. 1998. write for info. (*0-9662056-0-X*) Jeb Pubng.

Dickerson, O. Bruce, jt. ed. see Erdil, Michael.

Dickerson, Oliver M., ed. Boston under Military Rule 1768-1769. LC 70-118029. (Era of the American Revolution Ser.). 1970. reprint ed. 22.50 (*0-306-71943-6*) Da Capo.

Dickerson, P. W., et al, eds. Trans-Pecos Region: West Texas. (Guidebook Ser.: No. 31). (Illus.). 308p. 1980. 35.00 (*1-58546-062-1*); pap. 12.00 (*1-58546-063-X*) NMex Geol Soc.

Dickerson-Putman, Jeanette, ed. Women, Age, & Power: The Politics of Age Difference among Women in Papua New Guinea & Australia. (Pacific Studies: Vol. 19, No. 4). 152p. (C). 1997. pap. text 15.00 (*0-939154-62-5*) Inst Polynesian.

Dickerson-Putman, Jeanette & Brown, Judith K., eds. Women among Women: Anthropological Perspectives on Female Age Hierarchies. LC 97-31988. xvii, 147p. 1998. pap. text 14.95 (*0-252-06683-9*) U of Ill Pr.

Dickerson, R., et al. Chemical Principles. 4th ed. 1984. teacher ed. 9.95 (*0-685-42650-5*); text 49.50 (*0-8053-2422-4*) Benjamin-Cummings.

Dickerson, Reed. Products Liability & the Food Consumer. LC 77-139130. 339p. 1972. reprint ed. lib. bdg. 69.50 (*0-8371-5746-3*, DIPL, Greenwood Pr) Greenwood.

Dickerson, Richard. Nevada Angler's Guide: Fish Tails in the Sagebrush. LC 98-132820. (Illus.). 156p. 1997. pap. 14.95 (*1-57188-100-X*) F Amato Pubns.

Dickerson, Roger V. War on Waste II. 120p. 46.00 (*0-614-25583-X*, 00GM52102) Print Indus Am.

Dickerson, Ron & Peterson, James. 101 Defensive Back Drills. 1997. pap. 16.95 (*1-57167-089-0*) Coaches Choice.

Dickerson, Sharon L. Bicycling San Luis Obispo County. (Illus.). 128p. (Orig.). 1988. pap. 6.95 (*0-945092-03-2*) EZ Nature.

— Mountains of Fire: San Luis Obispo County's Famous Nine Sisters - A Chain of Ancient Volcanic Peaks. (Illus.). 128p. (Orig.). 1990. pap. 8.95 (*0-945092-14-8*) EZ Nature.

Dickerson, Stella M. Of People & Things. Leih, Janet, ed. (Illus.). 120p. 1990. pap. 8.00 (*1-877649-09-0*) Tesseract SD.

Dickerson, Thomas A. Class Actions: The Law of 50 States. 400p. 1988. ring bd. 85.00 (*0-318-37786-1*) NY Law Pub.

— Travel Law. 700p. 1986. reprint ed. ring bd. 98.00 (*0-318-21442-3*, 00565) NY Law Pub.

Dickerson-Thompson. The Dance of the Rain Gods. per. 8.95 (*0-86543-259-7*) Africa World.

Dickerson, Vanessa D. Victorian Ghosts in the Noontide: Women Writers & the Supernatural. 192p. (C). 1996. 34.95 (*0-8262-1081-3*) U of Mo Pr.

Dickerson, Vanessa D., ed. Keeping the Victorian House: A Collection of Essays. LC 94-30414. (Origins of Modernism Ser.: No. 7). 408p. 1994. text 30.00 (*0-8153-1575-9*, H1818) Garland.

Dickerson, Vanessa D., jt. ed. see Bennett, Michael

Dickerson, Victoria C., jt. auth. see Zimmerman, Jeffrey L.

Dickerson, Wayne B. Stress in the Speech Stream: The Rhythm of Spoken English. 312p. 1989. pap. text, teacher ed. 19.95 (*0-252-06096-2*) U of Ill Pr.

Dickerson, Wayne B. Stress in the Speech Stream: The Rhythm of Spoken English. 608p. 1989. pap. text, student ed. 24.95 (*0-252-06097-0*); audio, digital audio 39.95 (*0-252-06098-9*) U of Ill Pr.

Dickerson, Wayne B. & Dickerson, Lonna J. Tips on Taping: Language Recording in Social Sciences. LC 76-50023. (Applied Cultural Anthropology Ser.). 198p. 1977. pap. 5.95 (*0-87808-147-X*) William Carey Lib.

Dickerson, Wayne B., jt. auth. see Hahn, Laura D.

Dickes, E. W., tr. see Kohn, Hans.

Dickes, E. W., tr. see Nowak, Karl F.

Dickes, E. W., tr. see Rauschning, Hermann.

Dickes, E. W., tr. see Ruppin, Arthur.

Dickes, E. W., tr. see Stieve, Friedrich.

Dickes, E. W., tr. see Vallentin, Antonina.

Dickeson, Donna, et al, eds. Gathering Our Own: New Work from the Institute of American Indian Arts. 147p. (Orig.). (C). 1996. pap. text 8.00 (*1-881396-12-4*) IOA Indian Arts.

Dickeson, Robert C. Prioritizing Academic Programs & Services: Reallocating Resources to Achieve Strategic Balance. LC 98-40254. (Higher & Adult Education Ser.). 1999. 26.95 (*0-7879-4816-0*) Jossey-Bass.

Dickeson, Roger V. War on Waste II. Scharpf, Norman W., ed. 125p. 1991. 38.40 (*0-933505-18-3*) Graph Comm Assn.

Dickey. Laboratory Investigations for Biology. (C). 1997. spiral bd., lab manual ed. write for info. (*0-201-30463-5*) Addison-Wesley.

Dickey, A. Family Law. 2nd ed. civ, 756p. 1990. 110.00 (*0-455-21002-0*, Pub. by LawBk Co); pap. 85.00 (*0-455-21003-9*, Pub. by LawBk Co) Gaunt.

Dickey, Adam H. & Girtin, Tom. Memoirs of Mary Baker Eddy. 54p. 1986. 49.00 (*1-869832-00-0*) St Mut.

Dickey, Anthony, jt. auth. see Davies, Martin.

Dickey, Barbara, jt. ed. see Sederer, Lloyd I.

Dickey, Boyd. The Country Preacher. LC 84-52661. (Illus.). 63p. 1984. pap. 3.95 (*0-931117-01-1*) Univ Pub.

Dickey, Bruce, jt. auth. see Collver, Michael.

Dickey, Burton F., ed. see Aktories, K., et al.

Dickey, Christopher. Expats: Travels in Arabia, from Tripoli to Teheran. LC 90-151. 240p. 1991. pap. 10.95 (*0-87113-463-2*, Atlntc Mnthly) Grove-Atltic.

— Innocent Blood. LC 97-6778. 1997. 22.50 (*0-684-84200-9*) S&S Trade.

— Innocent Blood. 336p. 1998. pap. 11.00 (*0-684-85261-6*, Scribner Pap Fic) S&S Trade Pap.

— Summer of Deliverance: A Memoir of Father & Son. LC 98-23452. (Illus.). 288p. 1998. 24.00 (*0-684-84202-5*) S&S Trade.

— Summer of Deliverance: A Memoir of Father & Son. (Illus.). 288p. 1999. pap. 14.00 (*0-684-85537-2*, Touchstone) S&S Trade Pap.

***Dickey, David N.** A Study of the Place of Women in the Poetry & Prose Works of John Milton. LC 00-21121. (Women's Studies: Vol. 24). 212p. 2000. text 89.95 (*0-7734-7730-6*) E Mellen.

Dickey, Eleanor. Greek Forms of Address: From Herodotus to Lucian. LC 96-13439. (Oxford Classical Monographs). (Illus.). 358p. 1996. text 80.00 (*0-19-815054-7*, Clarendon Pr) OUP.

Dickey, Eleanor & Hamilton, Richard. New Selected Odes of Pindar. (Bryn Mawr Greek Commentaries Ser.). 112p. (Orig.). (C). 1991. pap. text 8.00 (*0-929524-72-1*) Bryn Mawr Commentaries.

***Dickey, Eric Jerome.** Cheaters. LC 99-13678. 362p. 1999. 24.95 (*0-525-94386-2*) NAL.

— Cheaters. 448p. 2000. mass mkt. 6.99 (*0-451-19407-1*, Sig) NAL.

Dickey, Eric Jerome. Friends & Lovers. LC 97-23040. 416p. 1997. 23.95 (*0-525-94127-4*) NAL.

— Friends & Lovers. 1998. mass mkt. 6.99 (*0-451-18803-9*, Sig) NAL.

***Dickey, Eric Jerome.** Friends & Lovers. 2000. pap. 12.95 (*0-451-20102-7*, Sig) NAL.

— Liar's Game. LC 99-87739. 336p. 2000. 23.95 (*0-525-94483-4*) NAL.

— Milk in My Coffee. 2000. pap. 12.95 (*0-451-20100-0*, Sig) NAL.

— Milk in My Coffee. LC 98-5258. 320p. 1998. 23.95 (*0-525-94385-4*, Dutton Child) Peng Put Young Read.

Dickey, Eric Jerome. Milk in My Coffee. 1999. reprint ed. mass mkt. 6.99 (*0-451-19406-3*, Sig) NAL.

— Sister, Sister. 1996. 22.95 (*0-614-25355-1*, Dutt) Dutton Plume.

— Sister, Sister. 368p. 1997. mass mkt. 6.99 (*0-451-18802-0*, Sig) NAL.

***Dickey, Eric Jerome.** Sister Sister. 2000. pap. 12.95 (*0-451-20101-9*, Sig) NAL.

Dickey, Esther. Skills for Survival: How Families Can Prepare. LC 78-52124. 224p. 1989. pap. 17.98 (*0-88290-093-5*) Horizon Utah.

Dickey, Esther, jt. auth. see Bingham, Rita.

Dickey, Eugene, jt. auth. see Wellner, Pamela.

***Dickey, Fern.** Last Minute Meetings. 160p. 2000. pap. 11.99 (*1-56414-497-6*) Career Pr Inc.

Dickey, Fred. Burial in Moscow. 384p. 1988. mass mkt. 3.95 (*0-373-97053-6*) Harlequin Bks.

***Dickey, Gary, ed.** Techniques & Projects III. LC 99-461822. (Techniques & Projects Ser.). (Illus.). 112p. 1999. pap. 19.95 (*0-9673163-0-8*) American Assn.

Dickey, George E. Money, Prices & Growth: The American Experience, 1869-1896. Bruchey, Stuart, ed. LC 76-39828. (Nineteen Seventy-Seven Dissertations Ser.). (Illus.). 1977. lib. bdg. 23.95 (*0-405-09907-X*) Ayer.

Dickey, Gilbert B. And Rose Makes Three. unabridged ed. 203p. 1998. pap. 14.95 (*1-892896-20-6*) Buy Books.

— And They Called Us Nancys. unabridged ed. 158p. 1998. pap. 16.95 (*1-892896-24-9*) Buy Books.

***Dickey, Glenn.** Inside the 49ers: A Behind-the-Scenes Look at America's Greatest Football Team. LC 00-27434. (Illus.). 288p. 2000. 25.00 (*0-7615-2232-8*) Prima Pub.

Dickey, Glenn. Just Win, Baby: Al Davis & His Raiders. 264p. 1991. 19.95 (*0-15-146580-0*) Harcourt.

— San Francisco Giants: Forty Years. LC 96-6180. (Illus.). 208p. (Orig.). 1997. pap. 19.95 (*0-942627-48-2*) Woodford Pubng.

— Sports Great Jerry Rice. LC 93-19997. (Sports Great Bks.). (Illus.). 64p. (J). (gr. 4-10). 1993. lib. bdg. 17.95 (*0-89490-419-1*) Enslow Pubs.

Dickey, Glenn, jt. auth. see Tunney, Jim.

Dickey, Grover. John & Alexander Dickey - Immigrants, 1772. LC 76-3239. 1976. 7.00 (*0-686-17281-7*) G C Dickey.

Dickey, Harris B. Original Land Entries in Montgomery County. (Illus.). 45p. 1997. reprint ed. pap. 9.00 (*0-8328-6853-1*) Higginson Bk Co.

Dickey, J., ed. Clusters of Galaxies & Large Scale Structure: The Minnesota Lectures. (ASP Conference Series Proceedings: Vol. 5). 250p. 1988. 34.00 (*0-937707-22-8*) Astron Soc Pacific.

***Dickey, Jacqueline.** When the Believer's Chin Points Toward the Moon. 52p. 1999. pap. 8.95 (*0-9636224-6-3*) Rose Hill Bks.

D

Dickey, James. Buckdancer's Choice: Poems. LC 65-21079. (Wesleyan Poetry Program Ser.: Vol. 28). 79p. (C). 1965. pap. 12.95 (*0-8195-1028-9*, Wesleyan Univ Pr) U Pr of New Eng.

***Dickey, James.** Crux: The Letters of James Dickey. Bruccoli, Matthew & Baughman, Judith S., eds. LC 99-15608. 576p. 1999. 35.00 (*0-375-40419-8*) Knopf.

Dickey, James. Deliverance. 1976. 25.95 (*0-8488-0476-7*) Amereon Ltd.

— Deliverance. 278p. 1994. pap. 12.95 (*0-385-31387-X*, Delta Trade) Dell.

— The Eagle's Mile. (Poster Poem Ser.). 1981. 20.00 (*0-89723-028-0*) Bruccoli.

— The Eagle's Mile. LC 89-49257. (Wesleyan Poetry Ser.). 76p. 1990. pap. 12.95 (*0-8195-1187-0*, Wesleyan Univ Pr) U Pr of New Eng.

— The Eagle's Mile. limited ed. (Poster Poem Ser.). 1981. 90.00 (*0-89723-029-9*) Bruccoli.

— God's Images: A New Vision. LC 78-17465. (Illus.). 110p. (Orig.). 1984. reprint ed. 7.95 (*0-8164-2194-3*) Harper SF.

— James Dickey: The Selected Poems. Kirschten, Robert, ed. & intro. by. LC 98-24045. (Wesleyan Poetry Ser.). 200p. 1998. pap. 16.95 (*0-8195-2260-0*, Wesleyan Univ Pr); text 35.00 (*0-8195-2259-7*, Wesleyan Univ Pr) U Pr of New Eng.

***Dickey, James.** The James Dickey Reader. Hart, Henry, ed. LC 99-23976. 528p. 1999. pap. 16.00 (*0-684-86435-5*, Touchstone) S&S Trade Pap.

Dickey, James. Night Hurdling. 1983. 50.00 (*0-89723-038-8*) Bruccoli.

— Night Hurdling. limited ed. 1983. 100.00 (*0-89723-040-X*) Bruccoli.

— Starry Place Between the Antlers: Why I Live in South Carolina. deluxe limited ed. 1981. 60.00 (*0-89723-031-0*) Bruccoli.

— Striking In: The Early Notebooks of James Dickey. Van Ness, Gordan, ed. & intro. by. 304p. (C). 1996. 39.95 (*0-8262-1056-2*) U of Mo Pr.

— Summons. deluxe limited ed. (Poster Poem Ser.). 1988. 100.00 (*0-89723-051-5*) Bruccoli.

— To the White Sea. 288p. 1994. pap. 11.95 (*0-385-31309-8*, Delta Trade) Dell.

— To the White Sea. large type ed. LC 93-47354. 1994. 24.95 (*1-56895-046-2*) Wheeler Pub.

— The Water-Bug's Mittens. limited ed. 1980. 80.00 (*0-89723-021-3*) Bruccoli.

— The Whole Motion: Collected Poems, 1945-1992. LC 91-50811. (Wesleyan Poetry Ser.). 494p. 1992. pap. 19.95 (*0-8195-1218-4*, Wesleyan Univ Pr) U Pr of New Eng.

— The Zodiac. deluxe limited ed. 1976. boxed set 1000.00 (*0-89723-018-3*) Bruccoli.

Dickey, James. In Pursuit of the Grey Soul. limited ed. 1978. 100.00 (*0-89723-004-3*) Bruccoli.

Dickey, Jerry. Sophie Treadwell: A Research & Production Sourcebook, 12. LC 96-43986. (Modern Dramatists Research & Production Sourcebooks: Vol. 12). 288p. 1997. lib. bdg. 79.50 (*0-313-29388-0*, Greenwood Pr) Greenwood.

***Dickey, John L., II.** A Family Saga: Flush Deck Destroyers 1917-1955. (Illus.). 279p. 2000. pap. 32.50 (*0-9679826-0-X*) J L Dickey.

Dickey, John S. On the Rocks: Earth Science for Everyone. LC 95-46167. (Illus.). 280p. 1996. pap. 16.95 (*0-471-13234-9*) Wiley.

Dickey, John S., ed. The United States & Canada. LC 64-21215. 1964. 3.95 (*0-317-02965-7*, C-93839); pap. 1.95 (*0-317-02966-5*, P-93838) Am Assembly.

Dickey, John W. CyberQuest: Problem Solving & Innovation Support System, Conceptual Background & Experiences. (Creativity Research Ser.). (Illus.). 328p. 1993. pap. 39.50 (*1-56750-117-6*); text 73.25 (*1-56750-113-3*) Ablx Pub.

Dickey, John W. & Miller, Leon H. Road Project Appraisal for Developing Countries. LC 83-10270. (Illus.). 293p. reprint ed. pap. 90.90 (*0-8357-3519-2*, 203422200089) Bks Demand.

Dickey, John W., et al. Metropolitan Transportation Planning. 2nd ed. 607p. 1983. pap. 75.00 (*0-89116-922-9*) Taylor & Francis.

Dickey, Karlene N. Denmark: A Study of the Educational System of Denmark & A Guide to the Academic Placement of Students in Educational Institutions in the United States. LC 94-33741. (PIER World Education Ser.). 1995. 50.00 (*0-929851-24-2*) Am Assn Coll Registrars.

— Slovenia: A Study of the Educational System of the Republic of Slovenia. Wakefield, Henny, ed. (PIER Working Paper Ser.). 126p. (C). 1995. 25.00 (*0-929851-34-X*) Am Assn Coll Registrars.

— Switzerland: A Study of the Educational System of Switzerland & a Guide to the Academic Placement of Students from Switzerland in Educational Institutions of the United States. LC 81-1240. (World Education Ser.). 142p. reprint ed. pap. 44.10 (*0-608-18336-9*, 203301300082) Bks Demand.

Dickey, Karlene N. & Bevis, Desmond, eds. The Admission & Placement of Students from the Republic of Hungary. (PIER Reports (Projects in International Education Research Workshop Reports)). (Illus.). 128p. (Orig.). 1990. pap. 30.00 (*0-929851-03-X*) Am Assn Coll Registrars.

— The Admission & Placement of Students from Yugoslavia. (PIER Reports (Projects in International Education Research Workshop Reports)). (Illus.). 112p. (Orig.). 1990. pap. 30.00 (*0-929851-04-8*) Am Assn Coll Registrars.

Dickey, Karlene N. & Lukas, Karen. Swiss Higher Schools of Engineering & Swiss Higher Schools of Economics & Business Administration. 1991. pap. 20.00 (*0-910054-95-9*) Am Assn Coll Registrars.

Dickey, Karlene N., jt. auth. see Feagles, Shelley M.

Dickey, Karlene N., jt. auth. see Zanotti, Kathleen.

Dickey, L. A. Soliton Equations & Hamiltonian Systems. 320p. (C). 1991. text 44.00 (*981-02-0215-6*) World Scientific Pub.

— String Figures from Hawaii, Including Some from New Hebrides & Gilbert Islands. (BMB Ser.: No. 54). 1974. reprint ed. 35.00 (*0-527-02160-1*) Periodicals Srv.

Dickey, Larry L. Clinician's Handbook of Preventive Services: Put Prevention into Practice. 2nd ed. (Illus.). 524p. (C). 1998. pap. text 60.00 (*0-7881-7246-8*) DIANE Pub.

Dickey, Larry W. Kids Travel on Commodore 64. write for info. (*0-318-59631-8*) S&S Trade.

***Dickey, Laurel.** Balloon. (Illus.). 1999. pap. 3.75 (*1-58453-028-6*) Pioneer MA.

— Hard at Work. (Illus.). 1999. pap. 3.75 (*1-58453-029-4*) Pioneer MA.

— I Love Camping. (Illus.). 1999. pap. 3.75 (*1-58453-025-1*) Pioneer MA.

— Where Are We? (Illus.). 1999. pap. 3.75 (*1-58453-026-X*) Pioneer MA.

— Zack's House. (Illus.). 1999. pap. 3.75 (*1-58453-036-7*) Pioneer MA.

***Dickey, Laurel & Dufresne, Michele.** Early Emergent, Set 2. (Illus.). 1999. pap. 16.25 (*1-58453-030-8*) Pioneer MA.

— Early Emergent Set 2: Classroom Collection. (Illus.). 1999. pap. 90.00 (*1-58453-071-5*) Pioneer MA.

— Early Emergent Books, Set 1. (Illus.). 1998. pap. 22.50 (*1-58453-032-4*) Pioneer MA.

— Emergent Set 1: Classroom Collection. (Illus.). 1998. pap. 135.00 (*1-58453-070-7*) Pioneer MA.

— Emergent Set 2: Classroom Collection. (Illus.). 1999. pap. 90.00 (*1-58453-074-X*) Pioneer MA.

— Emergent Books, Set 2. (Illus.). 1999. pap. 16.50 (*1-58453-033-2*) Pioneer MA.

Dickey, Laurel, jt. auth. see Dufresne, Michele.

Dickey, Lawrence, ed. see Hegel, Georg Wilhelm Friedrich.

Dickey, Lew. The Franchise (Book) Building Radio Brands. 150p. 1994. pap. 39.95 (*0-89324-221-7*, 3671) Natl Assn Broadcasters.

***Dickey, Lois.** His Sneakers Didn't Match My Formal. LC 00-190066. 313p. 2000. pap. 9.95 (*0-9678882-2-0*) MBrio Bks.

— My Bunny Slippers Didn't Match His Career. 319p. 2000. pap. 9.95 (*0-9678882-5-5*) MBrio Bks.

Dickey, Lynn E. & Weihrauch, John L. Composition on Foods: Fast Foods (Raw, Processed, Prepared) (Illus.). 193p. 1998. reprint ed. pap. text 30.00 (*0-7881-4328-X*) DIANE Pub.

Dickey, Page. Breaking Ground: Portraits of Ten Garden Designers. LC 97-15288. (Illus.). 208p. 1997. 45.00 (*1-885183-37-2*) Artisan.

***Dickey, Page.** Inside Out. 2000. 35.00 (*1-58479-046-6*) Stewart Tabori & Chang.

Dickey, Page. Vines & Climbers. (Taylor's Weekend Gardening Guide Ser.). 1999. pap. write for info. (*0-395-82941-0*) HM.

Dickey, Parke A. Petroleum Development Geology. 3rd ed. LC 81-11943. 544p. 1986. 25.00 (*0-87814-307-6*) PennWell Bks.

Dickey, Parke A., jt. ed. see Mason, John F.

Dickey, R. P. Self-Liberation: How to Face up to Reality & Enjoy It. LC 98-85386. 325p. 1998. 25.00 (*0-9663501-6-2*); pap. 15.00 (*0-7388-0024-4*) Xlibris Corp.

Dickey, R. P. & O'Brien, Mary K. Exercise Anytime: The Complete Don't Take Time Out to Exercise Plan. LC 98-86294. 325p. 1998. 25.00 (*0-7388-0059-7*); pap. 15.00 (*0-7388-0060-0*) Xlibris Corp.

Dickey, Richard P. Managing Contraceptive Pill Patients. 9th ed. LC 98-194210. 351p. 1998. pap. write for info. (*0-929240-84-7*) EMIS.

***Dickey, Richard P.** Managing Contraceptive Pill Patients. 9th ed. LC 76-29294. 1999. 17.95 (*0-917634-00-4*) EMIS.

— Managing Contraceptive Pill Patients. 10th rev. ed. (Illus.). 245p. 2000. pap. 17.95 (*0-917634-05-5*) EMIS.

Dickey, Richard P. Managing Danazol Patients. 2nd ed. 137p. 1992. pap. 12.95 (*0-929240-35-9*) EMIS.

Dickey, Roland F. New Mexico Village Arts. LC 90-33107. (Illus.). 280p. 1990. reprint ed. pap. 86.80 (*0-608-04130-0*, 206486300011) Bks Demand.

Dickey, Sara, jt. ed. see Adams, Kathleen M.

Dickey, Stephanie, ed. The Illustrated Bartsch Vol. 50: Rembrandt van Rijn. (Illus.). 1993. lib. bdg. 149.00 (*0-89835-048-4*) Abaris Bks.

***Dickey, Stephen M.** Parameters of Slavic Aspect. (Dissertations in Linguistics Ser.: Vol. 19). 225p. (C). 2000. text 59.95 (*1-57586-235-2*, Pub. by CSLI) Cambridge U Pr.

— Parameters of Slavic Aspect. (Dissertations in Linguistics Ser.: Vol. 192). 225p. (C). 2000. pap. 22.95 (*1-57586-236-0*, Pub. by CSLI) Cambridge U Pr.

Dickey, Terry. The Basics of Budgeting: A Practice Guide to Better Business Planning. Hicks, Tony, ed. LC 91-76241. (Fifty-Minute Ser.). 139p. 1992. pap. 10.95 (*1-56052-134-1*) Crisp Pubns.

— Budgeting for a Small Business: A Primer for Entrepreneurs. Manber, Beverly, ed. LC 92-54352. (Small Business & Entrepreneurship Ser.). 235p. (Orig.). 1993. pap. 15.95 (*1-56052-171-6*) Crisp Pubns.

— Using Business Statistics: A Guide for Beginners. Carrigan, Chris, ed. LC 93-72980. (Fifty-Minute Ser.). (Illus.). 115p. (Orig.). 1994. pap. 10.95 (*1-56052-250-X*) Crisp Pubns.

Dickey, Terry P., ed. see Carlo, Jean F. & Fosdick, Rose A.

Dickey, Terry P., ed. see Goodwin, Mary.

Dickey, Terry P., ed. see Yarber, Yvonne & Choy, Carol E.

Dickey, Thomas S. & George, Peter C. Field Artillery Projectiles of the American Civil War. McRae, Floyd W., Jr., ed. (Illus.). 505p. 1982. 29.95 (*0-686-35978-X*) Arsenal Pubns.

Dickey, Tina, jt. auth. see Friedel, Helmut.

Dickey, W. The Sacrifice Consenting. 60p. 1982. ring bd. 100.00 (*0-931757-10-X*); boxed set 17.00 (*0-931757-09-6*) Pterodactyl Pr.

Dickey, W. L. Fiscal Aspects of American Federalism: The Case of South Dakota. 1964. 1.00 (*1-55614-042-8*) U of SD Gov Res Bur.

Dickey, Walter L., jt. auth. see Schneider, Robert R.

Dickey, William. The Education of Desire. LC 96-1888. (Wesleyan Poetry Ser.). 83p. 1996. pap. 12.95 (*0-8195-2236-8*, Wesleyan Univ Pr); text 25.00 (*0-8195-2235-X*, Wesleyan Univ Pr) U Pr of New Eng.

— In the Dreaming: Selected Poems. LC 93-1098. 1994. pap. 12.00 (*1-55728-286-2*) U of Ark Pr.

— The King of the Golden River. 76p. (Orig.). 1985. 25.00 (*0-931757-17-7*); pap. 15.00 (*0-931757-18-5*) Pterodactyl Pr.

— Of the Festivity. LC 70-144759. (Yale Series of Younger Poets: No. 55). reprint ed. 18.00 (*0-404-53855-X*) AMS Pr.

— Six Philosophical Songs. 16p. 1983. 10.00 (*0-931757-13-4*) Pterodactyl Pr.

Dickey, William L. The New Federalism: The Administration's Approach to Intergovernmental Relations. 1970. 1.00 (*1-55614-068-1*) U of SD Gov Res Bur.

Dickhardt, R. Homakaryotisierung von Basidiomyceten. (Bibliotheca Mycologica Ser.: No. 95). (Illus.). 136p. 1985. pap. text 40.00 (*3-7682-1427-3*) Lubrecht & Cramer.

Dickhaut, Sebastian, jt. auth. see Saelzer, Sabine.

Dickhoff, Robert E. The Eternal Fountain. 128p. 1996. spiral bd. 12.50 (*0-7873-0288-0*) Hlth Research.

— Homecoming of the Martians. 175p. 1996. reprint ed. spiral bd. 11.50 (*0-7873-0289-9*) Hlth Research.

Dickhoff, Wilfred, jt. auth. see Diacono, Mario.

***Dickhoff, Wilfried.** After Nihilism: Essays on Contemporary Art. (Contemporary Artists & Their Critics Ser.). (Illus.). 304p. (C). 2000. 74.95 (*0-521-59294-1*); pap. 29.95 (*0-521-59698-X*) Cambridge U Pr.

Dickhoff, Wilfried, text. George Condo: Recent Paintings. LC 91-60368. (Illus.). 42p. 1991. pap. write for info. (*1-878283-15-4*) PaceWildenstein.

Dickhoner, Elaine M. Le Gourmet Microwave. Mattingly, Mary, ed. (Illus.). 204p. (Orig.). 1982. pap. 7.95 (*0-910601-00-3*) Creat Res OH.

Dickich, Nadja. Catalina Island Book AAA. Miller, Kristine, ed. 1999. 4.95 (*1-56413-390-7*) Auto Club.

***Dickie, Carl D.** Corporate Life to Small Business with Reduced Risk. 48p. 1999. pap. 9.95 (*0-9674307-0-4*) C D Dickie Assocs.

Dickie, George. The Art Circle: A Theory of Art. 116p. 1997. pap. 12.95 (*1-886094-70-5*) Chicago Spectrum.

— The Art Circle: A Theory of Art. LC 83-83295. 1984. 45.00 (*0-930586-37-9*) Haven Pubns.

— The Century of Taste: The Philosophical Odyssey of Taste in the Eighteenth Century. 168p. 1996. text 45.00 (*0-19-509680-0*) OUP.

— Evaluating Art. LC 88-29541. 208p. (C). 1988. 32.95 (*0-87722-597-4*) Temple U Pr.

— Evaluating Art. 208p. 1989. pap. 19.95 (*0-87722-683-0*) Temple U Pr.

— Introduction to Aesthetics: An Analytic Approach. 208p. (C). 1997. text 44.00 (*0-19-511303-9*); pap. text 23.95 (*0-19-511304-7*) OUP.

Dickie, George, et al, eds. Aesthetics: A Critical Anthology. 669p. (C). 1989. text. write for info. (*0-318-68122-6*) St Martin.

Dickie, George & Sclafani, Richard J. Aesthetics: A Critical Anthology. 2nd ed. Roblin, Ronald, ed. LC 88-60543. 678p. (C). 1989. pap. text 65.95 (*0-312-00309-9*) St Martin.

Dickie, John. Boys on the Bongo Bus. 1997. 24.95 (*1-86020-534-8*, Pub. by U of Luton Pr) Bks Intl VA.

— The Boys on the Bongo Bus. 1997. 40.00 (*1-86020-543-7*, Pub. by U of Luton Pr) Bks Intl VA.

— Darkest Italy. LC 99-23083. 209p. 1999. text 45.00 (*0-312-22168-1*) St Martin.

***Dickie, John.** Internet & Electronic Commerce Law in the European Union. 224p. 1999. pap. 54.00 (*1-84113-031-1*, Pub. by Hart Pub) Intl Spec Bk.

Dickie, Julie S. & Hoffman, Catherine S. Bobcat Meets Pippy Gordon. (Series of Tuck Ins). (Illus.). (J). (gr. k-5). 1996. pap. 8.95 (*0-938985-17-5*) Mntn Memories Bks.

— Bobcat's Magical Adventure. (Series of Tuck Ins). (Illus.). 15p. (Orig.). (J). (ps-4). 1996. reprint ed. pap. 8.95 (*0-938985-18-3*) Mntn Memories Bks.

Dickie, Margaret. Lyric Contingencies: Emily Dickinson & Wallace Stevens. LC 90-48495. 192p. (C). 1991. text 28.50 (*0-8122-3077-9*) U of Pa Pr.

— On the Modernist Long Poem. LC 85-20958. 190p. 1986. pap. text 24.95 (*0-87745-140-0*) U of Iowa Pr.

— Stein, Bishop, & Rich: Lyrics of Love, War, & Place. LC 96-9615. 272p. (C). 1997. 17.95 (*0-8078-4622-8*) U of NC Pr.

— Stein, Bishop, & Rich: Lyrics of Love, War, & Place. LC 96-9615. 272p. (C). (gr. 13). 1997. 49.95 (*0-8078-2308-2*) U of NC Pr.

Dickie, Margaret & Travisano, Thomas J., eds. Gendered Modernisms: American Women Poets & Their Readers. (Illus.). 352p. 1996. text 44.95 (*0-8122-3312-3*) U of Pa Pr.

— Gendered Modernisms: Women Poets & Their Readers. (Illus.). 352p. 1996. pap. text 18.95 (*0-8122-1550-8*) U of Pa Pr.

Dickie, Margaret, jt. ed. see Warren, Joyce W.

Dickie, Mark. Routing in Today's Internetworks: The Routing Protocols of IP, DECnet, NetWare, & AppleTalk. 273p. 1993. 48.95 (*0-471-28620-6*, VNR) Wiley.

Dickie, Mark. Routing in Today's Internetworks: The Routing Protocols of IP, DECnet, NetWare, & AppleTalk. (Illus.). 273p. 1993. 48.95 (*0-442-01811-8*, VNR) Wiley.

Dickie, Matthew, jt. ed. see Andersen, Oivind.

***Dickie, Paul M., frwd.** Regional Workshop on Solar Power Generation Using Photovoltaic Technology: Proceedings. (Illus.). 402p. (C). 1999. reprint ed. pap. text 35.00 (*0-7881-8264-1*) DIANE Pub.

Dickie, Phil. The Road to Fitzgerald & Beyond. rev. ed. 1989. pap. 16.95 (*0-7022-2244-5*, Pub. by Univ Queensland Pr) Intl Spec Bk.

Dickie, R. A., jt. ed. see Labana, S. S.

Dickie, R. A., ed. & tr. see Goldman, A. Ya.

Dickie, Ray A., et al, eds. Cross-Linked Polymers: Chemistry, Properties, & Applications. LC 88-3327. (Symposium Ser.: No. 367). (Illus.). 504p. 1988. text 110.00 (*0-8412-1471-9*, Pub. by Am Chemical) OUP.

Dickie, Ray A. & Floyd, F. Louis, eds. Polymeric Materials for Corrosion Control. LC 86-20646. (ACS Symposium Ser.: No. 322). (Illus.). ix, 359p. 1986. 76.95 (*0-8412-0998-7*) Am Chemical.

— Polymeric Materials for Corrosion Control. LC 86-20646. (ACS Symposium Ser.: Vol. 322). 384p. 1986. reprint ed. pap. 119.10 (*0-608-03526-2*, 206424500008) Bks Demand.

Dickie, Robert B. Financial Statement Analysis & Business Valuation for the Practical Lawyer. LC 98-8104. xiii, 269p. 1998. 119.00 (*1-57073-499-2*) Amer Bar Assn.

Dickie, Robert B. & Rouner, Leroy S., eds. Corporations & the Common Good. LC 85-40597. 160p. 1986. text 23.00 (*0-268-00754-3*); pap. text 10.50 (*0-268-00761-6*) U of Notre Dame Pr.

Dickie, Ruth S. Time of Transition: Women in Science: History of Sigma Delta Epsilon - Graduate Women in Science, Inc., 1979-1986 Supplement. LC 88-61097. (Orig.). 1988. pap. 2.00 (*0-9620513-3-0*) Sigma Delta Epsilon.

Dickie, Steve & Pearson, Darrell. Creative Junior High Programs from A to Z Vol. 1: 13 Complete, Ready-to-Use Topical Meetings, Vol. 1 (A-M) LC 96-20119. 96p. 1996. pap. 14.99 (*0-310-20779-7*) Youth Spec.

Dickins, Anthony S. & Ebert, Hilmar. One Hundred Classics of the Chessboard. (Chess Ser.). 208p. 1983. 25.90 (*0-08-026921-4*, Pergamon Pr); pap. 13.90 (*0-08-026920-6*, Pergamon Pr) Elsevier.

Dickins, Barry. The Crookes of Epping. 156p. (C). 1990. 35.00 (*0-9592104-3-1*, Pub. by Pascoe Pub) St Mut.

— Guts & Pity: The Hanging That Ended Capital Punishment in Australia. (Illus.). 100p. 1995. 14.95 (*0-86819-424-7*, Pub. by Currency Pr) Accents Pubns.

— Ron Truffle: His Life & Bump Out. 140p. (C). 1990. 30.00 (*0-947087-10-9*, Pub. by Pascoe Pub) St Mut.

Dickins, Bruce & Ross, Alan S., eds. The Dream of the Rood. (Old English Ser.). 1966. pap. text 9.95 (*0-89197-567-5*) Irvington.

***Dickins, Douglas.** In Granpa's Footsteps: A World Traveler's Autobiography. (Illus.). 176p. 2000. 29.50 (*1-85776-459-5*, Pub. by Book Guild Ltd) Trans-Atl Phila.

Dickins, Guy. Hellenistic Sculpture. Date not set. write for info. (*0-8434-0129-X*, Pub. by McGrath NH) Ayer.

— Hellenistic Sculpture. (Select Bibliographies Reprint Ser.). 1972. reprint ed. 19.75 (*0-8369-9960-6*) Ayer.

Dickins, J. M., et al, eds. Late Palaeozoic & Early Mesozoic Circum-Pacific Events & Their Global Correlation. (World & Regional Geology Ser.: No. 10). (Illus.). 255p. (C). 1997. text 115.00 (*0-521-47175-3*) Cambridge U Pr.

Dickins, James. Extended Axiomatic Linguistics. LC 98-23957. (Trends in Linguistics Ser.: No. 111). 512p. 1998. 132.00 (*3-11-016086-2*) De Gruyter.

***Dickins, James & Watson, Janet.** Standard Arabic: An Advanced Course. 612p. (C). 1999. 15.95 incl. audio (*0-521-63531-4*) Cambridge U Pr.

Dickins, James & Watson, Janet. Standard Arabic: An Advanced Student's Book. LC 98-21906. (Illus.). 612p. (C). 1999. text, teacher ed. 74.95 (*0-521-63211-0*); pap. text, teacher ed. 29.95 (*0-521-63558-6*) Cambridge U Pr.

Dickins, James & Watson, Janet C. E. Standard Arabic: An Advanced Course: Teacher's Handbook & Key to the Exercises. LC 98-38447. 192p. 1999. text 59.95 (*0-521-63161-0*) Cambridge U Pr.

Dickins, Roberts, jt. auth. see Brown, Hayden.

Dickinson. Annual Editions: Dying, Death, & Bereavement. 4th ed. 1997. pap. text 11.10 (*0-697-39295-3*) McGraw.

— Dallas Oil, Incorporated. (KM - Office Proceudres Ser.). 1985. pap. 16.95 (*0-538-25950-7*) S-W Pub.

— Dallas Oil, Incorporated. 2nd ed. (KM - Office Procedures Ser.). 1989. mass mkt. 11.25 (*0-538-60170-1*) S-W Pub.

— Fire Service Emergency Care. LC 98-25811. 1998. 48.00 (*0-8359-5279-7*); pap. text 57.00 (*0-8359-5133-2*) P-H.

— Plate Tectonics. 384p. (C). 1999. write for info. (*0-02-329640-2*, Macmillan Coll) P-H.

— Retailing. (SB - Marketing Education Ser.). 1997. pap., wbk. ed. 12.95 (*0-538-82687-8*) S-W Pub.

— A Summer in the Twenties. 1987. 4.95 (*0-07-541648-4*) McGraw.

— Understanding Family. 2nd ed. (C). 1994. pap. text, teacher ed. 33.75 (*0-15-502144-3*) Harcourt Coll Pubs.

Dickinson, jt. auth. see Czaja, Albert J.

D

An Asterisk (*) at the beginning of an entry indicates that the title is appearing for the first time.

Dickinson, A. & Boakes, R. A., eds. Mechanisms of Learning & Motivation: A Memorial Volume to Jerzy Konorski. 460p. 1979. 79.95 (*0-89859-460-X*) L Erlbaum Assocs.

Dickinson, Addie M. & Dickinson Association Staff. Dickinson: Descendants of Nathaniel Dickinson. (Illus.). 387p. 1997. reprint ed. pap. 58.00 (*0-8328-8290-9*); reprint ed. lib. bdg. 68.00 (*0-8328-8289-5*) Higginson Bk Co.

Dickinson, Alan E. Bach's Fugal Works. LC 78-25706. 280p. 1979. reprint ed. lib. bdg. 65.00 (*0-8371-6817-1*, DIBF, Greenwood Pr) Greenwood.

— A Study of Mozart's Last Three Symphonies. 58p. 1990. reprint ed. lib. bdg. 59.00 (*0-7812-0231-0*, 10,163) Rprt Serv.

— A Study of Mozart's Last Three Symphonies. LC 73-181142. 1927. reprint ed. 49.00 (*0-403-01543-X*) Scholarly.

— Vaughan Williams. 1988. reprint ed. lib. bdg. 79.00 (*0-7812-0245-0*) Rprt Serv.

— Vaughan Williams. LC 70-181141. 540p. 1963. reprint ed. 79.00 (*0-403-01542-1*) Scholarly.

Dickinson, Alaric, et al, eds. International Yearbook of History Education, Vol. 1. (Woburn Education Ser.). 232p. (C). 1995. 47.50 (*0-7130-0188-7*, Pub. by Woburn Pr) Intl Spec Bk.

Dickinson, Alis, jt. ed. see Adkins, Cecil.

Dickinson, Alyce M., jt. auth. see Redmon, William K.

Dickinson, AmieBeth & George, Denise. Who Moved the Line? Buck, William et al, eds. LC 96-86502. (Illus.). 175p. (Orig.). 1996. pap. 12.95 (*0-934530-10-6*) Buck Pub.

***Dickinson, Amy.** Web Design for Journalism. (Illus.). 320p. 2000. pap. 37.95 (*0-240-51626-5*, Focal) Buttrwrth-Heinemann.

Dickinson, Amy, jt. ed. see Garchow, Karen.

Dickinson, Andy, jt. auth. see Ward, Mike.

***Dickinson, Anna E.** A Ragged Register. (Illus.). 2000. pap. 12.95 (*1-928878-09-1*) Temporal Mech Pr.

Dickinson, Anna E. What Answer? LC 71-138646. (Black Heritage Library Collection). 1977. reprint ed. 22.95 (*0-8369-9004-8*) Ayer.

Dickinson Association Staff, jt. auth. see Dickinson, Addie M.

Dickinson, B. W., ed. see Bohlin, T., et al.

Dickinson, B. W., ed. see Brogliato, Bernard.

Dickinson, B. W., ed. see Chen, Ben M.

Dickinson, B. W., ed. see De Wilde, Philippe.

Dickinson, B. W., ed. see Isidori, Alberto.

Dickinson, B. W., ed. see Kaufman, H. & Bar-Kana, I.

Dickinson, B. W., ed. see Krstic, M., et al.

Dickinson, B. W., ed. see Landau, I. D., et al.

Dickinson, B. W., ed. see Luo, Zheng-hua, et al.

***Dickinson, Barbara M.** A Rebellious House. LC 97-23505. (Illus.). 242p. 1999. pap. 19.95 (*1-55618-185-X*) Brunswick Pub.

Dickinson, Barbara M. A Rebellious House: A Novel. LC 97-23505. (Illus.). 242p. 1997. 24.95 (*1-55618-165-5*) Brunswick Pub.

— Small House, Large World. LC 99-29306. (Illus.). 237p. 1999. pap. 19.95 (*1-55618-182-5*) Brunswick Pub.

Dickinson, Bill. Diggin' for Roots in Old Virginia. LC 95-142199. 165p. 1999. pap. 24.95 (*0-8063-4532-2*, 9101) Clearfield Co.

Dickinson, Bill, jt. auth. see Aspin, Lee.

Dickinson, Bob. Imprinting the Sticks: The Alternative Press Beyond London. LC 97-17223. (Popular Cultural Studies). 1997. 73.95 (*1-85742-234-1*, Pub. by Arena); pap. 36.95 (*1-85742-235-X*, Pub. by Arena) Ashgate Pub Co.

— Music & the Earth Spirit. (Orig.). 1999. pap. write for info. (*1-898307-89-X*, Pub. by Capall Bann Pubng) Holmes Pub.

Dickinson, Brian. The Business Engineering Methodology. (Business Engineering Ser.). (Illus.). 200p. 1999. pap. text 29.95 (*0-9629276-4-3*) LCI Pr.

— Creating Customer Focused Organizations. (The Business Engineering Ser.). Orig. Title: Risk Free Business Re-Engineering. (Illus.). 280p. 1998. pap. text 29.95 (*0-9629276-3-5*) LCI Pr.

— Developing Structured Systems: A Methodology Using Structured Techniques. LC 80-54609. (Illus.). 360p. 1986. pap. 39.95 (*0-917072-23-5*, Yourdon) P-H.

— Logical Business Engineering Analysis. (Business Engineering Ser.). (Illus.). 250p. 1999. pap. text 29.95 (*0-9629276-5-1*) LCI Pr.

— Risk-Free Business Re-Engineering: How to Re-Engineer Your Organization Using Business Event Partitioning to Achieve Ultimate Customer Satisfaction. (Business Re-Engineering Methodology Ser.). (Illus.). 296p. Date not set. text 39.95 (*0-9629276-2-7*) LCI Pr.

— Strategic Business Engineering: A Synergy of Software Engineering & Information Engineering. LC 91-60471. (Illus.). 236p. (Orig.). 1992. pap. text 27.95 (*0-9629276-0-0*) LCI Pr.

Dickinson, C. C., ed. see Lane, Byron.

Dickinson, C. E. History of Belpre, Washington County. (Illus.). 243p. 1995. reprint ed. lib. bdg. 34.00 (*0-8328-5092-6*) Higginson Bk Co.

Dickinson, C. H., jt. auth. see Lucas, John A.

Dickinson, C. J. Neurogenic Hypertension: A Synthesis & Review. 1991. 94.95 (*0-442-31414-0*) Chapman & Hall.

Dickinson, Calvin W. & Whiteaker, Larry. Tennessee in American Histroy. 2nd ed. (C). 1991. pap. text 35.00 (*0-536-58007-3*) Pearson Custom.

Dickinson, Charles. Crows. 304p. 1993. reprint ed. pap. 11.00 (*0-380-71950-9*, Avon Bks) Morrow Avon.

— One Thing Necessary. (C). 1989. 29.00 (*0-7223-2274-7*, Pub. by A H S Ltd) St Mut.

— Waltz in Marathon. 272p. 1993. reprint ed. pap. 10.00 (*0-380-71949-5*, Avon Bks) Morrow Avon.

***Dickinson, Charles.** The Widows' Adventures. 400p. 1999. reprint ed. pap. 12.50 (*0-380-70847-7*, Avon Bks) Morrow Avon.

Dickinson, Charles. With or Without. 160p. 1993. reprint ed. pap. 9.00 (*0-380-71951-7*, Avon Bks) Morrow Avon.

Dickinson, Charles R. & Vance, David. Texas Angler's Guide: Your Personal Guide to Fishing Texas' Top Lakes. Dickinson, T., ed. 200p. (Orig.). 1994. pap. 14.00 (*0-9639724-0-5*) Print Comm.

Dickinson, Christine. Low Vision in Optometric Practice. LC 98-28062. (Illus.). 320p. 1998. pap. text 65.00 (*0-7506-2262-8*) Buttrwrth-Heinemann.

Dickinson, Christine, et al, eds. John Dalton's Colour Vision Legacy. LC 97-139108. 784p. 1997. text 115.00 (*0-7484-0310-8*, Pub. by Tay Francis Ltd) Taylor & Francis.

Dickinson, Clarence E. Flying Guns: Cockpit Record of a Naval Pilot from Pearl Harbor Through Midway. LC 79-21837. 1980. reprint ed. 15.95 (*0-89201-090-8*) Zenger Pub.

Dickinson, Curtis. What the Bible Teaches about Immortality & Future Punishment. 1992. 6.99 (*0-87377-974-6*) GAM Pubns.

Dickinson, Curtis, jt. auth. see Dabney, R. L.

Dickinson, David & Mullineux, Andrew W., eds. Finance, Governance & Economic Performance in Pacific & South East Asia. 320p. 2000. write for info. (*1-85898-973-6*) E Elgar.

Dickinson, David G., et al, eds. Risk & Uncertainty in Economics: Essays in Honour of James L. Ford. 240p. 1995. 95.00 (*1-85278-736-8*) E Elgar.

Dickinson, David K., intro. Bridges to Literacy: Children, Families & Schools. LC 93-27158. (Illus.). 288p. 1994. pap. text 26.95 (*1-55786-373-3*) Blackwell Pubs.

Dickinson, Debbi. Heartsongs. 20p. (Orig.). 1995. pap. text 6.00 (*0-9647108-8-9*) D Dickinson.

— Whispers in the Wind. 20p. 1995. pap. text 6.00 (*0-9647108-5-4*) D Dickinson.

Dickinson, Dee, ed. Creating the Future. (Illus.). 240p. (Orig.). (C). 1991. pap. text 15.95 (*0-905553-32-2*, Pub. by Accel Lrn Sys) McClelland & Stewart.

***Dickinson, Dolly.** Moving On: Quiet Moments for the Divorced. 2000. pap. 10.99 (*1-56955-232-0*) Servant.

Dickinson, Don. Blue Husbands. 128p. 1991. pap. write for info. (*0-88984-123-3*) Porcup Quill.

Dickinson, Donald C. Dictionary of American Antiquarian Bookdealers. LC 97-40856. 288p. 1998. lib. bdg. 75.00 (*0-313-26675-1*, Greenwood Pr) Greenwood.

— Dictionary of American Book Collectors. LC 85-5580. 399p. 1986. lib. bdg. 75.00 (*0-313-22544-3*, DBC/, Greenwood Pr) Greenwood.

— George Watson Cole, 1850-1939. LC 90-31210. (Great Bibliographers Ser.: No. 8). 266p. 1990. 34.50 (*0-8108-2261-X*) Scarecrow.

— Henry E. Huntington's Library of Libraries. LC 95-10396. (Illus.). 286p. 1995. 24.95 (*0-87328-153-5*) Huntington Lib.

Dickinson, Donald J. Matching Consultation, Assessment, & Intervention. LC 93-79581. (Illus.). 310p. (C). 1993. pap. text 18.00 (*0-9637951-4-7*) Hart-Whitlow Pubs.

Dickinson, Duo. Expressive Details: Materials, Selection, Use. LC 96-12959. (Illus.). 192p. 1996. 49.95 (*0-07-016833-4*) McGraw.

— The Small House for the Next Century. 2nd ed. 272p. 1995. 44.95 (*0-07-016828-8*) McGraw.

Dickinson, E. Life Time Eternity. pap. 10.95 (*0-8027-2601-1*) Walker & Co.

Dickinson, E. & Bergenstahl, B., eds. Food Colloids Proteins, Lipids & Polysaccharides. (Special Publication Ser.: No. 192). x, 418p. 1997. 198.00 (*0-85404-776-X*) Am Chemical.

Dickinson, E. & Lorient, D., eds. Food Macromolecules & Colloids: Proceedings. 380p. 1995. 169.95 (*0-85404-700-X*, R4700) CRC Pr.

***Dickinson, E. & Patino, J. M. Rodriguez, eds.** Food Emulsions & Foams: Interfaces, Interactions & Stability. 420p. 1999. 198.00 (*0-85404-753-0*, Pub. by Royal Soc Chem) Spr-Verlag.

Dickinson, E. & Walstra, Pieter, eds. Food Colloids & Polymers: Stability & Mechanical Properties. 438p. 1993. 142.00 (*0-85186-325-6*, R6325) CRC Pr.

Dickinson, Edward. Music in the History of the Western Church. LC 77-127454. reprint ed. 37.50 (*0-404-02127-1*) AMS Pr.

— Music in the History of the Western Church. LC 68-25286. (Studies in Music: No. 42). 1969. reprint ed. lib. bdg. 75.00 (*0-8383-0301-3*) M S G Haskell Hse.

— Music in the History of the Western Church: With an Introduction in Religious Music among the Primitive & Ancient Peoples. 426p. 1990. reprint ed. lib. bdg. 89.00 (*0-7812-9120-8*) Rprt Serv.

— Music in the History of the Western Church, with an Introduction in Religious Music among the Primitive & Ancient Peoples. 1977. reprint ed. 49.00 (*0-403-08194-7*) Scholarly.

— The Spirit of Music: How to Find It & How to Share It. (Select Bibliographies Reprint Ser.). 1977. reprint ed. 20.95 (*0-8369-6683-X*) Ayer.

Dickinson, Edward R. The Politics of German Child Welfare from the Empire to the Federal Republic. LC 95-38644. (Historical Studies). 384p. 1996. 45.00 (*0-674-68862-7*) HUP.

***Dickinson, Edward T. & Wieder, Michael A.** Emergency Incident Rehabilitation. LC 99-39052. 129p. 1999. pap. text 27.80 (*0-8359-5375-0*) Globe Fearon.

Dickinson, Edward T., ed. see Limmer, Daniel & Grill, Michael.

Dickinson, Edward T., ed. see O'Keefe, Michael F., et al.

Dickinson, Edwin D. The Equality of States in International Law. LC 72-4270. (World Affairs Ser.: National & International Viewpoints). 440p. 1972. reprint ed. 29.95 (*0-405-04566-2*) Ayer.

Dickinson, Emily. A Brighter Garden. LC 88-5849. (Illus.). 64p. (YA). 1990. 17.95 (*0-399-21490-9*, Philomel) Peng Put Young Read.

— Collected Poems of Emily Dickinson. 288p. 1988. 6.99 (*0-517-36242-2*) Random Hse Value.

— Collected Works. 1990. reprint ed. lib. bdg. 75.00 (*0-7812-2627-9*, 1507); reprint ed. lib. bdg. write for info. (*0-318-67687-7*); reprint ed. lib. bdg. write for info. (*0-318-67688-5*); reprint ed. lib. bdg. write for info. (*0-318-67689-3*); reprint ed. lib. bdg. write for info. (*0-318-67690-7*); reprint ed. lib. bdg. write for info. (*0-318-67691-5*); reprint ed. lib. bdg. write for info. (*0-318-67692-3*); reprint ed. lib. bdg. write for info. (*0-318-67693-1*) Rprt Serv.

— Complete Letters. (Notable American Authors Ser.). 1992. reprint ed. lib. bdg. 75.00 (*0-7812-2635-X*) Rprt Serv.

— Complete Poems. (Notable American Authors Ser.). 1992. reprint ed. lib. bdg. 75.00 (*0-7812-2633-3*) Rprt Serv.

— Complete Poems of Emily. 1997. pap. 16.45 (*0-316-18441-2*, Back Bay) Little.

— Complete Poems of Emily. 1998. mass mkt. 17.00 (*0-316-19146-9*, Back Bay) Little.

— The Complete Poems of Emily Dickinson. Johnson, Thomas H., ed. 770p. (gr. 8). 1960. 32.50 (*0-316-18414-4*) Little.

— The Complete Poems of Emily Dickinson. Johnson, Thomas H., ed. LC 97-219964. 770p. 1976. pap. 18.00 (*0-316-18413-6*) Little.

— Complete Poems of Emily Dickinson. 1976. 40.95 (*0-8488-1281-6*) Amereon Ltd.

— Complete Poems of Emily Dickinson. 1990. reprint ed. lib. bdg. 49.95 (*0-89966-713-9*) Buccaneer Bks.

— Concordance to the Poems of Emily Dickinson. Rosenbaum, Stanford P., ed. LC 64-25335. (Cornell Concordances Ser.). 921p. 1964. text 157.50 (*0-8014-0362-6*) Cornell U Pr.

— Eleven Poems. deluxe limited ed. (Illus.). 1988. pap. 15.00 (*0-937686-19-0*) Turtles Quill.

— Eleven Poems, a Sequel To. deluxe limited ed. (Illus.). 1992. pap. 15.00 (*0-937686-20-4*) Turtles Quill.

— Emily Dickinson: A Collection of Critical Essays. Farr, Judith, ed. LC 94-48010. (New Century Views Ser.). 268p. (C). 1995. pap. text 12.95 (*0-13-033524-X*) P-H.

— Emily Dickinson: Selected Letters. Johnson, Thomas J., ed. 384p. 1990. pap. text 17.95 (*0-674-25070-2*) Belknap Pr.

— Emily Dickinson: Selected Letters. Johnson, Thomas H., ed. LC 78-129120. 1971. reprint ed. text 39.95 (*0-674-25060-5*) Belknap Pr.

— Emily Dickinson: Selected Poems. 96p. 1993. pap. 2.99 (*0-8125-2338-5*, Pub. by Tor Bks) St Martin.

— Emily Dickinson: Selected Poems. 2nd ed. (Bloomsbury Poetry Classics Ser.). 1993. text 9.95 (*0-312-09752-2*) St Martin.

***Dickinson, Emily.** Emily Dickinson Collected Poems. LC 91-71089. 1999. 8.98 (*0-7624-0562-7*) Running Pr.

Dickinson, Emily. Emily Dickinson's Open Folios: Scenes of Reading, Surfaces of Writing. Werner, Marta L., ed. LC 95-8858. 328p. 1995. text 52.50 (*0-472-10586-8*, 10586) U of Mich Pr.

— The Essential Dickinson. Oates, Joyce Carol, ed. LC 96-21314. (Essential Poets Ser.: No. 23). 144p. 1996. 18.00 (*0-88001-494-6*) HarpC.

— Essential Dickinson. Oates, Joyce Carol, ed. LC 96-21314. (Essential Poets Ser.). 112p. 1998. pap. 12.00 (*0-88001-520-9*) HarpC.

— Final Harvest. 1997. pap. 13.95 (*0-316-18443-8*) Little.

— Final Harvest. 1998. mass mkt. 13.95 (*0-316-19147-7*, Back Bay) Little.

— Final Harvest: Emily Dickinson's Poems. Johnson, Thomas H., ed. LC 97-219955. 331p. 1964. pap. 14.00 (*0-316-18415-2*) Little.

— Further Poems. (Notable American Authors Ser.). 1992. reprint ed. lib. bdg. 75.00 (*0-7812-2634-1*) Rprt Serv.

— I'm Nobody! Who Are You? Poems of Emily Dickinson for Children. LC 78-6828. (Poetry for Young People Ser.). (Illus.). 96p. (J). (gr. 1 up). 1978. 21.95 (*0-916144-21-6*); pap. 14.95 (*0-916144-22-4*) Stemmer Hse.

— I'm Nobody! Who Are You? Poems of Emily Dickinson for Young People. (J). 1978. 20.15 (*0-606-04391-8*, Pub. by Turtleback) Demco.

— Letters, 3 vols. Johnson, Thomas H. & Ward, Theodora, eds. LC 58-5594. (Illus.). 1042p. 1958. boxed set 74.50 (*0-674-52625-2*) Belknap Pr.

— Letters of Emily Dickinson. (Notable American Authors Ser.). 1992. reprint ed. lib. bdg. 75.00 (*0-7812-2630-9*) Rprt Serv.

— Listen & Read Emily Dickinson's Selected Poems. (Illus.). 64p. (Orig.). (YA). 1996. pap. text 5.95 incl. audio (*0-486-29118-9*) Dover.

— The Manuscript Books of Emily Dickinson: A Facsimile Edition, 2 vols. Franklin, Ralph W., ed. LC 80-17861. 1480p. 1981. 173.00 (*0-674-54828-0*) Belknap Pr.

— New Poems of Emily Dickinson. Shurr, William H., ed. LC 93-20353. x, 126p. 1993. 24.95 (*0-8078-2115-2*); pap. 12.95 (*0-8078-4416-0*) U of NC Pr.

— Open Me Carefully: Emily Dickinson's Intimate Letters to Susan Huntington Dickinson. Hart, Ellen L. & Smith, Martha N., eds. LC 98-31033. 352p. 1998. pap. 19.95 (*0-9638183-6-8*, Pub. by Paris Pr MA) Consort Bk Sales.

— Open Me Carefully: Emily Dickinson's Intimate Letters to Susan Huntington Dickinson. Hart, Ellen L. & Smith, Martha N., eds. LC 98-31033. 352p. 1998. 39.95 (*0-9638183-7-6*, Pub. by Paris Pr MA) Consort Bk Sales.

— Poems. LC 94-45647. (Pocket Classics Ser.). 208p. 1995. pap. 6.00 (*1-57062-099-7*, Pub. by Shambhala Pubns) Random.

Dickinson, Emily. Poems. (Notable American Authors Ser.). 1992. reprint ed. lib. bdg. 75.00 (*0-7812-2628-7*) Rprt Serv.

— Poems, 3rd Series. (Notable American Authors Ser.). 1992. reprint ed. lib. bdg. 75.00 (*0-7812-2631-7*) Rprt Serv.

Dickinson, Emily. Poems: Dickinson. LC 93-14360. (Pocket Poets Ser.). 256p. 1993. 12.50 (*0-679-42907-7*) Everymns Lib.

Dickinson, Emily. Poems: Second Series. (Notable American Authors Ser.). 1992. reprint ed. lib. bdg. 75.00 (*0-7812-2629-5*) Rprt Serv.

Dickinson, Emily. Poems, 1890-1896, 3 Vols. in 1. LC 67-25640. 624p. 1967. 75.00 (*0-8201-1014-0*) Schol Facsimiles.

— Poem's 1890. fac. ed. (Library of American Poets). 1994. reprint ed. 50.00 (*1-56515-002-3*) Collect Reprints.

— Poems for Youth. LC 95-33497. (Illus.). 128p. (J). (gr. k-3). 1996. 15.95 (*0-316-18435-7*) Little.

— Poems of Emily Dickinson. Plotz, Helen, ed. LC 64-12111. (Harper Poets Ser.). (Illus.). (J). (gr. 4 up). 1964. 12.95 (*0-690-63365-3*) HarpC Child Bks.

***Dickinson, Emily.** The Poems of Emily Dickinson. Franklin, R. W., ed. LC 99-11821. 704p. 1999. 29.95 (*0-674-67624-6*) HUP.

Dickinson, Emily. The Poems of Emily Dickinson, 3 vols. variorum ed. Franklin, R. W., ed. LC 98-20854. 1680p. 1998. 125.00 (*0-674-67622-X*) HUP.

— Selected Poems. (Dover Thrift Editions Ser.). 64p. 1991. pap. 1.00 (*0-486-26466-1*) Dover.

— Selected Poems. 1998. lib. bdg. 13.95 (*1-56723-037-7*) Yestermorrow.

— Selected Poems. (BCL1-PS American Literature Ser.). 231p. 1993. reprint ed. lib. bdg. 79.00 (*0-7812-6957-1*) Rprt Serv.

— Selected Poems & Letters of Emily Dickinson. LC 59-12052. 352p. 1959. pap. 8.95 (*0-385-09423-X*, Anchor NY) Doubleday.

— Selected Poems & Letters of Emily Dickinson: Together with Thomas Wentworth Higginson's Account. 1959. 14.05 (*0-606-02367-4*, Pub. by Turtleback) Demco.

— The Selected Poems of Emily Dickinson. LC 96-10466. 1996. write for info. (*0-614-13397-1*) Modern Lib NY.

— The Single Hound. (Notable American Authors Ser.). 1992. reprint ed. lib. bdg. 75.00 (*0-7812-2632-5*) Rprt Serv.

— The Works of Emily Dickinson. (Poetry Library). 416p. 1998. pap. 7.95 (*1-85326-419-9*, 4199WW, Pub. by Wrdsworth Edits) NTC Contemp Pub Co.

Dickinson, Emily & Cook, Ferris. A Murmur in the Trees. LC 97-40413. (Illus.). 128p. (gr. 8). 1998. 19.95 (*0-8212-2500-6*) Little.

Dickinson, Emily, et al. Acts of Light: Emily Dickinson, Small ed. (Illus.). 168p. 1995. 19.95 (*0-8212-2175-2*, Pub. by Bulfinch Pr) Little.

— This Way, That Way, Set 1. (Illus.). 1990. pap. 6.88 (*0-8123-6215-2*); pap. 6.88 (*0-8123-6216-0*); pap. 6.88 (*0-8123-6217-9*); pap. 6.88 (*0-8123-6218-7*); pap. 6.88 (*0-8123-6219-5*) McDougal-Littell.

— This Way, That Way, Set 2. (Illus.). 1990. pap. 8.80 (*0-8123-6220-9*); pap. 8.80 (*0-8123-6221-7*); pap. 8.80 (*0-8123-6222-5*); pap. 8.80 (*0-8123-6223-3*) McDougal-Littell.

Dickinson, Emily, jt. auth. see Herman, Carol.

Dickinson, Emily, jt. auth. see Modern Library Staff.

Dickinson, Emily N. A Poet's Parents: The Courtship Letters of Emily Norcross & Edward Dickinson. Pollak, Vivian R., ed. LC 87-35868. (Illus.). 274p. reprint ed. pap. 85.00 (*0-608-06013-5*, 206634100008) Bks Demand.

Dickinson, Eric. An Introduction to Food Colloids. (Illus.). 216p. 1992. 85.00 (*0-19-855224-6*); pap. text 45.00 (*0-19-855223-8*) OUP.

Dickinson, Eric, ed. Food Polymers, Gels & Colloids, No. 82. 1991. 259.00 (*0-85186-657-3*) CRC Pr.

Dickinson, Frank G. The Changing Position of Philanthropy in the American Economy. (Occasional Papers: No. 110). 236p. 1970. reprint ed. 61.40 (*0-87014-209-7*) Natl Bur Econ Res.

Dickinson, Frank G., ed. Philanthropy & Public Policy. (Fiscal Studies Ser.: No. 7). 159p. 1962. reprint ed. 41.40 (*0-87014-468-5*) Natl Bur Econ Res.

Dickinson, G. Creative Candles. 128p. 1996. 14.98 (*0-7858-0605-9*) Bk Sales Inc.

Dickinson, G. Lowes. Causes of International War. LC 84-12797. 110p. 1984. reprint ed. lib. bdg. 38.50 (*0-313-24565-7*, DICI, Greenwood Pr) Greenwood.

Dickinson, G. Lowes. The Greek View of Life. 20.00 (*0-8196-2870-0*) Biblo.

Dickinson, G. Lowes. The Greek View of Life. LC 78-12661. 261p. 1979. reprint ed. lib. bdg. 35.00 (*0-313-21195-7*, DIGV, Greenwood Pr) Greenwood.

Dickinson, G. Lowes & Meredith, H. O., eds. Temple Greek & Latin Classics, 5 vols. reprint ed. 120.00 (*0-404-07900-8*) AMS Pr.

Dickinson, G. W. Warp & Weft: In Search of the I Ching. (Orig.). 1997. pap. 23.95 (*1-86163-006-9*, Pub. by Capall Bann Pubng) Holmes Pub.

Dickinson, Gary & Wrigglesworth, Linda. Imperial Wardrobe. (Illus.). 204p. 1990. 112.50 (*1-870076-07-9*, Pub. by Bamboo Pub) Antique Collect.

***Dickinson, Gary, et al.** Imperial Wardrobe. LC 00-23175. 208p. 2000. 40.00 (*1-58008-188-6*) Ten Speed Pr.

Dickinson, George, et al, eds. Annual Editions: Dying, Death, & Bereavement. 3rd ed. 256p. (C). 1995. per. (*1-56134-439-7*) Brown & Benchmark.

D

***Dickinson, George, et al.** Dying, Death & Bereavement 2000-2001: Dying, Death, & Bereavement 00/01. 5th ed. (Annual Editions Ser.). 240p. (C). 1999. pap. 16.56 (*0-07-233374-X*) McGrw-H Hghr Educ.

Dickinson, George, jt. auth. see Leming, Michael.

Dickinson, Gill. Creative Gift Wrapping. LC 97-3432. 128p. 1997. 29.95 (*0-89577-962-5*, Pub. by RD Assn) Penguin Putnam.

— Gift Wrapping for Every Occasion. 128p. 1994. 14.98 (*0-7858-0155-3*) Bk Sales Inc.

— Green Gifts: How to Turn Flowers & Plants into Original & Lasting Gifts. LC 97-23567. (Illus.). 128p. 1998. 27.95 (*1-55591-397-0*) Fulcrum Pub.

Dickinson, Gill & Palmer, Mike. Gift Wrapping & Greeting Cards. (Illus.). 192p. 19.98 (*0-7858-0700-4*) Bk Sales Inc.

Dickinson, Gordon & Murphy, K. J. Ecosystems. LC 97-18303. (Routledge Introductions to Environment Ser.). (Illus.). 208p. (C). 1997. 65.00 (*0-415-14512-0*) Routledge.

Dickinson, Gordon & Murphy, Kevin J. Ecosystems. LC 97-18303. (Routledge Introductions to Environment Ser.). (Illus.). 208p. (C). 1997. pap. 18.99 (*0-415-14513-9*) Routledge.

Dickinson, H. T. Caricatures & the Constitution, 1760-1832. LC 85-5957. (English Satirical Print Ser.). 340p. 1986. lib. bdg. write for info. (*0-85964-171-6*) Chadwyck-Healey.

— The Politics of the People in Eighteenth-Century Britain. 358p. 1996. pap. 19.95 (*0-312-16033-X*) St Martin.

Dickinson, Harriett C. Cory. Some Chronicles of the Cory Family Relating to Eliakim & Sarah Sayre & Their Descendants, Westfield, New Jersey, Ballston Spa, New York, with Others from "John of Southold," with Supplement. (Illus.). 134p. 1997. reprint ed. pap. 19.00 (*0-8328-8070-1*); reprint ed. lib. bdg. 29.00 (*0-8328-8069-8*) Higginson Bk Co.

Dickinson, Harry D., et al. SeaSide Marina. (Computer-Based Collegiate Accounting Practice Set Ser.). 48p. (C). 1986. 19.95 (*0-934427-09-7*) Ivy Soft.

Dickinson, Helena. A Study of Henry D. Thoreau. 1972. 59.95 (*0-8490-1152-3*) Gordon Pr.

Dickinson, Helena, jt. auth. see Snyder, Helena A.

Dickinson, Henry D. The Economics of Socialism. (Select Bibliographies Reprint Ser.). 1977. reprint ed. 21.95 (*0-8369-5834-9*) Ayer.

— Institutional Revenue: A Study of the Influence of Social Institutions on the Distribution of Wealth. LC 66-21368. (Reprints of Economic Classics Ser.). 264p. 1966. reprint ed. 39.50 (*0-678-00160-X*) Kelley.

Dickinson, Henry W. Robert Fulton, Engineer & Artist. LC 77-148879. (Select Bibliographies Reprint Ser.). 1977. reprint ed. 29.95 (*0-8369-5649-4*) Ayer.

***Dickinson, Hugh.** Salisbury. 64p. 2000. pap. 6.50 (*1-85311-180-5*) Canterbury Press Norwich.

Dickinson, Jack L. Eighth Virginia Cavalry. (Virginia Regimental Histories Ser.). (Illus.). 119p. 1986. 19.95 (*0-930919-28-9*) H E Howard.

— Sixteenth Virginia Cavalry. (Virginia Regimental Histories Ser.). (Illus.). 123p. 1989. 19.95 (*0-930919-86-6*) H E Howard.

Dickinson, Jack L., ed. Diary of a Confederate Sharpshooter: The Life of James Conrad Peters. LC 97-69569. (Illus.). 160p. 1997. pap. 12.95 (*1-57510-033-9*) Pictorial Hist.

Dickinson, Jan. Complete Guide to Establishing an Effective Relocation Department. 64p. 1990. 250.00 (*0-934701-08-3*) Wheatherstone Pr.

— Complete Guide to Family Relocation. LC 83-91431. 246p. 1983. pap. 19.95 (*0-9613011-0-4*) Wheatherstone Pr.

— The Group Move. 130p. 1984. 250.00 (*0-934701-07-5*) Wheatherstone Pr.

— Obtaining the Highest Price for Your Home. 60p. 1986. 4.95 (*0-934701-05-9*) Wheatherstone Pr.

Dickinson, Joan D. Bill Gates: Billionaire Computer Genius. LC 96-44529. (People to Know Ser.). (Illus.). 104p. (YA). (gr. 6 up). 1997. lib. bdg. 20.95 (*0-89490-824-3*) Enslow Pubs.

Dickinson, Joan Y., ed. see Cordasco, Francesco.

Dickinson, John. Collected Works. 1990. reprint ed. lib. bdg. 75.00 (*0-7812-2636-8*, 1508); reprint ed. lib. bdg. write for info. (*0-318-67694-X*) Rprt Serv.

— Letters from a Farmer in Pennsylvania to the Inhabitants of the British Colonies. LC 03-20873. 49.00 (*0-403-00186-2*) Scholarly.

— Letters from a Farmer in Pennsylvania to the Inhabitants of the British Colonies. 1988. reprint ed. lib. bdg. 59.00 (*0-7812-0534-4*) Rprt Serv.

— Letters from a Farmer in Pennsylvania to the Inhabitants of the British Colonies. 1993. reprint ed. lib. bdg. 89.00 (*0-7812-5446-9*) Rprt Serv.

— The Political Writings of John Dickinson, Esq. (Notable American Authors Ser.). 1992. reprint ed. lib. bdg. 75.00 (*0-7812-2638-4*) Rprt Serv.

Dickinson, John, et al. Empire & Nation: Letters from a Farmer in Pennsylvania (John Dickinson), Letters from the Federal Farmer (Richard Henry Lee) 2nd ed. LC 98-2833. 1998. 17.00 (*0-86597-202-8*); pap. 8.50 (*0-86597-203-6*) Liberty Fund.

Dickinson, John C. Monastic Life in Medieval England. LC 78-25804. (Illus.). 160p. 1979. reprint ed. lib. bdg. 35.00 (*0-313-20774-7*, DIML, Greenwood Pr) Greenwood.

Dickinson, John N. To Build a Canal: Sault Ste. Marie, 1853-1854 & After. LC 80-27693. (Illus.). 222p. reprint ed. pap. 68.90 (*0-608-09666-0*, 206978100006) Bks Demand.

Dickinson, John T., jt. ed. see Conley, John.

***Dickinson, Jonathan, ed.** Sail Tall Ships! A Directory of Sail Training & Adventure at Sea. 12th ed. (Illus.). 372p. 2000. pap. 14.95 (*0-9636483-5-7*) Am Sail Trng.

Dickinson, Joy. Haunted City: An Unauthorized Guide to the Magical, Magnificent New Orleans of Anne Rice. rev. ed. LC 98-4427. (Illus.). 288p. 1998. pap. text 15.95 (*0-8065-1994-0*, Citadel Pr) Carol Pub Group.

Dickinson, Joycelyne G. The Congress of Arras, Fourteen Thirty-Five. 1973. reprint ed. 32.00 (*0-8196-0281-7*) Biblo.

Dickinson, Karen, jt. auth. see Etzel, Michael.

Dickinson, Karle. Love Notes: Boys on the Brain & Other Junior-High Stories. LC 93-44343. (Illus.). 128p. (YA). (gr. 6-9). 1994. pap. 3.50 (*0-8167-3468-2*) Troll Communs.

Dickinson, Kendell A., ed. Short Papers of the U. S. Geological Survey Uranium Workshop. (Illus.). 56p. (Orig.). (C). 1993. pap. text 30.00 (*1-56806-325-3*) DIANE Pub.

Dickinson, Linda. Price Guide to Cookbooks & Recipe Leaflets. 1995. pap. 9.95 (*0-89145-426-8*, 2080) Collector Bks.

Dickinson, Louise. Peninsula. 1976. 22.95 (*0-8488-0984-X*) Amereon Ltd.

— State O'Maine. 317p. Date not set. 24.95 (*0-8488-2589-6*) Amereon Ltd.

Dickinson, Lynda. Why Vegetarian? A Healthy, Humane, & Environmentally Friendly Approach to Food, Vol. 1. LC 95-153522. 111p. (Orig.). 1997. pap. 11.95 (*0-919574-89-0*) Gordon Soules Bk.

Dickinson, Malcolm M. Who Invented What 1992: With a Focus on Top Ten Technologies: Advanced Materials, Biotechnology, Computer-Aided Manufacturing, & Robotics, Computer Software, Electronics, Environmental Remediation, Medical Products, Photonics, Scientific & Technical Instrumentation, & Telecommunications. LC 93-12095. (Who Invented What Ser.). (Illus.). 160p. (Orig.). 1993. pap. 9.95 (*0-940983-03-6*); pap. 199.00 incl. cd-rom (*0-940983-04-4*) OPUS Pubns.

***Dickinson, Mandy.** Out of Bounds. (Orig.). 1999. mass mkt. 6.95 (*0-352-33431-2*) London Brdge.

Dickinson, Margaret. Abbeyford. 192p. 1998. 22.00 (*0-7278-5314-7*) Severn Hse.

***Dickinson, Margaret.** Abbeyford Inheritance. 192p. 1999. 24.00 (*0-7278-2227-6*, Pub. by Severn Hse) Chivers N Amer.

Dickinson, Margaret. Abbeyford Remembered. 192p. 1999. 24.00 (*0-7278-2290-X*, Pub. by Severn Hse) Chivers N Amer.

— Adelina. large type ed. (Illus.). 295p. 1996. 27.99 (*0-7505-0788-8*) Ulverscroft.

— Beloved Enemy. large type ed. 1995. 11.50 (*0-7505-0790-X*, Pub. by Mgna Lrg Print) Ulverscroft.

— Carrie. large type ed. (Magna Large Print Ser.). 278p. 1997. 27.99 (*0-7505-0789-6*) Ulverscroft.

— Lifeboat! large type ed. 336p. 1995. 27.99 (*0-7505-0784-5*, Pub. by Mgna Lrg Print) Ulverscroft.

— Portrait of Jonathan. large type ed. (Magna Large Print Ser.). 272p. 1997. 27.50 (*0-7505-0785-3*) Thorndike Pr.

— Pride of the Courtneys. large type ed. (Magna Large Print Ser.). 262p. 1997. 27.99 (*0-7505-0786-1*) Ulverscroft.

***Dickinson, Margaret.** Rogue Reels: Oppositional Film Making in Britain, 1945-1990. 288p. 1999. pap. text 27.95 (*0-85170-727-0*) Ind U Pr.

Dickinson, Margaret. Sarah. large type ed. 1996. 27.99 (*0-7505-0787-X*, Pub. by Mgna Lrg Print) Ulverscroft.

Dickinson, Marquis F., ed. John Marshall: The Tribute of Massachusetts Being the Addresses Delivered at Boston & Cambridge, February 4, 1901 in Commemoration of the One Hundredth Anniversary of His Elevation to the Bench as Chief Justice of the Supreme Court of the United States. xvii, 120p. 1988. reprint ed. 37.50 (*0-8377-2305-1*, Rothman) W S Hein.

Dickinson, Martin B., ed. Federal Income Tax Code & Regulations: Selected Sections, (1997-1998 Edition) rev. ed. 1575p. (C). 1997. pap. text 55.00 (*0-8080-0185-X*) CCH INC.

— Federal Income Tax Code & Regulations - Selected Sections: 1998-1999 Edition. 1568p. 1998. pap. text 34.00 (*0-8080-0263-5*) CCH INC.

— Federal Income Tax Code & Regulations - Selected Sections 1999-2000 Edition. 1999. pap. text 35.50 (*0-8080-0370-4*) CCH INC.

Dickinson, Mary & Charlotte. Alex's Bed. (J). Date not set. pap. text. write for info. (*0-05-004389-7*) Addison-Wesley.

***Dickinson, Matt.** The Other Side of Everest. (Illus.). 272p. 2000. pap. 13.00 (*0-8129-3340-0*, Times Bks) Crown Pub Group.

Dickinson, Matt. The Other Side of Everest: Climbing the North Face Through the Killer Storm. large type ed. LC 99-22830. (Basic Ser.). 1999. pap. 25.95 (*0-7862-1965-3*) Mac Lib Ref.

***Dickinson, Matt, pref.** The Other Side of Everest: Climbing the North Face Through the Killer Storm. LC 98-48850. (Illus.). 240p. 1999. 23.00 (*0-8129-3159-9*, Times Bks) Crown Pub Group.

Dickinson, Matthew J. Bitter Harvest: FDR, Presidential Power & the Growth of the Presidential Branch. 279p. (C). 1997. text 49.95 (*0-521-48193-7*) Cambridge U Pr.

— Bitter Harvest: FDR, Presidential Power & the Growth of the Presidential Branch. 279p. (C). 1999. pap. text 19.95 (*0-521-65395-9*) Cambridge U Pr.

***Dickinson, Michael.** The Confession of Judas. 124p. 2000. pap. 18.00 (*0-7388-2066-0*) Xlibris Corp.

Dickinson, O. P., jt. auth. see Simpson, R. H.

Dickinson, O. T. The Origins of Mycenaean Civilisation. (Studies in Mediterranean Archaeology: Vol. XLIX). (Illus.). 127p. 1977. pap. 49.50 (*91-85058-74-2*, Pub. by P Astroms) Coronet Bks.

Dickinson, Oliver. The Aegean Bronze Age. LC 93-2666. (World Archaeology Ser.). (Illus.). 364p. (C). 1994. pap. text 30.95 (*0-521-45664-9*) Cambridge U Pr.

***Dickinson, Pat.** Money. 280p. 2000. pap. write for info. (*1-893162-79-6*) AmErica.

Dickinson, Patric. A Round of Golf Courses: A Selection of the Best Eighteen. (Illus.). 159p. 1998. pap. text 15.00 (*0-7881-5245-9*) DIANE Pub.

Dickinson, Patric, tr. see Virgil.

Dickinson, Patti. Hollywood the Hard Way: A Cowboy's Journey. LC 99-18423. (Illus.). 218p. 1999. pap. 13.95 (*0-8032-6619-7*, Bison Books) U of Nebr Pr.

***Dickinson, Paul, et al.** Beautiful Corporations. (Illus.). 256p. 2000. 40.00 (*0-273-64233-2*, Pub. by F T P-H) Trans-Atl Phila.

Dickinson, Peter. AK. 240p. (YA). 1993. mass mkt. 3.99 (*0-440-21897-7*) Dell.

— AK. (J). 1992. 9.09 (*0-606-05727-7*, Pub. by Turtleback) Demco.

— The Blue Hawk. (J). (gr. 5-9). 1991. 22.00 (*0-8446-6478-2*) Peter Smith.

— A Bone from a Dry Sea. 208p. (YA). (gr. 7 up). 1995. mass mkt. 4.99 (*0-440-21928-0*) Dell.

***Dickinson, Peter.** A Bone from a Dry Sea. 1999. pap. 12.25 (*0-7857-6244-2*) Econo-Clad Bks.

Dickinson, Peter. A Bone from a Dry Sea. (J). 1995. 9.60 (*0-606-07311-6*, Pub. by Turtleback) Demco.

— A Bone from a Dry Sea. large type ed. LC 93-43769. (J). 1994. lib. bdg. 15.95 (*0-7862-0154-1*) Thorndike Pr.

— Chuck & Danielle. 1996. 20.95 (*0-385-31720-4*) Doubleday.

Dickinson, Peter. Chuck & Danielle. 115p. (J). (gr. 3-5). pap. 3.99 (*0-8072-1504-X*) Listening Lib.

Dickinson, Peter. Chuck & Danielle. (J). 1997. 9.09 (*0-606-11206-5*, Pub. by Turtleback) Demco.

— Eva. 224p. (YA). (gr. 7-12). 1990. reprint ed. mass mkt. 5.50 (*0-440-20766-5*, LLL BDD) BDD Bks Young Read.

— Here Is Queer: Nationalisms, Sexualities & the Literatures of Canada. 280p. 1999. text 50.00 (*0-8020-4403-4*); pap. text 19.95 (*0-8020-8210-6*) U of Toronto Pr.

— King & Joker. 224p. 1993. mass mkt. 4.99 (*0-446-40309-1*, Mysterious Paperbk) Warner Bks.

— The Lion Tamer's Daughter & Other Stories. (YA). (gr. 7 up). 1997. 15.95 (*0-614-28684-0*, Delacorte Pr Bks) BDD Bks Young Read.

***Dickinson, Peter.** The Lion Tamer's Daughter & Other Stories. 1998. 10.09 (*0-606-13572-3*, Pub. by Turtleback) Demco.

Dickinson, Peter. The Lion Tamer's Daughter & Other Stories. 304p. (YA). (gr. 7 up). 1998. reprint ed. mass mkt. 4.99 (*0-440-22690-2*, LLL BDD) BDD Bks Young Read.

— Mana's Story. (Kin Ser.). (Illus.). 160p. (J). (gr. 5-9). 1998. 14.99 (*0-399-23350-4*, G & D) Peng Put Young Read.

— Mana's Story: The Kin. (Kin Ser.). (Illus.). 211p. (YA). (gr. 5-9). 1998. pap. 3.99 (*0-448-41712-X*, G & D) Peng Put Young Read.

— Marigold: The Music of Billy Mayerl. (Illus.). 328p. 2000. 45.00 (*0-19-816213-8*) OUP.

— Noli's Story. LC 97-51182. 211p. (J). (gr. 4-8). 1998. pap. text 3.99 (*0-448-41710-3*, G & D) Peng Put Young Read.

— Po's Story. LC 98-33908. (Kin Ser.). (Illus.). 224p. (J). (gr. 5 up). 1998. mass mkt. 3.99 (*0-448-41711-1*, G & D) Peng Put Young Read.

— Shadow of a Hero. 1995. 9.09 (*0-606-09847-X*, Pub. by Turtleback) Demco.

— Skeleton-in-Waiting. large type ed. LC 90-34615. 281p. 1990. lib. bdg. 8.95 (*1-56054-004-4*) Thorndike Pr.

***Dickinson, Peter.** Some Deaths Before Dying. LC 00-22425. (Core Ser.). 2000. 28.95 (*0-7838-9016-8*, G K Hall Lrg Type) Mac Lib Ref.

— Some Deaths Before Dying. 256p. 2000. pap. 13.95 (*0-446-67612-8*, Mysterious Paperbk) Warner Bks.

Dickinson, Peter. Suth's Story. LC 98-14226. (Kin Ser.). 211p. (J). (gr. 4-6). 1998. 14.99 (*0-399-23327-X*, G & D); pap. 3.99 (*0-448-41709-X*, G & D) Peng Put Young Read.

— The Yellow Room Conspiracy. 256p. 1995. mass mkt. 5.99 (*0-446-40373-3*, Pub. by Warner Bks) Little.

— The Yellow Room Conspiracy. large type ed. LC 94-13806. (Cloak & Dagger Ser.). 395p. 1994. lib. bdg. 20.95 (*0-7862-0261-0*) Thorndike Pr.

Dickinson, Peter, ed. Chuck & Danielle, Set. unabridged ed. (J). (gr. 8 up). 1997. 21.98 incl. audio (*0-8072-7835-1*, YA929SP) Listening Lib.

Dickinson, Peter A. Sunbelt Retirement: The Complete State-by-State Guide to Retiring in the South & West of the United States. LC 91-30748. 399p. 1992. pap. 16.95 (*0-89526-736-5*, Pub. by Regnery Pub) Natl Bk Netwk.

— Sunbelt Retirement: The Complete State-by-State Guide to Retiring in the South & West of the United States. LC 91-30748. (Illus.). 399p. 1998. 29.95 (*0-89526-525-7*, Pub. by Regnery Pub) Natl Bk Netwk.

Dickinson, Peter S. Civil RICO: A Research Guide to Civil Liability for Business Crimes. LC 89-2099. (Legal Research Guides Ser.: Vol. 8). iii, 32p. 1989. lib. bdg. 32.00 (*0-89941-668-3*, 305780) W S Hein.

Dickinson, Philip. Employment Discrimination: Quick Answers to Everyday Questions. LC 98-173132. 600p. 1998. text 119.00 (*0-8080-0213-9*) CCH INC.

Dickinson, Philip D. Employee Privacy Rights & Wrongs. LC 96-23942. 80p. 1996. spiral bd. 47.00 (*0-925773-29-8*) M Lee Smith.

— Hiring Smart: How to Conduct Background Checks. LC 97-25347. 84p. 1997. spiral bd. 47.00 (*0-925773-39-5*) M Lee Smith.

— Workplace Violence & Employer Liability. LC 97-20822. 76p. 1997. spiral bd. 47.00 (*0-925773-37-9*) M Lee Smith.

Dickinson, R. J. Officers Mess: Life & Customs in the Regiments. 144p. (C). 1987. 125.00 (*81-7002-028-X*, Pub. by Himalayan Bks) St Mut.

***Dickinson, Rebecca.** Boo! A Halloween Sticker Book & Story. (Illus.). 16p. (J). (ps-3). 2000. pap. 4.95 (*0-8167-6529-4*) Troll Communs.

— Monster Cake. LC 00-21112. (Illus.). 32p. (J). (ps-3). 2000. 4.99 (*0-439-06752-9*) Scholastic Inc.

Dickinson, Rebecca. The 13 Nights of Halloween. LC 95-30065. (J). (ps-3). 1996. 4.99 (*0-590-47586-X*) Scholastic Inc.

***Dickinson, Richard & Royer, France.** Weeds of the Northern U. S. & Canada: A Guide for Identification. 434p. 1999. pap. 21.95 (*1-55105-221-0*) Lone Pine.

Dickinson, Richard, jt. auth. see Royer, France.

Dickinson, Richard L., jt. auth. see West, Bill W.

Dickinson, Robert. God Does Heal Today: Pastoral Principles & Practice of Faith-Healing. xv, 343p. 1995. reprint ed. pap. 25.00 (*0-946068-56-9*, Pub. by Paternoster Pub) OM Literature.

Dickinson, Robert E. The Geophysiology of Amazonia: Vegetation & Climate. LC 86-11015. (Climate & the Biosphere Ser.). 526p. 1987. 220.00 (*0-471-84511-6*) Wiley.

Dickinson, Robert H. & Vladimir, Andrew. Selling the Sea: An Inside Look at the Cruise Industry. LC 96-20420. 384p. 1996. 44.95 (*0-471-12001-4*) Wiley.

Dickinson, Robert L. Atlas of Human Sex Anatomy. LC 50-5564. (Illus.). 382p. 1971. reprint ed. 54.50 (*0-88275-014-3*) Krieger.

Dickinson, Robert L. & Beam, Lura. Thousand Marriages: A Medical Study of Sex Adjustment. LC 76-95093. 1970. reprint ed. lib. bdg. 75.00 (*0-8371-3085-9*, DIMA, Greenwood Pr) Greenwood.

Dickinson, Roger, et al, eds. Approaches to Audience: A Reader. LC 98-8038. (Foundations in Media Ser.). (Illus.). 336p. 1998. pap. text 19.95 (*0-340-69225-1*) OUP.

— Approaches to Audiences: A Reader. LC 98-8038. (Foundations in Media Ser.). (Illus.). 336p. 1998. text 75.00 (*0-340-69224-3*) OUP.

Dickinson, Rosemary, jt. auth. see Brown, Mary.

Dickinson, Rosemary, jt. auth. see Brown, Mary H.

Dickinson, Samuel D., ed. see Bossu, Jean-Bernard.

Dickinson-Shutz, Amy. Wacky Songs. LC 98-126697. (Looney Tunes Song & Sound Bks.). 24p. (J). (ps-2). 1997. 14.98 (*0-7853-2379-1*, PI25) Pubns Intl Ltd.

Dickinson, Susan. Brer Rabbit & the Peanut Patch. rev. ed. (Quality Time Easy Readers Ser.). (Illus.). 32p. (J). (gr. 1-3). 1990. reprint ed. lib. bdg. 12.95 (*1-878363-18-2*) Forest Hse.

Dickinson, T., ed. see Dickinson, Charles R. & Vance, David.

***Dickinson, Tania & Griffiths, David, eds.** The Making of Kingdoms. (Anglo-Saxon Studies in Archaeology & History: Vol. 10). (Illus.). 224p. 1999. pap. 60.00 (*0-947816-93-3*, Pub. by Oxford Univ Comm Arch) David Brown.

Dickinson, Tania & Harke, Heinrich. Early Anglo-Saxon Shields. (Archaeologia Ser.: Vol. 110). (Illus.). 94p. 1992. 45.00 (*0-85431-260-9*, Pub. by Soc Antiquaries) David Brown.

Dickinson, Terence. Exploring the Night Sky: The Equinox Astronomy Guide for Beginners. (Equinox Children's Science Book Ser.). (Illus.). 72p. (YA). (gr. 5 up). 1989. reprint ed. 17.95 (*0-920656-64-1*); reprint ed. pap. 9.95 (*0-920656-66-8*) Firefly Bks Ltd.

— Exploring the Sky by Day: The Equinox Guide to Weather & the Atmosphere. (Illus.). 72p. 1989. reprint ed. 17.95 (*0-920656-73-0*) Firefly Bks Ltd.

— Exploring the Sky by Day: The Equinox Guide to Weather & the Atmosphere. (Illus.). 72p. 1997. reprint ed. pap. 9.95 (*0-920656-71-4*) Firefly Bks Ltd.

Dickinson, Terence. Extraterrestrials: A Field Guide for Earthlings. 1994. 15.15 (*0-606-06976-3*, Pub. by Turtleback) Demco.

Dickinson, Terence. From the Big Bang to Planet X: The Fifty Most-Asked Question about the Universe ... & Their Answers. LC 93-94507. (Illus.). 152p. 1993. pap. 12.95 (*0-921820-71-2*, Pub. by Camden Hse) Firefly Bks Ltd.

— Nightwatch: A Practical Guide to Viewing the Universe. 3rd rev. expanded ed. (Illus.). 176p. 1998. 45.00 (*1-55209-300-X*); pap. 29.95 (*1-55209-302-6*) Firefly Bks Ltd.

— Nightwatch: An Equinox Guide to Viewing the Universe. rev. ed. (Illus.). 159p. 1999. reprint ed. pap. text 22.00 (*0-7881-6407-4*) DIANE Pub.

— Other Worlds: A Beginner's Guide to Planets & Moons. (Illus.). 64p. (J). (gr. 5-9). 1995. pap. 9.95 (*1-895565-70-7*); lib. bdg. 19.95 (*1-895565-71-5*) Firefly Bks Ltd.

— Summer Stargazing: A Practical Guide for Recreational Astronomers. (Illus.). 64p. 1996. 18.95 (*1-55209-014-0*) Firefly Bks Ltd.

— The Universe & Beyond. 3rd rev. ed. (Illus.). 168p. 1999. pap. 29.95 (*1-55209-361-1*) Firefly Bks Ltd.

***Dickinson, Terence.** The Universe & Beyond. 3rd rev. ed. (Illus.). 168p. 1999. lib. bdg. 40.00 (*1-55209-377-8*) Firefly Bks Ltd.

Dickinson, Terence & Dyer, Alan. The Backyard Astronomer's Guide. rev. ed. Estabrook, Barry, ed. (Illus.). 298p. 1991. 39.95 (*0-921820-11-9*) Firefly Bks Ltd.

Dickinson, Terence & Newton, Jack. Splendors of the Universe: A Practical Guide to Photographing the Night Sky. (Illus.). 144p. 1997. 40.00 (*1-55209-141-4*) Firefly Bks Ltd.

Dickinson, Terence & Schaller, Adolf. Extraterrestrials: A Field Guide for Earthlings. (Illus.). 64p. (YA). (gr. 4 up). 1994. pap. 9.95 (*0-921820-87-9*) Firefly Bks Ltd.

D

An Asterisk (*) at the beginning of an entry indicates that the title is appearing for the first time.

Dickinson, Terence & Schaller, Adolf. Extraterrestrials: A Field Guide for Earthlings. (Illus.). 64p. (YA). (gr. 4 up). 1994. lib. bdg. 17.95 (*0-921820-86-0*) Firefly Bks Ltd.
Dickinson, Thomas H. The Insurgent Theatre. LC 72-83277. 1972. reprint ed. 23.95 (*0-405-08445-5*) Ayer.
— An Outline of Contemporary Drama. LC 70-88059. 1969. reprint ed. 32.00 (*0-8196-0249-3*) Biblo.
— Playwrights of the New American Theater. LC 67-26731. (Essay Index Reprint Ser.). 1977. 23.95 (*0-8369-0373-0*) Ayer.
— Playwrights of the New American Theater. (BCL1-PS American Literature Ser.). 331p. 1992. reprint ed. lib. bdg. 89.00 (*0-7812-6634-3*) Rprt Serv.
Dickinson, Thomas H., ed. Chief Contemporary Dramatists. LC 76-6588. reprint ed. 52.50 (*0-404-15281-3*); reprint ed. 52.50 (*0-404-15282-1*) AMS Pr.
Dickinson, Thomas S. & Erb, Thomas O. We Gain More Than We Give: Teaming in Middle Schools, LC 96-47731. 1997. pap. write for info. (*1-56090-103-9*) Natl Middle Schl.
Dickinson, Thorold & De La Roche, Catherine. Soviet Cinema. Manvell, Roger, ed. LC 77-169327. (National Cinema Ser.). (Illus.). 140p. 1974. reprint ed. 20.95 (*0-405-03891-7*) Ayer.
Dickinson, Timothy, jt. ed. see Leebaert, Derek.
Dickinson, Tom, ed. Readings in Middle School Curriculum: A Continuing Conversation. 232p. (C). 1993. pap. text 25.00 (*1-56090-078-4*) Natl Middle Schl.
Dickinson, Torry D. CommonWealth: Self-Sufficiency & Work in American Communities, 1830 to 1993. LC 94-23739. (Illus.). 244p. (C). 1995. lib. bdg. 46.00 (*0-8191-9802-1*) U Pr of Amer.
Dickinson, V. M., et al. Health Studies of Free-Ranging Mojave Desert Tortoises in Utah & Arizona. (Arizona Game & Fish Department Technical Report: No. 21). (Illus.). 70p. (Orig.). 1995. pap. 5.00 (*0-917563-28-X*) AZ Game & Fish.
Dickinson, Vanessa M., et al. Health Studies of Free-Ranging Sonoran Desert Tortoises in Arizona: A Final Report. (Research Branch Technical Report Ser.: No. 24). (Illus.). 79p. 1996. pap. 5.00 (*0-917563-31-X*) AZ Game & Fish.
Dickinson, W. C. Solar Energy Technology Handbook: Pt. B: Applications, System Designs & Economics. (Energy, Power & Environment Ser: Vol. 6). (Illus.). 848p. 1980. text 295.00 (*0-8247-6927-9*) Dekker.
Dickinson, W. Calvin & Hitchcock, Eloise R., eds. A Bibliography of Tennessee History 1973 - 1996. LC 98-40195. 392p. 1999. text 40.00 (*1-57233-032-5*) U of Tenn Pr.
Dickinson, W. Calvin, jt. auth. see Whiteaker, Larry H.
Dickinson, W. Clavin & Hitchcock, Eloise R., compiled by. The War of the Spanish Succession, 1702-1713: A Selected Bibliography, 15. LC 95-41984. (Bibliographies of Battles & Leaders Ser.: No. 15). 160p. 1996. lib. bdg. 65.00 (*0-313-28302-8*, Greenwood Pr) Greenwood.
Dickinson, W. Croft. Scotland from the Earliest Times to 1603. 3rd ed. Duncan, Archibald A., ed. (Illus.). 1977. text 69.00 (*0-19-822453-2*) OUP.
Dickinson, W. R. Tectonic Setting of Faulted Tertiary Strata Associated with the Catalina Core Complex in Southern Arizona. (Special Papers: No. 264). (Illus.). 120p. 1991. pap. 18.00 (*0-8137-2264-0*) Geol Soc.
Dickinson, W. R., et al. The To'aga Site: Three Millennia of Polynesian Occupation in the Manu'a Islands, American Samoa. (Contributions of the University of California Archaeological Research Facility Ser.: No. 51). 249p. 1993. pap. text 24.00 (*1-882744-01-2*) U CA Arch Res Fac.
Dickinson, Wharton. Fowler: Genealogy of the Fowlers in England & America. (Illus.). 65p. 1997. reprint ed. pap. 13.00 (*0-8328-8634-3*); reprint ed. lib. bdg. 23.00 (*0-8328-8633-5*) Higginson Bk Co.
Dickinson, William. A Glossary of Words & Phrases Pertaining to the Dialect of Coumberland. (English Dialect Society Publications: Nos. 20 & 24). 1969. reprint ed. pap. 25.00 (*0-8115-0450-6*) Periodicals Srv.
Dickinson, William, et al. The School Personnel Management System. rev. ed. Harrington-Lueker, Donna, ed. 572p. 1996. ring bd. 215.00 (*0-88364-122-4*, 02-103) Natl Sch Boards.
Dickinson, William C. Sidney Godolphin, Lord Treasurer, 1702-1710. LC 89-12979. (Studies in British History: Vol. 18). 300p. 1990. lib. bdg. 89.95 (*0-88946-469-3*) E Mellen.
Dickinson, William C. & Cheremisinoff, Paul N., eds. Solar Energy Technology Handbook Pt. 1: Engineering Fundamentals. LC 80-10266. (Energy, Power, & Environment Ser.: Vol. 6). (Illus.). 896p. reprint ed. pap. 200.00 (*0-608-06267-7*, 206659600001) Bks Demand.
Dickinson, William R. Kinematics of Transrotational Tectonism in the California Transverse Ranges & Its Contribution to Cumulative Slip along the San Andreas Transform Fault System. (Special Papers: No. 305). (Illus.). 50p. 1996. pap. 26.50 (*0-8137-2305-1*) Geol Soc.
Dickinson, William R., ed. Tectonics & Sedimentation: Based on a Symposium Sponsored by the Society of Economic Paleontologists & Mineralogists: Papers. LC 75-302534. (Society of Economic Paleontologists & Mineralogists, Special Publication Ser.: No. 22). (Illus.). 210p. reprint ed. pap. 65.10 (*0-8357-6634-9*, 203528700094) Bks Demand.
Dickinson, William R. & Yarborough, Hunter. Plate Tectonics & Hydrocarbon Accumulation. LC TN0871.E38. (Education Course Note Ser.: Vol. 1). (Illus.). 218p. reprint ed. pap. 67.60 (*0-608-08722-X*, 206936100004) Bks Demand.
Dickison, Arthur. Crash Dive: In Action with HMS Safari 1942-43. 1999. 36.95 (*0-7509-2089-0*) A Sutton.
Dickison, Gill. Mask Making. 1995. 7.98 (*0-7858-0314-9*) Bk Sales Inc.
Dickison, Richard, jt. auth. see Brein, Michael.
Dickison, Roland & Gruner, Carolyn. Causes, Cures, Sense & Nonsense. LC 87-71853. (Illus.). 300p. (Orig.). 1987. pap. 10.00 (*0-9618946-1-X*) Bishop Publishing.
Dickison, Sheila K. & Hallett, Judith P., eds. Rome & Her Monuments: Essays on the City & Literature of Rome in Honor of Katherine A. Geffcken. xv, 616p. 2000. pap. 60.00 (*0-86516-457-6*) Bolchazy-Carducci.
***Dickison, William C.** Integrative Plant Anatomy. LC 99-68568. (Illus.). 544p. 2000. 69.95 (*0-12-215170-4*) Acad Pr.
Dickkerson, Kenneth. How to Win Games of Chance. LC 91-93044. 226p. (Orig.). 1992. mass mkt. 5.99 (*0-345-36317-5*) Ballantine Pub Grp.
Dickler, Howard & Ledbetter, Cathy. dBASE IV for the First-Time User. (Illus.). 300p. 1988. pap. 19.95 (*0-318-37393-9*) P-H.
Dickman. Thoracoscopic Spine Surgery. LC 99-19799. (Illus.). 360p. 1999. 199.00 (*0-86577-785-3*) Thieme Med Pubs.
Dickman, Alan. Designing Applications with MSMQ. LC 98-25737. 400p. (C). 1998. pap. text 42.95 (*0-201-32581-0*) Addison-Wesley.
Dickman, B. A. The Freon Fiasco. LC 94-96522. 117p. 1995. 14.95 (*0-932984-01-0*) Gracelaine.
Dickman, Barbara J., jt. auth. see Walters, Elizabeth R.
Dickman, Byron A. You're Fired. LC 76-73206. 1978. write for info. (*0-932984-00-2*) Gracelaine.
Dickman, Charleen R. Memories of Me, Baby. (Illus.). 86p. (J). (ps). 1994. 29.95 (*1-882237-20-X*) Life Time Pubs.
— Memories of Me, Baby. deluxe ed. (Illus.). 86p. (J). (ps). 1992. 39.95 (*1-882237-01-3*) Life Time Pubs.
Dickman, Chris, et al. Mastering CorelDRAW 4. (Illus.). 776p. 1999. pap. 34.95 incl. disk (*1-56609-099-7*) Peachpit Pr.
Dickman, Curtis, et al. Surgery of the Craniovertebral Junction. LC 97-25003. (Illus.). 784p. 1997. 249.00 (*0-86577-681-4*) Thieme Med Pubs.
Dickman, Curtis A., et al. Surgery of the Craniovertebral Junction. LC 97-25003. 1997. write for info. (*3-13-107181-8*, Pub. by G Thieme) Thieme Med Pubs.
Dickman, David, jt. auth. see Lowry, Robert W.
Dickman, David, ed. see Taylor, Charlie.
Dickman, Howard, ed. The Imperiled Academy. LC 92-41461. (Studies in Social Philosophy & Policy: No. 17). 250p. (C). 1993. text 39.95 (*1-56000-097-X*); pap. text 24.95 (*1-56000-675-7*) Transaction Pubs.
Dickman, Howard, jt. ed. see Paul, Ellen F.
Dickman, Irving R. Making Life More Livable. large type ed. LC 83-6412. (Illus.). 96p. 1983. pap. 19.95 (*0-89128-115-0*) Am Foun Blind.
— Outreach to the Aging Blind: Some Strategies for Community Action. LC 77-155406. 174p. reprint ed. pap. 54.00 (*0-7837-0133-0*, 204042100016) Bks Demand.
— Winning the Battle: Developing Support for Sexuality & HIV/AIDS Education. LC 82-61000. 58p. (Orig.). 1991. pap. 12.95 (*0-9609212-0-6*) SIECUS.
Dickman, Irving R., ed. Sex Education & Family Life for Visually Handicapped Children & Youth: A Resource Guide. LC HV1598.. 96p. reprint ed. pap. 30.00 (*0-608-16883-1*, 202735200055) Bks Demand.
Dickman, Jaqueline. As I Have Loved You. pap. 2.75 (*0-687-01926-5*) Abingdon.
***Dickman, Mike, tr.** The Sayings of Old Ch'eng: On the Nature of the Original Mind. 30p. 2000. 10.95 (*1-887276-22-X*, Pub. by Cool Grove Pub) LPC Group.
Dickman, Mike, tr. A Treasure-Trove of Protection & Blessings: The Seven Chapter Prayer of Orgyen Rinpoche. 288p. (Orig.). 1997. pap. 12.95 (*1-887276-05-X*, Coolgrve Pr) Cool Grove Pub.
***Dickman, Miriam.** My Family. 1999. pap. write for info. (*1-58235-018-3*) Watermrk Pr.
Dickman, R. L., et al, eds. Molecular Clouds in the Milky Way & External Galaxies. (Lecture Notes in Physics Ser.: Vol. 315). xvi, 475p. 1988. 70.95 (*0-387-50438-9*) Spr-Verlag.
Dickman, R. Thomas. Corporate Body. LC 82-90980. 1983. 9.95 (*0-87212-168-2*) Libra.
— In God We Should Trust. LC 76-53146. 1977. 6.95 (*0-87212-071-6*) Libra.
— Of Sex & Sin. LC 85-91068. 1986. 10.00 (*0-87212-195-X*) Libra.
— Potpourri. LC 88-91415. 1989. 12.95 (*0-87212-223-9*) Libra.
Dickman, Ronald, jt. auth. see Marro, Joaquin.
Dickman, Thomas. Some Light Remarks. LC 79-92087. 1980. 7.95 (*0-87212-120-8*) Libra.
Dickman, Tom, tr. see Beaud, Michel.
Dickman, William J. Battery Rodgers. 35p. (Orig.). 1980. pap. 12.00 (*0-89126-094-3*) MA-AH Pub.
Dickmann, Catherine H., jt. auth. see Carlebach, Diane.
***Dickmann, M. A. & Miraglia, Francisco.** Special Groups: Boolean-Theoretic Methods in the Theory of Quadratic Forms. LC 00-20862. (Memoirs of the American Mathematical Society Ser.). 2000. write for info. (*0-8218-2057-5*) Am Math.
Dickmann, Zeev. The Ultimatum to Mankind: An Unprecedented Social Revolution or Extinction. LC 96-95143. 150p. (Orig.). 1997. pap. 15.95 (*0-9655244-1-8*) AIT-ORN Pr.
Dickmeyer, Nathan & Cirino, Anna M. Comparative Financial Statistics for Public Two-Year Colleges: FY 1993. 1993. 30.00 (*0-685-62917-1*); 100.00 (*0-685-62918-X*) NACUBO.
— Comparative Financial Statistics for Public Two-Year Colleges: FY 1995. 1993. 30.00 (*0-685-62916-3*) NACUBO.
Dickneider. Teacher's Guide Learn to Earn. 1997. write for info. (*0-684-00643-X*, Fireside) S&S Trade Pap.
Dicko, Modibo, et al. Rural Lighting: A Guide for Development Workers. (Illus.). 120p. (Orig.). 1993. pap. 24.50 (*1-85339-200-6*, Pub. by Intermed Tech) Stylus Pub VA.
Dickoff, Robert E. Agharta. 106p. 1996. reprint ed. spiral bd. 12.50 (*0-7873-1239-8*) Hlth Research.
Dickonson, j Richard. Metabolism & Molecular Physiology of Saccharomyces Cerevisiae. LC 99-173817. 1998. 74.95 (*0-7484-0731-6*) Taylor & Francis.
Dickos, Andrew. Intrepid Laughter: Preston Sturges & the Movies. LC 85-2512. 186p. 1985. 27.50 (*0-8108-1815-9*) Scarecrow.
***Dickreiter, Michael.** Score Reading: A Key to the Musical Experience. Pauly, Reinhard G., tr. LC 00-29319. (Illus.). 272p. 2000. pap. 19.95 (*1-57467-056-5*, Amadeus Pr) Timber.
Dickretter, Michael. Tonmeister Technology: Recording Environments, Sound Sources, & Microphone Techniques. Temmer, Stephen F., tr. (GER.). 142p. 1989. 34.95 (*0-9617200-0-X*); pap. 19.95 (*0-9617200-1-8*) Temmer Enterps.
Dicks, B., jt. ed. see Gordon, G.
Dicks, Brian. Greece. (Focus On Ser.). (Illus.). 32p. (J). (gr. 4-6). 1991. write for info. (*0-237-60192-3*) EVN1 UK.
Dicks, Henry V. Marital Tensions: Clinical Studies Towards a Psychological Theory of Interaction. 368p. 1993. pap. text 33.00 (*1-85575-064-3*, Pub. by H Karnac Bks Ltd) Other Pr LLC.
— Marital Tensions: Clinical Studies Towards a Psychological Theory of Interaction. 189p. 1984. reprint ed. pap. 13.95 (*0-7102-0037-4*, Routledge Thoemms) Routledge.
***Dicks, Ian & Watton, Nick.** God's Earth Forces. (Zoomers Ser.). (J). (ps). 1999. 2.99 (*0-7847-1123-2*, 03533) Standard Pub.
— God's Fantastic Frogs. (J). (ps). 1999. 2.99 (*0-7847-1124-0*, 03534) Standard Pub.
— God's Solar System. (Zoomers Ser.). 4p. (J). (gr. 3-7). 1999. 2.99 (*0-7847-1121-6*, 03531) Standard Pub.
— The Human Body God Made. (Zoomers Ser.). (ps). 1999. 2.99 (*0-7847-1122-4*, 03532) Standard Pub.
***Dicks, J. W.** Form Your Own Corporation & Launch a Business in Any State. LC 99-49008. 288p. 1999. pap. 19.95 (*1-58062-192-9*) Adams Media.
Dicks, J. W. How to Incorporate & Start a Business in Alabama. LC 98-18324. 320p. 1998. pap. 16.95 (*1-58062-012-4*) Adams Media.
— How to Incorporate & Start a Business in Arizona. LC 98-18353. 320p. 1998. pap. 16.95 (*1-58062-0?-3*) Adams Media.
— How to Incorporate & Start a Business in Colorado. LC 97-41106. 1997. pap. 16.95 (*1-55850-767-1*) Adams Media.
— How to Incorporate & Start a Business in Connecticut: A Simple 6-Part Program. LC 97-41107. (How to Incorporate & Start a Business Ser.). 320p. 1997. pap. 16.95 (*1-55850-768-X*) Adams Media.
— How to Incorporate & Start a Business in Delaware. LC 98-18352. 320p. 1998. pap. 16.95 (*1-58062-013-2*) Adams Media.
— How to Incorporate & Start a Business in Florida. LC 97-11177. 320p. 1996. pap. 16.95 (*1-55850-587-3*) Adams Media.
— How to Incorporate & Start a Business in Georgia. LC 97-32369. 1997. pap. 16.95 (*1-55850-769-8*) Adams Media.
— How to Incorporate & Start a Business in Illinois. LC 97-11182. 320p. 1996. pap. 16.95 (*1-55850-588-1*) Adams Media.
— How to Incorporate & Start a Business in Indiana. LC 97-41108. 1997. pap. 16.95 (*1-55850-770-1*) Adams Media.
— How to Incorporate & Start a Business in Kentucky. LC 98-4076. 320p. 1998. pap. 16.95 (*1-58062-014-0*) Adams Media.
— How to Incorporate & Start a Business in Maryland. LC 98-4067. 320p. 1998. pap. 16.95 (*1-58062-020-5*) Adams Media.
— How to Incorporate & Start a Business in Massachusetts. LC 97-11172. 320p. 1996. pap. 16.95 (*1-55850-589-X*) Adams Media.
— How to Incorporate & Start a Business in Michigan. LC 97-11181. 320p. 1996. pap. 16.95 (*1-55850-590-3*) Adams Media.
— How to Incorporate & Start a Business in Minnesota. LC 97-42926. 1997. pap. 16.95 (*1-55850-772-8*) Adams Media.
— How to Incorporate & Start a Business in Mississippi. LC 98-4065. 320p. 1998. pap. 16.95 (*1-58062-016-7*) Adams Media.
— How to Incorporate & Start a Business in Missouri. LC 98-20869. 320p. 1998. pap. 16.95 (*1-58062-015-9*) Adams Media.
— How to Incorporate & Start a Business in Nevada. LC 97-35316. xviii, 289 p. 1997. pap. 16.95 (*1-55850-771-X*) Adams Media.
— How to Incorporate & Start a Business in New Jersey. LC 97-11178. 320p. 1996. pap. 16.95 (*1-55850-591-1*) Adams Media.
— How to Incorporate & Start a Business in New York. LC 97-11175. 320p. 1996. pap. 16.95 (*1-55850-592-X*) Adams Media.
— How to Incorporate & Start a Business in North Carolina. LC 97-11173. 320p. 1996. pap. 16.95 (*1-55850-593-8*) Adams Media.
— How to Incorporate & Start a Business in Ohio. LC 98-4066. 320p. 1998. pap. 16.95 (*1-58062-019-1*) Adams Media.
— How to Incorporate & Start a Business in Oregon. LC 97-35320. 1997. pap. 16.95 (*1-55850-773-6*) Adams Media.
— How to Incorporate & Start a Business in Pennsylvania. LC 97-11176. 320p. 1996. pap. 16.95 (*1-55850-594-6*) Adams Media.
— How to Incorporate & Start a Business in South Carolina. LC 98-4085. 320p. 1998. pap. 16.95 (*1-58062-017-5*) Adams Media.
— How to Incorporate & Start a Business in Tennessee. LC 97-35319. 1997. pap. 16.95 (*1-55850-774-4*) Adams Media.
— How to Incorporate & Start a Business in Texas. LC 97-11179. 320p. 1996. pap. 16.95 (*1-55850-595-4*) Adams Media.
— How to Incorporate & Start a Business in Virginia. LC 97-35317. 1997. pap. 16.95 (*1-55850-775-2*) Adams Media.
— How to Incorporate & Start a Business in Washington. LC 97-35318. 1997. pap. 16.95 (*1-55850-776-0*) Adams Media.
— How to Incorporate & Start a Business in Wisconsin. LC 98-4075. 320p. 1998. pap. 16.95 (*1-58062-018-3*) Adams Media.
— Moonlight Investing: A Simple Four Phase Program for Starting Small, Making Smart Choices, Insuring a Stress-Free Financial Future, Becoming You Own Savvy Money Manager. 256p. 1998. 17.95 (*1-886284-28-8*, Pub. by Chandler Hse) Natl Bk Netwk.
— Mutual Fund Investment Strategies. 1997. 17.95 (*0-02-861441-0*) Macmillan.
— Mutual Fund Strategies. 1997. 17.95 (*0-614-19918-2*) Macmillan Gen Ref.
— The Six Laws of Business Success: The Parable of American Entrepreneurship. LC 95-16189. 1995. write for info. (*1-881209-01-6*) Crown Oak Pub.
— The Small Business Legal Kit. (Small Business Ser.). 1997. 16.95 (*1-55850-699-3*) Adams Media.
Dicks, J. W. & Paris, James L. The American Dream: The Ten Power Principles for Financial Freedom. LC 92-25907. 1992. write for info. (*1-881209-00-8*) Crown Oak Pub.
***Dicks, Joseph E.** A Lonely Heart: A Collection of Poetry. 48p. 2000. pap. 8.00 (*0-8059-4722-1*) Dorrance.
Dicks, M. J. The Demographics of Housing Demand: Household Formations & the Growth of Owner-Occupation. LC HG1582.E53. (Bank of England. Discussion Papers: No. 32). 71p. 1988. reprint ed. pap. 30.00 (*0-8357-6088-X*, 203432700089) Bks Demand.
— A Simple Model of the Housing Market. LC HD7333.A4. (Bank of England - Discussion Papers: No. 49). 60p. 1990. reprint ed. pap. 30.00 (*0-608-03151-8*, 206360400007) Bks Demand.
Dicks, M. J. & Brown, R. G. Heating Controls in Large Spaces. 1997. pap. 80.00 (*0-86022-476-7*, Pub. by Build Servs Info Assn) St Mut.
Dicks, M. J. & Hatch, N. The Relationship Between Employment & Unemployment. LC HG0136.D57. (Bank of England, Discussion Papers: Vol. 39). (Illus.). 56p. 1989. reprint ed. pap. 30.00 (*0-608-01648-9*, 206230000002) Bks Demand.
Dicks, M. J. & Singh, S. Secondary Market Prices of LDC Debt. LC 92-24302. (Bank of England, Discussion Papers: Vol. 48). 48p. 1991. reprint ed. pap. 30.00 (*0-608-00542-8*, 206142100008) Bks Demand.
Dicks, Richard. Catch the Vision: Your Roadmap to Successful Network Marketing. 1997. pap. text 12.95 (*0-9658795-1-8*) Red Pt Publ.
Dicks, Shirley. From Vietnam to Hell: Interviews with Victims of Post-Traumatic Stress Disorder. LC 89-43647. (Illus.). 144p. 1990. pap. 26.50 (*0-89950-487-6*) McFarland & Co.
— They're Going to Kill My Son: A Man He Didn't Know a Murder He Didn't See a Death Sentence He Doesn't Deserve. Dunphy, Joan S., ed. LC 92-60563. 297p. 1992. 22.95 (*0-88282-112-1*) New Horizon NJ.
Dicks, Shirley, ed. Congregation of the Condemned: Voices Against the Death Penalty. LC 94-39969. (Illus.). 290p. 1991. pap. 17.95 (*0-87975-970-4*) Prometheus Bks.
— Young Blood: Juvenile Justice & the Death Penalty. LC 95-6336. 295p. 1995. 26.95 (*0-87975-953-4*) Prometheus Bks.
Dicks, Terrance. Catastrophe. (Doctor Who Ser.). 1998. pap. 5.95 (*0-563-40584-8*) BBC.
— Doctor Who & the Android Invasion. 17.95 (*0-8488-0150-4*) Amereon Ltd.
— Doctor Who & the Day of the Daleks. 18.95 (*0-8488-0151-2*) Amereon Ltd.
— Doctor Who & the Genesis of the Daleks. 17.95 (*0-8488-0152-0*) Amereon Ltd.
— Doctor Who & the Giant Robot. 17.95 (*0-8488-0153-9*) Amereon Ltd.
— Doctor Who & the Image of the Fendall. 17.95 (*0-8488-0154-7*) Amereon Ltd.
— Doctor Who & the Loch Ness Monster. 17.95 (*0-8488-0155-5*) Amereon Ltd.
— Doctor Who & the Revenge of the Cybermen. 17.95 (*0-8488-0156-3*) Amereon Ltd.
— Eight Doctors. (Doctor Who Ser.). 1998. pap. 5.95 (*0-563-40563-5*) BBC.
— Making of Doctor Who. 1976. 17.95 (*0-8488-0262-4*) Amereon Ltd.
— Mean Streets. (New Adventures Ser.). 1998. mass mkt. 5.95 (*0-426-20519-7*, Pub. by Virgin Bks) London Brdge.
***Dicks, Terrance.** Players. 1999. mass mkt. 9.99 (*0-563-55573-4*) BBC Worldwide.
Dicks, Terrance. True Stories: Horror. LC 96-50252. 352p. (J). 1997. pap. 7.95 (*0-8069-9655-2*) Sterling.

D

An Asterisk (*) at the beginning of an entry indicates that the title is appearing for the first time.

Dicks, W. Groups, Trees & Projective Modules. (Lecture Notes in Mathematics Ser.: Vol. 790). 127p. 1980. 18.00 (*0-387-09974-3*) Spr-Verlag.

Dicks, W., jt. ed. see Castellet, M.

Dicks, Warren & Dunwoody, M. J. Groups Acting on Graphs. 2nd ed. (Cambridge Studies in Advanced Mathematics: No. 17). (Illus.). 304p. 1989. text 90.00 (*0-521-23033-0*) Cambridge U Pr.

Dicks, Warren & Ventura, Enric. The Group Fixed by a Family of Injective Endomorphisms of a Free Group. LC 96-7228. (Contemporary Mathematics Ser.: Vol. 195). 81p. 1996. pap. 19.00 (*0-8218-0564-9*, CONM/195) Am Math.

Dicks, Xavier C. Survival Guide for Black Men in America: You Don't Have to Be Extinct. 300p. 1997. 24.95 (*0-9647003-2-8*) Farry Bell.

— The Time Has Come. LC 95-90487. (Illus.). 260p. 1995. 19.95 (*0-9647003-0-1*) Farry Bell.

Dicksee, Lawrence R. Advanced Accounting: Appendix on the Law Relating to Accounts by J. E. G. Dep Montmorency. LC 75-18464. (History of Accounting Ser.). (Illus.). 1979. reprint ed. 31.95 (*0-405-07547-2*) Ayer.

— Auditing: A Practical Manual for Auditors. 1979. 26.95 (*0-405-07548-0*, 14231) Ayer.

— Auditing: Practical Manual for Auditors, Authorized American Edition. Montgomery, Robert H., ed. LC 75-18466. (History of Accounting Ser.). 1979. reprint ed. 29.95 (*0-405-07549-9*) Ayer.

— Business Methods & the War: The Fundamentals of Manufacturing Costs & Published Balance Sheets & Window Dressing, 3 Vols. Brief, Richard P., ed. LC 80-1487. (Dimensions of Accounting Theory & Practice Ser.). 1981. reprint ed. lib. bdg. 18.00 (*0-686-73167-0*) Ayer.

— Business Methods & the War with the Fundamentals of Manufacturing Costs & Published Balance Sheets & Window Dressing. 1980. 23.95 (*0-405-13517-3*) Ayer.

— Business Organisation. Brief, Richard P., ed. LC 80-1488. (Dimensions of Accounting Theory & Practice Ser.). 1980. reprint ed. lib. bdg. 31.95 (*0-405-13518-1*) Ayer.

— Depreciation, Reserves, & Reserve Funds. LC 75-18467. (History of Accounting Ser.). (Illus.). 1979. reprint ed. 17.95 (*0-405-07550-2*) Ayer.

— Fraudulent Accounting. 1980. 19.95 (*0-405-13519-X*) Ayer.

— Fraudulent Accounting & Fraud in Accounts, 2 Vols. Brief, Richard P., ed. LC 80-1489. (Dimensions of Accounting Theory & Practice Ser.). 1981. reprint ed. lib. bdg. 15.00 (*0-686-73168-9*) Ayer.

— Goodwill & Its Treatment in Accounts. 2nd ed. LC 75-18468. (History of Accounting Ser.). (Illus.). 1979. 17.95 (*0-405-07551-0*) Ayer.

Dicksing. Unique & Unusual Pens: From the Wood Lathe. LC 97-67030. (Schiffer Book for Woodturners Ser.). (Illus.). 64p. 1997. pap. 14.95 (*0-7643-0359-7*) Schiffer.

Dickson. Alien Way. 1990. mass mkt. write for info. (*0-8125-0322-8*) Tor Bks.

Dickson. Chemistry 8th ed. 285p. 1999. pap., student ed. 26.95 (*0-471-36321-9*) Wiley.

***Dickson.** Chemistry 8th ed. 261p. 1999. pap., lab manual ed. 38.95 (*0-471-36319-7*) Wiley.

D

Dickson. Dawn of Belief: Religion in the Upper Paleolithic of Southwestern Europe. LC 89-38911. (Illus.). 259p. 1992. reprint ed. pap. 17.95 (*0-8165-1336-8*) U of Ariz Pr.

— Marketing Management. 2nd ed. (C). 1997. pap. text 33.50 (*0-03-018093-7*) Harcourt.

— Marketing Management. 2nd ed. (C). 1997. pap. text, teacher ed. 70.00 (*0-03-018094-5*) Harcourt.

— Marketing Management. 2nd ed. (C). 1998. teacher ed. 29.50 (*0-03-019554-3*) Harcourt.

— Marketing Management. 2nd ed. 1996. 246.00 (*0-03-018084-8*) Harcourt Coll Pubs.

Dickson, ed. see Scarron, Paul.

Dickson, A. D. & Treble, J. H. People & Society in Scotland, Vol. 3. (People & Society of Scotland Ser.). (Illus.). 300p. (C). 1998. pap. 48.00 (*0-85976-212-2*, Pub. by J Donald) St Mut.

Dickson, Albert J. Covered Wagon Days: A Journey Across the Plains in the Sixties, & Pioneer Days in the Northwest; from the Private Journals of Albert Jerome Dickson. (American Biography Ser.). 287p. 1991. reprint ed. lib. bdg. 69.00 (*0-7812-8108-3*) Rprt Serv.

Dickson, Albert J. Covered Wagon Days: From the Private Journals of Albert Jerome Dickson. Dickson, Arthur J., ed. LC 89-4934. 285p. 1989. pap. 12.00 (*0-8032-6582-4*, Bison Books) U of Nebr Pr.

Dickson, Andrew. Thoughts, Words & Deeds: Poems, Vol. 1. LC 94-18616. 64p. 1995. pap. 14.95 (*0-7734-0009-5*, Mellen Poetry Pr) E Mellen.

Dickson, Anna. Development & International Relations: A Critical Introduction. LC 97-23195. 220p. (C). 1997. 55.95 (*0-7456-1494-9*, Pub. by Polity Pr); pap. 23.95 (*0-7456-1495-7*, Pub. by Polity Pr) Blackwell Pubs.

Dickson, Anne & Henriques, Nikki. Hysterectomy: The Positive Recovery Plan. 240p. 1987. 7.95 (*0-7225-2162-6*) Harper SF.

— Menopause: A Woman's View. large type ed. 21.95 (*1-85695-097-2*, Pub. by ISIS Lrg Prnt) Transaction Pubs.

— Women on Menopause: A Change for the Better. 160p. (Orig.). 1989. pap. 9.95 (*0-89281-237-0*, Heal Arts VT) Inner Tradit.

Dickson, Antonia, jt. auth. see Dickson, W. K.

Dickson, Ardie, jt. auth. see Zukowski, Ginger.

Dickson, Arthur. Valentine & Orson: A Study in Late Medieval Romance. LC 75-153315. reprint ed. 32.50 (*0-404-02128-X*) AMS Pr.

Dickson, Arthur J., ed. see Dickson, Albert J.

Dickson, Athol. Whom Shall I Fear? A Garr Reed Mystery. (Garr Reed Ser.). 352p. 1996. pap. 10.99 (*0-310-20760-6*) Zondervan.

— Whom Shall I Fear? A Garr Reed Mystery. large type ed. (Christian Mystery Ser.). 465p. 1997. 21.95 (*0-7862-1179-2*) Thorndike Pr.

Dickson, Barry. Afraid Of The Dark. (Kids of Canada Ser.). (Illus.). 32p. (J). 1980. bds. 5.95 (*0-88862-255-4*, Pub. by J Lorimer) Formac Dist Ltd.

Dickson, Barry & Seonida. About Nellie & Me. (Where We Live Ser.). (Illus.). 88p. (J). 1985. pap. 5.95 (*0-88862-174-4*, Pub. by J Lorimer); bds. 12.95 (*0-88862-183-3*, Pub. by J Lorimer) Formac Dist Ltd.

Dickson, Brice & Carmichael, Paul, eds. The House of Lords: Its Parliamentary & Judicial Roles. 304p. 1998. 54.00 (*1-84113-020-6*) Hart Pub.

Dickson, Brice, et al. Introduction to French Law. 288p. (Orig.). 1994. pap. 57.50 (*0-273-60140-7*, Pub. by Pitman Pub) Trans-Atl Phila.

***Dickson, Bruce & Carleson, David.** Ancient Preludes. 300p. 1999. pap. 36.95 (*1-57879-001-8*) E Bowers Pub.

Dickson, Bruce & Harding, Harry, eds. Economic Relations in the Asian-Pacific Region: Trends & Prospects. (Dialogues on Public Policy Ser.). 91p. 1987. pap. 10.95 (*0-8157-1841-1*) Brookings.

Dickson, Bruce, jt. auth. see Lieberthal, Kenneth.

Dickson, Bruce J. Democratization in China & Taiwan: The Adaptability of Leninist Parties. (Studies on Contemporary China). (Illus.). 290p. 1998. text 69.00 (*0-19-829269-4*) OUP.

Dickson, C., tr. see Dib, Mohammed.

Dickson, C., tr. see Nadir, Shams.

Dickson, Carolyn. Creating Balance: Moving Out of Conflict into Compatibility. LC 97-12490. (Illus.). 160p. 1997. pap. 12.95 (*1-886939-16-0*) OakHill Pr VA.

Dickson, Carolyn & DePasquale, Paula. Speaking Magic: Performance Strategies for Winning Your Business Audience. LC 94-2834. 190p. 1994. pap. 14.95 (*0-9619590-8-8*) OakHill Pr VA.

Dickson, Carter, pseud. The Cavalier's Cup. 1987. mass mkt. 3.50 (*0-8217-2170-4*, Zebra Kensgtn) Kensgtn Pub Corp.

— The Curse of the Bronze Lamp. 192p. 1997. mass mkt. 4.95 (*0-7867-0440-3*) Carroll & Graf.

— Merrivale Holds the Key: Two Classic Locked-Room Mysteries. 628p. 1995. pap. 14.95 (*1-55882-027-2*) Intl Polygonics.

— Nine & Death Makes Ten. LC 87-82442. 175p. 1987. reprint ed. pap. 5.95 (*0-930330-69-2*) Intl Polygonics.

— The Peacock Feather Murders. LC 87-82443. 192p. 1987. reprint ed. pap. 5.95 (*0-930330-68-4*) Intl Polygonics.

— The Reader Is Warned. LC 89-85728. 192p. 1989. pap. 5.95 (*1-55882-019-1*, Lib Crime Classics) Intl Polygonics.

— The Unicorn Murders. 192p. 1989. reprint ed. pap. 5.95 (*1-55882-015-9*, Lib Crime Classics) Intl Polygonics.

Dickson, Charles. Beating the Chemical Cop-Out. Nelson, Becky, ed. 22p. (Orig.). (YA). (gr. 7-12). 1992. pap. text 1.95 (*1-56309-036-8*, C926107, Wrld Changers Res) Womans Mission Union.

— Medicinal Chemistry: Investigations in Biological & Pharmaceutical Chemistry. LC 98-24742. 224p. 1998. spiral bd., lab manual ed. 44.95 (*0-8493-1888-2*, 1888) CRC Pr.

— Please Help Me Hold On. Nelson, Becky, ed. 22p. (Orig.). (YA). (gr. 7-12). 1992. pap. text 1.95 (*1-56309-037-6*, C926106, Wrld Changers Res) Womans Mission Union.

— A Protestant Pastor Looks at Mary. LC 96-68286. 112p. 1996. pap. 7.95 (*0-87973-727-1*, 721) Our Sunday Visitor.

— The Revolt in the North: Antrim & down in 1798. (Illus.). 256p. 1998. 35.00 (*0-09-477260-6*, Pub. by Constable & Co) Trafalgar.

— The Wexford Rising in 1798: Its Causes & Its Course. (Illus.). 274p. 1998. 35.00 (*0-09-477250-9*, Pub. by Constable & Co) Trafalgar.

Dickson, Charles B. A Moon in Each Eye. (Illus.). 80p. (Orig.). 1993. pap. 7.00 (*0-944676-95-2*) AHA Bks.

Dickson, Charles C. Croydon Airport Remembered: An Aviation Artist Looks Back. 1985. 45.00 (*0-907335-12-8*, Pub. by Sutton Libs & Arts) St Mut.

Dickson, Curt, jt. auth. see Hill, Dickie.

Dickson, D. A Scout with Custer. 1976. 30.95 (*0-8488-0224-1*, J M C & Co) Amereon Ltd.

Dickson, D. A., et al. Communication Skills Training for Health Professionals. (Illus.). 368p. 1996. pap. 45.00 (*1-56593-766-X*, 1490) Singular Publishing.

Dickson, D. Bruce. Prehistoric Pueblo Settlement Patterns: The Arroyo Hondo, New Mexico, Site Survey. LC 79-21542. (Arroyo Hondo Archaeological Ser.: Vol. 2). (Illus.). 150p. 1983. pap. 14.95 (*0-933452-02-0*) Schol Am Res.

Dickson, D. C. M., jt. auth. see Atkinson, M. E.

Dickson, D. E., ed. Improve Your Business-Handbook & Workbook. 1994. 6.75 (*92-2-105340-7*); student ed. 11.25 (*92-2-105341-5*) Intl Labour Office.

— Improve Your Business-Handbook & Workbook. 1994. reprint ed. 15.75 (*92-2-105342-3*) Intl Labour Office.

Dickson, D. G. Expansions in Series of Solutions of Linear Difference-Differential & Infinite Order Differential Equations with Constant Coefficients. LC 52-42839. (Memoirs Ser.: No. 1/23). 72p. 1991. reprint ed. pap. 19.00 (*0-8218-1223-8*, MEMO/1/23) Am Math.

Dickson, D. P. & Berry, F. J., eds. Mossbauer Spectroscopy. (Illus.). 286p. 1987. text 69.95 (*0-521-26101-5*) Cambridge U Pr.

***Dickson, David.** New Foundations: Ireland, 1660-1800. rev. ed. LC 99-36787. (Illus.). 264p. 2000. 49.50 (*0-7165-2632-8*, Pub. by Irish Acad Pr); pap. 24.50 (*0-7165-2637-9*, Pub. by Irish Acad Pr) Intl Spec Bk.

Dickson, David. The New Politics of Science. (Illus.). 416p. 1988. pap. text 15.95 (*0-226-14763-0*) U Ch Pr.

— Psalms. (Geneva Commentaries Ser.). 1064p. 1985. reprint ed. 35.99 (*0-85151-481-2*) Banner of Truth.

— The Utterance of America: Emersonian Newness in Dos Passos' U. S. A. & Pynchon's Vineland. LC 98-210386. (Gothenburg Studies in English: No. 71). 215p. 1998. pap. 57.50 (*91-7346-330-2*, Pub. by Almqvist Wiksell) Coronet Bks.

Dickson, David & Keogh, Daire. The United Irishmen: Republicanism, Radicalism & Rebellion. 378p. 1993. pap. 31.95 (*1-874675-19-8*) Dufour.

Dickson, David & Maue-Dickson, Wilma. Anatomical & Physiological Bases of Speech. LC 90-21191. (Illus.). 338p. (C). 1982. text 49.50 (*0-7506-9760-1*, 1645) Buttrwrth-Heinemann.

Dickson, Denise, jt. auth. see Owen, Ted.

Dickson, Don R. The Albertson Site: A Deeply & Clearly Stratified Ozark Bluff Shelter. (Illus.). 307p. (Orig.). 1991. pap. 25.00 (*1-56349-071-4*, RS41) AR Archaeol.

Dickson, Donald J. Confidentiality & Privacy in Social Work: A Guide to the Law for Practitioners & Students. LC 97-34912. 224p. 1998. 34.95 (*0-684-82657-7*) Free Pr.

Dickson, Donald R. The Tessera of Antilia: Utopian Brotherhoods & Secret Societies in the Early Seventeenth Century. LC 98-16148. (Studies in Intellectual History: No. 88). (Illus.). 280p. 1998. 93.00 (*90-04-11032-1*) Brill Academic Pubs.

Dickson, Donald R., ed. see Donne, John.

Dickson, Donald T. Law in the Health & Human Services: A Guide for Social Workers, Psychologists, Psychiatrists, & Related Professionals. LC 94-23670. 1995. 35.00 (*0-02-907435-5*) Free Pr.

Dickson, Douglas G. Expansions in Series of Solutions of Linear Difference - Differential & Infinite Order Differential Equations with Constant Coefficients. LC 52-42839. (American Mathematical Society Ser.: No. 23). 74p. reprint ed. pap. 30.00 (*0-608-09171-5*, 205267500002) Bks Demand.

Dickson, E., jt. auth. see Woodman, M.

Dickson, E. M., ed. Raw Materials for the Refractory Industry. 3rd ed. pap. text. write for info. (*0-318-69936-2*) Metal Bulletin.

Dickson, E. M. & Harben, Peter W., eds. Phosphates: What Prospects for Growth. 357p. (Orig.). 1984. pap. text 35.00 (*0-913333-03-4*) Metal Bulletin.

Dickson, Edward. Knight of the Thistle. LC 99-216881. 1997. write for info. (*0-907616-62-3*) Able Publishing.

Dickson, Elizabeth. Computer Program Design. 256p. (C). 1995. text 20.75 (*0-697-26836-5*) Bus & Educ Tech.

Dickson, Elizabeth, ed. The English Garden Room. 1986. 24.95 (*0-316-18432-2*) Little.

Dickson, Frank & Smythe, Sandra, eds. The Writer's Digest Handbook of Short Story Writing, Vol. I. 238p. 1981. pap. 14.99 (*0-89879-049-2*, Wrtrs Digest Bks) F & W Pubns Inc.

Dickson, Fredrick R. War & the National Reinvention: Japan in the Great War, 1914-1919, Vol. 177. LC 99-23508. 1999. 40.00 (*0-674-94655-3*) HUP.

Dickson, G. C. C. I. I. Introduction to Insurance, No. 010. (C). 1984. suppl. ed. 240.00 (*0-7855-4290-6*, Pub. by Witherby & Co) St Mut.

— C. I. I. Quantitive Methods As Applied to Insurance, No. 110. (C). 1982. suppl. ed. 230.00 (*0-7855-4261-2*, Pub. by Witherby & Co) St Mut.

— Risk Analysis. 170p. (C). 1987. pap. 200.00 (*0-948691-78-6*, Pub. by Witherby & Co) St Mut.

— Risk Analysis. 170p. (C). 1990. 210.00 (*1-85609-014-0*, Pub. by Witherby & Co) St Mut.

Dickson, G. C. & Hastings, W. J. Corporate Risk Management. 180p. (C). 1989. pap. 275.00 (*0-948691-76-X*, Pub. by Witherby & Co) St Mut.

Dickson, Gary, ed. see Clowes, Kenneth W.

Dickson, Gary, ed. see Selig, Gad J.

***Dickson, Gary W. & DeSanctis, Gerardine.** Information Technology & the Future Enterprise: New Models for Managers. LC 00-44113. 2000. write for info. (*0-13-017854-3*) P-H.

Dickson, George L. The Direct Way: A Programmed Study of the English Sentence. 108p. (Orig.). 1979. pap. text 10.95 (*0-89641-023-4*) American Pr.

Dickson, Gladys, tr. from ARA. A Jerusalem Christian Treatise on Astrology. 1988. reprint ed. pap. text 8.95 (*1-55818-115-6*, Near Eastern) Holmes Pub.

Dickson, Gordon R., jt. auth. see Anderson, Poul.

Dickson, Gordon Rupert. Alien Art. (Illus.). 192p. 1986. reprint ed. pap. 2.95 (*0-8125-3577-4*, Pub. by Tor Bks) St Martin.

— The Chantry Guild. 1989. mass mkt. 5.50 (*0-441-10266-2*) Ace Bks.

***Dickson, Gordon Rupert.** The Chantry Guild: A Novel of the Dorsai. (Childe Cycle Ser.). 2000. mass mkt. 6.99 (*0-8125-7559-8*, Pub. by Tor Bks) St Martin.

Dickson, Gordon Rupert. Dickson! LC 84-60948. 193p. 1984. 13.00 (*0-915368-27-7*) New Eng SF Assoc.

— Dorsai! 288p. 1993. mass mkt. 4.99 (*0-8125-0398-8*, Pub. by Tor Bks) St Martin.

— The Dragon & the Djinn. 400p. 1998. mass mkt. 6.99 (*0-441-00495-4*) Ace Bks.

***Dickson, Gordon Rupert.** The Dragon & the Fair Maid of Kent. 416p. 2000. 26.95 (*0-312-86160-5*, Pub. by Tor Bks) St Martin.

Dickson, Gordon Rupert. The Dragon & the George. 288p. 1987. mass mkt. 5.99 (*0-345-35050-2*, Del Rey) Ballantine Pub Grp.

— The Dragon & the Gnarly King. LC 97-7024. 384p. 1997. text 24.95 (*0-312-86157-5*) St Martin.

— The Dragon & the Gnarly King. 472p. 1998. mass mkt. 6.99 (*0-8125-6270-4*, Pub. by Tor Bks) St Martin.

— The Dragon at War. (Dragon Knight Ser.). 1992. pap. 18.95 (*0-441-75698-0*) Ace Bks.

— The Dragon in Lyonesse. LC 98-23490. 384p. 1998. 25.95 (*0-312-86159-1*, Pub. by Tor Bks) St Martin.

— The Dragon in Lyonesse, 1 Vol. (Tor Fantasy Ser.). 1999. mass mkt. 6.99 (*0-8125-6271-2*) Tor Bks.

— The Dragon Knight. 1991. mass mkt. 5.99 (*0-8125-0943-9*, Pub. by Tor Bks) St Martin.

— The Dragon on the Border. 400p. 1993. mass mkt. 6.99 (*0-441-16657-1*) Ace Bks.

— The Dragon, the Earl & the Troll. LC 94-7538. (Dragon Knight Ser.). 448p. (Orig.). 1994. pap. 21.95 (*0-441-00098-3*) Ace Bks.

— The Dragon, the Earl & the Troll. (Orig.). 1996. mass mkt. 6.99 (*0-441-00282-X*) Ace Bks.

— The Far Call. 410p. 1989. mass mkt. 4.95 (*0-8125-3544-8*) Tor Bks.

— The Final Encyclopedia. LC 96-29217. 1996. 25.95 (*0-312-86288-1*, Pub. by Tor Bks) St Martin.

— The Final Encyclopedia, Vol. II. LC 96-29217. 1996. 25.95 (*0-312-86289-X*, Pub. by Tor Bks) St Martin.

— Final Encyclopedia 1. LC 96-29217. 1996. pap. 16.95 (*0-312-86186-9*) St Martin.

— Final Encyclopedia 2, Vol. II. LC 96-29217. 1996. pap. 16.95 (*0-312-86188-5*) St Martin.

— Guided Tour. 256p. 1988. pap. 3.50 (*0-8125-3589-8*, Pub. by Tor Bks) St Martin.

— Home from the Shore. (Illus.). 224p. 1988. pap. 3.50 (*0-8125-3592-8*, Pub. by Tor Bks) St Martin.

— The Last Master. 320p. (Orig.). 1984. pap. 2.95 (*0-8125-3562-6*, Pub. by Tor Bks) St Martin.

— Lost Dorsai. 288p. 1993. mass mkt. 4.99 (*0-8125-0404-6*, Pub. by Tor Bks) St Martin.

— Love Not Human. 256p. 1988. pap. 2.95 (*0-8125-3554-5*, Pub. by Tor Bks) St Martin.

— The Magnificent Wilf. 320p. 1995. 21.00 (*0-671-87664-3*) Baen Bks.

— The Magnificent Wilf. 304p. 1996. mass mkt. 5.99 (*0-671-87719-4*) Baen Bks.

— The Man the Worlds Rejected. 256p. (Orig.). 1986. pap. 2.95 (*0-8125-3572-3*, Pub. by Tor Bks) St Martin.

— Masters of Everon. 1992. mass mkt. 3.99 (*0-8125-0394-5*, Pub. by Tor Bks) St Martin.

— Mindspan. 288p. (Orig.). 1986. mass mkt. 4.99 (*0-671-65580-9*) Baen Bks.

— Naked to the Stars & The Alien Way. 1991. pap. 3.95 (*0-8125-0396-1*, Pub. by Tor Bks) St Martin.

— Necromancer. 1998. mass mkt. 5.99 (*0-8125-4530-3*, Pub. by Tor Bks) St Martin.

— Other. 576p. 1995. mass mkt. 6.99 (*0-8125-1599-4*, Pub. by Tor Bks) St Martin.

— The Outposter. 256p. 1992. mass mkt. 4.99 (*0-671-72140-2*) Baen Bks.

— Pritcher Mass. 256p. 1988. pap. 3.50 (*0-8125-3540-5*, Pub. by Tor Bks) St Martin.

— Pro. (Illus.). 192p. 1986. reprint ed. pap. 2.95 (*0-8125-3575-8*, Pub. by Tor Bks) St Martin.

— Sleepwalker's World. 256p. (Orig.). 1993. mass mkt. 4.99 (*0-671-72161-5*) Baen Bks.

— Soldier, Ask Not. 320p. 1993. mass mkt. 4.99 (*0-8125-0400-3*, Pub. by Tor Bks) St Martin.

— Space Winners. 256p. 1986. pap. 2.95 (*0-8125-3558-8*, Pub. by Tor Bks) St Martin.

— Spacepaw. (Illus.). 224p. 1988. pap. 3.50 (*0-8125-3542-1*, Pub. by Tor Bks) St Martin.

— The Spirit of Dorsai. 256p. 1993. mass mkt. 4.99 (*0-8125-0403-8*, Pub. by Tor Bks) St Martin.

— Steel Brother. (Orig.). 1991. mass mkt. 3.99 (*0-8125-1547-1*, Pub. by Tor Bks) St Martin.

— Tactics of Mistake. (Childe Cycle Ser.). 1998. pap. 5.99 (*0-8125-4531-1*, Pub. by Tor Bks) St Martin.

— Time Storm. 432p. 1992. per. 4.99 (*0-671-72148-8*) Baen Bks.

— The Way of the Pilgrim. LC 99-27540. 1999. pap. 15.95 (*0-312-86662-3*, Pub. by Tor Bks) St Martin.

— Wolf & Iron. 480p. 1993. mass mkt. 5.99 (*0-8125-3334-8*, Pub. by Tor Bks) St Martin.

— Wolfling. 256p. 1985. mass mkt. 5.99 (*0-671-55962-1*) Baen Bks.

— Young Bleys. 448p. 1992. mass mkt. 5.99 (*0-8125-0947-1*, Pub. by Tor Bks) St Martin.

Dickson, Gordon Rupert & Anderson, Poul. Hoka! Hoka! Hoka! 320p. 2000. mass mkt. 5.99 (*0-671-57774-3*) Baen Bks.

Dickson, Gordon Rupert, jt. auth. see Anderson, Poul.

Dickson, Gwen G. Johann Georg Hamann's Relational Metacriticism. LC 95-8276. (Theologische Bibliothek Toepelmann Ser.: Vol. 67). 1995. 198.55 (*3-11-014437-9*) De Gruyter.

Dickson, H. Climate & Weather. 1976. lib. bdg. 59.95 (*0-8490-1638-X*) Gordon Pr.

***Dickson, Harley.** The Real Miracle. LC 99-69305. (Illus.). 136p. 2000. 19.95 (*1-57736-176-8*) Providence Hse.

Dickson, Harold E. Land Grant Frescoes at The Pennsylvania State University by Henry Varnum Poor. (Illus.). 24p. 1981. pap. 1.00 (*0-911209-22-0*) Palmer Mus Art.

— Masterworks by Pennsylvania Painters in Pennsylvania Collections: Exhibition Catalogue. (Illus.). 72p. 1972. pap. 6.00 (*0-911209-00-X*) Palmer Mus Art.

— Portraits U. S. A., 1776-1976. (Illus.). 133p. 1976. pap. 10.00 (*0-911209-07-7*) Palmer Mus Art.

Dickson, Harris. Story of King Cotton. LC 79-107513. 309p. 1970. reprint ed. lib. bdg. 59.50 (*0-8371-3760-8*, DKC&) Greenwood.

Dickson, Harry E. Beating Time: A Musician's Memoir. (Illus.). 208p. 1995. text 24.95 (*1-55553-229-2*) NE U Pr.

Dickson, Heather, ed. see Goldding, Sylvia.

An Asterisk (*) at the beginning of an entry indicates that the title is appearing for the first time.

Dickson, Helen. An Illustrious Lord. large type ed. (Mills & Boon Large Print Ser.). 350p. 1998. 24.99 (*0-263-15451-3*, Pub. by Mills & Boon) Ulverscroft.

— Katherine. large type ed. (Mills & Boon Large Print Ser.). 350p. 1996. 23.99 (*0-263-14829-7*, Pub. by Mills & Boon) Ulverscroft.

— Lady Deceiver. large type ed. (Mills & Boon Large Print Ser.). 350p. 1997. 23.99 (*0-263-15147-6*, Pub. by Mills & Boon) Ulverscroft.

— The Rainborough Inheritance. 1999. per. 4.99 (*0-373-30333-5*, 1-30333-8) Harlequin Bks.

— The Rainborough Inheritance. large type ed. (Mills & Boon Large Print Ser.). 350p. 1997. 23.99 (*0-263-15017-8*) Ulverscroft.

— An Unpredictable Bride. 1998. mass mkt. 4.99 (*0-373-30311-4*, 1-30311-4) Harlequin Bks.

Dickson, Hugh, et al. Spinal Injuries Handbook. 2nd ed. 1992. pap. text 25.00 (*0-07-470001-4*) McGraw-Hill HPD.

Dickson, J. Wild Plants of Glasgow. 144p. 1989. 64.00 (*1-873644-09-4*, Pub. by Mercat Pr Bks) St Mut.

Dickson, J. H., ed. Conservation of Wild Plants in Glasgow. (Aberdeen University Press Bks.). (Illus.). 144p. 1991. 25.45 (*0-08-041200-9*, Pub. by Aberdeen U Pr) Macmillan.

Dickson, J. H & Mill, R. R., eds. Plants & People: Economic Botany in Northern Europe 800-1800 A.D. 198p. 1995. pap. 17.50 (*0-7486-0526-6*, Pub. by Edinburgh U Pr) Col U Pr.

***Dickson, J. H., et al.** The Changing Flora of Glasgow: Urban & Rural Plants Through the Centuries. 384p. 2000. text 45.00 (*0-7486-1397-8*) Col U Pr.

Dickson, J. Walter. Confessions of a Part-Time Seeker. LC 89-81144. (Illus.). 88p. (Orig.). 1991. pap. 8.95 (*0-89386-026-3*) Acorn NC.

***Dickson, Jack.** Banged Up. 225p. 1999. pap. 14.95 (*1-902852-04-4*, Pub. by Prowler GMP) LPC InBook.

— Crossing Jordan. 2000. pap. text 13.95 (*1-873741-41-3*) Millivres Bks.

Dickson, Jack. Freeform. 256p. 1997. pap. 12.95 (*0-85449-257-7*, Pub. by Gay Mens Pr) LPC InBook.

Dickson, James, ed. Seventh National Wild Turkey Symposium. LC 95-53675. 1996. write for info. (*0-8117-1105-6*) Stackpole.

Dickson, James G. The Politics of the Texas Sheriff: From Frontier to Bureaucracy. (Texas History Ser.). (Illus.). 68p. 1983. pap. text 9.95 (*0-89641-131-1*) American Pr.

Dickson, James G., ed. The Wild Turkey: Biology & Management. LC 92-11214. (Illus.). 496p. 1992. 69.95 (*0-8117-1859-X*) Stackpole.

Dickson, Jane. Peep Land: Paintings, 1983-1993. (Illus.). 64p. 1994. pap. 20.00 (*0-945558-21-X*) ISU Univ Galls.

Dickson, Jennifer. Gardener's Journal. 96p. 1991. boxed set. write for info. (*0-900946-37-7*) Porcup Quill.

— Hospital for Wounded Angels. 96p. 1987. write for info. (*0-88984-112-8*) Porcup Quill.

Dickson, Jo Ann, ed. see Turgeon, Bob.

Dickson, John. The Music of Solid Objects. LC 97-61511. (Illus.). 112p. 1997. pap. 7.95 (*0-939395-22-3*) Thorntree Pr.

— Sleeper. 72p. 1998. pap. 14.95 (*1-86940-187-5*, Pub. by Auckland Univ) Paul & Co Pubs.

— Waving at Trains. 96p. (Orig.). 1986. 9.95 (*0-939395-06-1*); pap. 5.95 (*0-939395-07-X*) Thorntree Pr.

Dickson, John, jt. auth. see Hosie, Gillian.

Dickson, Julie A. Forest Nectars: Poetry by Julie A. Dickson. 80p. (Orig.). 1997. pap. 5.95 (*1-57502-475-6*, P01427) Morris Pubng.

Dickson, K. & Maki, A. Fate & Effects of Sediment Bound Chems in Aquatic Systems: Proceedings of the 6th Pellston Workshop Florissant 8-84. LC 87-16210. (SETAC Special Publications). 1987. 206.00 (*0-08-034866-1*, Pub. by Pergamon Repr) Franklin.

Dickson, K. L., ed. Fate & Effects of Sediment-Bound Chemicals in Aquatic Systems. (Illus.). 450p. 65.00 (*0-317-66334-8*, Pergamon Pr) Elsevier.

Dickson, K. L. & Cairns, J., eds. Biological Data in Water Pollution Asses: Quantitative & Statistical Analyses - STP 652. 193p. 1982. 17.50 (*0-8031-0803-6*, STP652) ASTM.

Dickson, K. L., jt. ed. see Branson, D. R.

Dickson, K. L., jt. ed. see Cairns, John, Jr.

Dickson, Katharine. Downeast Dicksons: Forty-Two Lines of Early New England Settlers & All the Descendants, As of 1987, of Capt. Talbot Dickson & Susan Hayland of Harrington, Maine. LC 87-72754. (Illus.). xxvi, 208p. 1988. 30.00 (*0-9613959-1-5*) Brown Katharine.

— Stockman-Gallison Ancestral Lines: 114 Lines of Early New England Settlers & the Descendants, As of 1984 of John Gallison & Martha Moore. LC 84-72376. (Illus.). xxii, 285p. 1985. 30.00 (*0-9613959-0-7*) Brown Katharine.

Dickson, Katherine M. Katherine Mansfield's New Zealand Stories. LC 98-10528. 120p. 1998. 26.50 (*0-7618-1072-2*) U Pr of Amer.

— Sexism & Reentry: Job Realities for Women Librarians. LC 97-7884. 286p. 1997. 32.50 (*0-7618-0747-0*) U Pr of Amer.

Dickson, Keith. Nestor: Poetic Memory in Greek Epic. LC 95-12542. (Albert Bates Lord Studies in Oral Tradition: Vol. 16). (Illus.). 264p. 1995. text 57.00 (*0-8153-2073-6*, H1923) Garland.

Dickson, Keith, et al. Research Collaboration in Industry. 224p. 1990. text 35.00 (*0-86187-816-7*, Pub. by P P Pubs) Cassell & Continuum.

Dickson, Keith A. Towards Utopia: A Study of Brecht. 1978. 52.00 (*0-19-815750-9*) OUP.

Dickson, Kenneth L., jt. ed. see Cairns, John, Jr.

Dickson, Kwesi A. Uncompleted Mission: Christianity & Exclusivism. LC 91-11351. 150p. (Orig.). 1991. pap. 20.00 (*0-88344-751-7*) Orbis Bks.

Dickson, L. L. The Modern Allegories of William Golding. 160p. 1990. 49.95 (*0-8130-0971-5*) U Press Fla.

Dickson, L. M. Francis: Descendants of Joseph Francis of Maryland & Virginia. (Illus.). 201p. 1997. reprint ed. pap. 32.00 (*0-8328-8646-7*); reprint ed. lib. bdg. 42.00 (*0-8328-8645-9*) Higginson Bk Co.

Dickson, Lance E., intro. Treatise of Femme Coverts: or The Lady's Law. ix, viii, 280p. 1974. reprint ed. 42.00 (*0-8377-2129-6*, Rothman) W S Hein.

Dickson, Lance E., jt. ed. see Chiang, Win-Shin S.

Dickson, Lawrence J. The Book of Honor. LC 99-179145. 219p. 1998. pap. 10.00 (*0-9666440-0-X*) Fierce Pr.

Dickson, Leonard E. Collected Mathematical Papers, Set, Vols. I-VI. Albert, A. Adrian, ed. LC 69-19943. 4000p. 1983. text 295.00 (*0-8284-0273-6*) Chelsea Pub.

— History of the Theory of Numbers, 3 Vols. LC 66-26932. 85.00 (*0-8284-0086-5*) Chelsea Pub.

— Plane Trigonometry with Practical Applications. xii, 211p. 1992. text 14.95 (*0-8284-0230-2*) Chelsea Pub.

— Researches on Waring's Problem. LC 35-19856. (Carnegie Institution of Washington Publication Ser.: No. 464). 265p. reprint ed. pap. 82.20 (*0-608-10268-7*, 201571000095) Bks Demand.

***Dickson, Louise.** Crime Science. (Illus.). 40p. (J). (gr. 2-5). 1999. pap. text 5.95 (*1-55074-552-2*) Kids Can Pr.

Dickson, Louise. The Kids Guide to Fortune Telling. (Illus.). 40p. (J). (gr. 2-6). 1998. pap. 5.95 (*1-55074-479-8*, Pub. by Kids Can Pr) Genl Dist Srvs.

Dickson, Louise, jt. auth. see LeBlanc, Janet.

Dickson, Marcia. It's Not Like That Here: Teaching Academic Writing & Reading to Novice Writers. LC 94-36421. 206p. (Orig.). 1995. pap. text 22.00 (*0-86709-351-X*, 0351, Pub. by Boynton Cook Pubs) Heinemann.

Dickson, Marcia, jt. auth. see Belanoff, Patricia.

Dickson, Margaret, ed. National Women's Directory: Of Alcohol & Drug Abuse Treatment & Prevention Programs. 80p. 1988. pap. text 19.95 (*0-943519-07-1*, D1907) Sulzburger & Graham Pub.

Dickson, Marsha Ann, jt. auth. see Littrell, Mary Ann.

Dickson, Martin B. & Welch, S. Carey, intros. The Houghton Shahnameh: A Limited Facsimile Edition of the Shahnameh (Book of Kings), 2 vols., Set. 872p. 1982. 2500.00 (*0-674-40854-3*) HUP.

Dickson, Mary. The Americans with Disabilities Act: Hiring, Accommodating & Supervising Employees with... Keppler, Kay, ed. LC 94-68538. (Legal Issues in Business Ser.). 144p. (Orig.). 1995. pap. 15.95 (*1-56052-311-5*) Crisp Pubns.

— Supervising Employees with Disabilities: Beyond ADA Compliance. Machosky, Brenda, ed. LC 92-75714. (Fifty-Minute Ser.). 124p. (Orig.). 1993. pap. text 10.95 (*1-56052-209-7*) Crisp Pubns.

Dickson, Murray. Donde No Hay Dentista.Tr. of When There Is No Dentist. (SPA., Illus.). 208p. 1989. pap. 9.00 (*0-942364-19-8*) Hesperian Found.

— Where There Is No Dentist. Blake, Michael, ed. LC 82-84067. (Illus.). 192p. (Orig.). 1983. pap. 9.00 (*0-942364-05-8*) Hesperian Found.

Dickson, P. G. Finance & Government under Maria Theresia 1740-1780: Finance & Credit, Vol. II. (Illus.). 468p. 1987. text 95.00 (*0-19-822882-1*) OUP.

— Finance & Government under Maria Theresia 1740-1780: Society & Government, Vol. I. (Illus.). 510p. 1987. text 105.00 (*0-19-822570-9*) OUP.

— The Financial Revolution in England. (Modern Revivals in History Ser.). 500p. 1993. 92.95 (*0-7512-0010-7*, Pub. by Gregg Revivals) Ashgate Pub Co.

Dickson, Paul. Baseballs Greatest Q. LC 90-55531. (Illus.). 544p. 1992. reprint ed. pap. 21.00 (*0-06-272025-2*, Harper Ref) HarpC.

— The Book of Thanksgiving. LC 95-7694. 144p. (Orig.). 1995. pap. 9.00 (*0-399-52163-1*, Perigee Bks) Berkley Pub.

— Dickson's Joke Treasury: An Anthology of Gags, Bits, Puns & Jests - & How to Tell Them. LC 91-42415. 320p. 1992. pap. 16.95 (*0-471-55666-1*) Wiley.

— Family Words: The Dictionary for People Who Don't Know a Frone from a Brinkle. (Illus.). 144p. 1988. pap. 6.68 (*0-201-15593-1*) Addison-Wesley.

***Dickson, Paul.** From Elvis to E-Mail: Trends, Events & Trivia from the Postwar Era to the End of the Century. LC 99-62655. 416p. 1999. 9.98 (*1-892859-09-2*) Federal St Pr.

Dickson, Paul. The Future File: A Guide for People with One Foot in the 21st Century. LC 77-76998. 1977. 19.95 (*0-89256-031-2*) ETC Pubns.

— The Joy of Keeping Score: How Scoring the Game Has Influenced & Enhanced the History of Baseball. LC 97-14100. 128p. 1997. pap. 10.00 (*0-15-600516-6*) Harcourt.

— The Joy of Keeping Score: How Scoring the Game Has Influenced & Enhanced the History of Baseball. 1997. pap. write for info. (*0-614-27664-0*, Harvest Bks) Harcourt.

— The Joy of Keeping Score: How Scoring the Game Has Influenced & Enhanced the History of Baseball. (Illus.). 160p. 1996. 17.95 (*0-8027-1307-6*) Walker & Co.

— The New Dickson Baseball Dictionary. expanded rev. ed. LC 98-40700. (Illus.). 592p. 1999. pap. 20.00 (*0-15-600580-8*, Harvest Bks) Harcourt.

— The New Dickson Baseball Dictionary. expanded rev. ed. LC 98-40700. (Illus.). 592p. (C). 1999. 35.00 (*0-15-100380-7*, Harvest Bks) Harcourt.

— The New Official Rules: Maxims for Muddling Through to the 21st Century. 1989. pap. 8.95 (*0-685-25284-1*) Addison-Wesley.

***Dickson, Paul.** The Official Rules & Explanations: The Original Guide to Surviving the Electronic Age with Wit, Wisdom & Laughter. LC 99-62656. Orig. Title: The Official Rules, the Official Explanations. (Illus.). 512p. 1999. 9.98 (*1-892859-10-6*) Federal St Pr.

Dickson, Paul. The Official Rules at Home: The Laws That Determine What Can, & Probably Will, Go Awry in Your Daily Life. (Official Rules Ser.). 120p. 1996. 12.95 (*0-8027-1316-5*) Walker & Co.

— The Official Rules at Work: The Principles, Maxims, & Instructions That Define Your Life on the Job. (Official Rules Ser.). 120p. 1996. 12.95 (*0-8027-1317-3*) Walker & Co.

— The Official Rules for Golfers. LC 97-7816. 120p. 1997. 13.95 (*0-8027-1327-0*) Walker & Co.

— The Official Rules for Lawyers, Politicians . . . And Everyone They Torment. (Official Rules Ser.). (Illus.). 120p. 1996. 12.95 (*0-8027-1321-1*) Walker & Co.

— Slang! expanded rev. ed. LC 97-32543. 1998. 25.00 (*0-671-54920-0*) PB.

— Slang: The Authoritative Topic-by-Topic Dictionary of American Lingoes from All Walks of Life. expanded rev. ed. 480p. 1999. pap. 18.00 (*0-671-54919-7*) PB.

***Dickson, Paul.** Slang: The Authoritative Topic-by-Topic Dictionary of American Lingoes from All Walks of Life. rev. ed. 465p. 2000. 25.00 (*0-7881-9256-6*) DIANE Pub.

Dickson, Paul. Slang! The Topic-by-Topic Dictionary of Contemporary American Lingoes. McCarthy, Paul, ed. 320p. 1990. mass mkt. 10.00 (*0-671-67251-7*) S&S Trade.

— Timelines: Day by Day, Trend by Trend from the Dawn of the Atomic Age to the Close of the... 1991. pap. 10.95 (*0-201-56753-9*) HarperTrade.

— Toasts: Over Fifteen Hundred of the Best Toasts, Blessings, Sentiments, & Graces. rev. ed. (Illus.). 256p. 1991. 19.00 (*0-517-58412-3*, Crown) Crown Pub Group.

— War Slang: American Fighting Words & Phrases from the Civil War to the Gulf War. McCarthy, Paul, ed. 416p. 1995. pap. 18.00 (*0-671-75024-0*) PB.

***Dickson, Paul.** War Slang: American Fighting Words & Phrases from the Civil War to the Gulf War. 403p. 1999. reprint ed. pap. text 18.00 (*0-7881-6706-5*) DIANE Pub.

Dickson, Paul. The Worth Book of Softball: A Celebration of America's True National Pastime. LC 93-19312. (Illus.). 288p. 1994. 22.95 (*0-8160-2897-4*) Facts on File.

Dickson, Paul, compiled by. The Dickson Baseball Dictionary. 464p. 1991. pap. 14.95 (*0-380-71335-7*, Avon Bks) Morrow Avon.

Dickson, Paul & Clancy, Paul. The Congress Dictionary: The Ways & Meanings of Capitol Hill. 416p. 1995. pap. 19.95 (*0-471-11988-1*) Wiley.

***Dickson, Paul & Hickman, William.** Firestone: A Century, a Legend, a Celebration, 1900-2000. LC 99-52691. (Illus.). 124p. 1999. 28.95 (*0-8281-1338-6*) Forb Custom Pub.

Dickson, Paul & Skole, Robert. The Volvo Guide to Halls of Fame: The Traveler's Handbook of North America's Most Inspiring & Entertaining Attractions. (Illus.). 256p. (Orig.). 1995. pap. 12.95 (*1-879326-26-4*) Living Planet Pr.

Dickson, Paul, jt. auth. see Evelyn, Douglas E.

Dickson, Paul, jt. auth. see Mead, William B.

Dickson, Peter R. Marketing Management. 2nd ed. LC 96-83162. 852p. (C). 1996. text 101.50 (*0-03-017742-1*) Dryden Pr.

Dickson, Peter W. Kissinger & the Meaning of History. LC 78-5633. 207p. reprint ed. pap. 59.00 (*0-608-13314-0*, 2025581) Bks Demand.

Dickson, R. Gary. Divorce Guide for Alberta: Canadian Edition. 11th ed. (Legal Ser.). 144p. 1997. pap. 13.95 (*1-55180-169-8*) Self-Counsel Pr.

Dickson, R. J. Ulster Emigration to Colonial America, 1718-1775. 2nd rev. ed. 320p. 1997. pap. 29.95 (*0-901905-17-8*) Irish Bks Media.

***Dickson, Ray Clark.** Parlando: Selected Poems. xvii, 295p. 2000. 14.95 (*0-615-11586-1*) Kerouac Con.

Dickson, Rebecca, jt. auth. see Grady, Frank J.

Dickson, Richard J. The Christmas Story in Gospel & Tradition. (Dickson Study Ser.). 80p. 1992. teacher ed. 3.50 (*0-916010-14-7*); pap. text 6.95 (*0-916010-11-2*, DS-3) Crkside Weems.

— A Cruising Guide to the Corrotoman River: Including the Lower Rappahannock. (Bo-Ka Bks.). (Illus.). 80p. 1992. pap. text 9.95 (*0-916010-12-0*, BB-1) Crkside Weems.

— Letters from a Wandering Jew: A Study of the Pauline Epistles. (Dickson Study Ser.). 80p. 2001. pap. text 6.95 (*0-916010-13-9*, DS-6) Crkside Weems.

Dickson, Richard L. Warriner: The Colonial & European Ancestry of Julia Adelaide Warriner. (Illus.). 123p. 1991. reprint ed. pap. 19.50 (*0-8328-2057-1*); reprint ed. lib. bdg. 29.50 (*0-8328-2063-6*) Higginson Bk Co.

Dickson, Robert. Robert's of Charleston at Home. Colman, Beverly, ed. 58p. 1992. pap. 7.95 (*0-685-60201-X*) Roberts Charleston.

Dickson, Robert A. A Journal of Fine Cooking. 160p. 1988. write for info. (*0-318-64040-6*) Roberts Charleston.

Dickson, Robert A., jt. ed. see Torrens, Michael J.

Dickson, Robert B. Drug & Hormonal Resistance in Breast Cancer: Cellular & Molecular Mechanics. Lippman, M. E., ed. 448p. (C). 1995. 95.00 (*0-13-224858-1*) P-H.

Dickson, Robert B. & Lipman, Marc E., eds. Genes, Oncogenes & Hormones: Advances in Cellular & Molecular Biology of Breast Cancer. LC 92-15491. (Cancer Treatment & Research Ser.: Vol. 61). 464p. 1992. text 257.50 (*0-7923-1748-3*) Kluwer Academic.

Dickson, Robert B. & Lippman, Marc E., eds. Mammary Tumor Cell Cycle, Differentiation, & Metastasis: Advances in Cellular & Molecular Biology of Breast Cancer. LC 96-4654. 448p. 1996. text 345.00 (*0-7923-3905-3*) Kluwer Academic.

— Mammary Tumorigenesis & Malignant Progression: Advances in Cellular & Molecular Biology of Breast Cancer. LC 93-40375. (Cancer Treatment & Research Ser.: Vol. 71). 384p. (C). 1994. text 290.00 (*0-7923-2647-4*) Kluwer Academic.

Dickson, Robert B. & Salomon, David S., eds. Hormones & Growth Factors in Development & Neoplasia. LC 97-17442. 461p. 1998. 149.95 (*0-471-16899-8*, Wiley-Liss) Wiley.

Dickson, Robert B., jt. ed. see Lippman, Marc E.

Dickson, Robert H. Medical & Dental Negligence. LC 98-143898. xvii, 125p. 1997. write for info. (*0-567-00521-6*, Pub. by T & T Clark) Bks Intl VA.

Dickson, Roger E. Acts - Luke's Historical Defense of Christianity on Behalf of Paul. (Biblical Research Library: Vol. 2). 190p. (Orig.). 1996. pap. 8.95 (*1-56794-113-3*, C-2433) Star Bible.

— Baptism: Signing a Covenant with God. (Biblical Research Library: No. 6). 116p. (Orig.). 1997. pap. 6.95 (*1-56794-151-6*, C-2457) Star Bible.

— Eschatology: A Study of God's Judgments. (Biblical Reseach Library: No. 5). 140p. (Orig.). 1997. pap. 7.95 (*1-56794-150-8*, C-2456) Star Bible.

— Principles of Bible Interpretation, Vol. 3. 143p. (Orig.). 1996. pap. 7.95 (*1-56794-126-5*, C-2448) Star Bible.

— Servanthood Leadership, Vol. 4. (Biblical Research Library). 107p. (Orig.). 1996. pap. 5.95 (*1-56794-127-3*, C-2449) Star Bible.

— Sovereignty of the Father & Son. (Biblical Research Library: No. 1). 125p. (Orig.). 1996. pap. 7.95 (*1-56794-114-1*, C-2434) Star Bible.

Dickson, Ronald S. Homogeneous Catalysis with Compounds of Rhodium & Iridium. LC 85-18311. 1985. text 167.00 (*90-277-1880-6*) Kluwer Academic.

Dickson, Ruby Jones. The Holy Spirit Speaks: Poems. LC 98-50298. 1998. write for info. (*0-910683-39-5*) Townsnd-Pr.

***Dickson, Ruby Jones.** Taste & See: The Fruit of the Spirit. LC 98-54220. 1998. write for info. (*0-910683-40-9*) Townsnd-Pr.

Dickson, Ruby Jones. Think on These Things. LC 98-54135. 1998. write for info. (*0-910683-38-7*) Townsnd-Pr.

Dickson, S. Shattering the Icon of Abraham Lincoln: A New Look at the Lincoln Myth. 1987. lib. bdg. 79.00 (*0-8490-3956-8*) Gordon Pr.

Dickson, Samuel. Tales of San Francisco. viii, 711p. (C). 1992. pap. 19.95 (*0-8047-2097-5*) Stanford U Pr.

Dickson, Sandy. Kindred Threads--Loving Relationships: A Common Sense Layman's Guide. LC 98-129506. 1997. pap. 9.95 (*0-9661662-0-5*) Accolade Pub.

Dickson, T. R. Chemistry. 8th ed. pap. text. write for info. (*0-471-36317-0*) Wiley.

— Chemistry. 8th ed. 1999. pap. text, teacher ed. 25.00 (*0-471-36318-9*) Wiley.

Dickson, T. R. Introduction to Chemistry. 7th ed. LC 94-33544. 688p. 1995. pap. 43.95 (*0-471-04390-7*) Wiley.

***Dickson, T. R.** Introduction to Chemistry. 8th ed. LC 99-22865. 622p. 1999. pap. 48.95 (*0-471-18042-4*) Wiley.

Dickson, Thomas. Mass Media Education in Transition: Preparing for the 21st Century. LC 99-23014. (Communication Ser.). 296p. 1999. 59.95 (*0-8058-3097-9*) L Erlbaum Assocs.

Dickson, Tracy C. Dickson: Some of the Descendants of William Dickson & Elizabeth Campbell of Cherry Valley, N. Y. (Illus.). 367p. 1998. reprint ed. pap. 57.00 (*0-8328-8292-5*); reprint ed. lib. bdg. 67.00 (*0-8328-8291-7*) Higginson Bk Co.

Dickson, W. K. & Dickson, Antonia. History of the Kinetograph, Kinetoscope & Kinetophonograph. LC 79-124005. (Literature of Cinema, Ser. 1). 1973. reprint ed. 10.95 (*0-405-01611-5*) Ayer.

Dickson, W. K-L. The Biograph in Battle: Its Story in the South African War Related with Personal Experiences. (Illus.). 328p. 1995. 45.00 (*0-8386-3654-3*) Fairleigh Dickinson.

Dickson, W. Michael. Quantum Chance & Nonlocality: Probability & Nonlocality in the Interpretations of Quantum Mechanics. LC 97-8813. (Illus.). 264p. (C). 1998. text 69.95 (*0-521-58127-3*) Cambridge U Pr.

Dickson, William. Letters on Slavery. LC 79-111573. 1970. reprint ed. 25.00 (*0-8371-4598-8*, DLS&) Greenwood.

Dickson, William, ed. Mitigation of Slavery. LC 78-79013. (Black Heritage Library Collection). 1977. 26.95 (*0-8369-8655-5*) Ayer.

Dickson, William B., ed. Dickson. Genealogy of the Dickson Family & Its Immediate Collateral Branches, with Notes on the Scottish Emigration to N. Ireland. (Illus.). 189p. 1996. reprint ed. pap. 29.00 (*0-8328-5322-4*); reprint ed. lib. bdg. 39.00 (*0-8328-5321-6*) Higginson Bk Co.

Dickson, William J., jt. auth. see Roethlisberger, Fritz J.

Dickson-Wright, Clarissa, jt. auth. see Paterson, Jennifer.

Dickstein, Ellen, jt. auth. see Finley, Guy.

Dickstein, Esther, jt. auth. see Tiersky, Ethel.

Dickstein, Juliette, tr. see Jean, Raymond.

Dickstein, Leah J., et al, eds. American Psychiatric Press Review of Psychiatry, Vol. 15. 657p. 1996. 59.95 (*0-88048-442-X*, 8442) Am Psychiatric.

— American Psychiatric Press Review of Psychiatry, Vol. 16. 928p. 1997. text 59.95 (*0-88048-443-8*, 8443) Am Psychiatric.

Dickstein, Leah J., jt. ed. see Mogul, Kathleen M.

Dickstein, Mindi & Shapiro, Delilah. Israel: Triumph of the Spirit. LC 97-3645. (Illus.). 128p. 1997. 19.98 (*1-56799-446-6*, MetroBooks) M Friedman Pub Grp Inc.

Dickstein, Morris. Double Agent: The Critic & Society. 220p. 1996. reprint ed. pap. 21.00 (*0-19-511137-0*) OUP.

— Gates of Eden: American Culture in the Sixties. anniversary ed. LC 97-23295. 336p. 1997. pap. 15.95 (*0-674-34155-4*) HUP.

— Keats & His Poetry: A Study in Development. LC 74-136019. 288p. reprint ed. pap. 89.30 (0-608-16378-3, 202721000054) Bks Demand.
— Keats & His Poetry: A Study in Development. LC 74-136019. 288p. 1993. reprint ed. pap. text 4.25 (0-226-14796-7, P599) U Ch Pr.
— The Revival of Pragmatism: New Essays on Social Thought, Law, & Culture. LC 98-2992. 1998. 69.95 (0-8223-2228-5); pap. 23.95 (0-8223-2245-5) Duke.
Dickstein, Morris, jt. auth. see Cather, Willa.
Dickstein, Ruth & Brownmiller, Sara. Index to Women's Studies Anthologies: Research Across the Disciplines, 1985-1989. 725p. 1996. 165.00 (0-7838-1531-X, G K Hall Lrg Type) Mac Lib Ref.
Dickstein, Ruth, jt. auth. see Brownmiller, Sara.
DiClemente, R. J. & Peterson, J. L., eds. Preventing AIDS: Theories & Methods of Behavioral Interventions. (AIDS Prevention & Mental Health Ser.). (Illus.). 356p. (C). 1994. text 59.00 (0-306-44606-5, Kluwer Plenum) Kluwer Academic.
DiClemente, Ralph J. Adolescent & AIDS: Generation in Jeopardy: Epidemiology, Prevention & Policy. 312p. (C). 1992. text 46.00 (0-8039-4181-1); pap. text 21.95 (0-8039-4182-X) Sage.
DiClemente, Ralph J., et al, eds. Handbook of Adolescent Health Risk Behavior. (Clinical Child Psychology Library). (Illus.). 464p. 1996. 90.00 (0-306-45147-6, Kluwer Plenum) Kluwer Academic.
DiClemente, Ralph J., jt. ed. see Peterson, John L.
DiClemente, Ralph J., jt. ed. see Raczynski, James M.
DiClemente, Susan C., ed. see Arbeeny, Cynthia.
DiClemente, Susan C., ed. see Bassett, Pamela.
DiClemente, Susan C., ed. see Bisbee, Chester A.
DiClemente, Susan C., ed. see Goldin, Stan M.
DiClemente, Susan C., ed. see Goldin, Stan M. & Tankosic, Timothy.
DiClemente, Susan C., ed. see Hawkins, James W.
DiClemente, Susan C., ed. see Jain, Kewal.
DiClemente, Susan C., ed. see Rubenstein, Ken.
DiClemente, Susan C., ed. see Zavoico, George B.
Diclerico. Points of View. 8th ed. 2000. 25.00 (0-07-232268-3) McGraw.
Diclerico, James M. & Pavelec, Barry J. The Jersey Game: A History of Modern Baseball from Its Birth to the Big Leagues in the Garden State. (Illus.). 279p. (Orig.). (C). 1993. reprint ed. pap. 13.95 (0-8135-1943-8) Rutgers U Pr.
— The Jersey Game: The History of Modern Baseball from Its Birth to the Big Leagues in the Garden State. LC 90-44860. (Illus.). 224p. (C). 1991. 18.95 (0-8135-1652-8) Rutgers U Pr.
***DiClerico, Robert E.** American President. 5th ed. LC 99-12744. 432p. 1999. pap. text 45.00 (0-13-083575-7) P-H.
DiClerico, Robert E. Analyzing the Presidency. LC 85-71298. (Contemporary Focus Paperback Ser.). (Illus.). 300p. (C). 1987. per. 10.95 (0-87967-598-5, Dshkn McG-Hill) McGrw-H Hghr Educ.
— Analyzing the Presidency. 2nd ed. LC 85-71298. (Illus.). 276p. (C). 1989. per. 14.95 (0-87967-815-1, Dshkn McG-Hill) McGrw-H Hghr Educ.
***DiClerico, Robert E.** Political Parties, Campaigns & Elections. LC 99-48852. 299p. 2000. pap. 28.00 (0-13-040030-0) P-H.
DiClerico, Robert E. & Hammock, Allan S. Points of View: Readings in American Government & Politics. 4th ed. (Illus.). 352p. (C). 1989. pap. text. write for info. (0-318-62941-0) McGraw.
— Points of View: Readings in American Government & Politics. 5th ed. (C). 1991. text 25.25 (0-07-016849-0) McGraw.
— Points of View: Readings in American Government & Politics. 7th ed. LC 97-30864. 312p. 1997. pap. 34.06 (0-07-016870-9) McGraw.
DiClerico, Robert E. & Hammock, Allan S., eds. Points of View: Readings in American Government & Politics. 6th ed. LC 94-33042. 1994. pap. text 26.00 (0-07-016866-0) McGraw.
DiClerico, Robert E., jt. auth. see Davis, James W.
DiConti, Michael A. Entrepreneurship in Training: The Multinational Corporation in Mexico & Canada. Toyne, Brian, ed. LC 91-42535. (Critical Issues Facing the Multinational Enterprise Ser.). (Illus.). 180p. 1992. text 34.95 (0-87249-818-2) U of SC Pr.
DiConti, Veronica D. Interest Groups & Education Reform: The Latest Crusade to Restructure the Schools. LC 96-25405. 222p. 1996. lib. bdg. 36.50 (0-7618-0435-8) U Pr of Amer.
DiCosmo, F., jt. auth. see Nag, Raj T.
Dicosmo, Frank. Secondary Metabolites: Plant Cell & Tissue Cultures. Misawa, Masanaru, ed. LC 95-24670. 240p. 1996. lib. bdg. 209.95 (0-8493-5135-9) CRC Pr.
DiCosola, Cindy. Sing to the Lord. 1.75 (0-687-07105-4) Abingdon.
Dicou, Bert. Edom, Isreal's Brother & Antagonist: The Role of Edom in Biblical Prophecy & Story. LC 94-152796. (JSOTS Ser.: Vol. 169). 227p. 1994. 65.00 (1-85075-458-6, Pub. by Sheffield Acad) CUP Services.
Dicristina, Bruce. Method in Criminology: A Philosophical Primer. LC 94-23664. (C). 1995. text 30.00 (0-911577-28-9, Criminal Justice) Willow Tree NY.
DiCristo, Rose Marie, et al. A Guide to Judy Bolton Country. Carpentieri, Tony, ed. LC 98-131140. (Illus.). 726p. 1997. spiral bd. 39.95 (0-9639949-0-5) SynSine Pr.
Dicroce, Helen R., jt. auth. see Grohar-Murray, Mary Ellen.
Dicrola, Gerardo. Gerardo Dicrola: D'IO. (Illus.). 48p. 1999. pap. 16.95 (88-8158-173-6, Pub. by Charta) Dist Art Pubs.
Dict. Houghton Mifflin Picture Dictionary & Workbook, 001. 1986. 16.80 (0-395-41397-4) HM.
— Houghton Mifflin Student Dictionary & Workbook-Student, 001. 1986. 25.60 (0-395-38391-9) HM.
Dictionary of Literary Biography Editors Staff. Dictionary of Literary Biography Yearbook, 1987. 87th ed. (Illus.). 400p. 1993. text 155.00 (0-8103-1835-0) Gale.
Dictionary Staff. Random House Websters College Dictionary, No. 12. 2nd ed. 1997. write for info. (0-676-52705-1) Random Ref & Info.
— Random House Webster's Spell Checker & Abbreviations Dictionary. 1997. mass mkt. 4.99 (0-345-41440-3) Ballantine Pub Grp.
— Webster's American Family Dictionary. 1997. 23.95 (0-679-45801-8) Random Ref & Info.
Dictionnaires Robert, ed. Le Robert Mini: Langue Francaise et Noms Propres. (FRE.). 928p. 1995. 34.95 (0-7859-9310-X) Fr & Eur.
Dictor, Evan S. Visual Basic Controls in a Nutshell: The Controls of the Professional & Enterprise Editions. Petrusha, Ronald, ed. (Nutshell Handbook Ser.). (Illus.). 748p. (Orig.). 1999. pap. 24.95 (1-56592-294-8) OReilly & Assocs.
Dicum, Gregory & Luttinger, Nina. The Coffee Book: Anatomy of an Industry from Crop to the Last Drop. 196p. 1998. 14.95 (1-56584-508-0, Pub. by New Press NY) Norton.
— The Coffee Book: Industry from Crop to the Last Drop. LC 98-40702. 192p. 1999. pap. 14.95 (1-56584-452-1, Pub. by New Press NY) Norton.
DiCurcio, Robert A. Nantucket's Tried-Out Moby-Dick: Robert A. diCurcio's Companion Reader to Melville's Masterpiece. rev. ed. v, 136p. 1997. reprint ed. spiral bd. 18.00 (0-917358-11-2) Aeternium Pubng Co.
DiCyan, Erwin. A Beginner's Introduction to Trace Minerals. Passwater, Richard A. & Mindell, Earl R., eds. (Good Health Guide Ser.). 32p. 1984. pap. 3.95 (0-87983-362-9, 33629K, Keats Publng) NTC Contemp Pub Co.
Diczfalusy, E. & Griffin, P. Research in Human Reproduction: Biennial Report, 1986-1987. 346p. 1988. 25.00 (92-4-156120-3) World Health.
Diczfalusy, Egon. The Contraceptive Revolution: An Era of Scientific & Social Development. LC 96-34919. (Illus.). 256p. 1997. 75.00 (1-85070-748-0) Prthnon Pub.
Diczfalusy, Egon, jt. ed. see Benagiano, Giuseppe.
Did You Know Publishings Staff. Rosa Parks. LC 92-71756. 32p. (J). 1992. 11.99 (0-9633151-0-2) Did You Know Pub.
Didacta Inc. Staff. Workbook Pronunciation & Spelling. (Illus.). 1989. pap. text, student ed. 12.13 (0-8013-0235-8, 75891) Longman.
Didactic Systems, Inc. Staff & Didactic Systems Staff. Communications: Problems & Opportunities. (Simulation Game Ser.). 1971. pap. 26.25 (0-89401-008-5) Didactic Syst.
Didactic Systems Staff. Appraisal by Objectives: Coaching & Appraising. (Simulation Game Ser.). 1970. pap. 26.25 (0-89401-003-4) Didactic Syst.
— Appraising Employee Performance. (Study Units Ser.). 1978. pap. 9.00 (0-89401-107-3) Didactic Syst.
— Assigning Work. (Simulation Game Ser.). 1973. pap. 26.25 (0-89401-006-9); pap. 35.00 (0-89401-096-4) Didactic Syst.
Didactic Systems Staff. Communicating for Results. (Simulation Game Ser.). 1969. pap. 26.25 (0-89401-007-7); pap. 35.00 (0-89401-097-2) Didactic Syst.
Didactic Systems Staff. Constructive Discipline. 2nd ed. (Simulation Game Ser.). 1978. pap. 26.25 (0-89401-123-5) Didactic Syst.
— Effective Communications. (Study Units Ser.). 1977. pap. 9.00 (0-89401-138-3) Didactic Syst.
— Effective Delegation. Euro-Training & Garcia De Leon, Luis, trs. (Simulation Game Ser.). (FRE.). 1971. pap. 35.00 (0-89401-017-4) Didactic Syst.
— Effective Delegation. (Simulation Game Ser.). 1974. pap. 26.25 (0-89401-145-6) Didactic Syst.
— Effective Delegation. (Study Units Ser.). 1977. pap. 9.00 (0-89401-109-X) Didactic Syst.
— Effective Retail Selling & Customer Service. (Study Units Ser.). 1977. pap. 9.00 (0-89401-110-3) Didactic Syst.
— Effective Supervision. (SPA.). 1973. pap. 35.00 (0-89401-023-9) Didactic Syst.
— Effective Supervision. 1979. pap. 26.25 (0-89401-022-0) Didactic Syst.
— Grievance Handling: Industrial. 1970. pap. 26.25 (0-89401-027-1) Didactic Syst.
— Grievance Handling: Industrial. (FRE.). 1970. pap. 35.00 (0-89401-028-X) Didactic Syst.
— Grievance Handling: Non-Industrial. 1971. pap. 26.25 (0-89401-029-8); pap. 35.00 (0-89401-030-1) Didactic Syst.
— Handling Conflict in Law Enforcement Management: Conflict Among Peers. (Simulation Game Ser.). 1978. pap. 26.25 (0-89401-144-8) Didactic Syst.
— Handling Conflict in Law Enforcement Management: Superior Subordinate Conflict. (Simulation Game Ser.). 1978. pap. 26.25 (0-89401-040-9) Didactic Syst.
— Improving Labor Relations. (Study Units Ser.). 1977. pap. 9.00 (0-89401-111-1) Didactic Syst.
— The Instructor As Manager of Learning Experiences. (Simulation Game Ser.). 1975. pap. 26.25 (0-89401-044-1) Didactic Syst.
— Job Enrichment: Redesigning Jobs for Motivation. (Simulation Game Ser.). 1971. pap. 6.00 (0-89401-045-X) Didactic Syst.
— Long Range Planning. (Simulation Game Ser.). 1971. pap. 26.25 (0-89401-049-2) Didactic Syst.
— Management by Objectives. (Simulation Game Ser.). (POR.). 1970. pap. 35.00 (0-89401-053-0) Didactic Syst.
— Management by Objectives. 2nd ed. 1978. pap. 26.25 (0-89401-142-1) Didactic Syst.
— Management by Objectives for Insurance Companies. (Simulation Game Ser.). 1972. pap. 26.25 (0-89401-054-9) Didactic Syst.
— Management for Supervisors. 1970. pap. 26.25 (0-89401-056-5) Didactic Syst.
— Management for Supervisors. (FRE.). 1970. pap. 35.00 (0-89401-057-3); pap. 35.00 (0-89401-058-1) Didactic Syst.
— Management in Government. (Simulation Game Ser.). 1971. pap. 26.25 (0-89401-059-X) Didactic Syst.
— Managing in a Foreign Culture. (Simulation Game Ser.). 1974. pap. 26.25 (0-89401-062-X) Didactic Syst.
— Managing the Engineering Function. (Simulation Game Ser.). 1970. pap. 26.25 (0-89401-063-8); pap. 35.00 (0-89401-099-9) Didactic Syst.
— Managing the Manufacturing & Industrial Engineering Functions. (Simulation Game Ser.). 1970. pap. 26.25 (0-89401-064-6) Didactic Syst.
— Managing the Quality Control Function. 1970. pap. 26.25 (0-89401-065-4) Didactic Syst.
— Managing Through Face-to-Face Communication. (Simulation Game Ser.). (POR.). 1969. pap. 35.00 (0-89401-067-0) Didactic Syst.
— Managing Through Face-to-Face Communication. (Simulation Game Ser.). 1969. reprint ed. pap. 26.25 (0-89401-066-2) Didactic Syst.
— Managing Time Effectively. (Study Units Ser.). 1977. pap. 9.00 (0-89401-112-X) Didactic Syst.
— Market Planning. (Simulation Game Ser.). 1972. pap. 26.25 (0-89401-068-9) Didactic Syst.
— Market Strategy. (Simulation Game Ser.). 1970. pap. 26.25 (0-89401-069-7) Didactic Syst.
— Market Strategy. (Simulation Game Ser.). (POR.). 1970. pap. 35.00 (0-89401-118-9) Didactic Syst.
— Merchandising Challenges & Opportunities. (Study Units Ser.). 1977. pap. 9.00 (0-89401-113-8) Didactic Syst.
— Office Management. (Simulation Game Ser.). 1970. pap. 26.25 (0-89401-070-0) Didactic Syst.
— Optimum Delegation. (Simulation Game Ser.). 1973. pap. 26.25 (0-89401-019-0) Didactic Syst.
— Physical Distribution Management. (Simulation Game Ser.). (POR.). 1970. pap. 35.00 (0-89401-119-7) Didactic Syst.
— Physical Distribution Management. (Simulation Game Ser.). 1970. pap. 26.25 (0-89401-071-9) Didactic Syst.
— Planned Maintenance. (Simulation Game Ser.). 1969. pap. 26.25 (0-89401-072-7) Didactic Syst.
— Planning & Assigning Work. (Study Units Ser.). 1978. pap. 9.00 (0-89401-121-9) Didactic Syst.
— Planning for Growth. (Simulation Game Ser.). 1972. pap. 26.25 (0-89401-074-3) Didactic Syst.
— Positive Discipline. (Study Units Ser.). 1978. pap. 9.00 (0-89401-122-7) Didactic Syst.
— Practical On-the-Job Training. (Study Units Ser.). 1977. pap. 9.00 (0-89401-114-6) Didactic Syst.
— Principles of Effective Insurance Agents. (Simulation Game Ser.). 1973. pap. 26.25 (0-685-77372-8) Didactic Syst.
— Procurement Management. (Simulation Game Ser.). 1975. pap. 26.25 (0-89401-080-8) Didactic Syst.
— Productivity - Improving Performance. (Simulation Game Ser.). 1975. pap. 26.25 (0-89401-081-6) Didactic Syst.
— Recruiting Effective Insurance Agents. (Simulation Game Ser.). (FRE.). 1973. pap. 35.00 (0-89401-083-2) Didactic Syst.
— Recruiting Effective Insurance Agents. (Simulation Game Ser.). 1973. pap. 26.25 (0-89401-082-4) Didactic Syst.
— Retail Management. (Study Units Ser.). 1977. pap. 9.00 (0-89401-115-4) Didactic Syst.
Didactic Systems Staff. Sales Promotion. (Simulation Game Ser.). 1969. pap. 26.25 (0-89401-084-0) Didactic Syst.
Didactic Systems Staff. Sales Strategy. (Simulation Game Ser.). 1968. pap. 26.25 (0-89401-085-9) Didactic Syst.
— Selecting Effective Insurance Agents. (Simulation Game Ser.). 1973. pap. 26.25 (0-89401-090-5) Didactic Syst.
— Selecting Effective Insurance Agents. (Simulation Game Ser.). (FRE.). 1973. pap. 35.00 (0-89401-091-3) Didactic Syst.
— Selecting Effective People. (Simulation Game Ser.). (POR.). 1970. pap. 35.00 (0-89401-089-1) Didactic Syst.
— Selecting Effective People. (Simulation Game Ser.). 1970. pap. 26.25 (0-89401-087-5) Didactic Syst.
— Strategies for Motivation. (Study Units Ser.). 1970. pap. 9.00 (0-89401-116-2) Didactic Syst.
Didactic Systems Staff, jt. auth. see Didactic Systems, Inc. Staff.
Diday, E., ed. Data Analysis, Learning Symbolic & Numeric Knowledge. 538p. (C). 1989. text 245.00 (0-941743-64-0) Nova Sci Pubs.
Diday, E., et al, eds. New Approaches in Classification & Data Analysis. (Studies in Classification, Data Analysis, & Knowledge Organization). (Illus.). xii, 693p. 1994. 128.00 (3-540-58425-0) Spr-Verlag.
Diday, E. & Lechevallier, Y., eds. Symbolic-Numeric Data Analysis & Learning. 612p. (C). 1991. text 295.00 (1-56072-042-5) Nova Sci Pubs.
Diday, E., jt. ed. see Bock, H. H.
Didbin, Thomas F. Selections. LC 77-18012. (Great Bibliographers Ser.: No. 3). 253p. 1978. 18.50 (0-8108-1077-8, 2117) Scarecrow.
Didcott, Charles. St. Barth: French West Indies. LC 97-13684. (ENG & FRE., Illus.). 120p. 1997. 35.00 (0-393-04612-5) Norton.
Diddee, Dolly, tr. see Prem, Ma Ananda, ed.
Diddee, Jaymala, ed. Urbanisation: Trends, Perspectives & Challenges. (C). 1993. 30.00 (81-7033-185-4, Pub. by Rawat Pubns) S Asia.
Diddel, Margarita T. Thistle in Her Hand. (Illus.). 424p. (Orig.). 1988. pap. 14.95 (1-55787-035-7, MA20064, Windswept Books) Hrt of the Lakes.
Didenko, A. N., jt. ed. see Bystritskii, V. M.
Diderot, Denis. Anatomie-Chirurgie Encyclopedie Ou Dictionnaire Raissonne des Sciences. 2nd ed. (FRE.). 1977. 75.00 (0-7859-0857-9, M-7053) Fr & Eur.
— Architectural Plates from the "Encyclopedie" 128p. 1995. pap. 11.95 (0-486-27954-5) Dover.
— Les Bijoux Indiscrets. (FRE.). 1982. pap. 11.95 (0-7859-1946-5, 2070373436) Fr & Eur.
— Les Bijoux Indiscrets. unabridged ed. (FRE.). 1996. pap. 7.95 (2-87714-332-5, Pub. by Bookking Intl) Distribks Inc.
— Correspondance Complete de Didero Vol. 5: 1765-1766. (FRE.). 272p. 1958. pap. 24.95 (0-7859-5254-3, 2707304409) Fr & Eur.
— Correspondance Complete de Diderot, 16 vols. Incl. Vol. 1. 1713-1757. 1970. pap. 24.95 (0-8288-9582-1); Vol. 3. 1759-1761. 1970. pap. 24.95 (0-8288-9584-8); Vol. 5. 1765-1766. 1958. pap. 24.95 (0-8288-9586-4, 2707304409); Vol. 6. 1766. 1970. pap. 24.95 (0-8288-9587-2); Vol. 8. 1768. 1970. pap. 24.95 (0-8288-9589-9); Vol. 9. 1769. 1970. pap. 24.95 (0-8288-9590-2); Vol. 10. 1770-1771. 1970. pap. 24.95 (0-8288-9591-0); Vol. 11. 1771. 1970. pap. 24.95 (0-8288-9592-9); Vol. 13. 1773-1774. 1970. pap. 24.95 (0-8288-9594-5); Vol. 15. 1776-1784. 1970. pap. 24.95 (0-8288-9596-1); Vol. 16. Complement, Corrections, Listes et Index General. 1970. pap. 24.95 (0-8288-9597-X); (FRE.). 1970. pap. write for info. (0-318-51971-2) Fr & Eur.
— Correspondance Complete de Diderot Vol. 4: 1762-1764. (FRE.). 1958. pap. 24.95 (0-7859-5253-5, 2707304395) Fr & Eur.
— Correspondance Complete de Diderot Vol. 14: 1774-1776. (FRE.). 276p. 1968. pap. 24.95 (0-7859-5255-1, 2707304492) Fr & Eur.
— Denis Diderot, Wicked Philanthropy: A Translation of Est-il bon? Est-il Mechant? Brogyany, Gabriel J., tr. from FRE. 148p. 1986. pap. 19.50 (0-8191-5338-9); lib. bdg. 41.00 (0-8191-5337-0) U Pr of Amer.
— Diderot on Art, 2 vols. Goodman, John, tr. Incl. Vol. 1. Salon of 1765 & Notes on Painting. LC 95-10638. (Illus.). 250p. 1995. pap. 18.00 (0-300-06251-6); Vol. 1. Salon of 1765 & Notes on Painting. Goodman, John, ed. LC 95-10638. (Illus.). 250p. 1995. 42.00 (0-300-06248-6); Vol. 2. Salon of 1767. Goodman, John, ed. LC 95-10638. (Illus.). 344p. 1995. pap. 20.00 (0-300-06252-4); 85.00 (0-300-06250-8); Set pap. 38.00 (0-300-06253-2) Yale U Pr.
— Diderot's Early Philosophical Works. Jourdain, Margaret, ed. LC 70-147967. reprint ed. 34.50 (0-404-08219-X) AMS Pr.
— Diderot's Writings on the Theatre. Green, F. C., ed. LC 76-43916. (Music & Theatre in France in the 17th & 18th Centuries Ser.). reprint ed. 57.50 (0-404-60157-X) AMS Pr.
— L' Encyclopedia. (FRE.). 192p. 1967. 7.95 (0-8288-9598-8, F46920) Fr & Eur.
— Encyclopedia: Selections. Cassirer, Thomas & Hoyt, Nelly S., trs. LC 65-26535. 1965. pap. 8.80 (0-672-60479-5, Bobbs) Macmillan.
— Entretien Entre d'Alembert et Diderot. (FRE.). 1990. pap. 10.95 (0-7859-2958-4) Fr & Eur.
— Entretiens sur le Fils Naturel: Avec: Paradoxe sur le Comedien. (Cahiers Victor Hugo Ser.: No. 2). (FRE.). 190p. 1965. pap. 12.95 (0-7859-1171-5, 2082103013) Fr & Eur.
— Essai sur les Regnes de Claude et de Neron, 2 vols. (FRE.). 1972. 9.95 (0-685-73283-5) Fr & Eur.
— The Indiscreet Jewels. Hawkes, Sophie, tr. from FRE. LC 92-62369. 320p. (Orig.). 1993. 32.00 (0-941419-82-7) Marsilio Pubs.
— The Indiscreet Jewels. Hawkes, Sophie, tr. from FRE. LC 92-62369. 320p. (Orig.). 1993. pap. 16.00 (0-941419-83-5) Marsilio Pubs.
— Jacques le Fatalist et Son Maitre. (FRE.). 373p. 1977. pap. 11.95 (0-7859-1819-1, 2070367630) Fr & Eur.
— Jacques le Fataliste. Walter-Leutrat, ed. 1967. pap. 10.95 (0-7859-0382-8, M1797) Fr & Eur.
— Jacques le Fataliste. (Folio Ser.: No. 763). (FRE.). 320p. 1970. 9.95 (2-07-036763-0) Schoenhof.
— Jacques le Fataliste. unabridged ed. (FRE.). pap. 7.95 (2-87714-144-6, Pub. by Bookking Intl) Distribks Inc.
— Jacques the Fatalist. Coward, David, ed. LC 98-31240. (Oxford World's Classics Ser.). 304p. (Orig.). 1999. pap. 9.95 (0-19-283874-1) OUP.
— Lettre sur les Aveugles a l'Usage de ceux qui Voient. 2nd ed. (FRE.). 124p. 1973. 14.95 (0-8288-9956-8, F46880) Fr & Eur.
— Lettres a Sophie Volland. (FRE.). 416p. 1984. pap. 16.95 (0-7859-1993-7, 2070375471) Fr & Eur.
— Lettres a Sophie Volland. (Folio Ser.: No. 1547). (FRE.). 405p. 1984. pap. 14.95 (2-07-037547-1) Schoenhof.
— Lettres et de la Vie de Descartes par Baillet. (FRE.). 192p. 1967. 10.95 (0-7859-1170-7, 2080701649) Fr & Eur.
— Maximes et Pensees. (FRE.). 1993. pap. 13.95 (0-7859-3305-0, 2850552453) Fr & Eur.
— Memoirs of a Nun. Birrell, Francis, tr. 1992. 15.00 (0-679-41324-3) Everymns Lib.
— Le Neveu de Rameau. D'Adam, ed. (Coll. GF). (FRE.). 1966. pap. 10.95 (0-8288-9958-4, F46912) Fr & Eur.
— Le Neveu de Rameau - la Reve de d'Alembert... (FRE.). 438p. 1978. pap. 11.95 (0-7859-1818-3, 2070367614) Fr & Eur.
— Le Neveu de Rameau & le Reve d'Alembert, Supplement au Voyage de Bougainville, et Autres Dialogues. (Folio Ser.: No. 761). (FRE.). (Orig.). pap. 9.95 (2-07-036761-4) Schoenhof.

D

An Asterisk (*) at the beginning of an entry indicates that the title is appearing for the first time.

— The Nun. Tancock, Leonard W., tr. (Classics Ser.). 192p. 1981. pap. 15.99 (0-14-044300-2, Penguin Classics) Viking Penguin.

— Oeuvres. (FRE.). 1978. 95.00 (0-8288-3434-2, F46720) Fr & Eur.

— Oeuvres. deluxe ed. Billy, Andre, ed. (Pleiade Ser.). (FRE.). 1989. 75.95 (2-07-010173-8) Schoenhof.

— Oeuvres: Avec: Les Bijoux Indiscrets. (FRE.). 1480p. 1978. 105.00 (0-7859-1097-2, 2070101738) Fr & Eur.

— Oeuvres Completes: Le Modele Anglais, Vol. 1. 468p. 1975. 99.50 (0-686-56012-4) Fr & Eur.

— Oeuvres Esthetiques. Verniere, Paul, ed. (FRE.). 896p. 1988. pap. 59.95 (0-7859-4653-5) Fr & Eur.

— Oeuvres Philosophiques. Verniere, Paul, ed. 1961. 37.95 (0-8288-9951-7, F46750) Fr & Eur.

— Oeuvres Politiques. Verniere, Paul, ed. 1963. 28.95 (0-8288-9952-5, F46760) Fr & Eur.

— Oeuvres Romanesques. Benac, Henri, ed. 1962. 39.95 (0-8288-9953-3, F46772) Fr & Eur.

— Opinions et Paradoxes. 220p. 1963. 14.95 (0-686-56019-1) Fr & Eur.

— Le Paradoxe sur le Comedien: Avec: Danaud, Jean-Claude. Un Ouvrage de Dames. (Illus.). 49p. 1977. 10.95 (0-8288-9599-6, F46850) Fr & Eur.

— Le Paradoxe sur le Comedien: Paris, 1902. (FRE.). 125p. 1991. 10.95 (0-7859-1073-5, 2040192832) Fr & Eur.

— Pensees Philosophiques. 3rd ed. 75p. 1965. 10.95 (0-8288-9959-2, F46930) Fr & Eur.

— Pensees sur l'Interpretation de la Nature: Avec Varloot, Jean. La Pensee de Diderot dans l'Encyclopedie. 2nd ed. 9.95 (0-686-56023-X) Fr & Eur.

Diderot, Denis. Political Writings. Wokler, Robert & Mason, John H., eds. (Cambridge Texts in the History of Political Thought Ser.). 256p. (C). 1992. text 59.95 (0-521-36044-7); pap. text 19.95 (0-521-36911-8) Cambridge U Pr.

Diderot, Denis. Quatre Contes. 212p. 1964. 8.95 (0-686-56026-4) Fr & Eur.

— Rameau's Nephew & D'Alembert's Dream. Tancock, Leonard W., tr. (Classics Ser.). 240p. 1976. pap. 12.95 (0-14-044173-5, Penguin Classics) Viking Penguin.

— Rameau's Nephew & Other Works. Barzun, Jacques & Brown, Ralph H., trs. from FRE. LC 55-9755. 1964. 29.50 (0-672-51089-8) Irvington.

— La Religieuse. 1972. write for info. (0-318-63587-9); pap. 11.95 (0-7859-1689-X, 2070360571) Fr & Eur.

— La Religieuse. (Folio Ser.: No. 57). (FRE.). 1972. pap. 9.95 (2-07-036057-1) Schoenhof.

— La Religieuse. unabridged ed. (FRE.). pap. 5.95 (2-87714-189-6, Pub. by Bookking Intl) Distribks Inc.

— Selected Philosophical Writings. Lough, John, ed. LC 86-25774. 232p. 1987. reprint ed. lib. bdg. 59.50 (0-313-25228-9, DISE, Greenwood Pr) Greenwood.

— 1771-1772, Vol. 12. 1970. pap. 24.95 (0-8288-9593-7) Fr & Eur.

— 1767, Vol. 7. 1970. pap. 24.95 (0-8288-9588-0) Fr & Eur.

— Sur l'Art et les Artistes. (FRE.). 220p. 1967. 27.95 (0-8288-9954-1, F46790) Fr & Eur.

— Textes Politiques. (FRE.). 214p. 1971. 29.95 (0-8288-7428-X) Fr & Eur.

— This Is Not a Story & Other Stories. Furbank, P. N., tr. & intro. by. LC 92-26850. (World's Classics Ser.). 176p. 1993. pap. 9.95 (0-19-282958-0) OUP.

— This Is Not a Story & Other Stories. Furbank, P. N., tr. & intro. by. 176p. 1991. text 27.50 (0-8262-0815-0) U of Mo Pr.

***Diderot, Denis.** Thoughts on the Interpretation of Nature & Other Philosophical Works. Sandler, Lorna, tr. 200p. 2000. 75.00 (1-903083-06-0, Pub. by Clinamen Pr); pap. 35.00 (1-903083-05-2, Pub. by Clinamen Pr) Paul & Co Pubs.

Diderot, Denis. Le Turc sans Peine (Turkish for French Speakers) (FRE.). 476p. 1975. 99.50 incl. audio (0-7859-1190-1, 2705657932) Fr & Eur.

Diderot, Denis & Adam, Antoine. Bijoux Indiscrets. 320p. 1968. write for info. (0-318-63437-6) Fr & Eur.

— Les Bijoux Indiscrets. (Folio Ser.: No. 1343). (FRE.). 320p. 1968. pap. 9.95 (2-07-037343-6) Schoenhof.

— Supplement au Voyage de Bougainville: Avec: Pensees Philosophiques, Lettre sur les Aveugles. (FRE.). 192p. 1972. 10.95 (0-8288-9962-2, F46970) Fr & Eur.

Diderot, Denis & Alembert, Jean L. Theatre Architecture & Stage Machines: Engravings from the Encyclopedie, ou Dictionnaire Raisonne des Sciences, des Arts, et des Metiers. 1972. 27.95 (0-405-09139-7, 1713) Ayer.

Diderot, Denis & D'Alembert, Jean L., eds. Encyclopedie, 18 vols., Set. (FRE.). 1979. 3450.00 (0-685-03322-8, Pergamon Pr) Elsevier.

Diderot, Denis & Desne, R. Les Salons. 2nd ed. 9.95 (0-686-56029-9) Fr & Eur.

Diderot, Denis & Jean-Pierre. Oeuvres Completes: Avec: Philosophie et Mathematiques, Vol. 2. (FRE.). 320p. 1984. 19.95 (0-7859-1191-X, 2705659838) Fr & Eur.

Diderot, Denis & Perol, Lucette. Contes et Entretiens. (FRE.). 245p. 1977. 10.95 (0-8288-9961-4, F46960) Fr & Eur.

Diderot, Denis & Varloot, Jean. Le Reve d'Alembert. 2nd ed. (FRE.). 248p. 1962. 11.95 (0-8288-9745-X, 2253034738) Fr & Eur.

Diderot, Denis & Verniere, Paul. Memoires pour Catherine II. (FRE., Illus.). 420p. 1966. 29.95 (0-8288-9957-6, F46890) Fr & Eur.

Diderot, Denis, et al. Jacques le Fataliste et Son Maitre: Texte et Variantes Establis sur le ms de Leingrad. 664p. 1976. 14.95 (0-686-56008-6) Fr & Eur.

— Oeuvres Completes: Encyclopedie I (Lettre A), Vol. 5. 564p. 1977. 115.00 (0-686-56014-0) Fr & Eur.

— Oeuvres Completes: Encyclopedie II (Lettres B-C), Vol. 6. (Illus.). 564p. 1977. 115.00 (0-686-56015-9) Fr & Eur.

— Oeuvres Completes: Encyclopedie III (Lettres D-L), Vol. 7. 728p. 1977. 150.00 (0-686-56016-7) Fr & Eur.

— Oeuvres Completes: Encyclopedie IV (Lettres M-Z), Vol. 8. 564p. 1977. 135.00 (0-686-56017-5) Fr & Eur.

— Le Pour et le Contre: Correspondance Polemique sur le Respect de la Posterite. Pline et les Anciens Auteurs qui ont Parle de Peinture et de Sculpture. (FRE., Illus.). 384p. 1958. 10.95 (0-8288-9963-0, F47360) Fr & Eur.

Diderot, Denis, ed. see d'Holbach, Baron P.

Didi, Dolli, tr. see Osho.

Didi-Huberman, Georges. Fra Angelico: Dissemblance & Figuration. Todd, Jane M., tr. from FRE. LC 94-32177. (Illus.). 290p. 1995. 65.00 (0-226-14813-0) U Ch Pr.

Didi-Humberman, Georges & Tosatto, Guy, texts. Giuseppe Penone. (Illus.). 224p. 1998. pap. 45.00 (88-7757-069-5, 810933, Pub. by Hopefulmonster Editore) Dist Art Pubs.

Didier. Dictionnaire Bordas le Cadet. (FRE.). 1990. write for info. (0-7859-7706-6, 2040183604) Fr & Eur.

Didier, Beatrice. Dictionnaire Universel des Litteratures, 3 vols. (FRE.). 4544p. 1994. 1295.00 (0-7859-9265-0) Fr & Eur.

Didier, Beatrice, jt. auth. see Stendhal, pseud.

Didier, Beatrice, ed. see Marquis De Sade, pseud.

Didier, Bert, ed. B'98 - Recent Advances in the Development & Use of the B Method: Proceedings Second International B Conference, Montpellier, France, April 22-24, 1998. LC 98-18094. (Lecture Notes in Computer Science Ser.: Vol. 1393). viii, 313p. 1998. pap. 55.00 (3-540-64405-9) Spr-Verlag.

Didier, Charles. Sojourn with the Grand Sharif of Makkah. Boulind, Richard, tr. from FRE. (Arabia Past & Present Ser.: Vol. 18).Tr. of Sejour chez le Grand-Cherif de la Mekke. (Illus.). 176p. 1985. 45.00 (0-906672-11-2) Oleander Pr.

Didier, Don. Dictionnaire de L'EAO: With English-French Index. (ENG & FRE.). 248p. 1988. pap. 34.95 (0-7859-7930-1, 2708005847) Fr & Eur.

***Didier, Donna.** Intermediate CPT/HCPCS for Physician Office Coding: 2000 Edition. rev. ed. 144p. 2000. pap. text 60.00 (1-58426-036-X, AC401100) Am Hlth Info.

Didier, E. L. Life & Poems of Edgar Allen Poe. LC 73-16344. (Studies in Poe: No. 23). 1974. lib. bdg. 75.00 (0-8383-1726-X) M S G Haskell Hse.

Didier, Jean-Pierre. Dictionnaire de la Plongee Sous-Marine.Tr. of Dictionary of Skin-Diving. (ENG, FRE, GER, ITA & SPA.). 262p. 1985. pap. 110.00 (0-8288-2351-0, F71220) Fr & Eur.

Didier, Jean-Pierre & Barbarin, B. Enclaves & Granite Petrology. (Developments in Petrology Ser.: Vol. 13). xxiv,26p. 1991. 219.00 (0-444-89145-5) Elsevier.

Didier, Marcel. Dictionnaire Mes 10,000 Mots. (FRE.). write for info. (0-7859-7700-7, 2040161538) Fr & Eur.

Didier, Nicolas. Lexicon of Molecular Biology: English-French, French-English.Tr. of Lexique Biologie Moleculaire. (ENG & FRE.). 1990. pap. 39.95 (0-7859-3917-2) Fr & Eur.

Didier, Noel. Le Droit Des Fiefs Dans la Coutume De Hainaut Au Moyen Age. LC 80-2032. reprint ed. 29.50 (0-404-18561-4) AMS Pr.

***Didier, Pierre.** WTO Trade Instruments in EU Law. 1999. 198.00 (1-874698-27-9, Pub. by Cameron May) Gaunt.

Didier, Robert. Autour de l'Approximation Semi-Classique. (Progress in Mathematics Ser.: No. 68). 344p. 1987. 63.00 (0-8176-3354-5) Birkhauser.

Didik, Frank. Directory of American Businesses. 1992. 129.00 (1-56840-002-0) Am Directory.

— History & Guide Book to Lenticular Images. 1993. 129.00 (1-56840-003-9) Am Directory.

Didinger, Ray, ed. Game Plans for Success. (Illus.). 256p. 1996. pap. 14.95 (0-8092-3171-9, 317190, Contemporary Bks) NTC Contemp Pub Co.

DiDio, L. J., ed. see Motta, P. M.

Didio, L. J., jt. ed. see Motta, P. M.

***Didio, Roger J.** Atlantis: A Tale of the Earth. 586p. 1999. pap. 19.95 (0-9672760-0-4, Pub. by Atlantea Pr) ACCESS Pubs Network.

Didion, Joan. After Henry. LC 92-50640. 1993. pap. 13.00 (0-679-74539-4) Vin Bks.

— A Book of Common Prayer. 1995. pap. 13.00 (0-679-75486-5) Vin Bks.

— Democracy. 1995. pap. 13.00 (0-679-75485-7) Vin Bks.

— The Last Thing He Wanted. LC 96-17084. 227p. 1996. 23.00 (0-679-43331-7) Knopf.

— The Last Thing He Wanted. 240p. 1997. pap. 12.00 (0-679-75285-4) Vin Bks.

— Miami. LC 98-7127. 238p. 1999. pap. 12.00 (0-679-78180-3) Vin Bks.

— Play It As It Lays. 214p. 1990. pap. 11.00 (0-374-52171-9) FS&G.

— Run River. 1961. 18.95 (0-8392-1094-9) Astor-Honor.

— Run River. 1994. pap. 13.00 (0-679-75250-1) Vin Bks.

— Salvador. 1994. pap. 10.00 (0-679-75183-1) Vin Bks.

— Slouching Towards Bethlehem. 238p. 1990. pap. 12.00 (0-374-52172-7) FS&G.

***Didion, Joan.** Slouching Towards Bethlehem. LC 99-55156. 256p. 2000. 19.95 (0-679-64026-6) Random.

Didion, Joan. White Album. 224p. 1990. pap. 11.00 (0-374-52221-9) FS&G.

Didion, Joan & Fusco, Peter. Robert Graham: The Duke Ellington Memorial in Progress. LC 88-8214. (Illus.). 108p. (Orig.). 1988. pap. 14.95 (0-87587-149-6) LA Co Art Mus.

Didion, Julie, jt. ed. see Trzyna, Ted.

Didler, Julia. Diccionario de Filsofia. (SPA.). 328p. 1995. 59.95 (0-7859-9789-X) Fr & Eur.

Didominicis, Lynn. Early Childhood Units for Drama. (Illus.). 144p. 1997. pap., teacher ed. 14.95 (1-55734-207-5) Tchr Create Mat.

— Jumanji. (Literature Unit Ser.). (Illus.). 48p. (J). 1997. pap., teacher ed. 7.95 (1-55734-817-0, TCM817) Tchr Create Mat.

DiDona, Nancy, et al, eds. Introductory Maternal-Newborn Nursing. 6th ed. LC 94-39719. 480p. 1995. pap. text 25.95 (0-397-55008-1) Lppncott W & W.

DiDonata, Adrienne, ed. see Nily, Gisela, et al.

DiDonato, Robert, ed. Broadening the Frontiers of Foreign Language Education. LC 96-106402. (Central States Ser.). 1998. pap. 14.21 (0-8442-9353-9, VS9353-9) NTC Contemp Pub Co.

— Building Community Through Language Learning. LC 97-187908. (Central States Ser.). 205p. 1998. pap. 14.21 (0-8442-9344-X, VS9344-X) NTC Contemp Pub Co.

— Careers, Communication & Culture. (Central States Ser.). pap. 14.21 (0-8442-9302-4, VF9302-4) NTC Contemp Pub Co.

— Creating Opportunities for Excellence Through Language. LC 96-176118. (Central States Ser.). 1998. pap. 14.21 (0-8442-9358-X, VS9358-X) NTC Contemp Pub Co.

— Creative Approaches in Foreign Language Teaching. (Central States Ser.). pap. 14.21 (0-8442-9324-5, VF9324-5) NTC Contemp Pub Co.

— The Culture Revolution. (Central States Ser.). pap. 14.21 (0-8442-9303-2, VF9303-2) NTC Contemp Pub Co.

— Defining the Essentials for the Foreign Language Classroom. (Central States Ser.). pap. 14.21 (0-8442-9321-0, VF9321-0) NTC Contemp Pub Co.

— ESL & the Foreign Language Teacher. (Central States Ser.). pap. 14.21 (0-8442-9314-8, VF9314-8) NTC Contemp Pub Co.

— A Global Approach to Foreign Language Education. (Central States Ser.). pap. 14.21 (0-8442-9311-3, VF9311-3) NTC Contemp Pub Co.

— Meeting New Challenges in the Foreign Language Classroom. (Central States Ser.). pap. 14.21 (0-8442-9345-8, VF93458) NTC Contemp Pub Co.

— Meeting the Call for Excellence in the Foreign Language Classroom. (Central States Ser.). pap. 14.21 (0-8442-9317-2, VF9317-2) NTC Contemp Pub Co.

— New Frontiers in Foreign Language Education. (Central States Ser.). pap. 14.21 (0-8442-9308-3, VF9308-3) NTC Contemp Pub Co.

— Personalizing Foreign Language Instruction. (Central States Ser.). pap. 14.21 (0-8442-9305-9, VF9305-9) NTC Contemp Pub Co.

— Proficiency, Policy & Professionalism in Foreign Language Education. (Central States Ser.). pap. 14.21 (0-8442-9319-9, VF9319-9) NTC Contemp Pub Co.

— Realizing the Potential of Foreign Language Instruction. (Central States Ser.). pap. 14.21 (0-8442-9322-9, VF9322-9) NTC Contemp Pub Co.

— Shaping the Future of Foreign Language Education. (Central States Ser.). pap. 14.21 (0-8442-9320-2, VF9320-2) NTC Contemp Pub Co.

— Strategies for Foreign Language Teaching. (Central States Ser.). pap. 14.21 (0-8442-9316-4, VF9316-4) NTC Contemp Pub Co.

— Student Motivation & the Foreign Language Teacher. (Central States Ser.). pap. 14.21 (0-8442-9301-6, VF9301-6) NTC Contemp Pub Co.

— Teaching for Communication in the Foreign Language Classroom. (Central States Ser.). pap. 14.21 (0-8442-9304-0, VF9304-0) NTC Contemp Pub Co.

— Teaching for Tomorrow in the Foreign Language Classroom. (Central States Ser.). pap. 14.21 (0-8442-9306-7, VF9306-7) NTC Contemp Pub Co.

— Teaching the Basics in the Foreign Language Classroom. (Central States Ser.). 1998. pap. 14.21 (0-8442-9307-5, VS9307-5) NTC Contemp Pub Co.

— Visions & Reality in Foreign Language Teaching. (Central States Ser.). 1998. pap. 14.21 (0-8442-9342-3, VS9342-3) NTC Contemp Pub Co.

DiDonato, Robert, et al. Deutsch: Na klar! 2nd ed. (C). 1995. pap., wbk. ed. 24.69 (0-07-016971-3) McGraw.

DiDonato, Stefano, et al, eds. Molecular Genetics of Neurological & Neuromuscular Disease. LC 87-3531. (Advances in Neurology Ser.: Vol. 48). 286p. 1988. reprint ed. pap. 88.70 (0-608-04693-0, 206541400004) Bks Demand.

DiDonno, Lupe & Sperling, Phyllis. How to Design & Build Your Own House. rev. ed. LC 77-20352. (Illus.). 400p. 1987. pap. 26.95 (0-394-75200-7) Knopf.

Didpath, Ian. Diccionario Ilustrado de Astronomia y Astronautica. (SPA., Illus.). 264p. 1987. 19.95 (0-7859-5770-7) Fr & Eur.

Didsbury, Howard, Jr., ed. Creating a Global Agenda: Assessments, Solutions, & Action Plans. LC 84-50980. 346p. 1984. pap. 14.50 (0-930242-25-4) World Future.

Didsbury, Howard F., Jr. Challenges & Opportunities: From Now to 2001. 310p. 1986. pap. 16.95 (0-930242-31-9) World Future.

Didsbury, Howard F., Jr., ed. Communications & the Future. 400p. 1982. pap. 14.50 (0-930242-16-5) World Future.

— Communications Tomorrow: The Coming of the Post-Industrial Society. (Illus.). 160p. (C). 1982. pap. text 21.95 (0-930242-14-9) Transaction Pubs.

***Didsbury, Howard F., Jr., ed.** Frontiers of the 21st Century: Prelude to the New Millennium. 246p. 1999. pap. 29.95 (0-930242-55-6) World Future.

Didsbury, Howard F., Jr., ed. The Future: Opportunity Not Destiny. 302p. 1989. pap. 16.95 (0-930242-35-X) World Future.

— FutureVision: Ideas, Insights, & Strategies. 366p. (Orig.). 1996. pap. 25.00 (0-930242-53-X) World Future.

— The Global Economy: Today, Tomorrow, & the Transition. 1985. pap. 14.95 (0-930242-28-9) World Future.

— The Years Ahead: Perils, Problems, & Promises. 1993. pap. 21.00 (0-930242-46-7) World Future.

Didsbury, Peter. Butchers of Hull. 1982. pap. 12.95 (0-906427-42-8, Pub. by Bloodaxe Bks) Dufour.

— Classical Farm. LC 88-70229. 80p. 1988. pap. 11.95 (1-85224-012-1, Pub. by Bloodaxe Bks) Dufour.

— That Old-Time Religion: Poetry Book Society Recommendation. 64p. 1994. pap. 14.95 (1-85224-255-8, Pub. by Bloodaxe Bks) Dufour.

***Diduck, Alison & Kaganas, Felicity.** Family Law, Gender & the State: Text, Cases & Materials. 656p. 1999. 90.00 (1-84113-084-2, Pub. by Hart Pub); pap. 40.00 (1-84113-085-0, Pub. by Hart Pub) Intl Spec Bk.

***Didymus, Arius.** Arius Didymus, "Epitome of Stoic Ethics" Pomeroy, Arthur J., ed. LC 99-41529. (Texts & Translations Ser.: No. 44). (ENG & GRE.). 160p. 1999. 35.00 (0-88414-001-6, 06 02 44, Pub. by Soc Biblical Lit) Scholars Pr GA.

Die Gestalten Staff, ed. Surreality. (Localizer 1.2 Ser.). 160p. (Orig.). 1996. pap. 44.00 (3-931126-03-X, Pub. by Die Gestalten) Consort Bk Sales.

Die Gestalten Staff & Chromaparke, E. V., eds. Die Gestalten Verlag: Localizer 1.0. 304p. pap. 47.99 (3-931126-00-5, Pub. by Die Gestalten) Consort Bk Sales.

***Die Gestalten Verlag Staff.** Pop Tics with Other. 1999. pap. text 19.99 (3-931126-30-7, Pub. by Die Gestalten) Consort Bk Sales.

Die, Marguerite Van, see Van Die, Marguerite.

Dieatrick, Sheryl. The Bewilderment of Death & Life. 72p. 1999. pap. 14.95 (1-58244-020-4) Rutledge Bks.

***Diebboll, John.** John Diebboll: The Art of the Piano. 2000. 24.95 (1-56792-174-4); pap. 16.95 (1-56792-150-7) Godine.

Diebel. Computicon: German-English-German PC Version. (ENG & GER.). 600p. 1992. 150.00 (0-7859-7542-X, 3893622004) Fr & Eur.

Diebel, Anne & Newbold, Patt. Birds, Hat Patterns & Activities. (Illus.). 50p. (Orig.). (J). (ps-4). 1996. pap. text 8.95 (1-56422-988-2) Start Reading.

— Forest Animals, Hat Patterns & Activities. (Illus.). 50p. (J). (ps-4). 1996. pap. text 9.95 (1-56422-989-0) Start Reading.

— Hat Patterns to Help Teach Bible Stories. (Religious Ser.: Bk. A). (Illus.). 26p. (Orig.). 1994. pap. text 9.95 (1-56422-994-7) Start Reading.

— Hat Patterns to Help Teach Bible Stories. (Religious Ser.: Bk. B). (Illus.). 26p. (Orig.). 1994. pap. text 8.95 (1-56422-993-9) Start Reading.

— Insects & Dinosaurs, Hat Patterns & Activities. (Illus.). 50p. (J). (ps-4). 1996. pap. text 9.95 (1-56422-986-6) Start Reading.

— Noah's Ark Book of Hat Patterns. (Religious Ser.). (Illus.). 30p. 1997. pap. text 9.95 (1-56422-992-0) Start Reading.

— Paper Hat Tricks Vol. 3: A Big Book of Hat Patterns Zoo, Forest, & Dinosaur Hats. (Illus.). 39p. (Orig.). 1991. pap. text 15.95 (1-56422-997-1, Paper Hat) Start Reading.

Diebel, Anne, jt. auth. see Newbold, Patt.

Diebel, Don. The Complete Guide to Meeting Women. 2nd rev. ed. 136p. 1997. pap. 14.95 (0-937164-01-1) Gemini Pub Co.

— How to Pick up Women in Discos. LC 80-67924. (Illus.). 128p. 1981. pap. 6.95 (0-937164-00-3) Gemini Pub Co.

— 1001 Best Pick-Up Lines. 96p. 1999. pap. 14.95 (0-937164-05-4) Gemini Pub Co.

Diebel, Don, ed. see Evans, Derek.

Diebener, Wilhelm. Monograms & Decorations from the Art Nouveau Period. (Pictorial Archive Ser.). (Illus.). 144p. 1982. reprint ed. pap. 9.95 (0-486-24347-8) Dover.

Diebener, Wilhelm, ed. Monograms & Decorations from the Art Nouveau Period. 1983. 16.50 (0-8446-6007-8) Peter Smith.

Diebert, Linda. Motivational Magic. (Illus.). 128p. (J). (ps-2). 1990. 7.99 (0-86653-535-7, GA1137) Good Apple.

— Science for Me. 112p. (J). (ps-2). 1991. 12.99 (0-86653-597-7, GA1318) Good Apple.

***Diebold.** Elementos de Pronosticos. 1999. pap. 87.95 (968-7529-74-1) Thomson Learn.

Diebold. Seismic Velocity Analysis. (Handbook of Geophysical Exploration Ser.). 1999. write for info. (0-08-037218-X, Pergamon Pr) Elsevier.

Diebold, A. C., ed. see Bullis, W. Murray.

Diebold, A. Richard. The Evolution of Indo-European Nomenclature for Salmonid Fish. (Journal of Indo-European Studies: No. 5). 80p. 1986. pap. text 20.00 (0-941694-24-0) Inst Study Man.

Diebold, Francis. Elements of Forecasting. LC 97-23215. (HG - Cycles & Forecasting Ser.). 352p. 1997. mass mkt. 95.95 (0-538-86244-0) Sth-Wstrn College.

***Diebold, Francis X. & Rudebusch, Glenn D.** Business Cycles: Durations, Dynamics & Forecasting. LC 98-34877. xiii, 420p. 1999. 49.50 (0-691-01218-0, Pub. by Princeton U Pr) Cal Prin Full Svc.

Diebold, Grant V. Las Vegas Children's Coloring Book: A Family Adventure to Remember. (Illus.). 32p. (J). (gr. 1-5). 1995. 1.95 (0-9645900-7-7) Diebold Pubns.

Diebold Incorporated Staff. Word & Image. 2000. 40.00 (0-8133-3577-9) Westview.

Diebold Institute for Public Policy Studies, Inc.,. Healthcare Infostructures: The Development of Information-Based Infrastructures for the Healthcare Industry. LC 95-34413. 1995. 55.00 (0-275-95157-X, Praeger Pubs); pap. 18.95 (0-275-95158-8, Praeger Pubs) Greenwood.

Diebold, J., et al. CD-ROM Atlas of Pathology: Spleen. (ENG & FRE.). 1998. 149.00 incl. cd-rom (3-540-14640-7) Spr-Verlag.

Diebold, John. The Role of Business in Society. LC 82-71322. 144p. reprint ed. pap. 44.70 (0-608-12863-5, 202357600033) Bks Demand.

— Technology & Public Policy: Meeting Society's 21st Century Needs. unabridged ed. (Papers & Speeches of John Diebold: Vol. 7). (Illus.). 192p. (Orig.). 1997. pap. 12.95 (0-9658066-0-X) Mngmnt Science.

— Transportation Infostructures: The Development of

D

Intelligent Transportation Systems. LC 95-2213. 224p. 1995. 59.95 (*0-275-95155-3*, Praeger Pubs); pap. 18.95 (*0-275-95156-1*, Praeger Pubs) Greenwood.

Diebold, Michael A. A Family-Centered Way of the Cross. (Illus.). 32p. 1998. pap. text 1.00 (*0-7648-0163-5*) Liguori Pubns.

Diebold, William, Jr. Industrial Policy as an International Issue. (Nineteen Eighty's Project, Council on Foreign Relations Ser.). 1980. text 21.00 (*0-07-016809-1*) McGraw.

Diebold, William, Jr., ed. Bilateralism, Multilateralism, & Canada in U. S. Trade Policy. (Council on Foreign Relations Series on International Trade). 224p. 1988. text 19.95 (*0-88730-287-4*, HarpBusn) HarpInfo.

Diebolt, Thomas G., et al. California Election Code, 1999. abr. ed. 608p. (C). 1999. pap. 35.00 (*1-889056-02-2*) DFM Assoc.

— California Elections Code of 1997. rev. ed. 524p. (C). 1997. reprint ed. pap. text 35.00 (*1-889056-00-6*) DFM Assoc.

Diecidue, Gianni. Antinomie: Italian Poetry. 90p. 1981. pap. 10.00 (*0-89304-659-0*) Cross-Cultrl NY.

— Correspondence: Italian Poetry. 54p. 1988. pap. 7.50 (*0-89304-666-3*) Cross-Cultrl NY.

Dieck, H. Tom, jt. ed. see De Meijere, Armin.

Dieck, Margarete. Die Spanische Kapelle in Florenz: Das Trecenteske Bildprogramm des Kapitelsaals der Dominikaner von S. Maria Novella. (Europaische Hochschulschriften, Reihe 28: Bd. 298). (GER., Illus.). 219p. 1997. 42.95 (*3-631-31091-9*) P Lang Pubng.

Dieck, Ronald H. Measurement Uncertainty: Methods & Applications. LC 92-24674. (An Independent Learning Module from the Instrument Society of America Ser.). (Illus.). 238p. reprint ed. pap. 73.80 (*0-608-08597-9*, 206912000003) Bks Demand.

— Measurement Uncertainty: Methods & Applications : A Guide to Estimating & Understanding the Accuracy of Test & Experimental Data. 2nd ed. LC 97-22013. 1997. 76.00 (*1-55617-628-7*) ISA.

Dieck, Tom, ed. Algebraic Topology & Tranformation Groups. (Lecture Notes in Mathematics Ser.: Vol. 1361). vi, 298p. 1988. 56.95 (*0-387-50528-8*) Spr-Verlag.

Dieck, Tom, T., see Tom Dieck, T.

Dieck, Tammo Tom, et al. Homotopietheorie, Vol. 157. LC 96-15544. (Lecture Notes in Mathematics Ser.). 1996. 14.70 (*3-540-05185-6*) Spr-Verlag.

Dieck, Tom T., jt. auth. see Brocker, T.

Diecker, Mary L., ed. see Brady, Joan.

Diecker, Mary L., ed. see McCarthy, Laura J. & Zagury, Carolyn S.

Diecker, Mary L., ed. see Peluso, Samuel L.

Dieckhoff, Henry C., compiled by. A Pronouncing Dictionary of Scottish Gaelic. (C). 1989. 75.00 (*1-871901-18-9*, Pub. by Gairm Pubns) St Mut.

Dieckman & Selbst, Steven M. Textbook of Pediatric Emergency & Critical Care Procedures. LC 96-46924. (Illus.). 864p. (C). (gr. 13). 1996. text 150.00 (*0-8016-8102-2*, 08102) Mosby Inc.

Dieckman, Jane W. Wholesome Cookies. LC 98-10592. (Specialty Cookbook Ser.). 96p. 1998. pap. 6.95 (*0-89594-942-3*) Crossing Pr.

Dieckmann, Ed, Jr. Beyond Jonestown: 'Sensitivity Training' & the Cult of Mind Control. 191p. (Orig.). 1981. pap. 7.95 (*0-939482-02-9*, 0052, Noontide Pr) Legion Survival.

Dieckmann, Hans. Complexes: Diagnosis & Therapy in Analytical Psychology. Matthews, Boris, tr. from GER. LC 98-56173. (Illus.). 155p. 1998. pap. 24.95 (*1-888602-09-0*) Chiron Pubns.

— Methods in Analytical Psychology: An Introduction. Matthews, Boris, tr. from GER. 240p. (Orig.). 1991. pap. 24.95 (*0-933029-48-9*) Chiron Pubns.

***Dieckmann, Jane.** Easy & Hot from the Oven. LC 99-37376. (Specialty Cookbooks Ser.). 96p. 2000. pap. 6.95 (*0-89594-993-8*) Crossing Pr.

Dieckmann, Jane M. One-Dish Stovetop Meals. LC 98-26028. (Specialty Cookbook Ser.). (Illus.). 96p. 1998. pap. 6.95 (*0-89594-968-7*) Crossing Pr.

— A Short History of Tompkins County. LC 85-25440. (Illus.). 229p. 1986. pap. 7.95 (*0-942690-33-8*) DeWitt Hist.

Dieckmann, Jane M., et al. The Towns of Tompkins County: From Podunk to the Magnetic Springs. LC 98-12822. (Illus.). 256p. 1998. pap. 14.95 (*0-942690-39-7*) DeWitt Hist.

Dieckmann, Janna L., jt. auth. see Montagu, Gerald.

Dieckmann, L., tr. see Heuss, T., et al.

Dieckmann, Liselotte, tr. see Goethe, Johann Wolfgang Von & Schiller, Friedrich.

Dieckmann, Liselotte, tr. see Marc, Franz.

Dieckmann, Ronald A., jt. auth. see Grossman, Moses.

Dieckmann, U., et al. Male & Female, Feminine & Masculine. 1974. pap. 3.00 (*0-317-13546-5*) C G Jung Frisco.

***Dieckmann, Ulf, et al, eds.** Geometry of Ecological Interactions: Simplifying Spatial Complexity. LC 99-44951. (Studies in Adaptive Dynamics). 450p. (C). 1999. 80.00 (*0-521-64294-9*) Cambridge U Pr.

Dieckmann, Ulf & Metz, Johan A. J., eds. Adaptive Dynamics in Context. (Studies in Adaptive Dynamics). 400p. (C). 2000. 80.00 (*0-521-64293-0*) Cambridge U Pr.

Dieckow, Wanda S. Alliterations A-Z Potluck Poetry. 60p. 1993. 10.00 (*1-882560-10-8*) W Dieckow.

— Discreet Affections. 40p. 1993. 7.50 (*1-882560-00-0*) W Dieckow.

— Esoterically Speaking Not a Journey of Genetic Memory. (Illus.). 50p. 1994. 10.00 (*1-882560-21-3*) W Dieckow.

Diede, Alan. Best Choices along the Lakes (Erie & Ontario) (Best Choices Ser.). (Illus.). (Orig.). 1990. pap. 14.95 (*0-685-26995-7*) Monongahela PA.

— Best Choices in Western Pennsylvania. rev. ed. (Best Choices Ser.). (Illus.). 1989. reprint ed. pap. 14.95 (*0-685-26993-0*) Monongahela PA.

Diede, Pauline N. Homesteading on the Knife River Prairie. Hampsten, Elizabeth, ed. Rod Grantham Printing Staff, tr. (Pioneer Life Bks.: Vol. I). (Illus.). 88p. (Orig.). 1983. pap. text 6.95 (*0-685-26959-0*) P Neher Diede.

— North Dakota: In Grateful Homage. Brandt, C. Jane, ed. New Salem Journal Printing Staff, tr. (Pioneer Life Bks.: Vol. IV). (Illus.). 75p. (Orig.). 1987. pap. text 6.95 (*0-685-26962-0*) P Neher Diede.

— The Prairie Echoes. Brandt, C. Jane, ed. New Salem Journal Printing Staff, tr. Vol. V. (Illus.). (Orig.). 1989. pap. text. write for info. (*0-318-65406-7*) P Neher Diede.

— The Prairie Was Home. Abbey Press Printing Staff, tr. (Pioneer Life Bks.: Vol. II). (Illus.). 154p. (Orig.). 1986. pap. text 6.95 (*0-685-26960-4*) P Neher Diede.

— Speaking-out on Sod-House Times! Gengler, John H., ed. Abbey Press Printing Staff, tr. (Pioneer Life Bks.: Vol. III). (Illus.). 112p. (Orig.). 1985. pap. text 6.95 (*0-685-26961-2*) P Neher Diede.

Dieden, Robert C. Games to Keep Kids Moving! P. E. Activities to Promote Total Participation, Self-Esteem, & Fun for Grades 3-8. LC 95-111. (Illus.). 280p. (C). 1995. pap. text 28.95 (*0-13-352287-3*, Parker Publishing Co) P-H.

Diederen, A. M. Countercurrent Sorption Equipment Using Transported Open Sorbent Material. (Illus.). 260p. 1997. pap. 57.50 (*90-407-1527-0*, Pub. by Delft U Pr) Coronet Bks.

***Diederen, Paul, et al.** Innovation & Research Policies: An International Comparative Analysis. LC 99-34898. (New Horizons in the Economics of Innovation Ser.). 296p. 2000. 95.00 (*1-84064-027-8*) E Elgar.

Diederich. Vocabulary for College (A) 1989. pap. text, teacher ed. 6.25 (*0-15-329688-7*) Holt R&W.

— Vocabulary for College (A) (C). 1989. pap. text 15.25 (*0-15-329684-4*) Holt R&W.

— Vocabulary for College (B) 1989. pap. text, teacher ed. 6.25 (*0-15-329689-5*) Holt R&W.

— Vocabulary for College (B) (C). 1989. pap. text 15.25 (*0-15-329685-2*) Holt R&W.

— Vocabulary for College (C) 1989. pap. text, teacher ed. 6.25 (*0-15-329690-9*) Holt R&W.

— Vocabulary for College (C) (C). 1989. pap. text 15.25 (*0-15-329686-0*) Holt R&W.

— Vocabulary for College (D) 1989. pap. text, teacher ed. 6.25 (*0-15-329691-7*) Holt R&W.

— Vocabulary for College (D) (C). 1989. pap. text 15.25 (*0-15-329687-9*) Holt R&W.

Diederich, Adele. Intersensory Facilitation: Race, Superposition, & Diffusion Models for Reaction Time to Multiple Stimuli. LC 92-49247. (Illus.). 200p. 1992. 45.00 (*3-631-44946-1*) P Lang Pubng.

***Diederich, Bernard.** Trujillo: The Death of the Dictator. 264p. (C). 1999. pap. text 18.95 (*1-55876-206-X*) Wiener Pubs Inc.

Diederich, Francois. Cyclophanes. 1991. 153.00 (*0-85186-966-1*) CRC Pr.

Diederich, Francois & Eder, U. Recent Trends in Molecular Recognition. LC 98-50979. (Ernst Schering Research Foundation Ser.: Vol. 26). 250p. 1999. 89.95 (*3-540-65072-5*) Spr-Verlag.

***Diederich, Francois & Stang, Peter J., eds.** Templated Organic Synthesis. 430p. 2000. 170.00 (*3-527-29666-2*) Wiley.

Diederich, Francois, jt. ed. see Stang, Peter J.

Diederich, Paul. The Lichenicolous Heterobasidiomycetes. (Bibliotheca Lichenologica: No. 61). (Illus.). 198p. 1996. 82.60 (*3-443-58040-8*, Pub. by Gebruder Borntraeger) Balogh.

Diederichs, J. E. & Muller, Rainer H. Future Strategies for Drug Delivery with Particulate Systems. LC 97-46682. 194p. 1998. ring bd. 79.95 (*0-8493-3941-3*) CRC Pr.

***Diederichsen, Ulf, et al, eds.** New Aspects in Bioorganic Chemistry. 468p. 1999. pap. 85.00 (*3-527-29665-4*) Wiley.

Diederiks, H. A. & Reeder, D., eds. Cities of Finance. LC 97-104366. 328p. 1996. pap. 53.25 (*0-444-85800-8*) Elsevier.

Diederiks, Herman, et al, eds. The Visible Hand & the Fortune of Cities: Economic Planning in Europe Since the Late Middle Ages. (Illus.). 300p. 1992. text 55.00 (*0-7185-1347-9*) St Martin.

Diederiks-Verschoor, I. H. An Introduction to Air Law. 4th rev. ed. 224p. 1991. pap. 68.00 (*90-6544-539-0*) Kluwer Law Intl.

— An Introduction to Air Law. 5th rev. ed. LC 93-5895. 1993. 201.00 (*90-6544-720-2*) Kluwer Law Intl.

— An Introduction to Space Law. LC 93-15574. 1993. 205.00 (*90-6544-692-3*) Kluwer Law Intl.

***Diederiks-Verschoor, I. H.** An Introduction to Space Law. 2nd rev. ed. LC 99-48001. 1999. pap. 101.00 (*90-411-1261-8*) Kluwer Law Intl.

Diederiks-Vershoor, I. H. An Introduction to Air Law. 6th rev. ed. LC 97-8413. 1997. 92.50 (*90-411-0408-9*) Kluwer Law Intl.

Diedrich, Frank, jt. auth. see Koch, Harald.

***Diedrich, Jeff.** Monkey Business: Creation vs. Evolution. (Hot Shots Ser.). 40p. 1999. pap. 10.25 (*1-929784-01-5*) Psitive Action.

Diedrich, Karen K., jt. auth. see Lemke, Robert J.

Diedrich, Maria. Black Imagination & the Middle Passage. LC 98-24622. 336p. 1999. pap. 19.95 (*0-19-512641-6*) OUP.

Diedrich, Maria. Love Across Color Lines: Ottilie Assing & Frederick Douglass. LC 98-25224. (Illus.). 352p. 1999. 25.00 (*0-8090-1613-3*) Hill & Wang.

***Diedrich, Maria.** Love Across Color Lines: Ottilie Assing & Frederick Douglass. (Illus.). 512p. 2000. pap. 15.00 (*0-8090-6686-6*) Hill & Wang.

Diedrich, Maria, et al, eds. Black Imagination & the Middle Passage. LC 98-24622. 336p. 1999. text 55.00 (*0-19-512640-8*) OUP.

***Diedrich, Maria, et al, eds.** Mapping African America. (Forecast Forum for European Contributions to African American Studies). 252p. 1999. pap. 32.95 (*3-8258-3328-3*, Pub. by CE24) Transaction Pubs.

Diedrich, Maria & Fischer-Hornung, Dorothea, eds. Women & War. 176p. 1990. 19.50 (*0-85496-648-X*) Berg Pubs.

Diedrich, Maria & Sollors, Werner, eds. The Black Columbiad: Defining Moments in African American Literature & Culture. LC 94-19727. (Harvard English Studies: 19). (Illus.). 416p. 1995. text 39.95 (*0-674-07617-6*, SOLBLA) HUP.

Diedrich, Maria, ed. see Sollors, Werner.

Diedrich, Marjorie H. & Rivard, Catherine W., eds. Barker-Harland: A Genealogical Study. LC 89-51151. (Illus.). 318p. 1996. text 425.00 (*0-9616020-1-5*) Genealogic Ent.

— Family History of Bernard J. Diedrich, Vols. 1 & 2. (Illus.). 850p. 1996. text 425.00 (*0-9616020-2-3*) Genealogic Ent.

— Hoover-Thompson: A Genealogical Study. LC 85-73468. (Illus.). 300p. 1996. text 425.00 (*0-9616020-0-7*) Genealogic Ent.

Diedrich, Mark. Bright Lights in the Lord's Recovery Vol. 1: A Collection of Short Christian Biographies. (Illus.). 52p. (Orig.). 1984. pap. 12.95 (*0-9616901-5-1*) Coyote Bks MN.

— The Chiefs Hole-in-the-Day of the Mississippi Chippewa. LC 86-70921. (Illus.). 58p. (Orig.). 1986. pap. 14.95 (*0-9616901-0-0*) Coyote Bks MN.

***Diedrich, Mark.** Famous Dakota Chiefs. rev. ed. (Illus.). 148p. 1999. pap. 24.95 (*1-892415-01-1*) Coyote Bks MN.

Diedrich, Mark. The Odyssey of Chief Standing Buffalo (And the Northern Sisseton Sioux) LC 87-73501. (Illus.). 118p. (Orig.). 1988. pap. 18.95 (*0-9616901-2-7*) Coyote Bks MN.

***Diedrich, Mark.** Ojibway Chiefs: Portraits of Anishinaabe Leadership. LC 96-83324. (Illus.). 193p. (Orig.). 1999. pap. 29.95 (*0-9616901-8-6*) Coyote Bks MN.

Diedrich, Mark. Old Betsey: The Life & Times of a Famous Dakota Woman & Her Family. LC 94-71724. (Illus.). 170p. (Orig.). 1995. pap. 24.95 (*0-9616901-9-4*) Coyote Bks MN.

— Sitting Bull: The Collected Speeches. LC 98-92953. (Illus.). 190p. 1998. pap. 29.95 (*1-892415-00-3*) Coyote Bks MN.

Diedrich, Mark. Dakota Oratory. LC 88-71264. 102p. (Orig.). 1989. pap. 18.95 (*0-9616901-3-5*) Coyote Bks MN.

— Ojibway Oratory. LC 89-81116. 110p. (Orig.). 1990. pap. text 18.95 (*0-9616901-4-3*) Coyote Bks MN.

Diedrich, William L. & Gaus, William. Defense of Equal Employment Claims. LC 81-21339. (Individual Rights Ser.). 631p. 1982. text 105.00 (*0-07-016824-5*) Shepards.

Diedrick, James. Understanding Martin Amis. Bruccoli, Matthew J., ed. LC 95-4367. (Understanding Contemporary British Literature Ser.). 190p. 1995. text 29.95 (*1-57003-058-8*) U of SC Pr.

DiEdwardo, Maryann P., jt. auth. see Pasda, Patricia J.

DiEdwardo, Joseph. Minuet Opus I. 18p. (Orig.). (J). (gr. k-12). 1996. pap. 12.95 (*0-9641468-3-5*) M DiEdwardo Pubng.

DiEdwardo, Mary A., jt. auth. see Pasda, Patricia J.

***DiEdwardo, Mary Ann P. & Pasda, Patricia J.** Christian Coloring Book for Youth. (Illus.). 50p. (J). (gr. k-12). 2000. spiral bd. 19.95 (*0-9641468-7-8*) M DiEdwardo Pubng.

— Prayer Journal. (Illus.). 75p. (J). 2000. spiral bd. 19.95 (*0-9641468-5-1*) M DiEdwardo Pubng.

DiEdwardo, Mary Ann P. & Pasda, Patricia J. Write & Present a Speech. (Illus.). 35p. (J). (gr. k-12). 1998. wbk. ed. 15.95 (*0-9641468-6-X*) M DiEdwardo Pubng.

DiEdwards, Mary A., jt. auth. see Pasda, Patricia J.

Diefenbeck, James A. A Celebration of Subjective Thought. LC 83-20109. (Philosophical Explorations Ser.). 280p. 1984. 31.95 (*0-8093-1088-0*) S Ill U Pr.

Diefenbeck, James A. Rights, Politics, & Economics. 256p. (C). 1995. lib. bdg. 39.50 (*0-7618-0096-4*) U Pr of Amer.

— A Subjective Theory of Organism. 1995. 38.50 (*0-7618-0077-8*) U Pr of Amer.

— Wayward Reflections on the History of Philosophy. 322p. 1996. lib. bdg. 42.00 (*0-7618-0466-8*) U Pr of Amer.

Diefenderf. Principles of Electronic Instrumentation. 3rd ed. (C). 1994. pap. text, lab manual ed. 40.50 (*0-03-097263-9*) Harcourt Coll Pubs.

— Principles of Electronic Instrumentation. 3rd ed. (C). 1994. pap. text, teacher ed. 33.75 (*0-03-097262-0*) Harcourt Coll Pubs.

Diefenderf, jt. auth. see Garrett.

Diefenderfer, A. James & Holton, Brian E. Principles of Electronic Instrumentation. 3rd ed. LC 93-8672. (Golden Sunburst Ser.). (C). 1994. text 93.00 (*0-03-074709-0*, Pub. by SCP) Harcourt.

Diefenderfer, William M., 3rd, jt. auth. see Lilley, William, 3rd.

Diefendorf, Barbara. Beneath the Cross: Catholics & Huguenots in Sixteenth-Century Paris. (Illus.). 288p. (C). 1991. pap. text 23.95 (*0-19-507013-5*) OUP.

Diefendorf, Barbara B. Paris City Councillors in the Sixteenth Century: The Politics of Patrimony. LC 82-47591. 379p. 1983. reprint ed. pap. 117.50 (*0-7837-9330-8*, 206007100004) Bks Demand.

Diefendorf, Barbara B. & Hesse, Carla, eds. Culture & Identity in Early Modern Europe, 1500-1800: Essays in Honor of Natalie Zemon Davis. (Illus.). 300p. (C). 1993. text 57.50 (*0-472-10470-5*, 10470) U of Mich Pr.

Diefendorf, Elizabeth, ed. The New York Public Library's Books of the Century. (Illus.). 240p. (C). 1996. 19.95 (*0-19-510897-3*) OUP.

— The New York Public Library's Books of the Century. (Illus.). 240p. 1997. reprint ed. pap. 8.95 (*0-19-511790-5*) OUP.

Diefendorf, Jeffry M. Businessmen & Politics in the Rhineland, 1789-1834. LC 79-3200. 418p. reprint ed. pap. 129.60 (*0-8357-2923-0*, 203916200011) Bks Demand.

Diefendorf, Jeffry M., et al, eds. American Policy & the Reconstruction of West Germany, 1945-1955. (Publications of the German Historical Institute, Washington, D.C.). 559p. (C). 1994. text 89.95 (*0-521-43120-4*) Cambridge U Pr.

Diefendorf, Mary R. The Historic Mohawk. (Illus.). 321p. 1993. reprint ed. lib. bdg. 37.50 (*0-8328-3191-3*) Higginson Bk Co.

Diefendorf, R. Judd, ed. Advanced Composites in Japan. (JTEC Panel Reports). xvi, 139p. 1991. pap. write for info. (*1-883712-15-7*, JTEC) Intl Tech Res.

Diefer, D. Edward, et al, eds. XConnect, No. 2. 200p. 1998. 12.00 (*0-9651450-1-8*) CrossConnect.

Dieffenbach, Carl & Dveksler, Gabriela, eds. PCR Primer: A Laboratory Manual. (Illus.). 350p. (C). 1995. pap. 102.00 (*0-87969-448-3*) Cold Spring Harbor.

Diegel, Anna, tr. see Robles, Mireya.

Diego, Dominguez Fernandez, see Dominguez Fernandez, Diego.

Diego, Eliseo. Entre la Dicha y la Tiniebla (Between Joy & Darkness) Antologia Poetica, 1949-1985. (SPA.). 208p. 1986. pap. 13.99 (*968-16-2300-2*, Pub. by Fondo) Continental Bk.

Diego, Vicente Garcia De, see Garcia de Diego, Vicente.

***Dieguez, Carlos.** Growth Hormone Secretagogues. LC 99-36529. 340p. 1999. 99.00 (*0-444-82933-4*) Elsevier.

Dieguez, E., jt. auth. see Martin, C.

Dieguez, Sharlee. The Bearded Lady: A Novel. LC 98-75335. 312p. 1999. 25.00 (*1-892514-15-X*) Hill St Pr.

***Diehl.** Environmental Conflict. 2000. 70.00 (*0-8133-9753-7*, Pub. by Westview); pap. 35.00 (*0-8133-9754-5*, Pub. by Westview) HarpC.

Diehl, A. M., jt. ed. see Strain, A. J.

Diehl, Allison C., et al. Archaeological Investigations at El Dumpe, a Mid-Twentieth Century Dump, & the Embankment Site, Tuscon, Arizona. (Technical Report Ser.: No. 96-19). (Illus.). 180p. 1997. pap. 18.00 (*1-886398-25-9*) Desert Archaeol.

Diehl, Allison C., jt. auth. see Diehl, Michael W.

Diehl, Andrew K. Prevention & Screening in Office Practice. (Contemporary Management in Internal Medicine Ser.: Vol. 1, No. 4). (Illus.). 169p. 1991. text 36.00 (*0-443-08826-8*) Church.

Diehl, Andrew K., ed. Prevention & Screening in Office Practice. LC 92-34537. (Contemporary Management in Internal Medicine Ser.: Vol. 1, No. 5). (Illus.). 185p. reprint ed. pap. 57.40 (*0-7837-6236-4*, 204595000010) Bks Demand.

Diehl, Barbara W., ed. The Baltimore Review. 128p. 1998. pap. 7.95 (*1-891529-00-5*) Baltimore Review.

Diehl, Bryan. T. X. Margarita's: Guide to Modern Cocktails. 60p. 1992. pap. 8.95 (*0-9643225-0-1*) T X Margarita.

— T. X. Margarita's: New American Guide to Modern Cocktails. 102p. 1994. 18.50 (*0-9643225-1-X*) T X Margarita.

Diehl, Byron C. & Teter, D. Park. Vote Out Incumbents: Action Plan. 29p. 1992. 1.95 (*0-9634647-0-1*) Polis Pr CO.

Diehl, Carl. Americans & German Scholarship, 1770-1870. LC 77-12931. (Yale Historical Publications: Miscellany: No. 115). 205p. reprint ed. pap. 63.60 (*0-7837-3292-9*, 205769400006) Bks Demand.

Diehl, Carol. Altars & Icons: Patricia Nix. LC 97-215587. (Illus.). 1997. 20.00 (*0-9648340-4-9*) Dillon Gallery.

Diehl, Charles. Byzantine Empresses. 300p. (C). 1998. reprint ed. text 26.95 (*0-943670-04-7*) Studion Pubs Inc.

— Figures Byzantines, 2 vols., Set. vii, 695p. 1965. reprint ed. write for info. (*0-318-71338-1*) G Olms Pubs.

— History of the Byzantine Empire. LC 76-91295. reprint ed. 32.50 (*0-404-02129-8*) AMS Pr.

Diehl, Charles & Marcais, Georges. Le Monde Oriental de 395 a 1081. LC 80-2356. reprint ed. 72.50 (*0-404-18906-7*) AMS Pr.

Diehl, Cheryl J. Handbook of Mortgage Processing. Bray, Susan R., ed. (Mortgage Lending Handbook Ser.). 255p. (C). 1993. text 75.00 (*0-945359-16-0*) Mortgage Bankers.

Diehl, Daniel. Constructing Medieval Furniture: Plans & Instructions with Historical Notes. LC 96-28404. (Illus.). 192p. 1997. pap. 19.95 (*0-8117-2795-5*) Stackpole.

Diehl, Daniel & Donnelly, Mark. Medieval Furniture: Plans & Instructions for Historical Reproductions. LC 99-17160. (Illus.). 192p. 1999. pap. 19.95 (*0-8117-2854-4*) Stackpole.

— Siege: Castles at War. LC 98-37703. (Illus.). 184p. 1999. 29.95 (*0-87833-213-8*) Taylor Pub.

Diehl, Dennis R. Mat Power: Lehigh Wrestling Highlights, 1910-1997. Brownell, Gary, ed. LC 97-91579. (Illus.). 250p. 1997. 38.00 (*0-9656588-0-5*) Roby Pub.

Diehl, Digby. Tales from the Crypt. (Illus.). 256p. 1997. pap. 19.95 (*0-312-17040-8*) St Martin.

— Tales from the Crypt. limited ed. 256p. 2000. text 500.00 (*0-312-14866-6*) St Martin.

— Tales from the Crypt: The Official Archives. 1997. pap. 119.70 (*0-312-17203-6*, St Martin Griffin) St Martin.

Diehl, Digby, jt. auth. see Clarridge, Duane R.

Diehl, Digby, jt. auth. see Cole, Natalie.

D

Diehl, Digby, jt. auth. see Williams, Esther.

Diehl, E. H. Diehl: Addenda to Diehl Genealogy, 1915. 227p. 1997. reprint ed. pap. 33.50 (*0-8328-8298-4*); reprint ed. lib. bdg. 43.50 (*0-8328-8297-6*) Higginson Bk Co.

— Diehl Families of America: History, Genealogy, Reminiscences, Etc. (Illus.). 227p. 1997. reprint ed. pap. 34.00 (*0-8328-8294-1*); reprint ed. lib. bdg. 44.00 (*0-8328-8293-3*) Higginson Bk Co.

Diehl, Edith. Bookbinding: Its Background & Technique. (Illus.). 748p. 1980. pap. 16.95 (*0-486-24020-7*) Dover.

Diehl, Ernestus, ed. Inscriptiones Latinae Christianae Veteres, Bd. 1. xv, 488p. 1970. write for info. (*3-296-13501-4*) G Olms Pubs.

— Inscriptiones Latinae Christianae Veteres, Bd. 2. xii, 516p. 1970. write for info. (*3-296-13502-2*) G Olms Pubs.

— Inscriptiones Latinae Christianae Veteres, Bd. 3. viii, 620p. 1970. write for info. (*3-296-13503-0*) G Olms Pubs.

Diehl, F., et al. Field Guide to the Invertebrates of San Salvador Island, Bahamas. (Illus.). 105p. (Orig.). (C). 1988. pap. text 12.00 (*0-935909-17-6*) Bahamian.

Diehl, Gaston. Tarkhoff (Nicolas) (FRE., Illus.). 306p. 1982. 125.00 (*1-55660-281-2*) A Wofsy Fine Arts.

Diehl, Hans, jt. auth. see Ludington, Aileen.

Diehl, Harold S., et al. Health & Safety for You. 5th ed. (J). 1980. text 29.52 (*0-07-016863-6*) McGraw.

Diehl, Hermann. Sulla und Seine Zeit im Urteil Ciceros. (Beitrage Zur Altertumswissenschaft Ser.: Band 7). (GER.). xi, 253p. 1988. write for info. (*3-487-09110-0*) G Olms Pubs.

Diehl, Huston. An Index of Icons in English Emblem Books, 1500-1700. LC 85-40950. (Illus.). 288p. 1986. 47.50 (*0-8061-1989-6*) U of Okla Pr.

— Staging Reform, Reforming the Stage: Protestantism & Popular Theater in Early Modern England. LC 96-41169. (Illus.). 256p. 1996. text 39.95 (*0-8014-3303-7*) Cornell U Pr.

Diehl, J. F. Safety of Irradiated Foods. 2nd ed. (Food Science & Technology Ser.: Vol. 68). (Illus.). 464p. 1995. text 189.00 (*0-8247-9344-7*) Dekker.

Diehl, James M. The Thanks of the Fatherland: German Veterans after the Second World War. LC 92-50811. xiv, 346p. (C). 1993. 59.95 (*0-8078-2077-6*) U of NC Pr.

Diehl, Janet & Barrett, Thomas S. The Conservation Easement Handbook: Managing Land Conservation & Historic Preservation Easement Programs. 200p. (C). 1997. pap. text 35.00 (*0-943915-03-1*) Land Trust DC.

Diehl, Joanne F. Elizabeth Bishop & Marianne Moore: The Psychodynamics of Creativity. LC 92-23533. 136p. (C). 1993. text 24.95 (*0-691-06975-1*, Pub. by Princeton U Pr) Cal Prin Full Svc.

— Elizabeth Bishop & Marianne Moore: The Psychodynamics of Creativity. LC 92-23533. 129p. 1993. reprint ed. pap. 40.00 (*0-608-02554-2*, 206319900004) Bks Demand.

— Women Poets & the American Sublime. LC 89-45859. (Everywoman Studies in History, Literature & Culture; Blacks in the Diaspora Ser.). 224p. 1990. 31.50 (*0-253-31741-X*) Ind U Pr.

Diehl, John, jt. auth. see Barton, Ray.

Diehl, John, jt. ed. see Papp, Daniel S.

Diehl-Jones, Charlene. Fred Wah. (Canadian Author Studies). 55p. 1997. pap. 9.95 (*1-55022-328-3*, Pub. by ECW) LPC InBook.

***Diehl, Judy & Plumb, David.** What's the Difference? 10 Animal Look-Alikes. (Illus.). 24p. (J). (gr. k-3). 2000. lib. bdg. 19.95 (*1-55037-565-2*, Pub. by Annick Pr); per. 6.95 (*1-55037-564-4*, Pub. by Annick Pr) Firefly Bks Ltd.

Diehl, Katharine S. Hymns & Tunes: An Index. LC 66-13743. 1242p. 1979. lib. bdg. 97.50 (*0-8108-0062-4*) Scarecrow.

— Printers & Printing in the East Indies to 1850, 9 vols., Set. write for info. (*0-89241-384-0*) Caratzas.

Diehl, Katherine S. Batavia: 1600-1850. (Printers & Printing in the East Indies to 1850 Ser.: Vol. I). (Illus.). 445p. 1990. 100.00 (*0-89241-390-5*) Caratzas.

— Bombay Presidency & the Printing Press. (Printers & Printing in the East Indies to 1850 Ser.: Vol. IV). write for info. (*0-89241-393-X*) Caratzas.

— A Comprehensive & Systematic Bibliography. (Printers & Printing in the East Indies to 1850 Ser.: Vol. IX). write for info. (*0-89241-398-0*) Caratzas.

— Europeans & Ceylon, from Fifteen Hundred Five. (Printers & Printing in the East Indies to 1850 Ser.: Vol. II). 600p. 110.00 (*0-89241-391-3*) Caratzas.

— Four Studies: Madrasis, Armenians, Words, Music. (Printers & Printing in the East Indies to 1850 Ser.: Vol. VIII). write for info. (*0-89241-397-2*) Caratzas.

— Jesuits, Lutherans, & the Printing Press in South India. (Printers & Printing in the East Indies to 1850 Ser.: Vol. III). 384p. 100.00 (*0-89241-392-1*) Caratzas.

— Persian, Arabic, & Urdu Printing in Bengal from 1778. (Printers & Printing in the East Indies to 1850 Ser.: Vol. V). write for info. (*0-89241-394-8*) Caratzas.

— The Press Beyond Calcutta-North & East. (Printers & Printing in the East Indies to 1850 Ser.: Vol. VI). write for info. (*0-89241-395-6*) Caratzas.

— Scholarship & Education in Bengal. (Printers & Printing in the East Indies to 1850 Ser.: Vol. VII). write for info. (*0-89241-396-4*) Caratzas.

Diehl, L. W., jt. ed. see Berner, P.

Diehl, Lorraine B. The Late, Great Pennsylvania Station. 2nd ed. LC 96-21056. (Illus.). 168p. 1996. reprint ed. pap. 16.95 (*1-56858-060-6*) FWEW.

Diehl, Lorraine B., ed. see Morrison, David D.

Diehl, Marcia. Celtic Tunes for Recorder: Beginning-Intermediate Level. 32p. 1997. pap. 7.95 (*0-7866-1790-X*, 95735) Mel Bay.

Diehl, Marcy O. & Fordney, Marilyn T. Medical Keyboarding, Typing & Transcribing: Techniques & Procedures. 4th ed. Biblis, Margaret, ed. LC 96-41729. (Illus.). 544p. 1997. pap. text 43.00 (*0-7216-6858-5*, W B Saunders Co) Harcrt Hlth Sci Grp.

— Medical Typing & Transcribing: Techniques & Procedures. 2nd ed. (Illus.). 450p. 1984. teacher ed. 7.50 (*0-7216-2009-4*, W B Saunders Co) Harcrt Hlth Sci Grp.

Diehl, Marcy O. & Takahashi, Marilyn. Medical Typing & Transcribing Audiotapes. 3rd ed. 1980. pap. write for info. (*0-7216-9955-3*, W B Saunders Co) Harcrt Hlth Sci Grp.

Diehl, Marcy O., jt. auth. see Fordney, Marilyn T.

***Diehl, Margaret.** The Boy on the Green Bicycle. 312p. 2000. pap. 12.00 (*1-56947-201-7*) Soho Press.

— The Boy on the Green Bicycle: A Memoir. LC 99-12852. 320p. 1999. 25.00 (*1-56947-149-5*) Soho Press.

Diehl, Margaret. Me & You. LC 89-21958. 265p. 1990. 18.95 (*0-939149-31-1*) Soho Press.

— Men. LC 88-9691. 282p. 1988. 17.95 (*0-939149-14-1*) Soho Press.

— Men. LC 88-9691. 282p. 1997. pap. 13.00 (*1-56947-095-2*) Soho Press.

Diehl, Mary O. & Fordney, Marilyn T. Medical Keyboarding, Typing & Transcribing: Techniques & Procedures. 4th ed. (Illus.). 1997. pap., teacher ed. write for info. (*0-7216-6859-3*, W B Saunders Co) Harcrt Hlth Sci Grp.

— Medical Typing & Transcribing: Techniques & Procedures. 3rd ed. (Illus.). 1991. pap., teacher ed. write for info. (*0-7216-3736-1*, W B Saunders Co) Harcrt Hlth Sci Grp.

Diehl, Michael W. Archaeological Investigations of the Early Agricultural Period Settlement at the Base of A-Mountain, Tucson. (Technical Reports: No. 96-21). (Illus.). 145p. (Orig.). 1997. pap. 13.00 (*1-886398-23-2*) Desert Archaeol.

Diehl, Michael W., ed. Hierarchies in Action: Cui Bono? LC 98-71044. (Occasional Paper Ser.: No. 27). (Illus.). 350p. 2000. pap. 40.00 (*0-88104-084-3*) Center Archaeol.

Diehl, Michael W. & Diehl, Allison C. Archaeological Investigations of the Tucson Pressed Brick Company, Tucson, Arizona. (Technical Reports: No. 96-13). (Illus.). 111p. (Orig.). 1996. pap. 12.00 (*1-886398-22-4*) Desert Archaeol.

Diehl, P., et al, eds. NMR - Basic Principles & Progress Vol. 22: Solid-State NMR; Inorganic Matter, Vol. 31; Vol II. 162p. 1994. 219.95 (*0-387-57190-6*) Spr-Verlag.

— NMR - Basic Principles & Progress Vol. 23: Deuterium & Shift Calculation. (Illus.). x, 263p. 1991. 142.95 (*0-387-52949-7*) Spr-Verlag.

— NMR - Basic Principles & Progress Vol. 24: High Pressure NMR. (Illus.). x, 265p. 1991. 150.95 (*0-387-52938-1*) Spr-Verlag.

— NMR - Basic Principles & Progress Vol. 25: NMR at Very High Field. (Illus.). x, 168p. 1991. 111.95 (*0-387-52946-2*) Spr-Verlag.

— NMR - Basic Principles & Progress Vol. 27: In Vivo Magnetic Resonance Spectroscopy II: Localization & Spectral Editing. (Illus.). 298p. 1992. 130.95 (*0-387-55022-4*) Spr-Verlag.

— NMR - Basic Principles & Progress Vol. 28: In Vivo Magnetic Resonance Spectroscopy III: In-Vivo MR Spectroscopy: Potential & Limitations. (Illus.). 202p. 1992. 118.95 (*0-387-55029-1*) Spr-Verlag.

— NMR - Basic Principles & Progress Vol. 29: Special Applications. (Illus.). 176p. 1993. 119.95 (*0-387-56438-1*) Spr-Verlag.

— Solid-State NMR: Methods & Applications of Solid-State NMR, Vol. 4. (NMR-Basic Principles & Progress Ser.: Vol.33). 214p. 1994. 174.95 (*0-387-58212-6*) Spr-Verlag.

— Solid-State NMR: Organic Matter, Vol. 3. (NMR-Basic Principles & Progress Ser.: Vol.32). 223p. 1994. 174.95 (*0-387-57399-2*) Spr-Verlag.

— Spin-1 NMR. (NMR-Basic Principles & Progress Ser.: Vol. 34). (Illus.). 160p. 1996. 157.00 (*3-540-60581-9*) Spr-Verlag.

— Van der Waals Forces & Schielding Effects. LC 75-15821. (NMR-Basic Principles & Progress Ser.: Vol. 10). (Illus.). 140p. 1976. 47.95 (*0-387-07340-X*) Spr-Verlag.

Diehl, P. & Khetrapel, C. L. N M R Studies of Molecules Oriented in the Nematic Phase of Liquid Crystals. (NMR-Basic Principles & Progress Ser.: Vol. 1). (Illus.). v, 174p. 1970. 35.00 (*0-387-04665-8*) Spr-Verlag.

Diehl, P., ed. see Kanert, O. & Mehring, M.

Diehl, Paul F. The Dynamics of Enduring Rivalries. LC 97-21079. 264p. 1998. text 49.95 (*0-252-02369-2*); text 21.95 (*0-252-06673-1*) U of Ill Pr.

Diehl, Paul F., ed. The Politics of Global Governance: International Organizations in an Interdependent World. 421p. (Orig.). 1996. 55.00 (*1-55587-654-4*); pap. 24.95 (*1-55587-638-2*) L Rienner.

— A Road Map to War: Territorial Dimensions of International Conflict. LC 98-40129. (Illus.). 344p. 1999. pap. 21.95 (*0-8265-1329-8*); lib. bdg. 49.95 (*0-8265-1311-5*) Vanderbilt U Pr.

***Diehl, Paul F. & Goertz, Gary.** War & Peace in International Rivalry. LC 99-462011. (Illus.). 288p. (C). 2000. text 49.50 (*0-472-11127-2*, 11127) U of Mich Pr.

Diehl, Paul F., jt. auth. see Singer, J. David.

Diehl, Paul F., jt. ed. see Ku, Charlotte.

Diehl, Paul F., jt. ed. see Singer, J. David.

Diehl, Paul F., jt. ed. see Wayman, Frank W.

Diehl, Peter, jt. ed. see Waugh, Scott L.

***Diehl, R. D., ed.** High-Power Diode Lasers: Fundamentals, Technology, Applications. LC 00-28510. (Topics in Applied Physics Ser.: Vol. 78). (Illus.). xx, 380p. 2000. 159.00 (*3-540-66693-1*) Spr-Verlag.

Diehl, R. L. Articulatory Phonology. (Journal Phonetica: Vol. 49, No. 3-4, 1992). (Illus.). 108p. 1992. pap. 47.00 (*3-8055-5724-8*) S Karger.

Diehl, Richard, et al, eds. Tzeltal Tales of Demons & Monsters: Modern Folk Tales from the Tzeltal Maya Town of Tenejapa, Chiapas, Pt. 2. Stross, Brian, tr. LC 78-622530. (Museum Briefs Ser.: No. 24). iv, 40p. 1978. pap. 2.00 (*0-913134-24-4*) Mus Anthro MO.

Diehl, Richard A. & Berlo, Janet Catherine, eds. Mesoamerica after the Decline of Teotihuacan, A. D. 700-900. LC 88-30596. (Illus.). 500p. 1989. 60.00 (*0-88402-175-0*) Dumbarton Oaks.

Diehl, Richard A., jt. auth. see Coe, Michael D.

Diehl, Roger E., et al, eds. AAS/AIAA Spaceflight Mechanics Meeting, Feb. 24-26, 1992, Colorado Springs, CO. LC 57-43769. (Advances in the Astronautical Sciences Ser.: Vol. 79). (Illus.). 1512p. 1992. 240.00 (*0-87703-358-7*, Am Astronaut Soc) Univelt Inc.

Diehl, Stephan. Daten Programmierung mit Clipper 5.0 und C. 2nd ed. (GER.). (C). 1991. text. write for info. (*0-201-55992-7*) Addison-Wesley.

Diehl, V., et al, eds. New Aspects in the Diagnosis & Treatment of Hodgkin's Disease. (Recent Results in Cancer Research Ser.: Vol. 17). (Illus.). 305p. 1989. 137.00 (*0-387-51124-5*) Spr-Verlag.

Diehl, V., jt. ed. see Ackermann, A.

Diehl, William. Chameleon. 490p. 1982. mass mkt. 6.99 (*0-345-29445-9*) Ballantine Pub Grp.

— Chameleon. 1996. mass mkt. 5.99 (*0-345-90986-0*) Ballantine Pub Grp.

— Hooligans. 448p. 1985. mass mkt. 7.99 (*0-345-31201-5*, Ballantine) Ballantine Pub Grp.

— Hooligans. 1996. mass mkt. 5.99 (*0-345-90987-9*) Ballantine Pub Grp.

— The Hunt. LC 89-40200. 1991. mass mkt. 6.99 (*0-345-37073-2*) Ballantine Pub Grp.

— Primal Fear. 1993. mass mkt. 6.99 (*0-345-38391-5*) Ballantine Pub Grp.

— Primal Fear. 1994. mass mkt. 6.99 (*0-345-38877-1*) Ballantine Pub Grp.

— Primal Fear. 1998. pap. 6.99 (*0-345-91452-X*) Ballantine Pub Grp.

— Reign in Hell. 1998. mass mkt. 6.99 (*0-345-39506-9*) Ballantine Pub Grp.

— Sharky's Machine. 1995. mass mkt. 6.99 (*0-345-40239-1*) Ballantine Pub Grp.

— Show of Evil. 1995. mass mkt. 6.99 (*0-345-40133-6*) Ballantine Pub Grp.

— Show of Evil. 1996. mass mkt. 6.99 (*0-345-37535-X*) Ballantine Pub Grp.

— Show of Evil. 1998. pap. 6.99 (*0-345-91453-8*) Ballantine Pub Grp.

— Thai Horse. 1989. mass mkt. 6.99 (*0-345-32745-4*) Ballantine Pub Grp.

— Thai Horse. 1996. mass mkt. 5.99 (*0-345-90985-2*) Ballantine Pub Grp.

Diehl, William A., jt. auth. see Nist, Sherrie L.

Diehl, William E. Ministry in Daily Life: A Practical Guide for Congregations. LC 96-85342. 118p. 1996. pap. 14.25 (*1-56699-172-2*, AL174) Alban Inst.

— The Monday Connection: A Spirituality of Competence, Affirmation, & Support in the Workplace. LC 92-31436. 208p. 1992. reprint ed. pap. 14.00 (*0-06-061860-4*, Pub. by Harper SF) HarpC.

Diehm, C., et al, eds. Fluid Dynamics As a Localizing Factor for Atherosclerosis. (Illus.). 230p. 1983. 45.00 (*0-387-12393-8*) Spr-Verlag.

Diehm, C., et al. Color Atlas of Vascular Diseases. LC 99-43213. (Illus.). 450p. 1999. 189.00 (*3-540-62619-0*) Spr-Verlag.

Diehm, C., jt. ed. see Oenen, K.

Diehm, Philip J. How to Get More Private Practice Referrals: A Practical Marketing Guide for Mental Health Professionals. LC 96-69005. (Illus.). 187p. (Orig.). 1996. pap. 24.88 (*1-889423-00-9*) SMC Publng.

Diehm, William J. La Critica - Como Vencer la Autocritica: Criticizing - How to Overcome Self-Criticism. Smith, Josie H., tr. (SPA.). 112p. (Orig.). 1992. pap. 6.50 (*0-311-46130-1*) Casa Bautista.

— Sharpening Your People Skills: Twelve Tools for Success in Any Relationship. LC 96-11432. 176p. 1996. pap. 10.99 (*0-8054-6288-0*, 4262-88) Broadman.

Diehn, Carol. The Bridge Study Guide. 34p. (J). (gr. 4-6). 1993. student ed., ring bd. 12.99 (*1-58609-126-3*) Progeny Pr WI.

— Crown & Jewel Study Guide. 54p. (J). (gr. 4-6). 1993. student ed., ring bd. 12.99 (*1-58609-127-1*) Progeny Pr WI.

— The Hiding Place Study Guide. 46p. (YA). (gr. 6-8). 1993. student ed., ring bd. 12.99 (*1-58609-137-9*) Progeny Pr WI.

— The Two Collars Study Guide. 54p. (J). (gr. 4-6). 1993. student ed., ring bd. 12.99 (*1-58609-128-X*) Progeny Pr WI.

Diehn, Gwen. Geology Crafts for Kids. (Illus.). 144p. (J). 1998. 14.95 (*0-8069-8157-1*) Sterling.

— Making Books That Fly, Fold, Wrap, Hide, Pop Up, Twist, & Turn: Books for Kids to Make. LC 97-41037. (Illus.). 96p. (J). (gr. 4-7). 1998. 19.95 (*1-57990-023-2*, Pub. by Lark Books) Random.

***Diehn, Gwen.** Simple Printmaking. 2000. 24.95 (*1-57990-158-1*, Pub. by Lark Books) Sterling.

Diehn, Gwen & Krautwurst, Terry. Kid Style Nature Crafts: 50 Terrific Things to Make with Nature's Materials. (Illus.). 144p. (J). 1997. pap. 14.95 (*0-8069-0997-8*) Sterling.

— Nature Crafts for Kids: 50 Fantastic Things to Make with Mother Nature's Help. (Illus.). 144p. (J). 1997. pap. 14.95 (*0-8069-8373-6*) Sterling.

— Science Crafts for Kids: 50 Fantastic Things to Invent & Create. (Illus.). 144p. (J). 1997. pap. 14.95 (*0-8069-0284-1*) Sterling.

Dieijen-Visser, M. P. Van, see Kerkhof, P. L. & Van Dieijen-Visser, M. P., eds.

Diejomaoh, V. P., jt. ed. see Bienen, Henry S.

Diejomaoh, Victor P., jt. auth. see Damachi, Ukandi G.

Dieke, Gerhard H. Spectra & Energy Levels of Rare Earth Ions in Crystals. Crosswhite, H. M. & Crosswhite, Hannah, eds. LC 67-29453. 413p. reprint ed. pap. 128.10 (*0-608-10186-9*, 201196000080) Bks Demand.

Dieke, Ikenna. The Primordial Image: African, Afro-American & Caribbean Mythopoetic Text. LC 90-6299. (American University Studies: Comparative Literature: Ser. III, Vol. 37). XIV, 434p. (C). 1993. text 6.95 (*0-8204-1320-8*) P Lang Pubng.

Dieke, Ikenna, ed. Critical Essays on Alice Walker, 189. LC 98-37719. (Contributions in Afro-American & African Studies Ser.: Vol. 189). 240p. 1999. 59.95 (*0-313-30012-7*) Greenwood.

Dieke, Peter U., ed. The Political Economy of Tourism in Africa. (Tourism Dynamics Ser.). (C). 2000. 62.00 (*1-882345-26-6*); pap. text. write for info. (*1-882345-25-8*) Cognizant Comm.

Diekelmann, Nancy, et al. The NLN Criteria for Appraisal of Baccalaureate Programs: A Critical Hermeneutic Analysis. Moody, Linda & Shannon, Moira, eds. 80p. 1989. 17.95 (*0-88737-429-8*) Natl League Nurse.

Diekelmann, Nancy L. & Broadwell, Martin M. The New Hospital Supervisor. (Illus.). 1977. pap. text. write for info. (*0-201-00773-8*) Addison-Wesley.

Diekelmann, Nancy L., jt. auth. see Knopke, Harry J.

***Diekema, Anthony J.** Academic Freedom & Christian Scholarship. 232p. 2000. pap. 22.00 (*0-8028-4756-0*) Eerdmans.

Diekemper, Lou D. Women Who Take Care: Choosing to Live with Wisdom, Grace, & Power after Fifty-Five. LC 97-1374. (Illus.). 280p. 1997. pap. 14.95 (*1-57733-003-X*) B Dolphin Pub.

Dieker, Andrea & Steinkamp, Jutta. Dwarf Rabbits As a New Pet. (Illus.). 64p. 1992. pap. 6.95 (*0-86622-537-4*, TU-026) TFH Pubns.

Diekert, V. Combinatorics on Traces. Goos, G. & Hartmanis, J., eds. (Lecture Notes in Computer Science Ser.: Vol. 454). xii, 165p. 1990. 28.00 (*0-387-53031-2*) Spr-Verlag.

Diekhans, G., jt. auth. see Theissen, J.

Diekhans, Mark & Roseman, Mark, eds. The Fourth Annual TCL/TK Workshop '96 Proceedings. 240p. 1996. pap. 28.00 (*1-880446-78-2*) USENIX Assn.

Diekhoff, George M. Basic Statistics for the Social & Behavioral Sciences. LC 95-108031. 464p. 1995. 69.00 (*0-02-329524-4*, Macmillan Coll) P-H.

— Statistics for the Social & Behavioral Sciences. 448p. (C). 1994. text. write for info. (*0-697-28514-6*) Brown & Benchmark.

Diekman, Catherine H. Handling Student Conflicts: A Positive Approach: Participant's Manual. Burke, James A., II, ed. LC 98-146102. (Illus.). 82p. 1997. pap. text 23.95 (*1-878227-51-3*) Peace Educ.

— Handling Student Conflicts: A Positive Approach: Staff Development Manual. Burke, James A., II, ed. (Illus.). 32p. 1997. pap. text 16.95 (*1-878227-52-1*) Peace Educ.

Diekmann, A. & Mitter, P., eds. Paradoxical Effects of Social Behavior. (Illus.). xvi, 341p. 1986. 119.95 (*0-387-91285-1*) Spr-Verlag.

***Diekmann, O.** Mathematical Epidemiology of Infectious Diseases: Model Building, Analysis & Interpretation. (Illus.). 320p. 2000. 150.00 (*0-471-98682-8*) Wiley.

***Diekmann, O. & Heesterbeek, J. A.** Mathematical Epidemiology of Infectious Diseases: Model Building, Analysis & Interpretation. LC 99-52964. (Series in Mathematical & Computational Biology). 2000. pap., boxed set. write for info. (*0-471-49241-8*) Wiley.

***Diekmann, O., et al.** Mathematics Inspired by Biology: Lectures Given at the 1st Session of the Centro Internazionale Matematico Estivo (C.I.M.E.), Held in Martina Franca, Italy, June 13-20, 1997. LC 99-48772. (Lecture Notes in Mathematics Ser.). vii, 268p. 1999. pap. 52.80 (*3-540-66522-6*) Spr-Verlag.

Diekmann, O., jt. ed. see Metz, J. A.

Diekmann, Odo, et al. Delay Equations: Functional, Complex, & Nonlinear Analysis. LC 94-41858. (Applied Mathematical Sciences Ser.: Vol. 110). (Illus.). 508p. 1995. 59.95 (*0-387-94416-8*) Spr-Verlag.

Diekmannshenke, Hajo, jt. ed. see Klein, Josef.

Diekmayer, Ulrich, jt. auth. see Kirst, Werner.

Diekneite, Jorg & Eckhardt, Juliane. Kinder- und Jugendbucher/Kinder- und Jugendmedien: Auswahlbibliographie der Buchpublikationen. (GER.). 207p. 1996. 31.95 (*3-631-30242-8*) P Lang Pubng.

Dieks, Dennis G. & Vermaas, Pieter E. The Modal Interpretation of Quantum Mechanics. LC 98-35400. (Western Ontario Series in Philosophy of Science). 1998. 135.00 (*0-7923-5207-6*) Kluwer Academic.

Diekstra, F. N. The Middle English Weye of Paradys & the Middle French Voie de Paradis: A Parallel-Text Edition. LC 90-19288. (Medieval & Renaissance Authors Ser.: No. 1). (ENM & FEM., Illus.). xvi, 544p. 1991. 149.00 (*90-04-09118-1*) Brill Academic Pubs.

Diekstra, F. N., ed. Book for a Simple & Devout Woman: A Late Middle English Adaptation of Peraldus' Summa de Vittiis et Virtutibus & Friar Laurent's Somme le Roi. (Mediaevalia Groningana Ser.: Vol. XXIV). xi, 598p. 1998. pap. 85.00 (*90-6980-115-9*, Pub. by Egbert Forsten) Hodlder & Stoughton.

Diekstra, Rene F., ed. Preventive Strategies on Suicide. (Advances in Suicidology Ser.: Vol. 2). xii, 369p. 1995. pap. 83.00 (*90-04-10339-2*) Brill Academic Pubs.

Diekstra, Rene F. & Hawton, Keith E., eds. Suicide in Adolescence. 1987. text 111.00 (*0-89838-780-9*) Kluwer Academic.

D

***Diel.** Insurance Management. 100p. 1999. pap. text 19.00 (*0-536-02636-X*) S&S Trade.

Diel, Armin & Payne, Joel. German Wine Guide. LC 99-11481. (Illus.). 520p. 1999. 25.00 (*0-7892-0577-7*) Abbeville Pr.

Diel, I. J., et al, eds. Metastatic Bone Disease: Fundamental & Clinical Aspects. LC 93-46632. 1993. write for info. (*3-540-57356-9*); write for info. (*0-387-57356-9*) Spr-Verlag.

***Diel, Peter.** Surfing: In Search of the Perfect Wave. (Illus.). 2000. pap. text 17.95 (*1-84126-023-1*) Meyer & Meyer.

Diel, R. Kleines WFachwoerterbuch Wirtschaftsoerderung: Business Dictionary. (ENG & GER.). 132p. 1986. pap. 39.95 (*0-8288-7698-3*) Fr & Eur.

Diel, W. Rocks, Ridges & Glaciers: A Geologic Tour of the Denali Highway. (Illus.). 82p. 1995. pap. 7.00 (*0-930931-07-6*) Alaska Natural.

Dield, Eugene & Field, R. M. Echoes from the Sabine Farm. (Notable American Authors Ser.). 1992. reprint ed. lib. bdg. 75.00 (*0-685-49852-2*) Rprt Serv.

Diele, Joseph, ed. see Carretto, Carlo.

Dieleman, Frans M., jt. auth. see Clark, William A.

Dieleman, Frans M., jt. auth. see Gejl.

Dieleman, J., et al, eds. Photon-Assisted Processing of Surfaces & Thin Films: Proceedings of Symposium B on Photon-Assisted Processing of Surfaces & Thin Films of the 1994 E-MRS Spring Conference, Strasbourg, France, 24-27 May, 1994. (European Materials Research Society Symposia Proceedings Ser.: Vol. 47). 648p. 1995. 314.00 (*0-444-82162-7*, North Holland) Elsevier.

Dieling, et al. Die Tempora. 70p. 1989. 13.00 (*3-324-00510-8*) Langenscheidt.

Dieling, Helga. Phonetik im Fremdsprachenunterricht Deutsch. 134p. 1992. 22.50 (*3-468-49444-0*) Langenscheidt.

Dieling, Helga, et al. Phonothek. (GER.). 208p. 1996. wbk. ed. 23.50 (*3-324-00707-0*) Langenscheidt.

Diella, L. & Altarelli, Guido. Proton-Antiproton Collider Physics. (Advanced Series in Directions in High Energy Physics: Vol. 4). 416p. (C). 1989. text 99.00 (*9971-5-0562-2*); pap. text 52.00 (*9971-5-0563-0*) World Scientific Pub.

***Dielman.** Applied Regression Analysis for Business & Economics. 3rd ed. 2000. pap. 61.00 (*0-534-37955-9*) Wadsworth Pub.

Dielman. Applied Regression Analysis for Business Economics. (Business Statistics Ser.). 1990. student ed. 13.50 (*0-534-92590-1*) Brooks-Cole.

— Applied Regression Analysis with Applications. 2nd ed. (Business Statistics Ser.). 1995. pap., student ed. 28.00 (*0-534-26587-1*) PWS Pubs.

Dielman, Louis H., ed. see Marine, William M.

Dielman, Ted & Barton, Keith C. Child Personality Structure & Development: Multivariate Theory & Research. LC 82-16583. 204p. 1983. 49.95 (*0-275-90970-0*, C0970, Praeger Pubs) Greenwood.

Dielman, Terry E. Applied Regression Analysis for Business & Economics. 2nd ed. LC 95-24036. (C). 1995. text, mass mkt. 94.95 incl. 3.5 hd (*0-534-26586-3*) Wadsworth Pub.

— Pooled Cross-Sectional & Time Series Data Analysis. (Statistics: Textbooks & Monographs: Vol. 97). (Illus.). 264p. 1988. text 135.00 (*0-8247-7864-2*) Dekker.

Diels, H. & Kranz, Walther. Die Fragmente der Vorsokratiker, Band I. (GER.). xii, 504p. 1992. reprint ed. write for info. (*3-296-12201-X*) G Olms Pubs.

— Die Fragmente der Vorsokratiker, Band II. (GER.). 428p. 1992. reprint ed. write for info. (*3-296-12202-8*) G Olms Pubs.

— Die Fragmente der Vorsokratiker, Band III. (GER.). 660p. 1990. reprint ed. write for info. (*3-296-12203-6*) G Olms Pubs.

Diels, Hermann. Kleine Schriften Zur Geschichte der Antiken Philosophie. (GER.). xxvi, 467p. 1969. write for info. (*0-318-70453-6*) G Olms Pubs.

— Kleine Schriften Zur Geschichte der Antiken Philosophie. Burkert, Walter, ed. xxvi, 467p. 1969. write for info. (*0-318-70737-3*) G Olms Pubs.

Diels, Jean-Claude & Rudolph, Wolfgang. Ultrashort Laser Pulse Phenomena: Fundamentals, Techniques, & Applications on a Femtosecond Time Scale. (Optics & Photonics Ser.). (Illus.). 581p. 1996. text 110.00 (*0-12-215492-4*) Acad Pr.

DiElsi, John. Turbo Pascal 6.0: The Nuts & Bolts of Program Construction. 592p. (C). 1991. 60.00 (*0-07-557790-9*) McGraw.

Diem, Andrea G. The Gnostic Mystery: A Connection Between Ancient & Modern Mysticism. (Lost Horizon Book Ser.). 81p. (Orig.). 1992. pap. 9.95 (*1-56543-021-2*) Mt SA Coll Philos.

Diem, Bui & Chanoff, David. In the Jaws of History. LC 98-43865. (Vietnam War Era Classics Ser.). (Illus.). 400p. 1999. text 39.95 (*0-253-33539-6*) Ind U Pr.

Diem, Bui, et al. In the Jaws of History. LC 98-43865. (Vietnam War Era Classics Ser.). (Illus.). 400p. 1999. pap. 18.95 (*0-253-21301-0*) Ind U Pr.

Diem, Carl. Asiatische Reiterspiele. 291p. 1982. write for info. (*3-487-08241-1*) G Olms Pubs.

— Wesen und Lehre des Sports. (GER.). x, 271p. 1969. write for info. (*3-296-80200-2*, Pub. by Weidmann) Lubrecht & Cramer.

Diem, Gertrude. In the King's Service. (Illus.). 96p. 1987. reprint ed. pap. 4.50 (*0-910557-18-7*) Acad New Church.

Diem, Gordon. Politics, Sociology & Economics of the Municipal Area. 124p. (C). 1997. pap. text 21.35 (*1-56226-388-9*) CAT Pub.

— Social Science Research Methods. 218p. (C). 1997. pap. text 24.95 (*1-56226-387-0*) CAT Pub.

Diem, H. G., jt. ed. see Dommergues, Y. R.

Diem, Hermann. Kierkegaard's Dialectic of Existence. Knight, Harold, tr. from GER. LC 77-18886. 217p. 1978. reprint ed. lib. bdg. 35.00 (*0-313-20220-6*, DIKD, Greenwood Pr) Greenwood.

Diem, Kenneth L. & Diem, Lenore L. A Community of Scalawags, Renegades, Discharged Soldiers & Predestined Stinkers? A History of Northern Jackson Hole & Yellowstones Influence 1872-1920. LC 98-75034. 144p. 1999. pap. 14.95 (*0-931895-53-7*) Grand Teton NHA.

Diem, Lenore L., jt. auth. see Diem, Kenneth L.

Diem, Liselott. The Important Early Years. 88p. (Orig.). 1991. pap. 8.00 (*0-88314-491-3*, A4913) AAHPERD.

Diem, Max. Introduction to Modern Vibrational Spectroscopy. 285p. 1993. 95.00 (*0-471-59584-5*) Wiley.

Diemann, E., jt. auth. see Mueller, A.

Diemberger, Kurt. Kurt Diemberger Omnibus: Summits & Secrets, the Endless Knot, Spirits of the Air. (Illus.). 858p. 1998. 38.00 (*0-89886-606-5*) Mountaineers.

Diemberger, Kurt & Mantovani, Roberto. K2: Challenging the Sky. Davenport, Neil, tr. from UND. LC 97-223516. 144p. 1997. 35.00 (*0-89886-518-2*) Mountaineers.

Diemel, Earl. Meet Me in a Taxi. 88p. 1998. pap. 10.00 (*0-8059-4152-5*) Dorrance.

Diemer. Annotated Bibliography of Nineteenth Century Geology. 93.95 (*1-85928-131-1*) Ashgate Pub Co.

Diemer, Deedre. The ABC's of Chakra Therapy: A Workbook. LC 97-51637. (Illus.). 160p. 1998. pap., wbk. ed. 12.95 (*1-57863-021-5*) Weiser.

Diemer, Doug. The Eighteen Seventy-Five Baldwin 4-4-0. rev. ed. 12p. 1994. reprint ed. pap. 1.00 (*1-879897-02-4*) NV St Rail Mus.

Diemer, Emma L. Adventures in Sound for Piano. 32p. 1989. pap. text 5.95 (*0-87487-662-1*) Summy-Birchard.

***Diemer, Geert, ed.** The Social Negotiations of Technologies for Development. 192p. 1999. pap. text 23.95 (*3-8258-3026-8*, Pub. by CE24) Transaction Pubs.

Diemer, Geert & Huibers, Frans P., eds. Crops, People & Irrigation: Water Allocation Practices of Farmers & Engineers. 128p. 1996. pap. 19.50 (*1-85339-304-5*, Pub. by Intermed Tech) Stylus Pub VA.

Diemer, Hugo. Factory Organization & Administration. 1980. 37.95 (*0-405-13284-0*) Ayer.

Diemer, Hugo, Jr. Factory Organization & Administration, 2 vols. Chandler, Alfred D., ed. LC 79-7542. (History of Management Thought & Practice Ser.). 1980. reprint ed. lib. bdg. 35.95 (*0-405-12326-4*) Ayer.

Diemer, John, jt. auth. see Collie, Michael.

Diemer, Lorena. Magnolia Blossom. 88p. 1997. pap. 10.95 (*1-878406-11-6*, Paintbrsh) Parker Dstb.

Diemert, Brian. Graham Greene's Thrillers & the 1930s. LC 98-122715. 256p. 1996. 60.00 (*0-7735-1432-5*, Pub. by McG-Queens Univ Pr); pap. text 19.95 (*0-7735-1433-3*, Pub. by McG-Queens Univ Pr) CUP Services.

Dieminger, W., et al, eds. The Upper Atmosphere: Data Analysis & Interpretation. LC 94-6896. 1994. write for info. (*3-540-57562-6*) Spr-Verlag.

— The Upper Atmosphere: Data Analysis & Interpretation. LC 94-6896. (Illus.). 650p. 1996. 394.00 (*0-387-57562-6*) Spr-Verlag.

Dien, Albert E. Pei Ch'i Shu '45: Biography of Yen Chih-T'ui. (Wurzburger Sino-Japonica Ser.: Vol. 6). 184p. 1976. 38.00 (*3-261-01756-2*) P Lang Pubng.

Dien, Albert E., et al, eds. Chinese Archaeological Abstracts. Incl. Vol. 9. Prehistoric to Western Zhou. 618p. 1985. (*0-917956-55-9*); Vol. 10. Eastern Zhou to Han. 763p. 1985. (*0-917956-53-2*); Vol. 11. Post Han. 750p. 1985. (*0-917956-54-0*); (Monumenta Graeca et Romana Ser.: No. 9-11). (Illus.). 2131p. 1985. 75.00 (*0-685-11885-1*) UCLA Arch.

Dien, M. Izzi, ed. see Muhammad, Umar B.

Diender, Debra. The One Meal Cookbook: Cooking for Families with One or More Vegetarians. LC 98-53839. (Illus.). 240p. 1999. 18.95 (*1-55972-495-1*, Birch Ln Pr) Carol Pub Group.

Diendl, James P., tr. see Baroja, Y Nessi, Pio.

***Diendl, James Perry.** Simplified Retirement Planning for Baby Boomers. 41p. 2000. pap. 9.95 (*0-7414-0357-9*) Buy Books.

Dieneman, Debbie. The Easter Bunny. LC 92-32435. (Children's Classics Ser.). 32p. (J). 1993. 6.95 (*0-8362-4935-6*) Andrews & McMeel.

— Puss in Boots. 32p. (J). (ps-3). 1992. 6.95 (*0-8362-4932-1*) Andrews & McMeel.

— The Three Little Pigs. (Children's Classics Ser.). 32p. (J). 1991. 6.95 (*0-8362-4904-6*) Andrews & McMeel.

Dienemann, Jacqueline, ed. & intro. see American Nurses Association Staff.

Dienemann, Jaqueline A., ed. Nursing Administration: Managing Patient Care. 2nd ed. LC 97-14107. 544p. (C). 1997. pap. text 49.95 (*0-8385-6986-2*, A-6986-2) Appleton & Lange.

Diener, Dan. Introduction to Well Control. 2nd ed. McCann, Annes, ed. (Illus.). 30p. (C). 1999. pap. text 20.00 (*0-88698-185-9*, 5.10020) PETEX.

***Diener, Ed & Suh, Eunkook M., eds.** Culture & Subjective Well-Being. LC 00-35155. (Illus.). 384p. (C). 2000. 45.00 (*0-262-04182-0*, Bradford Bks) MIT Pr.

Diener, Edward & Crandall, Rick. Ethics in Social & Behavioral Research. LC 78-8881. 1993. pap. text 4.50 (*0-226-14824-6*) U Ch Pr.

Diener, Francine & Diener, Marc, eds. Nonstandard Analysis in Practice. LC 95-44955. 250p. 1995. 54.95 (*3-540-60297-6*) Spr-Verlag.

***Diener, H. C., ed.** Drug Treatment of Migraine & Other Headaches. x, 372p. 2000. 191.50 (*3-8055-6971-8*) S Karger.

Diener, H. C. & Wilkinson, M., eds. Drug-Induced Headache. (Advances in Applied Neurological Sciences Ser.: Vol. 5). (Illus.). 185p. 1988. 71.95 (*0-387-18762-6*) Spr-Verlag.

Diener, Marc. Insider's Guide to Dealmaking. LC 97-21591. 256p. 1998. pap. 9.95 (*0-8050-4108-7*) St Martin.

Diener, Marc, jt. ed. see Diener, Francine.

Diener, Michael. Lexikon des Zen von A-Z. (GER.). 264p. 1992. 45.00 (*0-7859-8681-2*, 350267406x) Fr & Eur.

Diener, Patricia & Peterson, Gail. Tears of Glass: Shattering of a Daughter's Heart. 85p. (Orig.). 1994. pap. text 14.95 (*0-9643323-0-2*) P Diener.

Diener, Paul W. Religion & Morality: An Introduction. LC 97-14698. 1997. pap. 15.00 (*0-664-25765-8*) Westminster John Knox.

Diener, Robert J. The Basics of Christianity. 98p. (Orig.). 1987. pap. 8.00 (*0-8100-0278-7*, 07N0756) Northwest Pub.

Diener, Roger. The House & the City: Diener & Diener - Urban Studies. (Illus.). 96p. 1995. pap. 35.00 (*3-7643-5223-X*, Pub. by Birkhauser) Princeton Arch.

Diener, Royce. How to Finance a Growing Business. 328p. 1995. pap. 24.95 (*1-56343-100-9*) Silver Lake.

Diener, Royce. How to Finance a Growing Business: An Insider's Guide to Negotiating the Capital Markets. 5th ed. 1997. pap. text 24.95 (*1-56343-162-9*) Silver Lake.

***Diener, Royce.** How to Finance a Growing Business: An Insider's Guide to Negotiating the Capital Markets. 5th ed. 2000. pap. 24.95 (*1-56343-700-7*) Silver Lake.

Diener, T. O. The Viroids. LC 87-13017. (Viruses Ser.). (Illus.). 366p. (C). 1987. text 110.00 (*0-306-42523-8*, Kluwer Plenum) Kluwer Academic.

Diener, Thomas. Growth of an American Invention: A Documentary History of the Junior & Community College Movement, 16. LC 85-9832. (Contributions to the Study of Education Ser.: No. 16). (Illus.). 267p. 1986. 57.95 (*0-313-24993-8*, DGR/) Greenwood.

Dienes, jt. auth. see Barron.

Dienes, B., et al, eds. Frontiers of Particle Beams: Factories with EP Plus SEP-S Rings: Proceedings of a Topical Course Held by the Joint U. S. - CERN School on Particle Accelerators at Benalmadena, Spain, 29 October-4 November, 1992. LC 93-39551. (Lecture Notes in Physics Ser.: Vol. 425). ix, 412p. 1994. 96.95 (*0-387-56588-4*) Spr-Verlag.

Dienes, C. Thomas, et al. Newsgathering & the Law. LC 97-70137. 1005p. 1997. text 105.00 (*1-55834-462-4*, 65190, MICHIE) LEXIS Pub.

***Dienes, C. Thomas, et al.** Newsgathering & the Law. 2nd ed. 1280p. 1999. 105.00 (*0-327-04972-3*, 6519011) LEXIS Pub.

Dienes, C. Thomas, jt. auth. see Barron, Jerome A.

Dienes, G. J., et al, eds. Molecular Crystals & Liquid Crystals Special Topics: Proceedings of the 8th International Liquid Crystals Conference, Kyoto, Japan, June 30-July 4, 1980, 6 vols., Pts. A-F, Vols. 63, 66, 67, 68, 70 & 74. 1955p. 1981. pap. 866.00 (*0-677-40295-3*) Gordon & Breach.

Dienes, G. J., jt. auth. see Borg, Richard J.

Dienes, Hans P. Viral & Autoimmune Hepatitis: Morphologic & Pathogenetic Aspects of Cell Damage in Hepatitis with Potential Chronicity. LC 88-38640. (Progress in Pathology Ser.: Vol. 132). 107p. 1989. pap. text 80.00 (*0-89574-280-2*, Pub. by Gustav Fischer) Balogh.

Dienes, Leslie. Locational Factors & Locational Developments in the Soviet Chemical Industry. LC 68-18023. (University of Chicago, Department of Geography, Research Paper Ser.: No. 119). 275p. reprint ed. pap. 85.30 (*0-7837-0396-1*, 204071700018) Bks Demand.

Dienes, Leslie, et al. Energy & Economic Reform in the Former Soviet Union: Implications for Production, Consumption & Exports, & for the International Energy Markets. LC 93-31487. 1994. text 85.00 (*0-312-12014-1*) St Martin.

Dienes, Margaret, jt. auth. see Month, Melvin.

Dienes, Margaret, jt. ed. see Month, Melvin.

Dienes, Sheila S. Learn WordPerfect 6.0 for Windows in a Day. LC 93-48168. (Popular Applications Ser.). 144p. (Orig.). 1994. pap. 15.95 incl. disk (*1-55622-416-8*) Wordware Pub.

Dienes, Sheila S. Mastering Lotus Word Pro 96 for Windows 95 Special Edition. 928p. 1996. pap. 34.99 (*0-7821-1390-7*) Sybex.

Dienes, Zoltan P. Memoirs of a Maverick Mathematician. LC 99-492151. 569p. 1998. write for info. (*0-7541-0350-1*, Pub. by Minerva Pr) Unity Dist.

***Dienes, Zoltan Paul.** Calls from the Past. 170p. 2000. write for info. (*0-7541-1347-7*, Pub. by Minerva Pr) Unity Dist.

Dieng, R., jt. ed. see Muller, H. J.

Dienhart, Anna. Reshaping Fatherhood: The Social Construction of Shared Parenting. LC 97-45392. (Understanding Families Ser.: Vol. 11). 245p. 1998. write for info. (*0-7619-0977-X*); pap. 23.50 (*0-7619-0978-8*) Sage.

Dienhart, John M. The Mayan Languages: A Comparative Vocabulary, 3 vols., Set. 1010p. 1989. 225.00 (*87-7492-722-1*) Coronet Bks.

Dienhart, John W. Business, Institutions & Ethics: A Text with Cases & Readings. LC 99-17556. (Illus.). 512p. (C). 1999. pap. text 39.95 (*0-19-508080-7*) OUP.

Dienhart, John W. & Curnutt, Jordan. Business Ethics: A Reference Handbook. LC 98-42277. (Contemporary Ethical Issues Ser.). (Illus.). 464p. 1998. lib. bdg. 55.00 (*0-87436-863-4*) ABC-CLIO.

Diening, J. A. On Reasonable Liability. 452p. pap. 32.00 (*90-6000-250-4*) Kluwer Academic.

Diensberg, B., jt. ed. see Zettersten, A.

Diensberg, Christoph. Betriebliche Weiterbildung, Vorschlagswesen und Unweltschutz: Lernprozesse Zwischen Mitarbeiter- und Unternehmensentwicklung. Geibler, Harald, ed. (Bildung und Organisation Ser.: Bd. 6). (GER., Illus.). 385p. 1997. 63.95 (*3-631-30311-4*) P Lang Pubng.

Dienst, Alex. The Navy of the Republic of Texas, 1835-1845. limited ed. (Source Texana Ser.: No. 2). 1987. reprint ed. 100.00 (*0-88342-066-X*) Old Army.

Dienst, Jill & Schaffer, Mark. Alexandre Iacovleff: Paintings & Drawings. LC 93-60177. (Illus.). 52p. (Orig.). 1993. 15.00 (*0-9611014-2-3*) A La Vieille.

Dienst, Richard. Still Life in Real Time: Theory after Television. LC 93-37942. (Post-Contemporary Interventions Ser.). 224p. (C). 1994. text 49.95 (*0-8223-1451-7*); pap. text 17.95 (*0-8223-1466-5*) Duke.

Dienstag, Jacob I. Eschatology in Maimonidean Thought: Messianism, Resurrection, & the World to Come-Jacob I. LC 82-17303. cxx, 281p. 1982. 59.50 (*0-87068-706-9*) Ktav.

Dienstag, Joshua F. Dancing in Chains: Narrative & Memory in Political Theory. LC 96-44652. 1997. write for info. (*0-8047-2818-6*); pap. 17.95 (*0-8047-2924-7*) Stanford U Pr.

Dienstbier, Richard, jt. ed. see Leger, Daniel W.

Dienstbier, Richard, ed. see Nebraska Symposium on Motivation Staff.

Dienstbier, Richard A., ed. Nebraska Symposium on Motivation, 1990: Perspectives on Motivation. LC 53-11655. (Nebraska Symposium on Motivation Ser.: Vol. 38). xiv, 369p. 1991. text 45.00 (*0-8032-1693-9*) U of Nebr Pr.

Dienstbier, Richard A., jt. ed. see Melton, Gary B.

Dienstbier, Richard A., ed. see Nebraska Symposium on Motivation Staff.

Dienstbier, Richard A., jt. ed. see Sonderegger, Theo B.

Dienstein, William. How to Write a Narrative Investigation Report. 128p. 1975. 29.95 (*0-398-00454-4*) C C Thomas.

Dienstfiey, Patricia, ed. see Rivera, Elena.

Dienstfrey, Pat, ed. see Frank, Thaisa.

Dienstfrey, Pat, ed. see Moriarty, Laura.

Dienstfrey, Pat, ed. see Rosenwasser, Rena.

Dienstfrey, Patricia. Newspaper Stories & Other Poems. 36p. (Orig.). 1979. pap. 9.95 (*0-917658-11-6*) BPW & P.

— Small Salvations. LC 87-14028. (Illus.). 36p. (Orig.). 1987. pap. 8.00 (*0-932716-22-9*) Kelsey St Pr.

— The Woman Without Experiences. Lawson, Denise & Rosenwasser, Rena, eds. LC 95-43687. 134p. (Orig.). 1995. pap. text 12.00 (*0-932716-37-7*) Kelsey St Pr.

Dienstfrey, Patricia, ed. see Berssenbrugge, Mei-mei.

Dienstfrey, Patricia, ed. see Berssenbrugge, Mei-Mei & Tuttle, Richard.

Dienstfrey, Patricia, ed. see Browne, Laynie.

Dienstfrey, Patricia, ed. see Einzig, Barbara.

Dienstfrey, Patricia, ed. see Going, Dale.

Dienstfrey, Patricia, ed. see Mullen, Laura.

Dienstfrey, Patricia, ed. see Robinson, Elizabeth.

Dienstfrey, Patricia, ed. see Roy, Camille.

Dienstfrey, Richard A., jt. ed. see Rivers, P. Clayton.

Diep, Bridgette. Trip Through Cambodia. LC 73-159478. (Illus.). 32p. (J). (ps-3). 14.95 (*0-87592-054-3*) Scroll Pr.

Diep, Do Ngoc. Non Commutative Geometry, 001. 351p. 1999. per. 64.95 (*1-58488-019-8*, Chap & Hall CRC) CRC Pr.

Diep, H. T. Magnetic Systems with Competing Interactions. 350p. 1994. text 99.00 (*981-02-1715-3*) World Scientific Pub.

Diepenbrock, Nancy H. Quick Reference to Critical Care. LC 98-44543. 336p. 1999. pap. text 24.95 (*0-7817-1862-7*) Lppncott W & W.

Diepenbrock, Wulf & Becker, Heiko. Physiological Potential of Yield Improvement of Annual Oil & Protein Crops. 291p. 1995. pap. 43.00 (*3-8263-3020-X*, Pub. by Blckwell Wissenschafts) Balogh.

Diepenbrook, Chloe. Gynecology & Textuality: Popular Representations of Reproductive Technology. LC 98-41890. (Studies in American Popular History & Culture). 200p. 1998. 50.00 (*0-8153-3222-X*) Garland.

Diepersloot, Jan. Qigong of the Center, the Essence of Taijiquan: The Teachings of Grandmaster Cai Song Fang, 3 vols. LC 95-96121. (Warriors of Stillness - Meditative Traditions in the Chinese Martial Arts Ser.: Vol. 1). (Illus.). 278p. (Orig.). 1996. pap. 24.95 (*0-9649976-0-6*) CCCFH & TA.

***Diepersloot, Jan.** Yiquan: The Method of Awareness in the Martial Arts. (Illus.). 2000. pap. 24.95 (*0-9649976-1-4*) CCCFH & TA.

Diepeveen, Leonard. Changing Voices: The Modern Quoting Poem. 224p. (C). 1993. text 47.50 (*0-472-10369-5*, 10369) U of Mich Pr.

***Diepeveen, Leonard & Van Laar, Timothy.** Art with a Difference: Looking at Difficult & Unfamiliar Art. LC 00-25676. (Illus.). 2000. write for info. (*1-55934-930-1*) Mayfield Pub.

Diepeveen, Leonard, jt. auth. see Van Laar, Timothy.

Diephouse, David J. Pastors & Pluralism in Wurttemberg, 1918-1933. LC 87-3293. 408p. 1987. reprint ed. pap. 126.50 (*0-608-02594-1*, 206325100004) Bks Demand.

Diephouse, David J., ed. & tr. see Riehl, Wilhelm H.

Diephouse, David J., tr. see Von Gerstner, Franz A.

Dieppe, P. A., et al. Arthritis & Rheumatism in Practice. (Illus.). 128p. (gr. 13). 1991. text 39.95 (*0-397-44588-1*, GM0036) Mosby Inc.

Dieppe, P. A., jt. auth. see Russell, R. G.

Dieppe, Paul, et al. Atlas of Clinical Rheumatology. LC 85-23129. 396p. reprint ed. pap. 122.80 (*0-7837-3277-5*, 205774200007) Bks Demand.

***Dier, Debra.** Beyond Forever. 368p. 1999. mass mkt. 5.50 (*0-8439-4623-7*, Leisure Bks) Dorchester Pub Co.

— Deceptions & Dreams. 448p. 1999. mass mkt. 5.99 (*0-8439-4582-6*, Pub. by Dorchester Pub Co) CMG.

Dier, Debra. Devil's Honor. 400p. 1998. mass mkt. 5.99 (*0-8439-4362-9*, Leisure Bks) Dorchester Pub Co.

Dier, Debra. Lord Savage. 320p. (Orig.). 1996. mass mkt. 4.99 (*0-8439-4119-7*) Dorchester Pub Co.

An Asterisk (*) at the beginning of an entry indicates that the title is appearing for the first time.

— Mac Laren's Bride. 368p. 2000. pap. 5.50 (*0-8439-4768-3*, Leisure Bks) Dorchester Pub Co.

Dier, Debra. Saint's Temptation. 400p. 1998. mass mkt. 5.99 (*0-8439-4459-5*, Leisure Bks) Dorchester Pub Co.

— Shadow of the Storm. 448p. (Orig.). 1998. mass mkt. 5.99 (*0-8439-4397-1*, Leisure Bks) Dorchester Pub Co.

— The Sorcerer's Lady. 448p. (Orig.). 1999. mass mkt. 5.50 (*0-505-52305-1*) Dorchester Pub Co.

Dier, Debra, et al. Holiday Inn. 400p. (Orig.). 1996. mass mkt. 5.99 (*0-8439-4107-3*) Dorchester Pub Co.

— Holiday Inn. 400p. (Orig.). 1998. mass mkt. 5.99 (*0-8439-4538-9*, Leisure Bks) Dorchester Pub Co.

Dier, John A. & Dier, Marcia L. Basic Electronic Calculator Operations. 2nd ed. (Illus.). 81p. (C). 1989. pap. text. write for info. (*0-9624253-0-3*) Comed Plus Inc.

Dier, Marcia L., jt. auth. see Dier, John A.

***Dier, Paul & Goralski, Richard.** Gas Assist Injection Molding. LC 99-462022. (Illus.). 2000. write for info. (*1-893677-05-2*) Abby Communs.

Dierbach, Johann H. Die Arzneimittel Des Hippokrates. xxiv, 270p. 1969. reprint ed. write for info. (*0-318-70910-4*) G Olms Pubs.

Dierben, K. Die Vegetation Nordeuropas (Vegetation of Northern Europe) (GER., Illus.). 830p. 1996. 88.00 (*3-8001-2700-8*, Pub. by Eugen Ulmer) Balogh.

Diercks, D. R. CNRA/CSNI Workshop on Steam Generator Tube Integrity in Nuclear Power Plants: Held in Oak Brook, Illinois, October 30-November 2, 1995. 618p. 1997. per. 53.00 (*0-16-063015-0*) USGPO.

— Steam Generator Tube Integrity Program: Annual Report, August 1995-September 1996. 195p. 1998. per. 16.00 (*0-16-062894-6*) USGPO.

— Steam Generator Tube Integrity Program: Semiannual Report, August 1995-March 1996. 112p. 1997. per. 10.00 (*0-16-062834-2*) USGPO.

— Steam Generator Tube Integrity Program: Semiannual Report, October 1996-March 1997. 123p. 1998. per. 10.00 (*0-16-062945-4*) USGPO.

***Diercks, Jon.** Mpe/Ix System Administrator's Handbook. 2000. pap. 50.00 (*0-13-030540-5*) P-H.

Diercks, Thelma C., ed. Foreign Book & Serial Vendors Directories, Vol. 1. LC 95-43416. 1995. 10.00 (*0-8389-7811-8*) ALA.

Diercksen, G. H., et al, eds. Molecular Astrophysics: State of the Art & Future Directions. 1985. text 318.00 (*90-277-2081-9*) Kluwer Academic.

Diercksen, G. H. & Wilson, S., eds. Methods in Computational Molecular Physics. 1983. text 171.00 (*90-277-1638-2*) Kluwer Academic.

Diercksen, G. H., jt. auth. see Wilson, S.

Diercksen, G. H., ed. see NATO Advanced Study Institute Staff.

Diercksen, G. H., jt. ed. see Wilson, S.

Diercksmeier, C. F., Jr., jt. auth. see Glossinger, John.

***Dierckx, Heidi M. C.** Africa. (Illus.). 96p. 1999. pap. text 10.95 (*1-58037-089-6*, Pub. by M Twain Media) Carson-Dellos.

— Greek & Roman Civilizations. 112p. (YA). (gr. 5-8). 1996. pap. text 11.95 (*1-58037-063-2*, Pub. by M Twain Media) Carson-Dellos.

Dierckx, Paul. Curve & Surface Fitting with Splines. (Monographs on Numerical Analysis). (Illus.). 302p. 1995. reprint ed. pap. text 65.00 (*0-19-853440-X*) OUP.

Dierdorf, Stephen F., jt. auth. see Stoelting, Robert K.

Dieren, Bernard Van, see Van Dieren, Bernard.

Dieren, Wouter Van, see Van Dieren, Wouter.

***Dierenbach, Karl.** Colorado Four-Wheel Drive Roads 2001 Calendar. (Illus.). 28p. 2000. pap. 11.95 (*0-9700293-0-6*) K Dierenbach.

Dierenfield, Bruce J. Keeper of the Rules: Congressman Howard W. Smith of Virginia. LC 86-19026. (Illus.). 320p. 1987. reprint ed. pap. 99.20 (*0-608-00255-0*, 206077200006) Bks Demand.

Dierhauf, Leslie A. M. D., ed. Handbook of Marine Mammal Medicine. 784p. 1990. boxed set 125.95 (*0-8493-2990-6*, SF997) CRC Pr.

Dierich, Manfred P., jt. ed. see Wuerzner, Reinhard.

***Dierich, Mary & Froe, Felicia.** Overcoming Incontinence: A Straightforward Guide to Your Options. LC 99-36372. 120p. 2000. pap. 14.95 (*0-471-34795-7*) Wiley.

Dierick, Augustinus P. Gottfried Benn & His Critics: Major Interpretations, 1912-1992. LC 92-18223. (LCGERM Ser.). 199p. 1992. 60.00 (*1-879751-25-9*) Camden Hse.

Dierick, Charles, jt. ed. see Lefevre, Pascal.

Dierikx, Marc. Fokker: A Transatlantic Biography. LC 97-4296. (History of Aviation Ser.). (Illus.). 360p. 1997. 35.00 (*1-56098-735-9*) Smithsonian.

Dierker, jt. auth. see Campbell.

Dierker, Paul & Voxman, William L. Discrete Mathematics: International Edition. 589p. (C). 1986. write for info. (*0-318-60393-4*) SCP.

Dierker, Robert H. & Mehan, Richard J. Missouri Contracts Litigation. Leahy, Monique C., ed. LC 96-76213. (Practitioner's Ser.). 800p. 1996. text. write for info. (*0-7620-0054-6*) West Group.

— Missouri Personal Injury & Torts. Leahy, Monique C., ed. LC 96-75996. (Practitioner's Ser.). 800p. 1996. text. write for info. (*0-7620-0053-8*) West Group.

Dierker, Robert H., jt. auth. see Mehan, Richard J.

***Dierkes, Meinolf & von Grote, Claudia, eds.** Between Understanding & Trust: The Public, Science & Technology. 398p. 2000. text 48.00 (*90-5823-007-4*, Harwood Acad Pubs) Gordon & Breach.

Dierkes, U., et al. Minimal Surface I: Boundary Value Problems. LC 90-27155. 507p. 1992. 135.95 (*0-387-53169-6*) Spr-Verlag.

Dierkheising, Judy, jt. auth. see Bulger, Leonaye.

Dierking, Connie C. & Anderson-McElveen, Susan. Teaching Writing Skills with Children's Literature. LC 98-36568. 156p. 1998. pap., teacher ed. 19.95 (*0-929895-27-4*) Maupin Hse.

Dierking, Lynn D., jt. auth. see Falk, John H.

Dierking, Lynn D., jt. ed. see Falk, John H.

Dierkins, Tony, jt. auth. see Anderson, Scott.

Dierks, Leslie. A Crafter's Book of Santas: More Than 50 Festive Projects. LC 96-1185. (Illus.). 144p. 1996. 27.95 (*0-8069-8164-4*) Lark Books.

— Crafter's Book of Santas: More Than 50 Festive Projects. (Illus.). 144p. 1997. pap. text 17.95 (*0-8069-8165-2*) Sterling.

— Creative Clay Jewelry: Extraordinary, Colorful, Fun Designs to Make from Polymer Clay. LC 93-37188. (Illus.). 144p. 1994. pap. 18.95 (*0-937274-74-7*) Lark Books.

— Everlasting Harvest: Making Distinctive Arrangements & Elegant Decorations from Nature. (Illus.). 144p. 1997. pap. text 16.95 (*0-8069-4867-1*) Sterling.

***Dierks, Leslie.** Making Mosaics: Designs, Techniques & Projects. 96p. 2000. 19.95 (*0-86573-168-3*) Creat Pub Intl.

Dierks, Leslie. Making Mosaics: Designs, Techniques & Projects. LC 96-31470. (Illus.). 128p. 1997. 24.95 (*0-8069-4872-8*) Sterling.

***Dierks, Leslie.** Making Pet Palaces: Princely Homes & Furnishings to Pamper Your Pets. (Illus.). 128p. 2000. reprint ed. text 25.00 (*0-7881-6912-2*) DIANE Pub.

Dierks, Leslie. Wreath Magic: Eighty-Six Magnificent Wreaths, Garlands & Swags to Make. LC 93-25678. (Illus.). 128p. 1994. 27.95 (*0-8069-0578-6*) Sterling.

— Wreath Magic: 86 Magnificent Wreaths, Garlands & Swags to Make. (Illus.). 128p. (Orig.). 1996. pap. 14.95 (*0-8069-0579-4*) Sterling.

— Wreaths from the Garden: Seventy-Five Fresh & Dried Floral Wreaths to Make. LC 93-40711. (Illus.). 128p. 1994. 27.95 (*0-8069-0604-9*) Sterling.

Dierks, Leslie, jt. auth. see Ford, Steven.

Dierks, Leslie, ed. see Blue Evening Star Staff.

Dierks, Leslie, ed. see Cooper, Kathy & Hersey, Jan.

Dierks, Leslie, ed. see Jenkins, Cindy.

Dierks, Leslie, ed. see Kellar, Casey.

Dierks, Leslie, ed. see LaPlantz, Shereen.

Dierks, Leslie, ed. see Nicholas, Kristin.

Dierks, Sheila D. Women Eucharist. LC 97-60762. 316p. (Orig.). 1997. pap. 16.95 (*0-9658137-9-7*) Woven Word.

Dierks, Sheila D., jt. auth. see Durkin, Mary C.

Dierks, T., jt. auth. see Maurer, Konrad.

***Dierlamm, Judith.** A Genetic Profile of Marginal Zone B-Cell Lymphoma. (Acta Biomedica Lovaniensia Ser.: Vol. 200). (Illus.). 120p. 1999. pap. 65.00 (*90-6186-965-X*, Pub. by Leuven Univ) Coronet Bks.

Dierman, Peter Van, see Van Dierman, Peter.

Dierolf, Susanne, et al, eds. Functional Analysis: Proceedings of the First International Workshop Held at Trier University, Germany, September 26-October 1, 1994. LC 96-34001. xii, 473p. (C). 1996. lib. bdg. 158.95 (*3-11-014617-7*) De Gruyter.

Diers-Caviness, Mary H., jt. ed. see Taylor, William J.

Diers, Rochelle K., et al. How to Buy a College Education. LC 96-96444. (Illus.). 128p. (Orig.). 1996. pap. 14.95 (*0-9652898-7-7*) Access Grp.

Diers, Tracy. Carbon & Carbro Tissue: You Can Make It! (Illus.). 72p. (Orig.). 1986. student ed. 19.95 (*0-9617656-0-7*) Tracy Diers.

— A Renaissance of Carbon & Carbro - The Pictorial Photographer's Handbook. (Illus.). 1980. write for info. (*0-9617656-1-5*) Tracy Diers.

Diers, Yves. Categories of Boolean Sheaves of Simple Algebras. (Lecture Notes in Mathematics Ser.: Vol. 1187). vi, 168p. 1986. 38.95 (*0-387-16459-6*) Spr-Verlag.

— Categories of Commutative Algebra. 280p. 1992. text 85.00 (*0-19-853586-4*) OUP.

***Diersch, Sandra.** Alicia's Challenge, Vol. 32. 101p. (J). (gr. 3-7). 1999. pap. 5.50 (*1-55028-650-1*, Pub. by J Lorimer) Orca Bk Pubs.

Diersche, Volker. Die Radiolarite des Oberjura Im Mittelabschnitt der Noerdlichen Kalkalpen. (Geotektonische Forschungen Ser.: Vol. 58). (GER.). ii, 217p. 1980. 91.00 (*3-510-50024-5*, Pub. by E Schweizerbartsche) Balogh.

Dierschke, Hartmut. Internationale Vereinigung Fuer Vegetationskunde: Berichte der Internationalen Symposien: Syntaxonomie (1980) (GER., Illus.). 614p. 1981. lib. bdg. 160.00 (*3-7682-1309-9*) Lubrecht & Cramer.

Dierschke, Hartmut, ed. Struktur und Dynamik Von Waeldern: Rinteln, April 1981, Berichte der Internationalen Symposien der Intern'len Vereinigung fuer Vegetationskunde. (GER., Illus.). 736p. (Orig.). 1983. lib. bdg. 120.00 (*3-7682-1334-X*) Lubrecht & Cramer.

Dierstein, R., et al, eds. Parallel Computing in Science & Engineering. (Lecture Notes in Computer Science Ser.: Vol. 295). vii, 180p. 1988. 30.00 (*0-387-18923-8*) Spr-Verlag.

***Dieruf, W. C., Jr.** Successful Entrepreneurship in the Twenty-First Century: The Successful Management of Independent Business. LC 99-66065. x, 100p. 1999. pap. 19.95 (*0-9651207-2-4*) Ray Pubng.

Dies, Auguste. Autour de Platon: Essais de Critique et d'Histoire. LC 75-13261. (History of Ideas in Ancient Greece Ser.). (FRE.). 1976. reprint ed. 42.95 (*0-405-07303-8*) Ayer.

Dies, Edward J. Behind the Wall Street Curtain. LC 73-86745. (Essay Index Reprint Ser.). 1977. 19.95 (*0-8369-1178-4*) Ayer.

— The Plunger: A Tale of the Wheat Pit. McCurry, Dan C. & Rubenstein, Richard E., eds. LC 74-30627. (American Farmers & the Rise of Agribusiness Ser.). (Illus.). 1975. reprint ed. 25.95 (*0-405-06789-5*) Ayer.

— Titans of the Soil: Great Builders of Agriculture. LC 76-49613. (Illus.). 216p. 1977. reprint ed. lib. bdg. 65.00 (*0-8371-9329-X*, DITS, Greenwood Pr) Greenwood.

Dies, Kathryn R., jt. auth. see MacLennan, Beryce W.

Dies, Martin. The Trojan Horse in America. Grob, Gerald N., ed. LC 76-46072. (Anti-Movements in America Ser.). 1977. reprint ed. lib. bdg. 31.95 (*0-405-09945-2*) Ayer.

Dies, Robert R. & MacKenzie, K. Roy, eds. Advances in Group Psychotherapy: Integrating Research & Practice. LC 83-206. (American Group Psychotherapy Association Monographs). xvii, 226p. 1985. 32.50 (*0-8236-0107-2*, 00107) Intl Univs Pr.

Diesbach, Ghislain De, see De Diesbach, Ghislain.

***Diesbergen, Clemens.** Radikal-Konstruktivistische Padagogik Als Problematische Konstruktion: Eine Studie Zum Radikalen Konstruktivismus und Seiner Anwendung in der Padagogik 2., Unveranderte Auflage. (Explorationen. Studien zur Erziehungswissenschaft Ser.). 318p. 2000. 44.95 (*3-906764-28-1*, Pub. by P Lang Pubng) P Lang Pubng.

Diesburg, Daniel E., ed. see Metallurgical Society of AIME Staff.

Diescho, Joseph. Born of the Sun: A Namibian Novel. 200p. 1988. 2.00 (*0-377-00188-0*) Friendship Pr.

Diesel, Alleyn & Maxwell, Patrick. Hinduism in Natal: A Brief Guide. (Illus.). 120p. 1993. pap. 24.95 (*0-86980-884-2*, Pub. by Univ Natal Pr) Intl Spec Bk.

Diesel, Anja A., et al, eds. "Jedes Ding hat seine Zeit..." Studien zur Israelitischen und Altorientalischen Weisheit Diethelm Michel zum 65. Geburtstag. (Beiheft zur Zeitschrift fuer die Alttestamentliche Wissenschaft Ser.: Vol. 241). (GER.). viii, 275p. (C). 1996. lib. bdg. 117.10 (*3-11-015052-2*) De Gruyter.

Diesel Era Staff & Sweetland, David R. Train Master: The Most Useful Locomotive Ever Built. LC 97-60477. 112p. 1997. pap. 29.95 (*1-881411-13-3*) Withers Pub.

Diesendorf, Mark & Hamilton, Clive, eds. Human Ecology, Human Economy. LC 97-185895. 400p. 1997. pap. 35.00 (*1-86448-288-5*, Pub. by Allen & Unwin Pty) Paul & Co Pubs.

Diesing, Molly. Indefinites. (Linguistic Inquiry Monographs: No. 20). (Illus.). 191p. 1992. pap. text 18.95 (*0-262-54066-5*) MIT Pr.

***Diesing, Paul.** Hegel's Dialectical Political Economy: Applied to Current Society. LC 99-20305. 200p. 1999. 65.00 (*0-8133-9131-8*, Pub. by Westview) HarpC.

Diesing, Paul. How Does Social Science Work? Reflections on Practice. LC 90-41706. (Policy & Institutional Studies). 432p. (C). 1992. pap. 19.95 (*0-8229-5475-3*) U of Pittsburgh Pr.

— Reason in Society: Five Types of Decisions & Their Social Conditions. LC 72-11328. 262p. 1973. reprint ed. pap. 4.95 (*0-8371-8941-1*, DIRPB); reprint ed. lib. bdg. 65.00 (*0-8371-6660-8*, DIRS) Greenwood.

Diesing, Paul, jt. auth. see Snyder, Glenn H.

Diessel, C. F. Coal Bearing Depositional Systems. (Illus.). 664p. 1993. 158.95 (*0-387-52516-5*) Spr-Verlag.

***Diessel, Holger.** Demonstratives: Form, Function & Grammaticalization. LC 99-46743. (Typological Studies in Language: Vol. 42). xii, 205p. 1999. 75.00 (*1-55619-656-3*) J Benjamins Pubng Co.

— Demonstratives: Form, Function & Grammaticalization. LC 99-46743. (Typological Studies in Language: Vol. 42). xii, 205p. 1999. pap. 29.95 (*1-55619-657-1*) J Benjamins Pubng Co.

Diesslin, Howard G. Agricultural Equipment Financing. (Occasional Papers: No. 50). 111p. 1955. reprint ed. 28.90 (*0-87014-364-6*) Natl Bur Econ Res.

Diessner. Sources. 384p. 2000. pap. 20.94 (*0-07-232334-5*) McGraw.

— Sources: Notable Selections in Human Development. 1997. pap., student ed. 20.94 (*0-697-31051-5*) McGraw.

Diessner, Don. Sitting Bull's Story: There Are No Indians Left but Me! (Native American Leaders Ser.: Vol. 1). (Illus.). 183p. 1993. 35.00 (*0-912783-13-3*) Upton & Sons.

Dieste, Rafael. De Los Archivos del Trasgo. Molina, Cesar A., tr. (Nueva Austral Ser.: Vol. 84). (SPA.). 1991. pap. text 24.95 (*84-239-1884-X*) Elliots Bks.

Diestel, H. Saturated Flow & Soil Structure: A Review of the Subject & Laboratory Experiments on the Basic Relationship. (Physical Environment Ser.: Vol. 14). (Illus.). vi, 125p. 1994. 118.95 (*0-387-55791-1*) Spr-Verlag.

Diestel, J. Sequences & Series in Banach Spaces. (Graduate Texts in Mathematics Ser.: Vol. 92). 280p. 1984. 49.00 (*0-387-90859-5*) Spr-Verlag.

Diestel, J. & Uhl, J. J., Jr. Vector Measures. LC 77-9625. (Mathematical Surveys Ser.: No. 15). 322p. 1991. reprint ed. pap. 50.00 (*0-8218-1515-6*, SURV/15) Am Math.

Diestel, Joe, et al. Absolutely Summing Operators. (Studies in Advanced Mathematics: No. 43). 490p. (C). 1995. text 74.95 (*0-521-43168-9*) Cambridge U Pr.

Diestel, Reinhard. Graph Decompositions: A Study in Infinite Graph Theory. (Illus.). 242p. 1990. text 55.00 (*0-19-853210-5*) OUP.

***Diestel, Reinhard.** Graph Theory. 2nd ed. LC 99-57468. (Graduate Texts in Mathematics Ser.: Vol. 173) (Illus.). 315p. 2000. 34.95 (*0-387-98976-5*) Spr-Verlag.

Diestel, Reinhard. Graph Theory, Vol. 173. LC 97-5932. (Graduate Texts in Mathematics Ser.). 1997. 59.95 (*0-387-98210-8*) Spr-Verlag.

Diestler, Dennis J., jt. auth. see Dence, Joseph B.

Diestler, Shery. Becoming a Critical Thinker: A User Friendly Manual. 2nd ed. LC 97-45965. 438p. 1997. pap. text 41.00 (*0-13-744335-8*) P-H.

Dietary Managers Assoc. Staff. Achieving Quality in Healthcare Nutrition Services. 178p. 1998. ring bd. 78.00 (*0-7872-4735-9*) Kendall-Hunt.

Dietch, Irene & Howell, Candace W., eds. Counseling the Aging & Their Families. LC 96-48067. (Family Psychology & Counseling Ser.). 155p. (Orig.). (C). 1997. pap. text 17.95 (*1-55620-163-X*, 72671) Am Coun Assn.

Dietel, Harvey M. & Dietel, Paul J. Microsoft IBM QuickBASIC. (C). 1989. pap. text 41.25 (*0-13-449422-9*) P-H.

Dietel, J. Edwin. Leading a Law Practice to Excellence. LC 91-76918. 517p. 1992. text 38.00 (*0-8318-0653-2*, B653) Am Law Inst.

— Sustaining Law Practice Excellence. LC 92-71400. 276p. 1992. text 18.00 (*0-8318-0688-5*, B688) Am Law Inst.

Dietel, Patricia, et al. The Best of Northern Monmouth: A Guide for Newcomers, Old-Timers, & Everyone-in-Between. (Illus.). 199p. 1997. pap. 18.95 (*0-9662309-0-6*) SW Pub Inc.

Dietel, Paul J., jt. auth. see Dietel, Harvey M.

Dieten, Ioannes Van, see Van Dieten, Ioannes, ed.

Dieten, V. E. Van, see Van Dieten, V. E.

Dieter. Engineering Design. 2nd ed. 1991. student ed. 30.00 (*0-07-016907-1*) McGraw.

***Dieter.** Engineering Design. 3rd ed. LC 99-24646. 816p. 1999. 86.88 (*0-07-366136-8*) McGraw.

Dieter. Mechanical Metallurgy. 3rd ed. 1986. student ed. 27.50 (*0-07-016894-6*) McGraw.

Dieter, Arnold. When the Pyramids Were Built. LC 99-33287. (Illus.). 144p. 1999. text 35.00 (*0-87099-908-7*) Metro Mus Art.

Dieter, Carol McCullough, jt. auth. see Hobuss, Jim.

Dieter, George. Engineering Design: Materials & Processing Approach. 2nd ed. 672p. (C). 1991. 96.88 (*0-07-016906-3*) McGraw.

— Mechanical Metallurgy. 3rd ed. (Materials Science & Engineering Ser.). 800p. (C). 1986. 99.38 (*0-07-016893-8*) McGraw.

Dieter, George E., ed. ASM Handbook Vol. 20: Materials Selection & Design. 900p. (C). 1997. 186.00 (*0-87170-386-6*, 6481) ASM.

Dieter, Hallie, ed. see Smith, Hannah W.

Dieter, Katherine, ed. see McDonald, John.

Dieter, Lance, tr. see Linden, G., ed.

Dieter Markert Staff. The Turbo-Protein Diet: Stop Yo-Yo Dieting Forever. (Illus.). 112p. 1998. pap. 7.95 (*0-9667285-1-3*) BioMed Intl.

Dieter, Melvin, ed. see Smith, Hannah W.

Dieter, Melvin E. The Holiness Revival of the Nineteenth Century. Dayton, Donald W. & Rowe, Kenneth E., eds. (Studies in Evangelicalism: No. 1). 324p. 1996. pap. 35.00 (*0-8108-3155-4*) Scarecrow.

— The Holiness Revival of the Nineteenth Century. rev. ed. LC 95-25919. (Studies in Evangelicalism: No. 1). 324p. 1996. 59.00 (*0-8108-3045-0*) Scarecrow.

Dieter, Michael P., jt. ed. see Goehl, Thomas J.

Dieter, Raymond A., Jr., ed. Thoracoscopy for Surgeons: Diagnostic & Therapeutic. LC 94-29082. (Illus.). 288p. 1995. 98.50 (*0-89640-269-X*) Igaku-Shoin.

Dieterich, et al. Urban Land Property Markets Germany. 256p. 1993. 75.00 (*1-85728-049-0*, Pub. by UCL Pr Ltd) Taylor & Francis.

Dieterich, Ernest. Solution of a Nondomestic Tame Classification Problem from Integral Representation Theory of Finite Groups (A equals RC3, v(3) equals 4) LC 91-15023. (Memoirs Ser.). 140p. 1991. pap. 24.00 (*0-8218-2521-6*, MEMO/92/450) Am Math.

Dieterich, Genoveva. Pequeno Diccionario de Teatro Mundial. (SPA.). 294p. 1976. pap. 19.95 (*0-8288-5748-2*, S31395) Fr & Eur.

Dieterich, Karl. Byzantinische Quellen Zur Lander- und Volkerkunde. 5-15. Jahrhundert, 2 vols. in 1. (Quellen und Forschungen Zur Geschichte der Erdkunde Ser.: No. 5). (GER.). xlix, 338p. 1973. reprint ed. write for info. (*3-487-04693-8*) G Olms Pubs.

— Untersuchungen zur Geschichte der Griechischen Sprache. xxiv, 326p. 1970. reprint ed. write for info. (*0-318-70911-2*) G Olms Pubs.

Dieterich, Thomas G. & Vosbinder, Anne S. English Grammar: Structure & Theme. 450p. (C). 1999. pap., teacher ed. 37.50 (*0-472-08453-4*, 08453); pap. text 42.50 (*0-472-06622-6*, 06622) U of Mich Pr.

Dieterici, Friedrich. Die Philosophie Bei den Arabern Im X. Jh. n. Chr. Gesamtdarstellung und Quellenwerke, 14 vols., Set. cxlii, 3174p. 1969. reprint ed. write for info. (*0-318-71500-7*) G Olms Pubs.

Dieterle, Martin, jt. text see Clark, Kenneth.

Dieterle, Regina. Vater und Tochter: Erkundung einer erotisierten Beziehung in Leben und Werk Theodor Fontanes. 1996. 50.95 (*3-906756-21-1*) P Lang Pubng.

Dieterlen, F. Zur Phaenologie des aequatorialen Regenwaldes im Ost-Zaire (Kivu) nebst Planzenliste und Klimadaten. (Dissertationes Botanicae Ser.: No. 47). (Illus.). 1979. pap. 18.00 (*3-7682-1215-7*) Lubrecht & Cramer.

Dietetic Practice Group Staff, jt. auth. see Dietitians in General Clinical Practice Staff.

Dieth, Eugen. Vademekum der Phonetik. 2nd ed. (GER.). 1968. 49.95 (*0-8288-6666-X*, M-7135) Fr & Eur.

Diethe, Carol. Aspects of Distorted Sexual Attitudes in German Expressionist Drama: With Particular Reference to Wedekind, Kokoschka & Kaiser. (American University Studies: Germanic Languages & Literature: Ser. I, Vol. 75). IV, 283p. (C). 1988. text 45.00 (*0-8204-0893-X*) P Lang Pubng.

— Historical Dictionary of Nietzscheanism. LC 98-26822. (Historical Dictionaries of Religions, Philosophies, & Movements Ser.: No. 21). (Illus.). 265p. 1998. 62.00 (*0-8108-3512-6*) Scarecrow.

— Nietzsche's Women: Beyond the Whip. LC 96-6241. (Monographien und Texte Zur Nietzsche-Forschung Ser.: No. 31). 1996. 88.90 (*3-11-014819-6*) De Gruyter.

— Nietzsche's Women: Beyond the Whip. (Illus.). xiv, 177p. (C). 1996. pap. text 19.95 (*3-11-014820-X*) De Gruyter.

D

— Towards Emancipation: German Women Writers of the Nineteenth Century. LC 97-31869. (Illus.). 192p. 1998. 39.95 (*1-57181-932-0*) Berghahn Bks.

— Towards Emancipation: German Women Writers of the Nineteenth Century. LC 97-31869. (Illus.). 192p. 1998. pap. 12.95 (*1-57181-933-9*) Berghahn Bks.

Diethe, Carol, ed. see Nietzsche, Friedrich Wilhelm.

Diethelm, Jerome. Designing in an Environmental Field: Essays, Metaphors, Kasinas. LC 97-94705. (Illus.). 116p. 1998. pap. 19.95 (*0-9660370-7-3*) Aurora Bks.

Diethelm, Oskar. Medical Dissertations of Psychiatric Interest. 1971. 36.75 (*3-8055-1201-5*) S Karger.

Diethelm, Walter. Saint Pius X: The Farm Boy Who Became Pope. LC 93-78530. (Illus.). 163p. (J). (gr. 4-9). 1996. pap. 9.95 (*0-89870-469-3*) Ignatius Pr.

Diethorn, Joe & Kaiser, David. The Beginner's PC Shopping Guide. (Illus.). 96p. (Orig.). 1992. pap. 9.95 (*0-9634208-0-1*) KD Info Systs.

Diethrich, Edward B. & Cohan, Carol. Women & Heart Disease: What You Can Do to Stop the Number One Killer of American Women. 320p. 1994. pap. 10.00 (*0-345-38620-5*) Ballantine Pub Grp.

Dietiker, Simone R. En Bonne Forme. 3rd ed. 416p. (C). 1983. pap. text 49.16 (*0-669-05255-8*) HM Trade Div.

— En Bonne Forme. 4th ed. LC 87-80701. 446p. (C). 1990. pap. text 49.16 (*0-669-12015-4*); pap. text 2.66 (*0-669-12020-0*); pap. text, student ed. 35.56 (*0-669-12016-2*); audio 2.66 (*0-669-12019-7*) HM Trade Div.

— En Bonne Forme. 5th ed. (FRE.). 497p. (C). 1992. pap. text 49.16 (*0-669-24235-7*); pap. text, student ed. 35.56 (*0-669-24237-3*); teacher ed. 2.76 (*0-669-24236-5*); teacher ed. 2.66 (*0-669-24239-X*); audio 31.16 (*0-669-24238-1*); audio 2.66 (*0-669-24241-1*) HM Trade Div.

Dietiker, Simone R. & Bugere, Gerard. Franc-Parler. 3rd ed. LC 84-80479. (FRE.). 470p. (C). 1985. text 61.16 (*0-669-07218-4*); teacher ed. 2.66 (*0-669-07220-6*); student ed. 29.16 (*0-669-07219-2*); 2.66 (*0-669-07224-9*); 2.66 (*0-669-07221-4*); audio 31.16 (*0-669-07223-0*) HM Trade Div.

Dietiker, Simone R. & Van Hooff, Dominique. En Bonne Forme. 6th ed. (FRE.). (C). 1996. pap. text, teacher ed. 50.36 (*0-669-41625-8*) HM Trade Div.

— En Bonne Forme. 6th ed. (FRE.). (C). 1996. pap. text, wbk. ed., lab manual ed. 35.56 (*0-669-41626-6*) HM Trade Div.

— En Bonne Forme. 6th ed. (FRE.). 512p. (C). 1997. pap. text 49.16 (*0-669-41624-X*) HM Trade Div.

Dietitians in College & University Food Service St & Allen, Susan D. Campus Favorites: Vegetarian Recipe Collection. 150p. 1991. 9.95 (*0-9629861-0-0*) Diet Col & U Food Srv.

Dietitians in General Clinical Practice Staff & Dietetic Practice Group Staff. Exchange Lists for Weight Management. (Illus.). 32p. (Orig.). 1995. pap. text 1.50 (*0-88091-045-3*, 0764) Am Dietetic Assn.

Dietl & Lorentz. English-German Dictionary of Legal, Commercial & Political Terms. 5th ed. (ENG & GER.). 936p. 1990. 265.00 (*3-406-34166-7*, Pub. by CH Beck Verlag) IBD Ltd.

Dietl, Bo & Cross, Ken. One Tough Cop: The Bo Dietl Story. 278p. 1998. mass mkt. 6.99 (*0-671-02841-3*) PB.

Dietl, C. Dictionary of Legal, Commercial & Political Terms Vol. 2: German-English. 4th ed. (ENG & GER.). 849p. 1992. 375.00 (*0-7859-7545-4*, 3406366546) Fr & Eur.

— Gabler Wirtschafts Woerterbuch: CD-ROM Version. (ENG & GER.). 1994. 295.00 (*0-7859-7543-8*, 3409198229); 295.00 (*0-7859-7544-6*, 3409198237) Fr & Eur.

Dietl, C. E. & Lorenz, E. German-English Dictionary of Legal, Commercial & Political Terms. 4th rev. ed. 850p. 1992. 250.00 (*3-406-36654-6*, Pub. by CH Beck Verlag) IBD Ltd.

Dietl, Clara-Erika. Dictionary Economics, Finance, Law Vol. 1: German to English. 3rd ed. (ENG & GER.). 423p. 1995. 150.00 (*0-320-00548-8*) Fr & Eur.

— Dictionary Economics, Finance, Law Vol. 2: English to German. 3rd ed. (ENG & GER.). 409p. 1996. 150.00 (*0-320-00498-8*) Fr & Eur.

— Dictionary of Legal, Commercial & Political Terms Vol. 1: English - German. 5th ed. (ENG & GER.). 937p. 1990. 350.00 (*0-8288-3876-3*, F132140) Fr & Eur.

— Wirtschaftsworterbuch, Vol. 1. (ENG & GER.). 409p. 1989. lib. bdg. 125.00 (*0-8288-3849-6*, M6940) Fr & Eur.

— Wirtschaftsworterbuch, Vol. 2: 1990. (ENG & GER.). 404p. 1990. lib. bdg. 125.00 (*0-8288-3875-5*, M6939) Fr & Eur.

— Worterbuch fur Recht Wirtschaft & Politik, Vol. 2. (ENG & GER.). lib. bdg. 375.00 (*0-685-48755-5*, M15095) Fr & Eur.

— Worterbuch fur Recht Wirtschaft & Politik Vol. 1: 1990 Edition. (ENG & GER.). lib. bdg. 300.00 (*0-685-48754-7*, F132140) Fr & Eur.

Dietl, Clara-Erika, et al. Dictionary of Legal, Commercial, & Political Terms, Vol. 2. 3rd rev. ed. (ENG & GER.). 821p. 1988. 375.00 (*0-8288-3877-1*, M 15095) Fr & Eur.

Dietl, Erhard. Glimatron Christmas: Sharing the Holiday Spirit. (Illus.). 24p. (J). (ps-2). 1997. 10.95 (*0-7641-5003-0*) Barron.

Dietl, Gudrun. Abhaengigkeit der Schwermetallaufnahme Hoeherer Pilze Von der Substratzusammensetzung und Von Standortsfaktoren. (Bibliotheca Mycologica: Vol. 110). (GER., Illus.). 178p. 1987. 42.00 (*3-443-59011-X*, Pub. by Gebruder Borntraeger) Balogh.

Dietl, Gulshan. The Dulles Era: America Enters West Asia. 260p. 1986. 34.00 (*0-8364-1639-2*, Pub. by Lancer India) S Asia.

— Through Two Wars & Beyond: A Study of Gulf Cooperation Council. xii, 312p. 1991. 40.00 (*81-7095-024-4*) Advent Bks Div.

Dietl, Helmut M. Capital Markets & Corporate Governance in Japan, Germany, & the United States: Organizational Responses to Market Inefficiencies. LC 97-21404. 208p. (C). 1997. 85.00 (*0-415-17188-1*) Routledge.

Dietl, J., ed. The Mammalian Egg Coat. (Illus.). 190p. 1989. 101.00 (*0-387-50272-6*) Spr-Verlag.

Dietl, L. Kay & Neff, Marsha J. Human Needs & Social Welfare Curriculum Project: Grades 9-12. Incl. New Directions: Alternatives to the United States Social Welfare System. 1983. 4.95 (*0-8077-6078-1*); New Directions: Alternatives to the United States Social Welfare System. 1983. teacher ed. 3.95 (*0-8077-6079-X*); Youth-Search for Identity. 1983. 9.95 (*0-8077-6074-9*); Youth-Search for Identity. 1983. teacher ed. 7.95 (*0-8077-6075-7*); Unit I. To Promote the General Welfare? An Introduction to the United States Social Welfare System. 1983. 4.95 (*0-8077-6070-6*); Unit I. To Promote the General Welfare? An Introduction to the United States Social Welfare System. 1983. teacher ed. 4.95 (*0-8077-6071-4*); Unit II. Aging Americans-Profiles, Programs & Possibilities. 1983. 6.50 (*0-8077-6072-2*); Unit II. Aging Americans-Profiles, Programs & Possibilities. 1983. teacher ed. 5.50 (*0-8077-6073-0*); Unit IV. Single Parent Families: Choice or Chance. 1983. 7.95 (*0-8077-6076-5*); Unit IV. Single Parent Families: Choice or Chance. 1983. teacher ed. 5.50 (*0-8077-6077-3*); 1983. write for info. (*0-318-56794-6*) Tchrs Coll.

Dietl, Ulla. The Plant-&-Grow Project Book. LC 93-24788. (Illus.). 48p. (J). (gr. 2-10). 1993. 14.95 (*0-8069-0456-9*) Sterling.

Dietliker, K. K., jt. auth. see Crivello, J. V.

Dietlin, Tracy. The Alphabet Passages: Poetry A - Z. 67p. 1999. mass mkt. 12.00 (*0-9670284-0-X*) T Dietlin.

Dietmann, J. L. Radiodiagnosis of the Skull. Wackenheim, M. T., tr. from FRE. (Exercises in Radiological Diagnosis Ser.). (Illus.). 200p. 1985. 35.95 (*0-387-13266-X*) Spr-Verlag.

Dietmar, Mieth & Vidal, Marciano, eds. Outside the Market No Salvation? LC 97-203360. (Concilium Ser.). 150p. 1997. pap. 15.00 (*1-57075-127-7*) Orbis Bks.

Dietrich. Accounting & Accountancy. (C). 1998. text 58.50 (*0-03-006637-9*); pap. text, student ed. 26.50 (*0-03-006638-7*) Harcourt Coll Pubs.

— Dada in Cologne & Hanover. 1997. 95.00 (*0-8161-7326-5*) Macmillan.

— Write Now! A Process Writing Program. (EC - HS Communication/English Ser.). 1991. mass mkt. 11.95 (*0-538-61166-9*) S-W Pub.

Dietrich, A. Spring Design with an IBM PC. 112p. 1985. 130.00 (*0-8247-7349-7*) Dekker.

***Dietrich, Alan J., frwd.** U. S. Navy Diving Manual Vol. 1: Air Diving. rev. ed. (Illus.). 300p. (C). 1999. reprint ed. pap. text 60.00 (*0-7881-8260-9*) DIANE Pub.

Dietrich, Albert J. Kants Begriff des Ganzen in Seiner Raumzeitlehre und Das Verhaltnis Zu Leibniz. (GER.). 1975. reprint ed. write for info. (*3-487-05638-0*) G Olms Pubs.

Dietrich, Amy. Babies Are Such a Nice Way to Start People. LC 98-141001. (Charming Petites Ser.). 80p. 1997. 4.95 (*0-88088-824-5*) Peter Pauper.

— Been There, Done That: Advice from Women in the Know. (Pocket Gift Editions Ser.). 64p. 1998. 4.95 (*0-88088-103-8*) Peter Pauper.

***Dietrich, Amy.** Best Friends Forever. (Charming Petites Ser.). 80p. 2000. 4.95 (*0-88088-516-5*) Peter Pauper.

Dietrich, Amy. First Aid for a Teenager's Soul. (Charming Petites Ser.). 80p. 1998. 4.95 (*0-88088-385-5*) Peter Pauper.

***Dietrich, Amy.** You Go Girl! A Very Cool Guided Journal. (Guided Journals). 128p. 1999. 11.99 (*0-88088-221-2*) Peter Pauper.

Dietrich, Ann Marie & Shaner, Steven. Pediatric Basic Trauma Life Support. American College of Emergency Physicians, Ohio Chapter Staff, ed. (Illus.). (C). 1995. pap. text 24.95 (*0-9647418-0-6*) Basic Trauma.

— Pediatric Basic Trauma Life Support Update. Campbell, John, ed. (Illus.). (C). 1998. pap. text 24.95 (*0-9647418-1-4*) Basic Trauma.

Dietrich, B. C. The Origins of Greek Religion. 314p. (C). 1973. 165.40 (*3-11-003982-6*) De Gruyter.

Dietrich, Bernard C. Cult Practice & Belief in Minoan Crete: Reconstructing an Aegean Religion. (Illus.). 272p. 1997. 118.00 (*3-11-015646-6*) De Gruyter.

— Tradition in Greek Religion. xvi, 213p. 1986. 86.15 (*3-11-010695-7*) De Gruyter.

Dietrich, Bill. Ice Reich. LC 97-39152. 375p. 1998. 25.00 (*0-446-52339-9*, Pub. by Warner Bks) Little.

Dietrich-Boorsch, Dorothea. German Drawings of the Sixties. (Illus.). 100p. (Orig.). 1982. pap. 4.50 (*0-89467-018-2*) Yale Art Gallery.

Dietrich, C. F. Uncertainty, Calibration & Probability: The Statistics of Scientific & Industrial Measurement. 2nd rev. ed. (Measurement Science & Technology Ser.). (Illus.). 556p. 1991. 249.00 (*0-7503-0060-4*) IOP Pub.

***Dietrich, Carole.** A Complete Handbook for Selling Your Own Home. ii, 200p. 1999. ring bd. 29.95 (*0-9671594-0-7*) AHomeForSale.

Dietrich, Craig. People's China: A Brief History. 3rd ed. LC 97-18948. (Illus.). 400p. (C). 1997. text 50.00 (*0-19-510628-8*); pap. text 22.95 (*0-19-510629-6*) OUP.

***Dietrich, D., et al, eds.** Fieldbus Technology: Systems Integration, Networking, & Engineering Proceedings of the Fieldbus Conference FeT'99 in Magdeburg, Federal Republic of Germany, September 23-24, 1999. (Illus.). xvi, 452p. 1999. pap. 75.95 (*3-211-83394-3*) Spr-Verlag.

Dietrich, D., jt. ed. see Zamrik, S. Y.

Dietrich, D. E., ed. see Energy Technology Conference Staff.

Dietrich, Dan. Bowhunting Big Game. LC 92-62494. (Hunter's Information Ser.). 250p. 1993. write for info. (*0-914697-53-6*) N Amer Outdoor Grp.

Dietrich, David R. & Shabad, Peter, eds. The Problem of Loss & Mourning: Psychoanalytic Perspectives. 500p. 1989. 67.50 (*0-8236-4349-2*, BN 04349) Intl Univs Pr.

Dietrich, Debra M., jt. auth. see Aitelli, Peter.

Dietrich, Donald J. Catholic Citizens in the Third Reich: Psyco-Social Principles & Moral Reasoning. 385p. 1988. 44.95 (*0-88738-131-6*) Transaction Pubs.

— God & Humanity in Auschwitz: Jewish-Christian Relations & Sanctioned Murder. LC 93-35689. 292p. (C). 1994. 39.95 (*1-56000-147-X*) Transaction Pubs.

Dietrich, Donald J. & Himes, Michael J., eds. The Legacy of the Tubingen School: The Relevance of Nineteenth-Century Theology for the Twenty-First Century. LC 97-30950. 228p. 1997. pap. text 24.95 (*0-8245-1700-8*) Crossroad NY.

Dietrich, Dorothea. The Collages of Kurt Schwitters: Tradition & Innovation. (Illus.). 256p. (C). 1995. pap. text 25.95 (*0-521-49891-0*) Cambridge U Pr.

Dietrich, Edgar & Schulze, Alfred. Statistical Procedures for Machine & Process Qualification. LC 98-53111. 1999. write for info. (*0-87389-447-2*) ASQ Qual Pr.

Dietrich, Eric & Markman, Arthur B., eds. Cognitive Dynamics: Conceptual & Representational Change in Humans & Machines. LC 99-30505. 392p. 1999. 89.95 (*0-8058-3408-7*) L Erlbaum Assocs.

Dietrich, frank H. The Basics of Statistics. 3rd ed. (C). 1989. text 57.80 (*0-02-328801-9*, Macmillan Coll) P-H.

Dietrich, Gabriele. Reflections on the Women's Movement in India: Religion, Ecology, Development. xiv, 145p. 1992. 25.00 (*81-85487-01-4*, Pub. by Horizon India Bks) Advent Bks Div.

Dietrich, Gaeir, et al. Critical Thinking Activities to Improve Writing Skills A1: Whatcha-Macallits. (Illus.). 50p. (YA). (gr. 7 up). 1991. pap. 11.95 (*0-89455-388-7*) Crit Think Bks.

Dietrich, Georg, jt. auth. see Haussermann, Ulrich.

Dietrich, Gunter. General Oceanography: An Introduction. 2nd ed. Roll, Susanne & Roll, Hans U., trs. LC 80-12919. (Illus.). 676p. reprint ed. pap. 200.00 (*0-608-18194-3*, 205659600078) Bks Demand.

Dietrich, Irvine T. & Hove, John. Conservation of Natural Resources: North Dakota. LC 62-63204. (Illus.). 1962. 3.00 (*0-911042-06-7*) NDSU Inst Reg.

Dietrich, J., et al. The Ultimate Authorware Tutorial. LC 99-32706. 255p. 1998. 79.00 incl. cd-rom (*3-540-64123-8*) Spr-Verlag.

Dietrich, J. Kimball. Financial Services & Institutions: Value Creation in Theory & Practice. LC 95-9669. 797p. 1994. 66.80 (*0-02-329545-7*, Macmillan Coll) P-H.

Dietrich, J. Kimball, jt. ed. see Canto, Victor A.

Dietrich, John, jt. auth. see Deutsch, Axel.

Dietrich, Julia. Hamlet in the Nineteen Sixties: An Annotated Bibliography. LC 91-29683. (Shakespeare Bibliographies Ser.: Vol. 18). 808p. 1991. text 40.00 (*0-8240-8990-1*, H00477) Garland.

— The Old Left. LC 95-6126. (Literature & Society Ser.: No. 8). 1995. 33.00 (*0-8057-8861-1*, Twyne) Mac Lib Ref.

— Old Left in History & Literature. 1995. pap. 20.00 (*0-8057-7819-5*, Twyne) Mac Lib Ref.

Dietrich, K., et al, eds. Winter College on Fundamental Nuclear Physics: Proceedings of the Winter College on Fundamental Nuclear Physics, Trieste, Italy, March 1984, 3 vols., Set. 2008p. 1985. 293.00 (*9971-978-25-3*) World Scientific Pub.

Dietrich, Linnea & Hurd, Diane S. Art: Discipline Analysis. (Women in the Curriculum Ser.: Vol. 7b). 40p. (Orig.). 1997. pap. 7.00 (*1-885303-17-3*) Towson St Univ.

Dietrich, Linnea S. Audrey Flack: Reflections in a Mirror. CarterSouthard, Edna, ed. LC 97-76292. (Illus.). 1998. pap. 7.00 (*0-940784-19-X*) Miami Univ Art.

Dietrich, Lisa C. Chicana Adolescents: Bitches, 'Ho's & Schoolgirls. LC 97-34750. 192p. 1998. 55.00 (*0-275-96154-0*, Praeger Pubs) Greenwood.

Dietrich, Luc. L'Apprentissage de la Ville. (FRE.). 1973. pap. 10.95 (*0-7859-1750-0*, 2070364186) Fr & Eur.

— Le Bonheur Des Tristes. (FRE.). 224p. 1980. pap. 10.95 (*0-7859-1921-X*, 2070372138) Fr & Eur.

Dietrich, Manfried, et al, eds. Ugarit - Forschungen, Vol. 9. (GER & ENG.). v, 428p. 1978. text 35.00 (*3-7887-0570-1*) NeukirchenerV.

— Ugarit - Forschungen, Vol. 10. (GER, FRE & ENG.). vi, 520p. 1979. text 50.00 (*3-7887-0605-8*) NeukirchenerV.

— Ugarit - Forschungen, Vol. 11. (GER, FRE & ITA.). xiv, 905p. 1980. text 85.00 (*3-7887-0606-6*) NeukirchenerV.

— Ugarit - Forschungen, Vol. 22. (GER & FRE.). vi, 536p. 1991. text 97.50 (*3-7887-1389-5*) NeukirchenerV.

Dietrich, Manfried & Loretz, Oswald. Analytic Ugaritic Bibliography, 1972-1988. (Alter Orient und Altes Testament Ser.: Vol. 20). (GER.). viii, 1077p. 1996. text 179.50 (*3-7887-1587-1*) NeukirchenerV.

— Jahwe und Seine Aschera: Anthropomorphes Kultbild in Mesopotamien, Ugarit und Israel - Das Biblische Bilderverbot. (Ugaritisch-Biblische Literatur Ser.: Vol. 9). (GER.). xi, 206p. 1992. text 55.00 (*3-927120-08-1*, Pub. by UGARIT) Eisenbrauns.

— Die Keilalphabete: Die Phonizisch-Kanaanaischen und Altarabischen Alphabete in Ugarit. (Abhandlungen Zur Literatur Alt-Syrien-Palastinas Ser.: Vol. 1). (GER., Illus.). xiv, 357p. 1988. text 66.00 (*3-927120-00-6*, Pub. by UGARIT) Eisenbrauns.

— Konig Idrimi Von Alalah. (Abhandlungen zur Literatur Alt-Syrien - Palastinas und Mesopotamiens Ser.: Vol. 4). write for info. (*0-318-70270-3*, Pub. by UGARIT) Eisenbrauns.

— Mantik in Ugarit: Keilalphabetische Texte der Opferschau - Omensammlungen Nekromantie. (Abhandlungen Zur Literatur Alt-Syrien-Palastinas Ser.: Vol. 3). x, 307p. 1990. text 71.00 (*3-927120-05-7*, Pub. by UGARIT) Eisenbrauns.

— Mesopotamica - Ugaritica - Biblica: Festchrift fur Kurt Bergerhof zur Vollendung Seines 70, Lebensjahres am 7. Mai 1992. (Alter Orient und Altes Testament Ser.: Vol. 232). (FRE & GER.). x, 515p. 1993. text 105.00 (*3-7887-1453-0*) NeukirchenerV.

— Ugarit-Forshungen, Vol. 28. (GER, ITA & FRE.). vi, 837p. 1997. text 92.00 (*3-927120-56-1*, Pub. by Ugarit-Verlag) Eisenbrauns.

— Word-List of the Cuneiform Alphabetic Texts from Ugarit, Ras Ibn Hani & Other Places. 2nd enl. ed. LC 97-216895. 232p. 1996. text 54.00 (*3-927120-40-5*, Pub. by Ugarit-Verlag) Eisenbrauns.

Dietrich, Manfried & Loretz, Oswald, eds. Beschreiben und Deuten Im der Archaologie Des Alten Orients: Festschrift Fur Ruth Mayer-Opificius Mit Beitragen von Freunden und Schulern. (Altertumskunde Des Vorderen Orients Ser.: Vol. 4). (ACE & GER.). xvii, 354p. 1994. text 83.00 (*3-927120-18-9*, Pub. by UGARIT) Eisenbrauns.

— Ugarit - Ein Ostmediterranes Kulturzentrum Im Alten Orient: Ugarit und Seine Altorientalioche Umwelt. (Abhandlungen Zur Literatur Alt-Syrien-Palastinas Ser.: Vol. 7/1). (GER.). xii, 298p. 1995. text 86.00 (*3-927120-17-0*, Pub. by UGARIT) Eisenbrauns.

— Ugarit - Forschungen, Vol. 23. (GER & ENG.). vii, 473p. 1992. text 102.50 (*3-7887-1434-4*) NeukirchenerV.

— Ugarit - Forschungen, Vol. 24. (GER & ENG.). v, 533p. 1993. text 102.50 (*3-7887-1476-X*) NeukirchenerV.

— Ugarit - Forschungen, Vol. 25. (GER, FRE & ENG.). v, 536p. 1994. text 102.50 (*3-7887-1506-5*) NeukirchenerV.

— Ugarit - Forschungen, Vol. 26. (GER & ENG.). v, 639p. 1995. text 102.50 (*3-7887-1537-5*) NeukirchenerV.

— Ugarit - Forschungen, Vol. 27. (GER, ENG & FRE.). vii, 771p. 1996. text 115.00 (*3-7887-1588-X*) NeukirchenerV.

***Dietrich, Manfried & Loretz, Oswald, eds.** Ugarit-Forschungen 30: Internationales Jahrbuch fur die Altertumskunde Syrien-Palastinas. (GER & ENG.). xiv, 972p. 1999. text 103.00 (*3-927120-74-X*, Pub. by Ugarit-Verlag) Eisenbrauns.

Dietrich, Manfried, et al. The Cuneiform Alphabetic Texts from Ugarit, Ras Ibn Hani & Other Places. (Abhandlungen zur Literatur Alt-Syrien - Palastinas und Mesopotamiens Ser.: No. 8). xvi, 666p. 1995. text 86.00 (*3-927120-24-3*, Pub. by UGARIT) Eisenbrauns.

— Ugarit - Bibliographie, 1928-1966: Teil 1: 1928-1950, Teil 2: 1950-1959, Teil 3: 1959-1966, Teil 4: Indizes, 4 vols. (GER.). 2129p. 1973. text 79.50 (*3-7887-0406-3*) NeukirchenerV.

Dietrich, Manfried, jt. ed. see Ahn, Gregor.

Dietrich, Marlene. Marlene. 304p. 1990. mass mkt. 4.95 (*0-380-71088-9*, Avon Bks) Morrow Avon.

Dietrich, Martin O. & Lehmann, Helmut T., eds. Luther's Works: Devotional Writings I, Vol. 42. LC 55-9893. 1969. 30.00 (*0-8006-0342-7*, 1-342, Fortress Pr) Augsburg Fortress.

Dietrich, Michael. Transaction Cost Economics & Beyond: Towards a New Economics of the Firm. LC 93-24592. 208p. (C). 1994. pap. 29.99 (*0-415-07156-9*) Routledge.

Dietrich, Michael, jt. ed. see Amin, Ash.

Dietrich, Mimi. Baltimore Bouquets. LC 92-10358. (Illus.). 72p. 1992. pap. 18.95 (*1-56477-010-9*, B142) Martingale & Co.

— Basic Quiltmaking Techniques for Borders & Bindings. (Basic Quiltmaking Techniques Ser.). (Illus.). 80p. 1998. pap. 14.95 (*1-56477-253-5*, B355, That Patchwrk Pl) Martingale & Co.

— Basic Quiltmaking Techniques for Hand Applique. Reikes, Ursula, ed. LC 98-4669. (Basic Quilting Techniques Ser.). (Illus.). 80p. 1998. pap. 14.95 (*1-56477-220-9*, B332, That Patchwrk Pl) Martingale & Co.

— Happy Endings: Finishing the Edges of Your Quilt. LC 87-51214. (Illus.). 52p. 1988. pap. 12.95 (*0-943574-44-7*, B93) Martingale & Co.

***Dietrich, Mimi.** Pink-Ribbon Quilts: A Book Because of Breast Cancer. LC 99-40527. (Illus.). 80p. 1999. pap. 19.95 (*1-56477-279-9*, B399, That Patchwrk Pl) Martingale & Co.

— Quilts: An American Legacy. (Illus.). 100p. 1996. reprint ed. pap. text 25.00 (*0-7881-9131-4*) DIANE Pub.

Dietrich, Mimi & Eppler, Roxi. The Easy Art of Applique. Hoffman, Kerry, ed. (Joy of Quilting Ser.). (Illus.). 64p. 1994. pap. 12.95 (*1-56477-081-8*, B207) Martingale & Co.

Dietrich, N. Kerr's Cost Data for Landscape Construction. 13th ed. 1993. pap. 54.95 (*0-442-01489-9*, VNR) Wiley.

— Kerr's Cost Data for Landscape Construction, 1994, 10 vols., Vol. 3. 14th enl. ed. (FRE.). 1400p. (J). (gr. 1-5). 1994. text 54.95 (*0-442-01808-8*, 6662315, VNR) Wiley.

Dietrich, Norman L. Kerr's Cost Data for Landscape Construction, 1994. 4th ed. (Landscape Architecture Ser.). 224p. 1994. pap. 64.95 (*0-471-28619-2*, VNR) Wiley.

Dietrich, Pablo T. Spanish & English Computer Dictionary: Diccionario de Informatica. (ENG & SPA.). 783p. 1985. 59.95 (*0-8288-0258-0*, F14700) Fr & Eur.

Dietrich, R. & Graumann, Carl F., eds. Language Processing in Social Context. (Linguistic Ser.: No. 54). (Illus.). x,302p. 1989. 195.50 (*0-444-87144-6*, North Holland) Elsevier.

Dietrich, R. F. & Sundell, Roger H., eds. The Art of Fiction. 4th ed. 453p. (C). 1983. pap. text 20.75 (*0-03-060546-6*) Harcourt Coll Pubs.

Dietrich, R. V. & Skinner, Brian J. Gems, Granites & Gravels: Knowing & Using Rocks & Minerals. (Illus.). 182p. (C). 1990. 29.95 (*0-521-34444-1*) Cambridge U Pr.

Dietrich, R. V., et al. Mineralogy. 2nd ed. LC 82-16008. 561p. (C). 1983. text 38.40 (*0-7167-1424-8*) W H Freeman.

D

Dietrich, Rainer, et al. The Acquisition of Temporality in a Second Language. LC 95-24437. (Studies in Bilingualism: No. 7). xii, 288p. 1995. 59.00 (*1-55619-537-0*) J Benjamins Pubng Co.

Dietrich, Richard. British Drama, Eighteen Ninety to Nineteen Fifty. (Critical History of British Drama Ser.). 330p. (C). 1989. 25.95 (*0-8057-8951-0*, Twyne) Mac Lib Ref.

— Untersuchungen Zum Fruhkapitalismus Im Mitteldeutschen Erzbergbau & Metallhandel. (GER.). 203p. 1991. reprint ed. write for info. (*3-487-09138-0*) G Olms Pubs.

Dietrich, Richard F. Bernard Shaw's Novels: Portraits of the Artist As Man & Superman. (Illus.). 240p. (C). 1996. 39.95 (*0-8130-1426-3*) U Press Fla.

— Portrait of the Artist as a Young Superman: A Study of Shaw's Novels. LC 75-77613. 209p. reprint ed. pap. 64.80 (*0-7837-5094-3*, 204479300004) Bks Demand.

Dietrich, Richard V. Geology & Virginia. LC 76-110752. (Illus.). 229p. reprint ed. pap. 71.00 (*0-608-18269-9*, 203299400082) Bks Demand.

— Stones: Their Collection, Identification, & Uses. rev. ed. LC 89-85070. (Illus.). 208p. 1989. reprint ed. pap. 9.95 (*0-945005-04-0*) Geoscience Pr.

— The Tourmaline Group. (Illus.). 228p. (gr. 13). 1985. text 60.95 (*0-442-21857-5*) Chapman & Hall.

Dietrich, Richard V. & Skinner, Brian J. Rocks & Rock Minerals. LC 79-12111. 336p. 1979. text 48.95 (*0-471-02934-3*) Wiley.

Dietrich, Robbi R. Local Income Taxes: One Solution to Fiscal Dilemmas Facing Local Governments Today. (Discussion Papers: No. 106). 1976. pap. 10.00 (*1-55869-069-7*) Regional Sci Res Inst.

Dietrich, Rosalind B., ed. Pediatric MRI. (MRI Teaching File Ser.). 256p. 1991. text 76.00 (*0-88167-708-6*) Lppncott W & W.

Dietrich, Rudiger. Untersuchungen Zum Einfluss der Kombinierten Nutzung Als Kuhl- und Abwasserteich Auf Den Stoffhaushalt eines Braunkohlerestgewaessers. (Dissertationes Botanicae Ser.: Band 129). (GER., Illus.). x, 175p. 1988. 48.00 (*3-443-64041-9*, Pub. by Gebruder Borntraeger) Balogh.

Dietrich, T. Stanton. Florida's Older Population Revisited. LC HQ1064.U6F63. 87p. (Orig.). reprint ed. pap. 30.00 (*0-7837-4913-9*, 204457800004) Bks Demand.

Dietrich, Volker J. Plattentektonik in den Ostalpen. (Geotektonische Forschungen Ser.: Vol. 50). (GER.). ii, 109p. 1976. 43.00 (*3-510-50016-4*, Pub. by E Schweizerbartsche) Balogh.

Dietrich, W. & Duddeck, H. Structure Elucidation of Modern NMR: A Workbook. 2nd enl. rev. ed. x, 274p. 1992. 44.00 (*0-387-91425-0*) Spr-Verlag.

Dietrich, W., jt. auth. see Duddeck, H.

Dietrich, W. D., jt. auth. see Globus, M. Y.

Dietrich, W. Dalton, ed. see Princeton Conference on Cerebrovascular Disease.

Dietrich, Waldemar, jt. auth. see Shepard, Orson.

Dietrich, Werner & Wagner, Warren L. Systematics of Oenothera Section Oenothera Subsection Raimannia & Subsection Nutantigemma (Onagraceae) Anderson, Christiane, ed. (Systematic Botany Monographs: Vol. 24). (Illus.). 91p. (Orig.). 1988. pap. 10.50 (*0-912861-24-X*) Am Soc Plant.

Dietrich, Werner, et al. Systematics of Oenothera Section Oenothera Subsection Oenothera (Onagraceae) Anderson, Christiane, ed. (Illus.). 234p. 1997. 30.00 (*0-912861-50-9*) Am Soc Plant.

Dietrich, William. The Final Forest: The Battle for the Last Great Trees of the Pacific Northwest. 304p. 1993. pap. 13.95 (*0-14-017750-7*, Penguin Bks) Viking Penguin.

— Getting Back. LC 99-19729. 384p. 2000. 24.95 (*0-446-52457-3*, Pub. by Warner Bks) Little.

***Dietrich, William.** Ice Reich. 448p. 2000. mass mkt. 7.50 (*0-446-60744-4*, Pub. by Warner Bks) Little.

Dietrich, William. Northwest Passage: The Great Columbia River. 448p. 1995. 26.00 (*0-671-79650-X*) S&S Trade.

— Northwest Passage: The Great Columbia River. LC 96-3972. (Illus.). 448p. 1996. reprint ed. pap. 18.95 (*0-295-97546-6*) U of Wash Pr.

Dietrich, William E. & Sposito, Garrison, eds. Hydrologic Processes from Catchment to Continental Scales. 1997. pap. 15.00 (*0-8243-2099-9*) Annual Reviews.

Dietrich, William S. In the Shadow of the Rising Sun: The Political Roots of American Economic Decline. 360p. 1991. 35.00 (*0-271-00765-6*) Pa St U Pr.

Dietrichson, J. W. Norwegian-English - English-Norwegian Dictionary. (Skolordbok Ser.). (ENG & NOR.). 331p. 1992. 33.75 (*82-573-0484-0*, Pub. by Kunnskapsforlaget) IBD Ltd.

***Dietsch, Deborah K.** Classic Modern: Midcentury Modern at Home. LC 00-37051. 2000. write for info. (*0-684-86744-3*) Simon & Schuster.

***Dietsch, John & Hubbell, Gary.** Shadowcasting: An Introduction to the Art of Flyfishing. (Illus.). 208p. 2000. pap. 21.00 (*1-893740-02-1*, SC112, Pub. by Clinetop) IPG Chicago.

Dietsche, Doreen, jt. auth. see Gerrick, David J.

Dietschi, Didier & Spreafico, Roberto. Adhesive Metal-Free Restorations: Current Concepts for the Esthetic Treatment of Posterior Teeth. LC 96-46353. 220p. 1997. text 98.00 (*0-86715-328-8*) Quint Pub Co.

Dietterich, Thomas & Shavlik, Jude W., eds. Readings in Machine Learning. (Machine Learning Ser.). (Illus.). 853p. 1990. pap. text 54.95 (*1-55860-143-0*) Morgan Kaufmann.

Dietvorst, jt. ed. see Ashworth, G. J.

Dietz. Dental Office Management. LC 99-28104. (C). 1999. 35.95 (*0-7668-0731-2*) Thomson Learn.

Dietz, ed. Prayers for Children. (Illus.). (J). (gr. 1-6). 1990. pap. 0.99 (*0-87509-121-0*) Chr Pubns.

Dietz, A. & Thayer, D. W., eds. Actinomycete Taxonomy: Procedures for Studying Aerobic Actinomytcetes with Emphasis on the Streptomycetes. 1980. 30.00 (*0-614-29704-4*) Society Indust Microb.

Dietz, A. & Thayer, W. D., eds. Actinomycete Taxonomy: Special Publ. No. 6. 380p. 1980. 30.00 (*0-318-16572-4*) Society Indust Microb.

Dietz, Albert G. Dwelling House Construction. 5th ed. (Illus.). 456p. 1990. 47.50 (*0-262-04108-1*) MIT Pr.

— Dwelling House Construction. 5th ed. (Illus.). 454p. 1992. reprint ed. pap. text 21.95 (*0-262-54069-X*) MIT Pr.

Dietz, Albert G., ed. Composite Engineering Laminates. 1969. 55.00 (*0-262-04017-4*) MIT Pr.

Dietz, Albert G. & Cutler, Laurence S., eds. Industrialized Building Systems for Housing. 1971. 45.00 (*0-262-04034-4*) MIT Pr.

Dietz, August, Sr. Presidents of the United States: Portraits & Biographies. 1988. pap. 2.50 (*0-87517-014-5*) Dietz.

Dietz, Betty W., contrib. by. Folk Melodies of the Orient. 1972. 4.00 (*0-913334-14-6*, CM1017) Consort Music.

Dietz, Charles H. Moving Towards the Standards: A National Action Plan for Mathematics Education Reform for the Deaf: A Report on the Recommendations of the NAPMERD Committee. (Report on the Recommendations of the NAPMERD Committee Ser.). (Illus.). 76p. 1995. pap. text, teacher ed. 8.95 (*0-88095-202-4*) Gallaudet U Pre Coll.

Dietz, Charles R. Ray's Light, Too. (Illus.). 168p. (Orig.). pap. 6.95 (*0-9618284-0-4*) Spirited Comns.

Dietz-Crawford, Debi, et al. Advice for a Happy Marriage: From Miss Dietz's Third-Grade Class. LC 97-151526. (Illus.). 64p. 1997. 7.95 (*0-446-91170-4*, Pub. by Warner Bks) Little.

Dietz, David. Science in Hawaii. (Illus.). 1968. 0.50 (*0-941200-03-5*) Aquarius.

Dietz, David, jt. auth. see Heider, Douglas.

***Dietz, Denise.** Beat up a Cookie: An Ellie Bernstein Mystery. 2000. per. 4.99 (*0-373-26340-6*) Harlequin Bks.

Dietz, Denise. Footprints in the Butter: An Ingrid Beaumont Mystery Co-Starring Hitchcock the Dog. 224p. 1999. 21.95 (*0-9663397-2-X*, 16579330) Delphi Bks.

***Dietz, Denise.** Throw Darts at a Cheesecake. 1999. per. 4.99 (*0-373-26334-1*) Harlequin Bks.

Dietz, Dennis A. Iowa Legal Forms: Commercial Real Estate. 170p. 1983. ring bd. 85.00 incl. disk (*0-250-40727-2*, MICHIE); suppl. ed. 35.00 incl. disk (*0-685-74344-6*, MICHIE) LEXIS Pub.

— Iowa Legal Forms: Commercial Real Estate. 170p. 1993. ring bd. 60.00 incl. disk (*0-86678-194-3*, 80989-10, MICHIE) LEXIS Pub.

Dietz, Elisabeth & Jonas, Shirley. Now Is the Hour: Native American Prophecies & Guidance for Earth Changes. LC 98-30958. (Illus.). 108p. 1998. pap. 10.00 (*1-57733-029-3*) B Dolphin Pub.

Dietz, Esther, ed. see Dietz, Greg.

Dietz, F. J. Environmental Policy in a Market Economy. (C). 1991. text 415.00 (*0-89771-596-9*, Pub. by Intl Bk Distr) St Mut.

Dietz, F. J., et al. Environmental Policy & the Economy. (Contributions to Economic Analysis Ser.: Vol. 206). xiv,332p. 1991. 128.50 (*0-444-88975-2*, North Holland) Elsevier.

Dietz, Frank. Restauracion del Ministerio Biblico.Tr. of Restoration of Biblical Ministry. (SPA.). 112p. 1994. pap. 4.99 (*1-56063-594-0*, 497718) Editorial Unilit.

Dietz, Frank J., et al, eds. Environment, Incentives, & the Common Market. LC 95-552. (Environment & Policy Ser.: Vol. 4). 186p. (C). 1995. lib. bdg. 118.00 (*0-7923-3602-X*) Kluwer Academic.

Dietz, Frederick C. The Industrial Revolution. LC 73-7193. 111p. (C). 1973. reprint ed. lib. bdg. 35.00 (*0-8371-6917-8*, DIIR, Greenwood Pr) Greenwood.

Dietz, Fredrick C. English Public Finance Vol. 1: English Government Finance, 1485-1558. 210p. 1964. reprint ed. 35.00 (*0-7146-1299-5*, Pub. by F Cass Pubs) Intl Spec Bk.

— English Public Finance Vol. 2: English Government Finance, 1558-1641. 478p. 1964. reprint ed. 42.50 (*0-7146-1300-2*, Pub. by F Cass Pubs) Intl Spec Bk.

Dietz, Greg. How to Make Where You Live More Secure: Easy Ways to Protect Your Residence & Its Contents. Dietz, Esther, ed. (Illus.). 95p. (Orig.). 1989. pap. text 15.95 (*0-685-29098-0*) Green Oaks Pub.

***Dietz, Heather.** The Great White Shark. LC 99-49767. (Underwater World of Sharks Ser.). (Illus.). (YA). 2000. lib. bdg. 18.60 (*0-8239-5583-4*, PowerKids) Rosen Group.

Dietz, Henry A. Urban Poverty, Political Participation, & the State: Lima, 1970-1990. LC 98-9054. (Latin American Ser.). 396p. 1998. pap. 22.95 (*0-8229-5667-5*); text 50.00 (*0-8229-4063-9*) U of Pittsburgh Pr.

Dietz, Henry A., et al, eds. Urban Elections in Democratic Latin America. LC 97-13454. (Latin American Silhouettes Ser.). 264p. (C). 1998. 50.00 (*0-8420-2627-4*, SR Bks); pap. 18.95 (*0-8420-2628-2*, SR Bks) Scholarly Res Inc.

Dietz, Henry A. & Moore, Richard J. Political Participation in a Non-Electoral Setting: The Urban Poor in Lima, Peru. LC 79-14218. (Papers in International Studies: Latin America Ser.: No. 6). 110p. reprint ed. pap. 34.10 (*0-7837-1329-0*, 204147700021) Bks Demand.

Dietz, James. African Animal Giants: A National Geographic Pop-Up Book. LC 94-25393. (Pop-Up Bks.). (Illus.). 12p. (J). (ps up). 1991. 16.00 (*0-7922-2783-2*, Pub. by Natl Geog) S&S Trade.

Dietz, James. Africa's Animal Giants. (Illus.). (J). (ps-3). 1997. 16.00 (*0-614-28873-8*) Natl Geog.

Dietz, James L. Economic History of Puerto Rico: Institutional Change & Capitalist Development. (Illus.). 608p. 1986. pap. text 22.50 (*0-691-02248-8*, Pub. by Princeton U Pr) Cal Prin Full Svc.

— Historia Economica de Puerto Rico. LC 89-84228. 359p. 1989. pap. 16.50 (*0-929157-01-X*) Ediciones Huracan.

Dietz, James L., ed. Latin America's Economic Development: Confronting Crisis. 2nd rev. ed. 401p. 1995. pap. 23.95 (*1-55587-600-5*) L Rienner.

Dietz, James L., jt. auth. see Cypher, James M.

Dietz, James M. Ecology & Social Organization of the Maned Wolf (Chrysocyon Brachyurus) LC 83-600292. (Smithsonian Contributions to Zoology Ser.: No. 392). 55p. reprint ed. pap. 30.00 (*0-608-11875-3*, 202300900030) Bks Demand.

Dietz, James S. Price Guide & Introduction to Movie Posters & Movie Memorabilia. 2nd ed. 175p. 1985. pap. 11.95 (*0-910041-02-4*) Baja Pr.

***Dietz, Janiz.** Yes, You Can!!! Positive Responses to Tough Challenges. 120p. 2000. pap. 15.95 (*1-888799-43-X*, Pub. by Demos Medical) SCB Distributors.

Dietz, Jim. Blow! Bugles! Blow! 60p. 1998. pap. 16.00 (*0-9658694-1-5*) Jolly Roger.

— Fire Brigade: World War Two in Miniature. (Illus.). 72p. 1998. pap. 20.00 (*0-9658694-2-3*) Jolly Roger.

— A Nation on Trial. (Illus.). 64p. Date not set. pap. 20.00 (*0-9658694-0-7*) Jolly Roger.

— Swashbuckler! (Illus.). 1998. pap. 20.00 (*0-9658694-3-1*) Jolly Roger.

Dietz, John D., ed. Environmental Engineering. 744p. 1987. 75.00 (*0-87262-607-5*) Am Soc Civil Eng.

Dietz, Jonathan M. & Stidinger, Dennis M. Evaluation of Wetlands Constructed for the Treatment of Acidic Mine Drainage. 265p. (Orig.). 1993. pap. 5.06 (*0-8182-0186-X*) Commonweal PA.

Dietz, K. Theory of the Interaction of Strong Laser Pulses with Atoms & Molecules. 250p. 1997. text 38.00 (*981-02-3202-0*) World Scientific Pub.

Dietz, K., jt. ed. see Rittenberg, V.

***Dietz, Kevin C., ed.** A+ Network + Certification. (Illus.). (YA). 1999. pap. write for info. (*0-7423-0365-9*, ACD36ANETKIT) ComputerPREP.

— Windows NT 4.0 Domains, 2 vols., Set. (Illus.). 1999. pap. write for info. (*0-7423-0366-7*, ACE36WNTDKIT) ComputerPREP.

— Windows 2000 Professional Certification, Vol. 1. (Illus.). (C). 1999. pap. write for info. (*0-7423-0377-2*) ComputerPREP.

— Windows 2000 Professional Certification, Vol. 2. (Illus.). (C). 1999. pap. write for info. (*0-7423-0378-0*) ComputerPREP.

***Dietz, Kevin C., et al, eds.** HTML 4.0 & Web Page Design: Module 2. (Illus.). 172p. 2000. pap. write for info. (*0-7423-0428-0*) ComputerPREP.

***Dietz, Kevin C. & Nigro, Linea, eds.** Network+ Accelerated Certification. (Illus.). 200p. (YA). 2000. pap. write for info. (*0-7423-0445-0*) ComputerPREP.

***Dietz, Kevin C. & Tillman, Jamie, eds.** Internet Explorer v5.0 Pt. A: Kit. (Illus.). 119p. (YA). 2000. pap. write for info. (*0-7423-0479-5*) ComputerPREP.

— Internet Explorer v5.0 Pt. B: Kit. (Illus.). 156p. (YA). 2000. pap. write for info. (*0-7423-0480-9*) ComputerPREP.

Dietz, Kevin C., jt. ed. see Carpentier, Charlotte.

Dietz, Kevin C., ed. see Cook, Jo.

Dietz, Kevin C., ed. see Mabee, Stephanie.

Dietz, Kevin C., ed. see Nelson, Paul & Lanier-Graham, Susan D.

Dietz, Lew. The Allagash. LC 78-8326. (Illus.). 264p. 1978. reprint ed. pap. 9.95 (*0-945980-34-5*) Nrth Country Pr.

— Camden Hills, Maine: An Informal History of the Camden-Rockport Region. (Illus.). 93p. 1997. reprint ed. pap. 17.00 (*0-8328-7103-6*); reprint ed. lib. bdg. 25.00 (*0-8328-7102-8*) Higginson Bk Co.

— Night Train at Wiscasset Station. LC 97-36446. (Illus.). 192p. 1998. reprint ed. pap. 21.95 (*0-89272-430-7*) Down East.

— The Story of Andre. LC 78-73269. (Illus.). 88p. (J). (gr. 2-3). 1979. pap. 10.95 (*0-89272-052-2*) Down East.

Dietz, Lew & Goodridge, Harry. A Seal Called Andre: The Two Worlds of a Maine Harbor Seal. LC 74-30996. 182p. 1980. pap. 9.95 (*0-89272-076-X*) Down East.

***Dietz, Lisa.** What Every Business Needs to Know about Sap. 1999. 29.99 (*0-7615-2025-2*) Prima Pub.

Dietz, M. De Virginia Hambook. Dietz, Meredith, ed. 1949. pap. 2.00 (*0-87517-001-3*) Dietz.

Dietz, M., jt. auth. see Shimizu, Fumio.

Dietz, Maggie, jt. ed. see Pinsky, Robert.

Dietz, Margaret N. Akron's Library: Commemorating Twenty-Five Years on Main Street. (Illus.). 148p. 1994. 9.40 (*0-9643208-0-0*) Akron-Summit.

Dietz, Mary E. Journals As Framework for Change. LC 98-60464. (Illus.). 160p. 1998. pap. 25.95 (*1-57517-082-5*, 1596) SkyLght.

Dietz, Mary G. Between the Human & the Divine: The Political Thought of Simone Weil. LC 87-20569. 224p. 1988. 58.00 (*0-8476-7574-2*); pap. 23.95 (*0-8476-7575-0*) Rowman.

Dietz, Mary G., ed. Thomas Hobbes & Political Theory. LC 89-37242. x, 214p. 1990. pap. 14.95 (*0-7006-0519-3*) U Pr of KS.

Dietz, Mary L. Killing for Profit: The Social Organization of Felony Homicide. LC 82-24571. (Illus.). 240p. 1983. text 31.95 (*0-8304-1008-2*) Burnham Inc.

Dietz, Matthias & Monninger, Michael. Japan Design. (Illus.). 176p. 1997. reprint ed. pap. text 40.00 (*0-7881-5027-8*) DIANE Pub.

Dietz, Max. Geschichte des Musikalischen Dramas in Frankreich Wahrend der Revolution bis zum Directorium (1787-95) viii, 472p. 1970. reprint ed. write for info. (*0-318-71451-5*) G Olms Pubs.

Dietz, Meredith. Photographic Studies of Old Virginia Homes & Gardens. 1953. 3.00 (*0-87517-029-3*) Dietz.

Dietz, Meredith, ed. see Dietz, M.

Dietz, Norman D. Fables & Vaudevilles & Plays: Theatre More-or-Less at Random. LC 68-16685. 176p. (Orig.). 1968. pap. 4.95 (*0-936520-00-0*) Norman & Sandra.

Dietz, Peter. The British in the Mediterranean. (Illus.). 250p. 1995. 49.00 (*0-08-037716-5*, Pub. by Brasseys) Brasseys.

Dietz, Philipp. Worterbuch zu Dr. Martin Luthers Deutschen Schriften. (GER.). xcii, 980p. 1997. reprint ed. 320.00 (*3-487-00145-4*) G Olms Pubs.

Dietz, Robert. Willful Injustice: A Post - O. J. Look at Rodney King, American Justice, & Trial by Race. 275p. 1996. 24.95 (*0-89526-457-9*) Regnery Pub.

Dietz, Robert E., 4th. Systematics & Biology of the Genus Macrocneme Hubner (Lepidoptera-Ctencuhidae) LC 93-49869. (Publications in Entomology: Vol. 113). 1994. pap. 25.00 (*0-520-09780-7*, Pub. by U CA Pr) Cal Prin Full Svc.

Dietz, Ruth M. Spanish-English Housekeeping. (ENG & SPA., Illus.). 156p. 1983. pap. 14.95 (*0-89015-379-5*) Sunbelt Media.

Dietz-Smith, Susan, et al, photos by. Color Me Cooking. (Illus.). 196p. 1997. 10.00 (*0-9668349-0-9*) St Louis Art.

Dietz, Soren. The Argolid at the Transition to the Mycenaean Age: Studies in the Chronology & Cultural Development in the Shaft Grave Period. (Illus.). 336p. (Orig.). (C). 1991. pap. 40.00 (*87-7288-501-7*, Pub. by Aarhus Univ Pr) David Brown.

— Asine II Fasc. 2: Results of the Excavations East of the Acropolis 1970-1974; the Middle Helladic Cemetary, the Middle Helladic & Early Mycenean Deposits. (Acta Instituti Atheniensis Regni Sueciae Ser.: Series 4, XXIV: 2). (Illus.). 144p. (Orig.). 1980. pap. 59.50 (*91-85086-24-X*, Pub. by P Astroms) Coronet Bks.

— Asine II - Results of the Excavations East of the Acropolis 1970-1974 Fasc. 1: General Stratigraphical Analysis & Architectural Remains. (Acta Instituti Atheniensis Regni Sueciae Ser.: Vol. XXIV:I). (Illus.). 144p. 1982. pap. 72.50 (*91-85086-55-X*, Pub. by P Astroms) Coronet Bks.

— Excavations & Surveys in Southern Rhodes: The Mycenaean Period. 120p. 1984. 32.00 (*87-480-0487-1*, Pub. by Aarhus Univ Pr) David Brown.

Dietz, Soren, ed. Proceedings of the Danish Institute at Athens, Vol. 1. (Illus.). 226p. (C). 1995. pap. 37.00 (*87-7288-721-4*, Pub. by Aarhus Univ Pr) David Brown.

Dietz, Soren, et al, eds. Africa Proconsularis Vols. I & II: Regional Studies in the Segermes Valley of Northern Tunisia, 2 vols., Nos. I-II. (Illus.). 800p. (C). 1996. text 80.00 (*87-7288-740-0*, Pub. by Aarhus Univ Pr) David Brown.

Dietz, Soren & Isager, Signe, eds. Proceedings of the Danish Institute at Athens II. (Illus.). 411p. 1998. pap. 37.00 (*87-7288-722-2*, Pub. by Aarhus Univ Pr) David Brown.

Dietz, Soren & Papachristopoulou, Ioannis, eds. Archaeology in the Dodecanese. (Illus.). 260p. (Orig.). (C). 1988. pap. 44.00 (*87-480-0626-2*, Pub. by Aarhus Univ Pr) David Brown.

Dietz, Soren & Trolle, Steffen, eds. Fouilles Danoises a Carthage: Premier Rapport Preliminaire. (Illus.). 146p. 1979. 3.95 (*87-480-0224-0*, Pub. by Aarhus Univ Pr) David Brown.

Dietz, Soren, ed. see Pentz, Peter.

Dietz, Soren, ed. & intro. see Sorensen, Lone W. & Pentz, Peter.

***Dietz, Southam.** Contemporary Business Mathematics. 13th ed. (General Business Ser.). (C). 2001. pap. 54.00 (*0-324-04299-X*) Sth-Wstrn College.

Dietz, Stephen A., ed. see Milliken, Randy.

Dietz, Steven. Halcyon Days. 1995. pap. 5.25 (*0-8222-1401-6*) Dramatists Play.

— Lonely Planet. 1994. pap. 5.25 (*0-8222-1404-0*) Dramatists Play.

— Private Eyes. 1998. pap. 5.25 (*0-8222-1619-1*) Dramatists Play.

— Still Life with Iris. 97p. 1998. pap. 5.50 (*0-87129-869-4*, SC4) Dramatic Pub.

— Trust. 1995. pap. 5.25 (*0-8222-1405-9*) Dramatists Play.

Dietz, T. Auto Sacramental & the Parable in Spanish Golden Age Literature. (North Carolina Studies in the Romance Languages & Literatures). 205p. 1973. 20.00 (*0-88438-932-4*) Spanish Lit Pubns.

Dietz, Terry. Republicans & Vietnam, 1961-1968, 146. LC 85-24764. (Contributions in Political Science Ser.: No. 146). (Illus.). 199p. 1986. 49.95 (*0-313-24892-3*, DRV/, Greenwood Pr) Greenwood.

Dietz, Thomas & Rycroft, Robert. The Risk Professionals. LC 87-19992. (Social Research Perspectives). 176p. 1988. pap. 9.95 (*0-87154-214-5*) Russell Sage.

Dietz, Ton. Entitlements to Natural Resources: Contours of Political Environmental Geography. 336p. (Orig.). 1997. pap. 9.95 (*90-5727-001-3*, Pub. by Uitgeverij Arkel) LPC InBook.

Dietz, Ulysses G. The Ballantine House: The Ballantine House & the Decorative Arts Galleries at the Newark Museum. Schwartz, Sheila, ed. LC 94-44419. (Illus.). 80p. (Orig.). 1994. pap. 19.95 (*0-932828-30-2*) Newark Mus.

— Desmond: A Novel about Love & the Modern Vampire. LC 98-12920. 300p. 1998. pap. 13.95 (*1-55583-470-1*) Alyson Pubns.

— The Newark Collection of American Art Pottery. Sweeney, Mary S., ed. LC 84-4818. (Illus.). 128p. (Orig.). 1984. pap. 19.95 (*0-932828-19-1*) Newark Mus.

***Dietz, Ulysses G.** The 1905-1906 Unger Bros. Supplemental Catalogue. Randolph, Benjamin A., ed. (Historical Catalogue Ser.: Vol. 9). (Illus.). 64p. 1999. pap. 29.95 (*0-9656139-5-X*) Eden Sterling.

Dietz, Ulysses G. Paul J. Stankard: Homage to Nature. LC 96-10850. (Illus.). 160p. 1996. 39.95 (*0-8109-4473-1*, Pub. by Abrams) Time Warner.

Dietz, Ulysses G., et al. The Glitter & the Gold: Fashioning America's Jewelry. (Illus.). 200p. 1997. 29.95 (*0-932828-35-3*) Newark Mus.
— The Glitter & the Gold: Fashioning America's Jewelry, May, 1997. LC 97-8038. (Illus.). 200p. (Orig.). 1997. pap. 50.00 (*0-932828-34-5*) Newark Mus.
Dietz-Wiley, Denise. Dream Dancer. 352p. 1997. mass mkt. 5.50 (*0-7860-0383-9*, Pinncle Kensgtn) Kensgtn Pub Corp.
Dietz Wiley, Denise. The Rainbow's Foot: A Novel of Danger, Greed, & Passion. 388p. 1998. pap. 15.95 (*0-9655668-1-1*) Voices Publishing.
Dietz, William. Teaching Woodwings. LC 97-17928. 1997. 39.00 (*0-02-864569-3*, Hall Reference) Macmillan.
Dietz, William C. Bodyguard. 240p. (Orig.). 1994. mass mkt. 5.99 (*0-441-00105-X*) Ace Bks.
***Dietz, William C.** By Force of Arms. 336p. 2000. mass mkt. 6.99 (*0-441-00735-X*) Ace Bks.
Dietz, William C. The Final Battle. 400p. (Orig.). 1995. mass mkt. 6.99 (*0-441-00217-X*) Ace Bks.
— Galactic Bounty. 256p. 1986. pap. 5.99 (*0-441-87346-4*) Ace Bks.
— Jedi Knight. LC 98-22691. (Star Wars: Bk. 2). (Illus.). 128p. 1998. 24.95 (*0-399-14452-8*) Dark Horse Comics.
— Legion of the Damned. 352p. (Orig.). 1993. mass mkt. 6.50 (*0-441-48040-3*) Ace Bks.
***Dietz, William C.** Rebel Agent. (Star Wars: Bk. 3). (Illus.). 128p. (YA). (gr. 5 up). 1999. reprint ed. pap. 14.95 (*0-425-16862-X*) Blvd Books.
Dietz, William C. Steelheart. 1998. mass mkt. 5.99 (*0-441-00542-X*) Ace Bks.
— Where the Ships Die. 1996. mass mkt. 5.99 (*0-441-00354-0*) Ace Bks.
***Dietz, William C. & Dorman, Dave.** Jedi Knight. (Star Wars: Bk. 2). (Illus.). 128p. (YA). (gr. 5 up). 1999. reprint ed. pap. 14.95 (*0-425-17051-9*) Berkley Pub.
Dietz, William C. & Zahn, Timothy. Soldier for the Empire. LC 96-48558. (Star Wars: Bk. 1). (Illus.). 128p. (YA). (gr. 5 up). 1997. pap. 24.95 (*0-399-14198-7*) Blvd Books.
Dietz, William C. & Zahn, Timothy. Soldier for the Empire. LC 96-48558. (Star Wars: Bk. 1). (Illus.). 126p. (YA). (gr. 5 up). 1997. 24.95 (*1-56971-155-0*) Dark Horse Comics.
Dietz, William C. & Zahn, Timothy. Soldier for the Empire. abr. ed. (Star Wars: Bk. 1). (YA). (gr. 5 up). 1997. pap. 16.95 incl. audio (*1-56511-202-4*, Pub. by D I Fine) Penguin Putnam.
— Soldier for the Empire. (Star Wars: Bk. 1). 128p. (YA). (gr. 5 up). 1998. reprint ed. pap. 14.95 (*0-425-16528-0*) Blvd Books.
Dietz, William H. & Stern, Loraine, eds. American Academy of Pediatrics Guide to Your Child's Nutrition: Making Peace at the Table & Building Healthy Eating Habits for Life. LC 98-14955. (Illus.). 256p. 1998. 23.95 (*0-375-50187-8*) Villard Books.
Dietze, G., et al, eds. Nutrition in Clinical Practice: Proceedings of the Congress of the European Society of Parenteral & Enteral Nutrition (ESPEN), Leipzig, August 1988, 10th. (Illus.). x, 308p. 1989. 101.75 (*3-8055-4894-X*) S Karger.
Dietze, G. & Kleinberger, G., eds. Clinical Nutrition & Metabolic Research. (Illus.). 400p. 1986. pap. 108.00 (*3-8055-4388-3*) S Karger.
Dietze, Gottfried. American Democracy: Aspects of Practical Liberlism. 304p. 1993. text 39.95 (*0-8018-4507-6*) Johns Hopkins.
— America's Political Dilemma: From Limited to Unlimited Democracy. LC 85-13338. 310p. 1985. reprint ed. pap. text 22.50 (*0-8191-4788-5*) U Pr of Amer.
— Federalist: A Classic on Federalism & Free Government. LC 99-191917. 390p. 1998. pap. text 18.95 (*0-8018-6091-1*) Johns Hopkins.
— The Federalist: A Classic on Federalism & Free Government. LC 60-11204. (Johns Hopkins Paperbacks Ser.: No. JH-8). 390p. reprint ed. pap. 120.90 (*0-8357-8131-3*, 203412500088) Bks Demand.
— In Defense of Property. 284p. (C). Date not set. reprint ed. pap. text 28.50 (*0-7618-0046-8*) U Pr of Amer.
— Liberalism Proper & Proper Liberalism. LC 98-24554. 292p. 1998. pap. 32.00 (*0-7618-1191-5*) U Pr of Amer.
Dietze, Joachim. Frequenzworterbuch der Russischen Schriftsprache des 18. Jahrhunderts. (GER.). 460p. 1996. write for info. (*3-487-10144-0*) G Olms Pubs.
Dietze, Wolfgang. German & Russian Dictionary of Mining & Processing: Bergbautechnik und Aufbereitung Russisch-Deutsch. (GER & RUS.). 428p. 1985. 95.00 (*0-8288-1921-1*, F69890) Fr & Eur.
Dietzel, Louise A. Parenting with Respect & Peacefulness: The Most Difficult Job in the World. LC 94-67445. 304p. 1995. pap. 10.95 (*0-914984-66-7*) Starburst.
Dietzel, M., jt. auth. see Usdowski, E.
Dietzel, Mary, jt. auth. see Stowell, Jo.
Dietzen, John J. The New Question Box: Catholic Life in a New Century. 11th rev. ed. LC 83-18540. 574p. 1997. pap. 15.95 (*0-940518-08-2*) Guildhall Pubs.
***Dietzer, M'Lou.** First Impressions, Theory, Vol. 2. 40p. 1999. pap. 7.50 (*0-7390-0733-5*, 17370) Alfred Pub.
Dietzer, M'Lou. First Impressions, Theory Book 1. 1998. pap. 7.50 (*0-88284-998-0*, 17369) Alfred Pub.
Dietzler, Jim. Camaro. LC 99-35325. 1999. 14.98 (*1-56799-816-X*, Friedman-Fairfax) M Friedman Pub Grp Inc.
Dietzmann, Harry E. Emissions Measurement Manual for Natural Gas Pipeline Compressor Engines. 137p. 1976. pap. 8.00 (*0-318-12606-0*, L22278) Am Gas Assn.
Dieu Mvuanda, Jean De. Inculturer pour Evangeliser en Profondeur: Des Initiations Traditionnelles Africaines a une Initiation Chretienne Engageante. (Etudes d'Histoire Interculturelle du Christianisme: Vol. 101). 451p. 1997. 62.95 (*3-906757-31-5*) P Lang Pubng.
Dieu, Nguyen T. The Mekong River & the Struggle for Indochina. LC 97-49488. 280p. 1999. 59.95 (*0-275-96137-0*, Praeger Pubs) Greenwood.
Dieu, Phan Dinh, jt. auth. see Dinh, P.
Dieudonne, Adeline & Roy, Martine. Broder les Saisons. (FRE., Illus.). 199p. 1997. 48.00 (*2-84229-020-8*) Lacis Pubns.
Dieudonne, J. Introduction to the Theory of Formal Groups. (Pure & Applied Mathematics Ser.: Vol. 20). (Illus.). 288p. 1973. text 125.00 (*0-8247-6011-5*) Dekker.
Dieudonne, J., ed. see Haraux, A.
Dieudonne, J., ed. see Wu, H. H.
Dieudonne, Jean. Special Functions & Linear Representations of Lie Groups. LC 79-22180. (CBMS Regional Conference Series in Mathematics: Vol. 42). 59p. 1980. reprint ed. pap. 14.00 (*0-8218-1692-6*, CBMS/42) Am Math.
Dieudonne, Jean & Hua, L. K. On the Automorphisms of the Classical Groups. LC 52-42839. (Memoirs Ser.: No. 1/2). 123p. 1989. reprint ed. pap. 21.00 (*0-8218-1202-5*, MEMO/1/2) Am Math.
Dieudonne, Jean A. A History of Algebraic & Differential Topology: (1900-1960) 624p. 1994. 82.50 (*0-8176-3388-X*) Birkhauser.
— History of Functional Analysis. (North Holland Mathematics Studies: Vol. 49). vi,312p. 1981. 111.50 (*0-444-86148-3*, North Holland) Elsevier.
— Mathematics - The Music of Reason: With Forty-One Figures. Dales, J. & Dales, H. G., trs. from FRE. LC 92-27390. (Illus.). 300p. 1992. 39.00 (*3-540-53346-X*); 42.95 (*0-387-53346-X*) Spr-Verlag.
— On the Automorphisms of the Classical Groups. LC 52-42839. (American Mathematical Society Ser.: No. 2). 129p. 1951. reprint ed. pap. 40.00 (*0-608-07822-0*, 205266700010) Bks Demand.
— Treatise on Analysis, Vol. 1. (Pure & Applied Mathematics Ser.). 1960. text 124.00 (*0-12-215550-5*) Acad Pr.
Dieudonne, Jean Alexandre. History of Algebraic Geometry. (Illus.). 256p. 1985. ring bd. 89.95 (*0-412-99371-6*, Chap & Hall CRC) CRC Pr.
DiEugenio, James. Destiny Betrayed: JFK, Cuba, & the Garrison Case. 436p. 1992. 19.95 (*1-879823-00-4*) Sheridan Sq Pr.
Dieulesaint, E. & Royer, D. Elastic Waves in Solids: Applications to Signal Processing. LC 80-49980. (Illus.). 531p. reprint ed. pap. 164.70 (*0-8357-6429-X*, 203580000097) Bks Demand.
Dieulesaint, E., jt. auth. see Royer, D.
Dievart, Roger. Teeth, Tusks & Fangs. Bogard, Vicki, tr. from FRE. LC 90-50778. (Young Discovery Library). (Illus.). 38p. (J). (gr. k-5). 1991. 5.95 (*0-944589-35-9*, 359) Young Discovery Lib.
Diewert, W. E., ed. Price Level Measurement. (Contributions to Economic Analysis Ser.: No. 196). viii,378p. 1991. 128.50 (*0-444-88108-5*, North Holland) Elsevier.
Diewert, W. Erwin, et al, eds. Mathematical Modelling in Economics: Essays in Honor of Wolfgang Eichhorn, Vol. XVIII. LC 93-34005. 713p. 1993. 159.00 (*0-387-57224-4*) Spr-Verlag.
Diewert, W. Erwin & Nakamura, Alice O., eds. Essays in Index Number Theory, Vol. 1. LC 93-18349. (Contributions to Economic Analysis Ser.: Vol. 217). x,552p. 1993. 130.00 (*0-444-87471-2*, North Holland) Elsevier.
Diez. Tres Cuentos: Unabridged Spanish Readers, Level D. text 8.95 (*0-8219-1209-7*) EMC-Paradigm.
Diez-Arguelles, Nicolas P. Pajarito Castano. LC 90-86231. 188p. 1991. 15.00 (*0-89729-594-3*) Ediciones.
Diez Borque, Jose M., ed. see de Vega, Lope.
Diez-Canedo, Joaquin, tr. see Keaney, Brian.
Diez Canseco, Maria R. De, see De Diez Canseco, Maria R.
Diez Canseco, Maria Rostworowski de, see Rostworowski de Diez Canseco, Maria.
Diez, Carlos. Bien Salud: A Guide to Baja's Medical Services. Warren, Sam, ed. (Illus.). 200p. (Orig.). Date not set. pap. 16.95 (*0-945949-08-1*) Warren Comns.
Diez De Revenga, Francisco J., ed. see Salinas, Pedro.
Diez de Revenga, Francisco J., ed. see Vallejo, Antonio B.
Diez, Friedrich. Etymologisches Worterbuch der Romanischen Sprachen. xxvi, 866p. 1969. reprint ed. write for info. (*0-318-71633-X*) G Olms Pubs.
— Grammatik der Romanischen Sprachen, 3 vols. xv, 1200p. reprint ed. write for info. (*0-318-71595-3*) G Olms Pubs.
Diez, Friedrich C. Etymologisches Worterbuch der Romanischen Sprachen. xxvi, 866p. 1969. reprint ed. write for info. (*0-318-71452-3*) G Olms Pubs.
— Grammatik der Romanischen Sprachen, 3 vols. xv, 1200p. reprint ed. write for info. (*0-318-71455-8*) G Olms Pubs.
— Leben und Werke der Troubadours. xvi, 506p. 1965. reprint ed. write for info. (*0-318-71453-1*) G Olms Pubs.
— Die Poesie der Troubadours. xxii, 314p. 1966. reprint ed. write for info. (*0-318-71454-X*) G Olms Pubs.
Diez, Klemens, pseud. Constanze, Formerly Widow of Mozart: Her Unwritten Memoir. Malloy, Joseph T., tr. from GER. LC 90-5760. 272p. 1991. lib. bdg. 89.95 (*0-88946-579-7*) E Mellen.
Diez, Luis Mateo, see Mateo Diez, Luis.
Diez, Mary E., ed. Changing the Practice of Teacher Education: Standards & Assessment As a Lever for Change. 1998. 25.00 (*0-89333-164-3*) AACTE.
Diez, Mary E., et al. Setting Standards & Educating Teachers: A National Conversation. 1994. 18.00 (*0-89333-116-3*) AACTE.
Diez Mateo, Felix. Diccionario Espanol Etimologico.Tr. of Spanish Etymological Dictionary. (SPA.). 396p. 1972. 16.95 (*0-8288-6362-8*, S-12291) Fr & Eur.
— Diccionario Manual Aleman-Espanol, Espanol-Aleman: German & Spanish. (GER & SPA.). 952p. 1978. pap. 14.95 (*0-8288-5142-5*, S50383) Fr & Eur.
— Illustrated Castilian Language Dictionary: Diccionario Castellano Ilustrado. (SPA.). 400p. 1980. 14.95 (*0-8288-2042-2*, S40776) Fr & Eur.
Diez Mateo, Felix & Hochleitner, Frida. Diccionario Manual Frances-Espanol, Espanol-Frances: French - Spanish, Spanish - French. (FRE & SPA.). 992p. 1971. 27.95 (*0-8288-6439-X*, S-50389) Fr & Eur.
— Diccionario Manual Ingles-Espanol, Espanol-Ingles. 3rd ed. (ENG & SPA.). 1008p. 1985. pap. write for info. (*0-7859-5116-4*) Fr & Eur.
Diez Medrano, Juan. Divided Nations: Class, Politics, & Nationalism in the Basque Country & Catalonia. (Wilder House Ser.). 256p. 1995. text 32.50 (*0-8014-3092-5*) Cornell U Pr.
Diez-Noguera, Antoni & Cambras, Trinitat, eds. Chronobiology & Chronomedicine: Basic Research & Applications: Proceedings of the 6th Annual Meeting of the European Society for Chronobiology, Barcelona, 1990. LC 92-15665. (Illus.). VIII, 415p. 1992. 63.00 (*3-631-44960-7*) P Lang Pubng.
***Diez, Octavio.** Anti-Tank Weapons & Military Vehicles. (Illus.). 96p. 2000. pap. 16.95 (*84-95323-30-3*) Lema Pubns.
— Artillery & Missiles. (Illus.). 96p. 2000. pap. 16.95 (*84-95323-29-X*) Lema Pubns.
— Assault Police. (Illus.). 96p. 2000. pap. 16.95 (*84-95323-41-9*) Lema Pubns.
— Commandos. (Illus.). 96p. 2000. pap. 16.95 (*84-95323-42-7*) Lema Pubns.
— Marines. (Illus.). 96p. 2000. pap. 16.95 (*84-95323-40-0*) Lema Pubns.
— Special Police Task Forces. (Illus.). 96p. 2000. pap. 16.95 (*84-95323-43-5*) Lema Pubns.
— Tanks & Bulletproff Vehicles. (Illus.). 96p. 2000. pap. 16.95 (*84-95323-28-1*) Lema Pubns.
DiFazio, Charles P. From Where Did You Come? Bhagavan Sri Sathya Saj Baba. 2nd ed. (C). 1999. reprint ed. pap. 14.00 (*81-207-1928-X*, Pub. by Sterling Pubs) S Asia.
DiFazio, William, jt. auth. see Aronowitz, Stanley.
DIFCO Laboratories Staff. DIFCO Manual: Dehydrated Culture Media & Reagents for Microbiology. 10th rev. ed. LC 84-70512. (Illus.). 1115p. 1984. reprint ed. 32.45 (*0-9613169-9-3*, X-100-30-8) Difco Labs.
Diffee, Nancy B., ed. see Tupelo Symphony League Staff.
Diffenbaugh, Dayanand, ed. see Dass, Baba Hari.
Diffenderfer, Susan, jt. auth. see Enz, Judith.
Differ, Philip. Only an Excuse? The Scripts. 192p. 1996. pap. 17.95 (*1-85158-699-7*, Pub. by Mainstream Pubng) Trafalgar.
Differding. Law Office Transcription. (KK - Legal Secretary Studies). (C). 1991. mass mkt. 21.50 (*0-538-70550-7*) S-W Pub.
Differding, Beverly. With Love, Bev: A Courageous Journey of Healing. 274p. 1994. pap. 14.95 (*0-9639586-1-5*) Gander Pubng.
Diffey, Myrna. Precious Spring. large type ed. (Linford Romance Library). 304p. 1997. pap. 16.99 (*0-7089-5184-8*) Ulverscroft.
— Uncertain Love. large type ed. (Linford Romance Library). 288p. 1997. pap. 16.99 (*0-7089-5172-4*) Ulverscroft.
Diffey, T. J. Republic of Art & Other Essays. LC 90-192. (New Studies in Aesthetics: Vol. 6). VIII, 347p. (C). 1991. text 49.95 (*0-8204-1433-6*) P Lang Pubng.
— Tolstoy's "What Is Art?" An Essay in the Philosophy of Art. LC 85-16667. 240p. 1986. 39.50 (*0-7099-0891-1*, Pub. by C Helm) Routldge.
Diffie, Bailey W. A History of Colonial Brazil: Fifteen Hundred to Seventeen Ninety-Two. LC 85-25605. 536p. 1987. 40.50 (*0-89874-685-X*); pap. 29.50 (*0-89464-214-6*) Krieger.
— Prelude to Empire: Portugal Overseas before Henry the Navigator. LC 60-14301. (Bison Book Original Ser.: No. BB108). (Illus.). 141p. reprint ed. pap. 43.80 (*0-7837-4660-1*, 204438400002) Bks Demand.
Diffie, Whitfield & Landau, Susan. Privacy on the Line: The Politics of Wiretapping & Encryption. LC 97-42347. (Illus.). 352p. 1998. 30.00 (*0-262-04167-7*) MIT Pr.
— Privacy on the Line: The Politics of Wiretapping & Encryption. 360p. 1999. pap. text 15.00 (*0-262-54100-9*) MIT Pr.
Diffily, Deborah & Morrison, Kathy, eds. Family-Friendly Communication for Early Childhood Programs. LC 96-71080. (Illus.). 118p. (Orig.). 1996. pap. text 7.00 (*0-935989-78-1*) Natl Assn Child Ed.
Diffley, P. B. Paolo Beni: A Biographical & Critical Study. (Oxford Modern Languages & Literature Monographs). 206p. 1988. 69.00 (*0-19-815855-6*) OUP.
Diffrient, Niels, et al. Humanscale Four-Five-Six. 1981. 60.00 (*0-262-04059-X*) MIT Pr.
— Humanscale One-Two-Three. 1974. 60.00 (*0-262-04042-5*) MIT Pr.
— Humanscale Seven-Eight-Nine. (Illus.). 1982. 60.00 (*0-262-04061-1*) MIT Pr.
DiFilippo, Anthony. Cracks in the Alliance: Science, Technology & the Evolution of U. S.-Japan Relations. LC 97-70885. (Illus.). 360p. 1997. text 73.95 (*1-85972-570-8*, Pub. by Ashgate Pub) Ashgate Pub Co.
Difilippo, Anthony. From Industry to Arms: The Political Economy of High Technology, 114. LC 90-38528. (Contributions in Economics & Economic History Ser.: No. 114). 216p. 1990. 57.95 (*0-313-27415-0*, DIB/, Greenwood Pr) Greenwood.
DiFilippo, Anthony. Military Spending & Industrial Decline: A Study of the American Machine Tool Industry, 68. LC 85-27144. (Contributions in Economics & Economic History Ser.: No. 68). (Illus.). 211p. 1986. 55.00 (*0-313-25179-7*, DMI/) Greenwood.
Difilippo, F. C., jt. ed. see Munoz-Cobo, J. L.
DiFilippo, Paul. Ribofunk. 256p. 1998. mass mkt. 3.99 (*0-380-73076-6*, Eos) Morrow Avon.
DiFino, Sharon M. The Intellectual Development of German Women in Selected Periodicals from 1725 to 1784. LC 90-6210. (American University Studies: Feminist Studies: Ser. XXVII, Vol. 2). X, 164p. (C). 1991. text 36.95 (*0-8204-1129-9*) P Lang Pubng.
DiFiore, Dante. Coming Forth to Carry Me Home: A Plumber's Guide. Scrivo, Bill & Gitlin, Lisa, eds. (Illus.). 72p. (Orig.). 1992. pap. 5.95 (*0-9634050-0-4*) DiFiore Wtrproof.
— Coming Forth to Carry Me Home: La Guida di un Idraulico. Scrivo, Bill & Gitlin, Lisa, eds. Berlitz Staff, tr. (ITA., Illus.). 72p. (Orig.). 1992. pap. 5.95 (*0-9634050-1-2*) DiFiore Wtrproof.
Difiore, Judy. Complete Guide to Postnatal Fitness. unabridged ed. (Illus.). 176p. pap. 16.95 (*0-7136-4852-X*, Pub. by A & C Blk) Midpt Trade.
DiFiori, Larry, jt. auth. see Foster, Kate.
DiFiori, Larry, jt. illus. see Redbank, Tennant.
DiFonzo, J. Herbie. Beneath the Fault Line: The Popular & Legal Culture of Divorce in Twentieth-Century America. 1997. text 35.00 (*0-8139-1707-7*) U Pr of Va.
DiFrancesco, Barbara L. His Window on the World: The Piscataqua & the Days of Hopley Yeaton. (Illus.). xii, 280p. 1997. pap. 20.95 (*0-9660822-0-6*) B L DiFrancesco.
— His Window on the World: The Piscataqua & the Days of Hopley Yeaton. braille ed. (Illus.). xii, 280p. 1997. pap. write for info. (*0-9660822-1-4*) B L DiFrancesco.
DiFranco, J. V. & Rubin, W. L. Radar Detection. fac. ed. LC 68-18248. (Artech Radar Library). (Illus.). 670p. 1980. pap. 200.00 (*0-7837-7627-6*, 204737900007) Bks Demand.
***DiFranco, Sue.** Secrets of Scrapbooking Success: Making Money, Making Memories: The Definitive Guide to Turning Your Passion into Profit. 144p. 1999. pap. 19.95 (*0-9676138-8-4*) Fun Facts.
DiFranza, Happy & DiFranza, Steve. Hooking Fine Gifts: Sixteen Projects for Rug Hookers. LC 92-11863. (Illus.). 168p. 1992. pap. 16.95 (*0-8117-2545-6*) Stackpole.
DiFranza, Steve, jt. auth. see DiFranza, Happy.
DiGaetani, John, ed. The Handbook of Executive Communication. 900p. 1986. 55.00 (*0-87094-526-2*, Irwn Prfssnl) McGraw-Hill Prof.
DiGaetani, John L. Carlo Gozzi: Translations of "The Love of Three Oranges", "Turandot", & "The Snake Lady" with a Bio-critical Introduction, 24. LC 87-17676. (Contributions in Drama & Theatre Studies: No. 24). 164p. 1988. 45.00 (*0-313-25676-4*, DCG/) Greenwood.
— An Invitation to the Opera. 304p. 1990. pap. 12.95 (*0-385-26339-2*, Anchor NY) Doubleday.
— An Invitation to the Opera. LC 83-16636. (Illus.). 303p. reprint ed. pap. 94.00 (*0-7837-1570-6*, 204186200024) Bks Demand.
— Richard Wagner & the Modern British Novel. 179p. 1978. 28.50 (*0-8386-1955-X*) Fairleigh Dickinson.
— A Search for a Postmodern Theatre: Interviews with Contemporary Playwrights, 41. LC 91-3936. (Contributions in Drama & Theatre Studies: No. 41). 336p. 1991. 62.95 (*0-313-27364-2*, DTS, Greenwood Pr) Greenwood.
Digaetani, John L., ed. A Companion to Pirandello Studies. LC 90-43377. 472p. 1991. lib. bdg. 105.00 (*0-313-25714-0*, DLP/, Greenwood Pr) Greenwood.
DiGaetani, John L., ed. Money: Lure, Lore & Literature, 55. LC 93-39359. (Contributions to the Study of World Literature Ser.: No. 55). 288p. 1994. 65.00 (*0-313-29219-1*, Greenwood Pr) Greenwood.
DiGaetani, John L. & Sirefman, Josef P., eds. Opera & the Golden West: The Present, Past, & Future of Opera in the U. S. A. LC 92-55065. 1994. 45.00 (*0-8386-3519-9*) Fairleigh Dickinson.
DiGaetani, John L., jt. auth. see Dervan, Peter A.
DiGaetani, John Louis. Carlo Gozzi: A Life in 18th Century Venetian Theatre, an Afterlife in Opera. LC 99-50037. (Illus.). 223p. 1999. lib. bdg. 49.95 (*0-7864-0077-3*) McFarland & Co.
DiGaetano, Alan & Klemanski, John S. Power & City Governance: Comparative Perspectives on Urban Development. LC 99-31736. (Globalization & Community Ser.: Vol. 4). 256p. 1999. pap. 22.95 (*0-8166-3219-7*, Pub. by U of Minn Pr); lib. bdg. 57.95 (*0-8166-3218-9*, Pub. by U of Minn Pr) Chicago Distribution Ctr.
Digan, James, jt. auth. see Cavadino, Michael.
Digan, Kathleen E. Herman N. Hesse's Narcissus & Goldmund: A Phenomenological Study. 1975. lib. bdg. 250.00 (*0-87700-238-X*) Revisionist Pr.
Digance, Richard. Another Animal Alphabet. 1983. 9.95 (*0-7181-2197-X*, M Joseph) Viking Penguin.
DiGangi, Mariano, ed. A Golden Treasury of Puritan Devotion: Selections from the Writings of Thirteen Puritan Divines. LC 98-35649. 200p. 1999. pap. 9.99 (*0-87552-173-8*) P & R Pubng.
DiGangi, Mario. The Homoerotics of Early Modern Drama. LC 96-37398. (Cambridge Studies in Renaissance Literature & Culture: Vol. 21). 230p. (C). 1997. text 59.95 (*0-521-58341-1*); pap. text 19.95 (*0-521-58701-8*) Cambridge U Pr.
Digby. Education. (C). 1998. pap. text 16.36 (*0-395-90257-6*) HM.
— Geography of Health. 1994. pap. text. write for info. (*0-582-07559-9*, Pub. by Addison-Wesley) Longman.
Digby, Anne. The Evolution of British General Practice, 1850-1948. LC R729.5.G4D54 1999. (Illus.). 390p. 1999. text 80.00 (*0-19-820513-9*) OUP.
— Making a Medical Living: Doctors & Patients in the English Market for Medicine, 1720-1911. (Cambridge Studies in Population, Economy & Society in Past Time: No. 24). (Illus.). 369p. (C). 1994. text 69.95 (*0-521-34526-X*) Cambridge U Pr.

D

An Asterisk (*) at the beginning of an entry indicates that the title is appearing for the first time.

Digby, Anne & Stewart, John, eds. Gender Health & Welfare. LC 98-5290. (Illus.). 256p. (C). 1998. pap. 24.99 (*0-415-18700-1*) Routledge.

Digby, Annette D., jt. auth. see Pedersen, Jon E.

Digby, Christine & Myers, John. Making Sense of Spelling & Pronunciation. LC 92-23301. 1993. 9.00 (*0-13-554205-7*) P-H.

Digby, Jenny. A Woman's Voice: Conversations with Australian Poets. 320p. 1996. pap. 29.95 (*0-7022-2732-3*, Pub. by Univ Queensland Pr) Intl Spec Bk.

***Digby, Joan.** Honors Programs 2000. 2nd ed. (Illus.). 576p. 1999. pap. 24.95 (*0-7689-0254-1*) Petersons.

Digby, Joan. Peterson's Honors Programs, 1998. Latimer, Jon, ed. LC 97-216918. 600p. 1997. pap. 21.95 (*1-56079-851-3*) Petersons.

Digby, John. Sailing Away from the Night. 56p. 1978. pap. 13.95 (*0-85646-040-0*, Pub. by Anvil Press) Dufour.

— To Amuse a Shrinking Sun. 70p. 1985. 21.95 (*0-85646-138-5*, Pub. by Anvil Press); pap. 14.95 (*0-85646-139-3*, Pub. by Anvil Press) Dufour.

Digby, John, tr. see Epicurus.

Digby-Junger, Richard. The Journalist As Reformer: Henry Demarest Lloyd & Wealth Against Commonwealth, 168. LC 95-50453. (Contributions in American History Ser.: No. 168). 208p. 1996. 59.95 (*0-313-29957-9*, Greenwood Pr) Greenwood.

Digby, K. H. Lawyer in the Wilderness. LC 81-109957. (Southeast Asia Program, Department of Asian Studies, Cornell University - Data Paper: No. 114). (Illus.). 123p. reprint ed. pap. 38.20 (*0-8357-3116-2*, 203937400012) Bks Demand.

Digby, Kenelm, ed. Journal of a Voyage into the Mediterranean, 1628. LC 72-164832. (Camden Society, London. Publications, First Ser.: No. 96). reprint ed. 32.50 (*0-404-50196-6*) AMS Pr.

***Digby, Simon.** Sufis & Soldiers in Awrangzeb's Deccan. 384p. 2000. text 29.95 (*0-19-564461-1*) OUP.

Digby, Tom, ed. Men Doing Feminism. LC 97-39468. 359p. (C). 1997. pap. 23.99 (*0-415-91626-7*) Routledge.

— Men Doing Feminism. LC 97-39468. 359p. (C). 1998. 80.00 (*0-415-91625-9*) Routledge.

Digby, William. Condemned Unheard: Government of India & H. H. the Maharaja of Kashmir, a Letter to the Ughtred Kay Shuttleworth. (C). 1994. reprint ed. 26.00 (*81-206-0879-8*, Pub. by Asian Educ Servs) S Asia.

DiGennaro, Jacqueline, jt. auth. see Pelton, Mary H.

DiGennaro, Joseph. Individualized Exercise & Optimal Physical Fitness: A Review Workbook for Men & Women. LC 73-9614. 152p. reprint ed. pap. 47.20 (*0-608-13673-5*, 205542000022) Bks Demand.

Digeorgia, James. The Clinton Silver Rush: A Second Chance for Silver Investors. Weiss, Martin D., ed. 69p. (Orig.). pap. text 72.00 (*0-941739-03-1*) M D Weiss Pub.

— Gold Fever! How to Cash in Big on Clinton Collapse. Weiss, Martin D., ed. 61p. (Orig.). pap. text 72.00 (*0-941739-05-8*) M D Weiss Pub.

— Insider's Guide to Buying Silver, Gold & Rare Coins: How Gold Dealers Lie, Cheat, & Rip You Off - All Within the Letter of the Law. Weiss, Martin D., ed. 120p. (Orig.). pap. text 49.00 (*0-941739-02-3*) M D Weiss Pub.

— Last Call for Gold! How to Cash in Big on the Coming Gold Fever. Weiss, Martin D., ed. 61p. (Orig.). pap. text 72.00 (*0-941739-06-6*) M D Weiss Pub.

— The Silver Frenzy: A Guide to Huge Profits in Silver. Weiss, Martin D., ed. 69p. (Orig.). pap. text 72.00 (*0-941739-04-X*) M D Weiss Pub.

DiGeorgio-Lutz, JoAnn, jt. ed. see McCoy, Melanie.

Digeronimo, Theresa. Insomnia: 50 Essential Things to Do. LC 96-53422. 192p. 1997. pap. 10.95 (*0-452-27636-5*, Plume) Dutton Plume.

DiGeronimo, Theresa, jt. auth. see Cameron, Myra.

Digeronimo, Theresa, jt. auth. see Di Salvo, Joe.

Digeronimo, Theresa, jt. auth. see Natural.

DiGeronimo, Theresa F. & Clement, Brian R. Living Foods for Optimum Health: A Highly Effective Program to Remove Toxins & Restore Your Body to Vibrant Health. (Illus.). 288p. 1996. boxed set 22.95 (*0-7615-0258-0*) Prima Pub.

DiGeronimo, Theresa F., jt. auth. see DiSalvo, Jack.

DiGeronimo, Theresa F., jt. auth. see Giuffre, Kenneth.

DiGeronimo, Theresa F., jt. auth. see Manginello, Frank P.

DiGeronimo, Theresa F., jt. auth. see Schaefer, Charles E.

Digeronimo, Theresa Foy & Gliksman, Michele Isaacs. The Complete Idiot's Guide to Pregnancy. (Complete Idiot's Guide Ser.). (Illus.). 332p. 1999. pap. 16.95 (*0-02-863104-8*, Pub. by Macmillan Gen Ref) S&S Trade.

Digeronimo, Theresa Foy, jt. auth. see Clement, Brian.

Digeronimo, Theresa Foy, jt. auth. see Schaefer, Charles E.

Digeronimo, Theresa Foy, jt. auth. see Tofler, Ian.

***Digeser, Elizabeth Depalma.** Making of A Christian Empire: Lactantius & Rome. LC 99-16168. 1999. 39.95 (*0-8014-3594-3*) Cornell U Pr.

Digeser, Peter. Our Politics, Our Selves? Liberalism, Identity & Harm. LC 94-23387. 296p. 1995. text 39.50 (*0-691-03716-7*, Pub. by Princeton U Pr) Cal Prin Full Svc.

Digeser, Peter, jt. auth. see David, Steven R.

Digest Readers Staff. How to Do Just about Anything: A Money Saving Guide to over 1200 Skills & Household Solutions. 1997. pap. text 16.95 (*0-89577-936-6*, Pub. by RD Assn) Penguin Putnam.

— Practical Problem Solver: Substitutes, Shortcuts & Ingenious Solutions to Make Life Easier. 1997. pap. text 16.95 (*0-89577-935-8*, Pub. by RD Assn) Penguin Putnam.

— Successful Gardening: A-Z of Annuals, Biennials & Bulbs. (Illus.). 176p. 1997. pap. text 24.95 (*0-89577-923-4*, Pub. by RD Assn) Penguin Putnam.

— Successful Gardening: The Garden Problem Solver. 1997. pap. text 24.95 (*0-89577-922-6*, Pub. by RD Assn) Penguin Putnam.

Digges, Deborah. Rough Music. 64p. 1997. pap. 15.00 (*0-679-76597-2*) Knopf.

— Rough Music. LC 95-15834. 80p. 1995. 20.00 (*0-679-44176-X*) Random.

— Vesper Sparrows. LC 95-67959. (Classic Contemporaries Ser.). 51p. (C). 1996. reprint ed. pap. 12.95 (*0-88748-228-7*) Carnegie-Mellon.

Digges, Deborah, tr. see Varela, Maria Elena Cruz.

Digges, Dick, ed. see Hart, Martha A. & Neblett, Hester.

Digges, Dudley. The Defence of Trade, in a Letter to Sir T. Smith. LC 68-54640. (English Experience Ser.: No. 26). 52p. 1968. reprint ed. 20.00 (*90-221-0026-X*) Walter J Johnson.

Digges, Jeremiah. In Great Waters: The Story of Portugese Fishermen. 1977. lib. bdg. 59.95 (*0-8490-2043-3*) Gordon Pr.

— In Great Waters: The Story of the Portuguese Fishermen. Cortes, Carlos E., ed. LC 79-6202. (Hispanics in the United States Ser.). 1981. reprint ed. lib. bdg. 29.95 (*0-405-13153-4*) Ayer.

Digges, Leonard. A Prognostication Euerlasting of Ryght Goode Effecte: Lately Corrected & Augmented by Thomas Digges, His Sonne. LC 74-28846. (English Experience Ser.: No. 727). 1975. reprint ed. 15.00 (*90-221-0727-2*) Walter J Johnson.

Digges, Leonard & Digges, Thomas. An Arithmeticall Militarie Treatise, Named Stratioticos. LC 68-27478. (English Experience Ser.: No. 71). 192p. 1968. reprint ed. 45.00 (*90-221-0071-5*) Walter J Johnson.

Digges, Mary, ed. see Hart, Martha A. & Neblett, Hester.

Digges, Mary-Dick. Bell Pull Finishing. (Illus.). 32p. (Orig.). 1988. pap. 9.95 (*0-929339-01-0*) Embroidery Research Pr Inc.

Digges, Mary-Dick, et al. Lady Evelyn's Needlework Collection. (Illus.). 198p. 1988. 39.95 (*0-929339-00-2*) Embroidery Research Pr Inc.

Digges, P., et al. International Markets for African Agricultural Exports: Agricultural Policy Reform & Agricultural Exports. 1997. pap. 60.00 (*0-85954-468-0*, Pub. by Nat Res Inst) St Mut.

Digges, Robert E., Jr. Behind the Walls. 112p. 1995. pap. 7.95 (*0-9645671-0-5*) Hi-Max Pub.

Digges, Thomas, jt. auth. see Digges, Leonard.

Digges, Thomas A. Adventures of Alonso: Containing Some Striking Anecdotes of the Present Minister of Portugal. (C). 1986. reprint ed. pap. text 5.95 (*0-8290-1896-4*) Irvington.

— Adventures of Alonso: Containing Some Striking Anecdotes of the Present Minister of Portugal. LC 43-13609. (Monographs: No. 18). 1943. reprint ed. 12.00 (*0-930060-01-6*) US Cath Hist.

— Adventures of Alonso: Continuing Some Striking Anecdotes of the Present Minister of Portugal. LC 74-104439. 1988. 14.00 (*0-8398-0362-1*) Irvington.

Diggin, Michael. Pocket Treasury of Irish Verse. 1998. pap. 7.99 (*1-85833-861-1*) Quadrillion Pubng.

Diggins. The Cunning of American History. Date not set. 24.50 (*0-684-82767-0*) Free Pr.

— The Cunning of American History. 1998. 23.00 (*0-02-874118-8*) Free Pr.

Diggins, Greg A. J.K. Lasser's Gay Finances in a Straight World: A Comprehensive Financial Plan. LC 97-80929. 228p. 1997. pap. 19.95 (*0-02-862222-7*) Macmillan.

Diggins, Gregory A. The Voluntary Tax Collections Process. 132p. (Orig.). 1995. pap. text 34.95 (*0-7811-0120-4*) Res Inst Am.

— What to Do When You Can't Pay Your Taxes. 14p. (Orig.). 1995. pap. text 14.95 (*0-7811-0126-3*) Res Inst Am.

Diggins, John P. The Liberal Persuasion: Arthur Schlesinger, Jr., & the Challenge of the American Past. LC 97-18920. 310p. 1997. text 35.00 (*0-691-04829-0*, Pub. by Princeton U Pr) Cal Prin Full Svc.

— The Lost Soul of American Politics: Virtue, Self-Interest, & the Foundations of Liberalism. LC 86-10594. 424p. (C). 1986. pap. text 32.00 (*0-226-14877-7*) U Ch Pr.

— Max Weber: Politics & the Spirit of Tragedy. 352p. 1996. pap. 16.00 (*0-465-01751-7*, Pub. by Basic) HarpC.

***Diggins, John P.** On Hallowed Ground: Abraham Lincoln & the Foundations of American History. LC 00-35915. 352p. 2000. 27.95 (*0-300-08237-1*) Yale U Pr.

Diggins, John P. The Promise of Pragmatism: Modernism & the Crisis of Knowledge & Authority. LC 93-11686. 530p. 1994. 29.95 (*0-226-14878-5*) U Ch Pr.

— The Promise of Pragmatism: Modernism & the Crisis of Knowledge & Authority. 528p. 1995. pap. 22.00 (*0-226-14879-3*) U Ch Pr.

— Proud Decades: America in War & Peace, 1941-1960. (Illus.). (Orig.). (C). 1989. pap. 17.95 (*0-393-95656-3*) Norton.

— Thorstein Veblen: Theorist of the Leisure Class LC 98-54179. 1999. 16.95 (*0-691-00654-7*, Pub. by Princeton U Pr) Cal Prin Full Svc.

— Up from Communism. 544p. 1994. 57.50 (*0-231-08488-9*); pap. 23.00 (*0-231-08489-7*) Col U Pr.

***Diggins, John Patrick.** Thorstein Veblen: Theorist of the Leisure Class. 1999. 55.00 (*0-691-00655-5*, Pub. by Princeton U Pr) Cal Prin Full Svc.

Diggle, J., ed. Tragicorum Graecorum: Fragmenta Selecta. (Oxford Classical Texts Ser.). 192p. 1998. text 47.50 (*0-19-814685-X*) OUP.

Diggle, James. Euripidea: Collected Essays. LC 93-29934. 576p. 1994. 98.00 (*0-19-814094-0*) OUP.

— Fabulae Vol. 2: Supplices, Hercules, Ion, Troiades. (Oxford Classical Texts Ser.). 388p. 1982. text 28.00 (*0-19-814590-X*) OUP.

— Studies on the Text of Euripides. 1981. 48.00 (*0-19-814019-3*) OUP.

— The Textual Tradition of Euripides' Orestes. (Illus.). 196p. 1991. text 69.00 (*0-19-814766-X*) OUP.

Diggle, James, ed. see Euripides.

Diggle, John W., ed. Oxides & Oxide Films. LC 72-83120. (Anodic Behavior of Metals & Semiconductors Ser.: Vol. 1). 560p. reprint ed. 173.60 (*0-8357-9090-8*, 205508200001) Bks Demand.

Diggle, John W., et al, eds. Oxides & Oxide Films, 2 vols., Vol. 2. LC 72-83120. (Anodic Behavior of Metals & Semiconductors Ser.). (Illus.). 416p. 1973. reprint ed. pap. 129.00 (*0-7837-0699-5*, 204103200002) Bks Demand.

— Oxides & Oxide Films, 2 vols., Vol. 4. LC 72-83120. (Anodic Behavior of Metals & Semiconductors Ser.). (Illus.). 295p. 1976. reprint ed. pap. 91.50 (*0-7837-0700-2*, 204103200004) Bks Demand.

Diggle, John W. & Vijh, Ashok K., eds. Oxides & Oxide Films, Vol. 3. LC 72-83120. (Anodic Behavior of Metals & Semiconductors Ser.). (Illus.). 351p. 1976. reprint ed. pap. 108.90 (*0-7837-4208-8*, 204103200003) Bks Demand.

— Oxides & Oxide Films, Vol. 5. LC 72-83120. (Anodic Behavior of Metals & Semiconductors Ser.). (Illus.). 201p. 1977. reprint ed. pap. 62.40 (*0-7837-4209-6*, 204103200005) Bks Demand.

— Oxides & Oxide Films, Vol. 6. LC 72-83120. (Anodic Behavior of Metals & Semiconductors Ser.). (Illus.). 359p. 1981. reprint ed. pap. 111.30 (*0-7837-4210-X*, 204103200006) Bks Demand.

Diggle, Martin. Riding Cross Country. 111p. 1990. 24.00 (*0-85131-426-0*, Pub. by J A Allen) Trafalgar.

— Riding from Scratch. 1997. 35.00 (*0-85131-682-4*, Pub. by J A Allen) Trafalgar.

— Riding over Jumps. 188p. 1990. 29.00 (*0-85131-423-6*, Pub. by J A Allen) Trafalgar.

— Teaching Basic Jumping. 141p. (C). 1990. pap. 30.00 (*0-85131-481-3*, Pub. by J A Allen) St Mut.

***Diggle, Martin.** Teaching Basic Jumping. 2000. 22.95 (*0-85131-706-5*, Pub. by J A Allen) Trafalgar.

Diggle, Martin. Teaching the Mature Rider. 125p. (C). 1990. pap. 30.00 (*0-85131-553-4*, Pub. by J A Allen) Trafalgar.

Diggle, Martin, jt. auth. see Colgate, Terry.

Diggle, Peter J. Time Series: A Biostatistical Introduction. (Oxford Statistical Science Ser.: No. 5). (Illus.). 268p. 1990. pap. text 45.00 (*0-19-852226-6*) OUP.

Diggle, Peter J., et al. The Analysis of Longitudinal Data. (Oxford Statistical Science Ser.: Vol. 13). (Illus.). 264p. 1994. text 65.00 (*0-19-852284-3*) OUP.

Diggles, Peter & Howis, Jill. Tolley's Tax Tables, 1993-94. 1993. 40.00 (*0-85459-695-X*, Pub. by Tolley Pubng) St Mut.

Diggory, Terence. William Carlos Williams & the Ethics of Painting. LC 90-8995. (Illus.). 181p. 1991. reprint ed. pap. 56.20 (*0-608-02562-3*, 206320700004) Bks Demand.

— Yeats & American Poetry: The Tradition of the Self. LC 82-15070. 283p. 1983. reprint ed. pap. 87.80 (*0-608-06386-X*, 206674700008) Bks Demand.

***Diggory, Terence & Miller, Stephen Paul, eds.** The Scene of My Selves: New Work on New York School Poets. 450p. 2000. pap. 24.95 (*0-943373-63-8*, Pub. by Natl Poet Foun); text 50.00 (*0-943373-50-6*, Pub. by Natl Poet Foun) U Pr of New Eng.

Diggs, Altha Y. Life, Learning, Love & Loss: Poems. 1998. pap. 8.95 (*0-533-12540-5*) Vantage.

Diggs, Anita & Paster, Vera S. Staying Married. LC 98-65137. 240p. 1998. 23.00 (*1-57566-248-5*, Knsington) Kensgtn Pub Corp.

Diggs, Anita D. Barrier Breaking Resumes & Interviews. LC 99-14789. 160p. 1999. pap. 12.00 (*0-8129-3130-0*, Times Bks) Crown Pub Group.

— Success at Work: A Guide for African-Americans. LC 92-36603. 128p. 1993. pap. 12.99 (*0-942637-85-2*) Barricade Bks.

***Diggs, Anita Doreen.** Staying Married. 288p. 1999. pap. 12.00 (*1-57566-422-4*, Knsington) Kensgtn Pub Corp.

Diggs, B. J., ed. The State, Justice, & the Common Good: An Introduction to Social & Political Philosophy. LC 98-73692. 256p. (C). 1998. pap. text 27.95 (*0-9658339-9-2*) Educ Intl Pr.

Diggs, Bernard J. Love & Being: An Investigation into the Metaphysics of St. Thomas Aquinas. 180p. 1947. 15.00 (*0-913298-45-X*) S F Vanni.

Diggs-Brown, Barbara, jt. auth. see Steinhorn, Leonard.

Diggs, Dorothy C. Working Manual for Altar Guilds. 3rd rev. ed. LC 87-31248. 80p. 1988. pap. 7.95 (*0-8192-1455-8*) Morehouse Pub.

Diggs, Elizabeth. Close Ties. 1982. pap. 5.25 (*0-8222-0220-4*) Dramatists Play.

— Dumping Ground. 1982. pap. 3.25 (*0-8222-0340-5*) Dramatists Play.

— Goodbye Freddy. 1986. pap. 5.25 (*0-8222-0460-6*) Dramatists Play.

Diggs, George, et al. Shinners & Mahler's Illustrated Flora of North Central Texas. (SIDA, Botanical Miscellany Ser.: Vol. 16). (Illus.). 1999. text 89.95 (*1-889878-01-4*) Botanical Res.

Diggs, J. Frank. Americans Behind the Barbed Wire. (Illus.). 208p. 1999. 24.95 (*0-918339-52-9*) Vandamere.

Diggs, Lawrence J. Allies: A Positive Approach to Racial Reconciliation. LC 98-84352. (Illus.). 96p. 1998. pap. 8.95 (*0-9621803-4-3*) Quiet Storm Trading.

— Vinegar: The User Friendly Standard Text, Reference & Guide to Appreciating, Making & Enjoying Vinegar. LC 88-92291. (Illus.). 320p. 1990. pap. 19.95 (*0-9621803-0-0*) Quiet Storm Trading.

Diggs, Nancy, jt. auth. see Lindsley, Evangeline.

Diggs, Nancy B. Steel Butterflies: Japanese Women & the American Experience. LC 97-11077. 160p. (C). 1997. text 56.50 (*0-7914-3623-3*); pap. text 18.95 (*0-7914-3624-1*) State U NY Pr.

Diggs, Rhunette, jt. ed. see Socha, Thomas J.

Diggs, Richard. Preventing Drop-Outs. LC 96-70272. 160p. (Orig.). 1996. pap. 19.95 (*0-937157-14-7*) Progressive Pubns.

Diggs, Richard & Clancey, Eleanor. Pretty Good Ain't Good Enough: The Dilemma of Education in the United States. (Orig.). 1991. pap. 9.95 (*0-937157-10-4*) Progressive Pubns.

Diggs, Richard N. Employ-Ability...Plus. 82p. (Orig.). 1987. pap. 6.95 (*0-937157-02-3*) Progressive Pubns.

— Finding Your Ideal Job: 1989-1990 Edition. rev. ed. Goeller, Ted, tr. & illus. by. Clancey, Noni, illus. 144p. (C). 1989. reprint ed. pap., student ed. 7.95 (*0-937157-05-8*) Progressive Pubns.

— Finding Your Ideal Job in the World of Electronics. (Illus.). 140p. (Orig.). (C). 1990. pap. text 7.95 (*0-937157-06-6*) Progressive Pubns.

— Great Businesses You Can Start on a Shoestring. 152p. (Orig.). 1991. pap. 8.95 (*0-937157-09-0*) Progressive Pubns.

— Keeping Students from Dropping Out of Post-Secondary Occupational Education. rev. ed. Hall, George J., ed. (Illus.). 176p. 1988. pap. 17.95 (*0-937157-04-X*) Progressive Pubns.

— Lessons for Living from an Ugly Old Man. (Illus.). 178p. 1997. pap. 12.95 (*0-937157-16-3*) Progressive Pubns.

— The Sex Education Handbook. (Illus.). 216p. (YA). (gr. 6-12). 1994. pap. text 17.95 (*0-937157-13-9*) Progressive Pubns.

Diggs, Steven F. Putting Your Best Foot Forward: How to Advertise & Promote Your Business. LC 89-85880. (Illus.). 1990. 17.95 (*0-9624293-0-9*) Boyd & Franklin.

Diggs-Tate, Tamara. Grandma's Teddy. (Illus.). 28p. (Orig.). (J). (gr. 4-8). 1995. pap. 7.95 (*1-885821-02-6*) Identity Toys.

Dighe, Anita, jt. auth. see Krishnan, Prabha.

***Dighton, G. L.** Consider the Lilies: Daily Inspirationals. LC 99-67509. 176p. 1999. pap. 10.95 (*1-57921-239-5*) WinePress Pub.

DiGiacomantonio, William C., et al, eds. Documentary History of the First Federal Congress Vol. 14: Debates in the House of Representatives: Third Session, December 1790-March 1791. 1002p. 1996. text 75.00 (*0-8018-5015-0*) Johns Hopkins.

***DiGiacomo, Anthony.** Crashpoint an X-Files Script. 25p. 2000. pap. 20.00 (*1-58265-024-1*, 0111) Orphan Press.

— The Falcon King. 200p. 2000. mass mkt. 6.99 (*1-58265-017-9*, 00022) Orphan Press.

— Girls of Power. (Illus.). 50p. (YA). (gr. 4-7). 2000. pap. 6.99 (*1-58265-018-7*, 00020) Orphan Press.

— Lanna: A Girls' Life. 100p. 2000. pap. 7.95 (*1-58265-020-9*, 00025) Orphan Press.

— Mr. Shadow. 200p. 2000. pap. 6.00 (*1-58265-022-5*, 0113) Orphan Press.

— Mortal Poetry. 20p. 1999. pap. 6.00 (*1-58265-010-1*, 00030) Orphan Press.

— Powerful Girls Adventures. (Illus.). 50p. (J). (gr. 5-7). 2000. pap. 6.00 (*1-58265-025-X*, 0112) Orphan Press.

— Screenwriting for Everyone. 50p. 2000. pap. 20.00 (*1-58265-003-9*, 00021) Orphan Press.

— The Starfleet Academy Course Catalogue. Date not set. pap. 10.00 (*1-58265-008-X*) Orphan Press.

— Starwars, The Void Riders. (Illus.). 50p. 2000. pap. 10.00 (*1-58265-023-3*, 0115) Orphan Press.

DiGiacomo, Anthony. The Voyage of the Sea Lion. (Illus.). 75p. 1998. pap. 6.00 (*1-58265-007-1*) Orphan Press.

DiGiacomo, Anthony W. All Our Alien Lovers. (Illus.). 25p. 1998. pap. 15.00 (*1-58265-006-3*) Orphan Press.

— Rachel's Stories for Tough Kids. (Illus.). 30p. (J). (gr. 1-4). 1998. pap. 7.95 (*1-58265-001-2*) Orphan Press.

— The Single Persons' Survival Manual. (Illus.). 35p. 1998. pap. 11.95 (*1-58265-000-4*) Orphan Press.

Digiacomo, Anthony W. Spacecraft, Starships & Hitech Vehicles: Blueprints & Deck Plans of the Future. (Illus.). 50p. 1998. pap. 15.00 (*1-58265-005-5*) Orphan Press.

***DiGiacomo, Anthony W.** Tarnished Images: A Superhero Story. 25p. 2000. pap. 6.00 (*1-58265-013-6*) Orphan Press.

Digiacomo, Anthony W. The True UFO Story: An Multi-Part Analysis. (Illus.). 100p. 1998. pap. 15.00 (*1-58265-002-0*) Orphan Press.

— The UFO Fighters = ADCOM. (Illus.). 25p. 1998. pap. 15.00 (*1-58265-004-7*) Orphan Press.

DiGiacomo, J. Handbook of Emerging Technology. (Computer Science Ser.). 1993. text. write for info. (*0-442-00487-7*, VNR) Wiley.

DiGiacomo, James. Do the Right Thing: A Guide to Christian Morality. LC 90-61957. 96p. (Orig.). (C). 1991. pap. 7.95 (*1-55612-374-4*, LL1374) Sheed & Ward WI.

— Morality & Youth: Fostering Christian Identity. LC 93-938. 160p. (Orig.). 1993. pap. 8.95 (*1-55612-652-2*) Sheed & Ward WI.

DiGiacomo, James & Walsh, John J. Christian Discovery: The Road to Justice. LC 91-41590. 1992. 12.00 (*0-88344-807-6*) Orbis Bks.

DiGiacomo, James, et al. The Longest Step: Searching for God. (Encounter Ser.). (Illus.). 1985. 5.95 (*0-86683-180-0*, 315) Harper SF.

DiGiacomo, James, jt. auth. see Walsh, John J.

DiGiacomo, James J. Teaching Religion in a Catholic Secondary School. (Keynote Ser.). 70p. 1989. pap. 3.00 (*1-55833-033-X*) Natl Cath Educ.

DiGiacomo, Joseph. The Design & Application of Digital Buses. (Illus.). 1991. 219.00 (*0-7803-0306-7*, HL4499) Inst Electrical.

Digiacomo, Kathy. Maltese. 1997. pap. 9.95 (*0-7938-2384-6*, KW-111S) TFH Pubns.

DiGiacomo, Louis J. The Clear & Simple Wine Guide. 160p. 1992. pap. 10.95 (*0-9633630-0-X*) Daylesford Pub.

***Digiacomo, Michael.** Apparently Unharmed: Riders of the Cresta Run. 2000. 22.95 (*1-58799-004-0*) Texere.

DiGiacomo, Mike. Classical Solos Arranged for the Guitar, Vol. II. 2nd ed. (C). 1991. reprint ed. pap. text 12.95 (*1-880462-05-2*); reprint ed. pap. text 22.95 incl. audio (*0-685-50701-7*) Mad Music.

— Classical Violin Solos Arranged for the Guitar. (Classical Solos Arranged for the Guitar Ser.: Vol. III). (C). 1991. pap. text 12.95 (*1-880462-08-7*); pap. text 22.95 incl. audio (*1-880462-10-9*) Mad Music.

— Music Theory for the Contemporary Guitarist Vol. 1: Note Reading Made Exciting. (C). 1989. pap. text 4.95 (*1-880462-11-7*); pap. text 10.95 incl. audio (*0-685-50700-9*) Mad Music.

***DiGiacomo, Tony.** How to Be a Mafiosi. (Illus.). 20p. 2000. pap. 10.00 (*1-58265-021-7*, 0114) Orphan Press.

***Digiacomo, Tony W.** Mash = The Role Playing Game. (Illus.). 25p. 2000. pap. 15.00 (*1-58265-016-0*, 00016) Orphan Press.

— New Amsterdam City: A Champions RPG Campaign Setting. (Illus.). 25p. 2000. pap. 10.00 (*1-58265-011-X*, 00011) Orphan Press.

— The Perchelli Chronicles. 200p. 2000. mass mkt. 6.99 (*1-58265-019-5*, 00024) Orphan Press.

— Starfleet = 2 = Keep the Faith. (Illus.). 100p. 2000. pap. 6.99 (*1-58265-015-2*, 00014) Orphan Press.

— Starfleet 1 = Have Faith. (Illus.). 100p. 2000. pap. 6.99 (*1-58265-014-4*, 00013) Orphan Press.

— Super People = A Champions RPG Characters Collection. (Illus.). 30p. 2000. pap. 10.00 (*1-58265-012-8*, 00012) Orphan Press.

DiGiano, Francis A., jt. auth. see Weber, Walter J., Jr.

Digilio, ed. GED Social Studies Test, No. 2. 1987. pap. 9.93 (*0-8092-5037-3*) NTC Contemp Pub Co.

Digilio, Karen S. Critical Thinking with Math: Reasoning & Problem Solving. 1988. pap. 10.26 (*0-8092-4455-1*) NTC Contemp Pub Co.

Digilio, Karen S., ed. GED Social Studies. 1988. pap., wbk. ed. 8.46 (*0-8092-4541-8*) NTC Contemp Pub Co.

DiGioanni, Caroline M., ed. Italian Canadian Voices: An Anthology of Poetry & Prose, 1946-1986. 208p. 1994. pap. 14.95 (*0-88962-255-8*) Mosaic.

DiGiovanna, Augustine G. Human Aging: Biological Perspectives. LC 93-16897. 336p. (C). 1994. pap. text 41.50 (*0-07-016915-2*) McGraw.

Digiovanna, Eileen. An Osteopathic Approach to Diagnosis & Treatment. 2nd ed. LC 96-41775. 500p. 1996. text 75.00 (*0-397-51581-2*, Lippnctt) Lppncott W & W.

DiGiovanna, Joseph J. Linguistic Phenomenology: Philosophical Method in J. L. Austin. (American University Studies: Philosophy: Ser. V, Vol. 63). XIV, 211p. (C). 1989. text 33.70 (*0-8204-0877-8*) P Lang Pubng.

DiGiovanni, George, ed. see Kant, Immanuel.

DiGiovanni, Nicholas, Jr. Age Discrimination: An Administrator's Guide. 180p. 1989. 25.00 (*0-910402-88-4*) Coll & U Personnel.

DiGiovanni, Nicholas, ed. see Freiday, Don.

DiGiovanni, P. R. & Adsit, N. R., eds. Testing Technology of Metal Matrix Composites STP 964. LC 88-15451. (Special Technical Publication (STP) Ser.). (Illus.). 472p. 1988. text 64.00 (*0-8031-0967-9*, STP964) ASTM.

D

DiGiovanni, Pauline G. The Golden Key to Reading: The Paula Di Intensive Phonics Method of Reading-Writing-Spelling, Bk. 1. rev. ed. (Illus.). 111p. (Orig.). 1985. pap. text, teacher ed. 9.99 (*0-936543-00-0*) Paula Di Ed.

— The Golden Key to Reading: The Paula Di Intensive Phonics Method of Reading-Writing-Spelling, Bk. 1. 2nd rev. ed. (Illus.). 111p. (Orig.). 1985. pap. text, student ed. 9.99 (*0-9613130-8-0*) Paula Di Ed.

— The Golden Key to Reading: The Paula Di Intensive Phonics Method of Reading-Writing-Spelling, Bk. 2. rev. ed. (Illus.). 189p. (Orig.). 1985. pap. text, teacher ed. 14.99 (*0-936543-01-9*) Paula Di Ed.

— The Golden Key to Reading: The Paula Di Intensive Phonics Method of Reading-Writing-Spelling, Bk. 2. 2nd rev. ed. (Illus.). 167p. (Orig.). 1985. pap. text, student ed. 14.99 (*0-9613130-7-2*) Paula Di Ed.

— The Golden Key to Reading: The Paula Di Intensive Phonics Method of Reading-Writing-Spelling, Bk. 3. rev. ed. (Illus.). 237p. (Orig.). 1985. pap. text, teacher ed. 19.99 (*0-936543-02-7*) Paula Di Ed.

— The Golden Key to Reading: The Paula Di Intensive Phonics Method of Reading-Writing-Spelling, Bk. 3. 2nd rev. ed. (Illus.). 237p. (Orig.). 1985. pap. text, student ed. 19.99 (*0-9613130-9-9*) Paula Di Ed.

— The Golden Key to Reading: The Paula Di Intensive Phonics Method of Reading-Writing-Spelling, Prog. 1 & 2: Writing Bklt. 48p. (Orig.). 1982. pap. text, student ed. 4.99 (*0-936543-03-5*); pap. text, student ed. 4.99 (*0-9613130-5-6*) Paula Di Ed.

— The Golden Key to Reading: The Paula Di Intensive Phonics Method of Reading-Writing-Spelling, 6 bks., Prog. Set. (Orig.). (J). (gr. k-3). 1985. pap. text, student ed. 59.94 (*0-936543-08-6*) Paula Di Ed.

— The Golden Key to Reading: The Paula Di Intensive Phonics Method of Reading-Writing-Spelling, Prog. Set, Bks. 1-3 & Reading Suppl. A. (Orig.). 1985. pap. text, teacher ed. 49.96 (*0-936543-04-3*) Paula Di Ed.

— The Golden Key to Reading: The Paula Di Intensive Phonics Method of Reading-Writing-Spelling, Reading Suppl. A. (Illus.). 60p. (Orig.). 1982. pap. text, teacher ed. 4.99 (*0-936543-05-1*); pap. text, student ed. 4.99 (*0-9613130-4-8*) Paula Di Ed.

— The Golden Key to Reading: The Paula Di Intensive Phonics Method of Reading-Writing-Spelling, 15 one-hr. audio tapes, Set. (Orig.). 1985. audio 124.99 (*0-936543-11-6*) Paula Di Ed.

— The Golden Key to Reading: The Paula Di Intensive Phonics Method of Reading-Writing-Spelling, Set. Bks. 1-3. 2nd rev. ed. (Orig.). 1985. pap. text, student ed. 44.97 (*0-9613130-6-4*) Paula Di Ed.

DigiPro Staff, tr. from ENG. Assepoester Het Sprookje. (Comes to Life Bks.).Tr. of Cinderella - The Fairy Tale. (DUT.). 16p. (J). (ps-2). 1994. write for info. (*1-883366-94-1*) YES Ent.

— La Bella Addormentata Nel Bosco. (Comes to Life Bks.).Tr. of Sleeping Beauty. (ITA.). 16p. (J). (ps-2). 1994. write for info. (*1-883366-98-4*) YES Ent.

— La Bella Durmiente. (Comes to Life Bks.).Tr. of Sleeping Beauty. (SPA.). 16p. (J). (ps-2). 1994. write for info. (*1-57234-010-X*) YES Ent.

— La Belle au Bois Dormant. (Comes to Life Bks.).Tr. of Sleeping Beauty. (FRE.). 16p. (J). (ps-2). 1994. write for info. (*1-883366-68-2*) YES Ent.

— Cendrillon - Le Conif de Fees. (Comes to Life Bks.).Tr. of Cinderella - The Fairy Tale. (FRE.). 16p. (J). (ps-2). 1994. write for info. (*1-883366-69-0*) YES Ent.

— Cenerentola. (Comes to Life Bks.).Tr. of Cinderella - The Fairy Tale. (ITA.). 16p. (J). (ps-2). 1994. write for info. (*1-883366-99-2*) YES Ent.

— La Cenicienta el Cuento de Hadas. (Comes to Life Bks.).Tr. of Cinderella - The Fairy Tale. (SPA.). 16p. (J). (ps-2). 1994. write for info. (*1-57234-011-8*) YES Ent.

— Un Club Construido para los Toons: Tiny Toon Adventures. (Comes to Life Bks.).Tr. of Clubhouse Built for Toons. (SPA.). 16p. (J). (ps-2). 1994. write for info. (*1-57234-013-4*) YES Ent.

— Doornroosje. (Comes to Life Bks.).Tr. of Sleeping Beauty. (DUT.). 16p. (J). (ps-2). 1994. write for info. (*1-883366-93-3*) YES Ent.

DigiPro Staff, tr. see Berenstain, Stan & Berenstain, Jan.

DigiPro Staff, tr. see Berenstain, Stan, et al.

DigiPro Staff, tr. see Goldsboro, Bobby.

DigiPro Staff, tr. see Hanshaw, Carol A.

DigiPro Staff, tr. see Hanshaw, Carol A. & YES! Entertainment Corporation Staff.

DigiPro Staff, tr. see Jablonsky, Alice.

DigiPro Staff, tr. see Murphy, Stephen.

Digirolamo, E. L. How to Choose a Husband. 1.98 (*0-931138-01-9*) Maiden Bks.

— A Med Cruise. 1978. pap. 1.50 (*0-931138-02-7*) Maiden Bks.

— Win Trots & Flats. 2.00 (*0-931138-00-0*) Maiden Bks.

Digirolamo, Eduardo L. Tear Drops of Love. 1978. 15.00 (*0-931138-03-5*) Maiden Bks.

DiGirolamo, Vinny, ed. Naval Command & Control: Policy, Programs, People & Issues. LC 91-36822. (Illus.). 396p. 1991. text 29.95 (*0-916159-23-X*) AFCEA Intl Pr.

Digital Avionics Systems Conference Staff, et al. 17th DASC: Proceedings of the AIAA/IEEE/SAE Digital Avionics Systems Conference: [Electronics in Motion], Belleview, Wa, Oct. 31-Nov. 7, 1998, 2 vols. LC 98-86916. 1998. pap. write for info. (*0-7803-5089-8*) IEEE Standards.

Digital Diagnostics Corp. Staff & Yale University Staff. Wavelet Packet Laboratory for Windows. (C). 1994. spiral bd. 350.00 incl. 3.5 hd (*1-56881-036-9*) AK Peters.

Digital Equipment Corporation, Corporate User Publ. Digital Guide to Developing International Software. (Software Design Ser.). (Illus.). 400p. 1990. pap. text 39.95 (*1-55558-063-7*, EY-F577E-DP, Digital DEC) Buttrwrth-Heinemann.

— The Digital Guide to Software Development. (Software Design Ser.). (Illus.). 239p. 1989. pap. text 39.95 (*1-55558-035-1*, EY-C178E-DP, Digital DEC) Buttrwrth-Heinemann.

Digital Focus Staff, jt. auth. see Berg, Clifford J.

Digital Maven LLC Staff. Digital Maven's Guide to Internet Success. 96p. 1998. pap. 19.95 (*0-9668427-0-7*) Digital Maven.

Digital Signal Processing Committee, ed. Programs for Digital Signal Processing. LC 79-89028. 592p. 1979. audio 85.00 (*0-686-96748-8*) Inst Electrical.

Digitalcre. Learning Microsoft Office 97: Online. (C). 1998. pap. text 74.00 (*0-03-023591-X*, Pub. by Harcourt Coll Pubs) Harcourt.

— Using Microsoft Works 4.0 online 98. (C). 1997. pap. text 66.50 (*0-03-023601-0*, Pub. by Harcourt Coll Pubs) Harcourt.

DiGiulio, Katherine. Natural Variations: Photographs by Colonel Stuart Wortley. (Illus.). 48p. 1994. pap. 6.95 (*0-87328-148-9*) Huntington Lib.

DiGiulio, Robert. Positive Classroom Management: A Step-by-Step Guide to Successfully Running the Show Without Destroying Student Dignity. LC 95-18298. (Illus.). 128p. 1995. pap. 19.95 (*0-8039-6289-4*) Corwin Pr.

— Positive Classroom Management: A Step-by-Step Guide to Successfully Running the Show Without Destroying Student Dignity. LC 95-18298. (Illus.). 128p. 1995. 45.95 (*0-8039-6288-6*) Corwin Pr.

***DiGiulio, Robert.** Positive Classroom Management: A Step-by-Step Guide to Sucessfully Running the Show Without Destroying Student Dignity. 2nd ed. LC 99-6664. (One-Off Ser.). (Illus.). 136p. 1999. pap. 21.95 (*0-8039-6816-7*); lib. bdg. 47.95 (*0-8039-6815-9*) Sage.

DiGiulio, Robert & Kranz, Rachel. Straight Talk about Death & Dying. LC 95-2488. (Straight Talk Ser.). 144p. (YA). (gr. 6-12). 1995. 19.95 (*0-8160-3078-2*) Facts on File.

— Straight Talk about Death & Dying. (Straight Talk Ser.). 144p. (YA). (gr. 6-12). 1996. pap. 9.95 (*0-8160-3553-9*) Facts on File.

***DiGiuseppe, David.** 100 Irish Tunes for Piano Accordion. 120p. 1999. pap. 24.95 incl. audio compact disk (*0-7866-3604-1*, 97211BCD) Mel Bay.

DiGiuseppe, Raymond, jt. auth. see Dryden, Windy.

Digman. Strategic Management: Cases. 5th ed. LC 98-70891. 1999. pap. 45.95 (*0-87393-793-7*) Dame Pubns.

— Strategic Management: Concepts, Processes, Decisions. 5th ed. LC 98-70892. 1998. pap. 51.95 (*0-87393-792-9*) Dame Pubns.

Digmedia Staff, et al. Computer Animation '94: Proceedings, May 25-28, 1994, Geneva, Switzerland. LC 94-75831. ix, 204p. 1994. pap. write for info. (*0-8186-6241-7*) IEEE Comp Soc.

Dignaga, jt. see Bhatt, S. R.

Dignam, John, jt. auth. see Sweetgall, Robert.

Dignan, James, jt. auth. see Cavadino, Michael.

Dignan, Ken. Til Healing Comes. 164p. (Orig.). 1993. pap. 8.95 (*1-883928-00-1*) Longwood.

Dignan, Mark. Measurement & Evaluation of Health Education. 3rd ed. LC 94-30631. (Illus.). 210p. (C). 1995. pap. 35.95 (*0-398-05958-6*) C C Thomas.

Dignan, Mark & Carr, Patricia A. Program Planning for Health Education & Promotion. 2nd ed. (Illus.). 176p. 1993. pap. 27.95 (*0-8121-1554-6*) Lppncott W & W.

Dignan, Mark, et al. Life & Health: Targeting Wellness. (C). 1991. text 44.54 (*0-07-037494-5*); pap. text, student ed. 19.00 (*0-07-037523-2*) McGraw.

Dignan, Mark B. Measurement & Evaluation of Health Education. 3rd ed. LC 94-30631. (Illus.). 210p. (C). 1994. text 51.95 (*0-398-05935-7*) C C Thomas.

Dignan, Patrick J. A History of the Legal Incorporation of Catholic Church Property in the United States (1784-1932) LC 73-3569. (Catholic University of America. Studies in Romance Languages & Literatures: No. 14). reprint ed. 42.50 (*0-404-57764-4*) AMS Pr.

Dignan, Pearline A. Heart Attacks & Rehabilitation: Index of New Information. 150p. 1994. 47.50 (*0-7883-0042-3*); pap. 44.50 (*0-7883-0043-1*) ABBE Pubs Assn.

— Heart Attacks-Real, Imagined & Suspicious: Index of New Information. 150p. 1994. 47.50 (*0-7883-0040-7*); pap. 44.50 (*0-7883-0041-5*) ABBE Pubs Assn.

Dignard, Margaret. Imagine. 1999. pap. write for info. (*1-58235-077-9*) Watermrk Pr.

D'Ignazio, F. Programming Your Texas Instruments Computer in TI BASIC. 256p. 1984. pap. 9.95 (*0-07-016897-0*, BYTE Bks) McGraw.

Digne, Francois & Michel, Jean. Representations of Finite Groups of Lie Type. (London Mathematical Society Student Texts Ser.: No. 21). 165p. (C). 1991. text 64.95 (*0-521-40117-8*); pap. text 25.95 (*0-521-40648-X*) Cambridge U Pr.

Digney, Marita. Mirrors of Transformation: The Self in Relationships. Brien, Dolores E., ed. LC 94-49053. (PAJA Papers). 1995. pap. write for info. (*1-882275-06-3*) Rnd Table Pr.

Digney, Phil. A Guide to Incubation & Handraising Parrots. 92p. 1998. pap. 24.95 (*0-9587102-1-X*) Avian Pubns.

Dignum, Frank, et al. Communication Modeling, the Language & Action Perspective: Proceedings of the First International Workshop on Communication Modeling, Tilburg, the Netherlands, 1-2 July, 1996. LC 96-48134. (Electronic Workshops in Computing Ser.). 1996. 59.95 (*3-540-76118-7*) Spr-Verlag.

Digo, Benjamin. Creator of Nikho. 201p. (Orig.). 1993. pap. 12.50 (*971-10-0513-1*, Pub. by New Day Pub) Cellar.

Digonnet, Michael J. & Ouellette, Francois, eds. Doped Fiber Devices II, Vol. 3542. 1999. 59.00 (*0-8194-3004-8*) SPIE.

Digonnet, Michael J. F. Rare Earth Doped Fiber Lasers & Amplifiers. (Optical Engineering Ser.: Vol. 37). (Illus.). 672p. 1993. text 215.00 (*0-8247-8785-4*) Dekker.

Digonnet, Michel. Hiking Death Valley: A Guide to Its Natural Wonders & Mining Past. LC 97-92255. (Illus.). 552p. 1999. reprint ed. pap. 17.95 (*0-9659178-0-0*) M Digonnet.

***Digonnet, Michel J., ed.** High Density Packaging & MCMS. 456p. 1999. pap. text 92.00 (*0-930815-57-2*) SPIE.

— Optical Devices for Fiber Communication. 1999. pap. text 72.00 (*0-8194-3440-X*) SPIE.

Digonnet, Michel J., ed. Rare-Earth-Doped Fiber Laser Sources & Amplifiers. (Milestone Ser.: Vol. MS37). 720p. 1991. pap. 45.00 (*0-8194-0735-6*) SPIE.

— Rare-Earth-Doped Fiber Laser Sources & Amplifiers. (Milestone Ser.: Vol. MS37/HC). 720p. 1991. 55.00 (*0-8194-0734-8*) SPIE.

Digonnet, Michel J. & Ouellette, Francois, eds. Doped Fiber Devices, Vol. 2841. 276p. 1996. 66.00 (*0-8194-2229-0*) SPIE.

DiGrado, Brian D. & Thorp, Gregory A. The Aboveground Steel Storage Tank Handbook. 350p. 1995. text 79.95 (*0-442-01845-2*, VNR) Wiley.

DiGrado, Brian D. & Thorp, Gregory A. The Aboveground Steel Storage Tank Handbook. (Industrial Health & Safety Ser.). 350p. 1995. 110.00 (*0-471-28629-X*, VNR) Wiley.

***DiGrado, Kimberly C., ed.** Pelican's Complete Guide to American Bed & Breakfasts. (Illus.). 480p. 2000. pap. 19.95 (*1-56554-735-7*) Pelican.

Digrappa, Carol, ed. Architecture: Theory. 132p. (Orig.). 1985. 17.95 (*0-912810-48-3*) Lustrum Pr.

***Digre & Corbett.** Viewing the Optic Disc: A Practical Guide. 2001. 99.00 (*0-7506-7289-7*) Buttrwrth-Heinemann.

Digre, Brian. Imperialism's New Clothes: The Repartition of Tropical Africa, 1914-1919. LC 89-28908. (American University Studies: History: Ser. IX, Vol. 79). XIV, 225p. 1990. text 44.95 (*0-8204-1120-5*) P Lang Pubng.

DiGregorio, Barry. Mars: The Living Planet. LC 96-37580. (Illus.). 300p. 1997. 25.00 (*1-883319-58-7*) Frog Ltd CA.

Digregorio, Charlotte. Beginner's Guide to Writing & Selling Quality Features: A Simple Course in Freelancing for Newspapers-Magazines. LC 89-91823. (Illus.). 156p. (Orig.). 1990. pap. 12.95 (*0-9623318-0-5*) Civetta Pr.

— You Can Be a Columnist: Writing & Selling Your Way to Prestige. LC 90-71020. (Illus.). 232p. (Orig.). 1993. pap. 13.95 (*0-9623318-1-3*) Civetta Pr.

— Your Original Personal Ad: The Complete Guide to Expressing Your Unique Sentiments to Find Your Dream Person. LC 94-71932. 156p. 1995. pap. 13.95 (*0-9623318-2-1*) Civetta Pr.

DiGregorio, G. J., et al. Handbook of Common Ocular Drugs. 153p. 1991. pap. 13.00 (*0-942447-07-7*) Med Surveill.

— Handbook of Commonly Rx Geriatric Drugs. 334p. 1993. pap. 15.00 (*0-942447-01-8*) Med Surveill.

DiGregorio, G. John. Handbook of Commonly Prescribed Drugs. 11th ed. 1996. pap. 15.50 (*0-942447-21-2*, D5668) Med Surveill.

Digregorio, G. John. Handbook of Commonly Prescribed Drugs. 13th ed. 1998. pap. 18.00 (*0-942447-25-5*) Med Surveill.

DiGregorio, G. John & Barbieri, E. Handbook of Commonly Prescribed Drugs. 15th ed. 300p. 2000. pap. 18.95 (*0-942447-35-2*) Med Surveill.

***DiGregorio, G John & Barbieri, Edward J.** Handbook of Commonly Prescribed Drugs. 14th ed. 312p. 1999. pap. 18.50 (*0-942447-29-8*) Med Surveill.

***DiGregorio, G. John, et al.** Travelers Guide to International Drugs: European, 4 vols., Vol. 1. (Travelers Guide To International Drugs: 1). 150p. 2000. pap. 8.95 (*0-942447-33-6*) Med Surveill.

— Travelers Guide to International Drugs: European Volume II, 4 vols., Vol. 1. (Travelers Guide To International Drugs). 150p. 2000. pap. 8.95 (*0-942447-34-4*) Med Surveill.

— Travelers Guide to International Drugs: Western Hemisphere I, 4 vols., Vol. 1. (Travelers Guide To International Drugs: 1). 125p. 2000. pap. 8.95 (*0-942447-30-1*) Med Surveill.

DiGregorio, Jennifer, ed. see Parkes, Brenda.

DiGregorio, Jennifer, ed. see Trumbauer, Lisa.

DiGregorio, Mario J., jt. auth. see Wallner, Jeff.

DiGregorio, Michael R. Urban Harvest: Recycling as a Peasant Industry in Northern Vietnam. LC 94-23197. (Occasional Papers: No. 17, September 1994). 1994. pap. 5.00 (*0-86638-164-3*) EW Ctr HI.

Digregorio, Robert V., jt. auth. see Singleton, Joanne K.

DiGregorio, Ron. 1992 Guide to Defense Cleanup. Rekenthaler, Doug, Jr., ed. 245p. 1992. pap. 390.00 (*0-935453-46-6*) Pasha Pubns.

DiGregorio, Ron, ed. The 1998-99 Guide to Superfund Sites. 864p. 1998. pap. 495.00 incl. cd-rom (*0-935453-87-3*) Pasha Pubns.

Diguet, Edouard J. Les Annamites. LC 71-179191. (Illus.). reprint ed. 54.50 (*0-404-54821-0*) AMS Pr.

— Les Montagnards du Tonkin. LC 77-87484. (Illus.). 176p. reprint ed. 39.50 (*0-404-16811-6*) AMS Pr.

DiGuiseppe, Raymond, jt. ed. see Bernard, Michael.

Diguiseppe, Sam. The Gray Lions. LC 97-68487. 176p. 1997. pap. 12.95 (*1-57087-346-1*) Stauker Ag.

Dihigo, Mario E., jt. auth. see Beguiristain, Rosa D.

Dihle, Albrecht. Greek & Latin Literature of the Roman Empire: From Augustus to Justinian. LC 93-11699. 640p. (C). (gr. 13). 1994. 90.00 (*0-415-06367-1*) Routledge.

— History of Greek Literature: From Homer to the Hellenistic Period. Krojzl, Clare, tr. LC 93-45284. 288p. (C). (gr. 13). 1994. 90.00 (*0-415-08620-5*, A9953) Routledge.

Dihn-Hoa, Nguyen. Vietnamese-English Dictionary. LC 66-17773. (VIE.). 584p. 1991. pap. 21.95 (*0-8048-1712-X*) Tuttle Pubng.

Dihoff, G. R., ed. Current Approaches to African Linguistics, Vol. 1. (Publications in African Languages & Linguistics). viii, 360p. 1983. pap. 90.80 (*90-70176-57-2*) Mouton.

Dihy. Merilainen Paleolimnology. 1983. 384.00 (*90-6193-766-3*, Pub. by Kluwer Academic) Kluwer Academic.

Dihy & Dokulil. Shallow Lakes. 1980. 221.00 (*90-6193-753-1*, Pub. by Kluwer Academic) Kluwer Academic.

Dihy & Forsberg, Curt. Forest Water Ecosystem. 1983. 240.00 (*90-6193-764-7*, Pub. by Kluwer Academic) Kluwer Academic.

DiIanni, Albert, jt. auth. see Griffin, James A.

DiIanni, Albert S. Religious Life As Adventure: Renewal, Refounding or Reform? LC 94-30399. 175p. (Orig.). 1994. pap. 9.95 (*0-8189-0716-9*) Alba.

***DiIonno, Mark.** A Guide to New Jersey's Revolutionary War Trail: For Families & History Buffs. LC 99-43167. (Illus.). 226p. 2000. pap. 19.00 (*0-8135-2770-8*); text 45.00 (*0-8135-2769-4*) Rutgers U Pr.

Diiorio, Frank C. SAS Applications Programming: A Gentle Introduction. 1997. pap. 40.95 (*0-534-49970-8*) Brooks-Cole.

DiIorio, Frank C. SAS Applications Programming: A Gentle Introduction. 704p. (C). 1991. pap. 51.95 (*0-534-92390-9*, BR56193) Thomson Learn.

Diiulio. The Truly Deviant Crime, Punishment & the Disadvantaged. 1994. 22.95 (*0-02-907884-9*) S&S Trade.

DiIulio, John, Jr. & Kettl, Donald F. Fine Print: The Contract with America, Devolution, & the Administrative Realities of American Federalism. 200p. (C). 1995. pap. 9.95 (*0-8157-8157-1*) Brookings.

DiIulio, John J. Governing Prisons: A Comparative Study of Correctional Management. 1990. pap. 18.95 (*0-02-907883-0*) Free Pr.

DiIulio, John J., Jr., ed. Courts, Corrections & the Constitution: The Impact of Judicial Intervention on Prisons & Jails. 352p. 1992. pap. text 24.95 (*0-19-507905-1*) OUP.
— Deregulating the Public Service: Can Government Be Improved? 308p. (C). 1994. 42.95 (*0-8157-1854-3*); pap. 18.95 (*0-8157-1853-5*) Brookings.
DiIulio, John J., Jr. & Nathan, Richard P., eds. Making Health Reform Work: The View from the States. 179p. (C). 1994. 34.95 (*0-8157-1852-7*) Brookings.
— Making Health Reform Work: The View from the States. 179p. (C). 1994. pap. 14.95 (*0-8157-1851-9*) Brookings.
DiIulio, John J., Jr., jt. auth. see Wilson, James Q.
DiIulio, John J., Jr., jt. ed. see Kettl, Donald F.
DiIulio, John J., Jr., jt. ed. see Thompson, Frank J.
Dijck, J. J. Van, see Van Dijck, J. J., ed.
Dijck, Jose van, see Van Dijck, Jose.
Dijck, Pitou Van, see Van Dijck, Pitou.
Dijin, Herman De, see De Dijin, Herman.
Dijk, A. Brikkenaar Van, see Maring, K. W. & Van Dijk, A. Brikkenaar, eds.
Dijk, C. G. Van, see Van Dijk, C. G.
Dijk, Frans Van, see Van Dijk, Frans.
Dijk, G. Van, see Van Dijk, G.
Dijk, Gert-Jan Van, see Van Dijk, Gert-Jan.
Dijk, H. A. Van, see Visser, H. & Van Dijk, H. A., eds.
***Dijk, Harrie F., et al.** Fate of Pesticides in the Atmosphere: Implications for Environmental Risk Assessment. LC 99-51826. 1999. write for info. (*0-7923-5994-1*) Kluwer Academic.
Dijk-Hemmes, Fokkelien Van, see Van Dijk-Hemmes, Fokkelien.
Dijk-Hemmes, Fokkelien Van, see Brenner, Athalya & Van Dijk-Hemmes, Fokkelien.
Dijk, Jouke Van, see Van Dijk, Jouke.
Dijk, Meine P. Van, see Van Dijk, Meine P., ed.
Dijk, Meine Pieter van, see Pieter van Dijk, Meine, ed.
Dijk, P. Van, see Bloed, Arie & Van Dijk, P., eds.
Dijk, P. Van, see Van Dijk, P.
Dijk, Robert Van, see Van Ham, Laurent & Van Dijk, Robert.
Dijk, T. A. Van, see Van Dijk, T. A., ed.
Dijk, Teun A. van. Ideology: A Multidisciplinary Approach LC 98-145596. x, 374 p. 1998. write for info. (*0-7619-5655-7*) Sage.
— Studies in the Pragmatics of Discourse. (Janua Linguarum, Series Major: No. 101). 332p. 1981. 65.40 (*90-279-3249-2*) Mouton.
Dijk, Teun A. Van, see Van Dijk, Teun A., ed.
Dijk, Teun A. Van, see Smitherman-Donaldson, Geneva, ed.
Dijk, Teun A. Van, see Smitherman-Donaldson, Geneva & Van Dijk, Teun A., eds.
Dijk, Teun A. Van, see Van Dijk, Teun A.
Dijk, Willibrord Christian van, see Rotzetter, Anton.
Dijkema, K. S. & Wolff, W. J., eds. Flora & Vegetation of the Wadden Sea Islands & Coastal Areas. (Illus.). 414p. 1983. pap. 128.00 (*90-6191-059-5*, Pub. by A A Balkema) Ashgate Pub Co.
Dijken, Suzan Van, see Van Dijken, Suzan.
Dijker, Barbara L., ed. A Guide to Writing Policies for Computer Sites. 72p. (Orig.). 1996. pap. text 7.50 (*1-880446-80-4*) USENIX Assn.
Dijkgraaf, R., et al, eds. The Moduli Space of Curves. LC 95-21641. (Progress in Mathematics Ser.: Vol. 129). 563p. 1995. 82.00 (*0-8176-3784-2*) Birkhauser.
Dijkgraff, R., et al. String Theory, Gauge Theory & Quantum Gravity, '93: Proceedings of the Spring School & Workshop. 352p. 1994. text 99.00 (*981-02-1806-0*) World Scientific Pub.
Dijkink, Gertjan. National Identity & Geopolitical Visions: Maps of Pride & Pain. (Illus.). 200p. (C). 1997. 75.00 (*0-415-13934-1*); pap. 24.99 (*0-415-13935-X*) Routledge.
Dijksma, A., et al, eds. Contributions to Operator Theory in Spaces with an Indefinite Metric: The Heinz Langer Anniversary Volume. LC 98-31196. (Operation Theory, Advances & Applications Ser.: Vol. 106). 432p. 1999. 130.00 (*3-7643-6003-8*) Birkhauser.
Dijksma, A., jt. auth. see Langer, Heinz.
Dijksma, Jan & Hoogendoorn, Martin. Netherlands. LC 92-40138. (European Financial Reporting Ser.). 255p. (C). (gr. 13). 1993. pap. 108.95 (*0-415-06316-7*, A9725) Thomson Learn.
Dijksman, F. J., et al, eds. IUTAM Symposium on Numerical Simulation of Non-Isothermal Flow of Viscoelastic Liquids: Proceedings of the IUTAM Symposium Held in Kerkrade, The Netherlands, 1-3 November 1993. LC 94-39298. (Fluid Mechanics & Its Applications Ser.: Vol. 28). 1995. text 110.50 (*0-7923-3262-8*) Kluwer Academic.
Dijksman, J. F., ed. Topics in Applied Mechanics: Integration of Theory & Applications in Applied Mechanics. LC 93-24466. 392p. (C). 1993. text 223.00 (*0-7923-2442-0*) Kluwer Academic.
Dijksman, J. F. & Nieuwstadt, F. T., eds. Integration of Theory & Applications in Applied Mechanics. (C). 1990. text 195.50 (*0-7923-0921-9*) Kluwer Academic.
Dijksterhuis, E. J., ed. Principal Works of Simon Stevin Vol. 1: General Introduction - Mechanism. v, 617p. 1955. text 211.00 (*90-265-0070-X*) Swets.
Dijksterhuis, Garmt B., ed. Multivariate Data Analysis in Sensory & Consumer Science. LC 97-61692. 309p. 1997. 100.00 (*0-917678-41-9*, 3312) Food & Nut Pr.
Dijkstra, Bouwe R. The Political Economy of Environmental Policy: A Public Choice Approach to Market Instruments. LC 98-53752. 400p. 1999. 100.00 (*1-85898-964-7*) E Elgar.
Dijkstra, Bram. Cubism, Stieglitz, & the Early Poetry of William Carlos Williams. 236p. 1989. pap. text 18.95 (*0-691-01345-4*, Pub. by Princeton U Pr) Cal Prin Full Svc.
— Evil Sisters: The Threat of Female Sexuality & the Cult of Manhood. LC 97-33585. 496p. 1998. pap. text 16.95 (*0-8050-5549-5*) H Holt & Co.
— Evil Sisters: The Threat of Female Sexuality & the Cult of Manhood. 480p. 1996. 30.00 (*0-394-56945-8*) Knopf.
— Evil Sisters: The Threat of Female Sexuality & the Cult of Manhood. LC 96-7448. 1996. write for info. (*0-614-14338-1*) Knopf.
— Georgia O'Keeffe & the Eros of Place. LC 98-3751. 272p. 1998. 29.95 (*0-691-01562-7*, Pub. by Princeton U Pr) Cal Prin Full Svc.
— Idols of Perversity: Fantasies of Feminine Evil in Fin-de-Siecle Culture. (Illus.). 480p. 1986. text 50.00 (*0-19-503779-0*) OUP.
— Idols of Perversity: Fantasies of Feminine Evil in Fin-de-Siecle Culture. (Illus.). 478p. 1988. pap. 21.50 (*0-19-505652-3*) OUP.
Dijkstra, D. Floating, Flowing, Flying: Pieter J. Zandbergen's Life As Innovator, Inspirator & Instigator in Nummerical Fluid Dynamics. LC 98-24603. 253p. 1998. write for info. (*0-7923-5128-2*) Kluwer Academic.
Dijkstra, E. W. Formal Development of Programs & Proofs. (Illus.). 224p. (C). 1990. text 37.95 (*0-201-17237-2*) Addison-Wesley.
Dijkstra, E. W. & Scholten, C. S. Predicate Calculus & Program Semantics. (Texts & Monographs in Computer Science). 224p. 1989. 71.95 (*0-387-96957-8*) Spr-Verlag.
Dijkstra, Edsger W. Selected Writings on Computing: A Personal Perspective. (Texts & Monographs in Computer Science). (Illus.). 272p. 1982. 89.95 (*0-387-90652-5*) Spr-Verlag.
Dijkstra, Edward W. A Discipline of Programming. (Illus.). 240p. 1976. text 65.20 (*0-13-215871-X*) P-H.
Dijkstra, Geske & Plantenga, Janneke. Gender & Economics: A European Perspective. LC 96-41437. 184p. (C). 1997. 65.00 (*0-415-15424-3*) Routledge.
Dijkstra, Geske & Plantenga, Janneke, eds. Gender & Economics: A European Perspective. LC 96-41437. 167p. (C). 1997. pap. 23.95 (*0-415-15425-1*) Routledge.
Dijkstra, Henk, ed. History of the Ancient & Medieval World, 12 vols. rev. ed. LC 95-35715. (YA). (gr. 8 up). 1996. lib. bdg. 657.07 (*0-7614-0351-5*) Marshall Cavendish.
Dijkstra, Jeanne & De Jager, C. P. Practical Plant Virology: Protocols & Exercises. LC 98-5845. (Illus.). 350p. 1998. pap. text 69.95 (*3-540-63759-1*) Spr-Verlag.
Dijkstra, Klaas. Life & Loyalty: A Study in the Socio-Religious Culture of Syria & Mesopotamia in the Graeco-Roman Period Based on Epigraphical Evidence. (Religions in the Graeco-Roman World Ser.: No. 128). 402p. 1995. 142.00 (*90-04-09996-4*) Brill Academic Pubs.
Dijkstra, Meindert, jt. ed. see Becking, Bob.
Dijkstra, S., et al. Research on Instruction: Design & Effects. LC 89-25682. 196p. 1990. 39.95 (*0-87778-221-0*) Educ Tech Pubns.
Dijkstra, Sanne, et al, eds. Instructional Design: International Perspectives, Vol. II. 1997. 135.00 (*0-8058-2868-0*); pap. 69.95 (*0-8058-2869-9*) L Erlbaum Assocs.
— Instructional Design: Solving Instructional Design Problems, Vol. II. LC 96-53459. 350p. 1997. pap. 49.95 (*0-8058-1398-5*); text 99.95 (*0-8058-1397-7*) L Erlbaum Assocs.
— Instructional Design: Theory, Research, & Models. LC 96-53459. 424p. 1997. text 89.95 (*0-8058-1399-3*) L Erlbaum Assocs.
— Instructional Design: Theory, Research, & Models, Vol. I. LC 96-53459. 350p. 1997. pap. 49.95 (*0-8058-1400-0*) L Erlbaum Assocs.
— Instructional Models in Computer-Based Learning Environments. LC 92-41419. (NATO ASI Series F: Computer & Systems Sciences, Special Programme AET: Vol. 104). 1992. 139.95 (*0-387-56159-5*) Spr-Verlag.
Dijkstra, T. K., ed. On Model Uncertainty & Its Statistical Implications. (Lecture Notes in Economics & Mathematical Systems Ser.: Vol. 307). 138p. 1988. 28.40 (*0-387-19367-7*) Spr-Verlag.
Dijkstra, Tjalling. Trading the Fruits of the Land. LC 98-141816. (African Studies Centre Leiden: Vol. 1). 272p. 1998. pap. 42.95 (*1-84014-353-3*, Pub. by Ashgate Pub) Ashgate Pub Co.
Dijkstra, Ton & De Smedt, Koenrad, eds. Computational Psycholinguistics: AI & Connectionist Models of Human Language Processing. 288p. 1996. 89.95 (*0-7484-0465-1*); pap. 34.95 (*0-7484-0466-X*) Taylor & Francis.
***Dijkzeul, Dennis.** Unops: Reforming for Results in the United Nations System. LC 99-86724. 2000. text 75.00 (*0-312-23223-3*) St Martin.
Dijkzeul, Lieneke. A Tiger under My Bed! Van Deventer, Eric, tr. from DUT. LC 97-23392. 25p. (J). 1998. 10.95 (*1-57379-069-9*, K1007) High-Scope.
Dijkzeut. The Management of Multiliberal Organizations, Vol. 26, NLSP. LC 96-52607. 1997. 94.00 (*90-411-0356-2*) Kluwer Law Intl.
Dijon, Jon. Who Is Robin? LC 93-84590. 248p. 1993. 21.95 (*0-938539-77-9*) Newmark Pub.
DiJoseph, John. Jacques Maritain & the Moral Foundation of Democracy. 196p. 1996. pap. text 23.95 (*0-8476-8247-1*); lib. bdg. 55.50 (*0-8476-8246-3*) Rowman.
Dijs, Bertha Van der, see Lechin, Fuad & Van der Dijs, Bertha, eds.
Dijs, Carla. Are You My Mommy? LC 90-216592. (Illus.). 12p. (J). (ps). 1990. 6.95 (*0-671-70226-2*) Litle Simon.
— Boy Who Cried Wolf. (My First Book of Fables Ser.: Vol. 4). (Illus.). 10p. (J). (ps-2). 1997. 5.99 (*0-689-81483-6*) Litle Simon.
— Daddy, Would You Love Me If . . .? LC 96-150685. (Illus.). 14p. (J). (ps-k). 1996. 8.99 (*0-689-80812-7*) Litle Simon.
— The Little Red Hen, Vol. 2. (My First Book of Fables Ser.). (Illus.). 10p. (J). (ps-2). 1997. 5.99 (*0-689-81481-X*) Litle Simon.
— Mommy, Would You Love Me If . . .? LC 96-147712. (Illus.). 14p. (J). (ps-k). 1996. 8.99 (*0-689-80813-5*) Litle Simon.
— Runaway Kitten. 16p. 1999. 8.99 (*0-85953-669-6*) Childs Play.
***Dijs, Carla.** Snail's Big Surprise. 1999. 8.99 (*0-85953-718-8*) Childs Play.
Dijs, Carla. Tortoise & the Hare. (My First Book of Fables Ser.: Vol. 3). (Illus.). 10p. (J). (ps-2). 1997. 5.99 (*0-689-81482-8*) Litle Simon.
***Dijs, Carla.** Truck One: On Safari in Africa, Europe A, Australia, The Poles, 4. 1999. 12.99 (*0-85953-830-3*) Childs Play.
— Truck Two: On Safari in North America, South America, Europe B, Asia, 4. 1999. 12.99 (*0-85953-831-1*) Childs Play.
Dijs, Carla. Up Pop the Monsters 1 2 3! A Pop-Up Counting Book. (Illus.). 22p. (J). (ps-k). 1996. 8.95 (*0-590-84762-7*, Cartwheel) Scholastic Inc.
— Who Loves You, Little Beetle? (Flap Bks.). (Illus.). (J). 1997. 8.99 (*0-85953-961-X*) Childs Play.
— Who's Afraid? A Pop-Up Counting Book. LC 95-78339. (Illus.). 89p. (J). (ps-1). 1995. 9.95 (*0-8050-4398-5*, B Martin BYR) H Holt & Co.
Dijs, Carla & Aesop. Lion & the Mouse, Vol. 1. (My First Book of Fables Ser.). (Illus.). 10p. (J). (ps-2). 1997. 5.99 (*0-689-81480-1*) Litle Simon.
Dijs, Carla & Moerbeek, Kees. Bee Says Buzz. 9p. (J). (gr. 3 up). 1990. 9.99 (*0-85953-222-4*) Childs Play.
— Hiding Places. 9p. (J). (gr. 4 up). 1990. 9.99 (*0-85953-223-2*) Childs Play.
— Let's Play. 9p. (J). (gr. 3 up). 1990. 9.99 (*0-85953-224-0*) Childs Play.
Dijstelberge, Paul & Noordegraaf, Leo. Plague & Print in the Netherlands: A Short-Title Catalogue of Publications in the University Library of Amsterdam. LC 98-163788. 360p. 1997. pap. 60.00 (*90-5235-126-0*, Pub. by Erasmus Pub) Balogh.
Dik & Gunsser. Diagnostic Radiology of the Horse Pt. 2: Diseases of the Hind Limb, Vol. 2. (Illus.). 148p. 1989. text 165.00 (*0-7216-2959-8*, W B Saunders Co) Harcrt Hlth Sci Grp.
— Diagnostic Radiology of the Horse Pt. 3: Diseases of the Head, Neck & Throat, Vol. 3. (Illus.). 172p. 1990. text 176.00 (*0-7216-3448-6*, W B Saunders Co) Harcrt Hlth Sci Grp.
Dik, Helma. Word Order in Ancient Greek: A Pragmatic Account of Word Order Variation in Herodotus. (Amsterdam Studies in Classical Philology: Vol. 5). 304p. 1995. lib. bdg. 90.00 (*90-5063-457-5*, Pub. by Gieben) J Benjamins Pubng Co.
Dik, Simon. Functional Grammar. 3rd ed. 230p. 1983. pap. 44.65 (*90-70176-42-4*) Mouton.
Dik, Simon & Conolly, John, eds. Functional Grammar & the Computer. (Functional Grammar Ser.). viii, 322p. (Orig.). (C). 1989. pap. 73.10 (*90-6765-433-7*) Mouton.
Dik, Simon C. Functional Grammar in Prolog: An Integrated Implementation for English, French & Dutch. LC 91-45020. (Natural Language Processing Ser.: No. 2). viii, 267p. (C). 1992. lib. bdg. 90.80 (*3-11-012979-5*) Mouton.
— The Theory of Functional Grammar. Hengeveld, Kees, ed. 1997. boxed set 175.00 (*3-11-015539-7*) Mouton.
— The Theory of Functional Grammar, Pt. 1. (Functional Grammar Ser.: No. 9). iv, 416p. 1989. pap. 29.95 (*90-6765-432-9*) Mouton.
— The Theory of Functional Grammar Pt. 1: The Structure of the Clause. 2nd rev. ed. Hengeveld, Kees, ed. LC 97-29611. (Functional Grammar Ser.). 509p. 1997. pap. text 49.00 (*3-11-015403-X*) Mouton.
— The Theory of Functional Grammar Pt. 2: Complex & Derived Constructions. 2nd ed. Hengeveld, Kees, ed. LC 97-29611. (Functional Grammar Ser.). 477p. 1997. pap. text 49.00 (*3-11-015405-6*) Mouton.
Dika, Vera. Games of Terror: Halloween, Friday the 13th & the Films of the Stalker Cycle. LC 88-46187. 160p. 1990. 32.50 (*0-8386-3364-1*) Fairleigh Dickinson.
Dikanov, Sergei A. Electron Spin Echo Envelope Modulation (ESEEM) Spectroscopy. 432p. 1992. lib. bdg. 210.00 (*0-8493-4224-4*, QC454) CRC Pr.
Dikansky, Nikolai, jt. auth. see Pestrikov, Dmitri.
Dikaois, Porphyrios, et al. Sotira: A Neolithie Settlement in Cyprus. (University Museum Monographs: No. 23). (Illus.). xiii, 252p. 1961. pap. 30.00 (*0-934718-15-6*) U Museum Pubns.
***Dikas, Susan U.** The New Spouse: For Better or for Worse. LC 99-93827. 1999. pap. 10.95 (*0-533-13160-X*) Vantage.
Dikau, Richard, et al, eds. Landslide Recognition: Identification, Movement & Causes. LC 95-52108. (Geomorphology Texts Ser.). 274p. 1996. 150.00 (*0-471-96477-8*) Wiley.
***Dikau, Richard & Saurer, Helmut.** GIS for Earth Surface Systems: Analysis & Modelling of the Natural Environment. (Illus.). vii, 197p. 1999. 45.00 (*3-443-01041-5*, Pub. by Gebruder Borntraeger) Balogh.
Dike, Catherine. Cane Curiosa: From Gun to Gadget. LC 83-670069. (Illus.). 378p. 1983. 68.00 (*2-85917-027-8*) Cane Curiosa.
— Cane Objet d'Art. (FRE., Illus.). 400p. 1988. 95.00 (*2-85917-074-X*) Cane Curiosa.
— Canes in the United States: Illustrated Mementoes of American History 1607-1953. LC 94-68262. (Illus.). 400p. 95.00 (*0-9642249-0-9*) Cane Curiosa.
— Walking Sticks. (Album Ser.: No. 256). (Illus.). 32p. 1989. pap. 25.00 (*0-7478-0079-0*, Pub. by Shire Pubns) Parkwest Pubns.
Dike, Donald A., ed. see Schwartz, Delmore.
Dike, Kenneth O. Trade & Politics in the Niger Delta, 1830-1885: An Introduction to the Economic & Political History of Nigeria. LC 81-13381. (Oxford Studies in African Affairs). 250p. 1982. reprint ed. lib. bdg. 65.00 (*0-313-23297-0*, DITR) Greenwood.
Dike, Phiner. Nigeria: World Development. (Illus.). 69p. (C). Date not set. pap. text 9.95 (*0-9643652-0-0*) Phiners Intl.
— Nigerian Cooking: Epicurean Delight of the Rich & Famous - Stay Slim & Healthy Forever! 2nd ed. (Stay Slim Forever Ser.). (Illus.). 90p. 1996. reprint ed. pap. 14.95 (*0-9643652-1-9*) Phiners Intl.
***Dike, Tina.** His Greatest Challenge. Schulman, Cory & Johnstone, Sandy, eds. 125p. (YA). (gr. 7-9). 2000. pap. 9.95 (*0-9642997-1-2*) Best Seller.
Dikeman, Karen J. & Kazandjian, Marta S. Communication & Swallowing Management of Tracheostomized & Ventilator Dependent Adults. (Illus.). 384p. (Orig.). (C). 1995. pap. text 59.95 (*1-56593-347-8*, 0645) Thomson Learn.
Diken, Bulent. Strangers, Ambivalence & Social Theory. LC 98-70994. (Research in Ethnic Relations Ser.). (Illus.). 360p. 1998. text 76.95 (*1-84014-522-6*, Pub. by Ashgate Pub) Ashgate Pub Co.
Dikengil, Angela & Kaye, Monique. Building Functional Social Skills: Group Activities for Adults. 211p. 1992. pap. text 51.50 (*0-7616-4280-3*) Commun Skill.
Dikengil, Angela T. Handbook of Home Health Care for the Speech-Language Pathologist. LC 98-9742. (Illus.). 210p. 1998. pap. 54.95 (*1-56593-969-7*, 1914) Thomson Learn.
Dikeogu, Rex N. Code of Life. LC 93-83441. 126p. (Orig.). 1993. 10.99 (*0-9636105-0-3*) Natty Pub.
Dikerson, John W., jt. auth. see Basu, Tapan K.
Diket, Read, jt. ed. see Kauppinen, Heta.
Diket, Susan O., jt. auth. see Yerger, Linda R.
Dikis, Eloise. The Twelve Powers of Animals. Wortman, Mary, ed. (Illus.). 44p. (J). (ps-5). 1989. spiral bd. 7.95 (*0-939339-06-4*) AFCOM Pub.
Dikken, Marcel den. Particles: On the Syntax of Verb-Particle, Triadic & Causative Constructions. (Oxford Studies in Comparative Syntax). (Illus.). 304p. 1995. text 65.00 (*0-19-509134-5*); pap. text 35.00 (*0-19-509135-3*) OUP.
Dikken, Marcel den, jt. ed. see Beukema, Frits.
Dikker, Scott, jt. auth. see Jim.
Dikkers, A. J. Geology in Petroleum Production. (Developments in Petroleum Science Ser.: No. 20). xiv,240p. 1985. 120.00 (*0-444-42450-4*) Elsevier.
Dikkers, Scott. I Feel Like a Grown-Up Now. (Jim's Journal Collection: No. 5). 1998. pap. text 7.95 (*0-8362-5184-9*) Andrews & McMeel.
— I Got Married If You Can Believe That: The Fourth Jim's Journal Collection. (Jim's Journal Collection). (Illus.). 128p. (Orig.). (C). 1996. pap. 7.95 (*0-8362-1029-8*) Andrews & McMeel.
***Dikkers, Scott.** Our Dumb Century: The Onion Presents One Hundred Years of Headlines from America's Finest New s Source. abr. ed. 1999. audio 12.00 (*0-694-52199-X*) HarperAudio.
Dikkers, Scott. The Pretty Good Jim's Journal Treasury: The Definitive Collection of Every Published Cartoon. 320p. 1999. pap. 14.95 (*0-7407-0007-3*) Andrews & McMeel.
Dikkers, Scott & Onion Writers Staff. Our Dumb Century: The Onion Presents 100 Years of Headlines from America's Finest News Source. (Illus.). 164p. 1999. pap. 16.00 (*0-609-80461-8*, Three Riv Pr) Crown Pub Group.
Dikkers, Scott & Pratt, Oswald T. You Are Worthless: Depressing Nuggets of Wisdom Sure to Ruin Your Day. LC 99-22170. 1999. pap. 9.95 (*0-7407-0025-1*) Andrews & McMeel.
***Dikkers, Scott & Siegel, Robert A., eds.** The Onion's Finest News Reporting, Vol. 1. LC 00-28650. 176p. 2000. pap. 16.00 (*0-609-80463-4*, HUM006000, Three Riv Pr) Crown Pub Group.
Dikobe, Modikwe. The Marabi Dance. (African Writers Ser.). 118p. (C). 1973. pap. 8.95 (*0-435-90124-9*, 90124) Heinemann.
Dikotter, Frank. The Discourse of Race in Modern China. LC 91-65999. 259p. (C). 1992. 45.00 (*0-8047-1994-2*) Stanford U Pr.
— Discourse of Race in Modern China. xiv, 252p. 1994. pap. 15.95 (*0-8047-2334-6*) Stanford U Pr.
***Dikotter, Frank.** Imperfect Conceptions: Medical Knowledge, Birth Defects & Eugenics in China. LC 98-15584. 288p. 1998. 27.50 (*0-231-11370-6*) Col U Pr.
Dikotter, Frank. Sex, Culture & Modernity in China. LC 94-46204. (Illus.). 200p. (C). 1995. text 22.50 (*0-8248-1676-5*) UH Pr.
Dikotter, Frank, ed. The Construction of Racial Identities in China & Japan. LC 96-44804. 192p. 1997. text 39.00 (*0-8248-1919-5*) UH Pr.
Dikranjan, D. & Tholen, W. Categorical Structure of Closure Operators with Applications to Topology, Algebra, & Discrete Mathematics. LC 95-39768. (Mathematics & Its Applications Ser.: No. 346). 356p. 1995. text 188.00 (*0-7923-3772-7*) Kluwer Academic.
Dikranjan, Dikran N. & Shakhmatov, Dmitri. Algebraic Structure of Pseudocompact Groups. LC 98-2683. (Memoirs of the American Mathematical Society Ser.: Vol. 133, No. 633). (Illus.). 83p. 1998. pap. 39.00 (*0-8218-0629-7*, MEMO/133/633) Am Math.
Diks, Cees. Nonlinear Time Series & Probability Measures. LC 99-16722. (Nonlinear Time Series & Chaos). (Illus.). 180p. 1998. 24.00 (*981-02-3505-4*) World Scientific Pub.

D

Dikshit, H. P. & Micchelli, C. A. Advances in Computational Mathematics. (Series on Approximations & Decomposition). 336p. 1994. text 95.00 (*981-02-1633-5*) World Scientific Pub.

Dikshit, K. R., et al, eds. India: Geomorphological Diversity: Essays in Honour of Professor A. B. Mukherji. (C). 1994. 68.00 (*81-7033-222-2*, Pub. by Rawat Pubns) S Asia.

Dikshit, R. D., ed. Geography of Electrons: Indian Context. (C). 1995. 49.50 (*81-7033-276-1*, Pub. by Rawat Pubns) S Asia.

Dikshit, Ramesh D., ed. Developments in Political Geography: A Century of Progress. LC 96-36650. 380p. (C). 1997. 39.95 (*0-8039-9357-9*, 93579) Sage.

Dikshit, Sudhakar, ed. see Balsekar, Ramesh S.

Dikshit, Sudhaker S., ed. see Maharaj, Nisargadatta.

Dikshitar, Ramachandra. Gupta Polity. (C). 1993. reprint ed. text 24.00 (*81-208-1024-4*, Pub. by Motilal Bnarsidass) S Asia.

— Mauryan Polity. (C). 1993. reprint ed. text 24.00 (*81-208-1023-6*, Pub. by Motilal Bnarsidass) S Asia.

Dikshitar, V. R. Lalita Cult. (C). 1991. reprint ed. 10.00 (*81-208-0919-X*, Pub. by Motilal Bnarsidass) S Asia.

— Purana Index, 3 vols., Set. (C). 1995. reprint ed. 110.00 (*0-614-13270-3*, Pub. by Motilal Bnarsidass) S Asia.

Dikshith, T. S. S. Toxicology of Pesticides in Animals. 264p. 1990. lib. bdg. 210.00 (*0-8493-6907-X*, RA1270) CRC Pr.

Diksic, Mirko. Radiopharmaceuticals & Brain Path Studied with Pet & Spect. Reba, Richard C., ed. 464p. 1990. lib. bdg. 249.95 (*0-8493-4863-3*, RC386) CRC Pr.

Dikstein, Grigori. And the Echo Will Reverberate. (RUS., Illus.). 238p. (Orig.). 1996. pap. 6.99 (*0-9643971-4-5*) Isometry.

Dikty, Alan S., ed. Buying Guide to Spirits: More Than 1000 Distilled Spirits & Fortified Wines Reviewed by the Beverage Testing Institute. 256p. 1999. pap. text 14.95 (*0-8069-2865-4*) Sterling.

***DIKU International Summer School on Partial Evaluation Staff.** Lectures on Partial Evaluation. Practice & Theory: DIKU 1998 International Summer School, Copenhagen, Denmark, July 1998. Hatcliff, John et al, eds. LC 99-52990. (Lecture Notes in Computer Science Ser.: Vol. 1706). ix, 433p. 1999. 49.95 (*3-540-66710-5*) Spr-Verlag.

Dil, Anwar, jt. auth. see Fuller, R. Buckminster.

Dil, Anwar S., ed. see Nida, Eugene A.

DiLalla, Lisabeth, jt. ed. see Dollinger, Stephanie M.

DiLalla, Lisabeth F., ed. see Clancy Dollinger, Stephanie M.

DiLallo, Kevin & Krumholtz, Jack. The Unofficial Gay Manual: Living the Lifestyle (or At Least Appearing To) LC 94-10769. (Illus.). 240p. 1994. pap. 13.95 (*0-385-47445-8*) Doubleday.

DiLascia, Paul. Windows++ Writing Reusable Windows Code in C++ LC 92-15872. 592p. (C). 1992. pap. 32.95 (*0-201-60891-X*) Addison-Wesley.

***Dilasser, Maurice.** The Symbols of the Church. Durken, Mary Cabrini et al, trs. from FRE. LC 99-31073. (Illus.). 167p. 1999. 39.95 (*0-8146-2538-X*) Liturgical Pr.

DiLauro, Stephen. Stephen Dilauros River Tales. 1996. 11.95 (*0-9651287-1-7*) Riv Tales Prod.

DiLavore, Phillip. The Bicycle: Force, Work & Energy. (Physics of Technology Ser.). 58p. 1975. 18.00 (*0-917853-69-5*, PT-2) Am Assn Physics.

Dilbert, Sheila, ed. Subject Index to Feature Articles & Special Reports in Encyclopedia Yearbooks: 1975-1991. 83p. (Orig.). 1992. pap. text 15.00 (*0-9625739-0-6*) Infodatafacts.

Dilcher, D. L., jt. ed. see Herendeen, P. S.

Dilcher, David L., ed. Botanical Society of America Membership Directory & Handbook, 1988. (Miscellaneous Series Publication: No. 165). (Orig.). 1988. 10.00 (*0-939201-03-8*) Botanical Soc.

Dilcher, K., tr. see Herman, J., et al.

Dilcher, Karl. Zeros of Bernoulli, Generalized Bernoulli, & Euler Polynomials. LC 88-6356. (Memoirs Ser.: No. 73/386). 94p. 1988. pap. 18.00 (*0-8218-2449-X*, MEMO/73/386) Am Math.

Dilcher, Karl, ed. Number Theory: Proceedings: Fourth Conference of the Canadian Number Theory Association, July 2-8, 1994, Dalhousie University, Halifax, Nova Scotia. LC 95-30722. (Canadian Mathematical Society Conference Proceedings Ser.: Vol. 15). 431p. 1995. pap. 89.00 (*0-8218-0312-3*, CMSAMS/15) Am Math.

Dilcher, Roman. Studies in Heraclitus. (Spudasmata Ser.: Vol. 56). (GER.). 206p. 1995. write for info. (*3-487-09986-1*) G Olms Pubs.

***Dilcock, Lesley.** Global Style: Exotic Elements in Contemporary Interiors. 2000. 27.50 (*1-84172-049-6*) Ryland Peters & Small.

Dilday, Russell H. I, II Kings. (Communicator's Commentary Ser.: Vol. 9). 512p. 22.99 (*0-8499-0414-5*) Word Pub.

Dilday, Russsell H. I, II Kings. (Mastering the Old & New Testament Ser.: Vol. 9). pap. 14.99 (*0-8499-3548-2*) Word Pub.

Dilea, Michael D., et al. Trauma to the Middle & Inner Ear. LC 96-50974. (Self-Instructional Package Ser.). (Illus.). 60p. (Orig.). 1997. pap. text 25.00 (*1-56772-054-4*, 5506300) AAO-HNS.

***Dilek, Yildirim.** Ophiolites & Oceanic Crust: New Insights from Field Studies & Ocean Drilling Program. LC 00-30831. (Special Paper Ser.). 2000. pap. write for info. (*0-8137-2349-3*) Geol Soc.

DiLella, Barbara. Jordan's Days Are Numbers. (Illus.). 32p. (J). (ps-k). 1994. pap. 5.95 (*1-55037-996-8*, Pub. by Annick) Firefly Bks Ltd.

Dilemma, Diana, pseud. Collecting Shrill Shadows. (Adult Poetry Ser.). (Illus.). 96p. (Orig.). 1987. pap. 6.95 (*0-915199-02-5*) Pen-Dec.

Dilendik, John R. Independent Mastery Testing System for Math Skills: Implementation Manual. Brett, Jennifer & Schenk, Brian, eds. 64p. 1988. pap. text 9.00 (*0-8428-9814-X*) Cambridge Bk.

Dilenschneider, Robert A. Briefing for Leaders: Communication As the Ultimate Exercise for Power. LC 92-52610. 288p. 1992. 23.00 (*0-88730-467-2*, HarpBusn) HarpInfo.

***Dilenschneider, Robert L.** Corporate Communications Bible. 2000. 24.95 (*1-893224-08-2*, New Millenn Pr) New Millenn Enter.

Dilenschneider, Robert L. Critical 14 Years of Your Professional Life. 208p. 1998. pap. 12.95 (*0-8065-2011-6*) Carol Pub Group.

— The Critical Fourteen Years of Your Professional Life: The Unsung Story. LC 97-621. (Illus.). 224p. 1998. pap. 19.95 (*1-55972-395-5*, Birch Ln Pr) Carol Pub Group.

— The Critical Second Phase of Your Professional Life: Keys to Success for Ages 35 to 50. LC 99-23287. 240p. 1999. 21.95 (*1-55972-509-5*, Birch Ln Pr) Carol Pub Group.

***Dilenschneider, Robert L.** Moses: C.E.O. 1999. text 19.95 (*1-893224-02-3*) New Millenn Enter.

Dilenschneider, Robert L. On Power. LC 93-5277. 256p. 1994. 25.00 (*0-88730-652-7*, HarpBusn) HarpInfo.

Dilenschneider, Robert L., ed. Dartnell's Public Relations Handbook. 4th ed. 465p. 1997. pap. 69.95 (*0-85013-313-0*) Dartnell Corp.

— Dartnell's Public Relations Handbook. 4th rev. ed. (Illus.). 465p. 1996. 69.95 (*0-85013-237-1*) Dartnell Corp.

***Dileo, Cheryl, ed.** Music Therapy & Medicine: Theoretical & Clinical Approaches. 1999. write for info. (*1-884914-00-4*) Amer Music Therapy.

DiLeo, Dale. Enhancing the Lives of Adults with Disabilities: An Orientation Manual. 2nd rev. ed. LC 93-61405. 104p. 1993. pap. 20.00 (*1-883302-02-1*) Trning Res.

— Reach for the Dream! Developing Individual Service Plans for Persons with Disabilities. 2nd ed. LC 95-119994. 50p. 1994. pap. 20.00 (*1-883302-01-3*) Trning Res.

— Trainer's Guide: For Enhancing the Lives of Adults with Disabilities. 2nd rev. ed. LC 93-61404. 112p. 1993. pap. 20.00 (*1-883302-04-8*) Trning Res.

DiLeo, Dale & Langton, Dawn. Get the Marketing Edge! A Job Developer's Toolkit for People with Disabilities. LC 93-60181. (Illus.). 131p. (Orig.). 1993. pap. 39.00 (*1-883302-00-5*) Trning Res.

DiLeo, Dale & Langton, Dawn, eds. Facing the Future: Best Practices in Supported Employment. unabridged ed. LC 96-24537. 131p. (Orig.). 1996. pap. 30.00 (*1-883302-09-9*) Trning Res.

DiLeo, Dale, et al. Natural Supports in Action: Strategies to Facilitate Employer Supports of Workers with Disabilities. LC 95-36639. 81p. (Orig.). 1995. pap. 25.00 (*1-883302-10-2*) Trning Res.

DiLeo, Dale, jt. auth. see Hagner, David.

DiLeo, David L. George Ball, Vietnam & the Rethinking of Containment. LC 90-12641. (Illus.). xxii, 265p. 1991. pap. 19.95 (*0-8078-4297-4*) U of NC Pr.

Dileo, Domenica, et al, eds. Curraggia: Writing by Women of Italian Descent. LC 99-208856. 400p. 1998. pap. write for info. (*0-88961-231-5*) Womens Pr.

Dileo, Frank. Euros. 10th ed. 1997. 16.95 (*3-86187-101-7*) LPC InBook.

DiLeo, John. And You Thought You Knew Classic Movies: 200 Quizzes for Golden Age Movie Lovers. LC 98-41595. 1999. pap. 13.95 (*0-312-19966-X*) St Martin.

DiLeo, Joseph. Child Development: Analysis & Synthesis. 192p. 1996. pap. 23.95 (*0-87630-834-5*) Brunner-Mazel.

— Young Children & Their Drawings. 384p. 1996. pap. text 29.95 (*0-87630-833-7*) Brunner-Mazel.

DiLeo, Joseph H. Children's Drawings As Diagnostic Aids. LC 73-79882. (Illus.). 240p. 1988. reprint ed. pap. text 23.95 (*0-87630-249-5*) Brunner-Mazel.

— Interpreting Children's Drawings. LC 83-2516. (Illus.). 240p. 1983. pap. text 23.95 (*0-87630-331-9*) Brunner-Mazel.

DiLeo, Vincent. Street Smart Estate Planning: A Complete Family Guide to Understanding Living Trusts, Probate, & How to Reduce or Eliminate Estate Taxes. Church, Paula, ed. (Illus.). 120p. (Orig.). 1993. pap. 19.95 (*1-880037-49-1*) Info Plus CA.

DiLeo, Virginia E. Exposing Drug Addiction in the Handwriting of Adolescents & Young Adults. 94p. 1992. pap. text 19.95 (*0-9633969-0-0*) Char Profile.

Dileonardo, Christopher. Methods & Principles in Physical Geology: A Laboratory Manual. 205p. 1993. pap., lab manual ed. 33.27 (*0-9649253-0-3*) Magellan Press.

Diles, Dave, jt. auth. see McCartney, Bill.

***Dilevko, Juris.** Unobtrusive Evaluation of Reference Service & Individual Responsibility: The Canadian Experience. LC 99-58739. (Contemporary Studies in Information Management, Policy & Services). 2000. pap. write for info. (*1-56750-507-4*) Ablx Pub.

— Unobtrusive Evaluation of Reference Service & Individual Responsibility: The Canadian Experience. 2000. write for info. (*1-56750-506-6*) Greenwood.

Dilg, Mary. Race & Culture in the Classroom: Teaching & Learning Through Multicultural Education. LC 98-55473. 6. 144p. 1999. text 40.00 (*0-8077-3823-9*) Tchrs Coll.

Dilg, Mary. Race & Culture in the Classroom: Teaching & Learning Through Multicultural Education. LC 98-55473. (Multicultural Education Ser.). 144p. 1999. pap. text 17.95 (*0-8077-3822-0*) Tchrs Coll.

Dilgard, David. Buildings of Early Everett: A Pictorial Survey of the Architecture of the Everett Boom, 1891-1894. (Illus.). 105p. 1994. pap. 16.95 (*1-881147-12-6*) Lowell Print.

— Dark Deeds. 1992. pap. 5.95 (*1-881147-01-0*) Lowell Print.

— Everett Chronology. 40p. 1992. pap. 5.95 (*1-881147-03-7*) Lowell Print.

Dilger, Robert J. Neighborhood Politics: Residential Community Associations in American Governance. 220p. (C). 1992. text 45.00 (*0-8147-1847-7*) NYU Pr.

Dilger, Robert J. & Witt, Tom S. West Virginia in the 1990s: Opportunities for Economic Progress. (Illus.). 347p. (C). 1993. pap. 13.00 (*0-937058-31-9*) West Va U Pr.

Dilherr, Johann M. & Harsdorffer, Georg P. Drei-Standige Sonn - & Festtag-Emblemata, Oder Sinnebilder. (GER.). 92p. 1994. write for info. (*3-487-09634-X*) G Olms Pubs.

Diliberto, Gioia. A Useful Woman: The Early Life of Jane Addams. LC 98-31853. 320p. 1999. 24.50 (*0-684-85365-5*) S&S Trade.

Diliberto, Ken, jt. auth. see Clark, Franklin.

Diligensky, G. Russia on the Threshold of an Uncertain Future. 249p. (C). 1995. lib. bdg. 115.00 (*1-56072-214-2*) Nova Sci Pubs.

Dilima, Sara N. & Eutsey, Dwayne E. Cardiovascular Patient Education Resource Manual. LC 97-30422. 1997. (*0-8342-1037-1*, 10371) Aspen Pub.

Dilima, Sara N., et al. Health Facilities Risk Management Forms, Checklists & Guidelines. LC 98-42526. 1998. 189.00 (*0-8342-1099-1*) Aspen Pub.

Dilima, Sara N., jt. auth. see Niemeyer, Suzanne.

Dilingham, Nancy. New Ground. LC 98-8790. 159p. 1998. pap. 9.95 (*1-56664-134-9*) WorldComm.

Dilip, Kadodwala. Holi. LC 96-42308. (World of Holidays Ser.). (Illus.). 32p. (J). 1997. lib. bdg. 22.83 (*0-8172-4610-X*) Raintree Steck-V.

Dilisio, ed. Human Geography & Global Understanding. (C). 1998. text. write for info. (*0-321-01210-0*) Addson-Wesley Educ.

Dilke, Annabel. Present from the Past. 240p. 1994. 23.95 (*0-233-98800-9*, Pub. by Andre Deutsch) Trafalgar.

Dilke, Emilia F. Book of the Spiritual Life. LC 70-37689. (Illus.). reprint ed. 39.50 (*0-404-56743-6*) AMS Pr.

Dilke, O. A. Greek & Roman Maps. LC 97-51607. (Illus.). 240p. 1998. reprint ed. pap. text 15.95 (*0-8018-5897-6*) Johns Hopkins.

— Mathematics & Measurement. (Reading the Past Ser.: Vol. 2). (Orig.). (C). 1987. pap. 13.95 (*0-520-06072-5*, Pub. by U CA Pr) Cal Prin Full Svc.

— The Roman Land Surveyors: An Introduction to the Agrimensores. (Illus.). 260p. 1993. pap. 60.00 (*90-256-1000-5*, Pub. by AM Hakkert) BookLink Distributors.

Dilke, O. A., ed. Lucan: De Bello Civili VII. (Bristol Latin Texts Ser.). (LAT.). 192p. 1978. reprint ed. 25.95 (*0-906515-04-1*, Pub. by Brist Class Pr) Focus Pub-R Pullins.

Dilke, O. A., jt. ed. see Connor, W. R.

Dilks, David, jt. ed. see Erickson, John.

Dill. Berkeley House Catering. (DF - Computer Applications Ser.). 1990. mass mkt. 18.95 (*0-538-60276-7*) S-W Pub.

— DOS 6.0: Quick Course. (DF - Computer Applications Ser.). 1994. mass mkt. 17.95 (*0-538-63492-8*) S-W Pub.

— Quattro Pro 6.O for Windows: Quick Course. (Quick Course Ser.). 192p. 1995. mass mkt. 15.95 (*0-538-65043-5*) S-W Pub.

— Quattro Pro 6.O for Windows: Standard Course. (DF - Computer Applications Ser.). 1995. mass mkt. 34.95 (*0-538-63946-6*) S-W Pub.

— A Quick Guide to Basic. (DF - Computer Applications Ser.). 1994. mass mkt. 19.95 (*0-538-62924-X*) S-W Pub.

— A Quick Guide to DOS. (DF - Computer Applications Ser.). 1992. mass mkt. 19.95 (*0-538-61778-0*) S-W Pub.

Dill, Barbara E., jt. auth. see H. W. Wilson Company.

Dill, Alonzo T. Carter Braxton, Virginia Signer: A Conservative in Revolt. LC 83-6513. (Illus.). 306p. (Orig.). 1983. pap. text 26.00 (*0-8191-3224-1*); lib. bdg. 58.00 (*0-8191-3223-3*) U Pr of Amer.

***Dill, Ann E. P.** Managing to Care: Case Management & Service System Reform. (Social Institutions & Social Change Ser.). 176p. 2000. pap. text 18.95 (*0-202-30612-7*); lib. bdg. 37.95 (*0-202-30611-9*) Aldine de Gruyter.

Dill, Barbara. At What Price? Privacy, Libel, & Freedom of the Press. 1993. pap. 9.95 (*0-87078-179-0*) Century Foundation.

Dill, Barbara & London, Martin. At What Price? Privacy, Libel, & Freedom of the Press. LC 93-2350. (Perspectives on the News Ser.). 1993. pap. 9.95 (*0-87078-356-4*) Century Foundation.

Dill, Bayard. Reminiscences of an Islander. 57p. (C). 1989. text 40.00 (*1-872795-19-6*, Pub. by Pentland Pr) St Mut.

Dill, Bonnie T. Across the Boundaries of Race & Class: An Exploration of Work & Family among Black Female Domestic Servamts. LC 93-6019. 2p. 1993. text 53.00 (*0-8153-1542-2*) Garland.

Dill, Bonnie T., jt. ed. see Zinn, Maxine B.

Dill, C. L. Early Peoples of North Dakota. 2nd rev. ed. Orig. Title: Early Peoples of North Dakota (Before 1858). (Illus.). 68p. 1990. pap. 6.00 (*1-891419-04-8*) State Hist ND.

Dill, Charles William. Monstrous Opera: Rameau & the Tragic Tradition. LC 97-31073. 240p. 1998. text 39.95 (*0-691-04443-0*, Pub. by Princeton U Pr) Cal Prin Full Svc.

Dill, Clarence C. Where Water Falls. LC 73-140147. 276p. 1970. 7.95 (*0-614-16725-6*) Ye Galleon.

Dill, David D. & Sporn, Barbara, eds. Emerging Patterns of Social Demand & University Reform. LC 95-37004. (Issues in Higher Education Ser.: Vol. 7). 250p. 1995. 90.00 (*0-08-042564-X*, Pergamon Pr) Elsevier.

Dill, David L., ed. see CAV '94 Staff.

Dill, Edith P. Perceptive Winds: From Bergen Beach to the Backwoods Trail. (Illus.). 124p. (Orig.). 1995. pap. 7.95 (*1-884707-11-4*) Lifestyles.

***Dill, Gilbert S.** The William Dill Family & Relatives in America, 3 vols., Set. (Illus.). 1520p. 1998. 150.00 (*0-944619-48-7*) Gregath Pub Co.

Dill, Harry F. African American Inhabitants of Rapides Parish, Louisiana: 1 June - 4 September, 1870. LC 98-166799. 373p. 1998. pap. 29.00 (*0-7884-0928-X*, D345) Heritage Bk.

— The Underground Railroad & the Picayune Connection. LC 99-190567. 159p. 1998. pap. 18.50 (*0-7884-1057-1*, D346) Heritage Bk.

Dill, Harry F. & Simpson, William. Some Slaveholders & Their Slaves, Union Parish Louisiana, 1839-1865. vi, 195p. (Orig.). 1997. pap. 20.00 (*0-7884-0617-5*, D344) Heritage Bk.

Dill, J. F., ed. see American Society of Mechanical Engineers Staff.

Dill, James H. Sixteen Days at Mungol-li. 1993. 24.00 (*0-943099-11-0*) M & M Pr.

Dill, Judith D. Cooking Everyday with Judy. large type ed. 187p. (Orig.). 1995. 14.95 (*1-888090-00-6*) Judyco.

— Cooking for the Holidays with Judy. 228p. (Orig.). 1995. 16.95 (*1-888090-01-4*) Judyco.

Dill, Ken A., jt. ed. see Nall, Barry T.

Dill, Marshall, Jr. Germany: A Modern History. rev. ed. LC 60-13891. (History of the Modern World Ser.). (Illus.). 528p. 1961. text 42.50 (*0-472-07101-7*, 07101) U of Mich Pr.

Dill, Raylene. DOS 6: Quick Course. large type ed. 1995. 52.50 (*0-614-09570-0*, L-83783-00) Am Printing Hse.

— DOS 6.0 Easy Reference Guide. (DF - Computer Applications Ser.). 1994. mass mkt. 9.95 (*0-538-63623-8*) S-W Pub.

— Quattro Pro 6.O for Windows: Standard Course. large type ed. 1995. 108.50 (*0-614-09605-7*, L-83782-00) Am Printing Hse.

Dill, Rosalie J. Dill: Mathew Dill Genealogy, a Study of the Dill Family of Dillsburg, York Co., Penna., 1698-1935, Pt. III. (Illus.). 67p. 1997. reprint ed. pap. 14.00 (*0-8328-8302-6*); reprint ed. lib. bdg. 24.00 (*0-8328-8301-8*) Higginson Bk Co.

— Dill: Mathew Dill Genealogy: Study of the Dill Family of Dillsburg, York Co., Pa., 1698-1935, Pts. I & II. (Illus.). 1997. reprint ed. pap. 27.50 (*0-8328-8304-2*); reprint ed. lib. bdg. 37.50 (*0-8328-8303-4*) Higginson Bk Co.

Dill, S. Roman Society from Nero to Marcus Aurelius. 1973. 300.00 (*0-87968-059-8*) Gordon Pr.

— Roman Society in the Last Century of Western Empire. 1973. 300.00 (*0-87968-060-1*) Gordon Pr.

Dill, Tom & Austin, Ed. Spokane Portland & Seattle. LC 95-72014. (Illus.). 376p. 1997. 74.50 (*0-915713-30-6*) Pac Fast Mail.

Dill, Tom & Grande, Walter R. The Red Electrics: Southern Pacific's Oregon Interurban. Pacific Fast Mail Staff, ed. (Illus.). 136p. 1994. 39.50 (*0-915713-28-4*) Pac Fast Mail.

Dill, Tom, jt. auth. see Austin, Ed.

***Dill, Vicky Schreiber.** A Peaceable School. 114p. 1998. pap. 12.00 (*0-87367-810-9*) Phi Delta Kappa.

Dill, William R., ed. Running the American Corporation. LC 78-16922. 1978. 10.95 (*0-13-783894-8*); pap. 4.95 (*0-13-783886-7*) Am Assembly.

Dilla, Harriette M. Politics of Michigan, 1865-1878. (Columbia University. Studies in the Social Sciences: No. 118). reprint ed. 37.50 (*0-404-51118-X*) AMS Pr.

Dillabough, Jo-Anne, jt. auth. see Arnot, Madeleine.

Dillala, David. Personality Theory Notes. (Adaptable Courseware Ser.). 1997. 6.25 (*0-534-49768-3*) Brooks-Cole.

Dillane, Christina & Dusharme, Susan. The Wonderful World of "Whey Lovers" 160p. (Orig.). 1983. pap. text 6.95 (*0-936744-08-1*) Country Bazaar.

Dillard. Emissary. (Star Trek: Deep Space Nine Ser.: No. 1). 1993. per. 5.50 (*0-671-78958-9*, Pocket Books) PB.

***Dillard, Angela D.** Guess Who's Coming to Dinner Now? Multicultural Conversation in America. 2001. 26.95 (*0-8147-1939-2*) NYU Pr.

Dillard, Annie. An American Childhood. LC 87-45042. 272p. 1999. pap. 13.50 (*0-06-091518-8*, Perennial) HarperTrade.

— An Annie Dillard Reader. 464p. 1995. pap. 15.00 (*0-06-092660-0*, Perennial) HarperTrade.

— Encounters with Chinese Writers. LC 84-7322. 117p. 1985. pap. 14.95 (*0-8195-6156-8*, Wesleyan Univ Pr) U Pr of New Eng.

***Dillard, Annie.** For the Time Being. LC 98-36720. 203p. 1999. 22.00 (*0-375-40380-9*) Knopf.

Dillard, Annie. For the Time Being. LC 99-15672. (Core Ser.). 1999. pap. 30.00 (*0-7838-8671-3*, G K Hall Lrg Type) Mac Lib Ref.

***Dillard, Annie.** For the Time Being. 204p. 2000. pap. 12.00 (*0-375-70347-0*) Vin Bks.

Dillard, Annie. Holy the Firm. LC 77-6883. 80p. 1999. pap. 13.00 (*0-06-091543-9*, Perennial) HarperTrade.

— The Living: A Novel. LC 91-58376. 464p. 1999. pap. 14.00 (*0-06-092411-X*, Perennial) HarperTrade.

— The Living: A Novel. large type ed. LC 92-19488. 693p. 1992. 23.95 (*1-56054-500-3*) Thorndike Pr.

— The Living: A Novel. large type ed. LC 92-19488. 693p. 1993. pap. 15.95 (*1-56054-925-4*) Thorndike Pr.

***Dillard, Annie.** Living by Fiction. LC 81-47882. 192p. 2000. pap. 12.00 (*0-06-091544-7*, Perennial) HarperTrade.

Dillard, Annie. Modern American Memoirs. 464p. 1996. pap. 16.00 (*0-06-092763-1*) HarpC.

— Mornings Like This: Found Poems. 96p. 1996. pap. 11.00 (*0-06-092725-9*) HarpC.

***Dillard, Annie.** Pilgrim at Tinker Creek. 1999. 24.75 (*0-8446-6986-5*) Peter Smith.

— Pilgrim at Tinker Creek. LC 99-88723. (Famous Authors Ser.). 2000. 28.95 (*0-7862-2325-1*) Thorndike Pr.

D

An Asterisk (*) at the beginning of an entry indicates that the title is appearing for the first time.

Dillard, Annie. Pilgrim at Tinker Creek. anniversary ed. LC 98-29765. 304p. 1998. pap. 13.00 (*0-06-095302-0*) HarpC.
— Pilgrim at Tinker Creek. 1998. reprint ed. 41.95 (*1-56849-706-7*) Buccaneer Bks.
— Teaching a Stone to Talk: Expeditions & Encounters. LC 82-45720. 176p. 1999. pap. 13.00 (*0-06-091541-2*, Perennial) HarperTrade.
— Three by Annie Dillard: Pilgrim at Tinker Creek, an American Childhood, & the Writing Life. LC 90-55495. 624p. 1990. reprint ed. pap. 19.00 (*0-06-092064-5*, Perennial) HarperTrade.
— Tickets for a Prayer Wheel: Poems. LC 73-86759. (Breakthrough Bks.). 128p. 1974. reprint ed. 18.95 (*0-8262-0156-3*) U of Mo Pr.
— The Writing Life. LC 89-45034. 128p. 1999. reprint ed. pap. 11.00 (*0-06-091988-4*, Harp PBks) HarpC.
Dillard, Annie & Atwan, Robert, eds. The Best American Essays, 1988. 336p. 1988. 17.95 (*0-89919-729-9*, Pub. by Ticknor & Fields) HM.
Dillard, Annie, et al. Hollins Celebrating 150 Years of Achievement, Tradition & Vision: A Photographic Portrait of Hollins College. (Illus.). 88p. 1991. text 44.00 (*0-9630170-0-4*) Hollins Coll.
Dillard, Dudley D. The Economics of John Maynard Keynes: The Theory of a Monetary Economy. LC 82-9219. 364p. 1983. reprint ed. lib. bdg. 69.50 (*0-313-23628-3*, DIEK, Greenwood Pr) Greenwood.
***Dillard, Elsie.** Good Bed & Breakfast Guide. (Illus.). 627p. 2000. pap. 25.00 (*1-56554-791-8*) Pelican.
Dillard, Elsie & Causin, Susan. Bed & Breakfast in Ireland. 3rd expanded rev. ed. LC 98-21565. 288p. 1999. pap. 14.95 (*0-8118-2275-3*) Chronicle Bks.
***Dillard, Gary E.** Common Freshwater Algae of the United States: An Illustrated Key to the Genera (Excluding Diatoms) (Illus.). 173p. 1999. spiral bd. 35.00 (*3-443-50026-9*, Pub. by Gebruder Borntraeger) Balogh.
Dillard, Gary E. Freshwater Algae of the Southeastern United States Pt. 1: Chlorophyceae: Volvocales, Tetrasporales & Chlorococcales. (Bibliotheca Phycologica Ser.: Vol. 81). (Illus.). 278p. 1989. 78.00 (*3-443-60008-5*, Pub. by Gebruder Borntraeger) Balogh.
— Freshwater Algae of the Southeastern United States Pt. 2: Chlorophyceae: Ulotrichales, Microsporales, Cylindrocapsales, Sphaeropleales, Chaetophorales, Cladophorales, Schizogoniales, Siphonales & Oedogoniales. (Bibliotheca Phycologica Ser.: Vol. 83). (Illus.). vi, 248p. 1989. reprint ed. 70.00 (*3-443-60010-7*, Pub. by Gebruder Borntraeger) Balogh.
— Freshwater Algae of the Southeastern United States Pt. 3, Section 1: Chlorophyceae: Zygnematales: Zygnemataceae, Mesotaeniaceae & Desmidiaceae. (Bibliotheca Phycologica Ser.: Vol. 85). (Illus.). vi, 276p. 1990. 80.00 (*3-443-60012-3*, Pub. by Gebruder Borntraeger) Balogh.
— Freshwater Algae of the Southeastern United States Pt. 4, Section 2: Chlorophyceae: Zygnematales: Desmidiaceae. (Bibliotheca Phycologica Ser.: Vol. 89). (Illus.). vi, 310p. 1991. 77.00 (*3-443-60016-6*, Pub. by Gebruder Borntraeger) Balogh.
— Freshwater Algae of the Southeastern United States Pt. 5, Section 3: Chlorophyceae: Zygnematales: Desmidiaceae. (Bibliotheca Phycologica Ser.: Vol. 90). (Illus.). vi, 231p. 1991. 65.00 (*3-443-60017-4*, Pub. by Gebruder Borntraeger) Balogh.
— Freshwater Algae of the Southeastern United States Pt. 6, Section 4: Chlorophyceae: Zygnematales: Desmidiaceae. (Bibliotheca Phycologica Ser.: Vol. 93). (Illus.). 166p. 1993. 71.00 (*3-443-60020-4*, Pub. by Gebruder Borntraeger) Balogh.
***Dillard, Gary E.** Freshwater Algae of the Southeastern United States Pt. 7: Pigmented Euglenophyceae. (Bibliotheca Phycologica Ser.: Vol. 106). (Illus.). iv, 176p. 2000. 48.60 (*3-443-60033-6*, Pub. by Gebruder Borntraeger) Balogh.
Dillard, Gavin G. A Day For a Lay: An Anthology of Gay Poetry. 1999. 22.00 (*1-56980-134-7*) Barricade Bks.
— In the Flesh: Undress for Success. LC 97-30649. 304p. 1998. 23.95 (*1-56980-118-5*) Barricade Bks.
— The Naked Poet. LC 89-90911. (Illus.). 86p. (Orig.). (C). 1989. pap. 7.95 (*0-944050-02-6*) Bhakti.
— Pagan Love Songs. LC 87-71217. (Illus.). 94p. (Orig.). (C). 1987. pap. 7.95 (*0-944050-00-X*) Bhakti.
— Satyriasis: Portraits of the Artist As a Young Pan. (Illus.). 104p. (Orig.). (C). 1994. pap. text 14.95 (*0-944050-04-2*) Bhakti.
— Yellow Snow: And Other Poems. LC 91-78118. (Illus.). 105p. (Orig.). (C). 1993. pap. 14.95 (*0-944050-03-4*) Bhakti.
Dillard, Gavin Geoffrey. Between the Cracks: The Daedalus Anthology of Kinky Verse. LC 96-86478. (Illus.). 360p. (Orig.). 1997. pap. 18.95 (*1-881943-10-0*) Daedalus Pub.
Dillard, George M., jt. auth. see Dillard, Robin A.
Dillard, J. L. Black English: Its History & Usage in the United States. 1973. pap. 12.00 (*0-394-71872-0*, V872) Random.
— Black Names. Fishman, Joshua A., ed. (Contributions to the Sociology of Language Ser.: No. 13). 1976. pap. text 19.25 (*90-279-7602-3*) Mouton.
— A History of American English. (Linguistics Library). 255p. (C). 1992. text 59.95 (*0-582-05298-X*, 79204) Longman.
— Toward a Social History of American English. (Contributions to the Sociology of Language Ser.: No. 39). xii, 301p. 1985. 98.50 (*3-11-010584-5*) Mouton.
Dillard, J. L., ed. Perspectives on American English. (Contributions to the Sociology of Language Ser.: No. 29). 468p. 1980. 84.65 (*90-279-3367-7*) Mouton.
— Perspectives on Black English. (Contributions to the Sociology of Language Ser.: No. 4). 391p. 1975. text 46.15 (*90-279-7811-5*) Mouton.
Dillard, J. M. Bloodthirst. Stern, Dave, ed. (Star Trek Ser.: No. 37). 1990. mass mkt. 5.50 (*0-671-70876-7*) PB.
— Demons. (Star Trek Ser.: No. 30). 1990. mass mkt. 4.50 (*0-671-70877-5*) PB.
Dillard, J. M. First Contact. abr. ed. (Star Trek, The Next Generation Ser.). 1996. 18.00 (*0-671-57391-8*, Audioworks) S&S Trade.
Dillard, J. M. Generations. (Star Trek: The Next Generation Ser.). 1994. pap. 17.00 incl. audio (*0-671-51996-4*, Audioworks) PB.
— The Lost Years. Stern, David, ed. (Star Trek Giant Novel Ser.). 448p. (Orig.). 1990. reprint ed. mass mkt. 5.99 (*0-671-70795-7*) PB.
— Mindshadow. (Star Trek Ser.: No. 27). 1989. mass mkt. 5.50 (*0-671-70420-6*, Pocket Star Bks) PB.
— Possession. (Star Trek Next Generation Ser.: No. 40). 1996. per. 5.99 (*0-671-86485-8*, PB Trade Paper) PB.
— Recovery. Ryan, Kevin, ed. (Star Trek Ser.: No. 73). 288p. 1995. mass mkt. 5.50 (*0-671-88342-9*) PB.
Dillard, J. M. Star Trek: The Lost Years. abr. ed. 1989. 15.95 (*0-671-68632-1*, Audioworks) S&S Trade.
Dillard, J. M. Star Trek: Where No One Has Gone Before. 192p. 1996. pap. 25.00 (*0-671-00206-6*, Pocket Books) PB.
— Star Trek Federation Passport: A Mini Travel Guide & Star Trek Passport. 1996. per. 6.00 (*0-671-00317-8*) PB.
— Star Trek V: The Final Frontier. 1989. mass mkt. 4.50 (*0-671-68008-0*) PB.
— Star Trek Generations II. 1996. 20.00 (*0-614-20656-1*, PB Hardcover) PB.
— Star Trek Movie 7. (Star Trek Generations Ser.). 1995. mass mkt. 5.99 (*0-671-53753-9*) PB.
— Star Trek VI: The Undiscovered Country. Stern, Dave, ed. 320p. (Orig.). 1992. per. 5.50 (*0-671-75883-7*) PB.
Dillard, J. M. & Berman, Rick. Star Trek Insurrection: A Novel. (Star Trek Ser.). 295p. 1998. 22.00 (*0-671-02447-7*) PB.
Dillard, Jack. 'Tis the Day after Christmas: The Christmas Curmudgeon. LC 91-61929. (Illus.). 32p. 1991. pap. 2.95 (*1-56352-010-9*) Longstreet.
***Dillard, James.** Alternative Medicine for Dummies: Dillard,&J.M. abr. ed. 1998. audio 12.00 (*0-694-52065-9*, CPN10165) HarperAudio.
Dillard, James & Ziporyn, Terra. Alternative Medicine for Dummies. (For Dummies Ser.). 384p. 1998. pap. 19.99 (*0-7645-5109-4*) IDG Bks.
Dillard, J.M., jt. auth. see Eaves, John.
Dillard, John E., Jr., jt. auth. see Davis, Grant M.
Dillard, John M. & Reilley, Robert R. Systematic Interviewing Communication Skills for Professional Effectiveness: Communication Skills for Professional Effectiveness. 384p. (C). 1990. pap. text 38.20 (*0-675-20824-6*, Merrill Coll) P-H.
Dillard, Joseph, jt. auth. see Krippner, Stanley.
Dillard, Julian. The United States vs. Hip Hop Music. (Orig.). 1992. pap. 4.95 (*1-56411-027-3*) Untd Bros & Sis.
Dillard, Kathryn, jt. auth. see Breeden, Terri.
Dillard, Kristine, jt. auth. see Gibson, Kathleen.
Dillard, Miladie L. Food & Diet: Reports of Harmful & Unfavorable Effects Including Illness & Cancer: Index of New Information with Authors & Subjects. rev. ed. LC 94-31245. 171p. 1994. 47.50 (*0-7883-0232-9*); pap. 44.50 (*0-7883-0233-7*) ABBE Pubs Assn.
— Food Sweeteners - Aspartame & Its Adverse Reactions, Strange Symptoms, Illness Behavior & Controversy: Index of New Information with Authors & Subjects. rev. ed. 157p. 1994. 47.50 (*0-7883-0446-1*); pap. 44.50 (*0-7883-0447-X*) ABBE Pubs Assn.
Dillard, Peggy N., ed. see Bourne, Tom & George, Jeannette Clift.
***Dillard, Philip D. & Hall, Randal L., eds.** The Southern Albatross: Race & Ethnicity in the American South. 268p. (C). 1999. pap. 19.00 (*0-86554-691-6*) Mercer Univ Pr.
Dillard, Philip H. How Quaint the Ways of Paradox! An Annotated Gilbert & Sullivan Bibliography. LC 91-3763. 216p. 1991. 27.50 (*0-8108-2445-0*) Scarecrow.
— Sir Arthur Sullivan: A Resource Book. LC 96-10157. (Illus.). 424p. 1996. 49.50 (*0-8108-3157-0*) Scarecrow.
Dillard, R. H. Just Here, Just Now. LC 94-17830. 64p. 1994. pap. 8.95 (*0-8071-1920-2*); text 15.95 (*0-8071-1919-9*) La State U Pr.
— Omniphobia: Stories. LC 94-27047. 208p. 1995. 22.95 (*0-8071-1839-7*) La State U Pr.
Dillard, Raymond B. Faith in the Face of Apostasy: The Gospel According to Elijah & Elisha. LC 99-28026. (The Gospel According to the Old Testament Ser.). 184p. 1999. pap. 12.99 (*0-87552-650-0*) P & R Pubng.
— Second Chronicles. (Biblical Commentary Ser.: Vol. 15). 29.99 (*0-8499-0214-2*) Word Pub.
Dillard, Raymond B. & Longman, Tremper, III. Introduction to the Old Testament. LC 94-32446. 512p. 1994. 24.99 (*0-310-43250-2*) Zondervan.
Dillard, Richard H. The First Man on the Sun: A Novel. LC 82-18649. 295p. 1983. pap. 91.50 (*0-7837-8450-3*, 204925500010) Bks Demand.
Dillard, Robin A. & Dillard, George M. Detectability of Spread-Spectrum Signals. LC 88-34286. (Artech House Radar Library). (Illus.). 157p. 1989. reprint ed. pap. 48.70 (*0-7837-9691-9*, 206042100005) Bks Demand.
Dillard, Scott W., jt. ed. see Kiraly, Bela K.
Dillard, Stephen C., ed. see State Bar of Texas, Pattern Jury Charges Committee.
Dillard, Tom W. & Thwing, Valerie. Researching Arkansas History: A Beginner's Guide. (Illus.). 64p. 1980. pap. 6.00 (*0-914546-25-2*) Rose Pub.
Dillard, W. O. Clearburning: (For Felonies Compounded by the F. B. I. Etcetera) (Illus.). 350p. (Orig.). 1993. pap. 19.95 (*0-9627737-2-7*) Persimmon Pr MS.
Dillard, Walter S., jt. ed. see Kiraly, Bela K.
Dillard, William L. Biblical Ancestry Voyage: In Search of Black Characters & References. 244p. 1992. 19.95 (*0-9636422-1-9*); pap. 12.95 (*0-9636422-0-0*); pap. 6.95 (*0-9636422-2-7*) RaLa-VenRue.
Dillavou, Essel R., jt. auth. see Simpson, Laurence.
Dillaye, Frederic. La Theorie, la Pratique et l'art en Photographie Avec le Procede au Gelatino Bromure d'Argent. Bunnell, Peter C. & Sobieszek, Robert A., eds. LC 76-23053. (Sources of Modern Photography Ser.). (FRE., Illus.). 1979. reprint ed. lib. bdg. 38.95 (*0-405-09618-6*) Ayer.
Dillbeck, Sandy, jt. auth. see Cope, Sandy.
Dille, Barbara. Standard Schnauzer: AKC Rank #100. (Rare Breed Ser.). (Illus.). 96p. 1997. 19.95 (*0-7938-C756-5*, RX-106) TFH Pubns.
Dille, Carolyn & Belsinger, Susan. Classic Southwest Cooking: Over 200 Succulent Recipes Celebrating America's Great Regional Cuisine. (Illus.). 272p. 1996. 9.98 (*0-9643600-3-9*) Biscuit Bks.
— Herbs in the Kitchen: A Celebration of Flavor. LC 91-46686. (Illus.). 356p. 1992. 26.95 (*0-934026-73-4*) Interweave.
— The Onion Book: A Bounty of Culture, Cultivation, & Cuisine. (Illus.). 96p. 1996. pap. 9.95 (*1-883010-10-1*) Interweave.
Dille, Carolyn, jt. auth. see Belsinger, Susan.
Dille, Carolyn, jt. auth. see Nims, Cynthia C.
Dille, Ed. Aegis - Guardian of the Fleet: Official Strategy Guide. LC 94-66677. (Illus.). 400p. 1994. pap. 19.95 (*1-55958-625-7*) Prima Pub.
— Doom II: Official Strategy Guide. (Secrets of the Games Ser.). 240p. 1994. pap. 19.95 (*1-55958-711-3*) Prima Pub.
Dille, Ed. Harpoon 2: The Official Strategy Guide, Vol. 1. (Illus.). 288p. 1994. pap. 19.95 (*1-55958-457-2*) Prima Pub.
Dille, Ed. Heretic: The Official Strategy Guide. 1995. pap. text 19.95 (*0-7615-0035-9*) Prima Pub.
— Ogre Battle the March of the Black Queen: Official Power Play Guide. LC 95-70452. 1995. pap. 14.95 (*0-7615-0289-0*) Prima Pub.
— Panzer General: Official Strategy Guide. 1995. pap. 19.95 (*1-55958-727-X*) Prima Pub.
— War Craft: Orcs & Humans Official Secrets & Solutions. LC 95-68590. 96p. 1995. pap. text 9.95 (*0-7615-0143-6*) Prima Pub.
— WarCraft II: Tides of Darkness: The Official Strategy Guide. 256p. 1996. pap. 19.95 (*0-7615-0188-6*) Prima Pub.
— Warlords II Deluxe: The Official Strategy Guide. 336p. 1995. pap. text 19.95 (*0-7615-0254-8*) Prima Pub.
Dillehay, James. Overcoming the Seven Devils That Ruin Success. LC 93-94313. 72p. (Orig.). 1994. pap. 6.95 (*0-9629923-1-3*) Warm Snow.
Dillehay, Ronald, jt. auth. see Johns, Krista.
***Dillehay, Thomas D.** The Settlement of the Americas: A New Prehistory. LC 00-27572. (Illus.). 352p. 2000. 40.00 (*0-465-07668-8*, Pub. by Basic) HarpC.
Dillehay, Thomas D. & Meltzer, David J. The First Americans: Search & Research. 280p. 1991. lib. bdg. 69.95 (*0-8493-8818-X*, E61) CRC Pr.
Dillehay, Tom D. Monte Verde: A Late Pleistocene Settlement in Chile: A Paleoenvironment & Site Context, Vol. 1. LC 88-23947. (Series in Archaeological Inquiry). 336p. 1989. text 60.00 (*0-87474-350-8*) Smithsonian.
— Monte Verde: A Late Pleistocene Settlement in Chile: The Archaeological Context & Interpretation, Vol. 2. (Smithsonian Series in Archaeological Inquiry). (Illus.). 1080p. 1996. text 155.00 (*1-56098-680-8*) Smithsonian.
Dillehay, Tom D., ed. Tombs for the Living: Andean Mortuary Practices: a Symposium at Dumbarton Oaks, 12th & 13th October, 1991. LC 93-29342. 1995. 28.00 (*0-88402-220-X*) Dumbarton Oaks.
Dillen, F. & Verstraelen, L. Geometry & Topology of Submanifolds VI. 300p. 1994. text 91.00 (*981-02-1813-3*) World Scientific Pub.
Dillen, F., et al. Geometry & Topology of Submanifolds V. 360p. 1993. text 121.00 (*981-02-1535-5*) World Scientific Pub.
— Geometry & Topology of Submanifolds, VII - Differential Geometry in Honour of Professor Katsumi Nomizu. 300p. 1995. text 99.00 (*981-02-2195-9*) World Scientific Pub.
***Dillen, Franki & Verstraelen, Leopold.** Handbook of Differential Geometry. LC 99-88735. 1060p. 1999. write for info. (*0-444-82240-2*, North Holland) Elsevier.
***Dillen, Frederick G.** Fool. LC 99-23456. 312p. 1999. 23.95 (*1-56512-234-8*) Algonquin Bks.
Dillen, Frederick G. Hero: A Novel. LC 94-13981. 134p. 1994. 17.00 (*1-883642-19-1*) Steerforth Pr.
— Hero: A Novel. LC 94-13981. 134p. 1996. pap. 10.00 (*1-883642-44-2*) Steerforth Pr.
Dillen, Lailee B. Van, see Van Dillen, Lailee B.
Dillenbeck, A. L. & Dallenbach, K. M. Dallenbach: The Dallenbach Family in America, 1710-1935. (Illus.). 439p. 1993. reprint ed. pap. 67.50 (*0-8328-3291-X*); reprint ed. lib. bdg. 77.50 (*0-8328-3290-1*) Higginson Bk Co.
Dillenberger, Jane D. The Religious Art of Andy Warhol. LC 98-8483. (Illus.). 128p. 1998. 39.95 (*0-8264-1112-6*) Continuum.
Dillenberger, John. Images & Relics: Theological Perceptions & Visual Images in Sixteenth-Century Europe. (The Oxford Studies in Historical Theology). (Illus.). 264p. 1999. text 45.00 (*0-19-512172-4*) OUP.
— Protestant Thought & Natural Science. LC 88-23214. (C). 1988. pap. text 16.50 (*0-268-01575-9*) U of Notre Dame Pr.
— Protestant Thought & Natural Science: A Historical Interpretation. LC 77-7200. 310p. 1977. reprint ed. lib. bdg. 35.00 (*0-8371-9670-1*, DIPT, Greenwood Pr) Greenwood.
Dillenberger, John, ed. John Calvin: Selections from His Writings. LC 75-26875. (American Academy of Religion, Aids for the Study of Religion Ser.). 590p. 1975. reprint ed. pap. 19.95 (*0-89130-025-2*, 010302) OUP.
Dillenberger, John & Welch, Claude. Protestant Christianity: Interpreted Through Its Development. 2nd ed. 537p. (C). 1988. pap. text 32.20 (*0-02-329601-1*, Macmillan Coll) P-H.
Dillenberger, John, ed. see Luther, Martin.
Dillenbourg, P., ed. Collaborative Learning: Cognitive & Computational Approaches. LC 98-38305. 1999. write for info. (*0-08-043073-2*, Pergamon Pr) Elsevier.
Dillenburger, Karola, et al. Advances in Behaviour Analysis. 236p. 1998. pap. 24.95 (*1-900621-08-8*, Pub. by Univ Coll Dublin Pr) Dufour.
Dillenburger, Karola, jt. auth. see O'Hagan, Kieran.
Diller. Cultural Diversity: A Primer for the Human Services. LC 98-37384. (Counseling Ser.). 1998. text 29.95 (*0-534-35584-6*) Brooks-Cole.
Diller & Quail. Off We Go Piano Book of Poetry Pieces. 48p. 1986. pap. 4.95 (*0-7935-5106-4*, 50326770) H Leonard.
— Second Solo Book for Piano: New Edition. 40p. 1986. pap. 5.95 (*0-7935-2856-9*, 50333260) H Leonard.
Diller, A. First Pedal Studies for Piano Progressive Ex & Pieces. 24p. 1986. pap. 7.95 (*0-7935-1145-3*, 50327800) H Leonard.
— The Textual Tradition of Strabo's Geography. iv, 222p. (Orig.). 1975. pap. text 64.50 (*0-317-57966-5*, Pub. by AM Hakkert) Coronet Bks.
— Twenty Five First Grade Piano Pieces. 24p. 1986. pap. 7.95 (*0-7935-5175-7*, 50327710) H Leonard.
Diller, Angela & Quail. First Solo Book for Piano. rev. ed. 48p. 1986. pap. 5.95 (*0-7935-2855-0*, 50332880) H Leonard.
Diller, Ann. The Gender Question in Education: Theory, Pedagogy & Politics. (C). 1996. pap. 28.00 (*0-8133-2563-3*, Pub. by Westview) HarpC.
Diller, Antoni. LATEX Line by Line: Tips & Techniques for Document Processing. 2nd ed. LC 98-47326. 528p. 1999. pap. 49.99 (*0-471-97918-X*) Wiley.
— Z: An Introduction to Formal Methods. 2nd ed. LC 94-4943. 394p. 1994. pap. 90.00 (*0-471-93973-0*) Wiley.
Diller, Daniel C. Russia & the Independent States. LC 92-33273. 252p. (YA). 1993. pap. 36.95 (*0-87187-617-5*) Congr Quarterly.
— Russia & the Independent States. LC 92-33273. 481p. 1993. text 32.97 (*0-87187-862-3*) Congr Quarterly.
Diller, Daniel C. & Moore, John L., eds. The Middle East. 8th ed. LC 94-17492. 438p. (C). (gr. 11). 1995. pap. text 34.95 (*0-87187-999-9*) Congr Quarterly.
Diller, Daniel C. & Robertson, Stephen L. The Presidents, First Ladies, & Vice Presidents: White House Biographies, 1789-1997. LC 96-37389. 180p. (YA). (gr. 11). 1996. pap. text 29.95 (*1-56802-311-1*) Congr Quarterly.
Diller, Edward. A Mythic Journey: Gunter Grass's Tin Drum. LC 73-86402. 224p. reprint ed. pap. 69.50 (*0-608-13085-0*, 201951600013) Bks Demand.
Diller, Edward, jt. ed. see Wishard, Armin.
Diller, Elizabeth & Scofidio, Ricardo. Back to the Front: Tourisms of War. LC 93-43548. (Illus.). 330p. (Orig.). 1994. pap. 29.95 (*1-56898-014-0*) Princeton Arch.
— Flesh. LC 94-36648. (Illus.). 256p. (Orig.). 1995. pap. 34.95 (*1-878271-37-7*) Princeton Arch.
Diller, George T., ed. Robert De Boron: The Grail Trilogy: Joseph, Merlin, & Perceval, 2 vols. (Library of Medieval Literature: Vol. MLA73). 1500p. 165.00 (*0-8240-5099-1*) Garland.
Diller, Harriet. The Big Band Sound, Vol. 1. LC 94-70682. (Illus.). 32p. (J). (gr. k-4). 1996. 14.95 (*1-56397-129-1*) Boyds Mills Pr.
Diller, Harriett. The Faraway Drawer. LC 95-80774. (Illus.). 32p. (J). (ps-3). 1996. 14.95 (*1-56397-190-9*) Boyds Mills Pr.
Diller, Howard, jt. auth. see Smith, Jill.
Diller, J., ed. see Proof Theory Symposium Staff.
Diller, Janelle. For the Love of Gold. 219p. (Orig.). (YA). (gr. 6 up). 1996. pap. 7.99 (*0-88092-268-0*, 2680) Royal Fireworks.
***Diller, Janelle.** Grammar Notebook - Parts of Speech. 2000. write for info. (*1-57022-237-1*) ECS Lrn Systs.
— Grammar Notebook - Punctuation. 2000. write for info. (*1-57022-239-8*) ECS Lrn Systs.
— Grammar Notebook - Sentence Structure. 2000. write for info. (*1-57022-238-X*) ECS Lrn Systs.
Diller, Janelle, jt. auth. see Diller, Stephen.
Diller, Jerry V. Ancient Roots & Modern Meanings. LC 77-99196. 1978. 12.50 (*0-8197-0457-1*); pap. 7.95 (*0-8197-0460-1*) Bloch.
— Freud's Jewish Identity: A Case Study in the Impact of Ethnicity. LC 89-45621. 248p. 1991. 38.50 (*0-8386-3374-9*) Fairleigh Dickinson.
Diller, Kenneth R., jt. ed. see Arinc, Faruk.
Diller, Lawrence H. Running On Ritalin. LC 99-20452. 400p. 1999. pap. 12.95 (*0-553-37906-2*) Bantam.
Diller, Phoebe. Let's Have a Musical Rhythm Band. 32p. 1976. pap., student ed. 5.95 (*0-7390-0609-6*, 270) Alfred Pub.
Diller, Robert. Farm Ownership, Tenancy & Land Use in the Nebraska Community. Bruchey, Stuart, ed. LC 78-56629. (Management of Public Lands in the U. S. Ser.). 1979. reprint ed. lib. bdg. 19.95 (*0-405-11330-7*) Ayer.

D

An Asterisk (*) at the beginning of an entry indicates that the title is appearing for the first time.

Diller, Stanley. The Seasonal Variation of Interest Rates. (Occasional Papers: No. 108). 128p. 1970. reprint ed. 33.30 (*0-87014-205-4*) Natl Bur Econ Res.

Diller, Stephen & Diller, Janelle. How to Succeed with Your Own Construction Business. (Illus.). 336p. 1990. pap. 28.50 (*0-934041-59-8*) Craftsman.

Diller, Steve. Dogs & Their People: Choosing & Training the Best Dog for You. LC 98-7014. (Illus.). 256p. (J). 1999. 21.95 (*0-7868-6361-7*, Pub. by Hyperion) Time Warner.

***Diller, Steven.** Dog & Their People: Choosing & Training the Best Dog for you. 256p. 2000. pap. 12.95 (*0-7868-8540-8*, Pub. by Disney Pr) Time Warner.

Dillery, John. Xenophon & the History of His Times. LC 94-30021. 344p. (C). (gr. 13). 1995. 85.00 (*0-415-09139-X*, C0190) Routledge.

Dilley, Becki & Dilley, Keith. Special Delivery. large type ed. (Niagara Large Print Ser.). (Illus.). 217p. 1996. 29.50 (*0-7089-5835-4*) Ulverscroft.

Dilley, Becki, et al. Sixty Fingers, Sixty Toes: See How the Dilley Sextuplets Grow! LC 97-23087. (Illus.). 32p. (J). (ps-3). 1998. 15.95 (*0-8027-8613-8*); lib. bdg. 16.85 (*0-8027-8614-6*) Walker & Co.

Dilley, Clyde H. Photography & Philosophy of Wynn Bullock. LC 81-65881. (Illus.). 129p. 1984. 35.00 (*0-87982-042-X*) Art Alliance.

Dilley, David D. Haeger Potteries Through the Years. LC 97-146321. (Illus.). 376p. 1997. 39.95 (*0-89538-083-8*) L-W Inc.

Dilley, Frank B. Teacher Certification in Ohio & a Proposed Plan of Reconstruction. LC 73-176720. (Columbia University. Teachers College. Contributions to Education Ser.: No. 630). reprint ed. 37.50 (*0-404-55630-2*) AMS Pr.

Dilley, Frank B., ed. Philosophical Interactions with Parapsychology: The Major Writings of H. H. Price on Parapsychology & Survival. LC 95-8229. 270p. 1995. text 65.00 (*0-312-12607-7*) St Martin.

Dilley, James P. The Solar Family. rev. ed. Craddock, Betty K. & Tigner, Thomas E., eds. (Illus.). 471p. (C). 1996. pap. text 30.00 (*0-9647223-3-X*) Ross Pub OH.

Dilley, James W. & Marks, Robert, eds. The UCSF AIDS Health Project Guide to Counseling: Perspectives on Psychotherapy, Prevention, & Therapeutic Practice. LC 98-18757. (Psychology Ser.). 384p. 1998. pap. 29.95 (*0-7879-4194-8*) Jossey-Bass.

Dilley, James W., et al. Face to Face: A Guide to AIDS Counseling. LC 89-20217. 350p. 1995. pap. 16.95 (*0-89087-583-9*) Celestial Arts.

Dilley, Josiah. And I Thought I Knew How to Communicate. Sorenson, Don L., ed. (Illus.). 168p. (Orig.). 1985. pap. text 8.95 (*0-932796-17-6*) Ed Media Corp.

Dilley, Keith, jt. auth. see Dilley, Becki.

Dilley, Kimberly J. Busybodies, Meddlers & Snoops: The Female Hero in Contemporary Women's Mysteries, 166. LC 97-45670. (Contributions in Women's Studies: 166). 192p. 1998. 55.00 (*0-313-30330-4*, Greenwood Pr) Greenwood.

Dilley, Marjorie R. British Policy in Kenya Colony 1937. 2nd ed. 300p. 1966. 45.00 (*0-7146-1655-9*, Pub. by F Cass Pubs) Intl Spec Bk.

Dilley, Michael F. Galahad: A History of the 5307th Composite Unit (Provisional) 2nd ed. (World War II Monograph: Vol. 220). (Illus.). 50p. 1997. pap. 10.95 (*1-57638-090-4*, M220S) Merriam Pr.

— Galahad: A History of the 5307th Composite Unit (Provisional) 2nd rev. ed. (World War II Monograph: Vol. 220). (Illus.). 50p. 1997. 20.95 (*1-57638-091-2*, M220H) Merriam Pr.

Dilley, Michael F., jt. auth. see Zedric, Lance Q.

***Dilley, R. M., ed.** The Problem of Context: Perspectives from Social Anthropology & Elsewhere. LC 99-35007. (Methodology & History in Anthropology Ser.: Vol. 4). 242p. 1999. 59.95 (*1-57181-700-X*); pap. 19.50 (*1-57181-773-5*) Berghahn Bks.

Dilley, Romilda. Mrrarr & Me. (Illus.). 48p. 1982. 24.00 (*0-88014-062-3*) Mosaic Pr OH.

Dilley, Roy, ed. Contesting Markets: The Anthropology of Ideology, Discourse, & Practice. 336p. 1993. text 79.00 (*0-7486-0371-9*, Pub. by Edinburgh U Pr) Col U Pr.

Dilliard, Irving, ed. see Hand, Learned.

Dilligan, Mary, jt. auth. see Piper, Eloise.

Dilligan, Robert, ed. Joseph & His Brethren: Three Ladino Poems. Lazar, Moshe, tr. & intro. by. LC 90-60869. (Sephardic Classical Library). (HEB & LAD.). 320p. 1990. text 70.00 (*0-911437-55-X*) Labyrinthos.

Dilligan, Robert, ed. see Halevi, Yehudah.

Dilligan, Robert, jt. ed. see Lazar, Moshe.

Dilligan, Robert, ed. see Maimonides.

Dilligan, Robert J. Computing in the Web Age: A Web-Interactive Introduction. LC 98-34957. (Illus.). 352p. (C). 1998. 28.50 (*0-306-45972-8*, Plenum Trade) Perseus Pubng.

Dillin, John. The Kentucky Rifle. 7th ed. LC 74-3685. (Longrifle Ser.). 1992. 50.00 (*0-87387-072-7*) Shumway.

Dillin, William & Simeone, Frederick A. Posterior Cervical Spine Surgery. LC 97-31574. (Principles & Techniques in Spine Surgery Ser.). 256p. 1997. text 120.00 (*0-7817-1005-7*) Lppncott W & W.

Dillinbe. Protestant Christianity College. 1985. pap. 12.95 (*0-684-14719-X*) S&S Trade.

Dilling. Psychiatry. 1990. 23.95 (*0-387-51980-7*) Spr-Verlag.

Dilling, Carole & Claster, Barbara L. Female Psychology: A Partially Annotated Bibliography. 326p. 1985. pap. text 25.00 (*0-9616028-0-5*) NYCCWMH.

Dilling, Cynthia C. & Jones, Carl A. Bicyclists' Touring Companion for the San Juan Islands. 12p. 1995. 4.95 (*0-9646580-0-3*) Cycle San Juans.

Dilling, Elizabeth. The Jewish Religion: Its Influence Today. rev. ed. (Illus.). 261p. (C). 1991. pap. text 11.00 (*0-939482-45-2*, 0217, Noontide Pr) Legion Survival.

***Dilling, Elizabeth.** The Plot Against Christianity. 310p. 1998. pap. 15.00 (*0-944379-10-9*) CPA Bk Pub.

— The Plot Against Christianity. unabridged ed. 310p. 1970. reprint ed. pap. 20.00 (*0-945001-71-1*) GSG & Assocs.

Dilling, Elizabeth. The Roosevelt Red Record & Its Background. 1985. lib. bdg. 79.95 (*0-87700-654-7*) Revisionist Pr.

Dilling, Elizabeth K. The Red Network: A "Who's Who" & Handbook of Radicalism for Patriots. LC 76-46073. (Anti-Movements in America Ser.). 1977. reprint ed. lib. bdg. 30.95 (*0-405-09946-0*) Ayer.

Dillinger, Hig R. How to Pursue Athletic Financial Aid. (Illus.). 63p. (Orig.). 1996. pap. 7.95 (*0-9653641-0-0*) OSS Inc.

Dillinger, Jesse A. Reasonably Thin: The Spiritual Aspects of Over & Undereating. LC 98-16303. 288p. 1998. pap. 12.99 (*0-7852-7062-0*) Nelson.

Dillinger, T. Handbook of Asic Design. (Electrical Engineering & Electronics Ser.). Date not set. write for info. (*0-8247-9431-1*) Dekker.

Dillinger, Thomas E. VLSI Engineering. (Illus.). 832p. (C). 1987. text 78.80 (*0-13-942731-7*) P-H.

Dillinger, William. Decentralization & Its Implications for Urban Service Delivery. LC 94-5013. (Urban Management Program Ser.: Vol. 16). 50p. 1994. pap. 22.00 (*0-8213-2792-5*, 12792) World Bank.

— Urban Property Tax Reform: Guidelines & Recommendations. 64p. 1992. pap. 22.00 (*0-8213-2065-3*, 12065) World Bank.

Dillinger, William C., ed. A History of the Lower American River. rev. ed. (Illus.). 176p. (Orig.). 1991. pap. 4.50 (*1-887815-00-7*) Amer River Nat Hist.

Dillingham. Microeconomics. Date not set. pap. text. write for info. (*0-314-61511-3*) West Pub.

Dillingham, jt. auth. see Newton.

Dillingham, Alan E., et al. Microeconomics: Individual Choice & Its Consequences. 576p. (C). 1992. pap. write for info. (*0-205-13528-5*) Allyn.

Dillingham, Catherine K., jt. auth. see Newton, Lisa H.

Dillingham, George A. The Foundation of the Peabody Tradition. 196p. (C). 1989. lib. bdg. 39.00 (*0-8191-7249-9*) U Pr of Amer.

***Dillingham, Gerald L., ed.** Air Traffic Control: FAA's Modernization Investment Management Approach Could Be Strengthened. 53p. (C). 1999. pap. text 20.00 (*0-7881-8388-5*) DIANE Pub.

Dillingham, John. Ease-Cruiser Waypoint Planner. (Illus.). pap. 19.95 (*0-9633561-0-0*) Easy Cruiser.

Dillingham, Louise B. The Creative Imagination of Theophile Gautier: A Study in Literary Psychology. (Psychological Monographs General & Applied: Vol. 37). 1972. reprint ed. 47.00 (*0-8115-1436-6*) Periodicals Srv.

Dillingham, Nancy, ed. see Boone, Don, et al.

Dillingham, Rick. Fourteen Families in Pueblo Pottery. LC 93-28021. (Illus.). 289p. 1994. pap. 39.95 (*0-8263-1499-6*) U of NM Pr.

Dillingham, Rick & Elliott, Melinda. Acoma & Laguna Pottery. O'Donnell, Joan K., ed. (Illus.). 256p. 1992. pap. 29.95 (*0-933452-32-2*) Schol Am Res.

***Dillingham, Ruth A.** Massachusetts Basic Practice Manual: Buying & Selling a Home. (Massachusetts Basic Practice Ser.). 150p. 1999. pap. write for info. (*1-57589-162-X*) Mass CLE.

***Dillingham, Timothy R.** Textbook of Military Medicine Surgical Combat Casualty Care Pt. 4: Rehabilitation of Injured Combatant, Vol.1. 478p. 2000. boxed set 45.00 (*0-16-059128-7*) USGPO.

Dillingham, William B. Melville & His Circle, 1877-1891. LC 96-767. 1996. 29.95 (*0-8203-1856-6*) U of Ga Pr.

— Melville's Later Novels. LC 85-1192. 448p. 1986. 40.00 (*0-8203-0799-8*) U of Ga Pr.

Dillingham, William B., jt. auth. see Cohen, Hennig.

Dillingham, William B., jt. auth. see Watkins, Floyd C.

Dillingham, William P. & Bennet, William S. Abstract of Reports of the Immigration Commission, with Conclusions & Recommendations & Views of the Minority Vol. 1: A Study of the Reports of the Immigration Commission, 1907-1910, 2 vols. 70.50 (*0-317-28306-5*, 19705) Ayer.

***Dillion, Dennis A.** Bitter Truth is Better Than Sweet Falsehood. Grainger, Karen, ed. & intro. by. 243p. 1998. pap. 14.95 (*0-9668730-0-9*) Bklyn Lantern.

Dillion, Diane, jt. auth. see Dillion, Leo.

Dillion, Leo & Dillion, Diane. What Am I? LC 93-48835. (J). (gr. 1 up). 1994. 13.95 (*0-590-47885-0*, Blue Sky Press) Scholastic Inc.

Dillion, Myles & Croinin, Donncha O. Teach Yourself Irish Complete Course. (IRI., Illus.). 320p. 1995. pap. 25.95 incl. audio (*0-8442-3865-1*, Teach Yrslf) NTC Contemp Pub Co.

Dillion, Myles & O'Croinin, Donncha. Teach Yourself Irish: A Complete Course for Beginners. (IRI.). 320p. 1995. pap. 11.95 (*0-8442-3800-7*, Teach Yrslf) NTC Contemp Pub Co.

Dillion, Tina. After the Quake. (Ten-Minute Thrillers Ser.). 32p. (YA). (gr. 6-12). 1995. pap. 2.95 (*0-7854-1062-7*, 40796) Am Guidance.

— After the Quake Readalong. (Ten-Minute Thrillers Ser.). 32p. (YA). (gr. 6-12). 1995. pap. 12.95 incl. audio (*0-7854-1073-2*, 40798) Am Guidance.

Dillistin, William H. Bank Note Reporters & Counterfeit Detectors, 1826-1866: With a Discourse on Wildcat Banks & Wildcat Bank Notes. LC 50-549. (Numismatic Notes & Monographs: Vol. 114). 118p. 1949. reprint ed. pap. 36.60 (*0-608-00467-7*, 206128600007) Bks Demand.

Dillman, Bradford. Are You Anybody? An Actor's Life. 208p. (Orig.). 1997. pap. 12.95 (*1-56474-199-0*) Fithian Pr.

***Dillman, Bradford L.** State & Private Sector in Algeria: The Politics of Rent-Seeking & Failed Development. LC 99-56858. (State, Culture & Society in Arab North Africa Ser.). 208p. 2000. 55.00 (*0-8133-3757-7*) Westview.

Dillman, Bruce. The CowBoy Handbook: A Guide to Your CowBoy Heritage. 2nd rev. ed. (Illus.). 308p. 1998. pap. 15.95 (*0-944112-24-2*, Lone Prairie) Outcomes.

— Results on Target. (Illus.). 180p. (Orig.). 1989. pap. 14.95 (*0-944112-12-9*) Outcomes.

Dillman, Caroline M. Days Gone by in Alpharetta & Roswell, Georgia, Vol. I. LC 92-73737. 1992. 50.00 (*0-9634253-0-7*) Chattahoochee.

— Southern Women. 226p. 1988. 63.95 (*0-89116-668-8*); pap. 29.95 (*0-89116-838-9*) Hemisp Pub.

***Dillman, Caroline Matheny.** Descendants of Edward Jefferson Maddox, Jr., North Georgia Pioneer. LC 00-130628. (Illus.). 584p. 2000. 60.00 (*0-9634253-5-8*) Chattahoochee.

Dillman, David R. Profiles of Progress: A Photographic Journal of Ketchikan-Saxman- Matlakatla Southeast Alaska. 240p. (C). 1989. 65.00 (*0-945848-02-1*); pap. 25.00 (*0-945848-01-3*) Prince Wales Pub.

— Profiles of Progress: A Photographic Journal of Prince of Wales Island Southeast Alaska. LC 88-60289. 144p. (C). 1988. pap. 15.00 (*0-945848-00-5*) Prince Wales Pub.

Dillman, Don A. Mail & Electronic Surveys: The Tailored Design Method. 2nd ed. LC 99-38738. 464p. 1999. 47.50 (*0-471-32354-3*) Wiley.

Dillman, Don A., jt. auth. see Salant, Priscilla.

Dillman, Don A., jt. auth. see Tremblay, Kenneth R., Jr.

***Dillman, Erika.** The Little Foot Care Book. LC 00-39898. 2000. write for info. (*0-446-67626-8*) Warner Bks.

Dillman, Erika. The Little Yoga Book. LC 98-21254. (Illus.). 189p. 1999. mass mkt. 9.99 (*0-446-67392-7*, Pub. by Warner Bks) Little.

Dillman, Everett. Spoils from the Sea. 400p. 1997. write for info. (*1-57502-600-7*, P01721) Morris Pubng.

Dillman, George & Thomas, Chris. Advanced Pressure Point Grappling-Tuite: Dillman Method of Instant Self-Defense. LC 94-92463. (Illus.). 360p. (Orig.). 1995. 59.95 (*0-9631996-5-X*); pap. 39.95 (*0-9631996-4-1*) G Dillman Karate.

— Kyusho Jitsu: The Dillman Method of Pressure Point Fighting. LC 92-90024. (Illus.). 272p. 1992. pap. 34.95 (*0-9631996-1-7*) G Dillman Karate.

Dillman, George A. & Thomas, Chris. Advanced Pressure Point Fighting of Ryukyu Kempo: Dillman Theory for All Systems. LC 93-91408. (Illus.). 272p. 1993. 49.95 (*0-9631996-2-5*); pap. 34.95 (*0-9631996-3-3*) G Dillman Karate.

***Dillman, George A. & Thomas, Chris.** Humane Pressure Point Self-Defense: Dillman Pressure Point Method for Law Enforcement, Medical Personnel, Business Professionals, Man & Woman. LC 00-91431. (Illus.). 264p. 2000. pap. 19.95 (*1-889267-03-1*) G Dillman Karate.

Dillman, George A. & Thomas, Chris. Pressure Point Karate Made Easy: A Guide to the Dillman Pressure Point Method for Beginners & Younger Martial Artists. LC 97-68274. (Illus.). 144p. (YA). (gr. 7 up). 1999. pap. 14.95 (*1-889267-02-3*, Pub. by G Dillman Karate) Assoc Pubs Grp.

Dillman, James R., jt. auth. see Phetsadasack, Thomas.

Dillman Laura, jt. auth. see Hiam, Alexander.

Dillman, Linda, ed. see Stewart, David.

***Dillman, Peter.** EMS Medication Pocket Guide. 2nd ed. (Illus.). 160p. (C). 1999. pap. text 16.00 (*0-7637-1225-6*) JB Pubns.

Dillman, Peter A. The EMS Drug Manual: A Field Guide for Emergency Care Personnel. LC 87-91752. 150p. (Orig.). 1987. pap. text 9.50 (*0-9619221-0-9*) Dillman Pub.

— The EMS Drug Manual: A Field Guide for Emergency Care Personnel. rev. ed. (Orig.). 1990. pap. text 9.50 (*0-9619221-1-7*) Dillman Pub.

— The EMS Pocket Drug Manual. 171p. 1991. pap. 16.25 (*0-86720-171-1*) Jones & Bartlett.

***Dillman, Phillip & Woestman, Larry.** Pepsi Memorabilia Then & Now: Unauthorized Handbook & Price Guide. (Illus.). 144p. 2000. pap. 29.95 (*0-7643-1105-0*) Schiffer.

Dillman, R., et al, eds. Distributed Autonomous Robotic Systems 3. (Illus.). xii, 416p. 1998. 159.00 (*3-540-64399-0*) Spr-Verlag.

Dillman, R. & Rembold, Ulrich, eds. Methods & Tools for Computer Integrated Manufacturing: Advanced CREST Course on Computer Integrated Manufacturing (CIM 83), Karlsruhe, Germany, Sept. 5-16, 1983. (Lecture Notes in Computer Science Ser.: Vol. 168). 555p. 1985. pap. 43.00 (*0-387-12926-X*) Spr-Verlag.

Dillman, R., jt. ed. see Rembold, Ulrich.

Dillman, Richard. Essays on Henry David Thoreau: Rhetoric, Style, & Audience. LC 92-39960. (Locust Hill Literary Studies: No. 13). 141p. (C). 1993. lib. bdg. 25.00 (*0-933951-50-7*) Locust Hill Pr.

— Thoreau's Comments on the Art of Writing. 66p. (Orig.). 1987. pap. text 14.00 (*0-8191-6601-4*) U Pr of Amer.

Dillman, Richard, ed. see Thoreau, Henry David.

Dillmann, Ed W., ed. The Endocrine Society Clinical Endocrinology Update: 1995 Syllabus. (Illus.). 382p. (C). 1995. pap. text 55.00 (*1-879225-20-4*) Endocrine Soc.

Dillmann, Eduard. Eine Neue Darstellung der Leibnizschen Monadenlehre Auf Grund der Quellen. (GER.). 1974. reprint ed. write for info. (*3-487-05152-4*) G Olms Pubs.

***Dillof, Mark.** Awakening with the Enemy: The Origin & End of Male/Female Conflict. 257p. 2000. pap. 14.95 (*0-9678252-0-2*) Philosophy Clinic Pr.

Dillon, Andrew. Designing Usable Electronic Text: Ergonomic Aspects of Human Information Usage. LC 94-1581. 1994. 37.50 (*0-7484-0112-1*, Pub. by Tay Francis Ltd); pap. 18.00 (*0-7484-0113-X*, Pub. by Tay Francis Ltd) Taylor & Francis.

Dillon, Andrew, et al, eds. Hypertext & Cognition. 192p. 1996. text 45.00 (*0-8058-2143-0*) L Erlbaum Assocs.

— Hypertext & Cognition. 192p. 1996. pap. 22.50 (*0-8058-2144-9*) L Erlbaum Assocs.

Dillon, Andrew P., tr. see Akiyama, Kaneo.

Dillon, Andrew P., tr. see Japan Institute of Plant Maintenance Staff, ed.

Dillon, Andrew P., tr. see Shigeo Shingo.

Dillon, Andrew P., tr. see Shingo, Shigeo.

Dillon, Authur O. Dillon: Ancestors of Arthur Orison Dillon & His Poems. (Illus.). 111p. 1997. reprint ed. pap. 18.50 (*0-8328-8314-X*); reprint ed. lib. bdg. 28.50 (*0-8328-8313-1*) Higginson Bk Co.

Dillon, Barbara. A Mom by Magic. LC 89-29410. (Trophy Bk.). (Illus.). 144p. (J). (gr. 3-7). 1991. pap. 3.95 (*0-06-440388-2*, HarpTrophy) HarpC Child Bks.

— Mrs. Tooey & the Terrible Toxic Tar. LC 87-45985. 96p. (J). (gr. 3-7). 1988. 10.95 (*0-397-32276-3*); lib. bdg. 11.89 (*0-397-32277-1*) HarpC Child Bks.

— My Stepfather Shrank! LC 91-23901. (Illus.). 128p. (J). (gr. 3-7). 1992. 13.00 (*0-06-021574-7*) HarpC Child Bks.

Dillon, Bev. Crochet from Start to Finishing. (Illus.). 20p. 1992. pap. 5.95 (*1-929512-04-X*) Delta Prod WA.

— Knitting from Start to Finish. (Illus.). 14p. 1989. 5.95 (*1-929512-05-8*) Delta Prod WA.

— Tatted Lace from Start to Finishing. (Illus.). 16p. 1990. pap. 5.95 (*1-929512-03-1*) Delta Prod WA.

Dillon, Brian. Archaeology & Historical Survey of Soguel Demonstration State Forest Santa Cruz County, California. (California Department of Forestry & Fire Protection Ser.: No. 6). (Illus.). 182p. (C). 1992. reprint ed. pap. text 19.38 (*1-55567-634-0*) Coyote Press.

— Excavations at the Sunset Point Site (CA-TUL-1052), Mountain Home Demonstration State Forest, Tulare County, California. (California Department of Forestry & Fire Protection Ser.: No. 11). (Illus.). 156p. (C). 1992. reprint ed. pap. text 16.88 (*1-55567-639-1*) Coyote Press.

— The Rancho Pavoreal Prescribed Burn Project, a 2,010 Acre Property near Sage Riverside County, California. (California Department of Forestry & Fire Protection Ser.: No. 10). 92p. (C). 1993. reprint ed. pap. text 10.31 (*1-55567-638-3*) Coyote Press.

Dillon, Brian D. History & Prehistory of Boggs Mountain Demonstration State Forest, Lake County, CA. (California Department of Forestry Archaeological Reports: Vol. 15). (Illus.). 245p. (C). 1995. pap. text 6.25 (*1-55567-651-0*) Coyote Press.

— Salinas de los Nueve Cerros Guatemala: Preliminary Archaeological Investigations. (Studies in Mesoamerican Art, Archaeology & Ethnohistory: No. 2). (Illus.). 94p. 1977. pap. 3.00 (*0-87919-070-1*) Ballena Pr.

— Timberland Historical Archaeology Notes. (California Department of Forestry Archaeological Reports: Vol. 16). (Illus.). 202p. (C). 1995. pap. text 21.25 (*1-55567-652-9*) Coyote Press.

Dillon, Brian D., ed. Practical Archaeology: Field & Laboratory Techniques & Archaeological Logistics. 3rd ed. LC 93-43422. (UCLA Institute of Archaeology Publications: No. 2). (Illus.). 85p. 1993. pap. 15.00 (*0-917956-80-X*) UCLA Arch.

— The Student's Guide to Archaeological Illustrating. 2nd rev. ed. LC 85-24066. (UCLA Institute of Archaeology Publications: No. 1). (Illus.). 185p. (C). 1985. pap. 25.00 (*0-917956-38-9*) UCLA Arch.

Dillon, Brian D. & Boxt, Mathew A., eds. Archaeology of the Three Springs Valley, California: A Study in Functional Cultural History. LC 88-28259. (UCLA Institute of Archaeology Publications: No. 30). (Illus.). 191p. (Orig.). 1989. pap. 19.00 (*0-917956-62-1*) UCLA Arch.

Dillon, C. A., et al. Haemodynamic Monitoring of the Critical Care Patient: A Practical Handbook. (Illus.). 100p. (Orig.). 1996. pap. text 19.95 (*1-85996-230-0*, Pub. by Bios Sci) Bks Intl VA.

Dillon, C. Douglas, intro. The John M. Crawford, Jr., Collection of Chinese Calligraphy & Painting in the Metropolitan Museum of Art. (Illus.). 61p. 1984. pap. 1.00 (*0-87099-390-9*) Metro Mus Art.

Dillon, C. P. Corrosion Control in the Chemical Process Industries, Pub. No. 45. LC 94-86176. (Illus.). 420p. 1994. 93.00 (*1-877914-58-4*) NACE Intl.

— Corrosion Resistance of Stainless Steels. (Corrosion Technology Ser.: Vol. 9). (Illus.). 384p. 1995. text 165.00 (*0-8247-9629-2*) Dekker.

— Materials Selector for Hazardous Chemicals: Concentrated Sulfuric Acid & Oleum. Pollock, Warren I., ed. (MS Ser.: Vol. 1). (Illus.). 276p. 1997. 89.00 (*1-57698-008-1*) Matrls Tech Inst.

— Materials Selector for Hazardous Chemicals: Formic, Acetic & Other Organic Acids. Pollock, Warren I., ed. (MS Ser.: Vol. 2). (Illus.). 184p. 1997. 69.00 (*1-57698-012-X*) Matrls Tech Inst.

Dillon, Carl F., Jr. Short Hikes in God's Country. LC 95-92730. (Explore Pennsylvania's North Central Highlands Ser.). (Illus.). 256p. (Orig.). 1995. pap. 10.95 (*0-9639328-3-7*) Pine Creek Pr.

Dillon, Carolyn, jt. auth. see Murphy, Bianca.

Dillon, Carrol F. A Domain of Heroes: An Airman's Life Behind Barbed Wire in Germany in World War II. LC 95-69460. (Illus.). 298p. 1995. 21.95 (*0-9646671-0-X*) Palm Islnd.

Dillon, Catherine. Beloved Prisoner. large type ed. 430p. 1980. 27.99 (*0-7089-0557-9*) Ulverscroft.

— Rockfire. large type ed. 1978. 27.99 (*0-7089-0170-0*) Ulverscroft.

Dillon, Charles R. Dillon Ancestors. (Illus.). 209p. 1997. reprint ed. pap. 32.00 (*0-8328-8310-7*); reprint ed. lib. bdg. 42.00 (*0-8328-8309-3*) Higginson Bk Co.

Dillon, Charles R. Eaten by the Gods. 424p. mass mkt. 5.99 (*1-55197-083-X*) Picasso Publ.

— Hell's Bells Are Ringing. 333p. mass mkt. 5.99 (*1-55197-081-3*) Picasso Publ.

***Dillon, Charlotte G.** Poems from the Heart: A Writer's Dreams Flow Like a River. Taylor, Kendrick & Searle, Helen W., eds. (Illus.). 52p. 1999. pap. 12.00 (*0-9664709-2-3*) Mountain Empire.

***Dillon, Christine.** Olympics. 2nd rev. ed. (My First Report Ser.). (Illus.). 50p. (J). (gr. 1-3). 1999. ring bd. 5.95 (*1-57896-049-5*, Hewitt Homeschl Res) Hewitt Res Fnd.

— Outdoor Activities. 2nd rev. ed. (My First Report Ser.). (Illus.). 56p. (J). 1999. ring bd. 5.95 (*1-57896-050-9*, 2573, Hewitt Homeschl Res) Hewitt Res Fnd.

— Sports. 2nd rev. ed. (My First Report Ser.). (Illus.). 56p. (J). 1999. ring bd. 5.95 (*1-57896-051-7*, 2572, Hewitt Homeschl Res) Hewitt Res Fnd.

Dillon, Christine. Weather. 2nd rev. ed. (My First Report Ser.). (Illus.). 40p. (J). (gr. 1-3). 1997. ring bd. 5.95 (*1-57896-004-5*, 1765) Hewitt Res Fnd.

Dillon, Christine J. Across America Language & Miscellaneous Worksheets. (Illus.). 104p. (J). (gr. k-2). 1998. ring bd. 10.00 (*1-57896-033-9*, 2518) Hewitt Res Fnd.

Dillon, Christine J. Keyboarding Syllabus. 39p. (YA). (gr. 9-12). Date not set. pap. text 4.95 (*1-57896-024-X*, 1920, Hewitt Homeschl Res) Hewitt Res Fnd.

Dillon, Christine J. Music. 2nd ed. (My First Report Ser.). (Illus.). 56p. (J). (gr. 1-3). 1997. reprint ed. ring bd. 5.95 (*1-57896-000-2*, 1763) Hewitt Res Fnd.

— My First Report: Set of Fourteen Unit Studies. (Illus.). (J). (gr. 1-4). 1998. ring bd. 49.95 (*1-57896-038-X*, 9212) Hewitt Res Fnd.

Dillon, Christine J., ed. Birds. (My First Report Ser.). (Illus.). 56p. (J). (gr. 1-3). 1995. ring bd. 5.95 (*1-57896-041-X*, 2223) Hewitt Res Fnd.

— Eastern United States. rev. ed. (My First Report Ser.). (Illus.). 60p. (J). (gr. 1-3). 1998. ring bd. 5.95 (*1-57896-020-7*, 1996) Hewitt Res Fnd.

— Famous People. (My First Report Ser.). (Illus.). 44p. (J). (gr. 1-3). 1993. ring bd. 5.95 (*1-57896-003-7*, 1767) Hewitt Res Fnd.

— Marine Life. (My First Report Ser.). (Illus.). 48p. (J). (gr. 1-3). 1995. ring bd. 5.95 (*1-57896-042-8*, 2224) Hewitt Res Fnd.

— Math Patterns. 70p. 1995. pap. 5.95 (*0-913717-73-8*, 2155) Hewitt Res Fnd.

— Me. (My First Report Ser.). (Illus.). 44p. (J). (gr. 1-3). 1993. ring bd. 5.95 (*1-57896-002-9*, 1766) Hewitt Res Fnd.

— Middle United States. rev. ed. (My First Report Ser.). (Illus.). 54p. (J). (gr. 1-3). 1998. ring bd. 5.95 (*1-57896-021-5*, 1998) Hewitt Res Fnd.

— Music for Minors. (Illus.). 130p. 1995. pap. 8.95 (*0-913717-81-9*, 2087) Hewitt Res Fnd.

— Pets & Farm Animals. (My First Report Ser.). (Illus.). 52p. (J). (gr. 1-3). 1995. ring bd. 5.95 (*1-57896-016-9*, 2170) Hewitt Res Fnd.

— Plants. (My First Report Ser.). (Illus.). 52p. (J). (gr. 1-3). 1997. ring bd. 5.95 (*1-57896-043-6*, 2344) Hewitt Res Fnd.

— Reptiles & Amphibians. (My First Report Ser.). (Illus.). 48p. (J). (gr. 1-3). 1995. ring bd. 5.95 (*1-57896-044-4*, 2225) Hewitt Res Fnd.

— The Solar System & Space. (My First Report Ser.). (Illus.). 58p. (J). (gr. 1-4). 1998. ring bd. 5.95 (*1-57896-019-3*, 2472) Hewitt Res Fnd.

— Southern United States. rev. ed. (My First Report Ser.). (Illus.). 54p. (J). (gr. 1-3). 1998. ring bd. 5.95 (*1-57896-022-3*, 1997) Hewitt Res Fnd.

— Teaching Writing Skills. (Illus.). 35p. 1993. pap. text 4.95 (*0-913717-24-X*) Hewitt Res Fnd.

— Transportation. (My First Report Ser.). (Illus.). 44p. (J). (gr. 1-3). 1993. ring bd. 5.95 (*1-57896-001-0*, 1764) Hewitt Res Fnd.

***Dillon, Christine J., ed.** Western United States. rev. ed. (My First Report Ser.). (Illus.). 60p. (J). (gr. 1-3). 1999. ring bd. 5.95 (*1-57896-023-1*) Hewitt Res Fnd.

Dillon, Christine J., ed. Wild Animals: Large Mammals. (My First Report Ser.). (Illus.). 44p. (J). (gr. 1-3). 1993. ring bd. 5.95 (*1-57896-012-6*, 1966) Hewitt Res Fnd.

— Wild Animals: Small Mammals. (My First Report Ser.). (Illus.). 48p. (J). (gr. 1-3). 1995. ring bd. 5.95 (*1-57896-015-0*, 2169) Hewitt Res Fnd.

Dillon, Christine J., jt. auth. see Fisher, Donna R.

Dillon, Christine J., jt. auth. see Purtell, April L.

Dillon, Curtis, ed. see McCrary, Jim.

***Dillon, David.** The Architecture of O'Neil Ford: Celebrating Place. LC 99-11908. 180p. 1999. 29.95 (*0-292-71602-8*) U of Tex Pr.

Dillon, David. Dan Kiley: The Miller Garden. (Land Marks Ser.). (Illus.). 64p. 1997. pap. text 19.95 (*1-888931-07-8*) Watsn-Guptill.

— The FDR Memorial: Lawrence Halprin. (Land Marks Ser.). (Illus.). 96p. 1998. pap. 29.95 (*1-888931-11-6*) Spacemkr Pr.

— Short-Term Counseling. (Contemporary Christian Counseling Ser.: Vol. 3). 18.99 (*0-8499-0775-6*) Word Pub.

Dillon, David, et al. Peter Walker: Experiments in Gesture, Seriality, & Flatness. (Illus.). 72p. 1990. 20.00 (*0-614-14659-3*) Harvard Univ Graduate Schl of.

Dillon, Debbie. Sheet Music Price Guide. 160p. 1990. pap. 9.95 (*0-89145-284-2*) L-W Inc.

***Dillon, Deborah A.** Kids Insight: Reconsidering How to Meet the Literacy Needs of All Students. 2000. pap., teacher ed. 19.95 (*0-87207-265-7*, 265) Intl Reading.

Dillon, Diane & Dillon, Leo. Award Puzzles: The Coretta Scott King Collection - Aida. (Illus.). 1992. 6.95 (*0-938971-73-5*) JTG Nashville.

Dillon, Diane, jt. auth. see Dillon, Leo.

Dillon, Diane, jt. illus. see Dillon, Leo.

Dillon, Dorothy R. New York Triumvirate: A Study of the Legal & Political Careers of William Livingston, John Morin Scott, & William Smith Jr. LC 68-58567. (Columbia University. Studies in the Social Sciences: No. 548). reprint ed. 20.00 (*0-404-51548-7*) AMS Pr.

Dillon, E., tr. see Krapf, Norbert, ed.

Dillon, E. S., jt. auth. see Dillon, L. S.

Dillon, Eilis. Lost Island. 1986. 16.95 (*0-86278-119-1*) Dufour.

— The Singing Cave. 259p. (YA). (gr. 6 up). 1992. reprint ed. pap. 8.95 (*1-85371-153-5*, Pub. by Poolbeg Pr) Dufour.

— Wild Geese. large type ed. 512p. 1983. 27.99 (*0-7089-1052-1*) Ulverscroft.

Dillon, Eilis, et al. The Sea Wall. LC 95-133562. 119p. (J). (gr. 4-10). 1994. reprint ed. pap. 8.95 (*1-85371-304-X*, Pub. by Poolbeg Pr) Dufour.

Dillon, Eilis, ed. see Mercier, Vivian.

Dillon, Elaine M., et al. Design Experiments. LC 92-25874. (Six Sigma Research Institute Ser.). 1992. pap. text 27.95 (*0-201-63401-5*) Addison-Wesley.

Dillon, Ella M., ed. see Edgar, Danny K. & Burgess, Craig E.

Dillon, Elsie B. Elsie's Poems of Faith. 80p. 1997. pap. 10.00 (*0-89896-172-6*) Larksdale.

Dillon, Emile J. Count Leo Tolstoy. LC 72-700. (Studies in European Literature: No. 56). 1972. reprint ed. lib. bdg. 75.00 (*0-8383-1420-1*) M S G Haskell Hse.

— Mexico on the Verge. 1976. lib. bdg. 59.95 (*0-8490-0631-7*) Gordon Pr.

— Mexico on the Verge: American Imperialism: Viewpoints of United States Foreign Policy 1898-1941. LC 78-111712. 1970. reprint ed. 23.95 (*0-405-02013-9*) Ayer.

— Sceptics of the Old Testament. LC 73-16064. (Studies in Comparative Literature: No. 35). 1974. reprint ed. lib. bdg. 75.00 (*0-8383-1723-5*) M S G Haskell Hse.

Dillon, Enoch. Love, from the Ends of the Earth: Poems. LC 90-3627. 64p. (Orig.). 1990. pap. 7.50 (*0-931832-64-0*) Fithian Pr.

Dillon, F. & Verstraelen, L. Geometry & Topology of Submanifolds, IV: Proceedings of the Conference on Differential Geometry & Vision. 296p. 1992. text 95.00 (*981-02-1045-0*) World Scientific Pub.

Dillon, G. M. Dependence & Deterrence. 206p. 1983. text 77.95 (*0-566-00588-3*, Pub. by Dartmth Pub) Ashgate Pub Co.

Dillon, G. M., ed. Defense Policy Making: A Comparative Analysis. 256p. 1989. text 14.50 (*0-7185-1268-5*, Pub. by Leicester U Pr) Cassell & Continuum.

Dillon, George, tr. see Racine, Jean.

Dillon, George L. Constructing Texts: Elements of a Theory of Composition & Style. LC 80-8377. 221p. reprint ed. pap. 68.60 (*0-7837-1748-2*, 205728200024) Bks Demand.

— Contending Rhetorics: Writing in Academic Disciplines. LC 90-25572. (Illus.). 196p. 1991. 14.95 (*0-253-31743-6*) Ind U Pr.

— Language Processing & the Reading of Literature: Toward a Model of Comprehension. LC 77-9861. 240p. reprint ed. pap. 74.40 (*0-8357-3964-3*, 205706000004) Bks Demand.

— Rhetoric As Social Imagination: Explorations in the Interpersonal Function of Language. LC 85-45069. 186p. (C). 1986. 26.95 (*0-253-35011-5*) Ind U Pr.

Dillon, H. Kenneth, jt. ed. see Ho, Mat H.

Dillon, Helen. Helen Dillon on Gardening. LC 99-175786. 280p. 1998. write for info. (*1-86059-085-3*) Town Hse.

Dillon, Helen & Robinson, Peter. The Flower Garden: A Practical Guide to Planning & Planting the Wayside Gardens Collection. LC 94-30696. (Wayside Gardens Collection). (Illus.). 128p. 1995. 19.95 (*0-8069-0847-5*) Sterling.

Dillon, Helen M. Exercises for the Computer User. Regis, Iester M., ed. (Illus.). 50p. (Orig.). 1989. pap. 10.95 (*0-317-93652-2*) Questar CA.

Dillon, Huw. Spiritual Journey of Aikido. 112p. 1996. pap. write for info. (*1-874250-35-9*, Pub. by P H Crompton) Midpt Trade.

Dillon, Ilene L. Exploring Fear with Your Child. (Emotional Literacy Ser.). 48p. (Orig.). 1994. pap. 4.95 (*1-56844-068-5*) Enchante Pub.

— Exploring Grief with Your Child. (Emotional Literacy Ser.). 48p. (Orig.). 1994. pap. 4.95 (*1-56844-064-2*) Enchante Pub.

— Exploring Guilt with Your Child. (Emotional Literacy Ser.). 48p. (Orig.). 1994. pap. 4.95 (*1-56844-069-3*) Enchante Pub.

— Exploring Hurt with Your Child. (Emotional Literacy Ser.). 48p. (Orig.). 1994. pap. 4.95 (*1-56844-070-7*) Enchante Pub.

— Exploring Jealousy with Your Child. (Emotional Literacy Ser.). 48p. 1994. pap. 4.95 (*1-56844-066-9*) Enchante Pub.

— Exploring Loneliness with Your Child. (Emotional Literacy Ser.). 48p. (Orig.). 1994. pap. 4.95 (*1-56844-067-7*) Enchante Pub.

***Dillon, Ilene L., et al.** Exploring Emotional Literacy: A Teacher's Guide to Anger, Fear, Grief, Guilt, Hurt, Jealousy, Loneliness, Love & Shame. LC 99-63339. (Illus.). 300p. 1999. pap. 34.95 (*0-9629123-7-9*) Six Seconds.

Dillon, Isaiah. Dillon: Ancestral Record of the Dillon, Hodgson, Risher & Leonard Families. (Illus.). 183p. 1997. reprint ed. pap. 26.00 (*0-8328-8312-3*); reprint ed. lib. bdg. 36.00 (*0-8328-8311-5*) Higginson Bk Co.

Dillon, J. Handbook of International Direct Marketing. 420p. 1976. 15.95 (*0-07-084473-9*) McGraw.

Dillon, J. F. The Law & Jurisprudence of England & America. LC 75-99475. (American Constitutional & Legal History Ser). 1970. reprint ed. lib. bdg. 49.50 (*0-306-71854-5*) Da Capo.

Dillon, J. L. & Hardaker, J. Brian. Farm Management Research for Small Farmer Development. Vol. 6. 1994. pap. 35.00 (*92-5-103305-6*, F33056, Pub. by FAO) Bernan Associates.

Dillon, J. M. & Long, A. A., eds. The Question of "Eclecticism" Studies in Later Greek Philosophy. (Hellenistic Culture & Society Ser.: Vol. 3). 286p. 1996. pap. 18.95 (*0-520-20696-7*, Pub. by U CA Pr) Cal Prin Full Svc.

Dillon, J. M., ed. & tr. see Chalcidensis, Iamblichus.

Dillon, J. T. Personal Teaching: Efforts to Combine Personal Love & Professional Skill in the Classroom. 178p. (C). 1990. reprint ed. pap. text 19.00 (*0-8191-7780-5*) U Pr of Amer.

Dillon, J. T., ed. Deliberation in Education & Society. LC 93-46340. 278p. 1994. pap. 39.50 (*1-56750-057-9*); text 73.25 (*1-56750-056-0*) Ablx Pub.

Dillon, Jacquelyn, et al. Bass: A Comprehensive String Method, Bk. 1. (Illus.). 40p. (J). (gr. 4-6). 1992. pap. 5.95 (*0-88284-533-0*, 5296) Alfred Pub.

— Cello: A Comprehensive String Method, Bk. 1. (Illus.). 40p. (J). (gr. 4-6). 1992. pap. 5.50 (*0-88284-532-2*, 5295) Alfred Pub.

— Conductor's Score, Bk. 1. (Strictly Strings Ser.). (Illus.). 216p. (J). (gr. 4-6). 1992. pap. 26.95 (*0-88284-534-9*, 5297) Alfred Pub.

— Piano Accompanioment, Bk. 1. (Strictly Strings Ser.). (Illus.). 64p. (J). (gr. 4-6). 1992. pap. 11.95 (*0-88284-535-7*, 5298) Alfred Pub.

— Strictly String, Violin a Comprehensive String Method, Bk. 1. (Strictly Strings Ser.). (Illus.). 40p. (J). (gr. 4-6). 1992. pap. 5.50 (*0-88284-530-6*, 5293) Alfred Pub.

— Viola: A Comprehensive String Method, Bk. 1. (Strictly Strings Ser.). (Illus.). 40p. (J). (gr. 4-6). 1992. pap. 5.50 (*0-88284-531-4*, 5294) Alfred Pub.

Dillon, James. Light My Fire. (My Private Eye Ser). 150p. (Orig.). 1984. pap. 6.95 (*0-915153-08-4*) Gold Star Pr.

Dillon, James T. Jesus As a Teacher: A Multidisciplinary Case Study. LC 94-21868. 211p. 1995. 64.95 (*1-883255-75-9*); pap. 44.95 (*1-883255-74-0*) Intl Scholars.

— Using Discussion in Classrooms. LC 94-11822. 160p. 1994. pap. 23.95 (*0-335-19324-2*) OpUniv Pr.

Dillon, James T., ed. Questioning & Discussion: A Multidisciplinary Study. LC 87-33355. 352p. 1988. pap. 39.50 (*0-89391-493-2*); text 73.25 (*0-89391-442-8*) Ablx Pub.

Dillon, Jana. Jeb Scarecrow's Pumpkin Patch. LC 91-16423. (Illus.). 32p. (J). (ps-3). 1992. 16.00 (*0-395-57578-8*) HM.

— Jeb Scarecrow's Pumpkin Patch. (Illus.). 32p. (J). (ps-3). 1995. pap. 5.95 (*0-395-74514-4*, Sandpiper) HM.

— Jeb Scarecrow's Pumpkin Patch. 1992. 11.15 (*0-606-07735-9*, Pub. by Turtleback) Demco.

— Lucky O'Leprechaun. LC 98-18304. (Illus.). 32p. (J). (gr. k-3). 1998. text 14.95 (*1-56554-333-5*) Pelican.

Dillon, Jana. Lucky O'Leprechaun Comes to America. 14.95 (*1-56554-816-7*) Pelican.

— Tashas Matrioshka Dolls. 2001. text. write for info. (*0-374-37387-6*) FS&G.

Dillon, Jana, jt. illus. see Dionne, Wanda.

Dillon, Jane. A Painter's Garden. 63p. 1996. pap. 10.50 (*1-56770-354-2*) S Scheewe Pubns.

— A Painters Garden, No. 3. (Illus.). 80p. 1999. pap. 10.50 (*1-56770-458-1*) S Scheewe Pubns.

Dillon, Janette. Geoffrey Chaucer. LC 92-26933. (Writers in Their Time Ser.). x, 212 p. 1993. text 39.95 (*0-312-09093-5*) St Martin.

— Language & Stage in Medieval & Renaissance England. LC 97-8795. 288p. (C). 1998. text 59.95 (*0-521-59334-4*) Cambridge U Pr.

***Dillon, Janette.** Theatre, Court & City, 1595-1610: Drama & Social Space in London. (Illus.). 197p. (C). 2000. text 54.95 (*0-521-66118-8*) Cambridge U Pr.

Dillon, Jeff R. IIS 4.0 & Proxy Server 2.0 MCSE Study Guide. (MCSE Certification Ser.). 500p. 1998. student ed. 49.99 (*0-7645-3118-2*) IDG Bks.

Dillon, Jim & Naylor, David. American Theaters: Performance Halls of the Nineteenth Century. LC 96-43764. 224p. 1997. 40.00 (*0-471-14393-6*) Wiley.

Dillon, John. Baby's First Picture. 1997. pap. write for info. (*0-7214-5527-1*) Viking Penguin.

— The Golden Chain: Studies in the Development of Platonism & Christianity. (Collected Studies: No. CS 333). 336p. 1991. text 109.95 (*0-86078-286-7*, Pub. by Variorum) Ashgate Pub Co.

— Inventory of the Ornaments, Reliques, Jewels, Vestments, Books, Etc. Belonging to the Cathedral Church of Glasgow. LC 76-168150. (Maitland Club, Glasgow. Publications: No. 13). reprint ed. 32.50 (*0-404-52945-3*) AMS Pr.

— The Middle Platonists: 80 B. C. to A. D. 220. rev. ed. 1996. pap. text 29.95 (*0-8014-8316-6*) Cornell U Pr.

— My First Blue Picture. 1997. pap. write for info. (*0-7214-5525-5*) Viking Penguin.

— My First Yellow Picture. 1997. pap. write for info. (*0-7214-5526-3*) Viking Penguin.

Dillon, John, ed. The Enneads. MacKenna, Stephen, tr. from GRE. 688p. 1991. pap. 14.95 (*0-14-044520-X*, Penguin Classics) Viking Penguin.

Dillon, John, tr. The Handbook of Platonism. (Clarendon Later Ancient Philosophers Ser.). 272p. 1996. pap. text 26.00 (*0-19-823607-7*) OUP.

Dillon, John, jt. ed. see Fischer, Joachim.

Dillon, John, tr. see Dexippus.

Dillon, John A. Foundations of General Systems Theory. (Systems Inquiry Ser.). 300p. (C). 1982. pap. 15.95 (*0-914105-05-1*) Intersystems Pubns.

Dillon, John A., Jr., ed. Mental Images, Values, & Reality: Proceedings of the Society for General Systems Research, 1986, Set, Vols. 1 & 2. 1100p. 1986. 86.00 (*0-685-14600-6*) Intersystems Pubns.

Dillon, John B. History of Indiana from Its Earliest Exploration by Europeans to the Close of Territorial Government in 1816. LC 73-146392. (First American Frontier Ser.). (Illus.). 1971. reprint ed. 49.95 (*0-405-02845-8*) Ayer.

— Notes on Historical Evidence in Reference to Adverse Theories of the Origin & Nature of the Government of the United States of America. 141p. 1985. reprint ed. 32.50 (*0-8377-0521-5*, Rothman) W S Hein.

Dillon, John F. Laws & Jurisprudence of England & America: Being a Series of Lectures Delivered Before Yale University. LC 94-17733. xvi, 431p. 1994. reprint ed. 52.50 (*0-8377-2039-7*, Rothman) W S Hein.

— Removal of Causes from State Courts to Federal Courts. 3rd ed. xxiii, 168p. 1981. reprint ed. 35.00 (*0-8377-0514-2*, Rothman) W S Hein.

Dillon, John J. A Path to Hope: For Parents of Aborted Children & Those Who Minister to Them. LC 90-70773. 80p. (Orig.). 1990. pap. 6.95 (*1-878718-00-2*, Resurrection Pr) Catholic Bk Pub.

Dillon, John L., jt. auth. see McConnell, Douglas J.

Dillon, John M. Edgar Allan Poe. LC 74-3420. (Studies in Poe: No. 23). 1974. lib. bdg. 75.00 (*0-8383-2069-4*) M S G Haskell Hse.

— The Great Tradition: Further Studies in the Development of Platonism & Early Christianity. LC 97-35614. (Variorum Collected Studies: Vol. 599). 352p. 1997. 111.95 (*0-86078-671-4*, B517.D535, Pub. by Ashgate Pub) Ashgate Pub Co.

Dillon, John M., jt. auth. see O'Hehir, Brendan.

Dillon, John M., tr. see Proclus.

Dillon, Justin & Maguire, Meg. Becoming a Teacher: Issues in Secondary Teaching. LC 96-51587. 1997. 94.00 (*0-335-19824-4*) OpUniv Pr.

Dillon, Justin, jt. ed. see Monk, Martin.

***Dillon, K. B., et al.** Phosphorous: The Carbon Copy - From Organophosphorous to Phospaorganic Chemistry. LC 97-29187. 376p. 1998. 265.00 (*0-471-97360-2*) Wiley.

Dillon, K. Burke & Oliveros, Gumersindo. Multilateral Official Debt Rescheduling: Recent Experience. (World Economic & Financial Surveys Ser.). 22p. 1987. pap. 10.00 (*0-939934-83-3*) Intl Monetary.

Dillon, K. Burke, et al. Officially Supported Export Credits: Developments & Prospects. LC 87-35493. (World Economic & Financial Surveys Ser.). vi, 47p. 1988. pap. 10.00 (*1-55775-006-8*) Intl Monetary.

— Recent Developments in External Debt Restructuring. (Occasional Paper Ser.: No. 40). vii, 68p. 1985. pap. 7.50 (*0-939934-52-3*) Intl Monetary.

Dillon, Karen & Brown, Gail. Sew a Beautiful Wedding. (Illus.). 128p. (C). 1980. pap. 8.95 (*0-935278-05-2*) Palmer-Pletsch.

Dillon, Katherine V. D-Day Normandy: The Story & Photographs. 1999. pap. text 19.95 (*1-57488-023-3*) Brasseys.

— Vietnam War: The Story & Photographs. 1999. pap. text 19.95 (*1-57488-210-4*) Brasseys.

Dillon, Katherine V., jt. auth. see Goldstein, Donald M.

Dillon, Katherine V., ed. see Goldstein, Donald M.

Dillon, Katherine V., jt. ed. see Goldstein, Donald M.

Dillon, Kathleen M. Living with Autism: The Parents' Stories. (Illus.). 265p. 1995. pap. 19.95 (*0-9635752-7-9*) Pkway Pubs.

Dillon, Kenneth, jt. auth. see Peters, Charles.

Dillon, Kenneth C., jt. auth. see Peters, Charles L.

Dillon, Kenneth J. Apprentice to Paracelsus: My Search for the Secrets of Healing. LC 94-68125. (Illus.). 200p. (Orig.). 1994. pap. 16.95 (*0-9642976-4-7*) Spectrum Biosci.

— Healing Photons: The Science & Art of Blood Irradiation Therapy. LC 97-62342. (Illus.). 180p. 1998. pap. 19.95 (*0-9642976-5-5*) Spectrum Biosci.

— Scholars' Guide to Washington, D. C., for Central & East European Studies: Albania, Austria, Bulgaria, Czechoslovakia, Germany (FRG & GDR), Greece (Ancient & Modern), Hungary, Poland, Romania, Switzerland, & Yugoslavia. David, Zdenek V., ed. LC 80-607019. 330p. 1991. 27.50 (*0-87474-368-0*); pap. text 11.95 (*0-87474-367-2*) W Wilson Ctr Pr.

Dillon-Krass, J. & Kjelland, James M. Strictly Strings, Violin, Bk. 3. (Strictly Strings Ser.). 40p. 1996. pap. 5.50 (*0-7390-0328-3*, 16859) Alfred Pub.

Dillon-Krass, Jacquelyn & Straub, Dorothy A., compiled by. Tips: Establishing a String & Orchestra Program. (Illus.). 25p. 1991. pap. 8.50 (*0-940796-66-X*) MENC.

Dillon, L. S. The Gene: Its Structure, Function & Evolution. LC 86-25291. (Illus.). 908p. (C). 1987. text 186.00 (*0-306-42319-7*, Kluwer Plenum) Kluwer Academic.

Dillon, L. S. & Dillon, E. S. Cerambycidae of the Fiji Islands. (BMB Ser.). 1952. 25.00 (*0-527-02314-0*) Periodicals Srv.

Dillon, Lacy A. I'll Remember You in the Morning. 167p. 1990. 12.95 (*0-9616811-1-X*) Coal Bks.

— They Died for King Coal. (Illus.). 172p. (C). 1992. reprint ed. 12.95 (*0-9616811-0-1*) Coal Bks.

— They Died in the Darkness. (Illus.). 280p. (C). 1992. reprint ed. 14.95 (*0-87012-230-4*) Coal Bks.

Dillon, Lawrence S. The Inconstant Gene. LC 82-20414. 590p. 1983. 125.00 (*0-306-41084-2*, Plenum Trade) Perseus Pubng.

— Ultrastructure, Macromolecules, & Evolution. LC 80-20550. 716p. 1981. 120.00 (*0-306-40528-8*, Plenum Trade) Perseus Pubng.

Dillon, Leo, ed. Aida. LC 89-36481. (Illus.). 32p. (J). (ps up). 1990. 19.00 (*0-15-200405-X*, Gulliver Bks) Harcourt.

Dillon, Leo & Dillon, Diane. East O' the Sun, West O' the Moon. (J). 1989. write for info. (*0-316-18560-4*) Little.

Dillon, Leo & Dillon, Diane. To Every Thing There Is a Season. LC 97-35124. (J). 1998. write for info. (*0-590-47893-1*) Scholastic Inc.

— To Every Thing There Is a Season. LC 97-35124. 40p. (J). (ps-3). 1998. 15.95 (*0-590-47887-7*, Pub. by Scholastic Inc) Penguin Putnam.

— To Every Thing There Is a Season. limited ed. 40p. 1998. 100.00 (*0-590-92340-4*, Pub. by Scholastic Inc) Penguin Putnam.

— Why Mosquitoes Buzz in People's Ears: A West African Tale. LC 74-2886. (Picture Puffin Ser.). 28p. (J). (ps-3). 1992. pap. 6.99 (*0-14-054905-6*, PuffinBks) Peng Put Young Read.

Dillon, Leo, jt. auth. see Dillon, Diane.

Dillon, Leo, jt. auth. see Willard, Nancy.

Dillon, Leo, ed. see Musgrove, Margaret W.

Dillon, Leo, ed. see Willard, Nancy.

Dillon, M. C. Ecart & Differance: Merleau-Ponty & Derrida on Seeing & Writing. LC 96-16192. 264p. 1997. 60.00 (*0-391-03989-X*) Humanities.

— Merleau-Ponty's Ontology. 2nd rev. ed. LC 97-35618. (Studies in Phenomenology & Existential Philosophy). 299p. 1997. pap. 19.95 (*0-8101-1528-X*) Northwestern U Pr.

— Semiological Reductionism: A Critique of the Deconstructionist Movement in Postmodern Thought. LC 94-13720. 241p. (C). 1995. text 59.50 (*0-7914-2375-1*); pap. text 19.95 (*0-7914-2376-X*) State U NY Pr.

Dillon, M. C., ed. Ecart & Differance: Merleau-Ponty & Derrida on Seeing & Writing. 264p. 1996. pap. 18.50 (*0-391-03990-3*) Humanities.

— Merleau-Ponty Vivant. LC 90-42946. (SUNY Series in Contemporary Continental Philosophy). 224p. (C). 1991. text 59.50 (*0-7914-0658-X*); pap. text 19.95 (*0-7914-0659-8*) State U NY Pr.

Dillon, M. C., jt. ed. see Dixon, R. A.

Dillon, M. M. Handbook on PCBS in Electrical Equipment. 3rd ed. (Illus.). 54p. (C). 1999. reprint ed. pap. text 20.00 (*0-7881-7665-X*) DIANE Pub.

Dillon-Malone, A., ed. Women on Women & on Age, Beauty, Love, Men, Marriage... 230p. 1999. pap. text 10.00 (*0-7881-6058-3*) DIANE Pub.

Dillon-Malone, A., jt. auth. see Behan, Brian.

***Dillon-Malone, Aubrey.** The Cynics Dictionary. LC 99-89682. 320p. 2000. 15.95 (*0-8092-2546-8*, 254680, Contemporary Bks) NTC Contemp Pub Co.

— I Was a Fugitive from a Hollywood Trivia Factory: A Book of Hollywood Trivia. 320p. 2000. 15.95 (*0-8092-9905-4*, 990540, Contemporary Bks) NTC Contemp Pub Co.

— Stranger Than Fiction. 2000. write for info. (*0-8092-9904-6*, Contemporary Bks) NTC Contemp Pub Co.

Dillon, Martin. The Dirty War. LC 98-49268. 2p. 1999. pap. 17.50 (*0-415-92281-X*) Routledge.

— God & the Gun: The Church & Irish Terrorism. LC 98-55579. 1999. pap. 17.99 (*0-415-92363-8*) Routledge.

— God & the Gun: The Church & Irish Terrorism. LC 97-48818. 244p. 1999. reprint ed. 17.50 (*0-415-92060-4*) Routledge.

— The Shankill Butchers: The Real Story of Cold-Blooded Mass Murder. LC 98-56518. (Illus.). 288p. 1999. pap. 16.00 (*0-415-92231-3*) Routledge.

Dillon, Martin, ed. Interfaces for Information Retrieval & Online Systems: The State of the Art. LC 91-8240. 368p. 1991. 65.00 (*0-313-27494-0*, DIF, Greenwood Pr) Greenwood.

Dillon, Martin, pref. OPACs & Beyond: Proceedings of a Joint Meeting of the British Library, DBMIST, & OCLC. (Library, Information, & Computer Science Ser.). 100p. (Orig.). 1989. pap. 12.50 (*1-55653-070-6*) OCLC Online Comp.

Dillon, Mary & Barclay, Shinan N. Flowering Woman: Moontime for Kory. LC 88-4921. (Illus.). 64p. (Orig.). 1988. pap. 7.95 (*0-945086-13-X*) Sunlight Prodns.

Dillon, Mary J. & Proctor, Custis N. The Women Golfer: A Beginner's Guide. 112p. 1996. pap. write for info. (*0-9650385-0-5*) Severn Grp.

Dillon, Matthew. Pilgrims & Pilgrimage in Ancient Greece. LC 97-205641. 336p. (C). 1997. 70.00 (*0-415-12775-0*) Routledge.

***Dillon, Matthew & Garland, Lynda.** Ancient Greece: Social & Historical Documents from Archaic Times to Death of Socrates. 2nd ed. LC 99-32499. 496p. (C). 2000. text 100.00 (*0-415-21754-7*) Routledge.

Dillon, Matthew & Garland, Lynda. Ancient Greece: Social & Historical Documents from Archaic Times to the Death of Socrates. LC 94-20490. (Classical Studies). 480p. (C). 1994. pap. 27.99 (*0-415-11367-9*, C0373) Routledge.

— Ancient Greece: Social & Historical Documents from Archaic Times to the Death of Socrates. LC 94-20490. (Classical Studies). 520p. (C). (gr. 13). 1994. 85.00 (*0-415-11366-0*, C0372) Routledge.

— Ancient Greece: Social & Historical Documents from Archaic Times to the Death of Socrates. 2nd ed. LC 99-32499. 496p. 1999. pap. 29.99 (*0-415-21755-5*) Routledge.

Dillon, Meighan, jt. auth. see Loustau, John.

Dillon, Melanie. Coffee & Clomid: The Art of Being Normal While Undergoing Infertility Treatment. 1998. 3.95 (*1-56123-107-X*) Centering Corp.

Dillon, Merrimac, jt. auth. see Williams, Anita.

Dillon, Merton L. Benjamin Lundy & the Struggle for Negro Freedom. LC 66-15473. 293p. reprint ed. pap. 90.90 (*0-8357-9663-9*, 201549700094) Bks Demand.

— Elijah P. Lovejoy, Abolitionist Editor. LC 80-11000. 190p. 1980. reprint ed. lib. bdg. 52.50 (*0-313-22352-1*, DIEJ, Greenwood Pr) Greenwood.

— Slavery Attacked: Southern Slaves & Their Allies, 1619-1865. LC 90-6067. 328p. 1990. pap. text 18.95 (*0-8071-1653-X*) La State U Pr.

— Ulrich Bonnell Phillips: Historian of the Old South. LC 85-10229. (Southern Biography Ser.). (Illus.). 190p. 1985. text 30.00 (*0-8071-1206-2*) La State U Pr.

Dillon, Michael. China's Hui Community: Migration, Settlement, & Sects. 288p. 1998. text 48.00 (*0-7007-1026-4*, Pub. by Curzon Pr Ltd) UH Pr.

— China's Muslims. (Images of Asia Ser.). (Illus.). 80p. (C). 1996. text 14.95 (*0-19-587504-4*) OUP.

— Dictionary of Chinese History. 240p. 1979. 35.00 (*0-7146-3107-8*, Pub. by F Cass Pubs) Intl Spec Bk.

— The Politics of Security: Towards a Political Philosophy of Continental Thought. LC 96-3435. 272p. (C). 1996. 85.00 (*0-415-12960-5*); pap. 24.99 (*0-415-12961-3*) Routledge.

Dillon, Michael, ed. China: A Cultural & Historical Dictionary. (Durham East Asia Ser.). 450p. (C). 1998. text 60.00 (*0-7007-0438-8*, Pub. by Curzon Pr Ltd); pap. text 32.95 (*0-7007-0439-6*, Pub. by Curzon Pr Ltd) UH Pr.

Dillon, Michael, jt. auth. see Herbach, Andrew.

Dillon, Michael, jt. auth. see Herbach, Andy.

Dillon, Michael, ed. see Platinum Media Inc. Staff.

Dillon, Michele. Catholic Identity: Balancing Reason, Faith, & Power. LC 98-50662. 288p. (C). 1999. 59.95 (*0-521-63044-4*); pap. 19.95 (*0-521-63959-X*) Cambridge U Pr.

— Debating Divorce: Moral Conflict in Ireland. LC 92-45297. 232p. 1993. text 27.50 (*0-8131-1822-0*) U Pr of Ky.

Dillon, Mike. Great Birdhouse Book: Fun, Fabulous Designs You Can Build. LC 98-46790. 1999. 24.95 (*0-8069-9334-0*) Sterling.

Dillon, Mike. Art of the Birdhouse: Flights of Fancy by Mike Dillon. LC 96-86715. 80p. 1997. 12.95 (*0-8362-2704-2*) Andrews & McMeel.

***Dillon, Millicent.** Harry Gold: A Novel. LC 99-86844. 288p. 2000. 26.95 (*1-58567-012-X*, Pub. by Overlook Pr) Penguin Putnam.

Dillon, Millicent. A Little Original Sin: The Life & Work of Jane Bowles. LC 97-33074. 476p. 1998. pap. 17.95 (*0-520-21193-6*, Pub. by U CA Pr) Cal Prin Full Svc.

Dillon, Millicent. You Are Not I: A Portrait of Paul Bowles. LC 97-26220. 340p. 1998. 40.00 (*0-520-21104-9*, Pub. by U CA Pr) Cal Prin Full Svc.

***Dillon, Millicent.** You Are Not I: A Portrait of Paul Bowles. LC 97-26220. (Illus.). 354p. 2000. pap. 17.95 (*0-520-22493-0*, Pub. by U CA Pr) Cal Prin Full Svc.

Dillon, Millicent, ed. see Bowles, Jane.

Dillon, Molly B., jt. ed. see DuWatt, Betsy.

Dillon, Myles. Cycles of the Kings. LC 95-140368. 132p. 1994. pap. 6.95 (*1-85182-178-3*, Pub. by Four Cts Pr) Intl Spec Bk.

— Early Irish Literature. LC 95-139083. 212p. 1994. pap. 9.95 (*1-85182-177-5*, Pub. by Four Cts Pr) Intl Spec Bk.

— Early Irish Literature. LC 48-6027. 210p. reprint ed. pap. 65.10 (*0-608-18220-6*, 205662700078) Bks Demand.

Dillon, Myles, ed. Irish Sagas. 176p. 1997. pap. 12.95 (*1-85635-174-2*, Pub. by Mercier Pr) Irish Amer Bk.

Dillon, Myles & O'Croinin, Connacha. Teach Yourself Irish. (Teach Yourself Ser.). 1992. 15.95 (*0-8288-8358-0*) Fr & Eur.

***Dillon, Neal B., ed.** A Dying Breed: The Courage of the Mighty Eighth Air Force. 210p. 2000. pap. 15.95 (*1-55571-529-X*, Pub. by PSI Resch) Midpt Trade.

Dillon, Paddy. In & Around Belfast. (Twenty-Five Walks Ser.). (Illus.). 112p. 1997. pap. text 16.95 (*0-11-495761-4*, Pub. by Statnry Office) Seven Hills Bk.

***Dillon, Patrick.** Lost at Sea. 288p. 2000. pap. 13.00 (*0-684-86909-8*, Touchstone) S&S Trade Pap.

Dillon, Patrick. Lost at Sea: An American Tragedy. LC 98-7013. 288p. 1998. 23.95 (*0-385-31421-3*, Dial Pr) Dell.

— Physiology 250: A Study Guide. (C). 1993. student ed. 12.00 (*1-881592-46-4*) Hayden-McNeil.

Dillon, Patrick M., jt. auth. see Leonard, David C.

***Dillon, Peter & Simmers, Ian, eds.** Shallow Groundwater Systems. (IAH International Contributions to Hydrogeology Ser.: Vol. 18). 250p. 1998. pap. 30.00 (*90-5410-443-0*, Pub. by A A Balkema) Ashgate Pub Co.

— Shallow Groundwater Systems. (IAH International Contributions to Hydrogeology Ser.: Vol. 18). (Illus.). 240p. (C). 1998. text 79.00 (*90-5410-442-2*, Pub. by A A Balkema) Ashgate Pub Co.

Dillon-Peterson, Betty, ed. Staff Development, Organization Development. fac. ed. LC 80-70653. 157p. 1981. reprint ed. pap. 48.70 (*0-608-01025-1*, 2082501) Bks Demand.

Dillon, Philip R. American Anniversaries: Every Day in the Year; Presenting Seven Hundred & Fifty Events in United States History from the Discovery of America to the Present Day. vi, 364p. 1991. reprint ed. lib. bdg. 48.00 (*1-55888-890-X*) Omnigraphics Inc.

***Dillon, Pradeep Ajit & Standish, Paul.** Lyotard: Just Education. LC 00-32830. 2000. write for info. (*0-415-21547-1*) Routledge.

Dillon, Richard. Arizona's Amazing Towns: From Wild West to High Tech. LC 92-70464. (Illus.). 112p. 1992. pap. 8.95 (*0-9632377-0-5*) Four Peaks.

— Captain John Sutter: Sacramento Valley's Sainted Sinner. LC 67-21511. (Illus.). 380p. 1981. reprint ed. pap. 12.95 (*0-934136-15-7*) Good Life.

— Meriwether Lewis. LC 65-10888. (Illus.). 363p. 1988. reprint ed. pap. 12.95 (*0-934136-39-4*) Good Life.

Dillon, Richard, ed. Western Quotations: Famous Words from the American West. LC 93-72249. 176p. (Orig.). 1993. pap. 9.95 (*0-9632377-1-3*) Four Peaks.

Dillon, Richard, et al. High Steel: Building the Bridges Across San Francisco Bay. (Illus.). 176p. 1998. reprint ed. pap. 24.95 (*0-89087-859-5*) Celestial Arts.

Dillon, Richard, jt. auth. see Egan, Ferol.

Dillon, Richard E. The Lawyer Who Doubled His Bets. LC 98-90582. 1999. pap. 11.95 (*0-533-12858-7*) Vantage.

Dillon, Richard G. Ranking & Resistance: A Precolonial Cameroonian Polity in Regional Perspective. 328p. 1990. 45.00 (*0-8047-1571-8*) Stanford U Pr.

Dillon, Richard H. Humbugs & Heroes: A Gallery of California Pioneers. (Illus.). 389p. 1983. reprint ed. pap. 9.95 (*0-911819-00-2*) Yosemite D.

Dillon, Richard H., ed. A Cannoneer in Navajo Country: Journal of Private Josiah M. Rice, 1851. limited ed. (Illus.). 1970. 25.00 (*0-912094-15-X*) Old West.

Dillon, Richard L. North American Indian Wars. 1993. 17.98 (*1-55521-951-9*) Bk Sales Inc.

Dillon, Richard S. Handbook of Endocrinology: Diagnosis & Management of Endocrine & Metabolic Disorders. LC 73-1948. (Illus.). 568p. 1973. reprint ed. pap. 176.10 (*0-8357-7645-X*, 205697000096) Bks Demand.

Dillon, Robert J. Reality & Value Judgment in Policymaking: A Study of Expert Judgments about Alternative Energy Technologies. Bruchey, Stuart, ed. LC 78-22674. (Energy in the American Economy Ser.). (Illus.). 1979. lib. bdg. 18.95 (*0-405-11977-1*) Ayer.

Dillon, Robert M., jt. auth. see Crawley, Stanley W.

***Dillon, Robert T.** The Ecology of Freshwater Molluscs. LC 99-15476. (Illus.). 528p. (C). 2000. 120.00 (*0-521-35210-X*) Cambridge U Pr.

Dillon, Robin S., ed. Dignity, Character, & Self-Regard: Essays on Self-Respect. LC 94-20565. 288p. (C). 1994. pap. 23.99 (*0-415-90709-8*, A9805) Routledge.

Dillon, Ronna F., ed. Handbook on Testing. LC 96-47430. 400p. 1997. lib. bdg. 95.00 (*0-313-28984-0*, Greenwood Pr) Greenwood.

Dillon, Ronna F. & Pellegrino, James W., eds. Instruction: Theoretical & Applied Perspectives. LC 90-42679. 208p. 1991. 55.00 (*0-275-92735-0*, C2735, Praeger Pubs) Greenwood.

Dillon, Ronna F. & Sternberg, Robert J., eds. Cognition & Instruction. 390p. 1988. reprint ed. pap. text 55.00 (*0-12-216406-7*) Acad Pr.

Dillon, Ronna R. & Pelligrino, James W., eds. Testing: Theoretical & Applied Perspectives. LC 88-316. 274p. 1989. 69.50 (*0-275-92759-8*, C2759, Praeger Pubs) Greenwood.

Dillon, Sally. Crossroads in Time: Archaeology Activity Book. LC 93-71694. (Illus.). 32p. (J). 1994. pap. 6.95 (*0-943872-73-1*) Andrews Univ Pr.

***Dillon, Sally.** Michael Asks Why Kids Activity Book. (Illus.). 77p. (J). 2000. pap. 1.99 (*0-8163-1793-3*) Pacific Pr Pub Assn.

***Dillon, Sally Pierson & White, Ellen Gould Harmon.** Michael Asks Why: Ellen G. White's Classic the Great Controversy Adapted for Children. LC 99-49058. (YA). 2000. pap. 10.99 (*0-8163-1759-3*) Pacific Pr Pub Assn.

Dillon, Steve, jt. auth. see Ennis, Garth.

***Dillon, Susan.** A True Love Story. 320p. 1999. 20.00 (*0-9676048-0-X*) Stone Post Pubng Co.

Dillon, Tharam, jt. auth. see Khosla, Rajiv.

Dillon, Tony, jt. auth. see Busch, Gladys.

Dillon, V. M. & Board, R. G., eds. Natural Antimicrobial Systems & Food Preservation. LC 97-181222. (Illus.). 300p. 1994. text 105.00 (*0-85198-878-4*) OUP.

Dillon, Valerie. Images of Grace: Makoto Fujimura. LC 97-214991. (Illus.). 1997. 20.00 (*0-9648340-3-0*) Dillon Gallery.

Dillon, Valerie, ed. see Kushner, Robert & Walstedt, Eric.

Dillon, Valerie R. Becoming a Woman: Basic Information, Guidance, & Attitudes on Sex for Girls. LC 89-52154. 168p. 1990. pap. 9.95 (*0-89622-433-3*) Twenty-Third.

Dillon, Valerie V., jt. auth. see Carotta, Michael.

Dillon, W. Tracy, jt. ed. see Wollner, Craig.

Dillon, William M. Business Mathematics. LC 84-16987. 320p. (C). 1985. disk 49.95 (*0-8273-2348-4*) Delmar.

— Business Mathematics. 2nd ed. 320p. (C). 1989. student ed. 68.95 incl. disk (*0-8273-3506-7*); suppl. ed. 60.95 incl. 5.25 hd (*0-8273-3503-2*) Delmar.

Dillon, William M. Business Mathematics. 3rd ed. LC 93-33699. 484p. 1994. pap. 55.95 (*0-8273-6011-8*) Delmar.

***Dillon, William P.** Teaching Atlas of Brain Imaging. LC 98-32391. 1999. write for info. (*3-13-116341-0*, Pub. by G Thieme) Thieme Med Pubs.

Dillon, William R. La Investigacion de Mercados en un Entorno de Marketing. 3rd ed. (C). 1996. text 38.40 (*84-8086-253-X*, Irwn McGrw-H) McGrw-H Hghr Educ.

— People Raising: A Practical Guide to Raising Support. wbk. ed. 15.99 (*0-8024-6447-5*, 246) Moody.

Dillon, William R. & Goldstein, Matthew. Multivariate Analysis: Methods & Application. LC 84-3584. (Probability & Mathematical Statistics Ser.: No. 1-346). 608p. (C). 1984. 109.95 (*0-471-08317-8*) Wiley.

Dillon, William R., et al. Essentials of Marketing Research. LC 92-30863. (Marketing Ser.). 700p. (C). 1992. text 65.25 (*0-256-08112-3*, Irwn McGrw-H) McGrw-H Hghr Educ.

— Essentials of Marketing Research. 2nd ed. 608p. (C). 1997. text 65.25 (*0-256-13911-3*, Irwn McGrw-H) McGrw-H Hghr Educ.

— Marketing Research in a Marketing Environment. 3rd ed. LC 93-24883. 784p. (C). 1993. text 67.50 (*0-256-10517-0*, Irwn McGrw-H) McGrw-H Hghr Educ.

— Marketing Research in a Marketing Environment: International. 3rd ed. (C). 1994. text, student ed. 32.50 (*0-256-10829-3*, Irwn McGrw-H) McGrw-H Hghr Educ.

— Marketing Research in a Marketing Environment: International Version. 2nd ed. (C). 1989. text 30.95 (*0-256-08403-3*, Irwn McGrw-H) McGrw-H Hghr Educ.

Dillon, Wilton S. & Kotler, Neil G., eds. The Statue of Liberty Revisited: Making a Universal Symbol. LC 92-37913. (Illus.). 192p. (Orig.). 1993. pap. text 17.95 (*1-56098-252-7*) Smithsonian.

Dillon, Zach. This One's for You! Thatch, Nancy R., ed. LC 99-19126. (Books for Students by Students). (Illus.). 29p. (J). (gr. 5-7). 1999. lib. bdg. 15.95 (*0-933849-72-9*) Landmark Edns.

Dillow, John. Baby's Day: Board Books. (S851 Ser.: No. 16). 10p. (J). (ps). 1991. pap. 3.50 (*0-7214-9136-7*, Ladybrd) Penguin Putnam.

— Baby's Toys: Little Ladybird Board Book. 8p. (J). (ps). 1991. pap. 3.50 (*0-7214-9137-5*, S851-15, Ladybrd) Penguin Putnam.

— Picture Atlas of the World. (SL Twenty One Ser.). 45p. (J). 1993. text 11.95 (*0-7214-5354-6*, Ladybrd) Penguin Putnam.

Dillow, Linda. Calm My Anxious Heart. LC 98-6268. 1998. pap. 10.00 (*1-57683-047-0*); pap. 10.00 (*1-57683-116-7*) NavPress.

— Creative Counterpart. rev. ed. LC 86-21648. 228p. 1986. pap. 11.99 (*0-8407-3067-5*) Nelson.

— La Esposa Virtuosa.Tr. of Creative Counterpart. (SPA.). 160p. 1992. 8.99 (*0-88113-064-8*) Caribe Betania.

— A Mother's Journey. 48p. 1998. 14.95 (*1-57856-041-1*); 119.60 (*1-57856-061-6*) Waterbrook Pr.

***Dillow, Linda & Pintus, Lorraine.** Intimate Issues: 21 Questions Christian Women Ask about Sex. LC 98-53167. 288p. 1999. 18.95 (*1-57856-149-3*) Waterbrook Pr.

Dillow, Louise B. Low Cal Country: Taking the Calories & Cholesterol Out of Hearty Country Cooking. LC 91-75620. (Illus.). 264p. 1992. pap. 13.95 (*0-931722-91-8*) Corona Pub.

Dillow, Louise B. & Carver, Dennie B. Mrs. Blackwell's Heart-of-Texas Cookbook. (Illus.). 130p. 1980. pap. 9.95 (*0-931722-06-3*) Corona Pub.

Dillow, Myron. Harvesttime on the Prairie: A History of Baptists in Illinois, 1796-1996. LC 96-70299. 640p. 1996. 29.95 (*1-57736-009-5*) Providence Hse.

Dillow, Rex O., ed. Facilities Management: A Manual for Plant Administration. 2nd ed. 1610p. 1989. 109.00 (*0-913359-50-5*) APPA VA.

Dilloway, C. Purchasing Computer Software Products. 126p. (C). 1985. 335.00 (*0-7855-5749-0*, Pub. by Inst Pur & Supply) St Mut.

Dilloway, James. From Cold War to Chaos? Reviving Humane Development - Or Remaking Market Man. LC 98-31367. 200p. 1999. 55.00 (*0-275-96474-4*) Greenwood.

Dills, Charles R. & Romiszowski, Alexander J., eds. Instructional Development Paradigms. LC 96-52249. (Illus.). 950p. 1997. 150.00 (*0-87778-294-6*); pap. 100.00 (*0-87778-295-4*) Educ Tech Pubns.

Dills, Michael J., ed. see Greenwood, John O.

Dills, R. S. History of Fayette County, Ohio. (Illus.). 1039p. 1993. reprint ed. lib. bdg. 99.50 (*0-8328-3459-9*) Higginson Bk Co.

— History of Greene County: Together with Historic Notes on the Northwest. (Illus.). 1018p. 1997. reprint ed. lib. bdg. 99.00 (*0-8328-6319-X*) Higginson Bk Co.

Dillworth, Ernest. Walter S. Landor. (Twayne's English Authors Ser.). 198p. 1968. pap. text 4.95 (*0-8290-1951-0*); lib. bdg. 20.95 (*0-8057-1312-3*) Irvington.

Dilman, Ilham. Existentialist Critiques of Cartesianism. LC 92-34116. 1993. lib. bdg. 49.75 (*0-389-21004-8*) B&N Imports.

— Free Will: An Historical & Philosophical Introduction. LC 98-35363. 1999. 75.00 (*0-415-20055-5*); pap. 24.99 (*0-415-20056-3*) Routledge.

— Mind Brain Behavior: Discussions of B. F. Skinner & J. R. Searle. 128p. (C). 1988. lib. bdg. 49.95 (*0-415-00006-8*) Routledge.

— Quine on Ontology, Necessity, & Experience: A Philosophical Critique. LC 83-4815. 138p. (C). 1984. pap. text 21.95 (*0-87395-760-1*) State U NY Pr.

***Dilman, Ilham.** Raskolinkov's Rebirth: Psychology & the Understanding of Good & Evil. 256p. 2000. pap. 26.95 (*0-8126-9416-3*) Open Court.

Dilman, Ilham. Studies in Language & Reason. LC 79-55527. 228p. 1981. text 53.00 (*0-389-20229-0*, N6436) B&N Imports.

Dilman, Ilham, ed. Philosophy & Life. LC 84-14685. 356p. 1984. text 185.50 (*90-247-2996-3*) Kluwer Academic.

Dilman, Victor V., jt. auth. see Polyanin, A. D.

Dilman, Victor V., jt. auth. see Polyanin, Andrei D.

Dilmore, John. Parts Unknown. 165p. 1999. pap. 13.95 (*0-88739-182-6*) Creat Arts Bk.

Dilnot, Andrew W. Reform of Social Security. 1984. pap. 9.95 (*0-19-877225-4*) OUP.

Dilonno, Mark. New Jersey's Coastal Heritage: A Guide. LC 96-26025. (Illus.). 224p. 1997. pap. 16.95 (*0-8135-2342-7*); text 38.00 (*0-8135-2341-9*) Rutgers U Pr.

DiLorenzo, J. J. The Miami Dolphins Football Team. LC 96-26414. (Great Sports Teams Ser.). 48p. (J). (gr. 4-10). 1997. lib. bdg. 18.95 (*0-89490-796-4*) Enslow Pubs.

DiLorenzo-Kearon, Maria. Spanish, Medical: A Conversational Approach. 256p. 1982. pap. text 195.00 incl. audio (*0-88432-079-0*, AFMS20) Audio-Forum.

Dilorenzo, Thomas, jt. auth. see Bennett, James T.

DiLorenzo, Thomas J., jt. auth. see Bennett, James T.

DiLorenzo, Vincent. Basic Legal Transactions. (General Law Ser.). 736p. 1985. 140.00 (*0-88712-353-8*) Warren Gorham & Lamont.

— Basic Legal Transactions, No. 1. (General Law Ser.). 736p. 1992. suppl. ed. 67.25 (*0-7913-1231-3*) Warren Gorham & Lamont.

DiLouie, Craig. The Lighting Management Handbook. LC 93-31081. 300p. 1994. 74.00 (*0-88173-169-2*) Fairmont Pr.

DiLouie, Craig & Marrano. Electrical System Design & Specification. 457p. (C). 1998. 72.00 (*0-13-387549-0*) P-H.

DiLouie, Craig, jt. auth. see Marrano, Steven J.

Dils, Tracey E. Cat Characters - A to Z. (Illus.). 1995. pap. 9.95 (*1-56189-397-8*) Amer Educ Pub.

— You Can Write Children's Books. LC 97-47235. (You Can Write It! Ser.). (Illus.). 128p. 1998. pap. 12.99 (*0-89879-829-9*, Wrtrs Digest Bks) F & W Pubns Inc.

***Dils, Tracy.** Mother Theresa. (Women of Achievement Ser.). 2000. 19.95 (*0-7910-5887-5*) Chelsea Hse.

— Mother Theresa. (Women of Achievement Ser.). (Illus.). 2001. pap. 9.95 (*0-7910-5888-3*) Chelsea Hse.

— Samuel L. Jackson: Actor. LC 99-37423. (Black Americans of Achievement Ser.). (Illus.). 144p. 1999. pap. 9.95 (*0-7910-5282-6*) Chelsea Hse.

— Samuel L. Jackson: Actor. LC 99-37423. (Black Americans of Achievement Ser.). (Illus.). 144p. 1999. 19.95 (*0-7910-5281-8*) Chelsea Hse.

Dilsaver, Lary M., ed. America's National Park System: The Critical Documents. 484p. 1997. pap. 31.95 (*0-8476-8440-7*) Rowman.

— America's National Park System: The Critical Documents. 484p. (C). 1994. reprint ed. 79.00 (*0-8476-7922-5*) Rowman.

Dilsaver, Lary M. & Tweed, William C. Challenge of the Big Trees: A Resource History of Sequoia & Kings Canyon National Parks. 1991. 16.95 (*1-878441-00-0*); pap. 9.95 (*1-878441-01-9*) Sequoia Nat Hist Assn.

Dilsaver, Lary M., jt. ed. see Wyckoff, William.

***Dilsaver, Paul.** Hardcore Haiku. 48p. 2000. pap. 6.00 (*0-9637000-5-7*) Acad & Arts.

Dilsaver, Paul. Medi-Phoria. (Illus.). 68p. 1998. pap. 9.00 (*0-9637000-3-0*) Acad & Arts.

Dilsaver, Paul L. A Cure for Optimism. 72p. 1993. pap. 8.00 (*0-9637000-0-6*) Acad & Arts.

— Nurtz! Nurtz! 206p. 1989. pap. 13.00 (*0-9637000-2-2*) Acad & Arts.

***Dilsizian, Vasken, ed.** Myocardial Viability: A Clinical & Scientific Treatise. LC 99-39509. (Illus.). 550p. 1999. 125.00 (*0-87993-437-9*) Futura Pub.

Dilthey, Wilhelm. Briefwechsel Zwischen Dilthey und Dem Grafen Paul Yorck Von Wartenburg 1877-1897. (GER.). xi, 280p. 1995. reprint ed. write for info. (*3-487-05171-0*) G Olms Pubs.

— Descriptive Psychology & Historical Understanding. 124p. 1978. pap. text 48.50 (*90-247-1951-8*) Kluwer Academic.

— Essence of Philosophy. Emery, Stephen A. & Emery, William T., trs. LC 76-164833. (North Carolina. University. Studies in the Germanic Languages & Literatures: No. 13). reprint ed. 37.50 (*0-404-50913-4*) AMS Pr.

— Hermeneutics & the Study of History. Makkreel, Rudolf A. & Rodi, Frithjof, eds. LC 95-39698. (Selected Works of Wilhelm Dilthey: No. 4). 432p. 1996. text 59.50 (*0-691-00649-0*, Pub. by Princeton U Pr) Cal Prin Full Svc.

— Historia de la Filosofia. (Breviarios Ser.). (SPA.). pap. 8.99 (*968-16-0131-9*, Pub. by Fondo) Continental Bk.

— Introduction to the Human Sciences: An Attempt to Lay a Foundation for the Study of Society & History. Betanzos, Ramon J., ed. & tr. by. LC 88-52. Orig. Title: Einleitung. (GER.). 388p. 1988. pap. 25.95 (*0-8143-1898-3*) Wayne St U Pr.

— Philosophy of Existence: Introduction to Weltanschauugslehre. LC 78-5673. 74p. 1978. reprint ed. lib. bdg. 47.50 (*0-313-20460-8*, DIPH, Greenwood Pr) Greenwood.

Dilts, ed. Aeschinis Orationes. (GRE.). 1997. 107.50 (*3-8154-1009-6*, T1009, Pub. by B G Teubner) U of Mich Pr.

— Scholia Demosthenica Vol. I: Scholia in Orationes 1-18. (GRE.). 1983. 69.50 (*3-322-00157-1*, T1258, Pub. by B G Teubner) U of Mich Pr.

— Scholia Demosthenica Vol. II: Scholia in Orationes 19-60. (GRE.). 1986. 99.50 (*3-322-00274-8*, T1259, Pub. by B G Teubner) U of Mich Pr.

— Scholia in Aeschinem. (GRE.). 1992. 82.50 (*3-8154-1011-8*, T1011, Pub. by B G Teubner) U of Mich Pr.

Dilts, Bryan L. Kentucky 1890 Veterans Census Index. 132p. lib. bdg. 33.00 (*0-945433-54-9*) Herit Quest.

Dilts, Bryan L., compiled by. District of Columbia 1870 Census Index: Heads of Households & Other Surnames in Households Index. LC 85-11829. xx, 180p. 1985. lib. bdg. 52.00 (*0-914311-36-0*) Herit Quest.

Dilts, David A. & Walsh, William J. Collective Bargaining & Impasse Resolution in the Public Sector. LC 88-4063. 253p. 1988. 62.95 (*0-89930-247-5*, DLI/, Quorum Bks) Greenwood.

Dilts, David A., et al. Assessing What Professors Do: An Introduction to Academic Performance Appraisal in Higher Education, 61. LC 93-30978. (Contributions to the Study of Education Ser.: Vol. 61). 220p. 1994. 55.00 (*0-313-26761-8*, Greenwood Pr) Greenwood.

— Getting Absent Workers Back on the Job: An Analytical Approach. LC 85-3540. (Illus.). 164p. 1985. 59.95 (*0-89930-025-1*, DWO/, Quorum Bks) Greenwood.

— Labor Relations Law in State & Local Government. LC 92-8405. 208p. 1992. 55.00 (*0-89930-414-1*, DSL, Quorum Bks) Greenwood.

Dilts, David A., jt. auth. see Deitsch, Clarence R.

Dilts, Es D. The Great Road: The Building of the Baltimore & Ohio, the Nation's First Railroad, 1828-1853. 1996. pap. 24.95 (*0-8047-2629-9*) Stanford U Pr.

Dilts, James D. The Great Road: The Building of the Baltimore & Ohio, the Nation's First Railroad, 1828-1853. LC 93-17074. (Illus.). 592p. (C). 1993. 60.00 (*0-8047-2235-8*) Stanford U Pr.

Dilts, James D. & Black, Catharine F., eds. Baltimore's Cast-Iron Buildings & Architectural Ironwork. LC 91-50583. 115p. 1991. reprint ed. pap. 35.70 (*0-608-02466-X*, 206311000004) Bks Demand.

Dilts, James D., jt. auth. see Dorsey, John.

Dilts, Joann, jt. auth. see Pozzo, Earlene Dal.

Dilts, Jon, jt. auth. see Counts, I. Wilmer.

Dilts, Mervin R. & Kennedy, George A., eds. Two Greek Rhetorical Treatises from the Roman Empire: Introduction, Text, & Translation of the Arts of Rhetoric Attributed to Anonymous Seguerianus & to Apsines of Gadara. LC 96-50247. (Memosyne, Bibliotheca Classica Batava Ser.: No. 168). (ENG & GRE.). 288p. 1997. 107.50 (*90-04-10728-2*) Brill Academic Pubs.

Dilts, Preston. Liability. LC 98-90665. 1999. 18.95 (*0-533-12875-7*) Vantage.

Dilts, Robert. Applications of NLP: '78-'84. LC 83-61049. 1983. 22.95 (*0-916990-13-3*) META Pubns.

— Changing Belief Systems with NLP. LC 90-60084. 1990. 22.95 (*0-916990-24-9*) META Pubns.

— Effective Presentation Skills. LC 94-76760. 1994. 24.95 (*0-916990-31-1*) META Pubns.

— Modeling with NLP. LC 98-66554. 324p. 1998. 27.95 (*0-916990-41-9*) META Pubns.

— Skills for the Future. LC 93-84504. 1993. 29.95 (*0-916990-27-3*) META Pubns.

***Dilts, Robert.** Sleight of Mouth. LC 99-74402. 352p. 1999. 32.95 (*0-916990-43-5*) META Pubns.

Dilts, Robert. Strategies of Genius, Vol. I. LC 94-77813. 1994. 24.95 (*0-916990-32-X*) META Pubns.

— Strategies of Genius, Vol. II. LC 94-7813. 1994. 21.95 (*0-916990-33-8*) META Pubns.

— Strategies of Genius, Vol. III. LC 94-7813. 1995. 29.95 (*0-916990-34-6*) META Pubns.

— Tools for Dreamers: Strategies for Creativity. LC 91-61373. 1991. 29.95 (*0-916990-26-5*) META Pubns.

— Visionary Leadership. LC 96-75856. 1996. 25.95 (*0-916990-38-9*) META Pubns.

Dilts, Robert & Epstein. Dynamic Learning. LC 95-78653. 1995. 29.95 (*0-916990-37-0*) META Pubns.

Dilts, Robert & Mc Donald, Robert. Tools of the Spirit. LC 97-72115. 320p. 1997. pap. 19.95 (*0-916990-40-0*) META Pubns.

Dilts, Robert, et al. Beliefs: Pathways to Health & Well-Being. 240p. (Orig.). 1990. pap. 13.95 (*1-55552-029-4*) Metamorphous Pr.

— Neuro-Linguistic Programming, Vol. 1. LC 80-50147. 1980. 24.95 (*0-916990-07-9*) META Pubns.

Dilts, Robert, jt. auth. see Marzuki, S.

***Dilts, Robert B. & DeLozier, Judith A.** The Encyclopedia of Systemic NLP & NLP New Coding, 2 vols., Set. LC 00-104098. (Illus.). xvi, 1626p. 2000. 399.95 (*0-9701540-0-3*) NLP Univ Pr.

Diltz, Russ, jt. auth. see Yunus, Ibrahim.

Diltz-Siler, Barbara. Understanding Avalanches: A Handbook for Snow Travelers in the Sierra & Cascades. (Illus.). 32p. 1977. pap. 3.95 (*0-913140-24-4*) Signpost Bk Pub.

Dilulio, John J., Jr., jt. ed. see Dionne, E. J., Jr.

Dilworth. Production & Operation Management. 5th ed. 1993. student ed. 28.75 (*0-07-016992-6*) McGraw.

Dilworth, Ann, jt. ed. see Steinberg, David.

Dilworth, Anne, jt. auth. see Blackwood, Susan.

Dilworth, Billy. Before the Pen Runs Dry... Smith, Sammy, ed. LC 96-70887. 150p. 1996. 14.95 (*0-9655242-0-5*) Rainmaker & Assocs Inc.

Dilworth, Collett B., Jr., jt. auth. see Kirkland, James W.

Dilworth, Craig. Laws, Theories & the Principles of Science. (Uppsala Philosophical Studies: No. 44). 108p. (Orig.). 1990. pap. 29.50 (*91-506-0787-1*) Coronet Bks.

— Scientific Progress. 2nd ed. 1986. pap. text 48.50 (*90-277-2216-1*); lib. bdg. 101.50 (*90-277-2215-3*) Kluwer Academic.

Dilworth, Craig, ed. Scientific Progress: A Study Concerning the Nature of the Relation Between Successive Scientific Theories. 3rd ed. LC 93-6199. (Synthese Library). 242p. (C). 1994. pap. text 43.50 (*0-7923-2488-9*, Pub. by Kluwer Academic); lib. bdg. 102.00 (*0-7923-2487-0*, Pub. by Kluwer Academic) Kluwer Academic.

Dilworth, David, ed. see Mori Ogai, pseud.

Dilworth, David A. & Viglielmo, Valdo H., eds. Sourcebook for Modern Japanese Philosophy: Selected Documents. Zavala, Agustin J., tr. LC 97-12763. (Resources in Asian Philosophy & Religion). 448p. 1998. lib. bdg. 95.00 (*0-313-27433-9*, Greenwood Pr) Greenwood.

Dilworth, David A., ed. see Mori Ogai, pseud.

Dilworth, David A., tr. see Nishida Kitaro.

Dilworth, Donald C. Embassies of the World: Five Walking Tours & Directory. (Illus.). (Orig.). 1986. pap. 7.95 (*0-89461-046-5*) Broadcasting Pubns.

Dilworth, Ernest, tr. see Voltaire.

Dilworth, Ernest N., tr. see Boileau-Despreaux, Nicolas.

Dilworth, James B. Operations Management. 2nd ed. LC 95-39692. (C). 1995. text 80.50 (*0-07-017021-5*) McGraw.

— Production & Operations Management. 5th ed. (C). 1992. text 70.00 (*0-07-016987-X*) McGraw.

Dilworth, James B., jt. auth. see Ettkin, Lawrence P.

Dilworth, Leah. Imagining Indians in the Southwest: Persistent Visions of a Primitive Past. LC 95-26790. (Illus.). 304p. 1996. 34.95 (*1-56098-641-7*) Smithsonian.

— Imagining Indians in the Southwest: Persistent Visions of a Primitive Past. 320p. 1998. pap. 16.95 (*1-56098-834-7*) Smithsonian.

Dilworth, M. J. & Glenn, A. R., eds. Biology & Biochemistry of Nitrogen Fixation. (Studies in Plant Science: No. 1). (Illus.). viii,38p. 1991. 154.50 (*0-444-88960-4*) Elsevier.

Dilworth, Mark. Scottish Monasteries: Monastic Life in the Sixteenth Century. LC 95-182030. (Illus.). 1985. (Orig.). 1995. pap. 25.00 (*0-7486-0527-4*, Pub. by Edinburgh U Pr) Col U Pr.

Dilworth, Mary E., ed. Being Responsive to Cultural Differences: How Teachers Learn. LC 97-21133. (Illus.). 224p. 1997. 65.95 (*0-8039-6669-5*); pap. 29.95 (*0-8039-6670-9*) Corwin Pr.

— Diversity in Teacher Education: New Expectations. LC 92-20123. (Education-Higher Education Ser.). 312p. 1992. text 36.45 (*1-55542-472-4*) Jossey-Bass.

— Of Course It Matters: Putting the National Commission Report into Action. 1998. 20.00 (*0-89333-165-1*) AACTE.

Dilworth, R. P., ed. see Pure Mathematics Symposium Staff.

Dilworth, Sharon. The Long White. LC 88-17307. (Iowa Short Fiction Award Ser.). 204p. 1988. 10.00 (*0-87745-216-4*) U of Iowa Pr.

— Women Drinking Benedictine. LC 98-26156. 220p. 1998. 22.00 (*0-8142-0812-6*, DILWOM) Ohio St U Pr.

— Women Drinking Benedictine. LC 98-26156. 168p. 2000. pap. 16.95 (*0-8142-5012-2*) Ohio St U Pr.

Dilworth, Thomas. A New Guide to the English Tongue. LC 78-14283. (American Linguistics Ser.). 176p. 1978. reprint ed. 50.00 (*0-8201-1322-0*) Schol Facsimiles.

— The Shape of Meaning in the Poetry of David Jones. 1988. text 50.00 (*0-8020-2613-3*) U of Toronto Pr.

Dilworths. Excerpts from the Diaries of Rev. Robert Dilworth & Blacksmith Dilworth. Lutes, Margaret D., ed. 11p. 1989. per. 5.00 (*0-933227-73-6*, 205) Closson Pr.

Dilys, Richard. Zodiac. large type ed. (Ulverscroft Large Print Ser.). 224p. 1996. 27.99 (*0-7089-3646-6*) Ulverscroft.

Dilys, Rosalind, tr. see Dubost, Thierry.

Dima, Nicholas. Bessarabia & Bukovina: The Soviet-Romanian Territorial Dispute. (East European Monographs: No. 110). 173p. 1983. text 40.00 (*0-88033-003-1*, Pub. by East Eur Monographs) Col U Pr.

— Cross Cultural Communication. (Illus.). 128p. (C). 1990. pap. text 16.00 (*0-941694-36-4*) Inst Study Man.

— Journey to Freedom. LC 89-62603. 1990. 22.95 (*0-944273-04-1*) Selous Found Pr.

DIMACS (Group) Staff. Parallel Algorithms: Third DIMACS Implementation Challenge, 1994. Bhatt, Sandeep N., ed. LC 96-52111. (DIMACS Series in Discrete Mathematics & Theoretical Computer Science: Vol. 30). 162p. 1997. text 45.00 (*0-8218-0447-2*, DIMACS/30) Am Math.

***DIMACS (Group) Staff & NSF Science & Technology Center in Discrete Mathem.** Robust Communication Networks: Interconnection & Survivability. Dean, Nathaniel et al, eds. LC 00-29958. (Series in Discrete Mathematics & Theoretical Computer Science: Vol. 53). 167p. 2000. 39.00 (*0-8218-1546-6*) Am Math.

DIMACS International Workshop Staff. Graph Drawing: Proceedings of the DIMACS International Workshop, GD '94, Held in Princeton, New Jersey, U. S. A., October 10-14, 1994. Tamassia, Roberto & Tollis, Ioannis G., eds. LC 94-47045. (Lecture Notes in Computer Science Ser.: Vol. 894). x, 471p. 1995. 68.00 (*0-387-58950-3*) Spr-Verlag.

DIMACS "Special Year" in Mathematical Support for Molecular Biology Staff & Farach-Colton, Martin. Mathematical Support for Molecular Biology: Special Year Workshops, 1994-1998. LC 98-32095. (DIMACS Series in Discrete Mathematics & Theoretical Computer Science). 1999. write for info. (*0-8218-0826-5*) Am Math.

DIMACS Staff, jt. auth. see NSF Science & Technology Center in Discrete Mathem.

***DIMACS Workshop Staff, et al.** External Memory Algorithms: DIMACS Workshop External Memory & Visualization, May 20-22, 1998. LC 99-43684. (Series in Discrete Mathematics & Theoretical Computer Science). 306p. 1999. write for info. (*0-8218-1184-3*) Am Math.

DiMaggio, Dom. Real Grass, Real Heroes. 320p. 1991. mass mkt. 4.95 (*0-8217-3409-1*, Zebra Kensgtn) Kensgtn Pub Corp.

Dimaggio, Edward. How to Write for Television. 304p. 1990. per. 12.00 (*0-671-76641-4*) S&S Trade Pap.

Dimaggio, Ken. T. V. Dinner Culture Poem. 6p. 1994. pap., per. 3.00 (*1-886206-09-0*) Venom Pr.

Dimaggio, Paul. Institutional Transformation of American Culture. Date not set. 19.95 (*0-465-03320-2*, Pub. by Basic); pap. 15.00 (*0-465-03321-0*, Pub. by Basic) HarpC.

DiMaggio, Paul. Managers of the Arts: Careers & Opinions of Administrators of U. S. Resident Theaters, Art Museums, Symphony Orchestras, & Community Arts Agencies. LC 87-9719. (Research Division Report, National Endowment for the Arts Ser.: No. 20). (Illus.). 104p. (Orig.). 1987. pap. 9.95 (*0-932020-56-X*) Seven Locks Pr.

Dimaggio, Paul, ed. Nonprofit Enterprise in the Arts: Studies in Mission & Constraint. (Illus.). 385p. 1987. text 70.00 (*0-19-504063-5*) OUP.

DiMaggio, Paul & Ostrower, Francie. Race, Ethnicity, & Participation in the Arts: Patterns of Participation by Hispanics, Whites, & African-Americans in Selected Activities from the 1982 & 1985 Surveys of Public Participation in the Arts. LC 92-31145. (Research Division Report, National Endowment for the Arts Ser.: No. 25). 112p. 1992. pap. text 11.95 (*0-929765-03-6*) Seven Locks Pr.

DiMaggio, Paul, jt. ed. see Powell, Walter W.

DiMagno, E. P., ed. see Lankisch, Paul G.

DiMagno, Eugene P., ed. Chronic Pancreatitis: Erice, Italy, 14-15 October 1996. (Science & Culture Ser.). 600p. 1998. 110.00 (*981-02-3440-6*) World Scientific Pub.

Dimai, Peter A., tr. see Bardon, Franz.

Dimaio, D. J. Forensic Pathology. (Practical Aspects of Criminal & Forensic Investigations Ser.). 1992. 65.00 (*0-444-01506-X*, RA1063) CRC Pr.

Dimamarca, Salvador. Estudio Del "Araudo Domado" De Pedro De Ona. (SPA.). 252p. 1952. 4.00 (*0-318-14262-7*) Hispanic Inst.

Diman, L. Jones: Leaves from a Family Tree, Being Random Records, Letters & Traditions of the Jones, Stimson & Clarke Families of Hopkinton, Medfield, Norton & Boston, Massachusetts, & Providence, Rhode Island. (Illus.). 121p. 1993. reprint ed. pap. 19.00 (*0-8328-3354-1*); reprint ed. lib. bdg. 29.00 (*0-8328-3353-3*) Higginson Bk Co.

Dimancescu, Dan. Seamless Enterprise. 1992. 30.00 (*0-88730-544-X*, HarpBusn) HarpInfo.

— The Seamless Enterprise: Making Cross-Functional Management Work. LC 93-61003. 249p. (Orig.). 1994. pap. 18.00 (*0-939246-51-1*) Wiley.

— The Seamless Enterprise: Making Cross-Functional Management Work. 250p. (Orig.). 1995. pap. 19.95 (*0-471-13193-8*) Wiley.

Dimancescu, Dan & Dwenger, Kemp. World Class New Product Development: Benchmarking Best Practices of Agile Manufacturers. (Illus.). 276p. 1995. 29.95 (*0-8144-0311-5*) AMACOM.

Dimancescu, Dan & Gerrity, Richard. Deferred Future: Corporate & World Debt & Bankruptcy. LC 83-15500. 192p. 1983. text 20.00 (*0-88410-360-9*, HarpBusn) HarpInfo.

Dimand, Mary Ann, et al, eds. Women of Value: Feminist Essays on the History of Women in Economics. LC 95-7191. 240p. 1995. 95.00 (*1-85278-959-X*) E Elgar.

Dimand, Mary Ann & Dimand, Robert W., eds. The Foundations of Game Theory, 3 vols. LC 96-39591. (Mini Ser.). 1896p. 1997. 630.00 (*1-85898-297-9*) E Elgar.

***Dimand, Robert W., et al.** A Biographical Dictionary of Women Economists. LC 00-28842. 2000. write for info. (*1-85278-964-6*) E Elgar.

Dimand, Robert W., jt. ed. see Dimand, Mary Ann.

Dimant, Devorah & Rappaport, Uriel, eds. The Dead Sea Scrolls: Forty Years of Research. LC 92-18573. (Studies on the Texts of the Desert of Judah: Vol. 10). 371p. 1992. 40.00 (*90-04-09679-5*, Pub. by Magnes Pr) Eisenbrauns.

Dimant, Devorah, ed. see Fellows of the Institute for Advanced Studies of t.

DiMarco. Moving Through Life Transitions with Power & Purpose. 2nd ed. LC 99-12702. (Illus.). 165p. 1999. pap. text 25.20 (*0-13-919465-7*) P-H.

Dimarco, Cara. Career Transitions: A Journey of Survival & Growth. 148p. (C). 1997. pap. text 23.80 (*0-13-776915-6*) P-H.

***DiMarco, Carol.** Alchemy. (Illus.). 20p. (J). 1999. 5.00 (*1-886383-65-0*, Little Blue) Pride & Imprints.

DiMarco, Carol. The Magical Child. (Illus.). 25p. (Orig.). (J). (gr. k-3). 1997. pap. 10.95 (*1-886383-19-7*) Pride & Imprints.

Dimarco, Donna. Natural Relief from Constipation. (Good Health Guides Ser.). 48p. 1999. pap. 3.95 (*0-87983-958-9*, 39589K, Keats Publng) NTC Contemp Pub Co.

DiMarco, Jennifer. At the Edge. 110p. (Orig.). 1994. pap. 9.95 (*1-886383-11-1*) Pride & Imprints.

***DiMarco, Jennifer.** Drinking Silver Wine. (Wind Triology Ser.: Bk. 3). 250p. 2000. pap. 12.95 (*1-886383-71-5*) Pride & Imprints.

DiMarco, Jennifer. Escape to the Wind. 238p. 1993. pap. 11.95 (*0-9628621-5-0*) Castillo Intl.

— Fall Through the Sky. 300p. (Orig.). 1997. pap. 12.95 (*1-886383-16-2*) Pride & Imprints.

DiMarco, Jennifer, et al. Wild Words. (Illus.). 100p. 1999. pap. 10.00 (*1-886383-31-6*) Pride & Imprints.

DiMarco, Jennifer, ed. see Tobin, Bette Lou.

DiMarco, John P. & Prystowsky, Eric N., eds. Atrial Arrhythmias: State of the Art. (American Heart Association Monographs). (Illus.). 448p. 1994. 70.00 (*0-87993-604-5*) Futura Pub.

DiMarco, Tony, ed. see Chelland, Patrick.

Dimarco, Wendy, jt. auth. see Turner, Tony.

DiMari, S., et al, eds. Microencapsulation - Microgels - Iniferters. (Advances in Polymer Science Ser.: Vol. 136). (Illus.). 210p. 1997. 179.00 (*3-540-64015-0*) Spr-Verlag.

DiMaria, Ernie. Fire: A War That Never Ends: An Introspective Account of the Fire That Killed 6 NYC Firefighters on Aug. 2, 1978. Cole, Victor, ed. LC 93-84762. (Illus.). 192p. 1993. 21.00 (*0-9637296-1-6*) Sunset Bkstore.

— Fire: A War That Never Ends: An Introspective Account of the Fire That Killed 6 NYC Firefighters on Aug. 2, 1978. Cole, Victor, ed. LC 93-84762. (Illus.). 192p. (YA). (gr. 9 up). 1995. pap. 7.95 (*0-9637296-2-4*) Sunset Bkstore.

***DiMarino, Anthony J., Jr. & Benjamin, Stanley B.** Gastrointestinal Disease Book. (Illus.). 1998. 499.95 incl. cd-rom (*0-632-04355-5*) Blackwell Sci.

DiMarino, Anthony J., Jr. & Benjamin, Stanley B., eds. Gastrointestinal Disease: An Endoscopic Approach, 2 vols. LC 97-678. (Illus.). 1504p. 1997. 395.00 (*0-86542-501-9*) Blackwell Sci.

D

Dimarogonas, Andrew, ed. Synopsis: An Annual Index of Greek Studies - 1992. 1997. text 81.00 incl. 3.5 hd (*90-5702-541-8*, ECU104, Harwood Acad Pubs) Gordon & Breach.

Dimarogonas, Andrew D. Vibrations for Engineers. 2nd ed. LC 95-34189. 825p. 1996. 95.00 (*0-13-456229-1*) P-H.

***Dimarogonas, Andrew D., ed.** Synopsis: An Annual Index of Greek Studies, 1994, Vol. 3. 408p. 1999. 65.00 incl. cd-rom (*90-5702-577-9*, Harwood Acad Pubs) Gordon & Breach.

DiMartini, Andrea, jt. ed. see Trzepacz, Paula.

DiMartino, Dave, jt. auth. see Crisafulli, Chuck.

DiMartino, David, et al. Health Care for the Poor in Omaha-Douglas County: Problems & Policy Options. 136p. (Orig.). 1985. pap. 9.50 (*1-55719-108-5*) U NE CPAR.

DiMartino, David R. A Needs Assessment of Older Hispanics in Omaha, Nebraska. 136p. (Orig.). 1979. pap. 9.00 (*1-55719-092-5*) U NE CPAR.

DiMartino, David R. & Davis, Carole M. Older Hispanics in Nebraska: Their Characteristics, Attitudes & Needs. 148p. (Orig.). 1980. pap. 8.50 (*1-55719-084-4*) U NE CPAR.

DiMartino, David R. & Frost, Murray. A Market Analysis for Nebraska City. 95p. (Orig.). 1985. pap. 7.50 (*1-55719-001-1*) U NE CPAR.

DiMartino, David R., et al. Geoprocessing for Grand Island & Hall County: Analysis & Recommendations. (Illus.). 68p. (Orig.). 1983. pap. 5.00 (*1-55719-016-X*) U NE CPAR.

— A Housing Allocation Formula for Nebraska Cities of the First Class: City of Bellevue, 1978. 128p. (Orig.). 1978. pap. 9.00 (*1-55719-098-4*) U NE CPAR.

DiMartino, David R., jt. auth. see Cervantes, Jesse.

DiMartino, David R., jt. auth. see Norris, Donald F.

DiMartino, E., jt. ed. see Cavalloro, R.

DiMartino, Nick. Christmas Ghost Story. 178p. (Orig.). 1996. pap. 12.95 (*0-9653918-0-9*) Rosebriar Pub.

— Seattle Ghost Story. (Illus.). 226p. (YA). 1998. pap. 12.95 (*0-9653918-2-5*) Rosebriar Pub.

— University Ghost Story. (Illus.). 226p. 1997. pap. 12.95 (*0-9653918-1-7*) Rosebriar Pub.

DiMarzio, Esther & Jacky, Gail. A Practical Guide to Building Your New Home: Decisions to Live With. (Illus.). 40p. (Orig.). 1996. pap. 12.00 (*0-9654464-0-9*) Sycamore Pr IL.

DiMarzio, Esther & Jacky, Gail D. A Practical Guide to Building Your New Home: The Financing Process. 20p. 1997. pap. 6.00 (*0-9654464-1-7*) Sycamore Pr IL.

DiMarzio, Nicholas, jt. auth. see Papademetriou, Demetrios G.

***Dimas, Pete R.** Progress & a Mexican American Community's Struggle for Existence: Phoenix's Gold Gate Barrio, Ser. 21. LC 97-48961. (American University Studies XXI: Vol. 10). XVIII, 175p. (C). 1999. pap. text 30.00 (*0-8204-2353-X*) P Lang Pubng.

Dimas, Peter, et al. Hacking the Internet: A Hacker's Guide to the Worldwide Web. 2nd ed. 30p. 1998. pap. 25.00 (*0-934274-54-1*) Consumertronics.

DiMassa, Diane. The Complete Hothead Paisan: Homocidal Lesbian Terrorist. LC 99-10937. (Illus.). 400p. 1999. pap. 24.95 (*1-57344-084-1*) Cleis Pr.

DiMassa, Joe. Readings in Humanities I. (C). pap. text. write for info. (*1-884155-08-1*) Day & Nite Pub.

— Readings in Religious Studies. (C). pap. text. write for info. (*1-884155-09-X*) Day & Nite Pub.

***Dimassi, M. & Sjostrand, J.** Spectral Asymtotics in the Semi-Classical Limit. (London Mathematical Society Lecture Note Ser.: Vol. 268). 240p. (C). 2000. pap. text 39.95 (*0-521-66544-2*) Cambridge U Pr.

***Dimatteo.** The Law of International Business Transactions. 2002. 65.00 (*0-324-04097-0*) Thomson Learn.

DiMatteo, Anthony. Natale Conti's Mythologies: A Select Translation. LC 94-13592. (Renaissance Imagination Ser.). (Illus.). 440p. 1994. text 25.00 (*0-8153-1464-7*) Garland.

DiMatteo, Larry A. Contract Theory: The Evolution of Contractual Intent. LC 98-20606. 270p. 1998. 43.95 (*0-87013-486-8*); pap. 24.95 (*0-87013-444-2*) Mich St U Pr.

***DiMatteo, Larry A.** The Law of International Contracting. LC 00-42438. 2000. write for info. (*90-411-9592-0*) Kluwer Law Intl.

DiMatteo, Richard, tr. see Parker, Roberta N. & Parker, Harvey C.

Dimattia, Dominic. Rational Effectiveness Training: Increasing Personal Productivity at Work. Mennen, Stacey, ed. (Illus.). 32p. (Orig.). 1990. pap. 2.50 (*0-917476-20-4*) A Ellis Institute.

DiMattia, Dominic & Ijzermans, Theo. Reaching Their Minds: A Trainers Manual to Rational Effectiveness Training. LC 95-82381. 112p. (Orig.). (C). 1996. pap., student ed. 10.95 (*0-917476-25-5*) A Ellis Institute.

Dimattia, Dominic & Lega, Leonor, eds. Will the Real Albert Ellis Please Stand Up: Anecdotes by His Colleagues, Students & Friends in Honor of His 75th Birthday. (Illus.). 144p. (Orig.). 1990. pap. 3.50 (*0-917476-19-0*) A Ellis Institute.

DiMattia, Philip, jt. auth. see Osborne, Allan G., Jr.

DiMattio, Joe. The Moon, the Grass & Us. LC 94-66847. 64p. 1994. pap. text 12.00 (*0-9641891-0-0*) Chelsea Lit.

— The Show in Destitute Times. Brooks, Noel, ed. (Illus.). 74p. (Orig.). Date not set. pap. text 12.00 (*0-9641891-1-9*) Chelsea Lit.

DiMauro. Twentieth Century Literary Criticism, Vol. 39. 500p. 1991. text 150.00 (*0-8103-2421-0*) Gale.

Dimauro. Twentieth Century Literary Criticism, Vol. 43. 1992. 150.00 (*0-8103-2425-3*) Gale.

DiMauro. Twentieth Century Literary Criticism, Vol. 46. 500p. 1992. text 150.00 (*0-8103-2428-8*) Gale.

DiMauro. Twentieth Century Literary Criticism, Vol. 47. 1993. 150.00 (*0-8103-7972-4*) Gale.

DiMauro. Twentieth Century Literary Criticism, Vol. 48. 500p. 1993. text 150.00 (*0-8103-7973-2*) Gale.

— Twentieth Century Literary Criticism, Vol. 49. 500p. 1993. text 150.00 (*0-8103-7974-0*) Gale.

DiMauro. Twentieth Century Literary Criticism, Vol. 51. 1993. 150.00 (*0-8103-2429-6*) Gale.

DiMauro. Twentieth Century Literary Criticism: Topic, Vol. 50. 500p. 1993. text 150.00 (*0-8103-7975-9*) Gale.

Dimauro, jt. auth. see Schapira, A. H.

DiMauro, Laurie. Twentieth Century Literary Criticism, Vol. 40. 500p. 1991. text 150.00 (*0-8103-2422-9*) Gale.

— Twentieth Century Literary Criticism, Vol. 41. 500p. 1991. text 150.00 (*0-8103-2423-7*) Gale.

— Twentieth Century Literary Criticism, Vol. 44. 500p. 1992. text 150.00 (*0-8103-2426-1*) Gale.

— Twentieth Century Literary Criticism, Vol. 45. 500p. 1992. text 150.00 (*0-8103-2427-X*) Gale.

— Twentieth Century Literary Criticism, Vol. 52. 500p. 1994. text 150.00 (*0-8103-2430-X*) Gale.

— Twentieth Century Literary Criticism, Vol. 53. 500p. 1994. text 150.00 (*0-8103-2431-8*) Gale.

— Twentieth Century Literary Criticism, Vol. 54. 500p. 1994. text 150.00 (*0-8103-2432-6*) Gale.

— Twentieth Century Literary Criticism: Topic, Vol. 42. 500p. 1991. text 150.00 (*0-8103-2424-5*) Gale.

DiMauro, Louis, et al, eds. Applications of High-Field & Short Wavelength Sources: Proceedings of the Optical Society of America Conference on Generation & Applications of High-Field & Short Wavelength Sources Held in Santa Fe, New Mexico, March 20-22, 1997. LC 98-35190. 300p. (C). 1999. text 110.00 (*0-306-45909-4*, Kluwer Plenum) Kluwer Academic.

***DiMauro, Louis F., et al, eds.** Multiphoton Processes: ICOMP VIII - 8th International Conference. LC 00-104278. (AIP Conference Proceedings Ser.: Vol. 525). (Illus.). xv, 686p. 2000. 195.00 (*1-56396-946-7*) Am Inst Physics.

DiMauro, Salvatore & Wallace, Douglas C., eds. Mitochondrial DNA in Human Pathology. LC 92-49034. 218p. 1993. text 58.00 (*0-7817-0006-X*) Lppncott W & W.

Dimbleby, David. An Ocean Apart: The Relationship Between Britain & America in the Twentieth Century. 1989. 9.95 (*0-07-558699-1*) McGraw.

Dimbleby, Geoffrey W. The Development of British Heathlands & their Soils. 1962. 65.00 (*0-7855-7177-9*) St Mut.

Dimbleby, Geoffrey W., ed. see Grayson, Donald K.

Dimbleby, Jonathan. The Last Governor: Chris Patten & the Handover of Hong Kong. LC 98-115639. xvi, 461p. 1997. write for info. (*0-316-64018-2*) Little.

— The Palestinians. 25.00 (*0-7043-2205-6*, Pub. by Quartet) Charles River Bks.

— The Prince of Wales. 640p. 1994. 32.95 (*0-385-25472-5*) Doubleday.

— The Prince of Wales: A Biography. large type ed. LC 95-2629. 894p. 1995. lib. bdg. 26.95 (*0-7862-0426-5*) Thorndike Pr.

Dimbleby, Richard. More Than Words: An Introduction to Communication. 3rd ed. (Illus.). 296p. (C). 1998. pap. 21.99 (*0-415-17007-9*) Routledge.

Dimbleby, Richard & Burton, Graeme. More Than Words: An Introduction to Communication. (Illus.). (C). 1985. pap. 10.95 (*0-416-38070-0*, 9574) Routledge.

— More Than Words: Introduction to Communication. 3rd ed. LC 97-38903. (Illus.). 296p. (C). 1998. 75.00 (*0-415-17006-0*) Routledge.

Dimbleby, Richard, jt. auth. see Burton, Graeme.

Dimblely, Richard. Elizabeth Our Queen. LC 78-12304. (Illus.). 1979. reprint ed. lib. bdg. 65.00 (*0-313-21096-9*, DIEQ, Greenwood Pr) Greenwood.

Dimca, A. Singularities & Topology of Hypersurfaces. (Universitext Ser.). xvi, 263p. 1992. 59.95 (*0-387-97709-0*) Spr-Verlag.

Dimcock, James F., ed. Adam of Eynsham: Magna Vita S. Hugonsi, Episcopi Lincolniensis. (Rolls Ser.: No. 37). 1972. reprint ed. 70.00 (*0-8115-1089-1*) Periodicals Srv.

Dimde, Manfred. Nostradamus: Predictions for the 21st Century. LC 98-18210. (Illus.). 160p. 1998. 12.95 (*0-8069-0757-6*) Sterling.

DiMedio, Annette M. Frances McCollin: Her Life & Music. LC 90-44831. (Composers of North America Ser.). (Illus.). 184p. 1990. 39.50 (*0-8108-2289-X*) Scarecrow.

Dimeff, Linda A., et al. Brief Alcohol Screening & Intervention for College Students Basics: A Harm Reduction Approach. LC 98-46593. 200p. 1999. pap. text 26.00 (*1-57230-392-1*) Guilford Pubns.

***Dimen, Muriel.** Storms in Her Head: Freud & the Construction of Hysteria. 300p. 1999. pap. 25.00 (*1-892746-23-9*) Other Pr LLC.

Dimen, Muriel. Surviving Sexual Contradiction. 1986. 19.95 (*0-02-531620-6*) Macmillan.

Dimen, Muriel & Goldner, Virginia, eds. Gender in Psychoanalytic Space. (C). (gr. 13). 1999. 55.00 (*0-415-91230-X*) Routledge.

Dimendberg, Edward, jt. auth. see Divola, John.

Dimenil, Annie, jt. auth. see Edmiston, William F.

DiMenna, Donna, jt. auth. see Maidman Joshua, Janice.

***Dimension Publishing Staff.** Gran Turismo 2: Prima's Official Strategy Guide. LC 99-68163. (Illus.). 165p. 2000. pap. 14.99 (*0-7615-2665-X*) Prima Pub.

— The Legend of Dragoon: Prima's Official Strategy Guide. 2000. pap. 14.99 (*0-7615-3007-X*) Prima Pub.

— MediEvil II: Prima's Official Strategy Guide. 2000. pap. 14.99 (*0-7615-3006-1*) Prima Pub.

— Resident Evil 3 Nemesis: Prima's Official Strategy Guide. LC 99-67346. (Illus.). 95p. 2000. pap. 14.99 (*0-7615-2617-X*) Prima Pub.

— Syphon Filter 2: Prima's Official Strategy Guide. (Official Strategy Guides Ser.). (Illus.). 128p. 2000. pap. 14.99 (*0-7615-2793-1*, Prima Tech) Prima Pub.

***Dimension Publishing Staff, ed.** Tomb Raider - The Last Revelation (DC) Prima's Official Strategy Guide. LC 99-61524. (Illus.). 176p. (YA). 2000. pap. 14.99 (*0-7615-2860-1*) Prima Pub.

Dimensional Illustrators Staff. Cyber Palette. (Illus.). 1998. 35.00 (*0-688-16391-2*, Wm Morrow) Morrow Avon.

— Extreme Graphics. 1998. 39.95 (*0-688-16392-0*, Wm Morrow) Morrow Avon.

***Dimensional Illustrators Staff.** Virtual Media. 1999. 35.00 (*0-688-17254-7*, Wm Morrow) Morrow Avon.

Dimensions for Living. Everyday Prayers for Techers. LC 94-223837. 96p. 1993. pap. 5.00 (*0-687-31695-2*) Dimen for Liv.

— Everyday Prayers for Women. 96p. 1993. pap. 5.00 (*0-687-31692-8*) Dimen for Liv.

Dimensions For Living. A Garden of Virtues. 1995. 249.00 incl. disk (*0-687-01763-7*) Dimen for Liv.

Dimensions for Living Staff. A Moment with God for Fathers: Prayers for Every Dad, Every Day. LC 98-234764. (Moment with God Ser.). 1997. pap. text 5.00 (*0-687-12183-3*) Abingdon.

***Dimensions for Living Staff.** A Moment with God for Men: Prayers for Every Man. LC 98-33957. 64p. 1998. pap. 5.00 (*0-687-08777-5*) Dimen for Liv.

Dimensions for Living Staff. A Moment with God for Women: Prayers for Every Woman. LC 98-33929. 64p. 1998. pap. 5.00 (*0-687-08787-2*) Dimen for Liv.

— My Daily Walk: Living a Life of Praise. 1999. write for info. (*0-687-07479-7*) Abingdon.

***Dimensions for Living Staff.** My Daily Walk, 1999: Living a Life of Hope. (Illus.). 264p. 1998. pap., spiral bd. 14.00 (*0-687-05723-X*) Dimen for Liv.

Dimensions for Living Staff. Simple Pleasures for Busy Couples. LC 98-168231. (Illus.). 64p. 1997. pap. 5.00 (*0-687-11109-9*) Abingdon.

— Simple Pleasures for Friends. (Illus.). 64p. 1997. pap. 5.00 (*0-687-11119-6*) Abingdon.

— Simple Pleasures for Teachers. LC 98-168217. (Illus.). 64p. 1997. pap. 5.00 (*0-687-11129-3*) Abingdon.

Dimenstein, Gilberto. Brazil: War on Children. 88p. 1994. pap. 12.00 (*0-85345-838-3*, Pub. by Lat Am Bur) Monthly Rev.

Diment, Eunice. Kidnapped. (Illus.). 80p. 1976. pap. 4.00 (*0-85364-199-4*) Attic Pr.

Diment, Galya. The Autobiographical Novel of Co-Consciousness: Goncharov, Woolf, & Joyce. LC 94-8385. (Florida James Joyce Ser.). 216p. 1994. 49.95 (*0-8130-1304-6*) U Press Fla.

— Goncharov's Oblomov: A Critical Companion. LC 97-50518. (AATSEEL Critical Companions to Russian Literature Ser.). 256p. 1998. pap. 17.95 (*0-8101-1405-4*) Northwestern U Pr.

— Pniniad: Vladimir Nabokov & Marc Szeftel. LC 97-10871. (McLellan Book Ser.). (Illus.). 256p. 1997. 35.00 (*0-295-97634-9*) U of Wash Pr.

Diment, Galya & Slezkine, Yuri, eds. Between Heaven & Hell: The Myth of Siberia in Russian Culture. LC 92-23337. 1993. text 39.95 (*0-312-06072-6*) St Martin.

Diment, Michael. The Lone Survivor: A Diary of the Lukacze Ghetto & Svyniukhy. Yahalom, Shmuel D., tr. 226p. 1992. pap. 13.95 (*0-89604-152-2*, Holocaust Library) US Holocaust.

DiMento, Joseph F. Environmental Law & American Business: Dilemmas of Compliance. LC 86-75. (Environment, Development, & Public Policy: Public Policy & Social Services Ser.). (Illus.). 244p. (C). 1986. 65.00 (*0-306-42168-2*, Plenum Trade) Perseus Pubng.

— Wipeouts & Their Mitigation: The Changing Context for Land Use & Environmental Law. fac. ed. LC 90-46451. (Illus.). 125p. 1990. reprint ed. pap. 38.80 (*0-7837-7828-7*, 204758400007) Bks Demand.

DiMento, Joseph F. & Graymer, LeRoy, eds. Confronting Regional Challenges: Approaches to LULUs, Growth, & Other Vexing Governance Problems. (Donald Hagman Memorial Conference Ser.: No. 6). 133p. (Orig.). (C). 1991. pap. text 17.50 (*1-55844-117-4*) Lincoln Inst Land.

DiMento, Joseph F., ed. see Donald G. Hagman Commemorative Conference Staff, et al.

Dimeo, Jean & Rudy, Theresa M. Wills: A Do-It-Yourself Guide. 256p. 1992. pap. 10.00 (*0-910073-16-3*) HALT DC.

Dimer, Eugenia. Molchalivaia Lubov: Collection of Stories. 1980. 5.00 (*0-685-44305-1*) RWCPH.

— Ogljadivays Nazad: Stories Out of the Past. 1987. 8.00 (*0-685-22667-0*) RWCPH.

— S Devjatogo Bala: Poems. 1981. 4.00 (*0-685-44307-8*) RWCPH.

DiMercurio, Michael. Attack of the Seawolf. 416p. 1994. reprint ed. mass mkt. 6.99 (*0-451-18051-8*, Onyx) NAL.

Dimercurio, Michael. Barracuda. 1997. mass mkt. 6.99 (*0-451-40742-3*, Onyx) NAL.

DiMercurio, Michael. Phoenix Sub Zero. 464p. (Orig.). 1995. mass mkt. 6.99 (*0-451-40603-6*, Onyx) NAL.

Dimercurio, Michael. Piranha Firing Point. 1 vols., Vol. 1. 1999. mass mkt. 6.99 (*0-451-40876-4*) NAL.

***DiMercurio, Michael.** Threat Vector. 2000. mass mkt. 6.99 (*0-451-40908-6*, Onyx) NAL.

DiMercurio, Michael. Voyage of the Devilfish. 400p. 1993. pap. 6.99 (*0-451-40392-4*, Onyx) NAL.

Dimermanas, Alon, ed. see Besancon, I.

Dimermanas, Alon, ed. & tr. see Nachman.

Dimermanas, Alon, ed. & tr. see Nachman, Rebbe.

Dimermanas, Alon, ed. & tr. see Nathan.

Dimermanas, Alon, tr. see Rabbi Nachman of Breslov.

Dimery, Robert, ed. The Story of Aqua. (Illus.). 32p. (YA). 1998. pap. 9.95 (*0-7119-6933-7*, OP48082) Omnibus NY.

Dimery, Robert, ed. see Omnibus Press Staff.

Dimes, F. G., jt. auth. see Ashurst, J.

***Dimes, John.** Tales of Home. (Illus.). 88p. 2000. pap. 12.95 (*0-9679731-0-4*) Bhatari.

Dimet, F. X. Le, see Le Dimet, F. X.

Dimey, Bernard. Je Ne Dirai Pas Tout. (FRE.). 1995. pap. 49.95 (*2-86808-050-2*) Intl Scholars.

— Sable et Cendre. (FRE.). 1995. pap. 49.95 (*2-86808-068-5*) Intl Scholars.

DiMichael, Eleanor, jt. auth. see King, Robert.

DiMichele, Bill. Capacity X. (Illus.). 38p. (Orig.). 1988. pap. 3.00 (*0-926935-08-9*) Runaway Spoon.

— Heart on the Right. 33p. (Orig.). 1992. pap. 7.00 (*0-926935-71-2*) Runaway Spoon.

DiMichele, Mary. Mimosa & Other Poems. 46p. 1995. reprint ed. pap. 9.95 (*0-88962-131-4*) Mosaic.

Dimick, M. T. Memphis: The City of the White Wall. (Illus.). 29p. 1956. pap. 5.00 (*0-318-01019-4*) U Museum Pubns.

Dimick, Paul S., ed. Cacao Biotechnology Symposium Proceedings. (Illus.). 154p. (Orig.). 1986. pap. text 25.00 (*0-9616407-0-7*) Penn State Food.

Dimidjian, Victoria J. Early Childhood at Risk: Actions & Advocacy for Young Children. 64p. 1989. pap. 8.95 (*0-8106-1481-2*) NEA.

— Play's Place in Public Education for Young Children. 96p. 1992. pap. 15.95 (*0-8106-0364-0*) NEA.

Dimier. Recueil de Plans d'Eglises Cisterciennes, 2 tomes. 100.75 (*0-685-34012-0*, F22250) Fr & Eur.

Dimier, Anselme. Stone Laid Before the Lord. (Illus.). 1997. 38.95 (*0-614-27494-X*); pap. 18.95 (*0-614-27495-8*) Cistercian Pubns.

— Stones Laid Before the Lord. Lavigne, Gilchrist, tr. LC 98-19022. (Cistercian Studies: No. 152). 1998. write for info. (*0-87907-552-X*); pap. write for info. (*0-87907-652-6*) Cistercian Pubns.

Dimier, Louis. French Painting in the Sixteenth Century. LC 74-88821. (Art Histories Collection). 1970. reprint ed. 20.95 (*0-405-02226-3*) Ayer.

Dimier, Paul. Love Without Measure: Extracts from the Writings of St. Bernard of Clairvaux. (Cistercian Studies: No. 127). 154p. 1990. pap. 10.95 (*0-87907-727-1*) Cistercian Pubns.

Dimiev, S. & Sekigawa, K. Complex Structures & Vector Fields. 160p. 1995. text 48.00 (*981-02-2340-4*) World Scientific Pub.

Dimiev, S. & Sekigawa, K., eds. Topics of Complex Analysis, Differential Geometry & Mathematical Physics. 230p. 1997. text 58.00 (*981-02-3194-6*) World Scientific Pub.

Dimiev, S., jt. auth. see Sekigawa, K.

Dimiev, Stancho. Aspects of Complex Analysis, Differential Geometry, Mathematical Physics & Applications: Proce. 250p. 1999. 58.00 (*981-02-3868-1*) World Scientific Pub.

Dimiris, Tasos. Born Beneath Measure: A Daily Spiritual Program Through the Advent Fast of the Orthodox Christian Church. (Illus.). 69p. (Orig.). (C). 1995. pap. text, student ed. 29.95 (*1-884090-13-3*) Ecumenics Intl.

— Circumcision & Anathema: The Orthodox Christian Sacred Tradition of Eros & Bodily Integrity. (Illus.). 125p. (Orig.). (C). 1995. pap. text 49.95 (*1-884090-11-7*) Ecumenics Intl.

— Taking on Death: A Daily Spiritual Program Through the Great & Holy Lenten Fast of the Orthodox Christian Church. (Illus.). 109p. (Orig.). 1995. pap. text, student ed. 37.95 (*1-884090-08-7*) Ecumenics Intl.

Dimit, Emma. In Black & White. 32p. 1989. pap. 4.00 (*0-614-24758-6*) Tesseract SD.

Dimitiriou, Harry. A Developmental Approach to Urban Transport Planning: An Indonesian Illustration. LC 94-74223. 224p. (C). 1995. 73.95 (*1-85972-004-8*, Pub. by Avebry) Ashgate Pub Co.

Dimitracopoulou, Ioanna. Conversational Competence & Social Development. (Illus.). 178p. (C). 1990. text 59.95 (*0-521-37551-7*) Cambridge U Pr.

Dimitrakopoulos, Roussos, ed. Geostatistics for the Next Century: An International Forum in Honour of Michel David's Contribution to Geostatistics, Montreal, 1993. LC 93-44969. (Quantitative Geology & Geostatistics Ser.: Vol. 6). 524p. (C). 1994. text 285.50 (*0-7923-2650-4*) Kluwer Academic.

Dimitras, Augustinos I., jt. auth. see Zopounidis, Constantin.

Dimitreas, Yiannis E. Transplanting the Agora: Hellenic Settlement in Australia. LC 99-487910. 336p. 1998. pap. 35.00 (*1-86448-430-6*, Pub. by Allen & Unwin Pty) Paul & Co Pubs.

Dimitrejevic, Dimitrije, jt. auth. see Macesich, George.

Dimitri, Michael A. The Daughter of Neoptolemus: A Biography of Olympias, the Mother of Alexander the Great. 400p. (Orig.). 1993. pap. 12.00 (*1-884191-01-0*) Alexandra Pub.

— In Search of the Macedonians of Pakistan. LC 95-83139. (Illus.). 80p. (Orig.). 1996. pap. 14.95 (*1-884191-03-7*) Alexandra Pub.

— The Radiance of Ancient Macedonia. 66p. 1993. pap. 15.00 (*1-884191-00-2*) Alexandra Pub.

Dimitri, Nicola, jt. ed. see Vercelli, Alessandro.

Dimitri Publications Staff, ed. see Galas, Philip-Dimitri.

Dimitric, R., tr. see Kostrikin, Alexei I. & Shafarevich, I. R., eds.

Dimitrienko, Yu I. Thermomechanics of Composites under High Temperatures. LC 98-31135. (Solid Mechanics & Its Applications Ser.). 1998. 159.00 (*0-7923-5309-9*) Kluwer Academic.

Dimitrijev, Sima. Understanding Semiconductor Devices. LC 99-35429. (Oxford Series in Electrical & Computer Engineering). (Illus.). 582p. (C). 2000. text 94.00 (*0-19-513186-X*) OUP.

Dimitrijev, Sima, jt. ed. see Chau, Kevin.

D

An Asterisk (*) at the beginning of an entry indicates that the title is appearing for the first time.

Dimitrijevic, Dimitrije & Macesich, George. Money & Finance in Contemporary Yugoslavia. LC 72-92889. (Special Studies in International Economics & Development). 1973. 42.95 (*0-275-28725-4*) Irvington.
— Money & Finance in Yugoslavia: A Comparative Analysis. LC 84-21162. 220p. 1983. 47.95 (*0-275-90971-9*, C0971, Praeger Pubs) Greenwood.
— The Money Supply Process: A Comparative Analysis. LC 90-39155. 192p. 1991. 52.95 (*0-275-93597-3*, C3597, Praeger Pubs) Greenwood.
Dimitrijevic, M. R., et al, eds. Altered Sensation & Pain. (Recent Achievements in Restorative Neurology Ser.: Vol. 3). (Illus.). xiv, 214p. 1990. 172.25 (*3-8055-5036-7*) S Karger.
— Progressive Neuromuscular Diseases. (Limited Volume Series 1-4: Recent Achievements in Restorative Neurology: Vol. 2). (Illus.). xii, 360p. 1986. 242.75 (*3-8055-4222-4*) S Karger.
Dimitrijevic, M. R., ed. see Eddy, B. E., et al.
Dimitrijevic, Milan R. & Halter, John A. Atlas of Human Spinal Cord Evoked Potentials. LC 95-12373. (Illus.). 180p. 1995. text 75.00 (*0-7506-9631-1*) Buttrwrth-Heinemann.
***Dimitriou, Demetrios & Johal, Jack S.** Selecting & Forming Business Entities - 6/99 Update. Peyerwold, David, ed. LC 96-85264. (California Business Start-Up Ser.). 410p. 1999. 55.00 (*0-7626-0343-7*, BU-32573) Cont Ed Bar-CA.
Dimitriou, Michael A., ed. Design Guidance Manual for Ozone Systems. 1990. 80.00 (*0-685-38312-1*) Pan Am Intl Ozone.
Dimitrious, Harry T. & Cook, Alison H., eds. Land-Use - Transport Planning in Hong Kong: The End of an Era: A Review of Principles & Practices. LC 98-71406. 404p. 1998. text 76.95 (*1-84014-171-9*, Pub. by Ashgate Pub) Ashgate Pub Co.
***Dimitrius, Jo-Ellan & Mazzarella, Mark.** Put Your Best Foot Forward: Make a Great Impression by Taking Control of How Others See You. LC 99-59604. 304p. 2000. 24.00 (*0-684-86406-1*) S&S Trade.
Dimitrius, Jo-Ellan & Mazzarella, Mark. Reading People: How to Understand People & Predict Their Behavior, Anytime, Anyplace. LC 98-4934. 295p. 1999. pap. 13.95 (*0-345-42587-1*) Ballantine Pub Grp.
Dimitroff, Thomas P., intro. Play of Light: The Glass Lamps of Frederick Carder. (Illus.). 20p. (Orig.). 1991. pap. 3.00 (*0-9622038-3-1*) Rockwell NY.
Dimitroff, Thomas P. & Hajdamach, Charles R. Frederick Carder & Steuben Glass: American Classics. LC 98-7851. (Books for Collectors Ser.). (Illus.). 330p. 1998. 125.00 (*0-7643-0486-0*) Schiffer.
Dimitrou, Jerry P., jt. auth. see Couture, Jacqueline A.
Dimitrou, Jerry Parrish, jt. auth. see Couture, Jacqueline Ann.
Dimitroulis & Avery. Oral Cancer: Synopsis of Pathology & Management. LC 98-4825. 176p. 1998. pap. text 42.50 (*0-7236-1022-3*) Buttrwrth-Heinemann.
Dimitroulis, George. A Synopsis of Minor Oral Surgery. LC 96-23371. 1997. 44.00 (*0-7236-1094-0*, Pub. by John Wright) Macmillan.
Dimitroulis, George, et al. Orthognathic Surgery: A Synopsis of Basis Principles & Surgical Techniques. (Illus.). 198p. 1994. pap. text 52.50 (*0-7236-1017-7*) Buttrwrth-Heinemann.
Dimitrov, Dimiter S. & Broder, Christopher C. HIV & Membrane Receptors. LC 97-22035. (Medical Intelligence Unit Ser.). 1997. text 99.00 (*1-57059-464-3*) Landes Bioscience.
Dimitrov, George. Against Fascism & War. LC 86-20121. 130p. (C). 1987. pap. 4.25 (*0-7178-0643-X*) Intl Pubs Co.
Dimitrov, Jerry P., jt. ed. see Hay, Charles C., III.
Dimitrov, L., ed. see IAEA Staff.
Dimitrov, Leonid I., jt. ed. see Wenger, Emanuel.
Dimitrova, Blaga. The Last Rock Eagle: Selected Poems. Walker, B. et al, trs. from BUL. LC 92-72166. 81p. 1993. pap. 16.95 (*1-85610-009-X*, Pub. by Forest Bks) Dufour.
Dimitrova, Blaga, ed. see Bagryana, Elisaveta.
Dimitrova, Ekaterina. The Gospels of Tsar Ivan Alexander. (Illus.). 64p. (C). 1995. pap. 21.95 (*0-7123-0349-9*, Pub. by B23tish Library) U of Toronto Pr.
Dimitrova, Stefana P. Iskliucheniya v Russkom Iazyke (Exceptions in the Russian Language) (RUS.). 246p. (Orig.). 1994. pap. 22.95 (*0-89357-248-9*) Slavica.
Dimitrova-Vulchanova, Mila & Hellan, Lars, eds. Topics in South Slavic Syntax & Semantics. LC 98-51652. (Current Issues in Linguistic Theory Ser.: Vol. 172). xxviii, 263p. 1999. 75.00 (*1-55619-889-2*) J Benjamins Pubng Co.
Dimitrovski, Dragan & Mijatovic, Mijat. A Series-Iteration Method in the Theory of Ordinary Differential Equations. (Illus.). 135p. (C). 1997. pap. text 60.00 (*1-57485-025-3*) Hadronic Pr Inc.
Dimitry of Rostov. Angels & the Other Heavenly Bodiless Powers. 1984. pap. 0.25 (*0-89981-003-9*) Eastern Orthodox.
— A Prayer of Daily Confession for a Person Entering on the Way of Salvation. 1996. pap. 0.50 (*0-89981-165-5*) Eastern Orthodox.
Dimler, G. Richard. Friedrich Spee's "Trutznachtigall" (Germanic Studies in America: Vol. 13). 158p. 1973. 32.00 (*3-261-00848-2*) P Lang Pubng.
Dimler, G. Richard, jt. ed. see Daly, Peter M.
Dimmel, Marlene, jt. ed. see Gillard, Carrie.
Dimmendaal, Gerrit J. The Turkana Language. (Publications in African Languages & Linguistics). xviii, 496p. 1983. 152.35 (*90-70176-83-1*); pap. 134.65 (*90-70176-82-3*) Mouton.
Dimmendaal, Gerrit J., ed. Current Approaches to African Linguistics, Vol. 3. ix, 297p. (C). 1986. pap. text 75.40 (*3-11-013285-0*) Mouton.
Dimmet, Cornelia, jt. ed. see Van Buitenen, J. A.
***Dimmick, Barbara.** In the Presence of Horses. large type ed. LC 00-22865. (Wheeler Large Print Bks.). 2000. pap. 22.95 (*1-56895-860-9*) Wheeler Pub.
Dimmick, Barbara. In the Presence of Horses: A Novel. LC 98-13556. 352p. 1998. 23.95 (*0-385-49297-9*) Doubleday.
— In the Presence of Horses: A Novel. LC 99-46542. 352p. 1999. pap. 14.00 (*0-312-24567-X*) St Martin.
Dimmick, J. E. & Singer, D. B., eds. Forensic Aspects in Pediatric Pathology. (Perspectives in Pediatric Pathology Ser.: Vol. 19). (Illus.). vi, 178p. 1995. 189.75 (*3-8055-6194-6*) S Karger.
Dimmick, James E. & Kalousek, Dagmar K. Developmental Pathology of the Embryo & Fetus. (Illus.). 896p. 1992. text 195.00 (*0-397-51040-3*) Lppncott W & W.
Dimmick, Mary L. The Rolling Stones: An Annotated Bibliography. LC 78-53599. 173p. reprint ed. pap. 53.70 (*0-8357-4637-2*, 203756800008) Bks Demand.
Dimmick, Ralph E., tr. see Ramos, Graciliano.
Dimmick, Ralph E., tr. see Sicre, Jose G.
***Dimmick, Roger.** Exploring IBM AS/400 Computers: The Instant Insider's Guide to IBM's Popular Mid-Range Computer Family. 10th ed. (Exploring IBM Ser.). 488p. 2000. pap. 39.95 (*1-885068-43-3*, Pub. by Maximum Pr) IPG Chicago.
Dimmick, Roger, jt. auth. see Hoskins, Jim.
Dimmick, Sally. Successful Communication Through NLP: A Trainer's Guide. LC 95-2772. 176p. 1995. 69.95 (*0-566-07579-2*, Pub. by Gower) Ashgate Pub Co.
Dimmitt, Cornelia, ed. Hindu Mythology: A Reader in the Sanskrit Puranas. Van Buitenen, J. A., tr. LC 77-92643. 388p. 1978. pap. 24.95 (*0-87722-122-7*) Temple U Pr.
***Dimmitt, Simon.** Medicine for Dentists. (Illus.). 156p. 1999. pap. 14.95 (*1-876268-12-3*, Pub. by Univ of West Aust Pr) Intl Spec Bk.
Dimmock, Clive. School Based Management & School Effectiveness. LC 93-2933. (Educational Management Ser.). 240p. (C). 1993. pap. 25.99 (*0-415-08314-1*, B0769) Routledge.
— School Based Management & School Effectiveness. LC 93-2933. (Educational Management Ser.). 240p. (C). (gr. 13). 1993. 80.00 (*0-415-08313-3*, B0765) Routledge.
Dimmock, N. J., ed. Immune Responses, Virus Infections & Disease. (Society for General Microbiology Special Publications: Vol. 27). (Illus.). 164p. 1990. 60.00 (*0-19-963030-5*) OUP.
Dimmock, N. J., et al, eds. Control of Virus Diseases. (Society for General Microbiology Symposium Ser.: No. 45). 383p. (C). 1990. text 100.00 (*0-521-38562-8*) Cambridge U Pr.
Dimmock, N. J. & Primrose, S. B. Introduction to Modern Virology. 4th ed. (Illus.). 464p. 1994. pap. 49.95 (*0-632-03403-3*) Blackwell Sci.
Dimnik, Martin. Mikhail, Prince of Chernigov & Grand Prince of Kiev, 1224-1246. (Illus.). xvi, 199p. pap. 18.29 (*0-88844-052-9*) Brill Academic Pubs.
Dimo, P. Nodal Analysis of Power Systems. (Abacus Bks.). 290p. 1975. text 82.00 (*0-85626-001-0*) Gordon & Breach.
Dimock, D. Limericks Naughty & Gay. 1997. pap. 6.50 (*0-9626531-9-5*) Factor Pr.
Dimock, Duane. My Official X-Files Pictorial Price Guide. 80p. 1995. pap. 13.00 (*1-888239-00-X*) E Finn Prods.
Dimock, E., et al. Introduction to Bengali. 1996. reprint ed. 22.50 (*81-7304-190-3*) S Asia.
Dimock, Edward C., Jr. Introduction to Bengali Pt. 1: A Basic Course in Spoken Bengali. 1991. 39.95 (*0-8288-8435-8*, F109540) Fr & Eur.
— The Place of the Hidden Moon: Erotic Mysticism in the Vaisnava-Sahajiya Cult of Bengal. LC 66-13865. xx, 332p. 1989. reprint ed. pap. text 23.00 (*0-226-15237-5*) U Ch Pr.
Dimock, Edward C., Jr., ed. Thief of Love: Bengali Tales from Court & Village. LC 63-11396. xiv, 306p. 1975. reprint ed. pap. text 3.95 (*0-226-15236-7*, P624) U Ch Pr.
Dimock, Edward C., Jr. & Levertov, Denise, trs. In Praise of Krishna: Songs from the Bengali. (Illus.). xii, 118p. 1981. pap. text 12.00 (*0-226-15231-6*) U Ch Pr.
Dimock, Edward C., Jr., et al. The Literatures of India: An Introduction. LC 73-87300. 1993. reprint ed. pap. text 6.95 (*0-226-15233-2*, P768) U Ch Pr.
Dimock, Edward C., Jr., tr. see Gangarama.
***Dimock, Edward Cameron.** Mr. Dimock Explores the Mysteries of the East: An American in India. LC 98-43901. 224p. 1999. 18.95 (*1-56512-153-8*, 72153) Algonquin Bks.
Dimock, Edward E., ed. Dimensions of Sociolinguistics in South Asia. (C). 1992. 39.50 (*81-204-0573-0*, Pub. by Oxford & IBH Pubng) Science Pubs.
Dimock, Elna M. Before You Step into That Classroom. 128p. 1988. pap. 9.95 (*0-914763-03-2*) Educ Development.
— Pass the CBEST. 2nd ed. LC 84-13794. (Illus.). 156p. (Orig.). (C). 1984. pap. 14.50 (*0-914763-01-6*) Educ Development.
— Pass the CBEST. 3rd ed. LC 88-16287. (Illus.). 256p. (Orig.). 1988. pap. 14.50 (*0-914763-02-4*) Educ Development.
— Teacher Certification Tests. 3rd ed. LC 92-31173. 256p. 1993. pap. 14.00 (*0-671-86526-9*, Arco) Macmillan Gen Ref.
— Teacher Certification Tests. 5th ed. LC 99-60589. 249p. 1999. pap. 15.95 (*0-02-862823-3*, Arc) IDG Bks.
Dimock, Elna Magnusson. California Basic Educational Skills Test (CBEST) (Professional Certification & Licensing Ser.). 256p. 1989. pap. 13.00 (*0-13-111949-4*, Arco) Macmillan Gen Ref.
Dimock, George E. Unity of the "Odyssey" LC 88-14824. 360p. (Orig.). (C). 1989. pap. 19.95 (*0-87023-721-7*, X1989) U of Mass Pr.
Dimock, George E., Jr., tr. see Euripides.
Dimock, Giles, jt. ed. see Alexander, Jon.
Dimock, Herbert & Dimork, Margaret. Golden Marriage: Secrets to a Long & Loving Union, 1. 1999. pap. 17.95 (*1-58501-002-2*) CeShore Pubg.
Dimock, M. E., jt. ed. see Haines, C. G.
Dimock, Marshall E. Congressional Investigating Committees. LC 72-155626. reprint ed. 37.50 (*0-404-02134-4*) AMS Pr.
— Law & Dynamic Administration. LC 80-12863. 156p. 1980. 45.00 (*0-275-90470-9*, C0470, Praeger Pubs) Greenwood.
Dimock, Marshall E., jt. ed. see Haines, Charles G.
Dimock, Peter. A Short Rhetoric for Leaving the Family. LC 98-22017. 128p. 1998. pap. 12.95 (*1-56478-210-7*) Dalkey Arch.
Dimock, Peter T., jt. auth. see Bear, Euan.
Dimock, Susan W., compiled by. Coventry Births, Marriages, Baptisms & Deaths, from the Records of the Town & Churches in Coventry, 1711-1844. (Illus.). 301p. 1997. reprint ed. lib. bdg. 35.00 (*0-8328-5630-4*) Higginson Bk Co.
Dimock, Wai-Chee. Empire for Liberty: Melville & the Poetics of Individualism. 248p. 1989. pap. text 15.95 (*0-691-01509-0*, Pub. by Princeton U Pr) Cal Prin Full Svc.
— Residues of Justice: Literature, Law, Philosophy. LC 95-39867. 291p. (C). 1996. 48.00 (*0-520-20242-0*, Pub. by U CA Pr) Cal Prin Full Svc.
Dimock, Wai Chee. Residues of Justice: Literature, Law, Philosophy. 1997. pap. text 18.95 (*0-520-20244-9*, Pub. by U CA Pr) Cal Prin Full Svc.
Dimock, Wai-chee & Gilmore, Michael T., eds. Rethinking Class: Literary Studies & Social Formations. LC 94-16980. (The Social Foundations of Aesthetic Forms Ser.). 285p. 1994. 57.50 (*0-231-07600-2*); pap. 19.50 (*0-231-07601-0*) Col U Pr.
Dimoff, Eleanor. Explorations of Visual Phenomena: A Curriculum for Young Children, Integrating Math, Art & Science. (Illus.). 1973. pap. 1.50 (*0-918374-06-5*) City Coll Wk.
Dimoff, Tim. The You in Business: How to Build a Strong Business from the Inside Out. LC 96-92916. 122p. 1997. pap. 15.95 (*0-7880-0922-2*) CSS OH.
Dimoff, Timothy & Carper, Steve. How to Tell If Your Kids Are Using Drugs. 160p. 1993. reprint ed. pap. 10.95 (*0-8160-2916-4*) Facts on File.
Dimoff, Timothy, jt. auth. see Carper, Steve.
Dimon, Elizabeth F., jt. auth. see Reynolds, Phyllis C.
Dimon, Theodore, Jr. The Undivided Self: Alexander Technique & the Control of Stress. LC 98-18328. (Illus.). 100p. 1998. pap. 15.95 (*1-55643-294-?*) North Atlantic.
Dimond. Pocket Salesman. 1993. pap. 4.95 (*0-9640173-0-X*) Stadot Pubns.
Dimond & Walters. Legal Aspects of Midwifery Workbook. LC 97-181671. 80p. 1997. pap. text, wbk. ed. 32.00 (*1-898507-43-0*) Buttrwrth-Heinemann.
Dimond, Bridgit. The Legal Aspects of Complementary Therapy Practice: A Guide for Health Care Professionals. LC 98-20834. (C). 1998. text. write for info. (*0-443-05615-3*) Church.
***Dimond, Bridgit.** Legal Aspects of Physiotherapy. LC 99-89275. 2000. pap. write for info. (*0-632-05108-6*) Blackwell Sci.
Dimond, Bridgit C. Legal Aspects of Occupational Therapy. LC 96-9284. (Illus.). 400p. (Orig.). 1997. pap. text 34.95 (*0-632-04074-2*) Blackwell Sci.
Dimond, Craig W. & Andersen, Borge B., photos by. Lion House Recipes. LC 80-19719. (Illus.). 122p. 1984. reprint ed. 21.95 (*0-87747-831-7*, Shadow Mount) Deseret Bk.
Dimond, Don, et al. Guide to Sea Kayaking Western Great Lakes: The Best Trips on Lakes Superior & Michigan. LC 99-12396. (Regional Sea Kayaking Ser.). (Illus.). 240p. 1999. pap. text 15.95 (*0-7627-0416-0*) Globe Pequot.
Dimond, E. Grey & Hattaway, Herman, eds. Letters from Forest Place: A Plantation Family's Correspondence, 1846-1881. LC 93-25041. (Illus.). 512p. 1993. text 35.00 (*0-87805-653-X*) U Pr of Miss.
***Dimond, Joni.** I'm in a Hateful (State) Territory. 148p. 1998. pap. 12.95 (*0-9678254-0-7*) Burroughs Pub.
Dimond, Paul R. Beyond Busing: Inside the Challenge to Urban Segregation. LC 84-29782. 424p. 1985. text 42.50 (*0-472-10062-9*, 10062) U of Mich Pr.
— The Supreme Court & Judicial Choice: The Role of Provisional Review in a Democracy. LC 88-26709. 176p. 1989. text 42.50 (*0-472-10103-X*, 10103) U of Mich Pr.
Dimond, Peter. A Mozart Diary: A Chronological Reconstruction of the Composer's Life, 1761-1791. 58. LC 96-29814. (Music Reference Collection: Vol. 58). 248p. 1997. lib. bdg. 65.00 (*0-313-30131-X*, Greenwood Pr) Greenwood.
Dimont, Max I. The Amazing Adventures of the Jewish People. LC 84-16806. 175p. (YA). (gr. 8 up). 1984. pap. 8.95 (*0-87441-391-5*) Behrman.
— Jews, God & History, 3 vols. 30.00 (*0-614-30547-0*) NAVH.
— Jews, God & History. rev. ed. 472p. 1994. mass mkt. 8.99 (*0-451-62866-7*, Ment) NAL.
Dimopoulos, George, tr. see Callinicos, Constantine.
Dimork, Margaret, jt. auth. see Dimock, Herbert.
Dimos, Duane, et al, eds. Solid Freeform & Additive Fabrication, Vol. 542. LC 99-20397. (Symposium Proceedings Ser.). 179p. 1999. 81.00 (*1-55899-448-3*) Materials Res.
DiMotto, Jean W., et al. Wisconsin Civil Procedure Before Trial. LC 96-386. 800p. 1996. ring bd. 125.00 (*0-945574-79-7*) State Bar WI.
Dimoula, Kiki & Stavrou, Theofanis G. Lethe's Adolescence. LC 96-72137. (Modern Greek History & Culture Ser.: Vol. 20). 102p. 1996. 25.00 (*0-932963-08-0*) Nostos Bks.
Dimov-Bogoev, Christo, jt. ed. see Decsy, Gyula.
Dimov, Ivan T. & McKee, Dean. Monte Carlo Methods for Applied Scientists. 240p. 1998. text 48.00 (*981-02-2329-3*) World Scientific Pub.
Dimov, Ivan T. & Tonev, O. Advances in Parallel Algorithms. LC 93-81158. 212p. (gr. 12). 1994. pap. 77.00 (*90-5199-151-7*) IOS Press.
Dimov, Ivan T., et al. Advances in Numerical Methods & Applications: Proceedings of the 3rd International Conference. LC 95-132496. 440p. 1994. text 109.00 (*981-02-1926-1*) World Scientific Pub.
Dimov, Ivan T., jt. auth. see Sendov, B. L.
Dimovski, Ivan H. Convolutional Calculus. (C). 1990. text 155.00 (*0-7923-0623-6*) Kluwer Academic.
D'Imperio, M. E. The Voynich Manuscript: An Elegant Enigma. 149p. 1976. pap. 20.80 (*0-89412-038-7*) Aegean Park Pr.
Dimples, Dolly, pseud. The Greatest Diet in the World. rev. ed. LC 74-15778. Orig. Title: Diet or Die. (Illus.). 239p. 1975. pap. 3.95 (*0-88435-002-9*) Chateau Pub.
***Dimri, V. P.** Application of Fractals in Earth Sciences. (Illus.). 248p. (C). 2000. text 58.00 (*90-5410-284-5*, Pub. by A A Balkema) Ashgate Pub Co.
Dimri, Vijay. Deconvolution & Inverse Theory: Application to Geophysical Problems. LC 92-12252. (Methods in Geochemistry & Geophysics Ser.: 29). xviii,230p. 1992. 170.00 (*0-444-89493-4*) Elsevier.
Dimsdale, Joel E., ed. Survivors, Victims & Perpetrators: Essays on the Nazi Holocaust. LC 79-24834. (Illus.). 474p. 1980. pap. text 49.95 (*0-89116-351-4*) Hemisp Pub.
Dimsdale, Joel E. & Baum, Andrew S., eds. Quality of Life in Behavioral Medicine Research. (Perspectives on Behavioral Medicine Ser.). 304p. 1995. text 59.95 (*0-8058-1653-4*) L Erlbaum Assocs.
Dimsdale, Marcus S. A History of Latin Literature. (Select Bibliographies Reprint Ser.). 1977. reprint ed. 30.95 (*0-8369-6684-8*) Ayer.
Dimsdale, Nicholas & Prevezer, Martha, eds. Capital Markets & Corporate Governance. (Illus.). 360p. 1994. text 79.00 (*0-19-828788-7*) OUP.
Dimsdale, Thomas J. Vigilantes of Montana. LC 53-9887. (Western Frontier Library: No. 1). 1977. reprint ed. pap. 12.95 (*0-8061-1379-0*) U of Okla Pr.
Dimson, Elroy & Mussavian, Massoud, eds. Foundations of Finance, Vols. I-III. LC 97-42949. (History of Management Thought Ser.). 1800p. 1998. text 288.95 (*1-85521-989-1*, Pub. by Ashgate Pub) Ashgate Pub Co.
Dimster, Frank & Steele, James. The New Austrian Architecture. LC 95-3185. (Illus.). 224p. 1995. pap. 35.00 (*0-8478-1758-X*, Pub. by Rizzoli Intl) St Martin.
Dimster, Frank, jt. auth. see Steele, James.
***DiMucci, Dion & Wiener, Andi L.** Chapters: Writing the Adventure of Your Life. LC 98-14165. 200p. 1998. pap. 10.95 (*1-55874-587-4*) Health Comm.
***DiMugno, John K.** California Insurance Law Handbook: A Reference & Guide. LC 99-213530. 1594 p. 1998. write for info. (*0-314-23367-9*) West Pub.
Din, Adel S. Aviation Insurance. rev. ed. (C). 1989. 850.00 (*0-7855-4317-1*, Pub. by Witherby & Co) St Mut.
— Reinsurance for the Professional, 2 vols. (C). 1986. 750.00 (*0-7855-4241-8*, Pub. by Witherby & Co) St Mut.
Din, Allan M., ed. Arms & Artificial Intelligence: Weapon & Arms Control Applications of Advanced Computing. (SIPRI Publication). (Illus.). 244p. 1988. text 65.00 (*0-19-829122-1*) OUP.
Din, Anne B., tr. see Marcos, Subcomandante.
Din, Gilbert C. Canary Islanders of Louisiana. LC 87-29941. 272p. 1999. pap. 17.95 (*0-8071-2437-0*) La State U Pr.
— Francisco Bouligny: A Bourbon Soldier in Spanish Louisiana. LC 92-23235. (Southern Biography Ser.). (Illus.). 288p. (C). 1993. text 45.00 (*0-8071-1795-1*) La State U Pr.
***Din, Gilbert C.** Spaniards, Planters & Slaves: The Spanish Regulation of Slavery in Louisiana, 1763-1803. LC 99-29227. 1999. 49.95 (*0-89096-904-3*) Tex A&M Univ Pr.
Din, Gilbert C. & Conrad, Glenn R., eds. The Spanish Presence in Louisiana, 1763-1803. LC 96-84494. (Louisiana Purchase Bicentennial: Vol. II). 579p. 1996. 40.00 (*1-887366-03-2*) Univ LA Lafayette.
Din, Gilbert C. & Harkins, John E. New Orleans Cabildo: Colonial Louisiana's First City Government, 1769-1803. LC 95-45715. (Illus.). 376p. (C). 1996. text 45.00 (*0-8071-2042-1*) La State U Pr.
Din, Gilbert C. & Nasatir, Abraham P. The Imperial Osages: Spanish-Indian Diplomacy in the Mississippi Valley. LC 82-40449. (Civilization of the American Indian Ser.: Vol. 161). (Illus.). 432p. 1983. 49.95 (*0-8061-1834-2*) U of Okla Pr.
Din, M. R., jt. auth. see Malik, Imam.
Din, Mata. Negotiable Instruments & Banking. (C). 1989. 350.00 (*0-7855-6034-3*) St Mut.
Din Quraishi, Salim A., jt. auth. see Burke, Samuel M.
***Din, Rasshied.** New Retail. (Illus.). 250p. 2000. 80.00 (*1-84091-042-9*, Pub. by Conran Octopus) Antique Collect.
***Din-Savva, Lena.** Iz Moskvy Da V Pekin? LC 00-20141. 2000. write for info. (*1-55779-123-6*) Hermitage Pubs.
Din, Shams U. Perestroika & the Nationality Question in the U. S. S. R. 1991. text 25.00 (*0-7069-4962-5*, Pub. by Vikas) Advent Bks Div.

D

An Asterisk (*) at the beginning of an entry indicates that the title is appearing for the first time.

Din, Shams U. & Ahmed, E. Legends of the Sufis. Shah, Idries, ed. Redhouse, James W., tr. 1977. pap. 10.95 (*0-7229-5051-9*) Theos Pub Hse.

Dinaburg, Kathy & Akel, D'Ann. Nutrition Survival Kit: A Wholefoods Recipe & Reference Guide. LC 76-28772. (Illus.). 256p. (C). 1976. 16.95 (*0-915572-18-4*); pap. 7.95 (*0-915572-17-6*) Panjandrum.

Dinackus, Thomas D. Order of Battle: Allied Ground Forces of Operation Desert Storm. LC 99-29407. (Illus.). 408p. 2000. pap. 17.95 (*1-55571-493-5*) PSI Resch.

Dinalay, D., tr. see Mayr, Helmut.

Dinallo, Greg. Final Answers. 320p. 1993. mass mkt. 5.50 (*0-671-73312-5*) PB.

— Red Ink. LC 93-49358. 1995. pap. 6.50 (*0-671-73314-1*, PB Trade Paper) PB.

— Red Ink. large type ed. 474p. 1995. 29.50 (*0-7089-5806-0*) Ulverscroft.

— Touched by Fire. 296p. 1998. mass mkt. 5.99 (*0-449-00295-0*, Crest) Fawcett.

Dinamation International Corp. Staff. Dinamation's Dinosaur's Alive! LC 92-82913. (Illus.). 32p. (J). (ps-2). 1993. pap. 3.95 (*0-590-47082-5*, Cartwheel) Scholastic Inc.

Dinan, Carolyn. Goodnight, Monster. (Illus.). 32p. (J). pap. 7.95 (*0-14-038281-X*, Pub. by Pnguin Bks Ltd) Trafalgar.

***Dinan, Desmond.** Encyclopedia of the European Union. LC 99-86544. (Illus.). 2000. 110.00 (*1-55587-904-7*) L Rienner.

— Ever Closer Union: An Introduction to European Integration. 2nd ed. LC 99-11101. 620p. 1999. pap. 23.50 (*1-55587-739-7*) L Rienner.

Dinan, Desmond. Historical Dictionary of the European Community. LC 93-2871. (International Organizations Ser.: No. 1). (Illus.). 319p. 1993. 46.00 (*0-8108-2666-6*) Scarecrow.

— The Politics of Persuasion: British Policy & French African Neutrality, 1940-1942. LC 88-10690. 320p. (Orig.). (C). 1988. pap. text 25.50 (*0-8191-6983-8*); lib. bdg. 55.00 (*0-8191-6982-X*) U Pr of Amer.

***Dinan, Desmond, ed.** Encyclopedia of the European Union. rev. ed. LC 99-86544. (Illus.). 565p. 2000. pap. 29.95 (*1-55587-926-8*) L Rienner.

Dinan, Desmond, ed. The Irish Question. (Special Issue of Conflict Ser.: Vol. 7, No. 3). 114p. 1987. 18.00 (*0-8448-1541-1*) Taylor & Francis.

***Dinan, John.** Sports in the Pulp Magazines. LC 98-26758. 210p. 1998. lib. bdg. 32.50 (*0-7864-0481-7*) McFarland & Co.

Dinan, John A. Chicago Ain't No Sissy Town! The Regional Detective Fiction of Howard Browne. LC 95-5338. (Brownstone Mystery Guides Ser.: Vol. 18). (Illus.). 96p. 1997. pap. 15.00 (*0-941028-24-0*) Millefleurs.

— The Pulp Western: A Popular History of the Western Fiction Magazine in America. LC 81-21697. (I. O. Evans Studies in the Philosophy & Criticism of Literature: Vol. 2). (Illus.). 128p. 1983. pap. 17.00 (*0-89370-261-7*) Millefleurs.

Dinan, John J. Keeping the People's Liberties. LC 98-13639. 272p. 1998. 35.00 (*0-7006-0905-9*) U Pr of KS.

Dinan, Susie & Sharp, Craig. Fitness For Life: The Y's Exercise Plan for Active Living & Better Health for the Rest of Your Life. (Illus.). 1998. pap. 14.95 (*0-7499-1577-3*, Pub. by Piatkus Bks) London Brdge.

Dinan, Terry. Federal Options for Reducing Waste Disposal. (Illus.). 85p. (C). 1995. pap. text 25.00 (*0-7881-2376-9*) DIANE Pub.

— The Safe Drinking Water Act: A Case Study of an Unfunded Federal Mandate. (Illus.). 46p. (Orig.). 1995. pap. text 20.00 (*0-7881-2612-1*) DIANE Pub.

Dinan, Terry & Tawil, Natalie. Federalism & Environmental Protection for Drinking Water & Ground Level Ozone: Case Studies. (Illus.). 63p. (C). 1998. pap. text 25.00 (*0-7881-4984-9*) DIANE Pub.

Dinan, Timothy M. The Legend of Hammie-Downz. large type ed. LC 97-94844. (Illus.). 33p. (J). (gr. 3-6). 1997. 14.95 (*0-9664361-0-5*, 9864) ITF Bks Co.

DiNapoli, Carlo. All I Ever Wanted to Know about Cooking I Learned from Momma. Constantine, R., ed. (Illus.). 188p. 1992. pap. 13.95 (*0-9627946-2-7*) Hawk FL.

— The Cajun Gourmet Afloat & on the Road: For a Society on the Move! DiNapoli, Renee C., ed. (Illus.). 272p. (Orig.). 1991. pap. 14.95 (*0-9627946-1-9*) Hawk FL.

— Cooking Country with Shotgun Red. Constantine, R., ed. (Illus.). 275p. (Orig.). 1993. pap. 15.95 (*0-9627946-8-6*) Hawk FL.

— The Damned Well Do's & Don'ts for a Perfect Lifestyle. Constantine, R., ed. LC 94-234903. (Illus.). 185p. (Orig.). 1994. pap. 9.95 (*0-9627946-9-4*) Hawk FL.

— Is This Country Cooking? This Is Country Cooking! Constantine, R., ed. (Illus.). 280p. (Orig.). 1992. pap. 14.95 (*0-9627946-7-8*) Hawk FL.

— The Upper Crud Cookbook: The Fine Art of Dining Rather Than Merely Eating. Constantine, R., ed. (Illus.). 275p. 1992. pap. 15.95 (*0-9627946-4-3*) Hawk FL.

— Yankee Cooking Conch & All Dem Other Sea Critters. Constantine, R., ed. (Illus.). 250p. (Orig.). 1993. pap. 14.95 (*0-9627946-5-1*) Hawk FL.

DiNapoli, Carlo & DiNapoli, Renee C. How to Own a Boat & Not Spend Any Money: The Misadventures of Bilge & Betty Scuppers. 165p. (Orig.). 1990. pap. 8.95 (*0-9627946-0-0*) Hawk FL.

DiNapoli, Dominic, ed. Workouts & Turnarounds II: Global Restructuring Strategies for the Next Century Insights from the Leading Authorities in the Field. LC 99-18780. 480p. 1999. text 95.00 (*0-471-24636-0*) Wiley.

DiNapoli, Joe. Applications Manual: For the Proportional Divider. 4th ed. (Illus.). 60p. 1987. reprint ed. pap. 60.00 (*1-891159-01-1*) Coast Invest.

— DiNapoli Levels: The Practical Application of Fibonacci Analysis to Investment Markets. Winfield, Lee & Winfield, David, eds. (Illus.). 295p. 1997. 162.00 (*1-891159-04-6*) Coast Invest.

— Fibonacci, Money Management, & Trend Analysis: In Home Trading Course. 3rd ed. (Illus.). 100p. 1989. reprint ed. 375.00 (*1-891159-03-8*) Coast Invest.

DiNapoli, Renee C., jt. auth. see DiNapoli, Carlo.

DiNapoli, Renee C., ed. see DiNapoli, Carlo.

DiNapoli, Robert. An Index of Theme & Image to the Homilies of the Anglo-Saxon Church. 128p. 1995. pap. 18.95 (*1-898281-05-X*) Paul & Co Pubs.

Dinar, Ariel. Modeling Economic Management & Policy Issues of Water in Irrigated Agriculture. LC 95-44596. 264p. 1996. 59.95 (*0-275-95017-4*, Praeger Pubs) Greenwood.

***Dinar, Ariel, ed.** The Political Economy of Water Pricing Reforms. LC 99-59024. (World Bank Publications). 412p. 2000. 50.00 (*0-19-521594-X*, 61594) OUP.

Dinar, Ariel & Loehman, Edna T., eds. Water Quantity - Quality Management & Conflict Resolution: Institutions, Processes & Economic Analyses. LC 94-13729. 552p. 1995. 75.00 (*0-275-94782-3*, Praeger Pubs) Greenwood.

Dinar, Ariel & Subramanian, Ashok. Water Pricing Experiences: An International Perspective. (Technical Paper Ser.: No. 386). 174p. 1998. pap. 22.00 (*0-8213-4060-3*, 14060) World Bank.

Dinar, Ariel, et al. Measuring the Impact of Climate Change on Indian Agriculture. LC 98-14309. (Technical Paper Ser.: No. 402). 280p. 1998. pap. 22.00 (*0-8213-4192-8*, 14192) World Bank.

— Restoring & Protecting the World's Lakes & Reservoirs. LC 95-22293. (Technical Papers: No. 289). 130p. 1995. pap. 22.00 (*0-8213-3321-6*, 13321) World Bank.

Dinar, Ariel, jt. auth. see Saleth, R. Maria.

Dinar, Nathan, jt. ed. see Kaplan, Gadassah.

Dinar, Nathan, jt. ed. see Kaplan, H.

DiNardi, Salvatore R. Calculation Methods for Industrial Hygiene. (Industrial Health & Safety Ser.). 304p. 1995. 69.95 (*0-471-28621-4*, VNR) Wiley.

— Calculation Methods for Industrial Hygiene. (Illus.). 304p. 1995. text 54.95 (*0-442-01821-5*, VNR) Wiley.

DiNardi, Salvatore R., ed. The Occupational Environment - Its Evaluation & Control. LC 98-108720. 1997. 125.00 (*0-932627-82-X*) Am Indus Hygiene.

Dinardo. Anesthesia for Cardiac Surgery. 2nd ed. LC 97-8137. 417p. (C). 1997. 115.00 (*0-8385-0253-9*, A-0253-3) McGraw.

Dinardo, Jeffrey. Timothy & the Night Noises. LC 86-9383. (J). 11.95 (*0-671-66807-2*) Litle Simon.

— Timothy & the Night Noises. LC 86-9383. (Illus.). 32p. (J). (ps-2). 1990. pap. 3.25 (*0-671-70298-X*) Litle Simon.

DiNardo, John N. Nanoscale Characterization of Surfaces & Interfaces. 174p. 1994. 150.00 (*3-527-29247-0*, Wiley-VCH) Wiley.

DiNardo, R. L. Mechanized Juggernaut or Military Anachronism? Horses & the German Army of World War II, 113. LC 91-9270. (Contributions in Military Studies Ser.: No. 113). 160p. 1991. 49.95 (*0-313-27810-5*, DMH/, Greenwood Pr) Greenwood.

Dinardo, R. L., jt. ed. see Syrett, David.

DiNardo, Richard. Germany's Panzer Arm, 166. LC 96-9025. (Contributions in Military Studies Ser.: No. 166). 176p. 1997. 55.00 (*0-313-30178-6*, Greenwood Pr) Greenwood.

Dinardo, Richard L. James Longstreet: The Man, the Soldier, the Controversy. LC 98-7366. 1998. 27.95 (*0-938289-96-9*, 289969) Combined Pub.

Dinari, G., et al, eds. Frontiers of Gastrointestinal Research. Vol. 15-16. (Illus.). xvi, 628p. 1989. 443.50 (*3-8055-4973-3*) S Karger.

— Newer Tests & Procedures in Pediatric Gastroenterology. (Frontiers of Gastrointestinal Research Ser.: Vol. 15). (Illus.). vii, 332p. 1989. 258.50 (*3-8055-4646-7*) S Karger.

— Newer Tests & Procedures in Pediatric Gastroenterology: Function & Laboratory Tests; Nutrition, 2. (Frontiers of Gastrointestinal Research Ser.: Vol. 16). (Illus.). viii, 296p. 1989. 233.25 (*3-8055-4900-8*) S Karger.

***Dinatale, Nancy & Shore, Hennie.** Lifeworks: Behavioral Health in the Classroom: A Guidebook for Educators, Counselors, School Professions & Families. unabridged ed. Barr, Catherine, ed. (Illus.). v, 200p. (YA). (gr. 6-12). 1999. pap. text 19.95 (*0-9676106-0-5*) Fnd Behavioral Hlth.

Dinavo, Jacques V. Privatization in Developing Countries: Its Impact on Economic Development & Democracy. LC 94-32925. 176p. 1995. 59.95 (*0-275-95007-7*, Praeger Pubs) Greenwood.

Dinawa. Sacred History & Earth Prophecies. Sindja, ed. LC 96-68507. (Illus.). 232p. (Orig.). 1997. pap. 13.95 (*1-886966-07-9*) In Print.

Dinca, C., ed. see Levenard, Jim, et al.

Dincauze, Dena F. The Neville Site: 8,000 Years at Amoskeag. LC 75-40771. (Peabody Museum Monographs: No. 4). (Illus.). 160p. 1976. pap. 12.00 (*0-87365-903-1*) Peabody Harvard.

***Dincauze, Dena Ferran.** Environmental Archaeology: Principles & Practice. LC 99-39090. (Illus.). 350p. (C). 2000. text. write for info. (*0-521-32568-4*); pap. text. write for info. (*0-521-31077-6*) Cambridge U Pr.

Dincer, Ibrahim. Heat Transfer in Food Cooling Applications. LC 97-13173. 1997. boxed set. write for info. (*1-56032-580-1*) Hemisp Pub.

***Dincer, Ibrahim & Ayhan, Teoman, eds.** Energy & the Environment: Proceedings: Trabzon International Energy & Environment Symposium (2nd: 1998: Trabzon, Turkey) 585p. 1999. 99.00 (*1-56700-127-0*) Begell Hse.

Dinchak, William G. & Mathis, Michael J., eds. Water Quality Issues at Fossil Fuel Plants: Proceedings of a Symposium Sponsored by the Energy Division. 90p. 1985. 5.00 (*0-87262-490-0*) Am Soc Civil Eng.

Dincher, Judith R., jt. auth. see Harkness, Gail.

Dincher, Judith R., jt. auth. see Harkness, Gail A.

Dinckney, La Verne. A Black Angel Delivers a Message. Gonzalez-Parker, Zulma, ed. (Illus.). (Orig.). 1989. pap. write for info. (*0-318-65768-6*) Heartfelt Pr.

***Dinculeanu, Nicolae.** Vector Integration & Stochastic Integration. (Pure & Applied Mathematics: A Wiley-Interscience Series of Texts, Monographs & Tracts). 448p. 2000. text 89.95 (*0-471-37738-4*, Wiley-Interscience) Wiley.

Dinda, Kara M. & Cranker, Lyle E. Growers Guide to Medicinal Plants. (Illus.). 1999. spiral bd. write for info. (*0-9629868-4-4*) HSMP Pr.

Dinda, Kara M., jt. auth. see Craker, Lyle E.

Dinda, R. J., tr. see Luther, Martin.

Dinda, Richard, tr. see Chytraeus, David & Melanchthon, Philip.

Dindi, Hasan, et al. Turkish Culture for Americans. LC 88-83130. 180p. 1989. pap. 19.95 (*0-924602-44-9*) Intl Concepts.

***Dindia, Kathryn.** Communication in Personal Relationships Across Cultures. 2000. pap. text. write for info. (*0-471-49133-0*) Wiley.

Dindia, Kathryn, jt. ed. see Canary, Daniel J.

Dindorf, et al, eds. Polybii, Vol. I. (GRE.). 1993. reprint ed. 57.50 (*3-519-01715-6*, T1715, Pub. by B G Teubner) U of Mich Pr.

— Polybii, Vol. II. (GRE.). 1995. reprint ed. 69.50 (*3-519-01716-4*, T1716, Pub. by B G Teubner) U of Mich Pr.

— Polybii, Vol. III. (GRE.). 1995. reprint ed. 62.50 (*3-519-01717-2*, T1717, Pub. by B G Teubner) U of Mich Pr.

— Polybii, Vol. IV. (GRE.). 1995. reprint ed. 79.50 (*3-519-01718-0*, T1718, Pub. by B G Teubner) U of Mich Pr.

— Polybii Vol. V: Appendix: Indices et Historiarum Conspectus. (GRE.). 1987. reprint ed. 43.50 (*3-519-01719-9*, T1719, Pub. by B G Teubner) U of Mich Pr.

Dindorf, W., ed. Aeschylus - Scholia Graeca Ex Codicibus Aucta et Emendata. (GER.). xviii, 548p. 1962. reprint ed. write for info. (*0-318-70530-3*) G Olms Pubs.

Dindorfii, Guilielmi, ed. Aristides, (Opera), 3 vols., Set. clxvii, 2541p. 1964. reprint ed. write for info. (*0-318-70854-X*) G Olms Pubs.

Dindub, L. Brief History of Mongolia in the Autonomous Period: Mongolian Text with an Introduction & Index in English by John G. Hangin. (Mongolia Society Special Papers: No. 6). spiral bd. 20.00 (*0-910980-26-8*) Mongolia.

D'Indy, Vincent. Beethoven. Baker, Theodore, tr. LC 74-107808. (Select Bibliographies Reprint Ser.). 1977. 20.95 (*0-8369-5184-0*) Ayer.

— Beethoven: A Critical Biography. LC 72-125054. (Music Ser.). (Illus.). 1970. reprint ed. lib. bdg. 22.50 (*0-306-70019-0*) Da Capo.

— Beethoven: A Critical Biography. 127p. 1990. reprint ed. lib. bdg. 59.00 (*0-7812-9043-0*) Rprt Serv.

— Cesar Franck. 286p. 1990. reprint ed. lib. bdg. 69.00 (*0-7812-9062-7*) Rprt Serv.

D'Indy, Vincent, ed. see Franck, Cesar.

Dine, Carol. Trying to Understand the Lunar Eclipse. LC 91-78221. 72p. (Orig.). (C). 1992. pap. 8.95 (*0-942582-17-9*) Erie St Pr.

Dine, Janet. Cases & Materials on the Theft Acts. 224p. (C). 1985. 120.00 (*0-906322-80-4*) St Mut.

— Criminal Law in the Company Context. 232p. 1995. text 87.95 (*1-85521-342-7*, Pub. by Dartmth Pub) Ashgate Pub Co.

***Dine, Janet.** The Governance of Corporate Groups. (Cambridge Studies in Corporate Law: Vol. 1). 232p. (C). 2000. text 59.95 (*0-521-66070-X*) Cambridge U Pr.

Dine, Janet & Gobert, James. Cases & Materials on Criminal Law. 2nd ed. 689p. 1998. pap. 56.00 (*1-85431-764-4*) Gaunt.

Dine, Janet & Gobert, James J. Cases & Materials on Criminal Law. 630p. 1993. pap. 50.00 (*1-85431-262-6*, Pub. by Blackstone Pr) Gaunt.

Dine, Janet & Watt, Bob, eds. Discrimination Law: Concepts, Limitations, & Justifications. xiii, 251p. 1996. pap. 48.50 (*0-582-28909-2*, 15718) Gaunt.

Dine, Jim. Diary of a Non-Deflector: Selected Poems. (Illus.). 80p. (Orig.). 1987. pap. text 10.00 (*0-910457-13-1*) Arion Pr.

— Jim Dine: Recent Work. LC 97-100457. (Illus.). 24p. (Orig.). 1996. pap. write for info. (*1-878283-64-2*) PaceWildenstein.

— Jim Dine: Some Greeks, Some Romans. (Illus.). 96p. (Orig.). 1996. pap. write for info. (*1-878283-61-8*) PaceWildenstein.

Dine, M., ed. String Theory in Four Dimensions: Current Physics Sources & Comments. (Current Physics Sources & Comments Ser.: Vol. 1). x, 476p. 1988. pap. 63.00 (*0-444-87102-0*, North Holland) Elsevier.

***Dine, Philip.** French Rugby Football: A Cultural History. (French Studies Ser.). (Illus.). 288p. 2001. 65.00 (*1-85973-322-0*, Pub. by Berg Pubs); pap. 19.50 (*1-85973-327-1*, Pub. by Berg Pubs) NYU Pr.

Dine, Philip D. Images of the Algerian War: French Fiction & Film, 1954-1992. 276p. 1995. text 59.00 (*0-19-815875-0*) OUP.

Dineen, Catherine. Michael Jackson: In His Own Words. (In Their Own Words Ser.). (Illus.). 96p. pap. 15.95 (*0-7119-3216-6*, OP 47188) Omnibus NY.

Dineen, Deborah. Selected Old Testament Themes As in Literature. (YA). (gr. 9-12). 1985. teacher ed. 13.50 (*1-881678-14-8*); student ed. 9.00 (*1-881678-15-6*) CSEE.

Dineen, Donal, jt. auth. see Deegan, James.

Dineen, Jacqueline. The Aztecs. LC 91-36169. (Worlds of the Past Ser.). (Illus.). 64p. (YA). (gr. 6 up). 1992. lib. bdg. 14.95 (*0-02-730652-6*, Mac Bks Young Read) S&S Childrens.

— Feasts & Festivals. Wilkinson, Philip, ed. LC 98-38117. (Illus.). 96p. (YA). (gr. 5 up). 1999. lib. bdg. 19.95 (*0-7910-5136-6*) Chelsea Hse.

— The Greeks. LC 91-512. (Worlds of the Past Ser.). (Illus.). 64p. (YA). (gr. 6 up). 1992. text 14.95 (*0-02-730650-X*, Mac Bks Young Read) S&S Childrens.

— Hunting, Harvesting, & Home. Wilkinson, Philip, ed. (Illus.). 96p. (YA). (gr. 5 up). 1999. lib. bdg. 19.95 (*0-7910-5134-X*) Chelsea Hse.

— Lift the Lid on Mummies: Unravel the Mysteries of Egyptian Tombs, & Make Your Own Mummy! (Lift the Lid Ser.). (Illus.). 24p. (J). 1998. pap. 19.95 (*0-7624-0208-3*) Running Pr.

— Living with the Gods. Wilkinson, Philip, ed. (Illus.). 96p. (YA). (gr. 5 up). 1999. lib. bdg. 19.95 (*0-7910-5135-8*) Chelsea Hse.

— Rites of Passage. Wilkinson, Philip, ed. (Illus.). 96p. (YA). (gr. 5 up). 1999. lib. bdg. 19.95 (*0-7910-5133-1*) Chelsea Hse.

— The Romans. LC 91-511. (Worlds of the Past Ser.). (Illus.). 64p. (YA). (gr. 6 up). 1992. lib. bdg. 17.95 (*0-02-730651-8*, Mac Bks Young Read) S&S Childrens.

Dineen, Jacqueline & Wilkinson, Philip. The Early Inventions. LC 94-36812. (Ideas That Changed the World). (Illus.). 96p. (YA). (gr. 5 up). 1995. lib. bdg. 19.95 (*0-7910-2766-X*) Chelsea Hse.

Dineen, Jacqueline, jt. auth. see Wilkinson, Philip.

***Dineen, Joe & Bndges, Mark, eds.** The Gig Bag Book of Theory & Harmony. 157p. 2000. pap. text 12.95 (*0-8256-1701-4*, AM948816) Music Sales.

Dineen, Joe, jt. compiled by see Bridges, Mark.

Dineen, Joe, jt. ed. see Bridges, Mark.

Dineen, Kimberly A., ed. see Schmidt, Gary E.

Dineen, Mark. Brazilian Woodcut Prints. (Illus.). 128p. 1997. 76.50 (*0-7103-0587-7*, Pub. by Kegan Paul Intl) Col U Pr.

Dineen, Patrick S. Irish-English Dictionary (Focloir Gaeilge Bearla) (IRI.). 1996. 75.00 (*1-870166-00-0*) Colton Bk.

***Dineen, Peter.** Ndugu's Boy. 160p. (YA). 1999. pap. 9.95 (*1-893302-06-7*) Dandelion Bks.

Dineen, Peter, ed. The Surgical Wound. LC 81-8163. (Illus.). 238p. reprint ed. pap. 73.80 (*0-8357-7646-8*, 205697100096) Bks Demand.

***Dineen, S.** Complex Analysis on Infinite Dimensional Spaces. LC 99-25273. (Monographs in Mathematics). xv, 543p. 1999. 112.00 (*1-85233-158-5*, Pub. by Spr-Verlag) Spr-Verlag.

Dineen, S. Multivariate Calculus & Geometry. LC 97-31752. (Undergraduate Mathematics Ser.). (Illus.). xii, 262p. 1998. pap. 29.95 (*3-540-76176-4*) Spr-Verlag.

Dineen, Sean. The Schwarz Lemma. (Oxford Mathematical Monographs). (Illus.). 264p. 1989. 55.00 (*0-19-853571-6*) OUP.

Dineen, Tana. Manufacturing Victims: How the Psychology Business Wants to Keep Your Dependent for Life. 320p. 1996. pap. text 16.99 (*1-895854-58-X*, Pub. by R Davies Pub) Genl Dist Srvs.

Dinehart, Randal L. Sediment Transport At Gaging Stations Near Mount St. Helens, Washington, 1980-90: Data Collection & Analysis. LC 97-14732. (U. S. Geological Survey Professional Papers). x, 105 p. 1998. write for info. (*0-607-88374-X*) USGPO.

Dineley, W. O., jt. auth. see Bole, A. G.

Dinelli, Mel. The Man: Manuscript Edition. 1950. pap. 13.00 (*0-8222-0721-4*) Dramatists Play.

— The Spiral Staircase. adapted ed. 1962. pap. 5.25 (*0-8222-1065-7*) Dramatists Play.

Dinelli, Raphael. Rescue from Beyond the Roaring Forties. (Illus.). 144p. 1998. pap. 29.95 (*0-7136-4882-1*) Sheridan.

Dineltsoi, Mazii. Ahi Ni Nikisheegiizh. (NAV.). 38p. (Orig.). 1988. pap. 5.00 (*0-317-91235-6*) Princeton Collects W Americana.

Diner, D. B. & Fender, D. H. Human Engineering & Stereoscopic Viewing Devices. LC 93-37838. (Advances in Computer Vision & Machine Intelligence Ser.). (Illus.). 206p. (C). 1993. 65.00 (*0-306-44667-7*, Plenum Trade) Perseus Pubng.

Diner, Dan. America in the Eyes of the Germans. Brown, Allison, tr. from GER. LC 96-11523. (Illus.). 196p. (C). 1996. text 44.95 (*1-55876-104-7*); pap. text 18.95 (*1-55876-105-5*) Wiener Pubs Inc.

***Diner, Dan.** Beyond the Conceivable. LC 99-47175. (Weimar & Now Ser.: Vol. 20). 290p. 2000. 45.00 (*0-520-21345-9*) U CA Pr.

Diner, Dudley S. Epilepsy & Sleep. 300p. 1999. 99.95 (*0-12-216770-8*) Acad Pr.

Diner, Hasia. Jews in America. LC 98-17645. (Religion in America Ser.). (Illus.). 160p. (YA). (gr. 6 up). 1999. text 22.00 (*0-19-510678-4*) OUP.

Diner, Hasia R. Erin's Daughters in America: Irish Immigrant Women in the Nineteenth Century. LC 83-183. (Studies in Historical & Political Science: No. 2). 208p. 1983. pap. 15.95 (*0-8018-2872-4*) Johns Hopkins.

— In the Almost Promised Land: American Jews & Blacks, 1915-1935. LC 94-35516. 288p. 1995. pap. text 16.95 (*0-8018-5065-7*) Johns Hopkins.

— In the Almost Promised Land: American Jews & Blacks, 1915-1935, 59. LC 76-46767. (Contributions in American History Ser.: No. 59). 271p. 1977. 57.95 (*0-8371-9400-8*, DIA/, Greenwood Pr) Greenwood.

— The Jewish People in America Vol. 2: A Time for Gathering: The Second Migration, 1820-1880. (Illus.). 344p. 1995. pap. 15.95 (*0-8018-5121-1*) Johns Hopkins.

An Asterisk (*) at the beginning of an entry indicates that the title is appearing for the first time.

***Diner, Hasia R.** Lower East Side Memories: A Jewish Place in America. LC 00-21148. (Illus.). 264p. 2000. 27.95 (*0-691-00747-0*) Princeton U Pr.

Diner, Hasia R. A Time for Gathering: The Second Migration, 1820-1880. (Jewish People in America Ser.: Vol. 2). (Illus.). 344p. 1992. 35.00 (*0-8018-4344-8*) Johns Hopkins.

***Diner, Hasia R., et al, eds.** Remembering the Lower East Side: American Jewish Reflections. LC 00-31042. (Modern Jewish Experience Ser.). 2000. 24.95 (*0-253-33788-7*) Ind U Pr.

Diner, Judith B., ed. from FRE. One Hundred New Tales: Les Cents Nouvelles Nouvelles. LC 89-23570. (Library of Medieval Literature). 394p. 1990. text 25.00 (*0-8240-8510-8*) Garland.

Diner, S., et al, eds. Dynamical Systems: A Renewal of Mechanism: Centennial of Georges David Birkhoff. 296p. 1986. text 58.00 (*9971-5-0150-3*, Z0300P-B) World Scientific Pub.

Diner, Steven J. A City & Its Universities: Public Policy in Chicago, 1892-1919. LC 79-16834. (Illus.). 275p. reprint ed. pap. 85.30 (*0-7837-3759-9*, 204357600010) Bks Demand.

— A Very Different Age: Americans of the Progressive Era. LC 97-3801. 320p. 1997. 25.00 (*0-8090-2553-1*) Hill & Wang.

— A Very Different Age: Americans of the Progressive Era. 336p. 1998. pap. 13.00 (*0-8090-1611-7*) Hill & Wang.

Diner, Steven J., jt. ed. see Breul, Frank R.

Dinerman, Ina R. Migrants & Stay-at-Homes: A Comparative Study of Rural Migration from Michoacan, Mexico. (Monographs: No. 5). 112p. (Orig.). (C). 1982. pap. 7.50 (*0-935391-43-6*, MN-05) UCSD Ctr US-Mex.

Dinerman, Miriam & Geismar, Ludwig L., eds. A Quarter-Century of Social Work Education. LC 84-6951. 272p. reprint ed. pap. 84.40 (*0-7837-6540-1*, 204567700007) Bks Demand.

Dinerman, Miriam, ed. see NASW Professional Symposium on Social Work Staff.

Dinero, Thomas E., ed. Selected Practical Problems in Health & Social Research. 107p. 1996. pap. 14.95 (*0-7890-0226-4*, Hawrth Medical) Haworth Pr.

— Selected Practical Problems in Health & Social Research. LC 96-30652. (Journal of Health & Social Policy: Vol. 8, No. 1). 107p. (C). 1996. 29.95 (*1-56024-832-7*) Haworth Pr.

Dinerova, E. Pocitajme Hravo (Arithmetics by Playing) (SLO.). 80p. 1997. pap. write for info. (*80-08-02587-5*, Pub. by Slov Pegagog Naklad) IBD Ltd.

Dinerstein, Eric, et al. A Conservation Assessment of the Terrestrial Ecoregions of Latin America & the Caribbean. LC 95-227. 148p. 1995. pap. 40.00 (*0-8213-3295-3*) World Bank.

— Una Evaluacion del Estado de Conservacion de las Eco-Regiones Terrestres de America Latina y el Caribe.Tr. of A Conservation Assessment of the Terrestrial Ecoregions of Latin America & the Caribbean. (SPA.). 154p. 1996. pap. 40.00 (*0-8213-3296-1*, 13296) World Bank.

Dinerstein, Herbert S. Fifty Years of Soviet Foreign Policy. LC 68-22278. (Washington Center of Foreign Policy Research, Studies in International Affairs: No. 6). 83p. reprint ed. pap. 30.00 (*0-608-30943-5*, 200495500048) Bks Demand.

— The Making of a Missile Crisis, October, 1962. LC 75-36943. 320p. reprint ed. pap. 99.20 (*0-608-18408-X*, 203057200069) Bks Demand.

— War & the Soviet Union. LC 75-45031. 265p. 1976. reprint ed. lib. bdg. 65.00 (*0-8371-8658-7*, DIWS, Greenwood Pr) Greenwood.

***Dinerstein, Robert D.** Get Consent. LC 98-47537. 125p. 1998. 39.95 (*0-940898-58-6*) Am Assn Meat Prcssrs.

Dines. Landscape Architects Portable. 2001. 59.95 (*0-07-134422-5*) McGraw.

Dines, Alison, ed. see Cribb, Alan.

Dines, Ann R. The Practical Gardener: An A-Z Guide to Techniques & Tips. LC 94-27977. (Illus.). 192p. 1995. 15.95 (*1-56799-157-2*, Friedman-Fairfax) M Friedman Pub Grp Inc.

Dines, Carol. Best Friends Tell. (J). 1990. mass mkt. 12.95 (*0-440-80153-2*) Dell.

— Talk to Me: Stories & a Novella. (YA). (gr. 7 up). 1997. 15.95 (*0-614-28683-2*, Delacorte Pr Bks) BDD Bks Young Read.

— Talk to Me: Stories & a Novella. LC 96-43114. 240p. (YA). (gr. 7). 1997. 15.95 (*0-385-32271-2*, Delacorte Pr Bks) BDD Bks Young Read.

— Talk to Me: Stories & a Novella. 240p. (YA). (gr. 7). 1999. mass mkt. 4.50 (*0-440-22026-2*) BDD Bks Young Read.

Dines-Cox, Elaine. Outerbridge. (Illus.). 252p. 1999. 39.99 (*3-8228-6618-0*) Taschen Amer.

Dines, Gail & Humez, Jean M. Gender, Race & Class in Media: A Critical Text-Reader. 450p. 1994. 75.00 (*0-8039-5163-9*); pap. 34.00 (*0-8039-5164-7*) Sage.

Dines, Gail & Jensen, Bob. Pornography: Production & Consumption of Male Supremacy. LC 97-18263. 224p. 1997. pap. 19.99 (*0-415-91813-8*) Routledge.

— Pornography: Production & Consumption of Male Supremacy. LC 97-18263. 224p. (C). 1997. 80.00 (*0-415-91812-X*) Routledge.

Dines, James. How Investors Can Make Money Using Mass Psychology: A Guide to Your Relationship with Money. (Illus.). 400p. 1996. 59.00 (*0-9649689-0-8*) J Dines.

Dines, Jess E. Choose the Right Mate, Lover or Friend Through Handwriting. 1992. pap. 10.95 (*0-9627666-1-5*) Pantex.

***Dines, Jess E.** Document Examiner Textbook LC 99-172607. 566 p. 1998. write for info. (*0-9627666-3-1*) Pantex.

Dines, Jess E. Handwriting Analysis Made Easy. 117p. 1990. pap. 15.00 (*0-9627666-0-7*) Pantex.

Dines, Nicholas T. & Brown, Kyle. Time-Saver Standards Concise Site Construction Details Manual. LC 99-169787. (Time-Saver Standards Concise Ser.). (Illus.). 384p. 1998. 49.95 (*0-07-017039-8*) McGraw-Hill Prof.

Dines, Nicholas T. & Harris, Charles W. Time-Saver Standards for Landscape Architecture. 2nd rev. ed. LC 97-31842. (Illus.). 928p. 1997. 150.00 (*0-07-017027-4*) McGraw.

***Dines, Patricia.** The Organic Traveler's Guide: Exploring Organics in Northern California's Sonoma, Napa &... (Illus.). 2000. pap. 9.95 (*0-9700941-0-8*) Comnity Actn.

Dinescu, T. A. & Radulescu, C. Slip Form Techniques. (Abacus Bks.). (Illus.). 488p. 1984. text 230.00 (*0-85626-307-9*) Gordon & Breach.

Dinesen, Isak. Anecdotes of Destiny. 1985. pap. 7.95 (*0-394-74215-X*) Vin Bks.

— Anecdotes of Destiny & Ehrengard. LC 92-50647. 1993. pap. 13.00 (*0-679-74333-2*) Vin Bks.

— Carnival. 1977. 17.95 (*0-226-15303-7*) U Ch Pr.

— Carnival: Entertainments & Posthumous Tales. LC 77-5666. 350p. 1979. pap. text 17.00 (*0-226-15304-5*) U Ch Pr.

— Contes d'Hiver. (FRE.). 416p. 1982. pap. 11.95 (*0-7859-1964-3*, 2070374114) Fr & Eur.

— Daguerreotypes & Other Essays. Mitchell, P. M. & Paden, William D., trs. LC 78-27543. 256p. 1984. pap. 15.95 (*0-226-15306-1*) U Ch Pr.

— Le Diner de Babette. (FRE.). 253p. 1989. pap. 11.95 (*0-7859-2107-9*, 2070380955) Fr & Eur.

— La Ferme Africaine. (FRE.). 512p. 1986. pap. 11.95 (*0-7859-1874-4*, 2070370372) Fr & Eur.

— Last Tales. LC 91-50031. (Vintage International Ser.). 352p. 1991. pap. 13.00 (*0-679-73640-9*) Vin Bks.

— Letters from Africa, 1914-1931. Lasson, Frans, ed. Born, Anne, tr. LC 80-25856. (Phoenix Fiction Ser.). (Illus.). xliii, 516p. (C). 1984. pap. 18.95 (*0-226-15311-8*) U Ch Pr.

— Letters from Africa, 1914-1931. Lasson, Frans, ed. Born, Anne, tr. LC 80-25856. (Phoenix Fiction Ser.). (Illus.). xliii, 530p. (C). 1992. 25.00 (*0-226-15309-6*) U Ch Pr.

— Nouveaux Contes d'Hiver. (FRE.). 416p. 1987. pap. 11.95 (*0-7859-2060-9*, 2070378217) Fr & Eur.

— On Modern Marriage & Other Observations. Born, Anne, tr. 144p. 1987. pap. 7.95 (*0-312-01074-5*) St Martin.

— Out of Africa. LC 92-50213. 420p. 1992. 16.50 (*0-679-60021-3*) Modern Lib NY.

— Out of Africa. 1993. reprint ed. lib. bdg. 18.95 (*0-89968-444-0*, Lghtyr Pr) Buccaneer Bks.

— Out of Africa & Shadows on the Grass. LC 89-40144. (Vintage International Ser.). 512p. 1989. pap. 13.00 (*0-679-72475-3*) Vin Bks.

— Seven Gothic Tales. LC 91-50030. (Vintage International Ser.). 432p. 1991. pap. 14.00 (*0-679-73641-7*) Vin Bks.

***Dinesen, Isak.** Shadows on the Grass. 2000. 6.95 (*0-226-15301-0*) U Ch Pr.

Dinesen, Isak. Les Voies du Vengeance. (FRE.). 440p. 1990. pap. 13.95 (*0-7859-2153-2*, 2070383202) Fr & Eur.

— Winter's Tales. LC 92-50615. 1993. pap. 13.00 (*0-679-74334-0*) Vin Bks.

— Winter's Tales. LC 70-169542. (Short Story Index Reprint Ser.). 1977. reprint ed. 19.95 (*0-8369-4003-2*) Ayer.

Dinesh, B. M. Economic Activities of Children. LC 88-901324. xi, 151 p. 1988. 100.00 (*81-7035-040-9*) S Asia.

Dinesh, Kamini. Between Spaces of Silence: Women Creative Writers. (C). 1994. write for info. (*81-207-1350-8*) Sterling Pubs.

Diness, Madelynne, ed. see Ames, Francis H.

Dineykhan, M., et al. Oscillator Representation in Quantum Physics. Ehlers, J. et al, eds. LC 95-7855. (Lecture Notes in Physics - Monographs: Vol. m26). ix, 279p. 1995. 57.95 (*3-540-59085-4*) Spr-Verlag.

Ding, M. Z. Proceedings of the 4th Experimental Chaos Conference: Boca Raton, Florida, USA, 6-8 August ,1997. 1999. 86.00 (*981-02-3743-X*) World Scientific Pub.

***Ding, C., et al, eds.** Sequences & Their Applications: Proceedings of SETA'98. LC 99-42725. (Series in Discrete Mathematics & Theoretical Computer Science). 405p. 1999. pap. 84.00 (*1-85233-196-8*, Pub. by Spr-Verlag) Spr-Verlag.

Ding, C. S., et al. The Stability Theory of Stream Ciphers. Goos, G. & Hartmanis, J., eds. (Lecture Notes in Computer Science Ser.: Vol. 561). ix, 187p. 1991. 31.00 (*0-387-54973-0*) Spr-Verlag.

Ding, George D. Prophecy & the World. LC 88-90464. (Illus.). 258p. (Orig.). 1988. pap. 8.95 (*0-9621732-0-7*); lib. bdg. 14.95 (*0-9621732-1-5*) G D D Ding.

Ding, L. Z. River Sedimentation, Vol. III. Shen, Hsieh W., ed. LC 31-25158. (Illus.). 1822p. 1986. 60.50 (*0-937099-07-4*) U MS Ctr Comput Hydrosci.

Ding, Li. Meridian Qigong: Transferring Qi along the Meridian. (Illus.). 261p. 1988. 12.95 (*0-8351-2322-7*) China Bks.

Ding-Ling Tai. Housing Policy & High-Rise Living: A Study of Singapore's Public Housing. (Illus.). 335p. 1988. text 75.00 (*9971-68-136-6*, Pub. by Chopmen Singapore) Advent Bks Div.

Ding Lu. Entrepreneurship in Suppressed Markets: Private-Sector Experience in China. LC 93-49426. (Studies in Entrepreneurship). 216p. 1994. text 20.00 (*0-8153-1643-7*) Garland.

Ding, Mae L., ed. Survey Sources: For U. S. & International Employee Pay & Benefit Surveys. rev. ed. 2000. pap. 365.00 (*0-9633931-3-8*, Pub. by Prsnl Systs Assocs) Am Compensation.

— Survey Sources: For U. S. & International Employee Pay & Benefit Surveys. 3rd rev. ed. 1997. pap. 265.00 (*0-9633931-2-X*) Prsnl Systs Assocs.

Ding, Qiulin & Davies, B. J. Surface Engineering Geometry for Computer-Aided Design & Manufacture. (Mechanical Engineering Ser.). 300p. 1988. text 79.95 (*0-470-20997-6*) P-H.

Ding, Shizhao. Ablaufplanung in Komplexen Systemen - Teilplane - Harmonisierung - Verknupfung. (GER.). 1997. 48.00 (*3-487-07764-7*) G Olms Pubs.

Ding, Shou-Qian & Wu, Bao G., eds. Display Devices & Systems II. LC 99-170357. (Proceedings of SPIE Ser.: Vol. 3560). 258p. 1998. 89.00 (*0-8194-3021-8*) SPIE.

Ding, X. L. The Decline of Communism in China: Legitimacy Crisis, 1977-1989. (Illus.). 246p. (C). 1994. text 54.95 (*0-521-45138-8*) Cambridge U Pr.

Ding, Xiaoqi. Maidenhome. Berry, Chris & Silber, Cathy, trs. LC 94-15414. 224p. 1994. pap. 8.95 (*1-879960-36-2*) Aunt Lute Bks.

— Maidenhome. Berry, Chris & Silber, Cathy, trs. 224p. 1996. 24.95 (*0-908569-77-7*, Pub. by Univ Otago Pr) Intl Spec Bk.

Ding Xiaxi. Theory of Ba Spaces & Its Applications. 168p. 1996. 29.90 (*7-03-003100-8*, Pub. by Sci Pr) Lubrecht & Cramer.

Ding, Ya. The Earth Sings. Rothschild, Jon, tr. 1990. 21.95 (*0-15-176140-X*) Harcourt.

Ding, Yihui. Monsoons over China. LC 92-12017. (Atmospheric Sciences Library). 432p. (C). 1994. text 264.50 (*0-7923-1757-2*) Kluwer Academic.

Ding, Yinong, ed. see Zhang, Pingping.

Ding-Zhu Du, ed. Gradient Projection Methods in Linear & Non-Linear Programming: Advances in Discrete Mathematics & Computer Science. 354p. (Orig.). (C). 1988. reprint ed. pap. 60.00 (*0-318-41158-X*) Hadronic Pr Inc.

Ding-Zhudu & Hsu, D. F., eds. Gradient Projection Method in Linear & Nonlinear Programming. 1988. 60.00 (*0-911767-45-2*) Hadronic Pr Inc.

Dingel, Dorthe Dahlgaard. Public Procurement: A Harmonization of the National Judicial Review Of The Application of European Community Law. LC 99-18786. (European Monographs). 1999. 99.00 (*90-411-1161-1*) Kluwer Law Intl.

Dingelstedt, Franz. Das Wesertal von Munden Bis Minden. (Malerische und Romantische Deutschland Ser.). (GER.). xxvi, 139p. 1996. reprint ed. 25.00 (*3-487-08050-8*) G Olms Pubs.

Dingemans, M. W. Water Wave Propagation Over Uneven Bottoms. LC 96-29860. 700p. 1997. text 99.00 (*981-02-0426-4*); pap. text 53.00 (*981-02-0427-2*) World Scientific Pub.

Dinger, jt. auth. see Black.

Dinger, Adeline S. Folk Life & Folklore of the Mexican Border. 98p. 1972. pap. text 0.75 (*1-888594-01-2*) Hidalgo Cty Hist Mus.

Dinger, Charlotte. Art of the Carousel. LC 82-90507. (Illus.). 223p. 1984. 40.00 (*0-914507-00-1*) Carousel Art.

***Dinger, Dennis R.** The Coming of the Lord Draweth Nigh. 165p. 2000. pap. 8.95 (*0-615-11209-9*) D R Dinger.

Dingerkus, Guido. The Shark Watcher's Guide. (Illus.). 144p. (YA). (gr. 7 up). 1989. pap. 5.95 (*0-671-68815-4*, Julian Messner) Silver Burdett Pr.

Dinges, David F. & Broughton, Roger J., eds. Sleep & Alertness: Chronobiological, Behavioral & Medical Aspects of Napping. LC 86-45981. (Illus.). 336p. reprint ed. pap. 104.20 (*0-608-07237-0*, 206746200009) Bks Demand.

Dinges, John, jt. ed. see Rosenbaum, Marcus D.

Dinges, Richard A. Two Tenebrae Readings & Services. 24p. (Orig.). 1997. pap. 5.25 (*0-7880-0757-2*) CSS OH.

Dinges, Susan & Thomas, Sue. Curtain Vol. II: Creative Drama for Children 9-12. (J). (ps-7). 1986. pap. 15.00 (*0-89824-168-5*) Trillium Pr.

Dinges, Susan, jt. auth. see Thomas, Sue.

Dinges, William D., et al. The Living Light Vol. 33, No. 3: Ministry to Young Adults. 96p. (Orig.). (C). 1997. pap. 8.95 (*1-57455-097-7*) US Catholic.

Dinghaus, Angela. Frauenwelten: Biographisch-Historische Skizzen Aus Niedersachsen. (GER.). xii, 371p. 1993. write for info. (*3-487-09727-3*) G Olms Pubs.

Dingle, Aylward E. Pipe All Hands! LC 74-101279. (Short Story Index Reprint Ser.). 1977. 23.95 (*0-8369-3216-1*) Ayer.

Dingle, Barbara, jt. auth. see Travis, Debbie.

Dingle, Brian. An Introduction to Programmable Controllers & Ladder Diagram Programming. 121p. 1988. 80.00 (*0-946796-22-X*) St Mut.

***Dingle, Derek T.** Black Enterprise Titans of the B. E. 100's: Black CEOs Who Redefined & Conquered American Business. LC 98-51031. (Illus.). 256p. 1999. 24.95 (*0-471-31853-1*) Wiley.

— First in the Field: The Life of Baseball Hero Jackie Robinson. 48p. 2000. pap. 7.99 (*0-7868-1230-3*, Pub. by Hyprn Ppbks) Little.

Dingle, Derek T. & Milestone Media Inc. Staff. First in the Field: Baseball Hero Jackie Robinson. LC 97-41333. 48p. (J). 1998. lib. bdg. 17.49 (*0-7868-2289-9*, Pub. by Hyprn Child) Little.

— First in the Field: Baseball Hero Jackie Robinson. LC 97-41333. (Illus.). 48p. (J). (gr. 3-7). 1998. 16.95 (*0-7868-0348-7*, Pub. by Hyprn Child) Time Warner.

Dingle, Edwin J. Breathing Your Way to Youth. 105p. 1998. reprint ed. pap. 16.95 (*0-7661-0321-8*) Kessinger Pub.

— China's Revolution, Nineteen Eleven to Nineteen Twelve. LC 72-3486. (World History Ser.: No. 48). (Illus.). 1972. reprint ed. lib. bdg. 75.00 (*0-8383-1565-8*) M S G Haskell Hse.

Dingle, H. & Hegmann, J. P. Evolution & Genetics of Life Histories. (Proceedings in Life Sciences Ser.). (Illus.). 256p. 1982. 136.00 (*0-387-90702-5*) Spr-Verlag.

Dingle, H., jt. ed. see Denno, R. F.

Dingle, Herbert. Scientific Adventure. LC 71-121462. (Essay Index Reprint Ser.). 1977. 26.95 (*0-8369-1749-9*) Ayer.

Dingle, Hugh. Migration: The Biology of Life on the Move. (Illus.). 480p. 1996. text 90.00 (*0-19-508962-6*); pap. text 45.00 (*0-19-509723-8*) OUP.

***Dingle, Hugh.** Migration: The Biology of Life on the Move. (Illus.). 474p. 1999. reprint ed. pap. text 20.00 (*0-7881-6751-0*) DIANE Pub.

Dingle, J. Project Management: Orientation for Decision Makers. LC 97-204382. 288p. 1997. pap. text 34.95 (*0-340-67770-8*, T56) Wiley.

Dingle, J. T., ed. How to Obtain Biomedical Research Funding. 64p. 1986. 10.00 (*0-317-45875-2*) Elsevier.

Dingle, John. Project Management: Orientation for Decision Makers. 279p. 1997. pap. 54.95 (*0-470-23759-7*) Wiley.

Dingle, John, jt. ed. see Davies, Elisabeth.

***Dingle, Lloyd & Tooley, Mike.** Aircraft Engineering Principles. 2001. pap. 59.95 (*0-7506-5015-X*, Newnes) Buttrwrth-Heinemann.

Dingle, R. V., et al. Mesozoic & Tertiary Geology of Southern Africa. 385p. (C). 1983. text 188.00 (*90-6191-099-4*, Pub. by A A Balkema) Ashgate Pub Co.

Dingle, Steven P., ed. see Booth, Jim & Sawyer, Steve.

Dingle, Tony, jt. auth. see McLeary, Ailsa.

Dingledine, D., ed. see Davis, Rebecca H.

Dingledine, Raymond, ed. Brain Slices. LC 83-22957. 460p. 1984. 89.50 (*0-306-41437-6*, Plenum Trade) Perseus Pubng.

Dingledy, David P. A Beer's Law Study. Neidig, H. Anthony, ed. (Modular Laboratory Program in Chemistry Ser.). 12p. (C). 1989. pap. text 1.50 (*0-87540-358-1*, ANAL 358-1) Chem Educ Res.

— Determining the Empirical Formula of a Compound. Neidig, H. Anthony, ed. (Modular Laboratory Program in Chemistry Ser.). 7p. (C). 1992. pap. text 1.50 (*0-87540-423-5*, STOI 423-5) Chem Educ Res.

Dingler, Hugo. Aufbau der Exakten Fundamentalwissenschaft. (GER.). 1997. 39.80 (*3-487-07634-9*) G Olms Pubs.

— Die Ergreifung des Wirklichen. (GER.). 1997. 39.80 (*3-487-07633-0*) G Olms Pubs.

— Geschichte der Naturphilosophie. (GER.). 1997. reprint ed. 39.80 (*3-487-07632-2*) G Olms Pubs.

— Die Grundlagen der Naturphilosophie. (GER.). 1997. reprint ed. 39.80 (*3-487-07635-7*) G Olms Pubs.

Dingles, Molly. Jinka, Jinka Jelly Bean. LC 96-60959. (Illus.). (J). (ps-6). 1998. 12.95 (*1-891997-03-3*) Dingles & Co.

***Dingles, Molly.** Little Lee Lee Goes Fishing. (Little Lee Lee Ser.). (Illus.). 32p. (J). (ps-1). 2000. 9.99 (*1-891997-13-0*) Dingles & Co.

— Little Lee Lee's Birthday Band. (Little Lee Lee Ser.). (Illus.). 32p. (J). (ps-1). 2000. 9.99 (*1-891997-12-2*) Dingles & Co.

Dingley, Bob, ed. see Brubeck, Dave.

Dingley, D. J., et al. Atlas of Backscattering Kikuchi Diffraction Patterns. (Microscopy in Materials Science Ser.). (Illus.). 148p. 1995. 189.00 (*0-7503-0212-7*) IOP Pub.

Dingley, Jame & Bekh, Olena. Teach Yourself Ukrainian Complete Course. (UKR., Illus.). 320p. 1996. pap. 14.95 (*0-8442-3680-2*) NTC Contemp Pub Co.

Dingley, James, jt. auth. see Bekh, Olena.

Dingley, Jim, jt. auth. see Bekh, Olena.

Dingley, Michael, jt. auth. see Hangay, George.

Dingley, Robert, jt. auth. see Sandison, Alan.

Dingley, Thomas. History from Marble. 2 vols. LC 70-164834. (Camden Society, London. Publications, First Ser.: Nos. 94 & 97). reprint ed. 165.00 (*0-404-50210-5*) AMS Pr.

Dingli-Attard-Inguanez, Marcel V. Einstein on Peace, Congress, Malta, 1984. 39p. (Orig.). 1984. pap. 25.00 (*0-9610740-4-3*) U Intel Data Bank.

— The Family of Inguanez. 2nd ed. LC 82-670117. (Illus.). 85p. 1979. pap. 25.00 (*0-685-10166-5*) U Intel Data Bank.

— The International Armorial Register. (Illus.). 380p. 1984. 27.50 (*0-9610740-0-0*) U Intel Data Bank.

Dingli-Attard-Inguanez, Marcel V., ed. Einstein on Peace, Congress, Malta, 1986. 71p. 1986. pap. 25.00 (*0-9610740-6-X*) U Intel Data Bank.

— Einstein on Peace, Congress, Malta, 1988. 120p. 1988. pap. 25.00 (*0-9610740-8-6*) U Intel Data Bank.

— International Register of Biographies. LC 83-80106. (Illus.). 364p. 1984. 103.50 (*0-9610740-1-9*) U Intel Data Bank.

— International Register of Biographies. 2nd ed. (Illus.). 608p. 1985. 103.50 (*0-9610740-3-5*) U Intel Data Bank.

— International Register of Biographies (Dedicated to Albert Einstein) 3rd ed. (Illus.). 756p. 1986. 125.50 (*0-9610740-5-1*) U Intel Data Bank.

— International Register of Biographies (Dedicated to Guglielmo Marconi) 4th ed. (Illus.). 810p. 1987. 125.50 (*0-9610740-7-8*) U Intel Data Bank.

Dingli-Attard-Inguanez, Marcel V., ed. see Bosredon de Ransijat, Chevalier.

Dingman, Larry. Bibliography of Limited & Signed Editions in Literature, Twentieth Century American Authors. 1973rd ed. 1973. 15.00 (*0-87018-069-X*) Ross.

Dingman, Lawrence. Physical Hydrology. LC 93-3301. 575p. (C). 1993. text 98.00 incl. disk (*0-02-329745-X*, Macmillan Coll) P-H.

Dingman, Monna. My Bicycle Trip. 232p. 1995. pap. 9.95 (*0-88961-212-9*) Womans Pr.

***Dingman, Richard.** Patterns: A Manual of Club Passing. 2nd ed. LC 99-31734. 1999. pap. 34.95 (*0-917643-11-9*) B Dube.

Dingman, Robert W. In Search of a Leader: The Complete Search Committee Guidebook. LC 94-75896. 262p. 1994. pap. 10.00 (*0-9641317-0-6*) Lakeside Bks.

D

An Asterisk (*) at the beginning of an entry indicates that the title is appearing for the first time.

Dingman, Roger. Ghost of War: The Sinking of the "Awa maru" & American-Japanese Relations, 1945-1995. LC 97-25742. (Illus.). 400p. 1997. 35.00 (*1-55750-159-9*) Naval Inst Pr.

Dingome, Jeanne N., ed. see Liking, Werewere.

Dings, Fred. After the Solstice. LC 93-18470. 64p. (Orig.). 1993. pap. 12.95 (*0-914061-34-8*) Orchises Pr.

— Eulogy for a Private Man. LC 99-35607. 72p. 1999. 39.95 (*0-8101-5093-X*, TriQuart) Northwestern U Pr.

***Dings, Fred.** Eulogy for a Private Man. 72p. 1999. pap. 14.95 (*0-8101-5094-8*, TriQuart) Northwestern U Pr.

Dingue, Jeffrey L. Essential Radio Guide 1997. 4th ed. (Illus.). 50p. (Orig.). 1996. pap. 9.95 (*0-9637162-3-9*) Peregrine MA.

Dingus. Age of Dinosaurs. 1998. 24.00 (*0-7167-3378-1*) W H Freeman.

— Soil Science. 195p. (C). 1998. pap., lab manual ed. 27.00 (*0-13-020080-8*) P-H.

***Dingus, Anne.** All Hat & No Cattle: A Guide for New Texans & the West of Us. LC 99-16451. 1999. pap. 12.95 (*0-87719-351-7*, 9351) Gulf Pub.

Dingus, Anne. More Texas Sayings. LC 96-16538. (Illus.). 128p. 1996. pap. 9.95 (*0-87719-292-8*, 9292) Gulf Pub.

— The Truth about Texas: Who Needs to Brag? We've Got the Facts. rev. ed. LC 95-12594. 190p. 1995. pap. 9.95 (*0-87719-282-0*, 9282) Gulf Pub.

Dingus, Bill N. Jeffrey the Jeep. (Illus.). 32p. (J). (gr. k-3). 1997. 9.95 (*1-57072-054-1*) Overmountain Pr.

***Dingus, Brenda L., et al, eds.** GeV-TeV Gamma Ray Astrophysics Workshop: Towards a Major Atmospheric Cherenkov Detector VI. LC 00-102242. (AIP Conference Proceedings Ser.: Vol. 515). (Illus.). xiii, 537p. 2000. 140.00 (*1-56396-938-6*, Pub. by Am Inst Physics) Spr-Verlag.

— 26th International Cosmic Ray Conference: ICRC XXVI, Invited, Rapporteur & Highlight Papers. LC 00-102543. (AIP Conference Proceedings Ser.: Vol. 516). (Illus.). xvii, 407p. 2000. 95.00 (*1-56396-939-4*, Pub. by Am Inst Physics) Spr-Verlag.

Dingus, C. Mary, jt. auth. see Sherlock, Richard.

Dingus, Lowell. Dead or Alive? The Search for Living Dinosaurs. LC 97-35749. 332p. 1997. pap. text 34.95 (*0-7167-2944-X*) W H Freeman.

— The Mistaken Extinction: Dinosaur Evolution & the Origin of Birds. 1998. 37.00 incl. cd-rom (*0-7167-3385-4*) St Martin.

— The Mistaken Extinction: Dinosaur Evolution & the Origin of Birds. 1998. 37.00 incl. cd-rom (*0-7167-3384-6*) W H Freeman.

— Next of Kin: Fossils in the Great Halls of the American Museum of Natural History. LC 95-48881. (Illus.). 160p. 1996. 40.00 (*0-8478-1929-9*, Pub. by Rizzoli Intl) St Martin.

— What Color Is That Dinosaur? Questions, Answers, & Mysteries. LC 93-10664. (Illus.). 80p. (J). (gr. 4-6). 1994. lib. bdg. 23.90 (*1-56294-365-0*) Millbrook Pr.

Dingus, Lowell & Norell, Mark A. Searching for Velociraptor. LC 95-22238. (Illus.). 32p. (J). (gr. 2 up). 1996. lib. bdg. 15.89 (*0-06-025894-2*) HarpC Child Bks.

***Dingus, Lowell & Rowe, Timothy.** The Mistaken Extinction: Dinosaur Evolution & the Origin of Birds. 2000. pap. 18.95 (*0-7167-4165-2*) W H Freeman.

Dingus, Lowell, et al. A Guide to the Halls of Mammals & Their Extinct Relatives. Maestro, Vittorio, ed. (Illus.). (Orig.). 1994. pap. text 7.50 (*0-913424-11-0*) Am Mus Natl Hist.

Dingus, Lowell, jt. auth. see Chiappe, Luis.

Dingus, Lowell, jt. auth. see Norell, Mark.

Dingus, Tom, jt. ed. see Barfield, Woodrow.

Dingus, Victor R. & Hauck, Warren C., eds. Achieving High Commitment Work Systems: A Practitioner's Guide to Sociotechnical System Implementation. 414p. 1990. pap. text 50.00 (*0-89806-115-6*, ACHHCW) Eng Mgmt Pr.

Dingwall, Cathie, jt. auth. see De La Haye, Amy.

***Dingwall, Cindy.** Bible Banquets with Kids. LC 99-59702. (Illus.). 192p. (J). 2000. pap. 20.00 (*0-687-08791-0*) Abingdon.

— Happy Birthday America! (Illus.). 80p. 2000. pap. text, teacher ed. 15.95 (*1-57950-048-X*, Alleyside) Highsmith Pr.

Dingwall, Cindy. Library Celebrations. LC 98-50401. 96p. (J). (gr. k-5). 1999. pap. 16.95 (*1-57950-027-7*, Alleyside) Highsmith Pr.

— Storybook Birthday Parties. LC 97-44990. (Illus.). 164p. 1998. pap. 19.95 (*1-57950-015-3*, 37684, Alleyside) Highsmith Pr.

Dingwall, Eric J., frwd. Racial Pride & Prejudice. LC 78-32177. 246p. 1979. reprint ed. lib. bdg. 59.50 (*0-8371-5940-7*, DIR&, Greenwood Pr) Greenwood.

Dingwall, Eric J., jt. auth. see Angoff, Allan.

Dingwall, Eric J., jt. auth. see Price, Harry.

***Dingwall, Gavin & Moody, Sue, eds.** Crime & Conflict in the Countryside. 176p. 1999. 75.00 (*0-7083-1510-0*, Pub. by Univ Wales Pr) Paul & Co Pubs.

Dingwall, Helen M. Late Seventeenth-Century Edinburgh: A Demographic Study. (Illus.). 336p. 1994. 86.95 (*1-85928-019-6*, Pub. by Scolar Pr) Ashgate Pub Co.

— Late Seventeenth-Century Edinburgh: A Demographic Study. LC 93-12545. 256p. 1993. write for info. (*0-7185-1460-2*) St Martin.

Dingwall, Robert & Eekelaar, John M., eds. Divorce Mediation & the Legal Process. (Oxford Socio-Legal Studies). 204p. 1988. text 46.00 (*0-19-825576-4*) OUP.

Dingwall, Robert, et al. The Protection of Children: State Intervention & Family Life. 320p. 1995. 72.95 (*1-85628-586-3*, Pub. by Avebry) Ashgate Pub Co.

Dingwall, Robert, jt. ed. see Kwak, Anna.

Dingwall, Robert, jt. ed. see Miller, Gale.

Dingwall, Ronald. The Management of Stress. 64p. (C). 1986. 75.00 (*0-86236-026-9*, Pub. by Granary) St Mut.

— Managing Time Effectively. 54p. (C). 1986. pap. 50.00 (*0-7855-2251-4*, Pub. by Granary) St Mut.

— Organise Your Mind. 72p. (C). 1986. 50.00 (*0-86236-001-3*, Pub. by Granary) St Mut.

— Personal Relationships & Communication. 54p. (C). 1986. 65.00 (*0-86236-000-5*, Pub. by Granary) St Mut.

— Tools for Team Development. 44p. (C). 1986. 60.00 (*0-86236-002-1*, Pub. by Granary) St Mut.

Dingwaney, Anuradha & Maier, Carol, eds. Between Languages & Cultures: Translation & Cross-Cultural Texts. (Series in Composition, Literacy, & Culture). (Illus.). 359p. (C). 1996. pap. 19.95 (*0-8229-5541-5*); text 49.95 (*0-8229-3858-8*) U of Pittsburgh Pr.

Dingwell, Eric J. Abnormal Hypnotic Phenomena, a Survey of Nineteenth-Century Cases Vol. 1: France. LC 68-85483. 344p. reprint ed. pap. 106.70 (*0-8357-5008-6*, 200309400019) Bks Demand.

Dingwell, Eric J., ed. see Zorab, G., et al.

Dingwell, Joyce. Nurse Smith, Cook. large type ed. 304p. 1984. 27.99 (*0-7089-1085-8*) Ulverscroft.

Dingwell, Ronald. How to Run a Successful Meeting. 40p. (C). 1986. 65.00 (*0-86236-010-2*, Pub. by Granary) St Mut.

***Dingyam Chen, Leslie H.** Chen Jiongming & the Chinese Federalist Movement: Regional Leadership & Nation Building in Early Republican China. LC 98-55065. (Michigan Monographs in Chinese Studies: No. 86). (Illus.). 365p. 1999. 50.00 (*0-89264-135-5*) Ctr Chinese Studies.

Dingzhu, Du & Guoding, Hu, eds. Combinatorics, Computing & Complexity. (C). 1989. text 160.00 (*0-7923-0308-3*) Kluwer Academic.

Dingzhu, Du, ed. see Yongging, Liu & Zhaoshu, Feng.

Dinh-Hoa, Nguyen. Essential English - Vietnamese Dictionary. LC 82-80014. (Tuttle Language Library). (ENG & VIE.). 316p. 1993. pap. 14.95 (*0-8048-1661-1*) Tuttle Pubng.

Dinh, Linh. Drunkard Boxing. (Philadelphia Publishing Project Ser.). 36p. 1998. pap. 8.00 (*0-935162-18-6*) Singing Horse.

***Dinh, Linh.** Fake House: Stories. 192p. 2000. 23.95 (*1-58322-039-9*, Pub. by Seven Stories) Publishers Group.

Dinh, Linh, ed. Night, Again: Contemporary Fiction from Vietnam. 176p. 1996. 25.00 (*1-888363-02-9*) Seven Stories.

— Night, Again: Contemporary Fiction from Vietnam. 176p. 1996. pap. 12.95 (*1-888363-07-X*) Seven Stories.

Dinh, P. & Dieu, Phan Dinh. Some Questions in Constructive Functional Analysis: Proceedings. LC 73-21929. 228p. 1974. pap. 93.00 (*0-8218-3014-7*, STEKLO/114) Am Math.

Dinh, Steven M., et al. Intelligent Materials for Controlled Release. LC 99-12879. (Illus.). 238p. 1999. text 100.00 (*0-8412-3595-3*, Pub. by Am Chemical) OUP.

Dinh, Steven M., jt. auth. see Berner, Bret.

Dinh, Tung Van & Hannigan, Edward V. Clinical Gynecologic Oncology Review. 2nd ed. LC 99-222782. 160p. (C). (gr. 13). 1997. pap. text 24.95 (*0-8151-2501-1*, 29173) Mosby Inc.

Dinham, Barbara. The Pesticide Hazard: A Global Health & Environmental Audit. LC 92-36319. (C). 1993. text 59.95 (*1-85649-201-X*, Pub. by Zed Books); text 25.00 (*1-85649-202-8*, Pub. by Zed Books) St Martin.

Dinham, Barbara, et al. Agribusiness in Africa. 224p. (C). 1984. 15.95 (*0-86543-003-9*); pap. text 6.95 (*0-86543-004-7*) Africa World.

Dini, Jack W. Electrodeposition: The Materials Science of Coatings & Substrates. LC 92-27804. (Illus.). 367p. 1993. 109.00 (*0-8155-1320-8*) Noyes.

Dini, Jane, jt. ed. see Brown, Elizabeth A.

Dini, Laura, tr. see Serena, Raffaella.

Dini, Luca, jt. ed. see Balari, Sergio.

Dini, Paul. Batman: War on Crime. (Illus.). 64p. 1999. pap. 9.95 (*1-56389-576-5*, Pub. by DC Comics) Time Warner.

— Batman & Superman Adventures: World's Finest. LC 98-125404. (Illus.). 64p. 1997. pap. 6.95 (*1-56389-386-X*) DC Comics.

***Dini, Paul.** Batman Beyond: Return of the Joker: The Official Screenplay. (Illus.). 128p. 2000. pap. 9.95 (*0-8230-7717-9*) Watsn-Guptill.

— Jingle Belle: Naughty & Nice. Rich, Jamie S., ed. (Illus.). 88p. 2000. pap. 8.50 (*1-929998-08-2*) Oni Pr Inc.

Dini, Paul. Superman: Adventures of the Man of Steel. LC 98-222987. (Illus.). 144p. 1998. pap. text 7.95 (*1-56389-429-7*, Pub. by DC Comics) Time Warner.

— Superman: Peace on Earth. LC 99-163043. (Illus.). 64p. 1998. pap. text 9.95 (*1-56389-464-5*, Pub. by DC Comics) Time Warner.

Dini, Paul & Kidd, Chip. Batman Animated. LC 99-169793. (Illus.). 164p. 1999. 50.00 (*0-06-757531-5*, HarperPrism); pap. 29.95 (*0-06-107327-X*) HarpC.

Dini, Paul & Timm, Bruce. The Batman Adventures: Mad Love. (Illus.). 64p. 1995. mass mkt. 5.95 (*1-56389-244-8*, Pub. by DC Comics) Time Warner.

Dini, Paul, jt. auth. see Busiek, Kurt.

Dinibutun, A. T., et al, eds. Measurement & Control - MECO '85: Proceedings, IASTED Symposium, Istanbul, Turkey, July 23-25, 1985. 226p. 1985. 80.00 (*0-88986-089-0*, 094) Acta Pr.

DiNicola, Albert. Dear David: Prisons & Capital Punishment-A Needed, Balanced Fresh Approach. 2nd ed. (Orig.). 1986. write for info. (*0-318-59204-5*) Lumen Series.

— Take a Break, Vol. 1. 2nd ed. (Orig.). 1986. pap. write for info. (*0-318-59205-3*) Lumen Series.

Dinin, Denise, ed. see Ritch, Barbara A. & Ficke, Mary M.

Dininio, Phyllis. The Political Economy of East German Privatization. LC 98-47764. 152p. 1999. 55.00 (*0-275-96484-1*, Praeger Pubs) Greenwood.

Dinio-Durkin, Cecilia. Easy MathArt Projects & Activities: Delightful Art Projects for Young Learners That Teach & Reinforce Math Concepts & Skills. 64p. (J). (gr. k-2). 1999. pap. text 9.95 (*0-590-37896-1*) Scholastic Inc.

— Hit the Trail! The Camping Kit for Kids. (J). 1998. pap. 16.95 (*0-8362-5450-3*) Andrews & McMeel.

Dinitto. Social Welfare: Politics & Public Policy. 5th ed. LC 99-13917. 450p. (C). 1999. 52.00 (*0-205-29454-5*) Allyn.

Dinitto, Diana M. & McNeece, C. Aaron. Social Work. 2nd ed. LC 96-23669. 432p. 1996. 67.00 (*0-13-063827-7*) P-H.

DiNitto, Diana M. & McNeece, C. Aaron. Social Work: Issues & Opportunities in a Challenging Profession. Incl. Test Bank. 2nd ed. (C). 1996. teacher ed. write for info. (*0-205-26422-0*, T6422-4) Allyn.

DiNitto, Diana M., jt. auth. see McNeece, C. Aaron.

Dinitz, Jeffrey H. & Stinson, Douglas R. Contemporary Design Theory: A Collection of Surveys. LC 91-24408. (Interscience Series in Discrete Mathematics). 656p. 1992. 162.00 (*0-471-53141-3*) Wiley.

Dinitz, Jeffrey H., jt. ed. see Colbourn, Charles J.

Dinitz, Sue, jt. ed. see Fulwiler, Toby.

Diniz, Paulo S. Adaptive Filtering: Algorithms & Practical Implementation. LC 97-6614. (International Series in Engineering & Computer Science). 1997. text 126.50 (*0-7923-9912-9*) Kluwer Academic.

Dinizulu, Nana Y. Nana Says. 73p. (Orig.). 1987. pap. 10.00 (*0-685-54579-2*) Aims Modzawe.

Dinkel, Alvin L. Glass Cutting Techniques. (Illus.). (Orig.). 1978. pap. 2.50 (*0-916552-18-7*) Acoma Bks.

Dinkel, Christoph. Kirche Gestalten - Schleiermachers Theorie des Kirchenregiments. (Schleiermacher-Archiv Ser.: Band 17). (GER.). ix, 295p. (C). 1995. lib. bdg. 152.30 (*3-11-014943-5*) De Gruyter.

***Dinkel, John.** The Road & Track Illustrated Automotive Dictionary. (Illus.). 286p. 2000. pap. 19.95 (*0-8376-0143-6*, GRAD) Bentley Pubs.

Dinkel, M. K. The Annapolis Guide to Weddings. 82p. 1995. 20.00 (*1-884878-01-6*) Annapol Pubng.

— The Annapolis Guide to Weddings & Banquets. 136p. 1995. pap. 24.00 (*1-884878-03-2*) Annapol Pubng.

Dinkel, R., et al, eds. Improving Drug Safety: A Joint Responsibility. (Health Systems Research Ser.). (Illus.). xxi, 338p. 1991. 79.95 (*0-387-53505-5*) Spr-Verlag.

Dinkelacker, Horst. Balduin Mollhausen (1825-1905) America Between Dream & Disillusionment in the Life & Works of a Best-Selling German Author of the 19th Century. (American University Studies: Germanic Languages & Literature: Ser. I, Vol. 86). XII, 189p. 1989. 34.50 (*0-8204-1133-7*) P Lang Pubng.

Dinkelspiel, John R., et al. Condominiums: The Effects of Conversion on a Community. LC 80-39894. 218p. 1981. 55.00 (*0-86569-059-6*, Auburn Hse) Greenwood.

Dinkey, G. F. Flory: Genealogy of Flory-Dinkey Family, with Direct Ancestors Including Boyd, Wallace, Carnahan, Cobb, et al, & Collateral Lines & Royal & Magna Carta Ancestors. 98p. 1992. reprint ed. pap. 19.00 (*0-8328-2657-X*); reprint ed. lib. bdg. 29.00 (*0-8328-2656-1*) Higginson Bk Co.

***Dinkgrfe, Daniel Meyer, ed.** Performance & Consciousness. (Performing Arts International Ser.: Vol. 1, Part 4). (Illus.). 132p. 1999. pap. text 21.00 (*90-5755-096-2*, Harwood Acad Pubs) Gordon & Breach.

Dinkin, Michael, jt. auth. see Lieberman, Michael.

Dinkin, Robert J. Before Equal Suffrage: Women in Partisan Politics from Colonial Times to 1920, 152. LC 95-19321. (Contributions in Women's Studies). 176p. 1995. 55.00 (*0-313-29482-8*, Greenwood Pr) Greenwood.

— Campaigning in America: A History of Election Practices, 135. LC 88-29627. 243p. 1989. 59.95 (*0-313-26167-9*, DCE/, Greenwood Pr) Greenwood.

— Voting in Provincial America: A Study of Elections in the Thirteen Colonies, 1689-1776, 64. LC 77-71861. (Contributions in American History Ser.: No. 64). (Illus.). 284p. 1977. 55.00 (*0-8371-9543-8*, DIV/, Greenwood Pr) Greenwood.

— Voting in Revolutionary America: A Study of Elections in the Original Thirteen States, 1776-1789, 99. LC 81-13266. (Contributions in American History Ser.: No. 99). (Illus.). 184p. 1982. 52.95 (*0-313-23091-9*, DVR/) Greenwood.

Dinkins, Larry. New Toes for Tia. 1987. pap. 2.95 (*9971-972-59-X*) OMF Bks.

***Dinkla, Soke.** Connected Cities: Processes of Art in the Urban Network. 2000. pap. 45.00 (*3-7757-0849-9*) Gerd Hatje.

Dinklage, Helen. Therapy Through Handwriting. (Illus.). 77p. (Orig.). 1978. pap. 10.00 (*0-936132-41-8*) Merc Pr NY.

Dinklin, Philip I. & Shrine, Jim, contrib. by. The Chartwell AMR Report, 1997-1998. 3rd ed. (Illus.). 373p. 1997. pap., spiral bd. 969.00 (*1-891790-08-0*) Chartwell Inc.

Dinkmeye, Don. Training in Marriage Environment Handbook. 1987. 14.95 (*0-913476-64-1*, 6002) Am Guidance.

***Dinkmeyer, Don.** Consultation: School Mental Health Professionals as Consultants. 2nd ed. 2000. pap. 36.95 (*1-56032-849-5*) Taylor & Francis.

Dinkmeyer, Don. Parenting Teenagers. rev. ed. 180p. 1998. pap. 15.95 (*0-8129-3014-2*, Times Bks) Crown Pub Group.

Dinkmeyer, Don, Sr. The Parent's Handbook. 1982. pap. 9.95 (*0-394-71031-2*) Random.

Dinkmeyer, Don. Raising a Responsible Child. 256p. 1996. per. 11.00 (*0-684-81516-8*) S&S Trade.

Dinkmeyer, Don, Sr. & Dinkmeyer, Don, Jr. Developing Understanding of Self & Others (DUSO) Storybook, No. 1. (J). (gr. k-4). 1982. pap. text 49.95 (*0-88671-278-5*, 5505) Am Guidance.

Dinkmeyer, Don & Losoncy, Lewis E. The Skills of Encouragement: Bringing Out the Best in Yourself & Others. 248p. 1995. per. 19.95 (*1-57444-004-7*) St Lucie Pr.

Dinkmeyer, Don & McKay, G. D. Parenting Young Children. rev. ed. 1997. pap. 15.95 (*0-679-77797-0*) Random.

— The Parent's Handbook: Systematic Training for Effective Parenting. rev. ed. (Illus.). 138p. 1997. pap. 15.95 (*0-679-77798-9*) Random.

Dinkmeyer, Don & McKay, Gary D. Padres Eficaces con Entrenamiento Sistematico. (SPA.). 1981. teacher ed. 45.95 (*0-913476-87-0*, 5461) Am Guidance.

Dinkmeyer, Don, Sr. & McKay, Gary D. The Parents Guide: The Step Approach to Parenting Your Teens. LC 82-74294. (Illus.). 192p. 1984. 10.95 (*0-394-72771-1*) Random.

— The Parents Handbook: Systematic Training for Effective Parenting. 1989. pap. 12.95 (*0-318-42598-X*) Random.

— Step-Teen Parents Guide - Parenting Teenagers. rev. ed. (Systematic Parenting for Effective Parenting of Teens Ser.). 1990. pap. 14.95 (*0-88671-404-4*, 5753) Am Guidance.

Dinkmeyer, Don & Sperry, Len. Counseling & Psychotherapy: An Intergrated, Individual Psychology Approach. 3rd ed. LC 99-16927. (Illus.). 313p. (C). 1999. pap. text 36.00 (*0-02-329671-2*, Macmillan Coll) P-H.

Dinkmeyer, Don, Sr., et al. Early Childhood STEP Leaders Manual. (Early Childhood STEP Ser.). 1989. pap. 39.95 (*0-88671-357-9*, 4301) Am Guidance.

Dinkmeyer, Don, et al. New Beginnings: Skills for Single Parents & Stepfamily Parents (Parent's Manual) LC 87-91035. (Illus.). 222p. 1987. pap. text 11.95 (*0-87822-286-3*, 2863) Res Press.

Dinkmeyer, Don, Sr., et al. The Next Step Leader's Guide. (Next Step Ser.). 1987. pap. text 42.95 (*0-913476-67-6*, 4801) Am Guidance.

— Parenting Young Children: Helpful Strategies Based on Systemic Training for Effective Parenting (Step) 1990. pap. 12.00 (*0-679-73220-9*) Random.

— Parenting Young Children: Parent's Handbook. (Early Childhood STEP Ser.). 1989. pap. 14.95 (*0-88671-356-0*, 4302) Am Guidance.

— PREP for Effective Family Living. (YA). (gr. 7 up). 1985. 134.95 (*0-88671-225-4*, 6400) Am Guidance.

— PREP for Effective Family Living: Student Handbook. (PREP Ser.). 1985. teacher ed. 42.95 (*0-88671-229-7*, 6401); student ed. 6.95 (*0-88671-228-9*, 6405); pap. 14.95 (*0-88671-226-2*, 6403); text 24.95 (*0-88671-227-0*, 6402) Am Guidance.

— Systematic Training for Effective Parenting of Teens - Step-Teen: Leader's Guide. rev. ed. (Systematic Training for Effective Parenting of Teens Ser.). 135p. 1990. pap. text 38.95 (*0-88671-403-6*, 5752) Am Guidance.

Dinkmeyer, Don, et al. Systematic Training for Effective Teaching: Teacher's Handbook. (Illus.). 291p. (Orig.). (C). 1980. pap. text 26.95 (*0-913476-75-7*, 5005) Am Guidance.

Dinkmeyer, Don, Jr., jt. auth. see Dinkmeyer, Don, Sr.

Dinkmeyer, Don, jt. auth. see Eckstein, Daniel G.

Dinkmeyer, Don, jt. auth. see McKay, Gary.

Dinkmeyer, Don, jt. auth. see Sherman, Robert.

Dinkmeyer, Don C. Dale Tiempo Al Amor. (SPA., Illus.). 215p. 1997. pap. text 19.98 (*968-13-3116-8*) Edit Diana.

Dinkmeyer, Don C. Parenting Teenagers: Systematic Training for Effective Parenting of Teens LC 98-231149. v, 154 p. 1998. write for info. (*0-7854-1468-1*) Am Guidance.

— Parenting Young Children: Systematic Training for Effective Parenting (step) of Children Under Six LC 98-231175. v, 138p. 1997. write for info. (*0-7854-1189-5*) Am Guidance.

Dinkmeyer, Don C. & Carlson, Jon. Consultation: A Book of Readings. LC 74-34048. 315p. (C). reprint ed. 97.70 (*0-8357-9866-6*, 201646500002) Bks Demand.

Dinkmeyer, Don C. & McKay, Gary D. The Parent's Handbook: Systematic Training for Effective Parenting LC 98-230528. v, 138 p. 1997. write for info. (*0-7854-1188-7*) Am Guidance.

— The Parent's Handbook: Systematic Training for Effective Parenting (STEP) LC 81-20481. 120 P. :p. 1982. 6.95 (*0-913476-77-3*) Am Guidance.

Dinkmeyer-Eckste, Don. Leadership by Encouragement. 208p. (C). 1993. pap. text 25.95 (*0-8403-8396-7*) Kendall-Hunt.

***Dinkmeyer, S.** Leadership by Encouragement. 1998. pap. 98.00 (*81-86982-02-7*, Pub. by Business Pubns) St Mut.

Dinnage, James D. The Constitutional Law of the European Union, 2 vols., set. 65.95 (*0-87084-262-5*) Anderson Pub Co.

Dinnage, James D. & Murphy, John F., eds. The Constitutional Law of the European Union: Documentary Supplement. 248p. (C). 1996. pap. 17.00 (*0-87084-256-0*) Anderson Pub Co.

Dinnage, James D., jt. auth. see Murphy, John F.

Dinnar, Uri. Cardiovascular Fluid Dynamics. 264p. 1981. 150.00 (*0-8493-5573-7*, QP105, CRC Reprint) Franklin.

Dinneen, Francis P. General Linguistics. LC 93-37008. 664p. 1995. 55.00 (*0-87840-278-0*) Georgetown U Pr.

— An Introduction to General Linguistics. LC 78-1323. 464p. 1967. reprint ed. pap. 143.90 (*0-7837-9390-1*, 206013500005) Bks Demand.

— Peter of Spain: Language in Dispute: An English Translation of Peter of Spain's "Tractatus" Called Afterwards Summulae Logicales, based by the Critical

D

Edition by L. M. DeRijk. (Studies in the History of the Language Sciences: No. 39). xl, 271p. 1990. 65.00 (*90-272-4524-X*) J Benjamins Pubng Co.

Dinneen, Francis P. & Koerner, E. F. K., eds. North American Contributions to the History of Linguistics. (Studies in the History of the Language Sciences: No. 58). xii, 238p. 1990. 59.00 (*1-55619-353-X*) J Benjamins Pubng Co.

Dinneen, Francis P., ed. see Georgetown University Round Table on Languages & L.

Dinneen, John. Super Challenge. 1990. pap. 1.95 (*0-8167-2252-8*) Troll Communs.

Dinneen, Joseph. Ward Eight. LC 76-6335. (Irish Americans Ser.). 1976. reprint ed. 29.95 (*0-405-09331-4*) Ayer.

Dinneen, L. Titles of Addresses in Christian Greek Epistolography. 114p. 1980. 15.00 (*0-89005-376-6*) Ares.

Dinneen, M. J., jt. ed. see Calude, C. S.

Dinneen, Mark. Listening to the People's Voice: Erudite & Popular Literature in North East Brazil. LC 95-44325. (Illus.). 280p. 1996. 93.50 (*0-7103-0545-1*, Pub. by Kegan Paul Intl) Col U Pr.

Dinneen, Patrick S. English-Irish Dictionary. rev. ed. Murcava, L. O., ed. (ENG & IRI.). 37.50 (*0-87559-072-1*) Shalom.

Dinneen, Patrick S., rev. Irish-English Dictionary. (ENG & IRI.). 37.50 (*0-87559-070-5*) Shalom.

Dinneen, Patrick S., ed. see O'Rahilly, Egan.

Dinnen. Faith on Fire. 1997. pap. 12.99 (*1-85792-321-9*, Pub. by Christian Focus) Spring Arbor Dist.

— You Can Learn to Lead. 1997. pap. 9.99 (*1-85792-282-4*, Pub. by Christian Focus) Spring Arbor Dist.

Dinnen, S. Rescue Shop Within a Yard of Hell. 8.50 (*1-85792-122-4*, Pub. by Christian Focus) Spring Arbor Dist.

***Dinnen, Stewart.** Learning about Union with Christ: You Can Live the Life You Should! 64p. 2000. pap. text 2.99 (*1-85792-424-X*) Christian Focus.

Dinner, Sherry H. Nothing to Be Ashamed Of: Growing up with Mental Illness in Your Family. 160p. (J). (ps-3). 1989. lib. bdg. 12.93 (*0-688-08482-6*) Lothrop.

***Dinner, Sherry H.** Nothing to Be Ashamed of: Growing up with Mental Illness in Your Family. 212p. (YA). (gr. 6-7). 2000. reprint ed. text 22.00 (*0-7881-9093-8*) DIANE Pub.

***Dinnerstein, Dorothy.** The Mermaid & the Minotaur: Sexual Arrangements & Human Malaise. LC 99-16337. (Illus.). 288p. 1999. reprint ed. pap. 15.95 (*1-892746-25-5*, 46255) Other Pr LLC.

Dinnerstein, Leonard. Antisemitism in America. 400p. 1995. pap. text 15.95 (*0-19-510112-X*) OUP.

— Ethnic Americans: A History of Immigration. 4th ed. LC 98-42643. 330p. 1999. pap. 16.50 (*0-231-11189-4*) Col U Pr.

***Dinnerstein, Leonard.** Ethnic Americans: A History of Immigration. 4th ed. 330p. 1999. 45.00 (*0-231-11188-6*) Col U Pr.

Dinnerstein, Leonard. A History of American Antisemitism. 400p. 1994. text 35.00 (*0-19-503780-4*) OUP.

— Leo Frank Case. 1999. pap. text 15.95 (*0-8203-2145-1*) U of Ga Pr.

— Uneasy at Home: Antisemitism & the American Jewish Experience. LC 87-521. 272p. 1987. text 50.00 (*0-231-06252-4*) Col U Pr.

Dinnerstein, Leonard & Jackson, Kenneth T., eds. American Vistas: 1877 to the Present, Vol. 2. 7th ed. (Illus.). 400p. (C). 1995. pap. text 22.95 (*0-19-508784-4*) OUP.

— American Vistas Vol. 1: 1607-1877. 7th ed. (Illus.). 352p. (C). 1995. pap. text 22.95 (*0-19-508783-6*) OUP.

Dinnerstein, Leonard, et al. Natives & Strangers: A Multicultural History of Americans. 3rd ed. (Illus.). 384p. (C). 1996. reprint ed. pap. text 23.95 (*0-19-509084-5*) OUP.

Dinnerstein, Myra. Kosher L. A. The Complete Guide to Jewish Los Angeles. LC 93-3245. (Illus.). 256p. (Orig.). 1993. pap. 9.95 (*0-9636381-5-7*, KLA-1) Whyte Rose Pr.

— Women Between Two Worlds: Midlife Reflections on Work & Family. (Women in the Political Economy Ser.). (C). 1992. 49.95 (*0-87722-884-1*); pap. 22.95 (*0-87722-885-X*) Temple U Pr.

Dinniah, D., et al, eds. Atlas of Pediatric Oncology. (Illus.). 256p. 1996. text 175.00 (*0-340-53592-X*, Pub. by E A) OUP.

Dinnis, Enid M. Traveller's Tales. LC 72-5908. (Short Story Index Reprint Ser.). 1977. reprint ed. 16.95 (*0-8369-4211-6*) Ayer.

D'Innocenza, Michael & Sirefman, Josef P., eds. Immigration & Ethnicity: American Society: "Melting Pot" or "Salad Bowl?", 97. LC 91-6281. (Contributions in Sociology Ser.: No. 97). 360p. 1992. 47.95 (*0-313-27759-1*, DIM, Greenwood Pr) Greenwood.

Dinnocenzo, Debra A. 101 Tips for Telecommuters: Successfully Manage Your Work, Team, Technology & Family. LC 99-35779. 250p. 1999. pap. 15.95 (*1-57675-069-8*) Berrett-Koehler.

D'Innocenzo, Len & Cullen, Jack. The Agile Manager's Guide to Coaching to Maximize Performance. LC 99-64995. (Agile Manager Ser.). (Illus.). 96p. 1999. pap. 9.95 (*1-58099-016-9*, Pub. by Velocity Busn) IPG Chicago.

***D'Innocenzo, Len & Cullen, Jack.** The Agile Manager's Guide to Customer-Focused Selling. 2nd ed. 128p. 2000. pap. 10.95 (*1-58099-021-5*, Pub. by Velocity Busn) IPG Chicago.

D'Innocenzo, Len, jt. auth. see Cullen, Jack.

Dinnseanchus. The Metrical Dindsenchas, 5 vols., bk.2, Set. LC 78-72687. (Royal Irish Academy. Todd Lecture Ser.: Vols. 8-12). reprint ed. 105.00 (*0-404-60570-2*) AMS Pr.

— Poems from the Dindshenchas. Gwynn, Edward, ed. & tr. by. LC 78-72686. (Royal Irish Academy. Todd Lecture Ser.: Vol. 7). reprint ed. 16.50 (*0-404-60567-2*) AMS Pr.

Dinnsen, Daniel A., ed. Current Approaches to Phonological Theory. LC 78-3241. 348p. reprint ed. pap. 107.90 (*0-8357-6674-8*, 205685200094) Bks Demand.

Dino, Pete. Rock Around the Keyboard with Just 4 Chords. pap. 15.95 (*0-943748-60-7*) Ekay Music.

Dino, Steven, jt. auth. see Baer, Nancy.

Dinoffer, Joe. Coach Tennis America: Issues 1.0-1.10. 205p. 1997. ring bd. 149.95 (*0-9642150-5-5*) Oncourt Offcourt.

***Dinoffer, Joe.** 101 Fun Skill Builders for Kids. 144p. 1999. pap. 16.95 (*1-57167-431-4*) Coaches Choice.

— 101 Team Games for Kids. 144p. 1999. pap. 16.95 (*1-57167-430-6*) Coaches Choice.

Dinoffer, Joe. Play Tennis in the Airzone: Air Target Training System & Drill Book. (Illus.). 80p. 1995. student ed. write for info. (*0-9642150-2-0*) Oncourt Offcourt.

— Play Tennis in the Ropezone: Target System & Drill Book. (Illus.). 64p. 1994. student ed. write for info. (*0-9642150-0-4*) Oncourt Offcourt.

DiNoia, J. Augustine. The Diversity of Religions: A Christian Perspective. LC 91-33001. 199p. 1992. pap. 17.95 (*0-8132-0769-X*) Cath U Pr.

DiNoia, J. Augustine, et al. The Love That Never Ends: A Key to the Catechism of the Catholic Church. LC 96-68289. 160p. 1996. 14.95 (*0-87973-852-9*, 852) Our Sunday Visitor.

Dinosaur Project Editors, jt. auth. see Owl Magazine Editors.

DiNoto, Andrea. Art Plastic: Designed for Living. LC 83-73418. (Illus.). 228p. 1984. 55.00 (*0-89659-437-8*); pap. 24.95 (*0-89659-696-6*) Abbeville Pr.

— Shop NY Jewelry. LC 97-160223. (Illus.). 240p. (Orig.). 1996. pap. 15.95 (*1-885492-34-0*) City & Co.

***DiNoto, Andrea & Winter, David.** The Pressed Plant: The Art of Botanical Specimens, Nature Prints & Sun Prints. LC 99-16501. (Illus.). 160p. 1999. text 29.95 (*1-55670-936-6*) STC Pubns.

Dinsay, Sid M. The Journey of Kumquathead Eli: Mile One. (Illus.). 100p. (Orig.). 1993. pap. 8.95 (*0-9636972-0-X*) Kumquat Bible.

Dinsdale, Alfred. First Principles of Television. LC 76-161141. (History of Broadcasting: Radio to Television Ser.). (Illus.). 1975. reprint ed. 23.95 (*0-405-03562-4*) Ayer.

Dinsdale, Allen. Pottery Science: Materials, Processes & Products. LC 85-29573. 276p. 1986. text 36.95 (*0-470-20276-9*) P-H.

Dinsdale, J., jt. auth. see Nicolello, L. G.

Dinsdale, Margaret. Skin Deep: Natural Recipes for Healthy Skin & Hair. (Illus.). 128p. 1994. 27.95 (*0-921820-88-7*); pap. 15.95 (*0-921820-81-X*) Firefly Bks Ltd.

Dinsdale, Tim. Loch Ness Monster. 1982. pap. 7.95 (*0-7100-9022-6*, Routledge Thoemms) Routledge.

— Loch Ness Monster. 4th ed. (Illus.). 230p. 1982. pap. 14.95 (*0-415-04550-9*) Routledge.

Dinsdale, W. A. Principles & Practice of Accident Insurance. 268p. 1975. 80.00 (*0-948691-06-9*, Pub. by Witherby & Co) St Mut.

***Dinse, James.** Thistlefoot's Gift. Wise, Noreen, ed. (Book-a-Day Collection). 32p. (YA). (ps up). 2000. pap. 5.95 (*1-58584-397-0*) Huckleberry CT.

Dinse, John M., et al, eds. Vermont Jury Instructions, Civil & Criminal. LC 93-28597. 1993. 85.00 (*0-562-57293-7*, MICHIE) LEXIS Pub.

Dinsen, Isak. Daguerreotypes & Other Essays. Mitchell, P. M. & Paden, William D., trs. LC 78-27543. 256p. 1997. 15.95 (*0-226-15305-3*) U Ch Pr.

Dinshah, Darius. Es Werde Licht: Praktischer Leitfaden fur Dinshahs 12-Farben Chromotherapie.Tr. of Let There Be Light. (GER., Illus.). 191p. 1989. 15.00 (*0-933917-03-1*) Dinshah Hlth Soc.

— Let There Be Light. 4th ed. (Illus.). 164p. 1997. 12.00 (*0-933917-17-1*) Dinshah Hlth Soc.

— Spectro-Chrome Guide. (Illus.). 104p. 1997. 9.00 (*0-933917-15-5*) Dinshah Hlth Soc.

Dinshah, Darius, ed. see Ghadiali, Dinshah P.

Dinshah, Freya. The Vegan Kitchen. 13th rev. ed. (Illus.). 96p. 1997. pap. 9.95 (*0-942401-17-4*) Am Vegan Soc.

— Vegetarian Cooking for One Hundred. 2nd ed. 1981. 24.95 (*0-942401-07-7*) Am Vegan Soc.

Dinshah, H. Jay. Health Can Be Harmless. 2nd ed. (Illus.). 80p. 1987. pap. 4.95 (*0-942401-09-3*) Am Vegan Soc.

— Out of the Jungle: The Way of Dynamic Harmlessness. 5th rev. ed. (Ahimsa Bks.). (Illus.). 96p. (Orig.). 1995. pap. 7.95 (*0-942401-14-X*) Am Vegan Soc.

— Song of India. (Illus.). 104p. 1973. 4.95 (*0-942401-01-8*); pap. 3.95 (*0-942401-02-6*) Am Vegan Soc.

Dinshah, H. Jay, ed. Here's Harmlessness: An Anthology of Ahimsa. 5th ed. (Ahimsa Bks.). (Illus.). 96p. 1993. pap. 7.95 (*0-942401-13-1*) Am Vegan Soc.

Dinshaw, Carolyn. Chaucer's Sexual Poetics. LC 89-40253. 272p. (C). 1990. pap. text 16.95 (*0-299-12274-3*) U of Wis Pr.

— Getting Medieval: Sexualities & Communities, Pre- & Postmodern. LC 98-32015. (Duke Monographs in Medieval & Renaissance Studies). 360p. 1999. pap. 18.95 (*0-8223-2365-6*) Duke.

***Dinshaw, Carolyn.** Getting Medieval: Sexualities & Communities, Pre- & Postmodern. LC 98-32015. 360p. 1999. 54.95 (*0-8223-2330-3*) Duke.

Dinsmoor, James. Brazil: Responses to the Debt Crisis. 163p. 1990. 13.50 (*0-940602-30-X*) IADB.

Dinsmoor, W. B. The Archons of Athens in the Hellenistic Age. (Illus.). 585p. 1931. reprint ed. lib. bdg. 137.50 (*0-685-13619-1*, Pub. by AM Hakkert) Coronet Bks.

Dinsmoor, W. Bell. The Architecture of Ancient Greece. LC 73-12401. 1973. pap. 30.00 (*0-8196-0283-3*) Biblo.

Dinsmoor, William B., Jr. The Propylaia to the Athenian Akropolis: The Predecessors, Vol. 1. LC 79-9232. (Illus.). xviii, 69p. 1980. 25.00 (*0-87661-940-5*) Am Sch Athens.

Dinsmoor, William B., Jr., jt. auth. see Camp, John M., II.

Dinsmore, Charles A. Great Poets & the Meaning of Life. LC 68-58786. (Essay Index Reprint Ser.). 1977. 20.95 (*0-8369-0109-6*) Ayer.

— Teachings of Dante. (Select Bibliographies Reprint Ser.). 1977. 19.95 (*0-8369-5521-8*) Ayer.

Dinsmore, Charles E., ed. A History of Regeneration Research: Milestones in the Evolution of a Science. (Illus.). 240p. (C). 1991. text 69.95 (*0-521-39271-3*) Cambridge U Pr.

Dinsmore, Christine. From Surviving to Thriving: Incest, Feminism, & Recovery. LC 90-40378. (SUNY Series, The Psychology of Women). 204p. (C). 1991. text 74.50 (*0-7914-0628-8*); pap. text 24.95 (*0-7914-0629-6*) State U NY Pr.

Dinsmore, Danika. Traffic. (Illus.). 64p. 1997. pap. 5.00 (*1-890051-01-2*) It Plays in Peoria.

Dinsmore, Danika, ed. see Nineteenth Draft Members.

Dinsmore, James J. A Country So Full of Game: The Story of Wildlife in Iowa. LC 93-34775. (Bur Oak Original Ser.). (Illus.). 261p. 1994. 32.95 (*0-87745-453-'*); pap. 15.95 (*0-87745-454-X*) U of Iowa Pr.

Dinsmore, John. The Inheritance of Presupposition. (Pragmatics & Beyond Ser.: II: 1). vi, 98p. (Orig.). 1981. pap. 29.00 (*90-272-2511-7*) J Benjamins Pubng Co.

— Partitioned Representations: A Study in Mental Representation, Language Understanding & Linguistic Structure. 352p. (C). 1991. lib. bdg. 122.00 (*0-7923-1348-8*) Kluwer Academic.

Dinsmore, John, ed. Closing the Gap: Symbolic vs Subsymbolic Processing. (Technical Monographs & Edited Collections in Cognitive Science). 280p. (C). 1992. pap. 36.00 (*0-8058-1080-3*); text 59.95 (*0-8058-1079-X*) L Erlbaum Assocs.

Dinsmore, Julia S. Verses & Sonnets of Julia Stockton Dinsmore. 200p. 1991. reprint ed. write for info. (*0-9624673-5-9*) Picture This Bks.

Dinsmore, Mark & Dinsmore, Wendy. Homeschool Guide to the Internet World: Your on Ramp to the Information Superhighway. 175p. 1996. pap. text 14.99 (*1-888306-20-3*, Home School Pr) Holly Hall.

— Homeschool Guide to the Online World: Everything You Need to Know to Start Making Great Connections. 112p. 1996. pap. text 12.99 (*1-888306-16-5*, Home School Pr) Holly Hall.

Dinsmore, Paul C. The AMA Handbook of Project Management. LC 93-6947. 452p. 1993. 85.00 (*0-8144-0106-6*) AMACOM.

— Managing Organizations by Projects: Winning Through Enterprise Project Management. LC 98-41020. 271p. 1999. 57.95 (*0-8144-0420-0*) AMACOM.

Dinsmore, Wendy, jt. auth. see Dinsmore, Mark.

Dinstein, Yoram. War, Aggression & Self Defence. 324p. (C). 1988. text 200.00 (*0-949009-15-6*, Pub. by Grotius Pubns Ltd) St Mut.

— War, Aggression & Self Defence. 2nd ed. LC 93-50563. 357p. (C). 1994. text 95.00 (*0-521-46526-5*) Cambridge U Pr.

***Dinstein, Yoram, ed.** Israel Yearbook on Human Rights Vol. 27: 1997. 376p. 1998. 149.00 (*90-411-1092-5*) Kluwer Law Intl.

Dinstein, Yoram, ed. Israel Yearbook on Human Rights, 1988, Vol. 18. (C). 1989. lib. bdg. 99.50 (*0-7923-0017-3*) Kluwer Academic.

— Israel Yearbook on Human Rights, 1989, Vol. 19. (C). 1990. lib. bdg. 132.50 (*0-7923-0450-0*) Kluwer Academic.

— Israel Yearbook on Human Rights, 1990, Vol. 20. 384p. 1991. lib. bdg. 124.50 (*0-7923-0943-X*) Kluwer Academic.

— Israel Yearbook on Human Rights, 1993, Vol. 23. 432p. (C). 1994. lib. bdg. 174.50 (*0-7923-2581-8*) Kluwer Academic.

— Models of Autonomy. LC 81-11479. 303p. (C). 1982. 44.95 (*0-87855-435-1*) Transaction Pubs.

— The Protection of Minorities & Human Rights. 544p. (C). 1992. lib. bdg. 185.50 (*0-7923-1437-9*) Kluwer Academic.

***Dinstein, Yoram & Domb, Fania, eds.** Israel Yearbook on Human Rights 1998, Vol. 28. 296p. 1999. text 165.00 (*90-411-1295-2*) Kluwer Law Intl.

Dinstein, Yoram & Tabory, Mala, eds. International Law at a Time of Perplexity: Essays in Honour of Shabtai Rosenne. (C). 1989. lib. bdg. 341.00 (*90-247-3654-4*) Kluwer Academic.

— War Crimes in International Law. LC 96-8151. 1996. lib. bdg. 151.00 (*90-411-0237-X*, Pub. by M Nijhoff) Kluwer Academic.

Dinstein, Yoram, jt. auth. see Iyhr.

Dintaman, Stephen F. Creative Grace: Faith & History in the Theology of Adolf Schlatter. LC 93-2966-. (American University Studies: Theology & Religion: Ser. VII, Vol. 152). XIII, 180p. 1993. 37.95 (*0-8204-2118-9*) P Lang Pubng.

Dinteman, Walter L. Anthracite Ghosts. LC 95-17313. (Illus.). 1995. write for info. (*0-940866-56-0*) pap. write for info. (*0-940866-57-9*) U Scranton Pr.

— Anthracite Ghosts. (Illus.). x, 112p. 1995. 35.00 (*0-940866-44-7*); pap. 25.00 (*0-940866-45-5*) U Scranton Pr.

Dintenfass, Leopold. Blood Viscosity. 1985. text 316.00 (*0-85200-413-3*) Kluwer Academic.

— Hyperviscosity in Hypertension. (Illus.). 192p. 1981. text 52.00 (*0-08-024816-0*) Elsevier.

— Hyperviscosity in Hypertension. (Illus.). 192p. 1982. pap. text 31.00 (*0-08-024815-2*, Pergamon Pr) Elsevier.

Dintenfass, Michael. The Decline of Industrial Britain: 1870-1980. LC 91-47996. (Historical Connections Ser.). 112p. (C). (gr. 13). 1992. pap. 16.99 (*0-415-05465-6*, A7882) Routledge.

Dintenfass, Michael, jt. ed. see Dormois, Jean-Pierre.

Dinter, Elmar. Hero or Coward. 1985. 42.50 (*0-7146-3230-9*, Pub. by F Cass Pubs); pap. 22.50 (*0-7146-4048-4*, Pub. by F Cass Pubs) Intl Spec Bk.

Dinter, F., et al. Thermal Energy Storage for Commercial Applications: A Feasibility Study on Economic Storage Systems. 400p. 1993. 103.95 (*0-387-53054-1*) Spr-Verlag.

Dinter-Gottlieb, Gail, ed. The Hepatitis Delta Virus. (Medical Intelligence Unit Ser.). 140p. 1995. text 79.00 (*1-57059-144-X*) Landes Bioscience.

Dinter, Ingrid. Unvollendete Trauerarbeit in der DDR-Literatur: Ein Studium der Vergangenheitsbewaltigung. LC 93-12391. (DDR Studien-East German Studies: Vol. 7). (GER.). 149p. (C). 1994. text 45.95 (*0-8204-2182-0*) P Lang Pubng.

Dinter, Wolfgang. Waldgesellschaften der Neiderrheinischen Sandplatten, No. 64. (Dissertationes Botanicae Ser.). (Illus.). 112p. 1982. pap. text 40.00 (*3-7682-1325-0*) Lubrecht & Cramer.

Dinter, Z. & Morein, B., eds. Virus Infections of Ruminants. (Virus Infections of Vertebrates Ser.: No. 3). 592p. 1990. 292.50 (*0-444-87312-0*) Elsevier.

Dintiman. Health Through Discovery. 4th ed. 1989. suppl. ed. 26.87 (*0-07-017000-2*) McGraw.

Dintiman, jt. auth. see Greenberg.

Dintiman, George B. How to Run Faster: A Do-It-Yourself Book for Athletes in All Sports. LC 76-54436. (Illus.). 60p. 1979. text 3.25 (*0-686-70704-4*) NASE VA.

Dintiman, George B., et al. Discovering Lifetime Fitness: Concepts of Exercise & Weight Control. 2nd ed. Marshall, ed. 312p. (C). 1988. mass mkt. 37.25 (*0-314-48120-6*) West Pub.

— Doctor Tennis: A Complete Guide to Conditioning & Injury Prevention for All Ages. LC 80-65623. (Illus.). 106p. (Orig.). 1980. text 8.95 (*0-938074-00-8*) NASE VA.

— Sports Speed. 2nd rev. ed. LC 96-47831. (Illus.). 256p. 1997. pap. 16.95 (*0-88011-607-2*, PDIN0607) Human Kinetics.

Dintiman, George B., jt. auth. see Greenberg, Jerrold S.

Dintino, Theresa. Ode to Minoa. LC 98-88534. 192p. 1999. pap. 11.95 (*1-56315-143-X*) SterlingHse.

Dintrone, Charles V. Television Program Master Index: Access to Critical & Historical Information on 1002 Shows in 341 Books. LC 96-11763. 143p. 1996. lib. bdg. 36.50 (*0-7864-0150-8*) McFarland & Co.

Dintzis, F. R. & Laszlo, J. A., eds. Mineral Absorption in the Monogastric GI Tract: Chemical, Nutritional, & Physiological Aspects. (Advances in Experimental Medicine & Biology Ser.). (Illus.). 208p. 1989. 69.50 (*0-306-43200-5*, Plenum Trade) Perseus Pubng.

Dinu. Gas Dynamics. 1996. write for info. (*0-582-20908-0*, Pub. by Addison-Wesley) Longman.

Dinu, Liviu. Mathematical Concepts in Nonlinear Gas Dynamics. 1994. write for info. (*0-318-70229-0*) Longman.

DiNucci, Darcy, et al. Elements of Web Design. 2nd ed. Hayes, Simon, ed. LC 98-213255. 240p. (C). 1998. pap. text 39.95 (*0-201-69698-3*, Pub. by Peachpit Pr) Addison-Wesley.

DiNunzio, Mario R., ed. Theodore Roosevelt: An American Mind: Selected Writings. (Illus.). 384p. 1995. pap. 13.95 (*0-14-024520-0*, Penguin Bks) Viking Penguin.

DiNunzio, Michael G. Adirondack Wildguide: A Natural History of the Adirondack Park. LC 84-70873. (Illus.). 160p. 1984. 20.95 (*0-9613403-0-4*); pap. 16.95 (*0-9613403-1-2*) ADK Mtn Club.

— Lake Champlain: Mirror on the Mountains. Sheehan, John J. & Trachtenberg, Anne, eds. (Illus.). 32p. 1995. pap. 5.00 (*0-614-13999-6*) Adirondack Council.

***Dinverno, James.** Sanctum. 2000. 17.95 (*0-7541-1006-0*, Pub. by Minerva Pr) Unity Dist.

D'Inverno, Ray A. Introducing Einstein's Relativity. (Illus.). 394p. (C). 1992. pap. text 49.95 (*0-19-859686-3*) OUP.

D'Inverno, Ray A., ed. Approaches to Numerical Relativity: Proceedings of the International Workshop on Numerical Relativity, Southhampton, December 1991. (Illus.). 398p. (C). 1993. text 90.00 (*0-521-43976-0*) Cambridge U Pr.

Dinwiddie-Boyd, Elza. 11001 Afro-Amer Baby Nam. 400p. 1994. mass mkt. 5.99 (*0-380-77340-6*, Avon Bks) Morrow Avon.

Dinwiddie-Boyd, Elza. Shortcuts to Increase Your Typing Speed. 1988. pap. 8.95 (*0-399-51489-9*, Perigee Bks) Berkley Pub.

— Typing Made Easy: Featuring the "See It, Say It, Strike It" Method. (Practical Handbook Ser.). 96p. 1991. pap. 8.95 (*0-399-51671-9*, Perigee Bks) Berkley Pub.

***Dinwiddie, Robert.** Creating Worksheets. (Essential Computers Ser.). 72p. 2000. pap. text 6.95 (*0-7894-5530-7*, D K Ink) DK Pub Inc.

Dinwiddie, Robert. The Diagnosis & Management of Paediatric Respiratory Disease. (Illus.). 299p. 1990. text 50.00 (*0-443-02744-7*) Church.

— The Diagnosis & Management of Paediatric Respiratory Disease. 2nd ed. 1997. text 70.00 (*0-443-05084-8*) Church.

— The Official Records of Robert Dinwiddie, Set, Vols. 1 & 2. LC 77-164836. (Illus.). reprint ed. 127.50 (*0-404-02135-2*) AMS Pr.

Dinwiddie, Sue. I Want It My Way! Problem-Solving Techniques with Children Two to Eight. (Illus.). 144p. 1997. spiral bd. 14.95 (*0-9660573-0-9*) Better World.

— Let Me Think! Activities to Develop Problem-Solving Abilities in Young Children. (Illus.). 70p. 1997. spiral bd. 10.95 (*0-9660573-1-7*) Better World.

D

Dinwiddy, Caroline. Elementary Mathematics for Economists. 370p. 1968. pap. text 14.95 (*0-19-644047-5*) OUP.

Dinwiddy, Caroline & Teal, Francis. Principles of Cost-Benefit Analysis for Developing Countries. 302p. (C). 1996. text 64.95 (*0-521-47358-6*); pap. text 20.95 (*0-521-47916-9*) Cambridge U Pr.

Dinwiddy, J. R. Radicalism & Reform in Britain, 1780-1850. 472p. 1992. 60.00 (*1-85285-062-0*) Hambledon Press.

Dinwiddy, John R. From Luddism to the First Reform Bill: Reform in England 1810-1832. 96p. 1986. pap. text 15.95 (*0-631-13952-4*) Blackwell Pubs.

Dinwiddy, John R., ed. see Bentham, Jeremy.

Dinwiddy, John R., jt. ed. see Dann, O.

***Dinwoodie, J. M.** Timber: Its Nature & Behavior. LC 99-87760. (Illus.). 232p. 2000. pap. 49.99 (*0-419-23580-9*) Routledge.

— Timber: Its Nature & Behavior. (Illus.). 232p. 2000. 115.00 (*0-419-25550-8*, E & FN Spon) Routledge.

Dinwoodie, J. M. Wood: Nature's Cellular, Polymeric, Fibre Composite. 140p. 1989. pap. text 40.00 (*0-901462-35-7*, Pub. by Inst Materials) Ashgate Pub Co.

Dinzelbacher, Peter. Dictionnaire de la Mystique. (FRE.). 786p. 1993. 135.00 (*0-7859-7908-5*, 2503503179) Fr & Eur.

— Woerterbuch der Mystik. (GER.). 530p. 1989. 49.95 (*0-7859-8682-0*, 352045601x) Fr & Eur.

Dinzes, Deborah. California Traveler: A Guide to California's Historic Sites & Museums. (American Traveler Ser.: Vol. 26). 1993. pap. 6.95 (*1-55838-134-1*) R H Pub.

Dio Cassius, jt. auth. see Mussies, G.

Dio Chrysostom. Discourses, 5 vols., 3. (Loeb Classical Library: No. 257, 339, 358, 376, 385). 490p. 1940. 19.95 (*0-674-99395-0*) HUP.

Dio Chrysoston. Hunters of Euboia. LC 53-10378. 1964. write for info. Macmillan.

Dio Cocceianus, Cassius. Cassius Dio: Roman History 53.1-55.9. Rich, J. W., ed. (Classical Texts Ser.). 272p. (C). 1991. 59.99 (*0-85668-383-3*, Pub. by Aris & Phillips); pap. 28.00 (*0-85668-384-1*, Pub. by Aris & Phillips) David Brown.

— Historiarum Romanarum Quae Supersunt, Vol. I: Liber 1-40. Boissevain, Philipp, ed. (GER.). iv, 540p. 1955. write for info. (*3-296-11401-7*) G Olms Pubs.

— Historiarum Romanarum Quae Supersunt, Vol. II: Liber 41-60. Boissevain, Philipp, ed. (GER.). xxxiv, 690p. 1955. write for info. (*3-296-11402-5*) G Olms Pubs.

— Historiarum Romanarum Quae Supersunt, Vol. III: Liber 61-80. Boissevain, Philipp, ed. (GER.). xx, 800p. 1955. write for info. (*3-296-11403-3*) G Olms Pubs.

— Historiarum Romanarum Quae Supersunt, Vol. IV: Index Historicus. Boissevain, Philipp, ed. (GER.). iv, 706p. 1955. write for info. (*3-296-11404-1*) G Olms Pubs.

— Historiarum Romanarum Quae Supersunt, Vol. V: Index Graecitatis. Boissevain, Philipp, ed. (GER.). vii, 880p. 1969. write for info. (*3-296-11405-X*) G Olms Pubs.

Diocese of Rapid City Staff, ed. see Family Life Ministries Staff & Young, Harriet.

Diodato, Virgil. Dictionary of Bibliometrics. LC 93-3952. (Illus.). 185p. 1994. lib. bdg. 39.95 (*1-56024-852-1*) Haworth Pr.

Diodato, Virgil P., jt. auth. see Freed.

Diogenes, jt. auth. see Heraclitus.

Diogenes, Allen. Traces of God: In a Frequently Hostile World. 1998. reprint ed. pap. 10.00 (*0-9653625-2-3*) Caroline Pr.

Diogenes Laertius. Lives of Eminent Philosophers, 2 vols., 1. Hicks, R. D., tr. (Loeb Classical Library: No. 184-185). 586p. 1925. 19.95 (*0-674-99203-2*) HUP.

— Lives of Eminent Philosophers, 2 vols., 2. Hicks, R. D., tr. (Loeb Classical Library: No. 184-185). 710p. 1925. 19.95 (*0-674-99204-0*) HUP.

Diogenes, Laertius. La Vie de Pythagore de Diogene Laerce. Vlastos, Gregory, ed. LC 78-19342. (Morals & Law in Ancient Greece Ser.). 1979. reprint ed. lib. bdg. 23.95 (*0-405-11537-7*) Ayer.

Diogenes, Laertius. Vitarum Philosophorum: Excerpta Byzantina Et Indices, Vol. 2. Marcovich, M., ed. (Illus.). 608p. (C). text 125.00 (*3-519-01317-7*) B G Teubner.

— Vitarum Philosophorum Libri. 10th ed. Marcovich, M., ed. (Illus.). 608p. (C). text 125.00 (*3-519-01316-9*, Pub. by B G Teubner) U of Mich Pr.

Dioguardi, Raffaele A. NTC's Beginners Italian & English Dictionary. Abate, Frank R., ed. LC 95-147735. (ENG & ITA., Illus.). 464p. 1995. 12.95 (*0-8442-8443-2*, 84432, Natl Textbk Co) NTC Contemp Pub Co.

Dioguardi, Raffaele A. & Abate, Frank R. NTC's Beginners Italian & English Dictionary. LC 97-47729. (Illus.). 464p. 1995. pap. 9.95 (*0-8442-8444-0*, 84440, Natl Textbk Co) NTC Contemp Pub Co.

Dioguardi, Raffaele A., ed. see National Textbook Company Staff, et al.

DioGuardi, Ralph. Roll Out the Barrel . . . The Tanks Are Coming: The Liberation of the Santo Tomas Internment Camp. 2nd ed. (World War II Monograph Ser.: Vol. 20). (Illus.). 34p. 1998. 17.95 (*1-57638-115-3*, M20); pap. 7.95 (*1-57638-114-5*, M20) Merriam Pr.

Dioguardi, Ralph, jt. ed. see Abate, Frank.

Diokno, Ananias & McCormick, Kathleen A. Urinary Incontinence in Adults: Clinical Practice Guideline. (Illus.). 125p. (C). 1997. reprint ed. pap. text 30.00 (*0-7881-4612-2*) DIANE Pub.

Diolata. Grammar. (Take Charge Ser.). 1997. wbk. ed. 10.00 (*0-07-044428-5*) McGraw.

Diolata, Edna. Voices of Tomorrow: An Introduction to English, Bk. 2. 176p. (C). 1997. pap. 12.81 (*0-07-044355-6*) McGraw.

— Voices of Tomorrow: An Introduction to English, Bk. 2. 1997. pap., wbk. ed. 10.00 (*0-07-044359-9*) McGraw.

Diolata, Edna T. Take Charge: A Student-Centered Approach to English, Bk. 1. 320p. (C). 1997. pap. 12.81 (*0-07-044427-7*) McGraw.

Diole, Philippe. L' Okapi. (FRE.). 352p. 1985. pap. 12.95 (*0-7859-2010-2*, 2070376419) Fr & Eur.

Dioli, M., jt. ed. see Schwartz, H. J.

Diomede, Matthew. Pietro DiDonato, the Master Builder. LC 94-38036. 1995. 32.50 (*0-8387-5289-6*) Assoc Univ Prs.

Diomedi, Alexander. Sketches of Indian Life in the Pacific Northwest. 96p. 1978. 19.95 (*0-87770-199-7*) Ye Galleon.

Dion & Paterson, Alexander H. G. Fundamental Problems. 1987. text 159.00 (*0-89838-863-5*) Kluwer Academic.

Dion & Polliack, Aaron. Human Leukemia. 1984. text 307.50 (*0-89838-585-7*) Kluwer Academic.

Dion, Conrad, tr. see Leberge, Albert.

Dion, Douglas. Turning the Legislative Thumbscrew: Minority Rights & Procedural Change in Legislative Politics. LC 97-22819. 312p. (C). 1997. text 52.50 (*0-472-10820-4*, 10820) U of Mich Pr.

Dion, Gerard. Canadian Dictionary of Labor Relations: Dictionnaire Canadien des Relations du Travail. 2nd ed. (ENG & FRE.). 993p. 1987. 95.00 (*0-8288-0416-8*, M6163) Fr & Eur.

— Vocabulaire Francais-Anglais des Relations Professionnelles. 2nd ed. (ENG & FRE.). 350p. 1975. 39.95 (*0-8288-5951-5*, M4655) Fr & Eur.

Dion, J. M. Linear Time Delay Systems. LC 98-55500. 222p. 1999. pap. 63.50 (*0-08-043047-3*) Elsevier.

Dion, Jim & Topping, Ted. Start & Run a Profitable Retail Business: A Step-by-Step Business Plan. 4th ed. (Business Ser.). 184p. 1997. pap. 16.95 (*1-55180-100-0*, 9520) Self-Counsel Pr.

Dion, Leon. Quebec: The Unfinished Revolution. Romer, Therese, tr. LC 77-352511. 232p. reprint ed. pap. 72.00 (*0-7837-1147-6*, 204167600022) Bks Demand.

Dion, Marc M. To Veronica's New Lover. LC 87-70660. (Target Midwest Poetry Ser.). 64p. 1987. 7.95 (*0-933532-60-1*) BkMk.

Dion, Mark, jt. ed. see Rockman, Alexis.

Dion, Robert L. Complicated Choices, Unacceptable Contracts: The 1992 Referendum in Quebec. (MacArthur Scholar Series, Occasional Paper). 89p. (Orig.). 1995. pap. 4.00 (*1-881157-31-8*) In Ctr Global.

— Crimes of the Secret Police. Orig. Title: Les Crimes de la Police Montee. 228p. 1982. pap. 12.99 (*0-919619-57-6*, Pub. by Black Rose) Consort Bk Sales.

Dion, Stephane. Straight Talk: Speeches & Writings on Canadian Unity. 55.00 (*0-7735-1853-3*); pap. 22.95 (*0-7735-1856-8*) McG-Queens Univ Pr.

Dion, Stephane, jt. ed. see Blais, Andre.

Dion, Susan F. Write Now: Maintaining a Creative Spirit While Homebound & Ill. 3rd rev. ed. (Illus.). 92p. 1997. pap. write for info. (*0-9657912-1-1*) Puffin Found.

Dion, Thomas R. Land Development for Civil Engineers. 664p. 1993. 120.00 (*0-471-54743-3*) Wiley.

Dione, Adela I. Women & Pelvic Inflammatory Diseases: Index of Modern Information. LC 88-47953. 150p. 1991. 47.50 (*1-55914-492-0*); pap. 44.50 (*1-55914-493-9*) ABBE Pubs Assn.

Dione, Arthur. Jungian Birth Charts. (Illus.). 256p. (Orig.). 1987. pap. 9.95 (*0-85030-642-6*, Pub. by Aqrn Pr) HarpC.

Dionetti, Michelle V. Mice to the Rescue! (Illus.). (J). (gr. 1-4). 1995. lib. bdg. 14.00 (*0-8167-3712-6*, Little Rainbow) Troll Communs.

— Mice to the Rescue! (J). (ps-3). 1997. pap. 3.95 (*0-8167-3515-8*, Little Rainbow) Troll Communs.

— Painting the Wind: A Story of Vincent van Gogh. LC 95-5301. (Illus.). 32p. (J). (gr. k-3). 1996. 15.95 (*0-316-18602-3*) Little.

Dionigi, R., et al, eds. European Society Surgical Research, 17th Congress, Stresa, May 1982: Abstracts. (Journal: European Surgical Research: Vol. 14, No. 2). (Illus.). 120p. 1982. pap. 39.25 (*3-8055-3558-9*) S Karger.

Dionigi, R. & Madariaga, Juan, eds. New Technologies for Liver Resections. LC 97-6443. (Medical Intelligence Unit Ser.). (Illus.). xiv, 268p. 1997. 98.00 (*3-8055-6564-X*) S Karger.

Dionigi, R., jt. ed. see Bozzetti, F.

Dionisi, David. Perfect Money Planning. Barrett, Joan, ed. (Illus.). 125p. (Orig.). 1995. pap. 12.95 (*0-9635770-7-7*) D Dionisi.

Dionisio, Marie, jt. auth. see Five, Cora L.

Dionisopoulos, George N., jt. auth. see Goldzwig, Steven R.

Dionisopoulos, P. Allan. Rebellion, Racism, & Representation: The Adam Clayton Powell Case & Its Antecedents. LC 76-125335. 175p. 1970. 25.00 (*0-87580-018-1*); pap. 15.00 (*0-87580-504-3*) N Ill U Pr.

Dionne. Pain & Anxiety Control in Dentistry. 2000. text. write for info. (*0-7216-7278-7*, W B Saunders Co) Harcrt Hlth Sci Grp.

***Dionne, Carla.** Sex, Lies & Uterine Fibroids. 2001. pap. 13.95 (*1-58333-070-4*, Avery) Penguin Putnam.

***Dionne, E. J.** Community Works: The Revival of Civil Society in America. 184p. 2000. pap. 16.95 (*0-8157-1867-5*) Brookings.

Dionne, E. J. They Only Look Dead. LC 97-3713. 1997. per. 13.00 (*0-684-82700-X*, Touchstone) S&S Trade Pap.

Dionne, E. J., Jr. The Vitality of Society Rests on the Nonprofit Sector. (Conversations with Leaders Ser.). 10p. Date not set. pap. 9.00 (*0-929556-22-4*) Ind Sector.

Dionne, E. J., Jr. Why Americans Hate Politics: The Death of the Democratic Process. rev. ed. 448p. 1992. per. 13.00 (*0-671-77877-3*, Touchstone) S&S Trade Pap.

Dionne, E. J., Jr., ed. Community Works: The Revival of Civil Society in America. LC 98-19685. 180p. 1998. 24.95 (*0-8157-1868-3*) Brookings.

***Dionne, E. J., Jr. & Dilulio, John J., Jr., eds.** What's God Got to Do with the American Experiment? Essays on Religion & Politics. 184p. 2000. pap. 16.95 (*0-8157-1869-1*) Brookings.

Dionne, Georges. Automobile Insurance: Road Safety, New Drivers, Risks, Insurance Fraud & Regulation. LC 98-46208. 11p. 1998. 129.95 (*0-7923-8394-X*) Kluwer Academic.

***Dionne, Georges.** Handbook of Insurance. LC 00-31342. (Huebner International Series on Risk, Insurance & Economic Security). 2000. write for info. (*0-7923-7870-9*) Kluwer Academic.

Dionne, Georges, ed. Contributions to Insurance Economics. (Huebner International Series on Risk, Insurance, & Economic Security). (Illus.). 524p. (C). 1991. lib. bdg. 138.00 (*0-7923-9175-6*) Huebner Foun Insur.

— Foundations of Insurance Economics: Readings in Economics & Finance. (Huebner International Series on Risk, Insurance, & Economic Security). (Illus.). 752p. (C). 1994. lib. bdg. 138.00 (*0-7923-9204-3*) Huebner Foun Insur.

— Foundations of Insurance Economics: Readings in Economics & Finance. (Hubner International Series on Risk, Insurance & Economic Security). 752p. (C). 1994. lib. bdg. 130.00 (*0-7923-9207-8*) Kluwer Academic.

***Dionne, Jean-Yves & Gazella, Karolyn A.** Protecting the Prostate: Relieving Symptoms Through the Integration of Diet & Lifestyle. 32p. 2000. pap. 3.95 (*1-890694-30-4*) IMPAKT Communs.

***Dionne, Jean-Yves & Torkos, Sherry.** The Secret of St. John's Wort Revealed. 32p. 1999. pap. 3.95 (*1-890694-20-7*) IMPAKT Communs.

Dionne, Joe. Heat Lightning. (Illus.). 30p. (Orig.). 1989. pap. 10.00 (*0-945950-03-9*) Canoe Pr MI.

Dionne, Joe, ed. see Drake, Albert.

Dionne, Joe, ed. see Drake, Barbara.

Dionne, Joe, ed. see Shaw, William.

Dionne, Joe, ed. see Thomas, F. R.

Dionne, Michele P., jt. auth. see TREDS Inc. Staff.

Dionne, Narcisse E. Champlain. LC 64-2614. (Canadian University Paperbooks Ser.: No. 13). 317p. reprint ed. pap. 98.30 (*0-8357-4154-0*, 203692800007) Bks Demand.

Dionne, Raymond A. & Phero, J. C. Management of Pain & Anxiety in Dental Practice. 420p. 1991. pap. 89.50 (*0-444-81749-2*) Elsevier.

Dionne, Rene. Propos sur la Litterature Outaouaise & Franco-Ontarienne. LC 79-361598. (Documents de Travail due Centre de Recherche en Civilisation Canadienne-Francaise Ser.: Vol. 11). (FRE.). 211p. 1978. reprint ed. pap. 65.50 (*0-608-02181-4*, 206285000004) Bks Demand.

Dionne, Rene & Fitzgerald, Michael. Catalysts. 308p. 1980. 5.95 (*0-318-14910-9*) Missionaries Africa.

Dionne, Wanda. The Couturiere of Galvez: Dressmaker of Galveston. LC 92-46147. (Illus.). (J). (gr. 6-9). 1993. pap. 9.95 (*1-57168-161-2*) Sunbelt Media.

Dionne, Wanda. Reyna's Reward. (American Dreams Ser.). 1996. 9.09 (*0-606-10294-9*, Pub. by Turtleback) Demco.

Dionne, Wanda. Reyna's Reward: American Dreams. 192p. (Orig.). (YA). 1996. mass mkt. 3.99 (*0-380-78476-9*, Avon Bks) Morrow Avon.

— A Yank among Us. LC 96-29633. 176p. (J). (gr. 6-6). 1997. pap. 12.95 (*1-57168-108-6*, Eakin Pr) Sunbelt Media.

***Dionne, Wanda & Dillon, Jana.** Little Thumb. LC 99-56098. (J). 2000. write for info. (*1-56554-754-3*) Pelican.

Dionysia, ed. see Shih, Bernadette.

Dionysius of Halicarnassus. Critical Essays, Vol. 1. Usher, Stephen, tr. from GRE. (Loeb Classical Library: No. 465). 670p. 1974. text 19.95 (*0-674-99512-0*) HUP.

— Critical Essays, Vol. II. (Loeb Classical Library: No. 466). 454p. 1985. text 19.95 (*0-674-99513-9*) HUP.

Dionysius Of Halicarnassus. Dionysius of Halicarnassus On Literary Composition. Roberts, W. Rhys, ed. & tr. by. LC 75-41075. reprint ed. 39.50 (*0-404-14533-7*) AMS Pr.

Dionysius of Halicarnassus. Roman Antiquities, Vols. 1-7. No. 319, 347, 357, 364, 372, 378, 388. 19.95 (*0-318-53176-3*) HUP.

— The Three Literary Letters. Roberts, William R., tr. & comment by. xi, 233p. reprint ed. write for info. (*0-318-70913-9*) G Olms Pubs.

Dionysius the Areopagite. Mystical Theology. Sire, Evelyn, ed. (Orig.). 1997. pap. 5.95 (*1-55818-381-7*) Holmes Pub.

Diop, Birago. Les Contes d'Amadou Koumba. (FRE.). 1969. pap. 12.95 (*0-7859-3454-5*) Fr & Eur.

— Les Nouveaux Contes d'Amadou Koumba. (FRE.). 188p. 1967. pap. 12.95 (*0-7859-3455-3*) Fr & Eur.

Diop, Cheikh Anta. The African Origin of Civilization: Myth or Reality. Cook, Mercer, ed. & tr. by. from FRE. LC 73-81746. (Illus.). 336p. 1974. pap. 14.95 (*1-55652-072-7*, Lawrence Hill) Chicago Review.

— Black Africa: The Economic & Cultural Basis for a Federated State. rev. ed. LC 87-17704. 146p. 1987. pap. 14.95 (*1-55652-061-1*, Lawrence Hill) Chicago Review.

— Civilization or Barbarism: An Authentic Anthropology. LC 90-4141. (Illus.). 464p. (C). 1991. pap. 17.95 (*1-55652-048-4*, Lawrence Hill) Chicago Review.

— Civilization or Barbarism: An Authentic Anthropology. Salemson, Harold J. & De Jager, Marjolijn, eds. Yaa-Lengi Meema Ngemi, tr. from FRE. LC 90-4141. (Illus.). 464p. (C). 1991. 35.00 (*1-55652-049-2*, Lawrence Hill) Chicago Review.

— The Cultural Unity of Black Africa. 2nd ed. LC 77-12276. 1987. reprint ed. pap. 14.95 (*0-88378-049-6*) Third World.

— Precolonial Black Africa. Salemson, Harold J., tr. from FRE. LC 86-22804. 240p. (C). 1987. pap. 13.95 (*1-55652-088-3*, Lawrence Hill) Chicago Review.

Diop, Momar-Coumba & Lavergne, Real, prods. L' Integration Regionale en l'Afrique de l Ouest: Resultats de la Conference Internationale Organisee Par le Centre de Recherche pour le Developpement International a Dakar (Senegal) du 11 au 15 Janvier 1993. LC 97-700559. (FRE.). 408p. 1996. pap. 20.00 (*0-88936-787-6*, Pub. by IDRC Bks) Stylus Pub VA.

Diop, Samba. The Oral History & Literature of the Wolof People of Waalo, Northern Senegal: The Master of the Word (Griot) in the Wolof Tradition. (African Studies: Vol. 36). 1995. write for info. (*0-7734-9031-0*) E Mellen.

Diorio, David, ed. see Bonny, Oscar.

DiOrio, Dorothy M. Leconte de Lisle: A Hundred & Twenty Years of Criticism, 1850-1970. (Romance Monographs: No. 1). 1972. pap. 24.00 (*84-400-5555-2*) Romance.

Diorio, Margaret. End of Summer. LC 92-72837. 80p. (Orig.). 1993. pap. 8.95 (*0-944806-03-1*) Icarus Press.

Diorio, Mary A. Selling Yourself on You: Discovering God's Will for Your Life. LC 88-70291. 214p. (Orig.). 1988. pap. 14.95 (*0-930037-02-2*) Daystar Comm.

Diorio, Mary Ann. Making Your Marriage Work. 1998. pap. 5.00 (*0-930037-05-7*, MYMW) Daystar Comm.

Diorio, MaryAnn L. Balancing Your Budget God's Way. 29p. (Orig.). 1987. pap. 1.00 (*0-930037-01-4*) Daystar Comm.

— Dating Etiquette for Christian Teens. (Illus.). 48p. (Orig.). (J). (gr. 6-12). 1984. pap. 3.95 (*0-930037-00-6*) Daystar Comm.

DiOrio, Ralph A. Called to Heal. LC 82-45354. 1982. 14.95 (*0-385-18226-0*) Doubleday.

Dios, Angel C. de, see Facelli, Julio C. & De Dios, Angel C., eds.

Diosa, Reina. Ebony Illusions, a Choreopoem. 80p. 1999. pap. 11.95 (*0-9671082-0-9*) Black Alchemist.

Diosdado, Ana. Yours for the Asking (Usted Tambien Podra Disfrutar de Ella) Halsey, Martha T., ed O'Connor, Patricia W., tr. from SPA. LC 94-72547. (Contemporary Spanish Plays Ser.: Vol. 7). x, 70p. 1995. pap. 6.00 (*0-9631212-6-X*) Estreno.

Diosdi, G. Contract in Roman Law. 230p. 1981. 85.00 (*0-569-08695-7*) St Mut.

Diosi, L. & Lukacs, B. Stochastic Evolution of Quantum States in Open Systems. 152p. 1994. text 68.00 (*981-02-1694-7*) World Scientific Pub.

Diosy, Andrew. There Must Be a Way: 52 Bridge Hands to Challenge Your Play & Defense. 1997. pap. text 9.95 (*0-9698461-1-8*) Master Pt Pr.

Dioszegi, Vilmos, ed. Popular Beliefs & Folklore Tradition in Siberia. (Uralic & Altaic Ser.: No. 57). 1968. text 78.50 (*3-11-000041-5*) Mouton.

Dioszegi, Vilmos & Hoppal, Mihaly, eds. Folk Beliefs & Shamanistic Traditions in Siberia (Valogatott Reprint) (Bibliotheca Shamanistica Ser.: No. 3). (Illus.). xvi, 248 p. 1996. 104.00 (*963-05-6965-5*, Pub. by Akade Kiado) St Mut.

***Diotalevi, David A.** God's Questions: Prayerful Answers for Daily Life. LC 98-9402. 119p. 1998. pap. 9.95 (*1-57249-112-4*, Ragged Edge) White Mane Pub.

Diotima. Dialectics of Diotima: Dialogues in the Greek Mode. 1969. 35.00 (*0-87556-079-2*) Saifer.

Diotte, Sharon, ed. see McGaa Eagle Man, Ed.

***Diou, Suzanne & Caldwell, Lois.** 12 Stepping Stones: For Young Children of Alcoholics & Other Addictive-Drug Users. (Illus.). 104p. (J). 1999. pap. 14.95 (*1-57543-077-0*) Mar Co Prods.

Dioudonnat, Pierre-Marie & Bragadir, Sabine. Dictionnaire des 10,000 Dirigeants Politiques Francais. (FRE.). 756p. 1978. 95.00 (*0-8288-5181-6*, M6164) Fr & Eur.

***Diouf, Sylviane.** Bintou's Braids. LC 99-50820. (Illus.). (J). 2000. 14.95 (*0-8118-2514-0*) Chronicle Bks.

Diouf, Sylviane, jt. auth. see Gravelle, Karen.

***Diouf, Sylviane A.** Growing up in Slavery. LC 00-38013. (Illus.). 2001. lib. bdg. write for info. (*0-7613-1763-5*) Millbrook Pr.

Diouf, Sylviane A. Servants of Allah: African Muslims Enslaved in the Americas. LC 98-19768. 248p. 1998. text 55.00 (*0-8147-1904-X*); pap. text 18.50 (*0-8147-1905-8*) NYU Pr.

DiPalma, Carolyn, jt. ed. see Winkler, Barbara Scott.

***DiPalma, Jim.** Covenant Keeping: Building Relationships That Last. Wallis, Scott, ed. 128p. 2000. pap. 7.95 (*0-9642211-8-7*) Lghthouse Pubns.

Dipalma, Joseph R. Pharmacology: PreTest Self-Assessment & Review. 5th ed. 1988. pap. text 15.95 (*0-07-051966-8*) McGraw.

DiPalma, Joseph R. The Sports Book. (Illus.). 52p. (YA). 1995. pap. 12.95 (*0-936459-30-1*) Stained Glass.

DiPalma, M. D., et al, eds. Basic Pharmacology in Medicine: Pharmacology in Medicine. 4th ed. (Illus.). 890p. 1994. pap. text 46.95 (*0-942447-04-2*) Med Surveill.

DiPalma, Ray. January Zero. (Morning Coffee Chapbook Ser.). (Illus.). 15p. (Orig.). 1984. pap. 15.00 (*0-915124-95-5*) Coffee Hse.

— Metropolitan Corridor. 1992. pap. 7.00 (*84-87467-13-X*, Pub. by Zasterle Pr) SPD-Small Pr Dist.

— Mock Fandango. 20p. 1991. pap. 5.00 (*1-55713-114-7*) Sun & Moon CA.

— Motion of the Cypher. 99p. (Orig.). 1995. pap. 10.95 (*0-937804-61-4*) Segue NYC.

— Numbers & Tempers: Selected Early Poems, 1966-1986. (Sun & Moon Classics Ser.: No. 24). 176p. 1992. pap. 11.95 (*1-55713-099-X*) Sun & Moon CA.

— Provocations. LC 95-134043. 1995. pap. 11.00 (*0-937013-55-2*) Potes Poets.

D

An Asterisk (*) at the beginning of an entry indicates that the title is appearing for the first time.

— Raik. LC 89-62801. (Roof Bks.). 108p. (Orig.). 1989. pap. 9.95 (*0-937804-37-1*) Segue NYC.

DiPalma, Ray, tr. see Hocquard, Emmanuel.

***DiPaola, Anthony M.** Scattered Thoughts. (Illus.). 80p. 2000. pap. 9.00 (*0-8059-4788-4*) Dorrance.

DiPaola, Anthony M. Walk with Me. (Orig.). 1997. pap. write for info. (*1-57553-495-9*) Watermrk Pr.

Dipaolo. Gore Vidal. 1995. text 26.95 (*0-8057-3984-X*) Macmillan.

***DiPaolo, Francesca.** Muffins: Over 300 Recipes & Variations to Accompany Any Meal. 224p. 2000. pap. 12.95 (*1-58062-252-6*) Adams Media.

DiPaolo-Healey, Antonette, ed. The Old English Vision of St. Paul. LC 77-89928. 1978. 20.00 (*0-910956-76-6*, SAM 2); pap. 12.00 (*0-910956-62-6*) Medieval Acad.

DiPaolo, Joseph, jt. auth. see Wallace, Adam.

DiPaolo, Joseph A., ed. see World Symposium on Model Studies in Chemical Carci.

***DiPaolo, Michael.** The Impact of Multiple Childhood Trauma on Homeless Runaway Adolescents. rev. ed. (Children of Poverty Ser.). (Illus.). 179p. 1999. 48.00 (*0-8153-3234-3*) Garland.

DiPaolo, Vincent. The Night & the Moon. LC 82-13724. 1987. pap. 13.95 (*0-87949-214-7*) Ashley Bks.

DiPardo, Anne. Teaching in Common: Challenges to Joint Work in Classrooms & Schools. LC 98-28699. (School Reform Ser.). 208p. 1999. text 40.00 (*0-8077-3764-X*); pap. text 18.95 (*0-8077-3763-1*) Tchrs Coll.

DiPasquale, Denise & Keyes, Langley C., eds. Building Foundations: Housing & Federal Policy. LC 90-30442. (Illus.). 512p. (C). 1990. 65.00 (*0-8122-8223-X*); pap. 27.95 (*0-8122-1309-2*) U of Pa Pr.

DiPasquale, Denise, jt. auth. see Wheaton, William.

DiPasquale, Emanuel. Genesis. 77p. 1997. reprint ed. pap. 12.00 (*0-9658221-0-9*, 199701) Jostro Pubns.

Dipasquale, Mark & Hewlett-Packard Company Staff. Thread Time: A Multi-Threaded Programming Guide. 560p. (C). 1996. pap. text 49.99 (*0-13-190067-6*) P-H.

DiPasquale, Theresa M. Literature & Sacrament: The Sacred & the Secular in John Donne. LC 99-6301. (Medieval & Renaissance Literary Studies). 300p. 1999. text 58.00 (*0-8207-0309-5*) Duquesne.

DiPaul, H. Bert. Focusing Industrial Arts on Career Education. LC 79-53500. (Illus.). 143p. (Orig.). (gr. 9-12). 1979. pap. 2.95 (*0-9605418-0-2*) DiPaul.

DiPaul, Margaret. The Chalk Dust Report. LC 93-11983. (Illus.). 176p. (Orig.). 1993. pap. 10.95 (*0-945213-11-5*) Rudi Pub.

Dipboye. Understanding Industrial & Organizational Psychology. 1997. text 90.00 (*0-03-051552-1*) H Holt & Co.

***Dipboye, Carolyn & Turrentine, Jan, contrib. by.** Women of Faith: Living Lives That Matter. 113p. 1999. pap. 8.99 (*1-56309-695-1*) Womans Mission Union.

Dipboye, Robert L. Understanding Industry & Organizations. (C). 1993. pap. text, teacher ed. 35.00 (*0-03-094857-6*) Harcourt Coll Pubs.

— Understanding Industry & Organizations. (C). 1994. pap. text, student ed. 29.00 (*0-03-094858-4*) Harcourt Coll Pubs.

Dipboye, Robert L., jt. auth. see Howell, William C.

Dipchand, Cecil R., et al. The Chinese Financial System, 157. LC 93-50539. (Contributions in Economics & Economic History Ser.: No. 157). 240p. 1994. 65.00 (*0-313-29282-5*, Greenwood Pr) Greenwood.

DiPego, Gerald. Cheevey. LC 97-13612. 304p. 1997. mass mkt. 12.99 (*0-446-67309-9*, Pub. by Warner Bks) Little.

DiPeri, Philip T. Business Planning: A Guidebook for Entrepreneurs & General Managers. 40p. (Orig.). 1985. pap. text 25.00 (*0-932797-00-8*) Stonehenge Intl.

DiPerna, Alan. Fender Classic Moments: 50 Years of Modern Music. 116p. 1996. per. 24.95 (*0-7935-5591-4*, 00330175) H Leonard.

Dipert, Brian. The PCI Handbook: For Hardware & Software Engineers. (Illus.). 96p. 1997. mass mkt. 14.95 (*0-929392-25-6*) Annabooks.

Dipert, Brian & Levy, Markus. Designing with Flash Memory. 421p. 1996. mass mkt. 49.95 (*0-929392-17-5*) Annabooks.

Dipert, Randall R. Artifacts, Art Works & Agency. (Arts & Their Philosophies Ser.). 288p. (C). 1993. 54.95 (*0-87722-990-2*) Temple U Pr.

DiPiazza, Domenica. Arkansas. LC 93-33391. (Hello U. S. A. Ser.). (Illus.). 72p. (J). (gr. 3-6). 1994. lib. bdg. 19.93 (*0-8225-2742-1*, Lerner Publctns) Lerner Pub.

— West Virginia. LC 93-46906. (Hello U. S. A. Ser.). (Illus.). 72p. (J). (gr. 3-6). 1995. lib. bdg. 19.95 (*0-8225-2745-6*, Lerner Publctns) Lerner Pub.

Dipiero, jt. auth. see Burr.

DiPiero, Thomas. Dangerous Truths & Criminal Passions: The Evolution of the French Novel, 1569-1791. LC 91-40396. 416p. (C). 1992. 39.50 (*0-8047-1999-3*) Stanford U Pr.

DiPiero, W. S. Shadows Burning. 80p. 1995. text 29.95 (*0-8101-5019-0*) Northwestern U Pr.

— Shadows Burning. 80p. (C). 1995. pap. 12.95 (*0-8101-5020-4*) Northwestern U Pr.

Dipierro, Joseph, jt. auth. see Ragonese, Roger R.

DiPietro, Joe. Over the River & Through the Woods. pap. 5.95 (*0-8222-1712-0*) Dramatists Play.

DiPietro, Joseph S., ed. A Primer for Health Care, Health Education & All Disciplines Amidst Change. LC 99-21013. (Studies in Health & Human Services: Vol. 33). 156p. 1999. 69.95 (*0-7734-7958-9*) E Mellen.

Dipietro, Marcie, ed. see Adams Media Corporation Staff.

DiPietro, Nicholas J. For the Gentle People. LC 86-91873. 1987. 10.00 (*0-87212-203-4*) Libra.

DiPietro, Robert, ed. see Williams, Stephanie.

DiPietro, Robert J., et al, eds. The First Delaware Symposium on Language Studies: Selected Papers. LC 80-71116. 420p. 1983. 45.00 (*0-87413-190-1*) U Delaware Pr.

DiPietro, Robert J. & Freedle, Roy O., eds. Linguistics & the Professions. LC 81-22905. (Advances in Discourse Processes Ser.: Vol. 8). 288p. (Orig.). (C). 1982. pap. 42.50 (*0-89391-120-8*); text 78.50 (*0-89391-092-9*) Ablx Pub.

DiPietro, Robert J. & Ifkovic, Edward, eds. Ethnic Perspectives in American Literature: Selected Essays on the European Contribution. LC 82-14265. 333p. 1983. lib. bdg. 19.75 (*0-87352-126-9*, B201C) Modern Lang.

DiPietro, Robert J., jt. auth. see Agard, Frederick B.

DiPietro, Robert J., ed. see Artigal, Josep M.

DiPietro, Robert J., ed. see Bernhardt, Elizabeth B.

DiPietro, Robert J., ed. see Georgetown University Round Table Meeting on Lingu.

DiPietro, Robert J., jt. ed. see Schweda-Nicholson, Nancy.

DiPietro, Robert J., ed. see Taeschner, Traute.

***DiPippa, John M. A., et al.** The Counselor-at-Law: A Collaborative Approach to Client Interviewing & Counseling. 290p. 1999. pap. 28.00 (*0-327-01517-9*, 1195010) LEXIS Pub.

***Dipiro.** Pharmacotherapy Interim Value Pak. 1999. 175.00 (*0-8385-8183-8*, Apple Lange Med) McGraw.

Dipiro. Pharmacotherapy Pathology Approach. 4th ed. 2912p. (C). 1999. 150.00 (*0-8385-7691-5*, Apple Lange Med) McGraw.

Dipiro, jt. auth. see Schwinghammer.

Dipiro, jt. auth. see Wells.

DiPiro, Joseph T. Pharmacotherapy. 3rd ed. 1998. text 175.00 (*0-8385-7686-9*) Appleton & Lange.

— Pharmacotherapy: A Pathophysiologic Approach. 3rd ed. LC 95-25685. (C). 1996. pap. text 150.00 (*0-8385-7892-6*, A7892-1) Appleton & Lange.

DiPiro, Joseph T., et al. Concepts in Clinical Pharmacokinetics. (Orig.). 1991. pap. text 69.00 (*0-930530-86-1*) Am Soc Hlth-Syst.

Dipl-Ling, V. & Bensch, Erhard. Dictionary of Shipbuilding, Shipping & Fisheries. 784p. 1980. vinyl bd. 150.00 (*0-7855-7152-3*) St Mut.

Dipleco, Daniel. Trackfacts: Examination of Data Bases. (Illus.). 178p. (Orig.). 1997. pap. write for info. (*1-57502-392-X*, PO1288) Morris Pubng.

Dipoko, M. S. Because of Women. (African Writers Ser.). 178p. (C). 1969. pap. 8.95 (*0-435-90057-9*, 90057) Heinemann.

Dipp. Monitoring Antagonistic Fungi Deliberately Released into the Environment. Jensen, Dan F., ed. LC 97-101122. (Developments in Plant Pathology Ser.). 188p. (C). 1996. text 95.50 (*0-7923-4077-9*) Kluwer Academic.

Dippel, David W. The August Bride: A Narrative Travelogue of a Short Stay in the People's Republic of China. (Illus.). 485p. 1990. ring bd. 75.00 (*0-9627693-0-4*) D.W.D. Pubn.

Dippel, Horst. Germany & the American Revolution, 1770-1800: A Sociohistorical Investigation of Late Eighteenth-Century Political Thinking. LC 77-367. (Illus.). 472p. reprint ed. pap. 146.40 (*0-8357-3885-X*, 203661700004) Bks Demand.

Dippel, John V. Two Against Hitler: Stealing the Nazis' Best-Kept Secrets. LC 91-25248. 272p. 1992. 55.00 (*0-275-93745-3*, C3745, Praeger Pubs) Greenwood.

Dippel, Raye L. & Hutton, J. Thomas, eds. Caring for the Alzheimer Patient: A Practical Guide. 3rd rev. ed. LC 96-29306. (Golden Age Books - Perspectives on Aging Ser.). 219p. 1996. pap. 17.95 (*1-57392-108-4*) Prometheus Bks.

— Caring for the Parkinson Patient: A Practical Guide. LC 89-10658. (Golden Age Books - Perspectives on Aging Ser.). (Illus.). 196p. 1989. 27.95 (*0-87975-478-8*); pap. 17.95 (*0-87975-562-8*) Prometheus Bks.

Dippel, Raye Lynne, jt. ed. see Hutton, J. Thomas.

Dippel, Stewart. The Professionalization of the English Church from 1560 to 1700: Ambassadors for Chirst. LC 99-23102. (Studies in Religion & Society: Vol. 44). 272p. 1999. text 89.95 (*0-7734-7982-1*) E Mellen.

Dipper, Andrew. Musical Instruments of the Violin Family & the Geometry of Positioning & Cutting Out Their F-Shaped Sound Holes. LC 98-108242. (Technical Studies in the Arts of Musical Instrument Making: Vol. 1). (Illus.). 80p. (Orig.). 1997. pap., spiral bd. 25.00 (*0-9657095-0-7*) Dipper Pr.

— Musical Instruments of the Violin Family & the Geometry of Positioning & Cutting Out Their F-Shaped Sound Holes. 4th ed. LC 98-108242. (Technical Studies in the Arts of Musical Instrument Making: No. 1). (Illus.). 80p. (Orig.). 1997. reprint ed. pap., spiral bd. 25.00 (*0-9657095-1-5*) Dipper Pr.

Dipper, Frances. The Ocean Deep. LC 95-40835. (Mysteries Of-- Ser.). (J). 1996. 12.15 (*0-606-09658-2*, Pub. by Turtleback) Demco.

— Oceans & Rivers, 6 vols. unabridged ed. LC 96-5009. (Changing World Ser.). (Illus.). 80p. (J). (gr. 3-7). 1996. 12.95 (*1-57145-027-0*, Silver Dolph) Advantage Pubs.

Dipper, Francis. New Book of Treasures under the Ocean. LC 97-24313. (Illus.). 32p. (J). (gr. 4-6). 1997. pap. 9.95 (*0-7613-0640-4*, Copper Beech Bks); lib. bdg. 23.90 (*0-7613-0703-6*, Copper Beech Bks) Millbrook Pr.

— The Ocean Deep. (Mysteries of...Ser.). (Illus.). 40p. (J). (gr. 4-6). 1996. lib. bdg. 22.90 (*0-7613-0454-1*, Copper Beech Bks) Millbrook Pr.

Dippie, Brian & Hassrick, Peter. Charles M. Russell: The Artist in His Heyday. LC 95-61424. (Illus.). 197p. (Orig.). 1995. pap. 45.00 (*0-935037-98-5*) G Peters Gallery.

Dippie, Brian W. Bards of the Little Big Horn. 1976. 37.95 (*0-8488-0248-9*, J M C & Co) Amereon Ltd.

— Catlin & His Contemporaries: The Politics of Patronage. LC 89-4963. (Illus.). xx, 569p. 1990. text 80.00 (*0-8032-1683-1*) U of Nebr Pr.

— Custer's Last Stand: The Anatomy of an American Myth. LC 94-26029. (Illus.). xxv, 226p. 1994. pap. 12.00 (*0-8032-6592-1*, Bison Books) U of Nebr Pr.

— Remington & Russell: The Sid Richardson Collection. rev. ed. LC 93-21260. (Illus.). 240p. 1994. 70.00 (*0-292-71569-2*); pap. 34.95 (*0-292-71568-4*) U of Tex Pr.

— The Vanishing American: White Attitudes & U. S. Indian Policy. LC 91-18772. (Illus.). 446p. 1991. reprint ed. pap. 15.95 (*0-7006-0507-X*) U Pr of KS.

— West-Fever. LC 98-13528. (Illus.). 128p. 1998. 35.00 (*0-295-97735-3*) U of Wash Pr.

Dippie, Brian W., compiled by. Custer's Last Stand 39.00 (*1-56696-081-9*) Jackdaw.

Dippie, Brian W., ed. Charlie Russell Roundup: Essays on America's Favorite Cowboy Artist. LC 98-56386. (Illus.). 300p. 1999. 39.95 (*0-917298-46-2*) MT Hist Soc.

Dippie, Brian W., ed. Charlie Russell Roundup: Essays on America's Favorite Western Artist. LC 98-56386. (Illus.). 360p. 1999. pap. 19.95 (*0-917298-47-0*) MT Hist Soc.

Dippie, Brian W. & Autry Museum of Western Heritage Staff. West-Fever. LC 98-13528. 1998. lib. bdg. write for info. (*1-882880-08-0*) Autry Mus Wstrn.

Dipple, Elizabeth. Iris Murdoch: Work for the Spirit. LC 81-52553. 366p. (C). 1992. 30.00 (*0-226-15363-0*) U Ch Pr.

— The Unresolvable Plot: Reading Contemporary Fiction. 288p. 1988. text 49.50 (*0-415-00661-9*); pap. text 14.95 (*0-415-00662-7*) Routledge.

Dipple, Geoffrey. Antifraternalism & Anticlericalism in the German Reformation: Johann Eberlin Von Gunzburg & the Campaign Against the Friars. (St. Andrews Studies in Reformation History). 256p. (C). 1996. 86.95 (*1-85928-267-9*, Pub. by Scolar Pr) Ashgate Pub Co.

Dipple, Geoffrey, ed. see Packull, Werner O., et al.

Dippman, Gerda. Practical Review of German Grammar. 514p. (C). 1987. teacher ed. write for info. (*0-318-59094-8*) P-H.

Dippmann. A Practical Review of German Grammar. 3rd ed. 397p. (C). 1999. 49.00 (*0-13-938143-0*) P-H.

***Dippo, Cathryn S.** Friedrichstal Church Records, 1698-1812. 429p. 1999. pap. 61.00 (*0-7884-1190-X*, D366) Heritage Bk.

Dippold, Joel. Picabo Sreet: Downhill Dynamo. LC 98-28467. (J). 1998. 5.95 (*0-8225-9839-6*) Lerner Pub.

— Picabo Street: Downhill Dynamo. LC 97-8848. (J). 1997. lib. bdg. 19.95 (*0-8225-3659-5*, Lerner Publctns) Lerner Pub.

— Picabo Street: Downhill Dynamo. LC 97-8848. (Illus.). 64p. (J). 1997. pap. 5.95 (*0-8225-9808-6*, Lerner Publctns) Lerner Pub.

— Troy Aikman, Quick-Draw Quarterback. LC 93-47909. (Sports Achievers Biographies Ser.). (Illus.). 64p. (J). (gr. 4-9). 1994. lib. bdg. 19.95 (*0-8225-2880-0*, Lerner Publctns) Lerner Pub.

— Troy Aikman, Quick-Draw Quarterback. LC 93-47909. (Achievers Ser.). (Illus.). 64p. (YA). (gr. 4-9). 1994. pap. 5.95 (*0-8225-9663-6*, Lerner Publctns) Lerner Pub.

DiPrete, T. A. The Bureaucratic Labor Market: The Case of the Federal Civil Service. (Studies & Work & Industry). (Illus.). 358p. (C). 1989. 55.00 (*0-306-43184-X*, Plenum Trade) Perseus Pubng.

DiPrima, Daniel. The Extra Nose. (Illus.). 32p. (J). (ps-3). 1994. 14.95 (*1-55933-151-8*) Zino Pr.

DiPrima, Diane. Pieces of a Song: Selected Poems of Diane DiPrima. 205p. (Orig.). 1989. pap. 12.95 (*0-87286-237-2*) City Lights.

Diprima, Liza, ed. see Pferdehirt, Julia & Schreiter, Dave.

DiPrima, Richard C., jt. auth. see Boyce, William.

DiPrima, Richard C., jt. auth. see Boyce, William E.

DiPrima, Richard O., ed. Modern Modeling of Continuum Phenomena. LC 77-9041. (Lectures in Applied Mathematics: Vol. 16). 251p. 1977. reprint ed. pap. 70.00 (*0-8218-1116-9*, LAM/16) Am Math.

DiPrince, Dawn. A Month of Fundays: A Whole Year of Games & Activities. 220p. (J). (gr. 5-12). 1996. pap. text 23.95 (*1-877673-29-3*, Fun) Cottonwood Pr.

Diprose. Cartographies: Poststructuralism & the Mapping of Bodies & Spaces. Ferrell, Robyn, ed. 176p. pap. 19.95 (*0-04-442291-1*) Paul & Co Pubs.

Diprose, Rosalyn. The Bodies of Women: Ethics, Embodiment & Sexual Difference. LC 93-37969. 176p. (C). 1994. pap. 22.99 (*0-415-09783-5*) Routledge.

DiPuccio, Denise M. Communicating Myths of the Golden Age "Comedia" LC 97-27146. 240p. (C). 1998. 39.50 (*0-8387-5372-8*) Bucknell U Pr.

DiPuccio, William. The Interior Sense of Scripture: The Sacred Hermeneutics of John W. Nevin. LC 97-45763. (Studies in American Biblical Hermeneutics: Vol. 14). 192p. 1998. pap. text 19.00 (*0-86554-568-5*, P167) Mercer Univ Pr.

Diqs, Isaak. A Bedouin Boyhood. LC 83-10451. 175p. (C). 1983. reprint ed. text 15.00 (*0-87663-430-7*, Pub. by Universe) St Martin.

Diquinzio, Patrice. Interrogating Maternal: Feminism, Individualism & the Problem of Mothering, 1 vol. LC 98-49163. 1999. 70.00 (*0-415-91022-6*); pap. 19.99 (*0-415-91023-4*) Routledge.

Diquinzio, Patrice & Young, Iris M. Feminist Ethics & Social Policy. LC 96-53431. (A Hypatia Bk.). 1997. 39.95 (*0-253-33296-6*); pap. 17.95 (*0-253-21125-5*) Ind U Pr.

Dirac, P. The Development of Quantum Theory: J. Robert Oppenheimer Memorial Prize Acceptance Speech. 76p. (C). 1971. text 112.00 (*0-677-02970-5*) Gordon & Breach.

Dirac, P. A. The Collected Works of P.A.M. Dirac: 1924-1948. Dalitz, R. H., ed. (Illus.). 1334p. (C). 1995. text 275.00 (*0-521-36231-8*) Cambridge U Pr.

— The Principles of Quantum Mechanics. 4th ed. (International Series of Monographs on Physics). 324p. 1982. pap. text 39.95 (*0-19-852011-5*) OUP.

Dirac, Paul Adrien Maurice. General Theory of Relativity. (Physics Notes Ser.). 68p. 1996. pap. text 10.95 (*0-691-01146-X*, Pub. by Princeton U Pr) Cal Prin Full Svc.

DiRaddo, Raymond S. & Kornfeld, Jerome M. New York Fire District Officer's Guide. 1998. write for info. (*1-58012-034-2*) James Pub Santa Ana.

Diran, Edward. Cow Palace: Great Moments. Compagno, Tony, ed. LC 91-65539. (Illus.). 224p. 1991. pap. 14.00 (*0-936029-27-7*) Western Bk Journ.

Diran, Richard K. The Vanishing Tribes of Burma. (Illus.). 240p. 1997. 45.00 (*0-8174-5559-0*) Watsn-Guptill.

Dirar, A. F. The Indigenous Fermented Foods of the Sudan: A Study in African Food & Nutrition. (Illus.). 576p. 1993. text 140.00 (*0-85198-858-X*) OUP.

Dirasse, Laketch. The Commoditization of Female Sexuality: Prostitution & Socio-Economic Relations in Addis Ababa, Ethiopia. LC 91-7792. (Studies in Anthropology: No. 11). 1991. 52.50 (*0-404-62611-4*) AMS Pr.

Dircks, Richard J., ed. The Letters of Richard Cumberland. LC 87-45799. (Studies in the Eighteenth Century: No. 13). 1989. 49.50 (*0-404-63513-X*) AMS Pr.

— The Unpublished Plays of Richard Cumberland, 2 vols., Set. (Studies in the Eighteenth Century: No. 17). 1992. 115.00 (*0-404-63517-2*) AMS Pr.

Dircks, Richard J., jt. auth. see Cumberland, Richard.

Dirckx, John. The Language of Medicine: Its Evolution, Structure, Dynamics. 2nd ed. LC 83-8863. 206p. 1983. 59.95 (*0-275-91388-0*, C1388, Praeger Pubs) Greenwood.

Dirckx, John H. H & P: A Nonphysicians Guide to the Medical History & Physical Examination. rev. ed. 152p. 1991. pap. 28.00 (*0-934385-04-1*) Hlth Prof Inst.

— Human Diseases. LC 98-234807. (Illus.). 350 p. (Orig.). 1997. pap. 28.00 (*0-934385-69-6*) Hlth Prof Inst.

— Laboratory Medicine: Essentials of Anatomic & Clinical Pathology. 2nd ed. 396p. 1995. pap. text 31.00 (*0-934385-61-0*) Hlth Prof Inst.

Dirckx, John H., ed. see Stedman, Thomas L.

***Dirda, Michael.** Readings: Essays & Literary Entertainments. 2000. 24.95 (*0-253-33824-7*) Ind U Pr.

Direccion de Salvamento Arqueologico Staff. Presencias y Encuentros: Investigaciones Arqueologicas de Salvamento. (SPA., Illus.). 394p. 1995. pap. 23.00 (*968-29-5222-0*, IN97, Pub. by Dir Gen Pubicaiones) UPLAAP.

Direccion General de Correos Staff. Itinerarios de los Dias en Que Se Recibe y Despacha Correspondencia. Ubico, Emilio, ed. (Guatemala Postal History Pamphlet Ser.: No. 2). 24p. 1984. reprint ed. pap. 3.75 (*0-913129-04-6*) La Tienda.

Directed Technologies, Inc. Staff. Hydrogen Infrastructure Report, 7-97. (Hydrogen Fuel Information Ser.: Vol. VII). (Illus.). 94p. 1997. lib. bdg. 135.00 (*0-89934-332-5*, BT981) Bus Tech Bks.

— Technology Development Goals for Automotive Fuel Cell Power Systems (Aug.-94) (Fuel Cell Information Ser.: Vol. VIII). (Illus.). 185p. 1996. lib. bdg. 135.00 (*0-89934-264-7*, BT939) Bus Tech Bks.

Directed Technologies, Inc. Staff, et al. Detailed Manufacturing Cost Estimates for Polymer Electrolyte (PEM) Fuel Cells for Light Duty Vehicles (8-98) (Fuel Cell Information Ser.: Vol. 18). (Illus.). 188p. 1997. lib. bdg. 155.00 (*0-89934-356-2*, BT 990) Bus Tech Bks.

Directions for Canadian Health Care Conference Staff, et al. Do We Care? Renewing Canada's Commitment to Health. 19.95 (*0-7735-1878-9*) McG-Queens Univ Pr.

Director, Aaron, jt. auth. see Douglas, Paul H.

Director, Anne. The Standard Wine Cookbook. (Culinary Arts Ser.). (Illus.). 192p. 1979. reprint ed. pap. 9.95 (*0-89496-013-X*) Ross Bks.

Director, S. W. & Maly, W., eds. Statistical Approach to VLSI. LC 93-46624. (Advances in CAD for VLSI Ser.: Vol. 8). 402p. 1994. 187.50 (*0-444-88371-1*, North Holland) Elsevier.

Director, Stephen W., et al. VLSI Design for Manufacturing: Yield Enhancement. (C). 1989. text 118.50 (*0-7923-9054-7*) Kluwer Academic.

Director, Stephen W., jt. auth. see Dewey, Allen M.

Director, Steven M. Strategic Planning for Human Resources. (Studies in Productivity: No. 42). 46p. 1985. pap. 55.00 (*0-08-029516-9*) Work in Amer.

Directorate-General Telecommunications Staff, jt. ed. see Commission of the European Communities Staff.

Directors & Curators Staff. The Brooklyn Museum of Art. (Illus.). 192p. 1997. 19.95 (*1-85759-171-2*) Scala Books.

Directors of Participating Schools Staff. The Preschool Report. Faison-Gardner, Kyra, ed. ii, 36p. (Orig.). 1996. pap. 5.50 (*0-9652127-0-X*) Fmly First Res.

Directors of the Japan Bonsai Association Staff. The Masters' Book of Bonsai. LC 67-12585. (Illus.). 144p. 1984. pap. 18.00 (*0-87011-453-0*) Kodansha.

Directory of Directors Staff, ed. Directory of Directors in the City of New York & Tri-State Area. 675p. 1998. 245.00 (*0-936612-19-3*) DODC.

Directx Team Staff. Inside DirectX. LC 97-35214. 550p. 1997. pap. text 44.99 incl. cd-rom (*1-57231-696-9*) Microsoft.

DiRenzo, Gordon J., ed. We, the People: American Character & Social Change, 24. LC 76-51926. (Contributions in Sociology Ser.: No. 24). (Illus.). 339p. 1977. 75.00 (*0-8371-9481-4*, DWP/, Greenwood Pr) Greenwood.

D

DiRenzo, Thomas G. Developing New Markets for Information Products. Cunningham, Ann M. & Wicks, Wendy, eds. (Report Series, 1993: No. 1). 144p. (Orig.). (C). 1993. pap. 50.00 (*0-942308-39-5*) NFAIS.

DiResta, David. Favorite Garlic Recipes. 62p. 1996. 4.95 (*1-55867-150-1*, Magnetic Bks) Bristol Pub Ent CA.

— The Garlic Cookbook. LC 95-128166. (Illus.). 176p. (Orig.). 1994. pap. 8.95 (*1-55867-108-0*, Nitty Gritty Ckbks) Bristol Pub Ent CA.

***DiResta, David.** The Garlic Cookbook. (Illus.). 160p. (Orig.). 2000. pap. 8.95 (*1-55867-253-2*, Nitty Gritty Ckbks) Bristol Pub Ent CA.

DiResta, David & Foran, Joanne. The Best 50 Flavored Oils & Vinegars. LC 97-117654. (Best 50 Ser.). 80p. (Orig.). 1996. pap. 4.95 (*1-55867-142-0*) Bristol Pub Ent CA.

— Oven & Rotisserie Roasting. LC 97-195760. (Illus.). 176p. (Orig.). 1997. pap. 8.95 (*1-55867-167-6*, Nitty Gritty Ckbks) Bristol Pub Ent CA.

— Sautes. (Illus.). 160p. (Orig.). 1996. pap. 8.95 (*1-55867-139-0*, Nitty Gritty Ckbks) Bristol Pub Ent CA.

— The Toaster Oven Cookbook. (Illus.). 160p. (Orig.). 1995. pap. 8.95 (*1-55867-124-2*, Nitty Gritty Ckbks) Bristol Pub Ent CA.

DiResta, David, et al. Favorite Last-Minute Meals. 62p. 1997. 4.95 (*1-55867-200-1*, Magnetic Bks) Bristol Pub Ent CA.

DiResta, Diane. Knockout Presentations: How to Deliver Your Message with Power, Punch & Pizzazz. 228p. 1998. pap. 15.95 (*1-886284-25-3*, Pub. by Chandler Hse) Natl Bk Netwk.

DiResta, John. Untitled John DiResta. 304p. 2000. 19.95 (*0-7868-6396-X*, Pub. by Hyperion) Little.

DiRezze, Deborah E., ed. see Spicer, S. Gary.

***Dirge, Roman.** Lenore: Noogies. (Illus.). 112p. (C). 1999. pap. 11.95 (*0-943151-03-1*) Slave Labor Bks.

— Lenore: Noogies. (Lenore Collection: No. 1). (Illus.). 112p. 1999. pap. 11.95 (*0-943151-16-3*) Slave Labor Bks.

— Monsters in My Tummy. (Illus.). 48p. 1999. pap. 5.95 (*0-943151-23-6*) Slave Labor Bks.

***Dirgo, Craig.** The Einstein Papers. 358p. 1999. 23.00 (*0-671-03489-8*, PB Hardcover) PB.

— The Einstein Papers. 400p. 2000. reprint ed. per. 6.99 (*0-671-02322-5*, Pocket Books) PB.

Dirgo, Craig, jt. auth. see Cussler, Clive.

Dirie, Waris & Miller, Cathleen. Desert Flower: The Extraordinary Journey of a Desert Nomad. 240p. 1999. pap. 14.00 (*0-688-17237-7*, Quil) HarperTrade.

— Desert Flower: The Extraordinary Journey of a Desert Nomad. LC 98-17480. (Illus.). 224p. 1998. 25.00 (*0-688-15823-4*, Wm Morrow) Morrow Avon.

DiRienzo, Madelyn. The Tale of Readalot. (Illus.). 24p. (J). 1995. 3.95 (*1-885110-01-4*) Devers Pubng.

Dirig, Robert, jt. auth. see Klass, Carolyn.

Diringer, David. The Alphabet: A Key to the History of Mankind. 1996. 47.50 (*0-614-31169-1*, Pub. by M Manoharial) Coronet Bks.

Diringer, David. The Book Before Printing: Ancient, Medieval & Oriental. (Illus.). 604p. (C). 1982. reprint ed. pap. 14.95 (*0-486-24243-9*) Dover.

Dirk, Alexandra. Origami Boxes: For Gifts, Treasures & Trifles. LC 96-46685. (Illus.). 64p. 1997. pap. 10.95 (*0-8069-9495-9*) Sterling.

Dirk, Carl W., jt. auth. see Kuzyk, Mark G.

Dirke, Sabine Von, see Von Dirke, Sabine.

Dirkes & Krause, John. The Route of the Erie Limited. (Illus.). 48p. 1989. pap. 7.95 (*0-911868-11-9*, C11) Carstens Pubns.

Dirkes, Ann. Self-Directed Problem Solving: Idea Production in Mathematics. 132p. (Orig.). (C). 1993. pap. text 19.50 (*0-8191-9130-2*) U Pr of Amer.

Dirkes, George R., jt. auth. see Hartog, John A.

Dirkes, M. Ann. Writing Activities to Develop Mathematical Thinking. 116p. 1990. pap. 14.99 (*0-89824-049-2*) Trillium Pr.

Dirkis, Michael, jt. auth. see Kobetsky, Michael.

Dirks, Christopher. The Gloria Estefan Scrapbook: A Celebration in Words & Pictures. (Illus.). 256p. 1999. pap. 21.95 (*0-8065-2107-4*, Citadel Pr) Carol Pub Group.

Dirks, Daniel, et al. Japanese Management in the Low Growth Era: Between External Shocks & Internal Evolution. LC 98-48119. ix, 438p. 1999. write for info. (*3-540-64035-5*) Spr-Verlag.

Dirks-Edmunds, Jane Claire. Not Just Trees: The Legacy of a Douglas-Fir Forest. LC 98-46721. (Illus.). 360p. 1999. 35.00 (*0-87422-169-2*); pap. 22.95 (*0-87422-170-6*) Wash St U Pr.

Dirks, G. Frederick. Walk: The Trees Are Marked for You. (Illus.). 238p. (Orig.). 1989. pap. 14.00 (*0-9621573-0-9*) G F Dirks.

Dirks, Gerald E. Art & Work: A Social History of Labour in the Canadian Graphic Arts Industry to the 1940s. LC 95-170474. (Illus.). 208p. 1994. 60.00 (*0-7735-1280-2*, Pub. by McG-Queens Univ Pr) CUP Services.

— Canada's Refugee Policy: Indifference or Opportunism? 1977. lib. bdg. 60.00 (*0-7735-0296-3*, Pub. by McG-Queens Univ Pr) CUP Services.

— Controversy & Complexity: Canadian Immigration Policy during the 1980s. 200p. 1995. 55.00 (*0-7735-1238-1*, Pub. by McG-Queens Univ Pr) CUP Services.

Dirks, Gerald E., et al. The State of the United Nations, 1993: North-South Perspectives. (Reports & Papers). 110p. (C). 1993. pap. 10.00 (*1-880660-07-5*) Acad Coun UN Syst.

Dirks, J. J. Centralized Litigation Practice Management. (Waterlow Practitioner's Library). 144p. 1990. pap. 29.95 (*0-08-040136-8*, Pergamon Pr) Elsevier.

— Making Legal Aid Pay. (Waterlow Practitioner's Library). 112p. 1989. pap. 19.95 (*0-08-036918-9*, Pergamon Pr) Elsevier.

Dirks, Jo. Sydney Downtown. (Illus.). 192p. (Orig.). 1993. pap. 14.95 (*0-86417-445-4*, Pub. by Kangaroo Pr) Seven Hills Bk.

Dirks, John H. & Sutton, Roger A. Diuretics: Physiology, Pharmacology & Clinical Use. (Illus.). 396p. 1986. text 104.00 (*0-7216-1243-1*, W B Saunders Co) Harcrt Hlth Sci Grp.

Dirks, Lana & Daniel, Sally. A Colorado Kind of Christmas. (Illus.). 128p. 1993. pap. 25.00 (*1-56579-049-9*) Westcliffe Pubs.

Dirks, Laura M., jt. auth. see Daniel, Sally.

Dirks, Laura M., jt. auth. see Daniel, Sally H.

Dirks, Lori, ed. Schizophrenia: Latest Advances in Understanding & Drug Development. (Biomedical Library). 296p. 1996. pap. 795.00 (*1-57936-016-5*) IBC USA.

Dirks, Moses, jt. ed. see Bergsland, Knut.

Dirks, Nicholas B. The Hollow Crown: Ethnohistory of an Indian Kingdom. 2nd ed. (Illus.). 488p. (C). 1993. pap. text 27.95 (*0-472-08187-X*, 08187) U of Mich Pr.

Dirks, Nicholas B., ed. Colonialism & Culture. LC 92-3315. (Comparative Studies in Society & History). 416p. (C). 1992. text 65.00 (*0-472-09434-3*, 09434); pap. text 23.95 (*0-472-06434-7*, 06434) U of Mich Pr.

— In Near Ruins: Cultural Theory at the End of the Century. LC 98-27833. (Illus.). 320p. 1998. 49.95 (*0-8166-3122-0*); pap. 19.95 (*0-8166-3123-9*) U of Minn Pr.

Dirks, Nicholas B., et al, eds. Culture-Power-History: A Reader in Contemporary Social Theory. LC 93-1795. (Studies in Culture - Power - History). (Illus.). 640p. 1993. pap. text 21.95 (*0-691-02102-3*, Pub. by Princeton U Pr) Cal Prin Full Svc.

Dirks, Patricia. The Failure of L' Action Libirale Nationale. 216p. 1991. 60.00 (*0-7735-0831-7*, Pub. by McG-Queens Univ Pr) CUP Services.

***Dirks, Raymond & Gross, Leonard.** The Great Wallstreet Scandal. 295p. 2000. 14.95 (*1-929925-03-4*) FirstPublish.

Dirks, Robert. The Black Saturnalia: Conflict & Its Ritual Expression on British West Indian Slave Plantations. LC 86-28931. (University of Florida Monographs: Vol. 72). (Illus.). 256p. 1987. reprint ed. pap. 79.40 (*0-608-04494-6*, 206523900001) Bks Demand.

— The Black Saturnalia: Conflict & Its Ritual Expression on West Indian Slave Plantations. (University of Florida Social Sciences Monographs: No. 72). (Orig.). (C). 1987. pap. 29.95 (*0-8130-0843-3*) U Press Fla.

Dirks, Ruthann. Computer Hardware: Standalone & Networked Systems. unabridged ed. (Illus.). 73p. (C). 1999. pap. text 22.00 (*1-881530-13-2*) Delta Pi Epsilon.

Dirkse, T. P. Copper, Silver, Gold, Et Cetera. (IUPAC Solubility Data Ser.). 1986. 130.00 (*0-08-032498-3*, Pergamon Pr) Elsevier.

Dirkse, Jan P., et al, eds. Development & Social Welfare: Indonesia's Experiences under the New Order. (KITLV Verhandelingen Ser.: No. 156). 306p. (Orig.). 1993. pap. 33.50 (*90-6718-056-4*, Pub. by KITLV Pr) Cellar.

Dirksen, D. & Von Bally, G., eds. Optical Technologies in the Humanities: Selected Contributions to the International Conference on New Technologies in the Humanities & Fourth International Conference on Optics Within Life Sciences, Owls IV, Munster, Germany, 9-13 July 1996. LC 97-30664. (Optics Within Life Sciences Ser.: Vol. 4). (Illus.). x, 267p. 1997. 99.95 (*3-540-63280-8*) Spr-Verlag.

Dirksen, D. J. Recreation Lakes of California. 11th ed. (Illus.). 256p. (Orig.). 1995. pap. text 16.95 (*0-943798-18-3*) Recreation Sales Pub.

Dirksen, Diane & McKinney, John. Colorado River Recreation. 3rd rev. ed. (Illus.). 176p. 1998. pap. 16.95 (*0-943798-19-1*) Recreation Sales Pub.

Dirksen, Diane, et al. Recreation Lakes of California. 12th ed. (Illus.). 1999. pap. 16.95 (*0-943798-20-5*) Recreation Sales Pub.

Dirksen, Everett M. The Education of a Senator. LC 97-46696. 1998. 29.95 (*0-252-02414-1*) U of Ill Pr.

Dirksen, H. A. & Linden, H. R. Pipeline Gas from Coal by Methanation of Synthesis Gas. (Research Bulletin Ser.: No. 31). vi, 137p. 1963. pap. 25.00 (*1-58222-038-7*) Inst Gas Tech.

Dirksen, H. A., et al. Autohydrogenation of Oil Gases. (Research Bulletin Ser.: No. 25). iv, 75p. 1955. pap. 25.00 (*1-58222-008-5*) Inst Gas Tech.

— Cracking Catalyst Activity in the Presence of Hydrogen Sulfide. (Research Bulletin Ser.: No. 4). iv, 27p. 1953. pap. 25.00 (*1-58222-014-X*) Inst Gas Tech.

Dirksen, P. B. An Annotated Bibliography of the Peshitta of the Old Testament. LC 88-31530. (Monographs of the Peshitta Institute Leiden: Vol. V). xiv, 119p. 1989. 51.00 (*90-04-09017-7*) Brill Academic Pubs.

Dirksen, P. B. & Mulder, M. J., eds. The Peshitta: Its Early Text & History: Papers Read at the Peshitta Symposium Held at Leiden 30-31 August 1988. (Monographs of the Peshitta Institute Leiden: Vol. IV). (Illus.). x, 310p. 1988. 82.00 (*90-04-08769-9*) Brill Academic Pubs.

Dirksen, P. B. & Van der Kooij, A., eds. Abraham Kuenen (1828-1891) His Major Contributions to the Study of the Old Testament. LC 92-40325. 1993. 67.00 (*90-04-09732-5*) Brill Academic Pubs.

Dirksen, P. B. & Van Der Kooij, A., eds. The Peshitta As a Translation: Proceedings; Peshitta Symposium (2nd: 1993: Leiden, Netherlands) LC 95-18530. (Monographs of the Peshitta Institute Leiden: Vol. 8). vii, 240p. 1995. 94.00 (*90-04-10351-1*) Brill Academic Pubs.

Dirksen, Shannon R., et al. Clinical Companion to Medical-Surgical Nursing. (Illus.). 768p. (C). (gr. 13). 1996. text 19.95 (*0-8151-5420-8*, 28204) Mosby Inc.

***Dirksen, Shannon R., et al.** Clinical Companion to Medical-Surgical Nursing. 2nd ed. LC 99-29383. (Illus.). 768p. (C). 1999. text. write for info. (*0-323-00404-0*) Mosby Inc.

Dirkx, J., jt. ed. see Singleton, W.

Dirkx, John M. & Prenger, Suzanne. A Guide for Planning & Implementing Instruction for Adults: A Theme-Based Approach. LC 96-51281. 1997. pap. 29.95 (*0-7879-0837-1*) Jossey-Bass.

Dirlam, Joel B. & Kahn, Alfred E. Fair Competition: The Law & Economics of Antitrust Policy. LC 73-100157. 307p. 1970. reprint ed. lib. bdg. 65.00 (*0-8371-2971-0*, DIFC, Greenwood Pr) Greenwood.

Dirlik, Arif. Anarchism in the Chinese Revolution. LC 90-21407. 336p. 1991. 50.00 (*0-520-07297-9*, Pub. by U CA Pr); pap. 17.95 (*0-520-08264-8*, Pub. by U CA Pr) Cal Prin Full Svc.

***Dirlik, Arif.** Chinese on the American Frontier. LC 00-34199. (Pacific Formation Ser.). (Illus.). 2000. write for info. (*0-8476-8532-2*) Rowman.

Dirlik, Arif. The Origins of Chinese Communism. (Illus.). 315p. (C). 1989. pap. text 23.95 (*0-19-505454-7*) OUP.

***Dirlik, Arif.** Postmodernism & China. LC 99-42240. (A Boundary Book Ser.). 464p. 2000. 69.95 (*0-8223-2506-3*) Duke.

— Postmodernism & China. LC 99-42240. (Boundary Book Ser.). (Illus.). 464p. 2000. pap. 23.95 (*0-8223-2544-6*) Duke.

— Postmodernity's Histories: The Past As Legacy & Project. 288p. 2000. 67.00 (*0-7425-0166-3*); pap. 23.95 (*0-7425-0167-1*) Rowman.

Dirlik, Arif. Revolution & History: Origins of Marxist Historiography in China, 1919-1937. LC 77-80469. 1978. pap. 16.95 (*0-520-06757-6*, Pub. by U CA Pr) Cal Prin Full Svc.

Dirlik, Arif, ed. What Is in a Rim? Critical Perspectives on the Pacific Region Idea. 2nd ed. LC 97-28861. (Dirlik - Pacific Formations Ser.). (Illus.). 392p. 1997. 70.00 (*0-8476-8468-7*); pap. 24.95 (*0-8476-8469-5*) Rowman.

Dirlik, Arif & Healy, Paul F. Critical Perspectives on Mao Zedong's Thought. LC 96-12006. 488p. (C). 1997. pap. 19.95 (*0-391-03994-6*); text 60.00 (*0-391-03993-8*) Humanities.

Dirlik, Arif & Meisner, Maurice, eds. Marxism & the Chinese Experience: Issues in Contemporary Chinese Socialism. LC 89-4251. (Socialism & Social Movements Ser.). 396p. (gr. 13). 1989. pap. text 42.95 (*0-87332-546-X*, East Gate Bk) M E Sharpe.

— Marxism & the Chinese Experience: Issues in Contemporary Chinese Socialism. LC 89-4251. (Socialism & Social Movements). 396p. (C). (gr. 13). 1989. text 87.95 (*0-87332-515-X*) M E Sharpe.

Dirlik, Arif & Wilson, Rob, eds. Asia - Pacific as Space of Cultural Production. 236p. 1994. pap. 12.00 (*0-8223-6416-6*) Duke.

Dirlik, Arif & Zhang, Xudong, eds. Chinese Postmodernism: Boundary 2 Special Issue, Vol. 24. 260p. 1997. pap. text 12.00 (*0-8223-6448-4*) Duke.

***Dirlik, Arif, et al.** History after the Three Worlds: Post-Eurocentric Historiographies. LC 00-33270. 2000. write for info. (*0-8476-9342-2*) Rowman.

Dirlik, Arif, jt. auth. see Chan, Ming K.

Dirlik, Arif, jt. ed. see Wilson, Rob.

Dirnagl, U., et al. Optical Imaging of Brain Function & Metabolism. LC 93-24703. (Advances in Experimental Medicine & Biology Ser.: Vol. 333). (Illus.). 308p. (C). 1993. text 95.00 (*0-306-44528-X*, Kluwer Plenum) Kluwer Academic.

Dirnagl, Ulrich, jt. ed. see Villringer, A.

Dirom, Major. A Narrative of the Campaign in India Which Terminated the War with Tippo Sultan in 1792. 1986. reprint ed. 32.00 (*0-8364-1846-8*, Pub. by Usha) S Asia.

***DiRoNa Award Program Staff.** The 2001 Guide to Distinguished Restaurants of North America: 400 Award-Winning Restaurants Independently & Anonymously. (Illus.). 464p. 2000. pap. 24.95 (*0-86730-808-7*) Lebhar Friedman.

Dirona Staff. Guide to Distinguished Restaurants of North America: 1998 Edition. 1998. pap. text 12.95 (*0-9662650-0-9*) Kostuch Pubns.

DiRosa, Veronica. Napa Town & Country Fair Red Hot Chili Cook Off. (Illus.). (Orig.). 1981. pap. 4.95 (*0-935360-04-2*) Napa Cnty Landmarks.

Dirr, Michael A. Dirr's Hardy Trees & Shrubs: An Illustrated Encyclopedia. LC 96-54032. (Illus.). 493p. 1997. 69.95 (*0-88192-404-0*) Timber.

— Manual of Woody Landscape Plants. 3rd ed. (Illus.). 1983. pap. text 26.80 (*0-87563-226-2*) Stipes.

***Dirr, Michael A.** Manual of Woody Landscape Plants: Their Identification, Ornamental Characteristics, Culture, Propagation & Uses. 5th ed. LC 98-61065. (Illus.). 1250p. 1998. 59.80 (*0-87563-800-7*); pap. text 50.80 (*0-87563-795-7*) Stipes.

Dirr, Michael A. Photographic Manual for Woody Landscape Plants. (Illus.). 1978. text 29.80 (*0-87563-156-8*); pap. text 19.80 (*0-87563-153-3*) Stipes.

Dirr, Michael A. & Heuser, Charles W. The Reference Manual of Woody Plant Propagation: From Seed to Tissue Culture. (Illus.). 240p. 1987. pap. 35.00 (*0-942375-00-9*) Varsity Pr.

Dirr, William P. The Most Asked Questions about Architecture & Building, Vol. 1. 258p. 1994. pap. 34.95 (*0-9638666-0-5*) Archi-Tech Pr.

***Dirro, Stephen.** Easy Classic Tunes for Alto Sax. 39p. 1999. pap. text 12.95 (*0-8256-1776-6*, AM961895) Music Sales.

Dirsch. Genus Schistocerca. (Sent Ser.). 1974. text 148.50 (*90-6193-120-7*) Kluwer Academic.

Dirsch, Sandra. Great Lengths, Vol. 26. 93p. (J). (gr. 3-8). 1999. text 5.50 (*1-55028-622-6*, Pub. by J Lorimer) Orca Bk Pubs.

Dirschedl, P. & Ostermann, R., eds. Computational Statistics: Papers Collected on the Occasion of the 25th Conference on Statistical Computing at Schlob Reisensburg. (Contributions to Statistics Ser.). (Illus.). viii, 553p. 1995. 129.00 (*3-7908-0813-X*) Spr-Verlag.

Dirschi, Douglas R. & LeCroy, C. Michael. On Call Orthopedics. Schmitt, Bill, ed. LC 98-3606. (On Call Ser.). (Illus.). 384p. (C). 1998. pap. text 21.95 (*0-7216-7990-0*, W B Saunders Co) Harcrt Hlth Sci Grp.

Dirt Merchants Staff & White Wolf Publishing Staff, Wolf. Buttery Wholesomeness. (TLOL Ser.). (Illus.). 1995. pap. 9.95 (*1-56504-585-8*, 5901) White Wolf.

***DiRuscio, Sarah.** Enhancing Science Curriculum with the Net: Grades 7-12. 140p. 1999. 19.95 (*1-893243-05-2*) Forefront.

***DiRuscio, Sarah A.** Enhancing Classroom Curriculum with the Net: Grades 7-12. 120p. 1999. 19.95 (*1-893243-02-8*) Forefront.

DiRuscio, Sarah A. Internet ABC's for Elementary Students: Grades K-6. 2nd ed. (Illus.). 72p. 1998. wbk. ed. 11.95 (*1-893243-00-1*) Forefront.

— Internet Skills for School Success: Grades 7-12. 2nd ed. (Illus.). 72p. 1998. wbk. ed. 11.95 (*1-893243-01-X*) Forefront.

***Dirven, Lucinda.** The Palmyrenes of Dura-Europos: A Study of Religious Interaction in Roman Syria. LC 99-44510. (Religions in the Graeco-Roman World Ser.). 1999. write for info. (*90-04-11589-7*) Brill Academic Pubs.

Dirven, Rene & Fried, V., eds. Functionalism in Linguistics. LC 87-8086. (Linguistic & Literary Studies in Eastern Europe: No. 20). xx, 489p. (C). 1987. 130.00 (*90-272-1524-3*) J Benjamins Pubng Co.

Dirven, Rene & Geiger, Richard. A User's Grammar of English Pt. B: Word, Sentence, Text, Interaction: The Structure of Sentences. (Duisburg Papers for Research in Language & Culture: Vol. 2). VII, 358p. 1989. pap. 24.00 (*3-631-40665-7*) P Lang Pubng.

Dirven, Rene & Putseys, Yvan. A User's Grammar of English Pt. A: Word, Sentence, Text, Interaction: The Structure of Words & Phrases. (Duisburg Papers for Research in Language & Culture: Vol. 1). VII, 245p. 1989. pap. 21.00 (*3-631-40664-9*) P Lang Pubng.

Dirven, Rene & Verspoor, Marjolijn, eds. Cognitive Exploration of Language & Linguistics. LC 98-44716. (Congnitive Linguistics in Practice Ser.: Vol. 1). xiv, 300p. 1999. 60.00 (*1-55619-197-9*) J Benjamins Pubng.

***Dirven, Rene & Verspoor, Marjolijn, eds.** Cognitive Exploration of Language & Linguistics. LC 98-44716. (Congnitive Linguistics in Practice Ser.: Vol. 1). xiv, 300p. 1999. pap. 24.95 (*1-55619-198-7*) J Benjamins Pubng.

Dirven, Rene, et al. The Scene of Linguistic Action & Its Perspectivization by Speak, Talk, Say, & Tell. (Pragmatics & Beyond Ser.: Vol. III:6). vi, 186p. 1983. pap. 53.00 (*90-272-2528-1*) J Benjamins Pubng Co.

Dirven, Rene, jt. ed. see Athanasiadou, Angeliki.

Dirven, Rene, jt. ed. see Niemeier, Susanne.

Dirven, Rene, jt. ed. see Puetz, Martin.

Dirvin, Joseph I. Mrs. Seton. 532p. 1993. pap. 10.00 (*0-9639851-0-8*) Nat Shrine St Eliz.

— St. Catherine Laboure of the Miraculous Medal. LC 84-50466. 245p. 1984. reprint ed. pap. 13.50 (*0-89555-242-6*) TAN Bks Pubs.

— The Soul of Elizabeth Seton: A Spiritual Portrait. LC 89-83260. (Illus.). 232p. (Orig.). 1990. pap. 11.95 (*0-89870-269-0*) Ignatius Pr.

DiRyals, Clyde. The Life of Robert Browning: A Critical Biography. (Critical Biographies Ser.). (Illus.). 304p. 1996. pap. 25.95 (*0-631-20093-2*) Blackwell Pubs.

Dirzhud-Rashid, Rajkhet. The Dream Book. (Illus.). 48p. Date not set. pap. write for info. (*1-878888-28-5*) Nine Muses Books.

Dis, Adriaan Van, see Van Dis, Adriaan.

Dis, Huib Van, see Van Dis, Huib, ed.

Disa, Dracula, et al. CITES Orchid Checklist for the Genera Cymbidium, Dendrobium (Selected Sections Only), Vol. 2. 300p. 1997. pap. 18.00 (*1-900347-34-2*, Pub. by Royal Botnic Grdns) Balogh.

DiSabato-Aust, Tracy. The Well-Tended Perennial Garden: Planting & Pruning Techniques. LC 97-29768. (Illus.). 338p. 1998. 29.95 (*0-88192-414-8*) Timber.

DiSabato, Giovanni, ed. Immunochemical Techniques Pt. M: Chemotoxins & Inflammation. (Methods in Enzymology Ser.: Vol. 163). 790p. 1988. text 146.00 (*0-12-182064-5*) Acad Pr.

— Immunochemical Techniques Vol. 150, Pt. K: In Vitro Models of B & T Cell Function & Lymphoid Cell Receptors. (Methods in Enzymology Ser.). 823p. 1987. text 149.00 (*0-12-182051-3*) Acad Pr.

DiSabato Traylor, Nadean, jt. auth. see Traylor, Jeff.

Disabilities in Ministry Committee. Ephphatha! Open Up! A Children's Curriculum for Understanding Disabilities. 80p. 1999. pap. 12.95 (*0-7880-1350-5*) CSS OH.

Disability Rag Staff & Johnson, Mary, eds. People with Disabilities Explain It All for You: Your Guide to the Public Accommodations Requirements of the Americans with Disabilities Act. 160p. (Orig.). 1992. pap. 15.95 (*0-9627064-2-6*) Advocado Pr.

Disaia, Philip J. Clinical Gynecologic Oncology. 5th ed. LC 97-11272. (Illus.). 720p. (C). (gr. 13). 1997. text 119.00 (*0-8151-2506-2*, 28279) Mosby Inc.

Disaia, Philip J., et al. Clinical Gynecologic Oncology, No. 5. (Illus.). 750p. (C). (gr. 13). 1997. text 139.95 (*0-8151-2387-6*, 31039) Mosby Inc.

Disaia, Philip J., jt. auth. see Brown, Stephen G.

Disalle, Michael V. The Power of Life or Death. LC 82-45662. (Capital Punishment Ser.). reprint ed. 28.50 (*0-404-62411-1*) AMS Pr.

DiSalvo, A. F., jt. auth. see Al-Doory, Y.

D

An Asterisk (*) at the beginning of an entry indicates that the title is appearing for the first time.

DiSalvo, Arthur F., ed. Occupational Mycoses. LC 83-765. 261p. reprint ed. pap. 81.00 (*0-7837-2700-3*, 204307900006) Bks Demand.

DiSalvo, Chris & Semas, Judith H. San Jose & Silicon Valley: Primed for the 21st Century. LC 97-16064. 336p. 1997. 45.00 (*1-885352-56-5*) Community Comm.

Disalvo, E. A. & Simon, Sidney A., eds. Permeability & Stability of Lipid Bilayers. LC 94-15447. 288p. 1995. boxed set 254.95 (*0-8493-4531-6*) CRC Pr.

DiSalvo, J., jt. ed. see Merlevede, E.

DiSalvo, J., jt. ed. see Merlevede, W.

DiSalvo, Jack & DiGeronimo, Theresa F. College Admissions for the High School Athlete. LC 93-16811. 176p. 1993. 21.95 (*0-8160-2760-9*) Facts on File.

DiSalvo, Jackie. War of Titans: Blake's Critique of Milton & the Politics of Religion. LC 82-11136. 403p. 1983. reprint ed. pap. 125.00 (*0-608-00903-2*, 206169700010) Bks Demand.

DiSalvo, Jacqueline, et al. Blake, Politics, & History. Cain, William, ed. LC 98-15870. (Wellesley Studies in Critical Theory: Vol. 17). (Illus.). 472p. 1998. 75.00 (*0-8153-1679-8*) Garland.

DiSalvo-Ryan, DyAnne. City Green. LC 93-27117. (Illus.). 32p. (J). (ps-3). 1994. 16.00 (*0-688-12786-X*, Wm Morrow) Morrow Avon.

***DiSalvo-Ryan, DyAnne.** A Dog Like Jack. LC 97-41949. (Illus.). 32p. (J). (ps-3). 1999. 15.95 (*0-8234-1369-1*) Holiday.

Disalvo-Ryan, Dyanne. Grandpa's Corner Store. LC 99-15504. (Illus.). 40p. (YA). (gr. k-3). 2000. 15.95 (*0-688-16716-0*, Wm Morrow); lib. bdg. 15.89 (*0-688-16717-9*, Wm Morrow) Morrow Avon.

DiSalvo-Ryan, DyAnne. A House on Viola Street. write for info. (*0-688-17690-9*, Wm Morrow); lib. bdg. write for info. (*0-688-17691-7*, Wm Morrow) Morrow Avon.

Disalvo-Ryan, Dyanne. Uncle Wille & the Soup Kitchen. LC 90-6375. (Illus.). 32p. (J). (gr. k up). 1997. mass mkt. 4.95 (*0-688-15285-6*, Wm Morrow) Morrow Avon.

DiSalvo-Ryan, DyAnne. Uncle Willie & the Soup Kitchen. (J). 1997. 10.15 (*0-606-12026-2*, Pub. by Turtleback) Demco.

DiSalvo-Ryan, DyAnne. Good Dog, Bonita. (Friends & Amigos Ser.). (J). (gr. 1-4). 1996. pap. 3.99 (*0-614-15576-2*, YB BDD) BDD Bks Young Read.

DiSalvo-Ryan, DyAnne, jt. auth. see Elste, Joan.

DiSalvo-Ryan, DyAnne, jt. auth. see Rosen, Michael J.

DiSalvo, Steven. The Loyola Freshman Experience. 2nd ed. 104p. (C). 1997. per. 32.95 (*0-7872-4163-6*, 41416301) Kendall-Hunt.

DiSanto, Joseph E., jt. auth. see Frideres, James S.

D'Isanto, Luca, tr. see Vattimo, Gianni.

DiSanto, Mark. My Parents Are Divorced. (J). (gr. 3-6). 1997. 8.95 (*0-533-12371-2*) Vantage.

DiSanza, James R. & Legge, Nancy J. Business & Professional Speaking: Plans, Processes, & Performance. LC 99-26282. 342p. (C). 1999. pap. text 42.67 (*0-205-29585-1*, Longwood Div) Allyn.

Disbrey, Claire. Innovation & Tradition in Religion: Toward a Philosophical Theory. (Avebury Series in Philosophy). 247p. 1994. 79.95 (*1-85628-852-8*, Pub. by Avebry) Ashgate Pub Co.

Disbro, William. 100 Things Every College Freshman Ought to Know. (Illus.). 226p. 1995. pap. text 9.95 (*0-935637-22-2*) Cambridge Strat.

Disbrow, Sarah, ed. see Holmes, Roger & Buchanan, Rita.

***Disch, Estelle.** Reconstructing Gender: A Multicultural Anthology. 2nd ed. LC 99-19056. xxvii, 591p. 1999. pap. text 37.00 (*0-7674-1002-5*) Mayfield Pub.

Disch, Estelle, ed. Reconstructing Gender: A Multicultural Anthology. LC 96-17516. 593p. (C). 1996. pap. text 37.95 (*1-55934-579-9*, 1579) Mayfield Pub.

Disch, Lisa J. Hannah Arendt & the Limits of Philosophy. LC 96-16196. 248p. 1995. text 37.50 (*0-8014-3013-5*) Cornell U Pr.

— Hannah Arendt & the Limits of Philosophy. LC 96-16196. 248p. 1996. pap. text 14.95 (*0-8014-8378-6*) Cornell U Pr.

Disch, Robert, ed. Ecological Conscience: Values for Survival. LC 71-130009. 1970. pap. 2.45 (*0-13-222810-6*, Spectrum IN) Macmillan Gen Ref.

Disch, Robert, intro. Twenty-Five Years of the Life Review: Theoretical & Practical Considerations. LC 88-14203. (Journal of Gerontological Social Work: Vol. 12, Nos. 3-4). (Illus.). 148p. 1989. text 39.95 (*0-86656-836-0*) Haworth Pr.

Disch, Robert, jt. ed. see Brabazon, Kevin.

Disch, Thomas M. Burn This: And Other Essays on Criticism. 126p. 1995. pap. 14.00 (*1-887478-05-1*, WiseAcre) Red Sea NY.

— Camp Concentration. LC 99-17866. 224p. 1999. pap. 12.00 (*0-375-70545-7*) Vin Bks.

— The Castle of Indolence. 240p. 1996. pap. 12.00 (*0-312-14559-4*) St Martin.

— A Child's Garden of Grammar. LC 97-23552. (Illus.). 94p. (J). 1997. pap. 9.95 (*0-87451-850-4*) U Pr of New Eng.

— Dark Verses & Light. LC 90-21344. (Poetry & Fiction Ser.). 120p. 1991. pap. 12.95 (*0-8018-4192-5*); text 26.00 (*0-8018-4191-7*) Johns Hopkins.

— The Dreams Our Stuff Is Made Of: How Science Fiction Conquered the World. LC 97-52068. 256p. 1998. 25.00 (*0-684-82405-1*) Free Pr.

***Disch, Thomas M.** The Dreams Our Stuff Is Made Of: How Science Fiction Conquered the World. 272p. 2000. pap. 13.00 (*0-684-85978-5*, Touchstone) S&S Trade Pap.

— The Genocides. 2000. pap. write for info. (*0-375-70546-5*) Vin Bks.

Disch, Thomas M. Haikus of a Pillow. deluxe ed. 1980. pap. 10.00 (*0-317-39744-3*) Bellevue Pr.

— Haikus of an AmPart. (Morning Coffee Chapbook Ser.). (Illus.). 14p. (Orig.). 1991. pap. 20.00 (*0-918273-68-4*) Coffee Hse.

— On Wings of Song. 359p. 1988. mass mkt. 3.95 (*0-88184-443-8*) Carroll & Graf.

— Orders of the Retina. LC 82-4728. 45p. (Orig.). 1982. pap. 30.00 (*0-915124-61-0*) Coffee Hse.

— The Priest: A Gothic Romance. 1995. 24.00 (*0-679-42880-1*) Knopf.

— The Silver Pillow: A Tale of Witchcraft. 1988. pap. 10.00 (*0-9612970-7-7*) Mark Ziesing.

— The Sub: A Study in Witchcraft. LC 98-50675. 384p. 1999. 24.00 (*0-679-44292-8*) Knopf.

— Yes, Let's: New & Selected Poems. LC 88-46116. (Johns Hopkins, Poetry & Fiction Ser.). 129p. 1989. reprint ed. pap. 40.00 (*0-608-03726-5*, 206455100009) Bks Demand.

Disch, Thomas M. & Naylor, Charles. Neighboring Lives. LC 80-19021. 351p. 1981. 25.00 (*0-684-16644-5*) Ultramarine Pub.

— Neighboring Lives. LC 90-25522. 368p. 1991. reprint ed. pap. 13.95 (*0-8018-4219-0*) Johns Hopkins.

Disch, Thomas M. & Sladek, John T. Black Alice. 186p. 1989. pap. 3.95 (*0-88184-506-X*) Carroll & Graf.

Disch, Thomas M., et al. Burning with a Vision: Poetry of Science & the Fantastic. Frazier, Robert, ed. & illus. by. Gaughan, Jack, illus. xvii, 139p. 1984. 14.75 (*0-913896-22-5*); pap. 8.75 (*0-913896-23-3*) Owlswick Pr.

Disch, Thomas M., ed. see Lupoff, Richard.

Dische. Doctor Needs a Home. Date not set. text. write for info. (*0-8050-4170-2*) St Martin.

Dische, Frederick, ed. Renal Pathology. 2nd ed. (Illus.). 230p. 1995. text 125.00 (*0-19-263032-6*) OUP.

Dische, Irene. Pious Secrets. 1999. pap. 8.95 (*0-14-013943-5*) Viking Penguin.

Discher, Clarence A. Modern Inorganic Pharmaceutical Chemistry. LC 64-14986. 648p. reprint ed. pap. 200.00 (*0-608-30493-X*, 200634700058) Bks Demand.

Discher, Clarence A., et al. Modern Inorganic Pharmaceutical Chemistry. 2nd ed. (Illus.). 631p. (C). 1985. text 43.95 (*0-88133-121-X*) Waveland Pr.

Dischinger, Mark, et al. Now. Sprvill, Shawn, ed. (Illus.). 128p. 1998. pap. 9.00 (*0-9652528-5-X*, 002) Neshui Pubng.

Dischler, Bernard & Wild, C. Low-Pressure Synthetic Diamond: Manufacturing & Applications. LC 98-2582. 193p. 1997. 109.00 (*3-540-63619-6*) Spr-Verlag.

DiScipio, Giuseppe C. The Presence of Pauline Thought in the Works of Dante. LC 94-40269. 366p. 1995. text 99.95 (*0-7734-9000-0*) E Mellen.

DiScipio, Giuseppe C. & Scaglione, Aldo, eds. The Divine Comedy & the Encyclopedia of Arts & Sciences: Acta of the International Dante Symposium, 13-16 Nov. 1983, Hunter College, New York. LC 88-14510. ix, 385p. (C). 1988. 106.00 (*1-55619-031-X*); pap. 27.95 (*1-55619-062-X*) J Benjamins Pubng Co.

DiScipio, Giuseppe C., ed. see Dante Alighieri.

Disciples of Donato the Christ. Healing: A Thought Away, Vol. 2. 438p. 1981. pap. 10.00 (*0-935146-61-X*) Morningland.

Disciples of Morningland. The Way to Oneness. 4th ed. 1979. pap. 3.95 (*0-935146-00-8*) Morningland.

Disciples of the Master Donato the Christ. Healing: As It Is, Vol. 4. 418p. (Orig.). pap. 10.00 (*0-935146-65-2*) Morningland.

***Discipleship Journal Staff, ed.** Nurturing a Passion for Prayer: A Discipleship Journal Bible Study. 96p. 2000. pap. text 6.00 (*1-57683-165-5*) NavPress.

— Redeeming Failure: A Discipleship Journal Bible Study. 2000. pap. text 6.00 (*1-57683-164-7*) NavPress.

DiSciullo, Alan M., jt. auth. see Wood, John B.

Disco, Cornelis & Van der Meulen, Barend, eds. Getting New Technologies Together: Studies in Making Sociotechnical Order. LC 98-28235. (Studies in Organization: No. 82). 376p. 1998. 111.00 (*3-11-015630-X*) De Gruyter.

Discover Staff. A Reader's Guide for Geology. (C). 1994. pap. text, lab manual ed. 8.50 (*0-03-010246-4*) Harcourt Coll Pubs.

— A Reader's Guide to Astronomy. (C). 1994. pap. text 14.50 (*0-03-008928-X*, Pub. by Harcourt Coll Pubs) Harcourt.

Discoveries Library Staff, jt. auth. see Craig, Claire.

Discoveries Library Staff, jt. auth. see Creagh, Carson.

Discoveries Library Staff, jt. auth. see Lynch, Anne.

Discoveries Library Staff, jt. auth. see Time-Life Books Editors.

Discovery Books Staff. Insects & Spiders. LC 99-87177. 2000. pap. 14.95 (*1-56331-841-5*, Pub. by Discovery) Random.

***Discovery Books Staff.** Reptiles & Amphibians. LC 99-59155. 2000. pap. 14.95 (*1-56331-839-3*, Pub. by Discovery) Random.

***Discovery Books Staff & Meyers, Philip.** Mammals: An Explore Your World Handbook. LC 00-27287. (Illus.). 192p. (J). 2000. pap. 14.95 (*1-56331-838-5*, Pub. by Discovery) Random.

Discovery Channel Staff. The Leopard Son. (Illus.). 29p. (J). (ps-3). 1996. 14.95 (*0-07-016061-9*) McGraw.

Discovery Communications Inc. Staff, jt. auth. see Watrous, Susan.

***Discovery Communications Staff.** Napoleon's Lost Fleet. 1999. write for info. (*0-8129-3281-1*, Times Bks) Crown Pub Group.

— Who's for Dinner? Predators & Prey. (Animal Planet Ser.). (J). 1998. 15.19 (*0-606-13914-1*, Pub. by Turtleback) Demco.

Discovery Communications Staff & Mitchell, Carolyn B. Cats: From Tigers to Tabbys. LC 97-43379. (Animal Planet Ser.). (Illus.). 64p. (J). 1998. lib. bdg. 13.99 (*0-517-80003-9*) C Potter.

— Predators & Who's for Dinner? LC 97-42899. (Animal Planet Ser.). (J). 1998. lib. bdg. 13.99 (*0-517-80005-5*) C Potter.

Discovery House Staff. Our Daily Times with God. 432p. 1988. pap. 12.99 (*0-929239-01-6*) Discovery Hse Pubs.

— Our Daily Times with God. large type ed. LC 96-17993. 432p. 1988. pap. 14.99 (*0-929239-03-2*) Discovery Hse Pubs.

***Discovery Kids.** Dangerous Dinosaurs. (Illus.). (J). 2000. 8.84 (*0-606-18465-1*) Turtleback.

— Terror under the Sea. (Illus.). (J). 2000. 8.84 (*0-606-18466-X*) Turtleback.

***Discovery Writers Staff.** Lewis & Clark on the Upper Missouri. LC 99-75624. (Illus.). 215p. 1999. 19.95 (*0-912299-85-1*); pap. 14.95 (*0-912299-84-3*) Stoneydale Pr Pub.

Disdier-Diaz, Orlando A. From P. R. to the U. S. A. & Then Africa & Europe. LC 97-90599. 68p. 1998. pap. 8.95 (*0-533-12434-4*) Vantage.

Dise, Craig. Physiology: Pretest Self-Assessment & Review. 5th ed. 1988. pap. text 15.95 (*0-07-051967-6*) McGraw.

Dise, Craig A. Physiology: Pretest Self-Assessment & Review. 4th ed. LC 85-12839. vii, 201p. 1985. write for info. (*0-07-051946-3*) McGraw-Hill HPD.

Dise, John H., Jr., et al. Searches of Students, Lockers & Automobiles. LC 96-86552. 110p. (Orig.). 1996. pap. 29.95 (*0-9630262-2-4*) Educ Risk.

Dise, John H., jt. auth. see Cody, Frank.

Dise, Robert L. Cultural Change & Imperial Administration: The Middle Danube Provinces of the Roman Empire. LC 90-24422. (American University Studies: History: Ser. IX, Vols. 99). (Illus.). XV, 205p. (C). 1991. text 37.95 (*0-8204-1465-4*) P Lang Pubng.

***Disegi, John A., et al, eds.** Cobalt-Base Alloys for Biomedical Applications. LC 99-40202. (Special Technical Publications: No. 1365). (Illus.). 230p. 1999. pap. text 80.00 (*0-8031-2608-5*) ASTM.

DiSessa. Toward Epist. (CI Ser.: Vol. 20, Nos. 2-3). 1993. 40.00 (*0-8058-9988-X*) L Erlbaum Assocs.

***DiSessa, Andrea.** Changing Minds: Computers, Learning & Literacy. LC 99-40215. (Illus.). 320p. 2000. 29.95 (*0-262-04180-4*, Bradford Bks) MIT Pr.

DiSessa, Andrea, jt. auth. see Abelson, Harold.

Disher, Garry. The Bamboo Flute. LC 92-39787. 96p. (J). (gr. 3-6). 1993. 14.00 (*0-395-66595-7*) Ticknor & Flds Bks Yng Read.

— The Fallout: A Wyatt Novel. 209p. (Orig.). 1997. pap. 5.95 (*1-86448-330-X*, Pub. by Allen & Unwin Pty) IPG Chicago.

— Paydirt. 176p. (Orig.). 1994. mass mkt. 5.95 (*1-86373-581-X*, Pub. by Allen & Unwin Pty) IPG Chicago.

— Port Vila Blues: A Wyatt Novel. 232p. (Orig.). 1996. pap. 6.95 (*1-86448-025-4*, Pub. by Allen & Unwin Pty) IPG Chicago.

— Ratface. LC 93-48131. 185p. (J). (gr. 5 up). 1994. 14.95 (*0-395-69451-5*) Ticknor & Flds Bks Yng Read.

— The Sunken Road. 214p. 1997. pap. 16.95 (*1-85702-485-0*, Pub. by Fourth Estate) Trafalgar.

***Disher, Garry.** The Sunken Road. 1999. pap. 13.00 (*1-85702-664-0*, Pub. by Fourth Estate) Trafalgar.

Disher, Garry. Switch Cat. large type ed. LC 94-21002. (Illus.). 32p. (J). (ps-2). 1995. 14.95 (*0-395-71643-8*, Pub. by Ticknor & Fields) HM.

Disher, M. W. Blood & Thunder. LC 73-21683. (English Literature Ser.: No. 33). 1974. lib. bdg. 75.00 (*0-8383-1761-8*) M S G Haskell Hse.

Disher, Maurice W. Clowns & Pantomimes. LC 68-21211. (Illus.). 362p. 1979. reprint ed. 40.95 (*0-405-08446-3*, Pub. by Blom Pubns) Ayer.

— Greatest Show on Earth. (Illus.). 316p. 1972. 20.95 (*0-405-18148-5*) Ayer.

Disher, Sharon H. First Class: Women Join the Ranks at the Naval Academy. LC 97-51652. (Illus.). 264p. 1998. 29.95 (*1-55750-165-3*) Naval Inst Pr.

Dishinger, Walter P. Language & Its Forms at Work & Play in the U. S. A. - Index of New Information Including Cultures, Science & Psychiatry. 160p. 1995. 47.50 (*0-7883-0492-5*); pap. 44.50 (*0-7883-0493-3*) ABBE Pubs Assn.

Dishion, Thomas J. & Patterson, Scot. Preventive Parenting with Love, Encouragement, & Limits: The Preschool Years. (Illus.). xiv, 130p. (Orig.). 1995. pap. 10.95 (*0-916154-13-0*) Castalia Pub.

Dishman, Madge. Wild Flowers & Untamed Women: 7 Plays about Women. 1999. pap. 4.50 (*1-57514-347-X*, 1183) Encore Perform Pub.

Dishman, Roberta C. Bulletin Board Brighteners. 56p. 1987. ring bd. 12.95 (*0-89265-121-0*) Randall Hse.

Dishman, Rod K., ed. Advances in Exercise Adherence. LC 93-47608. (Illus.). 416p. 1994. text 32.00 (*0-87322-664-X*, BDIS0664) Human Kinetics.

— Exercise Adherence: Its Impact on Public Health. LC 86-33731. (Illus.). 464p. 1987. text 42.00 (*0-87322-102-8*, BDIS0102) Human Kinetics.

Dishman, Ronald. Overton, TN. (Illus.). 575p. 1992. text 70.00 (*0-88107-210-9*) Curtis Media.

***Dishmon, James L., Jr.** Farm Service Agency: Characteristics of Small County Offices. 96p. (C). 2000. pap. text 20.00 (*0-7881-8811-9*) DIANE Pub.

Dishner, Ernest K. Reading in the Content Areas: Improving Classroom Instruction. 3rd ed. 480p. 1991. per. 42.95 (*0-8403-6408-3*) Kendall-Hunt.

Dishner, Kathee L. Ask Him into Your Heart. 76p. 1998. pap. 12.95 (*0-9667443-0-6*) K Dishner.

Dishon, Daniel, ed. Middle East Record, Vols. 1-4. Incl. Vol. 2. 826p. 1961. (*0-87855-165-4*); Vol. 4. 920p. 1968. (*0-87855-167-0*); 69.95 (*0-685-04921-3*) Transaction Pubs.

Dishon, David, jt. auth. see Zion, Noam.

Dishon, Dee & O'Leary, Pat W. Guidebook for Cooperative Learning. 3rd ed. 1994. pap. 24.95 (*1-55691-141-6*, 416) Learning Pubns.

Dishon, Dee, jt. auth. see Moorman, Chick.

***Dishongh, Burl E.** Essential Structural Technology for Construction & Architecture. 240p. 2000. 78.67 (*0-13-012858-9*, Prentice Hall) P-H.

Disi, Ahmad M., jt. auth. see Kahlaf, Maroof A.

DiSiano, Frank P. Presenting the Catholic Faith: A Modern Catechism for Inquirers. 144p. (Orig.). 1987. pap. 7.95 (*0-8091-2841-1*) Paulist Pr.

***Disilvester, Rob.** Hollywood Meals: Reel Menus from Classic Hollywood Films. (Illus.). 128p. 2000. 19.50 (*1-57223-311-7*) Willow Creek Pr.

DiSilvestro, Frank R. Sing along with Me. (Illus.). 52p. (YA). (gr. 8-10). 1985. pap. 7.95 (*0-934591-00-8*) Songs & Stories.

DiSilvestro, J. & Riley, Judy. Untrapping Your Inventiveness. 1992. pap. 19.95 (*0-936386-61-4*) Creative Learning.

DiSilvestro, Roger L. The African Elephant: Twilight in Eden. LC 90-24967. (Illus.). 224p. 1991. 34.95 (*0-471-53207-X*) Wiley.

— Audubon Perspectives: The Rebirth of Nature. LC 91-36848. (Illus.). 288p. 1992. 34.95 (*0-471-53208-8*) Wiley.

Disilvestro, Roger L. Biodiversity: A New Proposal for Protecting America's Wildlife. LC 92-46457. (Science Editions Ser.). 288p. 1993. 24.95 (*0-471-57244-6*) Wiley.

DiSilvestro, Roger L. The Endangered Kingdom: The Struggle to Save America's Wildlife. 241p. 1991. pap. 10.95 (*0-471-52822-6*) Wiley.

Disimini, Lisa. My House, Vol. 1. (Illus.). 32p. (J). 1997. reprint ed. pap. 5.95 (*0-8050-5516-9*) H Holt & Co.

Disinger, John F. & Monroe, Martha C. Defining Environmental Education. Cappaert, David, ed. (EEToolbox-Workshop Resource Manual Ser.). (Illus.). 40p. 1994. 8.00 (*1-884782-03-5*) Natl Consort EET.

Dision. Eske Nou Konprann: Text Comprehension Exercises in Haitian Creole. 20p. (J). (gr. 3-6). Date not set. wbk. ed. 2.00 (*1-881839-48-6*) Educa Vision.

Disk, Donald M. & Greiner, Mary M. Measuring State & Local Government Labor Productivity: Examples from Eleven Services. (Labor Statistics Bureau Bulletin Ser.: No. 2495). (Illus.). 206p. 1998. pap. 18.00 (*0-16-049663-2*) USGPO.

Diskavich, Laura, jt. auth. see Woods, Samuel G.

Diski, Jenny. Dream Mistress. LC 98-15806. 192p. 1999. reprint ed. 23.95 (*0-88001-611-6*) HarpC.

— Skating To Antarctica. LC 97-31154. 256p. 1998. 23.95 (*0-88001-603-5*) HarpC.

Diskin, Abraham. Elections & Voters in Israel. LC 90-24476. 232p. 1991. 59.95 (*0-275-92972-8*, C2972, Praeger Pubs) Greenwood.

Diskin, David, jt. auth. see Hecht, David.

Diskin, David, jt. auth. see Hecht, David B.

Diskin, Lahna. Theodore Sturgeon. Schlobin, Roger C., ed. LC 80-21423. (Starmont Reader's Guide Ser.: Vol. 7). (Illus.). 72p. 1981. pap. 15.00 (*0-916732-18-5*) Millefleurs.

Diskin, M. G., jt. ed. see Sreenan, J. M.

Diskin, Robert A. Alan's Fall. 213p. 1995. pap. 7.95 (*0-9647582-0-2*) R A Diskin.

***Diskin, Robert A.** A Falling Star. 278p. (Orig.). 2000. pap. 9.00 (*0-9647582-2-9*) R A Diskin.

Diskin, Robert A. Where All Roads End. 72p. (Orig.). 1996. pap. 6.95 (*0-9647582-1-0*) R A Diskin.

Diskin, Steve & Giovannini, Joseph. Los Angeles at 25 MPH. LC 92-19303. 219p. 1993. pap. 39.95 (*0-442-01319-1*, VNR) Wiley.

Diskin, Steve & Giovannini, Joseph. Los Angeles at 25 MPH. 219p. 1993. pap. 39.95 (*0-471-28526-9*, VNR) Wiley.

Diskit, K. R., ed. Contributions to Indian Geography: Geomorphology, Vol. 2. 1983. 37.50 (*0-8364-1038-6*, Pub. by Heritage IA) S Asia.

Disko, Mark Michael, ed. see Minerals, Metals & Materials Society Staff.

Diskul, Subhadrarus M., ed. The Art of Srivijaya. (Illus.). 1980. 55.00 (*0-19-580433-3*) OUP.

Disler, Jacqueline. Leopard Radio. 64p. (Orig.). 1989. pap. 6.00 (*0-942582-15-2*) Erie St Pr.

Disler, Mary J. Guitar QuickStart: A Guide to Playing & Understanding Music Reading & Chord Techniques. (Illus.). 96p. (C). 1994. pap. 15.95 (*0-9642229-0-6*) Lyra Hse Mus.

Dislis, Dick, et al. Test Economics & Design for Testability. 240p. 1995. 60.00 (*0-13-108994-3*, Prentice Hall) P-H.

Dismukes, J. P., et al, eds. Proceedings of the International Symposium on Diamond Materials, 3rd. LC 93-70063. (Proceedings Ser.: Vol. 93-17). 1120p. 1993. 66.00 (*1-56677-060-2*) Electrochem Soc.

Dismukes, John P., jt. ed. see Spear, Karl E.

***Disner, Eliot G.** Antitrust Law for Business Lawyers: Questions, Answers & Commentary. LC 99-34478. 1999. pap. write for info. (*1-57073-690-1*) Amer Bar Assn.

Disney. Disney's Mickey Mouse Classic. LC 99-43366. 128p. (ps-3). 1999. pap. text 18.99 (*0-7868-3253-3*, Pub. by Disney Pr) Time Warner.

***Disney.** How to Draw Tarzan. (gr. 4-7). 1999. pap. text 4.95 (*1-56010-515-1*) W Foster Pub.

Disney. Make Your Own Valentines. 40p. 1999. 7.99 (*0-7364-0100-8*, Pub. by Mouse Works) Time Warner.

***Disney.** Tarzan-Easy Piano. 48p. 1999. per. 16.95 (*0-634-00162-0*) H Leonard.

Disney. Toy Story 2. LC 99-55045. (Illus.). 128p. (J). 1999. pap. text 18.99 (*0-7868-3252-5*, Pub. by Disney Pr) Time Warner.

D

Disney, A. R. Twilight of the Pepper Empire: Portuguese Trade in Southwest India in the Early Seventeenth Century. LC 77-17376. (Historical Studies: No. 95). (Illus.). 272p. 1978. 18.50 (*0-674-91429-5*) HUP.

Disney, Anthony, ed. Historiography of Europeans in Africa & Asia: 1415-1800. LC 95-23892. (Expanding World Ser.: Vol. 4). 368p. 1995. 124.95 (*0-86078-503-3*, Pub. by Variorum) Ashgate Pub Co.

Disney Book Club Staff. Aladdin & the Wonderful Lamp. (J). 1999. lib. bdg. write for info. (*0-394-93937-9*) Random Bks Yng Read.

— Country Mouse, City Mouse. (J). 1999. lib. bdg. write for info. (*0-394-94026-1*) Random Bks Yng Read.

— Henny Penny & Big Bad Wolf. (J). 1999. lib. bdg. write for info. (*0-394-94008-3*) Random Bks Yng Read.

— Robin Hood & Golden Arrow. 1999. lib. bdg. 0.00 (*0-394-93928-X*) Random.

Disney, Diane M., jt. ed. see Paul, Robert D.

Disney, Doris M. The Day Miss Bessie Lewis Disappeared. 224p. 1987. mass mkt. 2.95 (*0-8217-2080-5*, Zebra Kensgtn) Kensgtn Pub Corp.

— Hospitality of the House. 1989. mass mkt. 3.50 (*0-8217-2738-9*, Zebra Kensgtn) Kensgtn Pub Corp.

— Last Straw. 1988. mass mkt. 2.95 (*0-8217-2286-7*, Zebra Kensgtn) Kensgtn Pub Corp.

— The Magic Grandfather. 224p. 1989. mass mkt. 2.95 (*0-8217-2584-X*, Zebra Kensgtn) Kensgtn Pub Corp.

— The Magic Grandfather. reprint ed. lib. bdg. 20.95 (*0-88411-842-8*) Amereon Ltd.

— Mrs. Meeker's Money. 1987. mass mkt. 2.95 (*0-8217-2212-3*, Zebra Kensgtn) Kensgtn Pub Corp.

— No Next of Kin. 1990. mass mkt. 3.50 (*0-8217-2969-1*, Zebra Kensgtn) Kensgtn Pub Corp.

— Only Couples Need Apply. 224p. 1988. mass mkt. 2.95 (*0-8217-2438-X*, Zebra Kensgtn) Kensgtn Pub Corp.

— Only Couples Need Apply. reprint ed. lib. bdg. 18.95 (*0-88411-841-X*) Amereon Ltd.

— Shadow of a Man. 1990. mass mkt. 3.50 (*0-8217-3077-0*, Zebra Kensgtn) Kensgtn Pub Corp.

— Shadow of a Man. reprint ed. lib. bdg. 20.95 (*0-88411-840-1*) Amereon Ltd.

— That Which Is Crooked. 1989. mass mkt. 3.50 (*0-8217-2848-2*, Zebra Kensgtn) Kensgtn Pub Corp.

— Three's a Crowd. 240p. 1987. mass mkt. 2.95 (*0-8217-2079-1*, Zebra Kensgtn) Kensgtn Pub Corp.

— Who Rides a Tiger? 1989. mass mkt. 3.50 (*0-8217-2799-0*, Zebra Kensgtn) Kensgtn Pub Corp.

***Disney Editions Staff.** The Walt Disney World Resort Millenium Pin Catalog. (Illus.). (J). 1999. pap. 10.95 (*0-7868-5308-5*, Pub. by Disney Pr) Time Warner.

Disney Enterprises, Inc. Staff. Aladdin: Wishful Thinking. (Disney's "Storytime Treasures" Library: Vol. 3). (Illus.). 44p. (J). (gr. 1-6). 1997. 3.49 (*1-885222-99-8*) Advance Pubs.

— Alice in Wonderland: It's About Time! (Disney's "Storytime Treasures" Library: Vol. 17). (Illus.). 44p. (J). (gr. 1-6). 1997. 3.49 (*1-57973-013-2*) Advance Pubs.

— Bambi: A Noisy Neighbor. (Disney's "Storytime Treasures" Library: Vol. 12). (Illus.). 44p. (J). (gr. 1-6). 1997. 3.49 (*1-57973-008-6*) Advance Pubs.

— Beauty & the Beast: The Perfect Party. (Disney's "Storytime Treasures" Library: Vol. 4). (Illus.). 44p. (J). (gr. 1-6). 1997. 3.49 (*1-57973-000-0*) Advance Pubs.

— The Bug Hunt. (Disney's "Out & about with Pooh" Library: Vol. 17). (Illus.). 44p. (J). (gr. 1-6). 1996. 3.49 (*1-885222-71-8*) Advance Pubs.

— Cinderella: The Runaway Wand. (Disney's "Storytime Treasures" Library: Vol. 8). (Illus.). 44p. (J). (gr. 1-6). 1997. 3.49 (*1-57973-004-3*) Advance Pubs.

— Count on Donald!/Parents Guide. (Walt Disney's Read & Grow Library: Nos. 2 & 19). (Illus.). 44p. (J). (gr. 1-6). 1997. 3.49 (*1-885222-95-5*) Advance Pubs.

— Cozy Beds. (Disney's "Out & about with Pooh" Library: Vol. 12). (Illus.). 44p. (J). (gr. 1-6). 1996. 3.49 (*1-885222-66-1*) Advance Pubs.

— Disney's "Out & About with Pooh" Library, 19 vols., Vols. 1-19. (Illus.). (J). (gr. 1-6). 1996. 66.60 (*1-885222-54-8*) Advance Pubs.

— Disney's "Storytime Treasures" Library, 19 vols., Vols. 1-19. (Illus.). 44p. (J). (gr. 1-6). 1997. 66.60 (*1-885222-96-3*) Advance Pubs.

— Dumbo: Not So Fast! (Disney's "Storytime Treasures" Library: Vol. 9). (Illus.). 44p. (J). (gr. 1-6). 1997. 3.49 (*1-57973-005-1*) Advance Pubs.

— Eeyore's Happy Tail. (Disney's "Out & about with Pooh" Library: Vol. 6). (Illus.). 44p. (J). (gr. 1-6). 1996. 3.49 (*1-885222-60-2*) Advance Pubs.

— Eeyor's Lucky Day. (Disney's "Out & about with Pooh" Library: Vol. 15). (Illus.). 44p. (J). (gr. 1-6). 1996. 3.49 (*1-885222-69-6*) Advance Pubs.

— The Friendship Garden, 3. (Disney's "Out & about with Pooh" Library: Vol. 3). (Illus.). 44p. (J). (gr. 1-6). 1996. 3.49 (*1-885222-57-2*) Advance Pubs.

— Fun Is Where You Find It. (Disney's "Out & about with Pooh" Library: Vol. 8). (Illus.). 44p. (J). (gr. 1-6). 1996. 3.49 (*1-885222-62-9*) Advance Pubs.

— Good As Gold. (Disney's "Out & About with Pooh" Library: Vol. 1). (Illus.). 44p. (J). (gr. 1-6). 1996. 3.49 (*1-885222-55-6*) Advance Pubs.

— Hercules: Lightning Strikes. (Disney's "Storytime Treasures" Library: Vol. 11). (Illus.). 44p. (J). (gr. 1-6). 1997. 3.49 (*1-57973-007-8*) Advance Pubs.

— The Honey Cake Mix-Up. (Disney's "Out & about with Pooh" Library: Vol. 5). (Illus.). 44p. (J). (gr. 1-6). 1996. 3.49 (*1-885222-59-9*) Advance Pubs.

— The Hunchback of Notre Dame: The Hidden Hero. (Disney's "Storytime Treasures" Library: Vol. 16). (Illus.). 44p. (J). (gr. 1-6). 1997. 3.49 (*1-57973-012-4*) Advance Pubs.

— The Jungle Book: A Friend for Life. (Disney's "Storytime Treasures" Library: Vol. 6). (Illus.). 44p. (J). (gr. 1-6). 1997. 3.49 (*1-57973-002-7*) Advance Pubs.

— Lady & the Tramp: A Trusty Old Pal. (Disney's "Storytime Treasures" Library: Vol. 15). (Illus.). 44p. (J). (gr. 1-6). 1997. 3.49 (*1-57973-011-6*) Advance Pubs.

— The Lion King: The Pal Patrol. (Disney's "Storytime Treasures" Library: Vol. 1). (Illus.). 44p. (J). (gr. 1-6). 1997. 3.49 (*1-885222-97-1*) Advance Pubs.

— The Little Mermaid: Treasures of Old. (Disney's "Storytime Treasures" Library: Vol. 7). (Illus.). 44p. (J). (gr. 1-6). 1997. 3.49 (*1-57973-003-5*) Advance Pubs.

— Look Before You Bounce. (Disney's "Out & about with Pooh" Library: Vol. 4). (Illus.). 44p. (J). (gr. 1-6). 1996. 3.49 (*1-885222-58-0*) Advance Pubs.

— 101 Dalmatians: Proud to Be a Pup. (Disney's "Storytime Treasures" Library: Vol. 2). (Illus.). 44p. (J). (gr. 1-6). 1997. 3.49 (*1-885222-98-X*) Advance Pubs.

— 101 Dalmatians & Parents Guide: Proud to Be a Pup. (Disney's "Storytime Treasures" Library: Vols. 2 & 19). (Illus.). 44p. (J). (gr. 1-6). 1997. 3.49 (*1-57973-016-7*) Advance Pubs.

— Owl's World. (Disney's "Out & about with Pooh" Library: Vol. 18). (Illus.). 44p. (J). (gr. 1-6). 1996. 3.49 (*1-885222-72-6*) Advance Pubs.

— Parents' Guide. (Disney's "Storytime Treasures" Library: Vol. 19). (Illus.). 44p. 1997. 3.49 (*1-57973-015-9*) Advance Pubs.

— Parent's Guide. (Disney's "Out & about with Pooh" Library: Vol. 19). (Illus.). 44p. (J). (gr. 1-6). 1996. 3.49 (*1-885222-73-4*) Advance Pubs.

— A Perfect Little Piglet. (Disney's "Out & about with Pooh" Library: Vol. 2). (Illus.). 44p. (J). (gr. 1-6). 1996. 3.49 (*1-885222-56-4*) Advance Pubs.

— A Perfect Little Piglet: Parent's Guide. (Disney's "Out & about with Pooh" Library: Vols. 2 & 19). (Illus.). 44p. (J). (gr. 1-6). 1996. 3.49 (*1-885222-74-2*) Advance Pubs.

— The Perfect Pet. (Disney's "Out & about with Pooh" Library: Vol. 11). (Illus.). 44p. (J). (gr. 1-6). 1996. 3.49 (*1-885222-65-3*) Advance Pubs.

— Peter Pan: Friends Ahoy! (Disney's "Storytime Treasures" Library: Vol. 18). (Illus.). 44p. (J). (gr. 1-6). 1997. 3.49 (*1-57973-014-0*) Advance Pubs.

— Pinocchio: Nose for Trouble. (Disney's "Storytime Treasures" Library: Vol. 13). (Illus.). 44p. (J). (gr. 1-6). 1997. 3.49 (*1-57973-009-4*) Advance Pubs.

— Pocahontas: An Unlikely Pair. (Disney's "Storytime Treasures" Library: Vol. 10). (Illus.). 44p. (J). (gr. 1-6). 1997. 3.49 (*1-57973-006-X*) Advance Pubs.

— Rabbit's Ears. (Disney's "Out & about with Pooh" Library: Vol. 16). (Illus.). 44p. (J). (gr. 1-6). 1996. 3.49 (*1-885222-70-X*) Advance Pubs.

— Sleeping Beauty: A Magic Plan. (Disney's "Storytime Treasures" Library: Vol. 14). (Illus.). 44p. (J). (gr. 1-6). 1997. 3.49 (*1-57973-010-8*) Advance Pubs.

— Snow White: What a Surprise! (Disney's "Storytime Treasures" Library: Vol. 5). (Illus.). 44p. (J). (gr. 1-6). 1997. 3.49 (*1-57973-001-9*) Advance Pubs.

— Sweet Dreams. (Disney's "Out & about with Pooh" Library: Vol. 9). (Illus.). 44p. (J). (gr. 1-6). 1996. 3.49 (*1-885222-63-7*) Advance Pubs.

— There's No Place Like Home. (Disney's "Out & about with Pooh" Library: Vol. 7). (Illus.). 44p. (J). (gr. 1-6). 1996. 3.49 (*1-885222-61-0*) Advance Pubs.

— Walt Disney's Read & Grow Library, 19 vols. Incl. Vol. 1. Mickey's Alphabet Soup. (Illus.). 44p. (J). (gr. 1-6). 1997. 3.49 (*1-885222-76-9*); Vol. 2. Count on Donald. (Illus.). 44p. (J). (gr. 1-6). 1997. 3.49 (*1-885222-77-7*); Vol. 3. Colors, Colors Everywhere! (Illus.). 44p. (J). (gr. 1-6). 1997. 3.49 (*1-885222-78-5*); Vol. 4. Missing Shapes Mix-Up. (Illus.). 44p. (J). (gr. 1-6). 1997. 3.49 (*1-885222-79-3*); Vol. 5. Amazing Muffin Search. (Illus.). 44p. (J). (gr. 1-6). 1997. 3.49 (*1-885222-80-7*); Vol. 6. Mickey's World of Words. (Illus.). 44p. (J). (gr. 1-6). 1997. 3.49 (*1-885222-81-5*); Vol. 7. Telling Time with Goofy. (Illus.). 44p. (J). (gr. 1-6). 1997. 3.49 (*1-885222-82-3*); Vol. 8. Follow Your Nose, Donald. (Illus.). 44p. (J). (gr. 1-6). 1997. 3.49 (*1-885222-83-1*); Vol. 9. Goofy Shapes Up. (Illus.). 44p. (J). (gr. 1-6). 1997. 3.49 (*1-885222-84-X*); Vol. 10. Look Before You Leap! (Illus.). 44p. (J). (gr. 1-6). 1997. 3.49 (*1-885222-85-8*); Vol. 11. Minnie's Small Wonders. (Illus.). 44p. (J). (gr. 1-6). 1997. 3.49 (*1-885222-86-6*); Vol. 12. Daisy's Nature Hunt. (Illus.). 44p. (J). (gr. 1-6). 1997. 3.49 (*1-885222-87-4*); Vol. 13. Mickey's Weather Machine. (Illus.). 44p. (J). (gr. 1-6). 1997. 3.49 (*1-885222-88-2*); Vol. 14. Donald Duck Directs. (Illus.). 44p. (J). (gr. 1-6). 1997. 3.49 (*1-885222-89-0*); Vol. 15. Minnie's Surprise Trip. (Illus.). 44p. (J). (gr. 1-6). 1997. 3.49 (*1-885222-90-4*); Vol. 16. All in a Day's Work. (Illus.). 44p. (J). (gr. 1-6). 1997. 3.49 (*1-885222-91-2*); Vol. 17. Uncle Scrooge Comes Home. (Illus.). 44p. (J). (gr. 1-6). 1997. 3.49 (*1-885222-92-0*); Vol. 18. Laugh-Along Mystery. (Illus.). 44p. (J). (gr. 1-6). 1997. 3.49 (*1-885222-93-9*); Vol. 19. Parents' Guide. (Illus.). 44p. (J). (gr. 1-6). 1997. 3.49 (*1-885222-94-7*); 1997. 66.60 (*1-885222-75-0*) Advance Pubs.

— Weather or Not. (Disney's "Out & about with Pooh" Library: Vol. 10). (Illus.). 44p. (J). (gr. 1-6). 1996. 3.49 (*1-885222-64-5*) Advance Pubs.

— A Wonderful Wind. (Disney's "Out & about with Pooh" Library: Vol. 13). (Illus.). 44p. (J). (gr. 1-6). 1996. 3.49 (*1-885222-67-X*) Advance Pubs.

Disney Enterprises, Inc. Staff & Pixar Animation Studios Staff. A Berry Brave Troop. (Disney-Pixar's "A Bug's Life" Library: Vol. 8). (Illus.). 44p. (J). (gr. 1-6). 1998. 3.99 (*1-57973-024-8*) Advance Pubs.

— Blueberries on Parade. (Disney-Pixar's "A Bug's Life" Library: Vol. 2). (Illus.). 44p. (J). (gr. 1-6). 1998. 3.99 (*1-57973-018-3*) Advance Pubs.

— Cake Mountain. (Disney-Pixar's "A Bug's Life" Library: Vol. 6). (Illus.). 44p. (J). (gr. 1-6). 1998. 3.99 (*1-57973-022-1*) Advance Pubs.

— Clowning Around. (Disney-Pixar's "A Bug's Life" Library: Vol. 5). (Illus.). 44p. (J). (gr. 1-6). 1998. 3.99 (*1-57973-021-3*) Advance Pubs.

— A Crown for Atta. (Disney-Pixar's "A Bug's Life" Library: Vol. 4). (Illus.). 44p. (J). (gr. 1-6). 1998. 3.99 (*1-57973-020-5*) Advance Pubs.

— Flick the Inventor. (Disney-Pixar's "A Bug's Life" Library: Vol. 1). (Illus.). 44p. (J). (gr. 1-6). 1998. 3.99 (*1-57973-017-5*) Advance Pubs.

— High Hopes. (Disney-Pixar's "A Bug's Life" Library: Vol. 10). (Illus.). 44p. (J). (gr. 1-6). 1998. 3.99 (*1-57973-026-4*) Advance Pubs.

— A Home for Aphie. (Disney-Pixar's "A Bug's Life" Library: Vol. 7). (Illus.). 44p. (J). (gr. 1-6). 1998. 3.99 (*1-57973-023-X*) Advance Pubs.

— Magical Memories. (Disney-Pixar's "A Bug's Life" Library: Vol. 12). (Illus.). 44p. (J). (gr. 1-6). 1998. 3.99 (*1-57973-028-0*) Advance Pubs.

— The Not-So-Perfect Picnic. (Disney-Pixar's "A Bug's Life" Library: Vol. 11). (Illus.). 44p. (J). (gr. 1-6). 1998. 3.99 (*1-57973-027-2*) Advance Pubs.

— Thinking Big. (Disney-Pixar's "A Bug's Life" Library: Vol. 3). (Illus.). 44p. (J). (gr. 1-6). 1998. 3.99 (*1-57973-019-1*) Advance Pubs.

— What a Team! (Disney-Pixar's "A Bug's Life" Library: Vol. 9). (Illus.). 44p. (J). (gr. 1-6). 1998. 3.99 (*1-57973-025-6*) Advance Pubs.

Disney, Francis. Shepton Mallet Prison: Three Hundred Eighty Years of Prison Regimes. 312p. (C). 1992. text 110.00 (*0-9511470-2-1*, Pub. by F J Disney) St Mut.

Disney, Jay. Let There Be Lite! An Illuminating Guide to Delicious Low-Fat Cooking. (Illus.). 300p. 1995. 23.95 (*0-87951-576-7*, Pub. by Overlook Pr) Penguin Putnam.

— Let There Be Lite! An Illuminating Guide to Delicious Low-Fat Cooking. LC 94-37368. (Illus.). 300p. 1997. reprint ed. pap. 15.95 (*0-87951-758-1*, Pub. by Overlook Pr) Penguin Putnam.

— The Middle Path Cookbook. LC 98-48796. (Illus.). 308p. 1999. text 26.95 (*0-87951-921-5*, Pub. by Overlook Pr) Penguin Putnam.

Disney, Jean A., jt. auth. see Ross, Annette L.

Disney, Jim. Line Finder: Rhyming Dictionary (Rhymes "Lines" Not Words) 4th rev. ed. LC 98-91425. 364p. 1998. 34.95 (*0-9664220-0-7*) JAD Music Grp.

Disney, Julian & Nethercote, J. R., eds. The House on Capital Hill: Parliament, Politics & Power in the National Capital. 245p. 1996. pap. 29.00 (*1-86287-223-6*, Pub. by Federation Pr) Gaunt.

Disney, M. Janelle & Stephens, Anthony M. Legal Issues in Clinical Supervision. LC 93-36194. (ACA Legal Ser.: Vol. 10). 90p. 1994. pap. text 18.95 (*1-55620-128-1*, 72310) Am Coun Assn.

***Disney Press Staff.** Disney Archive Noahs Ark. (Illus.). 32p. (J). (gr. k-2). 2000. trans. 14.99 (*0-7868-5310-7*, Pub. by Disney Pr) Time Warner.

— Disney Archive Sleeping Beauty. (Illus.). 32p. (J). (gr. k-2). 2000. trans. 14.99 (*0-7868-5311-5*, Pub. by Disney Pr) Time Warner.

Disney Press Staff. Disney Princess. (Disney's Chapters Ser.). (J). Date not set. pap. 3.99 (*0-7868-4311-X*, Pub. by Disney Pr) Little.

— Disney's Storybook Collection. Parent, Nancy, ed. LC 98-86249. (Illus.). 320p. (J). (ps-3). 1998. 14.99 (*0-7868-3234-7*, Pub. by Disney Pr) Time Warner.

***Disney Press Staff.** Easy-to-Read Stories: A Collection of Six Favorite Tales. (Illus.). 192p. (J). (gr. k-2). 1999. pap. text 9.99 (*0-7868-3244-4*, Pub. by Disney Pr) Time Warner.

— Fool's Gold. (Woody's Roundup Ser.: No. 4). (Illus.). 64p. (J). (gr. 2-5). 2000. pap. 4.99 (*0-7868-4445-0*, Pub. by Disney Pr) Time Warner.

— Giddy-Up Ghost Town. (Woody's Roundup Ser.: No. 2). (Illus.). 64p. (J). (gr. 2-5). 2000. pap. 4.99 (*0-7868-4443-4*, Pub. by Disney Pr) Time Warner.

— Hercules 3-D Mask Book, Vol. 1. LC 96-71094. 14p. (J). (ps-2). 1997. pap. 10.95 (*0-7868-4129-X*, Pub. by Disney Pr) Little.

Disney Press Staff. Play-Along Rhymes. 14p. 1999. 7.99 (*0-7364-0187-3*, Pub. by Mouse Works) Time Warner.

— Pooh Can, Can You?, Vol. 1. (Learn & Grow Ser.). 12p. (J). 1999. 6.99 (*0-7364-0135-0*, Pub. by Mouse Works) Time Warner.

— Pooh Plays Doctor Book & Kit. (Learn & Grow Ser.). 32p. (J). 1999. boxed set 11.99 (*0-7364-0144-X*, Pub. by Mouse Works) Time Warner.

— Pooh Says Please! 16p. (J). 1999. 3.50 (*0-7364-0150-4*, Pub. by Mouse Works) Time Warner.

— Pooh's Hero Party, No. 12. LC 98-86075. (Winnie the Pooh First Readers Ser.: No. 12). (Illus.). 40p. (J). (gr. k-3). 1999. pap. 3.99 (*0-7868-4270-9*, Pub. by Disney Pr) Time Warner.

— Pooh's Noisy Book. (Learn & Grow Ser.). 12p. (J). 1999. 6.99 (*0-7364-0136-9*, Pub. by Mouse Works) Time Warner.

***Disney Press Staff.** Ride'em Rodeo! (Woody's Roundup Ser.: No. 3). (Illus.). 64p. (J). (gr. 2-5). 2000. pap. 4.99 (*0-7868-4444-2*, Pub. by Disney Pr) Time Warner.

— Showdown at the Okey Dokey Corral. (Woody's Roundup Ser.: No. 1). (Illus.). 64p. (J). (gr. 2-5). 2000. pap. 4.99 (*0-7868-4442-6*, Pub. by Disney Pr) Time Warner.

Disney Press Staff. Stories to Tell a Three Year Old. (J). Date not set. pap. write for info. (*0-7868-4333-0*) Disney Pr.

— Toy Story. (Illus.). (J). 1996. pap. write for info. (*0-7868-4142-7*) Disney Pr.

— Toy Story II Picture Book. (Illus.). 48p. (J). 1999. lib. bdg. 11.49 (*0-7868-5095-7*, Pub. by Disney Pr) Little.

***Disney Press Staff.** Toy Story 2 Pull-Out Posters & Trading Cards Book. (Toy Story 2 Ser.). (Illus.). (J). 2000. 7.99 (*0-7364-0229-2*, Pub. by Mouse Works) Time Warner.

Disney Press Staff, ed. Toy Story II: Buzz's Story. (Illus.). 48p. (J). 1999. 10.99 (*0-7868-3233-9*, Pub. by Disney Pr) Time Warner.

Disney Publishing Group Staff. Big Things, Little Things. (Pooh's Learn & Grow Ser.: Vol. 9). (Illus.). 12p. (J). 1999. 3.49 (*1-57973-043-4*) Advance Pubs.

— Follow the Leader. (Pooh's Learn & Grow Ser.: Vol. 2). (Illus.). 12p. (J). 1999. 3.49 (*1-57973-036-1*) Advance Pubs.

— Fruity-Tooty Picnic. (Pooh's Learn & Grow Ser.: Vol. 5). (Illus.). 12p. (J). 1999. 3.49 (*1-57973-039-6*) Advance Pubs.

— Peek-a-Boo, Pooh! (Pooh's Learn & Grow Ser.: Vol. 7). (Illus.). 12p. (J). 1999. 3.49 (*1-57973-041-8*) Advance Pubs.

— Pooh Counts to Five. (Pooh's Learn & Grow Ser.: Vol. 4). (Illus.). 12p. (J). 1999. 3.49 (*1-57973-038-8*) Advance Pubs.

— Pooh's Colorful Shapes. (Pooh's Learn & Grow Ser.: Vol. 1). (Illus.). 12p. (J). 1999. 3.49 (*1-57973-035-3*) Advance Pubs.

***Disney Publishing Group Staff.** Pooh's Fast & Slow Days. (Illus.). 12p. (J). 2000. pap. text 6.99 (*0-7364-1005-8*, Pub. by Mouse Works) Time Warner.

Disney Publishing Group Staff. Pooh's Garden. (Pooh's Learn & Grow Ser.: Vol. 11). (Illus.). 12p. (J). 1999. 3.49 (*1-57973-045-0*) Advance Pubs.

— Pooh's Playful Pond. (Pooh's Learn & Grow Ser.: Vol. 6). (Illus.). 12p. (J). 1999. 3.49 (*1-57973-040-X*) Advance Pubs.

— Pooh's Rainy Day. (Pooh's Learn & Grow Ser.: Vol. 10). (Illus.). 12p. (J). 1999. 3.49 (*1-57973-044-2*) Advance Pubs.

— Pooh's Sunny Day. (Pooh's Learn & Grow Ser.: Vol. 3). (Illus.). 12p. (J). 1999. 3.49 (*1-57973-037-X*) Advance Pubs.

— Ready, Set, Go! (Pooh's Learn & Grow Ser.: Vol. 8). (Illus.). 12p. (J). 1999. 3.49 (*1-57973-042-6*) Advance Pubs.

— Sweet Dreams. (Pooh's Learn & Grow Ser.: Vol. 12). (Illus.). 12p. (J). 1999. 3.49 (*1-57973-046-9*) Advance Pubs.

Disney, R. H. A Key to the Larvae, Pupae & Adults of the British Dixidae (Diptera) 1975. 50.00 (*0-900386-23-1*) St Mut.

Disney, Ralph L. & Kiessler, Peter C. Traffic Processes in Queueing Networks: A Markov Renewal Approach. LC 86-46275. (Johns Hopkins Series in the Mathematical Sciences: No. 4). (Illus.). 272p. 1987. reprint ed. pap. 84.40 (*0-608-05950-1*, 206628700008) Bks Demand.

Disney, Ralph L., et al. Applied Probability - Computer Science: The Interface. LC 82-18506. (Progress in Computer Science Ser., Vol. 3). 1982. write for info. (*3-7643-3093-7*) Birkhauser.

Disney, Ralph L., jt. auth. see Clarke, A. Bruce.

Disney, Richard. Can We Afford to Grow Older? (Illus.). 356p. (C). 1996. 44.00 (*0-262-04157-X*) MIT Pr.

Disney, Richard, et al. The Dynamics of Retirement: Analyses of the Retirement Surveys : a Report of Research Carried Out by the Institute for Fiscal Studies & Age Concern Institute of Gerontology on Behalf of the Department of Social Security. LC 99-164932. (Illus.). 1997. write for info. (*0-11-762571-X*) Statnry Office.

Disney, Richard, jt. auth. see Creedy, John.

Disney, Rosemary. The Splendid Art of Decorating Eggs. 192p. 1986. reprint ed. pap. 6.95 (*0-486-25030-X*) Dover.

Disney Staff. Disney's My First Songbook: A Treasury of Favorite Songs to Sing. deluxe ed. LC 97-66885. (Illus.). 96p. (J). 1998. 16.95 (*0-7868-3147-2*, Pub. by Disney Pr) Time Warner.

Disney Staff. Disney's Princess Collection: The Music of Hopes, Dreams, & Happy Endings. 64p. 1996. pap. 8.95 (*0-7935-6749-1*) H Leonard.

— Disney's Princess Collection, 2nd ed. 2nd ed. 88p. 1998. pap. 9.95 (*0-7935-9771-4*) H Leonard.

Disney Staff. Dumbo Classic. (J). 1994. 7.98 (*1-57082-190-9*, Pub. by Mouse Works) Time Warner.

***Disney Staff.** Epcot Millenium 1999. 16.95 (*0-7868-6605-5*, Pub. by Disney Pr) Time Warner.

Disney Staff. Feel Better, Beast! (Illus.). (J). 1998. pap. text 2.99 (*0-307-15267-7*, 15267, Goldn Books) Gldn Bks Pub Co.

— Flounder the Fearless. LC 98-108374. (Disney's the Little Mermaid Ser.). 5p. (J). 1997. 7.98 (*1-57082-614-5*, Pub. by Mouse Works) Time Warner.

***Disney Staff.** Hang in There. (Illus.). 48p. (J). (ps-3). 2000. 4.95 (*0-7407-0079-0*) Andrews & McMeel.

Disney Staff. Hunting for Honey. (Pooh Ser.). (Illus.). (J). 1998. pap. text 2.99 (*0-307-25700-2*, 25700, Goldn Books) Gldn Bks Pub Co.

— The Lion King. (Illus.). 96p. (J). 1994. 7.98 (*1-57082-128-3*, Pub. by Mouse Works) Time Warner.

***Disney Staff.** Lion King. (SPA., Illus.). 64p. (ps-2). 1999. pap. text 4.99 (*0-7364-0130-X*, Pub. by Mouse Works) Time Warner.

— Lion King II; Simba's Pride. 48p. 1998. per. 14.95 (*0-634-00031-4*) H Leonard.

— Love. (Illus.). 48p. (J). (ps-3). 2000. pap. 4.95 (*0-7407-1039-7*) Andrews & McMeel.

Disney Staff. The Making of a Hero. (Mulan Ser.). (Illus.). (J). 1998. pap. text 2.99 (*0-307-25703-7*, 25703, Goldn Books) Gldn Bks Pub Co.

— The Many Adventures of Winnie the Pooh: A Classic Disney Treasury. LC 97-80021. (Illus.). 192p. (J). (ps-2). 1997. 19.95 (*0-7868-3138-3*, Pub. by Disney Pr) Time Warner.

— Merry Christmas to You: Hunny Pot Book. LC 97-220260. (Pooh Ser.). 5p. (J). 1997. 4.98 (*1-57082-630-7*, Pub. by Mouse Works) Time Warner.

***Disney Staff.** Millenium Pin Book Walt Disney World Exclusive. 1999. 8.95 (*0-7868-6612-8*, Pub. by Disney Pr) Time Warner.

Disney Staff. 101 Dalmatians: Illustrated Classic. (J). 1997. pap. 5.95 (*0-7868-4199-0*, Pub. by Disney Pr) Time Warner.

— Pirate's Cove: Paint with Water. (Walt Disney's Peter Pan Ser.). (Illus.). (J). 1998. pap. text 1.79 (*0-307-27000-9*, 27000, Goldn Books) Gldn Bks Pub Co.

***Disney Staff.** Pluto's Words of Wisdom. (Illus.). 48p. (J). (ps-3). 2000. pap. 4.95 (*0-7407-0080-4*) Andrews & McMeel.

Disney Staff. Sleeping Beauty. LC 98-141356. (Little Library). (Illus.). (J). 1997. 5.98 (*1-57082-608-0*, Pub. by Mouse Works) Little.

***Disney Staff.** Snow White & the Seven Dwarfs. (Disney's Read-Aloud Storybooks Ser.). 64p. 1999. pap. 4.99 (*0-7364-0131-8*, Pub. by Mouse Works) Time Warner.

Disney Staff. Snow White & the Seven Dwarfs. (Disney's Read-Aloud Storybooks Ser.). (SPA., Illus.). 64p. (J). (ps-2). 1999. 6.99 (*0-7364-0137-7*, Pub. by Mouse Works) Time Warner.

***Disney Staff.** Tarzan. 64p. 1999. per. 16.95 (*0-634-00161-2*) H Leonard.

Disney Staff. Tarzan Flip Book. 96p. (ps-3). 1999. pap. 3.99 (*0-7364-0143-1*) Mouse Works.

— Tarzan Jungle Adventure. LC 99-461945. (Illus.). 5p. (J). (ps). 1999. 8.99 (*0-7364-0066-4*, Pub. by Mouse Works) Time Warner.

— Tarzan, Me & You. (Illus.). 10p. (J). (ps). 1999. 3.99 (*0-7364-0132-6*, Pub. by Mouse Works) Time Warner.

***Disney Staff.** Toy Story Sketchbook. (Illus.). 112p. (J). 2000. 125.00 (*1-55709-340-7*) Applewood.

Disney Staff & Mouse Works Staff. Walt Disney's Winnie the Pooh & His Friends Friendship Box. (Illus.). (J). 1997. boxed set 9.98 (*1-57082-711-7*, Pub. by Mouse Works) Time Warner.

Disney Studio Archives. My Disney Princess Book: A Book for Keepsakes, Memories & Dreams. 96p. (J). (gr. 3 up). 1998. 10.95 (*0-7868-3159-6*, Pub. by Disney Pr) Time Warner.

Disney Studio Staff. Walt Disney's Bambi. limited ed. LC 97-162360. (Sketchbook Ser.). (Illus.). 104p. 1997. 100.00 (*1-55709-342-3*) Applewood.

***Disney Studios.** Holiday Greetings from Disney. (Illus.). 32p. 2000. pap. 9.95 (*1-55709-482-9*) Applewood.

Disney Studios Staff. Diccionario Disney. (SPA.). 112p. 1973. pap. 9.95 (*0-8288-6241-9*, S-24118) Fr & Eur.

— Disney's Silly Songs. 80p. (J). (ps-3). 1990. pap. 9.95 (*0-7935-1829-6*, 0290187) H Leonard.

Disney Studios Staff. The Lion King. (Classics Ser.). (Illus.). 96p. (J). 1994. 7.98 (*1-57082-087-2*, Pub. by Mouse Works) Little.

— The Lion King: Little Library. LC 96-232650. (Illus.). (J). 1994. 5.98 (*1-57082-088-0*, Pub. by Mouse Works) Little.

Disney Studios Staff. Simba Roars: The Lion King. LC 96-231735. (Squeeze Me Bks.). (Illus.). 18p. (J). (ps). 1994. 6.98 (*1-57082-090-2*) Mouse Works.

— Speak up, Patch! With 101 Dalmations. (Squeeze Me Bks.). 9p. (J). (ps). 1993. 6.98 (*0-453-03131-5*) Mouse Works.

— Squeak Abu! Aladdin. LC 97-101676. (Illus.). 9p. (J). (ps). 1994. 6.98 (*0-453-03243-5*) NAL.

— Tigger Bounces Back. LC 96-231771. (Winnie the Pooh Ser.). (Illus.). 10p. (J). (ps-3). 1994. 6.98 (*1-57082-095-3*, Pub. by Mouse Works) Time Warner.

— The Treasure Hunt. LC 96-231728. (Mickey Mouse Ser.). (Illus.). 5p. (J). (ps-3). 1994. 6.98 (*1-57082-094-5*, Pub. by Mouse Works) Little.

— Walt Disney Fairy Tale Treasury: Blue. (Penguin-Disney Ser.). (J). 1991. text 9.98 (*0-8317-9291-4*, Viking Child) Peng Put Young Read.

— Walt Disney Fairy Tale Treasury: Red. (Penguin-Disney Ser.). (J). 1991. text 9.98 (*0-8317-9292-2*, Viking Child) Peng Put Young Read.

Disney, Walt, Productions Staff. Beauty & the Beast. (Illus.). 96p. (J). (ps-3). 1991. 7.98 (*0-453-03037-8*) Mouse Works.

Disney, Walt, Studios Staff. Aladdin. (FRE.). 96p. (J). (gr. k-5). pap. 9.95 (*0-7859-8852-1*) Fr & Eur.

— Mickey Mouse & Minnie Mouse Pop-Up Boxed Collector's Set. deluxe ed. LC 93-31910. (Illus.). 32p. (J). 1999. reprint ed. 100.00 (*1-55709-215-X*) Applewood.

Disney, Walter Elias. Cinderella/Sleeping Beauty/Snow White. LC 98-102714. (Disney's Princess Treasury Collection Ser.). (Illus.). (J). 1997. 7.98 (*1-57082-024-4*, Pub. by Mouse Works) Time Warner.

— Feel the Pain, Pat the Panic: A Fun to Touch Book. LC 97-185333. (Hercules Ser.). (J). 1997. 6.98 (*1-57082-521-1*, Pub. by Mouse Works) Time Warner.

— Friends to the End: A Friendship Bracelet Book. (Barbie Ser.). 24p. (J). 1997. 7.98 (*1-57082-570-X*, Pub. by Mouse Works) Time Warner.

— The Illustrated Treasury of Disney Songs. (Illus.). 256p. (J). 1993. 34.00 (*1-56282-743-X*, Pub. by Hyperion) Time Warner.

Disney, Walter Elias. Jungle Book. (Illus.). 40p. (J). 1985. pap. 12.95 (*0-7935-3972-2*) H Leonard.

Disney, Walter Elias. The Little Mermaid: Makes a Splash Bath Book. (Illus.). (J). (ps). 1993. 5.98 (*0-453-03172-2*, Pub. by Mouse Works) Little.

— Mealtime Fun. (Illus.). 10p. (J). 1997. 7.98 (*1-57082-677-3*, Pub. by Mouse Works) Time Warner.

— Mickey's Treehouse Treasury. 1989. 17.50 (*0-88704-251-1*) Sight & Sound.

— Oh Bother! It's the Easter Bunny! A Honey Pot Book. LC 97-156040. (Pooh Ser.). 10p. (J). 1997. 4.98 (*1-57082-583-1*, Pub. by Mouse Works) Time Warner.

— 101 Dalmatians. LC 99-160962. (J). 1997. 9.98 (*1-57082-537-8*, Pub. by Mouse Works) Time Warner.

— Pumpkin Patch. LC 97-209626. (Illus.). 10p. (J). 1997. 5.98 (*1-57082-631-5*, Pub. by Mouse Works) Time Warner.

— Sp-la Bella y la Bestia (Beauty & the Beast) Orig. Title: Sp-la Bella y la Bestia. (SPA.). (J). 1996. 7.98 (*1-57082-372-3*, Pub. by Mouse Works) Time Warner.

Disney, Walter Elias. Star Wars. LC 97-117452. (Star Wars Ser.). 24p. (J). 1997. 8.98 (*1-57082-567-X*, Pub. by Mouse Works) Time Warner.

Disney, Walter Elias. Thank Heavens for Pegasus! A Squeeze Me Book. (Hercules Ser.). (J). 1997. 6.98 (*1-57082-536-X*, Pub. by Mouse Works) Time Warner.

— Very Best Mama: Peek-a-Pooh. LC 97-163609. (J). 1997. 6.98 (*1-57082-525-4*, Pub. by Mouse Works) Time Warner.

Dison, Jack E., jt. ed. see Murphy, John W.

Dison, Norma. Simplified Drugs & Solutions for Health Care Professionals. 11th ed. (Illus.). 352p. (C). (gr. 13). 1996. pap. text 21.00 (*0-8151-2505-4*, 28190) Mosby Inc.

Dispenza, Joseph. Live Better Longer: The Parcells Center 7-Step Plan for Health & Longevity. LC 96-39224. 240p. 1997. 22.00 (*0-06-251422-9*, Pub. by Harper SF) HarpC.

— The Magical Realism of Alyce Frank. Drabanski, Emily S., ed. (New Mexico Magazine Distinguished Artists Ser.: Vol. III). (Illus.). 76p. 1999. 38.95 (*0-937206-57-1*) New Mexico Mag.

***Dispenza, Joseph.** The Magical Realism of Alyce Frank. limited ed. Drabanski, Emily S., ed. (New Mexico Magazine Distinguished Artists Ser.: Vol. III). (Illus.). 76p. 1999. 195.00 (*0-937206-60-1*) New Mexico Mag.

Dispenza, Joseph. The Serigraphs of Doug West. Flores-Turney, Camille, ed. (Artist Ser.). (Illus.). 67p. 1995. pap. 40.00 (*0-937206-41-5*) New Mexico Mag.

Dispenza, Joseph. The Serigraphs of Doug West. limited ed. Flores-Turney, Camille, ed. (Artist Ser.). (Illus.). 67p. 1995. 190.00 (*0-937206-42-3*) New Mexico Mag.

Dispenza, Joseph. The Way of the Traveler: Making Every Trip a Journey of Self-Discovery. LC 99-28334. 128p. 1999. pap. 12.95 (*1-56261-488-6*) Avalon Travel.

Dispezio. Map Madness & Compass Caper. 1998. spiral bd. write for info. (*0-201-33998-6*) Addison-Wesley.

Dispezio, Michael. Awesome Adventures in Electricity & Magnetism. LC 98-22439. (Illus.). 160p. (J). (gr. 3-7). 1998. 17.95 (*0-8069-9819-9*) Sterling.

— Awesome Adventures in Forces & Motion. LC 98-22440. (Illus.). 160p. (J). (gr. 3-7). 1998. 17.95 (*0-8069-9821-0*) Sterling.

— Awesome Adventures in Light & Sound. LC 98-40845. (J). 1999. 17.95 (*0-8069-9823-7*) Sterling.

***Dispezio, Michael.** Awesome Experiments in Electricity & Magnetism. (Awesome Experiments Ser.). (Illus.). 160p. (J). 2000. pap. 7.95 (*0-8069-9820-2*) Sterling.

— Awesome Experiments in Force & Motion. (Awesome Experiments Ser.). (Illus.). (J). 2000. pap. 7.95 (*0-8069-9822-9*) Sterling.

Dispezio, Michael. Challenging Critical Thinking Puzzles. (J). Date not set. write for info. (*0-8069-3848-X*) Sterling.

— Challenging Critical Thinking Puzzles. LC 98-6167. (Illus.). 96p. 1998. 5.95 (*0-8069-3186-8*) Sterling.

— The Science of HIV. LC 96-72258. (Illus.). 184p. 1997. pap. 45.00 incl. VHS (*0-87355-160-5*, PB136X) Natl Sci Tchrs.

DiSpezio, Michael. Visual Thinking Puzzles. LC 98-6166. (Illus.). 96p. 1998. 5.95 (*0-8069-9975-6*) Sterling.

DiSpezio, Michael A. Critical Thinking Puzzles. LC 96-28211. (Illus.). 96p. 1996. pap. 4.95 (*0-8069-9430-4*) Sterling.

***DiSpezio, Michael A.** Optical Illusion Magic: Visual Tricks & Amusements LC 99-21113. 1999. 17.95 (*0-8069-6581-9*) Sterling.

DiSpezio, Michael A. The Science, Spread & Therapy of HIV Disease: Everything You Need to Know, but Had No Idea Who to Ask. LC 97-19710. (Science Fundamentals Ser.). (Illus.). 142p. (Orig.). (YA). (gr. 7 up). 1998. 26.95 (*1-882360-20-6*); pap. 13.95 (*1-882360-19-2*) ATL Pr Sci.

Dispezio, Michael A. & Miller, Myron. Great Critical Thinking Puzzles. LC 96-46532. (Illus.). 96p. 1997. 4.95 (*0-8069-9725-7*) Sterling.

***Dispirito, Mary Ann & Robinson.** Burlington, Vol. II. (Images of America Ser.). 128p. 1999. pap. 18.99 (*0-7385-0182-4*) Arcadia Publng.

Dispirito, Mary Ann, jt. auth. see Robinson, David E.

Displaced Homemakers Network Staff & Institute for Women's Policy Research Staff. Low Wage Jobs & Workers: Trends & Options for Change, Final Report. 348p. 1989. pap. 30.00 (*0-685-29929-5*) Inst Womens Policy Rsch.

— Low Wage Jobs & Workers: Trends & Options for Change: Summary of Findings. 23p. 1989. pap. 5.00 (*0-685-29942-2*) Inst Womens Policy Rsch.

Disque, Robert O. Applied Plastic Design in Steel. LC 79-153190. 255p. reprint ed. pap. 79.10 (*0-8357-5684-X*, 200724400063) Bks Demand.

Disraeli, Benjamin. Contarini Fleming: A Psychological Romance, etc., Vol. 6. LC 76-148746. 76.00 (*0-404-08806-6*) AMS Pr.

— Sybil. Smith, Sheila, ed. (Oxford World's Classics Ser.). 480p. 1999. pap. 9.95 (*0-19-283693-5*) OUP.

— Sybil. (Classics Library). 478p. pap. 3.95 (*1-85326-248-X*, 248XWW, Pub. by Wrdsworth Edits) NTC Contemp Pub Co.

— Tancred: Or, the New Crusade. LC 79-98811. 487p. 1971. reprint ed. lib. bdg. 35.00 (*0-8371-3072-7*, BATA, Greenwood Pr) Greenwood.

— Works of Benjamin Disraeli, 20 vols., Set. Incl. Vol. 5. Contarini Fleming: A Psychological Romance, etc. LC 76-148746. 76.00 (*0-404-08805-8*); Vol. 7. Alroy: Or, the Prince of the Captivity. LC 76-148746. 76.00 (*0-404-08807-4*); Vol. 8. Henrietta Temple: A Love Story, etc. LC 76-148746. 76.00 (*0-404-08808-2*); Vol. 9. Henrietta Temple: A Love Story, etc. 76.00 (*0-404-08809-0*); Vol. 12. Coningsby: Or, the New Generation & Selected Speeches. LC 76-148746. 76.00 (*0-404-08812-0*); Vol. 13. Coningsby: Or, the New Generation & Selected Speeches. 76.00 (*0-404-08813-9*); Vol. 14. Sybil: Tancred. LC 76-148746. 76.00 (*0-404-08814-7*); Vol. 15. Sybil: Tancred. 76.00 (*0-404-08815-5*); Vol. 17. Lothair & Letters to His Sister. LC 76-148746. 76.00 (*0-404-08817-1*); Vol. 18. Lothair & Letters to His Sister 76.00 (*0-404-08818-X*); Vol. 19. Endymion, Miscellania. LC 76-148746. 76.00 (*0-404-08819-8*); Vol. 20. Endymion, Miscellania. 76.00 (*0-404-08820-1*); Vols. 1-2. Vivian Grey: A Romance of Youth. LC 76-148746. 76.00 (*0-404-08801-5*); Vols. 3-4. Young Duke, Etc. LC 76-148746. 76.00 (*0-404-08804-X*); Vols. 10-11. Venetia, etc. LC 76-148746. 76.00 (*0-404-08810-4*); LC 76-148746. (Illus.). 1904. reprint ed. 1530.00 (*0-404-08800-7*) AMS Pr.

Disraeli, Benjamin & Disraeli, Sarah. A Year at Hartlebury: or The Election. 221p. 1983. text 24.95 (*0-8020-2439-4*) U of Toronto Pr.

Disraeli, Benjamin & Kamphuis, Robert W. Lord George Bentinck: A Political Biography. LC 89-34108. (Library of Conservative Thought). 396p. 1997. pap. text 24.95 (*1-56000-947-0*) Transaction Pubs.

Disraeli, Benjamin, ed. see Disraeli, Isaac.

Disraeli, Isaac. The Works, 6 vols., Set. Disraeli, Benjamin, ed. (Anglistica & Americana Ser.: No. 62). 1969. reprint ed. 323.70 (*0-685-66458-9*, 05102724) G Olms Pubs.

— The Works of Isaac Disraeli, 6 vols., Set. Disraeli, Benjamin, ed. 3333p. reprint ed. lib. bdg. 323.70 (*0-685-43591-1*, 05102724) G Olms Pubs.

Disraeli, Sarah, jt. auth. see Disraeli, Benjamin.

Diss-Greis, Theresa & Northrup, Herbert R., frwds. The Decline of Annual Hours Worked in the United States since 1947. LC 84-47551. (Manpower & Human Resources Studies: No. 10). 360p. 1984. 30.00 (*0-89546-044-0*) U PA Ctr Hum Res.

Diss, Ronald E. Recruiting & Training Volunteer Tutors of Emergent & Beginning Readers in the Primary Grades. (Illus.). 64p. 1998. 30.00 (*1-891677-03-9*) Appalachia Educ.

***Dissanayake, Ellen.** Art & Intimacy: How the Arts Began. LC 99-37639. (Illus.). 268p. 2000. 29.95 (*0-295-97911-9*) U of Wash Pr.

Dissanayake, Ellen. Homo Aestheticus: Where Art Comes from & Why. LC 95-14821. (Illus.). 320p. (C). 1995. pap. 16.95 (*0-295-97479-6*) U of Wash Pr.

— What Is Art For? LC 89-31648. (Illus.). 266p. 1990. pap. 17.95 (*0-295-97017-0*) U of Wash Pr.

Dissanayake, M. A., et al, eds. Solid State Physics - One. 325p. (C). 1989. text 175.00 (*0-941743-66-7*) Nova Sci Pubs.

— Solid State Physics Two. 292p. (C). 1993. pap. text 165.00 (*1-56072-030-1*) Nova Sci Pubs.

Dissanayake, Wimal, ed. Colonialism & Nationalism in Asian Cinema. LC 93-51497. 256p. 1994. 35.00 (*0-253-31804-1*); pap. 14.95 (*0-253-20895-5*) Ind U Pr.

— Melodrama & Asian Cinema. LC 92-23862. (Cambridge Studies in Film). 293p. (C). 1993. text 64.95 (*0-521-41465-2*) Cambridge U Pr.

— Narratives of Agency: Self-Making in China, India, & Japan. 1996. text 54.95 (*0-8166-2656-1*); pap. text 21.95 (*0-8166-2657-X*) U of Minn Pr.

Dissanayake, Wimal & Wickramagamage, Carmen. Self & Colonial Desire: Travel Writings of V. S. Naipaul. LC 92-43538. (Studies of World Literature in English: Vol. 2). VII, 160p. (C). 1993. text 45.95 (*0-8204-1975-3*) P Lang Pubng.

Dissanayake, Wimal, jt. auth. see Gokulsing, K. Moti.

Dissanayake, Wimal, jt. auth. see Tam, Kwok-kan.

Dissanayake, Wimal, jt. ed. see Ames, Roger T.

Dissanayake, Wimal, jt. ed. see Wilson, Rob.

Dissanyake, Wimal, jt. auth. see Gokulsing, K. Moti.

Disselkoen, Laura, ed. Semana de la Pasion Muerte y Resurreccion.Tr. of Week of the Death & Resurrection. (SPA.). 75p. 1967. reprint ed. pap. 5.99 (*0-311-08501-6*) Casa Bautista.

Dissell, Adis. Falling Between the Cracks. (Illus.). 135p. 1998. pap. 12.95 (*0-9644389-3-3*) Smoky Water Pr.

Dissemination Center for Bilingual-Bicultural Educ. Guide to Title VII ESEA Bilingual Bicultural Projects: 1973-1974. Cordasco, Francesco, ed. LC 77-90544. (Bilingual Bicultural Education in the U. S. Ser.). 1978. reprint ed. lib. bdg. 26.95 (*0-405-11084-7*) Ayer.

— Proceedings: National Conference on Bilingual Education. Cordasco, Francesco, ed. LC 77-90556. (Bilingual-Bicultural Education in the U. S. Ser.). 1978. reprint ed. lib. bdg. 34.95 (*0-405-11094-4*) Ayer.

Dissent (Periodical). Voices of Dissent. LC 77-99630. (Essay Index Reprint Ser.). 1977. 30.95 (*0-8369-1405-8*) Ayer.

Dissere, Jean. Dictionnaire Encyclopedique des Citations. (FRE.). 395p. 1970. 19.95 (*0-7859-0733-5*, M-6654) Fr & Eur.

Disston, Harry. Know All about Horses. 1975. pap. 5.00 (*0-87980-294-4*) Wilshire.

Distad, N. Merrill. Guessing at Truth: The Life of Julius Charles Hare 1795-1855. LC 78-11625. xiv, 258p. 1979. 23.50 (*0-915762-07-2*) Patmos Pr.

Distance Learning Consortium Staff. Definitive Guide Criminal Justice & Criminology on the World Wide Web. LC 98-8359. 154p. (C). 1998. pap. text 20.40 (*0-13-096251-1*) P-H.

Distant, W. L. Rhynchota: Heteroptera, Vol. 1. (Fauna of British India Ser.). xxxviii, 438p. 1977. reprint ed. 25.00 (*0-88065-048-6*) Scholarly Pubns.

— Rhynchota: Heteroptera, Vol. 2. (Fauna of British India Ser.). xviii, 504p. 1977. reprint ed. 25.00 (*0-88065-049-4*) Scholarly Pubns.

— Rhynchota: Heteroptera - Appendix, Vol. 5. (Fauna of British India Ser.). xii, 362p. 1977. reprint ed. 20.00 (*0-88065-077-X*) Scholarly Pubns.

— Rhynchota: Heteroptera-Homoptera, Vol. 3. (Fauna of British India Ser.). iiv, 504p. 1977. reprint ed. 25.00 (*0-88065-075-3*) Scholarly Pubns.

— Rhynchota: Homoptera - Appendix, Vol. 4. (Fauna of British India Ser.). xiv, 502p. 1977. reprint ed. 25.00 (*0-88065-076-1*) Scholarly Pubns.

— Rhynchota: Homoptera - Appendix, Vol. 6. (Fauna of British India Ser.). viii, 250p. 1977. reprint ed. 15.00 (*0-88065-078-8*, Pub. by Today Tomorrow) Scholarly Pubns.

— Rhynchota: Homoptera - Appendix, Heteroptera - Addenda, Vol. 7. (Fauna of British India Ser.). viii, 212p. 1977. reprint ed. 15.00 (*0-88065-079-6*) Scholarly Pubns.

DiStasio, Mario, et al, eds. Small Business Handbook: Laws, Regulations & Technical Assistance Services - U. S. Department of Labor. 87p. (Orig.). (C). 1994. pap. text 25.00 (*0-7881-1479-4*) DIANE Pub.

Distefano, Christine. Autonomy: Fate of an Ideal. (Thinking Gender Ser.). (C). (gr. 13). 1999. 75.00 (*0-415-90393-9*) Routledge.

DiStefano, Christine, jt. auth. see Hirschmann, Nancy J.

DiStefano, Christine, jt. ed. see Hirschmann, Nancy J.

DISTEFANO, DOMENIC. Painting Dynamic Watercolors: Capturing the Spontaneity of Nature. Rogoff, Herbert, ed. (Illus.). 128p. 1999. 27.99 (*0-929552-15-6*, 31508) Art Instr Assocs.

Distefano-Griffiths, Kathy. Heartfelt Ways to Say Thank You. LC 97-44355. (Illus.). 80p. 1998. 7.95 (*0-8069-0821-1*) Sterling.

Distefano, Joseph J. Schaum's Outline Feedback & Control Systems. 1994. pap. text 38.95 incl. disk (*0-07-842709-6*) McGraw.

DiStefano, Joseph J. & Stubberud, Allen J. Schaum's Outline of Feedback & Control Systems. 2nd ed. LC 96-224787. (Schaum's Outline Ser.). 496p. 1994. pap. 15.95 (*0-07-017052-5*) McGraw.

DiStefano, Joseph J., et al. Schaum's Outline of Feedback & Control Systems. 2nd ed. 572p. (C). 1997. pap. 14.95 (*0-07-017047-9*) McGraw.

Distefano, Joseph K. & Searl, James A. Music & Materials for Analysis: An Anthology. 412p. (C). 1995. pap. text 34.95 (*1-880157-19-5*) Ardsley.

DiStefano, Lynne D., jt. auth. see Tausky, Nancy Z.

Distel, Anne. Renoir: A Sensuous Vision. Frankel, Lory, tr. (Discoveries Ser.). (Illus.). 176p. 1995. pap. 12.95 (*0-8109-2875-2*, Pub. by Abrams) Time Warner.

Distel, Anne & Stein, Susan A. Cezanne to Van Gogh: The Collection of Doctor Gacher. (Illus.). 336p. 1999. 70.00 (*0-8109-6538-0*, Pub. by Abrams) Time Warner.

Distel, Anne, et al. Cezanne to Van Gogh: The Collection of Doctor Gachet. LC 99-20464. 1999. write for info. (*0-87099-904-4*) Metro Mus Art.

— Gustave Calillebotte: Urban Impressionist. LC 94-34903. (Illus.). 374p. 1995. 75.00 (*0-7892-0041-4*) Abbeville Pr.

***Distel, R.** Graph Theory. 2nd ed. (Graduate Texts in Mathematics Ser.: Vol. 173). (Illus.). 315p. 2000. 69.95 (*0-387-95014-1*) Spr-Verlag.

Distelbarth, Paul H. Das Andere Frankreich. 537p. 1997. 33.95 (*3-906754-93-6*, Pub. by P Lang) P Lang Pubng.

Distelberger, Rudolf, jt. auth. see Leithe-Jasper, Manfred.

Dister, Alain. It's Only Rock & Roll. 1993. pap. text 21.95 (*2-86234-040-5*, Pub. by Marval) Dist Art Pubs.

— The Story of Rock: Smash Hits & Superstars. Ballas, Toula, tr. (Discoveries Ser.). (Illus.). 176p. 1993. pap. 12.95 (*0-8109-2831-0*, Pub. by Abrams) Time Warner.

Disterheft, Dorothy. The Syntactic Development of the Infinitive in Indo-European. 220p. (Orig.). 1980. pap. 22.95 (*0-89357-058-3*) Slavica.

Disterheft, Dorothy, ed. see Levin, P., et al.

Disterhoft, John F., et al, eds. Calcium Hyphothesis of Aging & Dementia. LC 94-41979. (Annals Ser.: No. 747). 1995. 130.00 (*0-89766-878-2*) NY Acad Sci.

DiStilio, Veronica, tr. see Plaut, Thomas F.

***Distlehorst, Linda H., et al.** Teaching & Learning in Medical Surgical Education: Lessons Learned for the 21st Century. LC 99-52564. 2000. write for info. (*0-8058-3542-3*) L Erlbaum Assocs.

Distler, A. & Molzahn, M., eds. Gesellschaft fuer Nephrologie 27th Scientific Meeting, September, Berlin 1996. (Journal: Kidney & Blood Pressure Research: Vol. 19, Nos. 3 & 4, 1996). (Illus.). 84p. 1996. pap. 44.50 (*3-8055-6377-9*) S Karger.

Distler, A., jt. ed. see Philip, T.

Distler, Betsy, ed. see Bernstein, Doris.

Distler, Jed. Jazz Masters: Art Tatum. 1981. pap. 14.95 (*0-8256-4085-7*, AM30719) Music Sales.

Distler, Paul A., ed. Drugs, Society, & the Law: Societal Aspects of the Drug Crisis. LC 93-29318. (President's Symposium Ser.: Vol. 3). 1993. 10.00 (*0-929900-07-3*) VPI St Univ Pr.

Distler, Paul A., jt. ed. see Wallace, Bruce.

Distravalo. Spanish Glossary for Lial Mathematics Books. 48p. (C). 1997. pap. text 25.00 (*0-321-01647-5*) Addson-Wesley Educ.

***Distribooks Inc. Staff.** Answer Key to A Practice Grammar of German. 1999. pap. text 12.95 (*3-88532-623-X*) Distribks Inc.

D

Distribooks, Inc. Staff. Asterix Bind-Ups: Asterix & Friends. (Asterix Ser.). (J). 1998. 29.95 (*0-340-72755-1*, Pub. by Hodder & Stought Ltd) Trafalgar.
— Il Brutto Anatroccolo. 1999. pap. text 7.95 (*88-8148-256-8*) Midwest European Pubns.
— Cappucceto Rossi. (SPA & ITA.). (ps up). 1999. pap. text 7.95 (*88-8148-254-1*) Midwest European Pubns.
***Distribooks Inc. Staff.** Computer Englisch. 1999. pap. 28.95 (*3-499-19804-5*) Midwest European Pubns.
Distribooks Inc. Staff. Diccionario Basico de la Lengua Espanola. 1999. pap. text 9.95 (*970-607-009-5*) Distribks Inc.
— Diccionario Basico Escolar. 1999. pap. text 9.95 (*970-607-011-7*) Larousse Eds.
— Diccionario Escolar. 1999. pap. text 9.95 (*970-607-010-9*) Distribks Inc.
— Diccionario Esencial de la Dengua Espanola. 1999. pap. text 9.95 (*970-607-425-2*) Distribks Inc.
— Diccionario Practico de Sinonimos. 1999. pap. text 8.95 (*970-607-020-6*) Larousse Eds.
— Diccionario Usual. 1999. pap. text 12.95 (*970-607-359-0*) Larousse Eds.
— Die Drei Kleinen Schweinchen. (Lesen Leicht Germacht Ser,). (GER.). (ps-3). 1999. pap. text 7.95 (*88-8148-245-2*) Midwest European Pubns.
Distribooks Inc., Staff. French For Everyday Life: Practical French For Use in Everyday Situations. 1999. pap. text 19.95 (*2-266-04739-6*) Hachette.
***Distribooks Inc. Staff.** Garzanti: Il Nuovo Dizionario Inglese. 1999. pap. text 49.95 (*88-11-50433-3*) Distribks Inc.
— German-English. 1999. 15.95 (*3-572-00771-2*) Midwest European Pubns.
Distribooks Inc. Staff. Gran Diccionario. 1999. 59.95 (*970-607-371-X*) Larousse Eds.
— Das Hassliche Entein. (Lesen Leicht Germacht Ser,). 1999. pap. text 7.95 (*88-8148-246-0*) Midwest European Pubns.
Distribooks, Inc. Staff. I Tre Porcellini. 1999. pap. text 7.95 (*88-8148-255-X*) Midwest European Pubns.
***Distribooks Inc. Staff.** Le Larousse Maxi-Debutants. (FRE., Illus.). 1999. 40.00 (*2-03-320159-7*, Larousse LKC) LKC.
— Melhoramentos Minidicionario De Sinonimos E Antonimos. 1999. pap. 18.95 (*85-06-01988-5*) Midwest European Pubns.
— Michaelis Tech: Dicionario Tecnico Multilingue; English, Portuguese, French, Italian, German & Spanish. 1999. 125.00 (*85-06-01990-7*) Midwest European Pubns.
***Distribooks Inc. Staff.** Pinocchio. 1999. pap. text 7.95 (*88-8148-258-4*) Midwest European Pubns.
Distribooks Inc. Staff. Pinocchio. (Lesen Leicht Germacht Ser,). (GER.). (ps up). 1999. pap. text 7.95 (*88-8148-248-7*) Midwest European Pubns.
Distribooks, Inc. Staff. Practice Grammar of German: English Language Edition Of The Famous Lehr- & Ubungsbuch Der Deutsc. 1999. pap. text 48.95 (*3-88532-630-2*) Distribks Inc.
Distribooks Inc. Staff. Rotkappchen. (Lesen Leicht Germacht Ser,). 1999. pap. text 7.95 (*88-8148-244-4*) Midwest European Pubns.
Distribooks, Inc. Staff. Il Topo Di Citta E Il Topo Di Campagna. 1999. pap. text 7.95 (*88-8148-257-6*) Midwest European Pubns.
Distribooks Incorporated, Staff. Hungarian with Ease. (HUN.). 1997. pap. text 59.95 incl. audio (*2-7005-1373-8*, Pub. by Assimil) Distribks Inc.
***Distribooks Incorporated, Staff.** Larousse Sinonimos y Antonimos. (SPA.). 1999. pap. 8.95 (*970-607-127-X*, Larousse LKC) LKC.
— Le Petit Robert Illustre des Noms Propres. (FRE., Illus.). 1999. 99.95 (*2-85036-413-4*) Robert.
Distribution Committee of Book Industry Study Grou. Shipping Container Code & Symbol Guidelines for the U. S. Book Industry. rev. ed. (Illus.). 22p. 1996. pap. 8.00 (*0-940016-58-3*) Bk Indus Study.
Distribution Media, jt. auth. see Paulsen, Gary.
Distribution Media, jt. auth. see Rylant, Cynthia.
Distribution Media Staff. CRP XMas Morris BOR1. 1986. pap. 17.27 (*0-676-31899-1*) Ballantine Pub Grp.
— Cra Br Brs Dentist. 1985. pap. 11.96 (*0-676-31512-7*) Ballantine Pub Grp.
Distribution Media Staff, jt. auth. see Wood, Audrey.
District of Columbia Bar. The District of Columbia Practice Manual, 2. 5th ed. LC 96-86557. 1996. write for info. (*0-944694-13-6*) DC Bar.
District of Columbia Bar Association Staff. The District of Columbia Practice Manual. LC 93-74794. 1994. ring bd. write for info. (*0-944694-09-8*) DC Bar.
District of Columbia Supreme Court Staff, et al. The United States vs. Charles J. Guiteau: Supreme Court Holding a Criminal Term No. 14056. 141.00 (*0-685-11341-8*) Ayer.
Dita, P., et al, eds. Gauge Theories: Fundamentals Interactions & Rigorous Results. (Progress in Physics Ser.: Vol. 5). 389p. 1982. 69.00 (*0-8176-3095-3*) Birkhauser.
DiTata, Mario, tr. from ITA. St. Leonard's Way of the Cross. (Illus.). 32p. 1998. pap. 2.95 (*0-87973-935-5*) Our Sunday Visitor.
***Ditch, John.** Introduction to Social Security: Policies, Benefits & Poverty. LC 99-26250. 272p. (C). 1999. text. write for info. (*0-415-21430-0*) Routledge.
Ditch, John. Introduction to Social Security: Policies, Benefits Poverty. LC 99-26250. 272p. 1999. pap. 27.99 (*0-415-21431-9*) Routledge.
Ditch, John, et al, eds. Comparative Social Assistance: Localisation & Discretion. LC 97-77553. 98p. 1998. text 59.95 (*1-84014-346-0*, Pub. by Ashgate Pub) Ashgate Pub Co.
Ditch, Walter. Getting the Most from Autocad LT. 256p. (gr. 13). 1996. pap. text 24.95 (*0-340-61421-8*) Chapman & Hall.
Ditch, Walter. Getting the Most from AutoCAD LT. 250p. 1997. pap. text 49.95 incl. disk (*0-470-24439-9*) Wiley.
Ditchburn, David, jt. ed. see Mackay, Angus.
Ditchburn, Elizabeth & Cenczyk, Mark. Stargazers: Tridebook. (Werewolf Ser.). (Illus.). (Orig.). 1997. pap. 10.00 (*1-56504-332-4*, 3061) White Wolf.
Ditchburn, Elizabeth & Grove, Heather. The Risen. (Wruith Ser.). (Illus.). 72p. (Orig.). (YA). 1996. pap., suppl. ed. 12.00 (*1-56504-663-3*, 6302) White Wolf.
Ditchburn, Elizabeth, jt. auth. see Dansky, Richard.
Ditchburn, R. W. Light. 692p. 1991. pap. 16.95 (*0-486-66667-0*) Dover.
Ditchburn, R. W., jt. auth. see Heavens, O. S.
Ditchey, Karen M. & Novak, Pamela K. Nutrition, Exercise & Weight Training Journal: A 12-Week Record. Ohnstad, Arik T., ed. (Illus.). 208p. 1997. ring bd. 9.95 (*0-9659908-0-X*) My Place Pub.
Ditchfield. Evangelical Revival. LC 98-178663. (Introductions to History Ser.). 1998. pap. 11.95 (*1-85728-481-X*, Pub. by UCL Pr Ltd) Taylor & Francis.
***Ditchfield, Christin.** Cycling. LC 99-28190. (True Bks.). (J). 2000. 21.50 (*0-516-21061-0*) Childrens.
— Cycling. (True Bks.). (Illus.). (YA). 2000. pap. 6.95 (*0-516-27024-9*) Childrens.
— Gymnastics LC 99-28208. (True Bks.). (J). 2000. 21.50 (*0-516-21063-7*) Childrens.
— Gymnastics. (True Bks.). (Illus.). (YA). 2000. pap. 6.95 (*0-516-27026-5*) Childrens.
— Kayaking, Canoeing, Rowing & Yachting. LC 99-28207. (True Bks.). (J). 2000. 21.50 (*0-516-21610-4*) Childrens.
— Kayaking, Canoeing, Rowing & Yachting. (True Bks.). (Illus.). (YA). 2000. pap. 6.95 (*0-516-27027-3*) Childrens.
— Martina Hingis. (Women Who Win Ser.). (Illus.). 2000. pap. 7.95 (*0-7910-6157-4*) Chelsea Hse.
— Martina Hingis. LC 00-22841. (Women Who Win Ser.). 2001. 17.95 (*0-7910-5797-6*) Chelsea Hse.
Ditchfield, Christin. Sports Great Michael Chang. LC 98-25712. (Sports Great Bks.). 64p. (J). (gr. 4-10). 1999. lib. bdg. 17.95 (*0-7660-1223-9*) Enslow Pubs.
***Ditchfield, Christin.** Swimming & Diving LC 99-28189. (True Bks.). (J). 2000. 21.50 (*0-516-21065-3*) Childrens.
— Swimming & Diving. (True Bks.). (Illus.). (J). 2000. pap. 6.95 (*0-516-27030-3*) Childrens.
— Top 10 American Women's Olympic Gold Medalists. LC 99-56060. (Sports Top 10 Ser.). (Illus.). 48p. (YA). (gr. 4-10). 2000. lib. bdg. 18.95 (*0-7660-1277-8*) Enslow Pubs.
— Wrestling LC 99-28191. (True Bks.). (J). 2000. 21.50 (*0-516-21611-2*) Childrens.
— Wrestling. (True Bks.). (Illus.). (YA). 2000. pap. 6.95 (*0-516-27033-8*) Childrens.
Ditchfield, G. M., et al, eds. British Parliamentary Lists, 1660-1800: A Register. 1995. 50.00 (*1-85285-131-7*) Hambledon Press.
Ditchfield, Michael & Bahr, Walter. Coaching Soccer the Progressive Way. (Illus.). 256p. (C). 1988. text 27.95 (*0-13-139262-X*, Parker Publishing Co); pap. text 15.95 (*0-13-139288-3*, Parker Publishing Co) P-H.
Ditchfield, P. H. Books Fatal to Their Authors. 1977. lib. bdg. 59.95 (*0-8490-1536-7*) Gordon Pr.
Ditchfield, Simon. Liturgy, Sanctity & History in Tridentine Italy: Pietro Maria Campi & the Preservation of the Particular. (Cambridge Studies in Italian History & Culture). (Illus.). 413p. (C). 1995. text 80.00 (*0-521-46220-7*) Cambridge U Pr.
Ditchoff, Pamela. The Mirror of Monsters & Prodigies. LC 95-18247. 250p. (Orig.). 1995. pap. 12.95 (*1-56689-035-7*) Coffee Hse.
Dite, Kurt & Salaquarda, Jorg. Nietzsche-Studien Gesamtregister der Bande 1-20. 504p. 1997. 124.00 (*3-11-013885-9*) De Gruyter.
***DiTerlizzi, Tony.** Jimmy Zangwow's Out-of-This-World Moon Pie Adventure. LC 98-16602. (Illus.). 40p. (J). 2000. per. 16.00 (*0-689-82215-4*) S&S Childrens.
Dith, Pran & Depaul, Kim. Children of Cambodia's Killing Fields: Memoirs of Survivors. LC 96-49804. (Yale Southeast Asia Studies Monograph Ser.). (Illus.). 224p. 1999. 27.00 (*0-300-06839-5*) Yale U Pr.
DiTiberio, John K. & Jensen, George H. Writing & Personality: Finding Your Voice, Your Style, Your Way. LC 94-24284. 248p. (Orig.). 1995. pap. 14.95 (*0-89106-071-5*, 7192, Davies-Black Pub) Consulting Psychol.
DiTiberio, John K., jt. auth. see Jensen, George H.
DiTillio, Larry. Isle of Darksmoke. (Illus.). 1984. 9.95 (*0-940244-56-X*) Flying Buffalo.
DiTillio, Larry, ed. Citybook 1: Butcher, Baker, Candlestick Maker. (Illus.). 1982. 14.95 (*0-940244-70-5*) Flying Buffalo.
Ditingo, Vincent M. The Remaking of Radio. (Illus.). 168p. 1994. pap. 32.95 (*0-240-80174-1*, Focal) Buttrwrth-Heinemann.
Ditka, Mike & Pierson, Don. Ditka: An Autobiography. LC 86-70706. (Illus.). 271p. 1986. 16.95 (*0-933893-07-8*); pap. 7.95 (*0-933893-38-8*) Bonus Books.
Ditkin, V. & Prudnikov, A. Integral Transforms & Operational Calculus. LC 63-10135. (International Series of Monographs on Pure & Applied Mathematics: Vol. 78). 1965. 237.00 (*0-08-010044-9*, Pub. by Pergamon Repr) Franklin.
— Operational Calculus in Two Variables & Its Applications. LC 62-9177. (International Series of Monographs on Pure & Applied Mathematics: Vol. 241). 1962. 85.00 (*0-08-009629-8*, Pub. by Pergamon Repr) Franklin.
Ditko, Steve. Steve Ditkos 80 Page Package, Vol. 2. Snyder, Robin, ed. (Package Ser.). (Illus.). 80p. 1999. pap. 9.00 (*0-9673173-1-2*) R Snyder & S Ditko.
Ditko, Steve, et al. Spider-Man: Unmasked. (Illus.). 64p. 1997. pap. 5.95 (*0-7851-0288-4*) Marvel Entrprs.
Ditko, Steve, jt. auth. see Lee, Stan.
Ditkoff, Beth Ann, jt. auth. see Lo Gerfo, Paul.
Ditlefsen, Charles E. Those Magnificent Trains: An American Anthology. rev. ed. (Illus.). 104p. 1997. pap. 17.95 (*1-55912-154-8*) CEDCO Pub.
Ditlev, Anders. Essential Volvo Amazon & P1800: The Cars & Their Stories 1956-73. (Illus.). 80p. 1996. pap. 15.95 (*1-870979-74-5*, Bay View Bks) MBI Pubg.
Ditlevsen, Ove & Madsen, Henrick O. Structural Reliability Methods. LC 95-19753. 384p. 1996. 190.00 (*0-471-96086-1*) Wiley.
Ditlevsen, Tove. Complete Freedom & Other Stories. Brondum, Jack, tr. LC 81-15124. 88p. 1982. pap. 9.95 (*0-915306-24-7*) Curbstone.
— Early Spring. Nunnally, Tiina, tr. from DAN. LC 85-2091. (Women in Translation Ser.). Orig. Title: Childhood & Youth. 227p. (Orig.). 1985. pap. 8.95 (*0-931188-28-8*) Seal Pr WA.
— The Faces. Nunnally, Tiina, tr. from DAN. LC 90-23402. 153p. (Orig.). 19.95 (*0-940242-12-5*) Fjord Pr.
— The Faces. Nunnally, Tiina, tr. from DAN. LC 90-23402. 153p. (Orig.). 1991. pap. 9.95 (*0-940242-11-7*) Fjord Pr.
Ditlow, Clarence, jt. auth. see Nader, Ralph.
***Ditman, Henry M.** The Ballad of Bird Hill. 80p. 2000. pap. 2.95 (*0-9700882-1-3*) Bird Hill Pr.
— Tales of a Country Rhymer. 80p. 1998. pap. 2.95 (*0-9700882-0-5*) Bird Hill Pr.
Ditmar, Mark F., jt. ed. see Polin, Richard A.
Ditmar, Raymond L. A Field Book of North American Snakes. 305p. 1985. pap. 175.00 (*0-7855-0355-2*, Pub. by Intl Bks & Periodicals) St Mut.
Ditmars, Elsa. California Traveler: A Traveler's Guide to California 's Beaches. (American Traveler Ser.: Vol. 32). 1994. pap. 4.95 (*1-55838-152-X*) R H Pub.
— California under Sail: A Guide to Beaches, Boat Trips, Maritime Museums, Islands & Coastal Adventures. LC 93-37047. (Under Sail Ser.). (Illus.). 112p. 1994. pap. 9.95 (*1-56626-042-6*, Cntry Rds Pr) NTC Contemp Pub Co.
Ditmars, Raymond L. Confessions of a Scientist. LC 75-121463. (Essay Index Reprint Ser.). 1977. 23.95 (*0-8369-1800-2*) Ayer.
Ditmer, Judith A. Basic Bowl Turning: With Judy Ditmer. Congdon-Martin, Douglas, ed. LC 94-65624. (Illus.). 64p. (Orig.). 1994. pap. 12.95 (*0-88740-627-0*) Schiffer.
— Turning Wooden Jewelry. Congdon-Martin, Douglas, ed. LC 94-65631. (Illus.). 64p. (Orig.). 1994. pap. 12.95 (*0-88740-611-4*) Schiffer.
Ditmore, Esteban, tr. see Sisson, Richard, et al.
Ditmore, Shirley, tr. see Neighbour, Ralph W., Jr.
DiTomaso, N., jt. auth. see Thompson, D. E.
DiTomasso, A., jt. ed. see Sih, G. C.
DiTommaso, Marie, jt. auth. see Larkin, Richard F.
DiTraglia, J. Fat Science: Basic Biology for Dieters. (Illus.). 125p. (C). 1999. write for info. (*0-306-46000-9*, Plenum Trade) Perseus Pubng.
DiTraglia, John. Fat Science: Basic Biology for a Nation of Dieters. 2nd ed. (Illus.). 105p. 1994. reprint ed. pap. 8.95 (*0-9634188-1-5*) College Pub.
Ditraglia, Robert M. Dead Hearts Don't Break. 207p. 1998. pap. 9.95 (*0-9655975-0-4*) Wynford Pr.
D'Itri, Frank M. Chemical Deicers & the Environment. 624p. 1992. lib. bdg. 95.00 (*0-87371-705-8*, L705) Lewis Pubs.
D'Itri, Frank M., ed. Wastewater Renovation & Reuse: Proceedings of the International Conference on the Renovation & Reuse of Wastewater Through Aquatic & Terrestrial Systems. LC 76-54588. (Pollution Engineering & Technology Ser.: Vol. 3). 736p. reprint ed. pap. 200.00 (*0-608-30353-4*, 205503600008) Bks Demand.
— Zebra Mussels & Aquatic Nuisance Species: Proceedings, International Zebra Mussel & Other Aquatic Nuisance Species Conference (6th, 1996, Dearborn, MI) 648p. 1997. boxed set 104.95 (*1-57504-036-0*) CRC Pr.
D'Itri, Frank M., jt. auth. see Belcher, H. W.
Ditripon, F. P., ed. Concordantiae Bibliorum Sacrorum Vulgatae Editionis ad Recognitionem Jussu Sixti V Pontif: Max. Bibliis Adhibitam Recensitae Atque Atque Plusquam Viginti Quinque Millibus Versiculis Auctae Insuper & Notis Histoticis Geographicis, Chronologicis Locupletatae. Cura & Studio. (LAT.). 1484p. 1986. reprint ed. 498.95 incl. 3.5 hd (*0-614-97983-8*) G Olms Pubs.
Ditsky, John. Critical Essays on Steinbeck's "The Grapes of Wrath" (Critical Essays on American Literature Ser.). 216p. 1989. 49.00 (*0-8161-8887-4*, G K Hall & Co) Mac Lib Ref.
***Ditsky, John.** John Steinbeck & the Critics. 170p. 2000. 59.00 (*1-57113-210-4*, Pub. by Camden Hse) Boydell & Brewer.
Ditsky, John. The Onstage Christ: Studies in the Persistence of a Theme. (Critical Studies). 188p. 1980. 44.00 (*0-389-20059-X*, N6829) B&N Imports.
Ditta, Joseph M. Natural & Conceptual Design: Radical Confusion in Critical Theory. LC 84-47541. (American University Studies: English Language & Literature: Ser. IV, Vol. 9). 202p. (C). 1984. text 30.00 (*0-8204-0119-6*) P Lang Pubng.
Dittberner-Jax, Norita. What They Always Were. LC 94-67067. (Minnesota Voices Project Ser.: Vol. 68). 76p. 1995. pap. 9.95 (*0-89823-160-4*) New Rivers Pr.
Dittberner-Jax, Norita, ed. The Ragged Heart. (Illus.). 164p. (Orig.). (J). 1989. pap. 8.00 (*0-927663-14-7*) COMPAS.
Dittborn, Eugenio, et al. Remota: Airmail Paintings. (ENG & SPA., Illus.). 1997. mass mkt. 37.95 (*0-614-25987-8*) New Mus Contemp Art.
Dittemore, Margaret R. & Hay, Fred, eds. Documenting Cultural Diversity in the Resurgent American South: Collectors, Collecting, & Collections. LC 97-3357. (Illus.). 128p. 1997. pap. 21.00 (*0-8389-7897-5*) Assn Coll & Res Libs.
Dittenberger, W. Inscriptiones Megaridis Oropiae Boeotiae. (Inscriptiones Graecae Ser.: Vol. VII). (GRE & LAT., Illus.). vi, 806p. (C). 1991. text 100.00 (*0-89005-525-4*) Ares.
Dittenberger, Wilhelm. Orientis Graeci Inscriptiones Selectae, 2 vols., Set. (GER.). x, 1408p. 1986. reprint ed. write for info. (*3-487-00030-X*) G Olms Pubs.
***Dittenberger, Wilhelm.** Sylloge Inscriptionum Graecarum, 4 vols., set. 3rd ed. 2447p. 1999. reprint ed. 250.00 (*0-89005-580-7*) Ares.
Dittenberger, Wilhelm. Sylloge Inscriptionum Graecarum, 4 vols., Set. (GER.). 2512p. 1960. reprint ed. write for info. (*0-318-70443-9*) G Olms Pubs.
***Dittenberger, Wilhelm, ed.** Orientis Graeci Inscriptiones Selectae, 2 vols.; set. 1408p. 2000. reprint ed. 150.00 (*0-89005-587-4*) Ares.
Dittenberger, Wilhelm, ed. Sylloge Inscriptionum Graecarum (Syll. 3) 1982. reprint ed. write for info. (*3-487-00023-7*) G Olms Pubs.
Dittenhaver, Sarah L., et al. Tune Time, 2 pts., Pt. A. rev. ed. Goss, Louise, ed. (Frances Clark Library for Piano Students). 48p. (J). (gr. k-6). 1973. pap. text 6.95 (*0-87487-194-8*) Summy-Birchard.
— Tune Time, 2 pts., Pt. B. rev. ed. Goss, Louise, ed. (Frances Clark Library for Piano Students). 48p. (J). (gr. k-6). 1973. pap. text 6.95 (*0-87487-195-6*) Summy-Birchard.
Dittenhofer, M., jt. auth. see Sawyer, Lawrence B.
Dittenhofer, Mortimer, jt. auth. see Brink, Victor Z.
Dittenhofer, Mortimer A. Applying Government Accounting Principles. 1990. ring bd. 175.00 (*0-8205-1680-5*, 680) Bender.
— Applying Government Auditing Standards. 1990. ring bd. 155.00 (*0-8205-1853-0*, 853) Bender.
— A Study of Legislation & Regulation of Internal Auditing in Selected Governments. LC 88-1126. (McQueen Accounting Monographs: Vol. 4). xvii, 67p. (Orig.). 1988. pap. text 10.00 (*0-935951-03-2*) U AR Acc Dept.
Dittenhofer, Mortimer A. & Sennetti, J. T. Ethics & the Internal Auditor: Ten Years Later. Campbell, Lee A., ed. LC 96-104111. 69p. 1995. pap. text 25.00 (*0-89413-330-6*, A894) Inst Inter Aud.
Ditteon, Richard. Modern Geometrical Optics. (C). 1997. text. write for info. (*0-201-54836-4*) Addison-Wesley.
— Modern Geometrical Optics. LC 97-24252. 439p. 1997. 79.95 (*0-471-16922-6*, Wiley-Interscience) Wiley.
Ditter, Bob. In the Trenches: Answers from the Expert to the Toughest Questions You Face. LC 96-49401. 208p. (Orig.). 1998. pap. 27.95 (*0-87603-154-8*, LT51) Am Camping.
***Ditter-Stolz, Edeltrud.** Zeitgenossische Musik Nach 1945 Im Dusikunterricht der Sekundarstufe. (GER., Illus.). xvi, 418p. 1999. 57.00 (*3-631-34132-6*) P Lang Pubng.
Dittersdorf, Karl D. Von, see Von Dittersdorf, Karl D.
Dittes, James E. Driven by Hope: Men & Meaning. LC 96-16037. 158p. 1996. pap. 16.00 (*0-664-25677-5*) Westminster John Knox.
— Men at Work: Life Beyond the Office. LC 96-21398. 120p. (Orig.). 1996. pap. 14.95 (*0-664-25481-0*) Westminster John Knox.
— Pastoral Counseling: The Basics. LC 98-33352. 184p. 1999. pap. 16.00 (*0-664-25738-0*) Westminster John Knox.
— Re-Calling Ministry. LC 99-38565. 192p. 1999. pap. 19.99 (*0-8272-3217-9*) Chalice Pr.
Dittes, James E., jt. auth. see Capps, Donald.
***Dittfurth, David.** The Concepts & Methods of Federal Civil Procedure. LC 99-65177. 296p. 1999. pap. text 20.00 (*0-89089-738-7*) Carolina Acad Pr.
Dittgen, Herbert, jt. ed. see Minkenberg, Michael.
Dittimus, Evelyn. You Are My Stronghold: Psalm 91. 98p. (Orig.). 1997. pap. 9.95 (*1-56550-030-X*) Vis Bks Intl.
Dittl, Barbara & Mallmann, Joanne. From Plain to Fancy: Story of Yellowstone's Lake Hotel. 32p. 1987. pap. 4.95 (*0-911797-31-9*) Roberts Rinehart.
Dittman. Heat & Thermodynamics. 7th ed. 1997. 15.31 (*0-07-017060-6*) McGraw.
— Physics in Everyday Life. 1979. teacher ed. 26.87 (*0-07-017057-6*) McGraw.
Dittman, Richard & Schmieg, Glenn. Physics in Everyday Life. Rogers, Janice L. & Zappa, C. Robert, eds. LC 78-13381. (Schaum's Outline Ser.). (Illus.). 512p. (C). 1979. 40.63 (*0-07-017056-8*) McGraw.
Dittman, Richard, jt. auth. see Zemansky, Mark W.
***Dittmann, Helena & Hardy, Jane.** Learn Library of Congress Classification. LC 99-42766. (Illus.). 176p. 1999. pap. 29.50 (*0-8108-3696-3*) Scarecrow.
Dittmann, Laura L. & Ramsey, Marjorie E., eds. Their Future Is Now: Today Is for Children. LC 82-22716. (Illus.). 48p. 1982. pap. 6.25 (*0-87173-102-9*) ACEI.
***Dittmann, Lee.** 100 Spring Wildflowers of Henry W. Coe State Park, California. (Illus.). 48p. 2000. pap. 4.75 (*0-9675548-1-0*) budda-nature.
Dittmann, Mariam, jt. auth. see Shaw, J. Scott.
Dittmann, Reidar. Eros & Psyche: Strindberg & Munch in the 1890s. Foster, Stephen, ed. LC 82-4923. (Studies in the Fine Arts: The Avant-Garde: No. 27). 231p. reprint ed. pap. 71.70 (*0-8357-1319-9*, 207020500064) Bks Demand.
***Dittmann, Sabine.** The Wadden Sea Ecosystem: Stability Properties & Mechanisms. LC 99-34031. (Illus.). xii, 309p. 1999. 102.00 (*3-540-65532-8*) Spr-Verlag.

An Asterisk (*) at the beginning of an entry indicates that the title is appearing for the first time.

***Dittmar, Friedrich W. & Wellmann, Jutta.** Enzyme Therapy Basics: Powerful Remedies for Women. LC 99-37531. 160p. 2000. pap. 14.95 (*0-8069-2031-9*) Sterling.

Dittmar, Heinrich. Aischines von Sphettos: Studien zur Literaturgeschichte der Sokratiker. LC 75-13262. (History of Ideas in Ancient Greece Ser.). (GER.). 1976. reprint ed. 23.95 (*0-405-07304-6*) Ayer.

Dittmar, Joseph J. Baseball Records Registry: The Best & Worst Single-Day Performances & the Stories Behind Them. LC 97-1472. (Illus.). 692p. 1997. 55.00 (*0-7864-0293-8*) McFarland & Co.

***Dittmar, Joseph J.** The 100 Greatest Baseball Games of the 20th Century Ranked. (Illus.). 263p. 2000. per. 30.00 (*0-7864-0915-0*) McFarland & Co.

Dittmar, Linda & Michaud, Gene, eds. From Hanoi to Hollywood: The Vietnam War in American Film. LC 90-32548. (Illus.). 400p. (Orig.). (C). 1990. pap. 19.95 (*0-8135-1587-4*) Rutgers U Pr.

Dittmar, Mark. Jumbo Art Yearbook: Grade 3 & 4. (Jumbo Art Ser.). 96p. (gr. 3-4). 1981. student ed. 18.00 (*0-8209-0046-X*, JAY-34) ESP.

— Jumbo Art Yearbook: Grade 5 & 6. (Jumbo Art Ser.). 96p. (gr. 5-6). 1981. student ed. 18.00 (*0-8209-0047-8*, JAY-56) ESP.

— Jumbo Art Yearbook: Grade 7 & 8. (Jumbo Art Ser.). 96p. (gr. 7-8). 1982. student ed. 18.00 (*0-8209-0048-6*, JAY-78) ESP.

Dittmar, N., jt. auth. see Klein, W.

Dittmar, Norbert, et al, eds. Sociolinguistics - Soziolinguistik: An International Handbook of the Science of Language & Society - Ein Internationales Handbuch zur Wissenschaft von Sprache und Gesellschaft. (Handbooks of Linguistics & Communication Science: Vol. 3/2). (GER.). xix, 1058p. 1988. lib. bdg. 534.65 (*3-11-011645-6*) De Gruyter.

Dittmar, Norbert & Penner, Zvi, eds. Issues in the Theory of Language Acquisition: Essays in Honor of Jurgen Weissenborn. LC 97-39296. XXIII, 245p. (C). 1998. text 49.95 (*0-8204-3417-5*) P Lang Pubng.

Dittmar, Norbert & Reich, Astrid, eds. Modality in Language Acquisition (Modalite et Acquisition des Langues) LC 93-45800. (Sociolinguistics & Language Contact Ser.: Band 6). (ENG & FRE.). xxiv, 382p. (C). 1993. lib. bdg. 145.00 (*3-11-012378-9*) De Gruyter.

Dittmar, Norbert & Rost-Roth, Martina. Deutsch Als Zweit - und Fremdsprache: Methoden und Perspektiven Einer Akademischen Disziplin 2., Durchgesehene Auflage. 2nd ed. (GER.). 316p. 1997. 57.95 (*3-631-31759-X*) P Lang Pubng.

Dittmar, Norbert & Schlobinski, Peter, eds. The Sociolinguistics of Urban Vernaculars: Case Studies & Their Evaluation. (Sociolinguistics & Language Contact Ser.: Vol. 1). 276p. (C). 1988. lib. bdg. 125.95 (*3-11-010534-9*) De Gruyter.

Dittmar, P. Woerterbuch der Chinesischen Revolution. (GER.). 224p. 1975. pap. 5.95 (*0-686-56644-0*) Fr & Eur.

Dittmar, Sharon & Gresham, Glen. Functional Assessment & Outcome Measures for the Rehabilitation Health Professional. LC 97-7201. 224p. 1997. 51.00 (*0-8342-0929-2*, 20929) Aspen Pub.

Dittmer. Food & Beverage Labor Cost Control. 1999. text 57.50 (*0-471-31783-7*) Wiley.

— Food Beverage Labor. 5th import ed. 1993. pap. text. write for info. (*0-471-29052-1*) Wiley.

— Food Beverage Labor. 6th import ed. pap. text. write for info. (*0-471-29324-5*) Wiley.

***Dittmer.** Food Beverage Labor Cost 6th ed. 256p. 1999. pap. 29.95 (*0-471-36928-4*) Wiley.

Dittmer. Keeping the Faith: God's Truth Today. LC 97-197613. 1997. pap. text 8.99 (*0-570-01548-0*, 22-2435) Concordia.

***Dittmer.** Principles of Food & Beverage Labor Cost: Set of Text & Workbook. 5th ed. 1999. 63.95 (*0-471-35979-3*) Wiley.

Dittmer. Principles of Food, Beverage & Labor Cost. 5th ed. (C). 1994. pap. text, wbk. ed. 22.95 (*0-442-01827-4*, VNR) Wiley.

***Dittmer, Allan.** The Power of Ideas: The University of Louisville Grawemeyer Awards in Music, Education, Religion & World Order. LC 99-58106. 1999. write for info. (*0-945084-78-1*) J Stuart Found.

Dittmer, Allan, jt. ed. see Rentel, Victor M.

Dittmer, Grace H. To Tell the Story: Mission Stories from the Alaska Territory. LC 98-67414. 183 P. ;p. 1998. write for info. (*1-878422-40-5*) Moravian Ch in Amer.

Dittmer, Howard J. Phylogeny & Form in the Plant Kingdom. (Illus.). 1974. reprint ed. text 17.50 (*0-88275-167-0*) Lubrecht & Cramer.

Dittmer, Howard J., ed. see Coulter, Merle C.

Dittmer, Ingeborg. Das Lebenuad Wirken Von James Marion Sims. (De Medicinae Rebus Ser.: Vol. 2). (GER.). 120p. 1983. 17.00 (*0-931902-36-3*) Inst Mediaeval Mus.

Dittmer, John. Black Georgia in the Progressive Era, 1900-1920. LC 77-24249. (Blacks in the New World Ser.). 251p. 1977. pap. text 14.95 (*0-252-00813-8*) U of Ill Pr.

— Black Georgia in the Progressive Era, 1900-1920. LC 77-24249. (Blacks in the New World Ser.). 251p. reprint ed. pap. 77.90 (*0-8357-6042-1*, 203443000090) Bks Demand.

— Local People: The Struggle for Civil Rights in Mississippi. LC 93-39632. (Blacks in the New World Ser.). (Illus.). 560p. 1994. 29.95 (*0-252-02102-9*) U of Ill Pr.

— Local People: The Struggle for Civil Rights in Mississippi. (Blacks in the New World Ser.). (Illus.). 560p. (C). 1995. pap. text 16.95 (*0-252-06507-7*) U of Ill Pr.

Dittmer, Kalogreant S. Etude d'une Methode Non-Invasive d'Enregistrement des Potentiels Hisiens et Pre-P. (De Medicinae Rebus Ser.: Vol. 1). (ENG, FRE, GER & LAT.). 160p. 1983. pap. 17.00 (*0-912024-19-4*) Inst Mediaeval Mus.

Dittmer, Lorraine S. Jane Long's Brazoria Inn, an Early Texas Cookbook: An Early Texas Cookbook. 2nd ed. (Illus.). 112p. reprint ed. 9.95 (*1-880384-02-7*) Coldwater Pr.

Dittmer, Lowell. China's Continuous Revolution: The Postliberation Epoch, 1949-1981. 1987. pap. 16.95 (*0-520-06599-9*, Pub. by U CA Pr) Cal Prin Full Svc.

— Liu Shaoqi & the Chinese Cultural Revolution. rev. ed. LC 97-41292. 400p. (YA). 1998. text 76.95 (*1-56324-951-0*, East Gate Bk) M E Sharpe.

— Liu Shaoqi & the Chinese Cultural Revolution. rev. ed. LC 97-41292. (Illus.). 400p. (C). (gr. 13). 1998. pap. text 25.95 (*1-56324-952-9*, East Gate Bk) M E Sharpe.

— Sino-Soviet Normalization & Its International Implications. LC 91-15770. (Jackson School Publications in International Studies). 352p. 1992. text 35.00 (*0-295-97118-5*) U of Wash Pr.

Dittmer, Lowell, et al, eds. Informal Politics in East Asia. LC 99-40245. 352p. (C). 2000. 59.95 (*0-521-64232-9*) Cambridge U Pr.

— Informal Politics in East Asia. LC 99-40245. 352p. (C). 2000. pap. 19.95 (*0-521-64538-7*) Cambridge U Pr.

Dittmer, Lowell & Kim, Samuel S., eds. China's Quest for National Identity. LC 92-27284. 320p. 1993. text 47.50 (*0-8014-2785-1*); pap. text 17.95 (*0-8014-8064-7*) Cornell U Pr.

Dittmer, Lowell & Ruoxi, Chen. Ethics & Rhetoric of the Chinese Cultural Revolution. LC 81-82595. (Current Chinese Language Project Ser.: No. 19). 127p. 1981. pap. text 4.00 (*0-912966-47-5*) IEAS.

Dittmer, Luther, ed. Firenze, Pluteo Twenty-Nine, One, Pt. 1. (Veroffentlichungen Mittelalterlicher Musikhandschriften - Publications of Mediaeval Musical Manuscripts Ser.: Vols. 10 & 11). (ENG & GER.). 250p. 1983. 94.00 (*0-912024-10-0*) Inst Mediaeval Mus.

— Firenze, Pluteo Twenty-Nine, One, Pt. 2. (Veroffentlichungen Mittelalterlicher Musikhandschriften - Publications of Mediaeval Musical Manuscripts Ser.: Vols. 10 & 11). (ENG & GER.). 250p. 1983. lib. bdg. 94.00 (*0-912024-11-9*) Inst Mediaeval Mus.

— Oxford Latin Liturgical D 20. (Veroffentlichungen Mittelalterlicher Musikhandschriften - Publications of Mediaeval Musical Manuscripts Ser.: Vol. 6). (ENG & GER.). 1961. pap. 32.00 (*0-912024-06-2*) Inst Mediaeval Mus.

— Paris, Nouv. Acg. Frc. 13531. (Veroffentlichungen Mittelalterlicher Musikhandschriften - Publications of Mediaeval Musical Manuscripts Ser.: Vol. 4). (ENG & GER.). 1961. pap. 20.00 (*0-912024-04-6*) Inst Mediaeval Mus.

— Robert De Handlo. (Musical Theorists in Translation Ser.: Vol. 2). 1961. pap. 19.00 (*0-912024-22-4*) Inst Mediaeval Mus.

— Worcester, Add. 68. (Veroffentlichungen Mittelalterlicher Musikhandschriften - Publications of Mediaeval Musical Manuscripts Ser.: Vol. 4). (ENG & GER.). 1961. pap. 24.00 (*0-912024-05-4*) Inst Mediaeval Mus.

Dittmer, Luther, jt. ed. see Anderson, Gordon A.

Dittmer, Luther, ed. see Goudimel.

Dittmer, Luther, ed. see Ludwig, Friedrich.

Dittmer, Luther A. Die Ludendorff Brucke in Remagen am 7, Merz 1945 - Im Lichte Bekannter und Neuer Ameinkanischer Quellen. (De Medicinae Rebus Ser.: No. 3). (GER & ENG.). 1996. pap. 8.00 (*0-931902-35-5*) Inst Mediaeval Mus.

Dittmer, Mary-Jane, ed. see Phillipps, Calvin C. & McFadden, David A.

Dittmer, Paul R. Accounting Practices for Hotels, Motels, & Restaurants. LC 79-142507. 1971. wbk. ed. write for info. (*0-672-96063-X*); text. write for info. (*0-672-96062-1*) Macmillan.

— Principles of Food, Beverage & Labor Cost Controls. 5th ed. 562p. 1993. text 48.95 (*0-442-01601-8*, VNR) Wiley.

Dittmer, Paul R. & Griffin, Gerald G. Dimensions of the Hospitality Industry: A College Introduction. LC 92-17463. 1993. text 48.95 (*0-442-00770-1*, VNR) Wiley.

Dittmer, Paul R. & Griffin, Gerald G. Dimensions of the Hospitality Industry: An Introduction. 272p. 1993. pap., wbk. ed. 27.50 (*0-471-29388-1*) Wiley.

— Dimensions of the Hospitality Industry: An Introduction. 2nd ed. 592p. 1997. 59.95 (*0-471-28711-3*, VNR) Wiley.

Dittmer, Paul R. & Griffin, Gerald G. Dimensions of the Hospitality Industry: An Introduction. 2nd ed. LC 96-14906. (Hospitality, Travel & Tourism Ser.). (Illus.). 573p. 1997. 49.95 (*0-442-02082-1*, VNR) Wiley.

***Dittmer, Paul R. & Griffin, Gerald G.** Principles of Food, Beverage, & Labor Cost Controls. 6th ed. LC 98-31455. 592p. 1999. 54.95 (*0-471-29325-3*) Wiley.

— Principles of Food, Beverage & Labor Cost Controls: For Hotels & Restaurants. 1999. wbk. ed. 76.50 (*0-471-37844-5*) Wiley.

Dittmer, Paul R. & Griffin, Gerald G. Principles of Food, Beverage, & Labor Cost Controls for Hotels & Restaurants. 5th ed. 576p. 1993. text 49.95 (*0-471-28577-3*, VNR) Wiley.

Dittmer, Terry K. Youth Ministry Sketchbook: 130 Practical Ideas for Ministry. LC 96-135514. 1995. 12.99 (*0-570-04827-3*, 12-3269) Concordia.

Dittmerp. Principles of Food, Beverage & Lab. 4th ed. (Hospitality, Travel & Tourism Ser.). 1989. teacher ed. 20.95 (*0-442-23433-3*, VNR) Wiley.

Dittmore. Matrix With Linear Programming. (C). 1997. pap. 13.00 (*0-06-501266-6*) Addson-Wesley Educ.

Ditto, Christopher. Webmaster Answers! Certified Tech Support. LC 98-127833. 1998. pap. text 24.99 (*0-07-882459-1*) Osborne-McGraw.

Ditto, Jerry, et al. Eichler Homes: Design for Living. LC 94-41851. (Illus.). 120p. 1995. 29.95 (*0-8118-0846-7*) Chronicle Bks.

Ditto, Laura, ed. see Gosselin, Kim.

Ditto, Tanya. English Springer Spaniels. (Complete Pet Owner's Manual Ser.). 64p. 1994. pap. 6.95 (*0-8120-1778-1*) Barron.

— The Longest Street: A History of Lafourche Parish & GrandIsle. Woolfolk, Doug, ed. (Illus.). 136p. 1980. 13.00 (*0-86518-013-X*) Moran Pub Corp.

Ditto, Tanya B. Dalmations: A Complete Pet Owners Manual. (Barron's Pet Owner's Manuals Ser.). (Illus.). 64p. 1991. pap. 6.95 (*0-8120-4605-6*) Barron.

— The Shar-Pei. (Complete Pet Owner's Manual Ser.). (Illus.). 64p. 1992. pap. 6.95 (*0-8120-4834-2*) Barron.

Ditto, W., et al, eds. Experimental Chaos: Proceedings of the 2nd Conference. 380p. 1995. text 109.00 (*981-02-1746-3*) World Scientific Pub.

Dittoe. Civil Litigation - PA Pocket Part. 2nd ed. (LQ-Paralegal Ser.). 56p. 1996. pap. text 14.95 (*0-8273-7577-8*) Delmar.

Dittoe, Marilyn. Pieces of Mind: Fragmented Commentary on Domestic Blisters & Living Laughably Ever After. LC 98-30175. 176p. 1998. pap. 12.95 (*1-888683-77-5*) Wooster Bk.

Dittoe, Thomas A. Pennsylvania Student Pocket Part to Accompany Civil Litigation for the Paralegal. 1993. 9.95 (*0-8273-5936-5*) Delmar.

Ditton, Jason & Ford, Roslyn. The Reality of Probation: A Formal Ethnography of Process & Practice. 116p. 1994. 61.95 (*1-85628-858-7*, Pub. by Avebry) Ashgate Pub Co.

Ditton, Jason & Hammersley, Richard. A Very Greedy Drug: Cocaine in Context. 150p. 1996. pap. text 18.00 (*3-7186-5904-2*, Harwood Acad Pubs) Gordon & Breach.

— A Very Greedy Drug: Cocaine in Context. 160p. 1996. text 23.00 (*3-7186-5903-4*, Harwood Acad Pubs) Gordon & Breach.

Ditton, Richard P., et al. Yosemite Road Guide. (Illus.). 84p. 1981. reprint ed. pap. 3.50 (*0-939666-24-3*) Yosemite Assn.

Dittrich, Christoph. Die Vortridentinische Katholische Kontroverstheologie und die Taufer: Cochlaus - Eck - Fabr.. (Europaische Hochschulschriften Ser.: Reihe 3, Bd. 473). (GER., Illus.). VII, 457p. 1991. 67.80 (*3-631-43640-8*) P Lang Pubng.

Dittrich, Echard J., et al, eds. Industrial Transformation in Europe: Process & Contexts. 272p. 1995. 69.95 (*0-8039-7488-4*) Sage.

Dittrich, H., jt. ed. see Briege, M.

Dittrich, J., et al, eds. Mathematical Results in Quantum Mechanics: Qmath 7th Conference, Prague, June 22-26, 1998. LC 99-20181. (Operator Theory Ser.). 408p. 1999. 125.00 (*3-7643-6097-6*) Birkhauser.

Dittrich, J. & Exner, P., eds. Rigorous Results in Quantum Dynamics. 344p. (C). 1991. text 110.00 (*981-02-0561-9*) World Scientific Pub.

***Dittrich, Jaroslav, et al.** Mathematical Results in Quantum Mechanics: Qmath7 Conference, Prague, June 22-26, 1998. LC 99-20181. (Operator Theory, Advances & Applications Ser.). x, 393p. 1999. 125.00 (*0-8176-6097-6*) Birkhauser.

Dittrich, John E. The General Manager & Strategy Formulation: Objectives, Missions, Strategies, Policies. LC 87-29523. 794p. 1988. reprint ed. pap. 200.00 (*0-7837-2831-X*, 205764100006) Bks Demand.

Dittrich, K. R., ed. Advances in Object-Oriented Database Systems. (Lecture Notes in Computer Science Ser.: Vol. 334). vii, 373p. 1989. 42.00 (*0-387-50345-5*, 2310) Spr-Verlag.

Dittrich, K. R., et al, eds. On Object-Oriented Database Systems. (Topics in Information Systems Ser.). (Illus.). x, 422p. 1991. 71.95 (*0-387-53496-2*) Spr-Verlag.

***Dittrich, Klaus R.** Component Database Systems. 2000. 49.95 (*1-55860-642-4*) Morgan Kaufmann.

Dittrich, W. & Reuter, M. Advanced Classical & Quantum Dynamics: From Classical Paths to Path Integrals. 368p. 1992. pap. text 39.00 (*0-387-51992-0*) Spr-Verlag.

— Classical & Quantum Dynamics: From Classical Paths to Path Integrals. enl. ed. 361p. 1996. pap. 39.00 (*3-540-56245-1*) Spr-Verlag.

— Classical & Quantum Dynamics: From Classical Paths to Path Integrals. 2nd enl. ed. (Illus.). ix, 361p. 1996. 39.00 (*0-387-56245-1*) Spr-Verlag.

— Effective Lagrangians in Quantum Electrodynamics. (Lecture Notes in Physics Ser.: Vol. 220). v, 244p. 1985. 28.95 (*0-387-15182-6*) Spr-Verlag.

***Dittrich, Walter & Gies, Holger.** Probing the Quantum Vacuum: Pertubative Effective Action Aproach in Quantum Electrodynamics & Its Applications. LC 00-30078. (Tracts in Modern Physics Ser.). (Illus.). 2000. write for info. (*3-540-67428-4*) Spr-Verlag.

Dittrich, Wilhelm. Englische Ubungsstoffe Zum Nacherzahlen. (GER.). 84p. 1969. 5.80 (*3-296-50300-5*, Pub. by Weidmann) Lubrecht & Cramer.

— Franzosische Ubungsstoffe Zum Nacherzahlen. (GER.). 80p. 1962. 5.80 (*3-296-60100-7*, Pub. by Weidmann) Lubrecht & Cramer.

— 33 Short Stories. 134p. 1963. 9.80 (*3-296-50800-7*, Pub. by Weidmann) Lubrecht & Cramer.

— Ubungen Zu Den Wichtigsten Kapiteln der Englischen Grammatik: Gross-Und Kleinschreibung. (GER.). 32p. 1968. 5.90 (*3-296-50401-X*, Pub. by Weidmann) Lubrecht & Cramer.

Dittrich, Wilhelm S. Ubungssatze zur Einpragung der Franzosischen Unregelmabigen Verban Teil 1: Deutscher Text. (GER.). 34p. 1959. 3.90 (*3-296-60201-1* Pub. by Weidmann) Lubrecht & Cramer.

— Ubungssatze zur Einpragung der Franzosischen Unregelmabigen Verban Teil 2: Franzosischer Text. (GER.). 26p. 1967. 3.90 (*3-296-60202-X*, Pub. by Weidmann) Lubrecht & Cramer.

Dittrich, Yvonne. Computeranwendungen und Sprachlicher Kontext: Zu Den Wechselwirkungen Zwischen Normaler und Formaler Sprache Bei Einsatz und Entwicklung Von Software. (Europaische Hochschulschriften, Reihe 41 Ser.: No. 27). (GER., Illus.). 266p. 1997. 51.95 (*3-631-32024-8*) P Lang Pubng.

Ditts, Russell & Fakih, Mansour. Community Newspapers. (Technical Notes Ser.: Vol. 27). 19p. (Orig.). 1989. pap. 2.00 (*0-932288-80-4*) Ctr Intl Ed U of MA.

Dittus, Janet, jt. auth. see Wibking, Ben.

Dittus, P., jt. auth. see Jaccard, J.

Dituri, Frank. Jubilos. (ENG & SPA., Illus.). 108p. 1982. 14.00 (*0-910463-01-8*) Edit Heliodor.

— Mossa. (Illus.). 70p. (Orig.). 1985. pap. text. write for info. (*0-318-68760-7*) Edit Heliodor.

Dituri, Frank, ed. Beautifully Old. (Illus.). 72p. (Orig.). 1984. pap. text. write for info. (*0-910463-04-2*) Edit Heliodor.

Ditz. Shipwrecked. 1993. 34.95 (*0-226-15381-9*) U Ch Pr.

Ditz, Daryl, et al, eds. Green Ledgers: Case Studies in Corporate Environmental Accounting. LC 95-18773. 120p. 1995. 25.00 (*1-56973-032-6*) World Resources Inst.

Ditz, Daryl & Ranganathan, Janet. Measuring Up: Toward a Common Framework for Tracking Corporate Environmental Performance. LC 97-80030. 48p. 1997. pap. 20.00 (*1-56973-225-6*) World Resources Inst.

Ditz, Hans P., jt. auth. see Westarp, Martin E.

Ditz, Toby L. Property & Kinship: Inheritance in Early Connecticut, 1750-1820. LC 86-5051. 230p. 1986. reprint ed. pap. 71.30 (*0-608-03297-2*, 206381500007) Bks Demand.

***Ditz, Uwe, photos by.** Redheads. (Illus.). 112p. 2000. 39.95 (*3-908163-17-X*, Pub. by Edit Stemmle) Abbeville Pr.

Ditzel, J., ed. see Conference on Microcirculation, 6th, Aalborg, 1970.

Ditzel, J., ed. see Conference on Microcirculation, 6th European, Aalb.

Ditzel, J., ed. see European Conference on Microcirculation Staff.

Ditzel, Paul. Fire Alarm! The Fascinating Story Behind the Red Box on the Corner. (Fire Service History Ser.). (Illus.). 168p. 1990. 24.95 (*0-925165-02-6*) Fire Buff Hse.

— Firefighting During World War II. (Illus.). 200p. (Orig.). 1994. pap. 9.95 (*0-925165-16-6*) Fire Buff Hse.

— Los Angeles Fire Department: A Century of Service. (Fire Service History Ser.). (Illus.). 263p. (Orig.). 1988. pap. 39.95 (*0-925165-21-2*) Fire Buff Hse.

— Quantrill: The Wildest Killer of the Civil War & Other Stories. (True Adventure Stories from the Civil War Ser.). (Illus.). 112p. (Orig.). 1991. pap. 9.95 (*0-925165-06-9*) Fire Buff Hse.

— The Ruthless Exploits of Admiral John Winslow: Naval Hero of the Civil War. (True Adventure Stories from the Civil War Ser.). (Illus.). 112p. (Orig.). 1991. pap. 9.95 (*0-925165-05-0*) Fire Buff Hse.

***Ditzel, Resi J.** Great Beginnings: Creating a Literacy-Rich Kindergarten Program. LC 00-36560. 2000. write for info. (*1-57110-322-8*) Stenhse Pubs.

Ditzel, Resi J. Rainbow Readers, 8 vols., Set 1. (Illus.). (Orig.). 1992. pap. 9.95 (*1-880188-17-1*) Bess Pr.

— Rainbow Readers, 8 vols., Set 2. (Illus.). (Orig.). 1993. pap. 9.95 (*1-880188-41-4*) Bess Pr.

Ditzen, Eleanor D. Born with a Golden Spoon: Memoirs of a Capital Lady. LC 96-50353. (Illus.). 416p. 1997. write for info. (*1-56833-096-0*) Madison Bks UPA.

Ditzenberger. Selling: Helping Customers Buy. 2nd ed. (SB - Marketing Education Ser.). 1986. 3.95 (*0-538-19203-8*) S-W Pub.

— Selling: Helping Customers Buy. 2nd ed. (SB - Marketing Education Ser.). 1989. mass mkt. 19.95 (*0-538-60416-6*) S-W Pub.

— Selling: Helping Customers Buy. 3rd ed. (SB - Marketing Education Ser.). 1991. mass mkt. 37.95 (*0-538-60531-6*) S-W Pub.

— Selling: Helping Customers Buy. 3rd ed. (SB - Marketing Education Ser.). 1991. pap., wbk. ed. 20.95 (*0-538-60532-4*) S-W Pub.

— Selling, Tests: Helping Customers Buy. 3rd ed. (SB - Marketing Education Ser.). 1991. 3.95 (*0-538-60533-2*) S-W Pub.

Ditzian, Z. & Totik, Vilmos. Moduli of Smoothness. (Computational Mathematics Ser.: Vol. 9). (Illus.). 240p. 1987. 89.95 (*0-387-96536-X*) Spr-Verlag.

Ditzler, Jinny S. Your Best Year Yet! A Proven Method for Making the Next Twelve Months the Most Successful Ever. LC 98-8605. 230p. 1998. 16.00 (*0-446-52532-4*, Pub. by Warner Bks) Little.

— Your Best Year Yet! Ten Questions for Making the Next 12 Months Your Most Successful Ever. 256p. 2000. mass mkt. 12.95 (*0-446-67547-4*, Pub. by Warner Bks) Little.

Diubaldo, Richard J. Stefansson & the Canadian Arctic. (Illus.). 296p. 1999. pap. 22.95 (*0-7735-1815-0*) McG-Queens Univ Pr.

— Stefansson & the Canadian Arctic. LC 79-304078. 296p. reprint ed. pap. 91.80 (*0-7837-1020-8*, 204133100020) Bks Demand.

Diuguid, Norah M., et al. The History of the Helping Hand Club. (YA). 1990. 8.95 (*0-87498-010-0*) Assoc Pubs DC.

Diuk, Nadia & Karatnycky, Adrian. New Nations Rising: The Fall of the Soviets & the Challenge of Independence. LC 92-40195. 304p. (Orig.). 1993. pap. 14.95 (*0-471-58263-8*) Wiley.

Diulio, Eugene. Schaum's Outline of Macroeconomics. 3rd ed. LC 97-37207. (Schaum's Outline Ser.). (Illus.). 333p. (C). 1997. pap. 15.95 (*0-07-017053-3*) McGraw.

Diulio, Eugene, jt. auth. see Savatore, Dominick.

D

An Asterisk (*) at the beginning of an entry indicates that the title is appearing for the first time.

Diulio, Eugene A. Schaum's Outline of Macroeconomic Theory. 2nd ed. (C). 1990. pap. 12.95 (*0-07-017051-7*) McGraw.

Diulio, Eugene A., jt. auth. see Salvator, Dominick.

Divakar, Ramesh & Blau, Peter J., eds. Wear Testing of Advanced Materials. LC 92-2357. (Special Technical Publication Ser.: No. 1167). (Illus.). 180p. 1992. text 45.00 (*0-8031-1476-1*, STP1167) ASTM.

Divakaruni, Chitra Banerjee. Arranged Marriage: Stories. 320p. 1996. pap. 11.95 (*0-385-48350-3*, Anchor NY) Doubleday.

— Black Candle: Poems about Women from India, Pakistan & Bangladesh. 128p. 2000. reprint ed. 26.95 (*0-934971-75-7*, Pub. by Calyx Bks) Consort Bk Sales.

— Black Candle: Poems about Women from India, Pakistan & Bangladesh. rev. ed. 105p. 2000. pap. write for info. (*0-934971-74-9*, Pub. by Calyx Bks) Consort Bk Sales.

Divakaruni, Chitra Banerjee. Leaving Yuba City: New & Selected Poems. LC 97-6308. 128p. 1997. pap. 13.95 (*0-385-48854-8*, Anchor NY) Doubleday.

— Leaving Yuba City: Poems. 1997. pap. 12.95 (*0-614-27477-X*, Anchor NY) Doubleday.

— The Mistress of Spices: A Novel. LC 96-23767. 388p. 1998. pap. 12.95 (*0-385-48238-8*, Anchor NY) Doubleday.

— Multitude: Cross-Cultural Readings for Writers. 2nd ed. LC 96-2699. 624p. (C). 1996. pap. 34.06 (*0-07-017086-X*) McGraw.

— Sister of My Heart. LC 98-30254. 336p. 1999. 23.95 (*0-385-48950-1*) Bantam.

— Sister of My Heart. LC 98-30254. 320p. 2000. pap. 13.00 (*0-385-48951-X*, Anchor NY) Doubleday.

— We Too Sing America. LC 97-17611. 408p. (C). 1997. pap. 29.06 (*0-07-017084-3*) McGraw.

***Divan, Shyam & Rosencranz, Armin.** Environmental Law & Policy in India: Cases, Materials & Statutes. 850p. 2000. text 24.95 (*0-19-565226-6*) OUP.

Divan, Vasilii A. The Great Russian Navigator, A. I. Chirikov. annot. ed. Fisher, Raymond H., tr. from RUS. & anno. by. LC 92-43962. (Rasmuson Library Historical Translation Ser.: Vol. VI).Tr. of Velikii Ruskii Moreplavatel A. I. Chirikov. 1993. pap. 20.00 (*0-912006-63-3*) U of Alaska Pr.

Divant, Kay. Body Velocity: Reproductions of Poems & Objects. (Illus.). 88p. (Orig.). 1989. pap. 22.00 (*0-9625038-1-9*) Geanie.

Divari, Nikolai B., ed. Atmospheric Optics, Vol. 1. Dresner, Stephen B., tr. from RUS. LC 69-18138. 184p. reprint ed. pap. 57.10 (*0-8357-5849-4*, 202068200018) Bks Demand.

Divaris, C. & Stein, M. L. Silke on South African Income Tax: Eleventh Memorial Edition, 2 vols. 1991. ring bd. 274.00 (*0-7021-2268-8*, Pub. by Juta & Co) Gaunt.

Divarkar, Parmananda R., tr. from ITA. A Pilgrim's Testament: The Memoirs of St. Ignatius of Loyola. LC 95-60352. (Jesuit Primary Sources in English Translation Ser.: Vol. 13). (Illus.). xxx, 150p. (Orig.). 1995. pap. 14.25 (*1-880810-09-3*) Inst Jesuit.

Divatia, N. B. Gujarati Language & Literature. (Wilson Reading System Ser.). (C). 1993. text 50.00 (*81-206-0648-5*, Pub. by Asian Educ Servs) S Asia.

Dive, Caroline, jt. ed. see Hickman, John A.

***DiVecchio, Don.** Earth Song. Holder, Doug & Robitaille, Dianne, eds. (Illus.). 34p. 1999. pap. 4.00 (*0-9678131-1-5*) Ibbetson St Pr.

Divecchio, Jerry A. New Easy Basics. LC 96-61701. 192p. 1997. 24.95 (*0-376-02089-X*) Sunset Books.

Divedi, R. K. Organizational Culture & Performance. 330p. 1995. pap. 225.00 (*81-85880-59-X*, Pub. by Print Hse) St Mut.

Divekar, Dileep A. Fet Modeling for Circuit Simulation. (C). 1988. text 91.00 (*0-89838-264-5*) Kluwer Academic.

Divekar, V. D. Social Reform Movements in India: A Historical Perspective. (C). 1991. 17.50 (*81-7154-561-0*, Pub. by Vintage) S Asia.

Dively, George S. The Power of Professional Management. LC 77-151052. 191p. reprint ed. pap. 59.30 (*0-608-13397-3*, 205574000034) Bks Demand.

Diven, Gail. The Complete Idiot's Guide to Knitting & Crocheting. (Complete Idiot's Guides (Lifestyle) Ser.). (Illus.). 284p. 1999. 16.95 (*0-02-862123-9*) Macmillan Gen Ref.

Diven, William A. In Search of Awareness. (Illus.). 96p. (Orig.). 1995. pap., teacher ed. 12.95 (*0-9645032-9-8*) Unique Crfts.

Divendal, Joost, jt. ed. see Campschreur, Willem.

Diver, Bradford B. Van, see Van Diver, Bradford B.

Diver, Colin S., jt. auth. see Cass, Ronald A.

Diver, Katherine H. Royal India. LC 76-142620. (Essay Index Reprint Ser.). 1977. 24.95 (*0-8369-2152-6*) Ayer.

Diver, Maud. Royal India. (Essay Index Reprint Ser.). (Illus.). 288p. reprint ed. lib. bdg. 21.00 (*0-8290-0780-6*) Irvington.

— Siege Perilous, & Other Stories. LC 78-122694. (Short Story Index Reprint Ser.). 1977. 19.95 (*0-8369-3527-6*) Ayer.

Diver-Stamnes, Ann, jt. auth. see Thomas, R. Murray.

Diver-Stamnes, Ann C. Lives in the Balance: Youth, Poverty, & Education in Watts. LC 94-46295. (SUNY Series, Urban Voices, Urban Visions). 172p. (C). 1995. pap. text 18.95 (*0-7914-2668-8*) State U NY Pr.

Diver's Alert Network Staff. Best of Alert Diver. LC 97-73096. 1997. 19.95 (*0-941332-62-4*, D937) Best Pub Co.

Divers, Consuelo, ed. see Bradley, Scott A.

Divers-Stamnes, Ann C. & Thomas, R. Murray. Prevent, Repent, Reform, Revenge: Adolescents' Aims of Sanctions for Crimes & Misdeeds, 30. LC 95-16145. (Contributions in Psychology Ser.: Vol. 30). 240p. 1995. 59.95 (*0-313-29730-4*, Greenwood Pr) Greenwood.

Divers, Thomas J., jt. auth. see Orsini, James A.

Dives, Robert F. Journey on a Higher Plain. (C). 1990. text 35.00 (*0-7223-2538-X*, Pub. by A H S Ltd) St Mut.

— Soliloquy of Prose. (C). 1988. 40.00 (*0-7223-2337-9*, Pub. by A H S Ltd) St Mut.

Divilbiss, J. L., ed. Public Access to Library Automation: Proceedings of the Clinic on Library Applications of Data Processing,1980. LC 81-11685. 128p. 1981. 15.00 (*0-87845-065-3*) U of Ill Grad Sch.

Divilbiss, J. L., ed. see Conrad, Deborah K., et al.

Divin, V. A., et al. To the American Coast: The Voyages & Exploration of M. S. Gvozdev, the Discoverer of Northwestern America. Perminov, A. M., tr. from RUS. (Illus.). 144p. 1997. 19.95 (*0-9626727-1-8*) Whitestone AK.

DiVincenti, Marie. Administering Nursing Service. 2nd ed. 350p. 1977. 20.50 (*0-316-18651-1*, Little Brwn Med Div) Lppncott W & W.

Divine. America Past & Present, Vol. I. 5th ed. (C). 1999. pap. text, student ed. 21.56 (*0-321-00562-7*) Addison-Wesley.

— America Past & Present, Vol. II. 5th ed. (C). 1999. pap. text, student ed. 21.56 (*0-321-00563-5*) Addson-Wesley Educ.

Divine, ed. America: Past & Present. (C). 1994. text. write for info. (*0-673-46827-5*) Addison-Wesley.

— America: Past & Present Brief Edition, Vol. 1. 4th ed. (C). 1998. pap. text, student ed. 17.81 (*0-321-01300-X*) Addson-Wesley Educ.

— America: Past & Present Brief Edition, Vol. 2. 4th ed. (C). 1997. pap. text, student ed. 21.00 (*0-321-01301-8*) Addison-Wesley.

Divine, ed. I'm America Past Present. 1997. text 11.00 (*0-673-55110-5*) P-H.

Divine, A. L. Columbia County, N. Y. Gravestone Inscriptions, Guide to Interpretation with Comprehensive Family Name Index. LC 93-159835. 210p. 1991. lib. bdg. 39.50 (*1-56012-119-X*, 112) Kinship Rhinebeck.

Divine, Albert L. An Alphabetical First & Last Name Index Vol. 1: History of Columbia Co. New York by Capt. Benjamin F. Ellis. LC 87-13746. 105p. 1991. lib. bdg. 22.00 (*1-56012-087-8*, 87) Kinship Rhinebeck.

Divine, Donna R. Politics & Society in Ottoman Palestine: The Arab Struggle for Survival & Power. LC 93-40820. 230p. 1994. lib. bdg. 45.00 (*1-55587-473-8*) L Rienner.

Divine, Gerda E. Old Tombstones & Unusual Cemeteries in Columbia County, New York Vol. 1: Eastern Columbia County. 148p. 1988. reprint ed. pap. 12.00 (*1-56012-088-6*, 88) Kinship Rhinebeck.

Divine, J. A. & Blachford, G. Stained Glass Craft. (Illus.). 115p. 1972. reprint ed. pap. 4.95 (*0-486-22812-6*) Dover.

Divine, John E. Eighth Virginia Infantry. (Virginia Regimental Histories Ser.). (Illus.). 89p. 1983. 19.95 (*0-930919-05-X*) H E Howard.

— Thirty-Fifth Battalion Virginia Cavalry. (Virginia Regimental Histories Ser.). (Illus.). 112p. 1985. 19.95 (*0-930919-19-X*) H E Howard.

Divine, John E., et al. To Talk Is Treason: Quakers of Waterford, Virginia on Life, Love, Death & War in the Southern Confederacy. (Illus.). 112p. 1997. pap. 12.95 (*0-9660485-0-4*) Waterford Found.

— When Waterford & I Were Young. LC 97-61707. (Illus.). x, 138p. 1997. 21.95 (*0-9660485-2-0*); pap. 12.95 (*0-9660485-1-2*) Waterford Found.

Divine Laboratories, ed. The Little Black Leather Book of Rock'n'Roll. 96p. 1994. per. 4.95 (*1-55152-003-6*, Pub. by Arsenal Pulp) LPC InBook.

Divine, M. J. The Peace Mission Movement. LC 82-90163. (Illus.). 192p. (Orig.). 1982. 8.00 (*0-9609078-0-7*); pap. 6.00 (*0-9609078-1-5*) Palace Mission.

Divine, M. J., ed. Michie's Jurisprudence 1998 Citator, 2 vols. Incl. Michie's Jurisprudence 1998 Citator: Vol. A-L. Legner, G. E., ed. 1998. (*0-327-00852-0*, 7491010); Michie's Jurisprudence1998 Citator: Vol. M-Z. Legner, Gary, ed. 1998. (*0-327-00853-9*, 7491210); 1400p. 1998. write for info. (*0-327-00851-2*, 7491010) LEXIS Pub.

Divine, M. J., et al, eds. Michie's Jurisprudence, 49 vols. Date not set. text 1200.00 (*0-327-00332-4*) LEXIS Pub.

***Divine, M. J., et al, eds.** Michie's Jurisprudence 99 Table of Statutes: A Complete Treatise of Virginia/West Virginia. 200p. 1999. pap. write for info. (*0-327-04960-X*, 7484211) LEXIS Pub.

— Michie's Jurisprudence, 1999 Citator Vols. A-L & M-Z: A Complete Treatise of Virginia/West Virginia. 1300p. 1999. write for info. (*0-327-04959-6*, 7491011) LEXIS Pub.

Divine, M. J. & Ernest, Paul, eds. Dunnell Minnesota Digest, 1998 Tables & Index Pamphlet Vol. 41: An Encyclopedia of Minnesota Law. 4th ed. 100p. 1999. write for info. (*0-327-00923-3*, 8431010) LEXIS Pub.

— Michie on Banks & Banking, 1999, 13 vols. rev. ed. 501p. 1999. write for info. (*0-327-00956-X*, 7468310); 440.00 (*0-327-00931-4*) LEXIS Pub.

— Michie on Banks & Banking, 1999, 13 vols., Vol. 7A. rev. ed. 507p. 1999. write for info. (*0-327-00955-1*, 7468210) LEXIS Pub.

Divine, M. J. & Ernest, Paul A., eds. Dunnell Minnesota Digest, 1999 Edition: An Encyclopedia of Minnesota Law, 52 vols., Set. 4th ed. Incl. Vol. 41. Dunnell Minnesota Digest, 1999: An Encyclopedia of Minnesota Law. 4th ed. LC 89-661. 500p. 1999. (*0-327-00915-2*, 8430910); LC 89-661. 500p. 1999. write for info. (*0-327-00086-4*, 8430910) LEXIS Pub.

Divine, M. J. & Hayes, Heather, eds. Michigan Law & Practice, 1999 Interim Supplement, 32 vols. 85p. 1999. pap. write for info. (*0-327-01053-3*, 6391510) LEXIS Pub.

Divine, M. J. & Legner, G. E., eds. Instructions for Virginia & West Virginia, 1999 Cumulative Supplement. 153p. 1998. pap., suppl. ed. write for info. (*0-327-00660-9*, 7307516) LEXIS Pub.

— Michie's Jurisprudence for Virginia & West Virginia Replacement Vol. 21B, Pt. 2: State Court Rules, 53 vols. 850p. 1999. write for info. (*0-327-00964-0*, 7482112) LEXIS Pub.

— Michie's Jurisprudence for Virginia & West Virginia, 1999 Replacement Vol. 4C: A Complete Treatise of Virginia & West Virginia Law, 53 vols. 557p. 1999. write for info. (*0-327-01054-1*, 7475410) LEXIS Pub.

— Michie's Jurisprudence for Virginia & West Virginia 1999 Replacement Vol. 21B, Pt. 1: State Court Rules, 53 vols. 550p. 1999. write for info. (*0-327-00944-6*, 7482012) LEXIS Pub.

— Tennessee Jurisprudence Table of Statutes. 70p. 1998. write for info. (*0-327-00179-8*, 7750710) LEXIS Pub.

Divine, M. J. & Legner, Gary, eds. Michie's Jurisprudence Table of Statutes: 1998 Cumulative Supplement, 50 vols. 125p. 1998. write for info. (*0-327-00175-5*, 7484210) LEXIS Pub.

Divine, M. J. & Rieseman, Steve, eds. Illinois Jurisprudence, Table of Cases A-L, 1998 Replacement Volume, 27 vols., Set. 625p. 1998. write for info. (*0-327-00654-4*, 6345311) LEXIS Pub.

Divine, M. J. & Riesenman, Steve, eds. Illinois Jurisprudence Table of Statutes, 27 vols., Set. 400p. 1998. write for info. (*0-327-00653-6*, 6345910) LEXIS Pub.

Divine, M. J. & Tucker, Bruce, eds. Callaghan's Michigan Digest, 1999 Replacement Volume, 42 vols., Vol. 3A. 900p. 1999. write for info. (*0-327-00930-6*, 7640611) LEXIS Pub.

Divine, M. J. & Wagoner, David C., eds. Pennsylvania Law Encyclopedia, Special Supplement, Vol. 1. 2nd ed. 500p. 1998. pap. write for info. (*0-327-00864-4*, 6369113) LEXIS Pub.

— Pennsylvania Law Encyclopedia, Special Supplement, Vol. 2. 2nd ed. 500p. 1998. pap. write for info. (*0-327-00865-2*, 6369213) LEXIS Pub.

Divine, M. J., jt. ed. see Tucker, Bruce.

Divine, Mary J., jt. ed. see Ernest, Paul.

Divine, Mary Jane, et al, eds. Michie on Banks & Banking: 1999 Cumulative Supplement, 14 vols. 1810p. 1999. suppl. ed. write for info. (*0-327-00355-3*, 7464816) LEXIS Pub.

***Divine, Mary Jane & Ernest, Paul.** Dunnell Minnesota Digest, 1999 Edition Vol. 45: An Encyclopedia of Minnesota Law. 4th ed. 400p. 1999. write for info. (*0-327-04971-5*, 8431710) LEXIS Pub.

***Divine, Mary Jane & Ernest, Paul, eds.** Dunnell Minnesota Digest: An Encyclopedia of Minnesota Law, Vol. 44. 4th ed. 400p. 1999. write for info. (*0-327-01579-9*, 8431510) LEXIS Pub.

— Dunnell Minnesots Digest Vol. 45: 1999 Edition, Tables & Index Phamphlet. 4th ed. 100p. 1999. pap. write for info. (*0-327-04991-X*, 8431810) LEXIS Pub.

Divine, Mary Jane & Tucker, Bruce, eds. Callaghan's Michigan Digest: 1999 Cumulative Supplement, 42 vols., Set. 1550p. 1999. suppl. ed. write for info. (*0-327-01086-X*, 76500-12) LEXIS Pub.

— Callaghan's Michigan Digest: 1999 Cumulative Supplement, Vol. 1. 1999. suppl. ed. write for info. (*0-327-01087-8*, 76501-12) LEXIS Pub.

— Callaghan's Michigan Digest: 1999 Cumulative Supplement, Vol. 1A. 1999. suppl. ed. write for info. (*0-327-01128-9*, 76502-12) LEXIS Pub.

— Callaghan's Michigan Digest: 1999 Cumulative Supplement, Vol. 2. 1999. suppl. ed. write for info. (*0-327-01088-6*, 76503-12) LEXIS Pub.

— Callaghan's Michigan Digest: 1999 Cumulative Supplement, Vol. 2A. 1999. suppl. ed. write for info. (*0-327-01089-4*, 76504-12) LEXIS Pub.

— Callaghan's Michigan Digest: 1999 Cumulative Supplement, Vol. 3. 1999. suppl. ed. write for info. (*0-327-01090-8*, 76505-12) LEXIS Pub.

— Callaghan's Michigan Digest: 1999 Cumulative Supplement, Vol. 3A. 1999. suppl. ed. write for info. (*0-327-01091-6*, 76506-12) LEXIS Pub.

— Callaghan's Michigan Digest: 1999 Cumulative Supplement, Vol. 4. 1999. suppl. ed. write for info. (*0-327-01092-4*, 76507-12) LEXIS Pub.

— Callaghan's Michigan Digest: 1999 Cumulative Supplement, Vol. 4A. 1999. suppl. ed. write for info. (*0-327-01093-2*, 76508-12) LEXIS Pub.

— Callaghan's Michigan Digest: 1999 Cumulative Supplement, Vol. 4B. 1999. suppl. ed. write for info. (*0-327-01094-0*, 76509-12) LEXIS Pub.

— Callaghan's Michigan Digest: 1999 Cumulative Supplement, Vol. 5. 1999. suppl. ed. write for info. (*0-327-01095-9*, 76510-12) LEXIS Pub.

— Callaghan's Michigan Digest: 1999 Cumulative Supplement, Vol. 5A. 1999. suppl. ed. write for info. (*0-327-01096-7*, 76511-12) LEXIS Pub.

— Callaghan's Michigan Digest: 1999 Cumulative Supplement, Vol. 5B. 1999. suppl. ed. write for info. (*0-327-01097-5*, 76512-12) LEXIS Pub.

— Callaghan's Michigan Digest: 1999 Cumulative Supplement, Vol. 6. 1999. suppl. ed. write for info. (*0-327-01098-3*, 76513-12) LEXIS Pub.

— Callaghan's Michigan Digest: 1999 Cumulative Supplement, Vol. 6A. 1999. suppl. ed. write for info. (*0-327-01099-1*, 76514-12) LEXIS Pub.

— Callaghan's Michigan Digest: 1999 Cumulative Supplement, Vol. 7. 1999. suppl. ed. write for info. (*0-327-01100-9*, 76515-12) LEXIS Pub.

— Callaghan's Michigan Digest: 1999 Cumulative Supplement, Vol. 8. 1999. suppl. ed. write for info. (*0-327-01101-7*, 76516-12) LEXIS Pub.

— Callaghan's Michigan Digest: 1999 Cumulative Supplement, Vol. 8A. 1999. suppl. ed. write for info. (*0-327-01102-5*, 76517-12) LEXIS Pub.

— Callaghan's Michigan Digest: 1999 Cumulative Supplement, Vol. 9. 1999. suppl. ed. write for info. (*0-327-01103-3*, 76518-12) LEXIS Pub.

— Callaghan's Michigan Digest: 1999 Cumulative Supplement, Vol. 9A. 1999. suppl. ed. write for info. (*0-327-01104-1*, 76519-12) LEXIS Pub.

— Callaghan's Michigan Digest: 1999 Cumulative Supplement, Vol. 10. 1999. suppl. ed. write for info. (*0-327-01105-X*, 76520-12) LEXIS Pub.

— Callaghan's Michigan Digest: 1999 Cumulative Supplement, Vol. 10A. 1999. suppl. ed. write for info. (*0-327-01106-8*, 76521-12) LEXIS Pub.

— Callaghan's Michigan Digest: 1999 Cumulative Supplement, Vol. 11. 1999. suppl. ed. write for info. (*0-327-01107-6*, 76522-12) LEXIS Pub.

— Callaghan's Michigan Digest: 1999 Cumulative Supplement, Vol. 11A. 1999. suppl. ed. write for info. (*0-327-01108-4*, 76523-12) LEXIS Pub.

— Callaghan's Michigan Digest: 1999 Cumulative Supplement, Vol. 12. 1999. suppl. ed. write for info. (*0-327-01109-2*, 76524-12) LEXIS Pub.

— Callaghan's Michigan Digest: 1999 Cumulative Supplement, Vol. 12A. 1999. suppl. ed. write for info. (*0-327-01110-6*, 76525-12) LEXIS Pub.

— Callaghan's Michigan Digest: 1999 Cumulative Supplement, Vol. 13. 1999. suppl. ed. write for info. (*0-327-01111-4*, 76526-12) LEXIS Pub.

— Callaghan's Michigan Digest: 1999 Cumulative Supplement, Vol. 13A. 1999. suppl. ed. write for info. (*0-327-01112-2*, 76527-12) LEXIS Pub.

— Callaghan's Michigan Digest: 1999 Cumulative Supplement, Vol. 14. 1999. suppl. ed. write for info. (*0-327-01113-0*, 76528-12) LEXIS Pub.

— Callaghan's Michigan Digest: 1999 Cumulative Supplement, Vol. 14A. 1999. suppl. ed. write for info. (*0-327-01114-9*, 76529-12) LEXIS Pub.

— Callaghan's Michigan Digest: 1999 Cumulative Supplement, Vol. 15. 1999. suppl. ed. write for info. (*0-327-01115-7*, 76530-12) LEXIS Pub.

— Callaghan's Michigan Digest: 1999 Cumulative Supplement, Vol. 16. 1999. suppl. ed. write for info. (*0-327-01117-3*, 76532-12) LEXIS Pub.

— Callaghan's Michigan Digest: 1999 Cumulative Supplement, Vol. 16A. 1999. suppl. ed. write for info. (*0-327-01118-1*, 76533-12) LEXIS Pub.

— Callaghan's Michigan Digest: 1999 Cumulative Supplement, Vol. 17. 1999. suppl. ed. write for info. (*0-327-01119-X*, 76534-12) LEXIS Pub.

— Callaghan's Michigan Digest: 1999 Cumulative Supplement, Vol. 17A. 1999. suppl. ed. write for info. (*0-327-01120-3*, 76535-12) LEXIS Pub.

— Callaghan's Michigan Digest: 1999 Cumulative Supplement, Vol. 17B. 1999. suppl. ed. write for info. (*0-327-01121-1*, 76536-12) LEXIS Pub.

— Callaghan's Michigan Digest: 1999 Cumulative Supplement, Vol. 18. 1999. suppl. ed. write for info. (*0-327-01122-X*, 76537-12) LEXIS Pub.

— Callaghan's Michigan Digest: 1999 Cumulative Supplement, Vol. 18A. 1999. suppl. ed. write for info. (*0-327-01123-8*, 76538-12) LEXIS Pub.

— Callaghan's Michigan Digest: 1999 Cumulative Supplement, Vol. 19. 1999. suppl. ed. write for info. (*0-327-01124-6*, 76539-12) LEXIS Pub.

— Callaghan's Michigan Digest: 1999 Cumulative Supplement, Vol. 19A. 1999. suppl. ed. write for info. (*0-327-01125-4*, 76540-12) LEXIS Pub.

— Callaghan's Michigan Digest: 1999 Cumulative Supplement, Vol. 19B. 1999. suppl. ed. write for info. (*0-327-01126-2*, 76541-12) LEXIS Pub.

— Callaghan's Michigan Digest: 1999 Cumulative Supplement, Vol. 20. 1999. suppl. ed. write for info. (*0-327-01127-0*, 76542-12) LEXIS Pub.

— Callaghan's Michigan Digest Vol. 15A: 1999 Cumulative Supplement, Vol. 15A. 1999. suppl. ed. write for info. (*0-327-01116-5*, 76531-12) LEXIS Pub.

Divine, Mary Jane, jt. ed. see Ernest, Paul.

Divine, R. A., et al. America Past & Present: Instructor's Guide to Teaching American History. 5th ed. 40p. 1998. 24.00 (*0-321-04251-4*) Addson-Wesley Educ.

— America Past & Present: Instructor's Manual. 5th ed. (*0-321-00557-0*) Addson-Wesley Educ.

Divine, Robert A. America: Past & Present, Vol. 2. 5th ed. LC 98-27312. 672p. (C). 1998. pap. text 50.63 (*0-321-00293-8*) Addson-Wesley Educ.

— America Through the Eyes of Its People. 4th ed. (C). 1999. 57.00 (*0-321-03674-3*) Addison-Wesley.

— America Through the Eyes of Its People, Vol. 2. 5th ed. (C). 1998. pap. text. write for info. (*0-321-03676-X*) Addison-Wesley.

— American Immigration Policy Nineteen Twenty-Four to Nineteen Fifty-Two. LC 70-166323. (Civil Liberties in American History Ser.). 200p. 1972. reprint ed. lib. bdg. 27.50 (*0-306-70244-4*) Da Capo.

— Eisenhower & Sputnik. 272p. 1993. 30.00 (*0-19-505008-8*) OUP.

Divine, Robert A. Eisenhower & the Cold War. 182p. 1981. pap. text 8.95 (*0-19-502824-4*) OUP.

Divine, Robert A. Eisenhower & the Cold War. (Illus.). 1981. pap. 7.95 (*0-685-03764-9*) OUP.

— The Illusion of Neutrality. LC 62-10993. 382p. reprint ed. pap. 118.50 (*0-608-10703-4*, 202005700016) Bks Demand.

***Divine, Robert A.** Perpetual War for Perpetual Peace. LC 00-20198. (Foreign Relations & the Presidency Ser.: Vol. 5). 128p. 2000. 29.95 (*0-89096-953-1*); pap. 14.95 (*1-58544-105-8*) Tex A&M Univ Pr.

Divine, Robert A. The Reluctant Belligerent: American Entry into World War II. 2nd ed. 179p. (C). 1979. pap. 15.94 (*0-07-554672-8*) McGraw.

An Asterisk (*) at the beginning of an entry indicates that the title is appearing for the first time.

— Since 1945: Politics & Diplomacy in Recent American History. 3rd ed. 320p. (C). 1985. pap. 24.38 (*0-07-554644-2*) McGraw.

Divine, Robert A., ed. America Past & Present Brief Integrator. 3rd ed. (C). 1994. write for info. (*0-673-55109-1*) Addison-Wesley.

— Exploring the Johnson Years. LC 81-2269. (Illus.). 288p. 1981. text 24.95 (*0-292-72031-9*) U of Tex Pr.

— Exploring the Johnson Years. LC 81-2269. (Illus.). 288p. reprint ed. pap. 89.30 (*0-608-20102-2*, 207137400011) Bks Demand.

— The Johnson Years Vol. II: Vietnam, the Environment, & Science. LC 86-32443. (Illus.). xii, 272p. 1987. pap. 12.95 (*0-7006-0464-2*) U Pr of KS.

— The Johnson Years Vol. III: LBJ at Home & Abroad. LC 86-32443. xii, 294p. 1994. 29.95 (*0-7006-0655-6*) U Pr of KS.

Divine, Robert A., et al. America: Past & Present. 5th ed. LC 98-27312. (Illus.). 1036p. (C). 1998. 78.00 (*0-321-00289-X*) Addison-Wesley.

— America: Past & Present, Vol. 1. 5th ed. LC 98-27312. Vol. 1. (Illus.). 582p. (C). 1998. pap. 60.00 (*0-321-00291-1*) Addson-Wesley Educ.

— America: Past & Present, Brief Edition. 4th ed. LC 97-37237. (Illus.). 622p. (C). 1997. pap. text 52.00 (*0-673-98483-4*) Addison-Wesley.

Divine, Robert C. Immigration Practice, 1998. LC 98-85342. 1998. 117.00 (*0-327-00182-8*, 61230-12) LEXIS Pub.

— Immigration Practice, 1999 Edition. 1350p. 1999. 125.00 (*0-327-01494-6*, 6123013) LEXIS Pub.

— Immigration Practice, 1997 Edition. 1251p. 1997. pap. 125.00 (*1-55834-546-9*, 61230-11) LEXIS Pub.

— Immigration Practice, 1997. 2nd ed. LC 97-157950. (Illus.). 1231p. 1997. pap. text 110.00 (*1-55834-515-9*, 61230-11, MICHIE) LEXIS Pub.

Divine, Robert D. America Past & Present. 5th ed. (C). 1998. pap. text. write for info. (*0-321-01860-5*) Addison-Wesley.

Divine, Thomas F. Interest, an Historical & Analytical Study in Economics & Modern Ethics. LC 58-7264. 1959. 15.00 (*0-87462-405-3*) Marquette.

Diviney, Ann E. From Sea to Shining Sea: A Hike Across America on Old U. S. 30. (Illus.). xiii, 239p. (Orig.). 1997. pap. 12.95 (*0-9658216-0-9*) A E Diviney.

Diviney, Glade & Murray, Keith. The OS/2 Warp Programmer's Sidekick: Functions & Structures: A Quick-Reference to OS/2 Functions, Macros & Structures. 592p. (Orig.). 1995. pap. 39.95 (*0-9647472-8-6*) Quarter Horse.

***Divinnie, Chuck.** First Aid for Sporting Dogs: An Orvis Guide, 1. (Orvis Guides Ser.). (Illus.). 128p. 2000. 16.95 (*1-57223-315-X*) Willow Creek Pr.

Divinsky, Nathan. Life Maps: Of the Great Chess Masters. Berry, Jonathan, ed. viii, 312p. 1994. 46.95 (*1-879479-17-6*) ICE WA.

Diviny, Sean. Halloween Motel. (Illus.). 32p. (J). (ps-1). 5.25 hd 5.95 (*0-06-443651-9*) HarpC.

— Halloween Motel. LC 99-89317. 32p. (J). (ps-3). 2000. lib. bdg. 15.89 (*0-06-028816-7*) HarpC Child Bks.

— Halloween Motel. LC 99-89317. (Illus.). 32p. (J). (ps-3). 2000. 15.95 (*0-06-028815-9*) HarpC Child Bks.

Diviny, Sean. Snow Inside the House. LC 96-30723. (Illus.). 32p. (J). (ps-3). 1998. 14.95 (*0-06-027354-2*) HarpC Child Bks.

Divinyi, Joyce E. Good Kids, Difficult Behavior. Fallon, Elizabeth, ed. LC 97-91444. (Illus.). 120p. 1997. pap. write for info. (*0-9656353-4-1*) Wellness Connect.

Divis, J. Poincons d'Argent du Monde Entier. 6th ed. (FRE.). 246p. 1991. 49.95 (*0-8288-7300-3*, 2859170820) Fr & Eur.

***Divis, Jan.** Guide to Silvermarks of the World. (Illus.). 246p. 1999. reprint ed. text 25.00 (*0-7881-6584-4*) DIANE Pub.

Division, et al. Introductory Biology Lab Manual. 2nd ed. 128p. (C). 1999. spiral bd., lab manual ed. 25.95 (*0-7872-5596-3*, 41559601) Kendall-Hunt.

Division for Ocean Affairs & the Law of the Sea Of. Concept of the Common Heritage of Mankind: Concept of the Common Heritage of Mankind: Legislative History of Articles 133-150 & 311(6) of the United Nations Convention on the Law of the Sea. LC 96-161743. (The Law of the Sea Ser.). 472p. 55.00 (*92-1-133507-8*, 70392) UN.

— The Law of the Sea. (Bulletin Ser.: No. 31). 96p. 1996. pap. 15.00 (*0-614-25030-7*) UN.

— Law of the Sea: Official Text of the United Nations Convention on the Law of the Sea of 10 December 1982 & of the Agreement Relating to the Implementation of Part XI of the United Nations Convention . . . LC 97-229152. 294p. 1997. pap. 25.00 (*92-1-133522-1*, JX4408) UN.

Division of Early Childhood, Council on Exceptiona & National Board for Professional Teaching Standards. Guidelines for the Preparation of Early Childhood Professionals. 1996. pap. 5.00 (*0-935989-77-3*) Natl Assn Child Ed.

Division of Mental Retardation Staff. Medication Administration for Unlicensed Personnel. (Illus.). 1998. pap. 29.95 (*1-928752-06-3*) Mc Gowan Pubns.

Division of Ocean Affairs & the Law of the Sea Off. National Legislation on Territorial Sea, Right of Innocent Passage & the Contiguous Zone. LC 95-209391. (The Law of the Sea Ser.). 440p. 48.00 (*92-1-133486-1*) UN.

Division of Planning, Distribution & Development S, compiled by. Health Facilities in Southern New York: A Guide to Inpatient, Outpatient, & Long-Term Care, 1983 Edition. (Health Care Information Ser.). 72p. 1983. 15.00 (*0-934459-82-7*) United Hosp Fund.

— Inpatient Hospital Use in New York City: Community Hospital Profiles, 3 vols., Set. (POIS Reports). 1980. 80.00 (*0-934459-75-4*) United Hosp Fund.

Division of Public Administration & Development Management Staff & Department of Economic & Social Affairs Division f. Rethinking Public Administration: An Overview. LC 99-168733. 221p. 1998. pap. 24.00 (*92-1-123126-4*) UN.

Division of Research, Analysis, & Planning Staff. Health Care Annual: An Update on Trends & Facilities in New York. 128p. 1991. 40.00 (*0-934459-91-6*) United Hosp Fund.

— Health Facilities in Southern New York: A Guide to Inpatient, Outpatient, & Long-Term Care. 70p. 1988. 20.00 (*0-934459-49-5*) United Hosp Fund.

Division of Research, Analysis, & Planning Staff, compiled by. Ambulatory Care in New York City 1984, 3 vols., Set. 1985. 60.00 (*0-934459-16-9*) United Hosp Fund.

— Health & Health Care in New York City: Local, State, & National Perspectives. LC 85-8598. 136p. 1985. 25.00 (*0-934459-04-5*) United Hosp Fund.

— Health Care Annual: An Update on Trends & Facilities in New York. 114p. 1990. 40.00 (*0-934459-69-X*) United Hosp Fund.

— Health Care Information Series, 3 vols. 1985. 45.00 (*0-934459-05-3*) United Hosp Fund.

— Health Facilities in Southern New York: A Guide to Inpatient, Outpatient, & Long-Term Care, Vol. I. 70p. 1985. 15.00 (*0-934459-06-1*) United Hosp Fund.

— Inpatient Hospital Use in New York City, 1985, 3 vols., Set. 1987. 125.00 (*0-934459-42-8*) United Hosp Fund.

— Inpatient Hospital Use in New York City, 1985, Vol. One: Service Patterns & Insurance Coverage. 220p. 1987. 30.00 (*0-934459-43-6*) United Hosp Fund.

— Inpatient Hospital Use in New York City, 1985, Vol. Three: Community Profiles: Utilization & Insurance Coverage. 370p. 1987. 50.00 (*0-934459-45-2*) United Hosp Fund.

— Inpatient Hospital Use in New York City, 1985, Vol. Two: Community Profiles: Utilization & Clinical Service. 370p. 1987. 50.00 (*0-934459-44-4*) United Hosp Fund.

— New York City Community Health Atlas. LC 85-675630. 1985. 40.00 (*0-934459-15-0*) United Hosp Fund.

— Profiles & Trends: Hospital Inpatient & Ambulatory Care in Southern New York, Vol. II. 43p. 1985. 15.00 (*0-934459-07-X*) United Hosp Fund.

Division of Space History, National Air & Space Museum, The Smithsonian Institution Staff, jt. auth. see Collins, Martin J.

Division Public Affairs Staff. 40th Infantry Division. (Divisional Ser.: No. 47). (Illus.). 184p. 1995. reprint ed. 49.95 (*0-89839-225-X*) Battery Pr.

Division Staff. The Second United States Infantry Division in Korea, 1951-1952. (Divisional Ser.: No. 41). (Illus.). 232p. reprint ed. 49.95 (*0-89839-173-3*) Battery Pr.

— The Second United States Infantry Division in Korea, 1953. (Divisional Ser.: No. 43). (Illus.). 248p. reprint ed. 49.95 (*0-89839-177-6*) Battery Pr.

Divita, James J. A History of St. Christopher Catholic Parish in Speedway, Indiana. LC 87-61261. (Illus.). 84p. 1987. 10.00 (*0-9618519-0-2*) St Christopher Parish.

Divita, S. F., ed. Advertising & the Public Interest: Selected Papers from the Conference on Advertising & the Public Interest Held in Washington D.C., May 1973. LC 74-82870. 280p. reprint ed. pap. 86.80 (*0-8357-5206-2*, 201778000008) Bks Demand.

Divitiis, Gigliola Pagano de, see Pagano de Divitiis, Gigliola.

Divitis, Antonius. Antonius Divitis: Collected Works. Nugent, B. A., ed. (Recent Researches in Music of the Renaissance Ser.: Vol. RRR94). (Illus.). xlv, 247p. 1993. pap. 90.00 (*0-89579-281-8*, RRR94) A-R Eds.

Divkovic, Mirko. Latinsko - Hrvatski Rjecnik. 6th ed. (CRO & LAT.). 1990. 195.00 (*0-8288-3950-6*, F107540) Fr & Eur.

Divo, E. & Kassab, A. J. A New Boundary Integral Method for Anisotropic Heat Conduction. (Topics in Engineering Ser.). 120p. 1999. 94.00 incl. cd-rom (*1-85312-771-X*, Pub. by WIT Pr) Computational Mech MA.

DIVO Institut fuer Wirtschaftsforschung, Sozialfor. German Election Study, October 1965. 1975. write for info. (*0-89138-109-0*) ICPSR.

Divock, Rosemary. Growing & Using Herbs in the Midwest: A Regional Guide for Home Gardeners. LC 96-19449. (Illus.). 248p. 1996. 18.95 (*0-942495-52-7*) Palmer Pubns Inc.

***Divola, John.** Isolated Houses. (Illus.). 48p. 2000. 60.00 (*3-923922-80-9*) Nazraeli Press.

Divola, John & Dimendberg, Edward. John Divola: Continuity. (Illus.). 72p. 1997. pap. 35.00 (*0-9630785-4-2*) RAM Publications.

Divon, M. Abnormal Fetal Growth. (Illus.). 408p. (C). (gr. 13). 1991. text 83.95 (*0-412-04541-9*) Chapman & Hall.

Divona, Marcia & Shaw, Barbara, eds. City Symbols. LC 93-71360. (Illus.). 184p. 1993. text 22.50 (*0-88108-115-9*); pap. text 16.95 (*0-88108-116-7*) Art Dir.

Divone, Judene. Chocolate Moulds: A History & Encyclopedia. LC 86-28571. (Illus.). 168p. (Orig.). 1987. pap. 21.95 (*0-939047-02-0*) Oakton Hills Pubns.

Divone, Louis. Wings of History: The Air Museums of Europe. LC 88-5158. (Illus.). 312p. (Orig.). 1989. pap. 21.95 (*0-939047-21-7*) Oakton Hills Pubns.

DiVono, Sharman. Blood Moon. 441p. 1999. mass mkt. 6.99 (*0-88677-853-0*, Pub. by DAW Bks) Penguin Putnam.

Divort, Joan E. Van, see Van Divort, Joan E.

Divry, George C. Divry's English-To-Greek Phrase & Conversation Pronouncing Manual. 1966. 10.00 (*0-685-09027-2*) Divry.

— Divry's Greek-English Dialogues. 1947. 10.00 (*0-685-09028-0*) Divry.

— Divry's New Modern Greek-English & English-Greek Handy Dictionary. 1983. 8.00 (*0-317-02288-1*); 12.00 (*0-317-02289-X*) Divry.

— Divry's New Self Taught English Method for Greeks. 1983. 10.00 (*0-685-09032-9*) Divry.

— Greek Made Easy. 3rd ed. 1953. 10.00 (*0-685-09037-X*) Divry.

— Modern English-Greek-English Desk Dictionary with Thumb Index. (ENG & GRE.). 768p. 1979. 29.95 (*0-8288-4822-X*, M9443) Fr & Eur.

— New English-Greek-English Handy Dictionary. (ENG & GRE.). 511p. 1978. 12.95 (*0-8288-5256-1*, M9439) Fr & Eur.

Divshikar, D. G., jt. auth. see Mandal, J. N.

***Divyabhanusinh.** The End of a Trial: The Cheetah in India. (Illus.). 272p. 2000. pap. text 24.95 (*0-19-564956-7*) OUP.

Diwan, Ishac & Rodrik, Dani. External Debt, Adjustment & Burden Sharing: A Unified Framework. LC 92-40298. (Studies in International Finance: No. 73). 54p. 1992. pap. 3.50 (*0-88165-245-8*) Princeton U Int Finan Econ.

Diwan, Ishac & Shaban, Radwan A. Development under Adversity: The Palestinian Economy in Transition. LC 99-12532. 256p. 1999. 30.00 (*0-8213-4418-8*) World Bank.

Diwan, Ishac, jt. ed. see Husain, Ishrat.

***Diwan, Milind V. & Jung, Chang Kee, eds.** Next Generation Nucleon Decay & Neutrino Detector, NNN99. (AIP Conference Proceedings Ser.: Vol. 533). (Illus.). ix, 248p. 2000. 115.00 (*1-56396-956-4*) Am Inst Physics.

Diwan, Parag. Management in Eighty Days: An Executive's Encyclopaedia of Management Practices, 10 vols. 1997. 3400.00 (*81-86830-10-3*, Pub. by Print Hse) St Mut.

Diwan, Paras. Dowry & Protection to Married Women. 1987. 37.50 (*0-8364-2086-1*, Pub. by Deep & Deep Pubns) S Asia.

— Dowry & Protection to Married Women: With up-to-Date Amendments. (C). 1990. 145.00 (*0-89771-153-X*) St Mut.

— Environment Protection: Problems, Policy, Administration, Law. (C). 1990. 200.00 (*0-89771-157-2*) St Mut.

— Law of Marriage & Divorce. (C). 1988. 200.00 (*0-7855-3558-6*) St Mut.

— Law of Parental Control, Guardianship & Custody of Minor Children. 837p. 1978. 160.00 (*0-7855-1292-2*) St Mut.

Diwan, Paras, ed. Environment Protection: Problems, Policy Administration, Law. 559p. 1987. 49.95 (*81-7100-003-7*) Asia Bk Corp.

Diwan, Paras & Diwan, Peeyushi. Amending Powers & Constitutional Amendments: The Fight to the Latest Amendment. (C). 1990. 175.00 (*0-89771-207-2*) St Mut.

— Women & Legal Protection. (C). 1994. 40.00 (*81-7100-659-0*, Pub. by Deep & Deep Pubns) S Asia.

Diwan, Peeyushi, jt. auth. see Diwan, Paras.

Diwan, Romesh & Chakraborty, Chandana. High Technology & International Competitiveness. LC 90-27810. 288p. 1991. 75.00 (*0-275-93032-7*, C3032, Praeger Pubs) Greenwood.

Diwan, Romesh & Lutz, Mark, eds. Essays in Gandhian Economics. (Illus.). 243p. 1987. text 22.50 (*0-942850-07-6*) Intermediate Tech.

Diwekar, Urmila M. Batch Distillation: Simulation, Optimal Design, & Control. LC 95-21973. (Series in Chemical & Mechanical Engineering). 211p. 1995. 75.00 (*1-56032-324-8*) Taylor & Francis.

Diwekar, Urmila M., jt. auth. see Sikdar, Subhas K.

Diwo, Jean. Les Dames Du Fauborg. (FRE.). 1987. pap. 16.95 (*0-7859-2064-1*, 2070378349) Fr & Eur.

— Les Diners de Calpurnia, Vol. 2. 375p. 1997. pap. 25.99 (*2-84011-180-2*) Ulverscroft.

— Le Genie de la Bastille. (FRE.). 660p. 1991. pap 16.95 (*0-7859-2167-2*, 2070383938) Fr & Eur.

— Le Lit d'Acajou. (Dames Du Fauborg Ser.: Vol. II). (FRE.). 563p. 1989. pap. 16.95 (*0-7859-2120-6*, 2070381498) Fr & Eur.

Dix. Criminal Law. 4th ed. LC 98-16978. (Criminal Justice Ser.). 1998. 83.95 (*0-534-54684-6*) Wadsworth Pub.

— Gilbert Criminal Law. 15th ed. 1996. pap. text 18.95 (*0-15-900217-6*) Harcourt Legal.

Dix & Dawson. Texas Criminal Procedure. 1988. suppl. ed. write for info. (*0-8205-0482-3*) Bender.

Dix, Alan, jt. auth. see Finlay, Janet.

Dix, Alan J. & Beale, Russell, eds. Remote Cooperation: CSCW Issues for Mobile & Tele-Workers. LC 96-12820. (Computer Supported Cooperative Work Ser.). (Illus.). 255p. 1996. pap. 64.50 (*3-540-76035-0*) Spr-Verlag.

***Dix, Alan J., et al.** Human-Computer Interaction. 2nd ed. LC 97-48380. 6385p. 1998. 59.00 (*0-13-239864-8*) P-H.

Dix, Andrew, et al. Law for the Medical Profession. 336p. 1988. 70.00 (*0-409-49318-X*) Buttrwrth-Heinemann.

Dix, Bernard. Serving the Public - Building the Union: The Forerunners, 1889-1928. (History of NUPE Ser.: Vol. 1). (C). 1987. pap. 19.50 (*0-85315-646-8*, Pub. by Lawrence & Wishart); text 42.50 (*0-85315-645-X*, Pub. by Lawrence & Wishart) NYU Pr.

Dix, Byron E., jt. auth. see Mavor, James W.

Dix, Carol. The New Mother Syndrome. 320p. 1988. mass mkt. 4.50 (*0-671-64485-8*) PB.

Dix, Carol, jt. auth. see Scher, Jonathan.

Dix, Charles Hewitt. Seismic Prospecting for Oil. 422p. 1988. text 54.20 (*0-13-799800-7*) P-H.

Dix, Daniel B. Large-Time Behavior of Solutions of Linear Dispersive Equations, Vol. 166. Dold, A. & Takens, F., eds. LC 97-29078. (Lecture Notes in Mathematics Ser.: Vol. 1668). xiv, 203p. 1997. pap. 41.00 (*3-540-63434-7*) Spr-Verlag.

Dix, Dom G. The Shape of the Liturgy. 816p. 1984. 25.95 (*0-8164-2418-7*) Harper SF.

Dix, Dorothea L. On Behalf of the Insane Poor: Selected Reports, 1843-1852. LC 78-137163. (Poverty U. S. A. Historical Record Ser.). 1975. reprint ed. 30.95 (*0-405-03101-7*) Ayer.

— Remarks on Prison & Prison Discipline in the United States: With Introduction & Index Added. 2nd ed. LC 84-7714. (Criminology, Law Enforcement, & Social Problems Ser.: No. 4). iv, 113p. (C). 1984. reprint ed. lib. bdg. 20.00 (*0-87585-705-1*) Patterson Smith.

Dix, Dorothy. How to Win & Hold a Husband. LC 74-3939. (Women in America Ser.). 288p. 1974. reprint ed. 24.95 (*0-405-06086-6*) Ayer.

Dix, Francis, jt. auth. see Hoosen, Chris.

Dix, G., jt. auth. see Huby, M.

Dix, George E. & Aaron, Richard I. Criminal Law: Adaptable to Courses Utilizing Materials by Dix. LC 87-116615. (Legalines Ser.). 100p. 9.95 (*0-685-18526-5*) Harcourt.

Dix, George E. & Sharlot, M. Michael. Basic Criminal Law: Cases & Materials. 3rd ed. 672p. (C). 1987. pap. 53.25 (*0-314-34733-X*) West Pub.

— Cases & Materials on Criminal Law. 4th ed. (Paralegal). 928p. (C). 1996. text 48.00 (*0-314-09009-6*) West Pub.

— Criminal Law: Cases & Materials. 3rd ed. (American Casebook Ser.). 837p. 1988. reprint ed. text 44.50 (*0-314-35159-0*) West Pub.

— Criminal Law, Cases & Materials: Teacher's Manual to Accompany. 4th ed. (American Casebook Ser.). 258p. (C). Date not set. pap. text, teacher ed. write for info. (*0-314-09877-1*) West Pub.

Dix, Herbert M. Environmental Pollution: Atmosphere, Land, Water & Noise. LC 80-40287. (Institution of Environmental Sciences Ser.). (Illus.). 296p. reprint ed. pap. 91.80 (*0-8357-8514-9*, 203481100091) Bks Demand.

Dix, J., et al, eds. Logic Programming & Nonmonotonic Reasoning: Proceedings, Fourth International Conference, LPNMR'97, Dagstuhl Castle, Germany, July 28-31, 1997. LC 97-27551. (Lecture Notes in Artificial Intelligence: Vol. 1265). x, 453p. pap. write for info. (*3-540-63255-7*) Spr-Verlag.

— Logics in Artificial Intelligence. LC 98-46038. (Lecture Notes in Artificial Intelligence: Vol. 1489). ix, 391p. 1998. 67.00 (*3-540-65141-1*) Spr-Verlag.

— Non-Monotonic Extensions of Logic Programming: Second International Workshop NMELP '96, Bad Honnef, Germany September 5-6, 1996, Selected Papers, Vol. 121. LC 97-12651. (Lecture Notes in Artificial Intelligence Ser.: No. 1216). xii, 224p. 1997. pap. 43.00 (*3-540-62843-6*) Spr-Verlag.

— Nonmonotonic & Inductive Logic: 1st International Workshop Karlsruhe, Germany, December 4-7, 1990 Proceedings. (Lecture Notes in Artifiical Intelligence Ser.: Vol. 543). x, 243p. 1991. 32.95 (*0-387-54564-6*) Spr-Verlag.

Dix, J., ed. see Van Leeuwen, J., et al.

***Dix, Jay.** Color Atlas of Forensic Pathology. 184p. 1999. boxed set 199.95 (*0-8493-0278-1*) CRC Pr.

Dix, Jay. Guide to Forensic Pathology. LC 99-21246. 272p. 1998. per. 34.95 (*0-8493-0267-6*) CRC Pr.

— Handbook for Death Scene Investigators. LC 99-206524. 124p. 1999. lib. bdg. 19.95 (*0-8493-0298-6*) CRC Pr.

***Dix, Jay.** Time of Death, Decomposition & Identification: An Atlas. (Cause of Death Atlas Ser.). 120p. 1999. per. 34.95 (*0-8493-2367-3*) CRC Pr.

Dix, Jay & Calaluce, Robert. Guide to Forensic Pathology. unabridged ed. (Illus.). 257p. 1998. pap. 30.00 (*0-9663422-0-8*) Acad Info Systs.

***Dix, Jay D.** Asphyxia & Drowning. (Cause of Death Atlas Ser.). 120p. 2000. per. 34.95 (*0-8493-2369-X*) CRC Pr.

— Investigation of Road Traffic Fatalities: An Atlas. (Cause of Death Atlas Ser.). (Illus.). 128p. 2000. pap. 34.95 (*0-8493-2368-1*) CRC Pr.

Dix, Jay D. & Ernst, Mary F. Handbook for Death Scene Investigators. (Illus.). 131p. 1998. pap. 15.00 (*0-9663422-1-6*) Acad Info Systs.

Dix, John A. Sketch of the Resources of the City of New York: With a View of Its Municipal Government, Population, Etc. LC 79-112538. (Rise of Urban America Ser.). 1976. reprint ed. 19.95 (*0-405-02447-9*) Ayer.

Dix, Katharine F. Berks County Pa. Archives, 1767. 33p. 1989. per. 6.00 (*1-55856-016-5*, 097) Closson Pr.

— Chester County - (PA) Archives, 1765. 105p. 1990. per. 8.00 (*1-55856-061-0*, 103) Closson Pr.

Dix, Katharine F., ed. Berks County Pa. Archives, 1784. 95p. 1989. per. 8.00 (*1-55856-015-7*, 099) Closson Pr.

Dix, Keith. What's a Coal Miner to Do? The Mechanization of Coal Mining. LC 88-1337. (Social & Labor History Ser.). (Illus.). 272p. 1988. text 49.95 (*0-8229-3585-6*) U of Pittsburgh Pr.

Dix, Linda S., ed. see National Research Council Staff.

Dix, M. C., et al. Car Use: A Social & Economic Study. LC 83-14177. 265p. 1983. text 97.95 (*0-566-00666-9*, Pub. by Avebry) Ashgate Pub Co.

Dix, M. R. & Hood, J. D., eds. Vertigo. LC 83-10393. (Wiley-Medical Publication). 501p. reprint ed. pap. 155.40 (*0-8357-3469-2*, 203973100013) Bks Demand.

***Dix, Margaret A. & Dix, Michael W.** Orchids of Guatemala: A Revised Annotated Checklist. rev. annot. ed. iii, 62p. 2000. pap. 20.00 (*0-915279-66-5*) Miss Botan.

***Dix, Mark.** Discovering Auto CAD2000. LC 99-39149. (Illus.). 676p. 1999. pap. 49.00 (*0-13-084264-8*, Prentice Hall) P-H.

Dix, Mark. Discovering Autocad, Release 14. LC 98-26045. 594p. 1998. pap. 56.00 (*0-13-080183-6*) P-H.

Dix, Mark & Riley, Paul. Discovering AutoCAD Release 13 for Windows. LC 97-77749. 519p. (C). 1997. pap. 56.00 (*0-13-739491-8*) P-H.

— Fundamentals of AutoCAD R.13 for Windows. LC 97-28518. 252p. 1997. pap. 26.80 (*0-13-860362-6*) P-H.

D

An Asterisk (*) at the beginning of an entry indicates that the title is appearing for the first time.

***Dix, Mark & Riley, Paul.** Introduction to AutoCAD R.14. LC 98-50975. (Illus.). 235p. 1998. pap. 21.33 (0-13-011001-9) P-H.

— Introduction to Autocad 2000. 235p. (C). 2000. pap. 21.33 (0-13-016732-0) P-H.

Dix, Mary S., ed. see Davis, Jefferson.

Dix, Michael W., jt. auth. see Dix, Margaret A.

***Dix, Minnie.** From My Front Porch. 450p. 1999. 29.95 (1-930392-00-1) Poole & Smith.

Dix, Minnie. From My Front Porch. 458p. 1997. reprint ed. pap. 16.95 (0-944514-20-0) Williams SC.

— 150 Reasons Why I Can't Serve on Jury Duty, 2 vols., Vol. 1. large type ed. LC 96-94614. (Illus.). 70p. 1999. pap. 7.95 (0-7392-0092-5, PO2968) Morris Pubng.

Dix, O. R. & Jackson, M. P. Lithology, Microstructures, Fluid Inclusions, & Geochemistry of Rock Salt & of the Cap-Rock Contact in Oakwood Dome, East Texas: Significance for Nuclear Waste Storage. (Reports of Investigations: RI 120). (Illus.). 59p. 1982. pap. 3.00 (0-318-03261-9) Bur Econ Geology.

Dix, Robert H. The Politics of Colombia. LC 86-21168. 265p. 1986. 59.95 (0-275-92315-0, C2315, Praeger Pubs) Greenwood.

***Dix, Robin.** Mark Akenside: A Reassessment. LC 00-33571. 2000. write for info. (0-8386-3882-1) Fairleigh Dickinson.

Dix, Robin, ed. The Poetical Works of Mark Akenside. LC 95-25560. (Illus.). 600p. 1996. 69.50 (0-8386-3535-0) Fairleigh Dickinson.

Dix, Samuel M. The Cost of Future Freedom: Energy Economics. 1982. 30.00 (0-918998-05-0) Energy Educ.

— Energy: A Critical Decision for the United States Economy. LC 77-78403. (Illus.). 1977. 20.00 (0-918998-01-8) Energy Educ.

Dix, Shane, jt. auth. see Williams, Sean.

Dix, Thelma. The Irishman. large type ed. (Dales Large Print Ser.). 213p. 1997. pap. 18.99 (1-85389-775-2, Dales) Ulverscroft.

Dix, Walter S. Recollections of the American Congress on Surveying & Mapping. 94p. 1991. 25.00 (0-614-06109-1, S294) Am Congrs Survey.

Dix, William, ed. see American Library Association Committee, on Intelle.

Dixen, Jean, jt. auth. see Guzman, John.

Dixey, Graham. Microprocessor Interfacing. Thomas, Andy, ed. 112p. (Orig.). (C). 1991. 36.50 (0-7487-0583-X, Pub. by S Thornes Pubs) Trans-Atl Phila.

Dixey, Kay. Judar & His Two Brothers. (Butterfly Collection). (J). (gr. 2-8). 1990. 8.95 (0-86685-483-5, Pub. by Librairie du Liban) Intl Bk Ctr.

— Khaled & Aida: Story in Arabic. (J). 1991. 9.95 (0-86685-571-8) Intl Bk Ctr.

Dixey, Kay. Ali Baba & Forty Thieves. (Ladybird Bks.). 52p. 1993. 9.95 (0-86685-590-4, LDL192) Intl Bk Ctr.

Dixhoorn, Jan J. Van, see Van Dixhoorn, Jan J., ed.

Dixie, Quinton H. Distinguished African American Religious Leaders. (Illus.). 344p. 2001. 54.95 (1-57356-239-4) Oryx Pr.

***Dixie, Quinton Hosford & West, Cornel, eds.** The Courage to Hope: From Black Suffering to Human Redemption. LC 99-29666. 288p. 1999. pap. 21.00 (0-8070-0953-9) Beacon Pr.

Dixin, Xu. Chinese Capitalism, 1522-1840. abr. ed. LC 98-20137. 528p. 1999. text 79.95 (0-312-21729-3) St Martin.

Dixion, Joan M. National Intelligencer & Washington Advertiser Newspaper Abstracts 1811-1813. vi, 370p. 1997. pap. 22.50 (0-7884-0658-2, D398) Heritage Bk.

Dixit, Avinash. The Art of Smooth Pasting. LC 92-45249. (Fundamentals of Pure & Applied Economics Ser.: Vol. 55). 82p. 1993. pap. text 25.00 (3-7186-5384-2) Gordon & Breach.

Dixit, Avinash. Games of Strategy: Instructor's Manual. (C). pap. text, teacher ed. write for info. (0-393-97463-4) Norton.

Dixit, Avinash. Optimization in Economic Theory. 2nd ed. (Illus.). 196p. 1990. pap. text 23.00 (0-19-877210-6) OUP.

— The Theory of Equilibrium Growth. (Illus.). 214p. (C). 1976. text 29.95 (0-19-877080-4) OUP.

Dixit, Avinash K. The Making of Economic Policy: A Transaction Cost Politics Perspective. (Munich Lectures). (Illus.). 210p. 1996. 25.50 (0-262-04155-3) MIT Pr.

Dixit, Avinash K. & Nalebuff, Barry J. Thinking Strategically: The Competitive Edge in Business, Politics & Everyday Life. 416p. 1993. pap. 15.95 (0-393-31035-3) Norton.

Dixit, Avinash K. & Norman, V. D. Theory of International Trade. (Cambridge Economic Handbook Ser.). 350p. 1980. pap. text 25.95 (0-521-29969-1) Cambridge U Pr.

Dixit, Avinash K. & Pindyck, Robert S. Investment under Uncertainty. LC 93-26321. 440p. (C). 1994. text 47.50 (0-691-03410-9, Pub. by Princeton U Pr) Cal Prin Full Svc.

Dixit, Avinosh K. The Making of Economic Policy: A Transaction Cost Politics Perspective. (Munich Lectures). (Illus.). 216p. 1998. pap. text 12.50 (0-262-54098-3) MIT Pr.

Dixit, J. N. Anatomy of a Flawed Inheritance: Indo-Pak Relations 1970-94. (C). 1995. 36.00 (81-220-0404-0, Pub. by Konark Pubs) S Asia.

Dixit, J. N. My South Block Years: Memoirs of a Foreign Secretary. 1997. pap. 18.50 (81-7476-183-7, Pub. by UBS Pubs) S Asia.

Dixit, K., jt. auth. see Tuting, L.

Dixit, K., jt. ed. see Rurinf, L.

***Dixit, K. M.** Adventures of Nepali Frog. 1998. pap. 23.00 (0-7855-7520-0) St Mut.

— Conflict in the Himalayas. 1998. pap. 30.00 (0-7855-7531-6) St Mut.

Dixit, Mani. Annapurna Fantasy. 1997. pap. 24.00 (0-7855-7358-5, Pub. by Ratna Pustak Bhandar) St Mut.

Dixit, R. D. Civil Disobedience. 104p. 1980. 13.95 (0-318-36847-1) Asia Bk Corp.

Dixit, R. K. Political History of Chandalas. 1977. 16.00 (0-8364-0446-7) S Asia.

Dixit, R. S. Geography of Marketing & Commercial Activities in India: Documentation on Research Information. 1990. 22.50 (81-7022-272-9, Pub. by Concept) S Asia.

Dixit, Skeath. Games of Strategy. LC 98-49972. 1999. 72.92 (0-393-97421-9) Norton.

***Dixit, Vishweshwar.** Shrimad Bhagavat Kannudi: Kannada Bhagavadgite. xvi, 178p. 2000. 36.00 (0-9679623-0-7) Chirag CA.

Dixit, Vivek, jt. ed. see Liu, Dean-Mo.

Dixler, Debby. Celebrate Everyday. 108p. 1987. pap. 10.95 (0-9615005-5-7) First Teacher.

Dixler, Esa. The Red Badge of Courage (Crane) (Barron's Book Notes Ser.). (C). 1984. pap. 3.50 (0-8120-3438-4) Barron.

Dixmier, J. General Topology. Berberian, S. K., tr. from FRE. (Undergraduate Texts in Mathematics Ser.). 125p. 1984. 46.95 (0-387-90972-9) Spr-Verlag.

Dixmier, Jacques. Enveloping Algebras: The 1996 Printing of the 1977 English Translation. LC 96-7198. (Graduate Studies in Mathematics: No. 11). 379p. 1996. reprint ed. text 59.00 (0-8218-0560-6, GSM/11) Am Math.

***Dixon.** Advances in Immunology Vol. 74. (Illus.). 344p. (C). 1999. text 99.95 (0-12-022474-7) Acad Pr.

Dixon. Baumgarten Corruption: From Sense to Nonsense in Art & Philosophy. LC 95-3932. 1995. 54.95 (0-7453-0993-3, Pub. by Pluto GBR); pap. 18.95 (0-7453-0992-5, Pub. by Pluto GBR) Stylus Pub VA.

— Body Mechanics & Self Care. 1999. pap. text 29.95 (0-8385-0747-6, Medical Exam) Appleton & Lange.

— Clarisworks 4.0 Macintosh: Quick Course. (DF - Computer Applications Ser.). 1995. mass mkt. 15.95 (0-538-64384-6) S-W Pub.

— Digital Electronics. 128p. 1999. pap. text, lab manual ed. 37.80 (0-13-833823-X) P-H.

— Encounter with Children. 3rd ed. 1999. pap. text 49.95 (0-323-00253-6) Mosby Inc.

— Operative Breast Surgery. 1999. text 159.00 (0-443-05066-X, W B Saunders Co) Harcrt Hlth Sci Grp.

— Radio Receiver Design, Vol. 104. LC 98-29981. (Illus.). 488p. 1998. text 175.00 (0-8247-0161-5) Dekker.

— Romantic Fiction Mills & Boon. LC 97-150551. 224p. 1998. 59.95 (1-85728-266-3, Pub. by UCL Pr Ltd); pap. 19.95 (1-85728-267-1, Pub. by UCL Pr Ltd) Taylor & Francis.

— Thirty. 1999. pap. write for info. (0-8050-5924-5, Owlet BYR) H Holt & Co.

***Dixon.** Ways of Researching the World. 1998. pap. write for info. (0-582-29333-2) Addison-Wesley.

Dixon & Blake. Handbook of Australian Languages: Volume 2, Vol. 2. (Australian National University Press Ser.). 1995. pap. write for info. (0-08-032994-2, Pergamon Pr) Elsevier.

Dixon, ed. see de Vega, Lope.

Dixon, tr. see Insingel, Mark, et al.

Dixon, Gale. Aspects of Infant Mortality & Ethnicity in Malaysia: Explorations Towards a Research Agenda. LC 97-191412. 29 p. 1989. write for info. (0-7326-0132-0) Monash Asia Inst.

Dixon, Ynonne Romney. "Designs from Fancy" George Romney's Shakespearean Drawings. LC 99-161693. (Illus.). 248p. 1999. pap. text 45.00 (0-295-97784-1) U of Wash Pr.

Dixon, A. E., ed. see Solar Energy Conversion Course, 5th, University of.

Dixon, A. F. G. Aphid Ecology: An Optimization Approach. 2nd ed. 1997. text. write for info. (0-412-74180-6) Kluwer Academic.

***Dixon, A. F. G.** Insect Predator-Prey Dynamics: Ladybird Beetles & Biological Control. LC 99-45440. (Illus.). 264p. (C). 2000. 74.95 (0-521-62203-4) Cambridge U Pr.

Dixon, Addie B. East of the River: The Story of Barretts' Settlement Founded by Ex Slaves Harrison Barrett & His Family. (Illus.). 267p. 1998. 25.00 (0-9669006-9-3) Barretts.

Dixon, Adrienne, tr. see Brouwers, Jeroen.

Dixon, Adrienne, tr. see Insingel, Mark.

Dixon, Adrienne, tr. see Nooteboom, Cees.

Dixon, Alan C., jt. auth. see Antonakos, James L.

Dixon, Althea, ed. see Runyon, Linda.

Dixon, Amy, jt. auth. see Moss, Jenny Jackson.

Dixon, Andrew D., et al. Fundamentals of Bone Growth: Methodology & Applications. (Illus.). 816p. 1991. lib. bdg. 119.00 (0-8493-8820-1, QP88) CRC Pr.

— Fundamentals of Craniofacial Growth. LC 96-38685. 512p. 1997. boxed set 149.95 (0-8493-4575-8) CRC Pr.

Dixon, Andy. Dragon Quest. (Fantasy Adventure Games Ser.). (Illus.). 32p. (J). (gr. 3 up). 1997. pap. 8.95 (0-7460-2345-6, Usborne) EDC.

— Dragon Quest. (Fantasy Adventure Games Ser.). (Illus.). 32p. (J). (gr. 3 up). 1999. 16.95 (0-88110-890-1, Usborne) EDC.

— King Arthur's Knight Quest. (Fantasy Adventures Ser.). (Illus.). 32p. 1999. pap. text 8.95 (0-7460-3394-X, Usborne) EDC.

— Knights of King Arthur. (Illus.). 32p. (gr. 4-7). 1999. 16.95 (1-58086-221-7) EDC.

— Star Quest. (Fantasy Adventures Ser.). (Illus.). 32p. 1999. pap. text 8.95 (0-7460-2989-6, Usborne) EDC.

— Star Quest. (Illus.). 32p. (gr. 3-7). 1999. 16.95 (1-58086-187-3) EDC.

— Sword Quest. (Illus.). 32p. (gr. 3 up). 1998. lib. bdg. 18.95 (0-88110-995-9, Usborne) EDC.

— Sword Quest. (Illus.). 32p. (J). (gr. 3 up). 1998. pap. 8.95 (0-7460-2707-9, Usborne) EDC.

Dixon, Andy, ed. En Busca del Dragon/Dragon Quest. (Fantasy Adventures Ser.). (Illus.). 32p. (YA). (gr. 3 up). 1999. pap. 8.95 (0-7460-3433-4, Usborne) EDC.

— La Espada Encantada/Sword Quest. (Fantasy Adventures Ser.). (Illus.). 32p. (YA). (gr. 3 up). 1999. pap. 8.95 (0-7460-3435-0, Usborne) EDC.

***Dixon, Ann.** The Blueberry Shoe. LC 98-49680. (J). (ps-2). 1999. 15.95 (0-88240-518-7, Alaska NW Bks) Gr Arts Ctr Pub.

Dixon, Ann. The Blueberry Shoe. (Illus.). (J). (ps-2). 1999. pap. 8.95 (0-88240-519-5, Alaska NW Bks) Gr Arts Ctr Pub.

— The Sleeping Lady. LC 94-9157. (Illus.). 32p. (J). (ps-5). 1994. 15.95 (0-88240-444-X, Alaska NW Bks) Gr Arts Ctr Pub.

— Trick or Treat. (Read with Me Ser.). (J). 1998. 8.70 (0-606-13868-4, Pub. by Turtleback) Demco.

— Trick-or-Treat! (Read with Me Paperback Ser.). (Illus.). 32p. (J). (ps-3). 1998. pap. 2.99 (0-590-28161-5, Pub. by Scholastic Inc) Penguin Putnam.

— Waiting for Noel: An Advent Story. LC 99-23230. (Illus.). 32p. (J). (ps-5). 2000. 16.00 (0-8028-5192-4, Eerdmans Bks) Eerdmans.

Dixon, Annabelle. Clay. Stefoff, Rebecca, ed. LC 90-40369. (Threads Ser.). (Illus.). 22p. (J). (gr. 3-5). 1990. lib. bdg. 15.93 (0-944483-69-0) Garrett Ed Corp.

— Wool. Stefoff, Rebecca, ed. LC 90-40366. (Threads Ser.). (Illus.). 32p. (J). (gr. 3-5). 1990. lib. bdg. 15.93 (0-944483-73-9) Garrett Ed Corp.

Dixon, Annette, et al. Monet at Vethevil: The Turning Point. LC 94-12045. (Illus.). 118p. 1998. pap. 29.95 (0-912303-52-2) Michigan Mus.

Dixon, B. Homer. The Border or Riding Clans: Followed by a History of the Clan Dixon & a Brief Account of the Family of the Author. vi, 224p. 1996. reprint ed. pap. 21.00 (0-7884-0561-6, D396) Heritage Bk.

Dixon, Barbara M. & Wilson, Josleen. Good Health for African-American Kids. LC 95-34601. 1996. pap. 18.00 (0-614-08092-4) Crown Pub Group.

Dixon, Bernard. Power Unseen: How Microbes Rule the World. LC 93-37697. 1994. text 18.40 (0-7167-4504-6) W H Freeman.

— Power Unseen: How Microbes Rule the World. LC 95-44746. (Illus.). 272p. 1998. reprint ed. pap. text 16.95 (0-7167-4550-X) OUP.

Dixon, Beverly & Guyan, Suzanne. Compsense: California's Workers' Compensation Step by Step Usage Guide. 125p. 1994. pap. write for info. (0-9644331-0-9) Comp Sense.

Dixon, Bob, jt. auth. see Doolin, James H.

Dixon, Bonnie, tr. see Martinez, Gayle R.

Dixon, Brandt V. A Brief History of H. Sophie Newcomb Memorial College, 1887-1919: A Personal Reminiscence. (Illus.). 208p. 1998. 27.50 (0-9646222-0-3) Pelican.

***Dixon, Brian & Dixon, Mary.** Sams Teach Yourself E-Banking Today. (Illus.). 300p. 2000. 17.99 (0-672-31882-2) Sams.

Dixon, C. & Grant, A. Robin: A Hero Reborn. Raspler, Dan & O'Neil, Dennis, eds. (Illus.). 192p. 1998. mass mkt. 4.95 (1-56389-029-1, Pub. by DC Comics) Time Warner.

Dixon, C., et al. Batman: Knightfall, Pt. 2: Who Rules the Night. Kahan, Bob, ed. (Illus.). 296p. 1993. pap. 12.95 (1-56389-148-4, Pub. by DC Comics) Time Warner.

Dixon, C., et al. Batman: Knightfall, Pt. 1: Broken Bat. Kahan, Bob, ed. Vol. 1. (Illus.). 288p. 1993. pap. 12.95 (1-56389-142-5, Pub. by DC Comics) Time Warner.

Dixon, C. Scott. The Reformation & Rural Society: The Parishes of Brandeburg-Ansbach-Kulmbach, 1528-1603. (Studies in Early Modern History). 243p. (C). 1996. text 59.95 (0-521-48311-5) Cambridge U Pr.

Dixon, C. Scott, ed. The German Reformation. LC 98-56639. (Essential Readings in History Ser.). 288p. 1999. 59.95 (0-631-20810-0); pap. 24.95 (0-631-20811-9) Blackwell Pubs.

Dixon, Canon, jt. auth. see Lock, John.

Dixon, Carol. Aradus. LC 93-49597. 176p. (Orig.). 1994. pap. 4.99 (1-56722-019-3) Word Aflame.

— Language Experience Approach to Reading & Writing. (Illus.). 136p. (C). 1990. pap. 14.80 (0-13-521352-5) Alemany Pr.

— Roll Call. LC 95-33242. 270p. (Orig.). 1995. pap. text 4.99 (1-56722-138-6) Word Aflame.

Dixon, Carol, jt. auth. see Goodwin, James.

Dixon, Cassandra. Can't Knock the Hustle: A Woman's Guide for Beating a Player at His Own Game. 104p. 1999. pap. 10.00 (0-7392-0311-8, PO3338) Morris Pubng.

Dixon, Cathy, et al. Gifted & at Risk. LC 96-67182. (Fastback Ser.: No. 398). 39p. (Orig.). 1996. pap. 3.00 (0-87367-598-3) Phi Delta Kappa.

Dixon, Charles. Life in the Spirit. 89p. 1996. pap., wbk. ed. 11.99 (1-889389-09-9) End-Time Wave.

— Life in the Spirit: Understanding the Gifts & Operations of the Holy Spirit. 179p. (Orig.). 1996. pap. 4.99 (1-889389-01-3) End-Time Wave.

— The Mechanics of True Worship. 155p. (Orig.). 1996. pap. 11.99 (0-9634306-7-X) End-Time Wave.

— The Mechanics of True Worship: A Practical Workbook. 146p. (Orig.). 1996. pap. 14.99 (1-889389-00-5) End-Time Wave.

Dixon, Charles, tr. see Barriero, Enrique & Alcatena, Quique.

Dixon, Charles, tr. see Trillo, Carlos.

Dixon, Charlotte. Beautiful America's Wyoming. rev. ed. LC 89-6519. (Illus.). 80p. 1998. 19.95 (0-89802-691-1); pap. 12.95 (0-89802-690-3) Beautiful Am.

***Dixon, Charlotte G. & Emener, William G., eds.** Professional Counseling: Transitioning into the Next Millennium. LC 99-30363. (Illus.). 178p. 1999. 36.95 (0-398-06985-9); pap. 24.95 (0-398-06986-7) C C Thomas.

***Dixon, Chris.** African Americans & Haiti: Emigration & Black Nationalism in the Nineteenth Century, 186. LC 99-43506. (Contributions in American History Ser.). 264p. 2000. write for info. (0-313-31063-7) Greenwood.

Dixon, Chris. Perfecting the Family: Antislavery Marriages in Nineteenth-Century America. LC 96-47627. 336p. 1997. text 45.00 (1-55849-068-X) U of Mass Pr.

— The Thai Economy: Uneven Development & Internationalization. LC 98-4882. xx, 316 p. (C). 1999. 85.00 (0-415-02442-0) Routledge.

Dixon, Chris & Drakakis-Smith, David, eds. Uneven Development in South East Asia. LC 97-70341. 288p. 1997. 73.95 (1-85972-555-4, Pub. by Ashgate Pub) Ashgate Pub Co.

Dixon, Chris & Heffernan, Michael, eds. Colonialism & Development in the Contemporary World. (Illus.). 240p. 1991. text 110.00 (0-7201-2072-1) Continuum.

Dixon, Christa K. Negro Spirituals: From Bible to Folk Song. LC 75-36444. 127p. reprint ed. pap. 39.40 (0-608-16317-1, 202687400053) Bks Demand.

Dixon, Christine, jt. auth. see Desmond, Michael.

Dixon, Chuck. Air Wars & Other Poems. large type ed. (Illus.). 99p. 1998. pap. 20.00 (0-9628801-8-3) Coyote Pub.

— Batman: Bane. LC 97-221826. (Illus.). 48p. (Orig.). 1997. pap. 4.95 (1-56389-303-7) DC Comics.

***Dixon, Chuck.** Batman: The Chalice. 96p. 1999. 24.95 (1-56389-592-7, Pub. by DC Comics) Time Warner.

Dixon, Chuck. Batman vs. Predator III: Blood Ties. LC 99-173182. (Illus.). 136p. 1998. pap. text 7.95 (1-56389-418-1, Pub. by DC Comics) Time Warner.

— Birds of Prey: Revolution. (Illus.). 48p. 1997. pap. 2.95 (1-56389-349-5) DC Comics.

— Justice Riders. LC 97-152306. 64p. 1997. pap. 5.95 (1-56389-257-X) DC Comics.

***Dixon, Chuck.** Nightwing: Love & Bullets. (Illus.). 144p. 2000. pap. 17.95 (1-56389-613-3, Pub. by DC Comics) Time Warner.

Dixon, Chuck. Nightwing: Rough Justice. (Illus.). 224p. 1999. text 17.95 (1-56389-523-4, Pub. by DC Comics) Time Warner.

***Dixon, Chuck.** Robin: Flying Solo. (Robin Ser.). 144p. (YA). 2000. pap. text 12.95 (1-56389-609-5) DC Comics.

Dixon, Chuck & Gorfinkel, Jordan. Birds of Prey. (Illus.). 208p. (Orig.). 1999. pap. text 17.95 (1-56389-484-X, Pub. by DC Comics) Time Warner.

Dixon, Chuck & Nolan, Graham. The Joker: Devil's Advocate. LC 96-134900. (Illus.). 96p. 1996. pap. 12.95 (1-56389-280-4, Pub. by DC Comics) Time Warner.

Dixon, Chuck, et al. Batman: Knightsend. LC 95-171505. (Illus.). 320p. 1995. pap. 14.95 (1-56389-191-3, Pub. by DC Comics) Time Warner.

Dixon, Chuck, et al. Batman: Legacy. LC 97-175312. (Illus.). 280p. 1997. pap. 17.95 (1-56389-337-1, Pub. by DC Comics) Time Warner.

— Catwoman: The Catfile. LC 96-226382. (Illus.). 128p. 1996. pap. 9.95 (1-56389-262-6, Pub. by DC Comics) Time Warner.

Dixon, Chuck, jt. auth. see Marz, Ron.

***Dixon, Clare & Fisher, Michael, eds.** Temporal Representation & Reasoning (TIME-99) Proceedings of the 6th International Workshop on Temporal Representation & Reasoningn Orlando, FL. LC 99-61665. 106p. 1999. pap. 110.00 (0-7695-0173-7) IEEE Comp Soc.

Dixon, Conrad. Start to Navigate. (Illus.). 120p. 1977. 11.95 (0-8464-1139-3) Beekman Pubs.

— Using GPS. 2nd rev. ed. LC 98-46569. (Illus.). 112p. 1999. pap. 16.50 (1-57409-059-3) Sheridan.

Dixon, D. L. & Dugdale, L. M. An Introduction to Clinical Imaging. (Illus.). 316p. 1988. pap. text 35.00 (0-443-03060-X) Church.

Dixon, D. Nomathande. Rumpelstiltskin. rev. ed. LC 93-72071. (Illus.). 32p. (J). (ps-2). 1995. pap. 9.95 (1-882171-01-2) Confetti Ent.

Dixon, Danny. Essential Christian Baptism. 120p. 1990. pap. 4.95 (0-940999-71-4, C-2171) Star Bible.

Dixon, Danny A. Baptism - Which One Did You Receive? 96p. (Orig.). 1996. pap. 4.95 (1-56794-095-1, C-2396) Star Bible.

— Standing to Change - Changing to Stand. 122p. (Orig.). 1993. pap. 5.95 (1-56794-034-X, C2293) Star Bible.

Dixon, David. From Prohibition to Regulation: Bookmaking, Anti-Gambling, & the Law. 422p. 1991. text 95.00 (0-19-825616-7) OUP.

— Hero of Beecher Island: The Life & Military Career of George A. Forsyth. LC 94-2225. (Illus.). xviii, 275p. 1994. pap. 14.00 (0-8032-6605-7, Bison Books) U of Nebr Pr.

— Law in Policing: Legal Regulation & Policing Practice. LC 97-226. (Clarendon Studies in Criminology). 384p. 1997. text 78.00 (0-19-826476-3, Clarendon Pr) OUP.

Dixon, David R. The Frontier Experience: An Evolutionary Perspective. Larkin, William, ed. (Illus.). 250p. 1999. pap. text 19.95 (0-9669717-1-X) Laser Print.

Dixon, Debra. Goal, Motivation & Conflict: The Building Blocks of Good Fiction. (Illus.). 164p. 1996. 18.95 (0-9654371-0-8) Gryphon Bks Writers.

— Writing Your Heritage: A Sequence of Thinking, Reading & Writing Assignments. Ylvisaker, Miriam, ed. (Illus.). 88p. (Orig.). 1993. pap. 8.00 (1-883920-08-6) Nat Writing Proj.

Dixon, Debra S. & Henry, Susan V. Our Earth Vol. 1: The Water Planet: An Introduction. Spence, Lundie & San Jose, Christine, eds. (Illus.). 45p. (Orig.). (J). (gr. 3-7). 1992. pap. 14.95 (0-9609506-2-1) Prescott Durrell & Co.

Dixon, Deirdre Falvey, jt. auth. see Dixon, Stephen.

***Dixon, Dennis.** Finding Hidden Profits A Guide for Custom Builders. LC 98-45914. 1998. write for info. (0-86718-451-5) Home Builder.

Dixon, Dennis. It's a Queer Bird, the Hedgehog. (C). 1989. text 60.00 (1-85821-015-1, Pub. by Pentland Pr) St Mut.

Dixon, Diane. The Everyday Potato. LC 92-16738. 1993. 20.00 (0-679-40918-1) Villard Books.

Dixon, Dick. Trails among the Columbine, 1995/1996: The Calumet Branch & the Turret Mining Area. Collman, Russ, ed. (Illus.). 320p. 1996. 37.00 (0-913582-62-X, 0255) Sundance.

Dixon, Don, jt. auth. see Bishop, Paul.

Dixon, Doris. Memoirs of a Compassionate Terrorist. LC 97-75370. 120p. 1998. pap. 9.95 (1-882792-56-4) Proctor Pubns.

Dixon, Dorothy. Leather & Lace No. 2: The Trembling Heart. (Orig.). 1982. mass mkt. 2.50 (0-686-97467-0, Zebra Kensgtn) Kensgtn Pub Corp.

— The Night of the Green Dragon. (Illus.). 32p. 1996. pap. text 4.95 (0-19-421947-X) OUP.

Dixon, Dougal. After Man. 124p. 1998. pap. 15.95 (0-312-19433-1) St Martin.

— Be a Dinosaur Detective. (Illus.). 36p. (J). (gr. k-4). 1988. pap. 6.95 (0-8225-9538-9, First Ave Edns) Lerner Pub.

— The Changing Earth. LC 93-6829. (Young Geographer Ser.). (Illus.). 32p. (J). 1993. lib. bdg. 5.00 (1-56847-052-5) Raintree Steck-V.

— Dino Dots. 20p. 1989. pap. 4.95 (0-671-67084-0) S&S Trade.

— Dinosaur: An Interactive Guide to the Dinosaur World. (DK Action Packs Ser.). (Illus.). 16p. (J). (gr. 3-7). 1994. pap. 19.95 (1-56458-683-9) DK Pub Inc.

— Dinosaurs. LC 95-43798. (Pocket Gem Ser.). (Illus.). 64p. (J). (gr. 1 up). 1996. 3.95 (0-8120-6589-1) Barron.

— Dinosaurs: A Closer Look. (Illus.). 32p. (J). (gr. 3 up). 1996. pap. 4.95 (1-56397-533-5) Boyds Mills Pr.

— Dinosaurs: A Closer Look. rev. ed. (New Dinosaur Dynasty Ser.). (Illus.). 32p. (J). (gr. 2-6). 1998. lib. bdg. 21.27 (1-884756-62-X) Davidson Titles.

— Dinosaurs: All Shapes & Sizes. (Illus.). 32p. (J). (gr. 3 up). 1995. pap. 4.95 (1-56397-535-1) Boyds Mills Pr.

— Dinosaurs: All Shapes & Sizes. (New Dinosaur Dynasty Ser.). (Illus.). 32p. (J). (gr. 2-6). 1998. lib. bdg. 21.27 (1-884756-60-3) Davidson Titles.

— Dinosaurs: Giants of the Earth. (Illus.). 32p. (J). (gr. 3 up). 1995. pap. 4.95 (1-56397-534-3) Boyds Mills Pr.

— Dinosaurs: Giants of the Earth. rev. ed. (New Dinosaur Dynasty Ser.). (Illus.). 32p. (J). (gr. 2-6). 1998. lib. bdg. 21.27 (1-884756-63-8) Davidson Titles.

— Dinosaurs: The Fossil Hunters. (Illus.). 32p. (J). (gr. 3 up). 1996. pap. 4.95 (1-56397-532-7) Boyds Mills Pr.

— Dinosaurs: The Fossil Hunters. rev. ed. (New Dinosaur Dynasty Ser.). (Illus.). 32p. (J). (gr. 2-6). 1998. lib. bdg. 21.27 (1-884756-61-1) Davidson Titles.

— Dinosaurs: The Real Monsters. (Illus.). 32p. (J). (gr. 3 up). 1995. pap. 4.95 (1-56397-536-X) Boyds Mills Pr.

— Dinosaurs: The Real Monsters. rev. ed. (New Dinosaur Dynasty Ser.). (Illus.). 32p. (J). (gr. 2-6). 1998. lib. bdg. 21.27 (1-884756-64-6) Davidson Titles.

***Dixon, Dougal.** Dougal Dixon's Amazing Dinosaurs: The Fiercest, the Tallest, the Toughest, the Smallest. LC 00-65298. (Illus.). 128p. (YA). (gr. 1 up). 2000. lib. bdg. 17.95 (1-56397-773-7) Boyds Mills Pr.

Dixon, Dougal. Dougal Dixon's Dinosaurs. (Illus.). 160p. (J). (gr. 4-8). 1998. 19.95 (1-56397-722-2) Boyds Mills Pr.

— Introduction to Rocks & Minerals. 1996. 6.98 (0-7858-0547-8) Bk Sales Inc.

— The Practical Geologist. Bernor, Raymond L., ed. (Illus.). 160p. (Orig.). 1992. per. 15.00 (0-671-74697-9) S&S Trade Pap.

— Prehistoric Life. (Spotlights Ser.). (J). (gr. 3-5). 1996. 9.95 (0-614-15688-2) OUP.

— Prehistoric Life. (Spotlights Ser.). (Illus.). 46p. (J). (gr. 3-5). 1996. 11.95 (0-19-521237-1) OUP.

— Questions & Answers about Dinosaurs. LC 94-31066. (Questions & Answers about Ser.). (Illus.). 40p. (J). (gr. 2-6). 1995. pap. 8.95 (1-85697-553-3) LKC.

— The Search for Dinosaurs. (Digging up the Past Ser.). (Illus.). 48p. (J). (gr. 4-6). 1995. lib. bdg. 24.26 (1-56847-396-6) Raintree Steck-V.

Dixon, Dougal, ed. The Macmillan Illustrated Encyclopedia of Dinosaurs & Prehistoric Animals. (Illus.). 312p. 1988. 39.95 (0-02-580191-0) Macmillan.

Dixon, Dougal, jt. auth. see Stace, Alexa.

***Dixon, Douglas, et al.** The Simon & Schuster Encyclopedia of Dinosaurs & Prehistoric Creatures: A Visual Who's Who of Prehistoric Life. LC 99-24588. (Illus.). 312p. 1999. 40.00 (0-684-86411-8) S&S Trade.

***Dixon, E. James.** Bones, Boats, & Bison: Archeology & the First Colonization of North America. LC 99-41913. (Illus.). 320p. 1999. 49.95 (0-8263-2057-0); pap. 24.95 (0-8263-2138-0) U of NM Pr.

Dixon, Edla & Dixon, James, eds. Antioch: The Dixon Era, 1959-1975. LC 91-70339. xii, 232p. (Orig.). 1991. pap. 9.95 (0-9621921-3-9) Bastille Bks.

Dixon, Edna. Understanding & Using Microsoft PowerPoint 4.0. LC 95-37993. (Microcomputing Ser.). 150p. (C). 1996. mass mkt. 8.75 (0-314-04655-0) West Pub.

Dixon, Edward L., Jr. The Franchise Annual Directory, 1998: The Original Franchise Directory & Handbook. 29th ed. 350p. 1998. pap. 39.95 (0-9692267-6-4) Info Franchise.

Dixon, Ella H. The Story of a Modern Woman. (Radical Fiction Ser.). 288p. 1990. reprint ed. lib. bdg. 25.00 (0-929587-40-5) I R Dee.

Dixon, Ellen B., jt. auth. see Nadeau, Kathleen G.

Dixon Eppley, Anita, jt. auth. see Eppley, George.

Dixon, Ervin. I'm Free! Reaching for Your Inner Desire to Free Yourself from Tobacco, Drugs, & Alcohol Addictions Forever! 40p. 1997. pap. 8.00 (0-8059-4296-3) Dorrance.

Dixon, Ethyl, jt. auth. see Tate, Bibby.

Dixon, Eustace A. Gospel Music: Vocal Cords & Related Issues. LC 93-75018. (Illus.). (Orig.). 1994. pap. text 19.95 (0-942848-07-1) Eureka Pubns.

— New Jersey: Environment & Cancer. Vivian, V. Eugene, ed. (Illus.). 410p. (C). 1982. pap. 19.95 (0-942848-01-2) Eureka Pubns.

— Syndromes for the Layperson: Now I Know What's Wrong with Me. 108p. 1988. 8.95 (0-942848-04-7) Eureka Pubns.

Dixon, Frank. Dixon & Northup Families: Genealogy of Descendants of John S. Dixon (ab. 1778) (etc.), Stephen Northup (ab. 1660), Nicholas Northup (ab. 1695) (etc.) 1997. reprint ed. pap. write for info. (0-8328-8318-2) Higginson Bk Co.

— Dixon & Northup Families: Genealogy of Descendantsof John S. Dixon (ab. 1778) (etc.), Stephen Northup (ab. 1660), Nicholas Northup (ab. 1695) (etc.) 1997. reprint ed. lib. bdg. write for info. (0-8328-8317-4) Higginson Bk Co.

Dixon, Frank H. State Railroad Control with a History of Its Development in Iowa. Bruchey, Stuart, ed. LC 80-1303. (Railroads Ser.). 1981. reprint ed. lib. bdg. 24.95 (0-405-13772-9) Ayer.

Dixon, Frank J. Advances in Immunology. (C). 1998. text 89.95 (0-12-022471-2) Acad Pr.

— Advances in Immunology. 400p. 1999. 89.95 (0-12-022472-0) Acad Pr.

— Advances in Immunology, Vol. 63. (Illus.). 468p. 1996. text 95.00 (0-12-022463-1) Acad Pr.

— Advances in Immunology, Vol. 70. (Illus.). 574p. (C). 1998. text. write for info. (0-12-022470-4) Harcourt.

***Dixon, Frank J., ed.** Advances in Immunology. (Advances in Immunology Ser.: Vol. 75). 325p. 2000. 99.95 (0-12-022475-5) Acad Pr.

Dixon, Frank J., ed. Advances in Immunology, Vol. 50. (Illus.). 343p. (C). 1991. text 104.00 (0-12-022450-X) Acad Pr.

— Advances in Immunology, Vol. 51. (Illus.). 397p. 1992. text 104.00 (0-12-022451-8) Acad Pr.

— Advances in Immunology, Vol. 53. (Illus.). 342p. 1993. text 104.00 (0-12-022453-4) Acad Pr.

— Advances in Immunology, Vol. 54. (Illus.). 443p. 1993. text 104.00 (0-12-022454-2) Acad Pr.

— Advances in Immunology, Vol. 55. (Illus.). 456p. 1993. text 104.00 (0-12-022455-0) Acad Pr.

— Advances in Immunology, Vol. 56. 501p. 1994. text 104.00 (0-12-022456-9) Acad Pr.

— Advances in Immunology, Vol. 57. (Illus.). 391p. 1994. text 94.00 (0-12-022457-7) Acad Pr.

— Advances in Immunology, Vol. 58. (Illus.). 472p. 1995. text 90.00 (0-12-022458-5) Acad Pr.

— Advances in Immunology, Vol. 59. (Illus.). 468p. 1995. text 94.00 (0-12-022459-3) Acad Pr.

— Advances in Immunology, Vol. 60. (Illus.). 388p. 1995. text 85.00 (0-12-022460-7) Acad Pr.

— Advances in Immunology, Vol. 61. (Illus.). 416p. 1996. text 85.00 (0-12-022461-5) Acad Pr.

— Advances in Immunology, Vol. 62. (Illus.). 316p. 1996. text 79.00 (0-12-022462-3, Vol. 62) Acad Pr.

— Advances in Immunology, Vol. 64. (Illus.). 365p. 1997. text 89.00 (0-12-022464-X) Morgan Kaufmann.

— Advances in Immunology, Vol. 65. (Illus.). 408p. 1997. text 89.00 (0-12-022465-8) Morgan Kaufmann.

— Advances in Immunology, Vol. 66. (Illus.). 322p. 1997. text 89.95 (0-12-022466-6) Morgan Kaufmann.

— Advances in Immunology, Vol. 68. (Illus.). 432p. 1998. text 89.95 (0-12-022468-2) Morgan Kaufmann.

— Advances in Immunology, Vol. 69. (Illus.). 462p. 1998. boxed set 89.95 (0-12-022469-0) Acad Pr.

— Advances in Immunology Vol. 67: Cumulative Subject Index, Vols. 37-65, Vol. 67. (Illus.). 326p. 1997. text 89.95 (0-12-022467-4) Morgan Kaufmann.

***Dixon, Frank J., ed.** Advances in Immunology Vol. 73. 530p. 1999. 105.00 (0-12-022473-9) Acad Pr.

Dixon, Franklin W. The Abracadabra Case. (Hardy Boys Are: The Clues Brothers Ser.: No. 7). (Illus.). (J). (gr. 2-4). 1998. pap. 3.99 (0-671-00408-5) PB.

— The Abracadabra Case. (Hardy Boys Are: The Clues Brothers Ser.: No. 7). (Illus.). (J). (gr. 2-4). 1998. 9.09 (0-606-13402-6, Pub. by Turtleback) Demco.

— Absolute Zero. (Hardy Boys Casefiles Ser.: No. 121). 160p. (YA). (gr. 6 up). 1997. pap. 3.99 (0-671-56121-9, Archway) PB.

Dixon, Franklin W. Absolute Zero, 121. (Hardy Boys Casefiles Ser.: No. 121). (YA). (gr. 6 up). 1997. 9.09 (0-606-11435-1, Pub. by Turtleback) Demco.

Dixon, Franklin W. Acting Up. (Hardy Boys Casefiles Ser.: No. 116). (YA). (gr. 7 up). 1996. pap. 3.99 (0-671-50488-6) PB.

— Acting Up. (Hardy Boys Casefiles Ser.: No. 116). (YA). (gr. 6 up). 1996. 9.09 (0-606-09388-5, Pub. by Turtleback) Demco.

— Against All Odds. Greenberg, Anne, ed. (Hardy Boys Casefiles Ser.: No. 96). 160p. (YA). (gr. 7 up). 1995. pap. 3.99 (0-671-88207-4, Archway) PB.

Dixon, Franklin W. Against All Odds. (Hardy Boys Casefiles Ser.: No. 96). (YA). (gr. 6 up). 1995. 9.09 (0-606-07618-2, Pub. by Turtleback) Demco.

Dixon, Franklin W. The Alaskan Adventure. (Hardy Boys Mystery Stories Ser.: No. 138). (J). (gr. 3-6). 1996. 9.09 (0-606-09378-8, Pub. by Turtleback) Demco.

— The Arctic Patrol Mystery. LC 69-12164. (Hardy Boys Mystery Stories Ser.: No. 48). (Illus.). 180p. (J). (gr. 4-7). 1969. 5.95 (0-448-08948-3, G & D) Peng Put Young Read.

— Attack of the Video Villians. Greenberg, Ann, ed. (Hardy Boys Mystery Stories Ser.: No. 106). 160p. (J). (gr. 3-6). 1991. pap. 3.99 (0-671-69275-5, Minstrel Bks) PB.

— Attack of the Video Villians. (Hardy Boys Mystery Stories Ser.: No. 106). (J). (gr. 3-6). 1991. 9.09 (0-606-04610-0, Pub. by Turtleback) Demco.

— Bad Chemistry. (Hardy Boys Casefiles Ser.: No. 110). (YA). (gr. 7 up). 1996. pap. 3.99 (0-671-50433-9, Archway) PB.

— Bad Chemistry. (Hardy Boys Casefiles Ser.: No. 110). (J). (gr. 6 up). 1996. 9.09 (0-606-09382-6, Pub. by Turtleback) Demco.

— Bad Rap. Greenberg, Ann, ed. (Hardy Boys Casefiles Ser.: No. 73). 160p. (J). (gr. 6 up). 1993. pap. 3.99 (0-671-73109-2, Archway) PB.

— Bad Rap. (Hardy Boys Casefiles Ser.: No. 73). (YA). (gr. 6 up). 1993. 9.09 (0-606-02668-1, Pub. by Turtleback) Demco.

***Dixon, Franklin W.** The Bike Race Ruckus. (Hardy Boys Are: The Clues Brothers Ser.: Vol. 17). (Illus.). 80p. (J). (gr. 2-4). 2000. per. 3.99 (0-671-04041-3, Minstrel Bks) PB.

Dixon, Franklin W. Blood Sport. LC 49-243270. (Hardy Boys Casefiles Ser.: No. 117). 155p. (YA). (gr. 7 up). 1996. per. 3.99 (0-671-56117-0) PB.

— Blood Sport. (Hardy Boys Casefiles Ser.: No. 117). (J). (gr. 6 up). 1996. 9.09 (0-606-10836-X, Pub. by Turtleback) Demco.

— Blown Away. (Hardy Boys Casefiles Ser.: No. 108). (YA). (gr. 6 up). 1996. 9.09 (0-606-09380-X, Pub. by Turtleback) Demco.

— Bombay Boomerang. (Hardy Boys Mystery Stories Ser.: No. 49). (Illus.). 180p. (J). (gr. 3-6). 1970. 5.95 (0-448-08949-1, G & D) Peng Put Young Read.

— Campaign of Crime. (Hardy Boys Casefiles Ser.: No. 103). (YA). (gr. 6 up). 1995. 9.09 (0-606-07616-6, Pub. by Turtleback) Demco.

— The Caribbean Cruise Caper. (Hardy Boys Mystery Stories Ser.: No. 154). 160p. (J). (gr. 4-7). 1999. pap. 3.99 (0-671-02549-X) PB.

— The Case of the Counterfeit Criminals. Winkler, Ellen, ed. (Hardy Boys Mystery Stories Ser.: No. 114). 160p. (J). (gr. 4-7). 1992. pap. 3.99 (0-671-73061-4, Minstrel Bks) PB.

Dixon, Franklin W. The Case of the Counterfeit Criminals. (Hardy Boys Mystery Stories Ser.: No. 114). (J) (gr. 3-6). 1992. 9.09 (0-606-02195-7, Pub. by Turtleback) Demco.

Dixon, Franklin W. Castle Fear. Greenberg, Ann, ed. (Hardy Boys Casefiles Ser.: No. 44). 160p. (YA). (gr. 7 up). 1991. per. 3.75 (0-671-74615-4, Archway) PB.

— Castle Fear. (Hardy Boys Casefiles Ser.: No. 44). (YA). (gr. 6 up). 1990. 8.85 (0-606-04630-5, Pub. by Turtleback) Demco.

— Cave Trap. (Hardy Boys Casefiles Ser.: No. 115). (YA). (gr. 7 up). 1996. pap. 3.99 (0-671-50462-2) PB.

— Cave Trap. (Hardy Boys Casefiles Ser.: No. 115). (YA). (gr. 6 up). 1996. 9.09 (0-606-09387-7, Pub. by Turtleback) Demco.

— The Chase for the Mystery Twister. (Hardy Boys Mystery Stories Ser.: No. 149). (J). (gr. 3-6). 1998. pap. 3.99 (0-671-00123-X, Minstrel Bks) PB.

— The Chase for the Mystery Twister. (Hardy Boys Mystery Stories Ser.: No. 149). (J). (gr. 3-6). 1998. 9.09 (0-606-13463-8, Pub. by Turtleback) Demco.

— Clean Sweep. (Hardy Boys Casefiles Ser.: No. 114). (YA). (gr. 6 up). 1996. 9.09 (0-606-09386-9, Pub. by Turtleback) Demco.

— The Clue in the Embers. (Hardy Boys Mystery Stories Ser.: No. 35). (Illus.). 196p. (J). (gr. 3-6). 1956. 5.99 (0-448-08935-1, G & D) Peng Put Young Read.

— The Clue of the Broken Blade. LC 73-119043. (Hardy Boys Mystery Stories Ser.: No. 21). (Illus.). 180p. (J). (gr. 4-7). 1942. 5.95 (0-448-08921-1, G & D) Peng Put Young Read.

— The Clue of the Hissing Serpent. LC 73-13373. (Hardy Boys Mystery Stories Ser.: No. 53). (Illus.). 196p. (J). (gr. 4-7). 1974. 5.95 (0-448-08953-X, G & D) Peng Put Young Read.

— The Clue of the Screeching Owl. (Hardy Boys Mystery Stories Ser.: No. 41). (Illus.). 180p. (J). (gr. 4-7). 1962. 5.95 (0-448-08941-6, G & D) Peng Put Young Read.

— The Cold Cash Caper. (Hardy Boys Mystery Stories Ser.: No. 136). (J). (gr. 3-6). 1996. per. 3.99 (0-671-50520-3) PB.

— The Cold Cash Caper. (Hardy Boys Mystery Stories Ser.: No. 136). (J). (gr. 3-6). 1996. 9.09 (0-606-09376-1, Pub. by Turtleback) Demco.

— Collision Course. (Hardy Boys Casefiles Ser.: No. 33). 160p. (YA). (gr. 6 up). 1991. pap. 3.50 (0-671-74666-9, Archway) PB.

— Competitive Edge. (Hardy Boys Casefiles Ser.: No. 111). (YA). (gr. 7 up). 1996. mass mkt. 3.99 (0-671-50446-0, PB Trade Paper) PB.

— Competitive Edge. (Hardy Boys Casefiles Ser.: No. 111). (YA). (gr. 6 up). 1996. 9.09 (0-606-09383-4, Pub. by Turtleback) Demco.

— Crime in the Kennel. (Hardy Boys Mystery Stories Ser.: No. 133). 160p. (J). (gr. 4-7). 1995. per. 3.99 (0-671-87217-6, Minstrel Bks) PB.

— Crime in the Kennel. (Hardy Boys Mystery Stories Ser.: No. 133). (J). (gr. 3-6). 1995. 9.09 (0-606-07612-3, Pub. by Turtleback) Demco.

— The Crimson Flame, No. 77. (Hardy Boys Mystery Stories Ser.: Vol. 77). (J). (gr. 3-6). 1987. pap. 3.99 (0-671-64286-3, Minstrel Bks) PB.

— The Crisscross Crime. (Hardy Boys Mystery Stories Ser.: No. 150). (J). (gr. 3-6). 1998. per. 3.99 (0-671-00743-2) PB.

— The Crisscross Crime, (Hardy Boys Mystery Stories Ser.: No. 150). (J). (gr. 3-6). 1998. 9.09 (0-606-13464-6, Pub. by Turtleback) Demco.

— The Crisscross Shadow. rev. ed. (Hardy Boys Mystery Stories Ser.: No. 33). (Illus.). 180p. (J). (gr. 4-7). 1953. 5.95 (0-448-08932-7, G & D) Peng Put Young Read.

Dixon, Franklin W. Crusade of the Flaming Sword. (Hardy Boys Mystery Stories Ser.: No. 131). (J). (gr. 3-6). 1995. 9.09 (0-606-07610-7, Pub. by Turtleback) Demco.

Dixon, Franklin W. Cult of Crime. (Hardy Boys Casefiles Ser.: No. 3). (YA). (gr. 6 up). 1989. mass mkt. 3.99 (0-671-68726-3, Archway) PB.

— Cult of Crime. (Hardy Boys Casefiles Ser.: No. 3). (YA). (gr. 6 up). 1987. 9.09 (0-606-02678-9, Pub. by Turtleback) Demco.

— Danger in the Extreme. (Hardy Boys Mystery Stories Ser.: No. 152). (J). (gr. 4-7). 1998. per. 3.99 (0-671-02173-7) PB.

— Danger on the Diamond. Greenberg, Anne, ed. (Hardy Boys Mystery Stories Ser.: No. 90). 160p. (J). (gr. 3-6). 1988. pap. 3.99 (0-671-63425-9, Minstrel Bks) PB.

— Danger on Vampire Trail. LC 70-130337. (Hardy Boys Mystery Stories Ser.: No. 50). (Illus.). 180p. (J). (gr. 4-7). 1971. 5.95 (0-448-08950-5, G & D) Peng Put Young Read.

— Danger Unlimited. Greenberg, Anne, ed. LC 94-115322. (Hardy Boys Casefiles Ser.: No. 79). 160p. (J). (gr. 7 up). 1993. mass mkt. 3.99 (0-671-79463-9, Archway) PB.

— Danger Unlimited. (Hardy Boys Casefiles Ser.: No. 79). (YA). (gr. 6 up). 1993. 9.09 (0-606-05340-9, Pub. by Turtleback) Demco.

— Danger Zone. (Hardy Boys Casefiles Ser.: No. 37). (YA). (gr. 6 up). 1991. pap. 3.75 (0-671-73751-1) PB.

***Dixon, Franklin W.** Daredevils. (Hardy Boys Mystery Stories Ser.: No. 159). 160p. (J). (gr. 3-6). 2000. pap. 3.99 (0-671-03861-3, Minstrel Bks) PB.

Dixon, Franklin W. Darkness Falls. (Hardy Boys Casefiles Ser.: No. 89). (J). (gr. 6 up). 1994. 9.09 (0-606-06446-X, Pub. by Turtleback) Demco.

— Darkness Falls. abr. ed. Ashby, Ruth, ed. LC 00-1864. (Hardy Boys Casefiles Ser.: No. 89). 160p. (YA). (gr. 7 up). 1994. mass mkt. 3.99 (0-671-79473-6, Archway) PB.

— Day of the Dinosaur. Ashby, Ruth, ed. (Hardy Boys Mystery Stories Ser.: No. 128). 160p. (J). (gr. 3-6). 1994. mass mkt. 3.99 (0-671-87212-5, Minstrel Bks) PB.

Dixon, Franklin W. Day of the Dinosaur. (Hardy Boys Mystery Stories Ser.: No. 128). (J). (gr. 3-6). 1994. 9.09 (0-606-06999-2, Pub. by Turtleback) Demco.

Dixon, Franklin W. Dead in the Water. (Hardy Boys Casefiles Ser.: No. 127). (YA). (gr. 6 up). 1998. pap. 3.99 (0-671-56242-8) PB.

— Dead in the Water. (Hardy Boys Casefiles Ser.: No. 127). (YA). (gr. 6 up). 1998. 9.09 (0-606-13468-9, Pub. by Turtleback) Demco.

— Dead Man in Deadwood. Greenberg, Anne, ed. (Hardy Boys Casefiles Ser.: No. 87). 160p. (YA). (gr. 6 up). 1994. pap. 3.99 (0-671-79471-X, Archway) PB.

— Dead Man in Deadwood. (Hardy Boys Casefiles Ser.: No. 87). (YA). (gr. 6 up). 1994. 9.09 (0-606-06444-3, Pub. by Turtleback) Demco.

— Dead of Night. (Hardy Boys Casefiles Ser.: No. 80). 160p. (YA). (gr. 6 up). 1993. mass mkt. 3.99 (0-671-79464-7, Archway) PB.

— Dead of Night. (Hardy Boys Casefiles Ser.: No. 80). (YA). (gr. 6 up). 1993. 9.09 (0-606-05341-7, Pub. by Turtleback) Demco.

— Dead on Target. LC 88-21496. (Hardy Boys Casefiles Ser.: No. 1). (J). (gr. 7 up). 1991. mass mkt. 3.99 (0-671-73992-1, Archway) PB.

— Dead on Target. (Hardy Boys Casefiles Ser.: No. 1). (YA). (gr. 6 up). 1987. 8.85 (0-606-02714-9, Pub. by Turtleback) Demco.

— The Dead Season. (Hardy Boys Casefiles Ser.: No. 35). (YA). (gr. 6 up). 1990. 8.60 (0-606-00681-8, Pub. by Turtleback) Demco.

— Deadfall. (Hardy Boys Casefiles Ser.: No. 60). (YA). (gr. 6 up). 1992. 8.85 (0-606-00388-6, Pub. by Turtleback) Demco.

— Deathgame. (Hardy Boys Casefiles Ser.: No. 7). 160p. (YA). (gr. 6 up). 1991. mass mkt. 3.99 (0-671-73672-8, Archway) PB.

— Deep Trouble. Greenberg, Anne, ed. (Hardy Boys Casefiles Ser.: No. 54). 160p. (YA). (gr. 6 up). 1991. pap. 3.99 (0-671-73090-8, Archway) PB.

Dixon, Franklin W. Deep Trouble. (Hardy Boys Casefiles Ser.: No. 54). (YA). (gr. 6 up). 1991. 9.09 (0-606-04905-3, Pub. by Turtleback) Demco.

Dixon, Franklin W. The Demon's Den. (Hardy Boys Mystery Stories Ser.: No. 81). (J). (gr. 3-6). 1986. pap. 3.50 (0-685-08795-6) PB.

— The Desert Thieves. (Hardy Boys Mystery Stories Ser.: No. 141). 160p. (J). (gr. 5-7). 1996. pap. 3.99 (0-671-50527-0, PB Trade Paper) PB.

Dixon, Franklin W. The Desert Thieves. (Hardy Boys Mystery Stories Ser.: No. 141). (J). (gr. 3-6). 1996. 9.09 (0-606-11428-9, Pub. by Turtleback) Demco.

Dixon, Franklin W. Dinosaur Disaster. (Hardy Boys Are: The Clues Brothers Ser.: No. 5). (Illus.). (J). (gr. 2-4). 1998. pap. 3.99 (0-671-00406-9) PB.

— Dinosaur Disaster, 5. (Hardy Boys Are: The Clues Brothers Ser.: No. 5). (Illus.). (J). (gr. 2-4). 1998. 9.09 (0-606-13400-X, Pub. by Turtleback) Demco.

— Dirty Deeds. Greenberg, Ann, ed. (Hardy Boys Casefiles Ser.: No. 49). 160p. (YA). (gr. 7 up). 1991. pap. 3.99 (0-671-70046-4, Archway) PB.

D

— Dirty Deeds. (Hardy Boys Casefiles Ser.: No. 49). (YA). (gr. 6 up). 1991. 9.09 (*0-606-04654-2*, Pub. by Turtleback) Demco.

— The Disappearing Floor. (Hardy Boys Mystery Stories Ser.: No. 19). (Illus.). 180p. (J). (gr. 4-7). 1940. 5.95 (*0-448-08919-X*, G & D) Peng Put Young Read.

— The Doggone Detectives. (Hardy Boys Are: The Clues Brothers Ser.: No. 8). (Illus.). (J). (gr. 2-4). 1998. pap. 3.99 (*0-671-00409-3*, Minstrel Bks) PB.

— Edge of Destruction. (Hardy Boys Casefiles Ser.: No. 5). 160p. (YA). (gr. 6 up). 1991. mass mkt. 3.99 (*0-671-73669-8*, Archway) PB.

— The Emperor's Shield. (Hardy Boys Casefiles Ser.: No. 119). 160p. (YA). (gr. 6 up). 1997. pap. 3.99 (*0-671-56119-7*) PB.

Dixon, Franklin W. The Emperor's Shield. (Hardy Boys Casefiles Ser.: No. 119). (YA). (gr. 6 up). 1997. 9.09 (*0-606-11433-5*, Pub. by Turtleback) Demco.

— The End of the Trail. (Hardy Boys Mystery Stories Ser.: No. 162). 160p. (J). (gr. 3-6). 2000. per. 3.99 (*0-671-04759-0*, Minstrel Bks) PB.

Dixon, Franklin W. Evil, Inc. LC 88-21373. (Hardy Boys Casefiles Ser.: No. 2). (YA). (gr. 7 up). 1991. pap. 3.99 (*0-671-73668-X*, Archway) PB.

— Evil, Inc. (Hardy Boys Casefiles Ser.: No. 2). (YA). (gr. 6 up). 1987. 9.09 (*0-606-02717-3*, Pub. by Turtleback) Demco.

— Eye on Crime. (Hardy Boys Mystery Stories Ser.: No. 153). 160p. (J). (gr. 4-7). 1998. pap. 3.99 (*0-671-02174-5*, Minstrel Bks) PB.

— False Alarm. Greenberg, Anne, ed. (Hardy Boys Casefiles Ser.: No. 84). 160p. (YA). (gr. 7-12). 1994. pap. 3.99 (*0-671-79468-X*, Archway) PB.

— False Alarm. (Hardy Boys Casefiles Ser.: No. 84). (YA). (gr. 6 up). 1994. 9.09 (*0-606-05865-6*, Pub. by Turtleback) Demco.

— Fast Break. (Hardy Boys Casefiles Ser.: Vol. 107). (J). (gr. 7 up). 1996. pap. 3.99 (*0-671-50430-4*, Pocket Books) PB.

— Fast Break. (Hardy Boys Casefiles Ser.: No. 108). (YA). (gr. 6 up). 1996. 9.09 (*0-606-08539-4*, Pub. by Turtleback) Demco.

— Fear on Wheels. Greenberg, Anne, ed. (Hardy Boys Mystery Stories Ser.: No. 108). 160p. (J). (gr. 3-6). 1991. per. 3.99 (*0-671-69277-1*, Minstrel Bks) PB.

Dixon, Franklin W. Fear on Wheels. (Hardy Boys Mystery Stories Ser.: No. 108). (J). (gr. 3-6). 1991. 9.09 (*0-606-04915-0*, Pub. by Turtleback) Demco.

Dixon, Franklin W. A Figure in Hiding. LC 65-14752. (Hardy Boys Mystery Stories Ser.: No. 16). (Illus.). 180p. (J). (gr. 4-7). 1937. 5.95 (*0-448-08916-5*, G & D) Peng Put Young Read.

— Fire in the Sky. (Hardy Boys Casefiles Ser.: No. 126). 160p. (YA). (gr. 1-12). 1997. pap. 3.99 (*0-671-56125-1*) PB.

— Fire in the Sky. (Hardy Boys Casefiles Ser.: No. 126). (YA). (gr. 6 up). 1997. 9.09 (*0-606-13467-0*, Pub. by Turtleback) Demco.

— Firebird Rocket. (Hardy Boys Mystery Stories Ser.: No. 5). (Illus.). 180p. (J). (gr. 3-6). 1978. 5.95 (*0-448-08957-2*, G & D) Peng Put Young Read.

— First Day, Worst Day. (Hardy Boys Are: The Clues Brothers Ser.: No. 3). (Illus.). (J). (gr. 2-4). 1997. 9.09 (*0-606-12935-9*, Pub. by Turtleback) Demco.

— First Day, Worst Day. 3rd ed. (Hardy Boys Are: The Clues Brothers Ser.: No. 3). (Illus.). 80p. (J). (gr. 2-4). 1997. per. 3.99 (*0-671-00404-2*) PB.

— The Fish-Faced Mask of Mystery. (Hardy Boys Are: The Clues Brothers Ser.: No. 16). (Illus.). 80p. (J). (gr. 2-4). 2000. pap. 3.99 (*0-671-03872-9*, Minstrel Bks) PB.

— The Flickering Torch Mystery. LC 71-158747. (Hardy Boys Mystery Stories Ser.: No. 22). (Illus.). 180p. (J). (gr. 4-7). 1943. 5.95 (*0-448-08922-X*, G & D) Peng Put Young Read.

— Footprints under the Window. LC no-na1498. (Hardy Boys Mystery Stories Ser.: No. 12). (Illus.). 180p. (J). (gr. 4-7). 1933. 5.99 (*0-448-08912-2*, G & D) Peng Put Young Read.

— Foul Play. Greenberg, Ann, ed. (Hardy Boys Casefiles Ser.: No. 46). 160p. (YA). (gr. 6 up). 1990. pap. 3.99 (*0-671-70043-X*, Archway) PB.

— Foul Play. (Hardy Boys Casefiles Ser.: No. 46). (YA). (gr. 6 up). 1990. 9.09 (*0-606-04675-5*, Pub. by Turtleback) Demco.

— Frame-Up. (Hardy Boys Casefiles Ser.: No. 99). 160p. (J). (gr. 7 up). 1995. mass mkt. 3.99 (*0-671-88210-4*) PB.

Dixon, Franklin W. Frame-Up. (Hardy Boys Casefiles Ser.: No. 99). (YA). (gr. 6 up). 1995. 9.09 (*0-606-07621-2*, Pub. by Turtleback) Demco.

— A Game Called Chaos. (Hardy Boys Mystery Stories Ser.: No. 160). 160p. (J). (gr. 3-6). 2000. pap. 3.99 (*0-671-03870-2*, Minstrel Bks) PB.

Dixon, Franklin W. The Ghost at Skeleton Rock. rev. ed. (Hardy Boys Mystery Stories Ser.: No. 37). (Illus.). 180p. (J). (gr. 3-6). 1958. 5.95 (*0-448-08937-8*, G & D) Peng Put Young Read.

— The Giant Rat of Sumatra. (Hardy Boys Mystery Stories Ser.: No. 143). 160p. (J). (gr. 3-6). 1997. pap. 3.99 (*0-671-00055-1*, Minstrel Bks) PB.

Dixon, Franklin W. The Giant Rat of Sumatra. (Hardy Boys Mystery Stories Ser.: No. 143). (J). (gr. 3-6). 1997. 9.09 (*0-606-11430-0*, Pub. by Turtleback) Demco.

Dixon, Franklin W. Grave Danger. Greenberg, Anne, ed. (Hardy Boys Casefiles Ser.: No. 61). 160p. (YA). (gr. 7 up). 1992. pap. 3.99 (*0-671-73097-5*) PB.

— Grave Danger. (Hardy Boys Casefiles Ser.: No. 61). (YA). (gr. 6 up). 1990. 9.09 (*0-606-02030-6*, Pub. by Turtleback) Demco.

— The Great Airport Mystery. LC 99-16572. (Hardy Boys Mystery Stories Ser.: No. 9). 228p. (J). (gr. 4-7). 1999. 14.95 (*1-55709-267-2*, Pub. by Applewood) Consort Bk Sales.

— The Great Airport Mystery. (Hardy Boys Mystery Stories Ser.: No. 9). (Illus.). 180p. (J). (gr. 4-7). 1930. 5.99 (*0-448-08909-2*, G & D) Peng Put Young Read.

— The Gross Ghost Mystery. (Hardy Boys Are: The Clues Brothers Ser.: No. 1). (Illus.). (J). (gr. 2-4). 1997. pap. 2.99 (*0-671-00402-6*) PB.

— The Gross Ghost Mystery. (Hardy Boys Are: The Clues Brothers Ser.: No. 1). (Illus.). (J). (gr. 2-4). 1997. 8.19 (*0-606-12705-4*, Pub. by Turtleback) Demco.

— The Hardy Boys Casefiles Boxed Set: Beyond the Law; Spiked; Open Season. (Hardy Boys Casefiles Ser.: Nos. 55, 58, & 59). 464p. (YA). (gr. 6-12). 1999. mass mkt., boxed set 4.99 (*0-671-02035-8*, Archway) PB.

— The Hardy Boys Casefiles Boxed Set: Diplomatic Deceit; Flesh & Blood; Fright Wave. (Hardy Boys Casefiles Ser.: Nos. 38, 39, & 40). (YA). (gr. 6 up). 1998. pap., boxed set 4.99 (*0-671-02033-1*) PB.

— The Hardy Boys Casefiles Boxed Set: Rock 'n' Revenge; Choke Hold; Uncivil War. (Hardy Boys Casefiles Ser.: Nos. 38, 39 & 40). (YA). (gr. 6 up). 1998. pap. 4.99 (*0-671-02018-8*, Archway) PB.

— The Hardy Boys Casefiles Boxed Set: Rock 'n' Revenge; Choke Hold; Uncivil War. (Hardy Boys Casefiles Ser.: Nos. 48, 51, 52). (YA). (gr. 6 up). 1998. boxed set 4.99 (*0-671-02034-X*, Archway) PB.

— The Hardy Boys Casefiles Gift Set: Dead on Target; The Genius Thieves; Perfect Getaway; The Borgia Dagger; Blood Relations, 5 vols. (Hardy Boys Casefiles Ser.: Nos. 1, 9, 12, 13, 15). (YA). (gr. 6 up). 1989. pap., boxed set 14.75 (*0-671-92250-5*) PB.

Dixon, Franklin W. Hardy Boys Digest. gif. ed. (J). (gr. 3-7). 1987. pap. 14.00 (*0-671-91514-2*, Minstrel Bks) PB.

Dixon, Franklin W. Hardy Boys Digest, 4 vols. gif. ed. (J). (gr. 3-7). 1989. boxed set 14.00 (*0-671-92234-3*) PB.

— The Hardy Boys Ghost Stories. Greenberg, Ann, ed. 144p. (J). (gr. 3-6). 1909. pap. 3.99 (*0-671-69133-3*, Minstrel Bks) PB.

— The Hardy Boys Ghost Stories. (J). (gr. 3-7). 1989. 9.09 (*0-606-01308-3*, Pub. by Turtleback) Demco.

— The Hardy Boys Gift Set, 3 vols., Set. (J). (gr. 3-7). boxed set 8.55 (*0-317-12424-2*) S&S Trade.

Dixon, Franklin W. The Hardy Boys Mystery Stories Boxed Set: Sky Blue Frame; Wipeout; The Crusade of the Flaming Sword; Crime in the Kennel. (Hardy Boys Mystery Stories Ser.: Nos. 89, 96, 131, & 133). (J). (gr. 3-7). 1997. boxed set 15.96 (*0-671-87830-1*, Minstrel Bks) PB.

— The Hardy Boys Mystery Stories Boxed Set: The Missing Chums; Hunting for Hidden Gold; The Shore Road Mystery. (Hardy Boys Mystery Stories Ser.: Nos. 4,5 & 6). 560p. (YA). (gr. 4-7). 2000. 9.98 (*0-7651-1767-3*) Smithmark.

— The Hardy Boys Mystery Stories Boxed Set: The Tower Treasure; The House on the Cliff; The Secret of the Old Mill. LC 99-20941. (Hardy Boys Mystery Stories Ser.: Nos. 1, 2, & 3). (Illus.). 560p. (YA). (gr. 4-7). 1999. 9.98 (*0-7651-1727-4*) Smithmark.

Dixon, Franklin W. The Hardy Boys Starter Set: The Tower Treasure; House on the Cliff; Secret of the Old Mill/Missing Chums/Shore Road Mystery. (Hardy Boys Mystery Stories Ser.). (J). (gr. 3-7). 1997. 19.98 (*0-448-41672-7*, G & D) Peng Put Young Read.

— The Haunted Fort. (Hardy Boys Mystery Stories Ser.: No. 44). (Illus.). 180p. (J). (gr. 4-7). 1964. 5.95 (*0-448-08944-0*, G & D) Peng Put Young Read.

— Height of Danger. Greenberg, Anne, ed. (Hardy Boys Casefiles Ser.: No. 56). 160p. (J). (gr. 6 up). 1991. per. 3.99 (*0-671-73092-4*, Archway) PB.

— Height of Danger. (Hardy Boys Casefiles Ser.: No. 56). (YA). (gr. 6 up). 1991. 9.09 (*0-606-04932-0*, Pub. by Turtleback) Demco.

— The Hidden Harbor Mystery. (Hardy Boys Mystery Stories Ser.: No. 14). (Illus.). 180p. (J). (gr. 4-7). 1935. 5.95 (*0-448-08914-9*, G & D) Peng Put Young Read.

— High-Speed Showdown. (Hardy Boys Mystery Stories Ser.: No. 137). (J). (gr. 3-6). 1996. 9.09 (*0-606-09377-X*, Pub. by Turtleback) Demco.

— High-Wire Act. (Hardy Boys Casefiles Ser.: No. 123). (YA). (gr. 6 up). 1997. 9.09 (*0-606-11437-8*, Pub. by Turtleback) Demco.

— High-Wire Act, Vol. 123. (Hardy Boys Casefiles Ser.: No. 123). (YA). (gr. 6 up). 1997. mass mkt. 3.99 (*0-671-56122-7*, Archway) PB.

— Highway Robbery. Greenberg, Ann, ed. (Hardy Boys Casefiles Ser.: No. 41). 160p. (YA). (gr. 6 up). 1990. mass mkt. 3.75 (*0-671-70038-3*, Archway) PB.

— Highway Robbery. (Hardy Boys Casefiles Ser.: No. 41). (YA). (gr. 6 up). 1990. 8.85 (*0-606-03538-9*, Pub. by Turtleback) Demco.

— The Hooded Hawk Mystery. rev. ed. LC 73-155243. (Hardy Boys Mystery Stories Ser.: No. 34). (Illus.). 180p. (J). (gr. 4-7). 1955. 5.99 (*0-448-08934-3*, G & D) Peng Put Young Read.

— Hot Wheels. Ashby, Ruth, ed. (Hardy Boys Casefiles Ser.: No. 91). 160p. (YA). (gr. 7 up). 1994. pap. 3.99 (*0-671-79475-2*, Archway) PB.

Dixon, Franklin W. Hot Wheels. (Hardy Boys Casefiles Ser.: No. 91). (YA). (gr. 6 up). 1994. 9.09 (*0-606-06448-6*, Pub. by Turtleback) Demco.

Dixon, Franklin W. The House on the Cliff. (Hardy Boys Mystery Stories Ser.: No. 2). 212p. (J). (gr. 3-6). 1991. 14.95 (*1-55709-145-5*) Applewood.

— The House on the Cliff. LC 59-2530. (Hardy Boys Mystery Stories Ser.: No. 2). (Illus.). 180p. (J). (gr. 4-7). 1927. 5.99 (*0-448-08902-5*, G & D) Peng Put Young Read.

— The Hunt for the Four Brothers. (Hardy Boys Mystery Stories Ser.: No. 155). (J). (gr. 3-6). 1999. pap. 3.99 (*0-671-02550-3*) PB.

— Hunting for Hidden Gold. LC 96-28378. (Hardy Boys Mystery Stories Ser.: No. 5). (Illus.). 210p. (J). (gr. 4-7). 1996. 14.95 (*1-55709-148-X*, Pub. by Applewood) Consort Bk Sales.

— The Hypersonic Secret. (Hardy Boys Mystery Stories Ser.: No. 135). (J). (gr. 3-6). 1995. 9.09 (*0-606-08535-1*, Pub. by Turtleback) Demco.

— The Ice Cold Case. (Hardy Boys Mystery Stories Ser.: No. 148). (J). (gr. 3-6). 1998. pap. 3.99 (*0-671-00122-1*) PB.

— The Ice Cold Case, 148. (Hardy Boys Mystery Stories Ser.: No. 148). (J). (gr. 3-6). 1998. 9.09 (*0-606-13462-X*, Pub. by Turtleback) Demco.

— Illegal Procedure. Ashby, Ruth, ed. LC 00-4208. (Hardy Boys Casefiles Ser.: No. 95). 160p. (J). (gr. 7 up). 1995. mass mkt. 3.99 (*0-671-88206-6*) PB.

Dixon, Franklin W. Illegal Procedure. (Hardy Boys Casefiles Ser.: No. 95). (YA). (gr. 6 up). 1995. 9.09 (*0-606-07617-4*, Pub. by Turtleback) Demco.

Dixon, Franklin W. In Self-Defense. Greenberg, Ann, ed. (Hardy Boys Casefiles Ser.: No. 45). 160p. (YA). (gr. 7 up). 1990. mass mkt. 3.75 (*0-671-70042-1*, Archway) PB.

— In Self-Defense. (Hardy Boys Casefiles Ser.: No. 45). (YA). (gr. 6 up). 1990. 8.85 (*0-606-04702-6*, Pub. by Turtleback) Demco.

— Jump Shot Detectives. (Hardy Boys Are: The Clues Brothers Ser.: No. 4). (Illus.). (J). (gr. 2-4). 1998. pap. 3.99 (*0-671-00405-0*) PB.

— Jump Shot Detectives. (Hardy Boys Are: The Clues Brothers Ser.: No. 4). (Illus.). (J). (gr. 2-4). 1998. 9.09 (*0-606-12936-7*, Pub. by Turtleback) Demco.

— The Jungle Pyramid. LC 76-14297. (Hardy Boys Mystery Stories Ser.: No. 56). (Illus.). 180p. (J). (gr. 4-7). 1976. 5.95 (*0-448-08956-4*, G & D) Peng Put Young Read.

— The Karate Clue. (Hardy Boys Are: The Clues Brothers Ser.: No. 2). (J). (gr. 2-4). 1997. pap. 2.99 (*0-671-00403-4*) PB.

— The Karate Clue. (Hardy Boys Are: The Clues Brothers Ser.: No. 2). (J). (gr. 2-4). 1997. 8.19 (*0-606-12706-2*, Pub. by Turtleback) Demco.

— King for a Day. (Hardy Boys Are: The Clues Brothers Ser.: No. 12). (Illus.). 80p. (J). (ps-3). 1999. per. 3.99 (*0-671-02719-0*) PB.

— The Last Leap. (Hardy Boys Casefiles Ser.: No. 118). (YA). (gr. 6 up). 1996. pap. 3.99 (*0-671-56118-9*) PB.

Dixon, Franklin W. The Last Leap. (Hardy Boys Casefiles Ser.: No. 118). (YA). (gr. 6 up). 1996. 9.09 (*0-606-11432-7*, Pub. by Turtleback) Demco.

Dixon, Franklin W. Law of the Jungle. LC 96-105832. (Hardy Boys Casefiles Ser.: No. 105). (J). (gr. 7 up). 1995. pap. 3.99 (*0-671-50428-2*) PB.

— Law of the Jungle. (Hardy Boys Casefiles Ser.: No. 105). (YA). (gr. 6 up). 1995. 9.09 (*0-606-08537-8*, Pub. by Turtleback) Demco.

— The Lazarus Plot. LC 88-21365. (Hardy Boys Casefiles Ser.: No. 4). (YA). (gr. 7 up). 1991. mass mkt. 3.75 (*0-671-73995-6*, Archway) PB.

— The Lazarus Plot. (Hardy Boys Casefiles Ser.: No. 4). (YA). (gr. 6 up). 1987. 8.85 (*0-606-02104-3*, Pub. by Turtleback) Demco.

— London Deception. (Hardy Boys Mystery Stories Ser.: No. 158). 160p. (J). (gr. 4-7). 1999. pap. 3.99 (*0-671-03496-0*) PB.

— Lost in Gator Swamp. (Hardy Boys Mystery Stories Ser.: No. 142). (J). (gr. 3-6). 1997. per. 3.99 (*0-671-00054-3*, Minstrel Bks) PB.

— The Lure of the Italian Treasure. (Hardy Boys Mystery Stories Ser.: No. 157). (J). (gr. 3-6). 1999. pap. 3.99 (*0-671-03445-6*) PB.

— The Mark of the Blue Tattoo. (Hardy Boys Mystery Stories Ser.: No. 146). (J). (gr. 3-6). 1997. per. 3.99 (*0-671-00058-6*) PB.

— The Mark of the Blue Tattoo. (Hardy Boys Mystery Stories Ser.: No. 146). (J). (gr. 3-6). 1997. 9.09 (*0-606-13460-3*, Pub. by Turtleback) Demco.

— The Mark on the Door. rev. ed. LC 67-20847. (Hardy Boys Mystery Stories Ser.: No. 13). (Illus.). 180p. (J). (gr. 4-7). 1934. 5.99 (*0-448-08913-0*, G & D) Peng Put Young Read.

— The Masked Monkey. LC 71-180994. (Hardy Boys Mystery Stories Ser.: No. 51). (Illus.). 196p. (J). (gr. 4-7). 1972. 5.95 (*0-448-08951-3*, G & D) Peng Put Young Read.

— Maximum Challenge. (Hardy Boys Mystery Stories Ser.: No. 132). (Illus.). (J). (gr. 3-6). 1995. pap. 3.99 (*0-671-87216-8*, Minstrel Bks) PB.

— Maximum Challenge. (Hardy Boys Mystery Stories Ser.: No. 132). (J). (gr. 3-6). 1995. 9.09 (*0-606-07611-5*, Pub. by Turtleback) Demco.

— Mayhem in Motion. Greenberg, Anne, ed. (Hardy Boys Casefiles Ser.: No. 69). 160p. (YA). (gr. 6 up). 1992. pap. 3.75 (*0-671-73105-X*, Archway) PB.

— Mayhem in Motion. (Hardy Boys Casefiles Ser.: No. 69). (YA). (gr. 6 up). 1992. 8.85 (*0-606-02665-7*, Pub. by Turtleback) Demco.

— The Melted Coins. LC 78-86722. (Hardy Boys Mystery Stories Ser.: No. 23). (Illus.). 180p. (J). (gr. 4-7). 1944. 5.95 (*0-448-08923-8*, G & D) Peng Put Young Read.

— The Million Dollar Nightmare. Greenberg, Ann, ed. (Hardy Boys Mystery Stories Ser.: No. 103). 160p. (Orig.). (J). (gr. 3-6). 1990. pap. 3.99 (*0-671-69272-0*, Minstrel Bks) PB.

— The Missing Chums. (Hardy Boys Mystery Stories Ser.: No. 4). (Illus.). 210p. (J). (gr. 3-6). 1996. reprint ed. 14.95 (*1-55709-147-1*, Pub. by Applewood) Consort Bk Sales.

— The Missing Chums. rev. ed. (Hardy Boys Mystery Stories Ser.: No. 4). (Illus.). 180p. (J). (gr. 4-7). 1930. 5.99 (*0-448-08904-1*, G & D) Peng Put Young Read.

— Mission: Mayhem. Ashby, Ruth, ed. LC 00-1314. (Hardy Boys Casefiles Ser.: No. 93). 160p. (YA). (gr. 7-12). 1994. pap. 3.99 (*0-671-88204-X*, Archway) PB.

Dixon, Franklin W. Mission: Mayhem. (Hardy Boys Casefiles Ser.: No. 93). (YA). (gr. 6 up). 1994. 9.09 (*0-606-07002-8*, Pub. by Turtleback) Demco.

Dixon, Franklin W. Moment of Truth. (Hardy Boys Casefiles Ser.: No. 109). (YA). (gr. 6 up). 1996. 9.09 (*0-606-09381-8*, Pub. by Turtleback) Demco.

— The Money Hunt. Greenberg, Ann, ed. (Hardy Boys Mystery Stories Ser.: No. 101). 160p. (J). (gr. 3-6). 1990. pap. 3.99 (*0-671-69451-0*, Minstrel Bks) PB.

— The Monster in the Lake. (Hardy Boys Are: The Clues Brothers Ser.: Vol. 11). (Illus.). 80p. (J). (ps-3). 1999. pap. 3.99 (*0-671-02662-3*) PB.

— The Mummy Case. (Hardy Boys Mystery Stories Ser.: No. 63). 192p. (J). (gr. 3-6). 1987. mass mkt. 3.99 (*0-671-64289-8*, Minstrel Bks) PB.

— Murder by Magic. (Hardy Boys Casefiles Ser.: No. 98). (YA). (gr. 6 up). 1995. 9.09 (*0-606-07620-4*, Pub. by Turtleback) Demco.

— The Mysterious Caravan. (Hardy Boys Mystery Stories Ser.: No. 54). (Illus.). 180p. (J). (gr. 3-6). 1975. 5.95 (*0-448-08954-8*, G & D) Peng Put Young Read.

— The Mystery at Devil's Paw. (Hardy Boys Mystery Stories Ser.: No.38). (Illus.). 192p. (J). (gr. 3-6). 1959. reprint ed. 5.99 (*0-448-08938-6*, G & D) Peng Put Young Read.

— The Mystery of Cabin Island. LC 98-56443. (Hardy Boys Mystery Stories Ser.: No. 8). 210p. (J). (gr. 2-5). 1999. 14.95 (*1-55709-266-4*, Pub. by Applewood) Consort Bk Sales.

— The Mystery of Cabin Island. (Hardy Boys Mystery Stories Ser.: No. 8). (Illus.). 180p. (J). (gr. 4-7). 1929. 5.99 (*0-448-08908-4*, G & D) Peng Put Young Read.

— The Mystery of the Aztec Warrior. (Hardy Boys Mystery Stories Ser.: No. 43). (Illus.). 180p. (J). (gr. 4-7). 1964. 5.95 (*0-448-08943-2*, G & D) Peng Put Young Read.

— The Mystery of the Chinese Junk. (Hardy Boys Mystery Stories Ser.: No. 39). (Illus.). 180p. (J). (gr. 3-6). 1959. 5.95 (*0-448-08939-4*, G & D) Peng Put Young Read.

— The Mystery of the Desert Giant. LC no-na1090. (Hardy Boys Mystery Stories Ser.: No. 40). (Illus.). 180p. (J). (gr. 4-7). 1960. 5.95 (*0-448-08940-8*, G & D) Peng Put Young Read.

— The Mystery of the Flying Express. LC 73-106327. (Hardy Boys Mystery Stories Ser.: No. 20). (Illus.). 180p. (J). (gr. 4-7). 1941. 5.95 (*0-448-08920-3*, G & D) Peng Put Young Read.

— The Mystery of the Spiral Bridge. (Hardy Boys Mystery Stories Ser.: No. 45). (Illus.). 180p. (J). (gr. 3-6). 1965. 5.95 (*0-448-08945-9*, G & D) Peng Put Young Read.

— The Mystery of the Whale Tattoo. LC 68-12750. (Hardy Boys Mystery Stories Ser.: No. 47). (Illus.). 180p. (J). (gr. 4-7). 1967. 5.95 (*0-448-08947-5*, G & D) Peng Put Young Read.

— Mystery with a Dangerous Beat. LC MLC R CP01285. (Hardy Boys Mystery Stories Ser.: No. 124). 160p. (J). (gr. 3-6). 1994. pap. 3.99 (*0-671-79314-4*, Minstrel Bks) PB.

— Mystery with a Dangerous Beat. (Hardy Boys Mystery Stories Ser.: No. 124). (J). (gr. 3-6). 1994. 9.09 (*0-606-05859-1*, Pub. by Turtleback) Demco.

— Night of the Werewolf. Greenberg, Ann, ed. (Hardy Boys Mystery Stories Ser.: No. 59). 192p. (J). (gr. 3-6). 1990. pap. 3.99 (*0-671-70993-3*, Minstrel Bks) PB.

— Night of the Werewolf. gif. ed. (Hardy Boys Mystery Stories Ser.:). (J). (gr. 3-6). 1984. pap., boxed set 8.85 (*0-685-09390-5*) PB.

— No Mercy. Greenberg, Anne, ed. (Hardy Boys Casefiles Ser.: No. 65). 160p. (Orig.). (YA). (gr. 6 up). 1992. pap. 3.99 (*0-671-73101-7*, Archway) PB.

— No Way Out. Greenberg, Anne, ed. (Hardy Boys Casefiles Ser.: No. 75). 160p. (J). (gr. 7 up). 1993. pap. 3.99 (*0-671-73111-4*, Archway) PB.

— No Way Out. (Hardy Boys Casefiles Ser.: No. 75). (YA). (gr. 6 up). 1993. 9.09 (*0-606-05336-0*, Pub. by Turtleback) Demco.

— Panic on Gull Island. (Hardy Boys Mystery Stories Ser.: No. 107). 160p. (J). (gr. 3-6). 1991. mass mkt. 3.99 (*0-671-69276-3*, Minstrel Bks) PB.

— Panic on Gull Island. (Hardy Boys Mystery Stories Ser.: No. 107). (J). (gr. 3-6). 1991. 9.09 (*0-606-04998-3*, Pub. by Turtleback) Demco.

— Peak of Danger. (Hardy Boys Casefiles Ser.: No. 101). (Illus.). 160p. (J). (gr. 6 up). 1995. per. 3.99 (*0-671-88212-0*) PB.

— Peak of Danger. (Hardy Boys Casefiles Ser.: No. 101). (YA). (gr. 6 up). 1995. 9.09 (*0-606-07614-X*, Pub. by Turtleback) Demco.

— The Pentagon Spy. (Hardy Boys Mystery Stories Ser.: No. 61). (J). (gr. 3-6). 1984. 8.85 (*0-685-42775-7*) PB.

— The Pentagon Spy. Greenberg, Anne, ed. (Hardy Boys Mystery Stories Ser.: No. 61). 192p. (J). (gr. 3-6). 1988. pap. 3.99 (*0-671-67221-5*, Minstrel Bks) PB.

— Perfect Getaway, No. 12. (Hardy Boys Casefiles Ser.: No. 12). (Orig.). (YA). (gr. 6 up). 1991. mass mkt. 3.50 (*0-671-73675-2*) PB.

— The Phantom Freighter. rev. ed. LC 75-115957. (Hardy Boys Mystery Stories Ser.: No. 26). (Illus.). 180p. (J). (gr. 4-7). 1947. 5.95 (*0-448-08926-2*, G & D) Peng Put Young Read.

— The Phoenix Equation. Greenberg, Anne, ed. (Hardy Boys Casefiles Ser.: No. 66). 160p. (Orig.). (YA). (gr. 6 up). 1992. pap. 3.99 (*0-671-73102-5*, Archway) PB.

— Pirates Ahoy!, 1, 13. (Hardy Boys Are: The Clues Brothers Ser.: No. 13). (Illus.). 80p. (J). (gr. 2-4). 1999. pap. 3.99 (*0-671-02786-7*) PB.

An Asterisk (*) at the beginning of an entry indicates that the title is appearing for the first time.

— Power Play. Greenberg, Anne, ed. (Hardy Boys Casefiles Ser.: No. 50). (Illus.). 160p. (YA). (gr. 7 up). 1991. pap. 3.99 (*0-671-70047-2*, Archway) PB.

— Power Play. (Hardy Boys Casefiles Ser.: No. 50). (YA). (gr. 6 up). 1991. 9.09 (*0-606-05003-5*, Pub. by Turtleback) Demco.

— The Prime-Time Crime. Greenberg, Anne, ed. (Hardy Boys Mystery Stories Ser.: No. 109). 160p. (Orig.). (J). (gr. 4-7). 1991. pap. 3.99 (*0-671-69278-X*, Minstrel Bks) PB.

— Program for Destruction. Greenberg, Ann, ed. (Hardy Boys Mystery Stories Ser.: No. 87). (J). (gr. 3-6). 1987. pap. 3.99 (*0-671-64895-0*, Minstrel Bks) PB.

— The Pumped-up Pizza Problem. (Hardy Boys Are: The Clues Brothers Ser.: No. 9). (Illus.). 80p. (J). (gr. 2-4). 1998. pap. 3.99 (*0-671-02142-7*, Minstrel Bks) PB.

— Pure Evil. Greenberg, Anne, ed. (Hardy Boys Casefiles Ser.: No. 97). 160p. (YA). (gr. 7 up). 1995. mass mkt. 3.99 (*0-671-88208-2*, Archway) PB.

Dixon, Franklin W. Pure Evil. (Hardy Boys Casefiles Ser.: No. 97). (YA). (gr. 6 up). 1995. 9.09 (*0-606-07619-0*, Pub. by Turtleback) Demco.

Dixon, Franklin W. Racing to Disaster. (Hardy Boys Mystery Stories Ser.: No. 126). 160p. (YA). (gr. 3-6). 1994. pap. 3.99 (*0-671-87210-9*, Minstrel Bks) PB.

— Racing to Disaster. (Hardy Boys Mystery Stories Ser.: No. 125). (J). (gr. 3-6). 1994. 9.09 (*0-606-06441-9*, Pub. by Turtleback) Demco.

— Real Horror. Greenberg, Anne, ed. (Hardy Boys Casefiles Ser.: No. 71). 160p. (Orig.). (J). (gr. 6 up). 1993. pap. 3.99 (*0-671-73107-6*, Archway) PB.

Dixon, Franklin W. Revenge of the Desert Phantom. (Hardy Boys Mystery Stories Ser.: No. 84). (J). (gr. 3-6). write for info. (*0-671-49730-8*) PB.

Dixon, Franklin W. River Rats. (Hardy Boys Casefiles Ser.: No. 122). 160p. (YA). (gr. 6 up). 1997. pap. 3.99 (*0-671-56123-5*, Archway) PB.

— River Rats. (Hardy Boys Casefiles Ser.: No. 122). (YA). (gr. 6 up). 1997. 9.09 (*0-606-11436-X*, Pub. by Turtleback) Demco.

— The Robot's Revenge. Winkler, Ellen, ed. (Hardy Boys Mystery Stories Ser.: No. 123). 160p. (J). (gr. 3-6). 1993. per. 3.99 (*0-671-79313-6*, Minstrel Bks) PB.

— The Robot's Revenge. (Hardy Boys Mystery Stories Ser.: No. 123). (J). (gr. 3-6). 1993. 9.09 (*0-606-05858-3*, Pub. by Turtleback) Demco.

— Rock 'n' Revenge. (Hardy Boys Casefiles Ser.: No. 48). (YA). (gr. 6 up). 1991. 8.60 (*0-606-04782-4*, Pub. by Turtleback) Demco.

— Rock 'n' Roll Renegades. Winkler, Ellen, ed. (Hardy Boys Mystery Stories Ser.: No. 116). 160p. (J). (gr. 3-6). 1992. pap. 3.99 (*0-671-73063-0*, Minstrel Bks) PB.

— The Rocky Road to Revenge. (Hardy Boys Mystery Stories Ser.: No. 151). (J). (gr. 3-6). 1998. per. 3.99 (*0-671-02172-9*, Minstrel Bks) PB.

— The Rocky Road to Revenge. (Hardy Boys Mystery Stories Ser.: No. 151). (J). (gr. 3-6). 1998. 9.09 (*0-606-13465-4*, Pub. by Turtleback) Demco.

— Sabotage at Sea. Ashby, Ruth, ed. (Hardy Boys Casefiles Ser.: No. 92). 160p. (YA). (gr. 7 up). 1994. pap. 3.99 (*0-671-79476-0*, Archway) PB.

— Sabotage at Sea. (Hardy Boys Casefiles Ser.: No. 92). (YA). (gr. 6 up). 1994. 9.09 (*0-606-07001-X*, Pub. by Turtleback) Demco.

— The Search for the Snow Leopard. (Hardy Boys Mystery Stories Ser.: No. 139). 160p. (J). (gr. 3-6). 1996. pap. 3.99 (*0-671-50525-4*) PB.

— The Search for the Snow Leopard. (Hardy Boys Mystery Stories Ser.: No. 139). (J). (gr. 3-6). 1996. 9.09 (*0-606-09379-6*, Pub. by Turtleback) Demco.

— The Secret Agent on Flight 101. LC 67-5471. (Hardy Boys Mystery Stories Ser.: No. 46). (Illus.). 180p. (J). (gr. 4-7). 1967. 5.95 (*0-448-08946-7*, G & D) Peng Put Young Read.

— The Secret of Pirate's Hill. rev. ed. (Hardy Boys Mystery Stories Ser.: No. 36). (Illus.). 196p. (J). (gr. 3-6). 1957. 5.99 (*0-448-08936-X*, G & D) Peng Put Young Read.

— The Secret of Sigma Seven. (Hardy Boys Mystery Stories Ser.: No. 110). 160p. (J). (gr. 3-6). 1991. pap. 3.99 (*0-671-72717-6*, Minstrel Bks) PB.

— The Secret of Skeleton Reef. (Hardy Boys Mystery Stories Ser.: No. 144). (J). (gr. 3-6). 1997. per. 3.99 (*0-671-00056-X*, Archway) PB.

Dixon, Franklin W. The Secret of Skeleton Reef. (Hardy Boys Mystery Stories Ser.: No. 144). (J). (gr. 3-6). 1997. 9.09 (*0-606-11431-9*, Pub. by Turtleback) Demco.

Dixon, Franklin W. The Secret of Skull Mountain. LC 66-31247. (Hardy Boys Mystery Stories Ser.: No. 27). (Illus.). 180p. (J). (gr. 4-7). 1948. 5.95 (*0-448-08927-0*, G & D) Peng Put Young Read.

— The Secret of the Caves. LC 98-19285. (Hardy Boys Mystery Stories Ser.: No. 7). (Illus.). 228p. (J). (gr. 4-7). 1998. reprint ed. 14.95 (*1-55709-150-1*, Pub. by Applewood) Consort Bk Sales.

— The Secret of the Caves. rev. ed. (Hardy Boys Mystery Stories Ser.: No. 7). (Illus.). 180p. (J). (gr. 4-7). 1929. 5.99 (*0-448-08907-6*, G & D) Peng Put Young Read.

— The Secret of the Lost Tunnel. rev. ed. LC 68-24655. (Hardy Boys Mystery Stories Ser.: No. 29). (Illus.). 180p. (J). (gr. 4-7). 1950. 5.95 (*0-448-08929-7*, G & D) Peng Put Young Read.

— The Secret of the Old Mill. (Hardy Boys Mystery Stories Ser.: No. 3). (Illus.). 180p. (J). (gr. 4-7). 1927. 5.99 (*0-448-08903-3*, G & D) Peng Put Young Read.

— The Secret of Wildcat Swamp. LC 69-14267. (Hardy Boys Mystery Stories Ser.: No. 31). (Illus.). 180p. (J). (gr. 4-7). 1952. 5.95 (*0-448-08931-9*, G & D) Peng Put Young Read.

— The Secret Panel. rev. ed. LC 74-86693. (Hardy Boys Mystery Stories Ser.: No. 25). (Illus.). 180p. (J). (gr. 4-7). 1946. 5.95 (*0-448-08925-4*, G & D) Peng Put Young Read.

— The Secret Warning. LC no-na1580. (Hardy Boys Mystery Stories Ser.: No. 17). (Illus.). 180p. (J). (gr. 4-7). 1938. 5.99 (*0-448-08917-3*, G & D) Peng Put Young Read.

— See No Evil. (Hardy Boys Casefiles Ser.: No. 8). (YA). (gr. 6 up). 1991. mass mkt. 3.50 (*0-671-73673-6*, Archway) PB.

— See No Evil. (Hardy Boys Casefiles Ser.: No. 8). (YA). (gr. 6 up). 1987. 8.60 (*0-606-02109-4*, Pub. by Turtleback) Demco.

— The Serpent's Tooth Mystery. (Hardy Boys Mystery Stories Ser.: No. 93). (Orig.). (J). (gr. 3-6). 1988. pap. 3.99 (*0-671-66310-0*, Minstrel Bks) PB.

— The Shadow Killers. (Hardy Boys Mystery Stories Ser.: No. 92). (J). (gr. 3-6). 1988. pap. 3.99 (*0-671-66309-7*, Minstrel Bks) PB.

— The Shattered Helmet. LC 72-90825. (Hardy Boys Mystery Stories Ser.: No. 52). (Illus.). 196p. (J). (gr. 4-7). 1973. 5.95 (*0-448-08952-1*, G & D) Peng Put Young Read.

— Shield of Fear. Greenberg, Ann, ed. (Hardy Boys Mystery Stories Ser.: No. 91). 160p. (J). (gr. 3-6). 1988. reprint ed. pap. 3.99 (*0-671-66308-9*, Minstrel Bks) PB.

— Shock Jock. (Hardy Boys Casefiles Ser.: No. 106). (J). (gr. 7 up). 1995. pap. 3.99 (*0-671-50429-0*, Archway) PB.

— Shock Jock. (Hardy Boys Casefiles Ser.: No. 106). (YA). (gr. 6 up). 1995. 9.09 (*0-606-08538-6*, Pub. by Turtleback) Demco.

— The Shore Road Mystery. (Hardy Boys Mystery Stories Ser.: No. 6). (Illus.). 180p. (J). (gr. 3-6). 1928. 5.99 (*0-448-08906-8*, G & D) Peng Put Young Read.

— The Shore Road Mystery. fac. ed. LC 97-14799. (Hardy Boys Mystery Stories Ser.: No. 6). (Illus.). 210p. (J). (gr. 4-6). 1997. 14.95 (*1-55709-149-8*) Applewood.

— The Short-Wave Mystery. rev. ed. LC 45-1618. (Hardy Boys Mystery Stories Ser.: No. 24). (Illus.). 180p. (J). (gr. 4-7). 1945. 5.95 (*0-448-08924-6*, G & D) Peng Put Young Read.

Dixon, Franklin W. Sidetracked to Danger. (Hardy Boys Mystery Stories Ser.: No. 130). (Orig.). (J). (gr. 3-6). 1995. pap. 9.09 (*0-606-07609-3*, Pub. by Turtleback) Demco.

Dixon, Franklin W. Sign of the Crooked Arrow. rev. ed. (Hardy Boys Mystery Stories Ser.: No. 28). (Illus.). 180p. (J). (gr. 3-6). 1949. 5.95 (*0-448-08928-9*, G & D) Peng Put Young Read.

— The Sinister Sign Post. LC 68-15296. (Hardy Boys Mystery Stories Ser.: No. 15). (Illus.). 180p. (J). (gr. 4-7). 1936. 5.95 (*0-448-08915-7*, G & D) Peng Put Young Read.

***Dixon, Franklin W.** Skin & Bones. (Hardy Boys Mystery Stories Ser.: No. 164). 160p. (J). (gr. 3-6). 2000. pap. 3.99 (*0-671-04761-2*, Minstrel Bks) PB.

Dixon, Franklin W. The Sky Blue Frame. (Hardy Boys Mystery Stories Ser.: No. 89). 160p. (J). (gr. 3-6). 1988. mass mkt. 3.99 (*0-671-64974-4*, Minstrel Bks) PB.

— The Sky Blue Frame. (Hardy Boys Mystery Stories Ser.: No. 89). (J). (gr. 3-6). 1988. 9.09 (*0-606-03919-8*, Pub. by Turtleback) Demco.

— Sky High. (Hardy Boys Casefiles Ser.: No. 113). (YA). (gr. 6 up). 1996. 9.09 (*0-606-09385-0*, Pub. by Turtleback) Demco.

— Slam Dunk Sabotage. LC 49-243260. (Hardy Boys Mystery Stories Ser.: No. 140). (J). (gr. 4-7). 1996. per. 3.99 (*0-671-50526-2*) PB.

— Slam Dunk Sabotage. (Hardy Boys Mystery Stories Ser.: No. 140). (J). (gr. 3-6). 1996. 9.09 (*0-606-10835-1*, Pub. by Turtleback) Demco.

— Slip, Slide & Slap Shot. (Hardy Boys Are: The Clues Brothers Ser.: No. 15). (Illus.). 80p. (J). (gr. k-3). 1999. pap. 3.99 (*0-671-03254-2*) PB.

— The Smoke Screen Mystery. Greenberg, Ann, ed. (Hardy Boys Mystery Stories Ser.: No. 105). 160p. (J). (gr. 4-7). 1990. mass mkt. 3.99 (*0-671-69274-7*, Minstrel Bks) PB.

— The Smoke Screen Mystery. (Hardy Boys Mystery Stories Ser.: No. 105). (J). (gr. 3-6). 1990. 9.09 (*0-606-04798-0*, Pub. by Turtleback) Demco.

Dixon, Franklin W. The Spy That Never Lies. (Hardy Boys Mystery Stories Ser.: No. 163). 160p. (J). (ps up). 1909. mass mkt. 3.99 (*0-671-04760-4*, Minstrel Bks) PB.

Dixon, Franklin W. The Sting of the Scorpion. LC 78-57930. (Hardy Boys Mystery Stories Ser.: No. 58). (Illus.). 180p. (J). (gr. 4-7). 1978. 5.95 (*0-448-08958-0*, G & D) Peng Put Young Read.

— Stress Point. (Hardy Boys Casefiles Ser.: No. 125). 160p. (YA). (gr. 6 up). 1997. pap. 3.99 (*0-671-56241-X*) PB.

— Stress Point. (Hardy Boys Casefiles Ser.: No. 125). (YA). (gr. 6 up). 1997. 9.09 (*0-606-13466-2*, Pub. by Turtleback) Demco.

— Survival of the Fittest. (Hardy Boys Casefiles Ser.: No. 120). (YA). (gr. 6 up). 1997. pap. 3.99 (*0-671-56120-0*, Archway) PB.

— Survival of the Fittest. (Hardy Boys Casefiles Ser.: No. 120). (YA). (gr. 6 up). 1997. 9.09 (*0-606-11434-3*, Pub. by Turtleback) Demco.

— Survival Run. Greenberg, Ann, ed. (Hardy Boys Casefiles Ser.: No. 77). 160p. (J). (gr. 6 up). 1993. pap. 3.99 (*0-671-79461-2*, Archway) PB.

— Survival Run. (Hardy Boys Casefiles Ser.: No. 77). (YA). (gr. 6 up). 1993. 9.09 (*0-606-05338-7*, Pub. by Turtleback) Demco.

— Tagged for Terror. Greenberg, Anne, ed. (Hardy Boys Casefiles Ser.: No. 76). 160p. (J). (gr. 7 up). 1993. pap. 3.99 (*0-671-73112-2*, Archway) PB.

— Tagged for Terror. (Hardy Boys Casefiles Ser.: No. 76). (YA). (gr. 6 up). 1993. 9.09 (*0-606-05337-9*, Pub. by Turtleback) Demco.

— A Taste for Terror. Ashby, Ruth, ed. (Hardy Boys Casefiles Ser.: No. 94). 160p. (J). (gr. 7 up). 1994. pap. 3.99 (*0-671-88205-8*, Archway) PB.

Dixon, Franklin W. A Taste for Terror. (Hardy Boys Casefiles Ser.: No. 94). (YA). (gr. 6 up). 1994. 9.09 (*0-606-07003-6*, Pub. by Turtleback) Demco.

Dixon, Franklin W. Terminal Shock. Greenberg, Ann, ed. (Hardy Boys Mystery Stories Ser.: No. 102). 160p. (J). (gr. 3-6). 1990. pap. 3.99 (*0-671-69288-7*, Minstrel Bks) PB.

— Terror at High Tide. (Hardy Boys Mystery Stories Ser.: No. 145). (J). (gr. 3-6). 1997. pap. 3.99 (*0-671-00057-8*) PB.

— Terror at High Tide. (Hardy Boys Mystery Stories Ser.: No. 145). (J). (gr. 3-6). 1997. 9.09 (*0-606-13459-X*, Pub. by Turtleback) Demco.

— Terror on Track. (Hardy Boys Casefiles Ser.: No. 57). (YA). (gr. 6 up). 1991. 9.09 (*0-606-00799-7*, Pub. by Turtleback) Demco.

— Too Many Traitors. (Hardy Boys Casefiles Ser.: No. 14). 160p. (YA). (gr. 7 up). 1991. mass mkt. 3.50 (*0-671-73677-9*, Archway) PB.

— The Tower Treasure. (Hardy Boys Mystery Stories Ser.: No. 1). 214p. (J). (gr. 3-6). 1991. 14.95 (*1-55709-144-7*) Applewood.

— The Tower Treasure. (Hardy Boys Mystery Stories Ser.: No. 1). (J). (gr. 3-6). 7.25 (*0-448-18901-1*, G & D) Peng Put Young Read.

— The Tower Treasure. (Hardy Boys Mystery Stories Ser.: No. 1). (Illus.). 180p. (J). (gr. 4-7). 1927. 5.99 (*0-448-08901-7*, G & D) Peng Put Young Read.

— The Tower Treasure; The House on the Cliff. (Hardy Boys Back to Back Mysteries Ser.: Nos. 1 & 2). (Illus.). 360p. (J). (gr. 4-7). 1987. 7.99 (*0-448-08964-5*) Putnam Pub Group.

— Toxic Revenge. (Hardy Boys Casefiles Ser.: No. 83). (YA). (gr. 6 up). 1994. pap. 3.99 (*0-671-79467-1*, Archway) PB.

— Toxic Revenge. (Hardy Boys Casefiles Ser.: No. 83). (YA). (gr. 6 up). 1994. 9.09 (*0-606-05864-8*, Pub. by Turtleback) Demco.

***Dixon, Franklin W.** Training for Trouble. (Hardy Boys Mystery Stories Ser.: No. 161). 160p. (J). (gr. 3-6). 2000. per. 3.99 (*0-671-04758-2*) PB.

Dixon, Franklin W. Trial & Terror. (Hardy Boys Mystery Stories Ser.: No. 147). 160p. (J). (gr. 3-6). 1997. per. 3.99 (*0-671-00059-4*) PB.

— Trial & Terror. (Hardy Boys Mystery Stories Ser.: No. 147). (J). (gr. 3-6). 1997. 9.09 (*0-606-13461-1*, Pub. by Turtleback) Demco.

— Tricks of the Trade. Greenberg, Ann, ed. (Hardy Boys Mystery Stories Ser.: No. 104). 160p. (J). (gr. 3-6). 1990. mass mkt. 3.99 (*0-671-69273-9*, Minstrel Bks) PB.

— Tricks of the Trade. (Hardy Boys Mystery Stories Ser.: No. 104). (J). (gr. 3-6). 1990. 9.09 (*0-606-04833-2*, Pub. by Turtleback) Demco.

— Tricky Business. Greenberg, Ann, ed. (Hardy Boys Mystery Stories Ser.: No. 88). 160p. (J). (gr. 3-6). 1988. per. 3.99 (*0-671-64973-6*, Minstrel Bks) PB.

— Tricky Business. (Hardy Boys Mystery Stories Ser.: No. 88). (J). (gr. 3-6). 1988. 9.09 (*0-606-03666-0*, Pub. by Turtleback) Demco.

— Trouble at Coyote Canyon. Winkler, Ellen, ed. (Hardy Boys Mystery Stories Ser.: No. 119). 160p. (Orig.). (J). (gr. 3-6). 1993. pap. 3.99 (*0-671-79309-8*, Minstrel Bks) PB.

— True Thriller. (Hardy Boys Casefiles Ser.: No. 100). (YA). (gr. 6 up). 1995. 9.09 (*0-606-07613-1*, Pub. by Turtleback) Demco.

— True Thriller, No. 100. (Hardy Boys Casefiles Ser.: No. 100). (Illus.). (YA). (gr. 6 up). 1995. pap. 3.99 (*0-671-88211-2*, Archway) PB.

— The Twisted Claw. rev. ed. LC 77-86667. (Hardy Boys Mystery Stories Ser.: No. 18). (Illus.). 180p. (J). (gr. 4-7). 1939. 5.99 (*0-448-08918-1*, G & D) Peng Put Young Read.

— The Vanishing Thieves. (Hardy Boys Mystery Stories Ser.: No. 66). (J). (gr. 3-6). 1987. mass mkt. 3.99 (*0-671-63890-4*) PB.

— The Viking Symbol Mystery. (Hardy Boys Mystery Stories Ser.: No. 42). (Illus.). 180p. (J). (gr. 4-7) 1962. 5.95 (*0-448-08942-4*, G & D) Peng Put Young Read.

— The Viking's Revenge. (Hardy Boys Casefiles Ser.: No. 124). (YA). (gr. 6 up). 1997. pap. 3.99 (*0-671-56124-3*, Archway) PB.

— The Viking's Revenge. (Hardy Boys Casefiles Ser.: No. 124). (YA). (gr. 6 up). 1997. 9.09 (*0-606-11438-6*, Pub. by Turtleback) Demco.

— Virtual Villainy. (Hardy Boys Casefiles Ser.: No. 86). (YA). (gr. 6 up). 1994. 9.09 (*0-606-06443-5*, Pub. by Turtleback) Demco.

— The Voodoo Plot. (Hardy Boys Mystery Stories Ser.: No. 72). (J). (gr. 3-6). 1987. pap. 3.99 (*0-671-64287-1*) PB.

— The Wailing Siren Mystery. rev. ed. (Hardy Boys Mystery Stories Ser.: No. 30). (Illus.). 180p. (J). (gr. 4-7) 1951. 5.95 (*0-448-08930-0*, G & D) Peng Put Young Read.

— The Walking Snowman. (Hardy Boys Are: The Clues Brothers Ser.: No. 10). (Illus.). 80p. (J). (gr. k-3). 1999. pap. 3.99 (*0-671-02560-0*, Minstrel Bks) PB.

— Web of Horror. Greenberg, Ann, ed. (Hardy Boys Casefiles Ser.: No. 53). 160p. (Orig.). (J). (gr. 6 up). 1991. pap. 3.99 (*0-671-73089-4*, Archway) PB.

***Dixon, Franklin W.** What Happened at Midnight. LC 00-20178. (Hardy Boys Mystery Stories Ser.: No. 10). (Illus.). 228p. (YA). (gr. 4-7). 2000. 14.95 (*1-55709-268-0*) Applewood.

Dixon, Franklin W. What Happened at Midnight. (Hardy Boys Mystery Stories Ser.: No. 10). (Illus.). 180p. (J). (gr. 3-6). 1931. 5.99 (*0-448-08910-6*, G & D) Peng Put Young Read.

***Dixon, Franklin W.** While the Clock Ticked. (Hardy Boys Mystery Stories Ser.: Vol. 11). (Illus.). 212p. (J). (gr. 4-7). 2000. 14.95 (*1-55709-269-9*) Applewood.

Dixon, Franklin W. While the Clock Ticked. (Hardy Boys Mystery Stories Ser.: No. 11). (Illus.). 180p. (J). (gr. 4-7). 1932. 5.99 (*0-448-08911-4*, G & D) Peng Put Young Read.

— Who Took the Book? (Hardy Boys Are: The Clues Brothers Ser.: No. 6). (Illus.). (J). (gr. 2-4). 1998. pap. 3.99 (*0-671-00407-7*) PB.

— Who Took the Book?, 6. (Hardy Boys Are: The Clues Brothers Ser.: No. 6). (Illus.). (J). (gr. 2-4). 1998. 9.09 (*0-606-13401-8*, Pub. by Turtleback) Demco.

— Wild Wheels. (Hardy Boys Casefiles Ser.: No. 104). (J). (gr. 6 up). 1995. pap. 3.99 (*0-671-88215-5*, Archway) PB.

— Wild Wheels. (Hardy Boys Casefiles Ser.: No. 104). (YA). (gr. 6 up). 1995. 9.09 (*0-606-08536-X*, Pub. by Turtleback) Demco.

— A Will to Survive. (Hardy Boys Mystery Stories Ser.: No. 156). 160p. (J). (gr. 3-6). 1999. per. 3.99 (*0-671-03464-2*) PB.

— Winner Take All. Ashby, Ruth, ed. (Hardy Boys Casefiles Ser.: No. 85). 160p. (YA). (gr. 7 up). 1994. pap. 3.99 (*0-671-79469-8*, Archway) PB.

— Winner Take All. (Hardy Boys Casefiles Ser.: No. 85). (YA). (gr. 6 up). 1994. 9.09 (*0-606-05866-4*, Pub. by Turtleback) Demco.

— Wipeout. (Hardy Boys Mystery Stories Ser.: No. 96). (J). (gr. 3-6). 1989. pap. 3.50 (*0-671-89513-3*, Pocket Books) PB.

— Wipeout. Ashby, Ruth, ed. (Hardy Boys Mystery Stories Ser.: No. 96). 160p. (J). (gr. 3-6). 1989. pap. 3.99 (*0-671-66306-2*, Minstrel Bks) PB.

— Wipeout. (Hardy Boys Mystery Stories Ser.: No. 96). (J). (gr. 3-6). 1989. 9.09 (*0-606-04369-1*, Pub. by Turtleback) Demco.

— Wrong Side of the Law. (Hardy Boys Casefiles Ser.: No. 102). (YA). (gr. 6 up). 1995. mass mkt. 3.99 (*0-671-88213-9*, Archway) PB.

— Wrong Side of the Law. (Hardy Boys Casefiles Ser.: No. 102). (YA). (gr. 6 up). 1995. 9.09 (*0-606-07615-8*, Pub. by Turtleback) Demco.

— The Yellow Feather Mystery. LC 78-158746. (Hardy Boys Mystery Stories Ser.: No. 32). (Illus.). 180p. (J). (gr. 4-7). 1954. 5.99 (*0-448-08933-5*, G & D) Peng Put Young Read.

Dixon, Franklin W. & Flynn, William F. The Hardy Boys Detective Handbook. rev. ed. (Illus.). 224p. (J). (gr. 4-7). 1972. 5.99 (*0-448-01990-6*, G & D) Peng Put Young Read.

Dixon, Franklin W. & Greenberg, Anne. Crusade of the Flaming Sword. (Hardy Boys Mystery Stories Ser.: No. 131). 160p. (J). (gr. 3-6). 1995. pap. 3.99 (*0-671-87215-X*, Minstrel Bks) PB.

— Terror on Track. (Hardy Boys Casefiles Ser.: No. 57). 160p. (YA). (gr. 6 up). 1991. pap. 3.99 (*0-671-73093-2*, Archway) PB.

Dixon, Franklin W., jt. auth. see Keene, Carolyn.

***Dixon-Fyle, Mac.** A Saro Community in the Niger Delta, 1912-1984: The Potts-Johnsons of Port Harcourt & Their Heirs. LC 98-54324. (Rochester Studies in African History & the Diaspora: Vol. 5). (Illus.). 224p. 1999. 65.00 (*1-58046-038-0*) Univ Rochester Pr.

Dixon-Fyle, Mac, jt. auth. see Conteh-Morgan, Earl.

Dixon, G. D. Records of Coal Center Methodist Church, 1873-1938: Washington County, PA. 75p. 1996. per. 8.50 (*1-55856-213-3*, 088) Closson Pr.

Dixon, G. R. Plant Pathogens & Their Control in Horticulture. (Science in Horticulture Ser.). (Illus.). 265p. (Orig.). (C). 1984. pap. text 30.00 (*0-333-35912-7*) Scholium Intl.

Dixon, Geoffrey M. Division Algebras: Octonions, Quartnions, Complex Numbers, & the Algebraic Design of Physics. LC 94-13948. (Mathematics & Its Applications Ser.: Vol. 290). 1994. text 140.00 (*0-7923-2890-6*) Kluwer Academic.

Dixon, George. What Works at Work: Lessons from the Masters. 328p. 1988. 39.95 (*0-943210-05-4*) Lakewood Pubns.

Dixon, George, jt. auth. see Byham, William C.

Dixon, George L., Jr. Exercise a la Carte: An Activity Menu to a Healthier Lifestyle. LC 94-77596. (Illus.). 140p. (Orig.). 1994. pap. 12.95 (*0-9642615-0-2*) Lane & Ford.

***Dixon-Gough, R. W.** Land Reform & Sustainable Development. 305p. 1999. 78.95 (*0-7546-1052-7*) Ashgate Pub Co.

Dixon-Gough, R. W., jt. auth. see Bullard, R. K.

Dixon, Graeme. Holocaust Island. 1990. pap. 14.95 (*0-7022-2320-4*, Pub. by Univ Queensland Pr) Intl Spec Bk.

Dixon, Hannah F. Inspiration in Poetry. (Orig.). 1997. pap. write for info. (*1-57553-461-4*) Watermark Pr.

***Dixon, Hannah Forsyth.** Inspiration in Poetry. 70p. 1999. pap. 9.95 (*1-58597-001-8*) Leathers Pub.

***Dixon, Hepworth.** Robert Blake: Admiral & General at Sea. (Illus.). 392p. 2000. lib. bdg. 69.95 (*0-9674826-1-5*, Pub. by Regatta Pr) CUP Services.

Dixon, Hollis M., tr. see Hubner, Kurt.

Dixon, Huw & Rankin, Neil, eds. The New Macroeconomics: Imperfect Markets & Policy Effectiveness. (Illus.). 402p. (C). 1995. pap. text 25.95 (*0-521-47947-9*) Cambridge U Pr.

***Dixon, Huw D., ed.** Controversies in Macroeconomics: Growth Trade & Policy. 350p. 1999. 64.95 (*0-631-21585-9*); pap. text 34.95 (*0-631-21586-7*) Blackwell Pubs.

Dixon, J. Gear Grinding. (Technical Papers: Vol. P203). (Illus.). 23p. 1939. pap. text 30.00 (*1-55589-229-9*) AGMA.

D

An Asterisk (*) at the beginning of an entry indicates that the title is appearing for the first time.

— A History Watch Companies of America. (Illus.). 156p. 1978. pap. 16.95 (0-930163-51-6) Arlington Bk.

Dixon, J. B. & Weed, S. B., eds. Minerals in Soil Environments. 2nd ed. (Book Ser.: No. 1). 1264p. 1989. 90.00 (0-89118-787-1) Soil Sci Soc Am.

Dixon, J. C., ed. see Southern Conference on Gerontology Staff.

Dixon, J. I., jt. auth. see Boggs, Ralph S.

Dixon, J. M., ed. Centennial History of Polk County. (Illus.). 361p. 1997. reprint ed. lib. bdg. 42.00 (0-8328-6699-7) Higginson Bk Co.

— Electropotentials in the Clinical Assessment of Breast Neoplasia. LC 95-39600. (ESO Monographs). 75p. 1995. 72.95 (3-540-60348-4) Spr-Verlag.

*Dixon, J. M. & Sainsbury, J. R. Handbook of Diseases of the Breast. 2nd ed. (Illus.). 208p. 1998. pap. write for info. (0-443-06185-8) Church.

Dixon, J. M., et al. From Nonlinearity to Coherence: Universal Features of Non-Linear Behaviour in Many-Body Physics. LC 96-36601. (Illus.). 624p. (C). 1997. text 175.00 (0-19-853972-X) OUP.

Dixon, J. M., jt. auth. see Upton, M.

Dixon, J. Robb, et al. The New Performance Challenge: Measuring Operations for World-Class Competition. 200p. 1990. 47.50 (1-55623-301-9, Irwn Prfssnl) McGraw-Hill Prof.

Dixon, James, jt. ed. see Dixon, Edla.

Dixon, James, jt. ed. see Plain, Deborah.

Dixon, James G., III, jt. auth. see Franklin, Miriam A.

Dixon, James H., & Associates Staff. National Security Policy Formulation: Institutions, Processes, & Issues. 246p. (Orig.). (C). 1985. pap. text 25.00 (0-8191-4935-7) U Pr of Amer.

Dixon, James R., jt. auth. see Werler, John E.

*Dixon, James Ray. Amphibians & Reptiles of Texas: With Keys, Taxonomic Synopses, Bibliography, & Distribution Maps. 2nd ed. LC 99-40452. 426p. 2000. 39.95 (0-89096-919-1); pap. 24.95 (0-89096-920-5) Tex A&M Univ Pr.

Dixon, Janet. Predicting Seniors' Use of Cyberspace. rev. ed. LC 96-36709. (Studies on the Elderly in America). (Illus.). 144p. 1996. text 51.00 (0-8153-2628-9) Garland.

Dixon, Janice T. The Art of Writing Scrapbook Stories. (Illus.). 25p. 1998. pap. 8.95 (0-9656919-7-7) Mt Olympus Pub.

— Family Focused: A Step-by-Step Guide to Writing Your Autobiography & Family History. LC 98-102671. (Illus.). 352p. 1997. lib. bdg. 19.95 (0-9656919-6-9) Mt Olympus Pub.

Dixon, Jean, tr. see Cox, Don.

Dixon, Jeane. Do Cats Have ESP? 1998. 14.95 (0-9665202-0-3) Running Pr.

*Dixon, Jeane. Do Cats Have ESP? 112p. 2000. 14.95 (0-7624-0768-9) Running Pr.

Dixon, Jeane. Yesterday, Today & Forever. 394p. 1987. pap. 8.95 (0-8362-7941-7) Andrews & McMeel.

Dixon, Jerry & Reeves, J. Scott. Windows NT Server Concise. 400p. Date not set. pap. 19.99 (1-56205-691-3) New Riders Pub.

Dixon, Jess. The Little Grey Partridge: The Diary of Ishobel Ross, Serbia, 1916-1917. (Illus.). 100p. 1988. pap. 14.00 (0-08-036419-5, Pub. by Aberdeen U Pr) Macmillan.

Dixon, Jesse T. Adapting Activities for Therapeutic Recreation Service: Concepts & Applications. (Illus.). 100p. (Orig.). 1981. pap. 14.50 (0-916304-48-5) SDSU Press.

Dixon, Jim. The Zoo Is Blue: And Should Be Read. (Personalized Children's Book Ser.). (Illus.). 36p. (J). (gr. k-2). 1991. 12.95 (1-880453-01-0) J Hefty Pub.

Dixon, Jim, jt. auth. see Sullivan, Jem.

Dixon, Joan B. & Cassidy, Eric. Virtual Futures. LC 97-19274. (Illus.). 144p. (C). 1998. 80.00 (0-415-13379-3); pap. 24.99 (0-415-13380-7) Routledge.

Dixon, Joan De Vee, see De Vee Dixon, Joan.

Dixon, Joan M. National Intelligence Newspaper Abstracts, 1824-1826, Vol. 7. 520p. 1999. 39.50 (0-7884-1086-5, D403) Heritage Bk.

— National Intelligencer & Washington Advertiser Newspaper Abstracts, 1800-1805. ii, 309p. 1996. pap. 26.00 (0-7884-0392-3, D395) Heritage Bk.

— National Intelligencer & Washington Advertiser Newspaper Abstracts, 1806-1810, Vol. 2. vi, 275p. (Orig.). 1996. pap. 22.00 (0-7884-0596-9, D397) Heritage Bk.

— National Intelligencer & Washington Advertiser Newspaper Abstracts, 1814-1817. vi, 382p. 1997. pap. 28.50 (0-7884-0707-4, D400) Heritage Bk.

*Dixon, Joan M. National Intelligencer Newspaper Abstracts: 1830-1831. 160p. 1999. pap. 37.50 (0-7884-1309-0, D399) Heritage Bk.

Dixon, Joan M. National Intelligencer Newspaper Abstracts, 1818-1820. 429p. 1998. pap. 30.00 (0-7884-0830-5, D401) Heritage Bk.

— National Intelligencer Newspaper Abstracts, 1821-1823. 523p. 1998. pap. 40.00 (0-7884-0948-4, D402) Heritage Bk.

*Dixon, Joan M. National Intelligencer Newspaper Abstracts, 1832-1833. 567p. 2000. pap. 34.00 (0-7884-1428-3, 1428) Heritage Bk.

Dixon, Joan M. Natural Intelligencer Newspaper Abstracts, 1827-1929. 572p. 1999. pap. 43.50 (0-7884-1185-3, D404) Heritage Bk.

Dixon, Joe C. Defeat & Disarmament: Allied Diplomacy & the Politics of Military Affairs in Austria, 1918-1922. LC 82-49193. 168p. 1986. 32.50 (0-87413-221-5) U Delaware Pr.

Dixon, John. Catastrophic Rights: Experimental Drugs & AIDS. 132p. 1990. pap. 10.95 (0-921586-07-8, Pub. by New Star Bks) Genl Dist Srvs.

— The Chinese Welfare System, Nineteen Forty-Nine to Nineteen Seventy-Nine. LC 81-2822. 437p. 1981. 95.00 (0-275-90605-1, C0605, Praeger Pubs) Greenwood.

— A Schooling in English: Critical Episodes in the Struggle to Shape Literary & Cultural Studies. 192p. 1991. 113.00 (0-335-09322-1); pap. 39.95 (0-335-09321-3) OpUniv Pr.

— Scots Baronial. 1991. 14.00 (0-7486-6124-7, Pub. by Polygon) Subterranean Co.

— The Shock Absorber Handbook. LC 98-37276. 275p. 1999. 55.00 (0-7680-0050-5, R-176) Soc Auto Engineers.

— Social Security in Global Perspective. LC 98-41090. 376p. 1999. 69.50 (0-275-96509-0, Praeger Pubs); pap. 27.95 (0-275-96510-4, Praeger Pubs) Greenwood.

— Trading in the European Union: A Guide to Business & Taxation. 2nd ed. 480p. (C). 1996. pap. 195.00 (0-85459-964-9, Pub. by Tolley Pubng) St Mut.

Dixon, John, ed. Fiction in Libraries. LC 86-14264. (Handbooks on Library Practice). 230p. reprint ed. pap. 71.30 (0-7837-5296-2, 204505000005) Bks Demand.

— Social Welfare in the Middle East. 256p. (C). 1986. 55.00 (0-7099-4502-7, Pub. by C Helm) Routldge.

*Dixon, John & Hydeman, Mark, eds. The Marketization of Social Security. 2001. write for info. (1-56720-325-6) Greenwood.

Dixon, John & Kim, Hyung S., eds. Social Welfare in Asia. LC 85-21279. 432p. 1986. 49.95 (0-7099-0853-9, Pub. by C Helm) Routldge.

Dixon, John & MacArov, David. Poverty: A Persistent Global Reality. LC 97-35431. 304p. (C). 1998. 85.00 (0-415-14681-X) Routledge.

Dixon, John & Macarov, David. Poverty: A Persistent Global Reality. LC 97-35431. 304p. (C). 1998. pap. 25.99 (0-415-14682-8) Routledge.

Dixon, John & Newman, David. Entering the Chinese Market: The Risks & Discounted Rewards. LC 98-4963. 160p. 1998. 55.00 (1-56720-137-7, Quorum Bks) Greenwood.

Dixon, John & Poli, Corrado. Engineering Design & Design for Manufacturing: A Structured Approach. 600p. (C). 1995. text 54.00 (0-9645272-0-0) Field Stone.

Dixon, John & Scheurell, Robert P. Social Welfare in Developed Market Countries. (Comparative Social Welfare Ser.). 320p. (C). 1989. lib. bdg. 67.50 (0-415-00532-9) Routledge.

Dixon, John & Scheurell, Robert P., eds. Social Security: A Cross-Cultural Perspective. (Orig.). 1993. pap. 15.00 (0-944285-36-8) Pol Studies.

Dixon, John & Stratta, Leslie. Writing Narrative & Beyond. 88p. (C). 1986. pap. text 16.00 (0-920472-07-9, 0190) Heinemann.

Dixon, John & Thorne, Kevin. Tolley's Taxation of Intellectual Property. 500p. (C). 1994. 175.00 (0-85459-926-6, Pub. by Tolley Pubng) St Mut.

Dixon, John, et al. Economic Analysis Environmental Impacts. 2nd ed. 1993. 40.00 (1-85383-185-9, Pub. by Escan Pubns) Island Pr.

Dixon, John, ed. see Scheurell, Robert P.

Dixon, John A. & Hufschmidt, Maynard M., eds. Economic Valuation Techniques for the Environment: A Case Study Workbook. LC 86-2730. 224p. 1986. pap. text 16.95 (0-8018-3308-6) Johns Hopkins.

Dixon, John A., jt. auth. see Hodgson, Gregor.

Dixon, John C. Tires, Suspension & Handling. 2nd ed. LC 96-27115. 435p. 1996. 69.00 (1-56091-831-4, R-168) Soc Auto Engineers.

— Tolley's Trading in Europe: A Guide to Business & Taxation. 448p. 1992. 140.00 (0-85459-569-4, Pub. by Tolley Pubng) St Mut.

Dixon, John D. Problems in Group Theory. LC 72-76597. 176p. 1973. reprint ed. pap. 8.95 (0-486-61574-X) Dover.

Dixon, John D. & Mortimer, Brian. Permutation Groups. Axler, S. et al, eds. LC 95-44880. (Graduate Texts in Mathematics Ser.: Vol. 163). (Illus.). 346p. (C). 1996. 49.00 (0-387-94599-7) Spr-Verlag.

Dixon, John M. Altoon + Porter Architects: Context & Consequence, 1. 1999. pap. text 40.00 (88-7838-050-4) L'Arca IT.

Dixon, John Morris, ed. Urban Spaces. 308p. 1999. text 59.95 (0-934590-32-X) Visual Refer.

Dixon, John P. The Spatial Child. (Illus.). 248p. 1983. pap. 33.95 (0-398-06096-7) C C Thomas.

— The Spatial Child. (Illus.). 248p. (C). 1983. 47.95 (0-398-04821-5) C C Thomas.

Dixon, John R. Harry's Last. LC 98-80645. 310p. 1999. pap. 14.95 (0-88739-214-8) Creat Arts Bk.

*Dixon, John Robert. Secret Losses. LC 00-190176. 239p. 2000. 25.00 (0-7388-1492-X); pap. 18.00 (0-7388-1493-8) Xlibris Corp.

Dixon, John W., Jr. Art & Theological Imagination. (Illus.). 1984. 13.45 (0-8164-0397-X) Harper SF.

Dixon, Joly. Towards a More Coherent Global Economic Order. 1998. pap. text 25.00 (0-7494-2712-4) Kogan Page Ltd.

Dixon, Joly & Vignon, Jerome, eds. Towards a More Coherent Global Economic Order. LC 98-17449. 110p. 1998. text 39.95 (0-312-21602-5) St Martin.

Dixon, Jonathan S. & Furst, D. E., eds. Second-Line Agents in the Treatment of Arthritis. (Inflammatory Disease & Therapy Ser.: Vol. 9). (Illus.). 640p. 1991. text 255.00 (0-8247-8541-X) Dekker.

Dixon-Jones, Lorraine A. The Child Care Guarantee in Welfare Reform. 52p. 1990. pap. 15.00 (1-55516-629-6, 6117) Natl Conf State Legis.

Dixon, Joseph. Swimming Coaching. (Illus.). 192p. 1996. pap. 35.00 (1-85223-998-0, Pub. by Crolwood) Trafalgar.

Dixon, K., et al. Papers on California Prehistory, Vol. 22, Pt. 2. (Archives of California Prehistory Ser.: Vol. 22). 118p. (Orig.). (C). 1988. pap. text 13.13 (1-55567-058-X) Coyote Press.

Dixon, Karen R. & Southern, Pat. Roman Cavalry: From the First to the Third Century A. D. (Illus.). 272p. (C). 1997. pap. 25.99 (0-415-17039-7) Routledge.

Dixon, Karen R., jt. auth. see Southern, Pat.

Dixon, Katharine L., jt. auth. see Pilkey, Orrin H.

Dixon, Katherine L., jt. auth. see Pilkey, Orrin H.

Dixon, Kathleen. Making Relationships: Gender in the Forming of Academic Community. LC 95-53029. (Studies in Composition & Rhetoric: No. 2). VIII, 172p. (C). 1997. text 41.95 (0-8204-3123-0) P Lang Pubng.

— Outbursts in Academe: Multiculturalism & Other Sources of Conflicts. LC 98-29882. (Crosscurrents Ser.). 1998. pap. text 22.00 (0-86709-477-X) Heinemann.

Dixon, Keith. Freedom & Equality: The Moral Basis of Democratic Socialism. 160p. (C). 1986. text 33.00 (0-7102-0643-7, Routledge Thoemms) Routledge.

Dixon, Keith A. La Cueva de la Pala Chica: A Burial Cave in the Guaymas Region of Coastal Sonora, Mexico. Fowler, William et al, eds. (Vanderbilt University Publications in Anthropology: No. 38). 97p. (Orig.). 1990. pap. 12.25 (0-935462-29-5) VUPA.

Dixon-Kennedy, Mike. Arthurian Myth & Legend: An A-Z of People & Places. 304p. 1998. pap. 16.95 (0-7137-2703-9, Pub. by Blandford Pr) Sterling.

— Celtic Myth & Legend: An A-Z of People & Places. 240p. 1996. 27.95 (0-7137-2571-0, Pub. by Blandford Pr) Sterling.

— Celtic Myth & Legend: An A-Z of People & Places. 320p. 1998. pap. 14.95 (0-7137-2613-X, Pub. by Blandford Pr) Sterling.

— Encyclopedia of Greco-Roman Mythology. LC 98-40666. 370p. 1998. write for info. (1-57607-129-4) ABC-CLIO.

— Encyclopedia of Greco-Roman Mythology. LC 98-40666. 392p. 1998. lib. bdg. 65.00 (1-57607-094-8, AD-GRMYC) ABC-CLIO.

— Encyclopedia of Russian & Slavic Myth & Legend. LC 98-20330. 375 p. 1998. pap. write for info. (1-57607-130-8) ABC-CLIO.

— Encyclopedia of Russian & Slavic Myth & Legend. LC 98-20330. (Illus.). 392p. 1998. lib. bdg. 65.00 (1-57607-063-8, AD-SLAMYC) ABC-CLIO.

— European Myth & Legend: An A to Z of People & Places. LC 97-224017. 288p. 1997. 29.95 (0-7137-2676-8, Pub. by Blandford Pr) Sterling.

— Heroes of the Round Table. LC 98-120481. (Illus.). 160p. 1997. 24.95 (0-7137-2619-9, Pub. by Blandford Pr) Sterling.

— Native American Myth & Legend: An A-Z of People & Places. 288p. 1996. 27.95 (0-7137-2623-7, Pub. by Blandford Pr) Sterling.

— Native American Myth & Legend: An A-Z of People & Places. (Illus.). 304p. 1998. pap. 17.95 (0-7137-2669-5) Blandford Pr.

Dixon, Kingsley, jt. auth. see Pate, John.

Dixon-Krauss, Lisbeth, ed. Vygotsky in the Classroom: Mediated Literacy Instruction & Assessment. LC 95-9276. 225p. (Orig.). (C). 1995. pap. text 36.56 (0-8013-1590-5) Longman.

*Dixon, Lance. Andominii: Journey to the Perfect World. 1999. pap. 18.95 (0-9673454-3-X) L Dixon Cos.

Dixon, Larry. Project Turn-Around. LC 84-61674. 61p. 1985. ring bd. 49.95 (0-914607-20-0) Master Tchr.

Dixon, Larry, jt. auth. see Lackey, Mercedes.

Dixon, Lauren, ed. see Graves, Jeanne R.

Dixon, Laurinda. Arts & Ideas: Student Manual. 128p. (C). 1994. pap. text, spiral bd. 15.95 (0-8403-8622-2) Kendall-Hunt.

Dixon, Laurinda, ed. Nicolas Flamel: His Exposition of the Hieroglypical Figures (1624) LC 94-8101. (Illus.). 208p. 1994. text 37.00 (0-8240-5838-0, H979) Garland.

Dixon, Laurinda S. Alchemical Imagery in Bosch's Garden of Delights. LC 81-14673. (Studies in the Fine Arts: Iconography: No. 2). (Illus.). 249p. reprint ed. pap. 77.20 (0-8357-1247-8, 207020400064) Bks Demand.

— Perilous Chastity: Women & Illness in Pre-Enlightenment Art & Medicine. LC 94-34911. (Illus.). 320p. 1995. text 57.50 (0-8014-3026-7); pap. text 25.00 (0-8014-8215-1) Cornell U Pr.

— Skating in the Arts of Seventeenth Century Holland. LC 87-50001. (Illus.). 44p. (Orig.). 1987. pap. 8.00 (0-915577-12-7) Taft Museum.

Dixon, Laurinda S., jt. ed. see Weisberg, Gabriel P.

Dixon, Leon, Jr. Future in Our Hands: Institution Building for Supplementary Education. 444p. (Orig.). 1994. pap. text 15.00 (0-9632951-0-1) W E B DuBois Lrn Ctr.

Dixon, Lisa B., intro. Families & Mental Health Treatment: A Compendium of Articles from Psychiatric Services & Hospital & Community Psychiatry. LC 99-192267. 72 p. 1998. write for info. (0-89042-413-6) Amer Psych Assn.

Dixon, Lisa B., jt. ed. see Lehman, Anthony F.

Dixon, Lloyd. Fixing Superfund: The Effect of the Proposed Superfund Reform Act of 1994 on Transaction Costs. 111p. 1994. pap. 15.00 (0-8330-1568-0, MR-455-ICJ) Rand Corp.

*Dixon, Lloyd S. The Financial Implications of Releasing Small Firms & Small-Volume Contributors from Superfund Liability. LC 00-38732. (Illus.). 85p. (C). 2000. pap. 12.00 (0-8330-2825-1) Rand Corp.

Dixon, Lloyd S. & Garber, Steven. California's Ozone-Reduction Strategy for Light-Duty Vehicles: Direct Costs, Direct Emission Effects, & Market Responses. LC 96-177882. 499p. 1996. pap. text 13.00 (0-8330-2392-6, MR-695-ICJ) Rand Corp.

Dixon, Lloyd S., et al. California's 1991 Drought Water Bank: Economic Impacts in the Selling Regions. LC 93-33576. 1993. pap. text 13.00 (0-8330-1466-8, MR-301-CDWR) Rand Corp.

— California's Ozone-Reduction Stretegy for Light-Duty Vehicles: An Economic Assessment. LC 96-177881. 74p. 1996. pap. text 15.00 (0-8330-2391-8, MR-695/1-ICJ) Rand Corp.

— Drought Management Policies & Economic Effects in Urban Areas of California, 1987-1992. LC 96-48491. 151p. 1996. pap. text 13.00 (0-8330-2467-1, MR813CUWACDWRNS) Rand Corp.

— Private Sector Cleanup Expenditures & Transaction Costs at 18 Superfund Sites. LC 93-39916. 1993. pap. text 13.00 (0-8330-1470-6, MR-204-EPA/RC) Rand Corp.

Dixon, Lloyd S., jt. auth. see Dale, Larry L.

Dixon, Louis M., et al. Playing the Cards That Are Dealt: Mead Dixon, the Law, & Casino Gaming. (Illus.). 276p. 1992. 19.95 (1-56475-365-4) U NV Oral Hist.

Dixon, Louisa. Next Chance to Last. LC 98-217129. 345p. 1998. 24.95 (1-885478-39-9, Pub. by Genesis Press) BookWorld.

— Outside Chance. unabridged ed. 420p. 1999. 24.95 (1-885478-63-1, Pub. by Genesis Press) BookWorld.

— What Did I Do Today? 42p. (J). (gr. k-3). pap. 12.95 (0-9635811-0-4) Rosemont Ltd.

Dixon, Louisa & Boshers, Martha. What Did I Do Today? For Young Writers. 42p. (J). (gr. 3-7). pap. 12.95 (0-9635811-1-2) Rosemont Ltd.

Dixon, Lugenia & Lugo, James. Living Psychology: An Introduction. 3rd ed. 462p. (C). 1996. pap. text 50.50 (1-56226-279-3) CAT Pub.

— Living Psychology Handbook: An Introduction. 142p. (C). 1996. pap. text 21.35 (1-56226-301-3) CAT Pub.

Dixon, M. & Engleman, L., eds. Humana Festival '96: The Complete Plays. (Contemporary American Playwrights Ser.). 320p. (Orig.). 1996. pap. 19.95 (1-57525-033-0) Smith & Kraus.

Dixon, Malcolm & Smith, Karen. The Body. LC 98-6973. (Young Scientists Ser.). (Illus.). 32p. (J). 1998. lib. bdg. 21.30 (1-887068-69-4) Smart Apple.

— Electricity. LC 98-6972. (Young Scientists Ser.). (Illus.). 32p. (J). 1998. lib. bdg. 21.30 (1-887068-67-8) Smart Apple.

— Forces & Movement. LC 98-6971. (Young Scientists Ser.). (Illus.). 32p. (J). 1998. lib. bdg. 15.95 (1-887068-68-6) Smart Apple.

— Light & Color. LC 98-6974. (Young Scientists Ser.). (Illus.). 32p. (J). 1998. lib. bdg. 21.30 (1-887068-70-8) Smart Apple.

— Plants Around Us. LC 98-6975. (Young Scientists Ser.). (Illus.). 32p. (J). 1998. lib. bdg. 21.30 (1-887068-71-6) Smart Apple.

— Sound & Music. LC 98-4218. (Young Scientists Ser.). (Illus.). 32p. (J). 1998. lib. bdg. 21.30 (1-887068-72-4) Smart Apple.

Dixon, Malcolm, jt. auth. see Crane, Robin.

Dixon, Marden G. & Woodside, Frank C. Drug Product Liability, 3 vols. 1974. ring bd. 680.00 (0-8205-1257-5) Bender.

Dixon, Margaret C. & Vann, Elizabeth C. Denny Genealogy. (Illus.). 565p. 1998. reprint ed. pap. 86.50 (0-8328-8268-2); reprint ed. lib. bdg. 96.50 (0-8328-8267-4) Higginson Bk Co.

— Denny Genealogy, Third Book: Descendants of David Denny, Sr, of Penna. & the Shenandoah Valley of Ve., & Allied Families of Brunk, Campbell, Davis, Gaither, Guthrie, Hubbard, Lockhart, Lunsford, Stone, Washington & Many Others. 489p. 1997. reprint ed. pap. 75.00 (0-8328-8270-4); reprint ed. lib. bdg. 85.00 (0-8328-8269-0) Higginson Bk Co.

Dixon, Margaret C., jt. auth. see Vann, Elizabeth C.

Dixon, Mark & Heidt, Bob. House Painting: Inside & Out. LC 97-13869. (Illus.). 160p. 1997. pap. 19.95 (1-56158-165-8, 070292) Taunton.

Dixon, Marlene. Things Which Are Done in Secret. 296p. 1976. 38.99 (0-919618-68-5, Pub. by Black Rose); pap. 9.99 (0-919618-92-8, Pub. by Black Rose) Consort Bk Sales.

Dixon, Martha I. The New Mid-Life Crisis: The Reality of Caring for Your Parents. vi, 110p. 1998. pap. 13.00 (0-9668125-0-6) Revelat Pr Inc.

Dixon, Martin. Equity & Trusts. (Questions & Answers Ser.). 288p. 1995. 18.00 (1-874241-21-X, Pub. by Cavendish Pubng) Gaunt.

— Land Law. (Lecture Notes Ser.). 280p. 1994. pap. write for info. (1-874241-64-3, Pub. by Cavendish Pubng) Gaunt.

— Land Law. 2nd ed. (Questions & Answers Ser.). 284p. 1995. 18.00 (1-85941-265-3, Pub. by Cavendish Pubng) Gaunt.

— Land Law. 2nd ed. (Lecture Notes Ser.). 271p. 1996. pap. 30.00 (1-85941-170-3, Pub. by Cavendish Pubng) Gaunt.

— Textbook on International Law. 2nd ed. 332p. 1993. pap. 36.00 (1-85431-257-X, Pub. by Blackstone Pr) Gaunt.

— Textbook on International Law. 3rd ed. LC 97-153765. 340p. 1996. pap. 38.00 (1-85431-444-0, Pub. by Blackstone Pr) Gaunt.

Dixon, Martin & McCorquodale, Robert. Cases & Materials on International Law. 2nd ed. 688p. 1995. pap. 52.00 (1-85431-408-4, Pub. by Blackstone Pr) Gaunt.

*Dixon, Martin & McCorquodale, Robert. Cases & Materials on International Law. 3rd ed. 653p. 2000. pap. 45.00 (1-85431-880-2, Pub. by Blackstone Pr) Gaunt.

Dixon, Martin & McCorquodale, Robert, eds. Cases & Materials on International Law. 582p. (C). 1991. 51.00 (1-85431-123-9, Pub. by Blackstone Pr) Gaunt.

Dixon, Martin & Tate, Greg. Brooklyn Kings: New York City's Black Bikers. LC 99-12028. (Illus.). 144p. 1999. 50.00 (1-57687-044-8) pwerHse Cultrl.

Dixon, Martyn R. Sylow Theory Formations & Fitting Classes in Locally Finite Groups. (Series in Algebra). 320p. 1994. text 48.00 (981-02-1795-1) World Scientific Pub.

Dixon, Marvin N. That Saved a Wretch Like Me. LC 93-20016. 152p. 1993. pap. 10.99 (0-8272-3631-X) Chalice Pr.

Dixon, Mary. A White Lady Doing Nothing in the Tropics: The Story of Herman & Mary Dixon. LC 95-71782. (Jaffray Collection Of Missionary Portraits: No. 15). 1996. pap. 9.99 (0-87509-641-7) Chr Pubns.

Dixon, Mary, jt. auth. see Dixon, Brian.

Dixon, Mary, jt. auth. see Jackman, Dianne.

Dixon, Max. The Wataugans. (Illus.). 80p. 1989. reprint ed. pap. 6.95 (0-932807-47-X) Overmountain Pr.

***Dixon, McDonald.** Season of Mist. LC 00-190841. 2000. 25.00 (0-7388-1987-5); pap. 18.00 (0-7388-1988-3) Xlibris Corp.

Dixon, Melvin. Love's Instruments. LC 95-68621. 80p. (Orig.). 1995. pap. 10.95 (1-882688-07-4) Tia Chucha Pr.

— Ride Out the Wilderness: Geography & Identity in Afro-American Literature. LC 86-30918. 200p. 1987. text 24.95 (0-252-01414-6) U of Ill Pr.

— Trouble the Water. 243p. 1989. 18.95 (0-932511-23-6); pap. 8.95 (0-932511-24-4) Fiction Coll.

Dixon, Melvin, tr. see Fabre, Genevieve E.

Dixon, Melvin, tr. & intro. see Senghor, Leopold S.

***Dixon, Michael.** Cardiovascular Disease, Potentiated Magnesium & the True Fountain of Youth. LC 99-97280. (Illus.). 150p. 1999. pap. 9.95 (0-9638681-1-X, BodySense Pubns) Legal Ease.

Dixon, Michael, ed. ABC of Breast Diseases. (Illus.). 80p. 1995. pap. text 26.00 (0-7279-0915-0, Pub. by BMJ Pub) Login Brothers Bk Co.

— Humana Festival, 1997: The Complete Plays. 320p. (Orig.). pap. 19.95 (1-57525-114-0) Smith & Kraus.

Dixon, Michael & Smith, Joel A., eds. Anne Bogart: Viewpoints. LC 94-46467. (Career Development Ser.). 208p. 1995. 35.00 (1-880399-94-6); pap. 14.95 (1-880399-80-6) Smith & Kraus.

Dixon, Michael & Volansky, Michele, eds. A Brave & Violent Theatre: Monologues, Scenes & Historical Context for 20th Century Irish Drama. 224p. 1995. pap. 11.95 (1-880399-71-7) Smith & Kraus.

— Kiss & Tell: Restoration Comedy of Manners: Scenes, Monologues, & Historical Context. (Monologue Audition Ser.). 186p. 1993. pap. 11.95 (1-880399-38-5) Smith & Kraus.

Dixon, Michael B. Tales from the Arabian Nights: Dramatizations. (Illus.). 52p. (J). (gr. k up). 1985. pap. 4.50 (0-88680-239-3) I E Clark.

Dixon, Michael B., ed. 500 Years of Theatre History: From the Actor's Theatre of Louisville Classics in Context History. LC 99-48120. 448p. 1999. 19.95 (1-57525-173-6) Smith & Kraus.

— Humana Festival '98: The Complete Plays. (Contemporary Playwrights Ser.). 384p. 1998. pap. 19.95 (1-57525-142-6) Smith & Kraus.

Dixon, Michael B. & Smith, Valerie. Big Trouble: Six Ten-Minute Plays from Actors Theatre of Louisville. (Illus.). 80p. (Orig.). 1990. pap. 5.00 (0-88680-324-1) I E Clark.

Dixon, Michael B. & Volansky, Michele, eds. By Southern Playwrights: Plays from Actors Theatre of Louisville. LC 95-42493. (Illus.). 256p. 1996. pap. 19.95 (0-8131-0877-2); text 42.95 (0-8131-1967-7) U Pr of Ky.

— A Decade of New Comedy Vol. 1: Plays from the Humana Festival, 2 vols., Vol. 1. LC 96-1884. 313p. 1996. pap. 19.95 (0-435-07013-4, 07013) Heinemann.

— A Decade of New Comedy Vol. 2: Plays for the Humana Festival, 2 vols., Vol. 2. LC 96-1884. 1996. pap. 19.95 (0-435-07017-7, 07017) Heinemann.

***Dixon, Michael B. & Wegene, Amy, eds.** Human Festival '99: The Complete Plays. 348p. 1999. pap. 19.95 (1-57525-207-4) Smith & Kraus.

Dixon, Michael B., et al. Striking Out! (J). (gr. k up). 1984. pap. 6.00 (0-87602-252-2) Anchorage.

Dixon, Michael B., jt. ed. see Volansky, Michele.

Dixon, Michael C. Family Abuse: A Sad Reality. Nelson, Becky, ed. 22p. (YA). (gr. 7-12). 1994. pap. text 1.95 (1-56309-098-8, C946103, Wrld Changers Res) Womans Mission Union.

Dixon, Michael E. Bread of Blessing, Cup of Hope. 144p. (Orig.). 1987. pap. 7.95 (0-8272-0450-7) Chalice Pr.

Dixon, Michael E. & Dixon, Sandy. Fed by God's Grace: Communion Prayers for Year B. LC 99-38104. 1999. pap. 9.99 (0-8272-1025-6) Chalice Pr.

Dixon, Michael F. The Polliticke Courtier: Spenser's the Faerie Queene As a Rhetoric of Justice. LC 97-200926. (UND.). 256p. 1996. 55.00 (0-7735-1425-2, PR2358, Pub. by McG-Queens Univ Pr) CUP Services.

Dixon, Michael F. & Quirke, Philip. Aids to Pathology. 4th ed. LC 93-18262. 1993. text 24.00 (0-443-04442-2) Church.

Dixon, Michael P. Alaska Bound: A Life of Travel & Adventure in the Far North. LC 94-93811. (Illus.). 208p. 1996. reprint ed. pap. 13.95 (0-9639981-0-2) Dixon Paperback.

Dixon, Mike, jt. auth. see Craze, Richard.

***Dixon, Mim.** Managed Care in American Indian & Alaska Native Communities LC 98-74063. ix, 195 p. 1998. write for info. (0-87553-238-1) Am Pub Health.

Dixon, Mim. What Happened to Fairbanks? The Effects of the Trans-Alaska Oil Pipeline on the Community of Fairbanks, Alaska. (Social Impact Assessment Ser.: No. 1). (Illus.). 337p. 1978. text 33.00 (0-89158-071-9) Westview.

— What Happened to Fairbanks? The Effects of the Trans-Alaska Oil Pipeline on the Community of Fairbanks, Alaska. (Social Impact Assessment Ser.: No. 1). (Illus.). 337p. 1980. pap. text 16.90 (0-89158-961-9) Westview.

Dixon, Monica A. Love the Body You Were Born With: A Ten-Step Workbook for Women. 192p. 1996. pap. 13.00 (0-399-51975-0, Perigee Bks) Berkley Pub.

Dixon-Mueller, Ruth. Population Policy & Women's Rights: Transforming Reproductive Choice. LC 92-28547. 304p. 1993. 59.95 (0-275-94504-9, C4504, Praeger Pubs); pap. 21.95 (0-275-94611-8, B4611, Praeger Pubs) Greenwood.

— Women's Work in the Third World Agriculture: Concepts & Indicators. (Women, Work & Development Ser.: No. 9). xi, 151p. (Orig.). 1994. reprint ed. pap. 22.50 (92-2-105107-2) Intl Labour Office.

***Dixon, Nancy M.** Common Knowledge: How Companies Thrive by Sharing What They Know. LC 99-48879. 2000. 29.95 (0-87584-904-0, HBS Pr) Harvard Busn.

Dixon, Nancy M. Dialogue at Work, 1. 1998. pap. text 17.95 (1-898001-41-3) Lemos & Crane.

— The Organizational Learning Cycle: How We Can Learn Collectively. LC 94-17076. 176p. 1994. pap. 24.95 (0-07-707937-X) McGraw.

— The Organizational Learning Cycle: How We Can Learn Collectively. 2nd ed. LC 98-30675. xxiv, 240 p. 1999. 74.95 (0-566-08058-3) Ashgate Pub Co.

— Perspectives on Dialogue: Making Talk Developmental for Individuals & Organizations. LC 95-50957. 46p. 1996. pap. 20.00 (1-882197-16-X) Ctr Creat Leader.

Dixon, Nancy W. Palatine Roots: The 1710 German Settlement in New York As Experienced by Johann Peter Wagner. 352p. 1994. 49.50 (0-89725-175-X, 1521) Picton Pr.

Dixon, Neill, et al. Learning with Readers Theatre. Greenberg, Annalee, ed. (Building Connections Ser.). (Illus.). 154p. 1996. pap., teacher ed. 19.00 (1-895411-80-7) Peguis Pubs Ltd.

Dixon, Olive K. Life of "Billy" Dixon: Plainsman, Scout & Pioneer. 2nd ed. LC 87-42528. (Illus.). 298p. 1987. reprint ed. pap. 16.95 (0-938349-12-0) State House Pr.

Dixon, Owen. Jesting Pilate. LC 96-77650. xii, 275p. 1996. reprint ed. 68.00 (1-57588-123-3, 310630) W S Hein.

— Jesting Pilate. 2nd ed. LC 97-80052. xii, 304p. 1997. lib. bdg. 85.00 (1-57588-284-1, 311190) W S Hein.

Dixon, P. Truth about Drugs. (Illus.). mass mkt. 13.95 (0-340-66505-X, Pub. by Hodder & Stought Ltd) Trafalgar.

Dixon, P. B., et al. Notes & Problems in Applied General Equilibrium Economics. (Advanced Textbooks in Economics Ser.: Vol. 32). xvi,392p. 1992. 84.75 (0-444-88449-1, North Holland); 170.00 incl. disk (0-444-89379-2) Elsevier.

Dixon, Pam. Be Your Own Headhunter Online, 1. pap. 16.00 (0-8129-6383-0, Times Bks) Crown Pub Group.

— Job Searching Online for Dummies. LC 98-85427. (For Dummies Ser.). 384p. 1998. pap. 24.99 incl. cd-rom (0-7645-0376-6) IDG Bks.

***Dixon, Pam.** Job Searching Online for Dummies. 2nd ed. (For Dummies Ser.). 384p. 2000. pap. 24.99 (0-7645-0673-0) IDG Bks.

Dixon, Pam. Virtual College: A Quick Guide to How You Can Get the Degree You Want with Computer, TV, Video, Audio, & Other Distance Learning Tools. LC 96-41971. 160p. (Orig.). 1996. pap. 9.95 (1-56079-629-4) Petersons.

— Web Browsing with Compuserve. 1996. 22.95 (0-7615-0345-5) Prima Pub.

Dixon, Patricia E. Nietzsche & Jung: Quest for Wholeness. LC 89-13134. (Contemporary Existentialism Ser.). XVI, 459p. (C). 1999. text 68.00 (0-8204-1161-2) P Lang Pubng.

Dixon, Paul B. Retired Dreams: Dom Casmurro, Myth & Modernity. LC 88-29081. 156p. 1989. pap. 19.95 (0-911198-98-9) Purdue U Pr.

Dixon, Paul R., Jr., tr. see Hubner, Kurt.

Dixon, Peter. Great Tales of Old. 1976. 24.95 (0-8488-0477-5) Amereon Ltd.

— Oliver Goldsmith Revisited. (Twayne's English Authors Ser.: TEAS No. 487). 200p. 1991. 24.95 (0-8057-7008-9, Twyne) Mac Lib Ref.

— The Olympian. LC 83-63198. 274p. 1984. 13.95 (0-915677-00-8) Roundtable Pub.

— Rhetoric. (Critical Idiom Ser.: Vol. 19). 1971. pap. 8.95 (0-416-66760-0, NO. 2166) Routledge.

Dixon, Peter, ed. see Swift, Jonathan.

Dixon, Peter, ed. see Vanbrugh, John & Cibber, Colley.

Dixon, Peter, ed. see Wycherley, William.

Dixon, Peter, ed. & pref. see Farquhar, George.

Dixon, Peter S. Biology of the Rhodophyta. (University Reviews in Botany Ser.: No. 4). (Illus.). xiii, 285p. 1977. reprint ed. pap. 45.00 (3-87429-124-3, 002961, Pub. by Koeltz Sci Bks) Lubrecht & Cramer.

Dixon, Peter S. & Irvine, Linda M. Rhodophyta Pt. 1: Introduction, Nemaliales, Gigartinales. (Seaweeds of the British Isles Ser.: Vol. 1). (Illus.). 263p. 1997. pap. 64.95 (0-11-310000-0, Pub. by Statnry Office) Bernan Associates.

Dixon, Peter W. The Law Library. 250p. (Orig.). 1988. pap. 4.95 (0-317-91056-6) Lantern Bks.

Dixon, Peter W., intro. Great Tales of Old. LC 87-83338. (Illus.). 312p. (J). (gr. k-3). 1988. pap. 9.95 (0-945161-00-X); text 15.95 (0-945161-01-8) Lantern Bks.

Dixon, Phil & Hannigan, Pat. The Negro Baseball Leagues: A Photographic History. (Illus.). 364p. 1992. 39.95 (0-8488-0425-2) Amereon Ltd.

Dixon, R. & Holmes, P. Financial Markets. 176p. 1994. mass mkt. 18.99 (0-412-62280-7) Chapman & Hall.

Dixon, R. A. & Dillon, M. C., eds. Aborigines & Diamond Mining: The Politics of Resource Development in the East Kimberley, Western Australia. 1996. pap. 5.95 (0-85564-302-1, Pub. by Univ of West Aust Pr) Intl Spec Bk.

Dixon, R. B. & Kroeber, A. L. Linguistic Families of California. fac. ed. (University of California Publications in American Archaeology & Ethnology: Vol. 16: 3). 73p. (C). 1919. reprint ed. pap. text 8.44 (1-55567-223-X) Coyote Press.

Dixon, R. Brian. The Federal Wage & Hour Laws. 90p. (Orig.). 1994. pap. 20.00 (0-939900-66-1, PB22) Soc Human Resc Mgmt.

Dixon, R. M. Ergativity. (Cambridge Studies in Linguistics: No. 69). 293p. (C). 1994. pap. text 20.95 (0-521-44898-0) Cambridge U Pr.

— A New Approach to English Grammar, on Semantic Principles. 416p. 1991. 95.00 (0-19-824272-7) OUP.

— A New Approach to English Grammar, on Semantic Principles. 416p. 1992. reprint ed. pap. text 29.95 (0-19-824057-0) OUP.

— The Rise & Fall of Languages. LC 97-23092. (Illus.). 176p. (C). 1998. text 54.95 (0-521-62310-3); pap. text 16.95 (0-521-62654-4) Cambridge U Pr.

— Searching for Aboriginal Languages: Memoirs of a Field Worker. LC 89-34383. (Illus.). 348p. 1998. reprint ed. pap. text 18.95 (0-226-15430-0) U Ch Pr.

— Words of Our Country: Stories, Place Names & Vocabulary in Yidiny. (C). 1991. pap. 19.95 (0-7022-2360-3, Pub. by Univ Queensland Pr) Intl Spec Bk.

***Dixon, R. M. & Aikhenvald, Alexandra V., eds.** The Amazonian Languages. LC 98-46270. (Cambridge Language Surveys Ser.). (Illus.). 467p. 1999. 69.95 (0-521-57021-2) Cambridge U Pr.

Dixon, R. M. & Blake, Barry J., eds. Handbook of Australian Languages, Vol. II. xxiv, 427p. (C). 1981. 97.00 (90-272-2004-2) J Benjamins Pubng Co.

— Handbook of Australian Languages, Vol. III. (Illus.). xxiv, 531p. 1983. 97.00 (90-272-2005-0) J Benjamins Pubng Co.

Dixon, R. M. & Duwell, Martin, eds. The Honey-Ant Men's Love Song & Other Aboriginal Song Poems. 1990. pap. 16.95 (0-7022-2278-X, Pub. by Univ Queensland Pr) Intl Spec Bk.

Dixon, R. M. & Koch, Grace. Dyirbal Song Poems. 382p. 1996. pap. 29.95 (0-7022-2593-2, Pub. by Univ Queensland Pr) Intl Spec Bk.

Dixon, R. M., et al. Australian Aboriginal Words in English: Their Origin & Meaning. (Illus.). 278p. 1991. 47.00 (0-19-553099-3) OUP.

Dixon, R. M. W. A Grammar of Boumaa Fijian. (Illus.). 396p. 1988. pap. text 32.50 (0-226-15429-7); lib. bdg. 72.00 (0-226-15428-9) U Ch Pr.

Dixon, R. M. W. Where Have All the Adjectives Gone & Other Essays on Semantics & Syntax. (Janua Linguarum, Series Major: No. 107). 256p. 1982. text 52.35 (90-279-3309-X) Mouton.

***Dixon, R. M. W. & Aikhenvald, Alexandra Y., eds.** Changing Valency: Case Studies in Transitivity. (Illus.). 429p. 2000. 69.95 (0-521-66039-4) Cambridge U Pr.

***Dixon, R. M. W. & Blake, Barry J.** Handbook of Australian Languages, Vol. 5. 400p. 2000. pap. text 45.00 (0-19-554998-8) OUP.

Dixon, R. M. W. & Blake, Barry J., eds. Handbook of Australian Languages, Vol. I. xiv, 392p. 1979. 97.00 (90-272-0512-4) J Benjamins Pubng Co.

Dixon, Ramon & Aromatorio, Dave. How Far Do You Wanna Go? The True Story of the Man Who Turned 16 Inner City Kids into a Team of Champions. LC 97-67227. (Illus.). 266p. 1997. 22.95 (0-88282-155-5) New Horizon NJ.

Dixon, Ramon T. & Deanes, Charles. How Far Do You Wanna Go. Layne, Helen, ed. (Illus.). 193p. (Orig.). (YA). (gr. 6 up). 1995. pap. text 10.00 (0-9650424-0-5) Next Level.

Dixon, Rand M. Client/Server & Open Systems: Technologies & the Tools That Make Them Work. LC 95-32268. 303p. 1995. pap. 34.95 (0-471-05007-5) Wiley.

Dixon, Richard, tr. see Turrini, Peter.

Dixon, Richard, tr. & afterword by see Canetti, Veza, et al.

Dixon, Richard A. & Gonzales, Robert A., eds. Plant Cell Culture: A Practical Approach. (The Practical Approach Ser.: No. 145). (Illus.). 256p. 1995. ring bd. 85.00 (0-19-963403-3) OUP.

— Plant Cell Culture: A Practical Approach. 2nd ed. (The Practical Approach Ser.: No. 145). (Illus.). 250p. 1995. pap. text 55.00 (0-19-963402-5) OUP.

Dixon, Richard S., tr. & afterword by see Turrini, Peter.

Dixon, Rob. Banking in Europe: The Single Market. 2nd ed. 1993. pap. write for info. (0-415-10377-0) Thomson Learn.

Dixon, Rob. The Management Task. 2nd ed. LC 97-199379. (Institute of Management Ser.). 176p. 1997. pap. text 34.95 (0-7506-3390-5, HF) Buttrwrth-Heinemann.

Dixon, Rob, jt. auth. see Nicholson, Kevin.

Dixon, Robby G. How to Keep Your Child Out of Prison. 90p. (Orig.). 1996. pap. 9.95 (0-9651834-0-8) C Lestial Pub.

Dixon, Robert. Concepts in College Physics, 1. 704p. (C). 1994. pap. text 86.95 (0-7872-0055-7, 41005501) Kendall-Hunt.

— The Course of Empire: Neo-Classical Culture in the English Colony of New South Wales 1788-1860. 224p. 1986. 34.50 (0-19-554663-6) OUP.

— Mathographics. (General Science Ser.). (Illus.). 224p. 1991. pap. 10.95 (0-486-26639-7) Dover.

— Physics & Technology for the Liberal Arts. 2nd ed. 208p. (C). 1998. per. 37.95 (0-7872-4634-4) Kendall-Hunt.

— Writing the Colonial Adventure: Race, Gender & Nation in Anglo-Australian Popular Fiction 1875-1914. (Illus.). 238p. (C). 1996. text 64.95 (0-521-48190-2) Cambridge U Pr.

Dixon, Robert C. Spread Spectrum Systems: With Commercial Applications. 3rd ed. LC 93-8378. 592p. 1994. 98.95 (0-471-59342-7) Wiley.

Dixon, Robert G. Benchwork. LC 80-66607. (Machine Trades-Machine Shop Ser.). (Illus.). 211p. 1981. teacher ed. 14.00 (0-8273-1744-1); pap. text 37.95 (0-8273-1743-3) Delmar.

***Dixon, Robert K., ed.** The U. N. Framework Convention on Climate Change Activities Implemented Jointly Pilot: Experiences & Lessons Learned. LC 99-51738. (Institute for Global Environmental Strategies Ser.: Vol. 1). 422p. 1999. 210.00 (0-7923-6056-7) Kluwer Academic.

Dixon, Robert K., ed. see Warren, William G.

Dixon, Robert L. The McGraw-Hill Thirty-Six Hour Accounting Course. 3rd ed. 448p. 1993. 50.00 (0-07-017093-2); pap. 19.95 (0-07-017094-0) McGraw.

— Winning with CASE: Managing Modern Software Development. 480p. 1991. 39.95 (0-8306-2558-5) McGraw-Hill Prof.

Dixon, Robert L., jt. auth. see Paton, William A.

Dixon, Robert L., jt. ed. see Thomas, Stephen R.

Dixon, Robert M. Physics II. 128p. (C). 1995. spiral bd. 19.95 (0-8403-8200-6) Kendall-Hunt.

Dixon, Robert M., et al, eds. Blues & Gospel Records: 1890-1943. 4th ed. LC 96-6715. 1,420p. 1997. text 95.00 (0-19-816239-1) OUP.

Dixon, Robert T. Dynamics. 5th ed. 464p. (C). write for info. (0-318-63663-8) P-H.

***Dixon, Robert W.** The Old Beaded Bag. 36p. 1999. pap. 8.95 (1-58535-000-1) In His Steps.

Dixon, Roger & Muthesius, Stefan. Victorian Architecture. 2nd ed. (World of Art Ser.). (Illus.). 208p. 1985. pap. 14.95 (0-500-20160-9, Pub. by Thames Hudson) Norton.

Dixon, Roger A. & Backman, Lars, eds. Compensation for Psychological Deficits & Declines: Managing Losses & Promoting Gains. 360p. 1995. text 59.95 (0-8058-1559-7) L Erlbaum Assocs.

Dixon, Roland. The Racial History of Man, 2 vols. 1973. 250.00 (0-87968-273-6) Gordon Pr.

Dixon, Roland B. The Building of Cultures 1977. lib. bdg. 59.95 (0-8490-1560-X) Gordon Pr.

— The Building of Cultures. LC 76-44709. 328p. reprint ed. 49.50 (0-404-15917-6) AMS Pr.

— The Chimariko Indians & Language. fac. ed. (University of California Publications in American Archaeology & Ethnology: Vol. 5: 5). 88p. (C). 1910. reprint ed. pap. text 10.00 (1-55567-173-X) Coyote Press.

— The Huntington California Expedition Vol. XVII, Pt. I: Basketry Designs of the Indians of Northern California. (Publications of American Museum in Natural History: Vol. XVII, Pt. I). (Illus.). 106p. 1996. reprint ed. pap. text 11.88 (1-55567-425-9) Coyote Press.

— The Huntington California Expedition Vol. XVII, Pt. II: Maidu Myths. (Publications of American Museum in Natural History: Vol. XVII, Pt. II). 85p. 1997. reprint ed. pap. text 9.69 (1-55567-426-7) Coyote Press.

— The Huntington California Expedition Vol. XVII, Pt. III: The Northern Maidu. (Publications of American Museum in Natural History: Vol. XVII, Pt. III). (Illus.). 227p. 1905. reprint ed. pap. text 24.38 (1-55567-427-5) Coyote Press.

— The Huntington California Expedition Vol. XVII, Pt. V: The Shasta. (Publications of American Museum in Natural History: Vol. XVII, Pt. V). (Illus.). 144p. 1907. reprint ed. pap. text 15.63 (1-55567-429-1) Coyote Press.

— Maidu Texts. LC 73-3539. (American Ethnological Society Publications: No. 4). reprint ed. 39.50 (0-404-58154-4) AMS Pr.

— The Northern Maidu. LC 76-43692. (AMNH. Bulletin Ser.: Vol. XVII, Pt. 3). 152p. 1983. reprint ed. 39.50 (0-404-15523-5) AMS Pr.

Dixon, Ruth B. Rural Women at Work: Strategies for Development in South Asia. LC 78-5825. 227p. 1978. 21.95 (0-8018-2124-X) Resources Future.

Dixon, Ruth P. Indexes to Seamen's Protection Certificate Applications & Proofs of Citizenship, Forts of New Orleans, LA; New Haven, CT & Bath, ME: Additional Ports of Alabama, Connecticut, District of Columbia, Maine, Massachusetts, New Hampshire & Rhode Island. 170p. 1997. pap. 17.50 (0-8063-4508-X) Clearfield Co.

— Indexes to Seamen's Protection Certificate Applications & Proofs of Citizenship, Ports of New Orleans, LA; New Haven, CT & Bath, ME: Additional Ports of Alabama, Connecticut, District of Columbia, Maine, Massachusetts, New Hampshire, & Rhode Island. 171p. pap. 18.50 (0-8063-4819-4) Clearfield Co.

Dixon, S. Codename Quicksilver. (Advanced Puzzle Adventures Ser.). (Illus.). 48p. (J). (gr. 7 up). 1992. pap. 4.95 (0-7460-0688-8, Usborne); lib. bdg. 12.95 (0-88110-517-1, Usborne) EDC.

— Mystery on Main Street. (Advanced Puzzle Adventures Ser.). (Illus.). 48p. (YA). (gr. 7 up). 1994. pap. 4.95 (0-7460-0660-8, Usborne); lib. bdg. 12.95 (0-88110-700-X, Usborne) EDC.

— The Vanishing Village. (Puzzle Adventures Ser.). (Illus.). 48p. (J). (gr. 3-8). 1990. text 5.95 (0-7460-0330-7) EDC.

— The Vanishing Village. (Puzzle Adventures Ser.). (Illus.). 48p. (J). (gr. 3-8). 1999. lib. bdg. 13.95 (0-88110-405-1) EDC.

Dixon, S. L. Fluid Mechanics: Thermodynamics of Turbomachinery: In SI/Metric Units. 3rd ed. 270p. 1979. pap. text 38.95 (0-7506-2867-7) Buttrwrth-Heinemann.

— Fluid Mechanics & Thermodynamics of Turbomachinery. 4th ed. LC 98-5206. 320p. 1998. pap. 39.95 (0-7506-7059-2) Buttrwrth-Heinemann.

Dixon, Sam H. Heros of San Jacinto. 1993. reprint ed. lib. bdg. 75.00 (0-7812-5925-8) Rprt Serv.

— Men Who Made Texas Free. 1993. reprint ed. lib. bdg. 75.00 (0-7812-5924-X) Rprt Serv.

D

An Asterisk (*) at the beginning of an entry indicates that the title is appearing for the first time.

Dixon, Sandra J. We Rejoice in the Light: Candlelighting Ceremonies for Advent. 64p. 1988. pap. 5.99 (*0-8272-4223-9*) Chalice Pr.

Dixon, Sandra L. Augustine: The Scattered & Gathered Self. LC 99-29766. 304p. 1999. pap. 29.99 (*0-8272-0024-2*) Chalice Pr.

***Dixon, Sandy.** Everlasting Light: A Resource for Advent Worship. LC 00-9353. 2000. pap. 10.99 (*0-8272-0816-2*) Chalice Pr.

Dixon, Sandy, jt. auth. see Dixon, Michael E.

Dixon, Sarah. Cobra Consignment. (Advanced Puzzle Adventures Ser.). (Illus.). 48p. (YA). (gr. 7 up). 1995. pap. 4.95 (*0-7460-0751-5*, Usborne); lib. bdg. 12.95 (*0-88110-516-3*, Usborne) EDC.

— Map & Maze Puzzles. (Superpuzzles Ser.). (Illus.). 48p. (J). (gr. 7-12). 1993. pap. 7.95 (*0-7460-1579-8*, Usborne) EDC.

— Map & Maze Puzzles. (Superpuzzles Ser.). (Illus.). 48p. (J). (gr. 7 up). 1993. lib. bdg. 15.95 (*0-88110-525-2*, Usborne) EDC.

— Puzzle Adventure Kit: The Message in the Mirror. (Illus.). (J). (gr. 4 up). 1997. pap. 8.95 (*0-7460-2829-6*, Usborne) EDC.

Dixon, Schuck. Nightwing: A Knight in Bludhaven. (Illus.). 192p. 1998. pap. text 14.95 (*1-56389-425-4*, Pub. by DC Comics) Time Warner.

Dixon, Sheila A. & Crowell, Richard D. The Contract Guide: DPIC's Risk Management Handbook for Architects & Engineers. Owens, Tom & Menmuir, Ruth, eds. 380p. (C). 1993. 49.95 (*0-932056-06-7*) Design Prof Ins.

***Dixon, Simon.** The Modernisation of Russia, 1676-1825. LC 98-46739. (New Approaches to European History Ser.: No. 15). (Illus.). 256p. (C). 1999. 54.95 (*0-521-37100-7*) Cambridge U Pr.

— The Modernisation of Russia, 1676-1825. LC 98-46739. (New Approaches to European History Ser.: No. 15). (Illus.). 267p. (C). 1999. pap. 16.95 (*0-521-37961-X*) Cambridge U Pr.

Dixon, Solon. The Dixon Legend. LC 82-60023. 1982. 9.95 (*0-87397-208-2*, Strode Pubs) Circle Bk Service.

Dixon, Stacey L., jt. auth. see Caldwell, H. Stephen.

Dixon, Stella, ed. Autonomy & Dependence in Residential Care: An Evaluation of a Project to Promote Self Determination in a Home for Older People. 128p. (C). 1991. 59.00 (*0-7855-6578-7*, Pub. by Age Concern Eng) St Mut.

— Towards Resident-Oriented Environments. (C). 1989. 60.00 (*0-86242-098-9*, Pub. by Age Concern Eng) St Mut.

Dixon, Stephen. All Gone: Eighteen Short Stories. 1990. 17.95 (*0-8018-4010-4*) Johns Hopkins.

— Fourteen Stories. LC 80-14911. (Johns Hopkins Poetry & Fiction Ser.). 160p. 1980. 16.95 (*0-8018-2445-1*) Johns Hopkins.

— Friends: More Will & Magna Stories. LC 90-80160. 104p. (Orig.). 1990. pap. 6.95 (*1-878580-19-1*) Asylum Arts.

— Frog: A Novel. LC 96-39842. 769p. 1997. pap. 16.00 (*0-8050-4883-9*) H Holt & Co.

— Garbage. LC 87-70931. 165p. (Orig.). 1988. 8.95 (*0-943433-00-2*) Cane Hill Pr.

— Gould: A Novel in Two Novels. LC 96-19778. 288p. 1995. 24.00 (*0-8050-4424-8*) H Holt & Co.

— Gould: A Novel in Two Novels. 320p. 1998. pap. text 14.00 (*0-8050-5605-X*) H Holt & Co.

— Interstate: A Novel. 88p. 1995. 25.00 (*0-8050-2654-1*) H Holt & Co.

— Interstate: A Novel. 384p. 1997. pap. 14.00 (*0-8050-5028-0*) H Holt & Co.

***Dixon, Stephen.** It Doesn't Take a Village: Putting Parents Back in Charge. 192p. 2000. pap. 18.95 (*1-58501-014-6*, Pub. by CeShore Pubg) Natl Bk Netwk.

Dixon, Stephen. Long Made Short. LC 93-11174. (Poetry & Fiction Ser.). 160p. (C). 1993. text 32.50 (*0-8018-4738-9*) Johns Hopkins.

— Man on Stage: Play Stories. LC 96-76625. (Illus.). 96p. 1996. pap. 12.00 (*1-57650-053-5*) Hi Jinx Pr.

— The Play & Other Stories. LC 88-30153. 224p. (Orig.). 1988. pap. 9.95 (*0-918273-45-5*) Coffee Hse.

— Sleep. LC 98-56280. 288p. 1999. pap. 15.95 (*1-56689-081-0*, Pub. by Coffee Hse) Consort Bk Sales.

— Stories of Stephen Dixon. 89p. 1995. 25.00 (*0-8050-2653-3*) H Holt & Co.

— 30. LC 98-27707. x, 672p. 1999. 30.00 (*0-8050-5923-7*) H Holt & Co.

— Time to Go. LC 83-22624. 192p. 1984. 17.95 (*0-8018-3234-9*) Johns Hopkins.

***Dixon, Stephen.** Tisch. 184p. 2000. pap. 14.95 (*1-888996-19-6*, Red Hen Press) Valentine CA.

***Dixon, Stephen & Dixon, Deirdre Falvey.** Gift of the Gag: The Explosion in Irish Comedy. 224p. 2000. pap. 29.95 (*0-85640-658-9*, Pub. by Blackstaff Pr) Dufour.

Dixon, Stern, ed. see Lockman, Barbara.

Dixon, Steve. The Hawaiian Voyages of the Ono Jimmy. Blair, Penny, ed. LC 98-90170. (Illus.). 148p. 1998. pap. 19.95 (*0-9663624-0-3*, Pub. by Hawaii Tradewinds) Booklines Hawaii.

Dixon, Suzanne. The Roman Family. LC 91-25876. (Ancient Society & History Ser.). (Illus.). 232p. 1992. text 48.50 (*0-8018-4199-2*); pap. text 16.95 (*0-8018-4200-X*) Johns Hopkins.

— The Roman Mother. LC 87-30027. (Illus.). 288p. 1988. 39.95 (*0-8061-2125-4*) U of Okla Pr.

Dixon, Suzanne D. & Stein, Martin. Encounters with Children: A Practical Guide to Pediatric Behavior & Development. 2nd ed. (Illus.). 480p. (C). (gr. 13). 1991. pap. text 59.95 (*0-8016-1432-5*, 01432) Mosby Inc.

Dixon, Suzy A. & Stahel, Paula. The Insiders' Guide to Tampa Bay. 3rd rev. ed. (Insiders' Guide Travel Ser.). (Illus.). 361p. 1998. pap. 16.95 (*1-57380-080-5*, The Insiders Guide) Falcon Pub Inc.

Dixon, Sylvia W. Sug Learns How to Cook. Angaza, Mai T., ed. (Illus.). 28p. (Orig.). (J). (gr. 3-10). 1991. pap. 5.00 (*0-9652951-0-9*) S W Dixon.

Dixon, T. A., tr. see Sighart, Joachim.

Dixon, T. J., et al. Microcomputers in Property: A Surveyor's Guide to Lotus 1-2-3 & dBASE IV. (Illus.). 319p. (C). 1991. pap. 45.00 (*0-419-15260-1*, E & FN Spon) Routledge.

Dixon, Tamecka & Cohen, Judith. You Can Be a Woman Basketball Player. (Illus.). 40p. (J). (gr. 4-8). 1999. 14.95 incl. audio compact disk (*1-880599-39-2*); pap. 7.00 (*1-880599-38-4*) Cascade Pass.

Dixon, Tamecka & Cohen, Judith L. You Can Be a Woman Basketball Player. LC 99-20653. (Illus.). (J). (gr. 4-8). 1999. 13.95 (*1-880599-40-6*) Cascade Pass.

***Dixon, Ted. The Franchise Annual Directory 2000. 2000. 39.95 (*0-9692267-8-0*) Info Franchise.**

Approximately 4,000 franchisor listings published annually by INFO FRANCHISE NEWS, INC. since 1969 & known as "The Bible of the Franchise World." Each listing includes a description of business; names, addresses & telephone numbers of contact people; number of company owned & franchised units; franchise fee, royalty, total investment requirements; & financing available. Guaranteed Accurate. Completely updated. There are 48 categorical sections. Geared toward the prospective franchisee, the Handbook section of the Directory tells how to investigate the franchisor, details problem areas in franchising, outlines state/provincial & federal regulations & discusses new trends. "...among franchising directories, THE FRANCHISE ANNUAL is unique because it includes Canadian & Foreign opportunities. It also differs from those other works in quantity of entries: the Annual covers more than 500 American firms not included in others. The monthly INFO FRANCHISE NEWSLETTER updates the Annual & features news items about franchising industry..."--Booklist, Reference Books Bulletin, American Library Association; "...excellent...Recommended for business collections."--Library Journal; "...a gold mine of franchising data."--Toronto Star. LIBRARY DISCOUNT. For further details, contact INFO FRANCHISE NEWS, INC. 728 Center St., P.O. Box 826, Lewiston, NY, 14092 Tel. 888-806-2665, FAX: 905-688-7728, E-mail: infopress@infonews.com, WWW Site: http://infonews.com/franchise

Publisher Paid Annotation.

Dixon, Ted. The Franchise Annual Directory, 1997: The Original Franchise Handbook & Directory. 28th ed. 350p. (Orig.). 1997. per. 39.95 (*0-9692267-5-6*) Info Franchise.

Dixon, Terrell F., jt. auth. see Slovic, Scott H.

Dixon, Thomas, Jr. Chesapeake & Ohio in the Coal Fields. (Illus.). 108p. 1996. 22.95 (*0-939487-24-1*) Ches & OH Hist.

— Chessie: The Railroad Kitten. (Illus.). 64p. 1996. pap. 11.95 (*0-9622003-1-X*) TLC VA.

— The Chessie Era. (Illus.). 64p. 1997. pap. 14.95 (*0-9622003-2-8*) TLC VA.

— Clansman. 1976. 27.95 (*0-8488-0263-2*) Amereon Ltd.

— The Clansman. 1973. reprint ed. lib. bdg. 250.00 (*0-87968-194-2*) Gordon Pr.

***Dixon, Thomas.** The Clansman: A Historical Romance of the Ku Klux Klan. (Illus.). 224p. 2000. 54.95 (*0-7656-0614-3*, Sharpe Prof) M E Sharpe.

***Dixon, Thomas, Jr.** The Clansman: An Historical Romance of the Ku Klux Klan. Wintz, Cary D., ed. 200p. 2000. text 56.95 (*0-7656-0616-X*) M E Sharpe.

***Dixon, Thomas.** The Clansman: An Historical Romance of the Ku Klux Klan. Wintz, Cary D., ed. 2000. pap. 22.95 (*0-7656-0617-8*) M E Sharpe.

Dixon, Thomas, Jr. The Clansman: An Historical Romance of the Ku Klux Klan. LC 71-104761. 392p. 1970. reprint ed. pap. 19.00 (*0-8131-0126-3*) U Pr of Ky.

— The Fall of a Nation: Sequel to the Birth of a Nation. LC 74-15965. (Science Fiction Ser.). (Illus.). 372p. 1975. reprint ed. 29.95 (*0-405-06286-9*) Ayer.

— The Leopard's Spots: A Romance of the White Man's Burden. LC 67-29265. (Americans in Fiction Ser.). (Illus.). 481p. 1979. reprint ed. lib. bdg. 49.50 (*0-8398-0366-4*) Irvington.

— The Reconstruction Trilogy: The Leopard's Spots; The Clansman; The Traitor. xx, 550p. (C). 1994. 24.95 (*0-939482-49-5*, 0291, Noontide Pr); pap. 12.95 (*0-939482-48-7*, 0290, Noontide Pr) Legion Survival.

Dixon, Thomas C. Communication, Organization, & Performance. (Communication, Culture & Information Studies Ser.). 308p. 1996. pap. 39.50 (*1-56750-239-3*); text 73.25 (*1-56750-240-7*) Ablx Pub.

***Dixon, Thomas Homer.** The Ingenuity Gap. 2000. 27.50 (*0-375-40186-5*) Random.

Dixon, Thomas W., Jr. Appalachian Coal Mines & Railroads. (Illus.). 74p. 1996. pap. 12.95 (*1-883089-08-5*) TLC VA.

— Chessie, the Railroad Kitten. (Illus.). 64p. (Orig.). 1988. pap. text 10.95 (*0-317-93275-6*) TLC VA.

Dixon, Thomas W., Jr., jt. auth. see Million, Arthur B.

Dixon, Tim. Computerised Information Systems for Surveyors. 190p. (C). 1988. text 90.00 (*0-85406-411-7*, Pub. by Surveyors Pubns) St Mut.

Dixon, Tim, jt. auth. see Ford, Andrew.

Dixon, Tim, jt. auth. see Hargitay, Stephen.

Dixon, Tim, ed. see Webby & Chang.

Dixon, Timothy, jt. auth. see Freyer, Tony.

Dixon, Tom, jt. auth. see Huddleston, Gene.

Dixon, Trisha. The Country Garden. (Illus.). 150p. 1993. 35.00 (*0-207-17481-4*, Pub. by HarpC) HarpC.

Dixon, Trudy, ed. see Suzuki, Shunryu.

Dixon, Victor, ed. see de Vega, Lope.

Dixon, Victor, tr. see de Vega, Lope.

Dixon, Victor F., ed. see de Vega, Lope.

Dixon, W. B. European Sporting Cartridges: German & Austrian, 1875 to 1995. Hoyem, George A., ed. (Illus.). 248p. 1997. 60.00 (*0-939683-10-5*) Armory Pubns.

Dixon, W. MacNeile. English Epic & Heroic Poetry. LC 65-15894. (Studies in Poetry: No. 38). 1969. reprint ed. lib. bdg. 75.00 (*0-8383-0540-7*) M S G Haskell Hse.

Dixon, W. Macneile. The Human Situation. 1973. 250.00 (*0-87968-062-8*) Gordon Pr.

Dixon, W. Macneile, ed. The Edinburgh Book of Scottish Verse, 1300-1900. LC 75-37012. (Granger Index Reprint Ser.). 1977. reprint ed. 56.95 (*0-8369-6311-3*) Ayer.

Dixon, W. MacNeile, ed. The Edinburgh Book of Scottish Verse, 1300-1900. LC 75-37012. (Granger Index Reprint Ser.). 939p. reprint ed. 52.50 (*0-8290-0510-2*) Irvington.

Dixon, W. Macneile, ed. see Dixon, William M.

Dixon, W. MacNeile. Primer of Tennyson. LC 70-130255. (Studies in Tennyson: No. 27). 1971. reprint ed. lib. bdg. 75.00 (*0-8383-1147-4*) M S G Haskell Hse.

Dixon, Warren, Jr. Holiday Hilarities: A Collection of Holiday Humor. LC 98-93402. 192p. 1998. pap. 11.95 (*0-9648321-1-9*) Five Hawks Pr.

***Dixon, Wheeler.** Disaster & Memory: Celebrity Culture & the Crisis of Hollywood Cinema. LC 98-27256. 224p. 1998. pap. 16.50 (*0-231-11317-X*); lib. bdg. 42.50 (*0-231-11316-1*) Col U Pr.

Dixon, Wheeler W. The Charm of Evil: The Life & Films of Terence Fisher. LC 91-7687. (Filmmakers Ser.: No. 26). (Illus.). 591p. 1991. 62.50 (*0-8108-2375-6*) Scarecrow.

— The Exploding Eye: A Re-Visionary History of 1960s American Experimental Cinema. LC 97-11382. (SUNY Series, Cultural Studies in Cinema - Video). (Illus.). 250p. (C). 1997. text 57.50 (*0-7914-3565-2*); pap. text 18.95 (*0-7914-3566-0*) State U NY Pr.

— The Films of Jean-Luc Godard. LC 96-26612. (SUNY Series, Cultural Studies in Cinema/Video). 290p. (C). 1997. text 59.50 (*0-7914-3285-8*); pap. text 19.95 (*0-7914-3286-6*) State U NY Pr.

— It Looks at You: The Returned Gaze of Cinema. LC 94-13343. (SUNY Series in Postmodern Culture). 238p. (C). 1994. pap. text 16.95 (*0-7914-2340-9*) State U NY Pr.

— It Looks at You: The Returned Gaze of Cinema. LC 94-13343. (SUNY Series in Postmodern Culture). 238p. (C). 1995. text 49.50 (*0-7914-2339-5*) State U NY Pr.

— The Transparency of Spectacle: Meditations on the Moving Image. LC 97-24037. (SUNY Series in Postmodern Culture). 224p. (C). 1998. text 59.50 (*0-7914-3781-7*); pap. text 19.95 (*0-7914-3782-5*) State U NY Pr.

Dixon, Wheeler W., ed. Re-Viewing British Cinema, 1900-1992: Essays & Interviews. LC 93-1548. 288p. (C). 1994. text 59.50 (*0-7914-1861-8*); pap. text 19.95 (*0-7914-1862-6*) State U NY Pr.

Dixon, Wheeler W. & Francis, Freddie, intros. The Films of Freddie Francis. LC 90-46968. (Filmmakers Ser.: No. 24). (Illus.). 318p. 1991. 39.50 (*0-8108-2358-6*) Scarecrow.

Dixon, Wheeler W., ed. see Fraser, Harry L.

Dixon, Wheeler W., ed. see LeBorg, Reginald.

***Dixon, Wheeler Winston, ed.** Film Genre 2000: New Critical Essays. LC 99-29901. (C). 2000. text 54.50 (*0-7914-4513-5*); pap. text 17.95 (*0-7914-4514-3*) State U NY Pr.

Dixon, Wheeler Winston, ed. The Second Century of Cinema: The Past & Future of the Moving Image. LC 99-29900. (Illus.). 256p. (C). 2000. pap. text 17.95 (*0-7914-4516-X*) State U NY Pr.

— The Second Century of Cinema: The Past & Future of the Moving Image. LC 99-29900. (Illus.). 256p. (C). 2000. text 54.50 (*0-7914-4515-1*) State U NY Pr.

Dixon, Wilfred J. & Massey, Frank J., Jr. Introduction to Statistical Analysis. 4th ed. (Illus.). 672p. (C). 1983. 91.88 (*0-07-017073-8*) McGraw.

Dixon, William H. New America, 2 vols. LC 79-134428. reprint ed. 72.50 (*0-404-08468-0*) AMS Pr.

— White Conquest, 2 Vols. LC 70-138335. (Black Heritage Library Collection). 1977. 42.95 (*0-8369-8727-6*) Ayer.

Dixon, William M. The Edinburgh Book of Scottish Verse, 1300-1900. Dixon, W. Macneile, ed. LC 76-164841. reprint ed. 64.50 (*0-404-08632-2*) AMS Pr.

— English Epic & Heroic Poetry. LC 76-144503. (Channels of English Literature Ser.: No. 2). reprint ed. 43.50 (*0-404-07812-5*) AMS Pr.

— English Epic & Heroic Poetry. (BCL1-PR English Literature Ser.). 339p. 1992. reprint ed. lib. bdg. 89.00 (*0-7812-7080-4*) Rprt Serv.

Dixon, Willie. Willie Dixon - Master Blues Composer: With Notes & Tablature. 288p. 1992. per. 24.95 (*0-7935-0305-1*, 00660178) H Leonard.

Dixon, Willie, jt. auth. see Snowden, Elizabeth M.

Dixon, Yvonne R. Positive Confessions: A Prayer & Praise Workbook. 63p. 1996. wbk. ed. 8.95 (*0-9651838-0-7*) Dixon Solutions.

Dixson. Complete Course in English: Course B3. 144p. 1987. pap. 16.20 (*0-13-158833-8*) P-H.

— Modern American English, Vol. 1. 1991. pap. text, wbk. ed. 10.40 (*0-13-593930-5*) P-H.

— Resumen Practico de la Gramatica Inglesa. (SPA.). 96p. 1995. pap. text 19.00 (*0-13-774910-4*) P-H.

— Tests & Drill English Grammer. 128p. 1987. pap. text 16.67 (*0-13-903733-0*) P-H.

Dixson, A. F. The Natural History of the Gorilla. LC 81-57. 236p. reprint ed. pap. 73.20 (*0-7837-0425-9*, 204074800018) Bks Demand.

Dixson, Alan. Primate Sexuality: Comparative Studies of the Prosimians, Monkeys, Apes, & Human Beings. LC 98-18400. (Illus.). 560p. 1999. pap. text 60.00 (*0-19-850182-X*) OUP.

***Dixson, Ellis.** Unspoken. 1999. pap. write for info. (*1-58235-337-9*) Watermrk Pr.

Dixson, Lolita. Elementary Reader in English. (C). 1987. 105.00 (*0-13-259466-8*, Macmillan Coll) P-H.

— Exercises in English Conversation, 2 bks., Bk. 1. (Illus.). (YA). (gr. 7 up). 1985. pap. text 15.13 (*0-13-294646-7*, 18011) Prentice ESL.

— Exercises in English Conversation, 2 bks., Bk. 2. (Illus.). (YA). (gr. 7 up). 1985. pap. text 15.13 (*0-13-294679-3*, 18012) Prentice ESL.

— Exercises in English Conversation, 2 bks., Bk. 2. (Illus.). (YA). (gr. 7 up). 1987. audio 105.00 (*0-13-294695-5*) Prentice ESL.

— Modern American English, Bk. 1. (C). 1991. pap. text, teacher ed. 24.40 (*0-13-593922-4*) P-H.

— Modern Short Stories in English. (C). 1987. 105.00 (*0-13-597659-6*, Macmillan Coll) P-H.

Dixson, Lolita & Hall, Eugene. Modern American English, Bk. 2. (C). 1991. pap. text, teacher ed. 24.40 (*0-13-593963-1*) P-H.

— Modern American English, Bk. 4. (C). 1992. pap. text, teacher ed. 24.40 (*0-13-594078-8*) P-H.

— Modern American English, Bk. 5. 4th ed. (C). 1992. pap. text, teacher ed. 24.40 (*0-13-594128-8*) P-H.

— Modern American English, Bk. 6. (C). 1992. pap. text, teacher ed. 24.40 (*0-13-595372-3*) P-H.

— Modern American English, Vol. 3. 1992. pap. text, teacher ed. 18.40 (*0-13-594029-X*) P-H.

Dixson, Lolita & Woods, Elizabeth. Pronunciation Exercises in English. (C). 1987. 53.00 (*0-13-730870-1*, Macmillan Coll) P-H.

Dixson, Lolita, jt. auth. see Boggs, Ralph S.

Dixson, Lolita, jt. auth. see Whitford, Harold C.

***Dixson, Miriam.** The Imaginary Australian: Anglo-Celts & Identity - 1788 to the Present. 224p. 1999. pap. 24.95 (*0-86840-665-1*, Pub. by New South Wales Univ Pr) Intl Spec Bk.

— The Real Matilda: Women & Identity in Australia - 1788 to Present. 4th ed. 320p. 1999. pap. 24.95 (*0-86840-737-2*, Pub. by New South Wales Univ Pr) Intl Spec Bk.

***Dixson, Nancy.** Fortune & Misery: Sallie Rhett Roman of New Orleans: A Biographical Portrait & Selected Fiction, 1891-1920. LC 99-23173. (Southern Literary Studies). (Illus.). 224p. 1999. 26.95 (*0-8071-2296-3*) La State U Pr.

Dixson, R. Complete Course in English, Bk. 1. 1986. pap. 16.20 (*0-13-158817-6*) P-H.

Dixson, Robert J. Complete Course in English, Bk. 2. 144p. 1987. pap. 16.20 (*0-13-158825-7*) P-H.

— Complete Course in English, Bk. 4. rev. ed. 176p. 1987. pap. 16.20 (*0-13-158841-9*) P-H.

— Las 2000 Palabras Usados. 64p. (C). 1987. pap. text 15.80 (*0-13-523416-6*) P-H.

— Easy Reading Selections in English. rev. ed. (Illus.). 112p. (C). 1987. pap. text 17.00 (*0-13-222902-1*, 21395) Prentice ESL.

— Elementary Reader in English. rev. ed. (Illus.). 112p. (C). 1987. pap. text 17.00 (*0-13-259458-7*, 21410) Prentice ESL.

— Essential Idioms in English. LC 93-1103. 240p. 1993. pap. text 19.53 (*0-13-582025-1*) Prentice ESL.

— Everyday Dialogues in English. rev. ed. (Illus.). 208p. (C). 1983. pap. text 16.60 (*0-13-292848-5*, 21369) Prentice ESL.

— Graded Exercises in English, New Edition. 2nd ed. LC 94-4779. 208p. 1994. pap. text 19.13 (*0-13-298903-4*) P-H.

— El Ingles en Accion. (Illus.). 1977. pap. text 4.50 (*0-88345-295-2*, 18490); audio 70.00 (*0-685-77025-7*, 38492) Prentice ESL.

— El Ingles en Accion. (C). 1987. pap. text 17.20 (*0-13-273756-6*) Prentice ESL.

Dixson, Robert J. Ingles on Accion. pap. text 7.50 (*0-13-273765-5*) P-H.

Dixson, Robert J. Ingles Practico Sin Maestro, 2 vols. (C). (gr. 9 up). 1972. audio 70.00 (*0-685-73420-X*) Prentice ESL.

— Ingles Practico Sin Maestro, 2 vols., Vol. 1. (YA). (gr. 9 up). 1972. pap. text 4.50 (*0-88345-069-0*, 18103) Prentice ESL.

— Ingles Practico Sin Maestro, 2 vols., Vol. 2. (YA). (gr. 9 up). 1972. pap. text 4.50 (*0-88345-070-4*, 18104) Prentice ESL.

— Modern American English, 2 bks. (YA). (gr. 7-12). 1987. audio 100.00 (*0-13-543190-5*) Prentice ESL.

— Modern American English, Bk. 1. 160p. (C). 1991. pap. 15.73 (*0-13-593914-3*) P-H.

— Modern American English, Bk. 2. 160p. (C). 1991. pap. 15.73 (*0-13-593955-0*) P-H.

— Modern American English, Bk. 2. (C). 1991. pap. text, student ed., wbk. ed. 10.40 (*0-13-593971-2*) P-H.

— Modern American English, Bk. 3. 160p. (C). 1991. pap. 15.73 (*0-13-593997-6*) P-H.

— Modern American English, Bk. 3. (C). 1991. pap. text, student ed., wbk. ed. 10.40 (*0-13-594045-1*) P-H.

— Modern American English, Bk. 4. 160p. (C). 1992. pap. 15.73 (*0-13-594060-5*) P-H.

— Modern American English, Bk. 5. 4th ed. 160p. (C). 1992. pap. 15.73 (*0-13-594110-5*) P-H.

— Modern American English, Bk. 6. 160p. (C). 1992. pap. 15.73 (*0-13-595364-2*) P-H.

— Modern American English, Bk. 6. (Illus.). 167p. (YA). (gr. 9-12). 1987. student ed. 4.25 (*0-88345-320-7*, 18731) Prentice ESL.

— Modern American English Skillbooks, Bk. 1. (Modern American English Ser.). (gr. 7 up). 1974. 1.25 (*0-88345-233-2*) Prentice ESL.

— Modern American English Skillbooks, Bk. 2. (Modern American English Ser.). (gr. 7 up). 1974. 1.25 (*0-88345-234-0*) Prentice ESL.

— Modern American English Skillbooks, Bk. 4. (Modern American English Ser.). (gr. 7 up). 1974. 1.25 (*0-88345-236-7*) Prentice ESL.

— Modern Short Stories. 96p. (C). 1987. pap. text 15.13 (*0-13-597642-1*) Prentice ESL.

— Practical Guide to the Teaching of English As a Foreign Language. (C). 1987. pap. text 9.00 (*0-13-691032-7*, 18132) Prentice ESL.

— Regents English, Vol. 1. 2nd ed. 160p. 1995. pap. text, wbk. ed. 15.33 (*0-13-199001-2*) P-H.

— Regents English, Vol. 2. 2nd ed. 160p. 1995. pap. text, wbk. ed. 15.33 (*0-13-199101-9*) P-H.

— Second Book in English. 128p. (C). 1987. pap. text 15.00 (*0-13-797283-0*, 21179) Prentice ESL.

— Test & Drill English Grammar, Bk. 2. 128p. 1987. pap. text 16.67 (*0-13-903741-1*) P-H.

— The U. S. A. The Land & the People, Bk. 1. rev. ed. (Illus.). 169p. (YA). (gr. 7 up). 1987. pap. text 15.00 (*0-13-939373-0*, 18435) Prentice ESL.

Dixson, Robert J. & Dart, Alan. Regents English: Advanced, Vol. 3. 2nd ed. LC 94-47009. 128p. 1995. pap. text, wbk. ed. 15.33 (*0-13-199268-6*, Pub. by P-H) S&S Trade.

Dixson, Robert J., jt. auth. see Andujar, Julio.

Dixson, Robert J., jt. auth. see Andujar, Julio I.

Dixson, Robert J., jt. auth. see Angel, Juvenal L.

Dixson, Robert J., jt. auth. see Clarey, M. Elizabeth.

Dixson, Robert J., jt. auth. see Fisher, Isobel Y.

Dixson, Robert J., ed. see Harte, Bret.

Dixson, Robert J., ed. see Howells, William Dean.

Dixson, Robert J., ed. see Melville, Herman.

***Dixson, Rosemary.** Between Love & Hate. 500p. 1998. 35.00 (*0-9661202-1-3*) Tanager Pub Co.

Dixson, Walter C. Richland Crossing: A Portrait of Texas Pioneers. 2nd ed. LC 94-212378. 386p. 1994. reprint ed. pap. 25.00 (*0-9649936-0-0*) Peppermill Pub.

***Diyanni.** Basic Reading. 2000. pap. write for info. (*0-312-13689-7*) St Martin.

— Beyond Basic Reading. 2000. pap. write for info. (*0-312-13688-9*) St Martin.

Diyanni. Critical Perspectives. 65p. 1995. pap. 8.75 (*0-07-017035-5*) McGraw.

— Humanities, Vol. 1. 1998. pap. text, student ed. 15.40 (*0-13-863184-0*) P-H.

— Literature. 4th ed. 1999. 37.74 (*0-07-234945-X*) McGraw.

DiYanni. Scribner Handbook for Writers. 2nd ed. 304p. 1997. pap. text, wbk. ed. 24.00 (*0-205-27501-X*) Allyn.

Diyanni, jt. auth. see Benton.

Diyanni, jt. auth. see Benton, Janetta Rebold.

Diyanni, jt. auth. see Hoy.

DiYanni, Robert. Connections: Reading, Writing & Thinking. LC 84-16825. 320p. (Orig.). (C). 1985. pap. text 22.00 (*0-86709-049-9*, 0049, Pub. by Boynton Cook Pubs) Heinemann.

Diyanni, Robert. How to Succeed in College. LC 96-10384. 207p. 1996. pap. text 30.00 (*0-205-17526-0*) Allyn.

***DiYanni, Robert.** Literature: Reading Fiction, Poetry, & Drama. LC 99-14165. (Illus.). 2000. write for info. (*0-07-229507-4*); write for info. (*0-07-229509-0*); write for info. (*0-07-229510-4*); write for info. (*0-07-229511-2*) McGrw-H Hghr Educ.

Diyanni, Robert. Literature: Reading Fiction, Poetry, Drama & the Essay. 4th ed. LC 96-54711. 2064p. (C). 1997. 48.13 (*0-07-017037-1*) McGraw.

— Literature: Reading Fiction, Poetry, Drama & the Essay. 4th ed. LC 96-54711. 1997. pap. write for info. (*0-07-017038-X*) McGraw.

DiYanni, Robert. Modern American Poets: Their Voices & Visions. 2nd ed. LC 93-14414. 848p. (C). 1993. pap. 45.31 (*0-07-016957-8*) McGraw.

— Perspectives: Readings for Writers. LC 95-8885. 480p. (C). 1995. pap. 34.69 (*0-07-016967-5*) McGraw.

***DiYanni, Robert.** Writing about the Humanities. LC 99-31940. 162p. 1999. pap. text 18.20 (*0-13-022994-6*) P-H.

— Writing about the Humanities. LC 99-31940. 2000. 13.00 (*0-13-088994-6*) P-H.

DiYanni, Robert & Hoy, Pat C. Scribner Handbook for Writers. 2nd ed. LC 97-18962. 894p. 1997. 39.00 (*0-205-19838-4*) P-H.

DiYanni, Robert & Hoy, Pat C., II. The Scribner Handbook for Writers. 2nd ed. 1088p. (C). 1997. text, teacher ed. write for info. (*0-205-27496-X*, T7496-7) Allyn.

***DiYanni, Robert & Hoy, Pat C.** The Scribner Handbook for Writers. 3rd ed. 894p. 2000. 35.00 (*0-205-31981-5*) Allyn.

Diyanni, Robert & Hoy, Pat C., II. The Scribner Handbook for Writers: Instructor's Annotated Editorial. (Illus.). 848p. (C). 1994. teacher ed. write for info. (*0-318-72457-X*) Macmillan.

***DiYanni, Robert & Hoy, Patrick C.** The Scribner Essentials for Writers. 244p. 2000. spiral bd. 12.00 (*0-205-31903-3*) Allyn.

DiYanni, Robert & Rompf, Kraft. The McGraw-Hill Book of Fiction. LC 94-11559. 1264p. (C). 1994. pap. 41.88 (*0-07-016949-7*) McGraw.

Diyanni, Robert & Rompf, Kraft. The McGraw-Hill Book of Poetry. LC 92-37243. 1268p. (C). 1993. pap. 41.88 (*0-07-016944-6*) McGraw.

DiYanni, Robert, jt. auth. see Clifford, John.

DiYanni, Robert, jt. auth. see Hoy, Pat C.

DiYanni, Robert, jt. auth. see Miller, Edmund.

Diyraney, Saleam, ed. see Nahed, Nicola.

Diz, M. Ana. Historias de Certidumbre: Los Milagros de Berceo. (SPA.). 274p. (Orig.). 1995. pap. write for info. (*0-936388-69-2*) Juan de la Cuesta.

Diz, Marta A., ed. Patronio y Lucanor: La Lectura Inteligente "en el Tiempo Que Es Turbio" LC 83-51708. (Scripta Humanistica Ser.). (SPA.). 183p. (C). 1984. 26.00 (*0-916379-01-9*) Scripta.

Dizard, Jan E. Going Wild: Hunting, Animal Rights, & the Contested Meaning of Nature. LC 99-17091. 248p. 1999. pap. 16.95 (*1-55849-190-2*) U of Mass Pr.

Dizard, Jan E., et al, eds. Guns in America: A Reader. LC 98-47896. 400 p. 1999. pap. 24.95 (*0-8147-1879-5*) NYU Pr.

***Dizard, Jan E., et al, eds.** Guns in America: A Reader. LC 98-47896. 400p. 1999. text 65.00 (*0-8147-1878-7*) NYU Pr.

Dizard, Jan E. & Gadlin, Howard. The Minimal Family. LC 90-10801. 304p. 1992. 35.00 (*0-87023-728-4*); pap. 17.95 (*0-87023-804-3*) U of Mass Pr.

Dizard, Wilson, Jr. Meganet: How the Global Communications Network Will Connect Everyone on Earth. LC 97-13218. 272p. 1997. text 29.00 (*0-8133-3017-3*, Pub. by Westview) HarpC.

— Meganet: How the Global Communications Network Will Connect Everyone on Earth. 272p. (C). 1998. pap. text 22.00 (*0-8133-3018-1*, Pub. by Westview) HarpC.

Dizard, Wilson. Old Media/New Media. 3rd ed. LC 99-29688. 233p. (C). 1999. pap. text 41.40 (*0-8013-3277-X*) Longman.

Dizard, Wilson P., III, jt. auth. see Betancourt, Ernesto F.

***DiZazzo, Ray.** Corporate Media Production. LC 99-40964. 244p. 2000. pap. 39.95 (*0-240-80365-5*, Focal) Buttrwrth-Heinemann.

DiZazzo, Ray. Corporate Scriptwriting: A Professional Guide. 224p. 1992. pap. 44.95 (*0-240-80115-6*, Focal) Buttrwrth-Heinemann.

— Corporate Television: A Producer's Handbook. 201p. 1989. pap. 36.95 (*0-240-80023-0*, Focal) Buttrwrth-Heinemann.

***DiZazzo, Raymond.** The Clarity Factor: The Four Secrets to Being Clearly Understood. Orig. Title: Saying the Right Thing. 128p. 2000. pap. 9.95 (*1-57071-531-9*) Sourcebks.

DiZazzo, Raymond. Clovin's Head. 1976. pap. 2.50 (*0-88031-027-8*) Invisible-Red Hill.

Dizdar, Barbara. Frames & Framing. 96p. (Orig.). 1999. pap. text 14.95 (*1-85368-844-4*) New5 Holland.

Dizdareivc, Zlatko. Sarajevo: A War Journal. Alcalay, Ammiel et al, eds. Hollo, Anselm, tr. from FRE. LC 94-26222.Tr. of Journal de Guerre. 89p. 1995. pap. 12.95 (*0-8050-3535-4*) H Holt & Co.

Dizdarevic, Zlatko. Portraits of Sarajevo. Ridjanovic, Midhat, tr. LC 94-43620. 164p. 1995. 19.95 (*0-88064-167-3*) Fromm Intl Pub.

— Sarajevo: A War Journal. Hollo, Anselm, tr. LC 93-36174. (Illus.). 208p. 1993. 19.95 (*0-88064-149-5*) Fromm Intl Pub.

Dizdaroglu, M. & Karakaya, A. E., eds. Advances in DNA Damage & Repair: Oxygen Radical Effects, Cellular Protection & Biological Consequences. LC 98-47311. (NATO ASI Ser.: 302). (Illus.). 524p. (C). 1999. text 185.00 (*0-306-46042-4*) Plenum.

Dize, Frances W. Smith Island: Chesapeake Bay. LC 89-40301. 222p. 1990. pap. 17.95 (*0-87033-492-1*, Tidewtr Pubs) Cornell Maritime.

Dizeno, Patricia. Why Me? The Story of Jenny. 144p. (J). (gr. 7 up). 1976. pap. 3.50 (*0-380-00563-8*, Avon Bks) Morrow Avon.

Dizenzo, Charles. The Drapes Come. 1966. pap. 3.25 (*0-8222-0327-8*) Dramatists Play.

— An Evening for Merlin Finch. 1968. pap. 3.25 (*0-8222-0364-2*) Dramatists Play.

— A Great Career. 1966. pap. 3.25 (*0-8222-0480-0*) Dramatists Play.

— The Last Straw & Sociability. 1970. pap. 5.25 (*0-8222-0639-0*) Dramatists Play.

Dizer, John T. Tom Swift, The Bobbsey Twins & Other Heroes of American Juvenile Literature. LC 97-4374. (Studies in American Literature: Vol. 25). 460p. 1997. text 109.95 (*0-7734-8641-0*) E Mellen.

Dizerega, Gere S. Pelvic Surgery: Adhesion Formation & Prevention. LC 96-35592. (Illus.). 304p. 1996. 135.00 (*0-387-94823-6*) Spr-Verlag.

— Peritoneal Surgery. LC 99-12449. 448p. 1999. write for info. (*0-387-98610-3*) Spr-Verlag.

DiZerega, Gere S. & Rodgers, Kathleen E. The Peritoneum. LC 92-2221. (Illus.). 340p. 1992. write for info. (*3-540-97830-5*) Spr-Verlag.

— The Peritoneum. LC 92-2221. (Illus.). 340p. 1994. 145.00 (*0-387-97830-5*) Spr-Verlag.

***DiZerega, Gus.** Pagans & Christians: The Personal Spiritual Experience. 2001. pap. 14.95 (*1-56718-228-3*) Llewellyn Pubns.

Dizick, Missy C. Test Your Cat's Psychic Powers. 1998. pap. text 41.70 (*1-58062-102-3*) Adams Media.

— Test Your Cat's Psychic Powers. LC 98-7884. (Illus.). 80p. 1998. pap. 6.95 (*1-58062-067-1*) Adams Media.

Dizik, A. Allen. The Estimator. 12.95 (*0-938614-03-7*) Stratford Hse.

— The Style Wheel of Furniture & Decoration. (Illus.). 12.95 (*0-686-86777-7*) Stratford Hse.

Dizik, Allen. Concise Encyclopedia of Interior Design. 320p. 1988. text 34.95 (*0-442-22109-6*, VNR) Wiley.

Dizikes, John. Opera in America: A Cultural History. 1995. pap. 19.00 (*0-300-06101-3*) Yale U Pr.

***Dizikes, John.** Yankee Doodle Dandy: The Life & Times of Tod Sloan. (Illus.). 256p. 2000. 22.50 (*0-300-08334-3*) Yale U Pr.

Dizon, Salud C., tr. see De Los Reyes, Isabelo.

DiZovi, Lonnie. Rockin' Rhythms & Rhymes: Musical Chants, Rhythms & Rhymes for the E. S. L. Classroom. (Illus.). 61p. 1996. pap. 28.50 incl. audio (*0-935301-71-2*) Vibrante Pr.

Djafari, Ali M., ed. Bayesian Inference for Inverse Problems. (Proceedings of SPIE Ser.: Vol. 3459). 388p. 1998. 80.00 (*0-8194-2914-7*) SPIE.

Djaferis, Theodore E. Automatic Controls: Power of Feedback. LC 97-24247. (Electrical Engineering Ser.). (C). 1997. mass mkt. 17.95 (*0-534-95051-5*) Wadsworth Pub.

— Automatic Controls: Power of Feedback (revision) LC 99-16223. (Electrical Engineering Ser.). 1999. 25.95 (*0-534-37171-X*) Brooks-Cole.

— Robust Control Design: A Polynomial Approach. 288p. (C). 1995. text 151.50 (*0-7923-9617-0*) Kluwer Academic.

Djakonov, Victor, et al. The Revolutionary Guide to QBasic. 550p. 1996. pap. 34.95 incl. disk (*1-874416-20-6*) Wrox Pr Inc.

Djakov, Yuri L. & Bushuyeva, Tatjana S. The Red Army & the Wehrmacht: How the Soviets Militarized Germany, 1922-33, & Paved the Way for Fascism. LC 94-37158. (Illus.). 348p. (C). 1995. 26.95 (*0-87975-937-2*) Prometheus Bks.

Djaladiningrat, Idrus N. The Beginnings of the Indonesian-Dutch Negotiations & the Hoge Veluwe Talks. LC 60-4142. (Cornell University, Modern Indonesia Project, Monograph Ser.). 138p. reprint ed. pap. 42.80 (*0-8357-7102-4*, 201063800068) Bks Demand.

***Djalili.** Tajikistan. LC 97-17189. 248p. 1998. text 39.95 (*0-312-16143-3*) St Martin.

Djamgoz, M. B. Principles of Microelectrode Techniques. 120p. 1997. pap. 16.00 (*1-86094-011-0*) World Scientific Pub.

Djamgoz, Mustafa B., jt. ed. see Douglas, Ron H.

Djamson. The Dynamics of Euro-African Co-Operation. 1977. lib. bdg. 221.50 (*90-247-1841-4*) Kluwer Academic.

Djanikian, Gregory. About Distance. LC 94-70463. (Poetry Ser.). 80p. 1995. pap. 11.95 (*0-88748-187-6*) Carnegie-Mellon.

— The Man in the Middle. LC 84-70176. (Poetry Ser.). 79p. 1984. pap. 11.95 (*0-88748-002-0*) Carnegie-Mellon.

***Djanikian, Gregory.** Years Later. (Poetry Ser.). 2000. 24.95 (*0-88748-316-X*); pap. 12.95 (*0-88748-301-1*) Carnegie-Mellon.

Djanikian, Gregory D. Falling Deeply into America. LC 88-70530. 80p. 1989. pap. 11.95 (*0-88748-085-3*) Carnegie-Mellon.

Djaparidze, David, ed. Mediaeval Slavic Manuscripts: A Bibliography of Printed Catalogues. LC 57-9659. (Medieval Academy Bks.: No. 64). 1957. 20.00 (*0-910956-38-3*) Medieval Acad.

Djata, Sundiata A. The Bamana Empire by the Niger: Kingdom, Jihad & Colonization, 1712-1920. LC 96-11512. (Illus.). 320p. (C). 1997. pap. text 18.95 (*1-55876-132-2*) Wiener Pubs Inc.

— The Bamana Empire by the Niger: Kingdom, Jihad & Colonization, 1712-1920. LC 96-11512. (Illus.). 320p. (C). 1998. text 39.95 (*1-55876-131-4*) Wiener Pubs Inc.

Djatschenko, Sergei. Aveli I Kainy (Canes & Ables) Roman (A Novel) LC 90-60636. (RUS.). 293p. (Orig.) 1990. pap. text 18.00 (*0-911971-51-3*) Effect Pub.

Djavadi, C. Dictionnaire des Dictions Meteorologicues. (FRE.). 1998. 95.00 (*0-320-00299-3*) Fr & Eur

Dje Dje, Jacqueline C. Distribution of the One String Fiddle in West Africa. LC 80-54180. (Monograph Series in Ethnomusicology: No. 2). (Illus.). 43p. (Orig.). 1980. pap. text 6.00 (*0-88287-014-9*) UCLA Dept Ethnom.

Dje Dje, Jacqueline C., jt. ed. see Nketia, J. H.

Djebar, Assia. Fantasia. 288p. 1993. 19.95 (*0-7043-2610-8*, Pub. by Quartet) Interlink Pub.

— Fantasia: An Algerian Cavalcade. Blair, Dorothy S., tr. LC 92-42700. 227p. (C). 1993. pap. 12.95 (*0-435-08621-9*, 08621) Heinemann.

— A Sister to Scheherazade. Blair, Dorothy S., tr. LC 92-42699. 116p. (C). 1993. pap. 12.95 (*0-435-08622-7*, 08622) Heinemann.

— A Sister to Scheherazade. 170p. 1991. 19.95 (*0-7043-2670-1*, Pub. by Quartet) Interlink Pub.

***Djebar, Assia.** So Vast the Prison. Wing, Betsy, tr. from FRE. LC 99-41329. Orig. Title: Vaste est la Prison. 320p. 1999. 24.95 (*1-58322-009-7*, Pub. by Seven Stories) Publishers Group.

Djebar, Assia. Women of Algiers in Their Apartment. De Jager, Marjolijn, tr. from FRE. LC 92-16856. (CARAF Ser.). 224p. (C). 1992. text 25.00 (*0-8139-1402-7*) U Pr of Va.

— Women of Algiers in Their Apartment. De Jager, Marjoli, tr. (African & Caribbean Literature Translated from French Ser.). 224p. 1999. pap. 15.95 (*0-8139-1880-4*) U Pr of Va.

DjeDje, Jacqueline C., ed. African Musicology Vol. 2: Current Trends. 1992. pap. 35.00 (*0-918456-64-9*) African Studies Assn.

Djedje, Jacqueline C. & Carter, William G., eds. African Musicology: Current Trends: A Festschrift Presented to J. H. Kwabena Nketia, Vol. 1. (Illus.). 1989. pap. 60.00 (*0-918456-62-2*, Crossroads) African Studies Assn.

Djedje, Jacqueline C. & Meadows, Eddie S. The Soul of California: Music of African Americans. LC 96-49288. 462p. 1998. 60.00 (*0-520-20627-4*, Pub. by U CA Pr); pap. 24.95 (*0-520-20628-2*, Pub. by U CA Pr) Cal Prin Full Svc.

***DjeDje, Jacqueline C.l, et al.** Turn up the Volume: A Celebration of African Music. LC 99-42125. (Illus.). 364p. 1999. pap. 39.00 (*0-930741-77-3*) UCLA Fowler Mus.

***DjeDje, Jacqueline Cogdell, et al.** Turn up the Volume: A Celebration of African Music. LC 99-42125. 1999. write for info. (*0-930741-76-5*) UCLA Fowler Mus.

Djeflat, Abdelkadar, jt. ed. see Zawdie, Girma.

Djelantik, A. A. The Birthmark: Memoirs of a Balinese Prince. (Illus.). 300p. 1997. pap. 24.95 (*962-593-165-1*, Periplus Eds) Tuttle Pubng.

Djelic, Marie-Laure. Exporting the American Model: The Post-War Transformation of European Business. LC 98-2541. (Illus.). 322p. 1998. text 68.00 (*0-19-829317-8*) OUP.

***Djerassi.** Pill & I. 2000. 28.00 (*0-465-01657-X*, Pub. by Basic); pap. 14.00 (*0-465-01658-8*, Pub. by Basic) HarpC.

Djerassi, Carl. The Bourbaki Gambit. LC 93-44392. 240p. (C). 1994. 19.95 (*0-8203-1652-0*) U of Ga Pr.

— The Bourbaki Gambit. 256p. 1996. pap. 12.95 (*0-14-025485-4*, Viking) Viking Penguin.

— Cantor's Dilemma. 240p. 1991. pap. 12.95 (*0-14-014359-9*, Penguin Bks) Viking Penguin.

— Carl Djerassi: Steroids Made It Possible. LC 90-906. (Illus.). 205p. 1990. text 36.00 (*0-8412-1773-4*, Pub. by Am Chemical) OUP.

— Clock Runs Backward: A Chapbook of Poetry. 55p. 1991. pap. 8.00 (*0-934257-75-2*) Story Line.

— From the Lab into the World: A Pill for People, Pets & Bugs. LC 94-17603. 230p. 1994. text 29.95 (*0-8412-2808-6*, Pub. by Am Chemical) OUP.

— El Gambito de Bourbaki (The Bourbaki Gambit) (SPA.). 240p. 1996. pap. 11.99 (*968-16-5113-8*, Pub. by Fondo) Continental Bk.

— Menachem's Seed: A Novel. LC 97-12749. 216p. 1997. 21.95 (*0-8203-1925-2*) U of Ga Pr.

— Menachem's Seed: A Novel. 224p. 1998. pap. 12.95 (*0-14-027794-3*) Viking Penguin.

***Djerassi, Carl.** No. (Illus.). (J). 2000. pap. 14.00 (*0-14-029654-9*) Penguin Putnam.

Djerassi, Carl. No: A Novel. LC 98-6748. xii, 270p. 1998. 24.95 (*0-8203-2032-3*) U of Ga Pr.

Djerassi, Carl. The Pill, Pygmy Chimps, & Degas' Horse: The Remarkable Autobiography of the Award-Winning Scientist Who Synthesized the Pill. LC 91-58599. (Illus.). 336p. 1993. reprint ed. pap. 16.00 (*0-465-05758-6*, Pub. by Basic) HarpC.

Djerassi, Carl, jt. auth. see Budzikiewicz, Herbert.

***Djerassi, Norma Lundholm.** Heart Notes: A Mingle-Mangle. LC 99-50905. 96p. 2000. 15.00 (*1-56474-336-5*) Fithian Pr.

Djidjev, H., ed. Optimal Algorithms. (Lecture Notes in Computer Science Ser.: Vol. 401). vi, 308p. 1989. 40.00 (*0-387-51859-2*) Spr-Verlag.

Djilas, Aleksa. The Contested Country: Yugoslav Unity & Communist Revolution, 1919-1953. LC 90-46006. (Russian Research Center Studies: No. 85). (Illus.). 304p. 1991. 51.95 (*0-674-16698-1*, DJICON) HUP.

— The Contested Country: Yugoslav Unity & Communist Revolution, 1919-1953. (Illus.). 272p. 1996. pap. 17.95 (*0-674-16699-X*) HUP.

Djilas, Milovan. Conversations with Stalin. Petrovich, Michael B., tr. LC 62-14470. 228p. 1963. pap. 12.00 (*0-15-622591-3*, Harvest Bks) Harcourt.

— Montenegro. Johnstone, Kenneth, tr. LC 63-8090. 367p. 1963. 9.95 (*0-15-162102-0*) Harcourt.

— Of Prisons & Ideas. Petrovich, Michael B., tr. from SER. 144p. 1986. 17.95 (*0-15-167979-7*) Harcourt.

— Prisons & Ideas. 1986. 14.95 (*0-15-173087-3*) Harcourt.

— Wartime. LC 80-16174. (Illus.). 496p. 1980. pap. 7.95 (*0-15-694712-9*, Harvest Bks) Harcourt.

Djin, Nodar, intro. Kniga Evreiskikh Aforizmov. LC 84-60080. (RUS.). 406p. (Orig.). 1984. pap. 16.00 (*0-89830-082-7*) Russica Pubs.

Djin, Yana. Bits & Pieces of Conversations, Poetry. 104p. (Orig.). 1994. pap. write for info. (*0-929647-04-1*) H A Frager & Co.

Djinis & Post. Securities Arbitration: Practice & Forms, Vol. 1. 1991. 125.00 (*0-8205-1696-1*) Bender.

Djiwandono, J. Soedradjad & Esmara, Hendra, eds. International Financial Instability & ASEAN Financial Cooperation. 164p. 1986. text 32.50 (*0-317-43156-0*, Pub. by Chopmen Singapore); pap. text 15.95 (*9971-68-122-6*, Pub. by Chopmen Singapore) Advent Bks Div.

Djoken, Guy P. What a Century. 1999. pap. 8.95 (*0-533-12872-2*) Vantage.

Djokovic, D. Z. & Malzan, Jerry G. Products of Reflections in U(P,Q) LC 81-20544. (Memoirs Ser.: No. 37/259). 82p. 1982. pap. 16.00 (*0-8218-2259-4*, MEMO/37/259) Am Math.

Djoleto, Amu. The Frightened Thief. (Junior African Writers Ser.). (Illus.). 80p. (J). (gr. 3 up). 1992. pap. 4.95 (*0-7910-2902-6*) Chelsea Hse.

Djoleto, Amu. The Strange Man. (African Writers Ser.). 279p. (C). 1968. pap. 9.95 (*0-435-90041-2*, 90041) Heinemann.

Djoleto, Amu. Twins in Trouble. (Junior African Writers Ser.). (Illus.). 80p. (J). (gr. 3 up). 1992. pap. 4.95 (*0-7910-2905-0*) Chelsea Hse.

Djonga Manya, K'Omalowete A. Evolution du Pouvoir Local au Sankuru: La Legitimite et le Role des Chefs de Groupements Ainsi Que Leur Place dans la Formation des Classes Sociales au Zaire. (Publications Universitaires Europeennes Ser.: Vol. 47). (FRE.). 540p. 1996. 63.95 (*3-906754-02-2*, Pub. by P Lang) P Lang Pubng.

Djordje, Cistogradov. Aeronautic Dictionary: English-Russian-Serbian. (ENG, RUS & SER.). 1989. 95.00 (*0-8288-8226-6*) Fr & Eur.

D

***Djordjeuc, B. Boro & Dos Reis, Henrique L., eds.** Topics on Nondestructive Evaluation: Nondestructive Testing & Evaluation of Infrastructure. LC 99-230081. (Illus.). 296p. 1998. 85.00 (*1-57117-073-1*, 187) Am Soc Nondestructive.
— Topics on Nondestructive Evaluation Vol. 3: Advances in Signal Processing for Nondestructive Evaluation of Materials. LC 99-230083. (Illus.). 400p. 1998. 85.00 (*1-57117-074-X*) Am Soc Nondestructive.
Djordjevic, Antonije R., et al. Linpar for Windows: Matrix Parameters for Multiconductor Transmission Lines. 234p. 1999. pap. 375.00 (*1-58053-061-3*) Artech Hse.
Djordjevic, B. Boro, et al, eds. Topics on Nondestructive Evaluation (TONE) No. 1: Sensing for Materials Characterization Processing, & Manufacturing. LC 99-230082. (Illus.). 476p. 1998. 120.00 (*1-57117-067-7*, 975) Am Soc Nondestructive.
Djordjevic, Branislav. Cybernetics in Water Resources Management. 641p. 1993. text 85.00 (*0-918334-82-9*) WRP.
Djordjevic, Dimitrije, jt. auth. see Kiraly, Bela K.
Djordjevic, Dimitrije, jt. ed. see Karaly, Bela K.
Djordjevic, Josip. German-Serbocroatian Dictionary of the Chemical Industry: Recnik Industrijske Hemije Nemacko-Srpskohrvatski. (GER & SER.). 620p. 1986. 75.00 (*0-8288-1312-4*, F114960) Fr & Eur.
Djordjevich, Dusan, jt. ed. see Conquest, Robert.
Djordjevich, Michael. About Happy Living. LC 84-21555. 184p. 1985. 9.95 (*0-917569-00-8*); pap. 5.95 (*0-917569-01-6*) Bks With Ideas.
Djorgovski, S. G. & Meylan, G., eds. Structure & Dynamics of Globular Clusters. (ASP Conference Series Proceedings: Vol. 50). 416p. 1993. 34.00 (*0-937707-69-4*) Astron Soc Pacific.
DJ'R. 7 Heavens: A Game of Consciousness. LC 95-90018. (Illus.). 360p. 1995. 25.00 (*1-886180-07-5*) For Unltd Nurturing.
Djrbashian, Mkhitar M. Harmonic Analysis & Boundary Value Problems in the Complex Domain. LC 93-34622. (Operator Theory: Advances & Applications Ser.: Vol. 65). 272p. 1993. 118.00 (*0-8176-2855-X*) Birkhauser.
Djubek, Jozef, et al. Limit State of the Plate Elements of Steel Structures. 216p. (C). 1984. 76.00 (*0-8176-1478-8*) Birkhauser.
***Djukanovic, R.** An Atlas of Sputum Cytology. (Illus.). 2001. 85.00 (*1-84214-005-1*) Prthnon Pub.
— Illustrated Handbook of Asthma. (Illus.). 2001. 38.00 (*1-84214-016-7*) Prthnon Pub.
Djukanovic, R. & Holgate, Stephen T. An Atlas of Asthma. (Encyclopedia of Visual Medicine Ser.). (Illus.). 100p. 1999. 75.00 (*1-85070-908-4*) Prthnon Pub.
Djulbegovi, Benjamin C. Decision Making in Oncology: Evidence-Based Management. LC 97-3873. 1997. text 79.00 (*0-443-08989-2*) Church.
Djulbegovic, Benjamin. Reasoning & Decision Making in Hematology. 253p. 1992. pap. text 60.00 (*0-443-08858-6*) Church.
Djumalieva, D. & Vassilev, Anton, eds. Cropping Systems in Intensive Agriculture. 214p. (C). 1993. pap. 175.00 (*81-85880-07-7*, Pub. by Print Hse) St Mut.
Djung, Lu-Dzai. History of Democratic Education in Modern China. LC 75-32317. (Studies in Chinese History & Civilization). 258p. 1977. reprint ed. lib. bdg. 62.50 (*0-313-27023-6*, U7023, Greenwood Pr) Greenwood.

D

Djurhuus, J. C., et al, eds. European Society for Surgical Research: Abstracts, 22nd Congress, Aarhus, Denmark, May 1987. (Journal: European Surgical Research: Vol. 19, Suppl. 1, 1987). 128p. 1988. pap. 41.75 (*3-8055-4624-6*) S Karger.
Djuric, Dusan. Weather Analysis. 304p. 1994. 61.60 (*0-13-501149-3*) P-H.
Djuric, Mihailo. Nietzsche und die Metaphysik. (Monographien und Texte zur Nietzscge-Forschung Ser.: Band 16). (GER.). viii, 326p. 1985. 130.80 (*3-11-010169-6*) De Gruyter.
Djurovic, Liliana & Black, Sara. The Supple Body: The Way to Fitness, Strength & Flexibility. LC 95-17429. (Illus.). 144p. 1995. 16.00 (*0-02-860441-5*, Pub. by Macmillan) S&S Trade.
Djwa, Sandra. F. R. Scott & His Works. (Canadian Author Studies). 55p. (C). 1990. pap. text 9.95 (*1-55022-025-X*, Pub. by ECW) Genl Dist Srvs.
Djwa, Sandra & Macdonald, R. S., eds. On F. R. Scott: Essays on His Contributions to Law, Literature, & Politics. LC 84-171017. 225p. reprint ed. pap. 69.80 (*0-7837-1155-7*, 204168400022) Bks Demand.
Djwa, Sandra & Moyles, R. G., eds. E. J. Pratt: Complete Poems, 2 vols., Pts. I & II. 983p. (C). 1989. text 80.00 (*0-8020-5775-6*) U of Toronto Pr.
Djwa, Sandra & St. J. Macdonald, R., eds. On F. R. Scott: Essays on His Contributions to Law, Literature, & Politics. 256p. 1983. pap. 24.95 (*0-7735-0398-6*, Pub. by McG-Queens Univ Pr) CUP Services.
DK Editors. ABC. (Bath Bks.). (Illus.). 10p. (J). (ps). 1998. 4.95 (*0-7894-2921-7*) DK Pub Inc.
— Animal Counting. LC 97-42617. (Henry Silhouettes Ser.). (Illus.). 12p. (J). (ps). 1998. bds. 4.95 (*0-7894-3028-2*) DK Pub Inc.
— Animals Colors. (Bath Bks.). (Illus.). 10p. (J). 1998. 4.95 (*0-7894-2920-9*) DK Pub Inc.
— Big Book of Baby Animals. (Illus.). 40p. (J). (ps-5). 1998. 12.95 (*0-7894-2855-5*) DK Pub Inc.
— Boat. (Illus.). 12p. (J). (ps-1). 1998. 7.95 (*0-7894-2909-8*) DK Pub Inc.
— Cartoons. (You Can Draw Ser.). 21p. (J). (gr. 4 up). 1998. pap. 4.95 (*0-7894-2822-9*) DK Pub Inc.
— Farm. LC 97-32132. (Touch & Feel Ser.). (Illus.). 12p. (J). (ps-2). 1998. 6.95 (*0-7894-2916-0*) DK Pub Inc.
— Henry's Opposites. LC 97-32188. (Henry Silhouettes Ser.). (Illus.). 10p. (J). (ps). 1998. bds. 4.95 (*0-7894-3030-4*) DK Pub Inc.
— Hurricane/Tornado. (Eyewitness Files Ser.). (Illus.). (J). (gr. 3-10). 1998. pap. 9.95 (*0-7894-2790-7*) DK Pub Inc.
— Monster Machines. LC 97-39624. (Illus.). 32p. (J). (gr. 1 up). 1998. 14.95 (*0-7894-2796-6*) DK Pub Inc.
— Mummy. (Eyewitness Activity Files Ser.). (Illus.). (J). (gr. 3-10). 1998. pap. 9.95 (*0-7894-2791-5*) DK Pub Inc.
— Numbers. (Bath Bks.). (Illus.). 10p. (J). (ps). 1998. 4.95 (*0-7894-2922-5*) DK Pub Inc.
— Play & Learn Colors. LC 97-38164. (Play & Learn Ser.). (Illus.). 24p. (J). (ps-1). 1998. pap. 3.95 (*0-7894-2912-8*) DK Pub Inc.
— Play & Learn Numbers. LC 97-38163. (Play & Learn Ser.). (Illus.). 24p. (J). (ps-1). 1998. pap. 3.95 (*0-7894-2914-4*) DK Pub Inc.
— Play & Learn Shapes. LC 97-38162. (Play & Learn Ser.). (Illus.). 24p. (J). (ps-1). 1998. pap. 3.95 (*0-7894-2913-6*) DK Pub Inc.
— Play & Learn Sizes. LC 97-38157. (Play & Learn Ser.). (Illus.). 24p. (J). (ps-1). 1998. pap. 3.95 (*0-7894-2915-2*) DK Pub Inc.
— Pocket Thesaurus. LC 97-80388. (Pocket Guides Ser.). (Illus.). 512p. (YA). (gr. 5 up). 1998. pap. 6.95 (*0-7894-2809-1*) DK Pub Inc.
— Ponies. LC 97-34425. (Illus.). 64p. (J). (gr. 3-7). 1998. 15.95 (*0-7894-2810-5*) DK Pub Inc.
— Sea Animals. (Bath Bks.). (Illus.). 10p. (J). (ps). 1998. 4.95 (*0-7894-2923-3*) DK Pub Inc.
— Shark. (Eyewitness Files Ser.). (Illus.). (J). (gr. 3-10). 1998. pap. text 9.95 (*0-7894-2955-1*) DK Pub Inc.
— Skeleton. LC 97-32187. (Pocket Guides Ser.). (Illus.). 128p. (YA). (gr. 5 up). 1998. pap. 6.95 (*0-7894-2833-4*) DK Pub Inc.
— Space. (Eyewitness Files Ser.). (Illus.). (J). (gr. 3-10). 1998. pap. 9.95 (*0-7894-2792-3*) DK Pub Inc.
DK Editors, jt. auth. see Hamilton, Jake.
DK Multimedia Staff. Eyewitness Encyclopedia of Space & the Universe. LC 99-25468. (Eyewitness Books). (J). (gr. 4-7). 1997. 29.95 incl. cd-rom (*0-7894-0881-3*) DK Pub Inc.
DK Multimedia Staff. Jolly Post Office. (Jolly Postman Ser.). (J). (ps-3). 1997. 19.95 incl. cd-rom (*0-7894-2379-0*) DK Pub Inc.
— My First Amazing Words & Pictures. 1997. 29.95 (*0-7894-1663-8*) DK Pub Inc.
— Pinball Science. (YA). (gr. 3 up). 1998. cd-rom 29.95 (*0-7894-3260-9*) DK Pub Inc.
— Ultimate 3D Skeleton. (YA). (gr. 4 up). 1997. 19.95 incl. cd-rom (*0-7894-1280-2*) DK Pub Inc.
***DK Publishing Staff.** ABC. (Touch & Feel Ser.). (Illus.). 12p. (J). 2000. 6.95 (*0-7894-5219-7*, D K Ink) DK Pub Inc.
— Africa. (Eyewitness Books). (gr. 4-7). 2000. 15.95 (*0-7894-6030-0*) DK Pub Inc.
DK Publishing Staff. AHS Great Plant Guide: Featuring over 2000 Plants. LC 98-41283. 1999. 16.95 (*0-7894-4120-9*) DK Pub Inc.
***DK Publishing Staff.** Airplane. (Mighty Machines Ser.). (Illus.). 24p. (J). (gr. k-3). 2000. pap. text 5.95 (*0-7894-6075-0*, D K Ink) DK Pub Inc.
— Alphabet. (All Aboard Bks.). (Illus.). (J). 2000. 6.95 (*0-7894-5327-4*, D K Ink) DK Pub Inc.
DK Publishing Staff. Amazing Facts. LC 97-15214. (You Can Draw Ser.). (J). (gr. 1). 1997. 9.95 (*0-7894-2023-6*) DK Pub Inc.
***DK Publishing Staff.** Amsterdam. (Eyewitness City Maps Ser.). 2000. pap. 7.95 (*0-7894-5636-2*) DK Pub Inc.
DK Publishing Staff. Ancient Greece. 1999. 9.95 (*0-7894-4275-2*) DK Pub Inc.
***DK Publishing Staff.** Animal Colors. (Touch & Feel Ser.). 12p. 2000. 6.95 (*0-7894-5221-9*, D K Ink) DK Pub Inc.
DK Publishing Staff. Animals of the World. LC 99-219662. (DK Pockets Ser.). 1999. pap. text 9.95 (*0-7894-3950-6*) DK Pub Inc.
— Arabic Phrase Book. LC 99-24362. (Eyewitness Travel Guide Phrase Bks.). 128p. 1999. pap. 6.95 (*0-7894-4865-3*) DK Pub Inc.
— Aromatherapy Massage. (DK Living Ser.). 112p. 1999. pap. 13.95 (*0-7894-4835-1*) DK Pub Inc.
— The Art of Hand Reading. (DK Living Ser.). 120p. 1999. pap. 13.95 (*0-7894-4837-8*) DK Pub Inc.
***DK Publishing Staff.** Astronomy. (Eyewitness Books). 64p. (J). (gr. 4-7). 1999. 15.95 (*0-7894-4888-2*, D K Ink) DK Pub Inc.
— Australia. (Eyewitness Travel Guides Ser.). (Illus.). 64p. 2000. pap. text 9.95 (*0-7894-5542-0*, D K Ink) DK Pub Inc.
DK Publishing Staff. Aztecs: The Fall of an Empire. LC 99-12002. (DK Discoveries Series). 1999. 14.95 (*0-7894-3957-3*) DK Pub Inc.
— Baby ABC. LC 98-182582. 10p. (J). 1998. 4.95 (*0-7894-3648-5*) DK Pub Inc.
— Baby Colors. LC 98-182599. 10p. (J). 1998. 4.95 (*0-7894-3651-5*) DK Pub Inc.
— Baby Faces. LC 98-182573. (Illus.). 10p. (YA). 1998. bds. 4.95 (*0-7894-3650-7*) DK Pub Inc.
***DK Publishing Staff.** Baby Faces. (Illus.). 16p. (ps-k). 2000. 4.95 (*0-7894-6658-9*) DK Pub Inc.
DK Publishing Staff. Baby 123. LC 98-182594. 10p. (J). 1998. 4.95 (*0-7894-3649-3*) DK Pub Inc.
— Ballet. 1999. 6.95 (*0-7894-4281-7*) DK Pub Inc.
— Bananas in Pajamas: It's Fun Time. (J). (ps-1). 1998. 19.95 incl. cd-rom (*0-7894-4202-7*) DK Pub Inc.
***DK Publishing Staff.** Barbie 1,2,3. LC 00-24559. (Illus.). 32p. (ps-3). 2000. write for info. (*0-7894-6665-1*, Pub. by DK Pub Inc) Pub Resources Inc.
DK Publishing Staff. Barcelona & Catalonia. LC 99-23491. (Eyewitness Travel Guides Ser.). 176p. 1999. pap. 19.95 (*0-7894-4620-0*) DK Pub Inc.
***DK Publishing Staff.** Bible Questions & Answers. 32p. (J). 1999. 8.95 (*0-7894-1899-1*) DK Pub Inc.
DK Publishing Staff. The Big Book of Baby Animals. LC 97-43088. (J). 1998. write for info. (*0-7894-3069-X*) DK Pub Inc.
***DK Publishing Staff.** Big Book of Bugs. (Illus.). 32p. (gr. 4-7). 2000. 14.95 (*0-7894-6520-5*) DK Pub Inc.
— Big Rig. (Mighty Machines Ser.). (Illus.). 24p. (J). (gr. k-3). 2000. pap. text 5.95 (*0-7894-6102-1*, D K Ink) DK Pub Inc.
DK Publishing Staff. Bird. (Eyewitness Virtual Reality Ser.). (YA). (gr. 3 up). 1995. 19.95 incl. cd-rom (*0-7894-0296-3*) DK Pub Inc.
— Bird. (Eyewitness Virtual Reality Ser.). (YA). (gr. 3 up). 1996. 19.95 incl. cd-rom (*0-7894-0292-0*) DK Pub Inc.
— Birds: And How They Live. LC 98-219781. (See & Explore Library). 64p. (J). 1998. pap. text 7.95 (*0-7894-3445-8*) DK Pub Inc.
— The Body & How It Works. LC 98-133912. (See & Explore Library). (J). 1998. pap. 7.95 (*0-7894-2965-9*) DK Pub Inc.
***DK Publishing Staff.** The Border Book. (Living Ser.). 160p. 2000. pap. text 13.95 (*0-7894-5116-6*, D K Ink) DK Pub Inc.
DK Publishing Staff. Bosch: Master of the Grotesque-His Life in Paintings. LC 98-86748. 1999. pap. text 12.95 (*0-7894-4139-X*) DK Pub Inc.
— Britain: Landscapes, Treasures, & Traditions. LC 99-31895. (Eyewitness Travel Guides Ser.). (Illus.). 720p. 1999. 40.00 (*0-7894-4608-1*) DK Pub Inc.
***DK Publishing Staff.** California. (Eyewitness Travel Guides Ser.). 64p. 2000. pap. text 9.95 (*0-7894-4847-5*, D K Ink) DK Pub Inc.
— Canada. (Eyewitness Travel Guides Ser.). 64p. 2000. pap. text 9.95 (*0-7894-4848-3*, D K Ink) DK Pub Inc.
DK Publishing Staff. Caravaggio: Art Book. LC 98-86749. 1999. pap. text 12.95 (*0-7894-4138-1*) DK Pub Inc.
— Cars. 1996. 4.99 (*0-7894-0681-0*) DK Pub Inc.
— Cartopedia: The Ultimate World Reference Atlas. 1995. text 49.95 (*0-7894-0045-6*) DK Pub Inc.
— Cat. (Eyewitness Virtual Reality Ser.). (YA). (gr. 3 up). 1996. 29.95 incl. cd-rom (*0-7894-0291-2*) DK Pub Inc.
— Cats. 1997. 4.99 (*0-7894-2370-7*) DK Pub Inc.
***DK Publishing Staff.** Cave Life. LC 92-53490. (Look Closer Ser.). (Illus.). 32p. (J). (gr. 1-5). 2000. pap. text 7.95 (*0-7894-6100-5*, D K Ink) DK Pub Inc.
DK Publishing Staff. Cezanne: Art Book. LC 98-86750. 1999. pap. text 12.95 (*0-7894-4145-4*) DK Pub Inc.
***DK Publishing Staff.** Charts & Graphics. 72p. 2000. pap. 6.95 (*0-7894-6371-7*) DK Pub Inc.
DK Publishing Staff. Chemistry. (Eyewitness Books). 64p. (J). (gr. 4-7). 1999. 15.95 (*0-7894-4881-5*, D K Ink) DK Pub Inc.
— Children Just Like Me. 16p. (J). (gr. 3-6). 1998. pap. text 6.95 (*0-7894-3626-4*) DK Pub Inc.
— Children's Illustrated Encyclopedia. 2nd rev. ed. LC 97-52096. (Illus.). 644p. (J). (gr. 4-7). 1998. 39.95 (*0-7894-2787-7*) DK Pub Inc.
— Chocolate. (DK Living Ser.). 144p. 1999. pap. 13.95 (*0-7894-4838-6*) DK Pub Inc.
— Christmas. 1996. 4.99 (*0-7894-1267-5*) DK Pub Inc.
— Christmas. 1997. 6.99 (*0-7894-2368-5*) DK Pub Inc.
— Christmas. (DK Sticker Gift Box Ser.). 1998. 9.99 (*0-7894-3631-0*) DK Pub Inc.
— Christmas Crafts: Activity Fun Pack. (Fun Pax Activity Ser.). (J). (gr. 1-7). 1998. pap. 4.95 (*0-7894-3716-3*) DK Pub Inc.
— Christmas Story. (J). 1998. pap. text 5.95 (*0-7894-3470-9*) DK Pub Inc.
***DK Publishing Staff.** The Christmas Story. LC 99-24615. 1999. write for info. (*0-7894-4740-1*) DK Pub Inc.
DK Publishing Staff. The Clothes Book. (Illus.). 10p. (J). (ps-k). 1998. pap. 7.95 (*0-7894-3458-X*) DK Pub Inc.
— Concise Encyclopedia. LC 98-52895. 1999. pap. 16.95 (*0-7894-3948-4*) DK Pub Inc.
***DK Publishing Staff.** Copycat Faces. LC 98-43052. (Copy Cat Ser.). 16p. 1999. 5.95 (*0-7894-4287-6*) DK Pub Inc.
— Coral Reef. (Look Closer Ser.). (Illus.). 32p. (J). (gr. 1-5). 2000. pap. text 7.95 (*0-7894-6101-3*, D K Ink) DK Pub Inc.
DK Publishing Staff. Coral Reef Stickers Playboard. 1996. 6.99 (*0-7894-0686-1*) DK Pub Inc.
***DK Publishing Staff.** Corythosaurus. 12p. (J). (gr. k-2). 2000. 6.95 (*0-7894-5405-X*, D K Ink) DK Pub Inc.
DK Publishing Staff. Creepy Crawlies. 1996. 4.99 (*0-7894-0685-3*) DK Pub Inc.
— Creepy Crawlies. (Ultimate Sticker Books Ser.). 20p. (J). (gr. k-7). 1997. pap. text 6.95 (*0-7894-2167-4*) DK Pub Inc.
— Da Vinci. LC 98-86754. 1999. pap. text 12.95 (*0-7894-4144-6*) DK Pub Inc.
— Danish Phrase Book. LC 99-21841. (Eyewitness Travel Guide Phrase Bks.). 128p. 1999. pap. 6.95 (*0-7894-4866-1*) DK Pub Inc.
***DK Publishing Staff.** Desktop Publishing. 72p. 2000. pap. 6.95 (*0-7894-6893-X*) DK Pub Inc.
DK Publishing Staff. Diggers & Dumpers. 1997. 4.99 (*0-7894-2372-3*) DK Pub Inc.
— Dinosaur. 1996. 4.99 (*0-7894-1373-6*) DK Pub Inc.
— Dinosaurs. LC 97-20873. (Really Horrible Guides Ser.). (Illus.). 24p. (J). (ps-6). 1997. 9.95 (*0-7894-2051-1*) DK Pub Inc.
— Dinosaurs: And How They Lived. (See & Explore Library). 64p. (J). 1998. pap. text 7.95 (*0-7894-3447-4*) DK Pub Inc.
***DK Publishing Staff.** DK Dictionary Thesaurus: Over 100,000 Definitions & Synonyms. LC 98-52899. 1999. pap. text 9.95 (*0-7894-3949-2*) DK Pub Inc.
DK Publishing Staff. DK Illustrated Oxford Dictionary. Abate, Frank, ed. LC 98-3664. (Illus.). 1008p. 1998. 50.00 (*0-7894-3557-8*) DK Pub Inc.
DK Publishing Staff. DK Millennium Encyclopedia. LC 97-18927. (J). (gr. 3 up). 1997. 149.95 (*0-7894-2216-6*) DK Pub Inc.
— DK Millennium Pack. (Illus.). (J). (gr. 4-7). 1999. pap. 18.95 (*0-7894-4715-0*) DK Pub Inc.
— DK Oxford American Dictionary. LC 00-27458. 2000. 40.00 (*0-7894-6367-9*) DK Pub Inc.
— DK Spanish Dictionary. (Illus.). (J). 1999. 15.30 (*0-606-18116-4*) Turtleback.
DK Publishing Staff. DK Student Atlas. LC 97-45730. (Illus.). 160p. (YA). (gr. 5 up). 1998. 19.95 (*0-7894-2399-5*) DK Pub Inc.
— DK Ultimate Visual Dictionary 2000. 2nd ed. LC 94-11173. (Illus.). 640p. 1999. 39.95 (*0-7894-4619-7*) DK Pub Inc.
— DK World Atlas: Millennium Edition. LC 99-23293. 528p. 1999. 125.00 (*0-7894-4604-9*) DK Pub Inc.
***DK Publishing Staff.** Dublin. (Eyewitness City Maps Ser.). 2000. pap. 7.95 (*0-7894-5637-0*) DK Pub Inc.
DK Publishing Staff. Ducks & Chickens. 1997. 4.99 (*0-7894-1783-9*) DK Pub Inc.
— Dump Truck. LC 98-202599. (Wheelies Ser.). 10p. (J). 1998. 4.95 (*0-7894-3710-4*) DK Pub Inc.
***DK Publishing Staff.** Dump Truck. (Illus.). 12p. (ps-k). 2000. 6.95 (*0-7894-6532-9*) DK Pub Inc.
— Dump Trunk. (Illus.). 16p. (ps-k). 2000. 4.95 (*0-7894-6659-7*) DK Pub Inc.
DK Publishing Staff. Durer: Master Draftsman of the Renaissance-His Life in Paintings. LC 98-86751. 1999. pap. text 12.95 (*0-7894-4137-3*) DK Pub Inc.
— Entertaining. (DK Living Ser.). 192p. 1999. pap. 13.95 (*0-7894-4836-X*) DK Pub Inc.
— Extraordinary Plants. LC 96-45925. (Inside Guides Ser.). (Illus.). 48p. (J). 1997. 15.95 (*0-7894-1505-4*) DK Pub Inc.
***DK Publishing Staff.** Eyewitness City Map New York. LC 99-465915. (DK Eyewitness City Maps Ser.). (Illus.). 12p. 1999. 7.95 (*0-7894-4857-2*) DK Pub Inc.
DK Publishing Staff. Eyewitness Encyclopedia of Science. 1994. 39.95 (*1-56458-904-8*) DK Pub Inc.
***DK Publishing Staff.** Eyewitness Travel Guide: Loire Valley. (Eyewitness Travel Guides Ser.). (Illus.). 2000. pap. text 19.95 (*0-7894-6203-6*) DK Pub Inc.
— Eyewitness Travel Guide: Provence. (Eyewitness Travel Guides Ser.). 2000. pap. text 29.95 (*0-7894-6202-8*) DK Pub Inc.
— Eyewitness Travel Guide: Rome. (Eyewitness Travel Guides Ser.). 2000. pap. text 22.95 (*0-7894-6230-3*) DK Pub Inc.
— Eyewitness Travel Guide: Seville & Andlucia. (Eyewitness Travel Guides Ser.). 2000. pap. text 29.95 (*0-7894-6223-0*) DK Pub Inc.
— Eyewitness Travel Guide: Spain. 2000. pap. text 29.95 (*0-7894-6204-4*) DK Pub Inc.
— Eyewitness Travel Guide: Thailand. 2000. pap. text 24.95 (*0-7894-6206-0*) DK Pub Inc.
— Eyewitness Travel Guide: Venice & Veneto. (Eyewitness Travel Guides Ser.). 2000. pap. text 24.95 (*0-7894-6218-4*) DK Pub Inc.
— Eyewitness Travel Guide: Vienna. (Eyewitness Travel Guides Ser.). 2000. pap. text 29.95 (*0-7894-6217-6*) DK Pub Inc.
— Eyewitness Travel Guide: Warsaw. (Eyewitness Travel Guides Ser.). 2000. pap. text 19.95 (*0-7894-6210-9*) DK Pub Inc.
— Eyewitness Travel Guide Amsterdam. (Eyewitness Travel Guides Ser.). (Illus.). 2000. pap. text. write for info. (*0-7894-6219-2*) DK Pub Inc.
— Eyewitness Travel Guide Australia. (Eyewitness Travel Guides Ser.). (Illus.). 2000. pap. text. write for info. (*0-7894-6209-5*) DK Pub Inc.
— Eyewitness Travel Guide Britain. (Eyewitness Travel Guides Ser.). (Illus.). 2000. pap. text. write for info. (*0-7894-6220-6*) DK Pub Inc.
— Eyewitness Travel Guide Florence & Tuscany. (Eyewitness Travel Guides Ser.). (Illus.). 2000. pap. text. write for info. (*0-7894-6214-1*) DK Pub Inc.
— Eyewitness Travel Guide Florida. (Eyewitness Travel Guides Ser.). (Illus.). 2000. pap. text. write for info. (*0-7894-6207-9*) DK Pub Inc.
— Eyewitness Travel Guide France. (Eyewitness Travel Guides Ser.). (Illus.). 2000. pap. text. write for info. (*0-7894-6216-8*) DK Pub Inc.
— Eyewitness Travel Guide Greece Athens. (Eyewitness Travel Guides Ser.). (Illus.). 2000. pap. text. write for info. (*0-7894-6226-5*) DK Pub Inc.
— Eyewitness Travel Guide Greek Islands. (Eyewitness Travel Guides Ser.). (Illus.). 2000. pap. text 24.95 (*0-7894-6227-3*) DK Pub Inc.
— Eyewitness Travel Guide Ireland. (Eyewitness Travel Guides Ser.). (Illus.). 2000. pap. text 24.95 (*0-7894-6221-4*) DK Pub Inc.
— Eyewitness Travel Guide Istanbul. (Eyewitness Travel Guides Ser.). (Illus.). 2000. pap. text 19.95 (*0-7894-6211-7*) DK Pub Inc.
— Eyewitness Travel Guide Italy. (Eyewitness Travel Guides Ser.). (SPA., Illus.). 2000. pap. text 29.95 (*0-7894-6222-2*) DK Pub Inc.
— Eyewitness Travel Guide Lisbon. (Eyewitness Travel Guides Ser.). (Illus.). 2000. pap. text 19.95 (*0-7894-6208-7*) DK Pub Inc.
— Eyewitness Travel Guide London. (Eyewitness Travel Guides Ser.). (Illus.). 2000. pap. text 24.95 (*0-7894-6224-9*) DK Pub Inc.
— Eyewitness Travel Guide Mexico. (Eyewitness Travel Guides Ser.). (Illus.). 2000. pap. text 24.95 (*0-7894-6234-6*) DK Pub Inc.
— Eyewitness Travel Guide Moscow. (Eyewitness Travel Guides Ser.). (Illus.). 2000. pap. text 19.95 (*0-7894-6212-5*) DK Pub Inc.

An Asterisk (*) at the beginning of an entry indicates that the title is appearing for the first time.

— Eyewitness Travel Guide Naples. (Eyewitness Travel Guides Ser.). (Illus.). 2000. pap. text 19.95 (*0-7894-6232-X*) DK Pub Inc.
— Eyewitness Travel Guide New York. (Eyewitness Travel Guides Ser.). (Illus.). 2000. pap. text 24.95 (*0-7894-6229-X*) DK Pub Inc.
— Eyewitness Travel Guide Paris. (Eyewitness Travel Guides Ser.). (Illus.). 2000. pap. text 24.95 (*0-7894-6228-1*) DK Pub Inc.
DK Publishing Staff. Eyewitness Travel Guide Phrase Book: Greek. LC 98-7157. (Eyewitness Travel Guides Ser.). 1998. pap. 6.95 (*0-7894-3591-8*) DK Pub Inc.
— Eyewitness Travel Guide Phrase Book: Portuguese. LC 98-8705. 128p. 1998. pap. 6.95 (*0-7894-3592-6*) DK Pub Inc.
— Eyewitness Travel Guide Phrase Book: Thai. LC 98-18241. (Eyewitness Travel Guides Ser.). 1998. pap. 6.95 (*0-7894-3593-4*) DK Pub Inc.
***DK Publishing Staff.** Eyewitness Travel Guide Portugal. (Eyewitness Travel Guides Ser.). (Illus.). 2000. pap. text 24.95 (*0-7894-6205-2*) DK Pub Inc.
— Eyewitness Travel Guide San Francisco. (Eyewitness Travel Guides Ser.). 2000. pap. text 22.95 (*0-7894-6201-X*) DK Pub Inc.
— Eyewitness Travel Guide Sardinia. (Eyewitness Travel Guides Ser.). 2000. pap. text 22.95 (*0-7894-6233-8*) DK Pub Inc.
— Eyewitness Travel Guide St. Petersburg. 2000. pap. text 19.95 (*0-7894-6213-3*) DK Pub Inc.
— File Management. 72p. 2000. pap. 6.95 (*0-7894-6853-0*) DK Pub Inc.
DK Publishing Staff. Fire Engine. LC 99-161940. (Shaped Board Bks.). 12p. (J). (ps-k). 1998. 7.95 (*0-7894-3464-4*) DK Pub Inc.
— Fire Engine. LC 98-202606. (Wheelies Ser.). 10p. (J). 1998. 4.95 (*0-7894-3711-2*) DK Pub Inc.
***DK Publishing Staff.** Fire Truck. (Mighty Machines Ser.). (Illus.). 24p. (J). (gr. k-3). 2000. pap. text 5.95 (*0-7894-6103-X*, D K Ink) DK Pub Inc.
DK Publishing Staff. First 100 Phrases, Spanish. LC 96-43961. (J). 1996. write for info. (*0-7894-1561-5*) DK Pub Inc.
***DK Publishing Staff.** Florence. (Eyewitness City Maps Ser.). 2000. pap. 7.95 (*0-7894-5638-9*) DK Pub Inc.
— Florida. (Eyewitness Travel Guides Ser.). 64p. 2000. pap. text 9.95 (*0-7894-5541-2*, D K Ink) DK Pub Inc.
DK Publishing Staff. Flowers. 1996. 4.99 (*0-7894-1374-4*) DK Pub Inc.
— Flowers. (Eyewitness Explorers Ser.). 64p. (J). (gr. k-3). 1997. pap. 5.95 (*0-7894-2213-1*) DK Pub Inc.
— Food. LC 99-209784. (Scratch & Sniff Ser.). 12p. 1999. 6.95 (*0-7894-3988-3*) DK Pub Inc.
***DK Publishing Staff.** Force & Motion. (Eyewitness Books). 64p. (J). (gr. 4-7). 1999. 15.95 (*0-7894-4882-3*, D K Ink) DK Pub Inc.
DK Publishing Staff. The Formula One Yearbook: Chronicle of the 1998 Grand Prix Year. (Illus.). 128p. 1998. 19.95 (*0-7894-3754-6*) DK Pub Inc.
***DK Publishing Staff.** France. (Eyewitness Travel Guides Ser.). (Illus.). 64p. 2000. pap. text 9.95 (*0-7894-5540-4*, D K Ink) DK Pub Inc.
DK Publishing Staff. French Dictionary. LC 97-213051. (DK Pockets Ser.). 512p. 1997. pap. text 6.95 (*0-7894-2194-1*) DK Pub Inc.
— French Dictionary. LC 98-52898. 1998. pap. text 9.95 (*0-7894-4494-1*) DK Pub Inc.
— Friedrich. LC 99-32114. (Artbook Ser.). 144p. 1999. pap. 12.95 (*0-7894-4854-8*) DK Pub Inc.
***DK Publishing Staff.** Friendship. (Funpax Ser.). (Illus.). (ps-3). 2000. pap. text 7.95 (*0-7894-4786-X*) DK Pub Inc.
DK Publishing Staff. Funny Animals. LC 97-35377. (Funfax Shaped Board Book Ser.). 10p. (J). 1998. 3.95 (*0-7894-3104-1*) DK Pub Inc.
— Garden. LC 99-209791. 1999. 6.95 (*0-7894-3989-1*) DK Pub Inc.
— Gaugin: The First "Moder" Painter-His Life in Paintings. LC 98-86752. 144p. 1999. pap. text 12.95 (*0-7894-4147-0*) DK Pub Inc.
— Giotto. LC 99-31207. (Artbook Ser.). 144p. 1999. pap. 12.95 (*0-7894-4851-3*) DK Pub Inc.
***DK Publishing Staff.** Goya. (Eyewitness Books). 64p. (J). (gr. 4-7). 1999. 15.95 (*0-7894-4877-7*, D K Ink) DK Pub Inc.
DK Publishing Staff. Goya: The First "Modern" Painter-His Life in Paintings. LC 98-86753. 1999. pap. text 12.95 (*0-7894-4140-3*) DK Pub Inc.
— Great Places to Stay in Europe. (Eyewitness Travel Guides Ser.). 432p. 2000. pap. 24.95 (*0-7894-4626-X*) DK Pub Inc.
— Greek. LC 98-27352. (GRE & ENG.). 1998. pap. 29.95 incl. audio (*0-7894-3588-8*) DK Pub Inc.
***DK Publishing Staff.** Greetings, Sun. LC 97-34108. (Illus.). 32p. (J). (ps-2). 2000. pap. text 5.95 (*0-7894-2660-9*, D K Ink) DK Pub Inc.
— Halloween Book. 2000. write for info. (*0-7894-6655-4*, Pub. by DK Pub Inc) Pub Resources Inc.
— Hawaii. (Guias Visuales Ser.). (SPA., Illus.). 2000. pap. text 19.95 (*0-7894-6231-1*) DK Pub Inc.
DK Publishing Staff. Hebrew. LC 98-27353. (Hugo Ser.). 282 p. 1998. pap. 29.95 incl. audio (*0-7894-3590-X*) DK Pub Inc.
— Hebrew. LC 98-53865. 1999. pap. text 6.95 (*0-7894-4186-1*) DK Pub Inc.
— Henry's Colors. LC 97-38619. (Henry Board Bks.). (J). 1998. bds. 4.95 (*0-7894-3027-4*) DK Pub Inc.
— Horse. 1996. 4.99 (*0-7894-1266-7*) DK Pub Inc.
***DK Publishing Staff.** Horse & Pony. (Funpax Ser.). (Illus.). (ps-3). 2000. pap. text 7.95 (*0-7894-4785-1*) DK Pub Inc.
DK Publishing Staff. Horse & Pony Breeds. LC 98-50742. (DK Riding Club Series). 1999. pap. 7.95 (*0-7894-4267-1*) DK Pub Inc.
— Horse & Pony Breeds. LC 98-50742. (DK Riding Club Series). (YA). (gr. 4-9). 1999. 12.95 (*0-7894-4268-X*) DK Pub Inc.
— Horse & Pony Care. LC 98-49618. 1999. 12.95 (*0-7894-4270-1*); pap. 7.95 (*0-7894-4269-8*) DK Pub Inc.
— Horses. 1997. 6.99 (*0-7894-2367-7*) DK Pub Inc.
— Horses: With Stickers. (J). 1997. pap. text 9.99 (*0-7894-2363-4*) DK Pub Inc.
***DK Publishing Staff.** Hugo Arabic in Three Months: Simplified Language Course. LC 98-31746. (ARA & ENG.). 1999. pap. 29.95 incl. audio (*0-7894-4432-1*) DK Pub Inc.
DK Publishing Staff. Hugo's French in Three Months. (FRE.). 1998. pap. 12.95 (*0-7894-3225-0*); pap. 29.95 incl. audio (*0-7894-3226-9*) DK Pub Inc.
— Hugo's German in Three Months. LC 97-47226. (GER.). 1998. pap. 12.95 (*0-7894-3229-3*) DK Pub Inc.
— Hugo's Italian in Three Months. LC 97-47223. (ITA.). 1998. pap. 12.95 (*0-7894-3231-5*) DK Pub Inc.
— Human Body. LC 96-44243. (Inside Guides Ser.). (Illus.). 48p. (J). 1997. 15.95 (*0-7894-1506-2*) DK Pub Inc.
***DK Publishing Staff.** Human Body. (Eyewitness Books). 64p. (J). (gr. 4-7). 1999. 15.95 (*0-7894-4883-1*, D K Ink) DK Pub Inc.
DK Publishing Staff. Hungarian Phrase Book. LC 99-21843. (Eyewitness Travel Guide Phrase Bks.). 128p. 1999. pap. 6.95 (*0-7894-4867-X*) DK Pub Inc.
— Insects. LC 91-58212. (Eyewitness Explorers Ser.). 64p. (J). (gr. k-3). 1997. pap. 5.95 (*0-7894-2215-8*) DK Pub Inc.
— Insects. (What's Inside? Ser.). 24p. 1999. pap. text 3.95 (*0-7894-4294-9*) DK Pub Inc.
— Interviewing Skills. LC 97-38890. (Essential Managers Handbks.). (Illus.). 72p. 1999. pap. 6.95 (*0-7894-2445-2*) DK Pub Inc.
— Japanese. LC 98-53864. 1999. pap. text 6.95 (*0-7894-4185-3*) DK Pub Inc.
— Jolly Postman's Party. (J). (ps-3). 1998. 19.95 incl. cd-rom (*0-7894-3283-8*) DK Pub Inc.
— Kandinsky. LC 99-32115. (Artbook Ser.). 144p. 1999. pap. 12.95 (*0-7894-4852-1*) DK Pub Inc.
— Kitten. LC 99-185639. (Touch & Feel Ser.). (Illus.). 12p. (ps-k). 1999. 6.95 (*0-7894-3990-5*) DK Pub Inc.
***DK Publishing Staff.** Kitten. (Illus.). 16p. (ps-k). 2000. 4.95 (*0-7894-6657-0*) DK Pub Inc.
DK Publishing Staff. Kittens. LC 97-18890. 40p. (J). (gr. k-5). 1997. 12.95 (*0-7894-2132-1*) DK Pub Inc.
— Latin American Spanish. LC 98-51187. (Eyewitness Travel Guide Phrase Bks.). 128p. 1999. pap. text 6.95 (*0-7894-4187-X*) DK Pub Inc.
— Lawns & Groundcovers. 80p. 1999. pap. text 8.95 (*0-7894-4160-8*) DK Pub Inc.
***DK Publishing Staff.** Lego City: Level 1. (Readers Ser.). (Illus.). 32p. (ps-3). 2000. 12.95 (*0-7894-6699-6*); pap. 3.95 (*0-7894-6700-3*) DK Pub Inc.
— Lego Game Books Mixed Counter Display. 1999. pap. text 118.80 (*0-7894-4993-5*) DK Pub Inc.
— Lego Space Port: Level 2. (Readers Ser.). (Illus.). 32p. (ps-3). 2000. 12.95 (*0-7894-6701-1*) DK Pub Inc.
— Lego Space Port: Level 2. (Illus.). 32p. (ps-3). 2000. pap. 3.95 (*0-7894-6702-X*) DK Pub Inc.
DK Publishing Staff. Life. (Eyewitness Books). 64p. (J). (gr. 4-7). 1999. 15.95 (*0-7894-4884-X*, D K Ink) DK Pub Inc.
— Light. (Eyewitness Books). 64p. (J). (gr. 4-7). 1999. 15.95 (*0-7894-4885-8*, D K Ink) DK Pub Inc.
— London. LC 92-53470. (Eyewitness Travel Guides Ser.). 432p. 1999. 40.00 (*0-7894-4975-7*, D K Ink) DK Pub Inc.
— London. rev. ed. (Eyewitness Travel Guides Ser.). 432p. 1999. pap. 24.95 (*0-7894-4890-4*) DK Pub Inc.
***DK Publishing Staff.** Los Angeles. (Eyewitness City Maps Ser.). 2000. pap. 7.95 (*0-7894-5639-7*) DK Pub Inc.
— Lost Temple. (LEGO Game Bks.). 32p. (J). (gr. k-5). 1999. pap. 4.95 (*0-7894-4706-1*) DK Pub Inc.
— Madrid. (Eyewitness City Maps Ser.). 2000. pap. 7.95 (*0-7894-5640-0*) DK Pub Inc.
DK Publishing Staff. Making Presentations. LC 97-38907. (Essential Managers Handbks.). (Illus.). 72p. 1999. pap. 6.95 (*0-7894-2449-5*) DK Pub Inc.
— Mandarin--Chinese. LC 98-53896. (Eyewitness Travel Guide Phrase Bks.). 1999. pap. text 6.95 (*0-7894-4188-8*) DK Pub Inc.
— Manet. (Eyewitness Books). 64p. (J). (gr. 4-7). 1999. 15.95 (*0-7894-4879-3*, D K Ink) DK Pub Inc.
— Matisse: Master of Pure Color-His Life in Paintings. LC 98-86755. 1999. pap. text 12.95 (*0-7894-4136-5*) DK Pub Inc.
***DK Publishing Staff.** Matter. (Eyewitness Books). 64p. (J). (gr. 4-7). 1999. 15.95 (*0-7894-4886-6*, D K Ink) DK Pub Inc.
DK Publishing Staff. Mexico. LC 99-22557. (Eyewitness Travel Guides Ser.). 384p. 1999. pap. 24.95 (*0-7894-4623-5*) DK Pub Inc.
***DK Publishing Staff.** Microsoft Excel: Using Graphics. (Illus.). 72p. 2000. pap. 6.95 (*0-7894-5536-6*, D K Ink) DK Pub Inc.
— Microsoft PowerPoint: Creating Presentations. (Essential Computers Ser.). (Illus.). 72p. 2000. pap. 6.95 (*0-7894-5537-4*, D K Ink) DK Pub Inc.
— Microsoft Word: Good-Looking Documents. (Essential Computers Ser.). (Illus.). 72p. 2000. pap. 6.95 (*0-7894-5534-X*, D K Ink) DK Pub Inc.
— Microsoft Word: Tables, Charts & Graphs. (Essential Computers Ser.). (Illus.). 72p. 2000. pap. 6.95 (*0-7894-5535-8*, D K Ink) DK Pub Inc.
— Millennium. (Dk Sticker Gift Box Ser.). 1999. 9.99 (*0-7894-4794-0*); pap. 6.99 (*0-7894-4796-7*) DK Pub Inc.
DK Publishing Staff. Monet. LC 98-86756. 144p. 1999. pap. text 12.95 (*0-7894-4142-X*) DK Pub Inc.
***DK Publishing Staff.** Monet. (Eyewitness Books). 64p. (J). (gr. 4-7). 1999. 15.95 (*0-7894-4880-7*, D K Ink) DK Pub Inc.
DK Publishing Staff. Moon Landings. LC 99-11937. (DK Discoveries Series). 1999. 14.95 (*0-7894-3958-1*) DK Pub Inc.
— Multiplication: Math Sticker Workbook. 1997. pap. 4.95 (*0-7894-2189-5*) DK Pub Inc.
— My Body. (What's Inside? Ser.). 24p. 1999. pap. text 3.95 (*0-7894-4293-0*) DK Pub Inc.
***DK Publishing Staff.** My First Body Board Book. (My First Bks.). (Illus.). 36p. (ps-k). 2000. 6.95 (*0-7894-6516-7*) DK Pub Inc.
— My First Boxed Set. (Illus.). 100p. (ps-k). 2000. 19.95 (*0-7894-5561-7*) DK Pub Inc.
— My First "Essential Preschool Learning Tools" Display. 2000. 750.00 (*0-7894-6906-5*) DK Pub Inc.
— My First Farm Book. LC 99-39924. (Illus.). 64p. (J). (gr. k-2). 2000. 16.95 (*0-7894-5214-6*, D K Ink) DK Pub Inc.
— My First Lift the Flap Animals. (My First Bks.). (Illus.). 12p. (ps-k). 2000. 9.95 (*0-7894-6515-9*) DK Pub Inc.
— My First Number Bath Book. (Bath Bks.). (Illus.) 10p. (ps-k). 2000. pap. 4.95 (*0-7894-6517-5*) DK Pub Inc.
DK Publishing Staff. My First Number Board Book. LC 99-209609. (My First Bks.). 1999. bds. 6.95 (*0-7894-3450-4*) DK Pub Inc.
***DK Publishing Staff.** My First Phonics Board Book. LC 99-39928. (Illus.). 36p. (J). (gr. k-2). 2000. 6.95 (*0-7894-5215-4*, D K Ink) DK Pub Inc.
DK Publishing Staff. My First Truck Board Book. LC 98-44421. (DK's "My First" Ser.). 36p. 1999. bds. 6.95 (*0-7894-3978-6*) DK Pub Inc.
— My First Word Bath Book. (DK's "My First" Ser.). 10p. 1999. 4.95 (*0-7894-4297-3*) DK Pub Inc.
— My First Word Book. rev. ed. LC 99-206690. (DK's "My First" Ser.). 64p. 1999. 16.95 (*0-7894-3977-8*) DK Pub Inc.
— My Pregnancy Record Book. 64p. 1999. 9.95 (*0-7894-4122-5*) DK Pub Inc.
— Negotiate Successfully. LC 97-38889. (Instant Managers Ser.). 1998. 6.95 (*0-7894-2448-7*) DK Pub Inc.
— New York: Deluxe Gift Edition. (Eyewitness Travel Guides Ser.). 432p. 1999. pap. 40.00 (*0-7894-4976-5*, D K Ink) DK Pub Inc.
***DK Publishing Staff.** NFL, Big & Small. LC 99-24167. (NFL Board Bks.). 22p. (J). (gr. k-2). 1999. 6.95 (*0-7894-4720-7*) DK Pub Inc.
— NFL Colors. (NFL Board Bks.). (Illus.). 22p. (J). (ps-k). 2000. 6.95 (*0-7894-5538-2*, D K Ink) DK Pub Inc.
DK Publishing Staff. NFL Mixed Display. 1999. 166.80 (*0-7894-4962-5*) DK Pub Inc.
— Night Sky. LC 93-644. (Eyewitness Explorers Ser.). 64p. (J). (gr. k-3). 1997. pap. 5.95 (*0-7894-2214-X*) DK Pub Inc.
***DK Publishing Staff.** No More Strangers Now. LC 97-47293. (Illus.). 112p. (YA). (gr. 5-9). 2000. pap. text 11.95 (*0-7894-2663-3*, D K Ink) DK Pub Inc.
DK Publishing Staff. Noah's Ark. (J). 1998. pap. text 5.95 (*0-7894-3469-5*) DK Pub Inc.
— Norwegian Phrase Book. LC 99-21844. (Eyewitness Travel Guide Phrase Bks.). 128p. 1999. pap. 6.95 (*0-7894-4868-8*) DK Pub Inc.
— On the Farm. 1996. 4.99 (*0-7894-1372-8*) DK Pub Inc.
— 1000 Makers of the Millennium. LC 99-14757. 224p. (YA). (gr. 3 up). 1999. 19.95 (*0-7894-4709-6*) DK Pub Inc.
***DK Publishing Staff.** 1, 2, 3. (Touch & Feel Ser.). 12p. (J). 2000. 6.95 (*0-7894-5220-0*, D K Ink) DK Pub Inc.
DK Publishing Staff. Paper Mache. (Fun Pax Activity Ser.). (J). 1998. pap. 4.95 (*0-7894-3801-1*) DK Pub Inc.
— Paris: Deluxe Gift Edition. (Eyewitness Travel Guides Ser.). 432p. 1999. pap. 40.00 (*0-7894-4977-3*, D K Ink) DK Pub Inc.
***DK Publishing Staff.** Party. (Scratch & Sniff Ser.). 12p. (J). 2000. 6.95 (*0-7894-5224-3*, D K Ink) DK Pub Inc.
DK Publishing Staff. Paths & Paving. LC 99-199902. 80p. 1999. pap. text 8.95 (*0-7894-4158-6*) DK Pub Inc.
***DK Publishing Staff.** Pests & Diseases: A Complete Guide to Preventing, Identifying & Treating Plant Problems. (Illus.). 2000. pap. 0.00 (*0-7894-5996-5*) DK Pub Inc.
DK Publishing Staff. Picturpedia: The Earth. 1997. 12.95 (*1-56458-138-1*) DK Pub Inc.
— Piero Della Francesca. LC 99-31209. (Artbook Ser.). 144p. 1999. pap. 12.95 (*0-7894-4853-X*) DK Pub Inc.
— Pirate. 1999. 9.95 (*0-7894-4276-0*) DK Pub Inc.
— Planes. (What's Inside? Ser.). 1999. pap. text 3.95 (*0-7894-4296-5*) DK Pub Inc.
***DK Publishing Staff.** Playing Music on Your PC. 72p. 2000. pap. 6.95 (*0-7894-6372-5*) DK Pub Inc.
DK Publishing Staff. Pockets Spelling Dictionary. LC 97-80395. (DK Pockets Ser.). 432p. (J). 1998. pap. 6.95 (*0-7894-3073-8*) DK Pub Inc.
— Polish Phrase Book. LC 99-21840. (Eyewitness Travel Guide Phrase Bks.). 128p. 1999. pap. 6.95 (*0-7894-4869-6*) DK Pub Inc.
— Pony. 10p. (J). 1998. 3.95 (*0-7894-3714-7*) DK Pub Inc.
***DK Publishing Staff.** Praga. (Eyewitness Travel Guides Ser.). (SPA.). 2000. pap. text 19.95 (*0-7894-6215-X*) DK Pub Inc.
DK Publishing Staff. Prague. LC 93-34987. (Eyewitness Travel Guides Ser.). (Illus.). 264p. 1994. pap. 22.95 (*1-56458-503-4*) DK Pub Inc.
— Puppies. LC 97-15459. 40p. (J). (gr. k-5). 1997. 12.95 (*0-7894-2133-X*) DK Pub Inc.
— Puppies & Kittens. 1997. 6.99 (*0-7894-2366-9*) DK Pub Inc.
***DK Publishing Staff.** Puppy. LC 99-185569. (Touch & Feel Ser.). (Illus.). 10p. (ps-k). 1999. 6.95 (*0-7894-3991-3*) DK Pub Inc.
— Puppy. (Illus.). 16p. (ps-k). 2000. 4.95 (*0-7894-6656-2*) DK Pub Inc.
DK Publishing Staff. Puppy Care. (101 Essential Tips Ser.: Vol. 29). 72p. (J). 1997. pap. 4.95 (*0-7894-1463-5*) DK Pub Inc.
— Race Car. LC 98-202595. (J). 1998. 4.95 (*0-7894-3712-0*) DK Pub Inc.
***DK Publishing Staff.** Race Car. (Mighty Machines Ser.). (Illus.). 24p. (J). (gr. k-3). 2000. pap. text 5.95 (*0-7894-6074-2*, D K Ink) DK Pub Inc.
DK Publishing Staff. Rembrandt. LC 98-86757. 1999. pap. text 12.95 (*0-7894-4146-2*) DK Pub Inc.
— Removing Stains. LC 96-6587. (101 Essential Tips Ser.: Vol. 25). 72p. 1997. pap. 4.95 (*0-7894-1459-7*) DK Pub Inc.
— Rock Garden Plants. LC 96-47941. (Eyewitness Garden Handbks.). 200p. 1997. 18.95 (*0-7894-1455-4*) DK Pub Inc.
— Rome. (Eyewitness Travel Guides Ser.). 432p. 1999. pap. 24.95 (*0-7894-4891-2*) DK Pub Inc.
— Rome: Deluxe Gift Edition. (Eyewitness Travel Guides Ser.). 432p. (Orig.). 1999. pap. 40.00 (*0-7894-4978-1*, D K Ink) DK Pub Inc.
— Russian. LC 98-16725. (Eyewitness Travel Guide Phrase Bks.). (RUS.). 126 p. 1998. 6.95 (*0-7894-3594-2*) DK Pub Inc.
— St. Petersburg. LC 98-3673. (Eyewitness Travel Guides Ser.). 1998. pap. 22.95 (*0-7894-3530-6*) DK Pub Inc.
***DK Publishing Staff.** San Francisco y Norte de California. (Guias Visuales Ser.). (SPA., Illus.). 2000. pap. text 29.95 (*0-7894-6225-7*) DK Pub Inc.
DK Publishing Staff. Scottish Gaelic in Three Months. LC 98-48004. (Hugo Three Month Language Courses Ser.). 240p. 1999. pap. text 14.95 (*0-7894-4430-5*) DK Pub Inc.
***DK Publishing Staff.** Shapes. (Touch & Feel Ser.). 12p. 2000. 6.95 (*0-7894-5222-7*) DK Pub Inc.
DK Publishing Staff. Sharks. LC 97-20872. (Really Horrible Guides Ser.). (J). (gr. k-6). 1997. 9.95 (*0-7894-2050-3*) DK Pub Inc.
— Sharks & Other Monsters of the Deep. LC 91-72484. (See & Explore Library). 64p. (J). 1998. pap. 7.95 (*0-7894-2967-5*) DK Pub Inc.
***DK Publishing Staff.** Shopping. (Scratch & Sniff Ser.). 12p. (J). 2000. 6.95 (*0-7894-5223-5*, D K Ink) DK Pub Inc.
— Shore Line. LC 92-53491. (Look Closer Ser.). (Illus.). 32p. (J). (gr. 1-5). 2000. pap. text 7.95 (*0-7894-6070-X*, D K Ink) DK Pub Inc.
DK Publishing Staff. Skeleton. (Ultimate Sticker Books Ser.). 20p. (J). (gr. k-7). 1997. pap. text 6.95 (*0-7894-2168-2*) DK Pub Inc.
— Small Gardens. LC 98-52152. 80p. 1999. pap. text 8.95 (*0-7894-4159-4*) DK Pub Inc.
***DK Publishing Staff.** Snake Book: A Breathtaking Close-Up Look at Splendid, Slithery Snakes. (Illus.). 32p. (J). (gr. 1-5). 2000. pap. text 7.95 (*0-7894-6068-8*, D K Ink) DK Pub Inc.
DK Publishing Staff. Soccer: The Ultimate World Cup Companion. LC 97-36602. (J). (gr. 3 up). 1998. pap. 12.95 (*0-7894-3071-1*) DK Pub Inc.
— South Africa. LC 99-34693. (Eyewitness Travel Guides Ser.). 408p. 1999. pap. 24.95 (*0-7894-4622-7*) DK Pub Inc.
— Spanish Dictionary. LC 97-213044. (DK Pockets Ser.). 512p. 1997. pap. 6.95 (*0-7894-2195-X*) DK Pub Inc.
***DK Publishing Staff.** Spanish Dictionary. LC 98-52897. 1999. pap. text 9.95 (*0-7894-4495-X*) DK Pub Inc.
— Spreadsheets: Formatting & Printing. (Eyewitness Computers Ser.). (Illus.). 72p. 2000. pap. text 6.95 (*0-7894-6117-X*, D K Ink) DK Pub Inc.
— Star Wars: The Power of Myth. (Star Wars Ser.). 2000. pap. 12.95 (*0-7894-5591-9*) DK Pub Inc.
— Stegosuarus. 12p. (J). (gr. k-2). 2000. 6.95 (*0-7894-5406-8*, D K Ink) DK Pub Inc.
DK Publishing Staff. Story of Jesus. 1999. 5.95 (*0-7894-3984-0*) DK Pub Inc.
— Story of Moses. 1999. 5.95 (*0-7894-3985-9*) DK Pub Inc.
— Stucker Fun Book: Puzzle Fun. 1997. pap. text 6.95 (*0-7894-1524-0*) DK Pub Inc.
***DK Publishing Staff.** Swamp Life. LC 92-53489. (Look Closer Ser.). (Illus.). 32p. (J). (gr. 1-5). 2000. pap. text 7.95 (*0-7894-6071-8*, D K Ink) DK Pub Inc.
DK Publishing Staff. Swedish Phrase Book. LC 99-21842. (Eyewitness Travel Guide Phrase Bks.). 128p. 1999. pap. 6.95 (*0-7894-4870-X*) DK Pub Inc.
***DK Publishing Staff.** Sydney. deluxe ed. (Eyewitness Travel Guides Ser.). 264p. 2000. pap. text 40.00 (*0-7894-5644-3*, D K Ink) DK Pub Inc.
DK Publishing Staff. Technology. (Eyewitness Books). 64p. (J). (gr. 4-7). 1999. 15.95 (*0-7894-4887-4*, D K Ink) DK Pub Inc.
— Teddy Bear. LC 98-204692. (Shaped Board Bks.). 10p. (J). 1998. 3.95 (*0-7894-3715-5*) DK Pub Inc.
— Teddy Bears. 1997. 6.99 (*0-7894-2365-0*) DK Pub Inc.
— 3-D Human Body. LC 99-219949. (Eyewitness Books). 56p. (J). (gr. 4-7). 1999. 16.95 (*0-7894-4279-5*) DK Pub Inc.
— 3-D Rocks & Minerals. LC 99-216885. 56p. 1999. 16.95 (*0-7894-4280-9*) DK Pub Inc.
***DK Publishing Staff.** Titian. LC 98-86758. 1999. pap. text 12.95 (*0-7894-4141-1*) DK Pub Inc.
— Touch & Feel. (All Aboard Bks.). (Illus.). 22p. (J). 2000. 6.95 (*0-7894-5328-2*, D K Ink) DK Pub Inc.
— Touch & Feel: Christmas. (Touch & Feel Ser.). (Illus.). 12p. (ps-k). 2000. 6.95 (*0-7894-6512-4*) DK Pub Inc.

D

An Asterisk (*) at the beginning of an entry indicates that the title is appearing for the first time.

— Touch & Feel Halloween. (Touch & Feel Ser.). (Illus.). 12p. (ps-k). 2000. 6.95 (*0-7894-6511-6*) DK Pub Inc.

DK Publishing Staff. Toy Story: The Essential Guide. LC 99-43270. (J). 1999. 14.95 (*0-7894-5312-6*) DK Pub Inc.

— Toy Story: The Ultimate Sticker Book. (Ultimate Sticker Books Ser.). 8p. (J). (ps-3). 1999. pap. 6.95 (*0-7894-5343-6*) DK Pub Inc.

— Tractor. 1999. 6.95 (*0-7894-4282-5*) DK Pub Inc.

***DK Publishing Staff.** Tractor. LC 64-24403. (Mighty Machines Ser.). (Illus.). 24p. (J). (gr. k-3). 2000. pap. text 5.95 (*0-7894-6073-4*, D K Ink) DK Pub Inc.

— Tractor. (Illus.). 12p. (ps-k). 2000. 6.95 (*0-7894-6533-7*) DK Pub Inc.

DK Publishing Staff. Training Your Dog. LC 96-6586. (101 Essential Tips Ser.: Vol. 26). 72p. 1997. pap. 4.95 (*0-7894-1460-0*) DK Pub Inc.

— Trains & Railroads. LC 98-224407. (See & Explore Library). 64p. (J). 1998. pap. text 7.95 (*0-7894-3444-X*) DK Pub Inc.

— Travel Fun. (My Sticker Bk. of... Ser.). 20p. (J). (gr. k-3). 1997. pap. text 6.95 (*0-7894-1525-9*) DK Pub Inc.

***DK Publishing Staff.** Triceratops. 12p. (J). 2000. 6.95 (*0-7894-5404-1*, D K Ink) DK Pub Inc.

DK Publishing Staff. Triumph. (DK Classic Motorcycles Ser.). 1998. 8.95 (*0-7894-3507-1*) DK Pub Inc.

— Truck. LC 98-202611. (J). 1998. 4.95 (*0-7894-3713-9*) DK Pub Inc.

***DK Publishing Staff.** Truck. LC 94-38034. (Mighty Machines Ser.). (Illus.). 24p. (J). (gr. k-3). 2000. pap. text 5.95 (*0-7894-6072-6*, D K Ink) DK Pub Inc.

DK Publishing Staff. Trucks. (What's Inside? Ser.). 1999. pap. text 3.95 (*0-7894-4295-7*) DK Pub Inc.

***DK Publishing Staff.** Truly Tasteless Scratch & Sniff Book. (Illus.). 24p. (gr. 4-7). 2000. 9.95 (*0-7894-6514-0*) DK Pub Inc.

DK Publishing Staff. Twentieth Century. 1999. 9.95 (*0-7894-4277-9*) DK Pub Inc.

***DK Publishing Staff.** Tyrannosaurus Rex. 12p. (J). (gr. k-2). 2000. 6.95 (*0-7894-5403-3*, D K Ink) DK Pub Inc.

DK Publishing Staff. Ultimate Pocket World Atlas, 2 vols. 1997. 24.95 (*0-7894-1826-6*) DK Pub Inc.

— The Ultimate Truck with Sticker. (Ultimate Sticker Books Ser.). 20p. (J). (ps-3). 1998. pap. 6.95 (*0-7894-3466-0*) DK Pub Inc.

— Ultimate Visual Dictionary. LC 97-11173. (Illus.). 640p. 1998. pap. 14.95 (*0-7894-2874-1*) DK Pub Inc.

***DK Publishing Staff.** Ultimate Visual Dictionary 2001. (Illus.). 640p. 2000. 40.00 (*0-7894-6111-0*) DK Pub Inc.

DK Publishing Staff. Using the Internet. LC 96-6497. (101 Essential Tips Ser.: Vol. 28). 72p. 1997. pap. 4.95 (*0-7894-1462-7*) DK Pub Inc.

— Van Gogh. LC 98-86848. (DK Art Book Ser.). 144p. 1999. pap. text 12.95 (*0-7894-4143-8*) DK Pub Inc.

— Van Gogh. (Eyewitness Books). 64p. (J). (gr. 4-7). 1999. 15.95 (*0-7894-4878-5*) DK Pub Inc.

— Velazquez. LC 99-31208. (Artbook Ser.). 144p. 1999. pap. 12.95 (*0-7894-4855-6*) DK Pub Inc.

***DK Publishing Staff.** Venice. (Eyewitness City Maps Ser.). 2000. pap. 7.95 (*0-7894-5641-9*) DK Pub Inc.

DK Publishing Staff. Vermeer. (Artbook Ser.). 144p. 1999. pap. 12.95 (*0-7894-4850-5*) DK Pub Inc.

***DK Publishing Staff.** Visual Encyclopedia of Science. 512p. (gr. 4-7). 2000. pap. 16.95 (*0-7894-6676-7*) DK Pub Inc.

D

DK Publishing Staff. Volcano. 1999. 9.95 (*0-7894-4278-7*) DK Pub Inc.

— Whales, Dolphins & Porpoises. LC 92-7624. (See & Explore Library). (J). 1998. pap. 7.95 (*0-7894-2968-3*) DK Pub Inc.

— Wild Animals. 1996. 4.99 (*0-7894-0684-5*) DK Pub Inc.

— Wonders of the World. LC 98-224412. (See & Explore Library). (J). 1998. pap. text 7.95 (*0-7894-3446-6*) DK Pub Inc.

— World Desk Reference. 3rd rev. ed. LC 94-49376. (World Atlas Ser.). (Illus.). 732p. 2000. pap. text 29.95 (*0-7894-4894-7*, D K Ink) DK Pub Inc.

***DK Publishing Staff, ed.** Barbie, Queen of Glamour. LC 00-26174. (Illus.). 128p. (J). (gr. 4-7). 2000. 19.95 (*0-7894-6664-3*) DK Pub Inc.

— Millennium Year by Year. rev. ed. (Illus.). 2000. 29.95 (*0-7894-6539-6*) DK Pub Inc.

— Summer Vacation Dinosaur!, 2 vols. (Illus.). (J). (gr. 3-7). 2000. pap. 25.00 (*0-7894-6065-3*, D K Ink) DK Pub Inc.

DK Publishing Staff, told to. Scotland. LC 99-18500. (Eyewitness Travel Guides Ser.). 224p. 1999. 24.95 (*0-7894-4621-9*) DK Pub Inc.

***DK Publishing Staff & American Horticultural Society Staff.** Fuchsias. LC 99-41068. (AHS Practical Guides Ser.). 80p. 2000. pap. 8.95 (*0-7894-5068-2*, D K Ink) DK Pub Inc.

— Hanging Baskets. LC 99-41066. (AHS Practical Guides Ser.). 80p. 2000. pap. 8.95 (*0-7894-5069-0*, D K Ink) DK Pub Inc.

— Small Trees. LC 99-41067. (AHS Practical Guides Ser.). 80p. 1999. pap. 8.95 (*0-7894-5070-4*, D K Ink) DK Pub Inc.

***DK Publishing Staff & Carlson, Laurie.** Boss of the Plains: The Hat That Won the West. LC 97-30995. (Illus.). 32p. (J). (ps-5). 2000. pap. text 5.95 (*0-7894-2657-9*, D K Ink) DK Pub Inc.

DK Publishing Staff & Cheshire, Charles. Clematis. LC 98-41494. (AHS Practical Guides Ser.). (Illus.). 72p. 1999. pap. 8.95 (*0-7894-4153-5*) DK Pub Inc.

DK Publishing Staff & Edwards, Ray. Perennials. LC 98-41493. (AHS Practical Guides Ser.). (Illus.). 80p. 1999. pap. 8.95 (*0-7894-4151-9*) DK Pub Inc.

***DK Publishing Staff & Hooper, Anne.** KISS: Sex. (Keep It Simple Ser.). 352p. 2001. pap. 18.95 (*0-7894-6985-5*) DK Pub Inc.

DK Publishing Staff & McGuinness, Diane. My First Phonics Book. LC 99-21465. (My First Bks.). (Illus.). 48p. (J). (ps-k). 1999. 16.95 (*0-7894-4737-1*) DK Pub Inc.

DK Publishing Staff & Rosenfeld, Richard. Herb Garden. LC 98-41495. (AHS Practical Guides Ser.). (Illus.). 80p. 1999. pap. 8.95 (*0-7894-4150-0*) DK Pub Inc.

DK Publishing Staff & Trist, Glenda. A Child's First Book of Prayers: New & Traditional Prayers for Children. LC 98-45043. (Illus.). 48p. (J). (ps-2). 1999. 12.95 (*0-7894-3976-X*) DK Pub Inc.

DK Publishing Staff, et al. Chronicle of the Olympics, 1896-2000: All the Stars, Events & Results of the Last 100 Years. LC 97-41746. (Illus.). 330p. (gr. 5 up). 1998. 29.95 (*0-7894-2312-X*) DK Pub Inc.

DK Publishing Staff, jt. auth. see Martin, Sigrid B.

DK Staff. The Alphabet Book. LC 97-14413. (Illus.). 24p. (J). 1997. 12.95 (*0-7894-2053-8*) DK Pub Inc.

— Junior Chronicle of the 20th Century: A Comprehensive Record of 20th-Century History Written Specially for Children. LC 97-5212. (Illus.). 336p. (J). (gr. 4). 1997. 39.95 (*0-7894-2033-3*) DK Pub Inc.

DK Staff & Hastings, Selina. Illustrated Bible Stories for Jewish Children. LC 97-18943. (Illus.). 192p. (J). (gr. 2-6). 1997. 19.95 (*0-7894-2063-5*) DK Pub Inc.

DK Stickers Staff. Cats. (DK Stickers Activity Pack Ser.). 1998. 6.99 (*0-7894-3722-8*) DK Pub Inc.

***Dkeke-Ibezim, Felicia.** Love Poems for You. LC 99-94658. 62p. 1999. per. 6.95 (*0-9661598-1-0*) Ekwike Bks & Pub.

Dlab, V. & Scott, L. L., eds. Finite Dimensional Algebras & Related Topics. LC 94-6563. (NATO Advanced Study Institutes Series C, Mathematical & Physical Sciences: Vol. 424). 1994. text 220.50 (*0-7923-2755-1*) Kluwer Academic.

Dlab, V. & Tachikawa, H. Representations of Finite Dimensional Algebras. LC 91-24244. (Canadian Mathematical Society, Conference Proceedings Ser.: Vol. 11). 322p. 1991. pap. 92.00 (*0-8218-6016-X*, CMSAMS/11) Am Math.

Dlab, V., tr. see Drozd, Y. A. & Kirichenko, V. V.

Dlab, Vlastimil & Lenzing, Helmut, eds. Representations of Algebras: 6th International Conference, August 19-22, 1992. LC 93-32528. (Canadian Mathematical Society, Conference Proceedings Ser.: No. 14). 478p. 1993. pap. 81.00 (*0-8218-6019-4*, CMSAMS/14) Am Math.

Dlab, Vlastimil & Marki, Laszl, eds. Trends in Ring Theory: Ring Theory Conference, 1996, Miskolc, Hungary. LC 97-30267. (Canadian Mathematical Society Ser.: Vol. 22). 239p. 1998. pap. 49.00 (*0-8218-0849-4*) Am Math.

Dlab, Vlastimil & Ringel, Claus M. Indecomposable Representations of Graphs & Algebras. LC 76-18784. (Memoirs Ser.: No. 6/173). 57p. 1987. reprint ed. pap. 19.00 (*0-8218-1873-2*, MEMO 6/173) Am Math.

Dlabacz, Gottfried J. Allgemeines Historisches Kunstler-Lexikon. (GER.). xii, 1752p. 1973. reprint ed. write for info. (*3-487-05014-5*) G Olms Pubs.

Dlabay. Business in a Global Economy. (GB - Basic Business Ser.). 1995. mass mkt. 49.95 (*0-538-62290-3*) S-W Pub.

— Business in a Global Economy. (GB - Basic Business Ser.). 1995. mass mkt., student ed., wbk. ed. 12.95 (*0-538-62292-X*) S-W Pub.

— Business in a Global Economy: Post Secondary Version. (GB - Basic Business Ser.). 1995. mass mkt. 40.95 (*0-538-71409-3*) S-W Pub.

— Business in a Global Economy, Apple Microexam. (GB - Basic Business Ser.). 1996. 187.95 (*0-538-62372-1*) S-W Pub.

Dlabay, Les, et al. Personal Finance English/Spanish Glossary. 4th ed. 32p. (C). 1995. text 15.00 (*0-256-18544-1*, Irwn McGrw-H) McGrw-H Hghr Educ.

Dlabay, Scott. Business in a Global Economy. 1997. pap. 40.50 (*0-538-68337-6*) Thomson Learn.

Dlacey, Chris. Juggling with Jeremy. (Blue Bananas Ser.). (Illus.). 48p. 1997. pap. 4.99 (*0-7497-2631-8*) London Brdge.

Dlamini, C. R. Human Rights in Africa: Which Way South Africa? LC 96-122844. 167p. 1995. pap. write for info. (*0-409-02412-0*, MICHIE) LEXIS Pub.

Dlamini, Moses. Robben Island, Hell-Hole: Reminiscences of a Political Prisoner in South Africa. LC 84-72593. 202p. (C). 1985. pap. 8.95 (*0-86543-009-8*); text 25.95 (*0-86543-008-X*) Africa World.

D'Larmessin, jt. auth. see Valck, G.

D'Lemos, R. S., et al, eds. The Cadomian Orogeny. (Geological Society Special Publications: No. 51). (Illus.). 242p. 1990. 94.00 (*0-903317-47-8*, 237, Pub. by Geol Soc Pub Hse) AAPG.

DLM Legacy Staff, ed. Tranction Collector's Library. (Illus.). 1993. pap. 12.00 (*0-00-000108-2*, Pub. by Boston Mills) Genl Dist Srvs.

Dlodlo, Mqhele E. Digital Land-Mobile Satellite Communications Systems: Overview, Performance Analysis & Application. (Illus.). 144p. (Orig.). 1996. pap. 43.50 (*90-407-1373-1*, Pub. by Delft U Pr) Coronet Bks.

Dlotko, Tomasz, jt. auth. see Cholewa, Jan W.

Dlovu, Nandi. A Bride for the King. (Heartbeats Ser.). 112p. (YA). (gr. 7 up). 1994. pap. 5.95 (*0-7910-2936-0*) Chelsea Hse.

***D'Ltri, Patricia W.** Cross Currents in the International Women's Movement, 1848-1948. LC 98-40947. 5p. 1999. 51.95 (*0-87972-781-0*); pap. 25.95 (*0-87972-782-9*) Bowling Green Univ Popular Press.

Dlug, Paul. PFS: First Choice - Applications Made Easy. (Illus.). 220p. 1987. pap. 15.95 (*0-8306-2913-0*, 2913P) McGraw-Hill Prof.

Dlugi, D. A., et al. Czech - Russian, Russian - Czech Dictionary: Pocket Sized. 4th ed. (CZE & RUS.). 476p. 1977. reprint ed. 9.95 (*0-8285-5438-2*) Firebird NY.

D'Lugo, Carol C. The Fragmented Novel in Mexico: The Politics of Form. LC 96-38728. 296p. 1997. 40.00 (*0-292-71587-0*); pap. 17.95 (*0-292-71588-9*) U of Tex Pr.

D'Lugo, Marvin. The Films of Carlos Saura: The Practice of Seeing. (Illus.). 274p. 1991. text 55.00 (*0-691-03142-8*, Pub. by Princeton U Pr); pap. text 17.95 (*0-691-00855-8*, Pub. by Princeton U Pr) Cal Prin Full Svc.

— Guide to the Cinema of Spain. LC 96-36529. (Reference Guides to the World's Cinema). 304p. 1997. lib. bdg. 75.00 (*0-313-29474-7*, Greenwood Pr) Greenwood.

Dlugokinski, Eric. The Boys' & Girls' Book of Dealing with Feelings. 31p. (J). (gr. k-6). 1988. pap. 10.95 (*1-882801-02-4*) Feelings Factory.

— Caring Connections: Without Co-Dependency. 88p. 1990. pap. 11.95 (*1-882801-01-6*) Feelings Factory.

Dlugokinski, Eric, jt. auth. see Allen, Sandra.

Dlugos, Gunter & Weiermair, Klaus, eds. Management under Differing Value Systems Vol. XIV: Political, Social & Economical Perspectives in a Changing World. 868p. 1981. 124.00 (*3-11-008553-4*) De Gruyter.

Dlugos, Gunther, et al, eds. Management under Differing Labour Market & Employment Systems. 486p. (C). 1988. lib. bdg. 161.55 (*3-11-010947-6*) De Gruyter.

Dlugos, Pamela J. Messages from Heaven: Be a Shining Star. (Illus.). 64p. (J). (gr. 4-6). Date not set. pap. 10.95 (*0-9661564-0-4*) Rejoyce Pubns.

Dlugos, Tim. Powerless: Selected Poems, 1973-1990. Trinidad, David, ed. (High Risk Ser.). 150p. (Orig.). 1996. pap. 12.99 (*1-85242-407-9*, High Risk Bks) Serpents Tail.

Dlugosch, Sharon. Baby Shower Fun. LC 83-72953. (Illus.). 138p. 1987. pap. 7.95 (*0-918420-14-8*) Brighton Pubns.

— Folding Table Napkins: A New Look at a Traditional Craft. 2nd rev. ed. LC 97-32254. (Illus.). 96p. 1998. pap. 8.95 (*0-918420-32-6*) Brighton Pubns.

— Games for Baby Shower Fun. LC 83-73599. (Illus.). 112p. 1987. pap. 6.95 (*0-918420-20-2*) Brighton Pubns.

— Games for Party Fun. rev. ed. LC 97-32254. 112p. (Orig.). 1997. pap. 7.95 (*0-918420-29-6*) Brighton Pubns.

— Tabletop Vignettes. LC 91-39054. 144p. 1991. pap. 9.95 (*0-918420-16-4*) Brighton Pubns.

— Wedding Hints & Reminders. LC 89-9741. 156p. (Orig.). 1989. pap. 8.95 (*0-918420-09-1*) Brighton Pubns.

— Wedding Plans: 50 Unique Themes for the Wedding of Your Dreams. 2nd rev. ed. LC 96-12326. 160p. 1996. pap. 10.95 (*0-918420-28-8*) Brighton Pubns.

Dlugosch, Sharon, jt. auth. see Nelson, Florence E.

Dlugosch, Sharon E. Table Setting Guide. rev. ed. LC 90-2353. (Illus.). 80p. (Orig.). 1990. pap. 8.95 (*0-918420-11-3*) Brighton Pubns.

Dlugosch, Sharon E. & Nelson, Florence E. Bridal Showers: 50 Great Ideas for a Perfect Shower. (Illus.). 160p. 1987. pap. 10.00 (*0-399-51344-2*, Perigee Bks) Berkley Pub.

Dlugoss, Eileen B., et al. Mastery Approach to Lotus 1-2-3, Release 2.3, 2.4. LC 92-47135. 1993. 27.95 (*1-56118-378-4*); teacher ed. 19.00 (*1-56118-379-2*) Paradigm MN.

Dlugoss, Eileen B., jt. auth. see Mazursky, Alan D.

Dlugoszewski, Lucia, jt. auth. see Celichowska, Renata.

Dlugozima, Hope, et al. Six Months Off: How to Plan, Negotiate, & Take the Break You Need Without Burning Bridges or Going Broke. LC 95-37728. 1995. pap. 12.95 (*0-8050-3745-4*, Owl) H Holt & Co.

Dlugy, Max. Nimzo Indian 4. Qc2. 230p. (Orig.). 1990. pap. 14.95 (*0-945470-07-X*) Chess Ent.

***Dluhosch, Barbara.** Industrial Location & Economic Integration: Centrifugal & Centripetal Forces in the New Europe. LC 99-53988. 208p. 2000. 80.00 (*1-84064-210-6*) E Elgar.

Dluhosch, Barbara, et al. International Competitiveness & the Balance of Payments: Do Current Account Deficits & Surpluses Matter? LC 95-40197. (Illus.). 256p. 1996. 90.00 (*1-85898-210-3*) E Elgar.

Dluhosch, Eric, jt. auth. see Svacha, Rostislav.

Dluhosch, Eric, tr. see Egorov, Iurii A.

Dluhosch, Erich & Svacha, Rostislav, eds. Karel Tiege: L'Enfant Terrible of the Czech Modernist Avant-Garde. LC 99-14923. (Getty Grant Ser.). (Illus.). 440p. 1999. 50.00 (*0-262-04170-7*) MIT Pr.

Dluhy, Milan J. Building Coalitions in the Human Services: Guidelines for Practice. (Human Services Guides Ser.: Vol. 60). (Illus.). 144p. (C). 1990. pap. text 18.95 (*0-8039-2604-9*) Sage.

— Changing the System: Political Advocacy for Disadvantaged Groups. LC 81-14331. (Sage Human Services Guides Ser.: No. 24). 119p. 1981. reprint ed. pap. 36.90 (*0-608-01096-0*, 205940500001) Bks Demand.

— Services for the Elderly: Case Studies in Administration & Management. Pelaez, Martha B., ed. LC 92-7395. 120p. reprint ed. pap. 37.20 (*0-608-08563-4*, 206908600002) Bks Demand.

Dluhy, Milan J. & Chen, Kan, eds. Interdisciplinary Planning: A Perspective for the Future. LC 86-6854. 235p. 1986. pap. text 1.00 (*0-88285-116-0*) Ctr Urban Pol Res.

Dluhy, Milan J. & Pelaez, Martha. Services for the Elderly: Case Studies in Administration & Management. 128p. (C). 1992. text 29.95 (*0-8039-4409-8*); pap. text 14.50 (*0-8039-4410-1*) Sage.

Dluhy, Robert. Dictionary for Marine Technology Vol. 1: German - English. 5th ed. (ENG & GER.). 776p. 1987. 275.00 (*0-8288-0417-6*, M15459) Fr & Eur.

— Dictionary for Marine Technology Vol. 2: English - German. 5th ed. (ENG & GER.). 776p. 1987. 295.00 (*0-8288-0418-4*, M15460) Fr & Eur.

Dluhy, Robert, ed. Dictionary for Marine Technology, 2 vols., 1. (ENG & GER.). 1982. 254.00 (*3-87870-188-8*) Adlers Foreign Bks.

— Dictionary for Marine Technology, Vol. 2. (ENG & GER.). 1987. 254.00 (*3-87870-360-0*) Adlers Foreign Bks.

Dluzynski, Janice, ed. see American Trucking Association Staff.

DMA Staff. Diet Therapy for the Dietary Manager. 416p. 1996. per. 47.50 (*0-8403-7856-4*) Kendall-Hunt.

— Diet Therapy for the Dietary Manager. 2nd ed. LC 97-168714. 506p. 1997. pap. text, per. 55.00 (*0-7872-3375-7*, 41337501) Kendall-Hunt.

— Managing Food Protection. LC 98-183743. 202p. 1998. per. 35.00 (*0-7872-4736-7*, 41473601) Kendall-Hunt.

***DMA Staff.** Managing Food Protection. 3rd ed. 218p. 2000. per. 35.00 (*0-7872-7273-6*) Kendall-Hunt.

DMA Staff. Professional Procurement Practices: A Guide for Dietary Managers. 220p. 1997. per. 35.00 (*0-7872-3755-8*, 41375501) Kendall-Hunt.

— Ready Reference for Nutrition Care Planning. 54p. 1998. vinyl bd. 19.95 (*0-7872-5130-5*) Kendall-Hunt.

***DMA Staff & D'Mar Shimun, Surma.** Winning Management: Six Fail-safe Strategies for Building High Performance Organizations. 292p. 1999. text 24.95 (*0-7872-5989-6*) Kendall-Hunt.

D'Mar Shimun, Surma, jt. auth. see DMA Staff.

D'Mello. Multiple Choice Questions in Pharmacology: With Answers & Explanatory Comments. 2nd ed. pap. text. write for info. (*0-340-54321-3*, Pub. by E A) Routldge.

— Toxic Substances: Crop Plants. 1991. 160.00 (*0-85186-863-0*) CRC Pr.

D'Mello, C., jt. ed. see Boswell, L. F.

D'Mello, J. P. Handbook of Plant & Fungal Toxicants. LC 96-27516. (Handbooks of Pharmacology & Toxicology Ser.). 368p. 1997. lib. bdg. 99.95 (*0-8493-8551-2*) CRC Pr.

D'Mello, J. P., ed. Amino Acids in Farm Animal Nutrition. (Illus.). 432p. 1994. text 120.00 (*0-85198-881-4*) OUP.

D'Mello, J. P. & Devendra, C., eds. Tropical Legumes in Animal Nutrition. (Illus.). 352p. (C). 1995. text 120.00 (*0-85198-926-8*) OUP.

***D'Mello, J. P. Felix.** Farm Animal Metabolism & Nutrition: Critical Reviews. LC 99-48241. 400p. 2000. write for info. (*0-85199-378-8*) OUP.

Dmitirev, L., et al. Thirteen Papers in Algebra. LC 86-17254. (Translations Ser.: Series 2, Vol. 132). 104p. 1986. 51.00 (*0-8218-3107-0*, TRANS2/132) Am Math.

Dmitrenko, A. Fifty Russian Artists. 248p. 1986. text 100.00 (*0-569-08907-7*, Pub. by Collets) St Mut.

Dmitrenko, V. P., et al, eds. New Economic Policy (NEP) The Closing Stage: The Correlation of Economics & Politics. LC 99-23935. (Studies in Russian Politics, Sociology, & Economics: Vol. 4). (RUS.). 276p. 1999. text 89.95 (*0-7734-3186-1*) E Mellen.

Dmitrichev, T. F. Russian-English Dictionary of Disarmament. (ENG & RUS.). 1990. 125.00 (*0-8288-3973-5*, F39625) Fr & Eur.

Dmitrienko, V. E., jt. auth. see Belyakov, V. A.

Dmitriev, V. G., et al. Handbook of Nonlinear Optical Crystals. Schawlow, Arthur L. et al, eds. (Optical Sciences Ser.: Vol. 64). (Illus.). 221p. 1995. 64.95 (*0-387-53547-0*) Spr-Verlag.

Dmitriev, V. V., jt. auth. see Dmitrieva, V. A.

Dmitriev, Valentine. Early Education for Children with Down Syndrome: Time to Begin. 2nd ed. LC 00-40283. Date not set. write for info. (*0-89079-860-5*) PRO-ED.

Dmitriev, Viktor A. Serebrianyi Gost' O Liricheskom Geroe Bal'monta. LC 92-4594. (RUS.). 192p. (Orig.). (C). 1992. pap. 15.00 (*1-55779-047-7*) Hermitage Pubs.

Dmitriev, Vladimir, jt. auth. see Toledano, Pierre.

Dmitrieva, V. A. & Dmitriev, V. V. Russian-English Dictionary of Microbiological Terms. (ENG & RUS.). 248p. (C). 1991. 21.95 (*0-8285-5310-6*) Firebird NY.

***Dmitrievsky, A. & Panfilov, M., eds.** Porous Media. 420p. 1999. 96.00 (*981-02-4126-7*) World Scientific Pub.

Dmitriew, Helen. Surviving the Storms: Memory of Stalin's Tyranny. LC 92-62075. (Illus.). 218p. 1992. text 21.95 (*0-912201-31-2*) CSU Pr Fresno.

Dmitzak, Lee, ed. see Giagnocavo, Gregory & McLain, Timothy.

***DMNC4 Associates Staff.** X-Connections: Internet Reference Guide. 100p. 2000. pap. 12.95 (*0-9674741-0-8*, Pub. by DMNC) ACCESS Pubs Network.

***D'Monte, Rebecca & Pohl, Nicole.** Female Communities, 1600-1800. LC 99-46991. 2000. text 59.95 (*0-312-23021-4*) St Martin.

Dmowska, R. & Eckstrom, G. Shallow Subduction Zones: Seismicity, Mechanics & Seismic Potential, Part II. LC 94-198347. 240p. 1994. 27.50 (*0-8176-2963-7*) Birkhauser.

Dmowska, R. & Eckstrom, G., eds. Shallow Subduction Zones: Seismicity, Mechanics & Seismic Potential, Pt. 1. (PAGEOPH Reprint from Pure & Applied Geophysics Ser.: Vol. 140, No. 2). 220p. 1993. 27.50 (*0-8176-2962-9*) Birkhauser.

***Dmowska, Renata.** Advances in Geophysics, Vol. 42. 1999. 99.95 (*0-12-018842-2*) Acad Pr.

Dmowska, Renata. Advances in Geophysics, Vol.41. 224p. 1999. 124.00 (*0-12-018841-4*) Acad Pr.

Dmowska, Renata & Saltzman, Barry, eds. Advances in Geophysics, Vol. 36. (Illus.). 217p. 1994. text. write for info. (*0-12-018836-8*) Acad Pr.

— Advances in Geophysics, Vol. 37. (Illus.). 203p. 1996. text 95.00 (*0-12-018837-6*) Acad Pr.

— Advances in Geophysics, Vol. 38. (Illus.). 275p. 1996. text 99.95 (*0-12-018838-4*) Acad Pr.

— Advances in Geophysics Vol. 35: Seismological Structure of Slabs. (Illus.). 185p. 1994. text 95.00 (*0-12-018835-X*) Acad Pr.

— Tsunamigenic Earthquakes & Their Consequences. (Illus.). 223p. (C). 1998. boxed set 115.00 (*0-12-018839-2*) Acad Pr.

***Dmowska, Renata & Salzman, Barry.** Advances in Geophysics Vol. 40: Long-Range Persistence in Geophysical Time Series. (Illus.). 175p. 1999. 89.95 (*0-12-018840-6*) Acad Pr.

Dmowska, Renata, jt. auth. see Sauber, Jeanne.

Dmowska, Renata, jt. auth. see Wyss, Max.

Dmowska, Renata, jt. ed. see Aki, Keiiti.

Dmowska, Renata, ed. see Kaufman, Alexander A.

Dmytryk, Edward. Odd Man Out: A Memoir of the Hollywood Ten. LC 94-39958. (Illus.). 224p. (C). 1995. 34.95 (*0-8093-1998-5*); pap. 14.95 (*0-8093-1999-3*) S Ill U Pr.

— On Film Editing. 148p. (C). 1984. pap. 27.95 (*0-240-51738-5*, Focal) Buttrwrth-Heinemann.

— On Screen Writing. 180p. 1985. pap. 24.95 (*0-240-51753-9*, Focal) Buttrwrth-Heinemann.

Dmytryshyn, Basil. Medieval Russia: A Source Book, 850-1700. 3rd ed. 550p. (C). 1991. pap. text 46.00 (*0-03-033422-5*, Pub. by Harcourt Coll Pubs) Harcourt.

Dmytryshyn, Basil, ed. Imperial Russia: A Source Book, 1700-1917. 3rd ed. 500p. (C). 1990. pap. text 22.75 (*0-03-033419-5*) Harcourt Coll Pubs.

Dmytryshyn, Basil, et al, eds. The Russian American Colonies: A Documentary Record, 1798-1867. (To Siberia & Russian America Ser.: Vol. 3). (Illus.). 650p. 1989. 40.00 (*0-87595-150-3*) Oregon Hist.

— Russian Penetration of the North Pacific Ocean: A Documentary Record, 1700-1797. (To Siberia & Russian America Ser.). 640p. 1988. 40.00 (*0-87595-149-X*) Oregon Hist.

— Russia's Conquest of Siberia, 1558-1700 Vol. 1: A Documentary Record. (To Siberia & Russian America Ser.: Vol. 1). (Illus.). 1986. 40.00 (*0-87595-148-1*) Oregon Hist.

Dmytryshyn, Basil, jt. tr. see E. A. P. Crownhart-Vaughan Staff.

Dmytryshyn, Basil, tr. see Golovin, Pavel N.

DNA Insertion Meeting Staff, et al. DNA Insertion Elements, Plasmids & Episomes. Bukhari, A. I., ed. LC 76-57904. 796p. reprint ed. pap. 200.00 (*0-7837-1997-3*, 204227100002) Bks Demand.

Dneprov, E. D. The Fourth School Reform. 230p. 1998. pap. text 20.00 (*0-9643332-5-2*) ACIE.

Dnes, A. W. The Economics of Law. (Illus.). 304p. 1996. mass mkt. 21.99 (*0-412-62800-7*) Chapman & Hall.

Dnes, Antony. Franchising: A Case-Study Approach. 331p. 1992. 97.95 (*1-85628-221-X*, Pub. by Avebry) Ashgate Pub Co.

Dnestrovskii, Y. N. & Kostomarov, D. P. Numerical Simulation of Plasmas. Deyneka, N. V., tr. from RUS. (Computational Physics Ser.). (Illus.). 320p. 1986. 135.95 (*0-387-15835-9*) Spr-Verlag.

Dnyansagar, V. R., et al, eds. Recent Trends & Contacts Between Cytogenetics Embryology & Morphology, 1976. (Current Trends in Life Sciences Ser.: Vol. 5). xiv, 592p. 1977. 50.00 (*0-88065-081-8*) Scholarly Pubns.

Do Amaral, Alberto C. Fatima & Its Pilgrims. (Queen of Apostles Ser.: Vol. VI). 19p. 1994. 0.65 (*0-911988-94-7*, 49733) AMI Pr.

Do Amaral, Joao F., et al, eds. The Portuguese Economy Towards Nineteen Ninety-Two: Proceedings of a Conference Sponsored by Junta Nacional de Investigacao Cientifica e Tecnologica & Banco de Portugal. 272p. 1992. lib. bdg. 101.00 (*0-7923-9193-4*) Kluwer Academic.

Do Carmo Bogo, Maria. Led by Love. 64p. 1996. pap. 39.95 (*0-85439-329-3*, Pub. by St Paul Pubns) St Mut.

Do Carmo, Manfredo P. Differential Forms & Applications. LC 94-21965. (Universitext Ser.). Orig. Title: Formas Differencias e Aplicacoes. (Illus.). 118p. 1997. 34.95 (*0-387-57618-5*) Spr-Verlag.

— Differential Geometry of Curves & Surfaces. LC 75-22094. 503p. (C). 1976. 90.67 (*0-13-212589-7*) P-H.

Do Carmo, R. J., ed. Spreading Depression. (Experimental Brain Research Ser.: Vol. 23). (Illus.). 125p. 1992. 82.95 (*0-387-55532-3*) Spr-Verlag.

Do Castelo, Viana, ed. see NATO Advanced Research Workshop on Recent Research.

Do Ceu, Pinto Maria. Political Islam & the United States, 1. 1999. 40.00 (*0-86372-245-8*) Garnet-Ithaca.

Do, Duong D. Absorption Analysis: Equilibria & Kinetics. (Chemical Engineering Ser.). 900p. 1998. 86.00 (*1-86094-130-3*) World Scientific Pub.

***Do, Duong D., ed.** Adsorption Science & Technology. 740p. 2000. 120.00 (*981-02-4263-8*) World Scientific Pub.

Do, Duong D., jt. auth. see Rice, Richard G.

Do, Kiem & Kane, Julie. Counterpart: A South Vietnamese Naval Officer's War. LC 98-12206. (Illus.). 280p. 1998. 29.95 (*1-55750-181-5*) Naval Inst Pr.

Do, Le, tr. see Hutchinson, Hanna.

Do Mau, Hoanh L. Vietnam Mau Lua Que Huong Toi: Bo-Tuc Ho-So Ve Su Sup Do Cua Viet-Nam Cong-Hoa. 2nd ed. Do, Tai H., ed. (VIE., Illus.). 1100p. 25.00 (*1-884129-31-5*) Van Nghe.

Do Nascimento, Abdias. Brazil Mixture or Massacre? Essays in the Genocide of a Black People. rev. ed. Nascimento, Elisa L., tr. from POR. xviii, 214p. 1989. reprint ed. pap. text 12.95 (*0-912469-26-9*) Majority Pr.

***Do-Nguyen, Mariette.** God's Purification - Not Easy: Bride of Christ in Action, Pt. II. (Revelations Ser.). (Illus.). 641p. 1999. pap. 35.00 (*0-9652169-2-6*) Rebuild My Church.

— The Only Petition at U. S. Tax Court. (Revelations Ser.). (YA). 1999. 35.00 (*0-9652169-3-4*) Rebuild My Church.

Do-Nguyen, Mariette & Nelson, Gerald E. My Patient God's Gift: Mariette, a Saint for Our Time. Trainer, Beverly, ed. (Revelations Ser.). (Illus.). 200p. (Orig.). 1996. pap. 25.00 (*0-9652169-0-X*, 1) Rebuild My Church.

***Do-Nquyen, Mariette.** "God's Purification - Not Easy" Part 1: Bride of Christ in Action, II. Pt I. (The Revelations Ser.). 289p. (YA). 1999. 25.00 (*0-9652169-4-2*) Rebuild My Church.

Do Piero, W. S. Gregory Gillespie: Exhibition Catalogue. (Illus.). 36p. 1992. pap. 20.00 (*0-8150-0008-1*) Wittenborn Art.

Do Rega Silva, J. J. Acoustic & Elastic Wave Scattering Using Boundary Elements. 148p. 1994. 83.00 (*1-85312-293-9*) Computational Mech MA.

Do, Tai H., ed. see Do Mau, Hoanh L.

do Valle, Gilberto, ed. International Conference Rio de Janeiro. (Illus.). 736p. (C). 1994. text 40.00 (*0-939493-11-X*) Coun Tall Bldg.

Doak, Carol. Easy Machine Paper Piecing: 65 Quilt Blocks for Foundation Piecing. LC 93-28648. 1994. pap. 21.95 (*1-56477-038-9*, B165) Martingale & Co.

— Easy Mix & Match Machine Paper Piecing. LC 95-18306. 1995. pap. 21.95 (*1-56477-128-8*, B246) Martingale & Co.

— Easy Paper-Pieced Keepsake Quilts: 72 New Blocks Including the Alphabet! LC 95-6594. (Illus.). 96p. 1995. pap. 21.95 (*1-56477-109-1*, B226) Martingale & Co.

— Easy Reversible Vests. Reikes, Ursula G., ed. (Illus.). 88p. 1995. pap. 21.95 (*1-56477-092-3*, B211) Martingale & Co.

— Easy Stash Quilts. LC 99-40528. (Illus.). 112p. 1999. pap. 26.95 (*1-56477-264-0*, B383, That Patchwrk Pl) Martingale & Co.

***Doak, Carol.** 50 Fabulous Paper-Pieced Stars. LC 99-89521. (Illus.). 128p. 2000. pap. 27.95 (*1-56477-271-3*, B392, Pub. by Martingale & Co) F & W Pubns Inc.

Doak, Carol. Show Me How to Paper Piece. LC 97-17357. 1997. pap. text 7.95 (*1-56477-204-7*) Martingale & Co.

— Your First Quilt Book: (Or It Should Be!) Reikes, Ursula, ed. LC 97-20672. (Illus.). 224p. 1997. pap. 21.95 (*1-56477-198-9*, B312) Martingale & Co.

Doak, Carol & Reikes, Ursula. Easy Paper-Pieced Miniatures. LC 97-48430. (Illus.). 112p. 1998. pap. 21.95 (*1-56477-209-8*, B324, That Patchwrk Pl) Martingale & Co.

Doak, Cecilia C., et al. Teaching Patients with Low Literacy Skills. 2nd ed. LC 95-11640. 224p. 1995. pap. text 27.95 (*0-397-55161-4*) Lppncott W & W.

Doak, Howard J., 2nd, ed. Tulsa, a Celebration. (Illus.). Date not set. 34.95 (*0-9659783-0-3*) Novel Idea.

Doak, James. Coming to Life: The Emergence of Self in the Human Life Cycle. LC 87-15801. 160p. (Orig.). 1987. pap. 9.95 (*0-931892-11-2*) B Dolphin Pub.

Doak, James T. & Kloetzeman, Christine H. Cumputerized Accounting Principles. LC 94-16743. 708p. (C). 1995. spiral bd. 39.75 (*0-314-01256-7*) West Pub.

Doak, Joe, jt. auth. see Nadin, Vincent.

Doak, Kevin M. Dreams of Difference: The Japan Romantic School & the Crisis of Modernity. LC 93-5626. 1994. 45.00 (*0-520-08377-6*, Pub. by U CA Pr) Cal Prin Full Svc.

Doak, Leonard, jt. ed. see Crouch, Margaret.

Doak, Robin. The Awakening. 1997. pap. 3.95 (*0-8167-4336-3*) Troll Communs.

Doak, Tom. The Anatomy of a Golf Course. LC 92-6212. (Illus.). 288p. 1992. 24.95 (*1-58080-071-8*, Pub. by Burford Bks) Natl Bk Netwk.

— The Confidential Guide to Golf Courses. (Illus.). 362p. 1996. boxed set 45.00 (*1-886947-09-0*) Sleepng Bear.

Doak, Wade. Deep Blue: A South Pacific Odyssey. 192p. 1998. 25.00 (*1-86950-203-5*) HarpC.

Doake, David B. Literacy Learning: A Revolution in Progress. LC 94-27467. (Illus.). 430p. (Orig.). (C). 1995. pap. text 25.95 (*0-7802-2680-1*) Wright Group.

Doake, Jill, jt. auth. see Britton, Carol.

DoAmaral, Alberto C. Voluntary Mortification for Today. 28p. 1988. 1.50 (*0-911988-91-2*, 51425) AMI Pr.

Doan, Alan, et al. Aesop's Fables. LC 75-122365. 61p. 1971. write for info. (*0-87529-115-5*) Hallmark.

Doan, Daniel. Indian Stream Republic: Settling a New England Frontier, 1785-1842. MacDougall, Ruth D., ed. LC 96-9836. (Illus.). 287p. 1997. pap. 19.95 (*0-87451-768-0*) U Pr of New Eng.

— Our Last Backpack: A Memoir. LC 93-15766. (Illus.). 224p. (Orig.). 1993. pap. 14.00 (*0-88150-273-1*, Pub. by Countryman) Norton.

Doan, Daniel & MacDougall, Ruth D. 50 Hikes in the White Mountains: Hikes & Backpacking Trips in the High Peaks Region of New Hampshire. 5th ed. LC 96-48312. (50 Hikes Ser.). (Illus.). 224p. 1997. pap. 14.95 (*0-88150-389-4*, Pub. by Countryman) Norton.

— 50 More Hikes in New Hampshire: Day Hikes & Backpacking Trips from Mount Monadnock to Mount Magalloway. 4th ed. LC 97-50014. (Fifty Hikes Ser.). (Illus.). 240p. 1998. pap. 14.95 (*0-88150-407-6*, Pub. by Countryman) Norton.

***Doan, Eleanor.** Libro de Consulta Para el Orador. 1999. pap. write for info. (*0-8297-0630-5*) Vida Pubs.

Doan, Eleanor Lloyd. A Child's Treasury of Verse. (Illus.). 208p. (J). (gr. 1-6). 1987. pap. 10.95 (*0-310-23801-3*, 9545P) Zondervan.

— Speaker's Sourcebook II. 416p. 1989. reprint ed. pap. 18.99 (*0-310-24201-0*) Zondervan.

Doan, Helen M. Every Girl. (Illus.). 80p. 1985. pap. 9.95 (*0-7737-5027-4*) Genl Dist Srvs.

Doan, James E. Cearbhall O'Dalaigh: An Irish Poet in Romance & Oral Tradition. LC 90-2975. (Folklore & Oral Tradition Ser.). (Illus.). 430p. 1990. text 30.00 (*0-8240-2672-1*) Garland.

— Romance of Caerbhall & Fearbhlaidh. 1984. 17.95 (*0-685-20031-0*, Pub. by Smyth) Dufour.

Doan, Jane, jt. auth. see Chase, Penelle.

Doan, John H. Hampton History: Account of the Pennsylvania Hamptons in America in the Line of John Hampton, Jr., of Wrightstown, with an Appendix Treating of Some Other Branches. (Illus.). 199p. 1997. reprint ed. pap. 30.00 (*0-8328-8940-7*); reprint ed. lib. bdg. 40.00 (*0-8328-8939-3*) Higginson Bk Co.

***Doan, Laura.** Fashioning Sapphism: The Origins of a Modern English Lesbian Culture. 288p. 2001. text 49.50 (*0-231-11006-5*); pap. text 16.50 (*0-231-11007-3*) Col U Pr.

Doan, Laura. The Lesbian Postmodern. LC 94-18096. (Between Men - Between Women Ser.). 267p. 1994. 61.00 (*0-231-08410-2*); pap. 19.00 (*0-231-08411-0*) Col U Pr.

Doan, Laura L., ed. Old Maids to Radical Spinsters: Unmarried Women in the Twentieth-Century Novel. 304p. 1991. text 39.95 (*0-252-01731-5*); pap. text 15.95 (*0-252-06134-9*) U of Ill Pr.

Doan, Laura L., jt. auth. see Bland, Lucy.

Doan, Mary A. & Stevens, Jim, eds. Dreaming History: A Collection of Wisconsin Native-American Writing. LC 95-1752. 128p. 1995. pap. 10.95 (*1-879483-26-2*) Prairie Oak Pr.

Doan, Mason C. American Housing Production 1880-2000: A Concise History. 224p. 1996. 39.50 (*0-7618-0587-7*) U Pr of Amer.

Doan, Peter, et al. Local Institutional Development for Natural Resource Management. (Special Series on Local Institutional Development: No. 2). 66p. (Orig.). (C). 1985. pap. 6.50 (*0-86731-109-6*) Cornell CIS RDC.

Doan, Robert E., jt. auth. see Parry, Alan.

Doan, Tran Van, see Van Doan, Tran.

Doan, Tran Van, see Shen, Vincent, ed.

Doan, Tran Van, see Shen, Vincent & Van Doan, Tran, eds.

Doan, Tran Van, see Shen, Vincent, ed.

Doan, Tran Van, see Shen, Vincent & Van Doan, Tran, eds.

Doan, Tran Van, see Shen, Vincent.

Doan, Tran Van, jt. ed. see Shen, Vincent.

Doane. Positive Benefits of Astrology. 88p. 1992. 12.00 (*0-86690-410-7*) Am Fed Astrologers.

Doane, A. Doane Family: Deacon John Doane of Plymouth & Dr. John Done of Maryland & Their Descendants with Notes on English Families of the Name, 2 pts. (Illus.). 554p. 1989. reprint ed. pap. 70.00 (*0-8328-0481-9*); reprint ed. lib. bdg. 80.00 (*0-8328-0480-0*) Higginson Bk Co.

Doane, A. N. The Saxon Genesis: An Edition of the West Saxon Genesis B & the Old Saxon Vatican Genesis. LC 90-50641. 416p. 1991. 55.00 (*0-299-12800-8*) U of Wis Pr.

Doane, A. N., et al, eds. Anglo-Saxon Manuscripts in Microfiche Facsimile, Vol. 6. (C). 1998. pap. 120.00 (*0-86698-228-0*) MRTS.

Doane, A. N. & Pasternack, Carol B., eds. Vox Intexta: Orality & Textuality in the Middle Ages. LC 91-3573. (Illus.). 304p. (Orig.). (C). 1991. pap. 24.95 (*0-299-13094-0*); lib. bdg. 45.00 (*0-299-13090-8*) U of Wis Pr.

Doane, A. N. & Pulsiano, Phillip, eds. Anglo-Saxon Manuscripts in Microfiche Facsimile, Vol. 7. 1998. pap. 120.00 (*0-86698-229-9*) MRTS.

Doane, Alger N. Genesis A: A New Edition. LC 77-77437. 430p. 1978. 55.00 (*0-299-07430-7*) U of Wis Pr.

Doane, Benjamin. Following the Sea. (Illus.). 272p. 1991. pap. 17.95 (*0-920852-90-4*) Nimbus Publ.

Doane, Benjamin, jt. ed. see Klein, Raymond.

Doane, Bonnie M. The Parrot in Health & Illness: An Owner's Guide. (Illus.). 320p. 1991. 24.95 (*0-87605-826-8*) Howell Bks.

— The Pleasure of Their Company. LC 97-46150. 224p. 1998. pap. 27.95 (*0-87605-594-3*) Howell Bks.

— The Pleasure of Their Company. 1998. 27.95 (*0-87605-614-1*) Macmillan.

Doane, Bonnie M. & Qualkinbush, Thomas. My Parrot, My Friend: An Owner's Guide to Parrot Behavior. (Illus.). 256p. 1995. 25.00 (*0-87605-970-1*) Howell Bks.

Doane, Colin, jt. auth. see Medlin, Eugene.

Doane, D. V. & Kirkaldy, J. S., eds. Hardenability Concepts with Applications to Steel: Proceedings of a Symposium Held at the Sheraton - Chicago Hotel, October 24-26, 1977. LC 78-60479. 636p. reprint ed. pap. 197.20 (*0-608-16018-0*, 203311200084) Bks Demand.

Doane, Daryl A. & Franzon, Paul D., eds. Multichip Module Technologies & Alternatives: The Basics. LC 92-29779. 1993. text 89.95 (*0-442-01236-5*, VNR) Wiley.

Doane, David P., et al. Visual Statistics. LC 96-35857. 1997. write for info. (*0-256-20876-X*, Irwn Prfssnl) McGraw-Hill Prof.

Doane, David P., et al. Visual Statistics. LC 96-35857. (Illus.). 1997. write for info. (*0-07-292467-5*) McGrw-H Hghr Educ.

***Doane, Doris.** A Book of Cape Cod Houses. (Illus.). 96p. 2000. reprint ed. pap. 18.95 (*1-56792-113-2*) Godine.

Doane, Doris. Exploring Old Cape Cod. rev. ed. (Illustrated Guide Ser.). (Illus.). 1985. pap. 7.95 (*0-85699-003-5*) Chatham Pr.

— Exploring Old Cape Cod. rev. ed. (Illus.). 48p. 1995. pap. 9.95 (*0-940160-62-5*) Parnassus Imprints.

Doane, Doris C. Accurate World Horoscopes. 353p. 1984. 33.00 (*0-86690-241-4*, D2351-014) Am Fed Astrologers.

— Astrologer's Question Box. 200p. 1984. 16.00 (*0-86690-284-8*, D2554-014) Am Fed Astrologers.

— Astrology: Thirty Years Research. 328p. 1956. 17.00 (*0-86690-070-5*, D1065-014) Am Fed Astrologers.

— Astrology As a Business. LC 85-73309. 96p. 1986. 11.00 (*0-86690-303-8*, D2344-014) Am Fed Astrologers.

— Astrology of Childbirth. 1988. pap. 19.95 (*0-86690-380-1*, 3035-014) Am Fed Astrologers.

— Blending Astrology, Numerology & Tarot. LC 98-127062. 1997. pap. 18.50 (*0-86690-462-X*) Am Fed Astrologers.

— Contest Charts. LC 85-73314. 88p. 1986. 10.00 (*0-86690-315-1*, D2343-014) Am Fed Astrologers.

— Doane's World-Wide Time Change Update, 1986-1990. 80p. 1991. 10.00 (*0-86690-393-3*, D3167-014) Am Fed Astrologers.

— Horoscopes Reveal Personalities. 176p. 1995. pap. 23.00 (*0-86690-447-6*, D3564-014) Am Fed Astrologers.

— How Body Language Defines Character. 1996. 14.00 (*0-86690-461-1*, D3616-014) Am Fed Astrologers.

— How to Prepare & Pass an Astrologer Certification Exam. 56p. 1973. spiral bd. 12.00 (*0-86690-072-1*, D1067-014) Am Fed Astrologers.

— How to Read Cosmodynes. 56p. 1974. spiral bd. 10.00 (*0-86690-073-X*, D1068-014) Am Fed Astrologers.

— Let's Read a Horoscope. 78p. 1994. 12.95 (*0-86690-440-9*, D3512-014) Am Fed Astrologers.

— Modern Horary Astrology. 254p. 1994. 19.95 (*0-86690-439-5*, D3462-014) Am Fed Astrologers.

— Profit by Electional Astrology. 1990. pap. 28.95 (*0-86690-340-2*, 3034-014) Am Fed Astrologers.

— Secret Symbolism of the Tarot. 112p. 1993. pap. 13.00 (*0-86690-430-1*) Am Fed Astrologers.

— Time Changes in Canada & Mexico. 80p. 1980. 12.00 (*0-86690-075-6*, D1070-014) Am Fed Astrologers.

— Time Changes in the U. S. A. 200p. 1981. 19.95 (*0-86690-076-4*, D1071-014) Am Fed Astrologers.

— Time Changes in the World. LC 94-209842. 112p. 1980. 14.00 (*0-86690-077-2*, D1072-014) Am Fed Astrologers.

— Vocational Selection & Counseling, 2 vols., Vol. 1. LC 81-71851. 158p. 1987. 18.00 (*0-86690-011-X*, D1073-014) Am Fed Astrologers.

— Vocational Selection & Counseling, 2 vols., Vol. 2. LC 81-71851. 176p. 1987. 18.00 (*0-86690-012-8*, D1074-014) Am Fed Astrologers.

Doane, Doris C. & Cramer, Earl H. New Age Conversation. LC 96-152458. 1996. 14.00 (*0-86690-454-9*, D3587-014) Am Fed Astrologers.

Doane, E. Aquarian Age Philosophy. 128p. 1969. 10.00 (*0-86690-078-0*, D1075-014) Am Fed Astrologers.

Doane, Gilbert H. & Bell, James B. Searching for Your Ancestors: The How & Why of Genealogy. 6th rev. ed. (Illus.). 352p. (C). 1992. pap. 19.95 (*0-8166-1990-5*) U of Minn Pr.

Doane, Gilbert H. & Doane, Gilbert J., eds. The Doane Family, Vol. 2. 587p. 1976. text 30.00 (*0-686-32800-0*) Doane Fam Assn.

Doane, Gilbert J., jt. ed. see Doane, Gilbert H.

Doane, Herbert. The Wit, Wisdom, Tall Tales & Philosophy of Herbert Doane: A 94-Year-Old Ozark Native. 144p. 1994. pap. write for info. (*1-884597-00-9*) Tinswac Pubng.

Doane, J. William, ed. Display Technologies in Russia, Ukraine, & Belarus. unabridged ed. LC 96-127655. (WTEC Panel Reports). (Illus.). 270p. (Orig.). 1994. pap. write for info. (*1-883712-36-X*) Intl Tech Res.

Doane, Janet & Doane, Rex. Almond Essence. (Illus.). 64p. (Orig.). 1997. pap. write for info. (*0-9649510-3-7*) Seed Pubng.

D

Doane, Janice & Hodges, Devon. From Klein to Kristeva: Psychoanalytic Feminism & the Search for the "Good Enough" Mother. LC 92-36505. (Critical Perspectives on Women & Gender Ser.). 112p. (C). 1993. pap. 14.95 (*0-472-06433-9*, 06433) U of Mich Pr.

— Nostalgia & Sexual Difference: The Resistance to Contemporary Feminism. 160p. 1987. 27.50 (*0-416-01531-X*, 1180); pap. 12.95 (*0-416-01541-7*, 1185) Routledge.

Doane, Janice L. Silence & Narrative: The Early Novels of Gertrude Stein, 62. LC 85-9854. (Contributions in Women's Studies: No. 62). 189p. 1986. 49.95 (*0-313-24936-9*, DSN/, Greenwood Pr) Greenwood.

Doane, Jeri A. & Diamond, Diana. Affect & Attachment in the Family: A Family-Based Treatment of Major Psychiatric Disorder. (Illus.). 224p. (C). 1998. text 30.00 (*0-7881-5278-5*) DIANE Pub.

Doane, Jim, Jr. Aerial America: From Sea to Shining Sea. (J). (ps-12). 1981. 2.95 (*0-936672-11-0*) Aerial Photo.

— America: An Aerial View. (J). (ps-12). 1986. 5.00 (*0-936672-01-3*) Aerial Photo.

Doane, Jim. North Carolina: From the Mountains to the Sea. LC 80-80955. 72p. (J). (ps-12). 1980. 3.50 (*0-936672-75-7*) Aerial Photo.

Doane, John F., jt. auth. see Probst, Louis E.

Doane, Mary A. The Desire to Desire: The Woman's Film of the 1940s. LC 85-45986. (Theories of Representation & Difference Ser.). (Illus.). 224p. 1987. 15.95 (*0-253-20433-X*, MB-433) Ind U Pr.

— Femmes Fatales. (Illus.). 320p. (C). (gr. 13). 1991. pap. 21.99 (*0-415-90320-3*, A4599) Routledge.

Doane, Michael. Bullet Heart. 448p. 1995. mass mkt. 6.99 (*0-425-15099-2*) Berkley Pub.

— Capturing the Whirlwind. LC 97-197718. (Illus.). 180p. 1997. pap. write for info. (*1-57579-030-0*) Pine Hill Pr.

— In the Path of the Whirlwind. 140p. 1996. reprint ed. pap. write for info. (*1-57579-028-9*) Pine Hill Pr.

— In the Path of the Whirlwind. 4th rev. ed. (Illus.). 140p. 1997. pap. write for info. (*1-57579-029-7*) Pine Hill Pr.

— SAP Blue Book: A Concise Business Guide to the World of SAP. rev. ed. LC 98-217258. (Illus.). 198p. 1998. pap. 24.95 (*1-57579-125-0*) Pine Hill Pr.

— The SAP Consultant Handbook. (Illus.). 268p. 1999. pap. 22.95 (*1-57579-150-1*) Pine Hill Pr.

Doane, Nancy L. Indian Doctor Book. 54p. (J). (ps-12). pap. text 2.95 (*0-936672-15-3*) Aerial Photo.

Doane, Randell C. & Doane, Rebecca G. Death & Taxes: The Complete Guide to Family Inheritence Planning. LC 98-23963. 320p. 1998. 28.95 (*0-8040-1010-2*); pap. 16.95 (*0-8040-1011-0*) Swallow.

Doane, Rebecca G., jt. auth. see Doane, Randell C.

Doane, Rex, jt. auth. see Doane, Janet.

Doane, Sharon. New Beginnings: A Creative Writing Guide for Women Who Have Left Abusive Partners. LC 96-13790. (New Leaf Ser.). 144p. (Orig.). 1996. pap. 10.95 (*1-878067-78-8*) Seal Pr WA.

Doane, T. W. Bible Myths & Their Parallels in Other Religions. 589p. 1996. pap. 32.00 (*0-7873-0290-2*) Hlth Research.

— Bible Myths & Their Parallels in Other Religions: Being a Comparison of the Old & New Testament Myths & Miracles with Those of Heathen Nations of Antiquity Considering Also Their Origin & Meaning, 2 vols. 7th ed. (Illus.). 1990. 50.00 (*0-936128-45-3*) De Young Pr.

— Bible Myths & Their Parallels in Other Religions (1882) 610p. 1996. reprint ed. pap. 30.00 (*1-56459-922-1*) Kessinger Pub.

Doanld, Ashurst, et al. Southern California Ordinal Scales of Development, Set. (Series in Six). 638p. 1985. 130.00 (*0-943292-16-6*) Foreworks.

Doanto, M. R. Philippine Cooking in America. 134p. 1991. 15.95 (*0-318-36299-6*) Asia Bk Corp.

Doare, H. Healthcare Card Systems. LC 95-79709. (Studies in Health Technology & Informatics). 218p. 1995. 70.00 (*90-5199-225-4*) IOS Press.

Doares, Robert G. Immanuel, God with Us: The Life of Christ in Art. LC 94-21921. (Illus.). 112p. 1994. 60.00 (*0-89107-792-8*) Crossway Bks.

Dobado, Antonio, et al. Effective Lagrangians for the Standard Model. Balian, R. et al, eds. LC 97-13124. (Texts & Monographs in Physics). (Illus.). xii, 335p. 1997. 57.00 (*3-540-62570-4*) Spr-Verlag.

Dobai, Johannes, jt. auth. see Novatny, Fritz.

Dobai, P. Budapest Photoguide. (Illus.). 64p. (C). 1988. 100.00 (*0-7855-6500-0*, Pub. by Collets) St Mut.

Dobak, William A. Fort Riley & Its Neighbors: Military Money & Economic Growth, 1853-1895. LC 98-13474. (Illus.). 264p. 1998. 29.95 (*0-8061-3071-7*) U of Okla Pr.

Dobard, Raymond G. & Tobin, Jacqueline L. Hidden in Plain View: The Secret Story of Quilts & the Underground Railroad. LC 98-49804. (Illus.). 224p. 1999. 27.50 (*0-385-49137-9*) Bantam.

Dobard, Raymond G., jt. auth. see Tobin, Jacqueline L.

Dobash, R. Emerson, et al, eds. Gender & Crime. 356p. 1995. pap. 27.95 (*0-7083-1301-9*) Paul & Co Pubs.

Dobash, R. Emerson & Dobash, Russell. Rethinking Violence Against Women. LC 98-9084. 276p. 1998. 57.95 (*0-7619-1186-3*); pap. 25.95 (*0-7619-1187-1*) Sage.

Dobash, R. Emerson & Dobash, Russell P. Violence Against Wives. LC 79-7181. 1983. pap. 16.95 (*0-02-907810-5*) Free Pr.

— Women, Violence & Social Change. 352p. (C). 1992. pap. 27.99 (*0-415-03610-0*, A6516) Routledge.

Dobash, R. Emerson & Wasoff, Fran. The Simulated Client: A Method for Studying Professionals Working with Clients. LC 96-83271. (Cariff Papers). 112p. (C). 1996. 58.95 (*1-85628-920-6*, Pub. by Avebry) Ashgate Pub Co.

Dobash, Russell, jt. auth. see Dobash, R. Emerson.

Dobash, Russell P., jt. auth. see Dobash, R. Emerson.

Dobb. Current Topics in Intensive Care, No. 1. 1994. pap. text 55.00 (*0-7020-1677-2*, W B Saunders Co) Harcrt Hlth Sci Grp.

***Dobb.** ISO 9000 Registration Step by Step. 2001. pap. 47.95 (*0-7506-4949-6*) Buttrwrth-Heinemann.

Dobb, A., jt. ed. see Williams, G. D.

Dobb, F. P. ISO 9000 Quality Registration Step By Step. 2nd ed. LC 99-11370. 1999. write for info. (*0-7506-4440-0*) Buttrwrth-Heinemann.

Dobb, Linda S. & Dick, Patrick. Human Resource Management for the Small Library. LC 93-20868. (Small Libraries Publications: No. 21). 1993. pap. 8.00 (*0-8389-5751-X*) ALA.

Dobb, Maurice. Russian Economic Development Since the Revolution. (Business Enterprises Reprint Ser.). xii, 415p. 1986. reprint ed. lib. bdg. 45.00 (*0-89941-502-4*, 304380) W S Hein.

Dobb, Maurice, ed. see Marx, Karl.

Dobb, Maurice H. Political Economy & Capitalism: Some Essays in Economic Tradition. LC 76-108389. 357p. (C). 1972. reprint ed. lib. bdg. 38.50 (*0-8371-3812-4*, DOPE, Greenwood Pr) Greenwood.

— Wages. LC 82-994. (Cambridge Economic Handbooks). (Illus.). 201p. 1982. reprint ed. lib. bdg. 55.00 (*0-313-23483-3*, DOWA, Greenwood Pr) Greenwood.

Dobb, Maurice H., ed. see Ricardo, David.

Dobbelaere, Karel, jt. auth. see Wilson, Bryan.

Dobbelaere, Karel, jt. auth. see Wilson, Bryan R.

Dobbels, William J. An Epistle of Comfort: Scriptural Meditations & Passage for Persons Suffering from AIDS. LC 90-60899. (Illus.). 150p. (Orig.). 1990. pap. 7.95 (*1-55612-364-7*) Sheed & Ward WI.

Dobber, Max C. Thalidomide: Index of New Information for Research, Reference & Therapy. 160p. 1998. 44.50 (*0-7883-1878-0*); pap. 39.50 (*0-7883-1879-9*) ABBE Pubs Assn.

Dobberpuhl, Daniel W., jt. auth. see Glasser, Lance A.

Dobberstein, Leroy A. Law & Gospel: Bad News, Good News. LC 96-67924. (People's Bible Teachings Ser.). 181 p. 1996. 9.99 (*0-8100-0612-X*) Northwest Pub.

Dobbert, Guido A. The Disintegration of an Immigrant Community: The Cincinnati Germans, 1870-1920. Cordasco, Francesco, ed. LC 80-853. (American Ethnic Groups Ser.). 1981. lib. bdg. 47.95 (*0-405-13416-9*) Ayer.

Dobberteen, Sara, ed. Eleventh Annual Exhibition: National Academy of Western Art, 1983. (Illus.). 80p. (Orig.). 1983. pap. 15.00 (*0-932154-13-1*) Natl Cowboy Hall of Fame.

— National Academy of Western Art: 13th Annual Exhibition. (Illus.). 93p. 1985. pap. 15.00 (*0-932154-16-6*) Natl Cowboy Hall of Fame.

— Twelfth Annual Exhibition: National Academy of Western Art, 1984. (Illus.). 100p. (Orig.). 1984. pap. 15.00 (*0-932154-14-X*) Natl Cowboy Hall of Fame.

***Dobbertin, John, Jr.** Gargoyle Laughs at the 20th Century: The University of Michigan Humor Magazine. (Illus.). 220p. 1999. pap. 24.99 (*0-9674238-0-5*) Percheron Inc.

Dobbertin, Richard F., jt. auth. see Hofstrand, Richard K.

Dobbie, jt. auth. see Krapp, George P.

Dobbie, A. M. & Litt, M. A. Comenius's Pampaedia. 216p. (C). 1988. 160.00 (*0-7212-0781-2*, Pub. by Regency Pr GBR) St Mut.

Dobbie-Bateman, A. F. & Krishnananda, Rama. The Spiritual Instructions of Saint Seraphim of Sarov: A Spirit-Baptizer in the Eastern Christian Church. rev. ed. LC 90-27069. (Basket of Tolerance Ser.). (Illus.). 200p. 1991. pap. 12.95 (*0-918801-25-7*) Dawn Horse Pr.

Dobbie, Elliot V., ed. The Anglo-Saxon Minor Poems. LC 43-1513. (Anglo-Saxon Poetic Records Ser.). 220p. 1942. text 54.00 (*0-231-08770-5*) Col U Pr.

Dobbie, Elliott V., ed. Beowulf & Judith. LC 53-13397. (Anglo-Saxon Poetic Records Ser.). 289p. 1953. text 57.50 (*0-231-08768-3*) Col U Pr.

Dobbie, Geraldine. Country Mouse. (Patchwork Mice Ser.). (J). 5.98 (*1-57717-108-X*) Todtri Prods.

— Farm Mouse. (Patchwork Mice Ser.). (J). 5.98 (*1-57717-111-X*) Todtri Prods.

— House Mouse. (Patchwork Mice Ser.). (J). 5.98 (*1-57717-109-8*) Todtri Prods.

— Town Mouse. (Patchwork Mice Ser.). 5.98 (*1-57717-110-1*) Todtri Prods.

Dobbin, Christine. Asian Entrepreneurial Minorities: Conjoint Communities in the Making of the World-Economy, 1570-1940. (NIAS Monographs in Asian Studies: No. 71). 240p. (C). 1996. text 45.00 (*0-7007-0404-3*, Pub. by Curzon Pr Ltd); pap. text 24.95 (*0-7007-0443-4*, Pub. by Curzon Pr Ltd) UH Pr.

Dobbin, Frank. Forging Industrial Policy: The United States, Britain & France in the Railway Age. LC 93-21458. 276p. (C). 1994. text 54.95 (*0-521-45121-3*) Cambridge U Pr.

— Forging Industrial Policy: The United States, Britain & France in the Railway Age. 276p. 1997. pap. text 19.95 (*0-521-62990-X*) Cambridge U Pr.

Dobbin, James D. The Jombee Dance of Montserrat: A Study of Trance Ritual in the West Indies. LC 85-10446. (Illus.). 210p. 1986. reprint ed. pap. 65.10 (*0-608-00914-8*, 206170800011) Bks Demand.

Dobbin, John. How to Take a Test: Doing Your Best. 120p. 1986. mass mkt. 5.95 (*0-446-38485-2*) Warner Bks.

Dobbin, Muriel. Going Public. 1991. 16.95 (*1-55972-062-X*, Birch Ln Pr) Carol Pub Group.

Dobbin, Murray. The Myth of the Good Corporate Citizen: Democracy under the Rule of Big Business. 320p. 1998. 23.95 (*0-7737-3087-7*) Stoddart Publ.

— Preston Manning & the Reform Party. 298p. 1992. mass mkt. 6.95 (*0-88780-161-7*, Pub. by Formac Publ Co) Formac Dist Ltd.

Dobbin, Robert, tr. see Fitterling, Thomas.

Dobbin, Robert, tr. see Wilson, Peter N.

Dobbin, Robert F., tr. Epictetus Bk. 1: Discourses. (Clarendon Later Ancient Philosophers Ser.). 280p. 1998. text 70.00 (*0-19-823664-6*) OUP.

Dobbing, J., ed. A Balanced Diet. (Illus.). 210p. 1988. 62.00 (*0-387-19527-0*) Spr-Verlag.

— Brain, Behaviour & Iron in the Infant Diet. 208p. 1990. 64.00 (*0-387-19605-6*) Spr-Verlag.

— Sweetness. (Illus.). 282p. 1987. 55.00 (*3-540-17045-6*, 170456) Spr-Verlag.

Dobbing, John, ed. Developing Brain & Behaviour: The Role of Lipids in Infant Formula. LC 97-44768. (Illus.). 544p. 1997. text 59.95 (*0-12-218870-5*) Morgan Kaufmann.

— Prevention of Spina Bifida & Other Neural Tube Defects. 1983. text 99.00 (*0-12-218860-8*) Acad Pr.

Dobbins, et al. Introduction to Observing & Photographing the Solar System. 1988. 24.95 (*0-943396-17-4*) Willmann-Bell.

Dobbins, Alan. Hoppin' for Joy: A Mystery Jigsaw Puzzle. 1998. 11.00 (*1-57561-094-9*) Bepuzzled.

Dobbins, Austin C. Milton & the Book of Revelation: The Heavenly Cycle. LC 73-22715. (Studies in the Humanities: No. 7). (Illus.). 176p. 1975. pap. 54.60 (*0-7837-8370-1*, 205918000009) Bks Demand.

Dobbins, Bill. The Women: Photographs of the Top Female Bodybuilders. LC 94-19145. (Illus.). 128p. 1994. 27.50 (*1-885183-01-1*) Artisan.

Dobbins, Bill, jt. auth. see Jenner, Bruce.

Dobbins, Bill, jt. auth. see Schwarzenegger, Arnold.

Dobbins, C. Richard. How to Screw the IRS. 160p. (Orig.). 1996. pap. 12.95 (*0-9650251-0-1*) Rustic Inn.

Dobbins, Carl J. Health Care Reform: Index of New Information with Authors, Subjects & References. 157p. 1997. 47.50 (*0-7883-1514-5*); pap. 44.50 (*0-7883-1515-3*) ABBE Pubs Assn.

***Dobbins, Charles J.** If Jesus Were a Sportswriter: Parables from Sports. 131p. 1999. pap. 11.95 (*0-7414-0313-7*) Buy Books.

***Dobbins, Craig.** Fingerpicking Gospel Solos Book/CD Set. 32p. 2000. 9.95 incl. audio compact disk (*0-7866-4798-1*) Mel Bay.

Dobbins, Dick. The Grand Minor League: An Oral History of the Old Pacific Coast League. Defendorf, Richard, ed. (Illus.). 304p. 1999. 32.95 (*0-942627-53-9*, Pub. by Woodford Pubng); pap. 27.95 (*0-942627-51-2*, Pub. by Woodford Pubng) Andrews & McMeel.

Dobbins, Dick & Twichell, Jon. Nuggets on the Diamond: Professional Baseball in the Bay Area from the Gold Rush to the Present. Rochmis, Jon, ed. LC 94-60296. (Illus.). 304p. (Orig.). 1994. 32.95 (*0-942627-00-8*); pap. 29.95 (*0-942627-01-6*) Woodford Pubng.

Dobbins, Durell C. The Rainbow: Teacher's Helper. pap., teacher ed. 19.95 (*0-9666578-1-0*, RTHv1.0) Begin Pub Hse.

Dobbins, Durell C. The Rainbow Science Curriculum. Bingham, Mark E., ed. (Illus.). vii, 347p. (J). (gr. 7-9). 1998. pap. text 50.00 (*0-9666578-0-2*, RT1) Begin Pub Hse.

Dobbins, Frank, ed. The Oxford Book of French Chansons. 322p. 1987. pap. text 19.95 (*0-19-343539-X*) OUP.

Dobbins, Gregory H., jt. auth. see Cardy, Robert L.

Dobbins, James T. & Boone, John M., eds. Medical Imaging, 1998: Physics of Medical Imaging. LC 98-227297. (Proceedings of SPIE Ser.: Vol. 3336). 856p. 1998. 132.00 (*0-8194-2781-0*) SPIE.

Dobbins, James T., jt. ed. see Boone, John M.

Dobbins, Joann H. Pineapple Gold. LC 83-90001. 304p. 1983. pap. 10.95 (*0-9610540-0-X*) J H Dobbins.

Dobbins, Norm, et al. Etched Glass: Techniques & Designs. (Illus.). 144p. 1998. 29.99 (*0-9658248-1-0*) GUILDcom.

Dobbins, Norman & Oxley, Debra F. Glass Etching: Surface Techniques & Designs. (Illus.). 96p. (Orig.). 1988. pap. 22.95 (*0-935133-23-2*) CKE Pubns.

Dobbins, Norman, jt. auth. see Oxley, Debra F.

Dobbins, Richard & Pettman, Barrie O. The Ultimate Entrepreneur's Book: The Straight-Talking Guide to Business Success & Personal Riches. 256p. 1998. pap. 19.95 (*1-900961-96-2*) Capstone Pub NH.

Dobbins, Richard, et al. Portfolio Theory & Investment Management: An Introduction to Modern Portfolio Theory. 2nd ed. 208p. 1994. pap. 37.95 (*0-631-19182-8*) Blackwell Pubs.

Dobbins, Richard A. Atmospheric Motion & Air Pollution: An Introduction for Students of Engineering & Science. LC 79-952. (Environmental Science & Technology Ser.). (Illus.). 343p. reprint ed. pap. 106.40 (*0-8357-5848-6*, 205660100078) Bks Demand.

***Dobbins, Richard D.** At the Table of the Lord. 205p. 1999. 14.95 (*1-890329-67-3*) Totally Alive.

Dobbins, Richard D. Bonds & Boundaries: In Your Relationship with God, Your Mate, & Your Children. (Illus.). 77p. 1989. pap. 15.00 (*1-890329-04-5*); pap., wbk. ed. 2.50 (*1-890329-05-3*) Totally Alive.

— A Christian Family or an American Family: Which Values Will You Choose? 28p. (Orig.). 1993. pap. 1.00 (*1-890329-12-6*) Totally Alive.

— From This Day Forward: Bride's Workbook. 1997. pap., wbk. ed. 2.50 (*1-890329-62-2*) Totally Alive.

— From This Day Forward: Groom's Workbook. 1997. pap., wbk. ed. 2.50 (*1-890329-63-0*) Totally Alive.

— From This Day Forward: Pastor's Guide for Re-Married - Re-Marrying Couples. 1997. pap. 15.00 (*1-890329-61-4*) Totally Alive.

— God's Man in Today's World: In the Church, Learning; in the Home, Loving; in the Community, Living. (Illus.). 144p. (Orig.). 1991. pap. 15.00 (*1-890329-00-2*) Totally Alive.

— God's Man in Today's World: In the Church...Learning, in the Home...Loving, in the Community...Living. (Illus.). 58p. 1991. pap., wbk. ed. 2.75 (*1-890329-01-0*) Totally Alive.

— Is There Life after Sell? 118p. 1980. pap. 5.00 (*1-890329-15-0*) Totally Alive.

— One World - Two Views. 17p. (Orig.). 1990. pap. 1.00 (*1-890329-13-4*) Totally Alive.

— Our Father Who Art on Earth. 19p. 1990. pap. 1.00 (*1-890329-10-X*) Totally Alive.

— Raising Healthy Children in a Sexually Sick World: Leader's Guide. (Illus.). 77p. 1987. pap., teacher ed. 15.00 (*1-890329-06-1*) Totally Alive.

— Raising Healthy Children in a Sexually Sick World: Parents' Guide. (Illus.). 67p. 1987. reprint ed. pap. 2.95 (*1-890329-07-X*) Totally Alive.

— Venturing into a Child's World. 2nd ed. 189p. 1992. pap. 8.00 (*1-890329-08-8*) Totally Alive.

— When Two Become One: Leader Guide - Pre-Marital Counseling. 1998. pap., teacher ed. 17.00 (*1-890329-64-9*) Totally Alive.

— When Two Become One: Pre-Marital Counseling Series - Workbook for Bride. 1998. pap., wbk. ed. 2.50 (*1-890329-65-7*) Totally Alive.

— When Two Become One: Pre-Marital Counseling Series - Workbook for (Groom) 1998. pap., wbk. ed. 2.50 (*1-890329-66-5*) Totally Alive.

— Your Family Is Your Fortune. 15p. (Orig.). 1989. pap. 1.00 (*1-890329-09-6*) Totally Alive.

— Your Feelings . . . Friend or Foe? Biblical Guidelines for Managing Your Emotions. (Illus.). 1993. pap. 14.95 (*1-890329-02-9*) Totally Alive.

— Your Feelings . . . Friend or Foe? Biblical Guidelines for Managing Your Emotions. 201p. 1994. pap. 14.95 (*1-890329-03-7*) Totally Alive.

Dobbins, Richard D. & Dobbins, Sharon K. What Every Pastor Should Know . . . How to Protect the Children & Keep the Church Out of Court. 18p. (Orig.). 1988. pap. 3.00 (*1-890329-11-8*) Totally Alive.

Dobbins, Rosie E. A Rose in Solitude: A Poetic Anthology. 45p. 1998. spiral bd. 21.95 (*0-9663552-0-2*) Jamarda NC.

Dobbins, Sharon K., jt. auth. see Dobbins, Richard D.

Dobbins, W. O. Diagnostic Pathology of the Intestinal Mucosa. (Illus.). x, 217p. 1989. 189.00 (*0-387-97059-2*, 3051) Spr-Verlag.

Dobbs-Allsopp, F. W. Weep, O Daughter of Zion: A Study of the City-Lament Genre in the Hebrew Bible. LC 93-156074. (Biblica et Orientalia Ser.). xiv, 228p. 1993. write for info. (*88-7653-346-X*) Biblical Inst Pr.

Dobbs, Annie C. Dictionnaire Abrege du Surrealisme. (FRE.). pap. 39.95 (*0-7859-0756-4*, M-6165) Fr & Eur.

Dobbs, Betty J. The Janus Faces of Genius: The Role of Alchemy in Newton's Thought. (Illus.). 373p. (C). 1992. text 54.95 (*0-521-38084-7*) Cambridge U Pr.

Dobbs, Betty J. T., jt. auth. see Jacob, Margaret C.

Dobbs, Betty Jo, et al. Newton & the Culture of Newtonianism. LC 98-52947. 1998. write for info. (*1-57392-545-4*) Prometheus Bks.

Dobbs, Carrie. Reading for a Reason. 283p. (C). 1989. pap. text 30.47 (*0-13-761123-4*) P-H.

Dobbs, Carrie & Dobbs, Frank. Good Reasons for Reading: A Basic Course. LC 93-46926. 208p. (C). 1994. pap. text 30.47 (*0-13-630963-1*) Prentice ESL.

Dobbs, Carrie S. More Reasons for Reading. 304p. (C). 1992. pap. text 30.47 (*0-13-594433-3*) P-H.

Dobbs, Charles M. The United States & East Asia since 1945. LC 90-20213. (Studies in American History: Vol. 5). 248p. 1991. lib. bdg. 89.95 (*0-88946-505-3*) E Mellen.

— The Unwanted Symbol: American Foreign Policy, the Cold War & Korea, 1945-1950. LC 81-6261. 253p. reprint ed. pap. 78.50 (*0-608-17819-5*, 203248200079) Bks Demand.

Dobbs, Dan B. Hornbook on Remedies. 2nd ed. (Hornbook Ser.). 972p. (C). 1993. 43.50 (*0-314-01123-4*) West Pub.

— Law of Remedies, 3 vols. 2nd ed. 1992. write for info. (*0-318-69573-1*) West Pub.

— Teacher's Manual to Accompany Torts & Compensation. 2nd ed. (American Casebook Ser.). 1050p. 1993. pap. text. write for info. (*0-314-02651-7*) West Pub.

— Torts & Compensation: Personal Accountability & Social Responsibility. 2nd ed. (American Casebook Ser.). 1082p. 1993. 50.50 (*0-314-02224-4*) West Pub.

Dobbs, Dan B. & Hayden, Paul T. Torts & Compensation: Person Accountability & Social Responsibility for Injury. 2nd ed. LC 97-6302. (Paralegal). 1005p. (C). 1997. text 44.50 (*0-314-21111-X*) West Pub.

— Torts & Compensation: Personal Accountability & Social Responsibility. 3rd ed. (American Casebook Ser.). 1030p. 1997. pap. text. write for info. (*0-314-22583-8*) West Pub.

Dobbs, Dan B. & Kavanagh, Kathleen. Problems in Remedies. 2nd ed. (American Casebook Ser.). 218p. (C). 1993. pap. 20.50 (*0-314-02619-3*) West Pub.

— Remedies Teacher's Manual to Accompany Problems In. 2nd ed. (American Casebook Ser.). 311p. 1993. pap. text. write for info. (*0-314-02793-9*) West Pub.

Dobbs, Darris & Fleming, Bill. TrueSpace 3 & 4: Creature Creations. (Illus.). 399p. 1999. pap. 49.95 (*1-886801-80-0*) Chrles River Media.

***Dobbs, David.** The Great Gulf: Fishermen, Scientists & the Struggle to Revive the World's Greatest Fishery. 256p. 2000. 24.95 (*1-55963-663-7*, Shearwater Bks) Island Pr.

— Professional Metadata: With DTDs, XML Schemas, Topic Maps, RDF, WebDav, XML Servers. 1000p. 2000. pap. 59.99 (*1-86100-451-6*) Wrox Pr Inc.

Dobbs, David & Hanks, Robert. A Modern Course on the Theory of Equations. 2nd ed. LC 92-7178. (Illus.). 263p. (C). 1992. 25.00 (*0-936428-14-7*) Polygonal Pub.

Dobbs, David & Ober, Richard. The Northern Forest. 288p. 1996. pap. 19.95 (*0-930031-81-4*) Chelsea Green Pub.

***Dobbs, David E., ed.** Advances in Commutative Ring Theory: Proceedings International Conference on Commutative Ring Theory. 3rd ed. LC 99-18800. (Lecture Notes in Pure & Applied Mathematics: Vol. 205). (Illus.). 576p. 1999. pap. text 195.00 (*0-8247-7147-8*) Dekker.

Dobbs, David E. & Peterson, John C. Precalculus. 720p. (C). 1992. text 56.25 (*0-697-16235-4*, WCB McGr Hill) McGrw-H Hghr Educ.

— Precalculus. 720p. (C). 1993. text, student ed. 21.88 (*0-697-16289-3*, WCB McGr Hill) McGrw-H Hghr Educ.

Dobbs, David E., jt. ed. see Anderson, David F.

Dobbs, E. R. Electricity & Magnetism. (Student Physics Ser.). (Illus.). 128p. 1984. pap. 11.95 (*0-7102-0157-5*, Routledge Thoemms) Routledge.

— Solid Helium Three. (Illus.). 222p. 1994. text 69.00 (*0-19-851382-8*) OUP.

Dobbs, Farrell. Counter-Mobilization: A Strategy to Fight Racist & Fascist Attacks. 23p. pap. 5.00 (*0-87348-675-7*) Pathfinder NY.

— Revolutionary Continuity: Birth of the Communist Movement, 1918-1922, Vol. 2. Barnes, Jack, ed. LC 80-84850. 240p. 1983. pap. 16.95 (*0-913460-93-1*); lib. bdg. 50.00 (*0-913460-92-3*) Pathfinder NY.

— Revolutionary Continuity: Birth of the Communist Movement, 1918-22. 1998. pap. 18.95 (*0-87348-842-3*) Pathfinder NY.

— Revolutionary Continuity Vol. 1: Marxist Leadership in the U. S., 1848-1917. LC 80-84850. 220p. 1980. pap. 16.95 (*0-913460-84-2*); lib. bdg. 50.00 (*0-913460-85-0*) Pathfinder NY.

— Teamster Bureaucracy. LC 76-52771. (Illus.). 304p. 1977. reprint ed. pap. 18.95 (*0-913460-53-2*); reprint ed. lib. bdg. 55.00 (*0-913460-52-4*) Pathfinder NY.

***Dobbs, Farrell.** Teamster Politics. 256p. 2000. pap. 18.95 (*0-87348-862-8*) Pathfinder NY.

Dobbs, Farrell. Teamster Politics. LC 75-17324. (Illus.). 256p. 1975. reprint ed. lib. bdg. 50.00 (*0-913460-38-9*) Pathfinder NY.

— Teamster Power. LC 73-78115. 255p. 1973. reprint ed. lib. bdg. 50.00 (*0-913460-20-6*) Pathfinder NY.

An Asterisk (*) at the beginning of an entry indicates that the title is appearing for the first time.

— Teamster Power. LC 73-78115. 255p. (ps up). 1973. reprint ed. pap. 17.95 (*0-87348-861-X*) Pathfinder NY.
— Teamster Rebellion. pap. 16.95 (*0-87348-845-8*) Pathfinder NY.
— Teamster Rebellion. LC 78-186690. (Illus.). 192p. 1972. reprint ed. lib. bdg. 45.00 (*0-913460-02-8*) Pathfinder NY.
— Teamster Rebellion. LC 78-186690. (Illus.). 218p. 1972. reprint ed. pap. 16.95 (*0-913460-03-6*) Pathfinder NY.
Dobbs, Farrell, jt. auth. see Hansen, Beatrice.
Dobbs, Frank, jt. auth. see Dobbs, Carrie.
Dobbs, Frank Q., jt. auth. see Pirtle, Caleb, III.
Dobbs, Frank Q., jt. auth. see Pirtle, Caleb.
Dobbs, Happy. Spiritual Being: A User's Guide. (Illus.). 200p. (Orig.). 1997. pap. 18.95 (*0-85398-415-8*) G Ronald Pub.
Dobbs, Holly J. Tales of Wonder. LC 93-16083. (Timeless Tales Ser.). (J). 1993. audio 10.00 (*0-88336-524-3*) New Readers.
— Tales of Wonder: Reading Level 2-3. LC 93-16083. (Timeless Tales Ser.). 48p. (J). 1993. 4.95 (*0-88336-459-X*) New Readers.
Dobbs, Horace. Journey into Dolphin Dreamtime. large type ed. (Illus.). 1995. 27.99 (*0-7089-3292-4*) Ulverscroft.
— Tale of Two Dolphins. large type ed. (Illus.). 352p. 1988. 27.99 (*0-7089-1757-7*) Ulverscroft.
Dobbs, Hugh J. History of Gage County: Narrative of the Past, with Special Emphasis upon the Pioneer Period of the County's History, Its Social...& Civic Development from the Early Days to the Present Time. (Illus.). 1100p. 1997. reprint ed. lib. bdg. 105.00 (*0-8328-6867-1*) Higginson Bk Co.
***Dobbs, Ian M.** Managerial Economics. LC 99-24058. 1999. write for info. (*0-19-877571-7*); write for info. (*0-19-877570-9*) OUP.
Dobbs, Jane & Barrett, Ann. Practical Radiotherapy Planning. 2nd ed. 320p. 1992. pap. text 48.00 (*0-340-54557-7*, Pub. by E A) OUP.
Dobbs, Jeannine, et al. Three Some Poems. LC 75-23819. 88p. 1976. pap. 3.95 (*0-914086-11-1*) Alice James Bks.
Dobbs, Joannie, et al. Computer Nutrient Analysis Handbook for Food Culinary & Health Professionals. (Methods in Nutrition Research Ser.). 1998. 79.95 (*0-8493-9613-1*, 9613) CRC Pr.
***Dobbs, John, ed.** Recollections of an Old 52nd Man. 112p. 2000. 80.00 (*1-86227-093-7*, Pub. by Spellmnt Pubs) St Mut.
Dobbs, K. The Eleventh Hour. LC 97-204468. 1997. 12.95 (*0-88962-637-5*, 734080Q) Mosaic.
Dobbs, Katy. My First Gamebook. LC 85-40524. (My First Bks.). (Illus.). 16p. (J). (ps-3). 1985. pap. 5.95 (*0-89480-945-8*, 945) Workman Pub.
Dobbs, L., et al. Road Traffic Law: A Practical Guide. (Waterlow Criminal Law Guides Ser.). (Illus.). 288p. 1990. pap. 60.00 (*0-08-036916-2*) Macmillan.
— Road Traffic Statutes. (Waterlow Criminal Law Guides Ser.). 1990. pap. 70.00 (*0-08-040132-5*) Macmillan.
Dobbs, Larry & Farr, Donald N. How to Restore Your Mustang. (Illus.). 148p. (Orig.). 1991. reprint ed. pap. 14.95 (*0-9624908-4-9*) CA Mustang Sales.
Dobbs, Larry, et al. Mustang Recognition Guide, 1965-1973. rev. ed. (Illus.). 226p. 1989. pap. 16.95 (*0-685-59726-1*) CA Mustang Sales.
***Dobbs, Liz & Wood, Sarah.** Garden Makeovers: The Complete Guide to Reviving & Replenishing Your Garden. LC 99-89107. (Illus.). 224p. (gr. 8). 2000. 29.95 (*0-7370-0609-9*) Time-Life.
Dobbs, Marian F., et al. Determining Child & Spousal Support. (Family Law Ser.). 1995. ring bd. write for info. (*0-318-42404-5*) West Group.
Dobbs, Michael. Buddha of Brewer Street. 1997. 27.00 (*0-00-225412-3*) Collins SF.
***Dobbs, Michael.** Buddha of Brewer Street. 1998. mass mkt. 13.95 (*0-00-649798-5*, Pub. by HarpC) Trafalgar.
Dobbs, Michael. Down with Big Brother: The Fall of the Soviet Empire. 502p. 30.00 (*0-614-26978-4*) Knopf.
— Down with Big Brother: The Fall of the Soviet Empire. 1998. pap. 16.00 (*0-679-75151-3*) Vin Bks.
***Dobbs, Michael.** Madeleine Albright: A Twentieth-Century Odussey, Vol. 1. 2000. pap. 16.00 (*0-8050-5660-2*, Owl) H Holt & Co.
Dobbs, Michael. Madeleine Albright: Against All Odds. LC 98-53592. (Illus.). 464p. 1999. 27.50 (*0-8050-5659-9*) H Holt & Co.
— Wall Games. large type ed. 1991. 27.99 (*0-7089-2551-0*) Ulverscroft.
Dobbs, Rix. UFOs: Aliens among Us. LC 96-86379. 1996. mass mkt., per. 12.95 (*1-889131-09-1*) CasAnanda.
Dobbs, Roland. Electromagnetic Waves. (Student Physics Ser.). (Illus.). 128p. (Orig.). 1985. pap. 13.95 (*0-7102-0506-6*, Routledge Thoemms) Routledge.
Dobbs, Stephen M. Learning in & Through Art: A Guide to Discipline-Based Art Education. LC 97-31849. 160p. 1998. pap. 20.00 (*0-89236-494-7*, Pub. by J P Getty Trust) OUP.
Dobbs, Stephen M., jt. auth. see Nanus, Burt.
Dobbs, Steve. Oklahoma Gardener's Guide: The What, Where, When, How & Why of Gardening in Oklahoma. LC 99-39389. (Illus.). 424p. 1999. pap. 19.95 (*1-888608-56-0*) Cool Springs Pr.
Dobbs, Thomas L. Enhancing Agricultural Sustainability Through Changes in Federal Commodity Policy: Marginal Versus Radical Change. (Policy Studies Program Report: No. 2). 35p. 1993. pap. 6.00 (*1-893182-05-3*) H A Wallace Inst.
Dobbs, Verne L. Delicious & Delitefull: Lowfat Cooking with Kentucky Author Verne Louise Dobbs. LC 98-85090. (Illus.). 256p. 1998. pap. 15.95 (*0-913383-61-9*, Commwlth Bk Co) McClanahan Pub.
Dobbs-Weinstein, Idit. Maimonides & St. Thomas on the Limits of Reason. LC 94-3369. (SUNY Series in Philosophy). 278p. (C). 1995. text 64.50 (*0-7914-2415-4*); pap. text 21.95 (*0-7914-2416-2*) State U NY Pr.
Dobbs, Zygmund. Keynes at Harvard. enl. rev. ed. 3.75 (*0-685-46997-2*) Veritas.
Dobby, G. S., jt. auth. see Finch, J. A.
Dobbyn, John F. Injunctions in a Nutshell. (Nutshell Ser.). 264p. (C). 1974. reprint ed. pap. 21.00 (*0-314-28423-0*) West Pub.
— Insurance Law in a Nutshell 3E. 3rd ed. LC 95-25324. (Paralegal). 400p. (C). 1996. pap. text 18.00 (*0-314-06651-9*) West Pub.
Dobek, Mariusz M. The Political Logic of Privatization: Lessons from Great Britain & Poland. LC 93-6770. 184p. 1993. 55.00 (*0-275-94618-5*, C4618, Praeger Pubs) Greenwood.
Dobek, Sandra & Ranschaert, Ryan. Modeling for AutoCAD Designer. LC 95-43381. 256p. (C). 1996. text 22.75 (*0-256-21376-3*, Irwn McGrw-H) McGrw-H Hghr Educ.
Dobel, Heinrich, jt. auth. see Bertali, Antonio.
Dobel, J. Patrick. Compromise & Political Action: Political Morality in Liberal & Democratic Life. LC 88-25953. 224p. (C). 1990. lib. bdg. 58.50 (*0-8476-7604-8*) Rowman.
— Public Integrity. LC 99-21569. 288p. 1999. 38.00 (*0-8018-5930-1*) Johns Hopkins.
Dobelbower, Ralph R., Jr. & Abe, Mitsuyuki, eds. Intraoperative Radiation Therapy. 384p. 1989. lib. bdg. 210.00 (*0-8493-6846-4*, RD652) CRC Pr.
Dobelis, M. C. Anonymous & Pseudononymous Publications of Twentieth Century Authors. 16.95 (*0-918230-06-3*) Barnstable.
— Bridging the Gap Between Computer Technicians & Users. (Illus.). 1976. reprint ed. pap. 0.50 (*0-918230-05-5*) Barnstable.
— The Three-Day Week-Offshoot of an EDP Operation. (Illus.). 1976. reprint ed. pap. 0.50 (*0-918230-04-7*) Barnstable.
Dobell, Bertram, ed. see Shelley, Percy Bysshe.
Dobell, Brandon. Quik-Ref Business Reference Guide. Dobell, Christopher & Dobell, Charmian, eds. 112p. (Orig.). (C). 1996. pap. 7.49 (*1-889904-00-7*) D&D Designs.
Dobell, Brandon, ed. see Dobell, Christopher.
Dobell, Charmian, ed. see Dobell, Brandon.
Dobell, Charmian, ed. see Dobell, Christopher.
Dobell, Christopher. Quik-Ref Science Reference Guide. Dobell, Brandon & Dobell, Charmian, eds. 64p. (Orig.). 1996. pap. 6.49 (*1-889904-01-5*) D&D Designs.
Dobell, Christopher, ed. see Dobell, Brandon.
Dobell, Peter. Travels in Kamtchatka & Siberia: With a Narrative of a Residence in China. LC 78-115529. (Russia Observed Ser., No. 1). 1970. reprint ed. 36.95 (*0-405-03021-5*) Ayer.
Dobell, Rod & Neufeld, Michael, eds. Learning for Life: Education for an Economically Competitive & Socially Responsible North America. 134p. 1992. pap. text 10.95 (*0-88982-123-2*, Pub. by Oolichan Bks) Genl Dist Srvs.
— Trans-Border Citizens: Networks & New Institutions in North America. 160p. 1994. pap. text 10.95 (*0-88982-142-9*, Pub. by Oolichan Bks) Genl Dist Srvs.
Dobell, Rodney, jt. ed. see Cutt, James.
Dobell, Steve, compiled by. The Seven Deadly Sins: A Wicked Anthology of Wit & Wisdom. (Illus.). 96p. 1998. 11.95 (*1-86205-073-2*, Pub. by Pavilion Bks Ltd) Trafalgar.
Dobelstein, Andrew W. Moral Authority, Ideology & the Future of American Social Welfare. LC 98-29480. 304p. 1998. text 79.00 (*0-8133-3311-3*, Pub. by Westview); pap. text 29.00 (*0-8133-3312-1*, Pub. by Westview) HarpC.
— Social Welfare: Policy & Analysis. 2nd ed. LC 96-4578. (Illus.). (Orig.). 1996. pap. text 42.95 (*0-8304-1428-2*) Thomson Learn.
Dobenik. Dictionary Marine Technique: English - French, French - English. (ENG & FRE.). lib. bdg. 195.00 (*0-8288-2490-8*, F34890) Fr & Eur.
Dobenik, R. & Hartline, G. French-English - English-French Dictionary of Naval Technology. (Illus.). 688p. 1989. 95.00 (*2-85608-031-6*) IBD Ltd.
Dobenik, R., jt. auth. see Brasseur, B.
Dober, Richard P. Campus Architecture: Building in the Groves of Academe. (Illus.). 258p. 1996. 69.95 (*0-07-017185-8*) McGraw.
***Dober, Richard P.** The Campus Landscape: Functions, Forms & Features. LC 99-56351. 288p. 2000. 64.95 (*0-471-35356-6*) Wiley.
Dober, Richard P. Campus Planning. (Illus.). 316p. (C). 1996. reprint ed. pap. text 50.00 (*0-9601608-1-7*) Soc Coll & Univ Planning.
Dobereiner, Peter. Dobereiner on Golf. (Illus.). 1998. 14.95 (*1-85410-589-2*, Pub. by Aurum Pr) London Brdge.
— Golf a la Carte. LC 98-16192. (Illus.). 224p. 1998. pap. 14.95 (*1-58080-058-0*) Burford Bks.
— I'll Be Deemed! (Illus.). 128p. 1997. pap. 14.95 (*1-85410-439-X*, Pub. by Aurum Pr) London Brdge.
Doberkat, E. E. Stochastic Automata: Stability, Nondeterminism, & Prediction. (Lecture Notes in Computer Science Ser.: Vol. 113). 135p. 1981. 20.00 (*0-387-10835-1*) Spr-Verlag.
Doberman, C. Dictionary of Aquatic Sports. (ENG & GER.). 875p. 1987. 150.00 (*0-8288-7701-7*, F26730) Fr & Eur.
***Doberneck, B.** Travel Journals. (Illus.). 1998. text 22.50 (*1-55670-839-4*) Stewart Tabori & Chang.
Doberneck, Elizabeth. Divinations: A Fortune-Telling Journal. (Illus.). 176p. 1997. 17.95 (*1-55670-566-2*) Stewart Tabori & Chang.
Doberstein, ed. The Notebook of a Colonial Clergyman. Tappert, tr. 1998. pap. 16.00 (*0-8006-3148-X*, Fortress Pr) Augsburg Fortress.
Doberstein, Dick. Communication Made Easy for Pilots. (Illus.). 98p. 1976. pap. text 8.95 (*0-9607866-2-7*) Simplified Reg.
— Regulations Made Easy for Private Pilots. pap. text 8.95 (*0-9607866-4-3*) Simplified Reg.
Doberstein, John W., ed. Minister's Prayer Book: An Order of Prayers & Readings. LC 85-16212. 512p. 1986. 22.00 (*0-8006-0760-0*, 1-760, Fortress Pr) Augsburg Fortress.
Doberstein, John W., jt. ed. see Lehmann, Helmut T.
Doberstein, John W., tr. see Schubert, Kurt.
Doberstein, John W., tr. see Thielicke, Helmut.
Doberstein, John W., tr. & intro. see Bonhoeffer, Dietrich.
Dobert, Raymond. Gene Expression in Cereal Crops: Bibliography: 1992-May 1994. 108p. (Orig.). (C). 1996. pap. text 35.00 (*0-7881-2737-3*) DIANE Pub.
— Herbicide Tolerance/Resistance in Plants: Bibliography: April 1991-March 1994. 113p. (Orig.). (C). 1996. pap. text 35.00 (*0-7881-2733-0*) DIANE Pub.
— Transgenic Animals: Bibliography January 1991-February 1994. 56p. (Orig.). (C). 1996. pap. text 30.00 (*0-7881-2804-3*) DIANE Pub.
— Viral Resistance in Plants - Viral Coat Proteins: Bibliography: January, 1991-July, 1996. 64p. (Orig.). (C). 1997. pap. text 25.00 (*0-7881-3872-3*) DIANE Pub.
Dobert, Raymond, ed. Biotechnology: Education & Training: a Bibliography. 44p. 1998. reprint ed. pap. text 20.00 (*0-7881-3865-0*) DIANE Pub.
— Biotechnology - Risk Assessment: Bibliography, January 1992-September 1995. 45p. (Orig.). 1996. pap. text 25.00 (*0-7881-3415-9*) DIANE Pub.
Dobert, Raymond & Guenther, Kim. Biotechnology: Ti-Plasmids & Other Plan Vectors: Bibliography January 1993-June 1994. 74p. (Orig.). (C). 1996. pap. text 35.00 (*0-7881-2808-6*) DIANE Pub.
Dobert, Raymond, jt. auth. see Guenther, Kim.
Dobert, Raymond, jt. auth. see Leonard, Scott A.
Dobert, Raymond, jt. ed. see Cabirac, Daniel.
Dobesch, Gerhard. Vom Aussern Proletariat Zum Kulturtrager Ein Aspekt Zur Rolle der Germanen in der Spantantike. (GER.). 141p. 1994. pap. 54.00 (*90-256-1039-0*, Pub. by AM Hakkert) BookLink Distributors.
Dobesh, Martina. Call from the Heart: A Woman's Journey Through Spiritual Awakening. LC 96-68848. (Illus.). 320p. 1996. pap. 14.95 (*0-9644950-0-7*) Rdiant Lght Pubns.
Dobey, Daniel C., et al. Essentials of Elementary Science. 2nd ed. LC 98-17348. 194p. 1998. pap. text 27.00 (*0-205-28365-9*) Allyn.
Dobhal, G. L. Development of the Hill Areas. 1987. 27.00 (*0-8364-2242-2*, Pub. by Concept) S Asia.
Dobias, B., et al. New Developments, Vol. 56. (Structure & Bonding Ser.). (Illus.). 160p. 1984. 66.95 (*0-387-13106-X*) Spr-Verlag.
Dobias, Bohuslav. Coagulation & Flocculation. (Surfactant Science Ser.: Vol. 47). (Illus.). 720p. 1993. text 260.00 (*0-8247-8797-8*) Dekker.
Dobias, Bohuslav & Von Rybinski, Wolfgang. Solid/Liquid Dispersions. LC 99-18799. (Surfactant Science Ser.). (Illus.). 576p. (C). 1999. text 195.00 (*0-8247-0014-7*) Dekker.
***Dobic, Mina.** My Beautiful Life: How Macrobiotics Brought Me from Cancer to Radiant Health. LC 99-67783. (Illus.). 198p. 2000. pap. 15.95 (*1-899171-13-4*, Pub. by Findhorn Pr) Words Distrib.
Dobie. Medical-Legal Evaluation of Hearing Loss. 2nd ed. 2001. pap. 61.50 (*0-7693-0052-9*) Singular Publishing.
Dobie, Ann B., ed. Something in Common: Contemporary Louisiana Stories. LC 90-20232. 302p. 1991. 19.95 (*0-8071-1644-0*) La State U Pr.
— Uncommonplace: An Anthology of Contemporary Louisiana Poets. LC 97-46685. 264p. 1998. pap. 19.95 (*0-8071-2255-6*); text 32.50 (*0-8071-2254-8*) La State U Pr.
Dobie, Bruce, ed. see Richardson, R. T.
Dobie, Charles C. San Francisco, a Pageant. 1992. reprint ed. lib. bdg. 75.00 (*0-7812-5026-9*) Rprt Serv.
— San Francisco Adventures. LC 70-101800. (Short Story Index Reprint Ser.). 1977. 19.95 (*0-8369-3188-2*) Ayer.
Dobie, Duncan. Georgia's Greatest Whitetails. 2nd ed. LC 86-70614. (Illus.). 464p. (YA). (gr. 8 up). 1985. 25.00 (*0-939801-00-0*) Bucksnort.
— If You've Ever Seen a Rhinoceros Charge. LC 93-74574. (Illus.). 40p. (J). (gr. 1 up). 1994. 15.95 (*0-939801-02-7*) Bucksnort.
— White Tales & Other Hunting Stories. (Illus.). 229p. (YA). (gr. 8 up). 1989. 15.95 (*0-939801-01-9*) Bucksnort.
Dobie, Edith. Malta's Road to Independence. LC 67-15591. 308p. reprint ed. pap. 95.50 (*0-8357-9733-3*, 201621000002) Bks Demand.
Dobie, J. Frank. Apache Gold & Yaqui Silver. (Illus.). 380p. 1985. reprint ed. pap. 15.95 (*0-292-70381-3*) U of Tex Pr.
— Ben Lilly Legend. 249p. Date not set. 22.95 (*0-8488-2583-7*) Amereon Ltd.
— The Ben Lilly Legend. 253p. (C). 1981. pap. 12.95 (*0-292-70728-2*) U of Tex Pr.
— Coronado's Children. 1993. reprint ed. lib. bdg. 75.00 (*0-7812-5927-4*) Rprt Serv.
— Coronado's Children: Tales of Lost Mines & Buried Treasures of the Southwest. (Barker Texas History Center Ser.: No. 3). (Illus.). 351p. 1978. reprint ed. pap. 12.95 (*0-292-71052-6*) U of Tex Pr.
— Cow People. (Illus.). 317p. (C). 1981. reprint ed. pap. 14.95 (*0-292-71060-7*) U of Tex Pr.
— Flavor of Texas. 1993. reprint ed. lib. bdg. 75.00 (*0-7812-5965-7*) Rprt Serv.
— Guide to Life & Literature of the Southwest: Revised & Enlarged in Both Knowledge & Wisdom. LC 52-11834. (Illus.). 232p. 1981. reprint ed. 15.95 (*0-87074-036-9*); reprint ed. pap. 9.95 (*0-87074-037-7*) SMU Press.
— I'll Tell You a Tale. 1960. 15.95 (*0-316-18794-1*) Little.
— I'll Tell You a Tale: An Anthology. (Illus.). 378p. 1981. reprint ed. pap. 14.95 (*0-292-73821-8*) U of Tex Pr.
— John C. Duval: First Texas Man of Letters: His Life & Some of His Unpublished Writings. LC 40-5152. (Illus.). 108p. 1965. reprint ed. 12.95 (*0-87074-038-5*) SMU Press.
— Legends of Texas. 1993. reprint ed. lib. bdg. 75.00 (*0-7812-5875-8*) Rprt Serv.
— Legends of Texas Vol. I: Lost Mines & Buried Treasure. LC 91-32367. 208p. 1992. reprint ed. pap. 4.95 (*0-88289-909-0*) Pelican.
***Dobie, J Frank.** Longhorns. 1999. 9.99 (*0-7858-1130-3*) Book Sales.
Dobie, J. Frank. The Longhorns. LC 79-67706. (Illus.). 440p. 1980. reprint ed. pap. 16.95 (*0-292-74627-X*) U of Tex Pr.
***Dobie, J Frank.** Mustangs. 1999. 9.99 (*0-7858-1131-1*) Book Sales.
Dobie, J. Frank. The Mustangs. (Illus.). 392p. 1984. reprint ed. pap. 14.95 (*0-292-75081-1*) U of Tex Pr.
— Rattlesnakes. 207p. 1982. pap. 12.95 (*0-292-77023-5*) U of Tex Pr.
***Dobie, J Frank.** Tales of Old-Time Texas. 1999. 9.99 (*0-7858-1132-X*) Book Sales.
Dobie, J. Frank. Tales of Old-Time Texas. (Illus.). 350p. 1984. reprint ed. pap. 12.95 (*0-292-78069-9*) U of Tex Pr.
— Vaquero of the Brush Country. 1993. reprint ed. lib. bdg. 75.00 (*0-7812-5926-6*) Rprt Serv.
Dobie, J. Frank. The Voice of the Coyote. LC 49-8879. (Illus.). xx, 386p. 1961. pap. 16.95 (*0-8032-5050-9*, Bison Books) U of Nebr Pr.
Dobie, J. Frank, ed. Coffee in the Gourd. (Texas Folklore Society Publications: No. 2). (Illus.). 110p. 1969. reprint ed. 11.95 (*0-87074-039-3*) UNTX Pr.
— Legends of Texas, Vol. 2: Pirates Gold & Other Tales. 208p. 1995. pap. 4.95 (*1-56554-073-5*) Pelican.
— Man, Bird, & Beast. LC 33-1132. (Texas Folklore Society Publications: No. 8). (Illus.). 185p. 1965. reprint ed. 12.95 (*0-87074-131-4*) UNTX Pr.
— Southwestern Lore. LC 33-1134. (Texas Folklore Society Publications: No. 9). (Illus.). 208p. 1965. reprint ed. 12.95 (*0-87074-042-3*) UNTX Pr.
— Spur-of-the-Cock. LC 34-1434. (Texas Folklore Society Publications: No. 11). 112p. 1965. reprint ed. 11.95 (*0-87074-043-1*) UNTX Pr.
— Texas & Southwestern Lore. LC 33-1131. (Texas Folklore Society Publications: No. 6). 259p. 1982. reprint ed. 13.95 (*0-87074-044-X*) UNTX Pr.
— Tone the Bell Easy. LC 33-1135. (Texas Folklore Society Publications: No. 10). (Illus.). 200p. 1965. reprint ed. 12.95 (*0-87074-045-8*) UNTX Pr.
Dobie, J. Frank, et al, eds. In the Shadow of History. LC 80-21632. (Texas Folklore Society Publications: No. 15). 186p. 1980. reprint ed. 12.95 (*0-87074-173-X*) UNTX Pr.
Dobie, J. Frank & Dykes, Jeff C. Forty-Four Range Country Books & 44 More Range Country Books. 35p. 1972. reprint ed. 30.00 (*0-88426-003-8*) Encino Pr.
Dobie, J. Frank, jt. auth. see Young, John D.
Dobie, James, ed. Happy Hunting Ground. LC 74-32310. (Texas Folklore Society, Publication Ser.: No. 4). 164p. reprint ed. pap. 50.90 (*0-608-17195-6*, 202700100053) Bks Demand.
Dobie, James F. Coronado's Children: Tales of Lost Mines & Buried Treasures of the Southwest. (BCL1 - United States Local History Ser.). 367p. 1991. reprint ed. text 89.00 (*0-7812-6332-8*) Rprt Serv.
— A Vaquero of the Brush Country: The Life & Times of John D. Young. (BCL1 - United States Local History Ser.). 314p. 1991. reprint ed. lib. bdg. 89.00 (*0-7812-6308-5*) Rprt Serv.
Dobie, Jeanne. Making Color Sing. (Illus.). 160p. 1986. 27.50 (*0-8230-2993-X*) Watsn-Guptill.
***Dobie, Jeanne.** Making Color Sing. (Illus.). 160p. 2000. pap. 19.95 (*0-8230-2992-1*) Watsn-Guptill.
Dobie, M. R., tr. see Toutain, Jules.
Dobie, Madeleine, tr. see Kofman, Sarah.
Dobie, Robert A. Medical-Legal Evaluation of Hearing Loss. LC 93-5118. 400p. 1993. text 81.95 (*0-442-01266-7*, VNR) Wiley.
— Medical-Legal Evaluation of Hearing Loss. (Illus.). 398p. 1998. reprint ed. pap. 69.95 (*0-7693-0023-5*, 2024) Thomson Learn.
Dobill, Daniel, jt. auth. see Schafer, John W.
Dobin, Denny, ed. Microcomputer Applications in Occupational Health & Safety. (Illus.). 228p. 1987. lib. bdg. 68.00 (*0-87371-078-9*, L078) Lewis Pubs.
Dobin, Howard. Merlin's Disciples: Prophecy, Poetry, & Power in Renaissance England. LC 89-26168. 272p. 1990. 37.50 (*0-8047-1783-4*) Stanford U Pr.
Dobin, Joel C. Kabbalistic Astrology: The Sacred Tradition of the Hebrew Sages. LC 99-18547. (Illus.). 272p. 1999. 14.95 (*0-89281-763-1*) Inner Tradit.
Dobinson, Charles H., ed. Education in a Changing World. LC 78-117783. (Essay Index Reprint Ser.). 1977. 19.95 (*0-8369-1801-0*) Ayer.
Dobkin, Bethami A. Tales of Terror: Television News & the Construction of the Terrorist Threat. LC 91-28772. (Media & Society Ser.). 144p. 1992. 52.95 (*0-275-93981-2*, C3981, Praeger Pubs) Greenwood.
Dobkin, Bonnie. Collecting. (Rookie Readers Ser.). (Illus.). 32p. (J). (ps-2). 1993. lib. bdg. 17.00 (*0-516-02015-3*) Childrens.
— Everybody Says. (Rookie Readers Ser.). (Illus.). 32p. (J). (ps-2). 1993. pap. 4.95 (*0-516-42019-4*) Childrens.

D

— Everybody Says. LC 93-7835. (Rookie Readers Ser.). (Illus.). 32p. (J). (ps-3). 1993. lib. bdg. 17.00 (*0-516-02019-6*) Childrens.

— Go-with Words. (Rookie Readers Ser.). (Illus.). 32p. (J). (ps-2). 1993. lib. bdg. 17.00 (*0-516-02016-1*) Childrens.

***Dobkin, Bonnie.** Go-With Words. rev. ed. (Rookie Readers Ser.). (Illus.). 32p. (J). (gr. 1-2). 2000. pap. 4.95 (*0-516-27048-6*) Childrens.

Dobkin, Bonnie. The Great Bug Hunt. LC 93-10333. (Rookie Readers Ser.). (Illus.). 32p. (J). (gr. k-2). 1993. lib. bdg. 17.00 (*0-516-02017-X*) Childrens.

— The Great Bug Hunt. LC 93-10333. (Rookie Readers Ser.). (Illus.). 32p. (J). (ps-3). 1993. pap. 4.95 (*0-516-42017-8*) Childrens.

— I Love Fishing. LC 92-38506. (Rookie Readers Ser.). (Illus.). 32p. (J). (ps-3). 1993. lib. bdg. 17.00 (*0-516-02013-7*) Childrens.

— Just a Little Different. LC 93-13024. (Rookie Readers Ser.). (Illus.). 32p. (J). (ps-2). 1994. lib. bdg. 17.00 (*0-516-02018-8*) Childrens.

— Truck Stop. (Rookie Readers Ser.). (Illus.). 32p. (J). (gr. k-2). 1994. lib. bdg. 17.00 (*0-516-02027-7*) Childrens.

***Dobkin, Bonnie & Payne, Tom.** Go-With Words rev. ed. LC 99-33427. (Rookie Readers Ser.). 32p. (gr. 1-2). 2000. 17.50 (*0-516-22031-4*) Childrens.

Dobkin, Bruce H. Neurologic Rehabilitation. LC 95-46567. (Contemporary Neurology Ser.: No. 47). (Illus.). 360p. (C). 1996. text 99.00 (*0-8036-0169-7*) OUP.

Dobkin, David S. Conservation & Management of Neotropical Migrant Landbirds in the Northern Rockies & Great Plains. 220p. 1994. pap. 29.95 (*0-89301-168-1*) U of Idaho Pr.

Dobkin, David S., jt. auth. see Craig, Lyda J.

***Dobkin de Rios, Marlene.** Brief Psychotherapy with the Latino Immigrant Client. LC 00-33531. 2000. pap. write for info. (*0-7890-1090-9*) Haworth Pr.

Dobkin de Rios, Marlene. Visionary Vine: Hallucinogenic Healing in the Peruvian Amazon. (Illus.). 161p. (C). 1984. reprint ed. pap. text 11.50 (*0-88133-093-0*) Waveland Pr.

Dobkin, Eva Z., tr. see Morevski, Abraham.

***Dobkin, Irma.** Gracious Spaces: Universal Design Interiors. LC 99-29311. 304p. 1999. 49.95 (*0-07-017151-3*) McGraw.

Dobkin, James A., et al, eds. Joint Ventures with International Partners: Structure & Negotiation, Vol. 3. 1994. write for info. (*0-250-40704-3*, MICHIE) LEXIS Pub.

Dobkin, James A. & Burt, Jeffrey A. Joint Ventures with International Partners, Vols. 1 & 2. 1991. ring bd. 200.00 (*1-56257-196-6*, MICHIE) LEXIS Pub.

Dobkin, James A. & Burt, Jeffrey A., eds. Joint Ventures with International Partners. 1994. ring bd., suppl. ed. 45.00 (*0-614-03611-9*, MICHIE) LEXIS Pub.

— Joint Ventures with International Partners, 3 vols., Set. 1000p. 1991. ring bd. 270.00 (*0-88063-267-4*, MICHIE) LEXIS Pub.

Dobkin, James A., ed. see Burt, et al.

Dobkin, Jeffrey. How to Market a Product for under $500. 416p. 1996. pap., per. 29.95 (*0-9642879-2-7*) Danielle Adams.

— Uncommon Marketing Techniques: Practical Real-Life Lessons in Marketing & Direct Marketing. Axelrod, Michelle, ed. LC 97-71742. (Illus.). 200p. (Orig.). 1997. pap. 17.95 (*0-9642879-3-5*) Danielle Adams.

Dobkin, Marjorie H., ed. The Making of a Feminist: Early Journals & Letters of M. Carey Thomas. LC 79-88605. 314p. 1980. pap. 19.95 (*0-87338-237-4*) New Mark Pr.

Dobkin, Matt. Getting Opera: A Guide for the Cultured but Confused. LC 99-45234. (Illus.). 264p. 2000. per. 12.95 (*0-671-04139-8*) PB.

Dobkin, Rachel & Sippy, Shana. The College Woman's Handbook. LC 83-1362. (Illus.). 656p. 1995. pap. 14.95 (*1-56305-559-7*, 3559) Workman Pub.

Dobkins, Claudia, jt. auth. see Grim Reaper Books Staff.

Dobkins, Eve, ed. see Armellini, Toby J.

Dobkins, Lucy M. Bad Back: Coping for Life. LC 94-41901. (Illus.). 208p. (Orig.). 1995. pap. 12.95 (*1-56554-062-X*) Pelican.

— Daddy, There's a Hippo in the Grapes. LC 92-20321. (Illus.). 88p. (J). (gr. 5-7). 1992. 13.95 (*0-88289-889-2*) Pelican.

Dobkins, Rebecca J., et al. Memory & Imagination: The Legacy of Maidu Indian Artist Frank Day. LC 96-49341. (Illus.). 120p. 1997. pap. 24.95 (*0-295-97612-8*) U of Wash Pr.

Dobkowski, Jan. My Lomzynskie Dzieci. (POL., Illus.). 360p. (Orig.). 1992. pap. text 14.95 (*0-930401-52-2*) Artex Pub.

Dobkowski, Michael, jt. ed. see Wallimann, Isidor.

Dobkowski, Michael N., ed. Jewish American Voluntary Organizations. LC 84-10734. 716p. 1986. lib. bdg. 89.50 (*0-313-21204-X*, RJA/, Greenwood Pr) Greenwood.

Dobkowski, Michael N. & Wallimann, Isidor, eds. The Coming Age of Scarcity: Preventing Mass Death & Genocide in the Twenty-First Century. LC 97-18715. (Studies on Peace & Conflict Resolution). 384p. 1997. pap. 34.95 (*0-8156-2744-0*) Syracuse U Pr.

— Genocide in Our Time: An Annotated Bibliography with Analytical Introductions. (Resources on Contemporary Issues Ser.: No. 6). 200p. 1992. pap. 40.00 (*0-87650-280-X*) Pierian.

— Radical Perspectives on the Rise of Fascism in Germany, 1919 to 1945. 320p. (C). 1988. 30.00 (*0-85345-757-3*); pap. 18.00 (*0-85345-758-1*, Pub. by Monthly Rev) NYU Pr.

— Towards the Holocaust: The Social & Economic Collapse of the Weimar Republic. LC 82-18388. (Illus.). 422p. 1983. 37.50 (*0-313-22795-0*, DHO/, Greenwood Pr) Greenwood.

Dobkowski, Michael N., jt. ed. see Wallimann, Isidor.

Dobkowski, Stanislaw. Serce, Krzyz i Karabin (a Heart, a Cross, a Rifle) (POL.). 80p. (Orig.). 1989. pap. text 9.00 (*0-930401-24-7*) Artex Pub.

Doble, Adam & Martin, Ian L. The GABA Benzodiazepine Receptor As a Target for Psychoactive Drugs. LC 95-37910. 248p. 1996. 89.95 (*1-57059-305-1*) Landes Bioscience.

Doble, Henry F., Jr. Medical Office Design: Territory & Conflict. 200p. (C). 1982. pap. 42.50 (*0-87527-243-6*) Green.

Doble, John. Crime & Punishment: The Public's View. 85p. (Orig.). 1987. pap. write for info. (*1-889483-32-X*) Public Agenda.

— Introduction to Radio Propagation for Fixed & Mobile Communications. LC 96-26605. 189p. 1996. 79.00 (*0-89006-529-2*) Artech Hse.

— The Nation Reacts to AIDS: A Report from 6 Cities. 77p. (Orig.). 1988. pap. 11.50 (*1-889483-28-1*) Public Agenda.

— Science & the Public, 3 vols. Incl. Vol. I. Searching for Common Ground on Issues Related to Science & Technology. Johnson, Jean. 76p. (Orig.). 1990. pap. 15.00 (*1-889483-34-6*); Vol. II. The Disposal of Solid Waste. Richardson, Amy & Danks, Allen. 109p. (Orig.). 1990. pap. 25.00 (*1-889483-35-4*); Vol. III. Global Warming Caused by the Greenhouse Effect. Richardson, Amy & Danks, Allen. 188p. 1990. pap. 25.00 (*1-889483-36-2*); 65.00 (*1-889483-42-7*) Public Agenda.

***Doble, John & Camp, Charles L.** John Doble's Journal & Letters from the Mines: Mokelumne Hill, Jackson, Volcano & San Francisco, 1851-1865 LC 98-46963. 1999. 24.95 (*1-884244-18-1*) Volcano Pr.

Doble, John & Klein, Josh. Punishing Criminals: The Public's View, an Alabama Study. 74p. (Orig.). 1989. pap. write for info. (*1-889483-31-1*) Public Agenda.

Doble, John & Melville, Keith. Options for Social Welfare Policy: The Public's View. 52p. (Orig.). 1986. pap. 6.50 (*1-889483-04-4*) Public Agenda.

Doble, John, et al. Public Opinion about Charitable Solicitation & the Law. 60p. (Orig.). 1990. pap. 15.00 (*1-889483-41-9*) Public Agenda.

— Punishing Criminals: The People of Delaware Consider the Options. 111p. (Orig.). 1991. pap. write for info. (*1-889483-30-3*) Public Agenda.

Doble, Peter. The Paradox of Salvation: Luke's Theology of the Cross. (Society for New Testament Studies Monographs: No. 87). 286p. (C). 1996. text 64.95 (*0-521-55212-5*) Cambridge U Pr.

Dobler, Donald W., et al. Purchasing & Supply Management: Text & Cases. 6th rev. ed. LC 95-36200. (Management Ser.). Orig. Title: Purchasing & Materials Management. 864p. (C). 1995. 86.88 (*0-07-037089-3*) McGraw.

Dobler, Joe & Roseta, Steve. Club Seattle: The Nightclub Guide & Passbooks, 1994-95. 2nd ed. (Illus.). 64p. (Orig.). 1994. write for info. (*0-9637266-1-7*) Green Star.

Dobler, Judith, ed. see Atticks, Kevin.

Dobler, Judy & Ciafalo, Andrew. Saved to Serve: The Life of George McManus, Jr. LC 97-36601. 160p. 1997. text. write for info. (*1-885938-11-X*) Cathdrl Fndtn Pr.

Dobler, Lavinia. I Didn't Know That about Wyoming! 3rd rev. ed. (Illus.). 152p. 1990. reprint ed. pap. 10.95 (*0-941875-12-1*) Wolverine Distrib.

— The Land & People of Uruguay. rev. ed. LC 72-3741. (Portraits of the Nations Ser.). (Illus.). (J). (gr. 5-9). 1972. lib. bdg. 11.89 (*0-397-31391-8*) HarpC Child Bks.

Dobler, Merri L. Food Allergies. 1991. pap. 5.50 (*0-88091-096-8*, 0882) Am Dietetic Assn.

— Gluten Intolerance. 1991. pap. 5.50 (*0-88091-098-4*, 0880) Am Dietetic Assn.

— Lactose Intolerance. 1991. pap. 5.50 (*0-88091-097-6*, 0881) Am Dietetic Assn.

Dobler, Patricia. Talking to Strangers. LC 86-40046. (Brittingham Prize in Poetry Ser.). 80p. 1986. pap. 11.95 (*0-299-10834-1*) U of Wis Pr.

— Uxb: Poems & Translations. Oresick, Peter & Petrosky, Anthony, eds. 64p. (C). 1991. pap. 10.00 (*0-9626023-3-7*); text 20.00 (*0-9626023-2-9*) Mill Hunk Bks.

***Dobler, Patricia, ed.** Voices from the Attic: Poetry & Fiction from the Women's Creative Writing Center at Carlow College, Vol. VII. unabridged ed. vi, 68p. 1999. per. 6.00 (*1-929706-10-3*) Anderson Pubng.

Dobler, Peggy R. Sincerely Peg. (Illus.). 1976. pap. 4.95 (*0-686-17611-1*) New Expressions.

Dobler, Roslyn. Opportunities in Fashion. (Illus.). 160p. 1990. 13.95 (*0-8442-6156-4*, VGM Career) NTC Contemp Pub Co.

— Opportunities in Fashion. (Illus.). 160p. 1993. pap. 10.95 (*0-8442-6157-2*, VGM Career) NTC Contemp Pub Co.

Dobles, Fabian. Years Like Brief Days. Henry, Joan, tr. from SPA. 128p. 1996. 29.00 (*0-7206-0987-9*, Pub. by P Owen Ltd) Dufour.

Dobles, Ricardo, jt. ed. see Segarra, Jose A.

Doblin, Alfred. Berlin Alexanderplatz. (FRE.). 640p. 1981. pap. 13.95 (*0-7859-1925-2*, 2070372391) Fr & Eur.

— Berlin Alexanderplatz: The Story of Franz Biberkopf. Jolas, Eugene, tr. 500p. 1984. pap. text 19.95 (*0-8044-6121-X*) F Ungar Bks.

— Destiny's Journey. 352p. 1994. 24.95 (*1-56924-990-3*) Marlowe & Co.

— Journey to Poland. 1994. 21.95 (*1-56924-964-4*) Marlowe & Co.

— Karl & Rosa: November 1918: A German Revolution. Woods, John E., tr. from GER. LC 83-16461.Tr. of Karl und Rosa. 547p. (C). 1983. pap. 15.95 (*0-88064-011-1*) Fromm Intl Pub.

— Men Without Mercy. Blewitt, Trevor & Blewitt, Phyllis, trs. from GER. LC 75-31978. 446p. 1976. reprint ed. 45.00 (*0-86527-277-8*) Fertig.

— A People Betrayed: November 1918, A German Revolution. Woods, John E., tr. from GER. LC 82-25133.Tr. of Verratenes Volk & Heimkehr der Fronttruppen. 642p. 1983. pap. 16.95 (*0-88064-008-1*) Fromm Intl Pub.

— Tales of a Long Night. Kimber, Robert & Kimber, Rita, trs. from GER. LC 84-18798.Tr. of Hamlet Oder die Lange Nacht Nimmt ein Ende. 486p. 1995. pap. 15.95 (*0-88064-017-0*) Fromm Intl Pub.

Doblin, Helga & Lynn, Mary C., trs. The American Revolution, Canadian Theater, French & Native American Life: Eyewitness Account by an Officer of the Prinz Friedrich Regiment, 1776-1783, 144. LC 92-42433. (Contributions in Military Studies Ser.: No. 144). 192p. 1993. 59.95 (*0-313-28887-9*, GM8887, Greenwood Pr) Greenwood.

Doblin, Helga, tr. see Lynn, Mary C., ed.

Doblins, Jim & Gordon, Ellie. The Ararat Conspiracy: A Novel. 168p. 1988. pap. 5.95 (*0-943247-03-9*) UCS Press.

Dobmeyer, Ann M. Interviewing & Investigation for Paralegals: A Practical Approach. LC 97-43295. 1998. pap. text 28.95 (*1-56706-640-2*) Aspen Law.

Dobney, Frederick J., ed. see Clayton, William.

Dobney, Stephen. Harry Seidler: Selected & Current Works. (Master Architect Ser.: Vol. 3). (Illus.). 256p. 1997. 59.95 (*1-875498-75-3*, Pub. by Conran Octopus) Antique Collect.

***Dobney, Stephen, ed.** Ken Woolley & Ancher Mortlock & Woolley: Selected & Current Works. (Illus.). 256p. 1999. text. write for info. (*90-5703-172-8*, Pub. by Craftsman House) Gordon & Breach.

Dobnick, Otto P. & Glischinski, Steve, photos by. Wisconsin Central: Railroad Success Story. LC 97-153282. (Illus.). 160p. 1997. 49.95 (*0-89024-562-2*, 01069, Kalmbach Books) Kalmbach.

***Dobnikar, A., et al, eds.** Artificial Neural Nets & Genetic Algorithms: Proceedings of the International Conference in Portoroz, Slovenia, 1999. 350p. 1999. pap. 78.00 (*3-211-83364-1*) Spr-Verlag.

Dobolek, Roberta, jt. ed. see Monday, D. Charone.

Dobos & Mastim. Family Portrait. 2nd ed. (Sociology - Introductory Level Ser.). 1980. pap. 9.75 (*0-534-00874-7*) Wadsworth Pub.

Dobos, David E., et al. Family Portrait: A Study of Contemporary Lifestyles (30 Lessons) 3rd ed. 192p. (C). 1983. pap. write for info. (*0-534-02733-4*) Wadsworth Pub.

Dobost, Viola T., jt. auth. see Kretzoi, Miklos.

Dobosz, I., jt. auth. see Vielrose, E.

Dobovsky, Eva V., jt. auth. see Tauxe, W. Newlon.

Dobozi, Istvan, jt. ed. see Brada, Josef C.

Dobozy, Maria. The Saxon Mirror: A Sachsenspiegel of the Fourteenth Century. LC 98-51171. (Middle Ages Ser.). (ENG & GER.). 263p. 1999. 55.00 (*0-8122-3487-1*) U of Pa Pr.

Dobra, John L. Congressional Testimony on the U. S. Mining Act of 1872. 8p. 1993. 10.00 (*1-886306-08-7*) Nevada Policy.

— Hardrock Mining Royalty Issues. 15p. 1993. 10.00 (*1-886306-09-5*) Nevada Policy.

Dobraczynski, J. Before the Earth Arose. 267p. 1981. 6.25 (*0-8199-0783-9*, Frncscn Herld) Franciscan Pr.

Dobran, F. Theory of Structured Multiphase Mixtures. (Lecture Notes in Physics Ser.: Vol. 372). vii, 223p. 1991. 31.95 (*0-387-53564-0*) Spr-Verlag.

Dobranowski, J., et al. Proceedings in Gastrointestinal Radiology. (Illus.). 265p. 1990. 110.00 (*0-387-97113-0*) Spr-Verlag.

***Dobranski, Stephen B.** Milton, Authorship & the Book Trade. LC 98-44373. (Illus.). 264p. (C). 1999. 54.95 (*0-521-64192-6*) Cambridge U Pr.

Dobranski, Stephen B., et al, eds. Milton & Heresy. LC 97-35243. 293p. (C). 1998. 59.95 (*0-521-63065-7*) Cambridge U Pr.

Dobratz, Betty A. & Shanks-Meile, Stephanie L. "White Power, White Pride!" The KKK Neo Nazis & Skinhead. LC 97-30615. 1997. 33.00 (*0-8057-3865-7*, Twyne) Mac Lib Ref.

***Dobratz, Betty A. & Shanks-Meile, Stephanie L.** The White Separatist Movement in the United States. LC 00-32011. 380p. 2000. pap. 18.95 (*0-8018-6537-9*) Johns Hopkins.

Dobratz, Betty A., jt. auth. see Kourvetaris, Geroge E.

Dobratz, Betty A., jt. ed. see Kourvetaris, George A.

Dobree, Bonamy. Alexander Pope. LC 72-94604. 125p. 1969. reprint ed. lib. bdg. 49.50 (*0-8371-2459-X*, DOAP, Greenwood Pr) Greenwood.

— As Their Friends Saw Them. LC 67-30183. (Essay Index Reprint Ser.). 1977. 18.95 (*0-8369-0375-7*) Ayer.

— The Broken Cistern. LC 72-6790. (Studies in Comparative Literature: No. 35). 1972. reprint ed. lib. bdg. 75.00 (*0-8383-1664-6*) M S G Haskell Hse.

— Essays in Biography, 1680-1726. LC 67-23203. (Essay Index Reprint Ser.). 1977. 23.95 (*0-8369-0376-5*) Ayer.

— Milton to Ouida: A Collection of Essays. 198p. 1970. 26.00 (*0-7146-2393-8*, Pub. by F Cass Pubs) Intl Spec Bk.

— Modern Prose Style. 2nd ed. LC 77-25320. 306p. 1978. reprint ed. lib. bdg. 55.00 (*0-313-20124-2*, DOMP, Greenwood Pr) Greenwood.

Dobree, Bonamy. Restoration Comedy, 1660-1720. LC 81-1230. 182p. 1981. reprint ed. lib. bdg. 42.50 (*0-313-22722-5*, DORC, Greenwood Pr) Greenwood.

Dobree, Bonamy. Variety of Ways: Discussion on Six Authors. LC 67-23204. (Essay Index Reprint Ser.). 1977. 15.95 (*0-8369-0377-3*) Ayer.

Dobree, Bonamy, ed. Five Heroic Plays, No. 576. LC 78-14410. 417p. 1979. reprint ed. lib. bdg. 38.50 (*0-313-21051-9*, DOFH, Greenwood Pr) Greenwood.

— From Anne to Victoria: Essays by Various Hands. LC 67-30184. (Essay Index Reprint Ser.). 1977. 30.95 (*0-8369-0378-1*) Ayer.

Dobree, Bonamy & Manwaring, George E. Floating Republic: The Mutinies at Spithead & the Nore, 1797. (Illus.). 299p. 1966. reprint ed. 30.00 (*0-7146-1197-2*, BHA-01497, Pub. by F Cass Pubs) Intl Spec Bk.

Dobree, Bonamy, ed. see Beljame, Alexandre.

Dobree, Bonamy, ed. see Radcliffe, Ann.

Dobree, Bonamy, ed. see Vanbrugh, John.

Dobree, John H. & Boulter, Eric. Blindness & Visual Handicap: The Facts. (Facts Ser.). (Illus.). 200p. 1982. 13.95 (*0-19-261328-6*) OUP.

Dobrenko, E. A. The Making of the State Reader: Social & Aesthetic Contexts of the Reception of Soviet Literature. Savage, Jesse M., tr. from RUS. LC 97-12325. 382p. 1997. 49.50 (*0-8047-2854-2*) Stanford U Pr.

Dobrenko, Evgeny, jt. ed. see Lahusen, Thomas.

Dobrer, Jonathan. Out of My Mind: Triple Axles, Sperm Tests, & Neutrinos. Wells, Susan L., ed. 92p. (Orig.). 1995. pap. 8.95 (*0-9621390-1-7*) DAnca-Wells.

***Dobres, Marcia-Anne.** Technology & Social Agency: Outlining an Anthropological Framework for Archaeology. (Illus.). 320p. 2000. 62.95 (*1-57718-123-9*) Blackwell Pubs.

— Technology & Social Agency: Outlining an Anthropological Framework for Archaeology. LC 99-43959. (Social Archaeology Ser.). 320p. 2000. pap. text 29.95 (*1-57718-124-7*) Blackwell Pubs.

Dobres, Marcia-Anne & Hoffman, Christopher R., eds. The Social Dynamics of Technology: Practice, Politics & World Views. LC 98-38120. (Illus.). 256p. 1999. 45.00 (*1-56098-909-2*) Smithsonian.

***Dobres, Marcia-Anne & Robb, John E.** Agency in Archaeology. LC 99-44275. 272p. 2000. pap. write for info. (*0-415-20761-4*) Routledge.

— Agency in Archaeology. LC 99-44275. 288p. (C). 2000. text 100.00 (*0-415-20760-6*) Routledge.

Dobretsov, N. L. & Kirdyashkin, A. G. Deep-Level Geodynamics. 328p. 1998. 87.00 (*90-5410-734-0*, Pub. by A A Balkema) Ashgate Pub Co.

Dobrev, V. K. Lie Theory & Its Applications in Physics II: Proceedings of the Workshop Arnold Sommerfield. 1998. 78.00 (*981-02-3539-9*) World Scientific Pub.

Dobrev, V. K., jt. ed. see Doebner, H. D.

Dobreva-Martinova, Tzvetanka, tr. see Bekhterev, V. M.

Dobrez, Livio. Parnassus Mad Ward: Michael Dransfield & the New Australian Poetry. 1990. pap. 14.95 (*0-7022-2330-1*, Pub. by Univ Queensland Pr) Intl Spec Bk.

Dobrian, Joseph. Business Writing Skills. LC 97-25274. (Take Charge Assistant Ser.: No. 2). 128p. 1997. pap. 12.95 (*0-8144-7973-1*) AMACOM.

***Dobrianowa-Bauer, Snegi.** Auf Den Spuren der Munchner Schule: Nicola Michailow und die Neue Bulgarische Malerei, 1878-1944. (Illus.). 453p. 1999. 67.95 (*3-631-32693-9*) P Lang Pubng.

Dobriansky, A. F., ed. see Pinkevich, A. & Amelin, B.

Dobriansky, Lev E. U. S. A. & the Soviet Myth. 9.50 (*0-8159-7005-6*) Devin.

Dobrich, Momcilo. Chetnik: The Story of the Royal Yugoslav Army of the Homeland, 1941-1945. Munoz, Antonio J., ed. (Illus.). 64p. 1998. pap. 18.00 (*1-891227-20-3*, Axis Europa Bks) Axis Europa.

Dobrich, Wanda & Dranoff, Steven. The First Line of Defense: A Guide to Protecting Yourself Against Sexual Harassment. 238p. 2000. pap. 18.95 (*0-471-35358-2*) Wiley.

Dobrilla, G., et al, eds. Advances in Hepatobiliary & Pancreatic Diseases: Special Clinical Topics: Proceedings of the Falk Symposium No. 83, Held in Bolzano, Italy, April 7-8, 1995. LC 95-24716. 288p. (C). 1995. text 118.00 (*0-7923-8892-5*) Kluwer Academic.

Dobrin, Adam, et al. Statistical Handbook on Violence in America. LC 95-42437. (Illus.). 424p. 1995. boxed set 65.00 (*0-89774-945-6*) Oryx Pr.

Dobrin, Arnold. Josephine's 'Magination. 48p. (J). (gr. 2-5). 1992. pap. 4.95 (*0-590-43494-2*) Scholastic Inc.

Dobrin, Arthur. Angles & Chambers. (Review Long Island Writers Chapbook Ser.: No. 2). 48p. 1991. 15.00 (*0-89304-257-9*); pap. 5.00 (*0-89304-258-7*); audio 10.00 (*0-89304-259-5*) Cross-Cultrl NY.

— Angles & Chambers: Mini Book. (Review Long Island Writers Chapbook Ser.: No. 2). 48p. 1991. 15.00 (*0-89304-255-2*); pap. 5.00 (*0-89304-256-0*) Cross-Cultrl NY.

— Being Good & Doing Right: Readings in Moral Development. 190p. (Orig.). (C). 1993. pap. text 23.50 (*0-8191-9268-6*) U Pr of Amer.

— Gentle Spears. Barkan, Stanley H., ed. (Cross-Cultural Review Chapbook Ser.: No. 3: American Poetry 2). 16p. 1980. 15.00 (*0-89304-829-1*, CCC128); pap. 5.00 (*0-685-01274-3*); audio 10.00 (*0-89304-827-5*) Cross-Cultrl NY.

— Little Heroes. (Ethical Humanist Society Monograph: No. 1). (Illus.). 1977. pap. 5.00 (*0-89304-200-5*, CCC111) Cross-Cultrl NY.

— Love Your Neighbor: Stories of Values & Virtues. LC 97-44212. (Illus.). 64p. (J). (ps-3). 1999. 16.95 (*0-590-04410-9*) Scholastic Inc.

— Saying My Name Out Loud. (Illus.). 1978. pap. 2.50 (*0-918870-05-4*) Pleasure Dome.

— Saying My Name Out Loud. deluxe limited ed. (Illus.). 1978. 3.50 (*0-918870-06-2*) Pleasure Dome.

— Sunbird. (Illus.). 64p. 15.00 (*0-89304-046-0*, CCC109); pap. 7.50 (*0-89304-012-6*) Cross-Cultrl NY.

Dobrin, Arthur, ed. Lace: Poetry from the Poor, the Homeless, the Aged, the Physically & Emotionally Disabled. LC 79-90011. (Illus.). (Orig.). 1979. 15.00 (*0-89304-036-3*, CCC123); pap. 7.95 (*0-89304-037-1*) Cross-Cultrl NY.

An Asterisk (*) at the beginning of an entry indicates that the title is appearing for the first time.

Dobrin, Lise, et al, eds. Papers from the 32nd Regional Meeting of the Chicago Linguistic Society Vol. 1: The Main Session. 1996. write for info. (*0-914203-50-9*) Chicago Ling.

Dobrin, Lise M. Parasession on Negation, Vol. 2. Nichols, Lynn et al, eds. 373p. 1991. pap. 16.00 (*0-914203-38-X*) Chicago Ling.

Dobrin, Lise M., et al, eds. Papers from the 27th Regional Meeting of CLS, Vol. 1. 491p. 1991. pap. 16.00 (*0-914203-37-1*) Chicago Ling.

Dobrin, Philip B., jt. auth. see Keen, Richard R.

Dobrin, Sidney I. Constructing Knowledges: The Politics of Theory-Building & Pedagogy in Composition. LC 96-21040. 181p. (C). 1997. text 49.50 (*0-7914-3343-9*); pap. text 16.95 (*0-7914-3344-7*) State U NY Pr.

Dobrin, Sidney I., jt. ed. see Olson, Gary A.

Dobrin, Sidney I., jt. ed. see Weisser, Christian.

Dobrinsky, Joseph. The Artist in Conrad's Fiction: A Psychocritical Study. Litz, A. Walton, ed. LC 88-39247. (Studies in Modern Literature: No. 92). 151p. reprint ed. 46.90 (*0-8357-1873-5*, 207070900004) Bks Demand.

Dobrinsky, Rumen, et al, eds. Transforming Economies & European Integration. LC 95-6825. 352p. 1995. 95.00 (*1-85898-204-9*) E Elgar.

Dobris, Joel C. Ritchie, Alford & Effland's Estates & Trusts: Cases & Materials : Teachers Manual. LC 98-153769. 335p. 1998. write for info. (*1-56662-620-X*) Foundation Pr.

Dobris, Joel C. & Sterk, Stewart E. Estates & Trusts, Cases & Materials On. LC 98-11442. (University Casebook Ser.). 1014p. 1998. text 41.25 (*1-56662-594-7*) Foundation Pr.

Dobris, Joel C., jt. auth. see Alford, Neill H., Jr.

***Dobrish, Jeremy.** Plays by Jeremy Dobrish. 148p. 1999. pap. 11.95 (*0-88145-157-6*) Broadway Play.

Dobrocyznski, Grzegorz. Einsicht und Bekehrung: Ausgangspunkt der Fundamentaltheologie Bei Bernard Lonergan. (Europaische Hochschulschriften Ser.: Reihe 23, Bd. 441). (GER.). 385p. 1992. 57.80 (*3-631-44276-9*) P Lang Pubng.

Dobrof, Rose, ed. Ethnicity & Gerontological Social Work. LC 86-29464. (Journal of Gerontological Social Work: Vol. 9, No. 4). 143p. 1987. text 39.95 (*0-86656-646-5*) Haworth Pr.

— Gerontological Social Work in Home Health Care. LC 84-10924. (Journal of Gerontological Social Work: Vol. 7, No. 4). 114p. 1984. 39.95 (*0-86656-337-7*) Haworth Pr.

— Gerontological Social Work with Families: A Guide to Practice Issues & Service Delivery. LC 86-14930. (Journal of Gerontological Social Work: Vol. 10, Nos. 1-2). 184p. 1987. text 49.95 (*0-86656-599-X*) Haworth Pr.

— Social Work & Alzheimer's Disease: Practice Issues with Victims & Their Families. LC 85-220269. (Journal of Gerontological Social Work: Vol. 9, No. 2). 126p. 1986. text 39.95 (*0-86656-402-0*) Haworth Pr.

Dobrof, Rose, et al, eds. Dignity & Old Age. LC 98-17892. (Journal of Gerontological Social Work Ser.: Vol. 29, Nos. 2-3). 185p. 1998. 49.95 (*0-7890-0534-4*) Haworth Pr.

Dobrolavsky, A., tr. see Nezlin, Mikhail V. & Snezhkin, E. N.

Dobroliubov, Aleksandr M. Iz Knigi Nevidimoi. Grossman, Joan D., ed. (Modern Russian Literature & Culture, Studies & Texts: Vol. (Eleven)). (RUS.). 230p. (Orig.). 1983. reprint ed. pap. 15.00 (*0-933884-34-6*) Berkeley Slavic.

— Natura Naturans, Natura Naturata; Sobranie Stikhov. (Modern Russian Literature & Culture, Studies & Texts: Vol. 10). (RUS.). 211p. 1981. pap. 10.00 (*0-933884-20-6*) Berkeley Slavic.

Dobronic, Ljelja. Zagreb Croatia. 232p. 1985. 30.00 (*0-918660-85-8*) Ragusan Pr.

Dobrosielski-Vergona, Kathleen. Biology of the Salivary Gland. 480p. 1992. lib. bdg. 210.00 (*0-8493-8847-3*, QP191) CRC Pr.

Dobroski, Ella M. Memorial Day & Always: A Mother Remembers. 185p. 1988. pap. 12.00 (*0-9619586-0-X*) Debo Pub Co.

Dobrosky, Nanette, et al. Records of the Bureau of Vocational Information, 1908-1932. LC 91-16870. (Research Collections in Women's Studies). 28 p. 1989. write for info. (*1-55655-104-5*) U Pubns Amer.

— Voices from Ellis Island: An Oral History of American Immigration : A Project Of the Statue of Liberty-ellis Island Foundation. LC 89-20158. (Research Collections in American Immigration). 8 p. 1988. write for info. (*1-55655-041-3*) U Pubns Amer.

Dobrosky, Nanette, jt. auth. see Schomburg, Arthur A.

Dobroslavic, Terese. Dictionary of Canadian Abbreviations. 2nd rev. ed. 400p. (C). 1993. text 70.00 (*1-55022-196-5*, Pub. by ECW) Genl Dist Srvs.

Dobroszycki, Lucjan. The Chronicle of the Lodz Ghetto. LC 84-3614. 565p. 1987. pap. 30.00 (*0-300-03924-7*, Y-637) Yale U Pr.

— Reptile Journalism: The Official Polish-Language Press under the Nazis, 1939-1945. LC 94-17013. 199p. 1995. 27.50 (*0-300-05277-4*) Yale U Pr.

— Survivors of the Holocaust in Poland: A Portrait Based on Jewish Community Records, 1944-1947. LC 94-17363. (Illus.). 164p. (C). (gr. 13). 1994. text 57.95 (*1-56324-463-2*) M E Sharpe.

Dobroszycki, Lucjan & Gurock, Jeffrey S., eds. The Holocaust in the Soviet Union: Studies & Sources on the Destruction of the Jews in Nazi-Occupied Territories of the U. S. S. R. 1941-1945. LC 93-15567. 272p. (gr. 13). 1993. pap. text 42.95 (*1-56324-174-9*) M E Sharpe.

Dobroszycki, Lucjan & Gurock, Jeffrey S., eds. The Holocaust in the Soviet Union: Studies & Sources on the Destruction of the Jews in Nazi-Occupied Territories of the U. S. S. R. 1941-1945. LC 93-15567. 272p. (C). (gr. 13). 1993. text 85.95 (*1-56324-173-0*) M E Sharpe.

Dobrot, Nancy L. & McCawley, Rosemary. Beyond Flexible Scheduling: A Workshop Guide. 75p. 1992. pap. text 20.00 (*0-931510-44-9*) Hi Willow.

Dobrov, Gregory, tr. see Verkhovsky, Abbess V.

Dobrov, Gregory W. Figures of Play: Greek Drama & Metafictional Poetics. 256p. 2000. text 49.95 (*0-19-511658-5*) OUP.

Dobrov, Gregory W., ed. Beyond Aristophanes: Transition & Diversity in Greek Comedy. LC 95-23502. (American Philological Association Philological Monographs: No. 38). 209p. (C). 1995. pap. 19.95 (*0-7885-0140-2*, 400438) OUP.

— The City As Comedy: Society & Representation in Athenian Drama. LC 97-9888. 376p. 1998. lib. bdg. 65.00 (*0-8078-2337-6*) U of NC Pr.

Dobrovie-Sorin, Carmen. The Syntax of Romanian: Comparative Studies in Romance. Vol. 40. 1993. 109.00 (*0-685-67322-7*) Mouton.

— The Syntax of Romanian: Comparative Studies in Romance. (Studies in Generative Grammar: No. 40). xx, 296p. (C). 1993. lib. bdg. 121.55 (*3-11-013541-8*) Mouton.

Dobrovitz, Peter. Rochestrivia: An Illuminating Look at Rochester. (Illus.). 226p. (Orig.). 1984. pap. 9.95 (*0-930249-00-3*) Big Kids Pub.

Dobrovolny, J. S., et al. Problems in Engineering Drawing & Geometry: Series 13 & 16. 1964. pap. 12.80 (*0-318-55874-2*) Stipes.

***Dobrovolski, S. G.** Stochastic Climate Theory: Models & Applications. (Illus.). xiv, 282p. 2000. 116.00 (*3-540-66310-X*) Spr-Verlag.

Dobrovolsky, Sergei P. Corporate Income Retention, 1915-43. (Financial Research Program III: Studies in Business Financing: No. 10). 142p. 1951. reprint ed. 37.00 (*0-87014-138-4*) Natl Bur Econ Res.

Dobrovolsky, V. N. & Litovchenko, V. G. Surface Electronic Transport Phenomena in Semiconductors. Pestryakov, E. M., tr. (Semiconductor Science & Technology Ser.: No. 2). (Illus.). 240p. 1991. 85.00 (*0-19-852034-4*) OUP.

Dobrow, G. M. & Engelbert, H. Dictionary of Science: Woerterbuch der Wissenschafts. (ENG, GER & RUS.). 560p. 1984. 39.95 (*0-8288-0682-9*, M14127) Fr & Eur.

Dobrow, Julia, ed. Social & Cultural Aspects of VCR Use. 232p. (C). 1990. text 65.00 (*0-8058-0499-4*) L Erlbaum Assocs.

Dobrow, Marty. Going Bigtime: The Spectacular Rise of UMass Basketball. LC 96-69142. (Illus.). 300p. 1996. 23.95 (*0-9645250-1-1*) Smmrst Pr.

Dobrow, Vicki. Johnny Tremain. Friedland, Joyce & Kessler, Rikki, eds. (Novel-Ties Ser.). (J). (gr. 6-8). 1993. pap. text 15.95 (*0-88122-025-6*) Lrn Links.

— The Phantom Tollbooth: A Study Guide. (Novel-Ties Ser.). (J). (gr. 4-6). 1986. pap. text, teacher ed., student ed. 15.95 (*0-88122-089-2*) Lrn Links.

Dobrowolski, Janusz. Computer-Aided Analysis, Modeling, & Design of Microwave Networks: The Wave Approach. LC 95-49607. 1996. 103.00 (*0-89006-669-8*) Artech Hse.

Dobrowolski, Joseph A. Concrete Construction Handbook. 4th ed. LC 98-24784. (Illus.). 64p. 1998. 99.95 (*0-07-017198-X*) McGraw.

***Dobrowolsky, Alexandra.** The Politics of Pragmatism: Women, Representation, & Constitutionalism in Canada. 2000. pap. 24.95 (*0-19-541379-2*) OUP.

Dobrowolsky, Helene. Law of the Yukon. LC 96-134759. (Illus.). 192p. 1995. pap. 24.95 (*0-9694612-6-7*, Pub. by Lost Moose) Genl Dist Srvs.

Dobrowski, George, jt. auth. see Minoli, Daniel.

Dobrozemsky, R., ed. Vacuum-Industry-Energy: Proceedings of Second Joint Meeting of the Roland Eotvos Physical Society (Vacuum Physics & Thin Films Section) & the Austrian Vacuum Society, held Niederosterreich, Austria, 27-29 October, 1981. 128p. 1983. pap. 31.00 (*0-08-029993-8*, Pergamon Pr) Elsevier.

Dobrushin, R., et al. Lectures on Probability Theory & Statistics: Ecole d'Ete de Probabilities de St. Flour XXIV - 1994, Vol. VII. (Lecture Notes in Mathematics Ser.: Vol. 1648). 300p. 1997. pap. 59.00 (*3-540-62055-9*) Spr-Verlag.

— Wulff Construction: A Global Shape from Local Interaction. LC 92-9200. (Translations of Mathematical Monographs: Vol. 104).Tr. of Konstruktsiia Vulfa. 204p. 1992. text 130.00 (*0-8218-4563-2*, MMONO/104) Am Math.

Dobrushin, R. L., ed. A Collection of Surveys. 1986. text 206.50 (*90-277-2183-1*) Kluwer Academic.

— Probability Contributions to Statistical Mechanics. LC 91-640741. (Advances in Soviet Mathematics Ser.: Vol. 20). 289p. 1994. 100.00 (*0-8218-4120-3*, ADVSOV/20C) Am Math.

Dobrushin, R. L., et al, eds. Contemporary Mathematical Physics: F. A. Berezin Memorial Volume. LC 91-640741. (American Mathematical Society translations ser.: Vol. 175). 236p. 1997. text 99.00 (*0-8218-0426-X*, TRANS2/175) Am Math.

— Topics in Statistical & Theoretical Physics: F. A. Berezin Memorial Volume. LC 91-640741. (Translations Ser. II: Vol. 177). 233p. 1996. text 99.00 (*0-8218-0425-1*) Am Math.

Dobrushin, R. L. & Kusukoa, S. Statistical Mechanics & Fractals. LC 93-44952. 1994. 27.95 (*0-387-57516-2*) Spr-Verlag.

Dobrushin, R. L. & Sinai, Ya G., eds. Multicomponent Random Systems. LC 80-17688. (Advances in Probability & Related Topics Ser.: No. 6). 622p. reprint ed. pap. 192.90 (*0-7837-7016-2*, 204683200004) Bks Demand.

***Dobrusin, Eric M. & White, Katherine E.** Intellectual Property Litigation: Pretrial Practice. LC 99-38519. 1999. ring bd. 160.00 (*0-7355-0693-0*) Panel Pubs.

Dobruskina, I. A. Triassic Floras of Eurasia. (Schriftenreihe der Erdwissenschaftlichen Kommissionen Ser.: Bd. 10). 425p. 1997. pap. 96.00 (*0-387-86557-8*) Spr-Verlag.

Dobry, Claira. Make Cloud Shades, Yes You Can! (Illus.). 126p. 1985. spiral bd. 19.95 (*0-9615218-1-3*); per. 19.95 (*0-9615218-0-5*) Dobry Enter.

— Make Custom Drapery, Yes You Can! (Illus.). 195p. 1982. spiral bd. 19.95 (*0-9615218-3-X*); per. 19.95 (*0-9615218-2-1*) Dobry Enter.

— Make Swags & Jabots, Yes You Can! (Illus.). 118p. 1986. spiral bd. 19.95 (*0-9615218-5-6*); per. 19.95 (*0-9615218-4-8*) Dobry Enter.

— No-Sew Drapery. 78p. 1986. spiral bd. 19.95 (*0-9615218-9-9*) Dobry Enter.

***Dobry, Michel.** Democratic & Capitalist Transitions in Eastern Europe: Lessons for the Social Sciences. LC 00-38630. (Geojournal Library). 2000. write for info. (*0-7923-6331-0*) Kluwer Academic.

Dobry, Ricardo, jt. ed. see O'Neill, Michael W.

Dobry, T. P. A High Performance Architecture for Frolog. (C). 1990. text 103.50 (*0-7923-9060-1*) Kluwer Academic.

Dobrynin, Aleksander & Kuzmickas, Bronius, eds. Personal Freedom & National Resurgence. LC 94-6871. (Cultural Heritage & Contemporary Change Series IVA: Vol. 8). 1994. 45.00 (*1-56518-038-0*); pap. 17.50 (*1-56518-039-9*) Coun Res Values.

***Dobrynin, Anatoly.** En Confianza. 694p. 1999. 36.99 (*968-16-5466-8*) Fondo CA.

Dobryshin, R. L., et al, eds. Locally Interacting Systems & Their Application in Biology: Proceedings of the School - Seminar on Markov Interaction Processes in Biology, Held in Pushchino, Moscow Region, March, 1976. (Lecture Notes in Mathematics Ser.: Vol. 653). 1978. 27.95 (*0-387-08450-9*) Spr-Verlag.

Dobrzycki, Jerzy, ed. see International Union of History & Philosophy of Sci.

Dobrzykowski, Edward A., Jr. Essential Readings in Rehabilitation Outcomes Measurement: Application, Methodology, & Technology. LC 98-20405. 304p. 1998. 49.00 (*0-8342-1194-7*) Aspen Pub.

Dobrzynski, Angelo, ed. Christ's Way. limited ed. LC 98-86038. (Illus.). 40p. (YA). (gr. 9-12). 1998. text 35.95 (*0-9665080-0-9*) Subiaco Abbey.

Dobschiner, Johanna. Selected to Live. pap. 5.99 (*0-7208-0212-1*) Zondervan.

Dobschiner, Johanna-Ruth. Selected to Live. LC 73-473109. 256p. 1969. write for info. (*0-7208-2044-8*, Pub. by M Pickering) Harper SF.

Dobsen, Kenneth M., jt. auth. see Donaldson, Hal.

Dobson. Conservation & Biodiversity. 264p. 1998. pap. text 19.95 (*0-7167-6032-0*) W H Freeman.

— Nelson Balanced Science: Physical World. (UK - Science Ser.). 1991. mass mkt. 35.95 (*0-17-438667-2*) S-W Pub.

Dobson & Stokoe, C. J. Self-Paced/Introduction to Mathematics. (Australian National University Press Ser.). 1986. pap. text 22.00 (*0-08-032985-3*, Pergamon Pr) Elsevier.

Dobson, Michael S. The Juggler's Guide to Managing Multiple Projects. LC 99-13074. 220p. 1999. pap. 32.95 (*1-880410-65-6*) Proj Mgmt Inst.

Dobson, Alan P. Anglo-American Relations in the Twentieth Century: The Politics & Diplomacy of Friendly Superpowers. LC 94-39922. 240p. (C). 1995. pap. 27.99 (*0-415-11943-X*) Routledge.

— Flying in the Face of Competition: The Policies & Diplomacy of Airline Regulatory Reform in Britain, the U. S. A. & the European Community. 258p. 1995. 67.95 (*0-291-39821-9*, Pub. by Avebury Technical) Ashgate Pub Co.

Dobson, Alan P. Peaceful Air Warfare: The United States, Britain, & the Politics of International Aviation. 328p. 1991. text 75.00 (*0-19-827531-5*) OUP.

***Dobson, Alan P. & Marsh, Steve.** U. S. Foreign Policy since 1945. LC 00-36897. (Making of the Contemporary World Ser.). 2000. pap. write for info. (*0-415-17293-4*) Routledge.

Dobson, Alan P., ed. see Evans, Graham & Malik, Shahin P.

Dobson, Andrew. Green Political Thought: An Introduction. 224p. (C). 1990. text 49.95 (*0-04-445244-6*); pap. text 15.95 (*0-04-445245-4*) Routledge.

— Green Political Thought: An Introduction. 2nd ed. LC 95-15797. 240p. (C). (gr. 13). 1995. pap. 22.99 (*0-415-12443-3*) Routledge.

***Dobson, Andrew.** Green Political Thought: An Introduction. 3rd ed. LC 99-53151. 2000. pap. 25.99 (*0-415-22204-4*) Routledge.

Dobson, Andrew. Justice & the Environment: Conceptions of Environmental Sustainability & Dimensions of Social Justice. LC 98-8745. 292p. 1999. text 55.00 (*0-19-829482-4*); pap. text 29.95 (*0-19-829495-6*) OUP.

Dobson, Andrew, ed. Fairness & Futurity: Essays on Environmental Sustainability & Social Justice. LC 98-49344. 339p. 1999. text 72.00 (*0-19-829488-3*); pap. text 19.95 (*0-19-829489-1*) OUP.

— The Green Reader: Essays Toward a Sustainable Society. LC 91-9957. 296p. 1991. 24.95 (*1-56279-017-X*); pap. 11.95 (*1-56279-010-2*) Mercury Hse Inc.

Dobson, Andrew & Lucardie, Paul, eds. The Politics of Nature. 256p. (C). 1995. pap. 25.99 (*0-415-12471-9*, C0556) Routledge.

Dobson, Andrew, jt. ed. see Grenfell, Bryan.

Dobson, Andrew P., jt. auth. see Landweber, Laura F.

Dobson, Andrew P., jt. ed. see Landweber, Laura F.

Dobson, Ann. Conducting Effective Interviews: How to Find Out What You Need to Know & Achieve the Right Results. (Business Basics Ser.). 127p. 1996. pap. 19.95 (*1-85703-223-3*, Pub. by How To Bks) Trans-Atl Phila.

— How to Communicate at Work: Making a Success of Your Working Relationships. 192p. 1995. pap. 19.95 (*1-85703-103-2*, Pub. by How To Bks) Trans-Atl Phila.

— How to Manage an Office: Planning & Creating a Successful Workplace. 160p. 1995. pap. 19.95 (*1-85703-049-4*, Pub. by How To Bks) Trans-Atl Phila.

— How to Return to Work: Building New Skills, New Confidence & a New Career. 128p. 1995. pap. 19.95 (*1-85703-144-X*, Pub. by How To Bks) Trans-Atl Phila.

— Managing Meetings: How to Prepare, How to Take Part & How to Follow up Effectively. (Business Basics Ser.). 128p. 1996. pap. 19.95 (*1-85703-222-5*, Pub. by How To Bks) Trans-Atl Phila.

***Dobson, Ann.** Writing Business Letters: How to Produce Day-to-Day Business Correspondence That Is Clear & Effective. 3rd ed. (Business & Management Ser.). (Illus.). 183p. 1999. pap. 19.95 (*1-85703-491-0*, Pub. by How To Bks) Trans-Atl Phila.

Dobson, Annette J. An Introduction to Generalized Linear Models. 2nd ed. LC 99-22932. (Texts in Statistical Science Ser.). Orig. Title: An Introduction to Statistical Modelling. 176p. (C). (gr. 13). 1990. per. 36.95 (*0-412-31110-0*, A4226, Chap & Hall CRC) CRC Pr.

— Introduction to Generalized Linear Models. 2nd ed. Orig. Title: An Introduction to Statistical Modelling. 250p. 1990. lib. bdg. 59.95 (*0-412-31100-3*, A4222, Chap & Hall CRC) CRC Pr.

Dobson, Austin. At Prior Park & Other Papers. LC 73-105007. (Essay Index Reprint Ser.). 1977. 23.95 (*0-8369-1567-4*) Ayer.

— Complete Poetical Works. LC 70-115236. 1971. reprint ed. 59.00 (*0-403-00421-7*) Scholarly.

— Eighteenth Century Vignettes, 3 vols. (Illus.). 1971. reprint ed. 19.00 (*0-318-68140-4*) Scholarly.

— Eighteenth Century Vignettes, 3 vols., Set. (BCL1-PR English Literature Ser.). 1992. reprint ed. lib. bdg. 225.00 (*0-7812-7040-5*) Rprt Serv.

— Eighteenth Century Vignettes, 3 vols., Set. (Illus.). 1971. reprint ed. 57.00 (*0-686-57480-X*) Scholarly.

— Eighteenth Century Vignettes: First, Second & Third Series, 3 vols., 1. LC 67-29812. (Illus.). 1968. reprint ed. 22.00 (*0-686-66382-9*, Pub. by Blom Pubns) Ayer.

— Eighteenth Century Vignettes: First, Second & Third Series, 3 vols., Set. 933p. Date not set. 72.95 (*0-405-19054-9*) Ayer.

— Eighteenth Century Vignettes: First, Second & Third Series, 3 vols., Vol. 1. LC 67-29812. (Illus.). 1972. reprint ed. 22.95 (*0-405-08447-1*, Pub. by Blom Pubns) Ayer.

— Eighteenth Century Vignettes: First, Second & Third Series, 3 vols., Vol. 2. LC 67-29812. (Illus.). 1972. reprint ed. 23.95 (*0-405-08448-X*, Pub. by Blom Pubns) Ayer.

— Eighteenth Century Vignettes: First, Second & Third Series, 3 vols., Vol. 3. LC 67-29812. (Illus.). 1972. reprint ed. 27.95 (*0-405-08449-8*, Pub. by Blom Pubns) Ayer.

— Fielding. Morley, John, ed. LC 73-100820. (English Men of Letters Ser.). reprint ed. 27.50 (*0-404-51708-0*) AMS Pr.

— Fielding. (BCL1-PR English Literature Ser.). 218p. 1992. reprint ed. text 79.00 (*0-7812-7352-8*) Rprt Serv.

— Four Frenchwomen. LC 72-6853. (Essay Index Reprint Ser.). 1977. reprint ed. 23.95 (*0-8369-7269-4*) Ayer.

— Four Frenchwomen. LC 72-6853. (Essay Index Reprint Ser.). 212p. reprint ed. lib. bdg. 14.50 (*0-8290-0523-4*) Irvington.

— Horace Walpole: A Memoir. LC 72-160127. (English Biography Ser.: No. 31). 1971. reprint ed. lib. bdg. 75.00 (*0-8383-1267-5*) M S G Haskell Hse.

— Horace Walpole: A Memoir. 4th enl. rev. ed. (Select Bibliographies Reprint Ser.). 1977. reprint ed. 23.95 (*0-8369-5883-7*) Ayer.

— Later Essays, 1917-1920. LC 68-22910. (Essay Index Reprint Ser.). 1977. 18.95 (*0-8369-0379-X*) Ayer.

— Life of Oliver Goldsmith. LC 72-38350. (Select Bibliographies Reprint Ser.). 1977. reprint ed. 20.95 (*0-8369-6767-4*) Ayer.

— Miscellanies. LC 67-28749. (Essay Index Reprint Ser.: Second Series). 1977. 20.95 (*0-8369-0380-3*) Ayer.

— Miscellanies. LC 73-100820. (Second Ser.). reprint ed. 27.50 (*0-404-02140-9*) AMS Pr.

— Miscellanies. (BCL1-PR English Literature Ser.). 364p. 1992. reprint ed. lib. bdg. 89.00 (*0-7812-7041-3*) Rprt Serv.

— Miscellanies. (BCL1-PR English Literature Ser.: Second Series). 277p. 1992. reprint ed. lib. bdg. 79.00 (*0-7812-7042-1*) Rprt Serv.

— Miscellanies. 1889. reprint ed. 10.00 (*0-403-00250-8*) Scholarly.

— Miscellanies, Second Series. LC 79-108474. 1970. reprint ed. 16.00 (*0-403-00206-0*) Scholarly.

— Old Kensington Palace, & Other Papers. LC 68-54344. (Essay Index Reprint Ser.). 1977. 20.95 (*0-8369-0110-X*) Ayer.

— Poetical Works. 1988. reprint ed. lib. bdg. 75.00 (*0-7812-0033-4*) Rprt Serv.

— Richard Steele. (BCL1-PR English Literature Ser.). 240p. 1992. reprint ed. lib. bdg. 79.00 (*0-7812-7408-7*) Rprt Serv.

— Richard Steele. Long, Andrew, ed. LC 72-108475. 1970. reprint ed. 39.00 (*0-403-00229-X*) Scholarly.

— Rosalba's Journal & Other Papers. LC 71-111827. (Essay Index Reprint Ser.). 1977. 23.95 (*0-8369-1605-0*) Ayer.

— Samuel Richardson. 7.00 (*0-403-00018-1*) Scholarly.

D

— Samuel Richardson. (BCL1-PR English Literature Ser.). 214p. 1992. reprint ed. lib. bdg. 79.00 (*0-7812-7397-8*) Rprt Serv.

Dobson, Austin, ed. Old English Songs. LC 70-116398. (Granger Index Reprint Ser.). 1977. 18.95 (*0-8369-6139-0*) Ayer.

Dobson, Barrie, jt. ed. see Biller, Peter.

Dobson-Burk, Bonnie & Hill, Everett W. An Orientation & Mobility Primer for Families & Young Children. LC 89-14878. 48p. 1989. pap. 14.95 (*0-89128-157-6*) Am Foun Blind.

Dobson, C. B., jt. auth. see Burns, R. B.

Dobson, C. M. & Fersht, A. R., eds. Protein Folding. LC 96-15183. (Illus.). 119p. (C). 1996. pap. text 29.95 (*0-521-57636-9*) Cambridge U Pr.

Dobson, Charles. Inspirations: A Book of Miracles. Bennett, Harris, ed. (Illus.). 60p. (Orig.). 1989. pap. 4.95 (*0-941513-03-3*) C & M Pubs & Distributors.

Dobson, Chris, jt. auth. see Mason, Florence M.

Dobson, Christopher. The Freelance Journalist. (Illus.). 159p. 1992. pap. 37.95 (*0-7506-0005-5*) Buttrwrth-Heinemann.

Dobson, Christopher & Payne, Ronald. Counterattack: The West's Battle Against the Terrorists. LC 82-1589. 220p. reprint ed. pap. 68.20 (*0-8357-4238-5*, 203702500007) Bks Demand.

— The Never-Ending War: Terrorism in the '80's. LC 86-24093. 392p. 1989. reprint ed. pap. 121.60 (*0-608-02854-1*, 206391800007) Bks Demand.

— The Terrorists: Their Weapons, Leaders & Tactics. LC 82-1438. (Illus.). 284p. reprint ed. pap. 88.10 (*0-7837-5347-0*, 204509000005) Bks Demand.

Dobson, Clive. Feeding Wild Birds in Winter. (Illus.). 128p. 1981. pap. 9.95 (*0-920668-17-8*) Firefly Bks Ltd.

— Fred's TV. (Illus.). 32p. (J). (gr. k-5). 1989. pap. 6.95 (*0-920668-59-3*) Firefly Bks Ltd.

***Dobson, Clive & Beck, Gregor.** Watersheds: A Practical Handbook for Healthy Water. (Illus.). 160p. (YA). (gr. 2-8). 1999. pap. 19.95 (*1-55209-330-1*) Firefly Bks Ltd.

Dobson, D. Atrevete a Disciplinar. 9th ed.Tr. of New Dare to Discipline. (SPA.). 304p. 1993. pap. 7.99 (*0-8297-1950-4*) Vida Pubs.

Dobson, D., jt. ed. see Dobson, K.

Dobson, Danae. The Baseball Game. (Sunny Street Kids' Club Ser.: Vol. 3). (Illus.). 32p. (J). (ps-3). 1996. pap. 4.99 (*0-8499-5114-3*) Tommy Nelson.

— The Best of Woof. LC 98-53874. (Illus.). 252p. (J). (gr. k-5). 1999. 12.99 (*0-8423-0058-9*) Tyndale Hse.

— The Pet-Sitting Service. (Sunny Street Kids' Club Ser.: Vol. 2). (Illus.). 32p. (J). (ps-3). 1996. pap. 4.99 (*0-8499-5113-5*) Tommy Nelson.

— The School Carnival. LC 95-42264. (Sunny Street Kids' Club Ser.: Vol. 4). (Illus.). 32p. (J). (ps-3). 1996. pap. 4.99 (*0-8499-5115-1*) Tommy Nelson.

Dobson, Danae & Dobson, James. Parables for Kids: Eight Contemporary Stories Based on Best-Loved Bible Parables. LC 98-33381. 1999. 14.99 (*0-8423-0637-4*) Tyndale Hse.

Dobson, Daniel & Forbus, Ken, eds. AI & Computer Games: Papers from the Spring Symposium. (Technical Reports: Vol. SS-99-02). (Illus.). 85p. 1998. spiral bd. 25.00 (*1-57735-074-X*) AAAI Pr.

Dobson, David. American Data from the "Aberdeen Journal," 1748-1783. (Illus.). 102p. pap. 14.00 (*0-8063-4766-X*, 9307) Clearfield Co.

— Can We Save Them? Endangered Species of North America. LC 96-17854. (Illus.). 32p. (J). (gr. k-5). 1997. 16.95 (*0-88106-823-3*); pap. 6.95 (*0-88106-822-5*) Charlesbridge Pub.

— Directory of Scottish Settlers in North America, 1625-1825, Vol. I. LC 83-82470. 267p. 1988. reprint ed. 20.00 (*0-8063-1054-5*) Genealog Pub.

— Directory of Scottish Settlers in North America, 1625-1825, Vol. II. LC 83-82470. 216p. 1993. reprint ed. 20.00 (*0-8063-1074-X*) Genealog Pub.

— Directory of Scottish Settlers in North America, 1625-1825, Vol. IV. LC 83-82470. 161p. 1985. 17.50 (*0-8063-1105-3*) Genealog Pub.

— Directory of Scottish Settlers in North America, 1625-1825, Vol. VI. 126p. 1986. 15.00 (*0-8063-1157-6*, 1487) Genealog Pub.

***Dobson, David.** The Jacobites of Angus, 1689-1746. LC 97-214709. 49p. 1999. pap. 10.00 (*0-8063-4716-3*) Clearfield Co.

Dobson, David. The Original Scots Colonists of Early America: Supplement, 1607-1707. LC 97-77224. 211p. 1997. suppl. ed. 22.50 (*0-8063-1442-7*) Genealog Pub.

***Dobson, David.** The Original Scots Colonists of Early America, Caribbean Supplement. 147p. 1999. 20.00 (*0-8063-1612-8*) Genealog Pub.

Dobson, David. The Original Scots Colonists of Early America, 1612-1783. 370p. 1999. 28.50 (*0-8063-1239-4*) Genealog Pub.

***Dobson, David.** Scots in Georgia & the Deep South, 1735-1845. 218p. 2000. 25.00 (*0-8063-1629-2*) Genealog Pub.

— Scots in the West Indies, 1707-1857. (Illus.). 150p. pap. 18.50 (*0-8063-4829-1*) Clearfield Co.

— Scots-Irish Links, 1757-1725, 2 vols. in 1. 58p. 1999. reprint ed. pap. 10.00 (*0-8063-4686-8*, Pub. by Clearfield Co) ACCESS Pubs Network.

Dobson, David. Scots on the Chesapeake, 1607-1830. 169p. 1992. 20.00 (*0-8063-1328-5*, 1476) Genealog Pub.

— Scottish-American Court Records, 1733-1783. 105p. 1991. 12.00 (*0-8063-1312-9*, 1477) Genealog Pub.

— Scottish-American Gravestones, 1700-1900. LC 99-199883. 105p. 2000. reprint ed. pap. 14.00 (*0-8063-4803-8*, Pub. by Clearfield Co) ACCESS Pubs Network.

— Scottish-American Heirs, 1683-1883. 165p. 1992. reprint ed. 14.00 (*0-8063-1278-5*, 1479) Genealog Pub.

Dobson, David. Scottish-American Wills, 1650-1900. 137p. 1991. 14.00 (*0-8063-1296-3*) Genealog Pub.

Dobson, David. Scottish Emigration to Colonial America, 1607-1785. LC 92-14211. (Illus.). 216p. 1994. 37.00 (*0-8203-1492-7*) U of Ga Pr.

***Dobson, David.** Scottish Maritime Records, 1600-1850: A Guide for Family Historians. LC 97-214711. 32 p. 1999. pap. 9.00 (*0-8063-4717-1*, Pub. by Clearfield Co) ACCESS Pubs Network.

Dobson, David. Scottish Quakers & Early America, 1650-1700. (Illus.). 52p. 2000. reprint ed. pap. 10.95 (*0-8063-4765-1*, Pub. by Clearfield Co) ACCESS Pubs Network.

— Scottish Soldiers in Colonial America, 2 vols. in 1. LC 97-214710. (Illus.). 63p. 1999. reprint ed. pap. 12.00 (*0-8063-4718-X*, Pub. by Clearfield Co) ACCESS Pubs Network.

***Dobson, David.** Ships from Ireland to Early America, 1623-1850. 153p. 1999. pap. 18.50 (*0-8063-4943-3*) Clearfield Co.

Dobson, David. Ships from Scotland to America, 1628-1828. LC 79-88259. 127p. 1998. 20.00 (*0-8063-0851-6*) Genealog Pub.

Dobson, David, photos by. Precious in His Sight: Prayers of the Children of the World. LC 98-109801. (Illus.). 112p. 1997. 14.99 (*0-8499-5334-0*) Word Pub.

Dobson, David, ed. see Brewer, Gary.

Dobson, David, ed. see Channer, Pat, et al.

Dobson, David, ed. see Hemenway, Michele & Buchanan, Sara A.

Dobson, David, ed. see Hill, Richard H.

Dobson, David, ed. see Robinson, Duke.

Dobson, Deborah S., jt. auth. see Dobson, Michael.

Dobson, Deborah S., jt. auth. see Dobson, Michael S.

Dobson, Deborah Singer, jt. auth. see Dobson, Michael.

Dobson, E. Foundations & Concrete Works. (Illus.). pap. 25.00 (*0-87556-771-1*) Saifer.

Dobson, E. Foundations & Concrete Works - Circa 1850. 130p. 1990. pap. 20.00 (*0-87556-080-6*) Saifer.

Dobson, E. J. English Pronunciation, Fifteen Hundred to Seventeen Hundred, 2 vols. 1985. 159.00 (*0-19-811931-3*) OUP.

— Moralities on the Gospels: A New Source of Ancrene Wisse. 192p. 1975. text 26.50 (*0-19-812056-7*) OUP.

— The Origins of Ancrene Wisse. (Illus.). 450p. (C). 1976. text 49.00 (*0-19-811864-3*) OUP.

Dobson, E. J., ed. The English Text of the Ancrene Riwle, BM Cleopatra Cotton Cleopatra Cvi. (EETS Original Ser.: Vol. 267). 1972. 50.00 (*0-19-722269-2*, Pub. by EETS) Boydell & Brewer.

— The Phonetic Writings of Robert Robinson. (EETS Original Ser.: Vol. 238). 1963. reprint ed. 20.00 (*0-19-722238-2*, Pub. by EETS) Boydell & Brewer.

Dobson, E. J., jt. ed. see D'Ardenne, S. R.

Dobson, Ed. The End: Why Jesus Could Return by A. D. 2000. LC 97-14457. 224p. 1997. 12.99 (*0-310-21373-8*) Zondervan.

***Dobson, Ed.** El Fin. (SPA.). 176p. 1999. pap. 7.99 (*0-8254-1172-6*, Edit Portavoz) Kregel.

Dobson, Ed. Starting a Seeker-Sensitive Service. 160p. 1993. pap. 12.99 (*0-310-38481-8*) Zondervan.

Dobson, Ed, et al, eds. Starting Fast: Ministry in an Unfriendly World. (Pressure Points Ser.). 154p. 1994. 15.99 (*0-88070-646-5*, Multnomah Bks) Multnomah Pubs.

Dobson, Ed, jt. auth. see Thomas, Cal.

Dobson, Edward D. The Trading Rule That Can Make You Rich. LC 79-64620. (Illus.). 67p. 1979. 29.95 (*0-934380-03-1*, 5) Traders Pr.

— Understanding Bollinger Bands. (Illus.). 32p. 1994. pap. 8.00 (*0-934380-25-2*, 580) Traders Pr.

— Understanding Fibonacci Numbers. 16p. 1984. pap. 5.00 (*0-934380-08-2*, 43-A) Traders Pr.

Dobson, Edward D. & Shuler, Sandra K. Understanding Andrews. (Illus.). 64p. 2001. pap. 25.00 (*0-934380-42-2*, 1220) Traders Pr.

Dobson, Edward G., et al, contrib. by. Complete Bible Commentary. LC 98-50365. 900p. 1999. 24.99 (*0-7852-0854-2*) Nelson.

Dobson, Eric. Creating an Action Strategy for Downtown Development. Murphy, Jenny, ed. 31p. (Orig.). 1988. pap. 18.00 (*0-317-04865-1*) Natl Coun Econ Dev.

— Higher Education - Economic Development Linkages. Murphy, Jenny, ed. 36p. (Orig.). 1988. pap. 18.00 (*0-317-04857-0*) Natl Coun Econ Dev.

Dobson, Eric N., jt. auth. see Clarke, Marianne K.

Dobson, Eric N., jt. auth. see Craft, Ralph.

Dobson, F., jt. auth. see Hasse, L.

Dobson, Frank E. The Race Is Not Given. LC 98-85361. 192p. 1999. pap. 11.95 (*1-56315-194-4*, Pub. by SterlingHse) Natl Bk Netwk.

Dobson, Fred. Fungus the Lincolnshire Cat. (Illus.). 112p. (C). 1989. text 40.00 (*0-902662-32-5*, Pub. by R K Pubns); pap. text 21.00 (*0-902662-33-3*, Pub. by R K Pubns) St Mut.

— Lincolnshire Folk. (Illus.). (C). 1989. text 30.00 (*0-902662-36-8*, Pub. by R K Pubns) St Mut.

Dobson, Fulton N. You Can Eliminate Stress from the IRS: Your Chance of Being Audited? At Least Once or Twice in Your Lifetime. LC 91-67059. 112p. 1992. pap. 7.95 (*0-914984-40-3*) Starburst.

Dobson, G. E. Catalogue of the Chiroptera in the Collection of the British Museum. (Illus.). 1966. 65.00 (*3-7682-0300-X*) Lubrecht & Cramer.

Dobson, Gavin. Global Investment Insider: Opportunities, Risks & Realities for Institutional Investors. LC 95-159269. 1994. text 55.00 (*1-55738-556-4*, Irwn Prfssnl) McGraw-Hill Prof.

Dobson, H., jt. auth. see Cooper, J.

Dobson, Hubert E. Power to Excel. LC 81-90553. 273p. 1982. 10.95 (*0-9607256-0-1*); pap. 4.95 (*0-9607256-1-X*) Rich Pub Co.

Dobson, J. Cuando lo Que Dios Hace No. (Meditacion Diaria Ser.).Tr. of When God Doesn't Make Sense. 7.99 (*0-7899-0485-3*, 496626) Editorial Unilit.

— Cuando lo Que Dios Hace No Tiene Sentido.Tr. of When God Doesn't Make Sense. 10.99 (*1-56063-509-6*, 498571) Editorial Unilit.

— Dr. Dobson Contesta/Familia.Tr. of Dr. Dobson Answers Questions/Family. (SPA.). 2000. 8.99 (*0-7899-0030-0*, 497460) Editorial Unilit.

Dobson, J. F. The Greek Orators. 336p. 1974. 25.00 (*0-89005-486-X*) Ares.

Dobson, James. Adolescente de Voluntad Firme.Tr. of Strong-Willed Adolescent. (SPA.). 1.79 (*0-685-74901-0*, 497418) Editorial Unilit.

— El Amor Debe Ser Firme.Tr. of Love Must Be Tough. (SPA.). 288p. 1990. pap. 6.99 (*0-8297-0394-2*) Vida Pubs.

— Amor Para Toda la Vida.Tr. of Love for a Lifetime. (SPA.). 128p. (Orig.). 1990. pap. 7.99 (*0-88113-021-4*) Caribe Betania.

— El Amor Romantico.Tr. of Romantic Love. (SPA.). 84p. 1995. pap. 4.99 (*1-56063-738-2*, 498406) Editorial Unilit.

— Coming Home: Timeless Wisdom for Families, 1, 1. LC 98-45171. 1999. pap. 14.99 (*0-8423-1442-3*) Tyndale Hse.

— Como Criar a un Nino de Voluntad Firme.Tr. of Strong Willed Child. (SPA.). 9.99 (*0-7899-0047-5*, 497495) Editorial Unilit.

— Como Preservar Su Matrimonio. (Serie Enfoque a la Familia - Focus on the Family Ser.).Tr. of How to Preserve Your Marriage. (SPA.). 1991. 1.99 (*1-56063-053-1*, 497415) Editorial Unilit.

— El Corazon del Hogar: Aliento para las Familias.Tr. of Home with a Heart. (SPA.). 8.99 (*0-7899-0328-8*, 497553) Editorial Unilit.

— Criemos Ninos Seguros de Si Mismos.Tr. of Hide or Seek. (SPA.). 1993. pap. 9.99 (*0-88113-136-9*) Caribe Betania.

— Cuando lo Que Dios Hace No Tiene Sentido.Tr. of When God Doesn't Make Sense. (SPA.). 1993. pap. 7.99 (*1-56063-458-8*, 498561) Editorial Unilit.

— Dare to Discipline. 1982. mass mkt. 3.50 (*0-553-25528-2*) Bantam.

— Discipline with Love. 62p. 1972. pap. 3.99 (*0-8423-0665-X*) Tyndale Hse.

— Dr. Dobson Contesta Sus Preguntas No. 1: Matrimonio.Tr. of Dr. Dobson Answers Questions: Marriage. (SPA.). pap. 8.99 (*0-7899-0031-9*, 497459) Editorial Unilit.

— Dr. Dobson Contesta Sus Preguntas No. 3: Criando Ninos.Tr. of Dr. Dobson Answers Questions: Raising Children. (SPA.). 301p. 1996. 8.99 (*0-7899-0032-7*, 497461) Editorial Unilit.

— Hablemos Con Franqueza.Tr. of Straight Talk. (SPA.). 1993. pap. 10.99 (*0-88113-133-4*) Caribe Betania.

— Home with a Heart: Ninety-Second Commentaries. LC 96-44908. 270p. 1996. 14.99 (*0-8423-1443-1*) Tyndale Hse.

— In the Arms of God. LC 98-118793. (Illus.). 153p. 1997. 14.99 (*0-8423-1826-7*) Tyndale Hse.

— Life on the Edge. write for info. (*0-614-24966-X*) Focus Family.

— Life on the Edge. 256p. 1995. 19.99 (*0-8499-0927-9*) Word Pub.

— Love for a Lifetime: Building a Marriage That Will Go the Distance. 143p. 1994. pap. 5.99 (*0-88070-683-X*, Multnomah Bks) Multnomah Pubs.

— Love for a Lifetime: Building a Marriage That Will Go the Distance. 1999. 19.99 (*1-57673-588-5*) Multnomah Pubs.

— Love Must Be Tough: Proven Hope for Families in Crisis. 256p. 1996. 19.99 (*0-8499-1341-1*) Word Pub.

— The New Dare to Discipline. 276p. 1992. 18.99 (*0-8423-0507-6*) Tyndale Hse.

— The New Dare to Discipline. (Christian Growth Self Help Ser.). 276p. 1996. pap. 12.99 (*0-8423-0506-8*) Tyndale Hse.

— The New Hide or Seek: Building Self-Esteem in Your Child. 3rd rev. ed. LC 98-27744. 240p. (C). 1999. 16.99 (*0-8007-1760-0*) Revell.

— Preparemonos Para la Adolescencia.Tr. of Preparing for Adolescence. 192p. 1981. 8.99 (*0-88113-253-5*) Caribe Betania.

— Preparing for Adolescence. 160p. 1984. mass mkt. 3.95 (*0-553-26445-1*) Bantam.

***Dobson, James.** Preparing for Adolescence. 186p. 1999. pap. 9.99 (*0-8307-2499-0*); pap. 9.99 (*0-8307-2497-4*, Regal Bks) Gospel Lght.

Dobson, James. Preparing for Adolescence. 1992. pap. 5.99 (*0-8423-5037-3*) Tyndale Hse.

— Preparing for Adolescence: Family Guide. 1999. pap. text 14.99 (*0-8307-2501-6*) Gospel Lght.

— Raising Teenagers Right. 96p. 1988. pap. 3.99 (*0-8423-5139-6*) Tyndale Hse.

Dobson, James. Respuestas Confiables.Tr. of Solid Answers. (SPA.). 13.99 (*0-7899-0431-4*, 495016) Editorial Unilit.

Dobson, James. Solid Answers. LC 97-23017. 500p. 1997. 16.97 (*0-8423-0623-4*) Tyndale Hse.

— Straight Talk: What Men Need to Know, What Women Should Understand. rev. ed. 222p. 1995. pap. 12.99 (*0-8499-3858-9*) Word Pub.

— The Strong-Willed Child. 240p. 1978. pap. 11.99 (*0-8423-6661-X*) Tyndale Hse.

— The Strong-Willed Child. (Illus.). 335p. 1992. mass mkt. 6.99 (*0-8423-5924-9*) Tyndale Hse.

— Temper Your Child's Tantrums. abr. ed. (Pocket Guides Ser.). 80p. 1986. pap. 3.99 (*0-8423-6994-5*) Tyndale Hse.

— Tener Hijos No es para Cobardes.Tr. of Parenting Isn't for Cowards. (SPA.). 168p. 1991. pap. 8.99 (*0-8297-0395-0*) Vida Pubs.

***Dobson, James.** Turn Your Heart Toward Home. 240p. 2000. 19.99 (*0-8499-1659-3*) Word Pub.

Dobson, James. La Vida Recta (The Straight Life) (SPA.). 1.79 (*0-685-74986-X*, 497417) Editorial Unilit.

— What Wives Wish Their Husbands Knew about Women. 192p. 1977. pap. 9.99 (*0-8423-7889-8*) Tyndale Hse.

— What Wives Wish Their Husbands Knew about Women. 192p. 1979. mass mkt. 5.99 (*0-8423-7896-0*) Tyndale Hse.

— When God Doesn't Make Sense. LC 93-24631. 250p. 1993. 18.99 (*0-8423-8227-5*) Tyndale Hse.

— When God Doesn't Make Sense. (Illus.). 250p. 1997. pap. 12.99 (*0-8423-8237-2*) Tyndale Hse.

— When God Doesn't Make Sense. (Mini Bk.). 80p. 1996. 4.99 (*0-8499-5141-0*) Word Pub.

— When God Doesn't Make Sense. large type ed. 350p. 1994. 19.99 (*0-8423-8242-9*) Tyndale Hse.

Dobson, James, et al. Raising Kids. 48p. 1993. pap., teacher ed. 5.50 (*0-8341-1450-X*) Beacon Hill.

Dobson, James, jt. auth. see Dobson, Danae.

Dobson, James C. Adolescente de Voluntad Firme. (Serie Enfoque a la Familia - Focus on the Family Ser.).Tr. of Strong-Willed Adolescent. (SPA.). 1991. 1.99 (*1-56063-049-3*, 497418) Editorial Unilit.

— Azote de la Rivalidad Entre Hermanos. (Serie Enfoque a la Familia - Focus on the Family Ser.).Tr. of Scourge of Sibling Rivalry. (SPA.). 1991. pap. 1.99 (*1-56063-127-9*, 497404) Editorial Unilit.

— Children at Risk: What You Need to Know to Protect Your Family. rev. ed. 1994. pap. 12.99 (*0-8499-3584-9*) Word Pub.

— Como Hacer Frente a la Frustracion. (Serie Enfoque a la Familia - Focus on the Family Ser.).Tr. of Coping with Frustration. (SPA.). 93p. 1991. pap. 1.99 (*1-56063-130-9*, 497403) Editorial Unilit.

— Como Preservar Su Matrimonio. (Serie Enfoque a la Familia - Focus on the Family Ser.).Tr. of How to Preserve Your Marriage. (SPA.). 89p. 1991. pap. write for info. (*0-614-27008-1*) Editorial Unilit.

— Comprendiendo Personalidad de Su Hijo. (Serie Enfoque a la Familia - Focus on the Family Ser.).Tr. of Understanding Your Child's Personality. (SPA.). 32p. 1989. pap. 1.99 (*1-56063-058-2*, 497419) Editorial Unilit.

— Controle las Rabietas de Su Hijo. (Serie Guia de Bolsillo - Pocket Guides Ser.).Tr. of Temper Your Child's Tantrum. (SPA.). 108p. 1987. pap. 2.79 (*0-8423-6514-1*, 498041) Editorial Unilit.

— Criando a los Hijos Con Plena Confianza. (Serie Enfoque a la Familia - Focus on the Family Ser.).Tr. of Parenting Isn't for Cowards. (SPA.). 28p. 1992. pap. 1.99 (*1-56063-258-5*, 497424) Editorial Unilit.

— Cuando Lo Que Dice No Tiene Sentido.Tr. of When God Doesn't Make Sense. (SPA.). 274p. 1993. pap. write for info. (*0-614-27024-3*) Editorial Unilit.

— Disciplina de Cuatro a Doce. (Serie Enfoque a la Familia - Focus on the Family Ser.).Tr. of Discipline from Four to Twelve. (SPA.). 25p. 1991. 1.99 (*1-56063-056-6*, 497412) Editorial Unilit.

***Dobson, James C.** Dobson 2-In-1, 1. 1999. write for info. (*0-8499-1641-0*) J Countryman.

Dobson, James C. Educando a los Adolescentes. (Serie Guia de Bolsillo - Pocket Guides Ser.).Tr. of Raising Teenagers Right. (SPA.). 1989. pap. 2.79 (*0-945792-76-X*, 498048) Editorial Unilit.

— Ensenando a los Ninos Ser Amables. (Serie Enfoque a la Familia - Focus on the Family Ser.).Tr. of Teaching Children to Be Kind. (SPA.). 25p. 1995. 1.99 (*1-56063-893-1*, 497433) Editorial Unilit.

— Firmeza Amorosa para Personas Solteras. (Serie Enfoque a la Familia - Focus on the Family Ser.).Tr. of Tough Love for Singles. (SPA.). 24p. 1992. pap. 1.99 (*1-56063-259-3*, 497425) Editorial Unilit.

— Haciendole Frente a la Depresion. (Serie Enfoque a la Familia - Focus on the Family Ser.).Tr. of Coping with Depression. (SPA.). 23p. 1991. pap. 1.99 (*1-56063-189-9*, 497405) Editorial Unilit.

— Haciendole Frente a la Ira. (Serie Enfoque a la Familia - Focus on the Family Ser.).Tr. of Coping with Anger. (SPA.). 95p. 1991. pap. 1.99 (*1-56063-129-5*, 497402) Editorial Unilit.

— Home with a Heart: Ninety-Second Commentaries. 1999. pap. text 5.99 (*0-8423-3513-7*) Tyndale Hse.

***Dobson, James C.** Life on the Edge: A Young Adult Guide to a Meaningful Future. gif. ed. 124p. 2000. 12.99 (*0-8499-1629-1*) Word Pub.

— Love Must Be Tough - Straight Talk. 14.99 (*0-8499-1654-2*) Word Pub.

Dobson, James C. Matrimonio en Toda Su Excelencia. (Serie Enriquezca a la Familia - Enriching the Family Ser.).Tr. of Marriage at Its Best. (SPA.). 229p. 1995. 1.99 (*0-7899-0056-4*, 498203) Editorial Unilit.

***Dobson, James C.** Night Light. 2000. 19.99 (*1-57673-674-1*, Multnomah Bks) Multnomah Pubs.

Dobson, James C. Parenting Isn't for Cowards. rev. ed. 240p. 1997. pap. 12.99 (*0-8499-4014-1*) Word Pub.

— Preguntas Que Hacen, Padres Sobre la Disciplina. (Serie Enfoque a la Familia - Focus on the Family Ser.).Tr. of Questions Parents Ask about Discipline. (SPA.). 39p. 1991. pap. 1.99 (*1-56063-188-0*, 497407) Editorial Unilit.

— Sobreproteccion: La Error de los Padres. (Serie Enfoque a la Familia - Focus on the Family Ser.).Tr. of Overprotection: The Error of Dedicated Parents. (SPA.). 55p. 1992. pap. 1.99 (*1-56063-257-7*, 497428) Editorial Unilit.

***Dobson, James C.** Straight Talk to Men: Recovering the Biblical Meaning of Manhood. 272p. 2000. pap. 12.99 (*0-8499-4210-1*) Word Pub.

— La Vida Recta. (Serie Enfoque a la Familia - Focus on the Family Ser.).Tr. of Straight Life. (SPA.). 1.99 (*1-56063-048-5*, 497417) Editorial Unilit.

Dobson, James C. La Vida Recta. (Serie Enfoque a la Familia - Focus on the Family Ser.).Tr. of Straight Life. (SPA.). 23p. 1991. pap. write for info. (*0-614-27158-4*) Editorial Unilit.

— La Vida Recta (The Straight Life) (Serie Enfoque a la Familia - Focus on the Family Ser.). (SPA.). 23p. 1991. write for info. (*0-614-24408-0*) Editorial Unilit.

Dobson, James C., jt. auth. see Palau, Luis.

Dobson, Jane M. & Gorman, Neil T. Cancer Chemotherapy in Small Animal Practice. LC 93-3434. (Library of Veterinary Practice). (Illus.). 224p. 1993. pap. 41.95 (*0-632-03694-X*) Blackwell Sci.

Dobson, Jenni. Beautiful Quilts, Art Decorations: Making Classic Quilts & Modern Variations. (Illus.). 128p. 1997. pap. text 14.95 (*0-8069-1327-4*) Sterling.

— Patchwork, Quilting & Applique: The Complete Guide to All the Essential Techniques. LC 97-8241. 1997. 27.95 (*0-89577-971-4*, Pub. by RD Assn) Penguin Putnam.

— Sweet & Simple Country Quilts. LC 96-5185. (Illus.). 144p. 1996. 27.95 (*0-8069-9497-5*) Sterling.

***Dobson, Joanne.** Cold & Pure & Very Dead. 288p. 2000. 22.95 (*0-385-49340-1*) Doubleday.

Dobson, Joanne. Dickinson & the Strategies of Reticence: The Woman Writer in Nineteenth-Century America. LC 88-46030. 184p. 1989. 25.00 (*0-253-31809-2*) Ind U Pr.

— Dickinson & the Strategies of Reticence: The Woman Writer in Nineteenth-Century America. LC 88-46030. 177p. Date not set. reprint ed. pap. 54.90 (*0-608-20538-9*, 205445200002) Bks Demand.

— The Northbury Papers. 352p. 1999. mass mkt. 5.99 (*0-553-57661-5*) Bantam.

— The Northbury Papers. LC 98-5895. 288p. 1998. 21.95 (*0-385-48693-6*) Doubleday.

— Quieter Than Sleep. 336p. 1998. reprint ed. mass mkt. 5.99 (*0-553-57660-7*) Bantam.

***Dobson, Joanne.** The Raven & The Nightingale. 320p. 2000. mass mkt. 5.99 (*0-553-57999-1*) Bantam.

Dobson, Joanne. Raven & the Nightingale: A Modern Mystery of Edgar Allen Poe. LC 99-30866. 288p. 1999. 21.95 (*0-385-49339-8*) Doubleday.

Dobson, Joanne, ed. see Southworth, E.D.E.N.

Dobson, John. The Art of Management & the Aesthetic Manager: The Coming Way of Business. LC 98-30541. 208p. 1999. 59.95 (*1-56720-232-2*, Quorum Bks) Greenwood.

Dobson, John, ed. Finance Ethics: The Rationality of Virtue. 204p. 1996. 66.00 (*0-8476-8401-6*); pap. 23.95 (*0-8476-8402-4*) Rowman.

Dobson, John, intro. Tennessee Beginnings. LC 74-583. (Illus.). 144p. 1974. 17.50 (*0-87152-152-0*) Reprint.

Dobson, John, jt. auth. see Lord-Smith, Peter J.

Dobson, John F. Ancient Education & Its Meaning for Us. LC 63-10297. (Our Debt to Greece & Rome Ser.). reprint ed. 57.50 (*0-8154-0060-8*) Cooper Sq.

— Greek Orators. LC 67-23205. (Essay Index Reprint Ser.). 1977. 21.95 (*0-8369-0381-1*) Ayer.

Dobson, John F., et al, eds. Electronic Density Functional Theory: Recent Progress & New Directions. LC 98-21007. (Illus.). 406p. (C). 1998. text 125.00 (*0-306-45834-9*, Kluwer Plenum) Kluwer Academic.

***Dobson, John H.** Learn Biblical Hebrew. 310p. 1999. pap. text 33.50 (*1-55671-088-7*, Pub. by S I L Intl) Eisenbrauns.

Dobson, John H. Learn New Testament Greek. 2nd ed. LC 92-45770. 328p. 1993. pap. 14.99 (*0-8010-3019-6*) Baker Bks.

Dobson, John M. America's Ascent: The United States Becomes a Great Power, 1880-1914. LC 77-90754. (Illus.). 251p. 1978. 30.00 (*0-87580-070-X*); pap. 15.00 (*0-87580-523-X*) N Ill U Pr.

— Reticent Expansionism: The Foreign Policy of William McKinley. LC 87-34541. 212p. 1988. text 26.50 (*0-8207-0202-1*) Duquesne.

Dobson, Julia M. & Hawkins, Gerald S. Conversation in English: Professional Careers. (Illus.). 108p. (YA). (gr. 9-12). 1978. pap. 19.00 (*0-278-46440-8*) Heinle & Heinle.

Dobson, Julian, ed. see Blaszczak, Mike.

Dobson, Justine. Baby Beautiful: A Handbook of Baby Head Shaping. LC 94-96024. (Illus.). 320p. (Orig.). 1994. pap. 19.95 (*0-9640646-3-4*) Heirs Pr.

Dobson, K. & Dobson, D., eds. Professional Psychology in Canada. (Illus.). 480p. 1993. text 49.00 (*0-88937-043-5*) Hogrefe & Huber Pubs.

Dobson, Keith & Kendall, Philip C., eds. Psychopathology & Cognition. LC 93-19571. (Personality, Psychopathology & Psychotherapy Ser.). (Illus.). 492p. 1993. text 65.00 (*0-12-404175-2*) Acad Pr.

Dobson, Keith S., ed. Handbook of Cognitive-Behavioral Therapies. LC 87-27. 426p. 1987. lib. bdg. 65.00 (*0-89862-704-4*) Guilford Pubns.

— Handbook of Cognitive-Behavioral Therapies. LC 87-27. 426p. 1990. reprint ed. pap. text 26.95 (*0-89862-524-6*) Guilford Pubns.

Dobson, Keith S. & Craig, Kenneth D. Empirically Supported Therapies: Best Practice in Professional Psychology. LC 98-19759. (Banff International Behavioral Science Ser.). 317p. 1998. 35.00 (*0-7619-1075-1*); pap. 17.99 (*0-7619-1076-X*) Sage.

Dobson, Keith S. & Craig, Kenneth D., eds. Advances in Cognitive-Behavioral Therapy. (Banff International Behavioral Science Ser.). 328p. 1996. pap. 24.95 (*0-7619-0643-6*) Sage.

— Advances in Cognitive-Behavioral Therapy. LC 95-50226. (Banff International Behavioral Science Ser.: Vol. 2). 328p. 1996. 54.00 (*0-8039-7006-4*, RC489) Sage.

Dobson, Keith S., jt. ed. see Craig, Kenneth D.

Dobson, Kenneth M., jt. auth. see Donaldson, Hal.

Dobson, Linda. The Art of Education: Reclaiming Your Family, Community, & Self. LC 95-4148. 256p. 1995. pap. 14.75 (*0-945097-26-3*) Home Educ Pr.

— The Art of Education: Reclaiming Your Family, Community & Self. 256p. 1997. reprint ed. pap. 18.95 (*0-913677-14-0*) Holt Assocs.

— Homeschooling: The Early Years: Your Complete Guide to Successfully Homeschooling the 3- to 7-Year-Old Child. LC 99-32262. 224p. 1999. pap. 16.00 (*0-7615-2028-7*) Prima Pub.

— The Homeschooling Book of Answers: The 88 Most Important Questions Answered by Homeschooling's Most Respected Voices. LC 98-18595. 320p. 2000. pap. 16.95 (*0-7615-1377-9*) Prima Pub.

Dobson, Linda, jt. auth. see Prima Staff.

Dobson, Lorna. More Than a Pastor's Wife: Setting Boundaries, Coping with Frustrations, Defining You Own Role. 176p. 1995. pap. 9.99 (*0-310-48551-7*) Zondervan.

Dobson, M. B. Anaesthesia at the District Hospital. (ENG, FRE & SPA., Illus.). 143p. 1988. pap. text 20.00 (*92-4-154228-4*, 1150289) World Health.

Dobson, M. Craig. Ultra-Wideband Sar Forest Experiment Near Raco, Michigan: April 4-12, 1992. LC SD0387.R4. (University of Michigan Reports: No. TR-029312-1). 70p. reprint ed. pap. 30.00 (*0-7837-4624-5*, 204434700002) Bks Demand.

— Ultra-Wideband SAR Forest Experiment Near Raco, Michigan: July 1992 Data & Radiative Transfer Model Results. LC TK6595.. (University of Michigan Reports: No. 029312-2-F). 62p. reprint ed. pap. 30.00 (*0-7837-6289-5*, 204600400010) Bks Demand.

Dobson, M. Craig, jt. auth. see Ulaby, Fawwaz T.

Dobson, Margaret J. & Sisley, Becky L. Softball for Girls. LC 79-24256. 232p. 1980. reprint ed. lib. bdg. 15.50 (*0-89874-103-3*) Krieger.

Dobson, Martha, ed. see Hoyer, Mark V. & Canfield, Daniel E.

Dobson, Mary. Greek Grime. (Smelly Old History Ser.). (Illus.). 32p. (J). (gr. 4-6). 1998. pap. 7.95 (*0-19-910493-X*) OUP.

— Medieval Muck. LC 99-209828. (Smelly Old History Ser.). (Illus.). 32p. (J). (gr. 2 up). 1999. pap. 7.95 (*0-19-910528-6*) OUP.

— Mouldy Mummies. LC 99-170346. (Smelly Old History Ser.). (Illus.). 32p. (J). 1998. pap. 7.95 (*0-19-910495-6*) OUP.

— Reeking Royals. LC 99-209418. (Smelly Old History Ser.). (Illus.). 32p. (J). (gr. 2 up). 1999. pap. 7.95 (*0-19-910529-4*) OUP.

— Roman Aromas. LC 97-144505. (Smelly Old History Ser.). (Illus.). 32p. (J). (gr. 2 up). 1997. pap. 7.95 (*0-19-910094-2*) OUP.

— Tudor Odors. LC 97-144508. (Smelly Old History Ser.). (Illus.). 32p. (J). (gr. 2). 1997. pap. 7.95 (*0-19-910096-9*) OUP.

— Victorian Vapors. LC 97-144501. (Smelly Old History Ser.). (Illus.). 32p. (J). (gr. 2 up). 1997. pap. 7.95 (*0-19-910095-0*) OUP.

— Vile Vikings. (Smelly Old History Ser.). (Illus.). 32p. (J). (gr. 4-6). 1998. pap. 7.95 (*0-19-910494-8*) OUP.

— Wartime Whiffs. LC 99-209812. (Smelly Old History Ser.). (Illus.). 32p. (J). (gr. 2 up). 1999. pap. 7.95 (*0-19-910530-8*) OUP.

Dobson, Mary J. Contours of Death & Disease in Early Modern England. (Studies in Population, Economy & Society in Past Time: No. 29). (Illus.). 670p. (C). 1997. text 95.00 (*0-521-40464-9*) Cambridge U Pr.

Dobson, Mary Lynn. The Somewhat True Tale of Robin Hood. 85p. Date not set. pap. 5.60 (*1-58342-013-4*, SE7) Dramatic Pub.

Dobson, Melanie, jt. auth. see Williams, Tosha.

Dobson, Michael. The Making of the National Poet: Shakespeare, Adaptation & Authorship, 1660-1769. (Illus.). 276p. 1995. reprint ed. pap. text 22.00 (*0-19-818323-2*) OUP.

— Practical Project Management: Secrets of Managing Any Project on Time & on Budget. Scanlon, Kelly, ed. LC 96-67864. (Lifelong Learning Library). (Illus.). 292p. 1996. pap. 18.95 (*1-57294-015-8*, 17-0002) SkillPath Pubns.

Dobson, Michael & Dobson, Deborah S. Coping with Supervisory Nightmares: 12 Common Nightmares of Leadership & What to Do about Them. Scanlon, Kelly, ed. LC 96-68883. (Self-Study Sourcebook Ser.). (Illus.). 199p. 1997. pap. 15.95 (*1-57294-067-0*, 13-0026) SkillPath Pubns.

***Dobson, Michael & Dobson, Deborah Singer.** Enlightened Office Politics: Understanding, Coping With & Winning the Game - Without Losing Your Soul. 2001. pap. 17.95 (*0-8144-7065-3*) AMACOM.

Dobson, Michael, jt. auth. see Niles, Douglas.

***Dobson, Michael S. & Dobson, Deborah S.** Managing Up! 59 Ways to Build a Career-Advancing Relationship with Your Boss. LC 99-43413. 176p. 1999. pap. 16.95 (*0-8144-7042-4*) AMACOM.

Dobson, Ned. Venison as You Like It. (Illus.). 112p. 1997. pap. 9.95 (*0-9641160-0-6*) Stoneydale Pr Pub.

Dobson, P., jt. auth. see Cape, B. F.

Dobson, P. J., ed. Interdisciplinary Surface Science: Proceedings of the ISSC6 Conference, Warwick, U. K., April 18-21, 1983, Vol. VI. 250p. 1984. pap. 45.00 (*0-08-031146-6*, Pergamon Pr) Elsevier.

Dobson, P. J., jt. auth. see Larsen, P. K.

Dobson, Paul & Reddy, Jo. Commercial Law. (Questions & Answers Ser.). 295p. 1994. 18.00 (*1-874241-29-5*, Pub. by Cavendish Pubng) Gaunt.

Dobson, Paul & Starkey, Ken. The Strategic Management Blueprint. LC 92-31273. 176p. 1993. pap. 37.95 (*0-631-18624-7*) Blackwell Pubs.

Dobson, Pauline R., jt. ed. see Brown, Barry L.

Dobson, Peter. Los Dinosaurios Gigantes.Tr. of Giant Dinosaurs. (ENG & SPA.). (J). (ps-2). 1989. 19.95 (*0-590-73764-3*) Scholastic Inc.

Dobson, Phyllis, jt. auth. see Trigg, Maggie.

Dobson, R. B. Church & Society in the Medieval North of England. LC 95-49428. 1996. 60.00 (*1-85285-120-1*) Hambledon Press.

Dobson, R. B. & Taylor, J. The Rymes of Robyn Hood: An Introduction to the English Outlaw. rev. ed. (History Paperbacks Ser.). (Illus.). 368p. 1997. pap. 26.95 (*0-7509-1661-3*, Pub. by Sutton Pub Ltd) Intl Pubs Mktg.

Dobson, Richard B. Durham Priory, Fourteen Hundred to Fourteen Fifty. LC 72-89809. (Cambridge Studies in Medieval Life & Thought: vol. 6). 442p. reprint ed. pap. 126.00 (*0-608-13569-0*, 2022444) Bks Demand.

Dobson, Rick. Programming Microsoft Access 2000. LC 99-13032. (Illus.). 550p. 1999. pap. 49.99 incl. cd-rom (*0-7356-0500-9*) Microsoft.

Dobson, Ross V. Bringing the Economy Home from the Market. LC 92-72629. 235p. 1993. 48.99 (*1-895431-51-4*, Pub. by Black Rose); pap. 19.99 (*1-895431-50-6*, Pub. by Black Rose) Consort Bk Sales.

Dobson, Russell, et al. Staff Development: A Humanistic Approach. LC 80-67254. 175p. 1980. pap. text 19.00 (*0-8191-1131-7*) U Pr of Amer.

Dobson, S. M. Spectrum. 32p. 1986. 20.00 (*0-7223-2010-8*, Pub. by A H S Ltd) St Mut.

Dobson Saltzwedel, Caroline, tr. see Kemp, Wolfgang.

***Dobson, Sean.** Authority & Upheaval in Leipzig, 1910-1920: The Story of a Relationship. 352p. 2000. text 45.00 (*0-231-12076-1*) Col U Pr.

Dobson, Shirley. God Loves You! A Read-Aloud Coloring Book about God's Plan for Salvation. (ps-3). 1998. pap. 0.99 (*0-8307-2329-3*) Gospel Lght.

Dobson, Terry. It's a Lot Like Dancing: An Aikido Journal. LC 93-37479. (Illus.). 178p. (Orig.). 1993. pap. 22.50 (*1-883319-02-1*) Frog Ltd CA.

Dobson, Terry & Miller, Victor. Aikido in Everyday Life: Giving in to Get Your Way. 2nd ed. (Illus.). 257p. (Orig.). 1992. reprint ed. pap. 14.95 (*1-55643-151-1*) North Atlantic.

— Giving in to Get Your Way: The Attack-Tics System for Winning Your Everyday Battles. 1978. 8.95 (*0-440-03247-4*) Dell.

Dobson, Theodore. Inner Healing. large type ed. 384p. 1985. 12.95 (*0-8027-2488-4*) Walker & Co.

Dobson, Theodore E., jt. auth. see Hurley, Kathleen V.

Dobson, Vernon G., jt. ed. see Rose, David.

Dobson, W. A. A Dictionary of the Chinese Particles: With a Prolegomenon in Which the Problems of the Particles Are Considered & They Are Classified by Their Grammatical Functions. LC 73-91242. 917p. reprint ed. pap. 200.00 (*0-608-15399-0*, 202932900060) Bks Demand.

— The Language of the Book of Songs. LC 68-92657. (Illus.). 351p. reprint ed. pap. 108.90 (*0-608-11066-3*, 202047300018) Bks Demand.

— Late Archaic Chinese: A Grammatical Study. LC 59-38059. 282p. reprint ed. pap. 87.50 (*0-608-10792-1*, 205546400022) Bks Demand.

Dobson, Wach. Late Han Chinese: A Study of the Archaic-Han Shift. LC 65-976. 162p. reprint ed. pap. 50.30 (*0-7837-0536-0*, 204086400019) Bks Demand.

Dobson, Wendy & Jacquet, Pierre. Financial Services Liberalization in the World Trade Organization. LC 97-39379. 1998. pap. 20.00 (*0-88132-254-7*) Inst Intl Eco.

The financial services agreement (FSA) was reached in the World Trade Organization in December 1997 & is to be implemented in early 1999 - but this will be only a modest first step toward creating efficient financial sectors worldwide. What other steps should government take? During the negotiations in the WTO in Geneva, the industrial & developing countries agreed to lock in series of reforms that had been achieved in many countries through unilateral action, regional cooperation & more recently, as a condition of IMF assistance. Dobson & Jacquet evaluate the WTO financial services negotiations agreement & analyze the basic rationale for FSA: that efficient financial sectors are important contributors to economic growth & stability, a conclusion that is highlighted by the pivotal role of weak financial sectors in triggering the impact of the Asian financial crisis. They assess the impact of the agreement & the financial crisis on financial-sector liberalization in several important emerging-market economies. The authors explain remaining obstacles to establishing efficient & open financial sectors & conclude with a blueprint for liberalizing financial services in the future. *Publisher Paid Annotation.*

Dobson, Wendy, jt. ed. see Safarian, A. E.

Dobson, William, tr. see Schleiermacher, Friedrich Daniel Ernst.

***Dobson, Wolf, ed.** Artificial Intelligence & Interactive Entertainment: Papers from the AAAI Spring Symposium. (Technical Reports: Vol. SS-00-02). (Illus.). 86p. 2000. spiral bd. 25.00 (*1-57735-108-8*) AAAI Pr.

Dobszay, Laszlo. A History of Hungarian Music. 236p. 1999. pap. 21.00 (*963-13-3498-8*, Pub. by Corvina Bks) St Mut.

Dobuzinskis, Laurent, et al, eds. Policy Studies in Canada: The State of the Art. 360p. 1996. text 55.00 (*0-8020-0528-4*); pap. text 24.95 (*0-8020-6966-5*) U of Toronto Pr.

Doby, T. & Alker, G. Origins & Development of Medical Imaging. LC 96-8134. (Medical Humanities Ser.). (Illus.). 176p. (C). 1996. 29.95 (*0-8093-2010-X*) S Ill U Pr.

Dobychin, Leonid. The Town of N. Borden, Richard C. & Belova, Natalia, trs. from RUS. LC 98-15528. (European Classics Ser.). 144p. 1998. pap. text 14.95 (*0-8101-1589-1*) Northwestern U Pr.

Dobyns. Programmed Guide T-A 6FAT. 6th ed. (C). 1986. mass mkt. 14.75 (*0-87150-984-9*, 33L2985) PWS Pubs.

— Programmed Guide T-A 6FCA. 6th ed. (C). 1986. mass mkt. 13.50 (*0-87150-920-2*, 33L3015) PWS Pubs.

— Stories. Date not set. pap. 12.00 (*0-8050-6023-5*, Owl) H Holt & Co.

Dobyns, Ann. The Voices of Romance: Studies in Dialogue & Character. 1989. 27.50 (*0-87413-351-3*) U Delaware Pr.

Dobyns, Ann, jt. auth. see Callaghan, Patsy.

***Dobyns, Beth.** Worship: Why, What, How. 2000. pap. text 5.99 (*0-8272-9043-8*) Chalice Pr.

Dobyns, Henry F. Spanish Colonial Tucson: A Demographic History. LC 75-10344. (Illus.). 256p. reprint ed. pap. 79.40 (*0-7837-5043-9*, 204472000004) Bks Demand.

Dobyns, Henry F., ed. Spanish Colonial Frontier Research. (Spanish Borderlands Research Ser.: No. 1). 1980. 20.00 (*0-932752-05-5*) Ctr Anthrop Studies.

Dobyns, Kenneth W. A History of the Early Patent Offices: The Patent Office Pony. LC 97-8337. (Illus.). 256p. 1997. 29.95 (*1-887901-13-2*) Sergeant Kirk.

Dobyns, Kenneth W. & Thorpe, Margaret S. Daniel Dobyns of Colonial Virginia: His English Ancestry & American Descendants. LC 73-20318. 188p. reprint ed. pap. 58.30 (*0-608-10027-7*, 200524700051) Bks Demand.

Dobyns, Lloyd & Crawford-Mason, Clare. Quality or Else: The Revolution in World Business. 320p. 1993. pap. 11.95 (*0-395-63749-X*) HM.

***Dobyns, Lloyd & Crawford-Mason, Clare.** Thinking about Quality: Progress, Wisdom & the Deming Philosophy. 280p. 2000. reprint ed. text 23.00 (*0-7881-6989-0*) DIANE Pub.

Dobyns, Roy A. Programmed Guide to Accompany Fundamentals of Algebra & Trigonometry. 4th ed. 1978. pap. text 6.75 (*0-87150-258-5*, PWS 2075) PWS Pubs.

Dobyns, Stephen. Best Words, Best Order: Essays on Poetry. 352p. 1996. text 26.95 (*0-312-12932-7*) St Martin.

— Best Words Best Order: Essays on Poetry. 352p. 1997. pap. 16.95 (*0-312-17229-X*) St Martin.

— Black Dog, Red Dog. LC 89-81709. (Classic Contemporaries Ser.). 1990. pap. 12.95 (*0-88748-102-7*) Carnegie-Mellon.

— Boy in the Water. LC 98-56106. 406p. 1999. 25.00 (*0-8050-6020-0*, Pub. by H Holt & Co) VHPS.

***Dobyns, Stephen.** Boy in the Water. 448p. 2000. mass mkt. 6.99 (*0-312-97522-8*, St Martins Paperbacks) St Martin.

Dobyns, Stephen. The Church of Dead Girls. LC 96-52525. 300p. 1997. 23.00 (*0-8050-5103-1*) H Holt & Co.

— The Church of Dead Girls. LC 96-52525. 388p. 1998. pap. 12.00 (*0-8050-5104-X*) H Holt & Co.

— The Church of Dead Girls. large type ed. LC 97-29618. (Large Print Book Ser.). 1997. 25.95 (*1-56895-478-6*) Wheeler Pub.

— Common Carnage. LC 95-30214. 132p. 1996. pap. 15.95 (*0-14-058748-9*, Penguin Bks) Viking Penguin.

— Eating Naked: Stories. LC 99-87733. 276p. 2000. 23.00 (*0-8050-6022-7*, Metropol Bks) H Holt & Co.

— The House on Alexandrine. LC 89-32237. 236p. (C). 1990. pap. text 15.95 (*0-8143-2183-6*) Wayne St U Pr.

— The House on Alexandrine. LC 89-32237. 235p. reprint ed. pap. 72.90 (*0-608-10565-1*, 2071185) Bks Demand.

***Dobyns, Stephen.** Pallbearers Envying the One Who Rides. LC 99-18492. 160p. 1999. pap. 15.95 (*0-14-058916-3*, Penguin Bks) Viking Penguin.

Dobyns, Stephen. Saratoga Backtalk: A Charlie Bradshaw Mystery. large type ed. LC 94-45328. (Large Print Bks.). 1995. pap. 21.95 (*1-56895-089-6*) Wheeler Pub.

— Saratoga Fleshpot: A Charlie Bradshaw Mystery. 220p. 1995. 21.00 (*0-393-03805-X*) Norton.

— Saratoga Fleshpot: A Charlie Bradshaw Mystery. 224p. 1996. pap. 5.95 (*0-14-025535-4*, Penguin Bks) Viking Penguin.

— Saratoga Haunting. 224p. 1994. pap. 6.95 (*0-14-017162-2*, Penguin Bks) Viking Penguin.

— Saratoga Hexameter. large type ed. (General Ser.). 391p. 1991. lib. bdg. 20.95 (*0-8161-5133-4*, G K Hall Lrg Type) Mac Lib Ref.

— Saratoga Strongbox: A Charlie Bradshaw Mystery. (Charlie Bradshaw Mysteries Ser.). 208p. 1999. pap. 5.99 (*0-14-028012-X*) Viking Penguin.

***Dobyns, Stephen.** Saratoga Strongbox: A Charlie Bradshaw Mystery. large type ed. LC 99-86697. 2000. pap. 22.95 (*1-56895-848-X*) Wheeler Pub.

Dobyns, Stephen. Skin Deep. Date not set. pap. 13.00 (*0-8050-6021-9*, Owl) H Holt & Co.

— Velocities: New & Selected Poems, 1966-1992. 320p. 1994. pap. 16.95 (*0-14-058651-2*, Penguin Bks) Viking Penguin.

D

— The Wrestler's Cruel Study. LC 92-40861. 448p. 1993. 22.95 (0-393-03511-5) Norton.
— The Wrestler's Cruel Study. 432p. 1995. pap. 13.00 (0-393-31212-7) Norton.

Dobyns, Winifred S. California Gardens. LC 96-18860. (Illus.). 240p. 1996. reprint ed. 59.00 (1-888310-88-X) A A Knoll Pubs.

Dobyns, Zipporah. Expanding Astrology's Universe. LC 83-70657. 256p. (Orig.). 1985. pap. 12.95 (0-917086-49-X) ACS Pubns.

Dobyns, Zipporah, jt. auth. see Pottenger, Maritha.

Dobzhansky, Theodosius. Dobzhansky's Genetics of Natural Populations: I-XLIII. Lewontin, Richard C. et al, eds. LC 81-2073. 1024p. 1981. text 112.00 (0-231-05132-8) Col U Pr.
— Genetics of the Evolutionary Process. LC 72-127363. 505p. 1972. pap. text 32.50 (0-231-08306-8) Col U Pr.

Dobzhansky, Theodosius & Boesiger, Ernest. Human Culture: A Moment in Evolution. Wallace, Bruce, ed. LC 82-22172. (Illus.). 175p. 1983. text 44.50 (0-231-05632-X) Col U Pr.
— Human Culture: A Moment in Evolution. Wallace, Bruce, ed. LC 82-22172. (Illus.). 175p. 1986. pap. text 19.00 (0-231-05633-8) Col U Pr.

Dobzhansky, Theodosius & Eldridge, Niles. Genetics & the Origin of Species. Gould, Stephen Jay, ed. LC 82-4278. (Classics of Modern Evolution Ser.). 416p. 1982. reprint ed. pap. text 27.50 (0-231-05475-0) Col U Pr.

Dobzhansky, Theodosius, et al. Evolution. LC 77-23284. (Illus.). 572p. (C). 1977. text 36.00 (0-7167-0572-9) W H Freeman.

Dobzhansky, Theodosius, ed. see Schmalhausen, Ivan I.

Dobzhansky, Theodosius G. The Roving Naturalist: Travel Letters of Theodosius Dobzhansky. Glass, Bentley, ed. LC 79-55229. (American Philosophical Society, Memoirs Ser.: No. 139). 337p. reprint ed. pap. 104.50 (0-7837-2683-X, 204306000006) Bks Demand.

Doc-Fai Wong. Internal Secrets of Tai Chi Chuan. 1991. pap. 12.95 (0-86568-147-3, 250) Unique Pubns.

Doc Fai Wong & Hallander, Jane. Tai Chi Chuan's Internal Secrets. (Illus.). 160p. (Orig.). 1991. pap. 12.95 (0-86568-138-4, 250) Unique Pubns.

Doc Time, see Tim, Doc.

Docagne, Maurice, et al. Le Calcul Simplifie. Howlett, J. & Williams, M. R., trs. from FRE. (Charles Babbage Institute Reprint Series for the History of Computing). (Illus.). 211p. 1986. 35.00 (0-262-15032-8) MIT Pr.

DoCampo, Domingo, et al, eds. Intelligent Methods in Signal Processing & Communications. LC 97-183. 318p. 1997. 69.95 (0-8176-3960-8) Birkhauser.

DoCampo, Domingo, et al. Intelligent Methods in Signal Processing & Communications. LC 97-183. 336p. 1997. write for info. (3-7643-3960-8) Birkhauser.

DoCarmo, Manfredo. Riemannian Geometry. 300p. 1994. 43.50 (0-8176-3490-8) Birkhauser.

Docef, Alen, jt. auth. see Smith, Mark J.

Docents, DeGolyer. The Garden Gourmet. 336p. 1994. 24.95 (0-9640249-0-X) Dallas Arboretum.

Docents of Nursery Nature Staff. Trails, Tails & Tidepools in Pails: Over 100 Fun & Easy Nature Activities for Families & Teachers to Share with Babies & Young Children. 3rd ed. (Illus.). 112p. (Orig.). 1996. reprint ed. pap. 10.95 (0-9632753-2-1) Child Nature Inst.

Docents of Nursery Nature Walks Staff. Trails, Tails & Tide Pools in Pails (&) Nature Songs for Walk Alongs. 3rd ed. (Illus.). 112p. (J). 1997. 15.95 incl. audio (0-9632753-5-6) Child Nature Inst.
— Trails, Tails & Tidepools in Pails: Over 100 Nature Activities for Families with Babies & Young Children. (Illus.). 112p. (Orig.). 1992. pap. 9.95 (0-9632753-0-5) Child Nature Inst.

D

Dochain, D., jt. ed. see Bastin, G.

Docherty, Brian, ed. Twentieth-Century European Drama. LC 92-43732. (Insights Ser.). 256p. 1993. text 39.95 (0-312-09526-0) St Martin.

Docherty, Brian, jt. auth. see Bloom, Clive.

Docherty, Brian, jt. ed. see Day, Gary.

Docherty, Dan. Complete Tai Chi Chuan. (Illus.). 160p. 1998. pap. 24.95 (1-86126-033-4, Pub. by Cro1wood) Trafalgar.

Docherty, David. Running the Show: Twenty-One Years of London Weekend Television. 208p. (C). 1990. 60.00 (1-85283-103-0, Pub. by Boxtree) St Mut.

Docherty, David, ed. Measurement in Pediatric Exercise Science. LC 96-23786. (Illus.). 360p. 1995. text 47.00 (0-87322-960-6, BDOC0960) Human Kinetics.

Docherty, George M. I've Seen the Day. LC 83-25439. 319p. reprint ed. 98.90 (0-608-16677-4, 202754100055) Bks Demand.

Docherty, Gerard, jt. ed. see Foulkes, Paul.

Docherty, Gerard J. The Timing of Voicing in British English Obstruents. LC 91-42837. (Netherlands Phonetic Archives Ser.: No. 9). x, 289p. (C). 1992. lib. bdg. 129.25 (3-11-013408-X) Mouton.

Docherty, Gerard J. & Ladd, D. Robert, eds. Papers in Laboratory Phonology II: Gesture, Segment, Prosody. 476p. (C). 1992. text 99.95 (0-521-40127-5) Cambridge U Pr.

Docherty, Gerard J., jt. ed. see Foulkes, Paul.

***Docherty, Iain.** Making Tracks: The Politics of Local Rail Transport. 324p. 1999. text 87.95 (1-84014-765-2, Pub. by Ashgate Pub) Ashgate Pub Co.

Docherty, J. C. Historical Dictionary of Socialism. LC 97-15782. (Historical Dictionaries of Religions, Philosophies & Movements Ser.). 376p. 1997. 48.00 (0-8108-3358-1) Scarecrow.

Docherty, J. P. Iraq: Major World Nations. LC 98-4310. (Major World Nations Ser.). (Illus.). 144p. (YA). (gr. 5 up). 1999. lib. bdg. 19.95 (0-7910-4979-5) Chelsea Hse.

Docherty, James C. Historical Dictionary of Australia. (Oceanian Historical Dictionaries Ser.: No. 1). (Illus.). 302p. 1992. 37.00 (0-8108-2613-5) Scarecrow.
— Historical Dictionary of Australia. 2nd ed. LC 98-41796. (Asian/Oceanian Historical Dictionaries Ser.: No. 32). (Illus.). 464p. 1999. 65.00 (0-8108-3592-4) Scarecrow.
— Historical Dictionary of Organized Labor. (Historical Dictionaries of Religions, Philosophies, & Movements Ser.: Vol. 10). 368p. 1996. 54.00 (0-8108-3181-3) Scarecrow.

Docherty, John. The Literary Products of the Lewis Carroll - George MacDonald Friendship. LC 94-45740. 420p. 1995. text 109.95 (0-7734-9038-8) E Mellen.

Docherty, John P., ed. Inpatient Psychiatry in the 1990s. LC 87-646993. (New Directions for Mental Health Services Ser.: No. MHS 63). 113p. (Orig.). 1994. pap. 25.00 (0-7879-9990-3) Jossey-Bass.

Docherty, John P., jt. ed. see Clarkin, John F.

Docherty, John P., jt. ed. see Jimerson, David C.

Docherty, K., ed. Gene Transcription: DNA Binding Proteins - Essential Techniques, Vol. 2. (Essential Techniques Ser.). 166p. 1997. pap. 52.95 (0-471-97016-6) Wiley.

Docherty, Kevin, ed. Gene Transcription, 2 vols., Vol. 2. (Essential Techniques Ser.). 302p. 1997. 79.95 (0-471-97097-2) Wiley.
— Gene Transcription, RNA Analysis: Essential Techniques. LC 96-28789. (Essential Techniques Ser.). 136p. 1996. pap. 48.00 (0-471-96147-7) Wiley.

Docherty, Linda J. Women As Readers: Visual Interpretations. (Illus.). 54p. 1998. pap. 8.50 (0-944026-91-5) Am Antiquarian.

Docherty, Linda J. & Montclair Art Museum Staff. Paris 1900: The "American School" at the Universal Exposition. Fischer, Diane P., ed. LC 98-45276. (Illus.). 256p. (C). 1999. 50.00 (0-8135-2640-X); pap. 30.00 (0-8135-2641-8) Rutgers U Pr.

Docherty, Mararet. Applique Masterpiece Little Brown Bird Patterns. LC 99-56546. 128p. 1999. pap. 21.95 (1-57432-734-8, Am Quilters Soc) Collector Bks.

Docherty, Pete. Humor Travels Well: Tours de Farce. (Illus.). 192p. 1991. pap. 9.95 (1-880090-00-7) Galde Pr.

Docherty, Peter, ed. Design for Performance: Diaghilev to the Pet Shop Boys. (Illus.). 240p. 1996. pap. 39.95 (0-85331-720-8, Pub. by Lund Humphries) Antique Collect.

Docherty, Peter & Nyhan, Barry, eds. Human Competence & Business Development Vol. XIV: Emerging Patterns in European Companies. LC 96-40898. 302p. 1996. pap. 79.95 (3-540-19972-1) Spr-Verlag.

Docherty, Thomas. After Theory. LC 97-159534. (Postmodern Theory Ser.). 1997. pap. text 28.00 (0-7486-0840-0) Col U Pr.
— Alterities: Criticism, History, Representation. LC 95-41326. 234p. (C). 1996. pap. text 16.95 (0-19-818358-5) OUP.
— Alterities: Criticism, History, Representation. 234p. (C). 1996. text 62.00 (0-19-818357-7) OUP.
— Criticism & Modernity: Aesthetics, Literature & Nations in Europe & Its Academies. LC 98-49303. 256p. 1999. text 70.00 (0-19-818501-4) OUP.

Docherty, Thomas, ed. Postmodernism: A Reader. LC 92-28779. 544p. (C). 1993. pap. 23.00 (0-231-08221-5); text 67.00 (0-231-08220-7) Col U Pr.

Dochniaikc, Jim, ed. see Goodhue, Horace R.

Dochniak, Jim, ed. see McAnally, Mary E.

Dochy, Filip J., jt. ed. see Birenbaum, Menucha.

***Docie, Ronald Louis, et al.** Royalties in Your Future: An Inventor's & Entrepreneur's Guide to Marketing & Licensing Inventions, Patents, & Technology. LC 97-94116. (Illus.). 1998. write for info. (0-914127-89-6) Univ Class.

Dock. Press Ideas. 679p. 1996. pap. 38.95 (0-312-13319-7) St Martin.
— Press Ideas/Online. 1997. pap. text 28.60 (0-312-18788-2) St Martin.
— Press of Ideas. 2nd ed. 2000. pap. text 31.95 (0-312-20182-6) St Martin.
— Pressing Ideas. 1996. pap. text, teacher ed. 5.00 (0-312-13318-9) St Martin.
— Twentieth Century Reader. 1995. pap. write for info. (0-312-16736-9) St Martin.
— Twentieth Century Reader. 2000. pap. text. write for info. (0-312-16735-0); pap. text. write for info. (0-312-16734-2) St Martin.

Dock, Christopher. A Hundred Necessary Rules of Conduct for Children. Pennypacker, Samuel W., tr. from GER. 20p. (Orig.). 1993. pap. 9.99 (0-9643012-0-2) Hazelwood Pr.

Dock, Julie B. & Willing, Karen B. Cotton Now & Then: Fabric Making from Boll to Bolt. (Illus.). 32p. (J). (gr. 1-6). 1996. 12.95 (0-9641820-2-5); pap. 8.95 (0-9641820-3-3) Now & Then.
— Quilting Now & Then. (Illus.). 36p. (Orig.). (J). (gr. 1-5). 1994. text 12.95 (0-9641820-0-9); pap. text 8.95 (0-9641820-1-7) Now & Then.

Dock, Julie B., jt. auth. see Gilman, Charlotte Perkins.

Dock, Julie B., jt. auth. see Willing, Karen B.

Dock, V. Thomas. Computer Information Systems for Business. 614p. (C). 1988. text 58.75 (0-314-93173-2) West Pub.
— Structured COBOL: American National Standard. 2nd ed. (Illus.). 240p. 1984. pap. text 49.25 (0-314-77896-9); pap. text. write for info. (0-314-77897-7) West Pub.

Dock, William. Prevention of Obstruction of Coronary & Vital Arteries. LC 79-50185. 200p. (C). 1983. 42.50 (0-87527-202-9) Green.

Dockar-Drysdale, Barbara. The Provision of Primary Experience: Winnicottian Work with Children & Adolescents. LC 91-4536. 232p. 1991. 45.00 (0-87668-525-4) Aronson.

Dockendorf, Margo. The Mahdi: A Millennium Thriller. LC 98-74708. 440p. 1999. 24.95 (1-879384-35-3) Cypress Hse.

Docker, John. Postmodernism & Popular Culture: A Cultural History. (Illus.). 335p. (C). 1995. pap. text 19.95 (0-521-46598-2) Cambridge U Pr.

Docker, John, jt. ed. see Fischer, Gerhard.

Docker, Julie & Thawley, Deborah. Parliamo Insieme: Communication Activities in Italian. (Illus.). 112p. (C). 1995. pap. 21.95 (0-521-35656-3) Cambridge U Pr.

Dockeray, James, jt. auth. see Husband, William.

Dockerill, Michael & Goold, J. Douglas. Peace Without Promise: Britain & the Peace Conferences, 1919-1923. 287p. 1981. 79.50 (0-208-01909-X) Elliots Bks.

Dockery, C. C., jt. auth. see Borders, Rebecca.

Dockery, David & Gushee, David, eds. Future of Christian Higher Education. LC 99-12631. 256p. 1999. pap. 19.99 (0-8054-1682-X) Broadman.

***Dockery, David S.** Best Of A.t. Robertson. 1998. pap. text 9.99 (0-8054-1894-6) Broadman.

Dockery, David S. The Holman Concise Bible Commentary. LC 98-27818. 1998. 19.99 (0-8054-9337-9) Broadman.

Dockery, David S., ed. The Challenge of Postmodernism: An Evangelical Engagement. LC 95-1614. 432p. (gr. 12). 1995. pap. 24.99 (0-8010-2121-9, Bridgept Bks) Baker Bks.

Dockery, David S., ed. Holman Bible Handbook. (Illus.). 912p. 1992. 26.99 (1-55819-332-4) Broadman.

Dockery, David S., ed. New Dimensions in Evangelical Thought: Essays in Honor of Millard J. Erickson. LC 97-50064. 448p. 1998. 34.99 (0-8308-1517-1, 1517) InterVarsity.

Dockery, Della. Cami & Other Familiar Friends. (Illus.). 20p. (J). (ps). 1987. pap. 2.95 (0-943487-05-6) Sevgo Pr.

Dockery, Emily C., ed. Putting on the Dog with Little Effort. 73p. (Orig.). 1985. pap. text. write for info. (0-9616053-0-8) Grand Strand.

Dockery, Gary L. Cutaneous Lesions of the Lower Extremity. Bralow, Lisette, ed. 304p. 1996. text 156.00 (0-7216-5034-1, W B Saunders Co) Harcrt Hlth Sci Grp.

Dockery, Gary L. & Crawford, Mary E. Color Atlas of Foot & Ankle Dermatology. LC 98-12982. 208p. 1998. text 170.00 (0-397-51519-7) Lppncott W & W.

Dockery, J. Lee, jt. ed. see Bashook, Philip G.

Dockery, J. T. & Woodcock, A. E., eds. The Military Landscape: Mathematical Models of Combat. 608p. 1995. boxed set 285.00 (1-85573-077-4, Pub. by Woodhead Pubng) Am Educ Systs.

***Dockery, J. Todd.** Twenty Shots. (Illus.). 30p. 1999. 3.00 (0-9664124-7-8) Sweet Lady Moon.

Dockery, Karen. Am I in Love? 12 Youth Studies on Guy Girl Relationships. LC 97-5452. 112p. (J). 1997. 12.99 (0-570-04979-2, 12-3329) Concordia.
— Junior High Retreats & Lock-Ins: A Dozen Complete Programs. 230p. 1990. pap. 16.99 (0-931529-73-5) Group Pub.

Dockery, Karen, et al. Facing Down the Tough Stuff: Life Giving You a Rough Time? Here's Real Help from Real Kids Like Yourself. LC 98-16944. 144p. (J). (gr. 3-7). 1998. pap. 5.99 (0-7814-3059-3) Chariot Victor.

Dockery, Kevin. Compendium of Modern Firearms. (Illus.). 224p. (Orig.). 1991. pap. 20.00 (0-937279-23-4, ES4001) Talsorian.

***Dockery, Kevin.** Free Fire Zones. (Seal Missions). 256p. 2000. mass mkt. 6.50 (0-380-80826-9) Morrow Avon.
— Seals in Action. 392p. 1991. mass mkt. 6.99 (0-380-75886-5, Avon Bks) Morrow Avon.

Dockery, Kevin. Special Warfare, Special Weapons: Up Close & Personal. Rapid Fire Weapons of the SEAL's & UDT. (Illus.). 29.99 (1-883476-17-8) Emperors Pr.

Dockery, Kevin & Fawcett, Bill, eds. The Teams: An Oral History of the U. S. Navy SEALs. LC 97-33133. 281p. 1998. 23.00 (0-688-14964-2, Wm Morrow) Morrow Avon.
— The Teams: An Oral History of the U. S. Navy SEALs. 304p. 1999. mass mkt. 6.50 (0-380-72874-5, Avon Bks) Morrow Avon.

Dockery, Kevin, jt. auth. see Watson, James, Jr.

***Dockery, Linda & Giordano, Jolene.** Three Little Words. 198p. 2000. pap. 6.99 (0-9700344-0-7) Angel Pubng.

Dockery, Wallene T. Home Again: A Celebration of Watson Brown's Return to Vanderbilt. LC 86-61417. (Motivational Sports Bks.). 112p. 1986. 9.95 (0-936169-02-8) Dockery Enter.
— Only As One: The Words & Wisdom of Rex Dockery. Phillips, Bob, ed. LC 85-63031. (Motivational Sports Bks.). (Illus.). 112p. 1985. reprint ed. pap. 9.95 (0-936169-00-1) Dockery Enter.

Dockery, Wallene T. & Williford, Steve. They Said It Couldn't Be Done! LC 86-61416. (Motivational Ser.). 96p. 1987. 11.95 (0-936169-03-6) Dockery Enter.

Dockes, Pierre. Medieval Slavery & Liberation. Goldhammer, Arthur, tr. from FRE. LC 81-11594. 304p. 1997. 32.50 (0-226-15482-3) U Ch Pr.
— Medieval Slavery & Liberation. Goldhammer, Arthur, tr. LC 81-11594. 299p. reprint ed. pap. 92.70 (0-608-09450-1, 205425000005) Bks Demand.

Dockett, Lauren & Beck, Kristin. Facing 30: Women Talk about Constructing a Real Life & Other Scary Rights of Passage. LC 98-66705. 160p. 1998. pap. 12.95 (1-57224-150-0) New Harbinger.

Dockham, Alexandra, tr. see St. Theophan the Recluse.

Docking, J. W. Control & Discipline in Schools: Perspectives & Approaches. 2nd ed. 272p. (C). 1987. pap. 50.00 (0-06-318374-9, Pub. by P Chapman) St Mut.

Docking, Jim. Managing Behavior in the Primary School. 2nd ed. 160p. 1996. pap. 24.95 (1-85346-397-3, Pub. by David Fulton) Taylor & Francis.

Docking, Jim, ed. Education & Alienation in the Junior School. (Education & Alienation Ser.). 230p. 1990. 79.95 (1-85000-571-0, Falmer Pr) Taylor & Francis.

— National School Policy: Major Issues in Education Policy for Schools in England & Wales, 1979 Onwards. LC 96-223579. (Roehampton Text Ser.). 176p. 1996. pap. text 27.95 (1-85346-396-5, Pub. by David Fulton) Taylor & Francis.

***Dockner, Engelbert, et al.** Differential Games in Economics & Management Science. LC 99-59881. (Illus.). 400p. (C). 2000. write for info. (0-521-63125-4); pap. Price not set. (0-521-63732-5) Cambridge U Pr.

***Dockner, Engelbert J., et al, eds.** Optimization, Dynamics & Economic Analysis: Essays in Honor of Gustav Feichtinger. LC 00-38558. (Illus.). x, 428p. 2000. 94.00 (3-7908-1295-1, Pub. by Physica-Verlag) Spr-Verlag.

Dockray, Graham J., jt. ed. see Walsh, John H.

Dockray, Keith. Edward IV: A Source Book. 1999. pap. text 24.00 (0-7509-1942-6) A Sutton.

***Dockray, Keith.** Henry VI & the Wars of the Roses: A Source Book. 192p. 2000. pap. 21.95 (0-7509-2163-3) Sutton Publng.

Dockray, Keith. Richard III: A Sourcebook. expanded rev. ed. LC 97-221465. 192p. 1997. pap. 22.95 (0-7509-1479-3, Pub. by Sutton Pub Ltd) Intl Pubs Mktg.

Dockray, Martin. Cases & Materials on the Carriage of Goods by Sea. 2nd ed. xxxiv, 574p. 1997. pap. 63.00 (1-85941-346-3, Pub. by Cavendish Pubng) Gaunt.

***Dockray-Miller, Mary.** Motherhood & Mothering in Anglo-Saxon England. LC 99-39680. 1999. text 39.95 (0-312-22721-3) St Martin.

Dockray, Tracy A. & Grimm, Wilhelm K. Grimm's Grimmest. Grimm, Jacob W., ed. Matzig, Stefan, tr. from GER. LC 97-20586. (J). 1997. 22.95 (0-8118-1675-3) Chronicle Bks.

Dockray, Tracy A., jt. auth. see Bridges, Margaret Park.

Dockrell, Julie & McShane, John. Children's Learning Difficulties: A Cognitive Approach. LC 92-19116. 1993. pap. 26.95 (0-631-17017-0) Blackwell Pubs.

Dockrell, Julie, jt. ed. see Messer, David.

Dockrell, Julie, jt. ed. see Smith, Leslie.

Dockrey, Emily & Dockrey, Karen. You'll Never Believe What They Told Me: Trusting God Through Serious Illness. Norton, LoraBeth, ed. LC 94-4729. (Kids Helping Kids Ser.). 48p. (J). (gr. 3-8). 1994. pap. 4.99 (0-7814-0111-9, Chariot Bks) Chariot Victor.

Dockrey, Karen. Alone but Not Lonely: Christian Living - Encouragement. Nelson, Becky, ed. 22p. (YA). (gr. 10-12). 1994. per. 1.95 (1-56309-070-8, C936108, Wrld Changers Res) Womans Mission Union.
— Are You There, God? 48p. (Orig.). (YA). 1993. pap., student ed. 3.50 (1-56476-090-1, 6-3090, Victor Bks) Chariot Victor.
— Are You There, God? Leaders Book. 72p. (Orig.). 1993. pap. 1.00 (1-56476-089-8, 6-3089, Victor Bks) Chariot Victor.
— Curing the Self Hate Virus: Christian Living - Encouragement. Nelson, Becky, ed. 20p. (YA). (gr. 10-12). 1994. per. 1.95 (1-56309-069-4, C936110, Wrld Changers Res) Womans Mission Union.
— Family Survival Guide (Leaders & Student) 96p. 1988. pap., student ed. 2.80 (0-89693-458-6, Victor Bks) Chariot Victor.
— From Frustration to Freedom. (Women's Inductive Bible Study Ser.). 96p. 1992. pap. 5.99 (0-89693-233-8, 6-1233, Victor Bks) Chariot Victor.
— Fun Friend-Making Activities for Adult Groups. Buller, Bob, ed. LC 97-13805. 112p. (Orig.). 1997. pap. 15.99 (0-7644-2011-9) Group Pub.
— Growing a Family Where People Really Like Each Other. LC 95-45077. 176p. (Orig.). 1996. pap. 8.99 (1-55661-671-6) Bethany Hse.
— I Thought You Were My Friend. 48p. (Orig.). (YA). 1994. pap., student ed. 3.50 (1-56476-290-4, 6-3290, Victor Bks) Chariot Victor.
— I Thought You Were My Friend: Leader's Guide. 96p. (Orig.). (YA). 1994. pap. 5.99 (1-56476-281-5, 6-3281, Victor Bks) Chariot Victor.

***Dockrey, Karen.** Innovative Worship: 95 Easy Worship-Enhancing Ideas. LC 99-21808. 1999. 16.99 (0-7644-2097-6) Group Pub.

Dockrey, Karen. It's Not Fair! Through Grief to Healing. Nelson, Becky, ed. 22p. (Orig.). (YA). (gr. 7-12). 1992. pap. text 1.95 (1-56309-035-X, C926110, Wrld Changers Res) Womans Mission Union.
— MissionsQuest Devotional Book: Character Questions. (MissionsQuest Ser.). 113p. (J). (gr. 10). 1998. pap. text 9.95 (1-56309-263-8, W986123) Womans Mission Union.
— Spiritual Gifts. 80p. 1999. pap. 4.99 (0-87788-732-2, H Shaw Pubs) Waterbrook Pr.
— Tuned up Parenting: Eight Studes (sic) to Invite Harmony in Your Home. LC 94-4073. (Tapestry Collection). 96p. 1994. pap. 6.50 (1-56476-211-4, 6-3211, Victor Bks) Chariot Victor.
— What's Your Problem? 96p. (YA). (gr. 7 up). 1987. pap. 2.80 (0-89693-381-4, Victor Bks) Chariot Victor.
— The Youth Worker's Guide to Creative Bible Study. expanded rev. ed. LC 98-45976. 176p. 1999. pap. 10.99 (0-8054-1837-7) Broadman.
— YouthCare: Giving Real Help That Makes a Real Difference. LC 97-178461. 144p. (YA). (gr. 7). 1997. pap. text 12.95 (1-56309-200-X, N974105, New Hope) Womans Mission Union.

Dockrey, Karen, jt. auth. see Dockrey, Emily.

Dockrey Young, Judy, jt. auth. see Young, Richard.

Dockrill. Cold War, 1945-1963. 1996. text 11.95 (0-333-40380-0, Pub. by Macmillan) St Martin.

Dockrill, Alick. Australian Indigenous Orchids, Vol. 1. 200p. (C). 1992. text 175.00 (0-949324-43-4, Pub. by Surrey Beatty & Sons) St Mut.

Dockrill, Michael & French, David, eds. Strategy & Intelligence: British Policy During the First World War. LC 95-47677. 1996. 60.00 (*1-85285-099-X*) Hambledon Press.

Dockrill, Michael & McKercher, Brian, eds. Diplomacy & World Power: Studies in British Foreign Policy, 189-1950. LC 96-27749. (Illus.). 291p. (C). 1996. text 64.95 (*0-521-46243-6*) Cambridge U Pr.

Dockrill, Saki. Eisenhower's New-Look National Security Policy, 1953-1961. 496p. 1996. text 65.00 (*0-312-15880-7*) St Martin.

Dockrill, Saki, ed. From Pearl Harbor to Hiroshima: The Second World War in Asia & the Pacific, 1941-1945. LC 93-14207. 1994. text 45.00 (*0-312-10246-1*) St Martin.

Dockrill, Saki, jt. ed. see Bischof, Gunter.

Docks, Les. American Premium Record Guide: 1900-1965. 5th ed. LC 97-162591. (Illus.). 496p. 1997. pap. 24.95 (*0-89689-124-0*, ARG05) Krause Pubns.

Dockstader, Frederick J. Kachina & the White Man: The Influence of White Culture on the Hopi Kachina Cult. enl. rev. ed. LC 85-968. (Illus.). 202p. 1985. reprint ed. pap. 18.95 (*0-8263-0790-6*) U of NM Pr.

— The Song of the Loom: New Traditions in Navajo Weaving. LC 86-27610. (Illus.). 132p. 1987. 39.95 (*0-933920-87-3*) Hudson Hills.

***Dockstader, Mary A.** A Labor of Love: A Baby's Lullabye. (Illus.). 24p. 1999. pap. write for info. (*0-9668751-1-7*) Tadd Instruct.

Dockter. Estate Settlements in Blount County, Tennessee Naming Heirs. 114p. (Orig.). 1996. pap. 16.00 (*0-7884-0395-8*, D515) Heritage Bk.

Dockter, Albert W., Jr. Blount County, Tennessee Chancery Court Records, Bk. 0 & Bk. 1: 1852-1865. LC 92-199806. 172p. (Orig.). 1992. pap. 17.50 (*1-55613-589-0*) Heritage Bk.

Docobo. Visual Double Stars. LC 97-31474. 508p. 1997. text 257.50 (*0-7923-4793-5*) Kluwer Academic.

Docter, R. F. Transvestites & Transsexuals: Toward a Theory of Cross-Gender Behavior. LC 88-19586. (Perspectives in Sexuality Ser.). (Illus.). 266p. (C). 1988. 45.00 (*0-306-42878-4*, Plenum Trade) Perseus Pubng.

Docter, Richard F., jt. auth. see Holmen, Milton G.

Doctor, Adi H. Political Thinkers of Modern India. vii, 141p. 1997. 22.00 (*81-7099-661-9*, Pub. by Mittal Pubs Dist) Nataraj Bks.

Doctor, Bernard A. Malcolm X for Beginners. (Illus.). 192p. (Orig.). 1992. 19.95 (*0-86316-145-6*); pap. 9.95 (*0-86316-146-4*) Writers & Readers.

Doctor, Bhupendra P., et al, eds. Structure & Function of Cholinesterases & Related Proteins. LC 98-40690. (Illus.). 660p. (C). 1998. text 165.00 (*0-306-46050-5*, Kluwer Plenum) Kluwer Academic.

***Doctor, Brad.** Installing Red Hat Linux. 300p. 2000. 24.99 (*0-672-31826-1*, Waite Grp Pr) Sams.

Doctor, Gary L. The Sinatra Scrapbook. (Illus.). 256p. (Orig.). 1991. pap. 17.95 (*0-8065-1250-4*, Citadel Pr) Carol Pub Group.

Doctor, Jan. Farewell to the Flesh: Renouncing Carnal Christianity. LC 97-91036. 1998. pap. 14.95 (*0-533-12537-5*) Vantage.

***Doctor, Jennifer.** The BBC & Ultra-Modern Music, 1922-1936: Shaping a Nation's Tastes. LC 98-45824. (Music in the Twentieth Century Ser.: No. 10). (Illus.). 450p. 2000. 74.95 (*0-521-66117-X*) Cambridge U Pr.

Doctor, Joseph E. Shotguns on Sunday. 1988. reprint ed. 22.95 (*1-892622-04-1*) Brewers Hist.

***Doctor, Ron & Kahn, Ada P.** Facing Fears: The Sourcebook of Phobias, Fears, & Anxieties. LC 99-48737. (Facts for Life Ser.). 256p. 2000. pap. 16.95 (*0-8160-3992-5*, Checkmark) Facts on File.

Doctor, Ronald M. & Kahn, Ada P. The Encyclopedia of Phobias, Fears & Anxieties. 500p. 1989. 50.00 (*0-8160-1798-0*) Facts on File.

Doctor, Steven R., et al, eds. Nondestructive Evaluation of Materials & Composites, Vol. 2944. 344p. 1996. 85.00 (*0-8194-2348-3*) SPIE.

— Nondestructive Evaluation of Materials & Composites II, Vol. 3396. LC 98-184991. 300p. 1998. 80.00 (*0-8194-2845-0*) SPIE.

Doctorovich, Fabio, et al. Bribage Cartooniano. (Illus.). 52p. (Orig.). 1994. pap. 9.00 (*0-935350-42-X*) Luna Bisonte.

Doctorow. Lives of the Poets. 1984. 75.00 (*0-394-54131-6*) Random.

***Doctorow, E. L.** Best American Short Stories 2000. 2000. 27.50 (*0-395-92687-4*); pap. text 13.00 (*0-395-92686-6*) HM.

Doctorow, E. L. Billy Bathgate. LC 98-19318. 323p. 1998. pap. 12.95 (*0-452-28002-8*, Plume) Dutton Plume.

— The Book of Daniel: A Novel. 320p. 1996. pap. 13.95 (*0-452-27566-0*, Plume) Dutton Plume.

— City of God. LC 99-53215. 320p. 2000. 25.00 (*0-679-44783-0*) Random.

***Doctorow, E. L.** City of God. large type ed. (Basic Ser.). 498p. 2000. 31.95 (*0-7862-2681-1*) Thorndike Pr.

— City of God. 2001. reprint ed. pap. 13.00 (*0-452-28209-8*, Plume) Dutton Plume.

— City of God: A Novel. large type ed. LC 00-32528. 2000. write for info. (*0-7862-2684-6*) Thorndike Pr.

Doctorow, E. L. Conversations with E. L. Doctorow. Morris, Christopher D., ed. LC 99-12235. (Literary Conversations Ser.). 256p. 1999. 45.00 (*1-57806-143-1*); pap. 18.00 (*1-57806-144-X*) U Pr of Miss.

— Drinks Before Dinner. LC 95-26576. 96p. 1996. pap. 10.95 (*1-55936-115-8*) Theatre Comm.

— Jack London, Hemingway & the Constitution: Selected Essays, 1977-1992. 206p. 1999. reprint ed. pap. text 11.00 (*0-7881-6227-6*) DIANE Pub.

— Lives of the Poets. LC 97-12746. 160p. 1997. reprint ed. pap. 10.95 (*0-452-27879-1*, Plume) Dutton Plume.

— Lives of the Poets: Six Stories & a Novella. 1986. mass mkt. 4.95 (*0-380-69996-6*, Avon Bks) Morrow Avon.

— Poets & Presidents: Selected Essays, 1977-1992. 206p. (Orig.). 1994. pap. 26.50 (*0-333-61606-5*, Pub. by Papermac) Trans-Atl Phila.

— Ragtime. 1984. mass mkt. 4.95 (*0-553-25736-6*) Bantam.

— Ragtime. LC 97-42251. 1997. 15.50 (*0-679-60297-6*) Modern Lib NY.

— Ragtime. 270p. 1997. pap. 11.95 (*0-452-27907-0*) NAL.

— The Waterworks. 400p. 1995. mass mkt. 6.99 (*0-451-18563-3*, Sig) NAL.

— The Waterworks. LC 96-29871. 352p. 1997. reprint ed. pap. 14.00 (*0-452-27549-0*, Plume) Dutton Plume.

— Welcome to Hard Times. 1994. lib. bdg. 24.95 (*1-56849-393-2*) Buccaneer Bks.

— Welcome to Hard Times. LC 96-681. 1996. pap. 12.95 (*0-452-27571-7*, Plume) Dutton Plume.

— World's Fair. 384p. 1996. pap. 13.95 (*0-452-27572-5*, Plume) Dutton Plume.

— World's Fair. 1993. 24.25 (*0-8446-6696-3*) Peter Smith.

Doctor's Licensure Group, Inc. Staff. 1998 Nursing Licensure Guidelines: State Information Manual for Nursing in U. S. 290p. 1998. 65.00 (*1-887617-57-4*) St Bart Pr Ltd.

***Doctors' Prescription Staff.** Healing Arthritis Naturally. 156p. 2000. pap. 6.95 (*1-893910-10-5*, 904-009, Pub. by Freedom Pr Inc) BookWorld.

— Healing Depression Naturally. 96p. 2000. pap. 4.95 (*1-893910-12-1*, 904-013, Pub. by Freedom Pr Inc) BookWorld.

— The Men's Essential Guide to Prostrate Health. 96p. 2000. pap. 4.95 (*1-893910-07-5*, 904-012, Pub. by Freedom Pr Inc) BookWorld.

— Super Sexual Potency for Men: How Natural Medicines Can Revitalize Them. 128p. 2000. 0.95 (*1-893910-08-3*, 904-008, Pub. by Freedom Pr Inc) BookWorld.

Doctrine Commission of the Church of England Staff. The Mystery of Salvation: The Story of God's Gift. 223p. (Orig.). 1996. pap. 17.95 (*0-8192-1671-2*) Morehouse Pub.

Document Management Industries Association Staff. The Business Forms Handbook. 4th ed. 609p. 69.95 (*0-614-25543-0*, 00PO44692) Print Indus Am.

***Documentary Arts Inc.** Masters of Traditional Arts: A Biographical Dictionary & Curriculum Guide, 2 Vols. 2001. lib. bdg. 175.00 (*1-57607-240-1*) ABC-CLIO.

Documentary Book Publishers. Graphic Design in Seattle. 1997. pap. text 24.95 (*0-935503-18-8*) Document Bk.

Documentation Committee of REHVA Staff, compiled by. The International Dictionary of Heating, Ventilating, & Air Conditioning. 2nd ed. LC 92-46393. 856p. (C). 1994. 175.00 (*0-419-15390-X*, E & FN Spon) Routledge.

Doczi, Gyorgy. The Power of Limits: Proportional Harmonies in Nature, Art & Architecture. 1981. pap. 24.95 (*0-394-73580-3*, Pub. by Shambhala Pubns) Random.

— The Power of Limits: Proportional Harmonies in Nature, Art & Architecture. LC 77-90883. (Illus.). 224p. 1994. pap. 27.00 (*0-87773-193-4*, Pub. by Shambhala Pubns) Random.

Doda, Nancy M., jt. auth. see Erb, Thomas O.

Dodaro, Gene L. High-Risk Program: Information on Selected High-Risk Areas (Federal Programs at Risk from Abusive or Wasteful Practices) (Illus.). 133p. (C). 1998. pap. text 35.00 (*0-7881-4836-2*) DIANE Pub.

Dodaro, Gene L., ed. Year 2000 Computing Crisis: Potential for Widespread Disruption Calls for Strong Leadership & Partnerships. (Illus.). 60p. (C). 1999. pap. text 20.00 (*0-7881-7788-5*) DIANE Pub.

***Dodaro, Robert & Lawless, George.** Augustine & His Critics LC 99-34141. 2000. write for info. (*0-415-20062-8*) Routledge.

Dodbe, Lee. Gay Happiness: How to Get It. LC 98-203468. 234 p. 1998. write for info. (*0-9663054-0-X*) Arete Publ.

DODC Staff. Directory of Directors in the City of New York & Tri-State Area. 88th rev. ed. 700p. 1999. 250.00 (*0-936612-20-7*) DODC.

***DODC Staff.** Directory of Directors in the City of New York & Tri-State Area. 89th rev. ed. 680p. 2000. 265.00 (*0-936612-21-5*) DODC.

Dodd. Dynamic Intercultural Communication. 4th ed. 1994. teacher ed. 10.93 (*0-697-20137-6*, WCB McGr Hill) McGrw-H Hghr Educ.

— Walk in Yard. 300p. (C). 2000. lib. bdg. 34.95 (*0-226-15496-3*) U Ch Pr.

Dodd, jt. auth. see Powers.

Dodd, A. H. Life in Elizabethan England. (Illus.). 230p. 1998. pap. 26.95 (*0-8464-4922-6*) Beekman Pubs.

Dodd, A. H. Life in Elizabethan England. (Illus.). 192p. pap. 17.95 (*1-871083-46-X*, Pub. by J Jones Pub) Dufour.

Dodd, A. H. Short History of Wales: Welsh Life & Customs from Prehistoric Times to the Present Day. Orig. Title: Life in Wales. (Illus.). 173p. 1998. pap. 24.95 (*0-8464-4887-4*) Beekman Pubs.

Dodd, A. H. A Short History of Wales: Welsh Life & Customs from Prehistoric Times to the Present Day. (Illus.). 178p. pap. 15.95 (*1-871083-36-2*, Pub. by J Jones Pub) Dufour.

Dodd, Alfred. Francis Bacon's Personal Life Story. 382p. 1996. reprint ed. pap. 29.95 (*1-56459-563-3*) Kessinger Pub.

Dodd, Ann W. & Konzal, Jean L. Making Our High Schools Better: How Parents & Teachers Can Work Together. 2nd ed. LC 98-46121. (Illus.). 304p. 1999. text 26.95 (*0-312-21335-2*) St Martin.

Dodd, Anna B. The Republic of the Future. 1968. reprint ed. lib. bdg. 22.75 (*0-8290-1922-7*) Irvington.

***Dodd, Annabel Z.** Essential Guide Telecommunications. 2nd ed. LC 99-55312. (C). 1999. write for info. (*0-13-017612-5*) P-H.

— Essential Guide to Telecommunications: Making Sense of New Technologies, the Internet & Wireless. 2nd ed. LC 99-36423. 365p. 1999. pap. text 34.99 (*0-13-014295-6*) P-H.

Dodd, Anne W. Beachcombing & Beachcrafting. Wilensky, Julius M., ed. LC 89-50754. (Illus.). 144p. (Orig.). 1989. pap. 12.95 (*0-918752-10-8*) Wescott Cove.

— A Handbook for Substitute Teachers. (Illus.). 154p. 1989. pap. 26.95 (*0-398-06097-5*) C C Thomas.

— A Handbook for Substitute Teachers. (Illus.). 154p. (C). 1989. text 40.95 (*0-398-05539-4*) C C Thomas.

— A Parent's Guide to Innovative Education: Working with Teachers, Schools, & Your Children for Real Learning. LC 91-51219. 288p. (Orig.). 1992. pap. 12.95 (*1-879360-16-0*) Noble Pr.

— The Story of the Sea Glass. LC 99-13120. (Illus.). 32p. (J). (gr. k-3). 1999. 15.95 (*0-89272-416-1*) Down East.

***Dodd, Anne Wescott.** Making our High Schools Better. 304p. 2000. pap. 16.95 (*0-312-23346-9*) St Martin.

Dodd, Anthony. PROLOG: A Logical Approach. (Illus.). 568p. 1990. pap. 39.95 (*0-19-853821-9*) OUP.

Dodd, Arthur E. Dictionary of Ceramics. 3rd rev. ed. 384p. 1995. 90.00 (*0-901716-56-1*, Pub. by Inst Materials) Ashgate Pub Co.

Dodd, B., jt. auth. see Bai, Y.

Dodd, Barbara. The Differential Diagnosis & Treatment of Children with Speech Disorders. (Illus.). 346p. (Orig.). (C). 1995. pap. 55.00 (*1-56593-366-4*, 0735) Thomson Learn.

— Illustrated Guide to Full Body Reflexology. 1996. 12.95 (*1-885670-07-9*) Woodland UT.

Dodd, Barbara, et al, eds. Evaluating Theories of Language: Evidence from Disordered Communication. (Illus.). 218p. (Orig.). 1996. pap. 49.95 (*1-56593-788-0*, 1538) Thomson Learn.

Dodd, Barbara E. Blood Group Topics. (Current Topics in Immunology Ser.: Vol. 3). (Illus.). 1978. pap. 21.25 (*0-8151-2710-3*) Mosby Inc.

Dodd, Bella V. School of Darkness. 1963. pap. 6.95 (*0-8159-6804-3*) Devin.

Dodd, Bill. Broken Dreams. (Orig.). 1992. pap. 12.95 (*0-7022-2428-6*, Pub. by Univ Queensland Pr) Intl Spec Bk.

Dodd, Bill, et al. Modern German Grammar: A Practical Guide. LC 95-35096. (GER.). 504p. (C). 1996. 75.00 (*0-415-09847-5*); pap. 25.99 (*0-415-09848-3*) Routledge.

Dodd, Bill, jt. auth. see Coles, Waltraud.

Dodd, Brian J. Paul's Paradigmatic 'I' Personal Example as Literary Strategy. (JSNTS Ser.: Vol. 177). 288p. 1999. 75.00 (*1-85075-914-6*, Pub. by Sheffield Acad) CUP Services.

— Praying Jesus' Way: A Guide for Beginners & Veterans. LC 96-48376. 129p. (Orig.). 1997. pap. 9.99 (*0-8308-1993-2*, 1993) InterVarsity.

Dodd, Brian J., jt. ed. see Martin, Ralph P.

Dodd, C. W., et al. How to Protect a Wind Turbine from Lightning. 2nd ed. LC 88-50453. 109p. 1988. pap. text 39.95 (*0-88016-072-1*) WindBks.

Dodd, Carley, et al. Shattering the Silence: Telling the Church the Truth about Kids & Sex. rev. ed. Date not set. pap. 14.95 (*0-89112-014-9*) Abilene Christ U.

Dodd, Carley H. Dynamics of Intercultural Communication. 4th ed. 352p. (C). 1994. text. write for info. (*0-697-20136-8*) Brown & Benchmark.

Dodd, Carley H. Dynamics of Intercultural Communication. 5th ed. LC 97-70817. 336p. (C). 1997. per. write for info. (*0-697-32725-6*, WCB McGr Hill) McGrw-H Hghr Educ.

Dodd, Carley H. & Lewis, Michael L. Human Communication: Developing Positive Life Experiences. 2nd ed. 416p. 1992. per. 31.95 (*0-8403-7335-X*) Kendall-Hunt.

Dodd, Charles H. California Trail: Voyage of Discovery. LC 96-75968. (Illus.). 64p. (Orig.). 1996. pap. 7.95 (*0-88714-112-9*) KC Pubns.

— Dodd's Church History of England, 1500-1688, 5 vols. Tierney, M. A., ed. LC 75-119152. reprint ed. 382.50 (*0-404-02150-6*) AMS Pr.

— Interpretation of the Fourth Gospel. 490p. (C). 1968. pap. text 29.95 (*0-521-09517-4*) Cambridge U Pr.

Dodd, Charles H., ed. see Reed, Virginia.

Dodd, Charles K. Industrial Decision Making & High-Risk Technology: Facility Siting for the Nuclear Power Industry in the U. S. S. R. LC 93-20253. 256p. (C). 1993. lib. bdg. 50.00 (*0-8476-7847-4*) Rowman.

Dodd, Christina. Candle in the Window. 448p. 1991. mass mkt. 3.99 (*0-06-104026-6*, Harp PBks) HarpC.

— Candle in the Window RI. 448p. 1999. mass mkt. 3.99 (*0-06-108560-X*) HarpC.

— Castles in the Air. 432p. 1998. mass mkt. 3.99 (*0-06-108565-0*) HarpC.

— Castles in the Air: Castles in the Air. LC 94-115251. 432p. 1993. mass mkt. 5.99 (*0-06-108034-9*, Harp PBks) HarpC.

— Greatest Lover in All England. 400p. 1994. mass mkt. 3.99 (*0-06-108153-1*, Harp PBks) HarpC.

— The Greatest Lover in All England. 400p. 1999. mass mkt. 3.99 (*0-06-108561-8*) HarpC.

— A Knight to Remember. 368p. 1997. mass mkt. 5.99 (*0-06-108488-3*, Harp PBks) HarpC.

— A Knight to Remember. 368p. 1999. mass mkt. 3.99 (*0-06-109872-8*) HarpC.

— Move Heaven & Earth. 400p. 1995. mass mkt. 5.50 (*0-06-108152-3*) HarpC.

— Move Heaven & Earth. 400p. 1999. mass mkt. 3.99 (*0-06-103000-7*) HarpC.

— Once a Knight. 416p. 1999. mass mkt. 3.99 (*0-06-109899-X*) HarpC.

— Once upon a Time. 416p. 1996. mass mkt. 5.99 (*0-06-108398-4*) HarpC.

— Outrageous. 384p. 1994. mass mkt. 3.99 (*0-06-108151-5*, Harp PBks) HarpC.

— Priceless. 384p. 1992. mass mkt. 5.99 (*0-06-104153-X*, Harp PBks) HarpC.

— Priceless. 384p. 1998. mass mkt. 3.99 (*0-06-108563-4*) HarpC.

— The Rays of the Sun. 448p. 1998. mass mkt. 3.99 (*0-06-108564-2*) HarpC.

***Dodd, Christina.** Rules of Engagement. 384p. 2000. mass mkt. 6.99 (*0-380-81198-7*, Avon Bks) Morrow Avon.

— Rules of Surrender. 384p. 2000. mass mkt. 6.99 (*0-380-81197-9*, Avon Bks) Morrow Avon.

Dodd, Christina. The Runaway Princess. LC 98-93539. 384p. 1999. mass mkt. 6.50 (*0-380-80292-9*, Avon Bks) Morrow Avon.

— Scandalous Evening. LC 98-92453. 384p. 1998. mass mkt. 6.50 (*0-380-79091-2*, Avon Bks) Morrow Avon.

***Dodd, Christina.** Someday My Prince. LC 98-94820. 384p. 1999. mass mkt. 6.50 (*0-380-80293-7*, Avon Bks) Morrow Avon.

Dodd, Christina. Treasure of the Sun. 448p. (Orig.). 1991. mass mkt. 5.99 (*0-06-104062-2*, Harp PBks) HarpC.

— Well Favored Gentleman. LC 97-94308. 400p. 1998. mass mkt. 5.99 (*0-380-79090-4*, Avon Bks) Morrow Avon.

— Well Pleasured Lady. 384p. 1997. mass mkt. 5.99 (*0-380-79089-0*, Avon Bks) Morrow Avon.

Dodd, Christina, et al. Scottish Brides. 1999. mass mkt. 6.50 (*0-380-80451-4*, Avon Bks) Morrow Avon.

Dodd, Christopher J., jt. auth. see Bennett, Robert F.

Dodd, Christopher J., jt. ed. see Bennett, Robert.

Dodd, Clement H. The Cyprus Imbroglio. LC 98-197719. 215p. 1998. pap. 29.95 (*0-906719-21-6*, Pub. by Eothen) Paul & Co Pubs.

— The Cyprus Issue: A Current Perspective. 2nd ed. LC 97-179072. 37p. 1997. pap. 8.95 (*0-906719-35-6*, Pub. by Eothen) Paul & Co Pubs.

— Politics & Government in Turkey. LC 78-85453. 351p. reprint ed. pap. 108.90 (*0-608-17469-6*, 202995100066) Bks Demand.

***Dodd, Clement H., ed.** Cyprus: The Need for New Perspectives. 305p. 1999. pap. 35.00 (*0-906719-23-2*, Pub. by Eothen) Paul & Co Pubs.

Dodd, Cora. The Country Undertaker's Wife. LC 93-83445. (Illus.). 112p. 1993. 15.00 (*0-9631855-5-1*) Still Waters Pr.

***Dodd, Craig.** Aphrodisiac Foods: Eat Your Way to Ecstasy. 2000. pap. 16.95 (*1-85868-772-1*, Pub. by Carlton Bks Ltd) Natl Bk Netwk.

Dodd, Craig. Ballet in Motion: A Three-Dimensional Guide to Ballet for Young People. LC 87-26047. (Illus.). 14p. (J). (gr. 2-6). 1988. 15.95 (*0-397-32257-7*) HarpC Child Bks.

Dodd, Curt. Running on Empty in the Fast Lane: Redefining Success. 137p. 1990. pap. 7.99 (*0-89636-260-4*, AC 211, LifeJourney) Chariot Victor.

Dodd, Damon C. All of Mine for Him. 1977. pap. 3.95 (*0-89265-045-1*) Randall Hse.

Dodd, David. Playing It Straight: Personal Conversations on Recovery, Transformation & Success. 300p. 1996. pap. 12.95 (*1-55874-388-X*) Health Comm.

***Dodd, David & Spaulding, Diana.** The Grateful Dead Reader. 352p. 2000. 25.00 (*0-19-512470-7*) OUP.

Dodd, David, jt. auth. see Graham, Benjamin.

Dodd, David G. & Weiner, Robert G. The Grateful Dead & the Deadheads: An Annotated Bibliography, 60. LC 97-5300. (Music Reference Collection: Vol. 60). 448p. 1997. lib. bdg. 75.00 (*0-313-30141-7*, Greenwood Pr) Greenwood.

***Dodd, Don.** Deep South Aviation. (Images of America Ser.). 128p. 1999. pap. 18.99 (*0-7385-0246-4*) Arcadia Publng.

Dodd, Don, jt. auth. see Rabin, Jack.

Dodd, Donald B., compiled by. Historical Statistics of the States of the United States: Two Centuries of the Census, 1790-1990. LC 93-25014. 504p. 1993. lib. bdg. 125.00 (*0-313-28309-5*, DHI/, Greenwood Pr) Greenwood.

Dodd, Ed & Elrod, Jack. Mark Trail in the Smokies: A Naturalists Look at GSMNP & the Southern Appalachians. Canter, Stan et al, eds. (Illus.). 48p. (Orig.). 1989. pap. text 1.95 (*0-937207-11-X*) GSMNH.

Dodd, Ed, jt. auth. see Osler, Tom.

Dodd, Edward. The Island World of Polynesia: A Survey of the Racial Family & Its Far-Flung Cultures. 1990. 27.95 (*0-9622505-0-3*) Windmill Hill.

Dodd, Edward, ed. see Martin, Henry B.

Dodd, Edwin M. American Business Corporations until 1860 with Special Reference to Massachusetts. LC 53-9043. 544p. 1954. 35.00 (*0-674-02000-6*) HUP.

Dodd, Elizabeth. Like Memory, Caverns: Poems. LC 92-32627. 72p. (C). 1992. pap. 12.95 (*0-8147-1855-8*); text 25.00 (*0-8147-1854-X*) NYU Pr.

— The Veiled Mirror & the Woman Poet: H. D., Louise Bogan, Elizabeth Bishop, & Louise Gluck. 256p. 1992. text 34.95 (*0-8262-0857-6*) U of Mo Pr.

***Dodd, Emily.** Calling All Friends with Cellphone. (Telephone Book-Barbie Ser.). (Illus.). 24p. (J). (ps-3). 2000. spiral bd. write for info. (*1-57584-701-9*, Pub. by Rdrs Digest) S&S Trade.

Dodd, Eugene, jt. auth. see Gordon, Maggie.

Dodd, Fred W. Number Theory in the Quadratic Field with Golden Section Unit. LC 83-17799. (Examples of Mathematical Structures Ser.: Vol. 3). 159p. 1984. 8.50 (*0-936428-08-2*) Polygonal Pub.

Dodd, George. The Food of London. LC 75-27635. (World Food Supply Ser.). 1976. reprint ed. 45.95 (*0-405-07777-7*) Ayer.

Dodd, George H., jt. ed. see Van Toller, Steve.

Dodd, Gerard. Business Basics: A Microbusiness Start-Up Guide. LC 97-52777. (Illus.). 250p. 1998. pap. 16.95 (*1-55571-430-7*, BUBAP, Oasis Pr) PSI Resch.

D

Dodd, H. M. Genealogy of the Brothers & Sisters & Family & Descendants of Israel, Abner, John, Polly, William, Wolcott, Lewis & Nathaniel Read. 301p. 1989. reprint ed. pap. 45.00 (*0-8328-1009-6*); reprint ed. lib. bdg. 53.00 (*0-8328-1008-8*) Higginson Bk Co.

Dodd, Henry P. The Epigrammatist: A Selection from the Epigrammatic Literature of Ancient, Medieval & Modern Times. 1977. lib. bdg. 59.95 (*0-8490-1782-3*) Gordon Pr.

***Dodd, Hudson.** Brewpub Explorer of the Pacific Northwest. 2nd ed. 2000. pap. 16.95 (*1-881409-25-2*) Jhnstn Assocs.

Dodd, J. History of the Canon Law in Conjunction with Other Branches of Jurisprudence: With Chapters on the Royal Supremacy & the Report of the Commission on Ecclesiastical Courts. (Illus.). xvi, 278p. 1987. reprint ed. 58.00 (*0-8377-2032-X*, Rothman) W S Hein.

Dodd, J. E., jt. auth. see Coughlan, G. D.

Dodd, J. M. & Rose, P. M. Faculty Handbook: Students with Learning Disabilities. 37p. 1991. pap. text. write for info. (*1-888557-48-6*) No Ariz Univ.

Dodd, J. M., et al. Vocational Readiness in American Indian Learning Disabled Adolescents. 89p. 1992. pap. text. write for info. (*1-888557-14-1*, 100108) No Ariz Univ.

Dodd, J. N. Atoms & Light: Interactions. (Physics of Atoms & Molecules Ser.). (Illus.). 260p. (C). 1991. text 79.50 (*0-306-43741-4*, Kluwer Plenum) Kluwer Academic.

Dodd, James. Idealism & Corporeity: An Essay on the Problem of the Body in Husserl's Phenomenology. LC 96-53320. (Phaenomenologica Ser.). 162p. (C). 1997. text 90.50 (*0-7923-4400-6*) Kluwer Academic.

Dodd, James, ed. see Patocka, Jan.

Dodd, James W. Paleoecology Concepts & Applications. 2nd ed. LC 89-22502. 528p. 1990. 210.00 (*0-471-85711-4*) Wiley.

Dodd, Jan. The Rough Guide to Vietnam. (Rough Guides Ser.). 400p. (Orig.). 1996. pap. 15.95 (*1-85828-191-1*, Penguin Bks) Viking Penguin.

Dodd, Jan & Lewis, Mark. Vietnam. 2nd ed. (Rough Guide Ser.). (Illus.). 544p. 1998. pap. text 18.95 (*1-85828-339-6*, Pub. by Rough Guides) Penguin Putnam.

Dodd, Jan & Richmond, Simon. Japan. (Rough Guide Ser.). (Illus.). 704p. 1999. pap. 23.95 (*1-85828-340-X*, Pub. by Rough Guides) Penguin Putnam.

— Tokyo. (Mini Rough Guide Ser.). (Illus.). 256p. 1998. pap. text 9.95 (*1-85828-347-7*, Pub. by Rough Guides) Penguin Putnam.

Dodd, Janet S., ed. The ACS Style Guide: A Manual for Authors & Editors. LC 85-21472. 200p. 1985. 34.95 (*0-8412-0917-0*); pap. 24.95 (*0-8412-0943-X*) Am Chemical.

— The ACS Style Guide: A Manual for Authors & Editors. 2nd ed. LC 96-49413. (An American Chemical Society Publication). 260p. 1997. 39.95 (*0-8412-3461-2*, Pub. by Am Chemical); pap. text 27.00 (*0-8412-3462-0*, Pub. by Am Chemical) OUP.

Dodd, Jeremy, ed. see Linsey, Adrian & Fieldhouse, Ken.

***Dodd, John & Helgason, Gail.** Canadian Rockies Access Guide. 3rd rev. ed. (Illus.). 400p. 1998. pap. 16.95 (*1-55105-176-1*) Lone Pine.

Dodd, John J. Diatoms. LC 86-17696. (Illustrated Flora of Illinois Ser.). (Illus.). 491p. 1987. text 41.95 (*0-8093-1154-2*) S Ill U Pr.

Dodd, Jordan, ed. see Liahona Research, Inc. Staff.

***Dodd, Julian.** An Identity Theory of Truth. 2000. text 59.95 (*0-312-23199-7*) St Martin.

Dodd, Julie E., ed. see Robinson, Judy L.

***Dodd, Karen E.** Carolina Comfort. LC 00-101839. 100p. 2000. pap. 10.00 (*1-884778-85-2*) Old Mountain.

Dodd, Kenneth N. Computer Programming & Languages. LC 71-462842. viii, 140 p. 1969. write for info. (*0-408-43734-0*) Buttrwrth-Heinemann.

— Computer Programming & Languages. LC 71-462842. 148p. reprint ed. pap. 45.90 (*0-608-16543-3*, 202629100049) Bks Demand.

***Dodd, Kyle.** A Cut Above: Biblical Leadership Principles for the 21st Century. 156p. (YA). 2000. pap. 9.95 (*1-929478-12-7*) Cross Trng.

Dodd, Kyle & Dodd, Sharon. Family Matters: 365 Daily Devotions for Families. 378p. 1998. 19.95 (*1-887002-54-5*) Cross Trng.

Dodd, Lamar. Lamar Dodd: A Retrospective Exhibition. LC 71-133620. 138p. 1970. pap. 20.00 (*0-8203-0307-0*) U of Ga Pr.

Dodd, Lawrence. Narcissa Whitman on the Oregon Trail. 19p. 1986. pap. 4.95 (*0-87770-369-8*) Ye Galleon.

Dodd, Lawrence & Jillson, Calvin. New Perspectives on American Politics. LC 93-38566. 360p. 1993. 44.95 (*0-87187-882-8*) Congr Quarterly.

— New Perspectives on American Politics. LC 93-38566. 360p. (YA). (gr. 11). 1994. pap. text 32.95 (*0-87187-877-1*) Congr Quarterly.

Dodd, Lawrence C. Coalitions in Parliamentary Government. LC 75-2986. 304p. 1976. reprint ed. pap. 94.30 (*0-7837-9331-6*, 206007200004) Bks Demand.

Dodd, Lawrence C. & Oppenheimer, Bruce I. Congress Reconsidered. 6th ed. LC 96-38960. 450p. (YA). (gr. 11). 1997. pap. text 33.95 (*1-56802-203-4*) Congr Quarterly.

Dodd, Lawrence C. & Schott, Richard L. Congress & the Administrative State. 2nd ed. 1998. pap. 42.00 (*0-8133-0929-8*) Westview.

— Congress & the Administrative State. 2nd ed. 1999. pap. 15.95 (*0-8133-0930-1*) Westview.

Dodd, Lawrence C., jt. ed. see Craig, Stephen C.

Dodd, Loring H. A Glossary of Wulfstan's Homilies. (Yale Studies in English: No. 35). 244p. 1968. reprint ed. 41.60 (*0-685-66459-7*, 05102093) G Olms Pubs.

Dodd, Lynley. Gold Star First Readers, 8 bks. Incl. Dragon in a Wagon. Dodd, Lynley. LC 00-29156. 32p. (J). (gr. 1 up). 2000. lib. bdg. 21.27 (*0-8368-2687-6*); Hairy Maclary & Zachary Quack. Dodd, Lynley. LC 00-29170. 32p. (J). (gr. 1 up). 2000. lib. bdg. 21.27 (*0-8368-2676-0*); Hairy Maclary from Donaldson's Dairy. Dodd, Lynley. LC 00-29176. 32p. (J). (gr. 1 up). 2000. lib. bdg. 21.27 (*0-8368-2688-4*); Hairy Maclary Scattercat. Dodd, Lynley. LC 00-29175. 32p. (J). (gr. 1 up). 2000. lib. bdg. 21.27 (*0-8368-2689-2*); Hairy Maclary, Sit. Dodd, Lynley. LC 97-35443. 32p. (J). (ps up). 1998. lib. bdg. 21.27 (*0-8368-2093-2*); Hairy Maclary's Caterwaul Caper. LC 00-29171. (Illus.). 32p. (J). (gr. 1 up). 2000. lib. bdg. 21.27 (*0-8368-2690-6*); Hairy Maclary's Rumpus at the Vet. Dodd, Lynley. LC 00-29172. 32p. (J). (gr. 1 up). 2000. lib. bdg. 21.27 (*0-8368-2691-4*); Hairy Maclary's Show Business. LC 91-50554. (Illus.). 32p. (J). (gr. 1-2). 1992. lib. bdg. 21.27 (*0-8368-0763-4*); Minister's Cat, ABC. LC 93-36139. 36p. (J). 1994. lib. bdg. 21.27 (*0-8368-1073-2*); Slinky Malinki Catflaps. LC 98-23890. (Illus.). 32p. (J). 1999. lib. bdg. 21.27 (*0-8368-2249-8*); Smallest Turtle. Dodd, Lynley. LC 00-29174. 32p. (J). (gr. 1 up). 2000. lib. bdg. 21.27 (*0-8368-2692-2*); Sniff - Snuff - Snap! Dodd, Lynley. LC 00-29173. 32p. (J). (gr. 1 up). 2000. lib. bdg. 21.27 (*0-8368-2677-9*); (J). Set pap. 159.47 (*0-8368-2142-4*) Gareth Stevens Inc.

Dodd, Lynley. Gold Star First Readers, 13 bks. Incl. Dragon in a Wagon. Dodd, Lynley. LC 00-29156. 32p. (J). (gr. 1 up). 2000. lib. bdg. 21.27 (*0-8368-2687-6*); Hairy Maclary & Zachary Quack. Dodd, Lynley. LC 00-29170. 32p. (J). (gr. 1 up). 2000. lib. bdg. 21.27 (*0-8368-2676-0*); Hairy Maclary from Donaldson's Dairy. Dodd, Lynley. LC 00-29176. 32p. (J). (gr. 1 up). 2000. lib. bdg. 21.27 (*0-8368-2688-4*); Hairy Maclary Scattercat. Dodd, Lynley. LC 00-29175. 32p. (J). (gr. 1 up). 2000. lib. bdg. 21.27 (*0-8368-2689-2*); Hairy Maclary, Sit. Dodd, Lynley. LC 97-35443. 32p. (J). (ps up). 1998. lib. bdg. 21.27 (*0-8368-2093-2*); Hairy Maclary's Caterwaul Caper. LC 00-29171. (Illus.). 32p. (J). (gr. 1 up). 2000. lib. bdg. 21.27 (*0-8368-2690-6*); Hairy Maclary's Rumpus at the Vet. Dodd, Lynley. LC 00-29172. 32p. (J). (gr. 1 up). 2000. lib. bdg. 21.27 (*0-8368-2691-4*); Hairy Maclary's Show Business. LC 91-50554. (Illus.). 32p. (J). (gr. 1-2). 1992. lib. bdg. 21.27 (*0-8368-0763-4*); Minister's Cat, ABC. LC 93-36139. 36p. (J). 1994. lib. bdg. 21.27 (*0-8368-1073-2*); Slinky Malinki Catflaps. LC 98-23890. (Illus.). 32p. (J). 1999. lib. bdg. 21.27 (*0-8368-2249-8*); Smallest Turtle. Dodd, Lynley. LC 00-29174. 32p. (J). (gr. 1 up). 2000. lib. bdg. 21.27 (*0-8368-2692-2*); Sniff - Snuff - Snap! Dodd, Lynley. LC 00-29173. 32p. (J). (gr. 1 up). 2000. lib. bdg. 21.27 (*0-8368-2677-9*); (J). (gr. 1 up). Set lib. bdg. 276.51 (*0-8368-2742-2*) Gareth Stevens Inc.

Dodd, Mary A. & Engquist, Jayson. Gardner Read: A Bio-Bibliography, 60. LC 96-10356. (Bio-Bibliographies in Music Ser.). 290p. 1996. lib. bdg. 75.00 (*0-313-29384-8*, Greenwood Pr) Greenwood.

Dodd, Marylin J. Managing the Side Effects of Chemotherapy & Radiation Therapy: A Guide for Patients & Their Families. 198p. (Orig.). 1996. pap. 20.00 (*0-943671-12-4*) UCSF Schl Nursing.

Dodd, Max. The Handbook of Hope. 134p. (C). 1989. text 40.00 (*1-872795-61-7*, Pub. by Pentland Pr) St Mut.

Dodd, Monroe, ed. see Montgomery, Rick & Kasper, Shirl.

Dodd, Monroe, ed. see Phelps, Dale.

Dodd, Nigel. Social Theory & Modernity. LC 99-25388. 290p. (C). 1999. text 59.95 (*0-7456-1313-6*, Pub. by Polity Pr) Blackwell Pubs.

— Social Theory & Modernity. LC 99-25388. 290p. (C). 1999. pap. text 24.95 (*0-7456-1314-4*, Pub. by Polity Pr) Blackwell Pubs.

Dodd, Nigel & Hickson, Winifred, eds. Drama & Theatre in Education. 175p. (C). 1971. pap. text 15.00 (*0-435-18271-4*, 18271) Heinemann.

***Dodd, Norris L., et al.** Tassel-Earned Squirrel Population Dynamics in Az: Index Techniques & Relationships to Habitat Condition: A Final Report. Research Branch Technical Report, No. 27. 49p. 1998. write for info. (*0-917563-35-2*) AZ Game & Fish.

Dodd, P., jt. ed. see Seikaly, S.

Dodd, Paul. If My People Who Are Called Baptists... A Layman's Challenge. 128p. (Orig.). 1996. pap. 11.95 (*1-881576-85-X*) Providence Hse.

Dodd, Peter, jt. auth. see Lawrance, Alan.

Dodd, Philip, ed. Art of Travel: Essays on Travel Writing. 172p. 1982. text 25.00 (*0-7146-3205-8*, Pub. by F Cass Pubs) Intl Spec Bk.

— Walter Pater: An Imaginative Sense of Fact. 104p. 1981. 32.50 (*0-7146-3183-3*, Pub. by F Cass Pubs) Intl Spec Bk.

Dodd, Philip, jt. ed. see Christie, Ian.

Dodd, Philip, jt. ed. see Cook, Pam.

***Dodd, Richard S.** Diversity & Function in Mangrove Ecosystems. LC 99-88825. (Developments in Hydrobiology Ser.). (Illus.). 152p. 2000. write for info. (*0-7923-6158-X*) Kluwer Academic.

Dodd, Robert H., tr. see Prokopetz, Andrew T.

Dodd, Robert S. Thunderstones & Shooting Stars: The Meaning of Meteorites. (Illus.). 272p. 1986. reprint ed. pap. text 13.50 (*0-674-89138-4*) HUP.

Dodd, Robert V. Helping Children Cope with Death. LC 84-6713. 56p. (Orig.). 1984. pap. 4.99 (*0-8361-3368-4*) Herald Pr.

— Three Avenues of Spiritual Development. 1990. pap. 6.50 (*1-877871-05-2*, 3337) Ed Ministries.

— When Someone You Love Dies: An Explanation of Death for Children. 16p. 1986. pap. text 2.95 (*0-687-45025-X*) Abingdon.

— When They All Go Home. 1989. pap. text 2.50 (*0-687-45042-X*) Abingdon.

Dodd, Roger J., jt. auth. see Pozner, Larry S.

Dodd, S. C., Jr., jt. auth. see Kuzmin, S. L.

Dodd, S. M., et al, eds. Tubulointerstitial & Cystic Disease of the Kidney. LC 95-3278. (Current Topics in Pathology Ser.: Vol. 88). (Illus.). 304p. 1995. 143.00 (*3-540-58842-6*) Spr-Verlag.

Dodd, Shari. The Emerald of Lastanzia: The Enchantress' Secret. 314p. 1999. pap. 12.95 (*1-881542-52-1*) Blue Star Prodns.

— Rhiannon. 2nd ed. 250p. (Orig.). 1999. pap. 10.95 (*1-881542-53-X*) Book World Inc.

Dodd, Sharon, jt. auth. see Dodd, Kyle.

Dodd, Stephen L., jt. auth. see Powers, Scott K.

Dodd, Stuart C. Social Relations in the Near East. 2nd enl. rev. ed. LC 75-180333. reprint ed. 110.00 (*0-404-56239-6*) AMS Pr.

Dodd, Susan. Mamaw. LC 87-40661. 1988. 18.95 (*0-670-82180-2*) Grossman.

— Mamaw. 1988. 18.95 (*0-318-37677-6*) Viking Penguin.

***Dodd, Susan.** Mamaw: A Novel of an Outlaw Mother. LC 99-36178. 368p. 1999. reprint ed. pap. 13.00 (*0-688-17001-3*, Wm Morrow) Morrow Avon.

Dodd, Susan. The Mourners' Bench: A Novel. LC 97-52564. 288p. 1998. 24.00 (*0-688-15799-8*, Wm Morrow) Morrow Avon.

— The Mourners' Bench: A Novel. LC 98-46989. 1999. 25.95 (*1-56895-599-5*) Wheeler Pub.

***Dodd, Susan.** The Mourners' Bench: A Novel. 288p. 1999. reprint ed. pap. 13.00 (*0-688-16973-2*, Wm Morrow) Morrow Avon.

— O Careless Love. 2000. pap. write for info. (*0-688-17773-5*, Perennial) HarperTrade.

Dodd, Susan. O Careless Love: Stories & a Novella. LC 99-11468. 288p. 1999. 22.00 (*0-688-16999-6*, Wm Morrow) Morrow Avon.

***Dodd, Susan.** O Careless Love: Stories & a Novella. large type ed. (G. K. Hall Core Ser.). 2000. 27.95 (*0-7838-8976-3*, G K Hall Lrg Type) Mac Lib Ref.

Dodd, Susan, et al. Insides Out. (Illus.). 140p. 1997. pap., per. 18.95 (*1-888832-04-5*) Kings Estate.

Dodd, Susan M. Old Wives' Tales. LC 84-8879. (Iowa Short Fiction Award Ser.). 192p. (Orig.). (C). 1984. pap. 3.25 (*0-87745-133-8*) U of Iowa Pr.

Dodd, Terri, ed. see Hagan, Robert.

Dodd, Terri, ed. see Lynch, Tom.

Dodd, Terri, ed. see Robinson, E. John.

Dodd, Terry G. Uncommon Influence. 1994. pap. 14.95 (*0-9641600-0-5*) DCG Pubng.

Dodd, Thomas J. Managing Democracy in Central America, a Case Study: United States Election Supervision in Nicaragua, 1927-1933. LC 92-26327. 176p. (C). 1992. pap. 18.95 (*1-56000-631-5*, Pub. by U Miami N-S Ctr) L Rienner.

Dodd, Tony. Computing: The Technology of Information. (New Encyclopedia of Science Ser.). (Illus.). 160p. 1995. 39.95 (*0-19-521139-1*) OUP.

— ISO Prolog. 192p. (Orig.). 1994. pap. text 29.95 (*1-871516-47-1*, Pub. by Intellect) Cromland.

— The Life & Thought of Siger of Brabant, Thirteenth-Century Parisian Philosopher: An Examination of His Views on the Relationship of Philosophy & Theology. LC 97-52349. 1998. 119.95 (*0-7734-8477-9*) E Mellen.

Dodd, Tricia. The Prevalence of Back Pain in Great Britain in 1996: A Report on Research for the Department of Health Using the ONS Omnibus Survey. (Omnibus Survey Publications Report: No. OS 8). 15p. 1997. 26.00 (*0-11-620968-2*, Pub. by Statnry Office) Balogh.

Dodd, Vickie. Tuning the Blues to Gold: Sound Prints. LC 99-70961. 256p. 1999. pap. 24.95 (*0-9658137-1-1*) Woven Word.

Dodd, Vincent A. & Grace, Patrick, eds. Agricultural Engineering: Proceedings of the 11th International Congress, Dublin,m 4 - 8 September 1989, 4 vols., Set. (Illus.). 3175p. (C). 1989. 485.00 (*90-6191-980-0*, Pub. by A A Balkema) Ashgate Pub Co.

Dodd, Virginia A. Henry County, Virginia, Marriage Bonds, 1778-1849. 132p. 1996. reprint ed. pap. 15.00 (*0-8063-0702-1*, 1490) Clearfield Co.

Dodd, W. A., jt. auth. see Cameron, J.

Dodd, W. Craig. Bouquet of Aromatheraphy. LC 97-171678. (Gift of Health Ser.). (Illus.). 96p. 1997. pap. text 7.95 (*1-85368-667-0*, Pub. by New5 Holland) Sterling.

— Compendium of Oriental Healing. LC 97-171680. (A Gift of Health Ser.). (Illus.). 96p. 1997. pap. text 7.95 (*1-85368-669-7*, Pub. by New5 Holland) Sterling.

— Cornucopia of Aphrodisiacs. LC 97-171677. (A Gift of Health Ser.). (Illus.). 96p. 1997. pap. text 7.95 (*1-85368-668-9*, Pub. by New5 Holland) Sterling.

— Garden of Herbal Remedies. LC 97-156489. (A Gift of Health Ser.). (Illus.). 96p. 1997. pap. text 7.95 (*1-85368-670-0*, Pub. by New5 Holland) Sterling.

Dodd, W. F. Revision & Amendment of State Constitutions. LC 73-120854. (American Constitutional & Legal History Ser.). 1970. reprint ed. lib. bdg. 42.50 (*0-306-71959-2*) Da Capo.

Dodd, W. J. Peapatch Politics: The Earl K. Long Era in Louisiana Politics. 1991. 25.00 (*0-87511-932-8*) Claitors.

Dodd, Walter A., Jr. Final Year Excavations at the Evans Mound Site. (Anthropological Papers: No. 106). 160p. (Orig.). 1982. pap. 15.00 (*0-87480-207-5*) U of Utah Pr.

Dodd, Walter F. The Revision & Amendment of State Constitutions, 1910. LC 98-50815. 1999. 65.00 (*1-886363-73-0*) Lawbk Exchange.

Dodd, Wayne. The Blue Salvages. LC 97-65562. (Poetry Ser.). 94p. 1998. pap. 11.95 (*0-88748-259-7*) Carnegie-Mellon.

— Echoes of the Unspoken. LC 89-37882. (Contemporary Poetry Ser.). 88p. 1990. pap. 14.95 (*0-8203-1198-7*) U of Ga Pr.

— The Names You Gave It: Poems. fac. ed. LC 80-14240. 79p. 1980. reprint ed. pap. 30.00 (*0-7837-7730-2*, 204748600007) Bks Demand.

— Of Desire & Disorder. LC 93-73477. (Poetry Ser.). 72p. (Orig.). 1994. pap. 11.95 (*0-88748-169-8*) Carnegie-Mellon.

— Toward the End of the Century: Essays into Poetry. LC 92-15692. 154p. 1992. pap. 13.95 (*0-87745-256-3*) U of Iowa Pr.

Dodd, Wayne D., ed. The Ohio Review, No. 30. 280p. 1983. 13.95 (*0-942148-00-2*) Ohio Review.

***Dodd, William.** 800 Decorative Woodcuts for Artists & Craftspeople. LC 99-43238. 128p. 1999. pap. text 10.95 (*0-486-40700-4*) Dover & Greer.

Dodd, William & Klapper, John. Modern German Grammar Workbook. 112p. (C). 1996. pap., wbk. ed. 12.99 (*0-415-12094-2*) Routledge.

Dodd, William, jt. auth. see Presley, John.

Dodd, William C. The Tai Race, Elder Brother of the Chinese. 1976. lib. bdg. 59.95 (*0-8490-2726-8*) Gordon Pr.

Dodd, William E. The Cotton Kingdom: A Chronicle of the Old South. (BCL1 - United States Local History Ser.). 161p. 1991. reprint ed. lib. bdg. 69.00 (*0-7812-6287-9*) Rprt Serv.

— Jefferson Davis. LC 97-12862. xlii, 391p. 1997. pap. 16.95 (*0-8032-6609-X*, Bison Books) U of Nebr Pr.

— Statesmen of the Old South. 1994. pap. 22.00 (*0-8196-1897-7*) Biblo.

— Woodrow Wilson & His Work. 1958. 16.50 (*0-8446-1156-5*) Peter Smith.

Dodd, William J. Der Prozeb, Kafka: Critical Monographs in English. 62p. 1993. pap. 32.00 (*0-85261-323-7*, Pub. by Univ of Glasgow) St Mut.

Dodd, William J., ed. Kafka: The Metamorphosis, the Trial, & the Castle. LC 95-11016. Date not set. text. write for info. (*0-582-21680-X*, Pub. by Addison-Wesley) Longman.

Doddapaneni, N. & Landgrebe, A. R., eds. Proceedings of the Symposium on Lithium Batteries. LC 93-72862. (Proceedings Ser.: Vol. 94-04). 312p. 1994. 43.00 (*1-56677-033-5*) Electrochem Soc.

Dodder, Laura, jt. auth. see Muhlbauer, Gene.

Doddridge, Carole J. 7 Ways for 7 Days. (Illus.). 342p. 1999. 18.95 (*0-9671685-9-7*) Feather Nest.

Doddridge, Joseph. Notes on the Settlement & Indian Wars. annot. ed. 1824. reprint ed. pap. 14.95 (*0-87012-001-8*) McClain.

— Notes on the Settlement & Indian Wars of the Western Parts of VA & PA from 1763 to 1783, Inclusive, Together with a Review of the State of Society & Manners of the First Settlers of the Western Country. 320p. 1991. reprint ed. pap. 22.50 (*1-55613-127-5*) Heritage Bk.

***Doddridge, Joseph.** Notes on the Settlement & Indian Wars of the Western Parts of Virginia: Inclusive, Together with a Review of the State of Society & Manners of the First Settlers of the West Country. 320p. 1998. reprint ed. pap. 28.50 (*0-8063-4767-8*, 9316) Clearfield Co.

Dodds. The American Northwest: A History of Oregon & Washington. 19.95 (*0-88295-239-0*) Forum Pr IL.

Dodds. Environmental Economics. (C). 1996. text. write for info. (*0-03-002268-1*) Harcourt Coll Pubs.

***Dodds.** Geopolitics in a Changing World. LC 99-49446. 192p. (C). 1999. pap. 24.95 (*0-582-27954-2*) Addison-Wesley.

Dodds. Making Cars. (Scotland's Past in Action Ser.). (Illus.). 88p. (Orig.). Date not set. pap. 6.95 (*0-948636-81-5*, 6815, Pub. by Natl Mus Scotland) A Schwartz & Co.

— Readings in Environmental Economics. (C). 1996. pap. text. write for info. (*0-03-002269-X*) Harcourt Coll Pubs.

***Dodds.** The Ready Reference Handbook. 2nd ed. LC 99-11167. 412p. 1999. student ed., spiral bd. 33.00 (*0-205-30020-0*, Longwood Div) Allyn.

Dodds. Rehabilitating Blind & Visually Impaired People: A Psychological Approach. 218p. 1993. pap. 47.75 (*1-56593-153-X*, 0465) Singular Publishing.

***Dodds, Alastair, ed.** Scottish Bicycles & Tricycles. (Illus.). 96p. 1999. pap. 8.95 (*1-901663-21-3*, 3213, Pub. by Natl Mus Scotland) A Schwartz & Co.

Dodds, Alister W. & Sim, Robert B., eds. Complement: A Practical Approach, Vol. 182. LC 96-52102. (The Practical Approach Ser.: No. 182). (Illus.). 296p. 1997. pap. text 55.00 (*0-19-963539-0*) OUP.

— Complement: A Practical Approach, Vol. 182. LC 96-52102. (The Practical Approach Ser.: No. 182). (Illus.). 296p. (C). 1997. text 110.00 (*0-19-963540-4*) OUP.

Dodds, Allan. Rehabilitating Blind & Visually Impaired People: A Psychological Approach. LC 93-16158. 1993. 34.95 (*0-412-46970-7*) Chapman & Hall.

Dodds, Annie E. The Romantic Theory of Poetry: An Examination in the Light of Croce's Aesthetic. LC 75-28996. reprint ed. 44.50 (*0-404-14007-6*) AMS Pr.

Dodds, Bill. Are You Middle-Aged Yet? Test Yourself in the Privacy of Your Own Home. 100p. 1994. 7.00 (*0-671-88445-X*) S&S Trade.

— Are You over the Hill? (Illus.). 96p. 1994. pap. 7.00 (*0-88166-207-0*) Meadowbrook.

— The Hidden Fortune. LC 91-60944. 128p. (YA). (gr. 9-12). 1991. pap. 4.95 (*0-89243-346-9*) Liguori Pubns.

— How to Outsmart Your Kids: The Parents Guide to Dirty Tricks. rev. ed. LC 92-40981. (Illus.). 96p. 1993. pap. 6.00 (*0-88166-196-1*) Meadowbrook.

— How to Survive Your Fortieth Birthday. LC 90-36859. 78p. 1990. pap. 6.00 (*0-88166-139-2*) Meadowbrook.

D

An Asterisk (*) at the beginning of an entry indicates that the title is appearing for the first time.

— How to Survive Your 40th Birthday. 100p. 1990. 7.00 (*0-671-72561-0*) S&S Trade.

— My Sister Annie. LC 91-77599. (Illus.). 96p. (J). (gr. 3-7). 1997. pap. 7.95 (*1-56397-554-8*) Boyds Mills Pr.

***Dodds, Bill.** What You Dont Know About Retirement: A Funny Retirement Quiz. (Illus.). 112p. 2000. per. 6.00 (*0-671-31817-9*) S&S Trade.

— Your One-Stop Guide to How Saints Are Made. 2000. pap. 9.99 (*1-56955-198-7*) Servant.

Dodds, Bill & Dodds, Michael J. Living the Beatitudes Today: Happily Ever after Begins Here & Now. LC 97-12467. (Seeker Ser.). 1997. pap. 10.95 (*0-8294-0970-X*) Loyola Pr.

— The Seeker's Guide to 7 Life-Changing Virtues. LC 98-30741. (Seeker Ser.). 200p. 1999. pap. 10.95 (*0-8294-1171-2*) Loyola Pr.

***Dodds, Bill & Fushek, Dale.** Your One-Stop Guide to the Mass. 150p. 2000. pap. 9.99 (*1-56955-219-3*) Servant.

Dodds, Bill, jt. auth. see Dodds, Monica.

Dodds, Bob, jt. auth. see Smith, Brian.

Dodds, David L., ed. Arthurian Poets: Charles Williams. 320p. (C). 1991. pap. 24.95 (*0-85115-291-0*) Boydell & Brewer.

— Arthurian Poets: Charles Williams. 312p. (C). 1991. 75.00 (*0-85991-327-9*) Boydell & Brewer.

— Arthurian Poets: John Masefield. (Arthurian Studies: Vol. 32). 410p. (C). 1994. pap. 29.95 (*0-85115-363-1*) Boydell & Brewer.

Dodds, Dayle A. The Color Box. (Illus.). 32p. (J). (gr. k-3). 1992. 14.95 (*0-316-18820-4*) Little.

— Do Bunnies Talk? LC 91-13434. (Illus.). 32p. (J). (ps-1). 1992. 15.00 (*0-06-020248-3*); lib. bdg. 14.89 (*0-06-020249-1*) HarpC Child Bks.

— Ghost & Pete. LC 94-43102. (Step into Reading Ser.: A Step 2 Book). (Illus.). 48p. (J). (ps-3). 1995. lib. bdg. 11.99 (*0-679-96199-2*) Random.

— Ghost & Pete. LC 94-43102. (Step into Reading Ser.: A Step 2 Book). (Illus.). 48p. (J). (ps-3). 1995. pap. 3.99 (*0-679-86199-8*, Pub. by Random Bks Yng Read) Random.

— The Great Divide: A Mathematical Marathon. LC 98-35833. (Illus.). 32p. (J). (gr. 1-4). 1999. 15.99 (*0-7636-0442-9*) Candlewick Pr.

— On Our Way to Market. LC 91-6436. (Illus.). 40p. (J). (ps). 1991. pap. 13.95 (*0-671-73567-5*) S&S Bks Yung.

— The Shape of Things. LC 93-47255. (Illus.). 32p. (J). 1996. pap. 5.99 (*1-56402-698-1*) Candlewick Pr.

— Sing Sophie. LC 96-22411. (Illus.). 32p. (J). (gr. k-3). 1997. 15.99 (*0-7636-0131-4*) Candlewick Pr.

— Sing Sophie. LC 96-2241. (Illus.). 32p. (J). 1999. text 6.99 (*0-7636-0500-X*) Candlewick Pr.

Dodds, Dayle Ann. Shape of Things. 1996. 12.00 (*0-606-09849-6*, Pub. by Turtleback) Demco.

— Someone Is Hiding. (J). 1994. lib. bdg. 8.95 (*0-671-75542-0*) Litle Simon.

Dodds, Dennis R. & Eiland, Murray L., III, eds. Oriental Rugs from Atlantic Collections. (Illus.). 304p. 1996. 95.00 (*1-889666-02-5*, 02) Phila Eighth ICOC.

Dodds, Dinah & Allen-Thompson, Pam, eds. The Wall in My Backyard: East German Women in Transition. LC 94-18664. (Illus.). 192p. (C). 1994. pap. 15.95 (*0-87023-933-3*) U of Mass Pr.

— The Wall in My Backyard: East German Women in Transition. LC 94-18664. (Illus.). 192p. (C). 1995. 30.00 (*0-87023-932-5*) U of Mass Pr.

Dodds, Don. Modern Cruising under Sail. LC 97-40749. (Illus.). 496p. 1997. pap. 33.00 (*1-55821-626-X*) Lyons Pr.

***Dodds, Don.** Modern Seamanship. 512p. 2000. 12.99 (*0-517-16252-0*) Random Hse Value.

Dodds, Don. Modern Seamanship: A Complete Guide for the Recreational Boater. (Illus.). 512p. 1995. pap. 30.00 (*1-55821-270-1*) Lyons Pr.

Dodds, Donald G., jt. auth. see Gilbert, Frederick F.

Dodds, E. R. The Greeks & the Irrational. 1990. 32.50 (*0-8446-6224-0*) Peter Smith.

— Select Passages Illustrating Neoplatonism. 128p. 1980. pap. 15.00 (*0-89005-302-2*) Ares.

Dodds, E. R. & Euripides. Bacchae. 2nd ed.Tr. of Bacchae. 320p. 1987. pap. text 26.00 (*0-19-872125-0*) OUP.

Dodds, E. R., ed. see Plato.

Dodds, Edwin L., ed. see Dodds, Joanne W.

Dodds, Elreta. The Trouble with Farrakhan & the Nation of Islam: Another Message to the Black Man in America. LC 97-92584. ix, 214p. 1997. pap. 12.95 (*0-9660390-0-9*, Pub. by Pr Toward Mark) Bookmen Inc.

***Dodds, Elreta.** What the Bible Really Says about Slavery: This & Other Information on the Issue of Slavery as It Applies to History & Religion. 2nd rev. ed. LC 99-93470. Orig. Title: Slaves Obey Your Masters: What the Bible Really Says about Slavery. (Illus.). 160p. 2000. per. 12.00 (*0-9660390-1-7*, Pub. by Pr Toward Mark) Bookmen Inc.

Dodds, Eric R. The Ancient Concept of Progress: And Other Essays on Greek Literature & Belief. 226p. 1986. pap. text 21.00 (*0-19-814377-X*) OUP.

— The Greeks & the Irrational. (Sather Classical Lectures: No. 25). 1951. pap. 17.95 (*0-520-00327-6*, Pub. by U CA Pr) Cal Prin Full Svc.

— Pagan & Christian in an Age of Anxiety: Some Aspects of Religious Experience from Marcus Aurelius to Constantine. 160p. (C). 1991. pap. text 18.95 (*0-521-38599-7*) Cambridge U Pr.

Dodds, Eric R., tr. & comment see Proclus.

Dodds, Felix, ed. The Way Forward: Beyond Agenda 21. 224p. 1997. pap. 32.00 (*1-85383-437-8*, Pub. by Escan Pubns) Island Pr.

Dodds, George. Voice Placing & Training Exercise, 2 vols. Incl. Contralto & Baritone. 1927. 10.95 (*0-19-322141-1*); Soprano & Tenor. 1927. 10.95 (*0-19-322140-3*); (YA). (gr. 9 up). 1927. write for info. (*0-318-54901-8*) OUP.

Dodds, Glen L. Battles in Britain 1066-1746. (Illus.). 224p. 1996. 29.95 (*1-85409-297-9*, Pub. by Arms & Armour) Sterling.

— The Zulus & Matabele Warrior Nations. (Illus.). 272p. 1998. 24.95 (*1-85409-381-9*, Pub. by Arms & Armour) Sterling.

Dodds, Gordon. The American Northwest: A History of Washington & Oregon. LC 85-2072. (Illus.). 374p. (Orig.). (C). 1986. text 27.95 (*0-88273-239-0*); pap. text 19.95 (*0-88273-238-2*) Forum Pr IL.

Dodds, Gordon, ed. Varieties of Hope: An Anthology of Oregon Prose. LC 93-11479. (Oregon Literature Ser.: Vol. 3). (Illus.). 352p. 1993. pap. 21.95 (*0-87071-374-4*); text 35.95 (*0-87071-373-6*) Oreg St U Pr.

Dodds, Gordon & Wollner, Craig. Silicon Forest: High Tech in the Portland Area, 1945-1986. LC 90-41708. 210p. 1990. 19.95 (*0-87595-230-5*) Oregon Hist.

Dodds, Gordon, et al. The World of William Notman: The Nineteenth Century Through a Master Lens. (Illus.). 240p. 1993. 75.00 (*0-87923-939-5*) Godine.

***Dodds, Gordon B.** The College That Would Not Die: The First Fifty Years of Portland State University, 1946-1996. LC 99-51802. 1999. write for info. (*0-87595-274-7*) Oregon Hist.

Dodds, Harold W. Out of This Nettle, Danger. LC 78-99631. (Essay Index Reprint Ser.). 1977. 17.95 (*0-8369-1406-6*) Ayer.

Dodds, Ian. Tolley's Tax Office Directory, 1996. 100p. 1995. pap. 95.00 (*1-86012-055-5*, Pub. by Tolley Pubng) St Mut.

Dodds, J. A., jt. ed. see Bideau, D.

***Dodds, J. C.** Article 2b: Commercial Lawyers Invade the Land of Intellectual Property. 101p. 1998. ring bd. 30.00 (*1-56986-025-4*, IPR-98-101) Federal Bar.

Dodds, J. C., jt. auth. see Puxty, A. G.

Dodds, J. Terry, jt. auth. see American Institute of Certified Public Accountants Staff.

***Dodds, Jack & Jewinski, Judi.** Ready Reference Handbook: Writing, Revising, Editing Canadian Edition. 2nd ed. 480p. 2000. pap. 43.93 (*0-205-31917-3*) Allyn.

Dodds, James E. The Gentleman from Heaven. 123p. 1962. reprint ed. 7.50 (*0-87516-464-1*) DeVorss.

Dodds, Jerrilynn. Architecture & Ideology in Early Medieval Spain. LC 88-43437. (Illus.). 256p. (C). 1994. pap. text 25.00 (*0-271-01325-7*); lib. bdg. 45.00 (*0-271-00671-4*) Pa St U Pr.

Dodds, Joanne W. They All Came to Pueblo: A Social History. Dodds, Edwin L., ed. LC 94-35440. (Illus.). 1994. write for info. (*0-89865-908-6*) Donning Co.

Dodds, John H., ed. Plant Genetic Engineering. 320p. 1985. text 69.95 (*0-521-25966-5*) Cambridge U Pr.

Dodds, John H. & Roberts, Lorin W. Experiments in Plant Tissue Culture. 3rd ed. (Illus.). 272p. (C). 1995. text 69.95 (*0-521-47313-6*); pap. text 27.95 (*0-521-47892-8*) Cambridge U Pr.

Dodds, Josiah. A Child Psychotherapy Primer: Suggestions for the Beginning Therapist. 166p. 1985. pap. 20.95 (*0-89885-310-9*, Kluwer Acad Hman Sci) Kluwer Academic.

Dodds, Karen, jt. auth. see Farber, Jeffrey M.

Dodds, Karen L., jt. ed. see Hauschild, Andreas H.

***Dodds, Kip.** Kip's Flowers for Diana: Flower Arrangements Created for Princess Diana. (Illus.). 128p. 1999. 35.95 (*0-283-06348-3*, Pub. by S1 & J) Trans-Atl Phila.

***Dodds, Klaus & Atkinson, David, eds.** Geopolitical Traditions: Critical Histories of a Century of Political Thought. LC 99-44347. 336p. (C). 2000. text. write for info. (*0-415-17248-9*) Routledge.

Dodds, Klaus J. Geopolitics of Antarctica. LC 97-14902. 270p. 1998. 100.00 (*0-471-96992-3*) Wiley.

***Dodds, Klaus J. & Atkinson, David.** Geopolitical Traditions: Critical Histories of Century of Political Thought. LC 99-44347. 336p. 2000. pap. 29.99 (*0-415-17249-7*) Routledge.

Dodds, Malcolm, ed. Family Law. 260p. (C). 1991. 72.00 (*1-85352-878-1*, Pub. by HLT Pubns); 72.00 (*1-85352-397-6*, Pub. by HLT Pubns) St Mut.

— Family Law. 480p. 1996. pap. 110.00 (*0-7510-0696-3*, Pub. by HLT Pubns) St Mut.

— Family Law Cases. 330p. 1996. pap. 110.00 (*0-7510-0662-9*, Pub. by HLT Pubns) St Mut.

Dodds, Michael J., jt. auth. see Dodds, Bill.

Dodds, Monica & Dodds, Bill. The Joy of Marriage. LC 94-7059. (Illus.). 110p. 1994. pap. 5.95 (*0-88166-211-9*) Meadowbrook.

— The Joy of Marriage: Inspiration & Encouragement for Couples. (Illus.). 110p. 1994. 7.00 (*0-671-89458-7*) Meadowbrook.

Dodds, Patricia, et al. Beyond the Rainbow: A Guide for Parents of Children with Dyslexia & Other Learning Disabilities. 1991. pap. write for info. (*0-9636054-0-2*) Educ Intervent.

Dodds, Peter F. Outer Search/Inner Journey: An Orphan & Adoptee's Quest. LC 96-97016. 280p. (Orig.). 1997. pap. 15.00 (*1-889702-24-2*) Aphrodite WA.

Dodds, Philip V., ed. The Digital Multimedia Cross-Industry Guide. 350p. 1995. text 56.95 (*0-240-80205-5*, Focal) Buttrwrth-Heinemann.

Dodds, Richard J. The Eastern Shore's Own Steamboat Company: The Wheeler Transportation Line of Maryland. (Illus.). 1990. pap. 5.00 (*0-614-04341-7*) Ches Bay Mus.

— Solomons Island & Vicinity: An Illustrated History & Walking Tour. (Illus.). 80p. 1996. pap. 4.95 (*0-941647-12-9*) Calvert MM Pr.

Dodds, Rosemary. Listen with Mother: Consulting Users of Maternity Services. 84p. 1996. pap. text 32.00 (*1-898507-48-1*) Buttrwth-Heinemann.

Dodds, S. W., jt. auth. see Trall, R. T.

Dodds, Siobhan. Grandpa Bud. LC 92-53135. (Illus.). 32p. (J). (ps-3). 1993. 13.95 (*1-56402-175-0*) Candlewick Pr.

— Grandpa Bud. LC 92-53135. (J). 1995. pap. 5.99 (*1-56402-489-X*) Candlewick Pr.

***Dodds, Siobhan.** Old MacDonald Had a Farm: Flip-Flap. LC 98-73052. (Illus.). 32p. (J). 1999. pap. 3.99 (*0-7636-0761-4*) Candlewick Pr.

— Ting-a-Ling! LC 99-20845. (Dk Toddler Story Book Ser.). (Illus.). 24p. (J). (ps). 1999. 9.95 (*0-7894-4841-6*) DK Pub Inc.

Dodds, Siobhan. Words & Pictures: Reading with Picture Clues. LC 91-71817. (Illus.). 32p. (J). (ps up). 1992. 14.95 (*1-56402-042-8*) Candlewick Pr.

— Words & Pictures: Reading with Picture Clues. LC 91-71817. (Illus.). 32p. (J). (ps up). 1994. pap. 4.99 (*1-56402-285-4*) Candlewick Pr.

Dodds, Siobhan & Bentley, Dawn. The Noisy Farm: A Picture Puzzle Board Book. (Picture Puzzle Board Bks.). (Illus.). 12p. (J). 1999. 6.95 (*1-58117-031-9*, Pub. by Intervisual Bks) Andrews & McMeel.

— Sherlock's Missing Bone: A Picture Puzzle Board Book, 2 vols. (Picture Puzzle Board Bks.). (Illus.). 12p. (J). 1999. 6.95 (*1-58117-032-7*, Pub. by Intervisual Bks) Andrews & McMeel.

Dodds, Vera W., jt. auth. see Perloff, Harvey S.

Dodds, W. Jean, ed. Advances in Veterinary Science & Comparative Medicine Vol. 39: Veterinary Medical Specialization: Bridging Science & Medicine, Vol. 39. (Illus.). 303p. (C). 1995. text 84.00 (*0-12-039240-2*) Acad Pr.

***Dodds, W. Jean & Schultz, Ronald D., eds.** Advances in Veterinary Medicine Vol. 41: Veterinary Vaccines & Diagnostics. LC 98-233668. (Illus.). xxxviii, 815p. (C). 1999. boxed set 149.95 (*0-12-039242-9*) Acad Pr.

Dodds, W. Jean & Womack, James E., eds. Advances in Veterinary Science & Comparative Medicine Vol. 40: From Molecular Genetics to Gene Transfer & Therapy. LC 97-201498. (Illus.). 227p. 1997. text 90.00 (*0-12-039241-0*) Morgan Kaufmann.

Dode, Leonard. Identification & Characterization of the Human Sarco/Endoplasmic Reticulum Ca2+ - ATPase 3 (SERCA3) Gene. (Acta Biomedica Lovaniensia Ser.). (Illus.). 145p. 1998. pap. 53.50 (*90-6186-889-0*, Pub. by Leuven Univ) Coronet Bks.

Dodenhoff, Carla. Mental Fatigue - Analysis, Procedures, Tests, Factors, Results & Advice: Index of New Information with Authors, Subjects, Research Categories & References. 160p. (Orig.). 1995. 47.50 (*0-7883-0688-X*); pap. 44.50 (*0-7883-0689-8*) ABBE Pubs Assn.

Doder, Dusko. Shadows & Whispers: Power Politics Inside the Kremlin from Brezhnev to Gorbachev. (Illus.). 339p. 1986. 19.95 (*0-685-17620-7*) Random.

***Doder, Dusko & Branson, Louise.** Milosevic: Portrait of a Tyrant. LC 99-41729. 291p. 1999. 25.00 (*0-684-84308-0*) Free Pr.

Doder, Dusko, jt. auth. see Weihmiller, Gordon R.

Doderer, Heimito Von, see Von Doderer, Heimito.

***Dodes, Lance.** Taking Control. 2000. 24.00 (*0-06-019811-7*) HarpC.

— Talking Control. 2000. pap. 14.00 (*0-06-095803-0*) HarpC.

Dodet, B., jt. ed. see Girard, M.

Dodge. Foundations of Business & Accounting. 2nd ed. 1997. pap. 19.99 (*1-86152-153-7*) Thomson Learn.

— Foundations of Business & Accounting. 2nd ed. 1998. pap. 57.95 (*1-86152-154-5*) Thomson Learn.

Dodge. Foundations of Cost & Management Accounting. (Illus.). 80p. (Orig.). (C). (gr. 13). 1996. mass mkt., teacher ed. 63.75 (*0-412-58830-7*, Chap & Hall NY) Chapman & Hall.

Dodge, A. D., ed. Herbicides & Plant Metabolism. (Society for Experimental Biology Seminar Ser.: No. 28). 288p. (C). 1990. text 85.00 (*0-521-34422-0*) Cambridge U Pr.

Dodge, A. J., jt. auth. see Myers, E.

Dodge, Abigail J. Great Fruit Desserts. LC 96-71422. (Illus.). 64p. 1997. 15.95 (*0-8478-2018-1*, Pub. by Rizzoli Intl) St Martin.

***Dodge, Abigail J.** The Kids Cookbook: A Great Book for Kids Who Love to Cook. LC 99-49736. (Illus.). 128p. (YA). (gr. 4 up). 2000. 19.95 (*0-7370-2041-5*) Time-Life Educ.

***Dodge, Andrew Ian.** Statism Sucks! A Treatise on Freedom. 133p. 2000. pap. 18.95 (*0-9678127-0-4*) Blue Enterprises.

Dodge, Bayard. Al-Azhar: A Millennium of Muslim Learning. (Illus.). 1974. 3.50 (*0-916808-11-4*) Mid East Inst.

— Muslim Education in Medieval Times. LC 63-144. 1962. 3.75 (*0-916808-02-5*) Mid East Inst.

Dodge, Bertha S. Tales of Vermont Ways & People. LC 84-61170. (Illus.). 192p. 1984. reprint ed. pap. 14.95 (*0-933050-22-4*) New Eng Pr VT.

— Vermont by Choice: The Earliest Years. LC 87-62158. 160p. (Orig.). 1987. pap. 9.95 (*0-933050-50-X*) New Eng Pr VT.

Dodge, Bill, jt. auth. see Duey, Kathleen.

Dodge, C. W. Some Lichens of Tropical Africa V: Lecanoraceae to Physiaceae. 1971. pap. 80.00 (*3-7682-5438-0*) Lubrecht & Cramer.

— Some Lichens of Tropical Africa IV: Dermatocarpaceae to Pertusariaceae. 1964. pap. 64.00 (*3-7682-5412-7*) Lubrecht & Cramer.

Dodge, Carroll W. Lichen Flora of the Antarctic Continent & Adjacent Islands. 399p. 1973. lib. bdg. 19.95 (*0-318-41528-3*) Lubrecht & Cramer.

Dodge, Charles & Jerse, Thomas A. Computer Music: Synthesis, Composition, & Performance. 383p. 1985. 42.00 (*0-02-873100-X*, Schirmer Books) Mac Lib Ref.

Dodge, Chris & DeSirey, Jan, eds. Everything You Always Wanted to Know about Sandy Berman but Were Afraid to Ask. LC 95-8078. (Illus.). 199p. 1995. lib. bdg. 25.00 (*0-7864-0081-1*) McFarland & Co.

Dodge, Clifford H. & Glover, Albert D. Coal Resources of Greene County, Pennsylvania Pt. 1: Coal Crop Lines, Mined--outAreas, & Structure Contours. (Mineral Resource Reports: No. 86). (Illus.). 67p. (Orig.). 1984. pap. 6.60 (*0-8182-0055-3*) Commonweal PA.

Dodge, Cole & Raundalen, Magne. Reaching Children in War: Sudan, Uganda & Mozambique. 146p. 1991. 19.95 (*91-7106-319-6*, Pub. by Nordic Africa) Transaction Pubs.

Dodge, Cole P. & Raundelen, Magne. Reaching Children in War: Sudan, Uganda & Mozambique. 160p. 1992. pap. 23.00 (*82-90373-61-9*) Taylor & Francis.

Dodge, Cole P., jt. ed. see Wiebe, Paul D.

Dodge, Consuelo. The Everly Brothers: Ladies Love Outlaws. LC 90-85691. 345p. (Orig.). 1991. pap. 14.95 (*1-879347-09-1*) Cin-Dav.

Dodge, D. A., jt. ed. see Lee, W. H.

***Dodge, Daniel K.** Abraham Lincoln: The Evolution of His Literary Style. LC 99-29887. 2000. pap. 9.95 (*0-252-06854-8*) U of Ill Pr.

Dodge, David L. War Inconsistent with the Religion of Jesus Christ. LC 75-137540. (Peace Movement in America Ser.). xxiv, 168p. 1972. reprint ed. lib. bdg. 24.95 (*0-89198-067-9*) Ozer.

Dodge, David O. & Kyriss, S. E. Seamanship: Fundamentals for the Deck Officer. 2nd ed. LC 80-5684. (Fundamentals of Naval Science Ser.: No. 2). (Illus.). 272p. 1981. text 19.95 (*0-87021-613-9*) Naval Inst Pr.

Dodge, Diane T. A Guide for Supervisors & Trainers on Implementing the Creative Curriculum for Early Childhood. 3rd ed. LC 92-62949. (Illus.). 240p. (Orig.). (C). 1993. otabind 29.95 (*1-879537-07-9*) Tchng Strtgs.

Dodge, Diane T. & Bickart, Toni S. Preschool for Parents: What Every Parent Needs to Know about Preschool. LC 98-17216. 192p. 1998. pap. 12.95 (*1-57071-172-0*) Sourcebks.

Dodge, Diane T. & Colker, Laura J. The Creative Curriculum for Early Childhood. 3rd ed. LC 91-67416. (Illus.). 380p. (Orig.). (C). 1992. pap. text 39.95 (*1-879537-06-0*) Tchng Strtgs.

— The Creative Curriculum for Family Child Care. LC 90-71845. (Illus.). 264p. (Orig.). (C). 1991. pap. text 29.95 (*0-9602892-7-5*) Tchng Strtgs.

— El Curriculo Creativo para Educacion Preescolar. Nunez, Claudia C., tr. LC 96-60574. (SPA., Illus.). 390p. (Orig.). (C). 1996. pap. text 39.95 (*1-879537-23-0*) Tchng Strtgs.

— A Trainer's Guide to the Creative Curriculum for Family Child Care. LC 90-71846. (Illus.). 128p. (Orig.). (C). 1991. spiral bd. 22.95 (*0-9602892-8-3*) Tchng Strtgs.

***Dodge, Diane T. & Heroman, Cate.** Building Your Baby's Brain: A Parent's Guide to the First Five Years, 10 bks., Set. (Illus.). 48p. 1999. pap. text 29.50 (*1-879537-41-9*, Pub. by Tchng Strtgs) Gryphon Hse.

Dodge, Diane T. & Koralek, Derry G. A Trainer's Guide to Caring for Infants & Toddlers. LC 91-90304. 190p. (Orig.). (C). 1991. otabind 23.95 (*1-879537-03-6*) Tchng Strtgs.

Dodge, Diane T. & Phinney, Joanna. Guia para los Padres Sobre Educacion Preescolar, 10 bks., Set. 2nd ed. (SPA., Illus.). (Orig.). (C). 1996. pap. text 22.50 (*1-879537-05-2*) Tchng Strtgs.

— A Parent's Guide to Early Childhood Education, 10 bks., Set. (Illus.). 22p. (Orig.). (C). 1990. pap. text 22.50 (*0-9602892-5-9*) Tchng Strtgs.

— A Parent's Guide to Early Childhood Education, 10 bks., Set. (CHI., Illus.). 22p. (Orig.). 1995. pap. text 22.50 (*1-879537-17-6*) Tchng Strtgs.

Dodge, Diane T., et al. Caring for Children in Family Child Care, Set, Vols. 1 & 2. LC 93-61317. (Orig.). (C). 1993. pap. text 69.90 (*1-879537-08-7*) Tchng Strtgs.

— Caring for Children in Family Child Care, Vol. 1. LC 93-61317. 386p. (Orig.). (C). 1993. pap. text 34.95 (*1-879537-09-5*) Tchng Strtgs.

— Caring for Children in Family Child Care, Vol. 2. LC 93-61317. 425p. (Orig.). (C). 1993. pap. text 34.95 (*1-879537-10-9*) Tchng Strtgs.

— Caring for Infants & Toddlers, Set, Vols. 1 & 2. LC 91-65115. (Orig.). (C). 1991. pap. text 69.90 (*1-879537-00-1*) Tchng Strtgs.

— Caring for Infants & Toddlers, Vol. 1. LC 91-65115. 354p. (Orig.). (C). 1991. pap. text 34.95 (*1-879537-01-X*) Tchng Strtgs.

— Caring for Infants & Toddlers, Vol. 2. LC 91-65115. 356p. (Orig.). (C). 1991. pap. text 34.95 (*1-879537-02-8*) Tchng Strtgs.

— Caring for Preschool Children, 2 vols., Set. 2nd rev. ed. LC 96-61070. (Illus.). (C). 1996. pap. text 69.90 (*1-879537-27-3*) Tchng Strtgs.

— Caring for Preschool Children, Vol. 1. 2nd rev. ed. LC 96-61070. (Illus.). 337p. (C). 1996. pap. text 34.95 (*1-879537-25-7*) Tchng Strtgs.

— A Trainer's Guide to Caring for Children in Family Child Care. LC 93-61834. 240p. (C). 1994. spiral bd. 23.95 (*1-879537-11-7*) Tchng Strtgs.

— A Trainer's Guide to the Creative Curriculum for Infants & Toddlers. LC 98-61562. 340p. 1998. otabind 27.95 (*1-879537-31-1*) Tchng Strtgs.

***Dodge, Diane Trister & Heroman, Cate.** Como Estimular el Cerebro Infantil: Una Guia para Padres de Familia. Nunez, Claudia Caicedo, tr. (SPA., Illus.). 50p. 1999. pap. text 29.50 (*1-879537-42-7*) Tchng Strtgs.

D

An Asterisk (*) at the beginning of an entry indicates that the title is appearing for the first time.

***Dodge, Diane Trister, et al.** Connecting Content, Teaching & Learning: A Supplement to the Creative Curriculum for Early Childhood. 100p. 2000. pap. 9.95 (*1-879537-53-2*) Tchng Strtgs.

Dodge, Diane Trister, jt. auth. see Bickart, Toni S.

Dodge, E. R., ed. see Wilder, Alexander.

Dodge, Early, ed. see Plotinus.

Dodge, Edward J. Relief Is Greatly Wanted: The Battle of Fort William Henry. LC 98-169954. (Illus.). 206p. 1998. pap. 22.00 (*0-7884-0932-8*, D513) Heritage Bk.

***Dodge, Ellen P., ed.** Survival Guide for School-Based Speech-Language Pathologists. LC 99-40697. 438p. 1999. pap. 49.95 (*0-7693-0045-6*) Singular Publishing.

Dodge, Ellin. Numerology Has Your Number. 352p. 1988. pap. 12.00 (*0-671-64243-X*, Fireside) S&S Trade Pap.

Dodge, Ernest S. Hawaiian & Other Polynesian Gourds. 1995. pap. 12.95 (*0-914916-34-3*) Ku Paa.

Dodge, Ernest S., ed. Thirty Years of the American Neptune. LC 72-82988. (Illus.). 313p. reprint ed. pap. 97.10 (*0-7837-4460-9*, 205799000012) Bks Demand.

Dodge, Frank E. Dodge Drum Chart for Reading Drum Music. (Illus.). 24p. 1998. pap. text 3.50 (*1-892764-02-4*) G B Stone.

Dodge, Frank O. Fletcher in a Circle. (Illus.). 48p. (Orig.). Date not set. pap. 4.99 (*0-9640168-6-9*) Pirate Writings.

Dodge, Fred. Antique Tins. (Illus.). 296p. 1996. 24.95 (*0-89145-604-X*, 3872) Collector Bks.

— Antique Tins Book II: Identification & Values. 1998. 29.95 (*1-57432-033-5*, 5030) Collector Bks.

— Antique Tins III. 272p. 1999. 29.95 (*1-57432-099-8*) Collector Bks.

— Under Cover for Wells Fargo: The Unvarnished Recollections of Fred Dodge. Lake, Carolyn, ed. LC 98-24222. (Western Frontier Library: No. 63). (Illus.). 336p. 1998. 28.95 (*0-8061-3099-7*) U of Okla Pr.

Dodge, Garen E., jt. auth. see Tysse, G. John.

Dodge, Gary & Gorman, Tim. Oracle8 Data Warehousing. 5th ed. LC 97-42035. 672p. 1998. pap. 44.99 (*0-471-19952-4*) Wiley.

***Dodge, Gary & Gorman, Timothy.** Essential Oracle8i Data Warehousing: Designing, Building & Managing Oracle Data Warehouses. 2nd ed. 832p. 2000. pap. 44.99 (*0-471-37678-7*) Wiley.

Dodge, George A. A Whaling Voyage in the Pacific Ocean & Its Incidents. 30p. 1982. pap. 5.95 (*0-87770-243-8*) Ye Galleon.

Dodge, Grenville M. The Battle of Atlanta: And Other Campaigns, Addresses, Etc. large type unabridged ed. LC 96-44048. (Illus.). 183p. (C). 1996. reprint ed. 24.95 (*1-889881-07-4*) Old Bks Pub.

Dodge, Grethel, tr. see Nykiel, Connie.

Dodge, Gwen H., jt. auth. see Kneedler, Julia A.

Dodge, H. Robert & Zikmund, William C. A Collection of Cases in Marketing Management. 344p. (C). 1987. pap. text, teacher ed. write for info. (*0-314-34765-8*) West Pub.

Dodge, H. Robert, jt. auth. see Hanna, Nessim.

Dodge, Harold. Bessie, Buntie & Beauty. (Illus.). 32p. 1994. pap. 6.95 (*0-929032-95-0*, Pub. by Wood Lake Bks) Logos Prods.

***Dodge, Harold F.** Sampling Inspection Tables: Single & Double Sampling. 2nd ed. LC 98-140491. (Wiley Classics Library). 240p. 1998. pap. 54.95 (*0-471-25549-1*) Wiley.

Dodge, Harold F. & Romig, Harry G. Sampling Inspection Tables: Single & Double Sampling. 2nd ed. (Probability & Mathematical Statistics Ser.). (Illus.). 224p. 1959. 119.95 (*0-471-21747-6*) Wiley.

Dodge, Hazel & Ward-Perkins, Bryan. Marble in Antiquity: Collected Papers of J. B. Ward-Perkins. (Archaeological Monographs). (Illus.). 182p. 1992. pap. 45.00 (*0-904152-20-0*, Pub. by British Schl Rome) David Brown.

Dodge, Hazel, jt. auth. see Connolly, Peter.

Dodge, Hiroko H. Poverty Transitions among Elderly Widows. LC 95-46138. (Studies on the Elderly in America). (Illus.). 164p. 1996. text 58.00 (*0-8153-2280-1*) Garland.

Dodge, Howard. How to Prepare for the SAT II: Math II C. 6th rev. ed. LC 98-18035. 240p. 1998. pap. 12.95 (*0-7641-0462-4*) Barron.

Dodge, J. A. Cystic Fibrosis--Current Topics, Vol. 3. LC 92-15773. 386p. 1996. 245.95 (*0-471-96353-4*) Wiley.

Dodge, J. A., ed. Topics in Pediatric Gastroenterology. (Illus.). 1976. pap. 40.00 (*0-8464-0931-3*) Beekman Pubs.

Dodge, J. A., et al, eds. Cystic Fibrosis--Current Topics Vol. 2: Current Topics, Vol. 2. LC 92-15773. 368p. 1995. 245.95 (*0-471-95166-8*) Wiley.

Dodge, J. D., et al, eds. Cystic Fibrosis--Current Topics, Vol. 1, Vol. 1. LC 92-15773. 370p. 1993. 235.95 (*0-471-93101-2*, Wiley-Interscience) Wiley.

Dodge, James W., ed. Leadership for Continuing Development. (Reports of the Northeast Conference on the Teaching of Foreign Languages). 150p. 1971. pap. 10.95 (*0-685-51936-8*) NE Conf Teach Foreign.

— Other Words, Other Worlds: Language in Culture. 1972. pap. 10.95 (*0-915432-72-2*) NE Conf Teach Foreign.

— Sensitivity in the Foreign Language Classroom. 142p. 1973. pap. 10.95 (*0-915432-73-0*) NE Conf Teach Foreign.

Dodge, Jerry, jt. auth. see Flores, Anthony.

Dodge, Jim. Fup. LC 83-178295. 64p. 1986. pap. 5.95 (*0-933944-04-7*) City Miner Bks.

— Not Fade Away. 304p. 1998. reprint ed. pap. 12.00 (*0-8021-3584-6*, Grove) Grove-Atltic.

— Stone Junction. 376p. 1998. reprint ed. pap. 12.00 (*0-8021-3585-4*, Grove) Grove-Atltic.

Dodge, Joseph M. Estate & Gift Tax by Joseph M. Dodge, W. H. Francis Professor of Law, University of Texas at Austin. Tenen, Peter et al, eds. (Law Outlines Ser.). (Orig.). (C). 1998. pap. text. write for info. (*0-87457-188-X*, 5800) Casenotes Pub.

— Federal Income Taxation. LC 99-216277. (Law Outlines Ser.). 320p. (Orig.). 1994. pap. text. write for info. (*0-87457-182-0*, 5210) Casenotes Pub.

— The Logic of Tax. (Miscellaneous Ser.). 343p. (C). 1989. pap. 27.00 (*0-314-55868-3*) West Pub.

— Wills, Trusts & Estate Planning - Law & Taxation, Cases & Materials. 2nd ed. (American Casebook Ser.). 665p. (C). 1988. 57.50 (*0-314-37038-2*) West Pub.

***Dodge, Joseph M., et al.** Federal Income Tax: Doctrine, Structure & Policy - Text, Cases, Problems. 2nd ed. 400p. 1999. pap., teacher ed. write for info. (*0-327-01279-X*, 1112611) LEXIS Pub.

Dodge, Joseph M., et al. Federal Income Tax: Doctrine, Structure & Policy--Text, Cases, Problems. 2nd ed. LC 99-62385. 900p. 1999. text 56.00 (*0-327-01256-0*, 1112511) LEXIS Pub.

Dodge, Judith. Study Skills Handbook: More Than 75 Strategies for Better Learning. 1994. pap. 12.95 (*0-590-49510-0*) Scholastic Inc.

Dodge, Kenneth A., jt. ed. see Garber, Judy.

Dodge, Kirsten. Government & Business: Prospects for Partnership. (Symposia Ser.). 238p. 1980. pap. 5.00 (*0-89940-409-X*) LBJ Sch Pub Aff.

Dodge, Liz, jt. auth. see Whaley, Liz.

Dodge, Louis L. & Hill, William C. Dodge Family (of Block Isl, RI) (Illus.). 40p. 1997. reprint ed. pap. 8.00 (*0-8328-8322-0*); reprint ed. lib. bdg. 18.00 (*0-8328-8321-2*) Higginson Bk Co.

Dodge, M. G. Ballard Genealogy: The Descendants of Israel Ballard & Alice Fuller. 375p. 1991. reprint ed. pap. 58.00 (*0-8328-2089-X*); reprint ed. lib. bdg. 68.00 (*0-8328-2088-1*) Higginson Bk Co.

Dodge, Marilyn S., jt. auth. see Wiebe, Viola C.

Dodge, Mark & Stinson, Craig. Running Microsoft Excel 2000. LC 98-52136. (Running Ser.). (Illus.). 994p. 1999. pap. 39.99 (*1-57231-935-6*) Microsoft.

Dodge, Mark, et al. Running Microsoft Excel for Windows 95: In-Depth Reference & Inside Tips from THE Software Experts. (Running Ser.). 1200p. 1995. pap. 29.95 (*1-55615-831-9*) Microsoft.

— Running Microsoft Excel 97. LC 96-39339. 1184p. 39.95 incl. cd-rom (*1-57231-321-8*) Microsoft.

Dodge, Marshall J. & Howe, Walter. Frost, You Say? A Yankee Monologue. LC 73-83355. (Illus.). 128p. 1973. 12.95 (*0-85699-078-7*) Chatham Pr.

***Dodge, Martin & Kitchin, Rob.** Mapping Cyberspace. LC 00-38247. 2000. pap. write for info. (*0-415-19884-4*) Routledge.

Dodge, Martin, jt. auth. see Dodge, Venus.

Dodge, Martin, jt. auth. see Dodge, Venus A.

Dodge, Mary A. The Battle of the Books. (Notable American Authors Ser.). 1992. reprint ed. lib. bdg. 90.00 (*0-7812-2659-7*) Rprt Serv.

— Biography of James G. Blaine. (Notable American Authors Ser.). 1992. reprint ed. lib. bdg. 149.00 (*0-7812-2663-5*) Rprt Serv.

— Country Living & Country Thinking. (Notable American Authors Ser.). 1992. reprint ed. lib. bdg. 75.00 (*0-7812-2656-2*) Rprt Serv.

— A Gail Hamilton Reader. LC 91-35821. (American Women Writers Ser.). 280p. 1992. pap. text 15.00 (*0-8135-1810-5*) Rutgers U Pr.

— Gail Hamilton's Life in Letters. (Notable American Authors Ser.). 1992. reprint ed. lib. bdg. 90.00 (*0-7812-2665-1*) Rprt Serv.

— A New Atmosphere. (Notable American Authors Ser.). 1992. reprint ed. lib. bdg. 75.00 (*0-7812-2657-0*) Rprt Serv.

— Our Common School System. (Notable American Authors Ser.). 1992. reprint ed. lib. bdg. 75.00 (*0-7812-2661-9*) Rprt Serv.

— Twelve Miles from a Lemon. LC 76-37512. (Essay Index Reprint Ser.). 1977. reprint ed. 23.95 (*0-8369-2544-0*) Ayer.

— A Washington Bible Class. (Notable American Authors Ser.). 1992. reprint ed. lib. bdg. 90.00 (*0-7812-2662-7*) Rprt Serv.

— Woman's Worth & Worthlessness. (Notable American Authors Ser.). 1992. reprint ed. lib. bdg. 90.00 (*0-7812-2660-0*) Rprt Serv.

— Woman's Wrongs: A Counter-Irritant. (Notable American Authors Ser.). 1992. reprint ed. lib. bdg. 75.00 (*0-7812-2658-9*) Rprt Serv.

— Wool-Gathering. 1977. text 20.95 (*0-8369-9241-5*, 9095) Ayer.

— X-Rays. (Notable American Authors Ser.). 1992. reprint ed. lib. bdg. 75.00 (*0-7812-2664-3*) Rprt Serv.

Dodge, Mary A., jt. auth. see Todd, John.

Dodge, Mary M. Hans Brinker. LC 87-15472. (Illus.). 48p. (J). (gr. 3-6). 1988. lib. bdg. 19.95 (*0-8167-1205-0*) Troll Communs.

— Hans Brinker. LC 87-15472. (Illus.). 48p. (J). (gr. 3-6). 1997. pap. 5.95 (*0-8167-1206-9*) Troll Communs.

— Hans Brinker. 336p. 1997. pap. 3.99 (*0-14-036784-5*) Viking Penguin.

— Hans Brinker: The Silver Skates. 24.95 (*0-89190-548-0*) Amereon Ltd.

— Hans Brinker: The Silver Skates. unabridged ed. 235p. 1997. reprint ed. pap. 14.95 (*1-57002-018-3*) Univ Publng Hse.

— Hans Brinker or the Silver Skates. (YA). 1993. pap. 2.50 (*0-8125-3342-9*, Pub. by Tor Bks) St Martin.

Dodge, Mary M. Hans Brinker or the Silver Skates, Set. (J). (gr. 4). 1996. pap. 77.75 incl. audio (*0-7887-1551-8*, 40114) Recorded Bks.

Dodge, Mary M. Hans Brinker or the Silver Skates - Musical. 1998. pap. 5.95 (*0-87129-789-2*, H04) Dramatic Pub.

Dodge, Mary Mapes. Hans Brinker. Hanft, Joshua, ed. (Great Illustrated Classics Ser.: Vol. 40). (Illus.). 240p. (J). (gr. 3-6). 1994. 9.95 (*0-86611-991-4*) Playmore Inc.

— Hans Brinker & the Silver Skates. 1993. 7.60 (*0-606-12322-9*, Pub. by Turtleback) Demco.

Dodge, Meredith D., jt. ed. see Kern, Robert W.

Dodge, Meredith D., ed. & tr. see De Galve, Gelvira.

Dodge, Nancy C., jt. auth. see Lamb, Jane M.

Dodge, Nancy L. Northern New Hampshire Graveyards & Cemeteries: Transcriptions & Indexes of Burial Sites in Clarksville, Colebrook, Columbia, Dixville, Pittsburg, Stewartstown & Stratford. 443p. 1988. reprint ed. lib. bdg. 39.00 (*0-8328-0038-4*, NH0001) Higginson Bk Co.

Dodge, Natt N. Flowers of the Southwest Deserts. rev. ed. Priehs, T. J. & Dodson, Carolyn, eds. LC 84-62857. (Illus.). 136p. 1985. pap. 9.95 (*0-911408-65-7*) SW Pks Mnmts.

Dodge, Nik & Heath, Jody. High-Speed Chase: Guilty of Love in the Lust Degree. (Illus.). 35p. 1996. 9.95 (*0-9652914-0-5*) Dodge & Heath.

Dodge, Norton, jt. ed. see Rosenfeld, Alla.

Dodge, Philip J., et al. Why & How We Work in a Political Party. (Illus.). 130p. (Orig.). 1997. 12.00 (*0-9657747-0-8*) P & N Dodge.

Dodge, Pryor. The Bicycle. (Illus.). 224p. 1996. 50.00 (*2-08-013551-1*, Pub. by Flammarion) Abbeville Pr.

Dodge, R. The Concise Guide to Auditing Standards & Guidelines. 224p. 1990. pap. text 20.95 (*0-412-02671-6*, A4464, Chap & Hall NY) Chapman & Hall.

— Foundations of Cost & Management Accounting. 448p. 1994. mass mkt. 25.95 (*0-412-58820-X*) Chapman & Hall.

— Group Financial Statements. (Illus.). 320p. 1995. pap. 32.95 (*0-412-63930-0*) Thomson Learn.

Dodge, Ralph E. The Revolutionary Bishop Who Saw God at Work in Africa: An Autobiography. LC 85-29092. (Illus.). 211p. (Orig.). 1986. pap. 8.95 (*0-87808-203-4*, WCL203-4) William Carey Lib.

Dodge, Richard H. How to Read & Write in College: A Complete Course. (Orig.). 1989. text 13.50 (*0-685-02048-7*) Addson-Wesley Educ.

Dodge, Richard I. The Black Hills Journals of Colonel Richard Irving Dodge. Kime, Wayne R., ed. LC 95-41149. (American Exploration & Travel Ser.: Vol. 74). (Illus.). 288p. 1996. 29.95 (*0-8061-2846-1*) U of Okla Pr.

— Our Wild Indians: Thirty Three Years' Personal Experience Among the Red Men of the Great West. (Select Bibliographies Reprint Ser.). 1977. 60.95 (*0-8369-5230-8*) Ayer.

— Our Wild Indians: Thirty Three Years Personal Experience Among the Red Men of the Great West. 657p. 1978. reprint ed. 39.95 (*0-87928-089-1*) Corner Hse.

— The Plains of North America & Their Inhabitants. Kime, Wayne R., ed. LC 87-40706. (Illus.). 1989. 65.00 (*0-87413-344-0*) U Delaware Pr.

— The Powder River Expedition Journals of Colonel Richard Irving Dodge. Kime, Wayne R., ed. LC 97-9315. (Illus.). 208p. 1997. 28.95 (*0-8061-2983-2*) U of Okla Pr.

***Dodge, Richard Irving & Kime, Wayne R.** The Indian Territory Journals of Colonel Richard Irving Dodge. LC 00-27413. (Illus.). 592p. 2000. 50.00 (*0-8061-3267-1*) U of Okla Pr.

Dodge, Richard W., jt. ed. see Gaquin, Deirdre A.

Dodge, Robert K. A Topical Index of Early U. S. Almanacs, 1776-1800, 26. LC 97-9374. (Bibliographies & Indexes in American Literature: Vol. 26). 432p. 1997. lib. bdg. 95.00 (*0-313-26049-4*, Greenwood Pr) Greenwood.

Dodge, Robert K., ed. Early American Almanac Humor. LC 87-70546. 163p. 1987. 26.95 (*0-87972-393-9*) Bowling Green Univ Popular Press.

Dodge, Robert K., jt. auth. see Stitt, J. Michael.

Dodge, Roy. Foundations of Business Accounting. LC 93-9802. 1993. mass mkt. 26.95 (*0-412-54560-8*) Chapman & Hall.

Dodge, Roy L. Michigan Ghost Towns: Lower Peninsula, 2 vols. in 1. rev. ed. (Illus.). 311p. (Orig.). 1995. reprint ed. 13.95 (*0-932212-64-6*) Glendon Pub.

— Michigan Ghost Towns: Upper Peninsula. (Illus.). 301p. (Orig.). 1996. reprint ed. 13.95 (*0-934884-02-1*) Glendon Pub.

Dodge, Russ. Water Measurement Manual: Effective Water Measurement Practices for Better Water Management. 486p. 1997. boxed set 39.00 (*0-16-061625-5*) USGPO.

Dodge, Steve. Abaco: The History of an Out Island & Its Cays. 2nd ed. (Illus.). 256p. 1995. pap. text 17.50 (*0-932265-34-0*) White Sound.

Dodge, Steve. Christopher Columbus & the First Voyages to the New World. (World Explorers Ser.). 1991. 14.05 (*0-606-07371-X*, Pub. by Turtleback) Demco.

— The Compleat Guide to Nassau. (Illus.). 116p. (Orig.). 1987. pap. 4.95 (*0-932265-04-9*) White Sound.

— The Cruising Guide to Abaco, Bahamas, 1999. (Illus.). 136p. 1998. pap. 12.95 (*0-932265-52-9*) White Sound.

***Dodge, Steve.** The Cruising Guide to Abaco, Bahamas 2000. (Illus.). 144p. 1999. pap. 14.95 (*0-932265-56-1*) White Sound.

Dodge, Steve, compiled by. The Bahamas Index: 1986. 537p. 1987. lib. bdg. 150.00 (*0-932265-02-2*); disk 150.00 (*0-932265-03-0*) White Sound.

Dodge, Steve, et al, eds. The Bahamas Index & Yearbook: 1991. 200p. 1992. text 100.00 (*0-932265-25-1*); pap. text 49.95 (*0-932265-26-X*) White Sound.

Dodge, Steve & Malone, Vernon. A Guide & History of Hope Town. 2nd ed. (Illus.). 60p. (Orig.). 1990. pap. 4.50 (*0-932265-19-7*) White Sound.

Dodge, Steve & McIntire, Robert C., compiled by. The Bahamas Index, 1987. 500p. 1988. lib. bdg. 150.00 (*0-932265-06-5*); disk 150.00 (*0-932265-07-3*) White Sound.

Dodge, Steve & Toote, Elaine, eds. The Bahamas Index: 1989. 434p. 1990. lib. bdg. 150.00 (*0-932265-16-2*); disk 150.00 (*0-932265-17-0*) White Sound.

Dodge, Steve, jt. ed. see Soltermann, Jeffrey.

Dodge, Steven C. Christopher Columbus & the First Voyages to the New World. Goetzmann, William H., ed. (World Explorers Ser.). (Illus.). 120p. (YA). (gr. 5 up). 1991. lib. bdg. 19.95 (*0-7910-1299-9*) Chelsea Hse.

Dodge, Thedore A. Gustavus Adolphus. LC 98-7699. (Illus.). 864p. 1998. reprint ed. pap. 21.95 (*0-306-80863-3*) Da Capo.

Dodge, Theodore A. Alexander: A History of the Origin & Growth of the Art of War from the Earliest Times to the Battle of Ipsus, 301 B.C., with a Detailed Account of the Campaigns of the Great Macedonian. 721p. 1994. 59.95 (*1-85367-178-9*, 5400) Stackpole.

— Alexander: A History of the Origin & Growth of the Art of War from the Earliest Times to the Battle of Ipsus, 301 BC, with a Detailed Account of the Campaigns of the Great Macedonian. LC 95-45156. (Illus.). 723p. 1996. reprint ed. pap. 19.95 (*0-306-80690-8*) Da Capo.

— A Bird's Eye View of Our Civil War. LC 97-32938. (Illus.). 376p. 1998. reprint ed. pap. 15.95 (*0-306-80845-5*) Da Capo.

— Caesar, 2 vols., Set. LC 63-12453. (Illus.). 1968. pap. 45.00 (*0-8196-0122-5*) Biblo.

— Caesar: A History of the Art of War among the Romans... LC 97-16027. (Illus.). 816p. 1997. reprint ed. pap. 22.50 (*0-306-80787-4*) Da Capo.

— Caesar: A History of the Art of War among the Romans down to the End of the Roman Empire, with a Detailed Account of the Campaigns of Caius Julius Caesar. (Illus.). 816p. 1995. 59.95 (*1-85367-216-5*, Pub. by Greenhill Bks) Stackpole.

— The Campaign of Chancellorsville. LC E475.35.D64 1999. 296p. 1999. reprint ed. pap. 14.95 (*0-306-80914-1*, Pub. by Da Capo) HarpC.

— Gustavus Adolphus. (Great Captains Ser.). (Illus.). 896p. 59.95 (*1-85367-234-3*, Pub. by Greenhill Bks) Stackpole.

— Hannibal. (Illus.). 702p. 1995. reprint ed. pap. 19.95 (*0-306-80654-1*) Da Capo.

— Hannibal: A History of the Art of War among the Carthaginians & Roman Down to the Battle of Pydna, 168 B.C., with a Detailed Account of the Second Punic War. 704p. 1994. 59.95 (*1-85367-179-7*, 5414) Stackpole.

— Napoleon: A History of the Art of War, 4 vols. reprint ed. 275.00 (*0-404-02160-3*) AMS Pr.

Dodge, Timothy. Crime & Punishment in New Hampshire, 1812-1914. (AUS IX: Vol. 164). XV, 406p. (C). 1995. text 63.95 (*0-8204-2516-8*) P Lang Pubng.

— Poor Relief in Durham, Lee, & Medbury, NH, 1732-1891. 135p. (Orig.). 1995. pap. text 14.00 (*0-7884-0150-5*) Heritage Bk.

Dodge, Tom. Oedipus Road: Searching for a Father in a Mother's Fading Memory. LC 95-26697. 209p. (Orig.). 1996. pap. 15.95 (*0-87565-153-4*) Tex Christian.

***Dodge, Tom.** Tom Dodge Talks about Texas: Radio Vignettes & Other Observations, 1989-1999. (Illus.). 275p. 2000. pap. 17.95 (*1-55622-779-5*, Rep of TX Pr) Wordware Pub.

Dodge, Venus. The New Dolls' House Do-It-Yourself Book. (Illus.). 192p. 1997. pap. 19.95 (*0-7153-0616-2*) Sterling.

Dodge, Venus & Dodge, Martin. Making Miniatures: Dolls' House Projects in One-Twelfth Scale. (Illus.). 192p. 1993. pap. 19.95 (*0-7153-9963-2*, Pub. by D & C Pub) Sterling.

Dodge, Venus A. The Doll's Dressmaker: The Complete Pattern Book. (Illus.). 192p. 1988. pap. 19.95 (*0-7153-9289-1*, Pub. by D & C Pub) Sterling.

— Dolls' House Needlecrafts: Over 250 Projects in 1-12 Scale. (Illus.). 192p. 1995. 29.95 (*0-7153-0169-1*, Pub. by D & C Pub) Sterling.

Dodge, Venus A. & Dodge, Martin. Doll's House Do-It-Yourself Book. (Illus.). 224p. 1991. pap. 14.95 (*0-7153-9858-X*, Pub. by D & C Pub) Sterling.

Dodge, Walter P. Piers Gaveston: A Chapter of Early Constitutional History. LC 74-173161. (Illus.). 259p. 1972. reprint ed. 23.95 (*0-405-08451-X*, Pub. by Blom Pubns) Ayer.

Dodge, William. Skilled Labour Supply Imbalances: The Canadian Experience. LC 77-93071. (British-North American Committee Ser.). 56p. 1977. 3.00 (*0-902594-31-1*) Natl Planning.

Dodge, William R. Structuring State & Local Tax Reform Commissions. LC HJ9150.D62. (Lincoln Institute Monograph: No. 86-2). 75p. (Orig.). reprint ed. pap. 30.00 (*0-7837-5775-1*, 204544000006) Bks Demand.

Dodge, Yadolah, ed. L1 - Statistical Procedures & Related Topics. LC 97-73621. (Lecture Notes - Monograph Ser.: No. 31). 1997. pap. 69.00 (*0-940600-43-9*) Inst Math.

***Dodge, Yadolah & Jureickova, Jana.** Adaptive Regression. LC 99-55979. 192p. 2000. 49.95 (*0-387-98965-X*) Spr-Verlag.

Dodge, Yadolah & Whittaker, J., eds. Computational Statistics: Proceedings of the 10th Symposium on Computational Statistics, COMPSTAT, Neuchatel, Switzerland, August 1992. (Illus.). xvi, 578p. 1992. 143.95 (*0-387-91429-3*); 107.95 (*0-387-91430-7*) Spr-Verlag.

Dodge, Yadolah, jt. auth. see Arthanari, T. S.

Dodge, Yadolah, jt. auth. see Birkes, David.

Dodgen, Charles. What Should I Know about Someone Who Abuses Alcohol & Other Drugs. rev. ed. 1998. pap. 5.95 (*1-55691-156-4*, 564) Learning Pubns.

An Asterisk (*) at the beginning of an entry indicates that the title is appearing for the first time.

D

Dodson, Laura S. & Gibson, Terrill L., eds. Psyche & Family: Jungian Applications to Family Therapy. LC 96-25236. 164p. 1997. pap. 17.95 (*1-888602-02-3*, 023) Chiron Pubns.

Dodson, Leonidas. Alexander Spotswood, Governor of Colonial Virginia, 1710-22. LC 76-91784. (BCL Ser. I). (Illus.). reprint ed. 47.50 (*0-404-02141-7*) AMS Pr.

***Dodson, Lisa.** Don't Call Us Out of Name: The Untold Lives of Women & Girls in Poor America. LC 98-16520. 272p. 1999. pap. 16.00 (*0-8070-4209-9*) Beacon Pr.

Dodson, Liz B. Count Your Way Through Brazil. (Illus.). 24p. (J). (gr. 1-4). 1996. pap. text 5.95 (*0-87614-971-9*) Lerner Pub.

Dodson, Lynne, jt. auth. see Inlander, Charles B.

Dodson, M. M., jt. auth. see Bernik, V. I.

Dodson, Marty, jt. auth. see Schott, Linda.

Dodson, Mary A. & Dodson, Ella E. Positive Thoughts Attract Success. 64p. 1993. pap. 5.50 (*0-89540-299-8*, SB-299) Sun Pub.

Dodson, Melvin G. Transvaginal Ultrasound. 2nd ed. LC 94-36305. (Illus.). 352p. 1994. text 102.00 (*0-443-08953-1*) Church.

Dodson, Michael & O'Shaughnessy, Laura N. Nicaragua's Other Revolution: Religious Faith & Political Struggle. LC 89-35448. xii, 280p. (C). 1990. pap. 18.95 (*0-8078-4266-4*) U of NC Pr.

Dodson, Milton A. The Shepherd Sings. LC 97-90936. 1998. 24.95 (*0-533-12515-4*) Vantage.

— The Subtle Apocalypse. 208p. 1998. 17.95 (*1-887750-78-9*) Rutledge Bks.

Dodson, Mo, jt. ed. see Palmer, Jerry.

Dodson, O. Ray. Mission on the Mesa: History of St. Paul United Methodist Church, Pueblo, Colorado. (Orig.). 1994. pap. text 10.95 (*0-9620550-6-9*, Prairie Heritage Pr) Dodson Assocs.

— The Promised Land: Homestead Memories. 191p. (Orig.). 1989. pap. 10.95 (*0-9620550-4-2*) Dodson Assocs.

Dodson, Owen. Boy at the Window. 212p. 1972. reprint ed. 15.00 (*0-911860-10-X*) Chatham Bkseller.

Dodson, Pat, ed. see Campbell, Richard L.

Dodson, Peggy R. Girl in the Gold Camp: A True Account of an Alaska Adventure, 1909-1910. LC 94-84283. (Illus.). 160p. (Orig.). (YA). (gr. 9-12). 1996. pap. 14.95 (*0-945397-53-4*) Epicenter Pr.

Dodson, Peter. An Alphabet of Dinosaurs. LC 94-15522. (Illus.). 64p. (J). (ps-3). 1995. 14.95 (*0-590-46486-8*) Scholastic Inc.

— Ceratopsia: A Natural History of the Horned Dinosaurs. (C). 1995. 21.00 (*0-201-40699-3*) Addison-Wesley.

— Discover Dinosaurs. (Discover Ser.). (Illus.). 48p. (J). (gr. 3-6). 1992. lib. bdg. 15.95 (*1-878363-68-9*, HTS Bks) Forest Hse.

— Doing Palentology. (C). 1998. write for info. (*0-201-40720-5*) Addison-Wesley.

— The Horned Dinosaurs: A Natural History. 360p. 1996. pap. 19.95 (*0-691-05900-4*, Pub. by Princeton U Pr) Cal Prin Full Svc.

— The Horned Dinosaurs: A Natural History. LC 96-105. 392p. 1996. text 45.00 (*0-691-02882-6*, Pub. by Princeton U Pr) Cal Prin Full Svc.

Dodson, Rita. My Rites of Passage. 52p. 1986. pap. 5.00 (*0-9615511-0-0*) R Dodson.

Dodson, Rob. Eastern Europe by Rail. (Bradt Rail Guides Ser.). (Illus.). 197p. (Orig.). 1994. pap. 14.95 (*1-56440-534-6*, Pub. by Bradt Pubns) Globe Pequot.

***Dodson, Ronald G.** Managing Wildlife Habitat on Golf Courses. LC 99-53028. (Illus.). 177p. 2000. 45.00 (*1-57504-028-X*, Ann Arbor Press) Sleepng Bear.

Dodson, Roy D., Jr. Flood Plain Management Handbook. 736p. 1999. 99.00 (*0-07-017389-3*) McGraw.

— Storm Water Pollution Control: Municipal, Industrial, & Construction NPDES Compliance. 2nd ed. LC 98-25762. (Illus.). 448p. 1998. 84.95 (*0-07-017388-5*) McGraw.

Dodson, Shireen. The Mother-Daughter Book Club: How 10 Busy Mothers & Their Daughters Came Together to Talk, Laugh, Learn, andShare Through Their Love of Reading. LC 97-3702. 304p. 1997. pap. 14.00 (*0-06-095242-3*) HarpC.

***Dodson, Shireen.** 100 Books for Girls to Grow on. LC 98-27606. 352p. 1998. pap. 14.00 (*0-06-095718-2*, Perennial) HarperTrade.

Dodson, Stanley I., et al, eds. Reading in Ecology. LC 99-17689. (Illus.). 480p. (C). 1999. pap. text 35.00 (*0-19-513309-9*) OUP.

Dodson, Stanley I., et al. Ecology. LC 97-39029. (Illus.). 464p. (C). 1998. text 55.00 (*0-19-512079-5*) OUP.

Dodson, Thomas. Music Creativity: Conductor Score & Manual, Alto/Baritone Sax. 84p. 1992. 4.95 (*0-8497-0491-X*, L205E) Kjos.

— Music Creativity: Conductor Score & Manual, Clarinet/Trumpet. 84p. 1992. 4.95 (*0-8497-0490-1*, L205TP) Kjos.

— Music Creativity: Conductor Score & Manual, Flute/Oboe. 84p. 1992. 4.95 (*0-8497-0489-8*, L205C) Kjos.

— Music Creativity: Conductor Score & Manual, French Horn. 84p. 1992. 4.95 (*0-8497-0492-8*, L205HF) Kjos.

— Music Creativity: Conductor Score & Manual, Mallet Percussion. 84p. 1992. 4.95 (*0-8497-0496-0*, L205M) Kjos.

— Music Creativity: Conductor Score & Manual, Percussion. 84p. 1992. 4.95 (*0-8497-0495-2*, L205PR) Kjos.

— Music Creativity: Conductor Score & Manual, Score & Manual. 84p. 1994. 19.95 (*0-8497-0487-1*, L205F) Kjos.

— Music Creativity: Conductor Score & Manual, Tenor Sax/Baritone TC. 84p. 1992. 4.95 (*0-8497-0497-9*, L205XB) Kjos.

— Music Creativity: Conductor Score & Manual, Trombone/Baritone BC/Bassoon. 84p. 1992. 4.95 (*0-8497-0493-6*, L205BC) Kjos.

— Music Creativity: Conductor Score & Manual, Tuba. 84p. 1992. 4.95 (*0-8497-0494-4*, L205BS) Kjos.

Dodson, Vance H. Concrete Admixtures. 208p. (C). (gr. 13). 1990. mass mkt. 59.50 (*0-442-00149-5*) Chapman & Hall.

Dodson, Vance H., ed. Alkalies in Concrete, STP 930. LC 86-20564. (Special Technical Publication (STP) Ser.). (Illus.). 90p. pap. text 24.00 (*0-8031-0498-7*, STP930) ASTM.

Dodson, W. Edward & Pellock, John M., eds. Pediatric Epilepsy: Diagnosis & Therapy. 464p. 1993. pap. 95.00 (*0-939957-33-7*) Demos Medical.

Dodson, W. Edwin, et al. The Assessment of Cognitive Function in Epilepsy. Kinsbourne, Marcel & Hiltbrunner, Beat, eds. 192p. 1991. 69.95 (*0-939957-45-0*) Demos Medical.

Dodson, W. Edwin, jt. ed. see Trimble, Michael R.

Dodsworth, Barbara W. The Area di San Domenico. LC 93-43459. (Intercultural Studies: Vol. 2). XI, 220p. (C). 1995. text 47.95 (*0-8204-2452-8*) P Lang Pubng.

Dodsworth, Clark. Digital Illusions. LC 96-5713. 576p. (C). 1997. pap. text 37.95 (*0-201-84780-9*) Addison-Wesley.

Dodsworth, J. R., et al. Vietnam: Transition to a Market Economy. (Occasional Papers: Vol. 135). 1996. pap. 15.00 (*1-55775-538-8*) Intl Monetary.

Dodsworth, John & Mihaljek, Dubravko. Hong Kong, China: Growth, Structural Change, & Economic Stability During the Transition, Vol. 152. LC 97-34146. (Occasional Paper Ser.). 1997. write for info. (*1-55775-672-4*) Intl Monetary.

Dodsworth, Martin. Hamlet Closely Observed. LC 85-6151. 316p. (C). 1985. text 29.95 (*0-485-11283-3*, Pub. by Athlone Pr) Humanities.

Dodsworth, Martin, ed. William Shakespeare. (Everyman's Poetry Ser.). 116p. 1997. pap. 1.95 (*0-460-87815-8*, Everyman's Classic Lib) Tuttle Pubng.

Dodsworth, Martin, ed. see Burton, Robert.

Dodsworth, Martin, ed. see Shakespeare, William.

Dodsworth, Roger. Glass & Glassmaking. (Album Ser.: No. 83). (Illus.). 32p. 1989. pap. 4.75 (*0-85263-585-0*, Pub. by Shire Pubns) Parkwest Pubns.

Dodt, Colleen K. Bathing with Essential Oils. LC 96-43193. (Storey Publishing Bulletin Ser.). 1996. pap. 2.95 (*0-88266-591-X*, Storey Pub) Storey Bks.

— Natural BabyCare: Pure & Soothing Recipes & Techniques for Mothers & Babies. LC 96-46122. 144p. (Orig.). 1997. pap. 12.95 (*0-88266-953-2*) Storey Bks.

Dodt, Lorette. Graphic Arts Production. (Illus.). 302p. 1989. 31.96 (*0-8269-2684-3*) Am Technical.

Dodu, Gaston J. Histoire des Institutions Monarchiques dans le Royaume Latin de Jerusalem, 1099-1291. LC 76-29820. (FRE.). reprint ed. 55.00 (*0-404-15415-8*) AMS Pr.

Dodwell, B. Managing Information Security - Achieving BS7799. (Financial Times Management Briefings Ser.). 1997. pap. 94.50 (*0-273-63305-8*, Pub. by F T P-H) Trans-Atl Phila.

Dodwell, C. R. Anglo-Saxon Art: A New Perspective. LC 82-71592. (Illus.). 368p. (C). 1985. pap. 27.50 (*0-8014-9300-5*) Cornell U Pr.

***Dodwell, C. R.** Anglo-Saxon Gestures & the Roman Stage. Graham, Timothy, ed. (Cambridge Studies in Anglo-Saxon England: No. 28). (Illus.). 240p. (C). 2000. 69.95 (*0-521-66188-9*) Cambridge U Pr.

Dodwell, C. R. The Pictorial Arts of the West, 800-1200. LC 92-32502. (Pelican History of Art Ser.). (Illus.). 494p. (C). 1993. 65.00 (*0-300-05348-7*) Yale U Pr.

— The Pictorial Arts of the West, 800-1200. 1995. pap. 35.00 (*0-300-06493-4*) Yale U Pr.

Dodwell, Christina. Beyond Siberia. large type ed. 1993. 39.95 (*0-7066-1027-X*, Pub. by Remploy Pr) St Mut.

— A Traveller on Horseback. large type ed. (Illus.). 1989. 27.99 (*0-7089-2102-7*) Ulverscroft.

— A Traveller on Horseback: In Eastern Turkey & Iran. (Illus.). 192p. 1989. 18.95 (*0-8027-1078-6*) Walker & Co.

— Travels with Pegasus: A Microlight Journey Across West Africa. 208p. 1990. 19.95 (*0-8027-1125-1*) Walker & Co.

Dodwell, Henry. Duplex & Clive: Beginning of Empire. 277p. 1967. 32.00 (*0-7146-1125-5*, Pub. by F Cass Pubs) Intl Spec Bk.

Dodwell, Henry H. The Founder of Modern Egypt. LC 74-15029. (BCL Ser. II). reprint ed. 39.50 (*0-404-12036-9*) AMS Pr.

Dodwell, Peter. Brave New Mind: A Thoughtful Inquiry into the Nature & Meaning of Mental Life. LC 98-31381. (Illus.). 256p. 2000. 35.00 (*0-19-508905-7*) OUP.

Dodwell, Peter C. & Caelli, Terrence M., eds. Figural Synthesis. 318p. (C). 1984. 49.95 (*0-89859-382-4*) L Erlbaum Assocs.

Dodworth, Allen. To Be in This Country: The Paintings of V. Douglas Snow. (C). 1995. pap. text 10.95 (*0-87480-475-2*) U of Utah Pr.

Dodziuk, H. Modern Conformational Analysis: Elucidating Novel Exciting Molecular Structures. (Methods in Stereochemical Analysis Ser.). 264p. 1995. 139.00 (*0-471-18611-2*, Wiley-VCH) Wiley.

Dodziuk, Helena. Modern Conformational Analysis: Elucidating Novel Exciting Molecular Structures. Marchand, Alan P., ed. LC 95-16397. (Methods in Stereochemical Analysis Ser.). (Illus.). 288p. 1995. 99.95 (*1-56081-689-9*, Wiley-VCH) Wiley.

Dodziuk, Jozef & Jorgenson, Jay. Spectral Asymptotics on Degenerating Hyperbolic 3-Manifolds. LC 98-26524. (Memoirs of the American Mathematical Society Ser.: Vol. 135, No. 643). 75p. 1998. pap. 39.00 (*0-8218-0837-0*) Am Math.

Dodziuk, Jozef & Keen, Linda, eds. Lipa's Legacy: Proceedings of the BERS Colloquium, October 19-20, 1995, Graduate School & University Center of CUNY. LC 97-25848. (Contemporary Mathematics Ser.: Vol. 211). 488p. 1997. pap. 71.00 (*0-8218-0671-8*) Am Math.

Doe. Business Math. 2nd ed. Date not set. pap. text, teacher ed. 50.75 (*0-314-63053-8*) West Pub.

— Energy & Climate Changes. 184p. 1990. lib. bdg. 79.95 (*0-87371-417-2*, L417) Lewis Pubs.

Doe, jt. auth. see Smith.

Doe, Andrew, jt. auth. see Tobler, John.

Doe, B. R. & Smith, D. K., eds. Studies in Mineralogy & Precambrian Geology: A Volume in Honor of John W. Gruner. LC 70-190173. (Geological Society of America, Memoir Ser.: No. 135). 372p. reprint ed. pap. 115.40 (*0-608-14460-6*, 202502900041) Bks Demand.

Doe, Brian. Monuments of South Arabia. 284p. (C). 1990. 150.00 (*0-7855-7019-5*, Pub. by IMMEL Pubng) St Mut.

— Socotra: Island of Tranquillity. 238p. (C). 1995. 150.00 (*0-907151-31-0*, Pub. by IMMEL Pubng) St Mut.

Doe, Carlton. Administering Informix Dynamic Server on Windows NT. LC 99-10785. (Informix Press Ser.). (Illus.). 752p. 1999. pap. 54.99 incl. cd-rom (*0-13-080533-5*) P-H.

***Doe, Carlton.** Enterprise Databases On Linux. 500p. 2000. pap. 49.99 (*0-13-014922-5*) P-H.

Doe, Carlton. Informix-Online Dynamic Server Handbook. LC 97-12291. 450p. (C). 1997. pap. text 49.95 (*0-13-605296-7*) P-H.

Doe Entertainment Staff. Windows Games Adventure Set. 1995. pap. 39.99 (*1-883577-43-8*) Coriolis Grp.

Doe, Jane. Abolishing Lawyer Tyranny. 200p. (Orig.). (C). 1993. pap. 19.95 (*1-884094-02-3*) Ft Dearborn.

— Anarchist Farm. (Illus.). 192p. (Orig.). 1996. pap. 10.00 (*1-886625-01-8*) III Pub.

Doe, John. How to Cut Your Property Taxes: An Insider's Guide. Behrman, David, ed. (Illus.). 200p. (Orig.). 1991. pap. 39.95 (*0-9630196-0-0*) Property Tax.

Doe, Mary R. Sacred Poetry on the Path. (Orig.). 1993. pap. 9.95 (*1-883448-00-X*) Rose Pr Pub.

Doe, Mimi & Walch, Marsha. 10 Principles for Spiritual Parenting: Nurturing Your Child's Soul. LC 97-35123. 400p. 1998. pap. 13.00 (*0-06-095241-5*, Perennial) HarperTrade.

Doe, Mimi & Waller, Garland. Drawing Angels Near: Children Tell of Angels in Words & Pictures. 1997. per. 6.00 (*0-671-01481-1*) PB.

Doe, Norman. Canon Law in the Anglican Communion: A Worldwide Perspective. 440p. 1998. text 115.00 (*0-19-826782-7*) OUP.

— The Legal Framework of the Church of England: A Critical Study in a Comparative Context. 618p. 1996. text 110.00 (*0-19-826220-5*, Clarendon Pr) OUP.

Doe, Norman, ed. Essays in Canon Law. xxv, 206p. 1992. 30.00 (*0-7083-1147-4*, Pub. by Univ Wales Pr) Paul & Co Pubs.

***Doe, Norman, et al, eds.** English Canon Law: Essays in Honor of Erik Kemp, Bishop of Chichester. LC 99-202563. 176p. 1999. 55.00 (*0-7083-1478-3*, Pub. by Univ Wales Pr) Paul & Co Pubs.

DOE Office of Scientific & Technical Information S. Radioactive Waste Management: Uranium Mill Tailings - A Bibliography, Supplement 1. 75p. 1985. pap. 9.75 (*0-87079-574-0*, DOE/TIC-3393, SUPPLEMENT 1, DE85006278); fiche 9.00 (*0-87079-575-9*, DOE/TIC-3393, SUPPLEMENT 1, DE85006278) DOE.

Doe, Peter E. Fish Drying & Smoking: Production & Quality. LC 98-85445. 264p. 1998. 94.95 (*1-56676-668-0*) Technomic.

Doe, R. F. Bob Doe - Fighter Pilot. 160p. (C). 1991. 100.00 (*0-946771-73-1*, Pub. by Spellmnt Pubs) St Mut.

DOE Technical Information Center, Jr. Handbook on Atmospheric Diffusion. Hanna, Steven R. et al, eds. LC 81-15149. 107p. 1981. 10.75 (*0-87079-127-3*, DOE/TIC-11223); fiche 9.00 (*0-87079-464-7*, DOE/TIC-11223) DOE.

DOE Technical Information Center. Transuranic Elements in the Environment: A Summary of Environmental Research on Transuranium Radionuclides Funded by the U. S. Department of Energy Through Calendar Year 1979. Hanson, Wayne C., ed. LC 80-607069. 744p. 1980. 26.75 (*0-87079-119-2*, DOE/TIC-22800); fiche 9.00 (*0-87079-331-4*, DOE/TIC-22800) DOE.

DOE Technical Information Center Staff. Acid Precipitation: A Bibliography. 734p. 1983. pap. 30.00 (*0-87079-500-7*, DOE/TIC-3399); fiche 9.00 (*0-87079-501-5*, DOE/TIC-3399) DOE.

— The Canine As a Biomedical Research Model: Immunological, Hematological & Oncological Aspects. Shifrine, Moshe & Wilson, Floyd D., eds. LC 80-24174. 436p. 1980. 19.00 (*0-87079-122-2*, DOE/TIC-10191); 9.00 incl. fiche (*0-87079-457-4*, DOE/TIC-10191) DOE.

— Coal Desulfurization: A Bibliography. 510p. 1983. pap. 24.75 (*0-87079-514-7*, DOE/TIC-3400); fiche 9.00 (*0-87079-515-5*, DOE/TIC-3400) DOE.

— Coal Processing: Gasification, Liquefaction, Desulfurization. A Bibliography, 1930-1974. 766p. 1974. pap. 34.00 (*0-87079-165-6*, TID-3349); fiche 9.00 (*0-87079-409-4*, TID-3349) DOE.

— Computer Codes: A Bibliography, Supplement 1. 924p. 1985. pap. 98.00 (*0-87079-560-0*, DOE/TIC-3386, SUPPLEMENT 1); fiche 9.00 (*0-87079-561-9*, DOE/TIC-3386, SUPPLEMENT 1) DOE.

— Developing Role of Short-Lived Radionuclides in Nuclear Medical Practice: Proceedings. Paras, Peter & Thiessen, J. W., eds. LC 84-26718. (Symposium Ser.). 571p. 1985. pap. 22.95 (*0-87079-518-X*, CONF-820523); fiche 9.00 (*0-87079-519-8*, CONF-820523) DOE.

— Ecological Studies of Disturbed Landscapes: Compendium of the Results of Five Years of Research Aimed at the Restoration of Disturbed Ecosystems. Dvorak, A. J., ed. 382p. 1984. pap. 17.50 (*0-87079-540-6*, DOE/NBM-5009372); fiche 9.00 (*0-87079-541-4*, DOE/NBM-5009372) DOE.

— Engineering Materials: A Bibliography. 60p. 1982. pap. 9.50 (*0-87079-488-4*, DOE/TIC-4628); fiche 9.00 (*0-87079-489-2*, DOE/TIC-4628) DOE.

— Flue Gas Desulfurization & Denitrification: A Bibliography. 818p. 1985. pap. 91.00 (*0-87079-562-7*, DOE/TIC-3402); fiche 9.00 (*0-87079-563-5*, DOE/TIC-3402) DOE.

— Fuel Cells: A Bibliography Covering July 1980 Through February 1985, Supplement 2. 440p. 1985. pap. 23.00 (*0-87079-564-3*, DOE-METC-85-15); fiche 9.00 (*0-87079-565-1*, DOE-METC-85-15) DOE.

— Models & Parameters for Environmental Radiological Assessments. Miller, Charles W., ed. LC 84-14255. (DOE Critical Review Ser.). 157p. 1984. pap. 12.00 (*0-87079-517-1*, DOE/TIC-11468); fiche 9.00 (*0-87079-516-3*, DOE/TIC-11468) DOE.

— Patents (DOE) Available for Licensing: A Bibliography Covering January, 1974 Through December 1980. 284p. 1982. pap. 17.00 (*0-87079-445-0*, DOE/TIC-3398); fiche 9.00 (*0-87079-456-6*, DOE/TIC-3398) DOE.

— Patents (DOE) Available for Licensing: A Bibliography for the Period, 1966-1974. 64p. 1983. pap. 9.25 (*0-87079-512-0*, DOE/TIC-3398 SU); fiche 6.50 (*0-87079-513-9*, DOE/TIC-3398 SUPPL. 1) DOE.

— Radioactive Waste Management: Airborne Radioactive Effluents: Releases & Processing: A Bibliography. 245p. 1982. pap. 16.00 (*0-87079-479-5*, DOE/TIC-3397); fiche 9.00 (*0-87079-480-9*, DOE/TIC-3397) DOE.

— Radioactive Waste Management: Decontamination & Decommissioning, A Bibliography, Supplement 1. 84p. 1985. pap. 10.25 (*0-87079-568-6*, DOE/TIC-3391 SUPPLEMENT 1); fiche 9.00 (*0-87079-569-4*, DOE/TIC-3391 SUPPLEMENT 1) DOE.

— Radioactive Waste Management: Decontamination & Decommissioning: Bibliography. 124p. 1982. pap. 13.00 (*0-87079-484-1*, DOE/TIC-3391); fiche 9.00 (*0-87079-485-X*, DOE/TIC-3391) DOE.

— Radioactive Waste Management: Formerly Utilized Sites-Remedial Action: A Bibliography. 47p. 1982. pap. 8.50 (*0-87079-486-8*, DOE/TIC-3392); fiche 9.00 (*0-87079-487-6*, DOE/TIC-3392) DOE.

— Radioactive Waste Management: Formerly Utilized Sites-Remedial Action, Supplement 1. 53p. 1985. pap. 8.50 (*0-87079-570-8*, DOE/TIC-3392 SUPPLEMENT 1) DOE.

— Radioactive Waste Management: High-Level Radioactive Wastes: A Bibliography. 247p. 1982. pap. 16.25 (*0-87079-475-2*, DOE/TIC-3389, DE82012272); fiche 9.00 (*0-87079-476-0*, DOE/TIC-3389, DE82012272) DOE.

— Radioactive Waste Management: High-Level Radioactive Wastes: A Bibliography, Supplement 1. McLaren, Lynda H., ed. 393p. 1984. pap. 44.50 (*0-87079-528-7*, DOE/TIC-3389 SUPPLEMENT 1, DE84013656); fiche 9.00 (*0-87079-529-5*, DOE/TIC-3389 SUPPLEMENT 1, DE84013656) DOE.

— Radioactive Waste Management: Low-Level Radioactive Waste: A Bibliography. 184p. 1984. pap. 12.50 (*0-87079-524-4*, DOE-TIC-3387 SUPPL. 2, DE84005533); fiche 9.00 (*0-87079-525-2*, DOE-TIC-3387 SUPPL. 2, DE84005533) DOE.

— Radioactive Waste Management: Low-Level Radioactive Waste: A Bibliography Covering January Through December 1982. 144p. 1983. pap. 14.50 (*0-87079-502-3*, DOE/TIC-3387 (SUPPL. 1), DE83007212); fiche 9.00 (*0-87079-503-1*, DOE/TIC-3387 (SUPPL. 1), DE83007212) DOE.

— Radioactive Waste Management: Nuclear Fuel Cycle: A Bibliography, Supplement 1. McLaren, Lynda H., ed. 138p. 1984. pap. 27.50 (*0-87079-532-5*, DOE/TIC-3396 SUPPLEMENT 1, DE84013561); fiche 9.00 (*0-87079-533-3*, DOE/TIC-3396 SUPPLEMENT 1, DE84013561) DOE.

— Radioactive Waste Management: Nuclear Fuel Cycle Reprocessing: A Bibliography. 248p. 1982. pap. 16.25 (*0-87079-506-6*, DOE/TIC-3396, DE82012265); fiche 9.00 (*0-87079-507-4*, DOE/TIC-3396, DE82012265) DOE.

— Radioactive Waste Management: Radioactive Waste Inventories & Projections: A Bibliography. 18p. 1982. pap. 7.00 (*0-87079-490-6*, DOE/TIC-3394, DE82012267); fiche 9.00 (*0-87079-491-4*, DOE/TIC-3394, DE82012267) DOE.

— Radioactive Waste Management: Spent Fuel Storage: A Bibliography. 154p. 1982. pap. 12.00 (*0-87079-477-9*, DOE/TIC-3395); fiche 6.50 (*0-87079-478-7*, DOE/TIC-3395) DOE.

— Radioactive Waste Management: Spent Fuel Storage: A Bibliography, Supplement 1. McLaren, Lynda H., ed. 156p. 1984. pap. 11.75 (*0-87079-534-1*, DOE/TIC-3395-S1, DE84005534); fiche 9.00 (*0-87079-535-X*, DOE/TIC-3395-S1, DE84005534) DOE.

— Radioactive Waste Management: Transuranic Wastes: A Bibliography. 147p. 1982. pap. 14.50 (*0-87079-481-7*, DOE/TIC-3390, DE82012271); fiche 9.00 (*0-87079-482-5*, DOE/TIC-3390, DE82012271) DOE.

— Radioactive Waste Management: Transuranic Wastes-A Bibliography, Supplement 1. 132p. 1985. pap. 11.25 (*0-87079-572-4*, DOE/TIC-3390, SUPPLEMENT 1, DE85006324) DOE.

— Radioactive Waste Management: Uranium Mill Tailings: A Bibliography. 106p. 1982. pap. 13.00 (*0-87079-492-2*, DOE/TIC-3393, DE85003092); fiche 9.00 (*0-87079-493-0*, DOE/TIC-3393, DE85003092) DOE.

— Radioactive Waste Management: Waste Isolation - A

An Asterisk (*) at the beginning of an entry indicates that the title is appearing for the first time.

Bibliography, Supplement 1. 93p. 1985. pap. 12.75 (*0-87079-576-7*, DOE/TIC-3388, SUPPLEMENT 1); fiche 6.50 (*0-87079-577-5*, DOE/TIC-3388, SUPPLEMENT 1) DOE.

— Radioactive Waste Management: Waste Isolation: A Bibliography. 297p. 1982. pap. 17.50 (*0-87079-504-X*, DOE/TIC-3388, DE82012273); fiche 9.00 (*0-87079-505-8*, DOE/TIC-3388, DE82012273) DOE.

— Radioactive Waste Processing & Disposal: A Bibliography Covering January 1981 through December 1981, Supplement 11. 866p. 1982. pap. 91.00 (*0-87079-395-0*, DOE/TIC-3311-S11, DE82012480); fiche 20.50 (*0-87079-460-4*, DOE/TIC-3311-S11) DOE.

— Radioactive Waste Processing & Disposal: A Bibliography Covering January 1982 through December 1982, Supplement 12. 1122p. 1983. pap. 40.00 (*0-87079-508-2*, DOE/TIC-311-S12, DE84013531); fiche 9.00 (*0-87079-509-0*, DOE/TIC-3311-S12, DE84013531) DOE.

— Single-Photon Ultrashort-Lived Radionuclides: Proceedings. Paras, Peter & Thiessen, J. W., eds. LC 84-26051. (Symposium Ser.). 362p. 1985. pap. 17.00 (*0-87079-520-1*, CONF-830504, DE83017017); fiche 9.00 (*0-87079-521-X*, CONF-830504, DE83017017) DOE.

DOE Technical Information Center Staff & Kocher, David C. Radioactive Decay Data Tables. LC 81-607800. 228p. 1981. pap. 36.50 (*0-87079-124-9*, DOE/TIC-11026); fiche 9.00 (*0-87079-496-5*, DOE/TIC-11026) DOE.

DOE Technical Information Center Staff & Taylor, Lauriston S. Organization for Radiation Protection: The Operations of the ICRP & NCRP, 1928. LC 79-607999. 2062p. 1979. lib. bdg. 59.75 (*0-87079-116-8*, DOE/TIC-10124) DOE.

Doe, Willo. Jephan de Villiers, Sculptures. (ENG & FRE., Illus.). 48p. 1999. pap. 18.00 (*0-9672487-2-8*) R Koener Art Gall.

Doebele-Fluegel, Verena. Die Lerche Motivgeschichtliche Untersuchung Zur Deutschen Literatur, Insbesondere Zur Deutschen Lyrik. (C). 1977. 167.70 (*3-11-005909-6*) De Gruyter.

Doebele, William A., ed. Land Readjustment: A Different Approach to Financing Urbanization. LC 82-47967. 247p. reprint ed. pap. 76.60 (*0-7837-5763-8*, 204542600006) Bks Demand.

Doebelin. Systems Dynamics Modeling, Analysis Simulation, Design. (Illus.). 768p. 1998. text 195.00 (*0-8247-0126-7*) Dekker.

Doebelin, Ernest O. Engineering Experimentation: Planning, Execution, Reporting. LC 94-21434. (Series in Mechanical Engineering). 464p. (C). 1995. 81.25 (*0-07-017339-7*) McGraw.

— Measurement Systems. 4th ed. 992p. (C). 1989. 102.19 (*0-07-017338-9*) McGraw.

Doebeling, Marion, ed. New Approaches to Theodor Fontane: Cultural Codes in Flux. (Studies in German Literature, Linguistics & Culture). 213p. 2000. 55.00 (*1-57113-143-4*, Pub. by Camden Hse) Boydell & Brewer.

Doeberl, Michael. Das Akademische Deutschland, 4 vols., Set. (GER.). reprint ed. write for info. (*0-318-71899-5*) G Olms Pubs.

Doebler, Alan D. Air Bags - Safety, Controversy, Adult-Child Deaths in Automobiles: Index of New Information. 160p. 1997. pap. 44.50 (*0-7883-1693-1*); text 47.50 (*0-7883-1692-3*) ABBE Pubs Assn.

Doebler, Bettie A. Rooted Sorrow: Dying in Early Modern England. LC 94-2935. 1994. 43.50 (*0-8386-3543-1*) Fairleigh Dickinson.

Doebler, John, ed. see Beaumont, Francis.

Doebner, H. D. Group 21: Physical Applications & Mathematical Aspects of Geometry, Groups & Algebras: Proceedings of the XXI International Colloquium on Group Theoretical Methods in Physics, 15-20 July, 1996, Goslar, Germany, Arnold Sommerfeld Institute. LC 97-22218. 1997. write for info. (*981-02-3983-1*); pap. write for info. (*981-02-3984-X*) World Scientific Pub.

— Infinite Dimensional Lie Algebras & Quantum Field Theory: Proceedings of the Varna Summer Sch., 1987. 144p. 1988. text 61.00 (*9971-5-0716-1*) World Scientific Pub.

— Quantum Symmetries. 392p. 1993. text 121.00 (*981-02-1475-8*) World Scientific Pub.

Doebner, H. D., et al, eds. Group Theoretical Methods in Physics. (Lecture Notes in Physics Ser.: Vol. 313). xi, 599p. 1988. 17.95 (*0-387-50245-9*) Spr-Verlag.

***Doebner, H. D. & Arnold-Sommerfeld-Institut FHUR Mathematische Physik Staff.** Quantum Theory & Symmetries: Proceedings of the International Symposium: Goslar, Germany, 18-22 July 1999. LC 00-35185. 2000. write for info. (*981-02-4237-9*) World Scientific Pub.

Doebner, H. D. & Dobrev, V. K., eds. Quantum Group Symposium at Group 21: Proceedings of the Quantum Group Symposium at the XXI International Colloquium on Group Theoretical Methods on Physics Goslar, 1996. 408p. 1997. 94.95 (*954-580-027-5*, Pub. by Heron Pr) Intl Scholars.

Doebner, H. D. & Hennig, J. D., eds. Differential Geometric Methods in Mathematical Physics. (Lecture Notes in Mathematics Ser.: Vol. 1139). vi, 337p. 1985. 49.95 (*0-387-15666-6*) Spr-Verlag.

— Differential Geometric Methods in Theoretical Physics: Proceedings of the XV International Conference 1986. 568p. 1988. text 133.00 (*9971-5-0328-X*) World Scientific Pub.

Doebner, H. D. & Palev, T. D., eds. Differential Geometric Methods in Theoretical Physics: Proceedings of the XIII International Conference, Shumen, Bulgaria, August 1984. 380p. 1986. pap. 52.00 (*9971-5-0071-X*); text 95.00 (*9971-5-0070-1*) World Scientific Pub.

Doebner, H. D., et al. Generalized Symmetries in Physics. 444p. 1994. text 109.00 (*981-02-1771-4*) World Scientific Pub.

— Nonlinear Deformed & Irreversible Quantum Systems: Proceedings of the International Symposium. 500p. 1995. text 143.00 (*981-02-2266-1*) World Scientific Pub.

— Particles & Fields: Proceedings. 308p. 1994. text 95.00 (*981-02-1698-X*) World Scientific Pub.

— Supermanifolds Geometrical Methods & Conformal Groups, Lectures on. 136p. 1989. text 74.00 (*9971-5-0808-7*) World Scientific Pub.

Doebner, H. D., jt. ed. see Andersson, S. I.

Doebner, H. D., jt. ed. see Barut, Asim O.

Doebner, H. D., jt. ed. see DeNardo, G.

Doebner, H. D., jt. ed. see Pasemann, F.

***Doedel, E. & Tuckerman, L. S., eds.** Numerical Methods for Bifurction Problems & Large-Scale Dynamical Systems. LC 99-88039. (Illus.). 496p. 2000. 89.95 (*0-387-98970-6*) Spr-Verlag.

***Doeden, Matt.** Mountaineering Adventures. (Dangerous Adventures Ser.). 48p. (YA). (gr. 5 up). 2000. lib. bdg. 21.26 (*0-7368-0575-3*, Capstone Bks) Capstone Pr.

Doee, Britany, jt. auth. see Doee, Jonn.

***Doee, Jonn & Doee, Britany.** Vows of Death: Mormonism Revealed. 165p. 1999. pap. 14.95 (*0-9668920-0-3*) Vow Pubg.

Doeffinger, Derek. The Art of Seeing: A Creative Approach to Photography. 4th ed. LC 88-81373. (Kodak Workshop Ser.). (Illus.). 96p. (Orig.). (C). 1998. pap. 17.95 (*0-87985-747-1*, KW-20, Kodak) Saunders Photo.

— Waterfalls & Gorges of the Finger Lakes. LC 96-8826. (Illus.). 128p. (Orig.). 1996. pap. 29.95 (*0-935526-24-2*) McBooks Pr.

Doeffinger, Derek & Boas, Keith. Waterfalls of the Adirondacks & Catskills. LC 99-14322. 128p. (Orig.). 1999. pap. 32.95 (*0-935526-62-5*, Pub. by McBooks Pr) LPC InBook.

Doeffinger, Mark. Coupon Clippers. 98p. (Orig.). 1985. pap. 4.95 (*0-9615463-0-1*) Ross St.

Doege, Claudia M. Paul Revere & the Raiders: History Rebeats Itself! (Illus.). 160p. (Orig.). 1985. pap. text 9.95 (*0-9615517-0-4*) Dia Press.

Doehle, Heinrich. Medals & Decorations of the Third Reich. Hammelman, William, tr. (Illus.). 160p. 1995. 35.00 (*0-9624883-4-8*) Reddick Enterp.

Doehring, Carrie. Internal Desecration: Traumatization & Representations of God. 186p. (Orig.). (C). 1993. pap. text 27.50 (*0-8191-9121-3*); lib. bdg. 49.50 (*0-8191-9120-5*) U Pr of Amer.

— Taking Care: Monitoring Power Dynamics & Relational Boundaries in Pastoral Care & Counseling. 192p. (Orig.). 1995. pap. 16.95 (*0-687-35934-1*) Abingdon.

Doehring, Donald G. Research Strategies in Human Communication Disorders. 2nd ed. LC 90-22481. 261p. (Orig.). (C). 1996. pap. text 29.00 (*0-89079-644-0*, 7803) PRO-ED.

Doehring, Fred, et al. Florida Hurricanes & Tropical Storms, 1871-1993: An Historical Survey. LC 95-620014. (Florida Sea Grant Technical Paper). 118p. 1994. per. 5.00 (*0-912747-08-0*) FL Sea Grant Coll.

Doeing, Dennis A. The Prophet's Return: God's Missions & the Manners of Men. LC 96-94680. iv, 666p. (Orig.). 1997. pap. 26.00 (*0-9654224-1-0*) Ionisus Pr.

Doek, Jaap, et al, eds. Children on the Move: How to Implement Their Right to Family Life. LC 95-43179. 1995. lib. bdg. 105.50 (*90-411-0156-X*, Pub. by M Nijhoff) Kluwer Academic.

Doeker, Gunther, et al. Federal Republic of Germany & German Democratic Republic in International Relations, 6 vols. LC 79-1334. (Series I & II). 1979. 360.00 (*0-379-20456-8*) Oceana.

***Doel, Fran & Doel, Geoff.** Robin Hood: Outlaw or Greenwood Myth. (Illus.). 160p. 2000. pap. 16.99 (*0-7524-1479-8*, Pub. by Tempus Pubng) Arcadia Publng.

— Worlds of Arthur. (Illus.). 1999. 27.50 (*0-7524-1414-3*, Pub. by Tempus Pubng) Arcadia Publng.

— Worlds of Arthur. (Illus.). 1999. pap. 16.50 (*0-7524-1475-5*, Pub. by Tempus Pubng) Arcadia Publng.

Doel, Geoff, jt. auth. see Doel, Fran.

Doel, Hans Van den, see Van den Doel, Hans.

***Doel, Marcus.** Poststructural Geographies: The Diabolical Art of Spatial Science. (Illus.). 1999. pap. 28.95 (*0-8476-9819-X*) Rowman.

***Doel, Mark.** Essential Groupworker. LC 99-41631. 286p. 1999. pap. 29.95 (*1-85302-823-1*) Jessica Kingsley.

Doel, Mark. Teaching Social Work Practice: A Programme of Exercises & Activities Towards the Practice Teaching Award. 222p. (Orig.). 1996. pap. 50.95 (*1-85742-327-5*, Pub. by Arena) Ashgate Pub Co.

Doel, Mark & Marsh, Peter. Task-Centered Social Work. 144p. 1992. pap. text 29.95 (*1-85742-070-5*, Pub. by Arena) Ashgate Pub Co.

Doel, Mark & Shardlow, Steven. Training & Developing Social Workers: Exercises & Activities. LC 97-28139. 1998. 51.95 (*1-85742-375-5*, Pub. by Arena) Ashgate Pub Co.

Doel, Mark & Shardlow, Steven, eds. Social Work in a Changing World: An International Perspective on Practice. 232p. 1996. text 69.95 (*1-85742-343-7*, Pub. by Arena) Ashgate Pub Co.

Doel, Ronald E. Solar System Astronomy in America: Communities, Patronage, & Interdisciplinary Science, 1920-1960. (Illus.). 304p. (C). 1996. text 59.95 (*0-521-41573-X*) Cambridge U Pr.

Doeleman, David & Rogers, Ronald C. Real Estate Financial Management. 2nd ed. LC 86-62851. 152p. 1987. 22.00 (*0-913652-61-X*) Realtors Natl.

Doeleman, J. A. Biological Control of Salvinia Molesta in Sri Lanka: An Assessment of Costs & Benefits. 1989. pap. 36.00 (*0-949511-97-8*, Pub. by ACIAR) St Mut.

Doeleman, Jacobus A., jt. ed. see Ahmed, Iftikhar.

Doelker, E., et al, eds. Biopolymers I. (Advances in Polymer Science Ser.: Vol. 107). (Illus.). 292p. 1993. 159.00 (*0-387-56148-X*) Spr-Verlag.

Doell, M. Christine. Gardens of the Gilded Age: Nineteenth-Century Gardens & Homegrounds of New York State. LC 86-1061. (York State Book Ser.). (Illus.). 223p. 1986. reprint ed. pap. 69.20 (*0-608-06955-8*, 206716300009) Bks Demand.

Doelle, H. W. Applied Microbiology. (Topics in Inclusion Science Ser.). (Orig.). 1986. text 105.00 (*90-277-2095-9*) Kluwer Academic.

— Microbial Process Development. 350p. 1994. text 44.00 (*981-02-1515-0*) World Scientific Pub.

Doelle, William H. & Fish, Paul R., eds. Recent Research on Tucson Basin Prehistory: Proceedings of the Second Tucson Basin Conference. (Anthropological Papers: No. 10). (Illus.). 430p. (Orig.). 1988. pap. 10.00 (*1-886398-01-1*) Desert Archaeol.

Doelle, William H. & Swartz, Deborah L. Archaeology in the Mountain Shadows: Exploring the Romero Ruin. (Illus.). 16p. (Orig.). 1996. pap. 4.00 (*1-886398-21-6*) Desert Archaeol.

Doelle, William H., et al. Research Design for the Roosevelt Community Development Study. (Anthropological Papers: No. 12). (Illus.). 184p. (Orig.). 1992. pap. 12.00 (*1-886398-10-0*) Desert Archaeol.

Doelling, Carol Nesslein, ed. Social Work Career Development: A Handbook for Job Hunting & Career Planning. LC 97-30573. 325p. (Orig.). (C). 1997. pap. text 24.95 (*0-87101-282-0*, NASW Pr) Natl Assn Soc Wkrs.

Doelling, Hellmut H. Geologic Map of the Dewey Quadrangle, Grand County, Utah. (Map of the Utah Geological Survey Ser.: Vol. 169). 20p. 1996. pap. 7.25 (*1-55791-571-7*, M169) Utah Geological Survey.

Doelling, Hellmut H. Geology & Antelope Island State Park, Utah. (Miscellaneous Publications: Vol. 88-2). (Illus.). 20p. 1988. pap. 2.50 (*1-55791-299-8*) Utah Geological Survey.

— Geology & Grand County. (Miscellaneous Publications). (Illus.). 16p. 1987. pap. 1.50 (*1-55791-376-5*) Utah Geological Survey.

— Geology & Mineral Resources of Box Elder County, Utah. (Bulletin Ser.: Vol. 115). (Illus.). 251p. 1980. pap. 20.00 (*1-55791-082-0*) Utah Geological Survey.

Doelling, Hellmut H. & Davis, Fitzhugh D. The Geology of Kane County, Utah: Geology, Mineral Resources, Geologic Hazards. (Bulletin of the Utah Geological Survey Ser.: No. 124). (Illus.). 192p. (Orig.). 1989. pap. 15.00 (*1-55791-091-X*, B-124) Utah Geological Survey.

***Doelling, Hellmut H. & Ross, Michael D.** Geologic Map of the Big Bend Quadrangle, Grand County, Utah. (Map Ser.: Vol. 171). (Illus.). 29p. 1998. pap. 7.95 (*1-55791-573-3*, M-171) Utah Geological Survey.

Doelling, Hellmut H. & Willis, Grant C. Guide to Authors of Geologic Maps & Text Booklets of the Utah Geological Survey. (Circular of the Utah Geological Survey Ser.: No. 89). (Illus.). 98p. (Orig.). 1995. pap. 7.95 (*1-55791-368-4*, C-89) Utah Geological Survey.

Doelling, Hellmut H., et al. Geologic Map of the Grayback Hills Quadrangle, Tooele County, Utah. (Map of the Utah Geological Survey Ser.: Vol. 166). (Illus.). 22p. 1995. pap. 6.00 (*1-55791-568-7*, M-166) Utah Geological Survey.

— Salt Deformation in the Paradox Region. (Bulletin of the Utah Geological Survey Ser.: No. 122). (Illus.). 93p. (Orig.). 1988. pap. 9.50 (*1-55791-089-8*, B-122) Utah Geological Survey.

Doelling, Hellmut H., jt. auth. see Trimble, L. M.

Doelman, A. Nonlinear Dynamics & Pattern Formation in the Natural Environment. 1995. lib. bdg. 79.95 (*0-582-27371-4*, Pub. by Addison-Wesley) Longman.

***Doelman, James P.** King James I & the Religious Culture of England. (Studies in Renaissance Literature: Vol. 1465-6310). 240p. 2000. 75.00 (*0-85991-593-X*) Boydell & Brewer.

Doelp, R. & Loehlein, D., eds. Aktuelle Entwicklung und Standard der kuenstlichen Ernaehrung. (Beitraege zur Infusionstherapie und Klinische Ernaehrung Ser.: Vol. 16). (GER., Illus.). viii, 156p. 1986. 50.50 (*3-8055-4353-0*) S Karger.

Doemeny, Laurence J., jt. ed. see Scott, Ralph A., Jr.

Doemer, Patricia Martinez, see Martinez Doemer, Patricia.

Doemny, Laurence, jt. ed. see Scott, Ralph A., Jr.

D'Oench, Ellen. Prodigal Son Narratives, 1480-1980. LC 97-218076. 1995. pap. 5.00 (*0-89467-070-0*) Yale Art Gallery.

D'Oench, Ellen G. "Copper Into Gold" Prints by John Raphael Smith (1751-1812) LC 98-89216. 300p. 1999. 55.00 (*0-300-07630-4*) Yale U Pr.

Doenecke, Justus D. The Battle Against Intervention, 1939-1941. LC 96-18599. (Anvil Original Ser.). 222p. (Orig.). (C). 1997. pap. 14.95 (*0-89464-901-9*) Krieger.

— The Literature of Isolationism: Non-Interventionist Scholarship, 1930-1972. LC 72-80272. 90p. 1972. pap. 1.85 (*0-87926-016-5*) R Myles.

— The New Deal & Its Critics. Date not set. pap. write for info. (*1-57524-083-1*) Krieger.

— Not to the Swift: The "Old" Isolationists in the Cold War Era. LC 76-1030. 289p. 1978. 38.50 (*0-8387-1940-6*) Bucknell U Pr.

— The Presidencies of James A. Garfield & Chester A. Arthur. LC 80-18957. (American Presidency Ser.). xiv, 230p. 1981. 29.95 (*0-7006-0208-9*) U Pr of KS.

***Doenecke, Justus D.** Storm on the Horizon: The Challenge to American Intervention, 1939-1941. 752p. 2000. 39.95 (*0-7425-0784-X*) Rowman.

Doenecke, Justus D. When the Wicked Rise: American Public Opinion & the Manchurian Crisis. LC 82-45619. (Illus.). 192p. 1984. 29.50 (*0-8387-5048-6*) Bucknell U Pr.

Doenecke, Justus D., ed. In Danger Undaunted: The Anti-Interventionist Movement of 1940-1941 as Revealed in the Papers of the America First Committee. (Publication Series: Archival Documentaries: No. 384). 491p. 1990. 35.95 (*0-8179-8841-6*); pap. 25.95 (*0-8179-8842-4*) Hoover Inst Pr.

Doenecke, Justus D., jt. auth. see Wilz, John E.

Doenges, James M., et al. Carrying Capacity of Public Water Supply Watersheds: A Literature Review of Impacts on Water Quality from Residential Development. (Orig.). 1990. pap. 16.00 (*0-942085-00-0*) CT Dep Environ.

***Doenges, Judy.** What She Left Me: Stories & A Novella. LC 99-30945. (Bakeless Literary Publication Prize for Fiction, Bread Loaf Writer's Conference Ser.). 183p. 1999. 22.95 (*0-87451-937-3*) U Pr of New Eng.

Doenges, Marilyn E., et al. Application of Nursing Process & Nursing Diagnosis: An Interactive Text for Diagnostic Reasoning. 2nd ed. (Illus.). 331p. (Orig.). (C). 1995. pap. text 23.95 (*0-8036-2676-2*) Davis Co.

***Doenges, Marilyn E., et al.** Doenges & Moorhouse's Electronic Care Plan Maker. 1999. disk 49.95 (*0-8036-0494-7*) Davis Co.

Doenges, Marilynn E. & Moorhouse, Mary F. Maternal-Newborn Plans of Care: Guidelines for Planning & Documenting Client Care. 3rd ed. (Illus.). 592p. (C). 1999. pap. text 36.95 (*0-8036-0320-7*) Davis Co.

— Nurse's Pocket Guide: Nursing Diagnoses with Interventions. 6th ed. LC 97-29009. 670p. (C). 1997. spiral bd. 23.95 (*0-8036-0319-3*) Davis Co.

***Doenges, Marilynn E. & Moorhouse, Mary F.** Nurse's Pocket Guide: Nursing Diagnoses with Interventions. 7th ed. LC 97-29009. 710p. (C). 2000. spiral bd. 24.95 (*0-8036-0525-0*) Davis Co.

***Doenges, Marilynn E., et al.** Application of Nursing Process & Nursing Diagnosis: An Interactive Text for Diagnostic Reasoning. 3rd ed. LC 99-42874. 326p. 2000. 25.95 (*0-8036-0467-X*) Davis Co.

Doenges, Marilynn E., et al. Psychiatric Care Plans: Guidelines for Planning & Documenting Client Care. 3rd ed. LC 97-24117. (Illus.). 532p. (C). 1997. pap. text 36.95 (*0-8036-0322-3*) Davis Co.

Doenges, Marilynn E., jt. auth. see Moorhouse, Mary F.

Doenges, Norman A. The Letters of Themistokles. rev. ed. Connor, W. R., ed. LC 80-2648. (Monographs in Classical Studies). 1981. lib. bdg. 38.95 (*0-405-14035-5*) Ayer.

Doenhoff, Albert E. Von, see Abbott, Ira H.

Doenhoff, Albert E. Von, see Abbott, Ira H. & Von Doenhoff, Albert E.

Doenitz, Karl. Memoirs: Ten Years & Twenty Days. Stevens, R. H. & Woodward, David, trs. from GER. LC 96-37395. (Illus.). 554p. 1997. reprint ed. pap. 16.95 (*0-306-80764-5*) Da Capo.

Doepke, Frederick C. The Kinds of Things: A Theory of Personal Identity Based on Transcendental Argument. 292p. 1996. 41.95 (*0-8126-9319-1*); pap. 21.95 (*0-8126-9320-5*) Open Court.

***Doepp, Siegmar & Geerlings, Wilhelm, eds.** Dictionary of Early Christian Literature. 608p. 2000. text 75.00 (*0-8245-1805-5*, Pub. by Crossroad NY) Natl Bk Netwk.

Doeppers, Daniel F. Social Change in a Late Colonial Metropolis: Manila Nineteen Hundred to Nineteen Forty-One. LC 84-50326. (Monographs: No. 27). (Illus.). 194p. 1985. pap. 14.00 (*0-938692-06-2*) Yale U SE Asia.

Doeppers, Daniel F. & Xenos, Peter, eds. Population & History: The Demographic Origins of the Modern Philippines. (Wisconsin Monographs in Southeast Asian Studies: Vol. M16). (Illus.). 440p. 1998. 49.95 (*1-881261-22-0*); pap. 24.95 (*1-881261-23-9*) U Wisc Ctr SE Asian.

Doer, Bruno. Die Romische Namengebung. 230p. 1974. reprint ed. write for info. (*3-487-05159-1*) G Olms Pubs.

— Die Romische Namengebung: Ein Historischer Versuch. LC 75-7317. (Roman History Ser.). (GER.). 1975. reprint ed. 18.95 (*0-405-07081-0*) Ayer.

Doerberg, Donald L. & Wingate, C. Keith. Federal Courts, Federalism & Separation of Powers, Cases & Materials: Cases & Materials. LC 93-39479. (American Casebook Ser.). 935p. (C). 1994. 60.00 (*0-314-02996-6*) West Pub.

— Federal Rules of Civil Procedure. 866p. 1996. pap. 16.50 (*0-314-06764-7*) West Pub.

Doerberg, Richard L. International Taxation in a Nutshell. 2nd ed. LC 93-19664. (Nutshell Ser.). 394p. (C). 1993. pap. 17.00 (*0-314-02265-1*) West Pub.

Doerfel, Helen C. One Grain of Sand. 620p. 1991. lib. bdg. 73.50 (*1-880487-00-4*) Eldredge Hse.

Doerfelt, H. Lexikon der Mykologie. (GER., Illus.). 432p. 1989. lib. bdg. 33.00 (*3-437-20413-0*) Lubrecht & Cramer.

Doerfer, Gerhard. Khalaj Materials. LC 70-630301. (Uralic & Altaic Ser.: Vol. 115). (Illus.). (Orig.). 1971. pap. text 19.00 (*0-87750-150-5*) Res Inst Inner Asian Studies.

Doerfer, Gerhard, et al. Lamutisches Woerterbuch. (GER.). 1181p. 1980. 195.00 (*0-8288-1618-2*, F39233) Fr & Eur.

Doerfer, Jane. Going Solo in the Kitchen. 320p. 1998. pap. 15.95 (*0-375-70393-4*) Knopf.

Doerfer, Jane, jt. auth. see Berkowitz, George.

Doerfert, Regina. Die Substantivableitung Mit -Heit - -Keit, -Ida, -I Im Fruehneuhochdeutschen. (GER.). xvi, 340p. (C). 1994. lib. bdg. 141.55 (*3-11-014195-7*) De Gruyter.

D

An Asterisk (*) at the beginning of an entry indicates that the title is appearing for the first time.

Doerffer, J. W. Oil Spill Response in the Marine Environment. LC 92-580. 395p. 1992. 151.00 (0-08-041000-6, Pergamon Pr) Elsevier.

Doerfler. Foreign DNA in Mammalian System. 196p. 2000. 59.95 (3-527-30089-9) Wiley.

Doerfler, Christine. Vergleichende Untersuchungen Zum Biochemischen Aufbau der Zellwand an Hefestadien Von Niederen und Hoeheren Basidiomyceten. (Bibliotheca Mycologica: Vol. 129). (GER., Illus.). vi, 164p. 1990. 53.00 (3-443-59030-6, Pub. by Gebruder Borntraeger) Balogh.

Doerfler-Dall, Mary. Making Halleluwjah Hats! Crafts & Activities Based on Bible Stories. LC 98-197303. (Illus.). 160p. (J). (ps-3). 1998. pap. 14.95 (0-8091-3788-7, 3788-7) Paulist Pr.

Doerfler, H., ed. Das Internistische Gutachten. viii, 352p. 1991. pap. 42.75 (3-8055-5320-X) S Karger.

Doerfler, Ronald E. Dead Reckoning: Calculating Without Instruments. 182p. 1993. pap. 17.95 (0-88415-087-9, 5087) Gulf Pub.

Doerfler, W. & Bohm, P., eds. Virus Strategies: Molecular Biology & Pathogenesis. (Illus.). 543p. 1993. 236.00 (3-527-30027-9, Wiley-VCH) Wiley.

Doerfler, Walter, ed. Adenovirus DNA. (Developments in Molecular Virology Ser.). 1985. text 192.50 (0-89838-758-2) Kluwer Academic.

— Molecular Biology of the Cell: Final Report of the Sonderforschungsbereich, Molekularbiologie der Zelle, 1970-1988. LC 92-11241. (Sonderforschungsbereiche Ser.). 311p. 1992. 93.00 (3-527-27718-8, Wiley-VCH) Wiley.

Doerflinger, Thomas M. A Vigorous Spirit of Enterprise: Merchants & Economic Development in Revolutionary Philadelphia. LC 84-28036. (Institute of Early American History & Culture Ser.). (Illus.). xvi, 414p. 1986. 49.95 (0-8078-1653-1) U of NC Pr.

— A Vigorous Spirit of Enterprise: Merchants & Economic Development in Revolutionary Philadelphia. LC 84-28036. (Illus.). reprint ed. pap. 133.00 (0-608-08612-6, 2069135) Bks Demand.

Doerflinger, William M. Songs of the Sailor & Lumberman. 2nd ed. LC 72-81076. (Illus.). 397p. 1992. reprint ed. pap. 19.95 (0-916638-40-5) Meyerbooks.

Doerflor, Richard. Lucid Dreams. 240p. 1998. mass mkt. 5.99 (1-880090-68-6) Galde Pr.

Doering, Andrea. Winnie the Pooh's Colors Learn & Grow. (Learn & Grow Ser.). 20p. (J). 1999. 4.99 (0-7364-0119-9, Pub. by Mouse Works) Time Warner.

— Winnie the Pooh's Shapes. (Learn & Grow Ser.). 20p. 1999. 4.99 (0-7364-0118-0, Pub. by Mouse Works) Time Warner.

Doering, Bernard, ed. The Philosopher & the Provocateur: The Correspondence of Jacques Maritain & Saul Alinsky. LC 93-23924. (C). 1994. text 30.00 (0-268-03802-3) U of Notre Dame Pr.

Doering, Bernard, ed. see Maritain, Jacques.

Doering, Bernard, tr. see Bars, Henry, et al, eds.

Doering, Buzz. The Buzz on Leasing: How & When to Lease an Automobile. LC 98-226168. 240p. 1998. pap. 12.95 (0-915463-79-2) Jameson Bks.

Doering, Carol E. Reflections. (Illus.). 136p. 1996. pap. 12.95 (0-9652754-0-X) R A D Works.

***Doering, Carol E. R.** Gift of Words. (Illus.). 136p. 1999. pap. 14.98 (0-9652754-2-6) R A D Works.

Doering, Ch. R. & Kiss, L. B., eds. Unsolved Problems of Noise in Physics Biology. LC 98-175572. 348p. 1997. text 78.00 (981-02-3199-7) World Scientific Pub.

Doering, Charles R. & Gibbon, J. D. Applied Analysis of the Navier-Stokes Equations. (Cambridge Texts in Applied Mathematics Ser.: No. 12). (Illus.). 231p. (C). 1995. text 69.95 (0-521-44557-4); pap. text 27.95 (0-521-44568-X) Cambridge U Pr.

Doering, David. Guide to Novell NetWare 5: Network Administrator. (C). 1999. pap. 60.95 (0-7600-1078-1) Course Tech.

— Planning for NetWare 4.2. 416p. 1995. pap. 27.95 (1-55851-550-X, M&T Bks) IDG Bks.

Doering, G., et al, eds. Basic Research & Clinical Aspects of Pseudomonas Aeruginosa. (Antibiotics & Chemotherapy Ser.: Vol. 39). (Illus.). x, 314p. 1987. 221.00 (3-8055-4541-X) S Karger.

Doering, Otto, jt. ed. see Youngberg, Garth.

Doering, Otto C., jt. auth. see Schertz, Lyle.

Doering, Ronald L. & Runnalls, David. Prosperity & Sustainable Development for Canada: Advice to the Prime Minister of Canada. 37p. (Orig.). 1996. pap. text 20.00 (0-7881-2801-9) DIANE Pub.

Doering, Susan G., jt. auth. see Entwisle, Doris R.

Doering, William. Elliott Carter: A Bio-Bibliography, 51. LC 93-34079. (Bio-Bibliographies in Music Ser.: No. 51). 208p. 1993. lib. bdg. 59.95 (0-313-26864-9, Greenwood Pr) Greenwood.

Doeringer, Peter & Vermeulen, Bruce. Jobs & Training in the Eighties: Vocational Policy & the Labor Market. (Boston Studies in Applied Economics). 240p. 1981. lib. bdg. 69.00 (0-89838-062-6) Kluwer Academic.

Doeringer, Peter B., ed. Bridges to Retirement: Older Workers in a Changing Labor Market. LC 89-26789. 248p. 1990. text 37.50 (0-87546-159-X, ILR Press); pap. text 15.95 (0-87546-160-3, ILR Press) Cornell U Pr.

Doeringer, Peter B. & Piore, Michael J. Internal Labor Markets & Manpower Analysis. LC 85-2063. 248p. (gr. 13). 1985. reprint ed. pap. text 77.95 (0-87332-351-3) M E Sharpe.

Doeringer, Peter B., et al. The New England Fishing Economy: Jobs, Income, & Kinship. LC 86-7128. (Illus.). 160p. 1987. lib. bdg. 22.50 (0-87023-535-4) U of Mass Pr.

— Turbulence in the American Workplace. (Illus.). 272p. 1991. text 55.00 (0-19-506461-5) OUP.

Doerk, Klaus & Hawkes, Trevor. Finite Soluble Groups. (Expositions in Mathematics Ser.: No. 4). 900p. (C). 1992. lib. bdg. 159.95 (3-11-012892-6) De Gruyter.

***Doerken, Maurine.** Stepparenting Without Guilt. LC 99-55730. 144p. 2000. pap. 11.00 (1-57733-049-8) B Dolphin Pub.

Doerken, Nan. The First Family Car. (Sibling Ser.). 59p. (J). (gr. 1-4). 1986. pap. 3.95 (0-919797-53-9) Kindred Prods.

Doerksen, Daniel W. Conforming to the Word: Herbert, Donne, & the English Church Before Laud. LC 96-32252. (Illus.). 184p. 1997. 33.50 (0-8387-5334-5) Bucknell U Pr.

Doerksen, David P. Guide to Evaluating Teachers of Music Performance Groups. 72p. (Orig.). (C). 1990. pap., teacher ed. 14.50 (0-940796-74-0, 1017) MENC.

Doerksen, Lillian, jt. auth. see Wooding, Dan.

Doerksen, Nan. Bears for Breakfast: The Thiessen Family Adventures. (Kinderbook Ser.). (Illus.). 34p. (J). (ps-k). 1993. pap. 2.50 (0-919797-07-5) Kindred Prods.

Doerksen, Vernon. James. (Everyman's Bible Commentaries Ser.). 144p. 1983. pap. 9.99 (0-8024-0242-9, 495) Moody.

— Santiago. (Comentario Biblico Portavoz Ser.).Tr. of James. (SPA.). 144p. 1996. pap. 6.99 (0-8254-1166-1, Edit Portavoz) Kregel.

Doerksen, Victor G. Ludwig Uhland & His Critics. LC 94-26818. (Studies in German Literature, Linguistics & Culture). xii, 136p. 1994. 55.00 (1-57113-002-0) Camden Hse.

— A Path for Freedom: The Liberal Project of the Swabian School in Wuerttemberg, 1806-1848. LC 93-9961. (GERM Ser.). xvi, 244p. 1993. 65.00 (1-879751-70-4) Camden Hse.

Doern, Bruce. Global Change & Intellectual Property Agencies: An Institutional Perspective. LC 98-26010. (Science, Technology & the International Political Economy Ser.). 192p. 1998. 49.95 (1-85567-532-3, Pub. by P P Pubs) Cassell & Continuum.

Doern, Bruce G., et al, eds. Changing the Rules: Canadian Regulatory Institutions & Regimes. (Illus.). 464p. 1999. text 65.00 (0-8020-4163-9); pap. text 27.95 (0-8020-8025-1) U of Toronto Pr.

Doern, Bruce G. & MacDonald, Mark R. Free Trade Federalism: Negotiating the Canadian Agreement on Internal Trade. (Illus.). 240p. 1999. text 45.00 (0-8020-4223-6) U of Toronto Pr.

Doern, Bruce G. & Wilks, Stephen, eds. Changing Regulatory Institutions in Britain & North America. LC 99-189698. (Illus.). 448p. 1999. text 70.00 (0-8020-4260-0); pap. text 24.95 (0-8020-8100-2) U of Toronto Pr.

Doern, Bruce G., et al. Taxing & Spending: Issues of Process. 184p. 1995. pap. text 22.50 (0-8020-7194-5) U of Toronto Pr.

Doern, G. Bruce. Science & Politics in Canada. LC 79-180255. 252p. reprint ed. pap. 78.20 (0-608-12274-2, 202384200034) Bks Demand.

Doern, G. Bruce, ed. The Environmental Imperative: Market Approaches to the Greening of Canada. LC 90-94093. (Policy Study Ser.: No. 9). 150p. 1990. reprint ed. pap. 46.50 (0-608-01363-3, 206210200002) Bks Demand.

Doern, G. Bruce, et al, eds. Border Crossings: The Internationalization of Canadian Public Policy. 288p. 1996. pap. text 32.00 (0-19-541177-3) OUP.

Doern, G. Bruce & Conway, Thomas. The Greening of Canada: Federal Institutions & Decisions. 297p. 1995. text 50.00 (0-8020-0645-0) U of Toronto Pr.

Doern, G. Bruce & Conway, Tom. The Greening of Canada: Federal Institutions & Decisions. 312p. 1995. 50.00 (0-8020-6045-5); pap. text 19.95 (0-8020-7599-1) U of Toronto Pr.

Doern, G. Bruce & MacDonald, Mark R. Free Trade Federalism: Negotiating the Canadian Agreement on Interal Trade. (Illus.). 240p. 1999. pap. text 19.95 (0-8020-8072-3) U of Toronto Pr.

Doern, G. Bruce & Wilks, Stephen, eds. Comparative Competition Policy: National Institutions in a Global Market. LC 96-228163. (Illus.). 412p. 1996. text 85.00 (0-19-828062-9) OUP.

Doernbach, David. How to Survive ACLS. LC 97-47792. 304p. 1998. pap. text 27.95 (0-7817-1202-5) Lppncott W & W.

Doernbach, David P. Advanced Cardiac Treatment System (ACTS) (Illus.). 20p. (Orig.). 1996. pap., spiral bd. 65.00 (0-9638043-4-0) Vital Signs.

— How to Survive ACLS. (Illus.). 350p. (Orig.). 1996. pap. text, wbk. ed. 30.00 (0-9638043-3-2) Vital Signs.

Doernbach, David P. & Huff, Jane. Never Die Young: or How to Survive ACLS! 2nd ed. (Illus.). 195p. 1993. pap. text 24.00 (0-9638043-0-8) Vital Signs.

Doernberg. Federal Income Taxation of Corporations. 2nd ed. LC 94-75307. 768p. 1994. 52.00 (0-316-18838-7, Aspen Law & Bus) Aspen Pub.

Doernberg, Don & Wingate, C. Keith. Federal Courts, Federalism & Separation of Powers: Cases & Materials. (American Casebook Ser.). 160p. 1994. pap. text, teacher ed. write for info. (0-314-03993-7) West Pub.

— Federal Courts, Federalism & Separation of Powers, Cases & Materials, 1995 Supplement To. (American Casebook Ser.). 86p. 1995. pap. text, suppl. ed. 8.50 (0-314-07096-6) West Pub.

***Doernberg, Donald L.** Identity Crisis: Federal Courts in a Psychological Wilderness. LC 00-34291. 2000. write for info. (0-89089-741-7) Carolina Acad Pr.

Doernberg, Donald L. & Wingate, C. Keith. 1996 Supplement to Federal Courts, Federalism & Separation of Powers, Cases & Materials. (American Casebook Ser.). 166p. 1996. pap. text, suppl. ed. write for info. (0-314-20054-1) West Pub.

Doernberg, Myrna. Stolen Mind: The Slow Disappearance of Ray Doernberg. (Illus.). 224p. 1986. 14.95 (0-912697-32-6) Algonquin Bks.

***Doernberg, Richard L.** Federal Income Taxation of Corporations. LC 99-56001. 2000. text 64.00 (0-7355-1211-6) Panel Pubs.

Doernberg, Richard L. International Taxation in a Nutshell. 3rd ed. (Nutshell Ser.). 381p. (C). 1997. pap. text. write for info. (0-314-21202-7) West Pub.

— International Taxation in a Nutshell. 4th ed. LC 99-168221. (Nutshell Ser.). lxi, 465 p. 1999. pap. 22.50 (0-314-23156-0) West Pub.

Doernberg, Richard L. & Van Raad, C. The 1996 United States Model Income Tax Convention: Analysis, Commentary & Comparison. LC 97-5160. 1997. 85.00 (90-411-0998-6) Kluwer Law Intl.

Doernberg, Richard L., et al. Electronic Commerce & International Taxation. LC 98-49975. 1999. 94.50 (90-411-1053-4) Kluwer Law Intl.

— Federal Income Taxation of Corporations. 2nd ed. 768p. 1994. teacher ed. write for info. (0-316-18901-4, 89014) Aspen Law.

Doernberg, Richard L., jt. auth. see Abrams, Howard E.

Doernberg, Richard L., jt. auth. see Knight, W. Donald, Jr.

Doernberg, Richard L., jt. auth. see Van Raad, Kees.

Doernberg, Steven L. Clown Ambassador of Health Vol. 1: How to Relieve Stress at Home & in the Workplace. 17p. 1995. pap. write for info. (0-9648663-0-7) Clown Natural Hlth.

— Clown Ambassador of Health Vol. 2: Your Habits Are Knocking at Your Door. 9p. (Orig.). 1996. pap. write for info. (0-9648663-1-5) Clown Natural Hlth.

***Doernberg, Steven L.** Clown of Natural Health Vol. 1: Habit Busters, Stop Any Habit. 13p. 1999. mass mkt. 3.50 (0-9648663-2-3) Clown Natural Hlth.

— Clown of Natural Health Vol. 2: Work Is Play, Play Is Learning. 15p. (YA). (gr. 2-11). 1999. mass mkt. 3.50 (0-9648663-3-1) Clown Natural Hlth.

— Clown of Natural Health Vol. 3: Family Therapy, Non Ph.D. 41p. 1999. mass mkt. 5.00 (0-9648663-4-X) Clown Natural Hlth.

— Clown of Natural Health Vol. 4: Everyone Is Looking for Respect. 25p. 1999. mass mkt. 4.50 (0-9648663-5-8) Clown Natural Hlth.

Doerner, Andreas & Vogt, Ludgera, eds. Sprache des Parlaments und Semiotik der Demokratie: Studien zur Politischen Kommunikation in der Moderne. (Sprache, Politik, Oeffentlichkeit Ser.: Bd. 6). (GER.). iv, 400p. (C). 1995. lib. bdg. 144.60 (3-11-014496-4) De Gruyter.

Doerner, Carl. Ashes & Embers: Stories, Photographs & Poems. LC 98-34848. (Illus.). 192p. 1998. pap. 13.00 (1-888683-82-1) Wooster Bk.

Doerner, G. & McCann, S. M., eds. Systemic Hormones, Neurotransmitters & Brain Development. (Monographs in Neural Sciences: Vol. 12). (Illus.). x, 222p. 1986. 172.25 (3-8055-4287-9) S Karger.

Doerner, Max. The Materials of the Artist & Their Use in Painting with Notes of the Techniques of the Old Masters. rev. ed. Neuhaus, Eugen, tr. LC 84-10888. (Illus.). 458p. 1949. pap. 16.00 (0-15-657716-X, Harvest Bks) Harcourt.

Doerner, William G. An Introduction to Law Enforcement: An Insider's View. LC 97-20786. 340p. 1997. 44.95 (0-7506-9812-8, BH Security) Buttrwrth-Heinemann.

Doerner, William G. & Dantzker, Mark L. Contemporary Police Organization & Management: Issues & Trends. LC 99-17481. 282p. 1999. pap. 24.95 (0-7506-7137-8) Buttrwrth-Heinemann.

Doerner, William G. & Lab, Steven P. Victimology. 2nd ed. LC 98-12333. 335p. (C). 1998. pap. 36.95 (0-87084-226-9) Anderson Pub Co.

Doerner, William G. & Rushing, Charles W. Study Guide for the Florida Corrections Officer's Certification Examination. LC 97-28396. 144p. (Orig.). 1997. pap. 16.95 (1-56164-146-4) Pineapple Pr.

— Study Guide for the Florida Law Enforcement Officer's Certification Examination. LC 96-23269. 320p. (Orig.). 1996. pap. 16.95 (1-56164-109-X) Pineapple Pr.

Doerr, Arthur & Coling, Jerome F. Fundamentals of Physical Geography. 400p. (C). 1990. pap. write for info. (0-697-07905-8, WCB McGr Hill) McGraw-H Hghr Educ.

Doerr, Cathy A. Student Organizational Planbook. 112p. (J). (gr. 3-12). 1992. pap. 3.95 (0-9632893-0-6) Skills For Lrn.

Doerr, Christine. The Nature of Our Lives. LC 96-96394. (Illus.). vi, 72p. (Orig.). 1996. pap. 8.95 (0-9652677-0-9) Doerr Two Dr.

Doerr, Edd, ed. Timely & Timeless: The Wisdom of E. Burdette Backus. LC 98-70361. 251 p. 1998. write for info. (0-931779-10-3, Humanist Press) Am Humanist.

Doerr, Edd & Menendez, Al. Church Schools & Public Money: The Politics of Parochiaid. LC 91-22383. 156p. 1991. pap. 17.95 (0-87975-708-6) Prometheus Bks.

Doerr, Edd & Menendez, Albert J. Religious Liberty & State Constitutions. LC 93-5867. 117p. 1993. 21.95 (0-87975-839-2) Prometheus Bks.

Doerr, Edd, et al. The Case Against School Vouchers. LC 96-24370. 135p. (Orig.). 1996. pap. 17.95 (1-57392-092-4) Prometheus Bks.

Doerr, Hans O. & Carlin, Albert S., eds. Forensic Neuropsychology: Legal & Scientific Bases. LC 91-16389. 242p. 1991. lib. bdg. 35.00 (0-89862-770-2) Guilford Pubns.

Doerr, Hans W., et al, eds. Antiviral Chemotherapy. (Intervirology Ser.: Vol. 40, No. 5-6). (Illus.). 124p. 1998. pap. 51.50 (3-8055-6725-1) S Karger.

Doerr, Harriet. Consider This, Senora. LC 93-21471. 1993. 21.95 (0-15-193103-8) Harcourt.

— Consider This, Senora. 256p. (C). 1994. pap. 12.00 (0-15-600002-4) Harcourt.

— Stones for Ibarra. 224p. 1985. pap. 12.95 (0-14-007562-3, Penguin Bks) Viking Penguin.

— The Tiger in the Grass: Stories & Other Inventions. 224p. 1996. pap. 10.95 (0-14-025148-0) Viking Penguin.

— The Tiger in the Grass: Stories & Other Inventions. large type ed. LC 96-31685. (Large Print Bks.). 1996. 23.95 (1-56895-358-5, Compass) Wheeler Pub.

Doerr, Jeffrey. The Arming of a European Superstate. LC 97-21208. 1997. write for info. (1-57420-061-5) Chatelaine.

Doerr, Juergen C. The Big Powers & the German Question, 1941-1990: A Selected Bibliographic Guide. LC 91-45118. (Bibliographies on Nationalism Ser.: Vol. 9). 416p. 1992. text 20.00 (0-8240-0696-8, SS#518) Garland.

Doerr, Marilyn, jt. auth. see Owen, David.

Doerr, Mary B. For Better or Worse: For Couples Whose Child Has Died. (Illus.). 24p. (Orig.). 1992. pap. 3.25 (1-56123-053-7) Centering Corp.

Doerr, P. British Foreign Policy, 1919-1939. LC 98-13715. 224p. 1998. 74.95 (0-7190-4671-8, Pub. by Manchester Univ Pr); pap. 29.95 (0-7190-4672-6, Pub. by Manchester Univ Pr) St Martin.

Doerr, Robert. Grace in the Plaza. 86p. 1984. 6.95 (0-911819-03-7) Yosemite D.

***Doerr, Robert M.** Phelps County (MD) Marriages, 1857-1910. iv, 248p. 2000. write for info. (1-893474-19-4) Phelps Cnty Gene.

Doerr, Robert M., compiled by. Phelps County Missouri Will Books, 1857-1924. ii, 74p. 1998. pap. 32.00 (1-893474-00-3) Phelps Cnty Gene.

Doerr, Robert M., contrib. by. Marriages of Phelps County Missouri, 1880-1881, Bk. 2. 4p. Date not set. pap. write for info. (1-893474-13-5) Phelps Cnty Gene.

Doerr, W. & Seifert, Gerhard, eds. Tropical Pathology. 2nd ed. (Spezielle Pathologische Anatomie Ser.: Vol. 8). (Illus.). 1104p. 1995. 767.00 (0-387-57673-8) Spr-Verlag.

— Tropical Pathology. 2nd ed. (Illus.). xiv, 1379p. 1996. 698.00 (3-540-59391-8) Spr-Verlag.

Doerrer, Michael L. & Burkle-Young, Francis A. The Life of Cardinal Innocenzo del Monte, Together with Materials for a History of the House of Ciocchi del Monte: Scandal in Scarlet. LC 97-26519. (Renaissance Studies: Vol. 2). 264p. 1997. text 89.95 (0-7734-8581-3) E Mellen.

Doerrfuss, Ernst M. Mose in Den Chronikbuechern: Garant Theokratischer Zukunftserwartung. (Beiheft zur Zeitschrift fuer die Alttestamentliche Wissenschaft Ser.: Vol. 219). (GER.). xii, 302p. (C). 1994. lib. bdg. 113.85 (3-11-014017-9) De Gruyter.

Doerries, Reinhard R. Imperial Challenge: Ambassador Count Bernstorff & German-American Relations, 1908-1917. LC 88-20907. (Supplementary Volumes to the Papers of Woodrow Wilson). (Illus.). xx, 444p. (C). 1989. 70.00 (0-8078-1820-8) U of NC Pr.

***Doerries, Reinhard R.** Prelude to the Easter Rising. 288p. 2000. 59.50 (0-7165-2640-9, Pub. by Irish Acad Pr); 26.50 (0-7165-2707-3, Pub. by Irish Acad Pr) Intl Spec Bk.

— Prelude to the Easter Rising: Sir Roger Casement in Imperial Germany (New Directions in Irish History) LC 99-39128. (Case Studies in Intelligence). (Illus.). 256p. 2000. 59.50 (0-7146-5003-X, Pub. by F Cass Pubs); pap. 26.50 (0-7146-8070-2, Pub. by F Cass Pubs) Intl Spec Bk.

Doerry, Wulf. Baking Technology Vol. 2: Controlled Baking. (Illus.). 276p. 1995. 49.00 (1-880877-19-8) Am Inst Baking.

— Baking Technology - Breadmaking. (Illus.). 250p. (C). 1995. 49.00 (1-880877-16-3) Am Inst Baking.

Doerter, James M. The East-West Chronicles. 2nd ed. (Illus.). 80p. 1993. reprint ed. write for info. (0-9638485-0-X) Nussschale.

Doerzbacher, Darby. Enjoying Shrimp. 36p. (Orig.). 1986. pap. 3.25 (0-940844-27-3) Wellspring.

Does, Jaap Van Der, see Van Der Does, Jaap.

Does, Michael Vander, see Sisson, Michael & Vander Does, Michael.

Doescher, Rex A. Directory of Paleontologists of the World. 5th ed. 447p. (Orig.). 1989. pap. 20.00 (0-9622577-0-2) Intl Palaeontological.

Doeser, Linda. Best Ever Chinese & Asian: The Definitive Cook's Collection: 200 Step-by-Step Recipes. 1997. 19.98 (1-901289-54-0) Anness Pub.

— Classic Fish Cooking. 96p. 2000. pap. 12.95 (0-7548-0102-0) Anness Pub.

Doeser, Linda. More Than a Million Menus. 1994. 19.98 (0-7858-0134-0) Bk Sales Inc.

Doeser, Linda, ed. The Great Fish & Shellfish Cookbook: The Definitive Cook's Collection with over 200 Recipes. (Illus.). 256p. 1997. 24.95 (1-85967-549-2, Lorenz Bks) Anness Pub.

Doeser, M. C. & Kraay, J. N., eds. Facts & Values: Philosophical Reflections from Western & Non-Western Perspectives. 224p. 1986. text 132.50 (90-247-3384-7) Kluwer Academic.

Doesken, Nolan & Judson, Arthur. The Snow Booklet: A Guide to the Science, Climatology, & Measurement of Snow in the United States. 2nd ed. (Illus.). 86p. (C). 1998. pap. text 25.00 (0-7881-4801-X) DIANE Pub.

Doesken, Nolan J. & Judson, Arthur. The Snow Booklet: A Guide to the Science, Climatology & Measurement of Snow in the United States. (Illus.). 84p. (Orig.). (C). 1996. pap. text 10.00 (0-9651056-1-X) CSU Pub & Printing.

— The Snow Booklet: A Guide to the Science, Climatology, & Measurement of Snow in the United States. 2nd rev. ed. (Illus.). 88p. (C). 1997. pap. text. write for info. (0-9651056-2-8) CSU Pub & Printing.

Doets, Kees. Basic Model Theory. (Studies in Logic, Language & Information). 138p. (C). 1996. 59.95 (1-57586-049-X); pap. 20.95 (1-57586-048-1) CSLI.

D

— From Logic to Logic Programming. LC 93-6196. (Foundations of Computing Ser.). 228p. 1994. 35.00 (*0-262-04142-1*) MIT Pr.

Doetsch, G. Einfuhrung in Theorie und Anwendung der Laplace-Transformation. 3rd rev. ed. (Mathematische Reihe Ser.: No. 24). (GER.). 351p. 1980. 142.00 (*0-8176-0784-6*) Birkhauser.

— Theorie der Laplace Transformation. (Mathematische Reihe Ser.: Vol. 1). (GER.). 581p. 1980. 184.50 (*0-8176-0083-3*) Birkhauser.

Doeuff, Michele Le, see Le Doeuff, Michele.

Doeuff, R. Le, see Le Doeuff, R.

Doevendans, Peter A., et al. Cardiovascular Specific Gene Expression. LC 99-13442. (Developments in Cardiovascular Medicine Ser.). 1999. write for info. (*0-7923-5633-0*) Kluwer Academic.

Doezema, Jo, jt. auth. see Kempadoo, Kamala.

Doezema, Marianne. American Realism & the Industrial Age. LC 80-67347. (Themes in Art Ser.). (Illus.). 144p. 1981. pap. 5.00 (*0-910386-61-7*) Cleveland Mus Art.

— George Bellows & Urban America. (Illus.). 288p. (C). 1992. 50.00 (*0-300-05043-7*) Yale U Pr.

Doezema, Marianne & Milroy, Elizabeth. Reading American Art. LC 97-18004. 512p. 1998. 45.00 (*0-300-07348-8*); pap. 22.50 (*0-300-06998-7*) Yale U Pr.

Doezis, Michel. Diccionario de Sinonimos, Antonimos y Paronimos. 4th ed. (SPA.). 528p. 1990. pap. 13.95 (*0-7859-5034-6*) Fr & Eur.

Dofense Language Institute Staff. Headstart for the Philippines: Learn Tagalog or Philipino Quickly. (Intensive Cassette Ser.). (Illus.). 310p. 1998. spiral bd. 195.00 incl. audio (*1-58214-008-1*) Mltilingl Bks.

Doff, Adrian. Teach English: A Training Course for Teachers. (Illus.). 294p. 1988. pap. text, teacher ed. 22.95 (*0-521-34864-1*); pap. text, teacher ed. 17.95 (*0-521-34863-3*) Cambridge U Pr.

D'Offay, Danielle & Lionnet, G. Seychelles Creole-French Dictionary: Dictionnaire Creole (Seychellois)-Francais. (CRP & FRE.). 422p. 1982. 75.00 (*0-8288-1095-8*, F35790) Fr & Eur.

Dofflemyer, Trina. Timeline for Ancient Greece: A Companion to the Greenleaf Guide to Greece. 8p. (Orig.). (J). (gr. 3 up). 1995. pap. 4.95 (*1-882514-22-X*) Greenleaf TN.

— Timeline for Ancient Rome: A Companion to the Greenleaf Guide to Rome. 8p. (Orig.). (J). (gr. 3 up). 1995. pap. 4.95 (*1-882514-23-8*) Greenleaf TN.

— Timeline for Israel & Ancient Egypt: A Companion to the Greenleaf Guides to the Old Testament & Ancient Egypt. 8p. (Orig.). (J). (gr. 2 up). 1997. pap. 4.95 (*1-882514-21-1*) Greenleaf TN.

— Timeline for the Middle Ages: A Companion to the Greenleaf Guide to the Middle Ages. 8p. (Orig.). (J). (gr. 4 up). 1996. pap. 4.95 (*1-882514-24-6*) Greenleaf TN.

— Timeline for the Renaissance & Reformation: A Companion to the Greenleaf Guide to the Renaissance. 8p. (Orig.). (J). (gr. 5-12). 1997. pap. 4.95 (*1-882514-25-4*) Greenleaf TN.

Dofflemyer, Virginia. Southeast Asian Ceramics: From the Collection of Margot & Hans Ries. (Illus.). 100p. (C). 1989. 28.00 (*1-877921-27-0*) Pacific Asia.

Dofka, Charline M. Skills Competencies for the Dental Assistant. LC 94-24642. (Illus.). 576p. (C). 1995. mass mkt. 40.95 (*0-8273-6685-X*) Delmar.

Dofny, Jacques, jt. auth. see Arnaud, Nicole.

Doft, Peter S., jt. auth. see Mintz, Robert J.

Dog, Calvin T. Unleashed: The Wit & Wisdom of Calvin the Dog. Glaser, Chris, tr. LC 97-47377. 96p. 1998. 12.95 (*0-664-25773-9*) Westminster John Knox.

Dog, Leonard C., et al. Crow Dog: Four Generations of Sioux Medicine Men. (Illus.). 272p. 1996. pap. 13.00 (*0-06-092682-1*) HarpC.

Dog, Louise Lone, see Lone Dog, Louise.

Dog, Mary Crow, see Crow Dog, Mary.

Dog Museum Staff. Dogs of War. Date not set. 7.95 (*0-9615072-3-3*) Dog Museum.

Dogac, A., et al, eds. Workflow Management Systems & Interoperability. LC 98-26399. (NATO ASI Series F: Vol. 164). xvii, 481p. 1998. 119.00 (*3-540-64411-3*) Spr-Verlag.

Dogac, A., et al. Advances in Object-Oriented Databased Systems, Vol. 130. (Computer & Systems Sciences Ser.). 515p. 1994. 89.50 (*0-387-57825-0*) Spr-Verlag.

Dogac, Asuman, et al, eds. Current Trends in Data Management Technology. LC 98-55193. 275p. 1999. pap. text 64.95 (*1-878289-57-8*) Idea Group Pub.

Dogadina, A. V. Chemistry Reviews Vol. 15, Pt. 3: 1,3-Alkadiene-Phosphonates, Vol. 15. (Soviet Scientific Reviews Ser.: Section B). 57p. 1990. text 53.00 (*3-7186-5051-7*, Harwood Acad Pubs) Gordon & Breach.

Dogan, Mattei & Higley, John, eds. Elites, Crises, & the Origins of Regimes. LC 98-29685. 276p. 1998. 64.00 (*0-8476-9022-9*); pap. 22.95 (*0-8476-9023-7*) Rowman.

Dogan, Mattei & Kasarda, John D., eds. The Metropolis Era: A World of Giant Cities, Vol. 1. 400p. (C). 1988. 26.00 (*0-8039-3789-X*); text 55.00 (*0-8039-2602-2*) Sage.

— The Metropolis Era: Mega-Cities, Vol. 2. 400p. (C). 1988. 24.00 (*0-8039-3790-3*); text 52.00 (*0-8039-2603-0*) Sage.

Dogan, Mattei & Pelassy, Dominique. How to Compare Nations: Strategies in Comparative Politics. 2nd ed. LC 90-39431. (Sociologie Politique Comparative Ser.). 224p. (C). 1990. pap. text 24.95 (*0-934540-79-9*, Chatham House Pub) Seven Bridges.

***Dogan, Peter.** Instrument Flight Training Manual. 3rd ed. (Illus.). 279p. 1999. pap. text 26.95 (*0-916413-26-8*) Aviation.

Dogan, Z. M., jt. ed. see Yarar, Baki.

Doganalp-Votzi, Heidemarie. Der Gerber, der Kulturbringer: Politik, Okonomie, Zivilisation Im Osmanischen Vorderasien. 335p. 1997. 63.95 (*3-631-31604-6*) P Lang Pubng.

Doganis, Rigas. The Airport Business. LC 91-44797. 256p. (C). 1992. pap. 27.99 (*0-415-08117-3*, A7489) Routledge.

— Flying off Course: Economics of International Airlines. 2nd ed. (Illus.). 350p. (C). 1991. pap. 27.99 (*0-415-08439-3*) Routledge.

— Flying off Course: The Economics of International Airlines. 300p. (C). 1986. pap. text 18.95 (*0-04-387005-8*) Routledge.

— Flying off Course: The Economics of International Airlines. 300p. 1991. pap. 21.95 (*0-04-445983-1*, A8169) Routledge.

Doge, Polly. Color Your Hair Red. LC 95-77757. 144p. 1995. pap. 11.95 (*0-934252-59-9*, Pub. by Hohm Pr) SCB Distributors.

Dogen. Shobogenzo: Zen Essays by Dogen. Cleary, Thomas, tr. from JPN. LC 85-20979. 132p. (C). 1991. pap. text 14.00 (*0-8248-1401-0*) UH Pr.

Dogen, Eihei. Moon in a Dewdrop: Writings of Zen Master Dogen. Tanahashi, Kazuaki, ed. 356p. 1995. 16.00 (*0-374-47186-X*) FS&G.

Dogen, Eihei. Moon in a Dewdrop: Writings of Zen Master Dogen. Tanahashi, Kazuaki, ed. LC 84-62309. 356p. 1995. pap. 16.00 (*0-86547-186-X*) N Point Pr.

Dogen, Eihei. Zen Master Eihei Dogen's Monastic Regulations. ICHIMURA, Shohei, ed. & tr. by. from CHI. (Institute's Ser.: No. 1). 405p. (C). 1993. 50.00 (*0-9643788-1-7*) NAmer Inst Zen.

Dogen, Hosokawa. Omori Sogen: The Art of a Zen Master. LC 97-25743. (Illus.). 180p. 1997. 93.50 (*0-7103-0588-5*, Pub. by Kegan Paul Intl) Col U Pr.

***Dogg, Snoop.** Tha Doggfather: The Times, Trials, And Hardcore Truths Of Snoop Dogg. 2000. pap. 13.00 (*0-06-107607-4*, HarpEntertain) Morrow Avon.

Doggart, Sebastian, tr. Latin-American Plays. (International Collection). 256p. (Orig.). 1996. pap. 25.95 (*1-85459-249-1*, Pub. by N Hern Bks) Theatre Comm.

Doggart, Sebastian, tr. see Paz, Octavio.

Dogger, Barbara. Advanced Beginner's English Reader: Exploring Culture & Building Communication Skills. 80p. 1990. pap., student ed. 11.23 (*0-8442-5377-4*) NTC Contemp Pub Co.

— Advanced Beginner's English Reader: Exploring Culture & Building Communication Skills. 1992. pap., teacher ed. 5.58 (*0-8442-5378-2*) NTC Contemp Pub Co.

— Beginner's English Reader. 64p. 1990. pap. 8.40 (*0-8442-5363-4*); pap., teacher ed. 5.58 (*0-8442-5364-2*) NTC Contemp Pub Co.

— Listen & Learn Beginner's English Reader. 64p. 1995. pap. 42.32 incl. audio (*0-8442-5357-X*, 5357X, Natl Textbk Co) NTC Contemp Pub Co.

***Doggett, Annetta.** What Wondrous Love. 234p. 1999. pap. 13.95 (*0-9674821-0-0*) A Doggett.

Doggett, Decker, jt. auth. see Roth, Bob.

Doggett, Frank & Buttel, Robert, eds. Wallace Stevens: A Celebration. LC 79-18877. 384p. 1980. reprint ed. pap. 119.10 (*0-7837-8583-6*, 204939800011) Bks Demand.

Doggett, Frank A. Wallace Stevens, the Making of the Poem. LC 79-22772. 176p. reprint ed. pap. 54.60 (*0-8357-8368-5*, 203412300088) Bks Demand.

Doggett, G. Mathematics Chemistry. (C). 1996. pap. text 46.00 (*0-582-21970-1*) Addison-Wesley.

Doggett, Gerald, ed. see Brown, Clint.

Doggett, Martha. Death Foretold: The Jesuit Murders in El Salvador. LC 93-25209. 380p. 1993. 44.00 (*0-87840-545-3*); pap. 19.95 (*0-87840-546-1*) Georgetown U Pr.

— Underwriting Injustice: Aid & El Salvador's Judicial Reform Program. Posner, Michael & O'Neill, William, eds. (Illus.). 190p. (Orig.). 1989. pap. text 12.00 (*0-934143-24-2*) Lawyers Comm Human.

Doggett, Peter. Abbey Road - Let It Be: The Beatles. LC 97-29051. 138p. 1998. 14.95 (*0-02-864772-6*) Music Sales.

— Lou Reed: Growing up in Public. (Illus.). 216p. 1997. pap. 17.95 (*0-7119-3002-3*, OP 46820) Omnibus NY.

Doggett, Rachel, et al, eds. New World of Wonders: European Images of the Americas, 1492-1700. LC 92-28277. (Illus.). 1992. pap. 12.95 (*0-9629254-2-X*) Folger.

Doggett, Rachel, et al. Impressions of Wenceslaus Hollar. LC 97-176672. (Illus.). 128p. 1997. pap. 26.95 (*0-295-97594-6*) U of Wash Pr.

Doggett, S. B. A History of Doggett-Daggett Family. (Illus.). 696p. 1989. reprint ed. pap. 99.00 (*0-8328-0483-5*); reprint ed. lib. bdg. 107.00 (*0-8328-0482-7*) Higginson Bk Co.

***Doggett, Sandra L.** Beyond the Book: Technology Integration into the Secondary School Library Media Curriculum. LC 99-33151. 200p. 2000. pap. 29.50 (*1-56308-584-4*) Libs Unl.

***Doggett, Scott.** Las Vegas. (Lonely Planet Travel Guides Ser.). (Illus.). 256p. 2000. pap. 15.95 (*1-86450-086-7*) Lonely Planet.

Doggett, Scott. Lonely Planet Panama. (Illus.). 352p. 1999. pap. 16.95 (*0-86442-566-X*) Lonely Planet.

***Doggett, Scott.** Lonely Planet Yucatan. (Travel Guides Ser.). (Illus.). 320p. 2000. pap. 17.95 (*1-86450-103-0*) Lonely Planet.

Doggett, Scott & Gordon, Leah. Lonely Planet Dominican Republic & Haiti. 352p. 1999. pap. 15.95 (*0-86442-647-X*) Lonely Planet.

Doggett, Scott & Haddad, Annette, eds. Brazil. (Travelers' Tales Guides Ser.). 452p. 1997. pap. 17.95 (*1-885211-11-2*) Trvlers Tale.

Doggett, Sue. Bookworks: Books, Memory & Photo Albums, Journals & Diaries Made by Hand. LC 98-22960. 144p. 1998. 27.95 (*0-8230-0491-0*) Watsn-Guptill.

Doggett, Thomas, jt. auth. see Bacon, Terry R.

Doggett, Thomas, jt. auth. see Novak, Donald.

Doggett, Thomas B., jt. auth. see Bacon, Terry R.

Doggett, Thomas B., jt. auth. see Glidden, Stephanie R.

Doggett, Thomas B., jt. auth. see Herman, Stanley M.

Doggett, Thomas B., ed. see Herman, Stanley M.

Dogherty, Jennifer D., et al. Business Process Redesign for Higher Education. Reeder, Jefferson, ed. 194p. 1994. 59.00 (*0-915164-97-3*) NACUBO.

***Doghramji, Karl.** Psychotherapeutic & Pharmacological Treatment of Depression & Sleep Disorders. (LEA/DLN Mental Health Professionals Video Reference Library). 1999. VHS 129.95 (*0-8058-3304-8*) L Erlbaum Assocs.

***Doghri, I.** Mechanics of Deformable Solids: Linear & Nonlinear, Analytical & Computational Aspects. 580p. 2000. 84.95 (*3-540-66960-4*) Spr-Verlag.

Dogi, Fiametta. God Made Animal Families. (God Made Animals Ser.). (Illus.). 10p. (J). (ps). 1999. 3.99 (*0-7847-0883-5*, 03760) Standard Pub.

— God Made Baby Animals. (God Made Animals Ser.). (Illus.). 10p. (J). (ps). 1999. 3.99 (*0-7847-0882-7*, 03758) Standard Pub.

— God Made Jungle Animals. (God Made Animals Ser.). (Illus.). 10p. (J). (ps). 1999. 3.99 (*0-7847-0882-9*, 03757) Standard Pub.

— God Made Sea Animals. (God Made Animals Ser.). (Illus.). 10p. (J). (ps). 1999. 3.99 (*0-7847-0884-3*, 03761) Standard Pub.

Dogi, Fiammetta. Baby Animals. (My Little Book of Animals Ser.). 10p. (J). (gr. k-3). 1999. bds. 3.99 (*1-57584-268-8*, Pub. by Rdrs Digest) Random.

— Sea Animals. (My Little Book of Animals Ser.: Vol. 4). 10p. (J). (gr. k-3). 1998. bds. 3.99 (*1-57584-271-8*, Pub. by Rdrs Digest) Random.

Dogiaux, R., ed. Prediction of Solar Radiation in Areas with a Specific Microclimate. 120p. (C). 1994. text 85.50 (*0-7923-2596-6*) Kluwer Academic.

Dogin, Yvette. Teen-Agers at Work. 64p. (YA). (gr. 8 up). 1988. pap. text 3.75 (*0-88323-244-8*, 164) Pendergrass Pub.

Dogizaemon, Chibinosuke. Samurai Bulldog. (Illus.). 96p. (Orig.). 1994. pap. 9.95 (*0-8348-0305-4*) Weatherhill.

Dogliotti, L., ed. Breast Cancer - Biological & Clinical Progress: Proceedings of the Conference of the International Association for Breast Cancer Research, St. Vincent, Aosta Valley, Italy, May 26-29, 1991. (Developments in Oncology Ser.). 336p. (C). 1992. text 163.50 (*0-7923-1655-X*) Kluwer Academic.

Dogliotti, Miro & Rosiello, Luigi, eds. Lo Zingarelli 1994: Vocabolario Della Lingua Italiana de Nicola Zingarelli. 12th ed. (Illus.). 2144p. 1994. 85.00 (*88-08-12500-5*) OUP.

Dogo, G., jt. ed. see May, S. R.

***Dogra, Archana.** Marital Discord & Family Pathology: Impact on Children. 119p. 1999. 15.00 (*81-241-0645-2*, Pub. by Har-Anand Pubns) Nataraj Bks.

Dogra, Ramesh C. Bhutan. LC 92-122227. (World Bibliographical Ser.). 160p. 1991. lib. bdg. 49.50 (*1-85109-128-9*) ABC-CLIO.

Dogra, Ramesh C. & Mansukhani, Gobind S. Encyclopaedia of Sikh Religion & Culture. LC 94-907549. (C). 1995. 54.00 (*0-7069-8368-8*, Pub. by Vikas) S Asia.

Dogramaci, Ali, ed. Measurement Issues & Behavior of Productivity Variables. (C). 1986. lib. bdg. 115.50 (*0-89838-171-1*) Kluwer Academic.

Dogramaci, Ali & Adam, Nabil R. Aggregate & Industry-Level Productivity Analysis. (Productivity Analysis Studies: Vol. 2). 204p. 1981. lib. bdg. 73.50 (*0-89838-037-5*) Kluwer Academic.

Dogramaci, Ali & Adam, Nabil R., eds. Managerial Issues in Productivity Analysis. 1985. lib. bdg. 98.00 (*0-89838-162-2*) Kluwer Academic.

Dogramaci, Ali & Fare, Ralph, eds. Applications of Modern Production Theory. (C). 1987. lib. bdg. 120.00 (*0-89838-182-7*) Kluwer Academic.

Dogramaci, Ali, jt. ed. see Adam, Nabil R.

Doh, Joon C. The Planning-Programming-Budgeting Systems in Three Federal Agencies. LC 74-149365. (Special Studies in U. S. Economic, Social & Political Issues). 1971. 32.00 (*0-89197-887-9*) Irvington.

Dohan, Edith H. Excavations in Eastern Crete: Sphoungaras. LC 14-12344. (University of Pennsylvania, University Museum, Anthropological Publications: Vol. 3, No. 2). 48p. reprint ed. pap. 30.00 (*0-608-12384-6*, 205212100037) Bks Demand.

— Italic Tomb-Groups in the University Museum. LC 42-17075. 182p. reprint ed. pap. 56.50 (*0-608-16748-7*, 205219000054) Bks Demand.

Dohan, Michael & Hewett, Edward. Two Studies in Soviet Terms of Trade (1918-1970) (Studies in East European & Soviet Planning, Development, & Trade: No. 21). 1973. pap. text 3.00 (*0-89249-001-2*) Intl Development.

Dohan, Michael R., ed. The Best in Moscow, 1998 (Luchshee V Moskve, 1998) 656p. 1998. pap. 12.95 (*1-881832-16-3*) InfoSrvs Int.

— The Best in Moscow, 1996-1997. (Best in Ser.). (RUS.). 1996. pap. 12.95 (*1-881832-11-2*) InfoSrvs Int.

— The Best in Saint Petersburg, 1998-1999 (Luchshee V Sankt-Peterburge, 1998-1999(520p. 1998. pap. 9.95 (*1-881832-17-1*) InfoSrvs Int.

— The Best in Saint Petersburg, 1996-1997. (Best in Ser.). (RUS.). 604p. 1996. pap. 9.95 (*1-881832-12-0*) InfoSrvs Int.

— The Traveller's Yellow Pages & Handbook for St Petersburg, 1997-1998. (Traveller's Yellow Pages Ser.). 456p. 1997. pap. 9.95 (*1-881832-07-4*) InfoSrvs Int.

— The Traveller's Yellow Pages & Handbook for Moscow, 1997-1998. (Traveller's Yellow Pages Ser.). 640p. 1997. pap. 12.95 (*1-881832-08-2*) InfoSrvs Int.

— The Traveller's Yellow Pages & Handbook for Northwest Russia, 1997-1998. (Traveller's Yellow Pages Ser.). 384p. 1997. pap. 9.95 (*1-881832-09-0*) InfoSrvs Int.

— The Traveller's Yellow Pages & Handbook for Saint Petersburg, 1998-1999. 588p. 1998. pap. 10.95 (*1-881832-18-X*) InfoSrvs Int.

Dohan, Michael R. & Lisyuk, Mikhail B., eds. The Best in Saint Petersburg 1997-1998. (Best in...Ser.). (RUS.). 500p. 1997. pap. 9.95 (*1-881832-15-5*) InfoSrvs Int.

Dohaney, M. T. The Corrigan Women. 192p. 1988. pap. 12.95 (*0-920304-67-2*, Pub. by Gynergy-Ragweed) U of Toronto Pr.

— A Marriage of Masks. LC 95-173288. 176p. 1995. pap. 10.95 (*0-921556-56-X*, Pub. by Gynergy-Ragweed) U of Toronto Pr.

— To Scatter Stones. 192p. 1992. pap. 10.95 (*0-921556-23-3*, Pub. by Gynergy-Ragweed) U of Toronto Pr.

***Dohanyos, Franklin.** The Cats of Our Lives: Funny & Heartwarming Remeninscences of Feline Companions. LC 00-31975. (Illus.). 2000. 25.95 (*0-7531-5474-9*) ISIS Lrg Prnt.

Dohanyos, Franklin. Cats of Our Lives: Heartwarming Reminiscences of Feline Companions. LC 98-35390. (Illus.). 256p. 1999. 19.95 (*1-55972-487-0*, Birch Ln Pr) Carol Pub Group.

— 501 Golf Jokes for Almost All Occasions: From the First Tee to the 18th Green & Everything. LC 99-44701. 1999. pap. text 10.95 (*0-8065-2155-4*) Carol Pub Group.

Dohanyos, Franklin, jt. auth. see Grimes, Karolyn.

Dohar, William, jt. ed. see Shinners, John.

Dohar, William J. The Black Death & Pastoral Leadership: The Diocese of Hereford in the Fourteenth Century. (Middle Ages Ser.). 192p. (C). 1995. text 35.00 (*0-8122-3262-3*) U of Pa Pr.

Dohari, Harish. The Healing Power of Gemstones: In Tantra, Ayurveda, & Astrology. (Illus.). 240p. 1996. reprint ed. pap. 14.95 (*0-89281-608-2*, Destiny Bks) Inner Tradit.

DoHarris, Brenda C. The Coloured Girl in the Ring: A Guyanese Woman Remembers. LC 97-90924. 260p. 1997. pap. 14.95 (*0-9659444-0-9*) Tantaria Pr.

Doheny, Catherine, ed. Apple Basic II: Course Code 191-1. (Illus.). 96p. (J). (gr. 6). 1986. reprint ed. pap. text 9.95 (*0-917531-47-7*) CES Compu-Tech.

— Apple Basics II: Course Code 193-2. (Illus.). 68p. (J). (gr. 6). 1986. reprint ed. pap. text 9.95 (*0-917531-48-5*) CES Compu-Tech.

— BASIC Programming One: Course Code 103-1. (Illus.). 112p. (gr. 5). 1989. reprint ed. pap. text 9.95 (*0-917531-45-0*) CES Compu-Tech.

— BASIC Programming One: Course Code 103-2. (Illus.). 81p. (gr. 5). 1989. reprint ed. pap. text 9.95 (*0-917531-46-9*) CES Compu-Tech.

— BASIC Programming 1: Lab Pack, Pt. 1. 179.95 (*1-56177-032-9*, L103-1) CES Compu-Tech.

— BASIC Programming 1: Lab Pack, Pt. 1, No. 1. Apple II 15.95 (*1-56177-030-2*) CES Compu-Tech.

— BASIC Programming 1: Lab Pack, Pt. 2. (Illus.). text 179.95 incl. Apple II (*1-56177-033-7*, L103-2) CES Compu-Tech.

— BASIC Programming 1: Lab Pack, Pt. 2, No. 2. (Illus.). Apple II 15.95 (*1-56177-031-0*, D103-2) CES Compu-Tech.

— BASIC Programming 2: Lab Pack, Pt. 1. text 179.95 incl. Apple II (*1-56177-036-1*, L193-1) CES Compu-Tech.

— BASIC Programming 2: Lab Pack, Pt. 1, No. 1. Apple II 6.95 (*1-56177-034-5*, D193-1) CES Compu-Tech.

— BASIC Programming 2: Lab Pack, Pt. 2. (Illus.). text 179.95 incl. Apple II (*1-56177-037-X*, L193-2) CES Compu-Tech.

— BASIC Programming 2: Lab Pack, Pt. 2, No. 2. (Illus.). Apple II 6.95 (*1-56177-035-3*, D193-2) CES Compu-Tech.

Doheny, Catherine, ed. see Anderson, Jill & Weinman, Susan.

Doheny, Catherine, ed. see Black, Jeanne & Forker, Vickie.

Doheny, Catherine, ed. see Black, Jeanne, et al.

Doheny, Catherine, ed. see Danziger, Irene & Weinberger, Paula.

Doheny, Catherine, ed. see Hofkin, Mary.

Doheny, Catherine, ed. see Hofkin, Mary, et al.

Doheny, Catherine, ed. see Mullen, Yvonne & Schroeder, Bonnie.

Doheny, Catherine, ed. see Novak, Dan & Weinberger, Paula.

Doheny, Catherine, ed. see Weinberger, Paula & Novak, Dan.

Doheny, Cathy, ed. see Anderson, Jill, et al.

Doheny, Cathy, ed. see Black, Jeanne, et al.

Doheny, Cathy, ed. see Cavanaugh, Leah.

Doheny, Cathy, ed. see Danziger, Irene, et al.

Doheny, Cathy, ed. see Harrour, Marcia.

Doheny, Cathy, ed. see Rothman, Paula.

Doheny, Cathy, ed. see Schroeder, Bonnie.

Doheny-Farina, Stephen. Rhetoric, Innovation, Technology: Case Studies of Technical Communication in Technology Transfers. (Illus.). 296p. 1992. 47.50 (*0-262-04129-4*) MIT Pr.

— The Wired Neighborhood. LC 96-12241. 256p. 1996. 32.00 (*0-300-06765-8*) Yale U Pr.

— The Wired Neighborhood. 256p. 1998. pap. 14.00 (*0-300-07434-4*) Yale U Pr.

Doheny-Farina, Stephen, ed. Effective Documentation: What We Have Learned from Research. (Information Systems Ser.). 364p. 1988. 55.00 (*0-262-04098-0*) MIT Pr.

Doheny, Margaret, et al. Discipline of Nursing: An Introduction. 4th ed. LC 96-20875. 300p. (C). 1996. pap. text 29.95 (*0-8385-1716-1*, A1716-8) Appleton & Lange.

D

Doheny, Marilyn. Cubic Pinwheels: Strata Art Quilt. Eng, Chuck, ed. & illus. by. 12p. (Orig.). 1991. pap. 10.95 (*0-945169-07-8*) Doheny Pubns.
— Cubic Ribbons. Eng, Chuck, ed. & illus. by. (Strata Art Ser.). 12p. (Orig.). 1991. pap. 10.95 (*0-945169-09-4*) Doheny Pubns.
— Op-Art Quilt Illusions: Fast, Fun & Fabulous 3-D Illusions. 80p. 1996. reprint ed. pap. 22.95 (*0-945169-18-3*) Doheny Pubns.
— Triad Interlock: Strata Art Quilt. Eng, Chuck, ed. & illus. by. 12p. (Orig.). 1991. pap. 10.95 (*0-945169-08-6*) Doheny Pubns.
— Woven Ribbons. Eng, Chuck, ed. & illus. by. (Strata Art Ser.). 12p. (Orig.). 1991. pap. 10.95 (*0-945169-10-8*) Doheny Pubns.
Doheny, Marilyn, ed. see Hill, Susan G.
Doheny, Marilyn, ed. see McGovern, Pat.
Doheny, Marilyn, ed. see Podolsky, Nancy.
Doheny, Marilyn S. Amish Sparkle Star. 1996. 10.95 (*0-945169-14-0*) Doheny Pubns.
— Bargello Tapestry Quilts. LC 92-76193. (Illus.). 134p. 1994. pap. 24.95 (*0-945169-12-4*) Doheny Pubns.
— Goosey Hearts. Kime, Janet, ed. (Illus.). 64p. (Orig.). 1988. pap. 14.95 (*0-945169-00-0*, GH1) Doheny Pubns.
— Maple Leaves. 1996. 10.95 (*0-945169-13-2*) Doheny Pubns.
***Doherty.** Annual Reports in Medicinal Chemistry. 384p. (C). 1999. pap. text 85.00 (*0-12-040534-2*) Harcourt.
Doherty. Color Atlas & Text of Osteoarthritis. 1995. 105.00 (*0-8151-2752-9*, 22853) Mosby Inc.
***DOHERTY.** Integrated Risk Management. LC 99-88282. 2000. 70.00 (*0-07-135861-7*, McGrw-H College) McGrw-H Hghr Educ.
Doherty. The Iroquois. (J). 1991. pap. text 5.95 (*0-516-95603-5*) Childrens.
***DOHERTY.** Popeye Puzzle Book. 1999. mass mkt. 1.95 (*0-8125-7547-4*) Tor Bks.
Doherty. Social Judgement Theory: A Special Double Issue of "Thinking & Reasoning", Vol. 2, Nos. 2 & 3, 1997. 1997. pap. 45.00 (*0-86377-951-4*) L Erlbaum Assocs.
Doherty, et al, eds. Delaware Genealogical Research Guide. 42p. 1989. pap. text 11.50 (*1-887061-03-7*) DE Geneal Soc.
Doherty & Mavil. Health Promotion in Nursing. (Professional Reference - Nursing Ser.). (C). 1996. pap. text, teacher ed. 10.00 (*0-8273-8009-7*) Delmar.
— Health Promotion in Nursing. (Professional Reference - Nursing Ser.). (C). 2001. mass mkt. 39.95 (*0-8273-8008-9*) Delmar.
Doherty & Mynatt. Things Known about Human Behavior. 2nd ed. 440p. (C). 1998. pap. text 35.00 (*0-536-01309-8*) Pearson Custom.
— Understanding Human Behavior. Date not set. pap. text, student ed. 16.00 (*0-205-29280-1*) Allyn.
Doherty, A. M., jt. auth. see Paquette, Leo A.
***Doherty, Amy.** Rory's Random Walk down Wall Street. 32p. (J). 2000. 16.95 (*0-9674572-0-3*, Pub. by Playgroup) ACCESS Pubs Network.
Doherty, Amy, ed. see Mena, Maria C.
Doherty, Ann, ed. see International Cneter of Photograpy Staff.
***Doherty, Annette M., ed.** Annual Reports in Medicinal Chemistry. (Annual Reports in Medicinal Chemistry: Vol. 35). 500p. 2000. pap. 85.00 (*0-12-040535-0*) Acad Pr.
Doherty, Barbara, jt. auth. see Jaffe, Charlotte.
Doherty, Barbara, jt. auth. see Jaffee, Charlotte.
***Doherty, Berlie.** Daughter of the Sea. 128p. (gr. 5). 2000. pap. 4.99 (*0-440-22794-1*, LLL BDD) BDD Bks Young Read.
Doherty, Berlie. Daughter of the Sea. LC 97-36080. 128p. (YA). (gr. 5-9). 1997. 14.95 (*0-7894-2469-X*) DK Pub Inc.
***Doherty, Berlie.** Daughter of the Sea. (Illus.). (J). 2000. 10.34 (*0-606-18102-4*) Turtleback.
Doherty, Berlie. Dear Nobody. LC 93-9626. 192p. (YA). (gr. 8 up). 1994. mass mkt. 4.95 (*0-688-12764-9*, Wm Morrow) Morrow Avon.
— Dear Nobody. LC 92-11651. 192p. (YA). (gr. 6 up). 1992. 16.95 (*0-531-05461-6*) Orchard Bks Watts.
— Dear Nobody. 1995. 19.50 (*0-8446-6808-7*) Peter Smith.
— Dear Nobody. (J). 1994. 10.05 (*0-606-05805-2*, Pub. by Turtleback) Demco.
— Dear Nobody. large type ed. LC 93-13531. (YA). (gr. 6 up). 1993. pap. 15.95 (*1-56054-769-3*) Thorndike Pr.
— Encantacornio (Spellhorn) Mansour, Monica, tr. (SPA., Illus.). 179p. (YA). 1992. pap. 6.99 (*968-16-3760-7*, Pub. by Fondo) Continental Bk.
***Doherty, Berlie.** Fairy Tales. LC 99-89380. (Illus.). 224p. (J). (gr. 3-7). 2000. 19.99 (*0-7636-0997-8*) Candlewick Pr.
Doherty, Berlie. The Midnight Man. LC 98-3457. (Illus.). 32p. (J). (gr. k-3). 1998. 15.99 (*0-7636-0700-2*) Candlewick Pr.
— Paddiwak & Cozy. 1999. pap. 4.99 (*0-14-055271-5*) NAL.
***Doherty, Berlie.** Paddiwak & Cozy. LC 98-46168. (Illus.). 32p. (J). (ps-1). 1999. 14.95 (*0-531-30180-X*) Orchard Books.
Doherty, Berlie. The Snake-Stone. LC 95-36070. 176p. (J). (gr. 6 up). 1996. 15.95 (*0-531-09512-6*) Orchard Bks Watts.
Doherty, Berlie. The Snake-Stone. LC 95-36070. 176p. (J). (gr. 6 up). 1996. lib. bdg. 16.99 (*0-531-08862-6*) Orchard Bks Watts.
Doherty, Berlie. The Snake-Stone. (J). 1998. 10.09 (*0-606-13086-1*, Pub. by Turtleback) Demco.
— Street Child. LC 94-5020. 160p. (J). (gr. 4-7). 1994. 17.95 (*0-531-06864-1*); lib. bdg. 18.99 (*0-531-08714-X*) Orchard Bks Watts.
— Street Child. LC 96-11041. 1996. 10.09 (*0-606-08883-0*, Pub. by Turtleback) Demco.
— Tales of Wonder & Magic. LC 97-670. (Illus.). 128p. (J). (gr. 5 up). 1998. 21.99 (*1-56402-891-7*) Candlewick Pr.
Doherty, Brendan. City-Smart Guidebook: Albuquerque. 2nd ed. (Illus.). 216p. 1999. pap. 12.95 (*1-56261-486-X*, City Smart) Avalon Travel.
Doherty, Brian. Democracy & Green Political Thought. 256p. (C). 1996. 85.00 (*0-415-14411-6*); pap. 25.99 (*0-415-14412-4*) Routledge.
— Father Malachy's Miracle: Manuscript Edition. 1948. pap. 13.00 (*0-8222-0389-8*) Dramatists Play.
— Pocahontas Coloring Book. (Illus.). (J). (gr. k-3). 1994. pap. 2.95 (*0-486-28040-3*) Dover.
— The Story of Pocahontas. (Illus.). 96p. (J). (gr. 3 up). 1994. pap. 1.00 (*0-486-28025-X*) Dover.
***Doherty, Cathal.** Clauses Without "That" The Case for Bare Sentential Complementation in English. LC 00-26132. (Outstanding Dissertations in Linguistics Ser.). 2000. write for info. (*0-8153-3775-2*) Garland.
Doherty, Catherine. Can of Worms. (Illus.). 88p. 1999. pap. 12.95 (*1-56097-363-3*) Fantagraph Bks.
Doherty, Catherine, jt. auth. see Doherty, Craig.
Doherty, Catherine D. Apostolic Farming. 1991. pap. 4.00 (*0-921440-03-0*) Madonna Hse.
— Bogoroditza: She Who Gave Birth to God. 145p. 1998. pap. 12.95 (*0-921440-48-0*) Madonna Hse.
— Dear Father: A Message of Love to Priests. rev. ed. 117p. 1988. pap. 8.95 (*0-921440-00-6*) Madonna Hse.
— Dear Parents: A Gift of Love for Families. 156p. 1997. pap. 11.95 (*0-921440-44-8*) Madonna Hse.
— Dear Seminarian. 87p. 1992. pap. 6.95 (*0-921440-05-7*) Madonna Hse.
— Dearly Beloved: Letters to the Children of My Spirit, Vol. I. 1989. pap. 19.95 (*0-921440-10-3*) Madonna Hse.
— Dearly Beloved: Letters to the Children of My Spirit, Vol. II. 1990. pap. 19.95 (*0-921440-11-1*) Madonna Hse.
— Dearly Beloved: Letters to the Children of My Spirit, Vol. III. 1990. pap. 19.95 (*0-921440-21-9*) Madonna Hse.
— Donkey Bells: Advent & Christmas. Bazzett, Mary, ed. (Illus.). 158p. 1994. 11.95 (*0-921440-38-3*) Madonna Hse.
— Doubts, Loneliness, Rejection. 1993. pap. 8.95 (*0-921440-33-2*) Madonna Hse.
— Fragments of My Life. (Illus.). 206p. 1996. pap. 12.95 (*0-921440-41-3*) Madonna Hse.
— The Gospel of a Poor Woman. 1992. pap. 12.95 (*0-921440-27-8*) Madonna Hse.
— The Gospel Without Compromise. 150p. 1989. 11.95 (*0-921440-15-4*) Madonna Hse.
— Grace in Every Season: Through the Year with Catherine Doherty. Bazzett, Mary, ed. 320p. 1992. 14.95 (*0-921440-31-6*) Madonna Hse.
— Molchanie: The Silence of God. 100p. 1991. 9.95 (*0-921440-28-6*) Madonna Hse.
— My Russian Yesterdays. 136p. 1990. pap. 11.95 (*0-921440-18-9*) Madonna Hse.
— Not Without Parables: Stories of Yesterday, Today & Eternity. 187p. 1989. 13.95 (*0-921440-16-2*) Madonna Hse.
— The People of the Towel & the Water. 1991. pap. 12.95 (*0-921440-22-7*) Madonna Hse.
— Poustinia: Christian Spirituality of the East for Westerners. 224p. 1993. pap. 13.95 (*0-921440-35-9*) Madonna Hse.
— Season of Mercy: Lent & Easter. LC 96-900654. 160p. 1996. 16.95 (*0-921440-43-X*) Madonna Hse.
— Sobornost: Eastern Unity of Mind & Heart for Westerners. 164p. 1992. 12.95 (*0-921440-25-1*) Madonna Hse.
— Strannik: The Call to Pilgrimage for Westerners. (Russian Spirituality Ser.). 85p. 1991. 9.95 (*0-921440-24-3*) Madonna Hse.
— Urodivoi: Fools for God. 104p. 1993. 9.95 (*0-921440-34-0*) Madonna Hse.
— Welcome Pilgrim. 126p. 1991. pap. 9.95 (*0-921440-23-5*) Madonna Hse.
Doherty, Craig & Doherty, Catherine. Arnold Schwarzenegger: Larger Than Life. 128p. (J). (gr. 5 up). 1993. 14.95 (*0-8027-8236-1*); lib. bdg. 15.85 (*0-8027-8238-8*) Walker & Co.
Doherty, Craig A. & Doherty, Katherine M. The Apaches & Navajos. (Full-Color First Bks.). (Illus.). 64p. (J). (gr. 4-6). 1991. pap. 6.95 (*0-531-15602-8*) Watts.
— The Cahuilla. LC 93-31863. (Native American People Ser.). 32p. (J). (gr. 4-8). 1994. lib. bdg. 22.60 (*0-86625-527-3*) Rourke Pubns.
— The Chickasaw. LC 93-42163. (Native American People Ser.: Set IV). 32p. (J). (gr. 4-8). 1994. lib. bdg. 22.60 (*0-86625-531-1*) Rourke Pubns.
— The Crow. LC 93-35660. (Native American People Ser.: Set IV). 32p. (J). (gr. 4-8). 1994. lib. bdg. 22.60 (*0-86625-529-X*) Rourke Pubns.
— The Empire State Building. LC 96-40483. (Building America Ser.). (Illus.). 48p. (J). (gr. 5-7). 1997. lib. bdg. 17.95 (*1-56711-116-5*) Blackbirch.
— The Erie Canal. Bowman, Nicole, ed. LC 95-25104. (Building America Ser.). (Illus.). 48p. (J). (gr. 5-7). 1996. lib. bdg. 17.95 (*1-56711-112-2*) Blackbirch.
— The Golden Gate Bridge. Glassman, Bruce S., ed. LC 94-29996. (Building America Ser.). (Illus.). 48p. (J). (gr. 5-7). 1995. lib. bdg. 17.95 (*1-56711-106-8*) Blackbirch.
— Hoover Dam. Glassman, Bruce, ed. LC 94-23267. (Building America Ser.). (Illus.). 48p. (J). (gr. 5-7). 1995. lib. bdg. 17.95 (*1-56711-107-6*) Blackbirch.
— The Huron. LC 93-32667. (Native American People Ser.: Set IV). 32p. (J). (gr. 4-8). 1994. lib. bdg. 22.60 (*0-86625-528-1*) Rourke Pubns.
— The Iroquois. LC 89-33055. (First Bks.). (Illus.). 64p. (J). (gr. 3-5). 1989. lib. bdg. 22.00 (*0-531-10747-7*) Watts.
— The Iroquois. (First Bks.). (Illus.). 64p. (J). (gr. 5-8). 1991. pap. 6.95 (*0-531-15603-6*) Watts.
— Mount Rushmore. Glassman, Bruce, ed. LC 94-24757. (Building America Ser.). (Illus.). 48p. (J). (gr. 5-7). 1995. lib. bdg. 17.95 (*1-56711-108-4*) Blackbirch.
— The Narragansett. LC 93-32669. (Native American People Ser.: Set IV). 32p. (J). (gr. 4-8). 1994. lib. bdg. 22.60 (*0-86625-525-7*) Rourke Pubns.
— The Statue of Liberty. Bowman, Nicole, ed. LC 95-20921. (Building America Ser.). (Illus.). 48p. (J). (gr. 5-7). 1996. lib. bdg. 17.95 (*1-56711-111-4*) Blackbirch.
— The Ute. LC 93-37999. (Native American People Ser.: Set IV). 32p. (J). (gr. 4-8). 1994. lib. bdg. 22.60 (*0-86625-530-3*) Rourke Pubns.
— The Washington Monument. Glassman, Bruce S., ed. LC 94-24477. (Building America Ser.). (Illus.). 48p. (J). (gr. 5-7). 1995. lib. bdg. 17.95 (*1-56711-110-6*) Blackbirch.
Doherty, Craig A., jt. auth. see Doherty, Katherine M.
Doherty, D., jt. auth. see Redfern, Darren.
Doherty, Donald. Sams Teach Yourself JavaBeans in 21 Days. LC 97-66203. (Teach Yourself Ser.). 418p. 1997. 29.99 (*1-57521-316-8*) Sams.
Doherty, Donald & Que Development Group Staff. Using Latte: Special Edition. 800p. 1998. pap. 49.99 (*0-7897-0892-2*) Que.
Doherty, Donald & Toupin, Ed. Hands on Visual C++ 6 for Web Development. LC 98-65161. (Illus.). 550p. 1998. per. 40.00 (*0-7615-1394-9*) Prima Pub.
Doherty, Eddie. A Cricket in My Heart. rev. ed. (Illus.). 290p. 1990. pap. 10.50 (*0-9628295-0-1*) Blue Hse NY.
Doherty, Eddie. Gall & Honey: The Story of a Newspaperman. (Illus.). 305p. 1989. pap. 14.95 (*0-921440-13-8*) Madonna Hse.
— Getting to Know God. 145p. 1997. pap. 12.95 (*0-921440-47-2*) Madonna Hse.
— Splendor of Sorrow: For Sinners Only. 90p. 1990. 11.95 (*0-921440-20-0*) Madonna Hse.
Doherty, Eddie. True Devotion to Mary. 135p. 1956. pap. 4.95 (*0-910984-02-6*) Montfort Pubns.
Doherty, Eddie. Tumbleweed: A Biography. (Illus.). 203p. 1988. pap. 12.95 (*0-921440-12-X*) Madonna Hse.
Doherty, Eddie. Wisdom's Fool. 1976. pap. 4.95 (*0-910984-09-3*) Montfort Pubns.
Doherty, Edward J. & Quinn-Musgrove, Sandra L. Auctions for Amateurs. LC 93-71299. 166p. (Orig.). 1993. pap. 9.95 (*0-9628295-2-8*) Blue Hse NY.
Doherty, Edward J., ed. see Harum, Peggy.
Doherty, Eileen M., jt. ed. see Sil, Rudra.
Doherty, Elizabeth. Playing by the Rules: The Mitterrand Government & the International Economy. (Political Economy of Global Interdependence Ser.). (C). 2000. pap. 49.95 (*0-8133-2992-2*) Westview.
Doherty, F. The Art & Science of Interdental Cleaning. LC 99-20516. (Illus.). 62p. 1999. 29.00 (*1-85070-099-0*) Prthnon Pub.
Doherty, F., ed. see Plato.
Doherty, Fergus J. & Mayer, R. John. Intracellular Protein Degradation: In Focus. (In Focus Ser.). (Illus.). 80p. (C). 1992. pap. text 19.95 (*0-19-963293-6*) OUP.
Doherty, Filomena. Pugs. (Illus.). 1997. pap. 9.95 (*0-7938-2391-9*, KW-104S) TFH Pubns.
Doherty, Francis. A Study in Eighteenth-Century Advertising Methods: The Anodyne Necklace. LC 92-34967. 476p. 1992. text 109.95 (*0-7734-9177-5*) E Mellen.
***Doherty, Gabriel & Keogh, Dermot, eds.** Michael Collins & the Making of the Irish State. (Illus.). 200p. 1998. pap. 15.95 (*1-85635-211-0*, Pub. by Mercier Pr) Irish Amer Bk.
Doherty, Geoffrey D., ed. Developing Quality Systems & Educational Organisations. LC 93-47624. 320p. (C). 1994. pap. 29.99 (*0-415-09829-7*, B4101) Routledge.
Doherty, George. Peter & the Wolf. (J). 1994. 7.98 (*1-57042-224-9*) Warner Bks.
Doherty, Gerald. Theorizing Lawrence: Nine Meditations on Tropological Themes. LC 97-47418. (Studies in Twentieth-Century British Literature: Vol. 1). X, 201p. 1999. text 46.95 (*0-8204-3976-2*, 39762) P Lang Pubng.
Doherty, Gerard M. & Skogseid, Britt. Surgical Endocrinology: A Clinical Syndromes Approach. 350p. text 120.00 (*0-7817-1922-4*) Lppncott W & W.
Doherty, Gerard M. & Washington University, Saint Louis Staff. Washington Manual of Surgery. 2nd ed. LC 98-49850. 1999. write for info. (*0-7817-1640-3*) Lppncott W & W.
Doherty, Gerard M., jt. auth. see Washington University Department of Medicine.
Doherty, Gillian. Ghosts? (Illus.). 48p. (gr. 4-7). 1999. 13.95 (*1-58086-197-0*) EDC.
— Ghosts. (Illus.). 48p. (gr. 4-7). 1999. pap. 5.95 (*0-7460-3056-8*, Usborne) EDC.
— 101 Things to Do with Your Computer. (Computer Guides Ser.). (Illus.). 64p. (YA). (gr. 5-9). 1998. lib. bdg. 18.95 (*1-58086-123-7*, Usborne) EDC.
***Doherty, Gillian.** 101 Things to Do with Your Computer. (Computer Guides Ser.). (Illus.). 64p. (YA). (gr. 5-9). 2000. pap. 10.95 (*0-7460-2935-7*, Usborne) EDC.
— 1001 Cosas que Buscar en la Granja (1001 Things to Spot on the Farm) (One Thousand One Things to Spot Ser.). (SPA., Illus.). 32p. (J). (ps up). 1999. pap. 6.95 (*0-7460-3652-3*, Usborne) EDC.
Doherty, Gillian. 1001 Things to Spot Long Ago. (1001 Things to Spot Ser.). 1999. 14.95 (*1-58086-194-6*) EDC.
— Quality Matters: Excellence in Early Childhood Programs. 202p. 1995. pap. text 23.96 (*0-201-76614-0*) Addison-Wesley.
Doherty, Gillian, ed. 1001 Things to Spot on the Farm. (1001 Things to Spot Ser.). (Illus.). 32p. (J). (ps-3). 1999. pap. text 6.95 (*0-7460-2955-1*, Usborne); lib. bdg. 14.95 (*1-58086-152-0*, Usborne) EDC.
***Doherty, Gillian, et al, eds.** The Usborne Book of the Paranormal. (Paranormal Guides Ser.). (Illus.). 192p. (YA). (gr. 4-7). 2000. pap. 16.95 (*0-7460-3390-7*, Pub. by Usbrne Pbng UK) EDC.
***Doherty, Gillian, et al.** Book of the Paranormal. (Usborne Paranormal Guides Ser.). (Illus.). 192p. (gr. 4-7). 2000. 24.95 (*1-58086-231-4*) EDC.
Doherty, Gillian, et al. 1001 Things to Spot Long Ago. (One Thousand One Things to Spot Ser.). (Illus.). 32p. (J). (ps-3). 1999. pap. text 6.95 (*0-7460-3318-4*, Usborne) EDC.
Doherty, H., tr. see Fourier, Francois M.
Doherty, Herbert J. The Whigs of Florida, 1845-1854. LC 59-62570. (University of Florida Monographs: Social Sciences: No. 1). 79p. reprint ed. pap. 30.00 (*0-7837-4936-8*, 204460200004) Bks Demand.
Doherty, J. C. The Shock of War: Unknown Battles That Ruined Hitler's Plan for a Second Blitzkrieg in the West, December-January 1944-45, 3 vols. LC 95-60258. (Illus.). 875p. 1998. pap. 34.95 (*0-9613980-7-8*) Vert Milon Pr.
— The Shock of War Vol. II: Unknown Battles That Ruined Hitler's Plan for a Second Blitzkrieg in the West, December-January, 1944-45. Adda, Lionel, ed. (Illus.). 442p. (Orig.). 1996. pap. 13.95 (*0-9613980-5-1*) Vert Milon Pr.
— The Shock of War, Picture Annex, Unknown Battles That Ruined Hitler's Plan for a Second Blitzkrieg in the West, December-January 1944-45. 2nd ed. LC 95-60258. (Illus.). 52p. (Orig.). 1997. pap. 7.50 (*0-9613980-6-X*) Vert Milon Pr.
Doherty, J. Dennis, ed. see DeCamp, Graydon.
Doherty, J. E. & Hickey, D. J. A Chronology of Irish History since Fifteen Hundred. 352p. (C). 1989. lib. bdg. 52.50 (*0-389-20895-7*, N8453) B&N Imports.
***Doherty, James L.** In the Beginnings: Foundations for the Millennium Ahead. LC 99-28060. 144p. 1999. 24.95 (*1-55618-179-5*) Brunswick Pub.
Doherty, Jenni & Doherty, Liz. That Land Beyond. (Illus.). 47p. 1996. pap. 5.95 (*0-946451-24-9*, Pub. by Guildhall Pr) Irish Bks Media.
Doherty, John M. What's Wrong with Uncle Johnny? 36p. (J). (gr. 3-5). 1997. write for info. (*0-614-28392-2*, Power Hse) MYD Pubns.
Doherty, Johnny. Living the Sunday Liturgy. 288p. (Orig.). 1995. pap. 16.95 (*1-85607-137-5*, Pub. by Columba Press) Whitecap Bks.
Doherty, Jon & Hoehn, Robert G. The Magic of Thinking Big in Selling. 224p. 1983. pap. 7.95 (*0-13-545210-4*) P-H.
Doherty, Joseph C. Growth Management in Countryfied Cities Vol. 1: Change & Response. Doherty, Kristan & Grieg, Margot, eds. LC 84-51900. (Illus.). 100p. (Orig.). 1984. pap. 10.00 (*0-9613980-1-9*) Vert Milon Pr.
— Growth Management in Countryfied Cities Vol. 3: Six Perspectives on a Decade of Change. LC 84-51900. (Illus.). 204p. 1991. pap. 15.00 (*0-9613980-3-5*) Vert Milon Pr.
— The Shock of War: Unknown Battles That Ruined Hitler's Plan for a Second Blitzkrieg in the West, December-January 1944-45, Vol. 1. LC 95-60258. (Illus.). 381p. (Orig.). 1994. pap. 13.95 (*0-9613980-4-3*) Vert Milon Pr.
Doherty, Justin. The Acmeist Movement in Russian Poetry: Culture & the Word. (Modern Languages & Literature Monographs). 328p. 1995. 68.00 (*0-19-815888-2*) OUP.
Doherty, Katherine. The Penobscot. (First Bks., Indians of North America). (Illus.). 64p. (J). (gr. 4-6). 1996. reprint ed. pap. 6.95 (*0-531-15764-4*) Watts.
— The Wampanoag. (First Bks.). (Illus.). 64p. (J). (gr. 4-6). 1996. reprint ed. pap. 6.95 (*0-531-15765-2*) Watts.
Doherty, Katherine M. & Doherty, Craig A. The Gateway Arch. Glassman, Bruce S., ed. LC 94-36556. (Building America Ser.). (Illus.). 48p. (J). (gr. 5-7). 1995. lib. bdg. 17.95 (*1-56711-105-X*) Blackbirch.
— The Sears Tower. Glassman, Bruce S., ed. LC 94-40642. (Building America Ser.). (Illus.). 48p. (J). (gr. 5-7). 1995. lib. bdg. 17.95 (*1-56711-109-2*) Blackbirch.
— The Wampanoag. (First Bks.). (Illus.). 64p. (J). (gr. 4-6). 1995. lib. bdg. 22.00 (*0-531-20208-9*) Watts.
Doherty, Katherine M., jt. auth. see Doherty, Craig A.
Doherty, Kathleen, ed. see Koebner, Linda.
Doherty, Kieran. Congressional Medal of Honor Recipients. LC 97-23056. (Collective Biographies Ser.). (Illus.). 112p. (YA). (gr. 6 up). 1998. lib. bdg. 20.95 (*0-7660-1026-0*) Enslow Pubs.
— Explorers, Missionaries & Trappers: Trailblazers of the West. LC 98-54636. (Shaping America Ser.). (Illus.). 176p. (YA). (gr. 7-12). 1999. lib. bdg. 21.95 (*1-881508-52-8*) Oliver Pr MN.
— Puritans, Pilgrims & Merchants: Founders of the Northeastern Colonies. LC 98-10957. (Shaping America Ser.: Vol. 1). (Illus.). 176p. (YA). (gr. 7 up). 1999. lib. bdg. 21.95 (*1-881508-50-1*) Oliver Pr MN.
***Doherty, Kieran.** Ranchers, Homesteaders & Traders: Frontiersmen of the South -Central States. Johnson, Sylvia & Anderson, Jenna, eds. (Shaping America Ser.: No. 4). (Illus.). 176p. (YA). (gr. 7-12). 2001. lib. bdg. 21.95 (*1-881508-53-6*) Oliver Pr MN.
Doherty, Kieran. Soldiers, Cavaliers, & Planters: Settlers of the Southeastern Colonies. LC 98-10959. (Shaping America Ser.). (Illus.). 176p. (YA). (gr. 7-12). 1999. lib. bdg. 21.95 (*1-881508-51-X*) Oliver Pr MN.
— William Bradford: Rock of Plymouth. LC 99-10631. 192p. (YA). (gr. 5-9). 1999. lib. bdg. 22.90 (*0-7613-1304-4*) TFC Bks NY.
— Willian Penn: Quaker Colonist. LC 97-48504. (Illus.). 192p. (YA). (gr. 6-10). 1998. lib. bdg. 22.40 (*0-7613-0355-3*) Millbrook Pr.
Doherty, Kristan, ed. see Doherty, Joseph C.
***Doherty, LeeAnn.** The McClellan Legacy. LC 99-65323. 192p. 2000. pap. 11.95 (*1-56315-213-4*, Pub. by SterlingHse) Natl Bk Netwk.
Doherty, Lillian, tr. see DeRomilly, Jacqueline.

D

An Asterisk (*) at the beginning of an entry indicates that the title is appearing for the first time.

Doherty, Lillian E. Siren Songs: Gender, Audiences, & Narrators in the Odyssey. LC 95-19532. 232p. 1995. text 44.50 (*0-472-10597-3*, 10597) U of Mich Pr.

Doherty, Linda. Word Find Puzzles, No. 4. 1988. pap. 1.95 (*0-8125-7881-3*, Pub. by Tor Bks) St Martin.

— Word Finds Three. 96p. 1988. pap. 1.95 (*0-8125-7879-1*, Pub. by Tor Bks) St Martin.

Doherty, Liz, jt. auth. see Doherty, Jenni.

Doherty, Liz, jt. auth. see Yorke, Harvey.

Doherty, M. Epistemic Meaning. (Language & Communication Ser.: Vol. 21). (Illus.). 190p. 1987. 93.00 (*0-387-17236-X*) Spr-Verlag.

Doherty, M. Stephen. Business Letters for Artists. (Illus.). 128p. 1993. pap. 12.95 (*0-8230-0302-7*, Watson-Guptill Bks) Watsn-Guptill.

— Creative Oil Painting: The Step-by-Step Guide & Showcase. (Illus.). 144p. 1997. bds. 29.99 (*1-56496-323-3*, Quarry Bks) Rockport Pubs.

— Easy Solutions Color Mixing Watercolor: How to Mix the Right Colors for the Subject Every Time. (Illus.). 144p. 1998. 29.99 (*1-56496-417-5*, Quarry Bks) Rockport Pubs.

— Howard Behrens: An Artist's View of the World. 180p. 1994. 80.00 (*0-9638578-0-0*) Soho Editions.

— The Watson-Guptill Handbook of Landscape Painting. (Illus.). 128p. 1997. pap. 19.95 (*0-8230-5701-1*) Watsn-Guptill.

***Doherty, Martin.** Nazi Wireless Propaganda: Lord Haw-Haw & British Public Opinion. 256p. 2000. pap. text 25.00 (*0-7486-1363-3*) Col U Pr.

Doherty, Michael. Writing for Excellence: A Four-Stage Approach to Creating Maximum Impact in Business Writing. LC 92-17062. 1992. write for info. (*0-07-707654-0*) McGraw.

Doherty, Michael & George, Emmanuel. Self-Assessment Picture Tests in Rheumatology Medicine. (Illus.). 144p. (gr. 13). 1995. 15.95 (*0-7234-1968-X*) Mosby Inc.

Doherty, Michael, et al. Rheumatology Examination & Injection Techniques. (Illus.). 143p. 1992. text 93.00 (*0-7020-1442-7*, Pub. by W B Saunders) Saunders.

Doherty, Michael E., jt. auth. see Mynatt, Clifford R.

Doherty, Michael F., ed. see Fourth International Conference on Foundations of.

Doherty, N. S. Inflammation: Mechanisms & Therapeutics. LC 95-11482. (Agents & Actions Supplements Ser.: Vol. AAS 47). 1995. 79.50 (*0-8176-5129-2*) Birkhauser.

Doherty, Neil A., jt. auth. see D'Arcy, Stephen P.

Doherty, Oluwatoyin. Legal Practice & Management in Nigeria. xxv, 398p. 1998. pap. 54.00 (*1-85941-178-9*, Pub. by Cavendish Pubng) Gaunt.

Doherty, Oluwatoyin, ed. Criminal Procedure in Nigeria Law & Practice. 524p. (C). 1990. text 108.00 (*1-85431-114-X*, Pub. by Blackstone Pr); pap. text 63.00 (*1-85431-113-1*, Pub. by Blackstone Pr) Gaunt.

Doherty, P. C. An Ancient Evil: The Knight's Tale of Mystery & Murder as He Goes on Pilgrimage from London to Canterbury. large type ed. 1995. 27.99 (*0-7089-3409-9*) Ulverscroft.

***Doherty, P. C.** The Angel of Death. large type ed. 296p. 2000. pap. 18.99 (*0-7089-5671-8*, Linford) Ulverscroft.

Doherty, P. C. The Assassin in the Greenwood: A Medieval Mystery Featuring Hugh Corbett. large type ed. 384p. 1996. 27.99 (*0-7089-3535-4*) Ulverscroft.

***Doherty, P. C.** Crown in Darkness. large type ed. 304p. 1999. pap. 18.99 (*0-7089-5601-7*, Linford) Ulverscroft.

Doherty, P. C. The Devil's Hunt. LC 97-43668. 256p. 1998. text 21.95 (*0-312-18084-5*) St Martin.

***Doherty, P. C.** Ghostly Murders. large type ed. 368p. 1999. 31.99 (*0-7089-4059-5*) Ulverscroft.

Doherty, P. C. Ghostly Murders: The Priest's Tale of Mystery & Murder as He Goes on Pilgrimage from London to Canterbury. LC 98-26239. 256p. 1998. text 21.95 (*0-312-19418-8*) St Martin.

***Doherty, P. C.** Horus Killing. LC 99-88192. 288p. 2000. text 22.95 (*0-312-24263-8*) St Martin.

Doherty, P. C. Murder Wears a Cowl: A Medieval Mystery Featuring Hugh Corbett. large type ed. 400p. 1996. 27.99 (*0-7089-3495-1*) Ulverscroft.

— The Prince of Darkness. (WWL Mystery Ser.). 1995. per. 3.99 (*0-373-26164-0*, 1-26164-3) Harlequin Bks.

— The Prince of Darkness. large type ed. 400p. 1996. 27.99 (*0-7089-3482-X*) Ulverscroft.

***Doherty, P. C.** Satan in St. Mary's. large type ed. 320p. 1999. pap. 18.99 (*0-7089-5594-0*, Linford) Ulverscroft.

Doherty, P. C. The Song of a Dark Angel: A Medieval Mystery Featuring Hugh Corbett. large type ed. (Large Print Ser.). 400p. 1996. 27.99 (*0-7089-3611-3*) Ulverscroft.

***Doherty, P. C.** Spy in Chancery. large type ed. 304p. 2000. pap. 18.99 (*0-7089-5653-X*, Linford) Ulverscroft.

Doherty, P. C. A Tapestry of Murders. 256p. 1996. text 21.95 (*0-312-14052-5*) St Martin.

— A Tapestry of Murders. large type ed. 416p. 1996. 27.99 (*0-7089-3446-3*) Ulverscroft.

— A Tournament of Murders: The Franklin's Tale of Mystery & Murder as He Goes on Pilgrimage from London to Canterbury. large type ed. (Ulverscroft Large Print Ser.). 384p. 1998. 29.99 (*0-7089-3938-4*) Ulverscroft.

Doherty, P. J., et al, eds. Biomaterial-Tissue Interfaces: Proceedings of the Ninth European Conference on Biomaterials, Chester, U. K., September 9-11, 1991. LC 92-49135. (Advances in Biomaterials Ser.: Vol. 10). xii,534p. 1992. 315.50 (*0-444-89065-3*) Elsevier.

Doherty, Patricia. Marge Piercy: An Annotated Bibliography, 25. LC 96-53091. (Bibliographies & Indexes in American Literature Ser.: 25). 240p. 1997. lib. bdg. 67.95 (*0-313-30194-8*, Greenwood Pr) Greenwood.

Doherty, Patrick A., ed. Partiality, Modality & Nonmonotonicity. (Studies in Logic, Language & Information). 312p. (C). 1996. 64.95 (*1-57586-031-7*) CSLI.

— Partiality, Modality & Nonmonotonicity. (Studies in Logic, Language & Information). 312p. (C). 1996. pap. 23.95 (*1-57586-030-9*) CSLI.

Doherty, Paul. Building Telescopes & Observatories An Observer's Guide. (Illus.). 224p. 1998. 29.50 (*0-7503-0552-5*) IOP Pub.

Doherty, Paul & Cassidy, John. Magnetic Magic. 68p. 1994. 11.95 (*1-878257-86-2*) Klutz.

Doherty, Paul, jt. auth. see Murphy, Pat.

Doherty, Peter, ed. Post-Abortion Syndrome: Its Wide Ramifications. 128p. 1995. pap. 15.00 (*1-85182-159-7*, Pub. by Four Cts Pr) Intl Spec Bk.

Doherty, Peter & Sutton, Agneta, eds. Man-Made Man: The Genome Project: The Faustian Dream Come True? LC 98-120476. 128p. 1997. pap. 25.00 (*1-85182-278-X*, Pub. by Four Cts Pr) Intl Spec Bk.

Doherty, Richard. Clear the Way! A History of the 38th (Irish) Brigade, 1941-47. (Illus.). 352p. 1993. 39.50 (*0-7165-2504-6*, Pub. by Irish Acad Pr) Intl Spec Bk.

— Clear the Way! A History of the 38th (Irish) Brigade, 1941-47. (Illus.). 352p. 1994. pap. 22.95 (*0-7165-2542-9*, Pub. by Irish Acad Pr) Intl Spec Bk.

***Doherty, Richard.** Irish Men & Women in the Second World War. 320p. 1999. 35.00 (*1-85182-441-3*, Pub. by Four Cts Pr) Intl Spec Bk.

Doherty, Richard. Noble Crusade: The History of Eighth Army, 1941-1945. 1999. write for info. (*1-885119-63-1*) Sarpedon.

Doherty, Richard. A Noble Crusade: The History of Eighth Army 1941-1945. 352p. 1997. 100.00 (*1-86227-045-7*, Pub. by Spellmnt Pubs) St Mut.

— Only the Enemy in Front: The Recce Corps at War, 1940-1946. 288p. 1997. (*1-871085-18-7*) Donovan Pub.

Doherty, Richard. The Williamite War in Ireland. LC 98-189320. (Illus.). 256p. 1998. pap. 24.95 (*1-85182-375-1*, Pub. by Four Cts Pr); boxed set 55.00 (*1-85182-374-3*, Pub. by Four Cts Pr) Intl Spec Bk.

***Doherty, Richard & Truesdale, David.** Irish Winners of the Victoria Cross. 192p. 1999. 37.50 (*1-85182-491-X*, Pub. by Four Cts Pr); pap. 17.50 (*1-85182-442-1*, Pub. by Four Cts Pr) Intl Spec Bk.

Doherty, Robert. Area 51. 384p. 1997. mass mkt. 5.99 (*0-440-22073-4*) Dell.

— Area 51: The Reply. 384p. 1998. mass mkt. 5.99 (*0-440-22378-4*) Dell.

— Area 51: The Mission. (Area 51 Ser.: Vol. 3). 416p. 1999. mass mkt. 5.99 (*0-440-22381-4*) Dell.

— Psychic Warrior. 352p. 2000. mass mkt. 5.99 (*0-440-23625-8*) Dell.

Doherty, Robert. The Rock. 384p. 1995. mass mkt. 6.50 (*0-440-22072-6*) Dell.

— Society & Power: Five New England Towns, 1800-1860. LC 77-73477. 128p. 1977. 20.00 (*0-87023-242-8*) U of Mass Pr.

***Doherty, Robert.** Sphinx: A Novel. 384p. 2000. mass mkt. 5.99 (*0-440-23494-8*) Dell.

Doherty, Robert E. Industrial & Labor Relations Terms. 5th ed. (ILR Bulletin Ser.: No. 44). 40p. 1989. pap. text 5.95 (*0-87546-152-2*, ILR Press) Cornell U Pr.

Doherty, Robert J., ed. The Complete Photographic Work of Jacob A. Riis. (Illus.). 38p. 1987. 85.00 (*0-8161-1732-2*, Hall Reference) Macmillan.

Doherty, Robert W. The Foursome. 117p. mass mkt. 4.99 (*1-55197-214-X*) Picasso Publ.

Doherty, Sara & Schlemm, Betty L. Painting Color. (Best of Watercolor Ser.). (Illus.). 144p. 1998. 24.99 (*1-56496-349-7*, Quarry Bks) Rockport Pubs.

Doherty, Sara M., jt. auth. see Schlemm, Betty L.

Doherty, Stephen, jt. auth. see Viders, Sue.

Doherty, Sue. Kinergetics: Dancing with Your Baby. LC 93-19657. 1993. pap. 12.00 (*0-9623032-3-2*) Barricade Bks.

Doherty, Thomas. Pre-Code Hollywood: Sex, Immorality & Insurrection in American Cinema, 1930-1934. LC 99-11956. 416p. 1999. 49.50 (*0-231-11094-4*); pap. 19.50 (*0-231-11095-2*) Col U Pr.

— Projections of War: Hollywood, American Culture, & World War II. 1994. pap. 19.00 (*0-231-08245-2*) Col U Pr.

— Projections of War: Hollywood & American Culture. LC 99-461853. 1999. pap. 17.00 (*0-231-11635-7*) Col U Pr.

Doherty, Victor W. Talk Too Much? Who, Me? (Illus.). 71p. (Orig.). 1997. pap. 7.95 (*0-9656090-0-6*) Pickled Pepper.

Doherty, W. T., jt. auth. see Zaba, Joseph.

Doherty, William E. Tony's World. Champlin, Charles, ed. LC 98-36879. (Illus.). 288p. 1999. 29.95 (*1-56474-290-3*) Fithian Pr.

Doherty, William J. The Intentional Family: Simple Rituals to Strengthen Family Ties, 1. LC 96-40283. 240p. 1999. pap. 12.50 (*0-380-73205-X*, Avon Bks) Morrow Avon.

— Soul Searching: Why Psychotherapy Must Promote Moral Responsibility. 224p. 1996. pap. 12.00 (*0-465-00945-X*, Pub. by Basic) HarpC.

***Doherty, William J.** Take Back Your Kids: Confident Parenting in Turbulent Times. LC 99-67496. 160p. 2000. pap. 12.95 (*1-893732-07-X*) SORIN BKS.

Doherty, William J., et al, eds. Family Medicine: The Maturing of a Discipline. LC 86-29501. (Marriage & Family Review Ser.: Vol. 10, Nos. 3-4). 236p. 1987. text 49.95 (*0-86656-625-2*) Haworth Pr.

Doherty, William J. & Baird, Macaran A. Family Therapy & Family Medicine: Toward the Primary Care of Families. LC 82-3135. (Family Therapy Ser.). 302p. 1983. lib. bdg. 45.00 (*0-89862-041-4*) Guilford Pubns.

Doherty, William J. & Campbell, Thomas L. Families & Health. (Family Studies Text Ser.: Vol. 10). 160p. (C). 1988. text 42.00 (*0-8039-2992-7*); pap. text 18.95 (*0-8039-2993-5*) Sage.

Doherty, William T. West Virginia: Our Land - Our People. Buckalew, Marshall, ed. (Illus.). 320p. (J). (gr. 8). 1990. 25.00 (*0-914498-07-X*); teacher ed., ring bd. 25.00 (*0-914498-10-X*) WV Hist Ed Found.

— West Virginia Studies, Our Heritage. Buckalew, Marshall, ed. (Illus.). 306p. (gr. 8). 1984. 20.00 (*0-914498-04-5*); teacher ed. 10.00 (*0-914498-06-1*) WV Hist Ed Found.

— West Virginia University. LC 82-62028. 384p. 1982. 15.95 (*0-937058-16-5*) West Va U Pr.

Doherty, William T. & Conley, Phil. West Virginia History. (Illus.). 494p. (J). (gr. 8). 1974. 10.25 (*0-914498-00-2*) WV Hist Ed Found.

Dohla, Johann C. Hessian Diary of the American Revolution. LC 89-25029. (C). 1993. pap. 14.95 (*0-8061-2530-6*) U of Okla Pr.

Dohlen, Richard F. Von, see Von Dohlen, Richard F.

Dohler, K. D. & Pawlikowski, M. Progress in Neuropeptide Research. (Congress Reports: No. 3). 185p. 1989. 52.00 (*0-8176-2268-3*) Birkhauser.

Dohlman, Ebba. National Welfare & Economic Interdependence: The Case of Sweden's Foreign Trade Policy. (Illus.). 264p. 1989. text 65.00 (*0-19-827558-7*) OUP.

Dohm, Christian K. Von, see Von Dohm, Christian K.

Dohme, jt. auth. see Merck, Sharp.

Dohmen, Dieter. Neuordnung der Studienfinanzierung: Eine Kritische Bestandsaufnahme des Heutigen Systems & der Vorliegenden Reformvorschlage. (GER., Illus.). 239p. 1996. 51.95 (*3-631-30903-1*) P Lang Pubng.

Dohms, Jean E. Down Our Road: Nature Musings from the Northwoods. LC 95-94245. (Illus.). 144p. (Orig.). 1995. pap. 12.95 (*0-9645665-0-8*) Boulder Knob Bks.

— Northwood Rambles: Seasons of Wonder. LC 97-73814. (Illus.). 142p. (Orig.). 1997. pap. 12.95 (*0-9645665-1-6*) Boulder Knob Bks.

Dohn, Richard, jt. auth. see Stacy, Darryl.

***Dohnanyi, Erno.** Complete Rhapsodies & Other Works for Solo Piano. 1999. pap. text 16.95 (*0-486-40613-0*) Dover.

Dohney, Catherine, ed. see Black, Jeanne & Forker, Vickie.

Dohnke, K., et al, eds. Niederdeutsch im Nationalsozialismus. (GER.). 552p. 1994. write for info. (*3-487-09809-1*) G Olms Pubs.

Dohr, Donald A. El Camino Hacia el Amor. rev. ed. LC 81-71328. Orig. Title: Beginning Your Marriage. 128p. 1982. pap. 4.95 (*0-915388-14-6*, 152) ACTA Pubns.

***Dohree, Georgina, ed.** French Influence for Clarinet. 80p. 2000. pap. 14.95 (*0-7866-5811-8*, 99307) Mel Bay.

Dohren, Hans Von, see Kleinkauf, Horst & Von Dohren, Hans, eds.

Dohrenwend, Barbara S. & Dohrenwend, Bruce P., eds. Stressful Life Events & Their Contexts. (Monographs in Psychosocial Epidemiology). 287p. 1984. pap. text 15.00 (*0-8135-1004-X*) Rutgers U Pr.

Dohrenwend, Barbara S., jt. auth. see Dohrenwend, Bruce P.

Dohrenwend, Barbara S., jt. ed. see Ricks, David F.

Dohrenwend, Bruce P. Mental Illness in the United States: Epidemiological Estimates. LC 79-18725. 161p. 1980. 45.00 (*0-275-90471-7*, C0471, Praeger Pubs) Greenwood.

Dohrenwend, Bruce P., ed. Adversity, Stress & Psychopathology. (Illus.). 584p. 1998. text 89.50 (*0-19-512192-9*) OUP.

Dohrenwend, Bruce P. & Dohrenwend, Barbara S. Social Status & Psychological Disorder: A Causal Inquiry. LC 72-88310. (Personality Processes Ser.). 223p. (C). reprint ed. 69.20 (*0-8357-9978-6*, 201257000081) Bks Demand.

Dohrenwend, Bruce P., jt. ed. see Dohrenwend, Barbara S.

Dohrer, Timothy A., III & Evenwel, Gerard J. Realms of the Unknown Player's Manual. 24p. 1991. pap. 8.00 (*0-9630833-1-7*) Walnut Grp.

— Realms of the Unknown Realm Controller's Manual. 82p. 1991. pap. 15.00 (*0-9630833-0-9*) Walnut Grp.

Dohrman, H. T. California Cult: The Story of Mankind United. LC 76-42724. reprint ed. 29.50 (*0-404-60059-X*) AMS Pr.

Dohrman, Vicki S. Treating Memory Impairments: A Memory Book & Other Strategies. 207p. 1994. pap. text 49.00 (*0-7616-3041-4*) Commun Skill.

Dohrmann, Bernhard. Diamond Heart: My Father's Stories: an Adult Fairy Tale. LC 98-114519. 1997. write for info. (*1-890465-40-2*) ST Prodns.

Dohrmann, J., jt. auth. see Claridge, R. F.

Dohrmann, P., et al. Surgical Efficiency & Economy: Proceedings of the 3rd World-Conference. 1997. pap. 99.00 (*0-86577-733-0*) Thieme Med Pubs.

Dohrn, Lisa Uyehara. Hawaii: Heaven on Earth. LC 98-70099. 1998. pap. 19.95 (*0-9662571-0-3*) Ohara Pubns.

Dohrn-van Rossum, Gerhard. History of the Hour: Clocks & Modern Temporal Orders. LC 95-47660. 451p. (C). 1996. 29.95 (*0-226-15510-2*) U Ch Pr.

Dohrs, Fred E. & Sommers, Lawrence M. World Regional Geography: A Problem Approach. LC 76-3748. 700p. reprint ed. pap. 200.00 (*0-608-12021-9*, 202234100030) Bks Demand.

Doi & Kawakatsu. Computational Methods in Polymer Science: Modern Methods in Polymer Research & Technology. 350p. 1999. write for info. (*0-12-219770-4*) Acad Pr.

Doi, A. R. Hadith: An Introduction. 155p. (J). 1980. pap. 8.50 (*1-56744-031-2*) Kazi Pubns.

— Non-Muslims under Shari'ah. 1981. 6.50 (*1-56744-170-X*) Kazi Pubns.

— Quran, an Introduction. 1992. pap. 8.50 (*0-933511-25-6*) Kazi Pubns.

Doi, E., jt. auth. see Nishinari, K.

Doi, Joyce T., jt. auth. see Oae, Shigeru.

Doi, Kim, jt. auth. see West, Beverly.

Doi, Kunio, et al, eds. Recent Developments in Digital Imaging: Proceedings of the AAPM 1984 Summer School Held at the University of Notre Dame, South Bend, Indiana, July 22-27, 1984. (American Association of Physicists in Medicine Symposium Ser.: No. 12). 580p. 1985. 70.00 (*0-88318-463-X*, Pub. by Am Inst Physics) Med Physics Pub.

Doi, Kunio, jt. auth. see International Workshop on Computer-Aided Scheduling of Public Transport Staff.

Doi, Kunmio. Digital Mammography '96: Proceedings of the 3rd International Workshop on Digital Mammography, Chicago, 9-12 June 1996. LC 96-44173. (International Congress Ser.: Vol. 1119). 494p. 1996. 231.25 (*0-444-82431-6*) Elsevier.

Doi, M. Introduction to Polymer Physics. See, H., tr. (Illus.). 130p. 1996. reprint ed. pap. text 26.00 (*0-19-851789-0*) OUP.

Doi, M. & Edwards, S. F. The Theory of Polymer Dynamics. (International Series of Monographs on Physics). (Illus.). 408p. 1988. pap. text 55.00 (*0-19-852033-6*) OUP.

Doi, Takeo. The Anatomy of Dependence. Shaw, ed. Bester, John, tr. LC 72-76297. 180p. 1982. pap. 10.00 (*0-87011-494-8*) Kodansha.

— The Anatomy of Self: The Individual vs. Society. LC 88-80300. 168p. 1988. pap. 12.50 (*0-87011-902-8*) Kodansha.

— The Psychological World of Natsume Soseki. Tyler, William J., tr. & intro. by. (East Asian Monographs: No. 68). 250p. 1976. text 20.00 (*0-674-72116-0*) HUP.

Doi, Teruo & Shattuck, Warren L., eds. Patent & Know-How Licensing in Japan & the United States. LC 76-7785. (Asian Law Ser.: No. 5). 444p. 1977. 40.00 (*0-295-95513-9*) U of Wash Pr.

Doi, Tsugiyoshi. Momoyama Decorative Painting. LC 76-44338. (Heibonsha Survey of Japanese Art Ser.: Vol. 14). (Illus.). 168p. 1976. 20.00 (*0-8348-1024-7*) Weatherhill.

Doi, Y. Microbial Polyesters. 156p. 1990. 74.95 (*0-471-18732-1*, Wiley-VCH) Wiley.

Doi, Yoshiharu. Microbial Polyesters. LC 90-42419. 156p. 1990. 39.50 (*0-89573-746-9*, Wiley-VCH) Wiley.

Doi, Yoshiharu & Fukuda, Kazuhiko, eds. Biodegradable Plastics & Polymers: Proceedings of the Third International Scientific Workshop on Biodegradable Plastics & Polymers, Osaka, Japan, November 9-11, 1993. LC 94-20903. (Studies in Polymer Science: Vol. 12). (Illus.). 646p. 1994. 316.50 (*0-444-81708-5*) Elsevier.

***Doicu, Adrian.** Acoustic & Electromagnetic Scattering Analysis Using Discrete Sources. 280p. 2000. 79.95 (*0-12-219740-2*) Acad Pr.

Doidge, Spencer. Fingerpicking Ellington. (Illus.). 64p. pap. 14.95 (*0-8256-2412-6*, AM38464) Music Sales.

— Fingerpicking Joplin. 1984. pap. 14.95 (*0-8256-2310-3*, AM34802) Music Sales.

***Doig, Alan & Theobald, Robin, eds.** Corruption & Democratisation. LC 99-40344. 176p. 2000. 49.50 (*0-7146-4996-1*, Pub. by F Cass Pubs); pap. 24.50 (*0-7146-8057-5*, Pub. by F Cass Pubs) Intl Spec Bk.

Doig, Alison, tr. see Berg, Claude.

Doig, Alison G., jt. auth. see Kendall, Maurice.

Doig, Alistair. Military Metalurgy. (Illus.). 152p. 1998. 40.00 (*1-86125-061-4*, Pub. by Inst Materials) Ashgate Pub Co.

Doig, Allan. The Architectural Drawings Collection of King's College, Cambridge. (Illus.). 160p. 1980. 50.00 (*0-86127-501-2*) Eastview.

Doig, Brian, jt. auth. see Lokan, Jan.

Doig, Ivan. Bucking the Sun. 1997. pap. 12.98 (*0-671-04418-4*) PB.

Doig, Ivan. Bucking the Sun. 1997. per. 13.00 (*0-684-83149-X*, Scribner Pap Fic) S&S Trade Pap.

— Bucking the Sun. 412p. 1996. 23.00 (*0-684-81171-5*) Simon & Schuster.

— Bucking the Sun. large type ed. LC 96-20867. (Americana Series). 752p. 1996. lib. bdg. 23.95 (*0-7862-0814-7*) Thorndike Pr.

— Bucking the Sun: A Novel. 412p. 1998. text 23.00 (*0-7881-5700-0*) DIANE Pub.

— Dancing at the Rascal Fair. LC 96-23018. 416p. 1996. per. 13.00 (*0-684-83105-8*) S&S Trade.

— English Creek. 1992. 24.25 (*0-8446-6608-4*) Peter Smith.

— English Creek. (American Fiction Ser.). 352p. 1985. pap. 12.95 (*0-14-008442-8*, Penguin Bks) Viking Penguin.

— Heart Earth: A Memoir. 176p. 1994. reprint ed. pap. 11.95 (*0-14-023508-6*, Penguin Bks) Viking Penguin.

***Doig, Ivan.** Mountain Time. LC 99-14324. 320p. 1999. 24.50 (*0-684-83295-X*) Scribner.

— Mountain Time. large type ed. LC 99-45075. (Thorndike Americana Ser.). 1999. 28.95 (*0-7862-2216-6*) Thorndike Pr.

— Mountain Time: A Novel. 2000. pap. 13.00 (*0-684-86569-6*) Scribner.

Doig, Ivan. Ride with Me, Mariah Montana. 384p. 1990. text 18.95 (*0-689-12019-2*) Atheneum Yung Read.

— Ride with Me, Mariah Montana. (Contemporay American Fiction Ser.). 336p. 1991. reprint ed. pap. 12.95 (*0-14-015607-0*, Penguin Bks) Viking Penguin.

— The Sea Runners. 1992. 24.25 (*0-8446-6538-X*) Peter Smith.

— The Sea Runners. 288p. 1983. pap. 12.95 (*0-14-006780-9*, Penguin Bks) Viking Penguin.

— This House of Sky: Landscapes of a Western Mind. LC 79-18783. 336p. 1980. pap. 10.00 (*0-15-689982-5*, Harvest Bks) Harcourt.

— Winter Brothers: A Season at the Edge of America. LC 80-7933. (Illus.). 264p. 1982. pap. 10.00 (*0-15-697215-8*, Harvest Bks) Harcourt.

Doig, Ivan & Walker, Wendy. Whatcom Places. Keller, Robert H., ed. LC 97-190159. (Illus.). 96p. 1997. pap. 25.00 (*0-9657053-0-7*) Whatcom Land.

— Whatcom Places. Keller, Robert H., ed. (Illus.). 96p. 1997. 40.00 (*0-9657053-1-5*) Whatcom Land.

Doig, James C. In Defense of Cognitive Realism: Cutting the Cartesian Knot. LC 87-8327. 306p. (Orig.). (C). 1987. pap. text 27.00 (*0-8191-6359-7*); lib. bdg. 46.00 (*0-8191-6358-9*) U Pr of Amer.

Doig, Jameson, ed. Issues & Realities in Corrections: A Symposium. 1982. pap. 15.00 (*0-918592-58-5*) Pol Studies.

***Doig, Jameson W.** Empire on the Hudson: Entrepreneurial Vision & Political Power at the Port of New York Authority. LC 00-31609. (History of Urban Life Ser.). 2000. write for info. (*0-231-07677-0*) Col U Pr.

— Empire on the Hudson: Political Power & Progress at the Port of New York Authority. 2001. 49.50 (*0-231-07676-2*) Col U Pr.

Doig, Jameson W. & Hargrove, Erwin C., eds. Leadership & Innovation: A Biographical Perspective on Entrepreneurs in Government. LC 87-4155. 480p. 1987. text 55.00 (*0-8018-3442-2*) Johns Hopkins.

— Leadership & Innovation: Entrepreneurs in Government. LC 89-24685. 300p. reprint ed. pap. 93.00 (*0-608-08805-6*, 206944400004) Bks Demand.

Doig, Jameson W., jt. auth. see Danielson, Michael N.

Doig, Kenneth F. New Testament Chronology. LC 91-45430. 464p. 1992. pap. text 89.95 (*0-7734-9920-2*) E Mellen.

Doig, Melissa W., ed. see Swisher, Karen Gayton & Benally, AnCita.

Doig, P., ed. see Institute of Physics, Great Britain, Electron Micr.

Doignon, J. P. & Falmagne, Jean-Claude, eds. Mathematical Psychology: Current Developments. (Recent Research in Psychology Ser.). ix, 453p. 1991. 96.95 (*0-387-97665-5*) Spr-Verlag.

Doignon, Jean-Paul & Falmagne, Jean-Claude. Knowledge Spaces. LC 98-29442. (Illus.). 300p. 1998. pap. 59.95 (*3-540-64501-2*) Spr-Verlag.

***Doijad, P. S.** Transfer of Plant Protection Technology among Dryland Farmers. x, 117p. 1998. 13.00 (*81-7099-698-8*, Pub. by Mittal Pubns) Nataraj Bks.

***Doijode, S. D., ed.** Seed Storage of Horticultural Crops. LC 00-20623. 270p. (C). 2000. pap. text 49.95 (*1-56022-901-2*) Haworth Pr.

— Seed Storage of Horticultural Crops. LC 00-20623. 270p. 2000. 89.95 (*1-56022-883-0*, Food Products) Haworth Pr.

Doillon, Charles, jt. auth. see Silver, Frederik.

Doinas, Stefan, et al. Alibi & Other Poems. 32p. 1975. pap. 9.95 (*0-85646-021-4*, Pub. by Anvil Press) Dufour.

***Doinet, Mymi, et al.** The Dolphin. LC 00-22080. (My Animal Library). (J). 2000. 6.95 (*0-7892-0661-7*, Abbeville Kids) Abbeville Pr.

— The Elephant. LC 00-22081. (My Animal Library). (J). 2000. 6.95 (*0-7892-0662-5*, Abbeville Kids) Abbeville Pr.

***Doiron, Devra.** Well Behaved Children: 100 Tips from Parents Who Have Them. LC 99-91936. 108p. 2000. pap. 9.95 (*0-9678615-0-0*) Seaview Pr HI.

Doiron, Julie, jt. auth. see Roy, Ian.

Doiron, Lynn, ed. see Leenbouts, Keith J.

Doiron, Ray & Davies, Judy. Partners in Learning: Students, Teachers, & the School Library. LC 97-30591. (Illus.). 182p. 1998. text 28.00 (*1-56308-552-6*) Libs Unl.

Dois, Michael W. Majnun: The Madman in Medieval Islamic Society. 514p. 1996. 125.00 (*0-614-21552-8*, 751) Kazi Pubns.

Dois, Michael W., tr. see Ridwan, Ibn.

Doise, Willem & Clemence, Alain. The Quantitative Analysis of Social Represenations. 176p. 1994. pap. text 56.00 (*0-13-302142-4*) P-H.

Doise, Willem, et al. The Quantitiative Analysis of Social Representations. Kabeko, Julian, tr. (European Monographs in Social Psychology Ser.). 170p. 1996. pap. text 27.95 (*0-7450-1348-1*) Taylor & Francis.

Doise, Willem, jt. auth. see Moscovici, Serge.

Doisneau & Sage. The Boy & the Dove. pap. 6.95 (*0-89480-027-2*) Workman Pub.

Doisneau, Robert, photos by. Three Seconds of Eternity. (Illus.). 144p. 1997. pap. 29.95 (*3-8238-2124-5*) te Neues.

Doisneau, Sage. The Boy & the Dove. 12.95 (*0-89480-030-2*) Workman Pub.

***Dojcinovic, Uros.** Chamber Music for Guitar. 104p. 1999. spiral bd. 19.95 incl. audio compact disk (*0-7866-2792-1*, 96592BCD) Mel Bay.

Dojny, Brooke. The Best of New Orleans. LC 93-43039. (Illus.). 96p. 1994. 14.95 (*0-00-255477-1*) Collins SF.

— Full of Beans: Seventy-five Exciting, Tasty Recipes. LC 95-37126. 144p. 1996. pap. 12.50 (*0-06-095095-1*, Perennial) HarperTrade.

— The New England Cookbook: 350 Recipes from Town & Country, Land & Sea, Hearth & Home. LC 99-14393. (Illus.). 512p. 1999. pap. 18.95 (*1-55832-139-X*, Pub. by Harvard Common Pr) Natl Bk Netwk.

***Dojny, Brooke.** The New England Cookbook: 350 Recipes from Town & Country, Land & Sea, Hearth & Home. LC 99-14393. (Illus.). 512p. 1999. text 29.95 (*1-55832-138-1*, Pub. by Harvard Common Pr) Natl Bk Netwk.

Doka, Kenneth, jt. auth. see Lavin, Claire.

Doka, Kenneth A., ed. see Corr, Charles, et al.

Doka, Kenneth J. AIDS, Fear & Society: Challenging the Dreaded Disease. LC 96-44899. (Death Education, Aging & Health Care Ser.). 1997. 69.95 (*1-56032-248-9*) Hemisp Pub.

— AIDS, Fear & Society: Challenging the Dreaded Disease. LC 96-44899. (Death Education, Aging & Health Care Ser.). 1997. pap. 22.95 (*1-56032-681-6*) Taylor & Francis.

— Disenfranchised Grief. 347p. 1989. 46.95 (*0-669-17081-X*) Lxngtn Bks.

— Disenfranchised Grief: Recognizing & Treating Hidden Sorrow. LC 98-14145. 1998. pap. write for info. (*0-7879-4376-2*) Jossey-Bass.

***Doka, Kenneth J.** Grief-Beyond Gender. LC 99-47479. 180p. 1999. pap. text 22.95 (*0-87630-995-3*) Brunner-Mazel.

— Living with Grief: At Work, at School, at Worship. 320p. 1999. pap. text 18.95 (*1-58391-006-9*) Brunner-Mazel.

Doka, Kenneth J. Living with Grief: Who We Are, How We Grieve. LC 98-152429. 1998. pap. text 16.95 (*0-87630-898-1*) Brunner-Mazel.

— Living with Grief When Illness Is Prolonged. LC 97-6211. 1997. write for info. (*1-56032-703-0*) Hemisp Pub.

— Living with Life-Threatening Illness: A Guide for Patients, Their Families & Caregivers. LC 97-35541. 294p. 1998. pap. 26.95 (*0-7879-4048-8*) Jossey-Bass.

Doka, Kenneth J., ed. Children Mourning, Mourning Children. LC 95-12114. 180p. 1995. pap. 19.95 (*1-56032-447-3*) Taylor & Francis.

— Living with Grief: After Sudden Loss: Suicide, Homicide, Accident, Heart Attack, Stroke. 261p. 1996. pap. text 19.95 (*1-56032-578-X*) Taylor & Francis.

Doka, Kenneth J. & Morgan, John D., eds. Death & Spirituality. LC 92-31413. (Death, Value & Meaning Ser.). 416p. 1993. text 44.95 (*0-89503-106-X*) Baywood Pub.

Dokalskaite, Ona. Ona Dokalskaite: The Art of Ona Dokalskaite-Paskeviciene. LC 92-72672. (Illus.). 170p. 1993. 35.00 (*0-9617756-5-3*) Galerija.

Doke, Clement M. Lamba Folklore. LC 28-18358. (American Folklore Society Memoirs Ser.: Vol. 20). 1969. reprint ed. 70.00 (*0-527-01072-3*) Periodicals Srv.

Doke, E. Reed & Hardgrave, Bill C. An Introduction to Object COBOL. LC 97-13432. 208p. 1997. pap. 31.95 (*0-471-18346-6*) Wiley.

— Java for the COBOL Programmer. LC 99-24122. (Advances in Object Technology Ser.: No. 22). 360p. (C). 1999. pap. 39.95 (*0-521-65892-6*) Cambridge U Pr.

***Doke, E. Reed & Hardgrave, Bill C.** Java for the Visual Basic Programmer. (Illus.). 450p. 2000. pap. Price not set. (*0-521-79547-8*) Cambridge U Pr.

Doke E., Reed E. Getting Started with Micro Focus Personal COBOLT for Windows. 80p. 1997. pap. 20.95 (*0-471-18490-X*) Wiley.

Dokecki, Paul R. The Tragi-Comic Professional: Basic Considerations for Ethical Reflective-Generative Practice. LC 96-9981. 180p. (C). 1996. text 29.95 (*0-8207-0269-2*); pap. text 18.95 (*0-8207-0270-6*) Duquesne.

Dokey, Cameron. Carrie: Heart of Courage. (Hearts & Dreams Ser.). 224p. 1998. mass mkt. 3.99 (*0-380-78569-2*, Avon Bks) Morrow Avon.

— Charlotte: Heart of Hope. (Hearts & Dreams Ser.: No. 2). 192p. (YA). (gr. 5 up). 1997. mass mkt. 3.99 (*0-380-78566-8*, Avon Bks) Morrow Avon.

***Dokey, Cameron.** The Crimson Spell. (Charmed Ser.: No. 3). 192p. (YA). (gr. 7 up). 2000. per. 4.99 (*0-671-04164-9*, Pocket Pulse) PB.

Dokey, Cameron. Dance of Death. (Fear Street Sagas). Orig. Title: Les Simulachres & Historiees Faces Des La Mort. 1997. 9.09 (*0-606-12696-1*, Pub. by Turtleback) Demco.

***Dokey, Cameron.** Enchanted Hearts: Lost & Found, Vol. 3. (Enchanted Hearts Ser.: No. 3). 208p. (YA). (gr. 7 up). 1999. mass mkt. 4.50 (*0-380-80083-7*, Avon Bks) Morrow Avon.

— Here Be Monsters. (Buffy the Vampire Slayer Ser.: Vol. 16). 192p. (YA). (gr. 7 up). 2000. per. 5.99 (*0-671-03921-0*, Pocket Pulse) PB.

Dokey, Cameron. Hindenburg, 1937. 1999. per. 4.99 (*0-671-03601-7*) PB.

***Dokey, Cameron.** Hindenburg, 1937. (Illus.). (J). 1999. 10.34 (*0-606-18373-6*) Turtleback.

Dokey, Cameron. Katherine: Heart of Freedom. (Hearts & Dreams Ser.: Vol. 1). 192p. (YA). (gr. 5 up). 1997. mass mkt. 3.99 (*0-380-78565-X*, Avon Bks) Morrow Avon.

***Dokey, Cameron.** Lost & Found. (Enchanted Hearts Ser.). (Illus.). (J). 1999. 9.85 (*0-606-17965-8*) Turtleback.

Dokey, Cameron. Love Me, Love Me Not. 1995. mass mkt. 3.99 (*0-7860-4983-9*, Pinncle Kensgtn) Kensgtn Pub Corp.

— Stephanie: Heart of Gold. (Hearts & Dreams Ser.). 224p. 1998. mass mkt. 3.99 (*0-380-78567-6*, Avon Bks) Morrow Avon.

— Storm over Boston. (J). 1997. write for info. (*0-614-29167-4*, Avon Bks) Morrow Avon.

— Summer of Smoke. (J). 1997. write for info. (*0-614-29168-2*, Avon Bks) Morrow Avon.

***Dokey, Cameron.** Washington Avalanche, 1910. 256p. (J). 2000. per. 4.99 (*0-671-03604-1*, Archway) PB.

Dokey, Cameron. Winning Is Everything. (Full House Stephanie Ser.). (J). (gr. 4-6). 1999. pap. 3.99 (*0-671-01728-4*) PB.

Dokey, Cameron, et al. Be Mine: A Romantic Quartet of Special Valentines to Capture Your Heart. 144p. (gr. 8 up). 1997. mass mkt. 3.99 (*0-380-78704-0*, Avon Bks) Morrow Avon.

— New Year, New Love. 176p. (Orig.). (YA). 1996. mass mkt. 3.99 (*0-380-78663-X*, Avon Bks) Morrow Avon.

Dokey, Richard. The Funeral: A Play. (Review Ser.: No. 3). 80p. (Orig.). 1982. pap. 3.00 (*0-936044-03-9*) Pikestaff Pr.

— The Hollow Man. 243p. Date not set. 16.95 (*0-9628923-4-3*) Delta-West.

Dokic, Jerome, ed. European Review of Philosophy Vol. 2: Cognitive Dynamics, Vol. 2. (European Review of Philosophy Ser.). 186p. (C). 1997. 55.00 (*1-57586-073-2*); pap. 19.95 (*1-57586-072-4*) CSLI.

Dokiya, M., jt. ed. see Singhal, S. C.

Dokken, David, jt. ed. see Asrar, Ghassem.

Dokken, Kay. Will a Clownfish Make You Giggle? Answers to Some Very Fishy Questions. LC 95-34727. (Illus.). 32p. (J). (ps-2). 1995. boxed set 14.95 (*1-881652-07-6*) Aqua Quest.

Dokky, O. Daigaku. Directions in Functional Linguistics. Kamio, Akio, ed. LC 97-26691. (Studies in Language Companion Ser.: Vol. 36). (CHI & JPN.). xiii, 259p. 1997. lib. bdg. 74.00 (*1-55619-847-7*) J Benjamins Pubng Co.

Dokmaisot. A Secret Past. Strehlow, Ted, tr. from THA. (Southeast Asia Program Ser.: No. 9). 72p. 1992. pap. text 12.00 (*0-87727-126-7*) Cornell SE Asia.

Dokmecian, Adrian, tr. see Galeano Dominguez, Edgar.

Dokos, Thanos P. Negotiations for a CTBT, 1958-1994: Analysis & Evaluation of American Policy. LC 95-16819. 298p. (C). 1995. 44.50 (*0-8191-9985-0*) U Pr of Amer.

Dokshitzer, Y., jt. ed. see Cifarelli, L.

Doksum, K. A., jt. auth. see Bickel, P. J.

Doksum, Kjell A., jt. auth. see Bickel, P. J.

Dokter, Ditty. Arts Therapists Refugees & Migrants: Reaching Across Borders. LC 98-198529. 1998. pap. text 27.95 (*1-85302-550-X*) Taylor & Francis.

Dokter, Ditty, ed. Arts Therapies & Eating Disorders. 250p. 1995. pap. 29.95 (*1-85302-256-X*) Taylor & Francis.

Dokulil, jt. auth. see Dihy.

Dokulil, M., et al, eds. Shallow Lakes: Contributions to Their Limnology. (Developments in Hydrobiology Ser.: No. 3). 218p. 1981. lib. bdg. 59.50 (*0-686-28842-4*) Kluwer Academic.

***Dolainski, Stephen.** Arizona et Grand Canyon. 2nd ed. (Travel Guide (French Guides) Ser.). (FRE.). 1998. pap. text 23.95 (*2-89464-076-5*) Ulysses Travel.

Dolainski, Stephen. Hidden Arizona. 2nd rev. ed. (Hidden Travel Ser.). (Illus.). 360p. 1999. pap. 14.95 (*1-56975-173-0*) Ulysses Pr.

***Dolainski, Stephen.** Romantic Days & Nights in Los Angeles: Romantic Diversions in & Around the City. 2nd ed. LC 99-35753. (Illus.). 288p. 1999. pap. text 15.95 (*0-7627-0540-X*) Globe Pequot.

Dolainski, Steve. Disneyland & Beyond: Orlando Family Attractions. 4th rev. ed. (Illus.). 336p. 1998. pap. 12.95 (*1-56975-126-9*) Ulysses Pr.

Dolamore, Anne. A Buyer's Guide to Olive Oil. (Illus.). 128p. 1999. text 17.00 (*0-7881-6133-4*) DIANE Pub.

***Dolamore, Anne.** The Essential Olive Oil Companion. 160p. 1999. pap. 15.95 (*1-56656-334-8*) Interlink Pr.

Dolamore, James, ed. Making Connections: Essays in French Culture & Society in Honour of Philip Thody. 283p. 1999. 44.95 (*3-906760-69-3*, Pub. by P Lang) P Lang Pubng.

— Making Connections: Essays in French Culture & Society in Honour of Philip Thody. (Illus.). 283p. 1998. pap. text 44.95 (*0-8204-4206-2*) P Lang Pubng.

Dolan. Accident & Emergency Care. 1999. pap. text 25.00 (*0-7020-2239-X*, W B Saunders Co) Harcrt Hlth Sci Grp.

— Commercial Activities. 825p. 1991. 125.00 (*0-316-18903-0*) Little.

Dolan. Early Modern Englishwoman Part 2, Vol.13. 47.95 (*1-84014-226-X*) Ashgate Pub Co.

Dolan. Economic & Public Policy. 4th ed. Date not set. pap. text, teacher ed. write for info. (*0-314-52679-X*) West Pub.

— Economic Public Policy. 5th ed. Date not set. pap. text, teacher ed. write for info. (*0-314-06408-7*) West Pub.

— Economics. 7th ed. (C). 1994. pap. text 31.00 (*0-03-098775-X*, Pub. by Harcourt Coll Pubs) Harcourt.

— Global Organizational Behavior. (SWC-General Business Ser.). 2000. pap. 54.00 (*0-324-02052-X*) Thomson Learn.

— In Sports, Money Talks. 1996. write for info. (*0-8050-5275-5*) H Holt & Co.

***Dolan.** Managing New Product Development Process. 2nd ed. (C). 2000. pap. text. write for info. (*0-201-55569-7*) Addison-Wesley.

Dolan. Mathematical Activities for Elementary School Teachers, a Problem Solving Approach, to Accompany Long & Detemple's Mathematical Reasoning for Elementary Teachers. 3rd ed. 352p. (C). 1996. pap. text 26.00 (*0-201-85754-5*) Addison-Wesley.

— Nursing in Society. 15th ed. (Illus.). 417p. 1983. pap. text 45.00 (*0-7216-3135-5*, W B Saunders Co) Harcrt Hlth Sci Grp.

— Strategic Marketing Management. 400p. 1996. pap. 23.96 (*0-07-103361-0*) McGraw.

Dolan, A. G., jt. auth. see Balman, F. E.

Dolan, A. T. Imagery Treatment of Phobias, Anxiety States, & Other Symptom Complexes. LC 97-86462. 1997. pap. 40.00 (*0-913412-90-2*) Brandon Hse.

Dolan, Alan & Aldous, Joan M. Networks & Algorithms: An Introductory Approach. 556p. 1994. pap. 64.95 (*0-471-93993-5*) Wiley.

Dolan, Albert H. The Little Flower's Mother. 2nd ed. (Illus.). 96p. 1994. pap. 6.95 (*1-885553-36-6*) Firefly Press.

— Roses Fall Where Rivers Meet: A Description & Explanation of the Shower of Roses of the Little Flower. 176p. 1995. pap. 9.95 (*1-887548-03-3*) St Michael NC.

Dolan, Anthony J. The Kelsey Outrage: An American Story. LC 92-90639. 750p. 1992. write for info. (*0-9633239-0-3*) A J Dolan.

***Dolan, Brian.** Exploring European Frontiers: British Travellers in the Age of Enlightenment. LC 99-51808. 1999. text 59.95 (*0-312-23051-6*) St Martin.

Dolan, Bridget & Gitzinger, Inez, eds. Why Women? Gender Issues & Eating Disorders. 120p. (C). 1994. pap. 15.00 (*0-485-12106-9*, Pub. by Athlone Pr) Humanities.

Dolan, Bridget & Powell, Debra. The Mental Health Act, Explained. (Point of Law Ser.). 250p. 1999. pap. 50.00 (*0-11-702345-0*, Pub. by Statnry Office) Balogh.

Dolan, Charlotte L. The Counterfeit Gentleman. large type ed. LC 94-34005. 328p. (Orig.). 1994. pap. 18.95 (*0-7838-1140-3*, G K Hall Lrg Type) Mac Lib Ref.

— Fallen Angel. large type ed. LC 93-45636. 302p. 1994. lib. bdg. 20.95 (*0-8161-5947-5*, G K Hall Lrg Type) Mac Lib Ref.

Dolan, Chester. Blind Faith: Confronting Contemporary Religion. LC 94-40525. 367p. (C). 1995. 28.95 (*0-87975-931-3*) Prometheus Bks.

— Holy Daze: Coming to Grips with "Religion", the Holy Daze of Humanity. 3rd ed. LC 91-66373. 400p. 1992. text 29.85 (*0-9631042-8-4*); pap. text 19.85 (*0-9631042-7-6*) MOPAH Pubns.

Dolan, Chris. Ascension Day. 200p. Date not set. pap. 15.95 (*0-7486-6234-0*, Pub. by Polygon) Subterranean Co.

— Hazard-Wise: Classroom Resources for Teachers on Natural Hazards & Disasters. (Illus.). 112p. (Orig.). (C). 1996. pap. text 35.00 (*0-7881-2731-4*) DIANE Pub.

— Poor Angels: And Other Stories. 192p. (Orig.). 1995. pap. 15.95 (*0-7486-6206-5*, Pub. by Polygon) Subterranean Co.

Dolan, Christopher, tr. see Prieberg, Fred K.

Dolan, Dan. Mathematics Activities for Elementary School Teachers: A Problem Solving Approach. 3rd ed. Guardino, Karen, ed. LC 96-26206. 352p. (C). 1996. pap. text 28.00 (*0-201-44096-2*) Addison-Wesley.

— Mathematics Activities for Elementary School Teachers: A Problem Solving Approach. 3rd ed. (C). 1997. pap. text 23.66 (*0-201-84846-5*) Addison-Wesley.

Dolan, Dan & Williamson, Jim. Mathematics Activities for Elementary School Teachers: A Problem Solving Appproach. 4th ed. 300p. (C). 1990. pap. text 13.95 (*0-8053-0392-8*) Addison-Wesley.

Dolan, Daniel T. Teaching Problem-Solving Strategies. 1983. pap. text 18.35 (*0-201-10231-5*) Addison-Wesley.

Dolan, Daria, jt. auth. see Dolan, Ken.

Dolan, David. The End of Days. LC 96-51666. (Illus.). 336p. 1997. pap. 10.99 (*0-8007-5630-4*, The End of the) Revell.

Dolan, David M., et al, eds. Lake Huron 1980 Intensive Survey: Summary Report to the Surveillance Work Group. fac. ed. LC QH0541.5.L3L. (Illus.). 149p. 1986. pap. 46.20 (*0-7837-8621-2*, 207523100007) Bks Demand.

Dolan, Edward. The American Civil War: A House Divided. LC 97-6995. (Illus.). 112p. (J). (gr. 5-8). 1997. lib. bdg. 28.90 (*0-7613-0255-7*) Millbrook Pr.

Dolan, Edward F. America in the Korean War. LC 97-50460. 112p. (YA). (gr. 6-12). 1998. lib. bdg. 28.90 (*0-7613-0361-8*) Millbrook Pr.

— America in World War I. (Illus.). 96p. (J). (gr. 4-6). 1996. lib. bdg. 27.40 (*1-56294-522-X*) Millbrook Pr.

— America in World War II - 1941. (America in World War II Ser.). (Illus.). 72p. (J). (gr. 4-6). 1991. pap. 6.95 (*1-878841-81-5*) Millbrook Pr.

— America in World War II - 1942. LC 91-30808. (America in World War II Ser.). (Illus.). 72p. (J). (gr. 4-6). 1991. pap. 6.95 (*1-878841-82-3*) Millbrook Pr.

— America in World War II, 1941: 1941. (J). (gr. 4-7). 1992. pap. 6.70 (*0-395-65944-2*) HM.

— America in World War II, 1943. (J). (gr. 4-7). 1992. pap. 6.70 (*0-395-62463-0*) HM.

— The American Revolution: How We Fought the War of Independence. LC 94-44440. (Illus.). 112p. (J). (gr. 5-8). 1995. lib. bdg. 27.40 (*1-56294-521-1*) Millbrook Pr.

***Dolan, Edward F.** Beyond the Frontier: The Story of the Trails West. LC 98-43838. (Great Journeys Ser.). 112p. (J). (gr. 5-9). 2000. lib. bdg. 31.36 (*0-7614-0969-6*) Marshall Cavendish.

Dolan, Edward F. Child Abuse. rev. ed. LC 92-11355. (Issues Ser.). 112p. (YA). (gr. 9-12). 1992. lib. bdg. 24.00 (*0-531-11042-7*) Watts.

Dolan, Edward F., Jr. Starting Soccer. 1978. pap. 5.00 (*0-87980-352-5*) Wilshire.

Dolan, Edward F. Teenagers & Compulsive Gambling. LC 93-31956. (Teen Issues Ser.). (Illus.). 112p. (YA). (gr. 9-12). 1994. lib. bdg. 24.00 (*0-531-11100-8*) Watts.

Dolan, Edward F. & Scariano, Margaret M. Guns in the United States. (Impact Bks.). (Illus.). 128p. (YA). (gr. 7-12). 1994. lib. bdg. 24.00 (*0-531-11189-X*) Watts.

— Illiteracy in America. LC 93-29528. (Impact Bks.). (Illus.). 128p. (YA). (gr. 7-12). 1995. lib. bdg. 24.00 (*0-531-11178-4*) Watts.

— Shaping U. S. Foreign Policy: Profiles of Twelve Secretaries of State. (Democracy in Action Ser.). (Illus.). 128p. (YA). (gr. 7-12). 1996. lib. bdg. 24.00 (*0-531-11264-0*) Watts.

Dolan, Edwin G. & Goodman, John C. The Economics of Public Policy. 5th ed. LC 95-199398. 228p. (C). 1995. mass mkt. 44.95 (*0-314-04724-7*) West Pub.

Dolan, Edwin G. & Lindsey, David E. Economics. 7th ed. LC 93-71251. 861p. (C). 1993. text 75.00 (*0-03-096501-2*); teacher ed. 20.00 incl. disk (*0-685-71367-9*) Dryden Pr.

— Macroeconomics. 7th ed. LC 93-71249. 464p. (C). 1993. pap. text 51.00 (*0-03-097570-0*) Dryden Pr.

— Microeconomics. 7th ed. LC 93-71250. 496p. (C). 1994. pap. text 51.00 (*0-03-097569-7*) Dryden Pr.

Dolan, Edwin G., jt. auth. see Stoner, James A.

Dolan, Eileen. Winning over Asthma. 2nd rev. ed. LC 96-22124. (Illus.). 40p. (J). (ps-5). 1996. pap. 7.00 (*0-914625-17-9*) Pedipress.

D

An Asterisk (*) at the beginning of an entry indicates that the title is appearing for the first time.

Dolan, Ellen M. Susan Butcher & the Iditarod Trail. LC 92-36837. 1996. 12.05 (*0-606-10946-3*, Pub. by Turtleback) Demco.
— Susan Butcher & the Iditarod Trail. LC 92-36837. (J). 1993. 14.95 (*0-8027-8211-6*); lib. bdg. 15.85 (*0-8027-8212-4*) Walker & Co.
— Susan Butcher & the Iditarod Trail. (Illus.). 112p. (YA). (gr. 5 up). 1996. pap. 7.95 (*0-8027-7496-2*) Walker & Co.
— Thomas Alva Edison: Inventor. LC 97-37155. (Historical American Biographies Ser.). 128p. (YA). (gr. 6 up). 1998. lib. bdg. 20.95 (*0-7660-1014-7*) Enslow Pubs.
Dolan, Frances E. Dangerous Familiars: Representations of Domestic Crime in England, 1550-1700. LC 93-40060. (Illus.). 272p. 1994. text 42.50 (*0-8014-2901-3*); pap. text 17.95 (*0-8014-8134-1*) Cornell U Pr.
***Dolan, Frances E.** Timon of Athens. (Shakespeare Ser.). 176p. 2000. pap. 5.95 (*0-14-071487-1*) Penguin Putnam.
— Whores of Babylon: Catholicism, Gender, & Seventeenth-Century Print Culture. LC 99-15782. 1999. 39.95 (*0-8014-3629-X*) Cornell U Pr.
Dolan, Frances E., ed. Renaissance Drama: Renaissance Drama & the Law. 260p. 1996. text 59.95 (*0-8101-0688-4*) Northwestern U Pr.
Dolan, Frances E., ed. see Shakespeare, William.
Dolan, Frederick M. Allegories of America: Narratives, Metaphysics, Politics. (Contestations Ser.). 248p. 1994. text 39.95 (*0-8014-3006-2*); pap. text 16.95 (*0-8014-8200-3*) Cornell U Pr.
Dolan, Frederick M. & Dumm, Thomas L., eds. Rhetorical Republic: Governing Representations in American Politics. LC 92-41984. 304p. (C). 1993. pap. 18.95 (*0-87023-847-7*); lib. bdg. 40.00 (*0-87023-846-9*) U of Mass Pr.
Dolan, G. Keith. Athletes & Athletics: Sports Almanac-U. S. A. (Illus.). 383p. 1984. text 14.95 (*0-9613548-0-1*) Footprint Pub.
— Communication: A Way to Build Understanding About Schools: A Practical Guide for School Administrators. LC 95-21921. 335p. (C). 1995. pap. 72.95 (*0-534-25086-6*) Wadsworth Pub.
Dolan, Grace M., jt. ed. see Dolan, Paul J.
Dolan, Graham. The Greenwich Guide to Time & the Millenium. LC 98-43198. 1999. 24.22 (*1-57572-802-8*) Heinemann Lib.
***Dolan, J. D.** Phoenix: A Brother's Life. LC 99-33608. 224p. 2000. 22.00 (*0-375-40342-6*) Knopf.
Dolan, J. E. & Langer, S., eds. Explosives in the Service of Man: The Nobel Heritage. (Special Publication: No. 203). 254p. 1997. 134.00 (*0-85404-732-8*) Am Chemical.
Dolan, J. Michael. How to Care for Your Aging Parents... & Still Have a Life of Your Own. LC 92-60126. 208p. 1992. pap. 12.95 (*1-880867-13-3*) Mulholland Pac.
— Mastering Show Biz... from the Heart: 10 Timeless Principles. LC 97-92654. (Illus.). 192p. 1998. pap. 16.95 (*1-880867-20-6*) Mulholland Pac.
Dolan, James, jt. auth. see Rosen, Arnold.
Dolan, James C. The Tractatus Super Psalmum Vicesimum of Richard Rolle of Hampole. LC 91-23525. (Texts & Studies in Religion: Vol. 57). 124p. 1991. lib. bdg. 59.95 (*0-7734-9666-1*) E Mellen.
Dolan, James F. & Mann, Paul. Active Strike-Slip & Collisional Tectonics of the Northern Caribbean Plate Boundary Zone, Vol. 326. LC 98-28431. (Special Papers). 1998. write for info. (*0-8137-2326-4*) Geol Soc.
Dolan, James R. Meditations for Life: Meditations for Personal Prayer. (Illus.). 180p. 1992. pap. text. write for info. (*0-9632750-4-6*) McQuaid Jesuit.
Dolan, Jay P. The American Catholic Experience: A History from Colonial Times to the Present. LC 92-50409. (C). 1992. reprint ed. pap. text 18.50 (*0-268-00639-3*) U of Notre Dame Pr.
— Catholic Revivalism: The American Experience, 1830-1900. LC 77-89755. 1979. pap. text 16.50 (*0-268-00729-2*) U of Notre Dame Pr.
— The Immigrant Church: New York's Irish & German Catholics. LC 75-12552. 237p. reprint ed. pap. 73.50 (*0-608-30366-6*, 201981700014) Bks Demand.
— The Immigrant Church: New York's Irish & German Catholics, 1815-1865. LC 82-23827. (Illus.). xiv, 221p. (C). 1983. reprint ed. pap. text 11.50 (*0-268-01151-6*) U of Notre Dame Pr.
Dolan, Jay P., ed. The American Catholic Tradition. 1893.50 (*0-405-10810-9*) Ayer.
Dolan, Jay P. & Deck, Allan F., eds. Hispanic Catholic Culture in the U. S. Issues & Concerns. LC 94-15464. (Hispanic Catholics in the U. S. Ser.: Vol. 3). (C). 1994. text 38.00 (*0-268-01105-2*) U of Notre Dame Pr.
— Hispanic Catholic Culture in the U. S. Issues & Concerns. LC 94-15464. 472p. 1997. pap. 20.00 (*0-268-01111-7*) U of Notre Dame Pr.
Dolan, Jay P. & Hinojosa, Gilberto, eds. Mexican Americans & the Catholic Church, 1900-1965. LC 94-14003. 392p. 1997. pap. 16.00 (*0-268-01428-0*) U of Notre Dame Pr.
Dolan, Jay P. & Vidal, Jaime R., eds. Puerto Rican & Cuban Catholics in the U. S., 1900-1965. LC 94-15463. (Notre Dame History of Hispanic Catholics in the U.S. Ser.: Vol. 2). (C). 1994. text 29.00 (*0-268-03805-8*) U of Notre Dame Pr.
Dolan, Jill. The Feminist Spectator As Critic. Brockett, Oscar G., ed. LC 88-14219. (Theater & Dramatic Studies: No. 52). 168p. 1991. pap. text 16.95 (*0-472-08160-8*, 08160) U of Mich Pr.
— Presence & Desire: Essays on Gender, Sexuality, Performance. (Critical Perspectives on Women & Gender Ser.). 232p. (C). 1994. pap. text 17.95 (*0-472-06530-0*, 06530) U of Mich Pr.
Dolan, John. Leadership Strategies. 2nd ed. 288p. 1994. per., boxed set 32.95 (*0-8403-9423-3*) Kendall-Hunt.
— Movers, Shakers, & Changemakers. 336p. 1994. per., boxed set 32.95 (*0-8403-9422-5*) Kendall-Hunt.
***Dolan, John.** Poetic Occasion From Milton to Wordsworth. LC 98-54305. 242p. 2000. text 59.95 (*0-312-22094-4*) St Martin.
Dolan, John. Stuck Up. 72p. 1995. pap. 12.95 (*1-86940-120-4*, Pub. by Auckland Univ) Paul & Co Pubs.
Dolan, John, jt. auth. see Jedin, Hubert.
Dolan, John F. Commercial Activities. 1990. 125.00 (*0-316-18904-9*, Aspen Law & Bus) Aspen Pub.
— Commercial Law: Essential Terms & Concepts. 2nd ed. LC 96-79677. 600p. 1997. pap. 26.95 (*1-56706-505-8*, 65058) Panel Pubs.
— The Law of Letters of Credit. (Commercial Law Ser.). 616p. 1990. suppl. ed. 145.00 (*0-7913-0658-5*) Warren Gorham & Lamont.
— The Law of Letters of Credit. (Commercial Law Ser.). 616p. 1992. suppl. ed. 51.00 (*0-7913-1243-7*) Warren Gorham & Lamont.
— Secured Transactions & Payment Systems. 240p. 1995. 24.95 (*0-316-18910-3*) Little.
— Uniform Commercial Code. 1991. 25.95 (*0-316-18905-7*, Aspen Law & Bus) Aspen Pub.
Dolan, John F. & Donnolly, Lawrence. Basic Concepts in Commercial Law: Cases & Materials. (American Casebook Ser.). 758p. 1998. 57.50 (*0-314-21117-9*) West Pub.
Dolan, John M. Inference & Imagination. (Illus.). xiv, 396p. (C). 1994. text 35.00 (*0-9644114-0-7*) Archimedean Pt.
Dolan, John P. Negotiate Like the Pros. LC 92-9623. 176p. 1992. pap. 12.00 (*0-399-51775-8*, Perigee Bks) Berkley Pub.
Dolan, John P., tr. see Erasmus, Desiderius.
Dolan, John W. & Snyder, Lloyd R. Troubleshooting LC Systems: A Comprehensive Approach to Troubleshooting LC Equipment & Separations. LC 88-34722. (Illus.). 523p. 1989. 95.00 (*0-89603-151-9*) Humana.
Dolan, Joseph, tr. see Buttner, Gottfried.
Dolan, Kathleen. Business Computer Systems Design. 336p. 1984. pap. text 13.95 (*0-938188-20-8*) Mitchell Pub.
Dolan, Kathleen H. Cyclopean Song: Melancholy & Aestheticism in Gongora's Fabula de Polifemo y Galatea. LC 90-39387. (North Carolina Studies in the Romance Languages & Literatures: No. 236). 138p. reprint ed. pap. 42.80 (*0-608-20073-5*, 207134500011) Bks Demand.
Dolan, Ken. Smart Money: How to Be Your Own Financial Manager. 1990. pap. 12.95 (*0-425-12179-8*) Berkley Pub.
***Dolan, Ken & Dolan, Daria.** Sams Teach Yourself E-Personal Finance Today. (Illus.). 300p. 2000. 17.99 (*0-672-31879-2*) Sams.
Dolan, Ken & Dolan, Daria. The Smart Money Financial Planner. 208p. (Orig.). 1992. pap. 10.95 (*0-425-13477-6*) Berkley Pub.
— Straight Talk on Money: Ken & Daria Dolan's Guide to Family Money Management. 288p. 1993. 22.00 (*0-671-79808-1*) S&S Trade.
Dolan, Kevin. Ethics, Animals & Science. LC 99-12349. 320p. 1999. 42.95 (*0-632-05277-5*, Pub. by Blckwell Science) Iowa St U Pr.
***Dolan, Kevin.** Introduction to Laboratory Animal Law. LC 99-54972. 2000. write for info. (*0-632-05278-3*) Blackwell Sci.
Dolan, Kevin. U. S. Taxation of International Mergers, Acquisitions, & Joint Ventures, 2 vols., Set. 2000p. 1995. 345.00 (*0-7913-2569-5*) Warren Gorham & Lamont.
— U. S. Taxation of International Mergers, Acquisitions, & Joint Ventures, Vol. 1. 1995. write for info. (*0-7913-2586-5*) Warren Gorham & Lamont.
— U. S. Taxation of International Mergers, Acquisitions, & Joint Ventures, Vol. 2. 1995. write for info. (*0-7913-2587-3*) Warren Gorham & Lamont.
Dolan, Linda. Are Minnesotans Aware of the Dangers of Railroad Crossings? (Illus.). 80p. 1998. reprint ed. pap. text 20.00 (*0-7881-4190-2*) DIANE Pub.
Dolan, Marc. Modern Lives: A Cultural Re-Reading of "The Lost Generation" LC 95-30211. 246p. 1996. 36.95 (*1-55753-079-3*); pap. 19.95 (*1-55753-080-7*) Purdue U Pr.
Dolan, Maryanne. American Sterling Silver Flatware 1830's-1990's: An Identification & Value Guide. 222p. 1992. pap. 22.95 (*0-89689-095-3*, Bks Amrcana) Krause Pubns.
— Collecting Rhinestone & Colored Jewelry. 4th ed. LC 98-84636. (Illus.). 400p. 1998. pap. 24.95 (*0-87341-649-X*, RH504) Krause Pubns.
— Old Lace & Linens: Identification & Value Guide. 160p. 1989. pap. 10.95 (*0-89689-072-4*, Bks Amrcana) Krause Pubns.
— Vintage Clothing, 1880-1980: Identification & Value Guide. 3rd rev. ed. (Vintage Clothing 1880-1980 Ser.). (Illus.). 304p. 1995. pap. 22.95 (*0-89689-109-7*, Bks Amrcana) Krause Pubns.
— The World of Dolls: A Collectors' Identification & Price Guide. LC 98-84094. (Illus.). 368p. 1999. pap. 24.95 (*0-87341-570-1*, CHADO) Krause Pubns.
Dolan, Merrillee A. Favorite Flowers of the Cumbres & Toltec. (Illus.). 62p. (Orig.). 1996. pap. 12.00 (*0-9654329-0-4*) Dragonfly NM.
Dolan, Patricia A. Florida's Wildlife Coloring Book. (Illus.). 25p. (YA). (gr. 4 up). 1997. pap. text 2.75 (*0-9657376-2-4*) Creat By PAD.
— St. Augustine Coloring Book & Historical Text. rev. ed. (Illus.). 34p. 1991. pap. text 2.75 (*0-9657376-0-8*) Creat By PAD.
Dolan, Patricia G. Systematics of Middle American Mastiff Bats of the Genus Molossus. (Special Publications: No. 29). (C). 1989. pap. 12.00 (*0-89672-203-1*) Tex Tech Univ Pr.
Dolan, Patricia G., jt. auth. see Carter, Dilford C.
Dolan, Paul J. & Bennett, Joseph T., eds. An Introduction to Fiction. LC 73-18250. 533p. (C). reprint ed. 165.30 (*0-8357-9915-8*, 201236000081) Bks Demand.
Dolan, Paul J. & Dolan, Grace M., eds. Introduction to Drama. LC 73-18343. 656p. reprint ed. pap. 200.00 (*0-608-10993-2*, 201235900081) Bks Demand.
Dolan, Pavel, tr. see Tondl, Ales.
***Dolan, Richard M.** UFOs & the National Security State Vol. 1: An Unclassified History, 1941-1973. LC 00-90753. 564p. 2000. pap. 27.95 (*0-9677995-0-3*) Keyhole Pubng.
Dolan, Robert. Serial Murders. LC 97-8598. (Crime, Justice, & Punishment Ser.). (YA). (gr. 8 up). 1997. lib. bdg. 19.95 (*0-7910-4275-8*) Chelsea Hse.
Dolan, Robert J. Strategic Marketing Management. 1992. pap. 30.94 (*0-07-017810-0*) McGraw.
Dolan, Robert J., selected by. Strategic Marketing Management. (Practice of Management Ser.). 640p. 1992. pap. 29.95 (*0-87584-310-7*) Harvard Busn.
Dolan, Robert J. & Simon, Hermann. Power Pricing: How Managing Price Transforms the Bottom Line. LC 96-28203. 384p. 1997. 40.00 (*0-684-83443-X*) Free Pr.
Dolan, Ronald, ed. Japan: A Country Study. 4th ed LC 82-22835. (Area Handbook Ser.: DA Pam 550-30). 531p. 1992. 34.00 (*0-16-001592-8*, 008-020-01272-6) USGPO.
Dolan, Ronald E. Philippines: A Country Study. 418p. 1993. boxed set 35.00 (*0-16-061152-0*) USGPO.
Dolan, Ronald E., ed. Philippines: A Country Study. 4th ed. LC 92-39812. (Area Handbook Ser.). 1993. write for info. (*0-8444-0748-8*) Lib Congress.
Dolan, Sean. Bob Marley. 124p. (YA). (gr. 5 up). 1995. pap. 8.95 (*0-7910-3255-8*) Chelsea Hse.
— Bob Marley: Black Americans of Achievement. 124p. (YA). (gr. 5 up). 1996. lib. bdg. 19.95 (*0-7910-2041-X*) Chelsea Hse.
— Charles Barkley. (Basketball Legends Ser.). (Illus.). 64p. (YA). (gr. 3 up). 1995. lib. bdg. 15.95 (*0-7910-2433-4*) Chelsea Hse.
***Dolan, Sean.** Everything You Need to Know about Cults. LC 00-20959. (Need to Know Library). 2000. lib. bdg. 17.95 (*0-8239-3230-3*) Rosen Group.
Dolan, Sean. Gabriel Garcia Marquez: Colombian Writer. LC 93-9478. (Hispanics of Achievement Ser.). (Illus.). 120p. (YA). (gr. 5 up). 1994. lib. bdg. 19.95 (*0-7910-1243-3*) Chelsea Hse.
— Germany: Major World nations. LC 98-198528. (Major World Nations Ser.). (Illus.). 144p. (YA). (gr. 5 up). 1999. lib. bdg. 19.95 (*0-7910-4752-0*) Chelsea Hse.
— Julius Erving. LC 94-5777. (Basketball Legends Ser.). (Illus.). 64p. (J). (gr. 3 up). 1994. lib. bdg. 15.95 (*0-7910-2429-6*) Chelsea Hse.
— Junipero Serra: Spanish Missionary & Explorer. (Hispanics of Achievement Ser.). (Illus.). 120p. (YA). (gr. 5 up). 1991. lib. bdg. 19.95 (*0-7910-1255-7*) Chelsea Hse.
— Junipero Serra: Spanish Missionary & Explorer. (Hispanics of Achievement Ser.). (Illus.). 120p. (YA). (gr. 5 up). 1992. pap. 8.95 (*0-7910-1282-4*) Chelsea Hse.
— Larry Bird. LC 94-5776. (Basketball Legends Ser.). (Illus.). 64p. (J). (gr. 3 up). 1994. lib. bdg. 15.95 (*0-7910-2427-X*) Chelsea Hse.
— Magic Johnson: Basketball Great. Huggins, Nathan I., ed. LC 92-21378. (Black Americans of Achievement Ser.). (Illus.). 124p. (YA). (gr. 5 up). 1992. lib. bdg. 19.95 (*0-7910-1975-6*) Chelsea Hse.
— Michael Jordan. LC 94-5779. (Basketball Legends Ser.). (Illus.). 64p. (J). (gr. 3 up). 1994. lib. bdg. 15.95 (*0-7910-2432-6*) Chelsea Hse.
— Michael Jordan. (Black Americans of Achievement Ser.). (J). 1994. 13.15 (*0-606-07867-3*) Turtleback.
— Michael Jordan: Basketball Great. Huggins, Nathan I., ed. LC 93-16714. (Black Americans of Achievement Ser.). (Illus.). 124p. (YA). (gr. 5 up). 1994. lib. bdg. 19.95 (*0-7910-2150-5*) Chelsea Hse.
— Michael Jordan: Basketball Great. Huggins, Nathan I., ed. LC 93-16711. (Black Americans of Achievement Ser.). (Illus.). 124p. (YA). (gr. 5 up). 1994. pap. 8.95 (*0-7910-2151-3*) Chelsea Hse.
— The Polish Americans. LC 95-30995. (Immigrant Experience Ser.). 120p. (YA). (gr. 5 up). 1996. lib. bdg. 19.95 (*0-7910-3364-3*) Chelsea Hse.
— The Polish Americans. LC 95-30995. (Immigrant Experience Ser.). (Illus.). 120p. (YA). (gr. 7 up). 1996. pap. 9.95 (*0-7910-3386-4*) Chelsea Hse.
Dolan, Shimon D. & Schuler, Randall S. Personnel & Human Resource Management in Canada. 620p. (C). 1987. pap. text, teacher ed. write for info. (*0-314-34766-6*) West Pub.
Dolan, Shimon L. & Schuler, Randall S. Canadian Readings in Personnel & Human Resource Management. 467p. (C). 1987. pap. text 34.25 (*0-314-32487-9*) West Pub.
Dolan, Steve. Church & State. 232p. 1994. write for info. (*1-885845-00-6*) Leaflet Missal.
— Complete Visual Basic 4 Development. 1000p. (Orig.). 1996. pap. 49.95 (*1-881679-00-4*) ETN.
Dolan, Sylvia, ed. Nathan's Legal Markets, 1994: The Definitive Resource for Advertising to the Legal Profession. 700p. 1993. pap. write for info. (*0-9637775-0-5*) Dolan Media.
Dolan, Sylvia M., ed. Nathan's Legal Markets, 1995 Edition: The Definitive Resource for Marketing to the Legal Profession. rev. ed. 425p. 1994. pap. 159.95 (*0-9637775-1-3*) Dolan Media.
— Nathan's Legal Markets 1997 Edition. 4th ed. (Nathan's Legal Markets Ser.). 688p. 1997. write for info. (*0-614-28420-1*) Dolan Media.
— Nathan's Legal Markets 1996 Edition: The Definitive Resource for Marketing to Legal Professionals. rev. ed. 500p. 1996. pap. 159.95 (*0-9637775-2-1*) Dolan Media.
Dolan, T. J. & Broghamer, E. L. A Photoelastic Study of the Stresses in Gear Tooth Fillets. (Technical Papers: Vol. P224). (Illus.). 31p. 1941. pap. text 30.00 (*1-55589-269-8*) AGMA.
Dolan, T. M. Aim Before You Draw. large type ed. (Linford Western Large Print Ser.). 304p. 1998. pap. 17.99 (*0-7089-5268-2*, Linford) Ulverscroft.
— Black Days at Bull Run. large type ed. (Dales Large Print Ser.). 195p. 1996. pap. 18.99 (*1-85389-616-0*, Dales) Ulverscroft.
***Dolan, T. M.** Dark Dawn at Gisela. large type ed. 240p. 1999. pap. 20.99 (*1-85389-894-5*) Ulverscroft.
Dolan, T. M. Guns of the Pony Express. large type ed. (Linford Western Library). 304p. 1997. pap. 16.99 (*0-7089-5004-3*, Linford) Ulverscroft.
— The Trial of Sergeant Cimo. large type ed. 150p. 1996. pap. 18.99 (*1-85389-597-0*, Dales) Ulverscroft.
***Dolan, T. M.** West of Ash Hollow. large type ed. 240p. 1999. pap. 18.99 (*0-7089-5569-X*, Linford) Ulverscroft.
Dolan, T. P. & Muirithe, Diarmaid O. The Dialect of Forth & Bargy. 96p. 1996. 25.00 (*1-85182-200-3*, Pub. by Four Cts Pr) Intl Spec Bk.
***Dolan, Tanya.** High Art. (Sapphire Ser.). (Illus.). 2000. mass mkt. 10.95 (*0-352-33513-0*) Virgin Bks.
***Dolan, Terence, ed.** Dictionary of Hiberno-English. 320p. 1998. pap. 25.95 (*0-7171-2942-X*, Pub. by Gill & MacMill) Irish Bks Media.
Dolan, Terrance. Julio Cesar Chavez: Mexican Boxing Champion. LC 93-43867. (Hispanics of Achievement Ser.). (Illus.). 120p. (YA). (gr. 5 up). 1993. lib. bdg. 19.95 (*0-7910-2021-5*) Chelsea Hse.
— Probing Deep Space. Goetzmann, William H., ed. (World Explorers Ser.). (Illus.). 120p. (YA). (gr. 5 up). 1993. lib. bdg. 19.95 (*0-7910-1326-X*) Chelsea Hse.
— The Santee Sioux Indians. LC 96-25065. (Junior Library of American Indians). (Illus.). 76p. (J). (gr. 5-7). 1996. pap. 7.95 (*0-7910-4453-X*) Chelsea Hse.
Dolan, Therese. Inventing Reality: The Paintings of John Moore. LC 96-17760. (Illus.). 132p. 1996. 50.00 (*1-55595-134-1*) Hudson Hills.
Dolan, Therese A., et al. Elder Care Handbook. (Illus.). 1988. write for info. (*0-9618201-2-8*) Work Family Direct.
***Dolan, Timothy M.** Priests for the Third Millennium. LC 00-130467. 336p. 2000. 24.95 (*0-87973-319-5*) Our Sunday Visitor.
Dolan, Timothy M. Some Seed Fell on Good Ground: The Life of Edwin V. O'Hara. LC 91-7315. (Illus.). 300p. 1992. text 29.95 (*0-8132-0748-7*) Cath U Pr.
Dolan, W. Patrick. Restructuring Our Schools: A Primer on Systemic Change. LC 94-67028. 210p. 1994. pap. 19.95 (*0-9641690-0-2*) Systs & Organ.
Dolan, Yvonne. One Small Step: Moving Beyond Trauma & Therapy to a Life of Joy. LC 97-35072. 232p. (Orig.). 1998. pap. 11.95 (*1-57601-055-4*) Dolan.
Dolan, Yvonne M. A Path with a Heart: Ericksonian Utilization with Resistant & Chronic Clients. LC 85-4225. 224p. 1993. pap. text 28.95 (*0-87630-718-7*) Brunner-Mazel.
— Resolving Sexual Abuse. 1991. 29.95 (*0-393-70112-3*) Norton.
Dolan, Zak. Dolans Almanac of Magic. 560p. 1997. pap. 24.95 (*1-55622-562-8*) Wordware Pub.
Doland, Edmund, tr. see Duhem, Pierre.
Dolano, Sergio, ed. Santiago Calatrava: Complete Works. (Illus.). 326p. 1997. pap. 55.00 (*3-927258-37-7*) Gingko Press.
Dolara, Bobi. Vintage Peace. 80p. 1993. pap. 10.50 (*1-56770-270-8*) S Scheewe Pubns.
Dolayar, Mostafa & Gray, Tim. Water Politics in the Middle East: A Context for Conflict or Cooperation? LC 99-22104. 1999. text 65.00 (*0-312-22382-X*) St Martin.
Dolb, K. Danger at Demon's Cove. (Puzzle Adventures Ser.). (Illus.). 48p. (J). (gr. 3-8). 1988. pap. 5.95 (*0-7460-0179-7*) EDC.
— Danger at Demon's Cove. (Puzzle Adventures Ser.). (Illus.). 48p. (J). (gr. 3-8). 1999. lib. bdg. 13.95 (*0-88110-333-0*) EDC.
Dolbear, Geoffrey E., jt. auth. see Magee, J. S.
Dolbeare, Cushing N. Putting the Pieces Together: Controlling Lead Hazards in the Nation's Housing. (Illus.). 205p. 1997. reprint ed. pap. text 30.00 (*0-7881-4717-X*) DIANE Pub.
***Dolbeare, Kenneth & Cummings, Michael.** American Political Thought. 5th ed. 2001. pap. text 45.95 (*1-889119-58-X*, Chatham House Pub) Seven Bridges.
Dolbeare, Kenneth M. Democracy at Risk. LC 86-9607. (Chatham House Series on Change in American Politics). 255p. reprint ed. pap. 79.10 (*0-7837-2604-X*, 204276800006) Bks Demand.
Dolbeare, Kenneth M., ed. American Political Thought. 4th ed. LC 97-51407. 576p. (C). 1998. pap. text 42.95 (*1-56643-059-3*, Chatham House Pub) Seven Bridges.
Dolbeare, Kenneth M. & Edelman, Murray J. American Politics: Policies, Power, & Change. 5th ed. LC 84-81190. 572p. (C). 1985. pap. text 48.36 (*0-669-07323-7*) HM Trade Div.
Dolbeare, Kenneth M. & Gardiner, John A., eds. Public Policy Evaluation. LC 75-14631. (Sage Yearbooks in Politics & Public Policy Ser.: No. 2). 286p. 1975. reprint ed. pap. 88.70 (*0-608-01464-8*, 205950800001) Bks Demand.
Dolbeare, Kenneth M. & Hammond, Philip E. School Prayer Decisions: From Court Policy to Local Practice. LC 70-140461. 1994. lib. bdg. 8.00 (*0-226-15515-3*) U Ch Pr.

D

An Asterisk (*) at the beginning of an entry indicates that the title is appearing for the first time.

Dolbeare, Kenneth M. & Hubbell, Janette K. U. S. A. 2012: After the Middle-Class Revolution. LC 95-50207. (Illus.). 208p. (C). 1996. 25.00 (*1-56643-036-4*, Chatham House Pub); pap. text 22.95 (*1-56643-035-6*, Chatham House Pub) Seven Bridges.

Dolbeare, Kenneth M. & Medcalf, Linda J. American Ideologies Today: Shaping the New Politics of the 1990s. 2nd ed. LC 92-16441. 240p. (C). 1992. pap. 33.44 (*0-07-017411-3*) McGraw.

Dolbeare, Kenneth M., et al. American Politics. 572p. (C). 1985. teacher ed. 2.00 (*0-685-45690-0*); pap. text 23.00 (*0-685-45689-7*) HM Trade Div.

Dolbeare, Kenneth M., jt. ed. see Manley, John F.

***Dolbeault, P., et al, eds.** Complex Analysis & Geometry: International Conference in Honor of Pierre Lelong. (Progress in Mathematics Ser.: Vol. 188). 264p. 2000. 69.95 (*3-7643-6352-5*, Pub. by Birkhauser) Spr-Verlag.

Dolbeault, P., jt. auth. see Lelong, Pierre.

Dolber, Roslyn. College & Career Success for Students with Learning Disabilities. (Illus.). 224p. (Orig.). 1996. pap. 14.95 (*0-8442-4479-1*, 44791, VGM Career) NTC Contemp Pub Co.

— Opportunities in Fashion Careers. LC 92-16079. (Opportunities In . . . Ser.). (Illus.). 160p. pap. 11.95 (*0-8442-4023-0*, 40230, VGM Career) NTC Contemp Pub Co.

— Opportunities in Fashion Careers. LC 92-16079. (Opportunities in...Ser.). (Illus.). 160p. 1994. 14.95 (*0-8442-4022-2*, VGM Career) NTC Contemp Pub Co.

— Opportunities in Retailing Careers. (Illus.). 160p. 1993. pap. 10.95 (*0-8442-6521-7*, VGM Career) NTC Contemp Pub Co.

— Opportunities in Retailing Careers. (Illus.). 160p. 1994. 13.95 (*0-8442-6520-9*, VGM Career) NTC Contemp Pub Co.

— Opportunities in Retailing Careers. rev. ed. (Opportunities in... Ser.). (Illus.). 160p. pap. 11.95 (*0-8442-4642-5*, 46425, Natl Textbk Co) NTC Contemp Pub Co.

— Opportunities in Retailing Careers. rev. ed. (Opportunities in... Ser.). (Illus.). 160p. 1996. 14.95 (*0-8442-4641-7*, 46417) NTC Contemp Pub Co.

Dolbier, W. R. & Smart, B. Organofluorine Chemistry: Structure, Reactivity & Synthesis. Date not set. write for info. (*0-8247-9539-3*) Dekker.

Dolbow, Sandra W. Dictionary of Modern French Literature: From the Age of Reason Though Realism. LC 85-15492. (ENG & FRE.). 375p. 1986. lib. bdg. 69.50 (*0-313-23784-0*, Greenwood Pr) Greenwood.

Dolby, Cheryl. Woman Within the Web. Henderson, Karen, ed. (Illus.). 202p. (Orig.). 1996. pap. 24.95 incl. audio, audio compact disk (*0-9654898-2-5*) Earthlght Pr.

Dolby, George. Charles Dickens As I Knew Him. LC 79-130252. (English Literature Ser.: No. 33). 1970. reprint ed. lib. bdg. 75.00 (*0-8383-1142-3*) M S G Haskell Hse.

Dolby, K. The Ghost in the Mirror. (Puzzle Adventures Ser.). (Illus.). 48p. (J). (gr. 3-8). 1989. lib. bdg. 13.95 (*0-88110-369-1*) EDC.

— The Ghost in the Mirror. (Puzzle Adventures Ser.). (Illus.). 48p. (J). (gr. 3-8). 1989. pap. 5.95 (*0-7460-0334-X*) EDC.

— The Incredible Dinosaur Expedition. (Puzzle Adventures Ser.). (Illus.). 48p. (J). (gr. 3-8). 1987. pap. 5.95 (*0-7460-0149-5*) EDC.

— The Incredible Dinosaur Expedition. (Puzzle Adventures Ser.). (Illus.). 48p. (J). (gr. 3-8). 1999. lib. bdg. 13.95 (*0-88110-300-4*) EDC.

D

Dolby, K. & Church, C. Chocolate Island. (Young Puzzle Adventure Ser.). (Illus.). 32p. (J). (ps-1). 1995. lib. bdg. 13.95 (*0-88110-726-3*, Usborne) EDC.

— Chocolate Island. (Young Puzzle Adventure Ser.). (Illus.). 32p. (J). (ps-2). 1995. pap. 5.95 (*0-7460-1458-9*, Usborne) EDC.

— Lucy & the Sea Monster. (Puzzle Stories Ser.). (Illus.). 32p. (J). (ps-2). 1994. pap. 5.95 (*0-7460-1462-7*, Usborne); lib. bdg. 13.95 (*0-88110-679-8*, Usborne) EDC.

Dolby, Karen. Dragon in the Cupboard. (Young Puzzle Adventure Ser.). (Illus.). 32p. (J). (ps-2). 1995. pap. 5.95 (*0-7460-1355-8*, Usborne); lib. bdg. 13.95 (*0-88110-761-1*, Usborne) EDC.

— House of Shadows. (Spinechillers Ser.). (Illus.). 48p. (J). (gr. 4 up). 1993. lib. bdg. 13.95 (*0-88110-520-1*, Usborne) EDC.

Dolby, Karen. House of Shadows. (Spinechillers Ser.). (Illus.). 48p. (YA). (gr. 4 up). 1993. pap. 5.95 (*0-7460-0679-9*, Usborne) EDC.

Dolby, Karen. Lucy & the Sea Monster to the Rescue. Bates, Michelle, ed. (Young Puzzle Adventures Ser.). (Illus.). 32p. (Orig.). (J). (ps-2). 1997. pap. 5.95 (*0-7460-2292-1*, Usborne); lib. bdg. 13.95 (*0-88110-934-7*, Usborne) EDC.

— Spook's Surprise. (Young Puzzle Adventures Ser.). (Illus.). 32p. (J). (ps-2). 1996. pap. 5.95 (*0-7460-2296-4*, Usborne); lib. bdg. 13.95 (*0-88110-837-5*, Usborne) EDC.

— Young Puzzle Adventure. (Illus.). 96p. (J). (ps-2). 1996. pap. 11.95 (*0-7460-2290-5*, Usborne) EDC.

Dolby, Karen, ed. Wendy the Witch. (Young Puzzle Adventures Ser.). (Illus.). 32p. (J). (ps-2). 1999. pap. text 5.95 (*0-7460-2778-8*, Usborne); lib. bdg. 13.95 (*1-58086-121-0*, Usborne) EDC.

Dolby, R. E. & Kent, K. G., eds. Repair & Reclamation. (Illus.). 222p. 1986. pap. 125.00 (*0-85300-187-1*, Pub. by Woodhead Pubng) Am Educ Systs.

Dolby, R. G. Uncertain Knowledge: An Image of Science for a Changing World. (Illus.). 376p. (C). 1996. text 64.95 (*0-521-56004-7*) Cambridge U Pr.

Dolby, T. City Tripping: New York City: A Guide for Nighthawks, Foodies, Culture Vultures, Fashion Fetishists, Downtown Addicts & the Generally Style-Obsessed. LC 98-12835. 224p. 1997. pap. text 15.95 (*1-885492-51-0*) City & Co.

***Dolby, Tom.** City Tripping Los Angeles. (Illus.). 2000. pap. 15.95 (*1-885492-97-9*) City & Co.

Dolby, Victoria. Frequently Asked Questions All about Green Tea. (FAQs All about Health Ser.). 1998. mass mkt. 2.99 (*0-89529-890-2*, Avery) Penguin Putnam.

— Frequently Asked Questions All about Soy Isoflavones & Women's Health. (FAQs All about Health Ser.). 1998. mass mkt. 2.99 (*0-89529-940-2*, Avery) Penguin Putnam.

— Pregnenolone. (Good Health Guides Ser.). 1998. pap. 3.95 (*0-87983-885-X*, 3885XK, Keats Publng) NTC Contemp Pub Co.

Dolby, Victoria, jt. auth. see Challem, Jack.

Dolby, Victoria, jt. auth. see Challem, Jack J.

Dolc. Pre-Algebra. (C). 1991. pap., teacher ed., suppl. ed. 29.28 (*0-395-59675-0*) HM.

Dolce, Donna M. Metallurgy in Medicine & Industry: Index of New Information & Research Bible of Current Reviews. 150p. 1994. 47.50 (*0-7883-0006-7*); pap. 44.50 (*0-7883-0007-5*) ABBE Pubs Assn.

Dolce, Joe. Product Design 5, No. 5. LC 92-10433. 240p. 1992. 60.00 (*0-86636-185-5*) PBC Intl Inc.

Dolce, John E. Analytical Fleet Maintenance Management. 2nd ed. LC 97-41817. 550p. 1998. 59.00 (*1-56091-997-3*, R-197) Soc Auto Engineers.

Dolce, Laura. Australia: Major World Nations. LC 97-23404. (Major World Nations Ser.). (Illus.). 144p. (YA). (gr. 5 up). 1999. lib. bdg. 19.95 (*0-7910-4731-8*) Chelsea Hse.

— Suicide. (Encyclopedia of Health Ser.). (Illus.). 116p. (YA). (gr. 7 up). 1992. lib. bdg. 19.95 (*0-7910-0053-2*) Chelsea Hse.

Dolcetta, I., jt. auth. see Bardi, M.

Dolcetta, I. C., jt. auth. see Bardi, M.

Dolcetta, I. Capuzzo, et al, eds. Recent Mathematical Methods in Dynamic Programming. (Lecture Notes in Mathematics Ser.: Vol. 1119). vi, 202p. 1985. 37.95 (*0-387-15217-2*) Spr-Verlag.

Dolcetta, I. Capuzzo, ed. see Bardi, M., et al.

Dolch, Edward W., et al. Gulliver's Stories. (Illus.). (J). (gr. k-3). 1976. reprint ed. pap. 1.95 (*0-590-09850-0*) Scholastic Inc.

Dolch, Edward W., ed. see Defoe, Daniel.

Dolch, Norman A., jt. ed. see Peck, Dennis L.

Dolci, Danilo. Creature of Creatures: Selected Poems. Vitiello, Justin, ed. (Stanford French & Italian Studies: No. 22). Orig. Title: Creatura Di Creature, Poesie, 1949-1978. xxviii, 104p. 1980. pap. 56.50 (*0-915838-17-6*) Anma Libri.

— A New World in the Making. Munroe, R., tr. from ITA. LC 75-3990. 327p. 1976. reprint ed. lib. bdg. 69.50 (*0-8371-7419-8*, DONW, Greenwood Pr) Greenwood.

Dolciani. Algebra. (C). 1988. pap., suppl. ed. 33.88 (*0-395-45709-2*) HM.

— Algebra. (C). 1991. pap. 33.88 (*0-395-53591-3*) HM.

— Algebra & Trigonometry. (C). 1991. pap., suppl. ed. 41.68 (*0-395-53594-8*) HM.

— Algebra II & Trigonometry. (C). 1988. pap. 78.04 (*0-395-43059-3*) HM.

— Algebra II with Trigonometry. (C). 1988. pap., suppl. ed. 41.68 (*0-395-45710-6*) HM.

Dolciani. Algebra 1, 001. 1985. text, student ed. 61.76 (*0-395-34373-9*) HM.

Dolciani. Algebra 1. 1988. text, teacher ed. 72.00 (*0-395-43057-7*) HM.

— Algebra 1. 1991. text, teacher ed. 72.00 (*0-395-53590-5*); text, student ed. 59.24 (*0-395-53589-1*) HM.

Dolciani. Algebra 2 & Trigonometry, 001. 1985. text, student ed. 66.36 (*0-395-34378-X*) HM.

Dolciani. Algebra 2 & Trigonometry. 1991. text, teacher ed. 78.04 (*0-395-53593-X*); text, student ed. 62.36 (*0-395-53592-1*) HM.

Dolciani. Algebra 2 & Trigonometry Solution Key, 001. 1986. pap. 44.20 (*0-395-34380-1*) HM.

Dolciani. Introductory Analysis. 1990. text 68.04 (*0-395-52432-6*) HM.

— The Math Connection. (C). 1991. pap., student ed., suppl. ed. 29.28 (*0-395-56993-1*) HM.

— The Math Connection. (C). 1991. pap., student ed., suppl. ed. 29.28 (*0-395-57016-6*) HM.

Dolciani, Mary P. Introductory Analysis, 001. 1987. text, student ed. 75.36 (*0-395-40655-2*) HM.

Dold, et al, eds. Archimedis Vol. IV: Uber Einander Beruhrende Kreise. annot. ed. 1975. 54.50 (*3-519-01065-8*, T1065, Pub. by B G Teubner) U of Mich Pr.

Dold, A. Lectures on Algebraic Topology. LC 79-79062. (Grundlehren der Mathematischen Wissenschaften Ser.: Vol. 200). (Illus.). 377p. 1980. 79.00 (*0-387-10369-4*) Spr-Verlag.

— Lectures on Algebraic Topology. 2nd ed. LC 94-39729. (Classics in Mathematics Ser.). 376p. 1995. 35.00 (*3-540-58660-1*) Spr-Verlag.

Dold, A., et al, eds. Analytic Number Theory: Proceedings of the Japanese-French Symposium Held in Tokyo, Japan, October 10-13, 1988. (Lecture Notes in Mathematics Ser.: Vol. 1434). (Illus.). vi, 218p. 1990. 38.95 (*0-387-52787-7*) Spr-Verlag.

— Global Differential Geometry & Global Analysis: Proceedings, Berlin 1991. (Lecture Notes in Mathematics Ser.: Vol. 1481). (Illus.). viii, 282p. 1991. 45.95 (*0-387-54728-2*) Spr-Verlag.

— Stochastic Analysis & Related Topics II: Proceedings of a Second Workshop Held in Silivri, Turkey, July 18-30, 1988. (Lecture Notes in Mathematics Ser.: Vol. 1444). v, 268p. 1990. 46.95 (*0-387-53064-9*) Spr-Verlag.

— Topics in the Theory of Riemann Surfaces. LC 94-41550. (Lecture Notes in Mathematics Ser.: Vol. 1595). 105p. 1994. 29.95 (*3-540-58721-7*) Spr-Verlag.

— Topological Methods for Variational Problems with Symmetries. (Lecture Notes in Mathematics Ser.: Vol. 1560). 1993. 35.95 (*0-387-57378-X*) Spr-Verlag.

Dold, A., ed. see Alber, Hans D.

Dold, A., ed. see Arnold, L., et al.

Dold, A., ed. see Assing, Sigurd & Schmidt, W.

Dold, A., ed. see Biagioni, H. A.

Dold, A., ed. see Biane, P., et al.

Dold, A., ed. see Block, Louis S., et al.

Dold, A., ed. see Bouc, Serge.

Dold, A., ed. see Bujalance, E., et al.

Dold, A., ed. see Burstall, F. E. & Rawnsley, J. H.

Dold, A., ed. see Castillo, Jesus M. & Gonzales, Manuel.

Dold, A., ed. see Chabrowski, J.

Dold, A., ed. see Coornaert, Michel, et al.

Dold, A., ed. see Delfs, H.

Dold, A., ed. see Delort, Jean-Marc.

Dold, A., ed. see Dix, Daniel B.

Dold, A., ed. see Dovermann, K. H. & Schultz, R.

Dold, A., ed. see Dudley, R. M. & Norvaisa, R.

Dold, A., ed. see Ene, Vasile.

Dold, A., ed. see Erdmann, K.

Dold, A., ed. see Freitag, E.

Dold, A., ed. see Grosshans, Frank D.

Dold, A., ed. see Harder, G.

Dold, A., ed. see Hennequin, P. L.

Dold, A., ed. see Huber, Annette.

Dold, A., ed. see Inoue, Atsushi.

Dold, A., ed. see Isac, George.

Dold, A., ed. see Kaiser, Uwe.

Dold, A., ed. see Kajitani, K. & Nishitani, T.

Dold, A., ed. see Keimel, Klaus & Roth, Walter.

Dold, A., ed. see Knarr, Norbert.

Dold, A., ed. see Kochman, S. D.

Dold, A., ed. see Koshelev, Alexander A.

Dold, A., ed. see Kozlov, Vladimir & Maz'ya, V. G.

Dold, A., ed. see Krupkova, Olga.

Dold, A., ed. see Kuhnel, Wolfgang.

Dold, A., ed. see Lang, Serge A. & Cherry, W.

Dold, A., ed. see Lemaire, P. G.

Dold, A., ed. see Liu, P. D. & Qian, Min.

Dold, A., ed. see Ma, J. & Yong, J.

Dold, A., ed. see Mandal, Satya.

Dold, A., ed. see Metsch, K.

Dold, A., ed. see Meyer, P. A.

Dold, A., ed. see Meyer, Paul A.

Dold, A., ed. see Mielke, A.

Dold, A., ed. see Milman, Mario.

Dold, A., ed. see Mumford, David B.

Dold, A., ed. see Narkiewicz, Wladyslaw.

Dold, A., ed. see Neuberger, John W.

Dold, A., ed. see Nikolaeva, I. A. & Zhuzhoma, E.

Dold, A., ed. see Panchishkin, A. A., et al.

Dold, A., ed. see Pilyugin, Sergei Yu.

Dold, A., ed. see Proskurin, Nikolai.

Dold, A., ed. see Roussarie, R. H., et al.

Dold, A., ed. see Scedrov, Andrej, et al.

Dold, A., ed. see Schulz, F.

Dold, A., ed. see Serre, Jean-Pierre, et al.

Dold, A., ed. see Short, Mark W.

Dold, A., ed. see Simpson, C.

Dold, A., ed. see Soule, C., et al.

Dold, A., ed. see Tri-Jun Xiao & Liang, Jin.

Dold, A., ed. see Ustunel, Ali S.

Dold, A., ed. see Wahlbin, Lars B.

Dold, A., ed. see Wicks, K. R.

Dold, A., ed. see Wirsching, Gunther J.

Dold, A., ed. see Wolf-Gladrow, Dieter A.

Dold, A., ed. see Xue, Weimin.

Dold, A., ed. see Yurinsky, Vadim.

Dold, Gaylord. The Devil to Pay. LC 98-42392. 384p. 1999. text 24.95 (*0-312-19257-6*) St Martin.

— Moon Handbooks: Dominican Republic. (Illus.). 420p. 1997. pap. 15.95 (*1-56691-090-0*, Moon Handbks) Avalon Travel.

— The Wichita Mysteries Vol. 1: Three Complete Novels. 2nd ed. 640p. 1996. reprint ed. pap. 13.95 (*0-922820-17-1*) Watermark Pr.

Dolders, Arno, ed. The Illustrated Bartsch Vol. 56: Phillips Galle. 1987. lib. bdg. 149.00 (*0-89835-155-3*) Abaris Bks.

Doldinger, Klaus. European Labor Law. 59.95 (*1-85521-156-4*) Ashgate Pub Co.

Dole. Flight Theory Embry Riddle. 1998. pap. text 61.50 (*0-471-25443-6*) Wiley.

***Dole.** Flight Theory & Aerodynamics: A Practical Guide for Operational Safety. 2nd ed. LC 99-38912. 336p. 2000. 80.00 (*0-471-37006-1*) Wiley.

Dole, Anita S. Bible Study Notes, Vol. 1. Woofenden, William R., ed. LC 76-24081. 1978. lib. bdg. write for info. (*0-917426-01-0*) Am New Church Sunday.

— Bible Study Notes, Vol. 2. Woofenden, William R., ed. LC 76-24081. 1978. lib. bdg. write for info. (*0-917426-02-9*) Am New Church Sunday.

— Bible Study Notes, Vol. 3. Woofenden, William R., ed. LC 76-24081. 1978. lib. bdg. write for info. (*0-917426-03-7*) Am New Church Sunday.

— Bible Study Notes, Vol. 4. Woofenden, William R., ed. LC 76-24081. 1979. write for info. (*0-917426-04-5*) Am New Church Sunday.

— Bible Study Notes, Vol. 5. Woofenden, William R., ed. LC 76-24081. 1979. 8.95 (*0-917426-05-3*) Am New Church Sunday.

— Bible Study Notes, Vol. 6. Woofenden, William R., ed. LC 76-24081. 1979. write for info. (*0-917426-06-1*) Am New Church Sunday.

— Bible Study Notes, Vols. 1-3. Woofenden, William R., ed. LC 76-24081. 1978. lib. bdg. write for info. (*0-685-92171-9*) Am New Church Sunday.

***Dole, Bob.** Great Political Wit: Laughing (Almost) All the Way to the White House. (Illus.). 224p. 2000. pap. 9.95 (*0-7679-0667-5*) Broadway BDD.

— Great Presidential Wit. 2001. 22.00 (*0-7432-0392-5*) Scribner.

Dole, Bob, ed. Great Political Wit of the 20th Century. LC 98-20719. (Illus.). 208p. 1998. 16.95 (*0-385-49347-9*) Doubleday.

Dole, Bob & Dole, Elizabeth. Unlimited Partners: Our American Story. LC 96-217189. 384p. 1996. 24.00 (*0-684-83401-4*) S&S Trade.

Dole, Bob & Kemp, Jack. Trusting the People: The Dole-Kemp Plan to Free the Economy & Create a Better America. LC 96-35344. 1996. mass mkt. 15.00 (*0-06-101153-3*) HarpC.

Dole, Charles E. Flight Safety Technology Workbook. 302p. (Orig.). (C). 1994. pap. 25.00 (*0-9629524-2-7*) Wood Assocs.

— Flight Theory & Aerodynamics: A Practical Guide for Operational Safety. LC 81-3009. (Illus.). 320p. 1981. 135.00 (*0-471-09152-9*) Wiley.

— Flight Theory for Pilots. 3rd ed. LC 93-20618. (Illus.). 296p. (C). 1989. pap. 19.70 (*0-89100-338-X*, JS312681) Jeppesen Sanderson.

— Fundamentals of Aircraft Material Factors. 2nd ed. LC 92-46756. (Illus.). 201p. (C). 1989. pap. 16.60 (*0-89100-340-1*, JS312646) Jeppesen Sanderson.

— Mathematics & Physics for Aviation Personnel. 3rd ed. LC 93-24823. (Illus.). 94p. 1991. pap. text 12.45 (*0-89100-399-1*, JS312619) Jeppesen Sanderson.

Dole, Elizabeth, jt. auth. see Dole, Bob.

Dole, Frederick H. Sketches of the History of Windham, 1734-1935: The Story of a Typical New England Town. (Illus.). 157p. 1998. reprint ed. pap. 21.00 (*0-8328-7023-4*); reprint ed. lib. bdg. 29.00 (*0-8328-7022-6*) Higginson Bk Co.

Dole, Frederick H., ed. see Dole, Samuel T.

Dole, G. F., tr. see Swedenborg, Emanuel.

Dole, George. Introduction to Swedenborg's Theological Latin. 156p. 1984. pap. 8.95 (*0-87785-125-5*) Swedenborg.

Dole, George & Kirven, Robert. A Scientist Explores Spirit. LC 97-614. 112p. 1997. pap. 10.95 (*0-87785-241-3*) Swedenborg.

Dole, George, tr. see Swedenborg, Emanuel.

Dole, George F. Sorting Things Out. 273p. pap. (*0-9626795-3-4*) J Appleseed & Co.

Dole, George F. & Bonney, Charles C. With Absolute Respect: The Swedenborgian Theology of Charles Carroll Bonney. (Swedenborg Studies: No. 3). 58, vp. 1993. pap. text 6.95 (*0-87785-182-4*) Swedenborg.

Dole, George F., ed. see Swedenborg, Emanuel.

Dole, George F., ed. & tr. see Swedenborg, Emanuel.

Dole, George F., tr. see Horn, Friedemann.

Dole, George F., tr. see Swedenborg, Emanuel.

Dole, Helen B., jt. auth. see Spyri, Johanna.

Dole, Helen B., tr. see Spyri, Johanna.

Dole, Jim W. & Rose, Betty B. An Amateur Botanist's Identification Manual for the Shrubs & Trees of the Southern California Coastal Region & Mountains. (Illus.). vi, 184p. (Orig.). 1996. pap. 14.95 (*0-9654151-1-2*) Foot-loose.

— An Amateur Botanist's Identification Manual for the Shrubs & Trees of the Southern California Deserts. (Illus.). vi, 157p. (Orig.). 1996. pap. 14.95 (*0-9654151-0-4*) Foot-loose.

Dole, John M. & Wilkins, Harold F. Floriculture. LC 98-21537. 613p. (C). 1998. 100.00 (*0-13-374703-4*) P-H.

Dole, Nathan H. Famous Composers. LC 68-24848. (Essay Index Reprint Ser.). Orig. Title: Score of Composers. (Illus.). 1977. reprint ed. 44.95 (*0-8369-0382-X*) Ayer.

— Teacher of Dante, & Other Studies in Italian Literature. LC 67-26733. (Essay Index Reprint Ser.). 1977. 18.95 (*0-8369-0383-8*) Ayer.

Dole, Nathan H., ed. see Rambaud, Alfred N.

Dole, Nathan H., tr. see Tolstoy, Leo.

***Dole, Nathan Haskell, tr.** The Russian Fairy Book. LC 99-88108. 128p. 2000. pap. 4.95 (*0-486-41019-6*) Dover.

Dole, Patricia P. Children's Books about Religion. LC 98-33707. 230p. (YA). 1999. pap. 32.00 (*1-56308-515-1*) Teacher Ideas Pr.

— Religious Books for Children: An Annotated Bibliography. 3rd rev. ed. LC 93-4930. (Bibliography Ser.). 40p. 1993. reprint ed. pap. 8.50 (*0-915324-35-0*) CSLA.

Dole, Richard & Porteus, Elizabeth D. The Story of James Dole. 3rd rev. ed. (Illus.). 120p. 1999. pap. write for info. (*0-89610-162-2*) Island Heritage.

Dole, Richard F., Jr. Territorial Trademark Rights & the Antitrust Laws. LC 66-63307. (Michigan Legal Publications). vi, 150p. 1985. reprint ed. lib. bdg. 42.00 (*0-89941-381-1*, 303510) W S Hein.

Dole, Richard F., jt. auth. see Alderman, Richard.

Dole, Samuel T. Windham in the Past. Dole, Frederick H., ed. 611p. 1995. reprint ed. lib. bdg. 62.50 (*0-8328-4664-3*) Higginson Bk Co.

— Windham in the Past: With Genealogical Sketches. Dole, Frederick H., ed. (Illus.). 611p. 1997. reprint ed. lib. bdg. 64.00 (*0-8328-5928-1*) Higginson Bk Co.

Doleans-Dade, Catherine A., jt. auth. see Ash, Robert B.

***Dolecek, Kelli.** Month-to-Month Gardening, Colorado: Tips for Designing, Growing & Maintaining Your Colorado. 2nd rev. ed. (Month-to-Month Gardening Ser.). (Illus.). 156p. 1999. 22.95 (*0-9663566-0-8*) Four Sisters Pubg.

— Month-to-Month Gardening, New Mexico: Tips for

An Asterisk (*) at the beginning of an entry indicates that the title is appearing for the first time.

Desiging, Growing & Maintaining Your New Mexico Garden. (Month-to-Month Gardening Ser.). (Illus.). 156p. 1999. 22.95 (*0-9663566-2-4*) Four Sisters Pubg.
— Month-to-Month Gardening, Utah: Tips for Designing, Growing & Maintaining Your Utah Garden. (Month-to-Month Gardening Ser.). (Illus.). 156p. 1999. 22.95 (*0-9663566-1-6*) Four Sisters Pubg.
Dolecek, Rajko, et al. Endocrinology of Thermal Injury: Pathophysiologic Mechanisms & Clinical Interpretation. Vaughan, George, ed. LC 89-12668. (Illus.). 469p. 1990. text 85.00 (*0-8121-1127-3*) Lppncott W & W.
Dolecheck, Carolyn C. & Murphy, Danny W. Applied Word-Information Processing: An Introduction. 2nd ed. (C). 1988. mass mkt. 43.95 (*0-538-23960-3*, W96) S-W Pub.
Dolecki, M., ed. Optimization. (Lecture Notes in Mathematics Ser.: Vol. 1405). viii, 220p. 1989. 33.00 (*0-387-51970-X*) Spr-Verlag.
Dolejs, Ladislaw, jt. auth. see Sorm, Frantisek.
Dolejs, P., et al, eds. Reservoir Management & Water Supply - An Integrated System: Selected Proceedings of the 1st IAWQ - IWSA Joint Specialist Conference on Reservoir Management & Water Supply - An Integrated System, Held in Prague, Czech Republic 19-23 May, 1997. (Water Science & Technology Ser.: Vol. 37, No. 2). 370p. 1998. pap. 159.00 (*0-08-043380-4*, Pergamon Pr) Elsevier.
Doleman, Bill. The Big Red Adventure: University of Nebraska Football. (Illus.). 192p. 1996. 39.95 (*0-9652267-0-0*) Anderson Ent.
Doleman, E., jt. ed. see Boston Publishing Company Editors.
Dolen, Carolyn E. Rewiring the Brain: A Lifeline to New Connections. 1998. 59.92 (*1-57444-192-2*) St Lucie Pr.
Dolenc, V. V. Anatomy & Surgery of the Cavernous Sinus. (Illus.). 360p. 1989. 247.00 (*0-387-82155-4*, 3503) Spr-Verlag.
Dolenc, V. V., ed. The Cavernous Sinus. (Illus.). 400p. 1987. 192.00 (*0-387-82000-0*) Spr-Verlag.
Dolence, Michael G. Strategic Enrollment Management: A Primer for Campus Administrators. 1996. 10.00 (*0-614-23452-2*, 9906) Am Assn Coll Registrars.
Dolence, Michael G., ed. Strategic Enrollment Management: Cases from the Field. 96p. 1996. 20.00 (*0-614-23453-0*, 9914) Am Assn Coll Registrars.
Dolence, Michael G. & Norris, Donald M. Transforming Higher Education: A Vision for Learning in the 21st Century. unabridged ed. (Illus.). 100p. (Orig.). 1995. pap. 40.00 (*0-9601608-0-9*) Soc Coll & Univ Planning.
Dolence, Michael G., et al. Working Toward Strategic Change: A Step-by-Step Guide to the Planning Process. LC 96-35692. (Higher & Adult Education Ser.). 192p. 1997. 22.00 (*0-7879-0796-0*) Jossey-Bass.
Dolence, Michael G., ed. see American Association of Collegiate Registrars & Ad.
Dolenko, Marilyn. Auditing Human Resources Management. Campbell, Lee A., ed. 40p. 1990. pap. 15.00 (*0-89413-218-0*, A810) Inst Inter Aud.
Dolenko, Veronica N., jt. auth. see Townsend, Charles E.
Dolenska, Silva. Anaesthetic Data Interpretation. (Illus.). 180p. 1999. pap. text 47.50 (*1-84110-008-0*) OUP.
Doleski, Teddi. The Hurt. (Illus.). 32p. (J). (gr. 1-3). 1983. pap. 4.95 (*0-8091-6551-1*) Paulist Pr.
Dolev, D., et al, eds. Theory of Computing & Systems: Israel Symposium ISTCS, Haifa, Israel, May 27-28, 1992, Proceedings. LC 92-11112. (Lecture Notes in Computer Science Ser.: Vol. 601). viii, 220p. 1992. 41.95 (*0-387-55553-6*) Spr-Verlag.
***Dolev, Shlomi.** Self-Stabilization. LC 99-38297. (Illus.). 394p. 2000. 40.00 (*0-262-04178-2*) MIT Pr.
Doley, Christine R., jt. auth. see Tobin, Patrick R.
Doleys, Daniel M., et al, eds. Behavioral Medicine: Assessment & Treatment Strategies. LC 81-23376. 648p. (C). 1982. 90.00 (*0-306-40841-4*, Plenum Trade) Perseus Pubng.
Doleysh, Nancy, jt. auth. see Vogel, Gerry.
Dolezal. Achieving Your Aims. (Longman Tutorial Resources Ser.). 1993. pap. text. write for info. (*0-582-22508-6*, Pub. by Addison-Wesley) Longman.
Dolezal, Margaret. Smokey's Odyssey. 64p. (YA). (gr. 7 up). 1998. 12.00 (*0-8059-4137-X*) Dorrance.
***Dolezal, Robert J.** Great Political Wit: Laughing (Almost) All the Way to the White House. LC 99-31999. 1999. write for info. (*1-56895-754-8*, Compass) Wheeler Pub.

Dolezal, Sue & Butterfield, Perry M. A Curriculum Written for Partners in Parenting Education, 3 vols. Incl. Listen, Listen, Listen. rev. ed. Grimshaw, Julie. (Illus.). 1999. text (*1-889839-07-8*); Love Is Layers of Sharing. 2nd rev. ed. Knox, Richelle. (Illus.). 204p. 1997. text (*1-889839-01-9*); Playing Is Learning. Pagano, Barbara. Butterfield, Perry M., ed. (Illus.). 200p. 1997. text (*1-889839-02-7*); text. write for info. (*1-889839-06-X*) How to Read.
Partners in Parenting Education (PIPE) is a curriculum specifically designed to teach emotional development & attachment concepts & skills to high-risk parents & their children 0-3 years old. It uses the baby as a teacher, to validate & empower parents through experiential learning. The parenting educator or home visitor becomes the facilitator & consultant for learning. Eight emotional development concepts are addressed & interwoven throughout 3 curriculum units: interdependence (attachment) shared positive emotions, communication/negotiation, trust, regulation, temperament autonomy & emotional refueling. Each of the 3 units has a different focus. LISTEN, LISTEN, LISTEN focuses on communication, observation & interaction skills between parent & child. PLAYING IS LEARNING focuses on the shared learning & mastery skills, the power of play to promote learning & how parents can help or hinder that process. LOVE IS LAYERS OF SHARING focuses on relationship building & emotional development. Each of the 3 units contain 8-10 topics which include the lesson plan, conceptual material, strategies, activity cards, video & parent pages. Training is available. For information; call How to Read Your Baby @ 303-377-4584(www.howtoreadyourbaby.com. Curriculum orders - can also be taken by Child Development Media, 800-405-8942 & Zero to Three, 800-899-4301.
Publisher Paid Annotation.

Dolezalek, Hans & Dolezalek, Lotte. The East German Research Landscape in Transition: Information for Scientific Interaction with East Germany, Including Surveys on the Structure of Research in the Federal Republic of Germany. (Illus.). 52p. (Orig.). (C). 1993. pap. text 45.00 (*1-56806-379-2*) DIANE Pub.
Dolezalek, Lotte, jt. auth. see Dolezalek, Hans.
Dolezel, L., et al, eds. Language & Literary Theory. (Papers in Slavic Philology: No. 5). vii, 643 p. 1984. pap. 15.00 (*0-930042-59-X*) Mich Slavic Pubns.
Dolezel, Lubomir. Heterocosmica: Fiction & Possible Worlds. LC 97-28537. (Parallax Ser.). (Illus.). xii, 339 p. 1998. text 45.00 (*0-8018-5749-X*) Johns Hopkins.
— Narrative Modes in Czech Literature. LC 74-190343. 161p. reprint ed. pap. 50.00 (*0-608-16580-8*, 202636000049) Bks Demand.
— Occidental Poetics: Tradition & Progress. LC 89-32798. 271p. 1990. reprint ed. pap. 84.10 (*0-608-03491-6*, 206420600008) Bks Demand.
Dolezel, Lubomir, jt. auth. see Bailey, Richard W.
Dolezel, Stephan, jt. ed. see Short, K. R.
Dolezelova-Velingerova, Milena, ed. The Chinese Novel at the Turn of the Century. LC 79-22783. (Modern East Asian Studies: No. 1). (Illus.). 263p. reprint ed. pap. 81.60 (*0-8357-8071-6*, 203406000088) Bks Demand.
***Dolfe, Marie & Koritz, Anna.** European Cash Management. LC 99-40031. 236p. 1999. 89.00 (*0-471-86550-8*) Wiley.
***Dolfi, Bob, et al.** Be My Love: A Celebration of Mario Lanza. (Illus.). 188p. 1999. pap. 19.95 (*1-56625-129-X*) Bonus Books.
Dolgachev, I., ed. Algebraic Geometry. (Lecture Notes in Mathematics Ser.: Vol. 1008). 138p. 1983. 29.95 (*0-387-12337-7*) Spr-Verlag.
Dolgachev, I. V., jt. auth. see Cossec, F.
Dolgan, Jeffrey I. & Goodman, Sandra M. Dollar-A-Day Teenage Pregnancy Prevention Program. Segal, Gillian G., ed. 55p. (Orig.). 1989. pap., student ed. write for info. (*0-318-65177-7*) PP Rocky Mtns.
Dolge, Alfred. Pianos & Their Makers. (Illus.). 581p. 1972. reprint ed. pap. 11.95 (*0-486-22856-8*) Dover.
***Dolgener, Forrest.** Personal Wellness. Hensley, Larry, ed. 368p. (C). 1998. pap. text 34.95 (*0-945483-85-6*) E Bowers Pub.
Dolgin. Cupid's Valentine: Read-Along. (Illus.). 32p. (J). (ps-2). 1985. pap. 9.95 (*0-87386-264-3*) Jan Prods.
— A Halloween Dream: Read-Along. (Illus.). 32p. (J). (ps-2). 1985. pap. 9.95 (*0-87386-265-1*) Jan Prods.
— Yin's Special Thanksgiving: Read-Along. (Illus.). 32p. (J). (ps-2). 1985. pap. 9.95 (*0-87386-263-5*) Jan Prods.
Dolgin, ed. Climate of Antarctica. (C). 1988. 140.00 (*0-7855-7578-2*) St Mut.
Dolgin, I. M., ed. Climate of Antarctica. Datta, P., tr. from RUS. (ENG.). 224p. (C). 1986. text 123.00 (*90-6191-463-9*, Pub. by A A Balkema) Ashgate Pub Co.
Dolgin, Janet L. Defining the Family: Law, Technology, & Reproduction in an Uneasy Age. 1999. pap. text 19.50 (*0-8147-1917-1*) NYU Pr.
— Defining the Family: Law, Technology, & Reproduction in an Uneasy Age. LC 96-35617. 320p. (C). 1999. text 30.00 (*0-8147-1859-0*) NYU Pr.
Dolgin, Marina, tr. see Hutchinson, Hanna, ed.
Dolgin, Martin, ed. see Criteria Committee of the New York Heart Associati.
Dolginov, A. Z., et al. Propagation & Polarization of Radiation in Cosmic Media. 400p. 1995. text 154.00 (*2-88124-987-6*) Gordon & Breach.
Dolginow, J. & Kropatschjow, S. Abriss der Geologie Russlands und Angrenzender Staaten. viii, 174p. 1994. pap. 29.00 (*3-510-65158-8*, Pub. by E Schweizerbartsche) Balogh.
Dolgins, Adam. Rock Names: From ABBA to ZZ Top - How Rock Bands Got Their Names. (Illus.). 256p. 1992. pap. 10.95 (*0-8065-1363-2*, Citadel Pr) Carol Pub Group.
— Rock Names: From Abba to ZZ Top; How Rock Groups Got Their Names. rev. ed. LC 95-22309. 1995. pap. 10.95 (*0-8065-1617-8*, Citadel Pr) Carol Pub Group.
— Rock Names: How Rock Bands Got Their Names. 1998. pap. 95.70 (*0-8065-9808-5*, Citadel Pr) Carol Pub Group.
— Rock Names: How Rock Bands Got Their Names. rev. ed. LC 98-30717. (Illus.). 299p. 1998. pap. 15.95 (*0-8065-2046-9*, Citadel Pr) Carol Pub Group.
Dolgoff, Anatole. Physical Geology. (C). 1996. text, teacher ed. 2.66 (*0-669-33912-1*); pap. text 56.36 (*0-669-41685-1*) HM Trade Div.
— Physical Geology. (C). 1996. pap. text, student ed. 23.56 (*0-669-33911-3*) HM Trade Div.
— Understanding Social Welfare. 5th ed. LC 99-18226. 414p. (C). 1999. 63.00 (*0-8013-3036-X*) Allyn
Dolgoff, Anatole & Falcon, Mary. Essentials of Physical Geology Today. LC 97-72460. xxviii, 461p. 1998. write for info. (*0-669-33916-4*) HM Schl Div.
Dolgoff, Ralph & Feldstein, Donald. Understanding Social Welfare. 2nd ed. LC 83-20003. 400p. (C). 1983. pap. text 38.33 (*0-582-28462-7*, 71493) Longman.
Dolgoff, Ralph, jt. auth. see Loewenberg, Frank M.
Dolgoff, Sam. The Cuban Revolution: A Critical Perspective. 199p. 1976. 44.99 (*0-919618-36-7*, Pub. by Black Rose); pap. 15.99 (*0-919618-35-9*, Pub. by Black Rose) Consort Bk Sales.
Dolgoff, Sam, ed. The Anarchist Collectives: Workers Self-Management in Spain 1936-39. 195p. 1974. 45.99 (*0-919618-21-9*, 1974, Pub. by Black Rose); pap. 16.99 (*0-919618-20-0*, Pub. by Black Rose) Consort Bk Sales.
— Bakunin on Anarchism. 453p. 1980. 47.99 (*0-919619-06-1*, Pub. by Black Rose); pap. 18.99 (*0-919619-05-3*, Pub. by Black Rose) Consort Bk Sales.
Dolgopolsky, Aharon. The Nostratic Macrofamily & Linguistic Palaeontology. (Papers in the Prehistory of Languages). (Illus.). 116p. 1998. pap. 36.00 (*0-9519420-7-7*) McDonald Inst.
Dolgowich, Sheila, et al. Chances Are: Hands-On Activities in Probability & Statistics, Grades 3-7. xviii, 125p. 1995. pap. text 22.00 (*1-56308-314-0*) Teacher Ideas Pr.
Dolhinow, Phyllis & Fuentes, Augustin, eds. The Nonhuman Primates. LC 98-45272. 1999. pap. text 32.95 (*1-55934-974-3*) Mayfield Pub.
Doliana, Roberto, jt. auth. see Colombatti, Alfonso.
Dolibois, John E. Pattern of Circles: An Ambassador's Story. LC 89-8008. (Illus.). 333p. 1989. 26.00 (*0-87338-389-3*) Kent St U Pr.
Dolice, J. L. The Money Machine: Making Extra Income with Your Home Computer. (Illus.). 300p. (Orig.). 1997. pap. 29.95 (*0-935901-05-1*) Dolice Graphics.
— Techie Freelancing: Careers in Theatre & Business. (Illus.). 200p. (Orig.). 1997. pap. 29.95 (*0-935901-06-X*) Dolice Graphics.
Dolice, Joseph L. Free Computer Media: The Ultimate Guide to Free Computer Stuff. (Illus.). 230p. (Orig.). 1995. pap. 24.00 (*0-935901-02-7*) Dolice Graphics.
— Leon Dolice: Old New York Remembered & Other Etchings, 1920-1951. LC 85-91514. (Illus.). 24p. (Orig.). 1987. pap. 5.00 (*0-935901-01-9*) Dolice Graphics.
Doligez, B., ed. Migration of Hydrocarbons in Sedimentary Basins: 3rd IFP Exploration & Production Research Conference, Carcans, 1987. (Illus.). 712p. (C). 1987. 775.00 (*2-7108-0540-5*, Pub. by Edits Technip) Enfield Pubs NH.
Doligez, B., jt. auth. see Eschard, R.
Dolin, Eric J. Dirty Water, Clean Water: A Chronology of Events Surrounding the Degradation & Cleanup of Boston Harbor. (Illus.). (Orig.). 1990. pap. text 9.00 (*1-56172-001-1*) MIT Sea Grant.
Dolin, Eric J. & Pederson, Judith. Marine-Dredged Materials Management in Massachusetts: Issues, Options & the Future. 46p. (Orig.). 1992. write for info. (*1-56172-006-2*) MIT Sea Grant.
***Dolin, Eric Jay & Dumaine, Bob.** The Duck Stamp Story: Art, Conservation, History. LC 99-67653. (Illus.). 208p. 2000. 49.95 (*0-87341-815-8*); pap. 29.95 (*0-87341-814-X*, DUCK) Krause Pubns.
Dolin, Kieran. Fiction & the Law: Legal Discourses in Victorian & Modernist Literature. LC 98-38602. 300p. (C). 1999. text 54.95 (*0-521-62332-4*) Cambridge U Pr.
Dolin, Nick, et al. Basketball Stars: The Greatest Players in the History of the Game. LC 96-52612. (Illus.). 128p. (J). 1996. 24.98 (*1-884822-61-4*) Blck Dog & Leventhal.
***Dolin, Raphael & Wright, Peter F.** Viral Infections of the Respiratory Tract. LC 98-55495. (Lung Biology in Health & Disease Ser.). (Illus.). 464p. 1999. text 185.00 (*0-8247-0195-X*) Dekker.
Dolin, Raphael, et al. AIDS Therapy. Staruss, Marc, ed. LC 98-34773. 715p. (C). 1999. text 79.00 (*0-443-07592-1*) Church.
Dolin, Sharon. Climbing Mt. Sinai. 12p. 1996. pap. 15.00 (*1-891472-10-0*) Dim Gray.
— Heart Work: Poems. LC 95-39157. 96p. 1995. pap. 12.95 (*1-878818-42-2*, Pub. by Sheep Meadow) U Pr of New Eng.
***Dolin, Sharon.** Mistakes. (Poetry New York Pamphlet Ser.: No. 24). 18p. 1999. pap. 5.00 (*0-923389-40-7*) Meet Eyes Bind.
Dolin, Simon J., et al, eds. Pain Clinic Manual. LC 95-43195. 320p. 1996. text 75.00 (*0-7506-2036-6*) Buttrwrth-Heinemann.
Dolin, Tim. Mistress of the House: Women of Property in the Victorian Novel. LC 97-29550. (Nineteenth Century Ser.). 168p. 1997. text 61.95 (*1-85928-184-2*, Pub. by Ashgate Pub) Ashgate Pub Co.
Dolin, Tim, ed. & notes see Hardy, Thomas.
Dolinar, F. & Schmitt, S. The Osborne-McGraw-Hill 16-Bit CP-M User's Guide. (Osborne Books). 500p. 1984. pap. 18.95 (*0-88134-130-4*) McGraw.
Dolinar, Kathleen, et al. Learning Through Play: Curriculum & Activities for the Inclusive Classroom. LC 93-25976. 113p. 1994. teacher ed. 14.95 (*0-8273-5654-4*) Delmar.
Dolinar, Kathleen J., et al. Learning Through Play: Curriculum & Activities for the Inclusive Classroom. LC 93-25976. (C). 1994. mass mkt. 33.25 (*0-8273-5653-6*) Delmar.
Doling. Comparative Housing Policy. LC 96-30028. 1997. text 65.00 (*0-312-17410-1*) St Martin.
Doling, Annabel. Macau on a Plate. (Illus.). 126p. 1996. pap. 19.95 (*962-7992-01-1*, Pub. by Saqi) Intl Spec Bk.
— Vietnam on a Plate. (Illus.). 133p. 1996. pap. 19.95 (*962-7992-02-X*, Pub. by Saqi) Intl Spec Bk.
Doling, Tim. Asia Pacific Arts Directory: Vol. 1: Australasia & the Pacific; Vol. 2: South East Asia; Vol. 3: North East, Vols. 1-3. 1000p. 1996. 115.00 (*92-3-103292-5*, U3292, Pub. by UNESCO) Bernan Associates.
Dolinger, Jacob & Rosenn, Keith S., eds. A Panorama of Brazilian Law. 522p. (C). 1991. 89.95 (*0-935501-37-1*, Pub. by U Miami N-S Ctr) L Rienner.
***Dolinger, James A.** Selling in the Real World: Connect & Collect. Droke, Gina & Lee, Bunny, eds. 128p. 2000. pap. 19.95 (*0-9677272-0-0*) Real World.
Dolinger, Leah, tr. see Alfasi, E., et al.
Dolinin, A. S., jt. auth. see Suslova, Apollinaria P.
Dolinjak, Igor. Progulka V Durnoe Obshcestvo. Levin, Gina, ed. LC 90-61124.Tr. of A Walk into Bad Company. (RUS.). 66p. 1992. pap. text 14.98 (*0-914265-14-8*) New Eng Pub MA.
Dolinko, Caryl, jt. auth. see Smits, Wayne.
Dolins, Francine L., ed. Attitudes to Animals: Views in Animal Welfare. LC 97-32155. (Illus.). 275p. (C). 1999. text 64.95 (*0-521-47342-X*); pap. text 23.95 (*0-521-47906-1*) Cambridge U Pr.
Dolios, Demetrios. Screaming Poems: In the Night. 56p. (Orig.). 1996. pap. 5.00 (*1-885778-16-3*) Seaburn.
Dolis, John. The Style of Hawthorne's Gaze: Regarding Subjectivity. LC 92-33475. 288p. (C). 1993. text 39.95 (*0-8173-0681-1*) U of Ala Pr.
***Dolis, John.** Time Flies - Butterflies. 35p. 1999. pap. 5.00 (*1-57141-049-X*) Runaway Spoon.
Dolit, Alan. You Can Lose Weight. 130p. 1980. 7.95 (*0-8290-1571-X*) Irvington.
Dolitsky, Alexander B. Old Russia in Modern America: A Case from Russian Old Believers in Alaska. 3rd unabridged ed. (Alaska-Siberia Research Center Ser.: Vol. 10). (Illus.). 60p. 1988. pap. 12.00 (*0-9653891-2-X*, 94-3121266) Alaska-Siberia.
Dolitsky, Alexander B., ed. Fairy Tales & Myths of the Bering Strait Chukchi. unabridged ed. Michael, Henry N., tr. from RUS. (Alaska-Siberia Research Center Ser.: No. 8). (Illus.). 151p. (Orig.). (C). 1996. pap. 18.50 (*0-9653891-0-3*, 94-3121266) Alaska-Siberia.
— Fairy Tales & Myths of the Bering Strait Chukchi. 2nd unabridged ed. Michael, Henry N., tr. from RUS. (Alaska-Siberia Research Center, Publication: No. 9). (Illus.). 160p. (Orig.). 1997. pap. 18.00 (*0-9653891-1-1*, 94-3121266) Alaska-Siberia.
***Dolitsky, Alexander B., ed.** Tales & Legends of the Yupik Eskimos of Siberia. unabridged ed. Michael, Henry N., tr. from RUS. (Publication Ser.: No. 11). Orig. Title: Fairy Tales & Myths of the People of Chukotka & Kamchatka. (Illus.). 160p. 2000. pap. 18.00 (*0-9653891-3-8*, 94-3121266) Alaska-Siberia.
Dolitsky, Marlene. Under the Tumtum Tree: From Nonsense to Sense, a Study in Non-Automatic Comprehension. LC 84-28471. (Pragmatics & Beyond Ser.: Vol. V:1). vii, 118p. 1985. pap. 41.00 (*0-915027-39-9*) J Benjamins Pubng Co.
Dolitsky, Marlene, jt. ed. see Pieraut-Le Bonniec, Gilberte.
Dolive, David W. My God, My God, Why Hast Thou Forsaken Me. (Illus.). 192p. 1998. pap. write for info. (*0-9662785-0-X*) David Publng.
Dolive, Linda L. Electoral Politics at the Local Level in the German Federal Republic. LC 76-26473. (University of Florida Monographs: Social Sciences: No. 56). 120p. reprint ed. pap. 37.20 (*0-7837-5083-8*, 204478100004) Bks Demand.
***D'Oliveira, Basil & Goulder, Brian, eds.** The Macmillan Reeds Nautical Almanac 2000: European Edition. (Illus.). 1136p. 2000. pap. 69.50 (*0-333-80277-2*, Pub. by S1 & J) Trans-Atl Phila.
D'Oliveira, H. U., ed. Netherlands Reports to the 11th International Congress of Comparative Law. 465p. 1982. pap. 34.00 (*90-6544-073-9*) Kluwer Academic.
D'Oliveira, Manuela, jt. auth. see Greene, Judith.
D'Olivet, Antoine F. The Secret Lore of Music: The Hidden Power of Orpheus. Godwin, Joscelyn, tr. from FRE. LC 97-18293. 208p. 1997. pap. 12.95 (*0-89281-660-0*) Inner Tradit.
D'Olivet, Fabre. Cain: A Dramatic Mystery in Three Acts by Lord Byron. Redfield, Nayan L., tr. 275p. 1996. reprint ed. pap. 24.95 (*1-56459-615-X*) Kessinger Pub.
— The Golden Verses of Pythagoras: Explained & Translated into French & Preceded by a Discourse upon the Essence & Form of Poetry among the Principal Peoples of the Earth. Redfield, Nayan L., tr. (FRE.). 290p. 1992. reprint ed. pap. 27.00 (*1-56459-276-6*) Kessinger Pub.
— The Healing of Rudolphe Grivel: Congenital Deaf-Mute. Redfield, Nayan L., tr. 283p. 1995. reprint ed. pap. 24.95 (*1-56459-499-8*) Kessinger Pub.
— The Hebraic Tongue Restored: And the True Meaning of the Hebrew Words Re-Established & Proved by Their Radical Analysis. Redfield, Nayan L., tr. 824p. 1992. reprint ed. pap. 49.95 (*1-56459-281-2*) Kessinger Pub.
— Hermeneutic Interpretation of the Origin of the Social State of Man & of the Adamic Race. Redfield, Nayan L., tr. 607p. 1992. reprint ed. pap. 45.00 (*1-56459-277-4*) Kessinger Pub.
Doliveux, Paul. Driving a Tandem. 146p. 1997. pap. 60.00 (*0-85131-674-3*, Pub. by J A Allen) Trafalgar.
D'Olivo, J. C., et al, eds. Particles & Fields: Sixth Mexican Workshop. (Conference Proceedings Ser.: Vol. 445). (Illus.). 388p. 1998. 105.00 (*1-56396-791-X*) Am Inst Physics.
— Relativity & Gravitation - Classical & Quantum. 450p. (C). 1991. text 104.00 (*981-02-0715-8*) World Scientific Pub.
D'Olivo, J. C., et al. Particles & Fields: Proceedings of the Sixth Mexican School. 500p. 1995. text 122.00 (*981-02-2121-5*) World Scientific Pub.

D

An Asterisk (*) at the beginning of an entry indicates that the title is appearing for the first time.

D'Olivo, Juan C., et al, eds. The Fifth Workshop on Particles & Fields & the Workshop on Phenomenology of the Fundamental Interactions. (AIP Conference Proceedings Ser.: No. 359). (Illus.). 560p. 1996. 140.00 (*1-56396-548-8*, AIP Pr) Spr-Verlag.
— First Latin American Symposium on High Energy Physics & VII Mexican School of Particles & Fields. LC 97-73971. (Conference Proceedings Ser.: Vol. 400). (Illus.). xix, 578p. 1997. 135.00 (*1-56396-686-7*, AIP Pr) Spr-Verlag.

***D'Olivo, Juan Carlos, et al, eds.** Particles & Fields: 8th Mexican School. LC 99-67150. (Conference Proceedings Ser.: Vol. 490). (Illus.). 455p. 1999. 135.00 (*1-56396-895-9*) Am Inst Physics.

Dolk, Jann, jt. auth. see Sanders, Roger C.

Dolkark, Andrew. Gramercy, Its Architectural Surroundings: Preserving the Neighborhood's Important Contributing Buildings. Gramercy Neighborhood Associates Inc., Historic Pr, ed. (Illus.). 96p. (Orig.). 1996. pap. 30.00 (*0-9651763-0-4*) Gramercy Neighbrhd.

Dolkart, Andrew. Morningside Heights: A History of Its Architecture & Development. LC 97-44482. (History of Urban Life Ser.). (Illus.). 471p. 1998. 50.00 (*0-231-07850-1*) Col U Pr.

Dolkart, Andrew S. Touring Lower Manhattan: Walks in Three Historic Districts. 1999. pap. 12.00 (*0-9647061-4-8*, Pub. by NY Landmarks) City & Co.
— Touring the Upper East Side: Walks in Five Historic Districts. 128p. 1997. pap. 12.00 (*0-9647061-0-5*, Pub. by NY Landmarks) City & Co.

Dolkart, Andrew S. & Sorin, Gretchen S. Touring Historic Harlem: Four Walks in Northern Manhattan. 144p. 1997. pap. 12.00 (*0-9647061-1-3*, Pub. by NY Landmarks) City & Co.

Dolkart, Andrew S. & Tunick, Susan. George & Edward Blum: Texture & Design in New York Apartment House Architecture. (Illus.). 72p. 1993. pap. text 15.00 (*0-9636061-0-7*, Pub. by Frnds of TC) Kesend Pub Ltd.

Dolkas, jt. auth. see Bach.

Dolkhart, Ronald H., ed. The Argentine Right: Its History & Intellectual Origins, 1910 to the Present. LC 92-20368. (Latin American Silhouettes Ser.). 256p. (C). 1993. 45.00 (*0-8420-2418-2*, SR Bks); pap. text 17.95 (*0-8420-2419-0*, SR Bks) Scholarly Res Inc.

Doll, Amy & Rubin, Kenneth I. Significance in Environmental Project Planning: Resource Document. (Illus.). 84p. (C). 1997. pap. text 25.00 (*0-7881-4543-6*) DIANE Pub.

Doll, Beth & Doll, Carol. Bibliotherapy with Young People: Librarians & Mental Health Professionals Working Together. LC 96-51730. 125p. (Orig.). 1997. pap. 23.00 (*1-56308-407-4*) Libs Unl.

Doll, Bob. Instant Revenue: Low Maintenance High Profit Radio Telemarketing. (Illus.). 81p. (Orig.). 1998. pap. 117.00 (*1-886745-16-1*) Streamlne Pr.
— Sparks Out of the Plowed Ground. LC 95-67243. (Illus.). 322p. 1996. pap. 19.99 (*1-886745-05-6*) Streamlne Pr.

Doll, Carol, jt. auth. see Doll, Beth.

Doll, Carol A. Exploring the Pacific States Through Literature. LC 93-37447. (Exploring the United States Through Literature Ser.). 168p. 1994. pap. 27.50 (*0-89774-771-2*) Oryx Pr.
— Nonfiction Books for Children: Activities for Thinking, Learning, & Doing. x, 117p. 1990. pap. text 19.50 (*0-87287-710-8*) Teacher Ideas Pr.

Doll, Carol A. & Barron, Pamela P., eds. Collection Analysis for the School Library Media Center: A Practical Approach. LC 90-40208. (C). 1990. pap. text 17.00 (*0-8389-3390-4*, 3390-4) ALA.

Doll, Don, photos by. Creighton University. (Illus.). 112p. 1991. 39.00 (*0-916509-68-0*) Harmony Hse Pub.

***Doll, Elsie.** Essential Tremors. 32p. 1999. pap. 9.95 (*1-58374-010-4*) Chicago Spectrum.

Doll, J. D., jt. ed. see Gubernatis, J. E.

Doll, John G. The Battling Bastards of Bataan: A Chronology of the First Days of World War II in the Philippines. 3rd rev. ed. (World War II Monograph: Vol. 36). (Illus.). 69p. 1997. 24.95 (*1-57638-069-6*, M36H); pap. 14.95 (*1-57638-009-2*, M36S) Merriam Pr.
— Cloth Maps, Charts & Blood Chits of World War II. 3rd rev. ed. (World War II Monograph: Vol. 41). (Illus.). 32p. 1997. 14.95 (*1-57638-072-6*, M41H); pap. 4.95 (*1-57638-024-6*, M41S) Merriam Pr.

Doll, John P. & Orazem, Frank. Production Economics: Theory with Applications. 2nd ed. LC 92-18812. 480p. (C). 1992. reprint ed. lib. bdg. 56.50 (*0-89464-769-5*) Krieger.

Doll, Kathyrn, ed. see Beattie, Linda C.

Doll, Kathyrn, ed. see Inlow, Linda C.

Doll, Louis W. A History of the Newspapers of Ann Arbor, 1829-1920. LC 59-9322. (Wayne State University Studies: No. 5). 183p. reprint ed. pap. 56.80 (*0-7837-3787-4*, 204360700010) Bks Demand.

Doll, Mary A. To the Lighthouse & Back: Writings on Teaching & Living, Vol. 19. (Counterpoints Ser.). VIII, 172p. (C). 1995. pap. 29.95 (*0-8204-2777-2*) P Lang Pubng.

Doll, Nancy. Home Show 2. (Illus.). 28p. (Orig.). 1996. pap. 18.00 (*1-880658-11-9*) San Barb CAF.

Doll, Nancy, ed. see Moser, Joann & Dreishpoon, Douglas.

Doll, Nelly E., jt. auth. see Wilkinson, Helen M.

***Doll, Pancho.** Day Trips with a Splash: Swimming Holes of the Southwest. (Illus.). 216p. 2000. pap. 18.50 (*0-9657686-2-7*) Runnin Wtr Pubns.
— Day Trips with a Splash: The Swimming Holes of California. (Illus.). 256p. (Orig.). 1997. pap. 18.95 (*0-9657686-3-5*) Runnin Wtr Pubns.

***Doll, Pancho.** Day Trips with a Splash: The Swimming Holes of California. (Illus.). (Orig.). 1998. pap. 18.95 (*0-9657686-4-3*) Runnin Wtr Pubns.

***Doll, Peter M.** Revolution, Religion, & National Identity: Imperial Anglicanism in British North America, 1745-1795. LC 99-35775. 336p. 1999. 49.50 (*0-8386-3830-9*) Fairleigh Dickinson.

Doll, R., et al, eds. Trends in Cancer Incidence & Mortality. (Cancer Surveys Ser.: Vol. 19/20). (Illus.). 583p. (C). 1994. 108.00 (*0-87969-391-6*) Cold Spring Harbor.

Doll, R., ed. see International Agency for Research on Cancer Staff.

Doll, Richard, jt. ed. see Wald, Nicholas J.

Doll, Ronald C. Curriculum Improvement: Decision Making & Process. 7th rev. ed. 550p. 1989. boxed set 45.00 (*0-205-11851-8*, H1851-8) Allyn.
— Curriculum Improvement: Decision Making & Process. 9th ed. LC 94-48644. 544p. 1995. 79.00 (*0-205-16457-9*) Allyn.

Doll, Susan. The Films of Elvis Presley. (Illus.). 96p. 1993. 9.98 (*1-56173-278-8*, 3110000) Pubns Intl Ltd.

Doll, Susan M. Understanding Elvis: Southern Roots vs. Star Image. (Garland Studies in American Popular History & Culture). (Illus.). 224p. 1998. 56.00 (*0-8153-3164-9*) Garland.

Doll, Thomas. Marine Fighting Squadron 121: (VMF-121) (Illus.). 72p. (Orig.). 1996. pap. 12.95 (*0-89747-369-8*, 6177) Squad Sig Pubns.
— SBC Helldiver in Action. (Aircraft in Action Ser.). (Illus.). 50p. 1995. pap. 9.95 (*0-89747-331-0*) Squad Sig Pubns.
— SB2U Vindicator in Action. (Aircraft in Action Ser.). (Illus.). 50p. 1992. pap. 9.95 (*0-89747-274-8*, 1122) Squad Sig Pubns.

***Doll, Thomas.** USMC Night Fighters. 64p. 2000. pap. 11.95 (*0-89747-419-8*, 6083) Squad Sig Pubns.

Doll, William E., Jr. A Post-Modern Perspective on Curriculum. 232p. 1993. pap. 19.95 (*0-8077-3447-0*) Tchrs Coll.

Dollahite, David, jt. ed. see Card, Orson Scott.

***Dollahite, David C.** Strengthening Our Families: An In-Depth Look at the Proclamation on the Family. LC 00-37933. 2000. write for info. (*1-57345-824-4*) Deseret Bk.

Dollahite, David C., jt. ed. see Hawkins, Alan J.

Dollar. Color of Love. LC 97-218517. 304p. 1997. pap. 14.99 (*1-57794-024-5*, HH2-024) Harrison Hse.

Dollar, Alan. Secrets of Uechi Ryu Karate: And the Mysteries of Okinawa. Dollar, Alice & Davidson, Robert, eds. Shinjo, Kiyohide, tr. (Illus.). 512p. (Orig.). 1996. pap. 44.95 (*0-9651671-1-9*) Cherokee Pubng.

Dollar, Alice, ed. see Dollar, Alan.

Dollar, Bruce. Learning & Growing Through Tutoring. 130p. 1974. pap. 5.00 (*0-912041-07-2*) Natl Comm Res Youth.

Dollar, Cre. Anointing to Live. 1997. pap. 7.00 (*1-885072-10-4*) Wrld Chang Minist.

Dollar, Creflo. Answers Awaiting in the Presence of God. LC 96-108612. 96p. 1995. pap. 7.99 (*0-89274-794-3*, HH-794) Harrison Hse.

Dollar, Creflo A., Jr. Capturing the Reality of Heaven & Hell. 18p. (Orig.). 1993. pap. 1.99 (*0-9634781-2-5*) Wrld Chang Minist.
— Confidence: The Missing Substance. pap. 1.99 (*0-9634781-3-3*) Wrld Chang Minist.
— Confidence: The Missing Substance of Faith. 22p. (Orig.). 1993. pap. 1.99 (*0-9634781-6-8*, 004CX) Wrld Chang Minist.
— The Divine Order of Faith: How to Get from the Problem to the Answer. 80p. (Orig.). 1993. pap. 8.75 (*0-9634781-1-7*) Wrld Chang Minist.
— Exposing the Spirit of Competitive Jealousy. 28p. (Orig.). 1993. pap. 1.99 (*0-685-71361-X*) Wrld Chang Minist.
— The Force of Integrity. 20p. (Orig.). 1993. pap. 1.99 (*0-9634781-4-1*) Wrld Chang Minist.
— God's Purpose for the Anointing. 56p. 1992. pap. 7.95 (*0-9634781-0-9*) Wrld Chang Minist.
— Hearing from God & Walking in the Comfort of the Holy Spirit. 1994. write for info. (*0-9634781-9-2*) Wrld Chang Minist.
— How to Trouble Your Trouble. 1999. 17.99 (*1-57794-061-X*) Dake Pub.
— Lasciviousness: The Result of Neglect. 1994. write for info. (*0-9634781-7-6*) Wrld Chang Minist.

***Dollar, Creflo A., Jr.** Lord Teach Me How to Love: Learning from the Ultimate Example. 2000. 19.99 (*1-57794-295-7*) Harrison Hse.

Dollar, Creflo A., Jr. Rightness vs. Righteousness. 20p. (Orig.). 1993. pap. 1.99 (*0-9634781-5-X*) Wrld Chang Minist.
— Total Life Prosperity. LC 99-15324. 228p. 1999. pap. 12.99 (*0-7852-6900-2*) Nelson.
— Uprooting the Spirit of Fear. LC 95-195265. 96p. 1994. pap. 6.99 (*0-89274-686-6*) Harrison Hse.

Dollar, David & Wolff, Edward N. Competitiveness, Convergence & International Specialization. (Illus.). 232p. 1993. 37.50 (*0-262-04135-9*) MIT Pr.

Dollar, David, et al. Household Welfare & Vietnam's Transition. LC 97-46963. (Regional & Sectoral Studies). 352p. 1998. pap. 35.00 (*0-8213-4162-6*) World Bank.

Dollar, Harold E. A Biblical-Missiological Exploration of the Cross-Cultural Dimensions in Luke - Acts. LC 92-44979. 448p. 1993. text 109.95 (*0-7734-2212-9*) E Mellen.
— St. Luke's Missiology: A Cross-Cultural Challenge. LC 96-8292. 208p. (Orig.). 1996. pap. text 9.95 (*0-87808-267-0*, WCL267-0) William Carey Lib.

Dollar, Sam. The History of the Phoenix Mercury. LC 99-18891. (Women's Pro Basketball Today Ser.). 1999. lib. bdg. 21.30 (*1-58341-015-5*, Creat Educ) Creative Co.

Dollar, Susan E. The Freedmen's Bureau Schools of Natchitoches Parish Louisiana, 1865-1868. Cameron, Neill, ed. LC 98-66968. (Illus.). 148p. 1998. pap. 18.50 (*0-917898-20-6*) NSU Pr LA.

***Dollar, Taffi L.** A Woman after God's Own Heart: Fulfilling the Will of God for Your Life & Empowering Those Around You. LC 99-57357. 192p. 2000. pap. 12.99 (*0-7852-6999-1*) Nelson.

Dollar, Tom. Guide to Arizona's Wilderness Areas. LC 98-24594. (Illus.). 296p. 1999. pap. 24.95 (*1-56579-280-7*) Westcliffe Pubs.
— Indian Country: A Guide to Northeastern Arizona. 64p. 1994. pap. 9.95 (*0-916179-39-7*) Ariz Hwy.

Dollard, Jerry. Toward Spirituality: The Inner Journey. 17p. 1983. pap. 1.75 (*0-89486-193-X*, 1421B) Hazelden.

Dollard, John. Caste & Class in a Southern Town. LC 88-40430. 486p. 1988. reprint ed. pap. 150.70 (*0-608-07473-X*, 206769500009) Bks Demand.
— Criteria for the Life History, with Analyses of Six Notable Documents. (Select Bibliographies Reprint Ser.). 1977. reprint ed. 23.95 (*0-8369-6685-6*) Ayer.
— Fear in Battle. LC 75-41076. reprint ed. 22.50 (*0-404-14714-3*) AMS Pr.

Dollard, John, et al. Frustration & Aggression. LC 79-26458. 209p. 1980. reprint ed. lib. bdg. 35.00 (*0-313-22201-0*, DOFR, Greenwood Pr) Greenwood.

Dollard, John, jt. auth. see Miller, Neal E.

Dollard, Linda L. Hang-Ups! Ideas to Ignite Creativity & Imagination. 32p. 1995. teacher ed. 5.99 (*1-56417-830-7*, GA1547) Good Apple.
— Little Writers. 48p. (J). (gr. k-1). 1996. 6.99 (*1-56417-859-5*, FE7859) Fearon Teacher Aids.
— Writing Set, 3 bks., Set. (J). (gr. k-1). 25.99 (*1-56417-728-9*, FE0004) Fearon Teacher Aids.

Dollarhide, Colette. The Better Sentence. 200p. (C). 1987. pap. text 13.95 (*0-935920-36-6*, Ntl Pubs Blck) P-H.

Dollarhide, Kenneth. Nichiren's Senji-Sho: An Essay on the Selection of the Proper Time. LC 82-21687. (Studies in Asian Thought & Religion: Vol. 1). 184p. 1983. lib. bdg. 79.95 (*0-88946-051-5*) E Mellen.

Dollarhide, Louis D. Of Art & Artists: Selected Reviews of the Arts in Mississippi, 1955-1976. LC 80-52629. 176p. reprint ed. pap. 54.60 (*0-7837-1402-5*, 204158300021) Bks Demand.

***Dollarhide, William.** America's Best Genealogy Resource Centers. LC 99-212756. 139p. 1998. pap. 15.95 (*1-877677-90-6*, Precision Index) Herit Quest.
— British Origins of American Colonists, 1629-1775. 63p. 1997. pap. 12.95 (*1-877677-69-8*, Precision Index) Herit Quest.
— The Census Book: A Genealogist's Guide to Federal Census Facts, Schedules & Indexes. 183p. 1999. pap. 24.95 (*1-877677-98-1*) Herit Quest.

Dollarhide, William. Genealogy Starter Kit. 2nd ed. LC 98-72334. 48p. 1998. reprint ed. pap. 9.95 (*0-8063-1577-6*) Genealog Pub.
— Map Guide to American Migration Routes: 1735-1815. LC 98-145522. 1997. pap. text 9.95 (*1-877677-74-4*) Herit Quest.

Dollarhide, William. Seven Steps to a Family Tree. 26p. pap. 5.50 (*1-877677-68-X*) Herit Quest.

Dollarhide, William, jt. auth. see Thorndale, William.

Dollas, Apostolas. The Art of Microelectronic Systems. 350p. (C). 2000. text 49.95 (*1-56881-031-8*) AK Peters.

Dollase, Richard. Voices of Beginning Teachers: Visions & Realities. LC 92-13409. 192p. (C). 1992. pap. text 18.95 (*0-8077-3192-7*) Tchrs Coll.

Dollberg, Donald D. & Verstuyft, Allen W., eds. Analytical Techniques in Occupational Health Chemistry. LC 79-28460. (ACS Symposium Ser.: No. 120). 318p. 1980. 43.95 (*0-8412-0539-6*) Am Chemical.
— Analytical Techniques in Occupational Health Chemistry. LC 79-28460. (ACS Symposium Ser.: Vol. 120). 328p. 1980. reprint ed. pap. 101.70 (*0-608-03058-9*, 206351100007) Bks Demand.

Dolle, Raymond F. Anne Bradstreet: A Reference Guide. (Reference Guides to Literature Ser.). 300p. 1990. 45.00 (*0-8161-8974-9*, Hall Reference) Macmillan.

Dolleans, Edouard. Histoire du Mouvement Ouvrier, 3 vols., Set. Mayer, J. P., ed. LC 78-67350. (European Political Thought Ser.). (FRE.). 1980. reprint ed. lib. bdg. 92.95 (*0-405-11693-4*) Ayer.
— Histoire du Mouvement Ouvrier, 3 vols., Vol. 1. Mayer, J. P., ed. LC 78-67350. (European Political Thought Ser.). (FRE.). 1980. reprint ed. lib. bdg. 46.95 (*0-405-11694-2*) Ayer.
— Histoire du Mouvement Ouvrier, 3 vols., Vol. 3. Mayer, J. P., ed. LC 78-67350. (European Political Thought Ser.). (FRE.). 1980. reprint ed. 46.95 (*0-405-11696-9*) Ayer.

Dollemore, Doug. Age Erasers for Men. (Illus.). 596p. 1996. pap. 17.95 (*0-87596-405-2*) Rodale Pr Inc.

Dollemore, Doug & Prevention Editors. The Doctors Book of Home Remedies for Seniors: An A-to-Z Guide to Staying Physically Active, Mentally Sharp & Disease Free. LC 99-11451. (Illus.). 500p. 1999. 27.95 (*1-57954-011-2*) Rodale Pr Inc.

Dollemore, Doug & Prevention Health Books for Seniors Staff, eds. The Doctors Book of Home Remedies for Seniors: An A-to-Z Guide to Staying Physically Active, Mentally Sharp & Disease-Free. LC 99-11451. 592p. 2000. pap. 17.95 (*1-57954-012-0*) Rodale Pr Inc.

***Dollemore, Doug & Prevention Health Books Staff.** The Senior's Guide to Pain-Free Living. 2000. pap. 17.95 (*1-57954-295-6*) Rodale Pr Inc.

Dollemore, Doug & Raymond, Cathy. Disease-Free at 60 Plus: Hundreds of Life-Preserving Tips & Techniques to Defy Heart Trouble, Cancer, & Stroke. LC 96-46765. 416p. 1997. 27.95 (*0-87596-342-0*) Rodale Pr Inc.

***Dollen, B. L.** Collector's Encyclopedia of Red Wing Art Pottery: Identification & Values. (Illus.). 2000. 24.95 (*1-57432-192-7*) Collector Bks.

Dollen, B. L. Red Wing Art Pottery Bk. II: Identification & Value Guide. LC 96-209690. 1998. pap. text 19.95 (*1-57432-058-0*, 5055) Collector Bks.

Dollen, Charles. Listen, Mother of God! Reflections on the Litany of Loreto. LC 89-60266. 227p. (Orig.). 1989. pap. 6.95 (*0-87973-427-2*, 427) Our Sunday Visitor.
— Traditional Catholic Prayers. LC 89-62496. 176p. 1990. 13.95 (*0-87973-440-X*, 440) Our Sunday Visitor.

Dollen, Charles, ed. Introduction to the Devout Life: St. Francis DeSales. LC 92-10914. 204p. (Orig.). 1992. pap. 10.95 (*0-8189-0634-0*) Alba.

Dollen, Charles, ed. see St. Bernard of Clairvaux Staff.

Dollen, Charles J. Prayerbook of the King: The Psalms: A Commentary. LC 97-20173. 320p. 1998. pap. 16.95 (*0-8189-0751-7*) Alba.

Dollenmayer, David, ed. A Companion to Doblin's "Berlin Alexanderplatz" (Studs German Lit. Ser.). 2002. 55.00 (*1-57113-124-8*) Camden Hse.

Dollenmayer, David B. The Berlin Novels of Alfred Doblin: Wadzek's Battle with the Steam Turbine, Berlin Alexanderplatz, Men Without Mercy, & November, 1918. 1988. 42.50 (*0-520-06000-8*, Pub. by U CA Pr) Cal Prin Full Svc.
— Neue Horizonte: A First Course in German Language & Culture. 2nd ed. LC 87-81430. (ENG & GER.). (C). 1988. text 61.16 (*0-669-13917-3*); student ed. 34.36 (*0-669-13919-X*); audio 32.76 (*0-669-13922-X*) HM Trade Div.

Dollenmayer, David B. & Hansen, Thomas S. Neue Horizonte: A First Course in German Language & Culture. 3rd ed. (ENG & GER.). 550p. (C). 1992. audio 32.76 (*0-669-24249-7*) HM Trade Div.
— Neue Horizonte: A First Course in German Language & Culture. 3rd annot. ed. (ENG & GER.). 550p. (C). 1992. text, teacher ed. 56.76 (*0-669-24246-2*) HM Trade Div.
— Neue Horizonte: A First Course in German Language & Culture. 4th ed. (GER.). 545p. (C). 1996. text 61.16 (*0-669-35528-3*); pap. text, wbk. ed., lab manual ed. 34.36 (*0-669-35530-5*) HM Trade Div.
— Neue Horizonte: A First Course in German Language & Culture. 4th annot. ed. (GER.). (C). 1996. text, teacher ed. 56.76 (*0-669-35529-1*) HM Trade Div.

Dollens, Dennis. Exodesic: Structures, Tumbleweeds, Electronics: The Tumbletruss Project. 64p. 1998. pap. 15.00 (*0-930829-41-7*) Lumen Inc.

Dollens, Dennis, ed. Sites 24. 120p. (Orig.). 1992. pap. 15.00 (*0-930829-22-0*) Lumen Inc.

Dollens, Dennis & Christ, Ronald J., eds. Sites 11: Essays on Jujol & Gaudi. 58p. 1983. pap. 5.00 (*0-930829-25-5*) Lumen Inc.

Dollens, Dennis L. Josep Maria Jujol: Five Major Buildings, 1913-1923. LC 95-212007. 96p. 1994. pap. 20.00 (*0-930829-35-2*) Lumen Inc.
— Sites 25, No. 25. 120p. 1993. pap. 15.00 (*0-930829-33-6*) Lumen Inc.
— Sites 26. 96p. 1995. pap. text 20.00 (*0-930829-37-9*) Lumen Inc.

***Dollens, Dennis L.** The Tumble Truss Project. 2000. pap. 30.00 (*84-921103-4-1*, Pub. by Galeria HTwoO) Lumen Inc.

***Dollerup, Cay.** Tales & Translation: The Grimm Tales from Pan-Germanic Narratives to Shared International Fairytales. LC 99-21420. (Benjamins Translation Library: Vol. 30). 384p. 1999. 85.00 (*1-55619-789-6*) J Benjamins Pubng Co.

Dollerup, Cay & Appel, Vibeke, eds. Teaching Translation & Interpreting 3: New Horizons, Papers from the Third Language International Conference, Elsinore, Denmark 9-11 June 1995. LC 96-20500. (Benjamins Translation Library: Vol. 16). viii, 338p. 1996. lib. bdg. 69.00 (*1-55619-698-9*) J Benjamins Pubng Co.

Dollerup, Cay & Lindegaard, Annette, eds. Teaching Translation & Interpreting 2: Insights, Aims, Visions. Papers from the Second Language International COnference Elsinore, 1993. LC 94-10141. (Benjamins Translation Library: Vol. 5). viii, 358p. 1994. 69.00 (*1-55619-682-2*) J Benjamins Pubng Co.

Dollery. Therapeutic Drugs, 2 vols. 2nd ed. LC 98-40969. (C). 1999. text 850.00 (*0-443-05148-8*) Church.

Dollery, Brain & Marshall, Neil. Australian Local Government: Reform & Renewal. LC 97-153674. 272p. 1997. 64.95 (*0-7329-2903-2*, Pub. by Macmill Educ); pap. 32.95 (*0-7329-2904-0*, Pub. by Macmill Educ) Paul & Co Pubs.

Dollery, Colin, ed. Therapeutic Drugs. (Illus.). 3000p. 1991. text 660.00 (*0-443-02846-X*) Church.
— Therapeutic Drugs, Supplement 1. 2nd ed. (Illus.). 272p. 1993. text 250.00 (*0-443-04676-X*) Church.

Dollevoet, George D. The Dollevoet Theory Vol. 1: The All Universal Hyper Correlative Domain of Electromagnetic Correlative Principles & Laws. LC 87-73316. (Illus.). 100p. (Orig.). (C). 1988. pap. 6.50 (*0-9619823-0-6*) G D Dollevoet.

Dolley, M. The Norman Conquest & the English Coinage. 1966. 5.00 (*0-685-51535-4*) S J Durst.

Dolley, M., jt. auth. see Brown, I. D.

Dollfus, A., ed. see C.O.S.P.A.R International Space Science Symposium - London - Jul 26-27 1967, et al.

Dollfus, A., ed. see Steiner, Rudolf.

Dollfus, Audouin, jt. auth. see De Callatay, Vincent.

Dollfus, Charles & Bouche, Henri. Histoire de l'Aeronautique: The History of Aeronautics. Gilbert, James B., ed. LC 79-7246. (Flight: Its First Seventy-Five Years Ser.). (FRE., Illus.). 1980. reprint ed. lib. bdg. 98.95 (*0-405-12158-X*) Ayer.

Dollfus-Mieg, E. Cie. Crochet Designs for the Home: Full-Size Templates for Twelve Patchwork Projects. (Illus.). 48p. 1990. pap. 2.95 (*0-486-26168-9*) Dover.

Dollimore, D., jt. auth. see Keattch, Cyril J.

Dollimore, Jean, jt. auth. see Coulouris, George.

Dollimore, Jonathan. Death, Desire, & Loss in Western Culture. LC 98-4041. 416p. 1998. 35.00 (*0-415-92174-0*) Routledge.

— Radical Tragedy: Religion, Ideology, & Power in the Drama of Shakespeare & His Contemporaries. LC 83-18290. viii, 312p. (C). 1986. pap. text 12.50 (*0-226-15539-0*) U Ch Pr.

— Radical Tragedy: Religion, Ideology, & Power in the Drama of Shakespeare & His Contemporaries. 2nd ed. LC 93-9775. 380p. (C). 1993. pap. text 19.95 (*0-8223-1398-7*) Duke.

— Sexual Dissidence: Augustine to Wilde, Freud to Foucault. (Illus.). 398p. 1991. pap. text 19.95 (*0-19-811269-6*) OUP.

Dollimore, Jonathan & Sinfield, Alan, eds. Political Shakespeare: Essays in Cultural Materialism. 2nd ed. LC 94-15983. 304p. 1994. 45.00 (*0-8014-3091-7*); pap. text 16.95 (*0-8014-8243-7*) Cornell U Pr.

Dollimore, Jonathan, ed. see Orkin, Martin.

Dolling, Dieter, jt. auth. see Brunner, Rudolf.

***Dolling, Margaret, et al.** Introducing the European System of Accounts 1995 in the UK: The Changes to the UK Accounting System & the Reasoning Behind Them. LC 98-229358. 1998. write for info. (*0-11-621061-3*) Statnry Office.

Dolling, Susan W. A River in Springtime: My Story of Li Yu in Myth & Poetry. LC 97-27126. (Illus.). 72p. 1997. pap. 16.00 (*0-9655255-0-3*) Pucks Gold Proj.

Dolling, Susan W., ed. Feast of Cultures: A Doss Family Recipe - Storybook. 120p. 1999. pap., per. 12.00 (*0-9655255-1-1*) Pucks Gold Proj.

Dolling, Susan W., tr. from CHI. Family Catastrophe. LC 94-33940. (Fiction from Modern China Ser.). 280p. 1995. pap. 11.75 (*0-8248-1710-9*) UH Pr.

Dolling, Susan W., tr. see Wang Wen-hsing.

Dolling, W. R., et al. Catalog of the Names of Cimex Linnaeus, with Comments on Early Works Concerning the Heteroptera. (Monographs, Thomas Say Publications in Entomology Ser.). 154p. 1999. pap. 35.00 (*0-938522-84-1*) Entomol Soc.

Dolling, Yolanda & Cooper, Polly, eds. Who's Who of Women in World Politics: Biographies of Women Currently in Government or Legislatures. 320p. 1991. 95.00 (*0-86291-627-5*) Bowker-Saur.

Dollinger. Entrepreneurship: Strategies & Resources. 2nd ed. LC 98-23829. 562p. 1998. pap. text 63.00 (*0-13-745993-9*) P-H.

Dollinger, A., ed. Dictionary of Metallurgy. (ENG, FRE, GER, POL & RUS.). 767p. 1974. 150.00 (*0-8288-6006-8*, M9893) Fr & Eur.

Dollinger, Genora J. Not Automatic: Women & the Left in the Forging of the Auto Workers' Union. LC 99-38833. 1999. pap. 18.00 (*1-58367-018-1*, Pub. by Monthly Rev) NYU Pr.

Dollinger, Genora J., jt. auth. see Dollinger, Sol.

Dollinger, Johann J. Von, see Von Dollinger, Johann J.

Dollinger, Malin, et al. Everyone's Guide to Cancer Therapy: How Cancer Is Diagnosed, Treated & Managed Day to Day. Hasselback, Richard, ed. (Illus.). 672p. 24.95 (*0-921051-63-8*) Somerville Hse.

— Everyone's Guide to Cancer Therapy: How Cancer Is Diagnosed, Treated & Managed Day to Day. 2nd rev. ed. Hasselback, Richard, ed. (Illus.). 740p. pap. 34.95 (*1-895897-40-8*) Somerville Hse.

Dollinger, Malin, et al. Everyone's Guide to Cancer Therapy: How Cancer Is Diagnosed, Treated & Managed Day to Day. 3rd rev. ed. LC 97-34123. (Illus.). 848p. 1998. 29.95 (*0-8362-3617-3*); pap. 21.95 (*0-8362-3709-9*) Andrews & McMeel.

Dollinger, Marc J. Entrepreneurship: Strategies & Resources. LC 94-13717. 736p. (C). 1994. text 66.95 (*0-256-11980-5*, Irwn McGrw-H) McGrw-H Hghr Educ.

***Dollinger, Marc J.** Quest for Inclusion: Jews & Liberalism in Modern American. LC 99-89426. (Illus.). 288p. 2000. 35.00 (*0-691-00509-5*, Pub. by Princeton U Pr) Cal Prin Full Svc.

Dollinger, Marc J. & Daily, Catherine M. Purchasing from Small Minority-Owned Firms: Corporate Problems. Ketchum, Carol L., ed. LC 89-60726. 72p. (Orig.). (C). 1989. pap. text 20.00 (*0-945968-03-5*) Ctr Advanced Purchasing.

Dollinger, Martin E. New Jersey Real Estate Leasing Forms, 2 vols. 1991. disk 75.00 (*1-56257-356-X*, 83011-10, MICHIE) LEXIS Pub.

— New Jersey Real Estate Leasing Forms, 2 vols., Set. 1040p. 1991. spiral bd. 229.00 (*0-8342-0182-8*, 83007-10, MICHIE) LEXIS Pub.

Dollinger, Russell. Doctor-in-My-Pocket. (SPA.). 264p. 1995. spiral bd. 11.25 (*0-945585-05-5*) Booksmythe.

— 100 Thanks! 112p. 1995. 8.95 (*0-945585-06-3*) Booksmythe.

— Pocket Medical French. (FRE & ENG.). 262p. 1995. spiral bd. 11.95 (*0-945585-03-9*) Booksmythe.

— Pocket Medical Russian. (FRE & ENG.). 1995. spiral bd. 11.95 (*0-945585-04-7*) Booksmythe.

— Pocket Medical Spanish. (Medical Interpreting Aid Ser.). (ENG & SPA.). 262p. 1991. spiral bd. 11.95 (*0-945585-02-0*) Booksmythe.

— Pocket Pre-Hospital Spanish. (SPA.). Date not set. spiral bd. write for info. (*0-945585-07-1*) Booksmythe.

Dollinger, Russell & Uyeda, Carolyn. The Imperative Aid: General Medicine-Spanish. 2nd ed. LC 87-83658. (Medical Interpreting Aid Ser.). 210p. 1987. 29.95 (*0-945585-00-4*) Booksmythe.

***Dollinger, Sol & Dollinger, Genora J.** Not Automatic: Women & the Left in Forging the Auto Workers Union. LC 99-38833. 220p. 1999. 48.00 (*1-58367-017-3*, Pub. by Monthly Rev) NYU Pr.

Dollinger, Stephanie M. & DiLalla, Lisabeth, eds. Assessment & Intervention Issues across the Life Span. LC 96-27362. 320p. (C). 1997. text 79.95 (*0-8058-2164-3*) L Erlbaum Assocs.

Dollinger, Susan B. & Lockshin, Jane R. The New York Edge 1998 Savvy Shoppers' Survey: Everything from Pearls to Plumbers, Rated for Quality, Style, Service & Value. 2nd unabridged ed. 500p. 1997. pap. 14.95 (*1-889782-51-3*) Custom Databanks.

— The New York Edge 1997 Savvy Shoppers' Survey: Everything from Pearls to Plumbers, Rated for Quality, Style, Service & Value, Vol. 1. 478p. (Orig.). 1996. pap. 14.95 (*1-889782-50-5*) Custom Databanks.

Dollinger, Susan B. & Lockshiv, Jane R. The New York Edge Savvy Shopper's Survey: Everything from Pearls to Plumbers Rated for Quality, Style, Service & Value. (Illus.). 418p. 1998. pap. 14.95 (*1-889782-52-1*) Custom Databanks.

***Dolliver, B. Kemp, et al.** Equity Research & Valuation Techniques: Proceedings of the AIMR Seminar "Equity Research & Valuation Techniques", December 9, 1997, Philadelphia, Pennsylvania. LC 99-208094. (Illus.). 1998. write for info. (*0-935015-21-3*) Inst Charter Finan Analysts.

Dollman, J. G., jt. auth. see Lydekker, Richard.

Dolloff, Francis W. & Perkinson, Roy L. How to Care for Works of Art on Paper. 3rd ed. LC 77-2121. (Illus.). 48p. 1985. pap. 3.95 (*0-87846-254-6*) Mus Fine Arts Boston.

D'Ollone, Vicomte & Miall, Bernard. In Forbidden China: The D'Ollone Mission 1906-1909. (C). 1995. reprint ed. 52.00 (*81-206-1045-8*, Pub. by Asian Educ Servs) S Asia.

Dollot, Rene. L' Afghanistan. LC 75-179192. (Illus.). reprint ed. 52.50 (*0-404-54822-9*) AMS Pr.

Dolly, Edward D. & Mullarkey, James C., eds. Hydrocarbon Production from Low Contrast, Low Resistivity Reservoirs, Rocky Mountain & Mid-Continent Regions, Log Examples of Subtle Pays. (Illus.). 287p. 1996. write for info. (*0-933979-19-3*) Rocky Mtn Assoc Geol.

Dolly, Helen, ed. see Ashton, John, et al.

***Dolly, Martha.** On Purpose: A Writer's Guide to Rhetorical Situation. 2nd ed. 116p. (C). 1999. pap. text 23.95 (*0-7872-6508-X*, 41650801) Kendall-Hunt.

Dolman, Anthony J., ed. Global Planning & Resource Management: Toward International Decision Making in a Divided World. (Policy Studies on International Development). 272p. 1980. 52.00 (*0-08-026309-7*, Pergamon Pr); pap. 20.00 (*0-08-026320-8*, Pergamon Pr) Elsevier.

Dolman, Antony J. & van Ettinger, Jan. Ports As Nodal Points in a Global Transport System. 492p. 1992. 132.00 (*0-08-040994-6*, Pergamon Pr) Elsevier.

Dolman, Bob, jt. auth. see Howard, Ron.

Dolman, C. L. Ultrastructure of Brain Tumors & Biopsies: A Diagnostic Atlas, 5. LC 84-3469. (Methods in Laboratory Medicine Ser.: Vol. 5). 266p. 1984. 59.95 (*0-275-91426-7*, C1426, Praeger Pubs) Greenwood.

***Dolman, Carol & Saunders, Marcus.** Managing Your First Computer: How to Perform Core Tasks & Gain Knowledge & Confidence. 2nd ed. (Computer Basics Ser.). (Illus.). 144p. 1999. pap. 19.95 (*1-85703-502-X*, Pub. by How To Bks) Trans-Atl Phila.

— Moving on from Computer Basics: Improve Your Skills & Get More from Your Computer. (Computer Basics Ser.). (Illus.). 160p. 1999. pap. 19.95 (*1-85703-507-0*, Pub. by How To Bks) Trans-Atl Phila.

Dolman, John. Art of Acting. LC 79-109289. 313p. 1971. reprint ed. lib. bdg. 65.00 (*0-8371-3832-9*, DOAA, Greenwood Pr) Greenwood.

Dolman, Paul H. Dolman Compendium, A. D. 1340-1940. Inskeep, Annie D., ed. (Illus.). 139p. 1997. reprint ed. pap. 22.00 (*0-8328-8324-7*); reprint ed. lib. bdg. 32.00 (*0-8328-8323-9*) Higginson Bk Co.

Dolman, Paul S. What Matters Most. Kaufman, Mark, ed. 240p. (Orig.). 1996. pap. 20.00 (*0-614-30446-6*) South Beach.

— What Matters Most: Intimate Interviews with Notable Nashvillians. 1997. pap. text 20.00 (*1-890115-00-2*) South Beach.

Dolmat-Connell, Jack. AMA Salary Survey Guidebook: Understanding & Using Critical Competitive Information. LC 96-16784. 1996. write for info. (*0-8144-6251-0*) AMACOM.

***Dolmatch.** Stent-Grafts. (Illus.). 272p. 1999. 145.00 (*0-86577-893-0*) Thieme Med Pubs.

Dolmatz, Malvin, jt. auth. see Wong, Harry.

Dolmetsch, A., ed. Select English Songs & Dialogues of the 16th & 17th Centuries, 2 vols. in 1. LC 74-24070. reprint ed. 45.00 (*0-404-12897-1*) AMS Pr.

Dolmetsch, Arnold. The Interpretation of the Music of the 17th & 18th Centuries. 1988. reprint ed. lib. bdg. 75.00 (*0-7812-0415-1*) Rprt Serv.

Dolmetsch, Christopher. The German Press in the Shenandoah Valley. LC 81-69881. (GERM Ser.: Vol. 4). (Illus.). 180p. 1984. 35.00 (*0-938100-01-7*) Camden Hse.

Dolmetsch, Mabel. Personal Recollections of Arnold Dolmetsch. LC 79-24413. (Music Reprint Ser.). (Illus.). 1980. reprint ed. lib. bdg. 29.50 (*0-306-76022-3*) Da Capo.

Dolmetsch, Rudolph. Air & Minuet for Three Recorders: SAT: Composed 1928. (Contemporary Consort Ser.: No. 29). 3p. 1994. pap. text 1.00 (*1-56571-099-1*) PRB Prods.

— Caprice, for Solo Bass Viola da Gamba. Rose, Adrian, ed. (Contemporary Instrumental Ser.: No. 7). (Illus.). i, 2p. 1994. pap. text 3.50 (*1-56571-082-7*, CI007) PRB Prods.

Dolmetsch, Rudolph & Ring, Layton. Concertino for Viola Da Gamba & Small Orchestra (1941) (Contemporary Instrumental Ser.: No. 8). i, 35p. 1996. pap. text. write for info. (*1-56571-106-8*) PRB Prods.

Dolnick, Amy. Between Deep Valley & the Great World: Maud Hart Lovelace in Minneapolis. 38p. 1993. pap. 10.00 (*0-9640846-0-0*) M H Lovelace.

***Dolnick, Barrie.** The Executive Mystic: Intuitive Tools for Cultivating the Winning Edge in Business. 224p. 1999. pap. 12.00 (*0-88730-954-2*, HarpBusn) HarpInfo.

Dolnick, Barrie. The Executive Mystic: Psychic Power Tools for Success. LC 97-40275. 224p. 1998. 22.00 (*0-88730-903-8*, HarpBusn) HarpInfo.

***Dolnick, Barrie.** Simple Spells for Hearth & Home: Ancient Practices for Residing in Harmony. LC 99-34145. 192p. 1999. 18.00 (*0-609-60427-9*) Harmony Bks.

Dolnick, Barrie. Simple Spells for Love: Ancient Practices for Emotional Fulfillment. LC 94-31885. 1995. 15.00 (*0-517-79995-2*) Harmony Bks.

— Simple Spells for Success. 1996. 18.00 (*0-517-70338-6*) Random.

***Dolnick, Barrie & Baacke, Don.** How to Write a Love Letter: Putting What's in Your Heart on Paper. 2001. 15.00 (*0-609-60727-8*) Harmony Bks.

Dolnick, Barrie, et al. Sexual Bewitchery & Other Ancient Feminine Wiles. LC 97-33167. 176p. 1998. 18.00 (*0-380-97573-4*, Avon Bks) Morrow Avon.

Dolnick, Edward. Madness on the Couch: Blaming the Victim in the Heyday of Psychoanalysis. LC 98-23737. (Illus.). 352p. 1998. 25.00 (*0-684-82497-3*) Simon & Schuster.

Dolnick, Sandy. Friends of Libraries Sourcebook. 3rd ed. LC 96-3384. xiii, 313p. 1996. pap. 35.00 (*0-8389-0685-0*, 0685-0-2045) ALA.

Dolnick, Sandy & Stueart, Robert D., eds. Fundraising for Nonprofit Institutions. LC 87-31200. (Foundations in Library & Information Science: Vol. 19). 268p. 1988. 78.50 (*0-89232-387-6*) Jai Pr.

Dolnikowski, Edith W. Thomas Bradwardine: A View of Time & a Vision of Eternity in Fourteenth Century Thought. LC 95-2091. (Studies in the History of Christian Thought: Vol. 65). ix, 250p. 1995. 101.50 (*90-04-10226-4*) Brill Academic Pubs.

Dolo, Emmanuel. Democracy Versus Dictatorship: The Quest for Freedom & Justice in Africa's Oldest Republic - Liberia. 198p. (C). 1996. lib. bdg. 39.00 (*0-7618-0228-2*) U Pr of Amer.

Dologite, D. G., jt. auth. see Mockler, Robert J.

Dologite, Dorothy G. & Mockler, Robert J. Developing Knowledge Based Systems Using VP-Expert. (Illus.). 384p. (Orig.). (C). 1992. teacher ed. write for info. (*0-318-69334-8*) Macmillan.

Dolora, Bobi. Santa & Sams. 96p. 1992. pap. text 10.50 (*1-56770-258-9*) S Scheewe Pubns.

Dolores, Juan. Papago Nominal Stems. fac. ed. Mason, Alden, ed. (University of California Publications in American Archaeology & Ethnology: Vol. 20: 2). 14p. (C). 1923. reprint ed. pap. text 1.88 (*1-55567-238-8*) Coyote Press.

— Papago Verb Stems. fac. ed. (University of California Publications in American Archaeology & Ethnology: Vol. 10: 5). 23p. (C). 1913. reprint ed. pap. text 2.81 (*1-55567-191-8*) Coyote Press.

Dolors, Maria, jt. ed. see Monk, Janice.

Dolot, Miron. Execution by Hunger: The Hidden Holocaust. LC 84-16568. 248p. 1987. pap. 11.95 (*0-393-30416-7*) Norton.

Dolowitz, David P. Learning from America: Policy Transfer & the Development of the British Workfare State. LC 97-26461. 224p. 1997. 69.95 (*1-898723-73-7*, Pub. by Sussex Acad Pr) Intl Spec Bk.

***Dolowitz, David P.** Policy Transfer & British Social Policy: Learning from the U. S. A.? LC 99-29252. (Public Policy & Management Ser.). 1999. pap. 32.95 (*0-335-19991-7*) OpUniv Pr.

Dolph, Andrea & Clemens, Lynda. How to Hit the Ground Running in Your New Job. Kennedy, Sarah, ed. LC 94-12510. (Illus.). 160p. (Orig.). (C). 1994. pap. 9.95 (*0-8442-4391-4*, 43914, VGM Career) NTC Contemp Pub Co.

Dolph, Harry A. Evader: An Airman's 8 Months with the Dutch Underground. Eakin, Ed, ed. (Illus.). 320p. 1991. pap. 18.95 (*0-89015-974-2*, Eakin Pr) Sunbelt Media.

Dolph, James & Donohoe, Ronan. Around Portsmouth in the Victorian Era. LC 97-158067. (Images of America Ser.). 1997. pap. 16.99 (*0-7524-0281-1*) Arcadia Publng.

Dolph, Jerry. Fire in the Hole: The Untold Story of Hardrock Miners. LC 94-25176. (Illus.). 184p. 1994. 32.00 (*0-87422-112-9*) Wash St U Pr.

***Dolph, Jerry.** Wyatt Earp & Coeur D'Alene Gold Stampede to Idaho Territory. 1999. pap. 16.95 (*0-9671058-0-3*) Eagle City.

Dolphin. Biology Lab Manual Lab Prep. Guide. 3rd ed. 1991. 11.25 (*0-697-12958-6*) McGraw.

— Lab Prep Guide - Biology. 4th ed. 1997. lab manual ed. 11.00 (*0-697-15904-3*, WCB McGr Hill) McGrw-H Hghr Educ.

Dolphin Circle of the International Order of the K. Gourmet by the Bay: The Virginia Beach Cookbook. 324p. 1989. reprint ed. 18.95 (*0-9621080-0-6*) Dolphin VA.

Dolphin, David, ed. B12, 2 vols., Vol. 1: Chemistry. LC 81-10300. (Illus.). 687p. 1982. reprint ed. pap. 200.00 (*0-7837-3531-6*, 205786100001) Bks Demand.

— B12, 2 vols., Vol. 2: Biochemistry & Medicine. LC 81-10300. (Illus.). 521p. 1982. reprint ed. pap. 161.60 (*0-7837-3532-4*, 205786100002) Bks Demand.

Dolphin, David, et al, eds. Biomimetic Chemistry. LC 80-22864. (ACS Advances in Chemistry Ser.: No. 191). 437p. 1980. 65.95 (*0-8412-0514-0*, Pub. by Am Chemical) OUP.

— Biomimetic Chemistry. LC 80-22864. (Advances in Chemistry Ser.: Vol. 191). 448p. 1980. reprint ed. pap. 138.90 (*0-608-03498-3*, 206421700008) Bks Demand.

Dolphin, Harry A., jt. auth. see Haberman, David A.

Dolphin, Ida R. Life on Hold. LC 92-11891. 1992. 16.95 (*0-87770-506-2*) Ye Galleon.

Dolphin, Jack & Fitzgerald, Ted. The Vig & Wild Card. Lovisi, Gary, ed. (Gryphon Double Novel Ser.: No. 1). (Illus.). 50p. (Orig.). 1991. pap. 5.95 (*0-936071-20-6*, Gryp Grap Nov) Gryphon Pubns.

Dolphin, Johnny. The Collected Works of the Caravan of Dreams Vol. 2: Billy the Kid, Metal Woman, Tin Can Man. 152p. 1984. pap. 5.95 (*0-907791-02-6*) Synerg CA.

— The Collected Works of the Caravan of Dreams Theater Vol. I: Gilgamesh, Marouf the Cobbler, Faust: Part One. 224p. 1983. pap. 5.95 (*0-907791-01-8*) Synerg CA.

— The Dream & Drink of Freedom. 84p. 1987. pap. 5.00 (*0-907791-15-8*) Synerg CA.

— Journey Around an Extraordinary Planet. 96p. 1990. pap. 5.95 (*0-907791-23-9*) Synerg CA.

— Thirty-Nine Blows on a Gone Trumpet. 194p. 1985. pap. 5.95 (*0-907791-07-7*) Synerg CA.

— Uncommon Quotes: The Dream & Drink of Freedom. Hoffman, Kathelin, ed. & intro. by. Vol. II. (C). 1989. audio. write for info. (*0-318-63725-1*) Caravan Dreams Prodns.

— Uncommon Quotes: The Dream & Drink of Freedom. Hoffman, Kathelin, ed. & intro. by. (Uncommon Quotes Ser.: Vol. II). (Illus.). (C). 1989. 12.50 (*0-929856-03-1*) Caravan Dreams Prodns.

Dolphin, Johnny. Wild: Poems, Aphorisms, Short Stories. 144p. 1992. pap. text 7.95 (*0-907791-26-3*) Synerg CA.

Dolphin, Johnny & MacNeice, Corinna. Kabuki Blues. (Illus.). 46p. 1984. pap. 1.50 (*0-907791-03-4*) Synerg CA.

Dolphin, Laurie. Magical Objects. 1999. 15.99 (*0-525-45904-9*) NAL.

Dolphin, Laurie, ed. see Jernigan, Candy, et al.

Dolphin, Warren D. Biology. 3rd ed. 512p. (C). 1991. text, lab manual ed. write for info. (*0-697-12788-5*, WCB McGr Hill) McGrw-H Hghr Educ.

— Biology. 5th ed. 512p. 1998. spiral bd., lab manual ed. 54.06 (*0-697-36049-0*) McGraw.

— Biology Lab Manual. 6th ed. 2001. pap. text, lab manual ed. 37.74 (*0-07-303141-0*) McGraw.

— Biology Laboratory Manual. 4th ed. 496p. (C). 1996. text, lab manual ed. write for info. (*0-697-15903-5*, WCB McGr Hill) McGrw-H Hghr Educ.

Dols, Michael W. The Black Death in the Middle East. LC 76-3254. 408p. reprint ed. pap. 126.50 (*0-8357-3301-7*, 203952400013) Bks Demand.

***Dolseobe, Orogee.** Coherent Nature: The Structure & Process of Consciousness. LC 00-102035. (Illus.). 368p. 2000. pap. 16.95 (*1-56167-611-X*) Am Literary Pr.

Dolskaya, Olga, ed. Vasily Titov & the Russian Baroque: Selected Choral Works. (Monuments of Russian Sacred Music Ser.: Series XIII, Vol. 1). (Illus.). xxix, 204p. (C). 1995. 49.00 (*0-9629460-3-6*) Musica Russica.

Dolson, jt. auth. see Myers.

Dolson, Edward M., jt. auth. see Myers, Charles F.

Dolson, Frank. Always Young: A Biography. LC 75-20961. (Illus.). 206p. (Orig.). 1975. pap. 3.95 (*0-89037-072-9*); student ed. 4.95 (*0-89037-073-7*) Anderson World.

— Jim Bunning: Baseball & Beyond. LC 98-14655. (Baseball in America Ser.). (Illus.). 320p. 1998. 27.95 (*1-56639-636-0*) Temple U Pr.

Dolson, Hildegarde. We Shook the Family Tree. 71p. 1947. pap. 5.50 (*0-87129-765-5*, W13) Dramatic Pub.

Dolson, John C., et al, eds. Unconformity-Related Hydrocarbons in Sedimentary Sequences: A Guidebook for Exploration & Exploitation in Clastic & Carbonate Sediments. LC 94-66180. (Illus.). 298p. 1994. write for info. (*0-933979-16-9*) Rocky Mtn Assoc Geol.

Dolson, Leo R. Van, see Van Dolson, Leo R.

Dolson, Marianne & Curl, Wade. Total Quality Management Using FOCUS-PDCA: A Self Study for: Leadership. (Illus.). 88p. 1995. pap. text 15.95 (*1-880610-75-2*) PRO-ACT Pub.

Dolson, Marianne & Fritch, Nancy E. Teaching TQM/CQI Concepts in 20 Minute Sessions. (Illus.). 324p. 1996. pap. text 74.95 (*1-880610-76-0*) PRO-ACT Pub.

— Total Quality Management Using FOCUS-PDCA. (Illus.). 55p. 1997. pap. text 13.00 (*1-880610-77-9*) PRO-ACT Pub.

— Total Quality Management Using FOCUS-PDCA, Team Member Training Manual. (Illus.). 38p. 1997. pap. text 10.00 (*1-880610-78-7*) PRO-ACT Pub.

Dolson, Scott W. Professional Service Corporations in Kentucky. x, 186p. 1993. pap. 41.00 (*1-58757-004-1*, BM015) Univ of KY.

***Dolson, Scott W., et al.** Business Succession Planning. Greenwell, F. Gerald et al, eds. 298p. 1998. pap. 43.00 (*1-58757-022-X*, EM039) Univ of KY.

— Kentucky Corporation Law. (Illus.). xx, 932p. 1997. 98.00 (*1-58757-019-X*, BH031) Univ of KY.

— Limited Liability Companies in Kentucky. 2nd ed. (Illus.). 358p. 2000. pap. 45.00 (*1-58757-031-9*, BM035) Univ of KY.

***Dolson, William F.** Resolution of Labor & Employment Disputes: The Choices of Process in the 1990s & Beyond. LC 98-54236. 1999. write for info. (*0-8377-0566-5*, Rothman) W S Hein.

Dolson, William F., ed. First Annual Labor & Employment Law Institute: New Dimensions in Labor & Employment Relations (University of Louisville School of Law, May 1-2, 1984) LC 85-1976. viii, 255p. 1985. 52.50 (*0-8377-0520-7*, Rothman) W S Hein.

— 9th Annual Labor & Employment Law Institute: New Directions for Labor & Management in a Changing Economic Environment (University of Louisville School of Law, June 11-12, 1992) LC 97-37614. ix, 275p. 1997. 72.50 (*0-8377-0564-9*, Rothman) W S Hein.

— 2nd Annual Labor & Employment Law Institute: New

D

Directions in the Labor & Employment Law Field (University of Louisville School of Law, May 1-2, 1985) viii, 420p. 1986. 57.50 (*0-8377-0550-9*, Rothman) W S Hein.

Dolson, William F., et al. Labor Arbitration: Cases & Materials for Advocates. LC 97-2056. 1997. 45.00 (*1-57018-036-9*) BNA Books.

Dolson, William F., Labor & Employment Law Institu, et al. Eleventh Annual Carl A. Warns Jr. Labor & Employment Law Institute, Vol. 11. LC 98-13676. vii, 191p. 1999. lib. bdg. 880.00 (*0-8377-0565-7*, 110570, Rothman) W S Hein.

***Dolt, Thomas, et al.** The Complete Idiot's Guide for Dumies: The Fun & Easy Way to Achieve Total Stupidity. 128p. 1999. pap. 9.95 (*1-58008-174-6*) Ten Speed Pr.

Dolto, Francoise & Howe, John. Flower Dolls: Essays in Child Psychotherapy. 224p. (Orig.). 1998. pap. 22.95 (*0-7145-3026-3*) M Boyars Pubs.

Dolton, Alan & Saunders, Glyn. Tolley's Tax Cases, 1995. 750p. 1995. 195.00 (*0-85459-972-X*, Pub. by Tolley Pubng) St Mut.

— Tolley's Tax Cases, 1993. 760p. 1993. 93.00 (*0-85459-696-8*, Pub. by Tolley Pubng) St Mut.

Dolton, Alan & Wareham, Robert. Tolley's VAT Cases, 1995. 990p. 1995. 195.00 (*0-85459-975-4*, Pub. by Tolley Pubng) St Mut.

— Tolley's VAT Cases, 1993. 850p. 1993. 195.00 (*0-85459-697-6*, Pub. by Tolley Pubng) St Mut.

Dolton, Alan, jt. auth. see Bowen, Nicholas.

Dolton, Alan, jt. auth. see Saunders, Glyn.

Dolton, Allan, ed. see Hamilton, Penny.

***Doltsinis, Ioannis.** Elements of Plasticity: Theory & Computation. (High Performance Structures & Materials Ser.). 328p. 2000. 183.00 (*1-85312-702-7*, 7027, Pub. by WIT Pr) Computational Mech MA.

Dolukhanov, Pavel & Chapman, John, eds. Cultural Transformations & Interactions in Eastern Europe. (Worldwide Archaeology Ser.: Vol. 5). 272p. 1993. 72.95 (*1-85628-704-1*, Pub. by Avebry) Ashgate Pub Co.

Dolukhanov, Pavel M. Environment & Ethnicity in the Ancient Middle East. (Worldwide Archaeology Ser.). 416p. (C). 1994. 91.95 (*1-85628-706-8*, Pub. by Avebry) Ashgate Pub Co.

Dolvers, Horst. Fables Less & Less Fabulous: English Fables & Parables of the Nineteenth Century & Their Illustrations. LC 96-38210. (Illus.). 208p. 1997. 36.50 (*0-87413-584-2*) U Delaware Pr.

Dolvik, Jon E., jt. ed. see Steen, Arild H.

Dolwick. Surgical Approach to Head & Neck Anatomy. 1993. write for info. (*0-397-50970-7*) Lppncott W & W.

Dolwick, M. Franklin, jt. auth. see Bush, Francis M.

***Dolz, Joaquim & Meyer, Jean-Claude, texts.** Activites Metalangagieres et Enseignement du Francais. xiii, 283p. 1998. 32.95 (*3-906760-64-2*, Pub. by P Lang) P Lang Pubng.

Dom, Ann. Strategic Environmental Assessment in the Transport Sector. LC 98-144650. 92p. 1998. pap. 19.00 (*92-821-1223-3*, 75-98-05-1, Pub. by Org for Econ) OECD.

Domac, Dragutin. Sailor - The Bitter Years. 1987. 13.95 (*0-940168-10-3*) Boxwood.

Domain Independent Services Technical Committee St. Inter-Tool Communication Programming Interface, Vol. 2. 175p. 1993. pap. text 150.00 (*1-882750-02-0*) CAD Framewk.

— Tool Encapsulation Specification, Vol. 3. 140p. 1993. pap. text 100.00 (*1-882750-03-9*) CAD Framewk.

Domain, Public. Travel Journal. 160p. 1994. pap. 9.95 (*0-89815-647-5*) Ten Speed Pr.

Domain Public Staff. This Old Man. 14.89 (*0-06-028267-3*); pap. 4.95 (*0-06-443544-X*) HarpC.

***Domain 456 Staff.** Growing as a Christian, School, Leisure Time: 13 Bible-Based Sessions. (Domain 456 Ser.). 2000. pap. 18.99 (*0-7814-5515-4*) Cook.

— Invisible World, My Values, Sin: 13 Bible-Based Sessions. (Domain 456 Ser.). 2000. pap. 18.99 (*0-7814-5462-X*) Cook.

— Peer Pressure, Pain & Death, Heroes: 13 Bible-Based Sessions. (Domain 456 Ser.). 2000. pap. 18.99 (*0-7814-5516-2*) Cook.

— Self-Esteem, Differences, Authority: 13 Bible-Based Sessions. (Domain 456 Ser.). 2000. pap. 18.99 (*0-7814-5518-9*) Cook.

— Why Believe? Change, Fun: 13 Bible-Based Sessions. (Domain 456 Ser.). 2000. pap. 18.99 (*0-7814-5461-1*) Cook.

Domalain, Jean-Yves. The Animal Connection: The Confessions of an Ex-Wild Animal Trafficker. Barnett, Marguerite, tr. from FRE. (Illus.). 255p. 1978. 25.00 (*0-8464-1181-4*) Beekman Pubs.

Doman, Don, et al. Look Before You Leap: Market Research Made Easy. (Business Ser.). 144p. 1993. pap. 14.95 (*0-88908-292-8*) Self-Counsel Pr.

Doman, Glenn. How to Multiply Your Baby's Intelligence. 1992. 24.95 (*0-944349-51-X*) Inst Achieve Human Pot.

— How to Teach Your Baby Math. 1992. 15.95 (*0-944349-52-8*) Inst Achieve Human Pot.

— How to Teach Your Baby to Read. 1991. 18.95 (*0-944349-47-1*) Inst Achieve Human Pot.

— Nose Is Not Toes. LC 81-67340. (Gentle Revolution Ser.). (Illus.). 84p. 1963. 15.95 (*0-944349-62-5*) Inst Achieve Human Pot.

— Nose Is Not Toes. (Illus.). 144p. (J). Date not set. 15.95 (*0-89529-718-3*, Avery) Penguin Putnam.

— What to Do about Your Brain-Injured Child. 1990. 19.95 (*0-944349-24-2*) Inst Achieve Human Pot.

— What to Do about Your Brain-Injured Child. 3rd ed. LC 95-130868. 320p. pap. 11.95 (*0-89529-598-9*, Avery) Penguin Putnam.

Doman, Glenn & Armentrout, J. Michael. The Universal Multiplication of Intelligence. LC 80-66236. (Gentle Revolution Ser.). 223p. 1980. 12.50 (*0-936676-02-7*) Inst Achieve Human Pot.

Doman, Glenn & Doman, Janet. How to Multiply Your Baby's Intelligence: More Gentle Revolution. 2nd ed. 400p. pap. 12.95 (*0-89529-600-4*, Avery) Penguin Putnam.

— How to Teach Your Baby Math. 4th ed. LC 93-1273. 232p. pap. 12.95 (*0-89529-595-4*, Avery) Penguin Putnam.

— How to Teach Your Baby to Read. 4th ed. LC 93-21525. 280p. pap. 12.95 (*0-89529-597-0*, Avery) Penguin Putnam.

Doman, Glenn, et al. How to Give Your Baby Encyclopedic Knowledge. LC 83-73584. (Gentle Revolution Ser.). (Illus.). 325p. 1984. 19.95 (*0-936676-34-5*) Inst Achieve Human Pot.

— How to Give Your Baby Encyclopedic Knowledge: More Gentle Revolution. 2nd ed. LC 93-21713. 320p. pap. 12.95 (*0-89529-602-0*, Avery) Penguin Putnam.

— How to Teach Your Baby to Be Physically Superb. (Gentle Revolution Ser.). (Illus.). 296p. 1988. 24.95 (*0-936676-92-2*) Inst Achieve Human Pot.

— How to Teach Your Baby to Be Physically Superb. 320p. Date not set. 24.95 (*0-89529-672-1*, Avery) Penguin Putnam.

Doman, Janet. Enough Inigo Enough. 1991. 15.95 (*0-944349-57-9*) Inst Achieve Human Pot.

Doman, Janet, jt. auth. see Doman, Glenn.

Doman, Regina. Snow White & Rose Red: A Modern Fairy Tale. LC 96-80078. (Morning Gate Bks.). 280p. (Orig.). (YA). (gr. 9 up). 1997. 15.95 (*1-883937-23-X*, 23-X) Bethlehem ND.

Domandl, Sepp. Goethe, Kant, W. V. Humboldt: Zur Aktualitat der Deutschen Klassik. (GER., Illus.). 300p. 1997. 57.95 (*3-631-31037-4*) P Lang Pubng.

Domangue, Barbara B., jt. ed. see Field, Howard L.

Domangue, Edward J. Domingue of Louisiana: Immigrants to Spanish Colonial Louisiana. (Illus.). 221p. (C). 1991. pap. text 29.95 (*0-9631109-0-X*) E J Domangue.

***Domangue, Herman, ed.** A Seminarian's Journal. 64p. 1999. pap. 7.00 (*0-9666115-3-5*, Our Ladys Pr) Eureka Pub.

Domanick, Joe. Faking it in America: Barry Minkow & the Great ZZZZ Best Scam LC 99-26405. 1999. write for info. (*1-893122-11-5*) Beard Bks.

— To Protect & Serve: The L. A. P. D. at War. (Illus.). 448p. 1994. 23.00 (*0-671-75111-5*) PB.

Domanick, Joe A. To Protect & to Serve: The LAPD's Century of War in the City of Dreams. 1995. pap. 6.99 (*0-671-75113-1*) PB.

Domanovszky, A. Functions & Objects of Author & Title Cataloguing: A Contribution to Cataloguing Theory. 174p. (C). 1974. pap. text 30.00 (*963-05-0381-6*, Pub. by Akade Kiado) St Mut.

Domanovszky, S. & Glatz, F. Palatin Joseph's Schriften. 804p. (C). 1991. 216.00 (*963-05-4831-3*, Pub. by Akade Kiado) St Mut.

Domanska, Ewa. Encounters: Philosophy of History after Postmodernism. LC 98-10323. 294p. 1998. pap. 19.50 (*0-8139-1767-0*); text 55.00 (*0-8139-1766-2*) U Pr of Va.

Domanska, Janina. If All the Seas Were One Sea. LC 96-159016. (J). 1996. mass mkt. 5.95 (*0-689-80343-5*) Aladdin.

— If All the Seas Were One Sea. LC 73-146621. 1996. 11.15 (*0-606-09456-3*, Pub. by Turtleback) Demco.

Domanska, Janina. If All the Seas Were One Sea. LC 73-146621. 32p. (J). (ps-2). 1987. lib. bdg. 15.00 (*0-02-732540-7*, Mac Bks Young Read) S&S Childrens.

Domanski, Boleslaw. Industrial Control Over the Socialist Town: Benevolence or Exploitation? LC 96-24381. 272p. 1997. 65.00 (*0-275-95633-4*, Praeger Pubs) Greenwood.

Domanski, Don. Hammerstroke. 90p. (Orig.). 1986. pap. 8.95 (*0-88784-150-3*, Pub. by Hse of Anansi Pr) Genl Dist Srvs.

— Heaven. 62p. (Orig.). 1978. pap. 5.95 (*0-88784-069-8*, Pub. by Hse of Anansi Pr) Genl Dist Srvs.

— Parish of the Psychic Moon. LC 98-151609. 120p. 1998. pap. 9.95 (*0-7710-2874-1*) McCland & Stewart.

— War in an Empty House. 70p. (Orig.). 1982. pap. 6.95 (*0-88784-094-9*, Pub. by Hse of Anansi Pr) Genl Dist Srvs.

Domanski, George. For the Life of the World: St. Maximilian & the Eucharist. Fehlner, Peter D., tr. from ITA. (Studies & Texts: No. 2). 159p. (Orig.). 1993. pap. 12.95 (*0-9635345-1-3*) Acad Immaculate.

***Domanski, Henryk.** On the Verge of Convergence: Social Stratification in Eastern Europe. LC 00-31472. 200p. (C). 2000. 44.95 (*963-9116-81-5*); pap. 21.95 (*963-9116-82-3*) Ctrl Europ Univ.

Domanski, Jim. Profiting by Phone: No Nonsense Skills & Techniques for Selling & Getting Leads by Telephone. 248p. 1997. pap. 29.00 (*1-881081-08-7*, PBP) Busn By Phone.

Domanski, Michael J., jt. auth. see Nanda, Navin C.

Domanus, J. C., ed. Practical Neutron Radiography. LC 92-18023. 288p. (C). 1992. text 193.50 (*0-7923-1860-9*) Kluwer Academic.

Domany, E., ed. see Muller, B. & Reinhardt, J.

Domany, Eytan, ed. see Van Hemmen, J. L.

Domar, Alice D. & Dreher, Henry. Healing Mind, Healthy Woman: Domar,&Alice. abr. ed. 1996. audio 18.00 (*0-694-51698-8*, CPN 2573) HarperAudio.

Domar, Alice D. & Dreher, Henry. Healing Mind, Healthy Woman: Using the Mind-Body Connection. 448p. 1997. 13.95 (*0-385-31894-4*) Doubleday.

***Domar, Alice D. & Dreher, Henry.** Healing Mind, Healthy Woman: Using the Mind-Body Connection to Manage Stress & Take Control of Your Life. 422p. 1999. reprint ed. text 25.00 (*0-7881-6491-0*) DIANE Pub.

— Self-Nurture: Learning to Care for Yourself as Effectively as You Care for Everyone Else. LC 99-16823. 256p. 1999. 23.95 (*0-670-88286-0*, Viking) Viking Penguin.

Domar, Evsey D. Capitalism, Socialism, & Serfdom: Essays. 316p. (C). 1989. text 89.95 (*0-521-37091-4*) Cambridge U Pr.

— Essays in the Theory of Economic Growth. LC 82-6262. 272p. 1982. reprint ed. lib. bdg. 41.50 (*0-313-23592-9*, DOET, Greenwood Pr) Greenwood.

Domaracki, Joseph W., jt. ed. see Woolcock, William W.

Domaret, E., jt. auth. see Coleman, M. P.

Domart, Andre, ed. Larousse Dictionnaire de la Medecine. (FRE.). 690p. 1991. pap. 16.95 (*0-7859-3944-X*, 2035010063) Fr & Eur.

Domart, Andre & Bourneuf, Jacques. Larousse de la Medecine, 3 vols. 480p. 1982. pap. 34.95 (*0-7859-4820-1*) Fr & Eur.

— Nouveau Larousse de la Medecine, No. 2. 1152p. 1988. 155.00 (*0-7859-4827-9*) Fr & Eur.

Domart, Andre & Bourneuf, Jacques, eds. Nouveau Larousse de la Medecine, No. 2. (FRE.). 515p. 150.00 (*0-686-56993-8*, M-6333) Fr & Eur.

Domart, Andre, ed. see Bourneuf, Jacques.

Domarus, Max. Hitler: Speeches & Proclamations, 1932-1945, Vol. 1. (GER.). 464p. 1988. reprint ed. 91.00 (*0-86516-325-1*) Bolchazy-Carducci.

— Hitler: Speeches & Proclamations, 1932-1945, Vol. 2. (GER.). 536p. 1988. reprint ed. 100.00 (*0-86516-326-X*) Bolchazy-Carducci.

— Hitler: Speeches & Proclamations, 1932-1945, Vol. 3. (GER.). 642p. 1988. reprint ed. 116.00 (*0-86516-327-8*) Bolchazy-Carducci.

— Hitler: Speeches & Proclamations, 1932-1945, Vol. 4. (GER.). 682p. 1988. reprint ed. 123.00 (*0-86516-328-6*) Bolchazy-Carducci.

— Hitler: Speeches & Proclamations 1932-1945: The Years 1935-1938, Vol. II. (Illus.). 600p. 1991. 160.00 (*0-86516-229-8*) Bolchazy-Carducci.

— Hitler: Speeches & Proclamations 1932-1945: The Years 1939-1940, Vol. III. (Illus.). 600p. 1996. 180.00 (*0-86516-230-1*) Bolchazy-Carducci.

— Hitler: Speeches & Proclamations 1932-1945: The Years 1941-1945, Vol. IV. (Illus.). 600p. 1997. 185.00 (*0-86516-231-X*) Bolchazy-Carducci.

— Hitler Vol. I: Speeches & Proclamations, 1932-1945: The Chronicle of a Dictatorship: The Years, 1932-1934. (Illus.). 700p. 1989. text 135.00 (*0-86516-227-1*) Bolchazy-Carducci.

***Domash, Harry.** Everything Online Investing Book. 304p. 2000. pap. 12.95 (*1-58062-338-7*) Adams Media.

Domaszewski, Alfred. Abhandlungen Zur Romischen Religion. 240p. 1977. reprint ed. write for info. (*3-487-06448-0*) G Olms Pubs.

Domaszewski, Alfred V., jt. auth. see Brunnow, Rudolf E.

Domaszewski, Alfred Von, see Von Domaszewski, Alfred.

Domat, Jean. Civil Law in Its Natural Order, 2 vols., Set. Strahan, William, tr. from FRE. 1763p. 1981. reprint ed. 110.00 (*0-8377-0511-8*, Rothman) W S Hein.

Domatob, Jerry K. Contemporary Issues in Sub-Saharan African Political & Economic Development. LC 98-18493. 124p. 1998. 74.95 (*1-57309-292-4*, U Pr W Africa) Intl Scholars.

Domatob, Jerry Komia. African Higher Education Policy: A Survey of Sub-Saharan Africa: Education & Sustainable Development in Sub-Saharan Africa. LC 98-18060. 124p. 1998. 74.95 (*1-57309-293-2*, U Pr W Africa) Intl Scholars.

— Contemporary Issues in Sub-Saharan African Political & Economic Development. LC 98-18493. 124p. 1998. pap. 54.95 (*1-57309-291-6*, U Pr W Africa) Intl Scholars.

Domb, A. J., ed. Polymeric Site-specific Pharmacotherapy. LC 93-39724. 476p. 1994. 350.00 (*0-471-93824-6*) Wiley.

Domb, Abraham J., et al, eds. Handbook of Biodegradable Polymers. (Drug Targeting & Delivery Ser.: Vol. 7). 512p. 1997. text 101.00 (*90-5702-153-6*, Harwood Acad Pubs) Gordon & Breach.

***Domb, C.** Phase Transitions & Critical Phenomena, Vol. 18. 350p. 2000. 125.00 (*0-12-220318-6*) Acad Pr.

***Domb, C., ed.** Phase Transitions & Critical Phenomena. (Phase Transitions & Critical Phenomena Ser.: Vol. 19). 576p. 2000. 145.00 (*0-12-220319-4*) Acad Pr.

Domb, C., jt. ed. see Domb, Cyril M.

Domb, Cyril. The Critical Point: A Historical Introduction to the Modern Theory of Critical Phenomena. LC 96-141603. 392p. 1996. 110.00 (*0-7484-0435-X*) Taylor & Francis.

— Transitions in Critical Phenomena. 1983. text 195.00 (*0-12-220308-9*) Acad Pr.

Domb, Cyril, jt. ed. see Carmell, Aryeh.

Domb, Cyril M. & Domb, C., eds. Second Bar-Ilan Conference on the Physics of Disordered Systems: Special Issue of Philosophical Magazine, Pt. B, Vol. 56, No. 6. 414p. 1988. pap. 34.00 (*0-85066-907-3*) Taylor & Francis.

Domb, Cyril M. & Lebowitz, Joel L., eds. Phase Transitions & Critical Phenomena, Vol. 10. 363p. 1987. text 184.00 (*0-12-220310-0*) Acad Pr.

— Phase Transitions & Critical Phenomena, Vol. 11. 240p. 1987. text 147.00 (*0-12-220311-9*) Acad Pr.

— Phase Transitions & Critical Phenomena, Vol. 14. (Illus.). 376p. 1991. text 186.00 (*0-12-220314-3*) Acad Pr.

— Phase Transitions & Critical Phenomena, Vol. 15. (Illus.). 245p. 1992. text 138.00 (*0-12-220315-1*) Acad Pr.

Domb, Denise, ed. Natural Medicine Chest & Home Remedies Handbook. LC 94-220557. 72p. 1994. pap. 4.95 (*0-9636334-8-1*) AlternMed Bks.

Domb, Ellen, jt. auth. see Cowley, Michael.

Domb, Fania, jt. ed. see Dinstein, Yoram.

Domb, Risa. The Arab in Hebrew Prose. 180p. 1982. 32.50 (*0-85303-203-3*, Pub. by M Vallentine & Co) Intl Spec Bk.

— Home Thoughts from Abroad: Distant Visions of Israel in Contemporary Hebrew Fiction. LC 95-2681. 1995. 27.50 (*0-85303-303-X*, Pub. by M Vallentine & Co); pap. 16.50 (*0-85303-304-8*, Pub. by M Vallentine & Co) Intl Spec Bk.

Domb, Risa, ed. New Women's Writing from Israel. LC 96-21338. (Illus.). 235p. 1996. 42.50 (*0-85303-307-2*, Pub. by M Vallentine & Co); pap. 19.50 (*0-85303-308-0*, Pub. by M Vallentine & Co) Intl Spec Bk.

Dombal, Robert W. Appraising Condominiums: Suggested Data Analysis Techniques. 24p. 1981. pap. 5.00 (*0-685-16913-8*) Appraisal Inst.

Dombart, et al, eds. Augustini, S. Aurelii, Vol. I. (LAT.). 1993. reprint ed. 59.50 (*3-519-01104-2*, T1104, Pub. by B G Teubner) U of Mich Pr.

— Augustini, S. Aurelii, Vol. II. (LAT.). 1993. reprint ed. 59.50 (*3-519-01105-0*, T1105, Pub. by B G Teubner) U of Mich Pr.

Dombeck, Mary T. Dreams & Professional Personhood: The Contexts of Dream Telling & Dream Interpretation among American Psychotherapists. LC 90-9780. (SUNY Series in Dream Studies). 271p. (C). 1991. pap. text 21.95 (*0-7914-0589-3*) State U NY Pr.

Dombeck, T., et al. Detector Research & Development for the Superconducting Supercollider, Symposium on. 844p. 1991. text 173.00 (*981-02-0445-0*) World Scientific Pub.

Dombek, George. Airbrush Illustration for Architecture. (A Norton Book for Architects & Designe Ser.). (Illus.). 160p. 1997. 40.00 (*0-393-73022-0*) Norton.

Domberger, Simon. Contracting Organization: A Strategic Guide to Outsourcing. (Illus.). 248p. 1999. text 65.00 (*0-19-877458-3*); pap. text 24.95 (*0-19-877457-5*) OUP.

Domberger, Simon & Hall, Christine, eds. The Contracting Casebook: Competitive Tendering in Action. 193p. 1995. 45.50 (*0-644-43124-5*, Pub. by Aust Gov Pub) Accents Pubns.

Dombey, Henrietta & Moustafa, Margaret. Whole to Part Phonics: How Children Learn to Read & Spell. 1998. pap. text 9.00 (*0-325-00120-0*) Heinemann.

Dombey, Moshe, tr. see Epstein, Baruch H.

Dombey, Moshe, tr. see Fuchs, Yitzchak Y.

Dombey, Moshe, tr. see Grossman, Reuven.

Dombey, N. & Boudjema, F., eds. Radiative Corrections: Results & Perspectives. LC 90-7921. (NATO ASI Ser.: Vol. 233). (Illus.). 588p. (C). 1990. text 186.00 (*0-306-43670-1*, Kluwer Plenum) Kluwer Academic.

Dombhart, John M. History of Walker County, Alabama, Its Town & Its People. (Illus.). 382p. 1997. reprint ed. lib. bdg. 42.50 (*0-8328-7043-9*) Higginson Bk Co.

***Dombi, William A. & Houchen, Betsy J.** Home Care & Hospice Law: A Handbook for Executives. LC 00-130300. 508p. 2000. 250.00 (*1-886450-10-2*) Caring Pub.

***Dombinguez-Cristbobal, Carlos.** Panorama Histborico Forestal de Puerto Rico rev. ed. LC 99-35523. 2000. write for info. (*0-8477-0297-9*) U of PR Pr.

***Dombinguez, Jorge I.** The Future of Inter-American Relations. LC 99-35000. (Inter-American Dialogue Book Ser.). 1999. pap. 22.99 (*0-415-92216-X*) Routledge.

***Dombowsky, Greg.** Diver's Guide: Vancouver Island South. 1999. pap. 14.95 (*1-895811-88-0*) Heritage Hse.

Dombradi & Fenyes, T., eds. Proceedings of the International Symposium on In-Beam Nuclear Spectroscopy, Debrecen, Hungary, May 14-18, 1984. 820p. 1984. 520.00 (*0-569-08841-0*, Pub. by Collets) St Mut.

Dombradi, Z. S. & Fenyes, T. Proceedings of the International Symposium on InBeam Nuclear Spectroscopy, 2 vols., Set, Vols. 1 & 2. 820p. (C). 1984. 195.00 (*963-05-3993-4*, Pub. by Akade Kiado) St Mut.

Dombre, Irene, jt. auth. see Mills, Judy.

Dombrink, John & Thompson, William N. The Last Resort: Success & Failure in Campaigns for Casinos. LC 89-14821. (Wilbur S. Shepperson Series in History & Humanities). (Illus.). 232p. 1990. 29.95 (*0-87417-140-7*) U of Nev Pr.

Dombro, Amy, jt. auth. see Lerner, Claire.

Dombro, Amy L. Child Care Aware: A Guide to Promoting Professional Development in Family Child Care. 51p. 1995. pap. 9.00 (*1-888324-16-3*, C95-02) Families & Work.

Dombro, Amy L. & Modigliani, Kathy. Family Child Care Providers Speak about Training, Trainers, Accreditation, & Professionalism: Findings from a Survey of Family-to-Family Graduates. 37p. 1995. pap. 9.00 (*1-888324-20-1*, C95-01) Families & Work.

Dombro, Amy L., et al. The Creative Curriculum for Infants & Toddlers. rev. ed. (Illus.). 379p. (C). 1999. pap. text 34.95 (*1-879537-40-0*, Pub. by Tchng Strtgs) Gryphon Hse.

— Guia Para los Padres Sobre los Programas de Cuidado Infantil de 0-3 Anos, 10 bks. (SPA., Illus.). 27p. 1998. pap. text 22.50 (*1-879537-35-4*) Tchng Strtgs.

— A Journal for Using the Creative Curriculum for Infants & Toddlers. LC 97-62074. (Illus.). 139p. 1998. pap., wbk. ed. 5.00 (*1-879537-34-6*) Tchng Strtgs.

— A Parent's Guide to Infant - Toddler Programs, 10 bks. (Illus.). 24p. 1998. pap. text 22.50 (*1-879537-32-X*) Tchng Strtgs.

***Dombroff, Mark.** Evaluating & Recovering Wrongful Death & Personal Injury Cases. 75p. 2000. spiral bd. 45.00 (*0-913875-99-6*, 5996-N) Lawyers & Judges.

Dombroff, Mark, jt. auth. see Pope, Daniel J.

D

Dombroff, Mark A. Demonstrative Evidence. 1983. 25.00 incl. VHS (1-55917-115-4, 991); audio 125.00 (1-55917-113-8); VHS 450.00 (1-55917-114-6) Natl Prac Inst.
— Discovery with 1990 Cumulative Supplement. LC 86-20980. 687p. 1986. suppl. ed. 30.00 (0-930273-73-7, 61318-10, MICHIE) LEXIS Pub.
— Discovery with 1990 Cumulative Supplement. LC 86-20980. 687p. 1990. suppl. ed. 80.00 (0-930273-44-3, 61315-10, MICHIE) LEXIS Pub.
— Expert Witnesses in Civil Trials: Effective Preparation & Presentation. LC 87-82544. 1987. 103.00 (0-318-33006-7) West Group.
— Expert Witnesses in Civil Trials: Effective Preparation & Presentation. LC 87-82544. 1993. suppl. ed. 43.00 (0-317-04353-6) West Group.
— Key Trial Control Tactics: A Guide to Winning the Ultimate Verdict. enl. rev. ed. LC 84-8099. 1984. 99.50 (0-13-515073-6) Exec Reports.
— Litigation Management & Organization: The Winning Edge. 1985. 25.00 (1-55917-392-0, 5314); audio 125.00 (1-55917-390-4); VHS 395.00 (1-55917-391-2) Natl Prac Inst.
— Litigation Organization & Management, 2 vols. 2nd ed. 1338p. 1991. ring bd. 195.00 (0-13-072489-0) Aspen Law.
— Litigation Organization & Management: Effective Tactics & Techniques. LC 84-1257. 1984. 60.00 (0-15-004369-4, #H43694) Harcourt.
— Personal Injury Defense Techniques, 3 vols. 1987. ring bd. 610.00 (0-8205-1542-6) Bender.
— Trial Tactics. 1983. 25.00 (1-55917-750-0, 999); audio 125.00 (1-55917-748-9); VHS 395.00 (1-55917-749-7) Natl Prac Inst.
— Unfair Trial Tactics: Recognizing & Avoiding Them in Litigation. 1985. 25.00 (1-55917-781-0, 5315); audio 125.00 (1-55917-779-9); VHS 395.00 (1-55917-780-2) Natl Prac Inst.
Dombroff, Mark A., jt. auth. see Boltz, Howard O.
Dombroff, Mark A., jt. auth. see Conlon, John L.
Dombroski, Ken, pref. History of the Fifth Massachusetts Battery. (Army of the Potomac Ser.). (Illus.). 1100p. (C). 1996. reprint ed. 60.00 (0-935523-61-8) Butternut & Blue.
Dombroski, Paul, et al. The Employment Maze: Unlocking Doors to a New Job. (Illus.). 150p. (Orig.). 1989. 14.95 (0-9622443-1-7) Doubletake Prodns.
Dombroski, Robert S. Properties of Writing: Ideological Discourse in Modern Italian Fiction. LC 94-16037. 208p. 1995. text 35.00 (0-8018-4919-5) Johns Hopkins.
Dombrovskis, Peter, photos by. Wild Rivers. (Illus.). 128p. (C). 1983. 80.00 (0-9597530-4-4, Pub. by West Wind Pr) St Mut.
Dombrovsky, L. A. Radiation Heat Transfer in Disperse Systems. 256p. 1996. 112.50 (1-56700-057-6) Begell Hse.
— Radiation Heat Transfer in Disperse Systems. LC 96-5544. 1996. write for info. (0-614-13959-7) Begell Hse.
Dombrovsky, Yury. The Faculty of Useless Knowledge. Myers, Alan, tr. 1997. pap. text 16.00 (1-86046-343-6) Harvill Press.
Dombrowa, Regina. Strukturen in Shakespeares King Henry the Sixth. (BAS Ser.: No. 18). x, 320p. (Orig.). 1985. pap. write for info. (90-6032-267-3) B R Gruner.
Dombrower, Eddie. Zen & the Art of Interactive Entertainment Design. LC 97-23962. (Illus.). 400p. 1997. pap., pap. text 49.95 incl. cd-rom (0-07-017497-0) McGraw.
Dombrower, Jan. Getting to Know Your Emotional Needs. (Illus.). (J). Date not set. write for info. (1-55864-021-5) Kdsrghts.
— Getting to Know Your Feelings. (Orig.). (J). Date not set. teacher ed. write for info. (1-55864-022-3) Kdsrghts.
— Getting to Know Your Feelings. Johnson, Debbie, ed. (Illus.). 32p. (Orig.). (J). (ps-3). 1990. pap. text 4.95 (0-9626348-0-8) Kdsrghts.
Dombrowski, Daniel A. Analytic Theism, Hartshorne, & the Concept of God. LC 95-47051. (SUNY Series in Philosophy). 192p. (C). 1996. text 57.50 (0-7914-3099-5) State U NY Pr.
— Analytic Theism, Hartshorne, & the Concept of God. LC 95-47051. (SUNY Series in Philosophy). (Illus.). 192p. (C). 1996. pap. text 18.95 (0-7914-3100-2) State U NY Pr.
— Babies & Beasts: The Argument from Marginal Cases. LC 96-51232. 232p. 1997. 14.95 (0-252-06638-3); text 39.95 (0-252-02342-0) U of Ill Pr.
— Christian Pacifism. (Ethics & Action Ser.). 240p. 1991. 44.95 (0-87722-802-7) Temple U Pr.
— Hartshorne & the Metaphysics of Animal Rights. LC 87-16591. (SUNY Series in Philosophy). 159p. (C). 1988. text 65.50 (0-88706-704-2); pap. text 21.95 (0-88706-705-0) State U NY Pr.
— Kazantzakis & God. LC 96-48025. (SUNY Series in Constructive Postmodern Thought). 193p. (C). 1997. text 53.50 (0-7914-3491-5); pap. text 17.95 (0-7914-3492-3) State U NY Pr.
***Dombrowski, Daniel A.** Not a Sparrow Falls: The Philosophy of Stephen R. L. Clark. 352p. 2000. 39.95 (0-87013-549-X) Mich St U Pr.
Dombrowski, Daniel A. The Philosophy of Vegetarianism. LC 83-18125. 192p. 1984. pap. 15.95 (0-87023-431-5) U of Mass Pr.
— St. John of the Cross: An Appreciation. LC 90-28577. (SUNY Series in Latin American & Iberian Thought & Culture). 223p. (C). 1992. text 24.50 (0-7914-0887-6) State U NY Pr.
***Dombrowski, Daniel A. & Deltete, Robert John.** A Brief, Liberal, Catholic Defense of Abortion. LC 99-6707. 2000. 19.95 (0-252-02550-4) U of Ill Pr.
Dombrowski, Eric. German Leaders of Yesterday & Today. LC 67-23206. (Essay Index Reprint Ser.). 1977. 23.95 (0-8369-0384-6) Ayer.
Dombrowski, Lynn Blewett. Functional Needs Assessment Treatment Guide. 1998. pap. text 37.00 (0-12-784587-9) Acad Pr.
Dombrowski, Nicole A. Women & War in the Twentieth Century: Enlisted with or Without Consent. LC 98-36313. (Women's History & Culture Ser.: Vol. 13). (Illus.). 392p. 1998. 59.00 (0-8153-2287-9, H1969) Garland.
***Dombrowski, P. M.** Ethics in Technical Communications. LC 99-36590. 258p. 1999. pap. text 33.00 (0-205-27462-5, Longwood Div) Allyn.
Dombrowski, Paul M., ed. Humanistic Aspects of Technical Communication. (Technical Communications Ser.). 260p. (C). 1994. text 38.95 (0-89503-159-0); pap. text 30.72 (0-89503-160-4) Baywood Pub.
Dombrowski, Peter. Policy Responses Globalization: U. S. Foreign Policy & American Commercial Banks. (Policy & Institutional Studies). (Illus.). 247p. (C). 1996. text 34.95 (0-8229-3901-0) U of Pittsburgh Pr.
Dombrowski, Robert S. Antonio Gramsci. (World Authors Ser.). 176p. (C). 1989. 32.00 (0-8057-8245-1, TWAS 808, Twyne) Mac Lib Ref.
Dombrowski, Sharon A. A Concise Manual on the Theory of Music. (Illus.). 64p. (Orig.). (C). 1983. reprint ed. spiral bd. 10.00 (0-9610658-0-X) Blue Note.
Domburg, P. H. Van, see Van Domburg, P. H.
Dome Financial Services Staff. Saving Thousands on Your Mortgage. Picchione, Nick, ed. 256p. (Orig.). 1990. pap. 7.95 (0-02-028345-8) Macmillan.
Dome, Malcolm & Wall, Mick. Bon Jovi: In Their Own Words. (Illus.). 96p. pap. 15.95 (0-7119-6464-5) Omnibus Pr.
— Bon Jovi: Live! (Illus.). 32p. 1996. pap. 9.95 (0-7119-5700-2, OP47836) Omnibus NY.
Dome, Malcolm, jt. auth. see Wall, Mick.
Dome, Takuo. History of Economic Theory: A Critical Introduction. 360p. 1994. 95.00 (1-85898-114-X) E Elgar.
Domecq, Brianda. The Astonishing Story of the Saint of Cabora. Garcia, Kay, tr. from SPA. LC 98-2821.Tr. of La Insolita Historia de la Santa de Cabora. v, 362 p. 1998. pap. 14.00 (0-927534-78-9) Biling Rev-Pr.
— Eleven Days. LC 94-18711. 226p. (C). 1995. pap. 10.95 (0-8263-1606-9) U of NM Pr.
Domecq, Brianda, ed. Acechando Al Unicorno (Stalking the Unicorn) La Virginidad en la Literatura Mexicana (Virginity in Mexican Literature) (SPA.). 440p. 1988. pap. 13.99 (968-16-3030-0, Pub. by Fondo) Continental Bk.
***Domeier, Danja.** Gesundheitsschutz Und Leensmittelstrafrecht. 318p. 1999. 56.95 (3-631-34850-9) P Lang Pubng.
***Domeij, Bengt.** Pharmaceutical Patents in Europe. LC 00-35748. (Stockholm Studies in Law). 2000. write for info. (90-411-1348-7) Kluwer Law Intl.
Domeij, Scoti, jt. auth. see Arthur, Kay.
Domeisen, jt. auth. see Profos, P.
Domel. Builder's Portable Handbook. LC 00-22008. (McGraw-Hill Portable Handbooks Ser.). (Illus.). 400p. 1999. 54.95 (0-07-134654-6) McGraw-Hill Prof.
Domel, August W. Engineering for Contractors: Ready-to-Use Calculation. LC 96-33180. (Illus.). 306p. 1996. pap. 34.95 (0-07-018002-4) McGraw.
Domelen, J. Van, see Van Domelen, J.
Domellof, L., ed. Drug Delivery in Cancer Treatment II. (ESO Monographs). (Illus.). 120p. 1989. 108.00 (0-387-51055-9) Spr-Verlag.
Domellof, L. & Veronesi, U., eds. Drug Delivery in Cancer Treatment III: Home Care Symptom Control, Economy, Brain Tumours. (ESO Monographs). (Illus.). viii, 125p. 1990. 118.00 (0-387-52951-9) Spr-Verlag.
Domelsmith, Linda N., jt. ed. see Fischer, Janet J.
***Domen, Christoph.** No Trace of Christmas: Discovering Advent in the Old Testament. Maloney, Linda M., tr. 104p. 2000. pap. 11.95 (0-8146-2715-3) Liturgical Pr.
Domenach, Jean-Luc. Forgotten Gulag: China's Hidden Prison Camps. 1994. text 29.95 (0-02-907795-8) Free Pr.
Domenech, Ricardo, ed. see Del Valle-Inclan, Ramon.
Domenica, Michael F., ed. see ASCE, Boston Society of Civil Engineers Staff.
Domenicano, Aldo & Hargittai, Istvan, eds. Accurate Molecular Structures: Their Determination & Importance. (International Union of Crystallography Monographs on Crystallography: No. 1). (Illus.). 602p. 1992. text 135.00 (0-19-855556-3) OUP.
Domenici, Kathy. Mediation: Empowerment in Conflict Management. 137p. 1996. pap. text 11.95 (0-88133-894-X) Waveland Pr.
Domenici, Kathy, jt. auth. see Littlejohn, Stephen W.
Domenici, Pete V., ed. The Congressional Budget Process: An Explanation. 56p. (C). 1998. pap. text 20.00 (0-7881-7113-5) DIANE Pub.
***Domenici, Pete V., ed.** The Congressional Budget Process: An Explanation. rev. ed. 58p. (C). 2000. reprint ed. pap. text 20.00 (0-7881-8917-4) DIANE Pub.
— Social Security Reform: Congressional Hearings. (Illus.). 97p. (C). 1999. reprint ed. pap. text 25.00 (0-7881-8450-4) DIANE Pub.
Domenici, Thomas & Lesser, Ronnie C., eds. Disorienting Sexuality: Psychoanalytic Reappraisals of Sexual Identities. LC 95-38513. 314p. (C). 1995. pap. 24.99 (0-415-91198-2) Routledge.
— Disorienting Sexuality: Psychoanalytic Reappraisals of Sexual Identities. LC 95-38513. 313p. (C). (gr. 13 up). 1995. 75.00 (0-415-91197-4) Routledge.
***Domenico.** Masaje: Tecnica de Beard. 4th ed. (C). 1998. text 20.50 (84-8174-341-0) Mosby Inc.
Domenico, Giovanni De, see De Domenico, Giovanni.
Domenico, Patrick A. & Schwartz, Franklin W. Physical & Chemical Hydrogeology. 2nd ed. LC 97-21776. 528p. 1997. text 109.95 (0-471-59762-7) Wiley.
Domenico, Roy P. Italian Fascists on Trial, 1943-1948. LC 91-50251. (Illus.). xx, 295p. (C). 1992. 59.95 (0-8078-2006-7) U of NC Pr.
Domenico, S. N., jt. ed. see Danbom, S.
Domenig, Marc & Ten Hacken, Pius. Word Manager: A System for Morphological Dictionaries. (Informatik und Sprache: Bd. 1). (GER.). x, 212p. 1992. write for info. (3-487-09677-3) G Olms Pubs.
Domer, Dennis E., ed. Alfred Caldwell: The Life & Work of a Prairie School Landscape Architect. LC 96-49076. (Illus.). 336p. 1997. text 39.95 (0-8018-5551-9) Johns Hopkins.
Domeracki, Frank J., jt. auth. see Guyer, Richard S.
Domeraski, Regina, tr. see Ludwig, Christa.
Domes, Jurgen. P'eng Te-Huai: The Man & the Image. LC 85-50942. xii, 164p. 1985. 35.00 (0-8047-1303-0) Stanford U Pr.
— Socialism in the Chinese Countryside. 1980. 49.95 (0-7735-0532-6, Pub. by McG-Queens Univ Pr) CUP Services.
Domestic & Foreign Writers Staff, et al. Taproot's Osage Orange Tree: Taproot Literary Review, 1998. 1 th ed. (Taproots Tree Ser.: No. 1). 90p. 1998. pap. 6.95 (1-890269-02-6) Taproot Press.
Domestici, Fiamma. Della Robbia: A Family of Artists. Evans, Christopher, tr. from ITA. (Library of Great Masters). (Illus.). 80p. (Orig.). 1993. pap. 12.99 (1-878351-45-1) Riverside NY.
Dometrius. Politics & Policy: United States & Texas. 256p. (C). 1993. pap. text 13.95 (0-8403-8372-X) Kendall-Hunt.
Domhnallach, Tormod C. Call Na H-Iolaire. 1985. 40.00 (0-86152-000-9, Pub. by Acair Ltd) St Mut.
Domhoff, G. William. Finding Meaning in Dreams: A Quantitative Approach. LC 96-18169. (Emotions, Personality, & Psychotherapy Ser.). (Illus.). 372p. (C). 1996. 59.00 (0-306-45172-7, Plenum Trade) Perseus Pubng.
— The Mystique of Dreams: A Search for Utopia Through Senoi Dream Theory. 156p. 1985. pap. 14.95 (0-520-06021-0, Pub. by U CA Pr) Cal Prin Full Svc.
— The Power Elite & the State: How Policy Is Made in America. LC 90-393. (Social Institutions & Social Change Ser.). 334p. 1990. pap. text 29.95 (0-202-30373-X) Aldine de Gruyter.
— State Autonomy or Class Dominance? Case Studies on Policy Making in America. 307p. 1996. pap. text 25.95 (0-202-30512-0); lib. bdg. 51.95 (0-202-30511-2) Aldine de Gruyter.
— Who Really Rules? New Have & Community Power Reexamined. 190p. (C). 1978. pap. 32.95 (0-87620-965-7) Transaction Pubs.
— Who Rules America? Power & Politics in the Year 2000. 3rd ed. LC 97-31049. xi, 335p. 1998. pap. 22.95 (1-55934-973-5) Mayfield Pub.
— Who Rules America Now? A View for the Eighties. 230p. (Orig.). (YA). (gr. 9-12). 1983. pap. 7.95 (0-13-958405-6, Spectrum IN) Macmillan Gen Ref.
Domhoff, G. William, ed. Power Structure Research. LC 79-25255. (Sage Focus Editions Ser.: No. 17). 270p. reprint ed. pap. 83.70 (0-8357-8456-8, 203472000091) Bks Demand.
Domhoff, G. William & Dye, Thomas R., eds. Power Elites & Organizations. LC 85-30432. (Sage Focus Editions Ser.: No. 82). 292p. (Orig.). 1987. reprint ed. pap. 90.60 (0-608-01456-7, 205950000001) Bks Demand.
Domhoff, G. William, jt. auth. see Zweigenhaft, Richard L.
Domholdt, Elizabeth. Physical Therapy Research: Principles & Applications. LC 92-13390. (Illus.). 464p. 1992. pap. text 43.00 (0-7216-3611-X, W B Saunders Co) Harcrt Hlth Sci Grp.
— Physical Therapy Research: Principles & Applications. 2nd ed. LC 99-47086. (Illus.). 479p. 1998. pap. text. write for info. (0-7216-6963-8, W B Saunders Co) Harcrt Hlth Sci Grp.
Domi. La Senora Reganona (The Grouchy Woman) (SPA.). 20p. (J). (gr. 1-3). 1997. 12.99 (968-16-5212-6, Pub. by Fondo) Continental Bk.
Domico, Terry. Natural Areas of the San Juan Islands. rev. ed. (Illus.). 172p. 2000. pap. 19.95 (1-883385-00-8) Turtleback Bks.
— Wild Harvest: Edible Plants of the Pacific Northwest. (Illus.). 88p. 1979. reprint ed. pap. 8.95 (0-88839-022-X) Hancock House.
Domin, Hilde. Gesammelte Gedichte. (GER.). 435p. 1991. 38.00 (3-10-015304-9, Pub. by S Fischer) Intl Bk Import.
— Nur eine Rose als Stuetze, Gedichte. (GER.). 96p. 1994. pap. 11.75 (3-596-12207-4, Pub. by Fischer Tasch) Intl Bk Import.
— Von der Natur nicht vorgesehen. Autobiographisches. (GER.). 192p. 1993. pap. 13.50 (3-596-12203-1, Pub. by Fischer Tasch) Intl Bk Import.
Domin, Linda. Interpret Sus Manos. LC 98-41064. (SPA.). 256p. 1999. pap. 12.95 (1-56718-397-2) Llewellyn Pubns.
— Interprete Sus Manos: El Mapa de Su Vida. LC 97-13016.Tr. of Instant Palm Reader. (SPA., Illus.). 288p. 1999. pap. 12.95 (1-56718-232-1, K232-1) Llewellyn Pubns.
Domina, Bryant S. Principles of Success for the Classroom Teacher of the Autistic Impaired. 150p. 1998. pap. text 17.50 (0-9652495-5-7) Individual Educ.
Domina, Lyle, jt. auth. see Davis, Cathy H.
Domina, Lynn. Corporal Works. 80p. 94-71637. (Intro Ser.). 54p. 1995. pap. 11.95 (1-884800-03-3) Four Way Bks.
— Understanding A Raisin in the Sun: A Student Casebook to Issues, Sources & Historical Documents. LC 98-13975. (Greenwood Press Literature in Context Ser.). 176p. 1998. 39.95 (0-313-30349-5, Greenwood Pr) Greenwood.
***Domine, Andre.** Culinaria: France. (Culinaria Ser.). (Illus.). 460p. 1999. 39.95 (3-8290-2019-8, 520179) Konemann.
Domine, Andre. Die Kunst des Aperitif: Rezepte, Getranke, Philosophie. (GER., Illus.). 180p. (C). 1989. 40.00 (3-8170-0013-8, Pub. by Knstvrlag Weingrtn) Intl Bk Import.
— Organic & Whole Foods. (Culinaria Ser.). (Illus.). 460p. 1997. 39.95 (3-89508-472-7, 520074) Konemann.
Domine, Andre, et al. European Specialties, 2 Vols. (Culinaria Ser.). (Illus.). 736p. 1997. boxed set 79.95 (3-89508-234-1) Konemann.
Domineli, Lena. Anti-Racist Probation Practice. 160p. 1996. 64.95 (1-85742-328-3, Pub. by Arena); pap. 33.95 (1-85742-280-5, Pub. by Arena) Ashgate Pub Co.
Dominelli. Anti Racist Social Work. 1997. text 17.95 (0-333-30907-3, Pub. by Macmillan) St Martin.
Dominelli, Lena, ed. Community Approaches to Child Welfare: International Perspectives. (CEDR Ser.). 234p. 1999. text 65.95 (1-84014-942-6) Ashgate Pub Co.
Dominges da Silva, Alvaro A., jt. ed. see Banerjee, Timir.
***Domingo.** Death Famine Sword & Wild Beasts. LC 99-91658. 314p. 2000. 25.00 (0-7388-1162-9); pap. 18.00 (0-7388-1163-7) Xlibris Corp.
Domingo, Esteban. Origin & Evolution of Viruses. 496p. 1999. 120.00 (0-12-220360-7) Acad Pr.
Domingo, Esteban, et al, eds. RNA Genetics, Vol. I. 240p. 1988. 131.00 (0-8493-6666-6, QR395, CRC Reprint) Franklin.
— RNA Genetics, Vol. II. 240p. 1988. 148.00 (0-8493-6667-4, QR395, CRC Reprint) Franklin.
— RNA Genetics, Vol. III. 272p. 1988. 154.00 (0-8493-6668-2, QR395, CRC Reprint) Franklin.
***Domingo, Esteban & Holland, John J.** Quasispecies & RNA Virus Evolution: Principles & Consequences. (Molecular Biology Intelligence Unit Ser.). 233p. 2000. 99.00 (1-58706-010-8, Pub. by Eurekah) Landes Bioscience.
Domingo-Foraste, ed. Aeliani. (GRE.). 1994. 49.50 (3-8154-1005-3, T1005, Pub. by B G Teubner) U of Mich Pr.
Domingo, Margie. Let Me Walk Beside You. 60p. (Orig.). (C). 1993. pap. 10.00 (0-9631826-1-7) Exist InVerse.
— Let My Existence Be Born. LC 92-90122. 80p. (Orig.). (C). 1992. pap. 10.00 (0-9631826-0-9) Exist InVerse.
Domingo, Rene T. Quality Means Survival: Caveat Vendidor, Let the Seller Beware. LC 96-30052. (C). 1997. pap. text 24.95 (0-13-626780-7) P-H.
Domingo, Roger. Orphans in Babylon: Abortion in America. Where Are We Now? How Did We Get Here? Where Should We Be? How Can We Get There? LC 98-94109. 312p. 1998. pap. 29.95 (0-9668541-0-1) Turnstyle.
***Domingo, Santos Alfredo Garcia.** Raices de Esperanza. (MYN & SPA.). 85p. 2000. pap. 9.95 (1-886502-34-X) Yax Te Found.
Domingo, Zenaida T. The Community Advisory Board As the Grass Roots Planning Arm of Broadcasting in the Philippines. (Institute of Culture & Communication Case Studies: No. 10). (Illus.). xii, 137p. (Orig.). 1984. pap. 5.00 (0-86638-041-8) EW Ctr HI.
Domingue, Robert A. Phillips Academy - Andover, Massachusetts: An Illustrated History of the Property. (Illus.). 202p. (Orig.). 1990. pap. 17.95 (0-9620726-2-1) RAD Pub.
***Domingues, Jose M.** Social Creativity, Collective Subjectivity & Contemporary Modernity. LC 99-46785. 2000. text 65.00 (0-312-22987-9) St Martin.
Domingues, Jose M. Sociological Theory & Collective Subjectivity. 240p. 1995. text 65.00 (0-312-12976-9) St Martin.
Dominguez. Atajo 1.1: User's Manual for MAC. (College Spanish Ser.). (C). 1995. mass mkt. 12.95 (0-8384-6365-7) Heinle & Heinle.
— Complete Book of Sports Medicine. 1979. 2.95 (0-684-16384-5, Scribners Ref) Mac Lib Ref.
— Directory of Toxic & Related Test Labs. 1991. 68.95 (0-89116-904-0) Hemisp Pub.
— Murdos Hispanos Guide, Level 1. (College Spanish Ser.). 1996. pap. 36.95 (0-8384-6857-8) Heinle & Heinle.
Dominguez, jt. auth. see Noblitt, James S.
Dominguez, Abel M., ed. Comprehensive Index to the Journal of Forensic Sciences, 1972-1986. LC 87-17453. 1987. 35.00 (0-8031-0984-9, JOFSINDX87) ASTM.
Dominguez, Angel. Classic Animal Stories. 160p. (J). 1991. write for info. (1-85479-018-8, Pub. by M OMara) Assoc Pubs Grp.
***Dominguez, C. A. & Viollier, R. D., eds.** Win'99. 630p. 2000. 118.00 (981-02-4082-1) World Scientific Pub.
Dominguez Caparros. Diccionario de Metrica Espanola. 2nd ed. (SPA.). 1992. write for info. (0-7859-3681-5, 8428313660) Fr & Eur.
Dominguez, Catalina, tr. see Blackwood, Gary L.
Dominguez, Catalina, tr. see Oram, Hiawyn & Kitamura, Satoshi.
Dominguez, Catalina, tr. see Ross, Tony.
Dominguez, Catalina, tr. see Steadman, Ralph.
Dominguez, Catalina, tr. see Stone, Bernard.
Dominguez, Catalina, tr. see Swindells, Robert.
Dominguez, Catalina, tr. see Van Allsburg, Chris.
Dominguez, E. Outerelo, jt. auth. see Margalef-Roig, J.
Dominguez Fernandez, Diego. Diccionario de Contabilidad y Economia. (SPA.). 246p. 1988. pap. 14.95 (0-7859-5833-9, 8427115210) Fr & Eur.
Dominguez, Frances. Bulaklak ng Kaisipas. 145p. 1998. pap. 12.95 (1-57502-095-5, PO2378) Morris Pubng.

D

Dominguez, Francesc & Lopez, Nuria, compiled by. Language International World Directory of Sociolinguistic & Language Planning Organizations. LC 95-23742. (Language International World Directory Ser.: No. 1). xx, 530p. 1995. 130.00 (*1-55619-740-3*) J Benjamins Pubng Co.

Dominguez, Francisco J. Estranged: Poems from the Soul. 64p. 1999. pap. 8.00 (*0-8059-4548-2*) Dorrance.

***Dominguez, Francisco J., ed.** Identity & Discursive Practices. LC 99-59031. (Illus.). 328p. 2000. pap. 50.95 (*3-906763-67-6*) P Lang Pubng.

— Identity & Discursive Practices: Spain & Latin America. LC 99-59031. 328p. 2000. pap. text 50.95 (*0-8204-4621-1*) P Lang Pubng.

Dominguez, Frank A. Love & Remembrance: The Poetry of Jorge Manrique. LC 88-21627. 232p. 1988. 28.00 (*0-8131-1651-1*) U Pr of Ky.

Dominguez, Frank A., et al. Atajo 3.0 Dual-Platform CD-Rom Writing Assistant for Spanish (Individual Version) 18p. pap. 46.95 (*0-8384-0433-2*, Pub. by Heinle & Heinle) Thomson Learn.

Dominguez, G. S., ed. Guidebook: Toxic Substances Control Act, Vol. I. 448p. 1977. 186.00 (*0-8493-5321-1*, KF3958, CRC Reprint) Franklin.

— Guidebook: Toxic Substances Control Act, Vol. II. 240p. 1983. 136.00 (*0-8493-5322-X*, KF3958, CRC Reprint) Franklin.

Dominguez, George S. The Business Guide to Tosca: Effects & Actions. LC 79-20054. 383p. reprint ed. pap. 118.80 (*0-8357-7493-7*, 202518700042) Bks Demand.

— Government Relations: A Handbook for Developing & Conducting the Company Program. LC 81-11500. (Wiley-Interscience Publications). 438p. reprint ed. pap. 135.80 (*0-608-12361-7*, 202518200042) Bks Demand.

— Marketing in a Regulated Environment. LC 77-22099. (Marketing Management Ser.). 359p. reprint ed. 111.30 (*0-8357-9525-X*, 205525500011) Bks Demand.

Dominguez, George S. & Bartlett, Kenneth G., eds. Hazardous Waste Management: Law of Toxics & Toxic Substances, Vol. I. 272p. 1986. 126.00 (*0-8493-6356-X*, KF3879, CRC Reprint) Franklin.

Dominguez, Glenda, ed. see Hermann, Richard L. & Sutherland, Linda P.

Dominguez, Henry L. Edsel Ford & E. T. Gregorie: The Remarkable Design Team & Their Classic Fords of the 1930's & 1940's. LC 99-13062. 1999. 39.00 (*0-7680-0400-4*) Soc Auto Engineers.

Dominguez, Humberto S., tr. see Baldwin, Carl R.

Dominguez, Ivo, Jr. Beneath the Skins: The New Spirit & Politics of the Kink Community. LC 94-71572. 156p. (Orig.). 1994. pap. 12.95 (*1-881943-06-2*) Daedalus Pub.

— Castings: The Creation of Sacred Space. (Wheel of Trees Ser.: Vol. 1). (Illus.). 176p. (Orig.). 1996. pap. 14.95 (*0-9654198-0-0*) SapFire Prods.

***Dominguez, Ivo, Jr.** Of Spirits: The Book of Rowan. (Wheel of Trees Ser.: Vol. 2). (Illus.). 176p. 1998. pap. 14.95 (*0-9654198-1-9*) SapFire Prods.

Dominguez, J. Boundary Elements in Dymanics. 724p. 1993. 288.00 (*1-85312-258-0*) Computational Mech MA.

Dominguez, J., jt. auth. see Brebbia, C. A.

Dominguez, J., jt. auth. see Brebbia, Carlos A.

***Dominguez, Joe.** Your Money or Your Life: Transforming Your Relationship with Money & Achieving Financial Independence. 432p. 1999. pap. 13.95 (*0-14-028678-0*, Penguin Bks) Viking Penguin.

Dominguez, Joe & Robin, Vicki. La Bolsa o la Vida: Como Deja de ser Exclavo del Dinero y Mejorar la Calidad de Vida. 1997. pap. 12.95 (*0-14-026764-6*) Viking Penguin.

Dominguez, Jorge I. Cuba: Order & Revolution. LC 78-8288. 704p. 1978. 56.00 (*0-674-17925-0*) Belknap Pr.

— Democratic Politics in Latin America & the Caribbean. LC 97-28400. (Illus.). 216p. 1998. text 48.00 (*0-8018-5752-X*); pap. text 16.95 (*0-8018-5753-8*) Johns Hopkins.

— Democratic Transitions in Central America. (Political Economy & Economic Development in Latin America Ser.). 384p. (C). 1929. pap. text 48.50 (*0-8133-8693-4*) Westview.

— Democratizing Mexico: Public Opinion & Electoral Choices. 328p. 1998. pap. text 17.95 (*0-8018-6093-8*) Johns Hopkins.

— International Security & Democracy: Latin America & the Caribbean in the Post-Cold War Era. LC 97-33897. (Latin American Ser.). 422p. 1998. text 50.00 (*0-8229-4054-X*) U of Pittsburgh Pr.

— To Make a World Safe for Revolution: Cuba's Foreign Policy. LC 88-16556. (Center for International Affairs Ser.). (Illus.). 365p. 1989. 51.95 (*0-674-89325-5*) HUP.

Dominguez, Jorge I., ed. Cuba: Internal & International Affairs. LC 82-5700. (Sage Focus Editions Ser.: No. 50). 231p. reprint ed. pap. 71.70 (*0-8357-4780-8*, 203771700009) Bks Demand.

— Cuban Studies. LC 75-649635. (Latin American Ser.: Vol. 22). 328p. (C). 1992. text 39.95 (*0-8229-3723-9*) U of Pittsburgh Pr.

— Cuban Studies 26. 320p. 1997. text 39.95 (*0-8229-3954-1*) U of Pittsburgh Pr.

***Dominguez, Jorge I., ed.** Future of Inter-American Relations. LC 99-35000. 328p. (C). 1999. text. write for info. (*0-415-92215-1*) Routledge.

Dominguez, Jorge I., ed. International Security & Democracy: Latin America & the Caribbean in the Post-Cold War Era. LC 97-33897. (Pitt Series in Latin American Studies). 422p. 1998. pap. 22.95 (*0-8229-5659-4*) U of Pittsburgh Pr.

— Mexico's Political Economy: Challenges at Home & Abroad. LC 81-18472. (Sage Focus Editions Ser.: No. 47). 240p. reprint ed. pap. 74.40 (*0-8357-4781-6*, 203771800009) Bks Demand.

— Technopols: Freeing Politics & Markets in Latin America in the 1990s. LC 96-12003. (Illus.). 352p. 1996. 60.00 (*0-271-01613-2*); pap. 18.95 (*0-271-01614-0*) Pa St U Pr.

Dominguez, Jorge I., et al, eds. Democracy in the Caribbean: Political, Economic, & Social Perspectives. LC 92-28447. (World Peace Foundation Studies). 352p. 1993. text 48.00 (*0-8018-4450-9*) Johns Hopkins.

Dominguez, Jorge I., intro. Economic Strategies & Policies in Latin America. LC 93-43066. (Essays on Mexico, Central & South America Ser.: Vol. 1). 400p. 1994. text 77.00 (*0-8153-1485-X*) Garland.

— Latin America's International Relations & Their Domestic Consequences: War & Peace, Dependency & Autonomy, Integration & Disintegration. LC 93-45524. (Essays on Mexico, Central & South America Ser.: Vol. 6). 464p. 1994. text 84.00 (*0-8153-1490-6*) Garland.

— Parties, Elections, & Political Participation in Latin America. LC 93-42685. (Essays on Mexico, Central & South America Ser.: Vol. 5). 424p. 1994. text 79.00 (*0-8153-1489-2*) Garland.

— The Roman Catholic Church in Latin America. LC 93-45525. 424p. 1994. text 79.00 (*0-8153-1487-6*) Garland.

— Social Movements in Latin America: The Experience of Peasants, Workers, Women, the Urban Poor, & the Middle Sectors. LC 93-42736. (Essays on Mexico, Central & South America Ser.: Vol. 4). 400p. 1994. text 77.00 (*0-8153-1488-4*) Garland.

Dominguez, Jorge I. & Lindenberg, Marc, eds. Democratic Transitions in Central America. LC 96-21369. 240p. 1997. 49.95 (*0-8130-1486-7*) U Press Fla.

Dominguez, Jorge I. & Lowenthal, Abraham F., eds. Constructing Democratic Governance: Latin America & the Caribbean in the 1990's: Mexico, Central America, & the Caribbean. 248p. 1996. pap. text 15.95 (*0-8018-5404-0*) Johns Hopkins.

— Constructing Democratic Governance: Latin America & the Caribbean in the 1990s; South America. LC 96-220520. 240p. 1996. pap. text 15.95 (*0-8018-5403-2*) Johns Hopkins.

— Constructing Democratic Governance: Latin America & the Caribbean in the 1990's: Themes & Issues. 152p. 1996. pap. text 13.95 (*0-8018-5386-9*) Johns Hopkins.

Dominguez, Jorge I. & McCann, James A. Democratizing Mexico: Public Opinion & Electoral Choices. LC 95-16630. 328p. (C). 1996. text 45.00 (*0-8018-5146-7*) Johns Hopkins.

Dominguez, Jorge I. & Nozick, Robert, eds. Authoritarian & Democratic Regimes in Latin America. LC 93-45526. (Essays on Mexico, Central & South America Ser.: Vol. 2). 408p. 1994. text 77.00 (*0-8153-1486-8*) Garland.

Dominguez, Jorge I. & Poire, Alejandro, eds. Toward Mexico's Democratization: Parties, Campaigns, Elections & Public Opinion. LC 98-35528. 256p. (C). 1999. 75.00 (*0-415-92158-9*, D5940); pap. 22.99 (*0-415-92159-7*, D5944) Routledge.

Dominguez, Jorge I., jt. auth. see Dominguez, Virginia R.

Dominguez, Joseph F., jt. tr. see Livingston, Myra C.

Dominguez, Kathryn M. Does Foreign-Exchange Intervention Work? LC 93-2923. 170p. 1993. pap. 18.00 (*0-88132-104-4*) Inst Intl Eco.

— Exchange Rate Efficiency & the Behavior of International Asset Markets. rev. ed. LC 92-27792. (Financial Sector of the American Economy Ser.). 168p. 1992. text 20.00 (*0-8153-0961-9*) Garland.

Dominguez, Kathryn M., et al. Oil Markets Revisited. LC 90-62427. (International Energy Studies: No. 6). 70p. 1990. pap. 16.50 (*0-942781-06-6*) Harvard EEPC.

Dominguez, Marcela, et al. Claro Que Si! An Integrated Skills Approach, 3 vols. 3rd ed. (SPA.). (C). 1995. text, teacher ed. 11.96 (*0-395-74556-X*) HM.

— Claro Que Si! An Integrated Skills Approach, 3 vols. 3rd annot. ed. (SPA.). (C). 1995. text, teacher ed. 60.76 incl. audio (*0-395-74553-5*) HM.

— I Claro Gue Si, 3 vols. 3rd ed. (SPA.). 608p. (C). 1995. text 60.76 incl. audio (*0-395-74551-9*) HM.

Dominguez, Marcela, jt. auth. see Garner, Lucia C.

Dominguez, Margaret. Preparation for Eighth-Grade Math TAAS Test. Dominguez, Monica, ed. & illus. by. 53p. (J). (gr. 8). 1996. spiral bd. 19.95 (*1-889684-00-7*) Texas Testing.

— Preparation for Seventh-Grade Math TAAS Test. Dominguez, Monica, ed. & illus. by. 53p. (J). (gr. 7). 1996. spiral bd. 19.95 (*1-889684-01-5*) Texas Testing.

— TEKS Related Algebra 1 End-of-Course Test Packet. Dominguez, Monica, ed. & illus. by. 55p. (YA). (gr. 8-12). 1997. ring bd. 19.95 (*1-889684-04-X*) Texas Testing.

Dominguez, Margaret & Dominguez, Marissa. Algebra 1 End-of-Course Card Games. (Illus.). 90p. (YA). (gr. 9-12). 1995. ring bd. 19.95 (*0-9650840-5-1*) Texas Testing.

— Algebra 1 End-of-Course Test Packet. (Illus.). 54p. (YA). (gr. 9-12). 1995. ring bd. 19.95 (*0-9650840-4-3*) Texas Testing.

***Dominguez, Margaret & Dominguez, Marissa.** Eighth Grade Math TEKS-Based Worksheets Packet. 50p. (YA). (gr. 8-9). 2000. ring bd. 20.95 (*1-889684-13-9*) Texas Testing.

Dominguez, Margaret & Dominguez, Marissa. Eighth-Grade TAAS Math Card Games. (Illus.). 90p. (J). (gr. 8). 1996. ring bd. 19.95 (*0-9650840-8-6*) Texas Testing.

***Dominguez, Margaret & Dominguez, Marissa.** Exit Level Math TEKS-Based Worksheets Packet. 50p. (YA). (gr. 9 up). 2000. ring bd. 20.95 (*1-889684-14-7*) Texas Testing.

Dominguez, Margaret & Dominguez, Marissa. Exit Level TAAS Math Card Games. (Illus.). 90p. (J). (gr. 9-12). 1996. ring bd. 19.95 (*0-9650840-7-8*) Texas Testing.

— Exit Level TAAS Math Test Packet. (Illus.). 64p. (YA). (gr. 9-12). 1995. ring bd. 19.95 (*0-9650840-3-5*) Texas Testing.

— Health Topics Math TAAS Worksheets with Solutions. (Illus.). 105p. (YA). (gr. 7-12). 1997. ring bd. 24.95 (*1-889684-02-3*) Texas Testing.

— Math TAAS Cross Number/Crossword Puzzles for Exit Level. (Illus.). 50p. (YA). (gr. 9-12). 1997. ring bd. 19.95 (*1-889684-07-4*) Texas Testing.

— Math TAAS Cross Number/Crossword Puzzles for 8th & 9th Grades. (Illus.). 63p. (YA). (gr. 8-9). 1997. ring bd. 19.95 (*1-889684-06-6*) Texas Testing.

— Math TAAS Study Guide. (Illus.). 208p. (Orig.). (YA). (gr. 9-12). 1995. pap. text 9.99 (*0-9650840-0-0*) Texas Testing.

— Preparation for End-of-Year Algebra 1 Test. (Illus.). 74p. (YA). (gr. 9-12). 1994. spiral bd. 19.95 (*0-9650840-2-7*) Texas Testing.

— Preparation for TAAS Mathematics Test (Exit Level) (Illus.). 60p. (YA). (gr. 9-12). 1994. spiral bd. 19.95 (*0-9650840-1-9*) Texas Testing.

— Seventh-Grade Math TAAS Cross Number/Crossword Puzzles. (Illus.). 50p. (J). (gr. 7). 1997. ring bd. 19.95 (*1-889684-09-0*) Texas Testing.

***Dominguez, Margaret & Dominguez, Marissa.** Seventh Grade Math TEKS-Based Worksheets Packet. 50p. (YA). (gr. 7-8). 2000. ring bd. 20.95 (*1-889684-12-0*) Texas Testing.

Dominguez, Margaret & Dominguez, Marissa. TEKS Algebra 1 End-of-Course Cross Number/Crossword Puzzles. (Illus.). 50p. (YA). (gr. 8-12). 1997. ring bd. 19.95 (*1-889684-08-2*) Texas Testing.

— TEKS Related Algebra 1 End-of-Course Worksheet Packet. (Illus.). 48p. (YA). (gr. 8-12). 1997. ring bd. 19.95 (*1-889684-05-8*) Texas Testing.

Dominguez, Margaret, jt. auth. see Dominguez, Marissa.

Dominguez, Marissa. Geography Topics Math TAAS Worksheets with Solutions. (Illus.). 97p. (YA). (gr. 7-12). 1997. ring bd. 24.95 (*1-889684-03-1*) Texas Testing.

***Dominguez, Marissa.** Sixth Grade Math TEKS-Based Cross Number/Crossword Puzzles Packet. 50p. (YA). (gr. 6-7). 1999. ring bd. 20.95 (*1-889684-10-4*) Texas Testing.

— Sixth Grade Math TEKS-Based Worksheet Packet. 50p. (YA). (gr. 6-7). 1999. ring bd. 20.95 (*1-889684-11-2*) Texas Testing.

Dominguez, Marissa & Dominguez, Margaret. Seventh-Grade TAAS Math Card Games. (Illus.). 90p. (J). (gr. 7). 1996. ring bd. 19.95 (*0-9650840-9-4*) Texas Testing.

Dominguez, Marissa, jt. auth. see Dominguez, Margaret.

Dominguez, Michael. Antologia de la Narrativa Mexicana, 2 vols. (SPA.). 51.99 (*968-16-4394-1*, Pub. by Fondo) Continental Bk.

Dominguez, Monica, ed. & illus. see Dominguez, Margaret.

Dominguez, Natalio. Creatica Prenatal-Infancia. (SPA.). 214p. 1995. pap. write for info. (*0-929441-64-8*) Pubns Puertorriquenas.

— Macario, el Mono Sabio. (Fabulas Creaticas Ser.). (SPA.). 28p. (J). 1994. pap. write for info. (*0-929441-61-3*) Pubns Puertorriquenas.

— Manifiesto Educativo. (SPA.). 156p. 1992. pap. write for info. (*0-929441-34-6*) Pubns Puertorriquenas.

— Los Perros y el Hueso. (Fabulas Creaticas Ser.). (SPA.). 28p. (J). 1994. pap. write for info. (*0-929441-60-5*) Pubns Puertorriquenas.

Dominguez Ortiz, A. Andaluces en America. (Gran Enciclopedia de Espana y America Ser.). (SPA., Illus.). 1989. 200.00 (*84-87053-15-7*) Elliots Bks.

Dominguez, Reyes E. Soviet & Cuban interests in Latin America & the Caribbean. (WVSS on Latin America & the Caribbean Ser.). (C). 1996. text 35.95 (*0-8133-7564-9*) Westview.

Dominguez, Richard H. Caring for Your Wife in Sickness & in Health: A Husband's Guide to Understanding the Special Health Needs of a Woman. LC 94-43736. 224p. 1995. 14.99 (*0-929239-68-7*) Discovery Hse Pubs.

Dominguez, Rodrigo, ed. Diagnostic Imaging of the Premature Infant. (Illus.). 288p. 1991. text 127.00 (*0-443-08740-7*) Church.

Dominguez, Rosie, ed. see Mozeleski, Peter A.

Dominguez, Rosie, ed. & tr. see Mozeleski, Peter A.

Dominguez, Virginia. White by Definition: Social Classification in Creole Louisiana. 325p. (C). 1994. reprint ed. pap. text 16.95 (*0-8135-2088-6*) Rutgers U Pr.

Dominguez, Virginia R. People As Subject, People As Object: Selfhood & Peoplehood in Contemporary Israel. LC 89-40254. (New Directions in Anthropological Writing Ser.). 272p. 1989. pap. text 19.95 (*0-299-12324-3*) U of Wis Pr.

— White by Definition: Social Classification in Creole Louisiana. LC 85-14609. 343p. reprint ed. pap. 106.40 (*0-7837-5666-6*, 205909200005) Bks Demand.

Dominguez, Virginia R. & Dominguez, Jorge I. The Caribbean: Its Implications for the United States. LC 81-65441. (Headline Ser.: No. 253). (Illus.). 80p. (Orig.). 1981. pap. 5.95 (*0-87124-068-8*) Foreign Policy.

Dominguez, Virginia R. & Wu, David Y., eds. From Beijing to Port Moresby: The Politics of National Identity & Cultural Policies. 450p. 1998. pap. 60.00 (*90-5700-503-4*) Gordon & Breach.

— From Beijing to Port Moresby: The Politics of National Identity & Cultural Policies. 404p. 1998. text 39.00 (*90-5700-502-6*, Harwood Acad Pubs) Gordon & Breach.

Dominguez, Walter. Como Lograr Salud Financiera. Da Costa, Pedro, tr. (SPA.). 280p. 1999. pap. text 14.75 (*1-929236-01-8*) Salud Financiera.

Dominguez, Xorge A., tr. see McNair, Harold M.

***Domini, Amy L.** Socially Responsible Investing: Make Money While You Make a Difference. 2001. pap. 19.95 (*0-7931-4173-7*) Dearborn.

Domini, Amy L. & Kinder, Peter D. Ethical Investing. LC 84-2783. (Illus.). 256p. 1986. 17.95 (*0-201-10803-8*, 1726); pap. 12.95 (*0-201-10869-0*) Addison-Wesley.

Domini, Amy L., et al. The Challenges of Wealth: Mastering the Personal & Financial Conflicts. 420p. 1988. text 24.95 (*0-87094-960-8*, Irwn Prfssnl) McGraw-Hill Prof.

Domini, John. Bedlam: Short Stories. LC 81-71002. 136p. (Orig.). 1981. pap. 6.95 (*0-931362-03-2*) SDSU Press.

— Highway Trade. LC 97-76241. 192p. 1998. pap. 14.95 (*1-888996-07-2*, Red Hen Press) Valentine CA.

Dominiak. Managerial Accounting. 7th ed. (AB - Accounting Principles Ser.). (C). 1994. mass mkt., student ed. 26.50 (*0-538-82784-X*) S-W Pub.

— Managerial Accounting. 8th ed. LC 96-19924. (AQ - Managerial Accounting Ser.). 1996. mass mkt. 66.95 (*0-538-85612-2*); mass mkt., student ed. 19.95 (*0-538-85613-0*) S-W Pub.

Dominiak & Louderback. Managerial Accounting. 9th ed. LC 99-27838. (SWC-Accounting Ser.). 1999. pap. 91.95 (*0-324-01208-X*) Thomson Learn.

— Managerial Accounting, Chapters 1-7. 8th ed. 1996. 39.00 (*0-538-87226-8*) Thomson Learn.

Dominiak, George M., jt. auth. see Shapiro, Shanti.

Dominiak, Geraldine F. & Louderback, Joseph G., III. Managerial Accounting. 7th ed. LC 93-8305. (C). 1994. mass mkt. 59.00 (*0-538-82534-0*, AQ63CA) S-W Pub.

Dominiak, Geraldine J. & Louderback, Joseph G. Managerial Accounting. 9th ed. (SWC-Accounting). 1999. pap., student ed. 17.50 (*0-324-01209-8*) Thomson Learn.

Dominian, Jack. The Growth of Love & Sex. LC 84-1573. 95p. reprint ed. pap. 30.00 (*0-608-14490-8*, 202532000043) Bks Demand.

Dominian, Jack & Board of St. Paul Editorial Staff. Human Relationships. 80p. (C). 1996. pap. 39.95 (*0-85439-288-2*, Pub. by St Paul Pubns) St Mut.

Dominic, Catherine C., jt. ed. see Lazzari, Marie.

Dominic, Joseph F., jt. ed. see Whiteman, Marcia F.

Dominic, Raymond. Two Days a Week: Weight Loss for Real People. unabridged ed. LC 99-182855. (Illus.). 112p. 1998. mass mkt. 5.95 (*0-944327-07-9*) Design & Dev Engineering Pr.

Dominican Nuns of the Perpetual Rosary, tr. see Alonso, Joaquin M.

Dominican Nuns Staff. Memoir of Mary Ann. LC 88-43574. 112p. 1991. 16.95 (*0-913720-69-0*) Beil.

***Dominice, Pierre.** Learning from Our Lives: Using Educational Biographies with Adults. LC 99-50636. 208p. 2000. 27.95 (*0-7879-1031-7*) Jossey-Bass.

Dominicis. Mundo Unido Grammar Text & Workbook Set. 660p. 1995. pap. text 76.90 (*0-471-12855-4*) Wiley.

— Mundo Unido Grammar Text Workbook & Cassettes Set. 660p. 1995. pap. text 97.85 incl. audio (*0-471-12851-1*) Wiley.

Dominicis, Marbia Canteli, jt. auth. see Nicholas, Robert L.

Dominicis, Maria. Mundo Unido: Repaso y Conversacion, Vol. 2. 432p. 1995. pap. 46.95 (*0-471-58485-1*) Wiley.

Dominicis, Maria & Nicholas, Robert L. Mundo Unido Grammar Reader Workbook Cassettes Sets. 1080p. 1995. pap. 132.80 (*0-471-12856-2*) Wiley.

Dominicis, Maria C. Don Juan En el Teatro Espanol Del Siglo XX. LC 77-89033. 1978. pap. 10.00 (*0-89729-180-8*) Ediciones.

Dominicis, Maria C. & Cussen, Joseph A. Casos y Cosas. 3rd ed. (SPA.). 336p. (C). 1990. pap. 38.75 (*0-07-017409-1*) McGraw.

Dominicis, Maria C. & Reynolds, John J. Repase y Escriba: Curso Avanzado de Gramatica y Composicion. 3rd ed. LC 97-37366. 480p. 1997. pap. 81.95 (*0-471-17414-9*) Wiley.

— Repase y Escriba: Curso Avanzado de Gramatica y Composicion. 3rd ed. 192p. 1998. pap., wbk. ed. 33.95 (*0-471-17412-2*) Wiley.

Dominicis, Maria C., jt. auth. see Nicholas, Robert L.

Dominicis, Maria Canteli, jt. auth. see Nicholas, Robert L.

***Dominick.** Broadcasting, Cable, Internet & Beyond. 4th ed. LC 99-30379. 1999. 45.00 (*0-07-290441-0*, McGrw-H College) McGrw-H Hghr Educ.

Dominick. Dynamics of Mass Communication. 5th ed. 240p. 1997. pap. 24.06 (*0-07-018011-3*) McGraw.

Dominick, jt. auth. see Wimmer.

Dominick, ed. see Munroe, Eugene.

Dominick, Andie. Needles: A Memoir. LC 98-21415. 224p. 1998. 22.00 (*0-684-84232-7*) Scribner.

Dominick, Bayard. Joe, a Porpoise. (Illus.). (J). (gr. 3-5). 1968. 10.95 (*0-8392-3067-2*) Astor-Honor.

— Sam, a Goat. (Illus.). (J). (gr. 3-5). 1968. 9.95 (*0-8392-3062-1*) Astor-Honor.

Dominick, DeWitt & Chivers, Mary D. Doctor Dewey: Stories from the Life & Career of DeWitt Dominick of Cody, Wyoming. (Illus.). 224p. (Orig.). 1996. pap. 17.95 (*0-9652942-0-X*) WordsWorth.

Dominick, Jennifer. Poetry Alaska Women: Top of the World. 64p. (Orig.). 1993. pap. 10.00 (*0-9637003-0-8*) ArtsVenture.

Dominick, Joseph R. Broadcasting - Cable & Beyond: An Introduction to Modern Electronic Media. 4th ed. LC 94-27230. 749p. (C). 1995. 75.00 (*0-07-072158-0*) McGraw.

— The Dynamics of Mass Communication. 4th ed. (C). 1993. pap. text 47.50 (*0-07-017805-4*) McGraw.

— The Dynamics of Mass Communication. 5th ed. LC 95-40569. (Series in Mass Communication). (C). 1995. pap. text 43.25 (*0-07-017996-4*) McGraw.

D

An Asterisk (*) at the beginning of an entry indicates that the title is appearing for the first time.

— The Dynamics of Mass Communication. 6th ed. LC 98-16220. (Series in Mass Communication). 1998. 5.76 (*0-07-115685-2*) McGraw.

— The Dynamics of Mass Communication. 6th ed. LC 98-16220. (Series in Mass Communication). 1998. 52.25 (*0-07-290478-X*) McGraw.

— The Dynamics of Mass Communication, 1994. 4th ed. LC 93-47900. (C). 1994. pap. text 50.74 (*0-07-017882-8*) McGraw.

Dominick, Joseph R., et al. Broadcasting/Cable & Beyond: An Introduction to Modern Electronic Media. 3rd ed. LC 95-38837. (Series in Mass Communication). (C). 1995. text 52.00 (*0-07-017988-3*) McGraw.

Dominick, Joseph R., jt. auth. see Wimmer, Roger D.

Dominick, Mary F., ed. Human Rights & the Helsinki Accord. LC 81-80195. x, 411p. 1981. reprint ed. lib. bdg. 49.50 (*0-89941-095-2*, 300270) W S Hein.

***Dominick, Peter G., et al.** Tools & Tactics of Design. 304p. 2000. pap. write for info. (*0-471-38648-0*) Wiley.

Dominick, R. B., ed. see Ferguson, Douglas C.

Dominick, R. B., ed. see Franclemont, John G.

Dominick, R. B., ed. see Hodges, Ronald W.

Dominick, Raymond H., III. The Environmental Movement in Germany: Prophets & Pioneers, 1871-1971. LC 91-28558. (Illus.). 308p. 1992. 37.00 (*0-253-31819-X*) Ind U Pr.

Dominick, Raymond H. Wilhelm Liebknecht & the Founding of the German Social Democratic Party. LC 81-16329. 565p. reprint ed. pap. 175.20 (*0-7837-2466-7*, 204261900005) Bks Demand.

Dominick, Richard B., jt. auth. see Spong, John S.

Dominick, Richard B., ed. see Ferguson, Douglas C.

Dominick, Richard B., ed. see Hodges, Ronald W.

Dominick, William J. & Wehrle, William T. Roman Verse Satirists Lucilius to Juvenal: A Selection. LC 99-51347. 219p. 1999. pap. 24.00 (*0-86516-442-8*) Bolchazy-Carducci.

***Dominiczak.** Molecular Genetics of Hypertension. 269p. 1999. 115.00 (*0-12-220430-1*) Acad Pr.

Dominiek, Sandra. Morphology in the Reader's Mental Lexicon. LC 94-33477. (Illus.). II, 144p. 1994. write for info. (*3-631-44251-3*) P Lang Pubng.

Dominiguez, J. Boundary Elements in Dynamics. 724p. 1993. 272.00 (*1-85861-021-4*) Elsevier.

Dominik, Janet B. & Westphal, Ruth L., eds. American Scene Painting: California, 1930s & 1940s. (Illus.). 238p. 1991. 49.00 (*0-9610520-3-1*) Westphal Pub.

Dominik, Mark. Shakespeare-Middleton Collaborations. LC 87-37358. 184p. (C). 1988. 22.50 (*0-945088-01-9*) Alioth Pr.

— A Shakespearean Anomaly: Shakespeare's Hand in Sir John Oldcastle. LC 90-42562. 210p. (C). 1991. 22.50 (*0-945088-02-7*) Alioth Pr.

— William Shakespeare & "The Birth of Merlin" 2nd rev. ed. LC 90-1188. 290p. (C). 1991. reprint ed. 25.00 (*0-945088-03-5*) Alioth Pr.

Dominik, William J. The Mythic Voice of Statius: Power & Politics in Thebaid. LC 94-16658. (Mnemosyne, Bibliotheca Classica Batava. Supplementum: Vol. 136). 1994. 81.00 (*90-04-09972-7*) Brill Academic Pubs.

— Roman Eloquence: Rhetoric in Society & Literature. LC 96-52767. 280p. (C). 1997. pap. 25.99 (*0-415-12545-6*) Routledge.

— Speech & Rhetoric in Statius' Thebaid. LC 94-207302. (Altertumswissenschaftliche Texte und Studien: Bd. 27). (GER.). xii, 378p. 1994. write for info. (*3-487-09814-8*) G Olms Pubs.

Dominik, William J., ed. Roman Eloquence: Rhetoric in Society & Literature. LC 96-52767. 280p. (C). 1997. 80.00 (*0-415-12544-8*) Routledge.

Domininghaus, Hans. Plastics for Engineers: Materials, Properties, Applications.Tr. of Die Kunststoffe und Ihre Bigenschaften. 798p. (C). 1993. 98.00 (*1-56990-011-6*) Hanser-Gardner.

Dominique, C. Rene. The Economic Analysis of the Dynamics of Food Crop Production. (European University Studies: Economics & Management: Ser. 5, Vol. 188). 139p. 1979. 27.00 (*3-261-02455-0*) P Lang Pubng.

Dominique, C-Rene. Unfettered Globalization: A New Economic Orthodoxy. LC 98-25615. 288p. 1999. 65.00 (*0-275-96378-0*, Praeger Pubs) Greenwood.

Dominique Halbout & Assimil Staff. Le Turc sans Peine: Turkish for French Speakers. (FRE & TUR.). 529p. 1992. 31.95 (*0-7859-0999-0*, 2700501667) Fr & Eur.

Dominique-Rene de Lerma. Bibliography of Black Music: Geographical Studies, Vol. 3. LC 80-24681. (Encyclopedia of Black Music Ser.). 284p. 1982. lib. bdg. 65.00 (*0-313-23510-4*, DBI/03, Greenwood Pr) Greenwood.

***Dominitz, Ben.** How to Find the Love of Your Life. 224p. 2000. 6.98 (*1-56731-343-4*) Fine Comms.

Dominitz, Ben. How to Find the Love of Your Life. LC 93-9865. 224p. 1993. pap. 12.95 (*1-55958-321-5*) Prima Pub.

— How to Find the Love of Your Life: A Step-by-Step Program that Really Works. 224p. 1997. per. 13.00 (*0-7615-0839-2*) Prima Pub.

***Dominitz, Ben.** How to Find the Love of Your Life: A Step-by-Step Program that Really Works. 202p. 1999. reprint ed. text 11.00 (*0-7881-6594-1*) DIANE Pub.

Dominitz, Nancy D., ed. see Eddy, Jackie.

Domino & Machado. American Political Controversies. pap. text. write for info. (*0-312-24094-5*) St Martin.

Domino Books Ltd Staff. Business Letters Made to Measure. (C). 1988. 60.00 (*1-85122-047-X*, Pub. by Domino Bks Ltd) St Mut.

— A Comprehensive Guide to Careers. 350p. (C). 1988. 150.00 (*1-85122-046-1*, Pub. by Domino Bks Ltd); pap. 125.00 (*1-85122-041-0*, Pub. by Domino Bks Ltd) St Mut.

— A Comprehensive Guide to Educational Equipment & Resources. 280p. (C). 1988. 125.00 (*1-85122-044-5*, Pub. by Domino Bks Ltd); pap. 75.00 (*0-7855-2246-8*, Pub. by Domino Bks Ltd) St Mut.

— The Project File: (A Short Course on Project Work for Students & Their Teachers) (C). 1987. 150.00 (*0-7855-2247-6*, Pub. by Domino Bks Ltd); pap. 100.00 (*0-7855-2248-4*, Pub. by Domino Bks Ltd) St Mut.

— Resources for English As a Foreign Language (EFL) & English As a Second Language (ESL) a Guide. 400p. (C). 1988. 150.00 (*1-85122-050-X*, Pub. by Domino Bks Ltd); pap. 100.00 (*1-85122-024-0*, Pub. by Domino Bks Ltd) St Mut.

— Speak English Well: A Handbook of Spoken English for Foreign - Overseas Students. 250p. (C). 1988. 130.00 (*1-85122-030-5*, Pub. by Domino Bks Ltd); pap. 90.00 (*1-85122-011-9*, Pub. by Domino Bks Ltd) St Mut.

— Write English Well: A Handbook of Written English for Foreign - Overseas Students. 400p. (C). 1988. 140.00 (*1-85122-042-9*, Pub. by Domino Bks Ltd); pap. 100.00 (*1-85122-053-4*, Pub. by Domino Bks Ltd) St Mut.

***Domino, Christophe.** Contemporary Art. (Key Art/Selected Works). 2000. pap. 12.95 (*2-86656-222-4*) Scala Edit.

Domino, Christophe. Francis Bacon: Painter of a Dark Vision. Sharman, Ruth, tr. LC 96-46897. (Discoveries Ser.). (Illus.). 136p. 1997. pap. 12.95 (*0-8109-2811-6*, Pub. by Abrams) Time Warner.

***Domino, Christophe.** Modern Art. (Key Art/Selected Works). (Illus.). 2000. pap. 12.95 (*2-86656-221-6*) Scala Edit.

Domino, E. F., ed. Brain Imaging of Nicotine & Tobacco Smoking. LC 95-67172. (Illus.). 340p. 1995. 95.00 (*0-916182-10-X*) NPP Bks.

***Domino, E. F., ed.** Over Half a Century of Michigan Pharmacology, 1942-2001. (Illus.). 500p. 2001. 50.00 (*0-916182-12-6*) NPP Bks.

— PCP (Phencyclidine) Historical & Current Perspectives. LC 80-81498. (Illus.). 537p. 1981. 50.00 (*0-916182-03-7*) NPP Bks.

Domino, E. F., ed. Status of Ketamine in Anesthesiology: Pros & Cons. LC 89-92147. (Illus.). 583p. 1990. 95.00 (*0-916182-07-X*) NPP Bks.

Domino, E. F. & Davis, J. M., eds. Neurotransmitter Balances Regulating Behavior. LC 75-21131. (Illus.). 240p. 1975. 30.00 (*0-916182-00-2*) NPP Bks.

Domino, E. F. & Kamenka, J. M., eds. Sigma & Phencyclidine Like Compounds As Molecular Probes in Biology. LC 87-62521. (Illus.). 819p. 1988. 90.00 (*0-916182-05-3*) NPP Bks.

Domino, E. F., ed. see Adrianov, O. S. & Mering, T. A.

Domino, E. F., jt. ed. see Kamenka, J. M.

***Domino, Eward F. & Yanagita, Tomoji, eds.** Japanese Michigan Fellows in Pharmacology: 50 Years of Cooperation - An International Model. LC 98-68121. (Illus.). 255p. 1999. 25.00 (*0-916182-11-8*) NPP Bks.

Domino, Floyd. Baby Road. (J). 1989. 12.95 incl. audio (*0-938971-22-0*) JTG Nashville.

Domino, Floyd. The Four Tots: Mostly Motown: Soulful Songs Arranged & Performed for the Very Young. (J). 1990. 12.95 incl. audio (*0-938971-49-2*) JTG Nashville.

Domino, Floyd. The White Album. unabridged ed. (J). 1989. 12.95 incl. audio (*0-938971-29-8*) JTG Nashville.

Domino, George. Psychological Testing: An Introduction. LC 99-19524. 657p. (C). 1999. 88.00 (*0-13-020143-X*) P-H.

Domino, John C. Civil Rights & Liberties. LC 93-28161. 318p. (C). 1997. pap. 44.00 (*0-06-500612-7*) Addson-Wesley Educ.

— Longman Political Pamphleteer: Sexual Harassment & the Courts. (Political Pampheleteer Ser.). (C). 1997. pap. text 7.80 (*0-673-99781-2*) Addson-Wesley Educ.

Domino, Ruth. Search. (C). 1983. pap. 4.00 (*0-87574-052-9*) Pendle Hill.

Dominques, Manuel, jt. auth. see Laycock, Mary.

Dominquez, Humberto S., tr. see Baldwin, Carl R.

Dominquez, Jorge I. Insurrection of Loyalty: The Breakdown of the Spanish-American Empire. LC 78-8288. 456p. 1976. 47.50 (*0-674-45635-1*) HUP.

Dominquez, Jorge I., intro. Race & Ethnicity in Latin America. LC 93-47174. (Essays on Mexico, Central & South America Ser.: Vol. 7). 384p. 1994. text 77.00 (*0-8153-1491-4*) Garland.

Dominquez, Jose M. Las Arcillas: El Barro Noble. (Ciencia para Todos Ser.). (SPA.). pap. 6.99 (*968-16-3743-7*, Pub. by Fondo) Continental Bk.

Dominquez, Joseph F., tr. see Jimenez, Juan Ramon.

Dominy, Arthur L. & Morgenfrug, Rudolph A. Silver at Your Service: A Collectors Guide to Railroad Dining Car Flatware Patterns. LC 87-70565. (Illus.). 191p. 1995. 32.50 (*0-9626759-0-3*) D&M Pub CA.

Dominy, G. R., jt. auth. see Graham, S. D.

Domitrovic, Zalocar De, see De Domitrovic, Zalocar.

Domizio, Lucrezia De, see De Domizio, Lucrezia.

Domjan. Essentials of Conditioning & Learning. (Psychology Ser.). 1995. mass mkt. 32.00 (*0-534-23730-4*) Brooks-Cole.

— Principles of Learning & Behavior. 2nd ed. (Psychology Ser.). 1986. text, teacher ed. write for info. (*0-534-05209-6*) Brooks-Cole.

— Principles of Learning & Behavior. 4th ed. LC 97-21562. (Psychology Ser.). 435p. 1997. pap. 71.95 (*0-534-34670-7*) Brooks-Cole.

Domjan, Evelyn. Panorama of Hungarian Peasant Painting: Folk Art in Village Life from the Painted Easter Egg to the Tulip Chest. Skwerer, Lorry A., ed. (Illus.). Date not set. pap. 20.00 (*0-933652-19-4*) Domjan Studio.

— Parta: The Crown Jewels of the Village, Hungarian Folk Art Coronets. Magyar, Judith & Skwerer, Lory, eds. (Illus.). Date not set. pap. 20.00 (*0-913509-02-7*) Domjan Studio.

Domjan, Evelyn A. Edge of Paradise: A Collection of Color Woodcuts. Emig, Jane, ed. LC 78-73442. (Illus.). 108p. 1979. 30.00 (*0-933652-14-3*) Domjan Studio.

— Eternal Wool: A History of Spinning, Weaving, Tapestry. Brogan, Peggy, ed. (Illus.). 160p. 1980. 40.00 (*0-933652-15-1*) Domjan Studio.

— Pavologia: A Celebration of Peacocks Past. Stein, Rose & Skwerer, Lory, eds. (Illus.). 200p. 1984. 45.00 (*0-933652-17-8*) Domjan Studio.

Domjan, Evelyn A., jt. auth. see Domjan, Joseph.

Domjan, Joseph & Domjan, Evelyn A. Pacatus, a Trade-Mark from Antiquity: History of Art & Industry from Rome, Pompeii to the Present. Emig, Jane. ed. LC 78-73444. (Illus.). 1979. 20.00 (*0-933652-13-5*) Domjan Studio.

***Domjan, Michael.** Essentials of Conditioning & Learning. 2nd ed. LC 99-27558. (Psychology Ser.). 234p. 1999. pap. text 52.95 (*0-534-35642-7*) Wadsworth Pub.

Domjan, Michael & Burkhard-Ebin, Barbara. The Principles of Learning & Behavior. 3rd ed. LC 92-10828. 448p. (C). 1992. mass mkt. 52.25 (*0-534-18912-1*) Brooks-Cole.

Domjan, Michael P. & Burkhard, Barbara. Domjan & Burkhard's the Principles of Learning & Behavior. 2nd ed. LC 85-5276. (Psychology). 365p. (C). 1985. mass mkt. 46.00 (*0-534-05208-8*) Brooks-Cole.

Domke, Martin, ed. International Trade Arbitration: A Road to World-Wide Cooperation. LC 73-11852. 320p. 1973. reprint ed. lib. bdg. 75.00 (*0-8371-7075-3*, DOTA, Greenwood Pr) Greenwood.

Domke, Noelle, tr. see Navarre, Yves.

Domken, Carl-Heinz. Mahomed: Ghazals Erbe. (GER.). 104p. 1986. write for info. (*3-487-08338-8*) G Olms Pubs.

Domkowski, Dorothy, jt. auth. see Stair, Lila B.

Dommanger, jt. auth. see D'aguilar.

Dommanget, J., et al, eds. Wide Components in Double & Multiple Stars. (C). 1988. text 153.00 (*90-277-2737-6*) Kluwer Academic.

Dommasch, D., jt. auth. see Perkins, C.

Dommel, Darlene H. Collector's Encyclopedia of Howard Pierce Porcelain. LC 97-217919. (Illus.). 144p. 1997. 24.95 (*1-57432-019-X*, 4946) Collector Bks.

***Dommel, Darlene H.** Collectors Encyclopedia of Rosemeade Pottery: Identification & Values. (Illus.). 224p. 2000. 24.95 (*1-57432-180-3*) Collector Bks.

Dommel, Paul R. The Politics of Revenue Sharing. LC 74-376. (Illus.). 223p. reprint ed. 69.20 (*0-8357-9235-8*, 201761700007) Bks Demand.

Dommel, Paul R., et al. Decentralizing Urban Policy: Case Studies in Community Development. LC 81-70465. 271p. 1982. 34.95 (*0-8157-1888-8*); pap. 14.95 (*0-8157-1887-X*) Brookings.

Dommelen, Ad Van, see Van Dommelen, Ad.

Dommelen, Dom Van, see Van Dommelen, Dom.

Dommen, Caroline & Cullet, Philippe. Droit International de l'Environnement: Textes de Base et References. LC 98-36000. 1998. 230.00 (*90-411-0705-3*) Kluwer Law Intl.

Dommen, Edward, ed. Fair Principles for Sustainable Development: Essays on Environmental Policy & Developing Countries. (New Horizons in Environmental Economics Ser.). 192p. 1993. 85.00 (*1-85278-912-3*) E Elgar.

— Islands. (Illus.). 135p. 1981. 26.50 (*0-08-026799-8*, Pergamon Pr) Elsevier.

Dommergues, Y. R. & Diem, H. G., eds. Microbiology of Tropical Soils & Plant Productivity. 1982. 69.50 (*90-247-2405-8*) Kluwer Academic.

Dommergues, Y. R., jt. ed. see Subbarao, N. S.

Dommermuth-Costa, Carol. Agatha Christie: Writer of Mystery. LC 96-34435. (J). 1997. lib. bdg. 23.93 (*0-8225-4954-9*, Lerner Publctns) Lerner Pub.

Dommermuth-Costa, Carol. Emily Dickinson: Singular Poet. LC 97-40081. (Illus.). 112p. (YA). (gr. 8 up). 1998. lib. bdg. 23.93 (*0-8225-4958-1*) Lerner Pub.

Dommermuth-Costa, Carol. Nikola Tesla: A Spark of Genius. LC 93-43123. (Lerner Biography Ser.). (Illus.). 144p. (J). (gr. 5 up). 1994. lib. bdg. 23.95 (*0-8225-4920-4*, Lerner Publctns) Lerner Pub.

Dommermuth, William P. Promotion: Analysis,strategy ,creativity. LC 84-970. (SWC-Marketing). 745p. (C). 1984. mass mkt. 45.00 (*0-534-03106-4*) PWS Pubs.

Dommers, Richard. Here Kitty, Kitty: The Sequel, No. II. 160p. 1996. 5.99 (*0-7860-0244-1*, Pinncle Kensgtn) Kensgtn Pub Corp.

— Roll over, Rover. LC 97-104981. 128p. 1996. mass mkt. 5.99 (*0-7860-0317-0*, Pinncle Kensgtn) Kensgtn Pub Corp.

Dommes, Grit. Von Kunstlern und Lebenskunstlern. Kraft, Herbert, ed. (Historisch-Kritische Arbeiten Zur Deutschen Literatur Ser.: Bd. 22). (Illus.). 195p. 1998. pap. 37.95 (*3-631-33102-9*) P Lang Pubng.

Domnarski, William. In the Opinion of the Court. 208p. 1996. 14.95 (*0-252-06556-5*); text 32.50 (*0-252-02257-2*) U of Ill Pr.

Domning, Daryl P. Sirenian Evolution in the North Pacific Ocean. LC 77-83099. (University of California Publications in Social Welfare: No. 118). (Illus.). 208p. reprint ed. pap. 64.50 (*0-608-17443-2*, 202987400066) Bks Demand.

Domning, Denise. Autumn's Flame. 384p. 1995. mass mkt. 5.50 (*0-451-40612-5*, Topaz) NAL.

— Lady in Waiting. 1998. mass mkt. 5.99 (*0-451-40771-7*, Topaz) NAL.

***Domning, Denise.** Lady in Waiting. LC 98-51097. 1999. 26.95 (*0-7862-1785-5*) Thorndike Pr.

Domning, Denise. Lady in White. 1999. mass mkt. 3.99 (*0-451-40772-5*, Sig) NAL.

— A Love for All Seasons. 1996. mass mkt. 5.99 (*0-451-40704-0*, Onyx) NAL.

Domnitch, Larry. The Jewish Holidays: A Journey through History. LC 99-24287. 264p. 1999. 30.00 (*0-7657-6109-2*) Aronson.

Domnitz, Linda D. John Lennon Conversations. (Illus.). 286p. (Orig.). 1984. pap. 16.00 (*0-942494-85-7*) Coleman Pub.

Domokos, G., et al, eds. Nonperturbative Methods in Low Dimensional Quantum Field Theories. 500p. (C). 1991. text 118.00 (*981-02-0576-7*) World Scientific Pub.

***Domokos, G. & Khovesi-Domokos, S.** Neutrinos in the Next Millennium: Proceedings of the Johns Hopkins Workshop on Current Problems in Particle Theory 23, Baltimore, 1999, (June 10-12) LC 00-31993. 2000. write for info. (*981-02-4252-2*) World Scientific Pub.

Domokos, G. & Kovesi-Domokos, S. Lattice Gauge Theory, Supersymmetry & Grand Unification: Proceedings of the 7th Johns Hopkins Workshop on Current Problems in Particle Theory, Bad Honnef-Bonn, June 21-23, 1983. 300p. (C). 1983. 64.00 (*9971-950-63-4*); pap. 33.00 (*9971-950-62-6*) World Scientific Pub.

— Particle Physics from Underground to Heaven. 350p. 1992. text 98.00 (*981-02-0887-1*) World Scientific Pub.

Domokos, G. & Kovesi-Domokos, S., eds. Particles & Gravity: Proceedings of the Eighth Johns Hopkins Workshop on Current Problems in Particle Theory, Johns Hopkins University, June 20-22, 1984. 400p. 1984. 70.00 (*9971-966-90-5*); pap. 48.00 (*9971-966-91-3*) World Scientific Pub.

Domokos, G. & Kovsei-Domokos, S. TeV Physics: Proceedings of the Johns Hopkins Workshop on Current Problems in Particle Theory 12. 336p. 1989. text 89.00 (*9971-5-0822-2*) World Scientific Pub.

Domokos, G., jt. auth. see Casalbuoni, R.

Domoleczny, Jeanne. Chemistry 111 Laboratory Manual. 112p. (C). 1994. pap. text, spiral bd. 17.95 (*0-8403-9611-2*) Kendall-Hunt.

Domone, Dana J. Primer on ERISA Fiduciary Duties. LC 94-23864. 350p. 1994. trans. 45.00 (*0-87179-809-3*) BNA Books.

Domone, P. L. J. & Jefferis, S. A., eds. Structural Grouts. LC 93-73439. (Illus.). 240p. 1993. text 144.95 (*0-7514-0097-1*, Pub. by B Acad & Prof) Routldge.

Domoney, Lynette. Directory of Community Social Work Initiatives: England. (C). 1989. 40.00 (*0-7855-5892-6*, Pub. by Natl Inst Soc Work) St Mut.

Domoney, Lynette & Halves, Ruth. Directory of Practice Examples in Residential Care for Elderly People. (C). 1989. 75.00 (*0-902789-62-7*, Pub. by Natl Inst Soc Work); 40.00 (*0-7855-5885-3*, Pub. by Natl Inst Soc Work) St Mut.

Domoney, Lynette & Halves, Ruth, eds. Directory of Practice: Examples in Residential Care for Elderly People. (C). 1989. 50.00 (*0-7855-0085-5*, Pub. by Natl Inst Soc Work) St Mut.

Domoney, Lynette, jt. auth. see Miller, Clive.

Domoradzki, Stan. The Bridge over the Main. Caputo, Sal, ed. LC 98-37701. 150p. 1999. pap. 13.00 (*0-9667171-0-4*) Olympia Press.

Domoryad, A. & Moss, H. Mathematical Games & Pastimes. LC 63-16860. (Popular Lectures in Mathematics: Vol. 10). 1963. 142.00 (*0-08-013673-7*, Pub. by Pergamon Repr) Franklin.

Domosh, Mona. Invented Cities: The Creation of Landscape in Nineteenth-Century New York & Boston. (C). 1996. 35.00 (*0-614-95686-2*) Yale U Pr.

— Invented Cities: The Creation of Landscape in Nineteenth-Century New York & Boston. LC 95-6740. (Illus.). 200p. 1996. 42.00 (*0-300-06237-0*) Yale U Pr.

— Invented Cities: The Creation of Landscape in Nineteenth-Century New York & Boston. (Illus.). 200p. 1998. pap. 16.00 (*0-300-07491-3*) Yale U Pr.

Domosh, Mona, jt. auth. see Jordan, Terry G.

Domotor, Tekla. Hungarian Folk Customs. (Hungarian Folk Art Ser.). 124p. 1989. 24.00 (*963-13-2612-8*, Pub. by Corvina Bks) St Mut.

Dompere, Kofi K. Africentricity & African Nationalism: Philosophy & Ideology for Africa's Complete Emancipation. LC 92-82796. (Studies in the Development of the Afro-Diaspora). 215p. (C). 1992. 29.95 (*1-879893-01-0*) IAAS Pubs.

— The Theory of Aggregate Investment & Output Dynamics in Open Economic Systems, 204. LC 98-21666. (Contributions in Economics & Economic History Ser.: No. 204). 208p. 1999. 69.50 (*0-313-30794-6*, Greenwood Pr) Greenwood.

— Theory of Aggregate Investment in Closed Economic Systems, 202. LC 98-15327. (Contributions in Economics & Economic History Ser.: No. 202). 224p. 1999. 69.50 (*0-313-30796-2*, Greenwood Pr) Greenwood.

Dompere, Kofi Kissi & Ejaz, Manzur. Epistemics of Development Economics: Toward a Methodological Critique & Unity, 165. LC 94-47438. (Contributions in Economics & Economic History Ser.: No. 165). 224p. 1995. 67.95 (*0-313-29513-1*, Greenwood Pr) Greenwood.

Dompkowski, Judith A. Down a Spiral Staircase, Never Ending: Motion as Design in the Writing of Czeslaw Milosz. (American University Studies: Slavic Languages & Literature: Ser. XII, Vol. 6). XX, 180p. 1990. 38.95 (*0-8204-0979-0*) P Lang Pubng.

Dompnier, Robert. Bhutan: Kingdom of the Dragon. LC 99-14946. (Illus.). 152p. 1999. 59.95 (*1-57062-510-7*, Pub. by Shambhala Pubns) Random.

***Domroese, Margret C. & Sterling, Eleanor J.** Interpretando la Biodiversidad: Un Manual para Educadores Ambientales en los Tropicos. Calvo, Lorena, tr. (SPA., Illus.). 188p. 1999. spiral bd. write for info. (*1-930465-06-8*) Ctr Biodiv & Conserv.

— Interpreter la Biodiversite: Manual pour des Educateurs a

D

l'Environnement dans les Regions Tropicales. Guigue, Anne Marie, tr. (FRE., Illus.). 188p. 1999. spiral bd. write for info. (*1-930465-05-X*) Ctr Biodiv & Conserv.
— Interpreting Biodiversity: A Manual for Environmental Educators in the Tropics. (Illus.). 188p. 1999. spiral bd. write for info. (*1-930465-04-1*) Ctr Biodiv & Conserv.
Doms, Dennis & Weishaar, Tom. ProDOS Inside & Out. (Illus.). 270p. 1986. 24.95 (*0-8306-0245-3*) McGraw-Hill Prof.
Domsch, K. H., et al. Compendium of Soil Fungi, 2 vols., Set. (Illus.). 1264p. 1993. reprint ed. lib. bdg. 55.00 (*3-9803083-8-3*, Pub. by IHW) Lubrecht & Cramer.
Domschcke, Bernhard. Twenty Months in Captivity: Memoirs of a Union Officer in Confederate Prisons. Trautmann, Frederic, ed. LC 85-46015. 176p. 1987. 26.50 (*0-317-64558-7*) Fairleigh Dickinson.
Domschke, Bernhard. Twenty Months a Prisoner of War. LC 85-46015. 1987. 33.50 (*0-8386-3286-6*) Fairleigh Dickinson.
Domschke, Eliane M. & Goyer, Doreen S. The Handbook of National Population Censuses: Africa & Asia, 3 vols., Vol. 2. LC 85-31712. 1047p. 1986. lib. bdg. 235.00 (*0-313-25361-7*, GHK/, Greenwood Pr) Greenwood.
Domschke, Eliane M., jt. auth. see Goyer, Doreen S.
Domschke, W. & Drexl, A. Location & Layout Planning. (Lecture Notes in Economics & Mathematical Systems Ser.: Vol. 238). iv, 134p. 1985. 29.50 (*0-387-13908-7*) Spr-Verlag.
Domschke, W. & Konturek, S. J., eds. The Stomach. LC 93-21900. (Illus.). 1993. 137.00 (*0-387-56613-9*) Spr-Verlag.
— The Stomach. (Illus.). 420p. 1993. pap. write for info. (*3-540-56613-9*) Spr-Verlag.
Domsky, Irving I. & Perry, John A., eds. Recent Advances in Gas Chromatography. LC 72-145881. (Illus.). 430p. reprint ed. pap. 133.30 (*0-7837-0851-3*, 204116000019) Bks Demand.
Domson, Charles & Cohen, I. Bernard, eds. Nicolas Fatio de Duillier & the Prophets of Paris. LC 80-2086. (Development of Science Ser.). (Illus.). 1981. lib. bdg. 18.95 (*0-405-13852-0*) Ayer.
Domson, Joanne F., jt. ed. see Al-Doory, Yousef.
Domurat, George W., et al, eds. The California Coastal Zone Experience. (Coastlines of the World Ser.). 320p. 1991. pap. text 34.00 (*0-87262-837-X*) Am Soc Civil Eng.
Domville, Eric, ed. see Yeats, William Butler.
Domville, Eric W., ed. Editing British & American Literature, 1880-1920: Papers Given at the Tenth Annual Conference on Editorial Problems, University of Toronto, November, 1974. LC 76-7323. (Conference on Editorial Problems Ser.: No. 10). reprint ed. 42.50 (*0-404-63660-8*) AMS Pr.
Domville-Fife, Charles W. The United States of Brazil. 1976. lib. bdg. 59.95 (*0-8490-1243-0*) Gordon Pr.
Domzalski, John, ed. see Master Teachers Staff & Darlen-De.
Don Bosco Staff. Vocabulario de Artes de la Madera, Arquitectura y Decoracion. (SPA.). 152p. 1975. pap. 29.95 (*0-8288-5952-3*, S50084) Fr & Eur.
Don, C. B. Management by Vice: A Humorous Satire on R & D Life in a Fictitious Company. (Illus.). 232p. 1999. 19.95 (*0-9670084-4-1*) Sterling TL.
Don-chean Chu. Chairman Mao: Education of the Proletariat. LC 78-61107. 478p. 1980. 15.00 (*0-685-08149-4*) Inst Sino-Amer.
Don, D. Prodomus Flora Nepalensis. 256p. (C). 1976. text 100.00 (*0-89771-597-7*, Pub. by Intl Bk Distr) St Mut.
Don, D., ed. Prodromus Florae Nepalensis. 256p. 1976. reprint ed. 135.00 (*0-7855-5990-6*, Pub. by Intl Bk Distr) St Mut.
Don Guyon. One Way Pockets: The Book of Books on Wall Street Speculation. LC 65-18336. 1965. reprint ed. pap. 10.00 (*0-87034-013-1*) Fraser Pub Co.
Don, Henk, et al, eds. Applied General Equilibrium Modelling. 188p. 1991. lib. bdg. 118.00 (*0-7923-1376-3*) Kluwer Academic.
Don, M. Urban Jungle: The Simple Way to Tame Your Town Garden. (Illus.). 192p. 1999. text 35.00 (*0-7472-2190-1*, Pub. by Headline Bk Pub) Trafalgar.
Don, Montagu. Sensuous Garden. LC 97-17129. (Illus.). 160p. 1997. 32.50 (*0-684-83965-2*) Simon & Schuster.
Don, Monty. Gardening Mad. LC 97-53187. (Illus.). 192p. 1998. 25.00 (*1-57959-007-1*, SOMA) BB&T Inc.
***Don, Monty & Don, Sarah.** Fork to Fork. (Illus.). 224p. 2000. 35.00 (*1-85029-992-7*, Pub. by Conran Octopus) Antique Collect.
Don, Norma, jt. auth. see Krull, Sharron W.
Don Richard Roso. Personality Types at Work: Using the Enneagram to Understand the People You Deal With. 1999. 21.95 (*0-07-077997-X*) McGraw.
Don, Rosaline & Fonyam, John B., eds. Out of Torch: I Shot My Congressman. 1992. 19.95 (*0-910253-40-4*) Backwards & Backwards.
Don, Sarah. The Art of Shetland Lace. (Illus.). 119p. 1991. reprint ed. pap. 26.00 (*0-916896-34-X*) Lacis Pubns.
Don, Sarah, jt. auth. see Don, Monty.
Don-Yehiya, Eliezer, jt. auth. see Liebman, Charles S.
Don, Yehuda & Karady, Victor, eds. A Social & Economic History of Central European Jewry. 248p. 1989. 44.95 (*0-88738-211-8*) Transaction Pubs.
Donabedian, Avedis. Aspects of Medical Care Administration: Specifying Requirements for Health Care. LC 72-93948. (Commonwealth Fund Book Ser.). 662p. reprint ed. pap. 200.00 (*0-7837-3960-5*, 204379900011) Bks Demand.
— Benefits in Medical Care Programs. (Illus.). 456p. 1990. 51.95 (*0-674-06580-8*) HUP.
— The Definition of Quality & Approaches to Its Assessment. LC 80-15173. (Explorations in Quality Assessment & Monitoring Ser.: Vol. I). (Illus.). 178p. 1980. pap. text 30.00 (*0-914904-48-5*, 0824) Health Admin Pr.
Donabedian, Patrick, et al. Armenia & Karabagh: The Struggle for Unity. Walker, Chriatopher J., ed. 176p. pap. 17.95 (*1-873194-00-5*, Pub. by Minority Rts Pubns) Paul & Co Pubs.
— Armenia & Karabagh: The Struggle for Unity. 176p. 1991. 49.95 (*1-873194-20-X*, Pub. by Minority Rts Pubns) Paul & Co Pubs.
Donabedion, Charlotte, jt. auth. see Farrell, Thomas J.
Donachie, M. J., ed. Titanium: A Technical Guide. (Illus.). 469p. 1988. 124.00 (*0-87170-309-2*, 9606) ASM.
— Titanium: A Technical Guide. 1988. 83.00 (*0-614-23290-2*, 9606) Intl Titanium.
***Donachie, Matthew J.** Titanium: A Technical Guide. 2nd ed. LC 00-33134. (Illus.). 2000. write for info. (*0-87170-686-5*) ASM.
Donachie, Matthew J., Jr., ed. see American Society for Metals Staff.
Donachie, W., et al, eds. Haemophilus, Actinobacillus & Pasteurella: Proceedings of the Third International Conference Held in Edinburgh, Scotland, July 31-August 4, 1994. LC 95-35588. (Illus.). 254p. 1995. 95.00 (*0-306-45104-2*, Plenum Trade) Perseus Pubng.
Donadio, Stephen, et al, eds. Emerson & His Legacy: Essays in Honor of Quentin Anderson. LC 85-1763. 269p. 1986. text 31.95 (*0-8093-1218-2*) S Ill U Pr.
Donadio, Stephen, et al. The New York Public Library Book of Twentieth-Century American Quotations. 640p. 1992. 24.45 (*0-446-51639-2*, Pub. by Warner Bks) Little.
Donadoni, Sergio. The Egyptian Man. Bianchi, Robert, tr. LC 96-44074. 1997. pap. text 18.00 (*0-226-15556-0*); lib. bdg. 54.00 (*0-226-15555-2*) U Ch Pr.
Donaera, Patrizia, et al. Animals. LC 98-53222. (Around the World Ser.). 1998. 9.95 (*0-7641-5188-6*) Barron.
Donagan, Alan. Choice: The Essential Element in Human Action. (Studies in Philosophical Psychology). 192p. 1987. lib. bdg. 35.00 (*0-7102-1168-6*, Routledge Thoemms) Routledge.
— Human Ends & Human Actions: An Exploration in St. Thomas's Treatment. LC 84-63124. (Aquinas Lectures). 50p. 1985. 10.00 (*0-87462-153-4*) Marquette.
— The Later Philosophy of R. G. Collingwood. LC 85-16485. xvi, 332p. 1994. pap. text 20.00 (*0-226-15568-4*) U Ch Pr.
— The Philosophical Papers of Alan Donagan Vol. 1: Historical Understanding & the History of Philosophy. Malpas, J. E., ed. 298p. 1994. 39.95 (*0-226-15570-6*) U Ch Pr.
— The Philosophical Papers of Alan Donagan Vol. 2: Action, Reason & Value. Malpas, J. E., ed. 314p. 1994. 39.95 (*0-226-15571-4*) U Ch Pr.
— Reflections on Philosophy & Religion. Perovich, Anthony N., ed. LC 98-20754. 240p. 1999. text 45.00 (*0-19-512132-5*) OUP.
— Theory of Morality. LC 76-25634. 292p. 1979. pap. text 12.95 (*0-226-15567-6*, P838) U Ch Pr.
— Theory of Morality. LC 76-25634. 1994. lib. bdg. 20.00 (*0-226-15566-8*) U Ch Pr.
Donagan, Alan, et al, eds. Human Nature & Natural Knowledge. 396p. 1985. text 191.50 (*90-277-1974-8*, D Reidel) Kluwer Academic.
Donagan, Ann. Teaching with God's Heart for the World. 2nd rev. ed. (Illus.). 224p. 1995. ring bd. 49.95 (*0-9645420-0-5*) Fam Mission.
Donaghe, Robert T., et al, eds. Advanced Triaxial Testing of Soil & Rock, STP 977. LC 88-19070. (Special Technical Publication (STP) Ser.). (Illus.). 900p. 1988. text 120.00 (*0-8031-0983-0*, STP977) ASTM.
Donaghe, Ronald L. Letters in Search of Love: And Other Essays. LC 98-87848. 325p. 1998. 25.00 (*0-7388-0119-4*); pap. 15.00 (*0-7388-0120-8*) Xlibris Corp.
Donagher, Colleen P., tr. see Donagher, Fresco, ed.
Donagher, Fresco, ed. Renaut de Bage: Le Bel Inconnu (Li Biaus Descouneus; The Fair Unknown) Donagher, Colleen P., tr. LC 92-8114. (Library of Medieval Literature: Vol. MLA77). 496p. 1992. text 20.00 (*0-8240-0698-4*) Garland.
Donaghey, Bob. Bluegrass Yearbook. (Illus.). 150p. 1999. pap. 18.00 (*0-9670721-0-7*) Nectar Pub.
Donaghey, Lee F., ed. see International Conference on Chemical Vapor Deposit.
Donaghue, K. K. West Victoria Separation Movement. 1984. pap. 35.00 (*0-949759-40-6*, Pub. by Deakin Univ) St Mut.
***Donaghue, Mary M.** Smells of Childhood. large type unabridged ed. 198p. 1999. 23.95 (*0-7531-5077-8*, 150778, Pub. by ISIS Lrg Prnt) ISIS Pub.
***Donaghy, B.** Unzipped: Everything Teenagers Want to Know about Love, Sex & Each Other. 2000. pap. 12.95 (*0-7322-5780-8*) HarpC.
Donaghy, Greg & Kelly, Ted, eds. Documents on Canadian External Relations, 1954, Vol. 20. 1997. 99.95 (*0-660-60273-3*, Pub. by Canadian Govt Pub) Intl Spec Bk.
Donaghy, Henry J., ed. Conversations with Graham Greene. LC 91-33058. (Literary Conversations Ser.). 208p. 1992. text 39.50 (*0-87805-549-5*) U Pr of Miss.
Donaghy, James F. Superfund: Information on the Status of Sites. (Illus.). 117p. (C). 1999. text 25.00 (*0-7881-7905-5*) DIANE Pub.
— Superfund: Times to Complete the Assessment & Cleanup of Hazardous Waste Sites. (Illus.). 57p. (C). 1998. pap. text 25.00 (*0-7881-4791-9*) DIANE Pub.
Donaghy, Michael. Neurology. LC 97-11745. (Oxford Core Texts Ser.). (Illus.). 228p. 1997. pap. text 29.50 (*0-19-262795-3*) OUP.
Donaghy, Peter & Coopers & Lybrand. Diccionario de Informes Financieros: Ingles-Espanol, Espanol-Ingles. (ENG & SPA.). 365p. 1993. 75.00 (*0-7859-7480-6*, 8423407551) Fr & Eur.
Donaghy, Peter & Laidler, John. Understanding Spanish Accounts: Language & Terminology. Levy, Silvano, ed. 128p. (Orig.). 1994. pap. 42.50 (*0-273-60308-6*, Pub. by Pitman Pub) Trans-Atl Phila.
Donaghy, Peter, jt. auth. see Laidler, John.
Donaghy, Peter J., jt. auth. see Newton, Michael T.
Donaghy, Thomas J. My Guardian Angel: Helper & Friend. LC 97-203015. (Illus.). 32p. (J). 1994. 5.95 (*0-89942-125-3*, 125/22) Catholic Bk Pub.
— St. Joseph Catholic Manual. LC 98-107133. 1994. pap. 2.95 (*0-89942-268-3*, 268/04) Catholic Bk Pub.
Donaghy, Thomas J., jt. auth. see Catholic Book Staff.
***Donaghy, Tom.** The Beginning of August & Other Plays. 320p. 2000. pap. 15.00 (*0-8021-3724-5*, Grove) Grove-Atltic.
Donaghy, Tom. The Dadshuttle & Down the Shore: Two Plays in One Volume. 1995. pap. 5.25 (*0-8222-1432-6*) Dramatists Play.
— From Above. 1998. pap. 5.25 (*0-8222-1689-2*) Dramatists Play.
— Minutes from the Blue Route. LC 98-115338. 1997. pap. 5.25 (*0-8222-1608-6*) Dramatists Play.
— Northeast Local. LC 98-104351. 1996. pap. 5.25 (*0-8222-1550-0*) Dramatists Play.
Donagi, R., et al. Integrable Systems & Quantum Groups: Lectures Given at the 1st Session of the Centro Internazionale Matematico Estivo (C. I. M. E.) Held in Montecatini Terme, Italy, June 14-22, 1995. Francaviglia, M. & Greco, S., eds. (Lecture Notes in Mathematics Ser.: Vol. 1620). 488p. 1995. 94.95 (*3-540-60542-8*) Spr-Verlag.
Donagi, Ron, ed. Curves, Jacobians, & Abelian Varieties: (Proceedings of a Summer Research Workshop on the Schottky Problem) LC 92-20586. (Contemporary Mathematics Ser.: Vol. 136). 342p. 1992. pap. 62.00 (*0-8218-5143-8*, CONM/136) Am Math.
Donaho, Barbara A., et al. Transformational Leadership: Renewing Fundamental Values & Achieving New Relationships in Health Care. Linne, Eric B., ed. LC 95-35494. 275p. 1995. pap. 40.00 (*1-55648-144-6*, 001116) AHPI.
Donaho, Joe. Good News Travels Faster. 104p. (Orig.). 1990. pap. 8.00 (*1-885121-03-2*) CTS Press.
Donaho, Meyer. How to Get the Job You Want. 1976. 12.95 (*0-13-407254-5*) P-H.
Donahoe, Carol Cheney, jt. auth. see O'Neill, Robert J.
Donahoe, John W. & Dorsel, Vivian P. Neural-Network Models of Cognition: Biobehavioral Foundations, Vol. 121. LC 97-42861. (Advances in Psychology Ser.: 121). (Illus.). 600p. 1997. 155.00 (*0-444-81931-2*) Elsevier.
Donahoe, John W., et al. Learning & Complex Behavior. LC 93-22625. 480p. 1993. 88.00 (*0-205-13996-5*) Allyn.
Donahoe, J.W., ed. Neural Network Models of Cognition: Biobehavioral Foundations. 1996. write for info. (*0-614-17934-3*, North Holland) Elsevier.
Donahoe, Mary. You Are Mountain. 32p. 1984. 6.00 (*0-911051-11-2*) Plain View.
Donahoe, Myrna C. Resolving Discriminatory Practices Against Minorities & Women in Steel & Auto - Los Angeles, California, 1936-1982. 47p. (Orig.). 1991. pap. 8.50 (*0-89215-165-X*) U Cal LA Indus Rel.
Donahoe, Peter M., jt. auth. see Clancy, Ambrose.
Donahoe, Susan. The Magic of the Duck Pond. (J). (gr. k-3). 1999. pap. 6.95 (*0-533-12747-5*) Vantage.
Donahoo, Geo. Indian Villages & Place Names in Pennsylvania. LC 77-80384. 312p. 1995. reprint ed. 29.95 (*1-889037-05-2*, 6) Wennawoods.
Donahue. Answer Key to Exercises. 13th ed. (C). 1997. pap. text 26.75 (*0-15-508152-7*) Harcourt Coll Pubs.
— Exploring World Agriculture. (Agriculture Ser.). 1995. text 32.95 (*0-8273-6131-9*) Delmar.
— Exploring World Agriculture. (Agriculture Ser.). 1995. teacher ed. 10.00 (*0-8273-6132-7*) Delmar.
— Harbrace College Handbook. 12th ed. (C). 1994. pap. text, teacher ed. 34.00 (*0-15-501233-9*) Harcourt Coll Pubs.
Donahue & Quinn. Real Estate Practice in Ontario: Professional Edition. 4th ed. 336p. 1990. boxed set 81.00 (*0-409-80571-8*, MICHIE) LEXIS Pub.
Donahue, et al. Deutsch Zusammen. 2nd ed. 464p. (C). 1998. pap. 47.00 (*0-536-01167-2*) Pearson Custom.
Donahue, jt. auth. see Bowers.
Donahue, Alice K., ed. see Matsumoto, Sumiko.
Donahue, Anne M., ed. Ethics in Politics & Government. (Reference Shelf Ser.: Vol. 61, No. 2). 238p. (C). 1989. pap. text 25.00 (*0-8242-0781-5*) Wilson.
Donahue, Barbara. Farmington: New England Town Through Time. LC 89-84447. (Illus.). 176p. 1989. 29.95 (*0-9623090-0-1*) Farmington Land Trust.
Donahue, Bernard A., et al. Reclamation & Reprocessing of Spent Solvents. LC 89-22887. (Pollution Technology Review Ser.: No. 175). (Illus.). 190p. 1990. 42.00 (*0-8155-1222-8*) Noyes.
***Donahue, Bill.** Foundations: How We Got Our Bible. (Bible 101 Ser.). 64p. 2000. pap. 4.99 (*0-8308-2061-2*) InterVarsity.
— Parable & Prophecy: Unlocking the Bible's Mysteries. (Bible 101 Ser.). 64p. 2000. pap. 4.99 (*0-8308-2066-3*) InterVarsity.
Donahue, Bonnie K. Bankruptcy Concepts: A Desk Reference for Lenders. Geehr, Shelley W. & Tusler, Kathryn, eds. LC 94-18034. 96p. (Orig.). 1994. pap. 55.00 (*1-57070-003-6*, 32651) Robt Morris Assocs.
Donahue, Brian. Reclaiming the Commons: Community Farms & Forests in a New England Town. LC 98-49122. (Illus.). 324p. 1999. 27.50 (*0-300-07673-8*) Yale U Pr.
Donahue, Charles. Year Books Of Richard II: Richard II, 1382-1383. Thorne, Samuel E. & Peoples, Susan H., eds. Throne, Margaret M., tr. (Ames Foundation Publications: Vol. 2). (FRE, LAT & ENG., Illus.). 344p. 1996. 110.00 (*1-893606-01-5*) W S Hein.
Donahue, Charles, Jr., et al. Cases & Materials on Property, an Introduction to the Concept & the Institution. 3rd ed. (American Casebook Ser.). 1189p. (C). 1992. 65.00 (*0-314-00931-0*) West Pub.
— Property, an Introduction to the Concept & the Institution, Teacher's Manual to Accompany Cases & Materials On. 3rd ed. (American Casebook Ser.). 332p. 1993. pap. text, teacher ed. write for info. (*0-314-02806-4*) West Pub.
Donahue, David M. & Flowers, Nancy. The Uprooted: Refugees & the United States - A Multidisciplinary Teaching Guide. LC 95-5134. (Illus.). 224p. (Orig.). 1995. spiral bd. 22.95 (*0-89793-179-3*) Hunter Hse.
— The Uprooted: Refugees & the United States - A Multidisciplinary Teaching Guide. LC 95-5134. (Illus.). 224p. (Orig.). (YA). (gr. 7-12). 1995. pap. 15.95 (*0-89793-122-X*) Hunter Hse.
Donahue, Debra L. Conservation & the Law. LC 98-20225. (Contemporary Legal Issues Ser.). 347p. 1998. lib. bdg. 55.00 (*0-87436-771-9*) ABC-CLIO.
***Donahue, Debra L.** Western Range Revisited: Removing Livestock from Public Lands to Conserve Native Biodiversity. LC 99-35438. (Legal History of North America Ser.: Vol. 5). 388p. 1999. 47.95 (*0-8061-3176-4*) U of Okla Pr.
— Western Range Revisited: Removing Livestock from Public Lands to Conserve Native Biodiversity. Vol. 5. (Illus.). 352p. 2000. pap. 14.95 (*0-8061-3298-1*) U of Okla Pr.
Donahue, Dennis P. Layamon's "Brut", an Early Arthurian Poem: A Study of Middle English Formulaic Composition. LC 91-17743. (Studies in Medieval Literature: Vol. 9). 344p. 1991. lib. bdg. 99.95 (*0-7734-9768-4*) E Mellen.
Donahue, E. L., tr. see Pousset, Edouard.
***Donahue, Edward.** General Chemistry 3/4. 200p. (C). 2000. per. 28.95 (*0-7872-7300-7*) Kendall-Hunt.
Donahue, Eileen, jt. auth. see Harary, Keith.
Donahue, Elinor, et al. In the Kitchen with Elinor Donahue. LC 98-38072. (Illus.). 288p. 1998. pap. 16.95 (*1-888952-92-X*) Cumberland Hse.
Donahue, Frank E. & Watzinger, Johanna. Deutsch Zusammen: A Communicative Course in German. 624p. (C). 1990. text 66.00 (*0-13-204991-0*) P-H.
Donahue, Frank E. & Watzinger-Tharp, Johanna. Deutsch Zusammen: A Communicative Course in German. LC 89-34021. (ENG & GER.). lvi, 568 p. 1990. student ed. write for info. (*0-02-439955-8*) Macmillan.
Donahue-Gandy, Marlene M. Teaching Basic Aquatics . . . Especially to Those Who Have Difficulty Learning. LC 84-71097. (Illus.). 104p. (Orig.). 1984. pap. 10.00 (*0-9613514-0-3*) M M Donahue-Gandy.
Donahue-Gaudet. Le Vocalisme et le Consonantisme Francais. 26.15 (*0-685-36654-5*); 26.15 (*0-8288-7703-3*, F135030) Fr & Eur.
Donahue, Greg, jt. auth. see Zazarine, Paul.
Donahue, Hugh C. The Battle to Control Broadcast News: Who Owns the First Amendment? 254p. 1989. 30.00 (*0-262-04099-9*) MIT Pr.
Donahue, J., jt. ed. see Lasca, N. P.
Donahue, J. A. The Earhart Disappearance: The British Connection. LC 87-61635. (Aviation Heritage Library). (Illus.). 176p. 1987. 29.95 (*0-943691-01-X*) Aviation Heritage.
Donahue, James. Steamboats in Ice. Date not set. pap. 14.00 (*0-9626947-3-8*) J L Donahue.
— Terrifying Steamboat Stories. 2nd rev. ed. 209p. 1997. reprint ed. pap. 14.95 (*1-882376-36-6*) Thunder Bay Pr.
Donahue, James & Moser, M. Theresa, eds. Religion, Ethics & the Common Good. LC 96-60555. 272p. 1996. 14.95 (*0-89622-701-4*) Twenty-Third.
Donahue, James, tr. see Nunis, Doyce B., Jr., ed.
Donahue, James C. Blackjack-34: No Greater Love. 2000. mass mkt. 6.99 (*0-8041-1765-9*) Ivy Books.
— Blackjack-33. 1999. mass mkt. 6.99 (*0-8041-1764-0*) Ivy Books.
— Mobile Guerrilla Force. 1997. mass mkt. 6.99 (*0-312-96164-2*) St Martin.
— Mobile Guerrilla Force: With the Special Forces in War Zone D. LC 95-37395. (Naval Institute Special Warfare Ser.). (Illus.). 228p. 1996. 29.95 (*1-55750-172-6*) Naval Inst Pr.
Donahue, James L. Schooners in Peril: True & Exciting Stories about Tall Ships on the Great Lakes. 2nd ed. (Illus.). 237p. (Orig.). 1995. reprint ed. pap. 14.95 (*1-882376-23-4*) Thunder Bay Pr.
— Steaming Through Smoke & Fire: True Stories of Shipwreck & Disaster on the Great Lakes. 2nd ed. (Illus.). 192p. 1996. reprint ed. pap. 14.95 (*1-882376-30-7*) Thunder Bay Pr.
— Steaming Through Smoke & Fire, 1871: True Stories of Shipwreck & Disaster on the Great Lakes, Vol. 1. LC 90-93084. (Illus.). 192p. (Orig.). 1990. pap. text 12.00 (*0-9626947-0-3*) J L Donahue.
Donahue, Joanne, jt. auth. see Chandler, Elizabeth.
Donahue, JoElle C. Cranial Discrete Traits & Biological Distance in Prehistoric Northern California. fac. ed. (Illus.). xi, 147p. 1993. reprint ed. pap. 16.88 (*1-55567-585-9*) Coyote Press.
Donahue, John. The Gospel of Mark. (Sacra Pagina Ser.: No. 2). Date not set. write for info. (*0-8146-5804-0*, M Glazier) Liturgical Pr.
— An Island Far from Home. LC 94-9444. 180p. (J). (gr. 4-7). 1995. lib. bdg. 21.27 (*0-87614-859-3*, Carolrhoda) Lerner Pub.
— An Island Far from Home. 180p. (J). (gr. 6-8). 1997. pap. text 6.95 (*1-57505-076-5*, Carolrhoda) Lerner Pub.

D

An Asterisk (*) at the beginning of an entry indicates that the title is appearing for the first time.

— Prisons for Profit: Public Justice, Private Interests. 30p. (Orig.). 1988. 10.00 (*0-944826-02-4*) Economic Policy Inst.

Donahue, John C. & Jenkins, Linda W., eds. Five Plays from the Children's Theatre Company of Minneapolis. LC 73-91051. 262p. reprint ed. pap. 81.30 (*0-608-13268-3*, 205585500039) Bks Demand.

Donahue, John D. Confronting Inequality in an Era of Devolution. LC 98-41540. (Devolution Revolution Ser.). 120p. 1998. pap. 10.95 (*0-87078-428-5*) Century Foundation.

— Disunited States: What's at Stake as Washington Fades & the States Take the Lead. LC 97-3921. 272p. 1997. 25.00 (*0-465-01661-8*, Pub. by Basic) HarpC.

Donahue, John D. The Privatization Decision: Public Ends, Private Means. LC 89-42511. 285p. 1991. pap. 18.50 (*0-465-06357-8*, Pub. by Basic) HarpC.

Donahue, John D. Shortchanging the Workforce: The Job Training Partnership Act & the Overselling of Privatized Training. (Illus.). 40p. 1990. 12.00 (*0-944826-18-0*) Economic Policy Inst.

***Donahue, John D., ed.** Making Washington Work: Tales of Innovation in the Federal Government. LC 99-6552. 1999. pap. 18.95 (*0-8157-1895-0*) Brookings.

Donahue, John M. The Nicaraguan Revolution in Health: From Somoza to the Sandinistas. LC 85-31562. 188p. 1986. 55.00 (*0-89789-101-5*, Bergin & Garvey); pap. 17.95 (*0-89789-170-8*, Bergin & Garvey) Greenwood.

— Water, Culture & Power: Local Struggles in a Global Context. LC 97-41051. 430p. 1997. text 50.00 (*1-55963-521-5*); pap. text 30.00 (*1-55963-522-3*) Island Pr.

Donahue, John R. The Gospel in Parable: Metaphor, Narrative, & Theology in the Synoptic Gospels. LC 87-45888. 256p. 1988. pap. 19.00 (*0-8006-2480-7*, 1-2480, Fortress Pr) Augsburg Fortress.

— The Theology & Setting of Discipleship in the Gospel of Mark. LC 83-60749. (Pere Marquette Lectures). (C). 1983. 15.00 (*0-87462-538-6*) Marquette.

Donahue, John R., ed. see Brueggemann, Walter.

Donahue, Joseph. Monitions of the Approach. 14p. 1991. 3.00 (*0-87376-067-0*) Red Dust.

— Terra Lucida. (Illus.). 28p. 1998. pap. 5.95 (*1-891930-00-1*) Heaven Bone Pr.

***Donahue, Joseph.** Terra Lucida XVI-XX. (Poetry New York Pamphlet Ser.: No. 14). 23p. 1999. pap. 5.00 (*0-923389-29-6*) Meet Eyes Bind.

Donahue, Joseph. World Well Broken. viii, 64p. 1995. pap. 9.95 (*1-883689-22-8*); lib. bdg. 29.95 (*1-883689-23-6*) Talisman Hse.

Donahue, Joseph, jt. ed. see Foster, Edward.

Donahue, Judee C. From Whence It Came: The Book Lender's Logbook. 1993. pap. 6.95 (*0-9617426-9-0*) J N Townsend.

Donahue, Julian P., jt. auth. see Brown, Brian V.

***Donahue, Katherine M.** Business Compass - Comprehensive Guide to Organizational Effectiveness Assessment: Do-It-Yourself, Step-by-Step, Troubleshooting Toolkit. xii, 186p. 1999. ring bd. 89.99 (*0-9677446-0-1*) Mercury Group.

— Business Compass - Guide to Business Process Effectiveness Assessment: Do-It-Yourself, Step-by-Step Toolkit. v, 93p. 1999. ring bd. 29.99 (*0-9677446-1-X*) Mercury Group.

Donahue, Leigh R. Field Effect...The Pi Phase of Physics. rev. ed. (Illus.). 78p. (Orig.). 1993. pap. 11.95 (*0-943975-04-2*) Interdimens Sci.

Donahue, Leo O. Encyclopedia of Batik Designs. LC 80-67118. (Illus.). 520p. 1982. 60.00 (*0-87982-035-7*) Art Alliance.

— Encyclopedia of Batik Designs. LC 80-67121. (Illus.). 640p. 1982. 60.00 (*0-8453-4729-2*, Cornwall Bks) Assoc Univ Prs.

Donahue, M. Patricia. Nursing: The Fine Art: An Illustrated History. 2nd ed. (Illus.). 560p. (C). (gr. 13). 1995. text 56.95 (*0-8151-2727-8*, 26817) Mosby Inc.

Donahue, M. Patricia & American Organization of Nurse Executives Staff. Nursing & the Continuum of Care. LC 98-9874. (AONE Leadership Ser.). 138p. 1998. 36.00 (*1-55648-235-3*) AHPI.

— Nursing & the Continuum of Care. LC 98-9874. (AONE Leadership Ser.). 1998. write for info. (*1-55664-823-5*) Mosby Inc.

Donahue, Marie. The Old Academy on the Hill: A Bicentennial History, 1791-1991. LC 92-64437. 224p. 1992. 35.00 (*0-89725-093-1*, 1393) Picton Pr.

Donahue, Marilyn C. I'm Bailing as Fast as I Can. LC 91-32855. 96p. (YA). 1992. pap. 4.99 (*1-55513-274-X*, Chariot Bks) Chariot Victor.

— The Valley in Between. (J). 1987. 15.85 (*0-8027-6745-1*) Walker & Co.

— The Valley in Between. (YA). (gr. 5 up). 1987. 14.95 (*0-8027-6731-1*); lib. bdg. 15.85 (*0-8027-6733-8*) Walker & Co.

Donahue, Mary R., jt. auth. see Armstrong, Alexandra.

Donahue, Megan, jt. auth. see Bennett, Jeff.

Donahue, Michael. The Grandpa Tree. (Illus.). 24p. (J). (gr. 7 up). 1988. pap. 5.95 (*0-911797-42-4*) Roberts Rinehart.

Donahue, Michael J., et al. Money Matters: Personal Giving in American Churches. LC 96-22896. 240p. (Orig.). 1996. pap. 22.95 (*0-664-25687-2*) Westminster John Knox.

Donahue, Mike. Portland Rose Festival: For You a Rose in Portland Grows. LC 97-137014. (Illus.). 104p. (Orig.). 1996. pap. 19.95 (*1-56037-106-4*) Am Wrld Geog.

Donahue, Neil H. Forms of Disruption: Abstraction in Modern German Prose. LC 92-45215. 280p. 1993. text 49.50 (*0-472-10409-8*, 10409) U of Mich Pr.

Donahue, Neil H., ed. Invisible Cathedrals: The Expressionist Art of Wilhelm Worringer. LC 93-33979. (Illus.). 216p. 1995. 50.00 (*0-271-01306-0*) Pa St U Pr.

Donahue, Nick. Zelf, the Christmas Elf. LC 94-27167. (Illus.). (J). 1994. 6.95 (*0-9641502-0-4*) Wildbasin Pubng.

Donahue, P. J., ed. see O'Laughlin, Michael C.

Donahue, Patricia & Quandahl, Ellen, eds. Reclaiming Pedagogy: The Rhetoric of the Classroom. LC 88-39324. 216p. (C). 1989. 26.95 (*0-8093-1534-3*) S Ill U Pr.

***Donahue, Patricia L.** NAEP 1998 Reading Report Card for the Nation & the States. 293p. 1999. per. 25.00 (*0-16-050062-1*) USGPO.

— Reading Report Card for the Nation & the States, 1998 (NAEP) (Illus.). 285p. 1999. pap. text 35.00 (*0-7881-8119-X*) DIANE Pub.

***Donahue, Paul J., et al.** Mental Health Consultation in the Early Childhood Years. LC 99-37494. 2000. pap. 28.95 (*1-55766-449-8*) P H Brookes.

Donahue, Ray T. Japanese Culture & Communication: Critical Cultural Analysis. LC 98-14195. 400p. (C). 1998. 59.00 (*0-7618-1248-2*); pap. 39.50 (*0-7618-1249-0*) U Pr of Amer.

Donahue, Ray T. & Prosser, Michael H. Diplomatic Discourse: International Conflict at the United Nations. LC 96-30457. (Communication, Culture & Information Studies Ser.). (Illus.). 365p. 1997. pap. 42.50 (*1-56750-291-1*); text 78.50 (*1-56750-290-3*) Ablx Pub.

Donahue, Robert. Ten Tunes for Ten Fingers. 24p. 1988. pap. 6.95 (*0-938170-09-0*) Wimbledon Music.

— Thirty-Two Canons for Keyboard Instruments. 1975. pap. 5.95 (*0-934286-57-4*) Kenyon.

— What Shall I Be? 16p. 1993. pap. text 4.95 (*0-87487-669-9*) Summy-Birchard.

Donahue, Robert A. & Bookbinder, Jay A., eds. Cool Stars, Stellar Systems & the Sun, 10th Cambridge Workshop. LC 98-74164. (Conference Series Proceedings: Vol. 154). 646p. 1998. 52.00 (*1-886733-74-0*) Astron Soc Pacific.

Donahue, Roy L., et al. Our Soils & Their Management. 6th ed. LC 82-82462. 608p. 1990. 56.25 (*0-8134-2848-3*); teacher ed. 14.95 (*0-8134-2890-4*) Interstate.

Donahue, Roy L., jt. auth. see Camp, William G.

Donahue, Roy L., jt. auth. see Herren, Ray V.

Donahue, Shari F. The Zebra-Stripes Whale with the Polka-Dot Tail. (Illus.). 1999. 16.95 (*0-9634287-3-X*) Arimax.

Donahue, Shari Faden. Celebrate Hanukkah with Me. 1998. 15.95 (*0-9634287-2-1*) Arimax.

— My Favorite Family Haggadah: A Fun, Interactive Passover Service for Children & Their Families. (Illus.). 31p. (J). (ps-3). 1994. pap. 5.95 (*0-9634287-1-3*) Arimax.

— Philly's Favorites Recipe Collection: Delectable Recipes from Philadelphia's Finest Restaurants. 196p. 1992. 16.95 (*0-9634287-0-5*) Arimax.

Donahue, Suzanne M. American Film Distribution: The Changing Marketplace. Kirkpatrick, Diane, ed. LC 86-24900. (Studies in Cinema: No. 40). 393p. 1987. reprint ed. pap. 121.90 (*0-8357-1925-1*, 207068100017) Bks Demand.

Donahue, T. M., ed. see National Academy of Science Staff.

Donahue, Thomas. Gerhard Brunzema: His Work & His Influence. LC 97-25565. 360p. 1998. 60.00 (*0-8108-3366-2*) Scarecrow.

Donahue, Thomas J. Structure of Meaning: A Semiotic Approach to the Play Text. LC 91-58955. 184p. 1993. 35.00 (*0-8386-3476-1*) Fairleigh Dickinson.

Donahue, William H. & Cohen, I. Bernard, eds. The Dissolution of the Celestial Sphere. LC 80-2087. (Development of Science Ser.). (Illus.). 1981. lib. bdg. 30.95 (*0-405-13853-9*) Ayer.

Donahue, William H., tr. & illus. see Densmore, Dana.

Donahue, William P. Leading Life-Changing Small Groups: The Willow Creek Guide. LC 96-17624. 128p. 1996. pap. 14.99 (*0-310-20595-6*) Zondervan.

Donahue, Wilma, et al. Free Time: Challenge to Later Maturity. Stein, Leon, ed. LC 79-8667. (Growing Old Ser.). 1980. reprint ed. lib. bdg. 19.95 (*0-405-12807-X*) Ayer.

Donaill, Eamonn O. Irish on Your Own: A Self-Guided Course in the Irish Language. Set. (ENG & IRI., Illus.). 264p. 1997. pap. 49.95 incl. audio (*0-8442-2619-X*) NTC Contemp Pub Co.

Donais, Jeff. Official Tournament Player's Handbook. 1999. pap. 9.99 (*0-7869-1517-X*, Pub. by TSR Inc) Random.

Donald. Writing a Clear Paragraph. 5th ed. 1995. pap. text, teacher ed. write for info. (*0-13-180290-9*) Allyn.

***Donald.** Writing Clear Paragraphs. 6th ed. 1998. pap. text, teacher ed. write for info. (*0-13-095813-1*) P-H.

Donald, A. K., ed. see Scott, Alexander.

Donald, Alexander G., jt. ed. see Shah, Nandkumar S.

Donald, Alexander K., ed. see Jean D'Arras.

Donald, Allen, ed. see O'Hara, Frank.

Donald, Anabel. Smile, Honey. LC 89-32144. 256p. 1989. pap. 8.95 (*0-916515-88-5*) Mercury Hse Inc.

Donald, Anna & Stein, Michael. The Hands-On Guide for House Officers. LC 95-50825. (Illus.). 160p. 1996. pap. 28.95 (*0-86542-921-9*) Blackwell Sci.

Donald, Anna, jt. auth. see Cook, Elspeth.

Donald, Anna, jt. ed. see Greenhalgh, Trisha.

Donald, Anna, jt. ed. see Haines, Andrew.

Donald, B. R. Error Detection & Recovery in Robotics. (Lecture Notes in Computer Science Ser.: Vol. 336). xxiv, 314p. 1989. 48.95 (*0-387-96909-8*) Spr-Verlag.

Donald, Bruce, et al, eds. Symbolic & Numerical Computation for Artificial Intelligence. (Computational Mathematics & Applications Ser.). (Illus.). 369p. 1992. text 94.00 (*0-12-220535-9*) Acad Pr.

***Donald, Christopher J.** Waltzing at Midnight. LC 99-91436. 1999. 25.00 (*0-7388-0774-5*); pap. 18.00 (*0-7388-0775-3*) Xlibris Corp.

Donald, Daian. The Age of Caricature: Satirical Prints in the Reign of George III. (Paul Mellon Centre for Studies in British Art). (Illus.). 256p. 1998. pap. 30.00 (*0-300-07178-7*) Yale U Pr.

Donald, Dave, tr. see Barber, David W.

Donald, David. Aircraft Guide-Military Jets: From 1939 to the Present Day. 1998. 12.99 (*0-7858-0925-2*) Bk Sales Inc.

— Bombers of War II. 1998. 22.98 (*1-56799-683-3*, MetroBooks) M Friedman Pub Grp Inc.

— Civil War & Reconstruction. (C). pap. text. write for info. (*0-393-97427-8*) Norton.

***Donald, David.** Classic Civil Aircraft Guide: From 1920 to 1964, Vol. 1. 1999. 12.99 (*0-7858-1089-7*) Bk Sales Inc.

Donald, David. Fighters of World War II. 1998. 22.98 (*1-56799-684-1*, MetroBooks) M Friedman Pub Grp Inc.

Donald, David, ed. U. S. Air Force Air Power Directory. (Illus.). 232p. Date not set. reprint ed. pap. 24.95 (*1-880588-16-1*) AIRtime Pub.

Donald, David & Lake, Jon, eds. Encyclopedia of World Military Aircraft, 2 vols. in 1. (Illus.). 443p. 1994. reprint ed. 49.95 (*1-880588-24-2*) AIRtime Pub.

— U. S. Navy & Marine Corps Air Power Directory: World Air Power. (Illus.). 224p. 1992. pap. 24.95 (*1-880588-02-1*) AIRtime Pub.

Donald, David, ed. see Aerospace Publishing Ltd. Staff.

Donald, David H. Lincoln. abr. ed. 1995. audio. write for info. (*0-671-53681-8*, Pub. by S&S Audio) Lndmrk Audiobks.

Donald, David H. Why the North Won the Civil War. 128p. 1996. per. 10.00 (*0-684-82506-6*) S&S Trade.

Donald, David H., ed. see Alec Thomas Archives Staff.

Donald, David Herbert. Charles Sumner. LC 96-16124. Orig. Title: Charles Sumner & the Coming of the Civil War & Charles Sumner & the Rights of Man. (Illus.). 1152p. 1996. pap. 24.95 (*0-306-80720-3*) Da Capo.

— Liberty & Union. 318p. (C). 1978. pap. text 31.16 (*0-669-01152-5*) HM Trade Div.

— Lincoln. LC 95-4782. (Illus.). 599p. 1995. 35.00 (*0-684-80846-3*) S&S Trade.

— Lincoln. 720p. 1996. per. 17.00 (*0-684-82535-X*) S&S Trade.

— Lincoln. (Reading Group Guides Ser.). 1997. pap. write for info. (*0-684-00446-1*, Touchstone) S&S Trade Pap.

— Lincoln, Vol. 1. large type ed. (Niagara Large Print Ser.). 733p. 1996. 29.50 (*0-7089-5841-9*) Ulverscroft.

— Lincoln, Vol. 2. large type ed. (Niagara Large Print Ser.). 695p. 1996. 29.50 (*0-7089-5842-7*) Ulverscroft.

***Donald, David Herbert.** Lincoln at Home: Two Glimpses of Abraham Lincoln's Family Life. LC 00-41294. (Illus.). 2000. write for info. (*0-7432-0199-X*) S&S Trade.

Donald, David Herbert. Lincoln Reconsidered. 1956. pap. 5.95 (*0-685-02838-0*) Knopf.

— Lincoln Reconsidered: Essays on the Civil War Era. 1989. pap. 13.00 (*0-679-72310-2*) Vin Bks.

— Lincoln Reconsidered: Essays on the Civil War Era. LC 80-22804. (Illus.). 200p. 1981. reprint ed. lib. bdg. 38.50 (*0-313-22575-3*, DOLR, Greenwood Pr) Greenwood.

— The Nation in Crisis, 1861-1877. LC 74-79169. (Goldentree Bibliographies Series in American History). (C). 1969. pap. text 6.95 (*0-88295-511-X*) Harlan Davidson.

— The Politics of Reconstruction, 1863-1867. 128p. 1984. pap. 9.95 (*0-674-68953-4*) HUP.

— The Politics of Reconstruction, 1863-1867. LC 82-1015. (Walter Lynwood Fleming Lectures in Southern History). 105p. 1982. reprint ed. lib. bdg. 55.00 (*0-313-23481-7*, DONP, Greenwood Pr) Greenwood.

Donald, David Herbert, ed. Why the North Won the Civil War. (Paperbook Series in History). (Illus.). 128p. 1993. reprint ed. pap. text 2.25 (*1-877891-12-6*) Paperbook Pr Inc.

Donald, David Herbert, intro. Lincoln's Herndon. (Quality Paperbacks Ser.). (Illus.). 442p. 1989. pap. 13.95 (*0-306-80353-4*) Da Capo.

Donald, Diana. The Age of Caricature: Satirical Prints in the Reign of George III. LC 95-49193. (Illus.). 256p. 1996. 68.00 (*0-300-06605-8*) Yale U Pr.

Donald, Diana, jt. ed. see Banerji, Christiane.

Donald, E., et al. Writing Clear Sentences. (Illus.). 320p. (C). 1986. pap. text 57.00 (*0-13-970401-9*) P-H.

Donald, Elsie B. The French Farmhouse: It's History, Construction, & Regional Styles. (Illus.). 208p. 1995. 29.95 (*0-7892-0037-6*) Abbeville Pr.

Donald G. Hagman Commemorative Conference Staff, et al. Rental Housing in California: Market Forces & Public Policies, the Third Annual Donald G. Hagman Commemorative Conference. Graymer, LeRoy et al, eds. LC 86-28540. (Lincoln Institute of Land Policy Bk.). 127p. reprint ed. pap. 39.40 (*0-7837-5757-3*, 204541900006) Bks Demand.

— The Urban Caldron: The Second Annual Donald G Hagman Commemorative Conference. DiMento, Joseph F., ed. LC 85-21641. (Lincoln Institute of Land Policy Bk.). 160p. reprint ed. pap. 49.60 (*0-7837-5774-3*, 204543900006) Bks Demand.

Donald, Gertrude. Men Who Left the Movement. LC 67-23207. (Essay Index Reprint Ser.). 1977. 23.95 (*0-8369-0385-4*) Ayer.

Donald, Gordon, Jr. U. S. Foreign Aid & the National Interest. (Committee on Changing International Realities Ser.). 32p. (Orig.). 1983. pap. 4.00 (*0-89068-067-1*) Natl Planning.

Donald, Henderson H. Negro Freedom: Life Conditions of the American Negro in the Early Years after Emancipation. LC 70-160846. 1971. reprint ed. lib. bdg. 57.00 (*0-8154-0388-7*) Cooper Sq.

***Donald, J. Amelita.** The Horse Prevention Handbook. (Illus.). 62p. 1999. pap. 9.95 (*1-58150-021-1*, Eclipse Press) Blood-Horse.

Donald, J. Kay. Exploring the Golden West of New South Wales: Central Western New South Wales. (Illus.). 208p. (Orig.). 1993. pap. 12.95 (*0-86417-411-X*, Pub. by Kangaroo Pr) Seven Hills Bk.

Donald, Jack. Tell Pa I'm Dead. 1988. pap. 7.95 (*0-385-25068-1*) Doubleday.

***Donald, Jacquelyn.** Obsessive Sex: Resolving the Conflict of Loving Sex & Loving God. (YA). (gr. 8). 1998. reprint ed. 23.95 (*1-891809-07-5*) Pub by Devon.

Donald, James. Imagining the Modern City. LC 99-41606. 272p. 1999. pap. 24.95 (*0-8166-3555-2*, Pub. by U of Minn Pr); lib. bdg. 62.95 (*0-8166-3554-4*, Pub. by U of Minn Pr) Chicago Distribution Ctr.

— A Sentimental Education: Schooling, Popular Culture & the Regulation of Liberty. 192p. (C). 1992. pap. 18.00 (*0-86091-555-7*, A6409, Pub. by Verso) Norton.

Donald, James, ed. Fantasy & the Cinema. (Illus.). 304p. 1989. 11.50 (*0-85170-228-7*, Pub. by British Film Inst); 19.95 (*0-85170-229-5*, Pub. by British Film Inst) Ind U Pr.

Donald, James & Rattansi, Ali. Race, Culture & Difference. 336p. (C). 1992. text 59.95 (*0-8039-8579-7*); pap. text 21.95 (*0-8039-8580-0*) Sage.

Donald, James, et al. Close Up, 1927-1933: Cinema & Modernism. LC 98-24952. 1998. 65.00 (*0-691-00462-5*, Pub. by Princeton U Pr) Cal Prin Full Svc.

— Close Up, 1927-1933: Cinema & Modernism. LC 98-24952. 1999. pap. 19.95 (*0-691-00463-3*, Pub. by Princeton U Pr) Cal Prin Full Svc.

Donald, Janet G. Improving the Environment for Learning: Academic Leaders Talk about What Works. LC 96-44482. (Jossey-Bass Higher & Adult Education Ser.). 320p. 1997. 29.95 (*0-7879-0832-0*) Jossey-Bass.

Donald, Kathleen E., jt. ed. see Waterhouse, John A.

Donald, Kathy, ed. BASIC Programming One: Course Code 303-1. (Illus.). 106p. 1989. reprint ed. pap. text 9.95 (*0-917531-89-2*) CES Compu-Tech.

Donald, Ken. The Doping Game. (C). 1990. pap. 40.00 (*0-908175-73-6*, Pub. by Boolarong Pubns) St Mut.

Donald, Leland. Aboriginal Slavery on the Northwest Coast of North America. LC 96-46162. (Illus.). 379p. 1997. 42.50 (*0-520-20616-9*, Pub. by U CA Pr) Cal Prin Full Svc.

Donald, Lisa. MCSE JumpStart. LC 98-83172. (Illus.). 384p. 1999. pap. 19.99 (*0-7821-2462-3*) Sybex.

— MCSE Test Success: Internet Information Server 4. LC 98-86621. (MCSE Test Success Ser.). 400p. 1998. pap. 24.99 (*0-7821-2334-1*) Sybex.

— NT Network Solutions Kit. 1997. 59.99 incl. cd-rom (*0-7821-2122-5*) Sybex.

***Donald, Lisa.** NT Server 4 in the Enterprise Study Guide. 3rd ed. (MCSE Exam Preparation Guide Ser.). (Illus.). 720p. 1999. pap., student ed. 49.99 (*0-7821-2697-9*) Sybex.

Donald, Lisa, ed. MCSE NT Server 4 in the Enterprise Study Guide. 2nd ed. LC 97-81015. 800p. 1998. student ed. 54.99 incl. cd-rom (*0-7821-2221-3*) Sybex.

Donald, Lisa, et al. MCSE Test Success - NT Server 4. LC 97-61721. 368p. 1998. pap. text 39.99 incl. cd-rom (*0-7821-2148-9*) Sybex.

— MCSE Test Success - NT Server 4 in the Enterprise. LC 97-61722. 464p. 1998. pap. text 39.99 (*0-7821-2147-0*, Network Pr) Sybex.

***Donald, Lisa, et al.** MCSE 2000 Jumpstart. (Illus.). 416p. 2000. pap. text 19.99 (*0-7821-2749-5*, Network Pr) Sybex.

Donald, Mary Ellen. Doumbec Delight. 2nd ed. Munro, Jane, ed. (Illus.). 111p. (Orig.). 1976. pap. text 12.95 (*0-9606602-0-8*) Mary Ellen Bks.

Donald, Merlin. Origins of the Modern Mind: Three Stages in the Evolution of Culture & Cognition. (Illus.). 448p. (C). 1991. text 38.50 (*0-674-64483-2*) HUP.

— Origins of the Modern Mind: Three Stages in the Evolution of Culture & Cognition. (Illus.). 424p. (C). 1993. pap. text 16.95 (*0-674-64484-0*) HUP.

Donald-Mims, Jacquelyn. Faith Not Sight. 1998. pap. write for info. (*1-891809-02-4*) Pub by Devon.

— Move over Men: God Calls Women into the Pulpit for Boundless Preaching, Theological, Sociological & Logical Support for Women in Ministry. 1998. pap. 12.00 (*1-891809-00-8*) Pub by Devon.

— Not Sticks, Not Stones But Words: Women's Power Potential, Self-Esteem & Spirituality. 1998. pap. write for info. (*1-891809-04-0*) Pub by Devon.

— Obsessive Sex: Resolving the Conflict of Loving Sex & Loving God. 264p. (YA). 1999. pap. 21.95 (*1-891809-06-7*) Pub by Devon.

— Religious Robbers: Hundred Fold Return on an Investment of a Tenth, Theology, Spirituality & Praxi's for Giving God the Tithe. 1998. pap. 12.00 (*1-891809-01-6*) Pub by Devon.

***Donald, Moira.** Gender & Material Culture in Archaeological Perspective. LC 99-39504. 1999. text 55.00 (*0-312-22398-6*) St Martin.

— Gender & Material Culture in Historical Perspective. LC 99-46783. 1999. text 55.00 (*0-312-22399-4*) St Martin.

Donald, Moira. Marxism & Revolution. LC 93-60569. 336p. 1993. 45.00 (*0-300-04390-2*) Yale U Pr.

***Donald, Moira & Rees, Tim.** Reinterpreting Revolution in 20th Century Europe. LC 00-31129. (Illus.). 2000. write for info. (*0-312-23622-0*) St Martin.

Donald, Muireall. Glencoe: A Romance of Scotland. LC 97-73403. 272p. 1997. pap. 10.00 (*0-9659701-3-2*) Laughing Owl.

Donald, Paul J., et al, eds. The Sinuses. LC 94-13768. 688p. 1994. text 209.00 (*0-7817-0041-8*) Lppncott W & W.

Donald, R. Bullethead. LC 94-92347. 70p. 1994. pap. 4.95 (*1-882792-05-X*) Proctor Pubns.

D

An Asterisk (*) at the beginning of an entry indicates that the title is appearing for the first time.

Donald, Ralph & Spann, Thomas. Fundamentals of Television Production. LC 99-52243. (Illus.). 492p. 1999. 54.95 (*0-8138-2739-6*) Iowa St U Pr.

***Donald, Rhonda Lucas.** Frogs: Complete Cross-Curricular Theme Unit That Teaches about These Fasinating Amphibians. (Illus.). 32p. 2000. pap. 8.95 (*0-439-05178-9*) Scholastic Inc.

— The Ozone Layer. LC 00-38412. (True Bks.). (Illus.). (J). 2001. write for info. (*0-516-22195-7*) Childrens.

***Donald, Rhonda Lucas & Kranking, Kathleen W.** Spiders. 32p. 1999. pap. 8.95 (*0-590-64271-5*) Scholastic Inc.

Donald, Richard A. Endocrine Disorders: A Guide to Diagnosis. (Basic & Clinical Endocrinology Ser.: Vol. 4). (Illus.). 760p. 1984. text 250.00 (*0-8247-1913-1*) Dekker.

Donald, Robert B. Writing Clear Paragraphs. 6th ed. LC 98-13747. 359p. (C). 1998. pap. text 37.00 (*0-13-646571-4*) P-H.

Donald, Robert B., et al. Writing Clear Essays. 3rd ed. LC 95-35813. (Illus.). 418p. 1995. pap. text 42.00 (*0-13-454547-8*) P-H.

Donald, Robert Mc, see Dilts, Robert & Mc Donald, Robert.

Donald, Robyn. A Bitter Homecoming. (Presents Ser.: No. 1263). 1990. per. 2.50 (*0-373-11263-7*) Harlequin Bks.

***Donald, Robyn.** Une Captive a Seduire. 1999. mass mkt. 3.99 (*0-373-34800-2*) Silhouette.

Donald, Robyn. El Color la Medianoche-The Colour of Midnight. 1996. per. 3.50 (*0-373-33355-2*) Harlequin Bks.

— The Colour of Midnight. large type ed. 1994. 19.95 (*0-263-13929-8*) Thorndike Pr.

— Como Tu: Tiger, Tiger. (Bianca Ser.: Vol. 115).Tr. of Just Like You. (SPA.). 1998. per. 3.50 (*0-373-33465-6*, 1-33465-5) Harlequin Bks.

— Dark Fire. LC 95-7125. (Presents Ser.). 187p. 1995. per. 3.25 (*0-373-11735-3*, 1-11735-7) Harlequin Bks.

— Dark Fire. large type ed. (Harlequin Romance Ser.). 1994. lib. bdg. 19.95 (*0-263-13871-2*) Thorndike Pr.

— The Darker Side of Paradise. (Presents Ser.: No. 376). 1991. per. 2.75 (*0-373-11376-5*) Harlequin Bks.

— Decision Arriesgada. (Bianca Ser.). 1996. per. 3.50 (*0-373-33365-X*, 1-33365-7) Harlequin Bks.

— Element of Risk. LC 96-2352. 189p. 1996. per. 3.50 (*0-373-11803-1*, 1-11803-3) Harlequin Bks.

— Element of Risk. large type ed. (Harlequin Romance Ser.). 285p. 1995. lib. bdg. 18.95 (*0-263-14126-8*) Mac Lib Ref.

— La Fiancee Interdite. (Azur Ser.: No. 749). (FRE.). 1999. mass mkt. 3.50 (*0-373-34749-9*, 1-34749-1) Harlequin Bks.

— The Final Proposal. (Marriage Maker Ser.). 1997. per. 3.50 (*0-373-11877-5*, 1-11877-7) Harlequin Bks.

— Final Proposal. large type ed. (Harlequin Romance Ser.). 1997. 20.95 (*0-263-14993-5*) Mac Lib Ref.

— Forbidden Desire. large type ed. (Harlequin Romance Ser.). 1998. 20.95 (*0-263-15514-5*) Thorndike Pr.

— A Forbidden Desire. 50th ed. 1999. per. 3.75 (*0-373-12012-5*, Harlequin) Harlequin Bks.

***Donald, Robyn.** Forbidden Pleasure. (Presents Ser.: Vol. 2108). 2000. per. 3.99 (*0-373-12108-3*) Harlequin Bks.

Donald, Robyn. The Golden Mask. (Presents Ser.). 1993. per. 2.89 (*0-373-11537-7*, 1-11537-7) Harlequin Bks.

— The Golden Mask. large type ed. 1992. lib. bdg. 18.95 (*0-263-13120-3*) Thorndike Pr.

— Indiscretions. LC 95-23070. (Presents Ser.). 185p. 1996. per. 3.50 (*0-373-11794-9*, 1-11794-4) Harlequin Bks.

— Island Enchantment. 1994. per. 2.99 (*0-373-11699-3*, 1-11699-5) Harlequin Bks.

— La Magia de la Isla - Island Enchantment. (Bianca Ser.: No. 367). 1996. per. 3.50 (*0-373-33367-6*, 1-33367-3) Harlequin Bks.

***Donald, Robyn.** Mas Alla de la Ira. (Bianca Ser.: Bk. 207).Tr. of Beyond the Anger. (SPA.). 2000. per. 3.50 (*0-373-33557-1*, 1-33557-9) Harlequin Bks.

Donald, Robyn. A Matter of Will. (Presents Ser.: No. 1343). 1991. per. 2.75 (*0-373-11343-9*) Harlequin Bks.

— Meant to Marry. (Presents Ser.). 1997. per. 3.50 (*0-373-11871-6*, 1-11871-0) Harlequin Bks.

— Meant to Marry. large type ed. (Harlequin Ser.). 1997. 20.95 (*0-263-14966-8*) Mac Lib Ref.

— The Mirror Bride. 1997. per. 3.50 (*0-373-11865-1*, 1-11866-0) Harlequin Bks.

— The Nanny Affair: Nanny Wanted! (Presents Ser.: Vol. 1980). 1998. per. 3.75 (*0-373-11980-1*, 1-11980-9) Harlequin Bks.

— No Guarantees. 1990. per. 2.50 (*0-373-11303-X*) Harlequin Bks.

— No Place Too Far. (Presents Ser.: No. 434). 1992. pap. 2.79 (*0-373-11434-6*, 1-11434-7) Harlequin Bks.

— No Place Too Far. large type ed. 1991. reprint ed. 18.95 (*0-263-12675-7*) Mac Lib Ref.

— An Old Passion. large type ed. LC 94-13993. 220p. 1994. lib. bdg. 17.95 (*0-8161-5995-5*, G K Hall Lrg Type) Mac Lib Ref.

— Once Bitten Twice Shy. (Presents Ser.). 1993. per. 2.99 (*0-373-11565-2*, 1-11565-8) Harlequin Bks.

— Paraiso Perdido. (Bianca Ser.). 1996. per. 3.50 (*0-373-33363-3*, 1-33363-2) Harlequin Bks.

***Donald, Robyn.** The Paternity Affair. large type ed. 1999. write for info. (*0-263-16169-2*, Pub. by Mills & Boon) Ulverscroft.

Donald, Robyn. Prince of Lies. LC 96-283. 187p. 1995. per. 3.25 (*0-373-11783-3*, 1-11783-7) Harlequin Bks.

***Donald, Robyn.** El Principe de Sus Suenos. (Bianca Ser.).Tr. of Prince of Her Dreams. (SPA.). 2000. mass mkt. 3.50 (*0-373-33563-6*, 1-33563-7) Harlequin Bks.

— A Reluctant Mistress. large type ed. 288p. 2000. 25.99 (*0-263-16350-4*, Pub. by Mills & Boon) Ulverscroft.

Donald, Robyn. Some Kind of Madness. (Presents Ser.: No. 464). 1992. per. 2.89 (*0-373-11464-8*, 1-11464-4) Harlequin Bks.

— The Stone Princess Year down Under. (Presents Ser.). 1993. per. 2.99 (*0-373-11577-6*, 1-11577-3) Harlequin Bks.

— Storm over Paradise. (Presents Ser.). 1992. per. 2.89 (*0-373-11505-9*, 1-11505-4) Harlequin Bks.

***Donald, Robyn.** Storm over Paradise. large type ed. 352p. 1999. 31.99 (*0-7505-1408-6*, Pub. by Mgna Lrg Print) Ulverscroft.

Donald, Robyn. Such Dark Magic. large type ed. (Harlequin Ser.). 1993. lib. bdg. 18.95 (*0-263-13419-9*) Thorndike Pr.

— Such Dark Magic: Year down Under. 1993. per. 2.99 (*0-373-11611-X*, 1-11611-0) Harlequin Bks.

— A Summer Storm. (Presents Ser.: No. 1408). 1991. pap. 2.79 (*0-373-11408-7*) Harlequin Bks.

— A Summer Storm. large type ed. 1991. reprint ed. lib. bdg. 18.95 (*0-263-12593-9*) Thorndike Pr.

— Surrender to Seduction. (Presents Ser.: Bk. 107). 1999. mass mkt. 3.75 (*0-373-18707-6*, 1-18707-9) Harlequin Bks.

— Surrender to Seduction. 1999. 21.95 (*0-263-16054-8*, G K Hall & Co) Mac Lib Ref.

— Tiger Eyes. LC 95-13708. (Presents Ser.). 189p. 1995. per. 3.25 (*0-373-11755-8*, 1-11755-5) Harlequin Bks.

— Tiger Eyes. large type ed. 1995. lib. bdg. 18.95 (*0-263-13962-X*) Thorndike Pr.

— Tiger, Tiger. (Presents Ser.: No. 1931). 1998. per. 3.50 (*0-373-11931-3*, 1-11931-2) Harlequin Bks.

— Tiger, Tiger. large type ed. (Harlequin Ser.). 283p. 1998. 20.95 (*0-263-15373-8*) Thorndike Pr.

Donald, Roger J. The Fullness of Time. 310p. 1996. pap. 9.95 (*0-7610-0638-9*) Galaxy Redmond WA.

Donald Schmitt & Company Staff, jt. auth. see Diamond, A. J.

Donald, Sheena C., jt. auth. see Gordon, David S.

***Donald, Stephanie.** Public Secrets, Public Spaces: Cinema & Civility in China. LC 99-44346. 240p. 2000. pap. 24.95 (*0-8476-9877-7*); text 64.00 (*0-8476-9876-9*) Rowman.

Donald, Stephanie, jt. auth. see Benewick, Robert.

Donald, Stephanie, jt. ed. see Evans, Harriet.

Donald, Sydney G. Der Besuch der Alten Dame, Durrenmatt: Critical Monographs in English. 90p. 1993. pap. 32.00 (*0-85261-342-3*, Pub. by Univ of Glasgow) St Mut.

Donald, Tom. The Hunter & the Hunted. 256p. (Orig.). 1997. pap. 11.95 (*1-56167-376-5*) Am Literary Pr.

Donald, Vivian. The Lady Ambassador. 1978. mass mkt. 1.75 (*0-451-08268-0*, E8268, Sig) NAL.

— The Roots of Love. (Double Romance Ser.). 1977. mass mkt. 1.50 (*0-451-07297-9*, W7297, Sig) NAL.

Donaldon, S. S., jt. auth. see Order, S. E.

***Donalds.** Human Resource Development. 224p. 2000. pap. text 30.00 (*0-7382-0328-9*) Perseus Pubng.

Donaldson. Competing Voices: The American Novel 1865-1914. LC 98-39993. 218p. 1998. 32.00 (*0-8057-7854-3*) S&S Trade.

— Corporate Restructuring. 224p. 1994. 32.95 (*0-07-103584-2*) McGraw.

— Cultivating Successful Software Specialties. 1997. text 45.00 (*0-13-754268-2*) P-H.

— Engineering College Survival Guide. LC 98-38255. 192p. 1999. pap. 22.19 (*0-07-228647-4*) McGraw.

— Johnson & Shakespeare. (Australian National University Press Ser.). 1996. text. write for info. (*0-08-032844-X*, Pergamon Pr) Elsevier.

— Strategy for Financial Mobility. 1986. 14.95 (*0-07-103229-0*) McGraw.

— Transformation in Modern Europe. (Australian National University Press Ser.). 1996. pap. text. write for info. (*0-08-032843-1*, Pergamon Pr) Elsevier.

Donaldson & Thorburn. The Law of Canadian Corporate Directors. 425p. write for info. (*0-409-80593-9*, MICHIE) LEXIS Pub.

Donaldson, et al. Control of Fluid Power Analysis & Design. 2nd ed. LC 08-40027. (Engineering Science Ser.). 1987. pap. text 41.95 (*0-470-21016-8*) P-H.

— Ethical Issues in Business: A Philosophical Approach. 6th ed. LC 98-31341. 611p. (C). 1998. 49.00 (*0-13-290628-7*) P-H.

— Thin Thread. 64p. 1997. pap. 9.95 (*1-884778-34-8*) Old Mountain.

***Donaldson & Warn.** Donaldson & Warn: Crossing Midfield. (Illus.). 128p. 2000. pap. 49.95 (*3-7643-6334-7*) Birkhauser.

Donaldson, Aidan. The Thought of Lucien Goldmann: A Critical Study. LC 96-16094. (Problems in Contemporary Philosophy Ser.: Vol. 35). 348p. 1996. text 99.95 (*0-7734-8742-5*) E Mellen.

Donaldson, Alfred G. Some Comparative Aspects of Irish Law. LC 57-8815. (Duke University, Commonwealth-Studies Center, Publication Ser.: No. 3). 307p. reprint ed. pap. 95.20 (*0-608-18662-7*, 202337600032) Bks Demand.

Donaldson, Alfred L. A History of the Adirondacks, 2 vols., Set. 1993. reprint ed. lib. bdg. 180.00 (*0-7812-5172-9*) Rprt Serv.

— A History of the Adirondacks, 2 vols., Vols. I & II. LC 92-8106. (Illus.). 766p. 1996. pap. 45.00 (*0-935796-76-2*) Purple Mnt Pr.

Donaldson, B. C. Beyond the Dictionary in Dutch. (DUT.). 324p. 1990. pap. 45.00 (*90-6283-814-6*, Pub. by Coutinho Pub) IBD Ltd.

Donaldson, Barry, ed. Exterior Wall Systems: Glass & Concrete, Design & Construction. LC 91-8084. (Special Technical Publication Ser.: No. STP 1034). (Illus.). 220p. 1991. text 49.00 (*0-8031-1424-9*, STP1034) ASTM.

— New Stone Technology, Design, & Construction for Exterior Wall Systems. LC 88-2358. (Special Technical Publication Ser.: No. 996). (Illus.). 196p. 1988. text 34.00 (*0-8031-1164-9*, STP996) ASTM.

Donaldson, Bess A. The Wild Rue. LC 73-6277. (Middle East Ser.). 1977. reprint ed. 19.95 (*0-405-05332-0*) Ayer.

Donaldson, Beth. Block by Block: New Techniques for Machine Quilting & Assembly. 1995. pap. 19.95 (*1-56477-080-X*, B220) Martingale & Co.

— Charm Quilts: or Too Much Fun with a Stack of Squares & One Template! Penders, Mary C., ed. (Illus.). 104p. 1997. pap. 23.95 (*1-881588-19-X*, 882670158) EZ Quilting.

Donaldson, Bruce. Colloquial Dutch. (C). 1996. audio 27.99 (*0-415-13087-5*) Routledge.

— Colloquial Dutch: A Complete Language Course. LC 95-35857. (Colloquials Ser.). (Illus.). 320p. 1996. pap. 18.99 (*0-415-13086-7*) Routledge.

— Coloquial Dutch: A Complete Language Course Book. (Illus.). 288p. 1996. pap., pap. text 39.99 incl. audio (*0-415-13088-3*) Routledge.

— Dutch: Comprehensive Grammar. LC 97-210005. (Routledge Grammars Ser.). 368p. (C). 1997. 85.00 (*0-415-15418-9*); pap. 29.99 (*0-415-15419-7*) Routledge.

***Donaldson, Bruce C.** Colloquial Afrikaans: Complete Course for Beginners. LC 99-52355. (Colloquials Ser.). 304p. (C). 2000. pap. 27.95 (*0-415-20672-3*) Routledge.

Donaldson, Bruce C. A Grammar of Afrikaans. LC 92-9155. (Mouton Grammar Library: Vol. 8). xxi, 497p. 1993. lib. bdg. 190.80 (*3-11-013426-8*) Mouton.

Donaldson, Bruce K. Analysis of Aircraft Structures: An Introduction. 935p. (C). 1992. 103.44 (*0-07-017539-X*) McGraw.

Donaldson, Bryna. Bible Stories. (J). 1999. lib. bdg. write for info. (*0-394-93761-9*) Random Bks Yng Read.

Donaldson, Christina. Collecting China. (Illus.). 253p. 1997. pap. 8.00 (*0-00-471009-6*) Collins.

Donaldson, Christine. Patchwork Baby: Original Patchwork & Quilted Designs. (Illus.). 144p. 1995. 24.95 (*1-57076-017-9*, Trafalgar Sq Pub) Trafalgar.

Donaldson, Christine F. & Flynn, Elizabeth A. Alternative Careers for Ph.D.s in the Humanities: A Selected Bibliography. LC 82-3399. 48p. reprint ed. pap. 30.00 (*0-8357-5332-8*, 203078900074) Bks Demand.

Donaldson, Christopher. The Great English Pilgrimage from Rome to Canterbury: In the Footsteps of St. Augustine, 1400th Anniversary. LC 95-174587. 1995. pap. 17.95 (*1-85311-098-1*, 836, Pub. by Canterbury Press Norwich) Morehouse Pub.

— Martin of Tours: Parish Priest, Mystic & Exorcist. (Illus.). 196p. 1985. pap. 9.95 (*0-7102-0682-8*, Routledge Thoemms) Routledge.

— Martin of Tours: The Shaping of Celtic Spirituality. LC 99-170726. 176p. 1997. pap. 15.95 (*1-85311-157-0*, 1982, Pub. by Canterbury Press Norwich) Morehouse Pub.

Donaldson, Corey. Don't You Dare Get Married until You Read This. (Illus.). 142p. (gr. 11 up). 1998. pap. 24.95 (*0-9666559-0-7*) Sentinel Publishing.

Donaldson, Cyril & Le Cain, George. Tool Design. 3rd ed. (Illus.). 840p. 1973. text 59.95 (*0-07-017531-4*) McGraw.

Donaldson, D. & Panton, G. A., eds. The Gest Hystoriale of the Destruction of Troy, 2 vols., Vols. I & II. (EETS Original Ser.: Vol. 39). 1968. reprint ed. 40.00 (*0-19-722056-8*, Pub. by EETS) Boydell & Brewer.

— The Gest Hystoriale of the Destruction of Troy Parts I & II: 1869-1873. (EETS, OS Ser.: Nos. 39, 56). 1969. 40.00 (*0-527-00035-3*) Periodicals Srv.

Donaldson, D., jt. auth. see Lascelles, P. T.

Donaldson, D. J. Louisiana Fever. 288p. 1996. 21.95 (*0-312-14362-1*) St Martin.

— Louisiana Fever. 1997. mass mkt. 5.99 (*0-312-96257-6*) St Martin.

— New Orleans Requiem. LC 96-2377. (Mystery Ser.). 250p. 1996. per. 3.99 (*0-373-26188-8*, 1-26188-2, Wrldwide Lib) Harlequin Bks.

— No Mardi Gras for the Dead. (WWL Mystery Ser.). 1995. mass mkt. 3.99 (*0-373-26163-2*, 1-26163-5) Harlequin Bks.

— Sleeping with the Crawfish: An Andy Broussard & Kit Franklyn Mystery. LC 97-20036. 272p. 1997. text 21.95 (*0-312-17025-4*) St Martin.

— Sleeping with the Crawfish: An Andy Broussard & Kit Franklyn Mystery, Vol. 1. Date not set. 5.99 (*0-312-96681-4*, Pub. by Tor Bks) St Martin.

Donaldson, David. Psychiatric Disorders with a Biochemical Basis: Including Pharmacology, Toxicology & Nutritional Aspects. LC 97-7656. (Illus.). 252p. 1998. 45.00 (*1-85070-789-8*) Prthnon Pub.

Donaldson, David, ed. see Jamieson, John.

Donaldson, David J. & Wagle, Dileep M. Privatization: Principles & Practice. LC 95-24917. 96p. 1995. pap. 24.00 (*0-8213-3447-6*, 13447) World Bank.

Donaldson, Diana S., jt. auth. see Suplee, Dennis R.

***Donaldson, Don.** Do No Harm. 1999. mass mkt. 5.99 (*0-515-12650-0*, Jove) Berkley Pub.

Donaldson, Donna, ed. see Fox, John H.

Donaldson, Doris, ed. see McLaird, George L.

Donaldson, Dwight M. The Shi'ite Religion: A History of Islam in Persia & Iraq. LC 80-1933. 64.50 (*0-404-18959-8*) AMS Pr.

Donaldson, E. C., et al. Subsidence Due to Fluid Withdrawal. (Developments in Petroleum Science Ser.: Vol. 41). 516p. 1995. 210.00 (*0-444-81820-0*) Elsevier.

Donaldson, E. Lisbeth, ed. Caring for Your Voice: Teachers & Coaches. (Illus.). 144p. (Orig.). 1995. pap. text. write for info. (*1-55059-119-3*) Detselig Ents.

Donaldson, E. T., ed. & selected by see Chaucer, Geoffrey.

Donaldson, E. Talbot. MSS R & F in the B-Tradition of Piers Plowman. (Connecticut Academy of Arts & Sciences Ser., Trans.: Vol. 39). 1955. pap. 39.50 (*0-685-22799-5*) Elliots Bks.

— The Swan at the Well: Shakespeare Reading Chaucer. LC 84-21913. 192p. 1985. 32.00 (*0-300-03349-4*) Yale U Pr.

Donaldson, E. Talbot, tr. Beowulf: A New Translation. (C). 1966. pap. text 10.25 (*0-393-09687-4*) Norton.

Donaldson, E. Talbot, tr. see Langland, William.

Donaldson, E. Talbot, tr. see Tuso, Joseph F., ed.

Donaldson, Elisbeth. Making Transitions Work. 1980. pap. 19.95 (*1-55059-168-1*) Detselig Ents.

Donaldson, Enid. The Real Taste of Jamaica. LC 98-155492. (Illus.). 160p. (Orig.). pap. 15.95 (*976-8100-46-X*, Pub. by Ian Randle) Paul & Co Pubs.

— The Real Taste of Jamaica. (Illus.). 156p. (Orig.). 1996. pap. 18.95 (*1-895629-64-0*) Warwick Publ.

Donaldson, Erle C., jt. auth. see Tiab, Djebbar.

Donaldson, Erle C., jt. auth. see Tlab, Djebbar.

Donaldson-Evans, Lancelot K. Love's Fatal Glance: A Study of Eye Imagery in the Poets of the Ecole lyonnaise. LC 80-10415. (Romance Monographs: No. 39). 155p. 1980. 24.00 (*84-499-3694-2*) Romance.

***Donaldson-Evans, Mary.** Medical Examinations: Dissecting the Doctor in French Narrative Prose, 1857-1894. LC 00-37427. (Illus.). 256p. 2000. pap. text 49.95 (*0-8032-6628-6*, Bison Books) U of Nebr Pr.

Donaldson-Evans, Mary, jt. ed. see Cooper, Barbara T.

Donaldson, Everett. Raccoon John Smith: Frontiersman & Reformer. 2nd rev. ed. LC 93-72516. (Illus.). 199p. 1993. reprint ed. pap. 9.95 (*0-9636545-1-9*) Wind Pubns.

Donaldson, Frances, ed. see Wodehouse, P. G.

Donaldson, Francis Adams. Inside the Army of the Potomac: The Civil War Experience of Captain Francis Adams Donaldson. LC 98-17111. (Illus.). 480p. 1998. 34.95 (*0-8117-0901-9*) Kitch Keepsakes.

Donaldson, Frank. Catholic School Publications: Unifying the Image. 66p. 1991. 8.00 (*1-55833-074-7*) Natl Cath Educ.

***Donaldson, Fred.** Lure of the Sky. LC 99-91583. 326p. 2000. 25.00 (*0-7388-0906-3*); pap. 18.00 (*0-7388-0907-1*) Xlibris Corp.

Donaldson, G. Gilles Villeneuve: The Life of the Legendary Racing Driver. (Illus.). 352p. 1996. 34.95 (*0-947981-44-6*) Motor Racing.

Donaldson, Gary A. Abundance & Anxiety: America, 1945-1960. LC 96-43873. 208p. 1997. 57.95 (*0-275-95773-X*, Praeger Pubs) Greenwood.

— America at War since 1945: Politics & Diplomacy in Korea, Vietnam & the Gulf War. LC 96-11507. 248p. 1996. 62.95 (*0-275-95555-9*, Praeger Pubs); pap. 21.95 (*0-275-95660-1*, Praeger Pubs) Greenwood.

— The History of African Americans in the Military: Double V. 192p. (C). 1991. pap. 17.50 (*0-89464-514-5*) Krieger.

— The Second Reconstruction: A History of the Modern Civil Rights Movement. LC 99-31735. (Anvil Ser.). 153p. (C). 2000. pap. text 14.50 (*1-57524-066-1*) Krieger.

— Truman Defeats Dewey. LC 98-24424. (Illus.). 304p. 1998. 27.50 (*0-8131-2075-6*) U Pr of Ky.

***Donaldson, Gary A.** Truman Defeats Dewey. (Illus.). 280p. 2000. reprint ed. pap. 18.00 (*0-8131-9002-9*) U Pr of Ky.

***Donaldson, Gerald & Giansanti, Gianni.** British American Racing: From Dream to Reality. (Illus.). 160p. 2000. 39.95 (*1-874557-59-4*, 130063AE, Pub. by Hazelton Publishing) Motorbooks Intl.

Donaldson, Gordon. The Auld Alliance. 32p. 1986. 15.00 (*0-85411-031-3*, Pub. by Saltire Soc) St Mut.

— Corporate Restructuring: Managing the Change Process from Within. LC 93-30462. 1994. 29.95 (*0-87584-339-5*) Harvard Busn.

— The Edinburgh History of Scotland Vol. 3: James V.-James VII. 449p. (C). 1986. 75.00 (*0-901824-85-2*, Pub. by Mercat Pr Bks) St Mut.

— A Northern Commonwealth: Scotland & Norway. (C). 1993. pap. 21.00 (*0-85411-044-5*, Pub. by Saltire Soc) St Mut.

— Northwards by Sea. (Illus.). 1978. 27.00 (*0-8464-0677-2*) Beekman Pubs.

— Prime Ministers of Canada. 352p. 1994. pap. 19.95 (*0-385-25454-7*) Doubleday.

— Scottish Historical Documents. 300p. 1997. pap. 25.00 (*1-897784-41-4*, Pub. by N Wilson Pubng) Interlink Pub.

Donaldson, Gordon & Morpeth, Robert. Who's Who in Scottish History. 254p. 1997. pap. 19.95 (*1-86057-005-4*, Pub. by Welsh Acad) Intl Spec Bk.

Donaldson, Gordon, et al. A Dictionary of Scottish History. 234p. (C). 1996. pap. 30.00 (*0-85976-018-9*, Pub. by J Donald) Dufour.

Donaldson, Gordon A. Learning to Lead: The Dynamics of the High School Principalship. 45. LC 90-23094. (Contributions to the Study of Education Ser.: No. 45). 248p. 1991. 65.00 (*0-313-27743-5*, DSH, Greenwood Pr) Greenwood.

***Donaldson, Gordon A.** To Lead a School: A Collaborative Leadership Model for Teachers And Principals / LC 00-44336. 2000. pap. write for info. (*0-8077-4002-0*) Tchrs Coll.

Donaldson, Gordon A., Jr. & Marnik, George F. Becoming Better Leaders: The Challenge of Improving Student Learning. LC 95-3734. (Illus.). 176p. 1995. pap. 22.95 (*0-8039-6182-0*) Corwin Pr.

Donaldson, Gordon A., Jr. & Marnik, George F., eds. As Leaders Learn: Personal Stories of Growth in School Leadership. LC 95-7972. 112p. 1995. 43.95 (*0-8039-6301-7*); pap. 18.95 (*0-8039-6302-5*) Corwin Pr.

Donaldson, Gordon A., Jr. & Sanderson, David R. Working Together in Schools: A Guide for Educators. LC 96-10087. (Illus.). 184p. 1996. 61.95 (*0-8039-6377-7*); pap. 27.95 (*0-8039-6378-5*) Corwin Pr.

An Asterisk (*) at the beginning of an entry indicates that the title is appearing for the first time.

D

***Donaldson, Hal, et al, eds.** Family: How to Have a Healthy Christian Home. 119p. 2000. pap. 5.99 (*0-88243-342-3*, 02-1034) Gospel Pub.
— Strategies for Victorious Christian Living. 119p. 1999. pap. 5.99 (*0-88243-340-7*, 02-1032) Gospel Pub.
Donaldson, Hal & Dobsen, Kenneth M. Parenting: Successful Church Leaders Share Biblical Principles for Raising Kids in the Nineties. 280p. 1993. pap. 11.95 (*1-880689-02-2*) Onward Bks.
— Portraits of Success: Leaders Share Principles for Winning in the Nineties. 352p. 1994. pap. text 11.95 (*1-880689-03-0*) Onward Bks.
Donaldson, Hal & Dobson, Kenneth M. Huldah Buntain: Woman of Courage. 192p. 1995. pap. text 9.95 (*1-880689-04-9*) Onward Bks.
— Pleasing God, Pleasing You: Twenty Church Leaders Share Biblical Principles for Successful Christian Living. 200p. 1992. 14.95 (*1-880689-01-4*) Onward Bks.
— Power for Living: Christian Leaders Share Principles That Will Change Your Life. 250p. 1996. pap. text 11.95 (*1-880689-06-5*) Onward Bks.
— The Vow: One Man's Determination to Obey God. 192p. 1991. pap. 7.95 (*1-880689-00-6*) Onward Bks.
Donaldson, Hal, jt. auth. see Buntain, Fulton.
Donaldson, Harvey. Yours Truly, Harvey Donaldson. Wolfe, Dave, ed. 271p. 1981. text 19.50 (*0-935632-01-8*) Wolfe Pub Co.
Donaldson, Helen, jt. auth. see Goss, Lynn.
Donaldson, I. M. Life & Work of Samuel Rutherford Crockett. 1989. text 39.00 (*0-08-036597-3*, Pergamon Pr) Elsevier.
Donaldson, Ian. Jonson's Magic Houses: Essays in Interpretation. LC 97-163605. 250p. 1997. text 68.00 (*0-19-818394-1*) OUP.
— The Rapes of Lucretia: A Myth & Its Transformations. (Illus.). 214p. 1982. text 65.00 (*0-19-812638-7*) OUP.
Donaldson, Ian, ed. Ben Jonson. (Oxford Authors Ser.). 808p. 1985. pap. text 21.00 (*0-19-281339-0*) OUP.
Donaldson, Ian, ed. see Jonson, Ben.
Donaldson, Ivan & Cramer, Frederick. Fishwheels of the Columbia. LC 76-173928. (Illus.). 128p. 1971. 14.95 (*0-8323-0007-1*) Binford Mort.
Donaldson, J., jt. ed. see Roberts, A.
Donaldson, J. G. When Turkeys Talked & Politicians Were People. LC 98-94013. 1999. pap. 10.95 (*0-533-12948-6*) Vantage.
Donaldson, James. Woman: Her Position & Influence in Ancient Greece & Rome & Among the Early Christians. 1973. 300.00 (*0-87968-065-2*) Gordon Pr.
Donaldson, James & Roberts, Alexander, trs. Martyrdom of St. Polycarp: The Encyclical Epistle of the Church at Smyrna Concerning the Martyrdom of the Holy Polycarp. 1986. pap. 1.50 (*0-89981-056-X*) Eastern Orthodox.
Donaldson, James, jt. ed. see Roberts, Alexander.
Donaldson, James A., et al. Anson-Donaldson Surgical Anatomy of the Temporal Bone. 4th ed. 576p. 1992. text 154.00 (*0-88167-915-1*, 2393) Lppncott W & W.
Donaldson, Janet, ed. see Bingham, Marjorie W.
Donaldson, Janet M., ed. see Bingham, Marjorie W. & Gross, Susan H.
Donaldson, Janet M., ed. see Gross, Susan H. & Bingham, Marjorie W.
Donaldson, Jean. The Culture Clash. LC 97-200294. (Illus.). 224p. 1996. pap. 17.95 (*1-888047-05-4*) J & K Pubs.
Donaldson, Jeffery. Waterglass. 88p. pap. 12.95 (*0-7735-1900-9*) McG-Queens Univ Pr.
***Donaldson, Joan.** A Pebble & a Pen. LC 00-21777. 176p. (YA). (gr. 5 up). 2000. 15.95 (*0-8234-1500-7*) Holiday.
Donaldson, Joan. The Real Pretend. (Illus.). 32p. (J). (ps-3). 1992. 12.95 (*1-56288-158-2*) Checkerboard.
Donaldson, Joe F. & Kozoll, Charles E. Collaborative Program Planning: Principles, Practices, & Strategies. LC 98-30740. (Professional Practices in Adult Education & Human Resource Development Ser.). 155p. (C). 1999. text 22.50 (*1-57524-012-2*) Krieger.
Donaldson, John. A Legend on the Road: Bobby Fischer's 1964 SimulTour. Woro, Eric, ed. (Illus.). 128p. 1994. 26.95 (*1-879479-15-X*); pap. 16.95 (*1-879479-14-1*) ICE WA.
— Meran Defense. 111p. (Orig.). 1987. pap. 6.95 (*0-931462-64-9*) Chess Ent.
— A Strategic Opening Repertoire. (Illus.). 156p. 1998. pap. 14.95 (*1-879479-76-1*) ICE WA.
Donaldson, John & Minev, Nikolay. Akiba Rubinstein: The Later Years. Kleist, Fred, ed. (Illus.). 306p. 1995. 34.95 (*1-879479-27-3*); pap. 27.95 (*1-879479-26-5*) ICE WA.
— Akiba Rubinstein: Uncrowned King. Woro, Eric, ed. 336p. (Orig.). 1994. pap. 27.95 (*1-879479-19-2*) ICE WA.
***Donaldson, John & Tangborn, Eric.** The Unknown Bobby Fischer. (Illus.). 202p. 1999. pap. 19.95 (*1-879479-85-0*) ICE WA.
Donaldson, John, et al. Alekhine in Europe & Asia. Woro, Eric, ed. (Alekhine Ser.). (Illus.). ii, 118p. (Orig.). 1993. pap. 15.95 (*1-879479-12-5*) ICE WA.
— Alekhine in the Americas. Franett, Michael J., ed. (Alekhine Ser.). (Illus.). 48p. (Orig.). 1992. pap. 8.95 (*1-879479-06-0*) ICE WA.
Donaldson, John, jt. auth. see Hoffman, Asa.
Donaldson, John, jt. auth. see Silman, Jeremy.
Donaldson, John W. The Theatre of the Greeks. LC 72-2095. (Studies in Drama: No. 39). 1972. reprint ed. lib. bdg. 75.00 (*0-8383-1495-3*) M S G Haskell Hse.
— Theatre of the Greeks, 1836. (Illus.). 278p. 1998. reprint ed. pap. 35.00 (*0-87556-851-3*) Saifer.
Donaldson, Joseph C., et al. How To Manual for Volunteer Youth Leaders. LC 86-80688. (Equipping Ser.). (Illus.). 136p. (Orig.). 1986. pap. 6.95 (*0-935797-22-X*) Harvest IL.
Donaldson, Judith E. Doodles, Diddles, Puzzles, Quizzies & Fun Stuff, Vol. 2. (Illus.). 144p. (Orig.). (J). (gr. 2 up). 1981. pap. 2.25 (*0-939942-00-3*) Larkspur.
— Travel Games Vol. 2: 5 to 10 Years. Brown, George H., ed. (Illus.). 36p. (J). (gr. k-5). reprint ed. pap. text 1.50 (*0-939942-06-2*) Larkspur.
Donaldson, Judith E. & Brown, George H. Travel Games Vol. 1: Family. (Illus.). 36p. (Orig.). reprint ed. pap. text 1.50 (*0-939942-05-4*) Larkspur.
Donaldson, Judith E., ed. see Brown, George H.
Donaldson, Judith E., ed. & illus. see Brown, George H.
Donaldson, Judy P. Transcultural Education Model: A Guide for Developing ESL Bilingual & LEP Programs for K-12 & Adult Populations. LC 84-80658. 176p. (Orig.). 1988. pap. text 19.95 (*0-918452-60-0*, 600) Learning Pubns.
— Transcultural Picture Word List Vol. 1: For Teaching English to Children from Any of 35 Language Backgrounds. 2nd ed. LC 78-58532. 320p. 1998. pap. text 36.95 (*1-55691-132-7*, 327) Learning Pubns.
Donaldson, Julia. The Gruffalo. Skwarek, Skip, ed. LC 98-33893. (Illus.). 32p. (J). (ps-3). 1999. 15.99 (*0-8037-2386-5*, Dial Yng Read) Peng Put Young Read.
— Spirals Plays: Books & Crooks. Jackson, Anita, ed. 1998. pap. 22.00 (*0-7487-3656-5*, Pub. by S Thornes Pubs) Trans-Atl Phila.
Donaldson, Karen B. Through Students' Eyes: Combating Racism in United States Schools. LC 96-10432. 184p. 1996. pap. 18.95 (*0-275-95818-3*, Praeger Pubs) Greenwood.
Donaldson, Karen H. Haunted Houses of Michigan. (Illus.). 68p. 1998. pap. 8.95 (*0-9651497-9-X*) Whitechapel.
Donaldson, Kim, ed. see Dull, Terry R.
Donaldson, Kurt & Scott, Jamie. General Chemistry III. 308p. (C). 1994. pap. text, per. 57.95 (*0-7872-0223-1*) Kendall-Hunt.
— Organic Chemistry I & II: Lecture Notes & Workbook. 686p. (C). 1996. pap. text, per. 135.95 (*0-7872-1917-7*, 41191701) Kendall-Hunt.
Donaldson, Kurt D. & Scott, Jamie M. General Chemistry 1: Lecture Notes & Workbook. 524p. (C). 1995. per. 46.95 (*0-8403-8872-1*) Kendall-Hunt.
Donaldson, L. J., jt. auth. see Donaldson, R. J.
Donaldson, Laura E. Decolonizing Feminisms: Race, Gender, & Empire-Building. LC 92-54167. x, 176p. (C). 1992. 37.50 (*0-8078-2044-X*); pap. 14.95 (*0-8078-4382-2*) U of NC Pr.
Donaldson, Lee & Rand, Jonathan. Pushing up the Sky: Elevating Your Thinking, Learning & Communicating. 186p. 1997. pap. 12.95 (*0-9658105-1-8*) Candlewick Press.
Donaldson, Les. Behavioral Supervision: Practical Ways to Change Unsatisfactory Behavior & Increase Productivity. LC 79-25100. 1980. pap. text 17.95 (*0-201-01473-4*) Addison-Wesley.
— Conversational Magic: Key to Poise, Popularity & Success. 216p. 1981. text 27.95 (*0-13-172155-0*, Parker Publishing Co) P-H.
— Human Resource Developments: The New Trainer's Guide. 2nd ed. 1986. pap. 28.00 (*0-201-03087-X*) Addison-Wesley.
Donaldson, Les & Scannell, Edward. Human Resource Development: The New Trainer's Guide. 1978. pap. text 12.95 (*0-201-03081-0*) Addison-Wesley.
Donaldson, Lex. American Anti-Management Theories of Organization: A Critique of Paradigm Proliferation. (Cambridge Studies in Management: No. 25). (Illus.). 277p. (C). 1995. pap. text 20.95 (*0-521-47917-7*) Cambridge U Pr.
— For Positivist Organization Theory: Proving the Hard Core. 208p. 1996. 69.95 (*0-7619-5226-8*); pap. 26.95 (*0-7619-5227-6*) Sage.
— The Organizational Portfolio: A Theory of Performance-Driven Organizational Change. LC 98-25383. 320p. 1998. 32.00 (*0-7619-0354-2*) Sage.
— Performance-Driven Organizational Change: The Organizational Portfolio. LC 98-25383. 320p. 1998. pap. 14.99 (*0-7619-0355-0*) Sage.
Donaldson, Lex, ed. Contingency Theory. LC 93-47245. (History of Management Thought Ser.: Vol. 9). 448p. (C). 1994. text 163.95 (*1-85521-436-9*, Pub. by Dartmth Pub) Ashgate Pub Co.
Donaldson, Lex, jt. auth. see Hilmer, Frederick G.
Donaldson, Lloyd & Wilson, Drew. Russian Etiquette & Ethics in Business. (Etiquette & Ethics Ser.). (Illus.). 200p. 1995. pap. 16.95 (*0-8442-4216-0*, 42160, NTC Business Bks) NTC Contemp Pub Co.
Donaldson, Lynn, ed. see Kronour, David R.
Donaldson, Margaret. Children's Minds. (Illus.). (C). 1979. pap. text 13.25 (*0-393-95101-4*) Norton.
Donaldson, Mary A. Group Treatment of Adult Incest Survivors. LC 94-6852. (Interpersonal Violence: the Practice Ser.: Vol. 5). 1994. 48.00 (*0-8039-6165-0*); pap. 21.50 (*0-8039-6166-9*) Sage.
Donaldson, Mary Frances K., jt. auth. see Kendall, Katharine K.
Donaldson, Mary Frances K., jt. auth. see Kendall, Katherine K.
Donaldson, Maureen. Biology Lab Manual. 272p. (C). 1995. spiral bd., lab manual ed. 23.95 (*0-7872-1247-4*) Kendall-Hunt.
Donaldson, Maureen & Royce, William. An Affair to Remember: My Life with Cary Grant. large type ed. (General Ser.). (Illus.). 441p. 1990. lib. bdg. 19.95 (*0-8161-4896-1*, G K Hall Lrg Type) Mac Lib Ref.
Donaldson, Mel. Cornerstones. 1001p. (C). 1996. pap. 51.95 (*0-312-09530-9*) St Martin.
Donaldson, Michael & Donaldson, Mimi. Negotiating for Dummies. (For Dummies Ser.). 384p. 1996. pap. 19.99 (*1-56884-867-6*) IDG Bks.
— Negotiating for Dummies: A Reference for the Rest of Us! abr. ed. 1998. audio 12.00 (*0-694-51917-0*) HarperAudio.
Donaldson, Michael C. Clearance & Copyright: Everything the Independent Filmmaker Needs to Know. LC 96-43392. xvi, 276p. (Orig.). 1997. pap. 26.95 (*1-879505-30-4*) Silman James Pr.
Donaldson, Mike. Taking Our Time: Remaking the Temporal Order. LC 96-213815. 216p. (C). 1996. pap. 24.95 (*1-875560-64-5*, Pub. by Univ of West Aust Pr) Intl Spec Bk.
Donaldson, Mimi, jt. auth. see Donaldson, Michael.
Donaldson, Molla S., et al, eds. Medicare: New Directions in Quality Assurance: Proceedings of an Invitational Conference. LC 90-63821. 217p. 1991. reprint ed. pap. 67.30 (*0-608-02345-0*, 206298600004) Bks Demand.
Donaldson, Molla S., ed. see Institute of Medicine Committee on Regional Health.
Donaldson, Molla S., ed. see Institute of Medicine Staff.
Donaldson, Morag L. Children with Language Impairments: An Introduction. 144p. 1995. pap. write for info. (*1-85302-313-2*, Pub. by Jessica Kingsley) Taylor & Francis.
— Children's Explanations: A Psycholinguistic Study. (Illus.). 200p. 1986. text 64.95 (*0-521-32006-2*) Cambridge U Pr.
***Donaldson, Norman.** Donaldson on Freeman: Being the Introductions & Afterwords from the R. Austin Freeman Omnibus Volumes. 2000. pap. 16.00 (*1-55246-283-8*) Battered Silicon.
— How Did They Die? (Reference Bks.). 1999. 42.00 (*1-55246-142-4*) Battered Silicon.
— In Search of Dr. Thorndyke. (R. Austin Freeman Omnibus Edition Ser.). 1998. 28.00 (*1-55246-082-7*); pap. 18.00 (*1-55246-083-5*) Battered Silicon.
Donaldson, Norman. Life Begins. LC 98-52398. 1999. pap. 5.00 (*0-88734-826-2*) Players Pr.
Donaldson, Norman, jt. auth. see Freeman, R. Austin.
Donaldson, Peter. A Guide to Computer Music: An Introductory Resource. M. K. Graphic & Design Editorial Dept. Staff, ed. (Illus.). 88p. (Orig.). 1988. pap. 16.95 (*0-9621514-0-8*) Sound Mgmt Prodns.
Donaldson, Peter J. Nature Against Us: The United States & the World Population Crisis, 1965-1980. LC 89-38870. 223p. reprint ed. pap. 69.20 (*0-608-10497-3*, 207112600009) Bks Demand.
Donaldson, Peter S. Machiavelli & Mystery of State. 241p. (C). 1992. pap. text 19.95 (*0-521-43790-3*) Cambridge U Pr.
— Shakespearean Films - Shakespearean Directors. (Media & Popular Culture Ser.: No. 6). (Illus.). 240p. (C). 1990. pap. 19.95 (*0-04-445230-6*) Routledge.
— Shakespearean Films-Shakespearean Directors. (Illus.). 240p. 1990. 44.95 (*0-685-33056-7*); pap. 14.95 (*0-685-33057-5*) Routledge.
Donaldson-Pressman, Stephanie. The Narcissistic Family: Diagnosis & Treatment. LC 97-16678. 181p. 1997. 25.95 (*0-02-925435-3*) Free Pr.
Donaldson-Pressman, Stephanie & Pressman, Robert H. The Narcissistic Family: Diagnosis & Treatment. LC 97-16678. 192p. 1997. pap. 25.95 (*0-7879-0870-3*) Jossey-Bass.
Donaldson-Pressman, Stephanie & Pressman, Robert M. The Narcissistic Family: Diagnosis & Treatment. LC 93-40133. 1994. write for info. (*0-02-925434-5*) Free Pr.
Donaldson, R., ed. Experiments, Detectors & Experimental Areas for the Supercollider: Proceedings of the Workshop. 936p. (C). 1988. text 143.00 (*9971-5-0473-1*) World Scientific Pub.
Donaldson, R. & Gilchriese, M., eds. Calorimetry for the Supercollider. 736p. (C). 1990. text 173.00 (*9971-5-0918-0*) World Scientific Pub.
Donaldson, R. J. & Donaldson, L. J. Essential Community Medicine: Including Relevant Social Services. 600p. 1983. text 37.50 (*0-85200-373-0*) Kluwer Academic.
Donaldson, Robert H. Soviet Policy Toward India: Ideology & Strategy. LC 73-89708. (Russian Research Center Studies: No. 74). 355p. reprint ed. pap. 110.10 (*0-608-30176-0*, 202176900023) Bks Demand.
Donaldson, Robert H. & Nogee, Joseph L. The Foreign Policy of Russia: Changing Systems, Enduring Interests. LC 98-14390. 336p. (C). (gr. 13). 1998. text 66.95 (*0-7656-0046-3*); pap. text 26.95 (*0-7656-0047-1*) M E Sharpe.
Donaldson, Robert H., jt. auth. see Nogee, Joseph L.
Donaldson, S., jt. auth. see Order, S. E.
Donaldson, S. K. & Thomas, C. B., eds. Geometry of Low-Dimensional Manifolds, 1. (London Mathematical Society Lecture Note Ser.: Nos. 151 & 152). 273p. (C). 1991. pap. text 49.95 (*0-521-39978-5*) Cambridge U Pr.
— Geometry of Low-Dimensional Manifolds, 2. (London Mathematical Society Lecture Note Ser.: Nos. 151 & 152). 256p. (C). 1991. pap. text 49.95 (*0-521-40001-5*) Cambridge U Pr.
Donaldson, Sam A. The Really Big L. D. Block Book, Vol. 2. (Illus.). vii, 265p. (Orig.). (YA). (gr. 7-12). 1992. pap. text 47.00 (*1-889510-07-6*) Chmpionship Debate.
Donaldson, Sandra. Elizabeth Barrett Browning: An Annotated Bibliography of the Commentary & Criticism, 1826-1990. (G. K. Hall Reference Ser.). 550p. 1993. 70.00 (*0-8161-8910-2*, G K Hall & Co) Mac Lib Ref.
Donaldson, Scott. The Cambridge Companion to Hemingway. (Cambridge Companions to Literature Ser.). 335p. (C). 1996. text 64.95 (*0-521-45479-4*) Cambridge U Pr.
— Hemingway vs. Fitzgerald: The Rise & Fall of a Literacy Friendship. LC 99-37835. 320p. 1999. text 29.95 (*0-87951-711-5*, Pub. by Overlook Pr) Penguin Putnam.
— Poet in America: Winfield Townley Scott. LC 75-38568. 414p. reprint ed. pap. 128.40 (*0-8357-7736-7*, 203609300002) Bks Demand.
Donaldson, Scott, ed. The Cambridge Companion to Hemingway. (Cambridge Companions to Literature Ser.). 335p. (C). 1996. pap. text 18.95 (*0-521-45574-X*) Cambridge U Pr.
— Conversations with John Cheever. LC 87-17932. (Literary Conversations Ser.). 260p. 1987. 39.50 (*0-87805-331-X*); pap. 15.95 (*0-87805-332-8*) U Pr of Miss.
— Critical Essays on F. Scott Fitzgerald's "The Great Gatsby" (Critical Essays on American Literature Ser.). 304p. 1984. 49.00 (*0-8161-8679-0*, G K Hall & Co) Mac Lib Ref.
Donaldson, Scott & Siegel, Stanley. Cultivating Successful Software Systems Development: A Practitioners View. LC 96-36598. 548p. (C). 1997. 53.00 (*0-13-341678-X*) P-H.
Donaldson, Simon K. & Kronheimer, P. B. The Geometry of Four-Manifolds. (Oxford Mathematical Monographs). (Illus.). 456p. 1997. reprint ed. pap. text 55.00 (*0-19-850269-9*) OUP.
Donaldson, Stephanie. The Bath & Body Book: Creating a Private Oasis with Natural Fragrances, Scented Lotions & Decorative Effects. (Illus.). 128p. 1997. 19.95 (*1-85967-391-0*, Lorenz Bks) Anness Pub.
***Donaldson, Stephanie.** Complete Guide to Container Gardening. (Illus.). 2000. pap. 14.95 (*0-7548-0492-5*, Lorenz Bks) Anness Pub.
— Container Gardening: Inspirational Ideas & Projects for Creating Glorious Pots, Baskets & Bouquets. (Illus.). 2000. 14.95 (*0-7548-0571-9*, Lorenz Bks) Anness Pub.
Donaldson, Stephanie. Country Store: Traditional Food, Country Crafts, Natural Decorations. (Illus.). 160p. 1996. 27.50 (*1-85967-257-4*, Lorenz Bks) Anness Pub.
***Donaldson, Stephanie.** Decorating Pots: 25 Creative Projects to Make. 128p. 1999. 27.95 (*1-85585-663-8*) Collins & Br.
Donaldson, Stephanie. Dried Flower Gifts: Creating Decorative Arrangements. (Illus.). 128p. 1995. 24.95 (*0-7892-0005-8*) Abbeville Pr.
— From the Potting Shed: Inspired Projects for & from the Garden. (Illus.). 160p. 1997. 30.00 (*1-85967-383-X*, Lorenz Bks) Anness Pub.
***Donaldson, Stephanie.** Gardener's Gifts. 160p. 2000. pap. 14.95 (*1-84215-151-7*) Anness Pub.
Donaldson, Stephanie. Hanging Baskets. (Illus.). 96p. 1997. 16.95 (*1-85967-350-3*, Lorenz Bks) Anness Pub.
***Donaldson, Stephanie.** Household Wisdom. 2000. 24.95 (*1-57145-666-X*, Laurel Glen Pub) Advantage Pubs.
Donaldson, Stephanie. Scented Treasures: Aromatic Gifts from the Kitchen & Garden. LC 96-10642. (Illus.). 128p. 1996. 24.95 (*0-88266-930-3*) Storey Bks.
***Donaldson, Stephanie.** The Shaker Garden: Beauty Through Utility. 2000. 29.95 (*1-57076-163-9*, Trafalgar Sq Pub) Trafalgar.
Donaldson, Stephanie. Window Boxes. (Illus.). 96p. 1997. 16.95 (*1-85967-339-2*, Lorenz Bks) Anness Pub.
Donaldson, Stephanie & Berry, Susan. Plants for Small Spaces. LC 97-81350. (Illus.). 144p. 1998. 29.95 (*1-57076-117-5*, Trafalgar Sq Pub) Trafalgar.
Donaldson, Stephanie, jt. auth. see Walton, Sally.
Donaldson, Stephen. Prison Rape Education Project: Manual/Overview for Jail/Prison Administrators & Staff. 2nd rev. ed. Knopp, Fay H. & Bear, Euan, eds. 70p. (Orig.). 1997. pap. 15.00 (*1-884444-38-5*) Safer Soc.
Donaldson, Stephen, ed. Studies in Homosexuality: Anthology of Scholarly Articles, 13 vols., Set. 1992. 990.00 (*0-8153-0545-1*) Garland.
Donaldson, Stephen, jt. ed. see Dynes, Wayne R.
Donaldson, Stephen, jt. ed. see Rubin, Jerome.
Donaldson, Stephen R. Chaos & Order: The Gap into Madness. (Gap Ser.: No. 4). 688p. 1995. mass mkt. 6.99 (*0-553-57253-9*) Bantam.
— The Chronicles of Thomas Covenant, 3 vols. 1985. boxed set 14.85 (*0-345-32962-7*, Del Rey) Ballantine Pub Grp.
— The Chronicles of Thomas Covenant: The Unbeliever. LC 77-73868. 88p. 1995. 22.95 (*0-8050-1272-9*); 22.95 (*0-8050-1271-0*); 22.95 (*0-8050-1270-2*) H Holt & Co.
— A Dark & Hungry God Arises: The Gap into Power. (Gap Ser.: No. 3). 528p. 1993. mass mkt. 6.99 (*0-553-56260-6*) Bantam.
— Daughter of Regals. (Illus.). 1984. 50.00 (*0-937986-63-1*) D M Grant.
— Forbidden Knowledge: The Gap into Vision. (Gap Ser.: No. 2). 480p. 1992. mass mkt. 6.99 (*0-553-29760-0*) Bantam.
— The Illearth War: The Chronicles of Thomas Covenant, the Unbeliever, Vol. 2. (Del Rey Bk.). 528p. 1987. mass mkt. 6.99 (*0-345-34866-4*) Ballantine Pub Grp.
— Lord Foul's Bane: The Chronicles of Thomas Covenant, the Unbeliever, Vol. 1. (Del Rey Bk.). 496p. 1987. mass mkt. 3.99 (*0-345-34865-6*) Ballantine Pub Grp.
— The Mirror of Her Dreams. (The Wizards of Fantasy Promotion). 640p. 1987. mass mkt. 6.99 (*0-345-34697-1*, Del Rey) Ballantine Pub Grp.
— The One Tree. (Second Chronicles of Thomas Covenant Ser.: Bk. 2). 496p. 1987. mass mkt. 6.99 (*0-345-34869-9*, Del Rey) Ballantine Pub Grp.
— The One Tree. 1997. pap. 12.00 (*0-345-41847-6*, Del Rey) Ballantine Pub Grp.
— The Power That Preserves. 528p. 1987. mass mkt. 6.99 (*0-345-34867-2*, Del Rey) Ballantine Pub Grp.
— The Real Story: The Gap into Conflict. (Gap Ser.: No. 1). 272p. 1992. mass mkt. 6.99 (*0-553-29509-8*) Bantam.
***Donaldson, Stephen R.** Reave the Just & Other Tales. 496p. 2000. mass mkt. 6.99 (*0-553-58014-0*) Bantam.
Donaldson, Stephen R. Reave the Just & Other Tales: Stories. LC 98-24075. 400p. 1999. 23.95 (*0-553-11034-9*) Bantam.
— This Day All Gods Die: The Gap into Ruin. (Gap Ser.: No. 5). 704p. 1997. mass mkt. 6.99 (*0-553-57328-4*) Bantam.

D

An Asterisk (*) at the beginning of an entry indicates that the title is appearing for the first time.

— White Gold Wielder. 526p. 1987. mass mkt. 6.99 (*0-345-34870-2*, Del Rey) Ballantine Pub Grp.
— White Gold Wielder. 1997. pap. 12.00 (*0-345-41848-4*) Ballantine Pub Grp.
— The Wounded Land. 512p. 1987. mass mkt. 6.99 (*0-345-34868-0*, Del Rey) Ballantine Pub Grp.
Donaldson, Stuart, jt. auth. see Sella, Gabriel E.
***Donaldson, Susan V.** Summit's Courthouse - Its Past, Pictures & People. LC 00-131537. (Illus.). 108p. 2000. pap. 12.00 (*0-9701017-0-8*) Summit Hist Soc.
Donaldson, Susan V., jt. ed. see Jones, Anne G.
Donaldson, T. H. The Treatment of Intangibles: A Banker's View. LC 92-5286. 164p. 1993. text 69.95 (*0-312-07981-8*) St Martin.
Donaldson, Terence L. Jesus on the Mountain: A Study in Matthean Theology. (JSNT Supplement Ser.: No. 8). 326p. 1987. 85.00 (*0-905774-74-4*, Pub. by Sheffield Acad) CUP Services.
Donaldson, Terence L. Paul & the Gentiles: Remapping the Apostle's Convictional World. LC 97-202. 432p. 1997. pap. 34.00 (*0-8006-2993-0*, 1-2993, Fortress Pr) Augsburg Fortress.
***Donaldson, Terence L. & Canadian Corporation for Studies in Religion Staff.** Religious Rivalries & the Struggle for Success in Caesarea Maritime. LC 99-932480. (Studies in Christianity & Judaism: Vol. 8). 384p. 2000. pap. 29.95 (*0-88920-348-2*) Wilfrid Laurier.
Donaldson, Terry. The Dragon Tarot. (Illus.). 184p. 1996. pap. 9.95 (*0-88079-181-0*, BK64) US Games Syst.
— The Dragon Tarot, Set, incl. deck. (Illus.). 184p. 1996. pap. 26.00 (*0-88079-182-9*, DGS99) US Games Syst.
— The Lord of the Rings Oracle. (Illus.). 128p. 1998. 24.95 (*0-8069-2053-X*) Sterling.
— The Lord of the Rings Tarot. LC 97-36503. 1997. pap. text 14.00 (*1-57281-054-8*, BK169) US Games Syst.
— The Lord of the Rings Tarot Deck & Book Set. (Illus.). 224p. 1997. pap. 30.00 (*1-57281-055-6*, LRS99) US Games Syst.
— The Lord of the Rings Tarot Deck & Card Game. 1997. 15.00 (*1-57281-017-3*) US Games Syst.
Donaldson, Thomas. The Ethics of International Business. (Ruffin Series in Business Ethics). 224p. (C). 1991. reprint ed. pap. text 26.95 (*0-19-507471-8*) OUP.
— A Guide to Antiaging Drugs. LC 94-92224. (Illus.). 154p. 1994. ring bd. 24.00 (*0-9642190-0-X*) Periastron.
— A Laplace Transform Calculus for Partial Differential Operators. LC 74-7370. (Memoirs Ser.: No. 1/143). 166p. 1974. pap. 18.00 (*0-8218-1843-0*, MEMO/1/143) Am Math.
— The Six Nations of New York: Extra Census Bulletin. Indians. (Illus.). (C). reprint ed. pap. text 22.00 (*0-916141-01-2*) NY Hist Soc.
Donaldson, Thomas & Dunfee, Thomas W. Ties That Bind: A Social Contracts Approach to Business Ethics. 320p. 1999. 29.95 (*0-87584-727-7*) Harvard Busn.
Donaldson, Thomas & Dunfee, Thomas W., eds. Ethics in Business & Economics, 2 vols., Set. LC 97-34883. (International Library of Management). (Illus.). 992p. 1997. text 379.95 (*1-85521-585-3*, Pub. by Ashgate Pub) Ashgate Pub Co.
Donaldson, Thomas & Freeman, R. Edward, eds. Business as a Humanity. (Ruffin Series in Business Ethics). 268p. 1994. text 49.95 (*0-19-507156-5*) OUP.
Donaldson, Thomas & Gini, Al R., eds. Case Studies in Business Ethics. 4th ed. LC 95-34941. 336p. 1995. pap. text 36.20 (*0-13-382433-0*) P-H.
Donaldson, Thomas & Werhane, Patricia H., eds. Ethical Issues in Business: A Philosophical Approach. 5th ed. 1995. pap. text 47.00 (*0-13-504440-5*) P-H.
Donaldson, Thomas, jt. auth. see Behera, K. S.
Donaldson, Thomas, ed. see Mohapatra, Ramesh Prasad.
Donaldson, Weber D. French Reflexive Verbs: A Case Grammar Description. (Janua Linguarum, Series Practica: No. 194). 1973. pap. text 64.65 (*90-279-2503-8*) Mouton.
Donaldson, William. From Winchester to This. 1999. 39.95 (*0-7206-1063-X*) P Owen Ltd.
— The Jacobite Song: Political Myth & National Identity. (Illus.). 176p. (Orig.). (C). 1988. text 26.00 (*0-08-036576-0*, Pub. by Aberdeen U Pr); pap. text 16.00 (*0-08-036405-5*, Pub. by Aberdeen U Pr) Macmillan.
Donaldson, William, ed. The Language of the People. (Illus.). 246p. 1989. text 29.90 (*0-08-037730-0*, Pergamon Pr); pap. text 18.00 (*0-08-037731-9*, Pergamon Pr) Elsevier.
— Popular Literature in Victorian Scotland: Language, Fiction & the Press. (Illus.). 176p. 1986. text 27.95 (*0-08-034513-1*, Pub. by Aberdeen U Pr); pap. text 18.00 (*0-08-034515-8*, Pub. by Aberdeen U Pr) Macmillan.
Donaldson, William, ed. see Alexander, William.
Donaldson-Yarmey, Joan. Backroads of Alaska & the Yukon. 192p. 1999. pap. 11.95 (*1-55105-217-2*) Lone Pine.
— Backroads of Northern Alberta. 1992. pap. 9.95 (*0-919433-97-9*) Lone Pine.
***Donaldson-Yarmey, Joan.** Backroads of Northern & Central British Columbia. (Illus.). 224p. 2000. pap. 11.95 (*1-55105-225-3*) Lone Pine.
Donaldson-Yarmey, Joan. Backroads of Southern Alberta. 1992. pap. 9.95 (*1-55105-021-8*) Lone Pine.
— Backroads of Southern Interior British Columbia: Including Banff & Lake Louise, Alberta. (Illus.). 224p. 1996. pap. 11.95 (*1-55105-070-6*) Lone Pine.
— Backroads of Southwestern British Columbia. (Illus.). 168p. 1997. pap. 9.95 (*1-55105-097-8*) Lone Pine.
***Donaldson-Yarmey, Joan.** Backroads of the Yukon & Alaska. 192p. 1999. pap. 11.95 (*1-55105-213-X*) Lone Pine.
Donaldson-Yarmey, Joan. Backroads of Vancouver Island. (Illus.). 224p. 1998. pap. 11.95 (*1-55105-099-4*) Lone Pine.
Donalson, Malcolm D. The Domestic Cat in Roman Civilization. LC 98-53321. (Studies in Classics Ser.: Vol. 9). 15p. 1999. text 79.95 (*0-7734-8160-5*) E Mellen.
— A Translation of Jerome's Chronicon with Historical Commentary. LC 95-35398. 184p. (C). 1996. 79.95 (*0-7734-2258-7*) E Mellen.
Donaly, E. Brice. The Great Comanche Raid: Boldest Indian Attack of the Texas Republic. Roberts, Melissa, ed. (Illus.). 136p. 1988. 14.95 (*0-89015-594-1*) Sunbelt Media.
Donan, Hastings, jt. ed. see Ahmed, Akbar S.
***Donant, Alan E.** Colonel Arthur L. Conger. (Illus.). 32p. 1999. pap. 5.00 (*1-55700-139-1*) Theos U Pr.
***Donat, Alexander.** The Holocaust Kingdom. LC 99-22131. vi, 362p. (Orig.). 1998. reprint ed. pap. 15.95 (*0-89604-160-3*, Holocaust Library) US Holocaust.
Donat, James & Livernois, Jay, eds. Gateways to Identity Vol. 66: Eranos Yearbook, 1997. 160p. 1998. pap. 15.00 (*1-882670-12-4*, Pub. by Spring Jrnl) Continuum.
Donat, James, jt. ed. see Livernois, Jay.
Donat, James G., ed. see Kawai, Jayaa.
Donat, Pat, ed. History of Fayetteville City Hospital, 1912-1991. LC 99-72066. (Illus.). 200p. 1999. 25.00 (*0-938041-41-X*) Arc Pr AR.
Donat, Patricia. Chalk Dust Red Tape & Miracles: Teaching with Heart, Humor & Hope. unabridged ed. 1999. pap. write for info. (*0-9664351-0-9*) Tri-Star NY.
Donat, Peter C. & Gould, Barney. Sherlock Holmes & the Shakespeare Solution. 90p. 1997. 24.00 (*1-55246-016-9*); pap. 10.00 (*1-55246-017-7*) Battered Silicon.
Donatelle. Access to Health. 5th ed. (C). 1997. write for info. (*0-205-27940-6*, Macmillan Coll) P-H.
— Issues in Health: Readings from the Washington Post, Vol. 2. 4th ed. (C). 1995. pap. write for info. (*0-205-19926-7*, H9926-0) Allyn.
Donatelle & Davis. Health. 3rd ed. LC 98-22929. 444p. 1998. pap. text 48.00 (*0-205-28680-1*) Allyn.
— Self-Assessment Workbook with Review & Practice Tests. 3rd ed. 1998. pap. text, wbk. ed. write for info. (*0-205-29546-0*) Allyn.
— Take Charge Health Access. 6th ed. 1999. pap. text 7.50 (*0-205-30506-7*) Allyn.
— Think about Health Access. 6th ed. 1999. pap. text 12.75 (*0-205-30505-9*) Allyn.
— Thinking About Health. 3rd ed. 192p. 1998. pap. text, student ed. 20.00 (*0-205-29421-9*) Allyn.
Donatelle, Rebecca. Wellness. (C). 1995. pap. text 27.95 (*0-8053-0370-7*) Benjamin-Cummings.
— Wellness: Choices for Health & Fitness. (Health Sciences Ser.). 1995. mass mkt. 28.00 (*0-534-33951-4*) Brooks-Cole.
— Wellness: Choices for Health & Fitness. 2nd ed. LC 98-26394. (Health Sciences Ser.). 1998. pap. 40.95 (*0-534-34836-X*) Brooks-Cole.
***Donatelle, Rebecca J.** Health: The Basics. 2nd ed. 474p. 2000. pap. (*0-205-31764-2*) Allyn.
Donatelle, Rebecca J. & Davis, Lorraine G. Access to Health. 6th ed. LC 99-35425. 670p. 1999. pap. text 61.00 incl. audio compact disk (*0-205-30502-4*) P-H.
Donatelli, Betty. Clinical Cases Ortho/Sports Physical Medicine. 2000. pap. text Price not set. (*0-443-07553-0*) Church.
Donatelli, Carlo. The Gondola. 1994. 39.50 (*88-7743-137-7*, Pub. by Arsenale Editrice) Antique Collect.
Donatelli, Joseph M. Death & Life. LC 88-62571. (Speculum Anniversary Monographs: No. 15). (Illus.). xii, 136p. 1989. pap. 12.00 (*0-915651-02-5*) Medieval Acad.
— Death & Liffe. LC 88-62571. (Speculum Anniversary Monographs: No. 15). (Illus.). xii, 136p. 1989. 20.00 (*0-915651-01-7*) Medieval Acad.
Donatelli, Nancy S., et al. Organizational Restructuring in the Emergency Department. Greenberg, Linda, ed. 102p. 1995. pap. text 35.00 (*0-935890-53-X*) Emerg Nurses IL.
Donatelli, Robert. Biomechanics of the Foot & Ankle. 2nd ed. LC 95-24075. (Contemporary Perspectives in Rehabilitation Ser.). (Illus.). 391p. (C). 1995. 47.00 (*0-8036-0031-3*) Davis Co.
— Orthopaedic Physical Therapy. 3rd ed. (C). 1999. text. write for info. (*0-443-07993-5*) Church.
— Physical Therapy of the Shoulder. 3rd ed. LC 96-29475. (Clinics in Physical Therapy Ser.). 1996. pap. text 69.00 (*0-443-07591-3*) Church.
Donatelli, Robert, ed. Physical Therapy of the Shoulder. LC 86-20722. (Clinics in Physical Therapy Ser.: No. 11). (Illus.). 333p. reprint ed. pap. 103.30 (*0-8357-3068-9*, 203932400012) Bks Demand.
Donatelli, Robert & Wooden, Michael J., eds. Orthopaedic Physical Therapy. LC 88-25675. (Illus.). 613p. reprint ed. pap. 190.10 (*0-7837-6259-3*, 204597100010) Bks Demand.
Donatelli, Robert A. & Wooden, Michael J., eds. Orthopaedic Physical Therapy. 2nd ed. (Illus.). 864p. 1993. text 95.00 (*0-443-08835-7*) Church.
***Donatelli, S. & Kleijn, J.** Application & Theory of Petri Nets, 1999: Proceedings of the 20th International Conference, ICATPN'99, Williamsburg, Virginia, U. S. A., June 21-25, 1999. Goos, G. et al, eds. (Lecture Notes in Computer Science Ser.: Vol. 1639). viii, 425p. 1999. pap. 69.00 (*3-540-66132-8*) Spr-Verlag.
Donath, A. & Righetti, A., eds. Cardiovascular Nuclear Medicine. (Progress in Nuclear Medicine Ser.: Vol. 6). (Illus.). viii, 228p. 1980. 128.75 (*3-8055-0618-X*) S Karger.
Donath, A., jt. ed. see Juge, O.
Donath, Bob, et al. Managing Sales Leads. Knudsen, Anne, ed. LC 94-16180. (Illus.). 240p. 1995. 37.95 (*0-8442-3599-7*, NTC Business Bks) NTC Contemp Pub Co.
Donath, Emma B. Approximate Positions of Asteroids, Eighteen Fifty One to Two Thousand Fifty. LC 82-72518. 64p. 1981. 9.00 (*0-86690-037-3*, D2624-044) Am Fed Astrologers.
— Asteroids in Midpoints. LC 83-71149. 160p. 1982. 15.00 (*0-86690-242-2*, 2291-01) Am Fed Astrologers.
— Asteroids in Synastry. 96p. 1977. 12.00 (*0-86690-082-9*, D1080-024) Am Fed Astrologers.
— Asteroids in the Birthchart. 104p. 1979. 14.00 (*0-86690-081-0*, D1079-024) Am Fed Astrologers.
— Asteroids in the U. S. A. 144p. 1979. 13.00 (*0-86690-083-7*, D1081-024) Am Fed Astrologers.
— Houses: Which & When. 1989. pap. 16.00 (*0-86690-377-1*, 3033-014) Am Fed Astrologers.
— Patterns of Professions. LC 84-70084. 112p. 1984. 13.00 (*0-86690-265-1*, P2299-014) Am Fed Astrologers.
— Relocation. LC 88-70455. 284p. 1988. write for info. (*0-86690-335-6*, D2800-014) Am Fed Astrologers.
Donath, Fred A., et al, eds. Annual Review of Earth & Planetary Sciences, Vol. 1. LC 72-82137. (Illus.). 1973. text 55.00 (*0-8243-2001-8*) Annual Reviews.
— Annual Review of Earth & Planetary Sciences, Vol. 2. LC 72-82137. (Illus.). 1974. text 55.00 (*0-8243-2002-6*) Annual Reviews.
— Annual Review of Earth & Planetary Sciences, Vol. 3. LC 72-82137. (Illus.). 1975. text 55.00 (*0-8243-2003-4*) Annual Reviews.
— Annual Review of Earth & Planetary Sciences, Vol. 4. LC 72-82137. (Illus.). 1976. text 55.00 (*0-8243-2004-2*) Annual Reviews.
— Annual Review of Earth & Planetary Sciences, Vol. 5. LC 72-82137. (Illus.). 1977. text 55.00 (*0-8243-2005-0*) Annual Reviews.
— Annual Review of Earth & Planetary Sciences, Vol. 6. LC 72-82137. (Illus.). 1978. text 55.00 (*0-8243-2006-9*) Annual Reviews.
— Annual Review of Earth & Planetary Sciences, Vol. 8. LC 72-82137. (Illus.). 1980. text 55.00 (*0-8243-2008-5*) Annual Reviews.
Donath, Gyorgy. Utolso Szo Jogan: Mondott Beszede. LC 88-61575. (HUN., Illus.). 119p. 1998. pap. 12.00 (*963-7871-07-1*) Occidental.
Donath, M., et al, eds. Magnetism & Electronic Correlations in Local-Moment Systems: Rare-Earth Elements & Compounds: Proceedings of the Workshop Berlin, Germany. 400p. 1998. 84.00 (*981-02-3538-0*) World Scientific Pub.
Donath, M., jt. auth. see Bertel, E.
Donathan, David F. How Does Your Choir Grow? (Music Resources Ser.). 64p. (Orig.). 1995. pap. 9.95 (*0-687-01075-6*) Abingdon.
Donathan, Jean A. Single Mother. (Special Edition Ser.). 1993. per. 3.50 (*0-373-09858-8*, 5-09858-7) Silhouette.
Donati, Alyssa. Marzipan Pigeon. 1994. 21.00 (*0-671-86889-6*) S&S Trade.
Donati, Maria B., ed. Coagulation & Cancer. (Journal: Haemostasis: Vol. 18, No. 1, 1988). (Illus.). 72p. 1988. pap. 30.50 (*3-8055-4768-4*) S Karger.
— Vitamin K-Dependent Biological Processes. (Journal: Haemostasis: Vol. 16, No. 2, 1986). (Illus.). 132p. 1986. pap. 72.25 (*3-8055-4270-4*) S Karger.
Donati, Maria B., et al, eds. Malignancy & the Hemostatic System. LC 80-39949. (Monographs of the Mario Negri Institute for Pharmacological Research). 148p. 1981. reprint ed. pap. 45.90 (*0-608-00425-1*, 206114000007) Bks Demand.
Donati, Maria B., jt. ed. see Coccheri, S.
Donati, P. Manual de Sociologia de la Salud. (SPA.). 419p. 1994. pap. 29.75 (*84-7978-143-2*, Pub. by Ediciones Diaz) IBD Ltd.
Donati, Paolo, jt. auth. see Wilkinson, Philip.
Donati, Robert M., jt. ed. see Edwards, Janine C.
***Donati, Sara.** Dawn on a Distant Shore. LC 99-40438. 468p. 2000. 24.95 (*0-553-10748-8*) Bantam.
Donati, Sara. Into the Wilderness. LC 97-39051. 704p. 1998. 22.95 (*0-553-10736-4*) Bantam.
— Into the Wilderness. 912p. 1999. mass mkt. 6.50 (*0-553-57852-9*) Bantam.
***Donati, William.** Ida Lupino: A Biography. (Illus.). 344p. 2000. pap. 18.00 (*0-8131-0982-5*) U Pr of Ky.
Donati, William, jt. auth. see Wiles, Buster.
Donati, William J. Ida Lupino: A Biography. LC 95-35549. (Illus.). 344p. 1996. 27.50 (*0-8131-1895-6*) U Pr of Ky.
Donato, Clorinda, jt. ed. see Maniquis, Robert M.
Donato, Debora D. & Suhre, Terry. Photography Illinois. (Illus.). 26p. 1989. pap. 5.00 (*0-89792-122-4*) Ill St Museum.
Donato, Diane. Attitude by Design. (Illus.). 40p. 1996. 9.95 (*0-9652816-0-4*) Clothes Encounters.
— Integrating Technology into the Science Curriculum. 144p. (J). (gr. 3-5). 1997. pap. 14.95 (*1-57690-427-X*) Tchr Create Mat.
Donato, Eugenio, jt. ed. see Macksey, Richard.
Donato, Giuseppe & Seefried, Monique. The Fragrant Past: Perfumes of Cleopatra & Julius Caesar. (Illus.). 64p. 1995. pap. text 18.95 (*0-9638169-3-4*) M C Carlos Mus.
Donato, Gopi G. Lord Uranus. Morningland Publications, Inc. Staff, ed. (Astrology Ser.). (Illus.). 341p. (Orig.). 1981. spiral bd. 6.95 (*0-935146-52-0*) Morningland.
Donato, Gopi G., jt. auth. see Donato, Sri.
Donato, Gopi G., jt. auth. see Morningland Publications, Inc. Staff.
Donato, L. & Britton, K., eds. Immunoscintigraphy, Vol. 1. (Monographs in Nuclear Medicine). xviii, 378p. 1985. text 161.00 (*2-88124-076-3*) Gordon & Breach.
Donato, P., et al, eds. Symplectic Geometry & Mathematical Physics: Actes du Colloque en l'Honneur de Jean-Marie Souriau. (Progress in Mathematics Ser.: Vol. 99). xiii, 478p. 1991. 96.50 (*0-8176-3581-5*) Birkhauser.
Donato, Patrizia, jt. auth. see Cioranescu, Diona.
Donato, Riccardo Di, see Momigliano, Arnaldo D.
Donato, Ruben. The Other Struggle for Equal Schools: Mexican-Americans During the Civil Rights. LC 97-13021. (SUNY Series, the Social Context of Education). 210p. (C). 1997. text 59.50 (*0-7914-3519-9*); pap. text 19.95 (*0-7914-3520-2*) State U NY Pr.
Donato, Sri. The Day of Brahma. Morningland Publications, Inc. Staff, ed. (Illus.). 377p. 1981. pap. 10.00 (*0-935146-20-2*) Morningland.
— The Unicorn. Morningland Publications, Inc. Staff, ed. (Illus.). 207p. (Orig.). 1981. pap. 10.00 (*0-935146-16-4*) Morningland.
Donato, Sri & Donato, Gopi G. Oneness, Vol. III. Morningland Publications, Inc. Staff, ed. 167p. 1981. pap., spiral bd. 7.95 (*0-935146-58-X*) Morningland.
Donato, Vince & Poole, Gary. How to Laugh & Be Well. (Illus.). 105p. (Orig.). 1982. pap. 5.95 (*0-942106-00-8*) Feelgreat.
Donauer, Friedrich. Swords Against Carthage. Cooper, F. T., tr. LC 61-12878. (Illus.). (J). (gr. 7-11). 1932. 22.00 (*0-8196-0112-8*) Biblo.
Donavan, Laura, tr. see Cheek, Roland.
Donavan, Stephen K. & Paul, Christopher R. The Adequacy of the Fossil Record. LC 98-10110. 322p. 1998. 150.00 (*0-471-96988-5*) Wiley.
Donavich, Mike, ed. see Singh, Swayam P.
Donawa, Maria, ed. International Medical Device Registration. 488p. 1996. ring bd. 249.00 (*0-935184-85-6*) Interpharm.
Donaway, Mark & Shafer, Sue. Cucina Bella Cookbook. (Illus.). 160p. 1996. 45.00 (*0-9652960-0-8*) Cucina Bella.
Donawerth, Jane. Frankenstein's Daughters: Women Writing Science Fiction. LC 96-21139. 240p. 1996. 39.95 (*0-8156-2686-X*, DOWW); pap. 19.95 (*0-8156-0395-9*, DOWWP) Syracuse U Pr.
— Shakespeare & the Sixteenth Century Study of Language. LC 82-21740. 296p. 1984. text 29.95 (*0-252-01038-8*) U of Ill Pr.
Donawerth, Jane L. & Kolmerten, Carol A., eds. Utopian & Science Fiction by Women: Worlds of Difference. LC 93-33840. (Utopianism & Communitarianism Ser.). 296p. 1994. text 39.95 (*0-8156-2619-3*); pap. text 19.95 (*0-8156-2620-7*) Syracuse U Pr.
Donbaz, Veysel & Foster, Benjamin R. Sargonic Texts from Telloh in the Istanbul Archaeological Museums. (Occasional Publications of the Babylonian Fund: No. 5). (Illus.). xi, 17p. 1982. 20.00 (*0-934718-44-X*) U Museum Pubns.
Donbaz, Veysel & Grayson, A. Kirk. Royal Inscriptions on Clay Cones from Ashur Now in Istanbul. 144p. 1984. text 50.00 (*0-8020-5650-4*) U of Toronto Pr.
Donbaz, Veysel & Stolper, Matthew W. Istanbul Murasu Texts. LC 97-198802. xiv, 215 p. 1997. 32.00 (*90-6258-080-7*, Pub. by Netherlands Inst) Eisenbrauns.
Donbrow, M. Microcapsules & Nanoparticles in Medicine & Pharmacy. 360p. 1991. lib. bdg. 249.00 (*0-8493-6986-X*, RS201) CRC Pr.
Doncaster, William T., Jr. Legends from the Frosty Sons of Thunder. LC 98-30765. 156p. 1999. pap. 13.95 (*1-883911-25-7*) Brandylane.
Doncaster, Hugh L. The Quaker Message: A Personal Affirmation. LC 79-182982. (C). 1972. pap. 4.00 (*0-87574-181-9*) Pendle Hill.
Doncaster, Islay. Traditional China. Killingray, Margaret & O'Connor, Edmund, eds. (World History Program Ser.). (Illus.). (YA). (gr. 6-11). 1980. reprint ed. pap. text 5.90 (*0-89908-007-3*) Greenhaven.
Doncaster, Patrick, jt. auth. see Best, Pete.
Donceel, Joseph, ed. see Rousselot, Pierre.
Donceel, Joseph, tr. see Rahner, Karl.
Doncel, M. G., et al. Symmetries in Physics (1600-1980) Proceedings. 696p. 1988. text 75.00 (*84-7488-148-X*) World Scientific Pub.
Doncell, Joseph, tr. see Rahner, Karl.
Donchez, Bob, jt. auth. see Davidson, Todd.
Donchin, Anne & Purdy, Laura M., eds. Embodying Bioethics: Recent Feminist Advances. LC 98-28146. (New Feminist Perspectives Ser.). 288p. 1999. pap. 23.95 (*0-8476-8925-5*); text 63.00 (*0-8476-8924-7*) Rowman.
Donchin, E., ed. Cognitive Psychophysiology: Event-Related Potentials & the Study of Cognition, the Carmel Conferences, Vol. 1. (Illus.). 448p. (C). 1984. text 89.95 (*0-89859-150-3*) L Erlbaum Assocs.
D'Oncieu, Manek, jt. auth. see Mouravieff, Boris.
Donckels, Rik & Miettinen, Asko. Entrepreneurship & SME Research: On Its Way to the Next Millennium. LC 97-76953. (Illus.). 266p. 1998. text 69.95 (*1-84014-199-9*, Pub. by Ashgate Pub) Ashgate Pub Co.
Doncker, R. W. De, see De Doncker, R. W.
D'Oncley, Manek, tr. see Mouravieff, Boris.
Dondaine, Antoine. Les Heresies et L'Inquistion, XIIe - XIIe Siecles. Dossat, Yves, ed. (Collected Studies: No. CS314). 352p. 1990. lib. bdg. 124.95 (*0-86078-262-X*, Pub. by Variorum) Ashgate Pub Co.
Donde, Antoine. The Life, Death & Miracles of St. Francois de Paule. (Printed Sources of Western Art Ser.). (FRE., Illus.). 258p. 1981. reprint ed. boxed set 50.00 (*0-915346-64-8*) A Wofsy Fine Arts.
Dondelinger, E., comment. Papyrus Ani. fac. ed. (Codices Selecti D Ser.: Vol. LXII). (GER., Illus.). 84p. 1978. 617.00 (*3-201-01048-0*, Pub. by Akademische Druck-und) Balogh.

D

An Asterisk (*) at the beginning of an entry indicates that the title is appearing for the first time.

Dondelinger, R., et al, eds. Interventional Radiology. (Illus.). 800p. 1989. text 185.00 (*0-86577-286-X*) Thieme Med Pubs.
Dondelinger, Robert, et al, eds. Peripheral Musculoskeletal Ultrasound Atlas. LC 95-39513. (Illus.). 224p. 1996. text 115.00 (*0-86577-592-3*) Thieme Med Pubs.
***Donden, Yeshe.** Healing from the Source: The Science & Lore of Tibetan Medicine. Wallace, B. Alan, tr. (Illus.). 205p. 2000. pap. 16.95 (*1-55939-148-0*) Snow Lion Pubns.
Donden, Yeshi. Health Through Balance: An Introduction to Tibetan Medicine. Hopkins, Jeffrey, ed. Rabgay, Lobsang & Wallace, Alan, trs. LC 86-1879. (TIB., Illus.). 252p. (C). 1986. pap. 14.95 (*0-937938-25-4*) Snow Lion Pubns.
Donderi, Don. Pak: Textbook of Psychology. 112p. (C). 1995. pap., per. write for info. (*0-7872-1102-8*) Kendall-Hunt.
— Pak: Textbook of Psychology. 4th ed. LC 96-132348. 464p. (C). 1995. pap., per. write for info. (*0-7872-1101-X*) Kendall-Hunt.
Dondero, Don. Dateline: Reno. Stoess, Jean, ed. (Illus.). 128p. pap. 12.95 (*0-9631542-0-6*) Dondero-Stoess.
Dondero, John P. & Frary, Thomas D. New Pressures, New Responses in Religious Life. LC 76-26585. 1979. pap. 5.95 (*0-8189-0332-5*) Alba.
Donders, F. C. Accommodation & Refraction of the Eye. LC 78-27045. (Classics in Ophthalmology Ser.). 656p. 1979. reprint ed. lib. bdg. 49.50 (*0-88275-839-X*) Krieger.
Donders, Joseph G. Beyond Jesus: Reflections on the Gospels for the B-Cycle. LC 84-5088. 304p. reprint ed. pap. 94.30 (*0-8357-2672-X*, 204020800015) Bks Demand.
— Charged with the Spirit: Mission Is for Everyone? LC 93-1613. 133p. (Orig.). 1993. pap. 13.00 (*0-88344-915-3*) Orbis Bks.
— Christ, the Divine Network: Reflections on the Gospels for the A-Cycle. LC 86-718. 224p. reprint ed. pap. 69.50 (*0-8357-4053-6*, 203486900091) Bks Demand.
— Jesus, Hope Drawing Near: Reflections on the Gospel for the C-Cycle. LC 85-5125. 272p. (Orig.). reprint ed. pap. 84.40 (*0-8357-4062-5*, 203675200005) Bks Demand.
— Jesus the Stranger. rev. ed. LC 98-54140. x, 165 p. 1999. pap. 13.00 (*1-57075-254-0*) Orbis Bks.
— Jesus, the Stranger: Reflections on the Gospels. LC 77-21783. 303p. reprint ed. pap. 94.00 (*0-7837-5514-7*, 204528400005) Bks Demand.
— Non-Bourgeois Theology: An African Experience of Jesus. LC 84-16677. 224p. (Orig.). 1985. pap. 15.00 (*0-88344-352-X*) Orbis Bks.
— The Peace of Jesus: Reflections on the Gospel for the A-Cycle. LC 83-4240. 319p. (Orig.). reprint ed. pap. 98.90 (*0-8357-4069-2*, 203675900005) Bks Demand.
— Risen Life: Healing a Broken World. LC 90-47168. 127p. 1990. reprint ed. pap. 39.40 (*0-7837-9848-2*, 206057700005) Bks Demand.
— With Hearts on Fire: Reflections on the Weekday Readings of the Liturgical Year. LC 98-61777. 340p. 1999. pap. 19.95 (*0-89622-974-2*) Twenty-Third.
Donders, Joseph G., ed. see John Paul, II, pseud.
Donders, Josephs G. Empowering Hope. LC 85-51480. 112p. (Orig.). 1985. pap. 5.95 (*0-89622-281-0*) Twenty-Third.
Dondi, Beda, jt. auth. see Ray, Mary F.
Dondi, Francesco & Guiochon, Georges, eds. Theoretical Advancement in Chromatography & Related Separation Techniques. LC 92-32221. 1992. text 369.00 (*0-7923-1991-5*) Kluwer Academic.
Dondiego, Barbara. Start with Art. Iannetti, Marie, ed. LC 98-60797. (Start With . . . Ser.). (Illus.). 160p. (J). (gr. k up). 1998. pap. 3.95 (*1-57029-171-3*, W14601) Totline Pubns.
— Start with Science. Iannetti, Marie, ed. LC 98-60798. (Start With . . . Ser.). (Illus.). 160p. (J). (gr. k up). 1998. pap. 3.95 (*1-57029-172-1*, W14602) Totline Pubns.
Dondiego, Barbara, jt. auth. see Vansant, Rhonda.
Dondiego, Barbara L. After-School Crafts. (Anytime Crafts Bk.). (Illus.). 144p. (J). 1992. 22.95 (*0-8306-3868-7*, 4138); pap. 12.95 (*0-8306-3869-5*, 4138) McGraw-Hill Prof.
— After School Crafts. (Illus.). 144p. 1993. pap. 12.95 (*0-07-017578-0*) McGraw.
— Crafts for Kids: A Month-by-Month Idea Book. LC 84-16439. (Illus.). 304p. (Orig.). 1984. 17.95 (*0-8306-0784-6*); pap. 11.95 (*0-8306-1784-1*, 1784) McGraw-Hill Prof.
— Crafts for Kids: A Month-by-Month Idea Book. 2nd ed. (Illus.). 224p. (Orig.). 1990. pap. 14.95 (*0-8306-3573-4*) McGraw-Hill Prof.
— Crafts for Kids: A Month by Month Idea Book. 2nd ed. (Illus.). 240p. (J). (gr. 6-9). 1990. pap. 16.95 (*0-07-155890-X*) McGraw.
— Year-Round Crafts for Kids. (Illus.). 256p. (J). (ps-3). 1987. pap. 16.95 (*0-07-155774-1*) McGraw.
— Year-Round Crafts for Kids. (Illus.). 256p. 1987. 19.95 (*0-8306-0904-0*); pap. 13.95 (*0-8306-2904-1*) McGraw-Hill Prof.
Dondiego, Barbara L., jt. auth. see Vansant, Rhonda.
Dondis, Donis A. A Primer of Visual Literacy. (Illus.). 206p. 1973. pap. text 13.50 (*0-262-54029-0*) MIT Pr.
Dondlinger, Peter T. The Book of Wheat: An Economic History & Practical Manual of the Wheat Industry. LC 72-89073. (Rural America Ser.). 1973. reprint ed. 32.00 (*0-8420-1481-0*) Scholarly Res Inc.
Dondlinger, Sue-Ann K. Every One a Winner: Blue Ribbon Recipes. 96p. (Orig.). 1995. pap. 12.95 (*0-9638825-1-1*) SUESTA.
Dondoni, Alessandro, ed. Advances in the Use of Synthons in Organic Chemistry, Vol. 1. 227p. 1993. 109.50 (*1-55938-183-3*) Jai Pr.
— Advances in the Use of Synthons in Organic Chemistry, Vol. 2. 166p. 1995. 109.50 (*1-55938-833-1*) Jai Pr.
— Advances in the Use of Synthons in Organic Chemistry, Vol. 3. Date not set. 109.50 (*0-7623-0071-X*) Jai Pr.
Dondoux-Liberge, S., et al. Wirtschaft im Ohr: Lehrerheft. (GER.). 48p. (C). 1990. pap. text 14.50 (*3-12-675201-2*, Pub. by Klett Edition); pap. text 14.50 (*3-12-675204-7*, Pub. by Klett Edition) Intl Bk Import.
— Wirtschaft im Ohr Level 1: Uebungsbuch. (GER.). 48p. (C). 1990. pap. text 14.50 (*3-12-675200-4*, Pub. by Klett Edition); audio 45.00 (*3-12-675202-0*, Pub. by Klett Edition) Intl Bk Import.
— Wirtschaft im Ohr Level 2: Uebungsbuch. (GER.). 48p. (C). 1990. pap. text 14.50 (*3-12-675203-9*, Pub. by Klett Edition); audio 27.00 (*3-12-675205-5*, Pub. by Klett Edition) Intl Bk Import.
Done, John N., et al. Applications of High-Speed Liquid Chromatography. LC 74-16148. 246p. reprint ed. pap. 76.30 (*0-8357-5667-X*, 203039600069) Bks Demand.
Done, Ken. Ken Done - Paintings & Drawings, 1975-1987. (Illus.). 256p. 1996. pap. text 27.00 (*976-8097-47-7*) Gordon & Breach.
Done, Malcolm. The AC/DC Story: The Kerrang! Files. (Illus.). 256p. 1995. pap. 16.95 (*0-86369-908-1*, Pub. by Virgin Bks) London Brdge.
***Done, S. T., et al, eds.** The Proceedings of the 15th International Pig Veterinary Society Congress, 4 vols. & CD, Set. 1999. pap. 400.00 incl. cd-rom (*1-897676-84-0*, Pub. by Nottingham Univ Pr) St Mut.
Done, William J., jt. ed. see Kirlin, R. Lynn.
Donea, J. & Jones, P. M., eds. Experimental & Numerical Methods in Earthquake Engineering. 392p. (C). 1991. text 185.50 (*0-7923-1434-4*) Kluwer Academic.
Donecker, J. & Rechenberg, I., eds. Defect Recognition & Image Processing in Semiconductors: Proceedings of the Seventh Conference on Defect Recognition & Image Processing, Berlin, September 1997. (Conference Ser.: No. 160). 486p. 1998. 270.00 (*0-7503-0500-2*) IOP Pub.
Donegan, Francis. Paint Your Home: Skills, Techniques, & Tricks of the Trade for Professional Looking Interior Painting. LC 96-46950. 1997. 18.95 (*0-89577-838-6*, Pub. by RD Assn) Penguin Putnam.
Donegan, Greg. Atlantis. 1999. mass mkt. 6.99 (*0-425-16936-7*) Berkley Pub.
***Donegan, Greg.** Atlantis: Bermuda Triangle. Vol. 2. 304p. 2000. mass mkt. 6.99 (*0-425-17429-8*) Berkley Pub.
Donegan, Jane B. Hydropathic Highway to Health: Women & Water-Cure in Antebellum America. 17. LC 85-10083. (Contributions in Medical Studies: No. 17). (Illus.). 249p. 1986. 55.00 (*0-313-23816-2*, DWH/, Greenwood Pr) Greenwood.
— Women & Men Midwives: Medicine, Morality, & Misogyny in Early America. 2. LC 77-87968. (Contributions in Medical History Ser.: No. 2). (Illus.). 316p. 1978. 39.95 (*0-8371-9868-2*, DMA/, Greenwood Pr) Greenwood.
Donegan, Lawrence. Maybe It Should Have Been a Three Iron: My Years As Caddy for the World's 438th Best Golfer. LC 98-6152. 256p. 1998. text 21.95 (*0-312-18584-7*) St Martin.
— Maybe It Should Have Been a Three Iron: My Years As Caddy for the World's 438th Best Golfer. 2nd ed. 1999. pap. 12.95 (*0-312-20422-1*) St Martin.
***Donegan, Lawrence.** No News at Throat Lake. LC 99-89574. 250p. 2000. 23.95 (*0-671-78540-0*, PB Hardcover) PB.
Donegan, Nancy. The Forked Rivers. LC 89-35793. 72p. 1989. pap. 9.95 (*0-914086-89-8*) Alice James Bks.
Donegan, Patricia. Without Warning. 96p. 1990. per. 8.00 (*0-938077-32-5*) Parallax Pr.
Donegan, Patricia & Ishibashi, Yoshie, trs. from JPN. Chiyo-ni: Woman Haiku Master. (Illus.). 184p. 1998. pap. 14.95 (*0-8048-2053-8*) Tuttle Pubng.
Donegan, Thomas & Beckley, Catherine, eds. CTFA Labeling Manual: A Guide to Labeling & Advertising Cosmetics & OTC Drugs. 6th rev. ed. LC 96-86141. (Illus.). 250p. 1997. pap. 250.00 (*1-882621-18-2*, 8060) Cosmetic T&FA.
Donegan, William L. & Spratt, John S. Cancer of the Breast. 4th ed. LC 94-12235. (Illus.). 720p. 1995. text 173.00 (*0-7216-4694-8*, W B Saunders Co) Harcrt Hlth Sci Grp.
Donehoo, Beverly, tr. see Gellert, S., et al.
Donehoo, George. A History of the Indian Villages & Place Names of Pennsylvania: Geo. Donahoo. LC 77-80384. 312p. 1998. pap. 19.95 (*1-889037-11-7*, 12) Wennawoods.
Donehower, Kim, ed. see Lunsford, Andrea A.
Donehower, Kim, ed. see McLeod, Susan.
Donehower, Kim, ed. see Smitherman, Geneva.
Donelan, Charles. Romanticism & Male Fantasy. LC 99-15892. 195p. 1999. text 59.95 (*0-312-22491-5*) St Martin.
Donelan, M. D. & Grieve, M. J. International Disputes: Case Histories, 1945-70. 1973. 40.00 (*0-900362-39-1*) St Mut.
Donelan, M. D., jt. auth. see Northedge, F. S.
Donelan, Michael. Elements of International Political Theory. 224p. (C). 1993. reprint ed. pap. 19.95 (*0-19-827884-5*) OUP.
Donell, S. T. & Lettin, A. W. Fundamental Anatomy for Operative Orthopaedic Surgery, Vol. 2. (Fundamental Anatomy Ser.). (Illus.). ix, 90p. 1991. pap. 30.00 (*0-387-19669-2*) Spr-Verlag.
Donelley, C. A. Statistical Aspects of BSE & VCJD: Models for an Epidemic. LC 99-35812. 256p. 1999. boxed set 69.95 (*0-8493-0386-9*, Chap & Hall CRC) CRC Pr.
***Donelly, G. L.** A Quest for Wings. (Illus.). 160p. 2000. 27.99 (*0-7524-2014-3*, Pub. by Tempus Pubng) Arcadia Publng.
Donelly, James H., et al. Fundamentals of Management. 7th ed. (C). 1990. 13.95 (*0-317-99811-0*, Irwn McGrw-H) McGrw-H Hghr Educ.
Donelly, Patrick & Teske, Ronald J., eds. Robert Bellarmine: Spiritual Writings. (Classics of Western Spirituality Ser.). 1989. 19.95 (*0-8091-0389-3*); pap. 14.95 (*0-8091-2875-6*) Paulist Pr.
***Donelson, Dave.** Creative Selling: Unleash Your Sales Potential. 2000. pap. 17.95 (*1-891984-15-2*, Pub. by Entrepreneur) Natl Bk Netwk.
Donelson, Frances E. Women's Experiences: A Psychological Perspective. LC 97-45772. xxvi, 747p. 1998. pap. 42.95 (*0-7674-0043-7*, 0043-7) Mayfield Pub.
***Donelson, Frances E. & Galupo, M. Paz.** Women's Experience Instructor's Resource Guide. v, 99p. (C). 1998. pap. text. write for info. (*0-7674-0050-X*, 0050-X) Mayfield Pub.
Donelson, Ken & Sebesta, Sam L., eds. Inspiring Literacy: Literature for Children & Young Adults. LC 92-42713. 220p. 1993. 24.95 (*1-56000-668-4*) Transaction Pubs.
Donelson, Kenneth L., jt. auth. see Nilsen, Aleen P.
Donelson, Kenneth L., jt. auth. see Nilsen, Alleen P.
Donelson, Lewis R. Colossians, Ephesians, First & Second Timothy, & Titus. LC 95-46676. (Westminster Bible Companion Ser.). 192p. 1996. pap. 16.00 (*0-664-25264-8*) Westminster John Knox.
***Donelson, Lewis R.** From Hebrews to Revelation: A Theological Introduction. 175p. 2000. pap. 19.95 (*0-664-22236-6*) Westminster John Knox.
Donelson, Lewis R. Pseudepigraphy & Ethical Arguments in the Pastoral Epistles. 260p. 1986. lib. bdg. 82.50 (*3-16-145009-4*, Pub. by JCB Mohr) Coronet Bks.
Donelson, Linda. Out of Isak Dinesen in Africa: Karen Blixen's Untold Story. 2nd rev. ed. LC 98-72165. (Illus.). 440p. 1998. pap. 19.95 (*0-9643893-9-8*, SAN 298-6043) Coulsong List.
Doner, Kalia. The Restaurant Lovers' Fat Gram Counter. 128p. (Orig.). 1995. mass mkt. 6.99 (*0-425-14919-6*) Berkley Pub.
— Spa at Home. LC 97-217069. 224p. 1997. pap. 12.95 (*0-425-15769-5*) Berkley Pub.
Doner, Kalia, jt. auth. see Cohen, Misha R.
Doner, Kalla. The Restaurant Lover's Fat Gram Counter. 1995. pap. 6.99 (*0-425-14994-3*) Berkley Pub.
***Doner, Kim.** Buffalo Dreams. LC 99-22577. (J). (gr. k-4). 1999. pap. 9.95 (*1-55868-476-X*, West Winds Pr) Gr Arts Ctr Pub.
Doner, Kim. Buffalo Dreams. LC 99-22577. 40p. (YA). (gr. 2-4). 1999. 16.95 (*1-55868-475-1*, West Winds Pr) Gr Arts Ctr Pub.
Doner, Lynn, jt. auth. see Siegel, Michael.
Donersberger. Lab Text in Anatomy & Physiology. 5th ed. 1996. pap., spiral bd. 42.50 (*0-7637-3985-5*) Jones & Bartlett.
Dones, John, jt. auth. see Amos, Janet.
Donesky, Finlay. David Hare: Moral & Historical Perspectives, 75. LC 96-5803. (Contributions in Drama & Theatre Studies: No. 75). 232p. 1996. 59.95 (*0-313-29734-7*, Greenwood Pr) Greenwood.
Doneson, Patricia A. Songs of Silence. LC 97-76808. (Illus.). 80p. 1997. 19.95 (*1-57914-021-1*) Campbell-Smith.
Donethower, Kim, ed. see Bazerman, Charles.
Donetz, J. M., tr. see Zubov, V. I.
Donev, A. N., jt. auth. see Atkinson, A. C.
Doney. El Gorrion Muy Preocupado.Tr. of Very Worried Sparrow. (SPA.). (J). write for info. (*950-841-003-5*) Editorial Unilit.
***Doney.** Our Wedding. 1999. 16.95 (*0-7459-4057-9*, Pub. by Lion Pubng) Trafalgar.
Doney, Dennis & Arnot, Paul. Labworks Flight Manual: Windows Version. LC 98-139878. (Chemistry Ser.). 88p. 1998. spiral bd. 10.00 (*0-7637-0680-9*) Jones & Bartlett.
Doney, M. Prayers for Home & School. (Illus.). 16p. (J). 1982. reprint ed. 0.99 (*0-86683-652-7*, AY8231) Harper SF.
Doney, Meryl. All in the Ark: A Learning-by-Doing Pocket Book. (Illus.). 1997. pap. 9.99 (*1-85608-088-9*) Hunt GBR.
Doney, Meryl. Baskets. LC 97-6589. (World Crafts Ser.). (J). (gr. 4-7). 1997. 21.00 (*0-531-14445-3*) Watts.
— Baskets. (World Crafts Ser.). 1998. pap. 6.95 (*0-531-15328-2*) Watts.
— Festivals. LC 96-15838. (World Crafts Ser.). (J). (gr. 4-7). 1997. lib. bdg. 21.00 (*0-531-14431-3*) Watts.
— Festivals. (World Crafts Ser.). (J). 1998. pap. 6.95 (*0-531-15329-0*) Watts.
— Games. LC 95-46273. (World Crafts Ser.). (Illus.). 32p. (J). (gr. 4-7). 1996. lib. bdg. 21.00 (*0-531-14405-4*) Watts.
— Games. (World Crafts Ser.). (J). (gr. 4-7). 1997. pap. text 6.95 (*0-531-15868-3*) Watts.
— How the Bible Came to Us. (Illus.). 48p. (J). (gr. 3-7). 1997. pap. 7.99 (*0-7459-2098-5*, Lion) Chariot Victor.
— Jesus, the Man Who Changed History. (Illus.). 44p. (J). (gr. 3-7). 1997. pap. 7.99 (*0-7459-2099-3*, Lion) Chariot Victor.
— Jewelry. 32p. (J). 1996. lib. bdg. 21.00 (*0-531-14406-2*) Watts.
— Jewelry. (World Crafts Ser.). (J). (gr. 4). 1997. pap. text 5.95 (*0-531-15869-1*) Watts.
— Masks. (World Crafts Ser.). (J). (gr. 4). 1997. pap. text 5.95 (*0-531-15870-5*) Watts.
— Musical Instruments. LC 95-18099. (World Crafts Ser.). (Illus.). 32p. (J). (gr. 4-7). 1996. lib. bdg. 21.00 (*0-531-14398-8*) Watts.
— Musical Instruments. (World Crafts Ser.). (J). (gr. 4). 1997. pap. text 5.95 (*0-531-15871-3*) Watts.
— Now I Am Big. (Illus.). 16p. (J). 1983. reprint ed. 0.99 (*0-86683-705-1*, AY8301) Harper SF.
— Papercraft. LC 96-35495. (World Crafts Ser.). 32p. (J). (gr. 4 up). 1998. lib. bdg. 21.00 (*0-531-14446-1*) Watts.
— Papercrafts. (World Crafts Ser.). (J). 1998. pap. 6.95 (*0-531-15330-4*) Watts.
— Puppets. LC 95-11433. (World Crafts Ser.). (Illus.). 32p. (J). (gr. 4-7). 1996. lib. bdg. 21.00 (*0-531-14399-6*) Watts.
— Puppets. (World Crafts Ser.). (J). (gr. 4). 1997. pap. text 6.95 (*0-531-15872-1*) Watts.
— Textiles. (J). 1998. pap. 6.95 (*0-531-15331-2*) Watts.
— Toys. LC 95-10735. (World Crafts Ser.). (Illus.). 32p. (J). (gr. 4-7). 1996. lib. bdg. 21.00 (*0-531-14400-3*) Watts.
— Toys. (World Crafts Ser.). (J). (gr. 4). 1997. pap. text 6.95 (*0-531-15873-X*) Watts.
Doney, Meryl, ed. Now We Have a New Baby. (Illus.). 16p. (J). 1983. reprint ed. 0.99 (*0-86683-707-8*, AY8302) Harper SF.
Doney, Todd L. Sleeping Beauty: The Ballet Story. LC 93-14399. 32p. (J). (gr. 1-5). 1994. 14.95 (*0-689-31885-5*, Pub. by Ctrl Bur voor Schimmel) Macmillan.
Doney, Willis, tr. see Malebranche, Nicolas.
Donfried, Karl P., ed. The Romans Debate. expanded rev. ed. LC 91-13252. 372p. 1991. 19.95 (*0-943575-42-7*) Hendrickson MA.
Donfried, Karl P. & Marshall, I. Howard. The Theology of the Shorter Pauline Letters. LC 92-41218. (New Testament Theology Ser.). 220p. (C). 1993. text 54.95 (*0-521-36491-4*); pap. text 16.95 (*0-521-36731-X*) Cambridge U Pr.
Donfried, Karl P. & Richardson, Peter, eds. Judaism & Christianity in First-Century Rome. LC 98-15906. 277p. 1998. pap. 24.00 (*0-8028-4265-8*) Eerdmans.
***Donfried, Karl P., et al.** The Thessalonians Debate: Methodological Discord or Methodological Synthesis? LC 00-27977. 2000. pap. write for info. (*0-8028-4374-3*) Eerdmans.
Dong. Rapid Response Manufacturing. LC 97-75215. 384p. 1998. 99.95 (*0-412-78010-0*, Chap & Hall NY) Chapman & Hall.
Dong-A. Dong-A's Basic English Grammar for Korean Speakers. (ENG & KOR.). 1985. 24.95 (*0-8288-3957-3*, F52740) Fr & Eur.
— Dong-A's Junior English Dictionary. (ENG & KOR.). 1981. 29.95 (*0-8288-3959-X*, F130750) Fr & Eur.
— Dong-A's Korean Dictionary. (KOR.). 1991. 24.95 (*0-8288-3951-4*, F96270) Fr & Eur.
— Dong-A's New Little English Dictionary. (ENG & KOR.). 1984. 29.95 (*0-8288-3955-7*, F99520) Fr & Eur.
— Dong-A's Present Day English-Korean Dictionary. (ENG & KOR.). 1983. 24.95 (*0-8288-3958-1*, F139480) Fr & Eur.
— Dong-A's Present Day Korean-English Dictionary. (ENG & KOR.). 1984. 24.95 (*0-8288-3956-5*, F81170) Fr & Eur.
— Dong-A's Prime English - Korean Dictionary. (ENG & KOR.). 1989. 59.95 (*0-8288-3952-2*, F116290) Fr & Eur.
— Dong-A's Prime Korean-English Dictionary. (ENG & KOR.). 1981. 49.95 (*0-8288-3954-9*, F92260) Fr & Eur.
— New Korean Dictionary. (KOR.). 1988. 59.95 (*0-8288-3953-0*, F117800) Fr & Eur.
Dong, Chong-Ying & Lepowsky, James. Generalized Vertex Algebras & Relative Vertex Operators. LC 93-21608. (Progress in Mathematics Ser.: Vol. 112). 208p. 1993. 54.00 (*0-8176-3721-4*) Birkhauser.
Dong, Chongying & Mason, Geoffrey, eds. Moonshine, the Monster, & Related Topics: Proceedings, AMS-IMS-SIAM Summer Research Conference on Moonshine, the Monster, & Related Topics, Mount Holyoke College, 1994. LC 95-40534. (Contemporary Mathematics Ser.: No. 193). 368p. 1995. pap. 70.00 (*0-8218-0385-9*, CONM/193) Am Math.
Dong, Collin H. The Arthritic's Cookbook. 1995. pap. 8.95 (*0-8217-4883-1*, Zebra Kensgtn) Kensgtn Pub Corp.
***Dong, Eugene.** Schaum's Outline of Mathematica. (Schaum's Outlines Ser.). (Illus.). 368p. 2000. pap. text 16.95 (*0-07-135719-X*, Schaums Outlne) McGraw-Hill Prof.
Dong, Guangchang. Nonlinear Partial Differential Equations of Second Order. LC 91-27853. (Translations of Mathematical Monographs: Vol. 95). 251p. 1991. text 136.00 (*0-8218-4554-3*, MMONO/95) Am Math.
Dong, H. Collin. Arthritic's Cookbook. 1996. pap. 9.95 (*1-57566-158-6*) Kensgtn Pub Corp.
Dong, He. Ask the Sun: Stories of Childhood in the Cultural Revolution. Hanson, Katherine, tr. from CHI. LC 97-18111.Tr. of Spor Solen. 112p. (Orig.). 1997. pap. 12.95 (*1-879679-10-8*) Women Translation.
Dong-hwa, Huh, jt. ed. see Roberts, Clare.
Dong, Jason W., jt. auth. see Sullivan, Paul J.
Dong, Kim. Insight Jesus: From Bultmann to the Third World. 272p. 1993. pap. 36.00 (*0-86153-173-6*, Pub. by St Andrew) St Mut.
Dong, Mike, jt. auth. see Chen, Simon K.
***Dong, Paul.** Allure of Falun Gong. 2000. 24.95 (*1-56649-159-2*) Welcome Rain.
— China's Major Mysteries: Paranormal Phenomena & the Unexplained in the People's Republic. rev. ed. (Illus.). 224p. 2000. pap. 16.95 (*0-8351-2676-5*) China Bks.
Dong, Paul. China's Super Psychics. LC 97-74218. (Illus.). vi, 248 p. 1997. pap. text 12.95 (*1-56924-715-3*) Marlowe & Co.
Dong, Paul & Esser, Aristide H. Chi Gong: The Ancient Chinese Way to Health. (Illus.). 212p. (C). 1995. pap. 13.00 (*1-56924-856-7*) Marlowe & Co.
Dong, Paul & Raffill, Thomas. Empty Force. 160p. 1996. pap. 14.95 (*1-85230-783-8*, Pub. by Element MA) Penguin Putnam.

D

An Asterisk (*) at the beginning of an entry indicates that the title is appearing for the first time.

Dong, Ronald Y. Nuclear Magnetic Resonance of Liquid Crystals. 2nd ed. LC 97-10095. (Partially Ordered Systems Ser.). (Illus.). 328p. 1997. 69.95 (*0-387-98230-2*) Spr-Verlag.

— Nuclear Magnetic Resonance of Liquid Crystals: Partially Ordered Systems. LC 93-5261. 1993. 64.95 (*0-387-94121-5*) Spr-Verlag.

***Dong, Stella.** Shanghai: The Rise & Fall of a Decadent City. LC 99-41902. (Illus.). 320p. 2000. 27.50 (*0-688-15798-X*, Wm Morrow) Morrow Avon.

Dong, Tong-Ren, et al. Qualitative Theory of Differential Equations. LC 91-23961. (Translations of Mathematical Monographs). 461p. 1992. text 288.00 (*0-8218-4551-9*, MMONO/101) Am Math.

Dong Van Khuyen, jt. auth. see Cao Van Vien.

Dong, Wei. Color Rendering: A Guide for Interior Designers & Architects. LC 96-47591. (Illus.). 141p. 1997. 59.95 (*0-07-018007-5*) McGraw.

Dong, Wei & Gibson, Kathleen. Digital Graphics: For Architecture & Interior Visualization. LC 97-48510. (Illus.). 192p. 1998. pap. 39.95 (*0-07-018012-1*) McGraw.

***Dong, Wonmo.** The Two Koreas & the United States: Issues of Peace, Security & Economic Cooperation. LC 99-37183. (Illus.). 328p. 2000. pap. text 27.50 (*0-7656-0534-1*, East Gate Bk) M E Sharpe.

***Dong, Wonmo, ed.** The Two Koreas & the United States: Issues of Peace, Security & Economic Cooperation. LC 99-37183. (Illus.). 328p. 1999. text 66.95 (*0-7656-0533-3*, East Gate Bk) M E Sharpe.

Dong, Y. P. Still As a Mountain, Powerful As Thunder: Simple Taoist Exercises for Healing, Vitality, & Peace of Mind. LC 92-50442. (Illus.). 128p. (Orig.). 1993. pap. 15.00 (*0-87773-688-X*, Pub. by Shambhala Pubns) Random.

Dong-Yuan, Li. The Treatise on the Spleen & Stomach: A Translation of the Pi Wei Lun. Flaws, Bob, ed. Shou-Zhong, Yang & Jian-Yong, Li, trs. from CHI. LC 92-75135. 275p. 1993. pap. 22.95 (*0-936185-41-4*) Blue Poppy Pr.

Dong, Z. M. Dinosaurian Faunas of China. 200p. 1992. 148.95 (*0-387-52084-8*) Spr-Verlag.

Dong, Z. W. High T-c Superconducting Thin-Film Devices. 152p. 1995. pap. 97.50 (*90-407-1113-5*, Pub. by Delft U Pr) Coronet Bks.

***Dongala, Emmanuel.** The Fire of Origins: A Novel. 256p. 2000. 25.00 (*1-55652-420-X*, Pub. by Chicago Review) IPG Chicago.

— Little Boys Come from the Stars. Rejouis, Joel et al, trs. from FRE. 256p. 2001. 22.00 (*0-374-18496-8*) FS&G.

***Dongarra, J., et al, eds.** Recent Advances in Parallel Virtual Machine & Message Passing Interface: 6th European PVM/MPI Users' Group Meeting, Barcelona, Spain, September 26-29, 1999, Proceedings. LC 99-48580. (Lecture Notes in Computer Science Ser.: Vol. 1697). xvii, 551p. 1999. pap. 85.00 (*3-540-66549-8*) Spr-Verlag.

Dongarra, J. & Wasniewski, Jerry, eds. Parallel Scientific Computing. LC 94-40217. (Lecture Notes in Computer Science Ser.: Vol. 879). 577p. 1994. 79.95 (*3-540-58712-8*) Spr-Verlag.

Dongarra, J. J., et al, eds. High Performance Computing: Technology, Methods & Applications. 436p. 1995. 187.50 (*0-444-82163-5*) Elsevier.

Dongarra, J. J., jt. auth. see Palma, Jose M.L.M. Rence on Vector & Parallel Proc.

Dongarra, Jack, et al, eds. Applied Parallel Computing: Computations in Physics, Chemistry, & Engineering Science: Second International Workshop, PARA '95, Lyngby, Denmark, August 21-24, 1995, Proceedings. LC 96-1593. (Lecture Notes in Computer Science Ser.: Vol. 1041). xii, 562p. 1996. pap. 87.00 (*3-540-60902-4*) Spr-Verlag.

— Proceedings of the Fifth SIAM Conference on Parallel Processing for Scientific Computing. LC 92-26416. (Proceedings in Applied Mathematics Ser.: No. 62). xvii, 648p. 1992. pap. 112.00 (*0-89871-303-X*) Soc Indus-Appl Math.

— Vector & Parallel Computing: Issues in Applied Research & Development. 1989. text 49.95 (*0-470-21571-2*) P-H.

Dongarra, Jack, et al. Numerical Linear Algebra for High-Performance Computers. LC 98-44444. (Software, Environments & Tools Ser.: Vol. 7). (Illus.). xviii, 342p. 1998. pap. 37.00 (*0-89871-428-1*, BKSE0007) Soc Indus-Appl Math.

Dongarra, Jack, ed. see First International Workshop Staff.

Dongarra, Jack B. & Tourancheau, Bernard, eds. Environments & Tools for Parallel Scientific Computing. LC 93-16380. (Advances in Parallel Computing Ser.: Vol. 6). (Illus.). xviii,362p. 1993. 153.50 (*0-444-89963-4*, North Holland) Elsevier.

Dongarra, Jack J., et al, eds. Parallel Processing for Scientific Computing: Proceedings of the Fourth SIAM Conference. LC 90-10356. (Proceedings in Applied Mathematics Ser.: No. 44). xxii, 454p. 1990. pap. 52.50 (*0-89871-262-9*) Soc Indus-Appl Math.

Dongarra, Jack J. & Gentzsch, Wolfgang, eds. Computer Benchmarks. LC 93-4236. (Advances in Parallel Computing Ser.: Vol. 8). 364p. 1993. 146.50 (*0-444-81518-X*, North Holland) Elsevier.

Dongarra, Jack J. & Tourancheau, Bernard, eds. Proceedings of the Second Workshop on Environments & Tools for Parallel Scientific Computing. LC 94-36849. (Proceedings in Applied Mathematics Ser.: Vol. 74). x, 292p. 1994. pap. 43.50 (*0-89871-343-9*) Soc Indus-Appl Math.

Dongarra, Jack J., et al. LINPACK Users' Guide. LC 78-78206. (Miscellaneous Bks.: No. 8). viii, 367p. 1979. pap. 40.50 (*0-89871-172-X*) Soc Indus-Appl Math.

Dongarra, Kathryn, ed. see Stuart, Sally E. & Young, Woody.

Dongarra, Kathy, ed. see Young, Woody.

Dongelewicz-Milner, Carol. Effective Customer Service in a Mortgage Servicing Environment. 114p. 1998. pap. 30.00 (*0-945359-10-1*) Mortgage Bankers.

Dongell, Joseph. John: A Bible Commentary in the Wesleyan Tradition. Higle, David A., ed. LC 98-125224. 260p. 1997. text 24.95 (*0-89827-168-1*) Wesleyan Pub Hse.

Dongen, Emma Van, see Van Dis, Huib & Van Dongen, Emma, eds.

Dongen, J. J. Van, see Van Dongen, J. J.

Dongen, R. J. Van, see Herberer, G. & Van Dongen, R. J., eds.

Dongerson, Debbie, jt. auth. see Cofield, Lisa.

Donges, Juegen B., et al. The Second Enlargement of the European Community: Adjustments Requirements & Challenges for Policy Reform. 263p. 1982. lib. bdg. 62.50 (*3-16-344571-3*, Pub. by JCB Mohr) Coronet Bks.

Donges, Juergen B. Deregulating the German Economy: German Economy. 39p. 1991. pap. 9.95 (*1-55815-149-4*) ICS Pr.

Donghi, Antonio. Actions & Words: Symbolic Language in the Liturgy. McDonough, William & Serra, Dominic, trs. from ITA. LC 96-51699. 104p. (Orig.). 1997. pap. text 8.95 (*0-8146-2345-X*, Liturg Pr Bks) Liturgical Pr.

Donghi, Tulo H., et al. Sarmiento, Author of a Nation. LC 93-16613. 400p. 1994. 58.00 (*0-520-07531-5*, Pub. by U CA Pr); pap. 22.50 (*0-520-07532-3*, Pub. by U CA Pr) Cal Prin Full Svc.

Dongo, Thomas A. The Alien Tide - UFO-ET. (Illus.). 128p. (Orig.). 1990. pap. 7.95 (*0-9622748-1-X*) T Dongo.

Dongo, Tom. Merging Dimensions Vol. 1: The Opening Portals of Sedona. (Illus.). 189p. (Orig.). 1995. pap. 14.95 (*0-9622748-4-4*) T Dongo.

— The Mysteries of Sedona: The New Age Frontier. 2nd ed. (Illus.). 84p. 1988. reprint ed. pap. 6.95 (*0-9622748-0-1*) T Dongo.

— The Mysteries of Sedona Bk. III: The Quest. (Illus.). 146p. (Orig.). 1993. pap. 9.95 (*0-9622748-2-8*) T Dongo.

— Unseen Beings Unseen Worlds Vol. 1: A Look at the Realms of the Great Unknown. (Illus.). 122p. (Orig.). 1994. pap. 9.95 (*0-9622748-3-6*) T Dongo.

Dongwuxue & Cihui, Y. English-Chinese Biology Dictionary. (CHI & ENG.). 477p. 1975. 49.95 (*0-8288-5880-2*, M9277) Fr & Eur.

***Donham, Donald L.** History, Power, Ideology: Central Issues in Marxism & Anthropology. LC 98-50668. 242p. 1999. pap. 16.95 (*0-520-21337-8*, Pub. by U CA Pr) Cal Prin Full Svc.

— Marxist Modern: An Ethnographic History of the Ethiopian Revolution. LC 98-43144. 284p. 1999. 45.00 (*0-520-21328-9*, Pub. by U CA Pr); pap. 17.95 (*0-520-21329-7*, Pub. by U CA Pr) Cal Prin Full Svc.

— Marxist Modern: An Ethnographic History of the Ethiopian Revolution LC 98-43144. xxvi, 236 p. 1999. pap. write for info. (*0-85255-264-5*) J Currey.

Donham, Donald L. Work & Power in Maale, Ethiopia. 227p. 1994. pap. 19.00 (*0-231-10047-7*) Col U Pr.

Donham, K. J., jt. auth. see Mutel, C. F.

Donham, Kelly J. & Rautiainen, Risto. Agricultural Health & Safety: Recent Advances. LC 97-20493. (Journal of Agromedicine Ser.: Vol. 4, Nos. 1/2/3/4). 428p. 1997. 79.95 (*0-7890-0312-0*, Hawrth Medical) Haworth Pr.

Donhoffer, S. Z. Homeothermia of the Brain Cerebral Blood Flow, Metabolic Rate & Brain Temperature in the Cold: The Possible Role of Neuroglia. 140p. (C). 1980. pap. 34.50 (*963-05-2405-8*, Pub. by Akade Kiado) St Mut.

Donia, Robert J. Islam under the Double Eagle: The Muslims of Bosnia & Hercegovina, 1878-1914. (East European Monographs: No. 78). 237p. 1981. text 44.00 (*0-914710-72-9*, Pub. by East Eur Monographs) Col U Pr.

Donia, Robert J. & Fine, John V., Jr. Bosnia & Hercegovina: A Tradition Betrayed. 318p. 1995. pap. 18.95 (*0-231-10161-9*) Col U Pr.

Donia, Robert J. & Vine, John V., Jr. Bosnia & Hercegovina: A Tradition Betrayed. LC 94-16223. 1994. 42.00 (*0-231-10160-0*) Col U Pr.

Doniach, N. & Kahane, A., eds. The Oxford English-Hebrew Dictionary. 1,114p. 1998. reprint ed. pap. 22.50 (*0-19-860172-7*) OUP.

Doniach, N. S. Concise Oxford English: Arabic Dictionary of Current Usage. (ARA & ENG.). 1992. reprint ed. 29.95 (*0-8288-8436-6*) Fr & Eur.

Doniach, N. S., ed. The Concise Oxford English-Arabic Dictionary. (ARA & ENG.). 472p. (C). 1983. 32.00 (*0-19-864321-7*) OUP.

— Oxford English-Arabic Dictionary of Current Usage. (ARA & ENG.). 1,406p. 1972. text 95.00 (*0-19-864312-8*) OUP.

Doniach, S. Statistical Mechanics, Protein Structure & Protein Substrate Interactions. (NATO ASI Series B, Physics: Vol. 325). (Illus.). 416p. (C). 1994. text 150.00 (*0-306-44728-2*) Plenum.

Doniach, S. & Sondheimer, E. H. Green's Functions for Solid State Physicists. rev. ed. LC 98-23903. 300p. 1998. reprint ed. 74.00 (*1-86094-078-1*, Pub. by Imperial College); reprint ed. pap. 38.00 (*1-86094-080-3*, Pub. by Imperial College) World Scientific Pub.

Doniach, Seb, jt. ed. see Winick, Herman.

Donigan, Linda J. & Horwitz, Michael. Alligators Always Dress for Dinner: An Alphabet Book of Vintage Photographs. LC 97-25481. (Illus.). 64p. 1997. 25.00 (*1-884592-08-2*) Images from the Past.

Doniger, Anthony M. Massachusetts Litigation Forms & Analysis. Fleury, Ronald E., ed. LC 95-76594. 1500p. 1995. text. write for info. (*0-7620-0010-4*) West Group.

Doniger, David D. The Law & Policy of Toxic Substances Control: A Case Study of Vinyl Chloride. LC 78-24624. 179p. 1979. pap. 15.95 (*0-8018-2235-1*) Resources Future.

Doniger, Nancy. Morning, Noon & Night: Poems to Fill Your Day. LC 95-25527. 24p. (J). (ps-2). 1996. 14.95 (*1-57255-128-3*) Mondo Pubng.

Doniger, Simon, ed. The Nature of Man in Theological & Psychological Perspective. LC 72-10819. (Essay Index Reprint Ser.). 1977. reprint ed. 20.95 (*0-8369-7213-9*) Ayer.

***Doniger, Wendy.** Bed Trick. LC 99-50887. 1999. 35.00 (*0-226-15642-7*) U Ch Pr.

Doniger, Wendy. The Implied Spider: Politics & Theology in Myth. LC 97-26476. (Lectures on the History of Religions: Vol. 16). 200p. 1998. 28.50 (*0-231-11170-3*) Col U Pr.

— The Implied Spider: Politics & Theology in Myth. 256p. 1999. pap. 17.50 (*0-231-11171-1*) Col U Pr.

— Splitting the Difference Gender & Myth in Ancient Greece & India. LC 98-47996. 1999. pap. text 20.00 (*0-226-15641-9*) U Ch Pr.

***Doniger, Wendy.** Splitting the Difference: Gender & Myth in Ancient Greece & India. (Jordan Lectures in Comparative Religion). 1999. lib. bdg. 55.00 (*0-226-15640-0*) U Ch Pr.

Doniger, Wendy, ed. Purana Perennis: Reciprocity & Transformation in Hindu & Jaina Texts. LC 92-25322. 352p. (C). 1993. pap. text 21.95 (*0-7914-1382-9*) State U NY Pr.

— Purana Perennis: Reciprocity & Transformation in Hindu & Jaina Texts. LC 92-25322. 352p. (C). 1993. text 64.50 (*0-7914-1381-0*) State U NY Pr.

Doniger, Wendy, et al, trs. from FRE. American, African, & Old European Mythologies. LC 92-39231. (Illus.). xxiv, 280p. (C). 1993. pap. 27.50 (*0-226-06457-3*) U Ch Pr.

— Asian Mythologies. LC 92-39077. (Illus.). xxiv, 400p. (C). 1993. pap. 28.95 (*0-226-06456-5*) U Ch Pr.

Doniger, Wendy, jt. ed. see Eilberg-Schwartz, Howard.

Doniger, Wendy, ed. see Elizarenkova, Tatyana J.

Doniger, Wendy, ed. see Merriam-Webster Editors.

Doniger, Wendy, jt. ed. see Patton, Laurie L.

Doniger, Wendy, tr. see Bonnefoy, Yves, ed.

Doniger, Wendy, jt. tr. see Honigsblum, Gerald.

Doniger, Wendy, tr. see Wyatt, Thomas.

Doniger, Wendy, tr. see Zola, Emile.

Donigi, Peter. Indigenous or Aborginal Rights to Property: A Papua New Guinea Perspective. LC 94-226169. 1994. pap. text 19.95 (*90-6224-988-4*, Pub. by Uitgeverij Arkel) LPC InBook.

Donigian, George. Thank You God. (Storytelling Bks.). (Illus.). 8p. (J). (ps-3). 1995. pap. text 1.95 (*0-687-00658-9*) Abingdon.

— Thank You God for Baby Jesus. (Storytelling Bks.). (Illus.). 8p. (J). (ps-3). 1995. pap. 1.95 (*0-687-01701-7*) Abingdon.

— Thank You God for Jesus. (Storytelling Bks.). (Illus.). 8p. (J). (ps-3). 1995. pap. 1.95 (*0-687-00447-0*) Abingdon.

— Thank You God for Me. (Storytelling Bks.). (Illus.). 8p. (J). (ps-3). 1995. pap. 1.95 (*0-687-00445-4*) Abingdon.

Donigian, George, ed. Discipline & Recovery: 100 Meditations for Persons in Recovery. LC 97-9335. 128p. 1997. pap. 10.00 (*0-8358-0817-3*, UR 817) Upper Room Bks.

— Pathways to Discovery, No. 1. 1992. 99.95 (*0-687-30342-7*) Abingdon.

— Pathways to Discovery, No. 2. 1993. 99.95 (*0-687-30362-1*) Abingdon.

— Pathways to Discovery, No. 3. 1994. 99.95 (*0-687-30368-0*) Abingdon.

Donigian, George, ed. see Hinson, E. Glenn.

Donigian, George, ed. see Ives, Jane.

Donigian, George, ed. see Morris, Danny E. & Olsen, Charles M.

Donigian, Jeremiah & Hulse-Killacky, Diana. Critical Incidents in Group Therapy. 2nd ed. (Counseling Ser.). 378p. 1998. pap. 42.95 (*0-534-35727-X*) Brooks-Cole.

Donigian, Jeremiah & Malnati, Richard. Critical Incidents in Group Therapy. LC 86-1011. (Psychology Ser.). 239p. (C). 1986. 27.75 (*0-534-06282-2*) Brooks-Cole.

— Systemic Group Therapy: A Triadic Model. LC 96-17211. (Counseling Ser.). 115p. (C). 1996. mass mkt. 21.95 (*0-534-34518-2*) Brooks-Cole.

***Donihue, Anita C.** Selections from When I'm on My Knees. 96p. 2000. 9.97 (*1-57748-718-4*) Barbour Pub.

— When I'm on My Knees: Devotional Thoughts on Prayer for Women. 213p. 1997. pap. 4.97 (*1-55748-976-9*) Barbour Pub.

Donihue, Anita C. When I'm Praising God: Devotional Thoughts on Worship for Women. LC 99-194883. 221p. 1999. pap. 4.97 (*1-57748-447-9*) Barbour Pub.

Donihue, Anita C., jt. auth. see Reece, Colleen L.

***Donihue, Anita Corrine.** When I'm in His Presence: Devotional Thoughts on Worship for Women. (Inspirational Library Ser.). 224p. 2000. lthr. 4.97 (*1-57748-665-X*) Barbour Pub.

— When I'm on My Knees Prayer Journal. 224p. 2000. 4.97 (*1-57748-836-9*) Barbour Pub.

Donin, Hayim H. To Be a Jew: A Guide to Jewish Observance in Contemporary Life. LC 72-89175. 368p. 1991. pap. 16.00 (*0-465-08632-2*, Pub. by Basic) HarpC.

— To Raise a Jewish Child: A Guide for Parents. LC 76-7679. 232p. 1991. pap. 13.00 (*0-465-08635-7*, Pub. by Basic) HarpC.

Donington, Margaret & Donington, Robert. Scales, Arpeggios, & Exercises for the Recorder. 80p. (YA). (gr. 9 up). 1968. 17.95 (*0-19-322160-8*) OUP.

Donington, Robert. Baroque Music: Style & Performance, A Handbook. (Illus.). (Orig.). 1982. pap. 16.95 (*0-393-30052-8*) Norton.

— The Interpretation of Early Music. rev. ed. 766p. (C). 1992. pap. text 35.50 (*0-393-96003-X*) Norton.

— The Opera. (Harbrace History of Musical Forms Ser.). (Illus.). 238p. (C). 1978. pap. text 17.50 (*0-15-567536-2*, Pub. by Harcourt Coll Pubs) Harcourt.

— Opera. LC 77-93589. 1978. pap. text 23.00 (*0-15-504407-9*, Pub. by Harcourt Coll Pubs) Harcourt.

— Opera & Its Symbols: The Unity of Words, Music, & Staging. 256p. (C). 1991. 40.00 (*0-300-04713-4*) Yale U Pr.

— Opera & Its Symbols: The Unity of Words, Music, & Staging. (Illus.). 256p. (C). 1992. reprint ed. pap. 16.00 (*0-300-05661-3*) Yale U Pr.

— Wagner's 'Ring' & Its Symbols: The Music & the Myth. 3rd ed. (Illus.). 342p. 1974. pap. 24.95 (*0-571-04818-8*, Pub. by Faber & Faber) Penguin Books.

Donington, Robert, jt. auth. see Donington, Margaret.

Donini, Marilynn, jt. auth. see Herzenberg, Jere.

Donini, Pier G. Arab Travellers & Geographers. (Illus.). 108p. (C). 1995. 80.00 (*0-907151-35-3*, Pub. by IMMEL Pubng) St Mut.

Doninik, John J. St. Cloud: The Triplet City. 1983. 22.95 (*0-89781-091-0*, 5072) Am Historical Pr.

Donio, Michael A., jt. auth. see Inlander, Charles B.

Donisch, Jean M., jt. auth. see Schroeder, Pamela J.

Donizetti, G. Daughter of the Regiment: Vocal Score. (ENG & FRE.). 1986. pap. 18.95 (*0-7935-5386-5*, 50338660) H Leonard.

— Don Pasquale: Vocal Score. (ENG & ITA.). 1986. pap. 24.95 (*0-7935-5383-0*) H Leonard.

— L' Elisir d'Amore Libretto. (ENG & ITA.). 44p. 1986. pap. 4.95 (*0-7935-4733-4*, 50340100) H Leonard.

— Elixir of Love - l'Elisir D'Amore: Vocal Score. (ENG & ITA.). 400p. 1986. pap. 21.95 (*0-7935-5372-5*, 50338160) H Leonard.

— La Favorita Libretto: 4 Acts. (ENG & FRE.). 44p. 1986. pap. 4.95 (*0-7935-2228-5*, 50340690) H Leonard.

— La Fille du Regiment Custom Print for Metropolitan Opera. 48p. 1993. pap. 2.46 (*0-7935-2977-8*) H Leonard.

— Lucia di Lammermoor: Vocal Score. (ENG & ITA.). 256p. 1986. pap. 24.95 (*0-7935-2862-3*, 50337150) H Leonard.

— Lucia di Lammermoor Libretto. (ENG & ITA.). 36p. 1986. pap. 4.95 (*0-7935-2829-1*, 50340290) H Leonard.

Donizetti, Gaetano. Lucia di Lammermoor in Full Score. 384p. 1992. reprint ed. pap. text 23.95 (*0-486-27113-7*) Dover.

Donjon, Richard P. Medicine Cabinet Medicines: Over-the-Counter Drugs. LC 99-174414. (Illus.). 134p. (C). (gr. 13). 1997. spiral bd. 12.95 (*0-8151-8053-5*, 27217) Mosby Inc.

Donjon, Richard P. & Goeckner, Bryon J. Mosby's OTC Drugs: A Resource for Health Professionals. LC 98-39429. (Illus.). 464p. (C). (gr. 13). 1998. text 29.95 (*0-8151-8395-X*, 31695) Mosby Inc.

Donk, H. Van de, see Van de Donk, H., ed.

Donk, M. A. The Generic Names Proposed for Agaricaceae. 1962. pap. 80.00 (*3-7682-5405-4*) Lubrecht & Cramer.

— The Generic Names Proposed for Hymenomycetes 1-9,12,13. 1966. pap. 40.00 (*3-7682-0347-6*) Lubrecht & Cramer.

— The Generic Names Proposed for Polyporaceae. 1968. reprint ed. pap. 23.00 (*3-7682-0557-6*) Lubrecht & Cramer.

— Revision der Niederlaendishen Heterobasidiomycetae und Homobasidiomycetae-Aphyllophoraceae, 2 parts in 1 vol. (Illus.). 1969. reprint ed. 64.00 (*3-7682-0621-1*) Lubrecht & Cramer.

Donk, Van De, see De Donk, Van.

Donka, Joseph. The End: Role Playing Game. Jones, Matthew, ed. (Illus.). 188p. (Orig.). Date not set. 20.00 (*0-9648557-0-4*) Scapegoat Games.

Donkel, Douglas L. The Understanding of Difference in Heidegger & Derrida. LC 92-22090. (American University Studies: Philosophy: Ser. V, Vol. 143). X, 221p. (C). 1992. text 44.95 (*0-8204-1961-3*) P Lang Pubng.

***Donkel, Douglas L., ed.** The Theory of Difference: Readings in Contemporary Continental Thought. (C). 2001. pap. text. write for info. (*0-7914-4928-9*) State U NY Pr.

— The Theory of Difference: Readings in Contemporary Continental Thought. (C). 2001. text. write for info. (*0-7914-4927-0*) State U NY Pr.

Donkelaar, H. J. Ten, see Van Domburg, P. H. & Ten Donkelaar, H. J.

Donkelaar, H. J. Ten, see Ten Donkelaar, H. J.

Donker, Eric. Test Yourself Electronic Devices & Circuits. LC 97-13865. (Test Yourself Ser.). (Illus.). 152p. (C). 1996. pap. 12.95 (*0-8442-2355-7*, 23557) NTC Contemp Pub Co.

Donker, Marjorie. Shakespeare's Proverbial Themes: A Rhetorical Context for the Sentenia as Res, 44. LC 92-175. (Contributions to the Study of World Literature Ser.: No. 44). 224p. 1992. 52.95 (*0-313-28410-5*, DSK/, Greenwood Pr) Greenwood.

Donker, Marjorie & Muldrow, George M. Dictionary of Literary-Rhetorical Conventions of the English Renaissance. LC 81-4266. 268p. 1982. lib. bdg. 55.00 (*0-313-23000-5*, DER/, Greenwood Pr) Greenwood.

Donker, Rogier. Of Faith, Miracles, Memories & Reflections. (Illus.). 160p. 1998. pap. 16.00 (*0-9663775-0-8*) Wabash River.

Donker, Ruth. Daffodils in the Bathtub: And Other Meditations. LC 94-7277. 166p. 1994. pap. 9.95 (*1-56212-058-1*, 1701-0650) CRC Pubns.

Donker, Ruth. Have You Looked at Your Tongue Lately? LC 95-43119. 1996. pap. 7.95 (*1-56212-137-5*) CRC Pubns.

Donkersgoed, William L., et al. Consensus Building Strategies for Productive CEO-Board Relationships. 98p. 1998. pap. 100.00 (*1-880572-30-3*, 1752-35) Filene Res.

Donkersloot, Mary. Simply Gourmet Diabetes Coobook. LC 99-18309. 1999. pap. 17.95 (*0-609-80514-2*) C Potter.

D

An Asterisk (*) at the beginning of an entry indicates that the title is appearing for the first time.

Donkersloot, Mary & Hyder-Ferry, Linda. The How to Quit Smoking & Not Gain Weight Cookbook. LC 99-25276. 256p. 1999. pap. 14.95 (*0-609-80363-8*, Crown) Crown Pub Group.

***Donkersloot, Sara Feriante.** Down by the River: An Alaska Counting Rhyme. (Illus.). 32p. (J). (gr. 3-6). 1999. pap. 14.95 (*1-888125-60-8*) Publ Consult.

Donkin, Andrew. Alien Encyclopedia, 1. 160p. 1999. pap. 6.95 (*1-901881-44-X*, Pub. by Element MA) Penguin Putnam.

***Donkin, Andrew.** Atlantis: The Lost City? LC 00-27359. (Eyewitness Readers). (Illus.). 48p. (gr. 2-4). 2000. write for info. (*0-7894-6681-3*, D K Ink); pap. text 3.95 (*0-7894-6682-1*, D K Ink) DK Pub Inc.

— Bermuda Triangle. LC 99-43643. (Eyewitness Readers). (Illus.). 48p. (J). (gr. 2-3). 2000. 12.95 (*0-7894-5416-5*, D K Ink); pap. 3.95 (*0-7894-5415-7*, D K Ink) DK Pub Inc.

— Bermuda Triangle. (Illus.). (J). 2000. 9.40 (*0-606-18113-X*) Turtleback.

Donkin, Andrew. Dead Giveaways. 256p. (J). pap. 4.95 (*1-901881-05-9*, Pub. by Element MA) Penguin Putnam.

***Donkin, Andrew.** Going For Gold. LC 99-26070. (Eyewitness Readers). 48p. (J). (gr. 2-4). 1999. 12.95 (*0-7894-4765-7*); pap. 3.95 (*0-7894-4764-9*) DK Pub Inc.

— Lock, Stock & Two Smoking Barrels - The Novel. 2000. pap. 7.95 (*1-85782-415-6*, Pub. by Blake Publng) Seven Hills Bk.

Donkin, Andrew. The Mark of Mandragora: A Doctor Who Graphic Novel. (Illus.). 90p. 1999. reprint ed. pap. text 20.00 (*0-7881-6062-1*) DIANE Pub.

***Donkin, Andrew.** Spooky Spinechillers. (Eyewitness Readers). (Illus.). 48p. (J). (gr. 2-4). 2000. pap. text 3.95 (*0-7894-6523-X*, D K Ink) DK Pub Inc.

— Spooky Spinechillers. (Eyewitness Readers). (Illus.). 48p. (YA). (gr. 2-4). 2000. 12.95 (*0-7894-6522-1*, D K Ink) DK Pub Inc.

— Weird Creatures Encyclopedia. 192p. 1999. pap. 6.95 (*1-902618-61-0*) Elemental Pubns.

— Zeppelin: The Age of the Airship. (Dorling Kindersley Readers). (Illus.). (J). (gr. 2-3). 1999. 12.95 (*0-7894-5714-8*, D K Ink); pap. 3.95 (*0-7894-5715-6*, D K Ink) DK Pub Inc.

Donkin, E., ed. Cicero: Pro Roscio Amerino. (Bristol Latin Texts Ser.). (LAT.). 1991. pap. 20.95 (*0-86292-184-8*, Pub. by Brist Class Pr) Focus Pub-R Pullins.

Donkin, Ellen. Getting into the Act: Women Playwrights in London, 1776-1829. LC 94-48735. (Gender & Performance Ser.). (Illus.). 256p. (C). 1995. 90.00 (*0-415-08249-8*); pap. 25.99 (*0-415-08250-1*) Routledge.

Donkin, Ellen & Clement, Susan, eds. Upstaging Big Daddy: Directing Theater As If Gender & Race Matter. LC 92-38338. (Illus.). 344p. 1993. text 47.50 (*0-472-09503-X*, 09503); pap. text 18.95 (*0-472-06503-3*, 06503) U of Mich Pr.

Donkin, Ellen, jt. ed. see Davis, Tracy C.

Donkin, R. A. Beyond Price: Pearls & Pearl-Fishing - Origins to the Age of Discovery. LC 94-78515. (Memoirs Ser.: No. 224). (Illus.). 448p. 1998. 45.00 (*0-87169-224-4*, M224-dor) Am Philos.

— Dragon's Brain Perfume: An Historical Geography of Camphor. LC 98-43143. (Indological Library). 1999. 94.50 (*90-04-10983-8*) Brill Academic Pubs.

— Manna: An Historical Geography. (Biogeographica Ser.: No. 17). (Illus.). vii, 160p. 1980. text 148.50 (*90-6193-218-1*) Kluwer Academic.

— The Muscovy Duck: Cairina Moschata Domestica: Origins Dispersal Associated Aspects of the Geography of Domestication. 194p. (C). 1989. text 99.00 (*90-6191-544-9*, Pub. by A A Balkema) Ashgate Pub Co.

— The Peccary: With Observations on the Introduction of Pigs to the New World. LC 84-45906. (Transactions Ser.: Vol. 75, Pt. 5). 150p. 1985. pap. 25.00 (*0-87169-755-6*, T755-DOR) Am Philos.

Donkin, Robin. Agricultural Terracing in the Aboriginal New World. LC 77-15120. (Viking Fund Publications in Anthropology: No. 56). (Illus.). 196p. 1979. pap. 8.50 (*0-8165-0453-9*) U of Ariz Pr.

Donkin, S. Rational Representation of Algebraic Groups. (Lecture Notes in Mathematics Ser.: Vol. 1140). vii, 254p. 1985. 42.95 (*0-387-15668-2*) Spr-Verlag.

— Representations of the Hyperalgebra of a Semisimple Group. (London Mathematical Society Lecture Note Ser.: No. 219). 250p. (C). 1999. pap. text 39.95 (*0-521-47251-2*) Cambridge U Pr.

Donkin, Scot W. Sitting on the Job: How to Survive the Stresses of Sitting Down to Work - a Practical Handbook. (Illus.). 160p. 1989. pap. 15.00 (*0-395-50089-3*) HM.

Donkin, Scott. Pain Free at Your Computer: Guided Relaxations to Reduce the Painful Effects of Computer Use. (Illus.). 12p. 1996. 9.95 incl. audio (*1-55961-347-5*, BP7507) Relaxtn Co.

Donkin, Scott W. Sitting on the Job: A Practical Survival Guide for People Who Earn Their Living While Sitting. Sweere, Joseph J., ed. LC 86-90503. (Illus.). 137p. 1987. pap. 8.95 (*0-9617281-0-8*) Parallel Integ.

Donkin, Stephen. The q-Schur Algebra. (London Mathematical Society Lecture Note Ser.: No. 253). 235p. (C). 1999. pap. text 39.95 (*0-521-64558-1*) Cambridge U Pr.

Donkor, Kwabena. Structural Adjustment & Mass Poverty in Ghana. LC 97-73380. (Making of Modern Africa Ser.). (Illus.). 288p. 1997. text 73.95 (*1-84014-122-0*, Pub. by Ashgate Pub) Ashgate Pub Co.

***Donlan, Chris.** Development of Mathematical Skills. (Studies in Developmental Psychology). (Illus.). 2000. pap. 29.95 (*0-86377-817-8*) Psychol Pr.

Donlan, Chris. Development of Mathematical Skills. LC 99-182503. (Studies in Developmental Psychology). 1998. 59.95 (*0-86377-816-X*) Taylor & Francis.

Donlan, Dan, jt. auth. see Singer, Harry.

Donlan, John. Baysville: Poems. 80p. (Orig.). 1993. pap. 12.95 (*0-88784-540-1*, Pub. by Hse of Anansi Pr) Genl Dist Srvs.

Donlan, John. Domestic Economy. 64p. 1990. pap. 9.95 (*0-919626-45-9*, Pub. by Brick Bks) Genl Dist Srvs.

Donlan, Walter. The Aristocratic Ideal & Selected Papers: Attitudes of Superiority from Homer to the End of the Fifth Century B.C. LC 98-14706. xvii, 364p. (C). 1999. pap. 40.00 (*0-86516-411-8*) Bolchazy-Carducci.

Donlay, Philip S. Shadow Crossing. Schlumpf, Heidi, ed. 250p. 1997. 24.95 (*1-889587-87-7*) Pure Play Pub.

Donleavy, Gabriel, jt. ed. see Stewart, Sally.

Donleavy, Gabriel D. Cash Flow Accounting: International Uses & Abuses. LC 93-18904. (Series on International Accounting & Finance). 240p. (C). (gr. 13). 1993. pap. 78.95 (*0-415-08677-9*) Thomson Learn.

Donleavy, J. P. The Beastly Beatitudes of Balthazar B. LC 88-3415. 420p. 1988. pap. 7.95 (*0-87113-225-7*, Atlntc Mnthly) Grove-Atltic.

— Les Beatitudes Bestiales De Balthazar B. (FRE.). 587p. 1977. pap. 12.95 (*0-7859-1864-7*, 2070369870) Fr & Eur.

— Un Conte De Fees New-Yorkais. (FRE.). 464p. 1988. pap. 13.95 (*0-7859-2098-6*, 2070380645) Fr & Eur.

Donleavy, J. P. The Destinies of Darcy Dancer, Gentleman. LC 89-28306. 416p. 1990. pap. 9.95 (*0-87113-289-3*, Atlntc Mnthly) Grove-Atltic.

Donleavy, J. P. A Fairy Tale of New York. LC 88-10325. 352p. 1989. pap. 12.00 (*0-87113-264-8*, Atlntc Mnthly) Grove-Atltic.

— Fairy Tales of New York. LC 61-14890. 118p. 1961. 16.95 (*0-910278-15-6*) Boulevard.

— Ginger Man. 1958. 17.95 (*0-8392-1037-X*); pap. 10.95 (*0-8392-5007-X*) Astor-Honor.

— The Ginger Man. LC 88-3417. 352p. 1988. pap. 11.95 (*0-87113-199-4*, Atlntc Mnthly) Grove-Atltic.

— L' Homme de Gingembre. (FRE.). 406p. 1979. pap. 11.95 (*0-7859-1901-5*, 2070371409) Fr & Eur.

— The Lady Who Liked Clean Restrooms: The Chronicle of One of the Strangest Stories Ever. 128p. 1998. pap. 9.95 (*0-312-18734-3*) St Martin.

— Leila: Further in the Life & Destinies of Darcy Dancer, Gentleman. LC 89-28307. 432p. 1990. 12.00 (*0-87113-288-5*, Atlntc Mnthly) Grove-Atltic.

— A Singular Man. LC 88-33780. 416p. 1989. pap. 12.00 (*0-87113-265-6*, Atlntc Mnthly) Grove-Atltic.

— Wrong Information is Being Given Out at Princeton. (Illus.). 336p. 1999. pap. 14.95 (*0-312-24499-1*) St Martin.

Donleavy, James Patrick. Wrong Information is Being Given Out at Princeton. LC 98-19411. (Illus.). 323p. 1998. 24.95 (*0-312-19372-6*, Thomas Dunne) St Martin.

Donley, Ann, et al. Almanac of Virginia Politics: 1995 Regular. 1995. 24.95 (*0-917560-29-9*) Woman Activist.

— Almanac of Virginia Politics: 1996 Supplement. 1996. 18.95 (*0-917560-30-2*) Woman Activist.

— Almanac of Virginia Politics: 1997 Regular. 1997. 24.95 (*0-917560-31-0*) Woman Activist.

Donley, Carol & Buckley, Sheryl, eds. The Tyranny of the Normal: An Anthology. LC 95-36898. (Literature & Medicine Ser.: No. 2). 406p. (Orig.). (C). 1995. pap. 29.00 (*0-87338-535-7*) Kent St U Pr.

***Donley, Carol C. & Buckley, Sheryl.** What's Normal? An Anthology: Narratives of Mental & Emotional Disorders. LC 99-48190. (Literature & Medicine Ser.). 2000. pap. 26.00 (*0-87338-653-1*) Kent St U Pr.

***Donley, Clayton.** LDAP Programming: Directory Management & Integration. 2000. pap. 44.95 (*1-884777-91-0*) Manning Pubns.

Donley, Dorothea. Doubting Lady. 1999. mass mkt. 4.99 (*0-8217-6219-2*) Kensgtn Pub Corp.

— Gentleman's Choice. 224p. 1996. mass mkt. 4.50 (*0-8217-5239-1*, Zebra Kensgtn) Kensgtn Pub Corp.

— Lady Decides. 1999. mass mkt. 4.99 (*0-8217-6389-X*, Zebra Kensgtn) Kensgtn Pub Corp.

— A Proper Match. 224p. 1998. mass mkt. 4.99 (*0-8217-5827-6*, Zebra Kensgtn) Kensgtn Pub Corp.

— A Single Season. 224p. 1997. mass mkt. 4.99 (*0-8217-5672-9*, Zebra Kensgtn) Kensgtn Pub Corp.

Donley, Elizabeth L., et al. Wisconsin Limited Liability Company Forms & Practice Manual. LC 96-1124. 654p. 1997. ring bd. 219.90 (*1-57400-028-4*) Data Trace Pubng.

Donley, Elizabeth M., ed. Air Quality Data Management Software Report. unabridged ed. (Illus.). iv, 159p. 1995. 195.00 (*1-891682-04-0*) Donley Tech.

— Environmental Management Information Systems Report. 2nd rev. unabridged ed. iv, 152p. 1996. 195.00 (*1-891682-00-8*) Donley Tech.

— Waste Manifest Software Report. unabridged ed. (Illus.). iv, 118p. 1996. 195.00 (*1-891682-01-6*) Donley Tech.

***Donley, Elizabeth M., et al, eds.** EH&S Compliance Auditing & Tracking Software Report. 2nd unabridged ed. (Illus.). 240p. 1999. 195.00 (*1-891682-08-3*) Donley Tech.

— MSDS Software Report. 4th rev. unabridged ed. (Illus.). 424p. 1999. lib. bdg. 299.00 (*1-891682-07-5*) Donley Tech.

Donley, Elizabeth M. & Donley, John W., eds. Environmental Compliance Auditing Software Report. unabridged ed. (Illus.). iv, 190p. 1997. 195.00 (*1-891682-03-2*) Donley Tech.

— Environmental Cost Estimating Software Report. unabridged ed. (Illus.). iv, 162p. 1996. 195.00 (*1-891682-05-9*) Donley Tech.

— MSDS Software Report. 3rd rev. unabridged ed. (Illus.). vi, 382p. 1997. 239.00 (*1-891682-02-4*) Donley Tech.

Donley, John W., jt. ed. see Donley, Elizabeth M.

Donley, K. Opening New Doors: Finding Families for Older & Handicapped Children. (C). 1989. 55.00 (*0-903534-33-9*, Pub. by Brit Ag for Adopt & Fost) St Mut.

Donley, Marshall O. Power to the Teacher: How America's Educators Become Militant. LC 75-31421. (Illus.). 254p. reprint ed. pap. 78.80 (*0-8357-3952-X*, 205704800004) Bks Demand.

Donley, Mike. The Alphabet by God: An ABC Approach to a Real Relationship with God. LC 99-72367. 130p. 1999. pap. 5.95 (*0-7392-0125-5*, P03038) Morris Pubng.

Donley, Richard, jt. auth. see Rutledge, Leigh W.

Donley, Stephanie, ed. see Auer, Jorg A. & Stick, John A.

Donley, Stephanie, ed. see Fowler, Murray E. & Miller, R. Eric.

Donley, Stephanie, ed. see Hinman, Frank, Jr.

Donley, Stephanie, ed. see Howard, Jimmy L. & Smith, Robert.

Donley, Stephanie, ed. see Jay, Richard M.

Donley, Stephanie, ed. see Kane, Robert A.

Donley, Stephanie, ed. see King, Lowell R.

Donley, Stephanie, ed. see Maniglia, Anthony J., et al.

Donley, Stephanie, ed. see Nitti, Victor W.

Donley, Stephanie, ed. see Nseyo, Unyime, et al.

Donley, Stephanie, ed. see Orsini, James A. & Divers, Thomas J.

Donley, Stephanie, ed. see Reef, Virginia B.

Donley, Stephanie, ed. see Rose, Reuben J. & Hodgson, David R.

Donley, Stephanie, ed. see Rupley, Agnes E.

Donley, Stephanie, ed. see Samper, Juan C.

Donley, Stephanie, ed. see Thawley, Stanley E., et al.

Donley, Stephanie, ed. see White, Nathaniel A. & Moore, James N.

Donley, Stephanie, ed. see Youngquist, Robert S.

Donley, Susan K., jt. auth. see Kowalski, Ann N.

Donley, Thomas & Oppenheimer, M. Labor Markets in Transition - International Dimensions. (International Review of Comparative Public Policy Ser.: Vol. 10). 320p. 1999. 78.50 (*0-7623-0375-1*) Jai Pr.

Donley, Thomas, jt. auth. see Alwitt, Linda F.

Donloe, Darlene. Gordon Parks: Photographer, Writer, Composer, Film Maker. (Black American Ser.). (Illus.). 192p. (YA). 1993. mass mkt. 3.95 (*0-87067-595-8*, Melrose Sq) Holloway.

— Katherine Dunham: Dancer & Choreographer. (Black American Ser.). (Illus.). 192p. (YA). 1993. mass mkt. 3.95 (*0-87067-775-6*, Melrose Sq) Holloway.

Donloe, Darlene. Mahalia Jackson: Gospel Singer. (Black American Ser.). (Illus.). 192p. (YA). 1992. mass mkt. 4.95 (*0-87067-893-0*, Melrose Sq) Holloway.

Donlon, E. T., jt. auth. see Curtis, W. S.

Donlon, James I., jt. ed. see Pedone, F. Stephen.

Donlon, James I., jt. ed. see Vann, Kevin W.

Donlon, Roger H. Beyond Nam Dong LC 98-68197. 227 p. 1998. write for info. (*0-9621374-8-0*) J H Johnston.

Donlon, William C., jt. ed. see Jacobson, Alan L.

Donmoyer, Robert, et al, eds. The Knowledge Base in Educational Administration: Multiple Perspectives. LC 94-25386. (SUNY Series, Educational Leadership). 319p. (C). 1995. text 64.50 (*0-7914-2385-9*); pap. text 21.95 (*0-7914-2386-7*) State U NY Pr.

Donmoyer, Robert & Kos, Raylene, eds. At-Risk Students: Portraits, Policies, Programs, & Practices. LC 92-5481. (SUNY Series, Youth Social Services, Schooling, & Public Policy). 429p. (C). 1993. pap. text 24.95 (*0-7914-1394-2*) State U NY Pr.

Donn-Byrne, Brian O., see Byrne, Donn B., pseud.

Donn, Clifford B. The Australian Council of Trade Unions: History & Economic Policy. LC 83-15951. 400p. (C). 1984. pap. text 28.50 (*0-8191-2729-9*) U Pr of Amer.

Donn, Elizabeth R. Spanish-English Comparative Dictionary of Cognates: Diccionario Comparativo de Cognados en Espanol e Ingles. Camacho De Rodas, Isabel & Lyle, Jean K., eds. LC 85-90321. (ENG & SPA., Illus.). 212p. (Orig.). 1985. pap. 12.95 (*0-932058-02-7*) RoDonn Pub.

Donn, Gari, ed. Missiles, Reactors & Civil Liberties: Against the Nuclear State. 1981. 20.00 (*0-906502-04-7*, Pub. by NCCL) St Mut.

Donn, M. A. Checklist of European Polypores. (Verhandelingen der Koninklijke Nederlandse Akademie van Wetenschappen, Afd. Natuurkunde Ser.: No. 62). 470p. 1974. pap. text 53.75 (*0-7204-8255-0*) Elsevier.

Donn, Steven M. The Michigan Manual: A Guide to Neonatal Intensive Care. 2nd ed. LC 97-20394. (Illus.). 464p. 1997. 37.50 (*0-87993-676-2*) Futura Pub.

Donn, Steven M., ed. Neonatal & Pediatric Pulmonary Graphics: Principle & Clinical Applications. LC 97-39522. (Illus.). 443p. 1997. 85.00 (*0-87993-645-2*) Futura Pub.

Donn, Steven M. & Fisher, Charles W., eds. Risk Management Techniques in Perinatal & Neonatal Practice. LC 96-12740. (Illus.). 720p. 1996. 115.00 (*0-87993-640-1*) Futura Pub.

Donn, Steven M. & Kuhns, Lawrence R. Pediatric Transillumination. LC 82-11035. (Illus.). 133p. reprint ed. pap. 41.30 (*0-8357-7612-3*, 205693500096) Bks Demand.

Donn, Steven M., jt. ed. see Sinha, Sunil K.

Donn, William. The Earth: Our Physical Environment. LC 79-37431. 639p. (C). reprint ed. 198.10 (*0-8357-9875-5*, 205511000008) Bks Demand.

Donn, William L. & Shimer, John A. Graphic Methods in Structural Geology. LC 58-5315. (Century Earth Science Ser.). 189p. reprint ed. pap. 58.60 (*0-608-12391-9*, 205568400030) Bks Demand.

Donna, Mehalko, jt. auth. see Walker, Cindy.

Donna, Rose B., tr. see Cyprian of Carthage, St.

Donna, Sylvie. Teach Business English. (Handbks. for Language Teachers). (Illus.). 320p. 1999. pap. write for info. (*0-521-58557-0*) Cambridge U Pr.

Donnachie, Ian. A History of the Brewing Industry in Scotland. 350p. 1998. pap. 48.00 (*0-85976-470-2*, Pub. by J Donald) St Mut.

Donnachie, Ian & Hewitt, George. Historic New Lanark: The Dale & Owen Industrial Community since 1785. (Illus.). 256p. 1994. pap. 16.50 (*0-7486-0420-0*, Pub. by Edinburgh U Pr) Col U Pr.

Donnachie, Ian, jt. ed. see Butt, John.

Donnachie, Whatley. The Manufacture of Scottish History. 1992. 20.00 (*0-7486-6120-4*, Pub. by Polygon) Subterranean Co.

Donnadieu, Gabe & Schuler, Robert A. Controlling Unemployment Insurance Costs: The Employer's Comprehensive Guide to the UIC System. LC 93-42763. 304p. 1994. 65.00 (*0-89930-831-7*, Quorum Bks) Greenwood.

Donnahoe, Alan S. What Every Manager Should Know about Financial Analysis. 224p. 1990. pap. 10.00 (*0-671-70640-3*) S&S Trade.

Donnai, D. & Winter, R., eds. Congenital Malformation Syndromes. (Illus.). 640p. (gr. 13). 1995. pap. 115.00 (*0-412-56590-0*, Pub. by E A) OUP.

***Donnan, Bob.** Fighting Back. 1999. text 35.00 (*1-84018-171-0*, Pub. by Mainstream Pubng) Trafalgar.

Donnan, Bob & Morton, Hugh, photos by. Return to the Top: The Inside Story of North Carolina's 1993 NCAA Championship. (Illus.). 128p. 1994. 29.95 (*1-880123-07-X*) VilCom Sports.

Donnan, Christopher B. Ceramics of Ancient Peru. LC 92-72522. (Illus.). 128p. (C). 1992. 40.00 (*0-930741-21-8*); pap. 22.00 (*0-930741-22-6*) UCLA Fowler Mus.

Donnan, Christopher B., ed. Early Ceremonial Architecture in the Andes. LC 84-10291. (Illus.). 300p. 1985. 18.00 (*0-88402-135-1*) Dumbarton Oaks.

Donnan, Christopher B. & Cock, Guillermo A. The Pacatnamu Papers: The Moche Occupation, Vol. 2. (ENG & SPA., Illus.). 300p. (Orig.). 1997. 50.00 (*0-930741-56-0*); pap. 29.00 (*0-930741-57-9*) UCLA Fowler Mus.

***Donnan, Christopher B. & McClelland, Donna.** Moche Fineline Painting: Its Evolution & Its Artists. (Illus.). 320p. (C). 1999. 70.00 (*0-930741-78-1*); pap. 39.00 (*0-930741-79-X*) UCLA Fowler Mus.

Donnan, Christopher B., jt. auth. see Alva, Walter.

Donnan, Christopher B., jt. ed. see Cock, Guillermo A.

Donnan, Frederick G., et al, eds. Commentary on the Scientific Writings of Josiah-Willard Gibbs: A Propos de la Publication Des Ses Memories Scientifiques, 3 vols., Set. LC 79-7963. (Three Centuries of Science in America Ser.). 1980. reprint ed. lib. bdg. 126.95 (*0-405-12544-5*) Ayer.

— Commentary on the Scientific Writings of Josiah-Willard Gibbs: A Propos de la Publication Des Ses Memories Scientifiques, 3 vols., Vol. 1. LC 79-7963. (Three Centuries of Science in America Ser.). 1980. reprint ed. lib. bdg. 63.95 (*0-405-12611-5*) Ayer.

— Commentary on the Scientific Writings of Josiah-Willard Gibbs: A Propos de la Publication Des Ses Memories Scientifiques, 3 vols., Vol. 2. LC 79-7963. (Three Centuries of Science in America Ser.). 1980. reprint ed. lib. bdg. 63.95 (*0-405-12612-3*) Ayer.

Donnan, Geoffrey, et al, eds. Lacunar & Subcortical Infarctions. (Illus.). 294p. 1995. text 98.00 (*0-19-262341-9*) OUP.

Donnan, Geoffrey A. & Burton, Carol. After a Stroke: A Support Book for Patients, Caregivers, Families & Friends. 2nd ed. LC 92-241764. (Illus.). 144p. 1992. reprint ed. pap. 11.95 (*1-55643-130-9*) North Atlantic.

Donnan, H. Marriage among Muslims. 250p. 1996. 60.00 (*0-614-21515-3*, 754) Kazi Pubns.

Donnan, Hasting & Selier, Frits, eds. Family & Gender in Pakistan: Domestic Organization in a Muslim Society. (C). 1997. 32.00 (*81-7075-036-9*, Pub. by Hindustan) S Asia.

Donnan, Hastings & McFarlane, Graham. Social Anthropology & Public Policy in Northern Ireland. 165p. 1989. text 69.95 (*0-566-05594-5*, Pub. by Avebry) Ashgate Pub Co.

***Donnan, Hastings & Wilson, Thomas M.** Borders: Frontiers of Identity, Nation & State. 224p. 1999. 65.00 (*1-85973-241-0*, Pub. by Berg Pubs); pap. 19.50 (*1-85973-246-1*, Pub. by Berg Pubs) NYU Pr.

Donnan, Hastings & Wilson, Thomas M., eds. Border Approaches: Anthropological Perspectives on Frontiers. LC 93-50652. 134p. (Orig.). 1994. pap. 19.50 (*0-8191-9454-9*); lib. bdg. 44.50 (*0-8191-9453-0*) U Pr of Amer.

Donnan, Hastings, jt. ed. see Wilson, Thomas M.

Donnan, Robert, ed. see Southern Technology Council Staff.

Donnan, Thomas M. French Lyric Diction. LC 93-49524. 158p. (Orig.). 1994. pap. 18.75 (*0-8191-9441-7*) U Pr of Amer.

Donnay, Albert, ed. The Investor's Guide to the Military Industry: Fiscal Year, 1988. 2nd ed. 842p. (Orig.). 1989. ring bd. 950.00 (*0-9621396-1-0*) Nuclear Free Am.

Donne, Brian K. Christ Ascended: A Study in the Significance of the Ascension of Jesus Christ in the New Testament. 1983. pap. text 11.95 (*0-85364-336-9*) Attic Pr.

Donne, Charles E. Essay on the Tragedy of Arden of Feversham. LC 77-164773. reprint ed. 21.50 (*0-404-02143-3*) AMS Pr.

Donne, John, II. Biathanatos, Sullivan, Ernest W., ed. LC 80-66387. 352p. 1984. 47.50 (*0-87413-175-8*) U Delaware Pr.

D

An Asterisk (*) at the beginning of an entry indicates that the title is appearing for the first time.

Donne, John. Biathanatos. Kastenbaum, Robert J., ed. LC 76-19567. (Death & Dying Ser.). 1977. reprint ed. lib. bdg. 25.95 (*0-405-09563-5*) Ayer.

— A Complete Concordance to the Poems of John Donne, 2 vols. Floren, Celia, ed. (Alpha-Omega, Series C, English Authors: Vol. 5). (GER.). 1010p. Date not set. write for info. (*3-487-10326-5*) G Olms Pubs.

— The Complete English Poems. Hamilton, Robin & Patrides, C. A., eds. 600p. 1994. 9.50 (*0-460-87441-1*, Everyman's Classic Lib) Tuttle Pubng.

— The Complete English Poems of John Donne. Smith, A. J., ed. (Poets Ser.). 6089p. 1977. pap. 13.95 (*0-14-042209-9*, Penguin Classics) Viking Penguin.

— Complete Poetry & Selected Prose of John Donne. LC 94-4354. 644p. 1994. 20.00 (*0-679-60102-3*) Modern Lib NY.

— Devotions upon Emergent Occasions. 246p. 1959. pap. text 17.95 (*0-472-06030-9*, 06030, Ann Arbor Bks) U of Mich Pr.

— Devotions upon Emergent Occasions. Raspa, Anthony, ed. LC 76-361973. 248p. reprint ed. pap. 76.90 (*0-608-12421-4*, 202426300036) Bks Demand.

— Devotions upon Emergent Occasions & Death's Duel. LC 99-23675. 288p. 1999. pap. 12.95 (*0-375-70548-1*) Vin Bks.

— The Divine Poems. 2nd ed. Gardner, Helen, ed. (Oxford English Texts Ser.). 1982. pap. 17.95 (*0-19-871100-X*) OUP.

— Donne: Complete Poems. Bennett, Roger, ed. 336p. 1992. spiral bd. 59.50 (*0-87532-103-8*) Hendricks House.

— Donne: Selected Poems. Hayward, John, ed. (Poets Ser.). 192p. (Orig.). (gr. 9 up). 1986. pap. 9.95 (*0-14-058518-4*, Penguin Bks) Viking Penguin.

— Donne's Prebend Sermons. Mueller, Janel M., ed. LC 77-143229. 377p. reprint ed. pap. 116.90 (*0-8357-9156-4*, 201465200093) Bks Demand.

— Going to Bed & Other Poems. 1996. pap. 1.99 (*0-679-77099-2*) Modern Lib NY.

— Ignatius His Conclave, or His Inthronisation in a Late Election in Hell. LC 77-6876. (English Experience Ser.: No. 868). 1977. reprint ed. lib. bdg. 20.00 (*90-221-0868-6*) Walter J Johnson.

— John Donne. Carey, John, ed. (Oxford Authors Ser.). 528p. 1990. pap. text 22.00 (*0-19-281341-2*) OUP.

— John Donne. (Bloomsbury Classic Poetry Ser.). 128p. 1994. text 9.95 (*0-312-11468-0*) St Martin.

***Donne, John.** John Donne: The Major Works. Carey, John, ed. (Oxford World's Classics Ser.). 488p. 2000. pap. 14.95 (*0-19-284041-X*) OUP.

Donne, John. John Donne's Sermons on the Psalms & Gospels: With a Selection of Prayers & Meditations. Simpson, Evelyn M., ed. & intro. by. LC 63-16249. 1963. pap. 15.95 (*0-520-00340-3*, Pub. by U CA Pr) Cal Prin Full Svc.

— Juvenilia: or Certaine Paradoxes & Problemes. LC 70-25438. (English Experience Ser.: No. 239). 64p. 1970. reprint ed. 20.00 (*90-221-0239-4*) Walter J Johnson.

— Letters to Several Persons of Honour. (Anglistica & Americana Ser.: No. 148). 318p. 1974. reprint ed. 63.70 (*3-487-04484-6*) G Olms Pubs.

— Letters to Several Persons of Honour. LC 77-10078. 352p. 1977. reprint ed. lib. bdg. 75.00 (*0-8201-1296-8*) Schol Facsimiles.

— Poems. 576p. 1991. 20.00 (*0-679-40558-5*) Everymns Lib.

— Poems. LC 95-15330. (Everyman's Library of Pocket Poets). 256p. 1994. 12.50 (*0-679-44467-X*) Knopf.

Donne, John. Poems: With Elegies on the Author's Death. (Anglistica & Americana Ser.: No. 94). 406p. 1974. reprint ed. 83.20 (*3-487-05441-8*) G Olms Pubs.

Donne, John. Poems: With Elegies on the Author's Death. LC 72-191. (English Experience Ser.: No. 240). 408p. 1970. reprint ed. 50.00 (*90-221-0240-8*) Walter J Johnson.

— Poetry & Prose. Warnke, Frank J., ed. (Modern Library College Editions). 437p. (C). 1967. pap. 8.44 (*0-07-553663-3*, T89) McGraw.

— Poetry & Prose, with Izaac Walton's Life, Appreciations by Ben Jonson, Dryden, Coleridge & Others. LC 75-41077. reprint ed. 20.00 (*0-404-14769-0*) AMS Pr.

— The Prayers of John Donne. Umbach, Herbert H., ed. 1962. pap. 7.95 (*0-8084-0252-8*) NCUP.

— Pseudo-Martyr. 528p. 1993. 70.00 (*0-7735-0994-1*, Pub. by McG-Queens Univ Pr) CUP Services.

— Pseudo-Martyr. LC 74-16215. 450p. 1974. 75.00 (*0-8201-1140-6*) Schol Facsimiles.

***Donne, John.** Religious Poetry & Prose. Carrigan, Henry L., Jr., ed. LC 99-34592. 112p. 1999. pap. 12.95 (*1-55725-235-1*, 930-027, Pub. by Paraclete MA) BookWorld.

Donne, John. Selected Poems. Shaaber, Matthias A., ed. (Crofts Classics). 128p. 1958. pap. text 4.95 (*0-88295-032-0*) Harlan Davidson.

— Selected Poems: John Donne. LC 93-21800. (Thrift Editions Ser.). 96p. 1993. reprint ed. pap. 1.50 (*0-486-27788-7*) Dover.

— Selected Poetry. Carey, John, ed. (Oxford World's Classics Ser.). 292p. 2001. pap. 9.95 (*0-19-283490-8*) OUP.

Donne, John. The Variorum Edition of the Poetry of John Donne Vol. 6: The Anniversaries & Epicedes & Obsequies. Dickson, Donald R. et al, eds. LC 93-11800. 754p. 1995. text 49.95 (*0-253-31811-4*) Ind U Pr.

Donne, John, et al. John Donne's 1622 Gunpowder Plot Sermon: A Parallel-Text Edition. LC 96-25367. (Language & Literature Ser.). 200p. 1996. pap. text 21.50 (*0-8207-0283-8*) Duquesne.

— John Donne's 1622 Gunpowder Plot Sermon: A Parallel-Text Edition. LC 96-25367. (Language & Literature Ser.: Vol. 22). (Illus.). 200p. (C). 1996. text 45.00 (*0-8207-0261-7*) Duquesne.

Donne, T. & Verhoeven, T. EC-10, Proceedings of the 10th Joint Workshop on Electron Cyclotron Emission & Electron Cyclotron Resonance. 650p. 1997. text 128.00 (*981-02-3219-5*) World Scientific Pub.

Donne, W. B., ed. Correspondence of King George the Third with Lord North, 1768-1783. LC 76-154697. (Era of the American Revolution Ser.). 1971. reprint ed. lib. bdg. 95.00 (*0-306-70155-3*) Da Capo.

Donnell, Alison & Welsh, Sarah L., compiled by. The Routledge Reader in Caribbean Literature. 560p. (C). 1996. pap. 27.99 (*0-415-12049-7*) Routledge.

— The Routledge Reader in Caribbean Literature. 560p. (C). 1996. 90.00 (*0-415-12048-9*) Routledge.

Donnell, Annie H. Rebecca Mary. LC 72-4455. (Short Story Index Reprint Ser.). (Illus.). 1977. reprint ed. 23.95 (*0-8369-4173-X*) Ayer.

Donnell, Augustus & Dellinger, Margaret. Analyzing Business Process Data: The Looking Glass. 2nd rev. ed. (AT&T Quality Library). (Illus.). 172p. (Orig.). 1990. pap. 24.95 (*0-932764-22-3*, 500-445) AT&T Customer Info.

Donnell, Camilla & Donnell, Emma A. Donnell Family: History of Genealogy of the Descendants of Thos. Donnell of Scotland. (Illus.). 174p. 1997. reprint ed. pap. 26.50 (*0-8328-8328-X*); reprint ed. lib. bdg. 36.50 (*0-8328-8327-1*) Higginson Bk Co.

Donnell, Courtney G., et al. Ivan Albright. LC 96-49866. (Illus.). 208p. 1997. pap. 29.95 (*0-86559-142-3*) Art Inst Chi.

Donnell, David. Dancing in the Dark. 124p. 1996. pap. 12.99 (*0-7710-2833-4*) McCland & Stewart.

Donnell, E. A. & Donnell, J. A. Donnell, the Donnells & Their MacDonald Ancestors: A History & Genealogy, 157-1927 A.D. (Illus.). 251p. 1992. reprint ed. pap. 48.00 (*0-8328-2651-0*); reprint ed. lib. bdg. 58.00 (*0-8328-2650-2*) Higginson Bk Co.

Donnell, Emma A., jt. auth. see Donnell, Camilla.

Donnell, J. A., jt. auth. see Donnell, E. A.

Donnell, James H., Jr. 25 Management Lessons from the Customer's Side of the Counter. 214p. 1991. 24.95 (*1-55623-569-0*, Irwn Prfssnl) McGraw-Hill Prof.

Donnell-Kotrozo, Carl. Critical Essays on Post Impressionism. LC 81-65879. (Illus.). 176p. 1983. 37.50 (*0-87982-041-1*) Art Alliance.

Donnell Media Center Staff. 1994 Video Supplement. 342p. 1994. pap. 20.00 (*0-87104-745-4*, Branch Libraries) NY Pub Lib.

Donnell, Nils. It's Not the Same Old Me. 1975. pap. 2.00 (*0-88027-007-1*) Firm Foun Pub.

Donnell, Radka, tr. see Vogt, Adolf M.

Donnell, Rich. The Hig: Penn State's Gridiron Legacy: The Bob Higgins & Steve Suhey Families. 336p. 1994. 23.95 (*0-9638568-2-0*) Owl Bay Pubs.

— Shug: The Life & Times of Auburn's Ralph 'Shug' Jordan. 336p. 1994. 22.95 (*0-9638568-0-4*) Owl Bay Pubs.

Donnell, Susan. Pocahontas. 416p. 1993. mass mkt. 6.50 (*0-425-13620-5*) Berkley Pub.

Donnell, Susan M., jt. auth. see Hall, Jay.

Donnellan, Craig. Rich Man, Poor Man. LC 94-147575. (Issues for the Nineties Ser.). 40p. 1993. write for info. (*1-872995-31-4*) Independence Educ.

Donnellan, Anne M., ed. Classic Readings in Autism. LC 85-2695. (Special Education Ser.). 454p. reprint ed. pap. 140.80 (*0-7837-3889-7*, 204373700010) Bks Demand.

Donnellan, Anne M. & Leary, Martha R. Movement Differences & Diversity in Autism-Mental Retardation: Appreciations & Accommodations People with Communications & Behavior Challenges. (Movin' On Ser.). 106p. 1994. pap. text 16.00 (*1-886928-00-2*) DRI Pr.

Donnellan, Anne M., et al. Progress Without Punishment: Effective Approaches for Learners with Behavior Problems. (Special Education Ser.). 192p. (C). 1988. pap. text 17.95 (*0-8077-2911-6*) Tchrs Coll.

Donnellan, Anne M., jt. auth. see Haskew, Paul.

Donnellan, Anne M., jt. auth. see LaVigna, Gary W.

Donnellan, John. Merchandise Buying & Management. 52p. 1998. teacher ed. write for info. (*1-56367-053-4*) Fairchild.

— Merchandise Buying & Management. (Illus.). 473p. 1998. 56.00 (*1-56367-052-6*) Fairchild.

***Donnellan, John & Moran, Martha.** Selling & Promoting Products: Building the Sale: Workbook. Woodbury, Debbie, ed. LC 99-75995. (Retailing Smarts Ser.: Vol. 6). (Illus.). 72p. 1999. pap., wbk. ed. 7.95 (*1-56052-571-1*) Crisp Pubns.

— Selling & Promoting Products: Explaining Features & Benefits: Workbook. Woodbury, Debbie, ed. LC 99-75994. (Retailing Smarts Ser.: Vol. 5). (Illus.). 72p. 1999. pap., wbk. ed. 7.95 (*1-56052-570-3*) Crisp Pubns.

Donnellan, John, jt. auth. see Moran, Martha.

Donnellan, Patrick E., jt. auth. see Kuriyama, Noriko.

Donnellan, Sean. Something Tastes Funny. LC 97-1856. (Illus.). 208p. (Orig.). 1997. mass mkt. 9.99 (*0-446-67322-6*, Pub. by Warner Bks) Little.

Donnellan, William L., et al, eds. Abdominal Surgery of Infancy & Childhood, 2 vols., Set. 1424p. 1996. text 225.00 (*3-7186-5409-1*, Harwood Acad Pubs) Gordon & Breach.

Donnelley, Adelaide, jt. auth. see Pachen, Ani.

***Donnelley, Karen J.** Electrician. LC 00-22446. (Career Explorations Ser.). 48p. (YA). (gr. 5 up). 2000. lib. bdg. 21.26 (*0-7368-0594-X*, Capstone Bks) Capstone Pr.

Donnelli, Rebecca, jt. auth. see Keffler, Christina.

Donnellon, Anne. Team Talk: The Power of Language in Team Dynamics. LC 95-36810. 320p. (C). 1996. 24.95 (*0-87584-619-X*) Harvard Busn.

— Team Talk: The Power of Language in Team Dynamics. 1995. 24.95 (*0-07-103634-2*) McGraw.

Donnellon, Anne, jt. ed. see Heckscher, Charles C.

Donnellon, Daniel J. Injunctions & Restraining Orders in Ohio. (Ohio Prctice Manual Ser.). 245p. (Orig.). 1992. pap. 38.50 (*0-87084-229-3*) Anderson Pub Co.

Donnelly. On Your Own, A Personal Budgeting Simulaltion. 1995. 1525.00 (*0-538-62328-4*) Thomson Learn.

— Skills for Consumer Success. 2nd ed. (HM - Consumer Education Ser.). 1986. mass mkt., wbk. ed. 19.95 (*0-538-08110-4*) S-W Pub.

— Skills for Consumer Success. 3rd ed. (HM - Consumer Education Ser.). 1992. 3.95 (*0-538-61090-5*); mass mkt., wbk. ed. 14.00 (*0-538-61089-1*) S-W Pub.

Donnelly, ed. Human Anatomy (C). 1985. pap., lab manual ed. write for info. (*0-06-041689-0*) Addison-Wesley.

Donnelly, jt. auth. see Donnelly, Colm J.

Donnelly, A. S., tr. see Fedorova, Svetlana G.

Donnelly, Alton S., tr. from RUS. The Wreck of the SV. Nikolai. (North Pacific Studies: No. 8). (Illus.). 128p. 1985. 19.95 (*0-87595-124-4*) Oregon Hist.

Donnelly, Alton S., ed. see Tikhmenev, Petr A.

Donnelly, Amy, jt. auth. see Mills, Heidi.

Donnelly, Andrew. Water Pollution. LC 97-31352. (Illus.). 32p. (J). 1998. lib. bdg. 22.79 (*1-56766-510-1*) Childs World.

— Waterfalls. LC 97-44403. (Illus.). 32p. (J). 1998. lib. bdg. 22.79 (*1-56766-487-3*) Childs World.

— Wetlands. LC 97-30408. (Biomes of Nature Ser.). (Illus.). 32p. (J). (gr. 2-6). 1998. lib. bdg. 22.79 (*1-56766-466-0*) Childs World.

Donnelly, Andrew J. Anesthesiology & Critical Care Drug Handbook: Including Select Disease States & Perioperative. 1998. pap. text 33.75 (*0-916589-17-X*) Lexi-Comp.

— Anesthesiology & Critical Care Drug Handbook: 1999-2000 Edition. 2nd ed. 1999. pap. 35.95 (*0-916589-73-0*) Lexi-Comp.

Donnelly, Anthony J. The Day the Trees Held Their Breath. (Illus.). 50p. (J). 1998. pap. write for info. (*1-888701-11-0*) Jarrett Pr.

Donnelly, Austin. More Wealth Through Beating the Money Traps. 195p. (C). 1990. pap. 60.00 (*0-86439-124-2*, Pub. by Boolarong Pubns) St Mut.

***Donnelly, Beth & Martin, Andrea.** New York's 50 Best Places to Find Spiritual Renewal: A Peace & Quiet Book. 128p. 2000. pap. 14.00 (*1-929439-00-8*) City & Co.

Donnelly, Brenda W., et al. The Challenge of Adolescent Health: Views from Catholic Social Teaching & the Social & Medical Sciences. LC 96-35135. 242p. 1996. pap. text 29.50 (*0-7618-0561-3*); lib. bdg. 57.00 (*0-7618-0560-5*) U Pr of Amer.

Donnelly, Brenda W., jt. auth. see Voydanoff, Patricia.

Donnelly, Brian, jt. auth. see Evans, Philip S.

Donnelly, C. N. Heirs of Clausewitz: Change & Continuity in the Soviet War Machine. (C). 1990. 35.00 (*0-907967-71-X*, Pub. by Inst Euro Def & Strat) St Mut.

***Donnelly, Charles & Stallman, Richard M.** The Bison Manual: Using the YACC - Compatible Parser Generator for Version 1.29. 104p. (C). 1999. per. 20.00 (*1-882114-44-2*) Free Software.

Donnelly, Colleen. Linguistics for Writers. LC 92-36122. 251p. (C). 1994. text 54.50 (*0-7914-1571-6*); pap. text 20.95 (*0-7914-1572-4*) State U NY Pr.

Donnelly, Colm J. & Donnelly. Living Places: Archaeology, Continuity & Change at Historic Monuments in Northern Ireland. LC 98-230937. xiv, 146 p. 1997. write for info. (*0-85389-475-2*) Queens U Belfast.

***Donnelly, Cynthia.** A Woman in Love: A Play on the Life of Catherine de Hueck Doherty. 1998. pap. 4.00 (*0-921440-49-9*) Madonna Hse.

Donnelly, D. Glossary of Plant Tissue Culture. 141p. 1989. pap. 225.00 (*81-7089-119-1*, Pub. by Intl Bk Distr) St Mut.

Donnelly, D., jt. auth. see Pitfield, P.

Donnelly, Dan. Stand Alone Acoustic Guitar. (Alfred's Handy Guide Ser.). 1996. pap. 12.95 incl. audio compact disk (*0-88284-725-2*) Alfred Pub.

— Stand Alone Tracks Tie-Dye Rock: Handy Guide. (Alfred's Handy Guide Ser.). 1997. pap. 12.95 incl. audio compact disk (*0-88284-780-5*) Alfred Pub.

Donnelly, Daniel. Cutting Edge Web Design: The Next Generation. (Illus.). 160p. 1998. 49.99 incl. cd-rom (*1-56496-419-1*) Rockport Pubs.

— GED Social Studies. 1989. pap. text 14.95 (*1-56030-008-6*) Comex Systs.

— In Your Face: The Best of Interactive Interface Design. (Illus.). 160p. 1998. pap. 35.00 incl. cd-rom (*1-56496-400-0*) Rockport Pubs.

***Donnelly, Daniel.** In Your Face Too: More of hte Best Interactive Design, 160p. 2000. 50.00 (*1-56496-677-1*) Rockport Pubs.

Donnelly, Daniel. Upload: From Print to the Web. (Illus.). 160p. 1998. pap. 49.99 incl. cd-rom (*1-56496-399-3*) Rockport Pubs.

— Web Works: Typography. (Illus.). 192p. 1998. pap. 45.00 (*1-56496-519-8*) Rockport Pubs.

Donnelly, Daniel. WWW Design: Web Pages from Around the World. (Illus.). 160p. 1997. 49.99 incl. cd-rom (*1-56496-335-7*) Rockport Pubs.

***Donnelly, Daniel.** WWW Design: Web Pages from Around the World. 160p. 2000. pap. 25.00 (*1-56496-684-4*) Rockport Pubs.

Donnelly, Danielle J. & Vidaver, William. Glossary of Plant Tissue Culture. LC 88-9591. 144p. 1988. 22.95 (*0-931146-12-7*, Dioscorides) Timber.

Donnelly, David, et al. Money & Politics: Financing Our Elections Democratically. LC 98-53710. (New Democracy Forum Ser.). 112p. 1999. pap. 11.00 (*0-8070-4315-X*) Beacon Pr.

Donnelly, David B. Creating Your Backyard Bird Garden: How to Make Your Yard Irresistible to Birds! Thompson, Bill, ed. LC 99-177556. (Illus.). 32p. 1998. pap. 3.95 (*1-880241-13-7*) Bird Watchers.

Donnelly de Romero, Kate. Cocinando des de la Fortaleza. (SPA., Illus.). 232p. reprint ed. ring bd. 24.95 (*0-89825-008-0*) Pub Resces PR.

— Cocinando Desde la Fortaleza. (SPA.). 1994. pap., spiral bd. 19.95 (*0-89882-500-8*) Pub Resces PR.

Donnelly, Denis, ed. The Computer Culture: A Symposium to Explore the Computer's Impact on Society. LC 83-49215. (Illus.). 176p. 1985. 27.50 (*0-8386-3220-3*) Fairleigh Dickinson.

Donnelly, Denise, jt. auth. see Donnelly, Michael.

Donnelly, Dennis M. & Nelson, Louis J. Net Economic Value of Deer Hunting in Idaho. (Illus.). 36p. 1997. reprint ed. pap. 4.60 (*0-89904-644-4*, Wildlife Resrch Grp) Crumb Elbow Pub.

Donnelly, Dody H. Radical Love: An Approach to Sexual Spirituality. 136p. 1992. reprint ed. pap. 10.00 (*0-9623086-2-5*) Dharma Cloud Pubs.

Donnelly, Doris. Learning to Forgive. (Festival Bks.). 144p. 1986. reprint ed. pap. 8.95 (*0-687-21324-X*) Abingdon.

— Retrieving Charisms for the Twenty-First Century. LC 99-18655. 1999. 14.95 (*0-8146-2540-1*) Liturgical Pr.

Donnelly, Dorothy. Kudzu & Other Poems: Poems. (Pourboire Ser.). 1979. pap. 6.00 (*0-930900-57-X*) Burning Deck.

Donnelly, Dorothy F. Augustine's De Civitate Dei: An Annotated Bibliography of Modern Criticism, 1960-1990. LC 91-26511. (Augustinian Historical Institute Series of Villanova University). 109p. (C). 1992. text 29.95 (*0-8204-1607-X*) P Lang Pubng.

— Patterns of Order & Utopia. LC 98-3794. 156p. 1998. text 45.00 (*0-312-16496-3*) St Martin.

Donnelly, Dorothy F., ed. The City of God: A Collection of Critical Essays. LC 94-15185. XIII, 458p. (C). 1995. pap. text 29.95 (*0-8204-1726-2*) P Lang Pubng.

Donnelly, Douglas R., jt. auth. see Strom, Kay M.

Donnelly, Edward A. Peter: Eyewitness of His Majesty. 100p. 1998. pap. 9.99 (*0-85151-744-7*) Banner of Truth.

Donnelly, Frances. Catch the Wind. 1996. mass mkt. 8.99 (*0-552-13313-2*) Bantam.

— Shake Down the Stars. 1996. mass mkt. 6.95 (*0-552-12887-2*) Bantam.

Donnelly, Francis P. How to Love as Jesus Loves: Unlocking the Treasures of Christ's Sacred Heart. rev. ed. LC 99-23355. Orig. Title: The Heart of the Gospel: Traits of the Sacred Heart. 172p. 1999. pap. 13.95 (*0-918477-99-9*) Sophia Inst Pr.

— Literature the Leading Educator. LC 79-107694. (Essay Index Reprint Ser.). 1977. 21.95 (*0-8369-1497-X*) Ayer.

Donnelly, Frank. Touch-Type the Computer in Four Hours. 64p. 1991. spiral bd. 8.00 (*0-936862-85-8*, CKP) DDC Pub.

Donnelly, Frank P. Touch 'n' Type: Twenty-Five Words to Success. 95p. 1981. 10.00 (*0-936862-11-4*, TNT) DDC Pub.

***Donnelly, Gabrielle.** The Girl in the Photograph. LC 98-14552. 288p. 1998. 22.95 (*0-399-14417-X*, G P Putnam) Peng Put Young Read.

— The Girl in the Photograph. 1999. reprint ed. pap. 12.95 (*0-425-17058-6*) Berkley Pub.

Donnelly, Graham. Foundation in Economics. 360p. 1991. 75.00 (*0-7487-0560-0*, Pub. by S Thornes Pubs) Trans-Atl Phila.

Donnelly, Ignatius. The American People's Money. (Notable American Authors Ser.). 1992. reprint ed. lib. bdg. 75.00 (*0-7812-2671-6*) Rprt Serv.

— Atlantis: The Antediluvian World. 1973. lib. bdg. 300.00 (*0-87968-055-5*) Krishna Pr.

— Atlantis: The Antediluvian World. Bleiler, Everett F., ed. LC 76-24138. (Illus.). 490p. 1976. reprint ed. pap. 10.95 (*0-486-23371-5*) Dover.

— Atlantis: The Antediluvian World. (Notable American Authors Ser.). 1992. reprint ed. lib. bdg. 75.00 (*0-7812-2667-8*) Rprt Serv.

— Caesar's Column. 318p. 1993. reprint ed. lib. bdg. 35.00 (*0-8328-3174-3*) Higginson Bk Co.

— Caesar's Column: A Story of the Twentieth Century. LC 76-42811. reprint ed. 42.50 (*0-404-60060-3*) AMS Pr.

— Caesar's Column: A Story of the Twentieth Century. (Notable American Authors Ser.). 1992. reprint ed. lib. bdg. 75.00 (*0-7812-2670-8*) Rprt Serv.

— The Cipher in the Plays & on the Tombstone. (Notable American Authors Ser.). 1992. reprint ed. lib. bdg. 75.00 (*0-7812-2672-4*) Rprt Serv.

— Collected Works. 1990. reprint ed. lib. bdg. 75.00 (*0-7812-2666-X*, 1509); reprint ed. write for info. (*0-318-67695-8*); reprint ed. write for info. (*0-318-67696-6*); reprint ed. write for info. (*0-318-67697-4*); reprint ed. write for info. (*0-318-67698-2*); reprint ed. write for info. (*0-318-67699-0*) Rprt Serv.

— Doctor Huguet. LC 75-92230. (American Negro: His History & Literature. Series 3). 1970. reprint ed. 18.95 (*0-405-01920-3*) Ayer.

— Doctor Huguet. 309p. 1993. reprint ed. lib. bdg. 35.00 (*0-8328-3173-5*) Higginson Bk Co.

— The Golden Bottle. LC 68-57523. (Muckrakers Ser.). reprint ed. lib. bdg. 27.00 (*0-8398-0368-0*) Irvington.

— The Great Cryptogram, 2 vols. LC 72-135730. reprint ed. 75.00 (*0-404-02144-1*) AMS Pr.

— The Great Cryptogram. (Notable American Authors Ser.). 1992. reprint ed. lib. bdg. 90.00 (*0-7812-2669-4*) Rprt Serv.

— The Great Cryptogram: Francis Bacon's Cipher in the So-Called Shakespeare Plays. 1000p. 1996. reprint ed. pap. 65.00 (*1-56459-539-0*) Kessinger Pub.

— Ragnarok: The Age of Fire & Gravel. 462p. 1997. reprint ed. pap. 29.95 (*0-7661-0017-0*) Kessinger Pub.

An Asterisk (*) at the beginning of an entry indicates that the title is appearing for the first time.

— Ragnarok: The Age of Fire & Gravel. (Notable American Authors Ser.). 1992. reprint ed. lib. bdg. 75.00 (*0-7812-2668-6*) Rprt Serv.

Donnelly, J., jt. auth. see Marks, D. J.

Donnelly, J. S., Jr., ed. Irish Agrarian Rebellion, 1760-1800. 240p. 1997. 49.50 (*0-7165-2550-X*, Pub. by Irish Acad Pr); pap. 22.95 (*0-7165-2562-3*, Pub. by Irish Acad Pr) Intl Spec Bk.

***Donnelly, J. S., Jr. & Miller, Kerby A., eds.** Irish Popular Culture, 1650-1850. 312p. 1999. pap. 26.50 (*0-7165-2712-X*, Pub. by Irish Acad Pr) Intl Spec Bk.

Donnelly, J. S., Jr. & Miller, Kerby A., eds. Irish Popular Culture, 1650-1850. 312p. (C). 1999. reprint ed. 52.50 (*0-7165-2551-8*, Pub. by Irish Acad Pr) Intl Spec Bk.

Donnelly, Jack. International Human Rights. 2nd ed. LC 98-119539. (Dilemmas in World Politics Ser.). 6p. (C). 1997. pap. 20.00 (*0-8133-9969-6*, Pub. by Westview) HarpC.

***Donnelly, Jack.** Realism & International Relations. LC JZ1307.D66 2000. (Themes in International Relations Ser.). 256p. (C). 2000. text 49.95 (*0-521-59229-1*); pap. text 17.95 (*0-521-59752-8*) Cambridge U Pr.

Donnelly, Jack. Universal Human Rights in Theory & Practice. LC 89-7057. 304p. 1989. pap. text 15.95 (*0-8014-9570-9*) Cornell U Pr.

Donnelly, Jack & Howard, Rhoda E. International Handbook on Human Rights. LC 87-7529. 505p. 1987. lib. bdg. 115.00 (*0-313-24788-9*, DIH/, Greenwood Pr) Greenwood.

Donnelly, James. Close to the Customer: 25 Management Tips from the Other Side of the Counter, Keystone Financial Special Edition. 1993. per. 15.35 (*0-7863-0208-9*, Irwn Prfssnl) McGraw-Hill Prof.

— The HP 48 Pocket Book. 50p. (Orig.). 1993. pap. text 6.95 (*1-879828-05-7*) Armstrong OR.

— The HP48 Database. 34p. 1992. pap. 50.00 (*1-879828-02-2*) Armstrong Pub.

— The HP48 Handbook. (Illus.). 195p. (Orig.). 1990. pap. 20.00 (*1-879828-00-6*) Armstrong Pub.

— An Introduction to HP48 System RPL & Assembly Language Programming. 230p. 1995. pap. 25.00 (*1-879828-06-5*) Armstrong OR.

***Donnelly, James.** Love & Knowledge: The Quest for Personal Meaning. 84p. 1999. pap. 12.95 (*0-9672775-0-7*) South Garden.

Donnelly, James. A Modern Difference Engine. 44p. 1992. pap. 20.00 (*1-879828-03-0*) Armstrong OR.

Donnelly, James & Peter, Paul J. Marketing Management: CPS-Select Cases. 4th ed. (C). 1994. 20.95 (*0-256-19023-2*, Irwn McGrw-H) McGrw-H Hghr Educ.

Donnelly, James, et al. Fundamentals of Management. 9th ed. 416p. (C). 1994. text, pap. text, student ed. 24.68 (*0-256-15115-6*, Irwn McGrw-H) McGrw-H Hghr Educ.

— Fundamentals of Management & Irwin Career. 9th ed. 1997. 69.95 (*0-256-17766-X*, Irwn McGrw-H) McGrw-H Hghr Educ.

— Fundamentals of Management, International. 8th ed. (C). 1991. text, student ed. 32.50 (*0-256-11270-3*, Irwn McGrw-H) McGrw-H Hghr Educ.

— Fundamentos de Direccion y Administracion de Empresas. 8th ed. (SPA.). (C). 1996. text 28.00 (*84-8086-187-8*, Irwn McGrw-H) McGrw-H Hghr Educ.

— Marketing Management & Wall Street Journal. 4th ed. (C). 1994. 62.95 (*0-256-19096-8*, Irwn McGrw-H) McGrw-H Hghr Educ.

Donnelly, James, jt. auth. see Peter, Paul J.

Donnelly, James H. Administracion de Empresas. (SPA.). 880p. (C). 1994. pap. text. write for info. (*0-201-60108-7*) Addison-Wesley.

Donnelly, James H., Jr. 25 Management Lessons from the Customer's Side of the Counter. 1996. text 16.95 (*0-7863-1004-9*, Irwn Prfssnl) McGraw-Hill Prof.

Donnelly, James H., Jr. & Peter, J. Paul. Marketing Management: Knowledge & Skills. 4th ed. LC 94-7621. (Marketing Ser.). 864p. (C). 1994. text 70.95 (*0-256-13727-7*, Irwn McGrw-H) McGrw-H Hghr Educ.

Donnelly, James H., Jr., et al. Fundamentals of Management. 8th ed. 864p. (C). 1991. text 68.95 (*0-256-09790-9*, Irwn McGrw-H) McGrw-H Hghr Educ.

Donnelly, James H., et al. Fundamentals of Management. 10th ed. LC 97-25992. 1997. write for info. (*0-07-115233-4*) McGraw.

— Fundamentals of Management. 10th ed. LC 97-25992. (C). 1997. text. write for info. (*0-256-23237-7*, Irwn McGrw-H) McGrw-H Hghr Educ.

Donnelly, James H., Jr., et al. The New Banker: Developing Leadership in a Dynamic Era. 200p. 1989. text 42.50 (*1-55623-177-6*, Irwn Prfssnl) McGraw-Hill Prof.

Donnelly, James H., Jr., jt. auth. see Peter, J. Paul.

Donnelly, James R., et al. Innovative Site Remediation Technology Vol. 5: Solvent - Chemical Extraction. Anderson, William C., ed. LC 93-20786. (Illus.). 160p. 1995. 79.95 (*1-883767-05-9*) Am Acad Environ.

Donnelly, James S. The Decline of the Medieval Cistercian Laybrotherhood. LC 50-14032. (Fordham University Studies. History Ser.: No. 3). 105p. reprint ed. pap. 32.60 (*0-7837-5573-2*, 204535500005) Bks Demand.

***Donnelly, James S., Jr.** The Land & the People of Nineteenth-Century Cork: The Rural Economy & the Land Question. 2nd ed. 440p. 1999. pap. 24.95 (*1-898256-79-9*, Pub. by Collins Press) Dufour.

Donnelly, James S., Jr., jt. ed. see Clark, Samuel.

Donnelly, Jane. Dear Caliban. large type ed. (Linford Romance Library). 360p. 1984. pap. 16.99 (*0-7089-6046-4*) Ulverscroft.

— The Devil's Flower. large type ed. 1995. 11.50 (*0-7505-0826-4*, Pub. by Mgna Lrg Print) Ulverscroft.

— A Man Apart. large type ed. 329p. 1982. 27.99 (*0-7089-0803-9*) Ulverscroft.

— Shadows from the Sea. large type ed. 329p. 1980. 11.50 (*0-7089-0479-3*) Ulverscroft.

Donnelly, Jean. The Julia Set. 24p. (Orig.). 1995. pap. 4.00 (*0-9619097-6-5*) Edge Bks.

Donnelly, Jo. 999 Lies for Every Occasion. LC 95-19917. 240p. 1995. pap. 8.95 (*0-8065-1672-0*, Citadel Pr) Carol Pub Group.

Donnelly, John. Logical Analysis & Contemporary Theism. LC 77-168693. 351p. reprint ed. pap. 108.90 (*0-7837-0443-7*, 204076600018) Bks Demand.

Donnelly, John, ed. Language, Metaphysics & Death: Death & Afterlife, a Metaphysical Reader. 2nd ed. LC 76-18463. viii, 381p. (C). 1994. reprint ed. 27.00 (*0-8232-1581-4*); reprint ed. pap. 19.00 (*0-8232-1582-2*) Fordham.

— Reflective Wisdom: Richard Taylor on Issues That Matter. LC 89-10303. 380p. 1989. 36.95 (*0-87975-522-9*) Prometheus Bks.

— Suicide: Right or Wrong? 2nd ed. LC 97-35042. (Contemporary Issues in Philosophy Ser.). 335p. (Orig.). 1998. pap. text 17.95 (*1-57392-186-6*) Prometheus Bks.

Donnelly, John, tr. see More, Thomas.

Donnelly, John J. Handloader's Manual of Cartridge Conversions. 1056p. 1987. 49.95 (*0-88317-138-4*); pap. 34.95 (*0-88317-136-8*) Stoeger Pub Co.

Donnelly, John P., ed. A Bibliography of the Works of Peter Martyr Vermigli. (Sixteenth Century Essays & Studies: Vol. 13). (Illus.). 215p. 1990. 40.00 (*0-940474-14-X*, SCJP) Truman St Univ.

Donnelly, John P., ed. A Dialogue on the Two Natures in Christ. (Peter Martyr Vermigli Library: Vol. 2). 214p. 1995. 40.00 (*0-940474-33-6*) Truman St Univ.

— Life, Letters, & Sermons Vol. 42: Works, English, 1999. LC 98-27725. (Sixteenth Century Essays & Studies: Vol. 5). 350p. 1999. 45.00 (*0-943549-61-2*) Truman St Univ.

— Philipp Melanchthon: Annotations on the First Epistle to the Corinthians. (Reformation Texts with Translation Ser.: No. 2). 178p. (C). 1995. pap. 20.00 (*0-87462-701-X*) Marquette.

Donnelly, John P. & Maher, Michael W., eds. Confraternities & Catholic Reform in Italy, France, Spain. LC 98-3779. (Sixteenth Century Essays & Studies: No. 44). (Illus.). 262p. 1998. 40.00 (*0-943549-60-4*) Truman St Univ.

Donnelly, John P., ed. see John XXIII, pseud.

Donnelly, Joseph, jt. ed. see Doyle, Mary.

Donnelly, Joseph E. Living Anatomy. 2nd ed. LC 89-26982. (Illus.). 248p. (C). 1990. spiral bd. 28.00 (*0-87322-290-3*, BDON0290) Human Kinetics.

Donnelly, Joseph L. & Lipscher, Randolph B. Mosby's USMLE Step 3 Reviews: Specialty Clinical Sciences. (Ace the Boards Ser.). (Illus.). 504p. (C). (gr. 13). 1996. pap. text 38.00 incl. disk (*0-8151-2734-0*, 27047) Mosby Inc.

***Donnelly, Joseph W., et al.** Mental Health: Dimensions of Self-Esteem & Emotional Well-Being. LC 00-42093. 2001. write for info. (*0-205-30955-0*) Allyn.

Donnelly, Judy. Moonwalk: The First Trip to the Moon. LC 88-23668. (Step into Reading Ser.: A Step 4 Book). (Illus.). 48p. (J). (gr. 2-5). 1989. pap. 3.99 (*0-394-82457-1*, Pub. by Random Bks Yng Read) Random.

— Moonwalk: The First Trip to the Moon. (Step into Reading Ser.: A Step 4 Book). (J). (gr. 2-4). 1989. 9.19 (*0-606-12429-2*, Pub. by Turtleback) Demco.

— The Titanic: Lost...& Found. LC 86-20402. (Step into Reading Ser.: A Step 3 Book). (Illus.). 48p. (J). (gr. 1-4). 1987. pap. 3.99 (*0-394-88669-0*, Pub. by Random Bks Yng Read) Random.

Donnelly, Judy. Titanic, Lost--And Found. (Step into Reading Ser.: A Step 3 Book). (J). 1987. 9.19 (*0-606-03491-9*, Pub. by Turtleback) Demco.

Donnelly, Judy. True-Life Treasure Hunts. LC 93-20203. (Step into Reading Ser.: A Step 4 Book). (Illus.). 48p. (J). (ps-3). 1993. pap. 3.99 (*0-679-83980-1*, Pub. by Random Bks Yng Read) Random.

— Tut's Mummy: Lost...& Found. LC 87-20790. (Step into Reading Ser.: A Step 3 Book). (Illus.). 48p. (J). (gr. 2-3). 1988. pap. 3.99 (*0-394-89189-9*, Pub. by Random Bks Yng Read) Random.

Donnelly, Judy. Tut's Mummy: Lost...& Found. (Step into Reading Ser.: A Step 3 Book). (J). (gr. 2-3). 1988. 9.19 (*0-606-03942-2*, Pub. by Turtleback) Demco.

— A Wall of Names: The Story of the Vietnam Veterans Memorial. (Step into Reading Ser.: A Step 4 Book). (J). (gr. 2-4). 1991. 8.70 (*0-606-05043-4*, Pub. by Turtleback) Demco.

Donnelly, Judy. Who Shot the President? The Death of John F. Kennedy. LC 88-4418. (Step into Reading Ser.: A Step 4 Book). (Illus.). 48p. (J). (gr. 2-4). 1988. pap. 3.99 (*0-394-89944-X*, Pub. by Random Bks Yng Read) Random.

Donnelly, Judy. Who Shot the President? The Death of John F. Kennedy. (Step into Reading Ser.: A Step 4 Book). (J). (gr. 2-4). 1988. 9.19 (*0-606-03954-6*, Pub. by Turtleback) Demco.

Donnelly, Judy & Kramer, Sydelle A. My Escape: Shipwrecked. Ashby, Ruth, ed. LC 94-152967. 112p. (Orig.). (J). (gr. 4-7). 1994. pap. 2.99 (*0-671-67895-7*, Minstrel Bks) PB.

Donnelly, Julie. How to Be Pain-Less: A Beginners Guide to the Self-Treatment of Muscle Spasms. Jones, Mimi, ed. (Illus.). Date not set. pap. 19.95 (*1-929632-03-7*) Julstro Pubns.

— Massage Therapy Healing Techniques Workbook. rev. ed. (Illus.). 57p. 1996. pap., wbk. ed. 15.95 (*1-929632-00-2*) Julstro Pubns.

Donnelly, K. Probate Procedure Notes. (Waterlow Practitioner's Library). 112p. 1988. pap. 21.95 (*0-08-036898-0*) Macmillan.

***Donnelly, Karen.** Everything You Need to Know about Lyme Disease. LC 99-86258. (Need to Know Library). 2000. pap. write for info. (*0-8239-3216-8*) Rosen Group.

Donnelly, Karen, jt. auth. see Water, Mark.

Donnelly, Karen J. & Bernstein, J. B., eds. Our Mothers, Our Selves: Writers & Poets Celebrating Motherhood. LC 95-36903. 280p. 1996. 19.95 (*0-89789-445-6*, Bergin & Garvey) Greenwood.

Donnelly, Katherine F. Recovering from the Loss of a Child. LC 94-150486. 304p. 1994. mass mkt. 5.99 (*0-425-13909-3*) Berkley Pub.

— Recovering from the Loss of a Loved One to AIDS: Help for Surviving Family, Friends & Lovers Who Grieve. 272p. 1995. pap. 10.00 (*0-449-90990-5*) Fawcett.

***Donnelly, Katherine F.** Recovering from the Loss of a Loved One to AIDS: Help for Surviving Family, Friends & Lovers Who Grieve. 252p. 1999. reprint ed. text 23.00 (*0-7881-6321-3*) DIANE Pub.

Donnelly, Kerry. Doberman Pinschers: AKC Rank #20. (Illus.). 1997. pap. 19.95 (*0-7938-2309-9*, KW-209S) TFH Pubns.

— Poodles, AKC Rank No. 5. (KW Dog Ser.). (Illus.). 1996. pap. 9.95 (*0-7938-2363-3*, KW010S) TFH Pubns.

— Yorkshire Terriers, AKC Rank No. 11. (Illus.). 1996. pap. 9.95 (*0-7938-2386-2*, KW007S) TFH Pubns.

Donnelly, Kerry V., jt. auth. see Bruette, William A.

Donnelly, Kevin. Crop Production. 308p. (C). 1998. per. 40.95 (*0-7872-5421-5*) Kendall-Hunt.

Donnelly, Kevin, jt. auth. see Biggs, Keith.

Donnelly, Kevin, jt. auth. see Sullivan, Amy.

Donnelly, Kyle, ed. Classical Monologues for Men: From 16th, 17th & 18th Century Plays. LC 92-29025. 130p. (C). 1992. pap. 7.95 (*0-435-08619-7*, 08619) Heinemann.

— Classical Monologues for Women: From 16th, 17th & 18th Century Plays. LC 92-29026. 141p. (C). 1992. pap. 7.95 (*0-435-08620-0*, 08620, Pub. by Heinemann) Natl Bk Netwk.

Donnelly, Laurie, jt. auth. see Laroche, Loretta.

Donnelly, Linda, jt. auth. see Lee, Kaiman.

Donnelly, Liza. Dinosaur Beach. (Illus.). 32p. (J). (ps-3). 1991. pap. 2.50 (*0-685-43744-2*) Scholastic Inc.

— Dinosaur Day. 32p. (J). (ps-3). 1987. pap. 2.99 (*0-590-41800-9*) Scholastic Inc.

— Dinosaur Garden. (Illus.). 32p. (J). (ps-3). 1991. pap. 2.99 (*0-590-43172-2*) Scholastic Inc.

Donnelly, Liza. Dinosaur Garden. 1990. 8.19 (*0-606-04908-8*, Pub. by Turtleback) Demco.

Donnelly, Liza. Dinosaur Valentine. LC 94-164619. (Illus.). 32p. (J). (ps-3). 1994. pap. 2.50 (*0-590-46415-9*, Cartwheel) Scholastic Inc.

— Dinosaurs' Christmas. 32p. (J). (ps-3). 1994. pap. 2.50 (*0-590-44798-X*) Scholastic Inc.

— Dinosaurs' Thanksgiving. LC 95-229184. (Read with Me Paperback Ser.). (Illus.). 32p. (J). (ps-2). 1995. pap. 2.50 (*0-590-22195-7*, Cartwheel) Scholastic Inc.

Donnelly, Liza & Maslin, Michael. Husbands & Wives. 112p. (Orig.). 1995. pap. 8.00 (*0-345-39041-5*) Ballantine Pub Grp.

Donnelly, Loraine B. California State Capitol Time Machine Coloring Book. (Illus.). 23p. (J). (gr. 4-9). 1996. reprint ed. pap. text 4.50 (*0-9626304-0-3*); reprint ed. pap. text, teacher ed. 5.50 (*0-9626304-1-1*) CA Capital Enter.

Donnelly, Loraine B. & Cray, Evelyn S. California's Historic Capitol. 4th ed. (Illus.). 48p. 1995. pap. text 6.00 (*1-878779-00-1*) CA Capital Enter.

— California's Historic Capitol. 4th ed. (JPN., Illus.) 48p. 1995. reprint ed. pap. 7.50 (*1-878779-02-8*); reprint ed. pap. 7.50 (*1-878779-03-6*); reprint ed. pap., teacher ed. 6.95 (*1-878779-01-X*) CA Capital Enter.

Donnelly, Lura, et al, contrib. by. CFRN Study Guide. 2nd ed. 217p. (Orig.). 1996. pap. text, student ed. 26.00 (*0-935890-01-7*) Emerg Nurses IL.

Donnelly, Mabel C. The American Victorian Woman: The Myth & the Reality, 71. LC 86-358. (Contributions in Women's Studies: No. 71). 179p. 1986. 49.95 (*0-313-25327-7*, DVI/) Greenwood.

Donnelly, Marcos. Prophets for the End of Time. 1998. mass mkt. 5.99 (*0-671-57775-1*) S&S Trade.

Donnelly, Margaret E., ed. Reinterpreting the Legacy of William James. LC 92-32729. 371p. 1992. pap. text 19.95 (*1-55798-180-9*) Am Psychol.

Donnelly, Margarita, jt. ed. see Baldwin, Barbara.

Donnelly, Margarita, jt. ed. see Calyx Editorial Collective Staff.

Donnelly, Marian C. Architecture in the Scandinavian Countries. 414p. 1991. 55.00 (*0-262-04118-9*) MIT Pr.

— The Oregon Bach Festival, 1970-1994. LC 94-17193. 1994. pap. 10.00 (*0-87114-116-7*) U of Oreg Bks.

Donnelly, Marjorie. Another Country Heard From. Herman, Ira, ed. LC 97-90177. 128p. 1998. pap. 10.00 (*1-56002-747-9*) T Donnelly.

Donnelly, Marjorie T. Seasoned with Love: Southern Cousins' Favorite Recipes. Fundcraft Staff, ed. (Illus.). 98p. 1990. 6.95 (*0-9626892-0-3*) T Donnelly.

Donnelly, Mark. Britain in Second World War. LC 99-11773. 1999. pap. write for info. (*0-415-17425-0*) Routledge.

***Donnelly, Mark.** Britain in Second World War. LC 99-11773. 112p. (C). 1999. text. write for info. (*0-415-17425-2*) Routledge.

Donnelly, Mark, jt. auth. see Diehl, Daniel.

Donnelly, Martin J. The Catalogue of Antique Tools, 1998 Edition. (Illus.). 180p. 1998. pap. 23.95 (*1-893949-04-4*) M J Donnelly Antique.

— The Catalogue of Antique Tools, 1997 Edition. (Illus.). 160p. 1997. pap. 22.95 (*1-893949-03-6*) M J Donnelly Antique.

— The Catalogue of Antique Tools, 1996 Edition. (Illus.). 80p. 1996. pap. 17.95 (*1-893949-02-8*) M J Donnelly Antique.

— The Catalogue of Antique Tools, 1995 Edition. (Illus.). 80p. 1995. pap. 17.95 (*1-893949-01-X*) M J Donnelly Antique.

— The Catalogue of Antique Tools, 1994 Edition. (Illus.). 60p. 1994. pap. 15.95 (*1-893949-00-1*) M J Donnelly Antique.

— The Catalogue of Antique Tools, 1999 Edition. (Illus.). 248p. 1999. pap. 23.95 (*1-893949-05-2*) M J Donnelly Antique.

***Donnelly, Martin J.** The Catalogue of Antique Tools, 2000 Edition. (Illus.). 320p. 2000. pap. 25.95 (*1-893949-06-0*) M J Donnelly Antique.

Donnelly, Mary, jt. auth. see Strid, George L.

Donnelly, Mary A. Our Lady of Mercy Hymnal. LC 91-40804. 108p. 1992. 50.00 (*0-8201-1461-8*) Schol Facsimiles.

Donnelly, Mary L. Arnold Livers Family in America (Lyvers, Lievers) LC 77-852223. (Illus.). 362p. 1977. 24.00 (*0-939142-02-3*) M L Donnelly.

— Beaven-Blanford-Clarkson-Mitchell & Allied Families of Maryland, Kentucky, U. S. A. LC 97-141603. (Illus.). 448p. 1997. 46.00 (*0-939142-18-X*) M L Donnelly.

— The Buckman Family - Maryland, Kentucky, Missouri. 2nd rev. ed. Orig. Title: The Buckman Family of Maryland & Kentucky in 1979. (Illus.). 488p. 1996. 48.00 (*0-939142-17-1*) M L Donnelly.

— Colonial Settlers (1634-1780) St. Clement's Bay, St. Mary's County, Maryland. 2nd rev. ed. LC 98-100494. (Illus.). 300p. 1996. reprint ed. 36.00 (*0-939142-16-3*) M L Donnelly.

— Craycrofts of Maryland & Kentucky Kin. LC 82-90280. (Illus.). 336p. 1982. 20.00 (*0-939142-06-6*) M L Donnelly.

— Genealogy: A Step-by-Step Approach for Beginners, Ages 10 to 80. LC 83-71116. (Illus.). 64p. (J). (gr. 4 up). 1983. pap. 5.00 (*0-939142-08-2*) M L Donnelly.

— Hayden - Rapier & Allied Families: Colonial Maryland, Kentucky, U. S. A. 2nd rev. ed. (Illus.). 524p. 1991. 50.00 (*0-939142-12-0*) M L Donnelly.

— John Medley, (1615-1660) St. Mary's County, Maryland His Descendants. (Illus.). 460p. 1995. 45.00 (*0-939142-14-7*) M L Donnelly.

— Major William Boarman (1630-1709) Charles County, Maryland: His Descendants. (Boarman - Bowman & Allied Families Ser.). (Illus.). 452p. 1991. 50.00 (*0-939142-11-2*) M L Donnelly.

— Meet the Donnellys - Enjoy Their History. limited ed. LC 98-174545. (Illus.). 127p. 1997. pap. 36.00 (*0-939142-19-8*) M L Donnelly.

— St. Mary's County, Maryland, Colonial Period Tenants & Owners "Beaverdam Manor" & Surrounding Manors. LC 98-174544. (Illus.). 314p. 1998. 40.00 (*0-939142-20-1*) M L Donnelly.

***Donnelly, Mary L.** St. Joseph's Catholic Community, Waxahachie, Texas: Our Parish History of 125 Years, 1874-1999. (Illus.). 173p. 1999. pap. 16.00 (*0-939142-21-X*) M L Donnelly.

Donnelly, Mary L. Texas Trails of Our Tollett Family. (Illus.). 288p. 1994. 33.00 (*0-939142-13-9*) M L Donnelly.

— Thomas Hill & Rebecca Miles: Ancestors & Descendants. 2nd rev. ed. LC 84-247052. (Illus.). 911p. 1984. 50.00 (*0-939142-09-0*) M L Donnelly.

— William Elder, Ancestors & Descendants. 2nd rev. ed. LC 86-180069. (Illus.). 640p. 1986. 45.00 (*0-939142-10-4*) M L Donnelly.

***Donnelly, Mary Louise.** Edward Willett, Colonial Maryland Pewterer County Clerk, Plantation Owner, His Anscestors & Descendants. rev. ed. Orig. Title: The Willett Family of Maryland, Colonial Pewterer, Kentucky Pioneers. (Illus.). 907p. 1999. 62.00 (*0-939142-22-8*) M L Donnelly.

Donnelly, Mary Louise. Imprints Sixteen Hundred Eight to Nineteen Eighty, Hamilton, Allied Families. LC 80-84574. (Illus.). 660p. 1980. 43.00 (*0-939142-05-8*) M L Donnelly.

Donnelly, Mary Q., jt. auth. see Markey, Daniel J., Jr.

Donnelly, Maureen. Preservation Guide No. 7: Silver. LC 84-106237. (Illus.). ii, 14p. 1994. pap. 3.95 (*0-917860-34-9*) Historic New Orleans.

Donnelly, Maureen A. Preservation Guide No. 4: Furniture. LC 84-106237. (Illus.). ii, 14p. (Orig.). 1987. pap. 3.95 (*0-917860-24-1*) Historic New Orleans.

Donnelly, Michael. Scottish Stained Glass: Making the Colours Sing. (Discovering Historic Scotland Ser.). (Illus.). 100p. 1997. pap. 26.00 (*0-11-495793-2*, Pub. by Statnry Office) Balogh.

Donnelly, Michael & Donnelly, Denise. Falcon's Cry: A Desert Storm Memoir. LC 98-19471. (Illus.). 272p. 1998. 27.95 (*0-275-96462-0*, Pub. by Greenwood) Natl Bk Netwk.

Donnelly, Morwenna. Founding the Life Divine. 176p. 1976. reprint ed. 9.95 (*0-685-10116-9*) Auromere.

— Founding the Life Divine: An Introduction to the Integral Yoga of Sri Aurobindo. LC 74-2430. 182p. 1976. reprint ed. pap. 7.95 (*0-913922-13-7*) Dawn Horse Pr.

Donnelly, Nancy D. Changing Lives of Refugee among Women. LC 94-5746. (Illus.). 208p. 1997. reprint ed. pap. 14.95 (*0-295-97621-7*) U of Wash Pr.

Donnelly, Nancy D., jt. ed. see Hopkins, MaryCarol.

Donnelly, Nisa. The Bar Stories: A Novel after All. 368p. 1989. pap. 10.95 (*0-312-03795-3*) St Martin.

Donnelly, Nora, ed. see Medvedow, Jill & McElreavy, Tim.

Donnelly, P. J. Blanc De Chine: The Porcelain of Tcehua in Fukien. LC 77-417633. (Faber Monographs on Pottery & Porcelain). 407p. 1969. write for info. (*0-571-08078-2*) Faber & Faber.

Donnelly, Patricia J., jt. auth. see Wistreich, George A.

Donnelly, Patrick, ed. & tr. see Savonarola, Girolamo.

Donnelly, Paul S., ed. see Boone, Louis E., et al.

***Donnelly, Peter.** Invitation to a Royal Wedding: Edward & Sophie June 19th 1999. 1999. 14.99 (*1-84100-221-6*) Quadrillion Pub.

D

Donnelly, Peter, jt. auth. see Coakley, Jay J.

Donnelly, Peter J. & Tavare, E. Simon, eds. Progress in Population Genetics & Human Evolution. LC 96-49167. (IMA Volumes in Mathematics & Its Applications Ser.: Vol. 87). (Illus.). 336p. 1997. 59.95 (0-387-94944-5) Spr-Verlag.

***Donnelly, R. E.** Managing Communication in Changing Organizations. (Management Briefings Ser.). (Illus.). 1998. pap. 89.50 (0-273-63807-6, Pub. by F T P-H) Trans-Atl Phila.

Donnelly, R. J., ed. High Reynolds-Number Flows Using Liquid & Gaseous Helium: A Discussion of Liquid & Gaseous Helium as Test Fluids. (Illus.). xi, 294p. 1991. 79.95 (0-387-97475-X) Spr-Verlag.

Donnelly, R. J. & Sreenivasan, K. R., eds. Flow at Ultra-High Reynolds & Reyleigh Numbers: A Status Report. LC 98-21387. (Illus.). 450p. 1998. 59.00 (0-387-98544-1) Spr-Verlag.

Donnelly, Ralph W. The Confederate States Marine Corps: The Rebel Leathernecks. rev. ed. LC 89-24824. (Illus.). 337p. 1990. 24.95 (0-942597-13-3) White Mane Pub.

Donnelly, Richard W. Artificial Lift. Kirkley, Charles & Leecraft, Jodie, eds. (Oil & Gas Production Ser.). (Illus.). 71p. (Orig.). 1985. pap. text 15.00 (0-88698-086-0, 3.31210) PETEX.

— Beam Pumping. Leecraft, Jodie, ed. (Oil & Gas Production Ser.). (Illus.). 103p. (Orig.). 1986. pap. text 15.00 (0-88698-123-9, 3.31310) PETEX.

— Project Development for Gas Processing Plants & Facilities. Stelzner, Karen I., ed. (Illus.). 347p. 1982. ring bd. 45.00 (0-88698-047-X, 3.80020) PETEX.

Donnelly, Robert, jt. auth. see Pitfield, Michael.

Donnelly, Robin. Biking & Hiking the American River Parkway: A Cultural & Natural History Guide. (Illus.). 148p. 1998. pap. 12.95 (1-887815-08-2) Amer River Nat Hist.

Donnelly, Rory. Sequence. 4th ed. (C). 1996. pap. text, teacher ed. write for info. (0-15-503585-1) Harcourt Coll Pubs.

— Sequence: A Basic Writing Course. 4th ed. (C). 1996. pap. text 36.50 (0-15-501996-1, Pub. by Harcourt Coll Pubs) Harcourt.

— Sequence: A Basic Writing Course. 4th ed. (C). 1996. pap. text, teacher ed. 28.00 (0-15-503446-4) Harcourt Coll Pubs.

***Donnelly, Ruah.** The Adventurous Gardener: Where to Buy the Best Plants in New England. (Illus.). 304p. 2000. pap. 19.95 (0-9677303-1-7) Horticultural Pr.

Donnelly, Russell J. Experimental Superfluidity. LC 66-23686. (Illus.). (Orig.). 1993. pap. text 7.00 (0-226-15757-1) U Ch Pr.

— Quantized Vortices in Helium, No. II. (Studies in Low Temperature Physics: No. 3). (Illus.). 364p. (C). 1991. text 115.00 (0-521-32400-9) Cambridge U Pr.

Donnelly, S. E. & Evans, J. H. Fundamental Aspects of Inert Gases in Solids. (NATO ASI Ser.: Vol. 279). (Illus.). 488p. (C). 1991. text 140.00 (0-306-44051-2, Kluwer Plenum) Kluwer Academic.

Donnelly, Samuel J. M. The Language & Uses of Rights: A Biopsy of American Jurisprudence in the Twentieth Century. LC 93-40757. 174p. (Orig.). (C). 1994. pap. text 24.50 (0-8191-9405-0) U Pr of Amer.

Donnelly, Susan. Eve Names the Animals: Poems. (Samuel French Morse Poetry Prize Ser.: Vol. 1). 81p. (Orig.). 1984. pap. text 11.95 (0-930350-64-2) NE U Pr.

Donnelly, T. W., ed. Intersections Between Particle & Nuclear Physics: Sixth Conference. LC 97-77178. (AIP Conference Proceedings Ser.: Vol. 412). (Illus.). 1056p. 1998. 225.00 (1-56396-712-X) Am Inst Physics.

***Donnelly, T. W. & Turchinetz, W., eds.** Bates 25: Celebrating 25 Years of Beam to Experiment. LC 00-103944. (AIP Conference Proceedings Ser.: Vol. 520). (Illus.). ix, 353p. 2000. 115.00 (1-56396-949-1) Am Inst Physics.

***Donnelly, Terry.** Heaven on Earth. 1999. 5.95 (0-7892-0588-2) Abbeville Pr.

Donnelly, Thomas C., jt. auth. see Peel, Roy V.

Donnelly, Thomas J. & Giza, Christopher C. Differential Diagnosis Mnemonics. (Illus.). 250p. 2000. pap. text 27.00 (1-56053-311-0) Hanley & Belfus.

Donnelly, Thomas W. The Earth Sciences: Problems & Progress in Current Research. LC 63-20901. (Rice University Semicentennial Publications). (Illus.). 203p. reprint ed. pap. 63.00 (0-608-09594-X, 205439800006) Bks Demand.

Donnelly, Thomas W., ed. Earth Sciences: Problems & Progress in Current Research. LC 63-20901. 1994. lib. bdg. 12.50 (0-226-15656-7) U Ch Pr.

Donnelly, Thomas W., ed. see Caribbean Geological Conference Staff.

***Donnelly, Tom.** Clash of Chariots: The Great Tank Battles. 320p. 1999. pap. 14.95 (0-425-16871-9) Berkley Pub.

Donnelly, Tom & Naylor, Sean. Clash of Chariots: The Great Tank Battles. Boyne, Walter J., ed. 1996. 31.95 (0-425-15307-X) Berkley Pub.

Donnelly, Tom, jt. auth. see Thoms, David.

Donnelly, V. M., et al, eds. Photon, Beam & Plasma Stimulated Chemical Processes at Surfaces. (MRS Symposium Proceedings Ser.: Vol. 75). 1987. text 17.50 (0-931837-41-3) Materials Res.

Donnelly, Vanessa. Next Generation Websites. (C). 2000. text. write for info. (0-201-67468-8) Addison-Wesley.

Donnelly, William A. The Econometrics of Energy Demand: A Survey of Applications. LC 86-25220. 324p. 1987. 80.00 (0-275-92610-9, C2610, Praeger Pubs) Greenwood.

Donnelly, William F., ed. American Economic Growth. LC 73-10339. 1973. 31.50 (0-8422-5110-3) Irvington.

Donnelly, William J. Planning Media. 333p. (C). 1995. 75.00 (0-13-567835-8) P-H.

Donnelly, William W. One Touch Guide. 64p. (Orig.). 1997. pap. 19.95 (0-9658924-9-2) OTG.

***Donnels, Johnny & O'Malley, Lurana Donnels.** Johnny Donnels into Photography: 50 Years - 50 Photographs - 50 Stories. LC 99-67554. (Illus.). 192p. 1999. 95.00 (0-9676034-0-4) J Donnels.

Donnely, Marcus. Guffy the Bear. (Illus.). 32p. (J). (ps). 1986. 4.50 (0-938715-00-3) Toy Works Pr.

— Squeak the Dinosaur. (Illus.). 32p. (J). (ps-2). 1987. 9.00 (0-938715-02-X) Toy Works Pr.

Donner, jt. auth. see Auerbach.

***Donner, Allan & Klar, Neil S.** Design & Analysis of Cluster Randomisation Trials: In Health Research. (Illus.). 320p. 2000. text 60.00 (0-340-69153-0) OUP.

Donner, C. F., et al, eds. From Alveoli Back to Bronchi: Contribution of Bronchoalveolar, BAL & Bronchial, BL Lavage to the Understanding of Bronchial Disease. (Journal: Respiration: Vol. 59, Suppl. 1, 1992). (Illus.). vi, 54p. 1952. pap. 26.25 (3-8055-5575-X) S Karger.

***Donner, Chris.** Confronting the Cow: A Young Family's Struggle with Breast Cancer, Loss & Rebuilding. LC 00-101674. 240p. 2000. 21.95 (0-9679637-9-6) Moonlight.

***Donner, Eric.** Planning for Retirement Distributions: Tax, Financial, & Personal Aspects with CD-ROM. 300p. 2000. pap. 109.00 incl. cd-rom (0-15-607232-7) Harcourt Prof.

Donner, Florinda. Being-in-Dreaming: An Initiation into the Sorcerer's World. LC 90-56444. 320p. 1992. pap. 14.00 (0-06-250192-5, Pub. by Harper SF) HarpC.

— Shabono. large type ed. 480p. 1984. 27.99 (0-7089-1126-9) Ulverscroft.

— Shabono: A Visit to a Remote & Magical World in the South American Rainforest. LC 91-55379. 320p. 1992. pap. 14.00 (0-06-250242-5, Pub. by Harper SF) HarpC.

Donner, Frank. Protectors of Privilege: Red Squads & Police Repression in Urban America. LC 89-20290. 496p. 1990. 45.00 (0-520-05951-4, Pub. by U CA Pr) Cal Prin Full Svc.

— Protectors of Privilege: Red Squads & Police Repression in Urban America. 1992. pap. 17.95 (0-520-08035-1, Pub. by U CA Pr) Cal Prin Full Svc.

Donner, Fred M. Narratives of Islamic Origins: The Beginnings of Islamic Historical Writing, Vol. 14. LC 97-36808. (Studies in Late Antiquity & Early Islam). 360p. 1998. lib. bdg. 29.95 (0-87850-127-4) Darwin Pr.

Donner, Fred M., tr. The History of al-Tabari Vol. 10: The Conquest of Arabia - The Riddah Wars, A. D. 632-633 - A. H. 11. LC 91-35989. (SUNY Series in Near Eastern Studies). 216p. (C). 1993. pap. text 21.95 (0-7914-1072-2) State U NY Pr.

— The History of al-Tabari Vol. 10: The Conquest of Arabia - The Riddah Wars, A. D. 632-633 - A. H. 11. LC 91-35989. (SUNY Series in Near Eastern Studies). 216p. (C). 1993. text 49.50 (0-7914-1071-4) State U NY Pr.

Donner, Fred M., tr. see Al-Tabari.

Donner-Grau, Florinda. The Witch's Dream. 320p. 1997. pap. 12.95 (0-14-019531-9, Penguin Bks) Viking Penguin.

Donner, H. W., ed. see Beddoes, Thomas L.

Donner, Henry W. Introduction to Utopia. LC 78-94268. (Select Bibliographies Reprint Ser.). 1977. 20.95 (0-8369-5042-9) Ayer.

Donner, Herbert. Aufsaetze Zum Alten Testament: Aus Vier Jahrzehnten. (Beiheft zur Zeitschrift fuer die Alttestamentliche Wissenschaft Ser.: Vol. 224). (GER.). x, 284p. (C). 1994. lib. bdg. 129.25 (3-11-014097-7) De Gruyter.

Donner, Irah. Patent Prosecution: Practice & Procedure Before the U. S Patent Office: Includes, 1998 Supplement. 1997. pap. 255.00 incl. disk (1-57018-086-5, 1087) BNA Books.

Donner, Irah H. Guidelines & Tips for Prosecuting Computer Inventions & Designs. LC 98-17843. 1998. write for info. (0-9661188-0-4) D B Pub.

Donner, J. H. The King: Chess Pieces.Tr. of Koning. (Illus.). 414p. 1998. lib. bdg. 65.00 (90-5691-027-2, New Chess) Chess Combi.

Donner, Jeffrey J. Catholicism Today. 36p. (Orig.). 1996. pap. 2.25 (1-889711-00-4) Cathedral Direct.

Donner, Joakim. The Quaternary History of Scandinavia. (World & Regional Geology Ser.: No. 7). (Illus.). 210p. (C). 1995. text 115.00 (0-521-41730-9) Cambridge U Pr.

Donner, Jorn. The Personal Vision of Ingmar Bergman. (Biography Index Reprint Ser.). (Illus.). 276p. 1964. pap. 4.95 (0-8290-1760-7) Irvington.

— Personal Vision of Ingmar Bergman. Lundbergh, Holger, tr. (Biography Index Reprint Ser.). 1980. reprint ed. 20.95 (0-8369-8119-7) Ayer.

— The Personal Vision of Ingmar Bergman. (Biography Index Reprint Ser.). (Illus.). 276p. reprint ed. lib. bdg. 22.25 (0-8290-0832-2) Irvington.

Donner, Marc. Real-Time Control of Walking. (Progress in Computer Science Ser.: No. 7). 192p. 1986. 48.50 (0-8176-3332-4) Birkhauser.

Donner, Martin W., jt. ed. see Jones, B.

Donner, Michael. I Love Me, Vol. I: S. Wordrow's Palindrome Encyclopedia. (Illus.). 400p. 1996. pap. 15.95 (1-56512-109-0, 72109) Algonquin Bks.

Donner, Naomi E. Color for Body & Soul: Discover Yourself & Your Temperament Through Color. (Illus.). 96p. (Orig.). 1991. pap. 19.95 (0-9631778-0-X) N E Donner.

Donner, Neal & Stevenson, Daniel B., eds. The Great Calming & Contemplation: A Study & Annotated Translation of the First Chapter of Chih-i's "Mo-ho chih-kuan" LC 92-41546. (Classics in East Asian Buddhism). 494p. (C). 1993. text 45.00 (0-8248-1514-9) UH Pr.

Donner, R. O. & Pal, L. Science & Technology Policies in Finland & Hungary: A Comparative Study. 372p. 1985. 225.00 (0-569-08860-7, Pub. by Collets) St Mut.

Donner, Richard L. L. A. Discount Shopper's Guide: How to Buy a Car at Fleet Prices, How to Shop & Save for Watches, Furniture, Cameras, etc., Where to Buy Top Quality Merchandise. LC 74-84287. 143 p. 1974. write for info. (0-8431-0269-1, Price Stern) Peng Put Young Read.

Donner, Ruth. Regulation of Nationality in International Law. 2nd ed. 450p. 1995. 95.00 (0-941320-77-4) Transnatl Pubs.

Donner, Ted A. & Crowe, Brian L. Attorney's Practice Guide to Negotiations. 2nd ed. LC 95-16622. 1995. write for info. (0-614-07454-1) West Group.

Donner, Wendy. The Liberal Self: John Stuart Mill's Moral & Political Philosophy. LC 91-55065. 256p. 1992. text 45.00 (0-8014-2629-4); pap. text 16.95 (0-8014-9987-9) Cornell U Pr.

Donner, William W., ed. see Davenport, William H., et al.

***Donnerberg, Hansjorg.** Atomistic Simulation of Electro- & Magnetooptic Oxide Materials. LC 98-46730. (Tracts in Modern Physics Ser.: 151). 1998. write for info. (3-540-65111-X) Spr-Verlag.

***Donnersberger, Anne B. & Lesak, Anne E.** Anatomy & Physics. 7th ed. (Illus.). (C). 1999. pap. text, teacher ed., lab manual ed. 18.00 (0-7637-1053-9) JB Pubns.

Donnersberger, Anne B. & Lesak, Anne E. Lab Text Anatomy & Phys. The CAT. 6th ed. (Life Science Ser.). 496p. 1997. spiral bd. 46.25 (0-7637-0659-0) Jones & Bartlett.

— A Laboratory Textbook of Anatomy & Physiology. 6th ed. (Life Science Ser.). (C). 1996. pap., teacher ed. 10.00 (0-669-39881-0) Jones & Bartlett.

— A Laboratory Textbook of Anatomy & Physiology. 7th ed. LC 99-14177. 1999. write for info. (0-7637-0915-8) Jones & Bartlett.

Donnersberger, Anne B., et al. A Manual of Anatomy & Physiology: Brief Version. (Life Science Ser.). 344p. (C). 1989. pap., teacher ed. 10.00 (0-669-18012-2) Jones & Bartlett.

Donnerstein, Edward, et al. The Question of Pornography: Research Findings & Policy Implications. 288p. 1987. 40.00 (0-02-907521-1) Free Pr.

Donnerstein, Edward, jt. auth. see Malamuth, Neil M.

Donnerstein, Edward, jt. ed. see Geen, Russell G.

Donnert, Erich. 2000 Planning for Retirement Asset Distributions: Tax, Financial & Personal Aspects. 300p. 1999. pap. text 99.00 (0-15-606969-5) Harcourt.

Donnet, Jean B. & Voet, Andries. Carbon Black: Chemistry & Elastomer Reinforcement. LC 75-16753. (Illus.). 363p. reprint ed. pap. 112.60 (0-608-30560-X, 202028300016) Bks Demand.

Donnet, Jean-Baptiste. Carbon Fibers. 3rd ed. LC 98-9327. (Illus.). 584p. 1998. text 195.00 (0-8247-0172-0) Dekker.

Donnet, Jean-Baptiste, et al, eds. Carbon Black: Science & Technology. 2nd rev. ed. LC 93-16640. (Illus.). 480p. 1993. text 235.00 (0-8247-8975-X) Dekker.

Donnet, Pierre-Antoine. Tibet: Survival in Question. Broch, Tica, tr. (Politics in Contemporary Asia Ser.). (Illus.). 256p. (C). 1994. text 19.95 (1-85649-130-7, Pub. by Zed Books) St Martin.

Donnet, Stoeckl, ed. see Bansal, Roop Chand.

Donnett, Kathleen A., jt. auth. see Kowalczyk, Nina.

Donnevert, M. TexTerm Four Wheel Drive: English/German-German/English. (TexTerm Ser.). (ENG & GER., Illus.). xii, 131p. 1989. pap. 30.00 (3-527-27869-9, Wiley-VCH) Wiley.

Donnez, J., jt. auth. see Nisolle, M.

Donnez, J., jt. ed. see Brosens, I.

Donnici, Jeffrey A., ed. see Hentzen, Whil.

Donnington, George A. History & Progress of the County of Marion, West Virginia. 175p. 1997. reprint ed. pap. 18.00 (1-888265-21-3) Willow Bend.

Donnini, Frank P. ANZUS in Revision: Changing Defense Features of Australia & New Zealand in the mid-1980s. LC 90-28081. (Illus.). 219p. 1991. pap. 14.00 (1-58566-037-X) Air Univ.

— Battling for Bombers: The U.S. Air Force Fights for Its Modern Strategic Aircraft Programs, 195. LC 99-54511. (Contributions in Military Studies Ser.). 248p. 2000. 62.50 (0-313-31221-4, Greenwood Pr) Greenwood.

Donnini, Frank P., jt. auth. see Davis, Richard L.

Donnino, William C. New York Court of Appeals on Criminal Law. LC 85-50869. 1985. 105.00 (0-318-18300-5) West Group.

— New York Court of Appeals on Criminal Law. LC 85-50869. 1993. suppl. ed. 52.50 (0-317-03275-5) West Group.

— New York Court of Appeals on Criminal Law. 2nd ed. LC 97-29386. 1997. write for info. (0-8366-1150-0) West Group.

Donnison, David. Social Policy & Administration Revised Studies in the Development of Social Services at the Local Level. 1970. 30.00 (0-7855-0579-2, Pub. by Natl Inst Soc Work) St Mut.

Donnison, David V. & Eversley, David, eds. London: Urban Patterns, Problems, & Policies. LC 73-80440. (Centre for Environmental Studies Ser.: Vol. 2). 464p. reprint ed. pap. 143.90 (0-608-14193-3, 202188800026) Bks Demand.

Donnithorne, Audrey G. China's Economic System. LC 67-23967. 592p. reprint ed. pap. 168.80 (0-608-14426-6, 2051762) Bks Demand.

Donnithorne, Audrey G., jt. auth. see Allen, George C.

Donnithorne, Larry. West Point Way of Leadership. 192p. 1993. 24.95 (0-385-41703-9) Doubleday.

Donno, Daniel, ed. see Machiavelli, Niccolo.

Donno, Daniel J., ed. see Campanella, Tommaso.

Donno, Elizabeth S., ed. Andrew Marvell: The Critical Heritage. (Critical Heritage Ser.). xvii, 385p. 1978. 69.50 (0-7100-8791-8, 87918, Routledge Thoemms) Routledge.

— Elizabethan Minor Epics. LC 63-20343. 361p. reprint ed. 112.00 (0-8357-9064-9, 201327700087) Bks Demand.

— Three Renaissance Pastorals: Tasso, Guarini, Daniel. LC 92-16043. (Medieval & Renaissance Texts & Studies: Vol. 102). 296p. 1993. 20.00 (0-86698-118-7, MR102) MRTS.

Donno, Elizabeth S., ed. see Marvell, Andrew.

Donno, Elizabeth S., ed. see Shakespeare, William.

Donnolly, Lawrence, jt. auth. see Dolan, John F.

Donoahue, Zoe, et al, eds. Research in the Classroom: Talk, Texts & Inquiry. 136p. 1996. pap. 18.00 (0-87207-146-4) Intl Reading.

Donoff, Craig. Avoiding Probate: A Lawyers's View. (Illus.). 200p. 1988. 16.60 (0-945891-01-6); pap. write for info. (0-945891-00-8) Phoenix Orlando.

Donoff, R. Bruce, ed. see Massachusetts General Hospital Staff.

***D'Onofrio, Anthony, et al.** Regents High School Mathematics A. (Illus.). 295p. (YA). (gr. 8-12). 1999. pap. text 13.50 (0-937820-75-X) WestSea Pub.

D'Onofrio, B., jt. ed. see Dell'Antonio, G. F.

***Donofrio, Beverly.** Looking for Mary: Or, the Blessed Mother & Me. 304p. 2000. 23.95 (0-670-88459-6, Viking) Viking Penguin.

Donofrio, Beverly. Riding in Cars with Boys: Confessions of a Bad Girl Who Makes Good. 208p. 1992. pap. 9.95 (0-14-015629-1, Penguin Bks) Viking Penguin.

Donofrio, Beverly, jt. auth. see Bonanno, Rosalie.

D'Onofrio, Carol N., jt. auth. see Rich, Ruth.

D'Onofrio, Elizabeth, jt. auth. see D'Onofrio, Mary A.

D'Onofrio, Giulio. History of Theology Vol. 3: The Renaissance. 656p. 1998. 99.95 (0-8146-5917-9) Liturgical Pr.

D'Onofrio, Giuseppe & Zini, Gina. Morphology of the Blood. Bain, Barbara J., tr. LC 97-51175. 384p. 1998. text 195.00 (0-7506-4055-3) Buttrwrth-Heinemann.

Donofrio, Linda & Sholl, Andrea. Solving Math Word Problems Bk. 1: Sums to 99 No Borrowing or Carrying. Womack, Rnady L., ed. (Solving Math Word Problems Ser.). Orig. Title: Story Problems Made Easy. (Illus.). 48p. (J). (gr. 1-3). 1996. pap. text 7.95 (1-56500-038-2) Gldn Educ.

— Solving Math Word Problems Bk. 2: Sums to 500 with Borrowing or Carrying. Womack, Randy L., ed. (Solving Math Word Problems Ser.). Orig. Title: Story Problems Made Easy. (Illus.). 48p. (J). 1996. pap. text 7.95 (1-56500-039-0) Gldn Educ.

D'Onofrio, Mary A. & D'Onofrio, Elizabeth. Psychiatric Words & Phrases. 2nd ed. LC 99-159101. Orig. Title: Psychiatric Words & Phrases: A Quick Reference Guide. 12p. 1997. pap. 36.00 (0-934385-70-X) Hlth Prof Inst.

Donofrio, Monica J., jt. auth. see Title, Monroe M.

Donofrio, Phyllis. The CICS - ESA Migration Notebook: An Inside Look at Versions 3 & 4. Mascomm Associates Circle Education Staff, ed. (Compuware Technology Update Ser.). pap. text 49.95 (0-923039-00-7) CompuWare MI.

D'Onofrio, Richard. Journey Through a Long Winters Night. 700p. mass mkt. 6.99 (1-896329-19-5) Picasso Publ.

Donofrio, William, jt. auth. see Barcena, Theresa L.

Donoghue, Daniel. Style in Old English Poetry: The Test of the Auxiliary. LC 87-13264. 256p. 1988. 40.00 (0-300-03956-5) Yale U Pr.

Donoghue, Denis. Connoisseurs of Chaos: Ideas of Order in Modern American Poetry. LC 83-20935. 1984. pap. text 21.00 (0-231-05735-0) Col U Pr.

— Emily Dickinson. LC 76-628284. (University of Minnesota Pamphlets on American Writers Ser.: No. 81). 47p. reprint ed. pap. 30.00 (0-608-16749-5, 205620900055) Bks Demand.

— Ferocious Alphabets. 211p. 1984. reprint ed. pap. text 20.00 (0-231-05823-3) Col U Pr.

— The Politics of Modern Criticism. (Chapbooks in Literature Ser.). 31p. 1981. pap. text 5.00 (0-9614940-5-0) Bennington Coll.

— The Practice of Reading. LC 97-42549. 320p. 1998. 35.00 (0-300-07466-2) Yale U Pr.

***Donoghue, Denis.** The Practice of Reading. LC 97-42549. 320p. 2000. pap. 15.95 (0-300-08264-9) Yale U Pr.

Donoghue, Denis. The Sovereign Ghost: Studies in Imagination. LC 75-27923. 239p. reprint ed. pap. 74.10 (0-608-18508-6, 203153200075) Bks Demand.

— Warrenpoint. (Irish Studies). 196p. (C). 1994. reprint ed. pap. 16.95 (0-8156-0303-7) Syracuse U Pr.

— Who Says What & the Question of Voice. 48p. 1992. pap. 8.95 (0-86140-365-7, Pub. by Smyth) Dufour.

***Donoghue, Denis.** Words Alone: The Poet T. S. Eliot. 288p. 2000. 26.95 (0-300-08329-7) Yale U Pr.

Donoghue, Denis, ed. Seven American Poets from MacLeish to Nemerov: An Introduction. LC 74-22560. (Minnesota Library on American Writers). 337p. 1975. reprint ed. pap. 104.50 (0-7837-2966-9, 205748800006) Bks Demand.

Donoghue, Denis, et al. Creation & Interpretation. 300p. 1984. 65.00 (0-930586-20-4); pap. 30.00 (0-614-13736-5) Haven Pubns.

Donoghue, Denis, ed. see Blackmur, Richard P.

Donoghue, Denis, ed. see James, Henry.

Donoghue, E. We Are Michael Field: Outlines. 152p. 1997. pap. text 9.95 (1-899791-66-3) Stewart Tabori & Chang.

Donoghue, E. A., ed. Safety Code for Elevators & Escalators: Handbook on A17.1. 372p. 1987. 95.00 (0-685-06265-1, A00112) ASME.

***Donoghue, Edward A.** ADA & Building Transportation: A Handbook on Accessibility Regulations for Elevators. 2nd ed. (Illus.). 181p. 2000. pap. 49.95 (1-886536-29-5) Elevator Wrld.

Donoghue, Edward A. ADA & Vertical Transportation. (Illus.). 144p. (Orig.). 1993. pap. text 45.00 (1-886536-05-8) Elevator Wrld.

An Asterisk (*) at the beginning of an entry indicates that the title is appearing for the first time.

Donoghue, Emma. Hood. LC 95-48437. 280p. 1998. pap. 11.95 (*1-55583-453-1*) Alyson Pubns.

— Kissing the Witch: Old Tales in New Skins. LC 96-43465. (Joanna Cotler Bks.). 240p. (YA). (gr. 7-12). 1997. 14.95 (*0-06-027575-8*) HarpC.

— Kissing the Witch: Old Tales in New Skins. LC 96-43465. (Joanna Cotler Bks.). 240p. (YA). (gr. 7 up). 1997. lib. bdg. 14.89 (*0-06-027576-6*) HarpC.

***Donoghue, Emma.** Kissing the Witch: Old Tales in New Skins. LC 96-43465. 240p. 1999. pap. 11.00 (*0-06-440772-1*) HarpC Child Bks.

Donoghue, Emma. Kissing the Witch: Old Tales in New Skins. (YA). (gr. 7 up). 1993. 56.00 (*1-85594-099-X*) St Mut.

— Poems Between Women: Four Centuries of Love, Romantic Friendship, & Desire. LC 96-49693. 272p. (C). 1997. 26.50 (*0-231-10924-5*) Col U Pr.

Donoghue, Emma, ed. The Mammoth Book of Lesbian Short Stories. (Mammoth Book Ser.). 624p. 1999. pap. 10.95 (*0-7867-0627-9*) Carroll & Graf.

— Poems Between Women: Four Centuries of Love, Romantic Friendship, & Desire. 1999. pap. 17.50 (*0-231-10925-3*) Col U Pr.

Donoghue, Frank. The Fame Machine: Book Reviewing & Eighteenth-Century Literary Careers. LC 95-22803. 256p. 1996. 39.50 (*0-8047-2563-2*) Stanford U Pr.

***Donoghue, Freda.** Defining the Nonprofit Sector: Ireland. (Working Papers of the Johns Hopkins Comparative Nonprofit Sector Project: Vol. 28). (Illus.). 25p. 1998. pap. text 6.00 (*1-886333-33-5*) JH Univ Inst Pol Studies.

Donoghue, George T. Casey Federal Tax Practice: 1977-1990, 6 vols., Set. LC 77-18109. 700.00 (*0-317-11936-2*) West Group.

Donoghue, Jack. The Edge of War. (Illus.). 149p. 1988. 19.95 (*0-920490-75-1*) Temeron Bks.

Donoghue, John. Alexander Jackson Davis, Romantic Architect, 1803-1892. 1981. 32.95 (*0-405-14078-9*) Ayer.

***Donoghue, John.** Precipice. LC 99-71363. 63p. 2000. pap. 13.95 (*1-884800-28-9*, Pub. by Four Way Bks) SPD-Small Pr Dist.

Donoghue, John F. CP Violation & the Limits of the Standard Model: Proceedings of TASI-94. 788p. 1995. text 94.00 (*981-02-2283-1*) World Scientific Pub.

Donoghue, John F., et al. Dynamics of the Standard Model. (Cambridge Monographs on Particle Physics, Nuclear Physics & Cosmology: Vol. 2). (Illus.). 558p. (C). 1994. pap. text 49.95 (*0-521-47652-6*) Cambridge U Pr.

Donoghue, Mildred. The Child & the English Language Arts. 5th ed. 576p. (C). 1989. text. write for info. (*0-697-10403-6*) Brown & Benchmark.

Donoghue, P. S. The Sankov Confession. 352p. 1992. mass mkt. 4.50 (*0-8217-3800-3*, Zebra Kensgtn) Kensgtn Pub Corp.

Donoghue, Paul J. Sick & Tired of Feeling Sick & Tired: Living with Invisible Chronic Illness. 1994. pap. 13.95 (*0-393-31154-6*) Norton.

***Donoghue, Paul J.** Sick & Tired of Feeling Sick & Tired: Living with Invisible Chronic Illness. 304p. 2000. pap. 14.95 (*0-393-32065-0*) Norton.

Donoghue, Paul J. & Siegel, Mary E. Sick & Tired of Feeling Sick & Tired: Living with Invisible Chronic Illness. 288p. 1992. 22.95 (*0-393-03408-9*) Norton.

Donoghue, Sheila, ed. see Killingstad, Kay.

Donoghue, Simon J., jt. auth. see Manera, Nancy.

Donoghue, Susanne C. Meditations for Single Moms. LC 96-51876. 112p. (Orig.). 1997. pap. 8.99 (*0-8361-9061-0*) Herald Pr.

Donoghue, W. F., Jr., ed. Monotone Matrix Functions & Analytic Continuation. LC 73-15293. (Grundlehren der Mathematischen Wissenschaften Ser.: Vol. 207). 210p. 1974. 54.00 (*0-387-06543-1*) Spr-Verlag.

Donoghue, William E. Fessor Mojo's "Don't Start Me to Talkin" 98p. 1997. pap. 19.95 (*0-9637899-5-3*) Elliott & James Pubs.

— Mutual Fund Superstars: Invest in the Best, Forget about the Rest. 1994. 24.95 (*0-9637899-0-2*) Elliott & James Pubs.

— Mutual Fund Superstars: Invest in the Best, Forget about the Rest, 1996 Edition. 2nd ed. (Illus.). 300p. 1995. 24.95 (*0-9637899-1-0*); pap. 14.95 (*0-9637899-2-9*) Elliott & James Pubs.

Donohew, L., et al, eds. Persuasive Communication & Drug Abuse Prevention. (Communication Ser.). 360p. (C). 1991. text 69.95 (*0-8058-0693-8*) L Erlbaum Assocs.

Donohew, L., jt. ed. see Ray, Eileen B.

Donohew, Lewis, et al, eds. Communication, Social Cognition & Affect. (Communication & Psychology Ser.). 272p. 1987. text 59.95 (*0-89859-975-X*) L Erlbaum Assocs.

Donoho, Annette L. Buy American - A How-to-Handbook: Who Owns What in the United States. 164p. (Orig.). 1991. per. 9.95 (*0-9631519-0-8*) LRH Ent Buy Am.

Donohoe. Teaching Atlas of Nuclear Medicine: Casebase. LC 99-40822. (Illus.). 544p. 1999. 99.00 (*0-86577-775-6*) Thieme Med Pubs.

Donohoe, James J., jt. auth. see Chaucer, Geoffrey.

Donohoe, James J., jt. auth. see Chauser, Geoffrey.

Donohoe, Joseph I., ed. Essays on Quebec Cinema. LC 91-52909. (Illus.). 250p. (C). 1991. 26.00 (*0-87013-294-6*) Mich St U Pr.

***Donohoe, Joseph I., Jr. & Koustas, Jane M., eds.** Theater Sans Frontieres: Essays on the Dramatic Universe of Robert Lepage. 200p. 2001. pap. 29.95 (*0-87013-568-6*) Mich St U Pr.

Donohoe, Joseph I., Jr. & Weiss, Jonathan M., eds. Essays on Modern Quebec Theater. 240p. 1995. 35.00 (*0-87013-388-8*) Mich St U Pr.

Donohoe, Kitty. Bunyan & Banjoes: Michigan Songs & Stories. 2nd rev. ed. (Illus.). 48p. (J). (gr. 1-9). 1997. reprint ed. pap. 19.95 incl. audio (*1-882376-51-X*) Thunder Bay Pr.

— Bunyan & Banjoes Vol. 1: Michigan Songs & Stories. 2nd rev. ed. (Illus.). 48p. (J). (gr. 1-9). 1997. reprint ed. pap. 10.95 (*1-882376-28-5*) Thunder Bay Pr.

Donohoe, Neil. Ramblings. 1998. pap. write for info. (*1-57553-872-5*) Watermrk Pr.

Donohoe, Patrick, jt. auth. see TC2 Working IFIP Conference on Software Architecture Staff.

Donohoe, Ronan, jt. auth. see Dolph, James.

Donohoe, Timothy. Oxidations & Reduction in Organic Synthesis. (Oxford Chemistry Primers Ser.: No. 6). (Illus.). 96p. (C). 2000. pap. text 9.95 (*0-19-855664-0*) OUP.

Donohue, Agnes M. Hawthorne: Calvin's Ironic Stepchild. LC 84-12550. 372p. 1985. reprint ed. pap. 115.40 (*0-608-07349-0*, 206757700009) Bks Demand.

Donohue, Alice A. Xoana & the Origins of Greek Sculpture. LC 86-6511. (American Philological Association, American Classical Studies). 509p. 1988. pap. 16.95 (*1-55540-154-6*, 40-04-15) OUP.

Donohue, Cecilia S. Robert Penn Warren's Novels: Feminine & Feminist Discourse. LC 96-51555. (Modern American Literature Ser.: Vol. 12). 141p. (C). 1999. text 41.95 (*0-8204-3738-7*, 37387) P Lang Pubng.

Donohue, Daniel P. An Analysis of Radiographic Quality: Lab Manual & Workbook. 3rd ed. 544p. 1995. 52.00 (*0-8342-0678-1*) Aspen Pub.

Donohue, Dorothy. Big & Little on the Farm. 7. 24p. (ps-4). 1999. 9.95 (*0-307-10225-4*) Gldn Bks Pub Co.

***Donohue, Dorothy.** Veggie Soup. LC 99-462307. (Illus.). 32p. (J). (ps-3). 2000. 16.95 (*1-890817-21-X*, Pub. by Winslow Pr) Publishers Group.

Donohue, Harold. The Song of the Swan: Lucretius & the Influence of Callimachus. LC 93-13876. 170p. (C). 1993. lib. bdg. 39.50 (*0-8191-9187-6*) U Pr of Amer.

Donohue, Jerry. The Structures of the Elements. LC 80-15363. 448p. 1982. reprint ed. lib. bdg. 47.50 (*0-89874-230-7*) Krieger.

Donohue, John, 3rd, ed. Foundations of Employment Discrimination Law. (Interdisciplinary Readers in Law Ser.). (Illus.). 416p. 1997. pap. text 24.95 (*0-19-509281-3*) OUP.

Donohue, John, et al. The Human Condition in the Modern Age. 2nd ed. 544p. (C). 1996. pap. text, per. 75.95 (*0-7872-2751-X*, 41275101) Kendall-Hunt.

Donohue, John, ed. see Wright, Bonnie L., et al.

Donohue, John H., et al, eds. Atlas of Surgical Oncology. LC 94-18165. (Illus.). 336p. 1995. 135.00 (*0-86542-422-5*) Blackwell Sci.

Donohue, John J. Complete Kendo. LC 99-23109. 1999. pap. 19.95 (*0-8048-3148-3*) Tuttle Pubng.

— The Forge of the Spirit: Structure, Motion & Meaning in the Japanese Martial Tradition. LC 90-20911. 272p. 1991. text 15.00 (*0-8240-7114-X*) Garland.

— Herding the Ox: The Martial Arts As Moral Metaphor. LC 97-49087. (Illus.). 144p. 1998. pap. 12.95 (*1-880336-18-9*, HTO) Turtle CT.

— Muslim-Christian Relations: Dialogue in Lebanon. (Occasional Papers Ser.). iii, 24p. 1996. pap. 3.95 (*1-929218-10-9*) Georgetwn U Ctr Muslim.

— Warrior Dreams: The Martial Arts & the American Imagination. LC 93-9019. 160p. 1994. 52.95 (*0-89789-346-8*, Bergin & Garvey) Greenwood.

Donohue, John J. & Esposito, John L., eds. Islam in Transition: Muslim Perspectives. 336p. 1982. pap. text 23.95 (*0-19-503023-0*) OUP.

Donohue, John K. Baffling Eyes of Youth. LC 74-9578. 251p. 1974. reprint ed. lib. bdg. 22.50 (*0-8371-7601-8*, DOBY, Greenwood Pr) Greenwood.

Donohue, John W. Jesuit Education: An Essay on the Foundations of Its Idea. LC LC0493.D62. 239p. reprint ed. pap. 74.10 (*0-7837-0444-5*, 204076700018) Bks Demand.

Donohue, Joseph, ed. see Wilde, Oscar.

Donohue, Joseph C., jt. ed. see Kochen, Manfred.

Donohue, Julie. Fancy Fish Coloring Book. 22p. (J). (gr. 3-5). 1990. pap. 3.95 (*0-943864-61-5*) Davenport.

Donohue, Kathleen. Kitchen & Bath Theme Design: An Architectural Styling Guide. LC 99-174436. (Illus.). 256p. 1998. pap. 39.95 (*0-07-018134-9*) McGraw.

Donohue, L. A. Stock Market Fundamentals for Beginners: A Stock Investment Primer. 1997. pap. 7.25 (*0-9662673-0-3*) LJD Pub.

***Donohue, Laura K.** Regulating Violence. (New Directions in Irish History Ser.). 256p. 2000. 52.50 (*0-7165-2687-5*, Pub. by Irish Acad Pr) Intl Spec Bk.

Donohue, Mark. A Grammar of Tukang Besi. LC 98-43668. (Grammar Library). 608p. 1999. 186.00 (*3-11-016188-5*) De Gruyter.

***Donohue, Mark.** The Unfair Advantage. 2000. 49.95 (*0-8376-0073-1*, GDDO); pap. 24.95 (*0-8376-0069-3*, GDDS) Bentley Pubs.

Donohue, Michael. The Golden Bean. (Illus.). 113p. 1996. pap. 8.95 (*1-57502-236-2*, P0908) Morris Pubng.

Donohue, Michael J. Attractive Nuisance: A Thorpe Branch Stone Harbor Mystery. 234p. 1999. pap. write for info. (*0-7392-0180-8*, PO3145) Morris Pubng.

Donohue, Millie, jt. auth. see Westfall, Douglas.

Donohue, Rebecca, et al. Women's Health Nurse Practitioner Certification Exam Review. LC 98-17718. 135p. (C). 1998. pap. text 39.95 (*0-8385-9819-6*, A-9819-2) Appleton & Lange.

Donohue, Robert J. An Introduction to Cashflow Analysis. LC 94-74922. (Illus.). 212p. (C). 1995. pap. text 29.75 (*1-886654-00-X*) Regent Sch Pr.

— An Introduction to Cashflow Analysis. 2nd rev. ed. LC 94-74922. 316p. 1995. pap. 29.75 (*1-886654-02-6*) Regent Sch Pr.

Donohue, Ron M., jt. auth. see Seldin, Maury.

Donohue, Shiobhan. Kristi Yamaguchi: Artist on Ice. LC 92-38272. (J). (gr. 4-9). 1993. lib. bdg. 18.60 (*0-8225-0522-3*, Lerner Publctns) Lerner Pub.

— Kristi Yamaguchi: Artist on Ice. (Illus.). 64p. (J). (gr. 4-9). 1993. pap. 4.95 (*0-8225-9649-0*, Lerner Publctns) Lerner Pub.

Donohue, Sylvia, jt. auth. see Donohue, Thomas.

Donohue, Teresa, ed. see Gahala, Charles L.

Donohue, Teresa, ed. see Scherr, Frederick C.

Donohue, Teresa G., ed. see Marroritis, Basil P.

Donohue, Thomas & Donohue, Sylvia. Born Lucky or Unlucky. LC 97-68381. 128p. 1997. 14.95 (*1-887750-72-X*) Rutledge Bks.

Donohue, Timothy. In the Open: Diary of a Homeless Alcoholic. 216p. 1996. 22.95 (*0-226-15767-9*) U Ch Pr.

Donohue, Timothy E. In the Open: Diary of a Homeless Alcoholic. vi, 204p. 1997. pap. 11.95 (*0-226-15768-7*) U Ch Pr.

Donohue, Timothy F. & Sprouse, Curtis R. Drug Formularies & Pharmaceutical Industry: Thriving in the Managed Care Era. 179p. (Orig.). 1995. pap. 175.00 (*1-882615-23-9*) Parexel Intl.

Donohue, Walter, ed. see Boorman, John.

Donohue, Walter, jt. ed. see Boorman, John.

Donohue, William A. Communication, Marital Dispute & Divorce Mediation. 256p. (C). 1991. text 49.95 (*0-8058-0387-4*) L Erlbaum Assocs.

— Managing Interpersonal Conflict. (Interpersonal CommTexts Ser.: Vol. 4). 168p. (C). 1992. text 44.00 (*0-8039-3311-8*); pap. text 19.95 (*0-8039-3312-6*) Sage.

— The New Freedom: Individualism & Collectivism in the Social Lives of Americans. 296p. (C). 1994. 39.95 (*0-88738-298-3*); pap. 24.95 (*1-56000-789-3*) Transaction Pubs.

— On the Front Line of the Culture War: Recent Attacks on the Boy Scouts of America. LC 99-229406. 32p. (Orig.). (C). 1993. pap. 5.00 (*0-930783-20-4*) Claremont Inst.

— Twilight of Liberty: The Legacy of the ACLU. 310p. (C). 1994. text 39.95 (*1-56000-049-X*) Transaction Pubs.

***Donohue, William A.** Twilight of Liberty: The Legacy of the ACLU. 2000. pap. 29.95 (*0-7658-0722-X*) Transaction Pubs.

Donohue, William A. & Wildavsky, Aaron. The Politics of the American Civil Liberties Union. 390p. 1985. pap. 24.95 (*0-87855-983-3*) Transaction Pubs.

Donohue, William A., jt. ed. see Ellis, Donald E.

Donohugh, Donald L. Practice Management for Physicians. (Illus.). 365p. 1986. pap. text 55.00 (*0-7216-1889-8*, W B Saunders Co) Harcrt Hlth Sci Grp.

Donomvan, J. F., et al, eds. Boundary Layer & Free Shear Flows. LC 94-71358. (Fluid Engineering Division Conference Ser.: Vol. 184). 243p. 1994. pap. 45.00 (*0-7918-1367-3*) ASME.

***Donoso Cortes, Juan & Johnson, Jeffrey P.** Selected Works of Juan Donoso Cortes, 389. LC 99-56465. (Contributions in Political Science Ser.). 144p. 2000. 55.00 (*0-313-31397-0*, Greenwood Pr) Greenwood.

Donoso, Eulalia. Apacible Vida Provinciana. LC 93-79289. (SPA.). 190p. (Orig.). 1993. pap. 16.00 (*0-9637939-1-8*) Edic Rio Claro.

— La Causa. LC 91-73416. 156p. 1991. 15.00 (*0-89729-615-X*) Ediciones.

Donoso, J. Alejandro, jt. ed. see Fernandez, Hugo L.

Donoso, Jose. Curfew. 320p. 1989. pap. 12.00 (*0-8021-3381-9*, Grove) Grove-Atltic.

***Donoso, Jose.** Curfew. LC 99-42839. 490p. 1999. 32.95 (*1-56000-450-9*) Transaction Pubs.

Donoso, Jose. The Garden Next Door: A Novel. LC 91-41842. 288p. 1992. pap. 12.00 (*0-8021-3368-1*, Grove) Grove-Atltic.

***Donoso, Jose.** Hell Has No Limits. Levine, Suzanne Jill, tr. (Green Integer Bks.: No. 28). 168p. 1999. pap. text 10.95 (*1-892295-14-8*, Pub. by Green Integer) Consort Bk Sales.

Donoso, Jose. El Jardin de al Lado. (SPA.). pap. 22.95 (*84-322-0387-4*, Pub. by E Seix Barral) Continental Bk.

— El Lugar Sin Limites (Hell Has No Limits) 208p. 1995. pap. 12.50 (*0-679-76527-1*) Vin Bks.

— El Mocho. 1998. pap. 19.95 (*968-19-0334-X*) Santillana.

— The Obscene Bird of Night. St. Martin, Hardie & Marcus, Leonard, trs. from SPA. (Verba Mundi Ser.). 448p. 1979. reprint ed. pap. 15.95 (*1-56792-046-2*) Godine.

— Taratuta & Still Life with Pipe. 1994. pap. 8.95 (*0-393-31164-3*) Norton.

Donougher, Christine, tr. see Bealu, Marcel.

Donougher, Christine, tr. see Boito, Camillo.

Donougher, Christine, tr. see Germain, Sylvie.

Donougher, Christine, tr. see Mirbeau, Octave.

Donougher, Christine, tr. see Potocki, Jan.

Donougher, Christine, tr. see Rezvani.

***Donoughue, Carol.** The Mystery of the Hieroglyphs. (Illus.). 48p. (YA). 1999. lib. bdg. 18.95 (*0-19-521553-2*) OUP.

Donoughue, Carol. The Mystery of the Hieroglyphs: The Story of the Rosetta Stone & the Race to Decipher Egyptian Hieroglyphs. (Illus.). 48p. (YA). 1999. pap. 16.95 (*0-19-521554-0*) OUP.

Donoughue, Carol, compiled by. The Development of Writing. 39.00 (*1-56696-140-8*) Jackdaw.

Donovan. Business Re-Engineering with Information Technology. 224p. (C). 1994. 29.99 (*0-13-311028-1*, Macmillan Coll) P-H.

— Chemicals in Action. 2nd ed. 1995. text, teacher ed. 61.00 (*0-03-922456-2*); text, student ed. 58.25 (*0-03-922455-4*) H Holt & Co.

— Feminist Readings of Native Literature: Coming to Voice. LC 97-21197. 192p. 1998. 35.00 (*0-8165-1632-4*) U of Ariz Pr.

— Mass Extinctions: Processes & Evidence. 256p. 1991. pap. text 65.00 (*0-471-94524-2*) Wiley.

— Palaeobiology of Trace Fossils. 1994. text 177.00 (*0-471-94843-8*) Wiley.

— Protection of Metals from Corrosion in Storage & Transit. 1986. text 71.95 (*0-470-20332-3*) P-H.

Donovan. Technical Mathematics. 1995. pap. text. write for info. (*0-13-455644-5*) Allyn.

Donovan. Women & the Rise of the Novel. LC 98-41947. 176p. 1998. text 39.95 (*0-312-21827-3*) St Martin.

Donovan & Lucas. Ethics Military Leaders. LC 99-164799. 648p. (C). 1998. pap. text 67.00 (*0-536-01162-1*) S&S Trade.

Donovan, et al. Sociology: Relationships That Make a World. 608p. (C). 1998. per. 52.95 (*0-7872-3269-6*, 41326901) Kendall-Hunt.

Donovan, jt. auth. see Bignell.

***Donovan, Aine, ed.** Ethics for Military Leaders. 2nd ed. 520p. 1999. pap. text 70.00 (*0-536-02376-X*) P-H.

Donovan, Alvin G., III & Northcroft, Meg. Make More Money Now: Dramatic New 21-Day Money Making System Guaranteed to Make Everything You Say & Write Powerful, Influential, Convincing & Instantly Lucrative. 200p. 1997. 19.95 (*0-9657077-0-9*) Pavillion.

Donovan, Amy, ed. see Viola, Herman J.

Donovan, Anna & Lizatovic, Josip. Cuchulainn: A Storybook to Color. (Illus.). 32p. (J). 1997. pap. 5.95 (*0-86278-454-9*) Irish Amer Bk.

Donovan, Anthony J. World Peace? A Work Based on Interviews with Foreign Diplomats. LC 86-71893. 128p. (Orig.). 1986. pap. write for info. (*0-9617258-0-X*) A J Donovan.

Donovan, Arthur. Antoine Lavoisier: Science, Administration & Revolution. (Science Biographies Ser.). (Illus.). 367p. (C). 1996. text 69.95 (*0-521-56218-X*) Cambridge U Pr.

***Donovan, Arthur.** Osiris, Vol. 4. 2000. lib. bdg. 39.00 (*0-934235-10-4*) U Ch Pr.

Donovan, Arthur, et al, eds. Scrutinizing Science: Empirical Studies of Scientific Change. 407p. 1992. reprint ed. pap. text 24.95 (*0-8018-4517-3*) Johns Hopkins.

Donovan, Arthur, et al. Scrutinizing Science. 400p. (C). 1988. text 195.50 (*90-277-2608-6*) Kluwer Academic.

Donovan, Arthur, jt. auth. see Gibson, Andrew.

Donovan, Arthur J., Jr. & Drury, Bob. Fatso: Football When Men Were Really Men. 256p. 1988. mass mkt. 4.99 (*0-380-70629-6*, Avon Bks) Morrow Avon.

Donovan, B. H., jt. auth. see Wilson, R. B.

Donovan, B. T. Hormones & Human Behaviour. LC 85-4230. (Scientific Basis of Psychiatry Ser.: No. 2). 224p. 1985. text 74.95 (*0-521-25881-2*) Cambridge U Pr.

***Donovan, Beatrice.** Some Family Stories. Donovan, Diana, ed. LC 99-66472. (Illus.). 160p. 2000. pap. 40.00 (*0-923687-53-X*) Celo Valley Bks.

Donovan, Bonnie. The Cesarean Birth Experience: A Practical, Comprehensive & Reassuring Guide for Parents & Professionals. LC 85-47520. 283p. reprint ed. pap. 87.80 (*0-7837-1383-5*, 204155900021) Bks Demand.

Donovan, Bruce E. Euripides Papyri. LC 70-82816. (American Studies in Papyrology: Vol. 5). (Illus.). 137p. 1969. reprint ed. pap. 42.50 (*0-608-05669-3*, 206618500001) Bks Demand.

Donovan, Caroline, jt. auth. see Rohan, Patrick J.

Donovan, Charles A., jt. auth. see Marshall, Robert G.

Donovan, Charles F. Boston College: Glimpses of the Past. LC 94-60470. (Illus.). 274p. (Orig.). (C). 1994. pap. 12.95 (*0-9625934-1-9*) Univ Pr Boston Coll.

***Donovan, Charles F., Jr.** Renewal: World's Finest Toys. (Illus.). 144p. 1999. pap. 24.95 (*0-89538-105-2*) L-W Inc.

Donovan, Charles F., et al. History of Boston College: From the Beginnings to 1990. 584p. 1990. 35.00 (*0-9625934-0-0*) Univ Pr Boston Coll.

Donovan, Christine T., ed. Air Emissions & Ash Disposal at Wood-Burning Facilities: A Sourcebook & Case Studies for the Great Lakes Region. (Illus.). 201p. (C). 1997. reprint ed. pap. text 45.00 (*0-7881-3745-X*) DIANE Pub.

Donovan, Claire. The De Brailes Hours: Shaping the Book of Hours in Thirteenth-Century Oxford. (Medieval Texts & Translations Ser.: No. 7). (Illus.). 211p. 1991. text 85.00 (*0-8020-5951-1*) U of Toronto Pr.

— The Winchester Bible. (Illus.). 64p. 1993. pap. 24.95 (*0-8020-6991-6*) U of Toronto Pr.

Donovan, Craig P., ed. The Directory of Journals in Public & Non-Profit Administration, Public Policy & Political Science. xii, 130p. 1999. pap. 29.95 (*1-57420-064-X*) Chatelaine.

Donovan, Cynthia, jt. auth. see Ahmed, Raisuddin.

Donovan, D. & Woodward, Jacob A. History of Lyndeborough, 1735-1905. 932p. 1997. reprint ed. lib. bdg. 92.50 (*0-8328-6007-7*) Higginson Bk Co.

Donovan, D., jt. auth. see Schend, S.

Donovan, D. T., ed. Geology & Shelf Seas: Proceedings of the Geological Inter-University Congress, 14th. 1968. 15.75 (*0-934454-43-4*) Lubrecht & Cramer.

Donovan, D. W. Heroes' Lorebook. 1996. 20.00 (*0-7869-0412-7*, Pub. by TSR Inc) Random.

Donovan, Dale. For Duty & Deity. 1998. 13.95 (*0-7869-1234-0*, Pub. by TSR Inc) Random.

— Skills & Powers. (AD&D Accessory Ser.). 1997. pap. 22.95 (*0-7869-1149-2*, Pub. by TSR Inc) Random.

— Villains Lorebook. 1998. 22.95 (*0-7869-1236-7*, Pub. by TSR Inc) Random.

Donovan, Daniel. Distinctively Catholic: An Exploration of Catholic Identity. LC 97-24108. 224p. 1998. pap. 14.95 (*0-8091-3750-X*, 3750-X) Paulist Pr.

— Preparing for Worship: Sundays & Feast Days, Cycle A. 224p. (Orig.). 1995. pap. 11.95 (*0-8091-3571-X*) Paulist Pr.

D

— Preparing for Worship: Sundays & Feast Days, Cycle B. LC 93-13704. 224p. (Orig.). 1993. pap. 11.95 (*0-8091-3424-1*) Paulist Pr.
— Preparing for Worship: Sundays & Feast Days, Cycle C. 176p. 1994. pap. 11.95 (*0-8091-3507-8*) Paulist Pr.
— Stained Glass to Go. (Illus.). 20p. 1989. pap. 7.95 (*0-935133-32-1*) CKE Pubns.
— A Time of Grace: One Family's Experience with Chronic Care. 1990. pap. 5.95 (*0-8091-3164-1*) Paulist Pr.
— What Are They Saying about the Ministerial Priesthood? LC 92-11649. (What Are They Saying about...Ser.). 160p. 1992. pap. 7.95 (*0-8091-3318-0*) Paulist Pr.
— The Zoo Crew. (Illus.). 36p. 1989. pap. 8.95 (*0-935133-30-5*) CKE Pubns.

Donovan, Daryl. Men Mentoring Men: A Men's Discipleship Course. 222p. 1998. pap. 29.95 (*0-7880-1184-7*) CSS OH.

Donovan, Daryl G. Able to Stand. LC 95-62011. 96p. 1996. pap. 8.95 (*0-7880-0643-6*, Fairway Pr) CSS OH.

***Donovan, Daryl G.** Men Mentoring Men - Again: Men's Discipleship Course. 122p. 2000. pap. 19.95 (*0-7880-1594-X*) CSS OH.

Donovan, David. Once a Warrior King: Memories of an Officer in Vietnam. 352p. 1986. mass mkt. 5.99 (*0-345-33316-0*) Ballantine Pub Grp.

Donovan, David J., II. The Speed of the Bishop Image. (Illus.). 5p. 1989. 60.00 (*0-685-26796-2*) dG Printers.

Donovan, David J., II. Small Iowa Plates. 9p. (Orig.). 1989. 100.00 (*1-877886-00-9*) dG Printers.

Donovan, David Michael. Evil Down in the Alley: A Novel. LC 99-60200. 438p. 1999. 26.00 (*0-9669259-3-9*) J-D Pub.

***Donovan, Denis & McIntyre, Deborah.** What Did I Just Say!?! How New Insights into Childhood Thinking Can Help You Communicate More Effectively with Your Child. (Illus.). 240p. 2000. pap. 14.00 (*0-8050-6502-4*, Owl) H Holt & Co.

Donovan, Denis M. & McIntyre, Deborah. Healing the Hurt Child: A Developmental-Contextual Approach. (C). 1990. 34.95 (*0-393-70093-3*) Norton.

***Donovan, Denis M. & McIntyre, Deborah.** What Did I Just Say!?! How New Insights into Childhood Thinking Can Help You Communicate More Effectively with Your Child. LC 99-11987. (Illus.). 288p. 1999. 23.00 (*0-8050-6079-0*) H Holt & Co.

Donovan, Dennis G., et al. Sir Thomas Browne & Robert Burton: A Reference Guide. (C). 1981. 60.00 (*0-8161-8018-0*, Hall Reference) Macmillan.

Donovan, Dennis M. & Marlatt, G. Alan, eds. Assessment of Addictive Behaviors. LC 87-19674. (Behavioral Assessment Ser.). 497p. 1988. lib. bdg. 55.00 (*0-89862-144-5*) Guilford Pubns.

Donovan, Dennis M. & Mattson, Margaret E. Alcoholism Treatment Matching Research: Methodological & Clinical Approaches. (Journal of Studies on Alcohol: Suppl. No. 12). 1994. pap. 26.95 (*0-911290-53-2*, AJS-107) Rutgers Ctr Alcohol.

Donovan, Diana, ed. see Donovan, Beatrice.

Donovan, Doe. Do You Speak Astrology? Learn the Language of the Skies to Help Understand Yourself, Your Career & Your Relationships. Donovan-Young, Marge, ed. (Illus.). 274p. 1991. pap. 12.95 (*0-945027-05-2*) Sparrow Hawk Pr.

Donovan, Edward. The Natural History of British Fishes: Scientific & General Descriptions of the Most Interesting Species, 2 vols., Set. Sterling, Keir B., ed. LC 77-81091. (Biologists & Their World Ser.). (Illus.). 1978. reprint ed. lib. bdg. 68.95 (*0-405-10668-8*) Ayer.
— The Natural History of British Fishes: Scientific & General Descriptions of the Most Interesting Species, 2 vols., Vol. 1. Sterling, Keir B., ed. LC 77-81091. (Biologists & Their World Ser.). (Illus.). 1978. reprint ed. lib. bdg. 34.95 (*0-405-10669-6*) Ayer.
— The Natural History of British Fishes: Scientific & General Descriptions of the Most Interesting Species, 2 vols., Vol. 2. Sterling, Keir B., ed. LC 77-81091. (Biologists & Their World Ser.). (Illus.). 1978. reprint ed. lib. bdg. 34.95 (*0-405-10670-X*) Ayer.

Donovan, Erin. Teens, Crime, & Rural Communities. Kirby, Judy & O'Neil, Jean, eds. 40p. 1995. pap. 9.95 (*0-934513-35-X*, M48) Natl Crime DC.

Donovan, Finbarr, ed. see Conbhuidhe, Colmcille O.

Donovan, Fiona I. The Wood Block Prints of B. J. O. Nordfeldt: A Catalogue Raisonne. Brown, Susan Taylor, ed. LC 90-71792. 72p. (Illus.). 72p. (Orig.). 1991. pap. 16.00 (*0-938713-08-6*) Univ MN Art Mus.

Donovan, Frances H., jt. auth. see Jackson, Alun C.

Donovan, Frances R. The Saleslady. LC 74-3942. (Women in America Ser.). 278p. 1974. reprint ed. 25.95 (*0-405-06088-2*) Ayer.
— The Schoolma'am. LC 74-3943. (Women in America Ser.). 368p. 1974. reprint ed. 29.95 (*0-405-06087-4*) Ayer.
— The Woman Who Waits. LC 74-3941. (Women in America Ser.: From Colonial Times to the 20th Century). 228p. 1974. reprint ed. 20.95 (*0-405-06089-0*) Ayer.

Donovan, Francis D. Medway, Massachusetts, Births, Marriages, & Deaths. 190p. (Orig.). 1995. pap. text 29.50 (*0-7884-0230-7*) Heritage Bk.

Donovan, Frank P., Jr. Harry Bedwell, Last of the Great Railroad Storytellers. (Illus.). 1959. 10.00 (*0-87018-016-9*) Ross.

Donovan, Frederick & Goodby, James E. Changing the Rules: President Ronald Reagan's Strategic Defense Initiative Decision. (Pew Case Studies in International Affairs). 50p. (C). 1991. pap. text 3.50 (*1-56927-320-0*) Geo U Inst Dplmcy.
— Choosing Zero: Origins of the INF Treaty. (Pew Case Studies in International Affairs). 87p. (C). 1988. pap. text 3.50 (*1-56927-319-7*) Geo U Inst Dplmcy.
— High Stakes, High Risks: The Reykjavik "Base Camp" (Pew Case Studies in International Affairs). 50p. (C). 1993. pap. text 3.50 (*1-56927-317-0*) Geo U Inst Dplmcy.

***Donovan, Gerard.** The Lighthouse. 2000. pap. 12.95 (*1-903392-03-9*, Pub. by Salmon Poetry) Dufour.

Donovan, Graeme & Casey, Frank. Soil Fertility Management in Sub-Saharan Africa. LC 98-24350. (Technical Paper Ser.: No. 408). 69p. 1998. pap. 22.00 (*0-8213-4236-3*, 14236) World Bank.

Donovan, Gregory. Calling His Children Home: Poems. LC 93-4057. 64p. (Orig.). (C). 1993. pap. 10.95 (*0-8262-0896-7*); text 18.95 (*0-8262-0895-9*) U of Mo Pr.
— Land Boom! An Amateur's Guide to Professional Wealth or ... Your Inalienable Right to Your Own Eldorado! LC 83-80389. (Illus.). 76p. (Orig.). 1985. pap. 10.00 (*0-9615229-0-9*) Gregg Inc.

***Donovan, Henny.** The Painted Kitchen: Over 60 Quick & Easy Ways to Transform Your Kitchen Cupboards. (Illus.). 128p. 2000. 29.95 (*1-55209-455-3*) Firefly Bks Ltd.
— The Painted Kitchen: Over 60 Quick & Easy Ways to Transform Your Kitchen Cupboards. (Illus.). 128p. 2000. pap. 19.95 (*1-55209-501-0*) Firefly Bks Ltd.

Donovan, Herbert D. The Barnburners: A Study of Internal Movements in the Political History of New York State & of the Resulting Changes in Political Affiliations, 1830-1852. LC 73-16337. (Perspectives in American History Ser.: No. 5). (Illus.). viii, 140p. 1974. reprint ed. lib. bdg. 29.50 (*0-87991-337-1*) Porcupine Pr.

Donovan, I. A., jt. auth. see Bevan, P. Gilroy.

Donovan, J. W. Modern Jury Trials & Advocates: Containing Condensed Cases with Sketches & Speeches of American Advocates; the Art of Winning Cases & Manner of Counsel Described, with Notes & Rules of Practice. 4th enl. rev. ed. xxi, 720p. 1985. reprint ed. 65.00 (*0-8377-0523-1*, Rothman) W S Hein.
— Skill in Trials: Containing a Variety of Civil & Criminal Cases Won by the Art of Advocates, with Some of the Skill of Webster, Choate, Beach, Butler, Curtis, Davis, Fountain & Others, Given in Sketches of Their Work & Trial Stories, with New Selections of Western Eloquence. 173p. 1982. reprint ed. 35.00 (*0-8377-0515-0*, Rothman) W S Hein.
— Tact in Court: Containing Sketches of Cases Won by Skill, Wit, Art, Tact, Courage & Eloquence, with Practical Illustrations in Letters of Lawyers Giving Their Best Rules for Winning Cases. 3rd ed. 135p. 1983. reprint ed. 35.00 (*0-8377-0517-7*, Rothman) W S Hein.
— Tact in Court or How Lawyers Win: Containing Sketches of Cases Won by Skill, Wit, Art, Tact, Courage & Eloquence with Trial Rules & Illustrations. LC 88-80856. 124p. 1988. reprint ed. 45.00 (*0-912004-66-5*) Gaunt.

Donovan, James A. 50 Ways to Motivate Your Board: A Guide for Nonprofit Executives. unabridged ed. (Illus.). 112p. (Orig.). 1997. pap. 19.95 (*0-9639875-2-6*) Donovan Mgmt.
— Outpost in the North Atlantic: Marines in the Defense of Iceland. (Illus.). 33p. 1996. reprint ed. pap. text 20.00 (*0-7881-3524-4*) DIANE Pub.
— Take the Fear Out of Asking for Major Gifts. 103p. (Orig.). 1994. pap. 24.95 (*0-9639875-1-8*) Donovan Mgmt.

Donovan, James D. You Don't Have to Be a Poet to Put Your Love into Words. (Illus.). 138p. 1989. 14.95 (*0-9621051-0-4*, DV0) J D Donovan.

Donovan, James M., ed. Short-Term Couple Therapy. LC 98-32163. (Family Therapy Ser.). 417p. 1999. lib. bdg. 43.00 (*1-57230-431-6*) Guilford Pubns.

***Donovan, Jane.** Do Breakfast! Recipes for Morning Gourmets. (Illus.). 80p. 2000. 16.95 (*2-921556-95-2*, Pub. by Modus Viv) ACCESS Pubs Network.

Donovan, Jane. Garlic, Garlic, Garlic. 1998. 15.99 (*0-7858-0922-8*) Bk Sales Inc.
— Herbs, Herbs, Herbs. 1998. 15.99 (*0-7858-0924-4*) Bk Sales Inc.
— Super Soups Cookbook. 1998. 15.99 (*0-7858-0923-6*) Bk Sales Inc.
— Very Vegetarian Cookbook. 1998. 15.99 (*0-7858-0921-X*) Bk Sales Inc.

***Donovan, Jane, ed.** Chocolate. (Essentials Ser.). 80p. 2000. 12.95 (*0-8092-2328-7*, 232790, Contemporary Bks) NTC Contemp Pub Co.
— Tomato. (Essentials Ser.). 80p. 2000. 12.95 (*0-8092-2327-9*, 232790, Contemporary Bks) NTC Contemp Pub Co.

***Donovan, Jane, et al.** Lafayette Life: Words & Images Since 1928. (Illus.). 175p. 1999. 30.00 (*0-9671720-0-4*) Lafayette Home.

Donovan, Jane, ed. see Congdon.

Donovan, Jenny, jt. auth. see Eyles, John.

Donovan, Jerry J., jt. auth. see Blake, Judith.

Donovan, Jim. Dallas: Shining Star of Texas. LC 93-47312. (Illus.). 72p. 1994. pap. 11.95 (*0-89658-239-6*) Voyageur Pr.
— Handbook to a Happier Life: A Simple Guide to Learning to Live the Life You've Always Wanted. 96p. 1995. pap. 9.95 (*0-9650534-0-7*) Lahaska Pr.
— This Is Your Life, Not a Dress Rehearsal: Proven Principles for Creating the Life of Your Dreams. 128p. 1999. pap. 11.95 (*0-9650534-2-3*) Lahaska Pr.

Donovan, Jim, ed. Fit & Sexy after Fifty: The Conspiracy of Aging - & How to Reverse It! 216p. 1996. pap. 16.95 (*0-9647526-0-3*) RTR Pubng.

Donovan, Jim, et al. The Dallas Cowboy Encyclopedia: The Ultimate Guide to America's Team. rev. ed. LC 99-25094. (Illus.). 304p. 1999. pap. 19.95 (*0-8065-2111-2*, Citadel Pr) Carol Pub Group.
— The Dallas Cowboys Encyclopedia: The Ultimate Guide to America's Team. LC 96-28736. (Illus.). 288p. 1996. pap. 19.95 (*0-8065-1835-9*, Citadel Pr) Carol Pub Group.

Donovan, Jim, jt. auth. see Waldman, Carl.

Donovan, Jim, ed. see Dover, Benjamin F.

Donovan, Jim, ed. see Olimpio, Sal.

Donovan, Joe. The Self-Help Directory: A Sourcebook to Self-Help in the United States & Canada. LC 93-12074. 176p. 1993. 29.95 (*0-8160-2621-1*) Facts on File.

Donovan, John. Bittersweet Temptation. (Orig.). 1979. mass mkt. 2.50 (*0-89083-445-8*, Zebra Kensgtn) Kensgtn Pub Corp.

Donovan, John, tr. & intro. see De Saint-Pierre, Bernardin J.

Donovan, John A. Gaelic Names for Celtic Dogs. LC 95-39371. (Illus.). 96p. 1995. reprint ed. pap. 11.95 (*0-931866-86-3*) Alpine Pubns.
— The Irish Wolfhound: Great Symbol of Ireland. (Illus.). 128p. 1986. 24.95 (*0-931866-22-7*) Alpine Pubns.

Donovan, John C. The Cold Warriors: A Policy-Making Elite. 288p. (C). 1974. pap. text 27.96 (*0-669-83931-0*) HM Trade Div.

Donovan, John C., et al. People, Power & Politics: An Introduction to Political Science. 3rd ed. 360p. 1993. pap. 27.95 (*0-8226-3025-7*) Rowman.

Donovan, John J. Second Industrial Revolution: Reinventing Your Business on the Internet. LC 97-5704. 240p. (C). 1997. pap. text 19.95 (*0-13-745621-2*) P-H.
— SWAT: Strategic Weapons & Tactics for Executives: Handbook for Implementing Strategic Advantage Through Technology. (Illus.). 180p. 1988. 15.95 (*0-685-24279-X*) Cambridge Tech Grp Inc.

Donovan, John M., jt. auth. see Doorley, Thomas L.

Donovan, Joseph. Massachusetts Sales & Use Tax Manual, Issue 7. 1995. ring bd. write for info. (*0-88063-356-5*, 83362-11, MICHIE) LEXIS Pub.

Donovan, Joseph P. Pelagius & the Fifth Crusade. LC 76-29822. reprint ed. 36.50 (*0-404-15416-6*) AMS Pr.

Donovan, Joseph X. The Massachusetts Sales & Use Tax Manual. 600p. 1994. ring bd., wbk. ed. 175.00 (*0-614-05897-X*, MICHIE) LEXIS Pub.
— The Massachusetts Sales & Use Tax Manual, 2 vols. rev. ed. 586p. 1994. ring bd., suppl. ed. 49.00 (*0-685-73824-8*, MICHIE) LEXIS Pub.

Donovan, Josephine. After the Fall: The Demeter-Persephone Myth in Wharton, Cather, & Glasgow. LC 88-19490. 207p. 1989. lib. bdg. 30.00 (*0-271-00649-8*) Pa St U Pr.

***Donovan, Josephine.** Beyond Animal Rights: A Feminist Caring Ethic for the Treatment of Animals. 2000. pap. text 18.95 (*0-8264-1259-9*) Continuum.
— Feminist Theory: The Intellectual Traditions. 3rd ed. LC 00-27957. (Illus.). 2000. write for info. (*0-8264-1248-3*) Continuum.

Donovan, Josephine. Feminist Theory: The Intellectual Traditions of American Feminism. 2nd ed. LC 91-38756. 288p. (C). 1992. pap. 16.95 (*0-8264-0617-3*) Continuum.
— New England Local Color Literature: A Women's Tradition. LC 72-81713. 168p. 1988. 9.95 (*0-8264-0415-4*) Continuum.
— Uncle Tom's Cabin: Evil, Affliction, & Redemptive Love. Lecker, Robert, ed. (Twayne's Masterworks Ser.). 144p. 1991. 25.95 (*0-8057-8095-5*, MWS 63) Macmillan.

Donovan, Josephine. Women & the Rise of the Novel 1405-1726. pap. 18.95 (*0-312-23097-4*) St Martin.

Donovan, Josephine, ed. Feminist Literary Criticism: Explorations in Theory. 2nd ed. LC 88-356030. 202p. 1989. pap. 12.50 (*0-8131-0190-5*) U Pr of Ky.

Donovan, Josephine & Adams, Carol J., eds. Beyond Animal Rights: A Feminist Caring Ethic for the Treatment of Animals. LC 95-17448. 216p. 1996. 24.95 (*0-8264-0836-2*) Continuum.

Donovan, Josephine, jt. ed. see Adams, Carol J.

Donovan, Josephine, ed. see Donovan, William N.

Donovan, Karen. Fugitive Red. LC 98-32203. (Juniper Prize for Poetry Ser.). 80p. 1999. pap. 11.95 (*1-55849-199-6*) U of Mass Pr.

Donovan, Kate. A Dream Apart. 416p. 1995. mass mkt. 4.99 (*0-8217-0123-1*, Zebra Kensgtn); mass mkt. 4.99 (*0-7860-0123-2*, Pinncle Kensgtn) Kensgtn Pub Corp.
— A Dream Embraced. 384p. 1996. mass mkt. 4.99 (*0-7860-0232-8*, Pinncle Kensgtn) Kensgtn Pub Corp.

***Donovan, Kate.** Happily Ever after Co. Game of Hearts. (Ballad Romances Ser.). 2000. mass mkt. 5.50 (*0-8217-6683-X*, Zebra Kensgtn) Kensgtn Pub Corp.
— Stolen Kisses. (Bouquet Ser.: Vol. 56). 2000. mass mkt. 3.99 (*0-8217-6652-X*, Zebra Kensgtn) Kensgtn Pub Corp.

***Donovan, Kathleen E.** Conscious Coaching: The Soccer Mom's Bible. 176p. 1999. pap. write for info. (*0-9679273-0-7*) Conscious Coaching.
— Conscious Coaching: The Soccer Mom's Bible. LC 99-70858. 170p. 1999. pap. 10.95 (*0-9669707-0-5*) Writ in Stone.

Donovan, Kathleen M. Feminist Readings of Native American Literature: Coming to Voice. LC 97-21197. 192p. 1998. pap. 15.95 (*0-8165-1633-2*) U of Ariz Pr.

Donovan, Katie. Entering the Mare. 80p. 1998. pap. 15.95 (*1-85224-429-1*, Pub. by Bloodaxe Bks) Dufour.
— Irish Women Writers: Marginalized by Whom? 40p. (Orig.). 1988. pap. 7.95 (*1-85186-046-0*) Dufour.

Donovan, Katie, et al, selected by. Ireland's Women: Writings Past & Present. 522p. 1996. pap. 15.95 (*0-393-31360-3*, Norton Paperbks) Norton.

Donovan, Katie & Kennelly, Brendan, eds. Dublines. LC 94-143646. 320p. 1996. 55.00 (*1-85224-256-6*, Pub. by Bloodaxe Bks); pap. 23.00 (*1-85224-257-4*, Pub. by Bloodaxe Bks) Dufour.

Donovan, Katie, et al. Watermelon Man. 64p. 1994. pap. 12.95 (*1-85224-215-9*, Pub. by Bloodaxe Bks) Dufour.

Donovan, Kent R., et al. Emergency Radiology (Second Series) Test & Syllabus. LC 97-33316. (Professional Self-Evaluation Program Ser.). 1997. write for info. (*1-55903-041-0*) Am Coll Radiology.

Donovan, Kevin. Billy & His Friends Tame the Wild Wolf. 28p. (YA). (gr. 3 up). 1996. 15.95 (*1-889279-03-X*) Best Small Pr.
— Billy & His Friends Witness a Miracle. 1997. 15.95 (*1-889279-08-0*) Best Small Pr.

Donovan, Kevin, ed. Capirotada: Eight El Paso Artists. (Illus.). 80p. 1992. 20.00 (*0-9630816-0-8*) El Paso Mus.

Donovan, Kevin M. Billy & His Friends Discover Their Mission. (Illus.). 30p. (J). (gr. 3 up). 1994. 15.95 (*0-9641338-0-6*) K M Donovan.

***Donovan, Leslie A., tr. from ANG.** Women Saints' Lives in Old English Prose. LC 99-40572. (Library of Medieval Women). 128p. 1999. 19.95 (*0-85991-568-9*, DS Brewer) Boydell & Brewer.

Donovan, Liz. Painting Sunlit Still Lifes in Watercolor. LC 96-49205. (Illus.). 144p. 1997. 28.99 (*0-89134-732-1*, North Lght Bks) F & W Pubns Inc.

Donovan, M. Suzanne, ed. see National Research Council Staff.

Donovan, Marilee I., jt. auth. see Watt-Watson, Judith H.

Donovan, Mark. A Colt for a Railroad. large type ed. (Dales Western Ser.). 195p. 1992. pap. 18.99 (*1-85389-315-3*) Ulverscroft.
— Gunshots in Hambone. large type ed. 267p. 1995. pap. 18.99 (*1-85389-567-9*, Dales) Ulverscroft.
— Gunsmoke in Crosbie. large type ed. 1995. pap. 18.99 (*1-85389-568-7*, Dales) Ulverscroft.
— Rattlesnake Railroad. large type ed. (Linford Western Library). 256p. 1993. pap. 16.99 (*0-7089-7307-8*) Ulverscroft.
— Rawhide Storm. large type ed. (Linford Western Library). 304p. 1995. pap. 16.99 (*0-7089-7762-6*, Linford) Ulverscroft.
— Third Man's Range. large type ed. (Linford Western Library). 240p. 1993. pap. 16.99 (*0-7089-7446-5*) Ulverscroft.
— Underwater Range. large type ed. 182p. 1994. pap. 18.99 (*1-85389-439-7*) Ulverscroft.

Donovan, Mark, ed. Italy, Vols. I & II. LC 97-25137. (International Library of Politics & Comparative Government). 970p. 1997. text 309.95 (*1-85521-637-X*, JN5451.I848, Pub. by Dartmth Pub) Ashgate Pub Co.

Donovan, Mark, jt. ed. see Broughton, David.

Donovan, Marlene, ed. see Chatelain, Maurice.

Donovan, Mary. Opportunities in Culinary Careers. LC 97-18166. (Opportunities in... Ser.). 160p. 1998. 14.95 (*0-8442-2333-6*, 23336) NTC Contemp Pub Co.

Donovan, Mary A. One Right Reading: A Guide to Irenaeus. LC 97-37792. 208p. (Orig.). 1997. pap. 18.95 (*0-8146-5875-X*) Liturgical Pr.

Donovan, Mary D. Careers for Gourmets: And Others Who Relish Food. LC 92-18846. (Careers for You Ser.). (Illus.). 160p. 1994. 14.95 (*0-8442-8138-7*, 81387, VGM Career) NTC Contemp Pub Co.

Donovan, Mary D. Careers for Gourmets: And Others Who Relish Food. LC 92-18846. (Careers for You Ser.). (Illus.). 160p. 1994. 9.95 (*0-8442-8139-5*, 81395, VGM Career) NTC Contemp Pub Co.

Donovan, Mary D. Culinary Careers. (Opportunities In . . . Ser.). 160p. pap. 12.95 (*0-8442-8620-6*, 297OICUL, VGM Career) NTC Contemp Pub Co.
— Culinary Careers. (Opportunities in...Ser.). 160p. 1991. 14.95 (*0-8442-8619-2*, VGM Career) NTC Contemp Pub Co.
— Eat Better, Feel Better: A Visual Directory of Foods & the Nutrients They Contain, Plus a Unique Section on Combating Common Ailments. LC 97-32143. 1998. 29.95 (*1-882606-68-X*); pap. 18.95 (*1-882606-28-0*) Peoples Med Soc.
— Opportunities in Culinary Careers. LC 97-18166. (Opportunities in...Ser.). (Illus.). 160p. 1997. pap. 11.95 (*0-8442-2334-4*, 23344, VGM Career) NTC Contemp Pub Co.

Donovan, Mary D., jt. auth. see Culinary Institute of America Staff.

Donovan, Mary D., ed. see Culinary Institute of America Staff.

Donovan, Mary D., ed. see Food & Beverage Institute Staff.

Donovan, Mary E., jt. auth. see Sanford, Linda T.

Donovan, Mary L. Snuffles Makes a Friend. LC 95-10693. (Gund Children's Library). (Illus.). 32p. (J). (ps-1). 1997. reprint ed. pap. 3.99 (*0-7636-0096-2*) Candlewick Pr.
— Won't You Come & Play with Me? LC 97-2529. (Illus.). 32p. (J). (ps-1). 1998. 16.00 (*0-395-84630-7*) HM.

Donovan, Mary S. A Different Call: Women's Ministries in the Episcopal Church. LC 86-18032. 236p. (Orig.). 1986. 19.95 (*0-8192-1396-9*) Morehouse Pub.

Donovan, Melissa. Research Challanges. (Illus.). 168p. (J). (gr. 4-8). 1985. student ed. 13.99 (*0-86653-271-4*, GA 660) Good Apple.
— Teaching Creative Writing. 144p. (J). (gr. 3-8). 1990. 13.99 (*0-86653-559-4*, GA1156) Good Apple.

Donovan, Michael L. The Name Game: Football, Baseball, Hockey & Basketball How Your Favorite Sports Teams Were Named. (Illus.). 256p. (Orig.). 1997. pap. 12.95 (*1-895629-74-8*) Warwick Publ.

Donovan, Michelle R. & Matson, Theodore A., eds. Outpatient Case Management: Strategies for a New Reality. LC 94-9597. 298p. 1994. pap. write for info. (*1-55648-119-5*, 027100) AHPI.

Donovan, Mike. The Science of Boxing. (Illus.). 126p. 1996. pap. 12.95 (*0-9652952-5-7*) Doyle Studio.

D

An Asterisk (*) at the beginning of an entry indicates that the title is appearing for the first time.

D

An Asterisk (*) at the beginning of an entry indicates that the title is appearing for the first time.

Doody, Michael F. The Trustee's Guide to Compensation for Healthcare Executives. LC 93-257. (Hospital Trustee Guide Ser.). 96p. 1993. per. 24.95 (*1-882198-16-6*) Hlthcare Fin Mgmt.

***Doody, Rachelle S., ed.** Impact of New Therapies on Alzheimer's Disease Management. (Illus.). 38p. 1999. 21.75 (*3-8055-6817-7*) S Karger.

Doody, Terrence. Among Other Things: A Description of the Novel. LC 98-23621. 304p. 1998. text 40.00 (*0-8071-2248-3*) La State U Pr.

Doogan, Kathy & Crandall, Cass. Alaska Wilderness Lodges. (Illus.). 190p. 1991. pap. 14.95 (*0-9626071-2-6*) Kachemak Pub.

Doogan, Mike. Fashion Means Your Fur Hat Is Dead: A Guide to Good Manners & Social Survival in Alaska. LC 96-86224. (Illus.). 160p. (Orig.). 1996. pap. 14.95 (*0-945397-54-2*) Epicenter Pr.

Doogan, Mike, ed. How to Speak Alaskan. LC 93-70541. (Illus.). 64p. (Orig.). 1993. pap. 4.95 (*0-945397-24-0*) Epicenter Pr.

Doogan, Mike, jt. auth. see Alaska Geographic Society Staff.

Dooge, J. C., et al, eds. An Agenda of Science for Environment & Development into the 21st Century. (Illus.). 339p. (C). 1992. text 130.00 (*0-521-43174-3*); pap. text 44.95 (*0-521-43761-X*) Cambridge U Pr.

Dooghe, G., ed. Sheltered Accommodations for Elderly People in an International Perspective. (NIDI-CBGS Publications, Population & Family Study Center Ser.: Vol. 29). xii, 152p. 1993. pap. 46.00 (*90-265-1352-6*) Swets.

Dooghe, Gilbert & Helander, Jan, eds. Family Life in Old Age. (Netherlands Demographic Institute & the Population & Family Study Center Ser.: No. 8). 1979. pap. text 78.50 (*90-247-2207-1*) Kluwer Academic.

Doogue, John. The Writer & the Law. 329p. (C). 1981. 60.00 (*0-86828-283-9*, Pub. by Deakin Univ) St Mut.

Doohan, Helen. The Corinthian Correspondence: Ministering in the Best & Worst of Times. (Scripture for Worshipped Education Ser.). 48p. (Orig.). 1996. pap., teacher ed. 7.95 (*0-89390-362-0*); pap. text 17.95 (*0-89390-361-2*) Resource Pubns.

Doohan, James & David, Peter. Beam Me up, Scotty. LC 96-38340. (Illus.). 224p. 1996. pap. 12.00 (*0-671-52056-3*) S&S Trade.

***Doohan, James & Stirling, S. M.** Privateer. 320p. 2000. mass mkt. 6.99 (*0-671-31949-3*) Baen Bks.

Doohan, James & Stirling, S. M. The Privateer: Volume 2 of the Flight Engineer. LC 99-38132. 264p. 1999. pap. 21.00 (*0-671-57832-4*) Baen Bks.

— The Rising: Flight Engineer, Bk. I. 384p. 1996. 21.00 (*0-671-87758-5*) Baen Bks.

— The Rising Flight Engineer. (Flight Engineer Ser.: Bk. 1). 384p. 1997. per. 6.99 (*0-671-87849-2*) Baen Bks.

Doohan, Jimmy. Beam Me up, Scotty. 1996. pap. 12.00 (*0-614-12562-6*, PB Trade Paper) PB.

Doohan, Julie, ed. see Jacobs, George & Kerrins, Joseph.

Doohan, Julie, ed. see Kerrins, Joseph & Jacobs, George W.

Doohan, Leonard. Acts of Apostles: Building Faith Communities. LC 93-47959. (Scripture for Worship & Education Ser.). 240p. 1994. pap. 14.95 (*0-89390-292-6*) Resource Pubns.

— Acts of Apostles: Leader's Guide. (Scripture for Worship & Education Ser.). 48p. 1994. pap., teacher ed. 7.95 (*0-89390-300-0*) Resource Pubns.

— The Contemporary Challenge of John of the Cross: An Introduction to His Life & Teaching. LC 94-41294. 152p. 1995. pap. 8.95 (*0-935216-55-3*) ICS Pubns.

— John: Gospel for a New Age. LC 88-17703. (Scripture for Worship Ser.). 240p. (Orig.). (C). 1993. pap. text 10.95 (*0-89390-263-2*) Resource Pubns.

— Luke: The Perennial Spirituality. LC 85-71858. (Scripture for Worship Ser.). 228p. (Orig.). (C). 1993. pap. text 10.95 (*0-89390-262-4*) Resource Pubns.

— Mark: Visionary of Early Christianity. LC 86-72485. (Scripture for Worship Ser.). 192p. (Orig.). (C). 1993. pap. text 10.95 (*0-89390-261-6*) Resource Pubns.

— Matthew: Spirituality for the 80s & 90s. LC 85-70838. (Scripture for Worship Ser.). 214p. (C). 1993. pap. text 10.95 (*0-89390-260-8*) Resource Pubns.

— Revelation: Leader's Guide. (Scripture for Worship & Education Ser.). 48p. (Orig.). 1994. pap., teacher ed. 7.95 (*0-89390-308-6*) Resource Pubns.

Doohovskoy, A. P., tr. see Landkof, N. S.

Doohovskoy, A. P., tr. see Mal'cev, A. I.

Dook. Euros 06: Desert Parol. 1997. 17.95 (*3-86187-075-4*) B Gmunder.

Dookeran, Winston C., ed. Choices & Change: Reflections on the Caribbean. (Inter-American Development Bk.). 232p. 1996. pap. 18.50 (*1-886938-07-5*) IADB.

Doolan, Chris. Applying Numbers & IT in Health & Social Care. 160p. 1999. pap. 21.95 (*0-304-33365-4*) Continuum.

— Applying Numbers & IT in Leisure & Tourism. 160p. 1999. pap. 21.95 (*0-304-33459-6*) Continuum.

***Doolan, Denise L., ed.** Malaria Methods & Protocols. 375p. 2000. 99.50 (*0-89603-823-8*) Humana.

***Doolan, Kevin M.** Two Guys Gourmet. (Illus.). 2000. pap. 16.95 (*0-936085-65-7*) Blue Heron OR.

Doolan, T. A. The Complete Fishing Guide to Deep Creek Lake: Maryland's Best Kept Secret. (Illus.). 96p. (Orig.). 1992. pap. 8.95 (*0-929915-07-0*) Headline Bks.

Doole. International Market Strategy. 2nd ed. (ITBP Textbooks Ser.). 576p. 1999. pap. 22.99 (*1-86152-472-2*) Thomson Learn.

Doole, Isobel, et al. International Marketing Strategy: Analysis, Development & Implementation. LC 94-20949. 450p. (C). 1994. pap. 32.95 (*0-415-08985-9*, B4174) Thomson Learn.

Doole, Isobel, et al. International Marketing Strategy: Contemporary Readings. 256p. 1996. pap. 59.00 (*0-415-14453-1*) Thomson Learn.

— International Marketing Strategy: Contemporary Readings. 256p. 1997. pap. 17.99 (*1-86152-233-9*) Thomson Learn.

Doole, Isobel, jt. auth. see Gorton, Keith.

***Doole, Kerry & Twomey, Chris.** Crowded House: Private Universe. (Illus.). 128p. 1999. pap. 17.95 (*0-7119-6653-2*) Omnibus Pr.

Doole, Louise E. Herbs for Health: How to Grow & Use Them. 1979. pap. 7.00 (*0-87980-052-6*) Wilshire.

Doolen, Gary D. Lattice Gas Methods: Theory, Applications & Hardware. LC 91-10010. (Physica D Ser.). (Illus.). 348p. 1991. pap. text 39.00 (*0-262-54063-0*) MIT Pr.

Doolen, Gary D., et al. Lattice Gas Methods of Partial Differential Equations. (Santa Fe Institute Ser.). (Illus.). 576p. (C). 1990. 54.95 (*0-201-15679-2*); pap. 34.95 (*0-201-13232-X*) Addison-Wesley.

***Dooley.** Social Research Methods. 4th ed. LC 99-57769. 400p. 2000. pap. text 56.00 (*0-13-955428-9*) P-H.

Dooley, jt. auth. see Zhang, Yanzhong.

Dooley, Allan C. Author & Printer in Victorian England. LC 92-10420. (Victorian Literature & Culture Ser.). 206p. reprint ed. pap. 63.90 (*0-608-08554-5*, 206907700002) Bks Demand.

Dooley, Ann, jt. tr. see Roe, Harry.

Dooley, Anne M. Plane Death. 250p. write for info. (*1-896300-14-6*) NeWest Pubs.

Dooley, Arch R., et al. Basic Problems, Concepts, & Techniques. rev. ed. LC 67-30438. 780p. 1968. reprint ed. pap. 200.00 (*0-7837-3438-7*, 205776000008) Bks Demand.

***Dooley-Awbrey, Betty, et al.** Why Stop? 4th ed. LC 99-29048. 1999. pap. 16.95 (*0-88415-229-4*, 5229) Gulf Pub.

Dooley, Beth. Good Country Cooking. 36p. (Orig.). 1989. pap. 3.25 (*0-940844-36-2*) Wellspring.

— Great Freshwater Fish Recipes. 36p. (Orig.). 1989. pap. 3.25 (*0-940844-35-4*) Wellspring.

— Peppers, Hot & Sweet: Over 100 Recipes for All Tastes. Oxley, Constance, ed. LC 90-55044. (Illus.). 144p. (Orig.). 1990. 16.95 (*0-88266-622-3*, Garden Way Pub) Storey Bks.

Dooley, Beth & Watson, Lucia. Savoring the Seasons of the Northern Heartland. LC 94-9629. (Cooks American Ser.: Vol. 14). 384p. 1994. 29.95 (*0-679-41175-5*) Knopf.

Dooley, Beth, jt. auth. see Anton, Liz.

Dooley, Brendan, jt. auth. see Plewman, Nicholas.

Dooley, Brendan M. A Social History of Skepticism: Experience & Doubt in Early Modern Culture. LC 99-11406. (Studies in Historical & Political Science). 213p. 1999. 39.95 (*0-8018-6142-X*) Johns Hopkins.

Dooley, Brian. Black & Green: Civil Rights Struggles in Northern Ireland & Black America. LC 97-32971. 192p. 1998. 55.00 (*0-7453-1211-X*, Pub. by Pluto GBR); pap. text 18.95 (*0-7453-1295-0*, Pub. by Pluto GBR) Stylus Pub VA.

— Learn Windows in a Day. (Popular Applications Ser.). (Illus.). 128p. (Orig.). 1992. pap. 12.95 (*1-55622-263-7*) Wordware Pub.

— Robert Kennedy: The Final Years. 196p. 1996. text 39.95 (*0-312-16130-1*) St Martin.

Dooley, Brian A., jt. auth. see Christy, Joe.

Dooley, Brian J. Warriors for the Working Day. (Illus.). 109p. (Orig.). 1991. pap. 12.50 (*1-55613-468-1*) Heritage Bk.

Dooley, Brian J., jt. auth. see Christy, Joe.

***Dooley, Cheryl.** Telephone Technique. 180p. 2000. per. 11.00 (*0-684-87206-4*) S&S Trade.

— Telephone Technique: How to Communicate Effectively on The Telephone. 1998. pap. text 12.95 (*0-7318-0354-X*, Pub. by Simon & Schuster) Distican.

Dooley, David. Reflections. (Illus.). 104p. write for info. (*1-878044-15-X*) Mayhaven Pub.

— The Revenge by Love. 90p. (Orig.). 1995. pap. 11.95 (*1-885266-06-5*) Story Line.

— Social Research Methods. 3rd ed. LC 94-6044. 448p. 1994. 79.00 (*0-13-126161-4*) P-H.

— The Volcano Inside. LC 88-60849. (Roerich Poetry Prize Winner Ser.). 64p. (Orig.). 1988. pap. 8.00 (*0-934257-15-9*) Story Line.

Dooley, David J. The Art of Sinclair Lewis. LC 65-17173. 302p. reprint ed. pap. 93.70 (*0-7837-6024-8*, 204583600008) Bks Demand.

Dooley, Deborah A. Plain & Ordinary Things: Reading Women in the Writing Classroom. LC 94-21538. (SUNY Series, Feminist Theory in Education). 273p. (C). 1995. pap. text 14.95 (*0-7914-2320-4*) State U NY Pr.

— Plain & Ordinary Things: Reading Women in the Writing Classroom. LC 94-21538. (SUNY Series, Feminist Theory in Education). 273p. (C). 1995. text 44.50 (*0-7914-2319-0*) State U NY Pr.

Dooley, Dennis & Engle, Gary, eds. Superman at Fifty! The Persistence. LC 87-15221. (Illus.). 192p. 1987. 16.95 (*0-940601-00-1*) Octavia Ohio.

Dooley, Dennis A., ed. Index to State Bar Association Reports & Proceedings. LC 76-48816. xii, 640p. 1976. reprint ed. lib. bdg. 55.00 (*0-930342-30-5*, 300280) W S Hein.

Dooley, Dolores. Equality in Community: Sexual Equality in the Writings of William Thompson & Anna Doyle Wheeler. 484p. 1996. 54.95 (*1-85918-004-3*, Pub. by Cork Univ); pap. 24.00 (*1-85918-005-1*, Pub. by Cork Univ) Stylus Pub VA.

Dooley, Dolores, jt. auth. see Thompson, William.

Dooley, Don R. Survival in the New Millennium: Toward a Civilized World. LC 97-92431. 420p. 1998. pap. 9.95 (*0-9659938-0-9*) Cosmplitan Pub.

Dooley, Edwin L., jt. auth. see Hunter, Robert F.

Dooley, Frank J. & Thoms, William E. Railroad Law a Decade after Deregulation. LC 94-8539. 208p. 1994. 59.95 (*0-89930-631-4*, Quorum Bks) Greenwood.

Dooley, Frank J., jt. auth. see Thoms, William E.

***Dooley, George.** Battle for the Central Highlands: A Special Forces Story. (Illus.). 288p. 2000. mass mkt. 6.99 (*0-8041-1939-2*) Ballantine Pub Grp.

Dooley, Jackie M., ed. Encoded Archival Description: Context, Theory, & Case Studies. LC 98-46827. 178p. 1998. pap. 40.00 (*0-931828-43-0*) Soc Am Archivists.

Dooley, James, jt. auth. see Bushnell, Richard.

Dooley, James, jt. auth. see Sherlock, Sheila.

Dooley, James H. Dem Good Ole Times. LC 72-6486. (Black Heritage Library Collection). (Illus.). 1977. reprint ed. 19.95 (*0-8369-9166-4*) Ayer.

Dooley, James W. Inside Huntsville Prison. 160p. (Orig.). (C). 1981. pap. 5.95 (*0-9605576-0-1*) Grace Pub House.

Dooley, Jean, ed. see Habgood, Dawn & Habgood, Robert.

Dooley, Jean, ed. see Habgood, Robert P. & Habgood, Dawn W.

Dooley, John. Build on Ice. 7.95 (*1-892061-07-4*, Cooking Rock) Future Tense.

Dooley, John P., jt. auth. see Denton, Jeffrey H.

Dooley, K., ed. see Marz, Ron.

Dooley, Kate. To Listen & Tell: Commentary on the Introduction to the Lectionary for Masses with Children. 83p. 1993. pap. 9.95 (*1-56929-014-8*, Pastoral Press) OR Catholic.

Dooley, Ken, jt. auth. see Auerbach, Red.

Dooley, Kevin, ed. & intro. see Giffen, Keith & Jones, Gerard.

Dooley, Kirk. Everything You Ever Wanted to Know about Texas. 228p. (Orig.). 1986. pap. text 8.95 (*0-937619-00-0*) Half Court Pr.

Dooley, Kirk & Price, Ben. Read My Lips: Classic Texas Political Quotes. (Classic Texas Quotes: the Ser.). (Illus.). 256p. (Orig.). 1995. pap. 12.95 (*0-89672-350-X*) Tex Tech Univ Pr.

Dooley, L. M. Paradise, God's Guest of Tomorrow: A Mystical Visit to Purgatory & a Consideration of the Sabbatine Privilege. 1986. 4.95 (*1-56036-002-X*, 40580) AMI Pr.

Dooley, M. P., jt. auth. see Pineda, M. H.

Dooley, Mark, jt. ed. see Kearney, Richard.

Dooley, Maura. Explaining Magnetism. 77p. (Orig.). 1991. pap. 14.95 (*1-85224-137-3*, Pub. by Bloodaxe Bks) Dufour.

— The Honey Gatherers: A Book of Love Poems. 1996. 39.95 (*1-85224-358-9*, Pub. by Bloodaxe Bks); pap. 19.95 (*1-85224-359-7*, Pub. by Bloodaxe Bks) Dufour.

— Kissing a Bone. LC 97-120582. 62p. 1997. pap. 15.95 (*1-85224-373-2*, Pub. by Bloodaxe Bks) Dufour.

***Dooley, Maura, ed.** How Novelists Work. 180p. 1999. pap. (*1-85411-192-2*, Pub. by Seren Bks) Dufour.

Dooley, Maura, ed. Making for Planet Alice: New Women Poets. LC 97-171758. (Illus.). 176p. 1997. pap. 19.95 (*1-85224-398-8*, Pub. by Bloodaxe Bks) Dufour.

Dooley, Michael. Lost in Space. LC 98-96508. 64p. 1998. pap. 5.95 (*0-9642168-2-5*) Totally Unique.

Dooley, Michael E. Totally Unique Thoughts: Reminders of Life's Everyday Magic. unabridged ed. LC 98-96084. 128p. 1998. pap. 8.95 (*0-9642168-1-7*, 007) Totally Unique.

Dooley, Michael P. Fundamentals of Corporation Law. (University Casebook Ser.). 1078p. 1994. pap. text 45.95 (*1-56662-191-7*) Foundation Pr.

Dooley, Michael P., et al, eds. The Political Economy of Policy-Making: Essays in Honor of Will E. Mason. LC 78-25960. (Comparative Political Economy & Public Policy Ser.: Vol. 4). (Illus.). 248p. reprint ed. pap. 76.90 (*0-608-10733-6*, 202188900026) Bks Demand.

Dooley, Michael P., et al. Debt Reduction & Economic Activity. (Occasional Papers: No. 68). v, 30p. 1990. pap. 10.00 (*1-55775-135-8*) Intl Monetary.

Dooley, Norah. Everbody Bakes Bread. LC 95-6054. (Illus.). 32p. (J). (-3). 1996. pap. 6.95 (*0-87614-895-X*, First Ave Edns) Lerner Pub.

— Everbody Bakes Bread. LC 95-6054. (Illus.). 32p. (J). (gr. 3). 1996. lib. bdg. 19.93 (*0-87614-864-X*, Carolrhoda) Lerner Pub.

— Everybody Cooks Rice. (Illus.). (J). (gr. 3). 1995. 8.60 (*0-395-73233-6*) HM.

— Everybody Cooks Rice. (Illus.). 32p. (J). (ps-3). 1991. lib. bdg. 19.93 (*0-87614-412-1*, Carolrhoda) Lerner Pub.

— Everybody Cooks Rice. (Illus.). 32p. (J). (ps-3). 1992. pap. 6.95 (*0-87614-591-8*, First Ave Edns) Lerner Pub.

— Everybody Cooks Rice. large type ed. (Illus.). 46p. (J). (gr. 3). 11.50 (*0-614-20588-3*, L-38176-00 APHB) Am Printing Hse.

***Dooley, Norah.** Everybody Serves Soup. LC 00-8091. (Picture Bks.). (Illus.). 48p. (J). (ps-3). 2000. 15.95 (*1-57505-422-1*, Carolrhoda) Lerner Pub.

Dooley, Patricia, ed. The First Steps: Best of the Early ChLA Quarterly. 148p. 1985. 5.25 (*0-937263-05-2*) CHLA Pubns.

Dooley, Patricia L. Taking Their Political Place: Journalist & the Making of an Occupation, 52. LC 97-16713. (Contributions to the Study of Mass Media & Communications: Vol. 52). 184p. 1997. 55.00 (*0-313-30062-3*, Greenwood Pr) Greenwood.

***Dooley, Patricia L.** Taking Their Political Place: Journalists & the Making of An Occupation. 2000. pap. write for info. (*0-275-97103-1*, Praeger Trade) Greenwood.

Dooley, Patrick, ed. Stephen Crane: An Annotated Bibliography of Secondary Scholarship. (Reference Ser.). 300p. 1992. 60.00 (*0-8161-7265-X*, Hall Reference) Macmillan.

Dooley, Patrick K. The Pluralistic Philosophy of Stephen Crane. (Illus.). 224p. (C). 1993. pap. text 17.95 (*0-252-06390-2*) U of Ill Pr.

Dooley, R. B. The Interaction of Non Iron-Based Materials with Water & Steam. 522p. 1997. pap. text 200.00 (*0-8033-5061-9*) Elec Power Res Inst.

— Turbine Steam Path Damage Vol. 1: Theory & Practice Fundamentals. Date not set. pap. text 1000.00 (*0-8033-5062-7*) Elec Power Res Inst.

— Turbine Steam Path Damage Vol. 2: Theory & Practice: Damage Mechanisms. Date not set. pap. text 1000.00 (*0-8033-5063-5*) Elec Power Res Inst.

Dooley, R. B. & Naughton, W. P. Boiler Tube Failures Vol. 1: Theory & Practice: Fundamentals. 1996. text 2000.00 (*0-8033-5058-9*) Elec Power Res Inst.

— Boiler Tube Failures Vol. 2: Theory & Practice: Water-Touched Tubes. 1996. text 2000.00 (*0-8033-5059-7*) Elec Power Res Inst.

— Boiler Tube Failures Vol. 3: Theory & Practice: Steam-Touched Tubes. 1996. text 2000.00 (*0-8033-5060-0*) Elec Power Res Inst.

Dooley, Sharon. Professional SQL Server 6.5 Admin. LC 96-60557. 800p. 1996. pap. 44.95 (*1-874416-49-4*) Wrox Pr Inc.

***Dooley, Sharon.** SQL Server 7.X Essential Reference. (Illus.). 2000. pap. 35.00 (*0-7357-0864-9*) New Riders Pub.

***Dooley, Susan & Garden Design Editors.** The World of Garden Design: Inspiring Ideas from Around the Globe to Your Backyard. (Illus.). 320p. 2000. 40.00 (*0-8118-2656-2*) Chronicle Bks.

***Dooley, Terry.** Sources for the History of Landed Estates in Ireland. (Maynooth Guides for Local History Research Ser.). (Illus.). 84p. 2000. pap. 14.50 (*0-7165-2697-2*, Pub. by Irish Acad Pr) Intl Spec Bk.

Dooley, Thomas W. & Dahlheimer, Charles M. Real Estate in the '90s: A Whole New World Ahead. 304p. 1989. pap. text 19.95 (*0-9623018-0-9*) NAC Group Inc.

Dooley, Tim. The Interrupted Dream. 96p. 1985. pap. 14.95 (*0-85646-143-1*, Pub. by Anvil Press) Dufour.

Dooley, Timothy R. Homeopathy: Beyond Flat Earth Medicine: An Essential Guide for the Homeopathic Patient. LC 95-60000. 128p. (Orig.). 1995. pap. 9.00 (*1-886893-00-4*) Timing CA.

Dooley, Tom. The Night They Burned the Mountain. 1993. reprint ed. lib. bdg. 21.95 (*1-56849-119-0*) Buccaneer Bks.

Dooley, Vince & Smith, Loran. Dooley's Dawgs. LC 89-84530. (Illus.). 192p. 1989. 24.95 (*0-929264-60-6*) Longstreet.

Dooley, Virginia. R. C. Gorman: Chinle to Taos. (Illus.). 63p. (Orig.). 1988. pap. 10.00 (*0-9622721-0-8*) Navajo Gallery.

— R. C. Gorman Vol. 2: Nudes & Foods. (Illus.). 96p. (Orig.). 1989. pap. 20.00 (*0-9622721-1-6*) Navajo Gallery.

— R. C. Gorman's Nudes & Foods, Vol. II. (Illus.). (Orig.). 1989. write for info. (*0-318-65110-6*) Navajo Gallery.

— Tubes in My Ears: My Trip to the Hospital. LC 95-39915. (Illus.). 24p. (J). (ps-2). 1996. pap. 4.95 (*1-57255-118-6*) Mondo Pubng.

— Turn to Learn. 64p. (J). 1997. pap. 9.95 (*0-590-70134-7*) Scholastic Inc.

***Dooley, Virginia.** Turn-to-Learn: Alphabet Wheels. (Illus.). 64p. 1998. pap. 9.95 (*0-590-37904-6*) Scholastic.

Dooley, Virginia, ed. R. C. Gorman's Nudes & Foods: In Good Taste. LC 94-28417. (Illus.). 142p. 1994. 34.95 (*0-940666-41-3*) Clear Light.

Dooley, W. E., tr. see Alexander of Aphrodisias.

Dooley, William E., tr. see Alexander of Aphrodisias.

Doolin, Brian F. & Martin, Clyde F. Introduction to Differential Geometry for Engineers. LC 90-41747. (Monographs & Textbooks in Pure & Applied Mathematics: Vol. 136). (Illus.). 183p. reprint ed. pap. 56.80 (*0-608-08929-X*, 206956400005) Bks Demand.

Doolin, Dennis J. & North, Robert C. The Chinese People's Republic. LC 65-19769. (Classic Ser.: No. 14). 68p. 1966. pap. 1.80 (*0-8179-3142-2*) Hoover Inst Pr.

Doolin, James H. Auto Air Conditioning. 48p. 1982. pap. 15.00 (*0-914626-03-5*) Doolco Inc.

— La Biblia Doolin para el Tecnico Reparador. Salverredy, Luis E., tr. from ENG. (Illus.). 156p. 1973. reprint ed. pap. text 35.00 (*0-914626-01-9*) Doolco Inc.

— Commercial Refrigeration. 72p. 1982. pap. 15.00 (*0-914626-08-6*) Doolco Inc.

— Frost Free & Conventional Refrigerators. 70p. 1982. pap. 15.00 (*0-914626-09-4*) Doolco Inc.

— Residential Cooling, Pt. 1. 50p. 1982. pap. 15.00 (*0-914626-04-3*) Doolco Inc.

— Residential Cooling, Pt. 2. 91p. 1982. pap. 15.00 (*0-914626-05-1*) Doolco Inc.

— Residential Gas Heating. 75p. 1982. pap. 15.00 (*0-914626-06-X*) Doolco Inc.

— Window Units. 39p. 1982. pap. 15.00 (*0-914626-07-8*) Doolco Inc.

Doolin, James H. & Dixon, Bob. Doolin's Trouble Shooters Bible. 3rd ed. 302p. 1996. 60.00 (*0-914626-11-6*) Doolco Inc.

Doolin, James P. Eighteen Ninety-Three Columbian Exposition, Admission & Concession Tickets. 22p. 1981. pap. 10.00 (*0-914626-02-7*) Doolco Inc.

Doolin, Leon. Heaven Forbid: Bible Skits with the Human Touch. large type ed. (Illus.). 137p. (Orig.). 1996. pap. text 7.50 (*0-9650207-4-6*) Victory Minist.

Doolin, Sean. Golfer's Little Book of Wisdom. LC 96-29840. (Little Books of Wisdom Ser.). 160p. (Orig.). 1997. pap. 6.95 (*1-57034-063-3*) Globe Pequot.

Dooling, Amy D. & Torgeson, Kristina M. Writing Women in Modern China: An Anthology of Literature by Chinese Women from the Early Twentieth Century. LC 97-19306. (Illus.). 320p. 1998. pap. 19.50 (*0-231-10701-3*); lib. bdg. 52.00 (*0-231-10700-5*) Col U Pr.

An Asterisk (*) at the beginning of an entry indicates that the title is appearing for the first time.

Dooling, D. M. Spirit of Quest: Essays & Poems. (Illus.). 96p. 1994. 12.00 (*0-930407-30-X*) Parabola Bks.

Dooling, D. M., ed. Sons of the Wind: The Sacred Stories of the Lakota. 136p. (Orig.). 1984. pap. 8.95 (*0-930407-00-8*) Parabola Bks.

Dooling, D. M. & Jordan-Smith, Paul, eds. I Become Part of It: Sacred Dimensions in Native American Life. (Illus.). 292p. (Orig.). 1989. pap. 14.95 (*0-930407-07-5*) Parabola Bks.

Dooling, D. M. & Travers, Pamela L., eds. Way of working: The Spiritual Dimension of Craft. 5th ed. 128p. 1986. reprint ed. pap. 8.95 (*0-930407-01-6*) Parabola Bks.

***Dooling, D. M. & Walker, J. R.** The Sons of the Wind: The Sacred Stories of the Lakota. LC 99-54969. 160p. (Orig.). 2000. pap. 11.95 (*0-8061-3224-8*) U of Okla Pr.

Dooling, D. M., tr. see Charbonneau-Lassay, Louis.

Dooling, Michael, jt. auth. see Kimmel, Eric A.

***Dooling-Plecki, Eileen M. & Ruddy, Christine A.** A Love-Centered Life: Eileen M. Dooling-Plecki & Christine A. Ruddy. (Illus.). 240p. 2000. 22.95 (*1-58151-071-3*, Pub. by BookPartners) Midpt Trade.

Dooling, R. J. & Hulse, S. H., eds. The Comparative Psychology of Audition: Perceiving Complex Sounds. 496p. 1989. 99.95 (*0-8058-0020-4*); pap. 55.00 (*0-8058-0384-X*) L Erlbaum Assocs.

Dooling, Richard. Brain Storm: A Novel. LC 97-23376. 416p. 1998. 25.00 (*0-679-45239-7*) Random.

— Brain Storm: A Novel. LC 99-22390. 401p. 1999. text 14.00 (*0-312-20399-3*, Picador USA) St Martin.

— Critical Care. 288p. 1993. mass mkt. 4.99 (*0-380-71759-X*, Avon Bks) Morrow Avon.

— Critical Care. 1996. pap. 12.00 (*0-614-97769-X*, Picador USA) St Martin.

— White Man's Grave: A Novel. LC 93-37427. 356p. 1994. 22.00 (*0-374-28951-4*) FS&G.

— White Man's Grave: A Novel. 3rd ed. LC 95-4279. 400p. 1995. pap. 14.00 (*0-312-13214-X*) St Martin.

***Dooling, Robert J., et al, contrib. by.** Comparative Hearing: Birds & Reptiles. LC 99-52789. (Handbook in Auditory Research Ser.). 400p. 2000. 98.00 (*0-387-94684-5*) Spr-Verlag.

Doolittle. The Competent Public Communicator. (C). 1996. pap. text. write for info. (*0-15-501539-7*) Harcourt Coll Pubs.

— Energy Conversion Systems. (C). 2001. text, teacher ed. write for info. (*0-06-361690-4*) Addson-Wesley Educ.

Doolittle, Bev. The Art of Bev Doolittle. 160p. 1990. 65.00 (*0-553-07009-6*) Bantam.

***Doolittle, Bev & Maclay, Elise.** The Earth Is My Mother. (Illus.). 176p. (J). (gr. 4-6). 2000. 17.95 (*0-86713-044-X*, 85163, Pub. by Greenwich Wrkshop) Workman Pub.

Doolittle, Bev & Maclay, Elise. New Magic: Bev Doolittle. LC 95-15087. 86p. 1995. 30.00 (*0-553-10104-8*) Bantam.

Doolittle, Bill. The Kentucky Derby: Run for the Roses. (Illus.). 180p. (YA). (gr. 11). 1999. pap. 24.95 (*0-7370-0048-1*) T-L Custom Pub.

— The Kentucky Derby: Run for the Roses. (Illus.). 180p. (YA). (gr. 11). 1999. 39.95 (*0-7370-0032-5*) T-L Custom Pub.

— The Kentucky Derby: Run for the Roses. LC 98-31311. (Illus.). 180p. 1998. lthr. 195.00 (*1-887656-15-4*) Tehabi Bks.

***Doolittle, Bill.** The Kentucky Derby: Run for the Roses. deluxe ed. (Illus.). 180p. 1998. 50.00 (*1-887656-22-7*) Tehabi Bks.

Doolittle, Duncan H. A Soldier's Hero: General Sir Archibald Hunter. (Illus.). 1991. text. write for info. (*0-9630635-0-2*) Anawan Pub.

Doolittle, Hiland B. The Last Parade. rev. ed. LC 98-91277. 320p. 1998. 25.00 (*0-9662742-0-2*) Rome Pub.

Doolittle, Hilda, see H. D., pseud.

Doolittle, Ian. Butterworths Environmental Regulation: A Guide to the Powers of the Environment Agency & Local Authorities. ring bd. write for info. (*0-406-99883-3*, BERGASET, MICHIE) LEXIS Pub.

Doolittle, James H. & Glines, Carroll V. I Could Never Be So Lucky Again: An Autobiography of James H. "Jimmy" Doolittle. LC 91-3353. (Illus.). 574p. 1995. 29.95 (*0-88740-737-4*) Schiffer.

Doolittle, Jerome. Bear Hug. Grose, Bill, ed. 240p. 1993. mass mkt. 4.99 (*0-671-74569-7*) PB.

— Body Scissors. Grose, Bill, ed. 240p. 1991. reprint ed. mass mkt. 5.50 (*0-671-70753-1*) PB.

— Half Nelson: A Tom Bethany Mystery. 1995. mass mkt. 5.50 (*0-671-79979-7*) PB.

— Head Lock. 1994. per. 4.99 (*0-671-50288-3*) S&S Trade.

— Kill Story. 1996. mass mkt. 5.99 (*0-671-79981-9*) PB.

— Stranglehold. Grose, Bill, ed. 304p. 1992. reprint ed. mass mkt. 4.99 (*0-671-74571-9*) PB.

— Tom Bethany, No. 2. 1994. pap. 4.99 (*0-671-74570-0*) S&S Trade.

Doolittle, Jesse S. Energy: A Crisis, a Dilemma, or Just Another Problem. 2nd ed. 316p. (C). pap. 34.95 (*0-916460-33-9*, Matrix Pubs Inc) Weber Systems.

Doolittle, John H. Creative Problem Solving Activities A1. 58p. (Orig.). (J). (gr. 3-6). 1995. pap. 12.95 (*0-89455-629-0*) Crit Think Bks.

— Creative Problem Solving Activities B1. 58p. (Orig.). (YA). (gr. 6-8). 1995. pap. 12.95 (*0-89455-630-4*) Crit Think Bks.

— Creative Problem Solving Activities C1. 64p. (Orig.). (YA). (gr. 7 up). 1995. pap. 12.95 (*0-89455-631-2*) Crit Think Bks.

— Dr. DooRiddles A1: Associative Reasoning Activities. 40p. (Orig.). (J). (gr. k-3). 1991. pap. 9.95 (*0-89455-437-9*) Crit Think Bks.

— Dr. DooRiddles B1: Associative Reasoning Activities. 40p. (Orig.). (J). (gr. 4-7). 1991. pap. 9.95 (*0-89455-438-7*) Crit Think Bks.

— Dr. DooRiddles C1: Associative Reasoning Activities. 40p. (Orig.). (YA). (gr. 7 up). 1991. pap. 9.95 (*0-89455-439-5*) Crit Think Bks.

Doolittle, Joyce, ed. Playhouse: Six Fantasy Plays for Children. (Illus.). 206p. (J). (gr. 1-9). 1991. pap. 12.95 (*0-88995-028-8*, Pub. by Red Deer) Empire Pub Srvs.

Doolittle, Joyce, ed. see Brooker, Blake.

Doolittle, Joyce, ed. see Murrell, John, et al.

***Doolittle, June.** All Aboard the Whistle Stop Train. (Lionel Trains Rail Tales Ser.: No. 2). (Illus.). 16p. (J). (ps-2). 1999. pap. 4.99 (*0-689-82837-3*) Litle Simon.

Doolittle, June. Circus Train: A Little Lionel Book about Counting. (Lionel Trains Shaped Board Bks.: No. 1). (Illus.). 12p. (J). (ps-k). 1999. bds. 4.99 (*0-689-82834-9*) Little Simon.

***Doolittle, June.** Red Caboose: A Little Lionel Book About Colors. (Lionel Trains Shaped Board Bks.: No. 2). (Illus.). (J). (ps-k). 1999. bds. 4.99 (*0-689-82835-7*) Litle Simon.

Doolittle, June. The Train That Rode on Water. (Lionel Trains Rail Tales Ser.: No. 1). (Illus.). 16p. (J). (ps-2). 1999. 4.99 (*0-689-82836-5*) Litle Simon.

***Doolittle, June, et al.** The Case Of The Great Elephant Escape. (New Adventures of Mary-Kate & Ashley Ser.). (Illus.). 96p. (J). (gr. 1-5). 1999. pap. 4.25 (*0-06-106583-8*, HarpEntertain) Morrow Avon.

Doolittle, Mark & Reue, Karen. Lipase & Phospholipase Protocols. LC 98-22766. (Methods in Molecular Biology Ser.: Vol. 109). 384p. 1998. 79.50 (*0-89603-546-8*) Humana.

Doolittle, Michael J., jt. auth. see Goodman, Susan E.

Doolittle, Rosalie. Southwest Gardening. rev. ed. LC 52-11535. (Illus.). 237p. 1968. reprint ed. pap. 12.95 (*0-8263-0027-8*) U of NM Pr.

Doolittle, Russell F. Of URFS & ORFS: A Primer on How to Analyze Derived Amino Acid Sequences. (Illus.). 100p. (Orig.). (C). 1987. pap. text 14.00 (*0-935702-54-7*) Univ Sci Bks.

Doolittle, Thomas. Love to Christ (Necessary to Escape the Curse at His Coming) 215p. 1994. reprint ed. 18.95 (*1-877611-84-0*) Soli Deo Gloria.

— A Treatise Concerning the Lord's Supper. rev. ed. Kistler, Don, ed. LC 98-170942. 200p. 1998. 19.95 (*1-57358-080-5*) Soli Deo Gloria.

Doolittle, W. F. Doolittle Family in America. (Illus.). 730p. 1989. reprint ed. pap. 92.00 (*0-8328-0485-1*); reprint ed. lib. bdg. 102.00 (*0-8328-0484-3*) Higginson Bk Co.

Doolittle, William E. Canal Irrigation in Prehistoric Mexico: The Sequence of Technological Change. (Illus.). 219p. (C). 1990. text 32.50 (*0-292-71558-7*) U of Tex Pr.

***Doolittle, William E.** Cultivated Landscapes of Native North America. (Oxford Geographical & Environmental Studies). (Illus.). 420p. 2000. text 112.00 (*0-19-823420-1*) OUP.

Doolittle, William E. Pre-Hispanic Occupance in the Valley of Sonora, Mexico: Archaeological Confirmations of Early Spanish Reports. LC 87-30040. (Anthropological Papers: No. 48). 88p. 1988. pap. 28.50 (*0-8165-1010-5*) U of Ariz Pr.

Doom, C., jt. auth. see De Loore, Camiel W.

Doomernik, Jeroen. Going West: Soviet Jewish Immigrants in Berlin Since 1990. (Research in Ethnic Relations Ser.). 178p. 1997. text 64.95 (*1-85972-633-X*, Pub. by Avebry) Ashgate Pub Co.

Dooms-Goossens, A. Allergic Contact Dermatitis to Ingredients Used in Topically Applied Pharmaceutical Products & Cosmetics. 212p. (Orig.). 1993. pap. 42.50 (*90-6186-147-0*, Pub. by Leuven Univ) Coronet Bks.

Doon, Ellen. Vermont Favorites: A Collection of Favorite Vermont Recipes. (Illus.). 48p. (Orig.). 1991. pap. 3.95 (*0-933050-94-1*) New Eng Pr VT.

Doonan, Delia & Holt, Richard. Law of International Trade in Practice. 2nd ed. 265p. 1999. pap. 50.00 (*1-85431-905-1*, Pub. by Blackstone Pr) Gaunt.

Doonan, Elmer. Drafting. Macfarlane, Julie, ed. (Legal Skills Ser.). 260p. 1995. pap. 22.00 (*1-874241-45-7*, Pub. by Cavendish Pubng) Gaunt.

— Equity & Trusts. rev. ed. 330p. (C). 1991. pap. 60.00 (*1-85352-372-0*, Pub. by HLT Pubns) St Mut.

Doonan, Elmer, ed. Equity & Trusts. rev. ed. 330p. (C). 1991. 60.00 (*1-85352-698-3*, Pub. by HLT Pubns); pap. 65.00 (*1-85352-834-X*, Pub. by HLT Pubns) St Mut.

Doonan, Elmer, et al, eds. Business Organisations & Insolvency. 210p. (C). 1990. 60.00 (*1-85352-086-1*, Pub. by HLT Pubns) St Mut.

— Company & Partnership Law. 320p. (C). 1991. pap. 76.00 (*1-85352-821-8*, Pub. by HLT Pubns) St Mut.

Doonan, Gladys. En el Cumplimiento del Tiempo. (SPA.). 24p. 1997. pap. 1.25 (*1-879892-73-1*) Editorial Bautista.

— La Luz Navidena de Dios. Hilliker, Bernice, ed. (SPA., Illus.). 24p. 1998. pap. 1.25 (*1-879892-49-9*, EP-101) Editorial Bautista.

***Doonan, John E.** Chastised But Not Forsaken: Maintaining Relationship When You're Out of Fellowship. Orig. Title: The Chastisement of God. 38p. 1998. pap. 6.00 (*1-893437-05-1*) Amazing Grace Pubg.

Doonan, John E. The Chastisement of God. 38p. 1998. 5.00 (*1-893437-02-7*) Amazing Grace Pubg.

— Eye of the Needle. 22p. 1996. 5.00 (*1-893437-03-5*) Amazing Grace Pubg.

***Doonan, John E.** The Gates of the City. (Illus.). 1999. pap. 6.00 (*1-893437-04-3*) Amazing Grace Pubg.

Doonan, John E. Justice. 20p. 1998. 4.00 (*1-893437-01-9*) Amazing Grace Pubg.

— The Precious Blood of Jesus. 37p. 1998. 5.00 (*1-893437-00-0*) Amazing Grace Pubg.

Doonan, Shawn, ed. Protein Purification Protocols, Vol. 59. LC 96-3250. (Methods in Molecular Biology Ser.). (Illus.). 416p. 1996. 74.50 (*0-89603-336-8*) Humana.

***Doonan, Simon, intro.** Through the Shopping Glass. (Illus.). 96p. 2000. 35.00 (*0-8478-2288-5*) Rizzoli Intl.

Doone, Lorna. Romance of Exmoor. 384p. Date not set. 26.95 (*0-8488-2548-9*) Amereon Ltd.

Dooner, David B. & Seireg, Ali A. The Kniematic Geometry of Gearing: A Concurrent Engineering Approach. LC 94-14049. (Design Engineering Ser.). 450p. 1995. 140.00 incl. disk (*0-471-04597-7*) Wiley.

Dooner, Kate. A Century of Handbags. LC 93-85219. (Illus.). 160p. 1993. pap. 29.95 (*0-88740-465-0*) Schiffer.

— Telephones: Antique to Modern. 176p. 1998. pap. 29.95 (*0-7643-0352-X*) Schiffer.

Dooner, Kate E. Plastic Handbags: Scupltura to Wear. LC 92-85176. (Illus.). 112p. (Orig.). 1993. pap. 24.95 (*0-88740-466-9*) Schiffer.

— Telephone Collecting: Seven Decades of Design. LC 92-63107. (Illus.). 128p. (Orig.). 1993. pap. 24.95 (*0-88740-489-8*) Schiffer.

Dooner, Kate E., jt. auth. see Steinberg, Sheila.

***Dooner, Mike.** Design for Manufacture. (C). 1999. pap. text. write for info. (*0-201-40392-7*) Addison-Wesley.

Dooner, W. Pierton. Last Days of the Republic. Daniels, Roger, ed. LC 78-54814. (Asian Experience in North America Ser.). 1979. reprint ed. lib. bdg. 21.95 (*0-405-11270-X*) Ayer.

Door, Harriet. The Restless Water. 70p. (Orig.). 1983. pap. 10.00 (*0-932662-47-1*) St Andrews NC.

Doordan, Ann M. Lippincott's Need-to-Know: Research Survival Guide. LC 97-13229. 144p. 1997. pap. text 14.95 (*0-7817-1040-5*) Lppncott W & W.

Doordan, Dennis P., ed. Design History: An Anthology. LC 95-24677. (Design Issues Reader Ser.). (Illus.). 288p. (Orig.). 1996. pap. text 19.00 (*0-262-54076-2*) MIT Pr.

Dooren, Paul Van, see Golub, Gene H. & Van Dooren, Paul, eds.

Dooren, Paul Van, see Van Dooren, Paul, ed.

Doorenbos, J. Sections of Begonia. LC 99-187225. (Wageningen Agricultural University Papers: No. 98.2). (Illus.). 266p. 1998. pap. 79.00 (*90-5782-007-2*) Balogh.

Doorgeest, T., et al. Elsevier's Paint Dictionary. (DUT.). 306p. 1990. 175.50 (*0-444-88068-2*) Elsevier.

— Elsevier's Paint Dictionary in English, German, French & Dutch. (DUT, ENG, FRE & GER.). 292p. 1990. 250.00 (*0-8288-9222-9*, F27100) Fr & Eur.

Doorlag, Donald H., jt. auth. see Lewis, Rena B.

Doorley, Mark J. The Place of the Heart in Lonergan's Ethics: The Role of Feelings in the Ethical Intentionality Analysis of Bernard Lonergan. LC 96-15003. 154p. 1996. lib. bdg. 44.50 (*0-7618-0367-X*) U Pr of Amer.

Doorley, Thomas L. & Donovan, John M. Value-Creating Growth: How to Life Your Company to the Next Level of Performance. LC 98-58116. 192p. 1999. 30.00 (*0-7879-4661-3*) Jossey-Bass.

Doorley, William J. Prophet of Love: Understanding the Book of Hosea. 1991. pap. 8.95 (*0-8091-3241-9*) Paulist Pr.

Doorly, Gerald S. The Voyages of the Morning. 1998. pap. 135.00 (*1-85297-040-5*, Pub. by Erskine Press) St Mut.

Doorly, William J. Isaiah of Jerusalem: An Introduction. LC 92-11648. 192p. 1992. pap. 9.95 (*0-8091-3337-7*) Paulist Pr.

— Obsession with Justice: The Story of the Deuteronomists. LC 94-15328. 224p. 1994. pap. 12.95 (*0-8091-3487-X*) Paulist Pr.

— Prophet of Justice: Understanding the Book of Amos. 1989. pap. 5.95 (*0-8091-3089-0*) Paulist Pr.

— The Religion of Israel: A Short History. LC 97-154. (Orig.). 1997. pap. 16.95 (*0-8091-3705-4*) Paulist Pr.

Doorman, Frans. Global Development - Problems, Solutions, Strategies: A Proposal for Socially Just, Ecologically Sustainable Growth. LC 98-204428. 240p. (Orig.). 1998. pap. 24.95 (*90-5727-008-0*, Pub. by Uitgeverij Arkel) LPC InBook.

Doorn, Cornelius Van, see Van Doorn, Cornelius.

Doorn, E. A. Van, see Van Doorn, E. A.

Doornbos, Daniel, ed. Farm Tractor 1985: Self Propelled Implement Lubrication Guide. (Illus.). 384p. 1984. pap., student ed. 37.85 (*0-88098-060-5*, H M Gousha) Prntice Hall Bks.

— Tractor & Self Propelled Farm Implement Guide, 1987. rev. ed. (Illus.). 192p. 1986. student ed. 41.35 (*0-88098-092-3*, H M Gousha) Prntice Hall Bks.

Doornbos, Durk J., ed. Seismological Algorithms: Computational Methods & Computer Programs. 469p. 1988. text 138.00 (*0-12-220770-X*) Acad Pr.

Doornbos, Martin, et al, eds. Beyond Conflict in the Horn: The Prospects for Peace, Recovery & Development in Ethiopia, Somalia Eritrea & Sudan. LC 92-53881. 250p. 1992. 49.95 (*0-932415-81-4*); pap. 16.95 (*0-932415-82-2*) Red Sea Pr.

Doornbos, Martin & Nair, K. N., eds. Resources, Institutions & Strategies: Operation Flood & Indian Dairying. (IDPAD Ser.). 360p. (C). 1990. text 35.00 (*0-8039-9648-9*) Sage.

Doornbos, Martin, et al. Dairy Aid & Development: India's Operation Flood. (Illus.). 344p. (C). 1990. text 35.00 (*0-8039-9641-1*) Sage.

Doornbos, Martin, jt. auth. see Tesfai, Alemseged.

Doornbos, Martin, ed. see Tesfai, Alemseged.

***Doornbos, Martin R.** Institutionalizing Development Policies & Resource Strategies in Eastern Africa & India: Developing Winners & Losers. LC 99-32871. (International Political Economy Ser.). 2000. text 75.00 (*0-312-22737-X*) St Martin.

Doornbos, Martin R. & Kaviraj, Sudipta. Dynamics of State Formation: India & Europe Compared. LC 96-48357. (Indo-Dutch Studies on Development Alternatives). 1997. 36.00 (*0-8039-9335-8*) Sage.

Doorne-Huiskes, Anneke Van, see Baker, Susan & Van Doorne-Huiskes, Anneke, eds.

Doorne-Huiskes, Anneke Van, see Van Doorne-Huiskes, Anneke.

Doornenbal, Baukje & Lemstra, Tjitske. Homemaking: A Bible Study for Women at Home. 72p. 1981. pap. 5.00 (*0-89109-033-9*) NavPress.

Doornenbal, Baukje, jt. auth. see Lemstra, Tjitske.

Doornik & Hendry. Empirical Econometric Modeling 9th ed. 1996. pap. text 46.95 (*1-86152-057-3*) Thomson Learn.

— Modeling Dynamic Systems 9th ed. 1997. pap. text 46.95 (*1-86152-058-1*) Thomson Learn.

Doornik, C. J. Van, see Van Doornik, C. J.

Doornik, Jurgen A. & Hendry, David F. PC Give 8.0. LC 95-153695. 256p. 1994. pap., mass mkt. 81.95 incl. disk (*0-534-25050-5*) Wadsworth Pub.

***Doornkaat-Koolman, J. Ten & Keeney, William E.** Dirk Philips: Friend & Colleague of Menno Simons, 1504-1568. xxvii, 236p. 1998. pap. 23.50 (*0-9698762-3-8*) Pandora Pr.

Doornkamp, John C., jt. auth. see Cooke, Ronald U.

Doorslaer, Georges V. La Vie et les Oeuvres de Philippe de Monte (1521-1603) (Academie Royale De Belgique Memoires, Cl. Des Beaux Arts Ser.). 309p. 1980. reprint ed. write for info. (*3-487-06919-9*) G Olms Pubs.

Doos, Bo R., jt. auth. see Bolin, Bert.

Doot, Martin C., jt. auth. see DeJong, Alexander.

Dooyeweerd, H. Essays in Legal, Social & Political Philosophy LC 96-52481. (Collected Works of Herman Dooyeweerd, Series B). (ENG.). ix, 169p. 1996. write for info. (*0-7734-8731-X*) E Mellen.

Dooyeweerd, Herman. Christian Philosophy & the Meaning of History. LC 96-46720. 136p. 1997. text 69.95 (*0-7734-8732-8*) E Mellen.

— Essays in Legal, Social, & Political Philosophy. LC 96-52481. (Collected Works of Herman Dooyeweerd, Series B: Vol. 2). 184p. 1996. text 79.95 (*0-7734-8734-4*) E Mellen.

— In the Twilight of Western Thought: Studies in the Pretended Autonomy of Philosophical Thought. LC 99-11270. 180p. 1999. text 79.95 (*0-7734-8717-4*) E Mellen.

— A New Critique of Theoretical Thought Vol. I: The Necessary Presuppositions of Philosophy. Freeman, David H. & Young, William S., trs. from DUT. LC 96-52511. 600p. 1997. reprint ed. text 119.95 (*0-7734-8707-7*) E Mellen.

— A New Critique of Theoretical Thought Vol. II: The General Theory of the Modal Spheres. Freeman, David H. & De Jongste, H., trs. from DUT. LC 96-52511. 624p. 1997. reprint ed. text 129.95 (*0-7734-8709-3*) E Mellen.

— A New Critique of Theoretical Thought Vol. III: The Structures of Individuality of Temporal Reality. Freeman, David H. & De Jongste, H., trs. from DUT. LC 96-52511. 816p. 1997. reprint ed. text 139.95 (*0-7734-8711-5*) E Mellen.

— A New Critique of Theoretical Thought Vol. IV: Index of Subjects & Authors. Freeman, David H. & Cirigliano, Marc, trs. from DUT. LC 96-52511. 262p. 1997. reprint ed. text 89.85 (*0-7734-8713-1*) E Mellen.

— Roots of Western Culture: Pagan, Secular & Christian Options. (C). 1979. 12.95 (*0-88906-104-1*) Shiloh Pubns.

Dopfer, K., ed. The Global Dimension of Economic Evolution: Knowledge Variety & Diffusion in Economic Growth & Development. (Illus.). vi, 159p. 1996. 75.00 (*3-7908-0909-8*) Spr-Verlag.

Dopfer, Kurt, jt. ed. see Delorme, Robert.

***Dopke, Susanne.** Cross-Linguistic Structures in Simultaneous Bilingualism. LC 00-34225. (Studies in Bilingualism). 2000. write for info. (*1-55619-953-8*) J Benjamins Pubng Co.

Dopke, Susanne. One Parent - One Language: An Interactional Approach. (Studies in Bilingualism: No. 3). xviii, 213p. 1992. 59.00 (*1-55619-346-7*) J Benjamins Pubng Co.

— One Parent - One Language: An Interactional Approach. LC 92-26142. (Studies in Bilingualism: No. 3). xviii, 213p. 1992. pap. 24.95 (*1-55619-535-4*) J Benjamins Pubng Co.

Doplicher, S., et al, eds. Operator Algebras & Quantum Field Theory. (Illus.). 688p. 1997. 42.00 (*1-57146-047-0*) Intl Pr Boston.

Dopp, Elisabeth, et al. Grains. LC 98-51590. 96p. 1999. pap. 14.95 (*0-7641-0930-8*) Barron.

Dopp, Peggy H. & Vroman, Barbara F. Tomorrow Is a River. LC 76-52054. 390p. (Orig.). 1977. 15.95 (*0-931762-00-6*) Phunn Pubs.

Dopp, Roy. Dopp "We're from Iowa?" Revisited: A Family History Tracing Dopp, Marr, Sandvig & Omundson Ancestors. 370p. 1993. reprint ed. pap. 56.00 (*0-8328-3251-0*); reprint ed. lib. bdg. 66.00 (*0-8328-3250-2*) Higginson Bk Co.

Doppelmayr, Johann G. Historische Nachricht Von Den Nurnbergischen Mathematicis und Kunstlern. (Documenta Technica Ser.: No. 11). 1972. reprint ed. write for info. (*3-487-04164-2*) G Olms Pubs.

Doppelt, Bob, et al. Entering the Watershed: A New Approach to Save America's River Ecosystems. Frissell, Chris & Karr, James, eds. LC 93-8895. 1993. text 60.00 (*1-55963-274-7*); pap. text 32.00 (*1-55963-275-5*) Island Pr.

***Doppelt, Jack C. & Shearer, Ellen.** Nonvoters: America's No-Shows. LC 99-6630. 272p. 1999. 59.95 (*0-7619-1900-7*); pap. 24.95 (*0-7619-1901-5*) Sage.

Doppler, A. F. Fantaisie Pastorale: For Hongroiseflute & Piano Opus 26. 16p. 1986. pap. 7.95 (*0-7935-5264-8*, 50291030) H Leonard.

Doppman, John L., et al. Selective Arteriography of the Spinal Cord. LC 68-58106. (Illus.). 157p. 1969. 14.50 (*0-87527-006-9*) Green.

Doppo, Kunikida. River Mist & Other Stories. Chibbett, David G., tr. 176p. (C). 1996. text 29.00 (*0-904404-40-4*, Pub. by Curzon Pr Ltd) UH Pr.

Dopson, Betty. Fruit of the Vine: Two Hundred Years of Winemaking in California. (Illus.). 135p. (Orig.). 1988. pap. 9.95 (*0-938530-44-5*) Lexikos.

Dopson, Sue, jt. auth. see Austin, Noel.

Dopuch, Nicholas, jt. auth. see Gonedes, Nicholas.

Dopyera, John & Lay-Dopyera, Margaret Z. Becoming a Teacher of Young Children. 5th ed. LC 92-14951. (C). 1993. text 59.50 (*0-07-036777-9*) McGraw.

Dor Bahadur Bista. People of Nepal. 5th ed. (Illus.). 210p. (gr. 9-12). 1987. 44.50 (*0-685-05884-0*) Asia Bk Corp.

Dor, I. & Juanico, M., eds. Reservoirs for Wastewater Storage & Reuse: Ecology, Performance & Engineering Design. LC 99-35528. (Environmental Science Ser.). (Illus.). 425p. 1999. 149.00 (*3-540-65598-0*) Spr-Verlag.

Dor, I., jt. ed. see Por, F. D.

***Dor, Joel.** The Clinical Lacan. LC 99-28373. (Lacanian Clinical Field Ser.). 160p. 1999. reprint ed. pap. 17.95 (*1-892746-05-0*, 46050) Other Pr LLC.

Dor, Joel. Introduction to the Reading of Lacan. (Lacanian Clinical Field Ser.). (Illus.). 268p. 1998. reprint ed. pap. 18.95 (*1-892746-04-2*, 46042) Other Pr LLC.

Dor, Joel & Gurewich, Judith F. The Clinical Lacan. LC 96-32060. (The Lacanian Clinical Field Ser.). 160p. 1997. pap. 22.00 (*0-7657-0042-5*) Aronson.

Dor, Milo. On the Wrong Track: Fragments of an Autobiography. Glenn, Jerry & Kelley, Jennifer, trs. LC 92-45251. (Studies in Austrian Literature, Culture, & Thought. Translation Ser.). 241p. 1993. pap. 23.50 (*0-929497-66-X*) Ariadne CA.

Dor, Milo & Federmann, Reinhard. International Zone. Glenn, Jerry & Kelley-Thierman, Jennifer, trs. from GER. LC 99-17143. 212p. 1999. pap. 18.50 (*1-57241-076-0*) Ariadne CA.

Dor, Moshe. Crossing the River: Selected Poems. Mayne, Seymour, ed. 126p. 1989. pap. 12.95 (*0-88962-418-6*) Mosaic.

— Khamsin: Memoirs & Poetry by a Native Israeli. 169p. 1994. 25.00 (*0-89410-763-1*, Three Contnts); pap. 15.00 (*0-89410-764-X*, Three Contnts) L Rienner.

Dor, Moshe, et al, eds. The Stones Remember: Native Israeli Poetry. LC 90-70198. 120p. (Orig.). 1991. pap. 15.00 (*0-915380-25-0*) Word Works.

Dor, Mosheh & Goldberg, Barbara. After the First Rain: Israeli Poems on War & Peace. LC 97-46012. 1998. 24.95 (*0-8156-0524-2*) Syracuse U Pr.

***Dorairajan, N.** Current Concepts in Surgery. (Illus.). 304p. 2000. text 39.95 (*0-19-565127-8*) OUP.

Dorais, Louis J., et al. Exile in Cold Land. LC 87-51584. (Lac-Viet Ser.: No. 6). x, 220p. 1988. pap. 15.00 (*0-938692-31-3*) Yale U SE Asia.

Dorais, Louis-Jacques. Quaqtaq: Modernity & Identity in an Inuit Community. LC 97-160570. (Illus.). 132p. 1997. text 45.00 (*0-8020-4105-1*, E99) U of Toronto Pr.

Dorais, Lucie, ed. J. W. Morrice. (Canadian Artists Ser.: No. 8). (Illus.). 80p. 1986. pap. 7.95 (*0-226-56426-6*) U Ch Pr.

Doraisingham, S., jt. auth. see Chan, Y. C.

Doraiswamy, jt. ed. see Krishnan, K. Ranga Rama.

***Doraiswamy, L. K.** Organic Synthesis Engineering. (Topics in Chemical Engineering Ser.). (Illus.). 720p. 2000. text 125.00 (*0-19-509689-4*) OUP.

Doraiswamy, L. K. & Kulkarni, B. D. Advances in Transport Processes, Vol. 7: Fluidized Bed Reactors. (C). 1988. 52.00 (*0-85226-171-3*) S Asia.

Doraiswamy, L. K. & Kulkarni, B. D., eds. The Analysis of Chemically Reacting Systems: A Stochastic Approach. (Topics in Chemical Engineering Ser.: Vol. 4). xxvi, 462p. 1987. text 323.00 (*0-677-21670-X*) Gordon & Breach.

***Doral, Francis.** Insight Guide Tokyo. 3rd rev. ed. 2000. pap. 22.95 (*1-58573-030-0*) Langenscheidt.

Doramajian, Astrid. Recycled Dishes for the 21st Century. vi, 203p. (Orig.). 1997. pap. 14.95 (*0-9656404-0-X*) A Doramajian.

Dorame, Anthony. Peril at Thunder Ridge. (Illus.). 128p. (YA). (gr. 7-11). 1993. pap. 9.95 (*1-878610-26-0*) Red Crane Bks.

Doran. Activities in Management Accounting. 96p. 1996. pap. text 15.60 (*0-13-264458-4*) P-H.

— Applied Regression Analysis in Econometrics. (Statistics: Textbooks & Monographs: Vol. 102). (Illus.). 392p. 1989. text 157.50 (*0-8247-8049-3*) Dekker.

Doran, jt. auth. see Sher.

Doran, Claire, jt. auth. see Haslam, Andrew.

Doran, Alan, jt. auth. see Bannock, Graham.

Doran, Bob. Evidence & Recovered Property: The Police Property Control Function. 2nd ed. 304p. 1998. pap. 16.95 (*0-9636835-0-0*) Public Mgmt.

Doran, Cahrles F. & Naftali, Timothy J. U. S.-Canadian Softwood Lumber: Trade Dispute Negotiations. (Pew Case Studies in International Affairs). 50p. 1988. pap. text 3.50 (*1-56927-141-0*) Geo U Inst Dplmcy.

Doran, Carol & Troeger, Thomas H. Open to Glory. LC 82-18753. 160p. 1993. pap. 14.00 (*0-8170-0981-7*) Judson.

Doran, Carol, jt. auth. see Troeger, Thomas H.

Doran, Charles, et al. Pacific Partners: Canada & the United States. (Institute for Foreign Policy Anaylsis Ser.). 143p. 1994. pap. 11.95 (*0-02-881076-7*) Brasseys.

Doran, Charles F. Forgotten Partnership: U. S.-Canada Relations Today. LC 83-48052. 304p. 1985. reprint ed. pap. text 19.95 (*0-8018-3001-X*) Johns Hopkins.

— Myth, Oil & Politics: Introduction to the Political Economy of Petroleum. LC 77-4571. (Illus.). 1977. 22.95 (*0-02-907580-7*) Free Pr.

— The Politics of Assimilation: Hegemony & Its Aftermath. LC 77-148241. 237p. reprint ed. pap. 73.50 (*0-608-12098-7*, 202413700035) Bks Demand.

— Systems in Crisis: New Imperatives of High Politics at Century's End. (Cambridge Studies in International Relations: No. 16). (Illus.). 312p. (C). 1991. text 64.95 (*0-521-40185-2*); pap. text 19.95 (*0-521-31237-X*) Cambridge U Pr.

Doran, Charles F., et al, eds. North-South Relations: Studies of Dependency Reversal. LC 83-13657. 257p. 1983. 65.00 (*0-275-90972-7*, C0972, Praeger Pubs) Greenwood.

Doran, Charles F. & Babby, Ellen R., eds. Being & Becoming Canada. LC 94-66218. (Annals of the American Academy of Political & Social Science Ser.: Vol. 538). 1995. 28.00 (*0-8039-5884-6*); pap. 18.00 (*0-8039-5885-4*) Am Acad Pol Soc Sci.

Doran, Charles F. & Drischler, Alvin, eds. A New North America: Cooperation & Enhanced Interdependence. LC 95-40576. 184p. 1996. 55.00 (*0-275-95406-4*, Praeger Pubs); pap. 17.95 (*0-275-95407-2*, Praeger Pubs) Greenwood.

Doran, Charles F. & Sigler, John H. Canada & the United States: Enduring Friendship, Persistant Stress. 264p. 1985. pap. 15.95 (*0-13-113812-X*); pap. 7.95 (*0-13-113804-9*) Am Assembly.

Doran, Charles F. & Tang, Puay. Canada: Unity in Diversity. LC 89-81592. (Headline Ser.: No. 291). 64p. 1990. pap. 5.95 (*0-87124-131-5*) Foreign Policy.

Doran, Clare. The Japanese. (Look into the Past Ser.). (Illus.). 32p. (J). (gr. 4-6). 1995. lib. bdg. 22.83 (*1-56847-173-4*) Raintree Steck-V.

Doran, Colleen. A Distant Soil I: The Gathering. (Illus.). 240p. 1997. pap. 18.95 (*1-887279-51-2*, Pub. by Image Comics) Midpt Trade.

— A Distant Soil II: The Ascendant. (Illus.). 240p. 1998. pap. 18.95 (*1-58240-018-0*, Pub. by Image Comics) Midpt Trade.

Doran, Denis. Get the Rubber Habit. (Postcard Book). 64p. 1994. 7.95 (*0-9523229-0-0*, Pub. by Cassell) LPC InBook.

Doran, Diana R., ed. see Rowe, Josiah P., Jr.

Doran, Edward. Finding Your Way Through College Algebra: Help When Your Textbook Isn't Enough. 344p. (Orig.). 1987. pap. text 16.95 (*0-941775-00-3*) Finesse Pub.

Doran, Edward & Boersema, Raymond. Fundamental Mathematics. 2nd ed. 510p. (C). 1989. pap. 34.95 (*0-941775-02-X*) Finesse Pub.

Doran, Genevieve, ed. see Fielding, Mantle.

Doran, J. W. & Jones, A. J. Methods for Assessing Soil Quality. (SSSA Special Publications: No. 49). 410p. 1996. 36.00 (*0-89118-826-6*) Soil Sci Soc Am.

Doran, J. W., et al. Defining Soil Quality for a Sustainable Environment. LC 94-6338. (SSSA Special Publications: No. 35). 244p. 1994. 30.00 (*0-89118-807-X*) Soil Sci Soc Am.

Doran, James E. & Hodson, Frank R. Mathematics & Computers in Archaeology. (Illus.). 382p. 1975. 42.00 (*0-674-55455-8*) HUP.

Doran, James M. Herman Chittison: A Bio-Discography. Raichelson, Richard, ed. LC 93-78860. (IAJRC Monograph: No. 2). (Illus.). 136p. (Orig.). (C). 1992. pap. 30.00 (*0-9625487-1-5*) Intl Assn Jazz Record.

Doran, John. History of Court Fools. LC 68-3844. (Studies in Comparative Literature: No. 35). 1969. reprint ed. lib. bdg. 75.00 (*0-8383-0656-X*) M S G Haskell Hse.

— Lady of the Last Century: Mrs. Elizabeth Montague. 2nd ed. LC 75-37690. (Illus.). reprint ed. 47.50 (*0-404-56744-4*) AMS Pr.

— Their Majesties' Servants: Or Annals of the English Stage, 3 vols. Lowe, R. W., ed. LC 68-58985. reprint ed. 185.00 (*0-404-02170-0*) AMS Pr.

Doran, John & Connolly, Joe. Red Doran: The Story of a Derryman. LC 96-140084. 240p. 1997. pap. 15.95 (*0-85640-573-6*, Pub. by Blackstaff Pr) Dufour.

Doran, K. J. Personal Bankruptcy & Debt Adjustment. 2nd ed. 172p. 1995. pap. 10.00 (*0-679-76976-5*) Random.

Doran, Kenneth J. Surviving Personal Bankruptcy & Debt Adjustment: Third Edition. 3rd rev. ed. 2000. pap. 12.00 (*0-375-70465-5*) Random Ref & Info.

Doran, Kevin. More Joy in Heaven! Confession, the Sacrament of Reconciliation. 112p. 1989. pap. 22.00 (*0-7855-6978-2*, Pub. by Veritas Pubns) St Mut.

— Solidarity: A Synthesis of Personalism & Communalism in the Thought of Karol Wojtyla/Pope John Paul II. (American University Studies: Vol. VII). XVII, 277p. (C). 1996. text 47.95 (*0-8204-3071-4*) P Lang Pubng.

— What Is a Person? The Concept & the Implications for Ethics. LC 89-33546. (Studies in Health & Human Services: Vol. 14). 192p. 1989. lib. bdg. 79.95 (*0-88946-140-6*) E Mellen.

Doran, Laura D. Candy! A Sweet Selection of Fun & Favorite Recipes. LC 98-9654. (Illus.). 128p. 1998. 24.95 (*1-57990-055-0*, Pub. by Lark Books) Random.

— The New Silk Flower Book: Making Stylish Arrangements, Wreaths & Decorations. LC 97-3614. (Illus.). 128p. 1997. 24.95 (*1-887374-41-8*); pap. 16.95 (*1-57990-010-0*, Pub. by Lark Books) Random.

***Doran, Laura D.** Scented Gifts: From Sachets to Soap, from Gingerbread to Potpourri. LC 97-45872. 128p. 1998. 24.95 (*1-57990-035-6*, Pub. by Lark Books) Random.

Doran, Laura D. Ultimate Candymaking Book & Kit. 1998. 39.95 (*1-57990-073-9*, Pub. by Lark Books) Random.

Doran, Laura D., ed. see Bergnian, Bo.

Doran, Laura D., ed. see Henderson, Stevie & Baldwin, Mark.

Doran, Laura D., ed. see King, Heidi T. & Worell, Nancy.

Doran, Laura D., ed. see Rannefeld, Clarence.

***Doran, Laura Dover.** Scented Gifts: From Sachets to Soap, from Gingerbread to Potpourri. LC 97-45872. (Illus.). 128p. 1999. pap. 16.95 (*1-57990-142-5*, Pub. by Lark Books) Random.

Doran, Laura Dover, ed. see Henderson, Stevie & Baldwin, Mark.

Doran, Madeleine. Endeavors of Art: A Study of Form in Elizabethan Drama. LC 53-13439. (Illus.). 497p. 1954. reprint ed. pap. 154.10 (*0-608-07454-3*, 206768100009) Bks Demand.

— Shakespeare's Dramatic Language: Essays. LC 75-32072. 264p. reprint ed. pap. 81.90 (*0-608-09906-6*, 206924400003) Bks Demand.

— Something about Swans. LC 73-2042. 133p. 1973. reprint ed. pap. 41.30 (*0-608-01953-4*, 206260800003) Bks Demand.

Doran, Madeleine, ed. see Shakespeare, William.

Doran, Margie. What the Public School Doesn't Tell You. 219p. 1991. pap. 5.95 (*0-9629270-7-4*) Doran Prods.

***Doran, Marianne.** Breast Cancer: Diagnosis & Treatment: A Special Report from the Editors of Women's Health Advisor. Etingin, Orli & Weiner, Gabrielle, eds. (Illus.). 59p. 2000. pap. 19.95 (*1-929942-06-0*) Torstar.

— Breast Cancer: Risk Factors & Prevention Strategies: A Special Report from the Editors of Women's Health Advisor. Etingin, Orli & Weiner, Gabrielle, eds. 43p. 2000. pap. 19.95 (*1-929942-02-8*) Torstar.

Doran, Martha. Activities in Financial Accounting. 82p. (C). 1996. pap. text 15.60 (*0-13-228966-0*) P-H.

Doran, Martha S., et al. Keys to Business Success. LC 99-15637. (Illus.). 302p. 1999. pap. text 30.00 (*0-13-013304-3*) P-H.

Doran, Meredith, ed. The Neural Basis of Consciousness, the Dalai Lama, & a Glorious Piece of Meat: An Interview with Professor Patricia Smith Churchland. (Living Philosophy Ser.). 52p. 1992. pap. 2.00 (*1-56543-002-6*) Mt SA Coll Philos.

***Doran, Michael.** Pan-Arabism before Nasser: Egyptian Power Politics & the Palestine Question. LC 98-23001. (Studies in Middle Eastern History). 240p. 1999. text 35.00 (*0-19-512361-1*) OUP.

Doran, Michael, ed. see Cezanne, Paul.

Doran, Michael, jt. ed. see Landis, Joshua.

Doran, Nigel. Doran: Taxation of Corporation Joint Ventures. 193p. 1993. 150.00 (*0-406-01880-4*, U.K., MICHIE) LEXIS Pub.

— Taxation of Corporate Joint Ventures. 2nd ed. LC 95-114769. 193p. 1996. 134.00 (*0-406-07916-1*, MICHIE) LEXIS Pub.

Doran, Pauline M. Bioprocess Engineering Principles. (Illus.). 439p. 1995. text 137.00 (*0-12-220855-2*); pap. text 42.00 (*0-12-220856-0*) Acad Pr.

Doran, Pauline M., ed. Hairy Roots: Culture & Applications. 220p. 1997. text 65.00 (*90-5702-117-X*, Harwood Acad Pubs) Gordon & Breach.

Doran, R. S. & Belfi, V. A. Characterizations of C Algebras: The Gelfand Naimark Theorems. (Pure & Applied Mathematics Ser.: Vol. 101). (Illus.). 448p. 1986. text 175.00 (*0-8247-7569-4*) Dekker.

Doran, R. W., jt. ed. see Carpenter, B. E.

Doran, Robert. Birth of a Worldview: Early Christianity in Its Jewish & Pagan Context. LC 99-11556. 200p. 1999. pap. 25.95 (*0-8476-9371-6*) Rowman.

***Doran, Robert.** Birth of a Worldview: Early Christianity in Its Jewish & Pagan Context. LC 99-11556. 200p. 1999. text 65.00 (*0-8476-9370-8*) Rowman.

Doran, Robert. Temple Propaganda: The Purpose & Character of 2 Maccabees. LC 81-10084. (Catholic Biblical Quarterly Monographs: No. 12). ix, 124p. 1981. pap. 4.50 (*0-915170-11-6*) Catholic Bibl Assn.

Doran, Robert, tr. from GRE. Stylites: The Biographies. (Cistercian Studies: No. 112). 250p. 1992. write for info. (*0-87907-412-4*) Cistercian Pubns.

Doran, Robert M. Subject & Psyche. 2nd rev. ed. (Studies in Theology). 1995. pap. 25.00 (*0-87462-627-7*) Marquette.

— Theological Foundations, Vol. 1. LC 95-41772. (Studies in Theology: No. 8). 500p. (C). 1995. pap. 50.00 (*0-87462-632-3*) Marquette.

— Theological Foundations, Vol. 2. LC 95-41772. (Studies in Theology: No. 9). 550p. (C). 1995. pap. 55.00 (*0-87462-633-1*) Marquette.

— Theology & the Dialectics of History. 752p. 1989. text 95.00 (*0-8020-2713-X*); pap. text 45.00 (*0-8020-6777-8*) U of Toronto Pr.

Doran, Robert M., jt. ed. see Crowe, Frederick E.

Doran, Robert M., ed. see Lonergan, Bernard.

Doran, Robert M., ed. see Lonergan, Bernard J.

Doran, Robert M., ed. see Sala, Giovanni B.

Doran, Robert S., ed. C Algebras, 1943-1993 - A Fifty Year Celebration: Proceedings of an AMS Special Session Held January 13-14, 1993 at the San Antonio Convention Center in San Antonio, Texas. LC 94-17615. (Contemporary Mathematics Ser.: Vol. 167). 399p. 1994. pap. 65.00 (*0-8218-5175-6*, CONM/167) Am Math.

— Selfadjoint & Nonselfadjoint Operator Algebras & Operator Theory: Proceedings of the CBMS Regional Conference Held May 19-26, 1990 at Texas Christ. LC 91-19767. (Contemporary Mathematics Ser.: Vol. 120). 215p. 1991. pap. 51.00 (*0-8218-5127-6*, CONM/120) Am Math.

***Doran, Robert S., et al, eds.** Automorphic Forms, Automorphic Representations, & Arithmetic: Proceedings of the NSF-CBMS Regional Conference in Mathematics on Euler Products & Eisenstein Series Held at Texas Christian University, 1996, 2 vols., Set. LC 99-28916. (Proceedings of Symposia in Pure Mathematics Ser.: Vol. 66, Pts. 1-2). 608p. 1999. 121.00 (*0-8218-0659-9*) Am Math.

***Doran, Robert S. & Varadarajan, V. S., eds.** The Mathematical Legacy of Harish-Chandra: A Celebration of Representation Theory & Harmonic Analysis. (PSPUM Ser.: Vol. 68). 549p. 2000. 110.00 (*0-8218-1197-5*) Am Math.

Doran, Robert S., jt. ed. see Fell, James M.

Doran, Sandra F. Every Time I Say Grace We Fight. 94p. 1992. pap. 7.99 (*0-8280-0645-8*) Review & Herald.

Doran, Sandra F. & Slongwhite, Dale F. Gathering: A Search for Balance & Fulfillment. LC 98-50106. 1999. 10.99 (*0-8163-1696-1*) Pacific Pr Pub Assn.

Doran, Sean, jt. auth. see Jackson, John.

Doran, Serge Le, see Le Doran, Serge.

***Doran-Smith, Eileen J.** The Cloud Painter, No. 2. Smith, Douglas M., ed. LC 99-96214. (Illus.). 32p. (J). (ps-3). 2000. 14.99 (*1-929489-50-1*) Platinum Medallion.

— How the Youngest Angel Learned to Fly, No. 1. Smith, Douglas M., ed. LC 99-93488. (Illus.). 32p. (J). (ps-3). 2000. 14.99 (*1-929489-64-1*) Platinum Medallion.

***Doran, Susan.** Elizabeth I & Foreign Relations. LC 99-48895. 96p. 2000. pap. 11.99 (*0-415-15355-7*) Routledge.

Doran, Susan. England & Europe 1485 to 1603. 2nd ed. LC 96-28643. (Seminar Studies in History). 152p. (C). 1997. pap. 16.80 (*0-582-28991-2*) Longman.

— England & Europe in the Sixteenth Century. LC 98-21297. 168p. 1998. text 55.00 (*0-312-21706-4*) St Martin.

— Monarchy & Matrimony: The Courtships of Elizabeth I. LC 95-9080. (Illus.). 296p. (C). 1996. 50.00 (*0-415-11969-3*) Routledge.

Doran, Susan & Durston, Christopher. Princes, Pastors & People: The Church & Religion in England, 1529-1689. (Illus.). 224p. (C). 1991. pap. 18.99 (*0-415-05964-X*, A5674) Routledge.

***Doran, Thomas.** At the Crossroads: A Vision of Hope. 2000. 19.95 (*0-910941-26-2*) JGC.

Doran, Valerie C., tr. see Chang Shiang-hua.

Dorandi, Tiziano, ed. Filodemo, Storia dei Filosofi La Stoa da Zenone a Panezio, PHerc. 1018. (Philosophia Antiqua Ser.: No. 60). 212p. 1993. 77.50 (*90-04-09963-8*, NLG110) Brill Academic Pubs.

Dorans, Neil J., jt. auth. see Wainer, Howard.

***Dorat, Jean & Slavitt, David R.** The Latin Odes of Jean Dorat. LC 00-21664. 96p. 2000. 20.00 (*0-914061-80-1*) Orchises Pr.

Dorati, Antal. Notes of Seven Decades. rev. ed. LC 80-27568. (Illus.). 379p. reprint ed. pap. 117.50 (*0-608-10523-6*, 205443400009) Bks Demand.

***Dorato.** Analytic Feedback System Design: An Interpolation Approach. LC 99-36881. (Electrical Engineering Ser.). 1999. 21.95 (*0-534-36917-0*) Brooks-Cole.

Dorato, Mauro. Time & Reality: Spacetime Physics & the Objectivity of Temporal Becoming. 238p. 1996. pap. 24.00 (*88-8091-172-4*) Paul & Co Pubs.

Dorato, P., et al. Robust Control for Unstructured Perturbations: An Introduction. Thoma, M. & Wyner, A., eds. (Lecture Notes in Control & Information Sciences: Vol. 168). vi, 118p. 1992. 43.95 (*0-387-54920-X*) Spr-Verlag.

Dorato, Peter. Robust Control. LC 87-12448. 528p. 1987. 89.95 (*0-87942-233-5*, PCO2204) Inst Electrical.

Dorato, Peter & Yedavalli, R. K., eds. Recent Advances in Robust Control. LC 90-4563. (Illus.). 512p. 1990. text 79.95 (*0-87942-266-1*, PC02584) Inst Electrical.

***Dorato, Peter, et al.** Linear-Quadratic Control: An Introduction. (Illus.). (C). 2000. reprint ed. text. write for info. (*1-57524-156-0*) Krieger.

Dorau, Herbert B. & Hinman, Albert G. Urban Land Economics. 1982. 34.95 (*0-8434-0053-6*) McGrath NH.

Doray, Jocelyne & Samuel, Julian, eds. The Raft of the Medusa: Five Voices on Colonies, Nations, & Histories. LC 93-72751. 132p. 1994. 48.99 (*1-895431-77-8*, Pub. by Black Rose); pap. 19.99 (*1-895431-76-X*, Pub. by Black Rose) Consort Bk Sales.

Doray, S. J. Gateway to Islam, 4. (J). 1994. pap. 10.00 (*1-56744-019-3*) Kazi Pubns.

D'Orazio. Low Back Pain Handbook: Evaluation & Management. 336p. 1998. text 40.00 (*0-7506-9618-4*) Buttrwrth-Heinemann.

D'Orazio, Brian. Back Pain Rehabilitation. LC 93-11017. (Illus.). 282p. 1993. text 54.00 (*1-56372-029-9*) Buttrwrth-Heinemann.

D'Orazio, Leo, jt. auth. see Snook, I. Donald, Jr.

D'Orazio, Leo, jt. auth. see Snook, I. Donald.

D'Orazio, Paul, jt. contrib. by see Graham, Gary A.

***Dorazio, Sante.** Sante d'Orazio. 2000. pap. text 19.95 (*3-570-19242-3*) V C Bertelsman.

Dorazio, Sante. Sante Dorazio: A Private View: Photographs & Diary. 256p. 1998. pap. 30.00 (*0-14-027819-2*) Penguin Putnam.

***D'Orazio, Sante, photos by.** Sante D'Orazio: Photographs. (Illus.). 232p. 2000. 65.00 (*1-892041-30-8*) Arena Editions.

Dorazio, Sante, jt. auth. see Clemente, Francesco.

D'Orazio, T. B., jt. auth. see Tan, H. H.

Dorbad, Leo J. Sexually Balanced Relationships in the Novels of D. H. Lawrence. (American University Studies: Ser. IV, Vol. 76). 157p. (C). 1991. text 31.95 (*0-8204-1275-9*) P Lang Pubng.

Dorbe, Gustave, ed. see Coleridge, Samuel Taylor.

D'Orbessan, Marez E., compiled by. Walter Muir Whitehill, Director & Librarian, Boston Athenaeum, 1946-1973: A Bibliography & Verses by Friends Presented on His Retirement. (Illus.). 36p. (Orig.). 1974. pap. 1.50 (*0-934552-30-4*) Boston Athenaeum.

D'Orbigny, Alcide D. Cours Elementaire de Paleontologie et de Geologie Stratgraphiques, Vol. 2. (FRE.). 1980. 36.95 (*0-405-12744-8*) Ayer.

— Cours Elementaire de Paleontologie et de Geologie Stratigraphiques: Beginning Course in Paleontology & Stratigraphic Geology, 2 vols., Set. Gould, Stephen Jay, ed. LC 79-8339. (History of Paleontology Ser.). (FRE., Illus.). 1980. reprint ed. lib. bdg. 107.95 (*0-405-12725-1*) Ayer.

— Cours Elementaire de Paleontologie et de Geologie Stratigraphiques: Beginning Course in Paleontology &

D

An Asterisk (*) at the beginning of an entry indicates that the title is appearing for the first time.

D

Dorey, Annette K. Better Baby Contests: The Scientific Quest for Childhood Perfection in the Early Twentieth Century. LC 99-32146. (Illus.). 277p. 1999. boxed set 38.50 (0-7864-0617-8) McFarland & Co.

Dorey, Claire & Bianchini, Ellen, trs. from ITA. History of Italian Art, 2 vols.Tr. of Storia dell'Arte Italiana. (Illus.). 864p. 1997. pap. 52.00 (0-7456-1819-7) Blackwell Pubs.

— History of Italian Art, Vol. 1. 2nd ed.Tr. of Storia dell'Arte Italiana. (Illus.). 337p. 1996. pap. 26.95 (0-7456-1754-9) Blackwell Pubs.

— History of Italian Art, Vol. 2. 2nd ed.Tr. of Storia dell'Arte Italiana. (Illus.). 337p. 1996. pap. 26.95 (0-7456-1755-7) Blackwell Pubs.

Dorey, Claire, tr. see Burke, Peter, ed.

D'Orey, Leonor. Five Centuries of Jewellery: From the Collection of the Ancient Art Museum, Lisbon. LC 96-176275. (Illus.). 128p. 1996. 35.00 (0-302-00660-5) Scala Books.

Dorey, Peter. British Politics since 1945. LC 95-18884. (Making Contemporary Britain Ser.). 1995. 66.95 (0-631-19074-0) Blackwell Pubs.

— British Politics since 1945. LC 95-18884. (Making Contemporary Britain Ser.). 1996. pap. 27.95 (0-631-19075-9) Blackwell Pubs.

Dorey, Sasha. Decorative Stamping: Hundreds of Projects for Your Home. LC 95-10532. 96p. 1995. 18.95 (0-88266-809-9) Storey Bks.

Dorey, Thomas A. The Life & Times of the Hotel Athenaeum. 2nd ed. LC 90-93506. (Illus.). 85p. 1991. pap. 8.95 (0-9627431-1-9) T A Dorey.

Dorf. Electrical Engineering Handbook. LC 98-10884. 1998. cd-rom 129.00 (0-8493-9750-2) CRC Pr.

— Technology Management Handbook. 1998. cd-rom 129.00 (0-8493-9754-5) CRC Pr.

Dorf, Fran. Enemy Kissed. 1999. pap. 19.95 (0-525-93645-9) NAL.

— A Reasonable Madness. 1990. 18.95 (1-55972-045-X, Birch Ln Pr) Carol Pub Group.

***Dorf, Fran.** Saving Elijah. LC 99-88125. 400p. 2000. 25.95 (0-399-14630-X) Putnam Pub Group.

Dorf, Marilyn. Of Hoopoes & Hummingbirds. (Illus.). 30p. 1998. pap. 7.00 (0-9616211-2-5) Marilyn Dorf.

— Windmills Walk the Night. (Illus.). 48p. (Orig.). 1992. pap. 6.95 (0-9616211-1-7) Marilyn Dorf.

Dorf, Martin E. Restaurants That Work: Case Studies of the Best in the Industry. LC 92-11262. (Illus.). 224p. 1992. 55.00 (0-8230-4540-4, Whitney Lib) Watsn-Guptill.

Dorf, Michael. Knitting Music. 1992. pap. 10.00 (0-9632151-0-8) Knitt Fact Wrks.

Dorf, Michael C., jt. auth. see Tribe, Laurence H.

Dorf, Paul. What's Wrong With Compensation? How To Develop Better Pay Programs. 326p. 2000. 34.95 (0-471-32621-6) Wiley.

Dorf, Richard. Modern Control Systems. 6th ed. (C). 1994. pap. text. write for info. (0-201-59093-X) Addison-Wesley.

***Dorf, Richard C.** Business Design for E-Commerce. 132p. 2000. write for info. (1-58692-020-0) Copyright Mgmt.

Dorf, Richard C. The Electrical Engineering Handbook. 2nd ed. 2929p. 1997. 115.00 (0-7803-3467-1, PC5724-QOE) Inst Electrical.

— Energy, Resources & Policy. 1978. teacher ed. write for info. (0-318-50138-4); text. write for info. (0-201-01673-7) Addison-Wesley.

— Engineering Handbook. 1997. pap. 159.95 (0-8493-8590-3) CRC Pr.

— Investment Management with Microcomputers. (Illus.). 230p. 15.95 (0-317-13072-2) P-H.

***Dorf, Richard C.** Millenium Stocks. LC 99-45048. 239p. 1999. 39.95 (1-57444-250-3) St Lucie Pr.

Dorf, Richard C. Modern Control Systems. 4th ed. LC 85-7532. (Electrical Engineering Ser.). 550p. (C). 1986. text. write for info. (0-201-05326-8) Addison-Wesley.

— Modern Control Systems. 5th ed. (Electrical Engineering Ser.). (Illus.). (C). 1989. text 61.25 (0-201-14278-3); pap. text 34.25 (0-201-14279-1) Addison-Wesley.

— Modern Control Systems. 6th ed. (C). 1991. pap. text. write for info. (0-201-60701-8) Addison-Wesley.

— Modern Control Systems. 6th ed. (A-W Series in Electrical & Computer Engineering - Control Engineering). (Illus.). 603p. (C). 1992. text 69.95 (0-201-51713-2) Addison-Wesley.

— Modern Control Systems. 7th ed. (C). 1995. pap. text. write for info. (0-201-84559-8) Addison-Wesley.

— Modern Control Systems. 8th ed. LC 97-36632. 820p. (C). 1997. 100.00 (0-201-30864-9, Prentice Hall) P-H.

***Dorf, Richard C.** New & Small Business Ventures. 178p. 2000. write for info. (1-58692-021-9) Copyright Mgmt.

Dorf, Richard C. The New Mutual Fund Investment Advisor: Everything You Need to Know about Investing in No-Loads. 1991. text 24.95 (1-55738-157-7, Irwn Prfssnl) McGraw-Hill Prof.

— S/M Modern Control Sys. 4th ed. LC 85-7532. (Electrical Engineering Ser.). 550p. (C). 1986. teacher ed. 6.50 (0-201-05327-6) Addison-Wesley.

— The Technology Management Handbook. LC 98-22328. (Electrical Engineering Handbook Ser.). 1408p. 1998. lib. bdg. 95.00 (0-8493-8577-6) CRC Pr.

***Dorf, Richard C.** Technology Management Handbook. (Illus.). 1998. 94.95 (0-7803-4722-6) Inst Electrical.

Dorf, Richard C., ed. The Electrical Engineering Handbook. (Illus.). 2696p. 1993. lib. bdg. 115.00 (0-8493-0185-8, 185C2W) CRC Pr.

Dorf, Richard C., ed. The Electrical Engineering Handbook. 2nd ed. LC 97-35400. 2752p. 1997. boxed set 134.95 (0-8493-8574-1) CRC Pr.

Dorf, Richard C., ed. The Engineering Handbook. LC 95-32292. 2352p. 1995. boxed set 134.95 (0-8493-8344-7, 8344) CRC Pr.

— The Engineering Handbook on CD-ROM. LC 97-4535. (Illus.). 26p. 1997. 99.95 incl. cd-rom (0-8493-8576-8, 8576) CRC Pr.

***Dorf, Richard C. & Bishop, Robert H.** Modern Control Systems. 8th rev. ed. 1998. teacher ed. write for info. (0-201-30866-5) Addison-Wesley.

Dorf, Richard C. & Kusiak, Andrew, eds. Handbook of Manufacturing & Automation. 1064p. 1994. 210.00 (0-471-55218-6) Wiley.

Dorf, Richard C. & Nof, Shimon Y. International Encyclopedia of Robotics: Applications & Automation, 3 vols., Vol. 3. LC 87-37264. 2046p. 1988. 700.00 (0-471-87868-5) Wiley.

Dorf, Richard C. & Nof, Shimon Y., eds. Concise International Encyclopedia of Robotics: Applications & Automation. 1190p. 1990. 300.00 (0-471-51698-8) Wiley.

Dorf, Richard C. & Svoboda, James A. Introduction to Electric Circuits. 4th ed. LC 98-17816. 944p. 1998. 102.95 incl. cd-rom (0-471-19246-5) Wiley.

***Dorf, Richard C. & Svoboda, James A.** Introduction to Electric Circuits. 5th ed. LC 00-42290. 2000. write for info. (0-471-38689-8) Wiley.

Dorf, Richard C., jt. auth. see Oldfield, John V.

Dorf, Richard C., jt. auth. see Smith, Ralph J.

Dorf, Richard C., jt. auth. see Tallarida, Ronald J.

Dorfer, Ingemar. Arms Deal: The Selling of the F-16. LC 82-13132. 287p. 1983. 55.00 (0-275-91718-5, C1718, Praeger Pubs) Greenwood.

— The Nordic Nations in the New Western Security Regime. LC 97-8532. (Woodrow Wilson Center Press Ser.). 128p. 1997. text 32.50 (0-943875-83-8); pap. text 15.95 (0-943875-82-X) Johns Hopkins.

Dorff, Elliot. Jewish Law & Modern Ideology. 1970. pap. 6.50 (0-8381-0209-3) USCJE.

Dorff, Elliot N. Knowing God: Jewish Journeys to the Unknowable. LC 92-23253. 320p. 1997. pap. 40.00 (1-56821-964-4) Aronson.

— Matters of Life & Death: Jewish Bio-Ethics. LC 97-36295. 474p. 1998. 34.95 (0-8276-0647-8) JPS Phila.

Dorff, Elliot N. & Newman, Louis E., eds. Contemporary Jewish Ethics & Morality: A Reader. 488p. (C). 1995. text 57.00 (0-19-509065-9); pap. text 33.95 (0-19-509066-7) OUP.

— Contemporary Jewish Theology: A Reader. 544p. (C). 1998. text 55.95 (0-19-511466-3); pap. text 31.95 (0-19-511467-1) OUP.

Dorff, Elliot N. & Rossett, Arthur. A Living Tree: The Roots & Growth of Jewish Law. LC 86-14581. 680p. (C). 1987. pap. text 23.95 (0-88706-460-4) State U NY Pr.

Dorff, Elliot N., et al. The Poor among Us: Jewish Tradition & Social Policy. LC 86-72482. 63p. (Orig.). 1986. pap. 7.50 (0-87495-084-8) Am Jewish Comm.

Dorff, Francis & Praem, O. Journey from Misery to Ministry: Living Creatively in a Broken World. LC 97-40572. 184p. 1998. pap. 12.95 (0-87793-646-3) Ave Maria.

— Simply Soulstirring: Writing As a Meditative Process. LC 97-49222. 144p. 1998. 12.95 (0-8091-0496-2) Paulist Pr.

Dorff, Pat. File...Don't Pile. (Illus.). 224p. 1986. pap. 9.95 (0-312-28931-6) St Martin.

Dorff, Robert H., jt. auth. see Steiner, Jurg.

Dorff, Robert H., jt. ed. see Helms, Robert F.

Dorfler, M., jt. auth. see Becker, K. H.

Dorflinger, Carolyn. Tomorrow Is Mom's Birthday. LC 93-19607. (Illus.). 32p. (J). (ps-3). 1994. 14.95 (1-879085-84-4, Whispering Coyote) Charlesbridge Pub.

— Tomorrow Is Mom's Birthday. (Illus.). 32p. (J). (ps-2). 1996. pap. 5.95 (1-879085-67-4, Whispering Coyote) Charlesbridge Pub.

— Tomorrow is Mom's Birthday. 1994. 11.15 (0-606-08889-X, Pub. by Turtleback) Demco.

Dorfman & Czerniak. Bone Tumors. LC 97-36939. (Illus.). 1280p. (C). (gr. 13). 1997. text 225.00 (0-8151-2746-4, 24078) Mosby Inc.

Dorfman, Albert, ed. see Conference on Antenatal Diagnosis (1970: Universit.

***Dorfman, Allan.** A House at War: A Ship & a Family Do Battle Against the Sea & the Nazis. LC 00-191025. 2000. pap. 18.00 (0-7388-2201-9) Xlibris Corp.

Dorfman, Ariel. Death & the Maiden. 64p. (Orig.). 1994. pap. 8.95 (0-14-024684-3, Penguin Bks) Viking Penguin.

— The Empire's Old Clothes: What the Lone Ranger, Babar & Other Innocent Heroes Do to Our Minds. 240p. 1996. pap. 12.95 (0-14-025637-7, Penguin Bks) Viking Penguin.

— Hacia la Liberacion del Lector Latinoamericano. (Rama Ser.). (SPA.). 286p. 1984. pap. 15.00 (0-910061-21-1, 1503) Ediciones Norte.

— Hard Rain. Shivers, George, tr. from SPA. (Readers International Ser.). 220p. (Orig.). (C). 1990. 18.95 (0-930523-77-6); pap. 10.95 (0-930523-78-4) Readers Intl.

— Heading North, Looking South: A Bilingual Journey. 1999. pap. 13.95 (0-14-028253-X) Viking Penguin.

— Heading South, Looking North: A Bilingual Journey. LC 97-37364. 256p. 1998. text 24.00 (0-374-16862-8) FS&G.

— Konfidenz. LC 95-37600. 192p. 1996. pap. 11.00 (0-679-76716-9) Random.

— Konfidenz. 176p. 1995. pap. 12.50 (0-679-76333-3) Vin Bks.

— Konfidenz: A Novel. LC 94-25903. 177p. 1994. text 17.00 (0-374-18218-3) FS&G.

— Missing Continents. 1999. pap. 19.95 (0-670-84453-5) Viking Penguin.

***Dorfman, Ariel.** The Nanny & the Iceberg. LC 98-48371. 353p. 1999. 25.00 (0-374-21898-6) FS&G.

— Rumbo Al Sur, Deseando El Norte. 1999. pap. 28.95 (968-406-804-2) F Planeta.

— Rumbo Al Sur, Deseando el Norte: Un Romance Bilingue. (SPA.). 1999. pap. text. write for info. (84-08-02808-1) Planeta Edit.

Dorfman, Ariel. Some Write to the Future: Essays on Contemporary Latin American Fiction. Shivers, George, tr. LC 90-24936. 271p. 1991. pap. 17.95 (0-8223-1269-7) Duke.

Dorfman, Ariel & de la Parra, Marco Antonio. Chile: From Within, 1973-1988. Meiselas, Susan, ed. 1990. 39.95 (0-393-02817-8) Norton.

Dorfman, Ariel & Mattelart, Armand. How to Read Donald Duck: Imperialist Ideology in the Disney Comic. 2nd enl. ed. Kunzle, David, tr. from SPA.Tr. of Para Leer al Pato Donald. (Illus.). 120p. 1991. pap. 13.95 (0-88477-023-0) Intl General.

Dorfman, Ben-Zion, jt. auth. see Dorfman, Rivka.

Dorfman, Cynthia H., ed. Japanese Education Today. (Illus.). 92p. (C). 1993. pap. text 30.00 (1-56806-383-0) DIANE Pub.

Dorfman, Cynthia H., ed. see Kanter, Patsy F.

Dorfman, Gerald A. The British Election of 1992 & Why It Did Not Help George Bush. LC 93-3008. (Hoover Essays Ser.: No. 3). 1993. pap. text 5.00 (0-8179-3662-9) Hoover Inst Pr.

— British Trade Unionism Against the Trades Union Congress. LC 82-83300. (Publication Ser.: No. 281). vii, 165p. 1983. 9.98 (0-8179-7811-9) Hoover Inst Pr.

Dorfman, Gerald A. & Duignan, Peter J., eds. The Politics in Western Europe. 2nd ed. (Publication Ser.: No. 404). 438p. 1991. pap. 18.95 (0-8179-9122-0) Hoover Inst Pr.

Dorfman, Gilllian & Galbraith, Sheila. Plants. (World Wildlife Ser.: No. S864-3). (Illus.). (J). (gr. k-3). 1989. pap. 3.95 (0-7214-5214-0, Ladybrd) Penguin Putnam.

***Dorfman, Gladys E.** Hannah Mae, the Little Pelican of Sarasota Bay. LC 99-71679. (Illus.). (J). (gr. k-6). 1999. 10.95 (0-9671111-0-2) Hannah Mae Ent.

— The Little Pelican Alphabet Book. LC 99-95315. (Illus.). (J). (ps-2). 1999. 14.95 (0-9671111-1-0) Hannah Mae Ent.

***Dorfman, H. A.** The Mental ABC's of Pitching: A Handbook for Performance Enhancement. LC 99-47262. 2000. pap. 19.95 (1-888698-29-2) Diamond Communications.

Dorfman, H. A. & Kuehl, Karl. The Mental Game of Baseball: A Guide to Peak Performance. 2nd ed. LC 89-1407. (Orig.). 1994. pap. 19.95 (0-912083-78-6) Diamond Communications.

Dorfman, Irene. Dirac Structures & Integrability of Nonlinear Evolution Equations. LC 92-43294. (Nonlinear Science, Theory & Applications Ser.). 188p. 1993. 175.00 (0-471-93893-9) Wiley.

Dorfman, Irene, et al. Algebraic Aspects of Integrable Systems: In Memory of Irene Dorfman. LC 96-31350. (Progress in Nonlinear Differential Equations & Their Applications Ser.). 1996. write for info. (3-7643-3835-0) Birkhauser.

— Algebraic Aspects of Integrable Systems: In Memory of Irene Dorfman. LC 96-31350. (Progress in Nonlinear Differential Equations & Their Applications Ser.). 352p. 1996. 88.50 (0-8176-3835-0) Birkhauser.

Dorfman, J., jt. ed. see Mitchell, Wesley C.

Dorfman, Jeffrey H. Bayesian Economics Through Numerical Methods: A Guide to Econometrics & Decision Making with Prior Information. LC 97-12147. 1997. 49.95 (0-387-98233-7) Spr-Verlag.

Dorfman, Joseph. The Economic Mind in American Civilization, 1606-1933, 5 vols. LC 64-7764. (Reprints of Economic Classics Ser.). 1969. reprint ed. 45.00 (0-678-04007-9); reprint ed. 45.00 (0-678-04008-7) Kelley.

— The Economic Mind in American Civilization, 1606-1933, 5 vols., 1. LC 64-7764. (Reprints of Economic Classics Ser.). 1966. reprint ed. 45.00 (0-678-04004-4) Kelley.

— The Economic Mind in American Civilization, 1606-1933, 5 vols., 2. LC 64-7764. (Reprints of Economic Classics Ser.). 1966. reprint ed. 45.00 (0-678-04005-2) Kelley.

— The Economic Mind in American Civilization, 1606-1933, 5 vols., 3. LC 64-7764. (Reprints of Economic Classics Ser.). 1969. reprint ed. 45.00 (0-678-00539-7) Kelley.

— The Economic Mind in American Civilization, 1606-1933, 5 vols., Set. LC 64-7764. (Reprints of Economic Classics Ser.). 1966. reprint ed. 195.00 (0-678-00111-1) Kelley.

— The Thorstein Veblen & His America. LC 64-7662. (Reprints of Economic Classics Ser.). (Illus.). 572p. 1992. reprint ed. 49.50 (0-678-00007-7) Kelley.

Dorfman, Joseph & Tugwell, Rexford G. Early American Policy. LC 72-6758. (Essay Index Reprint Ser.). 1977. reprint ed. 29.95 (0-8369-7268-6) Ayer.

Dorfman, Joseph, ed. see Adams, Henry C.

***Dorfman, Josif.** Exchange Sacrifice. (Illus.). 200p. 2000. pap. 19.95 (1-879479-79-6) ICE WA.

Dorfman, L. Cavalcade of American Ballroom Dancing. (Ballroom Dance Ser.). 1985. lib. bdg. 250.00 (0-87700-764-0) Revisionist Pr.

Dorfman, Len. C++ by Example: Object-Oriented Analysis, Design & Programming. LC 94-23458. 1995. pap. text 39.95 incl. disk (0-07-911954-9) McGraw.

— Game Graphics in C++ LC 95-9681. (Illus.). 448p. 1995. pap. 34.95 (0-07-911951-4) McGraw.

— Lightning-Fast Animation Graphics. LC 93-50714. 1994. 48.95 (0-07-017940-9, Windcrest) TAB Bks.

— Object-Oriented Assembly Language. 1991. 29.95 (0-8306-6754-7) McGraw-Hill Prof.

— Optimizing Microsoft C Library, 5.25. 1991. 34.95 (0-8306-2567-4) McGraw-Hill Prof.

— Optimizing Microsoft C Library, 3.5. 1991. 34.95 (0-8306-2568-2) McGraw-Hill Prof.

— Structured Assembly Language. (Illus.). 464p. 1990. 34.95 (0-8306-9484-6); pap. 24.95 (0-8306-3484-3) McGraw-Hill Prof.

— Structured Assembly Language. 1991. 24.95 (0-8306-6745-8); 24.95 (0-8306-7744-5) McGraw-Hill Prof.

Dorfman, Len & Ghosh, Narendra K. Developing Games That Learn LC 96-146. xiv, 280 p. 1996. 34.95 (1-884777-15-5) Manning Pubns.

— Developing Games That Learn. 275p. (C). 1996. pap. text 35.50 (0-13-569617-8) P-H.

Dorfman, Len & Neuberger, Marc J. C Memory Management Techniques. 1992. 32.95 (0-07-017808-9) McGraw.

— C Memory Management Techniques. (Illus.). 320p. 1992. pap. 32.95 (0-8306-4058-4, 4191, Windcrest) TAB Bks.

Dorfman, Len, jt. auth. see Neuberger, Marc J.

Dorfman, Leonard & Ghosh, Narendra K. Developing Games That Learn. LC 96-146. 1996. pap. 34.95 (0-13-509617-0) P-H.

Dorfman, Lisa. Vegetarian Sports Nutrition Guide: Peak Performance for Beginners to Gold Medalists. 256p. 1999. pap. 16.95 (1-56561-179-9) Wiley.

Dorfman, Lisa & Gold. The Vegetarian Sports Nutrition Guide: Peak Performance for Beginners to Gold Medalists. LC 99-25294. 270p. 1999. pap. 16.95 (0-471-34808-2) Wiley.

Dorfman, Lorraine T. The Sun Still Shone: Professors Talk about Retirement. LC 97-16580. 218p. 1997. text 21.95 (0-87745-601-1) U of Iowa Pr.

Dorfman, Louis. Otters on the Loose: An Otter's Adventure Story. LC 98-60174. 147p. (J). (gr. 2-9). 1998. pap. 8.95 (1-881636-35-6) Windsor Hse Pub Grp.

Dorfman, Mark H., et al. Tracking Toxic Chemicals: The Value of Materials Accounting Data. LC 97-36146. 1997. write for info. (0-918780-68-3) INFORM NY.

Dorfman, Mark S. Introduction to Risk Management & Insurance. 6th ed. LC 97-19089. 622p. (C). 1997. 97.00 (0-13-752106-5) P-H.

Dorfman, Mary, jt. ed. see Abelson, Philip H.

Dorfman, Melody F., jt. auth. see Kundell, James E.

Dorfman, Merlin & Thayer, Richard H. Software Engineering. LC 96-15910. 696p. 1996. pap. 60.00 (0-8186-7609-4) IEEE Comp Soc.

Dorfman, Merlin, jt. auth. see Anderson, Christine.

Dorfman, Nancy S. Innovation & Market Structure: Lessons from the Computer & Semiconductor Industries. LC 86-21619. 280p. 1987. text 34.95 (0-88730-185-1, HarpBusn) HarpInfo.

Dorfman, Nancy S., jt. ed. see Dorfman, Robert.

Dorfman, Rachelle A. Aging into the Twenty-First Century: The Exploration of Aspirations & Values. LC 93-11673. 240p. 1993. text 35.95 (0-87630-643-1) Brunner-Mazel.

— Clinical Social Work: Definition, Practice, & Vision. LC 96-15973. (Basic Principles into Practice Ser.: Vol. 9). 224p. 1996. pap. text 24.95 (0-87630-808-6) Brunner-Mazel.

— Paradigms of Clinical Social Work, 2. (Paradigms of Clinical Social Work Ser.). 1998. 48.95 (0-87630-882-5) Brunner-Mazel.

Dorfman, Rachelle A., ed. Paradigms of Clinical Social work. LC 88-2879. 464p. 1988. text 48.95 (0-87630-512-5) Brunner-Mazel.

Dorfman, Ralph, ed. Methods in Hormone Research: A Multi-Volume Work, 5 vols. Incl. Pt. C. Steroidal Activity in Experimental Animals & Man. 1966. 65.00 (0-12-221105-7); Pt. A. Steroidal Activity in Experimental Animals & Man. 1964. 74.50 (0-12-221103-0); Pt. B. Steroidal Activity in Experimental Animals & Man. 1965. 65.00 (0-12-221104-9); Vol. 1. 2nd ed. 1969. 78.00 (0-12-221161-8); Vol. 2a. 2nd ed. 1969. 78.00 (0-12-221162-6); write for info. (0-318-50304-2) Acad Pr.

***Dorfman, Rivka & Dorfman, Ben-Zion.** Synagogues Without Jews. (Illus.). 2000. 50.00 (0-8276-0692-3) JPS Phila.

Dorfman, Robert. Economic Theory & Public Decisions: Selected Essays of Robert Dorfman. LC 96-35153. (Economists of the Twentieth Century Ser.). 512p. 1997. 100.00 (1-85898-212-X) E Elgar.

— An Introduction to Chaos in Nonequilibrium Statistical Mechanics. LC 98-50545. (Lecture Notes in Physics Ser.: No. 14). (Illus.). 300p. (C). 1999. pap. text 34.95 (0-521-65589-7) Cambridge U Pr.

Dorfman, Robert, ed. Measuring Benefits of Government Investments. LC 79-28577. (Brookings Institution, National Committee on Government Finance, Studies of Government Finance). (Illus.). 429p. 1980. reprint ed. lib. bdg. 79.50 (0-313-22307-6, DOMB) Greenwood.

— Measuring Benefits of Government Investments: Papers Presented at a Conference of Experts: November 7-9, 1963. LC 65-18313. (Brookings Institution Studies of Government Finance). 445p. reprint ed. pap. 138.00 (0-608-12176-2, 202537200043) Bks Demand.

Dorfman, Robert, et al, eds. Models for Managing Regional Water Quality. LC 72-87770. (Illus.). 471p. 1973. 43.00 (0-674-57825-2) HUP.

Dorfman, Robert & Dorfman, Nancy S., eds. The Economics of the Environment: Selected Readings. 3rd ed. LC 92-17707. (C). 1993. pap. 28.00 (0-393-96310-1) Norton.

Dorfman, Robert, et al. Linear Programming & Economic Analysis. ix, 525p. 1987. reprint ed. pap. text 14.95 (0-486-65491-5) Dover.

Dorfman, Ron, ed. see Yin, James & Young, Shi.

Dorfman, Ronald F., jt. ed. see Ziegler, John L.

***Dorfman, William I. & Hersen, Michel.** Understanding Psychological Assessment. LC 00-33114. (Perspectives on Individual Differences Ser.). 2000. pap. write for info. (0-306-46268-0, Kluwer Plenum) Kluwer Academic.

D

An Asterisk (*) at the beginning of an entry indicates that the title is appearing for the first time.

Dorfman, Yitzchak. Maggid of Mezritch. 133p. 1989. 13.95 (*0-944070-16-7*) Targum Pr.

***Dorfmann, Al & Muhr, Alan, eds.** Constitutive Models for Rubber: Proceedings of the First European Conference, Vienna, Austria, 9-10 September 1999. (Illus.). 316p. 1999. text 80.00 (*90-5809-113-9*) A A Balkema.

Dorfmueller, T. & Pecora, Robert, eds. Rotational Dynamics of Small & Macromolecules. (Lecture Notes in Physics Ser.: Vol. 293). 250p. 1987. 34.95 (*0-387-18688-3*) Spr-Verlag.

Dorfmuller, T., ed. Reactive & Flexible Molecules in Liquids. (C). 1989. text 245.00 (*0-7923-0469-1*) Kluwer Academic.

Dorfner. Neural Networks & a New Artificial Intelligence, Vol. 1. (ITCP-UK Computer Science Ser.). 1996. mass mkt. 39.95 (*1-85032-172-8*) ITCP.

Dorfner, John J. Kerouac - Visions of Lowell. 60p. 1993. pap. 11.95 (*0-9636046-7-8*) Cooper St Pubns.

— Kerouac - Visions of Rocky Mount. 65p. 1991. pap. 11.95 (*0-9636046-4-3*) Cooper St Pubns.

— Milkman's Matinee. 121p. (Orig.). 1994. pap. 9.95 (*0-9636046-8-6*) Cooper St Pubns.

Dorfner, Konrad, ed. Ion Exchangers. xxxii, 1495p. (C). 1990. lib. bdg. 523.10 (*3-11-010341-9*) De Gruyter.

Dorgan, et al. Remembrance, Reunion, & Revival: Celebrating a Decade of Appalachian Studies. (Proceedings of the Appalachian Studies Conference). (Orig.). (C). 1988. pap. text 10.95 (*0-913239-52-6*) Appalach Consortium.

Dorgan, Charity A. Job Seekers Guide to Private & Public Companies, 4 Vols. 2nd ed. 1993. 390.00 (*0-8103-8065-X*) Gale.

— Job Seekers Guide to Private & Public Companies, Vol. 1. 2nd ed. 1993. 99.00 (*0-8103-8066-8*) Gale.

— Job Seekers Guide to Private & Public Companies, Vol. 2. 2nd ed. 1993. 99.00 (*0-8103-8067-6*) Gale.

— Job Seekers Guide to Private & Public Companies, Vol. 3. 2nd ed. 1993. 99.00 (*0-8103-8068-4*) Gale.

— Job Seekers Guide to Private & Public Companies, Vol. 4. 2nd ed. 1993. 99.00 (*0-8103-8069-2*) Gale.

Dorgan, Charity Anne, ed. Statistical Record of Health & Medicine. 94th ed. (Illus.). 1218p. 1994. 109.00 (*0-8103-9745-5*) Gale.

— Statistical Record of the Environment. 3rd ed. LC 97-190579. 1118p. 1995. 109.00 (*0-8103-6432-8*) Gale.

Dorgan, Ethel J. Luther Halsey Gulick. LC 78-143055. 1982. 20.95 (*0-8434-0450-7*, Pub. by McGrath NH) Ayer.

Dorgan, Howard. The Airwaves of Zion: Radio & Religion in Appalachia. LC 92-40704. (Illus.). 248p. (Orig.). (C). 1993. pap. 18.95 (*0-87049-797-9*); text 34.00 (*0-87049-796-0*) U of Tenn Pr.

— Giving Glory to God in Appalachia: Worship Practices of Six Baptist Subdenominations. LC 87-5914. (Illus.). 254p. 1987. pap. 15.95 (*0-87049-666-2*) U of Tenn Pr.

— In the Hands of a Happy God: The "No-Hellers" of Central Appalachia. LC 96-25214. (Illus.). 224p. 1997. 34.00 (*0-87049-961-0*); pap. text 17.00 (*0-87049-962-9*) U of Tenn Pr.

— The Old Regular Baptists of Central Appalachia: Brothers & Sisters in Hope. LC 89-4832. (Illus.). 296p. 1989. 31.00 (*0-87049-616-6*) U of Tenn Pr.

Dorgan, Howard, jt. ed. see Logue, Calvin M.

Dorgan, Joseph V. The Guy Sleeping over Me Is Misty in the Peak: The World War One Naval Diaries of Joseph V. Dorgan. deluxe ed. Travers, Douglas N., ed. (Illus.). 373p. 1997. 65.00 (*1-929013-00-0*) Oakhill Pubg.

Dorgan, Theo, ed. Irish Poetry since Kavanagh. 176p. 1996. pap. 12.95 (*1-85182-240-2*, Pub. by Four Cts Pr); boxed set 35.00 (*1-85182-239-9*, Pub. by Four Cts Pr) Intl Spec Bk.

Dorge, Ray & Sibley, Gail. A Guide to Pet & Companion Birds. 124p. 1998. pap. 24.95 (*0-9587266-1-2*) Avian Pubns.

Dorge, Valerie & Howlett, F. Carey. Painted Wood History & Conservation: Proceedings of a Symposium at Williamsburg, Virginia, November 1994. LC 97-36527. (Symposium Proceedings). 576p. 1998. pap. 75.00 (*0-89236-501-3*, Pub. by J P Getty Trust) OUP.

***Dorge, Valerie & Jones, Sharon.** Building an Emergency Plan: A Guide for Museums & Other Cultural Institutions. LC 98-55487. (Illus.). 208p. (Orig.). 2000. pap. 39.95 (*0-89236-551-X*, Pub. by J P Getty Trust) OUP.

Dorgeloh, Heidrun, ed. Inversion in Modern English: Form & Function. LC 96-6511. (Studies in Discourse & Grammar: Vol. 6). x, 236p. 1997. lib. bdg. 69.00 (*1-55619-372-6*) J Benjamins Pubng Co.

Dorham, K. Blue Bossa Octet. 1995. pap. text 23.00 (*0-7935-4829-2*, 00000720) H Leonard.

— Monaco Sextet. 1995. pap. text 20.00 (*0-7935-4827-6*, 00000660) H Leonard.

***Dorhs, Michael.** Uber Den Tod Hinaus: Grundzuge Einer Individualeschatologie in der Theologie Rudolf Bultmanns. 397p. 1999. 56.95 (*3-631-34383-3*) P Lang Pubng.

Dori, D. & Bruckstein, A. Shape, Structure & Pattern Recognition. 400p. 1995. text 113.00 (*981-02-2239-4*) World Scientific Pub.

***Dori, Dov.** Object-Process Methodology: A Comprehensive Systems Development Approach. 300p. 1999. 59.95 (*3-540-65471-2*) Spr-Verlag.

Doria, Charles. Selected Poems, June 1988. 24p. 1990. pap. 9.00 (*0-916258-23-8*) Left Hand Bks.

— Short. 50p. (Orig.). 1981. pap. 10.00 (*0-915066-98-X*) Assembling Pr.

— Short. deluxe limited ed. 50p. (Orig.). 1981. 15.00 (*0-915066-97-1*) Assembling Pr.

— The Toy Palace: A Libretto for Animals, People & Machines. 32p. (Orig.). 1991. pap. 9.00 (*1-880516-02-0*) Left Hand Bks.

Doria, Charles, ed. The Tenth Muse: Classical Drama in Translation. LC 77-88695. vi, 587p. 1980. 30.00 (*0-8040-0781-0*) Swallow.

Doria, Charles, et al, eds. Assembling Thirteen Point One. (Thirteenth in Our Assembling Annual Ser.). (Illus.). 85p. 1987. 100.00 (*0-915066-51-3*) Assembling Pr.

— Assembling Thirteen Point Two. 850p. 1985. 100.00 (*0-915066-52-1*) Assembling Pr.

— Thirteenth Assembling Annual. (Illus.). 100p. (Orig.). 1987. pap. 50.00 (*0-915066-56-4*) Assembling Pr.

Doria, Charles, ed. see Lenowitz, Harris.

D'Oria, Domenico. Dictionnaire et Ideologie. (FRE.). 1989. 95.00 (*0-7859-8709-6*, 8875142858) Fr & Eur.

Doria, R. S. Environmental Impact of Narmada Sagar Project. (C). 1990. 29.00 (*81-7024-355-6*, Pub. by Ashish Pub Hse) S Asia.

Doria, R. S., et al. Man, Development & Environment. 1990. 47.50 (*81-7024-288-6*, Pub. by Ashish Pub Hse) S Asia.

Dorian, contrib. by. Lullabys for Starry Nights. (J). pap. 10.98 (*0-9647786-1-0*, 3001-4) Baby Music.

Dorian, A. & Osenton, J. Fachwoerterbuch der Luftfahrt. (ENG, FRE, GER, ITA & SPA.). 1964. 250.00 (*0-8288-6773-9*, M15468) Fr & Eur.

Dorian, A. F. Dictionary of Science & Technology. 2nd rev. ed. (ENG & GER.). 1130p. 1981. reprint ed. 263.00 (*0-444-41649-8*) Elsevier.

— Dictionary of Science & Technology: German-English. 2nd ed. (ENG & GER.). 1130p. 1981. 26300.00 (*0-444-41997-7*) Elsevier.

— Dorian's Dictionary of Science & Technology: English - French. (ENG & FRE.). 1586p. 1979. 350.00 (*0-8288-9273-3*, M7892) Fr & Eur.

— Dorian's Dictionary of Science & Technology: English - German. (ENG & GER.). 1402p. 1989. reprint ed. 350.00 (*0-8288-9275-X*, M7894) Fr & Eur.

— Dorian's Dictionary of Science & Technology: French - English. (ENG & FRE.). 1086p. 1980. 350.00 (*0-8288-9274-1*, F98320) Fr & Eur.

— Dorian's Dictionary of Science & Technology: German - English. (ENG & GER.). 1120p. 1981. 350.00 (*0-8288-9276-8*, M7895) Fr & Eur.

— Elsevier's Dictionary of Chemistry Including Terms from Biochemistry. (ENG, FRE, GER, ITA & SPA.). 692p. 1983. 244.00 (*0-444-42230-7*) Elsevier.

— Elsevier's Dictionary of Chemistry Including Terms from Biochemistry. (ENG, FRE, GER, ITA & SPA.). 686p. 1989. 295.00 (*0-8288-9223-7*, M13054) Fr & Eur.

— Elsevier's Dictionary of Mining & Mineralogy in English, French, German & Italian. (ENG, FRE, GER & ITA.). 300p. 1992. 295.00 (*0-8288-9247-4*) Fr & Eur.

— Elsevier's Encyclopaedic Dictionary of Medicine Vol. 1: General Medicine, Defined in English. (ENG, FRE, GER, ITA & SPA.). 1176p. 1989. reprint ed. 495.00 (*0-8288-9310-1*, M1710) Fr & Eur.

— Elsevier's Encyclopaedic Dictionary of Medicine Vol. 2: Anatomy, Defined in English. (ENG, FRE, GER, ITA & SPA.). 602p. 1988. 350.00 (*0-8288-9311-X*, M1715) Fr & Eur.

— Elsevier's Encyclopaedic Dictionary of Medicine Vol. 3: Biology, Genetics & Biochemistry, Defined in English. (ENG, FRE, GER, ITA & SPA.). 708p. 1989. 375.00 (*0-8288-9312-8*) Fr & Eur.

— Elsevier's Encyclopaedic Dictionary of Medicine Vol. 4: Therapeutic Substances, Defined in English. (ENG, FRE, GER, ITA & SPA.). 492p. 1990. 295.00 (*0-8288-9313-6*, M1730) Fr & Eur.

— Elsevier's Encyclopedic Dictionary of Medicine: In English (With Definitions), French, German, Italian, & Spanish; Part A: General Medicine. 1188p. 1987. 332.00 (*0-444-42823-2*) Elsevier.

— Elsevier's Encyclopedia Dictionary of Medicine Part B: Anatomy - in English (with definitions), French, German, Italian, & Spanish. 616p. 1988. 332.00 (*0-444-42824-0*) Elsevier.

— Elsevier's Encyclopedic Dictionary of Medicine: In English (with Definitions), French, German, Italian, & Spanish, Part C: Biology, Genetics & Biochemistry. 720p. 1989. 250.50 (*0-444-87293-0*) Elsevier.

— Elseviers's Encyclopaedic Dictionary of Medicine Pt. D: Therapeutic Substances. (ENG, FRE, GER, ITA & SPA.). 504p. 1990. 200.00 (*0-444-42826-7*) Elsevier.

Dorian, A. F., compiled by. Elsevier's Dictionary of Mining & Mineralogy. LC 92-35138. (ENG, FRE, GER & ITA.). 310p. 1993. 190.00 (*0-444-89039-4*) Elsevier.

Dorian, A. F., ed. Dorian's Dictionary of Science & Technology, Vol. I. 1596p. 1979. 263.00 (*0-444-41829-6*) Elsevier.

— Dorian's Dictionary of Science & Technology, Vol. II. 1096p. 1980. 263.00 (*0-444-41911-X*) Elsevier.

Dorian, David H. Shock Around the Clock. (KidBacks Ser.). (Illus.). (J). (gr. 3-7). 1997. pap. 5.99 (*0-614-28941-6*) Random Bks Yng Read.

Dorian, Frederick. The History of Music in Performance: The Art of Musical Interpretation from the Renaissance to Our Day. LC 80-28028. (Illus.). 387p. 1981. reprint ed. lib. bdg. 38.50 (*0-313-22893-0*, DOHM, Greenwood Pr) Greenwood.

— Musical Workshop. LC 77-138109. (Illus.). 368p. 1971. reprint ed. lib. bdg. 69.50 (*0-8371-5685-8*, DOMW, Greenwood Pr) Greenwood.

Dorian, James P. Minerals, Energy & Economic Development in China. (Illus.). 304p. 1994. text 75.00 (*0-19-828744-5*) OUP.

Dorian, James P., et al, eds. CIS Energy & Minerals Development: Prospects, Problems, & Opportunities for International Cooperation. LC 93-19530. (GeoJournal Library: Vol. 25). 388p. (C). 1993. lib. bdg. 174.50 (*0-7923-2323-8*) Kluwer Academic.

Dorian, M., tr. see Caraion, Ion.

Dorian, Margery & Gulland, Frances. Telling Stories Through Movement. LC 73-87493. vi, 66 p. 1974. write for info. (*0-8224-6940-5*) Fearon Teacher Aids.

Dorian, Mark. Keys of the Kingdom: Piano Interludes for Worship. 48p. 1999. pap. 9.95 (*0-687-07485-1*) Abingdon.

Dorian, Michael. The Nektonic Facteur. Bifsso, John, ed. LC 98-60067. 100p. 1998. pap. 10.95 (*0-9654452-1-6*) Silk City Pr.

Dorian, Nancy C., ed. Investigating Obsolescence: Studies in Language Contraction & Death. (Studies in the Social & Cultural Foundations of Language: No. 7). (Illus.). 464p. (C). 1989. text 80.00 (*0-521-32405-X*) Cambridge U Pr.

— Investigating Obsolescence: Studies in Language Contraction & Death. (Studies in the Social & Cultural Foundations of Language: No. 7). (Illus.). 459p. (C). 1992. pap. text 26.95 (*0-521-43757-1*) Cambridge U Pr.

Dorian, Robert H. Dead Without a Fight: Diseases & Their Treatment in the Mexican War. 43p. 1998. pap. 7.95 (*0-9647895-3-1*) FLPB Pr.

Dorian-Ross, David. Tai Chi Companion. pap. 8.90 (*0-9651502-1-4*) Tai Chi Paradise.

Dorian, Stacy W., compiled by. Homosexuality & the Law: An Annotated Bibliography. (Legal Bibliography Ser.: No. 32). 31p. 1989. 30.00 (*0-935630-30-9*) U of Tex Tarlton Law Lib.

Dorian, Terry. Health Begins in Him: Biblical Steps to Optimal Health & Nutrition. LC 94-79916. 224p. 1995. pap. 10.99 (*1-56384-081-2*) Huntington Hse.

— Hormonal Imbalance: The Madness & the Message. LC 98-75709. 208p. 1999. pap. 12.99 (*1-56384-156-8*) Huntington Hse.

Dorian, Terry & Thomas, Rita M. The Cookbook: Health Begins in Him. LC 96-61759. 208p. 1997. pap. 12.99 (*1-56384-127-4*, Vital Issue Pr) Huntington Hse.

Dorian, Terry & Tyler, Zan P. Anyone Can Homeschool: How to Find What Works for You. LC 95-76166. 224p. 1996. pap. 12.99 (*1-56384-095-2*, Pub. by Huntington Hse) BookWorld.

Doriani, Beth M. Emily Dickinson, Daughter of Prophecy. LC 95-11037. 248p. (C). 1996. 35.00 (*0-87023-999-6*) U of Mass Pr.

— For All You're Worth: Getting That Academic Job in Today's Market. (Illus.). 200p. 1999. pap. 30.00 (*0-938609-34-3*) Graduate Group.

Doriani, Daniel M. Getting the Message: A Plan for Interpreting & Applying the Bible. 227p. (Orig.). (C). 1996. pap. 14.99 (*0-87552-238-6*) P & R Pubng

Dorich, William. Kosovo. (Illus.). 208p. 1992. 100.00 (*1-882383-00-1*); pap. 50.00 (*0-317-05074-5*) Kosovo Charity.

Dorigato, A., jt. auth. see Mazzario, G.

Dorigato, Attila, jt. auth. see Mazzariol, Giuseppe

Dorigato, Attilia. Vetri Veneziani; Ohira: Collezione Pasta Vitrea. LC 98-202629. 1998. pap. text 19.95 (*88-7743-191-1*) Arsenale Editrice.

Dorigo, Joe. Mafia. 1992. 17.98 (*1-55521-788-5*) Bk Sales Inc.

Dorigo, Marco & Colombetti, Marco. Robot Shaping: An Experiment in Behavior Engineering. LC 97-16342. (Illus.). 300p. 1997. 37.50 (*0-262-04164-2*, Bradford Bks) MIT Pr.

Dorikens-Vanpraet, L., et al, eds. Positron Annihilation: Proceedings of the 8th International Conference. 1032p. (C). 1989. text 156.00 (*9971-5-0733-1*) World Scientific Pub.

***Dorin, Patrick C.** Chicago & North Western System Passenger Service. (Illus.). 128p. 2000. 26.95 (*1-883089-51-4*, 130610AE, Pub. by TLC VA) Motorbooks Intl.

— Missouri Pacific Lines. (Illus.). 160p. 2000. 28.95 (*1-883089-54-9*, 130613AE, Pub. by TLC VA) Motorbooks Intl.

Dorin, Patrick C. Western Pacific Locomotives - Cars. (Illus.). 112p. 1998. 24.95 (*1-883089-34-4*) TLC VA.

Doring, August. Die Kunstlehre Des Aristoteles. viii, 341p. 1972. reprint ed. write for info. (*3-487-04503-6*) G Olms Pubs.

***Doring, Brigitte, et al.** Uber Sprachhandeln im Spannungsfeld Von Reflektieren und Benennen. (GER.). 356p. 1999. 51.95 (*3-631-33887-2*) P Lang Pubng.

Doring, Denise, jt. auth. see Murphy, Robert J.

Doring, G. & Doring, Rudolphi. Tiefkuhl Lexikon. 19.95 (*0-8288-7713-0*, M7666) Fr & Eur.

Doring, G. & Rudolphi. Tiefkuhl Lexikon. (GER.). 239p. 19.95 (*3-87150-020-8*, M-7666) Fr & Eur.

Doring, P. F. Learn German for English Speakers. (ENG & GER.). pap. 20.95 (*0-87557-027-5*) Saphrograph.

Doring, Rudolphi, jt. auth. see Doring, G.

Dorinson, A. & Ludema, Kenneth C. Mechanics & Chemistry in Lubrication. (Tribology Ser.: Vol. 9). xvi, 634p. 1985. 288.50 (*0-444-42492-X*) Elsevier.

***Dorinson, Joseph.** Jackie Robinson: Race, Sports & the American Dream. 296p. 1999. pap. 19.95 (*0-7656-0318-7*) M E Sharpe.

Dorinson, Joseph & Warmund, Joram, eds. Jackie Robinson: Race, Sports & the American Dream. LC 98-38327. (Illus.). 296p. (gr. 13). 1998. text 36.95 (*0-7656-0317-9*) M E Sharpe.

Dorio, Marc. Complete Idiot's Guide to Getting the Job You Want. 2nd ed. (Complete Idiot's Guides Ser.). 1998. pap. text 16.95 (*0-02-862723-7*) Macmillan Gen Ref

— Complete Idiot's Guide to the Perfect Interview. LC 97-73155. 320p. 1997. 14.95 (*0-02-861945-5*) Macmillan Gen Ref.

***Dorio, Marc.** Complete Idiot's Guide to the Perfect Interview. 2nd ed. (Complete Idiot's Guides (Lifestyle) Ser.). 352p. 2000. pap. text 14.95 (*0-02-863890-5*, Alpha Ref) Macmillan Gen Ref.

Dorio, Marc. Staffing Problem Solver for Human Resource Professionals & Managers. 288p. 1994. 125.95 (*0-471-00630-0*) Wiley.

Dorion, Betty. Bay Girl. 160p. (J). 1999. pap. 5.95 (*1-55050-132-1*) Genl Dist Srvs.

Dorion, Betty F. Melanie Bluelake's Dream. LC 95-216575. 156p. (J). (gr. 4-7). 1995. pap. 4.95 (*1-55050-081-3*, Pub. by Coteau) Genl Dist Srvs.

Dorion, David H. Shock Around the Clock, Timely Tales of Terror. (Kidbacks Ser.). (J). 1997. 11.09 (*0-606-11839-X*, Pub. by Turtleback) Demco.

Dorion, Helene. The Edges of Light. (Essential Poets Ser.: No. 60). 108p. 1995. pap. 10.00 (*0-920717-95-0*) Guernica Editions.

Dorion, Henri & Poirier, Jean. Lexique des Termes Utiles a l'Etude des Noms de Lieux. (FRE.). 162p. 1975. pap. 24.95 (*0-8288-5931-0*, M6168) Fr & Eur.

Dorion, Theo. Manual of Ocular Fundus Examination. LC 98-2711. 576p. 1998. pap. text 65.00 (*0-7506-9987-6*) Buttrwrth-Heinemann.

Doriot, G., tr. see See, Henri E.

Doris. Listen . . . the Speaking Heart. LC 79-50254. 1979. pap. 3.75 (*0-87516-361-0*) DeVorss.

Doris, Carol, ed. see McKay, Cynthia.

Doris, Ellen. The Big Book of Nature Projects. (Illus.). (J). (gr. 3-9). 1997. 17.95 (*0-614-29118-6*) Thames Hudson.

— The Big Books of Nature Projects. LC 96-61458. (Real Kids/Real Science Ser.). (Illus.). 128p. (Orig.). (J). (gr. 3-8). 1997. pap. 17.95 (*0-500-01773-5*, Pub. by Thames Hudson) Norton.

— Doing What Scientists Do: Children Learn to Investigate Their World. LC 90-48126. (Illus.). 194p. (Orig.). (C). 1991. pap. text 22.00 (*0-435-08309-0*, 08309) Heinemann.

***Doris, Ellen.** Life at the Top: Discoveries in a Tropical Forest Canopy. (Turnstone Rain Forest Pilot Bks.). (Illus.). (J). 2000. 27.12 (*0-7398-2220-9*); pap. 7.95 (*0-7398-2229-2*) Raintree Steck-V.

Doris, Ellen. Meet the Arthropods. LC 95-61699. (Real Kids/Real Science Bks.). (Illus.). 64p. (J). (gr. 4-10). 1996. 16.95 (*0-500-19010-0*, Pub. by Thames Hudson) Norton.

— Ornithology. LC 93-61888. (Real Kids - Real Science Ser.). (Illus.). 63p. (J). 1994. 16.95 (*0-500-19008-9*, Pub. by Thames Hudson) Norton.

— Real Kids - Real Science Books: Entomology, Marine Biology, Invertebrate Zoology, Entomology. (Real Kids/Real Science Ser.). (Illus.). 48p. 1993. 16.95 (*0-500-19004-6*, Pub. by Thames Hudson) Norton.

— Real Kids - Real Science Books: Entomology, Marine Biology, Invertebrate Zoology, Invertebrate Zoology. (Real Kids/Real Science Ser.). (Illus.). 48p. 1993. 16.95 (*0-500-19005-4*, Pub. by Thames Hudson) Norton.

— Real Kids - Real Science Books: Entomology, Marine Biology, Invertebrate Zoology, Marine Biology. (Real Kids/Real Science Ser.). (Illus.). 48p. 1993. 16.95 (*0-500-19007-0*, Pub. by Thames Hudson) Norton.

— Vertebrates. Date not set. 16.95 (*0-500-19009-7*) Thames Hudson.

— Woods, Ponds, & Fields. LC 93-61889. (Real Kids - Real Science Ser.). (Illus.). 63p. (J). 1994. 16.95 (*0-500-19006-2*, Pub. by Thames Hudson) Norton.

Doris, John, ed. The Suggestibility of Children's Recollections: Implications for Eyewitness Testimony. 208p. 1991. pap. 19.95 (*1-55798-306-2*) Am Psychol.

Doris, Lillian, ed. The American Way in Taxation: Internal Revenue, 1862-1963. LC 94-76047. xiv, 301p. 1994. reprint ed. 45.00 (*0-89941-877-5*, 308230) W S Hein.

Doris, Lillian & Miller, Bessie M. Complete Secretary's Handbook. 5th ed. 596p. 1986. 24.95 (*0-13-163410-0*, Busn) P-H.

Doris, Stacy. Kildare. 99p. (Orig.). 1994. pap. 9.95 (*0-937804-59-2*) Segue NYC.

***Doris, Stacy.** Paramour. 134p. 2000. pap. 9.00 (*1-928650-05-8*, Pub. by Krupskaya) SPD-Small Pr Dist.

Doris, Stacy, jt. ed. see Cole, Norma.

Doriss, Barbara B. The Little Sister Jacket & Vest Book. (Illus.). 32p. 1985. pap. 8.00 (*0-932946-17-8*) Burdett CA.

Dorit. Zoology. (C). 1991. pap. text, teacher ed., suppl. ed. 34.00 (*0-03-030508-X*) Harcourt Coll Pubs.

Dorit, Robert, et al. Zoology. 1136p. (C). 1991. text 102.50 (*0-03-030504-7*, Pub. by SCP) Harcourt.

Dority, G. Kim, ed. A Guide to Reference Books for Small & Medium-Sized Libraries, 1984-1994. xviii, 372p. 1995. lib. bdg. 49.00 (*1-56308-103-2*) Libs Unl.

Doriver, ed. see Ibanez, Aniceto & Resano, Francisco.

Dorizas, H. The Greek Children Reader. 1976. pap., wbk. ed. 2.50 (*0-685-79097-5*) Divry.

Dorizas, H. & Aesop. Aesop's Fables Reader. 1976. pap., wbk. ed. 2.50 (*0-685-73008-5*) Divry.

***Dorizon, Jacques.** Chenard & Walcker: Le Constructeur a l'aigle. 1998. 44.95 (*2-908182-77-7*, Pub. by Histoire) Combined Pub.

Dorjahn, Alfred P. Political Forgiveness in Old Athens: The Amnesty of 403 B.C. (Northwestern University. Humanities Ser.: No. 13). reprint ed. 27.50 (*0-404-50713-1*) AMS Pr.

Dorjahn, Vernon R. & Isaac, Barry L., eds. Essays on the Economic Anthropology of Liberia & Sierra Leone. (Liberian Research Working Papers: No. 6). 24.00 (*0-686-33173-7*) Arden Assocs.

Dorje, Gyurme. Nepal & Tibet Handbook with Bhutan. (Handbooks of the World Ser.). (Illus.). 768p. 1996. 24.95 (*0-8442-4901-7*, Passprt Bks) NTC Contemp Pub Co.

***Dorje, Gyurme.** Tibet Handbook. 2nd ed. (Footprint Handbooks Ser.). (Illus.). 800p. 1999. pap. 21.95 (*0-8442-2190-2*, 21902) NTC Contemp Pub Co.

Dorje, Gyurme, ed. & tr. see Rinpoche, Dudjom & Dorje, Jigdrel Y.

D

Dorje, Jigdrel Y., jt. auth. see Rinpoche, Dudjom.

Dorje, Lama S., tr. Mahamudra Teachings of the Supreme Siddhas: The Eighth Situpa, Tanpa' Nyinchay on "The Aspiration Prayer on Mahamudra of Definitive Meaning" by the Third Karmapa, Rangjung Dorje. LC 93-40280. 208p. 1995. pap. 15.95 (*1-55939-025-5*) Snow Lion Pubns.

Dorje, Lotsawa T., tr. see Zongtse, Champa T.

Dorje, Rinjing. Tales of Uncle Tompa: The Legendary Rascal of Tibet. LC 97-12947. 160p. 1997. pap. text 13.95 (*1-886449-40-6*) Barrytown Ltd.

— Tales of Uncle Tompa: The Legendary Rascal of Tibet. LC 75-18105. (Illus.). 80p. 1975. pap. 15.00 (*0-915880-02-4*) Dorje Ling.

Dorjee, Pema. Stupa & Its Technology: A Tibeto-Buddhist Perspective. LC 96-905656. (C). 1996. 46.00 (*81-208-1301-4*, Pub. by Motilal Bnarsidass) S Asia.

Dorjee, Tenzin, tr. see Komito, David R.

Dorji, C. T. Blue Annals of Bhutan. LC 97-904769. 1998. 22.00 (*81-259-0436-0*, Pub. by Vikas) S Asia.

Dorji, C. T. An Introduction to Bhutanese Languages. LC 97-905524. (Illus.). 1997. 19.95 (*81-259-0437-9*, Pub. by Vikas) S Asia.

Dorken, Herbert. The Financing & Organization of Universal Healthcare. (Report to the National Academies of Practice Healthcare Utilization & Costs Ser.: Vol. 3). 1994. pap. text. write for info. (*0-9637577-1-7*) Fnd Behav Hlth.

Dorken, Herbert, et al. The Professional Psychologist Today: New Developments in Law, Health Insurance, & Health Practice. LC 75-24011. (Jossey-Bass Behavioral Science Ser.). 416p. reprint ed. pap. 129.00 (*0-608-15898-4*, 203081300070) Bks Demand.

— Professional Psychology in Transition: Meeting Today's Challenges. LC 85-45900. (Jossey-Bass Social & Behavioral Science Ser.). 440p. reprint ed. pap. 136.40 (*0-7837-2512-4*, 204267100006) Bks Demand.

Dorkenoo, Efua. Cutting the Rose: Female Genital Mutilation: the Practice & Its Prevention. (Illus.). 192p. 1995. 24.95 (*1-873194-60-9*, Pub. by Minority Rts Pubns) Paul & Co Pubs.

Dorkenou, Efuu. Cutting the Rose: Female Genital Mutilation: The Practice & its Prevention. 192p. pap. 18.95 (*1-873194-95-1*, Pub. by Minority Rts Pubns) Paul & Co Pubs.

Dorkin, C. M., jt. auth. see Munden, D. L.

Dorkin, Evan. Fun with Milk & Cheese. 96p. 1997. pap. 11.95 (*0-943151-07-4*) Slave Labor Bks.

— Hectic Planet Bk. 1: Dim Future. (Illus.). 120p. 1998. pap. 12.95 (*0-943151-21-X*) Slave Labor Bks.

— Hectic Planet Bk. 2: Checkered Past. (Illus.). 144p. 1998. pap. 14.95 (*0-943151-22-8*) Slave Labor Bks.

***Dorko, Ernest A., ed.** Gas & Chemical Lasers & Intense Beam Applications II. 194p. 1999. pap. text 72.00 (*0-8194-3082-X*) SPIE.

Dorko, Ernest A. & Moler, Jeffrey L., eds. Gas & Chemical Lasers & Intense Beam Applications, Vol. 3268. 370p. 1998. 116.00 (*0-8194-2707-1*) SPIE.

Dorko, Ernest A., jt. ed. see Sze, Robert C.

Dorko, William D., jt. ed. see Zielinski, Walter L., Jr.

Dorksen, Robert E., photos by. Strength Enough. (Illus.). 110p. 1980. pap. 10.95 (*0-911704-25-6*) Western Res.

Dorland. Diccionario Medico Dorland (Bolsillo) (SPA.). 900p. 1988. pap. 45.00 (*0-7859-6243-3*, 8476152825) Fr & Eur.

— Diccionario Medico Illustrado. 27th ed. (SPA., Illus.). 1991. text 55.00 (*0-07-104004-8*) McGraw.

— Dorland's Illustrated Medical Dictionary. 29th ed. (C). 2000. text 49.95 (*0-7216-6254-4*, W B Saunders Co) Harcrt Hlth Sci Grp.

***Dorland.** Dorland's Pocket Medical Dictionary. 26th ed. 2001. pap. text. write for info. (*0-7216-8281-2*) Harcrt Hlth Sci Grp.

Dorland. Dorland's Spanish English Illustrated Medical Dictionary. 27th ed. (ENG & SPA., Illus.). 1992. 250.00 (*0-7859-7485-7*, 8476158920) Fr & Eur.

— Illustrated Medical Dictionary. 28th deluxe ed. (Illus.). 1994. text 85.00 (*0-7216-5577-7*, W B Saunders Co) Harcrt Hlth Sci Grp.

Dorland, Frank. Holy Ice: Bridge to the Subconscious. LC 92-13885. (Illus.). 216p. 1992. pap. 12.95 (*1-880090-02-3*) Galde Pr.

Dorland, Gabrielle J. Scents Appeal: The Silent Persuasion of Aromatic Encounters. (Illus.). 324p. 1993. text 34.50 (*0-9603250-4-2*) Dorland Pub Co.

***Dorland, Gil.** Legacy of Discord: Voices of the Vietnam Era. 2001. 26.95 (*1-57488-215-5*) Brasseys.

Dorland, Gil. Path of Terror. 240p. 1996. pap. 10.95 (*0-9646531-9-2*) New Continents.

Dorland, Gil & Ospina, Clara. Profiles in Democracy: A New Generation of Latin American Leaders. 182p. 1995. 20.00 (*0-9646531-0-9*) New Continents.

— Profiles in Democracy: New Generation of Latin-American Leaders. Zalamea, Luis, tr. from ENG. 182p. 1995. pap. 12.00 (*0-9646531-1-7*) New Continents.

Dorland, James R., intro. When You're Teaching Adults. rev. ed. LC 59-15148. 1970. pap. text 1.00 (*0-686-00786-7*, 751-00798) A A A C E.

Dorland, Michael. So Close to the State/S: The Emergence of Canadian Feature Film Policy. LC 99-168716. 222p. 1998. text 60.00 (*0-8020-4182-5*); pap. text 19.95 (*0-8020-8043-X*) U of Toronto Pr.

Dorland, Michael, ed. The Cultural Industries in Canada: Policies, Problems & Prospects. LC 97-115937. (Illus.). 376p. 39.95 (*1-55028-495-9*, Pub. by J Lorimer); pap. 24.95 (*1-55028-494-0*, Pub. by J Lorimer) Formac Dist Ltd.

Dorland, Newman W. Dorland's Cardiology Speller. 287p. 1992. pap. text 26.00 (*0-7216-3748-5*, W B Saunders Co) Harcrt Hlth Sci Grp.

— Dorland's Dentistry Speller. LC 92-13389. 192p. 1993. pap. text 19.00 (*0-7216-4572-0*, W B Saunders Co) Harcrt Hlth Sci Grp.

— Dorland's Dermatology Speller. Date not set. pap. text. write for info. (*0-7216-4932-7*, W B Saunders Co) Harcrt Hlth Sci Grp.

— Dorland's Hematology - Oncology Speller. LC 92-13352. 255p. 1992. pap. text 19.95 (*0-7216-3750-7*, W B Saunders Co) Harcrt Hlth Sci Grp.

***Dorland, Newman W.** Dorland's Illustrated Medical Dictionary. 29th ed. 2000. text 95.00 (*0-7216-8261-8*, W B Saunders Co) Harcrt Hlth Sci Grp.

Dorland, Newman W. Dorland's Medical Abbreviations. LC 92-11623. 1992. pap. text 27.00 (*0-7216-3751-5*, W B Saunders Co) Harcrt Hlth Sci Grp.

— Dorland's Medical Speller. 1493p. 1991. pap. text 34.50 (*0-7216-3599-7*, W B Saunders Co) Harcrt Hlth Sci Grp.

— Dorland's Neurology Speller. 1999. pap. text. write for info. (*0-7216-4933-5*, W B Saunders Co) Harcrt Hlth Sci Grp.

Dorland, Norman W. Dorlands Gastroenterology Speller. LC 92-13353. 192p. 1993. pap. text 26.00 (*0-7216-4568-2*, W B Saunders Co) Harcrt Hlth Sci Grp.

— Dorland's Ob/Gyn Speller. 1999. pap. text. write for info. (*0-7216-4934-3*, W B Saunders Co) Harcrt Hlth Sci Grp.

— Dorland's Orthopedic Speller. LC 92-13380. 320p. 1993. pap. text 26.00 (*0-7216-3752-3*, W B Saunders Co) Harcrt Hlth Sci Grp.

— Dorland's Pathology Speller. 1999. pap. text. write for info. (*0-7216-4935-1*, W B Saunders Co) Harcrt Hlth Sci Grp.

— Dorland's Pocket Medical Dictionary. 25th ed. 816p. 1995. pap. text 24.00 (*0-7216-5738-9*, W B Saunders Co) Harcrt Hlth Sci Grp.

— Dorland's Podiatry Speller. 1999. pap. text. write for info. (*0-7216-4936-X*, W B Saunders Co) Harcrt Hlth Sci Grp.

— Dorland's Psychiatry/Psychology Speller. 272p. 1992. pap. text 23.00 (*0-7216-3749-3*, W B Saunders Co) Harcrt Hlth Sci Grp.

— Dorland's Radiology/Diagnostic Imaging Speller. 1999. pap. text. write for info. (*0-7216-4937-8*, W B Saunders Co) Harcrt Hlth Sci Grp.

— Dorland's Rheumatology Speller. 1999. pap. text. write for info. (*0-7216-4938-6*, W B Saunders Co) Harcrt Hlth Sci Grp.

Dorland, Wayne E. & Rogers, James A. The Fragrance & Flavor Industry. (Illus.). 1977. 30.00 (*0-9603250-1-8*) Dorland Pub Co.

Dorlands. Spanish-English Illustrated Medical Dictionary. 2 vols. 27th ed. (ENG & SPA., Illus.). 1992. 250.00 (*0-7859-8835-1*) Fr & Eur.

Dorlas, T. C. Statistical Mechanics: Fundamentals & Model Solutions. LC 99-19621. 1999. 40.00 (*0-7503-0540-1*) IOP Pub.

Dorlas, T. C., et al, eds. Statistical Mechanics & Field Theory: Mathematical Aspects. (Lecture Notes in Physics Ser.: Vol. 257). vii, 328p. 1986. 48.95 (*0-387-16777-3*) Spr-Verlag.

Dorling, Brian. Inside APPN & HPR: The Essential Guide to New SNA. 4th ed. LC 97-210124. (Illus.). 1997. write for info. (*0-11-376151-1*) Statnry Office.

Dorling, Brian. Inside APPN: The Essential Guide to the New SNA. 4th ed. 480p. (C). 1997. pap. 66.00 (*0-13-761511-6*) P-H.

Dorling, Brian, et al. Switch Virtual Networking. 1996. 40.00 (*0-614-20318-X*) P-H.

Dorling, Daniel. Mapping. 208p. (C). 1997. pap. text 24.60 (*0-582-28972-6*) Addison-Wesley.

Dorling, Daniel. A New Social Atlas of Britain. 286p. 1995. 125.00 (*0-471-94868-3*) Wiley.

***Dorling, Daniel & Simpson, Stephen C., eds.** Statistics in Society: The Arithmetic of Politics. LC 99-230472. (Illus.). 512p. 1999. pap. text 29.95 (*0-340-71994-X*) OUP.

Dorling, Daniel & Woodward, Rachel. Social Polarisation 1971-1991: A Micro-Geographical Analysis of Britain. (Progress in Planning Ser.: Vol. 45). 70p. 100.75 (*0-08-042890-8*, Pergamon Pr) Elsevier.

Dorling, Irene, ed. Twentieth Century Family. (C). 1986. 30.00 (*0-7300-0216-0*, Pub. by Deakin Univ) St Mut.

***Dorling, Kindersey Publishing.** Traffic Jam! 16p. 1999. 5.95 (*0-7894-4273-6*) DK Pub Inc.

***Dorling, Kindersley.** American Horticultural Society Gardening Manual. (Illus.). 424p. 2000. 40.00 (*0-7894-5952-3*) DK Pub Inc.

— Barbie Career Girl. LC 00-23244. (Illus.). 48p. (gr. 4-7). 2000. write for info. (*0-7894-6666-X*, Pub. by DK Pub Inc) Pub Resources Inc.

— Brussels. (DK Travel Guides Ser.). (Illus.). 192p. 2000. pap. 19.95 (*0-7894-5523-4*) DK Pub Inc.

Dorling, Kindersley. Castle Explorer. (YA). (gr. 4 up). 1997. 29.95 incl. cd-rom (*0-7894-0891-0*) DK Pub Inc.

***Dorling, Kindersley.** Diabetes Cookbook. 2000. pap. 13.95 (*0-7894-5175-1*) DK Pub Inc.

— Dinosaur! The Ultimate Guide. LC 99-86291. 64p. (J). 2000. 14.95 (*0-7894-5452-1*, D K Ink) DK Pub Inc.

— Dorling Kindersley World Atlas. (Illus.). 372p. 2000. 50.00 (*0-7894-5962-0*) DK Pub Inc.

— Dutch. 144p. 2000. pap. 9.95 (*0-7894-6260-5*) DK Pub Inc.

— A First Bible Story Book. LC 99-50388. (Read & Listen Ser.). 80p. (J). 2000. pap. text 7.95 (*0-7894-5464-5*, D K Ink) DK Pub Inc.

— French. 144p. 2000. pap. 9.95 (*0-7894-6253-2*) DK Pub Inc.

— German. 144p. 2000. pap. 9.95 (*0-7894-6254-0*) DK Pub Inc.

— Greek. 144p. 2000. pap. 9.95 (*0-7894-6258-3*) DK Pub Inc.

— Hebrew. 144p. 2000. pap. 9.95 (*0-7894-6259-1*) DK Pub Inc.

— Illustrated Book of Ballet Stories. LC 99-56153. (Read & Listen Ser.). (Illus.). 64p. (J). 2000. pap. text 7.95 (*0-7894-5466-1*, D K Ink) DK Pub Inc.

— Internet: Getting Connected. (Essential Computers Ser.). (Illus.). 72p. 2000. pap. 6.95 (*0-7894-5532-3*, D K Ink) DK Pub Inc.

— Internet: Parental Control. (Essential Computers Ser.). 72p. 2000. pap. text 6.95 (*0-7894-5528-5*, D K Ink) DK Pub Inc.

— Italian. 144p. 2000. pap. 9.95 (*0-7894-6255-9*) DK Pub Inc.

— James Bond: The Secret World of 007. LC 00-27165. 144p. (gr. 4-7). 2000. write for info. (*0-7894-6691-0*, Pub. by DK Pub Inc) Pub Resources Inc.

— Japan. (Travel Guides Ser.). 2000. pap. 24.95 (*0-7894-5545-5*) DK Pub Inc.

— Japanese. 144p. 2000. pap. 9.95 (*0-7894-6547-7*) DK Pub Inc.

— John Paul II: Chronicle of a Remarkable Life. (Illus.). 160p. 2000. 19.95 (*0-7894-6491-8*) DK Pub Inc.

— Latin American Spanish. 144p. 2000. pap. 9.95 (*0-7894-6544-2*) DK Pub Inc.

— Look Inside Cross-Sections: Tanks. (J). 1999. pap. 14.50 (*0-613-03015-X*) Econo-Clad Bks.

— Major League Baseball's Best Shots: The Greatest Baseball Photography of All Time. (Illus.). 2000. 30.00 (*0-7894-6119-6*) DK Pub Inc.

— Mandarin Chinese. 144p. 2000. pap. 9.95 (*0-7894-6546-9*) DK Pub Inc.

— NFL ABC Book. 36p. (ps-k). 2000. 6.95 (*0-7894-6374-1*) DK Pub Inc.

— NFL's Greatest: Pro Football's Best Players, Teams, & Games. 2000. 30.00 (*0-7894-5955-8*) DK Pub Inc.

— Olympic Games: Athens 1896-Sydney 2000. (Illus.). 352p. 2000. 29.95 (*0-7894-5975-2*) DK Pub Inc.

— Playtime Rhymes. LC 99-54784. (Read & Listen Ser.). (Illus.). 32p. (J). (ps-3). 2000. pap. text 7.95 (*0-7894-5465-3*, D K Ink) DK Pub Inc.

— Portuguese. 144p. 2000. pap. 9.95 (*0-7894-6257-5*) DK Pub Inc.

— Queen Mother: Chronicle of a Remarkable Life. (Illus.). 128p. 2000. 19.95 (*0-7894-5844-6*) DK Pub Inc.

— Robin Hood. LC 99-50013. (Read & Listen Ser.). (Illus.). 64p. (J). (gr. 4-7). 2000. pap. text 7.95 (*0-7894-5462-9*, D K Ink) DK Pub Inc.

— Russian. 144p. 2000. pap. 9.95 (*0-7894-6545-0*) DK Pub Inc.

— San Francisco. gif. deluxe ed. (Travel Guides Ser.). 2000. pap. 40.00 (*0-7894-5846-2*) DK Pub Inc.

— Singapore. (Travel Guides Ser.). (Illus.). 208p. 2000. pap. 19.95 (*0-7894-5544-7*) DK Pub Inc.

— Spanish. 144p. 2000. pap. 9.95 (*0-7894-6256-7*) DK Pub Inc.

— Ultimate WCW. LC 00-23238. (gr. 4-7). 2000. write for info. (*0-7894-6673-2*, Pub. by DK Pub Inc) Pub Resources Inc.

Dorling Kindersley Multimedia Staff. Cat. (Eyewitness Virtual Reality Ser.). (YA). (gr. 3 up). 1995. 19.95 incl. cd-rom (*0-7894-0295-5*) DK Pub Inc.

— Eyewitness World Atlas. (Eyewitness Books). (YA). (gr. 6 up). 1998. 19.95 incl. cd-rom (*0-7894-3264-1*) DK Pub Inc.

***Dorling, Kindersley Publishing.** Baby Animals. (Touch & Feel Ser.). 12p. 1999. 6.95 (*0-7894-4749-5*) DK Pub Inc.

— Bulldozer. 1999. pap. 6.95 (*0-7894-4719-3*) DK Pub Inc.

— Bus. 10p. (J). (gr. k-2). 1999. 4.95 (*0-7894-4731-2*) DK Pub Inc.

Dorling, Kindersley Publishing. Deadly Dinosaurs. 1999. pap. text 3.95 (*0-7894-4783-5*) DK Pub Inc.

***Dorling, Kindersley Publishing.** Drive a Fire Engine. 12p. (J). (gr. k-2). 1999. 12.95 (*0-7894-4744-4*) DK Pub Inc.

— Drive a Tractor. 12p. (J). (gr. k-2). 1999. 12.95 (*0-7894-4743-6*) DK Pub Inc.

— Fun Car. 10p. (J). (gr. k-2). 1999. 4.95 (*0-7894-4732-0*) DK Pub Inc.

Dorling, Kindersley Publishing. Mighty Dinosaurs. 1999. pap. text 3.95 (*0-7894-4784-3*) DK Pub Inc.

— Monster Truck. 1999. 4.95 (*0-7894-4734-7*) DK Pub Inc.

***Dorling, Kindersley Publishing.** Moon Landing. 1999. pap. 6.95 (*0-7894-4876-9*) DK Pub Inc.

— Motorcycle. 10p. (J). (gr. k-2). 1999. 4.95 (*0-7894-4733-9*) DK Pub Inc.

— My Big Alphabet Book. 8p. (J). (ps-k). 1999. 9.95 (*0-7894-4681-2*) DK Pub Inc.

— My Big Counting Book. 8p. (J). (ps-k). 1999. 9.95 (*0-7894-4682-0*) DK Pub Inc.

— My First Sticker Book. (My First Bks.). 16p. (J). (gr. k-2). 1999. pap. text 6.95 (*0-7894-4686-3*) DK Pub Inc.

— Ponies. (Touch & Feel Ser.). (Illus.). 12p. (ps-k). 1999. 6.95 (*0-7894-4748-7*) DK Pub Inc.

Dorling, Kindersley Publishing. Train. (Ultimate Sticker Books Ser.). 1999. pap. 6.95 (*0-7894-4718-5*) DK Pub Inc.

***Dorling Kindersley Publishing Co. Staff.** Atlas of World History: Mapping the Human Journey. Black, Jeremy, ed. LC 99-57342. (Illus.). 352p. 2000. 50.00 (*0-7894-4609-X*, D K Ink) DK Pub Inc.

— Bulgarian. LC 99-48549. (Eyewitness Travel Guide Phrase Bks.). (BUL & ENG.). 128p. 2000. pap. 6.95 (*0-7894-5180-8*, D K Ink) DK Pub Inc.

— Coronary Artery Disease. (ACP Home Medical Guides). 96p. 2000. pap. 6.95 (*0-7894-5154-9*, D K Ink) DK Pub Inc.

— Czech. LC 99-48547. (Eyewitness Travel Guide Phrase Bks.). (CHE & ENG.). 128p. 2000. pap. 6.95 (*0-7894-5181-6*, D K Ink) DK Pub Inc.

— Diabetes. (ACP Home Medical Guides). 80p. 2000. pap. 6.95 (*0-7894-5200-6*, D K Ink) DK Pub Inc.

— Dutch. LC 99-48545. (Eyewitness Travel Guide Phrase Bks.). (ENG & DUT.). 128p. 2000. pap. 6.95 (*0-7894-5182-4*, D K Ink) DK Pub Inc.

— Indonesian. LC 99-47486. (Eyewitness Travel Guide Phrase Bks.). (IND & ENG.). 128p. 2000. pap. 6.95 (*0-7894-5183-2*, D K Ink) DK Pub Inc.

— Memory Loss & Dementia. (ACP Home Medical Guides). 80p. 2000. pap. 6.95 (*0-7894-5201-4*, D K Ink) DK Pub Inc.

— My First Bible Board Book. LC 99-44314. (Illus.). 36p. (J). (gr. k-2). 2000. bds. 6.95 (*0-7894-5213-8*, D K Ink) DK Pub Inc.

— Romanian. LC 99-48548. (Eyewitness Travel Guide Phrase Bks.). (ENG & RUM.). 128p. 2000. pap. 6.95 (*0-7894-5184-0*, D K Ink) DK Pub Inc.

— Turkish. LC 99-47487. (Eyewitness Travel Guide Phrase Bks.). (TUR & ENG.). 128p. 2000. pap. 6.95 (*0-7894-5185-9*, D K Ink) DK Pub Inc.

***Dorling Kindersley Publishing Inc., Staff.** Barbie ABC Book. LC 99-56184. (Illus.). 32p. (J). (ps-3). 2000. 12.95 (*0-7894-5334-7*, D K Ink) DK Pub Inc.

— Barbie Fun-to-Make Activity Book. LC 99-48387. (Illus.). 48p. (J). 2000. pap. 9.95 (*0-7894-5333-9*, D K Ink) DK Pub Inc.

— Canada. LC 99-41075. (Eyewitness Travel Guides Ser.). (Illus.). 432p. 2000. pap. text 24.95 (*0-7894-5169-7*, D K Ink) DK Pub Inc.

— London. LC 99-55203. (Kids' Travel Guides Ser.). (Illus.). 64p. (J). (gr. 4-7). 2000. pap. 7.95 (*0-7894-5249-9*, D K Ink) DK Pub Inc.

— New York. LC 99-53294. (Kids' Travel Guides Ser.). (Illus.). 64p. (J). 2000. pap. 7.95 (*0-7894-5248-0*, D K Ink) DK Pub Inc.

***Dorling Kindersley Publishing Staff.** Alexander Technique. (Secrets of... Ser.). (Illus.). 224p. 2000. pap. 9.95 (*0-7894-6772-0*) DK Pub Inc.

— Alexander the Great. (Discoveries Ser.). (Illus.). 48p. (gr. 3-7). 2000. 14.95 (*0-7894-6166-8*, D K Ink) DK Pub Inc.

— Amazing Pop-Up, Pull-Out Mummy Book. (Illus.). 12p. (gr. 4-7). 2000. 19.95 (*0-7894-6507-8*) DK Pub Inc.

— Aromotherapy. (Secrets of... Ser.). 224p. 2000. pap. write for info. (*0-7894-6773-9*) DK Pub Inc.

— Bach Flower Remedies. (Secrets of... Ser.). (Illus.). 224p. 2000. pap. 9.95 (*0-7894-6774-7*) DK Pub Inc.

— Children's Illustrated Encyclopedia. (Illus.). 800p. (ps-3). 2000. 40.00 (*0-7894-6498-5*, D K Ink) DK Pub Inc.

— Dorling Kindersley Children's Atlas. (Illus.). 160p. (gr. 3-7). 2000. 24.95 (*0-7894-5845-4*, D K Ink) DK Pub Inc.

— Everest. (Discoveries Ser.). (Illus.). 48p. (gr. 3-7). 2000. 14.95 (*0-7894-6167-6*, D K Ink) DK Pub Inc.

— Hypnosis. (Secrets of... Ser.). 224p. 2000. pap. 9.95 (*0-7894-6776-3*) DK Pub Inc.

— Palm Reading. (Secrets of... Ser.). (Illus.). 224p. 2000. pap. 9.95 (*0-7894-6777-1*) DK Pub Inc.

— Reflexology. (Secrets of... Ser.). 2000. pap. 9.95 (*0-7894-6778-X*) DK Pub Inc.

— Shiatsu. (Secrets of... Ser.). 224p. 2000. pap. 9.95 (*0-7894-6779-8*) DK Pub Inc.

— Tarot. (Secrets of... Ser.). 2000. pap. 9.95 (*0-7894-6780-1*) DK Pub Inc.

— World War II. (Eyewitness Books). (Illus.). (gr. 4-7). 2000. 15.95 (*0-7894-6298-2*, D K Ink) DK Pub Inc.

— Yoga. (Secrets of... Ser.). 224p. 2000. pap. 9.95 (*0-7894-6781-X*) DK Pub Inc.

***Dorling Kindersley Publishing Staff & Fielding, Simon.** The Secrets of Energy Work. (Secrets of... Ser.). 224p. 2000. pap. 9.95 (*0-7894-6775-5*) DK Pub Inc.

Dorling Kindersley Staff. Aircraft. LC 97-164284. (Pockets Ser.). (Illus.). 128p. (J). (gr. 3 up). 1997. pap. 6.95 (*0-7894-1496-1*) DK Pub Inc.

— Amazing Addition. (My Math Sticker Work Bk.). (Illus.). 16p. (J). (ps-2). 1997. pap. 6.95 (*0-7894-1517-8*) DK Pub Inc.

— Angler's Guide to Fish. LC 96-30990. (Illus.). 96p. 1997. 14.95 (*0-7894-1438-4*) DK Pub Inc.

— Australia. LC 98-2810. (Eyewitness Travel Guides Ser.). 576p. 1998. 29.95 (*0-7894-3531-4*) DK Pub Inc.

— Chronicle Encyclopedia of History. (YA). (gr. 6 up). 1997. 29.95 incl. cd-rom (*0-7894-1734-0*) DK Pub Inc.

— Classic Makeup & Beauty. 1998. pap. 13.95 (*0-7894-3294-3*, D K Ink) DK Pub Inc.

— Container Gardening Through the Year. 1998. pap. 13.95 (*0-7894-3296-X*, D K Ink) DK Pub Inc.

— Dictionary of the Body. (J). (gr. 4-7). 1995. 19.95 (*0-7894-0011-1*) DK Pub Inc.

— The Dorling Kindersley Science Encyclopedia. LC 97-20881. 448p. (YA). (gr. 7-12). 1998. 39.95 (*0-7894-2190-9*) DK Pub Inc.

— English Dictionary. LC 97-167115. (Pockets Ser.). (Illus.). 512p. (J). 1997. pap. 6.95 (*0-7894-1497-X*) DK Pub Inc.

— French Phrase Book. LC 97-47222. (FRE.). 144 p. 1998. pap. 6.95 (*0-7894-3234-X*, D K Ink) DK Pub Inc.

— German Phrase Book. LC 97-47229. (GER.). 1998. pap. 6.95 (*0-7894-3235-8*, D K Ink) DK Pub Inc.

***Dorling Kindersley Staff.** Going for Goldberg. (Dorling Kindersley Readers). (Illus.). 48p. (J). (gr. 2-4). 2000. 12.95 (*0-7894-6675-9*); pap. 3.95 (*0-7894-6761-5*) DK Pub Inc.

Dorling Kindersley Staff. Introduction to Acrylics. 1998. pap. 9.95 (*0-7894-3287-0*, D K Ink) DK Pub Inc.

— Introduction to Drawing. 1998. pap. 9.95 (*0-7894-3288-9*, D K Ink) DK Pub Inc.

— Introduction to Oil Painting. 1998. pap. 9.95 (*0-7894-3289-7*, D K Ink) DK Pub Inc.

— Introduction to Pastels. 1998. pap. 9.95 (*0-7894-3290-0*, D K Ink) DK Pub Inc.

— Introduction to Watercolor. 1998. pap. 9.95 (*0-7894-3291-9*, D K Ink) DK Pub Inc.

An Asterisk (*) at the beginning of an entry indicates that the title is appearing for the first time.

— Introduction to Watercolor Color. 1998. pap. 9.95 (*0-7894-3292-7*, D K Ink) DK Pub Inc.
— Italian Phrase Book. LC 97-47227. (ITA.). 1998. pap. 6.95 (*0-7894-3236-6*, D K Ink) DK Pub Inc.
— Mindbenders Mirror. 1996. write for info. (*0-7894-1016-8*) HM.
— Mindbenders 3-D. 1996. write for info. (*0-7894-1017-6*) HM.
— My First Amazing Words & Pictures. 1997. 29.95 (*0-7894-1693-X*) DK Pub Inc.
— My Very First Word Book. LC 93-1112. (J). 1993. write for info. (*1-56458-375-9*) DK Pub Inc.
— Nature Facts. LC 97-164285. (Pockets Ser.). (Illus.). 128p. (J). 1997. pap. 6.95 (*0-7894-1494-5*) DK Pub Inc.
— New Gardener. 1998. pap. 13.95 (*0-7894-3298-6*, D K Ink) DK Pub Inc.
— Number Puzzles. (Math Sticker Work Bk.). (Illus.). 16p. (J). (ps-2). 1997. pap. 4.95 (*0-7894-1515-1*) DK Pub Inc.
— Nursery Rhymes. (Baby's Bk.). (J). 1994. write for info. (*1-56458-827-0*) DK Pub Inc.
— Opposites Sticker Activity Book. (Illus.). (J). (ps-3). 1993. pap. 6.95 (*1-56458-240-X*) DK Pub Inc.
— Out & About. (Treasure Hunt Board Bks.). (Illus.). 10p. (J). (ps-k). 1996. 4.95 (*0-7894-0626-8*) DK Pub Inc.
— Parker's Complete Book of Dreams. LC 98-164415. 1998. pap. 13.95 (*0-7894-3295-1*, D K Ink) DK Pub Inc.
— The Pattern Library: Crochet. 96p. 1985. pap. 9.00 (*0-345-32711-X*) Ballantine Pub Grp.
— Piglet. LC 97-136564. (Shaped Board Bks.). (Illus.). 10p. (J). 1997. bds. 3.95 (*0-7894-1542-9*) DK Pub Inc.
— Pocket Fisherman's Catch. 1995. pap. write for info. (*0-7894-0195-9*) HM.
— Spanish Phrase Book. LC 97-47228. (SPA.). 1998. pap. 6.95 (*0-7894-3233-1*, D K Ink) DK Pub Inc.
***Dorling Kindersley Staff.** Sting in the Tail. (Dorling Kindersley Readers). 48p. (J). (gr. 2-4). 2000. 12.95 (*0-7894-6674-0*) DK Pub Inc.
— Sting in the Tail. (Dorling Kindersley Readers). (Illus.). 48p. (J). (gr. 2-4). 2000. pap. 3.95 (*0-7894-6760-7*) DK Pub Inc.
Dorling Kindersley Staff. Subtraction. (My Math Sticker Work Bk.). (Illus.). 16p. (J). 1997. pap. 6.95 (*0-7894-1518-6*) DK Pub Inc.
— Sun Moon Compendium, 2 vols. 1995. write for info. (*0-7894-0368-4*) HM.
— Times Tables. (My Math Sticker Work Bk.). (Illus.). 16p. (J). (ps-2). 1997. pap. 6.95 (*0-7894-1516-X*) DK Pub Inc.
— Ultimate Golf Techniques. 1998. pap. 13.95 (*0-7894-3302-8*, D K Ink) DK Pub Inc.
— World Reference Atlas. 1998. pap. 29.95 (*0-7894-3251-X*, D K Ink) DK Pub Inc.
— Yan-Kit's Classic Chinese Cookbook. LC 98-166741. (CHI.). 1998. pap. 13.95 (*0-7894-3300-1*, D K Ink) DK Pub Inc.
— Yoga Mind & Body. 1998. pap. 13.95 (*0-7894-3301-X*, D K Ink) DK Pub Inc.
Dorling Kindersley Staff, ed. Complete Book of Rocks & Minerals. 1995. 29.95 (*0-7894-0169-X*) DK Pub Inc.
— Decorating Techniques. 1995. write for info. (*1-56458-874-2*) DK Pub Inc.
— Dinosaurs. (Pop Up Ser.). (J). 1995. write for info. (*0-7894-0208-4*) DK Pub Inc.
— Earth Facts. (Pocket Guides Ser.). (J). 1995. write for info. (*0-7894-0283-1*) DK Pub Inc.
— High Flyers. (Pop Up Ser.). (J). 1995. write for info. (*0-7894-0209-2*) DK Pub Inc.
— Insects. (Pop Up Ser.). (J). 1995. write for info. (*0-7894-0210-6*) DK Pub Inc.
— Inventions. (Pocket Guides Ser.). (J). 1995. write for info. (*0-7894-0282-3*) DK Pub Inc.
***Dorling Kindersley Staff, ed.** Leonardo & His Times. (Eyewitness Books). (Illus.). (J). (gr. 4-7). 2000. 19.99 (*0-7894-6819-0*) DK Pub Inc.
Dorling Kindersley Staff, ed. Truck. (Mighty Machines Ser.). (Illus.). (J). 1995. 9.95 (*0-7894-0299-8*) DK Pub Inc.
— Ultimate Pocket World Atlas. 192p. 1995. 12.95 (*0-7894-0192-4*) DK Pub Inc.
Dorling, P. R., jt. ed. see Colegate, S. M.
Dorm-Adzobu, Clement. New Roots: Institutionalizing Environmental Mechanisms in Africa. LC 95-45485. 57p. 1995. 20.00 (*1-56973-037-7*) World Resources Inst.
Dormady, Blanche. Greater Orlando Area: Hotel-Motel-Resort Accessibility Guide. Dormady, Dennis, ed. (Illus.). 15p. (Orig.). 1985. pap. text 10.00 (*0-933537-03-4*) Fleury Found.
Dormady, Dennis, ed. see Dormady, Blanche.
Dormael, Armand Van, see Van Dormael, Armand.
Dormagen, Robert L. Angel of Wealth. 164p. 1998. pap. 15.00 (*1-57502-723-2*) Morris Pubng.
Dorman, Adelle, jt. auth. see Duits, Carrie.
Dorman, Andrew M. & Otte, Thomas G. Military Intervention: From Gunboat Diplomacy to Humanitarian Intervention. (Illus.). 224p. 1995. text 81.95 (*1-85521-579-9*, Pub. by Dartmth Pub) Ashgate Pub Co.
Dorman, Andrew M. & Treacher, Adrian, eds. European Security: An Introduction to Security Issues in Post-Cold War Europe. (Issues in International Security Ser.). 224p. 1995. pap. 31.95 (*1-85521-611-6*, Pub. by Dartmth Pub) Ashgate Pub Co.
— European Security: An Introduction to Security Issues in Post-Cold War Europe. (Issues in International Security Ser.). 224p. (C). 1995. 82.95 (*1-85521-604-3*, Pub. by Dartmth Pub) Ashgate Pub Co.
Dorman, B. Hugh, jt. ed. see Conroy, Joanne M.
Dorman, Bennett W. Savin Rock: An Illustrated History. (Illus.). 270p. 1999. 49.95 (*0-9669159-0-9*) Photo Res Design.
Dorman, Caroline. Bird Talk. 1969. 12.50 (*0-87511-024-X*) Claitors.
Dorman, Casey & Katzir, Bilha. Cognitive Effects of Early Brain Injury. LC 94-6782. (Johns Hopkins Series in Psychiatry & Neuroscience). 1994. text 55.00 (*0-8018-4856-3*) Johns Hopkins.
Dorman, Dave. Star Wars: The Art of Dave Dorman, 1. (Orig.). 1999. pap. text 24.95 (*1-56649-019-7*) Welcome Rain.
Dorman, Dave, jt. auth. see Bissette, Steve.
Dorman, Dave, jt. auth. see Dietz, William C.
Dorman, Franklin A. Thomas Dorman of Topsfield, MA (1600-1670) Twelve Generations of Descendants. (Illus.). 733p. (Orig.). 1995. pap. text 46.50 (*0-7884-0108-4*) Heritage Bk.
— Twenty Families of Color in Massachusetts, 1742-1998. LC 99-195334. xxii, 524p. 1998. 35.00 (*0-88082-077-2*) New Eng Hist.
Dorman, Gayle. Middle Grades Assessment Program: Leader's Manual. rev. ed. Pulver, Robin, ed. 136p. 1995. pap., teacher ed. 17.50 (*1-57482-717-0*) Search Inst.
— Middle Grades Assessment Program: User's Manual. rev. ed. 175p. 1995. pap. 9.00 (*1-57482-718-9*) Search Inst.
Dorman, Gayle & Wheelock, Anne. Before It's Too Late: Dropout Prevention in the Middle Grades. 87p. 1988. reprint ed. pap. 7.50 (*1-57482-709-X*) Search Inst.
Dorman, Harry G. Toward Understanding Islam: Contemporary Apologetic of Islam & Missionary Policy. LC 79-176727. (Columbia University. Teachers College. Contributions to Education Ser.: No. 940). reprint ed. 37.50 (*0-404-55940-9*) AMS Pr.
Dorman, Janice, ed. Standardization of Epidemiological Studies of Host Susceptibility. LC 94-48569. (NATO ASI Ser.: Vol. 270). (Illus.). 298p. (C). 1995. text 95.00 (*0-306-44892-0*, Kluwer Plenum) Kluwer Academic.
Dorman, John, jt. auth. see Paschal, John.
Dorman, John F. Index to the Virginia Genealogist, Vols. 1-20. LC 81-83768. 941p. 1981. 50.00 (*0-89157-032-2*) GBIP.
— The Virginia Genealogist, Vol. 3, 1959. 235p. 1992. reprint ed. pap. 18.50 (*1-55613-599-8*) Heritage Bk.
— The Virginia Genealogist, Vol. 5. 234p. 1957. reprint ed. pap. 20.00 (*1-55613-714-1*) Heritage Bk.
— The Virginia Genealogist, Vol. 12, 1968. 235p. 1993. reprint ed. pap. text 20.00 (*1-55613-839-3*) Heritage Bk.
— The Virginia Genealogist, Vol. 17, 1973. 399p. 1994. reprint ed. pap. text 26.00 (*1-55613-968-3*) Heritage Bk.
— The Virginia Genealogist, 1970, Vol. 14. 233p. 1993. reprint ed. pap. text 21.00 (*1-55613-883-0*) Heritage Bk.
— The Virginia Genealogist, 1978, Vol. 22. 402p. 1994. reprint ed. pap. text 26.00 (*0-7884-0056-8*) Heritage Bk.
— The Virginia Genealogist, 1969, Vol. 13. 234p. (Orig.). 1993. pap. text 21.00 (*1-55613-882-2*) Heritage Bk.
— The Virginia Genealogist, 1967, Vol. 11. 240p. 1993. reprint ed. pap. text 20.00 (*1-55613-838-5*) Heritage Bk.
Dorman, John F., ed. The Virginia Genealogist, Vol. 15, 1971. 387p. 1994. reprint ed. pap. text 27.50 (*1-55613-920-9*) Heritage Bk.
— The Virginia Genealogist, Vol. 16, 1972. 386p. 1994. reprint ed. pap. text 27.50 (*1-55613-921-7*) Heritage Bk.
— The Virginia Genealogist, Vol. 18, 1974. 386p. 1994. reprint ed. pap. text 26.00 (*1-55613-969-1*) Heritage Bk.
— The Virginia Genealogist, Vol. 23, 1979. 397p. 1995. reprint ed. pap. text 26.00 (*0-7884-0086-X*) Heritage Bk.
— The Virginia Genealogist, Vol. 27, 1983. 384p. 1995. pap. 28.50 (*0-7884-2129-8*) Heritage Bk.
— The Virginia Genealogist, 1980, Vol. 26, 1982. 398p. (Orig.). 1980. reprint ed. pap. 29.00 (*0-7884-0211-0*) Heritage Bk.
— The Virginia Genealogist, 1981. 397p. 1995. reprint ed. pap. text 26.00 (*0-7884-0212-9*) Heritage Bk.
— The Virginia Genealogist, 1975, Vol. 19. 391p. (Orig.). 1994. pap. text 26.00 (*0-7884-0027-4*) Heritage Bk.
— The Virginia Genealogist, 1977, Vol. 2. 391p. 1994. reprint ed. pap. text 26.00 (*0-7884-0055-X*) Heritage Bk.
— The Virginia Genealogist, 1976, Vol. 20. 389p. (Orig.). 1994. pap. text 26.00 (*0-7884-0028-2*) Heritage Bk.
— The Virginia Genealogist, 1965, Vol. 9. ii, 241p. (Orig.). 1993. reprint ed. pap. text 21.00 (*1-55613-784-2*) Heritage Bk.
— The Virginia Genealogist, 1964, Vol. 8. 236p. 1993. reprint ed. pap. 20.00 (*1-55613-753-2*) Heritage Bk.
— The Virginia Genealogist, 1966, Vol. 10. ii, 256p. (Orig.). 1993. reprint ed. pap. text 21.00 (*1-55613-785-0*) Heritage Bk.
— The Virginia Genealogist, 1963, Vol. 7. ii, 243p. 1993. reprint ed. pap. 20.00 (*1-55613-752-4*) Heritage Bk.
— The Virginia Genealogist, 1962, Vol. 6. 237p. 1992. reprint ed. pap. text 20.00 (*1-55613-715-X*) Heritage Bk.
Dorman, John F. & Bentley, James R. The Prestons of Smithfield & Greenfield in Virginia. LC 80-2841. (Filson Club, Second Publications Ser.: No. 3). (Illus.). 441p. 1982. 28.75 (*0-9601072-1-5*) Filson Club.
Dorman, John Frederick, ed. The Virginia Genealogist, 1957, Vol. 1. 235p. 1992. reprint ed. pap. 18.50 (*1-55613-553-X*) Heritage Bk.
Dorman, Jon, jt. auth. see Carroll, David L.
***Dorman, Joseph.** Arguing the World: The New York Intellectuals in Their Own Words. 240p. 2000. 25.00 (*0-684-86279-4*) Free Pr.
Dorman, L. E., jt. auth. see Jamieson, James.
Dorman, L. I., ed. Cosmic Rays. 675p. 1974. 110.25 (*0-444-10480-1*, North Holland) Elsevier.
Dorman, L. S. & Rawlins, C. L. Leonard Cohen: Prophet of the Heart. (Illus.). 384p. pap. 24.95 (*0-7119-2774-X*, OP 46614) Omnibus NY.
Dorman, Larry. Ninety-Third U. S. Open. Norwood, Bev, ed. (Illus.). 64p. 1993. 20.00 (*1-878843-08-7*) Intl Merc OH.
Dorman, Lesley, jt. auth. see Todd, Robyn.
Dorman, Lewy. Party Politics in Alabama from 1850 Through 1860. LC 94-35291. (Library of Alabama Classics). (Illus.). 256p. 1995. pap. text 19.95 (*0-8173-0780-X*) U of Ala Pr.
Dorman, Marianne. The Coming of Christ. 104p. (C). 1989. text 45.00 (*1-872795-82-X*, Pub. by Pentland Pr) St Mut.
— A Life of Glory. 73p. (C). 1989. pap. text 39.00 (*1-872795-78-1*, Pub. by Pentland Pr) St Mut.
— Living Lent. 138p. (C). 1989. text 55.00 (*1-872795-79-X*, Pub. by Pentland Pr) St Mut.
— The Paschal Life. (C). 1989. text 60.00 (*0-7855-6365-0*, Pub. by Pentland Pr) St Mut.
— The Sermons of Lancelot Andrews Vol. 1: Nativity, Lentan & Passion. 275p. (C). 1989. text 70.00 (*1-872795-77-3*, Pub. by Pentland Pr) St Mut.
— The Sermons of Lancelot Andrews Vol. 11: Pascal & Pentecost. (C). 1989. text 75.00 (*1-85821-014-3* Pub. by Pentland Pr) St Mut.
Dorman, Marsha & Klein, Diane. How to Stay Two When Baby Makes Three. LC 83-62191. 156p. 1984. pap. 19.95 (*0-87975-253-X*) Prometheus Bks.
Dorman, Michael, jt. auth. see Blackman, Irving.
Dorman, Michael A., jt. auth. see Blackman, Irving L.
Dorman, N. B. Petey & Miss Magic. LC 92-11265. (Illus.). 99p. (J). (gr. 2-6). 1992. lib. bdg. 16.00 (*0-208-02345-3*, Linnet Bks) Shoe String.
Dorman, Peter. Markets & Mortality: Economics, Dangerous Work & the Value of Human Life. 286p. (C). 1996. text 54.95 (*0-521-55306-7*) Cambridge U Pr.
Dorman, Peter F. The Monuments of Senenmut: Problems in Historical Methodology. (Studies in Egyptology). 344p. (C). 1988. lib. bdg. 89.95 (*0-7103-0317-3*) Routledge.
Dorman, Rebekah L., et al. Planning, Funding & Implementing a Child Abuse Prevention Project. LC 98-24861. 200p. 1998. pap. 18.95 (*0-87868-562-6*) Child Welfare.
Dorman, Ricardo L. The Chili Line & Santa Fe the City Different. LC 96-93115. (Illus.). 224p. 1996. 44.95 (*0-9616656-0-2*) RD Pubns.
Dorman, Richard L. Alamosa, Salida & the Valley Line. LC 91-91427. (Illus.). 224p. 1992. 41.95 (*0-9616656-5-3*) RD Pubns.
Dorman, Richard L. Durango Always a Railroad Town. LC 87-90641. (Illus.). 218p. 1996. 42.95 (*0-9616656-1-0*) RD Pubns.
Dorman, Richard L. Gunnison: From Marshall Pass to Ouray. (Illus.). 224p. 1993. 44.95 (*0-9616656-6-1*) RD Pubns.
— The Rio Grande Southern: An Ultimate Pictorial Study. LC 90-91619. (Illus.). 280p. 1990. 46.00 (*0-9616656-4-5*) RD Pubns.
— The Rio Grande Southern II: An Ultimate Pictorial Study. LC 94-92171. (Illus.). 344p. 1994. 59.95 (*0-9616656-8-8*, 2500) RD Pubns.
— The Southern, a Narrow Gauge Odyssey. 2nd ed. (Illus.). 156p. 1988. 29.95 (*0-9616656-3-7*) RD Pubns.
Dorman, Robert L. The New Regionalism: Essays & Commentaries. Wilson, Charles R., ed. LC 97-9367. (Chancellor's Symposium Ser.). 184p. 1998. text 40.00 (*1-57806-013-3*) U Pr of Miss.
— Revolt of the Provinces: The Regionalist Movement in America, 1920-1945. LC 92-31234. (H. Eugene & Lillian Youngs Lehman Ser.). xvi, 366p. (C). 1993. 55.00 (*0-8078-2101-2*) U of NC Pr.
— A Word for Nature: Four Pioneering Environmental Advocates, 1845-1913. LC 97-23896. 272p. 1998. pap. 18.95 (*0-8078-4699-6*); lib. bdg. 49.95 (*0-8078-2396-1*) U of NC Pr.
Dorman, Sonya. Palace of Earth. Hunting, Constance, ed. 60p. 1984. pap. 5.95 (*0-913006-31-9*) Puckerbrush.
— A Paper Raincoat. (Illus.). 60p. 1979. pap. 3.50 (*0-913006-09-2*) Puckerbrush.
Dorman, Steve, ed. see Cairns, Carol.
Dorman-Stubbs, Lisa, ed. see Terrence, Chris.
Dorman, T. E. An African Experience: An Education Officer in North Rhodesia (Zambia) 240p. (C). 1993. text 39.50 (*1-85043-568-5*, Pub. by I B T) St Martin.
Dorman, Ted M. A Faith for All Seasons: Historic Christian Beliefs in Its Classical Expression. rev. ed. 400p. 1995. pap. 27.99 (*0-8054-1074-0*, 4210-74) Broadman.
Dorman, Theodore M. The Hermeneutics of Oscar Cullman. LC 91-30126. 208p. 1991. lib. bdg. 89.95 (*0-7734-9953-9*) E Mellen.
Dorman, Thomas A. & Ravin, Thomas. Diagnosis & Injection Techniques in Orthopaedic Medicine. (Illus.). 328p. 1991. 60.00 (*0-683-02630-5*) Lppncott W & W.
Dorman, William A. & Farhang, Mansour. The U. S. Press & Iran: Foreign Policy & the Journalism of Deference. LC 86-25032. 300p. 1987. pap. 16.95 (*0-520-06472-0*, Pub. by U CA Pr) Cal Prin Full Svc.
Dormand, John R. Numerical Methods for Differential Equations: A Computational Approach. Jeffrey, Alan, ed. (Library of Engineering Mathematics). 384p. 1996. lib. bdg. 94.95 incl. 3.5 hd, 5.25 hd, 3.5 ld (*0-8493-9433-3*, 9433) CRC Pr.
Dormand, John R. & Woolfson, Michael M. The Origin of the Solar System: The Capture Theory. 1989. text 49.95 (*0-470-21466-X*) P-H.
Dormandy, John A., ed. Blood Filtration & Blood Cell Deformability. 1985. pap. text 73.00 (*0-89838-774-0*) Kluwer Academic.
— Red Cell Deformability & Filterability. (Developments in Hematology & Immunology Ser.). 1983. text 14 .50 (*0-89838-578-4*) Kluwer Academic.
Dormandy, Klara, jt. auth. see van der Gaag, Anna.
Dormandy, Thomas. The White Death: A History of Tuberculosis. LC 98-38008. 1998. write for info. (*1-85285-169-4*) Hambledon Press.
***Dormandy, Thomas.** The White Death: A History of Tuberculosis. LC 99-32169. (Illus.). 440p. 2000. 29.95 (*0-8147-1927-9*) NYU Pr.
Dormann, Geneviaeve. Colette: A Passion for Life. LC 85-4074. 320p. 1985. write for info. (*0-89659-594-3*) Abbeville Pr.
Dormann, Genevieve. Remembering Paris. 255p. 1999. pap. text 29.95 (*2-08-013657-7*, Pub. by Flammarion) Abbeville Pr.
Dormann, Genvieve. Mauritius from the Air. 136p. 1999. 29.95 (*1-86812-455-X*) Menasha Ridge.
Dormann, Henry O. The Speaker's Book of Quotations. rev. ed. 304p. (Orig.). 2000. pap. 11.95 (*0-449-00560-7*) Ballantine Pub Grp.
Dormann, J. L. & Fiorani, D., eds. Studies of Magnetic Properties of Fine Particles & Their Relevance to Materials Science: Proceedings of the International Workshop, Rome, Italy, 4-8 November, 1991. LC 92-20648. (North-Holland Delta Ser.). xiv, 430p. 1992. 210.00 (*0-444-89552-3*, North Holland) Elsevier.
Dormann, Johannes. Pope John Paul II's Theological Journey to the Prayer Meeting of Religions at Assisi Pt. 2, Vol. 1: The Trinitarian Trilogy: "Redemptor Hominis", "Dives in Misericordia", "Dominum et Vivificantem" Brandler, Christopher, tr. from GER. 243p. (Orig.). 1996. pap. 11.45 (*0-935952-33-0*) Angelus Pr.
— Pope John Paul II's Theological Journey to the Prayer Meeting of Religions in Assisi Pt. 1: From the Second Vatican Council to the Papal Election. Society of St. Pius X Staff, ed. LC 94-25185. 8p. (Orig.). 1994. pap. 9.45 (*0-935952-52-7*) Angelus Pr.
— Pope John Paul II's Theological Journey to the Prayer Meeting of Religions at Assisi Pt. II, Vol. 2: The "Trinitarian Trilogy": Dives in Misericordia. Wall, Sebastian, tr. from GER. 200p. 1998. pap. 10.95 (*0-935952-72-1*) Angelus Pr.
Dormans, John P. & Pellegrino, Louis. Caring for Children with Cerebral Palsy: A Team Approach. LC 97-23367. 1997. 41.95 (*1-55766-322-X*) P H Brookes.
Dormant, Diane. Rolemaps. Langdon, Danny G., ed. LC 79-23398. (Instructional Design Library). 128p. 1980. 27.95 (*0-87778-153-2*) Educ Tech Pubns.
Dormay, Nadine & Lazar, Liliane. A Chacun sa France: Une Certaine Idee de l'Homme. LC 89-14545. (American University Studies: Romance Languages & Literature: Ser. II, Vol. 129). (FRE.). 195p. (C). 1990. text 43.00 (*0-8204-1155-8*) P Lang Pubng.
Dormen, Lesley, jt. auth. see Todd, Robyn.
Dorment, Richard. Alfred Gilbert. LC 84-52241. (Illus.). 320p. 1986. pap. 30.00 (*0-300-03698-1*) Yale U Pr.
— British Painting in the Philadelphia Museum of Art: From the Seventeenth Through the Nineteenth Century. LC 86-8105. (Illus.). 468p. 1986. 62.95 (*0-8122-8035-0*); pap. 18.00 (*0-87633-065-0*) Phila Mus Art.
Dorment, Richard & MacDonald, Margaret F. James McNeill Whistler. LC 94-40838. (Illus.). 336p. 1995. 85.00 (*0-8109-3976-2*, Pub. by Abrams) Time Warner.
Dormer. The Culture of Craft. LC 96-31364. 224p. 1997. text 50.00 (*0-7190-4617-3*, Pub. by Manchester Univ Pr) St Martin.
Dormer, Albert. Dormer on Deduction. (Illus.). 144p. 1996. pap. 13.95 (*0-575-06115-4*, Pub. by V Gollancz) Trafalgar.
— The New Complete Book of Bridge. 480p. 1996. 29.95 (*0-575-06084-0*, Pub. by V Gollancz) Trafalgar.
Dormer, Florence, ed. see Skinner, Louise, et al.
Dormer, K. J. Fundamental Tissue Geometry for Biologists. LC 79-14404. 155p. reprint ed. pap. 44.20 (*0-608-17094-1*, 2027288) Bks Demand.
Dormer, Peter. Design since Nineteen Forty-Five. LC 92-80335. (World of Art Ser.). (Illus.). 216p. 1993. pap. 14.95 (*0-500-20261-3*, Pub. by Thames Hudson) Norton.
— The New Ceramics: Trends & Traditions. 2nd rev. ed. LC 94-60277. (Illus.). 232p. 1994. pap. 24.95 (*0-500-27775-3*, Pub. by Thames Hudson) Norton.
Dormer, Peter & Turner, Ralph. The New Jewelry: Trends & Traditions. 2nd rev. ed. LC 94-60278. (Illus.). 216p. 1994. pap. 24.95 (*0-500-27774-5*, Pub. by Thames Hudson) Norton.
Dormer, Teresa & Reiser, Dee. Best of Friends. 2nd ed. 168p. 1987. pap. 9.95 (*0-9615950-4-3*) Best Friends.
Dormer, Teresa, jt. auth. see Reiser, Dee.
D'Ormesson, Jean. Un Amour pour Rien. (FRE.). 1978. pap. 10.95 (*0-7859-4099-5*) Fr & Eur.
— Du Cote de Chez Jean. (FRE.). 1978. pap. 10.95 (*0-7859-4106-1*) Fr & Eur.
— La Gloire de l'Empire, Tome II. (FRE.). 342p. 1977. pap. 10.95 (*0-7859-4074-X*, 2070368904) Fr & Eur.
— La Gloire de l'Empire, Vol. 1. 1977. pap. 10.95 (*0-7859-4073-1*) Fr & Eur.
— Le Vagabond Qui Passe sous une Ombrelle Trouee. (FRE.). 1981. pap. 8.95 (*0-7859-4158-4*) Fr & Eur.
***Dormeyer, Detlev.** The New Testament among the Writings of Antiquity. (Biblical Seminar Ser.: No. 55). 328p. 1998. pap. 28.50 (*1-85075-860-3*, Pub. by Sheffield Acad) CUP Services.
Dormeyer, Lavon. How I Weathered the Storm of Divorce: A 9 Session Program for Students in Grades 2-6. (Illus.). 20p. 1998. pap. 8.95 (*1-57543-064-9*) Mar Co Prods.
Dormidontov, E. A., et al. German-Russian Dictionary of Tractors & Construction Vehicles: Deutsch-Russisches Fachwoerterbuch Fuer Kraftwagen Und Traktoren. 3rd ed. (GER & RUS.). 776p. 1986. 95.00 (*0-8288-1188-1*, M1984) Fr & Eur.
Dorminey, John E. Dorminy/Dorminey: Descendants of John & Rachel Dorminey of Irwin County, Georgia. LC 98-84931. xiv, 905p. 1998. write for info. (*0-9663868-0-9*) MasterWorks Prodn.
Dorminy, Mark E., jt. auth. see Fletcher, James E.

D

Dormire, Byron T. Demo Details: Parachute Demonstration Performances. 2nd ed. LC 95-92241. 176p. 1995. pap. text 22.95 (*1-887260-07-2*) Blue Sun.

Dormois, Jean-Pierre & Dintenfass, Michael, eds. The British Industrial Decline. LC 98-22609. (Explorations in Economic History Ser.: 10). (Illus.). 248p. (C). (gr. 13). 1999. 95.00 (*0-415-17231-4*, D6038) Routledge.

Dormon. Wildflowers of L. A. 1997. pap. 20.00 (*1-57980-015-7*, DWILDF) Claitors.

Dormon, Caroline. Flowers Native to the Deep South. 1958. 25.00 (*0-87511-025-8*) Claitors.

— Natives Preferred. 1965. 25.00 (*0-87511-026-6*) Claitors.

— Southern Indian Boy. (Illus.). (J). 1967. 10.00 (*0-87511-027-4*) Claitors.

Dormon, James H. The People Called Cajuns: Introduction to an Ethnohistory. LC 83-71493. (Illus.). 110p. (C). 1983. 10.00 (*0-940984-09-1*) Univ LA Lafayette.

Dormon, James H., ed. Creoles of Color of the Gulf South. LC 95-4432. (Illus.). 224p. 1996. pap. text 16.00 (*0-87049-917-3*); lib. bdg. 32.00 (*0-87049-916-5*) U of Tenn Pr.

Dormuth, K. W. Canadian Nuclear Fuel Waste Management Program: Special Issue of the Journal Radioactive Waste Management & the Nuclear Fuel Cycle, Vol. 8, Nos. 2-3. 190p. 1987. pap. text 218.00 (*3-7186-0414-0*) Gordon & Breach.

Dorn. Building Essays: A Reader Centered Writing Guide. LC 99-19690. 357p. 1999. pap. text 35.40 (*0-13-758335-4*) P-H.

— Building World Order: Replacing the Law of Force with the Law of the New Millenium. LC 99-13634. 320p. 1999. text 49.95 (*0-312-21635-1*) St Martin.

— The Poet, the People, the Spirit. (NFS Canada Ser.). 1993. pap. 8.95 (*0-88922-101-4*) Genl Dist Srvs.

Dorn, Brian E. Eternal Strength: A Comprehensive Christian Guide to Strength & Fitness. LC 96-95207. (Illus.). xiii, 254p. (Orig.). 1997. pap. 18.95 (*0-9656198-0-X*) Lift & Run.

Dorn, Cecilia, jt. auth. see Dorn, Edward.

Dorn, Charles M. Mind in Art: Cognitive Foundations for Art Education. LC 98-35913. 272p. 1998. 69.95 (*0-8058-3078-2*); pap. 27.50 (*0-8058-3079-0*) L Erlbaum Assocs.

— Thinking in Art: A Philosophical Approach to Art Education. 180p. (Orig.). 1994. pap. 22.00 (*0-937652-69-5*, 227) Natl Art Ed.

Dorn, Charlotte & Becker, Peter. Mother Holle. (Illus.). 24p. (J). Date not set. 12.95 (*1-55082-042-7*, Pub. by Quarry Pr) LPC InBook.

— Mother Holle. (Illus.). 24p. 1993. per. 8.95 (*1-55082-043-5*, Pub. by Quarry Pr) LPC InBook.

Dorn, Dave, ed. see Shimp, Emily.

Dorn, Dennis & Shanda, Mark. Drafting for the Theatre. LC 89-20915. (Illus.). 224p. (C). 1991. pap. 24.95 (*0-8093-1508-4*) S Ill U Pr.

Dorn, Edward. Abhorrences. LC 90-34816. 178p. (Orig.). 1990. 20.00 (*0-87685-801-9*); pap. 12.50 (*0-87685-800-0*) Black Sparrow.

— By the Sound. LC 91-19033. 228p. (Orig.). 1991. 25.00 (*0-87685-841-8*) Black Sparrow.

— By the Sound. LC 91-19033. 228p. (Orig.). 1991. pap. 12.50 (*0-87685-840-X*) Black Sparrow.

— By the Sound, signed ed. deluxe ed. LC 91-19033. 228p. (Orig.). 1991. 30.00 (*0-87685-842-6*) Black Sparrow.

— Collected Poems: 1956-1974. LC 74-27227. (Writing Ser.: No. 34). 288p. 1975. 15.00 (*0-87704-030-3*); pap. 10.00 (*0-87704-029-X*) Four Seasons Foun.

— Gunslinger. LC 89-7901. 202p. 1989. text 39.95 (*0-8223-0964-5*); pap. text 16.95 (*0-8223-0932-7*) Duke.

— Interviews, 1961-1978. Allen, Donald, ed. LC 78-6100. (Writing Ser.: 38). 126p. 1980. pap. 5.00 (*0-87704-038-9*) Four Seasons Foun.

— Selected Poems. Allen, Donald, ed. LC 78-2925. 108p. 1978. pap. 3.50 (*0-912516-32-1*) Grey Fox.

— Views. Allen, Donald, ed. LC 79-25498. (Writing Ser.: No. 40). 144p. 1980. 12.00 (*0-87704-050-8*) Four Seasons Foun.

— Way West - Stories, Essays & Verse Accounts: 1963-1993. LC 93-24338. 281p. 1993. pap. 14.00 (*0-87685-905-8*) Black Sparrow.

Dorn, Edward & Brotherston, Gordon. Sun Unwound: Poems from Occupied America. LC 98-19843. (Illus.). 267p. 1999. pap. 14.95 (*1-55643-292-5*, Pub. by North Atlantic) SPD-Small Pr Dist.

Dorn, Edward & Dorn, Cecilia. An Illustrated RV & over the Coals Cookbook. Davis, Al, ed. LC 93-15441. (Illus.). 248p. 1994. pap. 19.95 (*0-9631806-4-9*) Cel Pubns.

Dorn, Edward G., II. Contracts for Protecting Your Advertising & Marketing Rights. LC 97-41636. 68p. (C). 1997. lib. bdg. 69.50 (*0-9631806-9-X*) Cel Pubns.

— How to Build an Agency New Business Swat Team. LC 98-53522. (Illus.). 145p. 1999. lib. bdg. 69.50 (*0-9631806-6-5*) Cel Pubns.

— How to Buy & Price Advertising Service. Davis, Al, ed. LC 97-40200. (How to Business Bks.). (Illus.). 104p. (Orig.). (C). 1997. pap. 69.50 (*0-9631806-8-1*) Cel Pubns.

— An Illustrated Handbook for Going Fishing at the Market. LC 92-10279. 1992. 6.95 (*0-9631806-3-0*) Cel Pubns.

— An Illustrated Handbook to Surviving Deli Counters: Selection Guides for Counting & Controlling Fats, Cholesterol, Calories, & Sodium Content in Delicatessen Foods. LC 92-13616. (Illus.). 43p. 1992. pap. 6.95 (*0-9631806-2-2*) Cel Pubns.

— An Illustrated Handbook to Surviving Family Campouts. (How to Bks.). 104p. 1992. 19.95 (*0-9631806-0-6*) Cel Pubns.

Dorn, Edward G. A Successful System for Pricing & Producing Advertising Services. LC 95-30851. 1995. write for info. (*0-9631806-7-3*) Cel Pubns.

Dorn, Edward G., II. Surviving Family Campouts. (How to Bks.). 104p. 1992. pap. 12.95 (*0-9631806-1-4*) Cel Pubns.

Dorn, Edwin. Rules & Racial Equality. LC 79-64228. 1979. 37.50 (*0-300-02362-6*) Yale U Pr.

Dorn, Georg & Weingartner, Paul, eds. Foundations of Logic & Linguistics. LC 84-26518. 726p. 1985. 125.00 (*0-306-41916-5*, Plenum Trade) Perseus Pubng.

Dorn, Georg J. Deductive, Probabilistic & Inductive Dependence: An Axiomatic Study in Probability Semantics. 61p. 1997. pap. 63.95 (*3-614-84429-3*) P Lang Pubng.

— Deductive, Probabilistic & Inductive Dependence: An Axiomatic Study in Probability Semantics. LC 97-3777. 361p. 1997. pap. 63.95 (*0-8204-3205-9*) P Lang Pubng.

Dorn, Georgette M., ed. Works by Miguel de Cervantes Saavedra in the Library of Congress. LC 92-34038. 1993. write for info. (*0-8444-0768-2*) Lib Congress.

Dorn, Gunther & Engelmann, Joachim. The Cavalry Regiments of Frederick the Great, 1756-1763. Force, Edward, tr. from GER. LC 88-64006. (Illus.). 160p. 1989. 95.00 (*0-88740-164-3*) Schiffer.

— The Infantry Regiments of Frederick the Great, 1756-1763. Force, Edward, tr. from GER. LC 88-64005. (Illus.). 160p. 1989. 95.00 (*0-88740-163-5*) Schiffer.

Dorn, H., et al. Theory of Elementary Particles: Proceedings of the 31st International Symposium Ahrenshoop, September 2-6 1997, Buckow, Germany. LC 98-229104. (Illus.). 508p. 1998. 185.00 (*3-527-40224-1*) Wiley.

Dorn, Harold. The Geography of Science. LC 90-25149. (Illus.). 264p. 1991. text 40.00 (*0-8018-4151-8*) Johns Hopkins.

Dorn, Harold, jt. auth. see McClellan, James E., III.

Dorn, Ileana. Back to School - A Guide for Returning Students. 2nd rev. ed. Breithaupt, Douglas J., ed. 103p. (Orig.). 1995. pap. text 23.95 (*1-880344-01-7*) Col Plan Netwk.

Dorn, Jacob H. Socialism & Christianity in Early 20th Century America, 181. LC 98-11104. 272p. 1998. 59.95 (*0-313-30262-6*, Greenwood Pr) Greenwood.

Dorn, James A. Economic Liberties & the Judiciary. Manne, Henry G. & Kozinski, Alex, eds. LC 87-8574. 414p. (Orig.). 1987. lib. bdg. 65.00 (*0-913969-16-8*) Univ Pub Assocs.

— Revolution in Development Economics. LC 97-53294. 1998. 22.95 (*1-882577-55-8*); pap. text 14.95 (*1-882577-56-6*) Cato Inst.

Dorn, James A., ed. China in the New Millennium: Market Reforms & Social Development. LC 98-34592. 1998. 24.95 (*1-882577-60-4*); pap. 15.95 (*1-882577-61-2*) Cato Inst.

— The Future of Money in the Information Age. LC 97-686. 171p. 1997. pap. 12.95 (*1-882577-52-3*) Cato Inst.

Dorn, James A. & Schwartz, Anna J., eds. The Search for Stable Money: Essays on Monetary Reform. LC 86-25654. xviii, 410p. 1995. pap. text 17.00 (*0-226-15830-6*) U Ch Pr.

Dorn, James A. & Xi, Wang, eds. Economic Reform in China: Problems & Prospects. (Illus.). 384p. 1990. pap. text 22.00 (*0-226-15832-2*) U Ch Pr.

— Economic Reform in China: Problems & Prospects. (Illus.). 384p. 1990. lib. bdg. 48.00 (*0-226-15831-4*) U Ch Pr.

Dorn, James A., jt. ed. see Carpenter, Ted Galen.

Dorn, James M. & Hopkins, Barbara M. Thanatochemistry. 2nd ed. LC 97-17390. 356p. 1997. 74.00 (*0-13-654195-X*) P-H.

Dorn, John M. Prognosis: Fair. 1993. pap. 14.95 (*1-56883-004-1*) Colonial Pr AL.

Dorn, Katie, jt. auth. see Cavanaugh, Joe.

Dorn, Katie K. Briefcase to Diaper Bag: A Mother's Journey to Find Balance at Home. LC 94-9990. (Illus.). 112p. 1994. pap. text 10.99 (*0-9640435-1-3*) Nantucket Pubng.

Dorn, Linda J., et al. Apprenticeship in Literacy: Transitions Across Reading & Writing. LC 98-16570. (Illus.). 192p. 1998. pap. text 20.00 (*1-57110-088-1*) Stenhse Pubs.

Dorn, Marilyn A. The Administrative Partitioning of Costa Rica: Politics & Planners. (Research Papers: No. 222). (Illus.). 140p. 1989. pap. text 14.50 (*0-89065-126-4*) U Ch Pr.

Dorn, Miriam S. Children's Questions. (Occasional Papers). 22p. 1987. pap. 3.00 (*0-918374-24-3*) City Coll Wk.

Dorn, Nicholas. European Drug Policies & Enforcement. 1995. 69.95 (*5-550-50722-6*) St Martin.

Dorn, Nicholas, et al, eds. AIDS: Women, Drugs & Social Care. (Social Aspects of AIDS Ser.: Vol. 1). 224p. 1992. pap. 29.95 (*1-85000-874-4*, Falmer Pr) Taylor & Francis.

— European Drug Policies & Enforcement. 288p. 1996. text 75.00 (*0-312-12926-2*) St Martin.

Dorn, P. & Walter, Roland. Geologie von Mitteleuropa. ix, 566p. 1995. 58.00 (*3-510-65167-7*, Pub. by E Schweizerbartsche) Balogh.

Dorn, Pamela, jt. auth. see Monsour, Sally.

Dorn, Patrick R. Career Fair. 25p. (Orig.). (YA). (gr. 7-10). 1993. pap. 3.00 (*1-57514-150-7*, 1088) Encore Perform Pub.

***Dorn, Patrick Rainville.** The Gingerbread Man: Comedy for the Stage. 40p. (YA). (gr. 1-12). 1999. pap. 4.00 (*0-88680-462-0*) I E Clark.

Dorn, Paul K. Dining with the Stars: A Taste of the Best. (Illus.). 256p. 1998. 22.00 (*0-671-01749-7*) S&S Trade.

Dorn, Rich, jt. auth. see Keadle, Chris.

***Dorn, Roland, et al.** Van Gogh Face to Face: Portraits. LC 99-66191. (Illus.). 272p. 2000. 50.00 (*0-500-09290-7*, Pub. by Thames Hudson) Norton.

Dorn, Ronald I., ed. Rock Coatings. LC 98-10344. (Developments in Earth Surface Processes Ser.: 6). 442p. 1998. 207.00 (*0-444-82919-9*) Elsevier.

Dorn, Sherman. Creating the Dropout: An Institutional & Social History of School Failure. LC 95-45414. 176p. 1996. 57.95 (*0-275-95175-8*, Praeger Pubs) Greenwood.

Dorn, Susan, ed. see Huckstadt, Jurgen.

Dorn, Susan, ed. see Mollmann, Gerd.

Dorn, Susan, ed. see Steiner, Josef & Steiner, Gerhard.

Dorn, Susan E., jt. auth. see Zeitlin, Kim A.

Dorn, T. Felder. The Tompkins School, 1925-1953: A Community Institution. 114p. (Orig.). 1994. pap. 15.00 (*0-87921-085-0*) Attic Pr.

Dorn, William G. Van, see Van Dorn, William G.

Dorn, William J. & Derks, Scott. Dorn: Of the People, a Political Way of Life. 1988. 16.95 (*0-87844-082-8*) Sandlapper Pub Co.

Dorn, William J. & McLean, Kathleen, eds. Hurray! Minnesota: A Guide to Discovering & Rediscovering Minnesota. (Illus.). 496p. (Orig.). 1993. pap. 13.95 (*0-9635873-0-7*) Minnmedia.

Dorn, William S. Five Sherlockian Walks in London. (Illus.). 48p. (Orig.). 1996. pap. 8.00 (*1-896648-68-1*) Battered Silicon.

— The Parlour Games of Sherlock Holmes. (Illus.). 65p. 1996. pap. 8.00 (*1-896648-67-3*) Battered Silicon.

Dorn, William S. & McCracken, Daniel D. Numerical Methods with FORTRAN IV Case Studies. LC 86-20125. 462p. (C). 1987. reprint ed. text 53.95 (*0-89874-982-4*) Krieger.

***Dornacher, Karla.** Blessing of Friendship. 1999. 12.99 (*0-8499-5520-3*) J Countryman.

Dornacher, Karla. Down A Garden Path: To Places of Love & Joy, 1. 1999. 12.99 (*0-8499-5498-3*) CDI.

— Love in Every Room: The Heartbeat of the Home. 80p. 1998. 12.99 (*0-8499-5400-2*) Word Pub.

Dornan. The Brief English Handbook - A Writer's Workshop. 5th ed. 1997. text 17.00 (*0-673-54341-2*) Addison-Wesley.

— The Brief English Handbook- A Writer's Workshop. 5th ed. 1997. text 17.00 (*0-673-54342-0*) Addison-Wesley.

— Clinical Neuropsychopharmacology. 2000. pap. text 37.00 (*0-534-25698-8*) Thomson Learn.

— Longman Handbook for Writers & Readers. 5th ed. (C). 1996. pap. text 11.25 (*0-673-97363-8*) Addison-Wesley.

Dornan & Dees. Four in One: Thinking, Reading, Writing, Researching (Web Edition) 1999. 44.00 (*0-205-30267-X*) Allyn.

Dornan, jt. see Rosen.

Dornan, jt. auth. see Dees.

Dornan, Dimity & Cryle, Denis. The Petrie Family - Building Colonial Brisbane. 1992. pap. 17.95 (*0-7022-2346-8*, Pub. by Univ Queensland Pr) Intl Spec Bk.

Dornan, Edward A. & Dawe, Charles W. The Brief English Handbook. 3rd ed. (C). 1997. pap. text 29.06 (*0-673-52002-1*) Addson-Wesley Educ.

— The Brief English Handbook. 5th ed. LC 95-32726. 576p. (C). 1997. spiral bd. 33.53 (*0-673-52488-4*) Addison-Wesley Educ.

***Dornan, Edward A. & Dawe, Charles W.** The Brief English Handbook. 6th ed. 480p. 2000. spiral bd. write for info. (*0-321-08002-5*) Longman.

Dornan, Edward A. & Dawe, Charles W. The Brief English Workbook. (C). 1997. wbk. ed. 38.00 (*0-673-39252-X*) Addison-Wesley Educ.

***Dornan, Edward A. & Dawe, Charles W., eds.** The Longwood Reader. 4th ed. LC 99-27491. 742p. (C). 1999. pap. text 36.00 (*0-205-30801-5*) Allyn.

Dornan, Edward A., jt. auth. see Dawe, Charles W.

Dornan, Elaine, et al, eds. The Journal Project: Dialogues & Conversations Inside Women's Studies. 224p. 1995. pap. 12.95 (*0-929005-69-4*) LPC InBook.

Dornan, Jim, jt. auth. see Maxwell, John.

Dornan, Jim, jt. auth. see Maxwell, John C.

DORNAN, MARC, ed. Buying Guide to Beers: More Than 2000 Beers Reviewed by the Beverage Testing Institute. 256p. 1999. pap. text 14.95 (*0-8069-2863-8*) Sterling.

Dornan, Peter & Dunn, Richard. Sporting Injuries. 2nd ed. (Illus.). 256p. 1988. pap. text 19.95 (*0-7022-2064-7*, Pub. by Univ Queensland Pr) Intl Spec Bk.

Dornan, Reade W. Arnold Wesker Revisited. LC 94-1771. (Twayne's English Authors Ser.: No. 506). 192p. 1994. 23.95 (*0-8057-7031-3*, Twyne) Mac Lib Ref.

Dornan, Reade W. & King, Kimball, eds. Arnold Wesker: A Casebook. LC 98-5256. (Casebooks on Modern Dramatists Ser.: Vol. 17). 304p. 1998. reprint ed. 65.00 (*0-8153-1178-8*, H1672) Garland.

Dornan, Robert K., ed. Accounting for POW - MIAs from the Korean War & the Vietnam War: Hearing Before the Committee on National Security, U. S. House of Representatives. 181p. (C). 1998. pap. text 35.00 (*0-7881-7114-3*) DIANE Pub.

Dornan, Robert K. & Vedlik, Csaba, Jr. Judicial Supremacy: The Supreme Court on Trial. 124p. (Orig.). 1986. pap. 5.95 (*0-942516-08-7*) Plymouth Rock Found.

Dornand, J., jt. ed. see Mani, J. C.

Dornbach, Alajos. The Secret Trial of Imre Nagy. LC 94-16459. 216p. 1994. 65.00 (*0-275-94332-1*, Praeger Pubs) Greenwood.

Dornbaum, Neil & Goldblum, Jane, eds. 1996-97 Eastern Region Directory of the INS Offices. 174p. 1996. 36.00 (*1-57370-008-8*, 53.26) Amer Immi Law Assn.

Dornberg, John. Central & Eastern Europe. LC 95-16582. (International Government & Politics Ser.). (Illus.). 238p. (YA). (gr. 9 up). 1995. pap. 37.95 (*0-89774-942-1*) Oryx Pr.

— Western Europe. LC 95-43046. (International Government & Politics Ser.). (Illus.). 296p. 1996. pap. 37.95 (*0-89774-943-X*) Oryx Pr.

Dornberg, Martin. Angefragt: Sterbehilfe: Behandlungsbegrenzung und Sterbehilfe aus der Sicht Internistischer Krankenhausarzte - Ergebnisse Einer Befragung und Medizinethische Bewertung. (GER., Illus.). XIII, 139p. 1997. 31.95 (*3-631-32233-X*) P Lang Pubng.

Dornberg, Natasha, tr. see Levin, Itamar.

Dornberg, Natasha, tr. see Yalon-Fortus, Judith.

Dornblazer, Ann V. Healing a Catholic Girlhood. LC 96-43267. (Woman in History Ser.: Vol. 77). 196p. (Orig.). 1997. pap. 20.00 (*0-86663-218-2*) Ide Hse.

Dornbos, Karen L., jt. auth. see Kaminski, Lorraine B.

Dornbrand, Laurie, et al, eds. Manual of Clinical Problems in Adult Ambulatory Care: With Annotated Key References. 3rd ed. LC 97-1675. (Illus.). 784p. 1997. spiral bd. 34.95 (*0-316-19038-1*) Lppncott W & W.

***Dornbusch.** Macroeconomics. 8th ed. 2000. 63.25 (*0-07-231485-0*) McGraw.

Dornbusch. Macroeconomics Study Guide. 7th ed. 1997. pap., student ed. 23.44 (*0-07-109309-5*) McGraw.

Dornbusch, Charles E. Charles King, American Army Novelist: A Bibliography. 1963. pap. 5.00 (*0-910746-05-2*, CKA01) Hope Farm.

Dornbusch, Charles E., ed. Military Bibliography of the Civil War: General References, Armed Forces, & Campaigns & Battle, Vol. 3. LC 72-137700. xv, 224p. 1989. reprint ed. 25.00 (*0-87104-117-0*) NY Pub Lib.

— Military Bibliography of the Civil War: Regimental Publications & Personal Narratives, Vol. 1. LC 72-137700. 528p. 1971. reprint ed. 35.00 (*0-87104-504-4*) NY Pub Lib.

— Military Bibliography of the Civil War: Southern, Border, Western & Territories; Federal Troops; Union & Confederate Biographies, Vol. 2. LC 61-15574. 270p. 1971. reprint ed. 30.00 (*0-87104-514-1*) NY Pub Lib.

Dornbusch, Charles E. & Paszek, Lawrence J. Unit Histories of the United States Air Forces: Including Privately Printed Personal Narratives & United States Air Force History: a Guide to Documentary Sources. Gilbert, James B., ed. LC 79-7247. (Flight: Its First Seventy-Five Years Ser.). (Illus.). 1979. reprint ed. lib. bdg. 28.50 (*0-405-12159-8*) Ayer.

***Dornbusch, Daniel.** Untersuchung von Modellen der Fundamentalen und Technischen Aktienanalyse: Ein Empirischer Vergleich Am Deutschen Aktienmarkt. (Beitrage zum Rechnungs-, Finanz- und Revisionswesen Ser.: Bd. 42). 332p. 1999. 52.95 (*3-631-35414-2*) P Lang Pubng.

Dornbusch, Hans-Joachim. Gefuege-, Mikrostrukturund Texturuntersuchungen an HochtemperaturScherzonen in Granulitfaziellen Metabasiten der IvreaZone. (Geotektonische Forschungen Ser.: Vol. 83). (GER.). ii, 94p. 1995. 58.00 (*3-510-50049-0*, Pub. by E Schweizerbartsche) Balogh.

Dornbusch, Horst D. Altbier: History, Brewing Techniques, Recipes. LC 97-51327. (Classic Beer Style Ser.: No. 12). (Illus.). 144p. 1998. pap. 14.95 (*0-937381-62-4*) Brewers Pubns.

***Dornbusch, Horst D.** Bavarian Lager: Beerhall Helles History, Brewing Techniques, Recipes. 2000. pap. 14.95 (*0-937381-73-X*) Brewers Pubns.

Dornbusch, Horst D. Prost! The Story of German Beer. LC 97-18237. (Illus.). 160p. 1998. pap. 14.95 (*0-937381-55-1*, Siris Bks) Brewers Pubns.

Dornbusch, R. David. Treasuries Made Easy: How to Loan Money to Uncle Sam Just Like the Fat Cats. LC 95-92721. (Illus.). 120p. (Orig.). 1995. pap. 24.95 (*0-930627-14-8*) Paradigm Comm.

Dornbusch, Rudiger. Capital Flight: Theory, Measurement, & Policy Issues. 44p. 1990. pap. text 8.00 (*0-940602-31-8*) IADB.

— Inflation, Exchange Rates, & Stabilization. LC 86-20930. (Essays in International Finance Ser.: No. 165). 28p. 1986. pap. text 10.00 (*0-88165-072-2*) Princeton U Int Finan Econ.

***Dornbusch, Rudiger.** Keys to Prosperity: Free Markets, Sound Money & a Bit of Luck. LC 00-35156. (Illus.). 376p. (C). 2000. 27.95 (*0-262-04181-2*) MIT Pr.

Dornbusch, Rudiger. Latin American Trade Misinvoicing As an Instrument of Capital Flight & Duty Evasion. 32p. 1990. pap. text 8.00 (*0-940602-32-6*) IADB.

— Post-Communist Monetary Problems: Lessons from the End of the Austro-Hungarian Empire. LC 93-42767. (Occasional Papers: No. 49). 1994. pap. 9.95 (*1-55815-308-X*) ICS Pr.

Dornbusch, Rudiger, ed. Policymaking in the Open Economy: Concepts & Case Studies in Economic Performance. LC 92-33405. (World Bank Publications). (Illus.). 272p. 1993. text 18.95 (*0-19-520884-6*, 60884) OUP.

Dornbusch, Rudiger, et al, eds. Postwar Economic Reconstruction & Lessons for the East Today. LC 92-34804. (Illus.). 263p. 1993. 35.00 (*0-262-04136-7*) MIT Pr.

Dornbusch, Rudiger & Draghi, Mario, eds. Public Debt Management: Theory & History. (Illus.). 376p. (C). 1990. text 64.95 (*0-521-39266-7*) Cambridge U Pr.

Dornbusch, Rudiger & Edwards, Sebastian, eds. The Macroeconomics of Populism in Latin America. (National Bureau of Economic Research Project Report Ser.). (Illus.). 411p. 1991. pap. text 24.95 (*0-226-15844-6*) U Ch Pr.

— The Macroeconomics of Populism in Latin America. (National Bureau of Economic Research Project Report Ser.). (Illus.). 416p. 1994. lib. bdg. 65.00 (*0-226-15843-8*) U Ch Pr.

— Reform, Recovery, & Growth: Latin America & the Middle East. LC 94-27934. (National Bureau of Economic Research Project Reports). 436p. 1994. 65.00 (*0-226-15845-4*) U Ch Pr.

— Reforma, Recuperacion y Crecimiento: America Latina y

D

An Asterisk (*) at the beginning of an entry indicates that the title is appearing for the first time.

Medio Oriente.Tr. of Reform, Recovery, & Growth: Latin America & the Middle East. (SPA.). 500p. 1996. pap. text 18.50 (*1-886938-05-9*) IADB.

Dornbusch, Rudiger & Fischer, Stanley. Macroeconomics. 3rd ed. 1984. pap. text. write for info. (*0-07-017771-6*) McGraw.

— Macroeconomics. 6th ed. LC 93-20536. (C). 1993. text 63.25 (*0-07-017844-5*) McGraw.

Dornbusch, Rudiger & Frenkel, Jacob A., eds. International Economic Policy: Theory & Evidence. LC 78-8423. (Illus.). 358p. reprint ed. pap. 111.00 (*0-608-06043-7*, 206637500008) Bks Demand.

Dornbusch, Rudiger & Layard, Richard, eds. The Performance of the British Economy. (Illus.). 288p. 1988. 75.00 (*0-19-877272-6*) OUP.

Dornbusch, Rudiger & Marcus, Steve. International Money & Debt: Challenges for the World Economy. 200p. 1991. pap. 19.95 (*1-55815-084-6*); 6.95 (*1-55815-120-6*) ICS Pr.

Dornbusch, Rudiger & Poterba, James M. Global Warming: Economic Policy Responses. (Illus.). 402p. 1991. 49.50 (*0-262-04126-X*) MIT Pr.

Dornbusch, Rudiger, et al. Inflation Stabilization with Income Policy Support. (Report Ser.). 71p. 1987. pap. 10.00 (*1-56708-070-7*) Grp of Thirty.

— Macroeconomics. 7th ed. LC 97-30777. 576p. (C). 1997. 80.94 (*0-07-017985-9*) McGraw.

Dornbusch, Sanford M. The Military Academy As an Assimilating Institution. (Reprint Series in Social Sciences). (C). 1993. reprint ed. pap. text 1.00 (*0-8290-2724-6*, S-73) Irvington.

Dornbusch, Sanford M. & Scott, W. Richard. Evaluation & the Exercise of Authority. LC 74-9344. (Jossey-Bass Higher Education Ser.). 400p. reprint ed. pap. 124.00 (*0-608-14904-7*, 202566900045) Bks Demand.

Dornbusch, Sanford M. & Strober, Myra H., eds. Feminism, Children, & the New Families. LC 88-21350. (Perspectives on Marriage & the Family Ser.). 366p. 1988. pap. text 22.95 (*0-89862-514-9*); lib. bdg. 47.95 (*0-89862-078-3*) Guilford Pubns.

Dornbusch, Sanford M., jt. auth. see Schneider, Louis.

Dornbush, Jean M. Pygmalion's Figure: Reading Old French Romance. LC 89-81169. (Edward C. Armstrong Monographs on Medieval Literature: No. 5). 153p. (Orig.). 1990. pap. 14.95 (*0-917058-75-5*) French Forum.

Dornbush, Magaret, jt. auth. see Bender, Steve.

Dornbush, Marilyn P. & Pruitt, Sheryl K. Teaching the Tiger: A Handbook for Individuals Involved in the Education of Students with Attention Deficit Disorders, Tourette Syndrome or Obsessive-Compulsive Disorders. LC 95-2018. (Illus.). 200p. 1995. pap. 35.00 (*1-878267-34-5*) Hope Pr CA.

Dornbush, Rudiger. Exchange Rates & Inflation. 488p. 1991. pap. text 26.50 (*0-262-54060-6*) MIT Pr.

Dorndorf, W. & Marx, P., eds. Stroke Prevention. (Illus.). viii, 200p. 1994. 64.50 (*3-8055-5882-1*) S Karger.

Dorne, Clifford & Gewerth, Kenneth. American Juvenile Justice: Cases, Legislations & Comments. LC 98-5601. 256p. (C). 1998. pap. 32.95 (*1-57292-100-5*) Austin & Winfield.

Dorne, Clifford K. Child Maltreatment: A Primer in History, Public Policy & Research. 2nd ed. LC 97-26620. 200p. 1997. pap. text 25.50 (*0-911577-43-2*, Criminal Justice) Willow Tree NY.

Dorne, Wendell R. My Collection of Recipes & Memories in Culinary Arts. LC 97-90567. (Illus.). 239p. 1997. pap. 15.00 (*0-9658806-0-5*) W R Dorne.

Dornemann, Joan & Ciaccia, Maria. Complete Preparation: A Guide to Auditioning for Opera. 150p. (Orig.). (C). 1992. pap. 18.95 (*0-9627226-3-4*) Excalibur Pub.

Dornemann, Rudolph H. A Neolithic Village at Tell El Kowm in the Syrian Desert. LC 86-70319. (Studies in Ancient Oriental Civilization: No. 43). (Illus.). 89p. 1986. pap. 30.00 (*0-918986-45-1*) Orient Inst.

Dornenburg. Becoming Chef Jour Set. 1997. 93.95 (*0-442-02456-8*, VNR) Wiley.

Dornenburg, Andrew. Chefs Night Out: Where America's Leading Chefs Eat on Their Nights Off & How You Can Enjoy the Same Experience. pap. text 29.95 (*0-471-36345-6*) Wiley.

— Think Global Cook Local. pap. text 29.95 (*0-471-36344-8*) Wiley.

Dornenburg, Andrew & Page, Karen. The Becoming: A Chef Journal. 256p. 1996. pap. 18.95 (*0-471-28784-9*, VNR) Wiley.

— Becoming a Chef: With Recipes & Reflections from America's Leading Chefs. 288p. 1995. pap. 29.95 (*0-442-01513-5*, VNR) Wiley.

— Becoming a Chef: With Recipies & Reflections from America's Leading Chefs. 352p. 1995. pap. 29.95 (*0-471-28571-4*, VNR) Wiley.

— The Becoming a Chef Journal. (Illus.). 250p. 1996. text 18.95 (*0-442-02332-4*, VNR) Wiley.

Dornenburg, Andrew & Page, Karen. Culinary Artistry. 426p. 1996. pap. 29.95 (*0-471-28785-7*, VNR) Wiley.

Dornenburg, Andrew & Page, Karen. Culinary Artistry. (Illus.). 300p. (C). 1996. pap. 29.95 (*0-442-02333-2*, VNR) Wiley.

— Dining Out: Secrets from America's Leading Critics, Chefs, & Restauranteurs. LC 98-16705. 368p. 1998. pap. 29.95 (*0-471-29277-X*, VNR) Wiley.

Dornenburg, John, ed. see Hingeston, John.

Dorner, Alexander. The Way Beyond "Art" rev. ed. LC 59-3452. 156p. reprint ed. pap. 48.40 (*0-608-11071-X*, 205028200058) Bks Demand.

Dorner, Dietrich. The Logic of Failure. Kimber, Rita & Kimber, Robert, trs. LC 97-20511. 240p. 1997. pap. 15.00 (*0-201-47948-6*) Addison-Wesley.

— The Logic of Failure: Why Things Go Wrong & What We Can Do to Make Them Right. Kimber, Robert & Kimber, Rita, trs. 288p. 1995. 25.00 (*0-8050-4160-5*) H Holt & Co.

Dorner, Helene T., jt. auth. see Beeton, Douglas R.

Dorner, Isaak A. Divine Immutability: A Critical Reconsideration. LC 94-17160. 208p. 1994. pap. 22.00 (*0-8006-3213-3*, 1-3213, Fortress Pr) Augsburg Fortress.

— History of Protestant Theology, 2 vols. LC 72-133823. reprint ed. 135.00 (*0-404-02147-6*) AMS Pr.

Dorner, Marjorie. Blood Kin. large type ed. 608p. 1994. 27.99 (*0-7089-3108-1*) Ulverscroft.

— A Choice of Nightmares. large type ed. 521p. 1989. 27.99 (*0-7089-1942-1*) Ulverscroft.

— Freeze Frame. 1992. mass mkt. 4.99 (*0-8217-3766-X*, Zebra Kensgtn) Kensgtn Pub Corp.

— Nightmare. 384p. 1988. mass mkt. 3.95 (*0-446-35016-8*, Pub. by Warner Bks) Little.

— Seasons of Sun & Rain. LC 98-50092. 350p. 1999. 23.95 (*1-57131-027-4*) Milkweed Ed.

*__Dorner, Marjorie.__ Seasons of Sun & Rain. large type ed. LC 99-89092. (Senior Lifestyles Ser.). 2000. 26.95 (*0-7862-2414-2*) Thorndike Pr.

— Seasons of Sun & Rain. 370p. 2000. reprint ed. pap. 14.95 (*1-57131-033-9*) Milkweed Ed.

— Winter Roads, Summer Fields. (Illus.). 208p. 2000. reprint ed. pap. 13.95 (*1-57131-032-0*) Milkweed Ed.

Dorner, Nancy L. A Woman's Guide to Spiritual Power: Through Scriptural Prayer. LC 92-60587. 208p. 1992. pap. 9.95 (*0-914984-47-0*) Starburst.

Dorner, Patricia M., jt. auth. see Silber, Kathleen.

Dorner, Peter. Latin American Land Reforms in Theory & Practice: A Retrospective Analysis. LC 91-26440. 118p. (Orig.). 1992. pap. 12.95 (*0-299-13164-5*); lib. bdg. 25.00 (*0-299-13160-2*) U of Wis Pr.

Dorner, Peter, ed. Cooperative & Commune: Group Farming in the Economic Development of Agriculture. LC 76-53651. 407p. 1977. reprint ed. pap. 126.20 (*0-608-01912-7*, 206256400003) Bks Demand.

Dorner, Peter, ed. see Wisconsin Seminar on Natural Resource Policies Sta.

Dorner, Robert F. & Greenwald, Martin L. Electrical Theory & Control Systems in Heating & Air-Conditioning Technology. LC 93-33968. 448p. 1994. text 59.95 (*0-8273-5749-4*) Delmar.

— Electrical Theory & Control Systems in Heating & Air Conditioning Technology. 60p. 1994. teacher ed. 14.95 (*0-8273-5750-8*) Delmar.

Dorneus, Gerardus. Dictionarium Theopharasti Paracelsi. (LAT.). 94p. 1981. reprint ed. write for info. (*3-487-07066-9*) G Olms Pubs.

Dorney, Cay, jt. auth. see Frooks, Dorothy.

Dorney, James. Financial Strategies for Changing Jobs. 50p. 1995. pap. text 21.95 (*0-7811-0105-0*) Res Inst Am.

Dorney, R. S. The Professional Practice of Environmental Management. (Environmental Management Ser.). (Illus.). 220p. 1991. 96.95 (*0-387-96907-1*) Spr-Verlag.

Dornfeld, A. A. Hello, Sweetheart, Get Me Rewrite! The Story of the City News Bureau of Chicago. (Illus.). 331p. 1988. pap. 10.00 (*0-89733-262-8*) Academy Chi Pubs.

Dornfeld, Barry. Producing Public Television, Producing Public Culture. LC 97-39819. 248p. 1998. text 55.00 (*0-691-04468-6*, Pub. by Princeton U Pr); pap. text 17.95 (*0-691-04467-8*, Pub. by Princeton U Pr) Cal Prin Full Svc.

Dornfeld, David A. Sensors for Manufacturing. (C). 1994. text. write for info. (*0-201-19634-4*) Addison-Wesley.

Dornfest, Asha. Do It Yourself Web Publishing with Pagemill. 320p. 1996. pap. text 19.99 incl. disk (*0-7821-1957-3*) Sybex.

— FrontPage 98 for Dummies. LC 97-80412. 384p. 1997. pap. 24.99 incl. cd-rom (*0-7645-0270-0*) IDG Bks.

— FrontPage 2000 for Dummies Quick Reference. LC TK5105.8885.M53D67. (For Dummies Ser.). (Illus.). 400p. 1999. pap. 24.99 incl. cd-rom (*0-7645-0423-1*) IDG Bks.

Dornfield, D. A., jt. ed. see De Vries, W. R.

Dornfield, Margaret. W. E. B. Du Bois: Civil Rights Leader. (Junior Black Americans of Achievement Ser.). (Illus.). 76p. (J). (gr. 3-6). 1995. lib. bdg. 15.95 (*0-7910-2382-6*) Chelsea Hse.

Dornheim, John F. In Remembrance of Me: A Collection of Eucharistic Prayers for the Lesser Feasts & Festivals. Ronneberg, Prudence H., ed. 95p. 1998. spiral bd., wbk. ed. 16.95 (*1-892573-02-4*, 0003) Campanile Pr.

Dornheim, John F.C. And He Took a Loaf of Bread... A Collection of Communion Bread Recipes & Alter Bread Commentary. Ronneberg, Prudence H., ed. 125p. (Orig.). 1998. spiral bd. 12.95 (*1-892573-01-6*, 0002) Campanile Pr.

Dornhoff, Larry L. Group Representation Theory Pt. B: Modular Representation Theory. LC 74-176305. (Pure & Applied Mathematics Ser.: No. 7). 268p. reprint ed. pap. 83.10 (*0-7837-0760-6*, 204107400002) Bks Demand.

*__Dornhoffer, Mary K.__ Doctors. (Community Workers Ser.). (Illus.). 32p. (J). (gr. 1-2). 2000. write for info. (*0-7565-0008-7*) Compass Point.

Dornhorst, Anne & Hadden, David R., eds. Diabetes & Pregnancy: An International Approach to Diagnosis & Management. LC 96-13798. (Practical Diabetes Ser.). 424p. 1996. 125.00 (*0-471-96204-X*) Wiley.

Dornic, Dean. Ophthalmic Pocket Companion. 4th ed. LC 95-38750. 306p. 1995. pap. text 32.00 (*0-7506-9627-3*) Buttrwrth-Heinemann.

— Ophthalmic Pocket Companion. 5th ed. 368p. 1998. pap. text 32.50 (*0-7506-7120-3*) Buttrwrth-Heinemann.

Dornic, S., jt. ed. see Ljunggren, G.

Dornic, Stanislav, ed. see International Symposium on Attention & Performance.

Dornin, George D. Thirty Years Ago: 1849-1879 Gold Rush Memories of a Daguerrotype Artist. Palmquist, Peter, ed. (Illus.). 64p. 1995. pap. 14.95 (*1-887694-01-3*) C Mautz Pubng.

Dornin, Tom & Dornin, Velta. Breeding a Strain of Better Beagles. (Illus.). 112p. write for info. (*0-936365-50-7*) Son Rise Pubns.

Dornin, Velta, jt. auth. see Dornin, Tom.

Dorning, Stacee, jt. auth. see Reifers, Kate.

Dornisch, Loretta. Faith & Philosophy in the Writings of Paul Ricoeur. LC 91-7625. (Problems in Contemporary Philosophy Ser.: Vol. 29). 408p. 1991. lib. bdg. 109.95 (*0-88946-737-4*) E Mellen.

— Paul & Third World Women Theologians. LC 98-51061. 1999. 9.95 (*0-8146-2553-3*) Liturgical Pr.

Dornisch, Loretta C. A Woman Reads the Gospel of Luke. 232p. (Orig.). 1996. pap. 19.95 (*0-8146-2307-7*, Liturg Pr Bks) Liturgical Pr.

Dornon, Bela, ed. Gay Testaments: Old & New. LC 97-90960. 160p. 1997. pap. 12.95 (*0-9659828-0-6*) Wind-Up Pubns.

Dornquast, Shari A., jt. auth. see Swanson, Marie L.

Dornsbusch, Sanford M., jt. auth. see Schneider, Louis.

Dornseif, Allan. ASCD Pocket Guide to School-Based Management. 1996. pap. 15.95 (*0-87120-324-3*) ASCD.

Dornseiff, F. & Hansen, Bernard. Reverse Lexicon of Greek Proper Names. (GRE.). xiv, 340p. 1978. reprint ed. 35.00 (*0-89005-251-4*) Ares.

Dornseiff, Franz. Der Deutsche Wortschatz nach Sachgruppen. 7th ed. (C). 1983. 84.65 (*3-11-000287-6*) De Gruyter.

Dornsife. Toward Computer Composition. (C). 1998. pap. text 14.75 (*0-15-505395-7*) Harcourt Coll Pubs

Dornstein, Ken. Accidentally on Purpose. 452p. 1998. pap. 19.95 (*0-312-17683-X*) St Martin.

— Accidentally, on Purpose: The Making of a Personal Injury Underworld in America. (Illus.). 460p. 1996. text 26.95 (*0-312-12992-0*) St Martin.

Dornstein, Miriam. Boards of Directors under Public Ownership: A Comparative Perspective. (Studies in Organization: No. 15). x, 165p. (C). 1989. lib. bdg. 52.95 (*3-11-011740-1*) De Gruyter.

— Conceptions of Fair Pay: Theoretical Perspectives & Empirical Research. LC 91-8609. 240p. 1991. 62.95 (*0-275-93404-7*, C3404, Praeger Pubs) Greenwood.

Dornyei, Zoltan & Thurrell, Sarah. Conversation & Dialogues in Action. LC 92-12368. (C). 1992. pap. 18.75 (*0-13-175035-6*) P-H.

Dornyei, Zoltan, jt. auth. see Ehrman, Madeline E.

Doro, Ann. Twin Pickle. LC 95-38430. (Illus.). 32p. (J). (ps-2). 1995. 14.95 (*0-8050-3802-7*, B Martin BYR) H Holt & Co.

Doro, Marion & Legum, Colin, eds. Africa Contemporary Record Annual Survey & Documents 1988-89, Vol. XXI. 1200p. 1992. 375.00 (*0-8419-0559-2*, Africana) Holmes & Meier.

Doro, Marion, jt. ed. see Legum, Colin.

Doro, Marion E. & Legum, Colin, eds. Africa Contemporary Record Vol. XXII: 1989-1990. 1296p. 1996. 395.00 (*0-8419-0560-6*) Holmes & Meier.

Doro, Marion E. & Stultz, Newell M., eds. Governing in Black Africa: Perspectives on New States. 2nd rev. ed. LC 85-24959. 272p. (C). 1986. 39.50 (*0-8419-0997-0*); pap. 18.50 (*0-8419-0998-9*) Holmes & Meier.

Doro, Sue. Blue Collar Goodbyes. LC 92-8310. (Illus.). 86p. 1993. reprint ed. 12.00 (*0-918949-23-8*); reprint ed. pap. 8.00 (*0-918949-22-X*) Papier-Mache Press.

— Heart, Home & Hard Hats. LC 86-162211. 96p. (Orig.). 1986. pap. text 6.00 (*0-935697-01-2*) Midwest Villages.

Dorobat, Dumitru. Receptarea Literaturii Americane in Romania in Secolul al 19-lea Si Prima Jumatate a Sec. al 20-Lea: The Reception of American Literature in Romania. unabridged ed. (RUM.). 442p. (C). 1996. text 30.00 (*0-9653217-0-3*) D Durobat.

Dorobek, S. L. & Ross, G. M., eds. Stratigraphic Evolution of Foreland Basins. (SEPM Special Publications: No. 52). (Illus.). 320p. 1995. text 97.00 (*1-56576-016-6*) SEPM.

Dorobiala, James F. A Ten Minute Cure for the Common Cold: A Natural Approach. Martinez, Kerry A., ed. LC 87-18114. (Illus.). 160p. (Orig.). 1988. 24.95 (*0-944346-01-4*); pap. 9.95 (*0-944346-02-2*) Sun Eagle Pub.

Dorodnicyn, Anatoly A. & Chushkin, Pavel I. Modern Problems-Computational Aerohydrodynamics. 1991. 110.00 (*0-8493-7533-9*, Q) CRC Pr.

Dorofeeva, L., jt. ed. see Kaliazina, N.

Doroff, Larry, jt. auth. see Doroff, Steven.

Doroff, Steven & Doroff, Larry. WordStar in English I. (English I Computer Tutorials Ser.). (Illus.). 134p. reprint ed. pap. 12.95 (*0-915869-01-2*) Eng Comp Tut.

Dorogman, Gy. Spanish-Hungarian Concise Dictionary. 876p. 1992. 45.00 (*963-05-5987-0*, Pub. by Akade Kiado) St Mut.

Dorogostaiskaya, Eugenia V. How It Was: Prehistory of the Limnological Institue of the Academy of Sciences, U. S. S. R. at Lake Baikal. Forest, Herman S., ed. 65p. 1993. 2.00 (*1-883641-02-0*) St U NY Geneseo.

Dorogovtsev, A. A. Stochastic Analysis & Random Maps in Hilbert Space. 114p. 1994. 128.00 (*90-6764-163-4*, Pub. by VSP) Coronet Bks.

Dorogovtsev, A. I., et al. Probability Theory: Collection of Problems. Klesov, O. I. & Kotov, V. A., trs. from ENG. LC 97-5939. (Translations of Mathematical Monographs: Vol. 163). 347p. 1997. text 119.00 (*0-8218-0372-7*, MMONO/163) Am Math.

*__Doron, Gideon & Harris, Michael.__ Public Policy & Electoral Reform: The Case of Israel. 144p. 2000. 45.00 (*0-7391-0134-X*) Lxngtn Bks.

Doron, Gideon & Mintz, Alex, eds. Policy Sciences State of the Art. (Orig.). 1992. pap. 15.00 (*0-944285-30-9*) Pol Studies.

Doron, Gideon, jt. auth. see Peretz, Don.

Doron, Paul H. Development: The Eventful Life & Travels of an Engineer. (Illus.). 372p. (Orig.). 1993. pap. 12.95 (*965-229-090-4*, Pub. by Gefen Pub Hse) Gefen Bks.

Doron, Pinchas. Mystery of Creation According to Rashi. 154p. 1982. 12.00 (*0-940118-58-0*) Moznaim.

*__Doron, Pinchas.__ Rashi's Torah Commentary: Religious, Philosophical, Ethical & Educational Insights. LC 99-17463. Orig. Title: Perush Rashi 'al ha-Torah. 1999. 40.00 (*0-7657-6095-9*) Aronson.

Doron, Reuven. One New Man. 193p. (Orig.). 1993. pap. 10.00 (*0-9629049-9-6*, RD1-103) Arrow Publications.

Doron, Roland. Dictionnaire de Psychologie. (FRE.). 776p. 1991. pap. 175.00 (*0-7859-7744-9*, 2130435513) Fr & Eur.

Doronila, Amando. The State, Economic Transformation, & Political Change in the Philippines, 1946-1972. (Illus.). 224p. 1992. 39.95 (*0-19-588577-5*) OUP.

Doronila, Maria L. Canieso, see Canieso Doronila, Maria L.

Doros, Paul E. The Tiffany Collection of the Chrysler Museum at Norfolk. LC 77-4768. (Illus.). 160p. 1978. pap. 10.00 (*0-940744-13-9*) Chrysler Museum.

Dorosh, G., jt. auth. see Kennedy, P.

Dorosh, Michael A. Canuck Vol. 1: Clothing & Equipping the Canadian Soldier 1939-1945. LC 95-70835. (Illus.). 168p. 1995. pap. 10.95 (*1-57510-005-3*) Pictorial Hist.

Dorosh, Paul & Bernier, Rene. Agricultural & Food Policy Issues in Mozambique: A Multimarket Analysis. (Working Papers: No. 63). 81p. (C). 1994. pap. 7.00 (*1-56401-163-1*) Cornell Food.

Dorosh, Paul & Valdes, Alberto. Effects of Exchange Rate & Trade Policies on Agriculture in Pakistan. 114p. 1990. 10.00 (*0-89629-088-3*) Intl Food Policy.

Dorosh, Paul, et al. Food Aid & Poverty Alleviation in Mozambique: The Potential for Self-Targeting with Yellow Maize. (Working Papers: No. 50). 43p. (C). 1994. pap. 7.00 (*1-56401-150-X*) Cornell Food.

Dorosh, Paul A. Adjustment, External Shocks, & Poverty in Lesotho: A Multiplier Analysis. (Working Papers: No. 71). 45p. (C). 1994. pap. 7.00 (*1-56401-171-2*) Cornell Food.

— Implications of Macroeconomic Policy for the Poor in Nigeria: A CGE Analysis. (Working Papers: No. 75). (C). Date not set. pap. 7.00 (*1-56401-175-5*) Cornell Food.

— Macroeconomic Adjustment & the Poor in Madagascar: A CGE Analysis. (Working Papers: No. 61). 33p. (C). 1994. pap. 7.00 (*1-56401-161-5*) Cornell Food.

Dorosh, Paul A. & Haggblade, Steven. Growth Linkages in Madagascar: Implications for Sectoral Investment Priorities. (Working Papers: No. 60). 29p. 1994. pap. 7.00 (*1-56401-160-7*) Cornell Food.

Dorosh, Paul A. & Lundberg, Mattias K. Aid Flows & Policy Reforms: A General Equilibrium Analysis of Adjustment & the Poor in the Gambia. (Working Papers: No. 46). 72p. (C). 1993. pap. 7.00 (*1-56401-146-1*) Cornell Food.

Dorosh, Paul A., et al. Macroeconomic Adjustment & the Poor: The Case of Madagascar. (Monographs). (Illus.). 160p. (C). 1990. pap. text 12.00 (*1-56401-009-0*) Cornell Food.

— Une Matrice de Comptabilite Sociale pour Madagascar: Methodologie et Resultats. (Working Papers). (C). 1991. pap. text 7.00 (*1-56401-200-X*) Cornell Food.

— A Social Accounting Matrix for Madagascar: Methodology & Results. (Working Papers). (C). 1991. pap. text 7.00 (*1-56401-106-2*) Cornell Food.

— Terms of Trade & the Real Exchange Rate in the CFA Zone: Implications for Income Distribution in Niger. (Working Papers: No. 57). 38p. (C). 1994. pap. 7.00 (*1-56401-157-7*) Cornell Food.

Dorosh, Paul A., jt. auth. see Barrett, Christopher B.

Doroshenko, Dmytro. Het'man Petro Dorohenko. Omelchenko, William, ed. (UKR., Illus.). 520p. 1985. 35.00 (*0-916381-03-X*) Ukrainian Arts Sci.

Doroshenko, Peter. Margie Hughto: A Ten Year Survey, 1980-1990. Piche, Thomas E., ed. LC 91-70277. (Illus.). 64p. 1991. pap. 10.00 (*0-914407-15-5*) Everson Mus.

Doroshenko, Peter, text. Texas: Between Two Worlds. LC 93-72062. (Illus.). 82p. 1993. pap. 24.95 (*0-936080-33-7*) Cont Arts Museum.

Doroshenko, Peter & Druckrey, Timothy. Gretchen Bender: Work 1981-1991. Piche, Thomas E., ed. LC 91-70276. (Illus.). 58p. (Orig.). 1991. pap. write for info. (*0-914407-16-3*) Everson Mus.

Doroshkin, Milton. Yiddish in America: Social & Cultural Foundations. LC 72-78612. (Illus.). 281p. 1975. 38.50 (*0-8386-7453-4*) Fairleigh Dickinson.

Doroshov, S. I., jt. ed. see Binkowski, F. P.

Doroshow, Joanne & Wilkes, Adrian J. Lloyd's of London. 154p. 1988. 10.00 (*0-936758-22-8*) Ctr Responsive Law.

Dorosin, Jeremy. Balance at Middlefork: An Adventure in Human Freedom. LC 98-74052. 332p. (Orig.). 1999. pap. 24.95 (*0-89087-851-X*) Celestial Arts.

Dorossiev, D. Rehabilitation & Comprehensive Secondary Prevention after Acute Myocardial Infarction. (Euro Reports & Studies Ser.: No. 84). 99p. 1983. pap. text 8.00 (*92-890-1250-1*) World Health.

*__Dorosz, Jan & Romaniuk, Ryszard S., eds.__ Optical Fibers & Their Applications VI. 342p. 1999. pap. text 84.00 (*0-8194-3205-9*) SPIE.

Dorosz, P. Guide Pratique des Medicaments. 19th ed. (FRE.). 1800p. 1998. 125.00 (*0-320-00696-4*) Fr & Eur.

— Practical Guide to Medications: Guide Pratique des Medicaments. 13th ed. 1624p. 1993. 125.00 (*0-685-64733-1*, M15473) Fr & Eur.

D

Doroszewski, Witold. Elements of Lexicology & Semiotics. Taylor, Iain, tr. from POL. (Approaches to Semiotics Ser.: No. 46). 314p. 1973. text 36.95 (90-279-2699-9) Mouton.

Dorotheus of Gaza. Dorotheos of Gaza: Discourses & Sayings. LC 77-4295. (Cistercian Studies: No. 33). 1977. pap. 9.95 (0-87907-933-9) Cistercian Pubns.

Dorothy, Charles V. The Books of Esther: Structure, Genre & Textual Integrity. LC 97-202693. (JSOT Supplement Ser.: No. 187). 384p. 1997. 85.00 (1-85075-518-3, Pub. by Sheffield Acad) CUP Services.

Dorothy, Paul, et al. The Cheshire Cat & Other Eye-Popping Experiments on How We See the World. LC 94-47034. (Exploratorium Science Snackbook Ser.). (Illus.). 114p. (YA). (gr. 5 up). 1995. pap. 10.95 (0-471-11516-9) Wiley.

— The Magic Wand & Other Bright Experiments on Light & Color. (Exploratorium Science Snackbook Ser.). 144p. (YA). (gr. 5 up). 1995. pap. 10.95 (0-471-11515-0) Wiley.

Dorot'Iakova, V., et al. Russian - Slovak Dictionary. (RUS & SLO.). 747p. 1989. 32.95 (0-8285-5399-8) Firebird NY.

Dorough, Jan, ed. see Zike, Dinah.

Dorough, Prince. Popular-Music Culture in America. (Illus.). 352p. (C). 1992. text 39.95 (1-880157-04-7) Ardsley.

Dorough, Prince L. & Gordon, Christopher P. Music: The New Curriculum. 309p. (Orig.). (C). 1995. pap. text 20.80 (0-87563-577-6) Stipes.

Dorovsky, V. N., jt. auth. see Blokhin, A. M.

Dorow, Sara. When You Were Born in China: A Memory Book for Children Adopted from China. (Illus.). 44p. 1997. 16.00 (0-9638472-1-X) Yeong & Yeong.

Dorow, Sara, ed. I Wish for You a Beautiful Life: Letters from the Korean Birth Mothers of Ae Ran Won to Their. 135p. 1999. 18.95 (0-9638472-3-6) Yeong & Yeong.

Dorow, Wolfgang. The Business Corporation in the Democratic Society. Orig. Title: Die Unternehmung in der Demokratischen Gesellschaft. (Illus.). 388p. (C). 1987. lib. bdg. 112.00 (3-11-010293-5) De Gruyter.

Doroy, Jean Francois & Artigaud, Frank. Wine & Cheese of France, 2 vols. (Illus.). 72p. 1998. 29.95 (88-7301-268-X, Pub. by Gremese Intl) Natl Bk Netwk.

Dorpalen, Andreas. German History in Marxist Perspective: The East German Approach. LC 88-5784. 543p. reprint ed. pap. 168.40 (0-608-10557-0, 207117700009) Bks Demand.

Dorpat, Paul. Seattle Now & Then. (Illus.). 288p. (Orig.). 1984. 25.00 (0-9614357-0-4); pap. 12.95 (0-9614357-1-2) Tartu Pubns.

— Seattle Now & Then, Vol. 2. 240p. (Orig.). 1987. 19.95 (0-9614357-3-9); pap. 12.95 (0-9614357-2-0) Tartu Pubns.

Dorpat, Theodore L. Gaslighting, the Double Whammy, Interrogation & Other Methods of Covert Control in Psychotherapy & Analysis. LC 96-14098. 1996. 50.00 (1-56821-828-1) Aronson.

Dorpat, Theodore L. & Miller, Michael L. Clinical Interaction & the Analysis of Meaning: A New Psychoanalytic Theory. 344p. 1992. text 49.95 (0-88163-146-9) Analytic Pr.

***Dorr.** Bell P 39 Airacobra. (Illus.). 192p. 2000. 44.95 (1-86126-348-1, Pub. by Crolwood) Motorbooks Intl.

— Cancer Chemotherapy Handbook. 2nd ed. 1994. text 90.00 (0-8385-1068-X) McGraw-Hill Prof.

Dorr. Introductory Music Theory. (Music Ser.). 1995. wbk. ed. 16.50 (0-534-18859-1) Wadsworth Pub.

— Introductory Music Theory. (Music Ser.). 1995. pap., suppl. ed., wbk. ed. 13.25 (0-534-18861-3) Wadsworth Pub.

Dorr, Aim'ee. Television & Children: A Special Medium for a Special Audience. LC 85-19675. (Sage Commtext Ser.: No. 14). 160p. 1986. reprint ed. pap. 49.60 (0-608-01487-7, 205953100001) Bks Demand.

Dorr, B. F. The Surveyor's Guide. 1978. reprint ed. pap. 12.00 (0-686-25542-9, 514) CARBEN Survey.

Dorr, Bonnie, ed. Building Lexicons for Machine Translation: Papers from the 1993 Spring Symposium. (Technical Reports). (Illus.). 140p. (C). 1993. spiral bd. 25.00 (0-929280-39-3) AAAI Pr.

Dorr, Bonnie J. Machine Translation: A View from the Lexicon. LC 92-35158. (Artificial Intelligence Ser.). (Illus.). 456p. 1993. 52.50 (0-262-04138-3) MIT Pr.

Dorr, Dalton. Dorr: Records of Lineage in the Dorr, Dalton, Odin, Walter & Other Allied New England Families. 144p. 1995. reprint ed. pap. 26.00 (0-8328-4952-9); reprint ed. lib. bdg. 36.00 (0-8328-4951-0) Higginson Bk Co.

Dorr, Darwin, et al. The Psychology of Discipline: Six Approaches to Discipline. LC 81-20775. xi, 253p. 1981. 40.00 (0-8236-5581-4) Intl Univs Pr.

Dorr, David F. A Colored Man Around the World. Schueller, Malini J., ed. LC 99-31471. (Illus.). 240p. 1999. text 42.50 (0-472-09694-X, 09694); pap. text 15.95 (0-472-06694-3, 06694) U of Mich Pr.

Dorr, Dee, jt. auth. see Knapp, Renae R.

***Dorr, Donal.** Mission in Today's World. 308p. 2000. pap. 20.00 (1-57075-339-3) Orbis Bks.

Dorr, Donal. Option for the Poor: A Hundred Years of Vatican Social Teaching. LC 92-20785. 300p. (Orig.). (C). 1992. pap. 19.00 (0-88344-827-0) Orbis Bks.

— The Social Justice Agenda: Justice, Ecology, Power, & the Church. LC 90-49049. 1991. pap. 13.50 (0-88344-722-3) Orbis Bks.

Dorr, Eugene L., et al. Merchandising. 2nd ed. (Occupational Manuals & Projects in Marketing Ser.). 1977. text 12.28 (0-07-017615-9) McGraw.

Dorr, Eugene L., ed. see Antrim, William.

Dorr, Eugene L., ed. see Bikkie, James A.

Dorr, Eugene L., ed. see Crawford, Lucy.

Dorr, Eugene L., ed. see Ely, Vivian K. & Barnes, Michael.

Dorr, Eugene L., ed. see Ertel, Kenneth & Walsh, Lawrence A.

Dorr, Eugene L., ed. see Harris, E. Edward.

Dorr, Eugene L., ed. see Hiserodt, Donald.

Dorr, Eugene L., ed. see Klaurens, Mary K.

Dorr, Eugene L., ed. see Logan, William B.

Dorr, George B. The Story of Acadia. 3rd ed. 127p. 1997. reprint ed. pap. 8.95 (0-934745-21-8) Acadia Pub Co.

Dorr, Gregory P. Santa's Lil' Gimp: A Book Not for Children. LC 95-80767. (Illus.). 30p. 1995. pap. 9.95 (1-878044-47-8) Mayhaven Pub.

Dorr, Heiko & Van Leeuwen, J. Efficient Graph Rewriting & Its Implementation. Goos, G. & Hartmanis, J., eds. LC 95-30326. (Lecture Notes in Computer Science Ser.: Vol. 922). ix, 266p. 1995. pap. 49.00 (3-540-60055-8) Spr-Verlag.

Dorr, J. Bermuda. 1976. lib. bdg. 59.95 (0-8490-1490-5) Gordon Pr.

Dorr, John A., Jr. & Eschman, Donald F. Geology of Michigan. LC 69-17351. (Illus.). 488p. 1970. text 39.50 (0-472-08280-9, 08280) U of Mich Pr.

Dorr, Joyce. Introductory Music Theory. 340p. 1995. 56.95 (0-534-18858-3) Wadsworth Pub.

Dorr, Kathleen, ed. see Wilhelm, Gayle B.

Dorr, Laurence. Plant Collectors in Madagascar & the Comoro Islands. (Illus.). 524p. 1997. 116.00 (1-900347-18-0, Pub. by Royal Botnic Grdns) Balogh.

Dorr, Laurence J. A Revision of the North American Genus Callirhoe (Malvaceae) LC 89-13653. (Memoirs Ser.: No. 56). (Illus.). 84p. 1990. pap. 18.50 (0-89327-349-X) NY Botanical.

Dorr, Madeline. The Mask: He's Gone from Zero to Hero! (J). (gr. 3 up). 1994. pap. 3.99 (0-679-87115-2, Bullseye Bks) Random Bks Yng Read.

Dorr, Marianne, jt. auth. see Weber, Hartmut.

Dorr, Nell & Hardee, Covington. Life Dance: A Photography Album. (Illus.). 72p. 1975. pap. 9.75 (0-911726-21-7, CODE LDB) Alleluia Pr.

Dorr, Rheta C. Inside the Russian Revolution. LC 72-115530. (Russia Observed, Series I). (Illus.). 1970. reprint ed. 21.95 (0-405-03022-3) Ayer.

— Susan B. Anthony, The Woman Who Changed the Mind of a Nation. LC 74-100519. reprint ed. 47.50 (0-404-00626-4) AMS Pr.

— A Woman of Fifty. Baxter, Annette K., ed. LC 79-8787. (Signal Lives Ser.). 1980. reprint ed. lib. bdg. 50.95 (0-405-12835-5) Ayer.

Dorr, Robert & Lake, Jon. Korean War Aces. (Aircraft of the Aces Ser.: Vol. 4). (Illus.). 96p. 1995. pap. 17.95 (1-85532-501-2, Pub. by Ospry) Motorbooks Intl.

***Dorr, Robert C. & Munch, Christopher H.** Protecting Trade Secrets, Patents, Copyrights & Trademarks. 3rd ed. LC 99-51534. 1999. ring bd. 165.00 (0-7355-1155-1) Panel Pubs.

— Trade Dress Law. 2nd ed. LC 99-41725. 1999. write for info. (0-7355-0301-X) Panel Pubs.

Dorr, Robert F. B-24 Liberator Units of the Eighth Air Force. (Combat Aircraft Ser.: Vol. 15). (Illus.). 112p. 1999. pap. 17.95 (1-85532-901-8, 129059AE, Pub. by Ospry) Motorbooks Intl.

***Dorr, Robert F.** B-24 Liberator Units of the Fifteenth Air Force. (Combat Aircraft Ser.: Vol. 21). (Illus.). 96p. 2000. pap. 17.95 (1-84176-081-1, 130588AE, Pub. by Ospry) Motorbooks Intl.

Dorr, Robert F. B-24 Liberator Units of the Pacific War. (Combat Aircraft Ser.: No. 11). (Illus.). 96p. 1999. pap. 17.95 (1-85532-781-3, Pub. by Ospry) Motorbooks Intl.

— Inside the Great Jet Fighters. LC 96-232392. (Illus.). 128p. 1996. pap. 24.95 (0-7603-0306-1) MBI Pubg.

— P-51 Mustang. LC 95-6118. (Warbird History Ser.). (Illus.). 128p. 1995. pap. 19.95 (0-7603-0002-X) MBI Pubg.

Dorr, Robert F. & Bishop, Chris. Vietnam Air War Debrief. (Illus.). 253p. 1996. 34.95 (1-880588-22-6) AIRtime Pub.

***Dorr, Robert F. & Peacock, Lindsey.** B-52 Stratofortress: Boeing's Cold War Warrior. (Illus.). 272p. 2000. pap. 29.95 (1-84176-097-8, 130160AE, Pub. by Ospry) Motorbooks Intl.

Dorr, Robert T. Cancer Chemotherapy Handbook. 3rd ed. 1999. 80.00 (0-8385-1534-7, Medical Exam) Appleton & Lange.

Dorr, Robert T. & Von Hoff, Daniel D. Cancer Chemotherapy Handbook. 2nd ed. 1020p. (C). 1996. pap. text 115.00 (0-8385-1036-1, A1036-1, Apple Lange Med) McGraw.

Dorr, Roberta K. Abraham & Sarah. 1996. pap. 10.99 (0-345-40779-2, Moorings) Ballantine Pub Grp.

Dorr, Steven, jt. auth. see Reich, Bernard.

Dorr, Steven R. Scholars' Guide to Washington, D. C., for Middle Eastern Studies: Egypt, Sudan, Jordan, Lebanon, Syria, Iraq, the Arabian Peninsula, Israel, Turkey, & Iran. David, Zdenek V., ed. LC 81-607073. 564p. 1991. 29.95 (0-87474-372-9); pap. text 15.00 (0-87474-371-0) W Wilson Ctr Pr.

Dorra, Henri. Art in Perspective: A Brief History. (Illus.). 334p. (Orig.). (C). 1973. pap. text 57.50 (0-15-503475-8, Pub. by Harcourt Coll Pubs) Harcourt.

— Symbolist Art Theories: A Critical Anthology. LC 93-32264. (Illus.). 396p. (C). 1996. pap. 19.95 (0-520-07768-7, Pub. by U CA Pr) Cal Prin Full Svc.

Dorra, Mary. Beautiful American Vegetable Gardens. LC 96-26003. 1997. 40.00 (0-517-70304-1) C Potter.

Dorra, Mary T. Beautiful American Rose Gardens. LC 98-43389. 192p. 1999. 40.00 (0-609-60080-X) Crown Pub Group.

Dorraj, Manochehr. From Zarathustra to Khomeini: Populism & Dissent in Iran. LC 89-10973. 220p. 1990. lib. bdg. 37.00 (1-55587-181-X) L Rienner.

Dorraj, Manochehr, ed. The Changing Political Economy of the Third World. LC 94-31378. 490p. 1995. pap. text 19.95 (1-55587-577-7); lib. bdg. 48.00 (1-55587-554-8) L Rienner.

— Middle East at the Crossroads: The Changing Political Dynamics & the Foreign Policy. LC 99-24370. 320p. 1999. 52.00 (0-7618-1390-X) U Pr of Amer.

***Dorraj, Manochehr, ed.** Middle East at the Crossroads: The Changing Political Dynamics & the Foreign Policy. LC 99-24370. 320p. 1999. pap. 34.50 (0-7618-1391-8) U Pr of Amer.

Dorrance, Anson. Training Soccer Champions. Nash, Tim, ed. (Illus.). 1996. pap. 19.95 (1-887791-02-7) JTC Sports.

Dorrance, Bill & Desmond, Leslie. True Horsemanship Through Feel. (Illus.). 286p. 1999. 65.00 (1-892578-00-X) Diamond Lu.

Dorrance, John C. The United States & the Pacific Islands, 158. LC 92-19951. (Washington Papers: No. 158). 208p. 1992. 49.95 (0-275-94471-9, C4471, Praeger Pubs); pap. 16.95 (0-275-94472-7, B4472, Greenwood Pr) Greenwood.

Dorrance, Tom. True Unity: Willing Communication Between Horse & Human. Porter, Milly H., ed. LC 87-72039. (Illus.). 151p. 1994. reprint ed. 18.95 (1-884995-09-8) Word Dancer.

Dorrance, William H. O'ahu's Hidden History. (Illus.). 240p. 1998. pap. 13.95 (1-56647-211-3) Mutual Pub HI.

***Dorraswamy, Naganand.** Ipsec: The New Security Standard for the Internet, Intranets & Virtual Private Networks. LC 99-23833. 300p. 1999. 44.99 (0-13-011898-2, Prentice Hall) P-H.

Dorrbecker, Detlef W., ed. see Blake, William.

Dorre, E., et al. Alumina: Processing, Properties & Applications. (Materials Research & Engineering Ser.). (Illus.). 330p. 1984. 95.00 (0-387-13576-6) Spr-Verlag.

Dorre, Pamela. Wind over Stonehenge. (Bestsellers II Ser.). (J). 1977. 16.60 (0-606-02449-2, Pub. by Turtleback) Demco.

Dorrel, Ruth, compiled by. Pioneer Ancestors of Members of the Society of Indiana Pioneers. iv, 245p. 1983. pap. 20.00 (0-87195-076-6) Ind Hist Soc.

Dorrel, Ruth, ed. An Index to Records of the Indiana Soldiers' & Sailors' Children's Home. LC 99-29805. 1999. pap. 30.00 (0-87195-143-6) Ind Hist Soc.

— Indiana Source Book Vol. VI with Index: Genealogical Material from the Hoosier Genealogist, 1985-1988. vii, 372p. 1992. 25.00 (0-87195-090-1); pap. 15.00 (0-87195-091-X) Ind Hist Soc.

— Indiana Source Book Vol. VII with index: Genealogical Material from the Hoosier Genealogist, 1989-1990. vi, 500p. 1994. 25.00 (0-87195-107-X) Ind Hist Soc.

— Indiana Source Book Vol. VIII with Index: Material from the Hoosier Genealogist, 1991-1992. LC 82-109870. vi, 393p. 1997. 25.00 (0-87195-117-7) Ind Hist Soc.

Dorrel, Ruth & Hamm, Thomas D., eds. Abstracts of the Records of the Society of Friends in Indiana, Vol. 1. LC 96-18658. xiv, 318p. 1996. 60.00 (0-87195-113-4) Ind Hist Soc.

— Abstracts of the Records of the Society of Friends in Indiana, Vol. 2. rev. ed. 234p. 1999. 40.00 (0-87195-142-8) Ind Hist Soc.

Dorrell, Jean. The Answer Book: A Reference Manual for Office Personnel. 2nd rev. ed. LC 92-61272. (Illus.). 358p. (C). 1993. pap. text. write for info. (0-935732-43-8) Roxbury Pub Co.

— Answer Book Student Workbook: A Reference Manual for Office Personnel. 2nd ed. (Illus.). 130p. (C). 1994. pap. text. write for info. (0-935732-56-X) Roxbury Pub Co.

Dorrell, Julie. Resource Based Learning: Using Open & Flexible Learning Resources for Continuous Development. LC 93-15715. (Training Ser.). 1993. write for info. (0-07-707692-3) McGraw.

Dorrell, Peter G. Photography in Archaeology & Conservation. 2nd ed. (Cambridge Manuals in Archaeology Ser.). (Illus.). 282p. (C). 1994. pap. text 24.95 (0-521-45554-5) Cambridge U Pr.

— Photography in Archaeology & Conservation. 2nd ed. (Cambridge Manuals in Archaeology Ser.). (Illus.). 282p. (C). 1995. text 65.00 (0-521-45534-0) Cambridge U Pr.

Dorren, Gaston, jt. auth. see Maharaj, Niala.

***Dorresteijn, Adriaan W. C. & Westheide, Wilfried.** Reproductive Strategies & Developmental Patterns in Annelids. LC 99-50111. (Developments in Hydrobiology Ser.). 1999. write for info. (0-7923-6018-4) Kluwer Academic.

Dorrestein, Renate. Unnatural Mothers: A Novel. Boeke, Wanda, tr. LC 94-16877. 232p. 1994. pap. 11.95 (1-879679-06-X) Women Translation.

Dorrian, James G. Storming St. Nazaire. (Special Warfare Ser.). (Illus.). 320p. 1998. 29.95 (1-55750-849-6) Naval Inst Pr.

***Dorrian, Jean.** Educational Background of Systems Librarians. (Occasional Papers: Vol. 20). (Illus.). 49p. 1998. pap. 25.00 (0-918006-32-5) Assn Res Lib.

Dorrie, Doris. Look at Me. (Illus.). 128p. 1998. 35.00 (3-908161-14-2) Abbeville Pr.

Dorrie, Heinrich. One Hundred Great Problems of Elementary Mathematics: Their History & Solution. Antin, David, tr. from GER. 393p. 1965. pap. 9.95 (0-486-61348-8) Dover.

Dorrien, Gary. The Barthian Revolt in Modern Theology: Theology Without Weapons. LC 99-38148. 288p. 1999. pap. 29.95 (0-664-22151-3) Westminster John Knox.

— The Neoconservative Mind: Politics, Culture, & the War of Ideology. LC 92-11187. 512p. (C). 1993. 59.95 (1-56639-019-2) Temple U Pr.

— The Neoconservative Mind: Politics, Culture, & the War of Ideology. LC 92-11187. 512p. (C). 1993. pap. 24.95 (1-56639-144-X) Temple U Pr.

— Soul in Society: The Making & Renewal of Social Christianity. LC 95-4023. 352p. 1995. pap. 26.00 (0-8006-2891-8, 1-2891, Fortress Pr) Augsburg Fortress.

— The Word As True Myth: Interpreting Modern Theology. LC 97-16941. 1997. pap. 24.95 (0-664-25745-3) Westminster John Knox.

Dorrien, Gary J. The Democratic Socialist Vision. 192p. 1986. 50.00 (0-8476-7507-6) Rowman.

— Reconstructing the Common Good: Theology & the Social Order. LC 90-31698. 1992. reprint ed. pap. 20.00 (0-88344-797-5) Orbis Bks.

— The Remaking of Evangelical Theology. LC 98-23573. 264p. 1998. pap. 24.00 (0-664-25803-4) Westminster John Knox.

Dorries. Coroner's Courts. 418p. 1999. 60.00 (0-471-96721-1) Wiley.

***Dorril, Stephen.** M16: Inside the Convert World of Her Majesty's Secret Intelligence Service. LC 00-29385. 880p. 2000. 39.50 (0-7432-0379-8) Free Pr.

Dorrin, Karen. Perfect Partners, 1, 4. (Zebra Bouquet Ser.). 1999. mass mkt. 3.99 (0-8217-6277-X) Kensgtn Pub Corp.

Dorrington, Jeff. In Your Garden. 1997. pap. 19.95 (1-86368-202-3, Pub. by Fremantle Arts) Intl Spec Bk.

Dorris. Biology: The Realm of Life. 3rd ed. (Illus.). (C). 1995. teacher ed. write for info. (0-673-55042-7) Addson-Wesley Educ.

Dorris, Charles, ed. see Kay, Alan F.

Dorris, George E. Paolo Rolli & the Italian Circle in London, 1715-1744. (Studies in Italian Literature: No. 2). (Orig.). 1967. pap. text 50.00 (0-89925-329-6) Mouton.

Dorris, George E., ed. The Royal Swedish Ballet. (Illus.). 160p. pap. 21.95 (1-85273-069-2, Pub. by Dance Bks) Princeton Bk Co.

Dorris, Jonathon T. Pardon & Amnesty under Lincoln & Johnson: The Restoration of the Confederates to Their Rights & Privileges, 1861-1898. LC 77-5940. 459p. 1977. lib. bdg. 59.75 (0-8371-9646-9, Greenwood Pr) Greenwood.

Dorris, Michael. Broken Cord. 1990. 19.95 (0-606-16267-4) Turtleback.

Dorris, Michael. Broken Cord Tv Tie-I. LC 88-45893. (Illus.). 288p. 1992. reprint ed. pap. 14.00 (0-06-091682-6, Perennial) HarperTrade.

— Cloud Chamber. 1998. 17.10 (0-606-12660-0, Pub. by Turtleback) Demco.

***Dorris, Michael.** Cloud Chamber: A Novel. 1998. per. write for info. (0-684-00606-5) S&S Trade.

Dorris, Michael. Cloud Chamber: A Novel. 320p. 1998. per. 12.00 (0-684-83535-5, Scribner Pap Fic) S&S Trade Pap.

— Cloud Chamber: A Novel. LC 96-42544. 320p. 1997. 23.50 (0-684-81567-2) Scribner.

— Cloud Chamber: A Novel. large type ed. LC 96-37879. 1997. 25.95 (0-7862-0981-X) Thorndike Pr.

— Dorris. 5.25 hd. write for info. (0-7868-0221-9, Pub. by Disney Pr) Little.

— Guests. LC 94-26057. 128p. (gr. 4-7). 1999. pap. 4.99 (0-7868-1356-3, Pub. by Hyperion) Time Warner.

— Guests. 128p. (J). (gr. 3-7). 1994. 13.95 (0-7868-0047-X, Pub. by Hyprn Child) Time Warner.

— Guests. LC 94-26057. 128p. (J). (gr. 3-7). 1996. pap. 4.50 (0-7868-1108-0, Pub. by Hyprn Ppbks) Little.

— Guests. (J). 1996. 10.34 (0-606-08759-1) Turtleback.

— Morning Girl. 80p. (J). (gr. 4-7). 1999. pap. text 4.99 (0-7868-1372-5, Pub. by Hyperion) Time Warner.

— Morning Girl. LC 92-52989. 80p. (YA). (gr. 4-7). 1994. pap. 4.95 (1-56282-661-1, Pub. by Hyprn Child) Little.

Dorris, Michael. Morning Girl. LC 92-52989. (J). 1994. 9.15 (0-606-06583-0, Pub. by Turtleback) Demco.

Dorris, Michael. Morning Girl. rev. ed. LC 92-52989. 80p. (J). (gr. 4-7). 1999. pap. 4.99 (0-7868-1358-X, Pub. by Hyperion) Time Warner.

— Paper Trail: Essays. LC 93-41420. 384p. 1995. pap. 12.00 (0-06-092593-0, Perennial) HarperTrade.

— Sees Behind Trees. LC 96-15859. (Illus.). 128p. (YA). (gr. 4-7). 1996. lib. bdg. 14.89 (0-7868-2215-5, Pub. by Hyprn Child) Little.

Dorris, Michael. Sees Behind Trees. 104p. (J). (gr. 4-6). pap. 4.95 (0-8072-1516-3) Listening Lib.

Dorris, Michael. Sees Behind Trees. (J). 1997. 10.05 (0-606-12807-7, Pub. by Turtleback) Demco.

— Sees Behind Trees. LC 96-15859. 112p. (YA). (gr. 3-7). 1997. reprint ed. pap. 4.95 (0-7868-1252-4, Pub. by Hyprn Ppbks) Little.

— Sees Behind Trees. rev. ed. LC 96-15859. 128p. (YA). (gr. 4-7). 1999. pap. 4.99 (0-7868-1357-1, Pub. by Disney Pr) Time Warner.

***Dorris, Michael.** Sees Behind Trees. unabridged ed. (J). (gr. 4-6). 1998. pap. 21.98 incl. audio (0-8072-7957-9, YA949SP) Listening Lib.

Dorris, Michael. Tainos.Tr. of Morning Girl. (SPA.). (J). 1996. pap. text 10.95 (84-204-4757-9) Santillana.

— Tainos.Tr. of Morning Girl. (SPA.). 1995. 16.05 (0-606-10513-1, Pub. by Turtleback) Demco.

— The Window. LC 97-2822. 112p. (YA). (gr. 4-7). 1999. pap. 4.99 (0-7868-1317-2, Pub. by Disney Pr) Time Warner.

— The Window. 112p. (gr. 4-7). 1999. pap. 4.99 (0-7868-1373-3, Pub. by Hyperion) Time Warner.

— The Window. LC 97-2822. (Illus.). 112p. (YA). (gr. 5 up). 1997. lib. bdg. 16.89 (0-7868-2240-6, Pub. by Hyprn Child) Time Warner.

— The Window. LC 97-2822. (Illus.). 112p. (YA). (gr. 5 up). 1997. 16.95 (0-7868-0301-0, Pub. by Hyprn Child) Time Warner.

— Working Men: Stories. 240p. 1995. 19.95 (0-8050-2296-1) H Holt & Co.

— Working Men: Stories. 304p. 1994. reprint ed. mass mkt. 11.99 (0-446-67019-7, Pub. by Warner Bks) Little.

— A Yellow Raft in Blue Water. LC 86-26947. 356p. 1995. 16.95 (*0-8050-0045-3*) H Holt & Co.
— A Yellow Raft in Blue Water. (J). 1987. 15.09 (*0-606-04133-8*, Pub. by Turtleback) Demco.
Dorris, Michael. A Yellow Raft in Blue Water. 384p. 1988. reprint ed. mass mkt. 14.00 (*0-446-38787-8*, Pub. by Warner Bks) Little.
— Yellow Raft in Blue Water: Dewhurst,&Colleen. abr. ed. 1995. audio 18.00 (*1-55994-159-6*, CPN 2145) HarperAudio.
Dorris, Michael & Buchwald, Emilie, eds. The Most Wonderful Books: Writers on Discovering the Pleasures of Reading. LC 96-29624. 320p. (Orig.). 1997. pap. 14.95 (*1-57131-216-1*) Milkweed Ed.
Dorris, Michael & Erdrich, Louise. The Crown of Columbus. large type ed. (General Ser.). 591p. 1992. 18.95 (*0-8161-5283-7*, G K Hall Lrg Type) Mac Lib Ref.
— Route Two. deluxe ed. 40p. 1990. 50.00 (*0-935716-54-8*) Lord John.
Dorris, Michael & Roby, William C. A Yellow Raft in Blue Water. (Cliffs Notes Ser.). 85p. 1999. 4.95 (*0-7645-8511-8*) IDG Bks.
Dorris, Michele M., jt. ed. see Chesneau, Howard L.
Dorris, Paul. Irish Phrase Book. (Pocket Guide Ser.). 71p. (Orig.). 1983. pap. 7.95 (*0-86281-010-8*, Pub. by Appletree Pr) Irish Bks Media.
Dorris, Pearl. Step by Step We Climb to Freedom & Victory, Vol. 3. LC 88-18013. (Step by Step Ser.). (Illus.). 216p. 1990. pap. 9.95 (*0-9619770-3-5*) Pearl Publishing.
Dorris, Ronald. Race: Jean Toomer's Swan Song. (Occasional Publications: Vol. 7). xii, 86p. (Orig.). 1997. pap. 8.95 (*1-883275-06-7*) Xavier Rev.
***Dorritie, Frank.** Essentials of Music for Audio Professionals. 2000. pap. 39.95 (*0-87288-737-5*) Intertec Pub.
Dorroh, J. Robert, et al, eds. Applied Analysis: Proceedings of a Conference on Applied Analysis, April 19-21, 1996, Baton Rouge, Louisiana. LC 98-34483. (Contemporary Mathematics Ser.: Vol. 221). 284p. 1998. pap. 59.00 (*0-8218-0673-4*) Am Math.
Dorros, Arthur. Abuela. LC 90-21459. (Illus.). 40p. (J). (ps-2). 1991. 16.99 (*0-525-44750-4*, Dutton Child) Peng Put Young Read.
— Abuela. (Illus.). 40p. (J). (ps-1). 1997. pap. 5.99 (*0-14-056225-7*, PuffinBks) Peng Put Young Read.
— Abuela. (SPA.). 48p. (J). (ps-1). 1997. pap. 5.99 (*0-14-056226-5*) Penguin Putnam.
— Abuela. (Picture Puffin Ser.). (J). 1997. 10.19 (*0-606-11018-6*, Pub. by Turtleback) Demco.
— Abuela. (Picture Puffin Ser.). 1997. 10.19 (*0-606-11019-4*, Pub. by Turtleback) Demco.
— Alligator Shoes. 1992. pap. 4.99 (*0-14-054734-7*) NAL.
— Alligator Shoes. (J). 1982. 10.19 (*0-606-03994-5*, Pub. by Turtleback) Demco.
Dorros, Arthur. Ant Cities. (Let's-Read-And-Find-Out Book Ser.). (J). 1987. 10.15 (*0-606-03715-2*, Pub. by Turtleback) Demco.
— Ant Cities (Library Repackage) LC 85-48244. (Let's-Read-&-Find-Out Science Bks.). (Illus.). 32p. (J). (gr. k-4). 1987. lib. bdg. 15.89 (*0-690-04570-0*) HarpC Child Bks.
— Ant Cities (Trophy Repackage) LC 85-48244. (Trophy Let's Read-&-Find-Out Science Bk.). (Illus.). 32p. (J). (gr. k-4). 1998. reprint ed. pap. 4.95 (*0-06-445079-1*, HarpTrophy) HarpC Child Bks.
— City Chicken. 40p. (J). (ps-1). 14.89 (*0-06-028483-8*) HarpC.
Dorros, Arthur. City Chicken. 40p. (J). (ps-1). Date not set. pap. 14.95 (*0-06-028482-X*); pap. 5.95 (*0-06-443587-3*) HarpC Child Bks.
— Ciudades de Hormigas. Santacruz, Daniel M., tr. from ENG. LC 94-35266.Tr. of Ant Cities. (SPA., Illus.). 32p. (J). (ps-3). 1995. pap. 5.95 (*0-06-445137-2*, HarpTrophy) HarpC Child Bks.
— Ciudades de Hormigas. (Let's Read-&-Find-Out Science Ser.).Tr. of Ant Cities. (SPA.). 1995. 10.15 (*0-606-07373-6*) Turtleback.
— Elephant Families. LC 92-38972. (Let's-Read-&-Find-Out Science Bks.). (Illus.). 32p. (J). (gr. k-4). 1994. pap. 4.95 (*0-06-445122-4*, HarpTrophy) HarpC Child Bks.
Dorros, Arthur. Elephant Families. (Let's-Read-And-Find-Out Science. Stage 2 Ser.). 1994. 10.15 (*0-606-06358-7*, Pub. by Turtleback) Demco.
Dorros, Arthur. Esta Es Mi Casa.Tr. of This Is My House. (SPA.). 32p. (J). (ps-3). 1995. pap. 4.99 (*0-590-49444-9*) Scholastic Inc.
Dorros, Arthur. Feel the Wind. LC 88-18961. (Trophy Let's-Read-&-Find-Out Bk.). (Illus.). 32p. (J). (gr. k-4). 1990. pap. 4.95 (*0-06-445095-3*, HarpTrophy) HarpC Child Bks.
— Feel the Wind (Library repackage) LC 88-18961. (Let's-Read-&-Find-Out Science Bks.). (Illus.). 32p. (J). (gr. k-4). 1998. lib. bdg. 15.89 (*0-690-04741-X*) HarpC Child Bks.
Dorros, Arthur. Follow the Water from Brook to Ocean. LC 90-1438. (Let's-Read-&-Find-Out Science Bks.). (Illus.). 32p. (J). (gr. k-4). 1991. 15.00 (*0-06-021598-4*) HarpC Child Bks.
— Follow the Water from Brook to Ocean. LC 90-1438. (Let's-Read-&-Find-Out Science Bks.). (Illus.). 32p. (J). (gr. k-4). 2000. lib. bdg. 15.89 (*0-06-021599-2*) HarpC Child Bks.
— Follow the Water from Brook to Ocean. LC 90-1438. (Trophy Let's Read-&-Find-Out Science Bk.: Stage 2). (Illus.). 32p. (J). (gr. k-4). 2000. pap. 4.95 (*0-06-445115-1*, HarpTrophy) HarpC Child Bks.
— Follow the Water from Brook to Ocean. (Let's-Read-And-Find-Out Book Ser.). (J). 1993. 10.15 (*0-606-05295-X*, Pub. by Turtleback) Demco.
— Las Huellas de los Animales. (Mariposa Scholastica en Espanol Ser.). (SPA.). (J). 1993. 10.15 (*0-606-05417-0*, Pub. by Turtleback) Demco.
— Las Huellas de los Animales: Animal Tracks. Dorros, Sandra M., tr. from ENG. (SPA., Illus.). 32p. (J). (ps-2). 1993. pap. 4.95 (*0-590-46847-2*) Scholastic Inc.
— Isla. (ps-1). 1999. pap. 5.99 (*0-14-056505-1*, PuffinBks); pap. 6.99 (*0-14-056541-8*, PuffinBks) Peng Put Young Read.
— La Isla. (SPA., Illus.). (J). (ps-2). 1995. 16.99 (*0-525-45422-5*, Dutton Child) Peng Put Young Read.
Dorros, Arthur. Julio's Magic. 32p. (ps-1). 15.95 (*0-06-029004-8*); lib. bdg. 15.89 (*0-06-029005-6*); mass mkt. 5.95 (*0-06-443686-1*) HarpC.
Dorros, Arthur. Por Fin es Carnaval.Tr. of Tonight Is Carnival. (SPA.). 1995. 10.44 (*0-606-08033-3*) Turtleback.
— Radio Man: Don Radio: A Story in English & Spanish. Dorros, Sandra, tr. (ENG & SPA.). (J). (gr. 4). 1995. 9.00 (*0-395-73244-1*) HM.
— Radio Man: Don Radio: A Story in English & Spanish. (Trophy Picture Bks.). 1997. 11.15 (*0-606-11777-6*, Pub. by Turtleback) Demco.
— Radio Man: Don Radio: A Story in English & Spanish. large type ed. Dorros, Sandra, tr. (ENG & SPA.). 62p. (J). (gr. 4). 15.50 (*0-614-32389-4*, L-38181-00 APHB) Am Printing Hse.
— Radio Man/Don Radio. LC 92-28369. (Trophy Bk.). (SPA., Illus.). 40p. (J). (gr. 1-5). 1997. reprint ed. pap. 6.95 (*0-06-443482-6*, HarpTrophy) HarpC Child Bks.
***Dorros, Arthur.** Rain Forest Secrets. 40p. (gr. 1-4). 1999. pap. text 5.99 (*0-439-06394-9*) Scholastic Inc.
Dorros, Arthur. Rainforest Secrets. 40p. (J). (gr. 1-4). 1990. 15.95 (*0-590-43369-5*) Scholastic Inc.
— Ten Go Tango. LC 98-5723. (Illus.). 32p. (J). (ps-1). 2000. 15.95 (*0-06-027690-8*); lib. bdg. 15.89 (*0-06-027691-6*) HarpC Child Bks.
— Tonight Is Carnaval. (J). 1995. 10.19 (*0-606-08311-1*, Pub. by Turtleback) Demco.
— A Tree Is Growing. LC 96-10844. (Illus.). 32p. (J). (gr. k-3). 1997. 15.95 (*0-590-45300-9*) Scholastic Inc.
***Dorros, Arthur & Catrow, David.** The Fungus That Ate My School. LC 99-25350. 32p. (J). (gr. k-3). 2000. 15.95 (*0-590-47704-8*, Scholastic Ref) Scholastic Inc.
Dorros, Arthur, jt. auth. see Branley, Franklyn M.
Dorros, Sandra, tr. see Dorros, Arthur.
Dorros, Sandra M., tr. see Dorros, Arthur.
Dorros, Sandra M., tr. see Ryder, Joanne.
Dorros, Sidney. Parkinson's: A Patient's View. LC 89-10122. 1989. pap. 12.95 (*0-929765-20-6*) Seven Locks Pr.
Dorrough, Ardith. The Real Christmas Tree. 48p. (Orig.). 1983. pap. 2.50 (*0-88144-020-5*, CPS/020) Christian Pub.
Dorrough, Raymond. Latter Reign. 112p. (Orig.). 1993. pap. 8.99 (*1-56043-759-6*, Treasure Hse) Destiny Image.
Dorsaneo & Crump. Texas Civil Procedure: Pretrial Litigation. 3rd ed. 1989. write for info. (*0-8205-0471-8*, 709) Bender.
Dorsaneo, Despo, jt. auth. see Dorsaneo, William, III.
Dorsaneo, W., et al. Texas Litigation Guide, 26 vols. 1977. 2690.00 (*0-8205-1719-4*) Bender.
Dorsaneo, William, III & Dorsaneo, Despo. Texas Civil Procedure, 1993: Trial & Appellate Practices. 2nd ed. (C). 1993. suppl. ed. 9.95 (*0-8205-0463-7*, Irwn McGrw-H) McGrw-H Hghr Educ.
Dorsaneo, William, jt. auth. see Johnson, Earl.
***Dorsaneo, William V.** Texas Civil Procedure: Pretrial Litigation. 4th ed. LC 99-21944. (Casebook Ser.). 1999. 59.00 (*0-8205-3124-3*) Bender.
***Dorsaneo, William V., III.** Texas Civil Procedure: Trial & Appellate Practice 1998. annuals 3rd ed. 1998. text 58.00 (*0-8205-3138-3*) Bender.
Dorsaneo, William V., III, ed. Texas Torts Update. text 295.00 (*0-8205-2134-5*) Bender.
Dorsaneo, William V., jt. auth. see St. Claire, Frank A.
D'Orsay, Laurence R. Stories You Can Sell. LC 79-101280. (Short Story Index Reprint Ser.). 1977. 20.95 (*0-8369-3217-X*) Ayer.
Dorsch. Psychologisches Woerterbuch. 11th ed. (GER.). 921p. 1992. 135.00 (*0-7859-7546-2*, 3456816146) Fr & Eur.
Dorsch, Carole C., jt. auth. see Schweitzer, Glenn E.
Dorsch, Cathie. Confessions for Raising Winning Kids. pap. 1.00 (*0-89274-680-7*) Harrison Hse.
Dorsch, Friedrich. Dictionary of Psychology: Diccionario de Psicologia. 6th ed. (ENG & SPA.). 1040p. 1991. 125.00 (*0-7859-4966-6*) Fr & Eur.
— Psychologisches Woerterbuch. 9th ed. (GER.). 784p. 1976. 95.00 (*0-8288-5752-0*, M7595) Fr & Eur.
Dorsch, Jerry A & Dorsch, Susan E. Understanding Anesthesia Equipment. 4th ed. 1066p. 1998. 89.00 (*0-683-30487-9*) Lppncott W & W.
Dorsch, Nina G. Community, Collaboration, & Collegiality in School Reform: An Odyssey Toward Connections. LC 97-9047. (SUNY Series, Restructuring & School Change). 238p. (C). 1997. pap. text 19.95 (*0-7914-3598-9*) State U NY Pr.
— Community, Collaboration, & Collegiality in School Reform: An Odyssey Toward Connections. LC 97-9047. (SUNY Series, Restructuring & School Change). 238p. (C). 1998. text 59.50 (*0-7914-3597-0*) State U NY Pr.
Dorsch, Susan A., jt. auth. see Vargo, Karen D.
Dorsch, Susan E., jt. auth. see Dorsch, Jerry A.
Dorsch, T. S., ed. see Shakespeare, William.
***Dorsch, Thomas G.** Der Reichsgerichtsbau in Leipzig: Anspruch und Wirklichkeit einer Staatsarchitektur. (Europaische Hochschulschriften: Reihe 37, Ser.). (Illus.). 409p. 1999. 67.95 (*3-631-35060-0*) P Lang Pubng.
Dorsch, Tom, ed. see Koltavowski, George.
Dorsch, Walter, ed. Late Phase Allergic Reactions. 464p. 1990. lib. bdg. 129.00 (*0-8493-6743-3*, QR188) CRC Pr.
Dorscheid, P. Elsevier's Dictionary of Export Financing & Credit Insurance in English, German & French. (ENG, FRE & GER.). 314p. 1989. 250.00 (*0-8288-9258-X*) Fr & Eur.
Dorscheid, P., ed. Elsevier's Dictionary of Export Financing & Credit Insurance: A Trilingual Glossary of Technical Terms in English, German & French. (Illus.). 322p. 1989. 175.50 (*0-444-87496-8*) Elsevier.
Dorschell, Mary F. George Bernanos' Debt to Therese of Lisieux. LC 95-47721. (FRE & ENG.). xxi, 267p. 1996. write for info. (*0-7734-2266-8*) E Mellen.
***Dorschfeldt, Christop.** Algebras of Pseudodifferential Operators near Edge & Corner Singularities. (Mathematical Research Ser.). 204p. 1998. 105.00 (*3-527-40118-0*) Wiley.
Dorschner, Cheryl, jt. ed. see Jamieson, Patricia.
Dorschner, Jon P. Alcohol Consumption in a Village in North India. LC 83-4987. (Studies in Cultural Anthropology: No. 1). (Illus.). 262p. 1983. reprint ed. pap. 81.30 (*0-608-00162-7*, 206094300006) Bks Demand.
Dorscht, Susan R. Women, Reading, Kroetsch: Telling the Difference. 120p. (C). 1991. text 29.95 (*0-88920-205-2*) W Laurier U Pr.
Dorsel, Tom. Complete Golfer: Physical Skill & Mental Toughness. LC 96-170509. 192p. (C). 1996. pap. text 23.00 (*0-205-15503-0*) P-H.
Dorsel, Vivian P., jt. auth. see Donahoe, John W.
Dorsen, Norman. Rights of Racial Minorities. LC 97-36594. 208p. (gr. 8 up). 1998. pap. 9.99 (*0-14-037785-9*) Viking Penguin.
— Rights of Women. LC 97-36596. 132p. (YA). (gr. 9 up). 1998. pap. 9.99 (*0-14-037782-4*) Viking Penguin.
Dorsen, Norman, et al. Emerson, Haber & Dorsen's Political & Civil Rights in the United States, Vol. I. 1976. student ed. 34.00 (*0-316-19046-2*, Aspen Law & Bus) Aspen Pub.
— Emerson, Haber & Dorsen's Political & Civil Rights in the United States, Vol. I. 4th ed. 1976. 55.00 (*0-316-23624-1*, Aspen Law & Bus) Aspen Pub.
— Emerson, Haber & Dorsen's Political & Civil Rights in the United States, Vol. I. 4th ed. 1998. pap. 14.95 (*0-316-19105-1*, Aspen Law & Bus) Aspen Pub.
— Emerson, Haber & Dorsen's Political & Civil Rights in the United States: 1982 Supplement to Volume I. (C). 1982. 10.95 (*0-316-19052-7*, Aspen Law & Bus) Aspen Pub.
Dorsen, Norman, jt. auth. see Gillers, Stephen.
Dorsen, Peter. Dr. D's Handbook for Men over 40: A Guide to Health, Fitness, Living & Loving in the Prime of Life. 256p. 1998. 23.95 (*0-471-34681-0*) Wiley.
***Dorsen, Peter.** Dr. D's Handbook for Men over 40: A Guide to Health, Fitness, Living & Loving in the Prime of Life. LC 98-230244. 260p. 1998. 23.95 (*1-56561-130-6*) Wiley.
Dorsen, Peter. Handbook for Men: A Guide to Health, Fitness, Living & Loving in the Prime of Life. 233p. (C). 1999. pap. 16.95 (*0-471-34787-6*) Wiley.
Dorsen, Richard M., ed. see Busk, Rachel H.
Dorsen, Richard M., ed. see Christiansen, Reidar T.
Dorsen, Richard M., ed. see Clouston, William A.
Dorsen, Richard M., ed. see Colcord, Joanna C.
Dorsen, Richard M., ed. see MacDougall, James.
Dorsen, Richard M., ed. see Mather, Increase.
Dorset, D. L. Structural Electron Crystallography. LC 95-34721. (Illus.). 466p. (C). 1995. text 83.00 (*0-306-45049-6*, Kluwer Plenum) Kluwer Academic.
Dorset, Douglas, ed. Electron Crystallography. (Transactions of the American Crystallographic Association Ser.: Vol. 28). 182p. 1994. pap. 30.00 (*0-937140-37-6*) Am Crystallographic.
Dorset, Douglas L., et al, eds. Electron Crystallography. LC 97-43111. 456p. 1998. text 264.50 (*0-7923-4876-1*) Kluwer Academic.
Dorset, Douglas L., jt. ed. see Fryer, John R.
Dorset, Gerald. Aristocrat of Intellect. (Studies in Poe: No. 23). 1970. reprint ed. pap. 39.95 (*0-8383-0085-8*) M S G Haskell Hse.
Dorsett, Barbara H. Secret Betrayal. Kenyatta, Imani, ed. & tr. by. 208p. 1998. 13.95 (*1-886580-03-0*) Pinnacle-Syatt.
Dorsett, Barbara Harned, see Harned Dorsett, Barbara.
Dorsett, Dovalee, jt. auth. see Reichenstein, William.
Dorsett, Judy. Creative Bible Games. rev. ed. Ford, Linda, ed. LC 98-135629. (Illus.). 1998. teacher ed. 7.99 (*0-7847-0741-3*, 03070) Standard Pub.
Dorsett, Linda. Get a Life! One That Makes You Happy. (Illus.). 150p. 1999. pap. 12.00 (*1-886383-63-4*, Little Blue) Pride & Imprints.
Dorsett, Lyle W. And God Came In: The Extraordinary Story of Joy Davidman; Her Life & Marriage to C. S. Lewis. (Illus.). 192p. 1984. mass mkt. 2.95 (*0-345-31787-4*, Ballantine) Ballantine Pub Grp.
— Billy Sunday & the Redemption of Urban America. Hatch, Nathan O. & Noll, Mark A., eds. (Library of Religious Biography). 224p. (Orig.). 1991. pap. 15.00 (*0-8028-0151-X*) Eerdmans.
— A Love Observed: Joy Davidman's Life & Marriage to C. S. Lewis. LC 98-10029. 168p. 1998. pap. 11.99 (*0-87788-479-X*, H Shaw Pubs) Waterbrook Fr.
— A Passion for Souls: The Life of D. L. Moody. LC 98-122137. 464p. 1997. 24.99 (*0-8024-5194-2*, 10) Moody.
— A Passion for Souls: The Life of D. L. Moody. deluxe ed. 1997. lthr. 89.99 (*0-8024-5243-4*, 11) Moody.
— The Pendergast Machine. LC 80-11581. 179p. reprint ed. pap. 55.50 (*0-7837-0225-6*, 204053300017) Bks Demand.
Dorsett, Lyle W., jt. auth. see Lewis, C. S.
Dorsett, Mary, jt. auth. see Beougher, Sharon.
Dorsett, Thomas. Dance Fire Dance. LC 92-72838. 80p. (Orig.). 1993. pap. 8.95 (*0-944806-04-X*) Icarus Press.
Dorsett, Thomas, tr. see Miller, Jim W.
Dorsett, Thomas, tr. see Rosenfeld, Ruth.
***Dorsett, William S. & National Rural Electric Cooperative Association.** Supplemental Underground Construction Drawings & Specifications for Cable-in-conduit Systems (12.5/7.2 KV, 24.9/14.4 KV, & 34.5/19.9 KV Class Systems) : Project 96-25. LC 99-26809. (Illus.). 1999. write for info. (*0-917599-25-X*) Natl Rural.
Dorsey & Swanton. Dictionary of the Biloxi & Ofo Languages. (Bureau of American Ethnology Bulletins Ser.). 340p. 1995. lib. bdg. 99.00 (*0-7812-4047-6*) Rprt Serv.
Dorsey & Whitney Staff. Iowa Environmental Law Handbook, No. XVI. 336p. 1995. pap. text 89.00 (*0-86587-429-8*) Gov Insts.
— Minnesota Environmental Law Handbook. 2nd ed. 360p. 1994. pap. text 89.00 (*0-86587-377-1*) Gov Insts.
Dorsey, Anna H. The Flemmings: A True Story. 1978. 39.95 (*0-405-10817-6*) Ayer.
Dorsey, Anne, jt. auth. see Sciarra, Dorothy.
Dorsey, Brian. Who Stole the Soul? Blaxploitation Echoed in the Harlem Renaissance. 128p. 1997. pap. 19.95 (*3-7052-0077-1*, Pub. by Poetry Salzburg) Intl Spec Bk.
Dorsey, Candas Jane. Black Wine. 288p. 1997. pap. 13.95 (*0-312-86578-3*) St Martin.
Dorsey, Cathryn, ed. Classic Currents: Annual Giving. 67p. 1998. pap. 36.00 (*0-89964-322-1*, 28111) Coun Adv & Supp Ed.
— Classic Currents: Market Research. (Illus.). 32p. 1998. pap. 25.00 (*0-89964-325-6*, 28117) Coun Adv & Supp Ed.
— Classic Currents: Media Relations: Management. (Illus.). 56p. 1998. pap. 25.00 (*0-89964-323-X*, 28112) Coun Adv & Supp Ed.
— Classic Currents: Media Relations: Practice. (Illus.). 56p. 1998. pap. 25.00 (*0-89964-326-4*, 28113) Coun Adv & Supp Ed.
Dorsey, Cathryn, ed. see Phair, Judith & King, Roland.
Dorsey, Cathryn, ed. see Taylor, Gordy & Onion, Cathy.
Dorsey, Chris. Game Days: A Tribute to North American Big Game Hunting. LC 94-35383. (Illus.). 176p. 1994. 35.00 (*1-57223-013-4*, 0134) Willow Creek Pr.
— Pheasant Days. (Illus.). 240p. 1994. pap. 9.95 (*0-89658-259-0*) Voyageur Pr.
— Wildfowler's Season: Modern Methods for a Classic Sport. (Illus.). 240p. 1998. reprint ed. 37.95 (*1-55821-292-2*); reprint ed. pap. 19.95 (*1-55821-714-2*) Lyons Pr.
Dorsey, Chris, et al. North American Game Birds. LC 95-39431. (Hunting & Fishing Library). (Illus.). 128p. 1996. 19.95 (*0-86573-049-0*) Creat Pub Intl.
Dorsey, Christine. By the Book. large type ed. (Black Satin Romance Ser.). 283p. 1996. 27.99 (*1-86110-017-5*) Ulverscroft.
— My Savage Heart. 448p. 1994. mass mkt. 4.50 (*0-8217-4523-9*, Zebra Kensgtn) Kensgtn Pub Corp.
— My Seaswept Heart. 384p. 1996. pap. 2.99 (*0-8217-5487-4*) Kensgtn Pub Corp.
— The Rebel & the Lily. 256p. 1997. mass mkt. 5.50 (*0-8217-5704-0*, Zebra Kensgtn) Kensgtn Pub Corp.
— The Rogue & the Heather. 288p. 1998. pap. 5.99 (*0-8217-5883-7*, Zebra Kensgtn) Kensgtn Pub Corp.
Dorsey, Christine, et al. The Way to Man's Heart, Vol. 1. 1997. mass mkt. 5.99 (*0-312-96333-5*) St Martin.
Dorsey, David. The Cost of Living. 273p. 1997. 23.95 (*0-614-27946-1*, Viking) Viking Penguin.
Dorsey, David A. Literary Structure of the Old Testament: A Commentary on Genesis-Malachi. LC 99-40433. 352p. 1999. 34.99 (*0-8010-2187-1*) Baker Bks.
— The Roads & Highways of Ancient Israel. LC 89-32589. (Illus.). 288p. 1991. text 49.95 (*0-8018-3898-3*) Johns Hopkins.
Dorsey, David F., et al, eds. Design & Intent in African Literature. LC 82-50450. 137p. 1982. 22.00 (*0-89410-354-7*); pap. 14.00 (*0-89410-355-5*) Cornell AS&RC.
Dorsey, Dayna R. Guardian of Light. Carsola, Rita, ed. LC 95-60354. (Illus.). 128p. 1995. per. 22.00 (*1-886834-05-9*) Athena Arts.
— Guardian of Light. deluxe ed. Carsola, Rita, ed. LC 95-60353. (Illus.). 128p. 1995. per. 29.95 incl. audio (*1-886834-06-7*) Athena Arts.
***Dorsey, Ed L.** The Sowing Seeds: A Collection of Poems Written by Ed L. Dorsey. rev. ed. LC 00-90802. 69p. 2000. pap. 12.95 (*0-9678305-0-8*) E L Dorsey.
Dorsey, Eleanor M. & Pederson, Judith, eds. Effects of Fishing, Gear on the Sea Floor of New England. unabridged ed. (Illus.). 150p. 1998. pap. 25.00 (*1-892787-00-8*) Conservation Law.
Dorsey, Ernestine, ed. see Turner, Patricia L.
Dorsey, Eugene C. O Papel do Presidente do Conselho Diretor.Tr. of Role of the Board Chairperson. (POR.). 20p. (Orig.). 1996. pap. write for info. (*0-925299-63-4*) Natl Ctr Nonprofit.
Dorsey, G. A. & Kroeber, A. L. Traditions of the Arapaho. (Chicago Field Museum of Natural History Fieldiana Anthropology Ser.: Vol. 5). 1903. 55.00 (*0-527-01865-1*) Periodicals Srv.
Dorsey, G. A. & Voth, H. R. Oraibi Soyal Ceremony, & Oraibi Powamu Ceremony, & Mishongnovi Ceremonies of the Snake & Antelope Fraternities, & Oraibi Summer Snake Ceremony, 4 wks. in 1 vol. 1901-03. (Chicago Field Museum of Natural History Fieldiana Anthropology Ser.: Vol. 3). 1974. 80.00 (*0-527-01863-5*) Periodicals Srv.
Dorsey-Gaines, Catherine, jt. auth. see Taylor, Denny.

D

Dorsey, Gary. The Children of Daedalus. 1989. write for info. (*0-318-62969-0*) Viking Penguin.
— Congregation. 400p. 1999. pap. 9.95 (*0-14-023452-7*, Viking) Viking Penguin.
— Congregation: The Journey Back to Church. LC 98-36237. 400p. 1998. pap. 18.95 (*0-8298-1296-2*) Pilgrim OH.
Dorsey, Gary. Silicon Sky: How One Small Start-Up Went over the Top to Beat the Big Boys into Satellite Heaven. LC 99-60039. 352p. 1999. text 26.00 (*0-7382-0094-8*, Pub. by Perseus Pubng) HarpC.
***Dorsey, Gary.** Silicon Sky: How One Small Start-Up Went over the Top to Beat the Big Boys into Satellite Heaven. LC 99-60039. (Illus.). 352p. 2000. pap. text 17.00 (*0-7382-0312-2*) Perseus Pubng.
Dorsey, George A. An Aboriginal Quartzite Quarry in Eastern Wyoming. LC E 0078.W5. (Field Columbian Museum Anthropological Ser.: Vol. 2, No. 4). (Illus.). 40p. 1900. reprint ed. pap. 30.00 (*0-608-02697-2*, 206335000004) Bks Demand.
— The Arapaho Sun Dance: The Ceremony of the Offerings Lodge. LC 04-7725. (Field Columbian Museum Anthropological Ser.: Vol. 4). (Illus.). 784p. reprint ed. pap. 200.00 (*0-608-02700-6*, 206336500004) Bks Demand.
— The Cheyenne Vol. 2: The Sun Dance. LC 05-33518. (Field Columbian Museum Anthropological Ser.: Vol. 9, No. 1-2). (Illus.). 344p. 1905. reprint ed. pap. 106.70 (*0-608-02698-0*, 206335100002) Bks Demand.
— Indians of the Southwest. LC 74-7952. (Illus.). reprint ed. 41.50 (*0-404-11841-0*) AMS Pr.
— The Mythology of the Wichita. LC 95-2857. 368p. 1995. pap. 12.95 (*0-8061-2778-3*, 2778) U of Okla Pr.
— Observations on a Collection of Papuan Crania with Notes on Preservation & Decorative Features by William H. Holmes. 2nd ed. LC 04-12212. (Field Columbian Museum Anthropological Ser.: Vol. 2, No. 1). (Illus.). 67p. reprint ed. pap. 30.00 (*0-608-02716-2*, 206338100004) Bks Demand.
— The Pawnee Mythology. LC 97-12832. (Sources of American Indian Oral Literature Ser.). (Illus.). xxvii, 546p. 1997. pap. 22.00 (*0-8032-6603-0*, Bison Books) U of Nebr Pr.
— Traditions of the Caddo. LC 74-7956. reprint ed. 29.50 (*0-404-11845-3*) AMS Pr.
— Traditions of the Osage. LC 74-7957. reprint ed. 29.50 (*0-404-11846-1*) AMS Pr.
Dorsey, George A., compiled by. Traditions of the Caddo. LC 97-30481. (Sources of American Indian Oral Literature Ser.). (Illus.). xxiv, 132p. 1997. pap. text 8.95 (*0-8032-6602-2*) U of Nebr Pr.
Dorsey, George A. & Kroeber, Alfred L. Traditions of the Arapaho: Collected under the Auspices of the Field Columbian Museum & of the American Museum of Natural History. LC 04-12211. (Field Columbian Museum, Publication 81, Anthropological Ser.: Vol. 5). 485p. 1903. reprint ed. pap. 150.40 (*0-608-02120-2*, 206276900004) Bks Demand.
Dorsey, George A. & Kroeber, Alfred L., compiled by. Traditions of the Arapaho. LC 97-30302. (Sources of American Indian Oral Literature Ser.). (Illus.). xxxvi, 488p. 1997. pap. text 19.95 (*0-8032-6608-1*) U of Nebr Pr.
Dorsey, Gray L. American Freedoms: A Bicentennial Essay on the Bill of Rights. rev. ed. LC 74-20856. x, 54p. 1987. pap. 20.00 (*0-89941-539-3*, 300290) W S Hein.
— Jurisculture: Greece & Rome. 92p. 1988. 34.95 (*0-88738-237-1*) Transaction Pubs.
— Jurisculture Vol. 2: India. 125p. 1989. 34.95 (*0-88738-310-6*) Transaction Pubs.
— Jurisculture Vol. 3: China. 210p. (C). 1993. text 39.95 (*1-56000-090-2*) Transaction Pubs.

***Dorsey-Holton, Clara. From a Broken Wing to a Sailboat: The Musings of a Black Crone. 2000. pap. 12.95 (*0-9679263-0-0*) Kennard Pubng.**
The author of this exciting book of essays uses nautical concepts to reflect upon the ordinary experiences of life with its potential for both enhancement & diminishment of the human spirit. Readers can expect to gain insight into life's inward & outward journeys through the book's seven parts: Anchors, Tides, Currents, Drifts, Winds, Harbors & Disasters. The author, an Afro-American woman, uses the medium of personal essay to examine & reflect upon life through the essays in each part. In a highly creative, powerful & stimulating style, the author in Anchors, specifically addresses the foundation & fundamental essence of being & self exploration. In Tides, we begin to understand the physical cycles of life as it is revealed in nature through the ebb & flow of bodies of water. The section Drifts, discusses the nuances encountered when we lose focus & are out of touch with our purpose. The author's style is informal, but succinctly informative as she takes you on these personal excursions on a sailboat called life.
Publisher Paid Annotation.

Dorsey, Ida T. Ida Dorsey's Original "Just in Case" A Guide for My Care-Giver, Gift Edition. rev. ed. 80p. 1997. spiral bd. 12.00 (*0-9646803-5-1*) Plant Speak Prods.
Dorsey, J. & Slusallek, P., eds. Rendering Techniques '97: Proceedings of the Eurographics Workshop in St. Etienne, France, June 16-18, 1997. (Eurographics Ser.). (Illus.). ix, 342p. 1997. pap. 74.95 (*3-211-83001-4*) Spr-Verlag.
Dorsey, James. Up South: Blacks in Chicago's Suburbs, 1719-1983. LC 86-50583. (Illus.). 113p. 1986. pap. text 20.00 (*0-932269-93-1*) Wyndham Hall.
Dorsey, James E., jt. auth. see Rowland, Arthur R.
Dorsey, James O. Omaha & Ponka Letters. (Bureau of American Ethnology Bulletins Ser.). 127p. 1995. lib. bdg. 79.00 (*0-7812-4011-5*) Rprt Serv.
— Omaha & Ponka Letters. 1988. reprint ed. lib. bdg. 49.00 (*0-7812-0232-9*) Rprt Serv.
— Omaha & Ponka Letters. reprint ed. 45.00 (*0-403-03675-5*) Scholarly.
Dorsey, Jason. Graduate to Your Perfect Job in 6 Easy Steps. Campbell, Dee A., ed. LC 97-93471. (Golden Ladder Ser.: Vol. 1). (Illus.). 140p. (Orig.). 1997. pap. 14.95 (*0-9657725-1-9*) Golden Ladder.
***Dorsey, Jason.** 101 Ways to Stop School Violence. 1999. pap. 9.99 (*1-890900-18-4*) Insight Intl.
***Dorsey, Jason Ryan.** Can Students End School Violence? Solutions from America's Youth. Patton, Elota & Gardner, Greta, eds. (Illus.). 168p. (YA). (gr. 7 up). 2000. pap. 14.95 (*1-929749-00-7*) Archstone.
Dorsey, Jimmy, jt. auth. see Pointer, Lyle.
Dorsey, John & Dilts, James D. A Guide to Baltimore Architecture. 3rd ed. LC 96-31928. (Illus.). 480p. 1997. pap. 24.95 (*0-87033-477-8*, Tidewtr Pubs) Cornell Maritime.
Dorsey, John M. The Growth of Self-Insight. LC 61-18939. (Franklin Memorial Lectures Ser.: No. 10). (Illus.). 219p. reprint ed. pap. 67.90 (*0-7837-3798-X*, 204361800010) Bks Demand.
Dorsey, John M. & Seegers, Walter H. Living Consciously: The Science of Self. LC 59-12400. (Illus.). 187p. reprint ed. pap. 58.00 (*0-608-10584-8*, 207120500009) Bks Demand.
Dorsey, Kurkpatrick. The Dawn of Conservation Diplomacy: U. S.-Canadian Wildlife Protection Treaties in the Progressive Era. LC 98-3752. (Weyerhaeuser Environmental Classics Ser.). (Illus.). 344p. 1998. 35.00 (*0-295-97676-4*) U of Wash Pr.
Dorsey, Maxwell J., et al. Dorsey Family: Descendants of Edward Darcy-Dorsey of Va. & Md. for Five Generations, & Allied Families. (Illus.). 270p. 1997. reprint ed. pap. 42.00 (*0-8328-8332-8*); reprint ed. lib. bdg. 52.00 (*0-8328-8331-X*) Higginson Bk Co.
Dorsey, Megan & Rockwell, David L. Principles of California Real Estate Workbook. 265p. (Orig.). 1996. pap. text, wbk. ed. 27.45 (*1-887051-03-1*) Rockwell WA.
Dorsey, Megan, jt. auth. see Rockwell, David L.
Dorsey, Megan, ed. see Haupt, Kathryn J. & Rockwell, David L.
***Dorsey, Nell Dunlap.** A Tipple, a Whistle & Stuff: A Memoir. LC 99-93442. 270p. 1999. pap. 19.00 (*0-87012-627-X*) McClain.
Dorsey, Noah E. Properties of Ordinary Water-Substances in All Its Phases: Water-Vapor, Water, & All the Ices. rev. ed. LC 68-19563. (American Chemical Society Symposium Ser.: No. 81). 687p. reprint ed. pap. 200.00 (*0-608-10137-0*, 201523700094) Bks Demand.
Dorsey, Oscar L., jt. auth. see Pierson, Michael J.
***Dorsey, Paul.** Oracle 8I Data Migration Handbook. 576p. 2000. pap. text. write for info. (*0-07-212391-5*, Oracle Press) Osborne-McGraw.
Dorsey, Paul & Hudicka, Joseph R. Oracle 8 Design Using UML Object Modeling. LC 99-185351. 496p. 1998. pap. 49.99 (*0-07-882474-5*) Intl Marine.
Dorsey, Paul & Koletzke, Peter. Oracle Designer - 2000 Handbook: Master Oracle's Powerful CASE Tools. LC 97-138981. 512p. 1996. pap. text 34.95 (*0-07-882229-7*) Osborne-McGraw.
— Oracle Designer Handbook - 2nd Edition. 2nd ed. LC 99-174707. (Illus.). 1075p. 1998. pap. 44.99 (*0-07-882417-6*, Oracle Press) Osborne-McGraw.
***Dorsey, Paul & Koletzke, Peter.** Oracle Developer: Advanced Forms & Reports. 835p. 2000. pap. text 59.99 (*0-07-212048-7*) Osborne-McGraw.
Dorsey, Peter A. Sacred Estrangement: The Rhetoric of Conversion in Modern American Autobiography. LC 92-16589. 240p. 1993. 40.00 (*0-271-00902-0*) Pa St U Pr.
Dorsey, R. Stephen. Gun Tools: Their History & Identification, Vol. 2. unabridged ed. (Illus.). 396p. 1997. pap. 30.00 (*0-9631208-3-2*) Collect Lib.
— Guns of the Western Indian War. LC 95-67427. 1995. pap. 30.00 (*0-9631208-5-9*) Collect Lib.
— Indian War Cartridge Pouches, Boxes & Carbine Boots. LC 93-72940. (Illus.). 157p. (Orig.). 1993. pap. 28.00 (*0-9631208-2-4*) Collect Lib.
— U. S. Martial Web Belts & Bandoliers, 1903-1981. LC 92-74358. (Illus.). 143p. (Orig.). 1993. pap. 20.00 (*0-9631208-1-6*) Collect Lib.
Dorsey, R. Stephen & McPheeters, Kenneth L. The American Military Saddle, 1776-1945. unabridged ed. LC 98-73724. (Illus.). 444p. 1999. 59.95 (*0-9631208-4-0*) Collect Lib.
Dorsey, Reaney, ed. see Simmerling, Jack & Wolf, Wayne.
Dorsey, Reaney, ed. see Wolf, Wayne L. & Simmerling, Jack.
Dorsey, Robert E., et al. Bankruptcy Prediction Using Artificial Neural Systems. 54p. (Orig.). 1995. pap. text 20.00 (*0-943205-31-X*) RFICFA.
Dorsey, Robert W. Case Studies in Design & Construction. LC 98-8330. 238p. 1998. pap. text 52.00 (*0-13-079775-8*) P-H.
Dorsey, Scott. The Choral Journal: An Index to Volumes 19-32. (Monographs: No. 7). 134p. (C). 1992. pap. write for info. (*1-882648-06-4*) Am Choral Dirs.
Dorsey, Scott W. The Choral Journal: An Index to Volumes 19-32. (Monograph Ser.: No. 7). 134p. 1992. 15.00 (*0-614-05594-6*) Am Choral Dirs.
Dorsey, Stephen. American Military Cartridge Belts & Related Equipment. 1984. 13.95 (*0-913150-49-5*) Pioneer Pr.
Dorsey, Stuart, et al. Pensions & Productivity. LC 98-17997. 139p. (C). 1998. 33.00 (*0-88099-186-0*); pap. 14.00 (*0-88099-185-2*) W E Upjohn.
Dorsey, T. J. Tigermania & the OMYGA: (Orlando Minority Youth Golf Association) LC 99-167632. (Illus.). 160p. 1998. pap. text 12.95 (*1-885066-39-2*) Four-G Pubs.
Dorsey, Thomas A. Great Gospel Songs of Thomas A. Dorsey. 80p. (Orig.). 1988. pap. 8.95 (*0-7935-3338-4*, 00359946) H Leonard.
Dorsey, Thomas J. Point & Figure Charting: The Essential Application for Forecasting & Tracking Market Prices. LC 95-3091. (Finance Editions Ser.). 256p. 1995. 59.95 (*0-471-11961-X*) Wiley.
— Thriving as a Broker in the 21st Century. LC 99-28640. 304p. 1999. 39.95 (*1-57660-066-1*, Pub. by Bloomberg NJ) Norton.
***Dorsey, Tim.** Florida Roadkill. LC 98-50945. 240p. 1999. 24.00 (*0-688-16782-9*, Wm Morrow) Morrow Avon.
— Florida Roadkill: A Novel. 384p. 2000. mass mkt. 6.99 (*0-380-73233-5*, HarpTorch) Morrow Avon.
— Hammerhead Ranch Motel: A Novel. LC 99-55754. 304p. 2000. 24.00 (*0-688-16783-7*, Wm Morrow) Morrow Avon.
Dorsey, Tina & Robinson, Jayne, eds. Criminal Victimization in the United States, 1994. 22nd ed. (Illus.). 150p. (C). 1998. pap. text 40.00 (*0-7881-7557-2*) DIANE Pub.
Dorsey, William, ed. see Claus, James R. & Claus, Karen.
***Dorsinville, Max.** The Rule of Francois ("Papa Doc") Duvalier in Two Novels by Roger Dorsinville: Realism & Magic Realism in Haiti. LC 99-51798. (Caribbean Studies: Vol. 6). 328p. 2000. text 99.95 (*0-7734-7830-2*) E Mellen.
Dorskind, Cheryl M. The Art of Handpainting Photographs. LC 97-36327. (Illus.). 144p. 1998. pap. 24.95 (*0-8174-3310-4*, Amphoto) Watsn-Guptill.
Dorsky, Susan. Women of Amran: A Middle Eastern Ethnographic Study. LC 85-26534. (Illus.). 216p. 1986. 22.50 (*0-87480-250-4*) U of Utah Pr.
Dorsman, Jerry. How to Quit Drinking Without A.A. 2nd rev. ed. 336p. 1997. per. 15.00 (*0-7615-1290-X*) Prima Pub.
— How to Quit Drinking Without A.A. A Complete Self-Help Guide Revised 2 Edition. 2nd rev. ed. LC 93-23555. 336p. 1994. pap. 12.95 (*1-55958-418-1*) Prima Pub.
— How to Quit Drugs for Good: A Complete Self-Help Guide. 368p. 1998. per. 15.00 (*0-7615-1517-8*) Prima Pub.
Dorsman, Jerry & Davis, Bob. How to Achieve Peace of Mind: Your Guide for Attaining Physical, Mental, Emotional, & Spiritual Well-Being. LC 94-1606. (Illus.). 240p. 1994. pap. 10.95 (*1-55958-485-8*) Prima Pub.
— You Can Achieve Peace of Mind: Achieving Inner Peace No Matter What Life Brings. LC 98-29808. 240p. 1998. pap. 12.95 (*0-7615-1548-8*) Prima Pub.
D'Orso, Michael. Rosewood - Like Judgment Day. LC 97-107235. (Illus.). 384p. 1996. pap. 12.00 (*1-57297-256-4*) Blvd Books.
D'Orso, Michael, jt. auth. see Lewis, John.
D'Orso, Michael, jt. auth. see Lieberman, Joseph L.
D'Orso, Michael, jt. auth. see Phillips, Bill.
D'Orso, Michael, jt. auth. see Steinberg, Leigh.
Dorso, Michael A. Seeds of Hope: A Physician's Personal Triumph over Prostate Cancer. Skardarasy, Doreen L., ed. (Illus.). Date not set. write for info. (*0-9678801-6-5*) Acorn MI.
D'Orso, Mike. Fast Takes: Slices of Life Through a Journalist's Eye. 272p. 1990. pap. 8.95 (*0-9624375-6-5*) Hampton Roads Pub Co.
— Pumping Granite: And Other Portraits of People at Play. (Illus.). 288p. 1994. 25.00 (*0-89672-338-0*) Tex Tech Univ Pr.
Dorson, Edward, jt. ed. see Ives, Edward D.
***Dorson, John.** Panama Canal: The Greatest Giveaway. 2000. pap. 7.95 (*0-533-13285-1*) Vantage.
Dorson, Mercedes & Wilmot Carter, Jeanne, eds. Tales from Rain Forest. LC 97-19791. (Illus.). 160p. (J). (gr. 4-7). 1997. 18.00 (*0-88001-567-5*, Ecco Press) HarperTrade.
Dorson, Richard M. American Folklore. LC 59-12283. (Chicago History of American Civilization Ser.). 350p. 1961. pap. 17.95 (*0-226-15859-4*, CHAC 4) U Ch Pr.
— American Folklore & the Historian. LC 75-149093. 251p. reprint ed. pap. 77.90 (*0-8357-5369-7*, 202677000052) Bks Demand.
— Bloodstoppers & Bearwalkers: Folk Traditions of the Upper Peninsula. LC 52-5394. (Illus.). 311p. 1952. pap. 14.50 (*0-674-07665-6*) HUP.
— British Folklorists: A History. LC 68-16689. (Folktales of the World Ser.). 1992. lib. bdg. 27.50 (*0-226-15863-2*) U Ch Pr.
— Buying the Wind: Regional Folklore in the United States. LC 63-13010. 592p. 1972. pap. text 23.00 (*0-226-15862-4*) U Ch Pr.
— Davy Crockett: American Comic Legend. (BCL1-PS American Literature Ser.). 171p. 1993. reprint ed. lib. bdg. 69.00 (*0-7812-6596-7*) Rprt Serv.
— Folklore: Selected Essays. LC 72-76944. 319p. reprint ed. 98.90 (*0-8357-9212-9*, 201545400094) Bks Demand.
— Folklore & Fakelore: Essays Toward a Discipline of Folk Studies. LC 75-30734. 403p. reprint ed. pap. 125.00 (*0-7837-2252-4*, 205734000004) Bks Demand.
— Folklore of the Santal Parganas. Bompas, Cecil H., tr. LC 77-70579. (International Folklore Ser.). 1977. reprint ed. lib. bdg. 41.95 (*0-405-10080-9*) Ayer.
— Folktales Told Around the World. (Illus.). xxvi, 648p. 1978. pap. text 30.00 (*0-226-15874-8*, P781) U Ch Pr.
— Land of the Millrats. LC 81-2944. (Illus.). 265p. (C). 1981. 34.50 (*0-674-50855-6*) HUP.
— Man & Beast in American Comic Legend. LC 81-48622. 206p. 1982. reprint ed. pap. 63.90 (*0-7837-3696-7*, 205787400009) Bks Demand.
— Negro Folktales in Michigan. LC 73-21099. (Illus.). 245p. 1974. reprint ed. lib. bdg. 49.75 (*0-8371-5989-X*, DONF, Greenwood Pr) Greenwood.
Dorson, Richard M., ed. America Begins: Early American Writings. LC 72-5802. (Folklore of the World Ser.). (Illus.). 1981. reprint ed. lib. bdg. 49.95 (*0-8369-2986-1*) Ayer.
— Davy Crockett: American Comic Legend. LC 77-70590. (International Folklore Ser.). (Illus.). 1977. reprint ed. lib. bdg. 18.95 (*0-405-10091-4*) Ayer.
— Egyptian Tales & Romances. Budge, E. A. Wallis, tr. from EGY. LC 80-739. (Folklore of the World Ser.). (Illus.). 1981. reprint ed. lib. bdg. 49.95 (*0-405-13304-9*) Ayer.
— Folklore & Folklife: An Introduction. LC 77-189038. viii, 562p. (C). 1996. pap. text 22.50 (*0-226-15871-3*) U Ch Pr.
— Folklore in the Modern World. (World Anthropology Ser.). xii, 366p. 1978. 60.00 (*90-279-7740-2*) Mouton.
— Folklore of the World Series, 38 bks., Set. 1980. lib. bdg. 1516.00 (*0-405-13300-6*) Ayer.
— International Folklore Series, 48 bks. (Illus.). 1977. reprint ed. 1460.00 (*0-405-10077-9*) Ayer.
— Patriots of the American Revolution: True Accounts by Great Americans, from Ethan Allen to George Rogers Clark. LC 98-12871. 352p. 1998. 7.99 (*0-517-20274-3*) Random Hse Value.
— Peasant Customs & Savage Myths: Selections from the British Folklorists, 2 vols. LC 68-16690. 766p. 1969. lib. bdg. 72.00 (*0-226-15867-5*) U Ch Pr.
— Sixty Folk-Tales from Exclusively Slavonic Sources. Wratislaw, Albert H., tr. LC 77-70629. (International Folklore Ser.). 1977. reprint ed. lib. bdg. 26.95 (*0-405-10133-3*) Ayer.
— Studies in Folk Life: Essays in Honor of Iorwerth C. Peate, John G. Jenkins. LC 77-70603. (International Folklore Ser.). 1977. lib. bdg. 33.95 (*0-405-10102-3*) Ayer.
— Studies in Japanese Folklore. LC 80-744. (Folklore of the World Ser.). (Illus.). 1981. reprint ed. lib. bdg. 37.95 (*0-405-13310-3*) Ayer.
— Tales of the Sun: Folklore of Southern India. LC 77-70604. (International Folklore Ser.). 1977. reprint ed. lib. bdg. 26.95 (*0-405-10103-1*) Ayer.
Dorson, Richard M., et al, eds. Handbook of American Folklore. LC 82-47574. (Illus.). 608p. 1986. reprint ed. pap. 18.95 (*0-253-20373-2*, MB-373) Ind U Pr.
Dorson, Richard M., ed. see Aesop.
Dorson, Richard M., ed. see Allies, Jabez.
Dorson, Richard M., jt. ed. see Almquist, Bo.
Dorson, Richard M., ed. see Arewa, Erastus O.
Dorson, Richard M., ed. see Beck, Earl C.
Dorson, Richard M., ed. see Briggs, Katherine M.
Dorson, Richard M., ed. see Campbell, Charles G.
Dorson, Richard M., ed. see Carey, George.
Dorson, Richard M., ed. see Carpenter, Inta G.
Dorson, Richard M., jt. ed. see Carpenter, Inta G.
Dorson, Richard M., ed. see Childers, J. Wesley.
Dorson, Richard M., ed. see Christiansen, Reider T.
Dorson, Richard M., ed. see Davids, Rhys.
Dorson, Richard M., ed. see Dawkins, Richard M.
Dorson, Richard M., ed. see Degh, Linda.
Dorson, Richard M., ed. see Delarue, Paul.
Dorson, Richard M., jt. ed. see Douglas, George B.
Dorson, Richard M., ed. see Eberhard, Wolfram.
Dorson, Richard M., ed. see Elwin, Verrier.
Dorson, Richard M., ed. see Flowers, Helen L.
Dorson, Richard M., ed. see Gardner, E. E.
Dorson, Richard M., ed. see Georges, Robert A.
Dorson, Richard M., ed. see Gill, William W.
Dorson, Richard M., ed. see Gizelis, Gregory.
Dorson, Richard M., ed. see Gomme, George L.
Dorson, Richard M., ed. see Grimm, Jacob W. & Grimm, Wilhelm K.
Dorson, Richard M., ed. see Groome, Francis H.
Dorson, Richard M., ed. see Hambruch, Paul.
Dorson, Richard M., ed. see Hardwick, Charles.
Dorson, Richard M., ed. see Hector, Lee H.
Dorson, Richard M., ed. see Henri, Gaidoz & Sebillot, Paul.
Dorson, Richard M., ed. see Jansen, William H.
Dorson, Richard M., ed. see Kirtley, Bacil F.
Dorson, Richard M., ed. see Klein, Barbro S.
Dorson, Richard M., ed. see Klymasz, Robert B.
Dorson, Richard M., ed. see Knowles, James H.
Dorson, Richard M., ed. see Kongas-Maranda, Elli K.
Dorson, Richard M., ed. see Mattfield, Julius.
Dorson, Richard M., ed. see McNair, John F. & Barlow, Thomas L.
Dorson, Richard M., ed. see McPherson, Joseph M.
Dorson, Richard M., ed. see Menez, Herminia Q.
Dorson, Richard M., ed. see Miller, Hugh G.
Dorson, Richard M., ed. see Muller, Friedrich M.
Dorson, Richard M., ed. see Palmer, Abram S.
Dorson, Richard M., ed. see Parker, Henry.
Dorson, Richard M., ed. see Parkinson, Thomas.
Dorson, Richard M., jt. ed. see Parry, Adam M.
Dorson, Richard M., ed. see Penzer, Norman M.
Dorson, Richard M., ed. see Perrault, Charles.
Dorson, Richard M., ed. see Rael, Juan B.

Dorson, Richard M., ed. see Ralston, William S.

Dorson, Richard M., ed. see Ricks, George R.

Dorson, Richard M., ed. see Rooth, Anna B.

Dorson, Richard M., ed. see Sebillot, Paul.

Dorson, Richard M., ed. see Stern, Stephen.

Dorson, Richard M., ed. see Taliaferro, Harden E.

Dorson, Richard M., ed. see Taylor, Archer.

Dorson, Richard M., ed. see Temple, Richard C.

Dorson, Richard M., ed. see Teske, Robert T.

Dorson, Richard M., ed. see Thigpen, Kenneth A.

Dorson, Richard M., ed. see Tully, Marjorie F. & Rael, Juan B.

Dorson, Richard M., ed. see Von Sydow, Carl W.

Dorson, Richard M., ed. see Winner, Thomas G.

Dorson, Richard M., ed. see Yates, Norris W.

Dorson, Ron. The Indy Five Hundred. (Illus.). 229p. 1974. 9.95 (*0-393-60007-6*) Norton.

— Stay Tuned for the Greatest Spectacle in Racing. (Illus.). 260p. 1980. lib. bdg. 19.95 (*0-915088-21-5*) C Hungness.

***Dorst, Adrian.** Under the Rainbow: North America's Rainforest Coast. large type ed. (Illus.). 160p. 1999. 35.00 (*0-7737-3195-4*, Pub. by Stoddart Publ) Genl Dist Srvs.

Dorst, Adrian, jt. auth. see Backhouse, Frances.

Dorst, John D. Looking West LC 98-37212. (Contemporary Ethnography Ser.). 1999. 19.95 (*0-8122-1440-4*) U of Pa Pr.

— Looking West. LC 98-37212. 1999. 45.00 (*0-8122-3173-2*) U of Pa Pr.

***Dorst, John D.** Looking West: Excursions in a Landscape of Vision & Display. LC 98-37212. (Contemporary Ethnography Ser.). 1999. write for info. (*0-8122-1680-6*); write for info. (*0-8122-3500-2*) U of Pa Pr.

Dorst, John D. The Written Suburb: An American Site, an Ethnographic Dilemma. LC 88-37485. (Contemporary Ethnography Ser.). 232p. 1989. pap. 72.00 (*0-608-04820-8*, 206547700004) Bks Demand.

— The Written Suburb: An American Site, an Ethnographic Dilemma. LC 89-37485. (Contemporary Ethnography Ser.). (Illus.). 232p. (C). 1989. text 49.95 (*0-8122-8160-8*); pap. text 17.95 (*0-8122-1282-7*) U of Pa Pr.

Dorst, L., et al. Reasoning with Uncertainty in Robotics: Proceedings of the International Workshop, Rur 95, Amsterdam, the Netherlands, December 1995. LC 96-22126. (Lecture Notes in Computer Science: Lecture Notes in Artificial Intelligence: Vol. 109). 387p. 1996. pap. 62.00 (*3-540-61376-5*) Spr-Verlag.

Dorst, R. W., jt. auth. see Elliott, Austin M.

Dorsten, J. L. Van, see Van Dorsten, J. L.

Dorszynski, ed. see Eisen, Jonathan, et al.

Dorszynski, Alexia, ed. see Mandell, Margery.

Dort, Evelyn Van, see Van Dort, Evelyn.

Dort, Veronica McLoud, jt. auth. see Furton, Edward James.

Dorta, Charles, et al, eds. Twelfth Assembling Annual. (Illus.). 100p. (Orig.). 1986. pap. 100.00 (*0-915066-59-9*); pap., suppl. ed. 200.00 (*0-915066-60-2*) Assembling Pr.

Dorta, Jose M. Pepito, el Nino Que Nunca de Bio Nacer. (SPA.). 1998. pap. 10.00 (*0-938693-11-5*) Maya Pubns.

Dortch, Chris. Blue Ribbon College Basketball Yearbook, 19th 1999-2000 Ed. 19th ed. 1999. pap. text 19.95 (*0-9651550-3-X*) Blue Ribbon Bsktball.

***Dortch, Chris.** Blue Ribbon College Basketball Yearbook 2000-2001. 384p. 2000. pap. 19.95 (*0-9651550-5-6*, 471-008, Pub. by Blue Ribbon Bsktball) BookWorld.

Dortch, Chris & Lunardi, Joe, eds. Blue Ribbon College Basketball Yearbook. 17th ed. 386p. 1999. pap. 19.95 (*0-9651550-2-1*) Blue Ribbon Bsktball.

Dortch, Chris, jt. ed. see Lunardi, Joe.

***Dortch, Christopher M.** BL Ribbon College Football Yearbook. 2000. pap. 19.95 (*0-9651550-4-8*, Pub. by Blue Ribbon Bsktball) BookWorld.

Dortch, Richard. Caring Enough to Help the One You Love. LC 93-87252. 128p. (Orig.). 1994. 13.95 (*0-89221-259-4*) New Leaf.

— Fatal Conceit. LC 92-63373. 264p. 1993. 14.95 (*0-89221-245-4*) New Leaf.

— Integrity: How I Lost It & My Journey Back. 362p. 1993. pap. 10.95 (*0-89221-248-9*) New Leaf.

— Losing It All & Find Yourself: How to Pick up the Pieces & Start Anew. LC 93-85812. 112p. (Orig.). 1993. pap. 6.95 (*0-89221-239-X*) New Leaf.

Dortch, Richard W. Fatal Conceit. LC 92-63373. 264p. 1993. pap. 9.95 (*0-89221-234-9*) New Leaf.

— Secrets of the Heart: Finding the Key to a Joyous Heart. LC 95-69895. 192p. 1996. pap. text 11.95 (*0-89221-299-3*) New Leaf.

Dortch, Sammie M., jt. auth. see Jackson, Barbara M.

***Dortch, Thomas W., Jr.** The Miracles of Mentoring: The Joy of Investing in the Future. LC 99-89128. 224p. 2000. 22.95 (*0-385-49991-4*) Doubleday.

Dortenzio. Fashion Sketching. (Fashion Merchandising Ser.). 1997. teacher ed. 12.00 (*0-8273-7651-0*) Delmar.

D'Ortenzio, Alfred D. Fashion Sketching. LC 96-42410. (Fashion Merchandising Ser.). 192p. (C). 1997. mass mkt. 49.95 (*0-8273-7650-2*) Delmar.

Dorteous. Arthur's Eyes. (Literature Units Ser.). (Illus.). 48p. (J). 1996. pap., student ed., wbk. ed. 9.95 (*1-55734-533-3*) Tchr Create Mat.

Dorter, Kenneth. Form & Good in Plato's Eleatic Dialogues: The Parmenides, Theaetetus, Sophist & Statesman. LC 94-18930. 1994. 50.00 (*0-520-08331-8*, Pub. by U CA Pr) Cal Prin Full Svc.

— Plato's Phaedo: An Interpretation. LC 82-217526. 245p. reprint ed. pap. 76.00 (*0-8357-6378-1*, 203573200096) Bks Demand.

D'Ortigue, M. J. Dictionnaire Liturgique, Historique et Theorique de Plainchant et de Musique d'Eglise. LC 79-155353. (Music Ser.). (FRE.). 1971. reprint ed. lib. bdg. 110.00 (*0-306-70165-0*) Da Capo.

Dorton, Anne M., jt. auth. see Fyock, Catherine D.

Dorton, Karen Harper, jt. auth. see Herbert, Martin.

Dortort, Fred. Dialectic of Vision: A Contrary Reading of William Blakes's "Jerusalem" LC 97-8305. 464p. (Orig.). 1997. pap. 24.95 (*1-886449-49-X*, P949X) Barrytown Ltd.

Dortzbach, Richard K., ed. Ophthalmic Plastic Surgery: Prevention & Management of Complications. LC 92-48529. 448p. 1993. text 204.00 (*0-7817-0029-9*) Lppncott W & W.

Dorum, Eileen. Percy Grainger: The Man Behind the Music. 260p. 1989. 29.50 (*0-912483-63-6*) Pro-Am Music.

***Doruyter, Karel.** Sailboat Buyers' Guide: Conducting Your Own Survey. LC 99-50390. 96p. 1999. pap. 14.95 (*0-938665-72-3*) Fine Edge Prods.

Dorval, Bruce & Freedle, Roy O., eds. Conversational Organization & Its Development. LC 89-78241. (Advances in Discourse Processes Ser.: Vol. 38). 376p. (C). 1990. pap. 42.50 (*0-89391-663-3*); text 78.50 (*0-89391-582-3*) Ablx Pub.

D'Orval, Jean B. Les Entretiens de l'Eveil. (FRE.). 1996. 19.95 (*2-920083-97-X*) Edns Roseau.

Dorvault, F. L' Officine: The Pharmacy. 21st ed. (FRE.). 1958p. 1982. 250.00 (*0-8288-1800-2*, M15478) Fr & Eur.

D'Orville, Hans, ed. Denken und Handeln In Globaler Verantwortung: Festschrift Fur Helmut Schmidt Zum 75. Geburtstag, Vol. II. (Illus.). 176p. (Orig.). 1994. 15.00 (*1-885060-00-9*) H dOrville.

— Leadership for Africa: In Honor of Olusegun Obasanjo on His 60th Birthday. LC 96-170461. 350p. (Orig.). (C). 1995. 25.00 (*1-885060-03-3*) H dOrville.

— Perspectives of Global Responsibility - In Honor of Helmut Schmidt on the Occasion of His 75th Birthday. (Illus.). 546p. 1994. 25.00 (*1-885060-01-7*) H dOrville.

— Statesman & Pragmatic Humanist - In Honor of Takeo Fukuda on the Occasion of His 90th Birthday. 175p. (C). 1995. 15.00 (*1-885060-02-5*) H dOrville.

D'Orville, Hans, ed. Beyond Freedom: Letters to Olusegun Obasanjo. (Illus.). 500p. 1996. 40.00 (*1-885060-05-X*) H dOrville.

D'Orville, Hans & Najman, Dragoljub. Towards a New Multilaterialism: Funding Global Priorities: New & Innovative Financing Mechanisms for Internationally Agreed Programmes. 60p. 1995. 15.00 (*1-885060-04-1*) H dOrville.

D'Orville, Hans, jt. ed. see Obasanjo, Olusegun.

Dorward, A. & Kidd, J. Smallholder Cash Crop Production Under Market Liberalisation: A New Institutional Economics Perspective. LC 98-21253. (CAB International Publication Ser.). 300p. 1998. 75.00 (*0-85199-277-3*) OUP.

Dorward, Barbara & Barraga, Natalie C. Teaching Aids for Blind & Visually Limited Children. LC HV1666.D721. 142p. reprint ed. pap. 44.10 (*0-7837-0140-3*, 204042900016) Bks Demand.

Dorward, D. M. Mountain Wildflowers Date Book. (Illus.). 52p. (Orig.). pap. 5.50 (*0-9615729-1-4*) Dorward Photo.

— Sun Valley Idaho, Vol. I. (Illus.). 33p. 1995. write for info. (*0-614-13005-0*) Dorward Photo.

— The Sun Valley Story, Vol. I. (Illus.). 32p. (Orig.). 1996. reprint ed. pap., mass mkt. write for info. (*0-9615729-2-2*) Dorward Photo.

Dorward, David. Scotland's Place - Names. expanded ed. 256p. 1989. pap. 40.00 (*1-873644-50-7*, Pub. by Mercat Pr Bks) St Mut.

— Scotland's Place Names. 64p. (C). 1986. pap. 35.00 (*0-901824-73-9*, Pub. by Mercat Pr Bks) St Mut.

— Scottish Surnames. 64p. (C). 1986. pap. 40.00 (*0-901824-77-1*) Mercat Pr Bks.

— Scottish Surnames. 80p. 1989. pap. 30.00 (*1-873644-04-3*, Pub. by Mercat Pr Bks) St Mut.

Dorward-King, Elaine J., ed. see Society of Environmental Toxicology & Chemistry (S.

Dorward, Neil. The Pricing Decision: Economic Theory & Business Practice. 200p. (C). 1987. pap. 50.00 (*0-06-318369-2*, Pub. by P Chapman) St Mut.

Dorward, Rosemary, jt. tr. see Clark, John P.

Dorwart, Harold L. Configurations: Number Puzzles & Patterns for All Ages. 1972. 10.00 (*0-911624-32-5*) Wffn Proof.

— The Geometry of Incidence. 1972. reprint ed. pap. 5.00 (*0-911624-34-1*) Wffn Proof.

Dorwart, Jeffery M. Eberstadt & Forrestal: A National Security Partnership, 1909-1949. LC 91-8769. (Military History Ser.: No. 21). 248p. 1991. 39.95 (*0-89096-469-6*) Tex A&M Univ Pr.

— Fort Mifflin of Philadelphia: An Illustrated History. LC 98-5195. (Illus.). 264p. 1998. 37.50 (*0-8122-3430-8*); pap. text 18.50 (*0-8122-1644-X*) U of Pa Pr.

— The Pigtail War: American Involvement in the Sino-Japanese War of 1894-1895. LC 75-8446. (Illus.). 176p. 1975. reprint ed. pap. 54.60 (*0-608-04438-5*, 206497000012) Bks Demand.

Dorwart, Jeffrey M. Cape May County, New Jersey: The Making of an American Resort Community. LC 91-29058. (Illus.). 385p. (C). 1992. pap. 18.95 (*0-8135-1784-2*) Rutgers U Pr.

***Dorwart, Jeffrey M.** The Philadelphia Navy Yard: An Illustrated History. 2000. 45.00 (*0-8122-3575-4*) U of Pa Pr.

Dorwart, Reinhold A. Administrative Reforms of Frederick William First of Prussia. LC 70-138221. (C). 1971. reprint ed. lib. bdg. 69.50 (*0-8371-5578-9*, DOAR, Greenwood Pr) Greenwood.

Dorwart, Reinhold August. The Prussian Welfare State Before 1740. LC 77-134954. (Illus.). 342p. 1971 37.00 (*0-674-71975-1*) HUP.

***Dorwart, Reinhold August.** The Prussian Welfare State Before 1740. 344p. 1999. 28.95 (*0-7351-0177-9*) Replica Bks.

Dorwart, Robert A. & Epstein, Sherrie S. Privatization & Mental Health Care: A Fragile Balance. LC 92-33615. 208p. 1993. 55.00 (*0-86569-002-2*, T002, Auburn Hse) Greenwood.

Dorwick. Que Tal? 1994. 78.43 (*0-07-075123-4*) McGraw.

— Que Tal? An Intro Course. 5th ed. LC 98-34904. 1998. 49.95 (*0-07-013681-5*) McGraw.

***Dorwick, Thalia, et al.** Que Tal? 5th ed. 496p. (C). 1998. pap., student ed. 61.25 (*0-07-231140-1*); pap., student ed. 61.25 (*0-07-561954-7*) McGrw-H Hghr Educ.

Dorwick, Thalia, et al. Que Tal? An Introductory Course. 4th ed. LC 94-39641. 1995. text, teacher ed. write for info. (*0-07-017957-3*) McGraw.

— Que tal? An Introductory Course. 4th ed. (C). 1995. 18.25 incl. audio (*0-07-911989-1*) McGraw.

Dorwick, Thalia, jt. auth. see Kupferschmid, Gene S.

Dory, A., jt. auth. see Herckenrath, C.

Dory, Stewart, et al. Maine, a Peopled Landscape: Salt Documentary Photography, 1978-1995. French, Hugh T., ed. LC 95-5471. (Illus.). 170p. 1995. pap. 22.95 (*0-87451-717-6*) U Pr of New Eng.

Dorzorets, Zh., jt. auth. see Gurevich, V.

Dos, Dirk De, see De Dos, Dirk.

Dos Pasos, ed. see Macin, Enrique.

***Dos Passos, Benj. F.** The Law of Collateral & Direct Inheritance, Legacy, & Succession Taxes: Embracing All American & Many English Decisions with Forms for New York State ... 2nd ed. LC 99-73238. 654p. 1999. 170.00 (*1-56169-524-6*) Gaunt.

Dos Passos, John. Afterglow & Other Undergraduate Writings of John Dos Passos. Layman, Richard, ed. (Archive of Literary Documents Ser.). xviii, 277p. 1990. lib. bdg. 125.00 (*1-55888-265-0*) Omnigraphics Inc.

— The American Lawyer: As He Was - As He Is - As He Can Be. iv, 185p. 1986. reprint ed. 35.00 (*0-8377-0524-X*, Rothman) W S Hein.

— L' An Premier du Siecle. (FRE.). 1980. pap. 12.95 (*0-7859-1919-8*, 2070372081) Fr & Eur.

— Aventures d'un Jeune Homme. (FRE.). 480p. 1987. pap. 16.95 (*0-7859-2234-2*, 207037808X) Fr & Eur.

— The Big Money. 1976. 31.95 (*0-88411-534-8*) Amereon Ltd.

— The Big Money. 1989. pap. 5.95 (*0-317-02795-6*) NAL.

***Dos Passos, John.** The Big Money, Vol. 3. (U. S. A. Trilogy Ser.: Vol. 3). 528p. 2000. pap. 13.00 (*0-618-05683-1*) HM.

Dos Passos, John. Brazil on the Move. 205p. 1994. pap. 10.95 (*1-56924-958-X*) Marlowe & Co.

— Century's Ebb: The Thirteenth Chronicle. LC 75-920. 448p. 1975. 9.95 (*0-87645-089-3*, Gambit) Harvard Common Pr.

— Chosen Country. 30.95 (*0-88411-550-X*) Amereon Ltd.

— Commercial Trusts: The Growth & Rights of Aggregated Capital. An Argument Delivered Before the Industrial Commission at Washington, D. C., December 12, 1899. LC 77-38275. (Evolution of Capitalism Ser.). 152p. 1972. reprint ed. 18.95 (*0-405-04118-7*) Ayer.

— Effective Business Communication. Pizer, Donald, ed. LC 88-18090. 308p. reprint ed. pap. 95.50 (*0-608-10578-3*, 207119800009) Bks Demand.

— Facing the Chair: Story of the Americanization of Two Foreign-Born Workmen. LC 72-104066. (Civil Liberties in American History Ser.). 1970. reprint ed. 19.50 (*0-306-71871-5*) Da Capo.

— First Encounter. reprint ed. 19.50 (*0-404-20083-4*) AMS Pr.

— The Forty Second Parallel. 26.95 (*0-88411-344-2*) Amereon Ltd.

— The Forty Second Parallel. (FRE.). 512p. 1986. pap. 17.95 (*0-7859-2229-6*, 207037694X) Fr & Eur.

***Dos Passos, John.** The 42nd Parallel. (U. S. A. Trilogy Ser.: Vol. 1). 448p. 2000. pap. 13.00 (*0-618-05681-5*) HM.

Dos Passos, John. La Grosse Galette. (FRE.). 704p. 1986. pap. 10.95 (*0-7859-2021-8*, 2070376931) Fr & Eur.

— John Dos Passos' Correspondence with Arthur K. McComb. Landsberg, Melvin, ed. & narrated by by. (Illus.). 312p. 1991. text 45.00 (*0-87081-137-1*) Univ Pr Colo.

— John Dos Possos' Correspondence with Arthur K. McComb: or Learn to Sing the Carmagnole. Landsberg, Melvin, ed. & narrated by by. LC 89-24775. (Illus.). 358p. 1991. reprint ed. pap. 111.00 (*0-608-08359-5*, 206949800004) Bks Demand.

— Manhattan Transfer. Date not set. lib. bdg. 27.95 (*0-8488-0986-6*) Amereon Ltd.

— Manhattan Transfer. (FRE.). 499p. 1976. pap. 11.95 (*0-7859-1831-0*, 2070368254) Fr & Eur.

— Manhattan Transfer. 410p. 1991. pap. 14.95 (*0-395-57423-4*) HM.

— Manhattan Transfer. 1980. reprint ed. lib. bdg. 22.00 (*0-8376-0433-8*) Bentley Pubs.

— 1919. 27.95 (*0-88411-345-0*) Amereon Ltd.

***Dos Passos, John.** 1919, Vol. 2. (U. S. A. Trilogy Ser.: Vol. 2). 464p. 2000. pap. 13.00 (*0-618-05682-3*) HM.

Dos Passos, John. One Man's Initiation 1917: A Novel. 146p. (C). 1986. reprint ed. pap. text 17.50 (*0-8191-5360-5*) U Pr of Amer.

— State of the Nation. LC 73-718. (Illus.). 333p. 1973. reprint ed. lib. bdg. 38.50 (*0-8371-6782-5*, DOSN, Greenwood Pr) Greenwood.

— Streets of Night. Clark, Michael, ed. LC 88-43406. 224p. 1990. 39.50 (*0-945636-02-4*) Susquehanna U Pr.

— The Theme Is Freedom. LC 71-99632. (Essay Index Reprint Ser.). 1977. 24.95 (*0-8369-1460-0*) Ayer.

— Three Soldiers. 464p. 1997. mass mkt. 5.95 (*0-553-21456-X*, Bantam Classics) Bantam.

— Three Soldiers. 433p. 1988. pap. 9.95 (*0-88184-413-6*) Carroll & Graf.

— Three Soldiers. LC 96-70406. 416p. 1997. mass mkt. 6.95 (*0-451-52645-7*, Sig Classics) NAL.

— Three Soldiers. LC 97-18911. xix, 371p. (C). 2000. pap. 9.95 (*0-14-118027-7*) Viking Penguin.

— U. S. A. The 42nd Parallel; 1919; The Big Money. Ludington, Townsend & Aaron, Daniel, eds. LC 95-49282. 1288p. 1996. 40.00 (*1-883011-14-0*, Pub. by Library of America) Penguin Putnam.

***Dos Passos, John Roderigo.** Ground We Stand On. 2000. 34.95 (*0-7658-0781-5*) Transaction Pubs.

Dos Reis, Henrique L., ed. Nondestructive Testing & Evaluation for Manufacturing & Construction. 550p. 1989. 198.00 (*0-89116-926-1*) Hemisp Pub.

Dos Reis, Henrique L., jt. ed. see Djordjeuc, B. Boro.

***Dos Remedios, Cristobal G. & Thomas, David D.** Molecular Interactions of Actin: Actin Structure & Actin-Binding Proteins. LC 00-41288. (Results & Problems in Cell Differentiation Ser.). 2000. write for info. (*3-540-67110-2*) Spr-Verlag.

Dos Santos. Goal Book, Vol. 3. (C). 1996. pap., student ed. 19.38 (*0-07-018161-6*) McGrw-H Hghr Educ.

— Goal Book, Vol. 4. (C). 1996. pap., student ed. 19.38 (*0-07-018165-9*) McGrw-H Hghr Educ.

— Student Goal Book, Vol. 1. (C). 1996. pap., student ed. 19.38 (*0-07-018153-5*) McGrw-H Hghr Educ.

Dos Santos, Alice G., jt. ed. see Van Der Hammen, Thomas.

Dos Santos, Brian L. & Peffers, Ken. Rewards to Investors in Innovative Technology Applications: A Study of First Movers & Early Followers in ATMS. (Illus.). 50p. (Orig.). (C). 1993. pap. text 20.00 (*1-56806-917-0*) DIANE Pub.

dos Santos, Daniel. Soccer in Your Backyard: An Innovative Approcach to Improving Your Childs Soccer Skills While Enhancing Your Family & Quality Time. Zuker, Linda S., ed. (Illus.). 160p. 1999. pap. 12.50 (*0-9664114-0-4*) Reneda Pub Hse.

Dos Santos, J. F., et al, eds. The Proceedings of the Fifth (1995) International Offshore & Polar Engineering Conference, Vol. IV. LC 94-73796. (Orig.). 1995. pap. 100.00 (*1-880653-20-6*) ISOPE.

Dos Santos, Joao C., ed. Camilo Castelo Branco: No Centenario da Morte, Colloquium of Santa Barbara. LC 95-69013. (Publication Ser.: No. 8). (ENG & POR.). 296p. (C). 1995. pap. 20.00 (*0-942208-25-0*) Bandanna Bks.

Dos Santos, Joao C. & Williams, Frederick G., eds. O Amor das Letras e das Gentes: In Homage to Maria de Lourdes Belchior Pontes. LC 95-74795. (Publication Ser.: No. 9). (FRE & POR.). 504p. (Orig.). (C). 1995. pap. 35.00 (*0-942208-28-5*) Bandanna Bks.

Dos Santos, Joao C., jt. ed. see Dutra, Francis A.

Dos Santos, Jose. Occlusion: Principles & Concepts. 2nd ed. LC 96-77392. (Illus.). xi, 147p. 1996. pap. 34.50 (*1-56386-035-X*, Ishiyaku EuroAmerica) Med Dent Media.

Dos Santos, Jose, Jr. Occlusion: Principles & Concepts. 2nd rev. ed. (Illus.). xi, 147p. 1996. pap. text 34.50 (*1-891949-00-4*) Med Dent Media.

Dos Santos, Joyce A. Sand Dollar, Sand Dollar. LC 79-3019. (Illus.). (J). (gr. k-3). 1980. 11.95 (*0-397-31891-X*) HarpC Child Bks.

Dos Santos, Judite. Holding Together. 24p. 1992. pap. 8.00 (*0-89822-074-2*) Visual Studies.

Dos Santos Silva, Isabel, jt. auth. see Swerdlow, Anthony.

Dos Santos, Solvi, jt. auth. see Colborne, Desmond.

Dos Santos, Susan. Dictionary of Derivatives, English-Portuguese. (ENG & POR.). 222p. 1998. 59.95 (*0-320-00793-6*) Fr & Eur.

Dosa, Marta L. Across All Borders: International Information Flows & Applications: Collected Papers. LC 96-21269. 432p. 1996. 69.50 (*0-8108-3198-8*) Scarecrow.

Dosa, Marta L., tr. Libraries in the Political Scene: Georg Leyh & German Librarianship, 1933-53, 7. LC 72-5218. (Contributions in Librarianship & Information Science Ser.: No. 7). 226p. 1974. 59.95 (*0-8371-6443-5*, DGL/, Greenwood Pr) Greenwood.

Dosal, Paul J. Doing Business with the Dictators: A Political History of United Fruit in Guatamala, 1899-1944. (Latin American Silhouettes Ser.). (Illus.). 256p. 1993. pap. 17.95 (*0-8420-2590-1*) Scholarly Res Inc.

— Doing Business with the Dictators: A Political History of United Fruit in Guatemala, 1899-1944. LC 93-10118. (Latin American Silhouettes Ser.). (Illus.). 256p. 1993. 45.00 (*0-8420-2475-1*) Scholarly Res Inc.

— Industrial Oligarchies: The Rise of Guatamela's Ruling Elites, 1871-1994. LC 94-37195. 240p. 1995. 62.95 (*0-275-95136-7*, Praeger Pubs) Greenwood.

Dosani, Majid & Miller, John. Materials-Handling Technologies Used at Hazardous Waste Sites. LC 91-46546. (Pollution Technology Review Ser.: No. 208). (Illus.). 214p. 1992. 69.00 (*0-8155-1299-6*) Noyes.

Dosanjh, J. S. & Ghuman, Paul A. Singh. Child-Rearing in Ethnic Minorities. LC 96-29198. (Bilingual Education & Bilingualism Ser.). 200p. 1996. pap. 39.95 (*1-85359-365-6*, Pub. by Multilingual Matters) Taylor & Francis.

— Child-Rearing in Ethnic Minorities. LC 96-29198. (Bilingual Education & Bilingualism Ser.: No. 12). 228p. 1996. 89.00 (*1-85359-366-4*, Pub. by Multilingual Matters) Taylor & Francis.

Dosanjh, Sukhdev K. Robin with the Red Hat. (Orig.). (J). (ps-4). 1997. pap. 6.95 (*0-533-12227-9*) Vantage.

DosAnjos, Cyro. Diary of a Civil Servant. Brakel, Arthur, tr. LC 86-46325. (Illus.). 184p. 1988. 29.50 (*0-8386-3315-3*) Fairleigh Dickinson.

Dosch, Donald F. The Old Courthouse: Americans Build a Forum on the Frontier. Murphy, Dan, ed. LC 79-66506. (Gateway Ser.). (Illus.). 129p. (Orig.). (C). 1979. pap. 9.95 (0-931056-02-0) Jefferson Natl.

Dosch, H. Critical Phenomena at Surfaces & Interfaces: Evanescent X-Ray & Neutron Scattering. (Tracts in Modern Physics Ser.: Vol. 126). (Illus.). x, 145p. 1992. 82.00 (0-387-54534-4) Spr-Verlag.

Dosch, Hans-Michael, jt. ed. see Gelfand, Erwin W.

Dosch, J. Peter. Facts about Neural Therapy According to Huneke: Regulation Therapy - Brief Summary for Patients. (Illus.). 58p. 1985. pap. 8.00 (3-7760-0851-2) Medicina Bio.

Dosch, Mathias. Illustrated Atlas of the Techniques of Neural Therapy with Local Anesthetics. (Illus.). 207p. 1985. 98.00 (3-7760-0849-0, Pub. by K F Haug Pubs) Medicina Bio.

Dosch, Peter. Manual of Neural Therapy According to Huneke: Therapy with Local Anesthetics. (Illus.). 498p. 1985. 98.00 (3-7760-0702-8, Pub. by K F Haug Pubs) Medicina Bio.

Doscher, Barbara M. The Functional Unity of the Singing Voice. 2nd ed. LC 93-32829. (Illus.). 352p. 1994. 38.50 (0-8108-2708-5) Scarecrow.

Doscher, Henry, Jr. Little Wolf at Leyte: Story of the Heroic Men of the USS Samuel B. Roberts in the Battle of Leyte Gulf. (Illus.). 158p. 1996. 18.95 (1-57168-082-9, Eakin Pr) Sunbelt Media.

Doscher, J. Henry, Jr. Subchaser in the South Pacific: A Saga of the U. S. S. SC-761 During World War II. LC 94-2271. 124p. 1994. 15.95 (0-89015-947-5) Sunbelt Media.

***Doscher, Robert & Simms, Richard L.** The DialAmerica Teleservices Handbook: A Guide to Successful Outbound Telemarketing. LC 00-38662. 2000. 44.95 (0-658-00399-2) NTC Contemp Pub Co.

Doscherholmen, Alfred. Studies in the Metabolism of Vitamin B12. LC 65-12097. 279p. reprint ed. pap. 86.50 (0-608-13267-5, 205585600039) Bks Demand.

Doschka, Roland. L' Eternel Feminin: From Renoir to Picasso. LC 96-38387. (Illus.). 224p. 1996. 49.95 (3-7913-1730-X, Pub. by Prestel) te Neues.

— Marc Chagall: Origins & Paths. (Illus.). 232p. 1998. 65.00 (3-7913-1989-2) te Neues.

***Doschka, Roland.** Pablo Picasso: Human Form in the 20th Century. (Illus.). 2000. 65.00 (3-7913-2350-4) Prestel Pub NY.

Dose, Klaus, et al, eds. Origins of Life: Proceedings of the Seventh International Conference, Mainz, July 10-15, 1983 (A Special Issue of a Journal) 1984. text 364.50 (90-277-1694-3) Kluwer Academic.

Dose, Klaus, jt. auth. see Fox, Sidney W.

Dosen, Kosta. Substructural Logics. Schroeder-Heister, Peter, ed. LC 93-29307. (Studies in Logic & Computation: Vol. 2). (Illus.). 396p. 1994. text 65.00 (0-19-853777-8, Clarendon Pr) OUP.

***Doser, Torge.** Gegenseitigkeit und Anerkennung Auslandischer Entscheidungen: Dargestellt Am Beispiel Sudafrika. (GER.). lxxiii, 376p. 1999. 74.00 (3-631-34888-6) P Lang Pubng.

Doser, William R. Clergy Stoles: Needlepoint or Cross Stitch. 58p. 1981. 7.50 (0-9618948-0-6) Doser Designs.

Dosh, Robert M., et al. The Taking Charge of Menopause Workbook. 195p. (Orig.). 1997. pap. 17.95 (1-57224-060-1) New Harbinger.

Doshay, Lewis J. Boy Sex Offender & His Later Career. LC 69-14921. (Criminology, Law Enforcement, & Social Problems Ser.: No. 59). 1969. reprint ed. 20.00 (0-87585-059-6) Patterson Smith.

***Doshi, Darshan.** SMS 2.0 Administration. (Illus.). 500p. 2000. pap. 52.95 (0-7357-0082-6) New Riders Pub.

Doshi, Mahendra, ed. Recycled Paper Technology: An Anthology of Published Papers. 342p. (Orig.). 1994. pap. 90.00 (0-89852-282-X, 0101R237) TAPPI.

Doshi, Mahendra R. & Dyer, Jeffrey M. Management & Control of Stickies. LC 98-195027. (Illus.). 43p. 1998. pap. 40.00 (0-9657447-2-8) Doshi & Assocs.

— Paper Recycling Challenge Vol. II: Deinking & Bleaching, 4 vols. LC 97-213200. (Illus.). 320p. 1997. pap. write for info. (0-9657447-1-X) Doshi & Assocs.

***Doshi, Mahendra R. & Dyer, Jeffrey M.** Paper Recycling Challenge Vol. III: Process Technology. LC 97-213200. (Illus.). 300p. 1998. pap. 105.00 (0-9657447-3-6) Doshi & Assocs.

— Paper Recycling Challenge Vol. IV: Process Control & Mensuration. (Illus.). 210p. 1999. pap. 75.00 (0-9657447-4-4) Doshi & Assocs.

Doshi, Mahendra R. & Dyers, Jeffrey M. Paper Recycling Challenge: Stickies, Vol. 1. 349p. 1997. (0-9657447-0-1) CA66.

***Doshi, Malvi.** From the Ganges: Wonderful Indian Vegetarian Fare. (Illus.). 288p. 2000. pap. 14.95 (0-89407-125-4) Strawberry Hill.

Doshi, Malvi. A Surti Touch: Adventures in Indian Cooking. LC 80-21487. (Illus.). 224p. (Orig.). 1980. pap. 9.95 (0-89407-042-8) Strawberry Hill.

Doshi, N. M. Administrative Law on Misconduct, Departmental Inquiry, Major & Minor Punishments, Etc., 2 vols. (C). 1990. 300.00 (0-89771-291-9) St Mut.

Doshi, Nagin. Guidance from Sri Aurobindo: Letters to a Young Disciple, Vol. 3. 268p. 1987. pap. 11.95 (81-7058-069-2, Pub. by SAA) E-W Cultural Ctr.

Doshi, S. L. Anthropology of Food & Nutrition. (C). 1995. 32.00 (81-7033-278-8, Pub. by Rawat Pubns) S Asia.

— Processes of Tribal Unification & Integration: Case Study of the Bhils. 1978. 11.00 (0-8364-0291-X) S Asia.

— Tribal Ethnicity, Class & Integration. 1990. 29.00 (81-7033-093-9, Pub. by Rawat Pubns) S Asia.

Doshi, S. L., ed. Relevance in Sociological Research. (C). 1991. 22.50 (81-7033-135-8, Pub. by Rawat Pubns) S Asia.

Doshi, Sandip, jt. auth. see Evans, Bruce.

Doshi, Saryu. Dances of Manipur: The Classical Tradition. LC 89-900003. 128p. 1989. 15.95 (81-85026-09-2, 1044, Pub. by Mandala Pub Grp) Words Distrib.

— Dharna Vihara, Ranakpur, Vol. 17. (Opus Ser.). 1995. 44.50 (3-930698-17-X, Pub. by E J Wasmuth) Dist Art Pubs.

Doshi, Saryu, ed. India & Egypt: Influences & Interaction. (C). 1993. 76.00 (81-85026-23-8, Pub. by Marg Publns) Art Media Resources.

Doshida, S., et al, eds. Algorithmic Learning Theory: Third Workshop, ALT '92, Tokyo, Japan, October 20- 22, 1992 Proceedings. LC 93-33444. (Lecture Notes in Computer Science, Lecture Notes in Artificial Intelligence Ser.: Vol. 743). 1993. 44.95 (0-387-57369-0) Spr-Verlag.

Dosi, Cesare, ed. Nonpoint Source Pollution Regulation - Issues & Analysis: The FEEM-KLUWER International Series on Economics, Energy & Environment. LC 94-32311. (Economics, Energy & Environment Ser.). 192p. (C). 1994. lib. bdg. 106.00 (0-7923-3121-4) Kluwer Academic.

Dosi, Giovanni. Innovation, Market Organization & Economic Dynamics: Selected Essays. LC 99-56230. 720p. 1999. 130.00 (1-85898-591-9) E Elgar.

***Dosi, Giovanni, et al, eds.** The Nature & Dynamics of Organizational Capabilities. 420p. 2000. text 74.00 (0-19-829680-0) OUP.

Dosi, Giovanni, et al, eds. Technical Change & Economic Theory. 656p. 1988. text 79.00 (0-86187-949-X, Pub. by P P Pubs) Cassell & Continuum.

— Technical Change & Economic Theory. 656p. 1990. text 32.50 (0-86187-894-9) St Martin.

— Technology, Organization & Competitiveness: Perspectives on Industrial & Corporate Change. LC HD45.T3968 1998. (Illus.). 356p. 1998. pap. text 24.95 (0-19-829096-9) OUP.

— Technology, Organization & Competitiveness: Perspectives on Industrial & Corporate Change. LC 98-175567. (Illus.). 356p. (C). 1998. text 85.00 (0-19-829098-5) OUP.

Dosi, Giovanni, et al. Economics of Technical Change & International Trade. 336p. (C). 1990. text 70.00 (0-8147-1834-5) NYU Pr.

***Dosick, Wayne.** The Business Bible: 10 New Commandments for Bringing Spirituality & Ethical Values into the Workplace. 2000. pap. 14.95 (1-58023-101-2) Jewish Lights.

Dosick, Wayne. Golden Rules: The Ten Ethical Values Parents Need to Teach Their Children. LC 94-37098. 240p. 1996. pap. 13.00 (0-06-251249-8, Pub. by Harper SF) HarpC.

— Golden Rules: The Then Ethical Values Parents Need to Teach Their Children. 288p. 1998. mass mkt. 5.99 (0-06-101328-5) HarpC.

— Living Judaism: The Complete Guide to Jewish Belief, Tradition, & Practice. LC 95-22260. (Illus.). 400p. 1995. 27.50 (0-06-062119-2, Pub. by Harper SF) HarpC.

— Soul Judaism: Dancing with God into a New Era. LC 99-19193. 304p. 1999. pap. 16.95 (1-58023-053-9) Jewish Lights.

***Dosick, Wayne.** When Life Hurts: A Personal Journey from Adversity to Renewal. 204p. 1999. pap. 12.95 (1-56975-184-6, Pub. by Ulysses Pr) Publishers Group.

Dosick, Wayne D. Dancing with God. LC 96-47349. 2000. pap. 12.00 (0-06-061956-2) Harper SF.

— Living Judaism: The Complete Guide to Jewish Belief, Tradition & Practice. LC 95-22260. (Illus.). 400p. 1998. pap. 20.00 (0-06-062179-6, Pub. by Harper SF) HarpC.

— When Life Hurts: Finding the Strength to Build Anew When Your Whole Life Falls Apart. LC 97-33152. 208p. 1998. 19.00 (0-06-251527-6, Pub. by Harper SF) HarpC.

***Dosier, Susan.** Civil War Cooking: The Confederacy. LC 99-20749. (Exploring History Through Simple Recipes Ser.). 32p. (J). (gr. 2-7). 2000. lib. bdg. 22.60 (0-7368-0350-5, Blue Earth Bks) Capstone Pr.

— Civil War Cooking: The Confederacy. (Exploring History Through Simple Recipes Ser.). 32p. (gr. 2-7). 1999. 14.60 (0-516-21933-2) Childrens.

Dosier, Susan. Civil War Cooking: The Union. LC 99-27048. (Exploring History Through Simple Recipes Ser.). 32p. (J). (gr. 2-7). 2000. lib. bdg. 22.60 (0-7368-0351-3, Blue Earth Bks) Capstone Pr.

***Dosier, Susan.** Civil War Cooking: The Union. (Exploring History Through Simple Recipes Ser.). 32p. (gr. 2-7). 1999. 14.60 (0-516-21862-X) Childrens.

— Colonial Cooking. LC 99-24596. (Exploring History Through Simple Recipes Ser.). 32p. (J). (gr. 2-7). 2000. lib. bdg. 22.60 (0-7368-0352-1, Blue Earth Bks) Capstone Pr.

— Colonial Cooking. (Exploring History Through Simple Recipes Ser.). 32p. (gr. 2-7). 1999. 14.60 (0-516-21863-8) Childrens.

Dosier, Susan & Gunderson, Mary. Exploring History through Simple Recipes. (Illus.). 32p. 135.60 (0-7368-0446-3, Blue Earth Bks) Capstone Pr.

Dosier, Susan & Rutland, Julia Dowling. Discover Dinnertime: Your Guide to Building Family Time Around the Table. (Illus.). 192p. 1998. 15.95 (1-879958-32-5, Tradery) Wimmer Cos.

Dosiere, Marcel. Crystallization of Polymers. LC 93-8271. (NATO Advanced Study Institutes Series C, Mathematical & Physical Sciences: Vol. 405). 1993. text 357.00 (0-7923-2350-5) Kluwer Academic.

Dosker, Henry E., ed. The Dutch Anabaptists: Stone Lectures Delivered at Princeton Theological Seminary, 1918-1919. LC 83-45610. reprint ed. 36.50 (0-404-19828-7) AMS Pr.

Doskey, John. European Journals of William Maclure. LC 84-45901. (Memoirs Ser.: Vol. 171). 700p. (C). 1988. 40.00 (0-87169-171-X, M171-DOJ) Am Philos.

Doskocil, Bill. Cannons & Sails: Meeting the Challenges to Marriage. 164p. (Orig.). (C). 1989. pap. 5.95 (0-9629600-0-4) Rock Cornerstone.

Doskow, Minna. William Blake's Jerusalem. LC 81-65463. (Illus.). 388p. 1983. 50.00 (0-8386-3090-1) Fairleigh Dickinson.

Doskow, Minna, ed. & intro. see Gilman, Charlotte Perkins.

Dosman. Practical Solutions in Occupational Medicine. 1997. write for info. (0-87371-618-3, L618) Lewis Pubs.

Dosman, Edgar, jt. auth. see Daudelin, Jean.

Dosman, Edgar J., jt. ed. see Haar, Jerry.

Dosman, James A. & Cockrof. Principles of Health & Safety in Agriculture. 456p. 1989. lib. bdg. 129.00 (0-8493-0160-2, RC965) CRC Pr.

Doss, A. Rodger, et al. Shine: Moonshine, Murder, Birth of Stock Car Racing. large type ed. (Illus.). 200p. 1996. pap. 12.95 (0-9641867-1-3) Docar Pubng.

Doss, Bonnie. But . . . What about Me! How It Feels to Be a Kid in Divorce. (Illus.). 52p. 1998. pap. 16.99 (0-9653895-8-8) Bookmark Pubg.

***Doss, Bonnie.** But... What about Me? How It Feels to Be a Kid in Divorce. 2nd ed. 52p. 2000. pap. 16.99 (0-9653895-6-1) Bookmark Pubg.

Doss, Bonnie. My Name Is Sara. 24p. 1999. 5.00 (0-9653895-9-6) Bookmark Pubg.

***Doss, Charles W.** Led by the Master's Hand: Missionary Journeys of Signs, Wonders & Miracles. 144p. 2000. pap. 9.99 (1-884369-48-0) McDougal Pubng.

Doss, Cheryl R. African Professional Women in Agriculture: An Analysis of Two Roundtable Discussions. (Development Studies). 22p. (Orig.). 1991. pap. 6.00 (0-933595-58-1) Winrock Intl.

Doss, Cheryl R., jt. auth. see Brunet-Perrault, Nicole.

Doss, Danny L. Poems of the Heart. 16p. (Orig.). 1995. pap. write for info. (1-885206-27-5, Iliad Pr) Cader Pubng.

Doss, Erika. Benton, Pollock, & the Politics of Modernism: From Regionalism to Abstract Expressionism. (Illus.). 462p. 1991. 46.00 (0-226-15942-6) U Ch Pr.

— Benton, Pollock, & the Politics of Modernism: From Regionalism to Abstract Expressionism. 462p. 1995. pap. text 16.95 (0-226-15943-4) U Ch Pr.

— Elvis Culture: Fans, Faith & Image. LC 97-34373. (CultureAmerica Ser.). (Illus.). 280p. 1999. 24.95 (0-7006-0948-2) U Pr of KS.

— Spirit Poles & Flying Pigs: Public Art & Cultural Democracy in American Communities. (Illus.). 288p. 1995. pap. 17.95 (1-56098-534-8) Smithsonian.

— Spirit Poles & Flying Pigs: Public Art & Cultural Democracy in American Communities. LC 94-26010. (Illus.). 288p. 1995. text 45.00 (1-56098-464-3) Smithsonian.

Doss, George M. COBRA for XML Developers. LC 99-22029. 290p. 1999. pap. 39.95 (1-55622-668-3) Wordware Pub.

— CORBA Networking with JAVA. LC 98-48671. 1999. pap. text 36.95 (1-55622-654-3) Wordware Pub.

— DCOM Networking with Visual J++ LC 98-48781. 1999. pap. 36.95 (1-55622-655-1) Wordware Pub.

***Doss, George M.** IS Project Management Handbook. LC 99-59668. (C). 2000. 79.95 (0-13-086668-7) P-H.

Doss, George M. Learn Red Hat Linux OS Tips. LC 99-28560. 379p. 1999. pap. 36.95 incl. cd-rom (1-55622-715-9) Wordware Pub.

***Doss, George M.** Learn Red Hat Linux Server Tips. LC 99-59496. 400p. 2000. 36.95 incl. audio compact disk (1-55622-714-0) Wordware Pub.

— Learn XML Tips. LC 00-38180. (Illus.). 400p. 2000. pap. write for info. (1-55622-757-4) Wordware Pub.

Doss, George M. Pure XML. (Illus.). 600p. (Orig.). 2000. pap. text 24.99 (0-672-31601-3) Sams.

***Doss, James D.** Grandmother Spider. 2001. write for info. (0-380-97722-2, Wm Morrow) Morrow Avon.

Doss, James D. The Night Visitor: A Shaman Mystery. LC 99-25049. 400p. 1999. 23.00 (0-380-97721-4, Avon Bks) Morrow Avon.

***Doss, James D.** The Night Visitor: A Shaman Mystery. 384p. 2000. mass mkt. 5.99 (0-380-80393-3, Avon Bks) Morrow Avon.

Doss, James D. Shaman Laughs. LC 95-31795. 336p. 1997. mass mkt. 5.99 (0-380-72690-4, Avon Bks) Morrow Avon.

— Shaman Sings. 256p. 1995. mass mkt. 5.99 (0-380-72496-0, Avon Bks) Morrow Avon.

— The Shaman's Bones. LC 96-52148. 288p. 1997. mass mkt. 22.00 (0-380-97424-X, Avon Bks) Morrow Avon.

— The Shaman's Game. LC 98-4494. 384p. 1998. mass mkt. 22.00 (0-380-97425-8, Avon Bks) Morrow Avon.

— The Shaman's Game: A Shaman Mystery. LC 98-4494. 352p. 1999. mass mkt. 5.99 (0-380-79030-0, Avon Bks) Morrow Avon.

— The Shaman's Mistake. LC 96-52148. 352p. 1998. mass mkt. 5.99 (0-380-79029-7, Avon Bks) Morrow Avon.

Doss, M., ed. see International Porphyrin Meeting Staff.

Doss, Manfred, ed. see International Research Conference Staff.

Doss, Margot. Walker's Yearbook. 1989. pap. 9.95 (0-917583-15-9, Dont Call Frisco) Lexikos.

Doss, Margot P. The Bay Area at Your Feet. rev. ed. (Illus.). 270p. 1987. pap. 7.95 (0-917583-12-4, Dont Call Frisco) Lexikos.

— New San Francisco at Your Feet. 3rd rev. ed. LC 79-6170. (Illus.). 256p. 1990. pap. 12.95 (0-8021-1145-9, Grove) Grove-Atltic.

Doss, Marion T., jt. auth. see Roberts, Robert N.

Doss, Michael P. Plenty Coups. (Raintree-Rivilo American Indian Stories Ser.). (J). 1996. 10.15 (0-606-12480-2, Pub. by Turtleback) Demco.

Doss-Quinby, Eglal, ed. The Lyrics of the Trouveres: A Research Guide, 1970-1990. LC 93-38222. (Medieval Bibliographies Ser.: Vol. 17). 280p. 1994. text 20.00 (0-8153-0085-9, H1423) Garland.

***Doss-Quinby, Eglal, et al, eds.** Songs of the Women Trouveres. Grimbert, Joan T. et al, trs. (Illus.). 256p. 2000. 35.00 (0-300-08412-9); pap. 15.00 (0-300-08413-7) Yale U Pr.

***Doss, Richard B.** Performance Puzzles: And How to Put Them Together. limited ed. (Illus.). 235p. 1999. pap. 19.95 (0-9631680-1-0) Human Side Pr.

Doss, Richard B. Theory P: A Premise for Improvement. (Illus.). (Orig.). (C). pap. 19.50 (0-9631680-0-2) Human Side Pr.

Doss, Robert. How to Coach Tee Ball Without Going Insane. unabridged ed. (Illus.). 96p. 1998. 12.95 (0-9665944-0-1) Bullhorn Media Grp.

Doss, Rodger. Killing of a Court: 1912 Hillsville Massacre. 140p. (J). (gr. 5-12). 1994. pap. 12.95 (0-9641867-0-5) Docar Pubng.

Doss, Seale. If P Then Q: Basic Logic for Philosophy Students. 150p. (Orig.). (C). 1997. pap. text 10.95 (0-929331-05-2) Ripon Coll Pr.

Doss, Seale, et al. Critical Thinking as a Philosophical Movement. 140p. (Orig.). (C). 1989. pap. text 6.95 (0-929331-02-8) Ripon Coll Pr.

***Doss, Tammy.** A Commitment to Spiritual Excellence: The Inspirational Teachings of Pastor Michael J.Metters. 1999. pap. write for info. (0-7392-0341-X, PO3514) Morris Pubng.

***Doss, Yvette C., ed.** Frontera Literary Review: Prose, Poetry, Revolution. (Illus.). 160p. 1999. pap. 10.00 (0-9669232-0-0, Interstitial Pr) Frontera.

Dossa, Shiraz. The Public Realm & the Public Self: The Political Theory of Hannah Arendt. LC 88-94398. xiv, 154p. (C). 1989. text 29.95 (0-88920-967-7) W Laurier U Pr.

Dossado, L. A. & Fothergill, C. J., eds. Electrical Degradation & Breakdown in Polymers. (IEE Materials & Devices Ser.: No. 9). xix, 601p. 1992. 135.00 (0-86341-196-7, Pub. by Peregrinus) Dist Unknown.

Dossal, Mariam. Imperial Designs & Indian Realities: The Planning of Bombay City 1845-1875. (Illus.). 286p. 1997. pap. 11.95 (0-19-563138-2) OUP.

Dossal, Mariam & Maloni, Ruby. State Intervention & Popular Response. LC 99-932142. xxiii, 242 p. 1999. write for info. (81-7154-855-5) Asia Bk Corp.

Dossani, Nazir G. Duality Theories in Linear, Quadratic & Convex Programming: A Survey. (Discussion Papers: No. 44). 1971. pap. 10.00 (1-55869-028-X) Regional Sci Res Inst.

Dossani, Nazir G., jt. auth. see Miller, Ronald E.

Dossar, Yves. Evolution de la France Meridionale 1249-1328. (Collected Studies: No. CS295). 346p. (C). 1989. lib. bdg. 124.95 (0-86078-243-3, Pub. by Variorum) Ashgate Pub Co.

Dossat, Roy J. Principles of Refrigeration. 2nd ed. LC 78-2938. 98p. 1978. pap. text 9.00 (0-471-03771-0) P-H.

— Principles of Refrigeration. 4th ed. LC 96-18469. 512p. 1996. 92.00 (0-13-233371-6) P-H.

Dossat, Yves, ed. see Dondaine, Antoine.

Dosse, Francois. Empire of Meaning: The Humanization of the Social Sciences. Melehy, Hassan, tr. from FRE. LC 98-26755. 352p. 1998. 39.95 (0-8166-2964-1) U of Minn Pr.

— History of Structuralism. Glassman, Deborah, tr. LC 96-51477. 496p. 1997. 29.95 (0-8166-2241-8); 29.95 (0-8166-2371-6) U of Minn Pr.

— History of Structuralism Vol. 1: The Rising Sign, 1945-1966. Glassman, Deborah, tr. from FRE. LC 96-51477.Tr. of .. 512p. (C). 1997. 49.95 (0-8166-2239-6) U of Minn Pr.

— History of Structuralism Vol. 2: The Sign Sets 1967-Present. Glassman, Deborah, tr. from FRE. LC 96-51477.Tr. of .. 416p. (C). 1997. 49.95 (0-8166-2370-8) U of Minn Pr.

Dossen, Francois. History of Structuralism. Glassman, Deborah, tr. LC 96-51477. 1997. write for info. (0-8166-2254-X) U of Minn Pr.

Dossenbach, Hans D. Beware We Are Poisonous! How Animals Defend Themselves. LC 97-45490. (Illus.). 40p. (J). (gr. 4-6). 1998. 16.95 (1-56711-215-3) Blackbirch.

Dossenbach, Hans D., jt. auth. see Dossenbach, Monika.

***Dossenbach, Monika & Dossenbach, Hans D.** Eye Openers! All about Animal Vision. LC 97-32130.Tr. of Augen Auf!. (Illus.). 32p. (J). (gr. 4-6). 1998. 16.95 (1-56711-216-1) Blackbirch.

Dossetor, Frank. The Third Horizon. 1985. 30.00 (0-7855-1945-9) St Mut.

Dossetor, J. B., jt. ed. see Land, W.

***Dossett, Ellen.** Just As I Am: Americans with Disabilities. LC 99-33976. 184p. 1999. 48.00 (1-57587-114-9) Crane Hill AL.

Dossett, John & Juetje, Robert, eds. Heat Treating: Proceedings of the 16th Conference. LC 96-85240. 700p. 1996. 154.00 (0-87170-579-6, 6116) ASM.

Dossey. Modeling with Function, 6 vols., Vol. 5. 1996. pap. text 20.00 (0-435-07111-4) Heinemann.

Dossey, ed. Discrette Math. 2nd ed. 96p. 1997. text, student ed. 12.00 (0-673-53501-0) S&S Trade.

Dossey, Barbara, jt. auth. see Keegan, Lynn.

Dossey, Barbara M. Core Curriculum for Holistic Nursing. LC 96-36535. 800p. 1997. 39.00 (0-8342-0870-9, 20870) Aspen Pub.

— Imagery & Relaxation: Awakening the Inner Healer. (Orig.). 1989. pap. write for info. (0-318-64876-8) Bodymind Systs.

Dossey, Barbara M., et al. Critical Care Nursing: Body - Mind - Spirit. 3rd ed. LC 91-18392. (Illus.). 1058p. 1992. reprint ed. pap. 200.00 (0-608-07313-X, 206754100009) Bks Demand.

— Essentials of Critical Care Nursing: Body, Mind, Spirit. (Illus.). 684p. 1990. teacher ed. write for info. (0-318-69544-8) Lppncott W & W.

An Asterisk (*) at the beginning of an entry indicates that the title is appearing for the first time.

— Holistic Health Promotion: A Guide for Practice. LC 89-6794. 324p. (C). 1989. 63.00 (*0-8342-0069-4*) Aspen Pub.

— Holistic Nurses Association Standards. 330p. 2000. spiral bd. 39.00 (*0-8342-1045-2*, 10452) Aspen Pub.

— Holistic Nursing: A Handbook for Practice. 3rd ed. LC 99-27912. 848p. 1999. 45.00 (*0-8342-1629-9*) Aspen Pub.

***Dossey, Barbara Montgomery.** Florence Nightingale: Mystic, Visionary, Reformer. LC 99-23725. 1999. 54.95 (*0-87434-984-2*) Springhouse Corp.

Dossey, Donald E. Holiday Folklore, Phobias & Fun: Mythical Origins, Scientific Treatments & Superstitious "Cures" LC 92-2467. 232p. (Orig.). 1995. 18.95 (*0-925640-06-9*) Outcomes Unltd.

— Holiday Folklore, Phobias & Fun: Mythical Origins, Scientific Treatments & Superstitious "Cures" LC 92-2467. (Illus.). 232p. (Orig.). 1995. pap. 14.95 (*0-925640-07-7*) Outcomes Unltd.

— Keying: The Power of Positive Feelings. LC 89-60820. (Illus.). 201p. 1995. 16.95 (*0-925640-00-X*); pap. 14.95 (*0-925640-01-8*) Outcomes Unltd.

— Surviving Disaster Stress: What to Do Before, During & after Any Crisis to Prevent Pos-Traumatic Stress Disorders. (Illus.). 256p. 1997. pap. 14.95 (*0-925640-08-5*) Outcomes Unltd.

Dossey, Donald E. & Hillyer, John I. The Mountains-to-Sea Trail: Western North Carolina's Majestic Rival to the Appalachian Trail. LC 97-40303. (Illus.). 240p. (Orig.). pap. 15.95 (*0-925640-09-3*) Outcomes Unltd.

Dossey, John A. Essential Skills in Mathematics: A Comparative Analysis of American & Japanese Assessments of Eighth-Graders. LC 97-171789. 66p. 1997. pap. 4.75 (*0-16-049022-7*) USGPO.

Dossey, John A., ed. Confronting the Core Curriculum: Considering Change in the Undergraduate Mathematics Major. LC 97-74332. (Classroom Resource Materials Ser.: Vol. 45). 136p. (C). 1998. pap. 38.50 (*0-88385-155-5*) Math Assn.

Dossey, John A., et al. Discrete Mathematics. 2nd ed. LC 92-19327. (C). 1993. text 85.31 (*0-673-46287-0*) Addson-Wesley Educ.

— Discrete Mathematics. 3rd ed. LC 96-654. 580p. (C). 1997. 93.00 (*0-673-98039-1*) Addson-Wesley Educ.

— Essential Skills in Mathematics: A Comparative Analysis of American & Japanese Assessments of Eighth Graders. (Illus.). 60p. 1998. pap. text 25.00 (*0-7881-7023-6*) DIANE Pub.

— EXPLRNG DISC MATH TI 81. (Illus.). 200p. (C). 1992. pap. text 21.50 (*0-201-52433-3*) Addison-Wesley.

Dossey, Larry. Be Careful What You Pray For, You Might Just Get It: What We Can Do About the Unintentional Effects of Our Thoughts, Prayers & Wishes. LC 97-15085. 272p. 1998. pap. 13.00 (*0-06-251434-2*, Pub. by Harper SF) HarpC.

Dossey, Larry. Be Careful What You Pray For..You Just Might Get It: Dossey,&Larry. abr. ed. 1997. audio 18.00 (*0-694-51871-9*, CPN 2698) HarperAudio.

— Beyond Illness: Discovering the Experience of Health. 1985. pap. 15.95 (*0-394-74192-7*) Random.

Dossey, Larry. Healing Words. 432p. 1997. mass mkt. 6.50 (*0-06-104383-4*, Harp PBks) HarpC.

— Healing Words: The Power of Prayer & the Practice of Medicine. LC 92-56132. 320p. 1995. pap. 14.00 (*0-06-250252-2*, Pub. by Harper SF) HarpC.

— Prayer Is Good Medicine: How to Reap Healing Benefits of Prayer. LC 96-12273. 272p. 1997. pap. 13.00 (*0-06-251424-5*, Pub. by Harper SF) HarpC.

— Recovering the Soul: A Scientific & Spiritual Search. 336p. 1989. pap. 14.95 (*0-553-34790-X*) Bantam.

— Recovering the Soul: A Scientific & Spiritual Search. 1990. 10.95 incl. audio (*1-56176-152-4*) Mystic Fire.

— Reinventing Medicine: Beyond Mind-Body to a New Era of Healing. LC 99-27970. 288p. 1999. 14.00 (*0-06-251644-2*, HarpBusn) HarpInfo.

— Reinventing Medicine: Beyond Mind-Body to a New Era of Healing. LC 99-27970. 271p. 1999. 24.00 (*0-06-251622-1*, Pub. by Harper SF) HarpC.

***Dossey, Larry.** Reinventing Medicine: Beyond Mind-Body to a New Era of Healing, Set. abr. ed. 1999. audio 18.00 (*0-694-52167-1*) HarperAudio.

Dossey, Larry. Scientific & Pastoral Perspectives on Intercessory Prayer: An Exchange Between Larry Dossey, M. D. & Health Care Chaplains. VandeCreek, Larry, ed. LC 98-12323. 140p. 1998. 29.95 (*0-7890-0518-2*, Haworth Pastrl); pap. 14.95 (*1-56023-113-0*, Harrington Park) Haworth Pr.

Dossey, Larry, et al. The Angels: The Entities Trilogy. Sardello, Robert J., ed. LC 94-43577. 273p. (Orig.). 1994. pap. 20.00 (*0-911005-27-7*) Dallas Inst Pubns.

***Dossi, Barbara.** Albertina: The History of the Collection & Its Masterpieces. (Illus.). 2000. 65.00 (*3-7913-2340-7*) Prestel Pub NY.

Dossick, Jane. Creative Therapy: Fifty-Two Exercises for Groups. LC 88-42577. (Illus.). 124p. 1988. pap. 25.95 (*0-943158-50-8*, CTBP) Pro Resource.

— Creative Therapy II: Fifty-Two More Exercises for Groups. LC 88-42577. (Illus.). 118p. 1990. pap. 25.95 (*0-943158-60-5*, CT2BP) Pro Resource.

— Creative Therapy III: Fifty-Two More Exercises for Groups. LC 94-35064. (Illus.). 122p. 1995. pap. 25.95 (*1-56887-008-6*, CT3BP, Prof Resc Pr) Pro Resource.

Dossor, Howard. Colin Wilson: The Man & His Mind. 1993. pap. 16.95 (*1-85230-176-7*, Pub. by Element MA) Penguin Putnam.

Dost & Lambert, eds. Simulation Technology, Proceedings of International Conference on (SIMTEC '93) 400p. 1993. pap. 60.00 (*1-56555-060-9*, SIMTEC-93) Soc Computer Sim.

Dost, H. Acid Sulphate Soils. (C). 1991. text 395.00 (*0-89771-599-3*, Pub. by Intl Bk Distr) St Mut.

Dost, William & Botsai, Elmer. Wood-Detailing for Performance. LC 90-80940. (Illus.). 200p. (Orig.). 1990. pap. 42.00 (*0-9614808-7-4*) GRDA Pubns.

Dostal. Keyboard Lesson Plans. Date not set. write for info. (*0-314-04904-5*) West Pub.

— Keyboarding. Date not set. pap. text, teacher ed. 42.95 (*0-314-02580-4*) West Pub.

— Keyboarding. 1994. mass mkt. 37.25 (*0-314-02648-7*) West Pub.

— Keyboarding Carnival. 1993. mass mkt. 197.25 (*0-314-02978-8*) West Pub.

Dostal. Learning to Keyboard. 1992. mass mkt. 35.00 (*0-314-00070-4*) West Pub.

Dostal. Learning to Keyboard. (TA - Typing/Keyboarding Ser.). (C). 1992. mass mkt. 35.00 (*0-314-00072-0*) West Pub.

— Learning to Study. 1992. mass mkt. 22.50 (*0-314-01096-3*) West Pub.

Dostal, Jiri. Operational Amplifiers. 2nd ed. (EDN Ser.). (Illus.). 360p. 1993. text 72.95 (*0-7506-9317-7*) Buttrwrth-Heinemann.

Dostal, John, jt. auth. see Gillette, Ned.

Dostal, June. Keyboarding for Personal & Business Use. 10th ed. LC 93-2058. 1993. mass mkt. 37.25 (*0-314-02314-3*) West Pub.

Dostal, June & St. Vincent, Deborah. Technical Communication: A Guided Approach. LC 95-35122. 1996. mass mkt. 58.95 (*0-314-06935-6*) West Pub.

Dostal, Rudolf. On Integration in Plants. Thimann, Kenneth V., ed. Kiely, Jana M., tr. LC 67-27083. (Illus.). 239p. 1967. 31.50 (*0-674-63450-0*) HUP.

Dostaler, Gilles, jt. auth. see Beaud, Michel.

Doster, Alexis, III, ed. see Kopper, Philip.

Doster, D. Howard, et al. Small Business Planning & Management for the First-Time Entrepreneur. Stuts, Jacqueline A., ed. (Illus.). 268p. (Orig.). (C). 1996. pap. text 19.95 (*1-56502-010-3*, 8003M) Ohio Agri Educ.

Doster, Gary. East Central Georgia in Vintage Postcards. (Postcard History Ser.). (Illus.). 128p. pap. 18.99 (*0-7524-1379-1*) Arcadia Publng.

Doster, Gary. Northeast Georgia in Vintage Postcards. LC 98-86585. (Postcard History Ser.). (Illus.). 128p. 1998. pap. 18.99 (*0-7524-1377-5*) Arcadia Publng.

— Northwest Georgia in Vintage Postcards. LC 98-86669. (Postcard History Ser.). (Illus.). 128p. 1998. pap. 18.99 (*0-7524-1376-7*) Arcadia Publng.

***Doster, Gary.** Southeast Georgia in Vintage Postcards. LC 99-185138. (Postcard History Ser.). (Illus.). 128p. 1998. 18.99 (*0-7524-1375-9*) Arcadia Publng.

— Southwest Georgia in Vintage Postcards. LC 99-185129. (Postcard History Ser.). (Illus.). 128p. 1998. pap. 18.99 (*0-7524-1378-3*) Arcadia Publng.

Doster, Gary. West Central Georgia in Vintage Postcards. LC 98-88057. (Postcard History Ser.). (Illus.). 128p. 1998. pap. 18.99 (*0-7524-1380-5*) Arcadia Publng.

Doster, Gary L., ed. From Abbeville to Zebulon: Early Postcard Views of Georgia. LC 90-27741. (Illus.). 240p. 1999. pap. 18.00 (*0-8203-2113-3*) U of Ga Pr.

***Doster, Gary L. & Atlanta History Center Staff.** Central of Georgia Railway. LC 98-88306. (Images of America Ser.). (Illus.). 128p. 1998. pap. 18.99 (*0-7524-1387-2*) Arcadia Publng.

Doster, James F. & Weaver, David C. Tenn-Tom Country: The Upper Tombigbee Valley. LC 85-13974. (Illus.). 251p. reprint ed. pap. 77.90 (*0-608-09223-1*, 205272700005) Bks Demand.

Doster, Jennifer R. Mother Earth Messages: For Twenty-First Century Parenting. LC 92-90271. 80p. 1992. pap. 7.95 (*0-9633152-0-X*) Doster Pub.

Doster, Rebecca, jt. auth. see Whordley, Derek.

Doster, Wadsworth, ed. see Hill, Mrs. Ben.

Doster, William C., et al. How to Prepare for the CLEP - College Level Exam Program. 8th rev. ed. LC 98-37370. 800p. (YA). 1999. pap. 14.95 (*0-7641-0476-4*) Barron.

Doster, William E. A Brief History of the Fourth Pennsylvania Cavalry. Galli, Anthony P., ed. LC 98-219033. (Illus.). 151p. 1997. reprint ed. 20.00 (*0-944413-45-5*, 211) Longstreet Hse.

Dostert, P., et al, eds. Early Markers in Parkinson's & Alzheimer's Diseases. (New Vistas in Drug Research Ser.: Vol. 1). (Illus.). xx, 310p. 1991. 111.00 (*0-387-82223-2*) Spr-Verlag.

Dostert, Pierre E. Africa 1996. 31st ed. 247p. 1996. pap. 11.50 (*0-943448-96-4*) Stryker-Post.

— Latin America, 1996. 30th ed. 217p. 1996. pap. 11.50 (*0-943448-99-9*) Stryker-Post.

Dosti, Rose. Dear S. O. S. Dessert Recipe Requests to the Los Angeles Times. 1996. 18.95 (*1-883792-15-0*) LA Times.

— Dear Sos: Thirty Years of Recipe Requests to the Los Angeles Times. 272p. 1994. pap. 18.95 (*1-883792-06-1*) LA Times.

— Mideast & Mediterranean Cuisines. LC 93-37394. 144p. 1993. pap. 9.95 (*1-55561-055-2*) Fisher Bks.

***Dostoevsky, Fyodor.** Demons. Pevear, Richard, tr. 784p. 2000. 23.00 (*0-375-41122-4*) Knopf.

Dostourian, Ara E. Armenia & the Crusades: Tenth to Twelfth Centuries - The Chronicle of Matthew of Edessa. 392p. 1993. lib. bdg. 64.00 (*0-8191-8953-7*) U Pr of Amer.

Dostoyevsky, Aimee. Fyodor Dostoyevsky. A Study. LC 72-1329. (Studies in European Literature: No. 56). 1972. reprint ed. lib. bdg. 75.00 (*0-8383-1438-4*) M S G Haskell Hse.

***Dostoyevsky, Fedor M.** Devils. Katz, Michael R., tr. (Oxford World's Classics Ser.). 800p. (Orig.). 2000. pap. 9.95 (*0-19-283829-6*) OUP.

***Dostoyevsky, Fyodor.** An Accidental Family. 630p. 1999. pap. 11.95 (*0-19-283705-2*) OUP.

Dostoyevsky, Fyodor. The Adolescent. MacAndrew, Andrew R., tr. 608p. 1981. reprint ed. pap. 18.95 (*0-393-00995-5*) Norton.

— L' Adolescent, Etc. (FRE.). 1956. 89.95 (*0-8288-3435-0*, F90470) Fr & Eur.

— The Best Short Stories of Dostoyevsky. Magarshack, David, tr. LC 92-50214. 378p. 1992. 16.95 (*0-679-60020-5*) Modern Lib NY.

— The Brothers Karamazov. 1976. 38.95 (*0-8488-0797-9*) Amereon Ltd.

— The Brothers Karamazov. 960p. 1984. mass mkt. 6.95 (*0-553-21216-8*, Bantam Classics) Bantam.

— The Brothers Karamazov. Garnett, Constance, tr. (Modern Library College Editions). 940p. (C). 1950. pap. 8.44 (*0-07-553575-0*, T12) McGraw.

— The Brothers Karamazov. Pevear, Richard & Volokhonsky, Larissa, trs. 1992. 20.00 (*0-679-41003-1*) McKay.

— The Brothers Karamazov. Van Der Eng, Jan & Meijer, Jan M., eds. 1971. text 33.85 (*90-279-1758-2*) Mouton.

— The Brothers Karamazov. Matlaw, Ralph E., ed. LC 75-37792. (Critical Editions Ser.). 1000p. (C). 1976. pap. text 18.25 (*0-393-09214-3*) Norton.

— The Brothers Karamazov. 868p. 1996. 21.00 (*0-679-60181-3*) Random.

— The Brothers Karamazov. Volokhonsky, Larissa & Pevear, Richard, trs. LC 91-50046. (Vintage Classics Ser.). 832p. 1991. pap. 17.00 (*0-679-72925-9*) Vin Bks.

***Dostoyevsky, Fyodor.** Brothers Karamazov. Komroff, Manuel, ed. Garnett, Constance, tr. from RUS. LC 99-19312. (Signet Classics Ser.). 752p. 1999. mass mkt. 7.95 (*0-451-52734-8*, Sig) NAL.

Dostoyevsky, Fyodor. Brothers Karamazov. 1970. 11.05 (*0-606-02916-8*, Pub. by Turtleback) Demco.

— The Brothers Karamazov. 595p. 1983. reprint ed. lib. bdg. 45.95 (*0-89966-315-X*) Buccaneer Bks.

— The Brothers Karamazov. unabridged ed. (World Classic Literature Ser.). (RUS.). pap. 8.95 (*2-87714-268-X*, Pub. by Bookking Intl) Distribks Inc.

— The Brothers Karamazov: A Dramatization. 1995. pap. 5.95 (*0-8222-1425-3*) Dramatists Play.

— The Brothers Karamazov: A New Translation. McDuff, David, tr. & intro. by. 960p. 1993. pap. 11.95 (*0-14-044527-7*, Penguin Classics) Viking Penguin.

— The Brothers Karamazov: A Novel in Four Parts with Epilogue. Pevear, Richard & Volokhonsky, Larissa, trs. from RUS. LC 89-26583. 832p. 1990. 40.00 (*0-86547-422-2*) N Point Pr.

— Complete Letters of Fyodor Dostoyevsky Vol. 2: 1860-1867. Lowe, David A., tr. from RUS. 1989. 35.00 (*0-88233-926-5*) Ardis Pubs.

— Complete Letters, Vol. 3: 1868-1871. Lowe, David A., ed. & tr. by. from RUS. 1991. 35.00 (*0-88233-542-1*) Ardis Pubs.

— Complete Letters, Vol. 4: 1872-1877. Lowe, David A., ed. & tr. by. from RUS. (Illus.). 350p. (C). 1991. 35.00 (*0-88233-543-X*) Ardis Pubs.

— Complete Letters, Vol. 5: 1878-1881. Lowe, David A., ed. & tr. by. from RUS. (Illus.). 350p. (C). 1991. 35.00 (*0-88233-544-8*) Ardis Pubs.

— Crime & Punishment. (Airmont Classics Ser.). (Illus.). 1967. mass mkt. 3.95 (*0-8049-0145-7*, CL-145) Airmont.

— Crime & Punishment. (Illustrated Classics Collection 5). 64p. (J). 1994. pap. 4.95 (*0-7854-0775-8*, 40544) Am Guidance.

— Crime & Punishment. 522p. Date not set. 31.95 (*0-8488-2516-0*) Amereon Ltd.

— Crime & Punishment. 1994. mass mkt. 4.95 (*0-553-85015-6*) Bantam.

— Crime & Punishment. Pevear, Richard & Volokhonsky, Larissa, trs. from RUS. LC 92-54292. 1993. 20.00 (*0-679-42029-0*) Everymns Lib.

— Crime & Punishment, 2 vols. (Cloth Bound Pocket Ser.). 1000p. 1999. boxed set 14.95 (*3-8290-0904-6*, 520666) Konemann.

— Crime & Punishment. 492p. (C). 1950. 8.44 (*0-07-553574-2*) McGraw.

— Crime & Punishment. Garnett, Constance, tr. 658p. 1994. 18.50 (*0-679-60100-7*) Modern Lib NY.

— Crime & Punishment. Monas, Sidney, tr. from RUS. & afterword by by. LC 98-19279. 1999. mass mkt. 7.95 (*0-451-52723-2*, Sig Classics) NAL.

— Crime & Punishment. Coulson, Jessie, tr. LC 99-163023. (Illus.). 576p. 1998. pap. 10.95 (*0-19-283383-9*) OUP.

— Crime & Punishment. (Now Age Illustrated V Ser.). (Illus.). 64p. (J). (gr. 4-12). 1979. student ed. 1.25 (*0-88301-410-6*); pap. text 2.95 (*0-88301-386-X*) Pendulum Pr.

— Crime & Punishment. (Washington Square Press Enriched Classic Ser.). 1972. 13.05 (*0-606-00502-1*, Pub. by Turtleback) Demco.

— Crime & Punishment. McDuff, David, tr. & intro. by. 656p. 1996. pap. 11.95 (*0-14-044528-5*, Penguin Classics) Viking Penguin.

— Crime & Punishment. (Classics Library). 416p. 1997. pap. 3.95 (*1-85326-200-5*, 2005WW, Pub. by Wrdsworth Edits) NTC Contemp Pub Co.

Dostoyevsky, Fyodor. Crime & Punishment. abr. ed. Garnett, Constance, tr. LC 81-740216. 1982. audio 14.00 (*0-694-50356-8*, SWC 1691, Caedmon) HarperAudio.

Dostoyevsky, Fyodor. Crime & Punishment. large type ed. 1997. pap. 21.95 (*1-55701-214-8*) BNI Pubns.

— Crime & Punishment. 1982. reprint ed. lib. bdg. 37.95 (*0-89966-397-4*) Buccaneer Bks.

— Crime & Punishment. 605p. 1998. reprint ed. lib. bdg. 25.00 (*1-58287-087-X*) North Bks.

— Crime & Punishment. unabridged ed. (World Classic Literature Ser.). (RUS.). pap. 8.95 (*2-87714-263-9*, Pub. by Bookking Intl) Distribks Inc.

— Crime & Punishment. 3rd ed. Gibian, George, ed. (Critical Editions Ser.). (C). 1989. pap. text 16.00 (*0-393-95623-7*) Norton.

— Crime & Punishment, Vol. 1. 528p. 1984. mass mkt. 5.95 (*0-553-21175-7*, Bantam Classics) Bantam.

— Crime & Punishment: A Novel in Six Parts with Epilogue. Pevear, Richard & Volokhonsky, Larissa, trs. LC 92-56354. (Classics Ser.). 592p. 1993. pap. 15.00 (*0-679-73450-3*) Vin Bks.

— Crime & Punishment Readalong. (Illustrated Classics Collection 5). 64p. 1994. pap. 14.95 incl. audio (*0-7854-0791-X*, 40546) Am Guidance.

— Crime et Chatiment, Tome I. (FRE.). 512p. 1975. pap. 11.95 (*0-7859-1798-5*, 2070366529) Fr & Eur.

— Crime et Chatiment, Tome II. (FRE.). 512p. 1975. pap. 11.95 (*0-7859-1799-3*, 2070366537) Fr & Eur.

— Crime et Chatiment: Maison des Morts, Etc. (FRE.). 1978. 99.50 (*0-8288-3436-9*, F79860) Fr & Eur.

— Crime et Chatiment, Journal de Raskolnikov, Souvenirs de la Maison des Morts. 1280p. 39.95 (*0-686-56501-0*) Fr & Eur.

***Dostoyevsky, Fyodor.** Crimen y Castigo. 1998. pap. 14.95 (*84-08-01883-3*) Planeta.

Dostoyevsky, Fyodor. The Crocodile, an Extraordinary Event. Cioran, Samuel D., tr. from RUS. Orig. Title: Krokodil. 1984. pap. 10.95 (*0-88233-588-X*) Ardis Pubs.

— Demons: A Novel in Three Parts. Pevear, Richard & Volokhonsky, Larissa, trs. LC 93-33367. (ENG & RUS.). 1995. pap. 17.00 (*0-679-73451-1*) Knopf.

— Les Demons, les Pauvres Gens. (FRE.). 1952. 105.00 (*0-8288-3437-7*, F104442) Fr & Eur.

— Les Demons (les Possedes) & les Pauvres Gens. (FRE.). 1384p. pap. 17.95 (*0-8288-9741-7*, 2080704206) Fr & Eur.

— Devils. Magarshack, David, tr. (Classics Ser.). 704p. (Orig.). 1954. pap. 10.95 (*0-14-044035-6*, Penguin Classics) Viking Penguin.

— Dostoevsky's Occasional Writings. Magarshack, David, tr. & selected by by. LC 97-15418. 1997. pap. text 17.95 (*0-8101-1473-9*) Northwestern U Pr.

— Dostoyevsky: Letters & Reminiscences. Koteliansky, Samuel S. & Murray, J. Middleton, trs. (Select Bibliographies Reprint Ser.). 1977. reprint ed. 25.95 (*0-8369-5835-7*) Ayer.

— The Double. Harden, Evelyn, tr. from RUS. 1985. pap. 10.95 (*0-88233-757-2*) Ardis Pubs.

— Le Double. (FRE.). 288p. 1980. pap. 10.95 (*0-7859-1924-4*, 2070372278) Fr & Eur.

— The Double. LC 96-38924. (Dover Thrift Editions Ser.). 144p. 1997. reprint ed. pap. 1.50 (*0-486-29572-9*) Dover.

— L' Eternel Marie. (FRE.). 1972. pap. 10.95 (*0-7859-1695-4*, 2070360970) Fr & Eur.

— Les Freres Karamazov, Tome I. (FRE.). 512p. 1973. pap. 11.95 (*0-7859-1765-9*, 2070364860) Fr & Eur.

— Les Freres Karamazov, Tome II. (FRE.). 512p. 1973. pap. 11.95 (*0-7859-1766-7*, 2070364879) Fr & Eur.

— Les Freres Karamazov & Nietotchka Niezvanov. (FRE.). 1296p. 23.95 (*0-8288-9738-7*, 2070336480) Fr & Eur.

— Les Freres Karamazov, Etc. (FRE.). 1987. 95.00 (*0-8288-3438-5*, M5091) Fr & Eur.

— The Gambler. 192p. 1997. reprint ed. pap. 11.00 (*0-393-31649-1*) Norton.

— The Gambler. unabridged ed. LC 95-35852. (Thrift Editions Ser.). 112p. 1996. reprint ed. pap. text 1.50 (*0-486-29081-6*) Dover.

— The Gambler & The Diary of Polina Suslova. Wasiolek, Edward, ed. Terras, Victor, tr. 366p. 1995. pap. 12.95 (*0-226-15972-8*, P470) U Ch Pr.

— The Gambler-Bobok: Nasty Story. Coulson, Jessie, tr. (Classics Ser.). 240p. (Orig.). 1966. pap. 10.95 (*0-14-044179-4*, Penguin Classics) Viking Penguin.

***Dostoyevsky, Fyodor.** Gentle Creature & Other Stories: White Nights; A Gentle Creature; The Dream of a Ridiculous Man. Myers, Alan, tr. (Oxford World's Classics Ser.). 160p. 1999. pap. 8.95 (*0-19-283828-8*) OUP.

Dostoyevsky, Fyodor. The Gospel in Dostoyevsky. Bruderhof Communities Staff, ed. Garnett, Constance & MacAndrew, Andrew R., trs. from RUS. LC 86-30578. (Illus.). 272p. 1988. pap. 15.00 (*0-87486-187-X*, PG3326.A15) Plough.

— The Grand Inquisitor. LC 56-7503. (Milestones of Thought Ser.). 44p. (C). 1981. pap. text 3.50 (*0-8044-6125-2*) F Ungar Bks.

— The Grand Inquisitor: With Related Chapters from the Brothers Karamazov. Garnett, Constance, tr. LC 93-28077. (Hackett Classics Ser.). 160p. (C). 1993. pap. text 4.95 (*0-87220-193-7*); lib. bdg. 24.95 (*0-87220-228-3*) Hackett Pub.

— Grand Inquisitor on the Nature of Man: Dostoevsky. Garnett, Constance, tr. 48p. (C). 1948. pap. text 5.00 (*0-02-340600-3*, Macmillan Coll) P-H.

— Great Short Works Dost. LC 70-54. 768p. 1968. pap. 9.50 (*0-06-083081-6*) HarperTrade.

— An Honest Thief, & Other Stories. Garnett, Constance, tr. LC 74-15163. 404p. 1975. reprint ed. lib. bdg. 75.00 (*0-8371-7807-X*, DOHT, Greenwood Pr) Greenwood.

— The House of the Dead. McDuff, David, tr. & intro. by. LC 86-144949. (Classics Ser.). 368p. 1986. pap. 9.95 (*0-14-044456-4*, Penguin Classics) Viking Penguin.

— Idiot. 592p. Date not set. 34.95 (*0-8488-2528-4*) Amereon Ltd.

— Idiot. (Classic Ser.). 1986. mass mkt. 6.95 (*0-451-52492-6*, Sig Classics) NAL.

***Dostoyevsky, Fyodor.** Idiot. 592p. 1998. pap. 3.95 (*1-85326-175-0*, 1750WW, Pub. by Wrdsworth Edits) NTC Contemp Pub Co.

Dostoyevsky, Fyodor. The Idiot. Garnett, Constance, tr. 608p. 1983. mass mkt. 6.95 (*0-553-21352-0*, Bantam Classics) Bantam.

D

An Asterisk (*) at the beginning of an entry indicates that the title is appearing for the first time.

— The Idiot. Myers, Alan, ed. & tr. by. (Oxford World's Classics Ser.). (Illus.). 688p. 1998. pap. 7.95 (*0-19-283411-8*) OUP.

— The Idiot. Magarshack, David, tr. (Classics Ser.). 672p. 1956. pap. 10.95 (*0-14-044054-2*, Penguin Classics) Viking Penguin.

— The Idiot. 1989. reprint ed. lib. bdg. 45.95 (*0-89966-627-2*) Buccaneer Bks.

— L' Idiot, Tome I. (FRE.). 1972. pap. 11.95 (*0-7859-2197-4*, 207036271X) Fr & Eur.

— L' Idiot, Tome II. (FRE.). 1989. reprint ed. pap. 11.95 (*0-7859-1719-5*, 2070362728) Fr & Eur.

— The Idiot: A Dramatization - Full Length Acting Edition. 1995. pap. 5.95 (*0-8222-1424-5*) Dramatists Play.

— L' Idiot: Humilies et Offenses. (FRE.). 1953. 95.00 (*0-8288-3439-3*, M5092) Fr & Eur.

— L' Idiot & Humilies et Offenses. 1400p. 135.00 (*0-686-56503-7*) Fr & Eur.

— Insulted & Injured. 350p. Date not set. 25.95 (*0-8488-2529-2*) Amereon Ltd.

— The Insulted & Injured. Garnett, Constance, tr. from RUS. LC 75-19182. 333p. 1975. reprint ed. lib. bdg. 65.00 (*0-8371-8248-4*, DOII, Greenwood Pr) Greenwood.

— Le Joueur. (FRE.). 1973. pap. 10.95 (*0-7859-1839-6*, 2070368939) Fr & Eur.

— Journal d'Un Ecrivain. 1648p. 42.95 (*0-686-56507-X*) Fr & Eur.

— Journal d'Un Ecrivain. (FRE.). 1972. 99.50 (*0-8288-3440-7*, F89350) Fr & Eur.

— The Karamazov Brothers. Avsey, Ignat, tr. & intro. by. (Oxford World's Classics Ser.). (Illus.). 1,050p. 1998. pap. 10.95 (*0-19-283509-2*) OUP.

— Memoirs from the House of the Dead. Hingley, Ronald, ed. Coulson, Jessie, tr. (World's Classics Paperback Ser.). 384p. (C). 1983. pap. 7.95 (*0-19-281613-6*) OUP.

*__Dostoyevsky, Fyodor.__ Memoirs from the House of the Dead. Hingley, Ronald, ed. Coulson, Jessie, tr. (Oxford World's Classics Ser.). 384p. 2000. pap. 8.95 (*0-19-283868-7*) OUP.

Dostoyevsky, Fyodor. Netochka Nezvanova. Kentish, Jane, tr. & intro. by. (Classics Ser.). 192p. 1986. pap. 10.95 (*0-14-044455-6*, Penguin Classics) Viking Penguin.

— New Dostoyevsky Letters. Koteliansky, Samuel S., tr. LC 73-20335. (Studies in Dostoyevsky: No. 86). 1974. lib. bdg. 75.00 (*0-8383-1824-X*) M S G Haskell Hse.

— Notebooks for the Idiot. LC 67-25513. 1973. pap. text 2.95 (*0-226-15962-0*, P559) U Ch Pr.

— Notes from the Underground. 1976. 20.95 (*0-8488-0347-7*) Amereon Ltd.

— Notes from the Underground. (Thrift Editions Ser.). 96p. 1992. reprint ed. pap. 1.00 (*0-486-27053-X*) Dover.

— Notes from the Underground & The Double. 1991. pap. 10.95 (*0-452-01093-4*, Mer) NAL.

— Notes from the Underground & The Double. large type ed. 515p. 1997. reprint ed. lib. bdg. 24.00 (*0-939495-15-5*) North Bks.

— Notes from the Underground & The Gambler. Kentish, Jane, tr. (Oxford World's Classics Ser.). 320p. 1999. pap. 7.95 (*0-19-283626-9*) OUP.

*__Dostoyevsky, Fyodor.__ Notes from the Underground; The Double. 323p. 1998. reprint ed. lib. bdg. 24.00 (*1-58287-053-5*) North Bks.

Dostoyevsky, Fyodor. Notes from Underground. Ginsburg, Mirra, tr. from RUS. 192p. 1983. mass mkt. 4.95 (*0-553-21144-7*, Bantam Classics) Bantam.

— Notes from Underground. Pevear, Richard & Volokhonsky, Larissa, trs. LC 92-32581. 160p. 1994. pap. 10.00 (*0-679-73452-X*) Knopf.

— Notes from Underground. Katz, Michael R., ed. & tr. by. LC 88-1062. (Critical Editions Ser.). 256p. (C). 1989. pap. text 11.25 (*0-393-95744-6*) Norton.

— Notes from Underground & Selected Stories: White Nights, Dream of a Ridiculous Man, House of the Dead. MacAndrew, Andrew R., tr. 1961. mass mkt. 4.95 (*0-451-52376-8*, CE1823, Sig Classics) NAL.

— Notes from Underground & the Double. Coulson, Jessie, tr. (Classics Ser.). 288p. 1972. pap. 11.99 (*0-14-044252-9*, Penguin Classics) Viking Penguin.

— Les Nuit Blancues - Le sous Sol. (FRE.). 1982. pap. 11.95 (*0-7859-1951-1*, 2070373525) Fr & Eur.

Dostoyevsky, Fyodor. Poor Folk. Dessaix, Robert, tr.Tr. of Bednye Liudi. 143p. 1983. pap. 12.50 (*0-88233-755-6*) Ardis Pubs.

Dostoyevsky, Fyodor. Poor Folk & Other Stories. McDuff, David, tr. & intro. by. 288p. 1989. pap. 9.95 (*0-14-044505-6*, Penguin Classics) Viking Penguin.

— Poor Folk & the Gambler. Briggs, A. D., ed. Hogarth, C. J., tr. 320p. 1994. 5.50 (*0-460-87331-8*, Everyman's Classic Lib) Tuttle Pubng.

— Les Possedes, Tome I. (FRE.). 512p. 1974. pap. 11.95 (*0-7859-1784-5*, 2070365743) Fr & Eur.

— Les Possedes, Tome II. (FRE.). 512p. 1974. pap. 11.95 (*0-7859-1785-3*, 2070365751) Fr & Eur.

— The Possessed. 702p. 1989. reprint ed. lib. bdg. 49.95 (*0-89966-628-0*) Buccaneer Bks.

— Recit, Chroniques et Polemiques. (FRE.). 1969. 110.00 (*0-8288-3441-5*, F118460) Fr & Eur.

— Recits, Chroniques et Polemiques. 1872p. 45.00 (*0-686-56506-1*) Fr & Eur.

— Selected Letters of Fyodor Dostoyevsky. Frank, Joseph & Goldstein, David I., eds. MacAndrew, Andrew R., tr. 533p. (C). 1987. 50.00 (*0-8135-1185-2*) Rutgers U Pr.

— Souvenirs de la Maison des Morts. (FRE.). 446p. 1977. pap. 11.95 (*0-7859-1851-5*, 2070369250) Fr & Eur.

— Stavrogin's Confession & the Plan of the Life of a Great Sinner. LC 72-2556. (Studies in Fiction: No. 34). 1972. reprint ed. lib. bdg. 75.00 (*0-8383-1494-5*) M S G Haskell Hse.

Dostoyevsky, Fyodor. Three Short Novels of Dostoyevsky. Garnett, Constance, tr. Incl. Double. Yarmolinsky, Avrahm, ed. LC 60-57341. 1960. pap. Eternal Husband. Garnett, Avrahm, ed. LC 60-57341. 1960. pap. Notes from the Underground. Yarmolinsky, Avrahm, tr. LC 60-57341. 1960. pap. LC 60-57341. 1959. Set pap. 6.95 (*0-385-09435-3*, A193, Anchor NY) Doubleday.

Dostoyevsky, Fyodor. Uncle's Dream & Other Stories. McDuff, David, tr. & intro. by. 304p. 1989. pap. 10.95 (*0-14-044518-8*, Penguin Classics) Viking Penguin.

— Veliky Inkvisitor: The Grand Inquisitor. Garnett, Constance, tr. (Voices from Russia Ser.). (ENG & RUS.). 52p. 1997. pap. text 9.50 (*1-58085-008-1*) Interlingua VA.

— The Village of Stepanchikovo & Its Inhabitants. Avsey, Ignat, tr. from RUS. LC 86-47995. 256p. 1987. reprint ed. text 37.50 (*0-8014-2051-2*) Cornell U Pr.

— Winter Notes on Summer Impressions. Patterson, David, tr. 78p. 1988. 24.95 (*0-8101-0813-5*) Northwestern U Pr.

— Winter Notes on Summer Impressions. Patterson, David, tr. LC 97-15114. 1997. pap. text 14.95 (*0-8101-1518-2*) Northwestern U Pr.

— A Writer's Diary: 1873-76, Vol. 1. Lantz, Kenneth, tr. from RUS. 1000p. (Orig.). 1993. 49.95 (*0-8101-1094-6*) Northwestern U Pr.

— A Writer's Diary Vol. 2: 1877-1881. Lantz, Kenneth, tr. from RUS. 900p. 1994. 39.95 (*0-8101-1101-2*) Northwestern U Pr.

— A Writer's Diary, 1877-1881, Vol. 2. 1997. pap. text 22.50 (*0-8101-1517-4*) Northwestern U Pr.

— A Writer's Diary, 1873-1876, Vol. 1. 1997. pap. text 22.50 (*0-8101-1516-6*) Northwestern U Pr.

Dostoyevsky, Fyodor & Tolstoy, Leo. Notes from the Underground & A Confession. Briggs, A. D., ed. 256p. 1994. pap. text 6.50 (*0-460-87448-9*, Everyman's Classic Lib) Tuttle Pubng.

Dostrovsky, I. Energy & the Missing Resource. (Illus.). 208p. 1989. text 59.95 (*0-521-26592-4*); pap. text 18.95 (*0-521-31965-X*) Cambridge U Pr.

Dostrovsky, S., jt. auth. see Cannon, J. T.

Doswald-Beck, Louise, ed. San Remo Manual on International Law Applicable to Armed Conflicts at Sea. 267p. (C). 1995. pap. text 24.95 (*0-521-55864-6*) Cambridge U Pr.

— San Remo Manual on International Law Applicable to Armed Conflicts at Sea. 167p. (C). 1995. text 64.95 (*0-521-55188-9*) Cambridge U Pr.

Doswald, Beverly J. Learning about God & Jesus: An Overview of the Gospel in Simple English. LC 86-81297. 50p. (Orig.). 1986. pap. 4.25 (*0-938783-00-9*) Helpful Beginnings.

— To Know Him . . . Is to Love & Praise Him! A Bible Study of God's Attributes. LC 92-70785. 327p. (Orig.). 1992. pap. 14.85 (*0-938783-02-5*) Helpful Beginnings.

Doswald, C., jt. auth. see Bianchi, P.

*__Doswald, Christopho, ed.__ Missing Link: The Image of Man in Contemporary Photography. (Illus.). 328p. 2000. 65.00 (*3-908163-12-9*, Pub. by Edit Stemmle) Abbeville Pr.

Doswell, Andrew. Foundations of Business Information Systems. LC 85-3689. (Approaches to Information Technology Ser.). 234p. 1985. pap. 39.50 (*0-306-41796-0*, Plenum Trade) Perseus Pubng.

— Office Automation. LC 82-6988. (Wiley Series in Information Processing). 293p. reprint ed. pap. 90.90 (*0-7837-6371-9*, 204608300010) Bks Demand.

— Office Automation: Context, Experience & Future. 2nd ed. LC 89-21516. 318p. 1991. 170.00 (*0-471-92553-5*) Wiley.

Doswell, J. William. The Bottom Line. Carr, Martha R., ed. 340p. (Orig.). 1994. pap. 14.95 (*0-9638639-2-4*) Nimrod Hse.

Doswell, Roger. Tourism: How Effective Management Makes the Difference. LC 97-203572. 336p. 1997. pap. text 37.95 (*0-7506-2272-5*) Buttrwrth-Heinemann.

Dot, To. Ruined City. 1997. pap. 3.99 (*1-85792-308-1*, Pub. by Christian Focus) Spring Arbor Dist.

Dotdot, Edgar. The Truth of Creation & Speculation about Evolution. 448p. 1999. pap. 20.00 (*0-8059-4418-4*) Dorrance.

Dote, Yasuhiko & Hoft, Richard G. Intelligent Control: Power Electronic Systems. (Monographs in Electrical & Electronic Engineering: No. 43). (Illus.). 224p. 1998. text 89.00 (*0-19-856466-X*) OUP.

Dotevall, Gerhard. Stress & Common Gastrointestinal Disorders: A Comprehensive Approach. 3. LC 85-6565. (Gastroenterology Ser.: Vol. 3). 192p. 1985. 62.95 (*0-275-91310-4*, C1310, Praeger Pubs) Greenwood.

Dothan, Michael U. Prices in Financial Markets. (Illus.). 360p. (C). 1990. text 59.95 (*0-19-505312-5*) OUP.

Dothan Service League Members. Sterling Service. (Illus.). 256p. 1996. 19.95 (*0-9653997-0-2*) Dothan Serv Leag.

Dothan, Trude. People of the Sea: The Search for the Philistines. 256p. 1992. text 25.00 (*0-02-532261-3*) Macmillan.

Dothan, Trude K. The Philistines & Their Material Culture. LC 80-22060. (Illus.). 332p. reprint ed. pap. 94.70 (*0-7837-2501-9*, 2080202) Bks Demand.

Doti, Irene. Italian Desserts: Dolce Memories. rev. ed. LC 97-43016. (Illus.). 160p. 1998. pap. 12.95 (*1-55561-158-3*) Fisher Bks.

Doti, James L. & Lee, Dwight R., eds. The Market Economy: A Reader. LC 90-19524. 360p. (C). 1991. pap. text. write for info. (*0-935732-26-8*) Roxbury Pub Co.

Doti, Lynne & Schweikart, Larry E. Banking in the American West: From the Gold Rush to Deregulation. LC 91-50302. 336p. 1991. 45.00 (*0-8061-2373-7*) U of Okla Pr.

Doti, Lynne P. Banking in an Unregulated Environment: California 1878-1905. rev. ed. LC 95-14436. (Financial Sector of the American Economy Ser.). (Illus.). 184p. 1995. text 20.00 (*0-8153-1873-1*) Garland.

Dotlich, David & Noel, James. Action Learning: How Companies Are Transforming Themselves by Re-Creating Their Leadership. LC 98-8887. 208p. 1998. mass mkt. 27.00 (*0-7879-0349-3*) Jossey-Bass.

Dotlich, David L. & Cairo, Peter C. Action Coaching: How to Leverage Individual Performance for Company Success. LC 99-33631. 256p. 1999. 28.00 (*0-7879-4477-7*) Jossey-Bass.

Dotlich, Rebecca K. Away We Go! LC 99-63977. (Illus.). 24p. (J). (ps). 2000. 9.95 (*0-694-01393-5*, HarpFestival) HarpC Child Bks.

— Lemonade Sun: And Other Summer Poems. LC 97-74192. (Illus.). 32p. (J). (ps-3). 1998. pap. 15.95 (*1-56397-660-9*, Wordsong) Boyds Mills Pr.

— What Is a Triangle. LC 99-63085. (Illus.). 24p. (J). (ps). 2000. pap. 9.95 (*0-694-01392-7*, HarpFestival) HarpC Child Bks.

*__Dotlich, Rebecca Kai.__ Sweet Dreams of the Wild. LC 94-60259. (Illus.). 32p. (J). (ps-1). 2000. pap. 8.95 (*1-56397-924-1*) Boyds Mills Pr.

Dotsch, Hans. Identification for Control Design with Application to a Compact Disk Mechanism. (Illus.). 251p. 1998. pap. 55.00 (*90-407-1656-0*, Pub. by Delft U Pr) Coronet Bks.

Dotsenko, A. V., et al. Pysics & Chemistry of Photochromic Glasses. LC 97-20870. (Laser & Optical Science & Technology Ser.). 208p. 1997. boxed set 104.95 (*0-8493-3780-1*) CRC Pr.

Dotsenko, V. S. Physics Reviews Vol. 15, Pt. 1: Spin Glasses & Related Problems, Vol. 15. (Soviet Scientific Reviews Ser.: Section A). 250p. 1991. text 269.00 (*3-7186-5039-8*, Harwood Acad Pubs) Gordon & Breach.

*__Dotsenko, Viktor.__ Introduction to the Replica Theory of Disordered Statistical Systems. (Collection Alea - Saclay Ser.). (Illus.). 248p. (C). 2000. text Price not set. (*0-521-77340-7*) Cambridge U Pr.

Dotsenko, Viktor. An Introduction to the Theory of Spin Glasses & Neural Networks. LC 94-35624. (World Scientific Notes in Physics Ser.: Vol. 55). 164p. 1995. text 30.00 (*981-02-1873-7*) World Scientific Pub.

Dotson, Anne C. & Wisont, Karen D. Teaching Character: Parents Guide. 80p. 1997. pap. 12.00 (*0-9653163-5-1*) Character Dev.

— Teaching Character: Teacher's Idea Book. 150p. 1997. pap. 24.00 (*0-9653163-4-3*) Character Dev.

*__Dotson, Bob.__ Make It Memorable: Writing & Packaging TV News with Style. 225p. 2000. 29.95 (*1-56625-158-3*) Bonus Books.

Dotson, Charles O. & Humphrey, James H., eds. Exercise Physiology: Current Selected Research, Vols. 1-5. LC 85-45448. 1993. write for info. (*0-404-62800-1*) AMS Pr.

Dotson, Edisol W. Behold the Man: The Hype & Selling of Male Beauty in Media & Culture. LC 98-39345. 174p. (C). 1998. pap. 19.95 (*1-56023-953-0*) Haworth Pr.

*__Dotson, Edisol W.__ Behold the Man: The Hype & Selling of Male Beauty in Media & Culture. LC 98-39345. 174p. (C). 1998. 39.95 (*0-7890-0634-0*) Haworth Pr.

Dotson, Edisol W., ed. Putting Out: The Essential Publishing Resource Guide for Gay & Lesbian Writers. 4th rev. ed. LC 94-77798. 200p. 1998. pap. 14.95 (*1-57344-033-7*) Cleis Pr.

Dotson, Ines. A Nickel & a Dream. LC 97-92541. 54p. 1997. pap. write for info. (*0-9660537-0-2*) Dotson Pubns.

Dotson, Jack. Sixty-Seven Feet in the Air. 54p. (Orig.). 1994. pap. text 7.00 (*0-9641454-0-5*) Pleiades Pr.

Dotson, John, ed. Radiant Days: Writings by Enos Mills. (Illus.). 272p. (Orig.). 1994. pap. 15.95 (*0-87480-463-9*) U of Utah Pr.

Dotson, John E., tr. Merchant Culture in Fourteenth-Century Venice: The Zibaldone da Canal. (Medieval & Renaissance Texts & Studies: Vol. 98). 240p. 1994. 25.00 (*0-86698-112-8*, MR98) MRTS.

Dotson, Lester. Big Boys (& Girls) Do Cry. (Illus.). 123p. (Orig.). 1990. pap. text 8.95 (*0-9626664-0-8*) Halt Counseling.

Dotson, Lester A. Big Boys & Girls Do Cry: Self-Help. (Illus.). 123p. (Orig.). 1990. pap. 8.95 (*0-614-13051-4*) Halt Counseling.

Dotson, N. A. & Galvan, R. Polymerization Process Modeling. 371p. 1995. 115.00 (*0-471-18615-5*, Wiley-VCH) Wiley.

Dotson, Neil A., et al. Polymerization Process Modeling. Evans, D. Fennell, ed. LC 95-14939. (Center for Interfacial Engineering Ser.). (Illus.). 350p. 1995. 95.00 (*1-56081-693-7*, Wiley-VCH) Wiley.

Dotson, Raymond. And the Night Rambles Past. 45p. (Orig.). 1992. pap. 5.00 (*0-9627087-8-X*) Mt Olive Coll Pr.

Dotson, Rondalynne L. Basic Math for College Students. 2nd ed. 150p. (C). 1991. pap. text 18.50 (*1-881496-01-5*) Trning Point Pr.

Dotson, Samuel E. & Griffin, James A. Educating for Leadership: Laying a Solid Foundation. LC 97-97177. (Illus.). 164p. 1997. pap. 10.95 (*0-9662588-0-0*) DaySpring Lrdrship.

— Organizational Excellence: Achieving Excellence by Building Leaders & Improving Processes. (Illus.). 370p. 1997. ring bd. 275.00 (*0-9662588-3-5*) DaySpring Lrdrship.

— Profile of a Leader: A Facilitator's Resource Kit. (Illus.). 176p. 1996. ring bd. 195.00 (*0-9662588-1-9*) DaySpring Lrdrship.

Dott. Evolution of the Earth. 1998. 18.50 (*0-07-233268-9*) McGraw.

— Evolution of the Earth. 5th ed. 1993. teacher ed. 13.12 (*0-07-017804-6*) McGraw.

Dott, A. Eric. Hide a Book: They Meet. (Illus.). 22p. (J). (ps-1). 1987. lib. bdg. 5.95 (*0-939871-00-9*) Monarch Toy.

Dott, Robert H., ed. Eustasy: The Historical Ups & Downs of a Major Geological Concept. LC 92-25961. 111p. 1992. 22.50 (*0-8137-1180-0*) Geol Soc.

Dott, Robert H., Jr. & Prothero, Donald R. Evolution of the Earth. 5th ed. LC 93-25849. 664p. (C). 1994. 75.94 (*0-07-017803-8*) McGraw.

Dott, Robert H. & Shaver, Robert H., eds. Modern & Ancient Geosynclinal Sedimentation: Proceedings of a Symposium Dedicated to Marshall Key & Held at Madison, Wisconsin, 1972. LC 74-175858. (Society of Economic Paleontologists & Mineralogists, Special Publication Ser.: No. 19). 389p. reprint ed. pap. 120.60 (*0-608-12952-6*, 202474200038) Bks Demand.

Dott, Robert H., ed. see Davy, Humphry.

Dott, Robert Henry & Reynolds, Merrill J. Sourcebook for Petroleum Geology: Semicentennial Commemorative Volume. LC 73-91979. (American Association of Petroleum Geologists. Memoir Ser.: No. 5). (Illus.). 481p. reprint ed. pap. 149.20 (*0-608-18103-X*, 203223400078) Bks Demand.

D'Ottari, Francesca. The Legend of King Arthur: A Young Reader's Edition of the Classic Story by Howard Pyle. LC 94-74315. (Illus.). 56p. (J). 1996. 9.98 (*1-56138-503-4*, Courage) Running Pr.

Dottavio, F. Dominic, et al, eds. Protecting Biological Diversity in the National Parks: Workshop Recommendations. LC 90-6008. (NPS Transactions & Proceedings Ser.: No. 9). (Illus.). (Orig.). (C). 1990. pap. write for info. (*0-943475-04-X*) Natl Park GA.

*__Dotter, Earl & American Industrial Hygiene Association.__ The Quiet Sickness: A Photographic Chronicle of Hazardous Work in America. LC 98-70894. (Illus.). 1999. write for info. (*0-932627-85-4*) Am Indus Hygiene.

Dotterer, Betty & Davidson, Paul. Understanding Fibromyalgia: A Guide for Family & Friends. LC 96-77600. 60p. 1996. pap. 9.95 (*0-9653493-0-6*) HlthRd Prods.

Dotterer, Dick, ed. see Shakespeare, William.

Dotterer, Dick, ed. & selected by see Shakespeare, William.

Dotterer, Dick, ed. & tr. see Moliere.

Dotterer, Donald W. Living the Easter Faith: Sermons for the Easter Season. LC 93-30842. 68p. 1993. pap. 7.50 (*1-55673-522-7*) CSS OH.

— Up & down the Mountain. 1991. pap. 6.95 (*1-55673-391-7*, 9209) CSS OH.

Dotterer, Henry S. Dotterer Family. 164p. 1997. reprint ed. pap. 25.00 (*0-8328-8334-4*); reprint ed. lib. bdg. 35.00 (*0-8328-8333-6*) Higginson Bk Co.

Dotterer, Ray H. Philosophy by Way of the Sciences: An Introductory Textbook. (Select Bibliographies Reprint Ser.). 1977. reprint ed. 29.95 (*0-8369-6642-2*) Ayer.

— Philosophy by Way of the Sciences: An Introductory Textbook. 484p. reprint ed. lib. bdg. 26.50 (*0-8290-0823-3*) Irvington.

Dotterer, Ronald, ed. Shakespeare: Text, Subtext, & Context. LC 87-42893. (Illus.). 240p. 1989. 28.50 (*0-941664-92-9*) Susquehanna U Pr.

Dotterer, Ronald, et al, eds. Jewish Settlement & Community in the Modern Western World. LC 38-14370. 1991. 32.50 (*0-945636-13-X*) Susquehanna U Pr.

Dotterer, Ronald & Bowers, Susan R. Gender, Culture & the Arts: Women, the Arts & Society. LC 38-14370. (Susquehanna Studies). 176p. 1993. 29.50 (*0-945636-31-8*) Susquehanna U Pr.

Dotterer, Ronald & Bowers, Susan R., eds. Politics, Gender, & the Arts: Women, the Arts, & Society. LC 38-14370. (Susquehanna Studies). (Illus.). 216p. 1993. 34.50 (*0-945636-30-X*) Susquehanna U Pr.

— Sexuality, the Female Gaze, & the Arts: Women, the Arts, & Society. LC 38-14370. (Susquehanna Studies). 192p. 1993. 32.50 (*0-945636-32-6*) Susquehanna U Pr.

Dotterweich, Kass. Be-Good-to-Your-Family Therapy. LC 96-79960. (Illus.). 88p. (Orig.). 1997. pap. 4.95 (*0-87029-300-1*, 20154) Abbey.

— Be-Good-to-Your-Marriage Therapy. LC 89-82665. (Illus.). 68p. (Orig.). 1990. pap. 4.95 (*0-87029-224-2*, 20205-1) Abbey.

— Grieving As a Woman: Moving Through Life's Many Losses. LC 97-78045. 120p. 1998. pap. 5.95 (*0-87029-310-9*, 20135) Abbey.

— We're Running Late! Teachable Moments for Working Mothers. LC 96-4571. (Teachable Moment Bks.). (Illus.). 128p. (Orig.). 1996. pap. 8.95 (*0-89243-924-6*) Liguori Pubns.

Dotterweich, Kass & Perry, John. Friendship Therapy. LC 93-74868. (Illus.). 80p. 1994. 4.95 (*0-87029-270-6*) Abbey.

*__Dotterweich, Kass P.__ My Triduum Journey: Celebrating the Easter Mysteries. (Illus.). 32p. 1998. 1.95 (*0-7648-0332-8*) Liguori Pubns.

— Prayer Services for Teens: 34 Resources for Special Reasons & Church Seasons. Larkin, Jean, ed. (Illus.). 96p. 1999. pap. 19.95 (*0-937997-47-1*) Hi-Time Pflaum.

— 25 Stories for Sharing Faith with Teens: Making Connections. Cannizzo, Karen, ed. (Youth Ministry Resource Library). 96p. (YA). 1999. pap. 19.95 (*0-937997-58-7*, 3212) Hi-Time Pflaum.

Dotterweich, Kass P. You Break It, You Buy It: And Three Dozen More Opportune Moments to Teach Family Values. LC 94-77399. 64p. 1994. pap. 3.95 (*0-89243-678-6*) Liguori Pubns.

— You Break It, You Buy It: And Three Dozen More Opportune Moments to Teach Family Values. LC 95-21247. (Teachable Moment Bks.). 128p. 1995. pap. 8.95 (*0-89243-811-8*) Liguori Pubns.

Dottin, Erskine S. & Miller, Lynne D., eds. Teaching As Enhancing Human Effectiveness. LC 94-17669. 98p. (Orig.). (C). 1994. reprint ed. pap. text 19.50 (*0-8191-9576-6*) U Pr of Amer.

D

Dottin, G., ed. see D'Angouleme, Marguerite.

Dottlich, Rebecca K. Sweet Dreams of the Wild Vol. 1: Poems for Bedtime. LC 94-60259. (Illus.). 32p. (J). (ps-k). 1996. 15.95 (*1-56397-180-1*, Wordsong) Boyds Mills Pr.

Dotto, Gabriele, ed. see Rossini, Giachino.

Dotto, Jerel E. Del, see Rourke, Byron P. & Del Dotto, Jerel E.

Dotto, Lydia. The Astronauts: Canada's Voyageurs in Space. (Illus.). 176p. 1993. 22.95 (*0-7737-2707-8*) Genl Dist Srvs.

— Ethical Choices & Global Greenhouse Warming. 96p. (C). 1993. pap. 15.00 (*0-88920-234-6*) W Laurier U Pr.

— Planet Earth in Jeopardy: Environmental Consequences of Nuclear War (Scope 28) 142p. 1986. 80.00 (*0-471-99836-2*) Wiley.

***Dotto, Lydia.** Storm Warning: Gambling with the Climate of Our Planet. 344p. 2000. pap. 13.95 (*0-385-25790-2*, Pub. by Doubleday) Random House.

Dotton, Alan, jt. auth. see Wareham, Robert.

Dotts, Cecil K. & Sikkema, Mildred. Challenging the Status Quo: Public Education in Hawaii, 1840-1980. xxvi, 286p. (Orig.). 1994. pap. 14.95 (*0-9648963-0-3*) Hawaii Educ Assn.

Dotts, M. Franklin & Dotts, Maryann J. Clues to Creativity Vol. 1: Providing Learning Experiences for Children. LC 74-20622. (Illus.). 129p. 1974. reprint ed. pap. 40.00 (*0-608-00240-2*, 206074400001) Bks Demand.

— Clues to Creativity Vol. 2: Providing Learning Experiences for Children. LC 74-20622. (Illus.). 130p. 1975. reprint ed. pap. 40.30 (*0-608-00241-0*, 206074400002) Bks Demand.

— Clues to Creativity Vol. 3: Providing Learning Experiences for Children. LC 74-20622. (Illus.). 129p. 1976. reprint ed. pap. 40.00 (*0-608-00242-9*, 206074400003) Bks Demand.

Dotts, M. Franklin, ed. see Halverson, Delia T.

Dotts, Maryann. When Jesus Was Born. LC 93-49667. 32p. (J). 1994. pap. 1.49 (*0-687-45019-5*) Abingdon.

— You Can Have a Church Library. 1988. pap. 5.95 (*0-687-04604-1*) Abingdon.

Dotts, Maryann J. When Jesus Was Born. 1996. pap. text 5.95 (*0-687-02004-2*) Abingdon.

Dotts, Maryann J., jt. auth. see Dotts, M. Franklin.

Doty. Work Methods & Measurement for Management. (Mechanical Technology Ser.). 1989. text 52.95 (*0-8273-3830-9*) Delmar.

Doty, Alex M. What Choice Do We Have? How States Manipulate Ballot Rules to Restrict Voter Choice, 2 vols. LC 97-91750. Orig. Title: Military Counselors Manual. 650p. 1997. pap. 125.00 (*0-614-30326-5*) CCCO.

***Doty, Alexander.** Flaming Classics: Queering the Film Canon. (Illus.). 256p. 2000. pap. 18.99 (*0-415-92345-X*); text 75.00 (*0-415-92344-1*) Routledge.

Doty, Alexander. Making Things Perfectly Queer: Interpreting Mass Culture. LC 92-40036. 168p. 1993. pap. 15.95 (*0-8166-2245-0*); text 39.95 (*0-8166-2244-2*) U of Minn Pr.

Doty, Alexander, jt. ed. see Creekmur, Corey K.

Doty, Alexander M. Helping Out: A Guide to Military Discharges & GI Rights, 2 vols. 5th rev. ed. 650p. 1997. pap. 175.00 (*0-933368-25-9*) CCCO.

Doty, Andrew M. Backwards into Battle: A Tail Gunner's Journey in World War II. (Illus.). 156p. 1995. pap. 13.95 (*0-9646253-0-X*) Tall Tree CA.

Doty, Betty. Break the Anger Trap. LC 85-71508. (Illus.). 90p. (Orig.). 1985. pap. 8.95 (*0-930822-06-4*) Bookery.

— Getting Through to Others Without Anger: A Clear Way to Avoid the Most Common Problem in Human Relations. (Illus.). 224p. (Orig.). 1994. pap. 11.95 (*0-930822-17-X*) Bookery.

— Marriage Insurance. LC 77-92285. (Illus.). 1978. pap. 8.95 (*0-930822-01-3*) Bookery.

— One Hundred Things We Can Do about Anger & Violence. 212p. (Orig.). 1994. pap. 9.95 (*0-930822-18-8*) Bookery.

Doty, Betty & Meredith, Rebecca. Hey Look I Made a Book. 128p. (Orig.). 1995. pap. 7.95 (*0-89815-686-6*) Ten Speed Pr.

Doty, Betty & Rooney, Pat, Jr. The Anger Puzzle. LC 86-70419. (Illus.). 112p. 1986. pap. 8.95 (*0-930822-07-2*) Bookery.

— Shake the Anger Habit! rev. ed. LC 87-71633. (Illus.). 213p. (Orig.). 1990. reprint ed. pap. 11.95 (*0-930822-10-2*) Bookery.

Doty, Brad, jt. auth. see Argabright, Dave.

Doty, C. Stewart. Acadian Hard Times: The Farm Security Administration in Maine's St. John Valley, 1940-1943. LC 90-23304. (Illus.). xiii, 186p. 1991. pap. 26.95 (*0-89101-071-8*) U Maine Pr.

Doty, Carolyn. Whisper: A Novel. 288p. 1992. text 21.95 (*0-684-19287-X*) S&S Trade.

Doty, Catherine. Just Kidding: Cartoons for Grownups. LC 99-13057. (Illus.). 1999. pap. 9.95 (*0-9661072-6-8*) Avocet Pr.

Doty, Charles R. Preparing for High Technology: Model Programs in the U. S. A. 100p. 1985. 8.00 (*0-318-20416-9*, RD258) Ctr Educ Trng Employ.

Doty, Charles R., ed. Developing Occupational Programs. LC 85-644753. (New Directions for Community Colleges Ser.: No. CC 58). 1987. pap. 22.00 (*1-55542-959-9*) Jossey-Bass.

Doty, David. A Field Guide to Carnival Glass. LC 99-161886. (Illus.). viii, 374p. 1998. pap. 24.95 (*1-57080-051-0*) Antique Pubns.

— Frommer's New York City '97. 1996. 14.95 (*0-02-861296-5*) Prntice Hall Bks.

Doty, David, jt. auth. see Reynolds, Marilyn.

Doty, David B. Programmer's Guide to the Hercules Graphics Cards. 1988. pap. 24.95 (*0-201-11885-8*) Addison-Wesley.

Doty, David W. Essential Children's Services Planner: Managed Care Preparedness, Program Redesign & Business Development. 1996. 29.95 (*1-887452-09-5*) Manisses Communs.

Doty, Dennis. Model Car Building: Advanced Techniques. (Illus.). 128p. 1988. pap. 10.95 (*0-8306-9395-5*, 3095) McGraw-Hill Prof.

— Model Car Building: Getting Started. (Illus.). 128p. 1988. pap. 10.95 (*0-8306-9385-8*, 3085) McGraw-Hill Prof.

Doty, Donald B. Cardiac Surgery: Operative Technique. LC 96-2567. (Illus.). 448p. (C). (gr. 13). 1996. text 195.00 (*0-8151-2761-8*, 24295) Mosby Inc.

Doty, Dorothy I. Publicity & Public Relations. deluxe ed. (Barron's Business Library). 320p. 1990. pap. 18.95 (*0-8120-4413-4*) Barron.

***Doty, Dorothy I. & Pincus, Marilyn.** Publicity & Public Relations. 2nd rev. ed. LC 00-33727. (Business Library). 2001. write for info. (*0-7641-1401-8*) Barron.

Doty, E. A. Doty - Doten Family in America: Descendants of Edward Doty, an Emigrant by the Mayflower, 1620, 2 vols. 1035p. 1989. reprint ed. pap. 155.00 (*0-8328-0489-4*); reprint ed. lib. bdg. 165.00 (*0-8328-0488-6*) Higginson Bk Co.

Doty, Eldon, jt. auth. see Mann, Paul Z.

***Doty, F. P., ed.** Penetrating Radiation Systems & Applications. 1999. pap. text 72.00 (*0-8194-3255-5*) SPIE.

Doty, F. Patrick & Hoover, Richard B., eds. Hard X-Ray & Gamma-Ray Detector Physics & Applications, Vol. 3446. LC 99-170363. (Proceedings of SPIE Ser.: Vol.3446). 276p. 1998. 69.00 (*0-8194-2901-5*) SPIE.

Doty, F. Patrick, jt. ed. see Hoover, Richard B.

Doty, Francis C. Health Care Made Better by Disease Prevention Using Health Promotion: Index of New Information with Authors, Subjects & References. (Illus.). 183p. 1997. 47.50 (*0-7883-1294-4*); pap. 44.50 (*0-7883-1295-2*) ABBE Pubs Assn.

Doty, Gene. Nose to Nose. 40p. 1998. 5.00 (*0-913719-97-8*, High Coo Pr) Brooks Books.

Doty, Gresdna A. The Career of Mrs. Anne Brunton Merry in the American Theatre. LC 74-166970. (Louisiana State University Studies: No. 21). 192p. 1971. pap. 59.60 (*0-7837-8452-X*, 204925700010) Bks Demand.

Doty, Gresdna A. & Harbin, Billy J., eds. Inside the Royal Court Theatre, 1956-1981: Artists Talk. LC 89-13477. 296p. 1990. text 42.50 (*0-8071-1550-9*); pap. text 19.95 (*0-8071-1623-8*) La State U Pr.

Doty, Hope, ed. see Haugen, Janie.

Doty, Howard, jt. auth. see Lyle, Linda.

Doty, Howard G., jt. auth. see Lyle, Linda R.

Doty, James. Journal of Operations. 1979. 18.95 (*0-87770-204-7*) Ye Galleon.

Doty, James R. & Rengachary, Setti S., eds. Surgical Disorders of the Sacrum. LC 93-2421. 320p. 1993. 102.00 (*0-86577-494-3*) Thieme Med Pubs.

***Doty, Joe.** The Heartbeat of God: Angelic Ministries Proclaims. (Illus.). 72p. 1999. pap. 9.95 (*1-58107-019-5*, Pub. by New Forums) Booksource.

Doty, Leilani. Communication & Assertion Skills for Older Persons. (Death Education, Aging & Health Care Ser.). 110p. 1987. 46.95 (*0-89116-400-6*) Hemisp Pub.

Doty, Leonard A. Reliability for the Technologies. 2nd ed. (Illus.). 307p. 1989. 29.95 (*0-8311-3024-5*) Indus Pr.

— SPC for Short Run Manufacturing. LC 97-35838. 1997. 34.95 (*1-56990-239-9*) Hanser-Gardner.

— Statistical Process Control. 2nd ed. LC 95-44408. 352p. 1996. 39.95 (*0-8311-3069-5*) Indus Pr.

Doty, Lockwood L. A History of Livingston County, New York: From Its Earliest Traditions, to Its Part in the War for Our Union: With an Account of the Seneca Nation of Indians. (Illus.). 685p. 1992. reprint ed. lib. bdg. 65.00 (*0-8328-2251-5*) Higginson Bk Co.

Doty, Lockwood R., ed. History of Livingston County, from Its Earliest Traditions to the Present, Together with Early Town Sketches. (Illus.). 1242p. 1997. reprint ed. lib. bdg. 119.50 (*0-8328-6162-6*) Higginson Bk Co.

Doty, Lynda A. Help Me Heal. LC 98-17613. 272p. 1998. pap. 9.99 (*1-56722-213-7*) Word Aflame.

***Doty, Lynda A.** Lord, Why Am I Crying? A Christian Perspective on Depression. LC 99-38445. 142p. 1999. pap. 7.99 (*1-56722-234-X*) Word Aflame.

Doty, Mark. Atlantis: New Poems. LC 96-185822. 112p. 1995. pap. 12.00 (*0-06-095106-0*, Perennial) HarperTrade.

***Doty, Mark.** Firebird: A Memoir. LC 99-15619. 224p. 1999. 25.00 (*0-06-019374-3*) HarpC.

Doty, Mark. Firebird: A Memoir. 224p. 2000. pap. 13.00 (*0-06-093197-3*) HarpC.

— Heaven's Coast: A Memoir. 320p. 1997. pap. 13.00 (*0-06-092805-0*, Perennial) HarperTrade.

***Doty, Mark.** An Island Sheaf. deluxe ed. 32p. 1998. 175.00 (*1-891472-14-3*) Dim Gray.

Doty, Mark. My Alexandria: Poems. LC 92-21564. (National Poetry Ser.). 102p. (C). 1993. 11.95 (*0-252-06317-1*) U of Ill Pr.

— My Alexandria: Poems. 102p. (C). 1995. 18.95 (*0-252-02210-6*) U of Ill Pr.

***Doty, Mark.** Still Life with Oysters & Lemon: On Objects & Intimacy. 2001. 20.00 (*0-8070-6608-7*) Beacon Pr.

Doty, Mark. Sweet Machine: Poems. LC 97-33215. 128p. 1998. pap. 12.00 (*0-06-095256-3*) HarpC.

***Doty, Mark.** Turtle, Swan & Bethlehem in Broad Daylight: Poetry, 2 vols. LC 99-6643. 2000. pap. 14.95 (*0-252-06842-4*) U of Ill Pr.

***Doty, Mark, ed.** Ploughshares Spring 1999 Vol. 25, No. 1: Poems & Stories Edited by Mark Doty. 207p. 1999. pap. 9.95 (*0-933277-25-3*) Ploughshares.

***Doty, Mark & J. Paul Getty Museum Staff.** Murano: Poem. LC 00-22399. (Illus.). 56p. 2000. 14.95 (*0-89236-598-6*, J P Getty Museum) J P Getty Trust.

Doty, Michael, et al. Rock Island & Tennessee Pass. LC 70-102682. (Colorado Rail Annual Ser.: No. 17) (Illus.). 264p. 1987. 35.95 (*0-918654-17-3*) CO RR Mus.

Doty, Pamela. Guided Change of the American Health System: Where the Levers Are. LC 80-12484. (Center for Policy Research Monographs: Vol. II). 299p. 1980. 43.95 (*0-87705-472-X*, Kluwer Acad Hman Sci) Kluwer Academic.

Doty, Pamela S., et al. Introducing Miz Lilly Lotta Leggs & the Land of Big Windy Vol. 1: Tall, Tall, Tales from the Land of Big Windy. LC 96-92837. (Illus.). 44p. (J). (gr. k-3). 1996. 100.00 (*0-9655005-0-0*) Silverbird Studio.

Doty, R., ed. Xenophon: Oeconomicus VII-XIII. (Bristol Greek Texts Ser.). (GRE.). 96p. 1994. pap. 16.95 (*1-85399-394-8*, Pub. by Brist Class Pr) Focus Pub-R Pullins.

Doty, R. L. & Muller-Schwarze, D. Chemical Signals in Vertebrates, Vol. 6. LC 92-22006. (Illus.). 654p. (C). 1992. text 155.00 (*0-306-44250-7*, Kluwer Plenum) Kluwer Academic.

Doty, Ralph. The Criteria of Truth. LC 90-21079. (American University Studies: Philosophy: Ser. V, Vol. 108). 127p. (C). 1992. text 35.95 (*0-8204-1424-7*) P Lang Pubng.

Doty, Richard. America's Money-America's Story. LC 98-84438. (Illus.). 248p. 1998. pap. 34.95 (*0-87341-618-X*, TPAN) Krause Pubns.

Doty, Richard G., ed. The Token: America's Other Money, Vol. 3. (Coinage of the Americas Conference Ser.). (Illus.). 224p. 1995. 25.00 (*0-89722-260-1*) Am Numismatic.

Doty, Richard G., intro. America's Currency, 1789-1866. (Coinage of the Americas Conference at the American Numismatic Society, New York Ser.: No. 2). (Illus.). 142p. 1986. 15.00 (*0-89722-214-8*) Am Numismatic.

— America's Silver Coinage, 1794-1891: Coinage of the Americas Conference at the American Numismatic Society, New York, Proceedings, No. 3. 210p. 1987. 15.00 (*0-89722-219-9*) Am Numismatic.

Doty, Richard L., ed. Handbook of Olfaction & Gustation. LC 94-33916. (Neurological Disease & Therapy Ser.: Vol. 32). (Illus.). 906p. 1994. text 250.00 (*0-8247-9252-1*) Dekker.

Doty, Robert M. Paintspitter: Paintings & Constructions by Robert Warrens. LC 89-43674. (Illus.). 44p. (Orig.). 1990. pap. 14.95 (*0-89494-031-7*) New Orleans Mus Art.

— Will Barnet. LC 84-396. (Illus.). 172p. 1984. 49.50 (*0-8109-0731-3*, Pub. by Abrams) Time Warner.

Doty, Robert M., ed. New Hampshire Photographs: The Portrait & the Environment. (Illus.). 72p. (Orig.). 1985. pap. text 10.00 (*0-914339-07-9*) P E Randall Pub.

Doty, Robert M. & Berkson, Bill. John Button. (Illus.). 72p. (Orig.). 1989. pap. 12.00 (*0-929710-03-7*) Currier Gal.

Doty, Robert W., tr. see Rusinov, V. S., ed.

Doty, Roxanne L. Imperial Encounters: The Politics of Representation in North-South Relations. LC 95-46540. (Borderlines Ser.: Vol. 5). (C). 1996. pap. 19.95 (*0-8166-2763-0*); text 49.95 (*0-8166-2762-2*) U of Minn Pr.

Doty, Roy. Fleet of Nursery Rhymes. (Illus.). (J). (ps). 1991. pap. 4.95 (*0-671-72843-1*) S&S Bks Yung.

— Wonderful Circus Parade. (J). (ps). 1991. pap. 4.95 (*0-671-72842-3*) Litle Simon.

Doty, Ruth. Elizabeth, the Real Mother Goose. Stollman, Carolyn, ed. LC 97-93225. (Illus.). 32p. (Orig.). (J). (gr. 4-6). 1997. 14.95 (*0-9658089-0-4*); pap. 8.95 (*0-9658089-1-2*) Howell Pub Co.

Doty, Silas. Life of Silas Doty, 1800-1876: A Forgotten Autobiography; the Most Noted Thief & Daring Burglar of His Time. (American Biography Ser.). 288p. 1991. reprint ed. lib. bdg. 69.00 (*0-7812-8109-1*) Rprt Serv.

Doty, W. MacMillan Encyclopedic Numismatic Dictionary. (Illus.). lib. bdg. 45.00 (*0-02-532270-2*) S J Durst.

Doty, Walter. All about Vegetables. rev. ed. Smith, Mike, ed. LC 90-80068. 160p. 1990. reprint ed. pap. 9.95 (*0-89721-222-3*, Ortho Bks) Meredith Bks.

Doty, Walter L. All about Vegetables. Reilly, Ann, ed. (Illus.). 144p. 1996. 14.95 (*0-89721-356-4*, Ortho Bks) Meredith Bks.

Doty, William G. Mythography: The Study of Myths & Rituals. LC 85-991. 352p. 1987. pap. text 22.95 (*0-8173-0398-7*) U of Ala Pr.

***Doty, William G.** Mythography: The Study of Myths & Rituals. LC 99-6781. 2000. 54.95 (*0-8173-1005-3*) U of Ala Pr.

— Mythography: The Study of Myths & Rituals. 2nd ed. LC 99-6781. 2000. pap. 24.95 (*0-8173-1006-1*) U of Ala Pr.

Doty, William G., ed. Picturing Cultural Values in Postmodern America. LC 94-13361. 272p. 1995. pap. text 29.95 (*0-8173-0733-8*) U of Ala Pr.

Doty, William G., jt. ed. see Hynes, William J.

Doty, William G, jt. ed. see Klein, Julie T.

Doty, William G., tr. see Guttgemans, Erhard T.

Dotz, Warren. Advertising Character Collectibles: An Identification & Value Guide. (Illus.). 176p. 1993. pap. 17.95 (*0-89145-531-0*, 3427) Collector Bks.

Dotz, Warren & Morton, Jim. What a Character! Twentieth-Century American Advertising Icons. (Illus.). 132p. 1996. pap. 16.95 (*0-8118-0936-6*) Chronicle Bks.

Dotzauer, J. J. Sixty-Two Select Studies for Violoncello, Bk. 2. Girard, F., ed. (Carl Fischer Music Library: No. 456). 1914. pap. 9.50 (*0-8258-0181-8*, L456) Fischer Inc NY.

Dotzler, Frederick J. The Marketing Idea Generator. (Illus.). 76p. (Orig.). 1982. pap. 14.95 (*0-9609906-0-7*) Innovex.

Dou, Sindo. Welding Metallurgy. LC 87-2218. 432p. 1987. 155.00 (*0-471-84090-4*) Wiley.

Douady, Jules. Liste Chronologique des Oeuvres de William Hazlitt. LC 78-164776. reprint ed. 31.50 (*0-404-07305-0*) AMS Pr.

Douais, Celestin. Les Albigeois. 2nd ed. LC 78-63182. (Heresies of the Early Christian & Medieval Era Ser.: Second Ser.). reprint ed. 64.50 (*0-404-16221-5*) AMS Pr.

Douanchand Hayes, Margo, jt. auth. see Monsaur, Mary Ann.

Douarche, Aristide. Les Tribunaux Civils de Paris Pendant la Revolution, 1791-1800: 1791-1800, 2 vols., Set. LC 71-164777. (Collection de Documents Relatifs a l'Histoire de Paris Pendant la Revolution Francaise). reprint ed. 270.00 (*0-404-52553-9*) AMS Pr.

Douarin, Nicole Le, see Le Douarin, Nicole, ed.

Douay, L., jt. ed. see Gorin, N. C.

Doub, George, et al. Raising a Loving Family. LC 99-12632. (Orig.). 1999. pap. 9.95 (*1-58062-049-3*) Adams Media.

***Doub, Siri Lise.** A Taste of Latvia. 200p. 2000. 24.95 (*0-7818-0803-0*) Hippocrene Bks.

Douben, Peter E. Pollution Risk Assessment & Management. LC 98-12078. (Ecological & Environmental Toxicology Ser.). 478p. 1998. 190.00 (*0-471-97297-5*) Wiley.

Douber Levin, Sholom. TiKunei Mikvo'os Lefi Takonas Raboiseinu.Tr. of Establishing of Mikvaos According to the Lubuvicher Rebbes. (HEB.). 190p. 1998. 15.00 (*0-8266-5216-6*) Kehot Pubn Soc.

***Doubert, Bonnie L.** Where Are Your Socks? A Guide on How to Achieve Professional & Personal Success Through Attitude, Dress, Communication. (Illus.). 150p. 1998. 19.95 (*1-883294-72-X*) Masthof Pr.

Doubiago, Sharon. The Book of Seeing with One's Own Eyes. LC 87-81373. (Short Fiction Ser.). 352p. 1988. pap. 10.95 (*1-55597-101-6*) Graywolf.

***Doubiago, Sharon.** Hard Country. 274p. 1999. pap. 19.95 (*0-931122-94-5*, Pub. by West End) SPD-Small Pr Dist.

Doubiago, Sharon. El Nino: Stories by Sharon Doubiago, No. 35. 152p. 1988. pap. 9.95 (*0-918786-39-8*) Lost Roads.

— South America Mi Hija. LC 90-20875. (Poetry Ser.). 312p. (C). 1992. pap. 15.95 (*0-8229-5450-8*) U of Pittsburgh Pr.

Doubiago, Sharon, jt. auth. see Claypoole, Antoinette.

Doubilet, David. Magia del Mar. (SPA.). 1997. 38.99 (*3-8228-8533-9*) Benedikt Taschen.

Doubilet, David. Water, Light, Time. (Illus.). 240p. 1999. 49.95 (*0-7148-3828-4*, Pub. by Phaidon Press) Phaidon Pr.

Doubilet, Peter M. Educational Guidelines for Diagnostic Sonography. 58p. 1993. pap. 38.00 (*1-930047-31-2*) Am Inst Ultrasound.

Doubilet, Susan. Private Architecture: Masterpieces of the Twentieth Century. LC 98-20360. (Illus.). 360p. 1998. 75.00 (*1-58093-008-5*, Pub. by Monacelli Pr) Penguin Putnam.

Doubilet, Susan & Boles, Daralice. American House Now: Contemporary Architectural Directions. (Illus.). 240p. 1997. pap. 25.00 (*0-7893-0049-4*, Pub. by Universe) St Martin.

— European House Now: Contemporary Architectural Directions. LC 99-34203. (Illus.). 240p. 1999. pap. 25.00 (*0-7893-0359-0*, Pub. by Universe) St Martin.

Doubinsky, Claude, tr. see Genette, Gerard.

***Doublas, Gregory M.** Using QuickBooks & QuickBooks Pro: And Accounting Properly. (Illus.). 179p. 1999. pap. 29.95 (*0-9677690-0-0*) Syst Mgmt Serv.

Doublas, Libby. All about Peer Pressure. rev. ed. 1999. pap. 0.50 (*0-89230-216-X*) Do It Now.

Doublas, Pearce. Tourist Development. 2nd ed. 360p. (C). 1996. pap. 43.00 (*0-582-01435-2*) Addison-Wesley.

Doublas, Vincent F., ed. Enrichment: The Gifted Child, Math. (Illus.). 80p. (J). (gr. 5). 1995. wbk. ed. 4.95 (*1-56189-445-1*) Amer Educ Pub.

Double, Alex, jt. auth. see Double, Tamara.

Double B Publications Staff. Great with Clip Borders. 1993. pap. 4.95 (*0-929526-24-4*) Double B Pubns.

— Great with Clip Rodeos. 1993. pap. 4.95 (*0-929526-23-6*) Double B Pubns.

Double B Staff. Clip Art-Holidays. 1993. pap. text 4.95 (*0-929526-22-8*) Double B Pubns.

Double, Don. Life in a New Dimension. 192p. 1979. mass mkt. 5.99 (*0-88368-083-1*) Whitaker Hse.

***Double, John & Bibby, M. C., eds.** Telomeres & Telomerase. (Methods in Molecular Medicine Ser.). 400p. 2000. 89.50 (*0-89603-657-X*) Humana.

Double, Mary E. & McKendry, Maryann. Computer Validation Compliance: A Quality Assurance Perspective. 205p. 1993. 195.00 (*0-935184-48-1*) Interpharm.

Double, Oliver. Stand Up! On Being a Comedian. 1996. 25.95 (*0-413-70310-X*, Methuen Drama) Methn.

— Stand-Up: On Being a Comedian. 1997. pap. 25.95 (*0-413-70320-7*) Heinemann.

Double, Richard. Beginning Philosophy. (Illus.). 368p. (C). 1998. pap. 31.95 (*0-19-511781-6*) OUP.

— Metaphilosophy & Free Will. 192p. 1996. text 39.95 (*0-19-510762-4*) OUP.

— The Non-Reality of Free Will. 272p. 1990. text 55.00 (*0-19-506497-6*) OUP.

Double, Tamara & Double, Alex. Red Sea Divers Guide. 172p. 1995. pap. 100.00 (*1-898162-00-X*, Pub. by IMMEL Pubng) St Mut.

— Red Sea Divers Guide, 2 vols., Vol. 1. 192p. (C). 1995. 150.00 (*0-907151-94-9*, Pub. by IMMEL Pubng) St Mut.

— Red Sea Divers Guide, 2 vols., Vol. 2. 172p. (C). 1990. 150.00 (*0-907151-40-X*, Pub. by IMMEL Pubng) St Mut.

Doubleday, Abner. Chancellorsville & Gettysburg. LC 93-38773. (Illus.). 269p. 1994. reprint ed. pap. 12.95 (*0-306-80549-9*) Da Capo.

— Gettysburg Made Plain. 59p. 1987. reprint ed. pap. 8.50 (*0-94221-35-9*) Olde Soldier Bks.

D

— My Life in the Old Army: The Reminiscences of Abner Doubleday. Chance, Joseph E., ed. & anno. by. LC 97-34316. (Illus.). 1998. 27.95 (*0-87565-185-2*) Tex Christian.

— Reminiscences of Forts Sumter & Moultrie in 1860-61. LC 98-6565. (Illus.). 1998. 21.95 (*1-877853-54-2*) Nautical & Aviation.

Doubleday, Abner, tr. see Levi, Eliphas.

Doubleday, Neal. Hawthorne's Early Tales: A Critical Study. LC 76-185462. 272p. reprint ed. pap. 84.40 (*0-608-15088-6*, 202619600048) Bks Demand.

Doubleday, Neal F. Variety of Attempt: British & American Fiction in the Early Nineteenth Century. LC 75-38057. 228p. reprint ed. pap. 70.70 (*0-7837-1819-5*, 204201900001) Bks Demand.

Doubleday Publishing Staff & Catalano, Grace. Leonardo: A Scrapbook in Words & Pictures. LC 99-182116. (Illus.). 32p. (YA). 1998. pap. 7.95 (*0-440-22795-X*) Dell.

Doubleday, Sandy, jt. auth. see Downs, Hugh.

Doubleday Staff, ed. Anne Frank. 352p. 1995. mass mkt. 7.50 (*0-385-42695-X*) Doubleday.

— Catecismo de la Iglesia Catolica: Con Modificaciones Basadas en la Editio Typica. (SPA.). 880p. 1995. mass mkt. 7.99 (*0-385-47984-0*) Doubleday.

— Festive Folding. 1991. 15.00 (*0-385-25369-9*) Doubleday.

— Journey to Fattouma. 160p. 1993. pap. 7.99 (*0-385-40470-0*) Doubleday.

— Relief from Insomnia. 1996. pap. 15.95 (*0-385-42753-0*) Doubleday.

Doubleday Staff, ed. see Bildner, Jim & Dodson, James.

Doubleday, Thomas. Financial, Monetary & Statistical History of England, from the Revolution of 1688 to the Present Time. LC 68-28626. 1968. reprint ed. lib. bdg. 22.50 (*0-8371-0388-6*, DOFM, Greenwood Pr) Greenwood.

— True Law of Population: Shown to Be Connected with the Food of the People. 2nd ed. LC 67-17492. (Reprints of Economic Classics Ser.). xxi, 278p. 1967. reprint ed. 45.00 (*0-678-00244-4*) Kelley.

Doubleday, Veronica. Three Women of Herat. large type ed. (Illus.). 1990. 27.99 (*0-7089-2201-5*) Ulverscroft.

Doubledee, Martha J. Marvelous Grace. (Illus.). 327p. 1998. pap. 11.95 (*1-891635-13-1*) Moore Bks.

Doubler, Michael D. Closing with the Enemy: How GIs Fought the War in Europe, 1944-1945. LC 94-25067. (Modern War Studies). (Illus.). 368p. (Orig.). (C). 1995. pap. 17.95 (*0-7006-0744-7*) U Pr of KS.

Doubrovsky, Serge. The New Criticism in France. Coltman, Derek, tr. from FRE. 1995. lib. bdg. 24.00 (*0-226-16040-8*) U Ch Pr.

— Writing & Fantasy in Proust. Bove, Carol M. & Bove, Paul A., trs. LC 85-31823. 183p. 1986. reprint ed. pap. 56.80 (*0-7837-8861-4*, 204957200001) Bks Demand.

***Doubt, John J.** Make Things Happen. 126p. 1999. pap. write for info. (*0-7392-0494-7*, PO3855) Morris Pubng.

***Doubt, Keith.** Sociology after Bosnia & Kosovo: Recovering Justice. LC 99-49771. (Postmodern Social Futures Ser.). 192p. 2000. text 60.00 (*0-8476-9376-7*) Rowman.

— Sociology after Bosnia & Kosovo: Recovering Justice. LC 99-49771. (Postmodern Social Futures Ser.). 192p. 2000. pap. 24.95 (*0-8476-9377-5*) Rowman.

Doubt, Keith. Towards a Sociology of Schizophrenia: Humanistic Reflections. 144p. 1996. pap. 13.95 (*0-8020-7830-3*); text 30.00 (*0-8020-0845-3*) U of Toronto Pr.

Doubtfire, Diane. Teach Yourself Creative Writing. 2nd rev. ed. (Illus.). 160p. 1996. pap. 10.95 (*0-8442-4011-7*) NTC Contemp Pub Co.

Doubtfire, Dianne. Teach Yourself Creative Writing. 144p. 1994. pap. 8.95 (*0-8442-3762-0*, Teach Yrslf) NTC Contemp Pub Co.

Douce, F. Herbert, jt. auth. see Dunlevy, Crystal L.

Douce, Roland & Day, D. A., eds. Higher Plant Cell Respiration. (New Encyclopedia of Plant Physiology Ser.: Vol. 18). (Illus.). 525p. 1985. 295.95 (*0-387-13935-4*) Spr-Verlag.

Doucet. Woerterbuch Recht und Wirtschafts Vol. 2: German-French. 5th ed. (ENG & GER.). 656p. 1994. 135.00 (*0-7859-7547-0*, 3406359957) Fr & Eur.

Doucet & Mainka Staff. Operator Training for Medical & Other Solid Waste Incinerators. (Illus.). 408p. (Orig.). 1992. pap. 169.00 (*0-87258-596-4*, 055210) Am Hospital.

Doucet, Bob. Adventures: Reading Level 2-3. LC 93-12039. (Timeless Tales Ser.). 1993. 4.95 (*0-88336-458-1*); audio 9.95 (*0-88336-523-5*) New Readers.

***Doucet, Clive.** Notes from Exile: On Being Acadian. 320p. 1999. text 21.95 (*0-7710-2839-3*) McCland & Stewart.

Doucet, Elizabeth H., jt. auth. see Lightle, Juliana.

Doucet, Eugenie. Tapas: A Spanish Interlude. (Illus.). 224p. pap. 19.95 (*0-9698752-0-7*) Sh1oreline.

***Doucet, Francois.** Miguel. (Coffragants Ser.). Orig. Title: Mes Yeux de l'Interieur (Mes Yeux D'Enfant). (FRE.). 64p. 1998. 12.95 (*2-921997-66-5*) Penton Overseas.

Doucet, Francois. Miguel. 2nd rev. ed. Orig. Title: Mes Yeux de l'Interieur (Mes Yeux D'Enfant). 150p. 1998. reprint ed. pap. write for info. (*2-921892-47-2*) EAsa.

Doucet, Friedrich W. Diccionario de Psicoanalisis Clasico. (SPA.). 232p. 1974. pap. 24.95 (*0-8288-5985-X*, S50069) Fr & Eur.

Doucet, J. P. & Weber, J. Computer-Aided Molecular Design: Theory & Applications. (Illus.). 512p. 1996. text 89.95 (*0-12-221285-1*) Acad Pr.

Doucet, Jacques. Catalogue de Fonds Speciaux de la Bibliotheque Litteraire Jacques Doucet, (Paris, France) (Fonds Valery Ser.). (FRE.). 1972. 160.00 (*0-8161-0952-4*, G K Hall & Co); 160.00 (*0-8161-0954-0*, G K Hall & Co) Mac Lib Ref.

— Catalogue de Manuscrits de la Bibliotheque Litteraire Jacques Doucet, (Paris, France) 1972. 160.00 (*0-8161-0950-8*, G K Hall & Co) Mac Lib Ref.

***Doucet, Julie.** My New York Diary. 124p. 1999. 24.95 (*1-896597-23-8*, Pub. by Drawn & Quarterly) LPC InBook.

Doucet, Julie. New York Diary. 1999. pap. text 13.95 (*1-896597-24-6*) LPC InBook.

Doucet, Michael & Weaver, John. Housing the North American City. 608p. 1991. 65.00 (*0-7735-0825-2*, Pub. by McG-Queens Univ Pr) CUP Services.

Doucet, Michel. Dictionary of Law & Economics: Woerterbuch der Rechtssprache & Wirtschaftssprache, Vol. 1. 4th ed. (FRE & GER.). 624p. 1987. 150.00 (*0-8288-0976-3*, M15089) Fr & Eur.

— Dictionnaire Juridique et Economique: French-English, English-French. (ENG & FRE.). 769p. 1979. 150.00 (*0-7859-8103-9*, 2856080111) Fr & Eur.

— Dictionnaire Juridique et Economique Doucet, Vol. 1. 3rd ed.Tr. of Legal & Economic Dictionary. (ENG & FRE.). 625p. 1980. 150.00 (*0-8288-0382-X*, M6147) Fr & Eur.

Doucet, Paul & Sloep, Peter B. Mathematical Modeling in the Life Sciences. LC 92-36766. (Ellis Horwood Series in Mathematics & Its Applications). 450p. 1993. pap. text 45.00 (*0-13-562018-X*, Pub. by Tavistock-E Horwood) Chapman & Hall.

***Doucet, Sharon A.** Fiddle Fever. 176p. (gr. 4-7). 2000. 15.00 (*0-618-04324-1*, Clarion Bks) HM.

Doucette-Dudman, Deborah & Lacure, Jeffrey R. Raising Our Children's Children. 240p. 1996. 19.95 (*0-925190-91-8*) Fairview Press.

Doucette-Dudman, Deborah & LaCure, Jeffrey R. Raising Our Children's Children. 256p. 1997. reprint ed. pap. 12.95 (*1-57749-026-6*) Fairview Press.

Doucette, Eugene F. Beating up Daddy: A Year in the Life of an Amateur Father. Boucke, Laurie, ed. LC 99-27646. 1999. pap. 13.00 (*1-888580-09-7*) White-Boucke.

Doucette, L. E., ed. The Drama of Our Past: Major Plays from Nineteenth-Century Quebec. 327p. 1997. text 60.00 (*0-8020-4140-X*) U of Toronto Pr.

Doucette, Leonard E. The Drama of Our Past: Major Plays from Nineteenth Century Quebec. LC 97-160011. 300p. 1997. pap. text 24.95 (*0-8020-7985-7*) U of Toronto Pr.

***Doucette, Lorraine J.** Basic Mathematics for the Health-Related Professions. LC 99-49765. (Illus.). 295p. 2000. pap. text. write for info. (*0-7216-7938-2*, W B Saunders Co) Harcrt Hlth Sci Grp.

Doucette, Lorraine J. & Kaszczuk, Selma. Mathematics for the Clinical Laboratory. LC 96-21902. 352p. 1997. pap. text 31.50 (*0-7216-4458-9*, W B Saunders Co) Harcrt Hlth Sci Grp.

Doucette, Martin. Microsoft Project 98 for Dummies. LC 97-81230. (For Dummies Ser.). 384p. 1998. pap. 24.99 incl. cd-rom (*0-7645-0321-9*) IDG Bks.

— MS Project X for Dummies. 384p. 2000. pap. 24.99 incl. cd-rom (*0-7645-0517-3*) IDG Bks.

***Doucette, Paul F.** Controlled Growth: The Artistry of Business Management. LC 00-131712. 176p. 2000. write for info. (*0-9678412-4-0*) Biz Mgmt Pubng.

Doucette, Wendy C. Illusion & the Absent Other in Madame Riccoboni's "Lettres de Mistriss Fanni Butlerd" LC 96-23020. (Age of Revolution & Romanticism Ser.: Vol. 22). X, 157p. (C). 1997. text 40.95 (*0-8204-3394-2*) P Lang Pubng.

Doucey, Elisabeth, jt. ed. see Horton, Elizabeth.

Douch, John. Smuggling: The Wicked Trade. 1984. 25.00 (*0-906124-05-0*, Pub. by Regency Pr GBR) St Mut.

— Smuggling-Rough, Rude Men. 150p. (C). 1988. 35.00 (*0-906124-07-7*, Pub. by Regency Pr GBR) St Mut.

Douch, John, ed. Smuggling-Flogging Joey's Warriors. 165p. (C). 1988. 35.00 (*0-906124-08-5*, Pub. by Regency Pr GBR) St Mut.

Douch, Nick. The Economics of Foreign Exchange. LC 89-4033. 233p. 1989. 75.00 (*0-89930-499-0*, DFE/, Greenwood Pr) Greenwood.

— Managing Foreign Exchange Risks. 80p. 1996. pap. 34.95 (*92-842-1202-2*, 549) ICC Pub.

— Managing Interest Rate Risks. 68p. (C). 1997. pap. 34.95 (*92-842-1228-6*, 572) ICC Pub.

Douchant. Inside Sports Complete College Basketball. 2nd ed. LC 96-20071. (Illus.). 650p. 1996. 19.95 (*0-7876-1033-X*) Visible Ink Pr.

Douchant, Michael. Inside Sports College Basketball 1998. 3rd ed. LC 97-23449. (Illus.). 712p. 1997. 19.95 (*1-57859-009-4*, 00156975) Visible Ink Pr.

Douchant, Michael A. Encyclopedia of College Basketball. 615p. 1994. 19.95 (*0-8103-9483-9*) Visible Ink Pr.

Douchant, Michael A. The Encyclopedia of College Basketball, Vol. 1. LC 94-35209. 615p. 1994. 55.00 (*0-8103-9640-8*) Gale.

***Douchene, Laurent, et al.** Le Cordon Bleu Dessert Techniques: More Than 1,000 Photographs Illustrating 300 Preparation And Cooking TechniquesFor Making Tarts, Pi. LC 98-32164. (Illus.). 224p. 1999. 30.00 (*0-688-16907-4*, Grenwillow Bks) HarpC Child Bks.

***Douchet, Jean.** The French New Wave. LC 98-26522. (Illus.). 384p. 1998. 75.00 (*1-56466-057-5*) Archer Fields.

Douchkoff, Wayne. Purchasing Capital Equipment. LC 97-30475. (Orig.). 1998. pap. 14.95 (*0-945456-29-8*) PT Pubns.

Douchkoff, Wayne L. & Petroski, Thomas E. Reengineering Through Cycle Time Management. LC 95-26503. 174p. 1996. 29.95 (*0-945456-12-3*) PT Pubns.

Douchkoff, Wayne L., jt. auth. see Gozzo, Michael W.

Doucot, B. & Zinn-Justin, J., eds. Strongly Interacting Fermions & High Tc Superconductivity. (Houches Summer School Proceedings Ser.: Vol. 56). 624p. 1995. 250.00 (*0-444-82190-2*) Elsevier.

Doud, Ann, ed. Summer Folks 'n Year-Round Neighbors: The Bayshore's History Settlement to the 1950s. LC 92-61252. (Illus.). 340p. 1992. lib. bdg. 40.00 (*0-9633751-0-5*) TX Marquee Pub.

Doud, David T. Berlin 2000: The Center of Europe. (Illus.). 346p. (C). 1995. lib. bdg. 49.50 (*0-7618-0067-0*) U Pr of Amer.

Doud, Forrest. The Gray Whale Pocket Guide. (Modified Reprint Ser.). (Illus.). 32p. 1996. pap. 1.95 (*0-945092-30-X*) EZ Nature.

Doud, Guy. Joy in the Journey. 1992. 12.99 (*1-56179-092-3*) Focus Family.

Doud, Guy R. Molder of Dreams, 1. 263p. (Orig.). 1999. mass mkt. 5.99 (*1-56179-712-X*) Focus Family.

— Stuff You Gotta Know: Straight Talk about Real-Life. LC 93-25113. (Illus.). 152p. (Orig.). (YA). (gr. 8-12). 1993. pap. 6.99 (*0-570-04622-X*, 12-3203) Concordia.

***Doud, Laurel.** This Body: A Novel of Reincarnation. 304p. 2000. pap. 13.95 (*0-316-19661-4*, Back Bay) Little.

Doud, Laurel M. This Body: A Novel of Reincarnation. LC 97-45573. 304p. (gr. 8). 1998. 23.95 (*0-316-19675-4*, Back Bay) Little.

Doud, Laurel M., jt. auth. see Martin, Robert D.

Doud, Patrick. The Man in Green. 64p. (Orig.). 1996. pap. 10.00 (*1-889960-00-4*) First Intensity.

Doud, Richard K. Winterthur Portfolio, No. 5. 202p. 1978. lib. bdg. 24.00 (*0-226-92130-1*) U Ch Pr.

Doud, Richard K., ed. Winterthur Portfolio, No. 4. (Winterthur Bk.: Vol. 4). (Illus.). 232p. 1978. lib. bdg. 24.00 (*0-226-92129-8*) U Ch Pr.

Doud, Richard K. & Quimby, Ian M. Winterthur Portfolio, No. 6. (Winterthur Bk.). (Illus.). 232p. 1978. lib. bdg. 24.00 (*0-226-92132-8*) U Ch Pr.

Doud, Richard K., ed. see Quimby, Ian M.

Doudeijns, Marco & Pearson, Mark. Benefit Systems & Work Incentives in OECD Countries, 1998 Edition. LC 98-196455. 60p. 1998. pap. 16.00 (*92-64-16073-6*, 81 98 05 1 P, Pub. by European Conference Ministers Transp) OECD.

Doudera, Gerard. Fritz Bultman: Collages, Drawings & Sculptures from Two Decades, 1960-1980. (Illus.). 12p. Date not set. 3.00 (*0-614-10426-2*) W Benton Mus.

***Doudera, Victoria.** Moving to Maine: The Essential Guide to Get You There. 144p. 2000. pap. 14.95 (*0-89272-479-X*) Down East.

***Doudin, Pierre A., et al, eds.** Metacognition et Education. xii, 350p. 1999. 49.95 (*3-906762-48-3*) P Lang Pubng.

***Doudna, Kelly.** Aa. LC 00-28879. (Alphabet Ser.). (Illus.). (J). 2000. write for info. (*1-57765-394-7*) ABDO Pub Co.

— Bb. LC 00-28891. (Alphabet Ser.). (Illus.). (J). 2000. write for info. (*1-57765-395-5*) ABDO Pub Co.

— Big & Small. LC 99-46332. (Opposites Ser.). (Illus.). 24p. (J). 2000. lib. bdg. 17.27 (*1-57765-144-8*, SndCastle) ABDO Pub Co.

Doudna, Kelly. Bunnies. LC 98-28346. (Baby Animals Ser.). (Illus.). 24p. (J). (gr. k-1). 2000. lib. bdg. 18.50 (*1-57765-184-7*, SndCastle) ABDO Pub Co.

— Calves. LC 98-22060. (Baby Animals Ser.). (Illus.). 24p. (J). 2000. lib. bdg. 18.50 (*1-57765-186-3*, SndCastle) ABDO Pub Co.

***Doudna, Kelly.** Cc. LC 00-28890. (Alphabet Ser.). (Illus.). (J). 2000. write for info. (*1-57765-396-3*) ABDO Pub Co.

— Dd. LC 00-28889. (Alphabet Ser.). (Illus.). (J). 2000. write for info. (*1-57765-397-1*) ABDO Pub Co.

— Ee. LC 00-28888. (Alphabet Ser.). (Illus.). (J). 2000. write for info. (*1-57765-398-X*) ABDO Pub Co.

— Ff. LC 00-28887. (Alphabet Ser.). (Illus.). (J). 2000. write for info. (*1-57765-399-8*) ABDO Pub Co.

Doudna, Kelly. Foals. LC 98-21701. (Baby Animals Ser.). (Illus.). 24p. (J). 2002. lib. bdg. 18.50 (*1-57765-183-9*, SndCastle) ABDO Pub Co.

***Doudna, Kelly.** Gg. LC 00-28886. (Alphabet Ser.). (Illus.). (J). 2000. write for info. (*1-57765-400-5*) ABDO Pub Co.

— Hh. LC 00-28885. (Alphabet Ser.). (Illus.). (J). 2000. write for info. (*1-57765-401-3*) ABDO Pub Co.

Doudna, Kelly. I Feel Angry. LC 98-26679. (How Do You Feel? Ser.). (Illus.). 24p. (J). (gr. 1). 2000. lib. bdg. 18.50 (*1-57765-187-1*) ABDO Pub Co.

— I Feel Brave. LC 98-26677. (How Do You Feel? Ser.). (Illus.). 24p. (J). 2000. lib. bdg. 18.50 (*1-57765-190-1*, SndCastle) ABDO Pub Co.

— I Feel Happy. LC 98-26675. (How Do You Feel? Ser.). (Illus.). 24p. (J). 2000. lib. bdg. 18.50 (*1-57765-188-X*, SndCastle) ABDO Pub Co.

— I Feel Sad. LC 98-26676. (How Do You Feel? Ser.). (Illus.). 24p. (J). (ps-1). 2000. lib. bdg. 18.50 (*1-57765-189-8*, SndCastle) ABDO Pub Co.

— I Feel Safe. LC 98-26689. (How Do You Feel? Ser.). (Illus.). 24p. (J). 2000. lib. bdg. 18.50 (*1-57765-191-X*, SndCastle) ABDO Pub Co.

— I Feel Scared. LC 98-27402. (How Do You Feel? Ser.). (Illus.). 24p. (J). (ps-1). 2000. lib. bdg. 18.50 (*1-57765-192-8*, SndCastle) ABDO Pub Co.

***Doudna, Kelly.** Ii. LC 00-28884. (Alphabet Ser.). (Illus.). (J). 2000. write for info. (*1-57765-402-1*) ABDO Pub Co.

— Jj. LC 00-28883. (Alphabet Ser.). (Illus.). (J). 2000. write for info. (*1-57765-403-X*) ABDO Pub Co.

Doudna, Kelly. Kittens. LC 98-21703. (Baby Animals Ser.). (Illus.). 24p. (J). (gr. k-1). 2000. lib. bdg. 18.50 (*1-57765-182-0*, SndCastle) ABDO Pub Co.

***Doudna, Kelly.** Kk. LC 00-28882. (Alphabet Ser.). (Illus.). (J). 2000. write for info. (*1-57765-404-8*) ABDO Pub Co.

— Mm. LC 00-28880. (Alphabet Ser.). (Illus.). (J). 2000. write for info. (*1-57765-406-4*) ABDO Pub Co.

Doudna, Kelly. Piglets. LC 98-21702. (Baby Animals Ser.). (Illus.). 24p. (J). 2000. lib. bdg. 18.50 (*1-57765-185-5*, SndCastle) ABDO Pub Co.

— Puppies. LC 98-21704. (Baby Animals Ser.). (Illus.). 24p. (J). 2000. lib. bdg. 18.50 (*1-57765-181-2*, SndCastle) ABDO Pub Co.

Doudna, Martin K. Concerned about the Planet: The Reporter Magazine & American Liberalism, 1949-1968, 32. LC 77-10048. (Contributions in American Studies: No. 32). 197p. 1977. 49.95 (*0-8371-9698-1*, DCA/, Greenwood Pr) Greenwood.

— Have You Any Room for Us? 1975. pap. text 2.50 (*0-687-16659-4*) Abingdon.

Doudomis, Pete. Shame or Shameless? LC 96-90863. (Illus.). 68p. (Orig.). 1997. pap. 8.95 (*0-533-12198-1*) Vantage.

Doudoroff, Michael J. Moros y Cristianos in Zacatecas: Text of a Mexican Folk Play. LC 81-1558. 66p. (Orig.). 1981. pap. text 5.00 (*0-939448-00-9*) Amadeo Concha.

Doudoroff, Peter. A Critical Review of Recent Literature on Toxicity of Cyanides to Fish. LC 80-68588. 71p. (Orig.). 1980. pap. 20.00 (*0-89364-039-5*, API 847-87000) Am Petroleum.

Douds, Alex F., jt. auth. see Ittner, Penny L.

Douds, David D., jt. auth. see Kapulnik, Yoram.

Douds, David D., jt. ed. see Podila, Gopi K.

Doudt, Kenny. Surfing with the Great White Shark. LC 92-90967. 88p. (Orig.). (YA). pap. 8.95 (*0-9633342-7-1*) Shark-Bite.

Doueck, Howard J., jt. auth. see Levine, Murray.

***Doueck, Jack.** Chesed Boomerang: How the Acts of Kindness Enrich Our Lives. 2000. 19.95 (*0-9665372-1-1*) Yagdiyl Torah.

Doueck, Jack. Hessed Boomerang. 1998. pap. text 19.95 (*0-9665372-0-3*) Yagdiyl Torah.

Doueihi, Hector Y., tr. from ARA. Qurbono: The Book of Offering. (Season of Epiphany Ser.). 161p. (Orig.). 1993. pap. 10.95 (*0-9628727-8-4*); 2.50 (*0-9628727-9-2*) St Maron Pubns.

— Qurbono: the Book of Offering: Season of the Birth of the Lord. 190p. (Orig.). (C). 1993. 4.50 (*0-9628727-6-8*); pap. text 19.95 (*0-9628727-7-6*) St Maron Pubns.

Doueihi, Milad. A Perverse History of the Human Heart. LC 97-27437. (Illus.). 256p. 1997. 35.00 (*0-674-66325-X*); pap. 18.95 (*0-674-66327-6*) HUP.

Douet d'Arcq, L. C., ed. Inventaire de la Collection des Sceaux des Archives Nationales. 1990. reprint ed. 435.00 (*0-8115-3867-2*) Periodicals Srv.

Douet, James. British Barracks, 1600-1914: Their Architecture & Role in Society. xviii, 220p. 1998. pap. 80.00 (*0-11-772482-3*, Pub. by Statnry Office) Balogh.

Douet, Valerie C. Drawing for Pleasure. (Illus.). 128p. (Orig.). 1998. pap. 22.50 (*0-85532-705-7*) Srch Pr.

***Douet, Valerie C.** Drawing for Pleasure. (Illus.). 128p. (Orig.). 2000. pap. 13.95 (*0-85532-860-6*) Srch Pr.

Douet, Valerie J. Dollhouses - Collector's Guide. 1995. 12.98 (*0-7858-0220-7*) Bk Sales Inc.

Dougados, Venance. La Quete du Ble. Cazals, Remy, ed. (Exeter French Texts Ser.: Vol. CI). (FRE.). 80p. 1997. pap. 21.95 (*0-85989-535-1*, Pub. by Univ Exeter Pr) Northwestern U Pr.

Dougal, William. Off for California: American Autobiography. 62p. 1995. lib. bdg. 69.00 (*0-7812-8500-3*) Rprt Serv.

Dougall, Alan, ed. see Jwing-Ming Yang.

Dougall, Alan, ed. see Yang, Jwing-Ming.

Dougall, Alan, ed. see Yang, Jwing-Ming & Liang, Shou-Yu.

Dougall, David S. Mac, see Mac Dougall, David S., ed.

Dougall, E. Graham, ed. see IFIP TC11 Ninth International Conference on Inform.

***Dougall, Edwin.** T. V. Tangle. unabridged ed. LC 99-55862. 28p. (YA). (gr. 4-12). 1999. pap. 5.00 (*0-88734-834-3*) Players Pr.

***Dougall, Lucy.** Orkney Days. deluxe ed. Peaslee, Dixie, tr. LC 00-610. (Illus.). 45p. 2000. pap. 12.95 (*0-9660092-8-2*) Puget Sound.

Dougall, Lucy. War & Peace in Literature. 128p. 1981. 5.00 (*0-318-16880-4*) World Without War.

Dougall, Neil. Stallions: Their Management & Handling. 102p. 1990. pap. 30.00 (*0-85131-256-X*, Pub. by J A Allen) Trafalgar.

Dougan. Immunology of Infection. (C). 1998. 59.95 (*0-12-402305-3*) Harcourt.

Dougan, Andy. Martin Scorcese - Close Up: The Making of His Movies. (Illus.). 144p. 1998. pap. text 13.95 (*1-56025-161-1*, Thunders Mouth) Avalon NY.

— Robin Williams: A Biography. (Illus.). 312p. 1999. pap. text 13.95 (*1-56025-213-8*, Thunders Mouth) Avalon NY.

— Robin Williams--A Biography. LC 98-34078. (Illus.). 264p. 1998. 22.95 (*1-56025-196-4*, Thunders Mouth) Avalon NY.

— Untouchable: A Biography of Robert De Niro. LC 96-26805. (Illus.). 312p. 1997. 24.95 (*1-56025-136-0*, Thunders Mouth) Avalon NY.

— Untouchable: A Biography of Robert De Niro. (Illus.). 312p. 1998. pap. 14.95 (*1-56025-180-8*, Thunders Mouth) Avalon NY.

Dougan, Carol W., jt. auth. see Dougan, Michael B.

Dougan, Clark. TET: The Crucial Year of 1968. Boston Publishing Company Editors, ed. (Vietnam Experience Ser.). (Illus.). 192p. 1983. 16.30 (*0-201-11326-0*) Addison-Wesley.

Dougan, Clark, et al. Flags into Battle II. Boston Publishing Company Editors, ed. (Vietman Experience Ser.). (Illus.). 10p. 1987. 16.30 (*0-201-11677-4*) Addison-Wesley.

— A War Remembered. 1986. 16.30 (*0-201-11275-2*) Addison-Wesley.

D

An Asterisk (*) at the beginning of an entry indicates that the title is appearing for the first time.

Dougan, John. Memphis, Tennessee. (Images of America Ser.). (Illus.). 128p. 1998. pap. 16.99 (*0-7524-1331-7*) Arcadia Publng.

Dougan, John C. Know Your Ruger Single Action: The Second Decade 63-73. (Know Your Gun Ser.). (Illus.). 144p. (C). 1992. 19.95 (*0-941540-15-4*, 2003) Blacksmith Corp.

Dougan, Michael. Arkansas Odyssey: The Saga of Arkansas from Prehistoric Times to Present. Griffee, Carol, ed. LC 88-62036. (Illus.). 684p. (C). 1995. text 79.95 (*0-914546-65-1*) Rose Pub.

— East Texas: Tales from Behind the Pine Curtain. LC 87-36774. (Illus.). 96p. (Orig.). 1988. pap. 7.95 (*0-941104-25-7*) Real Comet.

Dougan, Michael B. Confederate Arkansas: The People & Policies of a Frontier State in Wartime. LC 76-40053. 176p. 1990. pap. text 15.95 (*0-8173-0522-X*) U of Ala Pr.

Dougan, Michael B., et al, compiled by. Arkansas History: An Annotated Bibliography, 5. LC 95-7477. (Bibliographies of the States of the United States Ser.: No. 5). 392p. 1995. lib. bdg. 79.50 (*0-313-28226-9*, Greenwood Pr) Greenwood.

Dougan, Michael B. & Dougan, Carol W. By the Cypress Swamp: The Arkansas Stories of Octave Thanet. 232p. 1980. 14.95 (*0-939130-03-3*) J W Bell.

Dougan, Pat. Professional Acting in Television Commercials: Techniques, Exercises, Copy & Storyboards. LC 94-33838. (Illus.). 214p. 1995. pap. 19.95 (*0-435-08659-6*, 08659) Heinemann.

Dougan, Sonya, ed. A Century of Cricket Jokes. (Joke Bks.). (Illus.). 64p. 1996. 8.50 (*1-85015-776-6*) Exley Giftbooks.

Dougan, William R., ed. see Campbell, Colin D.

Dougans, Inge. Complete Illustrated Guide to Reflexology: Therapeutic Foot Massage for Health & Wellbeing. (Illus.). 192p. 1996. pap. 24.95 (*1-85230-910-5*, Pub. by Element MA) Penguin Putnam.

— A Practical Introduction: Reflexology. LC 98-24940. (Illus.). 208p. 1998. pap. 14.95 (*1-86204-160-1*, Pub. by Element MA) Penguin Putnam.

— Reflexology: Foot Massage for Total Health. (Health Essentials Ser.). 128p. 1997. pap. 9.95 (*1-86204-045-1*, Pub. by Element MA) Penguin Putnam.

***Dougans, Inge.** Reflexology: Intro Guide to Foot Massage for Total Health. (New Perspectives Ser.). 2000. pap. 9.95 (*1-86204-665-4*, Pub. by Element MA) Penguin Putnam.

Dougans, Inge, et al. Art of Reflexology: A Step-by-Step Guide. LC 92-10025. 196p. 1992. pap. 16.95 (*1-85230-236-4*, Pub. by Element MA) Penguin Putnam.

Dough, Whitney J. Andy: Twenty-Four Years of Fowl Play with a Talking Crow. 3rd rev. ed. LC 97-17379. (Illus.). 128p. 1997. reprint ed. pap. 9.95 (*1-57736-040-0*) Providence Hse.

— The Hymnwriters: Our Unknown Friends: A Biographical Guide to British & American Sacred Song. LC 95-68372. 224p. 1995. pap. text 16.95 (*1-881576-35-3*) Providence Hse.

Dough, Whitney J., ed. Sayings of E. Stanley Jones: A Treasury of Wisdom & Wit. 144p. (Orig.). 1994. pap. 12.95 (*1-881576-29-9*) Providence Hse.

***Dougher, Mike.** Clinical Behavior Analysis. LC 99-43532. 1999. write for info. (*1-878978-38-1*) Context Pr.

Dougher, Rayola S. & Hogarty, Thomas F. Octane Requirements of the Motor Vehicle Fleet & Gasoline Grade Sales. (Illus.). 51p. (C). 1998. reprint ed. pap. text 25.00 (*0-7881-3816-2*) DIANE Pub.

Dougherty. Consultation. 2nd ed. (Counseling Ser.). 1994. pap., teacher ed. write for info. (*0-534-25129-3*) Brooks-Cole.

— Consultation: Practice & Perspectives. 3rd ed. (Counseling Ser.). 1999. pap., teacher ed. write for info. (*0-534-36619-8*) Brooks-Cole.

— Consultation: Practice & Perspectives: Case Studies. 3rd ed. LC 98-52230. (Counseling Ser.). 1999. pap. 28.95 (*0-534-36644-9*) Brooks-Cole.

— Digital Image Processing Methods. (Optical Engineering Ser.: Vol. 42). (Illus.). 504p. 1994. text 190.00 (*0-8247-8927-X*) Dekker.

Dougherty & Mott. Activities Field Studies & Other Fun Stuff. 218p. 1998. pap. text 14.96 (*0-536-01576-7*) Pearson Custom.

Dougherty, A. Michael. Consultation: Practice & Perspectives. LC 89-9724. 352p. (C). 1989. text 43.95 (*0-534-10362-6*) Brooks-Cole.

— Consultation: Practice & Perspectives. 3rd ed. LC 99-28748. (Counseling Ser.). 1999. mass mkt. 69.95 (*0-534-35555-2*) Brooks-Cole.

— Consultation: Practice & Perspectives in School & Community Settings. 2nd ed. LC 94-18259. 392p. 1994. pap. 52.25 (*0-534-25128-5*) Brooks-Cole.

Dougherty, Adelyn. A Study of Rhythmic Structure in the Verse of William Butler Yeats. (De Proprietatibus Litterarum, Ser. Practica: No. 38). (Illus.). 135p. 1973. pap. text 40.00 (*90-279-2506-2*) Mouton.

Dougherty, Barb. Barb Dougherty on Art Marketing: Don't Look down at Your Own Bare Feet. LC 98-30319. (Art Calendar Guide Ser.). (Illus.). 192p. 1999. pap. 17.95 (*1-55821-734-7*) Lyons Pr.

Dougherty, Barbara, jt. auth. see Carter, Michelle.

***Dougherty, Barbara L.** 101 Frequently Asked Art Marketing Questions... And Their Answers. Steis, Drew, ed. (Art Calendar Guide Ser.). 43p. 1999. pap. 9.95 (*0-945388-23-3*) Art Calendar.

***Dougherty, Barry.** New York Friars Club. 2000. 21.95 (*0-87131-918-7*) M Evans.

***Dougherty, Bill.** The Darker Side of Golf. (Illus.). 204p. 1999. pap. 16.96 (*1-55212-296-4*, 99-0047) Trafford Pub.

Dougherty, C. Mobile Bay: From 5 Sea Chanties for Voice & Piano. 12p. 1995. pap. 3.95 (*0-7935-3834-3*, 50482272) H Leonard.

Dougherty, Carol. The Poetics of Colonization: From City to Text in Archaic Greece. LC 92-41090. (Illus.). 224p. 1993. text 55.00 (*0-19-508399-7*) OUP.

Dougherty, Carol & Kurke, Leslie, eds. Cultural Poetics in Archaic Greece: Cult, Performance, Politics. (Illus.). 288p. 1998. reprint ed. pap. 19.95 (*0-19-512415-4*) OUP.

Dougherty, Charles J. American Health Care: Realities, Rights, & Reforms. 240p. 1988. text 35.00 (*0-19-505271-4*); pap. text 19.95 (*0-19-505272-2*) OUP.

— Back to Reform: Values, Markets, & the Health Care System. 192p. (C). 1996. 29.95 (*0-19-510397-1*) OUP.

Dougherty, Charles M. Electronic Technology. LC 67-15982. 275p. reprint ed. pap. 85.30 (*0-608-30663-0*, 200456100043) Bks Demand.

Dougherty, Christopher. Computer Video Graphics for Introduction to Econometrics, Set. (Illus.). 416p. 1992. text 67.95 incl. disk (*0-19-508004-1*) OUP.

— Introduction to Econometrics. (Illus.). 416p. (C). 1992. text 69.95 (*0-19-504346-4*); pap. text. write for info. (*0-19-507668-0*) OUP.

***Dougherty, Chrys.** Improving Early Literacy of Preschool Children: A Handbook for Prekindergarten Educators. (Public Service Handbooks Ser.). 23p. 2000. pap. 6.00 (*0-89940-331-X*) LBJ Sch Pub Aff.

Dougherty, Dale, ed. see Branagan, Linda & Sierra, Mike.

Dougherty, Dale, ed. see Lewine, Donald.

Dougherty, Darlene. Negotiation in Dietetic Practice. (Audio Cassette Ser.). 1990. student ed. 25.00 incl. audio (*0-88091-081-X*, 1213) Am Dietetic Assn.

Dougherty, David C. Stanley Elkin. (Twayne's United States Authors Ser.: No. 568). 168p. (C). 1990. 22.95 (*0-8057-7616-8*) Macmillan.

— Strategic Organization Planning: Downsizing for Survival. LC 88-11355. 271p. 1989. 65.00 (*0-89930-339-0*, DYS/, Quorum Bks) Greenwood.

Dougherty, David M. & Barnes, Eugene B., eds. Le Galien' de Cheltenham. (Purdue University Monographs in Romance Languages: No. 7). (FRE.). xxxvii, 203p. 1981. 59.00 (*90-272-1717-3*) J Benjamins Pubng Co.

Dougherty, Dean, jt. auth. see Bohner, Charles H.

Dougherty, Denis. John Elway. LC 98-19167. (Jam Sessions Ser.). (J). 1999. 14.95 (*1-57765-040-9*) ABDO Pub Co.

— Michael Jordan. LC 98-22325. (Jam Sessions Ser.). (J). 1998. write for info. (*1-57765-038-7*) ABDO Pub Co.

Dougherty, Dennis & Lexis Law Publishing Staff, eds. Annotated Revised Code of Washington 1998 Supplement, Vol. 1. 1998. write for info. (*0-327-07067-6*, 53087-14) LEXIS Pub.

Dougherty, Dennis, et al. The Financial Management of Intercollegiate Athletics Program. 45p. 1993. 29.95 (*0-614-17591-7*) NACUBO.

Dougherty, Devon. Crisis Communications: What Every Executive Needs to Know. 197p. 1992. 24.95 (*0-8027-1195-2*) Walker & Co.

Dougherty, Don. Bugs Bunny & Friends. (Look & Find Ser.). (Illus.). 24p. (J). (gr. k-6). 1996. lib. bdg. 14.95 (*1-56674-121-1*, HTS Bks) Forest Hse.

— Croakers. (Illus.). 192p. (Orig.). 1982. mass mkt. 4.95 (*0-446-37245-5*, Pub. by Warner Bks) Little.

Dougherty, Donald. Sams' Teach Yourself MS Frontpage 98 in a Week. 2nd ed. LC 97-68009. 480p. 1997. 29.99 (*1-57521-350-8*) Sams.

Dougherty, Dorothy P. How to Talk to Your Baby: A Guide to Maximizing Your Child's Language & Learning Skills. (Illus.). 140p. 1999. pap. 9.95 (*0-89529-932-1*, Avery) Penguin Putnam.

***Dougherty, Dru & Azevedo, Milton M., eds.** Multicultural Iberia: Language, Literature & Music. LC 99-22188. (Research Ser.: Vol. 103). 259p. 1999. pap. text 26.50 (*0-87725-003-0*) U of Cal IAS.

Dougherty, E. M. & Fragola, J. R. Human Reliability Analysis: A Systems Engineering Approach with Nuclear Power Plant Applications. LC 87-31703. 256p. 1988. 195.00 (*0-471-60614-6*) Wiley.

Dougherty, Edward, ed. Mathematical Morphology in Image Processing. LC 92-25560. (Optical Engineering Ser.: Vol. 34). (Illus.). 552p. 1992. text 215.00 (*0-8247-8724-2*) Dekker.

Dougherty, Edward R. Electronic Imaging Technology. LC 98-53084. 432p. 1999. pap. 48.00 (*0-8194-3037-4*) SPIE.

— An Introduction to Morphological Image Processing. (Tutorial Texts in Optical Engineering Ser.: Vol. TT 9). 150p. 1992. 42.00 (*0-8194-0845-X*) SPIE.

— Random Processes for Image & Signal Processing. LC 97-42909. (SPI/IEEE Series on Imaging Science & Engineering). 1998. 75.00 (*0-8194-2513-3*) SPIE.

Dougherty, Edward R., et al, eds. Statistical & Stochastic Methods for Image Processing, Vol. 2823. 296p. 1996. 66.00 (*0-8194-2211-8*) SPIE.

Dougherty, Edward R. & Astola, Jaakko. An Introduction to Nonlinear Image Processing. LC 93-1458. (Tutorial Texts in Optical Engineering Ser.: Vol. TT 16). 1994. 42.00 (*0-8194-1560-X*) SPIE.

— Nonlinear Filters for Image Processing. LC 99-17646. (Series on Imaging Science & Engineering). 16p. 1999. pap. 80.00 (*0-8194-3033-1*) SPIE.

Dougherty, Edward R. & Astola, Jaakko, eds. Mathematical Nonlinear Image Processing: A Special Issue of the Journal of Mathematical Imaging & Vision. LC 92-40136. 184p. (C). 1992. text 179.00 (*0-7923-9314-7*) Kluwer Academic.

Dougherty, Edward R. & Astola, Jaakko T., eds. Nonlinear Image Processing IX, Vol. 3304. 334p. 1998. 69.00 (*0-8194-2744-6*) SPIE.

— Nonlinear Image Processing VIII, Vol. 3026. 358p. 1997. 69.00 (*0-8194-2437-4*) SPIE.

***Dougherty, Edward R. & Astola, Jaakko T., eds.** Nonlinear Image Processing X. 348p. 1999. pap. text 72.00 (*0-8194-3117-6*) SPIE.

Dougherty, Edward R. & Laplante, Phillip A. Introduction to Real-Time Imaging. LC 94-44221. (Tutorial Texts in Optical Engineering Ser.: Vol. TT19). 1994. 20.00 (*0-8194-1789-0*) SPIE.

Dougherty, Edward R. & Society of Photo-Optical Instrumentation Engineers. Neural, Morphological & Stochastic Methods in Image & Signal Processing: 10-11 July, 1995, San Diego, California. LC 95-58583. vii, 304 p. 1995. write for info. (*0-8194-1927-3*) SPIE.

Dougherty, Edward R., jt. auth. see Giardina, Charles R.

Dougherty, Edward R., jt. auth. see Loce, Robert P.

Dougherty, Edward R., jt. auth. see Sinha, Divyendu.

Dougherty, Eugene P., ed. Temperature Control Principles for Process Engineers: A Guidebook for Chemical, Bio-Chemical, & Polymer Process Engineers Who Design Temperature Control Systems. LC 93-34840. 256p. 1993. 94.50 (*1-56990-152-X*) Hanser-Gardner.

Dougherty, F. C., tr. see Kazner, E., et al, eds.

Dougherty, Flavian, ed. The Meaning of Human Suffering. LC 81-6267. 349p. 1982. 45.95 (*0-89885-011-8*, Kluwer Acad Hman Sci) Kluwer Academic.

Dougherty, Gary R., ed. see Yacht Owners Register, Inc. Staff.

Dougherty, J. & McDermott, J. Academic Component of Priestly Formation: Average Superiority Will Do Faithful & Critical Reason in Theology. (Analecta Ser.: No. II). 26p. (C). 1988. pap. 3.50 (*0-910919-05-4*) Mariel Pubns.

Dougherty, J. J., jt. auth. see Rummel, K. G.

Dougherty, James. Walt Whitman & the Citizen's Eye. LC 92-14096. (Illus.). 344p. (C). 1993. text 47.50 (*0-8071-1772-2*) La State U Pr.

Dougherty, James E. The Horn of Africa: A Map of Political-Strategic Conflict. LC 82-80948. (Special Reports). 76p. 1982. 11.95 (*0-89549-041-2*) Inst Foreign Policy Anal.

— JCS Reorganization & U. S. Arms Control Policy. LC 86-166. (National Security Papers: No. 5). 32p. 1986. 7.50 (*0-89549-072-2*) Inst Foreign Policy Anal.

— The Secret Happiness of Marilyn Monroe. (Illus.) 166p. 1992. reprint ed. lib. bdg. 16.95 (*0-89966-908-5*) Buccaneer Bks.

Dougherty, James E. & Pfaltzgraff, Diane K. Eurocommunism & the Atlantic Alliance. LC 76-53142. (Special Reports). 66p. 1977. 11.95 (*0-89549-003-X*) Inst Foreign Policy Anal.

Dougherty, James E. & Pfaltzgraff, Robert L., Jr. Contending Theories of International Relations: A Comprehensive Survey. 3rd ed. 608p. (C). 1997 pap. text 60.00 (*0-06-041706-4*) Addson-Wesley Educ.

Dougherty, James E. & Pfaltzgraff, Robert L., Jr. Contending Theories of International Relations: A Comprehensive Survey. 4th ed. LC 96-14654. 608p. (C). 1997. pap. 60.00 (*0-673-99756-1*) Addson-Wesley Educ.

Dougherty, James E., jt. auth. see Cottrell, Alvin J.

Dougherty, James J. The Politics of Wartime Aid: American Economic Assistance to France & French Northwest Africa, 1940-1946, 71. LC 77-84770. (Contributions in American History Ser.: No. 71). 264p. 1978. 65.00 (*0-8371-9882-8*, DPW/, Greenwood Pr) Greenwood.

***Dougherty, James J.** Stone's Brigade on McPherson's Ridge. 2000. 29.95 (*1-58097-032-X*, 97032X) Combined Pub.

Dougherty, James L., Jr., jt. auth. see Mixon, John.

Dougherty, Janet W., ed. Directions in Cognitive Anthropology. fac. ed. LC 84-2494. (Illus.). 461p. 1985. pap. 143.00 (*0-7837-7621-7*, 204737300007) Bks Demand.

***Dougherty, Jayne H. & Robillard, Paula A., contrib. by.** The Spirit Sets Us Free, Catechist's Guide: Confirmation Preparation for Youth. (Illus.). 68p. (YA). (gr. 6-9). 1999. pap. 16.50 (*0-8215-5702-5*) Sadlier.

Dougherty, Jennifer D. & Hubbell, Loren L. Cost-Effective Control Systems: A New Paradigm. LC 92-34574. 1992. 31.95 (*0-915164-73-6*) NACUBO.

***Dougherty, John W.** Attending to Attendance. (Fastback Ser.: No. 450). 50p. 1999. pap. 3.00 (*0-87367-650-5*, FB# 450) Phi Delta Kappa.

Dougherty, John W. Ensuring Success for All Students: Programs That Work. LC 97-8717. 1997. write for info. (*1-56090-115-2*) Natl Middle Schl.

— Four Philosophies That Shape the Middle School. Walling, Donovan R., ed. LC 97-65148. (Fastback Ser.: Vol. 410). 46p. 1997. pap. 3.00 (*0-87367-610-6*) Phi Delta Kappa.

Dougherty, Joseph. Digby. 1986. pap. 5.25 (*0-8222-0308-1*) Dramatists Play.

***Dougherty, Jude P.** Western Creed, Western Identity: Essays in Legal & Social Philosophy. LC 99-49307. 2000. pap. 24.95 (*0-8132-0975-7*) Cath U Pr.

Dougherty, Jude P., ed. The Good Life & Its Pursuit. LC 83-62067. (Illus.). 296p. 1984. 12.95 (*0-913729-00-0*) Paragon Hse.

Dougherty, Jude P., jt. ed. see McLean, George F.

Dougherty, Karla & Rosenberg, Stephen J. Complete Idiot's Guide to First Aid. LC 95-83358. 352p. 1996. 16.95 (*0-02-861099-7*) Macmillan.

Dougherty, Karla, jt. auth. see Beakman, Claudia.

Dougherty, Karla, jt. auth. see Rosenberg, Stephen J.

Dougherty, Karla, jt. auth. see Senelick, Richard C.

Dougherty, Kevin J. The Contradictory College: The Conflicting Origins, Impacts, & Futures of the Community College. LC 93-30837. (SUNY Series, Frontiers in Education). 365p. (C). 1994. pap. text 22.95 (*0-7914-1956-8*) State U NY Pr.

***Dougherty, Lisa & Lambert, Julien.** Intravenous Therapy in Nursing Practice. LC 99-17032. 1999. write for info. (*0-443-05983-7*) Church.

Dougherty, Margaret M., et al. Instant Spelling Dictionary. 3rd ed. 384p. 1990. reprint ed. mass mkt. 4.99 (*0-446-36082-1*, Pub. by Warner Bks) Little.

— Instant Spelling Dictionary: 25,000 Words Spelled, Divided - Accented. LC 67-11788. 1993. 6.95 (*0-911744-01-0*) Career Pub IL.

Dougherty, Marijo, et al. Memory & Mourning: Shared Cultural Experience. LC 97-61742. (Illus.). 1997. write for info. (*0-910763-17-8*) U Albany Art Mus.

Dougherty, Mark, ed. Composting for Municipalities: Planning & Design Considerations. LC 98-48857. (NRAES Ser.: No. 94). (Illus.). 126p. 1998. pap. text 20.00 (*0-935817-20-4*, NRAES-94) NRAES.

— Field Guide to On-Farm Composting. LC 98-55088. 118p. 1999. pap. text 14.00 (*0-935817-39-5*, Nraes-114) NRAES.

Dougherty, Mark, et al. Liquid Manure Application Systems Design Manual, Vol. 89. (Illus.). 168p. 1998. pap. text 20.00 (*0-935817-24-7*, NRAES-89) NRAES.

Dougherty, Martin. Art of Surviving in Supply Teaching. LC 99-179994. 106p. 1998. pap. 25.95 (*1-85346-508-9*, Pub. by David Fulton) Taylor & Francis.

***Dougherty, Martin J.** Behind the Throne. LC 00-101159. 320p. 2000. pap. 19.95 (*0-9678832-0-2*) Highbridge Pr.

Dougherty, Mary A., ed. see Reese, Lyn.

Dougherty, Michael. Great Inspirations. 2nd rev. ed. 128p. (Orig.). 1996. per. 9.95 (*1-888550-01-5*) Champions Pubng.

— Montana Roadside Directory & Trip Planner. Gaffner, Corinne & Williams, Jennifer, eds. (Illus.). 304p. 1999. pap. 24.95 (*1-888550-06-6*, Kirke Ministries) Champions Pubng.

— To Steal a Kingdom: Probing Hawaiian History. 245p. (Orig.). 1995. pap. 12.95 (*0-9633484-0-X*) Island Style.

Dougherty, Michael A. Case Studies in Human Services Consultation. 2nd ed. LC 95-113391. 193p. 1994. pap. 12.75 (*0-534-25130-7*) Brooks-Cole.

Dougherty, Neil, et al. Illinois Corporations, Associations & Partnerships Law, 1993 Edition. 1993. 35.00 (*0-614-05842-2*, MICHIE) LEXIS Pub.

Dougherty, Neil J., ed. Physical Activity & Sport for the Secondary School Student. 4th rev. ed. (Illus.). 394p. (Orig.). 1993. pap. text 28.00 (*0-88314-526-X*, A526X) AAHPERD.

Dougherty, Neil J., IV, ed. Principles of Safety in Physical Education & Sport. 2nd ed. (Illus.). 256p. (Orig.). 1994. pap. text 35.00 (*0-88314-556-1*, A5561) AAHPERD.

Dougherty, Neil J., et al. Sport, Physical Activity, & the Law. LC 93-21763. (Illus.). 328p. 1993. text 40.00 (*0-87322-512-0*, BDOU0512) Human Kinetics.

Dougherty, Neil J., ed. see School & Community Safety Society of America Staff.

***Dougherty, Pamela M. & Radoms.** The Cognitive Rehabilitation Workbook. 336p. 1998. pap. 89.00 (*0-8342-1193-9*) Aspen Pub.

Dougherty, Pamela M. & Radomski, Mary V. The Cognitive Rehabilitation Workbook: A Dynamic Assessment for Adults with Brain Injury. 2nd ed. 330p. 1993. pap. 82.00 (*0-8342-0357-X*, 20357) Aspen Pub.

Dougherty, Percy H., ed. Environmental Karst. LC 84-80188. (Illus.). 178p. (Orig.). 1984. text 7.95 (*0-9613107-0-7*) Geo Speleo Pubns.

Dougherty, Phillip M., jt. auth. see Duryea, Mary L.

Dougherty, R. Duke, Jr. Free Men, Real Men: A Novel of American Masculinity. 220p. 1996. 20.95 (*0-9649864-0-X*) Marble Pubng.

Dougherty, Ray C. Natural Language Computing: An English Generative Grammar in Prolog. 400p. (C). 1994. pap. 39.95 (*0-8058-1526-0*); text 69.95 (*0-8058-1525-2*) L Erlbaum Assocs.

Dougherty, Raymond P. Archives from Erech, 2 vols., Set. LC 78-63529. (Goucher College Cuneiform Inscriptions Ser.: Vols. 1-2). reprint ed. 57.50 (*0-404-60140-5*) AMS Pr.

— Nabonidus & Belshazzar: A Study of the Closing Events of the Neo-Babylonian Empire. LC 78-63559. (Yale Oriental Series: Researches: No. 5). reprint ed. 41.50 (*0-404-60285-1*) AMS Pr.

— Records from Erech, Time of Nabonidus (555-538 B.C.) LC 78-63535. (Yale Oriental Series: Babylonian Texts: No. 6). (Illus.). 224p. reprint ed. 40.00 (*0-404-60256-8*) AMS Pr.

— The Sealand of Ancient Arabia. LC 78-63564. (Yale Oriental Series: Researches: No. 19). reprint ed. 40.00 (*0-404-60289-4*) AMS Pr.

— The Shirkutu of Babylonian Deities. LC 78-63548. (Yale Oriental Series: Researches: No. 5, Pt. 2). reprint ed. 25.00 (*0-404-60295-9*) AMS Pr.

Dougherty, Richard M., et al. Scientific Management of Library Operations. 2nd ed. LC 81-18200. 286p. 1982. 29.00 (*0-8108-1485-4*) Scarecrow.

Dougherty, Robert W. Experimental Surgery in Farm Animals. LC 81-3693. (Illus.). 156p. 1981. reprint ed. pap. 48.40 (*0-608-00052-3*, 206081800006) Bks Demand.

Dougherty, Sean T. Sunset by the Chain-Link Fence. 30p. 1993. 3.00 (*1-881168-38-7*) Red Dancefir.

***Dougherty, Sean Thomas.** Except by Falling. 84p. 2000. pap. 12.00 (*0-9671216-1-2*) Pinyon Pr CO.

Dougherty, T. Systems & Control: An Introduction to Linear Sampled & Nonlinear Systems. 672p. 1995. text 68.00 (*981-02-2346-3*) World Scientific Pub.

Dougherty, T. J., ed. Optical Methods for Tumor Treatment & Detection: Mechanisms & Techniques in Photodynamic Therapy. 1992. 20.00 (*0-8194-0791-7*, 1645) SPIE.

Dougherty, Terri. Barry Sanders. LC 98-7744. 1999. pap. 6.95 (*1-57765-339-4*) ABDO Pub Co.

— Brett Favre. LC 98-5174. 1999. pap. 6.95 (*1-57765-338-6*) ABDO Pub Co.

D

— Brett Favre. LC 98-5174. (Jam Sessions Ser.). (J). 1999. 13.98 (1-57765-036-0) ABDO Pub Co.

***Dougherty, Terri.** Derek Jeter. (Jam Session Ser.). 2000. pap. 6.95 (1-57765-367-X) ABDO Pub Co.

— Jeff Gordon LC 99-25021. (Jam Session Ser.). 1999. 6.95 (1-57765-357-2) ABDO Pub Co.

Dougherty, Terri. Jeff Gordon. LC 99-25021. (Jam Session Ser.). (Illus.). 32p. 1999. lib. bdg. 19.93 (1-57765-355-6, ABDO & Dghtrs) ABDO Pub Co.

— John Elway. LC 98-19167. 1999. pap. 6.95 (1-57765-342-4) ABDO Pub Co.

— Kevin Garnett. 1999. pap. 6.95 (1-57765-341-6) ABDO Pub Co.

***Dougherty, Terri.** Kurt Warner. LC 00-38611. (Jam Session Ser.). (Illus.). (J). 2000. pap. write for info. (1-57765-428-5) ABDO Pub Co.

Dougherty, Terri. Lisa Leslie. (Jam Sessions Ser.). 1999. pap. text 6.95 (1-57765-345-9) ABDO Pub Co.

— Mark McGwire. LC 98-43248. 1999. 6.95 (1-57765-347-5) ABDO Pub Co.

***Dougherty, Terri.** Mark McGwire. LC 98-43248. (Jam Session Ser.). (Illus.). 32p. 1999. lib. bdg. 19.93 (1-57765-349-1, ABDO & Dghtrs) ABDO Pub Co.

— Mia Hamm. LC 99-41950. (Jam Session Ser.). 2000. pap. 6.95 (1-57765-365-3) ABDO Pub Co.

Dougherty, Terri. Michael Jordan. LC 98-22325. 1999. pap. 6.95 (1-57765-340-8) ABDO Pub Co.

— Sammy Sosa. LC 98-43185. 1999. 6.95 (1-57765-346-7) ABDO Pub Co.

***Dougherty, Terri.** Sammy Sosa. LC 98-43185. (Jam Session Ser.). (Illus.). 32p. (J). 1999. lib. bdg. 19.93 (1-57765-348-3, ABDO & Dghtrs) ABDO Pub Co.

Dougherty, Terri. Tara Lipinski. LC 98-21920. (Jam Sessions Ser.). (J). 1999. 16.95 (1-57765-312-2) ABDO Pub Co.

***Dougherty, Terri.** Tara Lipinski, 1. LC 98-21920. (Jam Sessions Ser.). 1999. pap. text 6.95 (1-57765-344-0) ABDO Pub Co.

— Terrell Davis LC 99-23954. (Jam Session Ser.). 1999. 6.95 (1-57765-356-4) ABDO Pub Co.

Dougherty, Terri. Tiger Woods. LC 98-24548. 1999. pap. 6.95 (1-57765-343-2) ABDO Pub Co.

— Tiger Woods. LC 98-24548. (Jam Sessions Ser.). (J). 1999. 16.95 (1-57765-041-7) ABDO Pub Co.

Dougherty, Terry. Barry Sanders. LC 98-7744. (Jam Sessions Ser.). (J). 1998. write for info. (1-57765-037-9) ABDO Pub Co.

— Kevin Garnett. LC 98-7626. (Jam Sessions Ser.). (J). 1998. 14.95 (1-57765-039-5) ABDO Pub Co.

***Dougherty, Terry.** Lisa Leslie. LC 98-27129. (Jam Sessions Ser.). (J). 1999. 14.95 (1-57765-313-0) ABDO Pub Co.

***Dougherty, Thomas J., ed.** Optical Methods for Tumor Treatment & Detection. 120p. 1999. pap. text 62.00 (0-8194-3062-5) SPIE.

Dougherty, Thomas J., ed. Optical Methods for Tumor Treatment & Detection Vol. 2972: Mechanisms & Techniques in Photodynamic Therapy VI. 194p. 1997. 69.00 (0-8194-2383-1) SPIE.

— Optical Methods for Tumor Treatment & Detections Vol. 3247: Mechanisms & Techniques in Photodynamic Therapy VII. 162p. 1998. 69.00 (0-8194-2686-5) SPIE.

Dougherty, Thomas J., jt. ed. see Henderson, Barbara W.

Dougherty, William C. Dougherty: Family History of James Dougherty & Lineage of Descent. 50p. 1997. reprint ed. pap. 10.00 (0-8328-8340-9); reprint ed. lib. bdg. 20.00 (0-8328-8339-5) Higginson Bk Co.

Dougherty, William H., tr. see Golovin, I. N.

***Doughman, Gordon.** Programming the Motorola M68HC12 Family. (Illus.). 576p. 2000. pap. 39.95 (0-929392-67-1, Pub. by Annabooks) Coriolis Grp.

***Doughman, Paula & Malott, Valerie J.** The "At Home" Childbirth Education Program: A Complete Course for the Childbearing Year. (Illus.). 65p. 1999. 59.95 incl. audio, VHS, cd-rom (0-9677660-0-1) Childbirth Inst.

— The "At Home" Childbirth Education Program: Student Manual. (Illus.). 65p. 1999. student ed. 12.95 (0-9677660-1-X) Childbirth Inst.

***Doughten, Russell S., Jr., et al.** Share Your Faith Seminar Workbook. (Illus.). 120p. (YA). 2000. pap. 11.95 (1-888568-56-9) R Doughten Films.

Doughter, William N., jt. auth. see De Salas, Francis.

Doughtery, Casey, ed. see Geffken, Jack W.

Doughtery, Mary A., ed. see Reese, Lyn.

Doughtery, Rose Mary. Group Spiritual Direction: Community for Discernment. LC 95-20356. 128p. (Orig.). 1995. 8.95 (0-8091-3598-1) Paulist Pr.

Doughtie, Edward. Lyrics from English Airs, 1596-1622. LC 78-115474. 679p. reprint ed. pap. 200.00 (0-7837-6082-5, 205912800007) Bks Demand.

Doughtie, Edward, ed. Liber Lilliati. LC 84-40489. (Illus.). 232p. 1985. 40.00 (0-87413-267-3) U Delaware Pr.

Doughton, K. J. Metallica Unbound. (Illus.). 176p. (Orig.). 1993. mass mkt. 15.99 (0-446-39486-6, Pub. by Warner Bks) Little.

Doughty. Urinary & Fecal Incontinence: Nursing Management. 2nd ed. LC 99-40801. (Illus.). 456p. (C). (gr. 13). 2000. text 41.95 (0-8151-2912-2, 31812) Mosby Inc.

— Urinary & Fecal Incontinence: Nursing Management (IAET) (Illus.). 296p. (C). (gr. 13). 1991. text 45.00 (0-8016-1444-9, 01444) Mosby Inc.

Doughty, Andrew & Friedman, Harriett. Hawaii - The Big Island Revealed: The Ultimate Guidebook. 2nd ed. LC 98-61055. (Illus.). 272p. (Orig.). 1999. pap. 14.95 (0-9639429-6-4) Wizard Pubns.

— The Ultimate Kauai Guidebook. 3rd ed. LC 97-61168. (Illus.). 216p. (Orig.). 1998. pap. 12.95 (0-9639429-4-8) Wizard Pubns.

***Doughty, Anne.** Stranger in the Place. large type ed. 368p. 1999. 31.99 (0-7089-4069-2) Ulverscroft.

Doughty, Arthur G., jt. auth. see Shortt, Adam.

Doughty, Arthur G., ed. see Knox, John.

Doughty, Bix L. Noah & the Great Ark. (J). (gr. k up). 1978. 7.00 (0-87602-163-1) Anchorage.

Doughty, Carolyn & McGrath, Jim. The Winning Edge: A Guide for College Bound Athletes. 2nd ed. 120p. (Orig.). (YA). (gr. 9-12). 1988. pap. 15.00 (0-9620914-1-3) Sports Plan Consult.

Doughty, Carolyn, ed. see Schriebman, Robert S.

Doughty, Catherine & Williams, Jessica, eds. Focus on Form in Classroom Second Language Acquisition. (Cambridge Applied Linguistics Ser.). (Illus.). 320p. (C). 1998. text 64.95 (0-521-62390-1) Cambridge U Pr.

***Doughty, Catherine & Williams, Jessica, eds.** Focus on Form in Classroom Second Language Acquisition. LC 97-46568. (Cambridge Applied Linguistics Ser.). (Illus.). 320p. (C). 1998. pap. text 22.95 (0-521-62551-3) Cambridge U Pr.

Doughty, Charles M. Adam Cast Forth. LC 75-41078. reprint ed. 31.50 (0-404-14535-3) AMS Pr.

— Mansoul or the Riddle of the World. 1971. reprint ed. 29.00 (0-403-00574-4) Scholarly.

— Die Offenbarung Arabiens (Arabia Deserta) (Illus.). 613p. reprint ed. write for info. (0-318-71501-5) G Olms Pubs.

— Travels in Arabia Deserta, 2 vols. xxxiv, 1345p. reprint ed. write for info. (0-318-71502-3) G Olms Pubs.

— Wandering in Arabia, Vol. 2. (C). 1988. 135.00 (1-85077-191-X, Pub. by Darf Pubs Ltd) St Mut.

Doughty, Charles M., ed. Wandering in Arabia, Vol. 1. (C). 1988. 150.00 (1-85077-190-1, Pub. by Darf Pubs Ltd) St Mut.

***Doughty, Charles W.** God Forbid... That I Should Sin & Not Pray. Cussen, Debra T., ed. 181p. 2000. 8.00 (0-9700216-0-7) Christian Kingdom.

***Doughty, Chris.** Field Guide to the Birds of the Solomons, Vanuatu & Caledonia. (Illus.). 1999. pap. 26.95 (0-7136-4690-X) A & C Blk.

Doughty, D. H., et al, eds. New Materials for Batteries & Fuel Cells Vol. 575: Materials Research Society Symposium Proceedings. LC 99-85708. 439p. 2000. text 73.00 (1-55899-482-3) Materials Res.

***Doughty, David P.** Dreams: There Is More Here Than What We Just See & We Must Deal with It. 112p. 1999. pap. 10.00 (0-939513-28-5) Joy Pub SJC.

Doughty, David P. Visions: Now, Will You Believe? 128p. 1998. pap. 10.00 (0-939513-27-7) Joy Pub SJC.

Doughty, Dick & Aydi, Mohammed E. Gaza: Legacy of Occupation - a Photographer's Journey. LC 94-45892. (Books for a World That Works). (Illus.). 232p. (Orig.). 1995. pap. 15.95 (1-56549-044-4) Kumarian Pr.

Doughty, Dorothy, jt. auth. see Bryant, Ruth.

Doughty, Dorothy B. Gastrointestinal Disorders. (Illus.). 368p. (C). (gr. 13). 1993. text 37.00 (0-8016-2096-1, 02096) Mosby Inc.

Doughty, Doug, jt. auth. see Lazenby, Roland.

Doughty, Francis W. Mirrikh: or A Woman from Mars. Reginald, R. & Menville, Douglas A., eds. LC 75-46267. (Supernatural & Occult Fiction Ser.). (Illus.). 1976. lib. bdg. 23.95 (0-405-08125-1) Ayer.

Doughty, Geoffrey H. New Haven Railroad in the Streamline Era. (Illus.). 128p. 1998. 33.95 (1-883089-33-6) TLC VA.

***Doughty, Geoffrey H.** New Haven Railroad's Streamline Passenger Fleet, 1934-1953. (Illus.). 160p. 2000. 28.95 (1-883089-52-2, 130611AE, Pub. by TLC VA) Motorbooks Intl.

— New York Central Stations & Terminals. (Illus.). 160p. 2000. 28.95 (1-883089-47-6, 130061AE, Pub. by TLC VA) Motorbooks Intl.

Doughty, Geoffrey H. New York Central System: Great Steel Fleet 1948-1968. rev. ed. (Illus.). 160p. 1999. 28.95 (1-883089-46-8, Pub. by TLC VA) Motorbooks Intl.

— New York Central's Great Steel Fleet, 1948-1967. (Illus.). 120p. 1996. 22.95 (1-883089-18-2) TLC VA.

Doughty, Geofrey J. New York Central & the Trains of the Future. (Illus.). 112p. 1997. 25.95 (1-883089-27-1) TLC VA.

***Doughty, Harold.** The Penguin Guide to American Law Schools. LC 98-28969. 307p. 1999. pap. 17.95 (0-14-046994-X) Viking Penguin.

***Doughty, Harold R.** Guide to American Business Schools. LC 99-53076. 288p. 2000. pap. 17.95 (0-14-046995-8) Viking Penguin.

Doughty, Harold R. Guide to American Graduate Schools. 8th ed. xxvi, 635p. 1997. pap. 24.95 (0-14-046986-9) Viking Penguin.

Doughty, Heather. Ski British Columbia. 192p. 1991. pap. 9.95 (0-919433-94-4) Lone Pine.

Doughty, Howard. Francis Parkman. 420p. 1983. pap. 15.50 (0-674-31775-0) HUP.

Doughty, J. Geoffrey. New York Central's Lightweight Passenger Cars, Trains & Travel. (Illus.). 160p. 1996. 28.95 (1-883089-25-5) TLC VA.

Doughty, John, ed. see Clayton, K. Marshall.

***Doughty, Ken.** Business Continuity Planning: Protecting Your Organization's Life. LC 00-44202. (Best Practices Ser.). 2000. write for info. (0-8493-0907-7) Auerbach.

***Doughty, Louise.** Dance With Me. 256p. 2000. per. 12.00 (0-684-86842-3) S&S Trade.

— An English Murder. 240p. 2000. 23.00 (0-7867-0757-7, Pub. by Carroll & Graf) Publishers Group.

Doughty, Mark, ed. see Baker, Georgette.

***Doughty, Michael.** Ocular Therapeutics & Pharmacology: A Primary & Shared Care Guide. (Illus.). 224p. 2000. pap. 70.00 (0-7506-4520-2) Buttrwrth-Heinemann.

Doughty, Oswald. Perturbed Spirit: The Life & Personality of Samuel Taylor Coleridge. LC 78-66792. 365p. 1981. 45.00 (0-8386-2353-0) Fairleigh Dickinson.

Doughty, Robert, et al. The American Civil War: The Emergence of Total Warfare, Chpts. 10-14. 192p. (C). 1996. pap. text 21.16 (0-669-41680-0) HM Trade Div.

— American Military History & the Evolution of Western Warfare, Chpts. 4-5, 10-14, & 16-31. 793p. (C). 1996. pap. text 35.96 (0-669-41683-5) HM Trade Div.

— Limited Warfare in the Nuclear Age, Chpts. 27-31. 192p. (C). 1996. pap. text 21.16 (0-669-41682-7) HM Trade Div.

— Warfare in the Western World Vol. 1: Military Operations from 1600 to 1871. 532p. (C). 1996. text 37.16 (0-669-20939-2) HM Trade Div.

— Warfare in the Western World Vol. 2: Military Operations since 1871. LC 94-74302. 564p. (C). 1996. text 37.16 (0-669-20940-6) HM Trade Div.

— World War II: Total Warfare Around the Globe, Chpts. 21-26. 224p. (C). 1996. pap. text 21.16 (0-669-41681-9) HM Trade Div.

Doughty, Robert A. The Breaking Point: Sedan & the Fall of France, 1940. LC 90-32505. xiv, 374p. (C). 1990. lib. bdg. 42.50 (0-208-02281-3, Archon Bks) Shoe String.

— The Seeds of Disaster: The Development of French Army Doctrine, 1919-1939. LC 85-20473. 232p. (C). 1985. lib. bdg. 35.00 (0-208-02096-9, Archon Bks) Shoe String.

Doughty, Robin W. The Mockingbird. LC 88-736. (Corrie Herring Hooks Ser.: No. 11). (Illus.). 80p. (YA). (gr. 10-12). 1988. 17.95 (0-292-75099-4) U of Tex Pr.

— The Mockingbird. (Corrie Herring Hooks Ser.). (Illus.). 80p. 1995. pap. 8.95 (0-292-71584-6) U of Tex Pr.

— The Return of the Whooping Crane. (Corrie Herring Hooks Ser.: No. 15). (Illus.). 192p. 1989. 24.95 (0-292-79041-4) U of Tex Pr.

— Wildlife & Man in Texas: Environmental Change & Conservation. LC 83-45103. (Illus.). 268p. 1989. pap. 16.95 (0-89096-416-5) Tex A&M Univ Pr.

Doughty, Samuel. Basic Mechanics of Machines. LC 87-23042. 496p. 1988. text 109.95 (0-471-84276-1) Wiley.

— Solve It: Computer-Aided Mathematics for Science & Engineering. LC 95-30439. (Illus.). 162p. 1995. 29.95 (0-88415-266-9, 5266) Gulf Pub.

Doughty, Sherri, jt. auth. see Yohey, Fred.

Doughty, Sherri, jt. ed. see Baltzell, D. Catherine.

Doughty, Stephen. Portraits of Darkness. (Orig.). 1989. pap. 2.50 (1-55673-104-3, 9815) CSS OH.

Doughty, Stephen V. Discovering Community: A Meditation on Community in Christ. LC 98-20639. 176p. 1999. pap. 12.00 (0-8358-0870-X) Upper Room Bks.

Doughty, W. L., ed. The Prayers of Susanna Wesley. 80p. 1984. reprint ed. pap. 4.95 (0-310-36351-9, 12368P) Zondervan.

Doughty, Wayne D. Crimson Mocassins. LC 66-11497. (Trophy Bk.). 224p. (YA). (gr. 7 up). 1972. pap. 2.95 (0-06-440015-8, HarpTrophy) HarpC Child Bks.

Dougill, John. Oxford in English Literature: The Making, & Undoing, of "The English Athens" LC 98-8954. (Illus.). 400p. 1998. 34.50 (0-472-10784-4, 10784) U of Mich Pr.

Dougill, Peter & Knott, Richard. The Primary Language Book. 2nd ed. LC 92-33218. 1993. 31.95 (0-335-19021-9) OpUniv Pr.

Douglas. Automotive Emissions Trainer's Companion. (IT-Automotive Technology Ser.). 1996. teacher ed. 250.00 (0-8273-7875-0) Delmar.

— British Drama Explication: Restoration to Contemporary. 1995. 55.00 (0-8161-7333-8, G K Hall & Co) Mac Lib Ref.

— Humid Landforms. (Australian National University Press Ser.). 1995. text 20.00 (0-08-033019-3, Pergamon Pr); pap. text 10.00 (0-08-033018-5, Pergamon Pr) Elsevier.

Douglas. Inorganic & Microscale, Set. 3rd ed. 1312p. 1997. text 105.00 (0-471-25571-8) Wiley.

— John Douglas's Guide to the Chicago Police Exam. 432p. 2000. pap. 35.00 (0-684-85507-0) S&S Trade.

Douglas. John Douglas's Guide to the Los Angeles Police Exam. 352p. 2000. pap. 35.00 (0-684-85508-9) S&S Trade.

— Modern Real Estate & Mortgage Forms. rev. ed. 1008p. 1986. 130.00 (0-88712-578-6); suppl. ed. 54.00 (0-7913-1232-1); suppl. ed. 68.00 (0-685-55839-8) Warren Gorham & Lamont.

— The Secretarial Dental Assistant. (Dental Assisting Procedures Ser.). 1976. teacher ed. 9.00 (0-8273-0350-5) Delmar.

— Taliswoman, No. 3. 1999. text 23.95 (0-312-85148-0) St Martin.

— Taxation in Britain Since 1660. LC 99-18160. 1999. text 39.95 (0-312-22217-3) St Martin.

Douglas & Teglovic. Advanced Application Programming Using Cobol. 1994. pap. 64.95 (0-87393-280-3) Dame Pubns.

— Application Programming Using Cobol. 1994. pap. 64.95 (0-87393-250-1) Dame Pubns.

— Comprehensive Application Programming Using Cobol. 1994. pap. 73.95 (0-87393-291-9) Dame Pubns.

Douglas, et al. Four Irish Plays. (Short Play Ser.). 1982. pap. 3.95 (0-912262-80-X) Proscenium.

Douglas, jt. auth. see Flenley, David C.

Douglas, jt. auth. see Strumpf.

Douglas, ed. see Cicero, Marcus Tullius.

Douglas, A., jt. auth. see Brown, H.

Douglas, A. E., ed. see Cicero, Marcus Tullius.

Douglas, A. H. An Approach to Engineering Mathematics. 1971. pap. 76.00 (0-08-016016-6, Pub. by Pergamon Repr) Franklin.

Douglas, A. S., jt. auth. see Allan, T. M.

Douglas, Ab. On Foreign Assignment: The Inside Story of Journalism's Elite Corps. (Illus.). 191p. (Orig.). 1993. pap. 17.95 (1-55059-057-X) Temeron Bks.

Douglas, Adam. The Beast Within. 352p. 1994. mass mkt. 5.99 (0-380-72264-X, Avon Bks) Morrow Avon.

Douglas, Aileen. Uneasy Sensations: Smollett & the Body. LC 95-1786. 232p. 1995. 29.95 (0-226-16051-3); pap. text 14.95 (0-226-16052-1) U Ch Pr.

Douglas, Alan. The Electronic Musical Instrument Manual. 1977. lib. bdg. 59.95 (0-8490-1755-6) Gordon Pr.

— Radio Manufacturers of the 1920s Vol. 1: A-C Dayton to J. B. Ferguson, Inc. (Illus.). 225p. 1988. pap. 24.95 (1-886606-02-1) Sonoran Pub.

***Douglas, Alan.** Radio Manufacturers of the 1920's Vol. 3: RCA to Zenith. (Illus.). 285p. 1999. pap. 29.95 (1-886606-04-8) Sonoran Pub.

Douglas, Alan. Radio Manufacturers of the 1920's, 3 vols., Set. (Illus.). 1988. pap. 84.85 (1-886606-05-6) Sonoran Pub.

— Radio Manufacturers of the 1920's, Vol. 2. 266p. 1994. pap. 29.95 (1-886606-00-5) Sonoran Pub.

Douglas, Alban. Cien Lecciones Biblicas.Tr. of One Hundred Bible Lessons. write for info. (0-614-28323-X) Editorial Unilit.

Douglas, Alfred. The Autobiography of Lord Alfred Douglas. (Select Bibliographies Reprint Ser.). 1977. 21.95 (0-8369-5421-1) Ayer.

— The Autobiography of Lord Alfred Douglas. 1994. reprint ed. lib. bdg. 79.00 (0-7812-0316-3) Rprt Serv.

— The Autobiography of Lord Alfred Douglas. LC 71-144979. (Illus.). 340p. 1972. reprint ed. 69.00 (0-403-00796-8) Scholarly.

— The City of the Soul, 1899. LC 95-25529. (Decadents, Symbolists, Anti-Decadents Ser.). 1996. 48.00 (1-85477-141-8) Continuum.

— The Collected Poems of Lord Alfred Douglas. LC 75-41079. reprint ed. 29.50 (0-404-14659-7) AMS Pr.

— The Collected Satires of Lord Alfred Douglas. LC 75-41081. reprint ed. 27.50 (0-404-14730-5) AMS Pr.

— Extra-Sensory Powers: A Century of Psychical Research. LC 77-77807. 392p. 1977. 22.95 (0-87951-064-1, Pub. by Overlook Pr) Penguin Putnam.

— Extra-Sensory Powers: A Century of Psychical Research. LC 77-77807. 392p. 1983. pap. 10.95 (0-87951-160-5, Pub. by Overlook Pr) Penguin Putnam.

— Halcyon Days: Contributions to the Spirit Lamp. Wintermans, Caspar, ed. (Illus.). 48p. 1995. 60.00 (0-930126-49-1) Typographeum.

— Two Loves & Other Poems: A Selection. LC 89-81154. 63p. 1990. 10.00 (0-9624631-1-6) Bennett & Kitchel.

Douglas, Alfred, tr. see Beardsley, Aubrey & Wilde, Oscar.

Douglas, Alfred B. Collected Poems. (BCL1-PR English Literature Ser.). 125p. 1992. reprint ed. lib. bdg. 69.00 (0-7812-7519-9) Rprt Serv.

Douglas, Allen. Cien Lecciones Biblicas.Tr. of One Hundred Bible Lessons. (SPA.). pap. 15.99 (0-7899-0055-6, 497540) Editorial Unilit.

— From Fascism to Libertarian Communism: Georges Valois Against the Third Republic. LC 92-15114. 1992. 50.00 (0-520-07678-8, Pub. by U CA Pr) Cal Prin Full Svc.

Douglas, Allen & Malti-Douglas, Fedwa. Arab Comic Strips: Politics of an Emerging Mass Culture. LC 93-103. (Illus.). 296p. 1994. 39.95 (0-253-31814-9) Ind U Pr.

Douglas, Andrew. British Charitable Gambling 1956-1994: Towards a National Lottery. 320p. (C). 1995. text 80.00 (0-485-11472-0, Pub. by Athlone Pr) Humanities.

— A Trainer's Companion to Advanced Automotive Emissions Systems. (IT-Automotive Technology Ser.). 689p. 1996. teacher ed. 395.00 incl. VHS (0-8273-7876-9) Delmar.

Douglas, Andrew B., ed. Aviation Consumer's Used Aircraft Guide, 2 vols., Set. 7th ed. 1048p. 1995. 59.95 (1-879620-40-5) Belvoir Pubns.

Douglas, Andrew H. The Philosophy & Psychology of Pietro Pomponazzi. Douglas, C. & Hardie, R. P., eds. x, 318p. 1974. reprint ed. 57.20 (3-487-05323-3) G Olms Pubs.

Douglas, Andrew M. Church & School in Scotland. 104p. (C). 1988. pap. text 25.00 (0-7152-0584-6) St Mut.

Douglas, Ann. After. LC 89-25277. 72p. 1991. 16.95 (0-932576-80-X); pap. 9.95 (0-932576-81-8) Breitenbush Bks.

— Baby Science: How Babies Really Work! (Illus.). 32p. (J). (ps-3). 1998. 18.95 (1-895688-83-3, Pub. by Owl Bks) Firefly Bks Ltd.

***Douglas, Ann.** Baby Science: How Babies Really Work! (Illus.). 32p. (J). (ps-3). 1998. pap. 6.95 (1-895688-84-1, Pub. by Owl Bks) Firefly Bks Ltd.

— Before You Were Born: The Inside Story! (Illus.). 32p. (J). (ps-3). 2000. 18.95 (1-894379-01-2, Pub. by GDPB); pap. 6.95 (1-894379-02-0, Pub. by GDPB) Firefly Bks Ltd.

Douglas, Ann. The Family Tree Detective: Cracking the Case of Your Family's Story. LC 98-93228. (Illus.). 48p. (J). (gr. 2-7). 1999. 19.95 (1-895688-88-4, Owl) H Holt & Co.

— The Family Tree Detective: Cracking the Case of Your Family's Story. LC 98-93228. (Illus.). 48p. (J). (gr. 2-7). 1999. pap. 9.95 (1-895688-89-2, Owl) H Holt & Co.

— The Feminization of American Culture. LC 98-16732. 416p. 1998. pap. 15.00 (0-374-52558-7) FS&G.

***Douglas, Ann.** The Incredible Shrinking Woman: A Girlfriend's Guide to Losing Weight. 240p. 2000. 18.95 (0-13-017838-1) P-H.

Douglas, Ann. Terrible Honesty: Mongrel Manhattan in the 1920s. LC 94-10892. 606p. 1995. text 27.50 (0-374-11620-2) FS&G.

— Terrible Honesty: Mongrel Manhattan in the 1920s. 608p. 1996. pap. 15.00 (0-374-52462-9) FS&G.

— The Unofficial Guide to Childcare. LC 99-231513. 400p. 1998. pap. 22.95 (0-02-862457-2) Macmillan.

***Douglas, Ann & Sussman, John R.** Trying Again: A Guide to Pregnancy after Miscarriage, Stillbirth, & Infant Loss. 2000. pap. 16.95 (0-87833-182-4) Taylor Pub.

***Douglas, Ann & Weltman, Barbara.** Complete Idiot's Guide to Raising Money-Smart Canadian Kids. 352p. 2000. pap. write for info. (0-13-086882-5, Prentice Hall) P-H.

Douglas, Ann, ed. & intro. see Rowson, Susanna Haswell.

D

An Asterisk (*) at the beginning of an entry indicates that the title is appearing for the first time.

D

An Asterisk (*) at the beginning of an entry indicates that the title is appearing for the first time.

Douglas, David C. & Greenaway, G. W., eds. English Historical Documents, 1042-1189, Vol. 2. (Illus.). 1110p. (C). 1996. 265.00 (*0-415-14367-5*, D2251) Routledge.

Douglas, Davison M. Reading, Writing, & Race: The Desegregation of the Charlotte Schools. LC 94-39347. 1995. pap. text 18.95 (*0-8078-4529-9*); lib. bdg. 49.95 (*0-8078-2216-7*) U of NC Pr.

— School Busing - Constitutional & Political Developments Vol. 2: The Public Debate over School Busing & Attempts to Restrict Its Use, 2 vols. LC 94-27194. (Controversies in Constitutional Law Ser.). 992p. 1994. 130.00 (*0-8153-1853-7*) Garland.

Douglas, Davison M & Murray, Pauli. States' Laws on Race & Color. LC 96-9128. (Studies in the Legal History of the South). 1997. 65.00 (*0-8203-1883-3*) U of Ga Pr.

Douglas, Davison M., jt. ed. see Devins, Neal.

Douglas, Debbie, et al, eds. Ma-Ka: Diasporic Juks: Contemporary Writing by Queers of African Descent. LC 98-140945. 264p. 1997. pap. write for info. (*1-896705-14-6*) Sister Vis Pr.

Douglas, Deborah. Gone for the Day: Family Fun in Central Texas. LC 95-16181. (Illus.). 190p. (Orig.). (C). 1995. pap. 12.95 (*0-89096-650-8*) Tex A&M Univ Pr.

— Stirring Prose: Cooking with Texas Authors. LC 98-10810. (Illus.). 226p. 1998. 19.95 (*0-89096-829-2*) Tex A&M Univ Pr.

Douglas, Deborah G. United States Women in Aviation, 1940-1985. Orig. Title: Smithsonian Studies in Air & Space, No. 7. (Illus.). 152p. 1991. pap. 13.95 (*0-87474-382-6*) Smithsonian.

Douglas, Derek, jt. auth. see Armstrong, Gary.

Douglas, Derek, jt. auth. see Hastings, Scott.

Douglas, Diane & Van Wyk, Dirk. The Drawing Process: Rendering. 160p. (C). 1993. pap. text 36.60 (*0-13-219833-9*) P-H.

Douglas, Diane, et al. Jean Jongeward in the Northwest Design Tradition. LC 95-23038. (Illus.). 71p. 1996. pap. 18.95 (*0-295-97496-6*) U of Wash Pr.

Douglas, Dianne, tr. see Ribeyro, Julio R.

Douglas, Donald, jt. auth. see Gaddie, Ronald E.

Douglas, Donna I. God Stories: They're So Amazing, Only God Could Make Them Happen. 256p. 1999. 18.95 (*1-892016-11-7*) Starburst.

Douglas, Dorothy, jt. auth. see Roth, Julius A.

Douglas, Dorothy J. & Roth, Julian A. Pre-Hospital Emergency Care by Ambulance Services. 300p. 1989. text 39.50 (*0-8290-2391-7*) Irvington.

Douglas, Dorothy W. Transitional Economic Systems: The Polish-Czech Example. LC 73-178717. 407p. reprint ed. pap. 126.20 (*0-608-15882-8*, 203076100070) Bks Demand.

Douglas, Drake. Horrors! (Illus.). 400p. 1991. reprint ed. pap. 13.95 (*0-87951-349-7*, Pub. by Overlook Pr) Penguin Putnam.

Douglas, Drusilla. Crisis in Callasay. large type ed. 288p. 1996. 23.99 (*0-263-14643-X*, Pub. by Mills & Boon) Ulverscroft.

— A Double Dose. large type ed. 1995. 11.50 (*0-7505-0820-5*, Pub. by Mgna Lrg Print) Ulverscroft.

— Surgeon's Daughter. large type ed. 1994. 27.99 (*0-7505-0749-7*, Pub. by Mgna Lrg Print) Ulverscroft.

***Douglas-Duncan, David.** Picasso Paints a Portrait. (Illus.). 62p. 2000. reprint ed. text 30.00 (*0-7881-9009-1*) DIANE Pub.

Douglas, E. Chomolungma Sings the Blues: Travels Round Everest. (Illus.). 225p. 1999. text 40.00 (*0-09-476390-9*, Pub. by Constable & Co) Trafalgar.

***Douglas, Edward M. & Douglas, Sharon.** The Blended Family: Achieving Peace & Harmony in the Christian Home. LC 00-100573. 2000. pap. 14.95 (*1-57736-179-2*) Providence Hse.

Douglas, Edward M., jt. auth. see Rose, David.

Douglas, Eileen. Biography, Elizabeth Swift Brengle. 1990. reprint ed. 5.95 (*0-86544-060-3*) Salv Army Suppl South.

Douglas, Elizabeth. Scottish Kings & Queens. (Scottie Bks.). (Illus.). 40p. (J). 1998. pap. 8.95 (*0-11-495753-3*, Pub. by Statnry Office) Seven Hills Bk.

Douglas, Ellen. Apostles of Light. LC 94-32158. (Banner Bk.). 320p. 1994. reprint ed. pap. 16.95 (*0-87805-738-2*); reprint ed. lib. bdg. 37.50 (*0-87805-737-4*) U Pr of Miss.

— Black Cloud, White Cloud. limited ed. LC 89-5524. (Author & Artist Ser.). (Illus.). 260p. 1989. reprint ed. 60.00 (*0-87805-397-2*) U Pr of Miss.

— Black Cloud, White Cloud. LC 89-5524. (Author & Artist Ser.). (Illus.). 260p. 1989. reprint ed. 25.00 (*0-87805-393-X*) U Pr of Miss.

— Can't Quit You, Baby. 272p. 1989. pap. 12.95 (*0-14-012102-1*, Penguin Bks) Viking Penguin.

— A Family's Affairs. LC 96-50169. (Voices of the South Ser.). 456p. 1997. pap. 14.95 (*0-8071-2163-0*) La State U Pr.

— Lifetime Burning. LC 82-40141. (Voices of the South Ser.). 212p. 1995. pap. 10.95 (*0-8071-2007-3*) La State U Pr.

— The Rock Cried Out. LC 79-87474. (Voices of the South Ser.). 350p. 1994. pap. 11.95 (*0-8071-1931-8*) La State U Pr.

— Truth: Four Stories I Am Finally Old Enough to Tell. LC 98-7238. 238p. 1998. 18.95 (*1-56512-214-3*) Algonquin Bks.

***Douglas, Ellen.** Truth: Four Stories I Am Finally Old Enough to Tell. 240p. 1999. pap. 12.95 (*0-452-28102-4*, Plume) Dutton Plume.

— Where the Dreams Cross. (Voices of the South Ser.). 320p. 2000. pap. 15.95 (*0-8071-2639-X*) La State U Pr.

Douglas, Elmer, tr. see Al-Sabbagh, Ibn.

Douglas, Elmer H., tr. The Mystical Teachings of Al-Shadhili: Including His Life, Prayers, Letters, & Followers. A Translation from the Arabic of Ibn Al-Sabbagh's Durrat Al-Asrar Wa Tuhfat Al-Abrar. LC 92-33632. (SUNY Series in Islam). 274p. (C). 1993. pap. text 19.95 (*0-7914-1614-3*) State U NY Pr.

— The Mystical Teachings of Al-Shadhili: Including His Life, Prayers, Letters, & Followers. A Translation from the Arabic of Ibn Al-Sabbagh's Durrat Al-Asrar Wa Tuhfat Al-Abrar. LC 92-33632. (SUNY Series in Islam). 274p. (C). 1993. text 59.50 (*0-7914-1613-5*) State U NY Pr.

Douglas, Elmer H., tr. see Brother Lawrence.

Douglas, Elmer H., tr. see Sassower, Raphael.

Douglas, Eric. Straight Talk: Turning Communication Upside down for Strategic Results at Work. LC 97-49444. 296p. 1998. 26.95 (*0-89106-117-7*, 7786, Davies-Black Pub) Consulting Psychol.

***Douglas, Erin.** Get That Pest! LC 99-6801. (Green Light Readers Ser.). (Illus.). 20p. (J). (gr. 1-3). 2000. pap. 3.95 (*0-15-202554-5*) Harcourt.

— Get That Pest! (Green Light Readers Ser.). (Illus.). 20p. (J). (gr. 1-3). 2000. 10.95 (*0-15-202548-0*) Harcourt.

— Get That Pest! (Illus.). (J). 2000. 9.40 (*0-606-18174-1*) Turtleback.

Douglas, Evan J. Managerial Economics. 4th ed. (C). 1992. text 53.20 (*0-13-554346-0*) P-H.

— Managerial Economics: Analysis & Strategy. 4th ed. 704p. (C). 1992. text. write for info. (*0-318-68774-7*) P-H.

Douglas, Evan J. & Shepherd, Dean A. Attracting Equity Investors: Positioning, Preparing, & Presenting the Business Plan. LC 98-19760. (Entrepreneurship & the Management of Growing Enterprises Ser.). 174p. 1998. write for info. (*0-7619-1476-5*); pap. write for info. (*0-7619-1477-3*) Sage.

Douglas, Evelyn. Phantasmagoria. Fletcher, Ian & Stokes, John, eds. LC 82-49104. (Degeneration & Regeneration Ser.). 150p. 1984. lib. bdg. 25.00 (*0-8240-5567-5*) Garland.

Douglas, Flick, jt. auth. see Trueman, Bob.

Douglas, Frank, jt. auth. see Loosley, Chris.

Douglas Franzosa, Susan. Ordinary Lessons: Girlhoods of the 1950s. LC 96-47028. (Counterpoints Ser.: Vol. 43). (Illus.). XIV, 315p. (C). 1999. pap. text 32.95 (*0-8204-3669-0*) P Lang Pubng.

Douglas, Fred A., jt. auth. see Suckow, Mark A.

Douglas, Frederic H. & D'Harnoncourt, Rene. Indian Art of the United States. LC 74-86425. (Museum of Modern Art Publications in Reprint). (Illus.). 1970. reprint ed. 23.95 (*0-405-01534-8*) Ayer.

Douglas, G., et al. Systematic New Product Development. 2nd ed. 196p. 1983. text 61.95 (*0-566-02412-8*, Pub. by Gower) Ashgate Pub Co.

Douglas, G. A. The Nest. 1987. pap. 3.95 (*0-8217-2166-6*) NAL.

Douglas, G. H., ed. The Teaching of Business Communication II. 292p. 1987. pap. 9.95 (*0-931874-18-1*) Assn Busn Comm.

Douglas, Garry. The Devil's Own. 258p. 1998. 27.00 (*0-00-225481-6*, Pub. by HarpC) Trafalgar.

***Douglas, Garry.** The Devil's Own. large type ed. 464p. 1999. 31.99 (*0-7089-4000-5*, Linford) Ulverscroft.

— Soldier's in the Mist. 258p. 1999. 28.00 (*0-00-225483-2*, Pub. by HarpC) Trafalgar.

— The Valley of Death. large type ed. 392p. 1999. 31.99 (*0-7089-4132-X*) Ulverscroft.

Douglas, Garvin. The Palis of Honoure. LC 77-6155. (English Experience Ser.: No. 89). 80p. 1969. reprint ed. 25.00 (*90-221-0089-8*) Walter J Johnson.

Douglas, Gavin. The Palis of Honoure. Parkinson, David, ed. LC 92-32976. (Teams Middle English Text Ser.). 1992. pap. 8.00 (*1-879288-25-7*) Medieval Inst.

— The Poetical Works of Gavin Douglas, Bishop of Dunkeld, 4 vols. Small, John, ed. (Anglistica & Americana Ser.: No. 80). (Illus.). 1970. reprint ed. 193.70 (*0-685-66460-0*, 05103095) G Olms Pubs.

Douglas, Gawin. The Palice of Honour. Kinnear, John G., ed. LC 70-144417. (Bannatyne Club, Edinburgh. Publications: No. 17). reprint ed. 31.50 (*0-404-52717-5*) AMS Pr.

Douglas, Gawin, tr. see Virgil.

Douglas, Geoffrey. Class: The Wreckage of an American Family. (Illus.). 264p. 1994. mass mkt. 5.99 (*0-446-60065-2*) Warner Bks.

— Dead Opposite. 88p. 1995. 22.50 (*0-8050-2686-X*) H Holt & Co.

— The Game of their Lives. 224p. 1995. 23.00 (*0-8050-3875-2*) H Holt & Co.

***Douglas, George.** Dead on Delivery. large type ed. 288p. 1999. pap. 18.99 (*0-7089-5534-7*, Linford) Ulverscroft.

— Dead Reckoning. large type ed. 352p. 1999. pap. 18.99 (*0-7089-5461-8*, Linford) Ulverscroft.

— Death in Retreat. large type ed. 304p. 1999. pap. 18.99 (*0-7089-5482-0*, Linford) Ulverscroft.

— Double-Cross. large type ed. 304p. pap. 18.99 (*0-7089-5444-8*) Ulverscroft.

Douglas, George. The House with the Green Shutters. (C). 1986. pap. 35.00 (*0-901824-72-0*, Pub. by Mercat Pr Bks) St Mut.

***Douglas, George.** Luckless Lady. large type ed. 296p. 1999. pap. 18.99 (*0-7089-5560-6*, Linford) Ulverscroft.

— Murder Unmourned. large type ed. 328p. 1999. pap. 18.99 (*0-7089-5588-6*, Linford) Ulverscroft.

Douglas, George. Unholy Terror. large type ed. 304p. 1998. pap. 17.99 (*0-7089-5398-0*, Linford) Ulverscroft.

Douglas, George, jt. auth. see Taylor, Ronald J.

Douglas, George B. The Book of Scottish Poetry. LC 77-144506. reprint ed. 64.50 (*0-404-08635-7*) AMS Pr.

— Contemporary Scottish Verse. LC 70-144504. (Canterbury Poets Ser.). reprint ed. 49.50 (*0-404-08633-0*) AMS Pr.

Douglas, George B., ed. Poems of the Scottish Minor Poets. LC 73-144505. reprint ed. 44.50 (*0-404-08634-9*) AMS Pr.

Douglas, George B. & Dorson, Richard M., eds. Scottish Fairy & Folk Tales. LC 77-70591. (International Folklore Ser.). (Illus.). 1977. reprint ed. lib. bdg. 25.95 (*0-405-10092-2*) Ayer.

Douglas, George B., et al. Building Ship Models: Patterns & Instructions for a Clipper Ship & a Whaler. unabridged ed. LC 98-19937. (Illus.). 90p. 1998. pap. 7.95 (*0-486-40215-0*) Dover.

Douglas, George H. All Aboard! The Railroad in American Life. 462p. 1995. pap. 14.95 (*1-56924-876-1*) Marlowe & Co.

— Edmund Wilson's America. LC 83-19696. (Illus.). 272p. 1983. 32.00 (*0-8131-1494-2*) U Pr of Ky.

— Education Without Impact: How Our Universities Fail the Young. 288p. 1992. 19.95 (*1-55972-124-3*, Birch Ln Pr) Carol Pub Group.

— The Golden Age of the Newspaper. LC 98-50238. 328p. (YA). (gr. 9 up). 1999. 45.00 (*0-313-31077-7*) Greenwood.

— Postwar America: 1948 & the Incubation of Our Times. LC 97-31438. 295p. (C). 1998. pap. 28.50 (*1-57524-041-6*) Krieger.

— Skyscrapers: A Social History of the Very Tall Building in America. LC 95-39761. (Illus.). 280p. 1996. lib. bdg. 39.95 (*0-7864-0082-X*) McFarland & Co.

Douglas, George H. & Hildebrandt, Herbert W., eds. Studies in the History of Business Writing. 224p. (Orig.). 1985. pap. text 12.95 (*0-931874-16-5*) Assn Busn Comm.

Douglas, Gillian & Sebba, Leslie, eds. Children's Rights & Traditional Values. LC 97-51289. (Programme on International Rights of the Child Ser.). 335p. 1998. text 82.95 (*1-85521-956-5*, K639.A55, Pub. by Ashgate Pub) Ashgate Pub Co.

Douglas, Gillian, jt. auth. see Barton, Chris.

Douglas, Gillian, jt. ed. see Lowe, Nigel V.

Douglas, Gregory. GestapoChief: 1948 Interrogation of Heinrich Muller, Vol. 3. (Illus.). 288p. 1998. 35.95 (*0-912138-73-4*) Bender Pub CA.

— The Rite. (Orig.). 1979. mass mkt. 2.50 (*0-89083-529-2*, Zebra Kensgtn) Kensgtn Pub Corp.

Douglas, Gregory, ed. see Muller, Heinrich.

Douglas, H. The Burns Supper Companion. 1980. pap. 30.00 (*0-907526-74-8*, Pub. by Alloway Publ) St Mut.

Douglas-Hamilton, Jill, jt. auth. see Hamilton & Brandon Staff.

Douglas-Hamilton, Oria. The Elephant Family Book. LC 95-20725. (Animal Family Bks.). (Illus.). 56p. (J). (gr. 1-4). 1996. pap. 8.95 (*1-55858-549-4*, Pub. by North-South Bks NYC) Chronicle Bks.

— The Elephant Family Book. LC 89-77319. (Illus.). 56p. (J). (ps up). 1991. 15.95 (*0-88708-126-6*, Picture Book Studio) S&S Childrens.

Douglas, Harriet C. Handweaver's Instruction Manual. LC 76-24020. (Guild Monographs: No. 34). (Illus.). 41p. 1949. pap. 9.95 (*0-916658-30-9*) Shuttle Craft.

Douglas, Heather, jt. auth. see Banks, Cate.

Douglas, Henry K. The Douglas Diary: Student Days at Franklin & Marshall College 1856-1858. Klein, Frederic S. & Carrill, John H., eds. LC 73-89382. (Illus.). 1973. 7.95 (*0-910626-00-6*) Franklin & Marshall.

— I Rode with Stonewall. xiii, 401p. 1940. 34.95 (*0-8078-0337-5*) U of NC Pr.

— I Rode with Stonewall. 386p. 1993. reprint ed. pap. 7.95 (*0-89176-040-7*) R Bemis Pub.

Douglas-Home, Jessica. Violet: The Life & Loves of Violet Gordon Woodhouse. LC 97-174846. (Illus.). 320p. 1997. 28.00 (*1-86046-269-3*) Harvill Press.

— Violet: The Life & Loves of Violet Gordon Woodhouse. (Illus.). 320p. 1998. pap. 14.00 (*1-86046-360-6*, Pub. by Harvill Press) FS&G.

Douglas-Home, Sholto, ed. see Zagat Publishers Staff.

Douglas, Hope M. Basic Wildlife Rehabilitation Series, 7 vols. 3rd ed. Incl. First Aid for Wildlife: Basic Manual for Wildlife Rehabilitation. 2nd ed. Ruth, Irene & Carlson, Dale. LC 96-84058. (Illus.). 64p. 1997. pap. 9.95 (*1-884158-14-5*, Pub. by Bick Pub Hse); I Found a Baby Bird, What Do I Do? Basic Manuals Wildlife Rehabilitation. 3rd ed. Carlson, Dale. LC 96-79852. (Illus.). 64p. 1997. pap. 9.95 (*1-884158-00-5*, Pub. by Bick Pub Hse); I Found a Baby Duck, What Do I Do? Basic Manuals Wildlife Rehabilitation. 3rd ed. Carson, Dale. LC 96-79853. (Illus.). 64p. 1997. pap. 9.95 (*1-884158-02-1*, Pub. by Bick Pub Hse); I Found a Baby Opossum, What Do I Do? Basic Manuals Wildlife Rehabilitation. 3rd ed. Carlson, Dale. LC 96-79854. (Illus.). 64p. 1997. pap. 9.95 (*1-884158-06-4*, Pub. by Bick Pub Hse); I Found a Baby Rabbit, What Do I Do? Basic Manuals Wildlife Rehabilitation. 3rd ed. Carlson, Dale. LC 96-79855. (Illus.). 64p. 1997. pap. 9.95 (*1-884158-03-X*, Pub. by Bick Pub Hse); I Found a Baby Raccoon, What Do I Do? Basic Manuals Wildlife Rehabilitation. 3rd ed. Carlson, Dale. LC 96-79856. (Illus.). 64p. 1997. pap. 9.95 (*1-884158-05-6*, Pub. by Bick Pub Hse); I Found a Baby Squirrel, What Do I Do? Basic Manuals Wildlife Rehabilitation. 3rd ed. Carlson, Dale. LC 96-79857. (Illus.). 64p. pap. 9.95 (*1-884158-01-3*, Pub. by Bick Pub Hse); 1997. Set pap. 59.70 (*1-884158-04-8*, Pub. by Bick Pub Hse) BookWorld.

Douglas, Hugh. Flora MacDonald: The Most Loyal Rebel. 1999. pap. text 17.99 (*0-7509-2098-X*) Sutton Pub Ltd.

***Douglas, Hugh.** The Hogmanay Companion. (Illus.). 2000. pap. 15.00 (*1-897784-93-7*, Pub. by N Wilson Pubng) Interlink Pub.

Douglas, Hugh. Jacobite Spy Wars Moles, Rogues & Treachery. 1999. 34.95 (*0-7509-1425-4*) Bks Intl VA.

— Johnnie Walker's Burns Supper Companion. 116p. 1985. 35.00 (*0-907526-01-2*, Pub. by Alloway Pub) St Mut.

— The Private Passions of Bonnie Prince Charlie. LC 99-192829. (Illus.). 320p. 1999. pap. 21.95 (*0-7509-1902-7*, Pub. by Sutton Pub Ltd) Intl Pubs Mktg.

— Robert Burns: The Tinder Heart. LC 96-42553. (Illus.). 288p. 1996. 31.95 (*0-7509-1213-8*, Pub. by Sutton Pub Ltd) Intl Pubs Mktg.

— Robert Burns: The Tinder Heart. LC 99-188097. (Illus.). 320p. 1998. pap. 19.95 (*0-7509-1903-5*, Pub. by Sutton Pub Ltd) Intl Pubs Mktg.

Douglas, Hugh, ed. Coping with Life. (C). 1990. pap. 45.00 (*0-85305-282-4*, Pub. by Arthur James) St Mut.

***Douglas, Hugh & Stead, Michael J.** The Flight of Bonnie Prince Charlie. (Illus.). 224p. 2000. 32.95 (*0-7509-1989-2*) Sutton Publng.

***Douglas, Ian.** Europa Strike: Book Three of the Heritage Trilogy. (Heritage Trilogy Ser.: Vol. 3). 432p. 2000. mass mkt. 6.50 (*0-380-78830-6*, Avon Bks) Morrow Avon.

Douglas, Ian. Fertility of Soils: A Future for Farming in the West African Savannah. Barsch, Dietrich et al, eds. (Physical Environment Ser.: Vol. 10). (Illus.). 384p. 1992. 205.95 (*0-387-53283-8*) Spr-Verlag.

***Douglas, Ian.** Ht 1: Semper Mars. (Heritage Trilogy Ser.). 384p. 1998. mass mkt. 6.50 (*0-380-78828-4*, Avon Bks) Morrow Avon.

Douglas, Ian. Luna Marine: Book Two of the Heritage Trilogy. LC 98-94799. (Heritage Trilogy Ser.: Bk. 2). 416p. 1999. mass mkt. 5.99 (*0-380-78829-2*, Eos) Morrow Avon.

— System-Theoretical Modelling in Surface Water Hydrology. Barsch, Dietrich et al, eds. (Physical Environment Ser.: Vol. 6). (Illus.). 200p. 1991. 118.95 (*0-387-51272-1*) Spr-Verlag.

Douglas, Ian, et al, eds. Companion Encyclopedia of Geography: The Environment & Humankind. LC 96-6097. (Illus.). 1056p. (C). 1996. 165.00 (*0-415-07417-7*) Routledge.

Douglas, Ian & Hagedorn, J., eds. Geomorphology & Geoecology - Fluvial Geomorphology Vol. 10: Proceedings of the Second International Conference on Geomorphology, Frankfurt/Main, 1989. (Zeitschrift fuer Geomorphologie - Annals of Geomorphology Ser.: Supplementband 88). (Illus.). iv, 139p. 1993. pap. 40.00 (*3-443-21088-0*, Pub. by Gebruder Borntraeger) Balogh.

Douglas, Ian & Lorrain, R. D. Ice Composition & Glacier Dynamics. Barsch, Dietrich et al, eds. (Physical Environment Ser.: Vol. 8). (Illus.). 224p. 1991. 163.95 (*0-387-52521-1*) Spr-Verlag.

Douglas, Ian & Spencer, Tom, eds. Applied Geomorphology in the Tropics. (Annals of Gemorphology Supplement Ser.: No. 44). (Illus.). 132p. 1982. text 58.50 (*0-317-63481-X*) Lubrecht & Cramer.

— Environmental Change & Tropical Geomorphology. (Illus.). 400p. (C). 1985. text 95.00 (*0-04-551074-1*) Routledge.

Douglas, Ian H. Abul Kalam Azad: An Intellectual & Religious Biography. Minault, Gail & Troll, Christian W., eds. (Illus.). 386p. (C). 1993. reprint ed. pap. 14.95 (*0-19-563279-6*, 8971) OUP.

Douglas, Ian H., et al. Abul Kalam Azad: An Intellectual & Religious Biography. (Illus.). 386p. 1988. 29.95 (*0-19-562205-7*) OUP.

Douglas, Ian J. Computer Audit & Control Handbook. LC 95-169691. 240p. 1995. pap. text 62.95 (*0-7506-1926-0*) Buttrwrth-Heinemann.

— Computer Audit & Control Handbook. LC 95-169691. (Illus.). 252p. reprint ed. pap. 78.20 (*0-608-07412-8*, 206763900009) Bks Demand.

Douglas, J., Jr. & Hornung, U., eds. Flow in Porous Media: Proceedings of the Oberwolfach Conference, June 21-27, 1992. LC 93-39837. (International Series of Numerical Mathematics: Vol. 114). 1993. 79.50 (*0-8176-2949-1*) Birkhauser.

Douglas, J. A., et al. Estate & Gift Tax Digest. 880p. 1989. 130.00 (*0-7913-0262-8*); suppl. ed. 42.75 (*0-7913-0854-5*); suppl. ed. 45.50 (*0-7913-1035-3*) Warren Gorham & Lamont.

Douglas, J. B. Analysis with Standard Contagious Distributions. (Statistical Distributions in Scientific Work Ser.: Vol. 4). 530p. 1980. 35.00 (*0-89974-012-X*) Intl Co-Op.

Douglas, J. D. Illustrated Bible Dictionary. (Illus.). 1998. 27.99 (*0-8308-1461-2*); 27.99 (*0-8308-1462-0*); 27.99 (*0-8308-1463-9*) InterVarsity.

— NIV Compact Dictionary of the Bible. 1999. pap. text 7.97 (*0-310-22873-5*) Zondervan.

— Who's Who in Christian History. 768p. 1992. 24.99 (*0-8423-1014-2*) Tyndale Hse.

Douglas, J. D., ed. The New Greek-English Interlinear New Testament. Brown, Robert K. & Comfort, Philip W., trs. 928p. 1990. 39.99 (*0-8423-1213-7*) Tyndale Hse.

Douglas, J. D. & Hillyer, N., eds. The Illustrated Bible Dictionary. (Illus.). 1776p. 1998. reprint ed. 79.99 (*0-8308-1460-4*) InterVarsity.

Douglas, J. D. & Tenney. NIV Bible Compact Dictionary. 2000. 6.99 (*0-310-21496-3*) Zondervan.

Douglas, J. D. & Tenney, Merril C. Diccionario Biblico Mundo Hispano: NIV. Bartley, James & Zorzoli, Ruben O., eds.Tr. of Hispanic World Bible Dictionary, NIV. (SPA.). 800p. 1997. 29.99 (*0-311-03668-6*, Edit Mundo) Casa Bautista.

Douglas, J. D. & Tenney, Merrill, eds. The Zondervan Pictorial Bible Dictionary. (Illus.). 1993. 24.99 (*0-310-40138-0*) Zondervan.

Douglas, J. D. & Tenney, Merrill C., eds. New International Dictionary of the Bible. 1987. 29.99 (*0-88469-214-0*) BMH Bks.

— The New International Dictionary of the Bible, Pictorial Edition. rev. ed. (Illus.). 1216p. 1987. 29.99 (*0-310-33190-0*, 6751) Zondervan.

Douglas, J. D., et al. The Concise Dictionary of the Christian Tradition: Doctrine, Liturgy, History. 400p. 1989. 19.95 (*0-310-44320-2*, 12807) Zondervan.

Douglas, J. Leigh. The Free Yemini Movement, 1935-1962. Chimianti, Giovanni, ed. (Books from the American University of Beirut Press). (Illus.). 308p. (C). 1988. pap. 19.95 (*0-8156-6080-4*) Syracuse U Pr.

Douglas, J. Lufkin. Douglas Genealogy: Descendants of John Douglas of Middleborough, Ma., the First of This Branch in America. (Illus.). 226p. 1997. reprint ed. pap. 34.00 (*0-8328-8342-5*); reprint ed. lib. bdg. 44.00 (*0-8328-8341-7*) Higginson Bk Co.

Douglas, J. M. Blackthorn Lore & the Art of Making Walking Sticks. 96p. 1984. 40.00 (*0-907526-16-0*, Pub. by Alloway Pub) St Mut.

— Blackthorn Lore & the Art of Making Walking Sticks. 1980. spiral bd. 40.00 (*0-907526-66-7*, Pub. by Alloway Publ) St Mut.

Douglas, J. Sholto & Hart, Robert A. de J. Forest Farming: Towards a Solution to Problems of World Hunger & Conservation. 2nd ed. 208p. 1984. pap. 21.00 (*0-946688-30-3*, Pub. by Intermed Tech) Stylus Pub VA.

***Douglas, J. Yellowlees.** The End of Books or Books Without End? Reading Interactive Narratives. LC 99-6689. 216p. 2000. text 34.50 (*0-472-11114-0*, 11114) U of Mich Pr.

***Douglas, Jack.** Invisible Anonymous Untraceable. 2000. text 23.95 (*0-312-25250-1*) St Martin.

Douglas, Jack. Managing a Veterinary Practice in Canada. 265p. 1994. pap. text 39.00 (*0-920513-11-5*, Pub. by Sau1nders) Saunders.

Douglas, Jack & Muller, Kathleen. Historical Footnotes of Santa Clara Valley. (Illus.). 160p. 1993. pap. 18.95 (*0-914139-10-X*) Hist San Jose.

Douglas, Jack D. Creative Interviewing. LC 84-23715. (Sage Library of Social Research: No. 159). 159p. 1985. reprint ed. pap. 49.30 (*0-608-01123-1*, 205942700001) Bks Demand.

— Investigative Social Research: Individual & Team Field Research. LC 76-21663. (Sage Library of Social Research: No. 29). 247p. 1976. reprint ed. pap. 76.60 (*0-608-01160-6*, 205946000001) Bks Demand.

— The Myth of the Welfare State. 505p. (C). 1990. pap. 24.95 (*0-88738-874-4*) Transaction Pubs.

— The Social Meanings of Suicide. LC 67-14408. 412p. 1973. reprint ed. pap. 127.80 (*0-7837-8166-0*, 204787100008) Bks Demand.

Douglas, Jack D., ed. Crime & Justice in American Society. LC 74-126302. (C). 1971. pap. write for info. (*0-672-60809-X*, Bobbs) Macmillan.

— Impact of Sociology: Readings in the Social Sciences. LC 76-119991. (Orig.). (C). 1970. pap. text 4.95 (*0-89197-228-5*) Irvington.

— Introduction to Sociology: Situations & Structures. LC 75-163608. (C). 1973. 24.95 (*0-02-907540-8*) Free Pr.

Douglas, Jack D. & Atwell, Freda C. Love, Intimacy, & Sex. LC 87-20658. (Sociological Observations Ser.: No. 20). (Illus.). 304p. 1988. reprint ed. pap. 94.30 (*0-608-01166-5*, 205946600001) Bks Demand.

Douglas, Jack D. & Tenney, Merrill C. The NIV Compact Dictionary of the Bible. 640p. 1989. 17.99 (*0-310-33180-3*, 6752) Zondervan.

***Douglas, Jake.** A Corner of Boot Hill. large type ed. 240p. 2000. pap. 18.99 (*0-7089-5629-7*, Linford) Ulverscroft.

Douglas, Jake. Laredo's Land. large type ed. (Linford Western Library Ser.). 256p. 1997. pap. 16.99 (*0-7089-5125-2*, Linford) Ulverscroft.

***Douglas, Jake.** Quick on the Trigger. large type ed. 256p. 1999. pap. 18.99 (*0-7089-5516-9*, Linford) Ulverscroft.

— Rio Reprisal. large type ed. (Linford Western Large Print Ser.). 240p. pap. 18.99 (*0-7089-5415-4*) Ulverscroft.

Douglas, James. Bombay & Western India, Vols. I & II. (C). 1987. reprint ed. 75.00 (*0-8364-2095-0*, Pub. by Usha) S Asia.

— Building Condition Assessment in the U. S. A. (C). 1992. text 75.00 (*0-85406-548-2*, Pub. by R-I-C-S Bks) St Mut.

— North City Traffic, Straight Ahead. (Irish Play Ser.). 1968. pap. 1.25 (*0-912262-09-5*) Proscenium.

— The Savages. (Irish Play Ser.). 1979. 6.95 (*0-912262-60-5*); pap. 2.95 (*0-912262-61-3*) Proscenium.

— Theodore Watts-Dunton: Poet, Novelist, Critic. LC 72-1509. (English Literature Ser.: No. 33). (Illus.). 1972. reprint ed. lib. bdg. 73.95 (*0-8383-1447-3*) M S G Haskell Hse.

Douglas, James, et al. Employment Testing Manual. 848p. 1989. 136.00 (*0-7913-0138-9*) Warren Gorham & Lamont.

— Employment Testing Manual. 848p. 1991. suppl. ed. 48.00 (*0-7913-0820-0*) Warren Gorham & Lamont.

— Modern Construction & Development Forms: Cumulative Supplementation. 2nd ed. LC 82-50345. (Modern Real Estate & Mortgage Forms Ser.). 1612p. 1982. suppl. ed. 69.50 (*0-7913-1009-4*) Warren Gorham & Lamont.

Douglas, James A. Corporate Tax Digest. rev. ed. 688p. 1987. 130.00 (*0-88712-622-7*) Warren Gorham & Lamont.

Douglas, James A. & Benton, Donald S., eds. Criminal Law Digest, 2 vol. set. 3rd ed. (General Law Ser.). 1983. 135.00 (*0-88262-904-2*, 78-56429) Warren Gorham & Lamont.

— Criminal Law Digest, 2 vols., Vol. 1. 3rd ed. (General Law Ser.). 1992. suppl. ed. 70.00 (*0-7913-1187-2*) Warren Gorham & Lamont.

Douglas, James A. & Binder-Arain, Laurel. Computer & Information Law Digest. 464p. 1995. 140.00 (*0-7913-2217-3*) Warren Gorham & Lamont.

Douglas, James A. & Feld, Daniel E. Partnership Tax Digest. 1992. suppl. ed. 130.00 (*0-7913-0880-4*); suppl. ed. 130.00 (*0-7913-1010-8*) Warren Gorham & Lamont.

Douglas, James A. & Nembach, Paul A. Federal Environmental Regulation of Real Estate Law Digest. 336p. 1995. 135.00 (*0-7913-2219-X*) Warren Gorham & Lamont.

Douglas, James A., et al. Closely Held Corporations: Forms & Checklists. 1989. 115.00 (*0-685-32303-X*) Warren Gorham & Lamont.

— Closely Held Corporations: Forms & Checklists, No. 1. 1992. suppl. ed. 51.50 (*0-685-56112-7*) Warren Gorham & Lamont.

— Financing Forms for Real Estate. 832p. 1995. 165.00 (*0-7913-2485-0*) Warren Gorham & Lamont.

— Modern Construction & Development Forms: Cumulative Supplementation. 2nd ed. LC 82-50345. 1612p. 1982. 160.00 (*0-88262-775-9*) Warren Gorham & Lamont.

— Modern Corporation Checklists. 3rd ed. 838p. 1990. 140.00 (*0-7913-0566-X*); suppl. ed. 56.00 (*0-7913-1188-0*) Warren Gorham & Lamont.

— Real Estate Law Digest, 2 vols. 3rd ed. 1991. 135.00 (*0-7913-0749-2*); suppl. ed. 51.00 (*0-7913-1193-7*) Warren Gorham & Lamont.

— Real Estate Tax Digest: Federal Income, Estate & Gift Taxes. rev. ed. LC 83-51782. 464p. 1984. suppl. ed. 130.00 (*0-7913-0641-0*) Warren Gorham & Lamont.

— Real Estate Tax Digest: Federal Income, Estate & Gift Taxes, No. 1. rev. ed. LC 83-51782. 464p. 1991. suppl. ed. 42.00 (*0-7913-0884-7*) Warren Gorham & Lamont.

— Real Estate Tax Digest: Federal Income, Estate & Gift Taxes, No. 2. rev. ed. LC 83-51782. 464p. 1991. suppl. ed. 45.00 (*0-7913-1027-2*) Warren Gorham & Lamont.

Douglas, James M. Conceptual Design of Chemical Processes. 601p. (C). 1988. 111.25 (*0-07-017762-7*) McGraw.

***Douglas, Janet R.** Integrated Disability Management: An Employer's Guide. LC 99-64589. 222p. 1999. pap. 38.00 (*0-89154-534-4*) Intl Found Employ.

Douglas, Janice G., jt. auth. see Fray, John C.

Douglas, Jeannine G. Don't Drown in the Mainstream. rev. ed. 66p. (J). (gr. k-12). 1986. pap. text 5.50 (*0-9607872-1-6*) Vail Pub.

Douglas, Jed A. Fleh: A Childrens Story & Playmate. LC 93-91817. (Illus.). 50p. (Orig.). (J). (ps-5). 1994. pap. 9.95 (*0-9639609-0-3*) Kookadala.

Douglas, Jennifer, ed. Cooking with the Stars: Healthy, Delicious Recipes from Celebrities' Own Kitchens. (Illus.). 224p. (Orig.). 1993. pap. 12.95 (*0-89329-031-9*) Ctr Sci Public.

Douglas, Jennifer, jt. auth. see Fischer, Lynn.

Douglas, Jerry. Mantalk. (Illus.). 222p. (Orig.). 1991. pap. 12.95 (*0-943383-02-1*) FirstHand Ltd.

Douglas, Jerry, et al. Skip, Hop & Wobble/Dobro Edition. Phillips, Stacy, tr. 72p. 1997. pap. 9.95 (*0-7866-2560-0*, 95765) Mel Bay.

Douglas, Jerry, ed. see Cardini, Leo.

Douglas, Jim, ed. Contentment or, the Compleat Nutmeg-State Songster. (Illus.). 128p. (YA). (gr. 10-12). 1988. 9.50 incl. lp (*0-318-23885-3*); pap. text 12.95 (*0-318-23884-5*) Pedlar Pr.

Douglas, Jo. Highland Destiny. large type ed. (Dales Large Print Ser.). 224p. 1996. pap. 18.99 (*1-85389-648-9*, Dales) Ulverscroft.

Douglas, Joan M. No, a Zamboni Is Not a Pasta: Guide for the Beginning Skater. large type ed. Hanst, John H., ed. (Illus.). 50p. 1997. pap. 9.95 (*0-9657186-0-3*) J M Douglas.

***Douglas, John.** The Anatomy of Motive: The FBI's Legendary Mindhunter Explores the Key to Understanding & Catchin. 432p. 2000. reprint ed. per. 7.99 (*0-671-02393-4*) PB.

— Broken Wings: A Mindhunter Novel. 2000. mass mkt. 6.99 (*0-671-02392-6*, Pocket Star Bks) PB.

— Following in the Footsteps of Abraham: A Study in Discipleship. 200p. 1999. pap. 9.99 (*1-84030-072-8*, Ambassador-Emerald) Emerald House Group Inc.

Douglas, John. Medical Topography of Upper Canada. LC 85-14626. 1986. 9.95 (*0-88135-078-8*) Watson Pub Intl.

***Douglas, John & Olshaker, Mark.** Broken Wings. large type ed. LC 00-27590. (Core Ser.). 570p. 2000. 29.95 (*0-7838-9027-3*, G K Hall Lrg Type) Mac Lib Ref.

— Broken Wings: The Mindhunters. 448p. 2000. reprint ed. 6.99 (*0-671-00395-X*) PB.

— The Cases That Haunt Us. 2000. 25.00 (*0-684-84600-4*) Scribner.

Douglas, John E. John Douglas' Guide to the FBI Exams. 304p. 2000. pap. 25.00 (*0-684-85505-4*) S&S Trade.

— John Douglas' Guide to the Police Officer Exams. LC 99-56788. 432p. 2000. pap. 25.00 (*0-684-85506-2*) S&S Trade.

— John Douglas's Guide to Careers in the FBI: The Complete Guide to the Skills & Education Required. 684th ed. LC 98-35527. (Illus.). 288p. 1998. pap. 15.00 (*0-684-85504-6*) S&S Trade.

— Mindhunter: Inside the FBI's Elite Serial Crime Unit. 1997. mass mkt. 3.99 (*0-671-01375-0*) PB.

— Unabomber: On the Trail of America's Most-Wanted Serial Killer. LC 96-219380. 1996. mass mkt. 6.50 (*0-671-00411-5*) PB.

Douglas, John E. & Olshaker, Mark. The Anatomy of Motive: The FBI's Legendary Mindhunter Explores the Key to Understanding & Catching Violent Criminals. LC 99-22058. (Illus.). 320p. 1999. 25.00 (*0-684-84598-9*) Scribner.

***Douglas, John E. & Olshaker, Mark.** Broken Wings. 304p. 1999. 24.00 (*0-671-02391-8*, PB Hardcover) PB.

Douglas, John E. & Olshaker, Mark. Journey into Darkness: The FBI's Premier Investigator Penetrates the Minds & Motives of the Most Terrifying Serial Killers. (Lisa Drew Book Ser.). (Illus.). 382p. 1997. per. 6.99 (*0-671-00394-1*) PB.

— Mindhunter: Inside the FBI's Elite Serial Crime Unit. 416p. 1996. per. 6.99 (*0-671-52890-4*) PB.

— Mindhunter: Inside the FBI's Elite Serial Crime Unit. (Illus.). 384p. 1995. 24.00 (*0-684-80376-3*) Scribner.

— Obsession: The FBI's Legendary Profiler Probes the Psyches of Killers, Rapists & Stalkers, & Their Victims & Tells How to Fight Back. 1998. mass mkt. 6.99 (*0-671-01704-7*) PB.

— Obsession: The FBI's Legendary Profiler Probes the Psyches of Killers, Rapists & Stalkers, & Their Victims & Tells How to Fight Back. LC 97-48654. 384p. 1998. 25.50 (*0-684-84560-1*) Scribner.

Douglas, John E., et al. Crime Classification Manual. LC 97-17809. 1997. pap. 34.95 (*0-7879-3885-8*) Jossey-Bass.

Douglas, John F. Fluid Mechanics. 3rd ed. 832p. (C). 1996. pap. text 62.95 (*0-582-23408-5*) Addison-Wesley.

— Solve Problems Fluid Mechanic, Vol. 1. 3rd ed. 272p. (C). 1996. pap. text 28.95 (*0-582-23987-7*) Addison-Wesley.

— Solve Problems Fluid Mechanics, Vol. 2. 3rd ed. 304p. (C). 1996. pap. text 28.95 (*0-582-23988-5*) Addison-Wesley.

Douglas, Johnson E. Successful Seed Programs: A Planning & Management Guide. (Winrock Development Oriented Literature Ser.). 330p. (C). 1980. pap. text 63.00 (*0-89158-793-4*) Westview.

Douglas, Johnson E., jt. auth. see Bal, Sharanjit S.

Douglas, Judith V. Performance Improvement Through Information Management: Health Care's Bridge to Success. Hannah, K. J. & Ball, Marion J., eds. LC 98-24445. (Health Informatics Ser.). (Illus.). 264p. 1999. 49.95 (*0-387-98452-6*) Spr-Verlag.

***Douglas, Julie.** California: Fun Facts & Games. (Fun Facts & Games Bks.). (Illus.). 64p. (J). (ps-3). 2000. pap. text 5.95 (*1-892920-22-0*) G H B Pubs.

— M Is for Michigan. (Alpha Flight Bks.). (Illus.). 60p. (ps-3). 2000. 17.95 (*1-892920-43-3*) G H B Pubs.

Douglas, Julie M. Handbook for Spiritual Directors. LC 98-19893. 96p. 1998. pap. 7.95 (*0-8091-3802-6*) Paulist Pr.

Douglas, K. Desert Wisdom: Sacred Middle Eastern Writings from the Goddess Through the Sufis. LC 94-31792. 1999. pap. 12.00 (*0-06-061997-X*) HarpC.

Douglas, Kaaren, et al. A Practical Guide to Clinical Teaching in Medicine. (Medical Education Ser.). 208p. 1988. 29.95 (*0-8261-5940-0*) Springer Pub.

Douglas, Karen B. Coffee with Mama. 160p. 1994. 12.00 (*0-9639947-1-9*) Suomi-SVerige.

— Scandinavian Smorgasbord Recipes. 158p. 1991. spiral bd. 6.95 (*0-941016-85-4*) Penfield.

— Scandinavian Sweet Treats. (Illus.). 120p. 1992. spiral bd. 6.95 (*0-941016-88-9*) Penfield.

Douglas, Katherine A. Short Stories for Long Rainy Days: Simple Tales of Life & Love. LC 99-193786. 225p. 1998. 12.99 (*1-57748-449-5*) Barbour Pub.

Douglas, Katherine Anne. More Short Stories for Long Rainy Days: Simple Tales of Life & Love. 224p. 1999. 12.99 (*1-57748-572-6*) Barbour Pub.

***Douglas, Katherine Anne.** Short Stories from Days Gone By: Nostalgic Tales of Simpler Times. 224p. 2000. pap. 12.99 (*1-57748-676-5*) Barbour Pub.

Douglas, Kathleen M. The Therapeutic Superhighway. (Illus.). 120p. 1999. pap. 9.95 (*1-891929-09-7*) Four Seasons.

Douglas, Kathy. Calculation Station. Bittinger, Gayle, ed. LC 97-62223. (Kinderstation Ser.). (Illus.). 160p. (J). (ps). 1998. pap. 14.95 (*1-57029-158-6*, 4501) Totline Pubns.

Douglas, Kay. Invisible Wounds: A Self-Help Guide for Women in Destructive Relationships. LC 97-145869. 272p. 1997. pap. 15.95 (*0-7043-4450-5*, Pub. by Womens Press) Trafalgar.

Douglas, Keith. Alamein to Zem Zem. (Illus.). 156p. 1994. pap. 13.95 (*0-571-16264-9*) Faber & Faber.

***Douglas, Keith.** The Complete Poems. Graham, Desmond, ed. & pref. by. 208p. 2000. pap. 13.00 (*0-571-20258-6*, Pub. by Faber & Faber) Penguin Books.

Douglas, Keith. The Complete Poems. 3rd ed. Graham, Desmond, ed. (The Oxford Poets Ser.). 208p. 1998. pap. 18.95 (*0-19-288087-X*) OUP.

***Douglas, Keith.** The Letters. 360p. 2000. pap. 29.95 (*1-85754-477-3*, Pub. by Carcanet Pr) Paul & Co Pubs.

— Pacific Siege, 1 vol., Vol. 8. (Seal Team Seven Ser.). 1999. mass mkt. 5.99 (*0-425-16941-3*) Berkley Pub.

Douglas, Kelly B. The Black Christ. LC 93-35821. (Bishop Henry McNeal Turner Studies: Vol. 9). 140p. (Orig.). 1994. pap. 14.00 (*0-88344-939-0*) Orbis Bks.

— Sexuality & the Black Church: A Womanist Perspective. LC 98-32189. 155p. 1999. pap. 14.00 (*1-57075-242-7*) Orbis Bks.

Douglas, Kenneth, tr. see Wagner, Jean.

Douglas, Kiang. Microsoft Flight Simulator 98: Unauthorized Game Secrets. LC 97-69769. 400p. 1997. per. 19.99 (*0-7615-1250-0*) Prima Pub.

Douglas, Kirk. The Broken Mirror. LC 96-47863. (Illus.). 96p. (J). 1997. per. 13.00 (*0-689-81493-3*) S&S Trade.

***Douglas, Kirk.** Climbing the Mountain: My Search for Meaning. (Illus.). 272p. 2000. pap. 13.00 (*0-684-86584-X*, Touchstone) S&S Trade Pap.

Douglas, Kirk. Climbing the Mountain: My Search for Meaning. LC 97-21507. (Illus.). 240p. 1997. 24.00 (*0-684-84415-X*) Simon & Schuster.

— Climbing the Mountain: My Search for Meaning. aut. ed. LC 97-21507. 1997. 23.50 (*0-684-84702-7*) S&S Trade.

— Last Tango in Brooklyn. 384p. 1995. mass mkt. 6.50 (*0-446-60201-9*, Pub. by Warner Bks) Little.

— Last Tango in Brooklyn. large type ed. LC 94-25461. 392p. 1994. lib. bdg. 24.95 (*0-8161-7465-2*, G K Hall Lrg Type) Mac Lib Ref.

— The Ragman's Son. Grose, Bill, ed. 1990. per. 5.99 (*0-671-73789-9*) PB.

— Young Heroes of the Bible. LC 98-25718. (Illus.). 133p. (J). (gr. 4-6). 1999. per. 15.00 (*0-689-81491-7*) S&S Bks Yung.

Douglas-Klotz, Neil. The Hidden Gospel: Decoding the Spiritual Message of the Aramaic Jesus. LC 99-28524. 208p. 1999. 24.95 (*0-8356-0780-1*, Pub. by Theos Pub Hse) Natl Bk Netwk.

— Prayers of the Cosmos: Meditations on the Aramaic Words of Jesus. LC 89-46456. 112p. 1993. pap. 12.00 (*0-06-061995-3*, Pub. by Harper SF) HarpC.

Douglas-Klotz, Neil, jt. auth. see Lewis, Samuel L.

Douglas-Klotz, Neil, ed. see Lewis, Samuel L.

Douglas, Krystan V. Guide to British Drama Explication: Beginnings to 1640, Vol. 1. (Reference Publication in Literature Ser.). 552p. 1996. 55.00 (*0-8161-7372-9*, G K Hall & Co) Mac Lib Ref.

Douglas, L. A., ed. Micromorphology: A Basic & Applied Science: Proceedings of the VIIIth International Working Meeting, San Antonio, Texas, July 1988. (Developments in Soil Science Ser.: Vol. 19). xviii,716p. 1990. 221.50 (*0-444-88302-9*) Elsevier.

***Douglas, Lake & Hardy, Jeanette.** New Orleans Gardens. LC 00-43013. 2001. write for info. (*0-8118-2421-7*) Chronicle Bks.

Douglas, Lauren W. The Always Anonymous Beast. LC 87-20342. 224p. 1987. pap. 8.95 (*0-941483-04-5*) Naiad Pr.

— The Daughters of Artemis. (Caitlin Reece Mystery Ser.). 240p. (Orig.). 1991. pap. 9.95 (*0-941483-95-9*) Naiad Pr.

— Death at Lavender Bay: An Allison O'Neil Mystery. 256p. (Orig.). 1996. pap. 11.95 (*1-56280-085-X*) Naiad Pr.

— Goblin Market. LC 93-24910. (Caitlin Reece Mystery Ser.: No. 5). 224p. 1993. pap. 10.95 (*1-56280-047-7*) Naiad Pr.

— Ninth Life. LC 89-34012. 256p. 1990. pap. 9.95 (*0-941483-50-9*) Naiad Pr.

— A Rage of Maidens: Sixth Caitlin Reece Mystery. LC 94-16241. 224p. 1994. pap. 10.95 (*1-56280-068-X*) Naiad Pr.

— Swimming Cat Cove: An Allison O'Neil Mystery. LC 96-45477. 224p. (Orig.). 1997. pap. 11.95 (*1-56280-168-6*) Naiad Pr.

— A Tiger's Heart. LC 92-20903. (Caitlin Reece Mystery Ser.: No. 4). 240p. 1992. pap. 9.95 (*1-56280-018-3*) Naiad Pr.

Douglas, Lawrie. A Guide to Commercial Radio Journalism. 2nd ed. LC 98-45350. 176p. 1999. pap. text 29.95 (*0-240-51547-1*, Focal) Buttrwrth-Heinemann.

Douglas, Lee, Jr. Winning Blackjack Made Easy. LC 82-80758. (Illus.). 52p. (Orig.). 1982. pap. 3.95 (*0-88083-001-8*) Poverty Hill Pr.

Douglas, Lewis W. The Liberal Tradition: A Free People & a Free Economy. LC 77-171382. (FDR & the Era of the New Deal Ser.). 136p. 1972. reprint ed. lib. bdg. 19.50 (*0-306-70376-9*) Da Capo.

***Douglas-Lithgow, R. A.** Native American Place Names of Connecticut. 96p. 2000. pap. 9.95 (*1-55709-540-X*) Applewood.

— Native American Place Names of Maine, New Hampshire & Vermont. 2000. pap. 9.95 (*1-55709-541-8*) Applewood.

— Native American Place Names of Massachusetts. 2000. pap. 9.95 (*1-55709-542-6*) Applewood.

— Native American Place Names of Rhode Island. 2000. pap. 9.95 (*1-55709-543-4*) Applewood.

D

Douglas, Livingston G. Bond Markets, 1995: A Desktop Reference to World Debt Market Performance & Analysis. 300p. 1995. per. 35.00 (*1-55738-553-X*, Irwn Prfssnl) McGraw-Hill Prof.

— The Fixed Income Almanac, 1993: The Bond Investor's Compendium of Key Market, Product & Performance Data. 700p. 1993. 75.00 (*1-55738-429-0*, Irwn Prfssnl) McGraw-Hill Prof.

— Fixed Income Masterpieces: Insights from America's Great Investors. 2nd ed. 650p. 1992. text 67.50 (*1-55623-862-2*, Irwn Prfssnl) McGraw-Hill Prof.

— Yield Curve Analysis: The Fundamentals of Risk & Return. (Illus.). 622p. (C). 1988. 75.00 (*0-13-972456-7*) NY Inst Finance.

Douglas, Lloyd. Disputed Passage. 29.95 (*0-88411-535-6*) Amereon Ltd.

— Forgive Us Our Trespasses. 26.95 (*0-88411-536-4*) Amereon Ltd.

— White Banners. 27.95 (*0-88411-537-2*) Amereon Ltd.

Douglas, Lloyd C. Doctor Hudson's Secret Journal. large type ed. LC 93-13716. 393p. 1993. lib. bdg. 21.95 (*1-56054-776-6*) Thorndike Pr.

— Doctor Hudson's Secret Journal. 240p. 1992. reprint ed. lib. bdg. 21.95 (*0-89966-944-1*) Buccaneer Bks.

— Magnificent Obsession. large type ed. 1994. 65.95 (*0-7862-9981-9*, G K Hall Lrg Type) Mac Lib Ref.

— Magnificent Obsession. 1976. 23.95 (*0-8488-0479-1*) Amereon Ltd.

— Magnificent Obsession. 1982. lib. bdg. 27.95 (*0-89966-387-7*) Buccaneer Bks.

— Magnificent Obsession. LC 99-20071. 1999. pap. 12.00 (*0-395-95774-5*) HM.

— Magnificent Obsession. large type ed. LC 91-39205. 424p. 1992. reprint ed. lib. bdg. 19.95 (*1-56054-311-6*) Thorndike Pr.

— The Robe. 476p. Date not set. 30.95 (*0-8488-2252-8*) Amereon Ltd.

Douglas, Lloyd C. The Robe. 77p. 1952. pap. 5.25 (*0-87129-941-0*, R19) Dramatic Pub.

Douglas, Lloyd C. The Robe. 1986. pap. 9.95 (*0-395-40299-9*) HM.

— The Robe. LC 99-20072. 508p. 1999. pap. 13.00 (*0-395-95775-3*) HM.

— The Robe. large type ed. LC 95-8707. 889p. 1995. lib. bdg. 21.95 (*0-7838-1362-7*, G K Hall Lrg Type) Mac Lib Ref.

— White Banners. 1990. reprint ed. lib. bdg. 23.95 (*0-89968-502-1*) Buccaneer Bks.

Douglas, Louis H., jt. auth. see Rohrer, Wayne.

Douglas, M. Joanne, jt. auth. see Gambling, David R.

Douglas, Mack. How to Make a Habit of Succeeding. 192p. 1987. reprint ed. pap. 7.95 (*0-310-23861-7*, 9538P) Zondervan.

Douglas, Mack R. How to Raise Drug-Free Children. 50p. (Orig.). 1986. pap. 1.95 (*0-937199-00-1*) Discovery FL.

— How to Win with High Self-Esteem. LC 93-5874. 208p. 1994. pap. 9.95 (*0-88289-994-5*) Pelican.

***Douglas, Mack R.** Making a Habit of Success. 464p. 1999. 19.90 (*1-57866-071-8*) Galahad Bks.

Douglas, Malcolm, jt. auth. see Norman, David.

Douglas, Mannering. Degas. 80p. (YA). (gr. 7 up). 1997. 17.95 (*1-85813-506-0*) Chelsea Hse.

***Douglas, Marcia.** City Smart Guidebook: Toronto. (City Smart Ser.). (Illus.). 224p. 2000. pap. 12.95 (*1-56261-429-0*, City Smart) Avalon Travel.

— Electricity Comes to Cocoa Bottom. 80p. 1999. pap. (*1-900715-28-7*, Pub. by Peepal Tree Pr) Paul & Co Pubs.

Douglas, Marcia. Madam Fate. LC 98-20395. 272p. 1998. 24.00 (*1-56947-134-7*, Pub. by Soho Press) FS&G.

Douglas, Marion. Bending at the Bow. 272p. 1995. pap. 14.95 (*0-88974-051-8*, Pub. by Press Gang Pubs) LPC InBook.

Douglas, Marion, ed. see Matz, Nancy J.

Douglas, Marion K. The Real World of Engineering: Case History, No. 42. 3.50 (*0-614-05210-6*, CHN04205913.5M) ASFE.

— The Real World of Engineering: Case History, No. 62. 3.50 (*0-614-05231-9*, CHN06203943.5M) ASFE.

Douglas, Marjorie M. Barefoot on Crane Island. LC 98-15457. (Midwest Reflections Ser.). (Illus.). 233p. 1998. 24.95 (*0-87351-362-2*, 362-2); pap. 15.95 (*0-87351-363-0*, 363-0) Minn Hist.

— Eggs in the Coffee, Sheep in the Corn: My 17 Years As a Farmwife. LC 94-17244. (Midwest Reflections Ser.). (Illus.). xi, 247p. 1994. pap. 15.95 (*0-87351-299-5*) Minn Hist.

Douglas, Marjory S. The Everglades: River of Grass. (Illus.). 312p. 1986. pap. 6.95 (*0-89176-029-6*, 6029, Mckingbird) R Bemis Pub.

— The Everglades: River of Grass. 50th anniversary ed. LC 97-1594. (Illus.). 480p. 1997. 18.95 (*1-56164-135-9*) Pineapple Pr.

— Freedom River. LC 94-6832. (Illus.). 240p. (J). (gr. 4 up). 1994. 19.95 (*0-9633461-4-8*); pap. 14.95 (*0-9633461-5-6*) Valiant Pr.

— Marjory Stoneman Douglas: Voice of the River. LC 87-2242. (Illus.). 268p. 1990. pap. 9.95 (*0-910923-94-9*) Pineapple Pr.

— Nine Florida Stories: A Florida Sand Dollar Book. McCarthy, Kevin M., ed. 216p. 1990. 22.95 (*0-8130-0988-X*); pap. 17.95 (*0-8130-0994-4*) U Press Fla.

— A River in Flood: Other Florida Stories. McCarthy, Kevin, ed. LC 98-26234. (Florida Sand Dollar Bks.). (Illus.). 176p. 1998. 39.95 (*0-8130-1622-3*); pap. 17.95 (*0-8130-1623-1*) U Press Fla.

D

Douglas, Marjory S. & Rothchild, John. Marjory Stoneman Douglas: Voice of the River. 5th ed. LC 87-2242. (Illus.). 268p. 1990. 17.95 (*0-910923-33-7*) Pineapple Pr.

Douglas, Mark. The Disciplined Trader: Developing Winning Attitudes. 1990. 29.95 (*0-317-04755-8*) NY Inst Finance.

— The Disciplined Trader: Developing Winning Attitudes. 320p. (C). 1990. text 34.95 (*0-13-215757-8*, Busn) P-H.

***Douglas, Mark.** Trading in the Zone. 2001. 35.00 (*0-7352-0144-7*) PH Pr.

Douglas, Mary. Black Is Not a Color. Frances, Dee, ed. Date not set. lib. bdg. 10.00 (*1-885519-15-X*) DDDD Pubns.

Douglas, Mary. How Institutions Think. LC 86-5696. (Frank W. Abrams Lectures). 160p. 1986. pap. text 16.95 (*0-8156-0206-5*) Syracuse U Pr.

— Implicit Meanings: Essays in Anthropology. 348p. (C). 1978. pap. 27.99 (*0-415-06561-5*) Routledge.

— Implicit Meanings: Essays in Anthropology. (Illus.). 1978. reprint ed. pap. 13.95 (*0-7100-0047-2*, Routledge Thoemms) Routledge.

— Implicit Meanings: Essays in Anthropology. 2nd ed. LC 99-19937. 1999. pap. 25.99 (*0-415-20554-9*) Routledge.

— In the Wilderness: The Doctrine of Defilement in the Book of Numbers. (Journal for the Study of the Old Testament Supplement Ser.: Vol. 158). 272p. 1993. 75.00 (*1-85075-444-6*, Pub. by Sheffield Acad) CUP Services.

— The Lele of the Kasai. LC GN0654.D66. 309p. reprint ed. pap. 95.80 (*0-8357-6951-8*, 203901000009) Bks Demand.

***Douglas, Mary.** Leviticus As Literature. LC 99-24071. 304p. 2000. text 35.00 (*0-19-815092-X*) OUP.

Douglas, Mary. Natural Symbols: Explorations in Cosmology. 2nd ed. LC 96-203. 224p. (C). 1996. reprint ed. 80.00 (*0-415-13825-6*); reprint ed. pap. 22.99 (*0-415-13826-4*) Routledge.

— Purity & Danger: An Analysis of the Concepts of Pollution & Taboo. 208p. (C). 1984. pap. 21.99 (*0-415-06608-5*) Routledge.

— Risk Acceptability According to the Social Sciences. LC 85-60758. (Social Research Perspectives: Occasional Reports on Current Topics Ser.). 160p. (Orig.). 1986. pap. text 9.95 (*0-87154-211-0*) Russell Sage.

— Risk & Blame: Essays in Cultural Theory. 336p. (C). 1994. pap. 25.99 (*0-415-11999-5*) Routledge.

— Thought Styles & Everyday Life: The Gamut from Rude to Elegant. (C). 1996. 65.00 (*0-8039-7655-0*); pap. 19.95 (*0-8039-7656-9*) Sage.

Douglas, Mary & Hull, David L., eds. How Classification Works: Nelson Goodman among the Social Sciences. (Illus.). 256p. 1994. 76.50 (*0-7486-0351-4*, Pub. by Edinburgh U Pr) Col U Pr.

Douglas, Mary & Isherwood, Baron. The World of Goods: Towards an Anthropology of Consumption. rev. ed. LC 96-2582. 208p. (C). 1996. pap. 20.99 (*0-415-13047-6*) Routledge.

— The World of Goods: Towards an Anthropology of Consumption. rev. ed. LC 96-2582. 200p. (C). 1996. 85.00 (*0-415-13046-8*) Routledge.

Douglas, Mary & Ney, Steven. Missing Persons: A Critique of the Social Sciences. LC 98-12747. 237p. 1998. 24.95 (*0-520-20752-1*, Pub. by U CA Pr) Cal Prin Full Svc.

Douglas, Mary & Wildavsky, Aaron B. Risk & Culture: An Essay on the Selection of Technological & Environmental Dangers. LC 81-16318. 224p. 1982. pap. 16.95 (*0-520-05063-0*, Pub. by U CA Pr) Cal Prin Full Svc.

Douglas, McDonald, intro. The Billion Dollar Sale: Program Marketing. (Program Marketing - A New Phenomenum Ser.). (Illus.). 400p. 1986. spiral bd. 69.95 (*0-934487-53-7*) R M Greene.

Douglas McHenry International Symposium on Concret. Douglas McHenry International Symposium on Concrete & Concrete Structures. LC 78-51383. (ACI Publication Ser.: No. SP-55). (Illus.). 683p. reprint ed. pap. 200.00 (*0-7837-5220-2*, 204495100005) Bks Demand.

Douglas, Michael. Digital Logic Design: Tutorials & Laboratory Exercises. (Illus.). 128p. 1984. pap., suppl. ed. 58.95 (*0-471-60345-7*) Wiley.

Douglas, Mike, et al. I'll Be Right Back: Memories of TV's Greatest Talk Show. LC 99-46415. (Illus.). 320p. 1999. 25.00 (*0-684-85437-6*) S&S Trade.

***Douglas, Mike, et al.** I'll Be Right Back: Memories of TV's Greatest Talk Show. large type ed. LC 99-57112. (Biography Ser.). (Illus.). 2000. 26.95 (*0-7862-2358-8*) Thorndike Pr.

Douglas, Murray & Irvine, Chippy. Brunschwig & Fils Style. LC 94-40231. (Illus.). 208p. (gr. 8). 1995. 50.00 (*0-8212-2041-1*) Little.

Douglas, Nancy & Walker, Jackie. An Integrated Skills Course for Learners of English: Side Lines. LC 96-51584. (YA). 1997. pap. text. write for info. (*0-13-619909-7*); pap. text. write for info. (*0-13-619917-8*) P-H.

Douglas, Nancy, ed. see Walker, Jackie.

Douglas, Nancy A. Sam, the Adirondack Railroad Cat. LC 94-7690. (Illus.). 32p. (J). 1994. pap. 6.50 (*0-925168-28-9*) North Country.

Douglas, Nancy E. & Baum, Nathan. Library Research Guide to Psychology. LC 84-60640. (Library Research Guides Ser.: No. 7). 1984. pap. 15.00 (*0-87650-175-7*) Pierian.

Douglas, Nathan, et al. The Defiant Ones: A Screen Adaptation of the Story of "The Long Road" Garrett, George et al, eds. LC 71-135273. (Film Scripts Ser.). 1989. reprint ed. pap. text 19.95 (*0-89197-725-2*) Irvington.

Douglas, Neil & Wykowski, Terry. Beyond Reductionism: Gateways for Learning & Change. LC 99-17559. 1999. 39.95 (*1-57444-263-5*) St Lucie Pr.

Douglas, Neil, jt. auth. see Treble, Stephen.

Douglas, Neil H. Freshwater Fishes of Louisiana. 1974. 30.00 (*0-87511-028-2*) Claitors.

***Douglas, Nick & Slinger, Penny.** Sexual Secrets: 20th Anniversary Edition: The Alchemy of Ecstasy. anniversary ed. (Illus.). 416p. 1999. pap. 30.00 (*0-89281-805-0*) Inner Tradit.

Douglas, Nigel. The Joy of Opera. (Illus.). 375p. 1998. 40.00 (*0-233-98965-X*, Pub. by Andre Deutsch) Trafalgar.

***Douglas, Nigel.** The Joy of Opera. 2000. reprint ed. pap. 24.95 (*0-233-99840-3*, Pub. by Andre Deutsch) Trafalgar.

Douglas, Nigel. Legendary Voices. LC 94-23927. (Illus.). 306p. 1995. pap. 20.00 (*0-87910-187-3*) Limelight Edns.

— More Legendary Voices: With Recommended Recordings on CD. (Illus.). 342p. 1995. 35.00 (*0-87910-193-8*) Limelight Edns.

Douglas, Nik. Erotic Sentiment: In the Paintings of India & Nepal. (Illus.). 80p. 1998. pap. text 16.95 (*0-89281-685-6*) Inner Tradit.

— Spiritual Sex. LC 97-12494. (Illus.). 304p. 1997. per. 20.00 (*0-671-53739-3*) PB.

— Tantra Yoga. 1971. 24.00 (*0-685-40172-3*, Pub. by M Manoharial) S Asia.

Douglas, Nik & Slinger, Penny. The Erotic Sentiment: In the Paintings of China & Japan. (Illus.). 80p. 1990. 19.95 (*0-89281-379-2*) Inner Tradit.

— The Erotic Sentiment: In the Paintings of China & Japan. (Illus.). 80p. 1994. pap. 16.95 (*0-89281-495-0*, Park St Pr) Inner Tradit.

— The Secret Dakini Oracle. (Illus.). 224p. 1979. pap. 12.95 (*0-89281-005-X*, Destiny Bks) Inner Tradit.

— The Secret Dakini Oracle Deck: A Tantric Divination Deck. 1997. pap. 18.00 (*0-913866-89-X*) US Games Syst.

— Secretos Sexuales: La Alquimia del Extasis - El Arte Amatorio de las Civilizaciones Mas Exquisitas. (SPA., Illus.). 383p. 1998. pap. 19.95 (*0-89281-588-4*) Inner Tradit.

Douglas, Nik, ed. see Bhattacharyya, Bhaskar.

Douglas, Norman. Birds & Beasts of the Greek Anthology. LC 78-173162. 1977. reprint ed. 24.95 (*0-405-08461-7*, Pub. by Blom Pubns) Ayer.

— D. H. Lawrence & Maurice Magnus. LC 72-8663. (Studies in D. H. Lawrence: No. 20). 1973. reprint ed. lib. bdg. 75.00 (*0-8383-1673-5*) M S G Haskell Hse.

— Good-Bye to Western Culture: Some Footnotes on East & West. LC 70-184841. 241p. 1972. reprint ed. lib. bdg. 65.00 (*0-8371-6330-7*, DOWC, Greenwood Pr) Greenwood.

— In the Beginning. 1988. reprint ed. lib. bdg. 59.00 (*0-7812-0527-1*) Rprt Serv.

— In the Beginning. LC 76-144980. 1971. reprint ed. 55.00 (*0-403-00946-4*) Scholarly.

— Late Harvest. LC 75-41082. reprint ed. 27.50 (*0-404-14717-8*) AMS Pr.

— Looking Back. 1988. reprint ed. lib. bdg. 59.00 (*0-7812-0058-X*) Rprt Serv.

— Looking Back. LC 70-144981. 1971. reprint ed. 69.00 (*0-403-00795-X*) Scholarly.

— Old Calabria. LC 96-38229. 325p. 1996. pap. 15.95 (*0-8101-6022-6*, Marlboro) Northwestern U Pr.

— South Wind. 422p. 1976. 28.95 (*0-8488-0987-4*) Amereon Ltd.

Douglas, Norman, see Bey, Pilaff, pseud.

Douglas, O. Penny Plain. large type ed. 1974. 27.99 (*0-85456-302-4*) Ulverscroft.

Douglas, Oronto, jt. auth. see Okonta, Ike.

Douglas, P. German Market Survey. 1977. pap. 42.00 (*0-8464-0450-8*) Beekman Pubs.

Douglas, Pamela S., ed. Cardiovascular Health & Disease in Women. LC 92-48884. (Illus.). 368p. 1993. text 79.00 (*0-7216-4567-4*, W B Saunders Co) Harcrt Hlth Sci Grp.

Douglas, Patricia & Bay, Darlene. Test Bank to Accompany Governmental & Nonprofit Accounting. 2nd ed. 132p. (C). 1995. pap. text 40.00 (*0-03-007438-X*) Dryden Pr.

Douglas, Patricia P. Government & Nonprofit Accounting. 2nd ed. LC 94-70133. (C). 1994. text 103.00 (*0-03-006639-5*) Harcourt Coll Pubs.

Douglas, Paul. How to Win at Tennis: A Young Player's Guide. (Illus.). 192p. 1995. pap. 12.95 (*1-85253-322-6*) Cimino Pub Grp.

Douglas, Paul, jt. auth. see Driscoll, John.

Douglas, Paul H. Ethics in Government. LC 74-138222. 114p. 1972. reprint ed. lib. bdg. 49.75 (*0-8371-5579-7*, DOEG, Greenwood Pr) Greenwood.

— Know America: Its Ills & Cures. 1933. pap. 15.00 (*0-686-17412-7*) R S Barnes.

— Social Security in the United States: An Analysis & Appraisal of the Federal Social Security Act. LC 71-137164. (Poverty U. S. A. Historical Record Ser.). 1980. reprint ed. 23.95 (*0-405-03102-5*) Ayer.

— Social Security in the United States: An Analysis & Appraisal of the Federal Social Security Act. 2nd ed. LC 70-167847. (FDR & the Era of the New Deal Ser.). 1971. reprint ed. lib. bdg. 55.00 (*0-306-70323-8*) Da Capo.

— The Theory of Wages. LC 64-22237. (Reprints of Economic Classics Ser.). liv, 639p. 1964. reprint ed. 49.50 (*0-678-00062-X*) Kelley.

Douglas, Paul H. & Director, Aaron. The Problem of Unemployment. LC 75-17217. (Social Problems & Social Policy Ser.). (Illus.). 1976. reprint ed. 42.95 (*0-405-07488-3*) Ayer.

Douglas, Paul H., et al. The Worker in Modern Economic Society. LC 70-89730. (American Labor, from Conspiracy to Collective Bargaining Ser., No. 1). 929p. 1970. reprint ed. 46.95 (*0-405-02117-8*) Ayer.

Douglas, Paul H., jt. auth. see Pinsky, Laura.

Douglas, Pearl, jt. auth. see Douglas, Carl.

Douglas, Peter & Ong, Andy. Investing in Unit Trusts in Singapore. LC 98-945611. 256 p. 1997. write for info. (*981-00-9923-1*) Select Bks.

Douglas, Peter, jt. auth. see Lingard, Bob.

Douglas, Philip. Saint of Philadelphia: The Life of Bishop John Neumann. 1991. reprint ed. 13.95 (*0-911218-07-6*); reprint ed. pap. 7.95 (*0-911218-08-4*) Ravengate Pr.

Douglas, Philip A. & Stroud, Richard H., eds. A Symposium on the Biological Significance of Estuaries. 1971. 4.00 (*0-686-21854-X*) Sport Fishing.

Douglas, R. Confucianism & Taoism. 1973. 59.95 (*0-87968-930-7*) Gordon Pr.

Douglas, R., jt. ed. see Arveson, William B.

Douglas, R. C. Spiritual Evolution or Regeneration. 352p. 1998. reprint ed. pap. 24.95 (*0-7661-0464-8*) Kessinger Pub.

Douglas, R. G. Banach Algebra Techniques in the Theory of Toeplitz Operators. LC 73-1021. (CBMS Regional Conference Series in Mathematics: No. 15). 53p. 1973. reprint ed. pap. 23.00 (*0-8218-1665-9*, CBMS/15) Am Math.

Douglas, R. H., et al, eds. Light in Biology & Medicine, Vol. 1. (Illus.). 474p. 1988. 110.00 (*0-306-42918-7*, Plenum Trade) Perseus Pubng.

— Light in Biology & Medicine, Vol. 2. (Illus.). 582p. (C). 1991. text 186.00 (*0-306-44025-3*, Kluwer Plenum) Kluwer Academic.

Douglas, R. J., jt. ed. see Price, Raymond A.

Douglas, R. M. Feminist Freikorps. LC 98-15648. 200p. 1999. 55.00 (*0-275-96249-0*, Praeger Pubs) Greenwood.

Douglas, R. P. & Green, G. K. The Laws of Harbours & Pilotage. 4th ed. 344p. 1993. 120.00 (*1-85044-490-0*) LLP.

Douglas, R. W. & Ellis, Bryan, eds. Amorphous Materials: Papers Presented to the Third International Conference on the Physics of Non-Crystalline Solids, Sheffield University, September 1970. LC 77-162326. 568p. reprint ed. pap. 176.10 (*0-8357-5416-2*, 201615200098) Bks Demand.

Douglas, Rachel, tr. see Glazyev, Sergei.

Douglas, Ray. Dreams & the Inner Self. 1999. pap. text 10.95 (*0-7137-2776-4*) Blandford Pr.

— Palmistry. (Teach Yourself Ser.). 224p. 1998. pap. 11.95 (*0-8442-0278-9*, 02789, Teach Yrslf) NTC Contemp Pub Co.

— Palmistry & the Inner Self. (Illus.). 256p. 1995. pap. 12.95 (*0-7137-2520-6*, Pub. by Blandford Pr) Sterling.

Douglas, Richard, jt. ed. see Cossa, Ralph A.

Douglas, Richardo Keens. Nutmeg Princess. 1992. 11.15 (*0-606-05519-3*, Pub. by Turtleback) Demco.

Douglas, Robert & Wood, John P. The Peerage of Scotland, 2 vols. (Illus.). 1573p. 1994. reprint ed. 149.95 (*1-56869-061-4*) Oldbuck Pr.

Douglas, Robert B., ed. & tr. see De Pontgibaud, Chevalier.

Douglas, Robert C. Selected Indices of Industrial Characteristics for U. S. SMSA. (Discussion Papers: No. 20). 1967. pap. 10.00 (*1-55869-111-1*) Regional Sci Res Inst.

Douglas, Robert D., et al. Douglas' Forms, Vols. 1 & 4. 5th ed. LC 97-74261. 1997. write for info. (*1-55834-607-4*) LEXIS Pub.

***Douglas, Robert E.** Changing Your Identity. large type ed. 115p. (C). 1999. 24.95 (*0-9662335-4-9*) Info Res Pubs.

Douglas, Robert G., jt. ed. see Garrison, Robert.

Douglas, Robert K. Chinese Stories. rev. ed. (Illus.). 216p. 1990. reprint ed. pap. 9.95 (*9971-4-9165-6*) Heian Intl.

Douglas, Robin. Helping People Work Together: A Guide to Participative Working Practices. (C). 1988. 65.00 (*0-7855-0078-2*, Pub. by Natl Inst Soc Work) St Mut.

Douglas, Robin, et al, eds. Developing Residential Practice: A Source Book of References & Resources for Staff Development. (C). 1985. 59.00 (*0-7855-5887-X*, Pub. by Natl Inst Soc Work) St Mut.

Douglas, Robin & National Institute for Social Work Staff. Helping People Work Together: A Guide to Participative Working Practices. (C). 1988. pap. 21.00 (*0-902789-42-2*, Pub. by Natl Inst Soc Work) St Mut.

Douglas, Robin & Payne, Chris. Learning about Caring: An Introductory Package for Staff Development in Residential & Day Care. (C). 1988. 115.00 (*0-7855-3734-1*, Pub. by Natl Inst Soc Work); 99.00 (*0-902789-38-4*, Pub. by Natl Inst Soc Work); 188.00 (*0-7855-0088-X*, Pub. by Natl Inst Soc Work) St Mut.

— Organising for Learning: Staff Development Strategies for Residential & Day Services Work: A Theoretical & Practical Guide. (C). 1988. 50.00 (*0-7855-3733-3*, Pub. by Natl Inst Soc Work) St Mut.

— Organising for Learning: Staff Development Strategies for Residential & Day Services Work. A Theoretical & Practical Guide. (C). 1988. 95.00 (*0-7855-0077-4*, Pub. by Natl Inst Soc Work) St Mut.

— Organizing for Learning: Staff Development Strategies for Residential & Day Services Work: a Theoretical & Practical Guide. (C). 1988. 70.00 (*0-902789-53-8*, Pub. by Natl Inst Soc Work) St Mut.

Douglas, Robin & Payne, Chris, eds. Organising for Learning: Staff Development Strategies for Residential & Day Services Work. A Theoretical & Practical Guide. (C). 1988. 50.00 (*0-7855-5883-7*, Pub. by Natl Inst Soc Work) St Mut.

Douglas, Robin, et al. Supplement to Developing Residential Practice: A Source Book. (C). 1987. 49.00 (*0-7855-3731-7*, Pub. by Natl Inst Soc Work); 45.00 (*0-7855-5886-1*, Pub. by Natl Inst Soc Work) St Mut.

Douglas, Roger & Jones, Melinda. Administrative Law: Cases & Materials. 690p. 1993. pap. 64.00 (*1-86287-104-3*, Pub. by Federation Pr) Gaunt.

— Administrative Law: Commentary & Materials. 2nd ed. 674p. 1996. pap. 84.00 (*1-86287-190-6*, Pub. by Federation Pr) Gaunt.

***Douglas, Roger & Jones, Melinda.** Administrative Law: Commentary & Materials. 3rd ed. 797p. 1999. pap. 89.00 (*1-86287-325-9*, Pub. by Federation Pr) Gaunt.

Douglas, Ron H. & Djamgoz, Mustafa B., eds. The Visual System of Fish. 1990. 69.95 (*0-685-45312-X*) Chapman & Hall.

Douglas, Ronald G. Banach Algebra Techniques in Operator Theory. 2nd ed. Axler, S. et al, eds. LC 97-42889. (Graduate Texts in Mathematics Ser.: Vol. 179). 240p. 1998. text 49.00 (*0-387-98377-5*) Spr-Verlag.

— C*-Algebra Extensions & K-Homology. LC 80-424. (Annals of Mathematics Studies: No. 95). (Illus.). 93p. 1980. reprint ed. pap. 30.00 (*0-608-06617-6*, 206681400009) Bks Demand.

Douglas, Ronald G. & Schochet, Claude, eds. Operator Algebras & K-Theory. LC 82-4094. (Contemporary Mathematics Ser.: Vol. 10). 204p. 1982. reprint ed. pap. 23.00 (*0-8218-5011-3*, CONM/10) Am Math.

Douglas, Rosalie. The Circus Cage: A Journey of Transformation. (Illus.). 100p. (Orig.). (C). 1992. pap. 10.00 (*0-944164-02-1*) Moon Bear Pr.

Douglas, Roy. Great Nations Still Enchained: The Cartoonists' Vision of Empire 1878-1914. LC 92-40447. (Illus.). 232p. (C). (gr. 13). 1993. 70.00 (*0-415-06856-8*, B2417) Routledge.

— The Great War, 1914-1918: The Cartoonist's View. LC 94-48853. 168p. (C). (gr. 13). 1995. 90.00 (*0-415-11713-5*) Routledge.

— The World War, 1939-1945: The Cartoonist's Version. (Illus.). 312p. (C). 1991. pap. text 16.95 (*0-415-07141-0*, A6523) Routledge.

Douglas, Roy, et al. Drawing Conclusions: A Cartoon History of Anglo-Irish Relations, 1798-1998. LC 98-210295. (Illus.). 304p. 1998. pap. 24.95 (*0-85640-624-4*, Pub. by Blackstaff Pr) Dufour.

***Douglas, Roy, et al.** Ireland since 1690: A Concise History. LC 99-196643. 240p. 1999. pap. 18.95 (*0-85640-645-7*, Pub. by Blackstaff Pr) Dufour.

— Ireland since 1690: A Concise History. LC 00-35842. (Illus.). 2000. pap. 14.95 (*0-8092-9898-8*, Contemporary Bks) NTC Contemp Pub Co.

Douglas, Ruben H. & Macciomei, Nancy R., eds. Aphasia: Assessment & Treatment. (Special Education Ser.). 110p. (C). 1986. 24.95 (*0-582-28631-X*); pap. text 16.95 (*0-582-28617-4*) Longman.

Douglas, S. C. The Blue Rebels: Union Civilian & Military Treason, Sedition, & Subversion During the War Between the States. unabridged ed. 150p. 1997. pap. 17.45 (*0-9660312-2-9*) Shetland Pubns.

An Asterisk (*) at the beginning of an entry indicates that the title is appearing for the first time.

— The Fighting Boys of Wiregrass Vol. 1: A Short History of the Ben Hill Guards. unabridged ed. 78p. 1996. pap. 14.00 (*0-9660312-0-2*) Shetland Pubns.

— Genealogy Basics Vol. 1: A Step-by-Step Guide for Beginners. unabridged ed. 1997. pap. 10.00 (*0-9660312-3-7*) Shetland Pubns.

***Douglas, Sara.** Wayfarer Redemption: Battle Axe. 2000. text 24.95 (*0-312-87717-X*) Tor Bks.

Douglas, Sara U. Labor's New Voice: Unions & the Mass Media. Voigt, Melvin J., ed. LC 86-3373. (Communication & Information Science Ser.). 320p. 1986. text 78.50 (*0-89391-352-9*) Ablx Pub.

Douglas, Sarah A. & Mithal, Anant Kartik. The Ergonomics of Computer Pointing Devices. LC 96-49162. (Applied Computing Ser.). (Illus.). 233p. 1997. pap. 79.00 (*3-540-19986-1*) Spr-Verlag.

Douglas, Scott, jt. auth. see Pfitzinger, Pete.

Douglas, Scott, jt. auth. see Rodgers, Bill.

Douglas, Sharon, jt. auth. see Douglas, Edward M.

Douglas, Sheila. Lines upon the Water: A Collection of Original Songs. 112p. 1998. pap. 11.95 (*0-946005-89-3*, OS10496, Pub. by Ossian) Music Sales.

Douglas, Sheila, ed. The King o the Black Art & Other Folk Tales. 166p. 1987. text 26.00 (*0-08-035058-5*, Pub. by Aberdeen U Pr); pap. text 16.00 (*0-08-035059-3*, Pub. by Aberdeen U Pr) Macmillan.

Douglas-Smith, Basil. The Mystics Come to Harley St. 48p. 1984. 15.00 (*0-7212-0608-5*, Pub. by Regency Pr GBR) St Mut.

***Douglas Smith Wiggin, Kate.** Rebecca of Sunnybrook Farm. LC 00-40907. (Illus.). (J). 2001. write for info. (*0-694-01528-8*, HarpFestival) HarpC Child Bks.

Douglas, Spencer. The Secret of Sugarbush Hollow. LC 95-60395. (Spencer Douglas Presents Ser.). (Illus.). (J). (gr. 3-6). 1995. pap. 5.95 (*0-9645152-0-2*) Applchn Pub.

Douglas, Stephen. The Redhead Encyclopedia: The Complete Book on Redhead History, Facts, & Folklore. (Illus.). 240p. (Orig.). 1996. pap. 19.95 (*0-9645216-0-1*) Redheads Intl.

Douglas, Stephen, jt. auth. see Lincoln, Abraham.

Douglas, Stoneman. Suenglades, River of Grass. 308p. 1974. pap. 6.95 (*0-912451-44-0*) Florida Classics.

Douglas, Sue. Earth Music. 64p. 1981. 8.95 (*0-9607090-0-2*); pap. 4.95 (*0-9607090-1-0*) D&S Pubns.

Douglas, Susan. Where the Girls Are: Growing up Female with the Mass Media. 1995. pap. 16.00 (*0-8129-2530-0*, Times Bks) Crown Pub Group.

Douglas, Susan J. Inventing American Broadcasting, 1899-1922. LC 87-3717. (Studies in the History of Technology: No. 9). (Illus.). 400p. 1997. reprint ed. pap. text 18.95 (*0-8018-3832-0*) Johns Hopkins.

— Listening In. 2000. pap. 16.00 (*0-8129-3300-1*, Times Bks) Crown Pub Group.

Douglas, Susan J. Listening In: Radio & the American Imagination, from Amos 'n' Andy & Edward R. Murrow to Wolfman Jack & Howard Stern. (Illus.). 496p. 1999. 27.50 (*0-8129-2546-7*, Times Bks) Crown Pub Group.

Douglas, Susan P. & Craig, C. Samuel. Global Marketing Strategy. LC 94-22706. (Marketing Ser.). 576p. (C). 1994. 80.63 (*0-07-013447-2*) McGraw.

Douglas, Suzanne G., jt. auth. see Donow, Kenneth R.

Douglas, T. Survival in Groups: The Basics of Group Membership. LC 95-15367. 167p. 1995. 108.95 (*0-335-19413-3*) OpUniv Pr.

Douglas, T. H., ed. Pumped Storage. 449p. 1990. 16.00 (*0-7277-1586-0*) Am Soc Civil Eng.

Douglas, Tamsin, jt. auth. see Lazar, Barry.

Douglas, Tom. Basic Groupwork. LC 78-61491. 208p. 1978. 30.00 (*0-8236-0450-0*) Intl Univs Pr.

***Douglas, Tom.** Basic Groupwork. 2nd ed. LC 99-57246. 2000. pap. write for info. (*0-415-22479-9*) Routledge.

Douglas, Tom. Groupwork Practice. LC 76-1316. 217p. 1976. 32.50 (*0-8236-2245-2*) Intl Univs Pr.

— Intervention, Change & Consequence. LC 98-112204. 1997. 59.50 (*1-85343-376-4*, Pub. by Free Assoc Bks); pap. 23.50 (*1-85343-377-2*, Pub. by Free Assoc Bks) NYU Pr.

— Scapegoats: Transferring Blame. LC 95-30567. 224p. (C). 1995. pap. 25.99 (*0-415-11019-X*) Routledge.

— Scapegoats: Transferring Blame. LC 95-30567. 224p. (C). (gr. 13). 1995. 85.00 (*0-415-11018-1*) Routledge.

— Survival in Groups: The Basics of Group Membership. LC 95-15367. 176p. 1995. pap. 33.95 (*0-335-19412-5*) OpUniv Pr.

— Tom Douglas's Seattle Kitchen. 2001. 26.00 (*0-688-17242-3*, Wm Morrow) Morrow Avon.

Douglas, Tommy. Circus Dogs. 1983. pap. text 7.95 (*0-88982-092-9*, Pub. by Oolichan Bks) Genl Dist Srvs.

Douglas, Vincent. Brighter Child Grade Six: Math. 1993. pap. text 2.25 (*1-56189-076-6*) Amer Educ Pub.

— Comprehensive Curriculum Grade. (Comprehensive Curriculum of Basic Skills Ser.). (Illus.). 176p. (ps). 1994. pap., student ed. 10.95 (*1-56189-374-9*) Amer Educ Pub.

— Comprehensive Curriculum of Basic Skills Workbook Grade K. 176p. 1993. pap. text 10.95 (*1-56189-367-6*) Amer Educ Pub.

— Comprehensive Curriculum of Basic Skills Workbook Grade 1. 544p. 1993. pap. text 19.95 (*1-56189-368-4*) Amer Educ Pub.

— Comprehensive Curriculum of Basic Skills Workbook Grade 2. 544p. 1993. pap. text 19.95 (*1-56189-369-2*) Amer Educ Pub.

— Comprehensive Curriculum of Basic Skills Workbook Grade 3. 544p. 1993. pap. text 19.95 (*1-56189-370-6*) Amer Educ Pub.

— Comprehensive Curriculum of Basic Skills Workbook Grade 4. 544p. 1993. pap. text 19.95 (*1-56189-371-4*) Amer Educ Pub.

— Comprehensive Curriculum of Basic Skills Workbook Grade 5. 544p. 1993. pap. text 19.95 (*1-56189-372-2*) Amer Educ Pub.

— Comprehensive Curriculum of Basic Skills Workbook Grade 6. 544p. 1993. pap. text 19.95 (*1-56189-373-0*) Amer Educ Pub.

— Math. (Spectrum Ser.). (Illus.). 128p. (J). (gr. 1). 1997. pap., wbk. ed. 6.95 (*1-57768-111-8*) MG-Hill OH.

— Math. (Spectrum Ser.). (Illus.). 128p. (J). (gr. 2). 1997. pap., wbk. ed. 6.95 (*1-57768-112-6*) MG-Hill OH.

— Math. (Spectrum Ser.). (Illus.). 176p. (J). (gr. 3). 1997. pap., wbk. ed. 6.95 (*1-57768-113-4*) MG-Hill OH.

— Math. (Spectrum Ser.). (Illus.). 176p. (J). (gr. 4). 1997. pap., wbk. ed. 6.95 (*1-57768-114-2*) MG-Hill OH.

— Math. (Spectrum Ser.). (Illus.). 176p. (J). (gr. 5). 1997. pap., wbk. ed. 6.95 (*1-57768-115-0*) MG-Hill OH.

— Math. (Spectrum Ser.). (Illus.). 176p. (J). (gr. 6). 1997. pap., wbk. ed. 6.95 (*1-57768-116-9*) MG-Hill OH.

— Math. (Spectrum Ser.). (Illus.). 208p. (J). (gr. 7). 1997. pap., wbk. ed. 6.95 (*1-57768-117-7*) MG-Hill OH.

— Math. (Spectrum Ser.). (Illus.). 208p. (J). (gr. 8). 1997. pap., wbk. ed. 6.95 (*1-57768-118-5*) MG-Hill OH.

— Test Prep. (Spectrum Ser.). (Illus.). 160p. 1997. pap., wbk. ed. 8.95 (*1-57768-103-7*); pap., wbk. ed. 8.95 (*1-57768-104-5*); pap., wbk. ed. 8.95 (*1-57768-105-3*); pap., wbk. ed. 8.95 (*1-57768-106-1*); pap., wbk. ed. 8.95 (*1-57768-107-X*); pap., wbk. ed. 8.95 (*1-57768-108-8*) MG-Hill OH.

— Writing. (Spectrum Ser.). (Illus.). 88p. (J). (gr. 2). 1997. pap., wbk. ed. 6.95 (*1-57768-142-8*) MG-Hill OH.

— Writing. (Spectrum Ser.). (Illus.). 136p. (J). (gr. 3). 1997. pap., wbk. ed. 6.95 (*1-57768-143-6*) MG-Hill OH.

Douglas, Vincent F., ed. Enrichment: The Gifted Child: Math. (Illus.). 80p. (J). (gr. 1). 1995. wbk. ed. 4.95 (*1-56189-441-9*) Amer Educ Pub.

— Enrichment: The Gifted Child: Math. (Illus.). 80p. (J). (gr. 2). 1995. wbk. ed. 4.95 (*1-56189-442-7*) Amer Educ Pub.

— Enrichment: The Gifted Child: Math. (Illus.). 80p. (J). (gr. 3). 1995. wbk. ed. 4.95 (*1-56189-443-5*) Amer Educ Pub.

— Enrichment: The Gifted Child: Math. (Illus.). 80p. (J). (gr. 4). 1995. wbk. ed. 4.95 (*1-56189-444-3*) Amer Educ Pub.

— Enrichment: The Gifted Child: Math. (Illus.). 80p. (J). (gr. 6). 1995. wbk. ed. 4.95 (*1-56189-446-X*) Amer Educ Pub.

— Enrichment: The Gifted Child: Reading. (Illus.). 80p. (J). (gr. 1). 1995. wbk. ed. 4.95 (*1-56189-431-1*) Amer Educ Pub.

— Enrichment: The Gifted Child: Reading. (Illus.). 80p. (J). (gr. 2). 1995. wbk. ed. 4.95 (*1-56189-432-X*) Amer Educ Pub.

— Enrichment: The Gifted Child: Reading. (Illus.). 80p. (J). (gr. 3). 1995. wbk. ed. 4.95 (*1-56189-433-8*) Amer Educ Pub.

— Enrichment: The Gifted Child: Reading. (Illus.). 80p. (J). (gr. 4). 1995. wbk. ed. 4.95 (*1-56189-434-6*) Amer Educ Pub.

— Enrichment: The Gifted Child: Reading. (Illus.). 80p. (J). (gr. 5). 1995. wbk. ed. 4.95 (*1-56189-435-4*) Amer Educ Pub.

— Enrichment: The Gifted Child: Reading. (Illus.). 80p. (J). (gr. 6). 1995. wbk. ed. 4.95 (*1-56189-436-2*) Amer Educ Pub.

Douglas, Virginia. The Roadrunner (& His Cuckoo Cousin) LC 84-982. 48p. 1984. pap. 5.95 (*0-87961-147-2*) Naturegraph.

Douglas, Vivian, jt. auth. see Douglas, C. V.

Douglas, W. A. The Creation of a National Air Force: The Official History of the Royal Canadian Air Force, Vol. II. 1986. 49.95 (*0-8020-2584-6*) U of Toronto Pr.

Douglas, W. A. & Greenhous, Brereton. Out of the Shadows: Canada in the Second World War. 1977. 18.95 (*0-19-540257-X*) OUP.

Douglas, W. B. Carpentry & Joinery: A Comprehensive Self-Teaching Text in the Fine Art of Carpentry, Complete Home Building Instructions. 25.50 (*0-87559-109-4*) Shalom.

Douglas, W. L. Nevill's Wil Drafting Handbook. 4th ed. 149p. 1988. boxed set 63.00 (*0-409-70222-6*, NZ, MICHIE) LEXIS Pub.

***Douglas, W. M.** Andrew Murray & His Message: One of God's Choice Saints. 3rd ed. 244p. (Orig.). 1998. reprint ed. pap. 10.99 (*1-84030-042-6*) Ambassador Prodns Ltd.

Douglas, Walter B. Manuel Lisa. Nasatir, Abraham P., ed. (Illus.). 1964. reprint ed. 25.00 (*0-87266-006-0*) Argosy.

***Douglas, Warren.** Simply Human. 416p. 2000. mass mkt. 6.99 (*0-671-57882-0*) Baen Bks.

Douglas-Wiggins, Kate. Rebecca of Sunnybrook Farm. Hinkle, Don, ed. LC 87-15475. (Illus.). 48p. (J). (gr. 3-6). 1988. pap. 5.95 (*0-8167-1218-2*); lib. bdg. 19.95 (*0-8167-1217-4*) Troll Communs.

Douglas, William. Of Men & Mountains. 360p. 1990. pap. 10.95 (*0-87701-712-3*) Chronicle Bks.

Douglas, William & Smollett, Tobias George. The Cornutor of Seventy-Five, Being a Genuine Narrative of the Life, Adventures, & Amours, of Don Ricardo Honeywater: And Don Ricardo Honeywater Vindicated, in a Letter to Doctor Salguod, Pysician in Ordinary. LC 92-22023. (Augustan Reprints Ser.: Nos. 244-245). 1987. reprint ed. 21.50 (*0-404-70244-9*, R489) AMS Pr.

Douglas, William, jt. auth. see Jowett, Garth.

Douglas, William A., jt. ed. see Goldman, Ralph M.

Douglas, William A., ed. see O'Brien, Edward L. & Larkin, Mary C.

Douglas, William J. Environmental GIS, Application to Industrial Facilities. (Mapping Sciences Ser.). 144p. 1994. lib. bdg. 75.00 (*0-87371-991-3*, L991) Lewis Pubs.

Douglas, William O. Being an American. LC 77-134071. (Essay Index Reprint Ser.). 1977. reprint ed. 18.95 (*0-8369-2223-9*) Ayer.

— Douglas of the Supreme Court: A Selection of His Opinions. Countryman, Vern, ed. LC 73-719. 401p. 1973. reprint ed. lib. bdg. 35.00 (*0-8371-6790-6*, DODS, Greenwood Pr) Greenwood.

— My Wilderness. 256p. 1989. 5.95 (*0-89174-054-6*, Comstock Edns.

— The Right of the People. LC 80-19135. 238p. 1980. reprint ed. lib. bdg. 55.00 (*0-313-22640-7*, DORP, Greenwood Pr) Greenwood.

— Stare Decisis. (Reprint Series in Social Sciences). (C). 1993. reprint ed. pap. text 5.00 (*0-8290-2818-8*, PS-66) Irvington.

— Supreme Court & the Bicentennial. LC 77-77835. (Leverton Lectures: No. 4). 99p. 1978. 19.50 (*0-8386-2064-7*) Fairleigh Dickinson.

***Douglas, William O. & O'Fallon, James M.** Nature's Justice: Writings of William O. Douglas. LC 00-9322. (Northwest Readers Ser.). (Illus.). 320p. 2000. 35.00 (*0-87071-482-1*) Oreg St U Pr.

Douglas, William O. Symposium Staff. In Honor of Justice Douglas: Proceedings of the William O. Douglas Symposium on Individual Freedom & the Government, Fairhaven College, 1977, 12. Keller, Robert H., Jr., ed. LC 78-22723. (Contributions in Legal Studies: No. 12). 231p. 1979. 59.95 (*0-313-20959-6*, KJD/) Greenwood.

Douglas, William S., ed. Collected Works of Robert Burns, 6 vols., Set. (Collected Works Ser.). (Illus.). 2550p. (C). (gr. 13). 1993. text, boxed set 700.00 (*0-415-09918-8*, B3778) Routledge.

Douglas, William S., ed. see Lockhart, John G.

Douglas-Young, John. Illustrated Encyclopedic Dictionary of Electronic Circuits. LC 82-23067. 444p. 1983. 32.95 (*0-13-450734-7*) P-H.

— Practical Oscilloscope Handbook. (Illus.). 1979. 14.95 (*0-13-693549-4*, Parker Publishing Co) P-H.

Douglass. Battleground: Seal Team Seven. large type ed. LC 98-31304. 1999. 30.00 (*0-7838-0416-4*, G K Hall Lrg Type) Mac Lib Ref.

Douglass, A. E. Climatic Cycle & Tree Growth, 3 vols. in one, Vol. 1 & 2. 1971. 98.00 (*3-7682-0720-X*) Lubrecht & Cramer.

— Climatic Cycle & Tree Growth, 3 vols. in 1, Vol. 3. 1971. write for info. (*0-318-54135-1*) Lubrecht & Cramer.

Douglass, Amy A. Prehistoric Exchange & Sociopolitical Development in the Plateau Southwest. LC 90-49134. (Evolution of North American Indians Ser.). 396p. 1990. reprint ed. text 10.00 (*0-8240-2500-8*) Garland.

Douglass, Ann & Sussman, John R. The Unofficial Guide to Having a Baby. (Illus.). 864p. 1999. pap. 15.95 (*0-02-862695-8*, Pub. by Macmillan) S&S Trade.

Douglass, Ben. History of Wayne Co. Ohio: From the Days of the Pioneers & First Settlers to the Present Time. (Illus.). 911p. (Orig.). 1874. pap. text 51.00 (*1-55613-995-0*) Heritage Bk.

— History of Wayne County Ohio. 868p. 1993. reprint ed. lib. bdg. 87.00 (*0-8328-2834-3*) Higginson Bk Co.

Douglass, Bruce P. Doing Hard Time: Using Object-Oriented Programming Software Patterns in Real Time Application. LC 99-18093. 800p. (C). 1999. 64.95 (*0-201-49837-5*) Addison-Wesley.

— Numerical BASIC. 1984. write for info. (*0-318-57974-X*) Macmillan.

— Real-Time UML. LC 97-39889. 400p. (C). 1997. pap. 37.95 (*0-201-32579-9*) Addison-Wesley.

— Using TURBO, IBM, & MICROSOFT PASCAL: An Applications Approach. write for info. (*0-318-59639-3*) S&S Trade.

Douglass, Carrie B. Bulls, Bullfighting & Spanish Identities. LC 96-45806. (Illus.). 270p. 1997. 35.00 (*0-8165-1651-0*) U of Ariz Pr.

Douglass, Catherine J. & Lieberman, Ellen. Corporate Counseling Monography Series: New York Securities Law: Practice & Policy. Merritt, Raymond W. & Ennico, Clifford M., eds. 125p. 1990. pap. 25.00 (*0-942954-27-0*) NYS Bar.

Douglass, Chester W., jt. auth. see Gillings, Dennis B.

***Douglass-Chin, Richard J.** Preacher Woman Sings the Blues: The Autobiographies of Nineteenth-Century African American Evangelists. 288p. 2001. 34.95 (*0-8262-1311-1*) U of Mo Pr.

Douglass, Curran. Austin Overview. (Illus.). 244p. (Orig.). 1995. pap. 16.95 (*1-57168-068-3*) Sunbelt Media.

Douglass, D. H., ed. see American Institute of Physics.

Douglass, D. L. & Kunz, F. W., eds. Columbium Metallurgy: Proceedings. LC 61-9442. (Metallurgy Society Conferences Ser.: Vol. 10). 763p. reprint ed. pap. 200.00 (*0-608-11110-4*, 200067300038) Bks Demand.

Douglass, Darren. Lonely Planet Diving & Snorkeling Guide to California's Central Coast: Including Southern Monterey County, San Luis Obispo County, Santa Barbara County, Ventura County. LC 94-20895. (Pisces Diving & Snorkeling Guides Ser.). 80p. 1994. pap. 14.95 (*1-55992-079-3*, Pisces Books) Lonely Planet.

Douglass, Darren & Douglass, Stacey. Diving Offshore California. rev. ed. LC 91-71780. (Illus.). 128p. (Orig.). 1997. pap. 18.95 (*0-9623389-5-8*) Aqua Quest

Douglass, David H., ed. see Braginsky, Vladimir B.

Douglass, David H., ed. see Braginsky, Vladimir B. & Manukin, A. B.

Douglass, David J. Pit Sense vs. the State. 112p. (Orig.). 1993. pap. 9.95 (*0-948984-26-0*, Pub. by Phoenix Pr) AK Pr Dist.

Douglass, David L. Public Report of the White House Security Review. (Illus.). 106p. (C). 1998. reprint ed. pap. text 25.00 (*0-7881-4654-8*) DIANE Pub.

Douglass, Don. GPS Waypoints British Columbia Coast, 1997. LC 97-20242. 144p. 1997. pap. 9.95 (*0-938665-50-2*) Fine Edge Prods.

***Douglass, Don & Hemingway-Douglass, Reanne.** Exploring Southeast Alaska: Dixon Entrance to Skagway. LC 99-55655. 400p. 2000. pap. 59.95 (*0-938665-58-8*) Fine Edge Prods.

Douglass, Don & Hemingway-Douglass, Reanne. Exploring the Inside Passage to Alaska: A Cruising Guide from the San Juan Islands to Glacier Bay. 1996. pap. text 49.95 (*0-07-018010-5*) McGraw.

— Exploring the San Juan & Gulf Islands: Cruising Paradise of the Pacific Northwest. LC 98-16845. (Illus.). 250p. 1998. pap. 39.95 (*0-938665-51-0*) Fine Edge Prods.

— Exploring the South Coast of British Columbia: Gulf Islands & Desolation Sound to Port Hardy & Blunden Harbour. rev. ed. LC 99-22931. 480p. 1999. pap. 49.95 (*0-938665-62-6*) Fine Edge Prods.

— Exploring Vancouver Island's West Coast: A Cruising Guide. 2nd rev. ed. LC 99-11366. (Illus.). 288p. 1999. pap. 49.95 (*0-938665-57-X*) Fine Edge Prods.

Douglass, Don & Lombardo, Chris. Ski Touring the Eastern High Sierra. 1990. 8.95 (*0-938665-08-1*) Fine Edge Prods.

***Douglass, Don & Monahan, Kevin.** Proven Cruise Routes of Alaska's Inside Passage: Seattle to Ketchikan. (Illus.). 2000. 39.95 (*0-938665-49-9*) Fine Edge Prods.

Douglass, Don, jt. auth. see Monahan, Kevin.

Douglass, Donald C. & Hemingway-Douglass, Reanne. Exploring the North Coast of British Columbia: From Blunden Harbour to Dixon Entrance, Including the Queen Charlotte Islands. LC 96-48468. (Illus.). 400p. 1997. pap. 49.95 (*0-938665-45-6*) Fine Edge Prods.

Douglass, Donna. Accent on Rhythm: Music Activities for the Aged. 3rd rev. ed. (MMB Horizon Ser.: No. 1). 88p. 1985. pap. 16.00 (*0-918812-47-X*, ST 015) MMB Music.

Douglass, Donna N., jt. auth. see Douglass, Merrill E.

Douglass, E. P. Rebels & Democrats. LC 77-160853. (Era of the American Revolution Ser.). 368p. 1971. reprint ed. 45.00 (*0-306-70402-1*) Da Capo.

Douglass, Elisha P. Rebels & Democrats: The Struggle for Equal Political Rights & Majority Rule During the American Revolution. 384p. 1989. reprint ed. pap. text 9.95 (*0-929587-12-X*, Elephant Paperbacks) I R Dee.

Douglass, Fenner. Cavaillbe-Coll & the French Romantic Tradition. LC 98-41897. (Illus.). 272p. 1999. 35.00 (*0-300-07114-0*) Yale U Pr.

— The Language of the Classical French Organ: A Musical Tradition Before 1800. expanded rev. ed. LC 94-45846. 251p. 1995. pap. 19.00 (*0-300-06426-8*) Yale U Pr.

Douglass, Frederick. Autobiographies: Narrative of a Life, My Bondage & My Freedom, Life & Times. Gates, Henry Louis, Jr., ed. LC 93-24168. 1126p. 1994. 35.00 (*0-940450-79-8*, Pub. by Library of America) Penguin Putnam.

— Autobiographies: Narrative of the Life, My Bondage & My Freedom: Life & Times. Gates, Henry Louis, Jr., ed. LC 93-24168. (Library of America College Editions). 1126p. (C). 1996. pap. text 13.95 (*1-883011-30-2*, Pub. by Library of America) Penguin Putnam.

— Collected Works. 1990. reprint ed. lib. bdg. 75.00 (*0-7812-2673-2*, 1510); reprint ed. write for info. (*0-318-67700-8*); reprint ed. write for info. (*0-318-67701-6*) Rprt Serv.

— Escape from Slavery: The Boyhood of Frederick Douglass in His Own Words. McCurdy, Michael, ed. & illus. by. 1993. pap. 6.99 (*0-679-84651-4*) Knopf.

Douglass, Frederick. Escape from Slavery: The Boyhood of Frederick Douglass in His Own Words. (J). 1994. 12.19 (*0-606-05824-9*, Pub. by Turtleback) Demco.

Douglass, Frederick. The Frederick Douglass Papers, Series 1 Vol.4: Speeches, Debates, & Interviews, 1864-80. Blassingame, John W. & McKivigan, John R., eds. 744p. 1991. 95.00 (*0-300-05142-5*) Yale U Pr.

— Frederick Douglass: Selected Speeches & Writings. Foner, Philip S. & Taylor, Yuval, eds. LC 99-23180. (Library of Black America). 800p. 1999. 39.95 (*1-55652-349-1*, Pub. by Chicago Review) IPG Chicago.

— Frederick Douglass: The Narrative & Selected Writings. 391p. (C). 1983. pap. 8.44 (*0-07-554375-3*) McGraw.

— Frederick Douglass: The Narrative & Selected Writings. Meyer, Michael, ed. 448p. (C). 1983. pap. text. write for info. (*0-318-57305-9*) Random.

— Frederick Douglass on Women's Rights. 200p. 1992. reprint ed. pap. 13.95 (*0-306-80489-1*) Da Capo.

— Frederick Douglass on Women's Rights, 25. Foner, Philip S., ed. LC 76-5326. (Contributions in Afro-American & African Studies: No. 25). 190p. 1976. 35.00 (*0-8371-8895-4*, FFD/, Greenwood Pr) Greenwood.

— The Frederick Douglass Papers: Series 1: Speeches, Debates, & Interviews Vol. I: 1841-1846. Blassingame, John W., ed. LC 78-16687. Vol. 1. 1979. 90.00 (*0-300-02246-8*) Yale U Pr.

— The Frederick Douglass Papers: Speeches, Debates, & Interviews, 1855-1863, Vol. 3, Ser. 1. LC 78-16687. 720p. 1986. 90.00 (*0-300-02923-3*) Yale U Pr.

— Life & Times of Frederick Douglass. (American Biography Ser.). 640p. 1991. reprint ed. lib. bdg. 109.00 (*0-7812-8110-5*) Rprt Serv.

— Life & Times of Frederick Douglass. (Notable American Authors Ser.). 1992. reprint ed. lib. bdg. 75.00 (*0-7812-2676-7*) Rprt Serv.

— Life & Times of Frederick Douglass: The Complete Autobiography. LC 62-12834. 640p. 1962. pap. 14.95 (*0-02-002350-2*) Macmillan.

— The Life & Writings of Frederick Douglass: Supplementary Volume: 1844-1860, Vol. 5. Foner, Philip S., ed. LC 50-7654. 1975. 17.00 (*0-7178-0453-4*); pap. 7.95 (*0-7178-0454-2*) Intl Pubs Co.

— My Bondage & My Freedom. Andrews, William L., ed. & intro. by. LC 87-5002. (Blacks in the New World Ser.). 344p. (C). 1988. text 34.95 (*0-252-01409-X*); pap. text 16.95 (*0-252-01410-3*) U of Ill Pr.

D

An Asterisk (*) at the beginning of an entry indicates that the title is appearing for the first time.

— My Bondage & My Freedom. LC 68-28994. (American Negro: His History & Literature. Series 1). (Illus.). 480p. 1968. reprint ed. 37.95 (*0-405-01813-4*) Ayer.
— My Bondage & My Freedom. (Black Rediscovery Ser.). 1969. reprint ed. pap. 8.95 (*0-486-22457-0*) Dover.
— My Bondage & My Freedom. (American Biography Ser.). 464p. 1991. reprint ed. lib. bdg. 89.00 (*0-7812-8111-3*) Rprt Serv.
— My Bondage & My Freedom. (Notable American Authors Ser.). 1992. reprint ed. lib. bdg. 75.00 (*0-7812-2675-9*) Rprt Serv.
— Narrative Life of Frederick Douglass. 1976. 17.95 (*0-8488-0264-0*) Amereon Ltd.
***Douglass, Frederick.** Narrative of the Life & Times of Frederick Douglass. 2000. pap. 8.95 (*1-930097-11-5*) Lushena Bks.
Douglass, Frederick. Narrative of the Life of an American Slave. large type ed. LC 97-30820. 148p. 1997. text 22.95 (*1-56000-534-3*) Transaction Pubs.
— The Narrative of the Life of Frederick Douglass. (Thrift Editions Ser.). (Illus.). 96p. 1995. pap. text 1.00 (*0-486-28499-9*) Dover.
— The Narrative of the Life of Frederick Douglass: An American Slave. LC 97-69696. 127p. (C). 1998. mass mkt. 4.95 (*0-451-52673-2*) Addson-Wesley Educ.
— The Narrative of the Life of Frederick Douglass: An American Slave. 124p. 1963. pap. 5.95 (*0-385-00705-1*, Anchor NY) Doubleday.
— The Narrative of the Life of Frederick Douglass: An American Slave. McDowell, Deborah E., ed. (Oxford World's Classics Ser.). 176p. 2000. pap. 8.95 (*0-19-283250-6*) OUP.
— The Narrative of the Life of Frederick Douglass: An American Slave. Baker, Houston A., Jr., ed. & intro. by. (American Library). 159p. 1981. pap. 11.99 (*0-14-039012-X*, Penguin Classics) Viking Penguin.
— The Narrative of the Life of Frederick Douglass: An American Slave. large type ed. (Large Print Heritage Ser.). 178p. 1997. lib. bdg. 26.95 (*1-58118-016-0*, 21485) LRS.
— The Narrative of the Life of Frederick Douglass: An American Slave. (American Biography Ser.). 163p. 1991. reprint ed. lib. bdg. 59.00 (*0-7812-8112-1*) Rprt Serv.
— The Narrative of the Life of Frederick Douglass: An American Slave. (Notable American Authors Ser.). 1992. reprint ed. lib. bdg. 75.00 (*0-7812-2674-0*) Rprt Serv.
— Narrative of the Life of Frederick Douglass: An American Slave, Written by Himself. Quarles, Benjamin, ed. LC 59-11516. (John Harvard Library). (Illus.). 163p. 1960. pap. 8.95 (*0-674-60101-7*) HUP.
— Narrative of the Life of Frederick Douglass: An American Slave, Written by Himself. LC 92-61004. (Books in American History). 163p. (C). 1993. pap. text 11.95 (*0-312-07531-6*) St Martin.
Douglass, Frederick. Narrative of the Life of Frederick Douglass: Authoritative Text, Contexts, Criticism. Andrews, William L. & McFeely, William S., eds. LC 95-47594. (C). 1996. pap. text 6.50 (*0-393-96966-5*) Norton.
Douglass, Frederick. The Oxford Frederick Douglass Reader. Andrews, William L., ed. & intro. by. 384p. (C). 1996. pap. text 27.95 (*0-19-509118-3*) OUP.
— The Slave Narrative of Frederick Douglass. LC 97-128626. 176p. 1997. mass mkt. 5.99 (*0-440-22228-1*) Dell.
— Speeches, Debates & Interviews, 1881-1895. Blassingame, John W. & McKivigan, John R., eds. (Frederick Douglass Papers: Series One, Vol. 5). 832p. (C). 1992. 95.00 (*0-300-04877-7*) Yale U Pr.
— Thoughts for All Time Vol. 1: Selections from the Works of Frederick Douglass. 4th rev. ed. (Illus.). 32p. 1996. pap. 3.95 (*1-887878-04-1*) Pks & Hist.
— Why Is the Negro Lynched? Obaba, Al I., ed. 49p. (Orig.). (YA). 1991. pap. text 7.95 (*0-916157-78-4*) African Islam Miss Pubns.
***Douglass, Frederick & Jacobs, Harriet A.** Narrative of the Life of Frederick Douglass, an American Slave. LC 00-30534. 2000. 10.95 (*0-679-78328-8*) Modern Lib NY.
***Douglass, Frederick, et al.** The Frederick Douglass Papers. LC 98-26125. Vol. 1. (Illus.). 288p. 1999. 45.00 (*0-300-07196-5*) Yale U Pr.
Douglass, Frederick, et al. Three Classic African-American Novels. Andrews, William L., ed. 1990. mass mkt. 6.99 (*0-451-62788-1*, Ment) NAL.
Douglass, Frederick, IV, jt. auth. see Fullwood, Harlow, Jr.
Douglass, Frederick, jt. auth. see Jones, Edward L.
Douglass, Gladys. Oh Grandma, You're Kidding. (Illus.). 110p. 1983. pap. 7.95 (*0-934904-00-6*) J & L Lee.
Douglass, Harl R., jt. auth. see Gruhn, William T.
Douglass, Harlan P. The Little Town: Especially in Its Rural Relationships. LC 75-112553. (Rise of Urban America Ser.). (Illus.). 1970. reprint ed. 24.95 (*0-405-02448-7*) Ayer.
— The Little Town: Especially in Its Rural Relationships. (Select Bibliographies Reprint Ser.). 1977. reprint ed. 24.95 (*0-8369-6643-0*) Ayer.
— St. Louis Church Survey: A Religious Investigation with a Social Background. LC 77-112540. (Rise of Urban America Ser.). (Illus.). 1978. reprint ed. 23.95 (*0-405-02449-5*) Ayer.
— Suburban Trend. LC 73-124478. (Rise of Urban America Ser.). 1974. reprint ed. 25.95 (*0-405-02450-9*) Ayer.
Douglass, Harold O., Jr., ed. Gastric Cancer. (Contemporary Issues in Clinical Oncology Ser.: Vol. 8). (Illus.). 244p. 1988. text 63.00 (*0-443-08536-6*) Church.
— Gastric Cancer. fac. ed. LC 87-25592. (Contemporary Issues in Clinical Oncology Ser.: No. 8). (Illus.). 262p. 1988. reprint ed. pap. 81.30 (*0-7837-7902-X*, 204765800008) Bks Demand.

Douglass, Herbert E. The Faith of Jesus: Saying Yes to God's Love. 96p. 1991. pap. 6.95 (*0-945460-12-0*) Upward Way.
— Messenger of the Lord: The Prophetic Ministry of Ellen G. White. LC 98-15574. 1998. 24.99 (*0-8163-1622-8*) Pacific Pr Pub Assn.
— Why Jesus Waits: How the Sanctuary Message Explains the Mission of the Seventh-Day Adventist Church. rev. ed. LC 76-10925. 96p. (YA). (gr. 10 up). 1987. pap. 3.95 (*0-945460-00-7*) Upward Way.
Douglass, J. H., contrib. by. Cassell's French & English Dictionary. (ENG & FRE.). 658p. 1986. mass mkt. 5.00 (*0-02-013680-3*) Macmillan.
Douglass, Jack R. & Douglass, William A. Tap Dancing on Ice: The Life & Times of a Nevada Gaming Pioneer. (Illus.). xvi, 255p. 1996. 21.95 (*1-56475-373-5*) U NV Oral Hist.
Douglass, Jackie L. Peterson First Guide to Shells of North America. 1989. 10.05 (*0-606-04509-0*, Pub. by Turtleback) Demco.
Douglass, James W. The Nonviolent Coming of God. LC 91-23942. 250p. (Orig.). 1991. pap. 16.00 (*0-88344-753-3*) Orbis Bks.
Douglass, Jane D. Women, Freedom, & Calvin. LC 85-8778. 156p. 1985. pap. 18.95 (*0-664-24663-X*) Westminster John Knox.
Douglass, Jane D. & Kay, James F., eds. Women, Gender, & Community. LC 96-40009. 160p. (Orig.). 1997. pap. 17.95 (*0-664-25728-3*) Westminster John Knox.
Douglass, Janet. God Is Coming. Polk, Barbara, ed. (Illus.). 96p. 1998. pap., per. 22.00 (*0-9665147-0-X*) JD Assocs.
Douglass, Jessica. Montana Rogue. 1995. per. 3.75 (*0-373-07665-7*) Harlequin Bks.
Douglass, Joan H. Information Systems: Index of Modern Information. LC 88-48006. 150p. 1989. 47.50 (*1-55914-092-5*); pap. 44.50 (*1-55914-093-3*) ABBE Pubs Assn.
***Douglass, John Aubrey.** The California Idea & American Higher Education: 1850 to the 1960 Master Plan. LC 99-45668. (Illus.). 435p. 2000. 55.00 (*0-8047-3189-6*) Stanford U Pr.
Douglass, John J., ed. Roles & Functions of the Prosecutor, 4 vols. Incl. Discretionary Authority of the Prosecutor. 1977. 4.25 Pretrial Problems of the Prosecutor. 1977. 4.25 Prosecutorial Relationships in Criminal Justice. 1977. 4.25 Special Problems in Prosecution. 1977. 4.25 1977. 26.50 (*0-318-18680-2*) NCDA.
Douglass, John S. & Harnden, Glenn P. The Art of Technique: An Aesthetic Approach to Film & Video Production. LC 95-24513. 350p. 1995. pap. text 41.00 (*0-205-14248-6*) Allyn.
Douglass, Joseph D. Red Cocaine: The Drugging of America & the West. 1999. pap. 35.00 (*1-899798-04-8*) E Harle Ltd.
Douglass, Judith S., et al. Composition of Foods: Breakfast Cereals: Raw, Processed, Prepared. (Illus.). 160p. (Orig.). (C). 1995. pap. text 40.00 (*0-7881-2478-1*) DIANE Pub.
Douglass, Judy D. What Can a Mother Do? Finding Significance at Home & Beyond. LC 87-21753. 189p. Date not set. pap. 6.99 (*0-89840-201-8*) Integrtd Res.
Douglass, Karl. Last Phoenix: A Novel of Betrayal & Revenge, 2 vols. LC 96-72473. 984p. (Orig.). 1997. pap., boxed set 29.95 (*1-888125-02-0*) Publ Consult.
Douglass, Kathy, ed. see Krause, Danna J.
Douglass, Keith. Afterburn. (Carrier Ser.: No. 7). 336p. 1996. mass mkt. 6.99 (*0-515-11914-8*, Jove) Berkley Pub.
— Alpha Strike, Vol. 8. (Carrier Ser.: No. 8). 336p. 1997. mass mkt. 6.99 (*0-515-12018-9*, Jove) Berkley Pub.
— Arctic Fire. (Carrier Ser.). 336p. 1997. mass mkt. 5.99 (*0-515-12084-7*, Jove) Berkley Pub.
— Armageddon Mode. (Carrier Ser.: No. 3). 1992. mass mkt. 4.99 (*0-515-10864-2*, Jove) Berkley Pub.
— Arsenal. (Creed Ser.). 1998. mass mkt. 6.99 (*0-425-16345-8*) Berkley Pub.
— Battleground. (Seal Team Seven Ser.). 1998. mass mkt. 5.99 (*0-425-16375-X*) Berkley Pub.
***Douglass, Keith.** Brink of War, 1 vol., Vol. 13. (Carrier Ser.). 266p. 1999. mass mkt. 5.99 (*0-515-12470-2*, Jove) Berkley Pub.
Douglass, Keith. Carrier. 1991. mass mkt. 6.50 (*0-515-10593-7*, Jove) Berkley Pub.
— Carrier: Nuke Zone. (Carrier Ser.: Vol. 11). 305p. 1998. mass mkt. 5.99 (*0-515-12253-X*, Jove) Berkley Pub.
— Chain of Command, 12. (Carrier Ser.: Vol. 12). 313p. 1999. mass mkt. 5.99 (*0-515-12431-1*, Jove) Berkley Pub.
— Countdown. (Carrier Ser.: No. 6). 336p. (Orig.). 1994. mass mkt. 5.99 (*0-515-11309-3*, Jove) Berkley Pub.
— Deathrace, 1 vol. (SEAL Team Seven Ser.). 1999. mass mkt. 5.99 (*0-425-16741-0*) Berkley Pub.
— Direct Action. (Seal Team Seven Ser.: No. 4). 288p. (Orig.). 1997. mass mkt. 5.99 (*0-425-15605-2*) Berkley Pub.
— Flame Out. (Carrier Ser.: No. 4). 336p. (Orig.). 1992. mass mkt. 5.99 (*0-515-10994-0*, Jove) Berkley Pub.
***Douglass, Keith.** Flashpoint. (SEAL Team Seven Ser.: Vol. 11). (Illus.). 320p. (J). 2000. mass mkt. 5.99 (*0-425-17503-0*) Berkley Pub.
Douglass, Keith. Maelstrom. (Carrier Ser.: No. 5). 336p. (Orig.). 1993. mass mkt. 5.99 (*0-515-11080-9*, Jove) Berkley Pub.
— Seal Team 7. 336p. (Orig.). 1994. mass mkt. 5.99 (*0-425-14340-6*) Berkley Pub.
— Seal Team 7. (SEAL Team Seven Ser.: No. 5). 304p. (Orig.). 1997. mass mkt. 5.99 (*0-425-16139-0*) Berkley Pub.
***Douglass, Keith.** Seal Team Seven: Frontal Assault, 10. 2000. mass mkt. 5.99 (*0-425-17352-6*) Berkley Pub.

Douglass, Keith. Seal Team 7: Nucflash. 304p. (Orig.). 1995. mass mkt. 5.99 (*0-425-14881-5*) Berkley Pub.
— Seal Team 7: Specter. 304p. (Orig.). 1995. mass mkt. 5.99 (*0-425-14569-7*) Berkley Pub.
***Douglass, Keith.** Typhoon Season. (Carrier Ser.: Vol. 14). 2000. mass mkt. 5.99 (*0-515-12736-1*, Jove) Berkley Pub.
Douglass, Keith. Viper Strike. (Carrier Ser.: No. 2). 1991. mass mkt. 5.99 (*0-515-10729-8*, Jove) Berkley Pub.
— War Cry, Vol. 9. 1999. mass mkt. 5.99 (*0-425-17117-5*) Berkley Pub.
***Douglass, Keith C.** Enemies. (Carrier Ser.: Vol. 15). 2000. mass mkt. 5.99 (*0-515-12869-4*) Berkley Pub.
Douglass, Larry W. & Kramer, Amihud, eds. Statistical Methods for Food & Agriculture. (Illus.). 345p. 1989. reprint ed. pap. text 49.95 (*1-56022-000-7*) Haworth Jrnl Co-Edits.
Douglass, Laura M. The Effective Nurse: Leader & Manager. 5th ed. (Illus.). 448p. (C). (gr. 13). 1995. pap. text 36.00 (*0-8151-2779-0*, 25188) Mosby Inc.
Douglass, Lois, ed. see Van Peebles, Melvin.
Douglass, Malcolm P. The History, Psychology & Pedagogy of Geographic Literacy. LC 98-14489. 208p. 1998. 59.95 (*0-275-96138-9*, Praeger Pubs) Greenwood.
***Douglass, Malcolm P.** The History, Psychology & Pedagogy of Geographic Literacy. 208p. 1999. pap. 27.95 (*0-275-96804-9*, Praeger Pubs) Greenwood.
Douglass, Malcolm P. Learning to Read: The Quest for Meaning. 176p. 1989. text 26.00 (*0-8077-2970-1*) Tchrs Coll.
Douglass, Malcolm P., ed. Claremont Reading Conference Yearbook: Reading: A Literary Feast. 260p. (Orig.). 1989. pap. 20.00 (*0-941742-07-5*) Claremont Grad.
— Literacy: Signs for Our Times. (Claremont Reading Conference Yearbook Ser.). 178p. (Orig.). 1988. pap. 20.00 (*0-941742-06-7*) Claremont Grad.
— Reading: The Process of Creating Meaning for Sensed Stimuli. (Claremont Reading Conference Yearbook Ser.). 234p. 1987. pap. 20.00 (*0-941742-05-9*) Claremont Grad.
— Reading: The Quest for Meaning. (Claremont Reading Conference Yearbook Ser.). 379p. 1986. pap. 20.00 (*0-941742-04-0*) Claremont Grad.
— Reading in the Age of the Computer. (Claremont Reading Conference Yearbook Ser.). 255p. 1984. pap. 7.00 (*0-941742-02-4*) Claremont Grad.
— Reading Reading: 50th Anniversary Perspectives. (Claremont Reading Conference Yearbook Ser.). 241p. 1983. pap. 6.00 (*0-941742-01-6*) Claremont Grad.
— Writing & Reading in a Balanced Curriculum. (Claremont Reading Conference Yearbook Ser.). 222p. (Orig.). 1982. pap. 5.00 (*0-941742-00-8*) Claremont Grad.
Douglass, Malcolm P., ed. Writing & Reading Across the Curriculum. (Claremont Reading Conference Yearbook Ser.). 276p. (Orig.). 1985. pap. 15.00 (*0-941742-03-2*) Claremont Grad.
Douglass, Melvin I. Black Winners: History of Springarm Medalists, 1915-1983. 160p. 1984. pap. 7.95 (*0-912444-31-2*) DARE Bks.
Douglass, Merrill, ed. see Kenison, Fred.
Douglass, Merrill E. ABC Time Tips. LC 97-42113. 224p. 1998. pap. 12.95 (*0-07-021995-8*) McGraw.
— Ideas for Better Living. unabridged ed. 27p. pap. 34.50 incl. audio (*0-88432-178-9*, S13054) Audio-Forum.
— Make Time Work for You. unabridged ed. 23p. pap. 12.95 incl. audio (*0-88432-177-0*, S13050) Audio-Forum.
— Time Management 101. (In the Midst of Greatness Ser.). 1999. pap. text 6.99 (*1-57757-037-5*) Trade Life.
Douglass, Merrill E. & Douglass, Donna N. Manage Your Time, Your Work, Yourself. 2nd rev. ed. LC 92-37820. 176p. 1993. pap. 15.95 (*0-8144-7825-5*) AMACOM.
— Time Management for Teams. LC 92-22118. 192p. 1992. pap. 17.95 (*0-8144-7804-2*) AMACOM.
Douglass, Merrill E. & Goodwin, Phillip H. Successful Time Management for Hospital Administrators. LC 79-55063. 150p. reprint ed. pap. 46.50 (*0-608-12700-0*, 202351900033) Bks Demand.
***Douglass, Mike & Friedmann, John, eds.** Cities for Citizens: Planning & the Rise of Civil Society in a Global Age. LC 97-34186. 308p. 1998. 90.00 (*0-471-97708-X*); pap. 39.95 (*0-471-97709-8*) Wiley.
Douglass, Mike & Roberts, Glenda S. Japan & Global Migration: Foreign Workers & Advent of a Multicultural Society. LC 99-24302. 1999. text. write for info. (*0-415-19110-6*) Routledge.
Douglass, Paul. Bergson, Eliot, & American Literature. LC 86-9227. 224p. 1986. 28.00 (*0-8131-1597-3*) U Pr of Ky.
Douglass, Paul, ed. see Rivers, Thomas E.
Douglass, R. Bruce, ed. The Deeper Meaning of Economic Life: Critical Essays on the U. S. Catholic Bishops' Pastoral Letter on the Economy. LC 86-27148. 247p. reprint ed. pap. 76.60 (*0-7837-6318-2*, 204603300010) Bks Demand.
Douglass, R. Bruce & Hollenbach, David, eds. Catholicism & Liberalism: Contributions to American Public Philosophy. (Studies in Religion & American Public Life). 368p. (C). 1994. text 69.95 (*0-521-44528-0*) Cambridge U Pr.
***Douglass, R. Bruce & Mitchell, Joshua, eds.** A Nation under God? Essays on the Fate of Religion in American Public Life. 290p. 2000. 63.00 (*0-7425-0750-5*, Pub. by AltaMira Pr) Rowman.
— A Nation under God? Essays on the Fate of Religion in American Public Life. 290p. 2000. pap. 22.95 (*0-7425-0751-3*) Rowman.
Douglass, Ralph. Calligraphic Lettering. 3rd enl. rev. ed. 112p. 1967. spiral bd. 14.95 (*0-8230-0551-8*) Watsn-Guptill.
Douglass, Reanne, ed. see Shipley, Robert & Thibault, Allen.

Douglass, Robert W. Forest Recreation. 4th rev. ed. (Illus.). 373p. (C). 1993. text 38.95 (*0-88133-714-5*) Waveland Pr.
***Douglass, Robert W.** Forest Recreation. 5th ed. (Illus.). 392p. 2000. 41.95 (*1-57766-119-2*) Waveland Pr.
Douglass, Ruth C. Genealogy of a Douglass-Donaldson Family: Ancestors & Descendants of David Stuart Douglass & Louise Elinor Donaldson Married in Menands, NY 1915. 248p. 1996. text 27.00 (*0-9646770-0-8*) R C Douglass.
Douglass, Scott, ed. see Shakespeare, William.
Douglass, Stacey, jt. auth. see Douglass, Darren.
Douglass, Stephen B. & Janssen, Al. Managing Yourself: Practical Help for Christians in Personal Planning, Time Scheduling & Self-Control. LC 78-70647. 223p. Date not set. pap. 8.99 (*0-918956-49-8*) Integrtd Res.
Douglass, Steve & Janssen, Al. How to Get Better Grades & Have More Fun. 9th ed. (Illus.). 143p. (Orig.). (C). Date not set. reprint ed. pap. 7.99 (*1-57902-000-3*, 1201e) Integrtd Res.
— Making the Grade Seminars Student Notes. (Illus.). 42p. (C). Date not set. pap. 49.00 (*1-57902-008-9*) Integrtd Res.
Douglass, Steven. Enjoying Your Walk with God: How to Live above Your Everyday Circumstances. LC 89-32075. 127p. (Orig.). Date not set. pap. 7.99 (*0-89840-248-4*) Integrtd Res.
Douglass, Steven & Janssen, Al. How to Achieve Your Potential & Enjoy Life! LC 86-33665. 131p. Date not set. pap. 7.99 (*0-89840-184-4*) Integrtd Res.
Douglass, Steven A. Introduction to Mathematical Analysis. LC 95-47899. 737p. (C). 1996. 100.00 (*0-201-50897-4*) Addison-Wesley.
Douglass, Susan. Strategies & Structures of Presenting World History: With Islam & Muslim History As a Case Study. LC 94-42643. (ARA & ENG., Illus.). 238p. (Orig.). 1994. pap. text 18.95 (*0-915957-23-X*) amana pubns.
***Douglass, Susan L.** Beyond A Thousand & One Nights. Shaikh, Munir A., ed. (Illus.). 300p. 1999. ring bd. 50.00 (*1-930109-06-7*) Council on Islamic.
— Images of the Orient: Nineteenth-Century European & Muslim Perspectives. Shaikh, Munir A., ed. (Illus.). 86p. 1998. spiral bd. 15.00 (*1-930109-04-0*) Council on Islamic.
***Douglass, Susan L. & Alavi, Karima.** The Emergence of Renaissance: Cultural Interactions Between Europeans & Muslims. Shaikh, Munir A., ed. (Illus.). 350p. 1999. ring bd. 75.00 (*1-930109-05-9*) Council on Islamic.
Douglass, Thomas E. A Room Forever: The Life, Work, & Letters of Breece D'J Pancake. LC 97-21171. (Illus.). 280p. 1998. text 32.00 (*1-57233-001-5*) U of Tenn Pr.
Douglass, William. Collected Works. 1990. reprint ed. lib. bdg. 75.00 (*0-7812-2677-5*, 1511); reprint ed. write for info. (*0-318-67702-4*); reprint ed. write for info. (*0-318-67703-2*); reprint ed. write for info. (*0-318-67704-0*) Rprt Serv.
— A Discourse Concerning the Currencies of the British Plantations in America. (Notable American Authors Ser.). 1992. reprint ed. lib. bdg. 90.00 (*0-7812-2679-1*) Rprt Serv.
— Mercurius Nov-Anglicanus. (Notable American Authors Ser.). 1992. reprint ed. lib. bdg. 75.00 (*0-7812-2680-5*) Rprt Serv.
— The Practical History of a New Epidemical Eruptive Military Fever . . . in Boston New England in the Years 1735 & 1736. (Notable American Authors Ser.). 1992. reprint ed. lib. bdg. 75.00 (*0-7812-2678-3*) Rprt Serv.
— Sermons Preached in the African Protestant Episcopal Church of St. Thomas' Philadelphia. LC 79-157366. (Black Heritage Library Collection). 1977. 24.95 (*0-8369-8804-3*) Ayer.
— Summary, Historical & Political, of the First Planting, Progressive Improvements, & Present State of the British Settlements in North-America. LC 74-141084. (Research Library of Colonial Americana). 1972. reprint ed. 87.95 (*0-405-03279-X*) Ayer.
— A Summary, Historical & Political, of the First Planting, Progressive Improvements, & Present State of the British Settlements in North America. (Notable American Authors Ser.). 1992. reprint ed. lib. bdg. 75.00 (*0-7812-2681-3*) Rprt Serv.
***Douglass, William A., et al, eds.** Basque Cultural Studies. LC 99-50006. (Basque Studies Program Occasional Papers). 315p. 2000. 29.95 (*1-877802-03-4*) UNV Reno Basque.
— The Basque Diaspora. (Occasional Papers Ser.). 304p. 2000. 29.95 (*1-877802-05-0*) UNV Reno Basque.
— Basque Politics & Nationalism on the Eve of the Millennium. LC 99-51532. 231p. 2000. 29.95 (*1-877802-04-2*) UNV Reno Basque.
Douglass, William A., intro. Essays in Basque Social Anthropology & History. LC 89-15013. (Basque Studies Program Occasional Papers: No. 4). 327p. 1989. 27.50 (*1-877802-02-6*) UNV Reno Basque.
— An Interview with Joseph Mosconi: Reflections on Life in Truckee, Verdi, & Reno, 1900-1960s. (Illus.). 301p. 1985. lib. bdg. 52.50 (*1-56475-298-4*); fiche. write for info. (*1-56475-299-2*) U NV Oral Hist.
Douglass, William A., jt. auth. see Douglass, Jack R.
Douglass, William A., jt. auth. see Zulaika, Joseba.
Douglass, William A., ed. see Oddie, Tasker L.
Douglass, William A., tr. see Bereciartu, Gurutz J.
Douglass, William C. AIDS - The End of Civilization: The Greatest Biological Disaster in the History of Mankind. 256p. 1992. reprint ed. pap. text 9.95 (*1-881316-00-9*) A&B Bks.
Douglass, Winsome. Decorative Stuffed Toys for the Needle-Worker. (Sewing & Related Miscellaneous Ser.). (Illus.). 224p. 1984. reprint ed. pap. 8.95 (*0-486-24638-8*) Dover.

Dougon, Gordon, et al, eds. Methods in Microbiology Vol. 26: Yeast Gene Analysis. (Illus.). 502p. 1998. 59.95 (*0-12-136655-3*); text 99.95 (*0-12-521526-6*) Morgan Kaufmann.

Douhet, Giulio. The Command of the Air. Ferrari, Dino, tr. LC 72-4271. (World Affairs Ser.: National & International Viewpoints). 402p. 1979. reprint ed. 33.95 (*0-405-04567-0*) Ayer.

Douhet, Giulio & Ferrari, Dino. Command of the Air. 408p. 1998. reprint ed. pap. 25.00 (*0-16-049772-8*) USGPO.

Douie, Decima L. The Nature & the Effect of the Heresy of the Fraticelli. LC 77-84715. reprint ed. 41.50 (*0-404-16121-9*) AMS Pr.

Douie, Decima L. & Farmer, David H., eds. Magna Vita Sancti Hugonis: The Life of St. Hugh of Lincoln, I. (Oxford Medieval Texts Ser.). (Illus.). 190p. 1985. text 85.00 (*0-19-822207-6*) OUP.

— Magna Vita Sancti Hugonis: The Life of St. Hugh of Lincoln, II. (Oxford Medieval Texts Ser.). (Illus.). 256p. 1985. text 75.00 (*0-19-822208-4*) OUP.

Douie, James. North-West Frontier Province & Kashmir. (C). 1994. 14.00 (*81-85557-85-3*, Pub. by Low Price) S Asia.

Douillard, John. Body, Mind & Sport: The Mind-Body Guide to Lifelong Fitness & Your Personal Best. 1995. pap. 13.00 (*0-517-88383-X*, Crown) Crown Pub Group.

***Douillard, John.** The 3-Season Diet: Solving the Mysteries of Food Cravings, Weight Loss & Exercise. LC 99-58302. (Illus.). 288p. 2000. 23.00 (*0-609-60589-5*) Harmony Bks.

Douin, J. Dictionnaire de la Censure au Cinema. (FRE.). 1998. 110.00 (*0-320-00188-1*) Fr & Eur.

Douin, Joel, jt. ed. see Clement, Nicole.

Douin, Robert, jt. auth. see Bonnier, Gaston.

Doukas, John, compiled by. European Equity Markets & Corporate Financial Decisions. LC 93-48151. (Journal of Multinational Financial Management). (Illus.). 213p. 1994. 69.95 (*1-56024-662-6*) Haworth Pr.

Doukas, John & Mathur, Ike, eds. European Foreign-Exchange Movements & Financial Institutions. LC 94-1876. (Journal of International Financial Markets, Institutions & Money). (Illus.). 167p. 1994. 49.95 (*1-56024-663-4*) Haworth Pr.

Doukas, John, et al. Financial Sector Reform & Privatization in Transition Economies. LC 98-15131. (Advances in Finance, Investment, & Banking Ser.). 1998. 129.50 (*0-444-82653-X*) Elsevier.

Doukas, John A., jt. ed. see Choi, J. Jay.

Doukhan, Jacques. Ellen G. White & the Jews: An Interpretative Analysis of Her Writings & Their Significance for Our Time. Adar Publications Staff, ed. LC 85-70340. 35p. (Orig.). 1985. pap. 2.50 (*0-916169-01-4*) Adar Pubns.

Doukhan, Jacques B. Daniel: Vision of the End. LC 87-82339. 194p. 1987. pap. 15.99 (*0-943872-41-3*) Andrews Univ Pr.

— Hebrew for Theologians: A Textbook for the Study of Biblical Hebrew in Relation to Hebrew Thinking. 278p. (Orig.). (C). 1993. pap. text 29.50 (*0-8191-9269-4*) U Pr of Amer.

Doukhan, Moses J., jt. auth. see Goadby, Frederic M.

***Doukhan, Paul.** Long-Range Dependence: Theory & Applications. (Illus.). 2000. 64.95 (*0-8176-4168-8*) Birkhauser.

Doukhan, Paul. Mixing: Properties & Examples. LC 93-47442. (Lecture Notes in Statistics Ser.: Vol. 85). 160p. 1994. pap. 29.00 (*0-387-94214-9*) Spr-Verlag.

Doukhobor Research Committee. The Doukhobors of British Columbia. Hawthorn, Harry B., ed. LC 79-8711. (Illus.). 288p. 1980. reprint ed. lib. bdg. 65.00 (*0-313-20652-X*, DOBC, Greenwood Pr) Greenwood.

Doukidis & Smithson Staff. Information Systems in the National Context. 272p. 1995. 77.95 (*1-85972-014-5*) Ashgate Pub Co.

Doukidis, Georgios I. Knowledge Based Management Support Systems. 385p. 1989. text 51.95 (*0-470-21218-7*) P-H.

Doulis, T. Journeys to Orthodoxy. 1986. pap. 10.95 (*0-937032-42-5*) Light&Life Pub Co MN.

Doulis, Thomas, ed. Toward an Authentic Church: Orthodox Christians Discuss Their Conversion. LC 95-78283. 116p. (Orig.). 1996. pap. 14.95 (*1-880971-10-0*) Light&Life Pub Co MN.

Doulos, Bill. A Journey of Compassion: Letters from a Street Minister. 148p. (Orig.). 1989. pap. 6.95 (*0-685-29160-X*) Lizardi Comns.

Doulos, Bill L., jt. auth. see Jordon, Clarence.

Doulton, Harold. I Remember. (Illus.). 528p. 1999. 40.00 (*0-933380-03-8*) Olive Pr Pubns.

Douma. Transportation of Dangerous Goods in Canada: A Practical Guide to the Law. 144p. 1990. pap. 46.00 (*0-409-89390-0*, MICHIE) LEXIS Pub.

Douma, George. Together with God. 1959. pap. 0.70 (*0-686-23478-2*) Rose Pub MI.

***Douma, J.** Los Diez Mandamientos: Manual de Vida Cristiana. Pimentel, Alejandro, ed. Blanch, Jose Maria, tr.Tr. of Ten Commandments: Manual for the Christian Life. (SPA.). 2000. write for info. (*1-55883-120-7*) Libros Desafio.

Douma, J. The Ten Commandments: Manual for the Christian Life. Kloosterman, Nelson, tr. from DUT.Tr. of De Tien Geboden. 424p. 1996. 24.99 (*0-87552-237-8*) P & R Pubng.

Douma, S. W. & Schreuder, Hein. Economic Approaches to Organizations. 2nd ed. 224p. 1997. pap. 63.00 (*0-13-788761-2*) P-H.

Doumani, Beshara. Rediscovering Palestine: Merchants & Peasants of Jabal Nablus, 1700-1900. LC 94-30401. (Illus.). 340p. 1995. 55.00 (*0-520-08895-6*, Pub. by U CA Pr); pap. 24.95 (*0-520-20370-4*, Pub. by U CA Pr) Cal Prin Full Svc.

Doumani, Carol. Chinese Checkers. LC 95-61683. 368p. 1996. 25.00 (*0-9642359-7-8*) Wave Pubng.

— Good Enough to Eat: A Collection of Recipes. LC 99-18749. (Illus.). 124p. 1999. 30.00 (*0-9642359-5-1*) Wave Pubng.

— Indiscretions. LC 98-42992. 336p. 1999. 25.00 (*0-9642359-9-4*) Wave Pubng.

***Doumani, Carol.** Taking Heart. LC 99-23893. 400p. 2000. 25.00 (*0-9642359-1-9*, Pub. by Wave Pubng) Baker & Taylor.

Doumani, Carol. Untitled Nude: A Novel. LC 94-61117. (Illus.). 352p. 1995. 25.00 (*0-9642359-6-X*) Wave Pubng.

Doumani, George A. The Frigid Mistress. LC 99-60071. (Illus.). 320p. 1999. 24.95 (*1-56167-476-1*) Noble Hse MD.

Doumani, Lissa, jt. auth. see Sone, Hiro.

Doumanis, Nicholas. Myth & Memory in the Mediterranean: Remembering Fascism's Empire. 256p. 1997. text 65.00 (*0-312-17243-5*) St Martin.

Doumas, Alex, tr. see Doumas, Christos.

Doumas, Alexandra, tr. see Raftis, Alkis.

Doumas, Alexandra, tr. see Tzannetakis, Tzannis.

Doumas, Christos. The Wall Paintings of Thera. Zafiropoulou, Diana, ed. Doumas, Alex, tr. from GRE. (Illus.). 188p. (C). 1993. boxed set 60.00 (*960-220-274-2*, Pub. by Thera Fnd) DAP Assocs.

Doumas, Diana M., jt. auth. see Matano, Robert A.

Doumato, Eleanor A. The Arabic-Speaking People in Rhode Island: A Centenary Celebration. (Rhode Island Ethnic Heritage Pamphlet Ser.). (Illus.). 48p. (Orig.). 1987. pap. 6.75 (*0-917012-84-4*) RI Pubns Soc.

***Doumato, Eleanor A.** Getting God's Ear: Women, Islam & Healing in Saudi Arabia & the Gulf. LC 99-35113. 498p. 1999. pap. 18.50 (*0-231-11667-5*) Col U Pr.

***Doumato, Eleanor A., ed.** Getting God's Ear: Women, Islam & Healing in Saudi Arabia & the Gulf. LC 99-35113. 498p. 1999. 45.00 (*0-231-11666-7*) Col U Pr.

Doumerc, Beatriz. El Invisible Director de Orquesta (The Invisible Orchestra Conductor) (SPA.). 64p. (J). (gr. 3-4). 1994. pap. 5.99 (*968-16-4040-3*, Pub. by Fondo) Continental Bk.

Doumerc, Beatriz & Alcantara, Ricardo. Two of a Kind. large type ed. Perez, Laura M. & Corbett, Kathryn, trs. (Illus.). 1994. 13.50 (*0-614-09811-4*, L-34101-00) Am Printing Hse.

Doumet, Claude. Sceaux et Cylindres Orientaux: La Collection Chiha. (Orbis Biblicus et Orientalis Ser.: Vol. 9). (FRE.). 210p. 1990. text 60.25 (*3-7278-0816-0*, Pub. by Presses Univ Fribourg) Eisenbrauns.

Doumette, Hanna J. Petitions Celestial (1932) 220p. 1998. reprint ed. pap. 19.95 (*0-7661-0326-9*) Kessinger Pub.

Doumitt, Debbie. Weddings in the Wine Country: Beautiful Locations for Your Romantic Northern California Wedding. 200p. (Orig.). 1995. pap. 16.95 (*0-9643567-2-4*) Bird Rock Pr.

Doumitt, Donald P. Voices of Ulster: A Cry from the Heart. LC 99-22984. 1999. 34.00 (*1-56072-665-2*) Nova Sci Pubs.

Doumpos, Michael, jt. auth. see Zopounidis, Constantin.

Dounia, Christiani B., ed. see Ibsen, Henrik.

Dounis, D. The Artist's Technique of Violin Playing. (FRE & GER., Illus.). 81p. 1921. pap. 16.95 (*0-8258-0147-8*, 0-2695) Fischer Inc NY.

Dounuts, Kevin. Doomed to Die: A Lonely Walk. Anderson, Mignon H., ed. 70p. (Orig.). (YA). 1993. pap. 9.95 (*0-9636006-3-X*) Old Ctry Bks.

— How to Possibly Avoid Being a Carjacking Victim. Martinez, Yasmin, ed. 1994. pap. 2.95 (*0-9636006-8-0*) Old Ctry Bks.

— Sensational Beauty Vol. 1: Universal Controversy. Daiell, Saralyn, ed. LC 92-82046. (Illus.). 50p. (Orig.). (YA). (gr. 7 up). 1993. pap. 4.95 (*0-9636006-2-1*) Old Ctry Bks.

Doup, T. M. Simplicial Algorithms on the Simplotope. (Lecture Notes in Economics & Mathematical Systems Ser.: Vol. 318). viii, 262p. 1988. 38.70 (*0-387-50233-5*) Spr-Verlag.

Douple, E., jt. ed. see Urano, M.

Douple, E. B., jt. ed. see Urano, M.

Doupnik, J. R., jt. auth. see Banks, Peter M.

Doupnik, Timothy S., ed. Advances in International Accounting, Vol. 3. 249p. 1990. 78.50 (*1-55938-078-0*) Jai Pr.

Doupnik, Timothy S. & Most, Kenneth S., eds. Advances in International Accounting, Vol. 2. 310p. 1989. 78.50 (*0-89232-694-8*) Jai Pr.

— Advances in International Accounting, Vol. 4. 274p. 1991. 78.50 (*1-55938-248-1*) Jai Pr.

— Advances in International Accounting, Vol. 5. 312p. 1992. 78.50 (*1-55938-415-8*) Jai Pr.

— Advances in International Accounting, Vol. 6. 334p. 1994. 78.50 (*1-55938-599-5*) Jai Pr.

— Advances in International Accounting, Vol. 7. 310p. 1994. 78.50 (*1-55938-776-9*) Jai Pr.

— Advances in International Accounting, Vol. 8. 244p. 1995. 78.50 (*1-55938-917-6*) Jai Pr.

— Advances in International Accounting, Vol. 9. 1996. 78.50 (*1-55938-991-5*) Jai Pr.

Doupnik, Timothy S., jt. auth. see Evans, Thomas G.

Dourado, Autran. Bells of Agony. Parker, John M., tr. from POR. LC 88-51686. 236p. 1989. 30.00 (*0-7206-0681-0*, Pub. by P Owen Ltd) Dufour.

— Pattern for a Tapestry. Parker, John M., tr. from POR. 170p. 1984. 30.00 (*0-7206-0608-X*, Pub. by P Owen Ltd) Dufour.

— Voices of the Dead. 248p. 1980. 28.00 (*0-7206-0558-X*, Pub. by P Owen Ltd) Dufour.

Dourish, Colin T., et al, eds. Multiple Cholecystokinin Receptors in the CNS. (Illus.). 580p. 1992. text 130.00 (*0-19-857756-7*) OUP.

Dourish, Colin T., jt. ed. see Cooper, Steven J.

Dourish, Colin T., jt. ed. see Greenshaw, Andrew J.

Dourley, John, jt. auth. see Lenz, Lee W.

Dourley, John P. The Goddess, Mother of the Trinity: A Jungian Implication. LC 90-37579. (Studies in the Psychology of Religion: Vol. 4). 112p. 1990. lib. bdg. 59.95 (*0-88946-244-5*) E Mellen.

— Illness That We Are. 128p. 1985. pap. 16.00 (*0-919123-16-3*, Pub. by Inner City Bks) BookWorld.

— Jung & the Religious Alternative: The Rerooting. LC 95-23010. (Studies in the Psychology of Religion: Vol. 6). 1995. write for info. (*0-7734-9048-5*) E Mellen.

— Love, Celibacy & the Inner Marriage. 128p. 1987. pap. 16.00 (*0-919123-28-7*, Pub. by Inner City Bks) BookWorld.

— Psyche As Sacrament. 128p. 1995. pap. 16.00 (*0-919123-06-6*, Pub. by Inner City Bks) BookWorld.

— A Strategy for a Loss of Faith: Jung's Proposal. 144p. 1995. pap. 16.00 (*0-919123-57-0*, Pub. by Inner City Bks) BookWorld.

Dournon, Francois. Dictionnaire des Mots et Formules Celebres. (FRE.). 400p. 1994. 110.00 (*0-7859-9205-7*) Fr & Eur.

Dournon, Jean-Yves. Dictionnaire des Proverbs et des Dictions de France. (FRE.). 347p. 1988. pap. 16.95 (*0-7859-7856-9*, 2253046795) Fr & Eur.

— Dictionnaire d'Orthographe et des Difficultes du Francais. (FRE.). 1987. pap. 18.95 (*0-7859-7849-6*, 2253028851) Fr & Eur.

— Dictionnaires des Proverbes et Dictons de France. (FRE.). 75.00 (*0-8288-7714-9*) Fr & Eur.

— The Large Dictionary of French Citations: Le Grand Dictionaire des Citations Francaises. (FRE.). 906p. 1982. 75.00 (*0-8288-2284-0*, M14146) Fr & Eur.

Dournon-Taurelle, Genevieve & Wright, John. Les Guimbardes du Musee de l'Homme. (FRE., Illus.). 150p. 1978. pap. 37.50 (*0-317-28710-9*) Intl Fanorona.

Douros, Basil. Carved in Stone: The Greek Heritage. LC 98-95025. (Illus.). 268p. 1999. pap. 14.95 (*0-9670593-1-3*) Five & Dot.

Dourte, Ruth, jt. auth. see Jacobs, Joy.

Doury, P., et al. Algodystrophy. (Illus.). 190p. 1981. 166.00 (*0-387-10624-3*) Spr-Verlag.

Douse, James. The Voice of Bethel. 96p. 1997. pap. 10.00 (*0-8059-4046-4*) Dorrance.

Douse, R. T. The Gold Book: Your Guide to Real Estate Investment. LC 83-91208. (Illus.). 80p. (Orig.). 1983. pap. 10.00 (*0-915493-00-4*, Classic Press) Gold Bk.

Dousey, Elisabeth, jt. ed. see Horton, Elizabeth.

Dousias, Terri, jt. auth. see Graham, Dwight.

***Douskalis, Bill.** IP Telephony: The Integration of Robust VoIP Services. 356p. 1999. pap. text 55.00 (*0-13-014118-6*) P-H.

Dousset, H. Vademecum Encyclopedique du Medecin Praticien: Encyclopedic Vademecum of Medical Practice. 9th ed. 1266p. 1980. 110.00 (*0-8288-1801-0*, M15580) Fr & Eur.

Doust, Jonathan L., jt. auth. see Silvertown, Jonathan W.

Douthit, Gretchen Van Kleef, see Van Kleef Douthit, Gretchen.

Douthit, Nathan. A Guide to Oregon South Coast History: Traveling the Jedediah Smith Trail. LC 99-25339. (Illus.). 224p. 1999. pap. 22.95 (*0-87071-462-7*) Oreg St U Pr.

Douthitt & Fedyk. The Cost of Raising Children in Canada. 224p. 1990. pap. 56.00 (*0-409-88957-1*, MICHIE) LEXIS Pub.

Douthitt, Chris. Voice-Overs: Putting Your Mouth Where the Money Is. Wiecks, Tom, ed. LC 96-77899. (Illus.). 240p. (Orig.). 1996. pap. 19.95 (*0-935566-21-X*) Grey Heron.

Douthwaite, G. K. & Dunn, W. L. Introductory Engineering Problems by Computer Methods: Fortran 2. (Illus.). 160p. 1964. pap. text 14.95 (*0-87015-130-4*) Pacific Bks.

— Introductory Engineering Problems by Computer Methods: Fortran 4. rev. ed. (Illus.). 250p. (C). 1965. pap. text 19.95 (*0-87015-135-5*) Pacific Bks.

Douthwaite, Graham. Jury Instructions for Product Liability: 1989 Cumulative Supplement. 1989. write for info. (*0-87473-497-5*, 61427-10, MICHIE) LEXIS Pub.

— Jury Instructions in Real Estate Litigation. 3rd ed. 528p. 1991. 80.00 (*0-87473-800-8*, 61435-10, MICHIE) LEXIS Pub.

— Jury Instructions on Damages Tort Action: 1990 Supplement. 2nd ed. 1990. write for info. (*0-87473-495-9*, 61429-10, MICHIE) LEXIS Pub.

— Jury Instructions on Medical Issues. 4th ed. 850p. 1992. 90.00 (*0-87473-967-5*, MICHIE) LEXIS Pub.

— Jury Instructions on Medical Issues: 1991 Cumulative Supplement. 204p. 1991. pap. text. write for info. (*0-87473-826-1*, 61417-10, MICHIE) LEXIS Pub.

Douthwaite, Graham & Eades, Ronald W. Jury Instructions for Personal Injury & Tort Cases: Current Supplements, 4 vols., Set. 1991. 280.00 (*0-87473-393-6*, 61421-10, MICHIE) LEXIS Pub.

— Jury Instructions in Automobile Negligence Actions. 2nd ed. 733p. 1992. suppl. ed. 90.00 (*0-87473-821-0*, MICHIE) LEXIS Pub.

Douthwaite, Graham, jt. see Eades, Ronald W.

Douthwaite, Julia V. Exotic Women: Literary Heroines & Cultural Strategies in Ancien Regime France. LC 92-2548. (New Cultural Studies). (Illus.). 224p. (Orig.). (C). 1992. pap. text 17.95 (*0-8122-1357-2*) U of Pa Pr.

Douthwaite, R. J. & Tingle, C. C., eds. DDT in the Tropics: The Impact on Wildlife in Zimbabwe of Ground-Spraying for Tsetse Fly Control. 195p. 1994. pap. 60.00 (*0-85954-364-1*, Pub. by Nat Res Inst) St Mut.

***Douthwaite, Richard.** The Ecology of Money. (Schumacher Briefings Ser.: No. 4). 80p. 2000. pap. 10.95 (*1-870098-81-1*, Pub. by Green Bks) Chelsea Green Pub.

Douthwaite, Richard. The Growth Illusion. 1996. pap. 29.95 (*0-946640-88-2*, Pub. by Lilliput Pr) Irish Bks Media.

— The Growth Illusion: How Economic Growth Has Enriched the Few, Impoverished, the Many & the Endangered, the Planet. (Illus.). 400p. 1999. reprint ed. pap. 20.95 (*0-86571-396-0*, Pub. by New Soc Pubs) Consort Bk Sales.

— Short Circuit: Strengthening Local Economies for Security in an Unstable World. LC 96-202093. 386p. 1997. pap. 29.95 (*1-874675-60-0*) Dufour.

— Short Circuit: Strengthening Local Economies for Security in an Unstable World. (Illus.). 400p. 1998. pap. 21.95 (*1-870098-64-1*, Pub. by Green Bks) Chelsea Green Pub.

***Douthwaite, Wendy.** The Orange Pony. (J). 2000. mass mkt. 4.99 (*0-330-33631-2*) Mcm Child Bks.

— Summer Ponies. (Polly Ser.). (Illus.). 96p. (J). (gr. 3). 2000. mass mkt. 4.99 (*0-330-32540-X*) Mcm Child Bks.

Douthwaite, William R. Gray's Inn: Its History & Associations Compiled from Original & Unpublished Documents. (Illus.). xxiii, 283p. 1987. reprint ed. 42.50 (*0-8377-2031-1*, Rothman) W S Hein.

Doutremepuich, ed. Low Molecular Weight Heparins in Clinical Practice. (Illus.). 264p. 1992. text 160.00 (*0-8247-8640-8*) Dekker.

Doutremepuich, Christian, ed. Anticoagulation. LC 94-16729. 1994. 127.00 (*0-387-94318-8*) Spr-Verlag.

— Ultra Low Doses. 180p. 1991. 65.00 (*0-7484-0021-4*, Pub. by Tay Francis Ltd) Taylor & Francis.

Doutrich, Paul E. To Form a More Perfect Union: The Federal Constitution & Pennsylvania. (Illus.). 20p. 1986. pap. 1.95 (*0-89271-039-X*) Pa Hist & Mus.

Doutt, B., et al. Anthology: A Collection of Poems. Shephard, David, ed. LC 74-25359. 1974. 3.50 (*0-915176-04-1*) Woods Hole Pr.

Doutt, Richard L. Cape Bulbs: Their Collection, Cultivation & Conservation. LC 93-17655. (Illus.). 290p. 1994. 34.95 (*0-88192-245-5*) Timber.

Douty, Christopher M. The Economics of Localized Disasters: The 1906 San Francisco Catastrophe. Bruchey, Stuart, ed. LC 76-39827. (Nineteen Seventy-Seven Dissertations Ser.). (Illus.). 1977. lib. bdg. 37.95 (*0-405-09908-8*) Ayer.

Douty, Harry M. The Wage Bargain & the Labor Market. LC 79-3720. (Policy Studies in Employment & Welfare: No. 37). 160p. reprint ed. pap. 49.60 (*0-608-15142-4*, 202580600046) Bks Demand.

Douty, Norman F. Did Christ Die Only for the Elect? A Treatise on the Extent of Christ's Atonement. 2nd ed. 180p. 1998. reprint ed. pap. 18.00 (*1-57910-135-6*) Wipf & Stock.

***Douty, Sheila Cornell & Cohen, Judith Love.** You Can Be a Woman Softball Player. LC 00-20931. (Illus.). 40p. (YA). (gr. 4-9). 2000. 13.95 (*1-880599-47-3*); 7.00 (*1-880599-46-5*) Cascade Pass.

Douven, Igor & Horsten, Leon, eds. Realism in the Sciences: Proceedings of the Ernan McMullin Symposium, 1995. (Louvain Philosophical Studies: No. 10). 216p. 1996. pap. 52.50 (*90-6186-763-0*, Pub. by Leuven Univ) Coronet Bks.

Douville, Judith, compiled by. Environmental Studies. 164p. (Orig.). (C). 1995. pap. 38.00 (*0-8389-7808-8*) Assn Coll & Res Libs.

Douville, Judith A. Corrosion Technology: An Information Sourcebook. (Anticipate Annual Ser.). 188p. 1989. 76.95 (*0-89116-857-5*) Hemisp Pub.

***Douville, Judith A. & Douville, Philip R.** Calculating the Molar Volume of Carbon Dioxide. (Modular Laboratory in Chemistry Ser.). 12p. (C). 1999. pap. text 1.50 (*0-87540-608-4*, PROP 608-4) Chem Educ Res.

Douville, Judith A. & Douville, Philip R. Determining the Molar Volume of Carbon Dioxide. Stanitski, C. L., ed. (Modular Laboratory Program in Chemistry Ser.). 8p. (C). 1998. pap. text 1.50 (*0-87540-407-3*, PROP 407) Chem Educ Res.

Douville, Philip R., jt. auth. see Douville, Judith A.

Douvitsas-Gamst, J. & Xanthos-Kretzschmer, S. Mina und Otto: Ein Lese-und Schreiblehrgang in Deutsch als Fremdsprache. Deutsch als Zweitsprache fuer Kinder: Schuelerbuch. (GER.). 141p. (J). 1989. pap. text 18.00 (*3-12-675030-3*, Pub. by Klett Edition) Intl Bk Import.

— Mina und Otto: Lehrerhandbuch. (GER.). 93p. (J). 1989. pap. text 19.00 (*3-12-675033-8*, Pub. by Klett Edition); audio 22.50 (*3-12-675034-6*, Pub. by Klett Edition) Intl Bk Import.

— Mina und Otto: Schreiblehrgang 1, Vereinf. Ausgangs. (GER.). 64p. (J). 1990. pap. text 11.75 (*3-12-675035-4*, Pub. by Klett Edition) Intl Bk Import.

— Mina und Otto: Schreiblehrgang 2, Vereinf. Ausgangs. (GER.). 64p. (J). 1990. pap. text 11.75 (*3-12-675036-2*, Pub. by Klett Edition) Intl Bk Import.

— Mina und Otto Level 1: Schreiblehrgang. (GER.). 64p. (J). 1989. pap. text 11.75 (*3-12-675031-1*, Pub. by Klett Edition) Intl Bk Import.

— Mina und Otto Level 2: Schreiblehrgang. (GER.). 64p. (J). 1989. pap. text 11.75 (*3-12-675032-X*, Pub. by Klett Edition) Intl Bk Import.

Douvitsas-Gamst, J., et al. Das Deutschmobil Level 1: Arbeitsbuch. (GER.). 112p. (J). 1990. pap. text 15.25 (*3-12-675041-9*, Pub. by Klett Edition) Intl Bk Import.

— Das Deutschmobil Level 1: Lehrerhandbuch. (GER.). 57p. (J). 1990. pap. text 14.75 (*3-12-675042-7*, Pub. by Klett Edition) Intl Bk Import.

— Das Deutschmobil Level 2: Lehrbuch. (GER.). 128p. (J). 1991. pap. text 19.75 (*3-12-675050-8*, Pub. by Klett Edition) Intl Bk Import.

D

— Das Deutschmobil Level 2: Lehrerhandbuch. (GER.). (J). 1991. audio 33.50 (*3-12-675053-2*, Pub. by Klett Edition) Intl Bk Import.

— Das Deutschmobil Level 2: Lehrerhandbuch. (GER.). 96p. (J). 1993. pap. text 19.00 (*3-12-675052-4*, Pub. by Klett Edition) Intl Bk Import.

— Das Deutschmobil Level 3: Arbeitsbuch. (GER.). 128p. (J). 1992. pap. text 16.75 (*3-12-675061-3*, Pub. by Klett Edition) Intl Bk Import.

— Das Deutschmobil Level 3: Lehrbuch. (GER.). 128p. (J). 1992. pap. text 19.75 (*3-12-675060-5*, Pub. by Klett Edition) Intl Bk Import.

— Das Deutschmobil Level 3: Lehrerhandbuch. (GER.). 96p. (J). 1996. pap. text 19.00 (*3-12-675062-1*, Pub. by Klett Edition) Intl Bk Import.

— Das Deutschmobil. Deutsch als Fremdsprache fuer Kinder Level 1: Lehrbuch. (GER.). 128p. (J). 1989. pap. text 19.75 (*3-12-675040-0*, Pub. by Klett Edition) Intl Bk Import.

— Das Deutschmobil. Deutsch als Fremdsprache fuer Kinder Level 1: Lehrbuch. (GER.). (J). 1990. audio 30.75 (*3-12-675043-5*, Pub. by Klett Edition) Intl Bk Import.

— Das Deutschmobile Level 2: Arbeitsbuch. (GER.). 132p. (J). 1991. pap. text 16.75 (*3-12-675051-6*, Pub. by Klett Edition) Intl Bk Import.

Douw, L. M. & Post, P., eds. South China: State, Culture & Social Change During the 20th Century. LC 97-142908. 272p. 1996. pap. 47.00 (*0-444-85811-3*) Elsevier.

Douw, Leo, ed. Unsettled Frontiers & Transnational Linkages: New Tasks for the Historian of Modern Asia. (Comparative Asian Studies: No. 19). 120p. 1997. pap. 19.50 (*90-5383-536-9*, Pub. by VU Univ Pr) Paul & Co Pubs.

***Douw, Leo, et al, eds.** Qiaoxiang Ties: Interdisciplinary Approaches to 'Cultural Capitalism' in South China. 240p. 1999. 110.00 (*0-7103-0653-9*, Pub. by Kegan Paul Intl) Col U Pr.

Douwen, Eric K. Van, see Van Douwen, Eric K.

Douwes. Ottomans in Syria: A History of Justice & Oppression. 224p. 1999. text 55.00 (*1-86064-031-1*) St Martin.

Douwes-Dekker, L., et al. Community Conflict: The Challenge Facing South Africa. LC 97-160913. 160p. 1996. pap. 19.60 (*0-7021-3404-X*, Pub. by Juta & Co) Intl Spec Bk.

Douwes Dekker, Niels A. Tanah Air Kita: A Book of the Country & People of Indonesia. 2nd ed. LC 77-86970. reprint ed. 46.00 (*0-404-16705-5*) AMS Pr.

Doux, Joan Le, see Le Doux, Joan.

Douyere, Sylvia E., jt. auth. see Flaubert, Gustave.

Douzinas, Costas. The End of Human Rights. 256p. 2000. 50.00 (*1-901362-91-4*, Pub. by Hart Pub); pap. 30.00 (*1-84113-000-1*, Pub. by Hart Pub) Intl Spec Bk.

Douzinas, Costas & Warrington, Ronnie. Justice Miscarried: Ethics & Aesthetics in Law. (C). 1995. pap. text, teacher ed. 34.95 (*0-13-182882-7*, Prentice Hall) P-H.

Dov Ber Schneersohn, Shalom. Tract on Prayer. Danzinger, Lazer, tr. LC 92-19383. 1992. 12.00 (*0-8266-0436-6*) Kehot Pubn Soc.

Dov Ber Schneerson, Shalom. Kuntres Uma'ayon. Posner, Zalman I., tr. 144p. 1969. reprint ed. 12.00 (*0-8266-0420-X*) Kehot Pubn Soc.

Dov Por, Francis. The Pantanal of Mato Grosso (Brazil) World's Largest Wetlands. (Monographiae Biologicae). 120p. (C). 1995. text 92.50 (*0-7923-3481-7*) Kluwer Academic.

***Dov, Rav Yosef & Soloveitchik, Ber.** Beis Halevi. Herczeg, Visroel, tr. 1998. 17.95 (*1-56871-148-4*, Pub. by Targum Pr) Feldheim.

Doval, G. Diccionario General de Citas. (SPA.). 422p. 1998. 69.95 (*0-320-00646-8*) Fr & Eur.

[D]ovani. Italian/Serbian/Italian Dictionary Grammar (Cyrillic) 2nd ed. (CRO, ITA & SER.). 507p. 1997. 95.00 (*0-320-00043-5*) Fr & Eur.

Dovaz, Michel. Bordeaux: A Legendary Wine. Lee, John, tr. from FRE. LC 98-15672. (Illus.). 268p. 1999. 75.00 (*0-7892-0499-5*) Abbeville Pr.

— Encyclopedia of the Great Wines of Bordeaux. Julliard, ed. 254p. 1981. 95.00 (*0-8288-4448-8*, M11718) Fr & Eur.

Dove. Agile Enterprise. 304p. write for info. (*0-471-35018-4*) Wiley.

Dove, Allan B. Steel Wire Handbook, Vol. 3. (Illus.). 495p. 1972. 50.00 (*0-685-26425-4*) Wire Assn Intl.

Dove, Allan B., ed. Steel Wire Handbook, Vol. 1. (Illus.). 318p. 1965. 50.00 (*0-685-26423-8*) Wire Assn Intl.

— Steel Wire Handbook, Vol. 4. (Illus.). 202p. 1980. 50.00 (*0-685-26427-0*) Wire Assn Intl.

— Steel Wire Handbooks, 4 vols., Set. (Illus.). 1965. 170.00 (*0-685-26426-2*) Wire Assn Intl.

Dove, Allan B. & Lewis, Dartrey B., eds. Steel Wire Handbook, Vol. 2. (Illus.). 388p. 1969. 50.00 (*0-685-26424-6*) Wire Assn Intl.

Dove, Anthea. Beginning with Me. 120p. 1996. pap. 39.95 (*0-85439-518-0*, Pub. by St Paul Pubns) St Mut.

Dove, Arthur G., jt. auth. see Eldredge, Charles C.

Dove, Audrey, et al. Journeying Through Life: With a Pocketful of Sayings to Live By. LC 98-93523. 83p. 1998. 12.99 (*0-9667356-1-7*); pap. 10.99 (*0-9667356-0-9*) Dosine Pr.

Dove Books Staff. Alice in Wonderland. (gr. 4-7). 1999. 20.00 (*0-7871-1978-4*) NewStar Media.

Dove, D., jt. ed. see Hench, L.

Dove, Daniel. The Adventures of Baby Penrose-the Richest Infant in the World: Being the Tales of Life in Silicone City in the Early Nineteen Nineties. 2nd ed. (Orig.). 1980. pap. 10.00 (*0-686-27614-0*) Tetragrammaton.

Dove, Donald E. Prehistoric Subsistence & Population Change along the Lower Agua Fria River, Arizona: A Model Simulation. (Anthropological Research Papers: No. 32). (Illus.). viii, 139p. 1984. pap. 15.00 (*0-685-73908-2*) AZ Univ ARP.

Dove, George N. The Boys from Grover Avenue: Ed McBain's 87th Precinct Novels. LC 84-73512. 166p. 1985. 18.95 (*0-87972-321-1*); pap. 8.95 (*0-87972-322-X*) Bowling Green Univ Popular Press.

— The Police Procedural. LC 81-84214. 1982. 21.95 (*0-87972-188-X*) Bowling Green Univ Popular Press.

— The Reader & the Detective Story. LC 96-47340. 210p. 1997. 39.95 (*0-87972-731-4*); pap. 18.95 (*0-87972-732-2*) Bowling Green Univ Popular Press.

— Suspense in the Formula Story. LC 89-61585. 144p. (C). 1989. 25.95 (*0-87972-455-2*); pap. 12.95 (*0-87972-456-0*) Bowling Green Univ Popular Press.

Dove, George N., jt. auth. see Bargainnier, Earl F.

Dove, Jennifer. Into the Green. Lott, Clarinda H., ed. (New Poets Ser.: Vol. 15). (Illus.). 64p. 1987. pap. 5.95 (*0-932616-20-8*) Brick Hse Bks.

Dove, John. Strange Vagabond of God: The Story of John Bradburne. 302p. 1990. pap. 12.95 (*1-85371-082-2*, Pub. by Poolbeg Pr) Dufour.

***Dove, Kent E.** Conducting a Successful Capital Campaign. 2nd expanded rev. ed. LC 99-6681. (Nonprofit & Public Management Ser.). 608p. 1999. text 49.95 (*0-7879-4989-2*) Jossey-Bass.

Dove, Kent E. Conducting a Successful Capital Campaign: A Comprehensive Fundraising Guide for Nonprofit Organizations. LC 88-42786. (Nonprofit Sector-Public Administration Ser.). 314p. 1988. text 38.95 (*1-55542-104-0*) Jossey-Bass.

Dove, Lee. The Official Actor's Handbook: How to Become a Famous Actor & How to Deal with Stardom. (Illus.). 96p. 1987. pap. 4.95 (*0-942435-03-6*) Collegiate Pub.

Dove, Linda A. Teachers & Teacher Education in Developing Countries. 320p. 1986. 45.00 (*0-7099-0886-5*, Pub. by C Helm) Routldge.

Dove, Louise E., jt. auth. see Adams, Lowell W.

Dove, Marguerite. Forfeited Future: The Conflict over Congress Ministries in British India, 1933-1937. 492p. (C). 1987. 42.00 (*81-7001-029-2*, Pub. by Chanakya) S Asia.

Dove, Martin T. Introduction to Lattice Dynamics. (Cambridge Topics in Mineral Physics & Chemistry Ser.: No. 4). (Illus.). 276p. (C). 1993. text 74.95 (*0-521-39293-4*) Cambridge U Pr.

Dove, Mary, ed. see Stauffer, Titus.

Dove, Michael R. Swidden Agriculture in Indonesia: The Subsistence Strategies of the Kalimantan Kantu' (New Babylon Studies in the Social Sciences: No. 43). (Illus.). xx, 515p. 1985. 129.25 (*3-11-009592-0*) Mouton.

Dove, Nah. Afrikan Mothers: Bearers of Culture, Makers of Social Change. LC 97-41264. 280p. (C). 1998. text 59.50 (*0-7914-3881-3*); pap. text 19.95 (*0-7914-3882-1*) State U NY Pr.

Dove, Patrick E. The Revolver: Its Description, Management & Use: With Hints on Rifle Clubs & the Defense of the Country. LC 68-134401. 59p. 1968. reprint ed. write for info. (*0-85368-160-0*, Pub. by Arms & Armour) Sterling.

Dove, Peter, jt. auth. see King, Daniel.

Dove, Richard. He Was a German: A Biography of Ernst Toller. (Illus.). 320p. 1994. pap. 24.95 (*1-870352-25-4*, Pub. by Libris) Paul & Co Pubs.

— He Was a German: A Biology of Ernst Toller. (Illus.). xi, 320p. (C). 1990. text 49.95 (*1-870352-85-8*, Pub. by Libris) Paul & Co Pubs.

***Dove, Richard.** Journey of No Return: Five German-Speaking Literary Exiles in Britain, 1933-1945. (Illus.). 320p. 2000. 55.00 (*1-870352-36-X*, Pub. by Libris) Paul & Co Pubs.

Dove, Richard, tr. see Kruger, Michael.

Dove, Rick, jt. auth. see Nagel, Roger N.

***Dove, Rita.** Best American Poetry 2000. 320p. 2000. per. 16.00 (*0-7432-0033-0*) S&S Trade.

— Best American Poetry 2000. (Best American Poetry Ser.). 320p. 2000. 30.00 (*0-684-84281-5*) Scribner.

— The Darker Face of the Earth. 3rd rev. ed. 182p. 2000. pap. 14.00 (*1-885266-94-4*, Pub. by Story Line) Consort Bk Sales.

Dove, Rita. The Darker Face of The Earth: A Play. 21st rev. ed. LC 96-26121. 172p. 1996. pap. 12.00 (*1-885266-19-7*) Story Line.

— Darker Face of the Earth: A Verse Play. 140p. 1994. pap. text 10.95 (*0-934257-74-4*) Story Line.

— Fifth Sunday. (Orig.). 1985. pap. 8.95 (*0-912759-06-2*) Callaloo Fic Poetry.

— Grace Notes: Poems. 1991. pap. 9.95 (*0-393-30696-8*) Norton.

— Mother Love. 88p. 1995. 17.95 (*0-393-03808-4*) Norton.

— Mother Love. 78p. 1996. pap. 10.00 (*0-393-31444-8*, Norton Paperbks) Norton.

— Museum. LC 82-71663. 1983. pap. 12.95 (*0-88748-147-7*) Carnegie-Mellon.

***Dove, Rita.** On the Bus with Rosa Parks. (Illus.). 96p. 2000. pap. text 11.00 (*0-393-32026-X*) Norton.

Dove, Rita. The Poet's World. LC 95-5323. 107p. 1995. pap. 9.50 (*0-8444-0874-3*) Lib Congress.

— Selected Poems. LC 93-26112. 210p. 1993. pap. 12.00 (*0-679-75080-0*) Vin Bks.

— Thomas & Beulah. LC 85-71965. 1987. pap. 11.95 (*0-88748-021-7*) Carnegie-Mellon.

— Through the Ivory Gate: A Novel. LC 93-10509. (Vintage Contemporaries Ser.). 288p. 1993. pap. 12.00 (*0-679-74240-9*) Vin Bks.

— The Yellow House on the Corner. LC 80-65700. (Classic Contemporaries Ser.). 1980. pap. 12.95 (*0-88748-092-6*) Carnegie-Mellon.

***Dove, Roger M.** Don't Retire Broke: Are You Ready for the Best Years of Your Life? (Illus.). 126p. 1998. pap. 12.95 (*0-87527-532-X*) Green.

***Dove, Shawn & Johnson, Ronald.** A New Me in the New Millennium. iv, 60p. 2000. pap. 5.00 (*0-9678063-0-5*) Dove & Gibbons.

Dove, Tom. Cruising Sailor. O'Connor, John P., ed. LC 99-72229. (Illus.). 140p. 1999. spiral bd. 21.95 (*1-892216-15-9*) Bristol Fash.

Dove, Virginia. The Bridal Promise. (Desire Ser.: No. 1206). 1999. per. 3.75 (*0-373-76206-2*, 1-76206-1) Harlequin Bks.

Dove, W. F. & Rusch, H. P., eds. Growth & Differentiation in Physarum Polycephalum. LC 79-3202. 269p. 1980. reprint ed. pap. 83.40 (*0-608-02930-0*, 206399600008) Bks Demand.

Dove, William F., et al, eds. The Molecular Biology of Physarum Polycephalum. LC 86-4963. (NATO ASI Series A, Life Sciences: Vol. 106). 378p. 1986. 85.00 (*0-306-42267-0*, Plenum Trade) Perseus Pubng.

Dove, William F., jt. ed. see Crow, James F.

Dovell, Andrea. Struktur und Funktion Linearer Plasmide Bei Dem Phytopathogenen Ascomyceten Claviceps Purpurea. (Bibliotheca Mycologica Ser.: Vol. 126). (GER., Illus.). 118p. 1989. 42.00 (*3-443-59027-6*, Pub. by Gebruder Borntraeger) Balogh.

Dovell, Michael. The Dahlia Connection: A Deacon Davenport Mystery. Dunn, Brian, ed. LC 95-70990. (Illus.). 212p. 1995. 24.95 (*1-877882-19-4*); pap. 11.95 (*1-877882-18-6*) SCW Pubns.

Dover. Egyptian Address Book. 64p. pap. 1.00 (*0-486-27054-8*) Dover.

Dover, Benjamin F. Back Off! The Definitive Guide to Stopping Collection Agency Harassment. Donovan, Jim, ed. LC 94-71190. xx, 252p. 1994. 14.95 (*1-880925-04-4*) Equitable Media.

— Benjamin Dover's Book of Letters... That Really Work. 272p. 1997. pap. 17.95 (*1-880925-07-9*) Equitable Media.

— Life after Debt: The Blueprint for Surviving in America's Credit Society. Hallberg, Sharon & Vanderwold, Linda, eds. LC 93-21205. 336p. (Orig.). 1993. pap. 16.95 (*1-880925-03-6*) Equitable Media.

Dover, Benjamin F., jt. auth. see Simon, Henry W.

Dover, Beth & Joseph, Catherine D., eds. Great Smoky Mountains: A Complete Tour Book in Five Languages: Spanish, French, German, Japanese, English. (Illus.). 64p. (Orig.). (C). 1995. pap. 8.95 (*1-880970-16-3*) Aerial Photo.

***Dover, Caitlin.** Print's Best Letterheads & Business Cards 6. (Illus.). 176p. 2000. 35.00 (*1-883915-10-4*) RC Pubns.

— Print's Best Logos & Symbols 6. (Illus.). 176p. 2000. pap. 35.00 (*1-883915-09-0*) RC Pubns.

Dover, Cindy L. Van, see Van Dover, Cindy L.

Dover Doran, Laura. The Well-Decorated Garden: Making Outdoor Ornaments & Accents. LC 98-48216. (Illus.). 128p. 1999. 24.95 (*1-57990-106-9*, Pub. by Lark Books) Random.

Dover Doran, Laura, ed. see Czernecki, Stefan & Haijtink, Michael.

Dover Doran, Laura, ed. see Hoppe, Flo.

Dover, E. D. The Presidential Election of 1996: Clinton's Incumbency & Television. LC 98-4946. 216p. 1998. 57.95 (*0-275-96259-8*, Praeger Pubs) Greenwood.

— Presidential Elections in the Television Age, 1960-1992. LC 93-42803. 250p. 1994. 52.95 (*0-275-94840-4*, Praeger Pubs) Greenwood.

Dover, Ed. The Long Flight Home: Captain Ford's Epic Journey. (Illus.). 192p. 1998. 30.00 (*1-888962-07-0*) Paladwr Pr.

***Dover, Gabriel.** Dear Mr. Darwin: Letters on the Evolution of Life & Human Nature. (Illus.). 262p. 2000. 27.50 (*0-520-22790-5*) U CA Pr.

Dover, Harriet. Home Front Furniture: British Utility Design 1941-1951. 200p. 1991. text 69.95 (*0-85967-842-3*, Pub. by Scolar Pr) Ashgate Pub Co.

Dover, Hazel. Poems of Yesteryear. (Illus.). 2p. 1998. pap. write for info. (*1-887804-12-9*) Cent Mont Pubng.

***Dover Historical Society Staff.** Dover. (Images of America Ser.). 128p. 1999. pap. 18.99 (*0-7385-0119-0*) Arcadia Pubng.

Dover, Jeffrey, jt. auth. see Turkington, Carol A.

Dover, Jeffrey S., et al. Illustrated Cutaneous Laser Surgery. (Illus.). 142p. (C). 1989. pap. text 125.00 (*0-8385-1432-4*, A1432-2, Apple Lange Med) McGraw.

Dover, Jeffrey S., jt. auth. see Turkington, Carol A.

Dover, Jeffrey S., jt. ed. see Arndt, Kenneth A.

Dover, Jefrey S., et al. Illustrated Cutaneous & Aesthetic Laser Surgery. 2nd ed. (Illus.). 142p. 1999. pap. 195.00 (*0-8385-4257-3*, Apple Lange Med) McGraw.

Dover, K. Theocritus: Select Poems. (Bristol Greek Texts Ser.). 400p. 1985. reprint ed. pap. 33.95 (*0-86292-147-3*, Pub. by Brist Class Pr) Focus Pub-R Pullins.

Dover, K. J. Greek Homosexuality. LC 79-3576. (Illus.). 1980. pap. 9.95 (*0-394-74224-9*) Random.

Dover, K. J. Greek Homosexuality. 256p. 1997. reprint ed. 12.98 (*1-56731-221-7*, MJF Bks) Fine Comms.

— Greek Popular Morality in the Time of Plato & Aristotle. LC 93-42840. 352p. (C). 1994. reprint ed. pap. text 16.95 (*0-87220-245-3*); reprint ed. lib. bdg. 39.95 (*0-87220-246-1*) Hackett Pub.

Dover, K. J., ed. Ancient Greek Literature. 2nd ed. LC 98-120951. (Illus.). 198p. 1997. pap. text 20.95 (*0-19-289294-0*) OUP.

— Clouds. abr. ed. 256p. 1969. pap. text 17.95 (*0-19-912009-9*) OUP.

Dover, K. J., ed. see Denniston, J. D.

Dover, Kenneth. The Evolution of Greek Prose Style. LC 97-2022. (Illus.). 220p. (C). 1997. text 65.00 (*0-19-814028-2*) OUP.

— The Greeks. (Illus.). 172p. 1981. pap. 14.95 (*0-292-72724-0*) U of Tex Pr.

Dover, Kenneth, ed. & comment see Aristophanes.

Dover, Kenneth J. Aristophanic Comedy. LC 70-182681. 1972. pap. 17.95 (*0-520-02211-4*, Pub. by U CA Pr) Cal Prin Full Svc.

— Greek Homosexuality. (Illus.). 288p. 1989. pap. 17.50 (*0-674-36270-5*) HUP.

— Lysias & the Corpus Lysiacum. LC 68-63337. (Sather Classical Lectures: No. 39). 1968. 60.00 (*0-520-00351-9*, Pub. by U CA Pr) Cal Prin Full Svc.

Dover, Kenneth J., ed. Clouds. (Illus.). 414p. 1989. pap. text 29.95 (*0-19-814395-8*) OUP.

Dover, Kenneth J., ed. from GRE. Theocritus: Select Poems. (ENG & GRE.). 323p. (C). 1987. reprint ed. pap. 23.00 (*0-86516-204-2*) Bolchazy-Carducci.

Dover, Kenneth J., jt. auth. see Thucydides.

Dover, Kenneth J., ed. see Plato.

Dover, Kenneth J., jt. ed. see Thucydides.

Dover, Laura D. The Big Book of Halloween: Creative & Creepy Projects for Revellers of All Ages. LC 98-16054. (Illus.). 160p. 1998. 19.95 (*1-57990-063-1*, Pub. by Lark Books) Random.

Dover, Linda A., jt. auth. see Bamgaertner, Jill P.

Dover, Michael & Croft, Brian. Getting Tough: Public Policy & the Management of Pesticide Resistance. LC 84-52397. 92p. 1984. pap. text 10.00 (*0-915825-03-1*) World Resources Inst.

Dover, Michael J. A Better Mousetrap: Improving Pest Management for Agriculture, No. 4. LC 85-62028. (Illus.). 96p. 1985. pap. text 10.00 (*0-915825-09-0*) World Resources Inst.

Dover Publications. Scary Fun Books. 1997. pap. text 10.00 (*0-486-29753-5*) Dover.

— Seven Great English Victorian Poets, 7 vols. 592p. 1998. text 7.50 (*0-486-40204-5*) Dover.

— Six Favorite Novels for Girls: Little Women, Wizard of Oz, a Little Princess, Secret Garden, Ann. LC 99-188401. 1998. text 6.00 (*0-486-40346-7*) Dover.

Dover Publications Inc. Staff. Butterfly Collection Stickers, Bookmarks, Tattoos, More. (Illus.). 1997. 10.00 (*0-486-29750-0*) Dover.

— Celtic Frames & Borders. (Pictorial Archive Ser). (Illus.). 2000. pap. 9.95 (*0-486-99974-2*) Dover.

— Christmas Activity Books. (J). 1997. pap. text 9.00 (*0-486-26582-X*) Dover.

— Christmas-Blank Book. (Illus.). 1991. pap. text 1.00 (*0-486-25602-2*) Dover.

— Christmas Fun Books, Vol. 10. (Illus.). 1998. pap. text 10.00 (*0-486-40253-3*) Dover.

— Christmas Marbleized Boxed. 1992. pap. text 2.95 (*0-486-27144-7*) Dover.

— Dinosaur Fun Books. 1998. pap. text 10.00 (*0-486-40343-2*) Dover.

— 500 Full-Color Decorative Illustrations. (Full-Color Electronic Design Ser.). (Illus.). 2000. pap. 19.95 (*0-486-99970-X*) Dover.

— Flower Fun Books. (Illus.). (J). 1997. pap. 10.00 (*0-486-29751-9*) Dover.

— Full-Color Fruit & Flower Illustrations. (Full-Color Electronic Design Ser.). (Illus.). 2000. pap. 19.95 (*0-486-99971-8*) Dover.

— Fun with Birds Books. (Illus.). 1997. pap. text 9.00 (*0-486-29752-7*) Dover.

— Fun with Invisible Magic Pictures. (Illus.). 1996. pap. text 6.00 (*0-486-29204-5*) Dover.

— Jewish Fun Books, 10 bks. (Illus.). (J). 2000. pap. 10.00 (*0-486-41188-5*) Dover.

— My Tyrannosaurus Rex Notebook. (Illus.). (J). 1991. pap. text 1.00 (*0-486-25604-9*) Dover.

— Rose Wreath Quilt Notebook. (Illus.). 1988. pap. text 1.00 (*0-486-25601-4*) Dover.

— 7 Games & Puzzles Books, 7 vols. (Illus.). 1996. pap. text, boxed set 7.00 (*0-486-29461-7*) Dover.

— Space Fun Books. (Illus.). 1996. pap. text 7.00 (*0-486-29198-7*) Dover.

— Stencil Fun Books. (Illus.). 1991. pap. text 10.00 (*0-486-26969-8*) Dover.

— Sticker Fun Books. (Illus.). 1991. pap. text 10.00 (*0-486-26970-1*) Dover.

Dover Publications, N. Y. C. Staff. Cupid's Wedding Planner. 78p. (Orig.). 1996. pap. 15.95 (*0-9655997-0-1*) L T Pubns.

— Some Early Lloyd (Loyd) Families of New Jersey, Virginia, Tennessee, & Kentucky. unabridged ed. LC 97-71574. 165p. (Orig.). 1997. pap. 15.00 (*0-9622972-5-9*) G G Lloyd.

Dover Publications, N. Y. C. Staff, ed. see Santa Barbara Sun Bulletin Staff.

Dover Publications, N. Y. C. Staff, tr. see Wyss, Mitchell S.

Dover Publications Staff. Design Notebook. 1989. pap. 1.00 (*0-486-25898-X*) Dover.

Dover Publications Staff. Egyptian Designs: 390 Different Copyright-Free Designs. (Illus.). 64p. 1999. text 9.95 (*0-486-99958-0*) Dover.

— Heraldic Designs: 390 Different Copyright-Free Designs. (Illus.). 64p. 1999. text 9.95 incl. cd-rom (*0-486-99957-2*) Dover.

— Listen & Enjoy Spanish Poetry. (Listen & Enjoy Cassettes Ser.). 1991. pap. 9.95 incl. audio (*0-486-99928-9*) Dover.

Dover Publications Staff. Listen & Learn Japanese. 14.95 (*0-486-98880-5*) Dover.

Dover Publications Staff. Victorian Decorative Letters: 800 Complete Copyright-Free. (Illus.). 64p. 1999. pap. 9.95 incl. audio, cd-rom (*0-486-99959-9*) Dover.

Dover Publications Staff. Word Puzzle Fun Books. 1997. pap. 7.00 (*0-486-29749-7*) Dover.

D

An Asterisk (*) at the beginning of an entry indicates that the title is appearing for the first time.

Dover Publications Staff, ed. Little Book of Crossword Puzzles. (Little Activity Bks.). (Illus.). (J). 1995. pap. 1.00 (*0-486-28559-6*) Dover.
— Little Book of Tracing Paper. (Illus.). (J). 1990. pap. text 1.00 (*0-486-26394-0*) Dover.
— Old-Time Christmas Stickers. (Illus.). (J). 1997. pap. 1.00 (*0-486-27146-3*) Dover.
Dover, Robert V., et al, eds. Andean Cosmologies Through Time: Persistence & Emergence. LC 91-22250. (Caribbean & Latin American Studies). (Illus.). 292p. 1992. text 15.00 (*0-253-31815-7*) Ind U Pr.
Dover Staff. Animal Illustrations. (Illus.). 64p. 1998. pap. 9.95 incl. cd-rom (*0-486-99946-7*) Dover.
— Art Nouveau Frames & Borders. (Electronic Clip Art Ser.). (Illus.). 64p. 1997. spiral bd. 9.95 incl. cd-rom (*0-486-99938-6*) Dover.
— Best-Loved Children's Stories. adapted ed. (Illus.). (J). 1997. boxed set 7.00 (*0-486-29747-0*) Dover.
— Best Works of Mark Twain: Four Books. 624p. Date not set. pap., boxed set 6.00 (*0-486-40226-6*) Dover.
— Books, Reading & Writing Illustrations. (Illus.). 64p. 1998. pap. 9.95 incl. cd-rom (*0-486-99952-1*) Dover.
— Calligraphic Ornaments. (Electronic Clip Art Ser.). (Illus.). 64p. 1997. text 9.95 incl. cd-rom (*0-486-99939-4*) Dover.
— Celtic Alphabets. (Illus.). 64p. 1998. pap. 9.95 incl. cd-rom (*0-486-99953-X*) Dover.
— Celtic Collection. 1996. pap. text 10.00 (*0-486-29456-0*) Dover.
— Celtic Designs. (Electronic Clip Art Ser.). (Illus.). 64p. pap. 9.95 incl. cd-rom (*0-486-99940-8*) Dover.
— Cherub Illustrations. (Illus.). 64p. pap. 9.95 incl. cd-rom (*0-486-99947-5*) Dover.
— Christmas Collection Notebook. 1998. pap. 10.00 (*0-486-40240-1*, 884106Q) Dover.
— Christmas Designs. (Electronic Clip Art Ser.). (Illus.). 64p. 1997. spiral bd. 9.95 incl. cd-rom (*0-486-99941-6*) Dover.
— Christmas Stories & Songs, 5 vols., Set. 1994. pap., boxed set 5.00 (*0-486-28387-9*) Dover.
— Classic Novels for Young Readers, 4 vols., Set. (Children's Thrift Classics Ser.). (J). 1998. pap., boxed set 5.50 (*0-486-28664-9*) Dover.
— Cowboy & Western Cuts. (Illus.). pap. 9.95 incl. cd-rom (*0-486-99948-3*) Dover.
— Decorative Letters. (Electronic Clip Art Ser.). (Illus.). 64p. 1997. text 9.95 incl. cd-rom (*0-486-99942-4*) Dover.
— Easy French Phrase Book: Over 750 Basic Phrases for Everyday Use. Cohen, Leon J., tr. LC 94-12189. (ENG & FRE.). 64p. (Orig.). 1994. reprint ed. pap. 1.00 (*0-486-28083-7*) Dover.
— Easy German Phrase Book: Over 740 Basic Phrases for Everyday Use. Mathieu, Gustave B. & Stern, Guy, trs. LC 94-12190. (GER.). 80p. (Orig.). 1994. pap. 1.50 (*0-486-28084-5*) Dover.
— Easy Italian Phrase Book: Over 770 Basic Phrases for Everyday Use. LC 94-15609. (ITA.). 80p. (Orig.). 1994. pap. 1.50 (*0-486-28085-3*) Dover.
— Easy Spanish Phrase Book: Over 770 Basic Phrases for Everyday Use. (SPA.). 80p. (Orig.). 1994. pap. 1.00 (*0-486-28086-1*) Dover.
— Eight Great Greek Tragedies: Six Books. 480p. Date not set. text, boxed set 6.50 (*0-486-40203-7*) Dover.
***Dover Staff.** Fairies Fun Books, 10 vols. 1998. pap. text 10.00 (*0-486-40252-5*) Dover.
Dover Staff. Fairy Tales from Many Lands, 5 vols., Set. (Children's Thrift Classics Ser.). 480p. (J). 1995. pap. 5.00 (*0-486-28663-0*) Dover.
— Favorite Children's Stories, 5 vols., Set. (Children's Thrift Classics Ser.). (J). 1998. pap. 5.00 (*0-486-28182-5*) Dover.
— Favorite Stories for Early Readers. (J). 1996. boxed set 8.00 (*0-486-29202-9*) Dover.
— Five Great American Novels. (Thrift Editions Ser.). 720p. 1995. pap., boxed set 7.00 (*0-486-28665-7*) Dover.
— Five Great English Romantic Poets, 5 vols., Set. 496p. 1993. pap., boxed set 6.00 (*0-486-27893-X*) Dover.
— Five Great Plays of Shakespeare, 5 vols., Set. 496p. 1993. pap., boxed set 5.00 (*0-486-27892-1*) Dover.
— Five Great Poets: Poems by Shakespeare, Keats, Poe, Dickinson & Whitman. 416p. 1991. pap., boxed set 5.00 (*0-486-26942-6*) Dover.
— Floral Illustrations. (Electronic Clip Art Ser.). (Illus.). 64p. pap. 9.95 incl. cd-rom (*0-486-99943-2*) Dover.
— Food & Drink Illustrations. (Electronic Clip Art Ser.). (Illus.). 64p. 1997. text 9.95 incl. cd-rom (*0-486-99944-0*) Dover.
— 47 Great Short Stories: Stories by Poe, Chekhov, Maupassant, Gogol, O. Henry & Twain. 688p. 1992. pap., boxed set 6.50 (*0-486-27178-1*) Dover.
— Fun With Animal Origami: 12 Projects & 24 Sheets of Origami Paper. (Illus.). 48p. (Orig.). 1996. pap. text 4.95 (*0-486-29245-2*) Dover.
— Fun with Bird Origami, Incl. paper. (Illus.). 48p. 1995. pap. 4.95 (*0-486-28917-6*) Dover.
— Fun with Easy Origami, Incl. paper. (Illus.). 48p. 1993. pap. 4.95 (*0-486-27480-2*) Dover.
— Fun with Origami, Incl. paper. 16p. 1991. pap. 4.95 (*0-486-26664-8*) Dover.
— Great Adventure Novels for Children, 7 vols. (J). pap. text 7.00 (*0-486-29613-X*) Dover.
— Great Modern Writers, 5 bks. 720p. 1996. pap., boxed set 8.50 (*0-486-29458-7*) Dover.
— Great Women Poets: Four Complete Books, Set. 256p. 1994. pap., boxed set 4.00 (*0-486-28388-7*) Dover.
— Listen & Learn German. (Listen & Learn Ser.). (ENG & GER.). 1986. pap. 2.50 (*0-486-25275-2*) Dover.
— Listen & Learn Italian. (Listen & Learn Ser.). (ENG & ITA.). 1986. pap. 2.50 (*0-486-25276-0*) Dover.
— Listen & Learn Spanish. (Listen & Learn Ser.). (ENG & SPA.). 1986. pap. 2.50 (*0-486-25282-5*) Dover.
— Listen & Learn Swedish. (Listen & Learn Ser.). (ENG & SWE.). 1986. pap. 2.50 (*0-486-25283-3*) Dover.
— Mucha Notebook. 1988. text 1.00 (*0-486-25599-9*) Dover.
— Nine Great English Poets: Poemsby Shakespeare, Keats, Blake, Coleridge, Wordsworth, Mrs. Browning, Fitzgerald, Tennyson, & Kipling, 6 vols., Set. 704p. 1992. pap., boxed set 9.00 (*0-486-27633-3*) Dover.
— North American Indian Motifs. (Electronic Clip Art Ser.). (Illus.). 64p. pap. 9.95 incl. cd-rom (*0-486-99945-9*) Dover.
— Old-Fashioned Frames. (Illus.). 64p. 1998. pap. 9.95 incl. cd-rom (*0-486-99950-5*) Dover.
— Playtime Activity Books. 1991. text 8.00 (*0-486-26972-8*) Dover.
— Quilter's Delight, Set. (Illus.). 1996. pap., boxed set 8.00 (*0-486-29454-4*) Dover.
— Rainbow Patterned Origami Papers. Date not set. 4.50 (*0-486-29864-7*) Dover.
— Rainy Day Activity Books. 1991. pap. text 7.00 (*0-486-26583-8*) Dover.
— Sears, Roebuck Catalog of Houses, 1926. 160p. 1991. pap. 13.95 (*0-486-26709-1*) Dover.
— Seven ABC Fun Books. 1995. pap. text 7.00 (*0-486-28662-2*) Dover.
— 7 Childrens' Sticker Storybooks. (Illus.). 112p. (J). 1998. boxed set 7.00 (*0-486-29983-X*) Dover.
— 7 Peter Cottontail Activity Books. (Illus.). 116p. (J). 1999. boxed set 7.00 (*0-486-29982-1*) Dover.
— Six Great American Poets: Poems by Poe, Dickinson, Whitman, Longfellow, Frost & Millay, 6 vols. 512p. 1992. pap., boxed set 6.00 (*0-486-27425-X*) Dover.
— Stencil Designs. (Illus.). pap. 9.95 incl. cd-rom (*0-486-99951-3*) Dover.
— 10 Animal Sticker Paper Dolls. (Illus.). (J). 1993. boxed set 10.00 (*0-486-27890-5*) Dover.
— 10 Easter Fun Books. (J). boxed set 10.00 (*0-486-26971-X*) Dover.
— 38 Short Stories by American Women Writers, 5 bks., Set. 512p. 1996. pap., boxed set 6.00 (*0-486-29459-5*) Dover.
— 24 Celtic & Medieval Display Fonts: CD-ROM & Book. (Illus.). 48p. Date not set. pap. 14.95 incl. cd-rom (*0-486-99960-2*) Dover.
— Twenty-four Script & Cursive Display Fonts. (Illus.). 48p. 1999. pap. 14.95 incl. audio, cd-rom (*0-486-99961-0*) Dover.
— 26 Great Tales of Terror & the Supernatural, 6 vols., Set. 608p. 1993. pap., boxed set 6.00 (*0-486-27891-3*) Dover.
Dover Staff, ed. Easter Fun Books. 1999. pap. 10.00 (*0-486-40462-5*) Dover.
— Four Great English Novels. (Thrift Editions Ser.). 704p. 1995. boxed set 6.00 (*0-486-28666-5*) Dover.
— Great African-American Writers, 7 bks. 704p. 1998. pap., boxed set 9.00 (*0-486-29995-3*) Dover.
— Great Irish Writers, 5 bks. 672p. 1998. pap., boxed set 6.50 (*0-486-29996-1*) Dover.
— Masterpieces of Russian Literature, 7 bks. 880p. 1999. pap. text 9.50 (*0-486-40665-2*) Dover.
Dover Staff & Zedcor. Deskgallery Mega-Bundle. 64p. Date not set. 149.95 (*0-486-99937-8*) Dover.
Dover Staff, ed. see Cirker, Hayward & Cirker, Blanche.
Dover Staff, ed. see Ibsen, Henrik, et al.
Dover Staff, jt. ed. see Negri, Paul.
Dover Staff, ed. see Wells, H. G.
Dover, Victor. A Handbook to Marine Insurance. rev. ed. 870p. 1975. 162.00 (*0-900886-17-X*, Pub. by Witherby & Co) St Mut.
Dover, W. D. & Madhava Rao, A. G., eds. Fatigue in Offshore Structures. LC 99-227580. (Illus.). 758p. (C). 1997. text 207.00 (*90-5410-713-8*, Pub. by A A Balkema) Ashgate Pub Co.
Dover, Wendy. The Inclusion Facilitator. LC 94-75085. 130p. 1994. ring bd. 49.95 (*0-914607-35-9*) Master Tchr.
***Dover, Wendy.** Inclusion the Next Step: Managing the Diversity of Needs in the Classroom. (Illus.). xvii, 200p. 1999. ring bd. 49.95 (*0-914607-69-3*, 1749) Master Tchr.
Dover, Wendy. The Personal Planner & Training Guide for the Paraprofessional. 75p. 1996. 19.95 (*0-914607-39-1*) Master Tchr.
Dovermann, K. H., ed. Topology - Hawaii. 500p. (C). 1992. text 81.00 (*981-02-0683-6*) World Scientific Pub.
Dovermann, K. H. & Schultz, R. Equivariant Surgery Theories & Their Periodicity Properties. Dold, A. et al, eds. (Lecture Notes in Mathematics Ser.: Vol. 1443). vi, 227p. 1990. 40.95 (*0-387-53042-8*) Spr-Verlag.
Dovermann, Karl H. & Petrie, Ted. G Surgery II. LC 81-22829. (Memoirs Ser.: No. 37/260). 118p. 1987. reprint ed. pap. 17.00 (*0-8218-2260-8*, MEMO/37/260) Am Math.
Dovermann, Karl H. & Rothenberg, Melvin. Equivariant Surgery & Classification of Finite Group Actions on Manifolds. LC 87-31925. (Memoirs of the American Mathematical Society Ser.: No. 379). 117p. 1988. pap. 21.00 (*0-8218-2442-2*, MEMO/71/379C) Am Math.
Dovers, S. R., jt. ed. see Norton, T. W.
***Dovers, Stephen.** Environment, History & Policy: Still Settling Australia. 256p. 2000. pap. 29.95 (*0-19-550749-5*) OUP.
Dovers, Stephen, ed. Australian Environmental History: Essays & Cases. (Illus.). 272p. 1995. pap. text 45.00 (*0-19-553482-4*) OUP.
— Sustainable Energy Systems: Pathways for Australian Energy Reform. (Illus.). 236p. (C). 1995. text 64.95 (*0-521-43099-2*) Cambridge U Pr.
***Doverspike, Dennis & Tuel, Rhonda C.** The Difficult Hire: Finding & Retaining Unskilled & Entry-Level Employees. 2000. 14.95 (*1-57023-137-0*) Impact VA.
***Doverspike, Dennis, et al.** Affirmative Action: A Psychological Perspective. LC 99-55099. 1999. write for info. (*1-56072-762-4*) Nova Sci Pubs.
***Doverspike, Robert & Saniee, Iraj.** Heuristic Approaches for Telecommunications Network Management, Planning & Expansion. LC 00-22056. 2000. write for info. (*0-7923-7798-2*) Kluwer Academic.
***Doverspike, William F.** Ethical Risk Management: Guidelines for Practice. LC 99-28460. 112p. 1999. pap. 18.95 (*1-56887-057-4*, ERMBP, Prof Resc Pr) Pro Resource.
— MDI, Multiaxial Diagnostic Inventory: Professional Manual. rev. ed. LC 99-27193. 100p. 1999. pap. 44.45 (*1-56887-051-5*, Prof Resc Pr) Pro Resource.
Doveton, Dorothy M. The Human Geography of Swaziland. LC 74-15031. (Illus.). reprint ed. 41.50 (*0-404-12038-5*) AMS Pr.
Doveton, John H. Geologic Log Analysis Using Computer Methods. (Computer Applications Ser.: No. 2). (Illus.). ix, 169p. 1994. 42.00 (*0-89181-701-8*, 321) AAPG.
— Geological Log Interpretation: Reading the Rocks from Wireline Logs. LC 94-231838. (SEPM Short Course Notes Ser.: Vol. 29). (Illus.). 181p. reprint ed. pap. 56.20 (*0-608-20847-7*, 207194600003) Bks Demand.
***Dovey, Jon.** Freakshow: First Person Media & Factual Television. LC 00-26030. 226p. 2000. 59.95 (*0-7453-1455-4*, Pub. by Pluto GBR); pap. 19.95 (*0-7453-1450-3*, Pub. by Pluto GBR) Stylus Pub VA.
Dovey, Jon, ed. Fractal Dreams: New Media in Social Context. LC 97-187388. 256p. (C). 1996. pap. 18.50 (*0-85315-800-2*, Pub. by Lawrence & Wishart) NYU Pr.
Dovey, Ken & Graffam, Joe, eds. One in Eleven: Educational Needs of Catholic Schools in Victoria. 186p. 1995. pap. 40.00 (*0-909184-22-4*, Pub. by Deakin Univ) St Mut.
— Special Schools: Students, Parents, Teachers. 250p. 1995. pap. 80.00 (*0-909184-36-4*, Pub. by Deakin Univ) St Mut.
Dovey, Kim. Framing Places: Mediating Power in Built Form. LC 98-35335. (Architext Ser.). 1999. pap. 27.99 (*0-415-17368-X*, E & FN Spon); text. write for info. (*0-415-17367-1*, E & FN Spon) Routledge.
Dovey, Zillah. An Elizabethan Progress: The Queen's Journey into East Anglia 1578. LC 96-15114. (Illus.). 192p. 1996. 38.50 (*0-8386-3721-3*) Fairleigh Dickinson.
Dovey, Zillah M. Elizabethan Progress: The Queen's Journey into East Anglia 1578. 1999. pap. text 19.95 (*0-7509-2150-1*) Sutton Pub Ltd.
Dovgal, A. V. & Kozlov, Valery V. Separated Flows & Jets: IUTAM - Symposium, Novosibirsk, U. S. S. R., July 9-13, 1990. (Illus.). 912p. 1992. 287.95 (*0-387-53762-7*) Spr-Verlag.
***Dovi, Carol, ed.** Gifts from Our Grandmothers. LC 99-41285. (Illus.). 224p. 2000. 21.00 (*0-609-60488-0*, FAM022000, Crown) Crown Pub Group.
Doviak, Michael, jt. auth. see Aczel, Amir D.
Doviak, Richard J. & Zrnic, Dusan S. Doppler Radar & Weather Observations. 2nd ed. (Illus.). 562p. 1993. text 82.00 (*0-12-221422-6*) Acad Pr.
Dovich, Robert A. Quality Engineering Statistics. 111p. 1992. 25.00 (*0-87389-141-4*, H0679) ASQ Qual Pr.
— Reliability Statistics. (Reliability Ser.). 93p. (Orig.). 1990. pap. 24.00 (*0-87389-086-8*, H0601) ASQ Qual Pr.
Dovidio, J. F., jt. ed. see Ellyson, S. L.
Dovidio, John F., jt. auth. see Gaertner, Samuel L.
Dovitch, Dana, jt. auth. see De Puy, Candace.
Dovlatov, Sergei. Chemodan. LC 86-7540. (RUS.). 108p. (Orig.). 1986. pap. 7.50 (*0-938920-70-7*) Hermitage Pubs.
— The Compromise. Frydman, Anne, tr. from RUS. 148p. 1990. reprint ed. pap. 7.95 (*0-89733-353-5*) Academy Chi Pubs.
— Filial. LC 88-60721. (RUS.). 175p. (Orig.). 1989. pap. 28.50 (*0-89830-123-8*) Russica Pubs.
— Inostranka. LC 86-63326. 146p. (Orig.). 1987. pap. 9.50 (*0-89830-109-2*) Russica Pubs.
— Inostranka: A Russian Reader. Rashkovsky, Avigeil & Fiene, Donald, eds. (Orig.). (C). 1995. pap. text 12.95 (*0-87501-099-7*) Ardis Pubs.
— Marsh Odinokikh. limited ed. Sonynn, Roman, ed. LC 83-61816.Tr. of March of the Lonely. (RUS.). 100p. 1983. pap. text 20.00 (*0-914265-06-7*) New Eng Pub MA.
Dovlatov, Sergei. Predstavlenie I Drugie Rasskazy. LC 87-60054. 100p. (Orig.). 1987. pap. 8.50 (*0-89830-111-4*) Russica Pubs.
Dovner, Sylvia, ed. see Martin, Corinne.
Dovrat, A., et al. Irrigated Forage Production. (Developments in Crop Science Ser.: 24). 272p 1993. 196.50 (*0-444-88300-2*) Elsevier.
Dovring, Folke. Farming for Fuel: The Political Economy of Energy Sources in the United States. LC 87-38479. (Illus.). 158p. 1988. 52.95 (*0-275-93008-4*, C3008, Praeger Pubs) Greenwood.
— Inequality: The Political Economy of Income Distribution. LC 90-27556. 200p. 1991. 57.95 (*0-275-93963-4*, C3963, Praeger Pubs) Greenwood.
— Knowledge & Ignorance: Essays on Lights & Shadows. LC 97-33244. 176p. 1998. 55.00 (*0-275-96139-7*, Praeger Pubs) Greenwood.
— Land Economics. (Agriculture Ser.). 1987. pap. 48.95 (*0-8273-3905-4*) Delmar.
— Leninism: Political Economy As Pseudoscience. LC 95-43770. 168p. 1996. 52.95 (*0-275-95464-1*, Praeger Pubs) Greenwood.
— Productivity & Value: The Political Economy of Measuring Progress. LC 87-2347. 201p. 1987. 57.95 (*0-275-92668-0*, C2668, Praeger Pubs) Greenwood.
— Progress for Food or Food for Progress? The Political Economy of Agricultural Growth & Development. 330p. 1988. 65.00 (*0-275-92904-3*, C2904, Praeger Pubs) Greenwood.
— Riches to Rags: The Political Economy of Social Waste. 170p. 1984. 18.95 (*0-87073-514-4*); pap. 14.95 (*0-87073-515-2*) Schenkman Bks Inc.
Dovring, Karin. English As Lingua Franca: Double Talk in Global Persuasion. LC 96-52632. 168p. 1997. 52.95 (*0-275-95878-7*, Praeger Pubs) Greenwood.
Dovzhenko, Alexander. Alexander Dovzhenko: The Poet As Filmmaker. Carynnyk, Marco, tr. from RUS. LC 73-2934. 384p. 1975. pap. text 6.95 (*0-262-54019-3*) MIT Pr.
Dow, ed. see Linton, Mary Fox.
Dow, Alastair. Deprenyl: The Anti-Aging Drug. LC 92-74929. 280p. (Orig.). 1993. pap. 14.95 (*0-87319-036-X*) Hallberg Pub Corp.
— Deprenyl: The Inside Story. 220p. (C). reprint ed. 19.95 (*0-9629285-0-X*) Easton CA.
Dow, Alexander. The History of Hindostan, 3 vols., Set. 1000p. 1986. reprint ed. 100.00 (*0-88065-082-6*) Scholarly Pubns.
Dow, Andrew. Norfolk & Western Coal Cars, 1881-1997. (Illus.). 240p. 1998. 29.95 (*1-883089-36-0*) TLC VA.
Dow, Arthur W. Composition: A Series of Exercises in Art Structure for the Use of Students & Teachers. LC 97-2400. 160p. 1997. pap. 39.95 (*0-520-20749-1*, Pub. by U CA Pr) Cal Prin Full Svc.
Dow, Bill, jt. photos by see Hedren, Tippi.
Dow, Bonnie J. Prime-Time Feminism: Television, Media Culture, & the Women's Movement since 1970. (Feminist Cultural Studies, the Media, & Political Culture). 272p. 1996. pap. text 17.50 (*0-8122-1554-0*) U of Pa Pr.
— Prime-Time Feminism: Television, Media Culture, & the Women's Movement Since 1970. (Feminist Cultural Studies, the Media, & Political Culture). 296p. 1996. text 39.95 (*0-8122-3315-8*) U of Pa Pr.
***Dow, Bonnie J., ed.** Wise Women: Political Cartoons of the Woman Suffrage Movement. (Illus.). 2000. 19.95 (*1-892514-60-5*) Hill St Pr.
Dow, Carol. Afro-Brazilian Magick. LC 96-52081. (Illus.). 264p. (Orig.). 1997. pap. 14.95 (*1-56718-235-6*) Llewellyn Pubns.
— The Final Days of Planet Earth. 192p. (Orig.). pap. 5.75 (*0-9646007-0-6*) Prairie Books.
— Green Magic: The Healing Power of Herbs, Talismans & Stones. (Illus.). 176p. (YA). (gr. 10-13). 1994. pap. 16.95 (*0-924608-18-8*, Whitford) Schiffer.
Dow, Carol L., tr. & intro. see Neto, Teixeira A.
Dow Chemical Company Staff. Chempat: Evaluating & Managing Mixing Hazards in the Chemical Industries. 60p. 1996. pap. 195.00 incl. disk (*0-8169-0701-3*, Z-1) Am Inst Chem Eng.
— Dow's Fire & Explosion Index Hazard Classification Guide. 7th ed. LC 80-29237. (CEP Technical Manual Ser.). 74p. 1994. pap. 50.00 (*0-8169-0623-8*, T80) Am Inst Chem Eng.
Dow, Christopher. Major Recessions: Britain & the World, 1920-1995. LC 98-36848. (Illus.). 490p. 1999. text 98.00 (*0-19-828858-1*) OUP.
***Dow, Christopher.** Major Recessions: Britain & the World 1920-1995. 496p. 2000. pap. 24.95 (*0-19-924123-6*) OUP.
Dow, Clista. Lunchroom Waste: A Study of "How Much & How Come" Smith, Linda H., ed. (Triad Prototype Ser.). 44p. 1978. pap. 5.00 (*0-936386-04-5*) Creative Learning.
Dow, Crawford S., jt. ed. see Poole, Robert K.
Dow, David & Smyser, Craig. Texas Contracts Handbook. Date not set. pap. 75.00 (*1-884554-27-X*) J McClure Pubng.
Dow, David, jt. auth. see Cohn, Marjorie.
Dow, Deborah, jt. auth. see Clayton, Judy.
Dow, Dianne, jt. ed. see Dickerson, Lonna.
Dow, Dianne F., jt. auth. see Dickerson, Lonna J.
Dow, Eric. How to Build the Shellback Dinghy. (Illus.). 64p. 1993. pap. 15.00 (*0-937822-27-2*) WoodenBoat Pubns.
***Dow, Frances.** Cromwellian Scotland, 1651-1660. 384p. 2000. pap. 31.95 (*0-85976-510-5*, Pub. by J Donald) Dufour.
Dow, George F. Domestic Life in New England in the Seventeenth Century. LC 72-83087. (Illus.). 1972. reprint ed. 19.95 (*0-405-08462-5*, Pub. by Blom Pubns) Ayer.
— Every Day Life in the Massachusetts Bay Colony. (Illus.). 416p. 1988. reprint ed. pap. 9.95 (*0-486-25565-4*) Dover.
— Everyday Life in Massachusetts Bay Colony. 1988. 24.00 (*0-8446-6331-X*) Peter Smith.
— Everyday Life in the Massachusetts Bay Colony. LC 67-13326. (Illus.). 1972. reprint ed. 24.95 (*0-405-08463-3*, Pub. by Blom Pubns) Ayer.
— History of Topsfield, Mass. (Illus.). 517p. 1989. reprint ed. lib. bdg. 57.50 (*0-8328-0915-2*, MA102) Higginson Bk Co.
— Slave Ships & Slaving. LC 68-57116. (Illus.). 424p. reprint ed. pap. 131.50 (*0-7837-6849-4*, 204667800003) Bks Demand.
— Whale Ships & Whaling. (Illus.). 1967. reprint ed. 35.00 (*0-87266-007-9*) Argosy.
— Whale Ships & Whaling: A Pictorial History. (Antiques Series: Transportation). 288p. 1985. reprint ed. pap. 10.95 (*0-486-24808-9*) Dover.
Dow, George F., ed. Records & Files of the Quarterly Courts of Essex County. Complete Record of Wills, Inventories, Vital Records, Court Cases, Fines, Depositions, Etc., Presented in Abstracted but with All "Particulars" Needed for Research. (Illus.). 1995. reprint ed. lib. bdg. 325.00 (*0-8328-4593-0*) Higginson Bk Co.

D

Dow, George F. & Edmonds, John. The Pirates of the New England Coast, 1630-1730. (Illus.). 512p. 1993. pap. 15.00 (*0-87380-179-2*) Popular E Commerce.

Dow, George F. & Edmonds, John H. The Pirates of the New England Coast, 1630-1730. (Illus.). 1968. reprint ed. 30.00 (*0-87266-008-7*) Argosy.

— The Pirates of the New England Coast, 1630-1730. unabridged ed. (Illus.). 480p. 1996. reprint ed. pap. 11.95 (*0-486-29064-6*) Dover.

Dow, Helen J. The Sculptural Decoration of the Henry VII Chapel, Westminster Abbey. 118p. (C). 1989. text 65.00 (*1-872795-59-5*, Pub. by Pentland Pr) St Mut.

Dow, J. C. & Saville, Iain D. A Critique of Monetary Policy: Theory & British Experience. (Illus.). 286p. 1990. reprint ed. pap. text 24.00 (*0-19-828319-9*) OUP.

Dow, J. D. & Schuller, Ivan K., eds. Interfaces, Superlattices, & Thin Films. (MRS Symposium Proceedings Ser.: Vol. 77). 1987. text 17.50 (*0-931837-56-1*) Materials Res.

Dow, J. Kamal. Colombia's Foreign Trade & Economic Integration in Latin America. LC 71-631067. (Latin American Monographs: Ser. 2, No. 9). 95p. reprint ed. pap. 30.00 (*0-7837-4975-9*, 204464100004) Bks Demand.

Dow, J. M. Orbit Determination & Analysis. (Advances in Space Research Ser.: Vol. 19). 108.00 (*0-08-043288-3*, Pergamon Pr) Elsevier.

Dow, J. W., jt. auth. see Chasen, S. H.

Dow, James. The Arrow. 2nd rev. ed. (Illus.). 166p. 1997. pap. 15.95 (*1-55028-554-8*, Pub. by J Lorimer) Formac Dist Ltd.

— Nuclear Energy & Insurance. 465p. (C). 1989. 525.00 (*0-948691-58-1*, Pub. by Witherby & Co) St Mut.

Dow, James E. A Good German Conscience: The Life & Time of Ernst Moritz Arndt. 156p. (C). 1995. lib. bdg. 34.00 (*0-8191-9830-7*) U Pr of Amer.

Dow, James R., ed. Focus on Language & Ethnicity: Essays in Honor of Joshua A. Fishman, Vol. 2. LC 91-699. viii, 244p. 1991. 68.00 (*1-55619-117-0*) J Benjamins Pubng Co.

— Languages & Lives: Essays in Honor of Werner Enninger. VI, 325p. (C). 1996. text 69.95 (*0-8204-2713-6*) P Lang Pubng.

Dow, James R. & Lixfeld, Hannjost, eds. German Volkskunde: A Decade of Theoretical Confrontation, Debate, & Reorientation (1967-1977) LC 84-43175. (Folklore Studies in Translation). (Illus.). 388p. 1986. 37.50 (*0-253-32577-3*) Ind U Pr.

— The Nazification of an Academic Discipline: Folklore in the Third Reich. LC 93-17205. (Folklore Studies in Translation). 1994. 9.95 (*0-253-31821-1*) Ind U Pr.

— The Nazification of an Academic Discipline: Folklore in the Third Reich. LC 93-17205. (Folklore Studies in Translation). (Illus.). 374p. Date not set. reprint ed. pap. 116.00 (*0-608-20539-7*, 2054453) Bks Demand.

Dow, JaneAnn. Crystal Journey: Travel Guide for the New Shaman. (Illus.). 288p. 1994. pap. 20.00 (*0-9642385-0-0*) Jrny Bks.

— Crystal Journey Cards. Muhammad, Yolanda, ed. (Illus.). 36p. (Orig.). 1995. pap. 28.00 (*0-9642385-1-9*) Jrny Bks.

***Dow, Jill.** Hazel & Clover's Great Escape. (Windy Edge Farm Ser.). (Illus.). (J). (ps-2). 1999. pap. text 7.99 (*0-7112-0732-1*) F Lincoln.

— Hepzibah's Wooly Fleece. (Windy Edge Farm Ser.). (Illus.). (J). (ps-2). 1999. pap. text 7.99 (*0-7112-0616-3*) F Lincoln.

— Maggie's Holiday. (Windy Edge Farm Ser.). (Illus.). (J). (ps-2). 1999. pap. text 7.99 (*0-7112-0852-2*) F Lincoln.

— Moonbeam's Big Splash. (Windy Edge Farm Ser.). (Illus.). 32p. (J). 1999. pap. text 7.99 (*0-7112-1028-4*) F Lincoln.

Dow, Jocelyn, et al. Biochemistry: Molecules, Cells, & the Body. (C). 1995. pap. text 27.19 (*0-201-63187-3*) Addison-Wesley.

Dow, John O. A Unified Approach to the Finite Element Method & Error Analysis Procedures. LC 98-22147. (Illus.). 656p. (C). 1999. boxed set 79.00 (*0-12-221440-4*) Acad Pr.

Dow Jones & Co, Inc. Staff, ed. Dow Jones Guide to the Global Stock Market (1999 Edition), 3 vols. 6th ed. LC 98-71746. 930p. 1998. pap. 34.95 (*1-881944-13-1*) Dow Jones & Co.

***Dow Jones & Company Staff.** Guide to the Wall Street Journal. 2000. pap. write for info. (*0-13-028475-0*) P-H.

Dow, Joseph. History of the Town of Hampton, New Hampshire. 1104p. 1993. reprint ed. lib. bdg. 109.00 (*0-8328-6542-7*) Higginson Bk Co.

Dow, Julian, jt. auth. see Lackie, John M.

Dow, Karen H. Contemporary Issues in Breast Cancer - Custom. (Nursing Ser.). 336p. 1997. 15.00 (*0-7637-0618-3*) Jones & Bartlett.

— Pocket Guide to Breast Cancer. (Nursing Ser.). 320p. Date not set. pap. 31.25 (*0-7637-0683-3*) Jones & Bartlett.

Dow, Karen H., et al. Nursing Care in Radiation Oncology. 2nd ed. Cullen, Barnara N., ed. (Illus.). 400p. 1997. text 72.50 (*0-7216-2347-6*, W B Saunders Co) Harcrt Hlth Sci Grp.

Dow, Lesley. Alligators & Crocodiles. (Great Creatures of the World Ser.). (Illus.). 72p. (YA). 1990. 17.95 (*0-8160-2273-9*) Facts on File.

— Incredible Plants. LC 95-53786. (Nature Company Discoveries Library). (Illus.). 64p. (J). (gr. 4-7). 1999. 16.00 (*0-7835-4799-4*) Time-Life.

— Whales. (Great Creatures of the World Ser.). (Illus.). 72p. (J). (gr. 4-12). 1990. 17.95 (*0-8160-2271-2*) Facts on File.

Dow, Lesley, ed. see Morgan, Murray.

Dow, Leslie A. & Hendon, Fred N. Economics & Society. 512p. (C). 1990. pap. text 77.00 (*0-13-224551-5*) P-H.

Dow, Leslie S. Adele Hugo: La Miserable. (Illus.). 194p. 1993. pap. 14.95 (*0-86492-168-3*, Pub. by Goose Ln Edits) Genl Dist Srvs.

Dow, Martin. The Islamic Baths of Palestine. 176p. 1996. 60.00 (*0-614-21582-X*, 1433) Kazi Pubns.

— The Islamic Baths of Palestine. (British Academy Monographs in Archaeology: No. 7). (Illus.). 142p. 1996. text 70.00 (*0-19-727006-9*) OUP.

Dow, Michael & Cook, Elizabeth, eds. Annals of Nyingma Lineage in America, Vol. III. 255p. (Orig.). 1985. pap. 14.95 (*0-913546-99-2*) Dharma Pub.

Dow, Morris. Journey to the Fourth Season. (Illus.). 80p. (J). (gr. 3-5). 1998. pap. 10.95 (*0-9661700-0-8*) Ming Pubn.

Dow, Peter B. Schoolhouse Politics: Lessons from the Sputnik Era. 304p. (C). 1991. 44.00 (*0-674-79240-8*) HUP.

Dow, Philip. Paying Back the Sea. LC 78-71891. (Poetry Ser.). 1979. 20.95 (*0-915604-54-X*); pap. 11.95 (*0-915604-55-8*) Carnegie-Mellon.

Dow, R. S., jt. ed. see Smith, C. S.

Dow, Robert & Moruzzi, Giuseppe. The Physiology & Pathology of the Cerebellum. LC 58-8343. 689p. reprint ed. pap. 200.00 (*0-608-13261-6*, 205585700039) Bks Demand.

Dow, Robert P. Dow. The Book of Dow: Genealogical Memoirs of the Descendants of Henry Dow, 1537, Thomas Dow of 1639 & Others of the Name, Immigrants to America During Colonial Times, Also the Allied Family of Nudd. (Illus.). 1013p. 1995. reprint ed. pap. 139.00 (*0-8328-4774-7*); reprint ed. lib. bdg. 149.00 (*0-8328-4773-9*) Higginson Bk Co.

Dow, Roger. Turned On: Eight Vital Insights to Energize Your People, Customers & Profits. 336p. 1997. pap. 13.50 (*0-88730-861-9*, HarpBusn) HarpInfo.

***Dow, Roger & Cook, Susan.** Turned On: Eight Vital Insights to Energize Your People, Customers & Profits. 302p. 2000. text 25.00 (*0-7881-9013-X*) DIANE Pub.

Dow, Roger, et al. The Trust Imperative: The Competitive Advantage of Trust-Based Business Relationships. 1998. pap. 15.00 (*0-9657422-1-0*) SAMA.

Dow, Roger J. & Cook, Susan P. Turned On: Eight Timeless Principles for Energizing Your Customers, People, & Profits. LC 96-24998. 288p. 1996. 25.00 (*0-88730-766-3*, HarpBusn) HarpInfo.

Dow, Roger W. Business English. LC 78-18253. 451p. 1979. pap. text 17.50 (*0-471-36661-7*) P-H.

Dow, Rosalie, ed. see Odom-Winn, Danni & Dunagan, Dianne E.

Dow, Sheila & Hillard, John, eds. Keynes, Knowledge & Uncertainty. 448p. 1995. 100.00 (*1-85278-873-9*) E Elgar.

— Post Keynesian Econometrics, Microeconomics & the Theory of the Firm: Beyond Keynes. 256p. 1999. 85.00 (*1-85898-584-6*) E Elgar.

Dow, Sheila C. Financial Markets & Regional Economic Development: The Canadian Experience. (Illus.). 200p. 1990. text 82.95 (*0-566-07089-8*, Pub. by Avebry) Ashgate Pub Co.

— The Methodology of Macroeconomic Thought: A Conceptual Analysis of Schools of Thought in Economics. LC 96-922. Orig. Title: Macroeconomic Thought. 272p. 1996. 90.00 (*1-85278-980-8*) E Elgar.

— The Methodology of Macroeconomic Thought: A Conceptual Analysis of Schools of Thought in Economics. LC 96-922. Orig. Title: Macroeconomic Thought. 272p. 1998. pap. 25.00 (*1-85898-909-4*) E Elgar.

— Money & the Economic Process. LC 93-16076. 232p. 1993. 90.00 (*1-85278-566-7*) E Elgar.

***Dow, Sheila C. & Earl, Peter E., eds.** Contingency, Complexity & the Theory of the Firm Vol. II: Essays in Honour of Brian J. Loasby. LC 99-28338. 328p. 1999. 100.00 (*1-84064-187-8*) E Elgar.

— Economic Organization & Economic Knowledge: Essays in Honour of Brian J. Loasby, Vol. I. LC 97-39590. 328p. 1999. 95.00 (*1-85898-725-3*) E Elgar.

Dow, Sheila C. & Hillard, John, eds. Keynes, Uncertainty & the Global Economy: Beyond Keynes. 256p. 1999. 85.00 (*1-85898-797-0*) E Elgar.

Dow, Sterling T. Maine Postal History & Postmarks. LC 75-1790. (Illus.). 256p. 1976. reprint ed. 35.00 (*0-88000-065-1*) Quarterman.

Dow, Susan L. State Document Checklists: A Historical Bibliography. LC 90-33881. 224p. 1990. lib. bdg. 42.00 (*0-89941-739-6*, 306370) W S Hein.

***Dow, Susan L.** State Document Checklists: A Historical Bibliography. 2nd ed. LC 99-57327. l, 280p. 2000. 48.50 (*1-57588-617-0*) W S Hein.

***Dow, Thomas A. & Sohn, Alex, eds.** Proceedings from ASPE Spring Topical Meeting on Precision Fabrication & Replication. (Illus.). 80p. 1999. pap. write for info. (*1-887706-21-6*) Am Soc Prec Engr.

Dow, Wallace G., jt. auth. see Mukhopadhyay, Prasanta K.

Dow, Wallace G., jt. ed. see Magoon, Leslie B.

Dow, William H. Unconditional Demand for Health Care in Cote D'Ivoire: Does Selection on Health Status Matter? LC 96-34971. (Living Standards Measurement Study Working Papers: No. 127). 62p. 1996. pap. 22.00 (*0-8213-3757-2*, 13757) World Bank.

Dowaliby, Margaret. Practical Aspects of Ophthalmic Optics: Third Edition. 3rd ed. (Illus.). 581p. 1988. text 49.50 (*0-7506-9661-3*) Buttrwrth-Heinemann.

Dowall, David, et al. The Warsaw Economy in Transition. LC 96-83221. 224p. 1996. 68.95 (*1-85972-339-X*, Pub. by Avebry) Ashgate Pub Co.

***Dowall, David E.** California's Infrastructure Policy for the 21st Century: Issues & Opportunities. LC 00-28326. 2000. write for info. (*1-58213-023-X*) Pub Policy Inst.

Dowall, David E. The Land Market Assessment: A New Tool for Urban Management. LC 93-33937. 82p. 1995. pap. 22.00 (*0-8213-2703-8*, 12703) World Bank.

Dowall, David E. & Mingilton, Jesse. Effects of Environmental Regulations on Housing Costs. (CPL Bibliographies Ser.: No. 6). 67p. 1979. pap. 7.00 (*0-317-00022-5*, Sage Prdcls Pr) Sage.

Dowan, V. K. Indian Penal Code. 1989. 175.00 (*0-7855-3024-X*, Pub. by Capital Law Hse) St Mut.

Doward, Jan S. Even the Angels Must Laugh Again. LC 97-41211. 1997. pap. 5.99 (*0-8163-1408-X*) Pacific Pr Pub Assn.

— Finding the Right Path. 96p. (J). (gr. 5 up). 1990. pap. 7.99 (*0-8163-0938-8*) Pacific Pr Pub Assn.

Dowben, Peter A. Surface Segregation Phenomena. Miller, Allen, ed. 440p. 1990. lib. bdg. 295.00 (*0-8493-6893-6*, TN690) CRC Pr.

Dowbenko, Kateryna, jt. auth. see Humesky, Assya.

***Dowbiggin, Bruce.** Of Ice & Men: Steve Yzerman, Chris Chelios, Glen Sather, Dominik Hasek: The Craft of Hockey. (Illus.). 288p. 2000. pap. text 13.95 (*1-55199-042-3*) MW&R.

Dowbiggin, Bruce, et al. Of Ice & Men: Steve Yzerman, Chris Chelios, Glen Sather, Dominik Hasek: The Craft of Hockey. LC 98-233031. (Illus.). 288p. (J). (gr. 3-6). 2000. text 24.95 (*1-55199-028-8*) MW&R.

Dowbiggin, Ian. Inheriting Madness: Professionalization & Psychiatric Knowledge in Nineteenth-Century France. LC 90-10914. (Medicine & Society Ser.: No. 4). 227p. 1991. 48.00 (*0-520-06937-4*, Pub. by U CA Pr) Cal Prin Full Svc.

Dowbiggin, Ian R. Keeping America Sane: Psychiatry & Eugenics in the United States & Canada, 1880-1940. LC 97-3425. (Cornell Studies in the History of Psychiatry). (Illus.). 288p. 1996. text 37.50 (*0-8014-3356-8*) Cornell U Pr.

— Keeping America Sane: Psychiatry & Eugenics in the United States & Canada, 1880-1940. LC 97-3425. (Cornell Studies in the History of Psychiatry). 1997. pap. write for info. (*0-8014-8398-0*) Cornell U Pr.

Dowd. Competition & Finance. 580p. 1996. text 59.95 (*0-312-16218-9*) St Martin.

— Encyclopedia on Radiographic Positioning, Vol. 1. (Illus.). 625p. (C). 1995. text 85.00 (*0-7216-5745-1*) Harcourt.

— Encyclopedia on Radiographic Positioning, Vol. 2. (Illus.). 624p. (C). 1995. text 85.00 (*0-7216-5746-X*) Harcourt.

— Examaster to Radiographic Positioning. 1997. write for info. (*0-7216-5569-6*) Harcourt.

— Practical Radiation Protection. 1994. 260.00 (*0-7216-4920-3*) Harcourt.

— Quality Management Review. (Radiographic Technology Ser.). (C). 2000. pap. 24.95 (*0-7668-1258-8*) Delmar.

— Radiographic Positioning. (C). 1995. pap. text. write for info. (*0-7216-5566-1*, W B Saunders Co) Harcrt Hlth Sci Grp.

Dowd, Betty J., et al. The Apple Box Label Coloring Book. 40p. (J). (gr. k-3). 1981. pap. 1.95 (*1-928707-02-5*) Yakima Valley Mus.

Dowd, Bryan, et al. Competitive Pricing for Medicare. 200p. (Orig.). 1996. 29.95 (*0-8447-7067-1*, AEI Pr) Am Enterprise.

Dowd, Bryan E., et al. Competitive Pricing for Medicare. 180p. 1996. pap. 9.95 (*0-8447-7034-5*) Am Enterprise.

Dowd, Charles. A Funky Primer for the Rock Drummer. 48p. 1987. pap. 9.95 (*0-7390-0663-0*, 3333) Alfred Pub.

Dowd, Colleen E., jt. auth. see Fine.

Dowd, D. W., et al, eds. Medical, Moral & Legal Implications of Recent Medical Advances: A Symposium. LC 71-152124. (Symposia on Law & Society Ser.). 1971. reprint ed. lib. bdg. 19.50 (*0-306-70128-6*) Da Capo.

Dowd, David L. Pageant-Master of the Republic. LC 72-75507. (Select Bibliographies Reprint Ser.). 1977. 24.95 (*0-8369-5005-4*) Ayer.

Dowd, Douglas. Blues for America: A Critique, a Lament, & Some Memories. LC 96-30891. (Illus.). 320p. 1997. 38.00 (*0-85345-981-9*, Pub. by Monthly Rev) NYU Pr.

***Dowd, Douglas.** Capitalism & Its Economics. 376p. 2000. pap. 24.95 (*0-7453-1643-3*, Pub. by Pluto GBR) Stylus Pub VA.

Dowd, Douglas, jt. auth. see Brady, Robert A.

Dowd, Douglas F. Blues for America: A Critique, a Lament, & Some Memories. LC 96-30891. (Illus.). 320p. 1997. pap. 18.00 (*0-85345-982-7*, Pub. by Monthly Rev) NYU Pr.

— U. S. Capitalist Development Since 1976: Of, by & for Which People? LC 93-16219. 592p. (C). (gr. 13). 1993. text 85.95 (*1-56324-166-8*); pap. text 40.95 (*1-56324-167-6*) M E Sharpe.

Dowd, Douglas F., ed. Thorstein Veblen: A Critical Reappraisal-Lectures & Essays Commemorating the Hundredth Anniversary of Veblen's Birth. LC 77-9623. 328p. 1977. reprint ed. lib. bdg. 35.00 (*0-8371-9714-7*, DOTV, Greenwood Pr) Greenwood.

***Dowd, Douglas F. & Keaney, Michael.** Thorstein Veblen. 206p. 2000. pap. 24.95 (*0-7658-0638-X*) Transaction Pubs.

***Dowd, Douglas Fitzgerald.** Capitalism & Its Economics: A Critical History. LC 00-20283. 376p. 2000. 75.00 (*0-7453-1644-1*, Pub. by Pluto GBR) Stylus Pub VA.

***Dowd, E. Thomas.** Cognitive Hypnotherapy. LC 99-14701. 232p. 1999. 40.00 (*0-7657-0228-2*) Aronson.

Dowd, E. Thomas & Rugle, Loreen, eds. Comparative Treatments of Substance Abuse. LC 99-14661. (Comparative Treatments for Psychological Disorders Ser.). (Illus.). 304p. 1999. text 38.95 (*0-8261-1276-5*) Springer Pub.

Dowd, F. B. The Double Man. 303p. 1996. spiral bd. 18.50 (*0-7873-0293-7*) Hlth Research.

— The Double Man. 304p. 1996. reprint ed. pap. 17.95 (*1-56459-948-5*) Kessinger Pub.

— Regeneration: Being Part Two of the Temple of the Rosy Cross (1900) 158p. 1996. reprint ed. pap. 17.95 (*1-56459-554-4*) Kessinger Pub.

— The Temple of the Rosy Cross: The Soul, Its Powers & Migrations. 244p. 1994. reprint ed. pap. 12.95 (*1-56459-445-9*) Kessinger Pub.

— The Temple of the Rosy Cross: The Soul, Its Powers, Migrations & Transmigrations. 3rd ed. 167p. 1993. reprint ed. spiral bd. 14.50 (*0-7873-0292-9*) Hlth Research.

Dowd, Frances S. Latchkey Children in the Library & Community: Issues, Strategies, & Programs. LC 91-3580. 232p. 1991. pap. 29.95 (*0-89774-651-1*) Oryx Pr.

Dowd, Freeman B. The Way: A Text Book for the Student of Rosicrucian Philosophy. 152p. 1996. reprint ed. spiral bd. 12.00 (*0-7873-0294-5*) Hlth Research.

— The Way: A Text Book for the Student of the Rosicrucian Philosophy (1917) 152p. 1996. reprint ed. pap. 9.95 (*1-56459-661-3*) Kessinger Pub.

Dowd, Gregory E. The Indians of New Jersey. LC 92-34212. (New Jersey History Ser.: No. 3). 1992. 9.00 (*0-89743-079-4*) NJ Hist Com.

Dowd, Irene. Taking Root to Fly: Articles on Functional Anatomy. 3rd rev. ed. (Illus.). 96p. (C). 1995. pap. text 16.00 (*0-9645805-0-0*) I Dowd.

Dowd, James. Story of a French Homestead in the Old Northwest. (Illus.). 162p. 1999. pap. 19.00 (*0-7884-1189-6*, D592) Heritage Bk.

Dowd, James P. Built Like A Bear. 190p. 1979. 19.95 (*0-87770-212-8*) Ye Galleon.

— Custer Lives! 264p. 1982. 16.95 (*0-87770-268-3*) Ye Galleon.

— Thunders Speak: Biographies of Nine Special Original People. (Illus.). 178p. 1999. pap. 20.50 (*0-7884-1135-7*, D556) Heritage Bk.

Dowd, Jerome. Negro in American Life. LC 68-56331. 600p. 1969. reprint ed. lib. bdg. 35.00 (*0-8371-0389-4*, DON&) Greenwood.

Dowd, John. Abalone Summer. 144p. 1993. pap. 9.95 (*1-895714-24-9*) Raincoast Bk.

— Hogsty Reef. LC 98-36411. 192p. (YA). (gr. 6-10). 1999. pap. 5.95 (*1-56145-187-8*, 51878) Peachtree Pubs.

***Dowd, John.** Rare & Endangered. LC 99-86976. 160p. (YA). (gr. 6-10). 2000. pap. 5.95 (*1-56145-217-3*) Peachtree Pubs.

Dowd, John. Ring of Tall Trees. 128p. (YA). 1992. 14.95 (*0-920417-15-9*) Raincoast Bk.

— Sea Kayaking: A Manual for Long-Distance Touring. enl. rev. ed. LC 88-2744. (Illus.). 304p. 1988. pap. 18.95 (*0-295-96630-0*) U of Wash Pr.

— Sea Kayaking: A Manual for Long-Distance Touring. expanded rev. ed. LC 96-40297. (Illus.). 304p. 1997. pap. 18.95 (*0-295-97622-5*) U of Wash Pr.

Dowd, John D., jt. auth. see Wilkens, Ernest C.

Dowd, John F., jt. auth. see Gore, M. C.

Dowd, Joseph, jt. auth. see Pelegrimas, Marthayn.

Dowd, Kevin. Beyond Value at Risk: The New Science of Risk Management. LC 97-31514. (Wiley Series in Financial Engineering). (Illus.). 286p. 1998. 103.50 (*0-471-97621-0*) Wiley.

— Beyond Value at Risk: The New Science of Risk Management. LC 97-31514. (Wiley Series in Financial Engineering). 286p. 1999. pap. 46.50 (*0-471-97622-9*) Wiley.

— Getting Connected: The Internet at 56K & Up. Loukides, Mike, ed. 450p. (Orig.). 1996. pap. 29.95 (*1-56592-154-2*) Thomson Learn.

— Getting Connected: The Internet at 56K & Up; International Edition. Loukides, Mike, ed. 450p. (Orig.). 1996. pap. 29.95 (*1-56592-203-4*) Thomson Learn.

— High Performance Computing. Loukides, Mike, ed. (Management Information Systems). (Illus.). 398p. 1993. pap. 25.95 (*1-56592-032-5*) Thomson Learn.

— Laissez-Faire Banking. 400p. (C). 1996. pap. 29.99 (*0-415-13732-2*) Routledge.

***Dowd, Kevin.** Money & the Market: Essays on Free Banking. LC 00-32180. (Foundations of the Market Economy Ser.). 2000. write for info. (*0-415-24212-6*) Routledge.

Dowd, Kevin. Private Money: The Path to Monetary Stability. (IEA Hobart Paper Ser.: No. 112). 71p. 1996. pap. 19.95 (*0-255-36216-1*, Pub. by Inst Economic Affairs) Coronet Bks.

Dowd, Kevin & Timberlake, J. Richard, eds. Money & the Nation State: The Financial Revolution, Government & the World Monetary System. LC 97-40091. 320p. (Orig.). 1997. pap. text 19.95 (*1-56000-930-6*) Transaction Pubs.

Dowd, Kevin & Timberlake, Richard H., Jr., eds. Money & the Nation State: The Financial Revolution, Government, & the World Monetary System. LC 97-40091. (Illus.). 480p. 1997. pap. 24.95 (*1-56000-302-2*) Transaction Pubs.

Dowd, Merle E. Estate Planning Made Simple. 176p. 1991. pap. 11.00 (*0-385-41638-5*) Doubleday.

— Wall Street Made Simple. 240p. 1992. pap. 12.95 (*0-385-41786-1*) Doubleday.

Dowd, Michael. Earthspirit: A Handbook for Nurturing An Ecological Christianity. LC 91-65198. 128p. (Orig.). 1991. pap. 7.95 (*0-89622-479-1*) Twenty-Third.

Dowd, Mike. Managing to Be a Non-Smoker. 96p. 1991. pap. 9.95 (*0-9630260-9-7*) Dowd Hlthgrp.

Dowd, Nancy, jt. auth. see De la Questa, Barbara.

Dowd, Nancy E. In Defense of Single-Parent Families. LC 96-25268. 272p. (C). 1996. text 45.00 (*0-8147-1869-8*) NYU Pr.

— In Defense of Single-Parent Families. 1999. pap. text 18.50 (*0-8147-1916-3*) NYU Pr.

***Dowd, Nancy E.** Redefining Fatherhood. 2000. 28.95 (*0-8147-1925-2*) NYU Pr.

Dowd, Ned. That's a Wrap: How Movies Are Made. (Illus.). (J). (gr. 3-7). pap. 4.95 (*0-382-24376-5*, Silver Pr NJ) Silver Burdett Pr.

An Asterisk (*) at the beginning of an entry indicates that the title is appearing for the first time.

Dowd, Patrick W. Optical Interconnects for Computer System Design. (C). 2001. 25.33 (*0-13-124637-2*, Macmillan Coll) P-H.

Dowd, Patrick W., ed. Proceedings, 27th Annual Simulation Symposium. LC 71-149514. 264p. 1994. pap. 90.00 (*0-8186-5620-4*, ANSS-27) Soc Computer Sim.

Dowd, Robert H. The Enemy Is Us: How to Defeat Drug Abuse & End the "War on Drugs" LC 96-94697. 193p. 1996. 17.95 (*0-9653999-7-4*) Hefty Pr.

— The Enemy Is Us: How to Defeat Drug Abuse & End the War on Drugs. LC 96-94697. 193p. 1997. reprint ed. pap. 8.95 (*0-9653999-8-2*) Hefty Pr.

***Dowd, Sebastian.** Lightning. limited ed. 78p. 1999. 90.00 (*1-881119-46-7*) Pyncheon Hse.

— Lightning. unabridged ed. 78p. 1999. 60.00 (*1-881119-30-0*) Pyncheon Hse.

***Dowd, Sharyn E.** Reading Mark: A Literary & Theological Commentary. LC 00-41024. 2000. write for info. (*1-57312-288-2*) Smyth & Helwys.

Dowd, Siobhan, ed. This Prison Where I Live: The Pen Anthology of Imprisoned Writers. LC 97-100459. (Global Issues Ser.). 192p. 1996. 80.00 (*0-304-33304-2*); pap. 25.95 (*0-304-33306-9*) Continuum.

Dowd, Steven B. Practical Radiation Protection & Applied Radiobiology. LC 93-22594. 1994. text 34.50 (*0-7216-4917-3*, W B Saunders Co); text, teacher ed. write for info. (*0-7216-4918-1*, W B Saunders Co); 231.00 (*0-7216-4919-X*, W B Saunders Co) Harcrt Hlth Sci Grp.

— Radiologic Technology Registry Preparation: RT. 267p. (C). 1995. pap. text, spiral bd., wbk. ed. 29.95 (*0-925016-94-2*) Educ Sftware.

— Teaching in the Health Related Professions. LC 96-14014. 292p. 1996. per. 29.95 (*0-89089-732-8*) Carolina Acad Pr.

Dowd, Steven B. & Hulse, Stephen F. Teaching Techniques in the Radiologic Sciences. (Illus.). 200p. (Orig.). (C). 1996. pap. text. write for info. (*1-886800-01-4*) Am Soc Radiologic Techns.

***Dowd, Steven B. & Tilson, Elwin R.** Instructor's Manual to Accompany Practical Radiation Protection & Applied Radiobiology. 1999. teacher ed. write for info. (*0-7216-7660-X*, W B Saunders Co) Harcrt Hlth Sci Grp.

Dowd, Steven B. & Tilson, Elwin R. Practical Radiation Protection & Applied Radiobiology. 2nd ed. Allen, Andrew, ed. LC 98-43925. (Illus.). 365p. 1999. text 32.95 (*0-7216-7523-9*, W B Saunders Co) Harcrt Hlth Sci Grp.

Dowd, Steven B. & Wilson, Bettye G. Encyclopedia of Radiographic Positioning, 2 vols., Set. LC 94-13891. (Illus.). 2016p. 1995. text 145.00 (*0-7216-4202-0*, W B Saunders Co) Harcrt Hlth Sci Grp.

Dowd, Steven B. & Wilson, Bettye G., eds. Encyclopedia of Radiographic Positioning. (Illus.). 1249p. 1995. teacher ed. write for info. (*0-7216-4288-8*, W B Saunders Co) Harcrt Hlth Sci Grp.

Dowd, T. The Market for Lawn, Garden, & Snow Equipment. (Illus.). 400p. 1999. spiral bd. 1295.00 (*0-317-65738-0*) Busn Trend.

— The U. S. Pet Food Market. 430p. 1998. 1495.00 (*0-318-04173-1*) Busn Trend.

Dowd, Tom & Tierney, Jeff. Teaching Social Skills to Youth: A Curriculum for Child-Care Providers. rev. ed. 284p. (C). 1992. pap. 29.95 (*0-938510-30-4*, 45-006) Boys Town Pr.

Dowd, Tom, et al. Effective Skills for Child Care Workers: A Training Manual. LC 95-125685. 185p. (Orig.). 1994. pap. text 29.95 (*0-938510-43-6*, 45-001) Boys Town Pr.

Dowd, Tom, jt. auth. see Sterba, Michael.

Dowd, W. W. The Descendants of Henry Doude Who Came from England in 1639. 342p. 1989. reprint ed. pap. 44.00 (*0-8328-0491-6*); reprint ed. lib. bdg. 54.00 (*0-8328-0490-8*) Higginson Bk Co.

Dowdall, George W. Adventures in Criminal Justice Research: Data Analysis for Windows 95/98 : Using SPSS Versions 7.5, 8.0, or Higher LC 99-171749. 393p. 1999. write for info. (*0-7619-8625-1*) Sage.

— The Eclipse of the State Mental Hospital: Policy, Stigma, & Organization. LC 94-12517. (SUNY Series in the Sociology of Work). 262p. (C). 1996. text 64.50 (*0-7914-2895-8*); pap. text 21.95 (*0-7914-2896-6*) State U NY Pr.

Dowdall, Jennifer, jt. auth. see Berry, Melanie.

Dowdall, John. Traditionary Anecdotes of Shakespeare. Collier, J. Payne, ed. LC 70-164782. reprint ed. 37.50 (*0-404-02165-4*) AMS Pr.

***Dowdall, Katherine M.** Temporal Contrasts in Archaeological Site Usage on the Northern Sonoma Coast. (Illus.). 346p. (C). 1999. pap. text 36.25 (*1-55567-814-9*) Coyote Press.

Dowdall, Mike. Men Are Such Babies. (Illus.). 64p. 1997. 16.95 (*0-8362-5034-6*) Andrews & McMeel.

Dowdall, Mike & Meehan, Sheila, eds. Pep Talk: Inspiration from America's Great Coaches. LC 94-33742. (Illus.). 88p. 1995. pap. 5.95 (*0-8118-0542-5*) Chronicle Bks.

Dowdell, D. Secrets of the ABCs. LC 65-22301. (Illus.). 64p. (J). (gr. 2 up). 1968. lib. bdg. 10.95 (*0-87783-035-5*) Oddo.

Dowdell, Dorothy & Dowdell, Joseph. Your Career in the World of Travel. LC 70-143452. 1971. write for info. (*0-671-32405-5*) S&S Trade.

Dowdell, E. G. A Hundred Years of Quarter Sessions. LC 85-80814. (Cambridge Studies in English Legal History). 290p. 1986. reprint ed. 72.00 (*0-912004-43-6*) Gaunt.

Dowdell, John, III, jt. auth. see Zakia, Richard D.

Dowdell, Joseph, jt. auth. see Dowdell, Dorothy.

Dowdell, Rodger B., ed. see Flow, Its Measurement & Control in Science & Indus.

Dowden. State Flowers. (J). 1978. 13.95 (*0-690-01339-6*) HarpC Child Bks.

Dowden, A. From Flower to Fruit. (J). 1984. lib. bdg. 14.89 (*0-690-04403-8*) HarpC Child Bks.

Dowden, Angela & Lacey, Graham. A Consumer Guide to Vitamins. 96p. (Orig.). 1995. pap. 9.95 (*0-330-34436-6*, Pub. by Pan) Trans-Atl Phila.

***Dowden, Anne O.** The Blossom on the Bough: A Book of Trees. (Illus.). 71p. (YA). (gr. 6-8). 1999. text 17.00 (*0-7881-6658-1*) DIANE Pub.

Dowden, Anne O. Clover & the Bee. LC 87-30116. (Illus.). 96p. (J). (gr. 5 up). 1990. 18.00 (*0-690-04677-4*); lib. bdg. 17.89 (*0-690-04679-0*) HarpC Child Bks.

— From Flower to Fruit. LC 83-46163. (Illus.). 64p. (YA). (gr. 7 up). 1984. 14.95 (*0-690-04402-X*) HarpC Child Bks.

— Poisons in Our Path: Plants That Harm & Heal. LC 92-9518. (Illus.). 64p. (J). 1994. lib. bdg. 17.89 (*0-06-020862-7*) HarpC Child Bks.

Dowden, Anne O. The Blossom on the Bough: A Book of Trees. LC 93-22726. 80p. (J). (gr. 3 up). 1994. 16.95 (*0-395-68375-0*) Ticknor & Flds Bks Yng Read.

— From Flower to Fruit. LC 93-24972. 64p. (J). (gr. 3 up). 1994. 15.95 (*0-395-68376-9*) Ticknor & Flds Bks Yng Read.

Dowden, Anne Ophelia Todd. Blossom on Bough Book of Trees. (J). 1975. 14.95 (*0-690-00384-6*) HarpC Child Bks.

— Blossom on the Bough: A Book of Trees. LC 93-22726. 1994. 15.15 (*0-606-06240-8*, Pub. by Turtleback) Demco.

Dowden, C. James. Community Associations: A Guide for Public Officials. LC 79-57077. (Illus.). 95p. reprint ed. pap. 30.00 (*0-8357-3186-3*, 203945600012) Bks Demand.

— Creating a Community Association: The Developer's Role in Condominium & Homeowner Associations. 2nd rev. ed. LC 86-50785. (Illus.). 86p. reprint ed. pap. 30.00 (*0-8357-3188-X*, 203945800012) Bks Demand.

Dowden, E., ed. see Shelley, Percy Bysshe.

Dowden, Edward. Essays, Modern & Elizabethan. LC 71-117784. (Essay Index Reprint Ser.). 1977. 22.95 (*0-8369-1647-6*) Ayer.

— The French Revolution & English Literature: Lectures Delivered in Connection with the Sesquicentennial Celebration of Princeton. (BCL1-PR English Literature Ser.). 285p. 1992. reprint ed. lib. bdg. 79.00 (*0-7812-7024-3*) Rprt Serv.

— A History of French Literature. (Select Bibliographies Reprint Ser.). x, 444 p. 1977. reprint ed. 26.95 (*0-8369-6644-9*) Ayer.

— Introduction to Shakespeare. (Select Bibliographies Reprint Ser.). 1977. 19.95 (*0-8369-5254-5*) Ayer.

— Introduction to Shakespeare. (BCL1-PR English Literature Ser.). 136p. 1992. reprint ed. lib. bdg. 69.00 (*0-7812-7281-5*) Rprt Serv.

— The Life of Percy Bysshe Shelley, 2 vols., Set. (BCL1-PR English Literature Ser.). 1992. reprint ed. lib. bdg. 150.00 (*0-7812-7650-0*) Rprt Serv.

— Puritan & Anglican: Studies in Literature. LC 67-23208. (Essay Index Reprint Ser.). 1977. 23.95 (*0-8369-0386-2*) Ayer.

— Puritan & Anglican: Studies in Literature. (BCL1-PR English Literature Ser.). 341p. 1992. reprint ed. lib. bdg. 89.00 (*0-7812-7039-1*) Rprt Serv.

— Robert Browning. 1972. 59.95 (*0-8490-0960-X*) Gordon Pr.

— Southey. Morley, John, ed. LC 68-58377. (English Men of Letters Ser.). reprint ed. lib. bdg. 26.50 (*0-404-51709-9*) AMS Pr.

— Southey. (BCL1-PR English Literature Ser.). 205p. 1992. reprint ed. lib. bdg. 79.00 (*0-7812-7662-4*) Rprt Serv.

Dowden, Joe. Watercolor: Two Books in One. (Illus.). 128p. 1999. 24.95 (*0-8069-2875-1*) Sterling.

Dowden, John, tr. from LAT. Altus of St. Columba. 1989. pap. 1.25 (*0-89981-210-4*) Eastern Orthodox.

Dowden, K. Religion & the Romans. (Classical World Ser.). 110p. 1992. pap. 18.95 (*1-85399-180-5*, Pub. by Brist Class Pr) Focus Pub-R Pullins.

Dowden, Ken. Death & the Maiden: Girls' Initiation Rites in Greek Mythology. 256p. 1989. 35.00 (*0-415-01263-5*, A2518) Routledge.

***Dowden, Ken.** European Paganism: Realities of Cult from Antiquity to Middle Ages. 400p. 2000. 75.00 (*0-415-12034-9*) Routledge.

Dowden, Ken. The Uses of Greek Mythology. LC 91-38305. (Approaching the Ancient World Ser.). 216p. (C). 1992. pap. 20.99 (*0-415-06135-0*, A7500) Routledge.

Dowden, Leland A. One & One Half Missions. LC 89-50089. (Illus.). 248p. 1989. 19.95 (*0-936029-41-2*) Western Bk Journ.

Dowden, Lisa G. & McNurney, John M., eds. Municipal Environmental Compliance Manual. LC 94-31122. 256p. 1994. lib. bdg. 65.00 (*1-56670-098-1*, L1098) Lewis Pubs.

Dowden, Mark & Kassberg, Maria, eds. Planning Your Career: A Business Decision Guide for the Ob-Gyn Resident. 2nd ed. 244p. 1995. pap. text. write for info. (*0-9628716-2-1*) Dowden Pub.

Dowden, Nigel. Old Fishing Tackle. (Illus.). 32p. 1995. pap. 25.00 (*0-7478-0278-5*, Pub. by Shire Pubns) Parkwest Pubns.

Dowden, Robert M., jt. ed. see Shay, Jerry W.

Dowden, Stephen, ed. Hermann Broch: Literature, Philosophy, Politics - The Yale Broch Symposium. LC 87-70866. (GERM Ser.: Vol. 30). (Illus.). xvii, 358p. 1988. 39.95 (*0-938100-50-5*) Camden Hse.

Dowden, Stephen D. Kafka's Castle & the Critical Imagination. (LCGERM Ser.). xiii, 112p. 1995. 55.00 (*1-57113-004-7*) Camden Hse.

— Understanding Thomas Bernhard. Hardin, James N., ed. LC 91-21970. (Understanding Modern European & Latin American Literature Ser.). 117p. 1991. text 29.95 (*0-87249-759-3*) U of SC Pr.

Dowden, Steven D., ed. A Companion to Thomas Mann's Magic Mountain. LC 98-21803. (Studies in German Literature & Culture). xix, 250 p. 1999. 65.00 (*1-57113-150-7*) Camden Hse.

Dowden, Wilfred S. Joseph Conrad: The Imaged Style. LC 74-112936. 200p. 1970. 17.95 (*0-8265-1153-8*) Vanderbilt U Pr.

Dowden, Wilfred S., ed. The Journal of Thomas Moore, Vol. 1. LC 79-13541. (Illus.). 400p. 1983. 65.00 (*0-87413-145-6*) U Delaware Pr.

— The Journal of Thomas Moore, Vol. 2. LC 79-13541. (Illus.). 488p. 1985. 65.00 (*0-87413-245-2*) U Delaware Pr.

— The Journal of Thomas Moore, Vol. 3. LC 79-13541. 472p. 1986. 70.00 (*0-87413-255-X*) U Delaware Pr.

— The Journal of Thomas Moore, 1831-1835, Vol. 4 LC 79-13541. (Illus.). 400p. 1987. 70.00 (*0-87413-256-8*) U Delaware Pr.

— The Journal of Thomas Moore, 1836-1842, Vol. 5 LC 79-13541. 544p. 1988. 70.00 (*0-87413-257-6*) U Delaware Pr.

Dowden, Wilfred S., ed. see Moore, Thomas.

Dowdeswell, E., jt. auth. see Obasi, G. O.

Dowdeswell, E. C., jt. ed. see Harland, W. B.

Dowdeswell, J. A. & Scourse, J. D., eds. Glacimarine Environments: Processes & Sediments. (Geological Society Special Publications: No. 53). (Illus.). 450p. 1990. 125.00 (*0-903317-54-0*, 255, Pub. by Geol Soc Pub Hse) AAPG.

Dowdey, C. Golden Age. 1976. 30.95 (*0-8488-0213-5*, J M C & Co) Amereon Ltd.

— Virginia Dynasties. 1976. 36.95 (*0-8488-0212-8*, J M C & Co) Amereon Ltd.

Dowdey, Clifford. Bugles Blow No More. LC 90-30891. 512p. 1990. reprint ed. 34.95 (*0-87797-176-5*) Cherokee.

— Experiment in Rebellion. LC 75-111828. (Essay Index Reprint Ser.). 1977. 46.95 (*0-8369-1648-4*) Ayer.

— Lee: A Biography of Robert E. Lee. (Illus.). 781p. 1991. reprint ed. 35.00 (*1-879664-09-7*); reprint ed. pap. 19.95 (*1-879664-10-0*) Stan Clark Military.

— Lee & His Men at Gettysburg: The Death of a Nation. LC 92-37872. (Illus.). 1999. pap. 16.95 (*0-8032-6616-2*) U of Nebr Pr.

— Lee's Last Campaign: The Story of Lee & His Men Against Grant - 1864. LC 92-37872. (Illus.). xxii, 415p. (C). 1993. pap. 15.95 (*0-8032-6595-6*, Bison Books) U of Nebr Pr.

— The Seven Days: The Emergence of Lee. LC 92-37791. (Illus.). xx, 380p. (C). 1993. pap. 15.95 (*0-8032-6594-8*, Bison Books) U of Nebr Pr.

Dowdey, Clifford & Manarin, Louis H., eds. The Wartime Papers of Robert E. Lee. (Quality Paperbacks Ser.). (Illus.). xiv, 994p. 1987. reprint ed. pap. 19.95 (*0-306-80282-1*) Da Capo.

Dowdey, Clifford, jt. auth. see Manarin, Louis H.

Dowdey, David, tr. see Sylvanus, Erwin.

Dowdey, Diane. The Researching Reader: Source-Based Writing Across the Disciplines. 608p. (C). 1990. teacher ed. write for info. (*0-03-028772-3*) Harcourt Coll Pubs.

Dowding, C. H., ed. Rock Masses: Modeling of Underground Openings-Probability of Slope Failure-Fracture of Intact Rock: Proceedings of a Symposium Sponsored by the Geotechnical Engineering Division. 189p. 1985. 27.00 (*0-87262-446-3*) Am Soc Civil Eng.

Dowding, Charles H. Blast Vibration Monitoring & Control. (Illus.). 297p. (C). 1995. pap. text 55.00 (*0-9644313-0-0*) C H Dowding.

— Construction Vibrations. LC 95-21237. 610p. (C). 1996. 100.00 (*0-13-299108-X*) P-H.

Dowding, Charles H., jt. auth. see O'Connor, Kevin M.

Dowding, D. Power. 112p. 1996. pap. 2.00 (*0-335-19440-0*) Taylor & Francis.

Dowding, Geoffrey. Finer Points in the Spacing & Arrangement of Type. LC 92-35936. (Illus.). 96p. 1995. pap. text 14.95 (*0-88179-119-9*) Hartley & Marks.

— An Introduction to the History of Printing Types: An Illustrated Summary of the Main Stages in the Development of Type Design from 1440 up to the Present Day: An Aid to Type Face Identification LC 97-43152. 1997. write for info. (*0-7123-4563-9*, Pub. by B23tish Library) U of Toronto Pr.

— An Introduction to the History of Printing Types: An Illustrated Summary of the Main Stages in the Development of Type Design from 1440 up to the Present Day: An Aid to Type Face Identification LC 97-43152. (Illus.). 304p. 1997. 39.95 (*1-884718-43-4*, 50314); pap. 29.95 (*1-884718-44-2*, 50320) Oak Knoll.

Dowding, Keith. Power. 112p. 1996. 9.00 (*0-335-19441-9*) Taylor & Francis.

— Power. (Concepts in Social Thought Ser.). 128p. 1996. pap. 14.95 (*0-8166-2941-2*); text 37.95 (*0-8166-2940-4*) U of Minn Pr.

Dowding, Keith & King, Desmond, eds. Preferences, Institutions, & Rational Choice. (Illus.). 304p. 1995. text 55.00 (*0-19-827895-0*) OUP.

Dowding, Keith M. Rational Choice & Political Power. 208p. 1991. text 90.00 (*1-85278-335-4*) E Elgar.

Dowding, Margaret, jt. ed. see Sanger, Frederick.

Dowding, Robert J. & Bose, Animesh, eds. Tungsten, Refractory Metals & Alloys 4: Processing, Properties & Applications. (Illus.). 420p. 1998. pap. 160.00 (*1-878954-65-2*, C2607) Metal Powder.

Dowding, Robert J., jt. ed. see Bose, Animesh.

Dowding, Robert J., ed. see International Conference on Tungsten & Refractory.

Dowding, Robert J., ed. see International Conference on Tungsten & Tungsten Al.

***Dowding, Robert L. & Liska, Julie.** A Few Survived LC 99-35482. 1999. write for info. (*1-886225-48-6*) Dageforde Pub.

***Dowdle, J.** The Independent Medical Examination. (Illus.). 256p. 1998. write for info. (*0-443-07650-2*) Church.

Dowdle, Walter & Hopkins, David. The Eradication of Infectious Diseases: Report of the Dahlem Workshop on the Eradication of Infectious Diseases, Berlin, March 16-22, 1997. LC 97-41829. (Dahlem Workshop Reports). 238p. 1998. 159.95 (*0-471-98089-7*) Wiley.

Dowdney, Donna L., jt. auth. see Sheridan, Donna R.

Dowdy, Carol, et al. Attention-Deficit/Hyperactivity Disorder in the Classroom: A Practical Guide for Teachers. LC 96-39435. 250p. (Orig.). (C). 1997. pap. 29.00 (*0-89079-665-3*, 6961) PRO-ED.

Dowdy, Dru, compiled by. National Portrait Gallery Permanent Collection Illustrated Checklist: 25th Anniversary Edition. rev. ed. (Illus.). 480p. 1978. 29.95 (*0-87474-674-4*) Smithsonian.

Dowdy, Edwin, ed. Marxist Policies Today in Socialist & Capitalist Countries. LC 85-8481. 234p. 1986. text 44.95 (*0-7022-1927-4*, Pub. by Univ Queensland Pr) Intl Spec Bk.

Dowdy, Gerald S., Jr. The Biliary Tract. LC 73-78536. (Illus.). 330p. reprint ed. 102.30 (*0-8357-9396-6*, 201454100090) Bks Demand.

Dowdy, Homer E. Speak My Words unto Them: A History of Unevangelized Fields Mission (UFM International) Nesbitt, James H., ed. 317p. (Orig.). 1997. pap. 10.00 (*0-9656830-0-1*) UFM Intl.

Dowdy, J. & Archer, J. Introduction to Chemistry 1: Lab Guide. 1996. pap. text 15.63 (*1-56870-241-8*) RonJon Pub.

***Dowdy, Linda.** Barney's Puppet Show. Davis, Guy, ed. LC 98-60909. (Barney Ser.). (Illus.). 20p. (J). (ps-k). 1999. 6.95 (*1-57064-597-3*, Barney Publ) Lyrick Pub.

— Freddi Fish What's Different? LC 00-105051. (Humongous Ser.). (Illus.). 32p. (J). (ps-1). 2001. 3.99 (*1-58668-063-3*) Lyrick Studios.

— Pajama Sam What's Different? LC 00-105050. (Humongous Ser.). (Illus.). 32p. (J). (ps-1). 2001. 3.99 (*1-58668-064-1*) Lyrick Studios.

— Putt Putt. (Illus.). 112p. (J). (ps-2). 2000. pap. 2.99 (*1-57064-943-X*, 73110, Humongous Bks) Lyrick Pub.

Dowdy, Linda, ed. see White, Stephen.

Dowdy, Linda C. Barney Goes to the Dentist. LC 96-86247. (Barney's Go to Ser.). (Illus.). 24p. (J). (ps-3). 1997. pap. 3.25 (*1-57064-116-1*) Lyrick Pub.

— Barney Goes to the Zoo. Hartley, Linda, ed. LC 93-77868. (Barney's Go to Ser.). (Illus.). 18p. (J). (ps-k). 1993. bds. 5.95 (*1-57064-011-4*) Lyrick Pub.

— Make Believe with Barney. LC 96-83767. (Barney Ser.). (Illus.). 14p. (J). (ps-3). 1996. bds. 7.95 (*1-57064-094-7*) Lyrick Pub.

Dowdy, Linda C., ed. see Bernthal, Mark S.

Dowdy, Linda C., ed. see Dudko, Mary A. & Larsen, Margie.

Dowdy, Linda C., ed. see White, Stephen.

Dowdy, Shirley & Wearden, Stanley. Statistics for Research. 2nd ed. LC 90-42104. (Series in Probability & Mathematics). 656p. 1991. 99.95 (*0-471-85703-3*) Wiley.

Dowdy, Thomas E. & McNamara, Patrick H. Religion: North American Style. 3rd ed. LC 96-18514. 250p. (C). 1997. text 48.95 (*0-8135-2343-5*); pap. text 16.95 (*0-8135-2344-3*) Rutgers U Pr.

Dowdy, William L. & Schneider, Barry R., eds. Pulling Back from the Nuclear Brink: Reducing & Countering Nuclear Threat. LC 97-53200. 328p. 1998. 52.50 (*0-7146-4856-6*, Pub. by F Cass Pubs); pap. 19.50 (*0-7146-4412-9*, Pub. by F Cass Pubs) Intl Spec Bk.

Dowdy, William L. & Trood, Russell B. The Indian Ocean. 638p. (C). 1987. 140.00 (*81-7002-025-5*, Pub. by Himalayan Bks) St Mut.

Dowdy, William L. & Trood, Russell B., eds. The Indian Ocean: Perspectives on a Strategic Arena. LC 85-20606. (Duke Press Policy Studies). (Illus.). xvii, 614p. 1985. pap. text 29.95 (*0-8223-0691-3*) Duke.

***Dowe, Dieter, et al, eds.** Europe in 1848: Revolution & Reform. 2000. 79.95 (*1-57181-164-8*) Berghahn Bks.

***Dowe, Phil.** Physical Causation. (Cambridge Studies in Probability, Induction & Decision Theory). (Illus.). 248p. 2000. 54.95 (*0-521-78049-7*) Cambridge U Pr.

Doweiko, Harold. Concepts of Chemical Dependency. 384p. (C). 1990. pap. 28.00 (*0-534-12834-3*) Brooks-Cole.

Doweiko, Harold E. Concepts of Chemical Dependency. 1997. mass mkt. 37.00 (*0-534-49969-4*) Brooks-Cole.

— Concepts of Chemical Dependency. 3rd ed. (Counseling Ser.). 608p. 1995. pap. 37.00 (*0-534-33904-2*) Brooks-Cole.

— Concepts of Chemical Dependency. 4th ed. LC 97-51593. 1998. pap. 51.95 (*0-534-35755-5*) Brooks-Cole.

— Concepts of Chemical Dependency: Test Items. 3rd ed. 1995. pap. write for info. (*0-534-33905-0*) Brooks-Cole.

Dowel, Earl H., et al. A Modern Course in Aeroelasticity. enl. rev. ed. (C). 1989. pap. text 148.50 (*0-7923-0185-4*) Kluwer Academic.

— A Modern Course in Aeroelasticity. 2nd enl. rev. ed. (C). 1989. lib. bdg. 261.00 (*0-7923-0062-9*) Kluwer Academic.

Dowell, Andrea C. & Rokke, Kathi R. Miguel & Sarah: Close Friends & Cystic Fibrosis. large type ed. (Illus.). 22p. (J). (gr. k-4). 1999. pap. 8.00 (*0-9644972-1-2*) Chldrns Hosps.

Dowell, Carol. California Perspectives Vol. 2: An Anthology from California Tomorrow Education for a Diverse Society Project. Kam, Katherine, ed. 58p. 1991. pap. 12.00 (*1-887039-05-8*) Calif Tomorrow.

Dowell, Carol, ed. see Chang, Hedy N., et al.

Dowell, Carol, jt. ed. see Kam, Katherine.

D

Dowell, Cassius. Military Aid to the Civil Power. Kavass, Igor I. & Sprudzs, Adolf, eds. LC 72-75030. (International Military Law & History Ser.: Vol. 1). 330p. 1972. reprint ed. lib. bdg. 42.00 (*0-930342-38-0*, 300300) W S Hein.

Dowell, Clifton, ed. Out on the Porch: An Evocation in Words & Pictures. (Illus.). 128p. 1992. 17.95 (*0-945575-93-9*) Algonquin Bks.

Dowell, Coleman. Island People. LC 96-4906. 309p. 1996. reprint ed. pap. 12.95 (*1-56478-093-7*) Dalkey Arch.

— Mrs. October Was Here. LC 73-89479. 224p. 1974. 9.25 (*0-8112-0518-5*, Pub. by New Directions); pap. 3.75 (*0-8112-0519-3*, NDP368, Pub. by New Directions) Norton.

— A Star-Bright Lie. LC 92-30873. (Illus.). 192p. 1993. 19.95 (*1-56478-022-8*) Dalkey Arch.

— Too Much Flesh & Jabez. LC 86-73236. 160p. 1987. pap. 9.95 (*0-916583-21-X*) Dalkey Arch.

— White on Black on White. 272p. 1991. pap. 14.95 (*1-85242-160-6*) Serpents Tail.

***Dowell, Coleman & Morrow, Bradford.** The House of Children. 199p. 2000. pap. 11.95 (*1-56478-257-3*) Dalkey Arch.

Dowell, David H., jt. ed. see Bennett, Harold E.

Dowell, E. H. Aeroelasticity of Plates & Shells. (Mechanics: Dynamical Systems Ser.: No. 1). 154p. 1974. text 82.50 (*90-286-0404-9*) Kluwer Academic.

Dowell, E. H. & Curtiss, H. C., Jr. A Modern Course in Aeroelasticity. (Mechanics: Dynamical Systems Ser.: No. 4). 479p. 1978. lib. bdg. 230.50 (*90-286-0057-4*) Kluwer Academic.

— A Modern Course in Aeroelasticity. (Mechanics: Dynamical Systems Ser.: No. 4). 479p. 1980. pap. text 82.50 (*90-286-0737-4*) Kluwer Academic.

Dowell, E. H. & Ilgamov, M. Studies in Non-Linear Aeroelasticity. (Illus.). 475p. 1988. 85.00 (*0-387-96791-5*) Spr-Verlag.

Dowell, Earl H., et al, eds. A Modern Course in Aeroelasticity. LC 94-9743. (Mechanics, Dynamical Systems Ser.: Vol. 11). 1995. lib. bdg. 260.00 (*0-7923-2788-8*) Kluwer Academic.

Dowell, Earl H., frwd. A Modern View of Theodore Theodorsen. (Illus.). 372p. 1992. 30.00 (*0-930403-85-1*, 85-1) AIAA.

* **Dowell, Frances O'Roark.** Dovey Coe. LC 99-46870. (J). (gr. 4-6). 2000. 16.00 (*0-689-83174-9*) Atheneum Yung Read.

Dowell, Ian, jt. auth. see Hoorweg, Jan.

Dowell, Jack D., ed. The Unity of Western Europe. LC 76-13400. 65p. reprint ed. pap. 30.00 (*0-608-18350-4*, 203303100083) Bks Demand.

***Dowell, Jennifer M. & Want, Robert S., eds.** Writer's Guide to Online Resources. 2nd ed. (Best of the Web Ser.). 90p. 2000. spiral bd. 15.95 (*0-942008-96-0*) Want Pub.

Dowell, Jennifer M., jt. ed. see Want, Robert S.

***Dowell, Jerry.** The Art of Living & Dying. LC 99-98125. (Illus.). 96p. 1999. pap. 9.95 (*1-58597-012-3*) Leathers Pub.

Dowell, Jesse, frwd. The Appraisal of Rural Property. (Illus.). 434p. 1983. 29.95 (*0-911780-66-1*) Appraisal Inst.

Dowell, Karen. Cooking with Dogs. LC 97-91290. (Illus.). 64p. 1998. 19.95 (*1-891090-01-1*, Pub. by Two Dog Pr) LPC Group.

Dowell, Ken, jt. auth. see Johnson, Ian.

Dowell, Linus J. Didactic Strategies in Physical Education. (Illus.). 232p. (Orig.). 1980. pap. text 19.95 (*0-89641-047-1*) American Pr.

Dowell, Linus J. & Grice, William A. Racquetball. 2nd ed. (Illus.). 128p. (C). 1983. pap. text 12.95 (*0-89641-123-0*) American Pr.

Dowell, Linus J. & Mamaliga, Emil. Anaerobics. (Illus.). 298p. 1982. pap. text 19.95 (*0-89641-086-2*) American Pr.

Dowell, Lynne. The Vinegar Year. Lott, Clarinda H., ed. (New Poets Ser.: Vol 7). (Illus.). 50p. 1980. pap. 2.95 (*0-932616-05-4*) Brick Hse Bks.

Dowell, Michael. State & Local Government Responsibilities to Provide Medical Care for Indigents. (Illus.). 384p. (Orig.). 1985. pap. 25.00 (*0-941077-02-0*, 40,275) NCLS Inc.

Dowell, Olivia S. The First Adventure of Peter Nelson Panda. (Illus.). 16p. (J). (gr. 2-4). 1986. pap. 5.95 (*0-9617624-0-3*) Bear Tracks Pub.

Dowell, Robert. Apple Maggot in the West. 104p. 1990. pap. 5.50 (*0-931876-95-8*, 3341) ANR Pubns CA.

Dowell, Roy, et al, contrib. by. Variations II: Seven Los Angeles Painters. LC 83-80463. (Illus.). 51p. 1983. pap. 15.00 (*0-911291-08-3*, Pub. by Fellows Cont Art) RAM Publications.

Dowell, Ruth I. Alphabet-ter Letter Rhymes Activity Book. (Move Over, Mother Goose Ser.). (J). (ps-2). 1991. pap. 8.00 (*0-945842-14-7*) Pollyanna Prodns.

— Busy Being Me: Fitness, Fun & Fundamentals. (Illus.). 40p. (Orig.). (J). (ps-3). 1988. pap. 10.00 (*0-945842-07-4*) Pollyanna Prodns.

— I Say...You Say! (Illus.). 104p. (J). (ps-2). 1991. pap. 9.95 (*0-945842-12-0*) Pollyanna Prodns.

— Let's Talk! (Illus.). 24p. (J). (ps-6). 1986. pap. 8.00 (*0-945842-03-1*) Pollyanna Prodns.

— Mother Ruth's Rhymes. (Illus.). 104p. (J). (ps-6). 1996. pap. 12.95 (*0-945842-13-9*) Pollyanna Prodns.

— Move over, Mother Goose! Finger Plays, Action Verses & Funny Rhymes. Charner, Kathleen, ed. (Illus.). 126p. (Orig.). (J). (ps-1). 1987. pap. 12.95 (*0-87659-113-6*) Gryphon Hse.

— Move over, Mother Goose Young Readers Edition. (Illus.). (J). (ps-6). 1991. reprint ed. pap. 8.00 (*0-945842-17-1*) Pollyanna Prodns.

— Pollyanna Herself. (Illus.). 44p. (J). (ps-6). 1988. pap. 6.00 (*0-945842-09-0*) Pollyanna Prodns.

— Think about It! (Illus.). 36p. (Orig.). (J). (ps-6). 1996. pap. 6.00 (*0-945842-04-X*) Pollyanna Prodns.

Dowell, Spright. Columbus Roberts: Christian Steward Extraordinary. LC 83-887. xvi, 171p. 1996. text 13.95 (*0-86554-071-3*, 4067) Mercer Univ Pr.

Dowell, Stephen. A History of Taxation & Taxes in England, 4 Vols, Set. 2nd ed. LC 67-5737. (Reprints of Economic Classics Ser.). 1965. reprint ed. 250.00 (*0-678-05167-4*) Kelley.

Dowell, Susan. They Two Shall Be One: Monogamy in History & Religion. 221p. (C). 1998. pap. text 13.00 (*0-7881-5824-4*) DIANE Pub.

Dowell, Susan S., jt. auth. see Kitching, Frances.

Dowell, William C. The Webley Story. (Illus.). 337p. 1987. 59.95 (*0-939683-04-0*) Armory Pubns.

Dowell, Yvonne L. 1411 Park Avenue: Dear God Book of Girl from the Projects. (Illus.). 52p. (J). (gr. 6-8). 1999. 24.95 (*1-893025-03-9*) P & F Pubg.

Dowen, Ken. Suburban Poems. 2nd ed. 1986. pap. 8.00 (*0-933967-05-5*) North Am Edit.

Dower, Catherine. Alfred Einstein on Music: Selected Music Criticisms, 21. LC 90-13997. (Contributions to the Study of Music & Dance Ser.: No. 21). 328p. 1991. 59.95 (*0-313-27363-4*, DEK/, Greenwood Pr) Greenwood.

— Yella Pessl, First Lady of the Harpsichord: A Life of Fire & Conviction. LC 92-37521. (Studies in the History & Interpretation of Music: Vol. 21). (Illus.). 212p. 1993. text 89.95 (*0-88946-446-4*) E Mellen.

Dower, Gordon E. EASI 12-Lead Electrocardiography. (Illus.). 135p. (Orig.). 1996. pap. 19.50 (*0-9651424-0-X*) Totemite.

Dower, J. W. Empire & Aftermath: Yoshida Shigeru & the Japanese Experience, 1878-1954. (East Asian Monographs: No. 84). 618p. 1988. reprint ed. pap. 19.95 (*0-674-25126-1*) HUP.

Dower, John. Japan in Peace & War. LC 92-50821. (Illus.). 384p. 1994. 30.00 (*1-56584-067-4*, Pub. by New Press NY) Norton.

— Japan in War & Peace: Selected Essays. 384p. 1995. pap. 14.95 (*1-56584-279-0*, Pub. by New Press NY) Norton.

— War Without Mercy: Race & Power in the Pacific War. LC 85-43462. 416p. 1987. pap. 15.00 (*0-394-75172-8*) Pantheon.

Dower, John W. Embracing Defeat: Japan in the Wake of World War II. LC 98-22133. (Illus.). 676p. 1999. 29.95 (*0-393-04686-9*) Norton.

***Dower, John W.** Embracing Defeat: Japan in the Wake of World War II. (Illus.). 680p. 2000. reprint ed. pap. text 15.95 (*0-393-32027-8*) Norton.

Dower, John W. Japan in War & Peace: Selected Essays. (Illus.). 368p. (C). 1999. text 30.00 (*0-7881-5564-4*) DIANE Pub.

Dower, John W. & George, Timothy S. Japanese History & Culture from Ancient to Modern Times: 7 Basic Bibliographies. 2nd ed. 486p. (C). 1995. text 59.95 (*1-55876-097-0*); pap. text 34.95 (*1-55876-098-9*) Wiener Pubs Inc.

***Dower, Laura.** Monkey See, Doggy Doo. (Powerpuff Girls Ser.). (Illus.). (J). 2000. pap. 3.50 (*0-439-16013-8*) Scholastic Inc.

— Paste Makes Waste. (Powerpuff Girls Ser.). (Illus.). (J). 2000. pap. 3.50 (*0-439-19105-X*) Scholastic Inc.

— Peace. (J). 2001. pap. write for info. (*0-06-440811-6*, HarpTrophy) HarpC Child Bks.

Dower, Laura. Scooby-Doo's Guide to Life - Just Say "Ruh-Roh!" 80p. (J). (gr. 3-7). 1999. pap. 3.99 (*0-590-63109-8*) Scholastic Inc.

***Dower, Laura.** Superstars: Britney Spears. (Illus.). 112p. (gr. 3-7). 2000. pap. text 4.50 (*0-439-22222-2*) Scholastic Inc.

Dower, Nigel. Ethics & Environmental Responsibility. 155p. 1989. text 82.95 (*0-566-05764-6*, Pub. by Avebry) Ashgate Pub Co.

— World Poverty: Challenge & Response By. (C). 1988. 50.00 (*0-900657-78-2*, Pub. by W Sessions) St Mut.

Dower, Roger, et al. Frontiers of Sustainability: Environmentally Sound Agriculture, Forestry, Transportation, & Power Production. LC 97-5206. (Illus.). 415p. 1997. pap. text 34.00 (*1-55963-546-0*, Shearwater Bks) Island Pr.

Dower, Roger C. & Zimmerman, Mary Beth. The Right Climate for Carbon Taxes: Creating Economic Incentives to Protect the Atmosphere. 48p. 1992. pap. 10.00 (*0-915825-78-3*, DODPP) World Resources Inst.

Dowers, Michael. Tijuana Bibles, Vol. 2. pap. 12.95 (*1-56097-238-6*, Pub. by Fantagraph Bks) Seven Hills Bk.

— Tijuana Bibles, vOL. 3. pap. 12.95 (*1-56097-318-8*, Pub. by Fantagraph Bks) Seven Hills Bk.

— Tijuana Bibles: Art & Wit in America's Forbidden Funnies, 1930-1950. pap. 12.95 (*1-56097-223-8*, Pub. by Fantagraph Bks) Seven Hills Bk.

Dowgiallo, Jan. From Science to Diplomacy: A Pole's Experiences in Israel. 81p. 1995. 25.00 (*1-888521-00-7*); pap. 10.00 (*1-888521-01-5*) Brunswick Pr.

Dowgiewicz, Mike & Dowgiewicz, Sue. Christian Halakhahs: Loving Jesus Through the Way You Apply His Word. 40p. 1998. pap. 5.00 (*1-890592-04-8*) Restrtion Minist.

— Demolishing Strongholds: God's Way to Mental Freedom. (Illus.). 72p. (Orig.). 1995. pap., spiral bd., wbk. ed. 15.00 (*1-888582-00-6*) Aslan Pubng.

— Demolishing Strongholds: God's Way to Mental Freedom. 2nd ed. (Illus.). 68p. (Orig.). 1997. reprint ed. pap. 10.00 (*1-890592-00-5*) Restrtion Minist.

— God's Instruments for War: Discovering & Coordinating Spiritual Gifts As Weapons of Warfare. LC 98-216992. 80p. 1998. pap. 8.00 (*1-890592-06-4*) Restrtion Minist.

— Growing Relationships Through Confrontation. 38p. 1998. pap. 5.00 (*1-890592-05-6*) Restrtion Minist.

— Pastoring by Elders: Reflecting the Heart of the Father. LC 98-209934. 162p. 1998. pap. 10.00 (*1-890592-07-2*) Restrtion Minist.

— Prodigal Church: How You Can Restore the Power & Intimacy Shared by Early Christians. (Illus.). 38p. 1997. pap. 3.00 (*1-890592-01-3*) Restrtion Minist.

— Restoring the Early Church: Returning Intimacy & Power to the Modern Day Church. 1997. pap. 15.00 (*1-890592-02-1*) Restrtion Minist.

Dowgiewicz, Sue, jt. auth. see Dowgiewicz, Mike.

***Dowie.** James Salter. LC 98-27006. 1998. text. write for info. (*0-8057-1604-1*, Twyne) Mac Lib Ref.

Dowie, Albert. Management & Practice of Low Visual Acuity. (C). 1989. 85.00 (*0-900099-24-0*, Pub. by Assn Brit Dispen Opticians) St Mut.

***Dowie, Clair.** Why Is John Lennon Wearing a Skirt? 2000. pap. 10.95 (*0-413-71090-4*) Methn.

Dowie, J. & Elstein, Arthur S., eds. Professional Judgment: A Reader in Clinical Decision Making. (Illus.). 584p. 1988. pap. text 38.95 (*0-521-34696-7*) Cambridge U Pr.

Dowie, J., jt. ed. see Ranke, M. B.

Dowie, J. Iverne & Tredway, J. Thomas, eds. Immigration of Ideas: Studies in the North Atlantic Community. LC 68-28713. (Augustana Historical Society Publications: No. 21). ix, 214p. 1968. 1.00 (*0-910184-21-6*) Augustana.

Dowie, James. Once a Londoner. unabridged ed. Szivos, Frank, ed. (Illus.). 157p. 1989. pap. 15.95 (*0-9637705-4-3*) Benchmark UT.

Dowie, Mark. Losing Ground: American Environmentalism at the Close of the Twentieth Century. (Illus.). 335p. 1996. pap. text 15.95 (*0-262-54084-3*) MIT Pr.

Dowie, Menie M. Gallia. rev. ed. Small, Helen, ed. (Everyman Paperback Classics Ser.). 304p. (C). 1995. pap. 6.50 (*0-460-87719-4*, Everyman's Classic Lib) Tuttle Pubng.

Dowie, Nancy M. From Womb to Tomb: The Generational Conspiracy. 280p. (Orig.). 1994. pap. 15.95 (*0-9637705-3-5*) Benchmark UT.

Dowie, Robin. General Practitioners & Consultants: A Study of Outpatient Referrals. 1984. 22.95 (*0-19-724624-9*) OUP.

Dowie, William. Peter Matthiessen. (Twayne's United States Authors Ser.: No. 587). 152p. (C). 1991. 28.95 (*0-8057-7635-4*, Twyne) Mac Lib Ref.

***Dowis, Richard.** The Lost Art of the Great Speech: How to Write One - How to Deliver It. LC 99-35742. 224p. 1999. pap. 14.95 (*0-8144-7054-8*) AMACOM.

Dowis, Richard, jt. auth. see Lederer, Richard.

Dowla, Farid U. & Rogers, Leah L. Solving Problems in Environmental Engineering & Geosciences with Artificial Neural Networks. (Illus.). 249p. (C). 1996. 44.00 (*0-262-04148-0*) MIT Pr.

Dowlah, Abu F. Perestroika: An Inquiry into Its Historical, Ideological & Intellectual Roots. 274p. (Orig.). 1990. pap. 72.50 (*91-86702-04-1*) Coronet Bks.

— Soviet Political Economy in Transition: From Lenin to Gorbachev, 130. LC 91-28147. (Contributions in Economics & Economic History Ser.: No. 130). 296p. 1992. 59.95 (*0-313-27944-6*, DPF, Greenwood Pr) Greenwood.

Dowlah, Alex F. & Elliott, John E. The Life & Times of Soviet Socialism. LC 96-24358. 296p. 1997. 65.00 (*0-275-95629-6*, Praeger Pubs) Greenwood.

Dowland, David A. Nineteenth-Century Anglican Theological Training: The Redbrick Challenge. LC 97-9923. (Oxford Theological Monographs). (Illus.). 250p. 1998. text 72.00 (*0-19-826929-3*) OUP.

Dowland, John. Lute Songs of John Dowland. 1997. 10.95 (*0-486-29935-X*) Dover.

Dowlatabadi, Hadi & Toman, Michael A. Technology Options for Electricity Generation: Economic & Environmental Factors. LC 91-6324. 87p. 1991. pap. 12.95 (*0-915707-58-6*) Resources Future.

Dowlatabadi, Zahra, jt. auth. see Winder, Catherine.

Dowlatshahi, Ali. Persian Designs & Motifs for Artists & Craftsmen. (Illus.). 120p. 1979. pap. 7.95 (*0-486-23815-6*) Dover.

Dowlding, William J. Beatlesongs. 448p. 1989. per. 12.95 (*0-671-68229-6*) S&S Trade Pap.

Dowlen, Lane. Ode to Oliver: The Adventures of a Sea Otter. LC 95-71191. (Illus.). 160p. (Orig.). (YA). (gr. 4 up). 1996. pap. 9.95 (*1-885884-99-0*) Cormorant Pr.

Dowler, Lawrence, ed. Gateways to Knowledge: The Role of Academic Libraries in Teaching, Learning & Research. (Illus.). 264p. (C). 1997. 38.50 (*0-262-04159-6*) MIT Pr.

Dowler, Lorraine. Think Locally, Act Globally! Linking Local & Global Communities Through Democracy & Environment. (Active Learning Modules on the Human Dimensions of Global Change Ser.). (Illus.). 151p. (C). 1997. pap., teacher ed. 20.00 (*0-89291-237-5*); pap., student ed., wbk. ed. 8.75 (*0-89291-238-3*) Assn Am Geographers.

Dowley. La Casa Llena de Gente. (Serie Pueblo Junto al Lago - Lakeside Town Ser.).Tr. of House Full of People. (SPA.). 5p. (J). 1.99 (*1-56063-408-1*, 493995) Editorial Unilit.

Dowley & Bishop. La Casa Llena de Gente. (Pueblo Junto al Lago Ser.).Tr. of House Full of People. (SPA.). (J). 2.99 (*1-56063-412-X*, 493999) Editorial Unilit.

Dowley, Mark W., ed. DPSS Lasers: Applications & Issues. LC 97-75574. (Trends in Optics & Photonics Ser.: Vol. 17). 215p. 1998. pap. 55.00 (*1-55752-520-X*) Optical Soc.

Dowley, T. Descubre los Errores, No. 1.Tr. of Spot the Mistakes. (SPA.). (J). 1.99 (*0-7899-0433-0*, 497764) Editorial Unilit.

— Descubre los Errores, No. 2.Tr. of Spot the Mistakes. (SPA.). (J). 1.99 (*0-7899-0434-9*, 497765) Editorial Unilit.

— Encuentra la Solucion, No. 1.Tr. of Seek & Find Bible Mazes. (SPA.). (J). 1.99 (*0-7899-0435-7*, 497766) Editorial Unilit.

— Encuentra la Solucion, No. 2.Tr. of Seek & Find Bible Mazes. (SPA.). (J). 1.99 (*0-7899-0436-5*, 497767) Editorial Unilit.

Dowley, Tim. Atlas Biblico Portavoz. (SPA., Illus.). 32p. 1991. pap. 8.99 (*0-8254-1168-8*, Edit Portavoz) Kregel.

— Atlas de la Biblia: Y de la Historia des Christianismo. 1998. 60.00 (*0-311-15045-4*) Baptist Spanish.

— Bach. (Illustrated Lives of the Great Composers Ser.). (Illus.). 144p. 1996. 17.95 (*0-7119-0262-3*, OP 42480) Omnibus NY.

— El Burrito de Belen. (Serie Libros de Carton - Animal Board Bks.).Tr. of Bethlehem Donkey. (SPA.). 6p. (J). 1991. bds. 2.99 (*1-56063-223-2*, 490389) Editorial Unilit.

— El Camello y la Estrella. (Serie Libros de Carton - Children's Bible Story Bks.).Tr. of Queen Esther Saves Her People. (SPA.). 8p. (J). 1991. 2.99 (*1-56063-222-4*, 490388) Editorial Unilit.

— The Collegeville Bible Time-Line. LC 93-19614. (Illus.). 32p. 1993. pap. 7.95 (*0-8146-2275-5*) Liturgical Pr.

— El Gran Pez. (Libros de Carton).Tr. of Big Fish. (SPA.). (J). 1991. bds. 2.99 (*1-56063-221-6*, 490387); bds. write for info. (*0-614-27049-9*) Editorial Unilit.

— Guia Biblica Portavoz. Orig. Title: Student Guide to the Bible. (SPA., Illus.). 32p. 1993. pap. 8.99 (*0-8254-1169-6*, Edit Portavoz) Kregel.

***Dowley, Tim.** La Guin Portavoz de la Vida en los Tiempos Biblicos. 32p. 1999. pap. text 8.99 (*0-8254-1171-8*, Edit Portavoz) Kregel.

— The Kregel Pictorial Guide to Everyday Life in Bible Times. (Illus.). 32p. 1999. pap. 8.99 (*0-8254-2465-8*) Kregel.

Dowley, Tim. La Oveja Perdida. (Serie Libros de Carton - Board Bks.).Tr. of Lost Sheep. (SPA.). 8p. (J). 1991. bds. write for info. (*0-614-27090-1*) Editorial Unilit.

— Schumann. (Illustrated Lives of the Great Composers Ser.). (Illus.). 144p. 1996. 17.95 (*0-7119-0261-5*, OP 42472) Omnibus NY.

— The Student Bible Atlas. LC 95-43345. (Illus.). 32p. (J). 1996. pap. 6.99 (*0-8066-2038-2*, 9-2038, Augsburg) Augsburg Fortress.

— The Student Bible Guide. LC 95-47644. (Illus.). 32p. (J). 1996. pap. 6.99 (*0-8066-2040-4*, 9-2040, Augsburg) Augsburg Fortress.

— El Viaje de la Jirafa. (Serie Libros de Carton - Board Bks.).Tr. of Giraffe's Voyage. (SPA.). 6p. (J). 1992. bds. 2.99 (*1-56063-220-8*, 490386) Editorial Unilit.

— El Viaje Especial del Burrito. (Serie Libros de Carton - Board Bks.).Tr. of Donkey's Special Ride. (SPA.). 6p. (J). 1992. bds. 2.99 (*1-56063-225-9*, 490391) Editorial Unilit.

— El Viaje Especial del Burrito - Donkey's Special Ride. (Serie Libros de Carton - Board Bks.). pap. write for info. (*1-56063-956-3*) Editorial Unilit.

Dowley, Tim, ed. Discovering the Bible: Archaeologists Look at Scripture. LC 86-218402. (Illus.). 144p. reprint ed. pap. 44.70 (*0-7837-0512-3*, 204083600018) Bks Demand.

— Introduction to the History of Christianity. 688p. 1995. 45.00 (*0-8006-2935-3*, 1-2935) Augsburg Fortress.

Dowley, Tim, jt. auth. see Bishop.

Dowlin, Kenneth E. The Electronic Library: The Promise & the Process. LC 83-21957. (Applications in Information Management & Technology Ser.). (Illus.). 199p. 1984. pap. 45.00 (*0-918212-75-8*) Neal-Schuman.

Dowling. Business Concepts. 2nd ed. (College ESL Ser.). (J). 1993. mass mkt., teacher ed. 9.95 (*0-8384-4210-2*) Heinle & Heinle.

***Dowling.** Creating Mind: How the Brain Works. 2000. pap. text. write for info. (*0-393-97446-4*) Norton.

Dowling. International Dimensions of Human Resource Management. 3rd ed. LC 98-28947. (GJ - Human Resources Management Ser.). 1998. pap. 33.95 (*0-538-86137-1*) S-W Pub.

***Dowling.** Introduction to Mathematical Economics. 3rd ed. (Illus.). 496p. 2000. 15.95 (*0-07-135896-X*, Schaums Outlne) McGraw-Hill Prof.

— John Fisher 1469-1535 LC 99-10939. 1999. text 65.00 (*0-312-22367-6*) St Martin.

Dowling. The Mechanical Behavior of Materials: Engineering Methods for Deformation, Fracture & Fatigue. 2nd ed. LC 98-33811. 830p. 1998. 105.00 (*0-13-905720-X*) P-H.

Dowling, jt. auth. see Evanson.

Dowling, jt. auth. see Foley.

***Dowling, Alfred E. P. Raymund.** The Flora of the Sacred Nativity. 222p. 2000. text 110.00 (*0-7103-0684-9*) Col U Pr.

***Dowling, Andrew.** Godless Pilgrim. 220p. 2000. pap. 14.95 (*1-58394-022-7*, Pub. by Frog Ltd CA) Publishers Group.

Dowling, Ann & Williams, John E. Sound & Sources of Sound. LC 82-15687. 321p. 1983. pap. text 36.95 (*0-470-27388-7*) P-H.

Dowling, Anthony, ed. see Dowling, James S.

Dowling, Barbara T. & Arden, Marianne M. Business Concepts: A Text for English Practice. 2nd rev. ed. LC 92-31120. Orig. Title: Business Concepts for English Practice. 202p. (J). 1992. mass mkt. 25.95 (*0-8384-4077-0*) Heinle & Heinle.

Dowling, Barbara T. & McDougal, Marianne. Business Concepts for English Practice. 200p. (J). 1982. mass mkt. 17.75 (*0-8384-2968-8*, Newbury); mass mkt. 10.50 (*0-8384-2969-6*, Newbury) Heinle & Heinle.

D

An Asterisk (*) at the beginning of an entry indicates that the title is appearing for the first time.

Dowling, Bary. Mudeye: An Australian Boyhood & Beyond. LC 95-214460. 1999. pap. text 14.95 (*1-86254-345-3*) Wakefield Pr.

***Dowling, Bernard.** GPs & Purchasing in the NHS: The Internal Market & Beyond. 276p. 2000. text 70.95 (*0-7546-1157-4*, Pub. by Ashgate Pub) Ashgate Pub Co.

Dowling, Brenda, ed. see Dowling, James.

***Dowling, Carolyn Wadley.** Through Silent Country. 2000. pap. 19.95 (*1-86368-281-3*, Pub. by Fremantle Arts) Intl Spec Bk.

Dowling, Christopher, ed. see Allen, Louis.

Dowling, Christopher, ed. see Bond, Brian.

Dowling, Christopher, ed. see Cruickshank, Charles.

Dowling, Christopher, ed. see Upton, Anthony F.

Dowling, Christopher, ed. see Warner, Geoffrey.

Dowling, Claudia. Explorers of Light. 1996. pap. text 27.95 (*0-922826-90-0*) Canon USA.

Dowling, Colette. The Cinderella Complex: Woman's Hidden Fear of Independence. 288p. 1990. per. 5.99 (*0-671-73334-6*) PB.

***Dowling, Colette.** The Frailty Myth. LC 00-28093. 304p. 2000. 24.95 (*0-375-50235-1*) Random.

Dowling, Colette. Maxing Out: Why Women Sabotage Their Financial Security. LC 97-49409. 304p. (gr. 8). 1998. 23.95 (*0-316-19120-5*) Little.

Dowling, Colette. Red Hot Mamas: Coming Into Our Own at Fifty. 304p. 1997. reprint ed. pap. 14.95 (*0-553-37495-8*) Bantam.

Dowling, Colette. You Mean I Don't Have to Feel This Way? New Help for Depression, Anxiety, & Addiction. 384p. 1992. text 19.95 (*0-684-19257-8*) S&S Trade.

— You Mean I Don't Have to Feel This Way? New Help for Depression, Anxiety, & Addiction. LC 92-46657. 320p. 1993. reprint ed. pap. 14.95 (*0-553-37169-X*) Bantam.

Dowling, Cornelia E., et al, eds. Recent Progress in Mathematical Psychology. LC 97-31138. (Scientific Psychology Ser.). 350p. 1998. write for info. (*0-8058-1975-4*) L Erlbaum Assocs.

Dowling, Curtis F., ed. see Morton, Julia F.

Dowling, D. McDonald. In Darkness. Abraham, Jo Ann, ed. LC 94-61628. 216p. 1995. pap. 12.95 (*1-880254-20-4*) Vista.

Dowling, David. Mrs. Dalloway: Mapping Streams of Consciousness. (Masterwork Studies: No. 67). 152p. 1991. 29.00 (*0-8057-9414-X*, Twyne) Mac Lib Ref.

***Dowling, David W.** Tire. Costalas, Nicholas & Clark, Danielle, trs. 96p. 1999. pap. (*0-9674934-0-4*) Weird Long.

Dowling, Donald, jt. ed. see Campbell, Christian.

Dowling, Donna, et al. Breastfeeding the Infant with Special Needs. LC 96-51893. (March of Dimes Nursing Modules Ser.). 1997. write for info. (*0-86525-075-8*) March of Dimes.

Dowling, Edward T. Calculus for Business, Economics, & the Social Sciences. 288p. (C). 1990. pap. 14.95 (*0-07-017673-6*) McGraw.

— Schaum's Outline of Mathematical Economics. 2nd ed. 485p. (C). 1992. pap. 15.95 (*0-07-017674-4*) McGraw.

— Schaum's Outline of Mathematical Methods for Business & Economics. 384p. (C). 1993. pap. 15.95 (*0-07-017697-3*) McGraw.

Dowling, Emilia & Osborne, Elsie, eds. The Family & the School: A Joint Systems Approach to Problems with Children. 2nd ed. LC 93-44329. 224p. (C). 1994. pap. 22.99 (*0-415-10128-X*, B3922); text 49.95 (*0-415-10127-1*, B3918) Routledge.

Dowling, Finuala. Fay Weldon's Fiction. LC 98-3146. 194 p. 1998. 36.50 (*0-8386-3750-7*) Fairleigh Dickinson.

***Dowling, Grahame.** Creating Corporate Reputations: Brands, Identity, & Performance. (Illus.). 256p. 2000. text 45.00 (*0-19-924163-5*) OUP.

Dowling, Harry F. The City Hospitals: The Undercare of the Underprivileged. (Illus.). 256p. 1982. 40.50 (*0-674-13197-5*) HUP.

— Fighting Infection: Conquests of the Twentieth Century. LC 77-8307. 336p. 1977. 41.00 (*0-674-30075-0*) HUP.

Dowling, J. M., Jr., jt. ed. see Quibria, M. G.

Dowling, J. Malcolm & Glahe, Fred R., eds. Readings in Econometric Theory. LC 79-128867. 586p. reprint ed. pap. 181.70 (*0-8357-5523-1*, 203513900093) Bks Demand.

Dowling, J. P. Chemistry & Technology of UV & EB Formulation for Coatings, Inks & Paints, Vol. 5. (Illus.). 185p. 1994. text 120.00 (*0-947798-37-4*, Pub. by SITA Tech) Scholium Intl.

— Electron Theory & Quantum Electrodynamics: 100 Years Later. LC 97-2807. (NATO ASI Series B, Physics: No. 358). (Illus.). 368p. (C). 1997. 125.00 (*0-306-45514-5*, Plenum Trade) Perseus Pubng.

***Dowling, James.** Animal Ark Bk. 1: In the Beginning. 2nd large type ed. Dowling, Brenda, ed. (Illus.). 48p. (J). (gr. 3-5). 1998. text 19.95 (*1-57087-381-X*) Prof Pr NC.

Dowling, James. In the Beginning, 1. 1998. write for info. (*0-9666535-0-5*) Animal Ark Inc.

— Suzy Saves Elysha, the Baby Elephant. (J). 1999. write for info. (*0-9666535-1-3*) Animal Ark Inc.

Dowling, James M. & Hess, Jeffrey P. Rolex Wristwatches: The Best of Times. LC 96-9370. (Illus.). 320p. 1996. 125.00 (*0-7643-0011-3*) Schiffer.

Dowling, James R. Keeping Busy: A Handbook of Activities for Persons with Dementia. LC 94-42721. 192p. 1995. pap. text 12.95 (*0-8018-5059-2*) Johns Hopkins.

Dowling, James S. Reminiscences of a Colonial Judge. Dowling, Anthony, ed. 218p. 1996. 44.00 (*1-86287-175-2*, Pub. by Federation Pr) Gaunt.

Dowling, John & Harrell, Evans M., intros. Civil Defense: A Choice of Disasters. LC 86-28785. (Monograph Ser.). (Illus.). 256p. 1987. text 45.00 (*0-88318-512-1*) Am Inst Physics.

Dowling, John, jt. auth. see Marlock, Dennis.

Dowling, John E. Creating Mind: How the Brain Works. LC 98-9365. (Illus.). 224p. 1998. 24.95 (*0-393-02746-5*) Norton.

— Neurons & Networks: An Introduction to Neuroscience. (Illus.). 447p. (C). 1992. 56.00 (*0-674-60820-8*) HUP.

— The Retina: An Approachable Part of the Brain. LC 87-152. (Illus.). 368p. 1987. 60.00 (*0-674-76680-6*) HUP.

Dowling, John E., jt. ed. see Cone, Richard A.

Dowling, Kenneth W. Guide to Curriculum Planning in Science. 183p. (C). 1986. pap. text 27.00 (*1-57337-010-X*) WI Dept Pub Instruct.

Dowling, Kim Y. & Dowling, Robert J. Korean Phrasebook: A Language Survival Kit. 2nd ed. (KOR., Illus.). 208p. 1995. pap. 5.95 (*0-86442-302-0*) Lonely Planet.

Dowling, Levi H. The Aquarian Gospel of Jesus Christ. 270p. 1972. pap. 14.95 (*0-87516-168-5*) DeVorss.

— The Aquarian Gospel of Jesus the Christ. 270p. 1997. pap. 14.95 (*0-932813-41-0*) Adventures Unltd.

Dowling, Linda. Hellenism & Homosexuality in Victorian Oxford. LC 93-32781. (Illus.). 192p. 1994. text 32.50 (*0-8014-2960-9*) Cornell U Pr.

— Hellenism & Homosexuality in Victorian Oxford. (Illus.). 192p. 1996. pap. text 12.95 (*0-8014-8170-8*) Cornell U Pr.

— The Vulgarization of Art: The Victorians & Aesthetic Democracy. (Victorian Literature & Culture Ser.). 192p. (C). 1996. text 35.00 (*0-8139-1634-8*) U Pr of Va.

Dowling, Linda C. Language & Decadence in the Victorian Fin de Siecle. LC 86-15135. 311p. reprint ed. pap. 96.50 (*0-608-06373-8*, 206673400008) Bks Demand.

Dowling, LuAnne, jt. auth. see Evanson, Jane.

Dowling, Maria. Humanism in the Age of Henry VIII. 288p. 1986. 57.50 (*0-7099-0864-4*, Pub. by C Helm) Routldge.

Dowling, Maria, jt. auth. see Lake, Peter.

Dowling, Marion. Education Three-Five. 2nd ed. 240p. 1992. pap. 32.00 (*1-85396-166-3*, Pub. by P Chapman) Taylor & Francis.

— Starting School at 4: A Joint Endeavor. LC 95-193731. 192p. 1995. pap. 19.95 (*1-85396-270-8*, Pub. by P Chapman) Taylor & Francis.

Dowling, Mark. Bike with a View: Easy - Moderate Mountain Bike Rides to Scenic Destinations. LC 93-91041. (Colorado's Front Range & Central Mountains Ser.). 104p. 1994. pap. 10.00 (*0-9639697-0-6*) Concept Writing.

Dowling, Martin W. Tenant Right & Agrarian Society in Ulster, 1600-1850. LC 98-43172. 488p. 1999. 59.50 (*0-7165-2592-5*, Pub. by Irish Acad Pr) Intl Spec Bk.

— Tenant Right & Agrarian Society in Ulster, 1600-1870. 1999. write for info. (*0-7165-2656-5*) Irish Acad Pr.

Dowling, Mary, ed. The Kylemore Abbey Cookbook. (Illus.). 139p. 1997. pap. 19.95 (*0-7171-2540-8*, Pub. by Gill & MacMill) Irish Bks Media.

Dowling, Monica. Social Work & Poverty: Attidues & Actions. LC 99-72361. 206p. 1999. text 61.95 (*1-85972-402-7*, Pub. by Ashgate Pub) Ashgate Pub Co.

Dowling, P. J. The Hedge Schools of Ireland. 128p. 1997. pap. 10.95 (*1-85635-181-5*, Pub. by Mercier Pr) Irish Amer Bk.

Dowling, Patrick J. California: The Irish Dream. (Illus.). xxx, 429p. (Orig.). 1989. 25.00 (*0-9620974-1-1*); pap. 17.00 (*0-9620974-0-3*) Gold Gate Pubs.

— California: The Irish Dream. 2nd ed. (Illus.). xxxi, 442p. (Orig.). 1989. write for info. (*0-9620974-3-8*) Gold Gate Pubs.

— Irish Californians: Historic, Benevolent, Romantic. (Illus.). 500p. 1998. 27.95 (*0-942087-16-X*) Scottwall Assocs.

Dowling, Patrick J., et al, eds. Constructional Steel Design: An International Guide. LC 92-24325. 1992. mass mkt. 254.50 (*1-85166-895-0*) Elsevier.

— Constructional Steel Design: World Developments. LC 92-30059. 1992. mass mkt. 290.50 (*1-85166-953-1*) Elsevier.

Dowling, Paul. Beans on Toast: Level Three, Blue. LC 98-88066. (Reading Together Ser.). (Illus.). (J). 1999. pap. write for info. (*0-7636-0875-0*) Candlewick Pr.

— Elvis: The Ultimate Album Cover Book. (Illus.). 160p. 1996. 24.95 (*0-8109-3268-7*, Pub. by Abrams) Time Warner.

— Elvis: The Ultimate Album Cover Book. 1996. 24.95 (*0-614-21956-6*) Abrams.

***Dowling, Paul.** Sally's Amazing Colour Book. (Illus.). 32p. 1999. 17.95 (*0-86264-801-7*, Pub. by Andersen Pr) Trafalgar.

— Sally's Fantastic Counting Book. (Illus.). 8p. (J). 2000. 15.95 (*0-86264-802-5*, Pub. by Andersen Pr) Trafalgar.

Dowling, Paul. Sociology of Mathematics Education: Mathematical Myths/Pedagogic Texts. LC 98-145863. (Studies in Mathematics Education). 1997. pap. text 27.95 (*0-7507-0792-5*, Falmer Pr) Taylor & Francis.

— The Sociology of Mathematics Education: Mathematical Myths/Pedagogic Texts. LC 98-145863. 335p. 1997. 85.00 (*0-7507-0791-7*, Falmer Pr) Taylor & Francis.

Dowling, Paul & Noss, Richard, eds. Mathematics Versus the National Curriculum. 258p. 1990. 79.95 (*1-85000-891-4*, Falmer Pr); pap. 39.95 (*1-85000-892-2*, Falmer Pr) Taylor & Francis.

Dowling, Paul, jt. auth. see Brown, Andrew.

Dowling, Paul M. Polite Wisdom: Heathen Rhetoric in Milton's Areopagitica. 146p. (C). 1995. pap. text 24.95 (*0-8476-8053-3*); lib. bdg. 58.50 (*0-8476-8052-5*) Rowman.

Dowling, Peter J., et al. Int'l Dimensions Of Human Resource Mgmt. 2nd ed. (SWC-Management). 267p. 1993. pap. 21.95 (*0-534-21366-9*) S-W Pub.

Dowling, R. H., ed. Dowling Folsch Loser Polyamines: Polyamines in the Gastrointestinal Tract. 544p. (C). 1992. text 251.00 (*0-7923-8976-X*) Kluwer Academic.

Dowling, Robert J., jt. auth. see Dowling, Kim Y.

Dowling, Scott, ed. Child & Adolescent Analysis: Its Significance for Clinical Work with Adults. LC 90-5089. (Workshop Series of the American Psychoanalytic Association: Monograph 6). 240p. 1990. 37.50 (*0-8236-0750-X*) Intl Univs Pr.

— Conflict & Compromise: Therapeutic Implications. LC 91-30989. (Workshop Series of the American Psychoanalytic Association: Monograph 7). 248p. (C). 1991. 37.50 (*0-8236-1038-1*) Intl Univs Pr.

— The Psychology & Treatment of Addictive Behavior. No. 8. (Workshop Series of the American Psychoanalytic Association: Monograph 8). 207p. 1995. 35.00 (*0-8236-5562-8*) Intl Univs Pr.

Dowling, Scott & Rothstein, Arnold, eds. Significance of Infant Observational Research for Clinical Work with Children, Adolescents, & Adults. (Workshop Series of the American Psychoanalytic Association: Monograph 5). 300p. 1989. 40.00 (*0-8236-6073-7*) Intl Univs Pr.

Dowling, Scott T. Tobacco: Index of Modern Information with Bibliography. LC 90-32063. 160p. 1990. 47.50 (*1-55914-154-9*); pap. 44.50 (*1-55914-155-7*) ABBE Pubs Assn.

***Dowling, Shelley L. & Custy, Mary C.** The Jurisprudence of United States Constitutional Interpretation: An Annotated Bibliography. LC 99-36067. xvii, 574p. 1999. 89.95 (*0-8377-0567-3*, 323100, Rothman) W S Hein.

Dowling, Terry. Blue Tyson. 238p. (Orig.). 1992. pap. 10.00 (*1-875346-05-8*, Pub. by Aphelion) Firebird Dist.

— An Intimate Knowledge of the Night. LC 96-135533. 285p. (Orig.). 1995. pap. 10.00 (*1-875346-15-5*, Pub. by Aphelion) Firebird Dist.

— Twilight Beach. (Greatwinter Ser.). 270p. (Orig.). 1993. pap. 10.00 (*1-875346-08-2*, Pub. by Aphelion) Firebird Dist.

— Wormwood. 253p. (Orig.). 1991. pap. 10.00 (*1-875346-02-3*, Pub. by Aphelion) Firebird Dist.

Dowling, Terry, ed. see Ellison, Harlan.

Dowling, Theodore E. Armenian Church. LC 71-131511. reprint ed. 39.50 (*0-404-02167-0*) AMS Pr.

Dowling, W. Jay & Harwood, Dane L. Music Cognition. (Cognition & Perception Ser.). 1985. text 59.95 (*0-12-221430-7*) Acad Pr.

Dowling, W. Jay, jt. ed. see Tighe, Thomas.

Dowling, W. Jay, tr. see Frances, Robert, ed.

Dowling, William C. The Epistolary Moment: The Poetics of the Eighteenth-Century Verse Epistle. 210p. 1991. text 39.50 (*0-691-06891-7*, Pub. by Princeton U Pr) Cal Prin Full Svc.

— The Epistolary Moment: The Poetics of the Eighteenth-Century Verse Epistle. LC 90-22540. 228p. reprint ed. pap. 70.70 (*0-608-20143-X*, 207141500011) Bks Demand.

— Jameson, Althusser, Marx: An Introduction to The Political Unconscious. LC 84-7032. 152p. 1984. text 35.00 (*0-8014-1714-7*) Cornell U Pr.

— Language & Logos in Boswell's Life of Johnson. LC 80-8545. 206p. reprint ed. pap. 63.90 (*0-8357-6928-3*, 203798700009) Bks Demand.

— Literary Federalism in the Age of Jefferson: Joseph Dennie & the Port-Folio. LC 97-45469. 160p. 1999. 24.95 (*1-57003-243-2*) U of SC Pr.

— The Senses of the Text: Intensional Semantics & Literary Theory. LC 98-36118. xv, 120p. 1999. pap. 15.00 (*0-8032-6617-0*) U of Nebr Pr.

Dowling, William C., contrib. by. The Senses of the Text: Intensional Semantics & Literary Theory. LC 98-36118. 1999. text 45.00 (*0-8032-1711-0*) U of Nebr Pr.

Dowling, William F., ed. Effective Management & the Behavioral Sciences: Conversations from Organizational Dynamics. LC 78-6695. 291p. reprint ed. pap. 90.30 (*0-608-12836-8*, 202355300033) Bks Demand.

Dowman, Keith. Buddhist Masters of Enchantment: The Lives & Legends of the Mahasiddhas. rev. ed. LC 98-6106. 208p. 1998. pap. 20.00 (*0-89281-784-4*) Inner Tradit.

— Masters of Mahamudra: Songs & Histories of the Eighty-Four Buddhist Siddhas. LC 85-20771. (SUNY Series in Buddhist Studies). 454p. (C). 1986. text 64.50 (*0-88706-158-3*); pap. text 21.95 (*0-88706-160-5*) State U NY Pr.

— Sky Dancer: The Secret Life & Songs of the Lady Yeshe Tsogyel. (Illus.). 379p. 1996. reprint ed. pap. 18.95 (*1-55939-065-4*) Snow Lion Pubns.

Dowman, Keith, tr. The Divine Madman: The Sublime Life & Sonas of Drukpa Kunley. 2nd ed. (Illus.). 169p. 1998. reprint ed. pap. 12.95 (*0-913922-75-7*) Dawn Horse Pr.

— Masters of Enchantment: The Lives & Legends of the Mahasiddhas. (Illus.). 192p. 1989. pap. 19.95 (*0-89281-224-9*, Destiny Bks) Inner Tradit.

Dowman, Keith, tr. Flight of the Garuda: Teachings of the Dzokchen Tradition of Tibetan Buddhism. LC 90-26418. 240p. 1994. pap. 15.00 (*0-86171-085-1*) Wisdom MA.

Dowman, Ketih, tr. see Tenzin, T. & Olishey, O.

Dowmans. Sacred Life of Tibet. 1997. pap. 21.00 (*0-7225-3375-6*, 758290Q) Thorsons PA.

Dowmunt, Tony, ed. Channels of Resistance: Global Television & Local Empowerment. (Illus.). 208p. (C). 1993. pap. 22.95 (*0-85170-388-7*, Pub. by British Film Inst) Ind U Pr.

Down, A. Graham & Mahlmann, John J., intros. The Vision for Arts Education in the 21st Century: The Ideas & Ideals Behind the Development of the National Standards for Education in the Arts. (Music Educators National Conference Ser.). 104p. 1993. pap. 19.50 (*1-56545-025-6*, 1617) MENC.

Down, Brian. Lymington: A Pictorial Past. (C). 1989. 39.00 (*1-85455-074-8*, Pub. by Ensign Pubns & Print) St Mut.

***Down, Chris.** Celtic Dreams: Visions of a Past. LC 99-475892. 1999. 24.95 (*0-7137-2741-1*) Blandford Pr.

***Down, Denis, ed.** Family Spending: A Report on the 1998-99 Family Expenditure Survey. 193p. 1999. 79.00 (*0-11-621251-9*, Pub. by Statnry Office) Balogh.

***Down, Down.** Drinking Games 2000. 1999. pap. 7.95 (*1-873668-22-8*, Pub. by Take That Bks) Trafalgar.

Down, Heather. Angel-Grams: Messages & Miracles by Special Delivery. 1999. pap. text 5.95 (*1-56245-357-2*) Great Quotations.

— Ignorance Is Bliss: The Things Men Don't Know & Don't Want to . . . Caton, Patrick, ed. LC 97-77637. (Illus.). 168p. 1998. pap. 5.95 (*1-56245-332-7*) Great Quotations.

— The Perfect Man: And Other Great Works of Fiction. Caton, Patrick, ed. LC 97-71658. 168p. 1997. pap. 5.95 (*1-56245-301-7*) Great Quotations.

Down, Ivy M. & Schnurr, Lorraine. Between Home & Nursing Home: The Board & Care Alternative. LC 91-21157. (Golden Age Books - Perspectives on Aging Ser.). 216p. (Orig.). (C). 1990. pap. 17.95 (*0-87975-620-9*) Prometheus Bks.

— Between Home & Nursing Home: The Board & Care Alternative. LC 91-21157. (Golden Age Books - Perspectives on Aging Ser.). 216p. (Orig.). (C). 1991. 26.95 (*0-87975-619-5*) Prometheus Bks.

Down, J. Langdon. Mental Affections of Childhood & Youth. (Classics in Developmental Medicine Ser.: No. 5). 185p. (C). 1991. text 19.95 (*0-521-41330-3*, Pub. by Mc Keith Pr) Cambridge U Pr.

Down, Jack. Basic Statistics for High School. 2nd rev. ed. (Illus.). 194p. (Orig.). 1985. pap. text 12.50 (*0-918907-00-4*) Golden Poplar Pr.

— Basic Statistics for Non-Math People. 2nd ed. (Illus.). 194p. (Orig.). 1984. pap. text 12.50 (*0-918907-01-2*) Golden Poplar Pr.

— Fate & the Power. (Illus.). 1990. pap. 9.50 (*0-918907-02-0*) Golden Poplar Pr.

Down, Kendall. Bethlehem Love Story. 144p. 1995. pap. 8.99 (*1-873796-51-X*) Review & Herald.

Down, Mike. Bear. LC 91-44726. (Life Story Ser.). (Illus.). 32p. (J). (gr. 4-6). 1993. pap., teacher ed. 4.95 (*0-8167-2766-X*) Troll Communs.

— Bear. LC 91-44726. (Life Story Ser.). (Illus.). 32p. (J). (gr. 4-6). 1997. text 17.25 (*0-8167-2765-1*) Troll Communs.

Down, Norman E. Saugus. LC 97-191434. (Images of America Ser.). 1997. pap. 16.99 (*0-7524-0469-5*) Arcadia Publng.

Down, R. D. Environmental Control Systems. 246p. 1992. 40.00 (*1-55617-333-4*, A333-4) ISA.

Down, Reg. Leaving Room for the Angels: Eurythmy & the Art of Teaching. Mitchell, David, ed. & illus. by. 176p. 1996. pap. 18.00 (*1-888365-00-5*) Assn Waldorf Schls.

Down, Tim. In the Heat of the Night: Setting & Keeping Sexual Standards. (Life Skills Ser.). (Illus.). 4p. (C). 1994. teacher ed., ring bd. 1.50 (*1-885702-55-8*, 742-005t); student ed., ring bd. 3.25 (*1-885702-54-X*, 742-005s) WSN Pr.

Downame, George. The Christian's Freedom: The Doctrine of Christian Liberty. 131p. 1993. reprint ed. 15.95 (*1-877611-75-1*) Soli Deo Gloria.

Downame, John. The Christian Warfare. LC 74-80174. (English Experience Ser.: No. 653). 674p. 1974. reprint ed. 85.00 (*90-221-0653-5*) Walter J Johnson.

Downard, Catherine, et al. Italianamerican. large type ed. LC 97-13078. (Spec-Hall Ser.). 164p. 1997. lib. bdg. 26.95 (*0-7838-8212-2*, G K Hall Lrg Type) Mac Lib Ref.

Downard, Georgia C. & Righter, Evie. Reasons to Roast. 1998. 25.00 (*0-8446-6940-7*) Peter Smith.

— Reasons to Roast: More Than 130 Simple & Intensely Flavorful Recipes. Martin, Rux, ed. LC 97-13760. (Illus.). 304p. (Orig.). 1997. pap. 15.00 (*1-57630-061-7*, Chapters Bks) HM.

Downard, William L. Dictionary of the History of the American Brewing & Distilling Industries. LC 79-6826. (Illus.). 268p. 1980. lib. bdg. 69.50 (*0-313-21330-5*, DOD/, Greenwood Pr) Greenwood.

Downe, Lisa. The Soft Signature. LC 97-158691. 80p. 1997. pap. 12.00 (*1-55022-314-3*, Pub. by ECW) Genl Dist Srvs.

Downe, Lise. A Velvet Increase of Curiosity. 76p. 1993. pap. 12.00 (*1-55022-199-X*, Pub. by ECW) Genl Dist Srvs.

***Downe, Solomon.** Confessions of a Social Climber. 300p. 1999. pap. 19.95 (*1-58444-009-0*, Looking Glass Pr) DiscUs Bks.

Downen, Robert, jt. ed. see Chiu, Hungdah.

Downer, Alan S. British Drama: A Handbook & Brief Chronicle. (Illus.). 1950. 47.50 (*0-89197-047-9*); pap. text 24.50 (*0-89197-048-7*) Irvington.

— The Eminent Tragedian William Charles Macready. LC 66-14441. 418p. 1966. reprint ed. pap. 129.60 (*0-7837-4137-5*, 205796000011) Bks Demand.

Downer, Alan S., ed. American Drama & Its Critics: A Collection of Critical Essays. LC 65-24424. (Midway Reprint Ser.). 1994. pap. text 15.00 (*0-226-16061-0*) U Ch Pr.

Downer, Alan S., ed. see Jefferson, Joseph.

Downer, Alan S., ed. see Sheridan, Richard Brinsley.

Downer, Alan S., ed. see Tarkington, Booth.

Downer, Alan S., ed. & tr. see Ibsen, Henrik.

Downer, Ann. The Spellkey Trilogy. 640p. 1995. mass mkt. 5.99 (*0-671-87644-9*) Baen Bks.

Downer, Ann H. Physical Therapy Procedures: Selected Techniques. 5th ed. LC 95-35460. (Illus.). 406p. (C). 1996. pap. text 49.95 (*0-398-06556-X*) C C Thomas.

Downer, Carol, jt. auth. see Chalker, Rebecca.

Downer, Deborah A. Classic American Ghost Stories. 214p. 1990. 19.95 (*0-87483-115-6*); pap. 9.95 (*0-87483-118-0*) August Hse.

Downer, Harry E. History of Davenport & Scott County, 2 vols. (Illus.). 2046p. 1997. reprint ed. lib. bdg. 169.50 (*0-8328-6677-6*) Higginson Bk Co.

D

***Downer, John.** Supernatural: The Unseen Powers of Animals. LC 99-54391. 1999. pap. 17.95 (*0-8069-7134-7*) Sterling.

Downer, Kate, ed. see Adams, Clinton, et al.

Downer, Lesley. At the Japanese Table: New & Traditional Recipes. LC 92-31597. (Illus.). 224p. 1993. pap. 14.95 (*0-8118-0319-8*) Chronicle Bks.

— Japan. (Modern Industrial World Ser.). (Illus.). 48p. (J). (gr. 6-8). 1995. 24.26 (*1-56847-241-2*) Raintree Steck-V.

***Downer, Leslie.** Geisha. 2000. 25.00 (*0-7679-0489-3*) Broadway BDD.

***Downer, Phil.** Finding True Success. 2000. pap. 12.99 (*0-8024-3388-X*) Moody.

Downer, Roger G., ed. Energy Metabolism in Insects. LC 81-11839. 256p. 1981. 55.00 (*0-306-40697-7*, Plenum Trade) Perseus Pubng.

Downes. Excavations at Esna 1905-1906. 1974. 65.00 (*0-85668-006-0*, Pub. by Aris & Phillips) David Brown.

— Soy Source. 1988. pap. 8.95 (*1-85327-001-6*, Pub. by Prism Pr) Assoc Pubs Grp.

Downes & Fatouros. Learning in an Electronic World. 154p. 1996. pap. text 22.00 (*0-435-07220-X*) Heinemann.

Downes & Goodman. Dictionary Finance, Investment, English to German. (ENG & GER.). 1249p. 1993. 150.00 (*0-320-00591-7*) Fr & Eur.

Downes, A. H., tr. see Gilson, Etienne.

Downes, Anne M. The Pilgrim Soul. unabridged ed. LC 97-204871. (Illus.). 288p. (Orig.). 1997. pap. 15.00 (*0-9633560-9-7*) Durand Pr.

Downes, Belinda. Every Little Angel. 1999. pap. 14.99 (*0-8037-2260-5*, Dial Yng Read) Peng Put Young Read.

Downes, Belinda. Silent Night: A Christmas Carol Sample. 32p. 1995. 18.00 (*0-679-86959-X*) Random.

Downes, Brenda & Miller, Steve. Media Studies. (Illus.). 192p. 1998. pap. 14.95 (*0-8442-0036-0*, 00360, Teach Yrslf) NTC Contemp Pub Co.

Downes, C. P. Cellular Responses to Stress. Vol. 64. LC 98-89203. 1999. 85.00 (*0-691-00951-1*, Pub. by Princeton U Pr) Cal Prin Full Svc.

Downes, C. P., et al, eds. Cellular Responses to Stress. (Biochemical Society Symposia Ser.: No. 64). (Illus.). 176p. 1998. text 110.50 (*1-85578-123-9*, Pub. by Portland Pr Ltd) Ashgate Pub Co.

Downes, Cathy. Special Trust & Confidence: The Making of an Officer. 270p. 1991. text 45.00 (*0-7146-3354-2*, Pub. by F Cass Pubs) Intl Spec Bk.

Downes, Celia. Separation Revisited: Adolescents in Foster Family Care. 210p. 1992. pap. 59.95 (*1-85742-042-X*, Pub. by Arena) Ashgate Pub Co.

Downes, Charles & Downes, Peggy. Dialogue of Hope: Talking Our Way Through Cancer. LC 93-84083. (Illus.). 136p. 1993. pap. 10.00 (*0-931104-37-8*) SunInk Pubn.

Downes, David. Contrasts in Tolerance: Post-War Penal Policy in the Netherlands & England & Wales. (Oxford Socio-Legal Studies). (Illus.). 240p. 1988. 69.00 (*0-19-825608-6*) OUP.

— Contrasts in Tolerance: Post-War Penal Policy in the Netherlands & England & Wales. (Oxford Socio-Legal Studies). (Illus.). 238p. (C). 1993. reprint ed. pap. text 21.00 (*0-19-825833-X*, 14319) OUP.

Downes, David & Rock, Paul. Understanding Deviance: A Guide to the Sociology of Crime & Rule-Breaking. 3rd ed. 438p. 1998. text 55.00 (*0-19-876534-7*); pap. text 24.95 (*0-19-876533-9*) OUP.

Downes, David, ed. see Davis, John.

Downes, David A. Hopkins' Achieved Self. 220p. (Orig.). (C). 1996. pap. text 34.00 (*0-7618-0190-1*); lib. bdg. 48.00 (*0-7618-0189-8*) U Pr of Amer.

— The Ignatian Personality of Gerard Manley Hopkins. LC 89-24977. 234p. (C). 1990. lib. bdg. 49.00 (*0-8191-7664-8*) U Pr of Amer.

— Temper of Victorian Belief: Studies in the Religious Novels of Pater, Kingsley, & Newman. LC 76-147189. 159p. 1972. 32.50 (*0-8290-0209-X*) Irvington.

Downes, David A., jt. auth. see Allsopp, Michael E.

Downes, Donald, ed. The Menu: Phoenix-Scottsdale, the Best Restaurants. (Illus.). 448p. (Orig.). 1995. pap. 12.95 (*0-9628274-9-5*) D Thomas Pub.

Downes, Edward. The Guide to Symphonic Music. LC 76-13813. (Illus.). 1058p. 1981. pap. 29.95 (*0-8027-7177-7*) Walker & Co.

— New York Philharmonic Guide to the Symphony. LC 76-13813. 1976. 65.00 (*0-8027-0540-5*) Walker & Co.

Downes, Edward, tr. see Werfel, Franz & Stefan, Paul, eds.

Downes, Ellisa & O'Donovan, P. J., eds. Advances in Gynaecologic Surgery, Vol. 1. (Greenwich Medical Media Ser.). (Illus.). 200p. 2000. text 89.50 (*1-900151-49-9*) OUP.

Downes, Frank. The Long Snake Tattoo. (Frontlines Ser.). 192p. 1998. pap. 12.95 (*1-899344-35-7*, Pub. by Do-Not Pr) Dufour.

Downes, G., et al, eds. Sampling Plantation Eucalypts for Wood & Fibre Properties. (Illus.). 144p. 1997. 100.00 (*0-643-06284-X*, Pub. by CSIRO) Accents Pubns.

***Downes, Gile R., Jr., et al.** Institutional Investors & Corporate Behavior. 1999. pap. 9.95 (*0-8447-7143-0*, Pub. by Am Enterprise) Pub Resources Inc.

Downes, Jeremy M. Recursive Desire: Rereading Epic Poetry. LC 96-9789. 336p. 1997. text 46.95 (*0-8173-0841-5*) U of Ala Pr.

Downes, John. Roscius Anglicanus. Summers, Montague, ed. LC 68-20220. 1972. reprint ed. 24.95 (*0-405-08464-1*) Ayer.

— Roscius Anglicanus: An Historical Review of the Stage. LC 92-22031. (Augustan Reprints Ser.: No. 134). 1969. reprint ed. 14.50 (*0-404-70134-5*, PN2592) AMS Pr.

Downes, John & Goodman, Jordan E. Dictionary of Finance & Investment Terms. 5th rev. ed. LC 98-38302. 600p. (Orig.). 1998. pap. 12.95 (*0-7641-0790-9*) Barron.

— Finance & Investment Handbook. 5th rev. ed. LC 98-36776. 140p. 1998. 35.00 (*0-7641-5099-5*) Barron.

Downes, John & Paton, Tricia. Travel Agency Law. viii, 211p. 1993. pap. 34.00 (*0-582-36847-2*, 15744) Gaunt.

Downes, John, jt. auth. see Amos, Janet.

Downes, John, jt. auth. see O'Higgins, Michael.

Downes, Jonathan J., ed. Ohio Civil Service & Collective Bargaining Laws & Rules Annotated, 1996-97. 751p. 1997. 55.00 (*0-8322-0672-5*) Banks-Baldwin.

Downes, Karen, jt. auth. see White, Judith.

Downes, Kate, et al, contrib. by. Fundamentals of 3D Studio Max 1.0 Student Guide. (Version 1.0 Ser.). (Illus.). 1997. pap. text, student ed. 25.00 (*1-890484-28-8*, KnowledgeWorks) HTR Inc.

Downes, Kerry. Vanbrugh. Harris, John & Laing, Alastair, eds. (Studies in Architecture: No. XVI). (Illus.). 280p. 1986. 125.00 (*0-302-02769-6*, Pub. by Zwemmer Bks) Intl Spec Bk.

Downes, Kevin & Boyles, Tim. CLSC Exam Certification Guide. 672p. 1999. 60.00 (*0-7357-0875-4*) Macmillan Tech.

Downes, Kevin, et al. Internetworking Technologies Handbook. 2nd ed. LC 98-86495. 1998. 50.00 (*1-57870-102-3*) Cisco Press.

Downes, Kevin, jt. auth. see GOUGH, CLARE.

Downes, Larry & Gillbert, D. Bruce. Baseball Intellect. 144p. 1996. pap. 6.95 (*0-7710-2830-X*) McCland & Stewart.

***Downes, Larry & Mui, Chunka.** Unleashing the Killer App. Digital Strategies for Market Dominance. LC 99-88674. 2000. pap. 16.95 (*1-57851-261-1*, Pub. by Harvard Busn) Random.

Downes, Larry, et al. Unleashing the Killer App. Digital Strategies for Market Dominance. LC 98-11311. 243p. 1998. 24.95 (*0-87584-801-X*, HBS Pr) Harvard Busn.

Downes-Le Guin, Theodore & Hoffman, Bruce R. The Impact of Terrorism on Public Opinion, 1988 to 1989. LC 93-15805. 1993. pap. text 13.00 (*0-8330-1379-3*, MR-225-FF) Rand Corp.

Downes, Leonard. Downes: Researches into the Genealogical History of Families Bearing the Name of Downes, Early Records of the Downes Families, Downes in Shropshire. 69p. 1997. reprint ed. pap. 13.50 (*0-8328-8352-2*); reprint ed. lib. bdg. 23.50 (*0-8328-8351-4*) Higginson Bk Co.

Downes, M. W. Murphy Family: Genealogy, History, Biography, with Official Statistics of the Part Played by Members of This Numerous Family in the Making & Maintenance of This Great American Republic. (Illus.). 363p. 1989. reprint ed. pap. 54.50 (*0-8328-0895-4*); reprint ed. lib. bdg. 62.50 (*0-8328-0894-6*) Higginson Bk Co.

Downes, Martin. The Doctrine of the Trinity: God in Three Persons. (Library of Religious Beliefs & Practices). 192p. 1999. pap. 19.95 (*1-902210-05-0*) Intl Spec Bk.

Downes, Michael, ed. see Harvey, Jonathan.

Downes, Nick. Whatever Happened to "Eureka"? Cartoons on Science. (Illus.). 155p. (Orig.). (C). 1994. pap. 10.95 (*0-8135-2146-7*) Rutgers U Pr.

Downes, Norma. Ethnic Americans for the Health Professional. 2nd ed. LC 97-178620. 256p. (C). 1997. per. 41.95 (*0-7872-3653-5*, 41365301) Kendall-Hunt.

Downes, Norma J. Ethnic Americans for the Health Professional. 192p. (C). 1994. pap. text, per. 25.95 (*0-8403-9752-6*) Kendall-Hunt.

Downes, Olin. Symphonic Masterpieces. LC 72-5560. (Essay Index Reprint Ser.). 1977. reprint ed. 24.95 (*0-8369-2987-X*) Ayer.

— Symphonic Masterpieces. (Music Book Index Ser.). 294p. 1992. reprint ed. lib. bdg. 79.00 (*0-7812-9479-7*) Rprt Serv.

Downes, P. G. The Story of Chakapas. 32p. (J). (ps-8). 1987. 7.95 (*0-920806-91-0*, Pub. by Penumbra Pr) U of Toronto Pr.

Downes, Patrick & Reza-Vaez-Zadeh, eds. The Evolving Role of Central Banks. ix, 458p. 1991. pap. 28.50 (*1-55775-185-4*) Intl Monetary.

Downes, Paul, ed. C-LECT Jr. rev. ed. 12p. (Orig.). (J). (gr. 7-10). 1992. student ed. 1.25 (*1-55631-202-4*) Chron Guide.

— Chronicle Agricultural Occupations Guidebook. rev. ed. (Illus.). 1994. 78.75 (*1-55631-013-7*) Chron Guide.

— Chronicle Artistic Occupations Guidebook. rev. ed. (Illus.). 1994. 81.80 (*1-55631-014-5*) Chron Guide.

— Chronicle Business Occupations Guidebook. rev. ed. (Illus.). 1994. 133.00 (*1-55631-015-3*) Chron Guide.

— Chronicle Health Occupations Guidebook. rev. ed. (Illus.). 1994. 100.65 (*1-55631-017-X*) Chron Guide.

— Chronicle Home Economics Occupations Guidebook. rev. ed. (Illus.). 1994. 90.35 (*1-55631-016-1*) Chron Guide.

— Chronicle Math & Science Occupations Guidebook. rev. ed. (Illus.). 1994. 109.25 (*1-55631-018-8*) Chron Guide.

— Chronicle of Sports Careers. 1994. 24.00 (*1-55631-019-6*) Chron Guide.

— Training Today: Careers Tomorrow. 1994. 122.95 (*1-55631-020-X*) Chron Guide.

Downes, Paul, ed. see Development Team Staff.

Downes, Paul A., ed. Chronicle Career Quest Career Crosswalk, 1993. rev. ed. 40p. 1993. pap. text 12.00 (*1-55631-219-9*) Chron Guide.

— Chronicle Career Quest Interpretation Guide: Form L, 1993, Set. rev. ed. 16p. 1993. pap. text 3.50 (*1-55631-218-0*) Chron Guide.

Downes, Peggy, jt. auth. see Downes, Charles.

***Downes, Rackstraw.** Under the Gowanus & Razor-Wire Journal: The Making of Two Paintings, 5.9.99-11.15.99. (Illus.). 108p. 2000. pap. 12.00 (*0-9700873-0-6*) Turn the Head.

Downes, Randolph C. Council Fires on the Upper Ohio. LC 40-34394. (Illus.). 384p. (C). 1969. reprint ed. pap. 14.95 (*0-8229-5201-7*) U of Pittsburgh Pr.

— Frontier Ohio: 1788-1803. 1993. reprint ed. lib. bdg. 89.00 (*0-7812-5357-8*) Rprt Serv.

— The Rise of Warren Gamaliel Harding, 1865-1920. rev. ed. LC 68-31421. 744p. 1970. pap. 200.00 (*0-608-00915-6*, 206170900011) Bks Demand.

Downes, Richard, jt. auth. see Marcella, Gabriel.

Downes, Richard, jt. auth. see Rosenn, Keith S.

Downes, Robin N., ed. Computing, Electronic Publishing & Information Technology: Their Impact on Academic Libraries. LC 88-23594. (Journal of Library Administration: Vol. 9, No. 4). (Illus.). 99p. 1989. text 39.95 (*0-86656-788-7*) Haworth Pr.

Downes, Stephen. Charming up Profits. 1996. pap. text 12.95 (*1-86351-171-7*, Pub. by Sally Milner) Seven Hills Bk.

Downes, Stephen C. Szymanowski As Post-Wagnerian: The Love Songs of Hafiz, Op. 24. LC 93-41942. (Outstanding Dissertations in Music from British Universities Ser.). 376p. 1994. text 25.00 (*0-8153-1634-8*) Garland.

Downes, Steven & Mackay, Duncan. Running Scared: How Athletics Lost Its Innocence. (Illus.). 224p. 1997. 29.95 (*1-85158-855-8*, Pub. by Mainstream Pubng) Trafalgar.

Downes, T. Antony & Ellison, Julian. The Legal Control of Mergers in the European Communities. 316p. 1991. pap. 58.00 (*1-85431-071-2*, Pub. by Blackstone Pr) Gaunt.

Downes, Valerie J. A Japanese Experience, 1993-1996. (Illus.). 28p. 1998. pap. write for info. (*0-9660583-0-5*) Sakura Pr.

Downes, William. Language & Society. 2nd rev. ed. LC 97-40832. (Approaches to Linguistics Ser.). (Illus.). 350p. (C). 1998. 64.95 (*0-521-45046-2*); pap. 24.95 (*0-521-45663-0*) Cambridge U Pr.

Downes, William L., Jr. The Nearctic Melanomya & Relatives: Dypeter, Calliphoridae: A Problem in Calyptrate Classification. (Bulletin Ser.: No. 460). (Illus.). (Orig.). 1986. pap. 3.00 (*1-55557-000-3*) NYS Museum.

Downey. U. S. History. Date not set. teacher ed. write for info. (*0-314-09865-8*) West Pub.

— U. S. History Plan Guide. Date not set. write for info. (*0-314-09860-7*) West Pub.

Downey. United States History: In the Course of Human Events. 1996. 26.25 (*0-314-09867-4*, Pub. by West Pub); 12.00 (*0-314-20298-6*, Pub. by West Pub) Thomson Learn.

Downey, ed. Themistii, Vol. I. (GRE.). 1965. 53.50 (*3-322-00839-8*, T1849, Pub. by B G Teubner) U of Mich Pr.

Downey & Giese. Great Trials in American History: In the Course of Human Events. LC 97-113615. 1996. mass mkt. 23.25 (*0-314-20131-9*) West Pub.

Downey, et al. Historical Maps, US History: In Course of Human Events. 1996. pap. 26.25 (*0-314-09864-X*) West Pub.

Downey, jt. auth. see Giese.

Downey & Lau Staff, et al. Boston Dog Lover's Companion: The Inside Scoop on Where to Take Your Dog. 2nd ed. (Dog Lover's Ser.). (Illus.). 450p. 1999. pap. 17.95 (*1-57354-074-9*) Avalon Travel.

Downey, Anne. Dear Stephen: A Mother's Letters to Her Teenage Son, Following His Suicide. (C). 1990. pap. 35.00 (*0-85305-281-6*, Pub. by Arthur James) St Mut.

Downey, Aurelia R. Addresses for Women's Day. 53p. (YA). (gr. 9-12). 1978. pap. 3.00 (*0-9641602-0-X*) A R Downey.

— A Tale of Three Women: God's Call & Their Response. 104p. (YA). (gr. 9-12). 1993. pap. 10.00 (*0-9641602-1-8*) A R Downey.

— A Tree Is Known by Its Fruit. 200p. (YA). (gr. 9-12). 1996. pap. write for info. (*0-9641602-2-6*) A R Downey.

Downey, Bill. Uncle Sam Must Be . . . Losing the War: Black Marines of the 51st. LC 82-5879. (Illus.). 224p. (Orig.). 1982. pap. 7.95 (*0-89407-050-9*) Strawberry Hill.

Downey, C. C. Downey: A History of the Protestant Downeys of the Counties of Sligo, Leitrim, Fermanagh & Donegal, & Their Descendants; Also the Hawksby Family of Counties Leitrim & Sligo. 173p. 1992. reprint ed. pap. 27.00 (*0-8328-2603-0*); reprint ed. lib. bdg. 37.00 (*0-8328-2602-2*) Higginson Bk Co.

Downey, Carolyn J., et al. The Quality Education Challenge. LC 94-5964. (Total Quality Education for the World's Best Schools Ser.: Vol. 1). 152p. 1994. pap. 21.95 (*0-8039-6129-4*) Corwin Pr.

Downey, Carolyn J., jt. auth. see Latta, Raymond F.

Downey, Charlotte, jt. auth. see Channing, Edward T.

Downey, Cynthia, ed. see Downey, Tiffany.

Downey, D. G. Downey Families of Kentucky: Ancestors of Donald G. Downey. 89p. 1996. reprint ed. pap. 18.00 (*0-8328-5280-5*); reprint ed. lib. bdg. 28.00 (*0-8328-5279-1*) Higginson Bk Co.

Downey, David & Erickson, Steven. Agribusiness Management. 2nd ed. 480p. (C). 1987. 81.56 (*0-07-017667-1*) McGraw.

Downey, David, ed. see Downey, Martha Kate.

Downey, Dennis B. & Bremer, Francis J., eds. A Guide to the History of Pennsylvania: Reference Guides to State History & Research. LC 93-305. 504p. 1993. lib. bdg. 95.00 (*0-313-25085-5*, BGP/, Greenwood Pr) Greenwood.

Downey, Dennis B. & Hyser, Ramond M. No Crooked Death: Coatesville, Pennsylvania, & the Lynching of Zachariah Walker. (Blacks in the New World Ser.). (Illus.). 200p. 1991. 28.95 (*0-252-01739-0*) U of Ill Pr.

***Downey, Donald L.** Lice & Pediculosis: Index of New Information with Authors, Subjects & Bibliographical References. rev. ed. 149p. 1999. 47.50 (*0-7883-2136-6*); pap. 44.50 (*0-7883-2137-4*) ABBE Pubs Assn.

Downey, Dorothy E., jt. auth. see Geier, John G.

***Downey, Douglas C., et al.** Cost-Effective Remediation & Closure of Petroleum-Contaminated Sites. LC 99-14314. 320p. 1999. pap. 65.00 (*1-57477-071-3*) Battelle.

Downey, Durbin H. The Gift & the Promise: In the Fourth Dimension. LC 82-90787. (Illus.). 176p. (Orig.). 1983. pap. 9.95 (*0-9610006-0-0*) Four D Pub Co.

Downey, Earl. How to Fish for Snook. rev. ed. 64p. (Orig.). 1985. pap. 2.95 (*0-8200-0104-X*) Great Outdoors.

Downey, Elizabeth A., et al, eds. Civil Engineering in the Asia Region: Asian Infrastructure, Sustainable Development, & Project Management: Proceedings of the First International Civil Engineering Conference. LC 97-43899. 296p. 1998. pap. text 39.00 (*0-7844-0313-9*, 40313-9) Am Soc Civil Eng.

Downey, Fairfax. Clash of Cavalry. 1976. 30.95 (*0-8488-0988-2*) Amereon Ltd.

— Clash of the Cavalry: Battle of Brandy Station. 238p. 1959. reprint ed. 25.00 (*0-942211-18-9*) Olde Soldier Bks.

— The Color-Bearers. (Illus.). 26.95 (*0-8488-0014-1*, J M C & Co); 2.95 (*0-685-10902-X*, J M C & Co) Amereon Ltd.

— The Color-Bearers. deluxe ed. (Illus.). 182.00 (*0-685-57993-X*, J M C & Co) Amereon Ltd.

— Guns at Gettysburg. 1976. 27.95 (*0-8488-0989-0*) Amereon Ltd.

— The Guns of Gettysburg. 290p. 1958. reprint ed. 25.00 (*0-942211-17-0*) Olde Soldier Bks.

Downey, Fairfax D. Our Lusty Forefathers: Being Diverse Chronicles of the Fervors, Frolics, Fights, Festivities, & Failings of Our American Ancestors. LC 74-179725. (Biography Index Reprint Ser). (Illus.). 1977. reprint ed. 23.95 (*0-8369-8093-X*) Ayer.

Downey, Gary L. The Machine in Me: An Anthropologist Sits among Computer Engineers. LC 97-45228. 270p. (C). 1998. pap. 22.99 (*0-415-92022-1*) Routledge.

— The Machine in Me: An Anthropologist Sits among Computer Engineers. LC 97-45228. (Illus.). 270p. (C). 1998. 80.00 (*0-415-92021-3*) Routledge.

Downey, Gary L. & Dumit, Joseph, eds. Cyborgs & Citadels: Anthropological Interventions in Emerging Sciences & Technologies. LC 97-20296. (Advanced Seminar Ser.). 328p. 1998. 55.00 (*0-933452-96-9*); pap. 24.95 (*0-933452-97-7*) Schol Am Res.

Downey, Glanville. Antioch in the Age of Theodosius the Great. LC 62-16481. (Centers of Civilization Ser.: No. 6). 176p. reprint ed. pap. 54.60 (*0-8357-5634-3*, 201009000068) Bks Demand.

— The Late Roman Empire. LC 76-18145. (Berkshire Studies). 158p. 1976. reprint ed. pap. 11.50 (*0-88275-441-6*) Krieger.

Downey, James. Lenihan: His Life & Loyalties LC 98-229543. xii, 251p. 1998. write for info. (*1-874597-34-0*) New Island Books.

***Downey, James.** Lenihan: His Life & Loyalties. (Illus.). 1999. pap. (*1-874597-97-9*, Pub. by New Island Books) Dufour.

Downey, James, ed. see Thomas Gray Bicentenary Conference Staff.

Downey, James M. Colorado Dependency Cases. 204p. 1988. ring bd. 75.00 (*0-9617390-0-2*) J M Downey.

Downey, Jean, ed. see Longfellow, Henry Wadsworth.

Downey, Jean, ed. see Whitman, Walt.

Downey, Jennifer I., jt. auth. see Friedman, Richard C.

Downey, Jim, jt. auth. see Connor, Tim.

Downey, Jim, jt. auth. see Connor, Tom.

Downey, Jim, jt. auth. see Street, Eddy.

Downey, Jim, ed. see Kramer, Russell.

Downey, Joel, et al. Successful Interior Projects Through Effective Contract Documents. 1995. 69.95 (*0-87629-383-6*, 67313) R S Means.

Downey, John, ed. see MacHovec, et al.

Downey, John A., et al, eds. Bereavement of Physical Disability: Recommitment to Life, Health & Function. 1982. 20.95 (*0-405-14214-5*) Ayer.

— The Physiological Basis of Rehabilitation Medicine. 2nd ed. LC 93-37020. (Illus.). 766p. 1994. text 140.00 (*1-56372-080-9*) Buttrwrth-Heinemann.

Downey, John A. & Low, Niels L. The Child with Disabling Illness: Principles of Rehabilitation. 2nd ed. LC 81-19891. (Illus.). 701p. reprint ed. pap. 200.00 (*0-608-00614-9*, 206120100007) Bks Demand.

***Downey, John K., ed.** Love's Strategy: The Political Theology of Johann Baptist Metz. LC 99-40925. 192p. 1999. pap. 25.00 (*1-56338-285-7*) TPI PA.

Downey, June E. Control Process in Modified Handwriting. (Psychological Monographs General & Applied: Vol. 9). 1972. reprint ed. 35.00 (*0-685-09929-6*) Periodicals Srv.

Downey, Laura L. Usability Engineering: Industry-Government Collaboration for System Effectiveness & Efficiency, Held February 26, 1996 at the National institute of Standards & Technology. 265p. 1997. per. 22.00 (*0-16-054669-9*) USGPO.

Downey, Lawrence L. Water Resources Policy & the Nineteen Seventy-Seven South Dakota Legislature. 1977. 1.00 (*1-55614-015-0*) U of SD Gov Res Bur.

Downey, Lorne W. Policy Analysis in Education. 107p. (Orig.). (C). 1988. pap. text 14.95 (*0-920490-83-2*) Temeron Bks.

Downey, Lynn. Sing, Henrietta! Sing! LC 96-38638. (Illus.). 32p. (J). (ps-3). 1997. 14.95 (*1-57102-103-5*, Ideals Child) Hambleton-Hill.

***Downey, Lynn.** This is the Earth That God Made. LC 99-47554. (Illus.). 32p. (J). (ps-3). 2000. pap. 8.99 (*0-8066-3960-1*) Augsburg Fortress.

***Downey, Lynn & Firehammer, Karla.** The Flea's Sneeze LC 99-33613. 32p. (J). (ps-1). 2000. 17.00 (*0-8050-6103-7*) H Holt & Co.

D

Downey, Lynn, et al. This Is a Pair of Levi's Jeans: The Official History of the Levi's Brand. Goldstein, Steve, ed. (Illus.). 318p. 1995. 75.00 (0-9617460-1-7) Gingko Press.

Downey, Margie. Diamonds: Ancestors & Descendants of Roy Monroe Cooper & Margie Helena Crawford Cooper, Vols. 1-5. LC 98-70461. (Illus.). 1200p. 1998. 250.00 (0-9663485-1-6); ring bd. 250.00 (0-9663485-0-8) Diamonds Pubs.

— Twins & Home School. 16p. 1998. pap. 2.00 (0-9663485-3-2) Diamonds Pubs.

Downey, Mariah. The Nylon Frog Goes for a Swim. 1998. pap. 6.95 (0-533-12725-4) Vantage.

***Downey, Martha Kate.** If You've Ever Wanted to Crawl in the Closet with an Oreo: Tips for Parenting a Child with Special Needs. Downey, David & Messner, Abby, eds. 144p. 2000. spiral bd. 11.95 (0-9650700-5-0) Potential Unltd.

Downey, Matthew T., ed. History in the Schools. LC 84-63085. (Bulletin Ser.: No. 74). 54p. (Orig.). 1985. pap. text 7.95 (0-87986-049-9) Nat Coun Soc Studies.

Downey, Matthew T., et al. United States History: In the Course of Human Events. LC 95-50644. 1996. mass mkt. write for info. (0-314-04021-8) West Pub.

— Working Workbook/ Historical Maps, American Century: History of U.S. Modern Time. 1999. pap. 2175.00 (0-538-42541-5) Thomson Learn.

Downey, Maureen E. Revision of the Atlantic Brisingida: Echinodermata: Asteroidea, with Description of a New Genus & Family. LC 86-6579. (Smithsonian Contributions to Zoology Ser.: No. 435). 61p. reprint ed. pap. 30.00 (0-608-15316-8, 202955300061) Bks Demand.

***Downey, Michael.** Altogether Gift: A Trinitarian Spirituality. 128p. 2000. pap. 12.00 (1-57075-333-4) Orbis Bks.

Downey, Michael. At the Margins: Spirituality & Liturgy. (Worship Ser.). (C). 1994. pap. text 14.95 (1-56929-021-0, Pastoral Press) OR Catholic.

— Hope Begins Where Hope Begins. LC 97-46451. 140p. (Orig.). 1998. pap. 12.00 (1-57075-185-4) Orbis Bks.

— Trappist: Living in the Land of Desire. LC 97-19977. (Illus.). 176p. 1997. 35.00 (0-8091-0491-1, 0491-1) Paulist Pr.

— Understanding Christian Spirituality. LC 96-41355. 192p. (Orig.). 1997. reprint ed. pap. 12.95 (0-8091-3680-5) Paulist Pr.

Downey, Michael, ed. The New Dictionary of Catholic Spirituality. 1120p. (Orig.). 1993. 79.50 (0-8146-5525-4, M Glazier) Liturgical Pr.

Downey, Michael & Fragomeni, Richard, eds. A Promise of Presence: Studies in Honor of David N. Power, OMI. 283p. (Orig.). 1992. pap. 24.95 (0-912405-92-9, Pastoral Press) OR Catholic.

Downey, Michael, jt. auth. see Pierce, Joanne M.

Downey, Michael, ed. see Kelty, Matthew.

Downey, Michael, ed. see Kramer, Victor A.

Downey, Michael J. & Edgington, Bobbie G. Engineer's Handbook for Earth Station Design & Implementation. 2nd ed. (Illus.). 195p. 1994. pap. 45.00 (0-9644428-0-9) MR Comm.

***Downey, Myles.** Effective Coaching. 160p. 1999. 13.95 (0-7528-2108-3, Pub. by Orion Pubng Grp) Trafalgar.

Downey, Ned. Just Plain Bridge: A Book for the Average Player (Who Would Like to Play Better Than Average) LC 98-162784. 150p. (Orig.). 1997. pap. 10.00 (0-9659893-0-5) Snug Harbor.

Downey, Pat. Top 40 Music on Compact Disc, 1955-1997. 700p. 1998. 49.95 (0-9633718-6-X) P Downey Ent.

— Top 40 Music on Compact Disc, 1955-1998. 810p. 1999. 59.95 (0-9633718-7-8) P Downey Ent.

***Downey, Pat.** Top 40 Music on Compact Disc, 1955-1999. 940p. 2000. 59.95 (0-9633718-8-6) P Downey Ent.

Downey, Pat. Top Forty Music on Compact Disc, 1955-1981. xii, 658p. (Orig.). 1994. lib. bdg. 49.50 (1-56308-307-8) Libs Unl.

***Downey, Patrick.** Serious Comedy: The Philosophical & Theological Significance of Tragic & Comic Writing in the Western Tradition. 304p. 2000. 70.00 (0-7391-0116-1) Lxngtn Bks.

Downey, Paul. Homoeopathy for the Primary Health Care Team. LC 97-29166. 224p. 1997. pap. text 37.50 (0-7506-2999-1) Buttrwrth-Heinemann.

***Downey, Peter.** Dads, Toddlers & the Chicken Dance. (Illus.). 208p. 2000. pap. 10.95 (1-55561-242-3) Fisher Bks.

— So You're Going to Be a Dad. LC 00-25709. (Illus.). 208p. 2000. pap. 10.95 (1-55561-241-5) Fisher Bks.

Downey, R. & Powell, Garth. Manson Family Picnic. large type rev. ed. (Illus.). 44p. 1998. pap. 6.50 (0-9660958-0-4) Playroom Pr.

Downey, Ray. The Rescue Company. 328p. 1992. 35.95 (0-912212-25-X) Fire Eng.

Downey, Richard. Critical & Constructive Essays. LC 68-8455. (Essay Index Reprint Ser.). 1977. reprint ed. 19.95 (0-8369-0387-0) Ayer.

Downey, Richard, et al. Communications Technology Guide for Business. LC 97-32245. 1997. 83.00 (0-89006-827-5) Artech Hse.

***Downey, Robert E.** Beverly Hills Detective: Memoirs of a Former Beverly Hills Detective. 2000. 25.00 (0-7388-0728-1); pap. 18.00 (0-7388-0729-X) Xlibris Corp.

Downey, Rod & Fellows, M. F. Parameterized Complexity. Gries, D. & Schneider, F., eds. LC 97-22882. (Monographs in Computer Science). xv, 533p. 1999. 49.95 (0-387-94883-X) Spr-Verlag.

***Downey, Roger.** Riddle of the Bones: Politics, Science, Race, & the Story of Kennewick Man. LC 99-40567. (Illus.). 216p. 2000. 25.00 (0-387-98877-7, Copernicus) Spr-Verlag.

Downey, Roger, tr. see Kroetz, Franz X.

Downey, Scott, jt. auth. see Bennett, Jeff.

Downey, Susan B. Architectural Terracottas from the Regia. (Papers & Monographs of the American Academy in Rome Ser.). 152p. 1995. text 44.50 (0-472-10571-X, 10571) U of Mich Pr.

— The Heracles Sculpture: Final Report III, Part 1, Fascicle 1. LC 43-2669. pap. 28.00 (0-685-71741-0) J J Augustin.

— Mesopotamian Religious Architecture: Alexander Through the Parthians. LC 87-3336. (Illus.). 216p. reprint ed. pap. 67.00 (0-7837-6762-5, 204659200003) Bks Demand.

Downey, T. W., et al. Willamette River Salmon Studies, 1992. (Illus.). 120p. 1998. reprint ed. pap. 3.80 (0-89904-789-0, Cascade Geog Soc) Crumb Elbow Pub.

Downey, Tiffany. Spelling Fitness: One Thousand One of the Most Frequently Misspelled Words. Downey, Cynthia, ed. 102p. (Orig.). (YA). (gr. 7-12). 1988. 29.95 (0-685-22519-4) Infini Educ.

Downey, W. David, ed. see Lincoln Institute of Land Policy Staff.

Downham, John, jt. auth. see Worcester, Robert M.

Downham, Marie-Clare. Lace for Church Use. 1989. 24.95 (0-7134-5836-4) Robin & Russ.

Downhower, Jerry F., ed. The Biogeography of the Island Region of Western Lake Erie. LC 87-20986. (Illus.). 288p. reprint ed. pap. 89.30 (0-608-09667-9, 206978200006) Bks Demand.

— Biogeography of the Island Region of Western Lake Erie Abstracts: A Laboratory for Experiments in Ecology & Evolution. LC 85-61221. (Informative Circular Ser.: No. 15). (Illus.). 15p. 1985. pap. text 2.00 (0-86727-101-9) Ohio Bio Survey.

Downie. The Buffalo Boy & the Weaver Girl. (Illus.). (J). 1996. 12.95 (0-919627-31-5, Pub. by Quarry Pr) LPC InBook.

— How the Devil Got His Cat. (Illus.). (J). 1996. 12.95 (0-919627-84-6, Pub. by Quarry Pr) LPC InBook.

— Pharmacology & Drug Management for Nurses. 2nd ed. (C). 1999. pap. text 30.00 (0-443-05968-3, W B Saunders Co) Harcrt Hlth Sci Grp.

Downie, . The Buffalo Boy & the Weaver Girl. (Illus.). (J). 1996. pap. 7.95 (0-919627-33-1, Pub. by Quarry Pr) LPC InBook.

— How the Devil Got His Cat. (Illus.). (J). 1996. pap. 7.95 (0-919627-86-2, Pub. by Quarry Pr) LPC InBook.

Downie, Alex M., jt. auth. see Forster, R. Roy.

Downie, David. Enchanted Liguria: The Glorious Lifestyle & Food of the Italian Riviera. LC 96-47013. (Illus.). 208p. 1997. 40.00 (0-8478-2007-6, Pub. by Rizzoli Intl) St Martin.

***Downie, David.** Frommer's Irreverent Guide to Amsterdam. 3rd ed. (Illus.). 240p. 2000. 12.95 (0-02-863791-7) Macmillan.

Downie, Diane, et al. Math for Girls & Other Problem Solvers. (Equals Ser.). (Illus.). 108p. (J). (gr. k-8). 1997. pap. 11.95 (0-912511-01-X, EQUALS) Lawrence Science.

Downie, Don & Downie, Julia. Air Camping. (Illus.). 160p. (Orig.). 1985. pap. 12.95 (0-8306-2380-9, 2380P) McGraw-Hill Prof.

Downie, Freda. Collected Poems. Szirtes, George, ed. 176p. 1996. pap. 19.95 (1-85224-301-5, Pub. by Bloodaxe Bks) Dufour.

Downie, George, et al. Pharmacology & Drug Management for Nurses. LC 94-8716. 1995. pap. text 30.00 (0-443-04477-5) Church.

Downie, Hugh D. Harvest Festivals. 160p. 1995. pap. 9.95 (1-882701-15-1) Uplook Min.

Downie, J. A., intro. Swift, Temple, & the Du Cros Affair, Letter from Monsieur de Cros...Being an Answer to Sir Wm. Temple's Memoirs, Concerning What Passed from the Year 1672 until the Year 1679 Pt. 2: And Reflections upon Two Pamphlets...Lately Published; One Called, a Letter from Monsieur de Cros, Concerning the Memoirs of Christendom, & the Other, an Answer. (Augustan Reprints Ser.: Nos. 241-242). 1987. reprint ed. 21.50 (0-404-70241-4) AMS Pr.

Downie, J. A. & Corns, Thomas N., eds. Telling People What to Think: Early Eighteenth-Century Periodicals from the Review to the Rambler. LC 92-36615. 1992. 35.00 (0-7146-4508-7, Pub. by F Cass Pubs) Intl Spec Bk.

***Downie, J. A. & Parnell, J. T., eds.** Constructing Christopher Marlowe. (Illus.). 246p. 2000. 59.95 (0-521-57255-X) Cambridge U Pr.

Downie, Jean. By Order of Adoption. LC 91-41048. 80p. 1992. pap. 9.95 (0-942963-18-0) Distinctive Pub.

Downie, Jill. A Passionate Pen: The Life & Times of Faith Fenton. (Illus.). 337p. 1998. text 27.00 (0-7881-5354-4) DIANE Pub.

Downie, John, jt. auth. see Alice, Mary.

Downie, Julia, jt. auth. see Downie, Don.

Downie, Mary A. The Cat Park. (Illus.). 32p. (J). 1993. 17.95 (1-55082-058-3, Pub. by Quarry Pr); pap. 8.95 (1-55082-059-1, Pub. by Quarry Pr) LPC InBook.

— Cathal the Giant Killer. (Illus.). (J). 1996. 12.95 (1-55082-008-7, Pub. by Quarry Pr) LPC InBook.

— Snow Paws. unabridged ed. LC 99-236453. (Illus.). 24p. (J). (ps-3). 1997. 16.95 (0-7737-2968-2) STDK.

Downie, Mary A. & Hamilton, Mary, eds. And Some Brought Flowers: Plants in a New World. rev. ed. (Illus.). 168p. 1996. pap. 29.95 (1-55082-156-3, Pub. by Quarry Pr) LPC InBook.

Downie, Mary A. & Rawlyk, George. A Proper Acadian. 64p. (J). 1980. pap. 4.96 (0-919964-29-X) Kids Can Pr.

Downie, Mary A. & Thompson, M. A. Written in Stone. (Illus.). 264p. 1993. pap. 19.95 (1-55082-063-X, Pub. by Quarry Pr) LPC InBook.

***Downie, Mary Alice.** Bright Paddles. (First Flight Chapter Bk.). (Illus.). 120p. (J). (gr. 1-3). 2000. pap. 3.95 (1-55041-516-6) Fitzhenry & W Ltd.

Downie, Mary Alice. Honor Bound. (Illus.). 216p. (YA). Date not set. 12.95 (1-55082-026-5, Pub. by Quarry Pr); pap. 7.95 (1-55082-027-3, Pub. by Quarry Pr) LPC InBook.

Downie, Mary Alice & Gilliland, Jillian Halume. Cathal the Giant Killer: And the Dun Shaggy Filly. (Illus.). (J). 1996. pap. 7.95 (1-55082-009-5, Pub. by Quarry Pr) LPC InBook.

Downie, Mary Alice & Zola. How the Devil Got His Cat & Other Multicultural Folktales for Children. (Illus.). 144p. (J). Date not set. 16.95 (1-55082-100-8, Pub. by Quarry Pr) LPC InBook.

Downie, N. A. Industrial Gases. (Illus.). 352p. 1996. pap. 256.00 (0-7514-0352-0) Kluwer Academic.

Downie, Patricia A. Cash's Textbook of Orthopaedics & Rheumatology for Physiotherapists. LC 65-73208. 1984. text 19.75 (0-397-58293-5, Lippnctt) Lppncott W & W.

Downie, Peter. Healers at Work: Firsthand Accounts of the Difference Alternative Healing Makes. LC 96-913434. (Illus.). 224p. 1996. 23.95 (1-55145-080-1) NStone Publ.

Downie, R. S., ed. The Healing Arts: An Oxford Illustrated Anthology. (Illus.). 352p. 1995. 35.00 (0-19-262319-2) OUP.

Downie, R. S. & Calman, Kenneth C. Healthy Respect: Ethics in Health Care. 2nd ed. 312p. (Orig.). 1994. 59.50 (0-19-262409-1); pap. text 31.95 (0-19-262408-3) OUP.

Downie, R. S., et al. Health Promotion: Models & Values. 2nd ed. (Illus.). 238p. (C). 1996. 75.00 (0-19-262592-6); pap. text 39.95 (0-19-262591-8) OUP.

— The Making of a Doctor: Medical Education in Theory & Practice. LC 92-13057. (Oxford Medical Publications). (Illus.). 224p. 1992. 49.95 (0-19-262136-X) OUP.

Downie, Richard D. Learning from Conflict: Studies in Counterinsurgency & Low Intensity Warfare. LC 97-34728. 312p. 1998. 65.00 (0-275-96010-2, Praeger Pubs) Greenwood.

Downie, Robert A., ed. see Frazer, James George.

Downie, Robert S., ed. Medical Ethics. LC 96-608. (International Research Library of Philosophy). (Illus.). 520p. 1996. 163.95 (1-85521-631-0, Pub. by Dartmth Pub) Ashgate Pub Co.

***Downie, Robin & MacNaughton, Jane.** Clinical Judgement. (Illus.). 224p. 2000. pap. text 27.50 (0-19-263216-7) OUP.

Downie, Robin S., jt. auth. see Randall, Fiona.

Downie, V. J. A Doctor of Sorts. large type ed. 320p. 1996. 27.99 (0-7089-3236-3) Ulverscroft.

Downie, Virginia L. Together: A Relationship Survival Kit. iv, 132p. 1997. pap. 14.95 (0-9662177-0-5) Downie Commun.

Downing. Downing on Course. (C). Date not set. 26.76 (0-395-90551-6) HM.

***Downing.** History of Zen Center. 2000. 28.00 (1-58243-113-2, Pub. by Counterpt DC) HarpC.

Downing. Hush Little Baby. (J). 1996. 16.95 (0-02-732531-8) S&S Bks Yung.

Downing, Alfred. The Region of the Upper Columbia River & How I Saw It. 50p. 1980. 11.95 (0-87770-535-6); pap. 6.95 (0-87770-234-9) Ye Galleon.

Downing, Andrew J. Architecture of Country Houses. LC 68-16230. (Architecture & Decorative Art Ser.). (Illus.). 1968. reprint ed. 65.00 (0-306-71034-X) Da Capo.

— Architecture of Country Houses. (Illus.). 484p. 1969. reprint ed. pap. 12.95 (0-486-22003-6) Dover.

— Architecture of Country Houses. 484p. 1993. reprint ed. lib. bdg. 99.00 (0-7812-5293-8) Rprt Serv.

— Fruits & Fruit Trees of America. 594p. 1993. reprint ed. lib. bdg. 99.00 (0-7812-5230-X) Rprt Serv.

— Rural Essays. Curtis, George W., ed. LC 69-13713. (Architecture & Decorative Art Ser.). 640p. 1975. reprint ed. lib. bdg. 69.50 (0-306-71035-8) Da Capo.

— A Treatise on the Theory & Practice of Landscape Gardening Adapted to North America. (Illus.). 1976. reprint ed. 20.00 (0-913728-23-3) Theophrastus.

— Treatise on the Theory & Practice of Landscape Gardening, Adapted to North America. LC 91-4356. (Dumbarton Oaks Reprints & Facsimiles in Landscape Architecture Ser.: No. 2). (Illus.). 576p. 1991. reprint ed. 60.00 (0-88402-192-0, DOTR) Dumbarton Oaks.

— Treatise on the Theory & Practice of Landscape Gardening Adapted to North America. 576p. 1993. reprint ed. lib. bdg. 99.00 (0-685-61624-X) Rprt Serv.

— Victorian Cottage Residences. Harney, George E., ed. (Illus.). 352p. 1999. reprint ed. pap. 8.95 (0-486-24078-9) Dover.

— A Visit to Montgomery Place. (Illus.). 16p. 1988. pap. 4.95 (0-912882-75-1) Sleepy Hollow.

Downing, Angela & Locke, Philip. A University course in English Grammar. 1994. pap. text 54.00 (0-13-952490-8) P-H.

Downing, Barry. The Bible & Flying Saucers. 2nd ed. (Illus.). 224p. 1998. pap. 13.95 (1-56924-745-5) Marlowe & Co.

Downing, Betty M. EZ-2-C Cookbook. large type ec. 4.50 (0-317-01864-7) B M Downing.

***Downing Books Staff.** Kentucky Basketball Encyclopedia. (Illus.). 300p. 1999. 39.95 (1-58261-065-7) Sprts Pubng.

Downing, Charles. The Messiahship of Shakespeare. LC 76-57998. (Studies in Shakespeare: No. 24). 1977. lib. bdg. 59.00 (0-8383-2172-0) M S G Haskell Hse.

— Russian Tales & Legends. (Oxford Myths & Legends Ser.). (Illus.). 216p. (YA). (gr. 5-12). 1990. pap. 12.95 (0-19-274144-6) OUP.

— Russian Tales & Legends. (Oxford Myths & Legends Ser.). (J). 1989. 18.05 (0-606-04531-7, Pub. by Turtleback) Demco.

Downing, Christine. The Goddess: Mythological Images of the Feminine. LC 60-53138. 252p. 1996. pap. 15.95 (0-8264-0917-2) Continuum.

— Myths & Mysteries of Same-Sex Love. rev. ed. LC 82-40283. 348p. (C). 1996. pap. 19.95 (0-8264-0918-0) Continuum.

Downing, Cynthia. Triad: The Evolution of Treatment for Chemical Dependency. 1989. pap. 6.50 (0-8309-0543-X) Herald Pub Hse.

Downing, D. & Clark, J. Statistics the Easy Way. (Barron's Easy Way Ser.). 368p. 1983. pap. 8.95 (0-8120-2666-7) Barron.

***Downing, Danna & Erickson, Fritz J.** Sub Survival: A Handbook for the Substitute Elementary Teacher. 4th ed. 150p. 2000. pap. text 19.95 (1-55691-180-7) Learning Pubns.

Downing, David. Dictionary of American Spelling. LC 91-60024. 316p. 1994. pap. 9.95 (0-8442-5476-2, Natl Textbk Co) NTC Contemp Pub Co.

— A Dreamer of Pictures: Neil Young: The Man & His Music. LC 94-29686. (Illus.). 272p. (Orig.). 1995. pap. 14.95 (0-306-80611-8) Da Capo.

— NTC's Dictionary for Doubtful Spellers. LC 90-63166. (Illus.). 336p. 1995. pap. 5.95 (0-8442-5474-6, Natl Textbk Co) NTC Contemp Pub Co.

— NTC's Spell It Right Dictionary. (Illus.). 336p. 1994. pap. 6.95 (0-8442-5477-0, 54770, Natl Textbk Co) NTC Contemp Pub Co.

— O Que Voce Sabe Pode Nao Estar.Tr. of What You Know Might Not Be So. (POR.). 136p. 1991. pap. 6.95 (0-8297-1652-1) Vida Pubs.

***Downing, David.** Passovotchka: Moscow Dynamo in Britain 1945. 1999. 32.50 (0-7475-4456-5, Pub. by Blmsbury Pub) Trafalgar.

Downing, David. The Red Eagles. 256p. 1989. reprint ed. pap. 4.50 (0-373-97097-8) Harlequin Bks.

— 303 Dumb Spelling Mistakes. (Illus.). 128p. 1994. pap. 5.95 (0-8442-5475-4, 54754, Natl Textbk Co) NTC Contemp Pub Co.

Downing, David B. & Bazargan, Susan, eds. Image & Ideology in Modern/Postmodern Discourse. LC 90-10284. 349p. (C). 1991. pap. text 24.95 (0-7914-0716-0) State U NY Pr.

— Image & Ideology in Modern/Postmodern Discourse. LC 90-10284. 349p. (C). 1991. text 74.50 (0-7914-0715-2) State U NY Pr.

Downing, David C. Planets in Peril: A Critical Study of C. S. Lewis's Ransom Trilogy. LC 91-34369. 200p. 1995. pap. 15.95 (0-87023-997-X) U of Mass Pr.

Downing, David H., jt. auth. see Downing, Mildred H.

***Downing, Donald.** Hidden Treasures of the Heart. 2000. pap. 10.99 (1-56043-315-9) Destiny Image.

Downing, Donald L. A Complete Course in Canning & Related Processes, 3 vols. 13th ed. Incl. Bk. 1. Fundamental Information on Canning. 13th ed. LC 96-8381. 1996. 85.00 (0-930027-26-4); Bk. 2. Microbiology, Packaging, HAACP & Ingredients. 13th ed. LC 96-8381. 1996. 85.00 (0-930027-27-2); Bk. 3. Processing Procedures for Canned Food Products. 13th ed. LC 96-8381. 1996. 85.00 (0-930027-28-0); LC 96-8381. 1996. 199.00 (0-930027-25-6) CTI Pubns.

***Downing, Doug.** Play Guitar Today. 48p. 1999. pap. 9.95 incl. audio compact disk (0-634-00410-7) H Leonard.

Downing, Douglas. Algebra the Easy Way. 3rd ed. LC 96-15413. (Barron's Easy Way Ser.). (Illus.). 334p. 1996. pap. 12.95 (0-8120-9393-3) Barron.

— Calculus the Easy Way. 3rd ed. LC 95-21994. (Barron's Easy Way Ser.). 336p. 1996. pap. 12.95 (0-8120-9141-8) Barron.

— Dictionary of Mathematics Terms. 2nd ed. LC 95-12039. (Professional Guides Ser.). (Illus.). 400p. 1995. pap. 10.95 (0-8120-3097-4) Barron.

— Forgotten Statistics. 1996. pap. text 12.95 (0-8120-9713-0) Barron.

— Quantitative Methods. 1988. pap. 12.95 (0-8120-3947-5) Barron.

— Trigonometry the Easy Way. 2nd ed. (Barron's Easy Way Ser.). 288p. 1990. pap. text 11.95 (0-8120-4389-8) Barron.

Downing, Douglas & Clark, Jeff. Business Statistics. 3rd ed. LC 96-30454. (Barron's Business Review Ser.). 1997. pap. 12.95 (0-8120-9658-4) Barron.

— Statistics the Easy Way. 3rd ed. LC 96-41827. 1997. pap. 12.95 (0-8120-9392-5) Barron.

Downing, Douglas, et al. Dictionary of Computer & Internet Terms. 6th exp. rev. ed. LC 98-6984. (Illus.). 530p. 1998. 9.95 (0-7641-0094-7) Barron.

***Downing, Douglas, et al.** Dictionary of Computer & Internet Terms 7th ed. LC 99-35913. 2000. 10.95 (0-7641-1265-1) Barron.

***Downing, Douglas A.** Calculus. (EZ-101 Study Keys Ser.). 200p. 2000. pap. text 7.95 (0-7641-1326-7) Barron.

— Computer Programming in Java the Easy Way. LC 98-43741. (Barron's Easy Way Ser.). (Illus.). 366p. 1999. pap. 18.95 incl. disk (0-7641-0752-6) Barron.

Downing, Douglas D. Computers & Business Tasks. deluxe ed. (Barron's Business Library). 320p. 1991. pap. 14.95 (0-8120-4543-2) Barron.

Downing, E. F., et al, eds. Lasers in Neurosurgery. (Illus.). 130p. 1989. 71.95 (0-387-82067-1) Spr-Verlag.

Downing, Elisabeth. Guide to Owning a Yorkshire Terrier: AKC Rank #9. LC 98-15130. (Popular Dog Library Ser.). (Illus.). 64p. (YA). (gr. 3 up). 1999. 19.95 (0-7910-5478-0) Chelsea Hse.

Downing, Elizabeth. Guide to Owning a Yorkshire Terrier: AKC Rank #9. (Guide to Owning Ser.). (Illus.). 64p. 1995. pap. 6.95 (0-7938-1862-1, RE-312) TFH Pubns.

***Downing, Eric.** Double Exposures: Repetition & Realism in Nineteenth-Century German Fiction. (Illus.). 2000. write for info. (0-8047-3678-2, Pub. by Stanford U Pr) Cambridge U Pr.

Downing, F. G. Christ & the Cynics. (Journal for the Study of the Old Testament Supplement Ser.: Vol. 4). 246p. 1988. 33.00 (1-85075-150-1, Pub. by McG-Queens Univ Pr) CUP Services.

D

***Downing, Frances.** Remembrance & the Design of Place. LC 99-43690. 2000. write for info. (0-89096-938-8) Tex A&M Univ Pr.

— Remembrance & the Design of Place. LC 99-43690. 192p. 2000. 39.95 (0-89096-922-1) Tex A&M Univ Pr.

Downing, Francis G. Cynics, Paul, & the Pauline Churches. LC 97-18310. 336p. (C). 1998. 65.00 (0-415-17159-8) Routledge.

Downing, George. Massage Book. 1972. pap. 12.00 (0-394-70770-2) Random.

— The Massage Book. 25th anniversary ed. LC 97-27511. 1998. pap. 14.95 (0-679-77789-X) Random.

Downing, George, jt. ed. see Robbins, Daniel.

Downing, George J. Three Weeks to Better Kids: Making Rules That Stick, & Discipline with a Smile. 210p. (Orig.). 1996. pap. 19.95 (1-889565-06-7, 996) Omnipr.

Downing, Gerald F. Cynics & Christian Origins. 352p. 1992. text 49.95 (0-567-09613-0, Pub. by T & T Clark) Bks Intl VA.

Downing Hahn, Mary. Anna All Year Round. LC 98-19985. (Illus.). 144p. (J). (gr. 1-5). 1999. 15.00 (0-395-86975-7, Clarion Bks) HM.

Downing, Henry F. The American Cavalryman: A Liberian Romance. LC 78-164784. reprint ed. 37.50 (0-404-00148-3) AMS Pr.

Downing, J. Cinderella. (Illus.). 1993. text 19.95 (0-340-56233-1, Pub. by Hodder & Stought Ltd) Trafalgar.

Downing, J. & Valtin, R., eds. Language Awareness & Learning to Read. (Language & Communication Ser.: Vol. 17). (Illus.). 385p. 1984. 118.00 (0-387-90890-0) Spr-Verlag.

Downing, Jack. Dreams & Nightmares: A Book of Gestalt Therapy Sessions. 2nd ed. 192p. 1996. reprint ed. pap. 20.00 (0-939266-27-X) Gestalt Journal.

Downing, James P. Creative Teaching: Ideas to Boost Student Interest. LC 97-11676. 200p. 1997. pap. text 25.00 (1-56308-476-7) Teacher Ideas Pr.

***Downing, Jerry N.** Between Conviction & Uncertainty: Philosophical Guidelines for the Practicing Psycotherapist. (C). 2000. text 71.50 (0-7914-4627-1); pap. text 23.95 (0-7914-4628-X) State U NY Pr.

Downing, Joan, ed. see Kent, Deborah.

Downing, Joan, ed. see Stein, R. Conrad.

Downing, John. Internationalizing Media Theory: Transition, Power, Culture. (Media, Culture & Society Ser.). 304p. 1996. 85.00 (0-8039-8710-2); pap. 26.95 (0-8039-8711-0) Sage.

***Downing, John.** Radical Media: Rebellious Communication & Social Movements. LC 00-8781. 2000. write for info. (0-8039-5699-1) Sage.

Downing, John, et al, eds. Questioning the Media: A Critical Introduction. 2nd ed. LC 94-48241. 1995. 59.95 (0-8039-7196-6) Sage.

Downing, John, et al. Computers for Social Change & Community Organizing. (Computers in Human Services Ser.: Vol. 8, No. 1). 136p. 1994. text 39.95 (0-86656-865-4) Haworth Pr.

— Questioning the Media: A Critical Introduction. 2nd ed. 400p. 1995. text 56.00 (0-8039-7199-0); pap. text 28.95 (0-8039-7197-4) Sage.

Downing, John A., jt. auth. see Silva, Marina.

Downing, John D., ed. Film & Politics in the Third World. 317p. Date not set. 12.00 (0-936756-31-4) Autonomedia.

Downing, Julie. Come Aboard Noah's Ark. LC 98-45042. 12p. 1999. 7.95 (0-7894-3986-7) DK Pub Inc.

— Mozart Tonight. LC 93-27445. (Illus.). 40p. (J). (ps-9). 1994. pap. 5.95 (0-689-71808-X) Aladdin.

— Mozart Tonight. LC 90-34479. (Illus.). 40p. (J). 1991. lib. bdg. 15.95 (0-02-732881-3, Bradbury S&S) S&S Childrens.

— Mozart Tonight. large type ed. 1993. 11.50 (0-614-09846-7, L-34083-00) Am Printing Hse.

Downing, Julie. Where's My Mommy. 1924. write for info. (0-688-17824-3, Wm Morrow) Morrow Avon.

Downing, Julie. White Snow - Blue Feather. LC 89-815. (Illus.). 32p. (J). (ps-1). 1989. text 14.95 (0-02-732530-X, Bradbury S&S) S&S Childrens.

***Downing, Julie.** Come Aboard Noah's Ark. 10p. (J). 1999. bds. 7.99 (0-8423-3591-9) Tyndale Hse.

Downing, Julie. A First Bible Story Book. LC 96-38302. 80p. (YA). (gr. k-2). 1998. 12.95 (0-7894-1555-0) DK Pub Inc.

***Downing, Julie.** A First Bible Story Book. 80p. (ps-3). 1998. 12.99 (1-57727-119-X) Jubilee Pub Grp.

Downing, Julie. Lullaby & Good Night. LC 97-47306. 31p. (J). (ps). 1999. 15.00 (0-689-81085-7) S&S Bks Yung.

— The Magpies' Nest. LC 94-1773. 32p. (J). (ps-3). 1995. 15.95 (0-395-62155-0, Clarion Bks) HM.

Downing, June. Teaching Communication Skills to Students with Severe Disabilities. LC 98-52005. 1999. pap. text 34.95 (1-55766-385-8) P H Brookes.

Downing, June E. Including Students with Severe & Multiple Disabilities in Typical Classrooms: Practical Strategies for Teachers. LC 96-6331. 1996. 35.00 (1-55766-239-8) P H Brookes.

Downing, Karen E., et al. Reaching a Multicultural Student Community: A Handbook for Academic Librarians. LC 93-548. (The Greenwood Library Management Collection). 240p. 1993. lib. bdg. 59.95 (0-313-27912-8, DRD) Greenwood.

Downing, Kenneth L. Holy Gossip. LC 92-31524. 112p. 1993. pap. 12.95 (0-942963-27-X) Distinctive Pub.

Downing, Marilyn, jt. ed. see Gasser, Ann.

Downing, Martin. The House of Dracula: A Comedy-Horror LC 92-238118. 71 p. 1992. write for info. (0-573-01790-5) French.

Downing, Michael. Breakfast with Scot. LC 99-35584. 208p. 1999. text 24.00 (1-58243-027-6, Pub. by Counterpt DC) HarpC.

— Perfect Agreement. LC 97-25629. 224p. 1997. 22.00 (1-887178-45-7, Pub. by Counterpt DC) HarpC.

— Perfect Agreement. 288p. 1998. reprint ed. pap. 12.95 (0-425-16628-7) Berkley Pub.

Downing, Mildred H. & Downing, David H. Introduction to Cataloging & Classification. 6th ed. LC 91-51210. (Illus.). 336p. 1992. lib. bdg. 39.95 (0-89950-720-4) McFarland & Co.

***Downing, Neil.** Maximize Your Benefits. 2000. pap. 17.95 (0-7931-3700-4) Dearborn.

Downing, Neil. Maximize Your IRA. LC 98-13650. 200p. 1998. pap. text 18.95 (0-7931-2853-6) Dearborn.

Downing, Noel. Doctor Watson & the Invisible Man. 200p. 1992. 25.00 (0-86025-275-2, Pub. by I Henry Pubns) Empire Pub Srvs.

Downing-Orr, K. Rethinking Depression: Why Current Treatments Fail. LC 98-39719. (Illus.). 164p. (C). 1998. 42.50 (0-306-45940-X, Plenum Trade) Perseus Pubng.

Downing-Orr, Kristina. Alienation & Social Support: A Social Psychological Study of Homeless Young People in London & in Sydney. LC 96-83272. x, 193p. 1996. 68.95 (1-85972-347-0, Pub. by Avebry) Ashgate Pub Co.

***Downing-Orr, Kristina.** What to Do If You're Burned Out & Blue: The Essential Guide to Help You Through Depression. 2000. pap. 16.95 (0-7225-3876-6, Pub. by Thorsons PA) HarpC.

Downing, Pamela, et al, eds. The Linguistics of Literacy. LC 92-7341. (Typological Studies in Language: No. 21). xx, 334p. 1992. 97.00 (1-55619-406-4); pap. 32.95 (1-55619-407-2) J Benjamins Pubng Co.

Downing, Pamela & Noonan, Michael, eds. Word Order in Discourse. LC 94-44088. (Typological Studies in Language: No. 30). x, 595p. 1995. pap. 37.95 (1-55619-636-9); lib. bdg. 135.00 (1-55619-424-2) J Benjamins Pubng Co.

Downing, Pamela A. Numeral Classifier Systems: The Case of Japanese. LC 96-9444. (Studies in Discourse & Grammar: No. 4). xx, 336p. Date not set. 79.00 (1-55619-370-X) J Benjamins Pubng Co.

Downing, Paul B. Environmental Economics & Policy. (C). 1984. text 40.00 (0-673-39120-5, Scott Frsmn) Addson-Wesley Educ.

***Downing, Paul B.** Opal Advanced Cutting & Setting. (Illus.). 144p. 2000. pap. 15.95 (0-9625311-5-4) Majestic Pr.

Downing, Paul B. Opal Adventures. 2nd ed. (Illus.). 240p. 1993. 19.95 (0-9625311-3-8) Majestic Pr.

— Opal Cutting Made Easy. 2nd ed. (Illus.). 100p. (Orig.). 1993. pap. 8.95 (0-9625311-4-6) Majestic Pr.

— Opal Identification & Value. (Illus.). 214p. 1992. 38.95 (0-9625311-2-X) Majestic Pr.

Downing, Paul B., ed. Air Pollution & the Social Sciences: Formulating & Implementing Control Programs. LC 75-153390. (Special Studies in U. S. Economic, Social & Political Issues). 1971. 46.50 (0-89197-652-3) Irvington.

Downing, Paul B. & Hanf, Kenneth. International Comparisons in Implementing Pollution Laws. 1983. lib. bdg. 64.00 (0-89838-110-X) Kluwer Academic.

Downing, Paula E. A Whisper of Time. (Orig.). 1994. mass mkt. 4.99 (0-345-38195-5, Del Rey) Ballantine Pub Grp.

Downing, Peggy. Brill of Exitorn. LC 93-50904. (Pennant Ser.). (Illus.). 184p. (J). 1994. pap. 6.49 (0-89084-736-3, 078238) Bob Jones Univ.

— The Lost Prince. Orig. Title: Segra & Stargull. (Illus.). 216p. (J). (gr. 2-4). 1995. reprint ed. pap. 6.49 (0-89084-834-3, 088799) Bob Jones Univ.

Downing, R. A., et al, eds. The Hydrogeology of the Chalk of North-West Europe. LC 92-44648. (Illus.). 310p. (C). 1993. text 125.00 (0-19-854285-2, Clarendon Pr) OUP.

Downing, R. A. & Wilkinson, W. B., eds. Applied Groundwater Hydrology: A British Perspective. (Illus.). 352p. 1992. text 175.00 (0-19-852139-1) OUP.

Downing, Robbie. EC Information Technology Law. LC 94-195951. 286p. 1995. 174.95 (0-471-95049-1) Wiley.

Downing, Robert J., et al. RAINS-ASIA: An Assessment Model for Acid Deposition in Asia. LC 97-10470. (Directions in Development Ser.). 84p. 1997. pap. 22.00 (0-8213-3919-2, 13919) World Bank.

***Downing, Robin.** Pets Living with Cancer: A Pet Owner's Resource Guide. 144p. 2000. pap. 19.95 (1-58326-022-6, AAHA Pr) Am Animal Hosp Assoc.

Downing, S., et al, eds. Proceedings of the 1995 National Heat Transfer Conference: August 6-9, 1995, Portland, Oregon, Vol. 5. 156p. 1995. 88.00 (0-7918-1706-7, H00988) ASME.

***Downing, Skip.** On Course. 2nd ed. LC 98-72017. xviii, 219 p. 1999. write for info. (0-395-93422-2) HM.

Downing, Skip. On Course: Strategies for Creating Success in College in Life: A Guided Journal Approach. (C). 1995. pap. text, teacher ed. 11.96 (0-395-73879-2) HM.

Downing, Stephen. Histology: A Photographic Atlas. (Illus.). (C). 1992. text 500.00 incl. disk (1-56815-002-4) Mosby Inc.

Downing, Steve & Crumpecker, Christina. Basic Facilitation: Facilitator Guide. Date not set. spiral bd. write for info. (1-57740-046-1) Intl LrningWrk.

— Basic Facilitation: Participant Manual. unabridged ed. Date not set. spiral bd. write for info. (1-57740-047-X) Intl LrningWrk.

***Downing, Sue.** Hand in Hand: Growing Spiritually with Our Children. 96p. 1998. pap. 16.95 (0-88177-224-0, DR224) Discipleship Res.

Downing, Sue K. Prayers for the Seasons of Life. (Illus.). 96p. 1997. 14.95 (1-57736-041-9) Providence Hse.

Downing, Sybil. Beauty in the Rockies. (Colorado Heritage Ser.). 1994. pap. text 7.95 (1-878611-10-0) Silver Rim Pr.

— Fire in the Hole. 1998. pap. 13.95 (0-87081-515-6) Univ Pr Colo.

— Ladies of the Goldfield Stock Exchange. LC 97-730. 352p. 1997. text 23.95 (0-312-86331-4) St Martin.

— Ladies of the Goldfield Stock Exchange. 1998. mass mkt. 5.99 (0-8125-3927-3, Pub. by Tor Bks) St Martin.

— Settling Down. (Colorado Heritage Ser.). 1979. pap. text 7.95 (1-878611-08-9) Silver Rim Pr.

Downing, Sybil & Barker, Jane. Crown of Life: The Story of Mary Roberts Rinehart. (Illus.). 178p. (YA). 1992. 19.50 (1-879373-13-0); pap. 9.95 (1-879373-18-1) Roberts Rinehart.

Downing, Sybil & Barker, Jane V. Florence Sabin: Pioneer Scientist. (Women of the West Ser.). (Illus.). 100p. (J). 1981. pap. 7.95 (1-878611-11-9) Silver Rim Pr.

— Happy Harvest. (Colorado Heritage Ser.). (Illus.). 43p. (J). reprint ed. pap. text 7.95 (1-878611-02-X) Silver Rim Pr.

— Magic, Mystery, & Monsters. (Colorado Heritage Ser.). (Illus.). 47p. (J). reprint ed. pap. 7.95 (1-878611-06-2) Silver Rim Pr.

— Mesas to Mountains. (Colorado Heritage Ser.). (Illus.). 47p. (J). (ps-8). reprint ed. pap. 7.95 (1-878611-04-6) Silver Rim Pr.

Downing, Sybil, jt. auth. see Barker, Jane V.

Downing, Sybil, ed. see Barker, Jane V.

Downing, T. The Mexican Earth. 1976. lib. bdg. 59.95 (0-8490-2234-7) Gordon Pr.

Downing, Taylor. Olympia. (BFI Film Classics Ser.). (Illus.). 96p. 1993. pap. 10.95 (0-85170-341-0, Pub. by British Film Inst) Ind U Pr.

Downing, Taylor, jt. auth. see Isaacs, Jeremy.

Downing, Theodore E., ed. see Adams, Robert M.

Downing, Thomas E., ed. Climate Change & World Food Security. (NATO ASI Ser.: Series 1, Vol. 37). 672p. 1995. 328.95 (3-540-60562-2) Spr-Verlag.

Downing, Thomas E., et al. Climate, Change & Risk. LC 97-51582. (Illus.). 320p. (C). 1998. 115.00 (0-415-17031-1) Routledge.

Downing, Todd. The Mexican Earth. 2nd ed. LC 95-39840. (American Indian Literature & Critical Studies Ser.: Vol. 20). (Illus.). 384p. (Orig.). 1996. pap. 16.95 (0-8061-2788-0) U of Okla Pr.

Downing, Troy, jt. auth. see Fox, David.

Downing, Troy, jt. auth. see Meyer, Jon.

Downing, Troy B. Java Rmi: Remote Method Invocation. LC 97-73632. 320p. 1998. pap. 39.99 (0-7645-8043-4) IDG Bks.

Downing, Victoria L. Selling Remodeling: Nine Steps to Sales Success. LC 92-33760. (Illus.). 107p. 1992. pap. 22.50 (0-86718-381-0) Home Builder.

Downing, Victoria L., jt. auth. see Case, Linda W.

Downing, Warwick. Choice of Evils. Isaacson, Dana, ed. 400p. (Orig.). 1994. mass mkt. 5.50 (0-671-76035-1) PB.

— Kid Curry's Last Ride. (Trophy Bk.). 176p. (J). (gr. 5-7). 1992. pap. 3.95 (0-06-440421-8, HarpTrophy) HarpC Child Bks.

***Downing, Warwick.** Leonardo's Hand. LC 00-32034. (Illus.). (J). 2001. write for info. (0-618-07893-2) HM.

Downing, Warwick. A Lingering Doubt. Isaacson, Dana, ed. 320p. (Orig.). 1993. mass mkt. 4.99 (0-671-76034-3) PB.

Downs. Child Welfare & Family Services: Policies & Practice. 6th ed. 500p. (C). 1999. 60.00 (0-8013-3046-7) Allyn.

— Earth Science Series, 4 vols. 1999. 71.92 (0-8050-5904-0) H Holt & Co.

— Earths Hidden Treasures. 1999. 17.98 (0-8050-5905-9) H Holt & Co.

— Erosion. 1999. 17.98 (0-8050-5908-3) H Holt & Co.

— More Than Victims. 1998. pap. text 17.00 (0-226-16160-9) U Ch Pr.

— Playwriting. LC 97-72178. (C). 1997. pap. text 22.50 (0-15-503861-3, Pub. by Harcourt Coll Pubs) Harcourt.

***Downs, Alan.** Beyond the Looking Glass: Overcoming the Seductive Culture of Corporate Narcissism. 222p. 2000. reprint ed. text 25.00 (0-7881-9176-4) DIANE Pub.

Downs, Alan. Corporate Executions: The Ugly Truth about Layoffs. How Corporate Greed Is Shattering Lives, Companies, & Communities. LC 95-20455. 224p. 1995. 22.95 (0-8144-0307-7) AMACOM.

***Downs, Alan.** The Fearless Executive: Finding the Courage to Trust Your Talents & Be the Leader You Are Meant to Be. LC 00-22615. 224p. 2000. 22.95 (0-8144-0565-7) AMACOM.

Downs, Alan. The Seven Miracles of Management. LC 98-23861. 224p. 1998. text 23.00 (0-7352-0042-4) P-H.

Downs, Andrew S., et al. Teach Yourself Java 1.1 for Macintosh in 21 Days. 2nd ed. 550p. 1997. pap. 39.99 (1-56830-342-4) Hayden Bridge.

Downs, Anthony. Economic Theory of Democracy. 310p. (C). 1997. pap. 47.00 (0-06-041750-1) Addson-Wesley Educ.

— Inside Bureaucracy. (C). 1967. pap. text 28.20 (0-673-39432-8) Addson-Wesley Educ.

— Inside Bureaucracy. (Illus.). 292p. (C). 1994. reprint ed. pap. text 17.95 (0-88133-778-1) Waveland Pr.

— Neighborhoods & Urban Development. LC 81-66190. 189p. 1981. 32.95 (0-8157-1920-5); pap. 12.95 (0-8157-1919-1) Brookings.

— New Visions for Metropolitan America. LC 93-47483. (Integrating National Economies: Promise & Pitfalls Ser.). 272p. (Orig.). (C). 1995. 38.95 (0-8157-1926-4); pap. 16.95 (0-8157-1925-6) Brookings.

— Political Theory & Public Choice Vol. 1: The Selected Essays of Anthony Downs. LC 98-12621. 192p. 1998. 70.00 (1-85898-733-4) E Elgar.

— A Reevaluation of Residential Rent Controls. LC 96-61396. 212p. 1996. pap. text 36.95 (0-87420-801-7, R02) Urban Land.

— Rental Housing in the 1980s. LC 83-10124. 202p. 1983. 32.95 (0-8157-1922-1); pap. 12.95 (0-8157-1921-3) Brookings.

— The Revolution in Real Estate Finance. LC 85-14941. 345p. 1985. 36.95 (0-8157-1918-3); pap. 16.95 (0-8157-1917-5) Brookings.

— Stuck in Traffic: Coping with Peak-Hour Traffic Congestion. 210p. (C). 1992. 38.95 (0-8157-1924-8); pap. 16.95 (0-8157-1923-X) Brookings.

— Urban Affairs & Urban Policy Vol. 2: The Selected Essays of Anthony Downs. LC 98-13246. 288p. 1998. 90.00 (1-85898-734-2) E Elgar.

Downs, Anthony, jt. auth. see Bradbury, Katharine L.

Downs, Anthony, jt. ed. see Bradbury, Katharine L.

***Downs, Art, ed.** The Death of Albert Johnson: Mad Trapper of Rat River. 5th ed. (Illus.). 96p. 2000. reprint ed. pap. 8.95 (1-894384-03-2, Pub. by Heritage Hse) Midpt Trade.

Downs, Brian W., jt. auth. see Mortensen, Brita M.

Downs, Brian Westerdale. Richardson. LC 73-453631. 248p. 1969. write for info. (0-7146-2058-0) Intl Spec Bk.

Downs, Buck. Marijuana Softdrink. 1999. pap. 11.00 (1-890311-02-2, Pub. by Edge Bks) SPD-Small Pr Dist.

Downs, Buck, jt. ed. see Columbia Books Staff.

Downs, Catherine & Kirkbride, James. Test Yourself in Company Law. 105p. 1997. pap. 22.00 (1-85431-629-X, Pub. by Blackstone Pr) Gaunt.

Downs, Cathy. Becoming Modern: Willa Cather's Journalism. LC 98-55337. (Illus.). 176p. 1999. write for info. (1-57591-023-3) Susquehanna U Pr.

Downs, Cathy, jt. ed. see Ball, Desmond.

Downs, Charles. Negotiating Development Assistance: USAID & the Choice Between Public & Private Implementation in Haiti. (Pew Case Studies in International Affairs). 50p. (C). 1994. pap. text 3.50 (1-56927-207-7) Geo U Inst Dplmcy.

— Problem Drinking: How to Help a Friend. 128p. (Orig.). 1990. pap. 7.99 (0-87788-662-8, H Shaw Pubs) Waterbrook Pr.

Downs, Chuck. Over the Line: North Korea's Negotiating Strategy. 340p. 1999. pap. 19.95 (0-8447-4029-2, Pub. by Am Enterprise) Pub Resources Inc.

Downs, Chuck, jt. auth. see Lilley, James R.

Downs, David. The Actor's Eye: Seeing & Being Seen. 192p. 1996. pap. 18.95 (1-55783-212-9) Applause Theatre Bk Pubs.

Downs, David, jt. auth. see Beck, Ken.

Downs, Deeann & Orth, Jennifer. The Big Blue Eggventure: The Hatching of Baby Jay. (Illus.). 32p. (Orig.). (J). 1997. pap. 10.95 (0-9658392-0-6) KR Bk Cnslting.

Downs, Donald A. Cornell '69: Liberalism & the Crisis of the American University. LC 98-32348. (Illus.). 432p. 1999. 35.00 (0-8014-3653-2) Cornell U Pr.

— More Than Victims: Battered Women, the Syndrome Society & the Law. LC 96-16427. 320p. 1996. 27.50 (0-226-16159-5) U Ch Pr.

— The New Politics of Pornography. LC 89-34968. 290p. 1989. lib. bdg. 49.95 (0-226-16162-5) U Ch Pr.

— The New Politics of Pornography. LC 89-34968. 290p. 1989. pap. text 17.95 (0-226-16163-3) U Ch Pr.

Downs, Dorothy. Art of the Florida Seminole & Miccosukee Indians. LC 94-36021. (Illus.). 330p. 1995. 39.95 (0-8130-1335-6) U Press Fla.

— Art of the Florida Seminole & Miccosukee Indians. (Illus.). 319p. 1997. pap. 19.95 (0-8130-1536-7) U Press Fla.

Downs, Earl J., ed. & photos by see Downs, Janet B. & Ritchie, Pat T.

Downs, Florence & Brooten, Dorothy A. New Careers in Nursing. LC 82-18449. (Illus.). 192p. 1985. pap. 12.95 (0-668-05255-4, Arco) Macmillan Gen Ref.

Downs, Florence S. Handbook of Research Methodology. 161p. 1988. 12.95 (0-685-49188-9) Am Journal Nurse.

Downs, Floyd L., jt. ed. see Pfingsten, Ralph.

Downs, Frederick, Jr. Aftermath: A Soldier's Return from Vietnam. 222p. 1997. reprint ed. text 13.00 (0-7881-5014-6) DIANE Pub.

— The Killing Zone: My Life in the Vietnam War. 240p. 1993. pap. 12.95 (0-393-31089-2) Norton.

— No Longer Enemies, Not Yet Friends: An American Soldier Returns to Vietnam. Tobias, Eric, ed. 424p. 1993. reprint ed. mass mkt. 5.99 (0-671-79513-9) PB.

Downs, Frederick. No Longer Enemies, Not Yet Friends: An American Soldier Returns to Vietnam. 352p. 1998. reprint ed. text 23.00 (0-7881-5150-9) DIANE Pub.

Downs, Frederick S. Essays on Christianity in North-East India. LC 95-900022. (C). 1995. 31.00 (81-7387-021-7, Pub. by Indus Pub) S Asia.

***Downs, Gabriel N. & Downs, Michael C.** Marquette. (Images of America Ser.). 1999. pap. 18.99 (0-7385-0056-9) Arcadia Publng.

Downs, George W. Optimal Imperfection? Domestic Uncertainty & Institutions in International Relations. 215p. 1996. pap. text 17.95 (0-691-01625-9, Pub. by Princeton U Pr) Cal Prin Full Svc.

Downs, George W., ed. Collective Security Beyond the Cold War. 300p. (C). 1994. text 47.50 (0-472-10457-8, 10457) U of Mich Pr.

Downs, George W. & Rocke, David M. Optimal Imperfection? Domestic Uncertainty & Institutions in International Relations. 159p. 1996. text 45.00 (0-691-04460-0, Pub. by Princeton U Pr) Cal Prin Full Svc.

— Tacit Bargaining, Arms Races, & Arms Control. LC 90-33589. (Illus.). 256p. (C). 1990. pap. text 20.95 (0-472-06450-9, 06450) U of Mich Pr.

Downs, Harold. Alphabet of Attributes. LC 72-107695. (Essay Index Reprint Ser.). 1977. 20.95 (0-8369-1498-8) Ayer.

Downs, Hugh & Doubleday, Sandy. Greater Phoenix. LC 99-21337. (Urban Tapestry Ser.). (Illus.). 1999. 49.95 (1-881096-69-6) Towery Pub.

D

An Asterisk (*) at the beginning of an entry indicates that the title is appearing for the first time.

Downs, Ian. The Last Mountain: A Life in Papua New Guinea. LC 85-31585. (Illus.). 298p. 1987. text 29.95 (0-7022-1985-1, Pub. by Univ Queensland Pr) Intl Spec Bk.

Downs, Jacques M. The Golden Ghetto: The American Commercial Community at Canton & the Shaping of American China Policy, 1784-1844. LC 96-4167. (Illus.). 496p. (C). 1997. 69.50 (0-934223-35-1) Lehigh Univ Pr.

Downs, James F. The Navajo. (Illus.). 136p. 1984. reprint ed. pap. text 10.50 (0-88133-037-X) Waveland Pr.

— Washo Religion. fac. ed. Rowe, J. H. et al, eds. (University of California Publications: No. 16:9). 26p. (C). 1961. reprint ed. pap. 3.13 (1-55567-150-0) Coyote Press.

Downs, Jane B., jt. auth. see Downs, Robert B.

Downs, Janet, jt. ed. see Williams, Janice L.

Downs, Janet B., ed. The Family Dyer: A Complete Guide for Colouring Every Variety of Shade, on Woolen, Cotton, Linen, & Silk Goods. fac. ed. LC 98-71048. 45p. 1997. reprint ed. pap. 9.95 (0-9664149-1-8) Harrisonburg-Rockingham.

Downs, Janet B. & Ritchie, Pat T. Mills of Rockingham County. Downs, Earl J., ed. & photos by by. (Illus.). 464p. 1997. 35.00 (0-9664149-0-X) Harrisonburg-Rockingham.

— Mills of Rockingham County, Vol. II. Downs, Earl J., ed. & photos by by. LC 98-71290. (Illus.). 688p. 1998. 45.00 (0-9664149-2-6) Harrisonburg-Rockingham.

*Downs, Jill. The Awakening of the Heart: The Soul's Journey from Darkness into Light. 310p. 2000. pap. 14.95 (1-886028-42-7, Pub. by Savage Pr) Bookmen Inc.

Downs, Jim. The Book of Positive Qualities. 640p. (Orig.). 1996. mass mkt. 14.99 (0-446-67140-1) Warner Bks.

Downs, John. Horses. LC 98-43595. (MiniSeries). (Illus.). 192p. 1999. pap. 5.95 (0-7892-0526-2) Abbeville Pr.

Downs, John H. Negotiating with the Russians on Nuclear Arms: Lawyers Making a Difference. LC 96-49100. 294p. 1997. 64.50 (0-7618-0649-0); pap. 41.50 (0-7618-0650-4) U Pr of Amer.

Downs, John P. & Hedley, Fenwick Y., eds. History of Chautauqua County & Its People, 3 vols. (Illus.). 3177p. 1997. reprint ed. lib. bdg. 125.00 (0-8328-6113-8) Higginson Bk Co.

Downs, John W. Sprays of Salt: Reminiscences of a Native Shoaler. (Illus.). 177p. 1944. reprint ed. 24.95 (0-914339-59-1, Pub. by P E Randall Pub) U Pr of New Eng.

Downs, L. Vaughn. The Mightiest of Them All: Memories of Grand Coulee Dam. rev. ed. LC 93-37713. 160p. 1993. pap. 63.00 (0-87262-935-X, ASCE Press) Am Soc Civil Eng.

Downs, Laura L. Manufacturing Inequality: Gender Division in the French & British Metalworking Industries, 1914-1939. (Wilder House Ser.). (Illus.). 344p. 1995. text 42.50 (0-8014-3015-1) Cornell U Pr.

Downs, Laurajean. You're Going to Do What?! Helping You Understand the Homeschool Decision. 176p. (Orig.). 1997. pap. 8.99 (1-888306-17-3, Home School Pr) Holly Hall.

Downs, Linda. Diego Rivera: A Retrospective. (Illus.). 372p. 1998. reprint ed. 85.00 (0-393-04609-5) Norton.

— Diego Rivera: The Detroit Industry Murals. (Illus.). 256p. 1999. 49.95 (0-393-04529-3) Norton.

Downs-Lombardi, Judy, et al. FTCE - Florida Teacher Certification Examination. 300p. 1999. pap. 24.95 (0-87891-091-3) Res & Educ.

Downs, Marilyn. No Reservations Required: A Guide to Dining at Home. 256p. 1992. 16.00 (0-9632850-0-9) Assist Leag IA.

Downs, Marion P., jt. auth. see Northern, Jerry L.

Downs, Marion P., jt. ed. see Roeser, Ross J.

Downs, Martha B. Lest I Forget. 110p. 1997. pap. 7.00 (0-89540-401-X, SB-401) Sun Pub.

*Downs, Martin F. The Silver Trumpet. LC 98-96777. (Illus.). 24p. (J). (ps-6). 1999. 19.95 (0-9668215-0-5) Alicubi Pubns.

Downs, Matthew P. The Notice Concerning the Assessment of Cooperative Joint Ventures Pursuant to Article 85 of the EEC Treaty: An Assessment. (Leuven Law Ser.: Vol. 3). 60p. (Orig.). 1995. pap. 26.00 (90-6186-690-1, Pub. by Leuven Univ) Coronet Bks.

Downs, Michael. James Harrington. LC 77-21418. (Twayne's English Authors Ser.). 152p. 1977. lib. bdg. 20.95 (0-8057-6693-6) Irvington.

Downs, Michael C., jt. auth. see Downs, Gabriel N.

Downs, Norton. Basic Documents in Medieval History. LC 92-24092. (Anvil Ser.). 190p. (C). 1992. reprint ed. pap. 12.50 (0-89464-788-1) Krieger.

Downs, Patrick & Weiss, Debra. So You Think You're Good at Trivia: Take the Official NTN Trivia Challenge. LC 94-21256. 432p. mass mkt. 6.95 (0-89529-631-4, Avery) Penguin Putnam.

Downs, Peggy, et al. The New Older Woman: A Dialogue for the Coming Century. 196p. 1995. pap. 12.95 (0-89087-769-6) Celestial Arts.

Downs, Perry G. Teaching for Spiritual Growth. 224p. 1994. 22.99 (0-310-59370-0) Zondervan.

Downs, Philip G. Classical Music. (C). 1992. text 48.75 (0-393-95191-X) Norton.

Downs, Philip G., ed. Anthology of Classical Music. (Introduction to Music History Ser.). (C). 1992. pap. text 43.25 (0-393-95209-6) Norton.

Downs, R. E., ed. The Political Economy of African Famine, Vol. 9. (Food & Nutrition in History & Anthro Ser.). 389p. 1991. text 130.00 (2-88124-476-9); pap. text 49.00 (2-88124-477-7) Gordon & Breach.

Downs, R. E. & Reyna, Stephen P., eds. Studying War: Anthropological Perspectives. LC 93-32710. (War & Society Ser.: Vol. 2). 220p. 1993. text 47.00 (2-88124-633-8); pap. text 24.00 (2-88124-634-6) Gordon & Breach.

Downs, R. E., jt. ed. see Revna, S. P.

Downs, R. Kansas. Crapshooting Made Simple & Easy. (Illus.). 52p. (Orig.). 1994. pap. 9.95 (0-9650803-0-7) R KANSAS Downs.

Downs, Robert B. Books That Changed the World. expanded ed. 1956. mass mkt. 6.99 (0-451-62698-2, Ment) NAL.

— A Dictionary of Eminent Librarians. LC 90-84054. 256p. 1990. 25.00 (0-9623333-5-2) High Plns WY.

— Landmarks in Science: Hippocrates to Carson. LC 82-154. 305p. 1982. lib. bdg. 26.00 (0-87287-295-5) Libs Unl.

Downs, Robert B. & Downs, Jane B. Journalists of the United States: Biographical Sketches of Print & Broadcast News Shapers from the Late 17th Century to the Present. LC 91-52634. 400p. 1991. lib. bdg. 55.00 (0-89950-549-X) McFarland & Co.

Downs, Robert B. & Jenkins, Frances B., eds. Bibliography: Current State & Future Trends. LC 67-21851. (Illinois Contributions to Librarianship Ser.: No. 8). 619p. reprint ed. pap. 191.90 (0-8357-7172-5, 201901500010) Bks Demand.

Downs, Robert B. & Keller, Clara D. How to Do Library Research. 2nd ed. LC 74-28301. 306p. reprint ed. pap. 94.90 (0-608-11323-9, 202278000029) Bks Demand.

*Downs, Robert C. The Fifth Season. LC 99-45924. 256p. 1999. text 24.00 (1-58243-048-9, Pub. by Counterpt DC) HarpC.

Downs, Robert C. Going Gently. LC 93-70627. 118p. 1993. reprint ed. pap. 11.00 (1-881090-00-0) Confluence Pr.

— Peoples. LC 73-10704. 1974. 6.95 (0-672-51900-3, Bobbs) Macmillan.

Downs, Robert C. S. White Mama. 1980. mass mkt. 1.95 (0-345-28803-3) Ballantine Pub Grp.

Downs, Robert J., jt. auth. see Smith, Lyman B.

Downs, Roger M., et al, eds. Visions of Aesthetics, the Environment, & Development: The Legacy of Joachim F. Wohlwill. 352p. 1991. text 69.95 (0-8058-1000-5) L Erlbaum Assocs.

*Downs, Sandra. Earth's Fiery Fury. LC 00-24956. (Exploring Planet Earth Ser.). (Illus.). 2000. lib. bdg. write for info. (0-7613-1413-X) TFC Bks NY.

— The Earth's Hidden Treasures. LC 98-48502. (Earth Science Ser.). 64p. (J). (gr. 6-9). 1999. 23.40 (0-7613-1411-3) TFC Bks NY.

— Shaping the Earth. LC 99-45541. (Exploring Planet Earth Ser.). 64p. (YA). (gr. 6-8). 2000. lib. bdg. 23.40 (0-7613-1414-8) TFC Bks NY.

Downs, Sandra. When the Earth Moves. LC 99-23728. (Earth Science Ser.). 64p. (J). (gr. 5-8). 1999. 23.40 (0-7613-1412-1) TFC Bks NY.

Downs, Shirley. Streamlining & Integrating Human Resource Development for Adults. Feinstein, Gerry & Glass, Karen, eds. 51p. (Orig.). 1991. pap. text 15.00 (1-55877-134-4) Natl Governor.

Downs, Sylvia. Learning at Work. 130p. 1995. pap. 15.95 (0-7494-1526-6, Kogan Pg Educ) Stylus Pub VA.

Downs, T. Anthony. Textbook on Contract. 360p. (C). 1987. 160.00 (1-85185-076-7, Pub. by Blackstone Pr) St Mut.

— Textbook on Contract. 360p. (C). 1991. 40.00 (1-85431-150-6, Pub. by Blackstone Pr) Gaunt.

— Textbook on Contract. 3rd ed. 405p. 1993. pap. 36.00 (1-85431-285-5, Pub. by Blackstone Pr) Gaunt.

— Textbook on Contract. 4th ed. LC 97-134766. 464p. 1995. pap. 32.00 (1-85431-453-X, Pub. by Blackstone Pr) Gaunt.

Downs, T. Nelson. The Art of Magic. Hilliard, John N., ed. 352p. 1980. reprint ed. pap. 7.95 (0-486-24005-3) Dover.

— Classic Coin Tricks: An Unabridged Reprint of Modern Coin Manipulation. rev. unabridged ed. LC 99-14079. (Illus.). 256p. 1999. pap. text 9.95 (0-486-40616-4) Dover.

Downs, Theodore. Fossil Vertebrates of Southern California. LC 68-26065. (California Natural History Guides Ser.: No. 23). (Illus.). 69p. reprint ed. pap. 30.00 (0-608-17953-1, 202904200058) Bks Demand.

*Downs, Thomas. Installing Debian GNU/Linux. 208p. 1999. pap. 24.99 (0-672-31745-1, Waite Grp Pr) Sams.

Downs, Tim. Conflict Happens: The Art of Apology & Forgiveness. rev. ed. (Life Skills Ser.). (Illus.). 4p. (C). 1996. teacher ed., ring bd. 1.25 (1-57334-028-6, 742-003t); student ed., ring bd. 3.25 (1-57334-027-8, 742-003s) WSN Pr.

— Dealing with Setbacks: Detours on the Road to Success. (Life Skills Ser.). (Illus.). 4p. (C). 1996. teacher ed., ring bd. 1.25 (1-57334-022-7, 742-102t); student ed., ring bd. 3.25 (1-57334-021-9, 742-102s) WSN Pr.

*Downs, Tim. Finding Common Ground: How to Communicate with Those Outside the Christian Community. 1999. pap. 11.99 (0-8024-4096-7) Moody.

Downs, Tim. It's about Sex: Creating an Environment for Sex. (Life Skills Ser.). (Illus.). 4p. (C). 1994. teacher ed., ring bd. 1.25 (1-885702-53-1, 742-004t); student ed., ring bd. 3.25 (1-885702-52-3, 742-004s) WSN Pr.

— The Laylo Papers: The Complete Guide to Relationships. (Illus.). 136p. (Orig.). Date not set. pap. 8.99 (0-9623125-0-9) T Downs.

— Mad about You: Dealing with Anger in Relationships. rev. ed. 4p. (C). 1995. teacher ed., ring bd. 1.25 (1-57334-011-1, 742-002t); student ed., ring bd. 3.25 (1-57334-010-3, 742-002s) WSN Pr.

— Overcoming Obstacles: Barriers to Success. (Life Skills Ser.). (Illus.). 4p. (C). 1996. teacher ed., ring bd. 1.25 (1-57334-018-9, 742-101t); student ed., ring bd. 3.25 (1-57334-017-0, 742-101s) WSN Pr.

Downs, Tim & Kramer, Kent. When Worlds Collide: Communication Between the Sexes. (Life Skills Ser.). (Illus.). 4p. (C). 1994. teacher ed., ring bd. 1.25 (1-885702-19-1, 742-010t); student ed., ring bd. 3.25 (1-885702-18-3, 742-010s) WSN Pr.

Downs, Tim, et al. Reconcilable Differences: How Are Men & Women Different? (Life Skills Ser.). (Illus.). 5p. (C). 1995. teacher ed., ring bd. 1.25 (1-885702-17-5 742-009t); student ed., ring bd. 3.25 (1-885702-16-7, 742-009s) WSN Pr.

Downs, Timothy. Organizational Communication. (C). 2001. 40.00 (0-205-26523-5, Macmillan Coll) P-H.

*Downs, Tom & Edge, John T. New Orleans. 2nd ed. (Illus.). 288p. 2000. pap. 15.95 (0-86442-782-4) Lonely Planet.

Downs, Tom & Wheeler, Tony. Lonely Planet San Francisco: City Guide. 2nd ed. (Lonely Planet City Guides). (Illus.). 256p. 1999. pap. text 15.95 (0-86442-556-2) Lonely Planet.

Downs, W. G., jt. auth. see Theiler, Max.

Downs, W. Scott, jt. auth. see Carroll, Michael.

Downs, William M., jt. auth. see Russin, Robin.

Downs, Williams M. Coalition Government, Subnational Style: Multiparty Politics in Europe's Regional Parliaments. LC 97-26776. (Parliaments & Legislatures Ser.). 336p. 1997. text 52.50 (0-8142-0747-2); pap. text 19.95 (0-8142-0748-0) Ohio St U Pr.

Downsbrough, Peter. Around. LC 78-65770. (Illus.). 1978. pap. text 4.50 (0-9602192-0-X) P Downsbrough.

— As to Place. LC 78-65771. (Illus.). 1979. pap. 5.00 (0-9602192-1-8) P Downsbrough.

Downswell, P., jt. auth. see Claridge, M.

Downton, A. C. Computadores & Microprocesadores, Componentes & Sistemas. (SPA.). 304p. (C). 1993. pap. text 14.33 (0-201-60137-0) Addison-Wesley.

Downton, Andy C. Computers & Microprocessors. 3rd ed. 256p. 1992. pap. 26.95 (0-442-31536-8) Chapman & Hall.

Downton, Andy C., ed. Engineering the Human-Computer Interface. LC 92-24601. (Essex Series in Telecommunications & Information Systems). 1993. write for info. (0-07-707727-X) McGraw.

Downton, James, jt. auth. see Wehr, Paul.

Downton, Joanna H. Falls in the Elderly. 160p. 1993. pap. text 31.95 (0-340-54848-7, Pub. by E A) OUP.

Downum, Christian E., et al. A Class III Archaeological Survey of the Phase B Corridor, Tucson Aqueduct, Central Arizona Project: Late Archaic; Late Pioneer, Colonial, Sedentary, & Early Classic Period Tucson Basin Hohokam; & Sobaipuri Occupation in the Avra Valley, Southern Arizona. (Archaeological Ser.: No. 168). (Illus.). 248p. 1986. pap. 14.95 (1-889747-40-8) Ariz St Mus.

Downum, K. R., et al. Phytochemical Potential of Tropical Plants. (Recent Advances in Phytochemistry Ser.: Vol. 27). (Illus.). 308p. (C). 1993. text 95.00 (0-306-44527-1, Kluwer Plenum) Kluwer Academic.

Downum, Kelsey R., jt. ed. see Heitz, James R.

*Downward, Michael. Logic & Declarative Language. 1998. pap. text 49.95 (0-7484-0802-9) Tay Francis Ltd.

— Logic & Declarative Language, 1 vol. LC 98-179219. 1998. 85.00 (0-7484-0803-7) Taylor & Francis.

Downward, Paul. Pricing Theory in Post-Keynesian Economics: A Realist Approach. LC 98-6257. (New Directions in Modern Economics Ser.). 240p. 1999. 90.00 (1-85898-791-1) E Elgar.

*Downward, Paul & Dawson, Alistair. The Economics of Professional Team Sports. LC 00-29116. 2000. pap. write for info. (0-415-20874-2) Routledge.

Dowood, N. J., ed. see Khaldun, Ibn.

Dowrick, Brian, jt. auth. see Thomas, Meryl.

*Dowrick, Christopher & Frith, Lucy. General Practice & Ethics. LC 98-38318. (Professional Ethics Ser.). 1999. write for info. (0-415-16498-2); pap. write for info. (0-415-16499-0) Routledge.

Dowrick, David J. Earthquake Resistant Design: For Engineers & Architects. 2nd ed. LC 87-2030. 540p. 1988. 230.00 (0-471-91503-3) Wiley.

Dowrick, Peter W. Practical Guide to Using Video in the Behavioral Sciences. LC 90-19418. 335p. 1991. 125.00 (0-471-63613-4) Wiley.

Dowrick, Peter W. & Biggs, Simon J., eds. Using Video: Psychological & Social Applications. LC 82-20058. (Illus.). 251p. reprint ed. pap. 77.90 (0-7837-6372-7, 204608400010) Bks Demand.

Dowrick, Stephanie. Forgiveness & Other Acts of Love. LC 97-17814. 304p. 1997. 23.95 (0-393-04545-5) Norton.

— Forgiveness & Other Acts of Love. 368p. 1998. pap. 14.00 (0-393-31820-6, Norton Paperbks) Norton.

— Intimacy & Solitude. 1994. 21.00 (0-393-03627-8) Norton.

— The Intimacy & Solitude Workbook. 288p. 1996. pap. 12.50 (0-393-31364-6, Norton Paperbks) Norton.

— Intimacy & Solitude. 352p. 1996. pap. 13.95 (0-393-31361-1, Norton Paperbks) Norton.

Dowrick, Stephanie & Parkin, Jane, eds. Speaking with the Sun. 228p. 1991. pap. 12.95 (0-04-442296-2, Pub. by Allen & Unwin Pty) Paul & Co Pubs.

Dowrick, Steve, ed. Economic Approaches to Innovation. LC 95-5532. 240p. (C). 1995. 100.00 (1-85898-248-0) E Elgar.

Dowry Cookie Company Staff. The Dowry Cookbook. (Illus.). 100p. 1996. 29.95 (0-9654328-0-7) Dowry Cookie.

Dows, A. M. Dows or Dowse Family in America: A Genealogy of the Descendants of Lawrence Dows, Including the Genealogy of the Masterman Family, Two Branches of the Newman Family, a Branch of the Morse Family, & Many Genealogical Lines of Other Families, 1642-1890. (Illus.). 348p. 1995. reprint ed. pap. 51.00 (0-8328-4776-3); reprint ed. lib. bdg. 61.00 (0-8328-4775-5) Higginson Bk Co.

*Dowse. Biology: The Living Science. 990p. 2000. pap. text 48.00 (0-536-01821-9) Pearson Custom.

*Dowse, Eileen. The Naked Manager: Developing Open & Authentic Relationships. LC 98-19059. (Illus.). 130p. 1998. pap. 12.95 (1-886939-24-1, Pub. by OakHill Pr VA) ACCESS Pubs Network.

Dowse, R. E., ed. see Hardie, James K.

Dowse, Robert E. & Hughes, John A. Political Sociology. 2nd ed. LC 88-672451. 410p. reprint ed. pap. 127.10 (0-7837-4732-2, 204451700004) Bks Demand.

Dowsett, C. J., tr. see Kalankatuarci, Moses.

Dowsett, D. & Kennedy, P. Physics of Diagnostic Imaging. (Illus.). 520p. 1997. text 52.50 (0-412-46060-2, Pub. by E A) OUP.

Dowsett, D. J., et al. MCQs in the Physics of Diagnostic Imaging. (An Arnold Publication). 368p. 1999. pap. text 24.50 (0-340-74088-4, Pub. by E A) OUP.

*Dowsett, Dick. God, That's Not Fair! Understanding Eternal Punishment & the Christian's Urgent Mission. 134p. 1998. reprint ed. mass mkt. 9.99 (1-85078-284-9, Pub. by O M Pubng) OM Literature.

Dowsett, G. W., jt. ed. see Connell, R. W.

Dowsett, Gary, jt. auth. see Ariss, Robert.

Dowsett, Gary W. Practicing Desire: Homosexual Sex in Era of AIDS. LC 96-10879. 1996. 49.50 (0-8047-2711-2); pap. 16.95 (0-8047-2712-0) Stanford U Pr.

Dowsett, M., jt. auth. see Howell, A.

Dowsett, M. G. & Parker, E. H., eds. The Technology & Physics of Molecular Beam Epitaxy. (Illus.). 706p. (C). 1985. text 180.00 (0-306-41860-6, Kluwer Plenum) Kluwer Academic.

Dowsey, Stuart, tr. see Cho Chikun, Nine-Dan.

Dowsing. Computers Logic Architecture & Communication. 2nd ed. (ITCP-UK Computer Science Ser.). 2000. pap. 29.99 (1-85032-226-0) Thomson Learn.

Dowsing, R. D. & Woodhams, F. W. D. Computers: From Logic Architecture. (ITCP-UK Computer Science Ser.). (C). 1989. mass mkt. 39.95 (0-412-44650-2) Chapman & Hall.

Dowson, D. Tribology for Energy Conservation: Proceedings of the 24th Leeds-Lyon Symposium on Tribology, Held in the Imperial College of Science, Technology, & Medicine, London U. K., 4th-6th September, 1997. LC 98-24634. 1998. 215.50 (0-444-50033-2) Elsevier.

Dowson, D., et al, eds. Dissipative Processes in Tribology: Proceedings of the 20th Leeds-Lyon Symposium on Tribology, Held in the Laboratoire de Mecanique des Contacts, Institut National des Sciences Appliquees, Lyon, France, 7-10 September, 1993. LC 94-18428. (Tribology Ser.: Vol. 27). 586p. 1994. 250.50 (0-444-81764-6) Elsevier.

— Elastohydrodynamics 1996: Fundamentals & Applications in Lubrication & Traction. LC 97-23440. (Tribology Ser.: Vol. 32). 770p. 1997. 284.50 (0-444-82809-5) Elsevier.

Dowson, D., ed. see Leeds-Lyons Symposium on Tribology Staff.

Dowson, D., ed. see Taylor, C. M., et al.

Dowson, Duncan, et al, eds. Mechanics of Coatings: Proceedings of the 16th Leeds-Lyon Symposium on Tribology, Lyon, France, 5-8 September, 1989. (Tribology Ser.: Vol. 17). xii, 498p. 1990. 250.50 (0-444-88676-1) Elsevier.

Dowson, Duncan & Higginson, Gordon R. Elasto-Hydrodynamics Lubrication: SI Edition. 2nd ed. 1977. 108.00 (0-08-021303-0, Pub. by Pergamon Repr) Franklin.

Dowson, Ernest. The Letters of Ernest Dowson. Flower, Desmond & Maas, Henry, eds. LC 67-29136. (Illus.). 470p. 1975. 65.00 (0-8386-6747-3) Fairleigh Dickinson.

— Verses: Decorations. LC 93-31596. (Decadents, Symbolists, Anti-Decadents Ser.). 1994. 48.00 (1-85477-142-6) Continuum.

Dowson, Ernest C. Complete Poems. 1988. reprint ed. lib. bdg. 59.00 (0-7812-0263-9) Rprt Serv.

— Complete Poems. 1980. reprint ed. 49.00 (0-403-00576-0) Scholarly.

— Dilemmas: Stories & Studies in Sentiment. LC 71-157774. (Short Story Index Reprint Ser.). 1977. reprint ed. 16.95 (0-8369-3886-0) Ayer.

— Poetical Works. 1988. reprint ed. lib. bdg. 49.00 (0-317-90186-9) Rprt Serv.

— Poetical Works. 1980. reprint ed. 49.00 (0-403-00948-0) Scholarly.

Dowson, Ernest C., tr. see De Laclos, Choderlos.

Dowson, Godfrey & Kaplan, Stuart R. Hermetic Tarot. 1980. pap. 15.00 (0-913866-92-X, HM78) US Games Syst.

Dowson, Jane, ed. Women's Poetry of the 1930s: A Critical Anthology. LC 95-14810. 224p. (C). (gr. 13). 1995. 85.00 (0-415-13095-6); pap. 20.99 (0-415-13096-4) Routledge.

Dowson, Jane, jt. auth. see Cornford, Frances.

Dowson, Jane, jt. auth. see Davison, Jon.

Dowson, John. A Classical Dictionary of Hindu Mythology & Religion. 411p. (C). 1987. reprint ed. 27.00 (0-8364-2089-6, Pub. by Usha) S Asia.

Dowson, John, ed. History of India, As Told by Its Own Historians, 8 vols. 1996. 120.00 (81-7536-051-8, Pub. by Low Price) S Asia.

Dowson, John, ed. see Elliot, Henry M.

Dowson, Jonathan H. & Grounds, Adrian T. Personality Disorders: Recognition & Clinical Management. (Illus.). 414p. (C). 1996. text 95.00 (0-521-45049-7) Cambridge U Pr.

Dowson, Mary E. & Haggard, A. M. Michael Fairless. LC 76-30785. (Studies in Women's Rights: No. 51). 1977. lib. bdg. 57.00 (0-8383-2158-5) M S G Haskell Hse.

D

Dowson, Thomas A. Rock Engravings of Southern Africa. (Illus.). 140p. 1994. 57.50 (*1-86814-120-9*) Ind U Pr.

Dowson, Thomas A., jt. ed. see Lewis-Williams, David.

Dowson, Tracy D. Equi-Marketing: Marketing Principles Effectively Applied to the Horse Industry. Sullivan, Olive, ed. (Illus.). 141p. (Orig.). 1991. pap. text 14.95 (*0-9630558-7-9*) Pica Pub.

Dowswell, P. Tales of Real Escape. (Real Tales Ser.). (Illus.). 64p. (YA). (gr. 7-12). 1995. pap. 8.95 (*0-7460-1669-7*, Usborne) EDC.

Dowswell, P. Tales of Real Escape. (Real Tales Ser.). (Illus.). 64p. (YA). (gr. 7 up). 1999. lib. bdg. 16.95 (*0-88110-724-7*, Usborne) EDC.

Dowswell, P. & Claridge, M. Science Quizbook. (Quizbooks Ser.). (Illus.). 32p. (J). (gr. 4 up). 1994. text 7.95 (*0-7460-1357-4*, Usborne) EDC.

— Science Quizbook. (Quizbooks Ser.). (Illus.). 32p. (J). (gr. 4 up). 1999. lib. bdg. 15.95 (*0-88110-652-6*, Usborne) EDC.

Dowswell, Paul. Egyptian Echo. (Newspaper Histories Ser.). (Illus.). 32p. (J). (gr. 5-9). 1996. lib. bdg. 14.95 (*0-88110-903-7*, Usborne) EDC.

— Egyptian Echo. (Newspaper Histories Ser.). (Illus.). 32p. (J). (gr. 5 up). 1996. pap. 6.95 (*0-7460-2751-6*, Usborne) EDC.

***Dowswell, Paul.** First Encyclopedia of Animals. (Illus.). 64p. (ps-3). 2000. lib. bdg. 17.95 (*1-58086-275-6*) EDC.

— Genetics: The Impact on Our Lives. LC 00-33279. (21st Century Debates Ser.). 2001. write for info. (*0-7398-3174-7*) Raintree Steck-V.

Dowswell, Paul. Greek Gazette. (Newspaper Histories Ser.). (Illus.). 32p. (Orig.). (YA). (gr. 5-9). 1997. pap. 6.95 (*0-7460-2755-9*, Usborne) EDC.

— Greek Gazette. (Newspaper Histories Ser.). (Illus.). 32p. (Orig.). (YA). (gr. 5 up). 1997. lib. bdg. 14.95 (*0-88110-927-4*, Usborne) EDC.

— Medieval Messenger. (Newspaper Histories Ser.). (Illus.). 32p. (J). (gr. 5-9). 1997. pap. 6.95 (*0-7460-2749-4*, Usborne) EDC.

— Medieval Messenger. (Newspaper Histories Ser.). (Illus.). 32p. (J). (gr. 5 up). 1997. lib. bdg. 14.95 (*0-88110-904-5*, Usborne) EDC.

— Roman Record. (Newspaper Histories Ser.). (Illus.). 32p. (J). (gr. 5 up). 1998. pap. 6.95 (*0-7460-2753-2*, Usborne) EDC.

— Roman Record. (Newspaper Histories Ser.). (Illus.). 32p. (YA). (gr. 5 up). 1998. lib. bdg. 14.95 (*0-88110-976-2*, Usborne) EDC.

— Tales of Real Adventures. (Real Tales Ser.). (Illus.). 192p. (YA). (gr. 7-12). 1996. 19.95 (*0-7460-2362-6*, Usborne) EDC.

— Tales of Real Heroism. (Real Tales Ser.). (Illus.). 64p. (YA). (gr. 7 up). 1996. pap. 8.95 (*0-7460-2357-X*, Usborne); lib. bdg. 15.95 (*0-88110-849-9*, Usborne) EDC.

— Tales of Real Survival. (Real Tales Ser.). (Illus.). 48p. (YA). (gr. 7-12). 1995. pap. 8.95 (*0-7460-1725-1*, Usborne) EDC.

***Dowswell, Paul.** Tales of Real Survival. (Real Tales Ser.). (Illus.). 64p. (YA). (gr. 7 up). 1999. lib. bdg. 16.95 (*0-88110-779-4*, Usborne) EDC.

Dowswell, Paul. Viking Invader. (Newspaper Histories Ser.). (Illus.). 64p. (J). (gr. 5-9). 1998. pap. 6.95 (*0-7460-2957-8*, Usborne) EDC.

***Dowswell, Paul, ed.** First Encyclopedia of Animals. (First Encyclopedia Ser.). (Illus.). 64p. (ps-3). 2000. pap. 9.95 (*0-7460-3400-8*) Usbrne Pbng UK.

Dowswell, Paul & Fleming, Fergus. Stone Age Sentinel. (Newspaper Histories Ser.). (Illus.). 32p. (YA). (gr. 5 up). 1998. lib. bdg. 14.95 (*1-58086-135-0*, Usborne) EDC.

— Viking Invader. (Newspaper Histories Ser.). (Illus.). 64p. (YA). (gr. 5 up). 1998. lib. bdg. 14.95 (*0-88110-972-X*, Usborne) EDC.

Dowswell, Paul, jt. auth. see Fleming, Fergus.

Dowswell, Therese, jt. auth. see Hewison, Jenny.

Dowty, Alan. Closed Borders. LC 86-23399. 272p. 1987. 40.00 (*0-300-03824-0*) Yale U Pr.

Dowty, Alan. Closed Borders: The Contemporary Assault on Freedom of Movement. LC 86-23399. 287p. (C). 1989. reprint ed. pap. 20.00 (*0-300-04498-4*) Yale U Pr.

— The Jewish State: A Century Later. LC 97-6603. 371p. 1998. 35.00 (*0-520-20941-9*, Pub. by U CA Pr) Cal Prin Full Svc.

Dowty, Daryl, ed. see Blanchette, Christopher J.

Dowty, David, et al. Introduction to Montague Semantics. 324p. (C). 1980. lib. bdg. 97.00 (*90-277-1141-0*, D Reidel) Kluwer Academic.

Dowty, David R. Word Meaning & Montague Grammar. (Synthese Language Library: No. 7). 432p. 1979. pap. text 39.00 (*90-277-1009-0*, D Reidel); lib. bdg. 117.50 (*90-277-1008-2*, D Reidel) Kluwer Academic.

Dowty, David R., et al. Introduction to Montague Semantics. (Studies in Linguistics & Philosophy: No. 11). 324p. 1980. pap. text 43.00 (*90-277-1142-9*) Kluwer Academic.

Dowty, Robert R. Rebirth of the Jupiter & 119: Building the Replica Locomotives at Golden Spike. Houk, Rose & Priehs, T. J., eds. LC 94-66380. 52p. 1994. pap. 6.95 (*1-877856-43-6*) SW Pks Mnmts.

Dox, I. G. & Melloni, J. L. Melloni's Illustrated Dictionary of Obstetrics & Gynecology. LC 99-56573. (Illus.). 402p. 2000. pap. 39.95 (*1-85070-710-3*) Prthnon Pub.

***Dox, Ida G. & Melloni, B. John.** Melloni's Illustrated Medical Dictionary. 4th ed. (Illus.). 550p. 2001. 39.95 (*1-85070-094-X*) Prthnon Pub.

Dox, Ida G., et al. HarperCollins Illustrated Medical Dictionary. LC 92-53299. 592p. 1993. pap. 27.50 (*0-06-273142-4*, Harper Ref) HarpC.

Dox, Ida G., jt. auth. see Melloni, B. John.

Dox, Thurston J., compiled by. American Oratorios & Cantatas: A Catalog of Works Written in the United States from Colonial Times to 1985, 2 vols. LC 85-27629. 1330p. 1986. 105.00 (*0-8108-1861-2*) Scarecrow.

Doxey, Denise. Ancient Egypt Explorer's Kit. (Illus.). 64p. (J). 1996. 18.95 (*1-56138-750-9*) Running Pr.

Doxey, Denise M. Egyptian Non-Royal Epithets in the Middle Kingdom: A Social & Historical Analysis. LC 98-36391. (Probleme der Agyptologie Ser.). 1998. write for info. (*90-04-11077-1*) Brill Academic Pubs.

Doxey, W. S. A Winter in the Woods. (Illus.). pap. 3.00 (*0-686-12232-1*) Doxey.

— A Winter in the Woods. 1975. 4.00 (*0-685-67936-5*) Windless Orchard.

Doxey, William. Cousins to the Kudzu. Novel. LC 84-21317. 255p. 1985. 18.95 (*0-8071-1225-9*) La State U Pr.

Doxford, Colin, jt. auth. see Tampke, Jurgen.

***Doxiadis, Apostolos K.** Uncle Petros & Goldbachs Conjecture: A Novel of Mathematical Obsession. 208p. 2000. 23.95 (*1-58234-067-6*) Bloomsbury Pubg.

Doxiadis, C. A. Anthropopolis: City for Human Development. (Illus.). 398p. (C). 1975. pap. 7.00 (*0-393-08737-9*) Norton.

Doxiadis, Calliope. Visions of the King. 1966. pap. 10.00 (*0-685-62614-8*) Atlantis Edns.

Doxiadis, Euphrosyne. The Mysterious Fayum Portraits: Faces from Ancient Egypt. (Illus.). 256p. 1995. 85.00 (*0-8109-3331-4*, Pub. by Abrams) Time Warner.

Doxiadis, Spyros, ed. Early Influences Shaping the Individual. (NATO ASI Series A, Life Sciences: Vol. 160). (Illus.). 348p. 1989. 89.50 (*0-306-43140-8*, Plenum Trade) Perseus Pubng.

— Ethical Issues in Preventive Medicine. 120p. 1985. lib. bdg. 104.50 (*90-247-3232-8*, Pub. by M Nijhoff) Kluwer Academic.

Doxiadis, Spyros, ed. Ethics in Health Education. 230p. 1990. 325.00 (*0-471-92606-X*) Wiley.

Doxiadis, Spyros, et al, eds. Ethical Dilemmas in Health Promotion. LC 86-24573. 248p. reprint ed. pap. 76.90 (*0-7837-6373-5*, 204608500010) Bks Demand.

Doxon, Lynn E. High Desert Yards & Gardens. LC 98-47385. (Illus.). 230p. 1999. 29.95 (*0-8263-1909-2*) U of NM Pr.

Doxon, Lynn Ellen. High Desert Yards & Gardens. LC 98-47385. (Illus.). 230p. 1999. pap. 14.95 (*0-8263-1910-6*) U of NM Pr.

Doxtater, Dennis. Architecture, Ritual Practice & Co-Determination in the Swedish Office. (Ethnoscapes Ser.). 400p. 1994. 85.95 (*1-85628-558-8*, Pub. by Avebry) Ashgate Pub Co.

Doy, Gen. Black Visual Culture. 258p. 2000. pap. 24.50 (*1-86064-382-5*) St Martin.

— Materializing Art History. LC 98-218568. (Materializing Culture Ser.). (Illus.). 256p. 1998. 55.00 (*1-85973-933-4*, Pub. by Berg Pubs); pap. 19.50 (*1-85973-938-5*, Pub. by Berg Pubs) NYU Pr.

— Seeing & Consciousness: Marxism, Gender, & Representation. LC 94-33342. 1995. 49.50 (*0-85496-960-8*); pap. 19.50 (*1-85973-017-5*) Berg Pubs.

— Women & Visual Culture in Early Nineteenth-Century France, 1800-1852. LC 97-15449. (Illus.). 256p. 1998. 85.00 (*0-7185-0148-9*) Bks Intl VA.

Doyal, Guy T., jt. auth. see Friedman, Ronald J.

Doyal, Len & Gough, Ian. A Theory of Human Need. LC 91-18024. (Critical Perspectives Ser.). 350p. 1991. pap. 18.95 (*0-89862-419-3*); lib. bdg. 47.50 (*0-89862-413-4*) Guilford Pubns.

Doyal, Len & Harris, Roger. Empiricism, Explanation & Rationality: An Introduction to the Philosophy of the Social Sciences. 256p. 1987. text 44.00 (*0-7100-9646-1*, Routledge Thoemms) Routledge.

Doyal, Lesley. What Makes Women Sick: Gender & the Political Economy of Health. 320p. 1995. text 50.00 (*0-8135-2206-4*); pap. text 15.95 (*0-8135-2207-2*) Rutgers U Pr.

— Women & Health Services: An Agenda for Change. LC 98-4891. 1998. 89.00 (*0-335-20137-7*); pap. 26.95 (*0-335-20136-9*) OpUniv Pr.

Doyal, Lesley, et al, eds. AIDS: Setting a Feminist Agenda. LC 94-4132. (Gender & Society Ser.). 1994. write for info. (*0-7484-0162-8*, Pub. by Tay Francis Ltd) Taylor & Francis.

— AIDS: Setting a Feminist Agenda. LC 94-4132. (Gender & Society Ser.). 1994. pap. 29.95 (*0-7484-0163-6*) Taylor & Francis.

Doyal, Lesley & Pennell. The Political Economy of Health. (C). pap. 19.95 (*0-86104-074-0*, Pub. by Pluto GBR) Stylus Pub VA.

Doyal, Lesley, jt. auth. see Watson, Sophie.

Doyama, M., et al, eds. Advanced Materials '93, Pt. 1. 1228p. 1995. 580.25 (*0-444-81996-7*) Elsevier.

Doyama, Masao & Sho Yoshida, eds. Progress in the Study of Point Defects. LC 78-303785. (Illus.). 448p. 1977. reprint ed. pap. 138.90 (*0-608-01196-7*, 206188500001) Bks Demand.

Doychak, Joseph, ed. see Workshop on the Oxidation of High-Temperature Inte.

Doycheff, James. Excuse Me, I'm Going to Kill My Hairdresser! A Humorous Survival Guide for Women Who Visit Hair Salons. LC 93-79838. 100p. 1993. pap. 14.95 (*0-9638037-9-4*) Gadoda Adanta.

Doye, Peter. Typologie der Testaufgaben fur den Dt. Unterricht. 223p. 1988. 26.25 (*3-468-49437-8*) Langenscheidt.

***Doyel, Alice Weiss.** No More Job Interviews! Self-Employment Strategies for People with Disabilities. LC 00-23414. 184p. 2000. pap. 29.95 (*1-883302-36-6*) Trning Res.

Doyel, David E., ed. see Haury, Emil W.

Doyel, Gregg. Coach K: Building the Duke Dynasty: the Story of Mike Krzyzewski & the Winning Tradition at Duke University. LC 99-37819. (Illus.). 236p. 1999. pap. 14.95 (*1-886110-86-7*, Pub. by Addax Pubng) Midpt Trade.

***Doyen, Barbara Hartsock.** Back to Protein: The Low Carb/No Carb Meat Cookbook. LC 00-35328. (Illus.). 280p. 2000. 24.95 (*0-87131-912-8*) M Evans.

Doyen, G. & Drakova, D. The Physical Principles of STM & AFM Operation. (Illus.). 250p. 1996. 80.00 (*3-05-501616-5*, Pub. by Akademie Verlag) Wiley.

***Doyen, Gerold.** Physical Principles of STM & AFM Operation. 350p. 2000. 124.95 (*3-527-40037-0*) Wiley.

Doyle. Ancient Regime. 1996. text 11.95 (*0-333-38696-5*, Pub. by Macmillan) St Martin.

— Drugs & Society. LC 97-75312. (C). 1998. pap. text 16.36 (*0-395-90253-3*) HM.

— Exito Commercial. (C). 1996. pap. text 36.50 (*0-15-504251-3*) Harcourt Coll Pubs.

— Foodborne Bacterial Pathogens. (Food Science & Technology Ser.: Vol. 31). (Illus.). 816p. 1989. text 225.00 (*0-8247-7866-9*) Dekker.

— Jansenism LC 99-29986. 2000. pap. 11.95 (*0-312-22676-4*) St Martin.

— The Male Experience. 4th ed. 2001. 23.00 (*0-697-25284-1*, WCB McGr Hill) McGrw-H Hghr Educ.

— Nursing Assistant: Nursing Procedures Approach. 5th ed. (Home Care Aide Ser.). 1989. wbk. ed. 18.95 (*0-8273-3369-2*) Delmar.

— Nursing Assistant: Nursing Procedures Approach. 5th ed. (Home Care Aide Ser.). 1989. pap. 25.95 (*0-8273-3370-6*) Delmar.

***Doyle.** Process Control Modules: A Software Laboratory for Control Design. LC 99-56390. 174p. 1999. pap. text 49.00 (*0-13-021107-9*) P-H.

Doyle. Run with the Tigers. (J). 1998. write for info. (*0-7352-0027-0*) S&S Childrens.

— Sex & Gender. 3rd ed. 1994. teacher ed. 9.68 (*0-697-12736-2*) McGraw.

— Study Guide. 2nd ed. LC 94-30741. 1994. pap. text, student ed. 19.00 (*0-13-148578-4*) P-H.

Doyle, jt. auth. see Loftus.

Doyle, A. Alfreda's Academy - Curriculum Directory. (Illus.). 20p. 1999. ring bd. 48.95 (*1-56820-396-9*) Story Time.

— Alfreda's Coloring Books: A Directory to Reproduce. (Illus.). 62p. (J). (gr. 4-9). 1998. ring bd. 39.95 (*1-56820-247-4*) Story Time.

— Alfreda's Cooking School Cookbook. 50p. 1997. ring bd., wbk. ed. 42.95 (*1-890928-33-X*) Frieda Carrol.

— Alfreda's Reader's Theatre: Be Somebody Be Yourself. (Illus.). (J). Date not set. spiral bd. 15.95 (*1-56820-363-2*) Story Time.

— Alfreda's Reader's Theatre: Comedy Club. (Illus.). (J). Date not set. spiral bd. 19.95 (*1-56820-362-4*) Story Time.

— Alfreda's Reader's Theatre: Dialogues. (Illus.). (J). Date not set. spiral bd. 19.95 (*1-56820-361-6*) Story Time.

— Alfreda's Reader's Theatre: Public Transportation. (Illus.). (J). Date not set. spiral bd. 15.95 (*1-56820-360-8*) Story Time.

— Alfreda's Readers Theatre: Story Plays That Rhyme. (Illus.). 38p. (J). (gr. 5-8). 1998. ring bd., wbk. ed. 19.95 (*1-56820-356-X*) Story Time.

— Alfreda's Reader's Theatre - Barter 3: Theatre. 50p. 1998. 10.95 (*1-56820-358-6*) Story Time.

— Alfreda's Reader's Theatre - Black English: Chocolate Slang. 50p. 1998. 10.95 (*1-56820-359-4*) Story Time.

— Alfreda's Reader's Theatre- Recycling: Theatre. 50p. 1998. 10.95 (*1-56820-357-8*) Story Time.

— As Long As the Sun Do Shine. (Illus.). 20p. 1999. pap. 9.95 (*1-56820-392-6*) Story Time.

— Black American Food Festival - A Story with Recipes. 23p. (Orig.). (J). (gr. 3-7). 1997. pap. text 10.95 (*1-56820-180-X*) Story Time.

— Black American Inventors Workbook - Based on Black American Inventors - A Rhyme. (Illus.). 20p. 1999. pap., wbk. ed. 15.95 (*1-56820-389-6*) Story Time.

***Doyle, A.** Coursesmith - Directory of Courses. 60p. 1999. ring bd. 200.95 (*1-890928-60-7*) Frieda Carrol.

Doyle, A. Cowboy Poetry: Uncle Bud. (Illus.). 20p. 1999. spiral bd. 18.95 (*1-56820-249-0*) Story Time.

— Creole Food Festival - Stories & Recipes. 23p. (Orig.). (J). (gr. 3-7). 1997. pap. text 10.95 (*1-56820-178-8*) Story Time.

— Don't Pick No Shade Tree For Me. (Illus.). 20p. 1999. pap. 12.95 (*1-56820-394-2*) Story Time.

— Enterprise Solutions: A Report. 200p. 1998. ring bd. 349.95 (*1-890928-40-2*) Frieda Carrol.

— Entrepreneural Libraries - Possibilities & Info. 188p. 1999. ring bd. 286.00 (*1-890928-55-0*) Frieda Carrol.

— Fabric Farm Workbook Based on the Story Fabric Farm. (Illus.). 20p. 1999. pap., wbk. ed. 15.95 (*1-56820-388-8*) Story Time.

— Herbal Libraries - Possibilities & Info. 100p. 1999. ring bd. 79.00 (*1-890928-54-2*) Frieda Carrol.

— Ideas Make People Great. (Illus.). 20p. 1999. pap. 12.95 (*1-56820-393-4*) Story Time.

— Kwanzaa Food Festival - A Story with Recipes. 23p. (Orig.). (J). (gr. 3-7). 1997. pap. text 10.95 (*1-56820-179-6*) Story Time.

— Library Exhibits: Fish Convention. (Illus.). 20p. 1999. ring bd. 69.95 (*1-56820-395-0*) Story Time.

— Nature: Stories, Poetry & Education. (Story Course Ser.). (Illus.). 40p. 1998. pap., wbk. ed. 29.95 (*1-56820-375-6*) Story Time.

— Newspaper Recycling Workbook Based on the Story Newspaper Recycling Association. (Illus.). 20p. 1999. pap., wbk. ed. 15.95 (*1-56820-390-X*) Story Time.

— Penguins Workbook Based on the Story Rye the Rhyming Detective in the Missing Fairy Penguin. (Illus.). 20p. 1999. pap., wbk. ed. 15.95 (*1-56820-391-8*) Story Time.

— Poetheralogist: A Reference. 50p. 1998. pap., wbk. ed. 21.95 (*1-890928-41-0*) Frieda Carrol.

— Poetry Therapy - Notebook of Stories & Poetry to Duplicate & Use. 70p. (Orig.). 1996. ring bd. 34.95 (*1-56820-164-8*) Story Time.

— Reader's Theatre: Coats. (Illus.). 12p. (J). 1998. 8.95 (*1-56820-353-5*) Story Time.

— Reader's Theatre: The Missing Hammer Oyster Shell. (Illus.). 20p. (J). (gr. 5-8). 1998. pap. 8.95 (*1-56820-354-3*) Story Time.

— Reader's Theatre: The Missing Sugar Beet. (Illus.). (J). (gr. 5-8). Date not set. spiral bd. 8.95 (*1-56820-355-1*) Story Time.

— Reader's Theatre - Murphy the Mistletoe Adventures from the Garden of Eden to the Garden of Nede. 20p. (J). 1998. 8.95 (*1-56820-351-9*) Story Time.

— Reader's Threatre - Zuetoo Mask Go to the Gallery. (Illus.). 10p. (J). 1998. 8.95 (*1-56820-352-7*) Story Time.

— Recycling Stories, Poetry & Education. (Story Course Ser.). (Illus.). 40p. 1998. pap., wbk. ed. 29.95 (*1-56820-376-4*) Story Time.

— Recycling Word Mapping Games & Story Pages. (Illus.). 20p. 1999. spiral bd. 19.95 (*1-56820-248-2*) Story Time.

— Restaurant Greetings to Duplicate & Use. 1996. ring bd. 149.95 (*1-56820-181-8*) Story Time.

— Rhy the Rhyming Detective Story Series, Set. Vols. 1-4. (Orig.). (J). (gr. 4-11). 1996. pap. 59.95 (*1-56820-165-6*) Story Time.

— Story Course - Mask: Stories, Poetry & Color Therapy. (Illus.). 40p. (J). 1998. pap., wbk. ed. 29.95 (*1-56820-377-2*) Story Time.

***Doyle, A.** Storytelling Is... (Illus.). 70p. 1999. 29.95 (*1-56820-398-5*) Story Time.

Doyle, A. Storytelling 101: A Course for Educational Offerings. (Illus.). 200p. 1999. teacher ed. 125.00 (*1-56820-399-3*) Story Time.

— Teaching You about Plants, Animals, Science & More with Stories That Rhyme. (Illus.). 65p. (Orig.). (J). (gr. 4-10). 1997. ring bd. 25.95 (*1-56820-188-5*) Story Time.

— Teaching You about Recycling with Stories That Rhyme. (Illus.). 32p. 1996. ring bd. 17.95 (*1-56820-151-6*) Story Time.

— Telecommunications Libraries - Possibilities & Info. 68p. 1999. ring bd. 269.00 (*1-890928-53-4*) Frieda Carrol.

— Word Mapping for Business Info Mapping Success. 1999. spiral bd. 29.95 (*1-890928-52-6*) Frieda Carrol.

— Word Mapping for Distance Education Info Mapping Success. 1999. spiral bd. 19.95 (*1-890928-50-X*) Frieda Carrol.

— Word Mapping for Recycling Info Mapping Success. 1999. spiral bd. 19.95 (*1-890928-51-8*) Frieda Carrol.

— Zuetoo Masqke Stories. (Illus.). 28p. (J). (gr. 1-7). 1996. ring bd. 24.95 (*1-56820-157-5*) Story Time.

Doyle, A., ed. Candles As a Business: A Report. 100p. 1997. ring bd. 39.95 (*1-890928-02-X*) Frieda Carrol.

— Degrees Via Distance Education, Home Study: A Report. 190p. 1997. ring bd. 52.95 (*1-890928-04-6*) Frieda Carrol.

— Education Via Computer, Correspondence & More: A Report. 75p. 1997. ring bd. 49.95 (*1-890928-03-8*) Frieda Carrol.

***Doyle, A., ed.** Edutrain - Directory of Course Syllabus. 60p. 1999. ring bd. 150.00 (*1-890928-61-5*) Frieda Carrol.

Doyle, A., ed. Premium Incentives with Herbal Books: A Samphlet. (Illus.). 52p. (Orig.). 1997. pap. 29.95 (*1-890928-09-7*) Frieda Carrol.

— Premium Incentives with Story Books: Story Samphlet. (Illus.). 50p. (Orig.). 1997. pap. text 29.95 (*1-890928-06-2*) Frieda Carrol.

— Thimband - Uses & Ideas. (Illus.). 50p. (Orig.). 1997. pap. text 16.95 (*1-890928-08-9*) Frieda Carrol.

Doyle, A., ed. Advertising with Comics That Tell Stories. 120p. 1997. ring bd. 59.95 (*1-890928-07-0*) Frieda Carrol.

— Art(o)copy - Flowers: Commercial Use Edition. 50p. 1997. ring bd. 195.00 (*1-890928-05-4*) Frieda Carrol.

***Doyle, A.** Art Prints for Child Care Centers & Nurseries. 50p. 1999. spiral bd. 195.00 (*1-890928-59-3*) Frieda Carrol.

— Art Prints for Food Businesses. 50p. 1999. spiral bd. 325.00 (*1-890928-58-5*) Frieda Carrol.

Doyle, A. Comics for Non-Profit Children's Directory Publications: Story Rhymes. 1997. ring bd. 275.00 (*1-56820-205-9*) Story Time.

— Comics for Non-Profit Children's Museum Publications: Story Rhymes. (J). (gr. 4 up). 1997. ring bd. 375.00 (*1-56820-207-5*) Story Time.

— Comics for Non-Profit Day Care Publications: Story Rhymes. 1997. ring bd. 59.95 (*1-56820-200-8*) Story Time.

— Comics for Non-Profit Educational Convention Publications: Story Rhymes. 1997. ring bd. 79.95 (*1-56820-203-2*) Story Time.

— Comics for Non-Profit Fishing Publications: Story Rhymes. 1997. ring bd. 185.00 (*1-56820-204-0*) Story Time.

— Comics for Non-Profit Organization Publications: Story Rhymes. 1997. ring bd. 175.95 (*1-56820-206-7*) Story Time.

— Comics for Non-Profit School Publications: Story Rhymes. 1997. ring bd. 79.95 (*1-56820-202-4*) Story Time.

Doyle, A., jt. auth. see Doyle, Alfreda C.

Doyle, A., jt. auth. see Griffiths, B.

Doyle, A., jt. ed. see Doyle, A. E.

Doyle, A., ed. see Doyle, Alfreda C.

Doyle, A., ed. see Story Time Staff.

Doyle, A. C. Bimbo the Bumble Bee & Rose the Rose Bud. 20p. (J). (gr. 4-7). 1982. 3.50 (*0-939476-74-6*) Prosperity & Profits.
— Poetry for the Peace Movement. 17p. 1984. pap. text 7.00 (*0-913597-56-2*) Prosperity & Profits.
— Posie the Positive Train: Illustrated Edition. 60p. (J). (gr. 4-9). 1996. pap. 19.95 (*0-939476-96-7*) Prosperity & Profits.
— Recipe Greetings to Duplicate & Use. 79p. 1991. ring bd. 25.95 (*0-913597-15-5*) Prosperity & Profits.
— Story Rhyme Journal. 60p. (Orig.). (J). (gr. 6-9). 1991. pap. text 15.95 (*0-317-04222-X*) Prosperity & Profits.
— Story T(R)yme File - Notebook of 30 Stories. 50p. 1996. 32.95 (*1-56820-182-6*); 32.95 (*1-56820-183-4*) Story Time.
Doyle, A. C., compiled by. Posie, Positive History: Reference Guide. 1983. pap. 6.95 (*0-317-00636-3*) Prosperity & Profits.
Doyle, A. C. & Lamp Light Press Staff. Cookie Bag Greetings. rev. ed. (Illus.). 50p. Date not set. ring bd. 29.95 (*0-917593-25-1*, Lamp Light Pr) Prosperity & Profits.
Doyle, A. C., ed. see Center for Self-Sufficiency Staff.
Doyle, A. C., ed. see Data Notes Publishing Staff.
Doyle, A. E., et al, eds. Cell & Tissue Culture: Laboratory Procedures. 700p. 1999. 1375.00 (*0-471-92852-6*) Wiley.
Doyle, A. E. & Doyle, A., eds. Maintenance of Microorganisms, & Cultured Cells: A Manual of Laboratory Methods. 2nd ed. (Illus.). 308p. 1991. 58.00 (*0-12-410351-0*) Acad Pr.
Doyle, A. I., ed. see Offler, H. S.
Doyle, A. T., jt. ed. see MacGregor, I. J.
Doyle, Adrian Conan & Carr, John Dickson. The Exploits of Sherlock Holmes: A Collection of Sherlock Holmes Adventurs Based on Unsolved Cases from the Original Sir Arthur Conan Doyle Stories. LC 98-33251. 1999. 6.99 (*0-517-20338-3*) Random Hse Value.
Doyle, Aileen, ed. see Kelly, Patrick.
Doyle, Aileen A. More Youth Retreats: Creating Sacred Space for Young People. 124p. 1989. spiral bd. 12.95 (*0-88489-223-9*) St Marys.
Doyle, Alan, et al, eds. Safety in Cell & Tissue Culture. LC 99-182328. 248p. 1999. text 157.00 (*0-412-82790-5*) Kluwer Academic.
***Doyle, Alan & Griffiths, Bryan.** Cell & Tissue Culture for Medical Research. LC 99-89625. (Illus.). 2000. write for info. (*0-471-85213-9*) Wiley.
***Doyle, Alan & Griffiths, J. B.** Cell & Tissue Culture: Laboratory Procedures in Biotechnology. LC 98-24068. 332p. 1998. pap. 125.00 (*0-471-98255-5*) Wiley.
Doyle, Alfreda. Animals & Their Life Spans: Story Rhyme Coloring Book. (Illus.). 24p. (J). (gr. 3-8). 1998. pap. 8.95 (*1-56820-325-X*) Story Time.
— Christmas Tree Ornaments: Story Rhyme Coloring Book. (Illus.). 24p. (J). (gr. 3-8). 1998. pap. 8.95 (*1-56820-329-2*) Story Time.
— Christmas Wreath: Story Rhyme Coloring Book. (Illus.). 24p. (J). (gr. 3-8). 1998. pap. 8.95 (*1-56820-327-6*) Story Time.
***Doyle, Alfreda.** Easter Story Rhymes. unabridged ed. (Alfreda's Radio Ser.: Vol. 8). (J). (gr. 5-9). 1998. 16.95 incl. audio (*1-56820-312-8*) Story Time.
— Herbal Verbal Rhymes. unabridged ed. (Alfreda's Radio Ser.: Vol. 2). (J). (gr. 5-9). 1998. 25.95 (*1-56820-306-3*) Story Time.
Doyle, Alfreda. News Crew: Story Rhyme Coloring Book. (Illus.). 24p. (J). (gr. 3-8). 1998. pap. 8.95 (*1-56820-326-8*) Story Time.
— Posie Meets Sea Shells, Vol. 11. (Illus.). 25p. 1998. 8.95 (*1-56820-285-7*) Story Time.
— Posie Meets the Butterflies, Vol. 12. (Illus.). 25p. 1998. 8.95 (*1-56820-286-5*) Story Time.
— Posie Meets the Fabric Farm, Vol. 10. (Illus.). 25p. 1998. pap. 8.95 (*1-56820-284-9*) Story Time.
— Posie Meets the Frogs, Vol. 13. (Illus.). 25p. 1998. pap. 8.95 (*1-56820-287-3*) Story Time.
— Posie Meets the Junk Yard, Vol. 8. (Illus.). 25p. 1998. pap. 8.95 (*1-56820-282-2*) Story Time.
— Posie Meets the Sugar Farm, Vol. 9. (Illus.). 25p. 1998. pap. 8.95 (*1-56820-283-0*) Story Time.
— Posie Meets the Watermelon Patch, Vol. 7. (Illus.). 25p. 1998. pap. 8.95 (*1-56820-281-4*) Story Time.
— Teaching You about Self Sufficiency with Stories That Rhyme. (Illus.). 30p. (J). (gr. 5-9). 1998. 9.95 (*1-56820-384-5*) Story Time.
— Zuetoo Mask Go to the Gallery: Story Rhyme Coloring Book. (Illus.). 24p. (J). (gr. 3-8). 1998. pap. 8.95 (*1-56820-328-4*) Story Time.
Doyle, Alfreda C. Alfreda's Stories, Tales & Myths - 20 Plus. 64p. (Orig.). (J). (gr. 3-9). 1995. pap. text 19.95 (*1-56820-125-7*) Story Time.
— Bartering - Stories about Bartering. unabridged ed. Doyle, A., ed. (J). (gr. 3-6). 1996. ring bd. 14.95 incl. audio (*1-56820-155-9*) Story Time.
— ZueToo Masqke Stories. unabridged ed. Doyle, A., ed. (YA). 1996. ring bd. 9.95 incl. audio (*1-56820-154-0*) Story Time.
Doyle, Alfreda C. & Doyle, A. Recycling - Stories about Recycling. unabridged ed. (J). 1996. ring bd. 9.95 incl. audio (*1-56820-156-7*) Story Time.
Doyle, Alison L. & Sherry, Robert J. Multiple Award Schedules: A Guide for Business & Government. 419p. 1995. ring bd. 99.00 (*1-56726-037-3*, B560) Mgmt Concepts.
Doyle, Amanda. A Mist in Glen Torran. large type ed. 288p. 1984. 27.99 (*0-7089-1099-8*) Ulverscroft.
Doyle, Anne F. Visions. (Orig.). 1997. pap. write for info. (*1-57553-486-X*) Watermrk Pr.
Doyle, Anthony. English Toffee & Broken Hearts. 177p. pap. write for info. (*0-9677541-0-0*) A B Doyle.
Doyle, Arthur Conan. Adventure of the Dancing Men. (Sherlock Holmes Ser.). 18p. (Orig.). 1996. pap. 2.50 (*1-57514-202-3*, 3065) Encore Perform Pub.
— The Adventure of the Dancing Men & Other Sherlock Holmes Stories. LC 96-36038. 80p. (Orig.). 1997. pap. 1.00 (*0-486-29558-3*) Dover.
— The Adventure of the Priory School: A Facsimile of the Original Manuscript in the Marvin P. Epstein Sherlock Holmes Collection. 100p. 1987. 85.00 (*0-944166-00-8*) Santa Teresa Pr.
— The Adventure of the Speckled Band. (Sherlock Holmes Ser.). 28p. 1996. pap. 2.50 (*1-57514-263-5*, 3071) Encore Perform Pub.
***Doyle, Arthur Conan.** Adventures of Gerard. 252p. 2000. pap. 9.95 (*0-594-00888-3*) Eightn Hundrd.
Doyle, Arthur Conan. The Adventures of Sherlock Holmes. 304p. (YA). (gr. 10 up). 1986. pap. 4.99 (*0-425-09838-9*) Berkley Pub.
— The Adventures of Sherlock Holmes. 1982. lib. bdg. 31.95 (*0-89966-385-0*) Buccaneer Bks.
— The Adventures of Sherlock Holmes. LC 91-39632. (Books of Wonder: Vol. 1). (Illus.). 352p. (YA). (gr. 2 up). 1992. 22.00 (*0-688-10782-6*, Wm Morrow) Morrow Avon.
— The Adventures of Sherlock Holmes. 1997. pap. 2.95 (*0-89375-402-1*) NAL.
— The Adventures of Sherlock Holmes. (Wordsworth Classics). (YA). (gr. 6-12). 1998. 5.27 (*0-89061-033-9*, R0339WW, Jamestwn Pub) NTC Contemp Pub Co.
— The Adventures of Sherlock Holmes. (Sherlock Holmes Ser.). (Illus.). 172p. 1996. 9.98 (*1-879582-12-0*) Platinum Pr.
— The Adventures of Sherlock Holmes. Vogel, Malvina, ed. (Great Illustrated Classics Ser.: Vol. 25). (Illus.). 240p. (J). (gr. 3-6). 1993. 9.95 (*0-86611-976-0*) Playmore Inc.
— The Adventures of Sherlock Holmes. (Illus.). 272p. (YA). (gr. 9-12). 1989. pap. 2.50 (*0-8125-0424-0*, Pub. by Tor Bks) St Martin.
— The Adventures of Sherlock Holmes. 288p. 1981. pap. 6.95 (*0-14-005724-2*, Penguin Bks) Viking Penguin.
— The Adventures of Sherlock Holmes. (Classics Library). 1997. pap. 3.95 (*1-85326-033-9*, 0339WW, Pub. by Wrdsworth Edits) NTC Contemp Pub Co.
***Doyle, Arthur Conan.** The Adventures of Sherlock Holmes. large type ed. (Large Print Heritage Ser.). 497p. 2000. lib. bdg. 35.95 (*1-58118-067-5*, 23664) LRS.
— The Adventures Of Sherlock Holmes. large type ed. 400p. 1999. pap. 22.00 (*0-06-093322-4*) HarpC.
Doyle, Arthur Conan. The Adventures of Sherlock Holmes. large type ed. (Large Print Ser.). 494p. 1986. reprint ed. lib. bdg. 24.00 (*0-939495-30-9*) North Bks.
— The Adventures of Sherlock Holmes. 308p. 1998. reprint ed. lib. bdg. 24.00 (*1-58287-011-X*) North Bks.
— The Adventures of Sherlock Holmes. Green, Richard L., ed. & intro. by. (Oxford World's Classics Ser.). 438p. 1998. reprint ed. pap. 6.95 (*0-19-283508-4*) OUP.
— The Adventures of Sherlock Holmes. 2nd ed. (Illus.). 78p. 1993. pap. text 5.95 (*0-19-585257-5*) OUP.
— The Adventures of Sherlock Holmes, Vol. 2. abr. ed. 1997. audio 16.99 (*0-553-47778-1*) BDD Aud Pub.
***Doyle, Arthur Conan.** The Adventures of Sherlock Holmes, Vol. 3. large type ed. 2000. reprint ed. 28.00 (*1-55246-290-0*) Battered Silicon.
Doyle, Arthur Conan. The Adventures of Sherlock Holmes: A Scandal in Bohemia. 1970. 7.95 (*0-02-732920-8*) S&S Trade.
— The Adventures of Sherlock Holmes: Book 2, 2. (Illus.). 156p. (Orig.). (J). (gr. 4-7). 1981. pap. 2.95 (*0-380-78097-6*, Avon Bks) Morrow Avon.
— The Adventures of Sherlock Holmes: Book 3, 3. (Illus.). 112p. (Orig.). (J). (gr. 4-7). 1981. pap. 2.95 (*0-380-78105-0*, Avon Bks) Morrow Avon.
— The Adventures of Sherlock Holmes: Book 4, 4. (Illus.). 112p. (Orig.). (J). (gr. 4-7). 1981. pap. 3.50 (*0-380-78113-1*, Avon Bks) Morrow Avon.
Doyle, Arthur Conan. Alien Voices Presents Sir Arthur Conan Doyle's Lost World. abr. ed. 1997. 18.00 incl. audio (*0-671-57721-2*, Audioworks) PB.
Doyle, Arthur Conan. The Annotated Sherlock Holmes: The Four Novels & the Fifty-Six Short Stories Complete. Baromg-Gould, William S., ed. LC 92-14297. (Illus.). 1992. 29.99 (*0-685-57417-2*) Random Hse Value.
— Arthur Conan Doyle: Author Kit. (Jamestown Classics). (J). (gr. 1-7). 1976. pap. 353.33 (*0-89061-604-3*) NTC Contemp Pub Co.
— The Best Horror Stories of Arthur Conan Doyle. Greenberg, Martin H. et al, eds. LC 88-3436. 152p. 1989. pap. 8.00 (*0-89733-265-2*) Academy Chi Pubs.
— The Best of Sherlock Holmes. Keating, H. R. F., ed. 384p. 1993. pap. 8.95 (*0-460-87368-7*, Everyman's Classic Lib) Tuttle Pubng.
— The Best Science Fiction of Arthur Conan Doyle. Waugh, Charles G. & Greenberg, Martin H., eds. LC 81-8884. (Alternatives Ser.). 209p. 1981. 21.95 (*0-8093-1046-5*) S Ill U Pr.
— Best Sherlock Homes Stories: Chosen by the Author. LC 96-134056. 1995. 35.00 (*0-9520471-8-7*, Pub. by Hrthstone Pubns) Intl Spec Bk.
— Best Supernatural Tales of Arthur Conan Doyle. Bleiler, Everett F., ed. LC 78-66710. (Illus.). 302p. 1979. pap. 8.95 (*0-486-23725-7*) Dover.
***Doyle, Arthur Conan.** Beyond the Canon: Four Apocryphal Stories. 66p. 2000. pap. 8.00 (*1-55246-264-1*) Battered Silicon.
Doyle, Arthur Conan. Beyond the City. LC 80-67703. (Conan Doyle Centennial Ser.). (Illus.). 187p. 1982. 16.00 (*0-934468-44-3*, Pub. by Gaslight) Empire Pub Srvs.
— Brigadier Gerard. Date not set. 24.95 (*0-934468-20-6*) Gaslight.
— Captain of the Polestar, & Other Tales. LC 70-116950. (Short Story Index Reprint Ser.). 1977. 12.95 (*0-8369-3453-9*) Ayer.
***Doyle, Arthur Conan.** The Case-Book of Sherlock Holmes. (Oxford World Classics Ser.). 336p. 2000. pap. text 7.95 (*0-19-283917-9*) OUP.
Doyle, Arthur Conan. The Case-Book of Sherlock Holmes. (Classics Library). 1998. pap. 3.95 (*1-85326-070-3*, 0703WW, Pub. by Wrdsworth Edits) NTC Contemp Pub Co.
— Case of the Five Orange Pips. (Jamestown Classics Ser.). 1995. pap., teacher ed. 7.32 (*0-89061-063-0*, Jamestwn Pub); pap., student ed. 5.99 (*0-89061-062-2*, Jamestwn Pub) NTC Contemp Pub Co.
— Case of the Six Napoleans. (Jamestown Classics Ser.). 1995. pap., teacher ed. 7.32 (*0-89061-059-2*, Jamestwn Pub); pap., student ed. 5.99 (*0-89061-058-4*, Jamestwn Pub) NTC Contemp Pub Co.
— Charles Augustus Milverton. (Sherlock Holmes Ser.). 16p. (Orig.). 1996. pap. 2.50 (*1-57514-242-2*, 3072) Encore Perform Pub.
— Collected Brigadier Gerard Stories. LC 96-127611. 1995. 35.00 (*0-9520471-6-0*, Pub. by Hrthstone Pubns) Intl Spec Bk.
— The Complete Brigadier Gerard Stories. Edwards, Owen D., ed. & intro. by. 400p. 1995. pap. 13.95 (*0-86241-534-9*, Pub. by Canongate Books) Interlink Pub.
— Complete Sherlock Holmes. LC 65-6074. 1136p. (J). 1960. 27.95 (*0-385-00689-6*) Doubleday.
***Doyle, Arthur Conan.** Complete Sherlock Holmes, 2 vols., Set. 1998. mass mkt. 13.00 (*0-553-32825-5*, Bantam Classics) Bantam.
Doyle, Arthur Conan. The Doings of Raffles Haw. LC 80-67702. (Conan Doyle Centennial Ser.). (Illus.). 157p. 1981. 16.00 (*0-934468-43-5*, Pub. by Gaslight) Empire Pub Srvs.
— Doings of Raffles Haw, & Other Stories. LC 72-103507. (Short Story Index Reprint Ser.). 1977. 15.95 (*0-8369-3249-8*) Ayer.
— A Duet (...with an Occasional Chorus) LC 80-67707. (Conan Doyle Centennial Ser.). (Illus.). 270p. 1990. 20.00 (*0-934468-48-6*, Pub. by Gaslight) Empire Pub Srvs.
***Doyle, Arthur Conan.** The Exploits of the Brigadier Gerard. 252p. 2000. pap. 9.95 (*0-594-00210-9*) Eightn Hundrd.
Doyle, Arthur Conan. The Extraordinary Cases of Sherlock Holmes. (Classics for Young Readers Ser.). (Illus.). 288p. (YA). (gr. 4-7). 1995. pap. 4.99 (*0-14-036705-5*, PuffinBks) Peng Put Young Read.
— Further Adventures of Sherlock Holmes. 219p. Date not set. 21.95 (*0-8488-2582-9*) Amereon Ltd.
— The Further Adventures of Sherlock Holmes. Green, Richard L., ed. (Fiction Ser.). 256p. 1986. pap. 6.95 (*0-14-007907-6*, Penguin Bks) Viking Penguin.
Doyle, Arthur Conan. Die Gespikkelde Band: The Speckled Band in Afrikaans. Morrissey, Dean & Kent, Tri by, trs.Tr. of Adventure of the Speckled Band. (AFR., Illus.). 32p. 1997. pap. 8.00 (*1-55246-036-3*) Battered Silicon.
Doyle, Arthur Conan. The Great Adventures of Sherlock Holmes. (Illustrated Classics Collection 2). 64p. 1994. pap. 4.95 (*0-7854-0715-4*, 40391) Am Guidance.
— The Great Adventures of Sherlock Holmes. (Puffin Classics Ser.). (Illus.). 288p. (YA). (gr. 5 up). 1995. pap. 4.99 (*0-14-036689-X*, PuffinBks) Peng Put Young Read.
— The Great Adventures of Sherlock Holmes Readalong. (Illustrated Classics Collection 2). 64p. 1994. pap. 14.95 incl. audio (*0-7854-0681-6*, 40393) Am Guidance.
***Doyle, Arthur Conan.** The Great Shadow: And Other Napoleonic Tales. 252p. 2000. pap. 9.95 (*0-594-00480-2*) Eightn Hundrd.
Doyle, Arthur Conan. Great Tales of the Supernatural. 225p. 1994. reprint ed. pap. text 4.95 (*0-460-87165-X*, Everyman's Classic Lib) Tuttle Pubng.
— Green Flag & Other Stories of War & Sport. LC 70-101468. (Short Story Index Reprint Ser.). 1977. 21.95 (*0-8369-3201-3*) Ayer.
— His Last Bow: Some Reminiscences of Sherlock Holmes. Edwards, Owen D., ed. & intro. by. (World's Classics Ser.). 302p. 1995. reprint ed. pap. 5.95 (*0-19-282381-7*) OUP.
— His Last Bow: Some Reminiscenes of Sherlock Holmes. Edwards, Owen D., ed. (Oxford Sherlock Holmes Ser.). 304p. (C). 1993. 13.95 (*0-19-212315-7*) OUP.
***Doyle, Arthur Conan.** His Last Bow: Some Reminiscenes of Sherlock Holmes. Edwards, Owen Dudley, ed. (Oxford World Classics Ser.). 304p. 2000. pap. 6.95 (*0-19-283789-3*) OUP.
Doyle, Arthur Conan. His Last Row. 1976. 19.95 (*0-8488-1285-9*) Amereon Ltd.
— The History of Spiritualism, 2 vols. LC 75-7375. (Perspectives in Psychical Research Ser.). (Illus.). 1975. reprint ed. 44.95 (*0-405-07025-X*) Ayer.
— The Hound of Baskervilles. (Andre Deutsch Classics). 204p. (J). (gr. 5-8). 1996. 9.95 (*0-233-99035-6*, Pub. by Andre Deutsch) Trafalgar.
— The Hound of the Baskervilles. (Airmont Classics Ser.). (J). (gr. 8 up). 1965. mass mkt. 3.50 (*0-8049-0052-0*, CL-62) Airmont.
***Doyle, Arthur Conan.** The Hound of the Baskervilles. (Classics Ser.). 256p. (J). (gr. 4-11). 2000. per. 3.99 (*0-689-83571-X*) Aladdin.
Doyle, Arthur Conan. The Hound of the Baskervilles. (Illustrated Classics Collection 3). 64p. 1994. pap. 4.95 (*0-7854-0696-4*, 40450) Am Guidance.
— The Hound of the Baskervilles. 1976. 19.95 (*0-8488-1286-7*) Amereon Ltd.
— The Hound of the Baskervilles. 224p. (YA). (gr. 5 up). 1959. mass mkt. 4.50 (*0-440-93758-2*, LLL BDD) BDD Bks Young Read.
— The Hound of the Baskervilles. 192p. 1987. mass mkt. 5.99 (*0-345-35052-9*) Ballantine Pub Grp.
— The Hound of the Baskervilles. 1986. lib. bdg. 19.95 (*0-89966-229-3*) Buccaneer Bks.
— The Hound of the Baskervilles. Bennett, S. A., ed. (Adventures of Sherlock Holmes Ser.). (Illus.). 64p. 1992. pap. write for info. (*0-944099-17-3*) Comic Art.
— The Hound of the Baskervilles. 251p. (YA). (gr. 7 up). 1986. mass mkt. 4.95 (*0-451-52478-0*, Sig Classics) NAL.
— The Hound of the Baskervilles. 1997. pap. 3.95 (*0-89375-410-2*) NAL.
— The Hound of the Baskervilles. (Puffin Classics Ser.). (Illus.). 256p. (YA). (gr. 4-7). 1995. pap. 4.99 (*0-14-036699-7*, PuffinBks) Peng Put Young Read.
— The Hound of the Baskervilles. (Sherlock Holmes Ser.). (Illus.). 120p. 1996. 9.98 (*1-879582-15-5*) Platinum Pr.
Doyle, Arthur Conan. The Hound of the Baskervilles. 1986. 9.05 (*0-606-01869-7*, Pub. by Turtleback) Demco.
Doyle, Arthur Conan. The Hound of the Baskervilles. 192p. (C). 1981. pap. 5.95 (*0-14-000111-5*, Penguin Bks) Viking Penguin.
— The Hound of the Baskervilles. abr. ed. Fago, John N., ed. (Now Age Illustrated III Ser.). (Illus.). (J). (gr. 4-12). 1977. pap. text 2.95 (*0-88301-264-2*) Pendulum Pr.
— The Hound of the Baskervilles. adapted ed. 1977. pap. 5.25 (*0-8222-0536-X*) Dramatists Play.
— The Hound of the Baskervilles. large type ed. (Large Print Heritage Ser.). 282p. 1997. lib. bdg. 28.95 (*1-58118-001-2*, 21486) LRS.
***Doyle, Arthur Conan.** The Hound of the Baskervilles. large type ed. 2000. reprint ed. 24.00 (*1-55246-292-7*) Battered Silicon.
Doyle, Arthur Conan. The Hound of the Baskervilles. unabridged ed. 128p. 1994. pap. text 1.00 (*0-486-28214-7*) Dover.
— The Hound of the Baskervilles. 2nd ed. (Illus.). 94p. 1993. pap. text 5.95 (*0-19-585432-2*) OUP.
— The Hound of the Baskervilles: Another Adventure of Sherlock Holmes. Robson, W. W., ed. & intro. by. (Oxford World's Classics Ser.). 232p. 1998. reprint ed. pap. 7.95 (*0-19-283519-X*) OUP.
— The Hound of the Baskervilles Readalong. (Illustrated Classics Collection 3). 64p. 1994. pap. 14.95 incl. audio (*0-7854-0737-5*, 40452) Am Guidance.
Doyle, Arthur Conan. Lebanta le Matheba: The Adventure of the Speckled Bank in Sotho. Kent, Trilby, tr.Tr. of Adventure of the Speckled Band. 32p. 1997. 8.00 (*1-55246-018-5*) Battered Silicon.
Doyle, Arthur Conan. Listen & Read Sherlock Holmes Stories. unabridged ed. 112p. (J). 1997. 6.95 incl. audio (*0-486-29827-2*) Dover.
— The Lost World. 320p. 1989. pap. 5.95 (*0-89733-331-4*) Academy Chi Pubs.
— The Lost World. 1992. pap. text. write for info. (*0-17-556535-X*) Addison-Wesley.
— The Lost World. 1976. 21.95 (*0-8488-0990-4*) Amereon Ltd.
— The Lost World. 1988. lib. bdg. 18.95 (*0-89966-233-1*) Buccaneer Bks.
— The Lost World. 176p. 1998. pap. 1.50 (*0-486-40060-3*) Dover.
— The Lost World. (Twelve-Point Ser.). 1999. lib. bdg. 24.00 (*1-58287-112-4*) North Bks.
— The Lost World. Duncan, Ian, ed. (Oxford World's Classics Ser.). 768p. 1998. pap. 8.95 (*0-19-283352-9*) OUP.
— The Lost World. (Puffin Classics Ser.). (Illus.). 288p. (YA). (gr. 5 up). 1995. pap. 4.99 (*0-14-036748-9*, PuffinBks) Peng Put Young Read.
— The Lost World. Matthews, Sarah, ed. (Thornes Classic Novels Ser.). (Illus.). 243p. 1996. pap. 16.95 (*0-7487-2481-8*, Pub. by S Thornes Pubs) Trans-Atl Phila.
— The Lost World. 256p. 1993. mass mkt. 4.99 (*0-8125-3468-9*, Pub. by Tor Bks) St Martin.
— The Lost World. 256p. 1997. mass mkt. 4.99 (*0-8125-6483-9*, Pub. by Tor Bks) St Martin.
— The Lost World. large type ed. (Large Print Heritage Ser.). 340p. 1998. lib. bdg. 31.95 (*1-58118-034-9*, 22017) LRS.
***Doyle, Arthur Conan.** The Lost World, Set. unabridged ed. (YA). (gr. 8 up). 1998. 35.95 incl. audio (*1-55685-583-4*) Audio Bk Con.
Doyle, Arthur Conan. The Lost World: And Other Stories. (Classics Library). 480p. 1998. pap. 3.95 (*1-85326-245-5*, 2455WW, Pub. by Wrdsworth Edits) NTC Contemp Pub Co.
— Maajabu Ya Utepe Wenye Madoadoa: The Adventure of the Speckled Band in Kiswahili. Gateno, George, tr. (SWA., Illus.). 31p. (Orig.). 1993. pap. 8.00 (*0-9695673-3-2*) Battered Silicon.
— Man from Archangel & Other Tales of Adventure. LC 73-101801. (Short Story Index Reprint Ser.). 1977. 19.95 (*0-8369-3189-0*) Ayer.
Doyle, Arthur Conan. Mbwa Wa Familia Ya Baskerville: The Hound of the Baskervilles (Kiswahili) Mosotf, Zachary Mumbo & Ali, Hassan O., trs. (Sherlockian Scholarship Ser.).Tr. of Hound of the Baskervilles. (SWA.). pap. 12.00 (*1-55246-059-2*) Battered Silicon.
Doyle, Arthur Conan. The Medal Brigadier: Penguin Reader Level 1. 1998. pap. 7.00 (*0-14-081557-0*) Viking Penguin.
— The Memoirs of Sherlock Holmes. Roden, Christopher, ed. (Oxford Sherlock Holmes Ser.). 384p. (C). 1993. 13.95 (*0-19-212309-2*) OUP.
***Doyle, Arthur Conan.** The Memoirs of Sherlock Holmes. Roden, Christopher, ed. (Oxford World's Classics Ser.). 384p. 2000. pap. 7.95 (*0-19-283811-3*) OUP.

D

Doyle, Arthur Conan. The Memoirs of Sherlock Holmes. (Sherlock Holmes Ser.). (Illus.). 160p. 1996. 9.98 (*1-879582-14-7*) Platinum Pr.

— The Memoirs of Sherlock Holmes. large type ed. (Large Print Ser.). 421p. 1986. reprint ed. lib. bdg. 24.00 (*0-939495-31-7*) North Bks.

— The Memoirs of Sherlock Holmes. 270p. 1998. reprint ed. lib. bdg. 24.00 (*1-58287-049-7*) North Bks.

— The Memoirs of Sherlock Holmes. Roden, Christopher, ed. & intro. by. (World's Classics Ser.). 378p. 1995. reprint ed. pap. 6.95 (*0-19-282375-2*) OUP.

— Memories & Adventures. LC 84-73098. (Illus.). 250p. Date not set. 24.95 (*0-934468-23-0*) Gaslight.

— Memories & Adventures. (BCL1-PR English Literature Ser.). 410p. 1992. reprint ed. lib. bdg. 99.00 (*0-7812-7522-9*) Rprt Serv.

— The Musgrave Ritual. (Jamestown Classics Ser.). 1995. pap., teacher ed. 7.32 (*0-89061-057-6*, Jamestwn Pub) NTC Contemp Pub Co.

— The Musgrave Ritual. (Jamestown Classics Ser.). (J). 1995. pap., student ed. 5.99 (*0-89061-056-8*, Jamestwn Pub) NTC Contemp Pub Co.

— My Friend the Murderer: And Other Mysteries & Adventures. LC 76-37267. (Short Story Index Reprint Ser.). 1977. reprint ed. 18.95 (*0-8369-4078-4*) Ayer.

— The Mysteries of Sherlock Holmes. LC 96-6275. (Illustrated Junior Library). (Illus.). 240p. (YA). (gr. 4 up). 1996. 14.95 (*0-448-40957-7*, G & D) Peng Put Young Read.

— The Mysteries of Sherlock Holmes. (Bullseye Step into Classics Ser.). (Illus.). 96p. (J). (gr. 2-6). 1994. pap. 3.50 (*0-679-85086-4*, Bullseye Bks) Random Bks Yng Read.

— The Mysteries of Sherlock Holmes. Conaway, Judith, ed. LC 81-15751. (Step into Classics Ser.). (Illus.). 96p. (J). (gr. 4-7). 1994. pap. 3.99 (*0-394-85086-6*, Pub. by Random Bks Yng Read) Random.

— The Mysterious Adventures of Sherlock Holmes. (Classics for Young Readers Ser.). (Illus.). 256p. (YA). (gr. 5 up). 1996. pap. 3.99 (*0-14-037262-8*, PuffinBks) Peng Put Young Read.

— The New Revelation. 122p. 1983. pap. 10.00 (*0-89540-103-7*, SB-103) Sun Pub.

— Original Illustrated Arthur Conan Doyle. 1992. 7.98 (*0-89009-391-1*) Bk Sales Inc.

— The Original Illustrated Sherlock Holmes. 636p. 1985. 7.98 (*0-89009-057-2*) Bk Sales Inc.

— The Original Illustrated Sherlock Holmes. (Illus.). 656p. 1996. pap. 12.95 (*1-879582-25-2*) Platinum Pr.

***Doyle, Arthur Conan.** The Original Illustrated 'Strand' Sherlock Holmes: The Complete Facsimile Edition. (Illus.). 1126p. 2000. reprint ed. pap. text 25.00 (*0-7881-9173-X*) DIANE Pub.

Doyle, Arthur Conan. The Poison Belt. 1976. 22.95 (*0-8488-0991-2*) Amereon Ltd.

— The Poison Belt. (BCL1-PR English Literature Ser.). 252p. 1992. reprint ed. lib. bdg. 79.00 (*0-7812-7521-0*) Rprt Serv.

— The Professor Challenger Adventures: The Lost World & the Poison Belt. LC 89-7204. 300p. (C). 1989. pap. 9.95 (*0-87701-620-8*) Chronicle Bks.

— The Red-Headed League. (Sherlock Holmes Ser.). 27p. 1996. pap. 2.50 (*1-57514-260-0*, 3068) Encore Perform Pub.

— The Red-Headed League. (Jamestown Classics Ser.). 1995. pap., teacher ed. 7.32 (*0-89061-061-4*, Jamestwn Pub) NTC Contemp Pub Co.

— The Red-Headed League. (Jamestown Classics Ser.). (J). 1995. pap., student ed. 5.99 (*0-89061-060-6*, Jamestwn Pub) NTC Contemp Pub Co.

***Doyle, Arthur Conan.** The Refugees: A Tale of Two Continents. 252p. 2000. pap. 9.95 (*0-594-00213-3*) Eighth Hundrd.

Doyle, Arthur Conan. The Return of Sherlock Holmes. (Heritage Literary Ser.). Date not set. pap. text. write for info. (*0-582-34913-3*, Pub. by Addison-Wesley) Longman.

— The Return of Sherlock Holmes. Green, Richard L., ed. (Oxford Sherlock Holmes Ser.). 474p. (C). 1993. 13.95 (*0-19-212317-3*, 8952) OUP.

— The Return of Sherlock Holmes. (Sherlock Holmes Ser.). (Illus.). 200p. 1996. 9.98 (*1-879582-13-9*) Platinum Pr.

— The Return of Sherlock Holmes. (Classics Library). 320p. 1997. pap. 3.95 (*1-85326-058-4*, 0584WW, Pub. by Wrdsworth Edits) NTC Contemp Pub Co.

— The Return of Sherlock Holmes. large type ed. (Large Print Heritage Ser.). 278p. (YA). (gr. 7-12). 1998. lib. bdg. 29.95 (*1-58118-038-1*) LRS.

— The Return of Sherlock Holmes: The Oxford Sherlock Holmes. (Oxford World's Classics Ser.). 1999. pap. text 5.95 (*0-19-283761-3*) OUP.

***Doyle, Arthur Conan.** Rodney Stone. 252p. 2000. pap. 9.95 (*0-594-00354-7*) Eighth Hundrd.

Doyle, Arthur Conan. Round the Red Lamp. LC 77-101802. (Short Story Index Reprint Ser.). 1977. 18.95 (*0-8369-3190-4*) Ayer.

— A Scandal in Bohemia. (Sherlock Holmes Ser.). 20p. 1996. pap. 2.50 (*1-57514-261-9*, 3069) Encore Perform Pub.

— The Second Stain. (Sherlock Holmes Ser.), 27p. (Orig.). 1996. pap. 2.50 (*1-57514-262-7*, 3070) Encore Perform Pub.

— Selected Adventures of Sherlock Holmes. abr. ed. Marshall, Michael J., ed. (Core Classics Ser.: Vol. 5). (Illus.). 160p. (J). (gr. 4-6). 1997. pap. 5.95 (*1-890517-08-9*); lib. bdg. 10.95 (*1-890517-09-7*) Core Knowledge.

— Selected Adventures of Sherlock Holmes. large type ed. 12.00 (*0-85456-589-2*) Ulverscroft.

— Sherlock Holmes. 1996. 15.95 (*0-679-45104-8*) McKay.

— Sherlock Holmes. 1996. pap. 23.95 (*0-312-13824-5*) St Martin.

— Sherlock Holmes: Classic Mysteries, Set. unabridged ed. 1996. 16.95 incl. audio (*1-883049-67-9*, Pub. by Sound Room) Penton Overseas.

— Sherlock Holmes: Four Great Novels. (Works). 358p. 1996. pap. 6.99 (*1-57215-205-2*, JG1204) World Pubns.

— Sherlock Holmes: Selected Stories. Roberts, S. C., ed. & intro. by. (Oxford World's Classics Ser.). 460p. 1998. pap. 8.95 (*0-19-283537-8*) OUP.

— Sherlock Holmes: The Complete Novels & Stories, Vol. I. 944p. 1986. mass mkt. 6.50 (*0-553-21241-9*, Bantam Classics) Bantam.

— Sherlock Holmes: The Complete Novels & Stories, Vol. II. 688p. 1986. mass mkt. 6.50 (*0-553-21242-7*, Bantam Classics) Bantam.

— Sherlock Holmes: The Major Stories with Contemporary Critical Essays. Hodgson, John A., ed. 452p. 1993. pap. 19.95 (*0-312-08945-7*) St Martin.

Doyle, Arthur Conan. Sherlock Holmes Vol. I: The Complete Novels & Stories. (J). 1986. 11.05 (*0-606-03126-X*, Pub. by Turtleback) Demco.

Doyle, Arthur Conan. Sherlock Holmes Vol. II: The Complete Novels & Stories. (J). 1986. 11.05 (*0-606-03127-8*, Pub. by Turtleback) Demco.

— Sherlock Holmes - Selected Stories. Date not set. lib. bdg. 29.95 (*0-8488-1672-2*) Amereon Ltd.

— Sherlock Holmes - The Four Long Stories: A Study in Scarlet; The Sign of Four; The Hound of the Baskervilles; The Valley of Fear. large type ed. 650p. 1995. lib. bdg. 25.00 (*0-939495-89-9*) North Bks.

— Sherlock Holmes - The Four Long Stories: A Study in Scarlet; The Sign of Four; The Hound of the Baskervilles; The Valley of Fear. 583p. 1998. reprint ed. lib. bdg. 24.00 (*1-58287-036-5*) North Bks.

— Sherlock Holmes & the Curse of the Sign of Four. 1975. pap. 5.25 (*0-8222-1020-7*) Dramatists Play.

— The Sherlock Holmes Apocrypha. Date not set. pap. 18.95 (*0-934468-51-6*) Gaslight.

Doyle, Arthur Conan. Sherlock Holmes Audio Collection: Rathbone,&Basil, Set. unabridged ed. 1991. audio 25.00 (*1-55994-498-6*, SBN 107) HarperAudio.

Doyle, Arthur Conan. The Sherlock Holmes Mysteries: New Expanded Edition. expanded ed. (YA). 1985. mass mkt. 5.95 (*0-451-52431-4*, Sig Classics) NAL.

***Doyle, Arthur Conan.** Sherlock Holmes Reader. (Unabridged Classics Ser.). 224p. (YA). 2000. pap. 5.98 (*0-7624-0553-8*, Courage) Running Pr.

Doyle, Arthur Conan. The Sign of Four. (J). 1997. pap. 2.95 (*0-8167-0851-7*) Troll Communs.

— Sign of Four. 112p. Date not set. 16.95 (*0-8488-2550-0*) Amereon Ltd.

— The Sign of Four. large type ed. 1969. 12.00 (*0-7089-0190-5*) Ulverscroft.

— The Sign of the Four. LC 93-50112. 160p. 1994. 24.95 (*1-55709-301-6*) Applewood.

— The Sign of the Four. 1989. lib. bdg. 15.95 (*0-89966-230-7*) Buccaneer Bks.

— Sign of the Four: The Oxford Sherlock Holmes. (Oxford World Classics Ser.). 1999. pap. text 5.95 (*0-19-283736-2*) OUP.

— Sir Arthur Conan Doyle: Three Adventures. LC 96-2326. 1997. 9.99 (*0-517-15075-1*) Random Hse Value.

— Sir Nigel. 26.95 (*0-88411-538-0*) Amereon Ltd.

***Doyle, Arthur Conan.** Sir Nigel. 252p. 2000. pap. 9.95 (*0-594-00345-8*) Eighth Hundrd.

Doyle, Arthur Conan. Sir Nigel. 350p. 1998. pap. 3.95 (*1-85326-229-3*, Pub. by Wrdsworth Edits) NTC Contemp Pub Co.

***Doyle, Arthur Conan.** Sir Nigel. 172p. 2000. reprint ed. pap. text 17.00 (*0-7881-9153-5*) DIANE Pub.

Doyle, Arthur Conan. Six Great Sherlock Holmes Stories. (Thrift Editions Ser.). 112p. (Orig.). 1992. pap. 1.00 (*0-486-27055-6*) Dover.

— The Stark Munro Letters. LC 80-67705. (Conan Doyle Centennial Ser.). (Illus.). 224p. 1982. 19.00 (*0-934468-46-X*, Pub. by Gaslight) Empire Pub Srvs.

— The Stark Munro Letters. LC 79-8259. (Illus.). reprint ed. 44.50 (*0-404-61840-5*) AMS Pr.

— Strange Studies from Life & Other Narratives: The Complete True Crime Writings of Sir Arthur Conan Doyle. LC 82-83684. (Illus.). 124p. 1988. 19.00 (*0-934468-49-4*, Pub. by Gaslight) Empire Pub Srvs.

— A Study in Scarlet. 1989. lib. bdg. 15.95 (*0-89966-231-5*) Buccaneer Bks.

— A Study in Scarlet. Bennett, S. A., ed. (Adventures of Sherlock Holmes Ser.). (Illus.). 64p. 1992. pap. write for info. (*0-944099-18-1*) Comic Art.

— A Study in Scarlet. Edwards, Owen D., ed. (Oxford Sherlock Holmes Ser.). 254p. (C). 1993. 13.95 (*0-19-212313-0*, 14615) OUP.

— A Study in Scarlet. (J). 1997. pap. 1.95 (*0-8167-0850-9*) Troll Communs.

— A Study in Scarlet. 144p. 1982. pap. 6.95 (*0-14-005707-2*, Penguin Bks) Viking Penguin.

— Study in Scarlet. 121p. Date not set. 17.95 (*0-8488-2554-3*) Amereon Ltd.

— Study in Scarlet, 1. 1998. pap. text 6.95 (*0-9666443-1-X*) Thorby Enterp.

***Doyle, Arthur Conan.** A Study in Scarlet, Set. unabridged ed. (C). 1998. 24.95 incl. audio (*1-55685-608-3*) Audio Bk Con.

Doyle, Arthur Conan. A Study in Scarlet: The Oxford Sherlock Holmes. (Oxford World's Classics Ser.). 256p. 2000. pap. 5.95 (*0-19-283765-6*) OUP.

— A Study in Scarlet & the Sign of the Four. 256p. (YA). (gr. 10 up). 1986. mass mkt. 4.50 (*0-425-10240-8*) Berkley Pub.

— Supernatural Tales. 1995. 27.95 (*0-8488-0752-9*) Amereon Ltd.

— The Supernatural Tales of Sir Arthur Conan Doyle. Haining, Peter, ed. & intro. by. (Illus.). 272p. 1995. 21.95 (*0-572-01453-8*, Pub. by Foulsham UK) Assoc Pubs Grp.

— Tales for a Winter's Night. 207p. (Orig.). 1989. pap. 14.95 (*0-89733-309-8*) Academy Chi Pubs.

— Tales of Terror & Mystery. large type ed. (Large Print Heritage Ser.). 340p. (gr. 7-12). 1999. lib. bdg. 33.95 (*1-58118-047-0*, 22516) LRS.

— Tales of Terror & Mystery. 1982. reprint ed. lib. bdg. 16.95 (*0-89966-429-6*) Buccaneer Bks.

— Thirty-Three by Arthur Conan Doyle. 1986. 6.98 (*0-685-16821-2*, 625431) Random Hse Value.

— Three Sherlock Holmes Adventures. Date not set. pap. text. write for info. (*0-17-557037-X*) Addison-Wesley.

***Doyle, Arthur Conan.** Through the Magic Door. (Common Reader Edition Ser.). 2000. pap. 16.95 (*1-888173-98-X*, Pub. by Akadine Pr) Trafalgar.

— Uncle Bernac: A Memory of the Empire. 252p. 2000. pap. 9.95 (*0-594-00309-1*) Eighth Hundrd.

Doyle, Arthur Conan. Uncollected Stories. 1998. lib. bdg. write for info. (*1-56723-038-5*) Yestermorrow.

— The Valley of Fear. 1976. 17.95 (*0-8488-1288-3*) Amereon Ltd.

— The Valley of Fear. 1988. lib. bdg. 16.95 (*0-89966-232-3*) Buccaneer Bks.

— The Valley of Fear. Edwards, Owen D., ed. (Oxford Sherlock Holmes Ser.). 296p. (C). 1993. 13.95 (*0-19-212314-9*, 8951) OUP.

— The Vital Message. 164p. 1994. reprint ed. pap. 14.95 (*1-56459-450-5*) Kessinger Pub.

— When the World Screamed, & Other Stories. LC 68-143632. 173 p. 1968. write for info. (*0-7195-1779-6*) John Murray.

— The White Company. 374p. Date not set. 26.95 (*0-8488-2560-8*) Amereon Ltd.

***Doyle, Arthur Conan.** The White Company. 252p. 2000. pap. 9.95 (*0-594-00357-1*) Eighth Hundrd.

Doyle, Arthur Conan. The White Company. LC 87-62625. (Books of Wonder). (Illus.). 362p. (J). (gr. 2 up). 1988. 22.00 (*0-688-07817-6*, Wm Morrow) Morrow Avon.

— The White Company. (Classics Library). 1998. pap. 3.95 (*1-85326-289-7*, 2897WW, Pub. by Wrdsworth Edits) NTC Contemp Pub Co.

— The White Company. 1986. reprint ed. lib. bdg. 31.95 (*0-89966-517-9*) Buccaneer Bks.

***Doyle, Arthur Conan.** The White Company & Sir Nigel. (Common Reader Edition Ser.). 618p. 2000. pap. 24.95 (*1-888173-90-4*, Pub. by Akadine Pr) Trafalgar.

Doyle, Arthur Conan & Barry, William. Sherlock Holmes, a Graphic Novel: 100 Year Anniversary Edition. anniversary ed. Harryman, Joan, ed. (Illus.). 80p. (Orig.). 1987. pap. 8.95 (*0-944099-00-9*) Comic Art.

Doyle, Arthur Conan & Carr, John Dickson, intros. The Exploits of Sherlock Holmes. LC 75-157775. (Short Story Index Reprint Ser.). 1977. reprint ed. 27.95 (*0-8369-3887-9*) Ayer.

Doyle, Arthur Conan & Earlson, Ian M. Beeton's Christmas Annual--1987: Sherlock Holmes. (Illus.). 80p. 1987. pap. 9.95 (*0-9619318-1-7*) W S Dorn.

Doyle, Arthur Conan & Howe, D. H. The Further Adventures of Sherlock Holmes. 2nd ed. (Illus.). 94p. 1993. pap. text 5.95 (*0-19-585335-0*) OUP.

Doyle, Arthur Conan & Reyburn, Stanley. The Valley of Fear. Landes, William-Alan, ed. LC 98-4275. 55p. 1998. pap. 10.00 (*0-88734-742-8*) Players Pr.

***Doyle, Arthur Conan & Van Der Leun, Gerard.** The Quotable Sherlock Holmes. LC 00-40108. 2000. write for info. (*0-446-67727-2*) Mysterious Pr.

Doyle, Arthur Conan, et al. The Annotated Lost World. (Illus.). 288p. 1996. 34.95 (*0-938501-23-2*) Wessex.

Doyle, Arthur Conan, et al. Ritualia Musgraviensia. (Sherlockian Scholarship Ser.). (LAT.). 20.00 (*1-55246-137-8*) Battered Silicon.

— Waterloo: A Case-Book on Sir Arthur Conan Doyle's Historical Play. 1998. 25.00 (*1-55246-112-2*) Battered Silicon.

Doyle, Arthur Conan, jt. auth. see Center for Learning Network Staff.

Doyle, Averil M. Delusional Relationships: How They Are Formed, Why They Falter & Fail. LC 94-32926. 224p. 1995. 59.95 (*0-275-95010-7*, Praeger Pubs) Greenwood.

— The Sexually Disturbed: Treating Psychosexual Disorders. LC 91-45565. 168p. 1992. 47.95 (*0-275-94294-5*, C4294, Praeger Pubs) Greenwood.

Doyle, Bernard W. Comb Making in America. (Illus.). 158p. 1993. reprint ed. lib. bdg. 29.50 (*0-8328-3198-0*) Higginson Bk Co.

Doyle, Betty, ed. see Doyle, Donald C.

Doyle, Bill, jt. auth. see Muldoon, Paul.

Doyle, Billy. The Ultimate Directory of the Silent Screen Performers: A Necrology of Births & Deaths & Essays on 50 Lost Players. Slide, Anthony, ed. LC 94-36832. (Illus.). 368p. 1995. 55.00 (*0-8108-2958-4*) Scarecrow.

***Doyle, Billy H.** The Ultimate Directory of Film Technicians: A Necrology of Dates & Places of Births & Deaths of More Than 9,000 Producers, Directors, Screenwrites, Composers, Cinematographers, Art Directors, Costumes Designers, Choreographers, Executives, & Publicists. Slide, Anthony, ed. LC 98-50958. 320p. 1999. 65.00 (*0-8108-3546-0*) Scarecrow.

Doyle, Billy H. The Ultimate Directory of Silent & Sound Era Performers: A Necrology of Actors & Actresses. Slide, Anthony, ed. LC 98-51695. 623p. 1999. text 98.50 (*0-8108-3547-9*) Scarecrow.

Doyle, Brendan. Meditations with Julian of Norwich. LC 82-73955. (Meditations with Ser.). (Illus.). 156p. 1997. reprint ed. pap. 9.95 (*0-939680-11-4*) Bear & Co.

Doyle, Brian. Angel Square. 128p. (J). (gr. 4-7). 1991. pap. 4.95 (*0-88899-070-7*) Publishers Group.

— Angel Square. (J). (gr. 4-6). 1996. pap. 5.95 (*0-88899-230-0*) Publishers Group.

— Covered Bridge. 1999. 15.95 (*0-88899-122-3*) Gro1undwood-Douglas.

— Covered Bridge. (J). (gr. 4-6). 1996. pap. 4.95 (*0-88899-190-8*) Publishers Group.

— Credo. 136p. 1999. pap. 9.95 (*0-88489-622-6*) St Marys.

— Dam Lies. 128p. (J). (gr. 4 up). 1999. 15.95 (*0-88899-349-8*, Pub. by Gro1undwood-Douglas); pap. write for info. (*0-88899-350-1*, Pub. by Gro1undwood-Douglas) Publishers Group.

— Disability, Discrimination, & Equal Opportunities: A Comparative Study of the Employment Rights of Disabled Persons. LC 94-34931. (Studies in Labour & Social Law). 320p. 1995. 110.00 (*0-7201-2242-2*) Continuum.

— Easy Avenue. 128p. (YA). (gr. 3-7). 1996. pap. 4.95 (*0-88899-248-3*) Publishers Group.

— English & Englishness. (New Accents Ser.). 172p. 1989. 39.95 (*0-415-00981-2*); pap. 12.95 (*0-415-00982-0*) Routledge.

— Hey, Dad! (J). (gr. 4-6). 1996. pap. 4.95 (*0-88899-148-7*) Publishers Group.

— Spud in Winter. 144p. (J). (gr. 3-7). 1996. 14.95 (*0-88899-261-0*) Publishers Group.

— Spud in Winter. 144p. (J). (gr. 4-6). 1996. pap. 5.95 (*0-88899-250-5*) Publishers Group.

— Spud Sweetgrass. 128p. (J). (gr. 3-7). 1996. 14.95 (*0-88899-164-9*) Publishers Group.

— Spud Sweetgrass. 144p. (J). (gr. 4-6). 1996. pap. 5.95 (*0-88899-251-3*) Publishers Group.

— Uncle Ronald. LC 96-34401. (J). 1997. text. write for info. (*0-88899-266-1*) DGL.

— Uncle Ronald. 144p. (gr. 4-7). 1998. pap. 4.95 (*0-88899-309-9*, Pub. by Gro1undwood-Douglas) Publishers Group.

— Uncle Ronald. LC 96-34401. 144p. (J). 1997. pap. write for info. (*0-88899-267-X*) Publishers Group.

— Up to Low. 116p. (J). (gr. 4-7). 1991. pap. 4.95 (*0-88899-088-X*) Publishers Group.

— Up to Low. 120p. (J). (gr. 4-6). 1996. pap. 5.95 (*0-88899-264-5*) Publishers Group.

— You Can Pick Me up at Peggy's Cove. 120p. (J). (gr. 4-7). 1991. pap. 4.95 (*0-88899-116-9*) Publishers Group.

— You Can Pick Me up at Peggy's Cove. 120p. (J). (gr. 4-6). 1996. reprint ed. pap. 5.95 (*0-88899-231-9*) Publishers Group.

Doyle, Brian, jt. auth. see Doyle, Jim.

Doyle, Brian B., jt. ed. see Scheiber, Stephen C.

Doyle, Bruce I., III. Before You Think Another Thought: An Illustrated Guide to Understanding How Your Thoughts & Beliefs Create Your Life. rev. ed. 128p. 1997. pap. 11.95 (*1-57174-076-7*) Hampton Roads Pub Co.

Doyle, Bryan, jt. auth. see BGA Staff.

Doyle, Celia. Child Sexual Abuse: A Guide for Health Professionals. 304p. 1994. 40.99 (*1-56593-136-X*, 0448) Singular Publishing.

— Helping Strategies in Child Sexual Abuse. LC 95-218955. 224p. 1996. pap. text 24.95 (*1-871177-39-1*, Pub. by Whiting & Birch) Paul & Co Pubs.

Doyle, Charles. Richard Aldington: A Biography. LC 88-34922. (Illus.). 350p. (C). 1989. text 41.95 (*0-8093-1566-1*) S Ill U Pr.

— Wallace Stevens: The Critical Heritage. (Critical Heritage Ser.). 500p. 1985. 69.50 (*0-7100-9647-X*, Routledge Thoemms) Routledge.

— William Carlos Williams: The Critical Heritage. (Critical Heritage Ser.). 1980. 69.50 (*0-7100-8987-2*, Routledge Thoemms) Routledge.

Doyle, Charles H. & Stuart, Terrell. Stand in the Door. 2nd ed. Phillips, Jim M., ed. LC 79-13509. (Illus.). 428p. 39.95 (*0-932572-09-X*) Phillips Pubns.

***Doyle, Charlotte.** Where's Bunny's Mommy? (Illus.). 29p. (J). (ps-k). 1999. reprint ed. text 14.00 (*0-7881-6653-0*) DIANE Pub.

Doyle, Charlottw L. You Can't Catch Me. LC 96-42350. (Illus.). 24p. (J). (ps up). 1998. 9.95 (*0-694-01038-3*) HarpC.

Doyle, Chris. Cruising Guide to the Leeward Islands. 5th ed. Scott, Nancy et al, eds. (Illus.). 432p. 1998. pap. 24.95 (*0-944428-39-8*) Cruising Guide.

— Cruising Guide to the Leeward Islands: Anguilla to Dominica. 368p. 1997. pap. 125.00 (*0-944428-30-4*, Pub. by Laurie Norie & Wilson Ltd) St Mut.

— Cruising Guide to Trinidad & Tobago, 1997-1998. 142p. 1997. pap. 125.00 (*0-944428-37-1*, Pub. by Laurie Norie & Wilson Ltd) St Mut.

***Doyle, Chris.** Crusing Guide to the Leeward Islands: Complete Guide for Caribbean Yachtsment, Divers & Watersports Enthusiasts. 6th ed. (Illus.). 2000. pap. 24.95 (*0-944428-51-7*) Cruising Guide.

Doyle, Chris. Exploring the Windward Islands. (Illus.). 230p. 11.95 (*976-8063-04-1*) F Papy Cruising Guide.

— Sailors Guide to the Windward Island. 9th ed. (Illus.). 320p. 1998. pap. 19.95 (*0-944428-46-0*) Cruising Guide.

— Sailors Guide to the Windward Islands. 6th ed. (Illus.). 320p. 1992. pap. 17.95 (*976-8063-07-6*) F Papy Cruising Guide.

Doyle, Chris & Fisher, Jeff. Cruising Guide to Venezuela & Bonaire. (Illus.). 224p. 1997. pap. 26.95 (*0-944428-38-X*) Cruising Guide.

Doyle, Chris, jt. auth. see Barlow, Virginia.

Doyle, Christina. Information Literacy in an Information Society: A Concept for the Information Age. 84p. 1994. 8.00 (*0-937597-38-4*) ERIC Clear.

Doyle, Christina S. Information Literacy in an Information Society: A Concept for the Information Age. 80p. (C). 1999. reprint ed. pap. text 20.00 (*0-7881-7012-0*) DIANE Pub.

An Asterisk (*) at the beginning of an entry indicates that the title is appearing for the first time.

***Doyle, Christine.** Louisa May Alcott & Charlotte Bronte: Transatlantic Translations. LC 99-50721. 232p. (C). 2000. text 28.00 (*1-57233-083-X*, Pub. by U of Tenn Pr) U Ch Pr.

Doyle, Christopher. A Cloud in Trousers. (Illus.). 128p. 1998. pap. 25.00 (*1-889195-33-2*, Pub. by Smart Art Pr) RAM Publications.

Doyle, Claire & Hutchinson, Vina. The Insiders' Guide to North Carolina's Central Coast & New Bern. 8th ed. (Insiders' Guide Travel Ser.). 1999. pap. 14.95 (*1-57380-119-4*, The Insiders Guide) Falcon Pub Inc.

Doyle, Clar. Raising Curtains on Education: Drama As a Site for Critical Pedagogy. LC 92-32180. (Critical Studies in Education & Culture). 176p. 1993. 55.00 (*0-89789-273-9*, H273, Bergin & Garvey) Greenwood.

— Raising Curtains on Education: Drama As a Site for Critical Pedagogy. LC 92-32180. (Critical Studies in Education & Culture). 176p. 1993. pap. 18.95 (*0-89789-274-7*, G274, Bergin & Garvey) Greenwood.

Doyle, Connie, ed. see Barraclough, Geoffrey.

Doyle, Connie, ed. see Dawson, Richard.

Doyle, Connie, ed. see Parkinson, Eric.

Doyle, Connie, ed. see Peacock, Graham & Smith, Robin.

Doyle, Crane, ed. Twentieth Century Poets: William Carlos Williams. (Critical Heritage Ser.). 456p. (C). 1997. 140.00 (*0-415-15944-X*) Routledge.

— Wilford Stirling Wilford. LC 97-173837. (Critical Heritage Ser.). (Illus.). 208p. (C). 1997. pap. 39.99 (*1-901050-00-9*) Routledge.

Doyle, Cranes, ed. Wallace Stevens. (Critical Heritage Ser.). 520p. (C). 1997. 160.00 (*0-415-15943-1*) Routledge.

Doyle, D. J. Computer Programs in Clinical & Laboratory Medicine. (Illus.). 200p. 1989. 57.00 (*0-387-96879-2*) Spr-Verlag.

Doyle, Daniel E., Jr. Are You Watching, Adolph Rupp? 336p. 1989. 18.95 (*0-929938-00-3*) Stadia Pubs.

Doyle, Danny & Folan, Terence. Golden Sun of Irish Freedom: 1798 in Song & Story. LC 99-175546. (Illus.). 160p. 1998. pap. 12.95 (*1-85635-208-0*, Pub. by Mercier Pr) Irish Amer Bk.

Doyle, David M. The Hunger: Beyond the Fields of Influence. 124p. Date not set. pap. write for info. (*0-945704-06-2*) Genesis Comns.

Doyle, David M., tr. see Bazhanov, Boris.

Doyle, David N. Irish-Americans, Native Rights & National Empires: The Structure, Divisions, & Attitudes of the Catholic Minority in the Decade of Expansion, 1890-1901. LC 76-6336. (Irish Americans Ser.). 1976. 29.95 (*0-405-09332-2*) Ayer.

Doyle, David N. & Edwards, Owen D., eds. America & Ireland, 1776-1976: The American Identity & the Irish Connection. LC 79-7066. 348p. 1980. 59.95 (*0-313-21119-1*, DOA/, Greenwood Pr) Greenwood.

Doyle, David W. Adding Value to Marketing. 256p. 1998. pap. 35.00 (*0-7494-2175-4*) Kogan Page Ltd.

Doyle, Deborah, ed. The Chicago Architectural Journal, 1984, Vol. 4. LC 82-641459. (Illus.). 136p. 1984. 17.50 (*0-9614052-0-1*) Chicago Arch.

Doyle, Debra. The Knight's Wyrd. LC 92-53944. 320p. 1997. pap. 6.00 (*0-15-201520-5*) Harcourt.

Doyle, Debra. The Knight's Wyrd. (Magic Carpet Books Ser.). (J). 1997. 11.10 (*0-606-11539-0*, Pub. by Turtleback) Demco.

Doyle, Debra. Long Hunt. 1996. mass mkt. 5.99 (*0-8125-3496-4*, Pub. by Tor Bks) St Martin.

***Doyle, Debra.** Stars Asunder. (Mageworlds Ser.). 384p. 2000. mass mkt. 6.99 (*0-8125-7192-4*) Tor Bks.

— Working of Stars. 2000. text. write for info. (*0-312-86411-6*) St Martin.

Doyle, Debra & MacDonald, James D. By Honor Betray'd. 416p. (Orig.). 1994. mass mkt. 4.99 (*0-8125-1706-7*, Pub. by Tor Bks) St Martin.

***Doyle, Debra & MacDonald, James D.** Danger in the Palace. (Illus.). 32p. (J). (gr. 3-7). 2000. pap. 3.95 (*0-8167-6939-7*) Troll Communs.

Doyle, Debra & MacDonald, James D. The Gathering Flame: The Prequel to Mageworlds. (Mageworlds Ser.: No. 4). 448p. (Orig.). 1995. mass mkt. 5.99 (*0-8125-3495-6*, Pub. by Tor Bks) St Martin.

***Doyle, Debra & MacDonald, James D.** Gene Roddenberry's Earth No. 3: Final Conflict - Requiem for Boone. 320p. 2000. 23.95 (*0-312-87460-X*, Pub. by Tor Bks) St Martin.

Doyle, Debra & MacDonald, James D. Groogleman. LC 96-2022. 128p. (J). 1996. 15.00 (*0-15-200235-9*) Harcourt.

— The Knight's Wyrd. LC 92-53789. 176p. (YA). (gr. 7 up). 1992. 16.95 (*0-15-200764-4*, Harcourt Child Bks) Harcourt.

— The Price of the Stars. (MageWorlds Ser.: No. 1). 448p. (Orig.). 1992. mass mkt. 4.99 (*0-8125-1704-0*, Pub. by Tor Bks) St Martin.

***Doyle, Debra & MacDonald, James D.** Requiem for Boone. (Gene Roddenberry's Earth Ser.). 320p. 2000. pap. 13.95 (*0-312-87461-8*, Pub. by Tor Bks) St Martin.

— School of Wizardry. (Circle of Magic Ser.: Vol. 1). (Illus.). 144p. (J). (gr. 3-7). 2000. pap. 3.95 (*0-8167-6936-2*) Troll Communs.

— Secret of the Tower. (Circle of Magic Ser.: Vol. 2). (Illus.). 144p. (J). (gr. 3-7). 2000. pap. 3.95 (*0-8167-6937-0*) Troll Communs.

Doyle, Debra & MacDonald, James D. Starpilot's Grave. (MageWorlds Ser.: No. 2). 448p. (Orig.). 1993. mass mkt. 4.50 (*0-8125-1705-9*, Pub. by Tor Bks) St Martin.

— The Stars Asunder. LC 99-24561. 320p. 1999. 24.95 (*0-312-86410-8*, Pub. by Tor Bks) St Martin.

***Doyle, Debra & MacDonald, James D.** The Wizard's Statue. (Illus.). 144p. (J). (gr. 3-7). 2000. pap. 3.95 (*0-8167-6938-9*) Troll Communs.

Doyle, Debra, ed. see Shelley, Mary Wollstonecraft.

Doyle, Debra, ed. see Walker, Dot & Brown, Pamela.

***Doyle, Del R.** Ghost Creek Renegades. large type ed. 224p. 1999. pap. 18.99 (*0-7089-5517-7*, Linford) Ulverscroft.

Doyle, Denis, jt. auth. see Kearns, David T.

Doyle, Denis P. The Business of Our Schools. (Excellence in Education Ser.). 32p. 1992. pap. text 3.00 (*1-878802-09-7*) J M Ashbrook Ctr Pub Affairs.

Doyle, Denis P. & Cooper, Bruce S. Federal Aid to the Disadvantaged, What Future for Chapter 1? (Education Policy Perspectives Ser.). 276p. 1988. 75.00 (*1-85000-368-8*, Falmer Pr) Taylor & Francis.

Doyle, Denis P. & Hartle, Terry W. Excellence in Education: The States Take Charge. LC 85-15731. (AEI Studies: No. 424). 88p. reprint ed. pap. 30.00 (*0-7837-0359-7*, 204068100018) Bks Demand.

Doyle, Denis P. & Pimentel, Susan. Raising the Standard: An Eight-Step Action Guide for Schools & Communities. LC 97-33893. 184p. 1997. pap. 29.95 (*0-8039-6707-1*) Corwin Pr.

— Raising the Standard: An Eight-Step Action Guide for Schools & Communities. LC 97-33893. 184p. 1998. 69.95 (*0-8039-6706-3*) Corwin Pr.

— Raising the Standard: An Eight-Step Action Guide for Schools & Communities. 2nd ed. LC 99-6170. (One-Off Ser.). 200p. 1999. pap. 35.00 incl. cd-rom (*0-8039-6869-8*) Corwin Pr.

Doyle, Denis P., et al. Taking Charge: State Action on School Reform in the 1980s. 150p. (Orig.). (C). 1991. pap. text 18.50 (*1-55813-038-1*) Hudson Instit IN.

Doyle, Dennis. The Church Emerging from Vatican Two: A Popular Approach to Contemporary Catholicism. LC 91-67714. 368p. (Orig.). 1992. pap. 14.95 (*0-89622-507-0*) Twenty-Third.

***Doyle, Dennis.** Irish Harp Music. 48p. 1998. pap. 12.95 (*0-7866-2846-4*, 97853) Mel Bay.

***Doyle, Dennis & Doyle, Paula.** Be in My Heart: Celtic Hymns & Songs Through the Day. 1998. audio 9.95 (*0-87793-918-7*); audio compact disk 15.95 (*0-87793-919-5*) Ave Maria.

Doyle, Dennis & Doyle, Paula. Songs of Celtic Christianity. (Illus.). 64p. (Orig.). 1994. write for info. (*1-886314-00-4*) Incarnat Music.

***Doyle, Dennis M.** Communion Ecclesiology: Vision & Versions. 192p. 2000. pap. 25.00 (*1-57075-327-X*) Orbis Bks.

Doyle, Dennis M. Efficient Accounting & Record Keeping. LC 78-2474. (Small Business Ser.). 116p. 1978. pap. 16.95 (*0-471-05044-X*) Wiley.

Doyle, Derek. Domiciliary Palliative Care: A Guide for the Primary Care Team. (Oxford General Practice Ser.: No. 27). (Illus.). 160p. 1995. pap. text 39.95 (*0-19-262489-X*) OUP.

***Doyle, Derek, et al, eds.** Oxford Textbook of Palliative Medicine. 2nd ed. (Illus.). 1,309p. 1999. pap. text 95.00 (*0-19-263057-1*) OUP.

Doyle, Derek, et al, eds. Oxford textbook of Palliative Medicine. 2nd ed. LC 97-34659. (Illus.). 1,308p. 1997. text 139.50 (*0-19-262566-7*) OUP.

Doyle, Don. Heroes of the Heart: Treasured Stories of Hurt, Hate, Horror & Humor. LC 95-71707. (Going Sane Ser.). (Illus.). 162p. 1995. 17.95 (*1-57087-200-7*) Prof Pr NC.

Doyle, Don H. Nashville since the 1920s. LC 85-3562. (Illus.). 352p. 1985. 34.00 (*0-87049-470-8*) U of Tenn Pr.

— New Men, New Cities, New South: Atlanta, Nashville, Charleston, Mobile, 1860-1910. LC 89-34924. (Fred W. Morrison Series in Southern Studies). (Illus.). xxii, 369p. (C). 1990. 65.00 (*0-8078-1883-6*); pap. 19.95 (*0-8078-4270-2*) U of NC Pr.

— The Social Order of a Frontier Community: Jacksonville, Illinois, 1825-70. LC 78-5287. (Illus.). 304p. 1978. text 29.95 (*0-252-00685-2*) U of Ill Pr.

— The Social Order of a Frontier Community: Jacksonville, Illinois, 1825-70. LC 78-5287. (Illus.). 304p. 1983. pap. text 23.95 (*0-252-01036-1*) U of Ill Pr.

Doyle, Don H., jt. ed. see Griffin, Larry J.

Doyle, Donald C. The Portable Therapist. Doyle, Betty, ed. LC 95-92394. 280p. (Orig.). (C). 1995. pap. 14.95 (*0-9648370-0-5*) D&D Publns.

Doyle, Doris Carol & Doyle, Ian. Fine Art Children's Photography: Techniques & Images In Black & White. 1. 128p. 1999. pap. text 29.95 (*1-58428-010-7*, Pub. by Amherst Media) IPG Chicago.

Doyle, Dorothy. Journey Through Jess: A Novel. LC 88-51753. 352p. (Orig.). 1989. pap. 12.00 (*0-923145-04-4*) Ten Star Pr.

Doyle, Dorothy P. Dancing on the Edge: A Story of Cancer, Courage, & the Resurrection of Life. LC 95-94707. 256p. 1996. pap. 14.95 (*0-9647763-5-9*) Hibiscus FL.

Doyle, E. F., et al. Pediatric Cardiology. (Illus.). I, 1340p. 1985. 198.00 (*0-387-96204-2*) Spr-Verlag.

Doyle, Edith M. Drafting California Irrevocable Living Trusts: February 1992 Update. 2nd ed. Gamble, Carol, ed. LC 86-72863. 941p. 1992. ring bd. 55.00 (*0-88124-452-X*, ES-32343) Cont Ed Bar-CA.

— Drafting California Irrevocable Living Trusts: June 1993 Update. 2nd ed. Allison, Cherri, ed. LC 86-72863. 262p. 1993. 55.00 (*0-88124-662-X*, ES-32344) Cont Ed Bar-CA.

— Drafting California Irrevocable Living Trusts: June 1994 Update. 2nd ed. LC 86-72863. 250p. 1994. 57.00 (*0-88124-770-7*, ES-32345) Cont Ed Bar-CA.

Doyle, Edward & Goggin, Paul. MCQs & OSCEs for the Primary FRCA. LC 96-39853. 168p. 1997. pap. text 35.00 (*0-7506-2338-1*) Buttrwrth-Heinemann.

Doyle, Edward G. A Commemorative History of the Cambridge Public Library. LC 89-17441. 120p. (Orig.). 1989. pap. 6.95 (*0-9623982-0-9*) Cambridge Pub Lib.

Doyle, Edward G. & Lipsman, Samuel L. America Takes over the Big Build-Up (1965-1967) Boston Publishing Company Editors, ed. (Vietnam Experience Ser.). (Illus.). 192p. 1983. 16.30 (*0-201-11328-7*) Addison-Wesley.

— Raising the Stakes, 3 vols. Boston Publishing Company Editors & Manning, Robert, eds. (Illus.). 1982. write for info. (*0-318-50145-7*) Addison-Wesley.

— Raising the Stakes, 3 vols., Vol. I. Boston Publishing Company Editors & Manning, Robert, eds. (Illus.). 192p. 1981. 16.30 (*0-201-11260-4*) Addison-Wesley.

— Raising the Stakes, 3 vols., Vol. II. Boston Publishing Company Editors & Manning, Robert, eds. (Illus.). 208p. 1981. 16.30 (*0-201-11261-2*) Addison-Wesley.

— Raising the Stakes, 3 vols., Vol. III. Boston Publishing Company Editors & Manning, Robert, eds. (Illus.). 192p. 1982. 16.30 (*0-201-11262-0*) Addison-Wesley.

Doyle, Edward G., et al. North Vietnam. 1986. 16.30 (*0-201-11276-0*) Addison-Wesley.

Doyle, Edward G., jt. auth. see Weiss, Stephen.

Doyle, Eileen. A Pro-Life Primer on Euthanasia. (Illus.). 84p. (Orig.). 1993. pap. 3.00 (*1-890712-09-4*, IE3) Amer Life League.

***Doyle, Elizabeth.** Now & Forever. 2000. mass mkt. 4.99 (*0-8217-6528-0*, Zebra Kensgtn) Kensgtn Pub Corp.

— Precious Passion. 1999. mass mkt. 4.99 (*0-8217-6446-2*) Kensgtn Pub Corp.

Doyle, Eric. Song of Brotherhood. (Pathways Ser.). 205p. 1996. pap. 18.00 (*1-57659-003-8*) Franciscan Inst.

Doyle, Eric, tr. see St. Bonaventure.

***Doyle, Eva & Ward, Susan.** The Process of Community Health Education & Promotion. LC 00-33244. 2000. write for info. (*0-7674-1561-2*) Mayfield Pub.

***Doyle, F. J., et al.** Identification & Control Using Volterra Models. LC 99-87077. (Communications & Control Engineering Ser.). (Illus.). 2000. write for info. (*1-85233-149-6*) Spr-Verlag.

Doyle, Fiona M., et al, eds. Innovations in Materials Processing Using Aqueous, Colloid & Surface Chemistry: Proceedings of A Topical Sympoium on Innovations in Materials Processing Using Aqueous, Colloid, & Surface Chemistry Held at the 1989 TMS Annual Meeting in Las Vegas, Nevada, February 27-March 3, 1989. LC 88-63684. (Illus.). 311p. 1988. reprint ed. pap. 96.50 (*0-7837-9135-6*, 204993500004) Bks Demand.

Doyle, Fiona M., ed. see Western Regional Symposium Mining & Mineral Wastes.

Doyle, Francis R. Searching the Law: The States. 2nd ed. LC 94-8319. 1994. 250.00 (*0-941320-88-X*) Transnatl Pubs.

Doyle, Francis R. Searching the Law: The States. 3rd ed. LC 94-8319. 1999. 125.00 (*1-57105-042-6*) Transnatl Pubs.

***Doyle, Francis R.** Searching the Law: The States, 2 vols. 3rd ed. LC 99-56932. 2000. 250.00 (*1-57105-101-5*) Transnatl Pubs.

Doyle, Francis R. & Bander, Edward J. Searching the Law. 2nd ed. LC 98-49318. 1999. 125.00 (*0-941320-90-1*) Transnatl Pubs.

Doyle, Gail. City Smart: Richmond. (City Smart Ser.). (Illus.). 224p. 1998. pap. 12.95 (*1-56261-375-8*, City Smart) Avalon Travel.

***Doyle, Gail.** City Smart: Richmond. 2nd ed. (Illus.). 216p. 2000. pap. 12.95 (*1-56261-510-6*, City Smart) Avalon Travel.

Doyle, Gail. Travel Smart: Virginias: Includes Washington D. C. (Travel Smart Ser.). (Illus.). 256p. 1999. pap. 15.95 (*1-56261-453-3*, Travel Smart) Avalon Travel.

Doyle, Gary T. Dancing the Last Mazurka: A Care Givers Journal. xii, 224p. 1998. mass mkt. 7.95 (*1-892589-11-7*) Madjec Jet.

Doyle, Georgina R. Roxanne, Does Your Husband Travel? The Corporate Wife: For Bitters or Wurst. 196p. 1985. pap. write for info. (*0-931515-07-6*) Triumph Pr.

Doyle, Glen Caspers. IHC - Care of Patients with Alzheimer's Disease. (Home Care Aide Ser.). 1989. pap. 325.00 (*0-8273-3358-7*) Delmar.

Doyle, Helen M. Doctor Nellie: The Autobiography of Dr. Helen MacKnight Doyle. LC 83-5720. (Illus.). 384p. 1983. reprint ed. 17.50 (*0-931378-07-9*) Live Oak.

Doyle, Hilary. Flammpanzer German Flamethrowers 1939-45. (Elite Ser.). (Illus.). 48p. 1995. pap. 12.95 (*1-85532-547-0*, Pub. by Ospry) Stackpole.

Doyle, Hilary & Jentz, Tom. Panther Medium Tank, 1943-45. (New Vanguard Ser.: No. 21). (Illus.). 48p. 1996. pap. 12.95 (*1-85532-476-8*, Pub. by Ospry) Stackpole.

— Stug III: Assault Gun. (Illus.). 48p. 1996. pap. 12.95 (*1-85532-537-3*, Pub. by Ospry) Stackpole.

— Tiger One. (New Vanguard Ser.: Vol. 5). (Illus.). 48p. 1993. pap. 12.95 (*1-85532-337-0*, 9340, Pub. by Ospry) Stackpole.

Doyle, Hilary, jt. auth. see Jentz, Thomas.

Doyle, Hilary, jt. auth. see Jentz, Tom.

Doyle, Hilary L., jt. auth. see Jentz, Thomas L.

Doyle, Hugh A. Seismology. LC 95-9101. 234p. 1996. pap. 80.00 (*0-471-94869-1*) Wiley.

Doyle, Ian, jt. auth. see Doyle, Doris Carol.

Doyle, J. A., jt. ed. see Kurmann, M. H.

Doyle, J. G., jt. ed. see Butler, C. J.

Doyle, J. J., jt. ed. see Crisp, M. D.

Doyle, Jack. Crude Awakening: The Oil Mess in America: Wasting Energy, Jobs, & the Environment. (Illus.). 350p. (Orig.). 1994. pap. 35.00 (*0-913890-95-2*) Friends of Earth.

***Doyle, Jack.** Taken for a Ride: Detroit's Big Three & the Politics of Air Pollution. LC 99-88236. (Illus.). 550p. 2000. pap. 22.00 (*1-56858-147-5*, Pub. by FWEW) Publishers Group.

Doyle, James. Dyslexia: An Introductory Guide. (Illus.). 218p. (Orig.). 1995. pap. 39.95 (*1-56593-604-3*, 1254) Thomson Learn.

— The Fin-de-Siecle Spirit. LC 95-225872. (Illus.). 160p. 1995. pap. 15.95 (*1-55022-232-5*) LPC InBook.

— The Governor's Office. 1986. 2.00 (*0-932593-05-4*) Black Bear.

— Stephen Leacock: The Sage of Orillia. (Illus.). 79p. (Orig.). 1993. pap. 9.95 (*1-55022-155-8*, Pub. by ECW) LPC InBook.

— Stephen Leacock: The Sage of Orillia. large type ed. (Illus.). 107p. (Orig.). 1995. pap. 15.95 (*1-55022-238-4*, Pub. by ECW) Genl Dist Srvs.

Doyle, James, ed. Yankees in Canada. 231p. (C). 1980. pap. text 3.50 (*0-920802-28-1*, Pub. by ECW) Genl Dist Srvs.

Doyle, James A. The Male Experience. 3rd ed. 368p. (C). 1994. text. write for info. (*0-697-10458-3*) Brown & Benchmark.

— Sex & Gender: The Human Experience. 3rd ed. 384p. (C). 1994. text. write for info. (*0-697-12735-4*) Brown & Benchmark.

Doyle, James A. & Paludi, Michele A. Sex & Gender: The Human Experience. 4th ed. LC 97-12938. 368p. 1997. pap. 45.94 (*0-697-25282-5*) McGraw.

Doyle, James F. Static & Dynamic Analysis of Structures: With Emphasis on Mechanics & Computer Matrix Methods. (C). 1991. pap. text 82.50 (*0-7923-1208-2*); lib. bdg. 157.50 (*0-7923-1124-8*) Kluwer Academic.

— Wave Propagation in Structures. (Illus.). x, 258p. 1989. 69.95 (*0-387-97078-9*) Spr-Verlag.

— Wave Propagation in Structures: Spectral Analysis Using Fast Fourier Transforms. 2nd ed. LC 97-1015. (Mechanical Engineering Ser.). 344p. 1997. 69.00 (*0-387-94940-2*) Spr-Verlag.

Doyle, James M., jt. auth. see Loftus, Elizabeth F.

Doyle, James S. The Business Coach: A Game Plan for the New Work Environment. LC 98-35144. 191p. 1999. 24.95 (*0-471-29326-1*) Wiley.

Doyle, James T. Epitaph for a Loser. 1988. 17.95 (*0-8027-5713-8*) Walker & Co.

Doyle, Jamie K. & Schelhas, John. Forest Remnants in the Tropical Landscape: Benefits & Policy Implications. 104p. (Orig.). pap. write for info. (*0-318-71304-7*) Smiths Migratory.

Doyle, Janet, et al. Practical Audiology for Speech-Language Therapists. LC 98-205045. xi, 292p. 1998. write for info. (*1-86156-059-1*) Whurr Pub.

Doyle, Jean M. & Dennis, Robert L. The Complete Handbook for Medical Secretaries & Assistants. 2nd ed. 1978. pap. text 18.95 (*0-316-18082-3*, Little Brwn Med Div) Lppncott W & W.

Doyle, Jeannine. Managing the Mortgage Maze: A Professional's Guide. 196p. 1997. pap. 65.90 (*0-9672223-0-3*) D&S Pubns WI.

Doyle, Jeannine, ed. see Martinez, Gayle R.

Doyle, Jeff. CCIC Professional Development: Routing TCP/IP, 1. LC 98-84220. (CCIE Preparation Guides Ser.: Vol. 1). 1998. 70.00 (*1-57870-041-8*) Cisco Press.

— CCIE Professional Development: Routing TCP IP, Vol. 2. 512p. 2000. 70.00 (*1-57870-089-2*) Macmillan Tech.

Doyle, Jeff & Grey, Jeffrey, eds. Australia R & R: Representations & Reinterpretations of Australia's War in Vietnam. (Vietnam Generation Ser.). 176p. (Orig.). (C). 1991. pap. text 15.00 (*0-9628524-3-0*) Burning Cities Pr.

Doyle, Jennifer, et al, eds. Pop Out: Queer Warhol. LC 95-35410. (Series Q). (Illus.). 296p. 1996. text 49.95 (*0-8223-1732-X*); pap. text 17.95 (*0-8223-1741-9*) Duke.

Doyle, Jeremiah W., IV. Preparing Fiduciary Income Tax Returns. LC 96-80039. 600p. 1997. ring bd. 95.00 (*1-57589-064-X*) Mass CLE.

Doyle, Jerry. Chessie System Diesel Locomotives. (Illus.). 112p. 1999. 36.95 (*1-883089-42-5*, Pub. by TLC VA) Motorbooks Intl.

Doyle, Jim. Tales from a Real Life: Everyday Essays. 136p. 1999. pap. 9.95 (*0-88489-623-4*) St Marys.

Doyle, Jim & Doyle, Brian. Two Voices: A Father & Son Discuss Family & Faith. LC 96-11396. 192p. (Orig.). 1996. pap. 11.00 (*0-89243-934-3*) Liguori Pubns.

Doyle, Joanne M., jt. auth. see Doyle, John M.

Doyle, John. Michigan Citation Manual. LC 85-82097. 122p. 1986. lib. bdg. 32.00 (*0-89941-462-1*, 303780) W S Hein.

Doyle, John & Lischner, Ray. Shakespeare for Dummies. (For Dummies Ser.). (Illus.). 384p. 1999. pap. 16.99 (*0-7645-5135-3*) IDG Bks.

Doyle, John A. The English in America, 5 vols., Set. Incl. Pt. 1. Puritan Colonies. (*0-404-02181-6*); Pt. 2. Puritan Colonies. (*0-404-02182-4*); Vol. 3. Middle Colonies. (*0-404-02183-2*); Vol. 4. Virginia, Maryland & the Carolinas. (*0-404-02184-0*); Vol. 5. Colonies Under the House of Hanover. (*0-404-02185-9*); (Illus.). reprint ed. 345.00 (*0-404-02180-8*) AMS Pr.

Doyle, John J. & Persley, Gabrielle J., eds. Enabling the Safe Use of Biotechnology: Principles & Practice. LC 96-22061. (Environmentally Sustainable Development Studies & Monographs Ser.: No. 10). 84p. 1996. pap. 22.00 (*0-8213-3671-1*, 13671) World Bank.

Doyle, John M. & Doyle, Joanne M. Of Parks & People. 50p. 1999. 10.00 (*0-9672703-0-8*) Wild Geese Ent.

***Doyle, John M. & Doyle, Joanne M.** The Summer Country. 2000. 7.50 (*0-9672703-1-6*) Wild Geese Ent.

Doyle, John P. Care & Handling of Salmon: The Key to Quality. (Marine Advisory Bulletin Ser.: No. 45). 66p. (Orig.). 1992. pap. text 5.00 (*1-56612-010-1*) AK Sea Grant CP.

Doyle, John P., tr. Francis Suarez, SJ: On Being of Reason, Metaphysical Disputation LIV. LC 94-72904. (Medieval Philosophical Texts in Translation Ser.: No. 33). 140p. (C). 1994. pap. 15.00 (*0-87462-236-0*) Marquette.

An Asterisk (*) at the beginning of an entry indicates that the title is appearing for the first time.

D

Doyle, John P., tr. & intro. see De Vitoria, Francisco.

Doyle, Jon, et al, eds. Proceedings of the 4th International Conference on Principles of Knowledge Representation & Reasoning. LC 94-9421. (Morgan Kaufmann Series in Representation & Reasoning). 655p. (C). 1994. pap. text 59.95 (1-55860-328-X) Morgan Kaufmann.

Doyle, Joseph B. 20th Century History of Steubenville & Jefferson County, a Representative Citizens. (Illus.). 1190p. 1997. reprint ed. lib. bdg. 114.50 (0-8328-6365-3) Higginson Bk Co.

Doyle, Judith. Transcript. 12p. (Orig.). 1981. pap. 3.00 (0-917061-08-X) Top Stories.

Doyle, Judith A., ed. see Nielson, Palle.

Doyle, Julie A., et al, eds. This Wilderness of War: The Civil War Letters of George W. Squier, Hoosier Volunteer. LC 97-33835. (Voices of the Civil War Ser.). (Illus.). 160p. 1998. 30.00 (1-57233-006-6) U of Tenn Pr.

Doyle, Kathleen, ed. see Corporate Agents, Inc. Staff.

Doyle, Kathleen, ed. see Lynch, Francis.

Doyle, Kathleen, ed. see Priz, Edward J.

Doyle, Ken, jt. auth. see Schmitz, Eric.

Doyle, Kenneth O., Jr. Social Meanings of Money & Property: In Search of a Talisman. LC 98-40185. 6p. 1998. 65.00 (0-7619-0208-2); pap. 29.95 (0-7619-0209-0) Sage.

Doyle, Kevin. Dating Younger Women: Cosmopolitan Guide for the Third Millennium. unabridged ed. (Renaissance Bks.: Vol. 2). (Illus.). 80p. 1998. pap. 14.95 (0-9652952-7-3) Doyle Studio.

***Doyle, Kevin.** How to Meet Beautiful Women: A Renaissance Book. (Illus.). 96p. 1998. pap. 14.95 (0-9652952-6-5) Doyle Studio.

Doyle, Kevin. Pensions Around the World. 82p. 1983. 70.00 (0-900886-79-X, Pub. by Witherby & Co) St Mut.

Doyle, Larry. Educational Crossword Puzzles in Chemistry. 64p. (YA). (gr. 9-12). 1990. per. 4.90 (0-921369-05-0) J C George Ent.

Doyle, Larry. MTV's Beavis & Butthead: Huh Huh for Hollywood. LC 97-109795. 1984. pap. 1.95 (0-671-00655-X) PB.

— This Sucks, Change It! (MTV's Beavis & Butthead Ser.: No. 3). 1995. 20.00 (0-671-53633-8) PB.

Doyle, Larry J. & Pilkey, Orrin H., eds. Geology of Continental Slopes. LC 79-127588. (Society of Economic Paleontologists & Mineralogists Ser.: Vol. 27). (Illus.). 382p. 1979. reprint ed. pap. 118.50 (0-608-05670-7, 206618600006) Bks Demand.

Doyle, Larry R., et al. Living with the West Florida Shore. LC 84-13611. (Living with the Shore Ser.). 240p. 1985. pap. 16.95 (0-8223-0517-8); text 39.95 (0-8223-0516-X) Duke.

***Doyle, Laura.** The Surrendered Wife: A Practical Guide to Finding Intimacy, Passion & Peace with a Man. 2001. pap. 11.00 (0-7432-0444-1, Touchstone) S&S Trade Pap.

— The Surrendered Wife: A Woman's Spiritual Guide to True Intimacy with a Man. Gordon, Christine, ed. 147p. 1999. pap. 14.95 (0-9673058-0-2, Pub. by St Monday Pubng) ACCESS Pubs Network.

Doyle, Laurance R., ed. Circumstellar Habitable Zones: Proceedings of the 1st International Conference. 1996. pap. 75.00 (0-9650896-0-6) Travis Hse.

Doyle, Leo F. Computer Peripherals. 2nd ed. LC 98-56087. 264p. (C). 1999. 69.00 (0-13-779463-0) P-H.

Doyle, Leonard J., tr. St. Benedict's Rule for Monasteries. 106p. 1950. pap. 3.95 (0-8146-0644-X) Liturgical Pr.

Doyle, Lisa A., jt. auth. see Ryan, Ray.

Doyle, Liz. How to Make Raffia Hats, Bags, & Baskets. LC 94-30287. (Illus.). 64p. 1995. pap. 9.95 (0-88266-887-0, Storey Pub) Storey Bks.

Doyle, M. R., jt. auth. see Coleman, D.

Doyle, M. Timothea, tr. see Garrigou-Lagrange, Reginald.

Doyle, Malachy. Jody's Beans. LC 98-40634. (Illus.). 32p. (J). (ps-1). 1999. 15.99 (0-7636-0687-1, Pub. by Candlewick Pr) Penguin Putnam.

***Doyle, Malachy.** Tales from Old Ireland. (Illus.). 96p. (YA). (gr. 8 up). 2000. 19.99 (1-902283-97-X) Barefoot Bks NY.

— Well, a Crocodile Can. LC 98-33792. (Illus.). 16p. (J). (gr. k-2). 1999. 12.95 (0-7613-1032-0, Copper Beech Bks) Millbrook Pr.

Doyle, Marc. The Future of Television. (Illus.). 208p. 1993. 49.95 (0-8442-3461-3, NTC Business Bks) NTC Contemp Pub Co.

— The Future of Television. (Illus.). 208p. 1994. pap. 19.95 (0-8442-3462-1, NTC Business Bks) NTC Contemp Pub Co.

Doyle, Margaret. The A-Z of Non-Sexist Language. 112p. 1997. pap. 13.95 (0-7043-4430-0, Pub. by Womens Press) Trafalgar.

— Understanding Sex. (Collins Gem Ser.). 1996. pap. 8.00 (0-00-470850-4) Collins.

Doyle, Marian M. The Doyle, Massey, Maher & McCormick Families. (Illus.). 112p. (Orig.). 1989. pap. write for info. (0-9624481-0-9) M M Doyle.

Doyle, Mark, jt. auth. see Coleman, James.

Doyle, Mark, jt. auth. see Wyland Studios Staff.

Doyle, Mary & Donnelly, Joseph, eds. Freedom of Information Act: A Practical Guide. LC 99-209550. 1998. pap. 28.00 (1-901657-37-X) Gaunt.

Doyle, Mary A., jt. ed. see Irwin, Judith W.

Doyle, Mary B. The Paraprofessional's Guide to the Inclusive Classroom: Working As a Team. LC 97-14059. (Illus.). xiii, 146p. 1997. 23.95 (1-55766-312-2) P H Brookes.

Doyle, Mary E. The Sympathetic Response: George Eliot's Fictional Rhetoric. LC 80-65908. (Illus.). 192p. 1981. 29.50 (0-8386-3065-0) Fairleigh Dickinson.

***Doyle, Mary K.** Mentoring Heroes: 52 Fabulous Women's Paths to Success & the Mentors Who Empowered Them. LC 99-97451. 237p. 2000. 21.95 (0-9677449-2-X) ThreeE Press.

Doyle, Mary L., ed. see Mead, Sidney E.

Doyle, Mary P. Study of Play Selection in Women's Colleges. LC 72-176728. (Columbia University. Teachers College. Contributions to Education Ser.: No. 648). reprint ed. 37.50 (0-404-55648-5) AMS Pr.

Doyle, Maureen, ed. see Parisi, Helen.

Doyle, Michael. American West on Film: The Agrarian Frontier. 2nd ed. 144p. (C). 1996. pap. text, per. 29.95 (0-7872-1979-7, 41197901) Kendall-Hunt.

— The Art of the Amplifier. (Illus.). 80p. (Orig.). 1996. per. 22.95 (0-7935-3989-7, HL00330002) H Leonard.

— The History of Marshall: The Illustrated Story of "the Sound of Rock" (Illus.). 256p. 1993. per. 32.95 (0-7935-2509-8, 00330058) H Leonard.

— A History of Marshall Valve Guitar Amplifiers, 1962-1992. (Illus.). 256p. 32.95 (0-614-30327-3) H Leonard.

— How to Make Meetings Work. 1993. pap. 12.95 (0-425-13870-4) Berkley Pub.

Doyle, Michael & Straus, David. How to Make Meetings Work. (Illus.). 320p. 1986. mass mkt. 6.50 (0-515-09048-4, Jove) Berkley Pub.

Doyle, Michael, et al. Modern Catalytic Methods for Organic Synthesis with Diazo Compounds: From Cyclopropanes to Ylides. LC 97-16541. 652p. 1998. 135.00 (0-471-13556-9) Wiley.

Doyle, Michael, jt. auth. see Schroeder, Hattie.

Doyle, Michael, ed. see Anderson-Sannes, Barbara.

Doyle, Michael E. Color Drawing: A Marker-Colored Pencil Approach for Architects, Landscape Architects, Interior & Graphic Designers, & Artists. rev. ed. LC 92-34773. (Illus.). 320p. 1993. pap. 39.95 (0-442-01431-7, VNR) Wiley.

***Doyle, Michael E.** Color Drawing: Design Drawing Skills & Techniques for Architects, Landscape Architects, & Interior Designers. 2nd ed. LC 98-34054. 360p. 1999. 44.95 (0-471-29245-1) Wiley.

Doyle, Michael F., jt. auth. see Burt, David N.

Doyle, Michael P., ed. Advances in Catalytic Processes, Vol. 1. 196p. 1995. 109.50 (1-55938-700-9) Jai Pr.

— Advances in Catalytic Processes, Vol. 2. 290p. 1997. 109.50 (0-7623-0068-X) Jai Pr.

— Advances in Catalytic Processes, Vol. 3. Date not set. 109.50 (0-7623-0239-9) Jai Pr.

Doyle, Michael P., et al, eds. Food Microbiology: Fundamentals & Frontiers. LC 96-36638. (Illus.). 784p. 1997. 99.95 (1-55581-117-5) ASM Pr.

Doyle, Michael S., et al. Exito Comercial: Practicas Administrativas y Contextos Cultural. (Illus.). 336p. (C). 1991. pap. text 24.75 (0-03-029618-8) Harcourt Coll Pubs.

— Exito Comezical: Practices Administrativas y Contextos Culturales. 2nd ed. (SPA.). 416p. (C). 1996. pap. text 43.00 (0-03-017318-3) Holt R&W.

— W/B - Exito Commercial. 2nd ed. (SPA.). 232p. (C). 1996. wbk. ed. 37.00 (0-03-017319-1) Holt R&W.

Doyle, Michael S., tr. see Matute, Ana M.

Doyle, Michael V. Gerald R. Ford Selected Speeches. 1973. pap. 3.95 (0-87948-029-7) Beatty.

Doyle, Michael W. Empires. LC 85-24297. (Cornell Studies in Comparative History). (Illus.). 408p. 1986. 49.95 (0-8014-1756-2); pap. text 18.95 (0-8014-9334-X) Cornell U Pr.

— U. N. Peacekeeping in Cambodia: UNTAC's Civil Mandate. LC 94-43542. (IPA Occasional Paper Ser.). 64p. 1995. pap. text 10.95 (1-55587-497-5) L Rienner.

— Ways of War & Peace: Realism, Liberalism, & Socialism. LC 96-15090. 416p. 1997. 30.00 (0-393-03826-2) Norton.

— Ways of War & Peace: Realism, Liberalism, & Socialism. LC 96-15090. (C). 1997. pap. text 26.00 (0-393-96947-9) Norton.

Doyle, Michael W., et al, eds. Keeping the Peace: Multidimensional U. N. Operations in Cambodia & El Salvador. LC 96-39891. 448p. 1997. text 69.95 (0-521-58185-0); pap. text 27.95 (0-521-58837-5) Cambridge U Pr.

Doyle, Michael W. & Ikenberry, G. John, eds. New Thinking in International Relations Theory. LC 97-15796. 304p. (C). 1997. pap. 28.00 (0-8133-9966-1, Pub. by Westview) HarpC.

Doyle, Michael W., jt. ed. see Otunnu, Olara A.

Doyle, Mike. The Sound of Rock: Acoustic Six-String, Twelve-String, & Arched-Top Guitars. (Illus.). 68p. 1993. reprint ed. pap. 17.95 (0-933224-19-2, T038) Bold Strummer Ltd.

Doyle, Mike & Sorensen, Steve. Morning Glass: The Adventures of Legendary Waterman Mike Doyle. LC 93-78947. (Illus.). 272p. (Orig.). 1993. pap. 14.95 (0-9629418-2-4) Fuyu Pr.

Doyle, Mona. Packaging Strategy: Winning the Consumer. LC 96-60500. 185p. 1996. text 39.95 (1-56676-298-7) Technomic.

Doyle, Nicholas, ed. The Tiger Garden: A Book of Writers' Dreams. LC 96-69726. 256p. (Orig.). (C). 1997. pap. text 14.99 (1-85242-533-4) Serpents Tail.

Doyle, P. Las Marcas del Discipulo.Tr. of Mark of a Disciple. write for info. (1-56063-945-8, 497463) Editorial Unilit.

Doyle, P., ed. Baranskaya: A Week Like Any Other (Nedelya Kak Negelya) (Bristol Russian Texts Ser.). (RUS.). 126p. 1993. pap. 18.95 (1-85399-339-5, Pub. by Brist Class Pr) Focus Pub-R Pullins.

Doyle, P., jt. ed. see Bennett, Mathew.

Doyle, P. J. Glass-Making Today. (Illus.). 358p. (C). 1994. reprint ed. text 97.00 (1-878907-08-5, RAN) TechBooks.

***Doyle, Paddy.** God Squad. 2000. pap. 14.95 (0-552-13582-8, Pub. by Transworld Publishers Ltd) Trafalgar.

Doyle-Papadopoulou, Margie, tr. from GRE. How to Begin "Re-Evaluation Counseling" 16p. 1999. pap. 1.00 (1-58429-046-3) Rational Isl.

Doyle, Paul. Nioka: Bride of Bigfoot. 476p. 1991. pap. 14.95 (0-9630458-0-6) Daily Plnt Pr.

Doyle, Paul & Morandi, Larry. Financing Clean Water: Nonpoint Source Pollution Programs. Hansen, Karen, ed. 11p. 1991. pap. text 5.00 (1-55516-501-X, 4334) Natl Conf State Legis.

Doyle, Paul A. Liam O'Flaherty: An Annotated Bibliography. LC 71-161085. iv, 68p. 1972. 7.50 (0-87875-017-7) Whitston Pub.

— Paul Vincent Carroll. LC 70-126005. (Irish Writers Ser.). 115p. 1975. 8.50 (0-8387-7764-3); pap. 1.95 (0-8387-7659-0) Bucknell U Pr.

— Pearl S. Buck. rev. ed. (United States Authors Ser.: No. 85). 184p. 1980. 22.95 (0-8057-7325-8, Twyne) Mac Lib Ref.

— A Reader's Companion to the Novels & Short Stories of Evelyn Waugh. (Illus.). 233p. 1989. 39.95 (0-937664-78-2) Pilgrim Bks OK.

Doyle, Paul A., et al, eds. A Bibliography of Evelyn Waugh. xii, 473p. 1986. 49.50 (0-87875-313-3) Whitston Pub.

Doyle, Paula, jt. see Doyle, Dennis.

Doyle, Paula, jt. auth. see Doyle, Dennis.

Doyle, Peigin, jt. auth. see McDonald, Frank.

***Doyle, Peter.** Marketing Growth & Shareholder Value. 356p. 2000. pap. 47.95 (0-7506-4613-6) Buttrwrth-Heinemann.

— Marketing Management & Strategy. 2nd ed. 544p. (C). 1998. pap. 72.00 (0-13-262239-4) P-H.

Doyle, Peter. Understanding Fossils: An Introduction to Invertebrate Palaeontology. LC 95-49411. 426p. 1996. pap. 54.95 (0-471-96351-8) Wiley.

Doyle, Peter, ed. Butler's Lives of the Saints: October. rev. ed. 240p. 2000. 24.95 (0-8146-2386-7, Liturg Pr Bks) Liturgical Pr.

— Tendryakov: The Trial (Sud) (Bristol Russian Texts Ser.). (RUS.). 102p. (C). 1990. reprint ed. pap. 19.95 (0-631-15771-9) Blackwell Pubs.

Doyle, Peter & Bennett, Matthew. Unlocking the Stratigraphical Record: Advances in Modern Stratigraphy. LC 97-41823. 542p. 1998. 130.00 (0-471-97766-7) Wiley.

***Doyle, Peter & Bennett, Matthew, eds.** Unlocking the Stratigraphical Record: Advances in Modern Stratigraphy. LC 97-41823. 542p. 1998. pap. 69.95 (0-471-97463-3) Wiley.

***Doyle, Peter & Burns, Paul, eds.** Butler's Lives of the Saints: July. rev. ed. 288p. 2000. 24.95 (0-8146-2383-2) Liturgical Pr.

Doyle, Peter, et al. Calamus Lovers: Walt Whitman's Working-Class Camerados. Shively, Charley, ed. (Illus.). 224p. (Orig.). 1987. pap. 14.95 (0-917342-18-6); lib. bdg. 25.00 (0-917342-17-8) Gay Sunshine.

— The Key to Earth History: An Introduction to Stratigraphy. 244p. 1994. pap. 49.95 (0-471-94845-4) Wiley.

Doyle, Peter, jt. auth. see Bennett, Matthew.

Doyle, Peter G. & Snell, J. Laurie. Random Walks & Electric Networks. LC 84-61495. 159p. 1984. 28.95 (0-88385-024-9, CAM-22) Math Assn.

Doyle, Peter R. Ambushed in Africa. (Daring Adventure Ser.: Vol. 1). (J). (gr. 4). 1993. pap. 5.99 (1-56179-142-3) Focus Family.

— Bunker Hill. (Drums of War Ser.: Vol. 2). 172p. (YA). (gr. 4-12). 1999. pap. 7.95 (1-887456-08-2) Providence Found.

— Chased by the Jewel Thieves. LC 97-10870. (Daring Adventure Ser.: Bk. 11). (J). (gr. 4). 1997. pap. 5.99 (1-56179-547-X) Focus Family.

— Escape from Black Forest. LC 95-17602. (Daring Adventure Ser.: Vol. 8). (J). (gr. 4). 1995. pap. 5.99 (1-56179-397-3) Focus Family.

— Hot Pursuit on the High Seas. LC 94-14347. (Daring Adventure Ser.: No. 5). (J). (gr. 4). 1994. pap. 5.99 (1-56179-259-4) Focus Family.

— Hunted along the Rhine. LC 94-15365. (Daring Adventure Ser.: No. 6). (J). (gr. 4). 1994. pap. 5.99 (1-56179-260-8) Focus Family.

— Independence. LC 97-226258. (The Drums of War Ser.: Vol. 1). 170p. (Orig.). (J). (gr. 4-12). 1997. pap. 6.95 (1-887456-06-6) Providence Found.

— Kidnapped in Rome. LC 96-5781. (Daring Adventure Ser.: Vol. 9). (J). (gr. 4). 1996. pap. 5.99 (1-56179-480-5) Focus Family.

— Launched from the Castle. LC 95-2694. (Daring Adventure Ser.: Vol. 7). (J). (gr. 4). 1995. pap. 5.99 (1-56179-368-X) Focus Family.

— Lost in the Secret Cave. LC 96-7656. (Daring Adventure Ser.: Bk. 10). (J). (gr. 4). 1996. pap. 5.99 (1-56179-481-3) Focus Family.

— Stalked in the Catacombs. (Daring Adventure Ser.: Vol. 3). (J). (gr. 4). 1993. pap. 5.99 (1-56179-144-X) Focus Family.

— Surrounded by the Cross Fire. LC 94-10277. (Daring Adventure Ser.: No. 4). 1994. pap. 5.99 (1-56179-258-6) Focus Family.

— Trapped in Pharaoh's Tomb. (Daring Adventure Ser.: Vol. 2). (J). (gr. 4). 1993. pap. 5.99 (1-56179-143-1) Focus Family.

Doyle, Philip C. Foundations of Voice & Speech Rehabilitation Following Laryngeal Cancer. LC 94-7648. (Illus.). 309p. (Orig.). (C). 1994. pap. text 55.00 (1-56593-109-2, 0412) Thomson Learn.

Doyle, Phyllis. Portraits & Landscapes. LC 96-53848. 52p. 1997. pap. 14.95 (0-7734-2806-2, Mellen Poetry Pr) E Mellen.

Doyle, R. J. & Slifkin, Malcolm, eds. Lectin-Microorganism Interactions. (Illus.). 416p. 1994. text 195.00 (0-8247-9113-4) Dekker.

Doyle, R. W., et al, eds. Genetics in Aquaculture V. 368p. 1996. 169.50 (0-444-82386-7) Elsevier.

Doyle, Richard. Deluge. large type ed. 497p. 1980. 27.99 (0-7089-0457-2) Ulverscroft.

— The Foreign Tour of Messrs Brown, Jones & Robinson: Being the History of What They Saw & Did in Belgium, Germany, Switzerland, & Italy. LC 74-177503. (Illus.). 1972. reprint ed. 15.95 (0-405-08465-X, Pub. by Blom Pubns) Ayer.

***Doyle, Richard.** Jack the Giant Killer. (Everyman's Library Children's Classics). (Illus.). 96p. (J). 2000. 14.00 (0-375-41070-8, Pub. by Knopf Bks Yng Read) Random.

Doyle, Richard. On Beyond Living: Rhetorical Transformations of the Life Sciences. LC 96-38493. (Writing Science Ser.). 1997. write for info. (0-8047-2764-3); pap. 18.95 (0-8047-2765-1) Stanford U Pr.

***Doyle, Richard & Lang, Andrew.** Princess Nobody: A Tale of Fairyland. (Illus.). 64p. (J). 2000. pap. 9.95 (0-486-41020-X) Dover.

Doyle, Richard E. ATH: Its Use & Meaning: A Study in the Greek Poetic Tradition from Homer to Euripides. LC 83-80059. 200p. reprint ed. pap. 62.00 (0-7837-5596-1, 204550200005) Bks Demand.

Doyle, Richard F. A Manifesto of Men's Liberation. 4th rev. ed. 1995. pap. 4.00 (0-917212-03-7) Poor Richards.

Doyle, Robert A., ed. see Fields, Debbi.

Doyle, Robert A., ed. see Lewis, Shari.

***Doyle, Robert C.** Eschatology & the Shape of Christian Belief. x, 342p. 1999. reprint ed. pap. 30.00 (0-85364-818-2, Pub. by Paternoster Pub) OM Literature.

Doyle, Robert C. A Prisoner's Duty: Great Escapes in U. S. History. 480p. 1999. mass mkt. 6.50 (0-553-57973-8) Bantam.

— A Prisoner's Duty: Great Escapes in U. S. Military History. LC 97-16453. (Illus.). 400p. 1997. 34.95 (1-55750-180-7) Naval Inst Pr.

— Voices from Captivity: Interpreting the American POW Narrative. LC 93-41111. (Modern War Studies). (Illus.). 392p. 1994. 40.00 (0-7006-0663-7) U Pr of KS.

Doyle, Robert E. The Essential Skills & Strategies in the Helping Process. LC 91-24852. 336p. (C). 1992. text 53.95 (0-534-17328-4) Brooks-Cole.

— Essential Skills & Strategies in the Helping Process. 2nd ed. LC 97-18814. 308p. 1997. 45.95 (0-534-34879-3) Brooks-Cole.

Doyle, Robert P. Banned Books: 1998 Resource Book. 1998. pap. 20.00 (0-8389-7947-5) ALA.

— Banned Books Resource Guide. Date not set. 20.00 (0-8389-7791-X) ALA.

Doyle, Robert P., ed. Access to Library Resources Through Technology & Preservation: Proceedings of the 1988 U.S. - U.S.S.R. Seminar, July 5-8, 1988, Washington, DC. LC 89-6618. (Illus.). 165p. 1994. reprint ed. pap. 51.20 (0-7837-5949-5, 204574800007) Bks Demand.

Doyle, Robert P. & Grygel, Joan A., eds. Serving Our Public: Standards for Illinois Public Libraries. rev. ed. LC 97-25790. 100p. 1997. pap. write for info. (1-890249-01-7) IL Lib Assn.

Doyle, Robert S., jt. auth. see Wickman, Robert F.

Doyle, Roddy. The Barrytown Trilogy: The Commitments, the Snapper, the Van. LC 95-12323. 640p. 1995. pap. 17.95 (0-14-025262-2, Penguin Bks) Viking Penguin.

— Brownbread & War. 224p. 1994. pap. 12.00 (0-14-023115-3, Penguin Bks) Viking Penguin.

— The Commitments. LC 88-82388. (Vintage Contemporaries Ser.). 165p. 1989. pap. 11.00 (0-679-72174-6) Vin Bks.

***Doyle, Roddy.** The Giggler Treatment. LC 99-89032. (Illus.). 112p. (J). (gr. 4-7). 2000. 14.95 (0-439-16299-8) Scholastic Inc.

Doyle, Roddy. Paddy Clarke Ha Ha Ha. 288p. 1995. pap. 12.95 (0-14-023390-3, Penguin Bks) Viking Penguin.

— Paddy Clarke Ha Ha Ha. large type ed. LC 94-8218. 1994. 23.95 (1-56895-070-5) Wheeler Pub.

— The Snapper. 224p. 1992. pap. 11.95 (0-14-017167-3, Penguin Bks) Viking Penguin.

***Doyle, Roddy.** A Star Called Henry. (Illus.). 2000. pap. 14.00 (0-14-029613-1) Penguin Putnam.

— A Star Called Henry. LC 99-58825. (Illus.). (J). 2000. 25.95 (1-56895-818-8, Compass) Wheeler Pub.

Doyle, Roddy. The Van. 320p. 1993. pap. 11.95 (0-14-017191-6, Penguin Bks) Viking Penguin.

— The Van. 1997. pap. 11.95 (0-14-026002-1) Viking Penguin.

— The Woman Who Walked into Doors. 240p. 1997. pap. 12.95 (0-14-025512-5) Viking Penguin.

— The Woman Who Walked into Doors. large type ed. 288p. 1997. pap. 22.95 (0-614-25142-7, G K Hall Lrg Type) Mac Lib Ref.

— The Woman Who Walked into Doors. large type ed. LC 96-21104. 1996. pap. 22.95 (0-7862-0831-7) Thorndike Pr.

Doyle, Roddy, jt. auth. see Toibin, Colm.

Doyle, Rodger P. Atlas of Contemporary America: A Portrait of the Nation's Politics, Economy, Environment, Ethnic, & Religious Divesity. LC 93-38380. (Illus.). 256p. 1994. 45.00 (0-8160-2545-2) Facts on File.

***Doyle, Ronald J.** Glycomicrobiology. LC 99-44858. 1999. write for info. (0-306-46239-7, Kluwer Plenum) Kluwer Academic.

Doyle, Ronald J. & Rosenberg, Mel, eds. Microbial Cell Surface Hydrophobicity. (Illus.). 435p. 1990. text 65.00 (1-55581-028-4) ASM Pr.

Doyle, Rosa. Catholic Atmosphere in Marie Von Ebner Eschenbach: Its Use As a Literary Device. LC 70-140040. (Catholic University Studies in German: No. 6). reprint ed. 37.50 (0-404-50226-1) AMS Pr.

Doyle, Rose. Shiver! 15 Ghostly Stories. 170p. 1996. pap. 8.95 (1-85371-300-7, Pub. by Poolbeg Pr) Dufour.

Doyle, Rose, ed. Letters from Irish College. (Illus.). 128p. 1996. pap. 11.95 (1-86023-036-9, Pub. by Martello Bks) Irish Amer Bk.

An Asterisk (*) at the beginning of an entry indicates that the title is appearing for the first time.

Doyle, Ruth. Reconciled Through Christ: On Reconciliation & Greater Collaboration Between Hispanic American Catholics & African American Catholics. Herrera, Marina, ed. LC 97-131508. (ENG & SPA., Illus.). 88p. 1997. pap. 7.95 (*1-57455-025-X*) US Catholic.

Doyle, Ruth L., compiled by. Victor Hugo's Drama: An Annotated Bibliography, 1900 to 1980. LC 80-29680. 217p. 1981. lib. bdg. 55.00 (*0-313-22884-1*, DVH/, Greenwood Pr) Greenwood.

Doyle, Sharon E. In Other Words. (J). 1976. 6.00 (*0-87602-141-0*) Anchorage.

Doyle, Sifu G. The Martial Artist's Way: Achieve Your Peak Performance. LC 98-46199. (Orig.). 1999. pap. 14.95 (*0-8048-3195-5*) Tuttle Pubng.

Doyle, Stephanie. Undiscovered Hero. (Intimate Moments Ser.: No. 792). 1997. per. 3.99 (*0-373-07792-0*, 1-07792-4) Silhouette.

Doyle, Stephen. Advanced Information Technology. 600p. 1997. pap. 42.50 (*0-7487-2890-2*, Pub. by S Thornes Pubs) Trans-Atl Phila.

***Doyle, Stephen.** Information & Communication Technology for Advanced GNVQ. 2nd ed. (Illus.). 528p. 2000. pap. 59.50 (*0-7487-5317-6*, Pub. by S Thornes Pubs) Trans-Atl Phila.

— Information Systems for You: Skillbuilder. (Illus.). 256p. 2000. pap. 24.95 (*0-7487-5316-8*, Pub. by S Thornes Pubs) Trans-Atl Phila.

Doyle, Stephen. A Retreat with Mark: Embracing Discipleship. LC 98-200458. 96p. 1998. pap. 8.95 (*0-86716-324-0*) St Anthony Mess Pr.

— Thessalonians & Galatians. (Read & Pray Ser.). 1980. pap. 1.00 (*0-8199-0635-2*, Frncscn Herld) Franciscan Pr.

***Doyle, Stephen.** Understanding Information Technology. (Illus.). 512p. 2000. pap. 59.50 (*0-7487-3609-3*, Pub. by S Thornes Pubs) Trans-Atl Phila.

Doyle, Stephen. Understanding the New Testament. LC 88-82197. (Catholic Home Library). (Illus.). 128p. 1989. 4.95 (*1-55944-000-7*) Franciscan Comns.

Doyle, Stephen C. Pilgrim's New Guide to the Holy Land. 2nd ed. 1999. pap. text 14.95 (*0-8146-5955-1*) Liturgical Pr.

Doyle, Stephen E. Civil Space Systems: Implications for International Security. LC 93-39213. 288p. 1994. 72.95 (*1-85521-431-8*, Pub. by Dartmth Pub) Ashgate Pub Co.

Doyle, Stephen E., ed. History of Liquid Rocket Engine Development in the United States 1955-1980. (AAS History Ser.: Vol. 13). (Illus.). 176p. 1992. 50.00 (*0-87703-349-8*, Am Astronaut Soc) Univelt Inc.

Doyle, Susan B., ed. Journeys to the Land of Gold: Emigrants on the Bozeman Trail, 1863-1866, 2 vols., Set. (Illus.). 800p. 2000. 95.00 (*0-917298-48-9*) MT Hist Soc.

Doyle, Susan B., et al. Civilian. Military. Native American: Portraits of Fort Phil Kearny. (Illus.). 269p. (Orig.). 1993. pap. write for info. (*1-878856-14-6*) Ft P Kearney BT Assn.

Doyle, Suzannah C. A Fertility Awareness Self-Instruction Course. (Illus.). 185p. (Orig.). 1989. student ed. 45.00 (*0-9628284-2-4*) FA Services.

— Infertility Self-Help: What You Can Do to Regain Fertility. (Illus.). 55p. (Orig.). 1991. student ed. 15.00 (*0-9628284-3-2*) FA Services.

— The Ovulation Method Charting Booklet. 3rd rev. ed. (Illus.). 124p. 1991. pap. 10.00 (*0-9628284-0-8*) FA Services.

Doyle, Suzannah C., ed. A Fertility Awareness & Natural Family Planning Resource Directory, 1991. 2nd rev. ed. 200p. 1991. reprint ed. pap. 40.00 (*0-9628284-1-6*) FA Services.

Doyle, T. J. The Bend Sinister: A Mystery. LC 98-26424. 230p. 1998. 24.95 (*1-55618-174-4*) Brunswick Pub.

Doyle, Tara. All about the Seasons Activity Book. 32p. (J). (ps-3). 1993. 1.95 (*0-590-46296-2*) Scholastic Inc.

Doyle, Terence, et al. Procedures in Diagnostic Radiology. (Illus.). 248p. 1989. pap. text 35.00 (*0-443-02982-2*) Church.

Doyle, Terrence W., jt. ed. see Borders, Donald B.

Doyle, Terry, jt. auth. see Gatti-Doyle, Gigi.

Doyle, Thomas. Galatians: The Cost of Freedom. (God's Word for Today Ser.). 1994. pap. 5.50 (*0-570-09488-7*, 20-2644) Concordia.

Doyle, Thomas, jt. auth. see Schurby, Ken.

Doyle, Thomas J., jt. auth. see Delucia, Robert C.

Doyle, Thomas P., ed. Marriage Studies: Reflections in Canon Law & Theology, Vol. 1. 155p. 1980. pap. 3.00 (*0-943616-03-4*) Canon Law Soc.

***Doyle, Tim.** Green Power: The Environmental Movement in Australia. 224p. 2000. 35.00 (*0-86840-714-3*, Pub. by NSW U Pr) Intl Spec Bk.

Doyle, Tim, jt. auth. see Adamski, Tony.

Doyle, Timothy & Kellow, Aynsley. Environmental Politics & Policy Making in Australia. 296p. 1995. 64.95 (*0-7329-2794-3*, Pub. by Macmill Educ); pap. 32.95 (*0-7329-2793-5*, Pub. by Macmill Educ) Paul & Co Pubs.

Doyle, Timothy & McEachern, Doug. Environment & Politics. LC 97-17918. (Routledge Introductions to Environment Ser.). 224p. (C). 1998. pap. 18.99 (*0-415-14776-X*) Routledge.

— Environment & Politics. LC 97-17918. (Routledge Introductions to Environment Ser.). (Illus.). 224p. (C). 1998. 65.00 (*0-415-14775-1*) Routledge.

***Doyle, Tom.** The Glamour Chase. 256p. 1999. pap. 14.95 (*0-7475-4399-2*, Pub. by Blmsbury Pub) Trafalgar.

Doyle, Tracy. Patterns from Finished Clothes: Re-Creating the Clothes You Love. LC 95-46185. (Illus.). 128p. 1996. 27.95 (*0-8069-4874-4*) Sterling.

— Patterns from Finished Clothes: Re-Creating the Clothes You Love. (Illus.). 128p. 1997. pap. 14.95 (*0-8069-4875-2*) Sterling.

Doyle, Walter & Good, Thomas L., eds. Focus on Teaching: Readings from the Elementary School Journal. 290p. (C). 1982. pap. text 13.50 (*0-226-16178-1*) U Ch Pr.

Doyle, Wendy. Teach Yourself Healthy Eating. (Illus.). 224p. 1994. pap. 7.95 (*0-8442-3923-2*, Teach Yrslf) NTC Contemp Pub Co.

Doyle, William. Adventures in Time: Musical Experience. (C). 1991. 48.00 (*0-536-58010-3*) Pearson Custom.

Doyle, William. Inside the Oval Office: The Secret White House Tapes from FDR to Clinton. LC 98-47389. (Illus.). 356p. 1999. 28.00 (*1-56836-285-4*) Kodansha.

— Officers, Nobles, & Revolutionaries: Essays on Eighteenth-Century France. LC 95-38673. 238p. 1995. 55.00 (*1-85285-121-X*) Hambledon Press.

— The Old European Order 1660-1800. 2nd ed. (Short Oxford History of the Modern World Ser.). (Illus.). 438p. (C). 1993. pap. text 29.95 (*0-19-820387-X*) OUP.

— Origins of the French Revolution. 2nd ed. 256p. (C). 1988. pap. text 21.00 (*0-19-822284-X*) OUP.

— Origins of the French Revolution. 3rd ed. LC 98-39031. 248p. 1999. text 65.00 (*0-19-873175-2*); pap. text 19.95 (*0-19-873174-4*) OUP.

— The Oxford History of the French Revolution. (Illus.). 480p. 1989. 40.00 (*0-19-822781-7*) OUP.

— The Oxford History of the French Revolution. (Illus.). 478p. 1990. reprint ed. pap. text 15.95 (*0-19-285221-3*) OUP.

— Venality: The Sale of Offices in Eighteenth-Century France. LC 96-7432. (Illus.). 360p. 1997. text 89.00 (*0-19-820536-8*, Clarendon Pr) OUP.

Doyle, William & Perkins, William. Smash the Pyramid. 320p. 1996. mass mkt. 6.99 (*0-446-60367-8*, Pub. by Warner Bks) Little.

Doyle, William, jt. auth. see Failde, Augusto.

Doyle, William, jt. auth. see Failde, Augusto A.

Doyle, William, jt. auth. see Milburn, Josephine F.

Doyle, William, jt. ed. see Haydon, Colin.

Doyle, William, tr. see Chaussinand-Nogaret, Guy.

Doyle, William J., jt. ed. see Cushman, Robert F.

Doyle, William L. Fund Raising Ideas: For All Nonprofits: Charities, Churches, Clubs, Etc. LC 95-81573. 264p. 1995. 34.95 (*0-9639846-1-6*) AFRI.

— Fund Raising 101: How to Raise Money for Charities. 237p. 1993. 34.50 (*0-9639846-0-8*) AFRI.

Doyle, William S., jt. auth. see Failde, Augusto A.

Doyle, William T. Vermont Political Tradition. rev. ed. (Illus.). 288p. 1991. 20.00 (*0-9615486-0-6*); pap. 12.50 (*0-9615486-1-4*) W T Doyle.

Doylem. Color Drawing, Vol. 2. (Architecture Ser.). 1998. pap. 44.95 (*0-442-02534-3*, VNR) Wiley.

Doylesmith, Herb. An Outline of the Bible: Why the Religious Right Can't Call Itself Christian. LC 95-79025. 100p. (Orig.). 1995. pap. 18.95 (*0-9647891-5-9*) A Denburn Pubng.

D'Oyley, Vincent, et al, eds. Education & Development: Lessons from the Third World. 224p. (Orig.). (C). 1994. pap. text 20.95 (*1-55059-090-1*) Temeron Bks.

D'Oyley, Vincent & Shapson, Stan M., eds. Bilingual & Multicultural Education: Canadian Perspectives. 170p. 1984. 69.00 (*0-905028-36-8*, Pub. by Multilingual Matters); pap. 24.95 (*0-905028-35-X*, Pub. by Multilingual Matters) Taylor & Francis.

D'Oyly-Watkins, C., jt. ed. see Butlin, A. G.

Doyma, Libros. Diccionario Medicina/Medical Dictionary. (SPA.). 1996. text 68.00 (*84-8086-140-1*) Mosby Inc.

Doyno, Victor, ed. Mark Twain: American Skeptic. LC 82-60382. (Illus.). 450p. 1995. pap. 19.95 (*0-87975-972-0*) Prometheus Bks.

Doynova, Ralitsa, tr. see Aleksiev, Archimandrite S.

Doyon, Jacques. Love Before the Law. (C). 1988. 39.00 (*0-85439-250-5*, Pub. by St Paul Pubns) St Mut.

Doyon, R. R., jt. auth. see Suckling, P. W.

Doyon, Stephanie. Buying Time. LC 98-52155. 224p. (gr. 7 up). 1999. pap. 3.99 (*0-689-82108-5*, 076714004504) S&S Childrens.

— It Had to Be You. (Love Stories Ser.). 192p. (YA). (gr. 7-12). 1996. mass mkt. 4.50 (*0-553-56669-5*) BDD Bks Young Read.

***Doyon, Stephanie.** Leaving Home. LC 98-44736. (On the Road Ser.: 1). 224p. (YA). (gr. 7 up). 1999. pap. 3.99 (*0-689-82107-7*, 076714004504) Aladdin.

Doyon, Stephanie. Making Waves, 1, 4. (On the Road Ser.: No. 4). 224p. (gr. 7 up). 1999. per. 3.99 (*0-689-82110-7*, 076714004504) S&S Childrens.

Doyon, Stephanie & Nielsen, Cliff. Taking Chances. LC 99-21610. (On the Road Ser.: No. 3). 218p. (J). (gr. 6-10). 1999. per. 4.50 (*0-689-82109-3*, 076714004504) Aladdin.

Doz, Yves L. Government Power & Multinational Strategic Management: Power Systems & Telecommunication Equipment. LC 79-11793. (Praeger Special Studies). 277p. 1979. 59.95 (*0-275-90347-8*, C0347, Praeger Pubs) Greenwood.

Doz, Yves L. & Hamel, Gary. Alliance Advantage: The Art of Creating Value Through Partnering. LC 97-51446. 336p. 1998. 29.95 (*0-87584-616-5*) Harvard Busn.

Doz, Yves L., jt. auth. see Prahalad, C. K.

Doze, Andrew. Discovering Saint Joseph. (C). 1990. 39.00 (*0-85439-383-8*, Pub. by St Paul Pubns) St Mut.

— St. Joseph: Shadow of the Father. Audett, Florentine, tr. LC 92-15022. 196p. (Orig.). 1992. pap. 9.95 (*0-8189-0644-8*) Alba.

Dozeman, Thomas, jt. auth. see Soards, Marion L.

Dozer, Donald M. Portrait of the Free State: A History of Maryland. LC 76-47023. (Illus.). 654p. 1976. reprint ed. pap. 200.00 (*0-7837-9085-6*, 204983500003) Bks Demand.

Dozier. Fear Itself. 288p. 1999. pap. 13.95 (*0-312-24724-9*) St Martin.

***Dozier.** Manual De Gramatica. 2nd ed. 1998. pap., student ed. 34.00 (*0-8384-1025-1*) Heinle & Heinle.

***Dozier, Annette.** Country Pathways. (Illus.). 48p. 2000. 10.95 (*1-57377-100-7*, 0-19884-0238-8) Easl Pubns.

Dozier, Annette. It's Show Time. (Illus.). 70p. 1997. pap. 10.95 (*1-57377-020-5*) Easl Pubns.

Dozier, Bette. Everything's Peachy. lv, 116p. 1996. pap. write for info. (*0-9654132-0-9*) B Dozier.

Dozier, Craig L. Nicaragua's Mosquito Shore: The Years of British & American Presence. LC 84-237. (Illus.). 280p. 1985. pap. 86.80 (*0-7837-8371-X*, 205918100009) Bks Demand.

Dozier, Dan. Come Let Us Adore Him: Dealing with the Struggle over Style of Worship. 1996. pap. 13.99 (*0-89900-749-X*) College Pr Pub.

Dozier, David M., et al. Manager's Guide to Excellence in Public Relations & Communication Management. (LEA's Communication Ser.). 272p. 1995. pap. 34.50 (*0-8058-1810-3*); text 59.95 (*0-8058-1809-X*) L Erlbaum Assocs.

Dozier, Deborah. The Heart Is Fire: The World of the Cahuilla Indians of Southern California. LC 97-52347. (Illus.). 159p. 1997. pap. 16.00 (*0-930588-89-4*) Heyday Bks.

Dozier, Edward P. The Kalinga of Northern Luzon, Philippines. Spindler, Louise S. & Spindler, George D., eds. (Case Studies in Cultural Anthropology). (Illus.). 112p. 1983. reprint ed. pap. text 9.95 (*0-8290-0279-0*) Irvington.

— Mountain Arbiters: The Changing Life of a Philippine Hill People. LC 66-18530. (Illus.). 319p. reprint ed. pap. 98.90 (*0-608-11659-9*, 205537300017) Bks Demand.

— The Pueblo Indians of North America. (Illus.). 224p. 1983. reprint ed. pap. text 12.50 (*0-88133-059-0*) Waveland Pr.

Dozier, Eleanor. Manual de Gramatica. 2nd ed. (SPA.). 1998. pap. text 51.95 (*0-8384-9832-9*) Heinle & Heinle.

Dozier, Eleanor & Iguina, Zulma. Manual de Gramatica: A Reference Tool for Intermediate-Level Spanish Students. LC 94-26367. (SPA.). (C). 1995. pap. 31.25 (*0-8384-5888-2*) Heinle & Heinle.

Dozier, Gloria C. Kerrville (Texas) Mountain Sun & Kerrville Advance: Obituary & Death Notice Index, 1898-1965. LC 98-166797. 245p. 1998. pap. 20.50 (*0-7884-0898-4*, D593) Heritage Bk.

Dozier, Gloria Clifton, see Clifton Dozier, Gloria.

***Dozier, Graham T. & Virginia Historical Society Annual Meeting Staff.** Virginia's Civil War: A Guide to Manuscripts at the Virginia Historical Society. LC 98-157776. v, 307 p. 1998. pap. write for info. (*0-945015-17-8*) VA Hist Soc.

Dozier, Jeff & Asrar, Chassem. Science Strategy for the Earth Observing Systems. LC 94-31836. (Illus.). 128p. 1994. pap. text 24.95 (*1-56396-198-9*, AIP Pr) Spr-Verlag.

Dozier, Nathaniel E. Southern Justice. 147p. (Orig.). 1996. reprint ed. pap. 10.00 (*1-56411-134-2*) Untd Bros & Sis.

Dozier, Robert R. For King, Constitution & Country: The English Loyalists & the French Revolution. LC 83-1221. 224p. 1983. 28.00 (*0-8131-1490-X*) U Pr of Ky.

Dozier, Rush. Fear Itself: The Origin, Nature & Reality of Our Most Primal Emotion. LC 98-21122. 272p. 1998. text 23.95 (*0-312-19412-9*) St Martin.

Dozier, Rush W., Jr. Pure Joy: Searching for Our Most Powerful Emotion. 256p. 2000. text 24.95 (*0-7167-3557-1*, Sci Am Lib) W H Freeman.

Dozier, Terry K. Teacher's Guide to the U. S. Department of Education. 3rd ed. 140p. (C). 1996. pap. text, teacher ed. 25.00 (*0-7881-2618-0*) DIANE Pub.

Dozier, Verna. The Dream of God: A Call to Return. LC 91-22941. 151p. (Orig.). 1991. pap. 9.95 (*1-56101-046-4*) Cowley Pubns.

Dozman, Thomas B. God at War: A Study of Power in the Exodus Tradition. 240p. 1996. text 49.95 (*0-19-510217-7*) OUP.

***Dozois, Elin B.** Phippsburg. (Images of America Ser.). (Illus.). 128p. 1999. pap. 18.99 (*0-7385-0095-X*) Arcadia Publng.

***Dozois, Gardner.** Explorers: SF Adventures to Far Horizons. LC 99-87937. 464p. 2000. pap. 17.95 (*0-312-25462-8*) St Martin.

Dozois, Gardner. The Fiction of James Tiptree, Jr. 1977. pap. 3.50 (*0-916186-04-0*) Algol Pr.

***Dozois, Gardner.** Furthest Horizon: SF Adventures to the Far Future. 480p. 2000. pap. 17.95 (*0-312-26326-0*) St Martin.

Dozois, Gardner. The Good New Stuff. LC 98-42824. 384p. 1999. pap. 17.95 (*0-312-19890-6*) St Martin.

— Good Old Stuff. LC 98-23489. 384p. 1998. text 17.95 (*0-312-19275-4*) St Martin.

— Isaac Asimov's Camelot. 1998. mass mkt. 5.99 (*0-441-00527-6*) Ace Bks.

— Isaac Asimov's Detectives. 1998. mass mkt. 5.99 (*0-441-00545-4*) Ace Bks.

***Dozois, Gardner.** Isaac Asimov's Solar System. 1999. mass mkt. 6.50 (*0-441-00698-1*) Ace Bks.

Dozois, Gardner. Isaac Asimov's Vampires. 1996. mass mkt. 5.50 (*0-441-00387-7*) Ace Bks.

— Modern Classics of Fantasy. LC 96-32347. 688p. 1996. text 35.00 (*0-312-15173-X*) St Martin.

— The Year's Best Science Fiction. LC 85-645716. 624p. 1997. text 29.95 (*0-312-15702-9*) St Martin.

***Dozois, Gardner.** The Year's Best Science Fiction. 17th ed. 640p. 2000. pap. 17.95 (*0-312-26417-8*); text 29.95 (*0-312-26275-2*) St Martin.

Dozois, Gardner. The Year's Best Science Fiction: Fourteenth Annual Collection. 14th ed. LC 85-645716. 624p. 1997. pap. 17.95 (*0-312-15703-7*) St Martin.

— The Year's Best Science Fiction: Twelfth Annual Collection. 12th ed. LC 85-645716. 1995. pap. 17.95 (*0-312-13221-2*) St Martin.

Dozois, Gardner, ed. Isaac Asimov's SF Lite. 256p. (Orig.). 1993. mass mkt. 4.99 (*0-441-37389-5*) Ace Bks.

— Modern Classic Short Novels of Science Fiction. 672p. 1994. pap. 15.95 (*0-312-11317-X*) St Martin.

— Modern Classics of Fantasy. LC 97-17821. 672p. 1997. pap. 15.95 (*0-312-16931-0*) St Martin.

— Modern Classics of Science Fiction. LC 92-42586. 1993. pap. 17.95 (*0-312-08847-7*) St Martin.

***Dozois, Gardner, ed.** The Year's Best Science Fiction. 16th ed. 624p. 1999. pap. 17.95 (*0-312-20445-0*); text 29.95 (*0-312-20963-0*) St Martin.

Dozois, Gardner, ed. The Year's Best Science Fiction: Eleventh Annual Collection. 624p. 1994. pap. 17.95 (*0-312-11104-5*) St Martin.

— The Year's Best Science Fiction: Fifteenth Annual Collection. 624p. 1998. pap. 17.95 (*0-312-19033-6*) St Martin.

— The Year's Best Science Fiction: Ninth Annual Collection. 624p. 1992. pap. 17.95 (*0-312-07891-9*) St Martin.

— The Year's Best Science Fiction: Seventh Annual Collection. 624p. 1990. pap. 14.95 (*0-312-04452-6*) St Martin.

— The Year's Best Science Fiction: Thirteenth Annual Collection. 13th ed. 624p. 1996. 29.95 (*0-312-14451-2*); pap. 17.95 (*0-312-14452-0*) St Martin.

Dozois, Gardner & Schmidt, Stanley, eds. Roads Not Taken. 1998. mass mkt. 6.99 (*0-345-42194-9*, Del Rey) Ballantine Pub Grp.

Dozois, Gardner & Williams, Sheila, eds. Isaac Asimov's Christmas. 240p. 1997. mass mkt. 5.99 (*0-441-00491-1*) Ace Bks.

— Isaac Asimov's Ghosts. 240p. (Orig.). 1995. mass mkt. 5.50 (*0-441-00254-4*) Ace Bks.

***Dozois, Gardner & Williams, Sheila, eds.** Isaac Asimov's Mother's Day. 256p. 2000. mass mkt. 5.99 (*0-441-00721-X*) Ace Bks.

Dozois, Gardner & Williams, Sheila, eds. Isaac Asimov's Valentines. 1999. pap. 5.99 (*0-441-00602-7*) Ace Bks.

Dozois, Gardner, et al. Slow Dancing Through Time. (Illus.). 270p. 1990. 22.00 (*0-942681-03-7*) Ursus Imprints.

Dozois, Gardner, jt. auth. see Dann, Jack.

Dozois, Gardner, jt. ed. see Dann, Jack.

***Dozor, Allen J., ed.** Cardiac Pacing & Defibrillation. (Illus.). 450p. 2000. write for info. (*0-87993-464-6*) Futura Pub.

Dozy, R. Dictionnaire Detaille des Noms de Vetements Chez Les Arabes. (ARA & FRE.). 1985. 29.95 (*0-86685-404-5*) Intl Bk Ctr.

— Glossaire des Mots Espagnols et Portugais Derives de L'arabe. (ARA, POR & SPA.). 1974. 20.00 (*0-86685-105-4*) Intl Bk Ctr.

— Moslems in Spain. 816p. 1988. 350.00 (*1-85077-180-4*, Pub. by Darf Pubs Ltd) St Mut.

Dozy, Reinhard P. Historia Abbadidarum, 3 vols., Set. xxxvi, 970p. reprint ed. write for info. (*0-318-71503-1*) G Olms Pubs.

— Scriptorum Arabum Loci de Abbadidis, 3 vols. in 1. (GER.). xxxvi, 970p. 1992. reprint ed. write for info. (*3-487-09566-1*) G Olms Pubs.

Dozy, Reinhart. Detaille Des Noms Vetements. (ARA & FRE.). 445p. 29.95 (*0-86685-104-6*, LDL1045, Pub. by Librairie du Liban) Intl Bk Ctr.

— Supplement aux Dictionnaire Arabe, 2 vols., set. (ARA & FRE.). 1721p. 95.00 (*0-86685-106-2*, LDL1062, Pub. by Librairie du Liban) Intl Bk Ctr.

Dozzi, Marco, et al, eds. Stochastic Processes & Related Topics. (Mathematical Research Ser.: Vol. 61). 168p. 1991. lib. bdg. 29.00 (*3-05-501262-3*, Pub. by Akademie Verlag) Wiley.

DPG Staff. E. L. I. T. E. American Government (Illinois State University) 80p. (C). 1995. text. write for info. (*0-697-31473-1*) Brown & Benchmark.

— E. L. I. T. E. Global Awareness. 252p. (C). 1995. text. write for info. (*0-697-32968-2*) Brown & Benchmark.

— E. L. I. T. E. Library of American Government - University of Iowa. 216p. (C). 1995. text. write for info. (*0-697-33183-0*) Brown & Benchmark.

DPIC Companies Staff. Lessons in Professional Liability: A Notebook for Certified Public Accountants. Edwards, Alison E., ed. 76p. (Orig.). 1990. spiral bd. 20.00 (*0-932056-05-9*) Design Prof Ins.

D'Queue, Jay, jt. auth. see Kerl, Mary A.

***Dr. Amazing.** How Not to Forget: Master Your Memory with Dr. Amazing. unabridged ed. (Illus.). 273p. 1999. pap. 65.95 (*0-9673669-1-7*) MiTerre Prodns.

Dr. Dobb's Journal Editors, ed. Dr. Dobb's Journal of Software Tools Bound Vol. 12. (Dr. Dobb's Journal Bound Volume Ser.: Vol. 12). (Illus.). 1015p. (Orig.). 1995. pap. 39.75 (*0-934375-84-4*, M&T Bks) IDG Bks.

Dr. "H". Resolving the Illness Care Crisis. LC 95-47513. 257p. 1996. pap. 45.00 (*1-56072-271-1*, Nova Kroshka Bks) Nova Sci Pubs.

Dr. Mac. The Tooth Fairy Legend: How the Custom Came to Be. (Illus.). 40p. (J). (gr. k-5). 1994. 12.95 (*0-9638033-8-7*) Storybk Pub.

Dr. Mike. Francis A. Frog's First & Last Picnic. LC 95-60380. (Illus.). 24p. (Orig.). (J). (gr. k-3). 1995. pap. 6.00 (*0-9639450-1-7*) Joy Ent.

Dr. Oetker. Let's Cook. (Illus.). 48p. (J). (gr. 4-10). 1993. pap. 5.95 (*0-8069-8533-X*) Sterling.

Dr. Paul. Rinkle-Ronkle the Rhinocerwurst & the Big Chocolate Milk Spill. (Illus.). 36p. (J). (ps-2). 1997. 14.95 (*0-9659681-0-3*) FDI Grp.

Dr. Williams' Library, London Staff, ed. Early Nonconformity, Fifteen Sixty-Six to Eighteen Hundred: A Catalogue of Books in Dr. Williams' Library, London, 3 pts. Incl. Set. Author Catalogue., 5 vols. 1970. 570.00 (*0-8161-0797-1*, G K Hall & Co); 1968. write for info. (*0-318-52343-4*, G K Hall & Co) Mac Lib Ref.

Draaijer, Gera E., jt. auth. see Goyer, Doreen S.

D

Draaijers, G. P., jt. auth. see Erisman, J. W.

***Draaisma, Douwe.** Metaphors of Memory: A History of Ideas about the Mind. LC 99-88502. (Illus.). 270p. 2000. 29.95 (*0-521-65024-0*) Cambridge U Pr.

Draan, J. & Veld, R. J., eds. Environmental Protection: Public or Private Choice. (Ecology & Environment Ser.). (C). 1991. lib. bdg. 146.50 (*0-7923-1333-X*) Kluwer Academic.

Draayer, Donald, jt. auth. see Roehlkepartain, Eugene C.

Draayer, J. P., et al, eds. Group Theory & Special Symmetries in Nuclear Physics: Proceedings of the International Symposium, University of Michigan, Ann Arbor, 19-21 September 1991. 400p. (C). 1992. text 114.00 (*981-02-0744-1*) World Scientific Pub.

Draayer, Suzanne Rhodes. A Singer's Guide to the Songs of Joaquin Rodrigo. LC 99-31780. (Illus.). 288p. 1999. 35.00 (*0-8108-3676-9*) Scarecrow.

Drabanski, Emily S., ed. see Dispenza, Joseph.

Drabble, Brian, ed. Artificial Intelligence Planning Systems: Proceedings of the Third International Conference on Artificial Intelligence Planning Systems, 1996, Edinburgh, Scotland. (Illus.). 307p. (Orig.). (C). 1996. pap. text 50.00 (*0-929280-97-0*) AAAI Pr.

***Drabble, Brian & Jarvis, Peter, eds.** Agent Based Systems in the Business Context: Papers from the AAAI Workshop. (Technical Reports: Vol. WS-99-02). (Illus.). 90p. 1999. spiral bd. 25.00 (*1-57735-086-3*) AAAI Pr.

Drabble, G. E. Elementary Engineering Mechanics. (Illus.). 276p. (C). 1986. pap. text 25.00 (*0-333-39927-7*) Scholium Intl.

Drabble, J. & Goldsmid, H. J. Thermal Conduction in Semiconductors. LC 61-14037. (International Series of Monographs on Semiconductors: Vol. 4). 1961. 114.00 (*0-08-009541-0*, Pub. by Pergamon Repr) Franklin.

***Drabble, John H.** An Economic History of Malaysia, C. 1800-1990: The Transition to Modern Economic Growth. LC 99-53111. (Modern Economic History of Southeast Asia Ser.). 2000. text 75.00 (*0-312-23077-X*) St Martin.

Drabble, Margaret. Angus Wilson: A Biography. 1997. pap. 19.95 (*0-312-16774-1*) St Martin.

— Arnold Bennett: A Biography. LC 74-181674. xii, 396p. 1974. write for info. (*0-297-76733-X*) Weidenfeld & Nicolson.

— The Gates of Ivory. 1992. pap. write for info. (*0-7710-2861-X*) McCland & Stewart.

— The Millstone. LC 98-20928. (C). 1998. pap. 12.00 (*0-15-600619-7*, Harvest Bks) Harcourt.

— A Natural Curiosity. 1990. mass mkt. 6.95 (*0-7710-2866-0*) McCland & Stewart.

***Drabble, Margaret.** Oxford Companion to English Literature. 5th ed. LC 99-204339. 1,166p. 1999. 60.00 (*0-19-866233-5*) OUP.

Drabble, Margaret. The Radiant Way. 384p. 1989. reprint ed. mass mkt. 5.99 (*0-8041-0365-8*) Ivy Books.

— The Waterfall. 1989. pap. 8.95 (*0-317-02811-1*) NAL.

— The Witch of Exmoor. LC 97-10952. 288p. 1997. 23.00 (*0-15-100363-7*); write for info. (*0-670-87276-8*) Harcourt.

— The Witch of Exmoor. 288p. (C). 1998. pap. 13.00 (*0-15-600604-9*, Harvest Bks) Harcourt.

***Drabble, Margaret, ed.** The Oxford Companion to English Literature. 6th ed. 1216p. 2000. 55.00 (*0-19-866244-0*) OUP.

Drabble, Margaret & Stringer, Jenny, eds. The Concise Oxford Companion to English Literature. 2nd rev. ed. (Oxford Paperback Reference Ser.). 670p. (C). 1996. pap. 14.95 (*0-19-280039-6*) OUP.

Drabble, Margaret, ed. see Austen, Jane.

Drabble, Margaret, ed. see Bronte, Emily Jane.

Drabble, Margaret, ed. see Woolf, Virginia.

Drabble, Phil. A Voice in the Wilderness: An Autobiography. large type ed. (Illus.). 301p. 1992. 21.95 (*1-85089-548-1*, Pub. by ISIS Lrg Prnt) Transaction Pubs.

Drabeck, Bernard A., et al, eds. The Archibald MacLeish Symposium, May 7-8, 1982: Proceedings. LC 88-1290. 160p. (C). 1988. lib. bdg. 35.00 (*0-8191-6913-7*) U Pr of Amer.

Drabeck, Bernard A. & Ellis, Helen E., eds. Archibald MacLeish: Reflections. LC 85-28912. (Illus.). 312p. 1986. 35.00 (*0-87023-511-7*); pap. 18.95 (*0-87023-623-7*) U of Mass Pr.

Drabek, Gordon, jt. ed. see Sinha, Radha.

Drabek, Pavel. Topological & Variational Methods for Nonlinear Boundary Value Problems. 1997. pap. 47.95 (*0-582-30921-2*, Pub. by Addison-Wesley) Longman.

***Drabek, Pavel, et al.** Nonlinear Differential Equations, 404. LC 99-229206. 12p. 1999. per. 49.95 (*1-58488-036-8*, Chap & Hall CRC) CRC Pr.

Drabek, Pavel, et al. Quasilinear Elliptic Equations with Degenerations & Singularities. LC 97-17293. (Series in Nonlinear Analysis & Applications). 219p. 1997. text 98.95 (*3-11-015490-0*) De Gruyter.

Drabek, T. E. Emergency Management. ix, 281p. 1989. 63.95 (*0-387-97114-9*, 3223) Spr-Verlag.

— Human System Responses to Disaster. (Environmental Management Ser.). (Illus.). 570p. 1986. 116.95 (*0-387-96323-5*) Spr-Verlag.

Drabek, Thomas E. Disaster Evacuation & the Tourist Industry. (Program on Environment & Behavior Monograph Ser.: No. 57). 282p. 1994. 20.00 (*1-877943-12-6*) Natural Hazards.

— Disaster Evacuation Behavior: Tourists & Other Transients. (Environment & Behavior Monograph Ser.: Vol. 58). 370p. 1996. pap. text 20.00 (*1-877943-13-4*) Natural Hazards.

***Drabek, Thomas E.** Disaster-Induced Employee Evacuation. LC 99-35449. (Program on Environment & Behavior Ser.: Vol. 60). 1999. write for info. (*1-877943-15-0*) Natural Hazards.

Drabek, Thomas E. Microcomputers in Emergency Management: Implementation of Computer Technology. (Monograph: No. 51). 224p. 1991. pap. 20.00 (*1-877943-06-1*) Natural Hazards.

Drabek, Thomas E. & Hoetmer, Gerard J., eds. Emergency Management: Principles & Practice for Local Government. (Municipal Management Ser.). (Illus.). 368p. 1991. 35.95 (*0-87326-082-1*) Intl City-Cnty Mgt.

Drabek, Thomas E. & Key, William H. Conquering Disaster: Family Recovery & Long Term Consequences. 485p. 1985. text 49.50 (*0-8290-1000-9*); pap. text 29.50 (*0-8290-1536-1*) Irvington.

Drabek, Thomas E., et al. Earthquake Mitigation Policy: The Experience of Two States. (Program on Environment & Behavior Monograph Ser.: No. 37). 220p. (Orig.). (C). 1983. pap. 20.00 (*0-685-28111-6*) Natural Hazards.

— The Flood Breakers: Citizens Band Radio Use During the 1978 Flood in the Grand Forks Region. (Program on Environment & Behavior Monograph Ser.: No. 29). 101p. (Orig.). (C). 1979. pap. 20.00 (*0-685-28104-3*) Natural Hazards.

Drabek, Zdenek & Griffith-Jones, Stephany, eds. Managing Capital Flows in Turbulent Times: The Experience of Europe's Emerging Market. LC 99-11328. (Illus.). 264p. 1999. text 90.00 (*0-7656-0369-1*) M E Sharpe.

Drabek, Zdenek, jt. auth. see Jones, Stephany G.

Drabenstott, Karen M., ed. Subject Authorities in the Online Environment: Papers from a Conference Program Held in San Francisco June 29, 1987. LC 90-20824. (ALCTS Papers on Library Technical Services & Collections: No. 1). (C). 1991. pap. text 20.00 (*0-8389-0558-7*, 0558-7) ALA.

Drabenstott, Karen M. & Vizine-Goetz, Diane. Using Subject Headings for Online Retrieval: Theory, Practice & Potential. LC 93-42568. (Library & Information Science Ser.). (Illus.). 365p. 1994. text 64.95 (*0-12-221570-2*) Acad Pr.

Draber, Wilfried & Fujita. Rational Approaches to Structure, Activity & Ecotox Agrochem. 608p. 1992. lib. bdg. 229.00 (*0-8493-5859-0*, SB951) CRC Pr.

Drabick, Lawrence W., ed. Interpreting Education: A Sociological Approach. LC 77-153388. (C). 1971. 27.00 (*0-89197-235-8*) Irvington.

Drabik, Harry. Harry Drabik's Guide to Wilderness Canoeing. (Illus.). 143p. 1987. pap. 6.95 (*0-931714-31-1*, Pub. by Nodin Pr) Bookmen Inc.

— Real Log Cabin. (Illus.). 167p. 1994. pap. 14.95 (*0-931714-51-6*, Pub. by Nodin Pr) Bookmen Inc.

— The Spirit of Canoe Camping. (Illus.). 126p. 1981. pap. 5.95 (*0-931714-11-7*, Pub. by Nodin Pr) Bookmen Inc.

— The Spirit of Winter Camping. (Illus.). 104p. (Orig.). 1985. pap. 5.95 (*0-931714-24-9*, Pub. by Nodin Pr) Bookmen Inc.

Drabik, Jozef. Children & Sports Training: How Your Future Champions Should Exercise to Be Healthy, Fit, & Happy. LC 92-85419. (Illus.). 250p. 1996. pap. 29.95 (*0-940149-03-6*); lib. bdg. 39.95 (*0-940149-02-8*) Stadion Pub.

***Drabinski, John E.** Sensibility & Singularity: The Problem of Phenomenology in Levinas. LC 00-32227. (C). 2001. pap. text 22.95 (*0-7914-4898-3*) State U NY Pr.

— Sensibility & Singularity: The Problem of Phenomenology in Levinas. LC 00-32227. (C). 2001. text 68.50 (*0-7914-4897-5*) State U NY Pr.

Drabkin, I. E., jt. auth. see Cohen, Morris R.

Drabkin, I. E., jt. tr. see Drake, Stillman.

Drabkin, William. Beethoven: "Missa Solemnis" (Cambridge Music Handbooks Ser.). (Illus.). 132p. (C). 1991. pap. text 12.95 (*0-521-37831-1*) Cambridge U Pr.

Drabkin, William, ed. A Reader's Guide to Haydn's Early String Quartets, 1. LC 99-11131. (Musical Guides to Musical Genres: Vol. 1). 200p. 1999. lib. bdg. 69.50 (*0-313-30173-5*) Greenwood.

Drabkin, William, ed. see Schenker, Heinrich.

Drabman, R. S., jt. auth. see Gross, A. M.

***Drabovich, Konstantin N., et al, eds.** Fundamental Aspects of Laser-Matter Interaction & New Nonlinear Optical Materials & Physics of Low-Dimensional Structures. 448p. 1999. pap. text 92.00 (*0-8194-3208-3*) SPIE.

Drabowicz, J. Stereoselective Reactions at the -Carbon Atom in Organosulfur Compounds, Vol. 3. (Sulfur Reports). 439p. 1992. pap. text. write for info. (*3-7186-5316-8*, Harwood Acad Pubs) Gordon & Breach.

Drabowitch, S. & Ancona, C. Antennas Vol. 2: Applications. 305p. 1988. 154.00 (*0-89116-279-8*) Hemisp Pub.

Drabowitch, Serge. Modern Antennas. 656p. 1997. 109.95 (*0-7803-3473-6*) Inst Electrical.

Drabu, Vishva N. Saivagamas: A Study in the Socio-Economic Ideas & Institutions of Kashmir. (C). 1990. 52.00 (*81-85182-38-8*, Pub. by Indus Pub) S Asia.

Drach, Albert. The Massive File on Zwetschkenbaum: A Novel. Dunkle, Harvey I., tr. from GER. LC 95-34150. (Studies in Austrian Literature, Culture, & Thought). Orig. Title: Das Grosse Protokoll Gegen Zwetschkenbaum. 285p. (Orig.). 1996. pap. 21.50 (*1-57241-003-5*) Ariadne CA.

— Unsentimental Journey. Dunkle, Harvey I., tr. (Studies in Austrian Literature, Culture, & Thought. Translation Ser.). 352p. 1991. pap. 22.00 (*0-929497-47-3*) Ariadne CA.

Drach, Ivan. Orchard Lamps. Kunitz, Stanley, ed. LC 77-95136. (Illus.). 79p. 1978. pap. 12.95 (*0-8180-1541-1*, Pub. by Sheep Meadow); text 25.00 (*0-8180-1538-1*, Pub. by Sheep Meadow) U Pr of New Eng.

Drache, Daniel. Health Reform: Public Success, Private Failure. 1999. pap. 29.99 (*0-415-20236-1*) Routledge.

Drache, Daniel, ed. Getting on Track: Social Democratic Strategies for Ontario. 256p. 1992. 65.00 (*0-7735-0895-3*, Pub. by McG-Queens Univ Pr); pap. 24.95 (*0-7735-0897-X*, Pub. by McG-Queens Univ Pr) CUP Services.

Drache, Daniel & Gertler, Meric S., eds. The New Era of Global Competition: State Policy & Market Power. 472p. (C). 1991. text 65.00 (*0-7735-0817-1*, Pub. by McG-Queens Univ Pr); pap. text 22.95 (*0-7735-0818-X*, Pub. by McG-Queens Univ Pr) CUP Services.

Drache, Daniel, ed. see Innis, Harold Adams.

Drache, Hiram M. The Challenge of the Prairie. LC 70-632775. 260p. 1970. text 20.95 (*0-8134-1994-8*) Interstate.

— The Day of the Bonanza. LC 64-65044. (Illus.). 239p. 1964. text 20.95 (*0-8134-1995-6*, 1995) Interstate.

— The History of U. S. Agriculture & Its Relevance to Today. LC 95-76604. 520p. 1996. 49.95 (*0-8134-3072-0*) Interstate.

— Koochiching: Pioneering along the Rainy River Frontier. (Illus.). 341p. 1983. 20.95 (*0-8134-2287-6*) Interstate.

— Tomorrow's Harvest. LC 78-57250. 315p. 1978. 20.95 (*0-8134-2032-6*, 2032) Interstate.

Drache, Hiram R. Plowshares to Printouts. (Illus.). 263p. 1985. 20.95 (*0-8134-2459-3*, 2459) Interstate.

Drache, Sharon. Ritual Slaughter. 166p. 1989. pap. 12.95 (*0-919627-27-7*, Pub. by Quarry Pr) LPC InBook.

Drachkovitch, Milorad M. Marxism in the Modern World. LC 65-13109. (Hoover Institution Publications). 308p. 1965. reprint ed. pap. 30.00 (*0-608-02957-2*, 206342200006) Bks Demand.

Drachkovitch, Milorad M., ed. Marxist Ideology in the Contemporary World-Its Appeals & Paradoxes. LC 72-13359. (Essay Index Reprint Ser.). 1977. reprint ed. 21.95 (*0-8369-8154-5*) Ayer.

Drachkovitch, Milorad M., jt. auth. see Lazitch, Branko.

Drachler, Jacob, ed. see Drachler, Rose.

Drachler, Norman. A Bibliography of Jewish Education in the United States. LC 93-47221. 754p. 1996. 29.95 (*0-8143-2353-7*) Wayne St U Pr.

Drachler, Rose. The Choice. LC 77-70787. 1977. pap. 12.50 (*0-686-19541-8*) Tree Bks.

— The Collected Poems of Rose Drachler. Drachler, Jacob & Ratner, Rochelle, eds. (Illus.). 240p. 1983. 30.00 (*0-915066-61-0*) Assembling Pr.

Drachline, Pierre, ed. see Bernard, Tristan.

Drachman, A. B. Atheism in Pagan Antiquity. 168p. 1977. pap. 15.00 (*0-89005-201-8*) Ares.

Drachman, Bernard. From the Heart of Israel. LC 72-110183. (Short Story Index Reprint Ser.). 1977. 25.95 (*0-8369-3334-6*) Ayer.

— Looking at America. LC 76-107696. (Essay Index Reprint Ser.). 1977. 23.95 (*0-8369-1499-6*) Ayer.

— Unfailing Light: Memoirs of an American Rabbi. (American Autobiography Ser.). 456p. 1995. reprint ed. lib. bdg. 99.00 (*0-7812-8501-1*) Rprt Serv.

Drachman, Bernard, tr. see Hirsch, Somson R.

Drachman, Byron C., jt. auth. see Cloud, Michael J.

Drachman, David. Assorted Architecture & Design. 1998. pap. text 17.95 (*1-56799-714-7*, Friedman-Fairfax) M Friedman Pub Grp Inc.

Drachman, Edward, jt. auth. see Shank, Alan.

Drachman, Edward R. United States Policy Toward Vietnam, 1940-1945. LC 71-86293. 470p. 1975. 29.50 (*0-8386-7535-2*) Fairleigh Dickinson.

Drachman, Edward R. & Shank, Alan. Presidents & Foreign Policy: Countdown to Ten Controversial Decisions. LC 96-47514. (SUNY Series on the Presidency). 390p. (C). 1997. text 59.50 (*0-7914-3339-0*); pap. text 23.95 (*0-7914-3340-4*) State U NY Pr.

***Drachman, Roy.** From Cowtown to Desert Metropolis: Ninety Years of Arizona Memories. LC 99-62482. (Illus.). 248p. 1999. 27.95 (*1-888965-02-9*); pap. 16.95 (*1-888965-03-7*) Whitewing Pr.

Drachman, Virginia G. Hospital with a Heart: Women Doctors & the Paradox of Separatism at the New England Hospital, 1862-1969. LC 83-45930. (Illus.). 256p. 1984. 38.50 (*0-8014-1624-8*) Cornell U Pr.

— Hospital with a Heart: Women Doctors & the Paradox of Separatism at the New England Hospital, 1862-1969. LC 83-45930. (Illus.). 259p. reprint ed. pap. 80.30 (*0-608-20881-7*, 207198000003) Bks Demand.

— Sisters in Law: Women Lawyers in Modern American History. LC 97-23490. (Illus.). 384p. 1998. 35.00 (*0-674-80991-2*) HUP.

— Women Lawyers & the Origins of Professional Community in America: The Letters of the Equity Club, 1886-1890. 312p. (C). 1993. text 49.50 (*0-472-10305-9*, 10305) U of Mich Pr.

Drachmann, ed. Scholia Vetera in Pindari Carmina Vol. I: Scholia in Olympionicas. (GRE.). 1997. reprint ed. 89.50 (*3-519-01597-8*, T1597, Pub. by B G Teubner) U of Mich Pr.

— Scholia Vetera in Pindari Carmina Vol. II: Scholia in Pythionicas. (GRE.). 1997. reprint ed. 69.50 (*3-519-01598-6*, T1598, Pub. by B G Teubner) U of Mich Pr.

— Scholia Vetera in Pindari Carmina Vol. III: Scholia in Nemeonicas et Isthmionicas. (GRE.). 1997. reprint ed. 89.50 (*3-519-01599-4*, T1599, Pub. by B G Teubner) U of Mich Pr.

Drachmann, A. G. The Mechanical Technology of Greek & Roman Antiquity. (Illus.). 1963. 25.00 (*0-934454-61-2*) Lubrecht & Cramer.

Drachnik, Cay. Interpreting Metaphors in Children's Drawing. (Illus.). 96p. (C). 1995. pap. text 23.95 (*1-885762-00-3*) Abbeygate Pr.

Drachsler, Julius. Intermarriage in New York City: A Statistical Study of the Amalgamation of European Peoples. (Columbia University. Studies in the Social Sciences: No. 213). reprint ed. 20.00 (*0-404-51213-5*) AMS Pr.

— Intermarriage in New York City: A Statistical Study of the Amalgamation of European Peoples. LC 74-145477. (American Immigration Library). 204p. 1971. reprint ed. lib. bdg. 27.95 (*0-89198-009-1*) Ozer.

Drackley, Arthur K. Prairie in My Pocket. LC 92-80681. (Illus.). 64p. (Orig.). 1992. pap. 12.95 (*0-88100-076-0*) Natl Writ Pr.

Drackley, James, jt. auth. see Davis, Carl.

***Drackley, James K., ed.** Soy in Animal Nutrition. (Illus.). 328p. 2000. 50.00 (*1-884706-01-0*) Fed Animal Sci.

Dracontius. Index Nominumet Verborum Profani Dracontii Praeter Orestis Tragoediam. Wolff, E., ed. (Alpha-Omega, Reihe A Ser.: Vol. 94). (LAT.). 102p. 1989. lib. bdg. 52.50 (*3-487-09129-1*) G Olms Pubs.

Dracopoli, Nicholas C., et al, eds. Current Protocols in Human Genetics, Vol. 1. LC 94-14135. 1994. text 525.00 (*0-471-03420-7*) Wiley.

Dracopoulos, Dimitris C. Evolutionary Learning Algorithms for Neural Adaptive Control. LC 97-20720. (Perspectives in Neural Computing Ser.). (Illus.). xii, 212p. pap. 44.95 (*3-540-76161-6*) Spr-Verlag.

Dracopoulou, Souzy. Ethics & Values in Health Care Management. LC 98-16654. 224p. (C). 1999. 65.00 (*0-415-14644-5*); pap. 24.99 (*0-415-14645-3*) Routledge.

Dracos, Helen. The House on Palmer Street. LC 93-20851. 1993. 20.00 (*0-917653-41-6*) Hellenic Coll Pr.

Dracos, T. Transport & Reactive Processes in Aquifers: Proceedings of the International Symposium, Zurich, April 1994. (Illus.). 500p. (C). 1994. text 148.00 (*90-5410-368-X*, Pub. by A A Balkema) Ashgate Pub Co.

Dracos, T. A., ed. Three-Dimensional Velocity & Vorticity Measuring & Image Analysis Techniques: Lecture Notes from the Short Course Held in Zurich, Switzerland, 3-6 September 1996. LC 96-42043. (ERCOFTAC Ser.). 310p. (C). 1996. lib. bdg. 150.00 (*0-7923-4256-9*) Kluwer Academic.

Dracos, Themistoles A. & Tsinober, A., eds. New Approaches & Concepts in Turbulence. LC 93-8949. (Monte Verita Ser.). 1993. 116.00 (*0-8176-2924-6*) Birkhauser.

Dracott, Alice E. Folk Tales from Simla (Himalayan Region of India) (Library of Folklore). (Illus.). 225p. (YA). (gr. 4 up). 1998. 14.95 (*0-7818-0704-2*) Hippocrene Bks.

— Folk Tales from the Himalayas. (C). 1992. reprint ed. text 25.00 (*81-85326-60-6*, Pub. by Vintage) S Asia.

— Simla Village Tales: or Folk Tales from the Himalayas. 1976. lib. bdg. 59.95 (*0-8490-2606-7*) Gordon Pr.

Dracquer, Michael & McNally, P. Diabetes Management: Step by Step. LC 98-18760. (Illus.). 1997. pap. 19.95 (*0-632-04848-4*) Blackwell Sci.

Dracu, A. H. Census of India, 1931: Bombay Presidency, 2 vols. 1987. reprint ed. 175.00 (*0-8364-2017-9*, Pub. by Usha) S Asia.

Dracup, Angela. Dearest Pretender. large type ed. (Lythway Ser.). 208p. 1991. 21.95 (*0-7451-1252-8*, G K Hall Lrg Type) Mac Lib Ref.

Dracup, Joseph F. & Kelley, Carl F. Horizontal Control As Applied to Local Surveying Needs. 126p. 1973. pap. 13.00 (*0-614-06116-4*, S200) Am Congrs Survey.

Dracup, Joseph F., et al. Surveying Instrumentation & Coordinate Computation Workshop Lecture Notes. 3rd ed. 208p. 1979. 20.90 (*0-317-32471-3*, S260) Am Congrs Survey.

— Surveying Instrumentation-Coordinate Computation Workshop Lecture Note. 208p. 1979. pap. 25.00 (*0-614-06115-6*, S260) Am Congrs Survey.

Dracup, Kathleen. Meltzer's Intensive Coronary Care. 5th ed. (C). 1995. pap. text 39.95 (*0-8385-4276-X*, A4276-0) Appleton & Lange.

Dracup, Miles & Kirby, Michael. Lupin Development Guide. LC 97-106174. 112p. 1996. pap. 19.95 (*1-875560-66-1*, Pub. by Univ of West Aust Pr) Intl Spec Bk.

Draeger, Donn, jt. auth. see Ishikawa, Takahiko.

Draeger, Donn F. Classical Budo. LC 73-6613. (Martial Arts & Ways of Japan Ser.: Vol. 2). (Illus.). 128p. 1973. pap. 22.50 (*0-8348-0234-1*) Weatherhill.

— Ninjutsu: The Art of Invisibility. 2nd ed. (Illus.). 128p. 1992. pap. 7.95 (*0-8048-1597-6*) Tuttle Pubng.

— Weapons & Fighting Arts of Indonesia. (Illus.). 256p. 1992. pap. 21.95 (*0-8048-1716-2*) Tuttle Pubng.

Draeger, Donn F. & Otaki, Tadao. Judo Formal Techniques: A Complete Guide to Kodokan Randori No Kata. LC 82-50095. (Illus.). 452p. 1983. pap. 22.95 (*0-8048-1676-X*) Tuttle Pubng.

Draeger, Donn F. & Smith, Robert. Comprehensive Asian Fighting Arts. (Illus.). 1969. 21.95 (*0-685-21878-3*) Wehman.

Draeger, Donn F. & Smith, Robert W. Comprehensive Asian Fighting Arts. LC 80-82527. (Illus.). 208p. 1981. pap. 22.00 (*0-87011-436-0*) Kodansha.

Draeger, Donn F., jt. auth. see Khim, P'ng Chye.

Draeger, Erich. Project Management. 400p. (C). 2000. 49.95 (*0-201-39835-4*) Addison-Wesley.

Draeger, Fritz. Das Germanische Heldenlied. (GER.). vi, 66p. 1961. write for info. (*3-296-20100-9*, Pub. by Weidmann) Lubrecht & Cramer.

Draeger, J. Corneal Sensitivity: Measurement & Clinical Importance. (Illus.). 160p. 1984. 61.95 (*0-387-81794-8*) Spr-Verlag.

Draeger, J. & Winter, R., eds. New Microsurgical Concepts (Posterior & Anterior Segments) (Developments in Ophthalmology Ser.: Vol. 14). (Illus.). xii, 208p. 1987. 156.75 (*3-8055-4545-2*) S Karger.

— New Microsurgical Concepts II: Cornea, Posterior

D

An Asterisk (*) at the beginning of an entry indicates that the title is appearing for the first time.

Segment, External Microsurgery. (Developments in Ophthalmology Ser.: Vol. 18). (Illus.). x, 226p. 1989. 182.75 (*3-8055-4922-9*) S Karger.

Draeger, J. A., ed. Ophthalmic Microsurgery. (Illus.). xii, 184p. 1986. 149.75 (*3-8055-4028-0*) S Karger.

Draeger, Mary C., et al. Birthday Smiles. (Illus.). 10p. (J). (gr. k-6). 1994. 15.95 (*0-9643951-0-X*) Dream Keeper.

Draeger, Wolfhart. Lexikon der Gesundheit: Medizinisches Fachwoerterbuch. (GER.). 19.95 (*0-7859-8329-5*, 3404621190) Fr & Eur.

Draelos, Zoe D. Cosmetics in Dermatology. 2nd ed. LC 95-24705. 317p. 1995. text 73.00 (*0-443-08965-5*) Church.

Draelos, Zoe K. Cosmetics in Dermatology. (Illus.). 214p. 1990. pap. text 32.00 (*0-443-08644-3*) Church.

Draenert, K., et al. Manual of Cementing Technique. 2nd ed. LC 99-17758. 140p. 1999. 129.00 (*3-540-65437-2*) Spr-Verlag.

Draenger, Gusta D. Justyna's Narrative. Hirsch, Roslyn & Hirsch, David H., trs. LC 96-734. (Illus.). 168p. 1996. 40.00 (*1-55849-037-X*); pap. 15.95 (*1-55849-038-8*) U of Mass Pr.

Draetta, Ugo, jt. auth. see Lake, Ralph B.

Draf, W., jt. ed. see Stamm, A. J.

Draf, Wolfgang, jt. auth. see Samii, Madjid.

Draffan, George, jt. auth. see Jensen, Derrick.

Draffen, Andrew. Lonely Planet Rio de Janeiro. 2nd ed. (Lonely Planet Travel Guides Ser.). (Illus.). 200p. 1998. pap. text 14.95 (*0-86442-591-0*) Lonely Planet.

Drafke, Michael. The Human Side of Organizations. 7th ed. (C). 1998. pap. text. write for info. (*0-321-02878-3*) Addison-Wesley.

Drafke, Michael W. Trauma & Mobile Radiography. LC 89-17230. (Illus.). 347p. 1990. pap., spiral bd. 25.95 (*0-8036-2805-6*) Davis Co.

***Drafke, Michael W.** Trauma & Mobile Radiography. 2nd ed. 386p. 2000. 25.95 (*0-8036-0694-X*) Davis Co.

Drafke, Michael W. Working in Health Care: What You Need to Know to Succeed. LC 94-13881. (Illus.). 213p. 1994. pap. 21.95 (*0-8036-2808-0*) Davis Co.

Draft Horse Journal Staff, ed. see Telleen, Maurice.

Dragalin, A. Mathematical Intuitionism, Introduction to Proof Theory. LC 87-32766. (Translations of Mathematical Monographs: Vol. 67). 228p. 1988. text 93.00 (*0-8218-4520-9*, MMONO/67) Am Math.

Dragalov, V. V., jt. ed. see Buekens, A. G.

Dragan, Emil R. To Hire Or Not to Hire: A Manager's Guide To Interviewing Applicants. (Illus.). (Orig.). 1997. pap. 8.95 (*0-9632744-1-4*) Interview Cnslts.

Dragan, Emil R., ed. Job Winning Interviewing. 3rd rev. ed. (Illus.). 1992. pap. 7.95 (*0-9632744-0-6*) Interview Cnslts.

Dragan, Mary A. Well Preserved: Pickles, Jams, Salsas & Chutneys for the New Cook. (Illus.). 240p. 1998. pap. 14.95 (*1-55110-766-X*) Whitecap Bks.

Dragan, Radu & Ioan, Augustin. Symbols & Language in Sacred Christian Architecture. LC 95-38447. (Illus.). 136p. 1996. 69.95 (*0-7734-8870-7*) E Mellen.

Dragan, V. & Halanay, A. Stabilization of Linear Systems. LC 98-44617. (Systems & Control Ser.). 250p. 1997. 64.50 (*0-8176-3970-5*) Birkhauser.

***Dragani, Tommaso A., ed.** Human Polygenic Diseases: Animal Models. (Illus.). 264p. 1998. text 90.00 (*90-5702-336-9*, Harwood Acad Pubs) Gordon & Breach.

Draganic, Ivan G., et al. Radiation & Radioactivity on Earth & Beyond. 2nd ed. 368p. 1993. boxed set 94.95 (*0-8493-8675-6*, QC795) CRC Pr.

Dragastin, S. E. & Elder, G. H., Jr., eds. Adolescence in the Life Cycle: Psychological Change & the Social Context. LC 74-22002. 336p. reprint ed. 104.20 (*0-8357-9146-7*, 205070500082) Bks Demand.

Drager, Brett O. Hat Patterns. 3rd rev. ed. (Illus.). 179p. 1994. reprint ed. text 24.00 (*0-9646782-3-3*) Hat Patterns.

Drager, Jorg, jt. auth. see Silsbee, Robert H.

Drager, Kerry. Scenic Photography 101: A Crash Course to Shooting Better Pictures Outdoors. LC 99-29592. (Illus.). 144p. 1999. pap. 24.95 (*0-8174-5819-0*) Watsn-Guptill.

Drager, Kerry, photos by. The Golden Dream: California Gold Rush to Statehood. LC 97-70197. (Illus.). 112p. 1997. 32.50 (*1-55868-312-7*) Gr Arts Ctr Pub.

Dragesco, Jean. High Resolution Astrophotography. McKim, Richard, tr. (Practical Astronomy Handbooks Ser.: Vol. 7). (Illus.). 172p. (C). 1995. text 44.95 (*0-521-41588-8*) Cambridge U Pr.

Dragga & Gong. Writer's Repertoire. 176p. (C). 1997. pap. text, student ed. 30.00 (*0-06-502520-2*) Addson-Wesley Educ.

Dragga, S., jt. auth. see Gong, G.

Dragga, Sam, jt. auth. see Gong, Gwendolyn.

Dragga, Sam, jt. auth. see Jones, Dan.

Dragga, Sam, jt. auth. see Rude, Carolyn.

Dragga, Sam, ed. see Barker, Thomas T.

Dragga, Sam, ed. see Kostelnick, Charles & Roberts, David D.

Draggan, Sidney, et al, eds. Environmental Impacts on Human Health: The Agenda for Long-Term Research & Development. 264p. 1987. 62.95 (*0-275-92338-X*, C2338, Praeger Pubs) Greenwood.

— Environmental Monitoring, Assessment & Management: The Agenda for Long-Term Research & Development. LC 87-6941. 176p. 1987. 55.00 (*0-275-92336-3*, C2336, Praeger Pubs) Greenwood.

— Geochemical & Hydrologic Processes & Their Protection: Agenda for Long-Term Research & Development. LC 87-6974. 244p. 1987. 55.00 (*0-275-92339-8*, C2339, Praeger Pubs) Greenwood.

— Preserving Ecological Systems: The Agenda for Long-Term Research & Development. 327p. 1987. 45.95 (*0-275-92337-1*, C2337, Praeger Pubs) Greenwood.

Draggett, jt. auth. see Vanhuss.

Draggo, Sam, ed. see Rude, Carolyn D.

Draghi, Giovanni B. Giovanni Battista Draghi. Klakowich, Robert, ed. (Recent Researches in Music of the Baroque Era Ser.: Vol. RRB56). (Illus.). xxiv, 111p. 1986. pap. 45.00 (*0-89579-216-8*) A-R Eds.

Draghi, Mario, jt. ed. see Dornbusch, Rudiger.

Draghi, Paul A., ed. see Permanent International Altaistic Conference Staff.

Draghi, Suzanne C., jt. auth. see Flach, Frederic F.

Draghici, S., ed. & tr. see Cortes, Juan D.

Draghici, Simona, ed. see Campanella, Tommaso.

Draghici, Simona, ed. see Fortescue, John.

Draghici, Simona, ed. see Gombrowicz, Witold.

Draghici, Simona, ed. see Plutarch.

Draghici, Simona, ed. see Schmitt, Carl.

Draghici, Simona, ed. see Simmel, George.

Draghici, Simona, ed. see Swift, Jonathan.

Draghici, Simona, ed. & tr. see Benn, Gottfried.

Draghici, Simona, ed. & tr. see Freund, Julien.

Draghici, Simona, ed. & tr. see Goethe, Johann Wolfgang Von.

Draghici, Simona, ed. & tr. see Schmitt, Carl.

Draghici, Simona, ed. & tr. see Weber, Max.

Draghici, Simona, tr. see Benn, Gottfried.

Dragich, Martha J. & Schanck, Peter C., compiled by. Law Library Staff Organization & Administration. LC 90-9129. (AALL Publications Ser.: No. 39). xiv, 238p. 1990. 32.50 (*0-8377-0137-6*, Rothman) W S Hein.

Dragisic, Patricia. How to Write a Letter. LC 97-35265. (Speak Out, Write On! Ser.). 127p. (YA). (gr. 6 up). 1998. 24.00 (*0-531-11391-4*) Watts.

— How to Write a Letter. LC 97-35265. (Illus.). (YA). (gr. 7-12). 1999. pap. text 7.95 (*0-531-15931-0*) Watts.

Dragisic, Peggy. From the Medley. 12p. 1978. pap. 3.00 (*0-919626-07-6*, Pub. by Brick Bks) Genl Dist Srvs.

Dragnea, Gabriela, tr. see Sorescu, Marin.

Dragnich, Alex N. The Development of Parliamentary Government in Serbia. (East European Monographs: No. 44). 138p. 1978. text 60.00 (*0-914710-37-0*, Pub. by East Eur Monographs) Col U Pr.

— Serbs & Croats: The Struggle in Yugoslavia. LC 92-19786. 202p. 1992. 22.95 (*0-15-181073-7*) Harcourt.

— Serbs & Croats: The Struggle in Yugoslavia. (Illus.). 224p. 1993. pap. 10.95 (*0-15-680663-0*) Harcourt.

Dragnich, Alex N., ed. Serbia's Historical Heritage. 180p. 1994. text 39.00 (*0-88033-244-1*, 347, Pub. by East Eur Monographs) Col U Pr.

Dragnich, Alex N. & Todorovich, Slavko. The Saga of Kosovo: Focus on Serbian-Albanian Relationships. (East European Monographs). 1985. 22.50 (*0-317-18452-0*) Brooklyn Coll Pr.

Dragnich, Dartha, ed. see Killingstad, Kay.

Drago, Carl J. Implant Restorations: A Step by Step Guide for Dentists. Implant Innovations, Inc. Staff, ed. & illus. by. xiii, 200p. 1997. text 100.00 (*0-9655930-0-2*) C Drago.

Drago, Edmund L. Black Politicians & Reconstruction in Georgia: A Splendid Failure. LC 82-232. xii, 204p. (C). 1982. text 30.00 (*0-8071-1021-3*) La State U Pr.

Drago, Edmund L. Black Politicians & Reconstruction in Georgia: A Splendid Failure. LC 91-47033. (Brown Thrasher Bks.). (Illus.). 232p. 1992. reprint ed. pap. 19.95 (*0-8203-1438-2*) U of Ga Pr.

Drago, Edmund L. Hurrah for Hampton! Black Red Shirts in South Carolina During Reconstruction. LC 98-37819. 176p. 1999. 32.00 (*1-55728-541-1*) U of Ark Pr.

Drago, Gail. Etta Place: Her Life & Times with Butch Cassidy & the Sundance Kid. (Women of the West Ser.). 208p. 1995. pap. 12.95 (*1-55622-398-6*, Rep of TX Pr) Wordware Pub.

— Galveston. (Lone Star Guides Ser.). 1999. pap. 15.95 (*0-89123-038-6*, 3038) Gulf Pub.

— Texas Bed & Breakfast. LC 99-18138. (Lone Star Guides Ser.). 268p. 1999. pap. 15.95 (*0-89123-027-0*) Gulf Pub.

Drago, Harry S. Lone Wolf of Dryguich Trail & More Precious Than Gold. 1990. pap. 3.50 (*0-8125-0542-5*, Pub. by Tor Bks) St Martin.

— Outlaws on Horseback: The History of the Organized Bands of Bank & Train Robbers Who Terrorized the Prairie Towns of Missouri, Kansas, Indian Territory, & Oklahoma for Half a Century. LC 97-32634. (Illus.). xxix, 328p. 1998. pap. 15.00 (*0-8032-6612-X*, Bison Books) U of Nebr Pr.

— Top Hand with a Gun. 16.95 (*0-89190-162-0*) Amereon Ltd.

Drago, Joseph A. Critical Assessment of Radon Removal Systems for Drinking Water Supplies. LC 98-6321. 341p. 1998. pap. 195.00 (*0-89867-953-2*) Am Water Wks Assn.

drago, peter. Spreadsheet Exercises & Solutions for Principles of Physics: With IBM 3.5 Disk. pap. 15.00 (*0-393-96578-3*) Norton.

— With IBM 5.25 Disk. pap. 13.00 (*0-393-96579-1*) Norton.

— With Macintosh Disk. pap. 15.00 (*0-393-96588-0*) Norton.

***Drago, R. J. & Filax, A. F.** The Effect of Material Defects on Gear Performance - A Case Study. (Technical Papers: Vol. 99FTM14). 7p. 1999. pap. 30.00 (*1-55589-752-5*) AGMA.

Drago, Raymond J. Comparative Load Capacity Evaluation of CBN-Finished Gears. (Nineteen Eighty-Eight Fall Technical Meeting Ser.: Vol. 88FTM8). (Illus.). 10p. 1988. pap. text 30.00 (*1-55589-513-1*) AGMA.

— An Improvement in the Conventional Analysis of Gear Tooth Bending Fatigue Strength. (Technical Papers: Vol. P229.24). (Illus.). 36p. 1982. pap. text 30.00 (*1-55589-291-4*) AGMA.

— Limitations of Current Tooth Root Stress Analysis. (Technical Papers: Vol. P229.20). (Illus.). 20p. 1976. pap. text 30.00 (*1-55589-287-6*) AGMA.

— Preliminary Surface Load Capacity Evaluation of Precision, Integrally Forged Spiral Bevel Gears. (Technical Papers: Vol. P219.09). (Illus.). 11p. 1977. pap. text 30.00 (*1-55589-254-X*) AGMA.

— Results of an Experimental Program Utilized to Verify a New Tooth Strength Analysis. (Technical Papers: Vol. P229.27). 60p. 1983. pap. text 30.00 (*1-55589-073-9*) AGMA.

Drago, Raymond J. & Aronson, R. B. High Frequency Vibration - Monitoring Techniques for Incipient Fault Detection in Spiral Bevel Gear Systems. (AGMA Technical Paper: Vol. P109.38). (Illus.). 13p. 1977. pap. text 30.00 (*1-55589-375-9*) AGMA.

Drago, Raymond J. & Board, D. B. High Frequency Vibration - Monitoring Techniques for Gear/Bearing-System Failure Detection. (Technical Papers: Vol. P109.36). (Illus.). 8p. 1975. pap. text 30.00 (*1-55589-374-0*) AGMA.

Drago, Raymond J. & Lanski, Joseph W. Advanced Rotorcraft Transmission Program - A Status Review. (Nineteen Ninety Fall Technical Meeting Ser.: Vol. 90FTM7). (Illus.). 15p. 1990. pap. text 30.00 (*1-55589-559-X*) AGMA.

Drago, Raymond J. & Lenski, J. W. An Analytical & Experimental Investigation of the Contact Conditions at the Roller End/Cone Rib of a Tapered-Roller Bearing. (Technical Papers: Vol. P109.32). (Illus.). 8p. 1973. pap. text 30.00 (*1-55589-361-9*) AGMA.

Drago, Raymond J. & Lutthans, R. V. An Experimental Investigation of the Combined Effects of Rim Thickness & Pitch Diameter on Spur Gear Tooth Root & Fillet Stresses. (Technical Papers: Vol. P229.22). (Illus.). 25p. 1981. pap. text 30.00 (*1-55589-289-2*) AGMA.

Drago, Raymond J. & Margasahayam, R. N. Gear Tooth Load Sharing Using Non-Linear Finite Element Methods. (Nineteen Eighty-Nine Fall Technical Meeting Ser.: Vol. 89FTM2). (Illus.). 10p. 1989. pap. text 30.00 (*1-55589-546-8*) AGMA.

Drago, Raymond J. & Margasahayam, Ravi N. On the Strength of a Planet Gear with an Integral Bearing (A Re-evaluation) (Nineteen Eighty-Six Fall Technical Meeting Ser.: Vol. 86FTM9). (Illus.). 13p. 1986. pap. 30.00 (*1-55589-473-9*, 86FTM9) AGMA.

Drago, Raymond J. & Scott, L. The Design, Development & Manufacture of Advanced Technology Gearing for Hot Strip Rolling Mill Applications. (Nineteen Ninety-Two Fall Technical Meeting Ser.: Vol. 92FTM4). (Illus.). 21p. 1992. pap. text 30.00 (*1-55589-584-0*) AGMA.

Drago, Raymond J. & Uppaluri, B. R. Analytical & Experimental Tooth Strength Study of Spur Plane Gears with Integral Bearings. (1984 Fall Technical Meeting Ser.: Vol. 84FTM1). 8p. 1984. pap. text 30.00 (*1-55589-083-0*) AGMA.

Drago, Raymond J., et al. The F-22 AMAD Gear Drive Optimization of Resonance Characteristics by Detuning, Coulomb Damping & Damped Force Response Analyses. (Technical Papers: Vol. 96FTM6). (Illus.). 16p. 1996. pap. text 30.00 (*1-55589-673-1*) AGMA.

— The Relative Noise Levels of Parallel Axis Gears Sets with Various Contact Ratios & Gear Tooth Forms. (1993 Fall Technical Meeting Ser.: Vol. 93FTM11). (Illus.). 15p. 1993. pap. text 30.00 (*1-55589-623-5*) AGMA.

— UltraSafe Gear Systems for Critical Applications - Initial Development. (Technical Papers: Vol. 97FTM10). (Illus.). 22p. 1997. pap. text 30.00 (*1-55589-704-5*) AGMA.

Drago, Raymond J., jt. auth. see Pizzigati, G. A.

Drago, Russell, jt. ed. see Bertini, Ivano.

Drago, Russell S. General Chemistry Problem Solving I, Vol. 1. LC 78-68545. 263p. (C). 1984. pap. text 27.96 (*0-669-08214-7*) HM Trade Div.

Dragolea, C., tr. see Casement, Patrick.

Dragoman, Daniela & Dragoman, Mircea. Advanced Optoelectronic Devices. LC 98-45458. (Springer Series in Photonics). xii, 424p. 1998. 129.00 (*3-540-64846-1*) Spr-Verlag.

Dragoman, Mircea, jt. auth. see Dragoman, Daniela.

Dragomir, Sorin & Ornea, Liviu. Locally Conformal Kahler Geometry. LC 97-27397. (Progress in Mathematics Ser.). 1997. write for info. (*3-7643-4020-7*) Birkhauser.

— Locally Conformal Kahler Geometry. LC 97-27397. (Progress in Mathematics Ser.). 400p. 1997. write for info. (*0-8176-4020-7*) Birkhauser.

Dragomoschenko, Arkadii. Xenia. Hejinian, Lyn & Balashova, Elena, trs. from RUS. LC 93-31808. (Sun & Moon Classics Ser.: No. 29). 160p. (Orig.). 1993. pap. 12.95 (*1-55713-107-4*) Sun & Moon CA.

Dragomoschenko, Arkadil. Description. Hejinian, Lyn & Balashova, Elena, trs. from RUS. (Sun & Moon Classics Ser.: No. 9). 136p. 1989. 11.95 (*1-55713-075-2*) Sun & Moon CA.

Dragon, James. Soil Chemistry of Hazardous Materials. 2nd ed. LC 97-46900. (Illus.). 800p. 1997. text 59.95 (*1-884940-11-0*) Amherst Sci Pubs.

Dragon, Judy & Popp, Terry, eds. Multiple Journeys to One: Spiritual Stories of Integrating from Dissociative Identity Disorder. (Illus.). 240p. 1999. pap. 17.95 (*0-9672458-0-X*) Dancing Serpents.

Dragon, Osvaldo. Historias para Ser Contadas - Stories for the Theatre. Rosenberg, Joe & Rosenberg, Graciela, trs. (Multicultural Theatre Ser.). 21p. 1994. pap. 4.00 (*1-57514-101-9*, 1145) Encore Perform Pub.

Dragon, Richard E. Registered in R. I. Vol. 1: Motor Vehicle License Plates & the Registration of Motor Vehicles in Rhode Island since 1904. LC 97-94543. (Illus.). xii, 500p. 1998. pap. 39.95 (*0-9661362-0-9*) Eastern Seaboard.

Dragone, Carol. Out of Absence. Hettich, M. & Ahern, Colleen, eds. 25p. 1978. 1.50 (*0-686-38057-6*) MoonsQuilt Pr.

Dragonetti, Carmen, jt. auth. see Tola, Fernando.

Dragonia, Giorgio & Fichera, Giuseppe, eds. Fountains Pens. (Illus.). 192p. 1998. 49.50 (*1-85149-289-5*) Antique Collect.

Dragonson, Jabiya. Under a Melting Sky. Gonzalez-Parker, Zulma, ed. (Orig.). 1989. pap. write for info. (*0-318-65769-4*) Heartfelt Pr.

***Dragonstar Staff.** New Magik Handbook: Simple Spells for a Complex World. (Illus.). 150p. 2000. pap. 14.95 (*1-892062-19-4*) Inner Light.

Dragonsun, Jabiya. Behind the Mask. Gonzalez-Parker, Zulma, ed. (Orig.). 1989. pap. 5.00 (*0-685-28956-7*) Heartfelt Pr.

Dragonwagon, Crescent. Alligator Arrived with Apples: A Potluck Alphabet Feast. LC 86-37. (Illus.). 40p. (J). (gr. k-3). 1987. text, lib. bdg. 15.95 (*0-02-733090-7*, Mac Bks Young Read) S&S Childrens.

Dragonwagon, Crescent. Alligator Arrived with Apples: A Potluck Alphabet Feast. (J). 1992. 11.19 (*0-606-01996-0*, Pub. by Turtleback) Demco.

Dragonwagon, Crescent. Alligator Arrived with Apples: A Potluck Alphabet Feast. LC 91-38490. (Illus.). 40p. (J). (gr. k-3). 1992. reprint ed. mass mkt. 5.99 (*0-689-71613-3*) Aladdin.

— Alligators & Others All Year Long: A Book of Months. LC 91-2831. (Illus.). 32p. (J). (gr. k-3). 1993. text, lib. bdg. 14.95 (*0-02-733091-5*, Mac Bks Young Read) S&S Childrens.

— Alligators & Others All Year Long, a Book of Months. 1997. 11.19 (*0-606-12871-9*, Pub. by Turtleback) Demco.

— Annie Flies the Birthday Bike. LC 90-42861. (Illus.). 32p. (J). (gr. k-3). 1993. text, lib. bdg. 14.95 (*0-02-733155-5*, Mac Bks Young Read) S&S Childrens.

— The Bat in the Dining Room. LC 96-54894. (Illus.). 32p. (J). (gr. k-3). 1997. 15.95 (*0-7614-5007-6*) Marshall Cavendish.

Dragonwagon, Crescent. Brass Button. LC 95-43893. (Illus.). 40p. (J). (gr. k-4). 1997. 16.00 (*0-689-80582-9*) Atheneum Yung Read.

Dragonwagon, Crescent. Coconut. LC 83-47691. (Illus.). 32p. (J). (ps-3). 1984. 13.95 (*0-06-021759-6*) HarpC Child Bks.

— The Dairy Hollow House Cookbook. 1992. pap. 14.95 (*0-9632569-0-4*) Cato & Martin.

— Dairy Hollow House Soup & Bread Cookbook. LC 91-50956. (Illus.). 416p. 1992. pap. 13.95 (*0-89480-751-X*, 1751) Workman Pub.

Dragonwagon, Crescent. Half a Moon & One Whole Star. LC 89-18643. 1990. 11.19 (*0-606-03415-3*, Pub. by Turtleback) Demco.

Dragonwagon, Crescent. Half a Moon & One Whole Star. LC 89-18643. (Illus.). 32p. (J). (gr. k-3). 1990. reprint ed. mass mkt. 5.99 (*0-689-71415-7*) Aladdin.

— Home Place. LC 89-32911. (Illus.). 32p. (J). (gr. k-3). 1990. text 14.95 (*0-02-733190-3*, Mac Bks Young Read) S&S Childrens.

— Home Place. 1993. 10.05 (*0-606-12339-3*, Pub. by Turtleback) Demco.

— Home Place. LC 92-46366. (Illus.). 40p. (J). (gr. k-3). 1993. reprint ed. mass mkt. 5.99 (*0-689-71758-X*) Aladdin.

— If You Call My Name. LC 78-22480. (Illus.). 32p. (J). (gr. k-4). 1981. 11.95 (*0-06-021743-X*) HarpC Child Bks.

— The Itch Book. LC 89-2695. (Illus.). 32p. (J). (gr. k-3). 1990. lib. bdg. 13.95 (*0-02-733121-0*, Mac Bks Young Read) S&S Childrens.

— The Sun Begun. (J). 1997. 16.95 (*0-02-733185-7*) Atheneum Yung Read.

— This Is the Bread I Baked for Ned. LC 88-22619. (Illus.). 32p. (J). (gr. k-3). 1989. mass mkt. 14.95 (*0-02-733220-9*, Mac Bks Young Read) S&S Childrens.

***Dragonwagon, Crescent.** This Is the Bread I Baked for Ned. (Illus.). 32p. (J). (gr. k-3). 1999. reprint ed. pap. 5.99 (*0-689-82353-3*) Aladdin.

Dragonwagon, Crescent. Wind Rose. LC 75-25414. (Illus.). 32p. (J). (ps-3). 1976. 12.95 (*0-06-021741-3*) HarpC Child Bks.

— Winter Holding Spring. LC 88-13747. (Illus.). 32p. (J). (gr. 2-5). 1990. mass mkt. 15.00 (*0-02-733122-9*, Mac Bks Young Read) S&S Childrens.

— Your Owl Friend. LC 76-58725. (Illus.). (J). (gr. k-3). 1977. 8.95 (*0-06-021731-6*) HarpC Child Bks.

Dragonwagon, Crescent & Shaffer. The Sun Begun. LC 97-42241. (J). 1999. 16.00 (*0-689-81159-4*) S&S Childrens.

Dragonwagon, Crescent & Zindel, Paul. To Take a Dare. LC 80-8441. 256p. (YA). (gr. 7 up). 1982. 12.95 (*0-06-026858-1*) HarpC Child Bks.

Dragoo, Bob, jt. auth. see Ernst & Young LLP Staff.

Dragoo, Don W. Archaic Hunters of the Upper Ohio Valley. fac. ed. (Carnegie Museum, Anthropological Ser.: Vol. 35). (Illus.). 107p. (C). 1959. reprint ed. pap. text 11.88 (*1-55567-759-2*) Coyote Press.

Dragoo, Don W. Mounds for the Dead. (Annals of C.M.N.H. Ser.: Vol. 37). (Illus.). 315p. 1963. pap. 13.95 (*0-911239-09-X*) Carnegie Mus.

Dragoo, Jason L. Handbook of Sports Medicine. LC 93-92722. (Illus.). 192p. (Orig.). 1993. pap. 14.95 (*0-9637144-0-6*) Renaiss AZ.

Dragoo, M. M., jt. auth. see Mitchell, B. J.

Dragoumis, Julia D. Tales of a Greek Island. LC 76-110184. (Short Story Index Reprint Ser.). 1977. 23.95 (*0-8369-3335-4*) Ayer.

Dragoumis, Mark, jt. auth. see Veremes, Thanos M.

Dragoumis, Mark, jt. compiled by see Veremis, Thanos.

D

An Asterisk (*) at the beginning of an entry indicates that the title is appearing for the first time.

Dragovic, Ivan. German Serbocroatian Dictionary of Industrial Electronic Technology: Recnik Industrijske Elektrotehnike Nemacko-Srpskohrvatski. (GER & SER.). 1988. 125.00 (*0-8288-1379-5*, F114980) Fr & Eur.

Dragovic, Ivan & Pavicevic, M. German-Serbocroation Dictionary of Modern Electronics: Recnik Moderne Elektronike Nemacko-Srpskohrvatski. (GER & SER.). 400p. 1987. write for info. (*0-8288-1378-7*, F27980) Fr & Eur.

Dragovic, J. English-Russian-Serbocroatian Aviations Dictionary. (ENG, RUS & SER.). 460p. 1973. 49.95 (*0-8288-6291-5*, M-9632) Fr & Eur.

Dragowick, Marilyn E., ed. Metalwares Price Guide: Including Silver, Brass, Copper, Pewter & More. LC 95-76093. (Illus.). 240p. 1995. pap. 14.95 (*0-930625-39-0*, Antique Trader) Krause Pubns.

***Dragstra, Henk.** Betraying Ourselves. 2000. text 49.95 (*0-312-23149-0*) St Martin.

Draguet, Michael. Treasures of Art Nouveau: Painting, Sculpture, Decorative Arts in the Anne-Marie Gillion Crowet Collection. LC 99-510598. (Illus.). 304p. 1999. 75.00 (*88-8118-324-2*, Pub. by Skira IT) Abbeville Pr.

Draguet, Rene, ed. Julien d'Halicarnasse et Sa Controverse avec Severe d'Antioch sur l'Incorruptibilite du Corps du Christ. LC 82-45813. (Orthodoxies & Heresies in the Early Church Ser.). reprint ed. 45.00 (*0-404-62382-4*) AMS Pr.

Draguhn, Werner & Ash, Robert. China's Economic Security. (Institute for Asian Affairs, Hamburg Ser.). 288p. (C). 1999. text 55.00 (*0-7007-1167-8*, Pub. by Curzon Pr Ltd) UH Pr.

Dragun, Andrew, jt. auth. see Jakobsson, Kristin.

Dragun, Andrew K. & Jakobsson, Kristin M., eds. Sustainability & Global Environmental Policy: New Perspectives. LC 97-14363. 336p. 1997. 90.00 (*1-85898-630-3*) E Elgar.

***Dragun, Andrew K. & Tisdell, Clem, eds.** Sustainable Agriculture & Environment: Globalisation & the Impact of Trade Liberalisation. LC 99-15402. 308p. 1999. 100.00 (*1-84064-172-X*) E Elgar.

Dragun, James, et al. Chromium in Soil: Perspectives in Chemistry, Health, & Environmental Regulation. 256p. 1998. boxed set 64.95 (*0-8493-1157-8*) CRC Pr.

Dragun, James, jt. auth. see Mason, Sharon.

Dragutan, V. & Streck, R. Catalytic Polymerization of Cycloolefins. (Studies in Surface Science & Catalysis). 1999. text. write for info. (*0-444-89519-1*) Elsevier.

Dragutan, Valerian, et al. Olef in Metathesis & Ring-Opening Polymerization of Cyclo-Olefins. 2nd rev. ed. LC 83-10189. (Illus.). 544p. reprint ed. pap. 168.70 (*0-8357-5596-7*, 203523500093) Bks Demand.

Dragutinovic, Gordan D. & Baclic, Branislav S. Operation of Counterflow Regenerators. LC 97-81220. (Developments in Heat Transfer Ser.: Vol. 4). 208p. 1998. 95.00 (*1-85312-548-2*, 5482, Pub. by WIT Pr) Computational Mech MA.

Draham, Vicky. Fall Games: I Fall Games; II The Bridge in Winter. LC 94-70519. 1994. 21.50 (*0-9640864-0-9*) Draham.

Draheim, Alan, ed. see Bromberg, Sarah.

Draheim, Joachim, ed. see Cooper, Ruskin.

Draheim, Joachim von & Wille, Guenther. Horaz-Vertonungen vom Mittelalter bis zur Gegenwart, Eine Anthologie. (Heuremata Studien Zu Literatur, Sprachenn & Kultur der Antike: Vol. 7A). (GER.). iv, 221p. (Orig.). 1985. pap. 44.00 (*90-6032-180-4*, Pub. by B R Gruner) Humanities.

Draher, Patricia, ed. see Mexican Museum Staff.

Drahmann, Theodore. Governance & Administration in the Catholic School. 45p. 1986. 3.00 (*0-318-20563-7*) Natl Cath Educ.

Drahmann, Theodore, et al. Sponsorship, Colleagueship & Service: A Conversation about the Future of Religious Communities & American Catholic High Schools. McDonald, Dale, ed. 59p. (Orig.). 1996. pap. 16.00 (*1-55833-179-4*) Natl Cath Educ.

Drahms, August. Criminal, His Personnel & Environment: A Scientific Study. LC 72-108231. (Criminology, Law Enforcement, & Social Problems Ser.: No. 114). (Illus.). 1971. reprint ed. lib. bdg. 25.00 (*0-87585-114-2*) Patterson Smith.

Drahos, Mary. Angels of God, Our Guardians Dear: Today's Catholics Rediscover Angels. 180p. 1995. pap. 9.99 (*0-89283-925-2*, Charis) Servant.

Drahos, Peter. A Philosophy of Intellectual Property. LC 96-24900. (Applied Legal Philosophy Ser.). 272p. (C). 1996. text 82.95 (*1-85521-240-4*, Pub. by Dartmth Pub) Ashgate Pub Co.

Drahos, Peter, ed. Intellectual Property. LC 99-72417. (International Library of Essays in Law & Legal Theory). 520p. 1999. text 212.95 (*1-84014-740-7*, Pub. by Ashgate Pub) Ashgate Pub Co.

Drahos, Peter, jt. auth. see Braithwaite, John.

Drahovsky, D. & Kornhuber, B., eds. Human Malignancies. (Illus.). 160p. 1989. 35.95 (*0-387-19219-0*) Spr-Verlag.

Drai, Dalia. Supervenience & Realism. LC B841.2.D73 1999. (Avebury Series in Philosophy). 142p. (C). 1999. text 61.95 (*1-84014-861-6*, Pub. by Ashgate Pub) Ashgate Pub Co.

Drai, Martine, et al. Monologues: Includes: Another Story, Night Just Before the Forest, The Sifter, All It Takes Is Something Small, Madame Bertin's Testimony, Anatomy Lesson. Kourilsky, Francoise, ed. Miller, Judith G. et al, trs. from FRE. 246p. (Orig.). 1995. pap. 15.95 (*0-913745-44-8*) Ubu Repertory.

Draig, Diana. How to Draw & Paint Pets. (Art for Children Ser.). (Illus.). 32p. (YA). (gr. 3 up). 1997. pap. 4.95 (*1-56010-251-9*, AC01) W Foster Pub.

Draigh, David. Behind the Screen: The American Museum of the Moving Image Guide to Who Does What in Motion Pictures & Television. (Illus.). 144p. 1988. spiral bd. 7.95 (*0-89659-955-8*) Abbeville Pr.

— A Behind the Screen Guide to Who Does What in Motion Pictures & Television. Hasiotis, Georgette M., ed. (Illus.). (Orig.). 1988. write for info. (*0-318-62753-1*) Amer Mus Moving Image.

Draijer, Dirk W. Autism & Austistic-Like Conditions in Mental Retardation. LC 97-29573. 450p. 1997. 50.00 (*90-265-1463-8*) Swets.

Draijer, Nel, jt. auth. see Boon, Suzette.

Draiman, Barbara H. Drugs & AIDS. (Drug Abuse Prevention Library). 64p. (gr. 7-12). 1997. pap. 6.95 (*1-56838-172-7*, 1764 A) Hazelden.

Draimin, Barbara H. Coping When a Parent Has AIDS. LC 93-5070. (YA). (gr. 7-12). 1994. lib. bdg. 17.95 (*0-8239-1664-2*) Rosen Group.

— Drugs & AIDS. rev. ed. LC 94-2331. (Drug Abuse Prevention Library). (Illus.). 64p. (YA). (gr. 7-12). 1997. lib. bdg. 17.95 (*0-8239-2583-8*) Rosen Group.

— Everything You Need to Know When a Parent Has AIDS. LC 94-15969. (Need to Know Library). (Illus.). 64p. (YA). (gr. 7-12). 1994. lib. bdg. 17.95 (*0-8239-1690-1*) Rosen Group.

— Working Together Against AIDS. LC 94-15208. (Library of Social Activism). (Illus.). 64p. (YA). 1994. lib. bdg. 16.95 (*0-8239-1777-0*) Rosen Group.

Drain, Cecil B. Decision Making in the Post Anesthesia Care Unit. 288p. 1995. 29.95 (*0-8016-7875-7*) Mosby Inc.

— The Post Anesthesia Care Unit: A Critical Care Approach to Post Anesthesia Nursing. 3rd ed. LC 93-8029. (Illus.). 640p. 1994. text 52.50 (*0-7216-4571-2*, W B Saunders Co) Harcrt Hlth Sci Grp.

Drain, L. E., jt. auth. see Scruby, C. B.

Drain, Patricia N. Hire Me! Secrets of Job Interviewing. LC 92-11124. 1992. pap. 9.99 (*0-8431-3444-5*, Price Stern) Peng Put Young Read.

Drain, Richard. Renewing Theatre: A Twentieth Century Sourcebook. LC 94-40136. 408p. (C). 1995. pap. 25.99 (*0-415-09620-0*, B3144) Routledge.

— Renewing Theatre: A Twentieth Century Sourcebook. LC 94-40136. 408p. (C). (gr. 13). 1995. 90.00 (*0-415-09619-7*, B3140) Routledge.

Drain, Susan. The Anglican Church in Nineteenth Century Britain: Hyms Ancient & Modern 1860-1875. LC 89-34070. (Texts & Studies in Religion: Vol. 40). 552p. 1989. lib. bdg. 119.95 (*0-88946-829-X*) E Mellen.

Drain, Thomas A. A Sense of Mission: Historic Churches of the Southwest. LC 93-5122. (Illus.). 144p. 1994. pap. 19.95 (*0-8118-0404-6*) Chronicle Bks.

Draine, Betsy. Substance under Pressure: Artistic Coherence & Evolving Form in the Novels of Doris Lessing. LC 82-70556. 240p. 1983. 25.00 (*0-299-09230-5*) U of Wis Pr.

— Substance under Pressure: Artistic Coherence & Evolving Form in the Novels of Doris Lessing. LC 82-70556. 240p. reprint ed. pap. 74.40 (*0-608-20424-2*, 207167700002) Bks Demand.

Draine, Betsy, tr. see Toussaint, Jean-Luc.

Draine, Cathie & Hall, Barbara, eds. Culture Shock! Indonesia. LC 90-85621. (Illus.). 280p. 1991. pap. 12.95 (*1-55868-057-8*) Gr Arts Ctr Pub.

Draine, Edwin H. Import Traffic of Chicago & Its Hinterland. LC 63-15947. (University of Chicago, Department of Geography, Research Paper Ser.: No. 81). 152p. reprint ed. pap. 47.20 (*0-7837-0411-9*, 204073200018) Bks Demand.

Drainie, Bronwyn. My Jerusalem. 304p. 1995. pap. 14.95 (*0-385-25520-9*) Doubleday.

***Draitser.** Making War Not Love. LC 99-19094. 336p. 1999. text 45.00 (*0-312-22129-0*) St Martin.

Draitser, Emil. The Lost Boy & Other Stories. (RUS.). (Orig.). 1993. pap. 9.95 (*5-239-01632-1*) Maxims Bk NJ.

— Taking Penguins to the Movies: Ethnic Humor in Russia. LC 97-44214. (Humor in Life & Letters Ser.). 224p. 1998. 34.95 (*0-8143-2327-8*) Wayne St U Pr.

Draitser, Emil, ed. Forbidden Laughter. LC 79-89635. (Soviet Underground Jokes Ser.: No. 1). (ENG & RUS., Illus.). (Orig.). 1980. pap. 6.95 (*0-89626-045-3*) Maxims Bk NJ.

***Draitser, Emil, ed.** Russkie Poety Xix Veka: Antologiia Dlia Studentov, 2 vols. 144p. 1999. pap. 12.00 (*1-55779-119-8*) Hermitage Pubs.

Draitser, Emil & Aksyonov, Vassily, intros. Peshchera Neozhidannostei (The Fun House) LC 83-63368. (RUS.). 160p. 1984. pap. 7.95 (*0-911971-03-3*) Effect Pub.

Draitser, Emil A. Techniques of Satire: The Case of Saltykov-Shchedrin. LC 93-43693. (Humor Research Ser.: No. 2). xiii, 213p. (C). 1994. lib. bdg. 83.10 (*3-11-012624-9*) Mouton.

Drak, William J. Toward Sustainable Competition in Global Telecommunications: From Principle to Practice. (Communications & Society Ser.). 125p. pap. 12.00 (*0-89843-258-8*) The Aspen Inst.

Drakakis, J., ed. & intro. see Shakespeare, William.

Drakakis, John. Alternative Shakespeare. 1985. pap. text 14.95 (*0-416-36860-3*) Routledge.

— Shakespearean Tragedy. (Critical Readers Ser.). 304p. (C). 1995. pap. text 47.00 (*0-582-05114-2*, 79009) Longman.

— Tragedy. LC 97-43677. (Longman Critical Readers Ser.). 376p. 1998. 72.00 (*0-582-20998-6*) Longman.

Drakakis, John, ed. Alternative Shakespeares. LC 85-4984. 320p. (Orig.). (C). 1985. pap. 20.99 (*0-415-02528-1*, 9457) Routledge.

— Shakespearean Tragedy. (C). 1991. 96.00 (*0-582-05115-0*) Addison-Wesley.

Drakakis, John, ed. see Shakespeare, William.

Drakakis-Smith, David. The Third World City. (Introductions to Development Ser.). 160p. 1987. pap. text 9.95 (*0-416-91970-7*) Routledge.

Drakakis-Smith, David, jt. ed. see Dixon, Chris.

Drakard, David. Printed English Pottery: History & Humour in the Reign of George III, 1760-1820. (Illus.). 268p. 1992. 125.00 (*0-9512140-5-5*, Pub. by J Horne) Antique Collect.

Drakard, Jane. A Kingdom of Words: Language & Power in Sumatra. LC 98-18943. (South-East Asian Historical Monographs). (Illus.). 344p. 1999. text 45.00 (*983-56-0035-X*) OUP.

— A Malay Frontier: Unity & Duality in a Sumatran Kingdom. (Studies on Southeast Asia: No. 7). (Illus.). 215p. (Orig.). (C). 1990. pap. text 15.00 (*0-87727-706-0*) Cornell SE Asia.

Drake. Caught in the Crossfire. 1998. per. 6.99 (*0-671-87882-4*) S&S Trade.

— The Drake Beam Morin Guide to Resumes & Marketing Letters. 154p. 1994. pap. 10.95 (*1-880030-22-5*) DBM Pub.

***Drake.** Ondine. LC 98-44599. 1999. 30.00 (*0-7862-1715-4*) Thorndike Pr.

Drake. Princess of Fire. LC 97-50360. 1998. 24.95 (*0-7862-1386-8*) Thorndike Pr.

Drake & Chadwick. Massachusetts One Hundred Years Ago: The Northeast. (Historical Ser.). (Illus.). 1976. pap. 3.50 (*0-89540-017-0*, SB-017) Sun Pub.

Drake, jt. auth. see White.

Drake, Frederick D. & Nelson, Lynne R., eds. States' Rights & American Federalism: A Documentary History. LC 99-21705. (Primary Documents in American History & Contemporary Issues Ser.). 264p. 1999. 49.95 (*0-313-30573-0*) Greenwood.

Drake, A., ed. The Electoral Handbook of Wales, 1900-1997. 250p. 1997. pap. 24.95 (*1-86057-013-5*, Pub. by Welsh Acad) Intl Spec Bk.

Drake, Alan. Easter Island: The Ceremonial Center of Orongo. Lee, Georgia, ed. & illus. by. LC 91-90732. (Easter Island Foundation Ser.). 100p. (Orig.). 1992. pap. 12.00 (*1-880636-00-X*) Easter Isl Fnd.

Drake, Alan, ed. see Rapahango, Ana B. & Liller, William.

Drake, Albert. Beyond the Pavement. LC 80-53525. 175p. 1981. 9.95 (*0-917976-10-X*, White Ewe Pr) Thunder Baas Pr.

— Fifties Flashback: A Nostalgia Trip. LC 98-27391. (Illus.). 160p. 1998. pap. 19.95 (*1-55561-161-3*) Fisher Bks.

— Garage. (Rockbook Ser.: No. 8). 24p. (Orig.). 1980. pap. 3.00 (*0-930012-38-0*) J Mudfoot.

— Homesick. Dionne, Joe, ed. (Illus.). 16p. (Orig.). 1988. pap. 10.00 (*0-945950-00-4*) Canoe Pr MI.

— I Remember the Day James Dean Died & other Stories. LC 82-51027. 189p. (Orig.). 1983. pap. 7.95 (*0-917976-17-7*, White Ewe Pr) Thunder Baas Pr.

— In the Time of Surveys & Other Stories of Americans Abroad. LC 78-53998. 1978. pap. 3.00 (*0-917976-02-9*, White Ewe Pr) Thunder Baas Pr.

— One Summer. LC 79-63672. 1979. pap. 5.00 (*0-917976-06-1*, White Ewe Pr) Thunder Baas Pr.

Drake, Albert N., ed. see Drake, Daniel.

Drake, Albert N., ed. see Drake, J. Madison.

Drake, Alexandra B., ed. Mastering Reading: Comp. I. 156p. 1988. pap. text 7.35 (*0-8428-0189-8*) Cambridge Bk.

— Mastering Reading: Comp. II. 156p. 1988. pap. text 7.05 (*0-8428-0191-X*) Cambridge Bk.

Drake, Alice. Fat & Fabulous: Looking Good & Feeling Great. v, 120p. (Orig.). 1997. pap. 10.00 (*0-9657830-0-6*) Zaftig Images.

Drake, Alice, ed. see Clark, Gail.

Drake, Alice, ed. see Dahlquist, Kathleen C.

***Drake, Allen.** Fly & Bubble Fishing Techniques Revealed. (Illus.). 80p. 2000. pap. 8.95 (*1-57188-204-9*) F Amato Pubns.

Drake, Alvin W. Fundamentals of Applied Probability Theory. (Illus.). 256p. (C). 1967. 103.44 (*0-07-017815-1*) McGraw.

Drake, Alvin W., et al. The American Blood Supply: Issues & Policies of Blood Donation. (Health & Public Policy Ser.). 224p. 1982. 32.50 (*0-262-04070-0*) MIT Pr.

Drake, Angela. Betrayed. (Scarlet Ser.). (Orig.). 1997. mass mkt. 3.99 (*1-85487-962-6*, Pub. by Scarlet Bks) London Brdge.

— Love Child. (Scarlet Ser.). 1997. mass mkt. 3.99 (*1-85487-987-1*, Pub. by Scarlet Bks) London Brdge.

***Drake, Angela.** The Love Child. 496p. 2000. 31.99 (*0-7505-1509-0*) Ulverscroft.

— Master of Destiny. 320p. 1999. 26.00 (*0-7278-5502-6*, Pub. by Severn Hse) Chivers N Amer.

— The Mistress. large type ed. 496p. 2000. 31.99 (*0-7505-1508-2*, Pub. by Mgna Lrg Print) Ulverscroft.

Drake, Angela. Woman of Dreams. 400p. 1997. mass mkt. 3.99 (*1-85487-714-3*, Pub. by Scarlet Bks) London Brdge.

Drake, Annie. Help Me...I Have a Teenager!! The Nitty Gritty Guide to Parental Sanity. 1999. pap. text 16.95 (*0-9667490-9-X*) Duckworks.

Drake, Archie, jt. ed. see Gavitt, Loren.

Drake, Asa. Warrior Witch of Hel. 240p. 1985. pap. 2.95 (*0-445-20039-1*) Warner Bks.

Drake, B. The Drake Beam Morin Guide to Getting Started with Your Career. 126p. 1994. pap. 10.95 (*1-880030-23-3*) DBM Pub.

Drake, B., ed. Construction Economics in the Single European Market. (Illus.). 256p. (C). 1994. 130.00 (*0-419-18980-7*, E & FN Spon) Routledge.

Drake, Barbara. Bees in Wet Weather. Browning, Brian & Dionne, Joe, eds. (Illus.). 30p. 1992. pap. 12.00 (*0-945950-07-1*) Canoe Pr MI.

— Life in a Gothic Novel. (WEP Poetry Ser.: No. 4). 24p. (Orig.). 1981. pap. 2.50 (*0-917976-09-6*, White Ewe Pr) Thunder Baas Pr.

— Love at the Egyptian Theatre. LC 78-50183. 1978. pap. 2.50 (*0-686-09378-X*) Red Cedar.

— Peace at Heart: An Oregon Country Life. LC 98-23928. 192p. 1998. pap. 15.95 (*0-87071-455-4*) Oreg St U Pr.

— Space Before A. 26p. 1996. 5.00 (*0-614-30121-1*) Skydog OR.

— What We Say to Strangers. LC 86-8300. 76p. 1987. 14.95 (*0-932576-34-6*); pap. 6.95 (*0-932576-35-4*) Breitenbush Bks.

— Writing Poetry. 2nd ed. LC 93-77381. (C). 1994. pap. text 39.00 (*0-15-500154-X*, Pub. by Harcourt Coll Pubs) Harcourt.

Drake Beam Morin Editors. Healthy, Wealthy & Wise: A Guide to Retirement Planning. LC 97-20439. (Illus.). 208p. (Orig.). 1997. pap. 12.95 (*1-57112-081-5*, PO815) Park Ave.

Drake Beam Morin, Inc. Managing Stress in Turbulent Times. 120p. (Orig.). 1993. pap. 22.95 incl. audio (*1-880030-14-4*) DBM Pub.

— Performance Management Workbook. 50p. (Orig.). 1993. pap. 12.95 (*1-880030-15-2*) DBM Pub.

Drake Beam Morin, Inc. Staff. Selection Interviewing for the 21st Century. 57p. (Orig.). 1993. pap. 10.95 (*1-880030-03-9*) DBM Pub.

— Seven Imperatives for Fair, Legal & Productive Interviewing: A Guide for Anyone Who Makes or Influences Hiring Decision. 2nd ed. (Illus.). 80p. 1993. reprint ed. pap. 10.95 (*1-880030-09-8*) DBM Pub.

Drake Beam Morio, Inc. Staff. I-Speak Your Language Interviewing Strategy. (Illus.). 60p. (Orig.). 1992. pap., student ed. 12.95 (*1-880030-08-X*) DBM Pub.

Drake, Benjamin. Cincinnati in Eighteen Twenty. (Notable American Authors Ser.). 1992. reprint ed. lib. bdg. 75.00 (*0-7812-2683-X*) Rprt Serv.

— The Life & Adventures of Black Hawk: With Sketches of Keokuk, the Sac & Fox Indians, & the Late Black Hawk War. (Notable American Authors Ser.). 1992. reprint ed. lib. bdg. 75.00 (*0-7812-2685-6*) Rprt Serv.

***Drake, Benjamin.** The Life of Tecumseh an His Brother the Prophet: A History of the Shawnee. LC 99-91264. 236p. 1999. reprint ed. pap. text 19.95 (*1-889037-21-4*) Wennawoods.

Drake, Benjamin. Life of Tecumseh & His Brother . . . With an Historical Sketch of the Shawanoe Indians. (Notable American Authors Ser.). 1992. reprint ed. lib. bdg. 75.00 (*0-7812-2686-4*) Rprt Serv.

— Life of Tecumseh & of His Brother the Prophet: With a Historical Sketch of the Shawanoe Indians. LC 78-90173. (Mass Violence in America Ser.). 1977. reprint ed. 24.95 (*0-405-01307-8*) Ayer.

— Tales & Sketches from the Queen City. (Notable American Authors Ser.). 1992. reprint ed. lib. bdg. 75.00 (*0-7812-2684-8*) Rprt Serv.

Drake, Benjamin, jt. auth. see Todd, Charles S.

Drake, Betty. Alabama Eighteen Forty Census Index: Vol. 1, The Counties Formed from the Creek & Cherokee Sessions of the 1830s. 93p. 1983. reprint ed. 15.00 (*0-89308-331-3*) Southern Hist Pr.

Drake, Bill. Inside Domino Development. 1998. 59.99 (*1-56205-822-3*) New Riders Pub.

Drake-Brockman, D. L. Mathura: A Gazetteer. 1985. reprint ed. 32.00 (*0-8364-1324-5*, Pub. by Usha) S Asia.

***Drake-Brockman, Henrietta.** Voyage to Disaster. LC 96-139381. 324p. (C). 2000. pap. 26.95 (*1-875560-32-7*, Pub. by Univ of West Aust Pr) Intl Spec Bk.

Drake-Brockman, Henrietta, jt. selected by see Murdoch, Walter.

Drake, C. G., et al. Surgery of Vertebrobasilar Aneurysms: London, Ontario, Experience on 1,767 Patients. LC 97-10380. (Illus.). 400p. 1996. 185.00 (*3-211-82696-3*) Spr-Verlag.

Drake, C. L., jt. ed. see Watkins, J. S.

Drake, Caleb. Object-Oriented Programming with C++ & Smalltalk. LC 97-18141. 1010p. (C). 1997. pap. 74.00 (*0-13-103797-8*) P-H.

Drake, Carrie L. The Brain in the Jar: The Transparency of Deception. 239p. (Orig.). 1988. pap. 10.95 (*0-945408-13-7*) Mind Matters Pub.

Drake, Charles, jt. ed. see Pindell, James L.

Drake, Charles A. A Study of an Interest Test & Affectivity Test in Forecasting Freshman Success in College. LC 76-176729. (Columbia University. Teachers College. Contributions to Education Ser.: No. 504). reprint ed. 37.50 (*0-404-55504-7*) AMS Pr.

Drake, Charles D. Union & Anti-Slavery Speeches. LC 77-83961. (Black Heritage Library Collection). 1977. 20.95 (*0-8369-8552-4*) Ayer.

Drake, Charles D., ed. Pioneer Life in Kentucky: Series of Reminscential Letters from Daniel Dranke, M.D., of Cincinnati to His Children. (Ohio Valley Historical Ser.: No. VI). (Illus.). 263p. 1997. reprint ed. lib. bdg. 32.00 (*0-8328-6728-4*) Higginson Bk Co.

Drake, Chris & Brown, Kimberley. Panic! UNIX System Crash Dump Analysis. 496p. (C). 1995. pap. 60.00 incl. cd-rom (*0-13-149386-8*) P-H.

Drake, Christopher, tr. & intro. see Ryuichi, Tamura.

***Drake, Clif.** Technical Analysis Simplified. 1999. pap. 29.95 (*1-883272-47-5*) Traders Lib.

Drake, D., et al. Essays in Critical Realism. LC 67-30877. 244p. 1967. reprint ed. 45.00 (*0-87752-028-3*) Gordian.

Drake, Dana B. Don Quijote, 1894-1970: A Selective & Annotated Bibliography, Vol. 2. LC 74-8503. 1978. pap. 20.00 (*0-89729-186-7*) Ediciones.

Drake, Dana B. & Finello, Dominick L. An Analytical & Bibliographical Guide to Criticism on Don Quijote (1790-1893) (Documentacion Cervantina Ser.: Vol. 6). 248p. 1987. 23.50 (*0-936388-27-7*) Juan de la Cuesta.

D

An Asterisk (*) at the beginning of an entry indicates that the title is appearing for the first time.

D

Drake, Jane, jt. auth. see Love, Ann.

Drake, Jane B., jt. auth. see Gooze, Mitchell.

Drake, Jennifer, jt. auth. see Heywood, Leslie.

***Drake, Jim.** Computers All Around Us. LC 98-48091. 32p. (J). (gr. k-2). 1999. lib. bdg. 21.36 (1-57572-784-6) Heinemann Lib.

Drake, Jim. Computers & School. LC 98-48090. (Log on to Computers Ser.). 32p. (J). (gr. 2-4). 1999. 14.95 (1-57572-785-4) Heinemann Lib.

***Drake, Jim.** Log on to Computers Series, 4 bks. 32p. 1999. 85.44 (1-57572-788-9) Heinemann Lib.

Drake, Jim. Play with Computers. LC 98-48088. 32p. (J). 1999. lib. bdg. 21.36 (1-57572-786-2) Heinemann Lib.

— What Is a Computer? LC 98-48089. (J). (gr. 2-4). 1999. lib. bdg. 21.36 (1-57572-787-0) Heinemann Lib.

Drake, John. The Beginning of the River: Herman's Quest. (Illus.). 48p. (J). (gr. k-5). 1992. 16.95 (0-9633574-0-9) Little Turtle.

— Organogermanium Compounds, Pt. 4. (Gmelin Handbook of Inorganic & Organometallic Chemistry Ser.: Vol. 4). 364p. 1994. 1600.00 (0-387-93696-3) Spr-Verlag.

Drake, John C. Songs of the Nightingale: Poetry of the Heart. LC 93-83991. (Illus.). 132p. (Orig.). 1993. 17.95 (0-9636472-5-3); pap. 13.99 (0-9636472-9-6) Nghtngale Pub.

Drake, John D. The Perfect Interview: How to Get the Job You Really Want. 2nd ed. Glenn, Mary, ed. LC 96-9327. 208p. 1996. pap. 17.95 (0-8144-7919-7) AMACOM.

— Performance Appraisal. Christopher, Bill, ed. LC 97-68251. (Management Library). 90p. 1997. pap. 12.95 (1-56052-442-1) Crisp Pubns.

Drake, John W. Just Another Day. (Illus.). 40p. (J). (gr. k-4). 1994. 16.95 (0-9633574-1-7) Little Turtle.

Drake, Joseph. Life & Works of Joseph Rodman Drake (1795-1820) (BCL1-PS American Literature Ser.). 424p. 1993. reprint ed. lib. bdg. 99.00 (0-7812-6959-8) Rprt Serv.

Drake, Joseph H., tr. Law of Nations: or The Principles of Natural Law, Vol. 2. LC 95-77192. (Classics in International Law Reprint Ser.: No. 13). 1743p. 1995. reprint ed. 125.00 (1-57588-257-4, 310100) W S Hein.

Drake, Joseph H., ed. see von Jhering, Rudolf.

Drake, Joseph H., tr. see Von Wolff, Christian.

Drake, Joseph R. Collected Works of Joseph Rodman Drake: Life & Works. Pleadwell, F. L., ed. (Notable American Authors Ser.). 1992. reprint ed. lib. bdg. 75.00 (0-318-67705-9) Rprt Serv.

— Collected Works of Joseph Rodman Drake: The Culprit Fay & Other Stories. (Notable American Authors Ser.). 1992. reprint ed. lib. bdg. 75.00 (0-7812-2692-9, 1512) Rprt Serv.

— The Culprit Fay & Other Poems. (Notable American Authors Ser.). 1992. reprint ed. lib. bdg. 90.00 (0-7812-2693-7) Rprt Serv.

— Life & Works. Pleadwell, F. L., ed. (Notable American Authors Ser.). 1992. reprint ed. lib. bdg. 75.00 (0-7812-2694-5) Rprt Serv.

Drake, Joy & Tyler, Kathy. Angel Cards. (Illus.). 1981. 8.95 (0-934245-25-8) Narada Prodns.

— Angel Cards. (FRE., Illus.). 1992. pap. text 8.95 (0-934245-27-4); pap. text 8.95 (0-934245-28-2); pap. text 8.95 (0-934245-26-6) Narada Prodns.

Drake, Joy, jt. auth. see Tyler, Kathy.

***Drake, Keith A.** The Medical Transcription Career Handbook. LC 99-37072. 149p. 1999. pap. text 20.80 (0-13-011540-1) P-H.

Drake, Ken, ed. see International SAMPE Symposium & Exhibition Staff.

Drake, Kenneth. The Beethoven Sonatas & the Creative Experience. LC 93-27719. (Illus.). 336p. 1994. lib. bdg. 49.95 (0-253-31822-X) Ind U Pr.

***Drake, Kenneth.** The Beethoven Sonatas & the Creative Experience. (Illus.). 336p. 2000. pap. 22.95 (0-253-21382-7) Ind U Pr.

Drake, Kenneth. The Sonatas of Beethoven, As He Played & Taught Them. LC 80-8608. 223p. reprint ed. pap. 69.20 (0-608-17405-X, 205642000067) Bks Demand.

Drake, L. S. The Drake Family in England & America, 1360-1895 & the Descendants of Thomas Drake of Weymouth, MA, 1635-1691. (Illus.). 347p. 1989. reprint ed. pap. 42.00 (0-8328-0493-2); reprint ed. lib. bdg. 52.00 (0-8328-0492-4) Higginson Bk Co.

Drake-Lee. Clinical Otorhinolaryngology. 1996. pap. text 28.00 (0-443-04965-3, W B Saunders Co) Harcrt Hlth Sci Grp.

Drake, Lee, et al. Inner Voices Vol. 3: A New Collection of Prison Literature. Williams, C. N., ed. (Inner Voices Ser.). 60p. 1996. pap. 4.00 (0-9653634-2-2) I V Pr.

Drake, Lewis E. & Oetting, E. R. An MMPI Codebook for Counselors. LC 59-10187. 148p. reprint ed. pap. 45.90 (0-8357-3330-0, 203955500013) Bks Demand.

Drake, Linda S. An Annotated Bibliography & Index Covering CPL Bibliographies 254-328, 1990-1995. LC 96-129686. 25p. 1995. pap. 10.00 (0-86602-328-3, Sage Prdcls Pr) Sage.

Drake, Lon. Lab Manual for 12:24. 1992. 15.35 (0-88252-090-3) Paladin Hse.

Drake, M. Gastro-Esophageal Cytology. (Monographs in Clinical Cytology Ser.: Vol. 10). (Illus.). xii, 268p. 1985. 107.00 (3-8055-3931-2) S Karger.

Drake, Madeline & Biebuych, Tony. Policy & Provision for the Single Homeless: Research Paper. 1977. 30.00 (0-7855-0567-9, Pub. by Natl Inst Soc Work) St Mut.

***Drake-Major, Laurel & Ferguson, Jacqueline.** The Grantseeker's Answerbook. 2nd ed. 267p. 1999. pap. 88.00 (0-8342-1746-5) Aspen Pub.

Drake, Margaret. Crafts in Therapy & Rehabilitation. 2nd ed. LC 98-42014. (Illus.). 272p. 1998. pap. 33.00 (1-55642-396-9, 33969) SLACK Inc.

***Drake, Margaret.** Crafts in Therapy & Rehabilitation. 2nd ed. 64p. (C). 1999. pap. text, teacher ed. write for info. (1-55642-427-2) SLACK Inc.

Drake, Marie R. Sexology Encyclopedia Vol. 22: Rape: Index of Modern Information with Bibliography. (Illus.). 129p. 1995. 49.50 (0-7883-0892-0); pap. 39.95 (0-7883-0893-9) ABBE Pubs Assn.

Drake, Marsha. The Proverbs Thirty-One Lady & Other Impossible Dreams. LC 84-6453. 192p. (Orig.). 1984. pap. 8.99 (0-87123-595-1) Bethany Hse.

Drake, Mary F., et al. Retail Fashion Promotion & Advertising. (Illus.). 354p. (C). 1991. 47.20 (0-02-330029-9, Macmillan Coll) P-H.

Drake, Melba. Houston Handbook. 5th ed. (Illus.). 101p. (YA). (gr. 8-12). 1994. pap. 7.50 (0-939903-01-6) LWV Houston Ed Fund.

Drake, Michael. I Ching: The Tao of Drumming. LC 97-90098. (Illus.). 152p. (Orig.). 1997. pap. 14.95 (0-9629002-2-2) Talking Drum.

— Population & Society in Norway, 1735-1865. LC 69-14393. (Cambridge Studies in Economic History). 276p. reprint ed. pap. 78.70 (0-608-12223-8, 2024445) Bks Demand.

— The Shamanic Drum: A Guide to Sacred Drumming. LC 91-90824. 104p. 1991. pap. 9.95 (0-9629002-0-6) Talking Drum.

— Time, Family & Community: Perspectives on Family & Community History. (Illus.). 352p. (C). 1994. pap. 29.95 (0-631-19237-9) Blackwell Pubs.

Drake, Michael, et al, eds. Global Acronyms, Codes & Designations Directory. 1237p. 1999. 525.00 (1-892303-00-0) R & P Global.

Drake, Michael, jt. ed. see Finnegan, Ruth.

Drake, Michael E. The Search for the Ancestors & Descendants of Henry Brasater Drake of Coles County, Illinois. LC 96-145923. (Illus.). 141p. (Orig.). 1996. pap. 17.00 (0-7884-0423-7, D611) Heritage Bk.

Drake, Michael Y. Baldness (Alopecia) - Causes, Treatments & Chemotherapy: Index of New Information. 150p. 1998. 47.50 (0-7883-2048-3); pap. 44.50 (0-7883-2049-1) ABBE Pubs Assn.

Drake, Michelle, compiled by. The Go Manual: Global Opportunities in Youth with a Mission. 270p. 1998. pap. 3.99 (0-927545-77-2) YWAM Pub.

Drake, Nathan. Memorials of Shakespeare. LC 76-164789. reprint ed. 46.50 (0-404-02177-8) AMS Pr.

Drake, Nicholas. Fashion Illustration Today. 2nd rev. ed. LC 94-60272. (Illus.). 176p. 1994. pap. 24.95 (0-500-27773-7, Pub. by Thames Hudson) Norton.

***Drake, Nicholas, contrib. by.** The Poetry of W. B. Yeats. (Penguin Critical Studies). 136p. 2000. pap. 9.95 (0-14-077132-8, Pub. by Pnguin Bks Ltd) Trafalgar.

***Drake, Nick.** The Man in the White Suit. 64p. 1999. pap. (1-85224-488-7, Pub. by Bloodaxe Bks) Dufour.

Drake, Oliver, jt. auth. see Canutt, Yakima.

***Drake, Pat & Owen, Patricia.** Gender & Management Issues in Education. 120p. 1998. pap. 18.95 (1-85856-087-X, Trentham Bks) Stylus Pub VA.

Drake, Paul. Dimensioning & Tolerancing Handbook. LC 99-36311. 704p. 1999. 125.00 (0-07-018131-4) McGraw.

***Drake, Paul.** Genealogy: How to Find Your Ancestors. (Illus.). 153p. 2000. pap. 26.54 (0-7884-1476-3, 1476) Heritage Bk.

Drake, Paul. In Search of Family History: A Starting Place. (Illus.). (Orig.). 1992. pap. text 24.00 (1-55613-718-4) Heritage Bk.

— Now in Our Fourth Century: Some American Families: A Documentary & Pictorial History of More Than Twenty Families Who Were Well Settled in the American Colonies Before the Year 1700, & Many of Their Ancestors, Kin, & Descendants. (Illus.). 586p. (Orig.). 1995. pap. text 61.50 (0-7884-0146-7) Heritage Bk.

— What Did They Mean by That? A Dictionary of Historical Terms for Genealogists. (Illus.). 234p. (Orig.). 1994. pap. text 23.00 (1-55613-944-6) Heritage Bk.

— What Did They Mean by That? A Dictionary of Historical Terms for Genealogists. rev. ed. (Illus.). 236p. (Orig.). 1998. pap. 25.00 (0-7884-0934-4, D604) Heritage Bk.

— What Did They Mean by That? Vol. 2: A Dictionary of Historical Terms for Genealogists. Some More Words. LC 94-178729. 1998. pap. 13.00 (0-7884-0851-8, D613) Heritage Bk.

— You Ought to Write All That Down. rev. ed. LC 98-207486. (Illus.). 217p. 1998. pap. 32.50 (0-7884-0989-1, D612) Heritage Bk.

— You Ought to Write All That Down: A Guide to Organizing & Writing Genealogical Narrative. LC 96-160260. (Illus.). 196p. (Orig.). 1996. pap. 32.50 (0-7884-0445-8, D612) Heritage Bk.

Drake, Paul & Jaksic, Ivan, eds. The Struggle for Democracy in Chile. rev. ed. LC 95-1353. (Latin American Studies Ser.). xiv, 358p. 1995. pap. text 24.50 (0-8032-6600-6, Bison Books) U of Nebr Pr.

Drake, Paul W. Labor Movements & Dictatorships: The Southern Cone in Comparative Perspective. LC 96-790. 240p. 1996. text 47.50 (0-8018-5326-5); pap. text 15.95 (0-8018-5327-3) Johns Hopkins.

— The Money Doctor in the Andes: U. S. Advisors, Investors, & Economic Reform in Latin America from WWI to the Great Depression. LC 88-18045. xvi, 448p. (C). 1988. text 59.95 (0-8223-0880-0) Duke.

— Socialism & Populism in Chile, 1932-52. LC 77-17414. 416p. 1977. text 34.95 (0-252-00657-7) U of Ill Pr.

Drake, Paul W., ed. Money Doctors, Foreign Debts, & Economic Reforms in Latin America from the 1890s to the Present. LC 93-34563. (Jaguar Books on Latin America: No. 3). 304p. 1994. 45.00 (0-8420-2434-4) Scholarly Res Inc.

Drake, Paul W. & McCubbins, Mathew D. The Origins of Liberty: Political & Economic Liberalization in the Modern World. LC 97-37205. 208p. 1998. text 55.00 (0-691-05753-2, Pub. by Princeton U Pr); pap. text 17.95 (0-691-05755-9, Pub. by Princeton U Pr) Cal Prin Full Svc.

Drake Publishers Editors. Porsche 914/4 Workshop Maintenance & Repair Manual: Range: 1970-1972. LC 72-185632. 1972. write for info. (0-87749-298-0) Crescent Pubng.

— Toyota Celica, Range: 1972: Workshop Maintenance & Repair Manual. LC 72-4067. 140 p. 1972. write for info. (0-87749-300-6) Crescent Pubng.

Drake Publishers Staff. BMW 1600/2, 2002, 2002A, 2002TI & 2002TII, Range, 1967-1973: Workshop Maintenance & Repair Manual. LC 72-5567. 150 p. 1973. write for info. (0-87749-343-X) Crescent Pubng.

Drake, Randy, jt. auth. see Drake, Ellen.

Drake, Richard. The Aldo Moro Murder Case. (Illus.). 336p. (C). 1995. 50.95 (0-674-01481-2) HUP.

— Byzantium for Rome: The Politics of Nostalgia in Umbertian Italy, 1878-1900. LC 79-16578. 336p. reprint ed. pap. 104.20 (0-7837-2454-3, 204260700005) Bks Demand.

— The Revolutionary Mystique & Terrorism in Contemporary Italy. LC 87-46410. (Illus.). 240p. 1989. 32.50 (0-253-35019-0) Ind U Pr.

— The Revolutionary Mystique & Terrorism in Contemporary Italy. LC 87-46410. (Illus.). 238p. Date not set. reprint ed. pap. 73.80 (0-608-20540-0, 205445400002) Bks Demand.

Drake, Richard, ed. Let Us Have Music for Flute. (Illus.). 79p. 1963. pap. 9.95 (0-8258-0156-7, 0-4077) Fischer Inc NY.

***Drake, Richard B.** A History of Appalachia. (Illus.). 304p. 2000. 29.95 (0-8131-2169-8) U Pr of Ky.

Drake, Rick. Ornamental Grasses. 72p. 1996. pap. text 12.95 (1-56799-323-0, Friedman-Fairfax) M Friedman Pub Grp Inc.

Drake, Robert. Amazing Grace. LC 80-16873. 168p. reprint ed. 52.10 (0-8357-9121-1, 201932000011) Bks Demand.

***Drake, Robert.** For the Record: A Robert Drake Reader. Hendricks, Randy & Perkins, James A., eds. 2001. 32.95 (0-86554-682-7, H527) Mercer Univ Pr.

Drake, Robert. The Gay Canon: Great Books Every Gay Man Should Read. LC 98-24581. 512p. 1998. pap. 12.95 (0-385-49228-6, Anchor NY) Doubleday.

— The Home Place: A Memory & a Celebration: The Restored Text. LC 98-11048. 192p. 1998. pap. 19.95 (0-86554-594-4, P172) Mercer Univ Pr.

— My Sweetheart's House: Memories, Fictions. LC 93-46129. (C). 1994. 18.95 (0-86554-437-9, MUP/P105) Mercer Univ Pr.

***Drake, Robert.** The Picture Frame & Other Stories. 208p. 2000. 23.00 (0-86554-689-4) Mercer Univ Pr.

Drake, Robert. Survivors & Others. LC 87-5644. 208p. 1987. 24.95 (0-86554-253-8, MUP H-218); pap. 14.95 (0-86554-254-6, MUP/P041) Mercer Univ Pr.

— What Will You Do for an Encore? 168p. (Orig.). 1996. pap. 19.95 (0-86554-523-5, MUP/P147) Mercer Univ Pr.

***Drake, Robert & Wolverton, Terry, eds.** Circa 2000: Gay Fiction at the Millennium. 352p. 2000. pap. 14.95 (1-55583-517-1, Pub. by Alyson Pubns) Consort Bk Sales.

Drake, Robert & Wolverton, Terry, eds. His: Brilliant New Fiction by Gay Writers. 242p. (Orig.). 1995. pap. 14.95 (0-571-19866-X) Faber & Faber.

***Drake, Robert & Wolverton, Terry, eds.** His 3: Brilliant New Fiction by Gay Writers. LC 98-33107. 256p. 1999. pap. text 15.00 (0-571-19963-1) Faber & Faber.

Drake, Robert & Wolverton, Terry, eds. His 2: Brilliant New Fiction by Gay Writers. 2nd ed. LC 96-37876. 256p. (Orig.). 1997. pap. 15.95 (0-571-19908-9) Faber & Faber.

Drake, Robert, jt. ed. see Minkoff, Kenneth.

Drake, Robert, jt. ed. see Wolverton, Terry.

Drake, Robert E. & International Association of Psychosocial Rehabil. Readings in Dual Diagnosis. LC 97-37262. 1997. write for info. (0-9655843-2-1) Intl Assn Psych.

Drake, Robert M., Jr., ed. see Eckert, Ernest R.

Drake, Samuel. Biography & History of the Indians of North America. (Illus.). 628p. (Orig.). 1995. pap. 38.50 (0-7884-0308-7) Heritage Bk.

— Indian Captivities: or Life in the Wigwam. (Illus.). 395p. 1996. reprint ed. pap. 29.00 (0-7884-0366-4, D608) Heritage Bk.

— A Particular History of the Five Years French & Indian War. (Illus.). 312p. 1995. reprint ed. pap. 22.00 (0-7884-0294-3) Heritage Bk.

Drake, Samuel A. Burgoyne's Invasion of Nineteen Seventy-Seven: Etc. 1988. reprint ed. lib. bdg. 59.00 (0-7812-0035-0) Rprt Serv.

— Burgoyne's Invasion of Seventeen Seventy-Seven, Etc. 1977. reprint ed. 49.00 (0-403-06301-9) Scholarly.

— The Heart of the White Mountains: Their Legend & Scenery. (Illus.). 318p. 1995. reprint ed. lib. bdg. 39.50 (0-8328-4620-1) Higginson Bk Co.

— New England Legends & Folk Lore. 1993. 8.98 (1-55521-925-X) Bk Sales Inc.

Drake, Samuel G. Annals of Witchcraft in New England & Elsewhere in the United States. 306p. 1994. reprint ed. lib. bdg. 35.00 (0-8328-4351-2) Higginson Bk Co.

— Annals of Witchcraft in New England & Elsewhere in the United States from Their First Settlement. LC 67-13327. 1972. reprint ed. 25.95 (0-405-08466-8, Pub. by Blom Pubns) Ayer.

— The Book of the Indians. LC 74-7960. reprint ed. 49.00 (0-404-11848-8) AMS Pr.

— Indian Captivities: Or, Life in the Wigwam. LC 74-7961. reprint ed. 54.50 (0-404-11849-6) AMS Pr.

— Particular History of the Five Years French & Indian War in New England & Parts Adjacent. (Select Bibliographies Reprint Ser.). 1977. 21.95 (0-8369-5575-7) Ayer.

Drake, Samuel G., ed. The Old Indian Chronicle. LC 74-7963. reprint ed. 47.50 (0-404-11850-X) AMS Pr.

Drake, Sandra E. Wilson Harris & the Modern Tradition: A New Architecture of the World, 93. LC 85-9874. (Contributions in Afro-American & African Studies: No. 93). (Illus.). 229p. 1986. 55.00 (0-313-24783-8, DWI/, Greenwood Pr) Greenwood.

Drake, Sandra L. & Lynch, Mary J. Community Colleges, Public Libraries, & the Humanities: A Study of Cooperative Programs. LC 78-107550. 48p. reprint ed. pap. 30.00 (0-608-17101-8, 202729300055) Bks Demand.

***Drake, Shannon.** Beneath a Blood Red Moon. LC 00-24499. 2000. write for info. (0-7862-2500-9) Five Star.

Drake, Shannon. Beneath a Blood Red Moon. 256p. 1999. mass mkt. 6.99 (0-8217-6298-2, Zebra Kensgtn) Kensgtn Pub Corp.

— Blue Heaven, Black Night. rev. ed. 544p. 1995. mass mkt. 6.50 (0-8217-5982-5, Zebra Kensgtn) Kensgtn Pub Corp.

— Branded Hearts. 432p. (Orig.). 1995. mass mkt. 5.99 (0-380-77170-5, Avon Bks) Morrow Avon.

— Bride of the Wind. 416p. (Orig.). 1992. mass mkt. 6.99 (0-380-76353-2, Avon Bks) Morrow Avon.

— Come the Morning. LC 98-66230. 384p. 1999. 22.00 (1-57566-383-X) Kensgtn Pub Corp.

***Drake, Shannon.** Come the Morning. 2000. mass mkt. 6.99 (0-8217-6471-3, Zebra Kensgtn); mass mkt. 6.99 (0-8217-6971-5, Zebra Kensgtn) Kensgtn Pub Corp.

— Conquer the Night. 2000. mass mkt. 6.99 (0-8217-6639-2, Zebra Kensgtn) Kensgtn Pub Corp.

Drake, Shannon. Damsel in Distress. 416p. 1992. mass mkt. 6.50 (0-380-76352-4, Avon Bks) Morrow Avon.

— The King's Pleasure. 384p. 1998. pap. 6.50 (0-8217-5857-8, Zebra Kensgtn) Kensgtn Pub Corp.

— Knight of Fire. 448p. (Orig.). 1993. mass mkt. 5.99 (0-380-77169-1, Avon Bks) Morrow Avon.

— Lie down in Roses. 512p. 1994. mass mkt. 5.99 (0-8217-4794-0, Zebra Kensgtn) Kensgtn Pub Corp.

— No Other Love. 1997. mass mkt. 6.50 (0-614-27702-7, Avon Bks); mass mkt. 6.50 (0-380-78137-9, Avon Bks) Morrow Avon.

— No Other Man. 400p. (Orig.). 1995. mass mkt. 5.99 (0-380-77171-3, Avon Bks) Morrow Avon.

— No Other Woman. 377p. (Orig.). 1996. mass mkt. 6.50 (0-380-78136-0, Avon Bks) Morrow Avon.

— Ondine. 480p. 1996. mass mkt. 6.50 (0-8217-5414-9, Zebra Kensgtn) Kensgtn Pub Corp.

— Princess of Fire. 512p. 1994. mass mkt. 5.99 (0-8217-4796-7, Zebra Kensgtn) Kensgtn Pub Corp.

— Princess of Fire - Tomorrow the Glory. 1994. mass mkt. 5.99 (0-8217-8890-6, Zebra Kensgtn) Kensgtn Pub Corp.

— Tomorrow the Glory. 448p. 1994. mass mkt. 5.99 (0-7860-0021-X, Pinncle Kensgtn) Kensgtn Pub Corp.

***Drake, Shannon.** When Darkness Falls. 448p. 2000. mass mkt. 6.99 (0-8217-6692-9, Zebra Kensgtn) Kensgtn Pub Corp.

Drake, Shannon, et al. Avon Books Presents: Under the Mistletoe. 400p. (Orig.). 1993. mass mkt. 4.99 (0-380-77326-0, Avon Bks) Morrow Avon.

Drake, St. Clair. Black Folk Here & There: An Essay in History & Anthropology, Vols. 1 & 2. (Afro-American Culture & Society Monographs: Vols. 7 & 9). (Illus.). 766p. 1991. boxed set 58.95 (0-934934-28-2); boxed set 35.95 (0-934934-29-0) CAAS Pubns.

— Black Folk Here & There Vol. 1: An Essay in History & Anthropology. (Afro-American Culture & Society Monographs: Vol. 7). (Illus.). 389p. 1987. 29.95 (0-934934-20-7); pap. 18.95 (0-934934-21-5) CAAS Pubns.

— Black Folk Here & There Vol. 2: An Essay in History & Anthropology. (Afro-American Culture & Society Monographs: Vol. 9). (Illus.). 37p. 1991. 29.95 (0-934934-30-4); pap. 18.95 (0-934934-31-2) CAAS Pubns.

Drake, St. Clair & Cayton, Horace R. Black Metropolis: A Study of Negro Life in a Northern City. (Illus.). 912p. (C). 1993. pap. text 24.00 (0-226-16234-6) U Ch Pr.

Drake, Stan, jt. auth. see Young, Dean.

Drake, Stanley. The Path to Birth. 64p. 1990. pap. 7.95 (0-903540-32-0, 888, Pub. by Floris Bks) Anthroposophic.

Drake, Stillman. Cause, Experiment, & Science: A Galilean Dialogue Incorporating a New English Translation of Galileo's "Bodies That Stay Atop Water, Or Move in It" LC 81-2974. (Illus.). 288p. (C). 1981. 20.00 (0-226-16228-1) U Ch Pr.

— Cause, Experiment, & Science: A Galilean Dialogue Incorporating a New English Translation of Galileo's "Bodies That Stay Atop Water, Or Move in It" LC 81-2974. (Illus.). 272p. (C). 1996. pap. 11.95 (0-226-16230-3) U Ch Pr.

— Cause, Experiment, & Science: A Galiliean Dialogue, Incorporating a New English Translation of Galileo's Bodies That Stay Atop Water, or Move in It. LC 81-2974. 267p. reprint ed. pap. 82.80 (0-608-09014-X, 206964900005) Bks Demand.

— Essays on Galileo & the History & Philosophy of Science. (Illus.). 476p. 1999. text 60.00 (0-8020-0626-4); pap. text 21.95 (0-8020-7585-1) U of Toronto Pr.

— Essays on Galileo & the History & Philosophy of Science. (Illus.). 1231p. 1999. pap. text 60.00 (0-8020-8288-2) U of Toronto Pr.

***Drake, Stillman.** Essays on Galileo & the History & Philosophy of Science, 3 vols. (Illus.). 1231p. 1999. text 180.00 (*0-8020-4716-5*) U of Toronto Pr.

Drake, Stillman. Essays on Galileo & the History & Philosophy of Science, Vol. 2. (Illus.). 376p. 1999. text 60.00 (*0-8020-4343-7*); pap. text 21.95 (*0-8020-8164-9*) U of Toronto Pr.

— Essays on Galileo & the History & Philosophy of Science, Vol. 3. (Illus.). 379p. 1999. text 60.00 (*0-8020-4344-5*); pap. text 21.95 (*0-8020-8165-7*) U of Toronto Pr.

— Galileo: Pioneer Scientist. (Illus.). 262p. 1994. text 40.00 (*0-8020-2725-3*) U of Toronto Pr.

— Galileo: Pioneer Scientist. (Illus.). 280p. 1994. pap. text 19.95 (*0-8020-7607-6*) U of Toronto Pr.

— Gallileo at Work: His Scientific Biography. (Illus.). xxiii, 536p. 1995. pap. text 14.95 (*0-486-28631-2*) Dover.

— Telescopes, Tides, & Tactics: A Galilean Dialogue about the "Starry Messenger" & Systems of the World. LC 82-24790. 256p. 1983. 27.00 (*0-226-16231-1*) U Ch Pr.

Drake, Stillman & Drabkin, I. E., trs. Mechanics in Sixteenth-Century Italy: Selections from Tartaglia, Benedetti, Guido Ubaldo, & Galileo. LC 68-9015. (University of Wisconsin Publications in Medieval Science: No. 13). (Illus.). 442p. reprint ed. pap. 137.10 (*0-7837-1657-5*, 204195400024) Bks Demand.

Drake, Stillman, jt. auth. see Galilei, Galileo.

Drake, Stillman, tr. see Galilei, Galileo.

Drake, Susan. Hear No Evil. (Intimate Moments Ser.). 1994. per. 3.50 (*0-373-07588-X*, 1-07588-6) Harlequin Bks.

Drake, Susan L., jt. auth. see Bredahl, A. Carl, Jr.

Drake, Susan M. Creating Integrated Curriculum: Proven Ways to Increase Student Learning. LC 98-9034. (Illus.). 256p. 1998. 65.95 (*0-8039-6716-0*); pap. 29.95 (*0-8039-6717-9*) Corwin Pr.

— Planning Integrated Curriculum: The Call to Adventure. LC 93-9219. 1993. pap. 10.95 (*0-87120-208-5*) ASCD.

Drake, Susan M. & Jones, Glen A. Writing Your Way to Success: Finding Your Own Voice in Academic Publishing. (Faculty Development Ser.). 64p. (Orig.). 1997. pap. 7.95 (*0-913507-63-6*) New Forums.

Drake, Susan S. Fields of Courage: Remembering Cesar Chavez & the People Whose Labor Feeds Us. LC 98-68606. (Illus.). 192p. (YA). 1999. pap. 14.95 (*0-9652575-6-8*, Pub. by Many Names) Bookpeople.

Drake, Terri. At the Seams. LC 98-85442. 61p. 1998. pap. 12.00 (*0-9657177-1-2*) Bear Star.

— Singing in a Dark Language. 1968. 3.00 (*0-936814-08-X*) New Collage.

Drake, Thelbert L. Principalship. 5th ed. LC 98-17494. 482p. 1998. 76.00 (*0-13-263260-8*) P-H.

Drake, Thomas J., III, jt. auth. see Ross, Charles C.

Drake, Thomas N. A Japan Diary: Grandparents' Quest. LC 94-74572. 336p. 1996. pap. 12.95 (*1-885487-10-X*) Brownell & Carroll.

Drake, V. A. & Gatehouse, A. G., eds. Insect Migration: Tracking Resources Through Space & Time. (Illus.). 496p. (C). 1995. text 85.00 (*0-521-44000-9*) Cambridge U Pr.

Drake, W. Avon & Holsworth, Bert D. Affirmative Action & the Stalled Quest for Black Progress. LC 95-41799. (Illus.). 232p. 1996. 16.95 (*0-252-06539-5*) U of Ill Pr.

Drake, W. Magruder, ed. see King, Edward.

Drake, Warren. Liber Amicorum John Steele: A Musical Tribute. LC 96-39599. (Festschrift Ser.: No. 16). 1997. 54.00 (*0-945193-80-7*) Pendragon NY.

Drake, William. Cultivator's Handbook of Marijuana. 6th rev. ed. (Illus.). 224p. 1992. reprint ed. pap. 24.95 (*0-914171-53-4*) Ronin Pub.

— Magnetic Oxides, 2 pts., Pt. 2. Craik, Derek J., ed. LC 73-14378. 337p. reprint ed. pap. 104.50 (*0-608-08264-3*, 202667300002) Bks Demand.

— Sustainable Competition in Global Telecommunications: From Principle to Practice. 94p. 1998. pap. text 12.00 (*0-89843-224-3*) The Aspen Inst.

Drake, William & Morris, Jeffrey W. Chapter Thirteen: Practice & Procedure. 1124p. 1983. text 105.00 (*0-07-017822-4*) Shepards.

Drake, William A. Contemporary European Writers. 408p. 1977. 20.95 (*0-8369-0388-9*) Ayer.

— Contemporary European Writers. 1976. 69.95 (*0-87968-937-4*) Gordon Pr.

Drake, William A., ed. American Criticism, Nineteen Twenty-Six. LC 67-28734. (Essay Index Reprint Ser.). 1977. 23.95 (*0-8369-0389-7*) Ayer.

Drake, William A., tr. see Istrati, Panait.

Drake, William A., tr. see Schnitzler, Arthur.

Drake, William J., ed. The New Information Infrastructure: Strategies for U. S. Policy. 448p. (C). 1995. pap. 14.95 (*0-87078-366-1*) Century Foundation.

Drakeford, Brian. The Whole-School Audit: Development Planning for Primary & Special Schools. LC 97-204544. 112p. 1997. ring bd. 37.95 (*1-85346-501-1*, Pub. by David Fulton) Taylor & Francis.

Drakeford, Brian & Cooling, Jeffrey. The Secondary Whole-school Audit: Development Planning for Secondary Schools. LC 98-214450. viii, 100p. 1998. write for info. (*1-85346-558-5*) David Fulton.

Drakeford, Dale. Medley for J. 160p. 1997. pap. write for info. (*1-57502-506-X*, P01506) Morris Pubng.

Drakeford, Dale B. Boo: Boo's Blackboard Book. LC 99-171885. (Illus.). 46p. (J). (gr. 3-5). 1998. pap. 8.95 (*1-57502-938-3*, P02572) Morris Pubng.

Drakeford, Elaine D., jt. auth. see Rado, Leonard G.

Drakeford, Jackie. Working Ferrets: Techniques for Successful Results. (Illus.). 128p. 1997. pap. 18.95 (*1-85310-804-9*, Pub. by Swan Hill Pr) Voyageur Pr.

Drakeford, John W. Hechos el Uno Para el Otro: Made for Each Other. De Plou, Dafne C., tr. (Sexo en la Vida Cristiana Ser.). 1977. pap. 6.50 (*0-311-46256-1*) Casa Bautista.

— El Humor en la Predicacion: Humor in Preaching. Canclini, Arnoldo, tr. (SPA.). 112p. (Orig.). 1991. pap. 11.50 (*0-311-42085-0*) Casa Bautista.

Drakeford, John W. Humor in Preaching. 160p. 1986. mass mkt. 10.99 (*0-310-20121-7*, 11415P) Zondervan.

Drakeford, John W. & King, Claude V. WiseCounsel: Skills for Lay Counseling. 224p. 1988. pap. text 11.95 (*0-7673-2615-6*, LifeWy Press) LifeWay Christian.

Drakeford, Mark. Social Movement & Their Support. LC 96-43974. 256p. 1997. text 65.00 (*0-312-17245-1*) St Martin.

Drakeman, Donald L. Church-State Constitutional Issues: Making Sense of the Establishment Clause, 62. LC 90-45464. (Contributions in Legal Studies: No. 62). 152p. 1991. 49.95 (*0-313-27663-3*, DCS, Greenwood Pr) Greenwood.

Drakeman, Donald L., jt. ed. see Wilson, John F.

Drakenstein, Rheede T. & Van, H. A. Hortus Indicus Malabaricus, Continens Regni Malabarici Apud Indos Celeberrici Generis Plantas Rarioris Etc, 12 vols. (LAT., Illus.). 1403p. 1703. reprint ed. lib. bdg. 2400.00 (*0-685-47410-0*, Pub. by B Singh) Lubrecht & Cramer.

Drakesmith, Mary M. & Moerschel, Jane R. When I Leave & You Are Left. 68p. 1996. pap. 12.95 (*0-9655020-7-4*) M & J Enter.

Drakopoulos, S. A. Values & Economic Theory: The Case of Hedonism. 225p. 1991. 82.95 (*1-85628-200-7*, Pub. by Avebry) Ashgate Pub Co.

Drakova, D., jt. auth. see Doyen, G.

Drakpa, Tsongkhapa L. Tsongkhapa's Six Yogas of Naropa. (Illus.). 275p. 1996. pap. 18.95 (*1-55939-058-1*) Snow Lion Pubns.

Drakulic, Slavenka. Cafe Europa: Life after Communism. LC 96-46010. 192p. 1997. 21.00 (*0-393-04012-7*) Norton.

— Cafe Europa: Life after Communism. LC 96-46010. 213p. 1999. pap. 12.95 (*0-14-027772-2*) Viking Penguin.

— How We Survived Communism & Even Laughed. LC 92-54849. 224p. 1993. pap. 13.00 (*0-06-097540-7*, Perennial) HarperTrade.

***Drakulic, Slavenka.** S. A Novel about the Balkans. 208p. 2000. 22.95 (*0-670-89097-9*, Viking) Viking Penguin.

Drakulic, Slavenka. Taste of a Man. Zoric, Christina P., tr. LC 97-193246. 208p. 1997. pap. 10.95 (*0-14-026622-4*) Viking Penguin.

Drakulic, Slavenka, tr. & afterword by see Karahasan, Dzevad.

Drakulich, Stanley. Riepetown Serb. Shaw, Thomas E., ed. LC 96-84853. (Illus.). 84p. 1996. pap. 12.95 (*0-9633371-3-0*) Carson St Pub.

Draley, Daniel, ed. A Genealogy of the Amati Family of Violin Makers, 1500-1740: Including the Most Comprehensive Set of Amati Family Instruments Photographed in Color. Champe, Gertrud G., tr. LC 89-61698. 1989. 185.00 (*0-944266-05-3*) Maecenas Pr.

— A Genealogy of the Amati Family of Violin Makers, 1500-1740: Including the Most Comprehensive Set of Amati Family Instruments Photographed in Color. deluxe ed. Champe, Gertrud G., tr. LC 89-61698. 1989. 365.00 (*0-944266-04-5*) Maecenas Pr.

Dralle, Lee A., jt. auth. see Dralle, Lynn.

Dralle, Lee A., jt. auth. see Dralle Wilson, Lynn.

Dralle, Lee A., jt. auth. see Wilson, Lynn D.

Dralle, Lynn. Unauthorized Beanie Baby Guide. 1998. pap. text 79.60 (*0-590-63581-6*) Scholastic Inc.

— Unauthorized Beanie Baby Guide. LC 99-182083. (Illus.). 1998. pap. 9.95 (*0-590-63478-X*) Scholastic Inc.

Dralle, Lynn & Dralle, Lee A. The Book of Beanie Babies: September 1998 Set. 1999. pap. 2.95 (*0-9663077-5-5*) aka Publ.

Dralle Wilson, Lynn & Dralle, Lee A. Beyond the Book of Beanies: An Extra Binder for Cataloging Your Collection of Beanies. 1998. 8.95 (*0-9663077-3-9*) aka Publ.

— The Book of Beanies May, 1998 New Release: Fourteen Pages for the Book of Beanies for New Beanies Announced May, 1998. (Illus.). 32p. 1998. ring bd. 2.95 (*0-9663077-2-0*) aka Publ.

Drallmeier, Gail S., et al. Crop Science: A Laboratory Manual. (Illus.). 300p. (C). 1988. pap., spiral bd. 20.00 (*0-9620569-0-1*) U IL Voc Agric Serv.

Drame, K., ed. see Depestre, Rene.

Drame, K., ed. see Oyono-Mbia, Guillaume, et al.

Drame, Kandioura. The Novel As Transformation Myth: A Study of the Novels of Mongo Beti & Ngugi wa Thiong'o. LC 89-14005. (Foreign & Comparative Studies Program, African Ser.: No. 43). (Orig.). (C). 1990. pap. text 14.00 (*0-915984-68-7*) Syracuse U Foreign Comp.

Drame, Kandioura, ed. see Fantoure, Alioum.

Drame, Kandioura, ed. see Glissant, Edouard.

Drame, Kandioura, ed. see Juminer, Bertene.

Dramer, jt. auth. see Kravitz.

Dramer, Dan. Disasters! 2nd ed. (Critical Reading Ser.). 158p. (Orig.). (J). (gr. 6-8). 1995. pap. 12.64 (*0-89061-766-X*, 768, Jamestwn Pub) NTC Contemp Pub Co.

— Monsters. (Illus.). 160p. (YA). (gr. 6 up). 1985. pap. text 12.64 (*0-89061-451-2*, Jamestwn Pub) NTC Contemp Pub Co.

Dramer, Daniel L. Criminal Law for California Peace Officers. 3rd ed. LC 84-72353. 464p. 1988. pap. 21.95 (*0-9613903-2-8*) Aviary Pub Co.

— Evidence for California Peace Officers. 208p. 1989. 14.95 (*0-9613903-3-6*) Aviary Pub Co.

Dramer, Kim. China. LC 96-40972. (Games People Play Ser.). (J). 1997. lib. bdg. 23.50 (*0-516-20308-8*) Childrens.

— The Chipewyan. Porter, Frank W., 3rd, ed. (J). 1995. pap. write for info. (*0-7910-3480-1*) Chelsea Hse.

— Kublai Khan. (World Leaders Past & Present Ser.) (Illus.). 120p. (YA). (gr. 5 up). 1990. lib. bdg. 19.95 (*1-55546-812-8*) Chelsea Hse.

Dramer, Kim. Native Americans & Black Americans. LC 96-51521. (Indians of North America Ser.). 120p. (YA). (gr. 5 up). 1997. pap. 9.95 (*0-7910-4462-9*, Chelsea Juniors) Chelsea Hse.

Dramer, Kim. People's Republic of China. LC 98-17643. (Enchantment of the World Ser.). 144p. (J). (gr. 5-10). 1999. 32.00 (*0-516-21077-7*) Childrens.

— Shoshone: Indians of North America. LC 96-49702. 120p. (YA). (gr. 5 up). 1996. pap. 9.95 (*0-7910-4452-1*) Chelsea Hse.

***Dramer, Kim.** The Yellow River. LC 00-39925. 2001. write for info. (*0-531-11855-X*) Watts.

Dramesi, John A. Code of Honor. 1990. mass mkt. 4.95 (*0-446-36055-4*) Warner Bks.

Dramstad, Wenche E., et al. Landscape Ecology Principles in Landscape Architecture & Land-Use Planning Seeking a Balance in Western Water Use. LC 96-52477. (Illus.). 80p. 1997. pap. text 19.95 (*1-55963-514-2*, Shearwater Bks) Island Pr.

Drance, S. M., ed. Optic Nerve in Glaucoma. LC 95-8861. 1995. 91.50 (*90-6299-123-8*) Kugler Pubns.

— Update to Glaucoma, Ocular Blood Flow & Drug Treatment. LC 95-17698. (Illus.). 144p. 1995. text 43.00 (*90-6299-124-6*, Pub. by Kugler) Kugler Pubns.

Drance, Stephen M. Vascular Risk Factors & Neuroprotection in Glaucoma: Update, 1996. LC 97-17662. 1997. 74.50 (*90-6299-137-8*) Kugler Pubns.

Drance, Stephen M., et al. Pharmacology of Glaucoma. (Illus.). 356p. 1992. 125.00 (*0-683-02655-0*) Lppncott W & W.

Dranchak, John. Building Access Applications: Using Point-&-Click Programming. 398p. (Orig.). 1995. pap. 29.95 (*0-471-30361-5*) Wiley.

— Excel for Windows, Spreadsheet Database. 340p. 1994. pap. 24.95 (*0-471-30360-7*) Wiley.

***Drancsak, Marina.** Transit Planning & Research Reports: An Annotated Bibliography. 146p. (C). 1999. reprint ed. pap. text 35.00 (*0-7881-8000-2*) DIANE Pub.

Drancsak, Marina & Maddock, Jerome T., eds. Advanced Public Transportation Systems: A Bibliography with Abstracts 1985-1991. (Illus.). 49p. (Orig.). (C). 1993. pap. text 30.00 (*1-56806-609-0*) DIANE Pub.

Drandell, Milton. IBM The Other Side: One Hundred One Former Employees Look Back. 140p. (Orig.). (C). 1990. pap. 9.95 (*0-9626511-5-X*) Quail Pr.

Drane. New Testament Epistles. (Orig.). 1999. text. write for info. (*0-312-22514-8*) St Martin.

— Revelation. LC 99-29991. 96p. 1999. pap. 12.95 (*0-312-22106-1*, St Martins Paperbacks) St Martin.

***Drane.** Revelation 1999. text 29.95 (*0-312-22513-X*) St Martin.

Drane, Augustus T. The Life of St. Dominic. LC 88-50268. 1988. reprint ed. pap. 12.00 (*0-89555-336-8*) TAN Bks Pubs.

Drane, C. R. Positioning Systems: A Unified Approach. LC 92-26470. (Lecture Notes in Control & Information Sciences: Vol. 181). 175p. 1992. 53.95 (*0-387-55850-0*) Spr-Verlag.

Drane, Chris R. & Rizos, Chris. Positioning Systems in Intelligent Transportation Systems. LC 97-42069. 392p. 1998. 89.00 (*0-89006-536-5*) Artech Hse.

***Drane, David.** Swankiller. 160p. 2000. pap. 14.95 (*1-84002-100-4*) Theatre Comm.

Drane, James F. Becoming a Good Doctor: The Place of Virtue & Character in Medical Ethics. 2nd ed. LC 88-61721. 226p. (Orig.). 1988. pap. 12.95 (*1-55612-209-8*) Sheed & Ward WI.

— Clinical Bioethics: Theory & Practice in Medical-Ethical Decision Making. LC 93-46600. 300p. (Orig.). 1994. pap. 24.95 (*1-55612-612-3*) Sheed & Ward WI.

— The Possibility of God: A Reconsideration of Religion in a Technological Society. (Quality Paperback Ser.: No. 321). 194p. 1976. 9.95 (*0-8226-0321-7*) Littlefield.

Drane, John. Christians Fact Finder. LC 50-107. (Factfinder Ser.). (Illus.). 48p. (J). (gr. 3-6). 1994. 13.95 (*0-7459-2516-2*) Lion USA.

***Drane, John.** How Can I Understand the Bible? A Way into the World's Best-Seller. (Bible Answers Library). 48p. 2000. pap. 1.99 (*1-57748-816-4*) Barbour Pub.

Drane, John. Introducing the New Testament. LC 90-55058. (Illus.). 479p. 1990. reprint ed. pap. 27.00 (*0-06-062073-0*, Pub. by Harper SF) HarpC.

— Introducing the Old Testament. LC 90-55059. (Illus.). 376p. 1990. reprint ed. pap. 25.00 (*0-06-062072-2*, Pub. by Harper SF) HarpC.

Drane, John, ed. Gospel of St. John: The Story of the Son of God. 160p. 1999. text 24.95 (*0-312-22209-2*) St Martin.

***Drane, John, ed.** The New Testament Epistles: Early Christian Wisdom. LC 99-15307. 382p. 1999. pap. 13.95 (*0-312-22103-7*) St Martin.

***Drane, John W.** The Bible Phenomenon. LC 99-488019. 196p. 1999. write for info. (*0-7459-4164-8*) Lion USA.

Drane, John W. Nelson's Illustrated Encyclopedia of the Bible. LC 98-13164. 34.99 (*0-7852-0985-9*) Nelson.

Drane, John W., intro. Great Sayings of Jesus: Proverbs, Parables, & Prayers. LC 99-23289. 320p. 1999. text 29.95 (*0-312-22211-4*) St Martin.

Dranem, Walter, jt. auth. see Hughes, Kris.

Draney, Karen, jt. ed. see Wilson, Mark.

Drange, Theodore. Type Crossings: Sentential Meaninglessness in the Border Area of Linguistics & Philosophy. (Janua Linguarum, Ser. Minor: No. 44). (Orig.). 1966. pap. text 36.95 (*90-279-0578-9*) Mouton.

Drange, Theodore M. Nonbelief & Evil: Two Arguments for the Nonexistence of God. LC 98-24173. 340p. 1998. 39.95 (*1-57392-228-5*) Prometheus Bks.

Drangel, Jason M., jt. auth. see Bazerman, Steven H.

Dranoff, Steven, jt. auth. see Dobrich, Wanda.

Dranov, Paula, et al. Video in the '80s: Emerging Uses for Television in Business, Education, Medicine & Government. LC 80-15745. v, 186 p. 1980. write for info. (*0-914236-58-X*) Buttrwrth-Heinemann.

Dranova, Anna, tr. from RUS. Hogtown: A Gothic Tale about Political Correctness & Other Virtues as Told by Gabriel Choreb. 178p. 1999. pap. 14.95 (*0-936041-11-0*) Barbary Coast Bks.

***Dranove, David.** The Economic Evolution of American Health Care: From Marcus Welby to Managed Care. 2000. 27.95 (*0-691-00693-8*) Princeton U Pr.

Dranove, David & White, William D. Clinton's Specialist Quota: Shaky Premises, Questionable Consequences. (Special Studies in Health Reform). 32p. (Orig.). 1994. pap. 9.95 (*0-8447-7024-8*, AEI Pr) Am Enterprise.

***Dranove, David & White, William D.** How Hospitals Survived: Competition & the American Hospital. 75p. 1999. pap. 9.95 (*0-8447-7141-4*, Pub. by Am Enterprise) Pub Resources Inc.

Dranow, John. Life in the Middle of the Century. 150p. (Orig.). 1988. 15.95 (*0-913123-14-5*); pap. text 9.95 (*0-913123-15-3*) Galileo.

— The Magic Step. 128p. (Orig.). 1991. pap. text 11.95 (*0-913123-35-8*) Galileo.

Dransart, Penny, ed. Andean Art: Visual Expression & Its Relation to Andean Beliefs & Values. LC 95-77014. 336p. 1995. 101.95 (*1-85628-712-2*, Pub. by Avebry) Ashgate Pub Co.

Dransfield & Needham. Marketing: Everybody's Business. 2nd ed. 1997. 24.95 (*0-435-45025-5*) Heinemann.

Dransfield, J. & Manokaran, N., eds. Rattans. (PROSEA Ser.: No. 6). (Illus.). 137p. 1993. 80.00 (*90-220-1057-0*, Pub. by Backhuys Pubs); pap. 29.00 (*979-8316-20-7*, Pub. by Backhuys Pubs) Balogh.

Dransfield, J., et al. Plant Diversity in Malesia III Pt. III: Proceedings of the Third International Floras Malesiana Symposium, 1995. (Illus.). 449p. 1997. pap. 66.00 (*1-900347-42-3*, Pub. by Royal Botnic Grdns) Balogh.

Dransfield, John. The Rattans of Sarawak. (Illus.). 233p. 1992. pap. text 36.00 (*0-947643-41-9*) Lubrecht & Cramer.

Dransfield, John & Beentje, Henk. Palms of Madagascar. (Illus.). 520p. 1995. boxed set 99.00 (*0-947643-82-6*, Pub. by Royal Botnic Grdns) Balogh.

Dransfield, John, et al. Corybas West of Wallace's Line. (Illus.). 38p. 1986. pap. 12.00 (*1-878762-08-7*, Pub. by Royal Botnic Grdns) Balogh.

Dransfield, Michael. Michael Dransfield: Collected Poems. LC 84-21992. 401p. (Orig.). 1988. pap. text 19.95 (*0-7022-1828-6*, Pub. by Univ Queensland Pr) Intl Spec Bk.

Dransfield, Peter. Introducing Root Locus: A Programmed Instruction Text. 136p. reprint ed. pap. 38.80 (*0-608-12211-4*, 2024443) Bks Demand.

Dransfield, Rob, jt. auth. see Needham, David.

***Dransfield, Robert.** Essential Business Studies for You: Key Notes. (Illus.). 80p. 2000. pap. 11.95 (*0-7487-5495-4*, Pub. by S Thornes Pubs) Trans-Atl Phila.

Dransfield, Robert & Needham, David. Business Studies. 2nd ed. LC 94-21705. 1994. write for info. (*0-07-707954-X*) McGraw.

Dransfield, Robert, jt. auth. see Needham, David.

Dransfield, Robert, jt. ed. see Needham, David.

Dransfield, S. & Widjaja, E. A., eds. Bamboos. (PROSEA Ser.: No. 7). (Illus.). 189p. 1995. 67.00 (*90-73348-35-8*, Pub. by Backhuys Pubs) Balogh.

Drant, Thomas H., tr. see Horace.

Drantell, Jan J., jt. auth. see Simon, Leslie.

Draovitch, Pete & Westcott, Wayne. Complete Conditioning for Golf. LC 99-24207. (Complete Conditioning Ser.). (Illus.). 208p. 1999. pap. 15.95 (*0-88011-986-1*, PDRA0986) Human Kinetics.

Drapac, Vesna. War & Religion: Catholics in the Churches of Occupied Paris. LC 97-22673. xv, 302 p. (C). 1998. text 74.95 (*0-8132-0903-X*) Cath U Pr.

Drapaca, Robert V., photos by. A Portrait of the Outerbanks, N. C., Chapter 1. (Illus.). 80p. Date not set. pap. 25.95 (*0-9660586-3-1*) Aerial Perspect.

Drapala, Timothy J. Optical Fiber Connectors: An Interlaboratory Comparison of Measurements of Endface Geometry. 36p. 1998. pap. 3.00 (*0-16-056684-3*) USGPO.

Drapchinsky, L. V., ed. Fiftieth Anniversary of Nuclear Fission. 887p. 1994. text 195.00 (*1-56072-024-7*) Nova Sci Pubs.

Drape, Marian, ed. Insurance Regulatory Information System Ratio Results, 1995. 9th rev. ed. 258p. (Orig.). (C). 1996. ring bd. 125.00 (*0-89382-407-0*, IRS-ZM) Nat Assn Insurance.

Drape, Theodore. American Communism & Soviet Russia. 1986. pap. 12.95 (*0-318-60883-9*) Random.

Drapeau, Don, jt. auth. see Carlisle, Barbara.

Drapeau, Lynn. Dictionnaire Montagnais-Francais. (FRE.). 904p. 1991. 125.00 (*0-7859-1009-3*, 2760506614) Fr & Eur.

Drapeau, Patti. Great Teaching with Graphic Organizers: Lessons & Fun-Shaped Templates That Motivate Kids of A, 1 vol. (Illus.). 96p. (J). 1999. pap. text 12.95 (*0-590-12876-0*) Scholastic Inc.

***Drapeau, Pierre & Vanasse, Andre.** The Encyclopedia of Home Winemaking Vol. 1: Fermentation & Winemaking Methods. (Illus.). 238p. 1999. pap. 22.50 (*1-85486-199-9*, Pub. by Nexus Special Interests) Trans-Atl Phila.

Drapeau, Rasul E. The Art & Methods of Invention: How to Develop, Protect & Market Your Invention. (Illus.). 144p. 1998. pap. 17.95 (*0-9666203-0-5*) Flag Bks.

Drapela, Victor J. A Review of Personality Theories. 2nd ed. LC 94-36205. (Illus.). 184p. (C). 1994. text 38.95 (*0-398-05943-8*); pap. text 24.95 (*0-398-05957-8*) C C Thomas.

D

An Asterisk (*) at the beginning of an entry indicates that the title is appearing for the first time.

Draper. Karl Marx's Theory of Revolution: The State & Bureaucracy. 748p. 20.00 (*0-85345-405-1*) Monthly Rev.
Draper. Paris Commune. 1971. pap. text 10.00 (*0-85345-219-9*, Pub. by Monthly Rev) NYU Pr.
Draper. Shakespeare The Comedies LC 99-15881. 2000. pap. 19.95 (*0-312-22703-5*) St Martin.
— Sun, Storm & Stars. (J). (gr. 7). 2000. 16.00 (*0-689-82181-6*) S&S Childrens.
Draper & Bailey. Steps in Clothing Skills. (J). (gr. 7-9). 1978. teacher ed. 2.00 (*0-02-665720-1*) Glencoe.
— Steps in Clothing Skills. 2nd ed. (J). (gr. 7-9). 1978. text 31.64 (*0-02-665710-4*) Glencoe.
Draper, Alan. Conflict of Interests: Organized Labor & the Civil Rights Movement in the South, 1954-1968. LC 93-46081. (Cornell Studies in Industrial & Labor Relations: No. 29). 248p. 1994. text 45.00 (*0-87546-315-0*, ILR Press); pap. text 18.95 (*0-87546-316-9*, ILR Press) Cornell U Pr.
— A Rope of Sand: The AFL-CIO Committee on Political Education, 1955-1967. LC 88-11773. 176p. 1988. 45.00 (*0-275-93045-9*, C3045, Praeger Pubs) Greenwood.
Draper, Alec. Electrical Circuits: Including Machines. 2nd ed. LC 73-173070. (Electrical Engineering Ser.). 425p. reprint ed. pap. 131.80 (*0-608-11022-1*, 200638500058) Bks Demand.
— Electrical Machines. 2nd ed. LC 67-98866. (Electrical Engineering Ser.). 404p. reprint ed. pap. 125.30 (*0-608-13215-2*, 202525600043) Bks Demand.
Draper, Alfred. The Con Man. large type ed. 1989. 27.99 (*0-7089-2103-5*) Ulverscroft.
— The Great Avenging Day. large type ed. 1990. 27.99 (*0-7089-2117-5*) Ulverscroft.
— Operation Midas. large type ed. (Magna Large Print Ser.). 470p. 1996. 27.99 (*0-7505-0954-6*, Pub. by Mgna Lrg Print) Ulverscroft.
***Draper, Allison Stark.** America's First Traitor: Benedict Arnold Betrays the Colonies. LC 00-26175. (Illus.). (J). 2000. write for info. (*0-8239-5673-3*, PowerKids) Rosen Group.
— The Battle of Yorktown. LC 00-24771. (Headlines from History Ser.). 2000. write for info. (*0-8239-5674-1*) Rosen Group.
— The Boston Massacre: Five Colonists Killed by British Soldiers. LC 00-20955. (Headlines from History Ser.). (Illus.). (J). 2000. write for info. (*0-8239-5700-4*, PowerKids) Rosen Group.
— The Boston Tea Party: Angry Colonists Dump British Tea. LC 99-58708. (Headlines from History Ser.). (Illus.). (J). 2000. lib. bdg. write for info. (*0-8239-5671-7*) Rosen Group.
— George Washington Elected: How America's First President Was Chosen. LC 00-26176. (Headlines from History Ser.). (Illus.). (J). 2000. write for info. (*0-8239-5675-X*, PowerKids) Rosen Group.
— Polio. LC 00-9371. (Epidemics! Ser.). (Illus.). (J). 2000. write for info. (*0-8239-3348-2*, PowerKids) Rosen Group.
— The Start of the American Revolutionary War: Paul Revere Rides at Midnight. LC 00-24765. (Headlines from History Ser.). (Illus.). (J). 2000. write for info. (*0-8239-5672-5*) Rosen Group.
— What People Wore During the American Revolution. LC 00-39163. (Illus.). (J). 2000. write for info. (*0-8239-5666-0*, PowerKids) Rosen Group.
— What People Wore During the Civil War. LC 00-36713. (Clothing, Costumes, & Uniforms Throughout American History Ser.). (Illus.). (J). 2000. write for info. (*0-8239-5669-5*, PowerKids) Rosen Group.
— What People Wore During the Westward Expansion. LC 00-39162. (Clothing, Costumes, & Uniforms Throughout American History Ser.). 2001. write for info. (*0-8239-5667-9*) Rosen Group.
— What People Wore in Early America. LC 00-24764. (Clothing, Costumes & Uniforms Thoughout American History Ser.). (Illus.). (J). 2000. write for info. (*0-8239-5664-4*, PowerKids) Rosen Group.
Draper, C. G. Great American Stories 1: An ESL - EFL Reader: Beginning-Intermediate to Intermediate Levels. 2nd ed. LC 92-14753. 144p. 1992. pap. text 13.87 (*0-13-364381-6*) P-H.
Draper, C. Stark, jt. ed. see Bolger, Philip H.
***Draper, Catheryne.** The Algebra Game Conic Sections Teacher's Manual. (Algebra Game Ser.). (Illus.). 162p. (YA). (gr. 10 up). 1999. 25.00 (*1-929362-24-2*, AGC010) Math Studio.
— The Algebra Game Linear Equations Teacher's Manual. (Algebra Game Ser.). (Illus.). 142p. (YA). (gr. 7 up). 1999. teacher ed. 25.00 (*1-929362-05-6*, AGL010) Math Studio.
— The Algebra Game Quadratic Equations Teacher's Manual. (Algebra Game Ser.). (Illus.). 190p. (YA). (gr. 8 up). 1999. 25.00 (*1-929362-16-1*, AGQ010) Math Studio.
— The Algebra Game Trig Teacher's Manual. (Algebra Game Ser.). (Illus.). 154p. (YA). (gr. 10 up). 1999. 25.00 (*1-929362-31-5*) Math Studio.
***Draper, Charla L.** Cooking on Nineteenth-Century Whaling Ships. (Exploring History Through Simple Recipes Ser.). 32p. (J). (gr. 2-7). 2000. lib. bdg. 22.60 (*0-7368-0602-4*, Blue Earth Bks) Capstone Pr.
Draper, Charlotte W. American Farm School: A Family Album, 1904-1944. LC 94-70446. (Illus.). 144p. (Orig.). 1994. pap. 30.00 (*0-9640411-0-3*) Am Farm Schl.
Draper, Clifton W. & Mazzoldi, Paolo, eds. Laser Surface Treatment of Metals. 1986. text 326.50 (*90-247-3405-3*) Kluwer Academic.
***Draper, Dar.** What Is Love. 2000. 14.99 (*1-929125-18-6*, Pub. by Loyal Pubng) BookWorld.
Draper, David K. Cody: A Novel That Motivates Towards Success. 88p. (Orig.). (YA). (gr. 9-12). 1990. pap. 8.98 (*0-88290-409-4*) Horizon Utah.
Draper, Delbert M. Draper: The Mormon Drapers. 377p. 1996. reprint ed. pap. 55.00 (*0-8328-5609-6*); reprint ed. lib. bdg. 65.00 (*0-8328-5608-8*) Higginson Bk Co.
Draper, Dorrie. Animals All the Way. 72p. (C). 1988. 35.00 (*0-7212-0721-9*, Pub. by Regency Pr GBR) St Mut.
Draper, E. Linn, Jr., ed. Technology of Controlled Thermonuclear Fusion Experiments & the Engineering Aspects of Fusion Reactors: Proceedings. LC 74-600044. (AEC Symposium Ser.). 1040p. 1974. pap. 34.25 (*0-87079-221-0*, CONF-721111); fiche 9.00 (*0-87079-222-9*, CONF-721111) DOE.
Draper, Edgar. Psychiatry & Pastoral Care. LC 65-23861. (Successful Pastoral Counseling Ser.). 138p. reprint ed. pap. 42.80 (*0-608-16383-X*, 202689400053) Bks Demand.
Draper, Edith. Cool. 558p. (J). (gr. 3-7). 1994. pap. 9.99 (*0-8423-1302-8*) Tyndale Hse.
Draper, Edythe. Daily Light. 750p. 1999. 17.99 (*0-8423-3547-1*); pap. text 13.99 (*0-8423-3548-X*) Tyndale Hse.
Draper, Elle. Thoughts & Reflections. 40p. 1997. pap. 8.00 (*0-8059-4198-3*) Dorrance.
Draper, Ellen D. & Koralek, Jenny, eds. A Lively Oracle: A Centennial Celebration of P. L. Travers, Original Creator of Mary Poppins. (Illus.). 224p. 1999. pap. 15.95 (*0-943914-94-9*) Larson Pubns.
Draper, G. I., et al. Reflections on Law & Armed Conflicts: The Selected Works on the Laws of War by the Late Professor Colonel G. I. A. D. Draper, OBE. LC 97-51736. 1998. 95.00 (*90-411-0557-3*) Kluwer Law Intl.
Draper, George. Great American Stories: An ESL-EFL Reader, Vol. 2. 2nd ed. 144p. 1994. pap. text 13.87 (*0-13-097528-1*) P-H.
Draper, H. H. Advances in Nutritional Research, Vol. 8. LC 78-640645. (Illus.). 162p. (C). 1990. text 78.00 (*0-306-43512-8*, Kluwer Plenum) Kluwer Academic.
— Advances in Nutritional Research Vol. 9: Nutrition & Osteoporosis. (Illus.). 336p. (C). 1995. 89.50 (*0-306-44893-9*, Kluwer Plenum) Kluwer Academic.
Draper, Hal. The Adventures of the Communist Manifesto. Haberkern, Ernest E., ed. x, 358p. (Orig.). (C). 1995. pap. 24.95 (*0-916695-07-7*) Ctr Social Hist.
— The Dictatorship of the Proletariat from Marx to Lenin. LC 87-1677. 192p. 1987. pap. 15.00 (*0-85345-726-3*, Pub. by Monthly Rev); text 26.00 (*0-85345-727-1*, Pub. by Monthly Rev) NYU Pr.
— Karl Marx's Theory of Revolution Vol. 1: The State & Bureaucracy. LC 76-40467. 748p. 1978. pap. 17.00 (*0-85345-461-2*, PB-4612, Pub. by Monthly Rev) NYU Pr.
— Karl Marx's Theory of Revolution Vol. 2: The Politics of Social Classes. LC 76-40467. 756p. 1981. 20.00 (*0-85345-439-6*, Pub. by Monthly Rev); pap. 17.00 (*0-85345-566-X*, Pub. by Monthly Rev) NYU Pr.
— Karl Marx's Theory of Revolution Vol. 3: The "Dictatorship of the Proletariat" 480p. 1986. 28.00 (*0-85345-673-9*, Pub. by Monthly Rev); pap. 17.00 (*0-85345-674-7*, Pub. by Monthly Rev) NYU Pr.
— Karl Marx's Theory of Revolution Vol. 4: Critique of Other Socialisms. 288p. (C). 1989. 36.00 (*0-85345-797-2*, Pub. by Monthly Rev); pap. 22.00 (*0-85345-798-0*, Pub. by Monthly Rev) NYU Pr.
— War & Revolution: Lenin & the Myth of Revolutionary Defeatism. Haberkern, Ernest E., ed. LC 95-42979. (Revolutionary Studies). 256p. (C). 1996. text 49.95 (*0-391-03930-X*) Humanities.
— Zionism, Israel & the Arabs: Notes on the Historical Background of the Middle East Tragedy. viii, 235p. 1997. pap. 15.95 (*0-916695-09-3*) Ctr Social Hist.
Draper, Hal, tr. Heine, Heinrich: The Complete Poems, a Modern English Version. 1050p. 1984. reprint ed. pap. 20.00 (*3-518-03062-0*, Pub. by Suhr Verlag) Intl Bk Import.
Draper, Hal, tr. see Heine, Heinrich.
Draper, Harold A. Probate Administration in Michigan: A Systems Approach. 3rd ed. LC 84-82232. 654p. 1989. ring bd. 95.00 (*0-685-45473-8*, 89-015) U MI Law CLE.
— Probate Administration in Michigan: A Systems Approach. 3rd ed. LC 84-82232. 654p. 1991. suppl. ed. 49.00 (*0-685-45474-6*, 91-030) U MI Law CLE.
— Probate Administration in Michigan: A Systems Approach. 3rd ed. LC 84-82232. 654p. 1992. suppl. ed. 55.00 (*0-685-58670-7*, 92-022) U MI Law CLE.
Draper, Henry. Studying Children: Observing & Participating. 1977. pap. text 15.00 (*0-02-665770-8*) Glencoe.
Draper, Hunter, jt. auth. see Hall, Betty L.
Draper, Ivan T., jt. auth. see Ginsberg, Lionel.
Draper, J. L. Lubrication of Enclosed Gear Drives. (Technical Papers: Vol. P125). (Illus.). 9p. 1935. pap. text 30.00 (*1-55589-354-6*) AGMA.
Draper, J. W. The Intellectual Development of Europe. 200p. 1998. reprint ed. 90.00 (*0-936128-85-2*) De Young Pr.
Draper, James & Brooks, James. Interior Design for Libraries. fac. ed. LC 79-16635. 162p. (Orig.). 1994. pap. 50.30 (*0-7837-7316-1*, 204724300007) Bks Demand.
Draper, James A. & Taylor, Maurice C. Voices from the Literacy Field. LC 93-21016. 432p. (C). 1994. reprint ed. text 39.95 (*0-89464-861-6*) Krieger.
Draper, James A., jt. ed. see Barer-Stein, Thelma.
Draper, James A., jt. ed. see Taylor, Maurice C.
Draper, James D. Bertoldo di Giovanni, Sculptor of the Medici Household: Critical Reappraisal & Catalogue Raisonne. (Illus.). 320p. (C). 1992. 75.00 (*0-8262-0819-3*) U of Mo Pr.
— European Terracottas from the Arthur M. Sackler Collections. (Illus.). 32p. (Orig.). 1981. pap. 1.95 (*0-87099-265-1*) Metro Mus Art.
Draper, James D. & Pajou, Augustin. Augustin Pajou, Royal Sculptor. LC 97-32253. 1998. pap. 45.00 (*0-87099-841-2*) Metro Mus Art.
Draper, James D., et al. Augustin Pajou, Royal Sculptor. LC 97-32253. 1998. 65.00 (*0-87099-840-4*) Metro Mus Art.
— Augustin Pajou: Royal Sculptor, 1730-1809. LC 97-32253. (Illus.). 431p. 1998. 75.00 (*0-8109-6518-6*, Pub. by Abrams) Time Warner.
Draper, James D., ed. see Bode, Wilhelm.
Draper, James P. Black Literature Criticism, 3 vols., Set. 2nd ed. LC 98-27492. 1998. 85.00 (*0-8103-8574-0*, 101388) Gale.
Draper, James P. Contemporary Literary Citicism: Excerpts from Criticism of the Works of Today's Novelists, Poets, Playwrights, Short Story Writers, Scriptwriters, & Other Creative Writers, Vol. 84. 500p. 1994. text 150.00 (*0-8103-4993-0*) Gale.
Draper, James P. World Literary Criticism, Vol. 1. 1992. write for info. (*0-8103-8362-4*) Gale.
— World Literary Criticism, Vol. 2. 1992. write for info. (*0-8103-8363-2*) Gale.
— World Literary Criticism, Vol. 3. 1992. write for info. (*0-8103-8364-0*) Gale.
— World Literary Criticism, Vol. 4. 1992. write for info. (*0-8103-8365-9*) Gale.
— World Literary Criticism, Vol. 5. 1992. write for info. (*0-8103-8366-7*) Gale.
— World Literary Criticism, Vol. 6. 1992. write for info. (*0-8103-8367-5*) Gale.
Draper, James P., ed. Black Literature Criticism: Excerpts from Criticism of the Most Significant Works of Black Authors over the Past 200 Years, 3 vols., Set. 2078p. 1991. 285.00 (*0-8103-7929-5*) Gale.
Draper, James P., ed. Contemporary Literary Criticism: Excerpts from Criticism of the Works of Today's Novelists, Poets, Playwrights, Short Story Writers, Scriptwriters, & Other Creative Writers, Vol. 83. 500p. 1994. text 150.00 (*0-8103-4991-4*) Gale.
Draper, James P., ed. DISCovering Authors: British Edition DOS Package: Biographies & Criticism on 330 Most Studied Authors, 1995, Vol. 1. 94th ed. 1994. 700.00 (*1-873477-41-4*) Gale.
— World Literature Criticism, 1500 to the Present: A Selection of Major Authors from Gale's Literary Criticism, 6 vols. 4209p. 1992. 365.00 (*0-8103-8361-6*, 101204) Gale.
Draper, James P. & Person, James E., Jr., eds. Literature Criticism from 1400 to 1800, Vol. 13. (Illus.). 541p. 1990. text 150.00 (*0-8103-6112-4*) Gale.
Draper, James P., ed. see Lesniak, James.
Draper, James P., jt. ed. see Person, James E., Jr.
Draper, James T., Jr. Basic Bible Sermons on Psalms for Everyday Living. 128p. (Orig.). 1992. pap. 6.99 (*0-8054-2280-3*, 4222-80) Broadman.
***Draper, James T.** Donde Comienza la Verdadera Adoracion. (SPA.). 1999. pap. text 10.99 (*0-311-32047-3*) Casa Bautista.
Draper, James T., Jr. Where Real Worship Begins: Lessons from the Life of Job. LC 95-51512. 165p. 1996. pap. 9.99 (*0-87213-126-2*) Loizeaux.
Draper, Joan E., ed. see Burnham, Daniel.
Draper, John S. Shams or Uncle Ben's Experience with Hypocrites. LC 71-166712. (Illus.). 1971. reprint ed. 29.00 (*0-403-01430-1*) Scholarly.
Draper, John W. Collected Works. 1990. reprint ed. lib. bdg. 75.00 (*0-685-37638-9*, 1513); reprint ed. lib. bdg. 75.00 (*0-7812-2695-3*, 1513); reprint ed. write for info. (*0-318-67706-7*); reprint ed. write for info. (*0-318-67707-5*); reprint ed. write for info. (*0-318-67708-3*); reprint ed. write for info. (*0-318-67709-1*); reprint ed. write for info. (*0-318-67710-5*); reprint ed. write for info. (*0-318-67711-3*); reprint ed. write for info. (*0-318-67712-1*); reprint ed. write for info. (*0-318-67713-X*) Rprt Serv.
— Contributions to Chemistry. (Notable American Authors Ser.). 1992. reprint ed. lib. bdg. 90.00 (*0-7812-2703-8*) Rprt Serv.
— History of the American Civil war, 3 Vols. 1977. 128.95 (*0-8369-7159-0*, 7991) Ayer.
— History of the American Civil War. (Notable American Authors Ser.). 1992. reprint ed. lib. bdg. 90.00 (*0-7812-2702-X*) Rprt Serv.
— History of the Conflict Between Religion & Science. 116p. 1998. reprint ed. 20.00 (*0-936128-96-8*) De Young Pr.
— History of the Conflict Between Religion & Science. (Notable American Authors Ser.). 1992. reprint ed. lib. bdg. 75.00 (*0-7812-2704-6*) Rprt Serv.
— History of the Intellectual Development of Europe. Date not set. reprint ed. pap. text 90.00 (*1-58073-023-X*) BCP Bks.
— History of the Intellectual Development of Europe. (Notable American Authors Ser.). 1992. reprint ed. lib. bdg. 99.00 (*0-7812-2700-3*) Rprt Serv.
— Human Physiology: Statical & Dynamical. (Notable American Authors Ser.). 1992. reprint ed. lib. bdg. 90.00 (*0-7812-2699-6*) Rprt Serv.
— Humors & Shakespeare's Characters. LC 77-142248. reprint ed. 34.50 (*0-404-02178-6*) AMS Pr.
— Scientific Memoirs. LC 72-9194. (Literature of Photography Ser.). 1973. reprint ed. 35.95 (*0-405-04904-8*) Ayer.
— Scientific Memoirs. (Notable American Authors Ser.). 1992. reprint ed. lib. bdg. 75.00 (*0-7812-2705-4*) Rprt Serv.
— Stratford to Dogberry: Studies in Shakespeare's Earlier Plays. (Select Bibliographies Reprint Ser.). 1977. 31.95 (*0-8369-5255-3*) Ayer.
— Thoughts on the Future Civil Policy of America. (Notable American Authors Ser.). 1992. reprint ed. lib. bdg. 75.00 (*0-7812-2701-1*) Rprt Serv.
— Treatise on Chemistry. (Notable American Authors Ser.). 1992. reprint ed. lib. bdg. 75.00 (*0-7812-2697-X*) Rprt Serv.
— Treatise on Natural History. (Notable American Authors Ser.). 1992. reprint ed. lib. bdg. 75.00 (*0-7812-2698-8*) Rprt Serv.
— A Treatise on the Forces Which Produce the Organization of Plants. (Notable American Authors Ser.). 1992. reprint ed. lib. bdg. 75.00 (*0-7812-2696-1*) Rprt Serv.
Draper, Jonathan A., ed. The Didache in Modern Research. 445p. 1996. 149.00 (*90-04-10375-9*) Brill Academic Pubs.
Draper, Jonathan A., jt. auth. see Horsley, Richard A.
***Draper, Judith.** Complete Horse. 1999. 30.00 (*1-85868-675-X*, Pub. by Carlton Bks Ltd) Natl Bk Netwk.
— Horse Care. (Practical Handbook Ser.). 1999. pap. 8.95 (*0-7548-0020-2*, Lorenz Bks) Anness Pub.
Draper, Linda. Symphony of Creation: The Heavens. (Illus.). 200p. (Orig.). 1989. pap. 14.95 (*0-317-93518-6*) Camenae Twins.
Draper, Linda & Louise, Virginia. Flight of the Soul: The Teachings of Zanzoona. (Illus.). pap. 15.95 (*0-9622367-9-9*) Camenae Twins.
Draper, Lyman. Pennsylvania Manuscripts, 1747-1827, Pt. 1. Henderson, Mary L., ed. 85p. 1993. pap. 8.95 (*1-55856-154-4*, 075) Closson Pr.
Draper, Lyman C. Action at the Galudoghson Dec. 14, 1742: Col. James Patton, Capt. John McDowell & the 1st Battle with the Indians in the Valley of Virginia. Lobdell, Jared C., ed. & intro. by. 44p. (Orig.). 1995. pap. text 13.00 (*0-7884-0192-0*) Heritage Bk.
— King's Mountain & Its Heroes: History of the Battle of King's Mountain. (Illus.). 612p. 1996. reprint ed. 34.50 (*1-57072-060-6*) Overmountain Pr.
— King's Mountain & Its Heroes: History of the Battle of King's Mountain, October 7th, 1780, & the Events Which Led to It. LC 67-28623. (Illus.). 612p. 1997. reprint ed. 35.00 (*0-8063-0097-3*) Genealog Pub.
— Life of Daniel Boone. LC 98-27008. (Illus.). 576p. 1998. 39.95 (*0-8117-0979-5*) Kitch Keepsakes.
Draper, M. W., jt. ed. see Nissenson, Robert A.
Draper, Mary Wanda. Caring for Children. 2nd ed. 1979. teacher ed. 33.48 (*0-02-662840-6*); text 45.00 (*0-02-662810-4*); student ed. 10.20 (*0-02-662820-1*) Glencoe.
***Draper, Maureen McCarthy.** The Nature of Music: Beauty, Sound & Healing. 192p. 2000. 23.95 (*1-57322-170-8*) Putnam Pub Group.
Draper, Maurice L. Arthur A. Oakman: An Artist with Words LC 98-195155. (Makers of Church Thought Ser.). 150 p. 1997. write for info. (*0-8309-0779-3*) Herald Pub Hse.
— Footnotes: Excerpts from an Appointee's Diary & Elder's Expense Report. LC 96-41526. (Illus.). 240p. (Orig.). 1996. pap. text 15.00 (*0-8309-0738-6*) Herald Pub Hse.
— The Founding Prophet: An Administrative Biography of Joseph Smith, Jr. 250p. (Orig.). 1991. pap. text 5.00 (*0-8309-0596-0*) Herald Pub Hse.
Draper, Michael & Lozovskaya, Elana. Genetics: Principles & Analysis, Printed Test Bank & Solutions Manual. 1998. pap. 10.00 (*0-7637-0713-9*) Jones & Bartlett.
***Draper, Michael I.** Shadows: Airlift & Airwar in Biafra & Nigeria, 1967-1970. (Illus.). 2000. 49.95 (*1-902109-63-5*) Hikoki Pubns.
Draper, Monette & Stimson, Judith, eds. Indiana Alternative Dispute Resolution. LC 95-79443. 650p. 1995. text. write for info. (*0-7620-0004-X*) West Group.
Draper, Muriel G. Music at Midnight. 327p. 1990. reprint ed. lib. bdg. 79.00 (*0-7812-9028-7*) Rprt Serv.
Draper, N. R. & Smith, H. Applied Regression Analysis. 3rd ed. LC 97-17969. (Series in Probability & Statistics). 736p. 1998. 89.95 (*0-471-17082-8*, Wiley-Interscience) Wiley.
Draper, Paul. On Tap Dancing. Avallone, Fran, ed. LC 77-17886. (Dance Program Ser.: Vol. 8). 175p. reprint ed. pap. 54.30 (*0-608-16751-7*, 202782400054) Bks Demand.
Draper, Paula, jt. ed. see Troper, Harold.
Draper, Peter. Guitar & Flute Duets, MFM69. (Illus.). 96p. 1986. pap. 17.95 (*0-8256-4069-5*, AM41773) Music Sales.
Draper, Peter, et al, eds. Artistic Integration in Gothic Buildings. (Illus.). 384p. 1995. text 65.00 (*0-8020-0457-1*); pap. text 24.95 (*0-8020-7477-4*) U of Toronto Pr.
***Draper, R. P.** Shakespeare: The Comedies. LC 99-15881. 2000. text 55.00 (*0-312-22702-7*) St Martin.
Draper, R. P., ed. Mid Twentieth Century Novelists: D. H. Lawrence. (Critical Heritage Ser.). 394p. (C). 1997. 125.00 (*0-415-15922-9*) Routledge.
Draper, Richard. Commutative Algebra. (Lecture Notes in Pure & Applied Mathematics Ser.: Vol. 68). (Illus.). 308p. 1982. pap. text 145.00 (*0-8247-1282-X*) Dekker.
Draper, Richard D. Opening the Seven Seals: The Visions of John the Revelator. LC 91-26254. xii, 308p. 1991. 17.95 (*0-87579-547-1*) Deseret Bk.
***Draper, Robert.** Hadrian's Walls. LC 98-43203. 325p. 1999. 23.00 (*0-375-40369-8*) Knopf.
Draper, Ronald P. D. H. Lawrence. (English Authors Ser.: No. 7). 192p. 1964. 32.00 (*0-8057-1320-4*, Twyne) Mac Lib Ref.
— Hardy: The Tragic Novels : the Return of the Native, the Mayor of Casterbridge, Tess of the D'urbervilles, Jude the Obscure : A Casebook LC 75-321840. (Casebook Ser.). 256p. 1975. write for info. (*0-333-15501-7*) Macmillan.

An Asterisk (*) at the beginning of an entry indicates that the title is appearing for the first time.

— An Introduction to Twentieth Century Poetry in English. LC 98-38114. 304p. 1999. pap. 19.95 (*0-312-21981-4*); text 55.00 (*0-312-21979-2*) St Martin.

Draper, Ronald P., ed. D. H. Lawrence: The Critical Heritage. (Critical Heritage Ser.). xvi, 377p. 1970. text 69.50 (*0-7100-6591-4*, Routledge Thoemms) Routledge.

Draper, Roni J., jt. auth. see McIntosh, Margaret E.

Draper, Rosalind, jt. auth. see Dallos, Rudi.

Draper, Ross, et al. Teaching Family Therapy. 265p. 1992. pap. text 30.00 (*1-85575-021-X*, Pub. by H Karnac Bks Ltd) Other Pr LLC.

***Draper, Ruth.** The Letters of Ruth Draper: Self-Portrait of an Actress, 1920-1956. Warren, Dorothy M., ed. LC 99-25456. 374p. 1999. pap. 19.95 (*0-8093-2188-2*) S Ill U Pr.

Draper, Samuel. Research Papers: A New Guide. 140p. 1994. per. 16.95 (*0-8403-6675-2*) Kendall-Hunt.

Draper, Samuel & Brearley, Joan M. The Book of the Chow Chow. (Illus.). 600p. 1989. 39.95 (*0-86622-711-3*, H-965) TFH Pubns.

— The World of the Chow Chow. (TS Ser.). (Illus.). 528p. 1992. 89.95 (*0-86622-630-3*, TS-149) TFH Pubns.

Draper, Sharon. Forged by Fire. 176p. (YA). (gr. 5 up). 1998. per. 3.99 (*0-689-81851-3*) S&S Childrens.

— Forged by Fire. LC 96-2763. 160p. (J). (gr. 7 up). 1997. 16.00 (*0-689-80699-X*) S&S Trade.

— Lost in the Tunnel of Time. (Ziggy & the Black Dinosaurs Ser.). (Illus.). (YA). (gr. 5-9). 1996. 14.00 (*0-614-15661-0*) Just Us Bks.

— Teaching from the Heart: Reflections, Encouragement, & Inspiration. LC 99-39534. 133p. 2000. pap. 16.00 (*0-325-00131-6*) Heinemann.

— Tears of a Tiger. LC 94-10278. 192p. (J). (gr. 7 up). 1994. 16.00 (*0-689-31878-2*) Atheneum Yung Read.

Draper, Sharon M. Before the Dawn. (YA). 2000. 16.00 (*0-689-83080-7*) S&S Childrens.

— Jazzimagination: A Journal to Read & Write. LC 99-20040. 128p. (J). (gr. 3-7). 2000. 12.95 (*0-439-06130-X*) Scholastic Inc.

— Lost in the Tunnel of Time. LC 96-75037. (Ziggy & the Black Dinosaurs Ser.). (Illus.). 96p. (J). (gr. 3-7). 1996. pap. 6.00 (*0-940975-63-7*) Just Us Bks.

— Lost in the Tunnel of Time. (Ziggy & the Black Dinosaurs Ser.). (Illus.). (YA). (gr. 5-9). 1996. pap. 6.00 (*0-614-15662-9*) Just Us Bks.

— Romiette & Julio. LC 98-50218. (Illus.). 240p. (J). (gr. 7). 1999. 16.00 (*0-689-82180-8*) Atheneum Yung Read.

— Tears of a Tiger. (J). (gr. 7). 1996. mass mkt. 3.95 (*0-689-80698-1*) S&S Childrens.

— Tears of a Tiger. 1996. 9.05 (*0-606-09952-2*, Pub. by Turtleback) Demco.

— Ziggy & the Black Dinosaurs. (Black Dinosaurs Ser.). (Illus.). 96p. (J). (gr. 3 up). 1994. 14.00 (*0-940975-47-5*); pap. 6.00 (*0-940975-48-3*) Just Us Bks.

— Ziggy & the Black Dinosaurs. LC 97-73796. (Shadows of Caesar's Creek Ser.). 96p. (J). 1997. 15.95 (*0-940975-78-5*) Just Us Bks.

— Ziggy & the Black Dinosaurs. LC 97-73796. (Shadows of Caesar's Creek Ser.). 91p. (J). (gr. 3-5). 1997. pap. text 6.00 (*0-940975-76-9*) Just Us Bks.

Draper, Stephen, jt. auth. see Norman, Donald A.

Draper, Tani. Miss Mary Mack Big Book: Black & White Nellie Edge I Can Read & Sing Big Book. (J). (ps-2). 1994. pap. text 20.00 (*0-922053-36-7*) N Edge Res.

— Peanut Butter & Jelly Big Book: Black & White Nellie Edge I Can Read & Sing Big Book. (J). (ps-2). 1988. pap. text 21.00 (*0-922053-10-3*) N Edge Res.

— Playmate Big Book: Black & White Nellie Edge I Can Read & Sing Big Book. (J). (ps-2). 1994. pap. text 20.00 (*0-922053-31-6*) N Edge Res.

Draper, Theodore. The Eighty-Fourth Infantry Division in the Battle of Germany. (Divisional Ser.: No. 24). (Illus.). 260p. 1985. reprint ed. 39.95 (*0-89839-069-9*) Battery Pr.

***Draper, Theodore.** Present of Things Past. 2000. pap. 24.95 (*0-7658-0713-0*) Transaction Pubs.

Draper, Theodore. The Rediscovery of Black Nationalism. 1970. write for info. (*0-318-61740-4*) Viking Penguin.

— A Struggle for Power: The American Revolution. Date not set. 35.00 (*0-685-23291-3*, Times Bks) Crown Pub Group.

— A Struggle for Power: The American Revolution. 1997. pap. 17.00 (*0-679-77642-7*) Vin Bks.

Draper, Thomas. The Bemis History & Genealogy: An Account of the Descendants of Joseph Bemis of Watertown, Mass. 295p. 1988. reprint ed. pap. 37.50 (*0-8328-0233-6*); reprint ed. lib. bdg. 47.50 (*0-8328-0232-8*) Higginson Bk Co.

— The Drapers in America, Being a History & Genealogy of Those of That Name & Connection. (Illus.). 324p. 1989. reprint ed. pap. 45.00 (*0-8328-0495-9*); reprint ed. lib. bdg. 55.00 (*0-8328-0494-0*) Higginson Bk Co.

Draper, Thomas W. & Marcos, Anastasios C., eds. Family Variables: Conceptualization, Measurement & Use. LC 89-37646. (New Perspectives on Family Ser.). (Illus.). 250p. 1990. pap. 77.50 (*0-7837-8962-9*, 204974300003) Bks Demand.

— Family Variables: Conceptualization, Measurement & Use. (New Perspectives on Family Ser.). 320p. (C). 1989. text 48.00 (*0-8039-3111-5*) Sage.

Draper, Verden R., jt. auth. see Irving, Robert H.

***Draper, Vivienne.** The Children of Dunseverick. large type unabridged ed. 149p. 1999. 23.95 (*0-7531-5075-1*, 150751, Pub. by ISIS Lrg Prnt) ISIS Pub.

Draper, William M., ed. Environmental Epidemiology: Effects of Environmental Chemicals on Human Health. LC 94-28456. (Advances in Chemistry Ser.: No. 241). (Illus.). 272p. 1994. text 85.00 (*0-8412-2517-6*, Pub. by Am Chemical); pap. text 55.00 (*0-8412-2933-3*, Pub. by Am Chemical) OUP.

Drapkin, Martin. Developing Policies & Procedures for Jails: A Step-by-Step Guide. LC 96-24889. 233p. 1996. pap. 40.95 (*1-56991-051-0*) Am Correctional.

Drapkin, Martin & Collins, William C. Management & Supervision of Jail Inmates with Mental Disorders. 300p. 1999. ring bd. 133.50 (*1-887554-08-4*) Civic Res Inst.

Drapkin, Michael. OS/2 Warp Presentation Manager Mentor: Foundations of PM Programming. LC 95-35268. 368p. 1995. pap. text 39.95 incl. disk (*0-471-13167-9*) Wiley.

Drapnell, F. Mackay. Braving Those Angry Skies: An American Pilot in the Battle of Britain. (Orig.). 1993. pap. write for info. (*0-9639242-0-6*) Delfin Press.

Drasar, B. & Forrest, B. D. Cholera & the Ecology of Vibrio Cholerae. 368p. 1996. write for info. (*0-412-61220-8*) Kluwer Academic.

Drascic, Branka, tr. see Jackins, Harvey.

Drasdo, Harold, jt. ed. see Tobias, Michael C.

Drasgow, Fritz & Olson-Buchanan, Julie B., eds. Innovations in Computerized Assessment. LC 98-29600. 280p. 1999. 59.95 (*0-8058-2876-1*); pap. 29.95 (*0-8058-2877-X*) L Erlbaum Assocs.

Drasher, Norm. Index of Surnames Appearing in the Hazleton Semi-Weekly, Hazleton, Pennsylvania, Pt. 1. LC 98-71411. 1998. per. 10.00 (*1-55856-275-3*, 169) Closson Pr.

Drasher, Norm & Drasher, Peggy. Luzerne County, PA Tombstone Inscriptions, Vol. 3. 236p. 1995. per. 19.95 (*1-55856-207-9*, 043) Closson Pr.

— Luzerne County, PA Tombstone Inscriptions, Vol. IV. LC 94-177840. 1993. per. 18.95 (*1-55856-262-1*, 044) Closson Pr.

— Tombstone Inscriptions Luzerne County, Pt. 1. 128p. 1993. pap. text 14.95 (*1-55856-160-9*, 041) Closson Pr.

— Tombstone Inscriptions, Luzerne County, PA, Pt. 2. 157p. 1994. per. 14.95 (*1-55856-169-2*, 042) Closson Pr.

— Tombstone Inscriptions St. John's Lutheran & Reformed CEM St. Johns: Formerly Hughesville, Luzerne County, PA. 202p. 1993. per. 19.95 (*1-55856-116-1*, 028) Closson Pr.

Drasher, Peggy, jt. auth. see Drasher, Norm.

Drashkovicheva, K., et al. Ordered Sets & Lattices. LC 88-38112. (Translations Ser.: Series 2, Vol. 141). 203p. 1989. 82.00 (*0-8218-3121-6*, TRANS2/141) Am Math.

Drasin, D., et al, eds. Holomorphic Functions & Moduli I. (Mathematical Sciences Research Institute Publications: Vol. 10). (Illus.). xiii, 246p. 1988. 65.95 (*0-387-96766-4*) Spr-Verlag.

Draskhanakertetsi, Hovhannes. Patmowt'iwn Hayots: History of the Armenians. Maksoudian, Krikor, ed. LC 79-24542. (Classical Armenian Texts Ser.). 488p. 1980. reprint ed. 50.00 (*0-88206-028-7*) Caravan Bks.

Draskovich, Slobodan. Will America Surrender? 480p. 1972. 12.95 (*0-8159-7211-3*) Devin.

— Will America Surrender? 1976. pap. 9.95 (*0-8159-7217-2*) Devin.

Drass, Richard R. Archeological Resources in the Bird Creek Basin, Rogers, Tulsa, & Osage Counties, Oklahoma. (Archeological Resource Survey Report: No. 21). (Illus.). 165p. (C). 1985. pap. text 5.00 (*1-881346-14-5*) Univ OK Archeol.

— Culture Change on the Eastern Margins of the Southern Plains. (Studies in Oklahoma's Past, No. 19: No. 7). (Illus.). 197p. (Orig.). 1997. pap. 7.50 (*1-881346-31-5*) Univ OK Archeol.

Drass, Richard R. & Turner, Christopher L. An Archeological Reconnaissance of the Wolf Creek Drainage Basin, Ellis County, Oklahoma. (Archeological Resource Survey Report: No. 35). (Illus.). 205p. (C). 1989. pap. text 9.00 (*1-881346-23-4*) Univ OK Archeol.

Draszt, Joan M. Echo of Crosscuts & Rails. (Illus.). 304p. 1998. 39.95 (*0-9663914-0-3*); pap. 24.95 (*0-9663914-1-1*) J M Draszt.

Dratch, Gladys I., compiled by. Childs Gallery, Boston: Exhibition Chronology & Publications, 1937-1980. 1982. pap. 5.00 (*0-89073-092-X*, 266) Boston Public Lib.

Drate, Spencer. Rock Art: A Collection of CDs, Albums & Posters. LC 93-4834. (Illus.). 1994. pap. 27.50 (*0-86636-277-0*) PBC Intl Inc.

— Web Art: Including Complete Design Instructions on CD ROM. 144p. 1999. pap. 39.95 (*0-8230-6980-X*) Watsn-Guptill.

***Drate, Spencer, et al, eds.** Web Art. (Illus.). 144p. 1999. pap. 34.95 (*0-942604-64-4*) Madison Square.

***Drate, Spencer & Olejar, Thomas.** Labels of Distinction: Microbrewery Label Design. (Illus.). 144p. 1999. pap. 24.95 (*3-927258-64-4*) Gingko Press.

***Drate, Spencer & Salavetz, Jutka.** Cool Type 2wo. LC 99-32186. (Illus.). 160p. 1999. 35.00 (*0-89134-932-4*, 31377, North Lght Bks) F & W Pubns Inc.

***Drate, Spencer & Salavetz, Jutka, eds.** Extreme Fonts. (Illus.). 144p. 1999. 34.99 (*0-942604-74-1*) Madison Square.

Drate, Spencer, et al. Cool Type. LC 96-44180. (Illus.). 144p. 1997. 34.99 (*0-89134-728-3*, North Lght Bks) F & W Pubns Inc.

Dratfield, Jim. Pug Shots. (Illus.). 96p. 1999. 19.95 (*0-670-88726-9*) Studio Bks.

***Dratfield, Jim & Coughlin, Pam.** The Quotable Feline. 2000. pap. 12.00 (*0-375-70214-8*) Knopf.

Dratfield, Jim & Coughlin, Paul. The Quotable Feline. (Illus.). 1996. 20.00 (*0-614-15945-8*) Knopf.

— The Quotable Feline. LC 96-77836. 96p. 1996. 20.00 (*0-679-44699-0*) Random.

Drath, Wilfred H. Why Managers Have Trouble Empowering: A Theoretical Perspective Based on Concepts of Adult Development. LC 93-70892. 1993. pap. 15.00 (*0-912879-96-3*, 155) Ctr Creat Leader.

Drath, Wilfred H., ed. Reader's Choice: A Decade of Issues & Observations. (Technical Reports: No. 314G). 65p. pap. 7.50 (*0-912879-63-7*) Ctr Creat Leader.

Drath, Wilfred H. & Palus, Charles J. Making Common Sense: Leadership As Meaning-Making in a Community of Practice. LC 94-17583. 27p. 1994. pap. text 15.00 (*0-912879-97-1*) Ctr Creat Leader.

Drath, Wilfred H., jt. auth. see Palus, Charles J.

Dratler, Jay, Jr. Intellectual Property Law. 1100p. 1991. ring bd. 95.00 (*0-317-05388-4*, 00615) NY Law Pub.

— Licensing. (Intellectual Property Ser.). 1994. write for info. (*0-614-32056-9*) Law Journal.

Drattell, Alan. The Other Victim: How Caregivers Survive a Loved One's Chronic Illness. LC 96-7742. 116p. 1996. pap. 17.95 (*0-929765-43-5*) Seven Locks Pr.

***Dratva, Tomas & Buznova, Viktoria.** Slovencina pre Cudzincov (Slovak for Foreigners) Zigo, Pavol & Protasov, Taisa Nikolajevna, eds. (SLO & ENG., Illus.). 375p. 1998. 35.00 (*0-86516-446-0*) Bolchazy-Carducci.

Draucker, Claire B. Counseling Survivors of Childhood Sexual Abuse. (Counselling in Practice Ser.: Vol. 1). (Illus.). 160p. (C). 1992. 49.95 (*0-8039-8570-3*); pap. 21.50 (*0-8039-8571-1*) Sage.

Draud, Georg. Bibliotheca Librorum Germanicorum Classica. viii, 791p. reprint ed. write for info. (*0-318-71767-0*) G Olms Pubs.

Draudt, Susan. Sourdough Baking: Fabulous Recipes for Bread Machines & Traditional Methods. LC 94-34432. (Illus.). 144p. 1994. pap. 10.95 (*1-55561-067-6*) Fisher Bks.

Draughn, Robert A., jt. auth. see An, Yuehuei H.

Draughon, Clyde, Jr. & Kemmer, Richard G. Profitable Asset-Based Lending. 352p. 1990. per. 55.00 (*1-55520-077-X*, Irwn Prfssnl) McGraw-Hill Prof

Draughon, Dennis. The Line Is Draughon: Political Cartoons. (Illus.). 132p. (Orig.). (C). 1988. pap. 5.95 (*0-929133-00-5*) Barefoot Pr.

Draughon, Eleanor S. Abstracts of Duplin County, North Carolina, Deeds, 1784-1813, Vol. 1. 256p. 1986. reprint ed. pap. 27.50 (*0-89308-598-7*, NC 33) Southern Hist Pr.

Draughon, Henry. Student's Vision Guide. (Illus.). 160p. (J). (gr. 6-12). 1995. pap., student ed. 9.95 (*1-885147-03-1*) FamilyTalk.

— Student's Vision Guide: Parent's & Mentor's Supplement. (Illus.). 1995. pap., student ed. 2.95 (*1-885147-04-X*) FamilyTalk.

***Draughon, Stefan.** A Passion for Watercolor: Painting the Inner Experience. (Illus.). 144p. 2000. write for info. (*0-8230-0102-4*) Watsn-Guptill.

Draughon, Stefan, tr. see Szabo, Magda.

Draughon, Wallace R. History of the Church of Jesus Christ of Latter-Day Saints in North Carolina. (Illus.). 320p. reprint ed. lib. bdg. 18.95 (*1-881851-01-X*) Genealogy Pub.

***Draugsvold, Ottar G., ed.** Nobel Writers on Writing. 303p. 2000. lib. bdg. 45.00 (*0-7864-0629-1*) McFarland & Co.

Draulens, Dirk. Red Queen. Garrett, Sam, tr. LC 97-8806. 224p. 1997. text 21.95 (*0-312-15636-7*) St Martin.

Draus, Franciszek, ed. see Aron, Raymond.

Draus, Julia A., jt. auth. see Troiano, Edna M.

Dravecky, Dave & Neal, C. W. Worth of a Man. 208p. 1998. pap. 12.99 (*0-310-21942-6*) Zondervan.

Dravecky, Dave & Stafford, Tim. Comeback. 272p. 1992. pap. 11.99 (*0-310-52881-X*) Zondervan.

Dravecky, Dave, et al. Do Not Lose Heart: Devotions of Encouragement & Comfort. LC 97-34171. (Illus.). 160p. 1998. 17.99 (*0-310-21706-7*) Zondervan.

— Glimpses of Heaven: Reflections on Your Eternal Hope. LC 98-17624. 128p. 1998. 12.99 (*0-310-21626-5*) Zondervan.

— Portraits in Courage: Extraordinary Lessons from Everyday Heroes. LC 98-24703. 208p. 1998. 12.99 (*0-310-21664-8*) Zondervan.

— Standy by Me: A Guidebook of Practical Ways to Encourage a Hurting Friend. LC 98-10281. 128p. 1998. pap. 9.99 (*0-310-21646-X*) Zondervan.

Dravecky, Jan & Neal, Connie. Joy I'd Never Known: One Woman's Triumph over Panic Attacks & Depression. 208p. 1998. pap. 12.99 (*0-310-21941-8*) Zondervan.

***Draves, et al.** Quantitative Analysis Laboratories F/multi-component System. 2001. pap. 6.25 (*0-534-37868-4*) Thomson Learn.

Draves-Arpaia, Neil. Graciously Hear Us: General Intercessions for Cycles A, B, C. LC 98-19810. 224p. 1998. pap. 21.95 (*0-87793-657-9*) Ave Maria.

***Draves-Arpaia, Neil J.** Come Light Our Hearts: General Intercessions for Ritual Celebrations, Feast Days & Civic Holiday. LC 99-28693. 240p. 1999. pap. 22.95 (*0-87793-680-3*) Ave Maria.

Draves, Bill. Achieving Financial Self-Suffiency. 117p. 115.00 (*0-914951-53-X*) LERN.

— The Free University: A Model for Lifelong Learning. 314p. 1980. 19.95 (*0-318-14138-8*) LERN.

— How to Teach Adults. 124p. 7.95 (*0-914951-20-3*) LERN.

— How-to-Teach Adults in One Hour. 67p. 7.95 (*0-914951-33-5*) LERN.

Draves, Pamela, ed. Citizens Media Directory. 1977. pap. 3.50 (*0-9603466-3-5*) T R A C.

— Citizens Media Directory. 1980. write for info. (*0-318-54564-0*) T R A C.

Draves, William. Marketing Techniques for Office Staff. 32p. 5.98 (*0-914951-14-9*) LERN.

***Draves, William A.** Teaching Online. (Illus.). 125p. 1999. pap. 14.95 (*1-57722-016-1*) LERN.

Dravid, Kamalini. Acculturation of Anti-Culture: A Study of Trillings Beyond Culture. 64p. 1989. text 8.95 (*81-7045-034-9*, Pub. by Assoc Pub Hse) Advent Bks Div.

Dravilas, Paul. Understanding a Local Area Network. Jonas, Jacqueline & Young, Natalie B., eds. (Illus.). 150p. (C). pap. text 245.00 incl. audio (*0-917792-77-7*, 150) OneOnOne Comp Trng.

Dravnieks, Dzintar E., et al, eds. IBM Personal Computer Handbook. LC 83-9953. (Illus.). 448p. (Orig.). 1983. pap. 19.95 (*0-915904-66-7*) And-Or Bks.

Draw, K. The Creative State: A Guide to the Thought Processes of the Actor. LC 97-7589. 184p. 1997. pap. 19.95 (*0-435-07029-0*, 07029) Heinemann.

Drawbaugh, Charles C. Time & Its Use: A Self Management Guide for Teachers. LC 84-8578. (Illus.). 144p. 1984. reprint ed. pap. 44.70 (*0-7837-8877-0*, 204958800001) Bks Demand.

***Drawe, Judith Anderson & Greenstein, Kathleen Bridge.** Lithographed Paper Toys Books & Games: Eighteen Eighty to Nineteen fifteen. (Illus.). 192p. 2000. 49.95 (*0-7643-1124-7*) Schiffer.

Drawe, Lynn, jt. intro. see Roberson, Sheila F.

Drawson, Blair. Flying Dimitri. LC 96-49274. (Illus.). 40p. (J). (ps-2). 1997. 14.95 (*0-531-30037-4*) Orchard Bks Watts.

— Mary Margaret's Tree. LC 96-3998. (Illus.). 40p. (J). (ps-2). 1996. 15.95 (*0-531-09521-5*); lib. bdg. 16.99 (*0-531-08871-5*) Orchard Bks Watts.

Drawson, Maynard C. Treasures of the Oregon Country, No. IV. (Illus.). 1977. pap. 9.95 (*0-934476-03-9*) Dee Pub Co.

***Drax, Simon.** A Very Fast Descent into Hell. 256p. 1999. pap. 12.00 (*0-9673604-0-4*) Studio Phaedra.

Draxe, Thomas. Bibliotheca Scholastica Instructissima: Or a Treasure of Ancient Adagies. LC 76-57378. (English Experience Ser.: No. 796). 1977. reprint ed. lib. bdg. 30.00 (*90-221-0796-5*) Walter J Johnson.

Draxler, G. Technical Dictionary, German to Russian. (GER & RUS.). 480p. 1995. 125.00 (*0-320-00547-X*) Fr & Eur.

— Technical Dictionary, Russian to German. (GER & RUS.). 480p. 1997. 125.00 (*0-320-00468-6*) Fr & Eur.

Draxler, Laura. Windows Programming, under the Hood of MFC: A Quick Tour of Visual C++ Tools. LC 97-40627. 640p. (C). 1997. pap. text 44.95 (*0-13-488975-4*) P-H.

Draxler, P., et al, eds. Computational Methods for Representations of Groups & Algebras. LC 99-29078. (Progress in Mathematics Ser.: Vol. 173). 376p. 1999. 85.00 (*3-7643-6063-1*) Birkhauser.

Draxten, Nina. Kristofer Janson in America. 401p. 1976. 20.00 (*0-87732-057-8*) Norwegian-Am Hist Assn.

— The Testing of M. Falk Gjertsen. (Topical Studies: Vol. 4). (Illus.). 140p. 1988. 15.00 (*0-87732-074-8*) Norwegian-Am Hist Assn.

Dray, Bryan, jt. auth. see Bowler, Dave.

Dray, S. Judges & Ruth. 1997. pap. 11.99 (*1-85792-323-5*, Pub. by Christian Focus) Spring Arbor Dist.

Dray, William H. History As Re-Enactment: R. G. Collingwood's Idea of History. 358p. 1996. text 75.00 (*0-19-824293-X*) OUP.

— History As Re-Enactment: R. G. Collingwood's Idea of History. 347p. 1999. pap. 24.95 (*0-19-823881-9*) OUP.

— Laws & Explanation in History. LC 78-25936. 174p. 1979. reprint ed. lib. bdg. 38.50 (*0-313-20790-9*, DRLE, Greenwood Pr) Greenwood.

— On History & Philosophers of History. LC 89-15793. (Philosophy of History & Culture Ser.). viii, 237p. 1989. 107.00 (*90-04-09000-2*) Brill Academic Pubs.

— Philosophy of History. 2nd ed. LC 92-24133. 176p. (Orig.). (C). 1992. pap. text 14.20 (*0-13-012816-3*) P-H.

Dray, Williams H., ed. see Collingwood, R. G.

Draycott, A. T., et al, eds. Stone's Justices' Manual, 1994. 126th ed. 1994. write for info. (*0-406-03501-6*, U.K., MICHIE) LEXIS Pub.

— Stone's Justices' Manual, 1996, 3 vols., Set, incl. case. 128th ed. 7700p. 1996. write for info. (*0-406-06463-6*, MICHIE) LEXIS Pub.

— Stones Justices' Manual 1997. 1997. write for info. (*0-406-99595-8*, SJM1997SET, MICHIE) LEXIS Pub.

Drayer, Burton P., ed. Neurologic Radiology: The Brain, a Practical Approach. 750p. 1999. text 195.00 (*0-7817-0120-1*) Lppncott W & W.

***Drayer, David.** Strip Cuts. 292p. 2000. pap. 13.95 (*0-9675215-6-4*) Rowdy Hse Pubg.

***Drayer, Fred.** Bill Clinton & I Have the Same Father. LC 00-131674. (Illus.). 144p. 2000. write for info. (*1-57197-229-3*, Pub. by Pentland Pr) Assoc Pubs Grp.

Drayer, Jeffrey A. The Cost-Effective Use of Leeches & Other Musings of a Medical School Survivor. LC 98-25829. 1998. pap. 14.95 (*1-883620-13-9*) Galen AZ.

Drayer, Ruth. Numerology, the Power in Numbers: A Right & Left Brain Approach. rev. ed. LC 95-100125. 221p. (Orig.). 1994. pap. 14.95 (*0-9640321-0-4*) Jewels of Light.

Drayman-Weisser, T., intro. Dialogue - 89 - The Conservation of Bronze Sculpture in the Outdoor Environment: A Dialogue among Conservators, Curators, Environmental Scientists, & Corrosion Engineers. (Illus.). 398p. 1992. pap. text 24.00 (*1-877914-38-X*) NACE Intl.

Drayton. Dolly Dingle Paper Dolls. 1989. pap. text 4.95 (*0-486-23711-7*) Dover.

Drayton, Anne, tr. & intro. see Brillat-Savarin, Jean Anthelme.

Drayton, Geoffrey. Christopher. (Caribbean Writers Ser.). 192p. (C). 1972. pap. 7.95 (*0-435-98235-4*, 98235) Heinemann.

Drayton, Grace G. The Adventures of Dolly Dingle Paper Dolls. 81st ed. (J). 1985. pap. 4.95 (*0-486-24809-7*) Dover.

— Favorite Dolly Dingle Stickers & Seals. 81st ed. (Illus.). (J). (gr. k-3). 1985. pap. 3.50 (*0-486-24922-0*) Dover.

D

An Asterisk (*) at the beginning of an entry indicates that the title is appearing for the first time.

Drayton, H. S. Human Magnetism: Its Nature, Physiology & Psychology. 66p. 1996. reprint ed. spiral bd. 13.00 (*0-7873-0295-3*) Hlth Research.

Drayton-Hargrove, Shirlee, jt. auth. see Derstine, Jill B.

***Drayton, Joanne.** Edith Collier: Her Life & Work, 1885-1964. (Illus.). 88p. (Orig.). 1999. pap. 29.95 (*0-908812-90-6*, Pub. by Canterbury Univ) Accents Pubns.

Drayton, John. Memoirs of the American Revolution, 2 vols., 1. Decker, Peter, ed. LC 77-76244. (Eyewitness Accounts of the American Revolution Ser.). 1977. reprint ed. 19.95 (*0-405-01150-4*) Ayer.

— Memoirs of the American Revolution, 2 vols., Set. Decker, Peter, ed. LC 77-76244. (Eyewitness Accounts of the American Revolution Ser.). 1969. reprint ed. 50.95 (*0-405-01149-0*) Ayer.

— Memoirs of the American Revolution, 2 vols., Vol. 2. Decker, Peter, ed. LC 77-76244. (Eyewitness Accounts of the American Revolution Ser.). 1969. reprint ed. 19.95 (*0-405-01151-2*) Ayer.

Drayton, Kat. Nantucket's Night Magic. 32p. (J). (gr. k). 1998. 14.95 (*0-9667090-0-4*) Dionis Bound.

Drayton, Louise & Thomson, Jane. The Floral Stencil Book. LC 97-215503. (Illus.). 38p. 1997. pap. 19.95 (*0-7894-2080-5*) DK Pub Inc.

Drayton, Marta, ed. see Ullinskey, Nancy & Hibbert, Lorri.

Drayton, Michael. Minor Poems. (Select Bibliographies Reprint Ser.). 1977. reprint ed. 21.95 (*0-8369-6853-0*) Ayer.

— To the Majestie of King James, a Gratulatorie Poem. LC 71-25832. (English Experience Ser.: No. 169). 16p. 1969. reprint ed. 15.00 (*90-221-0169-X*) Walter J Johnson.

Drayton, Michael, et al. Sir John Oldcastle. LC 72-133657. (Tudor Facsimile Texts. Old English Plays Ser.: No. 89). reprint ed. 59.50 (*0-404-53389-2*) AMS Pr.

***Drayton, Richard.** Nature's Government: Science, British Imperialism & the Improvement of the World. LC 99-59158. 416p. 2000. 40.00 (*0-300-05976-0*) Yale U Pr.

Drayton, Richard, ed. see Lamming, George.

Drayton, William H. The Letters of Freeman, Etc. LC 75-31089. reprint ed. 19.50 (*0-404-13507-2*) AMS Pr.

Draz, M. A. Introduction to the Qur'an. text 45.00 (*1-86064-421-X*) St Martin.

Drazan, Frank. The Pressroom Manager's Guidebook. 3rd ed. (Illus.). 112p. 1989. pap. 20.00 (*0-318-21788-0*) F Drazan.

— The Textbook for Pressman Training. 2nd ed. (Illus.). 106p. 1986. pap. 20.00 (*0-318-21789-9*) F Drazan.

Drazan, Joseph G. The Pacific Northwest: An Index to People & Places in Books. LC 79-16683. 176p. 1979. 20.00 (*0-8108-1234-7*) Scarecrow.

Drazan, Joseph G., compiled by. An Annotated Bibliography of ERIC Bibliographies, 1966-1980. LC 82-6151. (Illus.). 520p. 1982. lib. bdg. 59.95 (*0-313-22688-1*, DRE/, Greenwood Pr) Greenwood.

Drazen, E. L., et al. Patient Care Information Systems: Successful Design & Implementation. (Computers in Health Care Ser.). (Illus.). 188p. 1995. text 48.00 (*0-387-94255-6*) Spr-Verlag.

Drazen, Erica & Metzger, Jane, eds. Strategies for Integrated Health Care: Emerging Practices in Information Management & Cross-Continuum Care. (Business & Management Ser.). 256p. 1998. 46.95 (*0-7879-4159-X*) Jossey-Bass.

Drazen, Jeffrey M. & Dahl, Sven-Erik, eds. Five-Lipoxygenase Products in Asthma. LC 98-26626. (Lung Biology in Health & Disease Ser.). (Illus.). 496p. 1998. text 150.00 (*0-8247-0167-4*) Dekker.

Drazga, Nancy, jt. auth. see Zahn, Barbara.

Drazil, J. V. Quantities & Units of Measurement. (ENG, FRE & GER.). 314p. 1983. 110.00 (*0-8288-0009-X*, M6719) Fr & Eur.

Drazin, Charles. Blue Velvet: The Ultimate A-Z. 1999. pap. 15.95 (*1-58234-029-3*) Bloomsbury Pubg.

***Drazin, Charles.** In Search of the Third Man. (Illus.). 224p. 2000. reprint ed. pap. 17.95 (*0-87910-294-2*) Limelight Edns.

***Drazin, David H.** Croquet: A Bibliography: Specialist Books & Pamphlets from 1853 to 1997. LC 99-46911. (Illus.). 528p. 1999. 99.95 (*1-58456-008-8*, 56712) Oak Knoll.

Drazin, Israel. Targum Onkelos on Deuteronomy, Vol. 5. 1981. 79.50 (*0-87068-755-7*) Ktav.

— Targum Onkelos on Exodus, Vol. 2. 1990. 79.50 (*0-88125-342-1*) Ktav.

— Targum Onkelos to Leviticus: An English Translation of the Text with Analysis & Commentary, Vol. 3. LC 93-34042. 1993. 75.00 (*0-88125-470-3*) Ktav.

Drazin, Israel, et al. Targum Onkelos to Leviticus: An English Translation of the Text with Analysis & Commentary (Based on A. Sperber's Edition), No. 4. 1998. 79.50 (*0-88125-530-0*) Ktav.

Drazin, Michoel. Their Hollow Inheritance: A Comprehensive Refutation of the New Testament & Its Missionaries. 210p. 1992. 18.00 (*965-229-070-X*, Pub. by Gefen Pub Hse) Gefen Bks.

Drazin, Nathan. History of Jewish Education from 515 B. C. E. to 220 C. E. 1979. 18.95 (*0-405-10598-3*) Ayer.

— Legends Worth Living. 14.95 (*0-88125-381-2*) Ktav.

Drazin, P. G. Nonlinear Systems. (Cambridge Texts in Applied Mathematics Ser.: No. 10). (Illus.). 331p. (C). 1992. pap. text 36.95 (*0-521-40668-4*) Cambridge U Pr.

Drazin, P. G. & Johnson, R. S. Solitons: An Introduction. (Cambridge Texts in Applied Mathematics Ser.: No. 3). (Illus.). 240p. (C). 1989. pap. text 33.95 (*0-521-33655-4*) Cambridge U Pr.

Drazin, P. G. & Reid, W. H. Hydrodynamic Stability. LC 80-40273. (Cambridge Monographs on Mechanics & Applied Mathematics). (Illus.). 539p. 1982. pap. text 49.95 (*0-521-28980-7*) Cambridge U Pr.

Draznin. Diabetes. (C). 1999. text. write for info. (*0-7216-8219-7*, W B Saunders Co) Harcrt Hlth Sci Grp.

Draznin, Boris & Le Roith, Derek, eds. The Molecular Biology of Diabetes Pt. II: Insulin Action, Effects on Gene Expression & Regulation & Glucose Transport. LC 94-27263. (Illus.). 568p. 1994. 125.00 (*0-89603-287-6*) Humana.

Draznin, Boris & LeRoith, Derek, eds. The Molecular Biology of Diabetes Pt. I: Autoimmunity & Genetics: Insulin Synthesis & Secretion. LC 94-27263. (Illus.). 424p. 1994. text 125.00 (*0-89603-286-8*) Humana.

Draznin, Boris & Rizza, Robert, eds. Clinical Research in Diabetes & Obesity Vol. 1: Methods, Assessment & Metabolic Regulation. LC 97-5726. (Contemporary Biomedicine Ser.: Vol. 14). (Illus.). 408p. 1997. 139.50 (*0-89603-350-3*) Humana.

— Clinical Research in Diabetes & Obesity Vol. 2: Diabetes & Obesity. LC 97-5726. (Contemporary Biomedicine Ser.: Vol. 15). (Illus.). 408p. 1997. 139.50 (*0-89603-492-5*) Humana.

Draznin, Sharon Z. Writing Math: Project-Based Activities to Integrate Math & Language Arts. 184p. (Orig.). 1995. pap. 12.95 (*0-673-36127-6*, GoodYrBooks) Addson-Wesley Educ.

Draznin, Sharron. Simple Cooking Fun: Creative Kids. LC 96-61507. 1997. pap. text 12.95 (*1-57690-091-6*) Tchr Create Mat.

Draznin, Yaffa C., ed. My Other Self: The Letters of Olive Schreiner & Havelock Ellis, 1884- 1920. LC 90-5906. XI, 583p. (C). 1993. text 79.95 (*0-8204-1360-7*) P Lang Pubng.

***Draznin, Yaffa Claire.** Victorian London's Middle-Class Housewife: What She Did all Day, 179. LC 99-55116. (Contributions in Women's Studies: Vol. 179). 232p. 2000. 65.00 (*0-313-31399-7*, Greenwood Pr) Greenwood.

Drazniowsky, Roman. Cataloging & Filing Rules for Maps & Atlases in the Society's Collection. 92p. 1969. pap. 12.00 (*0-318-12729-6*) Am Geographical.

Drdacky, M., ed. Lessons from Structural Failures. 160p. 1991. pap. text 59.00 (*0-685-59661-3*, CZ1) Am Soc Civil Eng.

Drdacky, M., jt. ed. see Krupka, V.

Drea, Edward J. In the Service of the Emperor: Essays on the Imperial Japanese Army. LC 97-40180. (Studies in War, Society, & the Military). (Illus.). xix, 300p. 1998. text 50.00 (*0-8032-1708-0*) U of Nebr Pr.

— MacArthur's ULTRA: Codebreaking & the War Against Japan, 1942-1945. LC 91-16842. (Modern War Studies). (Illus.). xvi, 296p. 1991. pap. 15.95 (*0-7006-0576-2*) U Pr of KS.

Drea, Edward J. New Guinea: United States Army Campaigns of World War 2. 31p. 1993. pap. 1.50 (*0-16-061299-3*) USGPO.

Dreachslin, Janice & Hunt, Portia L. Diversity Leadership. LC 96-16820. (Management Ser.). 256p. 1996. 42.00 (*1-56793-046-8*) Health Admin Pr.

Dream Light Inc. Middle School Keyboarding. (PB - Keyboarding Ser.). (J). (gr. k-8). 1997. pap., teacher ed. 15.95 (*0-538-66049-X*) S-W Pub.

Dream Works Staff. When You Believe: The Miraculous Story of Moses from Scripture. LC 98-39381. (Illus.). 144p. 1998. 14.99 (*0-7852-7017-5*) Nelson.

Dream Works Staff, prod. Miriam's Gift: Book & Keepsake. LC 98-30081. (Prince of Egypt Ser.). 32p. (J). (gr. 1-4). 1998. 9.99 (*0-525-46052-7*, PuffinBks) Peng Put Young Read.

***Dreamer, Sue.** Bee Happy on Your Birthday. (Illus.). (J). 2000. 4.95 (*0-7407-1040-0*) Andrews & McMeel.

Dreamer, Sue. Dear Daughter. LC 99-72683. (Illus.). 64p. 1999. 6.95 (*0-7407-0089-8*) Andrews & McMeel.

— Girl Talk: Women on Life, Love & Getting What You Want. LC 99-72682. 64p. 1999. 6.95 (*0-7407-0090-1*) Andrews & McMeel.

— A Teddy Bear Christmas. LC 91-77714. (Illus.). 10p. (J). (ps-1). 1992. bds. 7.95 (*1-56397-121-6*) Boyds Mills Pr.

***Dreamer, Sue.** Thanks! You're the Best. (Illus.). (J). 2000. pap. 4.95 (*0-7407-1041-9*) Andrews & McMeel.

Dreamwalker, Arwyn, et al. Rituals for Sacred Living: Tapping the Infinite Energy of the Universe. LC 98-32354. (Illus.). 128p. (gr. 4-7). 1999. wbk. ed. 24.95 (*0-8069-7093-6*) Sterling.

Dreamwalker, Richard. Four Winds Returning: A Novel. LC 95-38649. 190p. (Orig.). 1996. pap. write for info. (*1-887786-10-4*) Sky & Sage Bks.

***DreamWorks Inc. Staff.** Road to El Dorado: Adventure Activity Book. (Gold & Glory Ser.). (Illus.). 16p. (J). 2000. mass mkt. 7.99 (*0-14-130713-7*, PuffinBks) Peng Put Young Read.

***DreamWorks Staff, ed.** Road to El Dorado. (Gold & Glory Ser.). (Illus.). (J). 2000. pap. 9.99 incl. audio (*0-14-180128-X*) Penguin Putnam.

Drean, J. Y., et al. Relationships Between Mechanical Properties of Fibres & Mechanical Properties of Yarns. 1991. pap. 42.00 (*0-7855-2834-2*, Pub. by Textile Inst) St Mut.

Drean, Tamara & Souviney, Randall. Measurement Investigations. 152p. 1997. 13.50 (*0-86651-591-7*) Seymour Pubns.

Dreaver, Jim. Ultimate Cure: The Healing Energy Within You. LC 95-45883. 312p. 1999. pap. 14.95 (*1-56718-244-5*) Llewellyn Pubns.

— The Way of Harmony: Walking The Inner Path To Balance, Happiness, And Success, Vol. 1. LC 99-29548. 272p. 1999. pap. 12.50 (*0-380-80313-5*, Avon Bks) Morrow Avon.

Dreazen, Phyllis, jt. auth. see Zelzer, Sarah S.

Drebin, Allan R., et al, eds. Objectives of Accounting & Financial Reporting by Governmental Units: A Research Study, 2 vols. Incl. Vol. I. (Illus.). 128p. 1981. pap. Vol. II. (Illus.). 200p. 1981. pap. 7.50 1981. pap. write for info. (*0-318-56852-7*) Municipal.

***Drechsel, Edwin.** From Venezuela with Love. LC 99-69686. 384p. 2001. pap. 19.50 (*0-88739-328-4*) Creat Arts Bk.

Drechsel, Emanuel J. Mobilian Jargon: Linguistic & Sociohistorical Aspects of a Native American Pidgin. LC 96-20837. (Illus.). 412p. 1997. text 59.00 (*0-19-824033-3*) OUP.

Drechsel, H., et al, eds. Cataclysmic Variables. 1987. text 313.00 (*90-277-2435-0*) Kluwer Academic.

Drechsel, Willem, et al, eds. South Africa in Focus. Meyer, Jacky, tr. from DUT. LC 92-40867. (In Focus Ser.). (Illus.). 158p. 1993. 39.95 (*0-7103-0462-5*, B2339) Routledge.

Drechsler, Arthur J. The Weightlifting Encyclopedia: A Guide to World Class Performance. LC 97-40958. (Illus.). xxv, 549p. (Orig.). 1998. pap. 29.95 (*0-9659179-2-4*) A Is A Comns.

Drechsler, Charles. Some Hyphomycetes That Prey on Free-Living Terricolous Nematodes. (Mycologia Ser.: No. 29). (Illus.). 103p. 1937. pap. text 20.00 (*0-945345-05-4*) Lubrecht & Cramer.

Drechsler, Debbie. Daddy's Girl. 88p. 1996. pap. 9.95 (*1-56097-303-X*) Fantagraph Bks.

Drechsler, Lawrence. The Pirates. LC 85-52401. (Illus.). (Orig.). (J). (gr. 6 up). pap. write for info. (*0-935143-01-7*) Treadle Pr.

Drechsler, Rolf. Binary Decision Diagrams: Theory & Implementation. 200p. 1998. 105.00 (*0-7923-8193-9*) Kluwer Academic.

— Evolutionary Algorithms for VLSI CAD. LC 98-18459. 1998. 97.50 (*0-7923-8168-8*) Kluwer Academic.

***Drechsler, Rolf.** Formal Verification of Circuits. LC 00-34888. 2000. write for info. (*0-7923-7858-X*) Kluwer Academic.

Drederian, Robert. Lost Art of Scratch Cooking: Recipes from the Kitchen of Natha Adkins Parker, 1. LC 97-94703. 1997. pap. 12.00 (*0-9661872-0-2*) C Parker.

Drederian, Robert, ed. Commemorating Excellence. (Illus.). 160p. 1998. 49.95 (*1-885206-61-5*) Cader Pubng.

— Moments. (Illus.). 210p. 1998. 49.95 (*1-885206-56-9*) Cader Pubng.

— Pathways. (Illus.). 240p. 1998. 49.95 (*1-885206-60-7*) Cader Pubng.

— Treasures. (Illus.). 400p. 1998. 49.95 (*1-885206-55-0*) Cader Pubng.

Drederian, Robert, jt. ed. see Dererian.

Dredge, Frances, jt. auth. see Hayes, Jenny.

Dredge, Gale. Parent-Teacher Resource Book. (Illus.). 200p. (Orig.). 1989. per. 14.95 (*0-685-28887-0*) Parent-Teacher.

Dredge, Rhonda, jt. auth. see De Crespigny, Lachlan.

Dreeben, Robert. What Is Learned In School. pap. text 6.00 (*0-201-01610-9*) Addison-Wesley.

Dreele, W. H. Von, see Von Dreele, W. H.

Dreer, Herman. The Immediate Jewel of His Soul. LC 72-144596. reprint ed. 39.50 (*0-404-00149-1*) AMS Pr.

Drees, Bastiaan M., jt. auth. see Jackman, John A.

Drees, Burkhard & Pazarba Sio Glu Ceyla. The Nordic Banking Crises: Pitfalls in Financial Liberization, Vol. 161. LC 98-14799. (Occasional Papers). 1998. 15.00 (*1-55775-700-3*) Intl Monetary.

Drees, Clayton J. Authority & Dissent in the English Church: The Prosecution of Heresy & Religious Non-Conformity in the Diocese of Winchester, 1380-1547. LC 97-14950. (Texts & Studies in Religion: Vol. 73). 224p. 1997. text 89.95 (*0-7734-8613-5*) E Mellen.

***Drees, Clayton J., ed.** The Late Medieval Age of Crisis & Renewal, 1300-1500: A Biographical Dictionary. LC 00-22335. (Great Cultural Eras of the Western World Ser.). 520p. 2000. lib. bdg. 89.00 (*0-313-30588-9*, GR0588, Greenwood Pr) Greenwood.

Drees, M. Pacific Particle Physics Phenomenology. (High Energy Physics Conference Proceedings Ser.). 1998. 78.00 (*981-02-3623-9*) World Scientific Pub.

Drees, Manuel. Theory & Phenomenology of S Particles. 1999. 78.00 (*981-02-3739-1*) World Scientific Pub.

Drees, N. C. Devonian Succession in the Subsurface of the Great Slave & Great Bear Plains, Northwest Territories. (GSC Bulletin Ser.: No. 393). (Illus.). 222p. (Orig.). 1993. pap. 34.10 (*0-660-14404-2*, Pub. by Canadian Govt Pub) Accents Pubns.

Drees, Thomas. Blood Plasma: The Promise & the Politics. LC 82-11617. (Illus.). 1983. 29.95 (*0-87949-225-2*) Ashley Bks.

Drees, Willem B. Beyond the Big Bang: Quantum Cosmologies & God. LC 90-38498. 344p. 1990. 44.95 (*0-8126-9117-2*) Open Court.

— Religion, Science & Naturalism. 336p. (C). 1998. pap. text 21.95 (*0-521-64562-X*) Cambridge U Pr.

Drees, William B. Beyond the Big Bang: Quantum Cosmologies & God. LC 90-38498. 344p. 1990. pap. 19.95 (*0-8126-9118-0*) Open Court.

— Religion, Science & Naturalism. 330p. (C). 1996. text 69.95 (*0-521-49708-6*) Cambridge U Pr.

Dreese, Michael A. An Imperishable Fame: The Civil War Experience of George Fisher McFarland. (Illus.). ixx, 199p. 1997. pap. 17.00 (*0-9662417-2-X*) Juniata Cty Hist.

***Dreese, Michael A.** The 151st Pennsylvania Volunteers in Gettysburg: Ripe Apples in a Storm. LC 99-89289. (Illus.). 200p. 2000. 45.00 (*0-7864-0804-9*) McFarland & Co.

Dreesman, Gordon R., ed. see Southwest Foundation for Biomedical Research, Inte.

Dreeszen, Craig. The Artist in Business: Basic Business Practices. 3rd rev. ed. Wood, Clare et al, eds. 120p. (Orig.). 1996. pap. text 14.50 (*0-945464-01-0*) Univ MA Arts.

Dreeszen, Craig, et al. Fundamentals of Local Arts Management. LC 94-71905. (Illus.). 310p. 1994. reprint ed. pap. 25.00 (*0-945464-07-X*) Univ MA Arts.

Drefahl, Axel & Reinhard, Martin. Estimating Physico-Chemical Properties of Organic Compounds Using DESOC: Data Evaluation System for Organic Compounds 1.1. (Illus.). 54p. (C). 1995. ring bd. 89.95 incl. disk (*1-887981-02-0*) Stanford Bookstore.

— Handbook for Estimating Physico-Chemical Properties of Organic Compounds. (Illus.). 230p. (C). 1995. ring bd. 59.95 (*1-887981-01-2*) Stanford Bookstore.

Drefahl, Axel, jt. auth. see Reinhard, Martin.

Drefahl, Axel, jt. auth. see Reinhard, Michael.

Dreger, Alice D. Hermaphrodites & the Medical Invention of Sex. LC 97-40487. 320p. 1999. text 35.00 (*0-674-08927-8*) HUP.

***Dreger, Alice Domurat.** Hermaphrodites & the Medical Invention of Sex. 2000. pap. text 16.95 (*0-674-00189-3*) HUP.

***Dreger, Alice Domurat, ed.** Intersex in the Age of Ethics. (Ethics in Clinical Medicine Ser.). (Illus.). 240p. 1999. lib. bdg. 45.00 (*1-55572-125-7*) Univ Pub Group.

— Intersex in the Age of Ethics. (Ethics in Clinical Medicine Ser.). (Illus.). 240p. (C). 1999. pap. 19.95 (*1-55572-100-1*) Univ Pub Group.

Dreger, Amy. A Citizen's Guide to Cleveland. 3rd ed. (Illus.). 80p. 1999. pap. write for info. (*1-880746-08-5*) LOWV Cleve Educ.

Dreger, Georgia, ed. see Sutton, Tommy.

Dreger, Ralph, ed. Multivariate Personality Research. 1972. 17.50 (*0-87511-029-0*) Claitors.

Dreger, Ralph M., ed. Proceedings of the Convocation on the Status of the Bill of Rights after 200 Years. viii, 50p. (C). 1992. pap. text 2.00 (*0-9635887-0-2*) LA Coun Hum Relat.

Dregne, H. E. Desertification of Arid Lands. LC 83-83969. (Advances in Desert & Arid Land Technology & Development Ser.: Vol. 3). (Illus.). x, 242p. 1983. text 114.00 (*3-7186-0168-0*) Gordon & Breach.

Dregne, H. E. & Willis, W. O., eds. Dryland Agriculture. (Agronomy Monograph Ser.: No. 23). (Illus.). 622p. 1983. 35.00 (*0-89118-075-3*) Am Soc Agron.

Dregni, Eric. Scooter Mania. LC 98-29634. (Illus.). 96p. 1998. pap. 14.95 (*0-7603-0446-7*) Motorbooks Intl.

Dregni, Eric, et al. Bake My Pie by Vinnie & the Stardusters: The Pie's Gone Out. unabridged ed. (Vinnie & the Stardusters Road to Stardumb Ser.). (Illus.). 20p. (Orig.). 1997. pap. 5.00 (*1-890529-03-6*) Simple Sense.

— Vinnie & the Stardusters: The Girl from Ipanema Wants to Kill Me. (Illus.). 24p. (Orig.). 1996. pap. 5.00 (*1-890529-01-X*) Simple Sense.

***Dregni, Eric, et al.** XXXMas Song, Ode to a Pig: Plus: Vivaldi's Three Seasons. unabridged ed. (Vinnie & the Stardusters Ser.: Pt. 4). (Illus.). 20p. 1998. pap. 5.00 (*1-890529-07-9*) Simple Sense.

Dregni, Eric, jt. auth. see Dregni, Michael.

Dregni, Meredith S. Experiencing More with Less. LC 83-80954. 88p. (Orig.). 1983. pap. 4.99 (*0-8361-3334-X*) Herald Pr.

Dregni, Michael. Harley-Davidson Collectibles. LC 97-44769. (Illus.). 160p. 1998. 14.95 (*0-89658-367-8*) Voyageur Pr.

— The Indianapolis 500. (Motorsports Ser.). (Illus.). 48p. (J). (gr. 3-6). 1994. lib. bdg. 19.00 (*0-516-35205-9*) Childrens.

***Dregni, Michael.** The Spirit of the Motorcycle: The Legends, the Riders & the Beauty of the Beast. LC 99-86262. (Town Square Bk.). (Illus.). 160p. 2000. 35.00 (*0-89658-450-X*) Voyageur Pr.

Dregni, Michael, ed. Loons: Song of the Wild: An Anthology of Writing, Photography, & Art from Throughout the World on the Five Species of Loons. LC 95-40899. (Illus.). 108p. 1996. 9.95 (*0-89658-279-5*) Voyageur Pr.

— Minnesota Days: Our Heritage in Stories, Art & Photos. LC 99-20679. (Illus.). 1999. 35.00 (*0-89658-421-6*) Voyageur Pr.

***Dregni, Michael, ed.** 101 Uses for an Old Farm Tractor. (Illus.). 108p. 2000. 14.95 (*0-89658-496-8*) Voyageur Pr.

— 100 Years of Vintage Farm Tractors: A Century of Tractor Tales & Heartwarming Family Farm Memories. LC 99-42237. (Town Square Bks.). (Illus.). 160p. 2000. 29.95 (*0-89658-462-3*) Voyageur Pr.

— Our Florida: Heritage of the Sunshine State in Stories & Photos. LC 00-44771. (Illus.). 160p. 2000. 29.95 (*0-89658-483-6*) Voyageur Pr.

Dregni, Michael, ed. This Old Farm: A Treasury of Family Farm Memories. LC 98-37711. (Town Square Bks.). (Illus.). 160p. 1999. 29.95 (*0-89658-411-9*) Voyageur Pr.

***Dregni, Michael, ed.** This Old Harley: The Ultimate Tribute to the World's Greatest Motorcycle. LC 00-38155. (Illus.). 160p. 2000. 29.95 (*0-89658-443-7*) Voyageur Pr.

Dregni, Michael & Berger, Todd R., eds. Love of Labs: The Ultimate Triibute to Labrador Retrievers. LC 97-7939. (World's Greatest Dogs Ser.). (Illus.). 160p. 1997. 29.95 (*0-89658-356-2*) Voyageur Pr.

— This Old Tractor: A Treasury of Vintage Tractors & Family Farm Memories. LC 97-44770. (Illus.). 160p. 1998. 29.95 (*0-89658-368-6*) Voyageur Pr.

Dregni, Michael & Dregni, Eric. Illustrated Motorscooter Buyer's Guide. LC 93-13170. (Illustrated Buyer's Guide Ser.). (Illus.). 160p. 1993. pap. 17.95 (*0-87938-791-2*) MBI Pubg.

— Scooters! LC 95-24758. (Crestline Ser.). (Illus.). 160p. 1995. pap. 19.95 (*0-7603-0072-0*, Crestline Pub) MBI Pubg.

Dregni, Michael, ed. Loons: Song of the Wild. (Illus.). 108p. 1999. pap. 9.95 (*0-89658-425-9*) Voyageur Pr.

Drehbiel, Henry E. A Book of Operas: Their Histories, Plots, & Music: Music Book Index. 1993. reprint ed. lib. bdg. 99.00 (*0-7812-9720-6*) Rprt Serv.

An Asterisk (*) at the beginning of an entry indicates that the title is appearing for the first time.

Dreher. Employee Selection Decision Making. (GC - Principles of Management Ser.). 1997. text 26.95 (*0-538-81482-9*) S-W Pub.

Dreher, Anna U., jt. auth. see Sandler, Joseph.

***Dreher, Anna Ursula.** The Concept of Research in Psychoanalysis. 256p. 2000. pap. 33.00 (*1-85575-244-1*, Pub. by H Karnac Bks Ltd) Other Pr LLC.

Dreher, Barbara. Communication Skills for Working with Elders, No. 17. (Adulthood & Aging Ser.). 160p. (C). 1987. pap. 25.95 (*0-8261-5620-7*) Springer Pub.

Dreher, Barbara B. & Alter, Joseph D. Interdisciplinary Casebook in Geriatric Communication. 96p. 1992. pap. text 19.95 (*0-8261-8160-0*) Springer Pub.

Dreher, Christine. The Cleanse Cookbook. (Illus.). xii, 204p. 1997. pap. 15.95 (*0-9658687-7-X*) Christines Clnse Crnr.

Dreher, Denise. From the Neck Up: An Illustrated Guide to Hatmaking. LC 80-83507. (Illus.). 206p. 1982. pap. 25.00 (*0-941082-00-8*) Madhatter.

***Dreher, Diane.** Inner Gardening. 2001. write for info. (*0-688-17812-X*, Wm Morrow) Morrow Avon.

— The Tao of Inner Peace. 2000. reprint ed. pap. 14.00 (*0-452-28199-7*, Plume) Dutton Plume.

Dreher, Diane. The Tao of Inner Peace. LC 90-55632. 320p. 1991. reprint ed. pap. 13.50 (*0-06-097375-7*, Perennial) HarperTrade.

— The Tao of Womanhood. LC 97-36907. 224p. 1998. 22.00 (*0-688-15114-0*, Wm Morrow) Morrow Avon.

— The Tao of Womanhood: Ten Lessons for Power & Peace. 256p. 1999. pap. 11.00 (*0-688-16629-6*, Quil) HarperTrade.

Dreher, Diane & Tzu, Lao. The Tao of Personal Leadership. 224p. 1996. pap. 13.00 (*0-88730-837-6*, HarpBusn) HarpInfo.

Dreher, Diane, jt. auth. see Farrow, Genevieve.

Dreher, Diane E. Domination & Defiance: Fathers & Daughters in Shakespeare. LC 85-13482. 216p. 1986. 28.00 (*0-8131-1557-4*) U Pr of Ky.

Dreher, E. Der Mensch Zwischen Anschauungen und Abstraktion. (Schriftenreihe des Instituts fuer Konfliktforschung Ser.: Vol. 8). x, 54p. 1982. pap. 10.00 (*3-8055-3489-2*) S Karger.

Dreher, E., ed. Bernisches Mammasymposium: Festschrift fuer Max Berger Mammasymposium, Bern, September 1987. (Journal: Gynaekologische Rundschau: Vol. 28, Suppl. 1, 1988). (Illus.). vi, 94p. 1988. pap. 30.50 (*3-8055-4832-X*) S Karger.

— Schweizerische Gesellschaft fuer Gynaekologie, Bericht ueber die Jahresversammlung, Montreux, Juni 1979. (Journal: Gynaekologische Rundschau: Vol. 19, Suppl. 2). 1980. pap. 28.75 (*3-8055-0456-X*) S Karger.

— Schweizerische Gesellschaft fuer Gynaekologie Bericht ueber die Jahresversammlung, St. Gallen. J 1980. (Journal: Gynaekologische Rundschau: Vol. 20, No. 1). (Illus.). iv, 144p. 1981. pap. 28.75 (*3-8055-2126-X*) S Karger.

— Schweizerische Gesellschaft fuer Gynaekologie und Geburtshilfe: Societe Suisse de Gynecologie et Obstetrique , Bericht ueber die Jahresversammlung, St. Moritz, April 1984. (Journal: Gynaekologische Rundschau: Vol. 24, Suppl. 1). iv, 160p. 1985. pap. 41.75 (*3-8055-3964-9*) S Karger.

— Schweizerische Gesellschaft fuer Gynaekologie und Geburtshilfe: Societe Suisse de Gynecologie et Obstetrique, Bericht ueber die Jahresversammlung Lugano, Juni 1, 1985. (Journal: Gynaekologische Rundschau: Vol. 25, Suppl. 2, 1985). (Illus.). ii, 92p. 1986. pap. 24.50 (*3-8055-4242-9*) S Karger.

— Schweizerische Gesellschaft fuer Gynaekologie und Geburtshilfe, Bericht ueber die Jahresversammlung, Lausanne, Juni 1983. (Journal: Gynaekologische Rundschau: Vol. 23, Suppl. 4). (Illus.). iv, 116p. 1984. pap. 28.75 (*3-8055-3815-4*) S Karger.

— Schweizerische Gesellschaft fuer Gynaekologie und Geburtshilfe unter Mitkirkung der Schweizerischen Gesellschaft fuer Medizinische Genetik. Bericht ueber die Jahresversammlung, Zuerich, 1982. (Journal: Gynaekologische Rundschau: Vol. 22, Suppl. 3). (Illus.). xiv, 104p. 1983. pap. 34.00 (*3-8055-3656-9*) S Karger.

— Societe Suisse de Gynecologie, Bericht ueber die Jahresversammlung, Genf, 1981. (Gynaekologische Rundschau Journal: Vol. 21, Suppl. 3). (Illus.). iv, 88p. 1981. pap. 25.25 (*3-8055-3479-5*) S Karger.

Dreher, G. K. A Meditative Medley: Ourselves & One Other: Images Tied Together by a View-of-Faithful-Response-to-Jesus Theme. LC 91-77731. (Illus.). 64p. (Orig.). 1992. pap. 4.95 (*0-9601000-3-2*) Longshanks Bk.

Dreher, George K. Now the Dog Is Quiet: Romain Will Knock. LC 95-77979. 72p. (Orig.). 1995. pap. 4.95 (*0-9601000-4-0*) Longshanks Bk.

— Samuel Huntington, President of Congress "Longer Than Expected" A Narrative Essay on the Letters of Samuel Huntington, 1779-1781. LC 95-45949. (Illus.). 240p. (C). 1995. pap. 12.95 (*0-9601000-6-7*); lib. bdg. 24.50 (*0-9601000-5-9*) Longshanks Bk.

Dreher, George K., ed. see Peele, George.

Dreher, Henry, jt. auth. see Chiel, Samuel.

Dreher, Henry, jt. auth. see Domar, Alice D.

Dreher, Henry, jt. auth. see Temoshok, Lydia.

Dreher, Henry, jt. auth. see Torre, Joe.

Dreher, Jacob, jt. auth. see Perry, William W.

Dreher, Jean. Iron Horses-Iron Men. (Illus.). 130p. (J). (gr. 10 up). 1984. 12.95 (*0-912113-20-0*); pap. 5.95 (*0-912113-21-9*) Railhead Pubns.

Dreher, Luis H. Metaphors of Light: Philipp K. Marheineke's Method & the Ongoing Program of Mediating Theology. 240p. 1998. 86.00 (*3-11-015828-0*) De Gruyter.

— Metaphors of Light: Philipp K. Marheineke's Method & the Ongoing Program of Mediation Theology, Vol. 622. LC 98-33535. (European University Studies: No. 23). 245p. 1998. pap. text 40.95 (*0-8204-3435-3*) P Lang Pubng.

Dreher, M. & Gordon, D. T. Dietary Fiber Handbook. 2nd expanded rev. ed. (Food Science & Technology Ser.). (Illus.). Date not set. text. write for info. (*0-8247-9345-5*, 9345-5) Dekker.

***Dreher, Mariam Jean, et al, eds.** Engaging Young Readers: Promoting Achievement & Motivation. LC 99-56748. (Solving Problems in the Teaching of Literacy Ser.). 328p. 2000. pap. text 24.95 (*1-57230-535-5*, C0535) Guilford Pubns.

Dreher, Mark L. Handbook of Dietary Fiber: An Applied Approach. (Food Science & Technology Ser.: Vol. 25). (Illus.). 488p. 1987. text 165.00 (*0-8247-7655-0*) Dekker.

Dreher, Martin. Hegemon & Symmachoi: Untersuchungen Zum Zweiten Athenischen Seebund. (Untersuchungen zur Antiken Literatur und Geschichte: Bd 46). (GER.). xi, 316p. (C). 1995. lib. bdg. 152.30 (*3-11-014444-1*) De Gruyter.

Dreher, Sarah. Bad Company: A Stoner McTavish Mystery. LC 94-37032. 235p. 1995. pap. 10.95 (*0-934678-66-9*); trans. 19.95 (*0-934678-67-7*) New Victoria Pubs.

— A Captive in Time. LC 90-31304. (Stoner McTavish Mystery Ser.). 256p. (Orig.). 1990. pap. 10.95 (*0-934678-22-7*) New Victoria Pubs.

— Gray Magic. LC 93-33332. (Stoner McTavish Mystery Ser.). (Orig.). 1987. pap. 9.95 (*0-934678-11-1*) New Victoria Pubs.

— Lesbian Stages: Plays by Sarah Dreher. LC 88-61508. 300p. (Orig.). 1988. pap. 9.95 (*0-934678-15-4*) New Victoria Pubs.

— Otherworld. LC 93-6977. (Stoner McTavish Mystery Ser.). 256p. (Orig.). 1993. pap. 10.95 (*0-934678-44-8*) New Victoria Pubs.

— Shaman's Moon. LC 98-12883. (Stoner McTavish Mystery Ser.). 197p. 1998. pap. 12.95 (*0-934678-91-X*) New Victoria Pubs.

— Solitaire & Brahms. LC 97-19545. 292p. 1997. pap. 12.95 (*0-934678-85-5*) New Victoria Pubs.

— Something Shady. LC 86-61106. (Stoner McTavish Mystery Ser.). 272p. 1986. pap. 8.95 (*0-934678-07-3*) New Victoria Pubs.

— Stoner McTavish. LC 94-1758. (Stoner McTavish Mystery Ser.). 200p. 1985. pap. 9.95 (*0-934678-06-5*) New Victoria Pubs.

Drehobl. Pediatric Massage. 1998. pap. 36.00 (*0-12-784569-0*) Acad Pr.

Drehobl, Kathy F. & Fuhr, Mary G. Pediatric Massage Manual: For the Child with Special Needs. (Illus.). 128p. 1991. pap. text 38.00 (*0-7616-4703-1*) Commun Skill.

***Drehobl, Kathy Fleming & Fuhr, Mary Gengler.** Pediatric Massage for the Child with Special Needs. rev. ed. LC 00-8442. 2000. pap. write for info. (*0-7616-4092-4*, Thrpy Skill Bldrs) Commun Skill.

Drehsen, G. & Engel, J. Structure-Activity Relationships of Thiophene Derivatives of Biological Interest, Vol. 3. 46p. 1983. pap. text 85.00 (*3-7186-0181-8*) Gordon & Breach.

Drehsen, Volker, et al, eds. Der Ganze Mensch: Perspektiven Lebensgeschichtlicher Individualitaet. (Arbeiten Zue Praktischen Theologie Ser.: Vol. 10). (GER.). xii, 477p. (C). 1997. lib. bdg. 191.45 (*3-11-015494-3*) De Gruyter.

Drehwald, Uwe. Epiphytische Pflanzengesellschaften in NO-Argentinien. (Dissertationes Botanicae Ser.: Band 250). (Illus.). 182p. 1995. pap. 48.00 (*3-443-64162-8*, Pub. by Gebruder Borntraeger) Balogh.

***Dreibrodt, Stacie Champlin.** Heaven. Robbins, Dawn Michelle, ed. (YA). 1999. 9.95 (*1-58130-612-1*) Novel Units.

— Holes. (YA). 1999. 11.95 (*1-58130-615-6*); 9.95 (*1-58130-614-8*) Novel Units.

— Little Women. (YA). 2000. 9.95 (*1-58130-630-X*); 11.95 (*1-58130-631-8*) Novel Units.

— Man Who Was Poe. Robbins, Dawn Michelle, ed. (YA). 1999. 11.95 (*1-58130-617-2*); 9.95 (*1-58130-616-4*) Novel Units.

— Stranded. (J). 1999. 11.95 (*1-58130-609-1*); 9.95 (*1-58130-608-3*) Novel Units.

— Where the Lilies Bloom. (YA). 2000. 9.95 (*1-58130-634-2*); 11.95 (*1-58130-635-0*) Novel Units.

***Dreibrodt, Stacie Champlin & Robbins, Dawn Michelle.** Heaven. (YA). 1999. 11.95 (*1-58130-613-X*) Novel Units.

Dreicer, Gregory K., ed. Between Fences. LC 96-8436. (Illus.). 80p. (Orig.). 1996. pap. 17.95 (*1-56898-080-9*) Princeton Arch.

Dreier, John C. International Organization in the Western Hemisphere. Gregg, Robert W., ed. LC 68-15908. 272p. reprint ed. pap. 84.40 (*0-608-15213-7*, 202740700055) Bks Demand.

Dreier, Patricia, compiled by. The Gold of Friendship: A Bouquet of Special Thoughts. (Illus.). 1980. 8.95 (*0-8378-1707-2*) Gibson.

Dreier, Peter. Housing Policy & Devolution: A Delicate Balancing Act. (Devolution Revolution Ser.). 120p. 1998. pap. 10.95 (*0-87078-427-7*) Century Foundation.

Dreier, Peter, jt. auth. see Porter, Jack N.

Dreier, Susan & Moriarty, Phyllis A. Isa Dreler: Paintings & Drawings. LC 98-93515. (Illus.). 72p. 1998. pap. 20.00 (*0-9665818-0-6*) Flying Mtn.

Dreier, Ted. Moozie's Cow Wisdom for Grabbing Life by the Horns, Vol. 2. LC 99-90040. (Illus.). 96p. 1999. 4.95 (*0-9662268-2-8*, CWII) Best Frnds Bks.

— Moozie's Cow Wisdom for Life's Little Beefs. (Illus.). 96p. 1998. 4.95 (*0-9662268-0-1*, CW1) Best Frnds Bks.

Dreier, Ted, jt. auth. see Morton, Jane.

Dreier, William A. & Rose, Paul A. Guidebook to Chancery Practice in New Jersey (1991) 3rd ed. (Illus.). 463p. ring bd. 75.00 (*0-685-65970-4*) NJ Inst CLE.

Dreier, William A., et al. Products Liability & Toxic Tort Law in New Jersey: A Practitioner's Guide (1983) 639p. 1988. suppl. ed. 30.00 (*0-685-65976-3*) NJ Inst CLE.

— Products Liability & Toxic Tort Law in New Jersey: A Practitioner's Guide (1988) 6th ed. 639p. 1988. ring bd., suppl. ed. 75.00 (*0-685-65975-5*) NJ Inst CLE.

— Secured Transactions under the Revised Uniform Commercial Code, 1989. 3rd ed. LC 86-104417 228p. ring bd. 65.00 (*0-685-65979-8*) NJ Inst CLE.

Dreifelds, Juris. Latvia in Transition. LC 97-721. 224p. (C). 1996. text 59.95 (*0-521-47131-1*) Cambridge U Pr.

Dreifkluft, Jolanda, jt. auth. see Koops, Aaldrick.

Dreifort, John E. Myopic Grandeur: The Ambivalence of French Foreign Policy Toward the Far East, 1919-1945. LC 91-11434. 352p. 1992. 35.00 (*0-87338-441-5*) Kent St U Pr.

— Yvon Delbos at the Quai D'Orsay: French Foreign Policy During the Popular Front, 1936-1938. LC 72-85252. xiv, 274p. 1973. 29.95 (*0-7006-0094-9*) U Pr of KS.

***Dreifort, John E., ed.** Baseball History from Outside the Lines: A Reader. (Illus.). (C). 2001. pap. text 24 95 (*0-8032-6587-5*, Bison Books) U of Nebr Pr.

Dreifus, Claudia. Interview. LC 96-37549. (Illus.). 280p. 1997. 24.95 (*1-888363-42-8*) Seven Stories.

— Interview. (Illus.). 336p. 1999. pap. 16.95 (*1-888363-90-8*, Pub. by Seven Stories) Publishers Group.

Dreifus, D. L., et al, eds. Diamond for Electronic Applications: Materials Research Society Symposium Proceedings, Vol. 416. 477p. 1996. 81.00 (*1-55899-319-3*) Materials Res.

Dreifus, Henry N. Smart Cards: A Guide to Building & Managing Smartcard Applications. LC 97-36221. 352p. 1997. pap. 39.99 (*0-471-15748-1*) Wiley.

Dreifus, L. S., ed. Management of Cardiac Arrhythmias - Update, 1990: Journal: Cardiology, Vol. 77, No. 3, 1990. (Illus.). 124p. 1990. pap. 77.50 (*3-8055-5308-0*) S Karger.

Dreifus, Leonard S. & Brest, Albert N., eds. Clinical Applications of Cardiovascular Drugs. (Developments in Cardiovascular Medicine Ser.: No. 5). (Illus.). 275p. 1980. lib. bdg. 123.50 (*90-247-2295-0*) Kluwer Academic.

— Clinical Applications of Cardiovascular Drugs. (Developments in Cardiovascular Medicine Ser. No. 5). (Illus.). 1973. 275p. 1980. pap. text 85.50 (*90-247-2309-8*) Kluwer Academic.

Dreifuss, Gustav & Riemer, Judith. Abraham - The Man & the Symbol: A Jungian Interpretation of the Biblical Story. LC 95-14100. 148p. (Orig.). 1995. pap. 14.95 (*0-933029-94-2*) Chiron Pubns.

Dreifuss-Kattan, Esther. Cancer Stories: Creativity & Self-Repair. (Psychoanalytic Inquiry Book Ser.: Vol. 11). 288p. 1994. reprint ed. pap. 27.50 (*0-88163-204-X*) Analytic Pr.

Dreijer, Matts. History of the Aland People: From the Stone Age to Gustavus Wasa. (Illus.). 561p. (Orig.). 1986. pap. text 53.00 (*91-22-00799-7*) Coronet Bks.

Dreikausen, Margret. Aerial Perception. LC 82-65880. (Illus.). 1985. 35.00 (*0-87982-040-3*) Art Alliance.

Dreikorn, Michael J. Aviation Industry Quality Systems: ISO 9000 & the Federal Aviation Regulations. LC 94-43754. (Illus.). 337p. 1995. 67.00 (*0-87389-331-X*, H0888) ASQ Qual Pr.

Dreikurs, Rudolf. Adult-Child Relations. 1972. reprint ed. pap. 6.00 (*0-918560-13-6*) Adler Sch Prof Psy.

— Child Guidance & Education: Collected Papers. pap. 6.50 (*0-918560-11-X*) Adler Sch Prof Psy.

— Discipline Without Tears. 1991. pap. 11.95 (*0-452-26898-2*, Plume) Dutton Plume.

— Fundamentals of Adlerian Psychology. LC 72-18801. 117p. 1989. pap. 11.95 (*0-918560-08-X*) Adler Sch Prof Psy.

— Social Equality. LC 83-72318. 1971. pap. 9.95 (*0-918560-30-6*) Adler Sch Prof Psy.

Dreikurs, Rudolf, et al. Children: The Challenge. 1991. pap. 13.95 (*0-452-26655-6*, Plume) Dutton Plume.

— Maintaining Sanity in the Classroom: Classroom Management Techniques. 2nd ed. LC 97-43852 1998. pap. write for info. (*1-56032-727-8*) Hemisp Pub.

— Multiple Psychotherapy. LC 84-71164. 146p. (Orig.). 1984. pap. 10.00 (*0-918560-31-4*) Adler Sch Prof Psy.

Dreikurs, Rudolf, jt. auth. see Blumenthal, Erik.

Dreikurs, Sadie. Cows Can Be Purple. 1986. pap. 9 95 (*0-918560-32-2*) Adler Sch Prof Psy.

***Dreiling, Michael C.** Solidarity & Contention: The Politics of Security & Sustainability in the Nafta Conflict. LC 00-42691. (Studies in the History of American Labor). 2000. write for info. (*0-8153-3873-2*) Garland.

Dreilinger, Marilyn. How to Be a Confident Single Parent. (Family Forum Library). 16p. 1992. 1.95 (*1-56688-042-4*) Bur For At-Risk.

— School Attendance, Truancy & Dropping Out. (Family Forum Library). 16p. 1992. 1.95 (*1-56688-043-2*) Bur For At-Risk.

Dreilinger, Marilyn & Kerner, Ron. How to Help Children Succeed in School. (Family Forum Library). 16p. 1992. 1.95 (*1-56688-007-6*) Bur For At-Risk.

— Latchkey Kids: Their Safety & Care. (Family Forum Library). 16p. 1992. 1.95 (*1-56688-006-8*) Bur For At-Risk.

Dreilinger, Sigmund, ed. Indoor Bonsai. (Plants & Gardens Ser.). (Illus.). 1991. per. 7.95 (*0-945352-59-X*) Bklyn Botanic.

Dreimiller, David. Sports Officiating Career Handbook: You Call the Shots. unabridged ed. LC 99-71520. (Illus.). 476p. 1999. pap. 49.00 (*0-936217-49-9*) LR Pub.

Dreimiller, Jeannine, ed. Lawyers Register International by Specialties & Fields of Law: Including a Directory of Corporate Counsel. 15th rev. ed. 2088p. 1998. 329.00 (*0-936217-50-2*) LR Pub.

— Lawyer's Register International by Specialties & Fields of Law: Including a Directory of Corporate Counsel, 3 vols. 16th ed. 1978p. 1999. 329.00 (*0-936217-52-9*) LR Pub.

Dreinhofer, D. L., ed. see Lawless, Donald I.

Dreisbach, Ardis, tr. see Coppens, Christian, ed.

***Dreisbach, Bob.** Seattle Outdoors: Hiking & Cycling: Puget Sound & Cascades. LC 00-130197. 384p. 2000. pap. 20.00 (*0-942153-13-8*) Entropy Conserv.

Dreisbach, Carl. Middle Fork Guide: Seattle Local Mountain Day Trips. LC 96-95107. (Illus.). 124p. 1998. pap. 11.95 (*0-942153-01-4*) Entropy Conserv.

Dreisbach, Christopher, ed. R. G. Collingwood: A Bibliographic Checklist. 139p. 1993. 29.00 (*0-912632-93-3*) Philos Document.

Dreisbach, Daniel A. & Varallo, Gregory V. The Board of Directors. (Coporate Practice Ser.: No. 63). 1994. 95.00 (*1-55871-297-6*) BNA.

Dreisbach, Daniel A., jt. auth. see Varallo, Gregory V.

Dreisbach, Daniel L. Religion & Politics in the Early Republic: Jasper Adams & the Church-State Debate. LC 95-37861. (Illus.). 240p. 1996. pap. text 17.00 (*0-8131-0880-2*) U Pr of Ky.

— Religion & Politics in the Early Republic: Jasper Adams & the Church-State Debate. LC 95-37861. (Illus.). 240p. (C). 1996. text 34.95 (*0-8131-1950-2*) U Pr of Ky.

***Dreisbach, Daniel L. & Sheldon, Garrett Ward, eds.** Religion & Political Culture in Jefferson's Virginia. 288p. 2000. text 65.00 (*0-7425-0774-2*) Rowman.

— Religion & Political Culture in Jefferson's Virginia. 288p. 2000. pap. 24.95 (*0-7425-0775-0*) Rowman.

Dreisbach, Donald F. Symbols & Salvation: Paul Tillich's Doctrine of Religious Symbols & His Interpretation of the Symbols of the Christian Tradition. 250p. (Orig.). (C). 1992. lib. bdg. 54.50 (*0-8191-8788-7*) U Pr of Amer.

Dreisbach, Ftritz, ed. see Giberson, Dudley F.

***Dreisbach, R. H. & True, B.** Dreisbach's Handbook of Poisoning. 13th ed. (Illus.). 600p. 2001. 42.00 (*1-85070-038-9*) Prthnon Pub.

Dreisbach, Robert H. Guide to Northeast Oregon. LC 94-62219. 160p. (Orig.). 1995. pap. 8.95 (*0-942153-14-6*) Entropy Conserv.

— Handbook of the San Francisco Region. LC 71-105927. 564p. 1969. pap. 10.00 (*0-942153-16-2*) Entropy Conserv.

***Dreisbach, Robert H., ed.** Pyramid Building & Its Consequences. 48p. 2000. pap. text 5.00 (*0-942153-12-X*, 27388X) Entropy Conserv.

Dreisbach, Robert R. Physical Properties of Chemical Compounds - II: A Systematic Tabular Presentation of Accurate Data on the Physical Properties of 476 Organic Straight-Chain Compounds. LC QD0001.A355. (Advances in Chemistry Ser.: No. 22). 495p. 1959. reprint ed. pap. 153.50 (*0-608-03268-9*, 206378700007) Bks Demand.

— Physical Properties of Chemical Compounds - III. LC QD0001.A355. (Advances in Chemistry Ser.: No. 29). 495p. 1961. reprint ed. pap. 153.50 (*0-608-03270-0*, 206378900007) Bks Demand.

Dreiser, Theodore. An American Tragedy. Date not set. pap. text. write for info. (*0-17-557044-2*) Addison-Wesley.

— An American Tragedy. 832p. Date not set. 38.95 (*0-8488-2253-6*) Amereon Ltd.

Dreiser, Theodore. An American Tragedy. (Signet Classics Ser.). 1964. mass mkt. 9.95 (*0-451-52465-9*, Sig Classics) NAL.

Dreiser, Theodore. An American Tragedy. 1964. 14.05 (*0-606-00332-0*, Pub. by Turtleback) Demco.

***Dreiser, Theodore.** American Tragedy. 1999. 17.95 (*0-8085-0951-9*) Econo-Clad Bks.

— American Tragedy. 2000. mass mkt. 9.95 (*0-451-52770-4*, Sig Classics) NAL.

Dreiser, Theodore. An American Tragedy. LC 78-55741. 874 p. 1978. reprint ed. lib. bdg. 32.00 (*0-8376-0424-9*) Bentley Pubs.

— An American Tragedy. 1990. reprint ed. lib. bdg. 54.95 (*0-89966-709-0*) Buccaneer Bks.

***Dreiser, Theodore.** An American Tragedy. (Collected Works of Theodore Dreiser). 349p. 1998. reprint ed. lib. bdg. 98.00 (*1-58201-614-3*) Classic Bks.

Dreiser, Theodore. The Best Short Stories of Theodore Dreiser. 25.95 (*0-88411-539-9*) Amereon Ltd.

— The Best Short Stories of Theodore Dreiser. 348p. 1989. reprint ed. pap. 12.95 (*0-929587-03-0*, Elephant Paperbacks) I R Dee.

***Dreiser, Theodore.** A Book about Myself. (Collected Works of Theodore Dreiser). 502p. 1998. reprint ed. lib. bdg. 108.00 (*1-58201-615-1*) Classic Bks.

Dreiser, Theodore. The Color of a Great City. (Illus.). 210p. (C). 1996. pap. 19.95 (*0-8156-0336-3*, DRCGP) Syracuse U Pr.

***Dreiser, Theodore.** The Color of a Great City. (Collected Works of Theodore Dreiser). 287p. 1998. reprint ed. lib. bdg. 88.00 (*1-58201-616-X*) Classic Bks.

Dreiser, Theodore. Dawn: An autobiography of early youth. Nostwich, T. D., ed. LC 98-36735. 600p. 1998. 30.00 (*1-57423-074-3*) Black Sparrow.

— Dawn: An Autobiography of Early Youth. Nostwich, T. D., ed. LC 98-36735. 600p. 1998. pap. 17.50 (*1-57423-073-5*) Black Sparrow.

— Dawn: An autobiography of early youth. deluxe ed. Nostwich, T. D., ed. LC 98-36735. 600p. 1998. 35.00 (*1-57423-075-1*) Black Sparrow.

— Dreiser's Russian Diary. Riggio, Thomas P. & West, James L. W., III, eds. (Dreiser Edition Ser.). (Illus.). 320p. 1996. text 38.50 (*0-8122-8091-1*) U of Pa Pr.

D

An Asterisk (*) at the beginning of an entry indicates that the title is appearing for the first time.

— The Financier. 1976. 27.95 (*0-8488-0992-0*) Amereon Ltd.
— The Financier. 320p. 1967. pap. 14.95 (*0-452-00825-5*, Mer) NAL.
— The Financier. 1990. reprint ed. lib. bdg. 33.95 (*0-89966-710-4*) Buccaneer Bks.
***Dreiser, Theodore.** The Financier. (Collected Works of Theodore Dreiser). 779p. 1998. reprint ed. lib. bdg. 148.00 (*1-58201-617-8*) Classic Bks.
Dreiser, Theodore. The Financier. 1993. reprint ed. lib. bdg. 89.00 (*0-7812-5447-7*) Rprt Serv.
— Fine Furniture. LC 75-22164. (Studies in Fiction: No. 34). (C). 1975. lib. bdg. 75.00 (*0-8383-2107-0*) M S G Haskell Hse.
***Dreiser, Theodore.** Free & Other Stories. (Collected Works of Theodore Dreiser). 309p. 1998. reprint ed. lib. bdg. 88.00 (*1-58201-618-6*) Classic Bks.
Dreiser, Theodore. Free & Other Stories. 1988. reprint ed. lib. bdg. 69.00 (*0-7812-0130-6*) Rprt Serv.
— Free & Other Stories. LC 70-144984. 1971. reprint ed. 65.00 (*0-403-00949-9*) Scholarly.
— Fulfilment & Other Tales of Women & Men. Nostwich, T. D., ed. & intro. by. LC 92-25060. 410p. (C). 1992. pap. 15.00 (*0-87685-881-7*) Black Sparrow.
— The Genius. 1976. 27.95 (*0-8488-0994-7*) Amereon Ltd.
— The Genius. 463p. 1980. reprint ed. lib. bdg. 32.95 (*0-89968-206-5*, Lghtyr Pr) Buccaneer Bks.
***Dreiser, Theodore.** The Genius. (Collected Works of Theodore Dreiser). 736p. 1998. reprint ed. lib. bdg. 128.00 (*1-58201-619-4*) Classic Bks.
— The Hand of the Potter. (Collected Works of Theodore Dreiser). 209p. 1998. reprint ed. lib. bdg. 88.00 (*1-58201-620-8*) Classic Bks.
— Hey, Rub-a-Dub-Dub: A Book of the Mystery & Wonder & Terror of Life. (Collected Works of Theodore Dreiser). 312p. 1998. reprint ed. lib. bdg. 88.00 (*1-58201-621-6*) Classic Bks.
Dreiser, Theodore. A Hoosier Holiday. LC 96-51687. (Illus.). 560p. 1998. 25.00 (*0-253-33283-4*); pap. 14.95 (*0-253-21121-2*) Ind U Pr.
***Dreiser, Theodore.** A Hoosier Holiday. (Collected Works of Theodore Dreiser). 513p. 1998. reprint ed. lib. bdg. 88.00 (*1-58201-622-4*) Classic Bks.
Dreiser, Theodore. A Hoosier Holiday. (BCL1 - U. S. History Ser.). 513p. 1991. reprint ed. lib. bdg. 109.00 (*0-7812-6015-9*) Rprt Serv.
— A Hoosier Holiday. (American Biography Ser.). 513p. 1991. reprint ed. lib. bdg. 99.00 (*0-7812-8113-X*) Rprt Serv.
— Jennie Gerhardt. West, James L. W., III & Riggio, Thomas P., eds. (Dreiser Edition Ser.). (Illus.). 592p. (C). 1992. text 45.00 (*0-8122-8164-0*); pap. text 22.00 (*0-8122-1284-3*) U of Pa Pr.
— Jennie Gerhardt. West, James L. W., III, ed. & intro. by. LC 94-6634. 432p. 1994. pap. 11.95 (*0-14-018710-3*, Penguin Classics) Viking Penguin.
— Jennie Gerhardt. LC 88-12844. 431p. 1988. reprint ed. 29.25 (*0-933249-07-1*) Mid-Peninsula Lib.
— Jennie Gerhardt. 1993. reprint ed. lib. bdg. 89.00 (*0-7812-5358-6*) Rprt Serv.
***Dreiser, Theodore.** Jennie Gerhardt. rev. ed. (Collected Works of Theodore Dreiser). 432p. 1998. reprint ed. lib. bdg. 98.00 (*1-58201-623-2*) Classic Bks.
Dreiser, Theodore. Newspaper Days. Nostwich, T. D., ed. LC 91-30225. (Dreiser Edition Ser.). 840p. (C). 1991. text 54.95 (*0-8122-3095-7*) U of Pa Pr.
***Dreiser, Theodore.** Newspaper Days: An Autobiography. Nostwich, T. D., ed. 750p. 2000. 30.00 (*1-57423-139-1*); pap. 18.00 (*1-57423-138-3*) Black Sparrow.
Dreiser, Theodore. Plays of the Natural & the Supernatural. LC 73-97893. 1969. reprint ed. 32.50 (*0-404-02179-4*) AMS Pr.
***Dreiser, Theodore.** Plays of the Natural & the Supernatural. (Collected Works of Theodore Dreiser). 288p. 1998. reprint ed. lib. bdg. 88.00 (*1-58201-624-0*) Classic Bks.
Dreiser, Theodore. Plays of the Natural & the Supernatural. LC 74-131690. reprint ed. 69.00 (*0-403-00577-9*) Scholarly.
— Selected Magazine Articles of Theodore Dreiser. Hakutani, Yoshinobu, ed. & intro. by. LC 82-49316. (Illus.). 288p. 1985. 45.00 (*0-8386-3174-6*) Fairleigh Dickinson.
— Selected Magazine Articles of Theodore Dreiser: Life & Art in the American 1890s, Vol. 2. Hakutani, Yoshinobu, ed. LC 82-49316. (Illus.). 1987. 35.00 (*0-8386-3294-7*) Fairleigh Dickinson.
— Short Stories. unabridged ed. (Thrift Editions Ser.). 112p. (Orig.). 1994. reprint ed. pap. text 1.50 (*0-486-28215-5*) Dover.
— Sister Carrie. 474p. (C). 1957. pap. text 24.00 (*0-03-009075-X*, Pub. by Harcourt Coll Pubs) Harcourt.
***Dreiser, Theodore.** Sister Carrie. LC 99-51795. 2000. mass mkt. 5.95 (*0-451-52760-7*, Sig Classics) NAL.
— Sister Carrie. Mitchell, Lee Clark, ed. (Oxford World's Classics Ser.). 508p. 1999. pap. 10.95 (*0-19-283574-2*) OUP.
— Sister Carrie. (Penguin Twentieth-Century Classics). 1994. 18.05 (*0-606-04903-7*, Pub. by Turtleback) Demco.
Dreiser, Theodore. Sister Carrie. large type ed. 632p. 1997. reprint ed. lib. bdg. 25.00 (*0-939495-16-3*) North Bks.
— Sister Carrie. 557p. 1980. reprint ed. lib. bdg. 37.95 (*0-89968-207-3*, Lghtyr Pr) Buccaneer Bks.
***Dreiser, Theodore.** Sister Carrie. (Collected Works of Theodore Dreiser). 382p. 1998. reprint ed. lib. bdg. 98.00 (*1-58201-625-9*) Classic Bks.
— Sister Carrie. 453p. 1998. reprint ed. lib. bdg. 24.00 (*1-58287-071-3*) North Bks.
Dreiser, Theodore. Sister Carrie: An Authoritative Text, Backgrounds & Sources Criticism. LC 73-116120. (Norton Critical Editions Ser.). (Illus.). x, 591p. (J). 1970. write for info. (*0-393-04325-8*) Norton.
— Sister Carrie: One of Modern Library's 100 Best Novels. 1976. 27.95 (*0-8488-0993-9*) Amereon Ltd.
— Sister Carrie: One of Modern Library's 100 Best Novels. 432p. 1982. mass mkt. 4.95 (*0-553-21374-1*, Bantam Classics) Bantam.
— Sister Carrie: One of Modern Library's 100 Best Novels. LC 98-31433. 1999. pap. 9.95 (*0-375-75321-4*) Modern Lib NY.
— Sister Carrie: One of Modern Library's 100 Best Novels. 1962. mass mkt. 5.95 (*0-451-52273-7*, Sig Classics) NAL.
— Sister Carrie: One of Modern Library's 100 Best Novels. 496p. 1994. pap. 12.95 (*0-14-018828-2*, Penguin Classics) Viking Penguin.
— Sister Carrie: One of Modern Library's 100 Best Novels. LC 78-183140. 472p. 1971. reprint ed. lib. bdg. 20.00 (*0-8376-0401-X*) Bentley Pubs.
— Sister Carrie: One of Modern Library's 100 Best Novels. 2nd ed. Pizer, Donald, ed. (Critical Editions Ser.). 600p. (C). 1991. pap. text 16.75 (*0-393-96042-0*) Norton.
— Sister Carrie: The Edition. Berkey, John C. et al, eds. LC 97-48293. (University of Pennsylvania Dreiser Edition Ser.). 544p. 1997. pap. 19.95 (*0-8122-1638-5*) U of Pa Pr.
— Sister Carrie, Jennie Gerhardt, Twelve Men. Lehan, Richard, ed. LC 86-27583. 1168p. 1987. 40.00 (*0-940450-41-0*, Pub. by Library of America) Penguin Putnam.
— Theodore Dreiser: A Selection of Uncollected Prose. Pizer, Donald, ed. LC 77-771. 341p. reprint ed. pap. 105.80 (*0-7837-3658-4*, 204352900009) Bks Demand.
— Theodore Dreiser's Ev'ry Month. Barrineau, Nancy W., ed. LC 95-36582. 1996. 50.00 (*0-8203-1816-7*) U of Ga Pr.
— Theodore Dreiser's "Heard in the Corridors" Articles & Related Writings. LC 87-13095. 179p. 1988. reprint ed. pap. 55.50 (*0-608-00013-2*, 206077900006) Bks Demand.
— Theodore Dreiser's "Heard in the Corridors" Articles & Related Writings. Nostwich, T. D., ed. LC 87-13095. 179p. 1988. reprint ed. pap. 55.50 (*0-608-06878-0*, 2067086) Bks Demand.
— The Titan. LC 83-45747. reprint ed. 27.50 (*0-404-20084-2*) AMS Pr.
***Dreiser, Theodore.** The Titan. (Collected Works of Theodore Dreiser). 551p. 1998. reprint ed. lib. bdg. 118.00 (*1-58201-626-7*) Classic Bks.
— A Traveler at Forty. (Collected Works of Theodore Dreiser). 526p. 1998. reprint ed. lib. bdg. 118.00 (*1-58201-627-5*) Classic Bks.
Dreiser, Theodore. Twelve Men. Coltrane, Robert, ed. LC 97-48786. (University of Pennsylvania Dreiser Edition Ser.). 416p. (C). 1998. text 45.00 (*0-8122-3363-8*) U of Pa Pr.
— Twelve Men. (Collected Works of Theodore Dreiser). 360p. 1998. reprint ed. lib. bdg. 98.00 (*1-58201-628-3*) Classic Bks.
Dreiser, Theodore. Twelve Men. 1988. reprint ed. lib. bdg. 49.00 (*0-7812-0371-6*) Rprt Serv.
— Twelve Men. LC 74-144985. 1971. reprint ed. 69.00 (*0-403-00914-6*) Scholarly.
Dreiser, Theodore, et al, intros. Harlan Miners Speak: Report on Terrorism in the Kentucky Coal Fields. LC 70-107410. (Civil Liberties in American History Ser.). 1970. reprint ed. lib. bdg. 32.50 (*0-306-71889-8*) Da Capo.
***Dreiser, Theodore & Hakutani, Yoshinobu.** Art, Music, And Literature, 1897-1902. LC 00-9791. .p. 2001. write for info. (*0-252-02625-X*) U Pr of Amer.
Dreiser, Theodore, jt. auth. see Eastman, Yvette S.
Dreishpoon, Doug, jt. auth. see Lane, Alvin S.
Dreishpoon, Douglas. Artists Look at Themselves. Blundell, Jude, ed. (Illus.). 40p. (Orig.). 1996. pap. write for info. (*1-878293-11-7*) Tampa Mus Art.
— From a Curator's Point of View: Making Selections & Forging Connections. Schwartz, Sheila, ed. (Illus.). 44p. 1996. pap. text 16.00 (*0-9627541-8-8*) UNC Greensboro.
— Ronald Bladen (1918-1988) Drawings & Sculptural Models. Schwartz, Sheila, ed. (Illus.). 59p. (Orig.). 1996. pap. text 10.00 (*0-9627541-6-1*) UNC Greensboro.
Dreishpoon, Douglas, ed. Beth B: It's about Control. (Illus.). 16p. 1997. pap. text 5.00 (*1-890949-00-0*) UNC Greensboro.
Dreishpoon, Douglas & Fletcher, Valerie. Saul Baizerman's "The City & the People" Schwartz, Sheila, ed. LC 97-61175. (Illus.). 64p. (Orig.). 1997. pap. 15.00 (*0-9627541-9-6*) UNC Greensboro.
Dreishpoon, Douglas, jt. auth. see Moser, Joann.
Dreisinger, D. B., ed. Aqueous Electrotechnologies: Progress in Theory & Practice. (Illus.). 1200p. 1997. 114.00 (*0-87339-356-2*, 3562) Minerals Metals.
Dreisinger, D. B., jt. auth. see Cooper, W. C.
Dreismann, C. A., ed. New Frontiers in Theoretical Biology. (Illus.). 540p. (C). 1996. pap. text 85.00 (*1-57485-012-1*) Hadronic Pr Inc.
Dreiss, Joseph G. Gari Melchers, His Works in the Belmont Collection. Reid, Richard S., ed. LC 83-19775. 223p. 1984. reprint ed. pap. 69.20 (*0-608-05908-0*, 206624300007) Bks Demand.
Dreist, Edward R. Van, see Van Driest, Edward R., ed.
Dreistadt, Anne M. From the Bottom of My Heart: A Collection of Inspirational Poems & Writings. Glover, Jean, ed. LC 93-93690. 124p. (Orig.). 1993. pap. 5.95 (*0-9639128-0-1*) NIC Pubng.
Dreistadt, Steve H. Pests of Landscape Trees & Shrubs. LC 94-60514. (Illus.). 336p. 1994. pap. 32.00 (*1-879906-18-X*, 3359) ANR Pubns CA.
Dreisziger, N. F., ed. Ethnic Armies: Polyethnic Armed Forces from the Time of the Habsburgs to the Age of the Superpowers. 224p. (C). 1990. text 35.00 (*0-88920-993-6*) W Laurier U Pr.
Dreisziger, Nandor F., jt. ed. see Kiraly, Bela K.
Dreith, Rae L. Fares & Tickets. 10th ed. Scott, Sharon, ed. 242p. (C). 1995. spiral bd. 39.00 (*1-879982-44-7*) Educ Systs.
Dreitzler, James A. Don't Call Me Stupid: The Truth of Why Public Schools Fail! (Illus.). 210p. (Orig.). 1990. pap. 19.95 (*0-9627890-0-3*, TX3-006-244) Four D NV.
Dreizen, Laverne. Medical Assistant Examination Review. 4th ed. 267p. (C). 1989. pap. text 24.95 (*0-8385-5772-4*, A5772-7) Appleton & Lange.
Dreizen, S., jt. auth. see Levy, Barnet M.
***Dreizler, Bob & Armstrong, Robert.** Tending Your Money Garden. LC 98-91581. 136 p. 1998. 11.95 (*0-9663139-0-9*) Rossonya Bks.
Dreizler, Carl. 52 Maneras de Decir Te Amo. pap. 7.99 (*0-88113-175-X*) Caribe Betania.
— 52 Maneras de Perder Peso. (SPA.). pap. 7.99 (*0-88113-176-8*) Caribe Betania.
— Fun Things to Do with Your Child. (Illus.). 288p. 1995. 7.98 (*0-88365-895-X*) Galahad Bks.
Dreizler, Loch A. Princess Pickle Head. LC 88-80123. (Illus.). 42p. (Orig.). (J). (ps-4). 1988. pap. 2.95 (*0-9620053-0-4*) LAD Redondo Beach.
Dreizler, R. M., jt. auth. see Gross, E. K.
Dreizler, Reiner M. & Da Providencia, Joao, eds. Density Functional Methods in Physics. LC 85-3563. (NATO ASI Series B, Physics: Vol. 123). 542p. 1985. 120.00 (*0-306-41926-2*, Plenum Trade) Perseus Pubng.
Dreizler, Reiner M. & Gross, E. K. Density Functional Theory: An Approach to the Quantum Many-Body Problem. (Illus.). 320p. 1996. 109.50 (*0-387-51993-9*) Spr-Verlag.
Drek, Anton. Anton's Collected Drek. (Eros Graphic Novel Ser.: No. 2). 104p. 1992. pap. 16.95 (*1-56097-201-7*, Pub. by Fantagraph Bks) Seven Hills Bk.
Dreke & Lind. Wechselspiel. 160p. 1986. 37.00 (*3-468-49994-9*) Langenscheidt.
Dreke, et al. Deux a Deux. 128p. 1991. 35.00 (*3-468-49996-5*) Langenscheidt.
— Wechselspiel: Espanol en Pareja (Paired Activities) 136p. 1991. 35.00 (*3-468-49998-1*) Langenscheidt.
Dreke, Michael & Lind, Wolfgang. Wechselspiel: A Tu Per Tu. (ITA.). 112p. 1996. wbk. ed. 35.00 (*3-468-49997-3*) Langenscheidt.
— Wechselspiel: Espanol en Pareja (Paired Activities) (SPA.). 136p. 1996. wbk. ed. 33.50 (*3-468-44998-4*) Langenscheidt.
— Wechselspiel: Face to Face. 160p. 1996. wbk. ed. 35.00 (*3-468-49999-X*) Langenscheidt.
Drekmeier, Charles. Kingship & Community in Early India. LC 62-9565. 383p. 1962. reprint ed. pap. 30.00 (*0-7837-0005-9*, 200136200076) Bks Demand.
Dreksler, Sam, see Drexler, Sam, pseud.
***Drelich, J., et al, eds.** Apparent & Microscopic Contact Angles. (Illus.). 562p. 2000. 167.50 (*90-6764-321-1*, Pub. by Uppsala Universitet) Coronet Bks.
Drell, Persis S. & Rubin, David L., eds. Heavy Quark Physics. (AIP Conference Proceedings Ser.: No.196). 464p. 1991. lib. bdg. 75.00 (*0-88318-644-6*) Am Inst Physics.
Drell, S. D., et al, eds. Sakharov Remembered. 320p. 1991. 29.95 (*0-88318-853-8*) Am Inst Physics.
Drell, S. D., jt. auth. see Bjorken, James D.
Drell, Sidney D. In the Shadow of the Bomb: Physics & Arms Control. LC 92-46573. (Masters of Modern Physics Ser.). 1993. 34.95 (*1-56396-058-3*) Spr-Verlag.
***Drell, Sidney D., et al, eds.** The New Terror: Facing the Threat of Biological & Chemical Weapons. LC 99-41989. (Publication Series: Archival Documentaries: Vol. 462). 500p. 1999. pap. 24.00 (*0-8179-9702-4*) Hoover Inst Pr.
Drell, Sidney D. & Johnson, Thomas H. Technical Trends & Strategic Policy. (Occasional Paper of Center for International Security & Arms Control, Stanford University Ser.). 41p. (Orig.). 1988. pap. 9.00 (*0-935371-18-4*) CFISAC.
Dreller, Aletta, jt. auth. see Jeffrey, Anne E. F.
Dreller, Larry. A Beginner's Guide to Mediumship. LC 97-12765. 144p. (Orig.). 1999. reprint ed. pap. 9.95 (*1-57863-011-8*) Weiser.
***Drelos, Zoe Diana.** Atlas of Cosmetic Dermatology. (Illus.). 595p. 2000. text. write for info. (*0-443-06548-9*) Church.
Dreman, David N. Contrarian Investment Strategies, the Next Generation: Beat the Market Going Against the Crowd. LC 98-14660. 464p. (YA). 1998. 24.50 (*0-684-81350-5*) S&S Trade.
Dreman, Solly, ed. The Family on the Threshold of the 21st Century: Trend & Implications. LC 97-6089. 304p. (C). 1997. text 59.95 (*0-8058-2217-8*) L Erlbaum Assocs.
Dremann, Craig C. Cal-Oregon-Revegetation Notes: U. S. National Forests - Utilizing Locally Collected Seeds for Revegetation of Dry Forest Soils in California or Oregon. 3rd ed. (Illus.). 57p. (Orig.). (C). 1993. pap. 12.00 (*0-933421-40-0*) Redwood Seed.
— Chili Peppers in California. 2nd ed. (Illus.). 41p. (Orig.). 1986. pap. 6.00 (*0-933421-00-1*) Redwood Seed.
— Companion Plants: Carrots Really Detest Tomatoes. 7p. (Orig.). (YA). (gr. 6-12). 1994. pap. 2.50 (*0-933421-50-8*) Redwood Seed.
— Food Plants Used in Sardinia, Nineteen Hundred to Nineteen Twenty. (Illus.). 11p. (Orig.). 1986. reprint ed. pap. 2.50 (*0-933421-08-7*) Redwood Seed.
— Grasses of California: Dremann's Distribution Maps. (Illus.). 24p. (Orig.). (C). 1993. pap. 4.00 (*0-933421-27-3*) Redwood Seed.
— Grasses of European Origin & Their Impact upon California Bunchgrass: Stipa Pulchia. (Illus.). 6p. (Orig.). (C). 1993. pap. 3.50 (*0-933421-41-9*) Redwood Seed.
— Grasses to Grizzly Bears: Checklist for Revegetation & Reintroduction of the Valley Grassland & Oak Woodland Plants & Animals to the San Francisco Bay Area. 2nd ed. 28p. (Orig.). 1986. pap. 5.00 (*0-933421-04-4*) Redwood Seed.
— Ground Cherries, Husk Tomatoes & Tomatillos. (Illus.). 21p. (Orig.). 1986. pap. 5.75 (*0-933421-03-6*) Redwood Seed.
— Hippie Ethnobotany. 2000. pap. text. write for info. (*0-933421-09-5*) Redwood Seed.
— In Search of Bioregional Agriculture. 9p. (Orig.). (YA). (gr. 6-12). 1994. pap. 2.50 (*0-933421-51-6*) Redwood Seed.
— Organic Fertilizer: The Truth & the B. S. LC 86-30225. 40p. (Orig.). 1987. pap. 6.00 (*0-933421-17-6*) Redwood Seed.
— Peppers: Hotness Testing. (Illus.). 4p. (Orig.). 1993. pap. 2.50 (*0-933421-28-1*) Redwood Seed.
— Peppers: Seed Cleaning. (Illus.). 6p. (Orig.). 1993. pap. 2.50 (*0-933421-26-5*) Redwood Seed.
— Radical Vegetable Gardening. 19p. (Orig.). 1993. pap. 3.75 (*0-933421-37-0*) Redwood Seed.
— Redwood Forest & Native Grasses & Their Stories. (Orig.). 1987. pap. 3.00 (*0-933421-19-2*) Redwood Seed.
— San Bruno Mountain Habitat Conservation Scam. 2nd ed. 82p. 1987. pap. 85.00 (*0-933421-20-6*) Redwood Seed.
— Seed Testing Handbook. 1995. pap. write for info. (*0-933421-22-2*) Redwood Seed.
— Star Thistle Control with Grasses. 4p. (Orig.). (C). 1993. pap. 3.00 (*0-933421-49-4*) Redwood Seed.
— Vegetable Seed Production in the San Francisco Bay Area & Other Warm-Winter Areas in the United States. 4th ed. 1987. pap. 4.25 (*0-933421-24-9*) Redwood Seed.
Dremann, Craig C., ed. see Barry, James.
Dremann, Sue. Ristras. (Illus.). 8p. (Orig.). (gr. 6-12). 1993. pap. 2.25 (*0-933421-35-4*) Redwood Seed.
Dremann, Sue J. Peppers: Pickled, Sauces & Salsas. 54p. (Orig.). 1986. pap. 6.00 (*0-933421-05-2*) Redwood Seed.
Dremin, Anatolifi N. Toward Detonation Theory. LC 98-44698. (High Pressure Shock Compression of Condensed Matter Ser.). 176p. 1999. 79.95 (*0-387-98672-3*) Spr-Verlag.
Dremin, I. & Gulamov, K., eds. Multiparticle Dynamics, 1987: Proceedings of the 18th International Symposium on Multiparticle Dynamics. 832p. (C). 1988. text 147.00 (*9971-5-0507-X*) World Scientific Pub.
Drench, Meredith. Red Ribbons Are Not Enough: Health Caregivers' Stories about AIDS. LC 97-76822. 240p. 1998. pap. 14.95 (*1-885221-80-0*) BookPartners.
Drendel, J., jt. ed. see Reyerson, Kathryn L.
Drendel, Lou. A-6 Walk Around. LC 94-234328. (Walk Around Ser.). (Illus.). 80p. 1994. pap. 14.95 (*0-89747-327-2*) Squad Sig Pubns.
— And Kill Migs: Air to Air Combat from Vietnam to the Gulf War. 3rd ed. LC 97-225457. 104p. 1997. pap. 14.95 (*0-89747-381-7*) Squad Sig Pubns.
— B-52 Walk Around. (Walk Around Ser.). (Illus.). 80p. (Orig.). 1996. pap. 14.95 (*0-89747-358-2*, 5506) Squad Sig Pubns.
— B-17 Flying Fortress Walk Around. (Walk Around Ser.: Vol. 16). (Illus.). 80p. 1998. pap. 14.95 (*0-89747-397-3*, 5516) Squad Sig Pubns.
— Eagle. (Modern Military Aircraft Ser.). (Illus.). 72p. 1992. pap. 9.95 (*0-89747-271-3*, 5008) Squad Sig Pubns.
— F-14 Walk Around. (Walk Around Ser.). (Illus.). 80p. 1995. pap. 14.95 (*0-89747-337-X*) Squad Sig Pubns.
— The Intruder. (Modern Military Aircraft Ser.). (Illus.). 72p. 1991. pap. 9.95 (*0-89747-263-2*, 5007) Squad Sig Pubns.
— P-47 Thunderbolt Walk Around. LC 97-178717. (Walk Around Ser.: No. 11). (Illus.). 80p. (Orig.). 1997. pap. 14.95 (*0-89747-375-2*, 5511) Squad Sig Pubns.
— P-40 Warhawk Walk Around. (Walk Around Ser.: No. 8). (Illus.). 80p. (Orig.). 1996. pap. 14.95 (*0-89747-361-2*, 5508) Squad Sig Pubns.
***Drendel, Lou.** Space Shuttle Walk Around. (Walk Around Ser.: Vol. 20). (Illus.). 80p. 1999. pap. 14.95 (*0-89747-406-6*) Squad Sig Pubns.
Drendel, Lou. SR-71 Blackbird in Action. (Illus.). 50p. 1982. pap. 9.95 (*0-89747-136-9*, 1055) Squad Sig Pubns.
— USMC Phantoms in Combat. (Vietnam Studies Group). (Illus.). 80p. 1990. pap. 9.95 (*0-89747-235-7*, 6353) Squad Sig Pubns.
— Viper: F-16. (Modern Military Aircraft Ser.). (Illus.). 64p. 1992. pap. 9.95 (*0-89747-281-0*, 5009) Squad Sig Pubns.
Drendel, Lou. Walk Around: B-25 Mitchell. LC 98-170321. 1997. write for info. (*0-89747-379-5*) Squad Sig Pubns.
Drengson, Alan & Inoue, Yuichi, eds. The Deep Ecology Movement: An Introductory Anthology. LC 95-3367. 250p. (Orig.). 1995. pap. 14.95 (*1-55643-198-8*) North Atlantic.
Drengson, Alan & Taylor, Duncan, eds. Ecoforestry: The Art & Science of Sustainable Forest Use. (Illus.). 320p. (Orig.). (C). 1997. pap. 24.95 (*0-86571-365-0*) New Soc Pubs.
Drengson, Alan R. Beyond Environmental Crisis: From Technocrat to Planetary Person. (American University Studies: Philosophy: Ser. V, Vol. 74). 259p. (C). 1989. text 38.70 (*0-8204-0871-9*) P Lang Pubng.
— The Practice of Technology: Exploring Technology, Ecophilosophy, & Spiritual Disciplines for Vital Links. LC 95-1305. 218p. (C). 1995. text 59.50 (*0-7914-2669-6*); pap. text 19.95 (*0-7914-2670-X*) State U NY Pr.
Drengson, Alan R., jt. ed. see Beehler, Roger.
Drenkhahn, Betty Jo, ed. see MacKay, Susan E.
Drennan, Bryce W. Indigo E-Print 1000 Graphic Designer's Companion: The Essential Independent Guide to Digital Offset Printing. rev. ed. LC 96-42079. 1999. pap. 29.95 (*0-9642552-5-1*) Adams-Harmon.

D

An Asterisk (*) at the beginning of an entry indicates that the title is appearing for the first time.

Drennan, Daniel. The New York Diaries. LC 98-19282. 234p. 1998. pap. 11.95 (*0-345-41643-0*) Ballantine Pub Grp.

Drennan, David. 12 Ladders to World Class Performance: Practical Steps to Seizing the Competitive Edge. 1999. pap. 19.95 (*0-7494-3000-1*, Kogan Pg Educ) Stylus Pub VA.

Drennan, Geo. B. Voices - Circles - Echoes: A Ten Year Journey. LC 95-92857. (Illus.). 115p. 1996. 60.00 (*0-9651159-0-9*) Printing Corner.

Drennan, Hugh H. Aids to the Psalms, Cycle A. 1992. pap. 12.50 (*1-55673-435-2*, 9238) CSS OH.

— Aids to the Psalms, Cycle B, Cycle B. 1996. 12.50 (*1-55673-619-3*) CSS OH.

Drennan, James. Oswald Mosley & British Fascism. 1976. lib. bdg. 69.95 (*0-8490-2388-2*) Gordon Pr.

Drennan, James C., ed. The Child's Foot & Ankle. 576p. 1992. text 143.00 (*0-88167-879-1*) Lppncott W & W.

Drennan, James C. & Saxon, John L. Manual for North Carolina Jury Commissioners. 2nd ed. 46p. (C). 1993. pap. text 9.00 (*1-56011-215-8*, 92.08) Institute Government.

Drennan, James C., jt. auth. see Loeb, Ben F., Jr.

Drennan, Mathew & Nichols, Annie. Vegetarian Entertaining: 100 Tempting & Nutritious Ideas for Easy Vegetarian Dining. (Illus.). 192p. 1997. pap. 16.95 (*1-85967-528-X*, Lorenz Bks) Anness Pub.

Drennan, Matthew P. Readings in State & Local Public Finance. Netzer, Dick, ed. LC 96-16614. 500p. (C). 1997. pap. text 44.95 (*1-55786-713-5*) Blackwell Pubs.

Drennan, Mimi. Fashion Writing. LC 85-21870. 1985. 26.60 (*0-02-682860-X*) Macmillan.

Drennan, R. D. Statistics for Archaeologists: A Commonsense Approach. (Interdisciplinary Contributions to Archaeology Ser.). (Illus.). 273p. (C). 1996. 51.00 (*0-306-45327-4*, Plenum Trade); pap. 29.00 (*0-306-45326-6*, Plenum Trade) Perseus Pubng.

Drennan, Robert D. Excavations at Quachilco: A Report on the 1977 Season of the Palo Blanco Project in the Tehuacan Valley. (Technical Reports Ser.: No. 7). (ENG & SPA., Illus.). 1978. pap. 2.00 (*0-932206-16-6*) U Mich Mus Anthro.

— Fabrica San Jose & Middle Formative Society in the Valley of Oaxaca. Flannery, Kent V., ed. (Memoirs Series, Prehistory & Human Ecology of the Valley of Oaxaca: No. 8, Vol. 4). (Illus.). (Orig.). 1976. pap. 4.00 (*0-932206-70-0*) U Mich Mus Anthro.

Drennan, Robert D., ed. Prehispanic Social, Political, & Economic Development in the Area of the Tehuacan Valley: Some Results of the Palo Blanco Project. (Technical Reports Ser.: No. 11). (Illus.). (Orig.). 1979. pap. 3.00 (*0-932206-82-4*) U Mich Mus Anthro.

— Regional Archaeology in the Valle de la Plata, Colombia: A Preliminary Report on the 1984 Season of the Projecto Arqueologico Valle de la Plata. Kennedy, Veronica, tr. (Technical Reports Ser.: No. 16). (ENG & SPA., Illus.). 195p. 1985. pap. 8.00 (*0-915703-06-8*) U Mich Mus Anthro.

Drennan, Robert D., et al, eds. Prehispanic Chiefdoms in the Valle de la Plata Vol. 1: The Environmental Context of Human Habitation. (University of Pittsburgh Memoirs in Latin American Archaeology Ser.: No. 2). (ENG & SPA., Illus.). 1989. pap. 15.00 (*1-877812-01-3*, M002) UPLAAP.

— Prehispanic Chiefdoms in the Valle de la Plata Vol. 2: Ceramics - Chronology & Craft Production. (University of Pittsburgh Memoirs in Latin American Archaeology Ser.: No. 5). (ENG & SPA.). xxvi, 188p. 1993. pap. 19.00 (*1-877812-07-2*, M005) UPLAAP.

Drennan, Robert E., ed. The Algonquin Wits. (Illus.). 176p. 1985. pap. 8.95 (*0-8065-0937-2*, Citadel Pr) Carol Pub Group.

— The Algonquin Wits. 178p. 1999. reprint ed. 26.95 (*0-7351-0116-7*) Replica Bks.

Drennan, Susan R. Where to Find Birds in New York State: The Top 500 Sites. LC 81-16744. (New York State Bks.). (Illus.). 532p. 1981. pap. text 24.95 (*0-8156-0173-5*) Syracuse U Pr.

Drennen, J., jt. auth. see Ciurczak, E. W.

Drennen, Marcia, ed. see Segerberg, Osborn, Jr.

***Drennen, Sarah, ed.** Citizen's Guide for Environmental Issues: A Handbook for Cultivating Dialogue. 2nd ed. (Illus.). 82p. (C). 1999. reprint ed. pap. text 20.00 (*0-7881-8311-7*) DIANE Pub.

Drennen, Thomas E., jt. ed. see Kaiser, Harry M.

Drennon, Cassandra, jt. auth. see Fingeret, Hanna A.

Drennon-Gala, Don. Delinquency & High School Dropouts: Reconsidering Social Correlates. LC 95-17940. 176p. 1995. 38.00 (*0-8191-9979-6*) U Pr of Amer.

Drenowatz, Claire & Elrod, Charlie, eds. The Ratite Encyclopedia: Ostrich-Emu-Rhea. (Illus.). 488p. 1995. 84.95 (*0-9642940-2-8*) Ratite Records.

Drensky, Vesselin, et al. Methods in Ring Theory: Proceedings of the Trento Conference. LC 98-9447. (Lecture Notes in Pure & Applied Mathematics Ser.). (Illus.). 328p. 1998. pap. text 150.00 (*0-8247-0183-6*) Dekker.

***Drensky, Vesselin S.** Free Algebras & Pi-Algebras: A Graduate Course in Algebra. LC 99-26869. 240p. 1999. pap. 39.95 (*981-4021-48-2*) Spr-Verlag.

Drent, Ailsa. Parenting Today. (C). 1990. teacher ed. 60.00 (*0-86431-074-9*, Pub. by Aust Council Educ Res); teacher ed. 90.00 (*0-86431-073-0*, Pub. by Aust Council Educ Res) St Mut.

***Drent, Ailsa.** Parenting Today. 2nd ed. 100p. 2000. pap. 29.95 (*0-86431-334-9*, Pub. by Aust Council Educ Res) Stylus Pub VA.

Drenth, Don R. NATO Negotiations on the Intermediate-Range Nuclear Forces, 1977-1979. (Pew Case Studies in International Affairs). 50p. (C). 1993. pap. text 3.50 (*1-56927-305-7*) Geo U Inst Dplmcy.

Drenth, Jan. Principles of Protein X-Ray Crystallography. LC 93-6235. (Advanced Texts in Chemistry Ser.). (Illus.). 305p. 1995. 54.95 (*0-387-94091-X*) Spr-Verlag.

— Principles of Protein X-Ray Crystallography. 2nd ed. LC 98-26970. (Advanced Texts in Chemistry Ser.). (Illus.). 336p. 1999. 64.50 (*0-387-98587-5*) Spr-Verlag.

Drenth, P. J., et al, eds. Organizational Decision-Making under Different Economic & Political Conditions. LC 97-104977. 248p. pap. 47.00 (*0-444-85810-5*) Elsevier.

Drenth, P. J. D. Organizational Psychology. 2nd ed. LC 98-186244. (Work & Organizational Psychology Handbks.). 1998. 79.95 (*0-86377-526-8*, Pub. by Psychol Pr) Taylor & Francis.

— Personnel Psychology. 2nd ed. LC 98-186244. (Work & Organizational Psychology Handbks.). 1998. 69.95 (*0-86377-524-1*, Pub. by Psychol Pr) Taylor & Francis.

— Work & Psychology. 2nd ed. LC 98-186244. (Work & Organizational Psychology Handbks.). 1998. 54.95 (*0-86377-522-5*, Pub. by Psychol Pr) Taylor & Francis.

Drenth, Pieter J., et al, eds. Handbook of Work & Organizational Psychology, Vol. 1. LC 83-23316. 704p. reprint ed. pap. 200.00 (*0-7837-4876-0*, 204451400001) Bks Demand.

— Handbook of Work & Organizational Psychology, Vol. 2. LC 83-23316. 680p. reprint ed. pap. 200.00 (*0-7837-4877-9*, 204451400002) Bks Demand.

Drenth, Pieter J., jt. ed. see Bleichrodt, N.

Drenth, P.J.D. Handbook of Work & Organizational Psychology. 2nd ed. LC 98-186244. 1998. 200.00 (*0-86377-528-4*, Pub. by Psychol Pr) Taylor & Francis.

— Introduction to Work & Organizational Psychology. 2nd ed. LC 98-186244. (Work & Organizational Psychology Handbks.). 1998. 34.95 (*0-86377-520-9*, Pub. by Psychol Pr) Taylor & Francis.

Drenth, Wiendelt & Kwart, Harold. Kinetics Applied to Organic Reactions. LC 79-27452. (Studies in Organic Chemistry: No. 9). (Illus.). 219p. reprint ed. pap. 67.90 (*0-7837-0853-X*, 204116200019) Bks Demand.

Drenttel, William. Paul Auster: A Comprehensive Bibliographic Checklist of Published Work 1968-1994. (Illus.). 96p. 1995. pap. 40.00 (*1-884381-00-6*) W Drenttel Ed.

— Paul Auster Signed: A Comprehensive Bibliographic Checklist of Published Work 1968-1994. (Illus.). 96p. 1995. 125.00 (*1-884381-01-4*) W Drenttel Ed.

Dreosti, Ivor E., ed. Trace Elements, Micronutrients & Free Radicals. LC 91-13721. (Contemporary Issues in Biomedicine, Ethics, & Society Ser.). (Illus.). 239p. 1991. 99.50 (*0-89603-188-8*) Humana.

Dreosti, Ivor E. & Smith, Richard M., eds. Neurobiology of the Trace Elements Vol. 1: Trace Element Neurobiology & Deficiencies. LC 83-8412. (Contemporary Neuroscience Ser.). 374p. 1983. 99.50 (*0-89603-046-6*) Humana.

— Neurobiology of the Trace Elements Vol. 2: Neurotoxicology & Neuropharmacology. LC 83-8413. (Contemporary Neuroscience Ser.). 323p. 1983. 99.50 (*0-89603-047-4*) Humana.

Dresang & Gosling. Politics & Policy in America. 2nd ed. LC 98-27117. 488p. 1998. 65.00 (*0-205-29118-X*) Allyn.

Dresang, Dennis. Public Personnel Management & Public Policy. 3rd ed. LC 98-38626. 352p. (C). 1998. 65.00 (*0-8013-1694-4*) Addison-Wesley.

— Public Personnel Mangement & Public Policy. 3rd ed. (C). 1996. text. write for info. (*0-8013-1693-6*) Addison-Wesley.

Dresang, Dennis L., jt. ed. see Holden, Matthew, Jr.

Dresang, Eliza T. The Land & People of Zambia. LC 74-23108. (Portraits of the Nations Ser.). (J). (gr. 5-9). 1975. lib. bdg. 11.89 (*0-397-31561-9*) HarpC Child Bks.

–Radical Change: Books for Youth in a Digital Age. LC 98-34791. 344p. 1999. 45.00 (0-8242-0953-2) Wilson. "Thoughtful & thought-provoking...Professionals who work with youth will come away from this with a new understanding of contemporary youth literature & how to evaluate it." - Booklist. Radical Change: Books for Youth in a Digital Age presents a new way of looking at literature for children & young adults. It offers a conceptual framework for understanding & evaluating books that differ sharply from traditional expectations - books that appeal to savvy Net Generation readers. Dresang shows how printed books are changing in step with positive developments in the digital world, & how librarians, teachers, & parents can recognize & appreciate good books for youth that break barriers, with materials previously unavailable in children's & young adult literature; create connections for & among young people; & use digital design to open the way for a new kind of reading & understanding, with sophisticated graphics & multilayered, nonlinear stories & information. The book includes a thorough discussion of radical change, in-depth analyses of individual titles & illustrations, a guide to recognizing a good book in the digital age, & an extensive annotated bibliography - with a digital connection, for Dresang has established a web site for Radical Change at http://slis-one.lis.fsu.edu.radicalchange. ***Publisher Paid Annotation.***

Dresch, Maria & Sheffrin, Steven M. Who Pays for Development Fees & Exactions? LC 97-23718. (Illus.). xix, 80p. 1997. pap. 10.00 (*0-9653184-7-8*) Pub Policy Inst.

Dresch, Paul. Tribes, Government, & History in Yemen. (Illus.). 470p. 1994. pap. text 26.00 (*0-19-827790-3*) OUP.

***Dresch, Paul, et al.** Anthropologists in a Wider World: Essays on Field Research. LC 99-87034. (Methodology & History in Anthropology Ser.: Vol. 6). (Illus.) 288p. 2000. 49.95 (*1-57181-799-9*); pap. 25.00 (*1-57181-800-6*) Berghahn Bks.

Dresch, Stephen. Occupational Earnings, 1967-1981: Returns to Occupational Choice, Schooling & Physician Specialization. LC 86-63. (Contemporary Studies in Economic & Financial Analysis: Vol. 49). 296p. 1986. 78.50 (*0-89232-596-8*) Jai Pr.

Drescher. Bug Book. 32p. (J). Date not set. lib. bdg. 14.89 (*0-06-022712-5*) HarperTrade.

— Spike's Christmas. (J). 1997. write for info. (*0-15-200213-8*) Harcourt.

Drescher, Gary L. Made-Up Minds: A Constructivist Approach to AI. (Artificial Intelligence - Bobrow, Brady & Davis Ser.). 240p. 1991. 35.00 (*0-262-04120-0*) MIT Pr.

Drescher, Henrik. The Boy Who Ate Around. LC 93-40848. (Illus.). 40p. (J). (ps-3). 1996. pap. 4.95 (*0-7868-1128-5*, Pub. by Hyprn Ppbks) Little.

— The Boy Who Ate Around. 1996. 10.15 (*0-606-11164-6*, Pub. by Turtleback) Demco.

— Boy Who Ate Around. LC 93-40848. (Illus.). 40p. (J). (ps-3). 1994. 14.95 (*0-7868-0014-3*, Pub. by Hyprn Child); lib. bdg. 14.89 (*0-7868-2011-X*, Pub. by Hyprn Child) Little.

— Junto a la Bahia. 3rd ed. Ada, Alma F., tr. (Dejame Leer Ser.).Tr. of Down by the Bay. (SPA., Illus.). 16p. (J). (ps-2). 1995. bds. 2.95 (*0-673-36293-0*, GoodYrBooks) Addson-Wesley Educ.

— Pat the Beastie: A Pull-&-Poke Book. (Illus.). 18p. (YA). (ps up). 1993. 9.95 (*1-56282-407-4*, Pub. by Hyprn Child) Little.

— Pat the Beastie Book & Puppet. (Illus.). (J). (ps-2). 1997. pap. 10.95 (*0-7868-1228-1*, Pub. by Hyprn Ppbks) Little.

— Simon's Book. LC 82-24931. (Illus.). 32p. (J). (ps up). 1991. reprint ed. mass mkt. 5.95 (*0-688-10484-3*, Wm Morrow) Morrow Avon.

— Too Much Bliss. limited ed. (Illus.). 46p. 1992. 3500.00 (*1-887123-05-9*) Granary Bks.

— Tooth Decay. 32p. (J). 2000. 15.95 (*0-7868-03436*, Pub. by Disney Pr) Time Warner.

— Whose Furry Nose? LC 87-45151. (Illus.). 32p. (J). (gr. k-3). 1987. 11.95 (*0-397-32236-4*); lib. bdg. 11.39 (*0-397-32243-7*) HarpC Child Bks.

— Whose Scaly Tail? LC 87-45152. (Illus.). 32p. (J). (gr. k-3). 1987. 11.95 (*0-397-32237-2*); lib. bdg. 11.39 (*0-397-32244-5*) HarpC Child Bks.

Drescher, Henrik. Brer Rabbit & the Wonderful Tar Baby. abr. ed. LC 90-7166. (Storybook Classics Ser.). 40p. (J). (gr. k up). 1991. 19.95 incl. audio (*0-88708-145-2*, Rabbit Ears) Litle Simon.

Drescher, Henrik. Klutz. LC 95-43625. 32p. (J). (ps-3). 1996. 15.95 (*0-7868-0233-2*, Pub. by Hyprn Child); lib. bdg. 15.89 (*0-7868-2182-5*, Pub. by Hyprn Child) Little.

Drescher, Horst. Lexikon der Englischen Literatur. (GER.). 534p. 1979. 49.95 (*0-7859-8410-0*, 3520465015) Fr & Eur.

***Drescher, Horst W.** Literature & Literati: The Literary Correspondence & Notebooks of Henry Mackenzie. (Scottish Studies International). 287p. (C). 1999. text 52.95 (*0-8204-4360-3*) P Lang Pubng.

Drescher, Horst W. Transfer: 50 Jahre Fachbereich Angewandte Sprach- und Kulturwissenschaft der Johannes Gutenberg - Universitat Mainz in Germersheim. (GER., Illus.). 672p. 1997. 57.95 (*3-631-31881-2*) P Lang Pubng.

Drescher, Horst W., ed. James Hogg: Poetic Mirrors: Comprising the "Poetic Mirror" (1816) & "New Poetic Mirror" (1829-1831) (Publications of the Scottish Studies Centre of the Johannes-Gutenberg Universitat Mainz in Germersheim: Vol. 11). XXXIX, 199p. 1990. pap. 60.00 (*3-631-42959-2*) P Lang Pubng.

***Drescher, Horst W., ed.** Literature & Literati the Literary Correspondence & Notebooks of Henry MacKenzie: Notebooks, 1763-1824. (Scottish Studies International: Vol. 2). 287p. 1999. 52.95 (*3-631-46084-8*) P Lang Pubng.

Drescher, Horst W. & Hagemann, Susanne, eds. Scotland to Slovenia: European Identities & Transcultural Communication, Proceedings of the Fourth International Scottish Studies Symposium. (Scottish Studies International: Vol. 21). 277p. 1996. pap. 54.95 (*0-8204-3164-8*) P Lang Pubng.

— Scotland to Slovenia: European Identities & Transcultural Communication, Proceedings of the 4th International Scottish Studies Symposium. LC 97-136242. (Scottish Studies International: Vol. 21). 277p. 1996. pap 54.95 (*3-631-50061-0*) P Lang Pubng.

Drescher, Horst W., ed. see Diamond, Peter J.

Drescher, Horst W., jt. ed. see Schwend, Joachim.

Drescher, Horst W., ed. see Volkel, Hermann.

Drescher, Jack. Psychoanalytic Therapy & the Gay Man. LC 98-36101. 384p. 1998. 55.00 (*0-88163-208-2*) Analytic Pr.

Drescher, James. Why Johnny Can't (Doesn't) Behave & What to Do about It. (Illus.). 87p. 1998. pap. 9.95 (*1-883294-64-9*) Masthof Pr.

Drescher, Joan. Birth Order Blues. 1999. pap. 3.95 (*0-14-054338-4*) NAL.

— I'm in Charge. (Illus.). (J). (gr. 1-3). 1981. 9.95 (*0-316-19330-5*) Little.

— Your Doctor, My Doctor. 32p. (J). (gr. 1-3). 1987. 10.95 (*0-8027-6668-4*); lib. bdg. 11.85 (*0-8027-6669-2*) Walker & Co.

— Your Family, My Family. (Illus.). 32p. (J). (gr. 2-5). 1980. lib. bdg. 13.85 (*0-8027-6383-9*) Walker & Co.

***Drescher, John.** Triumph of Good Will: How Terry Sanford Beat a Champion of Segregation & Reshaped the South. LC 00-35925. (Illus.). 256p. 2000. 27.00 (*1-57806-310-8*) U Pr of Miss.

Drescher, John M. Blessings by Your Bedside. rev. ed. (Visitation Pamphlet Ser.). 16p. 1988. 2.99 (*0-8361-3476-1*) Herald Pr.

— By Still Waters. rev. ed. (Visitation Pamphlet Ser.). 16p. 1988. 2.99 (*0-8361-3477-X*) Herald Pr.

— Doing What Comes Spiritually. rev. ed. LC 93-4271. 328p. 1993. pap. 12.99 (*0-8361-3611-X*) Herald Pr.

— Facing Illness with Faith. 16p. 1969. pap. 2.99 (*0-8361-1598-8*) Herald Pr.

— For the Golden Years. rev. ed. 16p. 1989. pap. text 2.99 (*0-8361-3432-X*) Herald Pr.

— For the Love of Marriage. 244p. 1996. pap. 9.95 (*1-56148-168-8*) Good Bks PA.

— God's Presence in Time of Trouble. (Visitation Pamphlets Ser.). 16p. (Orig.). 1989. pap. 2.99 (*0-8361-3509-1*) Herald Pr.

— I Lift My Eyes. 16p. (Orig.). 1976. pap. 2.99 (*0-8361-1308-X*) Herald Pr.

— If I Were Starting My Family Again. 57p. 1996. pap. 4.95 (*1-56148-220-X*) Good Bks PA.

— If I Were Starting My Ministry Again: Timeless Instructions & Life-Changing Wisdom. 64p. (Orig.). 1995. pap. 5.95 (*0-687-01001-2*) Abingdon.

— In Grief's Lone Hour, 5 vols. rev. ed. (Visitation Pamphlet Ser.). 16p. 1986. 2.99 (*0-8361-3425-7*) Herald Pr.

— The Lord Is Near: Experiencing the Presence of God. (Visitation Pamphlets Ser.). 16p. (Orig.). 1989. pap. 2.99 (*0-8361-3508-3*) Herald Pr.

— May Your Marriage Be a Happy One. rev. ed. 16p. 1989. pap. text 2.99 (*0-8361-3484-2*) Herald Pr.

— Meditations for the Newly Married. 3rd rev. ed. LC 69-10835. 142p. 1995. pap. 10.99 (*0-8361-9017-3*) Herald Pr.

— Meditations for the Newly Married. 4th rev. ed. LC 96-52252. 144p. 1997. 19.99 (*0-8361-9069-6*) Herald Pr.

— Parents - Passing the Torch of Faith. LC 97-13311. 94p. (Orig.). 1997. pap. 7.99 (*0-8361-9076-9*) Herald Pr.

— Personal Prescriptions. 16p. 1969. pap. 2.99 (*0-8361-1596-1*) Herald Pr.

— Seven Things Children Need. 2nd rev. ed. LC 88-10173. 144p. 1988. pap. 7.99 (*0-8361-3475-3*) Herald Pr.

— Siete Necesidades Basicas Del Nino: Seven Things Children Need. (SPA.). 128p. 1983. reprint ed. pap. 7.99 (*0-311-46085-2*) Casa Bautista.

— Sources of Spiritual Strength. 16p. 1975. pap. 2.99 (*0-8361-1772-7*) Herald Pr.

— Strength for Suffering. 16p. 1989. pap. 2.99 (*0-8361-1599-6*) Herald Pr.

— Suffering & Gods Presence. 16p. 1971. pap. 2.99 (*0-8361-1644-5*) Herald Pr.

— When Your Child Is Six to Twelve. LC 93-23558. 96p. 1993. pap. 8.95 (*1-56148-094-0*) Good Bks PA.

Drescher, John M., ed. Invocations & Benedictions for the Revised Common Lectionary. LC 97-42472. 176p. 1998. pap. 14.95 (*0-687-04629-7*) Abingdon.

Drescher, John M., et al. When Your Child... LC 86-4831. 144p. (Orig.). 1986. pap. 8.99 (*0-8361-3416-8*) Herald Pr.

Drescher, Jon. Promoting Healthy Self-Esteem in Children. (Family Forum Library). 16p. 1992. 1.95 (*1-56688-011-4*) Bur For At-Risk.

Drescher-Lehman, Sandra. Meditations for New Moms. LC 94-32940. (Illus.). 302p. 1994. pap. 7.95 (*1-56148-132-7*) Good Bks PA.

***Drescher-Lehman, Sandra.** Meditations for Weary Parents. 204p. 2000. pap. 7.95 (*1-56148-302-8*) Good Bks PA.

Drescher-Lehman, Sandra. Waters of Reflection: Meditations for Every Day. LC 93-1433. 181p. (Orig.). 1993. pap. 8.95 (*1-56148-084-3*) Good Bks PA.

Drescher, Nancy. Which Business? Help in Selecting Your New Venture. LC 96-47509. (Successful Business Library). (Illus.). 376p. 1997. pap. 18.95 (*1-55571-390-4*) PSI Resch.

Drescher, Seymour. Dilemmas of Democracy: Tocqueville & Modernization. LC 68-12725. 316p. reprint ed. pap. 98.00 (*0-608-12642-X*, 202543700043) Bks Demand.

— Econocide: British Slavery in the Era of Abolition. LC 76-50887. 293p. reprint ed. pap. 90.90 (*0-7837-2477-2*, 204263100005) Bks Demand.

— From Slavery to Freedom: Comparative Studies in the Rise & Fall of Atlantic Slavery. LC 98-37693. 374p. 1999. text 45.00 (*0-8147-1918-X*) NYU Pr.

Drescher, Seymour, et al, eds. Political Symbolism in Modern Europe: Essays in Honor of George L. Mosse. LC 80-26544. (Illus.). 310p. 1982. 49.95 (*0-87855-422-X*) Transaction Pubs.

Drescher, Seymour & Engerman, Stanley L., eds. A Historical Guide to World Slavery. (Illus.). 456p. 1998. text 75.00 (*0-19-512091-4*) OUP.

Drescher, Seymour, jt. ed. see McGlynn, Frank, Jr.

Drescher, Seymour, tr. see De Tocqueville, Alexis.

Drescher, Seymour I. Tocqueville & England. LC 63-20764. (Historical Monographs: No. 55). 271p. 1964. 20.00 (*0-674-89430-8*) HUP.

Drescher, Timothy W. San Francisco Bay Area Murals: Communities Create Their Muses. 3rd rev. ed. LC 97-76508. (Illus.). 148p. 1998. pap. 19.95 (*1-880654-13-X*) Pogo Pr.

***Drescher, Timothy W.** Wall Power. 2000. pap. 20.00 (*0-88454-096-0*) U of Pa Contemp Art.

D

An Asterisk (*) at the beginning of an entry indicates that the title is appearing for the first time.

Drescher, U., et al, eds. Molecular Bases of Axonal Growth & Pathfinding. LC 97-40498. (Illus.). 260p. 1997. pap. 64.95 (*3-540-63522-X*) Spr-Verlag.

Dreschhoff, G. A. & Splettstoesser, John F., eds. Mineral Resources Potential of Antarctica. (Antarctic Research Ser.: No. 51). 327p. 1990. 53.00 (*0-87590-174-3*) Am Geophysical.

Drescher-Fischer, Leonie, jt. ed. see Nebel, Bernhard.

***Dresden, Eline Hoekstra.** Wishing upon a Star: A Tale of the Holocaust & Hope. (Illus.). 170p. 2000. pap. write for info. (*0-9666244-1-6*) Blackmore & Black.

Dresden, Judith, et al. Mr. Slaptail's Secret. rev. ed. (My Health My World Ser.). (Illus.). iv, 36p. (J). (gr. k-5). 1997. pap. write for info. (*1-888997-29-X*) Baylor Coll Med.

Dresden, M. H. A. Kramer. (Illus.). 625p. 1987. 98.95 (*0-387-96282-4*) Spr-Verlag.

Dresden, M., ed. Summer Scientific Soundings. 300p. (C). 1998. text 32.00 (*981-02-0011-0*) World Scientific Pub.

Dresden, Max. Field Theory & General Relativity. 420p. (C). 1993. text 85.00 (*9971-5-0821-4*) World Scientific Pub.

Dresden, S., et al. Erasmi Opera Omnia, Vol. V-1. viii, 410p. 1977. 408.50 (*0-7204-6158-8*) Elsevier.

***Dresden, Sean, ed.** Campfire Tales Vol. 1: The Most Terrifying Tales Ever Told. (Illus.). 96p. (J). (gr. 3-7). 2000. pap. 4.95 (*0-7373-0437-5*, 04375W, Pub. by Lowell Hse Juvenile) NTC Contemp Pub Co.

— Campfire Tales Vol. 2: The Most Terrifying Tales Ever Told. (Illus.). 96p. (J). (gr. 3-7). 2000. pap. 4.95 (*0-7373-0436-7*, 04367W, Pub. by Lowell Hse Juvenile) NTC Contemp Pub Co.

Dresden Technical University Staff. Electrotechnik, Elektronik: Russian-German. 5th ed. (GER & RUS.). 808p. 1990. 150.00 (*0-7859-7055-X*) Fr & Eur.

***Dresdner, A.** Die Entstehung der Kunstkritik. (GER.). 500p. 1998. text 20.00 (*90-5705-109-5*, Verlag Kunst) Gordon & Breach.

Dresdner, Albert. Kultur- und Sittengeschichte der Italienischen Geistlichkeit Im 10. und 11. Jahrhundert. (GER.). 408p. 1998. reprint ed. write for info. (*3-487-10533-0*) G Olms Pubs.

— Kultur und Sittengeschichte der Italienischen Geistlichkeit Im 10 und 11 Jahrhundert. 408p. reprint ed. write for info. (*0-318-71596-1*) G Olms Pubs.

Dresdner, Jorge D. The Structuralist Theory of Inflation & Structural Inflation in Chile, 1950-1972: The Lagging Food Supply Hypothesis Revisted. (Studia Oeconomica Upsaliensia: No. 19). 165p. (Orig.). 1990. pap. 41.00 (*91-554-2628-X*) Coronet Bks.

Dresdner, Michael. The New Wood Finishing Book. LC 99-13395. 1999. pap. 19.95 (*1-56158-299-9*) Taunton.

— The Woodfinishing Book. LC 92-14899. (Illus.). 224p. 1992. pap. 24.95 (*1-56158-037-6*, 70172) Taunton.

Dresdon, Anna. Amanda's Companion. 1999. pap. 4.00 (*1-57514-334-8*, 1139) Encore Perform Pub.

Dresen, L. & Ruter, Horst. Seismic Coal Exploration Pt. B: In-Seam Seismics. (Handbook of Geophysical Exploration Ser.: Vol. 16). 446p. 1994. 154.50 (*0-08-037226-0*) Elsevier.

Dreser, Elena. Manuela Color Canela (Manuela, Color of Cinnamon) (SPA.). 32p. (J). (gr. 1-3). 1994. 12.99 (*968-16-4572-3*, Pub. by Fondo) Continental Bk.

Dresher, M., ed. see Aumann, R. J.

Dresher, Melvin, pref. The Mathematics of Games of Strategy: Theory & Applications. viii, 184p. (C). 1981. reprint ed. pap. 6.95 (*0-486-64216-X*) Dover.

Dreska, Noel & Weisenthal, Leonard. Physics for Aviation Technology. LC 92-27173. (Illus.). 183p. 1992. pap. text 17.65 (*0-89100-411-4*, JS312620) Jeppesen Sanderson.

Dresner, Joanne, ed. It's up to You. (English As a Second Language Bk.). (Illus.). 1980. pap. text 16.17 (*0-582-79727-6*, 74987) Longman.

Dresner, L. Applications of Lie's Theory of Ordinary & Partial Differential Equations. (Illus.). 170p. 1998. 90.00 (*0-7503-0530-4*); pap. 27.00 (*0-7503-0531-2*) IOP Pub.

— Stability of Superconductors. LC 95-17274. (Selected Topics in Superconductivity Ser.). (Illus.). 246p. (C). 1995. text 59.00 (*0-306-45030-5*, Kluwer Plenum) Kluwer Academic.

Dresner, Mara. An Impeccable Larceny. (Orig.). 1997. pap. 5.00 (*0-87440-044-9*) Bakers Plays.

Dresner, Samuel & Siegel, Seymour. Jewish Dietary Laws. rev. ed. LC 83-235401. 110p. pap. 2.95 (*0-8381-2105-5*) USCJE.

Dresner, Samuel, jt. auth. see Sherwin, Byron L.

Dresner, Samuel H. Rachel. LC 94-2826. 272p. 1995. pap. 21.00 (*0-8006-2777-6*, 1-2777, Fortress Pr) Augsburg Fortress.

— Sabbath. 1970. pap. 2.95 (*0-8381-2114-4*) USCJE.

— The Zaddik: The Doctrine of the Zaddik According to the Writings of Rabbi Yaakov Yosef of Polnoy. LC 94-16799. 314p. 1996. pap. 35.00 (*1-56821-312-3*) Aronson.

Dresner, Samuel H., jt. auth. see Kaplan, Edward K.

Dresner, Samuel H., ed. see Heschel, Abraham Joshua.

Dresner, Stephen. Units of Measurement: An Encyclopaedic Dictionary of Units, Both Scientific & Popular, & the Quantities They Measure. LC 72-187346. 303p. reprint ed. pap. 94.00 (*0-608-12370-6*, 205207100033) Bks Demand.

Dresner, Stephen B., tr. see Divari, Nikolai B., ed.

Dresner, Zita, jt. ed. see Walker, Nancy.

Dress, A., et al, eds. Trees & Hierarchical Structures: Proceedings of a Conference Held at Bielefeld, FRG, Fall 1987. (Lecture Notes in Biomathematics Ser.: Vol. 84). vi, 137p. 1990. 34.95 (*0-387-52453-3*) Spr-Verlag.

Dress, Abby, jt. auth. see Innace, Joseph J.

Dress, Walter. Die Theologic Gersons: Eine Untersuchung Zur Verbindung von Nominalismus und Mystik Im Spaetmittelalter. (GER.). vi, 208p. 1977. reprint ed. write for info. (*3-487-06283-6*) G Olms Pubs.

Dresscher, T. G. Index of Names & Location of Algae & Some Groups of Micro-Organisms Found in the Netherlands Waters. 808p. 1976. pap. 22.00 (*0-7204-8328-X*) Elsevier.

Dressel, et al. The Luftwarfe Profile Series No. 5: Junkers JU 87A. LC 96-160359. (Illus.). 48p. (YA). (gr. 10-13). 1996. pap. 14.95 (*0-88740-920-2*) Schiffer.

Dressel, Donald. Planking Techniques for Model Ship Builders. 144p. 1988. pap. 14.95 (*0-07-155312-6*) McGraw.

— Planking Techniques for Model Ship Builders. (Illus.). 160p. 1988. pap. 10.95 (*0-8306-2868-1*) McGraw-Hill Prof.

Dressel, Heinrich. Die Romischen Medaillone Im Berliner Munzkabinett. xvi, 485p. 1973. write for info. (*3-296-12601-5*); write for info. (*3-296-12602-3*) G Olms Pubs.

Dressel, Holly, jt. auth. see Suzuki, David.

Dressel, Joachim. Luftwaffe Album: Bomber & Fighter Aircraft of the German Air Force 1933-1945. LC 97-185341. (Illus.). 352p. 1997. 34.95 (*1-85409-409-2*, Pub. by Arms & Armour) Sterling.

— The Luftwaffe Album: Bomber & Fighter Aircraft of the German Air Force 1933-1945. 352p. 1999. pap. text 24.95 (*1-85409-519-6*) Strlng Pub CA.

Dressel, Joachim & Griehl, Manfred. Luftwaffe Airfield Equipment. Cox, Don, tr. LC 92-62385. (Illus.). 52p. (Orig.). 1993. pap. 9.95 (*0-88740-482-0*) Schiffer.

— The Luftwaffe Profile Series No. 3: Heinkel HE 219 UHU. Johnston, David, tr. from GER. LC 95-67545. (Illus.). 52p. (Orig.). 1995. pap. 14.95 (*0-88740-819-2*) Schiffer.

***Dressel, Joachim & Griehl, Manfried.** Junkers Ju 86. LC 98-134096. (Illus.). 48p. 1998. pap. 9.95 (*0-7643-0391-0*) Schiffer.

Dressel, Joachim, jt. auth. see Griehl, Manfred.

Dressel, Joacim, et al. Heinkel HE 280: The World's First Jet Aircraft. Force, Edward, tr. from GER. LC 91-66338. (Illus.). 48p. 1991. pap. 9.95 (*0-88740-344-1*) Schiffer.

Dressel, Jon. The Road to Shiloh: Poems since 1984. 115p. 1994. pap. 26.95 (*0-8464-4756-8*) Beekman Pubs.

— The Road to Shiloh: Poems since 1984. 115p. 1994. pap. 35.00 (*1-85902-185-9*) St Mut.

Dressel, Paul L. Administrative Leadership. LC 81-81962. (Jossey-Bass Series in Higher Education). 263p. reprint ed. pap. 81.60 (*0-8357-4878-2*, 203781000009) Bks Demand.

Dressel, Paul L. & Faricy, William H. Return to Responsibility: Constraints on Autonomy in Higher Education. LC 70-186574. (Jossey-Bass Higher Education Ser.). 252p. reprint ed. pap. 78.20 (*0-8357-9344-3*, 201393600087) Bks Demand.

Dressel, Paul L. & Marcus, Dora. On Teaching & Learning in College. LC 82-48077. (Jossey-Bass Series in Higher Education). 271p. reprint ed. pap. 84.10 (*0-8357-4879-0*, 203781200009) Bks Demand.

Dressel, Paul L. & Mayhew, Lewis B. Higher Education As a Field of Study: The Emergence of a Profession. LC 73-21073. (Jossey-Bass Higher Education Ser.). 225p. reprint ed. pap. 69.80 (*0-608-15029-0*, 205216000045) Bks Demand.

Dressel, Paul L. & Pratt, Sally R. The World of Higher Education: An Annotated Guide to the Major Literature. LC 71-158562. (Jossey-Bass Higher Education Ser.). 256p. reprint ed. pap. 79.40 (*0-608-11534-7*, 201393400088) Bks Demand.

Dressel, Paul L. & Thompson, Mary M. Independent Study: A New Interpretation of Concepts, Practices, & Problems. LC 73-50. (Jossey-Bass Higher Education Ser.). 176p. reprint ed. pap. 54.60 (*0-8357-9327-3*, 201375500087) Bks Demand.

Dressel, Paul L., et al. The Confidence Crisis: An Analysis of University Departments. LC 70-110642. (Jossey-Bass Higher Education Ser.). 286p. reprint ed. 88.70 (*0-8357-9309-5*, 201394800087) Bks Demand.

Dresselhaus, M. S., ed. Intercalation in Layered Materials. LC 86-30680. (NATO ASI Series B, Physics: Vol. 148). 512p. 1986. 115.00 (*0-306-42483-5*, Plenum Trade) Perseus Pubng.

Dresselhaus, M. S., et al, eds. Graphite Fibers & Filaments. (Materials Science Ser.: Vol. 5). (Illus.). 360p. 1988. 110.95 (*0-387-18938-6*) Spr-Verlag.

— Science of Fullerines & Carbon Nanotubes: Their Properties & Applications. LC 95-20629. (Illus.). 965p. 1996. text 130.00 (*0-12-221820-5*) Acad Pr.

Dresselhaus, M. S. & Kalish, R. Ion Implantation in Diamond, Graphite & Related Materials. Gonser, U. et al, eds. LC 92-11325. (Materials Science Ser.: Vol. 22). (Illus.). 179p. 1992. 79.00 (*3-540-54956-0*); 64.95 (*0-387-54956-0*) Spr-Verlag.

Dresselhaus, Mildred S., ed. High Temperature Superconductivity in Japan. (JTEC Panel Reports). xii, 222p. 1989. pap. write for info. (*1-883712-23-8*, JTEC) Intl Tech Res.

Dresselhaus, Richard L. The Deacon & His Ministry. LC 77-73518. 84p. 1977. mass mkt. 4.95 (*0-88243-493-4*, 02-0493) Gospel Pub.

— The Joy of Belonging. LC 78-66868. (Radiant Life Ser.). 128p. 1978. pap. 4.99 (*0-88243-526-4*, 02-0526) Gospel Pub.

— Teaching for Decision. LC 89-80210. (Sunday School Staff Training Ser.). 126p. 1989. pap. 2.95 (*0-88243-620-1*, 02-0620) Gospel Pub.

Dressendorfer, Paul V., jt. auth. see Ma, T. P.

Dresser, Christopher. Authentic Victorian Decoration & Ornamentation in Full Color: 46 Plates from "Studies in Design" (Pictorial Archive Ser.). 48p. (Orig.). 1986. pap. 7.95 (*0-486-25083-0*) Dover.

***Dresser, Christopher.** Japan: Its Architecture, Art, & Art Manufacturers. 488p. 2000. text 110.00 (*0-7103-0686-5*) Col U Pr.

Dresser, Christopher. Principles of Victorian Decorative Design. unabridged ed. (Illus.). 176p. 1996. reprint ed. pap. text 7.95 (*0-486-28900-1*) Dover.

— Traditional Arts & Crafts of Japan. LC 93-23730. Orig. Title: Japan: Its Architecture, Art & Art Manufactures. (Illus.). 480p. 1994. reprint ed. pap. 11.95 (*0-486-27992-8*) Dover.

Dresser, Cynthia. The Rainmaker's Dog: International Folktales to Build Communicative Skills. 330p. (C). 1994. pap. text 16.95 (*0-521-65778-4*) Cambridge U Pr.

— The Rainmaker's Dog: International Folktales to Build Communicative Skills: Instructor's Manual. 61p. (C). 1994. pap., teacher ed. 6.00 (*0-521-65777-6*) Cambridge U Pr.

Dresser, George B., jt. auth. see Stephenson, Amy.

Dresser, Ginny, ed. see Andrews, Janice H.

Dresser, Ginny, ed. see Linse, Barbara B. & Knight, Marilyn.

Dresser, Horatio W., ed. The Quimby Manuscripts. 2nd ed. 480p. 1984. pap. 9.95 (*0-8065-0913-9*, Citadel Pr) Carol Pub Group.

Dresser, James. Escort Carriers & Their Air Unit Markings During WWII in the Pacific. (Illus.). 120p. 1980. pap. text 10.00 (*0-9604696-0-5*) J Dresser.

Dresser, Louisa, ed. Catalogue of European Paintings in the Worcester Art Museum, 2 vols., Set. LC 73-90538. (Illus.). 696p. 1974. 45.00 (*0-87023-169-3*) U of Mass Pr.

Dresser, Marianne, ed. Buddhist Women on the Edge: Contemporary Perspectives from the Western Frontier. LC 96-25436. 321p. 1996. pap. 16.95 (*1-55643-203-8*) North Atlantic.

Dresser, Marianne, ed. see Dalai Lama XIV.

Dresser, Mary, ed. see Whitmarsh, Katharine.

Dresser, Michelle, jt. auth. see Rosenbaum, Deborah.

Dresser, Norine. I Felt Like I Was from Another Planet: Writing from Personal Experience. (J). (gr. 4-7). 1993. pap. 14.95 (*0-201-86058-9*) Addison-Wesley.

— Multicultural Celebrations: Today's Rules of Etiquette for Life's Special Occasions. LC 98-29809. 320p. 1999. pap. 14.00 (*0-609-80259-3*) Crown Pub Group.

— Multicultural Manners: New Rules of Etiquette for a Changing Society. 304p. 1996. pap. 15.95 (*0-471-11819-2*) Wiley.

Dresser, Pat. Manchester Terrier: A Complete & Reliable Handbook. (Illus.). 96p. 1998. 19.95 (*0-7938-0755-7*, RX-105) TFH Pubns.

Dresser, Peter & Bellenir, Karen, eds. Diabetes Sourcebook. LC 94-39437. (Health Reference Ser.: Vol. 3). 825p. 1994. lib. bdg. 78.00 (*1-55888-751-2*) Omnigraphics Inc.

Dresser, Peter D. Cancer Sourcebook for Women, Vol. 10. Cook, Alan R., ed. (Health Reference Ser.). 524p. 1995. lib. bdg. 78.00 (*0-7808-0076-1*) Omnigraphics Inc.

Dresser, Peter D. & Bellenir, Karen, eds. AIDS Sourcebook. LC 95-5997. (Health Reference Ser.: Vol. 4). 831p. 1995. lib. bdg. 78.00 (*0-7808-0031-1*) Omnigraphics Inc.

Dresser, Peter D., jt. ed. see Bellenir, Karen.

Dresser, Peter D., jt. ed. see Cook, Allan R.

Dresser, Richard. Bait & Switch. LC 93-208129. 42p. 1991. write for info. (*0-573-69260-2*) S French Trade.

Dresser, Richard. Gun-Shy. LC 99-214700. 79p. 1998. pap. 5.60 (*0-87129-879-1*, G63) Dramatic Pub.

Dresser, William, jt. ed. see Hayakawa, Samuel I.

Dresslar, Jim. Folk Art of Early America: The Engraved Powder Horn. Cunningham, Sharon, ed. (Illus.). 230p. (Orig.). 1996. 95.00 (*0-9651039-0-0*) Dresslar Publishing.

Dressler. Botulinum Toxin Therapy. (Illus.). 128p. 1999. pap. 79.00 (*0-86577-816-7*) Thieme Med Pubs.

— Cases & Materials on Criminal Law. 2nd ed. LC 99-461801. (Paralegal Ser.). (C). 1999. pap. 43.75 (*0-314-23307-5*) West Pub.

— Woerterbuch Klinisches Medizin German-English. (ENG & GER.). 878p. 1991. 195.00 (*0-7859-7548-9*, 3527154647) Fr & Eur.

Dressler, Burkhard O., et al, eds. Large Meteorite Impacts & Planetary Evolution. LC 94-34436. (Special Papers: 293). 1994. pap. 72.75 (*0-8137-2293-4*) Geol Soc.

Dressler, Camille. Eigg: The Story of an Island. (Illus.). 256p. (Orig.). 1998. pap. 19.95 (*0-7486-6224-3*, Pub. by Polygon) Subterranean Co.

Dressler, Dennis E., jt. auth. see Brinkerhoff, Robert O.

Dressler, Dennis W. & Newsom, Ron, eds. Selected Speeches on Adult Education by A. A. Liveright, 1958-1968. LC 92-10798. 224p. 1992. 89.95 (*0-7734-9556-8*) E Mellen.

Dressler, H. Resorcinol: Its Uses & Derivatives. LC 94-30813. (Topics in Applied Chemistry Ser.). (Illus.). 516p. (C). 1994. text 125.00 (*0-306-44850-5*, Kluwer Plenum) Kluwer Academic.

Dressler, John C. Gerald Finzi: A Bio-Bibliography, 64. LC 96-32996. (Bio-Bibliographies in Music Ser.). 216p. 1997. lib. bdg. 69.50 (*0-313-28693-0*) Greenwood.

Dressler, Joshua. Criminal Law. (Law Outlines Ser.). 210p. (Orig.). 1996. pap. text. write for info. (*0-87457-178-2*, 5020) Casenotes Pub.

— Criminal Law, Cases & Materials On. LC 94-15665. (American Casebook Ser.). 1994. pap. text. write for info. (*0-314-04201-6*) West Pub.

— Criminal Law, Cases & Materials On. LC 94-15665. (American Casebook Ser.). 968p. (C). 1994. text. write for info. (*0-314-03791-8*) West Pub.

— Criminal Procedure, Vol. 5200. Tene, Peter & Goldenberg, Norman S., eds. (Law Outlines Ser.). (C). 1997. pap. write for info. (*0-87457-184-7*, 5200) Casenotes Pub.

— Criminal Procedure: Principles, Policies & Perspectives LC 99-160599. (American Casebook Ser). 1423 p. 1999. 49.25 (*0-314-21119-5*) West Pub.

Dressler, Joshua. Understanding Criminal Law 1995. annuals 1995. text 30.00 (*0-8205-2717-3*) Bender.

Dressler, Joshua. Understanding Criminal Procedure. 2nd ed. LC 96-50953. 1997. 30.00 (*0-8205-2824-2*) Bender.

— Understanding Criminal Procedures. 2nd ed. (Legal Text Ser.). 1996. text 20.76 (*0-256-22169-3*) McGraw.

Dressler, Kellie J., ed. Revitalizing Communities: Innovative State & Local Programs. (Illus.). 149p. 1998. pap. text 30.00 (*0-7881-7314-6*) DIANE Pub.

Dressler, Mylene. The Medusa Tree. LC 96-45547. 176p. 1997. 18.50 (*1-878448-75-7*) MacMurray & Beck.

Dressler, Rachel A., ed. The Art Institute of Chicago Museum Studies, Vol. 16, No. 1. (Illus.). 96p. 1990. pap. 10.50 (*0-226-02818-6*) U Ch Pr.

Dressler, Robert L. Field Guide to the Orchids of Costa Rica & Panama. (Comstock Bk.). (Illus.). 384p. 1993. pap. text 35.00 (*0-8014-8139-2*) Cornell U Pr.

— The Orchids: Natural History & Classification. LC 80-24561. (Illus.). 344p. (C). 1990. 51.95 (*0-674-87525-7*) HUP.

— The Orchids: Natural History & Classification. (Illus.). 344p. 1990. pap. text 15.95 (*0-674-87526-5*) HUP.

— Phylogeny & Classification of the Orchid Family. LC 92-24390. (Illus.). 332p. 1993. 49.95 (*0-931146-24-0*, Dioscorides) Timber.

Dressler, S. Dictionary Clinical Medicine English, German. (ENG & GER.). 400p. 1990. lib. bdg. 195.00 (*0-8288-3408-3*, 3527154639) Fr & Eur.

— German AIDS Dictionary. 3rd ed. (GER.). 160p. 1996. pap. 24.50 (*3-540-61293-9*, Pub. by Spr-Verlag) IBD Ltd.

Dressler, Stephan. Dictionary Clinical Medicine. (ENG & GER.). 841p. 1990. 115.00 (*0-89573-993-3*, Wiley-VCH) Wiley.

— Dictionary of Clinical Medicine. (ENG & GER.). 878p. 1991. lib. bdg. 115.00 (*0-89573-992-5*, Wiley-VCH) Wiley.

Dressler, Thomas D., jt. ed. see Brewer, James F.

Dressler, William W. Stress & Adaptation in the Context of Culture: Depression in a Southern Black Community. LC 89-26307. 354p. (C). 1991. pap. text 24.95 (*0-7914-0414-5*) State U NY Pr.

Dressler, Wolfgang, et al, eds. Phonologica, 1988: Proceedings of the 6th International Phonology Meeting. 308p. (C). 1992. text 80.00 (*0-521-40175-5*) Cambridge U Pr.

Dressler, Wolfgang U., ed. Current Trends in Textlinguistics. (Research in Text Theory Ser.: Vol. 2). (C). 1978. 65.40 (*3-11-006518-5*) De Gruyter.

Dressler, Wolfgang U., et al, eds. Advances in Morphology. LC 96-42275. (Trends in Linguistics, Studies & Monographs: Vol. 97). v, 207p. 1997. lib. bdg. 115.85 (*3-11-014853-6*) Mouton.

***Dressler, Wolfgang U., et al, eds.** Morphological Analysis in Comparison. LC 00-24553. (Current Issues in Linguistic Theory Ser.: Vol. 201). 250p. 2000. 65.00 (*1-55619-979-1*) J Benjamins Pubng Co.

Dressler, Wolfgang U. & Barbaresi, Lavinia M. Morphopragmatics: Diminutives & Intensifiers in Italian, German & Other Languages. LC 94-28594. (GER & ITA.). 690p. (C). 1994. 213.85 (*3-11-014041-1*, 169-94) Mouton.

— Morphopragmatics: Diminutives & Intensifiers in Italian, German, & Other Languages. (GER & ITA.). 690p. (C). 1994. lib. bdg. 191.75 (*0-614-00665-1*, 169-94) Mouton.

Dressler, Wolfgang U. & Stark, Jack A., eds. Linguistic Analyses of Aphasic Language. (Neuropsychology Ser.). (Illus.). 365p. 1988. 128.00 (*0-387-96692-7*) Spr-Verlag.

Dressler, Wolfgang U., et al. Leitmotifs in Natural Morphology. LC 87-21791. (Studies in Language Companion: No. 10). ix, 168p. 1988. 43.00 (*90-272-3009-9*) J Benjamins Pubng Co.

Dressler, Wolfgang V., et al, eds. Contemporary Morphology. (Trends in Linguistics, Studies & Monographs: No. 49). ix, 317p. (C). 1990. lib. bdg. 106.15 (*3-11-012349-5*) Mouton.

Dressman, Fran. Gus Wortham: Portrait of a Leader. LC 93-31049. (Illus.). 304p. 1994. 29.95 (*0-89096-580-3*) Tex A&M Univ Pr.

Dressman, Howard. A Practical Guide to Your Unemployment Insurance Rates. 76p. 1984. pap. 4.95 (*0-317-70028-6*) H Dressman.

Dressman, John. On the Cliffs of Acoma: A Story for Children. Ortega, Pedro R., tr. from SPA. LC 83-20177. (Illus.). 32p. (J). (gr. 2-4). 1984. pap. 5.95 (*0-86534-021-8*) Sunstone Pr.

Dressman, Mark. Literacy in the Library: Negotiating the Spaces Between Order & Desire. LC 97-18571. (Critical Studies in Education & Culture). 216p. 1997. 57.95 (*0-89789-495-2*, Bergin & Garvey) Greenwood.

***Dresziger, Nandor.** Hungary in the Age of Total War, 1938-1948. LC 98-71490. 384p. 1998. text 54.00 (*0-88033-407-X*, 509, Pub. by East Eur Monographs) Col U Pr.

Dretke, James P. A Christian Approach to Muslims: Reflections from West Africa. LC 79-11912. (Islamic Studies). 261p. 1979. pap. 5.95 (*0-87808-432-0*) William Carey Lib.

Dretske, Fred. Explaining Behavior: Reasons in a World of Causes. 184p. 1991. reprint ed. pap. text 13.50 (*0-262-54061-4*, Bradford Bks) MIT Pr.

— Naturalizing the Mind. LC 95-2229. (Jean Nicod Lectures: Vol. 1995). 1995. 25.00 (*0-262-04149-9*, Bradford Bks) MIT Pr.

— Naturalizing the Mind. (Jean Nicod Ser.). (Illus.). 232p. 1997. reprint ed. pap. text 12.50 (*0-262-54089-4*, Bradford Bks) MIT Pr.

An Asterisk (*) at the beginning of an entry indicates that the title is appearing for the first time.

***Dretske, Fred.** Perception, Knowledge & Belief: Selected Essays. (Cambridge Studies in Philosophy). (Illus.). 295p. (C). 2000. text 59.95 (*0-521-77181-1*); pap. text 19.95 (*0-521-77742-9*) Cambridge U Pr.

Dretske, Fred I. Knowledge & the Flow of Information. LC 99-12546. (David Hume Ser.). (Illus.). 288p. (C). 1999. pap. text 22.95 (*1-57586-195-X*) CSLI.

— Seeing & Knowing. 272p. 1988. pap. text 17.95 (*0-226-16245-1*, Midway Reprint) U Ch Pr.

Dretske, Fred I., jt. ed. see Bernecker, Sven.

Drettakis, G., et al, eds. Rendering Techniques '98: Proceedings of the Eurographics Workshop in Vienna, Austria, June 29-July 1, 1998. (Eurographics Ser.). (Illus.). xi, 339p. 1998. pap. 79.95 (*3-211-83213-0*) Spr-Verlag.

Dretzke, Beverly Jean. Statistics with Microsoft Excel. LC 98-162694. (Illus.). 164p. (C). 1998. pap. 18.00 (*0-13-956533-7*, Prentice Hall) P-H.

Dreu, Carsten K. De, see De Dreu, Carsten K., ed.

Dreuckhammer, David. Agricultural Sales & Services. 65p. (C). 1994. 14.78 (*1-56870-130-6*) RonJon Pub.

Dreuihe. English-French Political, Legal & Economic Dictionary with French-English Lexicon: Dictionnaire Anglais-Francais et Lexique Francais-Anglais des Termes Politiques Juridiques et Economiques. (ENG & FRE.). 356p. 1978. pap. write for info. (*0-7859-4866-X*) Fr & Eur.

Dreux, William B. No Bridges Blown. LC 72-165994. 336p. reprint ed. pap. 104.20 (*0-608-12682-9*, 202436900037) Bks Demand.

***Drever, Frances, et al.** Social Inequalities 2000 Edition. 110p. 2000. pap. 60.00 (*0-11-621269-1*, Pub. by Statnry Office) Balogh.

Drever, J., jt. auth. see Frohlich, W. D.

Drever, James I. The Geochemistry of Natural Waters: Surface & Groundwater Environments. 3rd ed. LC 96-51617. (Illus.). 436p. (C). 1997. 85.33 (*0-13-272790-0*) P-H.

Drever, James I., ed. The Chemistry of Weathering. 1985. text 178.50 (*90-277-1962-4*) Kluwer Academic.

***Drever, Mena.** Teaching English in Primary Classrooms. 1999. pap. text 22.50 (*1-85856-177-9*, Trentham Bks) Stylus Pub VA.

Drevet. Bibliographie de la Litterature Francaise (1940-1948) write for info. (*0-8288-7715-7*, F12520) Fr & Eur.

Drevon, Christian A., et al, eds. Omega-3 Fatty Acids: Metabolism & Biological Effcts. LC 93-17079. (Advances in Life Sciences Ser.). ix, 389p. 1993. 93.50 (*0-8176-2884-3*) Birkhauser.

Drevyanko, William. Breaking the "No" Barrier. 160p. 1995. pap. text, per. 19.95 (*0-7872-1365-9*) Kendall-Hunt.

Drew. Autobiographical Sketch of Mrs. John Drew. LC 76-81207. (Illus.). 112p. 1972. 19.95 (*0-405-18149-3*) Ayer.

— Symmetry Operator Program. 32p. 1992. disk 250.00 (*0-19-268034-X*) OUP.

Drew & Cooper. An Introduction to Communication: A Student Workbook. 3rd ed. 182p. 1998. student ed. 32.95 (*0-7872-4897-5*, 41489701) Kendall-Hunt.

Drew, et al. Guide for Writing Theses. 56p. (C). 1999. per. 30.95 (*0-7872-5720-6*, 41572001) Kendall-Hunt.

Drew, jt. auth. see Hardman.

Drew, Erin, ed. see Lewis, Monty & Lewis, Sara.

Drew, Erin, ed. see Lewis, Sara & Lewis, Monty.

Drew, A. J. Wicca for Men: A Handbook for Male Pagans Seeking a Spiritual Path. LC 98-29048. 192p. 1998. pap. 10.95 (*0-8065-2023-X*, Citadel Pr) Carol Pub Group.

Drew, A. V. Alternative Disposal Methods of Associated Gas from Marginal Fields. (C). 1989. 125.00 (*0-89771-736-8*, Pub. by Lorne & MacLean Marine) St Mut.

— Alternative Disposal Methods of Association Gas from Marginal Fields. 1989. 130.00 (*90-6314-561-6*, Pub. by Lorne & MacLean Marine) St Mut.

***Drew, Angela F., ed.** Atherosclerosis Methods & Protocols. (Methods in Molecular Medicine Ser.: Vol. 52). (Illus.). 250p. 2000. 89.50 (*0-89603-751-7*) Humana.

Drew, Anne M. The Innkeeper's Wife. 32p. 1990. pap. 4.95 (*0-687-19027-4*) Abingdon.

Drew, Anne M., ed. Past Crimson, Past Woe: The Shakespeare Beckett Connection. LC 93-17684. (Studies in Modern Drama: Vol. 4). 200p. 1993. text 15.00 (*0-8153-1383-7*, H1756) Garland.

Drew, Anne M., et al. 365 Meditations for Teachers. 336p. 1996. pap. 12.00 (*0-687-01025-X*) Dimen for Liv.

Drew, Anne Marie, ed. Letters from Annapolis: Midshipmen Write Home, 1848-1969. LC 98-4956. (Illus.). 256p. 1998. 29.95 (*1-55750-170-X*) Naval Inst Pr.

Drew, Barbara, ed. Financial Management of Scientific Journals. LC 89-7666. (Illus.). 101p. 1989. pap. text 24.95 (*0-914340-08-5*) Coun Biology Eds.

Drew-Bear, Annette. Painted Faces on the Renaissance Stage: The Moral Significance of Face-Painting Conventions. (C). 92-54668. (C). 1994. 29.50 (*0-8387-5230-6*) Bucknell U Pr.

Drew-Bear, Marie. Le Nome Hermopolite: Toponymes et Sites. LC 78-13005. (American Studies in Papyrology: No. 21). (Illus.). 432p. reprint ed. pap. 134.00 (*0-7837-5494-9*, 204525900005) Bks Demand.

Drew, Benjamin. Burial Hill, Plymouth, Massachusetts: Its Monuments & Gravestones Numbered & Briefly Described & the Inscriptions & Epitaphs Thereon Carefully Copied. 332p. 1994. pap. 25.00 (*0-8063-4504-7*) Clearfield Co.

Drew, Bernard A. Action Series & Sequels: A Bibliography of Espionage, Vigilante & Soldier-of-Fortune Novels. LC 88-11007. 330p. 1988. text 66.00 (*0-8240-8396-2*) Garland.

— Berkshire Further off the Trail. (Illus.). 56p. 1992. pap. 7.50 (*0-941583-19-8*) Attic Rev Pr.

— The Berkshire Photo Album: Historic Images: 1870s-1990s. LC 99-61640. (Illus.). 128p. 1999. pap. 19.95 (*0-9671427-0-9*, Berkshire Eagle) New England MA.

— Heroines: A Bibliography of Women Series Characters in Mystery, Espionage, Action, Science Fiction, Fantasy, Horror, Western, Romance & Juvenile Novels. LC 89-34233. 404p. 1989. text 30.00 (*0-8240-3047-8*, H878) Garland.

— Hopalong Cassidy: The Clarence E. Mulford Story. LC 91-33491. (Illus.). 307p. 1991. 34.50 (*0-8108-2516-3*) Scarecrow.

***Drew, Bernard A.** Hopalong Cassidy: The Clarence E. Mulford Story. 307p. 2000. pap. 19.95 (*0-8108-3532-0*) Scarecrow.

Drew, Bernard A. Hopalong Cassidy Rides the Airwaves of the Old West. 20p. (Orig.). 1995. pap. 5.00 (*0-941583-24-4*) Attic Rev Pr.

— The Night Riley Chase Fell in the Icy Housatonic River. 48p. 1994. pap. 6.50 (*0-941583-22-8*) Attic Rev Pr.

— The 100 Most Popular Young Adult Authors: Biographical Sketches & Bibliographies. rev. ed. LC 97-25882. 531p. 1997. 55.00 (*1-56308-615-8*) Libs Unl.

— Spanning Berkshire Waterways: A Personal Excursion into the History of Metal Truss Highway Bridge Construction in Western New England 1865-1905. (Illus.). 32p. (Orig.). 1990. pap. 5.00 (*0-941583-18-X*) Attic Rev Pr.

— Western Series & Sequels. 2nd ed. LC 92-22569. 304p. 1993. text 15.00 (*0-8240-9648-7*, H1399) Garland.

Drew, Bernard A., compiled by. Lawmen in Scarlet: An Annotated Guide to Royal Canadian Mounted Police in Print & Performance. LC 90-8388. (Illus.). 296p. 1990. 31.50 (*0-8108-2330-6*) Scarecrow.

Drew, Bernard A., ed. see Bryant, William C.

Drew, Bettina. Crossing the Expendable Landscape. LC 98-84452. 232p. 1998. pap. 15.00 (*1-55597-279-9*) Graywolf.

Drew, Bettina, ed. & intro. see Algren, Nelson.

Drew, Bonnie J. & Drew, Noel. Fast Cash for Kids. 2nd ed. LC 95-5746. (Illus.). 264p. (J). (gr. 2-12). 1995. pap. 13.99 (*1-56414-154-3*) Career Pr Inc.

Drew, Brian & Edwards, John. Viagra & the Quest for Potency: Answers & Solutions to Restore & Enhance Your Quality of Life. Markowski, Mike & Markowski, Marjie, eds. 168p. 1998. pap. 11.95 (*0-938716-55-7*) Markowski Intl.

Drew, Candy F. Advanced Technologies: Pros & Cons. (Illus.). 160p. 1993. pap. text 30.00 (*1-883355-15-X*) Odelle Pubns.

— It Was Rape: A Collection of Art, Poetry & Fiction. 116p. 1993. pap. 10.00 (*1-883355-46-X*) Odelle Pubns.

— Tips on Evaluating & Re-Engineering the Help Desk. (Illus.). 138p. (Orig.). 1993. pap. 30.00 (*1-883355-01-X*) Odelle Pubns.

***Drew, Charles.** A Public Faith. 2000. pap. 8.00 (*1-57683-215-5*) NavPress.

Drew, Charles S. An Account of the Origin & Early Prosecution of the Indian War in Oregon. 48p. 1973. reprint ed. 10.95 (*0-87770-046-X*) Ye Galleon.

***Drew, Charles S.** The Ancient Love Song: Finding Christ in the Old Testament. (Illus.). 208p. 2000. pap. 10.99 (*0-87552-175-4*) P & R Pubng.

Drew, Christopher. God Theories Mislead People. 1992. pap. 3.00 (*0-936128-16-X*) De Young Pr.

Drew, Christopher, jt. auth. see Sontag, Sherry.

***Drew, Christopher M.** Jesus & Moses Were Invented. 126p. 2000. pap. 8.00 (*1-57884-912-8*, 5592) Am Atheist.

***Drew, Clifford J., ed.** Mental Retardation: A Life Cycle Approach. 7th ed. LC 99-18772. (Illus.). 429p. (C). 1999. 73.00 (*0-13-010044-7*) P-H.

Drew, Clifford J. & Hardman, M. L. Designing & Conducting Behavioral Research. (General Psychology Ser.: No. 134). 311p. 1986. pap. write for info. (*0-08-033988-3*, Pergamon Pr) Elsevier.

Drew, Clifford J., et al. Designing & Conducting Research: Inquiry in Education & Social Science. 2nd ed. (C). 1996. teacher ed. write for info. (*0-205-18806-0*, H8806-5) Allyn.

— Designing & Conducting Research: Inquiry in Education & Social Science. 2nd rev. ed. LC 95-16474. 480p. 1995. 79.00 (*0-205-16699-7*) Allyn.

Drew, D. A. & Passman, S. L. Theory of Multicomponent Fluids. Marsden, J. E. & Sirovich, L., eds. LC 98-18392. (Applied Mathematical Sciences Ser.). 330p. 1998. 59.95 (*0-387-98380-5*) Spr-Verlag.

Drew, Daniel C., tr. see Volkov, Vladimir & Milner, Evgeny C.

Drew, David. Ah, Treasure! LC 92-21455. (Voyages Ser.). (Illus.). (J). 1993. 3.75 (*0-383-03611-9*) SRA McGraw.

— The Big Brown Box. LC 92-30673. (Voyages Ser.). (Illus.). (J). 1993. 2.50 (*0-383-03619-4*) SRA McGraw.

— Collections. LC 93-16141. (Illus.). (J). 1994. write for info. (*0-383-03683-6*) SRA McGraw.

— Does a Duck Eat Honey? LC 92-31917. (Voyages Ser.). (Illus.). (J). 1993. 4.25 (*0-383-03563-5*) SRA McGraw.

— How Many Legs? LC 92-34268. (Voyages Ser.). (Illus.). (J). 1993. 4.25 (*0-383-03631-3*) SRA McGraw.

— Jock Jerome. LC 92-31133. (Voyages Ser.). (Illus.). (J). 1993. 2.50 (*0-383-03636-4*) SRA McGraw.

***Drew, David.** Lost Chronicles of the Maya Kings. 384p. 2000. 29.95 (*0-520-22612-7*, Pub. by U CA Pr) Cal Prin Full Svc.

Drew, David. Make a Salad Face. LC 92-34335. (Illus.). (J). 1993. 2.50 (*0-383-03640-2*) SRA McGraw.

— Man-Environment Processes. (Processes in Physical Geography Ser.: No. 6). (Illus.). 152p. 1983. pap. text 16.95 (*0-04-551063-6*) Routledge.

— My House. LC 92-30424. (Voyages Ser.). (Illus.). (J). 1993. 2.50 (*0-383-03586-4*) SRA McGraw.

— Nibbly Mouse. LC 92-21397. (Voyages Ser.). (Illus.). (J). 1993. 4.25 (*0-383-03587-2*) SRA McGraw.

— The Python Caught the Eagle. LC 92-31134. (Voyages Ser.). (Illus.). (J). 1993. 2.50 (*0-383-03648-8*) SRA McGraw.

— Race, Education, & Work. 232p. 1995. 72.95 (*1-85972-111-7*, Pub. by Avebry) Ashgate Pub Co.

— The Seesaw. LC 92-21394. (Illus.). (J). (gr. 2 up). 1993. 2.50 (*0-685-69191-8*) SRA McGraw.

— Senses. LC 92-34162. (Illus.). (J). 1993. 3.75 (*0-383-03651-8*) SRA McGraw.

— Something Silver, Something Blue. LC 92-34256. (Voyages Ser.). (Illus.). (J). 1993. 4.25 (*0-383-03654-2*) SRA McGraw.

— The Storm. LC 92-30671. (Voyages Ser.). (Illus.). (J). 1993. write for info. (*0-383-03656-9*) SRA McGraw.

— Toenails. LC 92-31135. (Voyages Ser.). (Illus.). (J). 1993. 2.50 (*0-383-03661-5*) SRA McGraw.

— Two More. LC 92-31957. (Voyages Ser.). (Illus.). (J). 1993. 3.75 (*0-383-03600-3*) SRA McGraw.

— When I Turned Six. LC 93-26929. (Voyages Ser.). (Illus.). (J). 1994. 4.25 (*0-383-03784-0*) SRA McGraw.

Drew, David & Hotzl, Heinz, eds. Karst Hydrogeology & Human Activities: Impacts, Consequences & Implications. (Illus.). 3p. 1999. 79.00 (*90-5410-463-5*, Pub. by A A Balkema) Ashgate Pub Co.

— Karst Hydrogeology & Human Activities: Impacts, Consequences & Implications (IAH International Contributions to Hydrogeology 20) 286p. 1998. pap. write for info. (*90-5410-464-3*, Pub. by A A Balkema) Ashgate Pub Co.

***Drew, David, et al.** Resuscitation of the Newborn: A Practical Approach. (Illus.). 128p. 2000. pap. text 30.00 (*0-7506-4378-1*) Buttrwrth-Heinemann.

Drew, David E. Aptitude Revisited: Rethinking Math & Science Education for America's Next Century. LC 95-35256. 296p. (C). 1996. text 35.95 (*0-8018-5143-2*) Johns Hopkins.

Drew, Dennis M. & Snow, Donald M. The Eagle's Talons: The American Experience at War. 445p. 1988. pap. 16.00 (*1-58566-025-6*) Air Univ.

— Making Strategy: An Introduction to National Security Processes & Problems. (Illus.). 1988. pap. 10.00 (*1-58566-021-3*) Air Univ.

Drew, Dennis M., jt. auth. see Snow, Donald M.

Drew, Donald A., et al, eds. Particulate Flows: Processing & Rheology. LC 97-41795. (IMA Volumes in Mathematics & Its Applications Ser.: Vol. 98). (Illus.). 156p. 1997. 49.95 (*0-387-98378-3*) Spr-Verlag.

Drew, Donald A. & Flaherty, Joseph E., eds. Mathematics Applied to Fluid Mechanics & Stability: Proceedings of a Conference Dedicated to Richard C. DiPrima. LC 86-61597. (Proceedings in Applied Mathematics Ser.: No. 24). (Illus.). xii, 295p. 1986. text 42.50 (*0-89871-208-4*) Soc Indus-Appl Math.

Drew, Donald B. Uncle Don's Adventure down East Cookbook. (Illus.). 217p. 1987. pap. 8.95 (*0-9617940-0-3*) D B Drew.

Drew, Eileen. Blue Taxis: Stories about Africa. LC 89-12595. (Illus.). 160p. (Orig.). 1989. pap. 9.95 (*0-915943-41-7*) Milkweed Ed.

— The Ivory Crocodile. LC 96-3143. 288p. 1996. 21.95 (*1-56689-042-X*) Coffee Hse.

Drew, Eileen P. & Foster, Gordon F., eds. Information Technology in Selected Countries: Reports from Ireland, Ethiopia, Nigeria & Tanzania. LC 96-129074. 148p. 1993. pap. write for info. (*92-808-0831-1*, Pub. by UN Univ Pr) Brookings.

Drew, Eileen P., et al. Women, Work, & the Family in Europe. LC 97-45075. 248p. (C). 1998. 85.00 (*0-415-15350-6*); pap. 24.99 (*0-415-15351-4*) Routledge.

***Drew, Elizabeth.** The Corruption of American Politics: What Went Wrong & Why. LC 99-28684. 256p. 1999. 21.95 (*1-55972-520-6*, Birch Ln Pr) Carol Pub Group.

— The Corruption of American Politics: What Went Wrong & Why. 2000. pap. 15.95 (*1-58567-049-9*, Pub. by Overlook Pr) Penguin Putnam.

Drew, Elizabeth. On the Edge: The Clinton Presidency. 512p. 1995. per. 14.00 (*0-684-81309-2*, Touchstone) S&S Trade Pap.

— Showdown: The Struggle Between the Gingrich Congress & the Clinton White House. LC 97-193528. 443p. 1996. 24.50 (*0-684-81518-4*) Simon & Schuster.

— Whatever It Takes: The Real Struggle for Political Power in America. LC 97-10423. 300p. 1998. pap. 13.95 (*0-14-026858-8*) Viking Penguin.

Drew, Elizabeth A. Jane Welsh & Jane Carlyle. LC 72-3641. (English Literature Ser.: No. 33). 1972. reprint ed. lib. bdg. 75.00 (*0-8383-1555-0*) M S G Haskell Hse.

Drew, Elizabeth A. & Sweeney, J. L. Directions in Modern Poetry. LC 67-30307. 290p. 1967. reprint ed. 45.00 (*0-87752-029-1*) Gordian.

***Drew, Flowayne.** Serving from Your Kitchen. 1999. pap. 14.99 (*0-89225-389-4*) Gospel Advocate.

Drew, Fraser. John Masefield's England: A Study of the National Themes in His Work. LC 72-415. (Illus.). 261p. 1973. 24.50 (*0-8386-1020-X*) Fairleigh Dickinson.

Drew, George. The Beatitudes: Attitudes for a Better Future. 63p. (Orig.). 1980. pap. 7.95 (*0-940754-03-7*) Ed Ministries.

— Making the Bible Our Own. 65p. 1985. pap. 7.95 (*0-940754-29-0*) Ed Ministries.

— The Original Ideas of Jesus That Are Changing the World. 45p. (Orig.). 1980. pap. 7.95 (*0-940754-05-3*) Ed Ministries.

— The Parables in Depth. 55p. (Orig.). 1982. pap. 7.95 (*0-940754-18-5*) Ed Ministries.

— Portraits of Jesus Through the Ages. 1990. pap. 7.95 (*0-940754-94-0*) Ed Ministries.

— The Prophets Speak to Our Time. 62p. (Orig.). 1981. pap. 7.95 (*0-940754-09-6*) Ed Ministries.

— St. Paul: He Created Christianity from Jesus' Religion. 60p. (Orig.). 1984. pap. 7.95 (*0-940754-22-3*) Ed Ministries.

— The Ten Commandments in Today's World. 48p. (Orig.). 1979. pap. 7.95 (*0-940754-00-2*) Ed Ministries.

Drew, George E. More Parables in Depth. 1988. pap. 7.95 (*0-940754-52-5*, 6348) Ed Ministries.

— Mysteries of the Psalms. 55p. (Orig.). 1989. pap. 7.95 (*0-940754-68-1*) Ed Ministries.

— What Kind of God Is God? 65p. (Orig.). 1986. pap. 7.95 (*0-940754-33-9*) Ed Ministries.

Drew, Grady. Using Set for Secure Electronic Commerce. LC 98-44679. 304p. 1998. pap. text 44.99 (*0-13-099715-3*) P-H.

Drew, Helen. My First Music Book. LC 92-54306. (Illus.). 48p. (J). (gr. k-3). 1993. 12.95 (*1-56458-215-9*) DK Pub Inc.

Drew, Helen & Wilkes, Angela. Let's Bake a Cake. LC 97-12534. (Illus.). (J). 1997. write for info. (*0-7894-1560-7*) DK Pub Inc.

Drew, Horace R., jt. auth. see Calladine, Chris R.

Drew, J. E., ed. New Developments in X-Ray & Ultraviolet Astronomy: Proceedings of the E1.2 Meeting of the COSPAR Scientific Commission E Which Was Held During the 30th COSPAR Scientific Assembly, Hamburg, Germany, 11-21 July, 1994. (Advances in Space Research Ser.: Vol. 16). 168p. 1995. pap. 104.00 (*0-08-042623-9*, Pergamon Pr) Elsevier.

***Drew, J. M.** Farm Blacksmithing: Practical Hints for Handy-Men. (Illus.). 2000. pap. 12.95 (*1-58574-097-7*) Lyons Pr.

Drew, J. P. & Spevak, Elaine. Discount Travel U. S. A., America on Sale. LC 96-134273. (Illus.). 304p. (Orig.). 1996. 18.00 (*0-9640397-1-0*) Travelus Pubng.

Drew, James. Blues & Rags. (Illus.). 13p. 1989. 3.50 (*0-9625023-0-8*) Art Pr Intl.

— Rackstraw: The Magical Thoughts & Adventures of A Brilliant Young Art Mouse. George, Mary G., ed. LC 93-71718. (Illus.). 168p. (J). (gr. 2-9). 2000. 18.95 (*0-9625023-9-1*) Art Pr Intl.

Drew, James & George, Mary G. FormingReforming, Bk. 1. 23p. (C). 1992. pap. text, teacher ed. 6.00 (*0-9625023-4-0*) Art Pr Intl.

— FormingReforming Bk. 1: Projects in Classical Improvisation. 12p. 1992. pap. text 3.50 (*0-9625023-3-2*) Art Pr Intl.

Drew, James M. Clean Water & Sewage Disposal on the Farm. (Illus.). 43p. 1986. reprint ed. pap. 10.00 (*0-8466-6037-7*, U-37, Shorey Pubns) Shoreys Bkstore.

Drew, Jane B., jt. auth. see Fry, Maxwell E.

Drew, Jane M. Where Were You When I Needed You, Dad? A Guide for Healing Your Father Wound. LC 91-68455. (Illus.). 193p. (Orig.). 1992. pap. 19.95 (*1-880883-00-7*) Tiger Lily Pub.

Drew, Jennifer. The Bad-Girl Bride. (Yours Truly Ser.). 1998. per. 3.50 (*0-373-52077-8*, 1-52077-4) Harlequin Bks.

— Dear Mr. Right. (Yours Truly Ser.). 1996. per. 3.50 (*0-373-52028-X*, 1-52028-7) Silhouette.

— The Prince & the Bogus Bride. (Yours Truly Ser.). 1998. per. 3.50 (*0-373-52060-3*, 1-52060-0) Silhouette.

— Turn Back the Night. 1994. per. 2.75 (*0-373-19040-9*, 1-19040-4) Harlequin Bks.

***Drew, Jennifer & Thomas, Kate.** Baby Lessons; Too Lucky for Love. (Duets Ser.: Bk. 18). 2000. per. 5.99 (*0-373-44084-7*, 1-44084-1) Harlequin Bks.

Drew, Jennifer, jt. auth. see Gabriel, Kristin.

Drew, Joanna, ed. Aromatherapy. (Select Pocket Library). 96p. 1997. 4.98 (*0-7858-0446-3*) Bk Sales Inc.

Drew, John. India & the Romantic Imagination. 305p. 1998. reprint ed. pap. 16.95 (*0-19-564710-6*) OUP.

— Lesser Vehicle. 1986. pap. 10.95 (*0-906427-71-1*, Pub. by Bloodaxe Bks) Dufour.

Drew, John, ed. Readings in International Enterprise. 368p. (C). 1995. pap. 31.95 (*0-415-12317-8*, C0239) Thomson Learn.

— Readings in International Enterprise. LC 94-36316. 368p. (C). (gr. 13). 1995. pap. 74.95 (*0-415-12316-X*, C0238) Thomson Learn.

Drew, Joseph W. & Hague, W. Creation of Full Human Personality. pap. 1.00 (*0-8199-0383-3*, L38115, Frncscn Herld) Franciscan Pr.

Drew, Julie, jt. ed. see Olson, Gary A.

Drew, Katherine F. Law & Society in Early Medieval Europe: Studies in Legal History. (Collected Studies: No. CS271). 302p. (C). 1988. reprint ed. lib. bdg. 106.95 (*0-86078-219-0*, Pub. by Variorum) Ashgate Pub Co.

— The Lombard Laws. LC 72-80381. (Middle Ages Ser.). 302p. 1973. pap. 18.95 (*0-8122-1055-7*) U of Pa Pr.

Drew, Katherine F., tr. Burgundian Code: Book of Constitutions or Law of Gundobad Additional Enactments. LC 70-182499. (Middle Ages Ser.). (Illus.). 128p. (Orig.). 1972. pap. text 16.50 (*0-8122-1035-2*) U of Pa Pr.

Drew, Katherine F., tr. from LAT. The Laws of the Salian Franks. LC 90-21755. (Middle Ages Ser.). 276p. (C). 1991. text 39.95 (*0-8122-8256-6*); pap. text 17.95 (*0-8122-1322-X*) U of Pa Pr.

Drew, Katherine F. & Lear, Floyd S., eds. Perspectives in Medieval History. LC 63-20902. 105p. reprint ed. 32.60 (*0-8357-9653-1*, 201575300097) Bks Demand.

Drew, Ken. Camp Sumter, the Andersonville Chronology. (Illus.). 56p. (Orig.). 1989. pap. 2.50 (*0-9622714-0-3*) K Drew.

— Countdown to Manassas. (Illus.). 56p. (Orig.). 1989. pap. 2.35 (*0-9622714-1-1*) K Drew.

Drew, L. J. Undiscovered Petroleum & Mineral Resources: Assessment & Controversy. LC 97-1864. (Illus.). 224p. (C). 1997. text 59.50 (*0-306-45524-2*, Kluwer Plenum) Kluwer Academic.

D

An Asterisk (*) at the beginning of an entry indicates that the title is appearing for the first time.

Drew, Lawrence J. Oil & Gas Forecasting: Reflections of a Petroleum Geologist. (International Association for Mathematical Geology: Studies in Mathematical Geology: No. 2). (Illus.). 264p. 1990. text 65.00 (*0-19-506170-5*) OUP.

Drew, Leslie. Haida: Their Art & Culture. (Illus.). 111p. 1989. pap. 9.95 (*0-88839-132-3*) Hancock House.

Drew, Leslie & Wilson, Douglas. Argillite: Art of the Haida. (Illus.). 312p. 40.00 (*0-88839-037-8*) Hancock House.

Drew, Linda. The Business of Fashion. (Illus.). 96p. (C). 1992. pap. 18.95 (*0-521-40825-3*) Cambridge U Pr.

Drew, Louisa L. Autobiographical Sketch of Mrs. John Drew. (American Biography Ser.). 200p. 1991. reprint ed. lib. bdg. 69.00 (*0-7812-8114-8*) Rprt Serv.

Drew, Lucas & Barr, Raymond. Everything You Always Wanted to Know about the Symphony Orchestra. rev. ed. 1992. write for info. (*0-913402-05-2*) E F Kalmus.

Drew, Lucas, et al. Artist's Studio for Strings - Shifting Development Studies: String Bass. 40p. 1986. pap. text 3.95 (*0-8497-3229-8*, 81SB) Kjos.

Drew, Mabel. A Way of Seeing. 118p. 1993. pap. 12.95 (*1-55082-096-6*, Pub. by Quarry Pr) LPC InBook.

Drew, Mary. Acton, Gladstone & Others. LC 68-20294. (Essay Index Reprint Ser.). 1977. 17.95 (*0-8369-0390-0*) Ayer.

Drew, Mary A. The Diabolist. (Orig.). 1978. pap. 0.95 (*0-380-00235-3*, 21451, Avon Bks) Morrow Avon.

Drew, Melinda, jt. auth. see Cowdrey, Michael L.

Drew, Nancy, et al. LACE Ten Years Documented. Moss, Karen, ed. (Illus.). 112p. 1988. pap. 15.00 (*0-937335-03-7*) LA Contemp Exhib.

Drew, Nancy, jt. auth. see Williams, Bunny.

***Drew, Nancy Swan.** Be Your Own Angel: Snippets for Tough Cookies (Breast Cancer Soldiers) LC 00-21779. (Illus.). 112p. 2000. bds. 12.95 (*0-89087-966-4*) Celestial Arts.

Drew, Nancy Swan. First-Aid Kit for Mothers: Fill Your Pockets Full of Miracles. LC RG121.D775 2000. (Illus.). 256p. 2000. pap. 18.95 (*0-89087-861-7*) Celestial Arts.

***Drew, Nancy Swan.** Love Pearls: From a Mother to Her Daughter. (Illus.). 112p. 2000. 12.95 (*0-89087-983-4*) Celestial Arts.

Drew, Naomi. Learning the Skills of Peacemaking: A K-6 Activity Guide to Resolving Conflicts, Communicating, & Cooperating. 2nd rev. ed. Remkus, Susan, ed. 272p. 1995. pap. 29.95 (*1-880396-42-4*, JP9642-4) Jalmar Pr.

***Drew, Naomi.** The Peaceful Classroom in Action: How to Create One & How to Keep It! 154p. 1999. pap. 24.95 (*1-880396-61-0*) Jalmar Pr.

— Peaceful Parents, Peaceful Kids: Practical Ways to Create a Calm & Happy Home. 2000. pap. 14.00 (*1-57566-608-1*) Kensgtn Pub Corp.

Drew, Noel, jt. auth. see Drew, Bonnie J.

Drew, Paul. After the Storm: A Vietnam Veteran's Reflections. LC 99-23110. 131p. 1999. pap. 14.95 (*1-55571-500-1*) PSI Resch.

Drew, Paul & Heritage, John, eds. Talk at Work: Interaction in Institutional Settings. (Studies in Interactional Sociolinguistics: No. 8). 592p. (C). 1993. pap. text 37.95 (*0-521-37633-5*) Cambridge U Pr.

Drew, Philip. Church on the Water & Church of the Light: Hokkaido, Japan 1988 & Osaka, Japan 1989. LC 96-172993. (Architecture in Detail Ser.). (Illus.). 60p. 1996. pap. text 29.95 (*0-7148-3268-5*, Pub. by Phaidon Press) Phaidon Pr.

— The Meaning of Freedom. (Illus.). 500p. (C). 1985. pap. text 16.50 (*0-08-032450-9*, Pub. by Aberdeen U Pr) Macmillan.

— The Meaning of Freedom. 460p. 1982. text 32.00 (*0-08-025743-7*, Pergamon Pr) Elsevier.

— Sydney Opera House: Sydney, 1957-73 - Jorn Utzon. (Architecture in Detail Ser.). (Illus.). 60p. (Orig.). (C). 1995. pap. 29.95 (*0-7148-3297-9*, Pub. by Phaidon Press) Phaidon Pr.

Drew, Philip, jt. auth. see Frampton, Kenneth.

Drew, Phillip. The Museum of Modern Art, Gunma: Takasaki, Gunma Prefecture, Japan, 1971-74. (Architecture in Detail Ser.). (Illus.). 60p. (Orig.). 1996. pap. 29.95 (*0-7148-3549-8*, Pub. by Phaidon Press) Phaidon Pr.

Drew, R. M., jt. ed. see Kerr, Alistair.

Drew, Rad A., jt. auth. see Mikulecky, Larry.

Drew, Ralph. Ophthalmic Dispensing: Present Day Realities. (Illus.). 304p. 1990. text 74.95 (*0-409-90225-X*) Buttrwrth-Heinemann.

Drew, Rosa. The Block Party, Vol. 4410. Kupperstein, Joel, ed. (Learn to Read Social Studies). (Illus.). 16p. (J). (ps-2). 1998. pap. 2.75 (*1-57471-333-7*, 4410) Creat Teach Pr.

— Cat & Dog Go Shopping, Vol. 4476. Kupperstein, Joel, ed. (Learn to Read Math Ser.). (Illus.). 16p. (J). 1998. pap. 2.75 (*1-57471-383-3*, 4476) Creat Teach Pr.

— Lemonade, Vol. 4472. Kupperstein, Joel, ed. (Learn to Read Math Ser.). (Illus.). 16p. (J). 1998. pap. 2.75 (*1-57471-379-5*, 4472) Creat Teach Pr.

Drew, Rosa & Phillips, Heather. Celebrating Chinese New Year No. 4524: Nick's New Year. Kupperstein, Joel, ed. (Illus.). 16p. (J). (ps-2). 1999. pap. 2.99 (*1-57471-569-0*) Creat Teach Pr.

Drew, Rosa, jt. auth. see Bauer, Karen.

Drew, S. Nelson. The Future of NATO: Facing an Unreliable Enemy in an Uncertain Environment. LC 90-7799. 224p. 1991. 55.00 (*0-275-93802-6*, C3802, Praeger Pubs) Greenwood.

— NATO: From Berlin to Bosnia - Trans-Atlantic Security in Transition. 49p. (Orig.). (C). 1996. reprint ed. pap. text 25.00 (*0-7881-3680-1*) DIANE Pub.

Drew, S. Nelson. Nato from Berlin to Bosnia: Trans-Atlantic Security in Transition. 53p. 1995. pap. 3.00 (*0-16-061174-1*) USGPO.

Drew, Shirley & Cooper, Gil. An Introduction to Communication: A Student Workbook. 224p. (C). 1996. spiral bd. 20.95 (*0-7872-2466-9*) Kendall-Hunt.

Drew, Simon. A Book of Bestial Nonsense. (Illus.). 48p. 1986. 12.50 (*1-85149-041-8*) Antique Collect.

— Camp David: Nonsense in Art. (Illus.). 48p. 1992. 12.95 (*1-85149-162-7*) Antique Collect.

— Cat with Piano Tuna & Other Feline Nonsense. (Illus.). 48p. 1990. 12.95 (*1-85149-138-4*) Antique Collect.

— Dogsbodies. (Illus.). 48p. 1997. 12.95 (*1-85149-271-2*) Antique Collect.

— The Duck Stops Here. (Illus.). 48p. 1998. 12.95 (*1-85149-290-9*) Antique Collect.

— Great Mistakes of Civilisation: Mankind's Mistakes & Faux Pas. (Illus.). 48p. 12.95 (*1-85149-246-1*) Antique Collect.

— Handel's Warthog Music: Nonsense in Music. (Illus.). 48p. 1993. 12.95 (*1-85149-186-4*) Antique Collect.

— Nonsense in Flight. (Illus.). 48p. 1987. 12.50 (*1-85149-061-2*) Antique Collect.

— A Pig's Ear: Nonsense from the Pigsty. (Illus.). 48p. 1994. 12.95 (*1-85149-208-9*) Antique Collect.

— Puffin's Advice. 48p. 1988. 12.50 (*1-85149-102-3*) Antique Collect.

— Simon Drew's Beastley Birthday Book. LC 96-154084. (Illus.). 128p. 1995. 13.95 (*1-85149-220-8*) Antique Collect.

***Drew, Simon.** Spot the Book Title. (Illus.). 48p. 2000. 14.95 (*1-85149-356-5*) Antique Collect.

Drew, Simon. Still Warthogs Run Deep & Other Free Range Nonsense. (Illus.). 48p. 1987. 12.95 (*1-85149-087-6*) Antique Collect.

***Drew, Simon.** The Very Worst of Simon Drew. (Illus.). 48p. 2000. 12.95 (*1-85149-331-X*) Antique Collect.

Drew-Smith, J., et al. Fungal Diseases of Amenity of Turf Grasses. 416p. 1989. 160.00 (*0-419-11530-7*, A2404, E & FN Spon) Routledge.

Drew, Stephen, jt. ed. see Flickinger, Michael.

Drew, Sue & Bingham, Rosie. The Student Skills Guide. (Student Skills Project Ser.). 350p. 1996. pap. text 22.95 (*0-566-07847-3*, Pub. by Gower) Ashgate Pub Co.

— Student Skills Tutor's Handbook. (Student Skills Project Ser.). 350p. 1996. pap. text 43.95 (*0-566-07846-5*, Pub. by Gower) Ashgate Pub Co.

Drew, Sue, jt. auth. see Bingham, Rosie.

Drew, Thomas, compiled by. The John Brown Invasion: An Authentic History of the Harper's Ferry Tragedy. LC 72-8568. (Black Heritage Library Collection). 1977. reprint ed. 17.95 (*0-8369-9188-5*) Ayer.

Drew, Thomas B., et al, eds. Advances in Chemical Engineering, Vol. 11. LC 56-6600. (Serial Publication Ser.). 1981. text 167.00 (*0-12-008511-9*) Acad Pr.

Drew, Thomas B. & Hoopes, John W., Jr., eds. Advances in Chemical Engineering, Vol. 10. (Serial Publication Ser.). 1978. text 167.00 (*0-12-008510-0*) Acad Pr.

Drew, Wilfred. A Guide to Internet/Bitnet Resources in Agriculture & Related Sciences. 58p. (Orig.). (C). 1996. pap. text 20.00 (*0-7881-2742-X*) DIANE Pub.

Drew, Wilfred E., Jr. & Ensor, Pat, eds. Key Guide to Electronic Resources Vol. 1: Agriculture. (Key Guide Ser.). 124p. 1995. pap. 39.50 (*1-57387-000-5*) Info Today Inc.

Drew-Wilkinson, Kate. Basic Wire Work for Bead Jewelry. rev. ed. Haynes, Colin, ed. (Kate Drew-Wilkinson's Best Bead Bks.). (Illus.). 100p. 1994. pap. 9.95 (*1-884648-00-2*) Kate Drew-Wilkinson.

— How to Be Successful in the Bead Jewelry Business. (Kate Drew-Wilkinson's Best Bead Bks.). (Illus.). 100p. (Orig.). 1994. pap. 24.00 (*1-884648-02-9*) Kate Drew-Wilkinson.

Drew, William M. At the Center of the Frame: Leading Ladies of the Twenties & Thirties. LC 99-32498. (Illus.). 376p. 1999. 47.50 (*1-879511-42-8*, Vestal Pr) Madison Bks UPA.

***Drew, William M.** At the Center of the Frame: Leading Ladies of the Twenties & Thirties. LC 99-32498. (Illus.). 320p. 1999. pap. 29.95 (*1-879511-44-4*, Pub. by Madison Bks UPA) Natl Bk Netwk.

Drew, William M. Speaking of Silents: First Ladies of the Screen. LC 89-9025. (Illus.). 312p. 1989. 39.95 (*0-911572-81-3*, Vestal Pr); pap. 24.95 (*0-911572-74-0*, Vestal Pr) Madison Bks UPA.

Drewal, Henry J. The Traditional Art of the Nigerian Peoples: The Ratner Collection. (Illus.). 1977. 7.00 (*0-686-25965-3*) Mus African Art.

Drewal, Henry J. & Drewal, Margaret T. Gelede: Art & Female Power among the Yoruba. LC 82-48388. (Illus.). 322p. (Orig.). 1983. 47.50 (*0-253-32569-2*) Ind U Pr.

— Gelede: Art & Female Power among the Yoruba. LC 82-48388. (Illus.). 322p. (Orig.). 1990. pap. 29.95 (*0-253-20565-4*, MB-565) Ind U Pr.

Drewal, Henry J., et al. Beads, Body, & Soul: Art & Light in the Yoruba Universe. LC 97-49498. (Illus.). 188p. 1997. 70.00 (*0-930741-62-5*) UCLA Fowler Mus.

— Beads, Body & Soul: Art & Light in the Yoruba Universe. LC 97-49498. (Illus.). 188p. 1997. pap. 39.00 (*0-930741-63-3*) UCLA Fowler Mus.

— Yoruba: Nine Centuries of African Art & Thought. Wardwell, Allen, ed. LC 89-22182. (Illus.). 1989. pap. 38.00 (*0-945802-04-8*) Museum African.

Drewal, Margaret T. Yoruba Ritual: Performers, Play, Agency. LC 91-8414. (African Systems of Thought Ser.). (Illus.). 276p. 1992. pap. text 15.95 (*0-253-20684-7*, MB-684) Ind U Pr.

Drewal, Margaret T., jt. auth. see Drewal, Henry J.

***Drewe, Robert.** The Shark Net: Memories & Murder. LC 99-87551. 320p. 2000. 24.95 (*0-670-88809-5*, Viking) Viking Penguin.

Drewe, Sheryle B. Creative Dance: Enriching Understanding. (Illus.). 128p. (Orig.). 1996. pap. text. write for info. (*1-55059-130-4*) Detselig Ents.

Drewermann, Eugen. Open Heavens: Meditations for Advent & Christmas. Laflamme, Joan M. & Marz, Bernd, eds. Krieger, David J., tr. LC 91-28323. 232p. (Orig.). reprint ed. pap. 72.00 (*0-608-20252-5*, 207151100012) Bks Demand.

Drewery, Benjamin, ed. see Bauckham, Richard.

Drewery, Benjamin, jt. ed. see Cunliffe-Jones, Hubert.

Drewes, ed. Tectonics of the Eastern Part of the Cordilleran Orogenic Belt, Chihuahua, New Mexico, & Arizona. (IGC Field Trip Guidebooks Ser.). 88p. 1989. 21.00 (*0-87590-589-7*, T121) Am Geophysical.

Drewes, Athena A. & Drucker, Sally A. Parapsychological Research with Children: An Annotated Bibliography. LC 91-39046. 245p. 1991. 29.00 (*0-8108-2514-7*) Scarecrow.

Drewes, Dorothy J., jt. ed. see Drewes, John M.

Drewes, Frederick W. How to Study Science. 2nd ed. LC 96-84293. 128p. (C). 1996. text. write for info. (*0-697-15905-1*, WCB McGr Hill) McGrw-H Hghr Educ.

— How to Study Science. 2nd ed. 128p. (C). 1997. per. write for info. (*0-07-114279-7*, WCB McGr Hill) McGrw-H Hghr Educ.

Drewes, Jack C. The Restaurant Owner's Handbook: Success Through Management Awareness. LC 87-32697. 356p. (Orig.). (C). 1988. text 49.95 (*0-945034-01-6*); pap. text 29.95 (*0-945034-00-8*) Posh Pubng.

Drewes, Jeanne M. & Page, Julie A., eds. Promoting Preservation Awareness in Libraries: A Sourcebook for Academic, Public, School & Special Collections. LC 96-32981. (Greenwood Library Management Collection). 384p. 1997. lib. bdg. 75.00 (*0-313-30206-5*, Greenwood Pr) Greenwood.

Drewes, John M. The Best of AFN II. (Illus.). 200p. (Orig.). 1990. pap. 19.95 (*0-929931-06-8*) Amer Fireworks.

Drewes, John M., ed. Fireworks Yearbook, 1988. (Illus.). (Orig.). 1989. pap. 19.95 (*0-929931-04-1*) Amer Fireworks.

— Fireworks Yearbook 1991. (Illus.). 250p. 1991. pap. 19.95 (*0-929931-08-4*) Amer Fireworks.

***Drewes, John M. & Drewes, Dorothy J., eds.** The Best of AFN IV. (Illus.). 208p. 2000. pap. 19.95 (*0-929931-15-7*) Amer Fireworks.

Drewes, John M. & Drewes, Dorothy J., eds. The Best of AFN III. (Illus.). 200p. (Orig.). 1995. pap. 19.95 (*0-929931-11-4*) Amer Fireworks.

Drewes, L. R. & Betz, A. L. Frontiers in Cerebral Vascular Biology: Transport & Its Regulation. LC 93-16860. (Advances in Experimental Medicine & Biology Ser.: Vol. 331). (Illus.). 306p. (C). 1993. text 95.00 (*0-306-44416-X*, Kluwer Plenum) Kluwer Academic.

Drewes, Robert W. The Air Force & the Great Engine War. (Illus.). 179p. (Orig.). (C). 1995. pap. text 35.00 (*0-7881-2151-0*) DIANE Pub.

Drewes-Siebel, Renate, tr. see Veldhuis, Henri.

Drewett, Alan M. Railway Trivia. (C). 1992. text 30.00 (*0-9514591-0-4*, Pub. by A M Drewett) St Mut.

Drewett, John. Surrey. (Country Guide Ser.: No. 8). (Illus.). 120p. pap. 12.50 (*0-7478-0310-2*, Pub. by Shire Pubns) Parkwest Pubns.

— Surrey. 120p. 1996. pap. 35.00 (*0-7855-2796-6*, Pub. by Shire Pubns) St Mut.

Drewett, Peter. South East to Ad. LC 87-17144. (Illus.). 384p. (C). 1988. text 39.95 (*0-582-49271-8*) Longman.

Drewett, Peter, et al. The South East to AD 1000. LC 87-17144. (Regional History of England Ser.). 1988. pap. write for info. (*0-582-49272-6*) Longman.

Drewett, Peter, jt. auth. see Biscombe, Tony.

Drewey, Benjamin, jt. ed. see Cunliffe-Jones, Hubert.

Drewitt, Keith, intro. National Conference on Engineering Heritage, 6th, 1992: Conserving & Recording Engineering Heritage. (National Conference Publication Ser.: No. 92-17). (Illus.). 152p. (Orig.). 1992. pap. 77.00 (*0-85825-567-7*, Pub. by Inst Engrs Aust-EA Bks) Accents Pubns.

Drewitz, I., jt. auth. see Richling, C.

Drewniany, Bonnie L., jt. auth. see Jewler, A. Jerome.

Drewnowska-Vargane, Ewa. Ein Neues Textlinguistisches Instrumentarium: Und Seine Anwendung Im Aufbau der Schreibkompetenz Ungarischer Germanistikstudenten. (GER.). 300p. 1997. 57.95 (*3-631-31460-4*) P Lang Pubng.

Drewnowski, Glen. Red Tailed Boas, Their Care & Breeding. (Illus.). 64p. 1995. pap. 9.95 (*0-7938-0275-X*, RE122) TFH Pubns.

Drewry & O'Connor. America Is. annot. ed. 1995. teacher ed. write for info. (*0-02-823323-9*) Glencoe.

Drewry, Douglas L. The Definitive Performance Writing Guide. LC 89-92039. (Illus.). 496p. (Orig.). 1989. pap. 25.95 (*0-9623673-0-3*) Prof Mgmt Spectrum.

— Enlisted Eval & Officer Fitrep Writing Guide. 2nd ed. (Illus.). 348p. 1989. pap. 23.95 (*0-9623673-1-1*) Prof Mgmt Spectrum.

— Fitness Report Writing Guide for Marines. (Illus.). 294p. (Orig.). 1989. pap. 23.95 (*0-9623673-9-7*) Prof Mgmt Spectrum.

— Navy & Marine Corps Performance Writing Guide. (Illus.). 389p. (Orig.). 1986. pap. 23.95 (*0-9623673-7-0*) Prof Mgmt Spectrum.

— Writing Guide for Air Force Efficiency Reports. 389p. (Orig.). 1990. pap. 23.95 (*0-9623673-3-8*) Prof Mgmt Spectrum.

— Writing Guide for Army Efficiency Reports. 389p. (Orig.). 1990. pap. 23.95 (*0-9623673-2-X*) Prof Mgmt Spectrum.

Drewry, Gavin. The New Select Committees: A Study of the 1979 Reforms. 2nd ed. (Illus.). 496p. 1989. pap. write for info. (*0-19-822784-1*) OUP.

— The New Select Committees: A Study of the 1979 Reforms. 2nd ed. (Illus.). 496p. 1989. 85.00 (*0-19-827835-7*) OUP.

***Drewry, Gavin & Blake, Charles, eds.** Law & the Spirit of Inquiry: Essays in Honour of Sir Louis Blom-Cooper, QC. 240p. 1999. text 87.00 (*90-411-9761-3*) Kluwer Law Intl.

Drewry, Gavin & Butcher, Tony. The Civil Service Today. (Illus.). 256p. 1991. pap. 32.95 (*0-631-18172-5*) Blackwell Pubs.

Drewry, Gavin, jt. auth. see Oliver, Dawn H.

Drewry, Gavin, jt. ed. see Giddings, Philip.

Drewry, H. N., jt. auth. see Notterman, J. M.

Drewry, John E. Concerning the Fourth Estate. 2nd ed. LC 42-18567. 181p. reprint ed. pap. 56.20 (*0-608-14015-5*, 205553700028) Bks Demand.

— Writing Book Reviews. LC 73-17951. 230p. 1974. reprint ed. lib. bdg. 62.50 (*0-8371-7285-3*, DRWB, Greenwood Pr) Greenwood.

Drews, A. W., ed. Manual on Hydrocarbon Analysis. 5th ed. LC 92-38461. 840p. 1992. pap. 68.00 (*0-8031-1497-4*) ASTM.

— Manual on Hydrocarbon Analysis. 5th ed. LC 92-38461. (ASTM Manual Ser.: MNL 3). (Illus.). 840p. 1992. text 68.00 (*0-8031-1767-1*, MNL3) ASTM.

— Manual on Hydrocarbon Analysis. 6th ed. LC 98-25886. (Manual Ser.: Vol. 3). (Illus.). 1000p. 1998. reprint ed. pap. 129.00 (*0-8031-2080-X*, MNL3) ASTM.

Drews, A. W., ed. see American Society for Testing & Materials Staff.

Drews, Arthur. Christ Myth. Burns, C. Delisle, tr. LC 97-46443. 304p. 1998. 34.95 (*1-57392-190-4*) Prometheus Bks.

— The Legend of Saint Peter: A Contribution to the Mythology of Christianity. Zindler, Frank R., tr. from GER. LC 97-46189. Orig. Title: Die Petruslegende. (Illus.). vii, 182p. 1997. pap. 12.00 (*1-57884-951-9*, 5580) Am Atheist.

— The Witnesses to the Historicity of Jesus. McCabe, Joseph, tr. LC 70-161327. (Atheist Viewpoint Ser.). 332p. 1972. reprint ed. 25.95 (*0-405-03811-9*) Ayer.

Drews, Bob, jt. ed. see Rapoport, Roger.

Drews, Christine M. & Wilmore, Jack H. Physiology of Sport & Exercise Study Guide. 2nd ed. LC 99-22719. 1999. 16.00 (*0-7360-0090-9*) Human Kinetics.

Drews, Dale H., jt. auth. see Firestone, William A.

Drews, Danae, jt. auth. see Degoede, Daniel L.

Drews, G. & Dawes, E. A., eds. Molecular Biology of Membrane-Bound Complexes in Phototrophic Bacteria. LC 90-7068. (FEMS Symposium Ser.: No. 53). (Illus.). 500p. 1990. 135.00 (*0-306-43515-2*, Plenum Trade) Perseus Pubng.

Drews, George J. The Improved Mono Diet: One Course, Full Meal Recipes. 36p. 1996. reprint ed. spiral bd. 9.00 (*0-7873-0297-X*) Hlth Research.

— Unfired Food & Tropho Therapy, Food Cure. 324p. 1996. reprint ed. spiral bd. 21.00 (*0-7873-0296-1*) Hlth Research.

Drews, J. Immunopharmacology: Principles & Perspectives. (Illus.). 300p. 1990. 118.00 (*0-387-52370-7*) Spr-Verlag.

— In Quest of Tomorrow's Medicines. LC 98-27801. (Illus.). 320p. 1998. 29.95 (*0-387-98547-6*) Spr-Verlag.

Drews, J., ed. R-Factors: Their Properties & Possible Control: Symposium, Baden Near Vienna, April 27-29, 1977. (Topics in Infectious Diseases Ser.: Vol. 2). 1978. 53.95 (*0-387-81455-8*) Spr-Verlag.

Drews, J., ed. see Symposium, Vienna, Sept. 4-6, 1974.

Drews, Mark. New Ears: A Guide to Education in Audio & the Recording Sciences. 208p. (Orig.). 1989. pap. 11.95 (*0-9623502-0-6*) New Ear Prodns.

— New Ears: The Audio Career & Education Handbook. 2nd rev. ed. LC 93-92640. 285p. (YA). 1993. pap. 24.95 (*0-9623502-1-4*) New Ear Prodns.

Drews, Rainer. Zur Krise Katholischer Jugendverbandsarbeit: Eine Lokalstudie von Strukturen Kirchlicher Jugendarbeit in Berlin (West) (Europaische Hochschulschriften Ser.: Reihe 23, Bd. 421). (GER., Illus.). 398p. 1991. 65.80 (*3-631-43841-9*) P Lang Pubng.

Drews, Robert. Basileus: The Evidence for Kingship in Geometric Greece. LC 82-10915. (Yale Classical Monographs: No. 4). 160p. 1983. 40.00 (*0-300-02831-8*) Yale U Pr.

— Coming of the Greeks: Indo-European Conquests in the Aegean & the Near East. 276p. 1988. pap. text 15.95 (*0-691-02951-2*, Pub. by Princeton U Pr) Cal Prin Full Svc.

— End of the Bronze Age: Changes in Warfare & the Catastrophe Ca. 1200 B.C. 264p. 1993. pap. text 15.95 (*0-691-02591-6*, Pub. by Princeton U Pr) Cal Prin Full Svc.

Drews, Toby R. Getting Rid of Anxiety & Stress. LC 82-61228. 167p. 1983. pap. 9.99 (*0-88270-537-7*) Bridge-Logos.

— Getting Them Sober, 4 vols., Vol. 1. 3rd ed. 1998. pap. 9.95 (*0-9615995-9-6*) Recover Comns.

— Getting Them Sober, Vol. 4. 107p. 1992. pap. 9.95 (*0-9615995-1-0*) Recover Comns.

— Getting Them Sober: A Guide for Those Living with Alcoholism, Vol. 1. LC 80-82751. 203p. (Orig.). 1980. mass mkt. 5.99 (*0-88270-460-5*) Bridge-Logos.

— Getting Them Sober: A Guide for Those Living with Alcoholism, Vol. 2. LC 84-235843. 197p. (Orig.). 1983. mass mkt. 5.99 (*0-88270-560-1*) Bridge-Logos.

— Getting Them Sober: A Guide for Those Living with Alcoholism, Vol. 3. LC 85-73330. 193p. (Orig.). 1986. mass mkt. 5.99 (*0-88270-603-9*) Bridge-Logos.

— Getting Them Sober: Action Guide, Vol. 1. 90p. 1983. pap. 4.99 (*0-88270-559-8*) Bridge-Logos.

— Getting Your Children Sober. LC 87-71392. (Orig.). 1987. pap. 9.99 (*0-88270-637-3*) Bridge-Logos.

— Sex & the Sober Alcoholic. 180p. 1987. 9.95 (*0-9615995-0-2*) Recover Comns.

D

An Asterisk (*) at the beginning of an entry indicates that the title is appearing for the first time.

Drews, Ulrich. Color Atlas of Embryology. Meyer, David B., tr. LC 95-298. (Illus.). 384p. 1996. 29.90 (*0-86577-544-3*) Thieme Med Pubs.

Drexel, Henry W., tr. see Raeder, Erich.

Drexel Institute of Technology Staff. Sheet Formability of Alpha-Brass: Effect of Material Properties, Anisotrophy, & Processing Parameters. 127p. 1973. 19.05 (*0-317-34545-1*, 129) Intl Copper.

Drexel, Karl W. The Politically Incorrect Cookbook: The Facts, Fantasies & Fallacies of the Endangered Species Act. Wright, Roxanne, ed. (Illus.). 176p. (Orig.). 1996. pap. 12.95 (*0-9650435-0-9*) Whitney-Hill.

Drexel, Paul. Mango Shoes: And Other Stories. McIntyre, Cordelia, ed. (Illus.). (Orig.). 1995. pap. 8.95 (*0-9640300-8-X*) Galhattan Pr.

Drexel, Theodor. Catalog der Kochbucher-Sammlung. (GER.). 240p. 1995. reprint ed. 55.00 (*1-888262-25-7*) Martino Pubng.

Drexelius, Jeremias. Heliotropium: Conformity of the Human Will to the Divine. LC 84-51597. 416p. 1985. reprint ed. pap. 13.00 (*0-89555-245-0*) TAN Bks Pubs.

Drexhage, M. G., et al, eds. Halide Glasse IV. (Materials Science Forum Ser.: Vols. 19 & 20). 740p. 1987. text 233.00 (*0-87849-558-4*, Pub. by Trans T Pub) Enfield Pubs NH.

Drexl, A. & Kimms, A., eds. Beyond Manufacturing Resource Planning (MRP II) Advanced Models & Methods for Production Planning. LC 98-16866. (Illus.). viii, 419p. 1998. 90.00 (*3-540-64247-1*) Spr-Verlag.

Drexl, A., jt. auth. see Domschke, W.

Drexl, Josef. What Is Protected in a Computer Program? Copyright Protection in the United States & Europe. LC 95-158908. (IIC Studies Ser.: Vol. 15). 124p. 1994. pap. 110.00 (*3-527-28688-8*, Wiley-VCH) Wiley.

Drexler, et al. Delaware Corporate Law & Practice. 1988. 185.00 (*0-8205-1245-1*) Bender.

Drexler, Allan, jt. auth. see Sibbet, David.

***Drexler, Alois.** Was Ist Objektive Existenz? Zur Analyse Eines Fixpunktes Unserer Vorstellung. 348p. 1999. 48.95 (*3-631-34848-7*) P Lang Pubng.

Drexler, Art, jt. auth. see Ferino, Fred.

Drexler, Arthur. Architecture of Japan. LC 55-5987. (Museum of Modern Art Publications in Reprint). (Illus.). 1967. reprint ed. 19.95 (*0-405-01516-X*) Ayer.

Drexler, Arthur, ed. The Mies Van Der Rohe Archive, Vol. 1. LC 86-9980. Pt. 1. 383p. 1986. text 225.00 (*0-8240-4025-2*) Garland.

— The Mies Van Der Rohe Archive, Vol. 3. LC 86-9980. Pt. 1. 511p. 1986. text 250.00 (*0-8240-4027-9*) Garland.

— The Mies Van Der Rohe Archive, Vol. 4. LC 86-9980. Pt. 1. 568p. 1986. text 275.00 (*0-8240-4028-7*) Garland.

— The Mies Van Der Rohe Archive, 1910-1937, Vol. 2, Pt. I. LC 86-9980. 568p. 1987. text 303.00 (*0-8240-4026-0*) Garland.

Drexler, E. S. Electron-Beam Moire Technique: Advances, Verification, Application. 76p. 1998. pap. 6.00 (*0-16-056778-5*) USGPO.

Drexler, Eric. Engines of Creation. LC 85-25362. 320p. 1987. pap. 13.95 (*0-385-19973-2*, Anchor NY) Doubleday.

Drexler, E.S. Procedures for the Electron-Beam Moire Technique. 137p. 1998. per. 11.00 (*0-16-056694-0*) USGPO.

Drexler, G., jt. auth. see Wachsmann, F.

Drexler, H., et al, eds. Endothelial Mechanisms of Vasomotor Control: With Special Reference to the Coronary Circulation. 352p. 1991. 63.00 (*0-387-91392-0*) Spr-Verlag.

Drexler, Hans. Ammianstudien. (Spudasmata Ser.: Bd. 31). (GER.). 207p. 1974. write for info. (*3-487-05289-X*) G Olms Pubs.

— Ausgewahlte Kleine Schriften. (Collectanea Ser.: Vol. IX). viii, 436p. 1982. write for info. (*3-487-07143-6*) G Olms Pubs.

— Herodotstudien. 269p. 1972. write for info. (*3-487-04202-9*) G Olms Pubs.

— Die Iambenkurzung. (GER.). vi, 257p. 1969. write for info. (*0-318-70571-0*) G Olms Pubs.

— Die Lambenkurzung. vi, 257p. 1969. write for info. (*0-318-71111-7*) G Olms Pubs.

— Plautinische Akzentstudien, 2 vols. in 1. (GER.). xvi, 694p. 1967. reprint ed. write for info. (*0-318-70572-9*); reprint ed. write for info. (*0-318-71112-5*) G Olms Pubs.

— Thukydides-Studien. (Altertumswissenschaftliche Texte und Studien: No. 5). 288p. 1976. write for info. (*3-487-05945-2*) G Olms Pubs.

Drexler, K. Eric. Nanosystems: Molecular Machinery, Manufacturing & Computation. LC 92-30870. 576p. 1992. pap. 54.99 (*0-471-57518-6*) Wiley.

— Nanosystems: Molecular Machinery, Manufacturing & Computation. LC 92-30870. 576p. 1992. 59.99 (*0-471-57547-X*) Wiley.

Drexler, R. D. My Father Becomes the Wind. (CRP Chapbook Ser.: No. 1). (Illus.). 32p. (Orig.). 1995. pap. 4.00 (*0-9636959-1-6*) Coe Review Pr.

Drexler, Robert W. Colombia & the United States: Narcotics Traffic & a Failed Foreign Policy. LC 97-8548. 197p. 1997. lib. bdg. 36.50 (*0-7864-0324-1*) McFarland & Co.

Drexler, Rosalyn. Dear: A New Play. LC 96-40093. 96p. 1997. pap. 6.95 (*1-55783-274-9*) Applause Theatre Bk Pubs.

Drexler, Rosalyn & Sokolowski, Thomas W. Intimate Emotions: Rosalyn Drexler. LC 86-80995. (Illus.). 42p. (Orig.). 1986. pap. 8.00 (*0-934349-02-9*) Grey Art Gallery Study Ctr.

Drexler, Roslyn. Art Does (Not!) Exist. 170p. 1996. 19.95 (*0-932511-98-8*) Fiction Coll.

***Drexler, Sam, pseud & Shelby, Fay.** Lost in Spillville. LC 00-190005. (Erika & Oz Adventures in American History Ser.: Vol. 1). 144p. (YA). (gr. 9-12). 2000. pap. 6.99 (*0-9669988-1-2*) Aunt Straw.

Drey, James. Bigbang. 28p. (Orig.). 1995. pap. text 3.95 (*0-9641986-7-3*) Poetry Harbor.

Drey, Johann S. Brief Introduction to the Study of Theology: With Reference to the Scientific Standpoint & the Catholic System. Himes, Michael J., tr. from GER. LC 93-42343. (Studies in Theology: Vol. 1). 1994. text 38.00 (*0-268-01171-0*) U of Notre Dame Pr.

Dreybrodt, W. Processes in Karst Systems Physics, Chemistry, & Geology. (Physical Environment Ser.: Vol. 4). (Illus.). 325p. 1988. 185.95 (*0-387-18839-8*) Spr-Verlag.

***Dreyer.** China's Political System: Moderization & Tradition. 3rd ed. LC 98-55914. 347p. 1999. pap. text 48.00 (*0-205-29640-8*) Allyn.

Dreyer, Angela E. Taboo. LC 83-62045. 87p. 1983. pap. 3.95 (*0-914241-00-1*) Macanna-Rose.

Dreyer, Carl Theodor. Dreyer in Double Reflection: Carl Dreyer's Writings on Film. Skoller, Donald, tr. from DAN. (Quality Paperbacks Ser.). (Illus.). 205p. 1991. reprint ed. pap. 12.95 (*0-306-80458-1*) Da Capo.

Dreyer, E. & Dreyer, W. Der Kosmos-Waldfuehrer (The Kosmos Forest Guide) Okologie, Gefahrdung, Schutz (Ecology, Endangered Status, & Protection) (Kosmos Naturfuehrer (Nature Guides) Ser.). (GER., Illus.). 383p. 1990. 43.00 (*3-440-05981-2*, Pub. by Franckh-Kosmos) Balogh.

Dreyer, Edward L. China at War, 1901-1949. LC 94-32357. (Modern Wars in Perspective Ser.). 384p. (C). 1996. text 55.95 (*0-582-05125-8*, 76985) Addison-Wesley.

— China War 1901 - 1949. LC 94-32357. (Modern Wars in Perspective Ser.). 384p. (C). 1996. pap. text 34.69 (*0-582-05123-1*, 76984, Pub. by Addison-Wesley) Longman.

— Early Ming China: A Political History, 1355-1435. LC 80-51646. 336p. 1982. 45.00 (*0-8047-1105-4*) Stanford U Pr.

Dreyer, Eileen. Bad Medicine. 368p. 1997. mass mkt. 5.99 (*0-06-104276-5*, Harp PBks) HarpC.

— Brain Dead. 512p. 1998. mass mkt. 6.99 (*0-06-101096-0*, Harp PBks) HarpC.

— A Man to Die For. 480p. 1997. mass mkt. 5.50 (*0-06-104055-X*, Harp PBks) HarpC.

— Nothing Personal. 480p. 1997. mass mkt. 6.50 (*0-06-104275-7*, Harp PBks) HarpC.

Dreyer, Elizabeth. Manifestations of Grace. (Theology & Life Ser.: Vol. 29). 246p. 1990. pap. 19.95 (*0-8146-5759-1*, M Glazier) Liturgical Pr.

Dreyer, Elizabeth A. Earth Crammed with Heaven: A Spirituality of Everyday Life. LC 93-39808. 208p. (Orig.). 1994. pap. 12.95 (*0-8091-3450-0*) Paulist Pr.

— A Retreat with Catherine of Siena: Living the Truth in Love. 115p. 1998. pap. 8.95 (*0-86716-303-8*) St Anthony Mess Pr.

***Dreyer, Elizabeth A., ed.** The Cross in Christian Tradition: From Paul to Bonaventure. 2001. pap. 21.95 (*0-8091-4000-4*) Paulist Pr.

Dreyer, Ellen. Speechless in New York: Going to New York. (Illus.). 96p. 2000. pap. 7.95 (*1-893577-01-5*, Pub. by Four Corners Pubg) Seven Hills Bk.

— Wild Animals. LC 90-11163. (Illus.). 96p. (J). (gr. 2-5). 1991. pap. 7.95 (*0-8167-2243-9*) Troll Communs.

Dreyer, Frederick A. The Genesis of Methodism. LC 99-13975. 1999. write for info. (*0-934223-56-4*) Lehigh Univ Pr.

Dreyer, Gale R. Astrology & Your Health. (C). 1997. pap. 14.95 (*0-13-757154-2*, Macmillan Coll) P-H.

— Astrology & Your Health. (C). 1998. 24.95 (*0-13-757162-3*, Macmillan Coll) P-H.

Dreyer, Glenn, ed. see DeVito, Jill & Markow, Joseph.

Dreyer, Glenn D. Connecticut's Notable Trees. rev. ed. (Illus.). 96p. 1998. pap. 12.95 (*1-58066-014-2*, Covered Brdge Pr) Douglas Charles Ltd.

Dreyer, Glenn D. & Niering, William A., eds. Tidal Marshes of Long Island Sound: Ecology, History & Restoration. (Connecticut College Arboretum Bulletin Ser.: No. 34). (Illus.). 73p. (Orig.). 1995. pap. 5.00 (*1-878899-05-8*) CT Coll Arboretum.

Dreyer, Jacob S. Composite Reserve Assets in the International Monetary System. Altman, Edward I. & Walter, Ingo I., eds. LC 76-5757. (Contemporary Studies in Economic & Financial Analysis: Vol. 2). 206p. 1977. 78.50 (*0-89232-003-6*) Jai Pr.

Dreyer, Jacob S., et al, eds. The International Monetary System: A Time of Turbulence. LC 82-13799. (AEI Symposia Ser.: No. 82E). (Illus.). 544p. reprint ed. pap. 168.70 (*0-8357-4495-7*, 203734800008) Bks Demand.

Dreyer, Jacob S., ed. see Conference on Exchange Rate Flexibility & the Inte.

Dreyer, John L. History of Astronomy from Thales to Kepler. 438p. (C). 1953. pap. 10.95 (*0-486-60079-3*) Dover.

Dreyer, June. China's Forty Millions: Minority Nationalities & National Integration in the People's Republic of China. (East Asian Monographs: No. 87). 343p. 1976. 24.95 (*0-674-11964-9*) HUP.

Dreyer, June T. China's Political System. 3rd ed. (C). 1999. pap. 40.00 (*0-321-07054-2*) Addson-Wesley Educ.

— China's Political System: Modernization & Tradition. 2nd ed. 349p. (C). 1996. pap. text 46.00 (*0-02-330561-4*, U84006, Macmillan Coll) P-H.

Dreyer, June T., ed. Asian-Pacific Regional Security. LC 90-12832. (Illus.). 264p. 1990. pap. text 14.95 (*0-88702-053-4*) Washington Inst Pr.

Dreyer, June T., jt. ed. see Kim, Ilpyong J.

***Dreyer, June Teufel.** The PLA & the Kosovo Conflict. 26p. 2000. pap. write for info. (*1-58487-022-2*) SSI US Army.

***Dreyer, Keith J., et al.** PACS: A Guide to the Filmless Revolution. (Illus.). 500p. 1999. 79.95 (*1-929987-05-6*) Login Brothers Bk Co.

Dreyer, Lynn & Haseltine, Beth A. Woodrow Project: A Sexual Abuse Prevention Curriculum for the Developmentally Disabled. Savageau, Vicki S., ed. 86p. 1986. lab manual ed. 99.95 incl. VHS (*0-914633-11-2*) Rape Abuse Crisis.

Dreyer, Lynne. The White Museum. LC 86-6180. (Roof Bks.). 125p. 1986. pap. 10.00 (*0-937804-21-5*) Segue NYC.

Dreyer, Olega, et al. Ecological Problems of Developing Countries. 1989. 23.00 (*81-202-0263-5*, Pub. by Ajanta) S Asia.

Dreyer, Oskar. Untersuchungen zum Begriff des Gottgeziemenden in der Antike. (GER.). viii, 164p. 1970. write for info. (*0-318-70626-1*) G Olms Pubs.

Dreyer, Peter. A Gardener Touched with Genius: The Life of Luther Burbank. expanded ed. LC 93-72642. (Illus.). 424p. 1993. pap. 19.00 (*0-9637883-0-2*) L Burbank Home.

Dreyer, Philip, ed. Claremont Reading Conference: Vision & Realities in Literacy. 140p. (Orig.). 1996. pap. 20.00 (*0-941742-16-4*) Claremont Grad.

— Claremont Reading Conference Yearbook No. 61: Literacy: Building on What We Know. 177p. 1997. pap. text 20.00 (*0-941742-17-2*) Claremont Grad.

Dreyer, Philip H., ed. Creating Authentic Images: A Multicultural Perspective: Proceedings of the 60th Claremont Reading Conference Held March 18-19, 1994. 58th ed. 203p. 1994. pap. 20.00 (*0-941742-13-X*) Claremont Grad.

— Towards Multiple Perspectives on Literacy: Proceedings from the 61st Claremont Reading Conference Held March 17-18, 1995. 58th ed. 216p. 1995. pap. 20.00 (*0-941742-15-6*) Claremont Grad.

Dreyer, R. J., jt. auth. see Clarkson, R. W.

Dreyer, Ronald. Namibia & Southern Africa: Regional Dynamics of Decolonization, 1945-1990. LC 93-14190. (Publication of the Graduate Institute of International Studies, Geneva). 300p. 1994. 76.50 (*0-7103-0471-4*) Routledge.

Dreyer, Ronnie G. Vedic Astrology: A Guide to the Fundamentals of Jyotish. LC 97-5620. (Illus.). 336p. (Orig.). 1997. pap. 16.95 (*0-87728-889-5*) Weiser.

— Venus Rising: Rediscovering the Goddess & Her Planet. (Illus.). 1994. 15.00 (*1-85538-006-4*, Pub. by Aqrn Pr) Harper SF.

***Dreyer, Ronnie Gale.** Healing Signs: The Astrological Guide to Health & Well Being. LC 99-40920. 336p. 2000. pap. 12.95 (*0-385-49815-2*, Main St Bks) Doubleday.

Dreyer, Sharon S. Best of Bookfinder: A Guide to Children's Literature about Interests & Concerns of Youth. LC 91-76898. 1992. pap. text 49.95 (*0-88671-439-7*, 7592) Am Guidance.

— The Bookfinder, Vol. 4. 1989. text 89.95 (*0-913476-50-1*, 7581); pap. text 44.95 (*0-913476-51-X*, 7582) Am Guidance.

Dreyer, Stephan. Feeding Tropical Fish the Right Way: A Complete Authoritative Guide. (Illus.). 64p. 1998. 12.95 (*0-7938-0210-5*, WW044) TFH Pubns.

Dreyer, Stephen & Keppler, Rainer. How to Have a Successful Aquarium. (Illus.). 160p. 1996. 35.95 (*0-7938-2090-1*, TS225) TFH Pubns.

Dreyer, T. P. Modelling with Ordinary Differential Equations. LC 93-9636. 304p. 1993. per. 84.95 (*0-8493-8636-5*, QA401) CRC Pr.

Dreyer, Todd, ed. see Surbrook, Truman C.

Dreyer, W., jt. auth. see Dreyer, E.

***Dreyfack, Raymond.** Achieving Financial Success as a Freelance Writer. 224p. 1999. pap. 16.95 (*0-936085-47-9*, Pub. by Blue Heron OR) Consort Bk Sales.

Dreyfack, Raymond. Supervisor's Script Book. 352p. (C). 1996. text 39.95 (*0-13-460114-9*) P-H.

— Supervisor's Script Book. 352p. (C). 1996. pap. text 15.95 (*0-13-476052-2*) P-H.

Dreyfous, Leslie. Getting a Life: America's Challenge to Grow Up. LC 96-12053. 181p. 1996. 18.95 (*1-882723-13-9*, Pub. by Gold Leaf Pr) Origin Bk Sales.

Dreyfus, Alfred. Five Years of My Life. Mortimer, James, tr. (Select Bibliographies Reprint Ser.). 1977. reprint ed. 26.95 (*0-8369-5836-5*) Ayer.

— Five Years of My Life: The Diary of Captain Alfred Dreyfus. (Illus.). 253p. 1977. 27.95 (*0-8464-1184-9*) Beekman Pubs.

Dreyfus, B. Hematologie. (FRE., Illus.). 950p. 1984. lib. bdg. 99.00 (*2-257-12526-6*) S M P F Inc.

***Dreyfus Editorial Staff.** Netscape Devedge Web Developers Library. LC 99-46066. 744p. 1999. pap. 34.99 (*0-7645-4585-X*) IDG Bks.

***Dreyfus, Edward A.** Keeping Your Sanity: Practical Essays for Your Psychological Well-Being. 2000. pap. 18.00 (*0-7388-2207-8*) Xlibris Corp.

Dreyfus, Edward A. Someone Right for You. 224p. 1992. 17.95 (*0-8306-3969-1*); pap. 9.95 (*0-8306-3087-2*) McGraw-Hill Prof.

Dreyfus, Francois. Did Jesus Know He Was God? 154p. 1988. pap. 5.95 (*0-8199-0899-1*, Frncscn Herld) Franciscan Pr.

Dreyfus, Georges B. Recognizing Reality: Dharmakirti's Philosophy & Its Tibetan Interpretations. LC 96-14258. (SUNY Series in Buddhist Studies). 480p. (C). 1997. text 68.50 (*0-7914-3097-9*); pap. text 22.95 (*0-7914-3098-7*) State U NY Pr.

Dreyfus, Herbert L. What Computers Still Can't Do: A Critique of Artificial Reason. (Illus.). 420p. 1992. 27.50 (*0-262-04134-0*) MIT Pr.

Dreyfus, Herbert L., tr. see Merleau-Ponty, Maurice.

Dreyfus, Hubert L. Being-in-the-World: A Commentary on Heidegger's Being & Time, Division I. 384p. (Orig.). 1990. pap. text 20.00 (*0-262-54056-8*) MIT Pr.

***Dreyfus, Hubert L.** Mind over Machine. 2000. per. 16.95 (*0-7432-0551-0*) S&S Trade.

Dreyfus, Hubert L. What Computers Still Can't Do: A Critique of Artificial Reason. (Illus.). 409p. 1992. pap. text 18.50 (*0-262-54067-3*) MIT Pr.

Dreyfus, Hubert L. & Dreyfus, Stuart E. Mind over Machine: The Power of Human Intuition & Expertise in the Era of the Computer. 256p. 1988. pap. 17.95 (*0-02-908061-4*) Free Pr.

Dreyfus, Hubert L. & Rabinow, Paul. Michel Foucault: Beyond Structuralism & Hermeneutics. 2nd ed. LC 83-9316. (Illus.). 280p. 1983. pap. text 14.50 (*0-226-16312-1*) U Ch Pr.

— Michel Foucault: Beyond Structuralism & Hermeneutics. 2nd ed. LC 83-9316. (Illus.). 232p. 1992. lib. bdg. 25.00 (*0-226-16311-3*) U Ch Pr.

Dreyfus, Jack. A Remarkable Medicine Has Been Overlooked: Including an Autobiography, & the Clinical Section of the Broad Range of Use of Phenytoin. LC 97-34597. (Illus.). 427p. 1997. pap. 14.95 (*0-8264-1069-3*) Continuum.

Dreyfus, Jack J. The Lion of Wall Street: The Two Lives of Jack Dreyfus. LC 95-37523. (Illus.). 352p. 1996. 24.95 (*0-89526-461-7*) Regnery Pub.

Dreyfus, John. Diccionario de la Edicion y la Artes Graficas. (SPA.). 724p. 1990. 105.00 (*0-7859-5980-7*, 8436805127) Fr & Eur.

— Into Print: Selected Writings on Printing History, Typography, & Book Production. 410p. 1996. 75.00 (*1-56792-045-4*) Godine.

Dreyfus, John, jt. auth. see Zapf, Hermann.

Dreyfus, Kay. Sweethearts of Rhythm. (Illus.). (Orig.). pap. 35.00 (*0-86819-452-2*, Pub. by Currency Pr) Accents Pubns.

Dreyfus, Laurence. Bach & the Patterns of Invention. LC 96-32275. (Illus.). 256p. 1996. 48.00 (*0-674-06005-9*) HUP.

— Bach's Continuo Group: Players & Practices in His Vocal Works. (Studies in the History of Music: No. 3). 280p. 1990. pap. 22.00 (*0-674-06030-X*) HUP.

Dreyfus, Lawrence. Source Readings Vol. 4: Baroque Era. rev. ed. Vol. 4. (C). 1998. pap. text 21.75 (*0-393-96697-6*) Norton.

Dreyfus, Nancy. Talk to Me Like I'm Someone You Love: Flash Cards for Real Life. 150p. 1995. pap. 8.95 (*0-89087-816-1*) Celestial Arts.

Dreyfus, Patrica A, tr. see Merleau-Ponty, Maurice.

Dreyfus, Paul, jt. auth. see Williams, Greg.

Dreyfus, Raphael, ed. Tragiques Grecs: Eschyle - Sophocle. deluxe ed. (FRE.). 1552p. 1967. 125.00 (*0-7859-3801-X*, 2070105679) Fr & Eur.

Dreyfus, Renee & Schraudolph, Ellen, eds. Pergamon: The Telephos Frieze from the Great Altar, Vol. 1. LC 95-83343. (Illus.). 120p. 1996. pap. 29.95 (*0-88401-089-9*) U of Tex Pr.

— Pergamon: The Telephos Frieze from the Great Altar, Vol. 2. (Illus.). 224p. 1996. pap. 39.95 (*0-88401-091-0*) U of Tex Pr.

Dreyfus, Stuart E., jt. auth. see Dreyfus, Hubert L.

Dreyfuss, Carl. Occupation & Ideology of the Salaried Employee. Stein, Leon, ed. LC 77-70490. 1977. reprint ed. lib. bdg. 46.95 (*0-405-10162-7*) Ayer.

Dreyfuss, David, et al. Dual-Use Technology Program for a Passenger-Cargo Rotorcraft. LC 96-151412. 76p. 1995. pap. text 6.00 (*0-8330-1667-9*, DB-138-A) Rand Corp.

Dreyfuss, Hans S., jt. auth. see Rosenberg, Maurice.

Dreyfuss, Henry. Symbol Sourcebook: An Authoritative Guide to International Graphic Symbols. 288p. 1984. pap. 42.95 (*0-471-28872-1*, VNR) Wiley.

Dreyfuss, Henry. Symbol Sourcebook: An Authoritative Guide to International Graphic Symbols. LC 83-12514. (Illus.). 292p. 1984. pap. 36.95 (*0-442-21806-0*, VNR) Wiley.

Dreyfuss, Henry, Associates Staff. The Measure of Man & Woman: Human Factors in Design. (Illus.). 96p. 1993. 60.00 (*0-8230-3031-8*, Whitney Lib) Watsn-Guptill.

Dreyfuss, Hubert L. Being-in-the-World: A Commentary on Heidegger's Being & Time, Division I. 316p. (Orig.). 1990. 30.00 (*0-262-04106-5*) MIT Pr.

Dreyfuss, P. Poly (Tetrahydrofuran) (Polymer Monographs: Vol. 8). xiv, 306p. 1982. text 274.00 (*0-677-03330-3*) Gordon & Breach.

Dreyfuss, Richard & Turtledove, Harry. The Two Georges. 384p. 1996. 23.95 (*0-312-85969-4*, Pub. by Tor Bks) St Martin.

— The Two Georges, Vol. 1. 1997. mass mkt. 6.99 (*0-8125-4459-5*, Pub. by Tor Bks) St Martin.

Dreyfuss, Robert, jt. ed. see Bush, George P.

Dreyfuss, Rochelle C. & Kwall, Roberta R. Intellectual Property: Trademark, Copyright & Patent Law: Cases & Materials (University Casebook Series) (Paralegal). 849p. 1996. text 39.75 (*1-56662-331-6*) Foundation Pr.

— Intellectual Property, Cases & Materials on Trademark, Copyright & Patent Law: Teacher's Manual for. (University Casebook Ser.). 386p. (C). 1996. pap. text. write for info. (*1-56662-355-3*) Foundation Pr.

— Intellectual Property, Cases & Materials on Trademark, Copyright & Patent Law, 1997 Supplement To. (University Casebook Ser.). 49p. 1997. pap. text. write for info. (*1-56662-565-3*) Foundation Pr.

***Dreysee, H., ed.** Electronic Structure & Physical Properties of Solids: The Uses of the LMTO Method. (Lecture Notes in Physics: Vol. 535). (Illus.). xii, 458p. 2000. 115.80 (*3-540-67238-9*) Spr-Verlag.

Dreyzin, Diana, tr. see Smith, Louise A.

Drez, David, jt. ed. see DeLee, Jesse C., Jr.

Drez, Ronald E., ed. Voices of D-Day: The Story of the Allied Invasion, Told by Those Who Were There. LC 93-41311. (Eisenhower Center Studies on War & Peace). (Illus.). 312p. (C). 1996. pap. 16.95 (*0-8071-2081-2*) La State U Pr.

Drezdon, M. A., jt. auth. see Shriver, D. F.

D

Dreze, Jacques H. Underemployment Equilibria: Essays in Theory, Econometrics & Policy. (Illus.). 594p. (C). 1991. text 80.00 (*0-521-39318-3*) Cambridge U Pr.

— Underemployment Equilibria: Essays in Theory, Econometrics & Policy. (Illus.). 594p. (C). 1993. pap. text 30.95 (*0-521-43524-2*) Cambridge U Pr.

Dreze, Jacques H. & Bean, Charles R., eds. Europe's Unemployment Problem. (Illus.). 502p. 1991. 55.00 (*0-262-04111-1*) MIT Pr.

***Dreze, Jean.** India: Economic Development & Social Opportunity. (Illus.). 312p. 1999. pap. text 19.95 (*0-19-829528-6*) OUP.

Dreze, Jean, ed. The Economics of Famine. LC 98-31060. (International Library of Critical Writings in Economics: Vol. 101). 584p. 1999. 215.00 (*1-85898-689-3*) E Elgar.

Dreze, Jean, et al, eds. The Dam & the Nation: Displacement & Resettlement in the Narmada Valley. (Illus.). 348p. 1997. text 32.00 (*0-19-564004-7*) OUP.

Dreze, Jean & Sen, Amartya, eds. Indian Development: Selected Regional Perspectives. LC 97-221672. (UNU/WIDER Studies in Development Economics). (Illus.). 440p. 1997. text 78.00 (*0-19-829204-X*) OUP.

Dreze, Jean & Sen, Amartya K. Hunger & Public Action. (WIDER Studies in Development Economics). (Illus.). 392p. 1991. reprint ed. pap. text 19.95 (*0-19-828365-2*, Clarendon Pr) OUP.

— India: Economic Development & Social Opportunity. LC 96-219941. (Illus.). 306p. (C). 1996. text 49.95 (*0-19-829012-8*) OUP.

— The Political Economy of Hunger. (WIDER Studies in Development Economics). (Illus.). 642p. 1995. pap. text 24.00 (*0-19-828883-2*) OUP.

Dreze, Jean & Sen, Amartya K., eds. The Political Economy of Hunger Vol. 1: Entitlement & Well-Being. (WIDER Studies in Development Economics). (Illus.). 512p. 1991. text 79.00 (*0-19-828635-X*) OUP.

— The Political Economy of Hunger Vol. 2: Famine Prevention. (WIDER Studies in Development Economics). (Illus.). 420p. 1991. text 69.00 (*0-19-828636-8*) OUP.

— The Political Economy of Hunger Vol. 3: Endemic Hunger. (WIDER Studies in Development Economics). (Illus.). 408p. 1991. text 75.00 (*0-19-828637-6*, 12216) OUP.

Dreze, Jean, jt. auth. see Sen, Amartya.

***Drezner, Daniel W.** The Sanctions Paradox: Economic Statecraft & International Relations. (Studies in International Relations: Vol. 65). (Illus.). 362p. (C). 1999. 64.95 (*0-521-64332-5*); pap. 24.95 (*0-521-64415-1*) Cambridge U Pr.

Drezner, Jeffrey, et al. An Analysis of Weapon System Cost Growth. LC 93-26135. 1993. pap. text 9.00 (*0-8330-1432-3*, MR-291-AF) Rand Corp.

Drezner, Jeffrey A. & Bradley, Melissa. A Survey of DoD Facility Energy Management Capabilities. LC 97-52255. (Illus.). 110p. 1998. pap. 15.00 (*0-8330-2584-8*, MR-875-OSD) Rand Corp.

Drezner, Jeffrey A. & Camm, Frank. Using Process Redesign to Improve DoD's Environmental Security Program: Remediation Program Management. LC 98-49228. 99p. 1998. pap. 15.00 (*0-8330-2695-X*, MR-1024) Rand Corp.

Drezner, Jeffrey A. & Krop, Richard A. The Use of Baselining in Acquisition Program Management. LC 97-36326. 1997. pap. text 7.50 (*0-8330-2550-3*) Rand Corp.

Drezner, Jeffrey A., et al. Innovative Management in the DARPA High-altitude Endurance Unmanned Aerial Vehicle Program: Phase II Experience. LC 99-19844. 1999. pap. 15.00 (*0-8330-2717-4*) Rand Corp.

— Maintaining Future Military Aircraft Design Capability. LC 92-15886. 1992. pap. 7.50 (*0-8330-1254-1*, R-4199-AF) Rand Corp.

Drezner, Z., ed. Facility Location: A Survey of Applications & Methods. (Series in Operations Research). (Illus.). xviii, 571p. 1995. 65.95 (*0-387-94545-8*) Spr-Verlag.

Drhaxler, P., et al. Computational Methods for Representations of Groups & Algebras: Euroconference in Essen (Germany), April 1-5, 1997. LC 99-29078. (Progress in Mathematics Ser.). 1999. write for info. (*0-8176-6063-1*) Birkhauser.

DRI Staff. The Potential Benefits of Integration of Environmental & Economic Policies: An Incentive Based Approach to Policy Integration. 448p. (C). 1994. lib. bdg. 125.00 (*1-85966-108-4*, Pub. by Graham & Trotman) Kluwer Academic.

Driankov, D. & Palm, R., eds. Advances in Fuzzy Control. LC 98-14457. (Studies in Fuzziness & Soft Computing: Vol. 16). (Illus.). viii, 421p. 1998. 99.00 (*3-7908-1090-8*) Spr-Verlag.

Driankov, D., et al. An Introduction to Fuzzy Control. 2nd ed. LC 96-1576. 316p. 1996. 59.95 (*0-387-60691-2*) Spr-Verlag.

— An Introduction to Fuzzy Control. 2nd ed. 316p. 1996. 59.95 (*3-540-60691-2*) Spr-Verlag.

Driankov, Dimiter, et al. An Introduction to Fuzzy Control. LC 93-19195. 1994. 59.00 (*0-387-56362-8*) Spr-Verlag.

Driankov, Dimiter, jt. ed. see Hellendoorn, Hans.

Driben, Paul. Aroland Is Our Home: An Incomplete Victory in Applied Anthropology. LC 85-48006. (Studies in Anthropolgy: No. 2). 1986. 32.50 (*0-404-62602-5*) AMS Pr.

Driben, Paul. Portrait of Humankind: An Introduction to Human Biology & Prehistoric Cultures. 456p. 1994. pap. 41.33 (*0-13-064015-8*) P-H.

Driben, Paul. We Are Metis: The Ethnography of a Halfbreed Community in Northern Alberta. LC 83-45353. (Immigrant Communities & Ethnic Minorities in the U. S. & Canada Ser.: No. 2). (Illus.). 1985. 37.50 (*0-404-19406-0*) AMS Pr.

Driben, Paul & Trudeau, Robert S. When Freedom Is Lost: The Dark Side of the Relationship Between Government & the Fort Hope Band. LC 84-165129. 143p. reprint ed. pap. 44.40 (*0-7837-1046-1*, 204135800020) Bks Demand.

— When Freedom Is Lost: The Dark Side of the Relationship Between Government & the Fort Hope Band. 128p. 1983. pap. 15.95 (*0-8020-6526-0*) U of Toronto Pr.

Driberg, Jack H. People of the Small Arrow. LC 72-3367. (Short Story Index Reprint Ser.). (Illus.). 1977. reprint ed. 31.95 (*0-8369-4146-2*) Ayer.

Dribin, Lois & Ivankovich, Susan. The Not-Strictly Vegetarian Cookbook. 2nd ed. LC 89-16932. (Illus.). 248p. 1989. reprint ed. pap. 12.95 (*1-55561-029-3*) Fisher Bks.

Drickamer. Animal Behavior:mechanism,ecol. 5th ed. 2000. 49.00 (*0-07-012199-0*) McGraw.

Drickamer, John M., tr. see Walther, Carl F.

Drickamer, Karen D., jt. ed. see Drickamer, Lee C.

Drickamer, Lee C. Animal Behavior. 5th ed. 1999. text 46.00 (*0-697-34549-1*) McGraw.

Drickamer, Lee C. & Drickamer, Karen D., eds. Fort Lyon to Harpers Ferry: On the Border of North & South with Rambling Jour, a Civil War Soldier. LC 87-23113. (Illus.). 273p. 1988. 19.95 (*0-942597-01-X*) White Mane Pub.

Drickamer, Lee C. & Vessey, Stephen H. Animal Behavior: Mechanisms, Ecology & Evolution. 4th ed. 464p. (C). 1996. text. write for info. (*0-07-114168-5*, WCB McGr Hill) McGrw-H Hghr Educ.

Drickamer, Lee C., et al. Animal Behavior: Mechanisms, Ecology, & Evolution. 4th ed. 496p. (C). 1995. text. write for info. (*0-697-13642-6*, WCB McGr Hill) McGrw-H Hghr Educ.

Drickamer, Lee C., jt. ed. see Houck, Lynne D.

***Driebe, Dean J.** Fully Chaotic Maps & Broken Time Symmetry. LC 98-53213. (Nonlinear Phenomena & Complex Systems Ser.). 11p. 1999. write for info. (*0-7923-5564-4*) Kluwer Academic.

Driebe, Tom. In Search of the Wild Indian: Photographs & Lifeworks by Carl & Grace Moon. LC 96-77881. (Illus.). 432p. 1997. 85.00 (*0-9652691-0-8*, Pub. by Maurose Pub) Treas Chest Bks.

Drieci, Paula, ed. see Anderson, Robert C.

Driedger, Carolyn L. A Visitor's Guide to Mount Rainier Glaciers. Moore, Shirley T., ed. (Illus.). 80p. (Orig.). 1986. pap. text 4.95 (*0-914019-11-2*) NW Interpretive.

Driedger, Diane. Imprinting Our Image: An International Anthology by Women with Disabilities. 224p. 1992. pap. 12.95 (*0-921881-22-3*, Pub. by Gynergy-Ragweed) U of Toronto Pr.

***Driedger, Diane.** The Mennonite Madonna. 80p. 1999. pap. 10.95 (*0-921881-53-3*) gynergy Bks.

Driedger, Diane, et al. Across Borders: Women with Disabilities Working Together. (Illus.). 224p. 1996. pap. 14.95 (*0-921881-38-X*, Pub. by Gynergy-Ragweed) U of Toronto Pr.

Driedger, Leo. Mennonite Identity in Conflict. LC 87-24733. (Studies in Religion & Society: Vol. 19). 240p. 1988. lib. bdg. 89.95 (*0-88946-855-9*) E Mellen.

— Multi-Ethnic Canada: Identities & Inequalities. LC 97-120361. 352p. 1996. pap. text 42.00 (*0-19-541161-7*) OUP.

***Driedger, Leo.** Race & Racism: Canada's Challenge. 328p. 2000. 65.00 (*0-88629-362-6*, Pub. by McG-Queens Univ Pr) CUP Services.

Driedger, Leo & Harder, Leland, eds. Anabaptist-Mennonite Identities in Ferment. (Occasional Papers: No. 14). 194p. (Orig.). 1990. pap. 8.00 (*0-936273-17-8*) Inst Mennonite.

Driedger, Leo & Kraybill, Donald B. Mennonite Peacemaking from Quietism to Activism. LC 93-36827. 336p. (Orig.). 1994. pap. 16.99 (*0-8361-3648-9*) Herald Pr.

Driedger, Leo, jt. auth. see Kauffman, J. Howard.

Driedger, Patricia M. The Church: Our Story : Catholic Tradition, Mission, & Practice. 208p. (YA). (gr. 11-12). 1999. teacher ed., spiral bd. 24.95 incl. disk (*0-87793-669-2*) Ave Maria.

Driedger, Patricia Morrison. The Church: Our Story : Catholic Tradition, Mission, & Practice. LC 99-214633. 271p. (YA). (gr. 11-12). 1999. pap. text, student ed. 14.95 (*0-87793-667-6*) Ave Maria.

Drieenhuizen, Bert P. Van, see Van Drieenhuizen, Bert P.

Driehaus, Hans-Joachim. Die Neue Verfassung von Berlin Im Spiegel der Rechtsprechung des Verfassungsgerichtshofs: Eine um Kernaussagen Aus der Rechtsprechung des Verfassungsgerichtshofs Erweiterte Textausgabe. viii, 69p. 1996. write for info. (*3-11-015131-6*) De Gruyter.

Driel, Barry Van, see Buunk, Bram & Van Driel, Barry.

Driel, Barry Van, see Buunk, Bram P. & Van Driel, Barry.

Driel, G. J. Van, see Van Driel, G. J.

Driel, Hans Van, see Van Driel, Hans, ed.

Driel-Murray, C. Van, see Van Driel-Murray, C., ed.

Drielak, Steven C. Environmental Crime: Evidence Gathering & Investigative Techniques. LC 98-7742. (Illus.). 248p. 1998. 51.95 (*0-398-06888-7*); pap. 38.95 (*0-398-06889-5*) C C Thomas.

***Drielak, Steven C. & Brandon, Thomas R.** Weapons of Mass Destruction: Response & Investigation. LC 00-32613. (Illus.). 2000. pap. write for info. (*0-398-07092-X*) C C Thomas.

Driels, Morris. Linear Control Systems Engineering. LC 94-11331. (Series in Mechanical Engineering). 628p. (C). 1995. 88.44 (*0-07-017824-0*) McGraw.

— Linear Control Systems Management: Solutions Manual. 1995. text. write for info. (*0-07-017825-9*) McGraw.

Driem, George Van, see Van Driem, George.

Driemen, J. E. Winston Churchill: An Unbreakable Spirit. LC 89-26029. (People in Focus Ser.). (Illus.). 128p. (YA). (gr. 5 up). 1990. lib. bdg. 13.95 (*0-87518-434-0*, Dillon Silver Burdett) Silver Burdett Pr.

***Driemeyer, T.** Rendering with Mental Ray. (Mental Ray Handbks.: Vol. 1). (Illus.). 500p. 2000. 59.95 (*3-211-83403-6*) Spr-Verlag.

***Driemeyer, T. & Herken, R., eds.** Programming Mental Ray. (Mental Ray Handbks.: Vol. 2). (Illus.). 480p. 2000. 99.00 (*3-211-83404-4*) Spr-Verlag.

Drier & Rose. Guidebook to Chancery Practice in New Jersey. 463p. 1991. 75.00 (*0-685-67520-3*) NJ Inst CLE.

Drier, Ted. Take Your Life off Hold. LC 87-12065. 224p. 1987. 15.95 (*1-55591-020-3*); pap. 13.95 (*1-55591-038-6*) Fulcrum Pub.

Dries, Angelyn. The Missionary Movement in American Catholic History. LC 97-32083. (American Society of Missiology Ser.: No. 26). 400p. 1998. pap. 20.00 (*1-57075-167-6*) Orbis Bks.

Dries, Angelyn, jt. ed. see Chinnici, Joseph P.

Dries, D. R., ed. & illus. see Tartell, Patrick L.

Dries, David C., et al. Electroconvulsive Therapy: A Guide. rev. ed. 19p. 1998. pap. 4.95 (*1-890802-17-4*) Madison Inst of Med.

Dries, Inge. 200 New Food Combining Recipes: Tasty Dishes from Around the World. 1995. pap. 9.95 (*1-85230-579-7*, Pub. by Element MA) Penguin Putnam.

Dries, Inge, jt. auth. see Dries, Jan.

Dries, Jan. Complete Book of Food Combining: A New Approach to the Hay Diet & Healthy Eating. LC 97-45050. 1998. pap. 15.95 (*1-86204-239-X*, Pub. by Element MA) Penguin Putnam.

— Dries Cancer Diet: A Practical Guide to the Use of Fresh Fruit & Raw Vegetables in the Treatment of Cancer. 160p. 1997. pap. 12.95 (*1-86204-092-3*, Pub. by Element MA) Penguin Putnam.

— New Book of Food Combining: A Completely New Approach to Healthy Eating. 1995. pap. 9.95 (*1-85230-578-9*, Pub. by Element MA) Penguin Putnam.

***Dries, Jan & Dries, Inge.** The Food Combining Bible: The Complete Diet & Lifestyle Guide, with over 200 Recipes. (Illus.). 2001. pap. 29.95 (*1-86204-003-6*) Element MA.

Dries, Lou van den, see Van den Dries, Lou.

***Driesbach, Janice.** Material Witness: Masters from California Crafts. LC 99-75841. (Illus.). 124p. 1999. 39.95 (*0-9674288-1-5*); pap. 19.95 (*0-9674288-0-7*) Creat Arts Sacramento.

Driesbach, Janice T. & Landauer, Susan, eds. Obata's Yosemite: The Art & Letters of Chiura Obata from His Trip to the High Sierra in 1927. LC 93-8320. (Illus.). 1993. 44.95 (*0-939666-66-9*); pap. 24.95 (*0-939666-67-7*) Yosemite Assn.

Driesbach, Janice T., et al. Art of the Gold Rush. LC 97-29319. 168p. 1998. 50.00 (*0-520-21431-5*); pap. 24.95 (*0-520-21432-3*) U CA Pr.

— Direct from Nature: The Oil Sketches of Thomas Hill. LC 96-47648. 1997. pap. 19.95 (*0-939666-84-7*) Yosemite Assn.

Driesch, Angela von den. A Guide to the Measurement of Animal Bones from Archaeological Sites. LC 76-49773. (Peabody Museum Bulletins Ser.: No. 1). (Illus.). 148p. 1976. pap. 22.00 (*0-87365-950-3*) Peabody Harvard.

Driesch, Angela Von den, see LaBianca, Oystein S. & Von den Driesch, Angela.

Driesch, Hans. Psychical Research: The Science of the Super-Normal. Besterman, Theodore, tr. LC 75-7376. (Perspectives in Psychical Research Ser.). 1975. reprint ed. 23.95 (*0-405-07026-8*) Ayer.

Driesch, Hans A. The Science & Philosophy of the Organism, 2 vols., Set. LC 77-27217. (Gifford Lectures: 1907-08). reprint ed. 89.50 (*0-404-60500-1*) AMS Pr.

Driesche, Jason Van, see Van Driesche, Jason.

Driesche, R. Van, see Van Driesche, R.

Driesche, Roy G. Van, see Van Driesche, Roy G.

Driesche, Roy G. Van, see Van Driesche, Jason & Van Driesche, Roy G.

Driesen, W., et al, eds. Computerized Tomography-Brain Metabolism-Spinal Injuries. (Advances in Neurosurgery Ser.: Vol. 10). (Illus.). 420p. 1982. pap. 75.00 (*0-387-11115-8*) Spr-Verlag.

Driessche, R. Van Den, ed. Mineral Nutrition of Conifer Seedlings. 288p. 1990. lib. bdg. 239.00 (*0-8493-5971-6*, QP519) CRC Pr.

Driessche, T. Vanden, et al, eds. Membranes & Circadian Rhythms. (Illus.). 238p. 1995. pap. 104.00 (*3-540-60101-5*) Spr-Verlag.

Driessen, Alfred & Suarez, Antoine. Mathematical Undecidability, Quantum Nonlocality & the Question of the Existence of God. LC 96-36621. 1997. text 107.00 (*0-7923-4306-9*) Kluwer Academic.

Driessen, Henk. On the Spanish-Moroccan Frontier: A Study in Ritual, Power & Ethnicity. 249p. 1992. 30.00 (*0-85496-702-8*) Berg Pubs.

***Driessen, Henk & Otto, Ton, eds.** Perplexities of Identification: Anthropological Studies in Cultural Differentiation & the Use of Resources. (Illus.). 265p. (C). 2000. 29.95 (*87-7288-818-0*, Pub. by Aarhus Univ Pr) David Brown.

Driessen, Karen C. & Smyth, Sheila A. A Library Manager's Guide to the Physical Processing of Nonprint. LC 94-17983. (Library Management Collection). 272p. 1995. lib. bdg. 67.95 (*0-313-27930-6*, Greenwood Pr) Greenwood.

Driessens, F. & Woltgens, J. H. Tooth Development & Caries, Vol. 1. LC 85-27002. 108p. 1986. 132.00 (*0-8493-6503-1*, CRC Reprint) Franklin.

— Tooth Development & Caries, Vol. 2. LC 85-27002. 208p. 1986. 158.00 (*0-8493-6504-X*, CRC Reprint) Franklin.

Driessens, F. C. Mineral Aspects of Dentistry. (Monographs in Oral Science: Vol. 10). (Illus.). xvi, 216p. 1982. 128.75 (*3-8055-3469-8*) S Karger.

Driessens, F. C. & Woltgens, J. H. Tooth Development & Caries, 2 vols. 1986. 239.95 (*0-8493-6500-7*, RK331) CRC Pr.

Driessens, F. C. M., ed. Biominerals. 440p. 1990. lib. bdg. 259.00 (*0-8493-5280-0*, QP88) CRC Pr.

Driessle, Hannelore & Rognebakke, Myrtle. Deutsch Warum Nicht Auf Bk. 1: German Lessons for Beginners. (ENG & GRE.). 221p. 1972. 12.50 (*0-87559-206-6*) Shalom.

Driesum, Rob Van, see Van Driesum, Rob.

Drieth, Rae L. & Wade, Lisa. Computer Reservation Systems: Apollo. 5th ed. Scott, Sharon, ed. 170p. (C). 1997. spiral bd. 35.00 (*1-879982-62-5*) Educ Systs.

Drieu La Rochelle, Pierre. La Comedie De Charleroi. (FRE.). 1982. pap. 10.95 (*0-7859-1955-4*, 2070373665) Fr & Eur.

— Feu Follet, Adieu Gozague. (Folio Ser.: No. 152). (FRE.). pap. 6.95 (*2-07-036152-7*) Schoenhof.

— Le Feu Follet Suivi d'Adieu a Gonzague. (FRE.). 192p. 1972. pap. 10.95 (*0-7859-1704-7*, 2070361527) Fr & Eur.

— Gilles. (FRE.). 1973. pap. 14.95 (*0-7859-1758-6*, 2070364593) Fr & Eur.

— Gilles. (Folio Ser.: No. 459). (FRE.). pap. 13.95 (*2-07-036459-3*) Schoenhof.

— L' Homme a Cheval. (FRE.). 256p. 1973. pap. 13.95 (*0-7859-1763-2*, 2070364844) Fr & Eur.

— Journal d'Un Homme Trompe. (FRE.). 256p. 1986. pap. 11.95 (*0-7859-2045-5*, 2070377652) Fr & Eur.

— Memoires de Dirk Raspe. (FRE.). 338p. 1978. pap. 11.95 (*0-7859-1876-0*, 2070370429) Fr & Eur.

— Reveuse Bourgeoise. (FRE.). 1976. pap. 12.95 (*0-7859-1793-4*, 2070366200) Fr & Eur.

— Secret Journal & Other Writings. Hamilton, Alastair, tr. from FRE. 1974. 35.00 (*0-86527-300-6*) Fertig.

— Will O' the Wisp. Robinson, Martin, tr. from ENG. LC 98-11474. 144p. 1998. pap. 12.95 (*0-7145-0613-3*) M Boyars Pubs.

Drieux, J. P. & Jarlaud, A. Let's Talk D P: Dictionary of Data Processing. (ENG & FRE.). 160p. 1986. pap. 31.95 (*0-7859-4821-X*) Fr & Eur.

Driever, Steven L. Spanish English Dictionary of Human & Physical Geography. LC 93-29895. 736p. 1993. lib. bdg. 115.00 (*0-313-27920-9*, Greenwood Pr) Greenwood.

Drife. Clinical Obstetrics & Gynecology. (Illus.). 410p. 2000. text. write for info. (*0-7020-1775-2*, W B Saunders Co) Harcrt Hlth Sci Grp.

Drife, J. O., et al, eds. Micturition. (Illus.). 372p. 1990. 125.00 (*0-387-19614-5*) Spr-Verlag.

Drife, J. O. & Calder, A. A., eds. Prostaglandins & the Uterus. (Illus.). xiii, 301p. 1992. 159.00 (*0-387-19719-2*) Spr-Verlag.

Drife, J. O. & Studd, John W., eds. HRT & Osteoporosis. (Illus.). 456p. 1990. 136.00 (*0-387-19628-5*) Spr-Verlag.

Drife, J. O., jt. ed. see Templeton, A. A.

Drife, James O. The Benefits & Risks of Oral Contraceptives Today. 2nd ed. LC 96-6752. (Illus.). 48p. 1997. pap. 19.95 (*1-85070-707-3*) Prthnon Pub.

Drife, James O., jt. auth. see Lewis, Gwyneth.

Driffield, Nigel. Global Competition & the U. K. Labour Market. (Studies in Global Competition). 170p. 1996. text 34.00 (*3-7186-5625-6*, Harwood Acad Pubs) Gordon & Breach.

Driffill, jt. auth. see Stiglitz.

***Drifte, Reinhard.** Japan's Quest for a Permanent Security Council Seat: A Matter of Pride or Justice? LC 99-40402. (St. Antony's Ser.). 336p. 1999. text 79.95 (*0-312-22847-3*) St Martin.

Drifte, Reinhard. Japan's Rise to International Responsibilities: The Case of Arms Control. LC 89-48447. 120p. (C). 1990. pap. 19.95 (*0-485-12073-9*, Pub. by Athlone Pr) Humanities.

Drifte, Reinhard, jt. ed. see Daniels, Gordon.

Driga. Electromagnetic Accelerations: Theory & Applications. 1993. 139.95 (*0-8493-7191-0*) CRC Pr.

Drigalski, Dorte V. Flowers on Granite: An Odyssey Through Psychoanalysis. Bell, Anthea, tr. from GER. 336p. 1987. 16.95 (*0-88739-013-7*) Creat Arts Bk.

Drigani, Fuluio. Computerized Project Control. (Cost Engineering Ser.: Vol. 13). (Illus.). 240p. 1988. text 135.00 (*0-8247-7867-7*) Dekker.

Driggers. Life Management Skills: Taking Charge of Your Future. LC 98-20900. 320p. (C). 1998. 33.95 (*0-7668-0506-9*) Delmar.

Driggers, Joann, jt. auth. see Leet, Don R.

Driggers, Ronald G., et al. Introduction to Infrared & Electro-Optical Systems. LC 98-53327. 400p. 1999. 99.00 (*0-89006-470-9*) Artech Hse.

Driggers, Susan. Painted Finishes for Walls & Furniture. LC 97-51565. (Illus.). 128p. 1998. 24.95 (*0-8069-9441-X*) Sterling.

***Driggers, Susan Goans.** Floor Decor: Decorating Techniques for Beautiful Floors & Floorcloths. (Illus.). 128p. 2000. 24.95 (*0-8069-3937-0*) Sterling.

— Painted Finishes for Walls & Furniture: Easy Techniques for Great New Looks. (Illus.). 128p. 1999. pap. 14.95 (*0-8069-9416-9*) Sterling.

Driggs, Cheryl. Inspirations to a Woman in Need. Van Treese, James B., ed. (Illus.). 60p. 1993. pap. 5.95 (*0-9658909-3-7*) CFD Pubns.

***Driggs, Cheryl F.** Pantry Cooking: Unlocking Your Pantry's Potential. (Illus.). 160p. 2000. pap. 14.95 (*0-9658909-2-9*) CFD Pubns.

Driggs, Cheryl F. Simply Prepared. (Illus.). iv, 90p. (Orig.). 1995. pap. 9.95 (*0-9658909-0-2*) CFD Pubns.

— Simply Prepared: A Guide to Emergency Preparedness & Food Storage. 2nd rev. ed. (Illus.). 112p. 1999. pap. 12.95 (*0-9658909-1-0*) CFD Pubns.

An Asterisk (*) at the beginning of an entry indicates that the title is appearing for the first time.

Driggs, Don W. & Goodall, Leonard E. Nevada Politics & Government: Conservatism in an Open Society. LC 95-43756. (Politics & Governments of the American States Ser.). (Illus.). xxviii, 235p. 1996. text 50.00 (*0-8032-1703-X*); pap. text 22.00 (*0-8032-6604-9*) U of Nebr Pr.

Driggs, Frank & Lewine, Harris. Black Beauty, White Heat: A Pictorial History of Classic Jazz, 1920-1950. LC 95-44844. (Illus.). 360p. 1996. reprint ed. pap. 35.00 (*0-306-80672-X*) Da Capo.

Driggs, Gary. Camelback: Sacred Mountain of Phoenix. LC 98-88616. (Illus.). 161p. 1998. 45.00 (*0-910152-17-9*) AZ Hist Foun.

Driggs, Howard R., ed. see Hooker, William F.

Driggs, John H. & Finn, Stephen E. Intimacy Between Men: How to Find & Keep Gay Love Relationships. 256p. 1991. pap. 12.95 (*0-452-26696-3*, Plume) Dutton Plume.

Driggs, Lorin, ed. see Damerow, Gail.

***Dright, Jimi.** Static: My Tupac Shakur Story. 110p. 1999. 24.99 (*0-9673959-0-9*, Pub. by Herb N Soul) Bookpeople.

Drigo, Paola. Maria Zef. Kirschenbaum, Blossom S., tr. & intro. by. LC 88-37837. (European Women Writers Ser.). xiv, 182p. 1989. pap. 15.00 (*0-8032-6577-8*, Bison Books) U of Nebr Pr.

Driguez, H. & Thiem, J., eds. Glycoscience: Synthesis of Oligosaccharides & Glycoconjugates. (Topics in Current Chemistry Ser.: Vol. 186). (Illus.). 256p. 1997. 179.00 (*3-540-62033-8*) Spr-Verlag.

— Glycoscience: Synthesis of Oligosaccharides & Glycoconjugates. LC 99-25200. (Desktop Editions in Chemistry Ser.). 240p. 1999. pap. 54.95 (*3-540-65557-3*) Spr-Verlag.

— Glycoscience: Synthesis of Substrate Analoges & Mimetics. (Topics in Current Chemistry Ser.: Vol. 187). (Illus.). 352p. 1997. 236.00 (*3-540-62032-X*) Spr-Verlag.

— Glycoscience: Synthesis of Substrate Analogs & Mimetics. LC 99-13178. (Desktop Editions in Chemistry Ser.). 320p. 1999. pap. 54.95 (*3-540-65546-8*) Spr-Verlag.

Drijepondt, Henri L. Die Antike Theorie der "Varietas" (Spudasmata Ser.: Bd. XXXVII). (GER.). xiii, 256p. 1979. write for info. (*3-487-06947-4*) G Olms Pubs.

Drijvers, H. J. & Healey, John F. The Old Syriac Inscriptions of Edessa & Osrhoene: Texts, Translations & Commentary. LC 98-43667. (Handbuch der Orientalistik). xvi, 358p. 1998. 105.00 (*90-04-11284-7*) Brill Academic Pubs.

Drijvers, Han J. East of Antioch: Studies in Early Syriac Christianity. (Collected Studies: No. CS198). 340p. (C). 1984. reprint ed. lib. bdg. 120.95 (*0-86078-146-1*, Pub. by Variorum) Ashgate Pub Co.

— History & Religion in Late Antique Syria. (Collected Studies: CS 464). 330p. 1994. 106.95 (*0-86078-451-7*, Pub. by Variorum) Ashgate Pub Co.

Drijvers, J. W. & MacDonald, A. A., eds. Centres of Learning: Learning & Location in Pre-Modern Europe & the Near East. LC 94-46806. (Studies in Intellectual History: Vol. 61). 1995. 113.00 (*90-04-10193-4*) Brill Academic Pubs.

Drijvers, Jan W. Helena Augusta: The Mother of Constantine the Great & the Legend of Her Finding of the True Cross. (Studies in Intellectual History: No. 27). viii, 217p. 1991. 87.00 (*90-04-09435-0*) Brill Academic Pubs.

Drijvers, Jan W. & Hunt, David. Late Roman World & Its Historian: Interpreting Ammianus Marcellinus. LC 99-18312. 1999. text. write for info. (*0-415-20271-X*) Routledge.

Drijvers, Jan W., jt. ed. see Sancisi-Weerdenburg, Heleen.

***Drijvers, Jan Willem, ed.** Portraits of Spiritual Authority: Religious Power in Early Christianity, Byzantium & the Christian Orient. LC 99-45650. 137. 240p. 1999. text 130.00 (*90-04-11459-9*) Brill Academic Pubs.

Drikey, Kay. Positive Aging A to Z. 164p. (Orig.). 1996. pap. 14.95 (*1-56550-038-5*) Vis Bks Intl.

Driljvers, H. J., jt. ed. see Van Baaren, T. P.

Drill, Esther, et al. Deal with It! A Whole New Approach to Your Body, Brain & Life as a Gurl. (Illus.). 320p. 1999. per. 15.00 (*0-671-04157-6*, PB Trade Paper) PB.

***Driller, Joachim.** Breuer Houses. (Illus.). 272p. 1999. 49.95 (*0-7148-3893-4*) Phaidon Pr.

Drillien & Drummond. Neurodevelopmental Problems in Early Childhood: Assessment & Management. (Illus.). 512p. (gr. 13). 1978. 89.95 (*0-632-00409-6*, B-1475-9) Mosby Inc.

Drillien, Cecil M. & Drummond, Margaret. Developmental Screening & the Child with Special Needs. (Clinics in Developmental Medicine Ser.: No. 86). (Illus.). 284p. (C). 1991. text 54.95 (*0-521-41206-4*, Pub. by Mc Keith Pr) Cambridge U Pr.

Drillien, P., ed. Annuaire Europeen 1988 - European Yearbook 1988, Vol. XXXVI. (C). 1990. lib. bdg. 363.50 (*0-7923-0417-9*) Kluwer Academic.

— Annuaire Europeen 1989 - European Yearbook 1989, Vol. XXXVII. (C). 1991. lib. bdg. 363.50 (*0-7923-0839-5*) Kluwer Academic.

Drillien, P., ed. European Yearbook 1983 - Annuaire Europeen 1984, Volume XXXII. (C). 1986. lib. bdg. 292.00 (*90-247-3322-7*) Kluwer Academic.

— European Yearbook, 1987, Vol. 35. (C). 1989. lib. bdg. 299.00 (*0-7923-0089-0*) Kluwer Academic.

Drilling, Eileen, jt. auth. see Rothfork, Judy.

Drilling, Vern. Closing Doors, Opening Worlds: Looking Beyond the Retirement Horizon. 160p. 1993. pap. 9.95 (*0-925190-63-2*) Fairview Press.

Drillings, Michael & O'Neil, Harold F., eds. Motivation: Theory & Research. 328p. 1994. pap. 29.95 (*0-8058-1287-3*); text 69.95 (*0-8058-1286-5*) L Erlbaum Assocs.

Drillock, David, et al, eds. The Divine Liturgy. 368p. 1982. text 40.00 (*0-913836-95-8*) St Vladimirs.

Drillock, David & Erickson, John H., eds. Liturgy of the Presanctified Gifts. 264p. 1990. 40.00 (*0-88141-097-7*); pap. 20.00 (*0-88141-095-0*) St Vladimirs.

Drillock, David, et al. Holy Week. (Music Ser.: Vol. 1). 186p. (Orig.). 1980. 18.00 (*0-913836-67-2*); pap. 14.00 (*0-913836-66-4*) St Vladimirs.

— Holy Week. (Music Ser.: Vol. 2). 287p. (Orig.). 1983. 30.00 (*0-913836-88-5*); pap. 20.00 (*0-913836-87-7*) St Vladimirs.

— Pascha: The Resurrection of Christ. (Music Ser.). 274p. 1980. 25.00 (*0-913836-65-6*) St Vladimirs.

Drillon, M., jt. ed. see Delhaes, P.

Drillsma, Barbara. What's Inside the Human Body? LC 97-23416. (What's Inside Ser.). (Illus.). 48p. (YA). (gr. 3-7). 1997. lib. bdg. 17.95 (*0-87226-398-3*, 63983B, P Bedrick Books) NTC Contemp Pub Co.

Drimmer, Frederick. The Body Snatchers: Stiffs & Other Goulish Delights. (Illus.). 224p. 1992. pap. 12.95 (*0-8065-1285-7*, Citadel Pr) Carol Pub Group.

— Incredible People. LC 96-9082. (Illus.). 192p. (J). (gr. 5-9). 1997. 16.00 (*0-689-31921-5*) Atheneum Yung Read.

— Until You Are Dead: The Book of Executions in America. 1990. 19.95 (*0-8065-1184-2*, Citadel Pr) Carol Pub Group.

— Very Special People. (Illus.). 360p. reprint ed. pap. 12.95 (*0-8065-1253-9*, Citadel Pr) Carol Pub Group.

Drimmer, Frederick, ed. Captured by the Indians: Fifteen Firsthand Accounts, 1750-1870. (Illus.). 384p. 1985. reprint ed. pap. 8.95 (*0-486-24901-8*) Dover.

Drimmer, Harold. A Letter to My Grandchildren. (Illus.). 224p. 1989. write for info. (*0-318-66599-9*) Drimmer Pr.

Drimmer, Harold L., jt. auth. see Shargel, Baila R.

Drinan, Ann, jt. ed. see Slone, John P.

Drinan, Joanne, jt. auth. see Spellman, Frank R.

Drinan, Robert F. Religion, the Courts, & Public Policy. LC 78-6124. 261p. 1978. reprint ed. lib. bdg. 65.00 (*0-313-20444-6*, DRRE, Greenwood Pr) Greenwood.

Drinfield, V. G., jt. auth. see Belavin, A. A.

Dring, D. M. Clathraceae. (Illus.). 96p. 1980. reprint ed. pap. 15.00 (*0-614-21738-5*, Pub. by Royal Botnic Grdns) Balogh.

— Contributions Toward a Rational Arrangement of the Clthraceae. (Illus.). 96p. 1979. reprint ed. pap. 15.00 (*0-318-11896-3*) Lubrecht & Cramer.

Dring, Gerald J., et al. Fundamental & Applied Aspects of Bacterial Spores. 1985. text 125.00 (*0-12-222080-3*) Acad Pr.

Dring, Harry. The Donkey Man: Kaiulani Around Cape Horn. Thomas, W. Geraint & Rose, Mary, eds. (Illus.). 1998. pap. write for info. (*0-9631232-9-7*) Rose Wind Pr.

Dring, Matthew H. The Biology of Marine Plants. (Illus.). 208p. 1991. pap. text 29.95 (*0-521-42765-7*) Cambridge U Pr.

Dring, Matthew J., ed. see Geider, Richard J. & Osborne, Bruce A.

Dring, Matthew J., jt. ed. see Melkonian, Michael.

***Drings, P., ed.** Survival as a Response Criterion for Small-Cell Lung Cancer. (Onkologie Ser.: Vol. 23, Suppl. 3 (2000)). (Illus.). iv, 20p. 2000. pap. 28.75 (*3-8055-7088-0*) S Karger.

Drings, P. & Vogt-Moykopf, I., eds. Therapy of Lung Metastases. (Contributions to Oncology Ser.: Vol. 30). (Illus.). viii, 222p. 1988. 58.50 (*3-8055-4749-8*) S Karger.

Drini, P. Feature Interactions in Telecommunications Networks IV. LC 97-61056. 366p. Date not set. 98.00 (*90-5199-347-1*) IOS Press.

Drinka, Bridget. The Sigmatic Aorist in Indo-European: Evidence for the Space-Time Hypothesis. LC 95-159264. (Journal of Indo-European Studies: No. 13). 210p. (C). 1995. pap. text 40.00 (*0-941694-46-1*) Inst Study Man.

***Drinka, Theresa J. K. & Clark, Phillip G.** Health Care Teamwork: Interdisciplinary Practice & Teaching. LC 00-20903. 2000. write for info. (*0-86569-297-1*); pap. 25.00 (*0-86569-298-X*, R298, Aburn Hse Paperback) Greenwood.

Drinkall, Gail & Foreman, Michael A., eds. The Anglo-Saxon Cemetery at Castledyke South, Barton-on-Humber. (Sheffield Excavations Reports: Vol. 6). 437p. 1997. 85.00 (*1-85075-643-0*, Pub. by Sheffield Acad) CUP Services.

Drinkard. Illinois Freedom Fighters. 176p. (C). 1998. pap. text 22.45 (*0-536-01198-2*) S&S Trade.

***Drinkard, Charles A.** Drinkards in the United States: Their History & Genealogy. 161p. 2000. 37.00 (*0-7404-1250-7*) Higginson Bk Co.

***Drinkard, G. Lawson, III.** Old Wood - New Home. (Illus.). 135p. 2000. 39.95 (*0-87905-953-2*) Gibbs Smith Pub.

Drinkard, G. Lawson, III. Retreats: Handmade Hideaways to Refresh the Spirit. LC 97-1829. (Illus.). 164p. 1997. 39.95 (*0-87905-798-X*) Gibbs Smith Pub.

***Drinkard, Lawson.** Fishing in a Brook: Angling Activities for Kids. LC 99-36731. (Illus.). 64p. 2000. pap. 9.95 (*0-87905-940-0*) Gibbs Smith Pub.

Drinkard, Lawson. Hiding in a Fort: Backyard Retreats for Kids. LC 98-45270. (Illus.). 48p. (YA). (gr. 1 up). 1999. pap. 8.95 (*0-87905-865-X*) Gibbs Smith Pub.

Drinkard, Michael. Disobedience. LC 96-8414. (California Fiction Ser.). 349p. 1996. pap. 13.95 (*0-520-20683-5*, Pub. by U CA Pr) Cal Prin Full Svc.

— Disobedience: A Novel. LC 92-36920. 324p. 1993. 21.95 (*0-393-03478-X*) Norton.

— Green Bananas. 240p. 1992. reprint ed. pap. 9.95 (*0-9617681-4-2*) Otter B Bks.

Drinkenburg, A. A., jt. ed. see Weijnen, M. P.

Drinker, Frederick E. Booker T. Washington: The Master Mind of a Child of Slavery. LC 77-100288. 320p. 1970. reprint ed. lib. bdg. 35.00 (*0-8371-2939-7*, DRW&, Greenwood Pr) Greenwood.

Drinker, Henry S., tr. see Schubert, Franz.

Drinker, Sophie. Music & Women: The Story of Women in Their Relation to Music. LC 95-14816. (Diane Peacock Jezic Series on Women & Music). (Illus.). 394p. 1995. reprint ed. pap. 16.95 (*1-55861-116-9*); reprint ed. lib. bdg. 45.00 (*1-55861-120-7*) Feminist Pr.

Drinker, Sophie L. Music & Women: The Story of Women in Their Relation to Music. LC 75-35730. 1976. reprint ed. 27.95 (*0-89201-011-8*) Zenger Pub.

Drinkhouse, W. Bruce. Bethlehem Steel Corporation: A History from Origin to World War I. 19p. (Orig.). 1969. pap. text 3.00 (*1-877701-06-8*) NCH&GS.

Drinking Water-Health Effects Task Force Staff. Health Effects of Drinking Water Treatment Technologies. (Illus.). 168p. 1989. lib. bdg. 69.95 (*0-87371-222-4*, L223) Lewis Pubs.

Drinkwater, Barbara L., ed. Female Endurance Athletes. LC 85-30243. (Illus.). 176p. 1986. reprint ed. pap. 54.60 (*0-608-06446-7*, 206728200009) Bks Demand.

***Drinkwater, Barbara L. & International Federation of Sports Medicine.** Women in Sport Vol. VIII: The Encyclopedia of Sports Medicine. LC 99-57719. (International Olympic Committee Ser.). (Illus.). 680p. 2000. 125.00 (*0-632-05084-5*) Blackwell Sci.

Drinkwater, Carol. The Haunted School. (J). (gr. 5-9). 1988. pap. 3.95 (*0-317-69631-9*, PuffinBks) Peng Put Young Read.

Drinkwater, D., jt. auth. see Hargreaves, Harry.

Drinkwater, J. F. Roman Gaul. LC 83-45143. (Illus.). 272p. 1983. text 45.00 (*0-8014-1642-6*) Cornell U Pr.

Drinkwater, John. A Book for Bookmen: Being Edited Manuscripts & Marginalia with Essays on Several Occasions. 1977. 20.95 (*0-8369-0391-9*) Ayer.

— Discovery. 1988. reprint ed. lib. bdg. 75.00 (*0-685-55953-X*) Rprt Serv.

— Discovery, Being the Second Book of an Autobiography. LC 78-131691. 435p. 1983. reprint ed. lib. bdg. 13.00 (*0-403-00578-7*) Scholarly.

— English Poetry: An Unfinished History. 1977. 20.95 (*0-8369-5837-3*, 6901) Ayer.

— The Life & Adventures of Carl Laemmle. Jowett, Garth S., ed. LC 77-11374. (Aspects of Film Ser.). 1978. reprint ed. lib. bdg. 23.95 (*0-405-11130-4*) Ayer.

— The Muse in Council: Being Essays on Poets & Poetry. 303p. 1977. 23.95 (*0-8369-1649-2*) Ayer.

— The Pilgrim of Eternity: Byron - A Conflict. (BCL1-PR English Literature Ser.). 408p. 1992. reprint ed. lib. bdg. 99.00 (*0-7812-7477-X*) Rprt Serv.

— Prose Papers. 259p. 1969. 20.95 (*0-8369-1205-5*) Bks for Libraries.

— Swinburne: An Estimate. (BCL1-PR English Literature Ser.). 215p. 1992. reprint ed. lib. bdg. 79.00 (*0-7812-7678-0*) Rprt Serv.

— This Troubled World. 1977. 17.95 (*0-8369-0392-7*) Ayer.

— Victorian Poetry. (BCL1-PR English Literature Ser.). 236p. 1992. reprint ed. lib. bdg. 79.00 (*0-7812-7068-5*) Rprt Serv.

— William Morris, a Critical Study. (BCL1-PR English Literature Ser.). 201p. 1992. reprint ed. lib. bdg. 79.00 (*0-7812-7609-8*) Rprt Serv.

Drinkwater, John, ed. Way of Poetry. LC 73-116399. (Granger Index Reprint Ser.). 1977. 18.95 (*0-8369-6140-4*) Ayer.

Drinkwater, John, ed. see Cunnigham, Peter.

***Drinkwater, Nathaniel.** Drinkwater. 2000. pap. 14.95 (*1-57409-999-X*) Sheridan.

Drinnan, Neal. Glove Puppet. LC 98-28866. 236p. 1998. 22.95 (*0-312-19271-1*) St Martin.

— Glove Puppet. 256p. 1999. pap. 12.95 (*0-312-24444-4*) St Martin.

***Drinnan, Neal.** Pussy's Bow. 272p. 2000. text 23.95 (*0-312-25255-2*) St Martin.

Drinnon, Bobby & Cartwright, Michael. Petitioning Reality with Faith. (Illus.). 228p. 1988. 17.95 (*0-9621995-0-8*) B Drinnon.

Drinnon, Elizabeth. Stuckey: The Biography of Williamson Sylvester Stuckey. (Illus.). 1997. 27.95 (*0-86554-569-3*, MUP/H425) Mercer Univ Pr.

Drinnon, Janis Bolton, see Bolton Drinnon, Janis.

Drinnon, Richard. Facing West: The Metaphysics of Indian-Hating & Empire-Building. LC 96-38854. (Illus.). 608p. 1997. pap. 19.95 (*0-8061-2928-X*) U of Okla Pr.

— Keeper of Concentration Camps: Dillon S. Myer & American Racism. 1987. pap. 16.95 (*0-520-06601-4*, Pub. by U CA Pr) Cal Prin Full Svc.

— Rebel in Paradise. LC 82-8531. (Phoenix Fiction Ser.). (Illus.). xvi, 350p. (C). 1993. reprint ed. pap. 12.95 (*0-226-16364-4*) U Ch Pr.

Drioli, E. & Nakagaki, M., eds. Membranes & Membrane Processes. LC 86-5076. 676p. 1986. 130.00 (*0-306-42270-0*, Plenum Trade) Perseus Pubng.

Drioli, Enrico. Biocatalytic Membrane Reactors. 1999. 89.95 (*0-7484-0654-9*) Taylor & Francis.

Driot, Marcel. Fathers of the Desert. 123p. (C). 1990. 50.00 (*0-85439-398-6*, Pub. by St Paul Pubns) St Mut.

Drioton, Etienne. Le Musee de Caire. (ENG & FRE., Illus.). 1949. lib. bdg. 24.95 (*0-8288-3990-5*) Fr & Eur.

Dripps, Craig, jt. auth. see Styron, Rose.

Dripps, R. D. The First House: Myth, Paradigm, & the Task of Architecture. LC 97-8889. (Illus.). 168p. 1997. 27.50 (*0-262-04163-4*) MIT Pr.

— The First House: Myth, Paradigm & the Task of Architecture. (Illus.). 168p. 1999. pap. text 13.00 (*0-262-54101-7*) MIT Pr.

Drips, J. H. Three Years among Indians in Dakota. 1976. 22.95 (*0-8488-0220-9*, J M C & Co) Amereon Ltd.

Dris, Patricia A. Corporate Formation: A Primer for Legal Assistants. 1. LC 95-8233. 392p. 1996. boxed set 72.95 (*0-471-08646-0*) Wiley.

Drisceoll, Diarmuid O. & Drisceoll, Donal O. The Murphy's Story: The History of Lady's Well Brewery, Cork. (Illus.). 164p. 1997. 29.95 (*0-9531431-0-4*, Pub. by Mercier Pr) Irish Amer Bk.

Drisceoll, Donal O., jt. auth. see Drisceoll, Diarmuid O.

Drischler, Alvin, jt. ed. see Doran, Charles F.

***Driscoll.** Data Aquisition & Process Control. 2nd ed. LC 99-29964. (Illus.). 779p. 1999. 101.00 (*0-13-779976-4*) P-H.

Driscoll. Microprocessor-Micro Computer Technology. 2nd ed. (Electronics Technology Ser.). 1990. text 57.95 (*0-8273-4084-2*) Delmar.

— Microprocessor/Micro Computer Tech. 2nd ed. (Electronics Technology Ser.). 1990. pap., teacher ed. 16.00 (*0-8273-4085-0*) Delmar.

— Precalculus. 504p. 1997. pap. 54.69 (*0-07-017867-4*) McGraw.

— Professionalism. (PJE Ser.: Vol. 73, No. 1). 1998. pap. 20.00 (*0-8058-9837-9*) L Erlbaum Assocs.

— Psychological Learning for Instruction. 2nd ed. LC 99-35051. 448p. 1999. 52.00 (*0-205-26321-6*) Allyn.

***Driscoll.** The Spoils of War. 2000. pap. 8.95 (*0-552-13827-4*, Pub. by Transworld Publishers Ltd) Trafalgar.

Driscoll. Youth. 1984. pap. 2.00 (*0-86683-842-2*) Harper SF.

Driscoll, et al. Early Childhood Education Birth to 8. LC 98-26472. 560p. (C). 1998. 61.33 (*0-205-19984-4*) Allyn.

Driscoll, jt. auth. see Freiberg.

Driscoll, Amy. Cases in Early Education: Stories of Programs & Practices. LC 93-1562. 200p. 1994. pap. text 33.00 (*0-205-15021-7*) Allyn.

— Early Childhood Education, Birth-8: The World of Children, Families, & Educators, Web Edition. 1999. 78.00 (*0-205-30000-6*) Allyn.

Driscoll, Amy & Lynton, Ernest, eds. Making Outreach Visible: A Guide to Documenting Professional Service & Outreach. 244p. 1999. pap. 19.00 (*1-56377-045-8*, FR9901) Am Assn Higher Ed.

***Driscoll, Anne.** Girl to Girl: Boys & You! (Illus.). 128p. (gr. 4-7). 2000. pap. 5.95 (*1-84207-031-2*) Element MA.

***Driscoll, Anne M.** Girl to Girl: Friends & You! 2000. 5.95 (*1-902618-06-8*, Pub. by Element Childrns) Penguin Putnam.

— Girl to Girl: Sports & You. (J). 2000. pap. text 4.95 (*1-902618-92-0*, Pub. by Element Childrns) Penguin Putnam.

— Girl to Girl: The Real Deal on Being a Girl Today. 128p. 1999. pap. 4.95 (*1-901881-29-6*, Pub. by Element MA) Penguin Putnam.

***Driscoll, Anne M.** Girl to Girl: The Real Deal on Being a Girl Today. 1999. 29.70 (*1-902618-00-9*, Pub. by Element MA) Penguin Putnam.

Driscoll, Barbara A. The Tracks North: The Railroad Bracero Program of World War II. LC 97-49865. (CMAS Border & Migration Studies Ser.). 224p. 1997. 30.00 (*0-292-71593-5*); pap. 14.95 (*0-292-71592-7*) U of Tex Pr.

Driscoll, C. F., jt. ed. see Roberson, C. W.

Driscoll, Charles. Country Jake: American Autobiography. 256p. 1995. lib. bdg. 79.00 (*0-7812-8503-8*) Rprt Serv.

— Kansas Irish: American Autobiography. 320p. 1995. lib. bdg. 89.00 (*0-7812-8504-6*) Rprt Serv.

Driscoll, Charles E., et al, eds. The Family Practice Desk Reference. 3rd ed. LC 95-19477. (Illus.). 784p. (C). (gr. 13). 1995. text 54.95 (*0-8151-2201-2*, 24423) Mosby Inc.

Driscoll, Charles E. & Rakel, Robert E. Patient Care Procedures for Your Practice, 1991. 2nd ed. (Illus.). 320p. (C). 1991. text. write for info. (*1-878487-29-9*, 6584M) Practice Mgmt Info.

Driscoll, Chris. And God Blessed the Irish. LC 97-77057. (Illus.). 80p. (J). (gr. 4-5). 1997. 9.95 (*0-9646439-6-0*) Ambasdr Bks.

Driscoll, Colin L.W., jt. auth. see Jackler, Robert K.

Driscoll, Craig. The Coming Chastisement. LC 95-69962. 64p. 1995. pap. 1.95 (*1-882972-49-X*, 3342) Queenship Pub.

— Our Lady, an Angel & Sister Agnes. 48p. 1994. pap. 3.00 (*1-890137-32-4*) One Hund-One Fnd.

Driscoll, Cynthia B. One Woman's Gold Rush: Snapshots from Mollie Brackett's Lost Photo Album 1898-1899. Curl, David H., ed. LC 96-12942. (Illus.). 128p. (Orig.). 1996. pap. 12.00 (*0-88196-007-1*) Oak Woods Media.

Driscoll, D., et al, eds. Proceedings of the XIth Congress of the International Society of Biometeorology. (Illus.). xvi, 407p. 1989. pap. 125.00 (*90-5103-036-3*, Pub. by SPB Acad Pub) Balogh.

Driscoll, Daniel. Strengthening Policy Analysis: Econometric Tests Using SPSS/PC+, SAS PC, & GAUSS-386. LC 95-5179. (Micrcomputers in Policy Research Ser.: Vol. 2). 1995. write for info. (*0-89629-330-0*) Intl Food Policy.

Driscoll, Dawn-Marie, ed. Women & Economic Empowerment: Special Issue. 272p. (Orig.). 1990. pap. 17.95 (*0-87023-644-X*) U of Mass Pr.

Driscoll, Dawn-Marie & Goldberg, Carol R. Members of the Club: The Coming of Age of Executive Women. 250p. 1993. 24.95 (*0-02-908065-7*) Free Pr.

***Driscoll, Dawn-Marie & Hoffman, W. Michael.** Ethics Matters: How to Implement Values-Driven Management. LC 99-52887. 1999. pap. write for info. (*0-9675514-0-4*) Center for Busn.

Driscoll, Dawn-Marie, et al. The Ethical Edge: Tales of Organizations That Have Faced Moral Crises. (Illus.). 238p. 1998. text 25.00 (*0-7881-5678-0*) DIANE Pub.

D

— The Ethical Edge: Tales of Organizations That Have Faced Moral Crises. 256p. 1997. 24.95 (*1-57101-051-3*) MasterMedia Pub.

Driscoll, Debbie. Jenny Come Along. (J). 1995. 19.95 (*0-385-44626-8*) BDD Bks Young Read.

***Driscoll, Diana.** Year 2000. 1999. 19.95 (*0-9667727-3-3*) Priority Consult.

Driscoll, Diana, et al. Health Care in Crisis: Preparing the Eye Care Practitioner's Office for the Year 2000. (Illus.). 79p. 1998. pap. 89.95 (*0-9667727-0-9*) Priority Consult.

— Health Care in Crisis: Preparing the Medical Office for the Year 2000. (Illus.). 79p. 1998. pap. 89.95 (*0-9667727-1-7*) Priority Consult.

— Year 2000: Mom & Pop's Small Business Guide: How to Prepare Your Small Business for the Upcoming Y2K Computer Crisis. (Illus.). 75p. 1998. pap. 89.95 (*0-9667727-2-5*) Priority Consult.

Driscoll, Edward B., Jr., jt. auth. see Borland, Lee.

Driscoll, Edward F. Industrial Electronics: Devices, Circuits & Applications. LC 74-31899. (Illus.). 432p. reprint ed. pap. 134.00 (*0-608-18812-3*, 203023300067) Bks Demand.

Driscoll, Eileen H. Alzheimer's: A Handbook for the Caretaker. LC 94-4805. 1996. pap. 12.95 (*0-8283-1962-6*) Branden Bks.

Driscoll, Fletcher G. Groundwater & Well. 1108p. (C). 1988. 900.00 (*0-7855-6697-X*, Pub. by Scientific) St Mut.

— Groundwater & Wells. 2nd ed. LC 85-63577. (Illus.). 1089p. 1986. text 62.00 (*0-9616456-0-1*) US Filter.

Driscoll, Frances. The Rape Poems. LC 96-72150. 88p. (Orig.). 1997. pap. 12.95 (*0-9651413-1-4*, SAN 299-0075) Pleasure Boat.

Driscoll, Fred F., jt. auth. see Coughlin, Robert F.

Driscoll, Frederick F. Data Communications. 450p. (C). 1992. text 66.50 (*0-03-026637-8*, Pub. by SCP) Harcourt.

Driscoll, Frederick F., Jr. & Coughlin, Robert F. Solid State Devices & Applications. (Illus.). 384p. 1975. text 53.00 (*0-13-822106-5*) P-H.

Driscoll, Frederick F., jt. auth. see Coughlin, Robert F.

Driscoll, Geraldine, ed. see Goc, Michael J.

Driscoll, J. R., tr. see Rommel, Erwin.

Driscoll, Jack. Building the Cold from Memory. (Ithaca House Poetry Ser.). 80p. (Orig.). (C). 1989. pap. 9.95 (*0-87886-130-0*) Greenfld Rev Lit.

— Fishing the Backwash. LC 84-3843. 71p. 1984. pap. 5.00 (*0-87886-123-8*, Greenfld Rev Pr) Greenfld Rev Lit.

— Lucky Man, Lucky Woman. 272p. 2000. pap. 13.00 (*0-393-31945-8*) Norton.

— Lucky Man, Lucky Woman: A Love Story. 264p. 1999. 24.50 (*1-888889-08-X*, Pub. by Pushcart Pr) Norton.

***Driscoll, Jack.** Stardog. LC 98-44862. (Illus.). 256p. (J). 2000. 22.95 (*0-7894-2626-9*, D K Ink) DK Pub Inc.

Driscoll, Jack. Wanting Only to Be Heard. LC 92-5109. 208p. 1992. 25.00 (*0-87023-808-6*) U of Mass Pr.

Driscoll, Jack, jt. auth. see Meissner, Bill.

Driscoll, James. Driscoll: A Guide to the Housing Act 1996. (Butterworths Annotated Legislation Service Ser.). 1996. pap. write for info. (*0-406-99894-9*, DGHA1996, MICHIE) LEXIS Pub.

— Leashold Reform - The New Law: A Guide to the Housing & Urban Development Act 1993. 300p. 1993. 96.00 (*0-85459-820-0*, Pub. by Tolley Pubng) St Mut.

— Sharing the Good News: A Workbook on Personal Evangelism. 1998. pap. text 10.00 (*0-7880-0967-2*) CSS OH.

Driscoll, James, ed. Butterworths Residential Landlord & Tenant Guide. 1997. write for info. (*0-406-00252-5*, BRLTG, MICHIE) LEXIS Pub.

— Butterworth's Residential Landlord & Tenant Handbook. viii,949p. 1995. pap. write for info. (*0-406-08130-1*, MICHIE) LEXIS Pub.

Driscoll, James L., et al. Instrument Evaluation in Biomedical Sciences. LC 84-12673. (Clinical & Biochemical Analysis Ser.: Vol. 15). (Illus.). 325p. reprint ed. pap. 100.80 (*0-608-08930-3*, 206956500005) Bks Demand.

Driscoll, James P. Identity in Shakespearean Drama. LC 81-72027. 208p. 1983. 32.50 (*0-8387-5024-9*) Bucknell U Pr.

— The Unfolding God of Jung & Milton. LC 92-21769. (Studies in the English Renaissance). 248p. (C). 1992. text 33.00 (*0-8131-1809-3*) U Pr of Ky.

Driscoll, Jeanne W. & Walker, Marsha. Taking Care of Your New Baby: A Guide to Infant Care. (Illus.). 208p. Date not set. mass mkt. 5.95 (*0-89529-693-4*, Avery) Penguin Putnam.

Driscoll, Jeanne W., jt. auth. see Sichel, Deborah.

Driscoll, Jeremy. Some Other Morning. 112p. (Orig.). (C). 1992. pap. 10.95 (*0-934257-66-3*) Story Line.

Driscoll, Jerry. College Chemistry. 374p. (C). 1999. spiral bd. 37.95 (*0-7872-5735-4*, 41573503) Kendall-Hunt.

— Student Study Guide & Solution Manual to Introductory Chemistry. 180p. (C). 1996. pap. text, student ed. 28.95 (*0-7872-2912-1*) Kendall-Hunt.

Driscoll, John. The Artist & the American Landscape. (Illus.). 176p. 1998. 22.95 (*1-885440-37-5*) First Glance.

— Sailing: A Beginner's Manual. (C). 1990. text 59.00 (*0-906754-28-3*, Pub. by Fernhurst Bks) St Mut.

Driscoll, John & Douglas, Paul. Learn to Play Tennis in a Weekend. 1991. 16.00 (*0-394-58746-4*) Knopf.

Driscoll, John K. The Baraboo Guards. LC 95-35927. (Illus.). 320p. 1995. pap. 16.95 (*1-879483-29-7*) Prairie Oak Pr.

Driscoll, John P. All That Is Glorious Around Us: Paintings from the Hudson River School. LC 97-17686. (Illus.). 144p. 1997. text 30.00 (*0-8014-3489-0*) Cornell U Pr.

— American Paintings from the Collection of Daniel J. Terra: Exhibition Catalogue. (Illus.). 38p. 1977. pap. 2.50 (*0-911209-10-7*) Palmer Mus Art.

— Communicating on Film. 124p. 1983. pap. text 8.80 (*0-87563-238-6*) Stipes.

— Learn to Sail in a Weekend. LC GV811.D68. (Illus.). 96p. 1998. pap. 10.95 (*0-375-70321-7*) Random.

— Works by Arthur B. Davies: From the Collection of Mr. & Mrs. Herbert Brill. (Illus.). 36p. 1979. pap. 3.00 (*0-911209-15-8*) Palmer Mus Art.

Driscoll, John P., jt. auth. see Howat, John R.

Driscoll, Kerry. William Carlos Williams & the Maternal Muse. LC 87-13855. (Studies in Modern Literature: No. 72). 213p. reprint ed. pap. 66.10 (*0-8357-2068-3*, 207071000004) Bks Demand.

Driscoll, Laura. All about Dogs & Puppies. LC 98-2911. 1998. pap. text 2.99 (*0-448-41841-X*, G & D) Peng Put Young Read.

— The Bravest Cat! The True Story of Scarlett, Level 1. LC 97-10487. (All Aboard Reading Ser.). (Illus.). 32p. (J). (ps-1). 1997. pap. 3.95 (*0-448-41703-0*, G & D); lib. bdg. 13.89 (*0-448-41720-0*, G & D) Peng Put Young Read.

— Frogs, Level 1. LC 97-43359. (All Aboard Reading Ser.). (Illus.). 32p. (J). (ps-1). 1998. lib. bdg. 13.89 (*0-448-41868-1*, G & D) Peng Put Young Read.

***Driscoll, Laura.** Frogs, Level 1. LC 97-43359. (All Aboard Reading Ser.). (Illus.). 32p. (J). (ps-1). 1998. pap. 3.99 (*0-448-41839-8*, G & D) Peng Put Young Read.

Driscoll, Laura. Fuzzy Critters, Vol. 1. 12p. (J). 1999. 6.99 (*0-448-41898-3*, G & D) Peng Put Young Read.

***Driscoll, Laura.** Halloween Treats, 1 vol. 12p. (J). 1999. 6.99 (*0-448-41899-1*, G & D) Peng Put Young Read.

Driscoll, Laura. Kitties Busy Day. Date not set. pap. 4.95 (*0-448-40903-8*) Putnam Pub Group.

— Let's Look at Families (Poke & Look Learning Books) (Poke & Look Learning Ser.). (Illus.). 16p. (J). (ps-3). 1999. bds. 9.99 (*0-448-41990-4*, G & D) Peng Put Young Read.

— Let's Look at the Planets. (Poke & Look Learning Ser.). (Illus.). 16p. (J). (ps-3). 1999. bds. 9.99 (*0-448-42066-X*, G & D) Peng Put Young Read.

— Look Inside a Castle. LC 98-71534. (Poke & Look Learning Ser.). (Illus.). 16p. (J). (ps-3). 1998. mass mkt. 9.99 (*0-448-41889-4*, G & D) Peng Put Young Read.

***Driscoll, Laura.** Muppets from Space: Gonzo's Book of Out of This World Puzzles. 24p. (J). 1999. 3.99 (*0-448-42058-9*, G & D) Peng Put Young Read.

— Sammy Sosa: Home Run Hero. LC 99-13641. (All Aboard Reading Ser.). (Illus.). 48p. (gr. 2-4). 1999. 13.89 (*0-448-42069-4*) Putnam Pub Group.

— Sammy Sosa: Home-Run Hero, 1 vol. 3rd ed. LC 99-13641. (All Aboard Reading Ser.). (Illus.). 48p. (gr. 2-4). 1999. pap. text 3.99 (*0-448-42067-8*) Putnam Pub Group.

Driscoll, Laura. Shake It up, Bunny! LC 98-209949. (Illus.). 12p. (J). (ps). 1998. bds. 8.95 (*0-448-41629-8*, G & D) Peng Put Young Read.

— Shake It up, Chick! LC 98-141087. (Illus.). 12p. (J). (ps). 1998. bds. 8.95 (*0-448-41630-1*, G & D) Peng Put Young Read.

— Shake It up, Kitty! (Illus.). 12p. (J). (ps-2). 1997. bds. 8.95 (*0-448-41626-3*, G & D) Peng Put Young Read.

— Shake It up, Pup! (Illus.). 12p. (J). (ps-2). 1997. bds. 8.95 (*0-448-41625-5*, G & D) Peng Put Young Read.

— Slugger Season: McGwire & Sosa. LC 98-47879. (Illus.). 32p. 1998. pap. 3.99 (*0-448-42039-2*, G & D) Peng Put Young Read.

— Slugger Season: McGwire & Sosa. LC 98-47879. (Illus.). 32p. (gr. 2-4). 1998. 13.89 (*0-448-42040-6*, G & D) Peng Put Young Read.

Driscoll, Laura, jt. auth. see Lundell, Margo.

Driscoll, Laura A. Sammy Sosa. (All Aboard Reading Ser.). (Illus.). 48p. (J). (gr. 2-4). 1999. 3.99 (*0-448-42068-6*, G & D) Peng Put Young Read.

Driscoll, Laura A., jt. auth. see Goodwin, William L.

***Driscoll, Lawrence.** Telling Signs of Addiction: Drug Discourses from the Victorians. 1999. text. write for info. (*0-312-22272-6*) St Martin.

Driscoll, M. J., et al. The Linear Reactivity Model for Nuclear Fuel Management. 256p. 54.00 (*0-89448-035-9*, 350014) Am Nuclear Soc.

Driscoll, Marcy P., jt. auth. see Gagne, Robert M.

Driscoll, Margaret. Web-Based Training: Using Technology to Design Adult Learning Experiences. LC 98-25314. (Business Training Ser.). 288p. 1998. 44.95 incl. disk (*0-7879-4203-0*) Jossey-Bass.

***Driscoll, Mark.** Fostering Algebraic Thinking: A Guide for Teachers, Grades 6-10. LC 98-51138. 168p. 1999. pap. text 22.00 (*0-325-00154-5*) Heinemann.

Driscoll, Mark, jt. ed. see Cuevas, Gilbert J.

Driscoll, Mark, ed. see National Research Council Staff.

Driscoll, Mark J., jt. auth. see Bryant, Deborah.

***Driscoll, Marsha.** Harvest of Love. LC 98-96843. 192p. 1999. lib. bdg. 18.95 (*0-8034-9332-0*, Avalon Bks) Bouregy.

Driscoll, Marsha. A Nest of One's Own. LC 97-94273. 192p. 1997. 18.95 (*0-8034-9267-7*, Avalon Bks) Bouregy.

— On Eagles' Wings. LC 97-94014. 192p. 1997. 18.95 (*0-8034-9252-9*, Avalon Bks) Bouregy.

Driscoll, Martha. Silent Herald of Unity: The Life of Bl. Gabrielle Sagheddu. (Cistercian Studies: No. 119). 142p. 1990. 19.95 (*0-87907-619-4*); pap. 10.95 (*0-87907-919-3*) Cistercian Pubns.

Driscoll, Maryanne. All about Successful Parenting. (Family Forum Library). 16p. 1992. 1.95 (*1-56688-009-2*) Bur For At-Risk.

Driscoll, Maryanne, jt. auth. see Fromberg, Doris.

Driscoll, Maryanne, jt. auth. see Fromberg, Doris P.

Driscoll, Maryanne, jt. auth. see Gleason, Charles.

Driscoll, Matthew J. The Unwashed Children of Eve: The Production, Dissemination & Reception of Popular Literature in Post-Reformation Iceland. LC 97-158346. 356p. 1996. 60.00 (*1-874312-30-3*, Pub. by Hisarlik Pr) Intl Spec Bk.

Driscoll, Michael, ed. see Kostick, Anne, et al.

Driscoll, Michael, ed. see Kranes, Martha, et al.

Driscoll, Michael P., jt. auth. see Mays, Sandra C.

Driscoll, Michael S., tr. see Puglisi, James F.

Driscoll, P., ed. Genetically Defined Animal Models of Neurobehavioral Dysfunctions. xx, 304p. 1992. 109.00 (*0-8176-3460-6*) Birkhauser.

Driscoll, Peter. Spearhead: A Novel. 304p. 1989. 17.95 (*0-316-19341-0*) Little.

***Driscoll, Peter, et al, eds.** ABC of Major Trauma. 3rd ed. 181p. 2000. pap. text 34.95 (*0-7279-1378-6*) BMJ Pub.

Driscoll, Peter, et al. Simple Guide to Blood Gas Analysis. (Illus.). 191p. 1997. pap. text 35.00 (*0-7279-1107-4*, Pub. by BMJ Pub) Login Brothers Bk Co.

Driscoll, Peter, jt. ed. see Nicholson, David.

Driscoll, Peter A. & Skinner, David V., eds. Trauma Care Beyond the Resuscitation Room: Beyond Resuscitation Room. 312p. 1998. text. write for info. (*0-7279-0933-9*) Login Brothers Bk Co.

Driscoll, Pippa. Children Afloat. (Illus.). 96p. 1989. pap. 12.95 (*0-906754-42-9*) McGraw-Hill Prof.

Driscoll, R. B. Annex to Unified Theory of Ether, Field & Matter. ix, 161p. 1994. pap. 15.00i (*0-9601374-2-4*) R B Driscoll.

— Unified Theory of Ether, Field & Matter. 3rd ed. 310p. 1966. pap. 20.00i (*0-9601374-1-6*) R B Driscoll.

Driscoll, Richard. Mental Shielding to Brush off Hostility. 2nd unabridged ed. LC 93-74709. 88p. 1994. pap. 18.00 incl. audio (*0-9634126-1-2*) Frontiers Pr.

— Recovering Love: Overcoming Standoffs & Stalemates in a Valued Relationship. 1993. pap. 11.95 (*0-02-907755-9*) Free Pr.

— The Stronger Sex: Understanding & Resolving the Power Struggle Between Men & Women. LC 97-35044. 288p. 1998. 22.00 (*0-7615-1280-2*) Prima Pub.

Driscoll, S. T. & Nieke, M. R., eds. Power & Politics in Early Britain & Ireland. (Illus.). 200p. 1988. 45.00 (*0-85224-520-3*, Pub. by Edinburgh U Pr) Col U Pr.

Driscoll, Stephen B., ed. The Basics of Testing Plastics: Mechanical Properties, Flame Exposure, & General Guidelines. LC 98-22760. (Manual Ser.: Vol. 35). (Illus.). 61p. 1998. pap. text 39.00 (*0-8031-2079-6*, MNL35) ASTM.

Driscoll, Susan & Ridolphi, Margaret. How Does Your Garden Grow? 75p. 1993. write for info. (*0-9637418-0-2*) Blossoms Up.

***Driscoll, Susan, et al.** Termination Without Consequences. LC 99-183858. 143p. 1998. write for info. (*0-87622-775-2*) Aspen Pub.

***Driscoll, William.** Discovering the World Through Debate: A Practical Guide to Educational Debate for Debaters, Coaches & Judges. 160p. 2000. pap. text 29.95 (*0-9702130-0-X*) Inter Debate.

Driscoll, William & Robb, Donald W. Conexiones Resolucion de Problemas: Guia del Maestro - Nivel Anaranjado.Tr. of Problem Solving Connections. (SPA., Illus.). 1994. pap. text, teacher ed. 15.00 (*1-57091-009-X*) Charlesbridge Pub.

— Conexiones Resolucion de Problemas: Guia del Maestro - Nivel Azul.Tr. of Problem Solving Connections. (Illus.). 1994. pap. text, teacher ed. 15.00 (*1-57091-010-3*) Charlesbridge Pub.

— Conexiones Resolucion de Problemas: Guia del Maestro - Nivel Marron.Tr. of Problem Solving Connections. (SPA., Illus.). 1994. pap. text, teacher ed. 15.00 (*1-57091-011-1*) Charlesbridge Pub.

— Conexiones Resolucion de Problemas: Guia del Maestro - Nivel Oro.Tr. of Problem Solving Connections. (SPA., Illus.). 1994. pap. text, teacher ed. 15.00 (*1-57091-012-X*) Charlesbridge Pub.

— Conexiones Resolucion de Problemas: Libro del Estudiante - Nivel Anaranjado.Tr. of Problem Solving Connections. (SPA., Illus.). (J). (gr. 3). 1994. pap. text 5.00 (*1-57091-001-4*) Charlesbridge Pub.

— Conexiones Resolucion de Problemas: Libro del Estudiante - Nivel Azul.Tr. of Problem Solving Connections. (SPA., Illus.). (J). (gr. 4). 1994. pap. text 5.00 (*1-57091-002-2*) Charlesbridge Pub.

— Conexiones Resolucion de Problemas: Libro del Estudiante - Nivel Marron.Tr. of Problem Solving Connections. (SPA., Illus.). (J). (gr. 5). 1994. pap. text 5.00 (*1-57091-003-0*) Charlesbridge Pub.

— Conexiones Resolucion de Problemas: Libro del Estudiante - Nivel Oro.Tr. of Problem Solving Connections. (SPA., Illus.). (J). (gr. 6). 1994. pap. text 5.00 (*1-57091-004-9*) Charlesbridge Pub.

— Problem Solving Connections: Blue Level Student Book. (Illus.). (J). (gr. 4). 1992. pap. text, student ed. 5.00 (*0-88106-652-4*) Charlesbridge Pub.

— Problem Solving Connections: Blue Level Teacher Manual. (Illus.). 1992. pap. text, teacher ed. 15.00 (*0-88106-653-2*) Charlesbridge Pub.

— Problem Solving Connections: Gold Level Student Book. (Illus.). (J). (gr. 6). 1992. pap. text, student ed. 5.00 (*0-88106-656-7*) Charlesbridge Pub.

— Problem Solving Connections: Gold Level Teacher Manual. (Illus.). 1992. pap. text, teacher ed. 15.00 (*0-88106-657-5*) Charlesbridge Pub.

— Problem Solving Connections: Green Level Student Book. (Illus.). (J). (gr. 2). 1996. pap. text, student ed. 5.00 (*1-57091-027-8*) Charlesbridge Pub.

— Problem Solving Connections: Green Level Teacher Manual. (Illus.). 1996. pap. text, teacher ed. 30.00 (*1-57091-028-6*) Charlesbridge Pub.

— Problem Solving Connections: Orange Level Student Book. (Illus.). (J). (gr. 3). 1992. pap. text, student ed. 5.00 (*0-88106-650-8*) Charlesbridge Pub.

— Problem Solving Connections: Orange Level Teacher Manual. (Illus.). 1992. pap. text, teacher ed. 15.00 (*0-88106-651-6*) Charlesbridge Pub.

— Problem Solving Connections: Red Level Student Book. (Illus.). (J). (gr. 1). 1996. pap. text, student ed. 5.00 (*1-57091-025-1*) Charlesbridge Pub.

— Problem Solving Connections: Red Level Teacher Manual. (Illus.). 1996. pap. text, teacher ed. 30.00 (*1-57091-026-X*) Charlesbridge Pub.

— Problem Solving Connections: Tan Level Student Book. (Illus.). (J). (gr. 5). 1992. pap. text, student ed. 5.00 (*0-88106-654-0*) Charlesbridge Pub.

— Problem Solving Connections: Tan Level Teacher Manual. (Illus.). 1992. pap. text, teacher ed. 15.00 (*0-88106-655-9*) Charlesbridge Pub.

Drisdelle, Rheal. Mali. LC 98-131254. (Country Profiles Ser.). (Illus.). 64p. (C). 1997. pap. 9.95 (*0-85598-334-5*, Pub. by Oxfam Pub) Stylus Pub VA.

Drishna, H. C. & Sirohi, Rajpal S. Mechanical Measurement. 3rd ed. 284p. 1993. text 59.95 (*0-470-21953-X*) Halsted Pr.

***Driskall, Kathleen.** Laughing Sickness. LC 99-63909. 68p. (Orig.). 1999. pap. 10.00 (*0-9652520-2-7*) Fleur-de-lis Pr.

Driskel, Michael P. As Befits a Legend: Building a Tomb for Napoleon, 1840-1861. LC 93-12099. (Illus.). 280p. 1994. 32.00 (*0-87338-484-9*) Kent St U Pr.

— Representing Belief: Religion, Art, & Society in Nineteenth-Century France. (Illus.). 288p. 1992. text 55.00 (*0-271-00747-8*) Pa St U Pr.

Driskell, David C. Contemporary Visual Expressions. LC 87-600094. (Illus.). 80p. (Orig.). (C). 1987. pap. 19.95 (*0-87474-385-0*) Smithsonian.

Driskell, David C., ed. African American Visual Aesthetics: A Postmodernist View. LC 95-10256. (Illus.). 128p. 1996. pap. text 26.95 (*1-56098-605-0*) Smithsonian.

Driskell, James E. & Salas, Eduardo, eds. Stress & Human Performance. (Applied Psychology Ser.). 360p. 1996. text 65.00 (*0-8058-1182-6*) L Erlbaum Assocs.

Driskell, Judy A. Sports Nutrition. LC 99-26360. (Nutrition in Exercise & Sport Ser.). 296p. 1999. boxed set 59.95 (*0-8493-8197-5*) CRC Pr.

***Driskell, Judy A. & Wolinsky, Ira.** Energy-Yielding Macronutrients & Energy Metabolism in Sports Nutrition. LC 99-32452. (Nutrition in Exercise & Sport Ser.). 352p. 1999. boxed set 89.95 (*0-8493-0755-4*) CRC Pr.

Driskell, Judy A. & Wolinsky, Ira. Macronutrients, Electrolytes & Macroelements in Sports Nutrition. LC 99-234359. (Nutrition in Exercise & Sport Ser.). 1999. 89.95 (*0-8493-8196-7*) CRC Pr.

Driskell, Judy A., jt. auth. see Wolinsky, Ira.

Driskell, Judy A., jt. ed. see Kies, Constance V.

Driskell, Leon. Passing Through: A Novel. 10th ed. (Front Porch Paperbacks Ser.). 252p. 1993. pap. 8.95 (*1-56512-056-6*) Algonquin Bks.

Driskell, Les. Control Valve Sizing. LC TJ0223.V3D73. (Instrument Society of America Monographs). (Illus.). 206p. reprint ed. pap., student ed. 63.90 (*0-7837-9041-4*, 204979200003) Bks Demand.

— Control Valve Sizing: Instructor's Guide. LC TJ0223.V3D73. (Instructional Resource Package Ser.). (Illus.). 53p. reprint ed. pap. 30.00 (*0-7837-5150-8*, 204487900004) Bks Demand.

— Introduction to Control Valves & Other Final Control Devices: Instructor's Guide. LC 81-80513. (Instructional Resource Package Ser.). (Illus.). 37p. reprint ed. pap. 30.00 (*0-7837-5149-4*, 204487800004) Bks Demand.

— Introduction to Control Valves & Other Final Control Devices: Student Text. LC 81-80513. (Instructional Resource Package Ser.). 127p. 1981. reprint ed. pap. 39.40 (*0-7837-5135-4*, 204486300004) Bks Demand.

— Selection of Control Valves & Other Final Control Devices: Instructor's Guide. LC 81-80514. (Instructional Resource Package Ser.). (Illus.). 54p. reprint ed. pap., teacher ed. 30.00 (*0-7837-5151-6*, 204488000004) Bks Demand.

Driskell, T. Ken. How to Make Your Banker Say Yes: 50 Successful Strategies for Guaranteed Loan Approval. LC 96-69021. (Illus.). 204p. (Orig.). 1996. pap. 19.95 (*0-9653204-9-9*) PowerBnking.

Driskill. Laboratory Procedures for Vet Technology. pap. text. write for info. (*0-7216-4548-8*, W B Saunders Co) Harcrt Hlth Sci Grp.

Driskill, Frank, jt. auth. see Grisham, Noel.

Driskill, Frank A. & Casad, Dede W. Admiral of the Hills: Biography of Chester W. Nimitz. (Illus.). 312p. 1983. pap. 14.95 (*0-89015-364-7*) Sunbelt Media.

Driskill, J. Lawrence. Adventures in Senior Living: Learning How to Make Retirement Meaningful & Enjoyable. LC 97-18763. (Illus.). 180p. 1997. 29.95 (*0-7890-0253-1*, Haworth Pastrl); pap. 14.95 (*0-7890-0254-X*, Haworth Pastrl) Haworth Pr.

— Cross-Cultural Marriages & the Church: Living the Global Neighborhood. LC 94-41144. 114p. 1995. pap. 9.95 (*0-932727-80-8*); lib. bdg. 17.95 (*0-932727-81-6*) Hope Pub Hse.

— Mission Adventures in Many Lands: Stories for Children. LC 92-15689. (Illus.). 212p. (J). (gr. 3-8). 1992. pap. 11.95 (*0-932727-56-5*); lib. bdg. 19.95 (*0-932727-57-3*) Hope Pub Hse.

— Mission Stories from Around the World: Stories for Children. LC 93-39413. 178p. (J). (gr. 4-8). 1994. pap. 11.95 (*0-932727-71-9*); lib. bdg. 19.95 (*0-932727-72-7*) Hope Pub Hse.

— World-Wide Mission Stories for Young People. LC 95-50392. (SPA., Illus.). 131p. (J). 1996. 19.95 (*0-932727-86-7*) Hope Pub Hse.

D

An Asterisk (*) at the beginning of an entry indicates that the title is appearing for the first time.

— Worldwide Mission Stories for Young People. LC 95-50392. (Illus.). 131p. (J). (gr. 4-9). 1996. pap. 19.95 (*0-932727-85-9*) Hope Pub Hse.

Driskill, J. Lawrence, ed. Christmas Stories from Around the World: Honoring Jesus in Many Lands. LC 96-38177. (Illus.). 136p. (J). (gr. 3-9). 1997. pap. 11.95 (*0-932727-87-5*); lib. bdg. 19.95 (*0-932727-88-3*) Hope Pub Hse.

Driskill, J. Lawrence & Driskill, Lillian C. Japan Diary of Cross-Cultural Mission. LC 92-43636. (Illus.). 192p. 1993. pap. 11.95 (*0-932727-62-X*); lib. bdg. 19.95 (*0-932727-63-8*) Hope Pub Hse.

***Driskill, Joseph D.** Protestant Spiritual Exercises: Theology, History & Practice. LC 99-12527. 152p. 1999. pap. 12.95 (*0-8192-1759-X*) Morehouse Pub.

Driskill, Joseph D., jt. auth. see Lebacqz, Karen.

Driskill, Lillian C., jt. auth. see Driskill, J. Lawrence.

Driskill, Richard T. Madonnas & Maidens: Sexual Confusion in Lawrence & Gide. LC 96-32147. (Sexuality & Literature Ser.: Vol. 6). VIII, 303p. (C). 1999. text 55.95 (*0-8204-3493-0*) P Lang Pubng.

Drisko, Barbara L., jt. auth. see Harrison, Henry S.

Drisko, Frances S. MackIntosh, MacIntosh, McIntosh: Descendants of Alexander MacIntosh. (Illus.). 319p. (Orig.). 1993. pap. text 43.00 (*1-55613-876-8*) Heritage Bk.

Drisko, George W. Narrative of the Town of Machias, Maine: The Old & the New, the Early & the Late. (Illus.). 589p. 1988. reprint ed. lib. bdg. 62.00 (*0-8328-0030-9*, ME0020) Higginson Bk Co.

Drisko, R., jt. ed. see Rex, Janet.

Drissel, Nancy, ed. see Magee, Jeffrey L.

Drissen, L., et al, eds. Nonisotropic & Variable Outflows from Stars. (ASP Conference Series Proceedings: Vol. 22). 408p. 1992. 34.00 (*0-937707-41-4*) Astron Soc Pacific.

Drits, V. A. & Tchoubar, C. X-Ray Diffraction by Disordered Lamellar Structures. (Illus.). 450p. 1990. 214.95 (*0-387-51222-5*) Spr-Verlag.

Dritsas. Fundamentals of Math. 1989. teacher ed. 80.50 (*0-15-353017-0*) H Holt & Co.

— Fundamentals of Mathematics. 1989. teacher ed. 89.00 (*0-15-353002-2*) H Holt & Co.

Dritschel, David G. & Perkins, R. J., eds. The Mathematics of Deforming Surfaces. (Institute of Mathematics & Its Applications Conference Ser.; New Ser.: Vol. 56). (Illus.). 260p. (C). 1996. text 140.00 (*0-19-853643-7*) OUP.

Dritschel, Michael A. & Woerdeman, Hugo J. Model Theory & Linear Extreme Points in the Numerical Radius Unit Ball. LC 97-21323. (Memoirs of the American Mathematical Society Ser.: Vol. 129, No. 615). 62p. 1997. pap. 34.00 (*0-8218-0651-3*) Am Math.

Dritschilo, Anatoly, jt. ed. see Rhim, Johng S.

***Drivdahl, Cheryl Miller.** We Are Fire! Resource Manual: Discipleship Activities & Prayer Experiences for Teens. Singer-Towns, Brian, ed. 32p. (YA). 2000. pap. 12.95 (*0-88489-639-0*) St Marys.

Driver. Programming Assembly Language. Date not set. pap. text, teacher ed. write for info. (*0-314-01316-4*) West Pub.

— The Ventilator-Assisted Child. 1997. 59.00 (*0-7616-1533-4*) Commun Skill.

Driver, B. L., et al, eds. Benefits of Leisure. LC 91-67118. 483p. 1991. 35.95 (*0-910251-48-7*) Venture Pub PA.

— Nature & the Human Spirit: Toward an Expanded Land Management Ethic. LC 96-60358. 497p. 1996. text 39.95 (*0-910251-82-7*, NHS86) Venture Pub PA.

Driver, Christopher, ed. see Evelyn, John.

Driver, Ciaran. Towards Full Employment: A Policy Appraisal. (Illus.). 252p. 1988. lib. bdg. 49.00 (*0-7102-0918-5*, Routledge Thoemms) Routledge.

***Driver, Ciaran & Temple, Paul.** Investment Growth & Employment: Perspectives & Policy. LC 99-19536. 1999. pap. write for info. (*0-415-19780-5*) Routledge.

***Driver, Ciaran & Temple, Paul, eds.** Investment Growth & Employment: Perspectives & Policy. LC 99-19536. 336p. (C). 1999. text. write for info. (*0-415-19779-1*) Routledge.

Driver, Clive E. The Art of Claud Lovat Fraser. LC 72-179649. (Illus.). 78p. 1971. pap. 6.50 (*0-939084-01-5*) R Mus & Lib.

— Early American Maps & Views. (Illus.). 64p. 1972. pap. 4.00 (*0-939084-12-0*) R Mus & Lib.

— A Selection from Our Shelves: Books, Manuscripts & Drawings from the Rosenbach Foundation Museum. (Illus.). 140p. 1973. pap. 13.25 (*0-939084-08-2*) R Mus & Lib.

Driver, Clive E., compiled by. Passing Through: Letters & Documents Written in Philadelphia by Famous Visitors. (Illus.). 126p. 1982. pap. 10.00 (*0-939084-23-6*) R Mus & Lib.

Driver, Clive E., jt. ed. see Feldman, Evelyn.

Driver, David. The Good Heart Book: A Guide to Volunteering. 2nd rev. ed. LC 89-61442. 220p. 1991. pap. 9.95 (*0-9622683-1-3*) Noble Pr.

Driver, David E. Bronzeville. 288p. 1996. 21.95 (*1-879360-44-6*) Noble Pr.

— Defending the Left: An Individual's Guide to Fighting for Social Justice, Individual Rights, & the Environment. LC 91-51221. 228p. (Orig.). 1992. pap. 12.95 (*1-879360-14-4*) Noble Pr.

— The Good Heart Book: A Guide to Volunteering. LC 89-61442. (Volunteer Ser.). 1989. 18.95 (*0-9622683-0-5*) Noble Pr.

Driver, Donald. Status Quo Vadis. 1973. pap. 5.25 (*0-8222-1076-2*) Dramatists Play.

Driver, Dorothy, et al, compiled by. Nadine Gordimer: A Bibliography of Primary & Secondary Sources. LC 93-37446. (Bibliographical Research in African Literatures Ser.: No. 4). 360p. 1994. 75.00 (*1-873836-26-0*, Pub. by H Zell Pubs) Seven Hills Bk.

Driver, Edwin D., ed. see Du Bois, W. E. B.

Driver, Elizabeth. A Bibliography of Cookery Books Published in Britain 1875-1914. 747p. 1989. 85.00 (*0-907325-41-6*, Pub. by Prospect) Food Words.

Driver, Felix. Geography Militant: Geographical Knowledge in an Age of Empire. 320p. 1999. 64.95 (*0-631-20111-4*); pap. 29.95 (*0-631-20112-2*) Blackwell Pubs.

***Driver, Felix.** Imperial Cities: Landscape, Display & Identity. 1999. 69.95 (*0-7190-5413-3*, Pub. by Manchester Univ Pr) St Martin.

Driver, G. R. Witchcraft in the Old Testament. 1994. pap. 3.95 (*1-55818-307-8*, Near Eastern) Holmes Pub.

Driver, G. R., tr. see Nestorius Patriarch Of Constantinople.

Driver, Grace. A Doubtful Prospect. large type ed. 1991. 27.99 (*0-7089-2406-9*) Ulverscroft.

— Island of Blossoms. large type ed. 1991. 27.99 (*0-7089-2530-8*) Ulverscroft.

— Return to Balandra. large type ed. 1990. 27.99 (*0-7089-2310-0*) Ulverscroft.

Driver, H. E. & Kroeber, A. L. Quantitive Expression of Cultural Relationships. fac. ed. (University of California Publications in American Archaeology & Ethnology: Vol. 31: 4). (Illus.). 49p. (C). 1932. reprint ed. pap. text 5.31 (*1-55567-284-1*) Coyote Press.

Driver, Harold E. Culture Element Distribution No. VI: Southern Sierra Nevada. fac. ed. (University of California Publications: No. 1:2). 107p. (C). 1937. reprint ed. pap. 11.88 (*1-55567-114-4*) Coyote Press.

— Culture Element Distribution No. X: Northwest California. fac. ed. Lowie, Robert H. et al, eds. (University of California Publications: No. 1:6). 134p. (C). 1937. reprint ed. pap. 15.00 (*1-55567-118-7*) Coyote Press.

— Culture Element Distributions No. VIII: The Reliability of Culture Element Data. fac. ed. Lowie, Robert H. et al, eds. (University of California Publications: No. 1:4). 19p. (C). 1938. reprint ed. pap. 2.50 (*1-55567-116-0*) Coyote Press.

— Culture Element Distributions No. XVI: Girls Puberty Rites in Western North America. Kroeber, A. L. et al, eds. (University of California Publications: Vol. 6:2). 125p. (C). 1941. pap. 13.75 (*1-55567-087-3*) Coyote Press.

— Indians of North America. 2nd rev. ed. LC 79-76207. (Illus.). 704p. 1969. pap. 29.95 (*0-226-16467-5*, P388) U Ch Pr.

Driver, Harold E. & Driver, Wilhelmine. Ethnography & Acculturation of the Chichimeca-Jonaz of Northeast Mexico. LC 63-62521. (General Publications: Vol. 26). 265p. 1963. pap. text 9.95 (*0-87750-116-5*) Res Inst Inner Asian Studies.

Driver, Harold E., jt. auth. see Goldschmidt, Walter.

Driver, Hugh. The Birth of Military Aviation: Britain, 1903-1914. LC 97-4456. (Royal Historical Society). (Illus.). 384p. 1997. 75.00 (*0-86193-234-X*, Royal Historical Soc) Boydell & Brewer.

Driver, J. E., tr. see Stein, R. A.

Driver, J. H., et al. Aluminium Alloys: Their Physical & Mechanical Properties, 4 vols. 2354p. 1997. text 570.00 (*0-87849-758-7*, Pub. by Trans T Pub) Enfield Pubs NH.

Driver, Jessica S. Speak for Yourself: Essentials of Speaking & Reading Aloud. rev. ed. LC 55-11267. (Essentials of Speaking & Reading Aloud Ser.: No. 193-96). (Illus.). 245p. reprint ed. 15.95 incl. audio (*0-9614864-0-6*) Speak Yourself.

Driver, Jim. Rock Talk. 190p. 1994. pap. 12.95 (*1-899344-00-4*) Dufour.

Driver, Jim, ed. Funny Talk. 186p. 1995. pap. 13.95 (*1-899344-01-2*) Dufour.

Driver, John. How Christians Made Peace with War: Early Christian Understandings of War. LC 87-32908. (Peace & Justice Ser.: Vol. 2). 96p. (Orig.). 1988. pap. 6.99 (*0-8361-3461-3*) Herald Pr.

— Images of the Church in Mission. LC 97-4928. 240p. (Orig.). 1997. pap. 19.99 (*0-8361-9058-0*) Herald Pr.

***Driver, John.** Kingdom Citizens. 158p. (Orig.). 1998. pap. 17.00 (*1-57910-138-0*) Wipf & Stock.

Driver, John. Understanding the Atonement for the Mission of the Church. LC 86-3133. 288p. (Orig.). 1986. pap. 19.99 (*0-8361-3403-6*) Herald Pr.

***Driver, John & Snyder, Carrie A.** Radical Faith: An Alternative History of the Christian Church. 338p. 1999. pap. 32.00 (*0-9683462-8-6*) Pandora Pr.

Driver, John, jt. auth. see Kuklinski, Barbara.

Driver, Jonathan, jt. auth. see David, Nicholas.

Driver, Jonathan C. Zooarchaeology of Six Prehistoric Sites in the Sierra Blance Region, New Mexico. (Technical Reports Ser.: No. 17). (Illus.). 103p. (Orig.). 1985. pap. 5.00 (*0-915703-07-6*) U Mich Mus Anthro.

***Driver, Lee.** Full Moon - Bloody Moon: A Chase Dagger Mystery. 308p. 2000. 21.95 (*0-9666021-4-5*) Full Moon Pub.

— The Good Die Twice: A Chase Dagger Mystery. 315p. 1999. 21.95 (*0-9666021-1-0*) Full Moon Pub.

Driver, Marjorie, tr. & pref. see Ibanez, Aniceto & Resano, Francisco.

Driver, Marjorie G., tr. Description of the Marianas Islands: Manuel Sanz - Manila, 1827. (Educational Ser.: No. 10). (Illus.). 55p. 1991. write for info. (*1-878453-07-6*) Univ Guam MAR Ctr.

Driver, Marjorie G., ed. see Del Valle, Teresa.

Driver, Marjorie G., ed. see Pineda y Ramirez, Antonio de.

Driver, Marjorie G., tr. see Brunal-Perry, Omaira.

Driver, Marjorie G., tr. see De Ibanez Y Garcia, Luis.

Driver, Marjorie G., tr. see McGrath, Thomas B., ed.

Driver, Martha W., ed. Journal of the Early Book Society: For the Study of Manuscripts & Printing History. (Illus.). 176p. (C). 1998. 39.95 (*0-944473-35-0*); pap. 19.95 (*0-944473-36-9*) Pace Univ Pr.

Driver, Martha W., ed. Journal of the Early Book Society for the Study of Manuscripts & Printing, Vol. 3. pap. 20.00 (*0-944473-52-0*) Pace Univ Pr.

Driver, Michael J., et al. The Dynamic Decision Maker: Five Decision Styles for Management Success. 244p. 1990. text 24.95 (*0-88730-297-1*, HarpBusn) HarpInfo.

Driver, P. & Christiansen, R. Music & Text. (Contemporary Music Review Ser.: Vol. 5). vi, 304p. 1989. pap. text 25.00 (*3-7186-4980-2*) Gordon & Breach.

Driver, P. M. & Humphries, D. A. Protean Behaviour: The Biology of Anarchization. (Illus.). 360p. 1988. 69.00 (*0-19-857170-4*) OUP.

Driver, Phoebe B. Gardner Cox: Sketches from Life (1906-1988) LC 94-3435. (Illus.). 300p. 1995. 25.00 (*0-87233-112-1*) Bauhan.

— Penobscot Island & Other Poems: Saga of a Maine Lobsterman's Family. 1992. 15.00 (*0-87233-105-9*); pap. 9.95 (*0-87233-109-1*) Bauhan.

Driver, R. D. Why Math? Undergraduate Texts in Mathematics. (Undergraduate Texts in Mathematics Ser.). (Illus.). 248p. 1996. 26.95 (*0-387-94427-3*) Spr-Verlag.

Driver, R. J., Jr. 5th Cavalry. (Virginia Regimental Histories Ser.). (Illus.). 282p. 1997. 25.00 (*1-56190-098-2*) H E Howard.

Driver, Rob. Cooking & Entertaining with Beer. 160p. 1995. 24.95 (*0-9637285-2-0*) Prose Assocs.

Driver, Robert J. Fifty-Eighth Virginia Infantry. (Virginia Regimental Histories Ser.). (Illus.). 160p. 1990. 19.95 (*1-56190-004-4*) H E Howard.

Driver, Robert J., Jr. Fifty-Second Virginia Infantry (Virginia Regimental Histories Ser.). (Illus.). 174p. 1986. 19.95 (*0-930919-22-X*) H E Howard.

— 1st & 2nd Maryland Cavalry, C. S. A. LC 98-49753. (Illus.). 272p. 1999. 34.95 (*1-883522-24-2*, Rockbridge) Howell Pr VA.

Driver, Robert J. The First & Second Rockbridge Artillery. (Virginia Regimental Histories Ser.). (Illus.). 153p. 1987. 19.95 (*0-930919-35-1*) H E Howard.

— First Virginia Cavalry. (Virginia Regimental Histories Ser.). (Illus.). 268p. 1991. 19.95 (*1-56190-023-0*) H E Howard.

Driver, Robert J., Jr. Fourteenth Virginia Cavalry. (Virginia Regimental Histories Ser.). (Illus.). 206p. 1988. 19.95 (*0-930919-60-2*) H E Howard.

— Lexington & Rochbridge County in the Civil War. (Virginia Civil War Battles & Leaders Ser.). (Illus.). 177p. 1989. 19.95 (*0-930919-84-X*) H E Howard.

— The Staunton Artillery - McClanahan's Battery. (Virginia Regimental Histories Ser.). (Illus.). 127p. 1988. 19.95 (*0-930919-63-7*) H E Howard.

— Tenth Virginia Cavalry. (Virginia Regimental Histories Ser.). (Illus.). 186p. 1993. 19.95 (*1-56190-039-7*) H E Howard.

Driver, Robert J. & Howard, H. E. Second Virginia Cavalry. (Virginia Regimental Histories Ser.). (Illus.). 302p. 1995. 25.00 (*1-56190-084-2*) H E Howard.

Driver, Robert J. & Ruffner, Kevin C. 1st Battalion, Virginia Infantry, 39th Battalion, Virginia Cavalry, 24th Battalion Virginia Partisan Rangers. (Virginia Regimental Histories Ser.). (Illus.). 174p. 1996. 25.00 (*1-56190-093-1*) H E Howard.

Driver, Rosalind, ed. The Pupil as Scientist? 128p. 1983. pap. 38.95 (*0-335-10178-X*) OpUniv Pr.

Driver, Rosalind, et al, eds. Children's Ideas in Science. LC 85-7104. 256p. 1985. pap. 34.95 (*0-335-15040-3*) OpUniv Pr.

— Making Sense of Secondary Science: Research into Children's Ideas. 176p. (C). 1993. pap. 22.99 (*0-415-09765-7*, B2450) Routledge.

Driver, Rosalind, et al. Young People's Images of Science. 172p. 1995. pap. 28.95 (*0-335-19381-1*) OpUniv Pr.

Driver, S. R. Modern Research As Illustrating the Bible. (British Academy, London, Schweich Lectures on Biblical Archaeology Series, 1930). 1974. reprint ed. pap. 25.00 (*0-8115-1250-9*) Periodicals Srv.

Driver, Sam N. Pushkin: Literature & Social Ideas. 192p. 1989. text 44.00 (*0-231-06848-4*) Col U Pr.

Driver, Samuel R. Deuteronomy: Critical & Exegetical Commentary. LC 02-25926. (International Critical Commentary Ser.). 556p. 1999. reprint ed. 39.95 (*0-567-05003-3*, Pub. by T & T Clark) Bks Intl VA.

— Job: Critical Exegetical Commentary. Plummer, Alfred & Briggs, Charles, eds. LC 21-15647. (International Critical Commentary Ser.). 816p. 1995. 39.95 (*0-567-05010-6*, Pub. by T & T Clark) Bks Intl VA.

***Driver, Samuel R. & Neubauer, Adolf.** The "Suffering Servant" of Isaiah: According to the Jewish Interpreters. 650p. 1999. pap. 45.00 (*1-57910-255-7*) Wipf & Stock.

Driver, Samuel R., ed. see Abbott, T. K.

Driver, Samuel R., ed. see Barton, George A.

Driver, Samuel R., ed. see Batten, Loring W.

Driver, Samuel R., ed. see Bernard, J. H.

Driver, Samuel R., ed. see Bigg, Charles.

Driver, Samuel R., ed. see Briggs, Charles & Briggs, Emile G.

Driver, Samuel R., ed. see Brooke, A. E.

Driver, Samuel R., ed. see Burton, Ernest De Witt.

Driver, Samuel R., ed. see Cooke, G. A.

Driver, Samuel R., ed. see Curtis, Edward L. & Madsen, Albert A.

Driver, Samuel R., ed. see Frame, James E.

Driver, Samuel R., ed. see Gould, Ezra P.

Driver, Samuel R., ed. see Gray, George B.

Driver, Samuel R., ed. see Harper, William R.

Driver, Samuel R., ed. see Lock, Walter.

Driver, Samuel R., ed. see Moffatt, James.

Driver, Samuel R., ed. see Montgomery, James A.

Driver, Samuel R., ed. see Moore, George F.

Driver, Samuel R., ed. see Paton, Lewis B.

Driver, Samuel R., ed. see Plummer, Alfred.

Driver, Samuel R., ed. see Plummer, Alfred & Robertson, Archibald T.

Driver, Samuel R., ed. see Sanday, William & Headlam, Arthur C.

Driver, Samuel R., ed. see Skinner, John.

Driver, Samuel R., ed. see Smith, Henry P.

Driver, Samuel R., ed. see Smith, John M., et al.

Driver, Samuel R., ed. see Toy, Crawford H.

Driver, Samuel R., ed. see Vincent, Marvin R.

Driver, Sherri B., jt. auth. see Lister, Barbara T.

Driver, Stephen & Martell, Luke. New Labour - Polity Press: Politics after Thatcherism. LC 98-16531. 224p. 1998. 59.95 (*0-7456-2050-7*); pap. 29.95 (*0-7456-2051-5*) Blackwell Pubs.

Driver, Tom F. Liberating Rites: Understanding the Transformative Power of Ritual. LC 97-43296. 296p. (C). 1997. pap. 27.00 (*0-8133-3455-1*, Pub. by Westview) HarpC.

Driver, Wilhelmine, jt. auth. see Driver, Harold E.

Drivers License Guide Co. Staff. U. S. Identification Manual, 1986. (Illus.). 700p. 1986. text 103.50 (*0-938964-10-0*) Drivers License Guide.

***Driving Hawk Sneve, Virginia.** Grandpa Was a Cowboy & an Indian & Other Stories. LC 00-23483. (Illus.). 112p. 2000. 19.95 (*0-8032-4274-3*) U of Nebr Pr.

***Driving Standards Agency Staff.** The Official Bus & Coach Driving Manual. (Illus.). vi, 253p. 1999. 26.00 (*0-11-552194-1*, Pub. by Statnry Office) Balogh.

— The Official Goods Vehicle Driving Manual. (Illus.). vi, 224p. 1999. 30.00 (*0-11-552195-X*, Pub. by Statnry Office) Balogh.

— The Official Theory Test for Drivers Of Large Vehicles. LC 99-488367. 350p. 1999. write for info. (*0-11-552168-2*, Pub. by Statnry Office) Balogh.

Driving Tours. Austria. (Driving Tours Ser.). 120p. 1995. 18.00 (*0-02-860071-1*) Macmillan.

— Scandinavia. (Driving Tours Ser.). 120p. 1995. 18.00 (*0-02-860072-X*) Macmillan.

Driving, Virginia, jt. auth. see Sneve, Hawk.

Drix, Samuel. Witness to Annihilation: Surviving the Holocaust - A Memoir. (World War II Commemorative Ser.). (Illus.). 272p. 1994. 24.95 (*0-02-881087-2*) Brasseys.

***Driza, Scott.** Learn Word 2000 VBA Document Automation. (Illus.). 500p. 2000. pap. 54.95 (*1-55622-751-5*) Wordware Pub.

Drizari, N. Albanian-English, English-Albanian Dictionary. (ALB & ENG.). 1991. lib. bdg. 39.95 (*0-8288-2629-3*, F130650) Fr & Eur.

Drlica, Karl. Understanding DNA & Gene Cloning: A Guide for the Curious. 3rd ed. LC 96-23077. 352p. 1996. pap. 34.95 (*0-471-13774-X*) Wiley.

Drlica, Karl & Riley, Monica, eds. The Bacterial Chromosome. LC 89-48369. (Illus.). 485p. reprint ed. pap. 150.40 (*0-608-08630-4*, 206915300003) Bks Demand.

Drmota, Michael & Tichy, R. F. Sequences, Discrepancies, & Applications, Vol. 165. LC 97-7675. (Lecture Notes in Mathematics Ser.). 1997. write for info. (*3-540-62606-9*) Spr-Verlag.

Drnevich & Gray, eds. Acoustic Emissions in Geotechnical Engineering Practice - STP 750. 218p. 1981. 25.00 (*0-8031-0788-9*, STP750) ASTM.

***Drob, Sanford L.** Kabbalistic Metaphors: Jewish Mystical Themes in Ancient & Modern Thought. 350p. 2001. 40.00 (*0-7657-6125-4*) Aronson.

— Symbols of the Kabbalah: Philosophical & Psychological Perspectives. LC 99-48145. 300p. 2000. 40.00 (*0-7657-6126-2*) Aronson.

Drobak, John N., ed. The Frontiers of the New Institutional Economics. LC 96-35892. (Illus.). 374p. 1997. pap. text 45.00 (*0-12-222240-7*) Morgan Kaufmann.

Drobisch, Moritz W. Neue Darstellung der Logik. (GER.). xxiv, 240p. 1998. reprint ed. write for info. (*3-487-10522-5*) G Olms Pubs.

Drobizheva, Leokadia, et al, eds. Ethnic Conflict in the Post-Soviet World: Case Studies & Analysis. LC 95-35962. 384p. (C). (gr. 13). 1996. text 81.95 (*1-56324-740-2*) M E Sharpe.

— Ethnic Conflict in the Post-Soviet World: Case Studies & Analysis. LC 95-35962. 384p. (gr. 13). 1998. pap. text 35.00 (*1-56324-741-0*) M E Sharpe.

Droblos-Greenberg, Adela & Greenberg, Seth. Fundamental Photoshop: A Complete Introduction. 2nd ed. 648p. 1994. pap. 27.95 (*0-07-881994-6*) Osborne-McGraw.

Drobna, Olga & Drobny, Eduard. Slovensko Moje. (SLO., Illus.). 56p. 1995. 30.00 (*0-86516-318-9*) Bolchazy-Carducci.

Drobna, Olga, et al. Slovakia: The Heart of Europe. Styan, Martin C. & Paulikova, Zuzana, trs. from SLO. LC 96-25905. (Illus.). 56p. 1997. lib. bdg. 30.00 (*0-86516-319-7*) Bolchazy-Carducci.

***Drobner, Hubertus R.** Augustinus von Hippo: Sermones Ad Populum: Uberlieferung und Bestand - Bibliographie - Indices. (Vigiliae Christianae Ser.). 246p. 1999. text 94.00 (*90-04-11451-3*) Brill Academic Pubs.

Drobner, Hubertus R. Persons-Exegese und Christologie bei Augustinus: Zur Herkunft der Formel una Persona. (Philosophia Patrum Ser.: Vol. 8). xiii, 353p. 1986. 74.00 (*90-04-07875-4*) Brill Academic Pubs.

Drobner, Hubertus R. & Klock, Christoph, eds. Studien Zu Gregor Von Nyssa und der Christlichen Spatantike. (Supplements to Vigiliae Christianae Ser.: Vol. 12). (ENG, FRE, GER, ITA & SPA.). xii, 418p. 1989. 134.50 (*90-04-09222-6*) Brill Academic Pubs.

D

Drobney, J. George. Fluoropolymers in Technology Industries. 1999. 99.95 *(0-8493-0246-3)* CRC Pr.

Drobney, Jeffrey. Lumbermen & Log Sawyers: Life, Labor, & Culture in the North Florida Timber Industry, 1830-1930. LC 97-18523. (Illus.). 384p. 1997. 39.95 *(0-86554-546-4*, H417) Mercer Univ Pr.

Drobnic, Karl, et al. Sci Tech: Reading & Writing the English of Science & Technology. 132p. (Orig.). (gr. 10-12). 1981. pap. text 4.95 *(0-89285-156-2)* ELS Educ Servs.

***Drobnick, Jim.** Living Human Display. 1999. pap. text 25.00 *(0-226-16475-6)*; lib. bdg. 70.00 *(0-226-16474-8)* U Ch Pr.

Drobnick, Richard, jt. ed. see Agmon, Tamir.

Drobnig, K., jt. auth. see Holmstrom, Leif.

Drobnig, K., jt. auth. see Zweigert, K.

Drobnig, K., jt. ed. see Zweigert, Konrad E.

Drobnig, U., jt. ed. see Zweigert, K.

Drobnig, Ulrich. Private Law in the European Union, Vol. FOIN 22. LC 96-52811. (Forum Internationale Ser.). 1997. 29.00 *(90-411-0335-X)* Kluwer Law Intl.

Drobnig, Ulrich N. & Van Erp, Sjef. The Use of Comparative Law by Courts. LC 98-34311. (ENG & FRE.). 1998. 95.00 *(90-411-1044-5)* Kluwer Law Intl.

Drobny, Eduard, jt. auth. see Drobna, Olga.

Drobny, Stanislav. Sakramentale Rechtfertigung. VII, 212p. 1998. 37.95 *(3-631-33289-0)* P Lang Pubng.

Drobot, A. T., ed. Computer Applications in Plasma Science & Engineering. (Illus.). x, 457p. 1990. 96.95 *(0-387-97455-5)* Spr-Verlag.

Drobot, Adam. Principles & Applications of Visualization in Science & Engineering. (C). 1996. text. write for info. *(0-201-56740-7)* Addison-Wesley.

Drobot, Bruce A. Word Warrior: A Book of Poems. 128p. 1992. 14.95 *(0-9632706-0-5)* Word Warrior.

Drobot, D. V., jt. auth. see Lapidus, I. I.

Drochner, Karl Heinz & Foehr, Dieter. Eindruecke-Einblicke No. 2: Arbeitsbuch. 128p. 1994. pap. 12.25 *(3-468-49782-2)* Langenscheidt.

— Eindruecke-Einblicke No. 2: Hortextheft. 24p. 1994. 6.00 *(3-468-49784-9)* Langenscheidt.

— Eindruecke-Einblicke Level 2. 112p. 1994. text 15.95 *(3-468-49781-4)* Langenscheidt.

Droege, Alonda & Droege, Jim. Around Puget Sound by Ferry Boat & Bicycle. (Illus.). 40p. (Orig.). (YA). 1997. pap. 7.95 *(1-882614-25-9)* Globe Pubs.

Droege, Jim, jt. auth. see Droege, Alonda.

Droege, Peter. Intelligent Environments: Spatial Aspects of the Information Revolution. LC 97-6430. 746p. 1997. 169.50 *(0-444-82332-8)* Elsevier.

Droegemueller, Lee. Working Is Learning, Learning Is Working. (School-to-Work Implementation Ser.). 13p. 1995. pap. write for info. *(1-884037-09-7)* Coun Chief St Schl Offs.

Droegkamp, Janis & Munger, Fredi. Gender & Development: Women Centered Training. (Illus.). 51p. (Orig.). 1980. pap. 4.00 *(0-932288-56-1)* Ctr Intl Ed U of MA.

***Droeglazov, Valerie V., ed.** Photon: Old Problems in Lighter New Ideas. 278p. 2000. lib. bdg. 98.00 *(1-56072-810-8)* Nova Sci Pubs.

Droel, William. The Spirituality of Work: Business People. (Spirituality of Work Ser.). 64p. (Orig.). 1991. pap. 2.95 *(0-914070-75-4*, 134) ACTA Pubns.

— The Spirituality of Work: Homemakers. 64p. (Orig.). 1991. pap. 2.95 *(0-914070-74-6*, 133) ACTA Pubns.

— The Spirituality of Work: Lawyers. 64p. (Orig.). 1991. pap. 2.95 *(0-914070-73-8*, 132) ACTA Pubns.

— The Spirituality of Work: Nurses. (Spirituality of Work Ser.). 48p. (Orig.). 1991. pap. 2.95 *(0-914070-71-1*, 130) ACTA Pubns.

— The Spirituality of Work: Teachers. 64p. (Orig.). 1991. pap. 2.95 *(0-914070-72-X*, 131) ACTA Pubns.

Droessler, Earl G., jt. ed. see Blackadar, Alfred K.

Droessler, Judith B. Craniometry & Biological Distance. LC 81-11009. (Research Ser.: No. 1). (Illus.). 270p. 1981. 15.00 *(0-942118-11-1*, E78.13D76); pap. 10.00 *(0-942118-12-X)* Ctr Amer Arche.

Droffelaar, H. Van & Atkinson, J. T. Corrosion & Its Control: An Introduction to the Subject. LC 95-87424. 332p. 1995. 157.00 *(1-877914-71-1)* NACE Intl.

Droga, jt. ed. see Levinson.

Drogaris, G. Major Accident Reporting System: Lessons Learned from Accidents Notified. LC 93-29726. 254p. 1993. 193.00 *(0-444-81665-8)* Elsevier.

Drogas, John. Closing Doors Behind Me. White, Bradford, ed. LC 88-80001. (Illus.). 321p. (Orig.). 1988. pap. 7.90 *(0-9620016-0-0)* Grt Lakes MI.

Droge, Arthur J. Homer or Moses? Early Christian Interpretations of the History of Culture. 240p. 1988. lib. bdg. 62.50 *(3-16-145354-9*, Pub. by JCB Mohr) Coronet Bks.

Droge, Cornelia & Calantone, Roger, eds. AMA Educators' Proceedings, 1996 Vol. 7: Enhancing Knowledge Development in Marketing. 577p. 1996. pap. 50.00 *(0-87757-262-3)* Am Mktg.

***Droge, David, et al, eds.** Voices of Strong Democracy: Concepts & Models for Service Learning in Communication Studies. (Service Learning in the Disciplines Ser.). 232p. 1999. pap. 28.50 *(1-56377-012-1)* Am Assn Higher Ed.

Drogin, Elasah. Margaret Sanger: Father of Modern Society. 3rd rev. ed. (Illus.). 128p. 1985. pap. 4.00 *(1-892875-00-4*, 0101, Remnant Israel) New Hope Publicatns.

***Drogin, Karen.** Right Choice. (Zebra Bouquet Ser.: Vol. 50). 256p. 2000. pap. 3.99 *(0-8217-6624-4*, Zebra Kensgtn) Kensgtn Pub Corp.

Drogin, Marc. Biblioclasm: The Mythical Origins, Magic Powers, & Perishability of the Written Word. 224p. (C). 1989. text 60.00 *(0-8476-7502-5*, R 7502) Rowman.

— Calligraphy of the Middle Ages & How to Do It. unabridged ed. LC 98-4276. 96p. 1998. pap. 7.95 *(0-486-40205-3)* Dover.

— Medieval Calligraphy. (Illus.). 224p. 1989. pap. 12.95 *(0-486-26142-5)* Dover.

Drogo, jt. auth. see Jubenville.

Drogoul, Alexis, et al, eds. Collective Robotics: 1st International Workshop, CRW '98, Paris, France, July 4-5, 1998, Proceedings. LC 98-29458. (Lecture Notes in Computer Science Ser.: Vol. 1456). vii, 161p. 1998. pap. 37.00 *(3-540-64768-6)* Spr-Verlag.

Drogues, Valerie. Battleship Missouri. LC 93-10423. (Those Daring Machines Ser.). (Illus.). 48p. (J). (gr. 5-6). 1994. lib. bdg. 13.95 *(0-89686-825-7*, Crstwood Hse) Silver Burdett Pr.

Drogus, Carol A. Women, Religion, & Social Change in Brazil's Popular Church. LC 97-21492. 226p. 1997. 26.00 *(0-268-01951-7)* U of Notre Dame Pr.

Droh, R. & Spintge, R., eds. Innovations in Physiological Anaesthesia & Monitoring. (Illus.). 190p. 1989. 69.95 *(0-387-50331-5)* Spr-Verlag.

Droh, Roland, jt. ed. see Spintge, Ralph.

Drohan, Francis G. A Handbook of Japanese Usage. (ENG & JPN.). 352p. (Orig.). 1992. pap. 16.95 *(0-8048-1610-7)* Tuttle Pubng.

***Drohan, Heather.** False Alarm. LC 99-69455. 240p. 2000. pap. 14.95 *(0-88739-319-5)* Creat Arts Bk.

Drohan, Michele I. Avalanches. LC 98-15379. (Natural Disasters Ser.). 24p. (J). (gr. k-4). 1999. 19.33 *(0-8239-5283-5*, PowerKids) Rosen Group.

***Drohan, Michele I.** Earthquakes. LC 97-39480. (Natural Disasters Ser.). 24p. (J). (gr. k-4). 1999. 19.33 *(0-8239-5285-1*, PowerKids) Rosen Group.

Drohan, Michele I. Floods. LC 98-9267. (Nature's Disasters Ser.). 24p. (J). (gr. k-4). 1999. 18.00 *(0-8239-5288-6*, PowerKids) Rosen Group.

— Forest Fires. LC 98-9260. (Natural Disasters Ser.). 24p. (J). (gr. k-4). 1999. 19.33 *(0-8239-5287-8*, PowerKids) Rosen Group.

***Drohan, Michele I.** Tsunamis. LC 98-4579. (Natural Disasters Ser.). 24p. (J). (gr. k-4). 1999. 19.33 *(0-8239-5286-X*, PowerKids) Rosen Group.

Drohan, Michele I. Volcanoes. LC 97-43119. (Natural Disasters Ser.). 24p. (J). (gr. k-4). 1999. 18.00 *(0-8239-5284-3*, PowerKids) Rosen Group.

Drohan, Michele I., jt. auth. see Levchuck, Caroline M.

***Drohan, Michele Ingber.** Learning about Strength of Character from the Life of Muhammad Ali. LC 98-26483. (Character Building Book 1). (Illus.). 24p. (J). 1999. 17.26 *(0-8239-5347-5*, PowerKids) Rosen Group.

Drohan, Michele Ingber. Weight-Loss Programs: Weighing the Risks & Realities. LC 98-4418. (Teen Health Library of Eating Disorder Prevention). (Illus.). 64p. (YA). (gr. 6 up). 1998. lib. bdg. 17.95 *(0-8239-2770-9*, EDWEPR) Rosen Group.

Drohan, Michele Ingber, jt. auth. see Levchuck, Caroline M.

Drohan, Thomas. The Reagan-Suzuki Comminque. (Pew Case Studies in International Affairs). 50p. (C). 1993. pap. text 3.50 *(1-56927-152-6)* Geo U Inst Dplmcy.

Drohan, W. N., jt. ed. see Hoyer, Leon W.

Drohobycky, Maria, ed. Crimea: Dynamics, Challenges & Prospects. LC 95-12637. 306p. (C). 1996. pap. text 22.95 *(0-8476-8067-3)* Rowman.

— Crimea: Dynamics, Challenges & Prospects. LC 95-12637. 306p. (C). lib. bdg. 59.50 *(0-8476-8066-5)* U Pr of Amer.

Drohojowska-Philp, Hunter. Close Scrutiny: The Art of Joan Tanner. (Illus.). 40p. (Orig.). 1995. pap. 20.00 *(1-880658-07-0)* San Barb CAF.

***Droit, Roger-Pol.** Greeks & Romans in the Modern World. LC 98-61690. 300p. 1998. text 42.00 *(0-88033-975-6*, Pub. by East Eur Monographs) Col U Pr.

— What Is the Meaning of Money. LC 98-61691. 250p. 1998. text 35.00 *(0-88033-976-4*, Pub. by East Eur Monographs) Col U Pr.

***Droke, Clif.** Elliott Wave Simplified. 2000. pap. 29.95 *(1-883272-48-3)* Traders Lib.

— Elliott Wave Simplified: Making Stock Market Profits with R. N. Elliott's Simple Theory. (Illus.). 144p. 1999. pap. 19.95 *(0-9670697-0-X)* Pubg Concepts.

Droke, Clif. Technical Analysis of the Internet Stocks: Making Money on the Internets. (Illus.). 140p. 1999. pap. 19.95 *(0-9670697-4-2)* Pubg Concepts.

— Technical Analysis Simplified: Making Money Through Charting. unabridged ed. (Illus.). 140p. 1999. 19.95 *(0-9670697-9-3)* Pubg Concepts.

Droke, Gina, ed. see Dolinger, James A.

Droleskey, Thomas A. Christ in the Voting Booth. LC 98-71722. 208p. 1998. pap. 14.95 *(1-891431-01-3)* Hope St Monica.

Drolet, Bonita & Harvey, Thomas. Building Teams, Building People: Expanding the Fifth Resource. LC 93-61663. 220p. 1998. pap. text 34.95 *(1-56676-084-4)* Scarecrow.

Drolet, Cindy, ed. see Carey, Linda, et al.

Drolet, Cindy, ed. see Carlson, Daniel F.

Drolet, Cindy, ed. see Carlson, Daniel J.

Drolet, Cindy, ed. see Conway, Nancy.

Drolet, Cindy, ed. see Cottier, Cynthia, et al.

Drolet, Cindy, ed. see Fandray, Dayton & Nolan, Jack.

Drolet, Cindy, ed. see Gilles-Brown, C.

Drolet, Cindy, ed. see Guerrero, Julie.

Drolet, Cindy, ed. see Gustafson, Monica & Owen, Margaret.

Drolet, Cindy, ed. see Hardy, Edward.

Drolet, Cindy, ed. see Hardy, Edward & Robinson, Natalie M.

Drolet, Cindy, ed. see Johnson, Rachel P. & Orichowski, Rose M.

Drolet, Cindy, ed. see Kaufman, Beth A.

Drolet, Cindy, ed. see Lewis, Jan.

Drolet, Cindy, ed. see Nagai, Jeanette & George-Olsen, Becky.

Drolet, Cindy, ed. see Nolan, Jack & Fandray, Dayton.

Drolet, Cindy, ed. see O'Connor, Lisa C.

Drolet, Cindy, ed. see Sena, Laura.

Drolet, Cindy, ed. see Wise, Robbie.

Drolet, Cindy, ed. see Yardley, Kathleen.

Drolet, Cindy, ed. see Ziol, Elaine & Caputo, Susan.

Drolet, Cindy, ed. see Ziol, Elaine, et al.

Drolet-Dube, Doris, jt. auth. see Charbonneau, Andre.

Drolet, Judy C. & Clark, Kay. The Sexuality Education Challenge: Promoting Healthy Sexuality in Young People. LC 93-43183. 1994. 39.95 *(1-56071-130-2)* ETR Assocs.

Drolet, Michele, ed. see Maddux, Mike.

***Droller, Michael J., ed.** Bladder Cancer. 400p. 2000. 125.00 *(0-89603-818-1)* Humana.

Drollet, A., jt. auth. see Viller, M.

Drollinger, William C. Tax Shelters & Tax-Free Income for Everyone, Vol. 1. 4th ed. LC 81-125456. 1981. 21.95 *(0-914244-04-3)* Epic Pubns.

— Tax Shelters & Tax-Free Income for Everyone: Special Edition. LC 81-125456. 1981. 14.95 *(0-914244-08-6)* Epic Pubns.

— You Are a Money Brain. LC 81-67503. 1981. write for info. *(0-914244-07-8)* Epic Pubns.

Drollinger, William C. & Drollinger, William C. Jr. Tax Shelters & Tax-Free Income for Everyone, Vol II. 4th ed. LC 81-125456. 1981. 24.95 *(0-914244-06-X)* Epic Pubns.

Drollinger, William C. Jr., jt. auth. see Drollinger, William C.

Drolma, Delog D. Delog: Journey to Realms Beyond Death. Barron, Richard, tr. from TIB. LC 94-22389. 184p. 1995. pap. 13.95 *(1-881847-05-5)* Padma Pub CA.

Drolsbaugh, Mark. Deaf Again. LC 97-93346. 203p. (Orig.). 1997. pap. 16.95 *(0-9657460-1-1)* Handwave Pubns.

Dromberg, D. A., jt. auth. see Linder, Leo.

Dromey. Grunwick: The Workers Story. 207 p. (C). 1978. pap. 19.95 *(0-85315-413-9*, Pub. by Lawrence & Wishart) NYU Pr.

Dromey, R. Geoff. Program Derivation: The Development of Programs from Specifications. 432p. (C). 1989. pap. text 29.95 *(0-201-41624-7)* Addison-Wesley.

Dromgoole. Power of A Penny. LC 99-15885. 1999. text 13.95 *(0-312-24422-3)* St Martin.

Dromgoole, Dick, ed. see Stopple, Libby.

***Dromgoole, Glenn.** What Cats Teach Us-- Life's Lessons Learned from Our Feline Friends. LC 00-26386. (Illus.). 112p. 2000. 14.95 *(1-57223-296-X*, 296x) Willow Creek Pr.

Dromgoole, Glenn. What Dogs Teach Us: Life's Lessons Learned from Our Best Friends. LC 99-36472. (Illus.). 112p. 1999. 14.95 *(1-57223-268-4)* Willow Creek Pr.

Dromgoole, R. H., ed. see Stopple, Libby.

***Dromgoole, Sarah.** Legal Protection of the Underwater Cultural Heritage: National & International Perspectives. LC 99-36398. 1999. 96.00 *(90-411-9762-1)* Kluwer Law Intl.

Dromgoole, Will A. Heart of Old Hickory & Other Stories of Tennessee. LC 72-113658. (Short Story Index Reprint Ser.). 1977. 18.95 *(0-8369-3387-7)* Ayer.

Dromi, Esther. Early Lexical Development. LC 96-7532. (Illus.). 224p. (C). 1996. reprint ed. pap. text 45.00 *(1-56593-739-2*, 1438) Thomson Learn.

Dromi, Esther & Strauss, Sidney, eds. Language & Cognition: A Developmental Perspective. (Human Development Ser.). 240p. (C). 1986. text 73.25 *(0-89391-682-X)* Ablx Pub.

Droms. Droms: Finanzas & Contabilidad para Ejecutivos No Financieros. (SPA.). 264p. (C). 1994. pap. text 17.66 *(0-201-62181-9)* Addison-Wesley.

***Droms, Ralph E. & Lemons, Ted.** The DHCP Handbook: Understanding, Deploying & Managing Automated Configuration Services. (Network Architecture & Development Ser.). 560p. 1999. 55.00 *(1-57870-137-6)* New Riders Pub.

Droms, William. Finance & Accounting for Non-Financial Managers. 3rd ed. 1990. 22.95 *(0-201-55037-7)* Addison-Wesley.

— Finance & Accounting for Nonfinancial Managers. 4th ed. 256p. 1997. write for info. *(0-201-31141-0)* Addison-Wesley.

— Finance & Accounting for Nonfinancial Managers. 4th ed. LC 97-38925. 256p. 1998. pap. 20.00 *(0-201-31139-9)* Addison-Wesley.

Dron, Alexander, tr. see Tropp, Eduard A., et al.

Dron, Peter. Lamb Count - Auto Class: The Complete Story. (Crowood Autoclassics Ser.). (Illus.). 192p. 1995. pap. 24.95 *(1-85223-914-X*, Pub. by Crolwood) Motorbooks Intl.

Dronamraju, Krishna R. Biological & Social Issues in Biotechnology Sharing. LC 98-73402. 202p. 1998. text 59.95 *(1-84014-897-7*, Pub. by Ashgate Pub) Ashgate Pub Co.

— If I Am to Be Remembered: Correspondence of Julian Huxley. 320p. 1993. text 48.00 *(981-02-1142-2)* World Scientific Pub.

— Science & Society: An Indo-American Perspective. LC 97-47024. 92p. (C). 1998. text 21.50 *(0-7618-1007-2)* U Pr of Amer.

Dronamraju, Krishna R., ed. Haldane: The Life & Work of J. B. S. Haldane with Special Reference to India. (Illus.). 224p. 1985. text 33.00 *(0-08-032436-3)* Macmillan.

— Haldane's Daedalus Revisited. (Illus.). 162p. 1995. text 39.95 *(0-19-854846-X)* OUP.

— The History & Development of Human Genetics: Progress in Different Countries, Washington, DC, 6 October 1991. LC 92-14003. 400p. 1992. text 121.00 *(981-02-0900-2)* World Scientific Pub.

— Selected Genetic Papers of J. B. S. Haldane. LC 90-14125. 568p. 1991. text 40.00 *(0-8240-0473-6)* Garland.

Dronberger, Ilse. Political Thought of Max Weber: In Quest of Statesmanship. LC 70-133904. (Orig.). (C). 1971. 49.00 *(0-89197-349-4)*; pap. text 17.95 *(0-89197-350-8)* Irvington.

Drone, Eaton S. Treatise on the Law of Property in Intellectual Productions in Great Britain & the U. S. Embracing Copyright in Works of Literature & Art & Playwright in Dramatic & Musical Compositions. liv, 774p. 1972. reprint ed. 55.00 *(0-8377-2027-3*, Rothman) W S Hein.

Drone, Jeanette M. Index to Opera, Operetta & Musical Comedy Synopses in Collections & Periodicals. LC 77-25822. 177p. 1978. 24.00 *(0-8108-1100-6)* Scarecrow.

— Musical Theater Synopses: An Index. LC 98-12198. 352p. 1998. 75.00 *(0-8108-3489-8)* Scarecrow.

Drongowski, Paul J. A Graphical Engineering Aid for VLSI Systems. LC 85-1041. (Computer Science: Computer Architecture & Design Ser.: No. 4). (Illus.). 226p. reprint ed. pap. 70.10 *(0-8357-1656-2*, 207037500088) Bks Demand.

Dronke, Peter. The Medieval Lyric. rev. ed. 302p. 1996. pap. 29.95 *(0-85991-484-4)* Boydell & Brewer.

— Verse with Prose from Petronius to Dante: The Art & Scope of the Mixed Form. LC 93-4282. (Carl Newell Jackson Lectures). 160p. 1994. text 35.50 *(0-674-93475-X)* HUP.

— Women Writers of the Middle Ages: A Critical Study of Texts from Perpetua (203) to Marquerite Porete (1310) LC 83-7456. 348p. 1984. pap. text 22.95 *(0-521-27573-3)* Cambridge U Pr.

Dronke, Ursula. Myth & Fiction in Early Norse Lands. (Collected Studies: No. CS524). 336p. 1996. text 101.95 *(0-86078-545-9*, Pub. by Variorum) Ashgate Pub Co.

Dronke, Ursula, ed. The Poetic Edda: Mythological Poems, Vol. II. (Illus.). 458p. 1997. text 120.00 *(0-19-811181-9)* OUP.

***Dronkers, J. & Scheffers, M. B., eds.** Physics of Estuaries & Coastal Areas: Proceedings of an International Conference, 9-12 September 1996. 432p. (C). 1998. text 87.00 *(90-5410-965-3*, Pub. by A A Balkema) Ashgate Pub Co.

Dronko, Peter. Latin & Vernacular Poets of the Middle Ages. (Collected Studies: No. CS352). 350p. 1991. text 115.95 *(0-86078-303-0*, Pub. by Variorum) Ashgate Pub Co.

Droog, Inger, tr. see Haberly, Helen J.

Drooger, C. W. Radial Foraminifera: Morphometrics & Evolution. 250p. 1994. pap. 61.25 *(0-444-85768-0*, North Holland) Elsevier.

Drooger, C. W. & Kaasschieter, J. P. Foraminifera of the Orinoco-Trinidad-Paria Shelf. (Verhandelingen der Koninklijke Nederlandse Akademie van Wetenschappen, Afd. Natuurkunde Ser.: No. 22). 108p. pap. 28.25 *(0-7204-8360-3)* Elsevier.

Droogers, Andre. The Dangerous Journey: Symbolic Aspects of Boys' Initiation Among the Wagenia of Kisangani, Zaire. (Change & Continuity in Africa Ser.). 1979. pap. text 56.95 *(90-279-3357-X)* Mouton.

Droogleever, R. W. The Road to Isandhlwana: Col. Anthony Durnford in Natal & Zululand, 1873-1879. 192p. 1992. 37.50 *(1-85367-118-5*, 5578) Stackpole.

Drooker, Eric. Blood Song. 2001. pap. Price not set. *(0-15-600884-X)* Harcourt.

— Street Posters & Ballads: A Selection of Poems, Songs & Graphics. LC 98-34082. (Illus.). 80p. 1998. pap. 18.00 *(1-888363-77-0)* Seven Stories.

Drooker, Penelope B. Mississippian Village Textiles at Wickliffe. LC 92-4722. 312p. (C). 1992. pap. text 29.95 *(0-8173-0592-0)* U of Ala Pr.

— The View from Madisonville: Protohistoric Western Fort Ancient Interaction Patterns. LC 97-28211. (Memoirs of the Museum of Anthropology, University of Michigan Ser.). 1997. pap. 28.00 *(0-915703-42-4)* U Mich Mus Anthro.

Drooker, Penelope B., ed. Fleeting Identities: Perishable Material Culture in Archaeological Research. LC 98-74464. (Center for Archaeological Investigations Occasional Paper Ser.: No. 28). (Illus.). 400p. 2001. pap. write for info. *(0-88104-085-1)* Center Archaeol.

Drooker, Penelope B. & Maurel, Martine. Makers & Markets: The Wright Collection of Twentieth-Century Native American Art. LC 98-65658. (Peabody Museum Press Ser.). (Illus.). 184p. 1998. pap. 30.00 *(0-87365-825-6*, PRMAKE) Peabody Harvard.

***Drooker, Penelope B. & Webster, Laurie D., eds.** Beyond Cloth & Cordage: Archaeological Textile Research in the Americas. (Illus.). 352p. 2000. 60.00 *(0-87480-662-3)* U of Utah Pr.

Droop, Constanza, jt. auth. see Langen, Annette.

Drooyan. Intermediate Algebra. 7th ed. (Mathematics Ser.). 1991. pap., student ed. 17.50 *(0-534-14905-7)* PWS Pubs.

Drooyan, jt. auth. see Beckenbach.

Drooyan, jt. auth. see Yoshiwara.

Drooyan, Irving. Basic Mathematics for Technical Programs. LC 95-42881. 409p. (C). 1996. pap. text 62.00 *(0-13-206632-7)* P-H.

Drooyan, Irving & Franklin, Katherine. Intermediate Algebra. 7th ed. 498p. (C). 1991. text 51.95 *(0-534-14904-9)* PWS Pubs.

Drooyan, Irving & Rosen, William. Introductory Algebra: A Guided Worktext. LC 81-99. 410p. 1982. pap. text 22.25 *(0-471-86591-5)* P-H.

D

An Asterisk (*) at the beginning of an entry indicates that the title is appearing for the first time.

Drooyan, Irving & Wooton, William. Beginning Algebra: A Modular Approach, 8 Vols., 1. LC 75-29776. 68p. 1976. reprint ed. pap. 30.00 (*0-8357-7092-3*, 201243700081) Bks Demand.
— Beginning Algebra: A Modular Approach, 8 Vols., 2. LC 75-29776. 104p. 1976. reprint ed. pap. 32.30 (*0-8357-7093-1*, 201243700082) Bks Demand.
— Beginning Algebra: A Modular Approach, 8 Vols., 3. LC 75-29776. 97p. 1976. reprint ed. pap. 30.10 (*0-8357-7094-X*, 201243700083) Bks Demand.
— Beginning Algebra: A Modular Approach, 8 Vols., 4. LC 75-29776. 81p. 1976. reprint ed. pap. 30.00 (*0-8357-7095-8*, 201243700084) Bks Demand.
— Beginning Algebra: A Modular Approach, 8 Vols., 5. LC 75-29776. 143p. 1976. reprint ed. pap. 44.40 (*0-8357-7096-6*, 201243700085) Bks Demand.
— Beginning Algebra: A Modular Approach, 8 Vols., 6. LC 75-29776. 143p. 1976. reprint ed. pap. 44.40 (*0-8357-7097-4*, 201243700086) Bks Demand.
— Beginning Algebra: A Modular Approach, 8 Vols., 7. LC 75-29776. 82p. 1976. reprint ed. pap. 30.00 (*0-8357-7098-2*, 201243700087) Bks Demand.
— Beginning Algebra: A Modular Approach, 8 Vols., 8. LC 75-29776. 106p. 1976. reprint ed. pap. 32.90 (*0-8357-7099-0*, 201243700088) Bks Demand.
— Elementary Algebra with Geometry. 2nd ed. 467p. (C). 1984. text 46.50 (*0-471-09825-6*) P-H.
— Intermediate Algebra. 6th ed. (Math). 488p. (C). 1984. mass mkt. 36.75 (*0-534-01433-X*) PWS Pubs.
Drooyan, Irving, et al. Modeling, Functions & Graphs: Algebra for College Students. 2nd ed. (Mathematics Ser.). 1995. mass mkt. 81.95 (*0-534-94560-0*) PWS Pubs.
Drooyan, Irving, jt. auth. see Franklin, Katherine.
Drooyan, Irving, jt. auth. see Grady, Michael D.
Drooyan, Irving, jt. auth. see Hyatt, Herman R.
Drooz, Irma. Doctor of Medicine: American Autobiography. 308p. 1995. lib. bdg. 89.00 (*0-7812-8505-4*) Rprt Serv.
Drop, Mark. Dateline Hollywood: Sins & Scandals of Yesterday & Today. LC 94-7778. (Illus.). 160p. 1994. 14.95 (*1-56799-108-4*, Friedman-Fairfax) M Friedman Pub Grp Inc.
Dropick, A. M. The Authority of the Poet in Late Medieval France: The Example of Eustache Des Champs (c-1340-c-1406) 1997. write for info. (*0-9651027-0-X*, Autotelic Hse) East West Eidetic.
Dropka, Edwin. Toshiba Medium PLC Primer. (Illus.). 146p. 1995. pap. text 36.95 (*0-7506-9694-X*) Buttrwrth-Heinemann.
Dropkin, Murray, ed. The Nonprofit Report: Accounting, Taxation & Management. 112.00 (*0-685-69609-X*, NPR) Warren Gorham & Lamont.
Dropkin, Murray & LaTouche, Bill. Budget Building Book for Nonprofits: A Step by Step Guide for Managers & Boards. LC 98-17568. 1998. pap. text 25.00 (*0-7879-4036-4*) Jossey-Bass.
Dropkin, Ruth, ed. Changing Schools: Open Corridors & Teaching Centers. 1978. pap. 3.50 (*0-918374-02-2*) City Coll Wk.
— Cumulative Index to Notes from Workshop Center for Open Education. 1979. pap. 1.00 (*0-918374-04-9*) City Coll Wk.
Dropkin, Ruth & Tobier, Arthur, eds. Roots of Open Education in America: Reminiscences & Reflections on the Ways Americans Have Educated Themselves, in & Out of Schools. LC 76-53146. (Illus.). 1976. pap. 5.00 (*0-918374-01-4*) City Coll Wk.
Dropkin, Ruth, jt. ed. see Alberty, Beth.
Dropo, Dr. Juggling Made Simple: A Positively Guaranteed Surefire Juggling Method. (Orig.). 1989. pap. 7.00 (*0-941599-12-4*) Piccadilly Bks.
Droppa, Jill. Fun with Hidden Picture Puzzles Coloring Book. (Illus.). (J). 1995. pap. 2.50 (*0-486-28826-9*) Dover.
Dropper, G. Outlines of Economic History in the 19th Century. 1977. lib. bdg. 59.95 (*0-8490-2396-3*) Gordon Pr.
Droppo, Dr. Balancing Tricks & Stunts. unabridged ed. Fife, Bruce, ed. LC 98-32111. (Illus.). 64p. 1998. pap. 10.00 (*0-941599-37-X*, Pub. by Piccadilly Bks) Empire Pub Srvs.
Dropsie, Moses A. Roman Law of Testaments, Codicils, & Gifts in the Event of Death (Mortis Causa Donationes) LC 96-26114. xii, 198p. 1996. reprint ed. 37.50 (*0-8377-2042-7*, Rothman) W S Hein.
Dror, Eli. Spas: The International Spa Guide. 5th rev. ed. Bain, Joseph H., ed. Da Costa, Rafael S., tr. (Illus.). 460p. 1999. pap. 29.00 (*1-890618-00-4*) Bain Dror.
Dror, Eli, ed. see Bain, Joseph H.
Dror, Eli, jt. ed. see Bain, Joseph H.
Dror, Yehezkel. Crazy States: A Counterconventional Strategic Problem. LC 80-81613. 1980. reprint ed. lib. bdg. 29.00 (*0-527-25140-2*) Periodicals Srv.
— Policymaking under Adversity. 450p. 1987. pap. 29.95 (*0-88738-721-7*) Transaction Pubs.
— Public Policymaking Reexamined. LC 83-351. 415p. 1995. pap. text 24.95 (*0-87855-928-0*) Transaction Pubs.
***Drori, Israel.** Seam Line: Arab Workers & Jewish Managers in the Israeli Textile Industry. LC 99-86426. (Illus.). 2000. 49.50 (*0-8047-3785-1*); pap. 18.95 (*0-8047-3787-8*) Stanford U Pr.
Drori, J. B. Mister Bluefin. 180p. (Orig.). 1986. pap. 12.95 (*0-940391-00-7*) Scopus Bks.
Drory, M. D., et al, eds. Mechanical Behavior of Diamond & Other Forms of Carbon. (Symposium Proceedings Ser.: Vol. 383). 474p. 1995. text 77.00 (*1-55899-286-3*) Materials Res.
***Drory, Rina.** Models & Contacts: Arabic Literature & its Impact on Medieval Jewish Culture. 240p. 2000. 73.00 (*90-04-11738-5*) Brill Academic Pubs.
Drory, Rina, jt. ed. see Izre'el, Shlomo.
***Drosd, Nancy & Weil, Danielle.** 40 Most Wanted Cats. LC 97-62151. (Illus.). 88p. 1998. 7.98 (*0-7651-9062-1*) Smithmark.
Drosdowski. Duden Grosse Woerterbuch, Vol. 4. (GER.). 1994. 125.00 (*0-7859-7558-6*, 3411047720) Fr & Eur.
— Duden Grosse Woerterbuch, Vol. 5. (GER.). 1994. 125.00 (*0-7859-7559-4*, 3411047828) Fr & Eur.
— Duden Grosse Woerterbuch Vol. 1: A-Bim. (GER.). 1993. 125.00 (*0-7859-7555-1*, 3411047429) Fr & Eur.
— Duden Grosse Woerterbuch Vol. 2: Bl-Fe. (GER.). 1993. 125.00 (*0-7859-7556-X*, 3411047526) Fr & Eur.
— Duden Grosse Woerterbuch Vol. 3: Fe-Hi. (GER.). 1993. 125.00 (*0-7859-7557-8*, 3411047623) Fr & Eur.
— Duden Grosse Woerterbuch Deutsch Vol. 1: A-Ci. (GER.). 464p. 1976. 95.00 (*0-7859-7549-7*, 3411013559) Fr & Eur.
— Duden Grosse Woerterbuch Deutsch Vol. 2: Ci-F. (GER.). 463p. 1976. write for info. (*0-7859-7550-0*, 3411013567) Fr & Eur.
— Duden Grosse Woerterbuch Deutsch Vol. 3: G-Kal. (GER.). 479p. 1977. write for info. (*0-7859-7551-9*, 3411013575) Fr & Eur.
— Duden Grosse Woerterbuch Deutsch Vol. 4: Kam-N. (GER.). 495p. 1978. 95.00 (*0-7859-7552-7*, 3411013583) Fr & Eur.
— Duden Grosse Woerterbuch Deutsch Vol. 5: O-So. (GER.). 527p. 1980. 95.00 (*0-7859-7553-5*, 3411013605) Fr & Eur.
Drosdowski. Duden Woerterbuch Vol. 11: Idiomatik. (GER.). 864p. 1992. text 49.95 (*0-614-00347-4*, 3411041110) Fr & Eur.
Drosdowski, G., ed. Duden-Deutsches Universalworterbuch. 2nd ed. 1816p. 1989. 43.95 (*3-411-02176-4*, Pub. by Bibliogr Inst Brockhaus) Langenscheidt.
Drose, Julia A. Fetal Echocardiography. Allen, Andrew, ed. LC 97-18557. (Illus.). 352p. 1998. text 65.00 (*0-7216-6284-6*, W B Saunders Co) Harcrt Hlth Sci Grp.
Drosen, James, jt. auth. see Bharath, Ramachandran.
Droske, Susan C., jt. auth. see Ashwill, Jean W.
Droske, Susan C., jt. ed. see Ashwill, Jean W.
Drosler, J. Quantitative Psychology. LC 89-7457. (Illus.). 200p. (C). 1989. text 38.00 (*0-88937-028-1*) Hogrefe & Huber Pubs.
Drosnin, Michael. The Bible Code. LC 97-18821. 320p. 1997. 25.00 (*0-684-81079-4*) S&S Trade.
— The Bible Code. LC 97-18821. (Illus.). 272p. 1998. per. 14.00 (*0-684-84973-9*, Touchstone) S&S Trade Pap.
***Drosnin, Michael.** Codigo Secreto de la Biblia. 1998. 20.95 (*84-08-02234-2*) Planeta Edit.
Drossel-Brown, Cordula. Zeit und Zeiterfahrung in der Deutschsprachigen Lyrik der Funfziger Jahre: Marie Luise Kaschnitz, Ingeborg Bachmann und Christine Lavant. (Studies in Modern German Literature: Vol. 66). (GER.). X, 172p. (C). 1995. text 45.95 (*0-8204-2388-2*) P Lang Pubng.
Drossman, Douglas A., ed. Manual of Gastoenterologic Procedures. 2nd ed. LC 86-42509. 283p. reprint ed. pap. 87.80 (*0-7837-7119-3*, 204694800004) Bks Demand.
— Manual of Gastroenterologic Procedures. 3rd ed. LC 92-17142. (Illus.). 304p. 1992. spiral bd. 40.00 (*0-88167-944-5*, 2424) Lppncott W & W.
Drossman, Douglas A., et al, eds. The Functional Gastrointestinal Disorders: Diagnosis Pathophysiology & Treatment - a Multinational Consensus. 370p. 1994. pap. 49.95 (*0-9656837-0-2*, 00971) Degnon Assocs.
— The Functional Gastrointestinal Disorders: Diagnosis, Pathophysiology, & Treatment; a Multinational Consenus. LC 93-45247. 400p. 1994. text 103.00 (*0-316-19342-9*) Lppncott W & W.
***Drossman, Douglas A., et al, eds.** Rome II: The Functional Gastrointestinal Disorders: Diagnosis, Pathophysiology, & Treatment - A Multinational Consensus. 2nd rev. unabridged ed. LC 99-40667. Orig. Title: The Functional Gastrointestinal Disorders. 800 p. 2000. pap. text 99.95 (*0-9656837-2-9*) Degnon Assocs.
— Rome II: The Functional Gastrointestinal Disorders: Diagnosis, Pathophysiology, & Treatment - A Multinational Consensus. 2nd rev. unabridged ed. LC 99-40667. Orig. Title: The Functional Gastrointestinal Disorders. 800p. 2000. text 79.95 (*0-9656837-1-0*) Degnon Assocs.
***Drost, Bill, et al.** Bill Drost, the Pentecost. LC 00-26802. 2000. write for info. (*1-56722-245-5*) Word Aflame.
— Bill Drost the Pentecost. rev. ed. LC 00-26802. 200p. 2000. pap. 8.99 (*1-56722-246-3*) Word Aflame.
Drost, Billie F. & King, Karon. Upshur County, West Virginia Births, 1853-1897. 224p. (Orig.). 1993. pap. text 30.00 (*1-55613-877-6*) Heritage Bk.
Drost, Dan. A Choice to Live. (Illus.). 150p. 1998. pap. 14.95 (*1-57901-031-8*, CDR) ProMotion Pub.
Drost, Harry. What's What & Who's Who in Europe. LC 94-6211. 1995. 25.00 (*0-13-955097-6*) S&S Trade.
Drost, J., et al. New Writing from Drost, Hewett, Hilburger, Hopkins, Lulat, McGoldrick: Poetry & Prose. LC 92-8884. 309p. (Orig.). 1992. pap. 18.99 (*0-944265-09-X*) Librosmondiale.
Drost, Jerome, jt. compiled by see Hartman, Donald K.
***Drost, T. Wynn.** Dedicated to Revival! 150p. 2000. pap. 8.99 (*1-56722-426-1*) Word Aflame.
Drost, T. Wynn. Orchestrating Revival: A Story of Missions in Mexico. LC 96-5118. (Illus.). 132p. (Orig.). 1996. pap. 6.99 (*1-56722-142-4*) Word Aflame.
Drost, Walter H. David Snedden & Education for Social Efficiency. LC 67-25945. 254p. reprint ed. pap. 78.80 (*0-608-15096-7*, 202372000033) Bks Demand.
Droste, Conrad & Von Planta, Martin. Memorix Clinical Medicine. 384p. 1999. pap. text 19.50 (*0-412-56050-X*, Pub. by E A) OUP.
Droste, Flip G. & Joseph, John E., eds. Linguistic Theory & Grammatical Description: Nine Current Approaches. LC 91-34226. (Current Issues in Linguistic Theory Ser.: No. 75). viii, 354p. 1991. 112.00 (*1-55619-103-0*) J Benjamins Pubng Co.
Droste-Hulshoff, Annette Von. Die Judenbuche: Erzahlungen. unabridged ed. (World Classic Literature Ser.). (GER.). pap. 5.95 (*3-89507-026-2*, Pub. by Bookking Intl) Distribks Inc.
Droste, Kathleen, ed. Gale Book of Averages. 617p. 1993. 60.00 (*0-8103-9138-4*, 101790) Gale.
Droste, M. Bauhaus. 1994. pap. 24.99 (*3-8228-0295-6*) Taschen Amer.
Droste, M., jt. auth. see Bauhaus.
Droste, Manfred. Structure of Partially Ordered Sets with Transitive Automorphism Groups. LC 85-15625. (Memoirs of the AMS Ser.: No. 57/334). 100p. 1985. pap. 18.00 (*0-8218-2335-3*, MEMO/57/334) Am Math.
— Structure of Partially Ordered Sets with Transitive Automorphism Groups. LC 85-15625. (American Mathematical Society Ser.: Vol. 334). (Illus.). 107p. reprint ed. pap. 33.20 (*0-608-07559-0*, 205265900009) Bks Demand.
Droste, Manfred & Gobel, Rudiger, eds. Advances in Algebra & Model Theory: Selected Surveys Presented at Conferences in Essen 1994 & Dresden 1995. (Algebra, Logic & Applications Ser.: Vol. 9). 512p. 1997. text 62.00 (*90-5699-101-9*, QA, Harwood Acad Pubs) Gordon & Breach.
Droste, Manfred & Gurevich, Yuri, eds. Semantics of Programming Languages & Model Theory. LC 93-18657. (Algebra, Logic & Applications Ser.: Vol. 5). 416p. 1993. text 120.00 (*2-88124-935-3*) Gordon & Breach.
Droste, Ronald L. Theory & Practice of Water & Wastewater Treatment. LC 96-15477. 816p. 1996. text 95.95 (*0-471-12444-3*) Wiley.
Droste, Thorston & Mosler, Axel M. Chateaux of Loire. (Illus.). 208p. 1997. 45.00 (*1-86064-164-4*, Pub. by I B T) St Martin.
Drotar, David L. The Fire Curse & Other Medical Mysteries. LC 94-5659. (J). 1994. 15.85 (*0-8027-8327-9*) Walker & Co.
— The Fire Curse & Other Medical Mysteries. LC 94-5659. (Illus.). 96p. (J). 1994. 14.95 (*0-8027-8326-0*) Walker & Co.
Drotar, Dennis. Consulting with Pediatricians: Psychological Perspectives. (Issues in Clinical Child Psychology Ser.). (Illus.). 270p. (C). 1995. text 39.50 (*0-306-44955-8*, Kluwer Plenum) Kluwer Academic.
***Drotar, Dennis, ed.** Handbook of Research Methods in Pediatric & Clinical Child Psychology. (Issues in Clinical Child Psychology Ser.). 552p. 1999. 130.00 (*0-306-46229-X*, Kluwer Plenum) Kluwer Academic.
Drotar, Dennis, ed. Measuring Health-Related Quality of Life in Children & Adolescents: Implications for Research & Practice. LC 97-34793. 350p. 1998. write for info. (*0-8058-2479-0*); pap. write for info. (*0-8058-2480-4*) L Erlbaum Assocs.
— New Directions in Failure to Thrive: Implications for Future Research & Practice. 398p. 1986. 85.00 (*0-306-42216-6*, Plenum Trade) Perseus Pubng.
Drotner, Kirsten. English Children & Their Magazines, 1751-1945. LC 87-37156. (Illus.). (C). 1988. 37.00 (*0-300-04010-5*) Yale U Pr.
Drotsky, J. G. Strength of Materials for Technicians. (Illus.). 272p. 1985. pap. text 34.95 (*0-409-11082-5*) Buttrwrth-Heinemann.
Drotter, Stephen J., jt. auth. see Mahler, Walter R.
***Drouart, Michele.** Into the Wadi. 376p. 2000. pap. 19.95 (*1-86368-275-9*, Pub. by Fremantle Arts) Intl Spec Bk.
Drouet, F. Revision of the Nostocaceae with Constricted Trichomes. (Beiheft zur Nova Hedwigia Ser.: No. 57). (Illus.). 1978. text 120.00 (*3-7682-5457-7*) Lubrecht & Cramer.
— Revision of the Stigonematacaea: With a Summary of the Classification of Blue-Green Algae. (Nova Hedwigia Beiheft Ser.: No. 66). (Illus.). 300p. 1981. lib. bdg. 65.00 (*3-7682-5466-6*) Lubrecht & Cramer.
Drouet, Francis. Revision of the Classification of the Oscillatoriaceae. (Monograph: No. 15). (Illus.). 370p. 1968. lib. bdg. 8.00 (*0-910006-23-7*) Acad Nat Sci Phila.
Drouffe, Jean-Michel & Itzykson, Claude. Statistical Field Theory: Strong Coupling, Monte Carlo Methods, Conformal Field Theory, & Random Systems, Vol. 2. (Cambridge Monographs on Mathematical Physics). 432p. (C). 1989. text 105.00 (*0-521-37012-4*) Cambridge U Pr.
Drouffe, Jean-Michel, jt. auth. see Itzykson, Claude.
Drouillard, Richard, jt. auth. see Raynor, Sherry.
Drouin, F., et al. The Stereoscope & Stereoscopic Photography. fac. ed. Surface, Matthew, tr. from FRE. (Historical 3-D Reprint Ser.: No. 2). Orig. Title: Le Stereoscope et la Photographie Stereoscopique. (Illus.). 188p. 1995. reprint ed. pap. 14.95 (*0-939617-02-1*, 1050) Reel Three-D.
Drouin, M., et al. Control of Complex Systems: Methods & Technology. LC 89-26612. (Applied Information Technology Ser.). (Illus.). 190p. (C). 1991. 65.00 (*0-306-43400-8*, Plenum Trade) Perseus Pubng.
Drouin, Marie J., et al. Western European Adjustment to Structural Economic Problems. Albrecht, Catherine et al, eds. (Illus.). 282p. (Orig.). (C). 1987. lib. bdg. 49.50 (*0-8191-6527-1*, Pub. by Hudson Instit IN) U Pr of Amer.
— Western European Adjustment to Structural Economic Problems. Albrecht, Catherine et al, eds. (Illus.). 282p. (Orig.). (C). 1987. pap. text 24.00 (*0-8191-6528-X*) U Pr of Amer.
Drouin, Rene. Dictionnaire Extraordinaire des Mots Ordinaires. (FRE.). 1991. write for info. (*0-7859-7944-1*, 2-7144-2567-4) Fr & Eur.
Drov, Yehezkel, jt. auth. see Akzin, Benjamin.
Drover, Glenn & Kerans, Patrick, eds. New Approaches to Welfare Theory. 336p. 1993. 95.00 (*1-85278-881-X*); pap. 30.00 (*1-85278-981-6*) E Elgar.
Drover, Glenn, jt. ed. see Moscovitch, Allan.
Drowatzky, John N. Ethical Decision Making in Physical Activity Research. LC 95-42649. (Illus.). 112p. (Orig.). (C). 1996. pap. text 16.00 (*0-87322-473-6*, BDRO0473) Human Kinetics.
— Legal Issues in Sport & Physical Education Management. Zeigler, Earle F., ed. (Monograph Series on Sport & Physical Education Management). (Illus.). 44p. 1993. pap. text 4.80 (*0-87563-426-5*) Stipes.
— Physical Education for the Mentally Retarded. LC 70-157467. (Health Education, Physical Education, & Recreation Ser.). (Illus.). 201p. reprint ed. pap. 62.40 (*0-608-10889-8*, 205541900022) Bks Demand.
Drowatzky, John W. & Armstrong, Charles W. Exercise Science: Career Perspectives & Professional Foundations. 304p. (C). 1993. per. 34.95 (*0-8403-8188-3*) Kendall-Hunt.
Drower, E. S. Mandaean Book of Black Magic. 1990. pap. 5.95 (*1-55818-139-3*) Holmes Pub.
Drower, Ethel S. By Tigris & Euphrates. LC 77-87642. (Illus.). reprint ed. 29.50 (*0-404-16424-2*) AMS Pr.
— Folk-Tales of Iraq. LC 78-63226. (Illus.). reprint ed. 30.50 (*0-404-16165-0*) AMS Pr.
— Peacock Angel: Being Some Account of Votaries of a Secret Cult & Their Sanctuaries. LC 77-87643. reprint ed. 20.00 (*0-404-16425-0*) AMS Pr.
— Water into Wine: A Study of Ritual Idiom in the Middle East. LC 77-87663. reprint ed. 23.50 (*0-404-16401-3*) AMS Pr.
***Drower, George.** Gardeners, Gurus & Grubs: The Stories of Garden Inventors & Innovators. 2001. pap. 21.95 (*0-7509-2543-4*, Pub. by Sutton Publng) Intl Pubs Mktg.
Drower, George. John Hume: Peacemaker. (Illus.). 256p. 29.95 (*0-575-06217-7*, Pub. by V Gollancz) Trafalgar.
— John Hume: Peacemaker. (Illus.). 272p. 1996. pap. 15.95 (*0-575-60084-5*, Pub. by V Gollancz) Trafalgar.
Drower, Margaret S. Flinders Petrie: A Life in Archaeology. LC 94-42111. (Studies in Classics). (Illus.). 522p. (C). 1995. pap. text 24.95 (*0-299-14624-3*); lib. bdg. 40.00 (*0-299-14620-0*) U of Wis Pr.
Drower, Margaret S., tr. see Montet, Pierre.
Drower, William M. Our Man on the Hill: A British Diplomat Remembers. LC 93-29492. 163p. (Orig.). reprint ed. pap. 50.60 (*0-608-20123-5*, 207139500011) Bks Demand.
Drown, Harold J. You the Graduate. rev. ed. 1990. 8.95 (*0-687-46854-X*) Abingdon.
Drown, Merle. The Suburbs of Heaven. LC 99-27543. 320p. 2000. 24.00 (*1-56947-182-7*) Soho Press.
Drown, Ruth B. Drown Radio-Vision & Homo-Vibra Ray Instruments & Their Use. 96p. 1998. reprint ed. pap. 31.00 (*0-7873-1015-8*) Hlth Research.
— Theory & Technique of the Drown H. V. R. & Radio-Vision Instruments, Vol. 1. 152p. 1994. spiral bd. 31.00 (*0-7873-1235-5*) Hlth Research.
— Wisdom from Atlantis. 153p. 1981. pap. 14.00 (*0-89540-098-7*, SB-098) Sun Pub.
Drown, Simeon DeWitt. The Peoria Directory for 1844. 1978. reprint ed. 10.00 (*0-930358-02-3*) Spoon River.
Drowns. Juvenile Justice. Date not set. pap. text, teacher ed. write for info. (*0-314-68779-3*) West Pub.
Drowns, Robert W. & Hess, Karen M. Juvenile Justice. 2nd ed. LC 94-44142. 664p. (C). 1995. 47.00 (*0-314-04454-X*) West Pub.
Droy Advertising Staff, ed. see Tartakoff, Katy.
Droz, Eugene, jt. auth. see Klebs, Arnold C.
Droz, Eugenie, et al, eds. Trois Chansonniers Francais du XV Siecle. LC 77-26063. (Music Reprint Ser.). 1978. reprint ed. lib. bdg. 35.00 (*0-306-77561-1*) Da Capo.
Droz, Georges A. & Rodriguez. E Pluribus Unum: Liber Amicorum Georges A.L. Droz - on the Progressive Unification of Private International Law. LC 96-24929. 1996. lib. bdg. 198.00 (*90-411-0282-5*, Pub. by M Nijhoff) Kluwer Academic.
Droz, Michel, jt. auth. see Chopard, Bastine.
Droz, R. & Rahmy, M. Understanding Piaget. Diamanti, Joyce, tr. from FRE. LC 75-18509. Orig. Title: Lire Piaget. 212p. 1976. 35.00 (*0-8236-6690-5*) Intl Univs Pr.
Drozd, Taras, tr. see Olhovych, Orest, ed.
Drozd, V. N. & Zefirov, N. S. Sigmatropic Additions & Cyclosubstitutions in Five-Membered Heterocyclic Compounds Containing Exocyclic Double Bonds, Vol. 1. (Sulfur Reports). 45p. 1981. pap. text 75.00 (*3-7186-0081-1*) Gordon & Breach.
Drozd, Y. A. & Kirichenko, V. V. Finite-Dimensional Algebras. Dlab, V., tr. from RUS. 256p. 1994. 103.95 (*0-387-53380-X*) Spr-Verlag.
Drozda, Joe. The Golfer's Wagering Handbook. 1998. pap. text 55.60 (*1-57028-209-9*, Mstrs Pr) NTC Contemp Pub Co.
Drozda, T., ed. Composites Applications: The Future Is Now. 466p. 1989. 12.50 (*0-87263-355-1*) SME.
— SQC-SPC Manufacturing Experiences. LC 89-61109. 275p. 1989. 16.50 (*0-87263-362-4*) SME.
Drozda, T., ed. see Society of Manufacturing Engineers Staff.
Drozda, Thomas J., ed. Cutting Fluids & Industrial Lubricants: A Selection from the Tool & Manufacturing Engineers Handbook. LC 82-60312. (Illus.). 66p. 1988. reprint ed. pap. 30.00 (*0-7837-8191-1*, 204789600008) Bks Demand.
— Flexible Manufacturing Systems. 2nd ed. LC 88-61233. (Illus.). 449p. 1988. reprint ed. pap. 139.20 (*0-7837-9736-2*, 206046400005) Bks Demand.
— Machine Controls: A Selection from the Tool &

D

Manufacturing Engineers Handbook. LC 82-60312. (Illus.). 102p. 1988. reprint ed. pap. 31.70 (*0-7837-8190-3*, 204789500008) Bks Demand.

— Personal Computer Solutions for CAD-CAM. LC 89-60297. (Illus.). 236p. 1989. text 42.00 (*0-87263-357-8*) SME.

Drozdeck, Steven. Broker's Edge: How to Sell Securities in Any Market. LC 94-37830. 352p. (C). 1994. text 29.95 (*0-13-311044-3*) P-H.

Drozdek, Adam. Data Structures & Algorithms in C Plus Plus. LC 95-38032. (Computer Science Ser.). 528p. (C). 1995. mass mkt. 78.95 (*0-534-94974-6*) PWS Pubs.

***Drozdek, Adam.** Data Structures & Algorithms in Java. (C). 2001. 52.00 (*0-534-37668-1*) Thomson Learn.

Drozdek, Adam. Moral Dimension of Man in the Age of Computers. 162p. (C). 1995. pap. text 28.50 (*0-8191-9984-2*); lib. bdg. 47.00 (*0-8191-9983-4*) U Pr of Amer.

Drozdov, Aleksey D. Finite Elasticity & Viscoelasticity: A Course in the Nonlinear Mechanics of Solids. 300p. 1996. 68.00 (*981-02-2433-8*) World Scientific Pub.

— Mechanics of Viscoelastic Solids. LC 97-46065. 484p. 1998. 149.95 (*0-471-97512-5*) Wiley.

Drozdov, Aleksy D., ed. Viscoelastic Structures: Mechanics of Growth & Aging. LC 97-29072. (Illus.). 596p. 1997. text 69.95 (*0-12-222280-6*) Morgan Kaufmann.

Drozdov, Aleskey D. & Kolmanovskii, Vladimir B. Stability in Viscoelasticity. LC 94-39063. (Applied Mathematics & Mechanics Ser.: Vol. 38). 622p. 1994. 187.50 (*0-444-81951-7*, North Holland) Elsevier.

Drozdova, T. F., tr. see Alexandrov, Yu A.

Drozdowski, Ted, et al. The Best Music CD Art & Design. (Illus.). 160p. 1997. 34.99 (*1-56496-367-5*) Rockport Pubs.

Drozdowsky, Bohdan, ed. Twentieth-Century Polish Theatre. 256p. 1983. 14.95 (*0-7145-3738-1*) Riverrun NY.

Drozdyk, Charlie. Jobs That Don't Suck. LC 98-12736. 384p. 1998. pap. 12.95 (*0-345-42426-3*) Ballantine Pub Grp.

Droze, Wilmon H. High Dams & Slack Waters: TVA Rebuilds a River. LC 65-14533. 184p. reprint ed. pap. 57.10 (*0-608-10306-3*, 200717900062) Bks Demand.

Drpic, Ivo. Architectural Delineation: Professional Shortcuts. 1993. pap. 36.95 (*0-442-01352-3*, VNR) Wiley.

— Sketching & Rendering of Interior Spaces. (Illus.). 176p. 1988. pap. 27.50 (*0-8230-4853-5*, Whitney Lib) Watsn-Guptill.

Drpic, Ivo D. Architectural Delineation: Professional Shortcuts. 198p. 1993. pap. 44.95 (*0-471-28538-2*, VNR) Wiley.

***Drtikol, Frantisek.** The Photographer Frantisek Drtikol. (Illus.). 200p. 2000. 45.00 (*80-86217-20-5*, Pub. by Kant) Dist Art Pubs.

Drtina, Ralph E., jt. auth. see Brandon, Charles H.

Dru, A., tr. see Von Balthasar, Hans U.

Dru, Alexander, ed. & tr. see Kierkegaard, Soren.

Dru, Alexander, tr. see Burckhardt, Jacob.

Dru, Alexander, tr. see Pieper, Josef.

Dru, Jean-Marie. Disruption: A New Approach to Creativity in Advertising. LC 96-21256. 256p. 1996. 29.95 (*0-471-16565-4*) Wiley.

D

Druart, Therese A., ed. The Recovery of Form Vol. 69: Annual ACPA Proceedings, 1995. 1996. pap. 20.00 (*0-918090-29-6*) Am Cath Philo.

Druart, Therese-Anne, ed. Arabic Philosophy & the West: Continuity & Interaction. 156p. (Orig.). 1988. pap. text 12.95 (*0-932568-15-7*) GU Ctr CAS.

— Philosophy of Technology Vol. 70: Annual ACPA Proceedings, 1996. 1997. pap. 20.00 (*0-918090-30-X*) Am Cath Philo.

— Reason in History Vol. 68: Annual ACPA Proceedings, 1994. 1995. pap. 20.00 (*0-918090-28-8*) Am Cath Philo.

— Relations Vol. 66: From Having to Being Annual ACPA Proceedings, 1992. 1993. pap. 20.00 (*0-918090-26-1*) Am Cath Philo.

Druart, Therese-Anne & Rasevic, Marc, eds. Religions & the Virtue of Religion Vol. 65: Annual ACPA Proceedings, 1992. 1992. pap. 20.00 (*0-918090-25-3*) Am Cath Philo.

***Drubach.** Brain: An Owner's Manual. 168p. 1999. pap. 30.67 (*0-13-796194-4*) P-H.

***Drubek Meyer, Natascha & Murasov, Jurij.** Apparatur und Rhapsodie. 2000. 48.95 (*3-631-33076-6*) P Lang Pubng.

Druben, Laurel, jt. auth. see Lindblad, Carl.

Druben, Laurel, ed. see Chakroff, Marilyn.

***Drubin, David, ed.** Cell Polarity. (Frontiers in Molecular Biology Ser.: No. 28). (Illus.). 352p. 2000. text 110.00 (*0-19-963803-9*); pap. text 55.00 (*0-19-963802-0*) OUP.

Druc, I., jt. auth. see Velde, B.

Druce, Arden. Chalk Talk Stories. LC 93-37956. (School Library Media Ser.: No. 1). (Illus.). 160p. 1993. 26.00 (*0-8108-2781-6*) Scarecrow.

— Complete Library Skills Activities Program: Ready-to-Use Lessons for Grades K-6. 320p. 1990. pap. text 27.95 (*0-87628-240-0*) Ctr Appl Res.

— Library Lessons for Grades 7-9. (School Library Media Ser.: No. 8). (Illus.). 329p. 1989. teacher ed. 24.00 (*0-9617595-2-6*) D Whittington Pr.

— Library Lessons for Grades 7-9. rev. ed. LC 95-46644. (School Library Media Ser.: No. 8). (Illus.). 356p. 1996. text 55.00 (*0-8108-3100-7*) Scarecrow.

— Paper Bag Puppets. LC 97-37705. (School Library Media Ser.: No. 15). (Illus.). 224p. 1999. pap. 27.50 (*0-8108-3400-6*) Scarecrow.

— Witch, Witch. LC 91-29763. (Illus.). 32p. (J). 1991. 13.99 (*0-85953-780-3*) Childs Play.

— Witch, Witch. LC 91-29763. (Illus.). 32p. (J). 1991. pap. 6.99 (*0-85953-781-1*) Childs Play.

— Witch, Witch. (J). 1996. lib. bdg. 15.95 (*0-85953-887-7*) Childs Play.

Druce, Howard M., ed. Sinusitis: Pathogenesis & Treatment. LC 93-20821. (Clinical Allergy & Immunology Ser.: Vol. 1). (Illus.). 352p. 1993. text 145.00 (*0-8247-8845-1*) Dekker.

Druce, Nell & Hammond, Jenny, eds. Sweeter Than Honey: Ethiopian Women & Revolution: Testimonies of Tigrayan Women. LC 90-60727. (Illus.). 184p. (C). 1990. 35.00 (*0-932415-55-5*); pap. 11.95 (*0-932415-56-3*) Red Sea Pr.

Druck, Kalman B., ed. New Technology & Public Relations: A Guide for Public Relations & Public Affairs Practitioners. LC 87-105313. 188p. reprint ed. pap. 58.30 (*0-7837-0081-4*, 204033900016) Bks Demand.

Druck, Kitty, jt. ed. see Groth, Patricia C.

Druck, Mark. The Final Mission. (Orig.). 1978. mass mkt. 2.25 (*0-89083-386-9*, Zebra Kensgtn) Kensgtn Pub Corp.

***Druckenmiller, Bart.** Dreams in the Spirit, Vol. 1. 1999. pap. 10.99 (*1-56043-346-9*, Treasure Hse) Destiny Image.

— Dreams in the Spirit, Vol. 11. Vol. 11. 2000. pap. 8.99 (*1-56043-347-7*, Treasure Hse) Destiny Image.

Druckenmuelle. Knaurs Lexikon, A-Z. (GER.). 1056p. 1991. 59.95 (*0-8288-1961-0*, M7518) Fr & Eur.

Drucker. M. D. Mad's Show Stoppers, Vol. 1. 1985. mass mkt. 4.95 (*0-446-38179-9*, Pub. by Warner Bks) Little.

***Drucker & White.** Managing People in Construction. 272p. 2000. pap. 47.95 (*0-8464-5116-6*) Beekman Pubs.

Drucker, Al. Sai Baba Gita - The Way to Self-Realization & Liberation in This Age. (Wisdom Teachings Ser.). 384p. 1993. pap. 12.50 (*0-9638449-0-3*) ATMA Pr.

— Self-Realization - The Knowledge of the Absolute. (Wisdom Teachings Ser.). 54p. 1994. pap. 4.50 (*0-9638449-1-1*) ATMA Pr.

Drucker, Arno P. American Piano Trios. LC 98-45853. 416p. 1999. 60.00 (*0-8108-3608-4*) Scarecrow.

Drucker-Brown, Susan, ed. see Malinowski, Bronislaw & De La Fuente, Julio.

Drucker, Cecily Ann, jt. auth. see Weller, Louis S.

Drucker, Dan. Abortion Decisions of the Supreme Court, 1973 Through 1989: A Comprehensive Review with Historical Commentary. LC 89-43620. 220p. 1990. lib. bdg. 42.50 (*0-89950-459-0*) McFarland & Co.

Drucker, Daniel. Exceptional Lie Algebras & the Structure of Hermitian Symmetric Spaces. LC 78-15619. (Memoirs Ser.: No. 16/208). 207p. 1982. reprint ed. pap. 26.00 (*0-8218-2208-X*, MEMO/16/208) Am Math.

Drucker, Daniel C. & Gilman, J. J., eds. Fracture of Solids: Proceedings of an International Conference, Maple Valley, Washington, August 21-24, 1962. LC 63-13590. (Metallurgical Society Conference Ser.: Vol. 20). 718p. reprint ed. pap. 200.00 (*0-608-11774-9*, 200150800079) Bks Demand.

Drucker, Daniel C., jt. ed. see Wang, Ren.

Drucker, David, jt. auth. see Steinhauer, Lauren.

Drucker, E. Z. The IBM PC User's English-Russian Dictionary. 187p. 1992. pap. 39.95 (*0-7859-9091-7*) Fr & Eur.

Drucker Foundation Staff. How to Assess Your Nonprofit Organization: The Drucker Foundation Self-Assessment Tool for Nonprofit Organizations - Process Guide. rev. ed. LC 98-67792. (Nonprofit & Public Administration Ser.). 128p. 1998. pap. 19.95 (*0-7879-4436-X*) Jossey-Bass.

Drucker Foundation Staff, et al, eds. The Leader of the Future. 352p. 1997. mass mkt. 16.50 (*0-7879-0935-1*) Jossey-Bass.

— The Leader of the Future: New Essays by World-Class Leaders & Thinkers. (Management Ser.). 347p. 1996. mass mkt. 24.50 (*0-7879-0180-6*) Jossey-Bass.

Drucker Foundation Staff & Drucker, Peter F. The Five Most Important Questions You Will Ever Ask about Your Nonprofit: The Drucker Foundation Self-Assessment Tool for Nonprofit Organizations - Participant's Workbook. 2nd ed. (Nonprofit & Public Administration Ser.). 64p. 1998. pap., wbk. ed. 11.95 (*0-7879-4437-8*) Jossey-Bass.

Drucker, H. M., ed. Multi-Party Britain. LC 79-52940. (Praeger Special Studies). 256p. 1979. 65.00 (*0-275-90348-6*, C0348, Praeger Pubs) Greenwood.

Drucker, Hal. From the Desk Of. 1989. 29.95 (*0-15-133795-0*) Harcourt.

Drucker, Harvey & Wildung, Raymond E., eds. Biological Implications of Metals in the Environment: Proceedings. LC 77-1039. (ERDA Symposium Ser.). 692p. 1977. pap. 25.25 (*0-87079-104-4*, CONF-750929); fiche 9.00 (*0-87079-149-4*, CONF-750929) DOE.

Drucker, Henry M. & Brown, Gordon. The Politics of Nationalism & Devolution. LC 79-41025. 144p. reprint ed. pap. 44.70 (*0-608-13104-0*, 202521900043) Bks Demand.

Drucker, Jacki L. Silly Sights New York City. LC 96-70492. (Illus.). 32p. (J). (ps-4). 1997. 16.95 (*0-9647857-1-4*); pap. 9.95 (*0-9647857-2-2*) Peeking Duck Bks.

— Silly Sights Washington, DC. LC 95-74712. (Illus.). 32p. (Orig.). (J). (ps-4). 1996. pap. 8.95 (*0-9647857-0-6*) Peeking Duck Bks.

Drucker, Jane. Families of Value: Gay & Lesbian Parents & Their Children Speak Out. LC 98-12619. (Illus.). 284p. (C). 1998. 27.95 (*0-306-45863-2*, Plen Insight) Perseus Pubng.

Drucker, Janet & Jensen, Georg A. Georg Jensen: A Tradition of Splendid Silver. LC 97-11059. 312p. 1997. 79.95 (*0-88740-978-4*) Schiffer.

Drucker, Johanna. The Alphabetic Labyrinth: The Alphabet in History, Mysticism & Imagination. LC 93-61369. (Illus.). 328p. 1995. 45.00 (*0-500-01608-9*, Pub. by Thames Hudson) Norton.

— The Alphabetic Labyrinth: The Letters in History & Imagination. LC 93-61369. (Illus.). 320p. 1999. pap. 27.50 (*0-500-28068-1*, Pub. by Thames Hudson) Norton.

— The Century of Artists' Books. LC 95-79670. 377p. (C). 1995. 35.00 (*1-887123-01-6*) Granary Bks.

— The Century of Artists' Books. LC 95-79670. 377p. 1997. pap. 24.95 (*1-887123-02-4*) Granary Bks.

— Dark Decade. Deike, Marta & Sullivan, Gary, eds. LC 94-48128. 128p. (Orig.). 1995. pap. 10.95 (*1-886214-00-X*) Detour Pr.

***Drucker, Johanna.** Figuring the Word: Essays on Books, Writing & Visual Poetics. (Illus.). 312p. 1998. pap. 24.95 (*1-887123-23-7*) Granary Bks.

Drucker, Johanna. The History of the/My Wor(l)d. LC 95-80210. (Illus.). 40p. 1995. reprint ed. 50.00 (*1-887123-06-7*) Granary Bks.

— Italy. 1980. per. 5.00 (*0-935724-05-2*) Figures.

— Narratology. (Illus.). 40p. 1994. 950.00 (*1-887123-00-8*) Granary Bks.

— Prove Before Laying: Figuring the Word. (Illus.). 30p. 1997. 300.00 (*1-887123-24-5*, Druckwerk) Granary Bks.

— Theorizing Modernism: Visual Art & the Critical Tradition. (Illus.). 224p. 1996. pap. 18.00 (*0-231-08083-2*) Col U Pr.

— The Visible Word: Experimental Typography & Modern Art, 1909-1923. LC 93-39657. 306p. 1994. 35.00 (*0-226-16501-9*) U Ch Pr.

— The Visible Word: Experimental Typography & Modern Art, 1909-1923. vii, 298p. 1996. pap. text 15.95 (*0-226-16502-7*) U Ch Pr.

— The Word Made Flesh. fac. ed. (Illus.). 40p. 1996. 60.00 (*1-887123-09-1*) Granary Bks.

— The Word Returned: Artist Books by Ken Campbell. Fairman, Elisabeth, ed. LC 96-60902. (Illus.). 24p. 1996. pap. 10.00 (*0-930606-79-5*) Yale Ctr Brit Art.

Drucker, Johanna & Freeman, Brad. Otherspace: Martian Typography. 1992. 35.00 (*0-932526-41-1*) Nexus Pr.

Drucker, Johanna, et al. The Dual Muse: The Writer As Artist, the Artist As Writer. Neidhardt, Jane E. & Cudco, Lorin, eds. LC 97-40460. (Illus.). 144p. 1997. 45.00 (*1-55619-524-9*) J Benjamins Pubng Co.

Drucker, Joseph. Blood & Other Poems. 1971. write for info. (*0-318-64101-1*) Poets Pr.

***Drucker, Maika.** The Family Treasury of Jewish Holidays. (Illus.). 192p. (J). (gr. k-3). 1999. pap. 12.95 (*0-316-19313-5*) Little.

Drucker, Malka. The Family Treasury of Jewish Holidays. LC 93-7549. (Illus.). 192p. (J). (gr. k-3). 1994. 22.95 (*0-316-19343-7*) Little.

— Frida Kahlo. LC 95-13666. (Illus.). 159p. 1995. reprint ed. pap. 12.95 (*0-8263-1642-5*) U of NM Pr.

— Grandma's Latkes. LC 91-30086. (Illus.). 40p. (J). 1996. pap. 6.00 (*0-15-201388-1*) Harcourt.

— Grandma's Latkes. LC 91-30086. 1996. 11.45 (*0-606-10201-9*, Pub. by Turtleback) Demco.

— Jacob's Rescue: A Holocaust Story. 128p. (J). (gr. 4-7). 1994. pap. 4.50 (*0-440-40965-9*) Dell.

Drucker, Malka. Jacob's Rescue: A Holocaust Story. LC 92-30523. 1993. 9.60 (*0-606-06504-0*, Pub. by Turtleback) Demco.

Drucker, Malka. A Jewish Holiday ABC. LC 90-36791. (Illus.). 40p. (J). 1996. pap. 6.00 (*0-15-201366-0*) Harcourt.

— A Jewish Holiday ABC. LC 90-36791. 1996. 11.20 (*0-606-10232-9*, Pub. by Turtleback) Demco.

— The Sea Monster's Secret: A Tale from the Pacific Northwest. LC 96-5123. (Illus.). 32p. (J). 1999. 16.00 (*0-15-200619-2*) Harcourt.

Drucker, Malka, jt. auth. see Block, Gay.

Drucker, Margaret A.R., ed. Companion to My Tears: Working Through The Process of Bereavement. LC 94-23550. 96p. (Orig.). 1994. pap. 3.95 (*0-8189-0710-X*) Alba.

Drucker, Margaret R. Mangoes & Chappaties. LC 98-90664. (Orig.). 1999. pap. 14.95 (*0-533-12870-6*) Vantage.

Drucker, Marge B. Memories: The Story of Dick & Marge Bong (Major Richard Bong America's Ace of Aces) 2nd ed. (Illus.). 120p. 1995. 25.00 (*0-9647840-0-9*) Drucker Pubns.

Drucker, Mark, ed. Urban Decision Making . . . A Guide to Information Sources. LC 80-19252. (Urban Studies Information Guide Ser.: Vol. 13). 208p. 1981. 68.00 (*0-8103-1481-9*) Gale.

Drucker, Mindy & Finkelstein, Pierre. Recipes for Surfaces. 256p. 1990. pap. 20.00 (*0-671-68249-0*) S&S Trade.

Drucker, Mindy & Rosen, Nancy. Recipes for Surfaces Vol. II: New & Exciting Ideas for Decorative Paint Finishes, Vol. 2. 1995. per. 20.00 (*0-684-80179-5*, Fireside) S&S Trade Pap.

Drucker, Olga L. Kindertransport. 160p. (J). (gr. 4-7). 1995. pap. 7.95 (*0-8050-4251-2*) H Holt & Co.

— Kindertransport. LC 92-14121. 88p. (J). (gr. 5-8). 1995. 14.95 (*0-8050-1711-9*, Bks Young Read) H Holt & Co.

— Kindertransport. 1995. 13.05 (*0-606-08790-7*, Pub. by Turtleback) Demco.

Drucker, Peter. Drucker on Management. Date not set. pap. 18.00 (*0-88730-999-2*, HarpBusn) HarpInfo.

— Managing in Time. 1998. pap. 14.95 (*0-452-27837-6*, Plume) Dutton Plume.

— Max Shachtman & His Left: A Socialist's Odyssey Through the American Century. LC 93-12763. (Revolutionary Studies). 336p. (C). 1993. pap. 18.50 (*0-391-03816-8*) Humanities.

— Max Shachtman & His Left: A Socialist's Odyssey Through the American Century. LC 93-12763. (Revolutionary Studies). 336p. (C). 1993. text 49.95 (*0-391-03815-X*) Humanities.

— Peter Drucker on the Profession of Management. Stone, Nan, ed. LC 97-39984. 224p. 1998. 29.95 (*0-87584-836-2*) Harvard Busn.

Drucker, Peter. The Practice of Management: Bookspan,&Martin. abr. ed. 1990. audio 12.00 (*1-55994-278-9*, CPN 1866) HarperAudio.

Drucker, Peter, intro. Landmarks of Tomorrow: A Report on the New "Post-Modern" World. 280p. 1996. pap. text 24.95 (*1-56000-622-6*) Transaction Pubs.

Drucker, Peter, tr. see Samary, Catherine.

Drucker, Peter F. Adventures of a Bystander. LC 93-47313. 360p. (C). 1994. pap. 24.95 (*1-56000-738-9*) Transaction Pubs.

***Drucker, Peter F.** Adventures of a Bystander. LC 97-37798. (Trailblazers Ser.). 352p. 1998. 27.95 (*0-471-24739-1*) Wiley.

Drucker, Peter F. The Age of Discontinuity: Guidelines to Our Changing Society. 420p. (C). 1992. pap. 24.95 (*1-56000-618-8*) Transaction Pubs.

— America's Next Twenty Years. LC 72-6759. (Essay Index Reprint Ser.). 1980. reprint ed. 18.95 (*0-8369-7267-8*) Ayer.

— Concept of the Corporation. rev. ed. 319p. (C). 1993. pap. text 24.95 (*1-56000-625-0*) Transaction Pubs.

— The Ecological Vision: Reflections on the American Condition. LC 92-3967. 424p. (C). 1992. 44.95 (*1-56000-061-9*) Transaction Pubs.

***Drucker, Peter F.** Ecological Vision: Reflections on the American Condition. (Illus.). 2000. pap. 29.95 (*0-7658-0725-4*) Transaction Pubs.

— Effective Executive. 1999. 13.00 (*0-06-662019-8*) HarpC.

Drucker, Peter F. The Effective Executive. LC 84-48156. 178p. 1993. reprint ed. pap. 14.00 (*0-88730-612-8*, HarpBusn) HarpInfo.

— The Executive in Action: 3 Classic Works on Management. LC 96-6380. 720p. 1996. 32.00 (*0-88730-828-7*, HarpBusn) HarpInfo.

— Frontiers of Management: Where Tomorrow's Decicions Are Being Shaped Today, 1 vol. 368p. 1999. pap. 13.95 (*0-452-28055-9*) NAL.

— The Future of Industrial Man. rev. ed. 248p. (C). 1994. pap. 24.95 (*1-56000-623-4*) Transaction Pubs.

— Innovation & Entrepreneurship: Practice & Principles. LC 84-48593. 277p. 1986. pap. 14.50 (*0-88730-618-7*, HarpBusn) HarpInfo.

***Drucker, Peter F.** Management. 1999. 20.00 (*0-06-662021-X*) HarpC.

Drucker, Peter F. Management: Tasks, Practices, Responsibilities. LC 84-48157. 864p. 1993. reprint ed. pap. 20.00 (*0-88730-615-2*, HarpBusn) HarpInfo.

— Management Challenges for the 21st Century. LC 99-17087. 224p. 1999. 27.50 (*0-88730-998-4*, HarpBusn) HarpInfo.

***Drucker, Peter F.** Management Challenges for the 21st Century. unabridged ed. 1999. audio 25.00 (*0-694-52212-0*, 698412, Pub. by HarperAudio) Lndmrk Audiobks.

— Managing for Results. 1999. pap. 13.00 (*0-06-662024-4*, HarpBusn) HarpInfo.

Drucker, Peter F. Managing for Results: Economic Tasks & Risk-Taking Decisions. LC 85-45683. 240p. 1993. reprint ed. pap. 12.50 (*0-88730-614-4*, HarpBusn) HarpInfo.

— Managing for the Future: The 1990s & Beyond. LC 93-10126. 384p. 1993. pap. 14.95 (*0-452-26984-9*, Truman Talley) St Martin.

— Managing in a Time of Great Change. LC 95-13316. 371p. 1995. pap. 24.95 (*0-525-94053-7*, Truman Talley) St Martin.

***Drucker, Peter F.** Managing the Non-Profit Organization: Practices & Principles. 1999. pap. 13.50 (*0-06-662023-6*) HarpC.

Drucker, Peter F. Managing the Non-Profit Organization: Principles & Practices. LC 89-46525. 235p. 1992. pap. 13.50 (*0-88730-601-2*, HarpBusn) HarpInfo.

Drucker, Peter F. Managing the Nonprofit Organization: Drucker,&Peter F., Set. abr. ed. 1992. audio 17.00 (*1-55994-552-4*, CPN 2283) HarperAudio.

— New Realities. 1999. pap. 13.50 (*0-06-662027-9*, HarpBusn) HarpInfo.

Drucker, Peter F. The New Realities. LC 89-1192. 288p. 1994. reprint ed. pap. 14.00 (*0-88730-617-9*, HarpBusn) HarpInfo.

— The New Society: The Anatomy of Industrial Order. 365p. (C). 1993. pap. text 24.95 (*1-56000-624-2*) Transaction Pubs.

— The Pension Fund Revolution. 240p. (C). 1995. pap. text 21.95 (*1-56000-626-9*) Transaction Pubs.

***Drucker, Peter F.** Post-Capitalist Society. 1999. pap. 13.50 (*0-06-662025-2*, HarpBusn) HarpInfo.

Drucker, Peter F. Post-Capitalist Society. LC 92-54323. 240p. 1994. reprint ed. pap. 13.50 (*0-88730-661-6*, HarpBusn) HarpInfo.

***Drucker, Peter F.** Practice of Management. 1999. pap. 17.00 (*0-06-662026-0*, HarpBusn) HarpInfo.

Drucker, Peter F. Toward the Next Economics & Other Essays. LC HD0031.D775. 224p. reprint ed. pap. 69.50 (*0-608-10634-8*, 207125600009) Bks Demand.

Drucker, Peter F. & Nakauchi, Isao. Drucker on Asia: The Drucker-Nakauchi Dialogue. LC 97-144801. 200p. 1997. text 22.50 (*0-7506-3132-5*) Buttrwrth-Heinemann.

Drucker, Peter F., et al. Excellence in Nonprofit Leadership: A Three-in-One Development Program for Boards & Staff, 3 vols. (Nonprofit & Public Administration Ser.). pap., teacher ed., wbk. ed. 129.95 incl. vdisk (*0-7879-1081-3*); pap., wbk. ed. 11.95 (*0-7879-4298-7*) Jossey-Bass.

— Excellence in Nonprofit Leadership: A Three-in-One Development Program for Boards & Staff. LC 98-66557. (Nonprofit & Public Administration Ser.). 32p. 1998. pap., teacher ed. 19.95 (*0-7879-4398-3*) Jossey-Bass.

— Power & Democracy in America. D'Antonio, William V., ed. LC 79-28576. 181p. 1980. reprint ed. lib. bdg. 55.00 (*0-313-22319-X*, PDAM, Greenwood Pr) Greenwood.

Drucker, Peter F., jt. auth. see Drucker Foundation Staff.

Drucker, Peter Ferdinand. The Practice of Management. LC 85-45189. 404p. 1986. pap. 17.00 (*0-88730-613-6*, HarpBusn) HarpInfo.

Drucker, Philip. Ceramic Sequences at Tres Zapotes, Veracruz, Mexico. (Bureau of American Ethnology Bulletins Ser.). 148p. 1995. lib. bdg. 79.00 (*0-7812-4140-5*) Rprt Serv.

— Ceramic Stratigraphy at Cerro de las Mesas, Veracruz, Mexico. (Smithsonian Institution Bureau of American Ethnology Bulletins Ser.: No. 141). (Illus.). 164p. (C). 1943. pap. text 17.50 (*1-55567-749-5*) Coyote Press.

— Ceramic Stratigraphy at Cerro de las Mesas, Veracruz, Mexico. (Bureau of American Ethnology Bulletins Ser.). 95p. 1995. lib. bdg. 79.00 (*0-7812-4141-3*) Rprt Serv.

— Cultural Element Distributions No. XXVI: Northwest Coast. fac. ed. Gifford, Edward W. et al, eds. (University of California Publications: No. 9:3). (Illus.). 142p. (C). 1950. reprint ed. pap. 15.63 (*1-55567-096-2*) Coyote Press.

— Culture Element Distributions No. V: Southern California. fac. ed. (University of California Publications: No. 1:1). 55p. (C). 1937. reprint ed. pap. 6.56 (*1-55567-113-6*) Coyote Press.

— Culture Element Distributions No. XVII: Yuman-Piman. fac. ed. Kroeber, A. L. et al, eds. (University of California Publications: No. 6:3). (Illus.). 145p. (C). 1941. reprint ed. pap. 15.63 (*1-55567-088-1*) Coyote Press.

— Excavations at La Venta, Tabasco. (Bureau of American Ethnology Bulletins Ser.). 312p. 1995. lib. bdg. 99.00 (*0-7812-4170-7*) Rprt Serv.

— Kwakiutl Dancing Societies. fac. ed. Lowie, Robert H. et al, eds. (University of California Publications: No. 2:6). 35p. (C). 1940. reprint ed. pap. 4.06 (*1-55567-075-X*) Coyote Press.

— The Native Brotherhoods: Modern Inter-Tribal Organizations on the Northwest Coast. reprint ed. 59.00 (*0-403-03657-7*) Scholarly.

— The Native Brotherhoods: Modern Intertribal Organizations. (Bureau of American Ethnology Bulletins Ser.). 194p. 1995. lib. bdg. 79.00 (*0-7812-4168-5*) Rprt Serv.

— The Native Brotherhoods: Modern Intertribal Organizations on the Northwest Coast. (Bureau of American Ethnology Ser.). 200p. 1992. reprint ed. pap. text 39.00 (*1-878592-27-0*); reprint ed. lib. bdg. 59.00 (*1-878592-28-9*) Native Amer Bk Pubs.

— The Native Brotherhoods: Modern Intertribal Organizations on the Northwest Coast. 1988. reprint ed. lib. bdg. 79.00 (*0-7812-0755-X*) Rprt Serv.

— The Northern & Central Nootkan Tribes. (Bureau of American Ethnology Bulletins Ser.). 480p. 1995. lib. bdg. 109.00 (*0-7812-4144-8*) Rprt Serv.

— The Northern & Central Nootkan Tribes. fac. ed. (Smithsonian Institution, Bureau of American Ethnology Ser.: Bulletin 144). (Illus.). 492p. (C). 1951. reprint ed. pap. text 50.63 (*1-55567-680-4*) Coyote Press.

— The Northern & Central Nootkan Tribes. 1988. reprint ed. lib. bdg. 75.00 (*0-7812-0233-7*) Rprt Serv.

— The Tolowa & Their Southwest Oregon Kin. fac. ed. (University of California Publications in American Archaeology & Ethnology: Vol. 36: 4). (Illus.). 86p. (C). 1937. reprint ed. pap. text 9.69 (*1-55567-305-8*) Coyote Press.

— La Venta, Tabasco: A Study of Olmec Ceramics & Art. (Bureau of American Ethnology Bulletins Ser.). 257p. 1995. lib. bdg. 89.00 (*0-7812-4153-7*) Rprt Serv.

Drucker, Philip, et al. Excavations at La Venta Tabasco, 1955. fac. ed. (Smithsonian Institution, Bureau of American Ethnology Ser.: No. 170). (Illus.). 345p. (C). 1959. reprint ed. pap. text 36.25 (*1-55567-791-6*) Coyote Press.

Drucker, Philip, et al. Varia Anthropologica. fac. ed. (University of California Publications in American Archaeology & Ethnology: Vol. 35: 3-5). 27p. (C). 1936. reprint ed. pap. text 3.13 (*1-55567-299-X*) Coyote Press.

Drucker, Reuven. Joshua - Yehoshua. (ArtScroll Tanach Ser.). (Illus.). 480p. 1982. 24.99 (*0-89906-087-0*); pap. 20.99 (*0-89906-088-9*) Mesorah Pubns.

Drucker, Sally A., jt. auth. see Drewes, Athena A.

Drucker, Saul & Hexter, Maurice-Beck. Children Astray. LC 74-1681. (Children & Youth Ser.: Vol. 28). 450p. 1974. reprint ed. 36.95 (*0-405-05959-0*) Ayer.

Drucker, Stanley, compiled by. Easy Original Clarinet Solos, MFM26. (Illus.). 160p. 1998. pap. 16.95 (*0-8256-4026-1*, AM41534) Music Sales.

Drucker, Susan J. & Cathcart, Robert S. American Heroes in a Media Age. Becker, Lee, ed. LC 94-19788. (Communication Series: Mass Communications & Journalism). 368p. (C). 1994. text 72.50 (*1-881303-19-5*); pap. text 28.50 (*1-881303-20-9*) Hampton Pr NJ.

Drucker, Susan J. & Gumpert, Gary, eds. Real Law @ Virtual Space: Communication Regulation in Cyberspace. LC 99-19762. (Communication Ser.). 432p. (C). 1999. 85.00 (*1-57273-124-9*); pap. 35.00 (*1-57273-125-7*) Hampton Pr NJ.

— Voices in the Street: Explorations in Gender, Media & Public Space. LC 96-44098. (The Hampton Press Communication Ser.). 320p. (Orig.). (C). 1996. text 27.50 (*1-57273-017-X*) Hampton Pr NJ.

— Voices in the Street: Explorations in Gender, Media & Public Space. LC 96-44098. (Communication Ser.). 320p. (Orig.). (C). 1996. text 72.50 (*1-57273-016-1*) Hampton Pr NJ.

Drucker, Susan J., jt. ed. see Gumpert, Gary.

Drucker, Susan J., jt. ed. see Siegel, Paul.

Drucker, T., ed. Perspectives on the History of Mathematical Logic. (Illus.). 232p. 1991. 86.50 (*0-8176-3444-4*) Birkhauser.

Drucker, William. SAT I: The Answer Key. 1999. pap. text 24.95 (*1-890838-07-1*) Indus Pub.

Druckman, Daniel. In the Mind's Eye: Enhancing Human Performance. Bjork, Robert A., ed. LC 91-23941. (Illus.). 303p. reprint ed. pap. 94.00 (*0-608-10443-4*, 207107700008) Bks Demand.

Druckman, Daniel, ed. Negotiations: Social-Psychological Perspectives. LC 76-58353. (Illus.). 416p. reprint ed. pap. 129.00 (*0-8357-8457-6*, 203472200091) Bks Demand.

Druckman, Daniel & Bjork, Robert A. In the Mind's Eye: Enhancing Human Performance. 304p. 1992. pap. 19.95 (*0-309-04747-1*) Natl Acad Pr.

Druckman, Daniel & Green, Justin. Political Stability in the Philippines: Framework & Analysis. (Monograph Series in World Affairs: Vol. 22, Bk. 3). (Orig.). 1986. pap. 9.95 (*0-87940-082-X*) Monograph Series.

Druckman, Daniel & Mitchell, Christopher, eds. Flexibility in International Negotiation & Mediation. LC 95-69939. (The Annals of the American Academy of Political & Social Science Ser.: Vol. 542). 1995. 28.00 (*0-7619-0133-7*); pap. 18.00 (*0-7619-0134-5*) Am Acad Pol Soc Sci.

Druckman, Daniel, et al. Nonverbal Communication: Survey, Theory, & Research. LC 81-21309. (Sage Library of Social Research: No. 139). (Illus.). 264p. reprint ed. pap. 81.90 (*0-8357-4782-4*, 203771900009) Bks Demand.

Druckman, Daniel, ed. see National Research Council Staff.

Druckrey, Timothy, ed. Ars Electronica: Facing the Future. LC 99-14921. (Illus.). 400p. 1999. 40.00 (*0-262-04176-6*) MIT Pr.

— Iterations: The New Image. LC 93-31695. (Illus.). 199p. 1994. 42.50 (*0-262-04143-X*) MIT Pr.

Druckrey, Timothy & Lemmon, Nadine, eds. For a Burning World Is Come to Dance Inane: Essays by & about Jim Pomeray. (Revisioning Technology Ser.). (Illus.). 83p. (Orig.). 1993. pap. 15.00 (*1-883831-00-8*) Critical Pr.

Druckrey, Timothy, jt. auth. see Doroshenko, Peter.

Druckrey, Timothy, jt. auth. see Riddell, Jennifer.

Druckrey, Timothy, jt. ed. see Bender, Gretchen.

Druckrey, Timothy, ed. see Stone, Allucquere R.

Dructor, Robert M. Guide to Genealogical Sources at the Pennsylvania State Archives. expanded rev. ed. LC 99-234418. (Illus.). 374p. 1997. pap. 14.95 (*0-89271-077-2*, 1203) Pa Hist & Mus.

***Dructor, Robert M.** Guide to Genealogical Sources at the Pennsylvania State Archives. 2nd ed. (Illus.). 374p. (C). 1999. pap. text 40.00 (*0-7881-8377-X*) DIANE Pub.

Dructor, Robert M., compiled by. Guide to the Microfilmed Harmony Society Records, 1786-1951 in the Pennsylvania State Archives. LC 84-622821. 77p. 1983. pap. 6.00 (*0-89271-025-X*) Pa Hist & Mus.

Drude, Gunter, jt. auth. see Sachs, Wolfgang.

Drude, O., jt. ed. see Engler, A.

Drude, Oscar. Handbuch der Pflanzengeographie: Handbook of Phytogeography. Egerton, Frank N., 3rd, ed. LC 77-74213. (History of Ecology Ser.). (Illus.). 1978. reprint ed. lib. bdg. 51.95 (*0-405-10384-0*) Ayer.

***Drudge, Matt.** Drudge Manifesto. 2000. 22.95 (*0-451-20150-7*, Sig) NAL.

***Drudi, Dino.** Fatal Workplace Injuries in 1996: A Collection of Data & Analysis. (Illus.). 164p. (C). 1999. pap. text 30.00 (*0-7881-8277-3*) DIANE Pub.

Drue, Abby. Amy Spangler Lactania Una Guia para los Padres. 6th ed. LC 96-92059. (SPA.). 108p. (Orig.). 1995. pap. 5.75 (*0-9627450-8-1*) A Spangler.

Drue, Thomas. Bloody Banquet. (Tudor Facsimile Texts. Old English Plays Ser.: N0. 142). reprint ed. 59.50 (*0-404-53442-2*) AMS Pr.

Druee, Hermann. Psychologie aus dem Begriff. (C). 1976. 150.00 (*3-11-004603-2*) De Gruyter.

Drueke, Tilman B., jt. ed. see Van Ypersele, Charles.

Druelinger, Melvin L. & Schoffstall, Allen M. Organic Chemistry by Leroy Wade: Solutions Manual & Study Guide. 752p. (C). 1987. pap. text. write for info. (*0-318-62491-5*) P-H.

Druen, Dan. Sometimes We Flew. LC 95-61858. 200p. (C). 1995. text 14.95 (*0-9638455-3-5*) Warwick Hse.

***Druen, Dan.** Sometimes We Flew Too. LC 98-61882. (Illus.). 210p. 1999. 15.95 (*1-890306-17-7*) Warwick Hse.

Druesdow, John E., Jr. Library Research Guide to Music: Illustrated Search Strategy & Sources. LC 81-86634. (Library Research Guides Ser.: No. 6). (Illus.). 1982. 25.00 (*0-87650-138-2*) Pierian.

Druesedow, Jean, jt. auth. see Mechan, Norma Lu.

Druesedow, Jean L., ed. Authentic Art Deco Interiors & Furniture in Full Color. LC 97-21828. (Illus.). 80p. (Orig.). 1997. reprint ed. pap. text 15.95 (*0-486-29635-0*) Dover.

Druett. Hen Frigates. large type ed. LC 98-45068. 1999. 30.00 (*0-7838-0418-0*, G K Hall Lrg Type) Mac Lib Ref.

Druett, Joan. Hen Frigates: Passion & Peril, Nineteenth Century Women at Sea. (Illus.). 288p. 1999. pap. 13.00 (*0-684-85434-1*, Touchstone) S&S Trade Pap.

— Hen Frigates: Wives of Merchant Captains under Sail. LC 97-37624. 272p. 1998. 24.50 (*0-684-83968-7*) S&S Trade Pap.

— Petticoat Whalers: Whaling Wives at Sea, 1820-1920. (Illus.). 214p. 1992. 25.00 (*1-86950-043-1*, Pub. by HarpC) HarpC.

***Druett, Joan.** Rough Medicine: Surgeons at Sea in the Age of Sail. (Illus.). 256p. 2000. 27.50 (*0-415-92451-0*) Routledge.

Druett, Joan. She Captains: Heroines & Hellions of the Sea. LC 99-53592. (Illus.). 304p. 2000. 26.00 (*0-684-85690-5*) S&S Trade.

Druett, Joan, ed. She Was a Sister Sailor: The Whaling Journals of Mary Brewster, 1845-1851. (Illus.). xx, 449p. 1992. 39.95 (*0-913372-60-9*) Mystic Seaport.

Druett, Joan & Wallace, Mary A. The Sailing Circle 19th Century Seafaring Women from New York. (Illus.). 48p. 1995. 11.95 (*0-9636361-1-1*) Whaling Mus.

Druffel, Ann. How to Defend Yourself Against Alien Abduction. LC 98-6414. (Illus.). 256p. 1998. pap. 12.00 (*0-609-80263-1*) Harmony Bks.

Druffel, Ann & Marcotte, Armand. The Psychic & the Detective. 176p. (Orig.). 1995. pap. 10.95 (*1-57174-029-5*) Hampton Roads Pub Co.

Druffel, Ann, jt. auth. see Marcotte, Armand.

Drug Strategies Staff. Making the Grade: A Guide to School Drug Prevention Programs. (Illus.). 36p. 1996. pap. 12.95 (*0-9665342-0-4*) Drug Strtgies.

— Safe Schools, Safe Students: A Guide to Violence Prevention Strategies. LC 98-184961. (Illus.). 56p. 1998. pap. 12.95 (*0-9665342-1-2*) Drug Strtgies.

***Druga-Marchett, Jacqueline.** Siege of the Witches. 2000. pap. 17.95 (*0-87714-688-8*) Denlingers.

Druger, Marvin. Individualized Biology, Units 1-13 & Script 9. 4th ed. 590p. (C). 1997. pap. text 62.95 (*0-7872-4322-1*, 41432201) Kendall-Hunt.

— Individualized Biology, Units 1-13, Script No. 9. 3rd ed. 696p. (C). 1996. spiral bd. 45.95 (*0-8403-5525-4*) Kendall-Hunt.

— Individualized Biology, Units 14-18. 3rd ed. 398p. (C). 1998. pap. text 40.95 (*0-7872-4231-4*, 41423101) Kendall-Hunt.

Druger, Marvin, jt. ed. see Anderson, O. Roger.

Drugi, Tom. Prace I Pisma Ksiedza Biskupa Franciszka Hodura, 2 vols. (POL.). 145p. (Orig.). (C). 1986. pap. 20.00 (*0-944497-03-9*) Polish Natl Cath Ch.

Drugov, Yu S., jt. auth. see Berezkin, V. G.

Druguhn, Werner. China's Economy Security. LC 99-10721. 1999. text 59.95 (*0-312-22298-X*) St Martin.

Drugulin, Wilhelm E. Allgemeiner Portrait Katalog. (GER.). 1972. reprint ed. 150.00 (*0-8115-3751-X*) Periodicals Srv.

Druhan, Marlene M. Naked Soul: Astral Travel & Cosmic Relationships. LC 98-30546. (Illus.). 216p. 1999. 12.95 (*1-56718-247-X*, K247) Llewellyn Pubns.

Druhe, David N. Soviet Russia & Indian Communism. 1959. 19.95 (*0-8084-0385-0*) NCUP.

Druhot, George S. An American Topographer: The Working Years of George Stanley Druhot (1914-1983) Le…ers, Phyllis et al, eds. (Illus.). 238p. 1986. 55.00 (*0-910845-25-5*, 976) Landmark Ent.

Druick, Douglas W. Renoir: The Art Institute of Chicago, Artists in Focus. Salvesen, Britt, ed. LC 97-73867. (Artists in Focus Ser.). (Illus.). 112p. 1997. 19.95 (*0-8109-6325-6*) Art Inst Chi.

Druick, Douglas W., ed. Odilon Redon: Prince of Dreams. LC 94-10379. (Illus.). 472p. 1994. pap. 39.95 (*0-86559-126-1*) Art Inst Chi.

— Odilon Redon: Prince of Dreams. LC 94-10379. (Illus.). 472p. 1997. 60.00 (*0-8109-3769-7*) Art Inst Chi.

Druin, Allison, ed. The Design of Children's Technology: How We Design, What We Design & Why. LC 98-38500. (Series in Interactive Technologies). 368p. (C). 1998. pap. 39.95 (*1-55860-507-X*) Morgan Kaufmann.

***Druin, Allison & Hendler, Jim.** Robots for Kids: Exploring New Technologies for Learning Experiences. Neilsen, Jakob et al, eds. (Interactive Technologies Ser.). 350p. 2000. pap. 44.95 incl. cd-rom (*1-55860-597-5*, Pub. by Morgan Kaufmann) Harcourt.

Druin, Allison & Solomon, Cynthia. Designing Multimedia Environments for Children: Computers, Creativity & Kids. LC 95-37039. 288p. 1996. pap., pap. text 44.95 incl. cd-rom (*0-471-11688-2*) Wiley.

Druist, Miriam. Wildlife on the Farm. (Illus.). 153p. (J). (gr. 3-6). 1977. 7.67 (*0-7399-0101-X*, 2475) Rod & Staff.

Druitt, Ann, et al. All Year Round. (Illus.). 288p. 1995. 19.95 (*1-869890-47-7*, Pub. by Hawthorn Press) Anthroposophic.

Druitt, Liz. Gardening with Kids. 184p. 1998. pap. text 16.95 (*0-87833-969-8*) Taylor Pub.

***Druitt, Liz.** Liz Druitt's Guide to Little Roses. 2001. 24.95 (*0-87833-193-X*) Taylor Pub.

Druitt, Liz. Organic Rose Garden. LC 95-51682. 175p. 1996. 19.95 (*0-87833-906-X*) Taylor Pub.

Druitt, Liz & Shoup, G. Michael. Landscaping with Antique Roses. (Illus.). 240p. (C). 1992. 34.95 (*0-942391-64-0*) Taunton.

Druitt, Michael & Druitt, Montague. John F. Kennedy, Jr. A Life in the Spotlight. rev. ed. LC 96-6271. (Illus.). 128p. (Orig.). 1996. pap. 14.95 (*0-8362-1513-3*) Andrews & McMeel.

Druitt, Montague, jt. auth. see Druitt, Michael.

D'Ruiz, Carl D. Aqueous Cleaning As an Alternative to CFC & Chlorinated Solvent-Based Cleaning. LC 91-12464. (Illus.). 119p. 1991. 98.00 (*0-8155-1285-6*) Noyes.

Druk, V., jt. auth. see Balanshi, P.

Drukarev, Gregorii F., ed. Collisions of Electrons with Atoms & Molecules. Burke, P. G., tr. from RUS. LC 85-1699. (Physics of Atoms & Molecules Ser.). (Illus.). 252p. (C). 1987. text 102.00 (*0-306-42099-6*, Kluwer Plenum) Kluwer Academic.

Druke, Mary, ed. Iroquois Indians: A Documentary History-Guide to the Mircofilm Collection. LC 85-175112. 718p. 1985. lib. bdg. 425.00 (*0-89235-088-1*) Primary Srce Media.

Druker, Jan & White, Geoff. Managing People in Construction. 272p. 1996. pap. 64.00 (*0-85292-642-1*, Pub. by IPM Hse) St Mut.

***Druker, Paul.** Comprehensive Russian-English Dictionary of Computer Terms. (RUS & ENG.). 1999. 35.00 (*0-7695-0074-9*, IEEE Inst Elec) IEEE Comp Soc.

Drukier, Manny. Carved in Stone: Holocaust Years - A Boy's Tale. (Illus.). 264p. 1996. text 35.00 (*0-8020-0832-1*) U of Toronto Pr.

Drukker, jt. auth. see Knuppel, Robert A.

Drukker, A. & Gruskin, A. B., eds. Pediatric Nephrology. (Pediatric & Adolescent Medicine Ser.: Vol. 5). (Illus.). x, 242p. 1994. 238.50 (*3-8055-5835-X*) S Karger.

Drukman, Mason. Wayne Morse: A Political Biography. LC 97-3380. 1997. 35.00 (*0-87595-263-1*) Oregon Hist.

Druks, Herbert. The Failure to Rescue. 1977. 12.95 (*0-8315-0175-8*); pap. 7.95 (*0-8315-0198-7*) Speller.

— Jewish Resistance During the Holocaust. LC 83-14. 132p. 1983. pap. text 12.95 (*0-8290-1295-8*) Irvington.

— Truman & the Russians. 1981. pap. 12.50 (*0-8315-0183-9*) Speller.

***Druks, Herbert.** The Uncertain Friendship: The U. S. & Israel from Roosevelt to Kennedy, 80. (Contributions to the Study of World History Ser.: Vol. 80). 2000. write for info. (*0-313-31423-3*, Greenwood Pr) Greenwood.

Druks, Herbert, jt. ed. see Rose, Paul L.

Druks, Herbert J. U. S. & Israel, 1945-1986: A Diplomatic History. 2000. 15.00 (*0-8315-0193-6*) Speller.

***Druks, Judit.** Object & Action Naming Battery. 1999. pap. text. write for info. (*0-86377-888-7*) L Erlbaum Assocs.

Drukteinis, Albert M. The Psychology of Back Pain: A Clinical & Legal Handbook. (American Behavioral Science & Law Ser.). (Illus.). 208p. (C). 1996. text 41.95 (*0-398-06559-4*); pap. text 26.95 (*0-398-06560-8*) C C Thomas.

Druley, Ray M., jt. auth. see Cohen, Annette R.

Druliner, jt. auth. see Halio.

Drullinsky, Rafael. Lariega y el Labrador. Slusa Staff, ed. (SPA.). 72p. (Orig.). 1985. pap. 9.00 (*0-917129-01-6*) SLUSA.

Drulovic, Milojko. Self-Management on Trial: Yugoslavia's Attempt to Establish a Society. 346p. 1978. 44.50 (*0-85124-231-6*, Pub. by Spkesman) Coronet Bks.

Drum. Database Applications. (DF - Computer Applications Ser.). (C). 1987. mass mkt. 15.95 (*0-538-10037-0*) S-W Pub.

— Database Applications. 2nd ed. (DF - Computer Applications Ser.). 1989. mass mkt. 16.95 (*0-538-60228-7*) S-W Pub.

— Database Applications Reinforcement. 3rd ed. (DF - Computer Applications Ser.). 83.95 (*0-538-63258-5*) S-W Pub.

— Database Applications Reinforcement. 3rd ed. (DF - Computer Applications Ser.). 1994. mass mkt. 27.95 (*0-538-63255-0*) S-W Pub.

— Excel 4.0 for Mac: Tutorial & Applications. (DF - Computer Applications Ser.). 1994. mass mkt. 30.95 (*0-538-62274-1*) S-W Pub.

— Excel 4.0 for Windows: Tutorial & Applications. (DF - Computer Applications Ser.). 1994. mass mkt. 30.95 (*0-538-62275-X*) S-W Pub.

— Multimedia & Presentations Graphics Project Guide. (DF - Computer Applications Ser.). 1997. mass mkt. 13.95 (*0-538-71785-8*) S-W Pub.

Drum & Spear Collective Staff. Children of Africa: A Coloring Book. LC 92-63013. (Illus.). 24p. (J). (ps-3). 1993. reprint ed. pap. 5.95 (*0-88378-076-3*) Third World.

Drum, Alice & Kneedler, Richard. Funding a College Education: Finding the Right School for Your Child & the Right Fit for Your Budget. 256p. (C). 1996. 14.95 (*0-87584-628-9*) Harvard Busn.

Drum, B., ed. Colour Vision Deficiencies, No. 11: Proceedings of the Eleventh International Symposium, Sydney, Australia, 21-23 June 1991. LC 92-23627. (Documenta Ophthalmologica Proceedings Ser.: Vol. 56). (C). 1993. text 313.00 (*0-7923-1864-1*) Kluwer Academic.

Drum, B., et al, eds. Colour Vision Deficiencies Ten. (Documenta Ophthalmologica Proceedings Ser.). (C). 1991. text 375.00 (*0-7923-0948-0*) Kluwer Academic.

— Colour Vision Deficiencies Twelve: Proceedings of the Twelfth Symposium of the International Research Group on Colour Vision Deficiencies, Vol. XII, No. 57. LC 94-13946. (Documenta Ophthalmologica Proceedings Ser.: Vol. 57). 572p. (C). 1995. text 257.50 (*0-7923-2889-2*) Kluwer Academic.

Drum, B. & Verriest, Guy, eds. Colour Vision Deficiencies, IX. (Documenta Ophthalmologica Proceedings Ser.). (C). 1988. text 380.00 (*0-89838-403-6*) Kluwer Academic.

Drum, Dale D., jt. auth. see Drum, Jean.

Drum, David. Chronic Pain Management Sourcebook. LC 99-21948. 368p. 1999. pap. 18.95 (*0-7373-0101-5*, 01015W) NTC Contemp Pub Co.

— Making the Chemotherapy Decision. 288p. 1996. 27.00 (*1-56565-445-5*) Lowell Hse.

***Drum, David.** Making the Chemotherapy Decision. 3rd ed. 352p. 2000. pap. 16.95 (*0-7373-0383-2*, 03832W, Pub. by Lowell Hse) NTC Contemp Pub Co.

Drum, David & Zierenberg, Terry. The Type II Diabetes Sourcebook. 352p. 1998. pap. 16.00 (*1-56565-862-0*, 08620W, Pub. by Lowell Hse) NTC Contemp Pub Co.

Drum, David J. & Figler, Howard E. Outreach in Counseling: Applying the Growth & Prevention Model in Schools & Colleges. LC 77-8091. 242p. 1976. reprint ed. pap. 8.50 (*0-910328-11-0*) Sulzburger & Graham Pub.

Drum, Jan, et al. Global Winners: Seventy-Four Learning Activities for Inside & Outside the Classroom. LC 94-1404. (Illus.). 229p. (Orig.). 1994. pap. 16.95 (*1-877864-18-8*) Intercult Pr.

***Drum, Jean & Drum, Dale D.** My Only Great Passion: The Life & Films of Carl the Dreyer. LC 99-86373. (Filmmakers Ser.). 320p. 2000. 45.00 (*0-8108-3679-3*) Scarecrow.

D

An Asterisk (*) at the beginning of an entry indicates that the title is appearing for the first time.

Drum, Jonathan, et al. Top Executive Compensation in 1995. (Report Ser.: No. 1170-96-RR). (Illus.). 94p. (Orig.). 1996. pap. text 120.00 (0-8237-0619-2) Conference Bd.

Drum, Karl. Airpower & Russian Partisan Warfare. LC 68-22553. (German Air Force in World War 2 Ser.). (Illus.). 1968. reprint ed. 16.95 (0-405-00041-3) Ayer.

Drum, Ronald A. American Solutions Without Sacrifice: An End to Special Interests - A Return to the Interests of America's Middle-Class. rev. ed. LC 96-93009. 504p. (Orig.). 1997. pap. 17.95 (0-9654025-2-5) Pitbull Pr.

Drum, Sue & Whitely, H. Ellen. Women in Veterinary Medicine: Profiles of Success. LC 91-7050. (Illus.). 286p. 1991. pap. 24.95 (0-8138-0667-4) Iowa St U Pr.

Drum, William O. Using dBase for Database Applications. 1992. mass mkt. 27.95 (0-538-61589-3) S-W Pub.

Drum, William O., jt. auth. see Clark, James F.

Drumann, W. Geschichte Roms, 6 vols. in 2. xxxix, 3904p. 1964. reprint ed. write for info. (0-318-71114-1) G Olms Pubs.

Drumbeat Publishing Staff. Bush Toads. Date not set. pap. text. write for info. (0-582-78567-7, Drumbeat) Longman.

— Bushtrackers. Date not set. pap. text. write for info. (0-582-78525-1, Drumbeat) Longman.

— Cowrie Tears. Date not set. pap. text. write for info. (0-582-78566-9, Drumbeat) Longman.

— Laughing Shadows. Date not set. pap. text. write for info. (0-582-78574-X, Drumbeat) Longman.

— Mocking Stones. Date not set. pap. text. write for info. (0-582-78568-5, Pub. by Addison-Wesley) Longman.

— No Second Chance. Date not set. pap. text. write for info. (0-582-78578-2, Drumbeat) Longman.

— Nothing Is Impossible. Date not set. pap. text. write for info. (0-582-78570-7, Pub. by Addison-Wesley) Longman.

— Southern Circle. Date not set. pap. text. write for info. (0-582-78520-0, Drumbeat) Longman.

— Stillborn. Date not set. pap. text. write for info. (0-582-78600-2, Pub. by Addison-Wesley) Longman.

— Thought Tracks. Date not set. pap. text. write for info. (0-582-78560-X, Pub. by Addison-Wesley) Longman.

— The Whirlwind. Date not set. pap. text. write for info. (0-582-78543-X, Drumbeat) Longman.

Drumheller, D. S. Introduction to Wave Propagation in Nonlinear Fluids & Solids. LC 97-3266. (Illus.). 536p. (C). 1998. text 110.00 (0-521-58313-6); pap. text 49.95 (0-521-58746-8) Cambridge U Pr.

Drumheller, D. S., jt. auth. see Bedford, A.

Drumheller, Dan. Uncle Dan Drumheller Tells Thrills of Western Trails in 1854. 123p. 1985. 14.95 (0-87770-366-3) Ye Galleon.

Drumheller, Sidney J. Handbook of Curriculum Design for Individualized Instruction: A Systems Approach (How to Develop Curriculum Materials from Rigorously Defined Behavioral Objectives). LC 79-122812. 116p. 1971. pap. 37.95 (0-87778-004-8) Educ Tech Pubns.

— Teacher's Handbook for a Functional Behavior-Based Curriculum: Communicable Models & Guides for Classroom Use. LC 72-933. 138p. 1972. pap. 24.95 (0-87778-036-6) Educ Tech Pubns.

Drumm, Chris, compiled by. An Algis Budrys Checklist. (Booklet Ser.: No. 5). 16p. (Orig.). 1983. pap. 0.75 (0-936055-03-0) C Drumm Bks.

— A James Gunn Checklist. (Booklet Ser.: No. 16). 27p. (Orig.). 1984. pap. 1.25 (0-936055-13-8) C Drumm Bks.

— A Larry Niven Checklist. (Booklet Ser.: No. 10). 24p. (Orig.). 1983. pap. 1.00 (0-936055-07-3) C Drumm Bks.

— A Tom Disch Checklist. (Booklet Ser.: No. 4). 24p. 1983. pap. 1.00 (0-936055-02-2) C Drumm Bks.

Drumm, Russell. In the Slick of the Cricket: A Shark Odyssey. LC 98-198244. 352p. 1998. pap. 13.95 (0-14-027435-9) Viking Penguin.

— In the Slick of the Cricket: The Real Story of the "Jaws" Captain. LC 98-198244. (Editor's Book Award Ser.: No. 16). (Illus.). 315p. 1997. 25.00 (1-888889-05-5, Pub. by Pushcart Pr) Norton.

Drumm, Stella M., ed. see Magoffin, Susan S.

Drumm, Susan T. Study Skills Grades 5-8. Pedigo, Patricia & DeSanti, Roger, eds. (Kelley Wingate Ser.). 132p. (J). (gr. 5-8). 1996. pap. text 10.95 (0-88724-448-3, CD-3730) Carson-Dellos.

— Study Skills Grades 2-4. Pedigo, Patricia & DeSanti, Roger, eds. (Kelley Wingate Ser.). 140p. (J). (gr. 2-4). 1996. pap. text 10.95 (0-88724-447-5, CD-3729) Carson-Dellos.

Drumm, Walter. The Old Palace: The Catholic Chaplaincy at Oxford. 272p. 1989. pap. 40.00 (1-85390-192-X, Pub. by Veritas Pubns) St Mut.

Drummey, James J. Catholic Replies. 464p. (Orig.). 1995. pap. 17.95 (0-9649087-0-0) C R Publns.

Drummond. Dimensions of Hospital Industry Student Workbook. 1993. pap. 22.95 (0-442-01473-2, VNR) Wiley.

***Drummond.** Nutrition for Foodservice & Culinary Professionals. 4th ed. 656p. 2000. text 59.95 (0-471-34777-9) Wiley.

Drummond. Nutrition for the Foodservice Profession. 2nd ed. (Hospitality, Travel & Tourism Ser.). 1996. pap., teacher ed. write for info. (0-442-01866-5, VNR) Wiley.

— Nutrition for the Foodservice Professional. (Hospitality, Travel & Tourism Ser.). 1997. pap. write for info. (0-442-02474-6, VNR) Wiley.

— Purchasing & Provide Costs. (C). 1994. pap. text 33.50 (0-443-04946-7, W B Saunders Co) Harcrt Hlth Sci Grp.

Drummond, jt. auth. see Drillien.

Drummond, A. Research Methods for Therapists. (Illus.). 176p. (Orig.). 1996. pap. 47.75 (1-56593-207-2, 0521) Singular Publishing.

Drummond, A. L. A Curious Thievery at the Philadelphia Mint: A Tale from the 1890's. Bowers, Q. David, ed. (Bowers & Merena Galleries' Little Editions Ser.). (Illus.). 16p. 1997. pap. 5.95 (0-943161-72-X) Bowers & Merena.

Drummond, Alexander A. Enos Mills: Citizens of Nature. (Illus.). 384p. 1995. 34.95 (0-87081-407-9) Univ Pr Colo.

Drummond, Alfreda L. A. Hands of a Teacher: The Alfreda Drummond Story, Vol. 1. (Illus.). 168p. 1997. 14.95 (0-9643374-7-9) Pubng Connect.

Drummond, Allan. Casey Jones. LC 99-22385. (J). 2000. 16.00 (0-374-31175-7) FS&G.

— The Willow Pattern Story. LC 91-56239. (Illus.). 64p. (J). (gr. k-3). 1995. pap. 5.95 (1-55858-413-7, Pub. by North-South Bks NYC) Chronicle Bks.

Drummond, Allan. The Willow Pattern Story. 1995. 11.15 (0-606-08909-8, Pub. by Turtleback) Demco.

Drummond, Andrew L. & Bulloch, James. The Church in Late Victorian Scotland, 1874-1900. 352p. (C). 1988. text 80.00 (0-7152-0371-1) St Mut.

Drummond, Anthony, ed. see Schleit, Phillip.

Drummond, Anthony, ed. see Weeks, Christopher.

Drummond, Archie & Coles-Mogford, Anne. Applied Typing & Information Processing. 6th ed. 230p. (Orig.). 1994. pap. 49.50 (0-7487-1897-4, Pub. by S Thornes Pubs) Trans-Atl Phila.

— First Course-Keyboarding & Document Processing. 6th ed. 192p. 1995. pap. 32.50 (0-7487-2586-5, Pub. by S Thornes Pubs) Trans-Atl Phila.

— Typing: Two-in-One - Keyboarding & Document Processing. 3rd ed. 208p. 1996. pap. 32.50 (0-7487-2437-0, Pub. by S Thornes Pubs) Trans-Atl Phila.

Drummond, Archie & Coles-Mogford, Anne M. First Course: Keyboarding & Document Processing. 6th rev. ed. LC 92-30930. Orig. Title: Typing, First Course. 1993. write for info. (0-07-707605-2) McGraw.

— First Course Handbook, Solutions, & Resource Material. 6th ed. LC 93-12144. 1993. 35.00 (0-07-707612-5) McGraw.

Drummond, Betty. The Spiritual Woman: 10 Steps to Spirituality in a Demanding World. LC 99-18858. 1999. pap. 14.99 (0-8254-2469-0) Kregel.

Drummond, Betty, jt. auth. see Drummond, Lewis.

Drummond, Bill. Bad Wisdom. 288p. 1996. pap. 13.95 (0-14-026118-4, Pub. by Pnguin Bks Ltd) Trafalgar.

— How to Have a Number One the Easy Way Manual. 1999. pap. 15.00 (1-899858-65-2, Pub. by Ellipsis) Norton.

Drummond, Carl. Foundations in Earth Science: Adventures in Nature & Mathematics. 156p. (C). 1998. per. 25.95 (0-7872-5154-2) Kendall-Hunt.

Drummond, Connie M. The Power of Faith: A Mother's Prayers for Her Dying Son. Sample Enterprises, Inc., ed. & illus. by. 34p. 1997. mass mkt. 8.98 (1-930384-13-0, BB-42003) Sample Enter.

Drummond, D. A., et al. Dictionary of Russian Obscenities. (ENG & RUS.). 79p. (Orig.). 1980. pap. 12.95 (0-8288-1229-2, M14269) Fr & Eur.

Drummond, D. Colin, et al, eds. Addictive Behaviour: Cue Exposure Theory & Practice. LC 94-23956. 268p. 1995. 155.00 (0-471-94454-8) Wiley.

Drummond, David A. & Perkins, G. Dictionary of Russian Obscenities. (ENG & RUS.). 92p. (Orig.). 1987. pap. 5.95 (0-933884-54-0) Berkeley Slavic.

Drummond, Diane. Crewe: Railway Town, Company & People, 1840-1914. (Illus.). 224p. 1991. text 59.00 (0-7185-1382-7) St Martin.

Drummond, Diane K. Crewe: Railway Town, Company & People, 1840-1914. LC 94-14921. (Illus.). 273p. 1995. 86.95 (1-85928-020-X, Pub. by Scolar Pr) Ashgate Pub Co.

Drummond, Donald F. Passing of American Neutrality, 1937-1941, Vol. 20--20. LC 68-54416. (Illus.). 409p. 1969. reprint ed. lib. bdg. 35.00 (0-8371-0394-0, DRAN, Greenwood Pr) Greenwood.

Drummond, Edward H. Benzo Blues: A Groundbreaking Program for Overcoming Anxiety Without Tranquilizers. 320p. 1998. pap. 13.95 (0-452-27826-0, Plume) Dutton Plume.

***Drummond, Edward H.** The Complete Guide to Psychiatric Drugs: Straight Talk for Best Results. LC 99-50236. 352p. 2000. pap. 16.95 (0-471-35370-1) Wiley.

Drummond, Emma. Act of Valour. LC 98-14845. 1998. text 25.95 (0-312-18521-9) St Martin.

— The Burning Land. large type ed. 624p. 1987. 17.95 (0-7089-8379-0, Charnwood) Ulverscroft.

— A Question of Honour. large type ed. (Charnwood Large Print Ser.). 656p. 1995. 27.99 (0-7089-8834-2, Charnwood) Ulverscroft.

Drummond, Frederick A. The Power Manual: The Revival of Praise & Worship in the Church. (Illus.). 216p. (C). 1994. student ed., ring bd. 30.00 (1-885042-00-0) ESCA Triumphant.

Drummond, Gary, jt. auth. see Garofalo, Gene.

Drummond, George I. Cyclic Nucleotides in the Nervous System. LC 84-40127. 135p. 1984. reprint ed. pap. 41.90 (0-7837-9567-X, 206031600005) Bks Demand.

Drummond, George I., et al, eds. Advances in Cyclic Nucleotide Research: Second International Conference on Cyclic AMP, Vancouver, British Columbia, Canada, July 8-11, 1974, Vol. 5. fac. ed. LC 71-181305. (Illus.). 886p. pap. 200.00 (0-7837-7240-8, 204706200005) Bks Demand.

***Drummond, Glenn, ed.** The Heritage of Macon County, Alabama. (Heritage of Alabama Ser.: Vol. 44). 320p. 2001. 50.00 (1-891647-57-1) Herit Pub Consult.

Drummond, Graeme & Ensor, John. Strategic Marketing: Planning & Control. 176p. 1999. pap. text 34.95 (0-7506-4482-6) Buttrwrth-Heinemann.

Drummond, H. Evan, ed. see Grozinger, Jim & Thompson, Brian.

Drummond, H. Evan, ed. see Purcell, Wayne.

Drummond, H. J., compiled by. A Short-Title Catalogue of Books Printed on the Continent of Europe, Fifteen Hundred to Sixteen Hundred, in Aberdeen University Library. 1980. text 72.00 (0-19-714106-4) OUP.

Drummond, Harold P. Jurisprudence & Confidentiality: Index of Modern Information. rev. ed. LC 88-47586. 150p. 1991. 47.50 (1-55914-464-5); pap. 44.50 (1-55914-465-3) ABBE Pubs Assn.

— Psychology of Attempted Suicide: A Medical Subject Analysis with Reference Bibliography. rev. ed. 163p. (Orig.). 1992. 47.50 (1-55914-952-3); pap. 44.50 (1-55914-953-1) ABBE Pubs Assn.

— Schizophrenia: Medical & Psychological Subject Index with Bibliography. LC 87-31833. 150p. 1987. 47.50 (0-88164-496-X); pap. 44.50 (0-88164-497-8) ABBE Pubs Assn.

— Schizophrenic Psychology: Index of New Information with Authors, Subjects & Bibliography. 180p. 1993. 47.50 (1-55914-810-1); pap. 44.50 (1-55914-811-X) ABBE Pubs Assn.

— Sex & Prostitution: Index of Modern Information. LC 88-47978. 150p. 1990. 47.50 (1-55914-182-4); pap. 44.50 (1-55914-183-2) ABBE Pubs Assn.

— Sex Offenses: Medical & Psychological Subject Analysis with Research Index & Bibliography. LC 84-45994. 150p. 1987. 47.50 (0-88164-310-6); pap. 44.50 (0-88164-311-4) ABBE Pubs Assn.

— Sexology Encyclopedia Vol. 4: Sex Offenses: Index & Reference Books of New Information. Bartone, John C., ed. (Illus.). 157p. 1996. pap. 39.95 (0-7883-0857-2) ABBE Pubs Assn.

— Sexology Encyclopedia Vol. 4: Sex Offenses: Index & Reference Books of New Information, 25 vols., Set. Bartone, John C., ed. (Illus.). 157p. 1996. 49.95 (0-7883-0856-4) ABBE Pubs Assn.

— Sexual Deviations & Paraphilias: Medical Analysis Index with Research Bibliography. LC 85-47570. 150p. 1987. 47.50 (0-88164-314-9); pap. 44.50 (0-88164-315-7) ABBE Pubs Assn.

Drummond, Helga. Escalation in Decision-Making: The Tragedy of Taurus. LC 96-21020. (Illus.). 286p. 1997. text 60.00 (0-19-828953-7) OUP.

— Power & Involvement in Organizations: An Empirical Examination of Etzioni's Compliance Theory. 247p. 1993. 72.95 (1-85628-474-3, Pub. by Avebry) Ashgate Pub Co.

— The Quality Movement: What Total Quality Management Is Really All About. 128p. (C). 1992. pap. 14.95 (0-89397-383-1) Nichols Pub.

Drummond, Helga, tr. see Spuler, Bertold.

Drummond, Henry. Addresses. 375p. 1998. reprint ed. pap. 24.95 (0-7661-0521-0) Kessinger Pub.

— The Greatest Thing in the World. 64p. 1994. pap. 6.95 (0-87516-675-X) DeVorss.

— The Greatest Thing in the World. 1987. 8.95 (0-933062-21-4) R H Sommer.

— The Greatest Thing in the World. 64p. (gr. 11). 1983. mass mkt. 3.99 (0-8007-8018-3, Spire) Revell.

— The Greatest Thing in the World. 61p. 1981. mass mkt. 4.99 (0-88368-100-5) Whitaker Hse.

— The Greatest Thing in the World. 160p. 1988. 7.99 (0-529-05911-8, F4) World Publng.

— The Greatest Thing in the World: And Other Essays. 176p. 1997. pap. 9.99 (0-86347-221-4, Pub. by Eagle Bks) Shaw Pubs.

— The Greatest Thing in the World: Love. 64p. 1994. 5.97 (1-55748-547-X) Barbour Pub.

— The Greatest Thing in the World... Love. rev. ed. Chadwick, Harold J., ed. LC 98-74680. 100p. 1999. pap. 9.99 (0-88270-763-9, Bridge) Bridge-Logos.

— The Greatest Thing in the World (1888) 42p. 1998. reprint ed. pap. 3.75 (0-7661-0181-9) Kessinger Pub.

— Natural Law in the Spiritual World. 371p. 1981. pap. 32.00 (0-89540-082-0, SB-082) Sun Pub.

Drummond, Henry, jt. auth. see Drummond, Lewis A.

***Drummond, Ian & Marsden, Terry.** The Condition of Sustainability. LC 98-24232. (Research Global Environmental Change Ser.). 242p. 1999. 85.00 (0-415-19493-8) Routledge.

Drummond, Ian M. Progress Without Planning: The Economic History of Ontario from Confederation to the Second World War. (Ontario Historical Studies). 525p. 1987. pap. 19.95 (0-8020-6661-5); text 45.00 (0-8020-2614-1) U of Toronto Pr.

Drummond, Ian M. & Hillmer, Norman. Negotiating Freer Trade: The United Kingdom, the United States, Canada & the Trade Agreements of 1938. (Illus.). 200p. (C). 1989. text 35.00 (0-88920-970-7) W Laurier U Pr.

Drummond, Inez B., ed. see Paris, Lance K.

Drummond, Isobel. Spitze. 1989. pap. text 15.28 (0-582-33206-0, 72075); audio 22.61 (0-582-33207-9, 72076) Longman.

Drummond, J., ed. Onward & Upward: Extracts from the Magazine of the Onward & Upward Association Founded by Lady Aberdeen for the Material, Mental & Moral Elevation of Women. 1983. pap. text 3.80 (0-08-030354-4, Pergamon Pr) Elsevier.

Drummond, James. Via, Veritas, Vita: Lectures on "Christianity in Its Most Simple & Intelligible Form" 2nd ed. LC 77-27160. (Hibbert Lectures: 1894). reprint ed. 31.50 (0-404-60412-9) AMS Pr.

Drummond, James, ed. Upstairs to Downstairs: Advice to Servant Girls & Weary Mothers. (SWSS Ser.). 96p. 1991. pap. text 7.90 (0-08-041204-1, Pub. by Aberdeen U Pr) Macmillan.

Drummond, Jocelyn. The Essentials of Horsemanship. 112p. 1998. 19.95 (0-87605-669-9) Howell Bks.

Drummond, John. Managing Business Ethics. Bain, Bill, ed. 1994. pap. text 46.95 (0-7506-0663-0) Buttrwrth-Heinemann.

— Memoirs of Sir Ewen Cameron. Macknight, James, ed. LC 72-983. (Maitland Club, Glasgow. Publications: No. 59). reprint ed. 65.00 (0-404-53049-4) AMS Pr.

— Speaking of Diaghilev. (Illus.). 384p. 1999. pap. 20.00 (0-571-19549-0, Pub. by Faber & Faber) Penguin Books.

— Thirty Years in the Trenches Covering Crooks, Characters & Capers. LC 99-179141. (Illus.). 250p. 1998. pap. 14.95 (1-886094-77-2) Chicago Spectrum.

Drummond, John & Bain, Bill, eds. Managing Business Ethics: A Reader on Business Ethics for Managers & Students. LC 94-150795. (Management Readers Ser.). (Illus.). 223p. reprint ed. pap. 69.20 (0-608-07420-9, 206764700009) Bks Demand.

Drummond, John J. Husserlian Intentionality & Non-Foundational Realism: Noema & Object. (Contributions to Phenomenology Ser.: No. 4). 308p. (C). 1990. lib. bdg. 166.50 (0-7923-0651-1, Pub. by Kluwer Academic) Kluwer Academic.

Drummond, John J. & Embree, Lester, eds. The Phenomenology of the Noema. LC 92-30372. (Contributions to Phenomenology Ser.: Vol. 10). 264p. (C). 1992. lib. bdg. 138.00 (0-7923-1980-X, Pub. by Kluwer Academic) Kluwer Academic.

Drummond, John J., ed. see Sokolowski, Robert & Hart, James G.

Drummond, Josiah. Joshua Bean of Exeter, Brentwood & Gilmanton, N. H., & Some of His Descendants. 116p. 1988. reprint ed. pap. 20.50 (0-8328-0213-1); reprint ed. lib. bdg. 28.50 (0-8328-0212-3) Higginson Bk Co.

Drummond, Josiah H. Drummond: Descendants of Alexander Drummond of Georgetown ME, Including Those by the Name of Campbell, Chamberlain, Crane, Morse, Eves, Grace, Keith, Marshall, Rogers & Williams. (Illus.). 171p. 1997. reprint ed. pap. 25.00 (0-8328-8358-1); reprint ed. lib. bdg. 35.00 (0-8328-8357-3) Higginson Bk Co.

Drummond, June. Burden of Guilt. 192p. 1991. 23.95 (0-575-05149-3, Pub. by V Gollancz) Trafalgar.

— Burden of Guilt. large type ed. (Dales Large Print Ser.). 1994. pap. 18.99 (1-85389-481-8, Pub. by Mgna Lrg Print) Ulverscroft.

— Hidden Agenda. large type ed. (Dales Large Print Ser.). 1994. pap. 18.99 (1-85389-515-6, Pub. by Mgna Lrg Print) Ulverscroft.

— The Impostor. 224p. 1994. mass mkt. 3.99 (0-380-72358-1, Avon Bks) Morrow Avon.

— The Impostor. large type ed. 480p. 1994. 27.99 (0-7089-3074-3) Ulverscroft.

Drummond, Karen A. The Restaurant Training Program: An Employee Training Guide for Managers. LC 92-47. 432p. 1992. pap. 90.00 (0-471-55207-0) Wiley.

Drummond, Karen E. Developing & Conducting Training for Foodservice Employees: A Guide for Trainers. LC 92-19567. 1992. student ed. 25.00 incl. audio (0-88091-102-6) Am Dietetic Assn.

— Dictionary Nutrition Dietetics. (Culinary Arts Ser.). 391p. 1996. 49.95 (0-471-29370-9, VNR) Wiley.

Drummond, Karen E. Human Resource Management for Hospitality. 1990. text 55.95 (0-442-31859-6, VNR) Wiley.

Drummond, Karen E. Human Resource Management for the Hospitality Industry. 368p. 1990. 64.95 (0-471-28972-8, VNR) Wiley.

Drummond, Karen E. Retaining Your Foodservice Employees: 40 Ways to Better Employee Relations. 224p. 1991. pap. 44.95 (0-471-29062-9, VNR) Wiley.

Drummond, Karen E., et al. The Cook's Healthy Handbook: Good Nutrition & Safety in Your Kitchen. LC 92-21833. 320p. 1992. 32.95 (0-471-55608-4) Wiley.

Drummond, Karen E., jt. auth. see D'Amico, J.

Drummond, Karen E., jt. auth. see D'Amico, Joan.

Drummond, Karen E., jt. auth. see Miller, Jack E.

Drummond, Lee. American Dreamtime: A Cultural Analysis of Popular Movies & Their Implications for a Science of Humanity. 344p. (C). 1995. pap. text 24.95 (0-8226-3047-8); lib. bdg. 62.50 (0-8226-3046-X) Littlefield.

Drummond, Lewis & Drummond, Betty. Women of Awakenings: The Historic Contribution of Women to Revival Movements. 368p. 1997. pap. 15.99 (0-8254-2474-7) Kregel.

Drummond, Lewis A. Miss Bertha: Woman of Revival. 304p. 1996. 12.99 (0-8054-1164-X, 4211-64) Broadman.

— Ripe for Harvest: The Role of Spiritual Awakening in Church Growth. 2001. pap. 22.99 (0-8054-1656-0) Broadman.

— Spurgeon: The Prince of Preachers. LC 92-15242. (Illus.). 208p. 1992. 29.99 (0-8254-2472-0) Kregel.

Drummond, Lewis A. & Drummond, Henry. Love: The Greatest Thing in the World : A Classic Devotional Study On 1 Corinthians 13. rev. ed. LC 97-30340. 208p. 1998. pap. 6.99 (0-8254-2470-4) Kregel.

Drummond, Lorena, ed. see Texas University Staff.

Drummond, Lynne M., jt. auth. see Stern, Richard.

Drummond, M., tr. see Haberlandt, G.

Drummond, Maggie. Investor's Handbook: Proshare's No-Nonsense Guide to Sensible Investing. 1998. pap. text 16.95 (0-7134-8481-0, Pub. by B T B) Branford.

Drummond, Marcy. Horse Care & Stable Management. (Illus.). 160p. 1992. 34.95 (1-85223-712-0, Pub. by Cro1wood) Trafalgar.

— Horse Management. (Crowood Equestrian Guides Ser.). (Illus.). 96p. 1992. pap. 17.95 (1-85223-492-X, Pub. by Cro1wood) Trafalgar.

Drummond, Margaret, jt. auth. see Drillien, Cecil M.

D

An Asterisk (*) at the beginning of an entry indicates that the title is appearing for the first time.

Drummond, Mark, et al, eds. Practical Approaches to Scheduling & Planning: Papers from the 1992 Spring Symposium. (Technical Reports). (Illus.). 164p. (Orig.). 1993. spiral bd. 25.00 (*0-929280-32-6*) AAAI Pr.

***Drummond, Mary-Ellen.** A Woman's Way: Inspirational Advice & Real-Life Lessons from 34 Prominent Business Women. 352p. 2000. 24.95 (*1-58062-469-3*) Adams Media.

Drummond, Mary J. Assessing Children's Learning. (Primary Curriculum Ser.). 160p. 1993. pap. 26.00 (*1-85346-198-9*, Pub. by David Fulton) Taylor & Francis.

— Learning to See: Assessment Through Observation. LC 94-3581. (Illus.). 208p. (C). 1994. pap. text 18.00 (*1-57110-004-0*) Stenhse Pubs.

Drummond, Michael. Renegades of the Empire: How Three Software Warriors Started a Revolution Behind the Walls of Fortress Microsoft. LC 99-34657. 304p. 1999. 25.00 (*0-609-60416-3*) Crown Pub Group.

***Drummond, Michael.** Renegades of the Empire: How Three Software Warriors Started a Revolution Behind the Walls of Fortress Microsoft. 320p. 2000. reprint ed. pap. 14.00 (*0-609-80745-5*, Three Riv Pr) Crown Pub Group.

Drummond, Michael F. Studies in Economic Appraisal in Health Care, 2 vols., 1. 224p. 1981. text 39.95 (*0-19-261274-3*) OUP.

— Studies in Economic Appraisal in Health Care, 2 vols., 2. 304p. 1986. text 49.00 (*0-19-261398-7*) OUP.

Drummond, Michael F., et al. Methods for the Economic Evaluation of Health Care Programmes. 2nd ed. LC 97-10273. (Illus.). 316p. 1997. pap. text 42.50 (*0-19-262773-2*) OUP.

Drummond, Montagu, tr. see Haberlandt, G.

***Drummond, Nancy.** Few Laughs, Right God? 2000. pap. 8.99 (*1-930027-03-6*) Insght Pub.

Drummond, Oliver E., ed. Signal & Data Processing of Small Targets. 68p. 1997. pap. 107.00 (*0-8194-2585-0*) SPIE.

— Signal & Data Processing of Small Targets, 1998. (Proceedings of SPIE Ser.: Vol. 3372). 610p. 1998. 116.00 (*0-8194-2822-1*) SPIE.

***Drummond, Peter D.** Quantum Squeezing. 360p. 1999. 79.95 (*3-540-65989-7*) Spr-Verlag.

Drummond, Philip. High Noon. (Film Classics Ser.). (Illus.). 96p. 1998. pap. 10.95 (*0-85170-494-8*, Pub. by British Film Inst) Ind U Pr.

Drummond, R. O., ed. see George, J. E.

Drummond, R. S. Gear Lapping After Heat Treatment. (Technical Papers: Vol. P30). (Illus.). 9p. 1933. pap. text 30.00 (*1-55589-218-3*) AGMA.

— Rotary Crossed Axes Shaving of Spur & Helical Gears. (Technical Papers: Vol. P118). (Illus.). 11p. 1935. pap. text 30.00 (*1-55589-226-4*) AGMA.

— Sound Testing - Noises in Gears Due to the Design, Material, & Manufacture (Not Wear) (Technical Papers: Vol. P173). (Illus.). 14p. 1938. pap. text 30.00 (*1-55589-377-5*) AGMA.

Drummond, Richard H. A Broader Vision: Perspectives on the Buddha & the Christ. Skidmore, Kenneth M., ed. LC 95-19151. 341p. (Orig.). 1995. pap. 16.95 (*0-87604-348-1*, 447) ARE Pr.

— Life of Jesus the Christ: An Edgar Cayce Guide, Vol. 1. 1996. mass mkt. 5.99 (*0-312-96057-3*) St Martin.

— Toward a New Age in Christian Theology. LC 85-5155. (American Society of Missiology Ser.: No. 8). 272p. 1985. reprint ed. pap. 84.40 (*0-7837-9829-6*, 206055800005) Bks Demand.

— Unto the Churches: Jesus Christ, Christianity, & the Edgar Cayce Readings. 206p. 1978. pap. 7.95 (*0-87604-102-0*, 289) ARE Pr.

Drummond, Robert. Healing the Hurts of Resentment. (Christian Living Ser.). 44p. 1991. pap. 3.50 (*0-8341-1385-6*) Beacon Hill.

Drummond, Robert, jt. auth. see Colby, Robert.

***Drummond, Robert J.** Appraisal Procedures for Counselors & Helping Professionals. 4th ed. LC 99-24051. 540p. (C). 1999. 67.00 (*0-13-080590-4*) P-H.

Drummond, Robert J. & Ryan, Charles W. Career Counseling: A Developmental Approach. LC 94-16162. 544p. (C). 1994. 78.00 (*0-02-330675-0*, Macmillan Coll) P-H.

Drummond, Robert R. Early German Music in Philadelphia. LC 72-1596. reprint ed. 29.50 (*0-404-09917-3*) AMS Pr.

— Early German Music in Philadelphia. LC 74-125068. (Music Ser.). 1970. reprint ed. lib. bdg. 19.50 (*0-306-70005-0*) Da Capo.

Drummond, Roger. Ticks: And What You Can Do about Them. 2nd rev. ed. LC 98-9969. (Illus.). 72p. 1998. pap. 6.95 (*0-89997-222-5*) Wilderness Pr.

Drummond, Sandy, jt. auth. see Rhein, Betsy.

Drummond, Sarah E. The What in the World Are We Going to Have for Dinner? Cookbook. rev. ed. LC 88-82586. (Illus.). 192p. 1989. 11.95 (*0-9621600-0-8*) Essedee Enterprises.

Drummond, Steven K. & Nelson, Lynn H. The Western Frontiers of Imperial Rome. LC 93-3650. 288p. (C). (gr. 13). 1993. text 79.95 (*1-56324-150-1*); pap. text 34.95 (*1-56324-151-X*) M E Sharpe.

Drummond, Steven K., jt. auth. see Nelson, Lynn H.

Drummond, Stuart, tr. see Spuler, Bertold.

Drummond, Susan G. Incorporating the Familiar: An Investigation into Legal Sensibilities in Nunavik. LC 98-175068. 200p. 1997. text 39.95 (*0-7735-1671-9*, Pub. by McG-Queens Univ Pr) CUP Services.

Drummond, W. Poetical Works of William Drummond of Hawthornden, 2 Vols. Kastner, L. E., ed. LC 68-24906. (Studies in Poetry: No. 38). 1969. reprint ed. lib. bdg. 150.00 (*0-8383-0157-6*) M S G Haskell Hse.

Drummond, William. Academical Questions. LC 84-13925. 448p. 1985. reprint ed. 75.00 (*0-8201-1398-0*) Schol Facsimiles.

— Forth Feasting: A Panegyricke to the Kings Most Excellent Majestie. LC 79-25570. (English Experience Ser.: No. 138). 16p. 1969. reprint ed. 10.00 (*90-221-0138-X*) Walter J Johnson.

— Philosophical Sketches of the Principles of Society & Government. LC 86-17791. 192p. 1986. reprint ed. 50.00 (*0-8201-1418-9*) Schol Facsimiles.

— Poems. Maitland, Thomas, ed. LC 77-144419. (Maitland Club, Glasgow. Publications: No. 18). reprint ed. 67.50 (*0-404-52956-9*) AMS Pr.

— Poems. LC 76-6156. (English Experience Ser.: No. 83). 128p. 1969. reprint ed. 20.00 (*90-221-0083-9*) Walter J Johnson.

— The Poetical Works of William Drummond of Hawthornden, with "A Cypresse Grove" (BCL1-PR English Literature Ser.: 2 vols.). 1992. reprint ed. lib. bdg. 150.00 (*0-7812-7206-8*) Rprt Serv.

— The Works. (Anglistica & Americana Ser.: No. 60). xlviii, 303p. 1970. reprint ed. 76.70 (*0-685-66461-9*, 05102701) G Olms Pubs.

Drumtra, Stacy. Face-off. 128p. (Orig.). (YA). 1992. pap. 3.50 (*0-380-76863-1*, Avon Bks) Morrow Avon.

Druon, jt. auth. see Tistou.

Drury. Costing: An Introduction OHP Masters. 3rd ed. (Illus.). 150p. (Orig.). (C). (gr. 13). 1994. pap. text 48.00 (*0-412-58790-4*, Chap & Hall NY) Chapman & Hall.

***Drury.** Costing: An Introduction OHP Masters. 4th ed. (ITBP Textbooks Ser.). (Orig.). 1998. pap. write for info. (*1-86152-276-2*, Pub. by ITBP) Thomson Learn.

— Management & Cost Accounting. 4th rev. ed. (ITBP Textbooks Ser.). 1996. pap., student ed. 15.99 (*1-86152-510-9*) Thomson Learn.

— Mauch Chunk/Jim Thorpe. (Images of America Ser.). 128p. 1999. pap. 18.99 (*0-7524-1325-2*) Arcadia Publng.

Drury. Standard Costing. 1998. pap. 24.95 (*1-86152-433-1*) Thomson Learn.

Drury, A. C. & Ferrier, Charles W. Credit Cards. 1984. pap. 36.00 (*0-406-25940-2*, UK, MICHIE) LEXIS Pub.

Drury, A. W. History of the City of Dayton & Montgomery Co., Ohio. (Illus.). 1081p. 1993. reprint ed. lib. bdg. 99.00 (*0-8328-2798-3*); reprint ed. lib. bdg. 95.00 (*0-8328-2797-5*) Higginson Bk Co.

Drury, Allen. Advise & Consent. 1991. lib. bdg. 54.95 (*1-56849-060-7*) Buccaneer Bks.

— Preserve & Protect. large type ed. LC 99-48201. 690p. 1999. 34.95 (*1-56000-471-1*) Transaction Pubs.

Drury, Allen. Public Men: A Novel. LC 98-6729. 384p. 1999. 26.00 (*0-684-80703-3*) S&S Trade.

— A Senate Journal, 1943 to 1955. LC 76-38824. (FDR & the Era of the New Deal Ser.). 1972. reprint ed. lib. bdg. 59.50 (*0-306-70448-X*) Da Capo.

— A Thing of State: A Novel. LC 95-8857. 384p. 1995. 24.00 (*0-684-80702-5*) S&S Trade.

Drury, Aubrey. California, an Intimate Guide. 1992. reprint ed. lib. bdg. 75.00 (*0-7812-5028-5*) Rprt Serv.

***Drury, B. C.** Dreams of Perfection: A Collection of Verse. LC 99-97380. 2000. pap. 7.95 (*0-533-13427-7*) Vantage.

Drury, Beatrice, jt. ed. see Rex, John.

***Drury, Ben, des.** Futura. (Illus.). 176p. 2000. 45.00 (*1-86154-134-1*, Pub. by Booth-Clibborn) Dist Art Pubs.

Drury, Bob, jt. auth. see Donovan, Arthur J., Jr.

Drury, Bob, jt. auth. see Eppolito, Lou.

Drury, Bob, jt. auth. see Jones, Jerry.

Drury, C. Costing: An Introduction. 2nd ed. (Illus.). 160p. (Orig.). (C). (gr. 13). 1992. pap. text, student ed. 19.50 (*0-412-35810-7*) Chapman & Hall.

Drury, C. H. Useful Plants of India. 512p. 1991. pap. 500.00 (*81-7089-155-8*, Pub. by Intl Bk Distr) St Mut.

— The Useful Plants of India. 513p. 1978. reprint ed. 260.00 (*0-7855-6654-6*, Pub. by Intl Bk Distr) St Mut.

Drury, C. H., ed. The Useful Plants of India. 513p. (C). 1978. text 260.00 (*0-89771-600-0*, Pub. by Intl Bk Distr) St Mut.

— The Useful Plants of India. (C). 1988. 75.00 (*0-7855-2267-0*, Pub. by Scientific) St Mut.

Drury, Catherine, jt. auth. see Toth, Margo.

Drury, Chris. Chris Drury. LC 98-33490. (Illus.). 120p. 1998. 49.50 (*0-8109-3246-6*, Pub. by Abrams) Time Warner.

Drury, Clare, ed. see Davies, Douglas J.

Drury, Clifford M. Marcus & Narcissa Whitman & the Opening of Old Oregon. (Illus.). 911p. 1986. reprint ed. pap. 19.95 (*0-914019-08-2*) NW Interpretive.

Drury, Clifford M., ed. On to Oregon: The Diaries of Mary Walker & Myra Eells. LC 97-50202. (Illus.). iv, 382p. 1998. pap. 16.00 (*0-8032-6613-8*, Bison Books) U of Nebr Pr.

— Where Wagons Could Go: Narcissa Whitman & Eliza Spaulding. LC 96-38594. (Illus.). 280p. 1997. pap. 12.00 (*0-8032-6606-5*, Bison Books) U of Nebr Pr.

Drury, Clifford M. & Lewis, Bonnie Sue, intros. The Mountains We Have Crossed: Diaries & Letters of the Oregon Mission, 1838. LC 99-23583. (Illus.). 336p. 1999. pap. 15.00 (*0-8032-6621-9*, Bison Books) U of Nebr Pr.

***Drury, Cohn.** Management & Cost Accounting. 5th ed. (ITBP Textbooks Ser.). 2000. pap., student ed. 39.95 (*1-86152-537-0*) Thomson Learn.

Drury, Colin. Costing: An Introduction. 512p. 1996. mass mkt. 26.95 (*0-412-58780-7*) Chapman & Hall.

— Costing: An Introduction. 2nd ed. 416p. 1990. pap. 30.00 (*0-412-35800-X*, A4881) Chapman & Hall.

— Costing: An Introduction. 3rd ed. (Illus.). 192p. 1996. pap., teacher ed. 63.75 (*0-412-58810-2*) Thomson Learn.

— Management Accounting for Business Decisions. LC 97-21927. 1997. pap. 20.99 (*1-86152-102-2*) Thomson Learn.

— Management & Cost Accounting. 3rd ed. (Illus.) 308p. (C). 1994. pap. text, student ed. 22.00 (*0-412-46400-4*, Chap & Hall NY) Chapman & Hall.

— Management & Cost Accounting. 4th ed. 900p. 1996. pap., student ed. 26.95 (*1-86152-002-6*, Pub. by ITBP) Thomson Learn.

***Drury, Colin.** Management & Cost Accounting. 5th ed. (ITBP Textbooks Ser.). 2000. write for info. (*1-86152-596-6*, Pub. by ITBP); write for info. (*1-86152-597-4*, Pub. by ITBP) Thomson Learn.

— Management & Cost Accounting. 5th ed. (ITBP Textbooks Ser.). 2000. pap. 26.99 (*1-86152-536-2*) Thomson Learn.

Drury, Colin. Standard Costing. (Advanced Management Accounting & Finance Ser.). (Illus.). 198p. 1992. pap. text 19.95 (*0-12-222355-1*) Acad Pr.

Drury, Darrel, jt. auth. see Puma, Michael.

***Drury, Darrel W.** Reinventing School-Based Management: A School Board Guide to School-Based Improvement. 60p. 1999. pap. 20.00 (*0-88364-221-2*) Natl Sch Boards.

Drury, David. Iron Schoolmaster: Education, Employment & the Family in India. 1993. 24.00 (*81-7075-025-3*, Pub. by Hindustan) S Asia.

— Poor Man's Weapon. LC 97-91320. 1998. pap. 11.95 (*0-533-12639-8*) Vantage.

***Drury, E. J., Jr.** Close Eucounters of a Very Special Kind. 420p. 1999. pap. 14.95 (*0-934426-93-7*) NAPSAC Reprods.

Drury, Elizabeth & Lewis, Philippa. The Victorian Garden Album. (Illus.). 128p. 1995. 18.95 (*0-926684-12-4*) Eclectic Oregon.

Drury, G. Thorn, ed. see Waller, Edmund.

Drury, George & Model Railroad Magazine Staff. HO Trackside Structures You Can Build. (Model Railroad Handbook Ser.: No. 40). (Illus.). 120p. 1994. per. 14.95 (*0-89024-219-4*, 12143) Kalmbach.

Drury, George H. Guide to North American Steam Locomotives. LC 93-41472. (Railroad Reference Ser.: Vol. 8). 1993. pap. 27.95 (*0-89024-206-2*, 01051) Kalmbach.

— Historical Guide to North American Railroads. 2nd ed. 1999. pap. text 28.95 (*0-89024-356-5*) Kalmbach.

— The Railfan Guide to Austria. LC 99-174867. 112p. 1998. pap. 17.95 (*0-9665300-1-2*) G H Drury.

***Drury, George H.** The Railfan Guide to Switzerland. LC 99-174869. 160p. 1998. pap. 17.95 (*0-9665300-0-4*) G H Drury.

Drury, George H. The Reluctant Railfan's Introduction to Europe. LC 99-191974. 1p. 1998. 17.95 (*0-9665300-2-0*) G H Drury.

— Southern Pacific in the Bay Area: The San Francisco-Sacramento-Stockton Triangle. LC 97-119664. (Golden Years of Railroading Ser.: No. 3). (Illus.). 128p. 1996. pap. 18.95 (*0-89024-274-7*, 01070) Kalmbach.

Drury, George H., ed. see Lewis, Edward A.

Drury, George H., ed. see Marre, Louis A.

Drury, George H., ed. see Morgan, David P.

Drury, H. Hand Book of the Indian Flora, Vols. 1-3. (C). 1988. 65.00 (*0-7855-7062-4*, Pub. by Scientific) St Mut.

Drury, Herb. Pianist's Guide to Blues, Jazz, & Melodic Imp. 104p. 1994. spiral bd. 11.95 (*1-56222-905-2*, 95080) Mel Bay.

Drury, Horace B. Scientific Management. 2nd rev. ed. LC 68-56654. (Columbia University. Studies in the Social Sciences: No. 157). 1922. 37.50 (*0-404-51157-0*) AMS Pr.

Drury, Horace B., jt. auth. see Nourse, Edwin G.

Drury, Howard. Alpines & Rockplants. 96p. 1988. 60.00 (*1-85283-227-4*, Pub. by Boxtree) St Mut.

Drury, Ian. Confederate Infantryman 1861-1865. (Warrior Ser.). (Illus.). 64p. 1993. pap. 12.95 (*1-85532-401-6*, 9605, Pub. by Osprey) Stackpole.

— German Stormtrooper, 1915-1918. (Warrior Ser.). (Illus.). 64p. 1994. pap. 12.95 (*1-85532-372-9*, 9611, Pub. by Osprey) Stackpole.

— The Russo-Turkish, 1877. (Men-at-Arms Ser.: No. 277). (Illus.). 48p. 1994. pap. 11.95 (*1-85532-371-0*, 9249, Pub. by Osprey) Stackpole.

***Drury, Ian.** Stormtrooper. 2000. pap. 14.95 (*1-84176-038-2*) Osprey.

Drury, Jack. Camping. (Illus.). 128p. 1999. pap. 12.95 (*1-58382-010-8*) Sagamore Pub.

***Drury, Jack.** Canoeing. (Illus.). 128p. 1999. pap. 12.95 (*1-58382-011-6*) Sagamore Pub.

Drury, Jack & Holmlund, Eric. Camper's Guide to Outdoor Pursuits: Finding Safe, Nature-Friendly & Comfortable Passage Through Wild Places. Orig. Title: Camper's Bible. (Illus.). 200p. 1997. pap. 19.95 (*1-57167-074-2*) Sagamore Pub.

Drury, Jack K., jt. auth. see Bonney, Bruce F.

Drury, James W. The Government of Kansas. 5th rev. ed. (Illus.). 424p. 1997. pap. 20.00 (*0-936352-13-2*) U of KS Cont Ed.

Drury, Jennifer. The Athlete's Guide to Sponsorship. 2nd ed. LC 98-5582. 160p. (Orig.). 1998. pap. 14.95 (*1-884737-45-5*) VeloPress.

***Drury, Jennifer & Elliott, Cheri.** The Athlete's Guide to Sponsorship: How to Find an Individual, Team or Event Sponsor. 2nd ed. (Illus.). 160p. 2000. pap. 14.95 (*1-884737-78-1*) VeloPress.

Drury, Joan M. Closed in Silence. LC 98-24115. (Tyler Jones Feminist Mystery Ser.: No. 3). 224p. 1998. pap. 10.95 (*1-883523-29-X*) Spinsters Ink.

— The Other Side of Silence. LC 93-26211. 256p. (Orig.). 1993. pap. 9.95 (*0-933216-92-0*) Spinsters Ink

— Silent Words. 224p. 1996. pap. 10.95 (*1-883523-13-3*) Spinsters Ink.

***Drury, Joan M.** Those Jordan Girls. 224p. 2000. pap. 12.00 (*1-883523-36-2*, Pub. by Spinsters Ink) Words Distrib.

Drury, John. Creating Poetry. LC 90-48504. 224p. 1991. 18.99 (*0-89879-443-9*, Wrtrs Digest Bks) F & W Pubns Inc.

— Historic Midwest Houses. LC 77-78084. (Illus.). 1977. pap. 6.95 (*0-226-16551-5*) U Ch Pr.

— History of Upminster & Cranham. 1993. pap. 16.00 (*0-86025-405-4*, Pub. by I Henry Pubns) Empire Pub Srvs.

— Management Cost Accounting: Fall 1996. 4th ed. 1996. pap. text 24.99 (*1-86152-230-4*) Thomson Learn.

***Drury, John.** Painting the Word: Christian Pictures & Their Meanings. LC 99-25840. (Illus.). 201p. 1999. 25.00 (*0-300-07777-7*) Yale U Pr.

Drury, John. Parables in the Gospels. 192p. 1989. pap. 9.95 (*0-8245-0947-1*) Crossroad NY.

— The Poetry Dictionary. 352p. 1995. 18.99 (*1-884910-04-1*, Story Press) F & W Pubns Inc.

Drury, John, ed. see Segundo, Juan L.

Drury, John, ed. & tr. see Bellini, Enzo, et al.

Drury, John, ed. & tr. see Segundo, Juan L.

Drury, John, tr. see Alves, Rubem A.

Drury, John, tr. see Boff, Leonardo.

Drury, John, tr. see Christo, Carlos.

Drury, John, tr. see Cussianovich, Alejandro.

Drury, John, tr. see DaMatta, Roberto.

Drury, John, tr. see De Carvalho Azevedo, Marcello.

Drury, John, tr. see Dussel, Enrique D.

Drury, John, tr. see Eagleson, John & Scharper, Philip J., eds.

Drury, John, tr. see Elizondo, Virgilio P., ed.

Drury, John, tr. see Gutierrez, Gustavo, et al.

Drury, John, tr. see International Ecumenical Congress of Theology Staf.

Drury, John, tr. see Mesters, Carlos.

Drury, John, tr. see Metz, Johannes B.

Drury, John, tr. see Miranda, Jose P.

Drury, John, tr. see Motte, Ganzague.

Drury, John, tr. see Perez Esclarin, Antonio.

Drury, John, tr. see Ranciere, Jacques.

Drury, John, tr. see Segundo, Juan L.

Drury, John, tr. see Stella, Pietro.

***Drury, John P.** The Disappearing Town. LC 99-40609. 80p. 2000. 19.95 (*1-881163-31-8*, Pub. by Miami Univ Pr); pap. 11.95 (*1-881163-32-6*, Pub. by Miami Univ Pr) Pathway Bk Serv.

Drury, K. This Is the Newfoundland. 355p. 1978. 23.95 (*0-87666-340-4*, PS-666) TFH Pubns.

Drury, Keith. Disciplinas Espirituales para Todo Creyente.Tr. of Spiritual Disciplines for Ordinary People. (SPA.). 196p. 1997. pap. text 9.95 (*0-89827-169-X*) Wesleyan Pub Hse.

***Drury, Keith.** A Guide to Canoeing the Missouri River. 142p. 1999. pap. 4.99 (*0-9664049-3-9*) Premiere Publng.

Drury, Keith. Holiness for Ordinary People. rev. ed. 143p. 1995. reprint ed. 14.95 (*0-89827-132-0*, BKT12) Wesleyan Pub Hse.

— How to Establish Accountability. 40p. 1996. reprint ed. 1.35 (*0-89827-176-2*) Wesleyan Pub Hse.

— Money, Sex & Spiritual Power: Student Book. 128p. 1992. pap. text, student ed. 6.95 (*0-89827-103-7*, BKR82) Wesleyan Pub Hse.

— La Santidad para Todo Creyente. Crosby, Roberto et al, trs. 146p. 1995. pap. 9.95 (*0-89827-152-5*, BK799) Wesleyan Pub Hse.

— So, What Do You Think? Provocative Essays for Christians Who Think. 249p. 1998. pap. text 9.95 (*0-89827-190-8*) Wesleyan Pub Hse.

— Spiritual Disciplines for Ordinary People -- Leader's Guide. (Illus.). 180p. 1990. spiral bd. 14.95 (*0-89827-074-X*, BKM94) Wesleyan Pub Hse.

Drury, Keith, ed. Seize the Day: Your Church Can Survive Thrive! (Leader's Book) (Illus.). 112p. 1992. teacher ed., spiral bd., wbk. ed. 14.95 (*0-89827-102-9*, BKR79) Wesleyan Pub Hse.

Drury, Keith, ed. see DeNeff, Steve.

Drury, Keith W. Spiritual Development Guide: An In-Depth Guided Study for Your Spiritual Growth. (Illus.). 24p. (Orig.). 1991. reprint ed. pap., wbk. ed. 3.95 (*0-89827-068-5*, BKE61) Wesleyan Pub Hse.

— Successful Youth Mentoring: 24 Practical Sessions to Impact Lives. LC 98-16966. 128p. (YA). 1998. per. 16.99 (*0-7644-2104-2*, Vital Ministry) Group Pub.

Drury, Kiny & Linn, Bill. Newfoundlands: AKC Rank #50. (Illus.). 1997. pap. 9.95 (*0-7938-2318-8*, KW-174S) TFH Pubns.

Drury, M. O. The Danger of Words. rev. ed. Berman, David et al, eds. (Wittgenstein Studies). 278p. 1996. pap. 24.95 (*1-85506-490-1*) Bks Intl VA.

Drury, Michael. Advice to a Young Wife from an Old Mistress. 128p. 1996. pap. 8.00 (*0-380-72718-8*, Avon Bks) Morrow Avon.

— Advice to a Young Wife from an Old Mistress. large type ed. LC 96-49894. (Large Print Bks.). 1997. 23.95 (*1-56895-408-5*) Wheeler Pub.

— Advice to a Young Wife from an Old Mistress. 2nd ed. 204p. 1993. 17.95 (*0-9627659-5-3*) Four Directions.

— Medical Secretary & Receptionists. 6th ed. 1998. pap. text 21.00 (*0-7020-1643-8*) Harcourt.

Drury, N., ed. New Art 4. (Illus.). 230p. 1990. text 30.00 (*0-947131-33-7*) Gordon & Breach.

— New Art 3. (Illus.). 224p. 1989. text 37.00 (*0-947131-27-2*) Gordon & Breach.

Drury, Necill. Lexikon Esoterischen Wissens. (GER.). 29.95 (*0-7859-8678-2*, 342604160x) Fr & Eur.

***Drury, Nevil.** Shamanism: An Introductory Guide to Living in Harmony with Nature. (New Perspectives (Element) Ser.). (Illus.). 128p. 2000. pap. 9.95 (*1-86204-761-8*, Pub. by Onewrld Pubns) Penguin Putnam.

Drury, Nevill. Contemporary Aboriginal Painting: Poster Book. (Illus.). 32p. 1993. pap. text 19.00 (*976-8097-49-3*) Gordon & Breach.

D

— Contemporary Australian Women Artists: Poster Book. (Illus.). 32p. 1993. pap. text 19.00 (*976-8097-50-7*) Gordon & Breach.
— Dictionary of Mysticism & Esoteric Traditions. 2nd ed. LC 92-23484. (Mythology & Religion Ser.). 350p. 1992. lib. bdg. 55.00 (*0-87436-699-2*) ABC-CLIO.
— Echoes from the Void: Writings on Magic, Visionary Art & the New Consciousness. (Illus.). 176p. (Orig.). (C). 1994. pap. 14.95 (*1-85327-089-X*, Pub. by Prism Pr) Assoc Pubs Grp.
— Elements of Human Potential. (Illus.). 144p. 1993. pap. 9.95 (*1-85230-086-8*, Pub. by Element MA) Penguin Putnam.
— Elements of Shamanism. (Illus.). 144p. 1997. pap. 9.95 (*1-86204-038-9*, Pub. by Element MA) Penguin Putnam.
— Exploring the Labyrinth: Making Sense of the New Spirituality. LC 60-13991. 240p. 1999. pap. 18.95 (*0-8264-1182-7*) Continuum.
***Drury, Nevill.** The History of Modern Magic: The Quest for Personal Transformation. 288p. 2000. 25.00 (*0-7867-0782-8*, Pub. by Carroll & Graf) Publishers Group.
— Images 3: Contemporary Australian Painting. (Illus.). 276p. 1998. text 95.00 (*90-5703-451-4*, Harwood Acad Pubs) Gordon & Breach.
Drury, Nevill. Inner Visions: Explorations in Magical Consciousness. 160p. 1995. pap. 10.95 (*0-14-019283-2*, Arkana) Viking Penguin.
— New Art 8: Profiles in Contemporary Australian Art. (Illus.). 204p. 1993. text 37.00 (*976-8097-36-1*) Gordon & Breach.
— New Art 1: Profiles in Contemporary Australian Art. (Illus.). 160p. 1987. 65.00 (*0-947131-02-7*, Pub. by Craftsman House) Gordon & Breach.
— New Art 7: Profiles in Contemporary Australian Art. (Illus.). 204p. 1992. text 40.00 (*976-8097-18-3*) Gordon & Breach.
— New Sculpture: Profiles in Contemporary Australian Sculpture. (Illus.). 186p. 1993. text 35.00 (*976-8097-72-8*) Gordon & Breach.
— Shamanism. 96p. 1996. pap. 14.95 (*1-85230-794-3*, Pub. by Element MA) Penguin Putnam.
— The Visionary Human: Mystical Consciousness & Paranormal Perspectives. 144p. 1993. pap. 14.95 (*1-85230-206-2*, Pub. by Element MA) Penguin Putnam.
***Drury, Nevill.** The Visionary Human: Mystical Consciousness & Paranormal Perspectives. 151p. (C). 1998. reprint ed. pap. 21.95 (*1-85327-102-0*, Pub. by Prism Pr) Assoc Pubs Grp.
Drury, Nevill, ed. New Art 5: Profiles in Contemporary Australian Art. 204p. 1991. text 37.00 (*976-8097-03-5*) Gordon & Breach.
— New Art 2: Profiles in Contemporary Australian Art. (Illus.). 230p. 1989. text 37.00 (*0-947131-15-9*) Gordon & Breach.
Drury, Nevill & Voigt, Anna. Fire & Shadow: Spirituality in Contemporary Australian Art. LC 96-202224. (Illus.). 184p. 1996. text 37.50 (*976-641-042-9*, ECU46, Harwood Acad Pubs) Gordon & Breach.
Drury, Nevill, jt. auth. see Voigt, Anna.
Drury, Nevill, jt. auth. see Watson, Andrew.
***Drury, Neville.** Merlin's Book of Magic & Enchantment. LC 98-75035. (Illus.). 160p. 1999. 8.98 (*0-7651-1026-1*) Smithmark.
Drury, Patricia M., jt. auth. see Connors, Nellie Nally.
***Drury, Robert.** A Capital Childhood: Coming of Age in the Nation's Capital. (Illus.). vi, 178p. 1999. pap. 10.00 (*0-9671599-0-3*, Vintage Voices) Jo Atwater.
Drury, Robert & Defoe, Daniel. Madagascar: or Robert Drury's Journal During Fifteen Years' Captivity on That Island, & a Further Description of Madagascar by Alexis Rochon. LC 69-19359. (Illus.). 398p. 1970. reprint ed. lib. bdg. 35.00 (*0-8371-1403-9*, DRM&) Greenwood.
Drury, Robert & Xuereb, Peter. European Company Laws: A Comparative Approach. 350p. 1990. text 109.95 (*1-85521-172-6*, Pub. by Dartmth Pub) Ashgate Pub Co.
Drury, Ronan, ed. New Testament As Personal Reading. 158p. 1983. pap. 7.95 (*0-87243-122-3*) Templegate.
***Drury, Rose.** Looking at Early Years Education & Care. 2000. pap. 25.95 (*1-85346-659-X*) David Fulton.
Drury, Ruth. Tapping into Prosperity: The Universal Path to Success. Levine, Gene N., ed. 222p. (Orig.). 1992. pap. 18.95 (*0-9631383-0-8*) Prosperity Times.
Drury, S. A. Image Interpretation in Geology. 256p. (C). 1986. text 100.00 (*0-04-550037-1*); pap. text 39.95 (*0-04-550038-X*) Routledge.
— Images of the Earth: A Guide to Remote Sensing. 2nd ed. (Illus.). 212p. 1998. text 75.00 (*0-19-854998-9*); pap. text 45.00 (*0-19-854997-0*) OUP.
Drury, S. W., ed. see Herz, Carl S.
Drury, Sandra M., jt. auth. see Borders, L. DiAnne.
Drury, Shadia B. Alexandre Kojeve: The Roots of Postmodern Politics. 1994. text 49.95 (*0-312-12089-3*) St Martin.
— Leo Strauss & the American Right. LC 97-11580. 256p. 1997. text 35.00 (*0-312-12689-1*) St Martin.
***Drury, Shadia B.** Leo Strauss & the American Right. 256p. 1999. pap. 18.95 (*0-312-21783-8*) St Martin.
Drury, Shadia B. & Knopff, Rainer, eds. Law & Politics: Readings In Legal & Political Thought, Vol. 1. 270p. (Orig.). (C). 1980. pap. 13.95 (*0-920490-12-3*) Temeron Bks.
Drury, Sharon, ed. Money, Sex & Spiritual Power: Leader's Book. (Illus.). 136p. 1992. teacher ed., spiral bd. 14.95 (*0-89827-104-5*, BKR81) Wesleyan Pub Hse.
***Drury, Stephen.** Stepping Stones: The Making of Our Home World. LC 98-45284. (Illus.). 430p. 1999. 35.00 (*0-19-850271-0*) OUP.
Drury, Susan. Tea Tree Oil. 111p. 1991. pap. 7.95 (*0-85207-238-4*, Pub. by C W Daniel) Natl Bk Netwk.
— Tea Tree Oil. 3rd ed. 88p. pap. 11.95 (*0-8464-4299-X*) Beekman Pubs.
Drury, Tim. When I'm Big. LC 98-54912. (Illus.). 32p. 1999. 15.95 (*0-531-30189-3*) Orchard Bks Watts.
Drury, Tom. The Black Brook. LC 98-12843. 256p. 1998. 23.00 (*0-395-70194-5*) HM.
***Drury, Tom.** The Black Brook. 336p. 2000. pap. 13.00 (*0-395-95795-8*) HM.
Drury, Tom. The End of Vandalism. 336p. 1995. pap. 11.00 (*0-449-90982-4*) Fawcett.
***Drury, Tom.** Hunts in Dreams. LC 99-55519. 208p. 2000. 22.00 (*0-395-94113-X*) HM.
Drury, William Holland & Anderson, John G. Chance & Change: Ecology for Conservationists. LC 97-14859. 218p. 1998. 24.95 (*0-520-21155-3*, Pub. by U CA Pr) Cal Prin Full Svc.
Druse, Ken. The Collector's Garden: Designing with Extraordinary Plants. Roach, Margaret, ed. LC 95-30182. (Illus.). 248p. 1996. 45.00 (*0-517-79983-9*) C Potter.
— Eighty Great Natural Shade Garden Plants. LC 97-167213. 128p. 1997. pap. 15.00 (*0-609-80043-4*) Random Hse Value.
— Flowering Shrubs. (Burpee American Gardening Ser.). (Illus.). 96p. 1992. pap. 8.00 (*0-13-093717-7*, P-H Gardening) Prntice Hall Bks.
***Druse, Ken.** Making More Plants: The Science, Art & Joy of Propagation. (Illus.). 256p. 2000. 45.00 (*0-517-70787-X*) C Potter.
Druse, Ken. The Natural Garden. 1988. 40.00 (*0-517-55046-6*) C Potter.
— The Natural Shade Garden. 288p. 1992. 40.00 (*0-517-58017-9*) C Potter.
Druse, Ken & Roach, Margaret. The Natural Habitat Garden. LC 93-12558. 1994. 40.00 (*0-517-58989-3*) C Potter.
Drushal, Mary E. On Tablets of Human Hearts: Christian Education with Children. 224p. 1990. 17.99 (*0-310-36840-5*) Zondervan.
***Drushka, Ken.** In the Bight: The B. C. Forest Industry Today. 300p. 1999. 32.95 (*1-55017-161-5*) Harbour Pub Co.
***Druss, Richard G.** Listening to Patients: Relearning the art of Healing in Psychotherapy. 160p. 2000. 19.95 (*0-19-513593-8*) OUP.
Druss, Richard G. The Psychology of Illness: In Sickness & in Health. LC 94-23688. 144p. 1995. text 23.50 (*0-88048-661-9*, 8661) Am Psychiatric.
Drutchas, Geoffrey G. Is Life Sacred? LC 98-36257. 208p. 1998. pap. 18.95 (*0-8298-1275-X*) Pilgrim OH.
Drutman, Ava & Zuckerman, Susan. Protecting Our Planet (Intermediate) 144p. (J). (gr. 4-8). 1991. 10.99 (*0-86653-589-6*, GA1302) Good Apple.
Drutman, Ava D. Land (Primary) (Illus.). 48p. (J). (gr. 1-3). 1992. student ed. 6.99 (*0-86653-599-3*, 1406) Good Apple.
— Protecting Our Planet - Primary Grades. 144p. (J). (gr. 1-3). 1991. 10.99 (*0-86653-619-1*, GA1338) Good Apple.
— Water (Primary) (Illus.). 48p. (J). (gr. 1-3). 1992. student ed. 6.99 (*0-86653-604-3*, 1407) Good Apple.
Drutman, Ave D. & Deutsch, Evelyn. Protecting Our Planet (Early Childhood Version) (Illus.). 128p. (J). (ps-1). 1992. 9.99 (*0-86653-665-5*, GA1400) Good Apple.
Drutt, Matthew, ed. Motorcycle Mania: The Biker Book. 128p. 1998. 27.50 (*0-7893-0132-6*, Pub. by Universe) St Martin.
Drutt, Matthew & Torchia, Richard. William Daley: Ceramic Works & Drawings. LC 93-79842. (Illus.). 36p. 1993. pap. 25.00 (*1-58442-008-1*) Galleries at Moore.
Drutt, Matthew, jt. ed. see Bowlt, John E.
Drutt, Matthew J. William Daley: Ceramic Works & Drawings. LC 93-79842. (Illus.). 36p. (Orig.). 1993. pap. 21.00 (*0-8122-1541-9*) U of Pa Pr.
Druxes, Helga. The Feminization of Dr. Faustus: Female Identity Quests from Stendhal to Morgner. 160p. (C). 1993. 37.50 (*0-271-00759-1*) Pa St U Pr.
— Resisting Bodies: The Negotiation of Female Agency in Twentieth-Century Women's Fiction. (Kritik Ser.). 232p. 1996. 34.95 (*0-8143-2534-3*) Wayne St U Pr.
Druxes, Herbert. Physik Theorie/Experiment/Didautik. (GER.). (C). 1991. text. write for info. (*0-201-55946-3*) Addison-Wesley.
Druxman, Michael B. Cheyenne Warrior: The Original Screenplay with Author Commentary. Artof, Susan, ed. LC 97-46522. (Writing for Pleasure Ser.). 128p. 1998. 11.95 (*1-889198-03-X*) Ctr Pr CA.
— How to Write a Story...Any Story: The Art of Storytelling. LC 97-18517. (Writing for Pleasure Ser.). (Illus.). 128p. (C). 1997. pap. 11.95 (*0-9626888-8-6*) Ctr Pr CA.
— Nobody Drowns in Mineral Lake. LC 99-10203. 286p. 1999. pap. 12.95 (*1-889198-04-8*) Ctr Pr CA.
Druyan, Ann, jt. auth. see Sagan, Carl.
Druyan, Gerald. High Intensity Jazz: Jazz Handbook & Workbook. rev. ed. (Handbook & Workbook Ser.). (Illus.). 64p. (YA). (gr. 6-12). Date not set. pap., student ed. 14.00 (*0-9639983-0-7*) Druyan Pubng.
Druyanov, B. Technological Mechanics of Porous Bodies. LC 92-33960. (Illus.). 200p. 1993. 65.00 (*0-19-856364-7*) OUP.
Druyanov, B. & Nepershin, R. Problems of Technological Plasticity. LC 94-6654. (Studies in Applied Mechanics: Vol. 38). 426p. 1994. 196.50 (*0-444-81646-1*) Elsevier.
Druyfuss, Rochelle & Keavall, Roberta. 1998 Supplement to Intellectual Property Cases & materials on Trademark, Copyright & Patent Law. (University Casebks.). 50p. 1998. pap. text 5.50 (*1-56662-684-6*) Foundation Pr.
Druzhinin, Aleksandr. Polinka Saks & the Story of Aleksei Dmitrich. Katz, Michael R., tr. from RUS. & intro. by. (Studies in Russian Literature & Theory). 225p. (Orig.). 1992. 49.95 (*0-8101-1052-0*); pap. 16.95 (*0-8101-1077-6*) Northwestern U Pr.
Druzhnikov, Yuri. Collected Works, 6 vols. LC 98-60549. (RUS., Illus.). 2972p. 1998. 150.00 (*1-885563-16-7*) VIA Press MD.
— Collected Works Vol. 1: Micronovels & Short Stories. LC 98-60549. (RUS., Illus.). 567p. 1998. 25.00 (*1-885563-10-8*) VIA Press MD.
— Collected Works Vol. 2: Angels on the Head of a Pin. LC 98-60549. (RUS., Illus.). 567p. 1998. 25.00 (*1-885563-11-6*) VIA Press MD.
— Collected Works Vol. 3: Prisoner of Russia (Pushkin) LC 98-60549. (RUS., Illus.). 455p. 1998. 25.00 (*1-885563-12-4*) VIA Press MD.
— Collected Works Vol. 4: Literary Criticism. Informer 001. LC 98-60549. (RUS., Illus.). 519p. 1998. 25.00 (*1-885563-13-2*) VIA Press MD.
— Collected Works Vol. 5: Prose & Plays for Children. LC 98-60549. (RUS., Illus.). 464p. 1998. 25.00 (*1-885563-14-0*) VIA Press MD.
— Collected Works Vol. 6: Esseys Memoirs. LC 98-60549. (RUS., Illus.). 400p. 1998. 25.00 (*1-885563-15-9*) VIA Press MD.
***Druzhnikov, Yuri.** Contemporary Russian Myths: A Skeptical View of the Literary Past. LC 99-25319. (Studies in Slavic Language & Literature: Vol. 14). 340p. 1999. text 99.95 (*0-7734-8161-3*) E Mellen.
Druzhnikov, Yuri. Informer 001: The Myth of Pavlik Morozov. LC 96-42466. 214p. 1997. text 29.95 (*1-56000-283-2*) Transaction Pubs.
— Prisoner of Russia: Alexander Pushkin & the Political Uses of Nationalism. LC 98-52062. 10p. 1998. 39.95 (*1-56000-390-1*) Transaction Pubs.
Druzhnikov, Yuri I. Ia Rodilsia v Ocheredi. LC 95-3179. (RUS.). 256p. (Orig.). 1995. pap. 14.00 (*1-55779-073-6*) Hermitage Pubs.
Druzik, J. R., et al, eds. Materials Issues in Art & Archaeology III. (Materials Research Society Symposium Proceedings Ser.: Vol. 267). 1097p. 1992. text 62.00 (*1-55899-162-X*) Materials Res.
Druzik, James, ed. Research Abstracts of the Scientific Program. 3rd ed. (GCI Scientific Program Reports Ser.). 275p. 1995. pap. text 15.00 (*0-89236-244-8*, Pub. by J P Getty Trust) OUP.
Drvodelic, Milan. English-Croatian Or Serbian Dictionary. (CRO, ENG & SER.). 880p. 1988. 125.00 (*0-8288-0502-4*, M9707) Fr & Eur.
— Serbocroatian-English Dictionary: Hrvatsko Ili Srpsko-Engelski Rjecnik. (ENG & SER.). 848p. 1988. 49.95 (*0-8288-0503-2*, F36830) Fr & Eur.
Drwal, Frances. Polish Wycinanki Designs. (International Design Library). (Illus.). 48p. (Orig.). 1984. pap. 5.95 (*0-88045-058-4*) Stemmer Hse.
Dry Color Manufacturers' Association, Metal Oxides. Classification & Descriptions of Mixed Metal Oxide Inorganic Colored Pigments. 2nd ed. 68p. 1982. write for info. (*0-318-60068-4*) Dry Color Mfrs.
Dry, Dan. The College of William & Mary. (Illus.). 112p. 1987. 37.50 (*0-916509-12-5*) Harmony Hse Pub.
Dry, Dan, photos by. Barbados. (Illus.). 128p. 1988. 35.00 (*0-916509-50-8*) Harmony Hse Pub.
— Boston College. (First Edition Ser.). (Illus.). 112p. 1988. 39.00 (*0-916509-28-1*) Harmony Hse Pub.
— Miami University - Then & Now. (Illus.). 112p. 1993. 39.95 (*1-56469-007-5*) Harmony Hse Pub.
— Ohio University - Then & Now. (First Edition Ser.). (Illus.). 112p. 1992. 39.95 (*0-916509-87-7*) Harmony Hse Pub.
— University of Chicago. (Illus.). 112p. 1992. 39.95 (*0-916509-67-2*) Harmony Hse Pub.
— Wellesley. (First Edition Ser.). (Illus.). 112p. 1988. 39.00 (*0-916509-42-7*) Harmony Hse Pub.
— Woodberry Forest School. (Illus.). 112p. 1990. 40.00 (*0-916509-65-6*) Harmony Hse Pub.
Dry, Dan & Spears, Amy. Gardens of Kentucky. (Illus.). 160p. 1999. 39.95 (*1-891138-02-2*, Pub. by Sulgrave Pr) Howell Pr VA.
Dry, Helen A., jt. auth. see Lawler, John.
Dry, Murray, jt. ed. see Storing, Herbert J.
Dryander, Jonas. Catalogus Bibliothecae Historico-Naturalis Josephi Banks, 5 vols., Set. 1966. 240.00 (*90-6123-003-9*) Lubrecht & Cramer.
Dryansky, Amy. How I Got Lost So Close to Home. LC 99-11029. 65p. 1999. pap. 11.95 (*1-882295-22-6*, 95-22-6, Pub. by Alice James Bks) SPD-Small Pr Dist.
Dryansky, Amy, ed. see Ferris-Jenkins, Rachel, et al.
Drybrough, Anne. Red Bleeds the Sun. (C). 1990. 45.00 (*0-7223-2551-7*, Pub. by A H S Ltd) St Mut.
Dryburgh, Robert. So You're Thinking of Going to a Chiropractor. 160p. 1984. pap. 3.95 (*0-87983-355-6*, Keats Publng) NTC Contemp Pub Co.
Drydan, Deborah. Fabric Painting & Dyeing for the Theater. LC 93-31128. 256p. (C). 1993. pap. 34.95 (*0-435-08624-3*, 08624) Heinemann.
Dryden. Counseling Individuals: A Handbook. 2nd ed. 304p. 1993. 65.00 (*1-56593-524-1*, 0314) Singular Publishing.
— Current Regional Issues. LC 94-216983. (C). 1994. pap. text 19.00 (*0-03-001949-4*) Harcourt.
— Current Regional Issues: Alaska, Idaho, Montana. LC 94-178062. (C). 1994. pap. text 15.50 (*0-03-002053-0*, Pub. by Harcourt Coll Pubs) Harcourt.
— Current Regional Issues - California. LC 94-210486. (C). 1994. pap. text 13.75 (*0-03-001952-4*, Pub. by Harcourt Coll Pubs) Harcourt.
— Dictionary of Rational Emotive Behavior Therapy. 174p. 1994. pap. 39.95 (*1-56593-508-X*, 1174) Singular Publishing.
— The Dryden Interviews: Dialogues on the Psychotherapeutic Process. 152p. 1992. pap. 48.00 (*1-56593-526-8*, 0315) Singular Publishing.
— Dryden on Counseling, Vol. 3. 180p. 1991. pap. 47.75 (*1-56593-529-2*, 0309) Singular Publishing.
— Dryden on Counseling Vol. 1: Seminal Papers. 164p. 1991. pap. 47.75 (*1-56593-527-6*, 0307) Singular Publishing.
— Dryden on Counseling Vol. 2: A Dialogue. 84p. 1991. pap. 40.00 (*1-56593-528-4*, 0308) Singular Publishing.
— Essential Arnold Lazarus. 246p. 1991. pap. 48.00 (*1-56593-573-X*, 0305) Singular Publishing.
— Facilitating Client Change in Rational Emotive Behavior Therapy. 163p. 1995. pap. 35.00 (*1-56593-512-8*, 1182) Singular Publishing.
— Getting Started with the Internet. 1998. pap. text 40.50 (*0-03-027191-6*) Harcourt Coll Pubs.
— Marketing Image CD-ROM. (C). 1995. 246.00 (*0-03-018127-5*) Harcourt Coll Pubs.
— Preparing for Client Change in Rational Emotive Behavior Therapy. 149p. 1994. pap. 32.95 (*1-56593-511-X*, 1180) Singular Publishing.
— Reason & Therapeutic Change. 334p. 1991. pap. 48.95 (*1-56593-530-6*, 0306) Singular Publishing.
— Reflections on Counseling. 118p. 1993. pap. 48.00 (*1-56593-262-5*, 0552) Singular Publishing.
Dryden, tr. see Trotter, Catherine.
Dryden, Bob. Staging a Snazzy Senior Showcase. Trone, Mary, ed. LC 89-92203. (Illus.). 168p. (Orig.). 1989. pap. 9.95 (*0-9624834-0-0*) Cent Lakas Coll.
Dryden, Caroline. Being Married Doing Gender: Critical Analysis of Gender Relationships in Marriage. LC 98-29689. (Women & Psychology Ser.). 192p. (C). 1999. pap. 22.99 (*0-415-16559-8*) Routledge.
Dryden, Caroline, ed. Being Married Doing Gender: Critical Analysis of Gender Relationships in Marriage. LC 98-29689. (Women & Psychology Ser.). 192p. (C). 1999. 75.00 (*0-415-16558-X*) Routledge.
Dryden, Charles W. A-Train: Memoirs of a Tuskegee Airman. LC 96-24118. 432p. 1997. 29.95 (*0-8173-0856-3*) U of Ala Pr.
Dryden, Deborah M., jt. auth. see Sweet, Harvey.
Dryden, Dorothy G. Under the Shadows of Mt. Fanny: Life Was to Change. (Illus.). 83p. (Orig.). 1996. pap. 6.95 (*0-9644370-4-X*) Dryden Publ.
Dryden, Edgar A. The Form of American Romance. LC 88-6490. 271p. 1988. reprint ed. pap. 84.10 (*0-608-05951-X*, 206628800008) Bks Demand.
— Melville's Thematics of Form: The Great Art of Telling the Truth. LC 68-55612. (Illus.). 240p. 1968. reprint ed. pap. 74.40 (*0-608-04061-4*, 206479700011) Bks Demand.
Dryden, Emma. Christmas Surprise. (J). 1997. pap. 2.75 (*0-679-88876-4*) Random.
***Dryden, Gordon.** Learning Revolution. 2nd ed. 1999. 30.00 (*1-929284-00-4*) Learning Web.
Dryden, H., jt. auth. see Ovid.
***Dryden, I.** Statistical Analysis of Shape. LC 98-4092. 376p. 1998. 139.95 (*0-471-95816-6*) Wiley.
Dryden, J. L. Mona, Queen of Lost Atlantis. 169p. 1971. reprint ed. spiral bd. 10.00 (*0-7873-0298-8*) Hlth Research.
— Mona Queen of Lost Atlantis an Idyllic: Re-Embodiment of Long Forgotten History (1925) 109p. 1996. reprint ed. pap. 15.95 (*1-56459-918-3*) Kessinger Pub.
Dryden, Joan, tr. see Ovid & Dryden, H.
***Dryden, John.** All for Love. 96p. 1998. pap. 6.95 (*1-85459-372-2*, Pub. by N Hern Bks) Consort Bk Sales.
Dryden, John. All for Love: The World Well Lost. Andrew, Nicholas J., ed. (New Mermaids Ser.). (C). 1976. pap. text 9.75 (*0-393-90006-1*) Norton.
— All for Love: The World Well Lost. Landes, William-Alan, ed. & intro. by. LC 94-20321. 80p. 1994. pap. 7.00 (*0-88734-274-4*) Players Pr.
— All for Love: The World Well Lost. Vieth, David M., ed. LC 72-128912. (Regents Restoration Drama Ser.). 146p. 1972. reprint ed. pap. 7.95 (*0-8032-5379-6*, Bison Books) U of Nebr Pr.
— Aureng-Zebe. Link, Frederick M., ed. LC 78-123119. (Regents Restoration Drama Ser.). 155p. reprint ed. pap. 48.10 (*0-8357-7876-2*, 203629400002) Bks Demand.
— Dramatic Works, 6 Vols, Set. Summers, Montague, ed. LC 68-15208. 490p. 1968. reprint ed. 500.00 (*0-87752-030-5*) Gordian.
— An Essay of Dramatic Poesy & Other Critical Writings. Mahoney, John L., ed. LC 65-26522. 150p. 1993. reprint ed. pap. text 15.95 (*0-8290-1006-8*) Irvington.
— John Dryden: Four Tragedies. Beaurline, L. A. & Bowers, Fredson, eds. LC 67-26813. (Curtain Playwrights Ser.). 422p. reprint ed. pap. 130.90 (*0-608-13386-8*, 202409000035) Bks Demand.
— Letters. Ward, Charles E., ed. LC 74-164791. reprint ed. 27.50 (*0-404-02186-7*) AMS Pr.
— Literary Criticism of John Dryden. Kirsch, Arthur C., ed. LC 66-23019. (Regents Critics Ser.). 192p. reprint ed. 59.60 (*0-8357-9709-0*, 201265800083) Bks Demand.
— Longman Annotated English Poems 1649-1681, Vol. I. Hammond, Paul, ed. (Annotated English Poets Ser.). 480p. (C). 1995. 194.00 (*0-582-49213-0*, 76666) Longman.
— Longman Annotated Englsh Poems V2 1682-1685, Vol. II. Hammond, Paul, ed. 480p. (C). 1995. text 130.50 (*0-582-23944-3*, 76667) Addison-Wesley.
— Marriage a la Mode. Crane, David, ed. (New Mermaids Ser.). (C). 1991. pap. text 11.25 (*0-393-90064-9*) Norton.
— Marriage a la Mode. Auburn, Mark S., ed. LC 80-51043. (Regents Restoration Drama Ser.). xxxii, 144p. 1981. pap. text 7.95 (*0-8032-6556-5*) U of Nebr Pr.

D

— The Poems of John Dryden. Hammond, Paul, ed. LC 94-14270. (Longman Annotated English Poets Ser.). (C). 1995. text 251.25 (*0-8013-1430-5*, Pub. by Addison-Wesley) Longman.

— Selected Poems. 320p. 1993. pap. 7.95 (*0-460-87230-3*, Everyman's Classic Lib) Tuttle Pubng.

— The Selected Poetry & Prose. LC 69-17414. (Modern Library College Editions). 628p. (C). 1969. pap. 8.44 (*0-07-553553-X*) McGraw.

— The Works of John Dryden Vol. XIV: Plays: The Kind Keeper; The Spanish Fryar; The Duke of Guise; & The Vindication. 646p. (C). 1992. 80.00 (*0-520-07561-7*, Pub. by U CA Pr) Cal Prin Full Svc.

Dryden, John & Eliot, T. S. Of Dramatic Poesie: An Essay, 1668. LC 72-1308. (Studies in Dryden: No. 10). 1972. reprint ed. lib. bdg. 75.00 (*0-8383-1440-6*) M S G Haskell Hse.

Dryden, John & Mahoney, John L. Essays of Dramatic Poesy, a Defence of an Essay of Dramatic Poesy, & Preface to the Fables. LC 65-26522. 1965. 2.90 (*0-672-60298-9*, Bobbs) Macmillan.

Dryden, John & Shadwell, Thomas. Dryden & Shadwell: The Literary Controversy & MacFlecknoe 1668-1678. Oden, Richard L., ed. LC 77-5952. 328p. 1977. lib. bdg. 50.00 (*0-8201-1289-5*) Schol Facsimiles.

Dryden, John, jt. auth. see Gardner, William B.

Dryden, John, tr. see Clough, Arthur H.

Dryden, John, tr. see Clough, Arthur H., ed.

Dryden, John, tr. see Juvenal.

Dryden, John, tr. see Ovid.

Dryden, John, tr. see Virgil.

Dryden, Konrad C. Riccardo Zandonai, a Biography. LC 99-22681. (Illus.). 530p. 1999. pap. text 73.95 (*0-8204-3649-6*) P Lang Pubng.

***Dryden, Konrad Claude.** Riccardo Zandonai, a Biography. (Illus.). 530p. 1999. pap. 73.95 (*3-631-34374-4*) P Lang Pubng.

Dryden, Laurel, compiled by. Employment Creation Policies & Strategies: An Annotated Bibliography, 1980-86. (International Labour Bibliography Ser.: No. 3). ix, 400p. (Orig.). 1987. pap. 20.25 (*92-2-106173-6*) Intl Labour Office.

***Dryden, Linda.** Joseph Conrad & the Imperial Romance. LC 99-22232. (Illus.). 224p. 2000. text 65.00 (*0-312-22553-9*) St Martin.

***Dryden, Mack, et al.** Remember When... The Funniest Book with the Word "Millennium" on the Cover. LC 99-61759. (Illus.). 96p. 1999. pap. 7.95 (*1-56352-584-4*) Longstreet.

Dryden, Michael W., jt. ed. see Blagburn, Byron L.

Dryden, Ron S. Dance Before the Lord. rev. ed. 160p. 1996. pap. 9.95 (*1-887399-00-3*) Colbert Hse.

— Eleven Keys of the Kingdom. 160p. 2000. pap. write for info. (*1-887399-01-1*) Colbert Hse.

***Dryden, Stephen.** The Key to Repair Broken & Half-Broken Marriages. LC 99-93739. 70p. 2000. 13.95 (*0-533-13140-5*) Vantage.

Dryden, Stephen M. The Key to a Lasting & Happy Marriage. (Illus.). 77p. 1997. pap. write for info. (*0-9662720-4-8*) S Dryden.

***Dryden, Steve, ed.** Century of Hockey. (Illus.). 160p. 2000. 24.95 (*0-7710-4179-9*) McCland & Stewart.

— The Top 100 NHL Players of All Time. (Illus.). 160p. 1998. text 22.95 (*0-7710-4175-6*) McCland & Stewart.

— The Top 100 NHL Players of All Time. (Illus.). 160p. 1999. pap. 16.95 (*0-7710-4176-4*) McCland & Stewart.

— Total Gretzky: The Magic, the Legend, the Numbers. (Illus.). 176p. 1999. text 24.95 (*0-7710-4177-2*) McCland & Stewart.

— Total Gretzky: The Magic, the Legend, the Numbers. (Illus.). 176p. 2000. pap. 16.95 (*0-7710-4178-0*) McCland & Stewart.

Dryden, Wendy. Current Issues in Rational-Emotive Therapy. 220p. 1987. lib. bdg. 42.50 (*0-7099-4557-4*, Pub. by C Helm) Routldge.

— Individual Therapy Handbook. 1990. 113.00 (*0-335-09446-5*); pap. 36.95 (*0-335-09445-7*) OpUniv Pr.

— Marital Therapy in Britain Vol. 1: Context & Therapeutic Approaches. 368p. 1985. pap. 28.00 (*0-335-09812-6*) OpUniv Pr.

— Marital Therapy in Britain Vol. 2: Special Areas. 368p. 1985. pap. 28.00 (*0-335-09813-4*) OpUniv Pr.

***Dryden, Wendy.** Overcoming Jealousy. 1999. pap. text. write for info. (*0-85969-765-7*, Pub. by Sheldon Pr); pap. text 10.95 (*0-85969-756-8*) Sheldon Pr.

Dryden, Wendy, ed. Individual Therapy in Britain. 448p. 1984. pap. 32.00 (*0-335-09810-X*) OpUniv Pr.

— Therapists' Dilemmas. 192p. 1988. 49.95 (*0-89116-775-7*) Hemisp Pub.

Dryden, Wendy & Feltham, Colin, eds. Psychotherapy & Its Discontents. 256p. 1992. 123.00 (*0-335-09678-6*); pap. 38.95 (*0-335-09677-8*) OpUniv Pr.

Dryden, Wendy & Spurling, Laurence, eds. On Becoming a Psychotherapist. 272p. 1989. 52.50 (*0-415-01933-8*, A3639) Routledge.

— On Becoming a Psychotherapist. 272p. (C). 1989. pap. 25.99 (*0-415-03611-9*, A3643) Routledge.

Dryden, Wendy & Yankura, Joseph. Daring to Be Myself: A Case Study in Rational-Emotive Therapy. 224p. 1992. pap. 41.95 (*0-335-09341-8*) OpUniv Pr.

Dryden, Wendy, jt. auth. see Aveline, Mark.

Dryden, Wendy, jt. auth. see Cole, Martin.

Dryden, Wendy, jt. ed. see Heap, Michael.

Dryden, Wendy, jt. ed. see Hooper, Douglas.

Dryden, Wendy, jt. ed. see Thorne, Brian.

Dryden, Windy. Brief Rational Emotive Behaviour Therapy. 244p. 1995. pap. 59.95 (*0-471-95786-0*) Wiley.

***Dryden, Windy.** Counselling Individuals. 3rd ed. 1999. pap. text 44.95 (*1-86156-056-7*) Whurr Pub.

Dryden, Windy. Dealing with Anger Problems: Rational-Emotive Therapeutic Interventions. Smith, Harold H., Jr., ed. LC 90-52986. (Practitioner's Resource Ser.). 60p. 1990. pap. 15.45 (*0-943158-59-1*, DAPBP) Pro Resource.

— Developing Self-Acceptance: A Brief, Educational & Small Group Approach. LC 97-38900. (Series in Brief Therapy & Counselling). 240p. 1998. pap. 42.50 (*0-471-98099-4*) Wiley.

— Developments in Psychotherapy: Historical Perspectives. 256p. 1996. 69.95 (*0-8039-7911-8*); pap. 22.95 (*0-8039-7912-6*) Sage.

— Four Approaches to Counselling & Psychotherapy. LC 98-37422. 1999. 85.00 (*0-415-13992-9*); pap. 27.99 (*0-415-13993-7*) Routledge.

— Handbook of Individual Therapy. 416p. 1996. 79.95 (*0-8039-7842-1*); pap. 32.95 (*0-8039-7843-X*) Sage.

— Hard-Earned Lessons from Counselling in Action. (Counselling in Action Ser.: Vol. 15). 160p. (C). 1992. 49.95 (*0-8039-8668-8*); pap. 21.50 (*0-8039-8669-6*) Sage.

— Inquiries in Rational Emotive Behaviour Therapy. 160p. 1996. 49.95 (*0-7619-5130-X*); pap. 24.95 (*0-7619-5131-8*) Sage.

— Invitation to Rational Emotive Psychology. 170p. 1994. pap. text 49.95 (*1-56593-402-4*, 0764) Singular Publishing.

***Dryden, Windy.** Overcoming Procrastination. 2000. pap. 9.95 (*0-85969-815-7*) Sheldon Pr.

Dryden, Windy. Positive Thought for Every Day. 1999. 12.95 (*0-85969-744-4*) S C K Pubns.

— Progress in Rational Emotive Behavior Therapy. 150p. 1994. pap. 39.50 (*1-56593-369-9*, 0725) Singular Publishing.

— Rational Emotive Behavior Therapy: A Reader. 304p. 1995. text 65.00 (*0-8039-7858-8*); pap. text 26.95 (*0-8039-7859-6*) Sage.

***Dryden, Windy.** Rational Emotive Behavior Therapy: A Training Manual. LC 98-48400. 300p. 1999. 42.95 (*0-8261-1249-8*) Springer Pub.

Dryden, Windy. Rational Emotive Behavior Therapy: Learning from Demonstration Sessions. (Illus.). 250p. (Orig.). 1996. pap. 34.95 (*1-56593-784-8*, 1530) Singular Publishing.

— Rational-Emotive Counselling in Action. (Counselling in Action Ser.: Vol. 9). 112p. (C). 1990. text 49.95 (*0-8039-8269-0*); pap. text 21.50 (*0-8039-8270-4*) Sage.

Dryden, Windy, ed. The Essential Albert Ellis: Seminal Writings on Psychotherapy. LC 89-26338. 336p. 1990. 38.95 (*0-8261-6940-6*) Springer Pub.

— Key Issues for Counselling in Action. (Counselling in Action Ser.: Vol. 7). 118p. (C). 1989. text 49.95 (*0-8039-8051-5*); pap. text 21.50 (*0-8039-8052-3*) Sage.

— Questions & Answers on Counselling in Action. (Counselling in Action Ser.: Vol. 16). (Illus.). 192p. (C). 1993. text 49.95 (*0-8039-8858-3*); pap. text 21.50 (*0-8039-8859-1*) Sage.

— Research in Counseling & Psychotherapy: Practical Applications. LC 96-67700. 272p. 1996. 69.95 (*0-8039-7840-5*); pap. 24.95 (*0-8039-7841-3*) Sage.

— Therapists' Dilemmas. 208p. 1997. 55.00 (*0-7619-5393-0*); pap. 24.95 (*0-7619-5394-9*) Sage.

Dryden, Windy & DiGiuseppe, Raymond. A Primer on Rational-Emotive Therapy. LC 89-69838. 108p. (Orig.). 1990. pap. text 11.95 (*0-87822-319-3*, 4420) Res Press.

Dryden, Windy & Feltham, Colin. Brief Counselling: A Practical Guide for Beginning Practitioners. LC 92-8610. 1992. pap. 31.95 (*0-335-09972-6*) OpUniv Pr.

— Developing Counselor Training. LC 94-65540. (Developing Counselling Ser.: Vol. 3). 128p. 1994. 35.00 (*0-8039-8942-3*); pap. 16.95 (*0-8039-8943-1*) Sage.

— Developing the Practice of Counseling. LC 94-65695. (Developing Counselling Ser.: Vol. 1). 128p. 1994. 35.00 (*0-8039-8940-7*); pap. 16.95 (*0-8039-8941-5*) Sage.

Dryden, Windy & Hill, Larry K. Innovations in Rational-Emotive Therapy. (Illus.). 320p. (C). 1992. 48.00 (*0-8039-4300-8*); pap. 22.95 (*0-8039-4301-6*) Sage.

Dryden, Windy & Neenan, Michael. Dictionary of Rational Emotive Behaviour Therapy. 22.95 (*1-897635-71-0*, B152) Inst Rational-Emotive.

Dryden, Windy & Palmer, Stephen. Counselling for Stress Problems. LC 94-68660. (Counselling in Practice Ser.). 240p. 1995. text 49.95 (*0-8039-8862-1*); pap. text 21.50 (*0-8039-8863-X*) Sage.

Dryden, Windy & Thorne, Brian, eds. Training & Supervision for Counselling in Action. (Counselling in Action Ser.: Vol. 14). 192p. (C). 1991. 49.95 (*0-8039-8335-2*); pap. 21.50 (*0-8039-8336-0*) Sage.

Dryden, Windy & Trower, Peter, eds. Developments in Cognitive Psychotherapy. 288p. (C). 1988. text 47.50 (*0-8039-8134-1*) Sage.

Dryden, Windy & Varma, Ved P. The Stresses of Counselling in Action. (Counselling in Action Ser.). 208p. 1995. text 49.95 (*0-8039-8995-4*); pap. text 21.50 (*0-8039-8996-2*) Sage.

Dryden, Windy & Yankura, Joseph. Developing Rational Emotive Behavioural Therapy. LC 95-217342. (Developing Counselling Ser.). 144p. 1995. 39.95 (*0-8039-7754-9*); pap. 18.95 (*0-8039-7755-7*) Sage.

Dryden, Windy, et al. Issues in Professional Counselor Training. (Counselor Trainer & Supervisor Ser.). (Illus.). 176p. 1995. 100.00 (*0-304-32976-2*); pap. 33.95 (*0-304-32978-9*) Continuum.

— A Practitioner's Guide to Rational-Emotive Therapy. 2nd ed. (Illus.). 400p. (C). 1992. pap. text 33.95 (*0-19-507169-7*) OUP.

Dryden, Windy, jt. auth. see Ellis, Albert.

Dryden, Windy, jt. auth. see Feltham, Colin.

Dryden, Windy, jt. auth. see Neenan, Michael.

Dryden, Windy, jt. auth. see Tilney, Tony.

Dryden, Windy, jt. auth. see Traverse, John.

Dryden, Windy, jt. auth. see Yankura, Joe.

Dryden, Windy, jt. auth. see Yankura, Joseph.

Dryden, Windy, ed. see Charleton, Mary.

Dryden, Windy, jt. ed. see Mearns, Dave.

Dryden, Windy, jt. ed. see Palmer, Stephen.

Dryden, Windy, jt. ed. see Woolfe, Ray.

Dryden, Windy, jt. ed. see Yankura, Joseph.

Dryden, Windy Binding. Essential Arnold Lazarus. 248p. 1995. pap. 27.50 (*0-87668-002-3*) Aronson.

Drye, Stephen C. & Wake, William C. JAVA Foundation Classes: Swing Reference. LC 98-29935. 1085p. 1999. pap. 39.95 (*1-884777-67-8*) Manning Pubns.

***Dryenhaus, David, ed.** Recrafting the Rule of Law: The Limits of Legal Order. 340p. 1999. 54.00 (*1-901362-31-0*, Pub. by Hart Pub) Intl Spec Bk.

Dryer, Douglas P. Kant's Solution for Verification in Metaphysics. LC 66-77652. 528p. reprint ed. pap. 163.70 (*0-608-10151-6*, 201214400080) Bks Demand.

Dryer, Frederick L. & Sawyer, Robert F., eds. Physical & Chemical Aspects of Combustion: A Tribute to Irvin Glassman. (Combustion Science & Technology Ser.). 520p. 1997. text 69.00 (*90-5699-584-7*) Gordon & Breach.

Dryer, J. F. Dryer: Ancestry of Rufus K. Dryer. (Illus.). 280p. 1991. reprint ed. pap. 43.50 (*0-8328-2139-X*); reprint ed. lib. bdg. 53.50 (*0-8328-2138-1*) Higginson Bk Co.

Dryer, Murray & Tandberg-Hanssen, Einar, eds. Solar & Interplanetary Dynamics. (International Astronomical Union Symposia Ser.: No. 91). 570p. 1980. pap. text 78.00 (*90-277-1163-1*); lib. bdg. 165.00 (*90-277-1162-3*) Kluwer Academic.

Dryer, Raymond C. December 7, 1941 - Remembered: An Eyewitness Account. 96p. 1991. 15.95 (*0-9631304-0-4*) D&Ds Pub.

Dryer, Sharon Spred. The Bookfinder: A Guide to Children's Literature about the Needs & Problems of Youth Aged 2 to 15. 1993. pap. text 49.95 (*0-88671-169-X*) Am Guidance.

Dryer, Stan. The Antique Radio Boys & the Garrulous Grebe. 64p. 1992. 4.95 (*1-882452-00-3*) Antique Radio.

Dryfoos, Joy G. Adolescents at Risk: Prevalence & Prevention. (Illus.). 288p. 1991. reprint ed. pap. text 24.95 (*0-19-507268-5*) OUP.

— Full-Service Schools: A Revolution in Health & Social Services for Children, Youth & Families. 1998. pap. text 21.95 (*0-7879-4064-X*) Jossey-Bass.

— Safe Passage: Making It Through Adolescence in a Risky Society. LC 97-36424. (Illus.). 304p. (C). 1998. 27.50 (*0-19-511256-3*) OUP.

***Dryfoos, Joy G.** Safe Passage: Making It Through Adolescence in a Risky Society: What Parents, School & Communities Can Do. (Illus.). 304p. 2000. pap. 15.95 (*0-19-513785-X*) OUP.

Dryhurst, Dinah. Black Beauty Diary, 1. (Diaries Ser.). (J). 1999. 14.95 (*1-57145-106-4*) Advantage Pubs.

Dryhurst, G. & Niki, K., eds. Redox Chemistry & Interfacial Behavior of Biological Molecules. LC 88-29382. (Illus.). 672p. 1988. 145.00 (*0-306-43038-X*, Plenum Trade) Perseus Pubng.

***Dryhurst, James.** C. Michelet: La Grande Muraille. 72p. 1999. pap. 35.00 (*0-85261-527-2*, Pub. by U of Glasgow) St Mut.

Dryk, Marti. The Fraction Family Heads West. (Illus.). 32p. (J). (gr. 2-8). 1997. text 16.95 (*0-9658912-0-8*); pap. text 6.95 (*0-9658912-1-6*) Bookaloppy Pr.

Drymon, Kathleen. Blaze of Desire. 288p. 1999. mass mkt. 5.99 (*0-8217-6098-X*) Kensgtn Pub Corp.

— Gentle Savage. 1990. mass mkt. 4.50 (*0-8217-2915-2*, Zebra Kensgtn) Kensgtn Pub Corp.

— Legend of Desire. 320p. 1998. pap. 5.99 (*0-8217-5924-8*, Zebra Kensgtn) Kensgtn Pub Corp.

— Precious Amber. 1996. mass mkt. 4.99 (*0-8217-5328-2*, Zebra Kensgtn) Kensgtn Pub Corp.

Dryne, Jane. The Black Stallion: Teaching Methods & Materials. (Literature Units Ser.). (Illus.). 48p. (J). (gr. 5-8). 1995. pap. text, wbk. ed. 7.95 (*1-55734-416-7*) Tchr Create Mat.

Dryoff, George V., ed. Manual on Significance of Tests for Petroleum Products. 6th ed. LC 93-39717. (Manual Ser.: No. 1). 127p. 1993. 33.00 (*0-8031-2050-8*, MNL1) ASTM.

Drysdale. Holiness in the Parables. pap. 7.99 (*0-88019-044-2*) Schmul Pub Co.

— Problem Solving for Entrepreneurs: A Creative New Approach to Overcoming Your Business Problems. 1995. pap. text 15.95 (*0-9639506-1-4*) SMD Pubng.

Drysdale, Alan. Doing Aikido. (Illus.). 128p. 1996. pap. 15.00 (*0-9668244-0-7*) Spitz Pubg.

Drysdale, Alasdair & Blake, Gerald H. The Middle East & North Africa: A Political Geography. LC 84-1095. (Illus.). 382p. 1985. pap. text 33.95 (*0-19-503538-0*) OUP.

Drysdale, Alasdair & Hinnebusch, Raymond A. Syria & the Middle East Peace Process. LC 91-23949. 256p. 1991. reprint ed. pap. 79.40 (*0-608-02007-9*, 206266300003) Bks Demand.

Drysdale, Anne. A Pig in a Passage. large type ed. 250p. 1998. 24.95 (*0-7531-5059-X*, Pub. by ISIS Lrg Prnt) Transaction Pubs.

***Drysdale, Anne.** A Pig in a Passage. large type ed. 1998. 25.95 (*0-7531-5829-9*) T T Beeler.

— A Pig in a Passage. large type unabridged ed. 130p. 1999. pap. 19.95 (*0-7531-5067-0*, 150670, Pub. by ISIS Lrg Prnt) ISIS Pub.

Drysdale, Bryan & Blan, Julie. Never Give up, Never Give In: How to Achieve Your Goals Through the Power of Perseverance. LC 93-86783. 200p. 1994. pap. 14.95 (*0-9639506-7-3*) SMD Pubng.

Drysdale, Dougal. Introduction to Fire Dynamics. LC 98-26200. 460p. 1997. 119.95 (*0-471-97290-8*) Wiley.

Drysdale, Dougal. Introduction to Fire Dynamics. LC 98-26200. 470p. 1998. pap. 64.95 (*0-471-97291-6*) Wiley.

Drysdale, Eric C., tr. see Furtado, Celso.

Drysdale, John A. Profitable Menu Planning. 2nd ed. LC 97-26733. 378p. (C). 1997. pap. text 82.00 (*0-13-646944-2*) P-H.

Drysdale, Minerva House, jt. auth. see Hamilton, Robert W.

Drysdale, Patrick. The Journey to No-Self: A Personal Account of the Mystical Experience. LC 97-81138. 192p. 1999. pap. 14.95 (*1-56184-136-6*) New Falcon Pubns.

Drysdale, Peter. International Economic Pluralism: Economic Policy in East Asia & the Pacific. 368p. (C). 1990. text 75.00 (*0-04-335062-3*) Routledge.

Drysdale, Peter & Gower, Luke. The Japanese Economy. LC 98-2521. (Library of Modern Japan). 1592p. (C). 2000. 700.00 (*0-415-17435-X*) Routledge.

Drysdale, Peter & Gower, Luke, eds. Japanese Economy Pt. 1, Set. LC 98-2521. (Routledge Library of Modern Japan Ser.). 1400p. (C). 1998. 700.00 (*0-415-17430-9*) Routledge.

Drysdale, Peter & O'Hare, Martin, eds. The Soviets & the Pacific Challenge. LC 91-8373. 182p. (gr. 13). 1992. text 75.95 (*0-87332-866-3*); pap. text 42.95 (*0-87332-867-1*) M E Sharpe.

***Drysdale, Peter & Sung, Li-Kang.** China's Entry to the WTO: Strategic Issues & Quantitative Assessments. LC 00-42462. 2000. write for info. (*0-415-24101-4*) Routledge.

Drysdale, Peter & Vines, David, eds. Europe, East Asia & the APEC: A Shared Global Agenda. (Global Economic Institutions Ser.: No. 1). (Illus.). 322p. (C). 1998. text 59.95 (*0-521-63315-X*) Cambridge U Pr.

Drysdale, Rosemary. Miniature Crocheting & Knitting for Dollhouses. (Illus.). 48p. 1982. pap. 3.95 (*0-486-23964-0*) Dover.

Drysdale, Vera L., ed. The Gift of the Sacred Pipe: Based on Black Elk's Account of the Seven Rites of the Oglala Sioux As Originally Recorded & Edited by Joseph Epes Brown. LC 81-15949. 120p. 1995. pap. 27.95 (*0-8061-2311-7*) U of Okla Pr.

Drysdale, William. Pine Ridge Plantation. LC 75-38647. (Black Heritage Library Collection). 1977. reprint ed. 27.95 (*0-8369-9005-6*) Ayer.

Drysdall, A. R., et al, eds. Felsic Plutonic Rocks & Associated Mineralization of the Kingdom of Saudi Arabia. 292p. 1986. pap. 51.00 (*0-08-032634-X*, Pub. by PPL) Elsevier.

Drysdall, Denis L. & De Lavardin, Jacques, eds. La Celestine in the French Translation of 1578. (Textos B Ser.: Vol. XVIII). 266p. (Orig.). (C). 1974. pap. 51.00 (*0-900411-83-X*, Pub. by Tamesis Bks Ltd) Boydell & Brewer.

Dryuk, V. G. The Mechanism of Epoxidation of Olefins by Pelacids. 1977. pap. 32.00 (*0-08-021586-6*, Pergamon Pr) Elsevier.

Dryzek, John. Democracy in Capitalist Times: Ideals, Limits & Struggles. 192p. (C). 1996. pap. text 20.95 (*0-19-510600-8*) OUP.

Dryzek, John & Schlosberg, David, eds. Debating the Earth: The Environmental Politics Reader. (Illus.). 624p. (C). 1998. text 75.00 (*0-19-878228-4*); pap. text 31.95 (*0-19-878227-6*) OUP.

Dryzek, John S. Discursive Democracy: Politics, Policy & Political Science. (Illus.). 264p. (C). 1994. pap. text 19.95 (*0-521-47827-8*) Cambridge U Pr.

— The Politics of the Earth: Environmental Discourses. LC 97-7366. (Illus.). 234p. (C). 1997. text 71.00 (*0-19-878160-1*); pap. text 21.95 (*0-19-878159-8*) OUP.

***Dryzek, John S.** Rational Ecology: Environment & Political Economy. 270p. 2000. reprint ed. pap. 44.95 (*1-930665-09-1*) Blackburn Pr.

Dryzek, John S., jt. auth. see Bobrow, Davis B.

Dryzhakova, Elena, jt. auth. see Altshuller, Mark.

Drzaic, Paul S. Nematic Dispersions. (Liquid Crystals Ser.: Vol. 2). 200p. 1995. text 48.00 (*981-02-1745-5*) World Scientific Pub.

Drzal, Lawrence T., ed. see Astm Committee D-30 On High Modulus Fibers & Their.

Drzemczewski, Andrew Z. European Human Rights Convention in Domestic Law: A Comparative Study. 372p. 1998. pap. text 49.95 (*0-19-825525-X*) OUP.

Drzewiecki, Gary M. & Li, John K., eds. Analysis & Assessment of Cardiovascular Function. LC 97-22078. (Illus.). 352p. 1997. 79.95 (*0-387-98282-5*) Spr-Verlag.

Drzewiecki, T. M., ed. see American Society of Mechanical Engineers Staff.

Drzewiecki, Tadusz M., ed. see Fluidics Symposium Staff.

Drzewucki, Vincent, Jr. Gardening in Deer Country. Colby, J., ed. (Gardening Guides Ser.). (Illus.). 110p. (Orig.). 1998. pap. 9.95 (*1-883283-09-4*) Brick Tower.

Drzick, Lynn, jt. auth. see Gideon, Nancy.

D'Sa, Aires A., jt. auth. see Chant, Anthony D.

Dschulnigg, Peter, jt. auth. see Ruckstuhl, Eugen.

Dshalalow, Jewgeni H. Advances in Queuing: Theory, Methods & Open Problems. LC 95-31086. 528p. 1995. lib. bdg. 95.00 (*0-8493-8074-X*, 8074) CRC Pr.

— Applied Real Analysis. (Studies in Advanced Mathematics). 1999. 79.95 (*0-8493-7165-1*) CRC Pr.

Dshalalow, Jewgeni H., ed. Frontiers in Queueing: Models & Applications in Science & Engineering. LC 96-49563. (Probability & Stochastics Ser.). 480p. 1997. boxed set 89.95 (*0-8493-8076-6*) CRC Pr.

***Dsikszentmih.** Becoming Adult. 2000. pap. 15.00 (*0-465-01541-7*, Pub. by Basic) HarpC.

D

D'Silva, Emmanuel & Appanah, Simmathiri. Forestry Management for Sustainable Development. LC 93-6024. (EDI Policy Seminar Reports: Vol. 32). 52p. 1993. 6.95 (*0-8213-2597-3*, 12597) World Bank.

D'Silva, Emmanuel H. & Bysouth, Kaye. Poverty Alleviation Through Agricultural Projects: Report on a Seminar Held Jointly by the Asian Development Bank, the Centre on Integrated Rural Development for Asia & the Pacific, & the Economic Development Institute of the World Bank. LC 92-23284. (EDI Policy Seminar Reports: No. 30). 88p. 1992. pap. 22.00 (*0-8213-2200-1*, 12200) World Bank.

D'Silva, Joyce & Tansey, Geoff, eds. The Meat Business: Devouring a Hungry Planet. LC 99-30053. 249p. 1999. text 45.00 (*0-312-22686-1*) St Martin.

D'Sousa, Rudolf V. The Bhagavadgeitea & St. John of the Cross: A Comparative Study of the Dynamism of Spiritual Growth in the Process of God-Realisation. LC 96-225739. (Tesi Gregoriana Ser.). 483 p. 1996. write for info. (*88-7652-699-4*) Gregorian Univ Pr.

D'Sousa, Valerian. Bioorganic Chemistry of Enzymatic Catalysis: An Homage to Myron L. Bender. 208p. 1991. lib. bdg. 169.00 (*0-8493-6823-5*, QP601) CRC Pr.

D'Souza. Development Planning & Structural Inequalities: The Response of the Underprivileged. 208p. 1991. 27.50 (*0-8039-9664-0*) Sage.

— Toolbk Strat Bus Integrt. 3rd ed. 242p. 1999. pap. text 27.50 (*0-536-02334-4*) Pearson Custom.

***D'Souza, Aruna, ed.** Self & History: Essays in Honor of Linda Nochlin. LC 00-101149. (Illus.). 224p. 2001. pap. 24.95 (*0-500-28250-1*, Pub. by Thames Hudson) Norton.

D'Souza, Desmond. Objects, Components, & Frameworks with UML. LC 98-31109. 816p. (C). 1998. pap. text 49.95 (*0-201-31012-0*) Addison-Wesley.

D'Souza, Dinesh. The End of Racism: Principles for a Multiracial Society. 756p. 1996. per. 16.00 (*0-684-82524-4*) S&S Trade.

— Illiberal Education: Political Correctness & the College Experience. (Excellence in Education Ser.). 32p. (Orig.). 1992. pap. 3.00 (*1-878802-08-9*) J M Ashbrook Ctr Pub Affairs.

— Illiberal Education: The Politics of Race & Sex on Campus. 1992. pap. 13.00 (*0-679-73857-6*) Vin Bks.

***D'Souza, Dinesh.** The Moral Conundrum of Success: Searching for Values in an Age of Prosperity & Technology. 2000. 26.00 (*0-684-86814-8*) Free Pr.

D'Souza, Dinesh. Ronald Reagan: How an Ordinary Man Became an Extraordinary Leader. 304p. 1999. per. 13.00 (*0-684-84823-6*, Touchstone) S&S Trade Pap.

— Ronald Reagan: Spirit of a Leader. LC 97-31396. 289p. 1997. 24.50 (*0-684-84428-1*) Free Pr.

D'Souza, Dinesh & Fossedal, Gregory. My Dear Alex: Letters from the KGB. LC 87-9720. 160p. 1987. 14.95 (*0-89526-576-1*) Regnery Pub.

D'Souza, Gerard E. & Gebremedhin, Tesfa G., eds. Sustainability in Agricultural & Rural Development. LC 97-51331. 245p. 1998. text 72.95 (*1-85521-977-8*, Pub. by Dartmth Pub) Ashgate Pub Co.

D'Souza, Giles, et al, eds. Advances in the Use of NOAA AVHRR Data for Land Applications: Based on the Lectures Given During the Eurocourse Held at the Joint Research Centre, Ispra, Italy, December 6-12, 1993. LC 95-52287. (Eurocourses: Remoting Sensing Ser.: Vol. 5). 492p. (C). 1996. text 254.00 (*0-7923-3911-8*) Kluwer Academic.

D'Souza, I. & Kalman, C. S. Preons: Models of Leptons, Quarks & Gauge Bosons as Composite Particles. 100p. 1992. text 36.00 (*981-02-1019-1*) World Scientific Pub.

D'Souza, Natasha. Touching the Stars. 1997. pap. 56.95 (*1-57553-658-7*) Watermrk Pr.

D'Souza, Valerian T. Chymotrypsins: Real & Artificial. 352p. 1991. lib. bdg. 129.00 (*0-8493-6433-7*, RC267) CRC Pr.

D'Souza, Victor S. Inequality & Its Perpetuation. 1982. 18.50 (*0-8364-0873-X*, Pub. by Manohar) S Asia.

DSR Inc. Staff. Consequences English Discussion Guidelines. (Illus.). 4p. 1991. write for info. (*0-936731-09-5*) Devel Self Rel.

— Consequences Ndebele Discussion Guidelines. (Illus.). 4p. 1991. write for info. (*0-936731-12-5*) Devel Self Rel.

— Consequences Shona Discussion Guidelines. (Illus.). 4p. 1991. write for info. (*0-936731-11-7*) Devel Self Rel.

DSS Staff. Social Security Research Yearbook, 1993/1994. (DSS Research Report Ser.). 1994. 35.00 (*0-11-762302-4*, Pub. by Statnry Office) Bernan Associates.

— Social Security Research Yearbook, 1994/1995. (DSS Research Report Ser.). 1995. 40.00 (*0-11-762362-8*, Pub. by Statnry Office) Bernan Associates.

— Social Security Research Yearbook, 1995/96. (DSS Research Report Ser.). 1996. write for info. (*0-11-762446-2*, Pub. by Statnry Office) Bernan Associates.

***Dssouli, R., et al.** SDL '99, the Next Millennium: Proceedings of the 9th SDL Forum, Montreal, Quebec, Canada, 21-25, 1999. abr. ed. LC 99-29948. 502p. 1999. 124.50 (*0-444-50228-9*) Elsevier.

DST Staff. Robotics. (C). 1988. 47.50 (*81-204-0349-5*, Pub. by Oxford IBH) S Asia.

Dtr Business Systems Staff. Using Unix. 2nd ed. (Using... Ser.). 1998. pap. 29.99 (*0-7897-1632-1*) Que.

DTV Staff. DTV Junior Lexikon, 10 vols., Set. (GER.). 1974. pap. 69.95 (*0-8288-6029-7*, M7340) Fr & Eur.

— DTV Kindlers, 25 vols. (GER.). 1986. pap. 310.00 (*0-8288-1565-8*, M7341) Fr & Eur.

Du. Peptides Biology & Chemistry. 352p. 1993. text 154.00 (*90-72199-18-9*) Kluwer Academic.

Du Bartas, Guillaume D. Bartas: His Devine Weekes & Workes. LC 65-10398. 1965. reprint ed. lib. bdg. 90.00 (*0-8201-1265-8*) Schol Facsimiles.

Du Bellay. Les Regrets. (FRE.). (C). 1967. pap. 11.95 (*0-8442-1999-1*, VF1999-1) NTC Contemp Pub Co.

Du Bellay, Jean. Correspondance, 2 vols. (FRE.). 549p. 1969. 25.95 (*0-7859-0064-0*, M1364); 39.95 (*0-686-56035-3*) Fr & Eur.

Du Bellay, Joachim. Les Antiquitez de Rome... And Ruines at Rome. Smith, Malcolm C., ed. Spencer, Edmund, tr. LC 96-133461. 144p. 1994. pap. 10.95 (*0-86698-126-8*, P22) Pegasus Pr.

— Les Regrets et Autres Oeuvres Poetiques. Jolliffe, ed. (Textes Litteraires Francais Ser.). 8.75 (*0-685-34184-4*) Fr & Eur.

— Regrets, Les Antiquites de Rome, Defense et Illustration, Etc. (Poesie Ser.). (FRE.). 317p. 1967. pap. 9.95 (*2-07-032147-9*) Schoenhof.

Du Bellay, Joachim & Caldarini, E. L' Olive. (FRE.). 180p. 1975. 49.95 (*0-7859-0060-8*, M11796) Fr & Eur.

Du Bellay, Joachim & Nolhac, Pierre de. Lettres. (Illus.). 120p. 1974. 49.95 (*0-7859-5527-5*) Fr & Eur.

Du Bellay, Joachim & Saulnier, V. L. Divers Jeux Rustiques. 232p. 1965. 35.00 (*0-8288-9915-0*, F28915) Fr & Eur.

du Bellet, Louise P. Some Prominent Virginia Families, 2 vols. in 4. LC 76-13286. (Illus.). 1715p. 1994. reprint ed. pap. 135.00 (*0-8063-0722-6*) Clearfield Co.

Du Blanc, Bernardo. Relief in Recovery: A Guide to a Joyful Sobriety that Lasts. (Illus.). (Orig.). 1995. pap. 19.95 (*1-887195-15-7*) Visual Bks.

— Relief Recorder: Record Your Foods & Moods for Emotional Relief. (Illus.). 1995. pap. 10.95 (*1-887195-16-5*) Visual Bks.

Du Bocacho, Manuel M. De Barrosa, see De Barrosa Du Bocacho, Manuel M.

Du Boff, Richard B. Accumulation & Power: An Economic History of the United States. LC 88-39542. 252p. (C). (gr. 13). 1989. pap. text 35.95 (*0-87332-559-1*) M E Sharpe.

Du Bois, Anne, ed. see Dumond, K. J. & Merlin, Ann.

Du Bois, Charles G. The Custer Mystery. LC 86-5029. (Montana & the West Ser.: Vol. 4V). (Illus.). 198p. (C). 2000. 35.00 (*0-912783-06-0*) Upton & Sons.

— Kick the Dead Lion: A Casebook of the Custer Battle. LC 87-50695. (Echoes of the Little Big Horn Ser.: Vol. 1). (Illus.). 120p. (C). 1987. reprint ed. 35.00 (*0-912783-09-5*) Upton & Sons.

Du Bois, Cora A. Social Forces in Southeast Asia. LC 59-2120. (Smith College Lectures: No. 1947). (Illus.). 82p. 1959. reprint ed. pap. 30.00 (*0-7837-4143-X*, 205799100012) Bks Demand.

Du Bois, David A., jt. auth. see Gadbow, Nancy F.

Du Bois, Donna. Enteral Feedings in the Nursing Home. (Illus.). 111p. (Orig.). (C). 1988. 13.50 (*1-877735-20-5*, 2135PP) Prof Prnting & Pub.

— When the Nursing Home Is the Choice. 76p. 1991. 9.50 (*1-877735-17-5*, 2130pp) Prof Prnting & Pub.

Du Bois, Jack, jt. auth. see Darby, William.

Du Bois, Paul M., jt. auth. see Lappe, Frances M.

Du Bois, Paul Z., ed. see Nicholson, John B., Jr.

Du Bois, Rachel D. & Schweppe, Emma. The Germans in American Life. 1977. 17.95 (*0-8369-6928-6*, 7809) Ayer.

Du Bois-Reymond, Emil H. Two Great Scientists of the Nineteenth Century: Correspondence of Emil Du Bois-Reymond & Carl Ludwig. Ayes, Sabine L. & Cranefield, Paul F., trs. LC 79-24140. (Illus.). 203p. reprint ed. pap. 63.00 (*0-8357-6609-8*, 203525400094) Bks Demand.

du Bois-Reymond, Manuela, et al, eds. Childhood & Youth in Germany & the Netherlands: Transitions & Coping Strategies of Adolescents. (International Studies on Childhood & Adolescence: Vol. 1). xii, 352p. (C). 1995. lib. bdg. 74.95 (*3-11-014154-X*) De Gruyter.

Du Bois, Shirley G. His Day Is Marching on: Memoirs of W. E. B. Du Bois. LC 71-146693. 1971. 30.00 (*0-89388-156-2*); pap. 15.00 (*0-89388-157-0*) Okpaku Communications.

— Pictorial History of W. E. B. Du Bois. LC 77-16696. 174p. 14.95 (*0-87485-076-2*) Johnson Chicago.

Du Bois, W. E. B. Against Racism: Unpublished Essays, Papers, Addresses, 1887-1961. Aptheker, Herbert, ed. LC 84-16173. (Illus.). 304p. 1988. pap. 19.95 (*0-87023-624-5*) U of Mass Pr.

— Autobiography of W. E. Burghardt Du Bois: A Soliloquy on Viewing My Life from the Last Decade of Its First Century. Aptheker, Herbert, ed. LC 68-14103. 448p. (C). 1968. 19.00 (*0-7178-0235-3*) Intl Pubs Co.

— Autobiography of W. E. Burghardt Du Bois: A Soliloquy on Viewing My Life from the Last Decade of Its First Century. Aptheker, Herbert, ed. LC 68-14103. (Illus.). 448p. (C). 1968. pap. 14.95 (*0-7178-0234-5*) Intl Pubs Co.

— Black North in Nineteen One: A Social Study. LC 70-92229. (American Negro: His History & Literature. Series 2). 1970. reprint ed. 11.95 (*0-405-01921-1*) Ayer.

***Du Bois, W. E. B.** Black Reconstruction: An Essay Toward a History of the Part Which Black Folk Played in the Attempt to Reconstruct Democracy in America, 1860-1880. rev. ed. (African American Intellectual Heritage Ser.). 776p. 2001. pap. 24.95 (*0-268-02164-3*, Pub. by U of Notre Dame Pr); lib. bdg. 48.95 (*0-268-02165-1*, Pub. by U of Notre Dame Pr) Chicago Distribution Ctr.

Du Bois, W. E. B. Colonies & Democracy: Color & Race. (African Heritage Classical Research Studies). 143p. reprint ed. 20.00 (*0-938818-55-4*) ECA Assoc.

— The Correspondence of W. E. B. Du Bois Vol. 1: Selections, 1877-1934. Aptheker, Herbert, ed. LC 72-90496. (Illus.). 510p. 1973. 40.00 (*0-87023-131-6*) U of Mass Pr.

— The Correspondence of W. E. B. Du Bois Vol. 1: Selections, 1877-1934. Aptheker, Herbert, ed. LC 72-90496. (Illus.). 510p. 1997. pap. 20.95 (*1-55849-103-1*) U of Mass Pr.

— The Correspondence of W. E. B. Du Bois Vol. 2: Selections, 1934-1944. Aptheker, Herbert, ed. LC 72-90496. (Illus.). 512p. 1976. 40.00 (*0-87023-132-4*) U of Mass Pr.

— The Correspondence of W. E. B. Du Bois Vol. II: Selections, 1934-1944. Aptheker, Herbert, ed. LC 72-90496. (Illus.). 512p. 1997. pap. 20.95 (*1-55849-104-X*) U of Mass Pr.

— The Correspondence of W. E. B. Du Bois Vol. 3: Selections, 1944-1963. Aptheker, Herbert, ed. LC 72-90496. (Illus.). 512p. 1978. lib. bdg. 40.00 (*0-87023-133-2*) U of Mass Pr.

— The Correspondence of W. E. B. Du Bois Vol. III: Selections, 1944-1963. Aptheker, Herbert, ed. LC 72-90496. (Illus.). 512p. 1997. pap. 20.95 (*1-55849-105-8*) U of Mass Pr.

— Dark Princess: A Romance. LC 94-43867. (Banner Bk.). 1995. pap. 16.95 (*0-87805-765-X*); lib. bdg. 40.00 (*0-87805-764-1*) U Pr of Miss.

— Darkwater: Voices from Within the Veil. LC 99-32231. (Thrift Editions Ser.). 256p. 1999. pap. text 2.00 (*0-486-40890-6*) Dover.

— Darkwater: Voices from Within the Veil. LC 70-91785. reprint ed. 37.50 (*0-404-00151-3*) AMS Pr.

— Darkwater: Voices from Within the Veil. (BCL1 - U. S. History Ser.). 276p. 1991. reprint ed. lib. bdg. 79.00 (*0-7812-6084-1*) Rprt Serv.

— The Du Bois Reader: A Reader. Lewis, David L., ed. 1995. pap. 16.95 (*0-8050-3264-9*) H Holt & Co.

— Dusk of Dawn: An Essay Toward an Autobiography of a Race Concept. (Black Classics in Social Science Ser.). 355p. 1991. reprint ed. pap. 21.95 (*0-87855-917-5*) Transaction Pubs.

— The Education of Black People: Ten Critiques, 1906-1960. Aptheker, Herbert, ed. LC 72-90495. 176p. 1975. reprint ed. pap. 12.00 (*0-85345-363-2*, Pub. by Monthly Rev) NYU Pr.

— The Gift of Black Folk. LC 70-144598. reprint ed. 15.00 (*0-404-00152-1*) AMS Pr.

— John Brown. LC 96-48132. (American History Through Literature Ser.). 254p. (gr. 13). 1997. pap. text 21.95 (*1-56324-972-3*) M E Sharpe.

— John Brown. LC 96-48132. (American History Through Literature Ser.). 254p. (C). (gr. 13). 1997. text 74.95 (*1-56324-971-5*) M E Sharpe.

— Negro in Business. LC 70-153098. reprint ed. 37.50 (*0-404-00153-X*) AMS Pr.

— The Philadelphia Negro. 540p. 1972. 18.95 (*0-405-18100-0*) Ayer.

— The Philadelphia Negro: A Social Study. 560p. 1995. pap. 16.95 (*0-8122-1573-7*) U of Pa Pr.

— Prayers for Dark People. Aptheker, Herbert, ed. LC 80-12234. 88p. 1980. pap. 10.95 (*0-87023-303-3*) U of Mass Pr.

— Quest of the Silver Fleece. LC 71-83922. (Black Heritage Library Collection). (Illus.). 1977. 20.95 (*0-8369-8553-2*) Ayer.

— Quest of the Silver Fleece. LC 73-144599. reprint ed. 37.50 (*0-404-00154-8*) AMS Pr.

— Quest of the Silver Fleece. LC 73-86658. (American Negro: His History & Literature. Series 3). 1970. reprint ed. 20.95 (*0-405-01922-X*) Ayer.

— The Souls of Black Folk. 1976. 22.95 (*0-8488-0995-5*) Amereon Ltd.

— The Souls of Black Folk. 224p. 1989. mass mkt. 5.50 (*0-553-21336-9*) Bantam.

— The Souls of Black Folk. LC 93-1859. 1993. 15.00 (*0-679-42802-X*) Everymns Lib.

— The Souls of Black Folk. 322p. 1996. 14.50 (*0-679-60187-2*) Modern Lib NY.

— The Souls of Black Folk. 288p. 1995. mass mkt. 4.95 (*0-451-52603-1*, Sig) NAL.

***Du Bois, W. E. B.** The Souls of Black Folk. Gates, Henry Louis, Jr. & Oliver, Terri Hume, eds. LC 98-31634. 1999. pap. 11.25 (*0-393-97393-X*) Norton.

Du Bois, W. E. B. The Souls of Black Folk. Gooding-Williams, Robert & Blight, David W., eds. LC 96-86763. 224p. 1997. text 35.00 (*0-312-12806-1*) St Martin.

— The Souls of Black Folk. Blight, David W. & Gooding-Williams, Robert, eds. LC 96-86763. 184p. 1997. pap. text 11.95 (*0-312-09114-1*) St Martin.

— The Souls of Black Folk. LC 97-39940. (Isis Large Print Bks.). 257p. 1998. text 24.95 (*1-56000-524-6*) Transaction Pubs.

Du Bois, W. E. B. The Souls of Black Folk. LC 71-82444. (Signet Classics). (J). 1969. 10.05 (*0-606-03475-7*, Pub. by Turtleback) Demco.

Du Bois, W. E. B. The Souls of Black Folk. 288p. (C). 1996. pap. 9.95 (*0-14-018998-X*) Viking Penguin.

— The Souls of Black Folk. 228p. 1990. pap. 11.50 (*0-679-72519-9*) Vin Bks.

***Du Bois, W. E. B.** Souls of Black Folk. 2000. pap. 9.95 (*1-930097-13-1*) Lushena Bks.

Du Bois, W. E. B. The Souls of Black Folk. 280p. 1986. reprint ed. lib. bdg. 22.95 (*0-89966-535-7*) Buccaneer Bks.

— The Souls of Black Folk. (Thrift Editions Ser.). (Illus.). 176p. 1994. reprint ed. pap. 2.00 (*0-486-28041-1*) Dover.

— The Suppression of the African Slave-Trade. 27.95 (*0-8488-1289-1*) Amereon Ltd.

— The Suppression of the African Slave-Trade to the U. S., 1638-1870. (History - United States Ser.). 335p. 1992. reprint ed. lib. bdg. 89.00 (*0-7812-6153-8*) Rprt Serv.

— The Suppression of the African Slave-Trade to the United States of America. 344p. 1987. reprint ed. lib. bdg. 26.95 (*0-89966-588-8*) Buccaneer Bks.

— Suppression of the African Slave Trade to the United States of America, 1638-1870. LC 99-31505. 352p. 1999. pap. text 9.95 (*0-486-40910-4*) Dover.

— Suppression of the African Slave Trade, 1638-1870. LC 65-18803. xx, 336p. 1970. pap. text 19.95 (*0-8071-0149-4*) La State U Pr.

— W. E. B. Du Bois: A Reader. Paschal, Andrew G., ed. LC 92-30128. 376p. 1993. reprint ed. pap. 12.00 (*0-02-002351-0*) Macmillan.

— W. E. B. Du Bois on Sociology & the Black Community. Green, Dan S. & Driver, Edwin D., eds. LC 78-770. (Illus.). viii, 328p. (C). 1996. pap. text 21.00 (*0-226-16762-3*) U Ch Pr.

— W. E. B. Du Bois on Sociology & the Black Community. Green, Dan S. & Driver, Edwin D., eds. LC 78-770. 320p. 1980. reprint ed. pap. 17.95 (*0-226-16760-7*, 866) U Ch Pr.

— W. E. B. Du Bois Speaks, 2 vols. Incl. Vol. 1. W. E. B. Du Bois Speaks: Speeches & Addresses, 1890-1919. Foner, Philip S., ed. LC 78-108719. 289p. 1970. reprint ed. lib. bdg. 50.00 (*0-87348-181-X*); Vol. 1. W. E. B. Du Bois Speaks: Speeches & Addresses, 1890-1919. Foner, Philip S., ed. LC 78-108719. 289p. 1970. reprint ed. pap. 18.95 (*0-87348-125-9*); Vol. 2. W. E. B. Du Bois Speaks: Speeches & Addresses, 1920-1963. LC 78-108719. 1988. reprint ed. lib. bdg. 55.00 (*0-87348-182-8*); Vol. 2. W. E. B. Du Bois Speaks: Speeches & Addresses, 1920-1963. Foner, Philip S., ed. LC 78-108719. 346p. 1970. reprint ed. pap. 19.95 (*0-87348-126-7*); LC 78-108719. write for info. (*0-318-54959-X*) Pathfinder NY.

— World & Africa: Inquiry into the Part Which Africa Has Played in World History. rev. ed. LC 65-16392. (Illus.). 1965. pap. 8.95 (*0-7178-0221-3*) Intl Pubs Co.

— The World of W. E. B. Du Bois: A Quotation Sourcebook. Weinberg, Meyer, ed. LC 92-15481. 296p. 1992. lib. bdg. 75.00 (*0-313-28619-1*, WWJ, Greenwood Pr) Greenwood.

— Writings: The Suppression of the African Slave-Trade; The Souls of Black Folk; Dusk of Dawn; Essay; Articles from The Crisis. Huggins, Nathan I., ed. LC 86-10565. 1334p. 1987. 35.00 (*0-940450-33-X*, Pub. by Library of America) Penguin Putnam.

— Writings: The Suppression of the African Slave-Trade; The Souls of Black Folk; Dusk of Dawn; Essays; Articles from the Crisis. Huggins, Nathan I., ed. LC 86-10565. (Library of America College Editions). 1334p. (C). 1996. pap. text 15.95 (*1-883011-31-0*, Pub. by Library of America) Penguin Putnam.

Du Bois, W. E. B., ed. Black Reconstruction: An Essay Toward a History of the Part Which Black Folk Played in the Attempt to Reconstruct Democracy in America, 1860-1880. (History - United States Ser.). 746p. 1993. reprint ed. lib. bdg. 169.00 (*0-7812-4871-X*) Rprt Serv.

— The Negro-American Family. LC 68-55882. (Illus.). 156p. 1970. reprint ed. lib. bdg. 35.00 (*0-8371-1342-3*, DUF&) Greenwood.

Du Bois, W. E. B., et al. African American Political Thought, 1890-1930: Washington, Du Bois, Garvey, & Randolph. Wintz, Cary D., ed. LC 95-33287. (Illus.). 360p. (C). (gr. 13). 1996. 81.95 (*1-56324-178-1*) M E Sharpe.

Du Bois, W. E. B., jt. auth. see Washington, Booker T.

Du Bois, William P. The Twenty-One Balloons. (Puffin Newbery Library Ser.). (Illus.). 180p. (J). (gr. 3-7). 1986. pap. 4.99 (*0-14-032097-0*, PuffinBks) Peng Put Young Read.

— Twenty-One Balloons. (Puffin Newbery Library). (J). 1986. 10.09 (*0-606-05077-9*, Pub. by Turtleback) Demco.

Du Bois, William P. The Twenty-One Balloons, Set. unabridged ed. (J). (gr. 5). 1997. pap. 39.24 incl. audio (*0-7887-1715-4*, 40583) Recorded Bks.

Du Bois, William P., jt. auth. see Bowen, Otis R.

Du Bois, William Pene, see Pene Du Bois, William.

Du Bois, William Pene, see Caudill, Rebecca & Pene Du Bois, William.

Du Bos, Charles. Byron & the Need of Fatality. LC 78-95423. (Studies in Byron: No. 5). 1970. reprint ed. lib. bdg. 75.00 (*0-8383-0971-2*) M S G Haskell Hse.

Du Bosc, Jacques. The Compleat Woman. LC 68-54642. (English Experience Ser.: No. 12). 88p. 1968. reprint ed. 35.00 (*90-221-0012-X*) Walter J Johnson.

Du Bouchet, Andre. Where Heat Looms. Mus, David, tr. from FRE. (Sun & Moon Classics Ser.: No. 87). 110p. 1995. pap. 12.95 (*1-55713-238-0*) Sun & Moon CA.

Du Bouchet, Paule, jt. auth. see Bernadac, Marie-Laure.

Du Boulay, Benedict, jt. auth. see Thornton, Chris.

Du Boulay, Benedict, jt. auth. see Thornton, Christopher.

Du Boulay, F. R. The England of 'Piers Plowman' William Langland & His Vision of the Fourteenth Century. (Illus.). 176p. 1991. 60.00 (*0-85991-312-0*) Boydell & Brewer.

— Germany in the Later Middle Ages. (Illus.). 272p. (C). 1988. reprint ed. pap. 15.00 (*0-485-12042-9*, Pub. by Athlone Pr) Humanities.

Du Boulay, G. H., et al, eds. Proceedings of the 14th Symposium: or Neuroadiologicum: London, June, 17-23, 1990. (Illus.). 680p. 1991. 278.00 (*0-387-53726-0*) Spr-Verlag.

Du Boulay, Shirley. Beyond Darkness: A Biography of Bede Griffiths. LC 98-30173. (Illus.). 320p. 1998. 24.95 (*0-385-48946-3*) Bantam.

— The Road to Canterbury: A Modern Pilgrimage. LC 95-22775. (Illus.). 256p. 1995. reprint ed. pap. 14.95 (*0-8192-1645-3*) Morehouse Pub.

— Tutu: Voice of the Voiceless. LC 88-11037. (Illus.). 294p. 1988. reprint ed. pap. 91.20 (*0-7837-5564-3*, 204533900005) Bks Demand.

Du Brin, Andrew. Reengineering Survival Guide: Managing in the Changing Workplace. 320p. (C). 1995. pap. 44.95 (*0-538-84387-X*) S-W Pub.

Du Brul, Jack. Charon's Landing. LC 99-24566. 384p. 1999. 24.95 (*0-312-86816-2*, Pub. by Forge NYC) St Martin.

An Asterisk (*) at the beginning of an entry indicates that the title is appearing for the first time.

***Du Brul, Jack.** Charon's Landing. 512p. 2000. mass mkt. 7.99 (*0-8125-7550-4*) Tor Bks.
— The Medusa Stone. 464p. 2000. mass mkt. 6.99 (*0-451-40922-1*, Onyx) NAL.
Du Brul, Jack. Vulcan's Forge. 1999. mass mkt. 6.99 (*0-8125-6461-8*, Pub. by Tor Bks) St Martin.
Du Camp, Maxime. Convulsions De Paris, 1878-1879, 4 vols. LC 78-164792. reprint ed. 210.00 (*0-404-07180-5*) AMS Pr.
— Theophile Gautier. Gordon, J. E., tr. (Select Bibliographies Reprint Ser.). 1977. reprint ed. 20.95 (*0-8369-5732-6*) Ayer.
Du Cane, Hubert, tr. see Prussia Kriegministerium Staff.
Du Cann, Richard. Art of the Advocate. 1993. pap. 16.95 (*0-14-017931-3*, Pub. by Pnguin Bks Ltd) Trafalgar.
Du Castel, Christine. Here Begynneth the Booke Which Is Called "the Body of Polycye" LC 72-184. (English Experience Ser.: No. 304). 180p. 1971. reprint ed. 28.00 (*90-221-0304-8*) Walter J Johnson.
— The Morale Proberbes of Christyne. LC 73-25783. (English Experience Ser.: No. 241). 8p. 1970. reprint ed. 20.00 (*90-221-0241-6*) Walter J Johnson.
Du Chaillu, Paul B. The Viking Age, 2 vols. LC 75-118628. reprint ed. 155.00 (*0-404-02187-5*) AMS Pr.
Du Chaillu, Paul E. Explorations & Adventures in Equatorial Africa. LC 74-97364. (Illus.). 531p. 1970. reprint ed. lib. bdg. 35.00 (*0-8371-2407-7*, DUE&) Greenwood.
Du Charme, Jerome, tr. see Roguet, A. M.
Du Charme, Rita M. Bibliography of Media Management & Economics. 2nd ed. 131p. (C). 1988. pap. text 12.00 (*0-944866-01-8*) Media Mgmt & Econ.
Du Chazaud, H. B. Dictionary of Synonyms: Dictionnaire des Synonymes. (ENG & FRE.). 520p. 1983. 69.95 (*0-8288-1933-5*, M5227) Fr & Eur.
Du Chazaud, Henri B. Dictionnaire des Synonymes. (FRE.). 800p. 1992. 34.95 (*0-7859-9192-1*) Fr & Eur.
— Dictionnaire des Synonymes et Contraires: Nouvelle Edition Augmentee. (FRE.). 800p. 1992. 89.95 (*0-7859-9190-5*) Fr & Eur.
— Robert Dictionary Synonymes et Contraires. (FRE.). 768p. 1997. 69.95 (*0-320-00430-9*) Fr & Eur.
Du Claux, Agnes M. Twentieth Century French Writers. LC 67-22089. (Essay Index Reprint Ser.). 258p. 1982. reprint ed. lib. bdg. 21.50 (*0-8290-0484-X*) Irvington.
Du Clos, Alain T., jt. auth. see Sarkisov, A. A.
Du Cloux, Fokko. Representations de Longueur Finie des Groupes de Lie Resolubles. LC 89-14898. (Memoirs Ser.: Vol. 80/407). 78p. 1989. pap. 18.00 (*0-8218-2470-8*, MEMO/80/407) Am Math.
Du Colombies, Pierre. Alfred Sisley in the Musee du Louvre. (Illus.). 1947. lib. bdg. 9.95 (*0-8288-3979-4*) Fr & Eur.
Du Cret, Rene P., jt. auth. see Kuni, Christopher C.
Du Creux, Francois. History of Canada, or New France, 2 Vols, Vol. 2. Conacher, James B., ed. Robinson, Percy J., tr. LC 69-14507. 371p. 1969. reprint ed. lib. bdg. 75.00 (*0-8371-5071-X*, DUHJ) Greenwood.
— History of Canada, or New France, 2 Vols, Vol. 30. Conacher, James B., ed. Robinson, Percy J., tr. LC 69-14507. 404p. 1969. reprint ed. lib. bdg. 75.00 (*0-8371-5070-1*, DUHI) Greenwood.
Du Cross, Janet T. Divided Loyalties: A Scotswoman in Occupied France. (Classics Ser.). (Illus.). 342p. 1993. pap. 13.95 (*0-86241-375-3*, Pub. by Canongate Books) Interlink Pub.
Du, D. Z., et al, eds. Algorithms & Computation, 834. (Lecture Notes in Computer Science Ser.: Vol. 834). 687p. 1994. 96.00 (*0-387-58325-4*) Spr-Verlag.
Du, D. Z. & Hwang, F. K. Combinatorial Group Testing & Applications. LC 93-26812. (Series on Applied Mathematics). 264p. 1993. text 48.00 (*981-02-1293-3*) World Scientific Pub.
Du, D. Z. & Hwang, F. K., eds. Computing in Euclidean Geometry. LC 92-19668. (Lecture Notes in Computing Ser.: Vol. 1). 400p. 1992. text 91.00 (*981-02-0966-5*) World Scientific Pub.
Du, D. Z. & Pardalos, Panos M. Network Optimization Problems: Algorithms, Applications & Complexity. (Series on Applied Mathematics). 416p. 1993. text 109.00 (*981-02-1277-1*) World Scientific Pub.
Du, Ding-Zhu, et al, eds. Computing & Combinatorics: First International Conference, COCOON '95, Xi'an, China, August 24-26, 1995, Proceedings, Vol. XIII. LC 95-24802. (Lecture Notes in Computer Science Ser.: Vol. 959). (Illus.). 654p. 1995. 100.00 (*3-540-60216-X*) Spr-Verlag.
— Recent Advances in Nonsmooth Optimization. 400p. 1995. text 78.00 (*981-02-2265-3*) World Scientific Pub.
Du, Ding-Zhu & Hsu, D. Frank, eds. Combinatorial Network Theory. (Applied Optimization Ser.: Vol. 1). 220p. (C). 1996. text 114.50 (*0-7923-3777-8*) Kluwer Academic.
Du, Ding-Zhu & Hwang, Frank, eds. Computing in Euclidean Geometry. 2nd ed. LC 94-36694. (Lecture Notes in Computing Ser.: Vol. 4). 508p. 1995. text 99.00 (*981-02-1876-1*) World Scientific Pub.
Du, Ding-Zhu & Hwang, Frank K., eds. Advances in Switching Networks. LC 98-6284. (DIMACS Ser.: Vol. 42). 333p. 1998. 70.00 (*0-8218-0831-1*, DIMACS/42) Am Math.
***Du, Ding-Zhu & Ko, Ker-I.** Theory of Computational Complexity. 504p. 2000. 89.95 (*0-471-34506-7*, Wiley-Interscience) Wiley.
Du, Ding-Zhu & Sun, Jie, eds. Advances in Optimization & Approximation. LC 94-9739. (Nonconvex Optimization & Its Applications Ser.: Vol. 1). 404p. (C). 1994. text 204.50 (*0-7923-2785-3*) Kluwer Academic.
Du, Ding-Zhu, et al. Advances in Algorithms, Languages & Complexity. LC 96-52590. 1997. text 214.00 (*0-7923-4396-4*) Kluwer Academic.
Du Dingzhu. Convergence Theory of Feasible Direction Methods. (Applied Discrete Mathematics & Theoretical Computer Science Ser.: Vol. 1). 118p. 1991. text 31.00 (*1-880132-00-1*) Sci Pr NY.
***Du, Dingzhu & Hwang, Frank.** Combinatorial Group Testing & Its Applications. 2nd ed. LC 99-48251. (Series on Applied Mathematics). 2000. 67.00 (*981-02-4107-0*) World Scientific Pub.
Du Dingzhu & Pardalos, Panos M. Handbook of Combinatorial Optimization. LC 98-2942. (Combinatorial Optimization Ser.). 1998. write for info. (*0-7923-5018-9*) Kluwer Academic.
Du Dingzhu, jt. auth. see Panalos, P. M.
Du Dingzhu, ed. see NSF Science & Technology Center in Discrete Mathem.
Du Dingzhu, ed. see Qingde, Kang.
Du Dingzhu, ed. see Rosen, J. B., et al.
Du Faur, Curt V. German Baroque Literature, 2 vols. 681p. 1997. reprint ed. 95.00 (*1-57898-050-X*) Martino Pubng.
Du Feu, Veronica. Rapanui: A Descriptive Grammar. LC 94-19109. (Descriptive Grammars Ser.). 240p. (C). (gr. 13). 1995. 190.00 (*0-415-00011-4*, B2258) Routledge.
Du-Feu, Viv & Warnock, Owen. Employment Law in the NHS. (Medico-Legal Practitioner Ser.). 173p. 1995. pap. 40.00 (*1-85941-016-2*, Pub. by Cavendish Pubng) Gaunt.
Du Fresne, Jim. Lonely Planet Tramping in New Zealand: Walking Guide. 4th ed. (Lonely Planet Walking Guides). (Illus.). 352p. 1998. pap. text 17.95 (*0-86442-598-8*) Lonely Planet.
Du Fresnoy, Charles A. Art of Painting. LC 76-88819. (Art Histories Collection). 1969. reprint ed. 25.95 (*0-405-02221-2*) Ayer.
Du Gay, Paul. Consumption & Identity at Work. 256p. 1996. 65.00 (*0-8039-7927-4*); pap. 22.95 (*0-8039-7928-2*) Sage.
Du Gay, Paul, ed. Production of Culture, Cultures of Production. LC 97-65516. (Culture, Media & Identities Ser.). 368p. 1997. 75.00 (*0-7619-5435-X*); pap. 24.95 (*0-7619-5436-8*) Sage.
Du Gay, Paul, et al. Doing Cultural Studies: The Story of the Sony Walkman. (Culture, Media & Identities Ser.: Vol. 1). 192p. (C). 1997. 69.95 (*0-7619-5401-5*, 54015); pap. 21.50 (*0-7619-5402-3*, 54023) Sage.
Du Gay, Paul, jt. ed. see Hall, Stuart.
Du Goslin, B. Conversational Zulu for Beginners. 2nd ed. (ENG & ZUL.). 109p. 1988. 21.95 (*0-7859-7486-5*) Fr & Eur.
Du Gue Trapier, Elizabeth. Valdes Leal, Spanish Baroque Painter. (Illus.). 1960. 10.00 (*0-87535-112-3*) Hispanic Soc.
— Velazquez. (Illus.). 1948. 20.00 (*0-87535-062-3*) Hispanic Soc.
***Du Houx, Ramona, et al.** Manitou, a Mythological Journey in Time. unabridged ed. (Illus.). 196p. 1999. pap. 7.99 (*1-882190-77-7*, Pub. by Polar Bear ME) Maine Writers.
Du Jardin, Rosamond. Boy Trouble. LC 53-5423. 192p. (YA). (gr. 7 up). 1988. reprint ed. lib. bdg. 12.89 (*0-397-32263-1*) HarpC Child Bks.
— Class Ring. (J). (gr. 4-9). 1951. 14.95 (*0-397-30184-7*) HarpC Child Bks.
— Double Wedding. LC 59-12354. (J). (gr. 4-9). 1959. 14.95 (*0-397-30446-3*) HarpC Child Bks.
Du Jarric, Pierre. Akbar & the Jesuits: An Account of the Jesuits Missions to the Court of Akbar. 1996. 48.00 (*81-206-1069-5*, Pub. by Asian Educ Servs) S Asia.
Du Jonchay, Gilles, jt. auth. see Daoud, Abu.
Du Liban, Librarie. My First Dictionary of the Zoo in Arabic & English. 1981. 5.50 (*0-86685-297-2*) Intl Bk Ctr.
— Spoken Arabic of the Arabian Gulf. 1976. pap. 5.50 (*0-86685-042-2*) Intl Bk Ctr.
Du Maurier, Daphne. Echoes from the Macabre: Selected Stories. 25.95 (*0-88411-543-7*) Amereon Ltd.
— Frenchman's Creek. LC 70-184730. 320p. 1971. reprint ed. lib. bdg. 20.00 (*0-8376-0412-5*) Bentley Pubs.
— The Glass Blowers. 1999. reprint ed. 39.95 (*1-56849-561-7*) Buccaneer Bks.
— Golden Lads: Sir Frances Bacon, Anthony Bacon & Their Friends. 22.95 (*0-88411-544-5*) Amereon Ltd.
***Du Maurier, Daphne.** The House on the Strand. LC 99-89179. 304p. 2000. pap. 15.95 (*0-8122-1726-8*) U of Pa Pr.
Du Maurier, Daphne. The House on the Strand. 1993. reprint ed. lib. bdg. 35.95 (*0-89968-424-6*, Lghtyr Pr) Buccaneer Bks.
— Hungry Hill. LC 78-184732. 416p. 1971. reprint ed. lib. bdg. 20.00 (*0-8376-0414-1*) Bentley Pubs.
— Jamaica Inn. 304p. 1971. mass mkt. 4.95 (*0-380-00072-5*, Avon Bks) Morrow Avon.
— Jamaica Inn. 304p. 1995. mass mkt. 5.99 (*0-380-72539-8*, Avon Bks) Morrow Avon.
— Jamaica Inn. 1979. reprint ed. lib. bdg. 29.95 (*0-89966-432-6*) Buccaneer Bks.
— Jamaica Inn Longman Simp. (Longman Simplified English Ser.). 122p. 1995. pap. text 5.95 (*0-582-52823-2*) Addison-Wesley.
— The King's General. 1972. pap. 3.50 (*0-380-00210-8*, Avon Bks) Morrow Avon.
— The Loving Spirit. LC 71-184733. 384p. 1971. reprint ed. lib. bdg. 20.00 (*0-8376-0415-X*) Bentley Pubs.
— Mary Anne. LC 76-184729. 352p. 1971. reprint ed. lib. bdg. 20.00 (*0-8376-0411-7*) Bentley Pubs.
— My Cousin Rachel. adapted ed. 1980. pap. 5.25 (*0-8222-0797-4*) Dramatists Play.
— My Cousin Rachel. LC 74-184731. 352p. 1971. reprint ed. lib. bdg. 20.00 (*0-8376-0413-3*) Bentley Pubs.
— My Cousin Rachel. 1993. reprint ed. lib. bdg. 28.95 (*1-56849-142-5*) Buccaneer Bks.
Du Maurier, Daphne. The Parasites. LC 72-184728. 320p. 1971. reprint ed. lib. bdg. 20.00 (*0-8376-0410-9*) Bentley Pubs.
Du Maurier, Daphne. Rebecca. 384p. 1948. 27.50 (*0-385-04380-5*) Doubleday.
— Rebecca. 1946. pap. 5.25 (*0-8222-0933-0*) Dramatists Play.
— Rebecca. 384p. 1994. mass mkt. 6.99 (*0-380-77855-6*, Avon Bks) Morrow Avon.
— Rebecca. 1971. 12.09 (*0-606-04492-2*, Pub. by Turtleback) Demco.
— Rebecca, abr. ed. 1993. pap. 24.95 incl. audio (*1-55927-261-9*, 692908, Pub. by Audio Renaissance) Lndmrk Audiobks.
— Rebecca. 384p. 1988. reprint ed. mass mkt. 5.99 (*0-380-00917-X*, Avon Bks) Morrow Avon.
— Rebecca T. 416p. 1997. pap. 12.00 (*0-380-73040-5*, Avon Bks) Morrow Avon.
— The Scapegoat. 1976. 24.95 (*0-89233-037-6*) Queens Hse-Focus Serv.
***Du Maurier, Daphne.** The Scapegoat. LC 99-58082. 352p. 2000. pap. 15.95 (*0-8122-1725-X*) U of Pa Pr.
Du Maurier, Daphne. Scapegoat. 1976. 21.95 (*0-89190-154-X*, Queens House) Amereon Ltd.
— The Scapegoat. 1977. reprint ed. lib. bdg. 25.95 (*0-88411-149-0*, Queens House) Amereon Ltd.
— The Scapegoat. 1994. reprint ed. lib. bdg. 29.95 (*1-56849-550-1*) Buccaneer Bks.
— The Winding Stair: Sir Francis Bacon, His Rise & Fall. 21.95 (*0-88411-545-3*) Amereon Ltd.
Du Maurier, Daphne, jt. auth. see Quiller-Couch, Arthur.
Du Maurier, George. Trilby. Showalter, Elaine, ed. LC 98-34388. (Oxford World's Classics Ser.). (Illus.). 364p. 1999. pap. 6.95 (*0-19-283351-0*) OUP.
— Trilby. 390p. 1994. pap. 7.50 (*0-460-87447-0*, Everyman's Classic Lib) Tuttle Pubng.
— Trilby. unabridged ed. LC 94-29799. (Illus.). 384p. 1994. pap. text 9.95 (*0-486-28319-4*) Dover.
***Du Maurier, George.** Trilby, Set. unabridged ed. (YA). (gr. 9 up). 1998. 47.95 incl. audio (*1-55685-567-2*) Audio Bk Con.
Du Maurier, George. Trilby: A Novel. 447p. 1998. reprint ed. lib. bdg. 75.00 (*0-7812-7712-4*) Rprt Serv.
Du Maurier, George L. Martian. LC 77-144991. (Illus.). 1971. reprint ed. 69.00 (*0-403-00919-7*) Scholarly.
— Peter Ibbetson. 1971. reprint ed. 69.00 (*0-403-00920-0*) Scholarly.
— Trilby. 1976. 26.95 (*0-8488-0265-9*) Amereon Ltd.
Du Moncel, Theodore A. The Telephone, the Microphone, & the Phonograph. LC 74-4673. (Telecommunications Ser.). (Illus.). 282p. 1974. reprint ed. 25.95 (*0-405-06039-4*) Ayer.
Du Mont, J., jt. auth. see Tartakower, A.
Du Mont, J., tr. see Lasker, Edward.
Du Mont, J., tr. see Nimzowitsch, Aron.
Du Mont, J., tr. see Spielmann, Rudolf.
***Du Mont, Mary.** The Mozart-Da Ponte Operas: An Annotated Bibliography, 81. LC 00-21226. (Music Reference Collection: Vol. 81). 224p. 2000. lib. bdg. 79.50 (*0-313-30413-0*, GM0413, Greenwood Pr) Greenwood.
Du Mont, Rosemary R., et al. Multiculturalism in Libraries, 83. LC 93-49543. (Contributions in Librarianship & Information Science Ser.: No. 83). 256p. 1994. 59.95 (*0-313-28418-0*, Quorum Bks) Greenwood.
***Du Mortier, Gustavo.** Creacion de Macros en Office en Espanol - Spanish (en Visual Basic) Como Programarlos en Visual Basic para Aplicaciones. (Manuales de Soluciones Ser.). (SPA., Illus.). 222p. 1999. pap. 13.90 (*987-9131-92-4*, Pub. by MP Ediciones) Am Wholesale.
Du Nann Winter, Deborah, jt. ed. see Wessells, Michael.
Du Nay, Andre. The Early History of the Rumanian Language. LC 79-115770. (Edward Sapir Monographs in Language, Culture & Cognition: No. 3). (Illus.). xii, 275p. (Orig.). (C). 1977. pap. 32.00 (*0-933104-03-0*) Jupiter Pr.
Du Noyer, Paul. Clash. LC 98-231257. 93p. 1998. text 9.95 (*0-312-17939-1*) St Martin.
— John Lennon: Whatever Gets You through the Night; The Stories behind Every John Lennon Song 1970. 128p. 1999. pap. 22.95 (*1-56025-210-3*, Thunders Mouth) Avalon NY.
***Du Noyer, Paul.** We All Shine On: The Stories Behind Every John Lennon Song, 1970-80. (Illus.). 128p. 1999. reprint ed. pap. text 19.00 (*0-7881-6805-3*) DIANE Pub.
Du Pan, Jacques Mallet, see Mallet Du Pan, Jacques.
du Pasquier, Jacqueline, see Pasquier, Jacqueline du.
***Du Pasquier, L. & Litman, G. W., eds.** Origin & Evolution of the Vertebrate Immune System. (Current Topics in Microbiology & Immunology Ser.: Vol. 248). (Illus.). 340p. 2000. 199.00 (*3-540-66414-9*) Spr-Verlag.
Du Pasquier, Roger. Unveiling Islam. 138p. (Orig.). 1992. pap. 9.95 (*0-946621-32-2*, Pub. by Islamic Texts) Intl Spec Bk.
Du Paul, George J., et al. ADHD Rating Scale IV: Checklists, Norms & Clinical Interpretation. LC 98-35857. 80p. 1998. pap. text 36.00 (*1-57230-423-5*) Guilford Pubns.
Du Perron, E. Country of Origin. Beekman, E. M., ed. Daverman, Elizabeth, tr. from DUT. LC 83-18171. (Library of the Indies).Tr. of Het Land Van Herkomst. 464p. 1984. lib. bdg. 40.00 (*0-87023-429-3*) U of Mass Pr.
— Country of Origin: A Novel of the East Indies. (Library of the Indies).Tr. of Het Land Van Herkomst. 438p. 1999. pap. 16.95 (*962-593-510-X*) Tuttle Pubng.
Du Pices, Charles A. Roots of Strategy, Bk. 2. LC 86-23195. (Illus.). 560p. (Orig.). 1987. pap. 14.95 (*0-8117-2260-0*) Stackpole.
Du Pin Calmon, Paulo, jt. auth. see Galbraith, James K.
Du Plessis, A. G., jt. auth. see Du Plessis, L. M.
Du Plessis, A. G., jt. auth. see Du Plessis, Lourens M.
Du Plessis, Eric H., tr. & intro. see Balzac, Honore de.
***du Plessis, Heather.** Tourism Destinations Southern Africa. (Illus.). 231p. 2000. 40.00 (*0-7021-5272-2*) Juta & Co.
Du Plessis, Hugo. Fiberglass Boats. 3rd ed. LC 97-139541. 304p. 1997. 39.95 (*0-07-050317-6*) McGraw.
Du Plessis, J. & Kok, L. An Elementary Introduction to the Study of South African Law. 2nd ed. 165p. 1989. pap. write for info. (*0-7021-2234-3*, Pub. by Juta & Co) Gaunt.
Du Plessis, J. C., jt. auth. see De Jong, M.
Du Plessis, L. M. & Du Plessis, A. G. Inleiding tot die Reg. 241p. 1990. pap. write for info. (*0-7021-2552-0*, Pub. by Juta & Co) Gaunt.
Du Plessis, Lourens & Corder, Hugh. Understanding South Africa's Transitional Bill of Rights. 224p. 1994. pap. 25.00 (*0-7021-3333-7*, 15677, Pub. by Juta & Co) Gaunt.
Du Plessis, Lourens M. The Interpretation of Statutes. 165p. 1986. pap. 72.00 (*0-409-02508-9*, SA, MICHIE) LEXIS Pub.
***Du Plessis, Lourens M.** An Introduction to Law. 3rd ed. Hees, Edwin, tr. 250p. 1999. pap. 35.00 (*0-7021-4919-5*, Pub. by Juta & Co) Gaunt.
Du Plessis, Lourens M. & Du Plessis, A. G. An Introduction to Law. 230p. 1992. pap. 31.00 (*0-7021-2763-9*, Pub. by Juta & Co) Gaunt.
— An Introduction to Law. 2nd ed. 262p. 1995. pap. 30.00 (*0-7021-3381-7*, Pub. by Juta & Co) Gaunt.
Du Plessis, Roger. Poor Man's Explanation of Kalman Filtering: or How I Stopped Worrying & Learned to Love Matrix Inversion. (Illus.). 57p. 1997. pap. 19.95 (*0-9661016-0-X*) Taygeta Sci.
Du Plessis, Rosemary, et al, eds. Feminist Voices: Women's Studies Texts for Aotearoa-New Zealand. (Illus.). 376p. (C). 1993. pap. 39.95 (*0-19-558239-X*) OUP.
Du Plessis, Rosemary & Alice, Lynne, eds. Feminist Thought in Aotearoa/New Zealand: Differences & Connections. LC HQ1865.5.F45 1998. 326p. 1998. pap. text 39.95 (*0-19-558356-6*) OUP.
Du Plessis, Susan. The New Truth about Learning Disabilities. Heller, Robert J., ed. (Illus.). 160p. (Orig.). 1997. pap. 12.95 (*0-9657005-1-8*) Bobrich Pub.
Du Plessix Gray, Francine. Lovers & Tyrants. 1988. pap. 7.95 (*0-393-30547-3*) Norton.
Du Plock, Simon. Case Studies in Existential Psychotherapy & Counselling. LC 97-8659. (Wiley Series in Existential Psychotherapy & Counselling). 218p. 1997. 89.95 (*0-471-96192-2*) Wiley.
Du Plock, Simon, ed. Case Studies in Existential Psychotherapy & Counselling. LC 97-8659. 218p. 1997. pap. 45.00 (*0-471-97079-4*) Wiley.
Du Plooy, Gertruida M. 500 Communication Concepts English/Afrikaans. (Communicamus Ser.: Vol. 10). 177p. (C). 1995. text 29.00 (*0-7021-2650-0*, Pub. by Juta & Co) Intl Spec Bk.
— Understanding Television: Guidelines for Visual Literacy. 2nd ed. (Communicamus Ser.: Vol. 4). 111p. (C). 1994. reprint ed. text 29.00 (*0-7021-2255-6*, Pub. by Juta & Co) Intl Spec Bk.
Du Plooy, Susanna M., et al. Accounting for Attorneys. LC 98-110201. vii, 265p. 1997. write for info. (*0-409-06087-9*) Buttrwrth-Heinemann.
Du Plou, Dafne C., tr. see Edens, David.
Du Ponceau, Peter S. A Brief View of the Constitution of the United States. LC 72-124893. (American Constitutional & Legal History Ser). 1974. reprint ed. lib. bdg. 18.50 (*0-306-71986-X*) Da Capo.
— A Dissertation on the Nature & Extent of the Jurisdiction of the Courts of the U. S., Being a Valedictory Address Delivered... LC 79-37971. (American Law: The Formative Years). 296p. 1972. reprint ed. 24.95 (*0-405-04007-5*) Ayer.
— Dissertation on the Nature & Extent of the Jurisdiction of the Courts of the United States: Being a Valedictory Address Delivered to the Students of the Law Academy of Philadelphia, at the Close of the Academic Year, on the 22nd April, 1824 - To Which Are Added, a Brief Sketch of the National Judiciary Powers Exercised in the United States Prior to the Adoption of the Present Federal Constitution. xxxiii, 254p. 1993. reprint ed. 65.00 (*0-8377-2038-9*, Rothman) W S Hein.
Du Ponceau, Peter S., tr. see Zeisberger, David.
Du Pont De Nemours, Pierre S. Du Pont De Nemours on the Dangers of Inflation: An Address by Pierre Sanvel DuPont, 1790. Lincoln, Edmond E., tr. (Kress Library of Business & Economics Publication: No. 7). 58p. 1949. pap. 9.95 (*0-678-09902-2*) Kelley.
***Du Pont, Diana C. & Santa Barbara Museum of Art Staff.** Copywork: The Dictionary Pages & Other Diversions by Gilles Barbier. LC 99-48909. 1999. write for info. (*0-89951-104-X*) Santa Barb Mus Art.
Du Pont, Henry F., jt. auth. see Sweeney, John A.
Du Pont, M. Kay. Don't Let Your Participles Dangle in Public! 5th ed. (Illus.). 272p. (Orig.). 1990. reprint ed. pap. 14.95 (*0-9614927-1-6*) Comm Connect.
***Du Pont, Michael.** Foreign Direct Investment in Transitional Economies: A Case Study. 2000. text 69.95 (*0-312-23384-1*) St Martin.
Du Pont, Peter & Morrill, John. Residential Indoor Air Quality & Energy Efficiency. (Illus.). 267p. 1989. pap. 25.00 (*0-918249-08-2*) Am Coun Energy.
Du Pontet, R. L., ed. see Caesar, Julius.
Du Pool, Lif. Heute Hier, Morgen Dort. 144p. text 38.95 incl. audio (*3-468-49848-9*) Langenscheidt.
— Mein Gespraech, Meine Lieder, Set. 128p. text 38.95 incl. audio (*3-468-49847-0*) Langenscheidt.
***du-Pre, Athena.** Communicating about Health: Current Issues & Perspectives. LC 99-38413. xix, 376p. 2000. pap. text 34.95 (*0-7674-1081-5*) Mayfield Pub.

D

An Asterisk (*) at the beginning of an entry indicates that the title is appearing for the first time.

Du Pre, Athena. Humor & the Healing Arts: A Multimethod Analysis of Humor Use in Healthcare. LC 97-17943. (Communication Ser.). 250p. 1998. write for info. (*0-8058-2647-5*); pap. write for info. (*0-8058-2648-3*) L Erlbaum Assocs.

***du Pre, Hilary & du Pre, Piers.** Hilary & Jackie. LC 99-193246. 350p. 1998. pap. 12.95 (*0-345-43271-1*) Ballantine Pub Grp.

***Du Pre, Jon.** The Prodigal Father: A True Story of Tragedy, Survival & Reconciliation in an American Family. LC 99-59123. (Illus.). 304p. 2000. pap. 13.95 (*1-56170-674-4*, 5010) Hay House.

Du Pre, Peter D., jt. auth. see Haynes, J. H.

du Pre, Piers, jt. auth. see du Pre, Hilary.

Du Pre Thornton, F. Elementary Arabic. 238p. (C). 1989. pap. 30.00 (*1-85077-217-7*, Pub. by Darf Pubs Ltd) St Mut.

Du Pre Thornton, F. & Ghali, Wagdy R. Arabic Pocket Grammar: Arabic-English Pocket Dictionary. 245p. 1992. pap. 14.95 (*0-86685-551-3*, Pub. by Librairie du Liban) Intl Bk Ctr.

Du Preez, B. G., jt. ed. see National Industrial Council Staff.

Du Preez, Jan H., jt. auth. see Van den Heever, Louw W.

Du Preez, Peter. Genocide: Past, Present & Future. (Briefings Ser.). 160p. (Orig.). 1994. pap. 14.95 (*0-7145-2977-X*) M Boyars Pubs.

— A Science of Mind: The Quest of Psychological Reality. 228p. 1991. text 65.00 (*0-12-224960-7*) Acad Pr.

Du Preez, T. L., ed. Business Unusal - Wit Whims & Wealth. (Illus.). 160p. pap. write for info. (*0-620-25384-3*) Kuru Bks.

Du Prel, Carl. The Philosophy of Mysticism, 2 vols. 1977. lib. bdg. 250.00 (*0-8490-2434-X*) Gordon Pr.

— The Philosophy of Mysticism, 2 vols. Massey, Charles C., tr. LC 75-36838. (Occult Ser.). 1976. reprint ed. 56.95 (*0-405-07951-6*) Ayer.

Du Prey, Pierre D. John Soane, the Making of an Architect. LC 81-16453. (Illus.). 432p. reprint ed. pap. 134.00 (*0-608-09015-8*, 206965000005) Bks Demand.

— The Villas of Pliny from Antiquity to Posterity. LC 93-44209. 404p. 1994. 65.00 (*0-226-17300-3*) U Ch Pr.

Du Prey, Pierre De La Ruffiniere. John Soane: The Making of an Architect. LC 81-16453. 1982. 51.00 (*0-226-17298-8*) U Ch Pr.

— John Soane: The Making of an Architect. LC 81-16453. 432p. 1983. pap. 23.95 (*0-226-17299-6*) U Ch Pr.

du Puis, MD, Robert J. How to Avoid High Tech Stress. LC 98-75120. 192p. 1998. pap. 11.99 (*1-56384-159-2*) Huntington Hse.

Du Puitspelu, N. Dictionary Etymologique Patois Lyonnais. (FRE.). 595p. 1970. 195.00 (*0-320-00896-7*) Fr & Eur.

***Du Puy, David, et al.** The Orchids of Madagascar. (Illus.). 376p. 1999. 98.00 (*1-900347-70-9*, Pub. by Royal Botnic Grdns) Balogh.

Du Puy, William A. Hawaii & Its Race Problem. LC 75-35214. reprint ed. 39.50 (*0-404-14237-0*) AMS Pr.

Du, Qinghua & Tanaka, Masataka, eds. Theory & Applications of Boundary Element Methods. 495p. 1990. 139.95 (*0-387-50703-5*) Spr-Verlag.

Du, Qinghua, jt. ed. see Tanaka, Masataka.

Du Quette, Constance, jt. auth. see Du Quette, Lon.

Du Quette, Keith. Hotel Animal. 1996. 10.19 (*0-606-09434-2*, Pub. by Turtleback) Demco.

Du Quette, Lon & Du Quette, Constance. Tarot of Ceremonial Magick. 38p. 1995. pap. 15.00 (*0-88079-728-2*, TCM78) US Games Syst.

Du Rand, Le Clanche. Winnie-the-Pooh - Small Cast Musical. 1992. pap. 5.95 (*0-87129-182-7*, W72) Dramatic Pub.

Du Roi, Denyse. Filmmaking. 84p. 1991. pap. 8.95 (*1-880766-01-9*) Pantograph Pr.

Du Ru, Paul & Butler, Ruth L. Journal of Paul Du Ru, February 1 to May 8, 1700, Missionary Priest to Louisiana. LC 97-13260. 1997. 14.95 (*0-87770-607-7*); pap. 9.95 (*0-87770-606-9*) Ye Galleon.

Du Ruofu & Yip, Vincent F. The Ethnic Groups in China. 400p. 1996. 149.00 (*7-03-003325-6*, Pub. by Sci Pr) Lubrecht & Cramer.

Du Ry, Marc, tr. see Lefort, Rosine.

Du Ryer. Esther, Vol. XLVII. Campion, E. & Gethner, P., eds. (FRE.). 117p. (C). pap. text 19.95 (*0-85989-168-2*, Pub. by Univ Exeter Pr) Northwestern U Pr.

Du Sautoy, Marcus, et al. Analytic Pro-P Groups. 2nd ed. LC 99-11615. (Studies in Advanced Mathematics: Vol. 61). (Illus.). 380p. (C). 1999. text 59.95 (*0-521-65011-9*) Cambridge U Pr.

***du Soleil, Oz D.** All of That Meat Gone to Waste. (Illus.). vii, 180p. 1999. pap. 11.55 (*0-9674109-9-1*) Two-Two-B.

— Object Lessons. (Illus.). iii, 97p. 1999. pap. 9.50 (*0-9674109-0-8*) Two-Two-B.

Du St. Espirit, Julie. Spiritual Pastels. (Illus.). 10.00 (*0-8159-6821-3*) Devin.

Du Terme, Laurence. The Flower De Luce Planted in England, Wherein Is Contained the Pronuntiation & Understanding of the French Tongue. LC 72-5977. (English Experience Ser.: No. 505). 68p. 1973. reprint ed. 15.00 (*90-221-0505-9*) Walter J Johnson.

Du Toit, Brian M. Aging & Menopause Among Indian South African Women. LC 89-26107. (SUNY Series in Medical Anthropology). (Illus.). 343p. (C). 1990. pap. text 24.95 (*0-7914-0390-4*) State U NY Pr.

— The Boers in East Africa: Ethnicity & Identity. LC 98-18514. 224p. 1998. 59.95 (*0-89789-611-4*, Bergin & Garvey) Greenwood.

— Cannabis, Alcohol, & the South African Student: Adolescent Drug Use, 1974-1985. LC 91-25451. (Monographs in International Studies, Africa: No. 59A). 177p. (Orig.). (C). 1991. pap. text 17.00 (*0-89680-166-7*) Ohio U Pr.

— Colonia Boer, an Afrikaner Settlement in Chubut, Argentina: An Afrikaner Settlement in Chubut, Argentina. LC 94-39217. (Illus.). 488p. 1995. text 109.95 (*0-7734-8975-4*) E Mellen.

— Configurations of Cultural Continuity. 159p. 1976. pap. 47.00 (*90-6191-011-0*, Pub. by A A Balkema) Ashgate Pub Co.

— Content & Context of Zulu Folk-Narratives. LC 76-28522. (University of Florida Monographs: Social Sciences: No. 58). 104p. reprint ed. pap. 32.30 (*0-7837-4908-2*, 204457300004) Bks Demand.

Du Toit, Brian M. & Safa, Helen I., eds. Migration & Urbanization: Models & Adaptive Strategies. (World Anthropology Ser.). xii, 306p. 1975. 33.10 (*90-279-7579-5*) Mouton.

Du Toit, Brian M., jt. ed. see Safa, Helen I.

Du Toit, D., et al. The Labour Relations Act of 1995. LC 97-162573. 1996. pap. write for info. (*0-409-01280-7*, MICHIE) LEXIS Pub.

Du Toit, D. F., et al. Public Management: Its Grassroots. 310p. 1996. 38.95 (*0-7021-3833-9*, Pub. by Juta & Co) Intl Spec Bk.

Du Toit, Darcy. Capital & Labour in South Africa. (Monographs from the African Studies Centre, Leiden). 480p. 1981. 75.00 (*0-7103-0001-8*, 00018) Routledge.

Du Toit, E. Straf in Suid-Afrika. 600p. 1981. write for info. (*0-7021-1215-1*, Pub. by Juta & Co) Gaunt.

Du Toit, E., et al. Commentary on the Criminal Procedure Act. 1987. ring bd. 132.00 (*0-7021-1962-8*, Pub. by Juta & Co) Gaunt.

— Commentary on the Criminal Procedure Act. 1993. pap. write for info. (*0-7021-3010-9*, Pub. by Juta & Co) Gaunt.

***Du Toit, Herman.** Vision in the Desert: Tree of Utah - Sculpture by Momen. (Illus.). 120p. 2000. 25.00 (*1-888106-89-1*) Agreka Bks.

— Vision in the Desert: Tree of Utah - Sculpture by Momen. (Illus.). 120p. 2000. pap. 12.00 (*1-888106-86-7*) Agreka Bks.

***Du Toit, Herman, et al.** Presage of Passage: Sculpture for a New Century. (Illus.). 61p. 1999. pap. 15.00 (*0-8425-2456-8*, BYU Press) Brigham.

Du Toit, Johan. How to Paint Portraits from Photographs, a Combined Book & Video Art Course: Three: Paint a Man Sitting, His Head & Hands. (Illus.). 128p. 1993. 72.95 incl. VHS (*1-883707-20-X*) Protea Publng GA.

Du Toit, Johan, ed. & illus. see Passmore, Debbie.

Du Toit, Pierre. State Building & Democracy in Southern Africa: Botswana, Zimbabwe, & South Africa. LC 95-22653. 1995. 37.50 (*1-878379-50-X*); pap. text 19.95 (*1-878379-46-1*) US Inst Peace.

Du Toit, S. H., et al. Graphical Exploratory Data Analysis. (Texts in Statistics Ser.). (Illus.). 305p. 1986. 47.95 (*0-387-96313-8*) Spr-Verlag.

Du Toit, Stephen, et al. Interactive Lisrel: User's Guide. xx, 360p. 1999. pap. 35.00 (*0-89498-044-0*) Sci Ware.

Du V Florey, Charles, jt. ed. see Namekata, Tsukasa.

Du Vair, Guillaume. Oeuvres, 5 pts. in 1. vi, 1241p. 1973. reprint ed. write for info. (*3-487-04589-3*) G Olms Pubs.

Du Val, Miles P. And the Mountains Will Move: The Story of the Building of the Panama Canal. LC 69-10086. (Illus.). 374p. 1969. reprint ed. lib. bdg. 49.50 (*0-8371-0400-9*, DUBP, Greenwood Pr) Greenwood.

Du Vall, Dean F. Class Prophecy: Murder. LC 80-65177. (Derek Dax Adventure Ser.: No. 2). (Illus.). 228p. 1982. pap. 6.95 (*0-931232-25-2*) Du Vall Financial.

— The Du Vall Method for Acquiring Great Self-Publishing Wealth. 7th ed. 88p. 1980. pap. 25.00 (*0-931232-10-4*) Du Vall Financial.

— The Enchanted Cottage. LC 80-65176. (Derek Dax Adventure Ser.: No. 1). (Illus.). 228p. 1981. pap. 6.95 (*0-931232-21-X*) Du Vall Financial.

— Exactly How to Build a Fortune in Mail Order. 1978. pap. 10.00 (*0-931232-18-X*) Du Vall Financial.

— Grab Your Share of the Wealth. 1978. 100.00 (*0-931232-17-1*) Du Vall Financial.

— How I'm Creating a Fortune in Real Estate Using Other People's Money, Time & Talent. 1975. reprint ed. pap. 32.50 (*0-931232-12-0*) Du Vall Financial.

— How to Average a Thousand Dollars or More per Week in the Stock Market (Bear or Bull) 2nd ed. 100p. 1980. reprint ed. pap. text 100.00 (*0-931232-11-2*) Du Vall Financial.

— The Princely Profits of Party Plan. 12th ed. 84p. 1980. pap. 10.00 (*0-931232-08-2*) Du Vall Financial.

Du Vivier, Anthony, jt. auth. see Higgins, Elisabeth.

Du, Weichang. Agricultural Market Surplus Response in China. 216p. 1995. 72.95 (*1-85972-258-X*, Pub. by Avebry) Ashgate Pub Co.

***Du Wors, George Manter & Washington, Everett.** White Knuckles & Wishful Thinking: Learning from the Moment of Relapse in Alcoholism & Other Addictions. 2nd rev. expanded ed. LC 99-45881. (Illus.). 416p. 2000. pap. text 17.50 (*0-88937-224-1*) Hogrefe & Huber Pubs.

Du, Xiangwan, jt. ed. see Xie, Jialin.

Dua, Andre, jt. auth. see Esty, Daniel C.

Dua, Edward M., jt. auth. see Kuo, L. Jay.

Dua, Enakshi. Scratching the Surface: Canadian Anti-Racist Feminist Thought. 1999. pap. 24.95 (*0-88961-230-7*) Womens Pr.

Dua, Enakshi, et al, eds. On Women Healthsharing. 369p. pap. 17.95 (*0-88961-201-3*, Pub. by Womens Pr) LPC InBook.

Dua, I. S., ed. see Dhir, K. K., et al.

Dua, J. C. Glossary of Revenue & Allied Terms of South India. LC 98-908226. 1998. 52.00 (*81-7479-017-9*, Pub. by Kaveri Bks) S Asia.

Dua, Shiva S. Society & Culture in Northern India, 1850-1900. vi, 272p. 1985. 26.50 (*81-85004-04-8*) Nataraj Bks.

Duan, Jian J., jt. auth. see Follett, Peter A.

Duan, Lian, jt. auth. see Chen, Wai-Fah.

Duan, Zhi-Dao J. Journey Against One Current: The Spiritual Autobiography of a Chinese Christian. LC 97-27487. (Illus.). 208p. 1997. pap. 8.95 (*0-87808-273-5*, WCL273-5) William Carey Lib.

Duan, Zhongqiao. Marx's Theory of Social Formation. (Avebury Series in Philosophy). 144p. 1995. 66.95 (*1-85972-015-3*, Pub. by Avebry) Ashgate Pub Co.

***Duane.** Spider Man Lizard. 1999. pap. 9.98 (*0-671-04419-2*) PB.

Duane, Catherine J. & Duane, Orla. Pocket Prophecy. (Illus.). 64p. 1997. 7.95 (*1-86204-133-4*, Pub. by Element MA) Penguin Putnam.

Duane, Charles P. & Boessenecker, John. Against the Vigilantes: The Recollections of Dutch Charley Duane. LC 99-21450. 240p. 1999. 27.95 (*0-8061-3166-7*) U of Okla Pr.

Duane, Daniel. Caught Inside: A Surfer's Year on the California Coast. 1999. pap. text 0.00 (*0-86442-767-0*) Lonely Planet.

— Caught Inside: A Surfer's Year on the California Coast. 218p. 1996. 21.00 (*0-86547-494-X*) N Point Pr.

— Caught Inside: A Surfer's Year on the California Coast. 256p. 1997. pap. text 12.00 (*0-86547-509-1*) N Point Pr.

***Duane, Daniel.** El Capitan: Historic Feats & Radical Routes. LC 00-29459. 2000. 24.95 (*0-8118-2484-5*) Chronicle Bks.

Duane, Daniel. Looking for Mo. LC 97-43486. 224p. 1998. 22.00 (*0-374-19083-6*) FS&G.

— Looking for Mo. 229p. 1999. pap. 12.00 (*0-671-03483-9*, WSP) PB.

Duane, Daniel & Warshaw, Matt. Surfers: Photographs by Patrick Cariou. LC 97-27627. (Illus.). 144p. 1998. 60.00 (*1-57687-010-3*, pwerHse Bks) pwerHse Cultrl.

— Surfers: Photographs by Patrick Cariou. LC 97-27627. (Illus.). 144p. 1998. pap. 35.00 (*1-57687-040-5*, pwerHse Bks) pwerHse Cultrl.

Duane, Daniel K. Lighting Out: A Vision of California & the Mountains. LC 93-34067. 256p. 1994. 14.00 (*1-55597-210-1*) Graywolf.

Duane, Diane. Deep Wizardry. LC 96-860. 368p. (J). 1996. pap. 6.00 (*0-15-201240-0*) Harcourt.

— Deep Wizardry. LC 96-860. (J). 1996. 11.10 (*0-606-11248-0*, Pub. by Turtleback) Demco.

Duane, Diane. High Wizardry. (Magic Carpet Books Ser.). (J). 1997. 11.10 (*0-606-11461-0*, Pub. by Turtleback) Demco.

Duane, Diane. High Wizardry. LC 96-8456. 352p. (J). 1997. reprint ed. pap. 6.00 (*0-15-201241-9*) Harcourt.

***Duane, Diane.** Rihannsu Bk. 1: My Enemy, My Ally. (Star Trek Ser.: Vol. 18). 320p. 2000. mass mkt. 3.99 (*0-7434-0369-X*) PB.

— Rihannsu Book Four: Honor Blade. (Star Trek Ser.: No. 96). 288p. 2000. 6.99 (*0-671-04210-6*, Star Trek) PB.

— Rihennsu Book Three: Swordhunt. (Star Track Ser.: No. 95). 256p. 2000. 6.99 (*0-671-04209-2*, Star Trek) PB.

— So You Want to Be a Wizard. LC 95-33451. (J). 1996. 11.10 (*0-606-11854-3*, Pub. by Turtleback) Demco.

Duane, Diane. So You Want to Be a Wizard. LC 95-33451. 384p. (J). (gr. 7-9). 1996. reprint ed. pap. 6.50 (*0-15-201239-7*) Harcourt.

***Duane, Diane.** Spocks World. (Star Trek Ser.). 400p. 2000. mass mkt. 3.99 (*0-7434-0371-1*) PB.

Duane, Diane. A Wizard Abroad. LC 96-45406. 352p. (J). (gr. 5). 1997. 15.00 (*0-15-201209-5*) Harcourt.

— A Wizard Abroad. LC 96-45406. 352p. (J). 1999. pap. 6.00 (*0-15-201207-9*) Harcourt.

***Duane, Diane & Morwood, Peter.** Rihannsu Bk. 2: Romulan Way. (Star Trek Ser.: Vol. 35). 256p. 2000. per. 3.99 (*0-7434-0370-3*) PB.

***Duane, Drake D.** Reading & Attention Disorders: Neurobiological Correlates. LC 99-47193. (Illus.). 1999. pap. text 38.00 (*0-912752-55-6*) York Pr.

Duane E., Diane. The Book of Night with Moon. LC 97-14214. 400p. 1997. mass mkt. 12.99 (*0-446-67302-1*, Pub. by Warner Bks); mass mkt. 77.94 (*0-446-16579-4*) Warner Bks.

— The Book of Night with Moon. 446p. 1999. mass mkt. 6.50 (*0-446-60633-2*, Pub. by Warner Bks) Little.

— Dark Mirror. Ryan, Kevin, ed. (Star Trek: The Next Generation Ser.). 352p. 1994. reprint ed. mass mkt. 5.99 (*0-671-79438-8*, Pocket Star Bks) PB.

— Doctor's Orders. (Star Trek Ser.: No. 50). 288p. 1990. mass mkt. 5.50 (*0-671-66189-2*, Pocket Star Bks) PB.

— The Door into Sunset, Vol. 3. (Tales of the Five Ser.: No. 3). 384p. 1994. mass mkt. 4.99 (*0-8125-1431-9*) Tor Bks.

— Empire's End. (X-Men Ser.). (Illus.). 352p. 1998. reprint ed. mass mkt. 6.99 (*0-425-16448-9*) Blvd Books.

— Intellivore. (Star Trek Next Generation Ser.: No. 45). 1997. mass mkt. 5.99 (*0-671-56832-9*) PB.

— The Lizard Sanction. (Spider-Man Ser.). 1996. mass mkt. 6.50 (*1-57297-148-7*) Blvd Books.

— My Enemy, My Ally. Stern, Dave, ed. (Star Trek Ser.: No. 18). 320p. (Orig.). 1989. mass mkt. 5.50 (*0-671-70421-4*) PB.

***Duane E., Diane.** Nightfall at Algemron. (Harbinger Trilogy Ser.: Vol. 3). (Illus.). 352p. 2000. mass mkt. 5.99 (*0-7869-1563-3*) TSR Inc.

Duane E., Diane. The Romulan Way. (Star Trek Ser.: No. 35). 1991. mass mkt. 4.99 (*0-671-74357-0*) PB.

— Spider-Man: The Octopus Agenda. 272p. 1997. mass mkt. 6.50 (*1-57297-279-3*) Blvd Books.

— Spider-Man: The Venom Factor. 352p. 1995. mass mkt. 6.50 (*1-57297-038-3*) Blvd Books.

— Spock's World. 1989. mass mkt. 6.50 (*0-671-66773-4*) PB.

— Starrise at Corrivale. 1998. pap. 5.99 (*0-7869-1179-4*, Pub. by TSR Inc) Random.

***Duane E., Diane.** To Visit the Queen. 384p. 2000. mass mkt. 6.50 (*0-446-60855-6*, Aspect) Warner Bks.

Duane E., Diane. To Visit the Queen, Bk. II. LC 98-36598. (Cat Novel Ser.). 368p. 1999. mass mkt. 14.99 (*0-446-67318-8*, Pub. by Warner Bks) Little.

— The Wounded Sky, No. 13. (Star Trek Ser.). 224p. (Orig.). 1991. mass mkt. 5.50 (*0-671-74352-X*) PB.

— X-Com UFO Defense: A Novel. LC 95-74905. 264p. 1995. mass mkt. 5.99 (*0-7615-0235-1*) Prima Pub.

— X-Men: Empire's End. LC 97-24452. (X-Men Ser.). (Illus.). 352p. 1997. 23.95 (*0-399-14334-3*, G P Putnam) Peng Put Young Read.

Duane E., Diane & Morwood, Peter. Space Cops: High Moon. 256p. (Orig.). 1992. mass mkt. 3.99 (*0-380-75855-5*, Avon Bks) Morrow Avon.

— Space Cops: Kill Station. 256p. (Orig.). 1992. mass mkt. 3.99 (*0-380-75854-7*, Avon Bks) Morrow Avon.

— Space Cops: Mindblast. 256p. (Orig.). 1991. pap. 3.95 (*0-380-75852-0*, Avon Bks) Morrow Avon.

Duane, Edward. Integrative Studies in Social Science. (C). 1993. student ed. 15.00 (*1-881592-32-4*) Hayden-McNeil.

Duane, Edward A., jt. ed. see Bridgeland, William M.

Duane, James E. Media about Media: An Annotated Listing of Media Software. LC 80-21339. (Instructional Media Library: Vol. 6). 232p. 1981. 34.95 (*0-87778-166-4*) Educ Tech Pubns.

Duane, James E., ed. Individualized Instruction - Programs & Materials. LC 72-11990. 440p. 1973. 44.95 (*0-87778-043-9*) Educ Tech Pubns.

Duane, James E., ed. see Baker, Dan & Weisgerber, Bill.

Duane, James E., ed. see Beatty, LaMond F.

Duane, James E., ed. see Bullough, Robert V., Sr.

Duane, James E., ed. see Cluff, E. Dale.

Duane, James E., ed. see Flanagan, Cathleen C.

Duane, James E., ed. see Kueter, Roger A. & Miller, Janeen.

Duane, James E., ed. see Schneider, Edward W. & Bennion, Junius L.

Duane, James E., ed. see Soulier, J. Steven.

Duane, James E., ed. see Sparks, Jerry D.

Duane, James E., ed. see Wood, Rulon K.

Duane, Josann & Wilke, Robert. Solid Modeling in Engineering. (Illus.). 528p. (C). 1992. text. write for info. (*0-201-18344-7*) Addison-Wesley.

***Duane, Kelly, ed.** Radiance. LC 99-12754. (Illus.). 72p. 2000. 14.95 (*0-8118-2516-7*) Chronicle Bks.

Duane, Kit, ed. see Klusmire, John.

Duane, Michael. Molecular Biophysics: Structures & Dynamics. Duffin, W. D., tr. from FRE. LC 98-36756. (Illus.). 522p. (C). 1999. text 110.00 (*0-19-857783-4*) OUP.

Duane, Michael J. Customized Human Resource Planning: Different Practices for Different Organizations. LC 95-41388. 165p. 1996. 55.00 (*0-89930-911-9*, Quorum Bks) Greenwood.

— The Grievance Process in Labor-Management Cooperation. LC 92-44683. 176p. 1993. 52.95 (*0-89930-760-4*, DRK, Quorum Bks) Greenwood.

Duane, Orla, jt. auth. see Duane, Catherine J.

Duane, Thomas D. Thomas David Duane, MD: Wills Eye Hospital & Thomas Jefferson Medical College. (Ophthalmology Oral History Ser.). (Illus.). 178p. 1989. 35.00 (*0-926866-03-6*) FAAO.

***Duane, Timothy P.** Shaping the Sierra: Nature, Culture & Conflict in the Changing West. LC 98-4212. (Illus.). 623p. 2000. pap. 29.95 (*0-520-22676-3*, Pub. by U CA Pr) Cal Prin Full Svc.

Duane, Timothy P. Shaping the Sierra: Nature, Culture & Conflict in the Changing West. alternate ed. LC 98-4212. 623p. 1999. 50.00 (*0-520-21246-0*, Pub. by U CA Pr) Cal Prin Full Svc.

Duane, William, ed. Letters to Benjamin Franklin, from His Family & Friends, 1751-1790. (Select Bibliographies Reprint Ser.). 1977. 20.95 (*0-8369-5325-8*) Ayer.

Duane, William, jt. ed. see Marshall, Christopher D.

Duane, William, tr. see Blanchard, Claude.

Duane, William J. Letters Addressed to the People of Pennsylvania: Respecting the Internal Improvement of the Commonwealth by Means of Roads & Canals. LC 68-18218. (Reprints of Economic Classics Ser.). 125p. 1968. reprint ed. 35.00 (*0-678-00381-5*) Kelley.

***Duanmu, San.** The Phonology of Standard Chinese. (The Phonology of the World's Languages Ser.). (Illus.). 300p. 2000. text 74.00 (*0-19-824120-8*) OUP.

***Duany, Andrés, ed.** The New Civic Art: Elements of Town Planning. (Illus.). 320p. 2000. 75.00 (*0-8478-2186-2*) Rizzoli Intl.

***Duany, Andres, et al.** Suburban Nation: The Rise of Sprawl & the Decline of the American Dream. (Illus.). 283p. 2000. 30.00 (*0-86547-557-1*) N Point Pr.

Duany, Andres, et al. Towns & Townmaking Principles: Andres Duany & Elizabeth Platerzyberck, Architects. LC 91-71811. (Illus.). 120p. 1991. pap. 35.00 (*0-8478-1436-X*, Pub. by Rizzoli Intl) St Martin.

Duany, Jorge, ed. Dominicanos en Puerto Rico: Migracion en la Semi-Periferia. LC 90-81615. 132p. 1990. pap. 9.50 (*0-929157-08-7*) Ediciones Huracan.

Duany, Jorge, jt. auth. see Cobas, Jose.

Duany, Jorge, jt. auth. see Cobas, Jose A.

Duanzhi, She, tr. see Rusong, Wu, et al.

Duara, Prasenjit. Culture, Power, & the State: Rural North China, 1900-1942. LC 87-18173. 344p. 1988. 47.50 (*0-8047-1445-2*); pap. 16.95 (*0-8047-1888-1*) Stanford U Pr.

— Rescuing History from the Nation: Questioning Narratives of Modern China. LC 95-3205. 286p. 1995. 32.00 (*0-226-16721-6*) U Ch Pr.

— Rescuing History from the Nation: Questioning Narratives of Modern China. x, 276p. 1996. pap. text 17.95 (*0-226-16722-4*) U Ch Pr.

D

Duarte. Foundational Perspectives in Multicultural Education. LC 99-36610. 374p. (C). 1999. pap. text 54.00 (*0-321-02345-5*) Addson-Wesley Educ.

Duarte, Abigail D., ed. see Davis, John P.

Duarte, Alex. The Benefits of Velvet Antler: The 2000-Year-Old Health Food for All Resons. 39p. 1995. pap. text 6.00 (*1-891036-01-7*) Nutri Tapes.

— Cataract Breakthrough: The Booklet. 60p. 1994. pap. text 8.00 (*1-891036-00-9*) Nutri Tapes.

— The Collagen Type II Cure for Arthritis & Heart Disease: Chicken Sternal Collagen Type II, the Nuri-Medical Revelation of the Millennium LC 99-173621. 135 p. 1997. write for info. (*1-891036-11-4*) Nutri Tapes.

— Get Smart Eat Healthy: Add Years to Your Life & Life to Your Years! 112p. 1991. pap. text 20.00 (*1-891036-04-1*) Nutri Tapes.

— How to Obtain Miracle Medicines Off-Shore Legally. 84p. 1994. pap. text 15.00 (*1-891036-07-6*) Nutri Tapes.

— Jaws for Life: The Story of Shark Cartilage. 76p. 1994. pap. text 15.00 (*1-891036-06-8*) Nutri Tapes.

— The Magic of Melatonin. 41p. 1994. pap. text 6.00 (*1-891036-03-3*) Nutri Tapes.

— Muscle Mass, Strength & Endurance: The Ultimate Sports Nutrition Protocol with the Power-Sync System. 84p. 1994. pap. text 15.00 (*1-891036-05-X*) Nutri Tapes.

— Primal Fire. LC 98-231646. 197p. 1997. pap. text 15.00 (*1-891036-10-6*) Nutri Tapes.

Duarte, Alex & Witman, Wynn R. Colostrum Discovering the Motherlode. 75p. 1996. pap. text 9.00 (*1-891036-12-2*) Nutri Tapes.

Duarte, Carlota. Odella: A Hidden Survivor. (Illus.). 56p. (Orig.). 1990. pap. text 17.95 (*0-9624109-0-X*) C Duarte.

Duarte, Deborah L. Mastering Virtual Teams: Strategies, Tools & Techniques That Succeed. LC 98-53902. (Illus.). 256p. 1999. 28.95 (*0-7879-4183-2*) Jossey-Bass.

Duarte, F. J. Tunable Lasers Handbook. (Optics & Photonics Ser.). (Illus.). 477p. 1995. text 80.00 (*0-12-222695-X*) Acad Pr.

Duarte, F. J., ed. Tunable Laser Applications. LC 95-23394. (Optical Engineering Ser.: Vol. 50). (Illus.). 336p. 1995. text 140.00 (*0-8247-8928-8*) Dekker.

Duarte, Frank J., ed. Dye Lasers, Vol. 45. 682p. 1992. pap. 50.00 (*0-8194-0885-9*) SPIE.

— High-Power Dye Lasers. (Optical Sciences Ser.: Vol. 65). (Illus.). xiii, 253p. 1992. 75.95 (*0-387-54066-0*) Spr-Verlag.

— Selected Papers on Dye Lasers. 682p. 1992. 55.00 (*0-8194-0884-0*, MS45/HC) SPIE.

Duarte, Frank J. & Hillman, L. W., eds. Dye Laser Principles: With Applications. (Quantum Electronics - Principles & Applications Ser.). 456p. 1990. text 97.00 (*0-12-222700-X*) Acad Pr.

***Duarte, Joe & Burke, Roland.** After-Hours Trading Made Easy. 5th ed. 2000. 29.95 (*0-7615-2519-X*) Prima Pub.

***Duarte, John W.** Andres Segovia as I Knew Him. 136p. 1998. pap. text 10.95 (*0-7866-3319-0*, 96596) Mel Bay.

Duarte, Jose C., et al, eds. Perspectives in Biotechnology. LC 87-11015. (NATO ASI Series A, Life Sciences: Vol. 128). 218p. 1987. 69.50 (*0-306-42569-6*, Plenum Trade) Perseus Pubng.

Duarte, Lawrence. The Microcontroller Beginner's Handbook. 2nd ed. (Illus.). 272p. 1998. pap. 29.95 (*0-7906-1153-8*) Prompt Publns.

Duarte, Maria A. & Sousa, Ronald W. Reading the Harper: On a Portuguese Immigrant Poem from California, 1901. (ENG & POR.). 1997. pap. text 12.00 (*0-943722-22-5*) Gavea-Brown.

Duarte, Michael. Autumn Moons & Whitetail Dreams: A Portrait of an American Deer Hunter. (Illus.). 248p. 1998. 24.95 (*1-57157-109-4*) Safari Pr.

Duarte, R. L., jt. auth. see Duarte, Salvador R.

Duarte, Salvador R. & Duarte, R. L. Electronics Assembly & Fabrication Methods. 2nd ed. LC 72-6495. (C). 1973. text 49.23 (*0-07-017880-1*) McGraw.

Duarte, Stella P. Fragile Night. LC 97-23080. 160p. (Orig.). 1997. pap. 13.00 (*0-927534-71-1*) Biling Rev-Pr.

Duato, Jose, et al. Interconnection Networks: An Engineering Approach. LC 97-20502. 550p. 1997. 60.00 (*0-8186-7800-3*, BP07800) IEEE Comp Soc.

***Duax, Anne.** Hip Hop Hooray Easter. (J). 2000. pap. 2.99 (*0-375-80453-6*, Pub. by Random Bks Yng Read) Random.

Duax, William L., et al, eds. Atlas of Steroid Structure, Vol. 2. LC 75-22419. 760p. 1983. 150.00 (*0-306-66102-0*, Kluwer Plenum) Kluwer Academic.

Duba, A. G., et al, eds. The Brittle-Ductile Transition in Rocks: The Heard Volume. (Geophysical Monograph Ser.: Vol. 56). 243p. 1990. 42.00 (*0-87590-025-9*, GM0560259) Am Geophysical.

Duba, Ursula. Tales from a Child Enemy. LC 96-36893. 128p. 1997. pap. 9.95 (*0-14-058787-X*) Viking Penguin.

Dubach, U. C., jt. ed. see Obrecht, J. B.

DuBacher, Monique E., jt. auth. see Roes, Nicholas A.

Duback, Josef. Traditional Cheesemaking: An Introduction. 112p. (Orig.). 1988. pap. 13.50 (*0-942850-18-1*) Bootstrap Pr.

***Dubal, David.** Essential Canon of Classical Music. 2000. 35.00 (*0-86547-608-X*) N Point Pr.

Dubal, David. Evenings with Horowitz: An Intimate Portrait. LC 93-46588. 1994. pap. 14.95 (*0-8065-1513-9*, Citadel Pr) Carol Pub Group.

— Literature of Piano. 1992. pap. write for info. (*0-679-41225-5*) McKay.

Duban, James. Melville's Major Fiction: Politics, Theology, & Imagination. LC 83-2432. (Illus.). 284p. (C). 1983. 30.00 (*0-87580-086-6*) N Ill U Pr.

Duban, Jeffrey, tr. see Sebesta, Judith L., ed.

DuBane, Janet & Kuman, Alexandra, eds. Pillow Ideas. (Illus.). 64p. (Orig.). 1980. pap. 2.50 (*0-918178-19-3*) Simplicity.

Dubanevich. Big Chicken Express. 1999. pap. 13.99 (*0-670-85441-7*) Viking Penguin.

Dubanevich, Arlene. Calico Cows. LC 89-16062. (J). 1990. write for info. (*0-531-05823-9*); lib. bdg. write for info. (*0-531-08423-X*) Orchard Bks Watts.

— Pig William. LC 85-5776. (Illus.). 32p. (J). (ps-2). 1985. lib. bdg. 14.95 (*0-02-733200-4*, Bradbury S&S) S&S Childrens.

— The Piggest Show on Earth. LC 88-11742. (Illus.). 32p. (J). (ps-1). 1998. pap. 6.95 (*0-531-07105-7*) Orchard Bks Watts.

Dubanivich, Arlene. The Piggest Show on Earth. LC 88-11742. (Illus.). 32p. (J). (ps-1). 1989. 15.95 (*0-531-30122-2*) Orchard Bks Watts.

Dubansky, Mindell. Guess Who Died? Memories of Baltimore with Recipes. Pinkwas, Stan & Bindman, Catherine, eds. (Illus.). 50p. 1999. 100.00 (*1-893125-00-9*) Womens Studio Wrkshop.

Dubansky, Mindell, et al. Crossing Borders: The Kaldewey Press, NY. (Illus.). 120p. 1997. 35.00 (*3-89322-322-3*) Dist Art Pubs.

Dubard, Trip. A Visitor's Guide to Myrtle Beach & the Grand Strand. (Illus.). 146p. (Orig.). 1995. pap. 12.95 (*0-941711-22-6*) Wyrick & Co.

Dubas, M., jt. auth. see Schumann, W.

Dubash, P. N. Hindoo Art in Its Social Setting. (Illus.). 278p. 1986. reprint ed. 30.00 (*0-8364-1752-6*, Pub. by Usha) S Asia.

Dubashi, Jay. Snakes & Ladders: The Development Game. 299p. 1985. 24.95 (*0-317-39861-X*, Pub. by Allied Pubs) Asia Bk Corp.

DuBasky, Mayo. The Gist of Mencken: Quotations from America's Critic. LC 89-6385. (Illus.). 882p. 1990. 83.50 (*0-8108-2150-8*) Scarecrow.

***Dubats, Sally.** Natural Magic: Inside the Well-Stocked Witch's Cupboard, 1999. pap. 12.00 (*1-57566-461-5*, Knsington) Kensgtn Pub Corp.

Dubay, Bren. Beauty & the Beast. 19p. (Orig.). (J). (gr. 2 up). 1989. pap. 3.00 (*1-57514-241-4*, 1049) Encore Perform Pub.

— Rumpelstiltskin. 22p. (J). (gr. 2-7). 1989. pap. 3.00 (*1-57514-259-7*, 1050) Encore Perform Pub.

Dubay, Bren, adapted by. Just So Stories: Dramatizations of Stories by Rudyard Kipling. (Illus.). 36p. (J). (ps-7). 1990. pap. 3.50 (*0-88680-333-0*) I E Clark.

***DuBay, Connie.** Speak! The Best Quips, Quotes & Anecdotes for Dog Lovers. 2000. pap. 10.00 (*0-452-28205-5*, Plume) Dutton Plume.

Dubay, Inga, jt. auth. see Getty, Barbara.

Dubay, Ingay, jt. auth. see Getty, Barbara.

Dubay, Thomas. And You Are Christ's: The Charism of Virginity & the Celibate Life. LC 87-80793. 149p. (Orig.). 1987. pap. 9.95 (*0-89870-161-9*) Ignatius Pr.

— Authenticity: A Biblical Theology of Discernment. LC 96-78009. 1997. pap. text 14.95 (*0-89870-619-X*) Ignatius Pr.

***Dubay, Thomas.** Evidential Power of Beauty: Science & Theology Meet. 1999. pap. 14.95 (*0-89870-752-8*) Ignatius Pr.

Dubay, Thomas. Fire Within: St. Teresa of Avila, St. John of the Cross & the Gospel - on Prayer. LC 89-83653. 366p. (Orig.). 1989. pap. text 17.95 (*0-89870-263-1*) Ignatius Pr.

— Philosophy of the State As Educator. LC 78-6256. 237p. 1978. reprint ed. lib. bdg. 59.50 (*0-313-20416-0*, DUPH, Greenwood Pr) Greenwood.

— Seeking Spiritual Direction: How to Grow the Divine Life Within. LC 93-26747. 300p. 1994. pap. 11.99 (*0-89283-810-8*, Charis) Servant.

Dubb, Steve. Logics of Resistance: Globalization & Telephone Unionism in Mexico & British Columbia. LC 99-19513. 400p. 1999. 70.00 (*0-8153-3373-0*) Garland.

Dubbel, Heinrich. Handbook of Mechanical Engineers. Beitz, Wolfgang & Kuttner, K. H., eds. LC 94-16420. 1994. write for info. (*3-540-19868-7*) Spr-Verlag.

— Handbook of Mechanical Engineers. Beitz, Wolfgang & Kuttner, K. H., eds. LC 94-16420. (Illus.). 898p. 1994. 135.00 (*0-387-19868-7*) Spr-Verlag.

Dubbeldam, J. L., ed. Brainstem (PRE) Motor Mechanisms & the Stereotypy of Motor Patterns: 5th International Congress of Vertebrate Morphology, Bristol, July 1997. 5th ed. (Acta Anatomica Ser.: Vol. 163, No. 3). (Illus.). 52p. 1999. pap. 75.75 (*3-8055-6848-7*) S Karger.

Dubben, Nigel & Sayce, Sarah. Property Portfolio Management: An Introduction. 336p. (C). (gr. 13). 1991. pap. 75.95 (*0-415-05123-1*, A5779); pap. 27.95 (*0-415-05124-X*, A5783) Thomson Learn.

Dubberly, Sara, ed. Exhibition Planning & Management: Reprints from NAME's Recent & Recommended. (Professional Practice Ser.). (Illus.). 112p. 1992. pap. 29.00 (*0-931201-54-3*, XXT828) Am Assn Mus.

Dubberly, Susan. Social Forces: Great! They in the Sky. 210p. (C). 1996. text 31.40 (*0-536-59590-9*) Pearson Custom.

***Dubbini, Renzo.** Geographies of Seeing. 1999. 25.00 (*0-226-16736-4*) U Ch Pr.

Dubbins, Paul A. & Joseph, A. E. Ultrasound in Gastroenterology. LC 94-16246. (Clinics in Diagnostic Ultrasound Ser.: Vol. 29). 1994. text 109.00 (*0-443-08905-1*) Church.

Dubble, Curtis W. Real Families: From Patriarchs to Prime Time. LC 94-41676. (Covenant Bible Studies). 86p. 1995. pap. 5.95 (*0-87178-735-0*) Brethren.

Dubbs-Ball, Joanne. Costume Jewelers: The Golden Age of Design. rev. ed. (Illus.). 208p. 1997. 39.95 (*0-7643-0212-4*) Schiffer.

Dubbs, Chris. Quick & Easy Art of Smoking Food. 1991. pap. 13.95 (*0-8329-0462-7*, Winchester Pr) New Win Pub.

Dubbs Millbrook, Minnie, jt. auth. see Leland, Ottilie M.

Dubbs, William, ed. Diversity in Corporate America, 1996-1997 Edition. (Illus.). 464p. 1996. 179.00 (*0-9640975-1-6*) Inst Corp Diversity.

Dubcek, Alexander & Hochman, Jiri. Hope Dies Last - Dubcek by Dubcek: The Autobiography. De Angelis, Paul, ed. (Illus.). 386p. 1993. 27.50 (*1-56836-000-2*) Kodansha.

Dube & Fortin. Dictionnaire of Images in Words: French/English/French. (ENG & FRE.). 1998. 49.95 (*0-320-00398-1*) Fr & Eur.

Dube, Allison. The Theme of Acquisitiveness in Bentham's Political Thought. LC 91-11375. (Political Theory & Political Philosophy Ser.). 384p. 1991. text 10.00 (*0-8153-0132-4*) Garland.

Dube, Brian, ed. see Franco, Dick.

Dube, Dina N. Folk Tales of Rajasthan. 72p. 1985. 5.50 (*0-318-36949-4*) Asia Bk Corp.

Dube, Doris. Zulu. LC 96-79003. (Illus.). 26p. (J). 1997. 8.95 (*0-916035-78-6*) Evangel Indiana.

Dube, Gilberte. Images in Words Dictionary. 1998. 29.95 (*2-7604-0599-0*) Stanke.

Dube, H. C. Fungi & Biotechnology: Recent Advances. (International Bioscience Ser.: Vol. 16). (Illus.). 250p. 1991. 59.00 (*1-55528-257-1*, Pub. by Today Tomorrow) Scholarly Pubns.

— An Introduction to Fungi. 616p. 1983. text 45.00 (*0-7069-1897-5*, Pub. by Vikas) S Asia.

Dube, Hope. Heart of Love. (Heartbeats Ser.). 112p. (YA). (gr. 7 up). 1994. pap. 5.95 (*0-7910-2938-7*) Chelsea Hse.

— Love Is a Challenge. (Junior African Writers Ser.). (Illus.). 80p. (J). (gr. 3 up). 1992. pap. 5.00 (*0-7910-2923-9*) Chelsea Hse.

Dube, J. L. A Zulu Song Book (1911) Rycroft, David, ed. & tr. by. (Colin Webb Natal & Zululand Ser.: No. 7). 104p. 1996. reprint ed. pap. 24.00 (*0-86980-910-5*, Pub. by Univ Natal Pr) Intl Spec Bk.

Dube, Janet. In Praise of Carnivores. 1997. pap. 13.95 (*0-8464-4589-1*) Beekman Pubs.

— In Praise of Carnivores. 1997. pap. 22.00 (*1-85902-413-0*, Pub. by Gomer Pr) St Mut.

Dube, Jasmine. Les Deux Nazaire. (Premier Roman Ser.). (FRE., Illus.). 64p. (J). (gr. 2 up). 1996. pap. 8.95 (*2-89021-261-0*, Pub. by La Courte Ech) Firefly Bks Ltd.

— Fais un Voeu, Nazaire! (Novels in the Premier Roman Ser.). (FRE.). 64p. (J). (gr. 2-5). 1994. pap. 8.95 (*2-89021-215-7*, Pub. by La Courte Ech) Firefly Bks Ltd.

— Nazaire et les Mousquetaires. (Novels in the Premier Roman Ser.). (FRE.). 64p. (J). (gr. 2-5). 1995. pap. 8.95 (*2-89021-231-9*, Pub. by La Courte Ech) Firefly Bks Ltd.

Dube, Jasmine & Barrette, Doris. Grattelle au Bois Mordant. 24p. (*2-89021-332-3*) La Courte Ech.

Dube, Jasmine & Franson, Leanne. L' Ourson Qui Voulait une Juliette. (*2-89021-302-1*) La Courte Ech.

Dube, Kathy A., ed. see La\Maveleine Chefs & Loomis, Susan Herrmann.

Dube, Lawrence E., Jr. Employment References & the Law. 1989. pap. 29.95 (*1-55840-100-8*) Exec Ent Pubns.

Dube, Leela, et al, eds. Visibility & Power: Essays on Women in Society & Development. (Illus.). 361p. 1987. text 35.00 (*0-19-561682-0*) OUP.

Dube, Leela & Palrewala, Rajni, eds. Structures & Strategies: Women, Work & Family. (Women & the Household in Asia Ser.: Vol. 3). (Illus.). 284p. (C). 1990. text 26.00 (*0-8039-9621-7*) Sage.

Dube, Louis J., et al. The Physics of Electronic & Atomic Collissions: XIX International Conference, Whistler, Canada 1995. (AIP Press Conference Proceedings Ser.: No. 360). (Illus.). 928p. 1996. 175.00 (*1-56396-440-6*, CP 360, AIP Pr) Spr-Verlag.

Dube, Musa W., jt. ed. see West, Gerald O.

Dube, Philippe. Charlevoix: Two Centuries at Murray Bay. Martin-Sperry, Tony, tr. from FRE. (Illus.). 288p. (C). 1990. 55.00 (*0-7735-0726-4*, Pub. by McG-Queens Univ Pr) CUP Services.

Dube, Pierre H., ed. see Pascal, Blaise.

Dube, Pierrette. Sticks & Stones! (Illus.). 24p. (J). (gr. k-3). 1998. pap. 4.95 (*1-55209-234-8*) Firefly Bks Ltd.

— Sticks & Stones. (Illus.). 24p. (J). (gr. k-3). 1998. 14.95 (*1-55209-284-4*) Firefly Bks Ltd.

Dube, R. K., jt. auth. see Upadhyaya, G. S.

Dube, R. S. Agricultural Geography: Issues & Applications. 208p. 1987. 10.00 (*81-212-0083-0*, Pub. by Gian Publng Hse) S Asia.

— Population Pressure & Agrarian Change. 1990. 22.00 (*81-7033-075-0*, Pub. by Rawat Pubns) S Asia.

Dube, Rajiv. Tourism in the Economy of Madhya Pradesh. LC 87-900304. 164p. 1987. write for info. (*81-7035-029-8*, Pub. by Daya Pub Hse) S Asia.

Dube, Rani. The Evil Within. 9.95 (*0-7043-2161-6*, Pub. by Quartet) Charles River Bks.

Dube, Richard L. Natural Pattern Forms. (Landscape Architecture Ser.). 1997. pap. 42.95 (*0-442-02286-7*, VNR) Wiley.

Dube, Richard L. Natural Pattern Forms: A Practical Sourcebook for Landscape Design. 229p. 1996. 54.95 (*0-471-28768-7*, VNR) Wiley.

Dube, Richard L. & Campbell, Frederick C. Natural Stonescapes: The Art & Craft of Stone Placement. LC 98-31046. 1999. pap. 24.95 (*1-58017-092-7*) Storey Bks.

Dube, Richard L., jt. auth. see Campbell, Frederick C.

Dube, S. C. Explanation & Management of Change. 1974. text 3.95 (*0-07-096388-6*) McGraw.

— Tradition & Development. (C). 1995. text 32.00 (*0-7069-8956-2*, Pub. by Vikas); pap. text 12.00 (*0-7069-8339-4*, Pub. by Vikas) S Asia.

— Understanding Change: Anthropological & Sociological Perspectives. (C). 1992. pap. text 7.95 (*0-7069-6396-2*) Advent Bks Div.

Dube, S. C. & Indian Council of Social Science Research Staff. Antiquity to Modernity in Tribal India, 4 vols. LC 98-908105. (Tribal Studies of India Series T). 1998. write for info. (*81-210-0386-5*) Inter-India Pubns.

Dube, S. N. Cross Currents in Early Buddhism. 1981. 22.50 (*0-8364-0686-9*, Pub. by Manohar) S Asia.

Dube, Saurabh. Untouchable Pasts: Religion, Identity, & Power among a Central Indian Community, 1780-1950. LC 97-49929. (SUNY Series in Hindu Studies). (Illus.). 320p. (C). 1998. pap. text 23.95 (*0-7914-3688-8*) State U NY Pr.

— Untouchable Pasts: Religion, Identity, & Power among a Central Indian Community, 1780-1950. LC 97-49929. (SUNY Series in Hindu Studies). (Illus.). 320p. (C). 1998. text 71.50 (*0-7914-3687-X*) State U NY Pr.

***Dube Shomanah, Musa W.** Postcolonial Feminist Interpretation of the Bible. LC 00-8998. 2000. pap. 29.99 (*0-8272-2963-1*) Chalice Pr.

Dube, Siddharth. In the Land of Poverty: Memoirs of an Indian Family, 1947-97. LC 98-19800. 1998. pap. 25.00 (*1-85649-598-1*, Pub. by Zed Books); text 65.00 (*1-85649-597-3*, Pub. by Zed Books) St Martin.

Dube, Wolf-Dieter. The Expressionists. LC 87-50465. (World of Art Ser.). (Illus.). 216p. 1985. pap. 14.95 (*0-500-20123-4*, Pub. by Thames Hudson) Norton.

Dube, Wolf-Dieter, jt. auth. see Barron, Stephanie.

Dubec, George E. Find-a-Mate Personal Introduction Handbook (for Singles) 85p. (Orig.). 1988. pap. 4.95 (*0-925574-00-7*) GIO Enterps.

Dubeck, Leroy W., et al. Fantastic Voyages: Learning Science Through Science Fiction Films. LC 93-10039. 327p. 1993. pap. 29.95 (*1-56396-195-4*) Spr-Verlag.

— Science in Cinema: Teaching Science Fact Through Science Fiction Films. 204p. (C). 1988. pap. text 17.95 (*0-8077-2915-9*) Tchrs Coll.

***Dubeck, Paula & Dunn, Dana, eds.** Workplace/Women's Place: An Anthology. 2nd ed. 395p. 2000. pap. text. write for info. (*1-891487-51-5*) Roxbury Pub Co.

Dubeck, Paula, jt. ed. see Vannoy, Dana.

Dubeck, Paula J., et al, eds. Women & Work: A Handbook. LC 95-49853. (Illus.). 592p. 1996. text 80.00 (*0-8240-7647-8*, SS679) Garland.

Dubeck, Paula J. & Borman, Kathryn M., eds. Women & Work: A Reader. LC 97-22828. 550p. 1997. pap. 26.00 (*0-8135-2473-3*) Rutgers U Pr.

Dubeif, H., jt. auth. see Bernard, P.

***Dubel, Stefan & Breitling, Frank.** Recombinant Antibodies. LC 99-14610. 161p. 1999. pap. 64.95 (*0-471-17847-0*) Wiley.

Dubelaar, Thea. Looking for Vincent. (Illus.). 56p. (J). (gr. 2-8). 1992. 9.95 (*1-56288-300-3*) Checkerboard.

Dubell, Folke. Kenya - Fran Enpartistat Till Demokrati? (Afrikafakta Ser.: Nr. 1). 57p. 1994. write for info. (*91-7106-350-1*, Pub. by Nordic Africa) Transaction Pubs.

Dubelle, Beverley B. This Dumpster Leaks: Falling in Love with the South. (Illus.). 180p. 1999. pap. 7.50 (*1-892614-21-9*) Briarwood VA.

DuBelle, Lee. Internal Cleansing Is an Old Movement. 105p. (Orig.). 1988. pap. 12.00 (*0-9618703-2-X*) L DuBelle.

— Proper Food Combining Cookbook. rev. ed. 200p. 1987. pap. 20.00 (*0-9618703-0-3*) L DuBelle.

Dubelle, Lee. Proper Food Combining Works - Living Testimony. rev. ed. 115p. 1987. pap. 12.00 (*0-9618703-1-1*) L DuBelle.

Dubelman, Richard S. Adventures of Holly Hobbie. 1980. pap. 10.95 (*0-385-28019-X*) Doubleday.

Duben, Ipek A., tr. see Castle, Frederick T. & Sonmez, Necmi.

Dubendorf, Donald R. & Storey, M. John. The Insider Buyout. LC 84-52258. 272p. 1985. 19.95 (*0-88266-387-9*, Storey Pub) Storey Bks.

Duberman, Lucile. Reconstituted Family: A Study of Remarried Couples & Their Children. LC 75-8840. 200p. 1975. text 33.95 (*0-88229-168-8*) Burnham Inc.

Duberman, Lucille. Marriage Other Alternative. 2nd ed. (C). 1977. pap. write for info. (*0-03-038336-6*) Harcourt Coll Pubs.

Duberman, Martin. Black Mountain: An Exploration in Community. 576p. 1993. pap. 14.95 (*0-393-30953-3*) Norton.

— Black Mountain - An Exploration in Community. 1988. 25.50 (*0-8446-6338-7*) Peter Smith.

Duberman, Martin. Left Out: A Political Journey. 16.00 (*0-465-01745-2*) Basic.

— Left Out: A Political Journey. 466p. 1999. 30.00 (*0-465-01744-4*, Pub. by Basic) HarpC.

Duberman, Martin. Midlife Queer: Autobiography of a Decade, 1971-1981. LC 98-28098. 240p. 1998. pap. 18.95 (*0-299-16024-6*) U of Wis Pr.

— Paul Robeson. LC 94-43400. 816p. 1995. pap. 19.95 (*1-56584-288-X*, Pub. by New Press NY) Norton.

— Stonewall. LC 93-45838. (Illus.). 352p. 1994. pap. 14.95 (*0-452-27206-8*, Plume) Dutton Plume.

***Duberman, Martin, ed.** Contemporary Issues. (Illus.). 112-196p. (gr. 9). 1999. pap. 51.80 (*0-7910-3755-X*) Chelsea Hse.

Duberman, Martin, ed. Queer Representations: Reading Lives, Reading Cultures. LC 96-53042. 450p. (C). 1997. text 60.00 (*0-8147-1884-1*); pap. text 23.50 (*0-8147-1883-3*) NYU Pr.

— A Queer World: The Center for Lesbian & Gay Studies Reader. LC 96-53390. 600p. (C). 1997. text 65.00 (*0-8147-1874-4*); pap. text 25.00 (*0-8147-1875-2*) NYU Pr.

Duberman, Martin, ed. see Clausen, Jan.

Duberman, Martin, ed. see Herman, Ellen.

Duberman, Martin, ed. see Robson, Ruthann.

Duberman, Martin, ed. see Young, Perry D.

D

Duberman, Martin B., ed. The Antislavery Vanguard: New Essays on the Abolitionists. LC 65-10824. 518p. reprint ed. pap. 160.60 (*0-8357-5640-8*, 203263300080) Bks Demand.

Duberman, Martin B., et al. Hidden from History: Reclaiming the Gay & Lesbian Past. (Illus.). 580p. 1990. pap. 17.95 (*0-452-01067-5*, Plume) Dutton Plume.

Dubernard, J. M. & Sutherland, David E., eds. International Handbook of Pancreas Transplantation. (Developments in Surgery Ser.). (C). 1989. text 346.00 (*0-89838-399-4*) Kluwer Academic.

Duberstein, Larry. The Alibi Breakfast. LC 94-27512. 229p. 1995. 22.00 (*1-877946-59-1*) Permanent Pr.

— Carnovsky's Retreat. LC 87-62806. 273p. 1988. 22.00 (*0-932966-83-7*) Permanent Pr.

— Eccentric Circles. LC 91-40188. 191p. 1992. 22.00 (*1-877946-20-6*) Permanent Pr.

— The Handsome Sailor. LC 97-29805. 240p. 1998. 25.00 (*1-57962-007-8*) Permanent Pr.

— The Handsome Sailor. large type ed. LC 98-42687. 1999. 30.00 (*0-7862-1685-9*) Thorndike Pr.

— The Marriage Hearse. 1988. mass mkt. 4.50 (*0-440-20195-0*, LE) Dell.

— The Marriage Hearse. LC 86-62450. 160p. 1987. 22.00 (*0-932966-76-4*) Permanent Pr.

— Postcards from Pinsk. LC 90-53324. 224p. 1991. 22.00 (*1-877946-04-4*) Permanent Pr.

***Duberstein, Paul Raphael & Masling, Joseph M.** Psychodynamic Perspectives on Sickness & Health. LC 99-58549. 408p. 2000. 49.95 (*1-55798-668-1*) Am Psychol.

Dubesset, M. Glossaire des Unites, Graneurs Informatique. (FRE.). 1998. 24.95 (*0-320-00161-X*) Fr & Eur.

Dubetz, Anthony & Gellis, Willard. Making Nightmares Pay. rev. ed. 1987. 6.00 (*0-917455-03-7*) Big Foot NY.

Dubey, Abinash C., et al, eds. Detection & Remediation Technologies for Mines & Minelike Targets III. LC 98-226765. (Proceedings of SPIE Ser.: Vol. 3392). 1306p. 1998. 166.00 (*0-8194-2841-8*) SPIE.

***Dubey, Abinash C., et al, eds.** Detection & Remediation Technologies for Mines & Minelike Targets IV. 1488p. 1999. pap. text 171.00 (*0-8194-3184-2*) SPIE.

Dubey, Abinash C. & Barnard, Robert L., eds. Detection & Remediation Technologies for Mines & Minelike Targets II. 80p. 1997. pap. 116.00 (*0-8194-2494-3*) SPIE.

Dubey, Ajay K. Indo-African Relations in the Post-Nehru Era, 1965-1985. (Illus.). 96p. 1990. 12.00 (*81-85163-07-3*, Pub. by Kalinga) Nataraj Bks.

Dubey, Alok. Environmental Geomorphology: A Study of Trans-Yamuna Region. 1990. 94.00 (*81-210-0244-3*, Pub. by Inter-India Pubns) S Asia.

Dubey, Anju, jt. auth. see Kumari, Ranjana.

Dubey, D. P., ed. Rays & Ways of Indian Culture. LC 96-900661. 273p. 1996. pap. 250.00 (*81-85880-98-0*, Pub. by Print Hse) St Mut.

Dubey, J. P., ed. Cryptosporidiosis in Man & Animals. 208p. 1990. lib. bdg. 165.95 (*0-8493-6401-9*, RC136) CRC Pr.

Dubey, J. P. & Beattie, C. P. Toxoplasmosis of Animals & Man. 232p. 1988. boxed set 214.95 (*0-8493-4618-5*, SF809) CRC Pr.

Dubey, J. P. & Towle, A. Toxoplasmosis in Sheep: A Review & Annotated Bibliography. 152p. (C). 1996. pap. text 24.95 (*0-85198-562-9*) OUP.

Dubey, J. P., et al. Sarcocystosis of Animals. LC 88-15684. 224p. 1989. 130.00 (*0-8493-6364-0*, QR201, CRC Reprint) Franklin.

Dubey, K. N. Planning & Development in India. 1990. 47.50 (*81-7024-268-1*, Pub. by Ashish Pub Hse) S Asia.

— Process of Socio-Economic Development. (C). 1992. text 22.00 (*81-7033-164-1*, Pub. by Rawat Pubns) S Asia.

Dubey, Madhu. Black Women Novelists & the Nationalist Aesthetic. LC 93-14343. 208p. 1994. 35.00 (*0-253-31841-6*) Ind U Pr.

— Black Women Novelists & the Nationalist Aesthetic. LC 93-14343. 1994. pap. 35.00 (*0-253-20855-6*) Ind U Pr.

Dubey, Muchkund, ed. Communal Revivalism in India: A Study of External Implications. (C). 1994. 18.00 (*81-241-0197-3*, Pub. by Har-Anand Pubns) S Asia.

— Indian Society Today. (C). 1995. 44.00 (*81-241-0329-1*, Pub. by Har-Anand Pubns) S Asia.

— Subhas Chandra Bose: The Man & His Vision. 1998. 20.00 (*81-241-0582-0*) Har-Anand Pubns.

Dubey, Ravi K. Indo-Sri Lankan Relations with Special Reference to the Tamil Problem. 1993. 22.00 (*81-7100-492-X*, Pub. by Deep & Deep Pubns) S Asia.

Dubey, S. P., ed. Facets of Recent Indian Philosophy Vol. 2: Indian Philosophy & History. (C). 1996. 26.00 (*81-85636-25-7*, Pub. by M Manoharial) S Asia.

— Metaphysics of the Spirit: Facets of Recent Indian Philosophy, No. 1. (C). 1994. 19.50 (*81-85636-04-4*, Pub. by M Manoharial) S Asia.

— Problems of Indian Philosophy Vol. 3: Problems of Indian Philosophy. LC 96-902047. (C). 1997. 26.00 (*81-85636-21-4*, Pub. by M Manoharial) S Asia.

Dubhashi, P. R. Essays in Development Administration. 1987. 85.00 (*0-7855-1810-X*, Pub. by Archives Pubs) St Mut.

— Essays in Development Administrations. 1986. 120.00 (*0-7855-1811-8*, Pub. by Archives Pubs) St Mut.

Dubhoff, jt. auth. see Goold.

Dubie, Alan. Frank A. Golder. 278p. 1989. text 55.50 (*0-88033-165-8*, Pub. by East Eur Monographs) Col U Pr.

Dubie, Norman. Groom Falconer. 1990. pap. 7.95 (*0-393-30570-8*) Norton.

Dubie, Norman. Radio Sky. 64p. 1992. pap. 8.95 (*0-393-30852-9*) Norton.

Dubie, Norman. Selected & New Poems. LC 83-42686. 160p. 1983. pap. 5.95 (*0-393-30140-0*) Norton.

Dubiel, Hulmet. Theory & Politics: Studies in the Development of Critical Theory. Gregg, Benjamin, tr. from GER. (German Social Thought Ser.). (Illus.). 224p. 1985. 27.50 (*0-262-04080-8*) MIT Pr.

Dubin. Jewish Fun Set, 3 vols. pap. text 3.00 (*0-486-27191-9*) Dover.

— Puppies & Kittens, Miniature. (Itty Bitties Ser.). (Illus.). 20p. (J). (ps). 1991. bds. 2.50 (*0-8120-6265-5*) Barron.

— Spectacular Healing Foods. (C). 1998. pap. 13.95 (*0-13-621251-4*) P-H.

Dubin, A. Clinical Biochemistry of Lipids. Rafelson, Max E., ed. (Journal: Clinical Physiology & Biochemistry: Vol. 2, No. 2-3). (Illus.). 80p. 1984. pap. 69.75 (*3-8055-3859-6*) S Karger.

***Dubin, A.** Systems Engineering & Monte Carlo Applications. LC 99-35831. (Illus.). 288p. 2000. 110.00 (*0-471-98172-9*) Wiley.

Dubin, Alex, ed. see Jamar, Mary H.

Dubin, Andrew E., ed. The Principal As Chief Executive Officer. 224p. 1991. pap. 29.95 (*1-85000-806-X*, Falmer Pr) Taylor & Francis.

***Dubin, Cindy & Bernabe, Jan, eds.** Managing Logistics, 2000 Yearbook. annuals (Illus.). 200p. 2000. pap. 199.00 (*1-58673-019-3*) IOMA.

Dubin, D. A. & Hennings, M. A. Quantum Mechanics, Algebras & Distributions. LC 90-42157. (Pitman Research Notes in Mathematics Ser.: No. 238). 252p. 1990. pap. 78.20 (*0-608-05237-X*, 206577400001) Bks Demand.

Dubin, D. A., et al. Quantization & Phase. 350p. 1999. 60.00 (*981-02-3919-X*) World Scientific Pub.

Dubin, D. H. & Schneider, D., eds. Trapped Charged Particles & Fundamentals Physics. LC 98-89576. (Conference Proceedings Ser.: Vol. 457). (Illus.). 426p. 1999. (*1-56396-776-6*) Am Inst Physics.

Dubin, Dale. Rapid Interpretation of EKG's. 5th ed. LC 88-72108. (Illus.). 342p. 1996. pap. text 29.99 (*0-912912-02-2*) Cover Pub.

***Dubin, Dale.** Rapid Interpretation of EKG's. 6th ed. (Illus.). 368p. 2000. pap. text 34.95 (*0-912912-06-5*) Cover Pub.

Dubin, Daniel H., jt. ed. see Fajans, Joel.

Dubin, Debbie I., jt. auth. see Block, Linda F.

Dubin, Elliott, jt. auth. see Reid, J. Norman.

Dubin, Fraida. Encounter English: The Britannica Method, 4 vols. LC 92-154088. (English Communications Ser.). 1991. write for info. (*0-85229-560-X*) Ency Brit Inc.

— Reading by All Means. 2nd rev. ed. (Illus.). 224p. (C). 1990. pap. text 27.87 (*0-201-50352-2*) Addison-Wesley.

Dubin, Fraida & Olshtain, Elite. Course Design: Developing Programs & Materials for Language Learning. (New Directions in Language Teaching Ser.). (Illus.). 206p. 1986. pap. text 19.95 (*0-521-27642-X*) Cambridge U Pr.

— Reading by All Means. (Illus.). (C). 1981. pap. text. write for info. (*0-201-10077-0*) Addison-Wesley.

— Reading on Purpose: Cognitive Skills for Intermediate Learners. (Illus.). 240p. (C). 1987. pap. text 24.92 (*0-201-11671-5*) Addison-Wesley.

Dubin, Harry N., et al. Coping Successfully: A How-To Manual for Operational Improvement. 238p. (Orig.). 1981. text 27.50 (*0-8290-0262-6*); pap. text 15.95 (*0-8290-0270-7*) Irvington.

***Dubin, Jeffrey A.** Studies in Consumer Demand: Econometric Methods Applied to Market Data. LC 98-26792. 28p. 1998. 120.00 (*0-7923-8215-3*) Kluwer Academic.

Dubin, Jill. Chanukah Sticker Book. (Little Activity Bks.). (Illus.). (J). 1993. pap. 1.00 (*0-486-27154-4*) Dover.

Dubin, Jill. Create Your Own Noah's Ark Sticker Picture: With 52 Reusable Stickers. 25th ed. (Illus.). (J). (gr. k-3). 1994. pap. 3.50 (*0-486-27921-9*) Dover.

— Hebrew Alphabet Stickers. (Illus.). (J). (gr. k-3). 1992. pap. 1.00 (*0-486-27322-9*) Dover.

— Jewish Activity Book. (Illus.). (J). (gr. 4-7). 1992. pap. 1.00 (*0-486-27257-5*) Dover.

Dubin, Jill. Jewish Sticker Book. (Illus.). (J). 1991. pap. text 1.00 (*0-486-26604-4*) Dover.

— Kids at Play Sticker Book. (Little Activity Bks.). (Illus.). (J). 1995. pap. 1.00 (*0-486-28791-2*) Dover.

Dubin, Jill. Little Hebrew Alphabet Coloring Book. 81st ed. (HEB., Illus.). (J). 1992. pap. 1.00 (*0-486-27018-1*) Dover.

Dubin, Jill. Toys Sticker Book. (Little Activity Bks.). (Illus.). (J). 1994. pap. 1.00 (*0-486-28161-2*) Dover.

Dubin, Jill. Twelve Children's Bookmarks. 40th ed. (Illus.). (J). (gr. 4-7). 1993. pap. 1.00 (*0-486-27705-4*) Dover.

Dubin, Jill. ABC Bible Block Pop-Up. 12p. (J). 1998. 10.99 (*0-8054-1276-X*) Broadman.

— The Little Red Caboose. LC 98-24330. (My First Hello Reader Ser.). (J). 1998. 3.99 (*0-590-63598-0*) Scholastic Inc.

— My Mini ABC's: 24 Bible Alphabet Board Books. (Read to Me Mommy Ser.). 144p. (J). 1998. bds. 14.99 (*0-8499-5831-8*) Tommy Nelson.

Dubin, Jill, jt. auth. see Slier, Debby.

Dubin, Lawrence A. & Guernsey, Thomas F. Trial Practice. LC 92-167121. 200p. 1991. pap. 27.95 (*0-87084-248-X*) Anderson Pub Co.

Dubin, Lawrence A. & Schwartz, Michael A. Michigan Rules of Professional Conduct & Disciplinary Procedure. LC 89-80298. 632p. 1989. ring bd., suppl. ed. 85.00 (*0-685-38204-4*) U MI Law CLE.

— Michigan Rules of Professional Conduct & Disciplinary Procedure. 632p. 1991. suppl. ed. write for info. (*0-318-68095-5*, 89-012); suppl. ed. 45.00 (*0-685-47525-5*) U MI Law CLE.

— Michigan Rules of Professional Conduct & Disciplinary Procedure. LC 89-80298. 632p. 1992. suppl. ed. 50.00 (*0-685-58879-3*, 92-002) U MI Law CLE.

— Michigan Rules of Professional Conduct & Disciplinary Procedure. LC 89-80298. 632p. 1993. suppl. ed. 55.00 (*0-685-58880-7*, 93-004) U MI Law CLE.

Dubin, Lois C. The Port Jews of Habsburg Trieste: Absolutist Politics & Enlightenment Culture. (Studies in Jewish History & Culture). (Illus.). 2p. 1998. 49.50 (*0-8047-3320-1*) Stanford U Pr.

Dubin, Lois S. History of Beads: From 30,000 B. C. to the Present. (Illus.). 136p. 1998. pap. 17.98 (*0-8109-8178-5*, Pub. by Abrams) Time Warner.

— The History of Beads: From 30,000 B. C. to the Present. abr. ed. (Illus.). 136p. 1995. pap. 19.95 (*0-8109-2617-2*, Pub. by Abrams) Time Warner.

— The History of Beads: From 30,000 B.C. to the Present. (Illus.). 364p. 1987. 75.00 (*0-8109-0736-4*, Pub. by Abrams) Time Warner.

Dubin, Lois Sherr. North American Indian Jewelry & Adornment: From Prehistory to the Present. LC 98-37491. (Illus.). 608p. 1999. 75.00 (*0-8109-3689-5*, Pub. by Abrams) Time Warner.

Dubin, Marc. Lonely Planet Trekking in Spain: A Walking Guide. (Illus.). 208p. (Orig.). 1990. pap. 11.95 (*0-86442-088-9*) Lonely Planet.

— Pyrenees. 3rd ed. (Rough Guides Ser.). 1998. pap. 17.95 (*1-85828-308-6*, Penguin Bks) Viking Penguin.

— Rough Cyprus, No. 2. 2nd ed. LC 96-195330. (Illus.). 368p. 1996. pap. 16.95 (*1-85828-182-2*) NAL.

— The Rough Guide to Cyprus. 3rd ed. (Illus.). 432p. 1999. 16.95 (*1-85828-430-9*, Pub. by Rough Guides) Penguin Putnam.

Dubin, Michael. Foreign Acquisitions & the Spread of the Multinational Firm. Bruchey, Stuart, ed. LC 80-572. (Multinational Corporations Ser.). (Illus.). 1981. lib. bdg. 24.95 (*0-405-13366-9*) Ayer.

Dubin, Michael J. United States Congressional Elections, 1788-1997: The Official Results of the Elections of the 1st Through 105th Congresses. LC 96-9841. 1035p. 1998. lib. bdg. 235.00 (*0-7864-0283-0*) McFarland & Co.

Dubin, Murray. South Philadelphia: Mummers, Memories, & the Melrose Diner. (Illus.). 256p. (C). 1996. 29.95 (*1-56639-429-5*) Temple U Pr.

Dubin, P., et al. Macromolecular Complexes in Chemistry & Biology. LC 93-38677. 1994. 131.95 (*0-387-57166-3*) Spr-Verlag.

Dubin, Patricia B. Tweak & the Absolutely Right Whale. (Illus.). 48p. (Orig.). (J). (gr. k-3). 1993. pap. 9.95 (*1-880812-06-1*) S Ink WA.

Dubin, Paul, ed. Microdomains in Polymer Solutions. LC 85-24246. (Polymer Science & Technology Ser.: Vol. 30). 472p. 1986. 105.00 (*0-306-42110-0*, Plenum Trade) Perseus Pubng.

***Dubin, Paul & Farinato, Raymond S.** Colloid-Polymer Interactions: From Fundamentals to Practice. LC 98-50702. 417p. (C). 1999. 115.00 (*0-471-24316-7*) Wiley.

Dubin, Paul L. & Tong, Penger, eds. Colloid-Polymer Interactions: Particulate, Amphiphilic, & Biological Surfaces. LC 93-8495. (ACS Symposium Ser.: No. 532). (Illus.). 290p. 1993. text 85.00 (*0-8412-2696-2*, Pub. by Am Chemical) OUP.

Dubin, Paul L., jt. ed. see Potschka, Martin.

Dubin, Reese P. Healing Foods from the Bible. 320p. 1998. pap. 14.00 (*0-7352-0037-8*) PH Pr.

***Dubin, Reese P.** Milagrosos Alimentos Curativos de la Biblia. 2000. pap. 13.95 (*0-13-083425-4*) P-H.

— Milagrosos Alimentos Curativos de la Biblia. (SPA.). 2000. pap. 14.00 (*0-7352-0210-9*) PH Pr.

Dubin, Reese P. Miracle Food Cures from the Bible. LC 99-19393. xix, 410p. 1999. text 24.95 (*0-13-621269-7*) P-H.

Dubin, Rick & Van Cura, Kevin. Hottest Drinks of the 90's. 68p. Date not set. pap. text 15.00 (*0-9672345-0-6*) Hottest Drinks.

Dubin, Robert. Central Life Interests: Creative Individualism in a Complex World. 256p. (C). 1992. 39.95 (*1-56000-051-1*) Transaction Pubs.

Dubin, Stan. The Small Business Success Manual. LC 99-90469. 196p. 1998. pap. 28.95 (*0-9662555-0-X*) Workable Solns.

***Dubin, Stan.** When the Thrill Is Gone: How to Put the Life & Excitement Back into Any Relationship. 117p. 1999. pap. 28.95 (*0-9662555-1-8*) Workable Solns.

Dubin, Steven C. Arresting Images: Impolitic Art & Uncivil Actions. 368p. (C). (gr. 13). 1994. pap. 19.99 (*0-415-90893-0*, Pub. by Tavistock) Routldge.

— Bureaucratizing the Muse: Public Funds & the Cultural Worker. LC 86-30862. (Illus.). 248p. (C). 1987. 34.50 (*0-226-16748-8*) U Ch Pr.

***Dubin, Steven C.** Displays of Power: Controversy in the American Museum from the Enola Gay to Sensation! 2000. pap. 18.95 (*0-8147-1890-6*) NYU Pr.

Dubin, Steven C. Displays of Power: Memory & Amnesia in the American Museum. LC 98-58108. (Illus.). 300p. 1999. 24.95 (*0-8147-1889-2*) NYU Pr.

Dubin, W. R. & Stolberg, R. Emergency Psychiatry for the House Officer. (Illus.). 166p. (Orig.). 1981. pap. text 19.50 (*0-88331-139-9*) R B Luce.

Dubin, William R., et al, eds. Psychiatric Emergencies. (Clinics in Emergency Medicine Ser.: Vol. 4). (Illus.). 268p. 1984. text 42.00 (*0-443-08288-X*) Church.

Dubina, Babara, jt. auth. see Dubina, Phil.

Dubina, Phil & Dubina, Babara. Oregon Retirement & Relocation Guide. large type ed. LC 97-33597. (Retirement & Relocation Guides Ser.). (Illus.). 350p. (Orig.). 1999. pap. 24.95 (*1-56559-106-2*) HGI-Over Fifty.

Dubinin, G. N. Diffusion Chromizing of Alloys. Pai, K. M., tr. (RUS., Illus.). 526p. (C). 1987. 38.00 (*81-205-0069-5*, Pub. by Oxford IBH) S Asia.

Dubinin, G. N. & Avraamov, Yu S. Materials Technology for Electrical Appliances: Magnetic & Electrical Properties of Metals & Alloys. Patel, T. S., tr. from RUS. (Illus.). 282p. (C). 1987. 21.00 (*81-205-0030-X*, Pub. by Oxford IBH) S Asia.

Dubinky, Dinah. A Narrow Bridge. LC 91-43756. (ENG & HEB.). 1992. 16.95 (*0-87306-590-5*); pap. 13.95 (*0-87306-594-8*) Feldheim.

Dubino, Jeanne, jt. auth. see Rosenberg, Beth C.

Dubinskas, Frank A., ed. Making Time. LC 87-28411. 238p. (C). 1988. 34.95 (*0-87722-535-4*) Temple U Pr.

Dubinskas, Franks A. & McDonald, James H., eds. Electronic Technologies & Instruction: Tools, Users, & Power. LC 93-27139. (NAPA Bulletin Ser.: Vol. 12). 1993. write for info. (*0-913167-57-6*) Am Anthro Assn.

Dubinski, J., jt. ed. see Kidybinski, A.

Dubinski, Roman R., ed. see Brome, Alexander.

Dubinskii, A. V., jt. auth. see Bunimovich, A. I.

Dubinskii, Ju. A., et al. Nine Papers on Functional Analysis & Partial Differential Equations. (Translations Ser.: Series 2, Vol. 67). 288p. 1968. 50.00 (*0-8218-1767-1*, TRANS2/67) Am Math.

Dubinskii, Julii A. Analytic Pseudo-Differential Operators & Their Applications. (C). 1991. text 171.00 (*0-7923-1296-1*) Kluwer Academic.

— Sobolev Spaces of Infinite Order & Differential Equations. 1986. text 107.50 (*90-277-2147-5*) Kluwer Academic.

Dubinsky, E. & Leron, Uri. Learning Abstract Algebra with ISETL. 280p. 1993. 49.95 (*0-387-94104-5*) Spr-Verlag.

Dubinsky, Ed, et al, eds. Readings in Cooperative Learning for Undergraduate Mathematics. LC 97-71908. (MAA Notes Ser.: Vol. 44). 324p. (C). 1997. pap. text 34.95 (*0-88385-153-9*) Math Assn.

— Research in Collegiate Mathematics Education, I. (CBMS Issues in Mathematics Education Ser.: Vol. 4). 229p. 1994. pap. 42.00 (*0-8218-3504-1*, CBMATH/4) Am Math.

Dubinsky, Ed & Leron, Uri. Learning Abstract Algebra with ISETL. 1993. 59.95 (*0-387-94152-5*) Spr-Verlag.

Dubinsky, Ed & Ramanujan, M. S. On Lambda Nuclearity. LC 72-4515. (Memoirs Ser.: No. 1/128). 101p. 1972. pap. 17.00 (*0-8218-1828-7*, MEMO/1/128) Am Math.

Dubinsky, Ed, jt. auth. see Fenton, William N.

Dubinsky, Ed, jt. ed. see Kaput, James.

Dubinsky, Helene, jt. auth. see Bradley, Jonathan.

Dubinsky, Irwin. Reform in Trade Union Discrimination in the Construction Industry: Operation Dig & Its Legacy. LC 72-12974. (Special Studies in U. S. Economic, Social & Political Issues). 1973. 52.50 (*0-275-07080-8*) Irvington.

Dubinsky, James, ed. see Baer, Elizabeth H.

Dubinsky, Karen. Improper Advances: Rape & Heterosexual Conflict in Ontario, 1880-1929. LC 92-44673. (Chicago Series on Sexuality, History, & Society). (Illus.). 240p. (C). 1993. pap. text 14.95 (*0-226-16754-2*); lib. bdg. 39.95 (*0-226-16753-4*) U Ch Pr.

— The Second Greatest Disappointment: Honeymooners, Heterosexuality, & the Tourist Industry at Niagara Falls. LC 98-51533. (Illus.). 288p. (C). 1999. pap. 22.00 (*0-8135-2656-6*); text 52.00 (*0-8135-2655-8*) Rutgers U Pr.

Dubinsky, Z., ed. Coral Reefs. (Ecosystems of the World Ser.: No. 25). xii,550p. 1991. 296.00 (*0-444-87392-9*) Elsevier.

Dubis, Michael. The Hangman. 288p. 1998. pap. 10.95 (*0-9659308-6-6*) Erica Hse.

Dubisch, Jill. In a Different Place: Pilgrimage, Gender, & Politics at a Greek Island Shrine. LC 94-39673. (Modern Greek Studies). 352p. 1995. text 52.50 (*0-691-02968-7*, Pub. by Princeton U Pr) Cal Prin Full Svc.

Dubisch, Jill, ed. Gender & Power in Rural Greece. LC 86-3183. 277p. 1986. reprint ed. pap. 85.90 (*0-608-04595-0*, 206536500003) Bks Demand.

Dubisch, Roy. Basic Concepts: A Student Workbook. 2nd ed. LC 80-19446. (Mathematics Ser.). (Illus.). 483p. (C). 1981. pap. text, student ed. 14.25 (*0-201-03156-6*) Addison-Wesley.

— Basic Concepts of Mathematics for Elementary Teachers. 2nd ed. LC 80-19446. (Mathematics Ser.). (Illus.). 483p. (C). 1981. write for info. (*0-201-03170-1*) Addison-Wesley.

— Trigonometry. LC 55-6084. 410p. reprint ed. pap. 127.10 (*0-608-30370-4*, 201245100081) Bks Demand.

Duble, Richard L. Turfgrasses: Their Management & Use in the Southern Zone. 2nd rev. ed. LC 95-39690. (W. L. Moody, Jr., Natural History Ser.: No. 20). (Illus.). 356p. 1996. 49.95 (*0-89096-647-8*) Tex A&M Univ Pr.

Dubler, Martin. Taxation Law. (LBC Nutshell Ser.). 120p. 1995. pap. 14.95 (*0-455-21324-0*, Pub. by LawBk Co) Gaunt.

Dubler, Nancy N. & Mareus, Leonard J. Mediating Bioethical Disputes: Community Health Outreach Worker Programs. LC 94-14572. (Practical Guide Ser.). 40p. 1994. 20.00 (*1-881277-19-4*) United Hosp Fund.

Dubler, Nancy N., ed. see American Public Health Association, Jails & Prison.

Dubler, Nancy N., jt. ed. see Melnick, Vijaya L.

Dublin. Outpatient Invasive Radiologic Procedures: Diagnostic & Therapeutic. 1989. text 65.00 (*0-7216-1532-5*, W B Saunders Co) Harcrt Hlth Sci Grp.

— Taxes & Wealth of a Nation. 1996. 23.00 (*0-02-874024-6*) Free Pr.

Dublin, Aba, jt. auth. see Fallon, B. P.

Dublin, Arthur, jt. auth. see Dublin, William B.

Dublin City University, Dublin City, jt. auth. see Nuallain, Sean O.

Dublin, Jack & Dublin, Selma M. Credit Unions in a Changing World: The Tanzania-Kenya Experience. LC 83-1353. 302p. 1983. reprint ed. pap. 93.70 (*0-7837-3647-9*, 204351800009) Bks Demand.

An Asterisk (*) at the beginning of an entry indicates that the title is appearing for the first time.

D

Dublin, Jill. Mother Goose Rhymes. (Itty Bitties Ser.). (Illus.). 20p. (J). (ps). 1991. bds. 3.50 (*0-8120-6267-1*) Barron.

— Things That Go. (Little Bitty Ser.). (Illus.). 20p. (J). (ps). 1991. bds. 3.50 (*0-8120-6263-9*) Barron.

Dublin, Louis I. & Lotka, Alfred J. The Money Value of a Man. Rosenkrantz, Barbara G., ed. LC 76-25659. (Public Health in America Ser.). (Illus.). 1977. reprint ed. lib. bdg. 26.95 (*0-405-09814-6*) Ayer.

Dublin, Peter & Pressman, Harvey. Computers in Middle & Secondary English. 176p. (C). 1997. 28.00 (*0-06-501676-9*) Addson-Wesley Educ.

Dublin, Peter & Pressman, Harvey, eds. Elementary Language Arts. (Integrating Computers in Your Classrooms Ser.: 8 bks.). 160p. (C). 1994. pap. 18.00 (*0-06-501673-4*) Addson-Wesley Educ.

Dublin, Peter, jt. auth. see Clodfelter, Richard.

Dublin, Peter, jt. auth. see Perrin, Carl.

Dublin, Selma M., jt. auth. see Dublin, Jack.

Dublin, Thomas. Lowell: The Story of an Industrial City. LC 91-28814. (Official National Park Handbook Ser.: No. 140). (Illus.). 112p. 1993. pap. 8.00 (*0-912627-46-8*, 024-005-01097-1) Natl Park Serv.

— Transforming Women's Work: New England Lives in the Industrial Revolution. (Illus.). 344p. 1995. pap. text 16.95 (*0-8014-8090-6*) Cornell U Pr.

— When the Mines Closed: Stories of Struggles in Hard Times. LC 98-14330. 304p. 1998. pap. 16.95 (*0-8014-8467-7*) Cornell U Pr.

— When the Mines Closed: Stories of Struggles in Hard Times. LC 98-14330. (Illus.). 304p. 1998. text 55.00 (*0-8014-3462-9*) Cornell U Pr.

— Women at Work: The Transformation of Work & Community in Lowell, Massachusetts, 1826-1860. LC 79-10701. 360p. 1981. reprint ed. pap. text 21.00 (*0-231-04167-5*) Col U Pr.

Dublin, Thomas, ed. Becoming American, Becoming Ethnic: College Students Explore Their Roots. LC 96-3554. (Illus.). 224p. (C). 1996. pap. 22.95 (*1-56639-439-2*); lib. bdg. 69.95 (*1-56639-438-4*) Temple U Pr.

— Farm to Factory: Women's Letters, 1830-1860. 2nd ed. LC 92-34787. (Illus.). 208p. (C). 1993. pap. 19.00 (*0-231-08157-X*); text 50.00 (*0-231-08156-1*) Col U Pr.

— Immigrant Voices: New Lives in America: 1773-1986. LC 92-31748. 336p. 1993. text 49.95 (*0-252-01769-2*); pap. text 15.95 (*0-252-06290-6*) U of Ill Pr.

Dublin, Thomas & Marion, Paul. Lowell: The Story of an Industrial City: A Guide to Lowell National Historical Park & Lowell Heritage State Park, Lowell, Massachusetts. (Illus.). 111p. 1998. pap. text 20.00 (*0-7881-4825-7*) DIANE Pub.

Dublin, Thomas, jt. auth. see Sklar, Kathryn K.

Dublin, Wayne, jt. auth. see Parker, James W.

Dublin, William B. & Dublin, Arthur. Atlas of Neuroanatomy with Radiologic Correlation & Pathologic Illustration: Surface & Sectional, with CT Scanning Correlation. LC 79-50199. (Illus.). 252p. (C). 1982. 62.50 (*0-87527-204-5*) Green.

Dubner, Barry H. The Law of International Sea Piracy. (Developments in International Law Ser.: No. 2). 1980. lib. bdg. 70.50 (*90-247-2191-1*) Kluwer Academic.

— The Law of Territorial Waters of Midocean Archipelagos & Archipelagic States. 1977. pap. text 51.00 (*90-247-1893-7*) Kluwer Academic.

Dubner, Friedrich, ed. see Aristophanes.

Dubner, Julia, ed. see Rice, Anne, et al.

Dubner, Ronald B., jt. ed. see Fricton, James R.

***Dubner, Stephen J.** Turbulent Souls: A Catholic Son's Return to His Jewish Family. LC 98-34077. (Illus.). 288p. 1998. 24.00 (*0-688-15180-9*, Wm Morrow) Morrow Avon.

Dubner, Stephen J. Turbulent Souls: A Catholic Son's Return to His Jewish Family, Vol. 1. LC 98-34077. (Illus.). 368p. 1999. pap. 12.50 (*0-380-72930-X*, Avon Bks) Morrow Avon.

Dubnerum, F., tr. see Aristotle.

Dubnick, Mel, et al, eds. Public Policy & Economic Institutions, Vol. 10. LC 90-41571. (Public Policy Ser.). 408p. 1991. 73.25 (*0-89232-376-0*) Jai Pr.

Dubnick, Mel & Gitelson, Alan, eds. Regulatory Policy Analysis. (Orig.). (C). 1982. pap. 15.00 (*0-918592-51-8*) Pol Studies.

Dubnick, Melvin J. American Business & Public Politics. text. write for info. (*0-312-00333-1*) St Martin.

Dubnick, Randa. The Structure of Obscurity: Gertrude Stein, Language, & Cubism. LC 83-3603. (Illus.). 184p. 1984. 24.95 (*0-252-00909-6*) U of Ill Pr.

Dubnov-Erlich, Sophie. The Life & Work of S. M. Dubnov: Diaspora Nationalism & Jewish History. LC 89-46342. (Modern Jewish Experience Ser.). (Illus.). 298p. 1991. 12.95 (*0-253-31836-X*) Ind U Pr.

Dubnov, Simon. History of the Jews, Vol. 1. 18.00 (*0-8453-6410-3*, Cornwall Bks) Assoc Univ Prs.

— History of the Jews, Vol. 2. 18.00 (*0-8453-6659-9*, Cornwall Bks) Assoc Univ Prs.

— History of the Jews: From Cromwell's Commonwealth to the Napoleonic Era, Vol. 4. Spiegel, Moshe, tr. from RUS. 1980. 18.00 (*0-8453-7537-7*, Cornwall Bks) Assoc Univ Prs.

Dubnov, William L. How Shall I Know Thee, O King? The Collected Poems of William L. Dubnov. (Illus.). 96p. 1996. 15.00 (*0-9630976-6-0*) Morgin Pr.

Dubnov, William L., jt. auth. see Grisson, Grant R.

Dubnow, Semen M. Jewish History: An Essay in the Philosophy of History. LC 72-5481. (Select Bibliographies Reprint Ser.). 1977. reprint ed. 18.95 (*0-8369-6903-0*) Ayer.

***Dubnow, Simon & Friedlaender, Israel.** History of the Jews in Russia & Poland. LC 00-33175. 2000. write for info. (*1-886223-11-4*) Avotaynu.

DuBoff, Leonard. The Art Business Encyclopedia. LC 93-71921. (Illus.). 320p. (Orig.). 1994. pap. 18.95 (*1-880559-13-7*) Allworth Pr.

— The Law (in Plain English) for Photographers. LC 95-75286. 208p. 1995. pap. 18.95 (*1-880559-19-6*) Allworth Pr.

— The Law (in Plain English) for Small Businesses. 3rd rev. ed. LC 98-70406. 256p. 1998. pap. 19.95 (*1-880559-95-1*) Allworth Pr.

Duboff, Leonard. The Performing Arts Business Encyclopedia: For Individuals & Organizations As Well As the Attorneys & Business Advisors Who Assist Them. LC 95-83003. 256p. 1996. pap. 19.95 (*1-880559-42-0*) Allworth Pr.

DuBoff, Leonard D. Art Law in a Nutshell. 2nd ed. (Nutshell Ser.). 350p. (C). 1992. pap. 21.00 (*0-314-01335-0*) West Pub.

— Book Publishers' Legal Guide. 2nd ed. LC 91-39975. xv, 384p. 1992. reprint ed. 65.00 (*0-8377-0559-2*, Rothman) W S Hein.

— Business Forms & Contracts in Plain English for Craftspeople. 2nd ed. 128p. 1993. reprint ed. pap. 14.95 (*0-934026-83-1*) Interweave.

— The Law (in Plain English) for Art & Craft Galleries. Ligon, Linda C., ed. 156p. 1993. pap. 14.95 (*0-934026-87-4*) Interweave.

— The Law (In Plain English) for Crafts. 5th ed. LC 98-72766. 224p. 1999. pap. 18.95 (*1-58115-016-4*) Allworth Pr.

— The Law in Plain English for Craftspeople. 3rd ed. 139p. 1993. reprint ed. pap. 12.95 (*0-934026-82-3*) Interweave.

— The Law (In Plain English) for Galleries. 2nd ed. 208p. 1999. pap. text 18.95 (*1-58115-026-1*) Allworth Pr.

— The Law (in Plain English) for Health Care Professionals. LC 92-39745. 206p. 1993. 39.95 (*0-471-58001-5*); pap. 14.95 (*0-471-58002-3*) Wiley.

— The Law (in Plain English) for Small Businesses. 2nd ed. LC 91-10582. 240p. 1991. 49.95 (*0-471-53617-2*); pap. 14.95 (*0-471-53616-4*) Wiley.

— The Law (in Plain English) for Writers. 2nd ed. LC 91-24391. 272p. (Orig.). 1992. pap. 14.95 (*0-471-53615-6*) Wiley.

— The Photographers Business & Legal Handbook. 116p. 1989. pap. 18.95 (*0-929667-02-6*, 10255) Images NY.

DuBoff, Leonard D., ed. Art Law: Domestic & International. LC 75-7668. (Illus.). x, 627p. 1975. reprint ed. 37.50 (*0-8377-0503-7*, Rothman) W S Hein.

DuBoff, Leonard D., et al. The Deskbook of Art Law, 2 vols. 2nd ed. 1993. ring bd. 385.00 (*0-379-20157-7*) Oceana.

DuBoff, Richard B. Electric Power in American Manufacturing, Eighteen Eighty-Nine to Nineteen Fifty-Eight. Bruchey, Stuart, ed. LC 78-22675. (Energy in the American Economy Ser.). (Illus.). 1979. lib. bdg. 25.95 (*0-405-11978-X*) Ayer.

***Duboff, Robert S. & Spaeth, Jim.** Market Research Matters: Tools & Techniques for Aligning Your Business. 224p. 2000. text 34.95 (*0-471-36005-8*) Wiley.

***Dubofsky, Melvyn.** Hard Work: The Making of Labor History. LC 99-6862. (Working Class in American History Ser.). 2000. pap. 17.95 (*0-252-06868-8*) U of Ill Pr.

Dubofsky, Melvyn. Industrialism & the American Worker, 1865-1920. 3rd rev. ed. Eisenstadt, A. S. & Franklin, John H., eds. (American History Ser.). 167p. (C). 1996. pap. text 11.95 (*0-88295-925-5*) Harlan Davidson.

— Papers of the National War Labor Board, 1918-1919. LC 86-893393. (Research Collections on Labor Studies). 22 p. 1984. write for info. (*0-89093-711-7*) U Pubns Amer.

— The State & Labor in Modern America. LC 93-21404. xx, 322p. 1994. 45.00 (*0-8078-2125-X*); pap. 19.95 (*0-8078-4436-5*) U of NC Pr.

***Dubofsky, Melvyn.** We Shall Be All: A History of the Industrial Workers of the World. abr. ed. McCartin, Joseph A., ed. (The Working Class in American History Ser.). 296p. 2000. 49.95 (*0-252-02595-4*) U of Ill Pr.

Dubofsky, Melvyn. When Workers Organize: New York City in the Progressive Era. LC 68-19669. 240p. 1968. 30.00 (*0-87023-042-5*) U of Mass Pr.

Dubofsky, Melvyn, ed. Technological Change & Workers' Movements. LC 85-2173. (Explorations in the World-Economy Ser.: No. 4). 272p. reprint ed. pap. 84.40 (*0-8357-8458-4*, 203472300091) Bks Demand.

Dubofsky, Melvyn & Burwood, Stephen, eds. The American Economy During the Great Depression: Selected Articles. LC 89-25952. (Outstanding Articles on the Great Depression & the New Deal Ser.). 320p. 1990. reprint ed. text 20.00 (*0-8240-0895-2*) Garland.

— Labor: (Selected Articles on Workers & Unions During the Great Depression) LC 89-71389. (Great Depression & the New Deal Ser.: Vol. 2). 416p. 1990. text 20.00 (*0-8240-0894-4*) Garland.

— The Law & the New Deal: Selected Articles on Legal Issues Surrounding the Depression & Roosevelt's Policies. (Articles on the Great Depression Ser.). 344p. 1990. reprint ed. text 20.00 (*0-8240-0899-5*) Garland.

Dubofsky, Melvyn & Dulles, Foster R. Labor in America: A History. 6th ed. LC 99-17713. (Illus.). 475p. (C). 1999. pap. text 27.95 (*0-88295-979-4*) Harlan Davidson.

***Dubofsky, Melvyn & McCartin, Joseph Anthony.** We Shall Be All: A History of the Industrial Workers of the World. abr. ed. LC 00-8215. 296p. 2000. 17.95 (*0-252-06905-6*) U of Ill Pr.

Dubofsky, Melvyn & Theoharis, Athan G. Imperial Democracy: The United States Since 1945. 2nd ed. (Illus.). 288p. (C). 1988. pap. text 37.60 (*0-13-451766-0*) P-H.

Dubofsky, Melvyn & Van Tine, Warren R. John L. Lewis: A Biography. abr. ed. LC 85-20116. (Illus.). 408p. 1986. pap. text 16.95 (*0-252-01287-9*) U of Ill Pr.

Dubofsky, Melvyn & Van Tine, Warren R., eds. Labor Leaders in America. LC 86-4368. (Working Class in American History Ser.). 416p. 1987. text 39.95 (*0-252-01327-1*); pap. text 17.95 (*0-252-01343-3*) U of Ill Pr.

Dubofsky, Melvyn, et al. American Bureau of Industrial Research: Manuscript Collections on the Early American Labor Movement, 1862-1908. LC 86-890788. (Research Collections in Labor Studies). 12p. 1985. write for info. (*0-89093-899-7*) U Pubns Amer.

— Department of Justice Investigative Files. LC 90-12989. (Research Collections in American Radicalism). 43p. 1989. write for info. (*1-55655-056-1*) U Pubns Amer.

Dubofsky, Melvyn, jt. auth. see Schipper, Martin P.

Duboia, Page. Sappho Is Burning. 1997. pap. text 14.95 (*0-226-16756-9*) U Ch Pr.

Duboin, Alain-Marie. Life & Message of Sr. Mary of The Holy Trinity: Poor Clare of Jerusalem (1901-1942) Poor Clares of Rockford & Brown, Raphael, eds. Chomeau, Mary D., tr. from FRE. LC 87-50747. (Illus.). 254p. 1987. pap. 10.00 (*0-89555-318-X*) TAN Bks Pubs.

Dubois. Education JIT Suny Oneonta. 1996. pap. text. write for info. (*0-205-26743-2*) Allyn.

***DuBois.** Philadelphia Negro. 1999. pap. text 16.95 (*0-8122-1690-3*) U of Pa Pr.

Dubois. Sociology. 222p. (C). 1998. pap. text 18.49 (*0-536-01415-9*) Pearson Custom.

Dubois, ed. see Quinault.

Dubois, A. J. Hindu Manners, Customs & Ceremonies. 741p. 1985. 24.95 (*0-318-36960-5*) Asia Bk Corp.

Dubois, Abbe J. Letters on the State of Christianity in India: To Which Is Added a Vindication of the Hindus Male & Female. (C). 1995. reprint ed. 17.50 (*81-206-0624-8*, Pub. by Asian Educ Servs) S Asia.

DuBois, Abee J. A Description of the Character, Manners, & Customs of the People of India & of Their Institutions, Religious & Civil. (C). 1989. reprint ed. 25.00 (*81-206-0454-7*, Pub. by Asian Educ Servs) S Asia.

DuBois, Alan. Arkansas: Year of the American Craft 1993. 64p. 1993. pap. 15.00 (*1-884240-03-8*) Arkansas Art Ctr.

— Fifth National Objects Invitational, 1995. 64p. 1995. pap. 15.00 (*1-884240-09-7*) Arkansas Art Ctr.

— Fourth National Objects Invitational, 1993. 50p. 1993. pap. 16.00 (*1-884240-07-0*) Arkansas Art Ctr.

— National Objects Invitational, 1993. 50p. 1993. pap. 16.00 (*1-884240-02-X*) Arkansas Art Ctr.

— Working in Other Dimensions: Objects & Drawings II. 64p. 1994. pap. 20.00 (*1-884240-04-6*) Arkansas Art Ctr.

DuBois, Alan, jt. auth. see Loar, Steve.

Dubois, Alberic. Conversations in Umbria. 277p. 1980. 5.95 (*0-8199-0784-7*, Frncscn Herld) Franciscan Pr.

Dubois, Andre & Castell, Donald, eds. Esophageal & Gastric Emptying. LC 84-1895. 168p. 1984. 10?.00 (*0-8493-6367-5*, OP150, CRC Reprint) Franklin.

Dubois, Andre, et al. Radiation & the Gastrointestinal Tract. LC 94-27144. 304p. 1994. lib. bdg. 175.00 (*0-8493-7667-X*, 7667) CRC Pr.

DuBois, Andre, jt. auth. see Lewis, James.

Dubois, Anna. Organizing Industrial Activities Across Firm Boundaries. LC 97-21645. 176p. (C). 1998. 75.00 (*0-415-14707-7*) Routledge.

DuBois, Anson & DuBois, James G. DuBois: Documents & Genealogical Chart of the Family of Benjamin DuBois. 104p. 1997. reprint ed. pap. 17.00 (*0-8328-8362-X*); reprint ed. lib. bdg. 27.00 (*0-8328-8361-1*) Higginson Bk Co.

***DuBois, Bernard, et al, eds.** European Advances in Consumer Research Vol. 4: Proceedings of the 1999 Conference. 2000. 49.00 (*0-915552-43-4*) Assn Consumer Res.

DuBois, Bessie W. History of Juno Beach & Juno, Florida. (Illus.). 21p. 1978. pap. 2.95 (*0-912451-39-4*) Florida Classics.

— History of Jupiter Lighthouse. (Illus.). 29p. 1960. pap. 2.95 (*0-912451-40-8*) Florida Classics.

— History of the Loxahatchee River. (Illus.). 29p. 1980. pap. 2.95 (*0-912451-41-6*) Florida Classics.

— Shipwrecks in the Vicinity of Jupiter Inlet. (Illus.). 31p. 1981. pap. 3.50 (*0-912451-42-4*) Florida Classics.

Dubois, Betty L. & Crouch, Isabel. Regulatory Language Behavior. (Edward Sapir Monographs in Language, Culture & Cognition: No. 13). xiv, 96p. (Orig.). 1985. pap. 20.00 (*0-933104-19-7*) Jupiter Pr.

DuBois, Bonna L. Long Ago Love. LC 85-10451. 192p. 1985. 14.95 (*0-8027-0861-7*) Walker & Co.

Dubois, Brenda & Miley, Karla K. Social Work: An Empowering Profession. 3rd ed. LC 98-5165. 535p. 1998. pap. text 54.00 (*0-205-27705-5*) Allyn.

DuBois, Brendan. Black Tide: A Lewis Cole Mystery. 1996. mass mkt. 5.99 (*0-671-89999-6*) PB.

— Black Tide: A Lewis Cole Mystery. LC 94-28920. 1995. 21.50 (*1-883402-58-1*) S&S Trade.

— Dead Sand. 1996. mass mkt. 5.99 (*0-671-54521-3*) PB.

DuBois, Brendan. Dead Sand: A Lewis Cole Mystery. 304p. 1994. 21.00 (*1-883402-45-X*) S&S Trade.

DuBois, Brendan. Resurrection Day. LC 98-54888. 400p. (YA). 1999. 23.95 (*0-399-14498-6*, G P Putnam) Peng Put Young Read.

— Shattered Shell. LC 98-47005. 368p. 1999. text 24.95 (*0-312-19332-7*) St Martin.

Dubois-Charlier, F. Dictionnaire de l'Anglais Contemporain. (ENG & FRE.). 863p. 1980. 22.50 (*0-8288-0776-0*, M14141) Fr & Eur.

Dubois, Christine, ed. see Castillo, Obdulia R.

DuBois, Constance G. The Religion of the Luiseno Indians of Southern California. fac. ed. (University of California Publications in American Archaeology & Ethnology: Vol. 8: 3). 192p. (C). 1908. reprint ed. pap. text 20.63 (*1-55567-182-9*) Coyote Press.

DuBois, Cora. The 1870 Ghost Dance. fac. ed. Lowie, Robert H. et al, eds. (University of California Publications: No. 3:1). 158p. (C). 1939. reprint ed. pap. 16.88 (*1-55567-076-8*) Coyote Press.

— Wintu Ethnography. fac. ed. (University of California Publications in American Archaeology & Ethnology: Vol. 36: 1). (Illus.). 154p. (C). 1935. reprint ed. pap. text 16.88 (*1-55567-304-X*) Coyote Press.

Dubois, Cora & Demetracopoulou, Dorothy. Winter Myths. fac. ed. (University of California Publications in American Archaeology & Ethnology: Vol. 28: 5). 127p. (C). 1931. reprint ed. pap. text 14.38 (*1-55567-278-7*) Coyote Press.

Dubois, D. & Prade, H. Possibility Theory: An Approach to Computerized Processing of Uncertainty. LC 87-32179. (Illus.). 280p. (C). 1988. text 75.00 (*0-306-42520-3*, Kluwer Plenum) Kluwer Academic.

Dubois, D. W. & Recio, T., eds. Ordered Fields & Real Algebraic Geometry. LC 82-3951. (Contemporary Mathematics Ser.: Vol. 8). 360p. 1982. pap. 33.00 (*0-8218-5007-5*, CONM/8) Am Math.

Dubois, D. W., ed. see American Mathematical Society Special Session Staf.

Dubois-Dalco, M., et al. Assembly of Enveloped RNA Viruses. Kingsbury, D. W., ed. (Illus.). 250p. 1985. 111.00 (*0-387-81802-2*) Spr-Verlag.

Dubois, Daniel M., ed. Computing Anticipatory Systems: CASYS First International Conference. LC 98-72270. (Conference Proceedings Ser.: Vol. 437). (Illus.). 672p. 1998. 190.00 (*1-56396-827-4*) Spr-Verlag.

***Dubois, Daniel M., ed.** Computing Anticipatory Systems: CASYS '99 - Third International Conference. LC 00-101913. (AIP Conference Proceedings: Vol. 517). (Illus.). xi, 678p. 2000. 190.00 (*1-56396-933-5*, Pub. by Am Inst Physics) Spr-Verlag.

Dubois, Daniel M., ed. Computing Anticipatory Systems: CASYS'98 - 2nd International Conference. LC 99-60814. (AIP Conference Proceedings Ser.). (Illus.). 578p. 1999. 185.00 (*1-56396-863-0*) Am Inst Physics.

Dubois, David D. Competency-Based Performance Improvement: A Strategy for Organizational Change. 308p. 1993. 39.95 (*0-87425-223-7*) HRD Press.

— Competency-Based Performance Improvement: Organizational Assessment Package. 64p. 1995. 69.95 (*0-87425-269-5*) HRD Press.

DuBois, Dean C., Sr. Is It True What They Say about Dixie? An Unbiased, Objective Look at the South from a Southerner's Viewpoint. LC 97-90294. (Illus.), x, 118p. 1997. pap. 11.95 (*0-9657409-0-0*) Turkey Creek.

***Dubois, Diana.** In Her Sister's Shadow: An Intimate Biography of Lee Radziwill. (Illus.). 414p. 2000. reprint ed. 24.00 (*0-7881-9394-5*) DIANE Pub.

***Dubois, Didier, et al, eds.** Fuzzy Sets, Logics & Reasoning about Knowledge. LC 99-46159. (Applied Logic Ser.). 436p. 1999. text 173.00 (*0-7923-5977-1*) Kluwer Academic.

DuBois, Dina. In Her Sister's Shadow. 1997. mass mkt. 6.99 (*0-312-96237-1*) St Martin.

DuBois, Dorothy. Travelers Hotline Directory. 288p. (Orig.). 1991. pap. 15.95 (*1-880581-88-4*) Visions Res.

DuBois, Duane J. Benzene--Index of New Information & Medical Research Bible. rev. ed. 149p. 1998. 47.50 (*0-7883-1964-7*); pap. 44.50 (*0-7883-1965-5*) ABBE Pubs Assn.

Dubois-Dumee, Jean P. & Board of St. Paul Editorial Staff. Becoming Prayer. 72p. (C). 1996. pap. 39.95 (*0-85439-311-0*, Pub. by St Paul Pubns) St Mut.

Dubois, Ellen & Kearns, Karen. Votes for Women: A 75th Anniversary Album. (Illus.). 48p. 1995. pap. 9.50 (*0-87328-157-8*, Pub. by Huntington Lib) A Schwartz & Co.

DuBois, Ellen C. Feminism & Suffrage: The Emergence of an Independent Women's Movement in America 1848-1869. 224p. 1980. pap. text 14.95 (*0-8014-9182-7*) Cornell U Pr.

Dubois, Ellen C. Harriot Stanton Blatch & the Winning of Woman Suffrage. LC 97-7293. (Illus.). 384p. 1997. 37.50 (*0-300-06562-0*) Yale U Pr.

— Woman Suffrage & Women's Rights. LC 98-19698. (Illus.). 304p. 1998. text 55.00 (*0-8147-1900-7*); pap. text 18.50 (*0-8147-1901-5*) NYU Pr.

DuBois, Ellen C., ed. The Elizabeth Cady Stanton - Susan B. Anthony Reader: Correspondence, Writing, Speeches. rev. ed. 288p. 1992. reprint ed. text 45.00 (*1-55553-149-0*); reprint ed. pap. text 16.95 (*1-55553-143-1*) NE U Pr.

DuBois, Ellen C. & Ruiz, Vicki L., eds. Unequal Sisters: A Multicultural Reader in U. S. Women's History. 2nd ed. LC 94-2430. 576p. (C). (gr. 13 up). 1994. 75.00 (*0-415-90891-4*) Routledge.

— Unequal Sisters: A Multicultural Reader in U. S. Women's History. 2nd ed. LC 94-2430. 576p. (C). (gr. 13). 1994. pap. 29.99 (*0-415-90892-2*, Pub. by Tavistock) Routledge.

DuBois, Ellen C., et al. Feminist Scholarship: Kindling in the Groves of Academe. LC 84-2589. 240p. 1987. pap. text 14.95 (*0-252-01464-2*) U of Ill Pr.

Dubois, Ellen C., jt. auth. see Rubiz, Vicki.

DuBois, Ellen C., jt. ed. see Ruiz, Vicki L.

***Dubois, Ellen Carol.** Feminism & Suffrage: The Emergence of An Independent Women's Movement in America, 1848-1869. 1999. pap. text 15.95 (*0-8014-8641-6*) Cornell U Pr.

— Harriet Stanton Blatch & the Winning of Woman Suffrage. (Illus.). 384p. 1999. pap. 19.00 (*0-300-08068-9*) Yale U Pr.

Dubois, Emile. Le Feud de la Riviere-Du-Chene: Etude Historique sur le Mouvement Insurr. 1998. write for info. (*2-89415-234-5*) Edits Meridien.

D

DuBois, Eugene E. The City of Frederick Douglass: Rochester's African-American People & Places. (Illus.). 50p. (Orig.). 1995. pap. 6.95 (*0-9641706-0-4*) Landmark Soc.

Dubois, F. & Werny, P. Dictionnaire Francais-Allemand des Locutions. (FRE & GER.). 1976. 39.95 (*0-8288-5652-4*, M6172) Fr & Eur.

Dubois, Felix. Timbuctoo the Mysterious. White, Diana, tr. LC 70-94475. (Illus.). 377p. 1970. reprint ed. lib. bdg. 35.00 (*0-8371-2372-0*, DTI&, Greenwood Pr) Greenwood.

***Dubois, Ia & Hanson, Katherine, eds.** Echo: Scandinavian Stories about Girls. LC 99-55211. 312p. 2000. pap. 18.95 (*1-879679-14-0*) Women Translation.

Dubois, J. Dictionary Etymology, Historique du Francais. (FRE.). 1998. 59.95 (*0-320-00255-1*) Fr & Eur.

— Larousse Dictionnaire de Linguistique et des Sciences du Langage. (FRE.). 672p. 1994. 85.00 (*0-7859-7647-7*, 2033403343) Fr & Eur.

— Non-Linear Dynamics in Geophysics. LC 97-41824. 286p. 1998. 85.00 (*0-471-97853-1*) Wiley.

Dubois, J. A. & Beauchamp, Henry K. Hindu Manners, Customs & Ceremonies. 800p. 1986. reprint ed. 17.50 (*0-8364-1760-7*, Pub. by Manohar) S Asia.

Dubois, J. B., et al, eds. Immunopharmacologic Effects of Radiation Therapy. fac. ed. LC 80-5931. (Monograph Series of the European Organization for Research on Treatment of Cancer: No. 8). (Illus.). 566p. pap. 175.50 (*0-7837-7203-3*, 204709600005) Bks Demand.

Dubois, J. E. & Gershon, N. D., eds. Industrial Information & Design Issues. LC 96-30567. (Data & Knowledge in a Changing World Ser.). 312p. 1996. 117.50 (*3-540-61457-5*) Spr-Verlag.

— The Information Revolution: Impact on Science & Technology. LC 96-7195. (Data & Knowledge in a Changing World Ser.). (Illus.). xix, 276p. 1996. 115.00 (*3-540-60855-9*) Spr-Verlag.

DuBois, J. E. & Gershon, N. D., eds. Modeling Complex Data for Creating Information. LC 96-18690. (Data & Knowledge in a Changing World Ser.). (Illus.). 271p. 1996. 117.00 (*3-540-61069-3*) Spr-Verlag.

DuBois, J. Harry & Pribble, Wayne I. Plastics Mold Design Engineering Handbook. 4th ed. (Illus.). 704p. 1987. text 89.95 (*0-442-21897-4*) Chapman & Hall.

Dubois, J. O. & Gvishiani, A. D. Dynamic Systems & Dynamic Classification Problems in Geophysical Applications. LC 98-3585. (Data & Knowledge in a Changing World Ser.). (Illus.). 250p. 1998. 109.00 (*3-540-64238-2*) Spr-Verlag.

DuBois Jacobs, Paul, jt. auth. see Seeger, Pete.

Dubois, Jacque. Aspects de la Vie Monastique en France au Moyen Age. (Collected Studies: No. CS 395). 593p. 1993. 119.95 (*0-86078-360-X*, Pub. by Variorum) Ashgate Pub Co.

Dubois, Jacques. Dictionnaire du Francais Langue Etrangere, Niveau. (FRE.). 910p. 1988. 55.00 (*0-7859-4786-8*) Fr & Eur.

Dubois, Jacques, et al. A General Rhetoric. Burrell, Paul B. & Slotkin, Edgar M., trs. from FRE. LC 80-24495. (Illus.). 288p. 1981. text 42.00 (*0-8018-2326-9*) Johns Hopkins.

Dubois, Jacques, ed. see Zola, Emile.

Dubois, Jacques F., jt. auth. see Oates, Michael D.

Dubois, Jacques F., tr. see Sandstrom, Roy E., ed.

DuBois, James G., jt. auth. see DuBois, Anson.

DuBois, James M. Judgment & Sachverhalt: An Introduction to Adolf Reinach's Phenomenological Realism. LC 95-17979. (Phaenomenologica Ser.: Vol. 132). 176p. (C). 1995. lib. bdg. 99.50 (*0-7923-3519-8*, Pub. by Kluwer Academic) Kluwer Academic.

Dubois, James M., compiled by. The Nature & Tasks of a Personalist Psychology. LC 95-36961. 204p. (Orig.). (C). 1995. pap. text 28.50 (*0-7618-0101-4*); lib. bdg. 52.50 (*0-7618-0100-6*) U Pr of Amer.

DuBois, James M., ed. Moral Issues in Psychology: Personalist Contributions to Selected Problems. LC 96-36306. 182p. 1996. pap. text 28.50 (*0-7618-0543-5*); lib. bdg. 46.00 (*0-7618-0542-7*) U Pr of Amer.

Dubois, Jean. Diccionario de Linguistica: Dictionary of Linguistics. (SPA.). 1979. pap. 62.50 (*0-8288-4758-4*, S-50086) Fr & Eur.

— Dictionnaire du Francais Langue Etrangere, Niveau. 2nd ed. (FRE.). 1090p. 1986. lib. bdg. 55.00 (*0-7859-3943-1*) Fr & Eur.

— Larousse Dictionnaire du Francais Classique. (FRE.). 608p. 1971. 45.00 (*0-7859-7644-2*, 2033402150) Fr & Eur.

— Petit Dictionnaire Larousse de la Langue Francaise. (FRE.). 1095p. 1993. pap. 32.95 (*0-7859-7679-5*, 2037102216) Fr & Eur.

— The Same Sweet Yellow. 48p. (Orig.). 1994. pap. 12.50 (*0-9622932-2-9*) San Miguel Pr.

Dubois, Jean, ed. Lexis: Dictionnaire de la Langue Francaise. (FRE.). 2109p. 1992. 95.00 (*0-7859-4830-9*) Fr & Eur.

Dubois, Jean & Dubois, Lee. Silent Stones, Empty Passageways: Poetry & Photography from the Anasazi Homeland. (Illus.). 59p. (Orig.). 1992. pap. 7.95 (*0-9622932-8-8*) San Miguel Pr.

Dubois, Jean & Lagane, Rene. Dictionnaire du Francais Classique. (FRE.). 511p. 1992. pap. 85.00 (*0-8288-6451-9*, F-133960) Fr & Eur.

Dubois, Jean, et al. Dictionary of Linguistics: Diccionario de Linguistica. 3rd ed. (ENG & SPA.). 712p. 1986. 95.00 (*0-7859-4951-8*) Fr & Eur.

— Larousse: Dictionnaire de Francais. (FRE.). 1059p. 1986. 45.00 (*0-8288-1934-3*, F82260) Fr & Eur.

Dubois, Jean-Luc. Think Before Measuring: Methodological Innovations for the Collection & Analysis of Statistical Data. (Social Dimensions of Adjustment in Sub-Saharan Africa Working Paper Ser.: No. 7). 59p. 1992. pap. 22.00 (*0-8213-1703-2*, 11703) World Bank.

***DuBois, Jean M., et al, eds.** Quasicrystals, Vol. 553. LC 99-13855. (Symposium Proceedings Ser.). 524p. 1999. 88.00 (*1-55899-459-9*) Materials Res.

DuBois, Jean M. & Mitterand, Henri. Dictionnaire de Linguistique et des Sciences du Langage. rev. ed. (FRE.). 672p. 1994. write for info. (*0-7859-7680-9*, 2037102283) Fr & Eur.

Dubois, Jean-Marie & Janot, Christian. Useful Quasicrystals. 300p. 1998. 48.00 (*981-02-3254-3*) World Scientific Pub.

Dubois, Jennifer & Gutmann, Steve. Now Hiring! Outdoor Jobs: The Insider's Guide to Gaining Seasonal & Year-Round Employment in America's National Parks & Forests. Veith, Elliot, ed. (Illus.). 297p. (C). 1993. pap. 17.95 (*1-881199-50-9*) Perptual Pr.

Dubois, Jennifer, et al. Now Hiring! Jobs in Asia: The Insider's Guide to Gaining Seasonal & Year-round Employment Throughout Asia. LC 93-84884. (Illus.). 280p. (Orig.). (C). 1993. pap. 17.95 (*1-881199-23-1*) Perptual Pr.

Dubois, Jennifer, jt. auth. see Connley, Mark.

Dubois, John. April & Ty: The Story of Two Suburban Dogs. LC 97-91140. 1998. pap. 8.95 (*0-533-12575-8*) Vantage.

DuBois, John. Campaigns in the West: American Autobiography. 120p. 1995. lib. bdg. 69.00 (*0-7812-8506-2*) Rprt Serv.

— Sco Email Configuration Guide. 1994. pap. text 24.00 (*0-685-70621-4*) P-H.

Dubois, L. H., et al, eds. Chemical Perspectives of Microelectronic Materials Vol. 204: Materials Research Society Symposium Proceedings. 584p. 1991. text 17.50 (*1-55899-096-8*) Materials Res.

Dubois, Lee. Chaco Canyon: Sunrise to Sunset. 76p. (Orig.). 1993. pap. 9.95 (*0-9622932-0-2*) San Miguel Pr.

Dubois, Lee, jt. auth. see Dubois, Jean.

DuBois, Lindy. Basic Procedures. LC 98-12042. (The Basic Bookshelf for Eyecare Professionals). (Illus.). 128p. 1998. pap. text 30.00 (*1-55642-347-0*, 63470) SLACK Inc.

Dubois, Ludovic, jt. auth. see Kovach, Warren.

Dubois, M. M. Larousse Saturne French-English - English-French Dictionary. 1616p. 1988. 49.95 (*0-685-19997-5*) Fr & Eur.

Dubois, Marc. Philippe Samyn: Architecture & Engineering, 1900-2000. LC 99-26856. 1999. write for info. (*0-8176-6067-4*) Birkhauser.

***Dubois, Marc.** Philippe Samyn: Architecture & Engineering 1900-2000. LC 99-26856. (Illus.). 128p. 1999. pap. 49.95 (*3-7643-6067-4*) Birkhauser.

Dubois, Marguerite-Mari. Larousse's French-English, English-French Dictionary. (ENG & FRE.). 1971. 11.09 (*0-606-03767-5*, Pub. by Turtleback) Demco.

Dubois, Marguerite-Marie. Dictionnaire de Locutions, Francais-Anglais. (ENG & FRE.). 392p. 1973. 59.95 (*0-685-57711-2*, M-6173) Fr & Eur.

— Saturn Larousse French-English, English-French Dictionary: Dictionnaire Larousse Saturne Francais-Anglais-Francais. (ENG & FRE.). 1632p. 1981. 59.95 (*0-8288-0060-X*, M6174) Fr & Eur.

Dubois, Maurice. Home Buyer's Confidential: The Insider's Guide to Buying Your Dream House, Condo, or Co-op. 288p. 1991. pap. 16.95 (*0-07-157003-9*) McGraw.

— Home Buyer's Confidential: The Insider's Guide to Buying Your Dream House, Condo, or Co-op. (Illus.). 272p. 1991. pap. 16.95 (*0-8306-3446-0*, 3446, Liberty Hall Pr) TAB Bks.

Dubois, Michael. Readings in Fuzzy Sets for Intelligent Systems. LC 93-35702. 916p. (Orig.). (C). 1993. pap. text 58.95 (*1-55860-257-7*) Morgan Kaufmann.

Dubois, Michel. Dictionnaire de Sigles Nationaux et Internationaux.Tr. of Dictionary of National & International Siglas. (FRE.). 479p. 1977. pap. 125.00 (*0-8288-5384-3*, M6609) Fr & Eur.

Dubois, Michel & Thakkar, Shreekant S., eds. Cache & Interconnect Architectures in Multiprocessors. (C). 1990. text 134.00 (*0-7923-9074-1*) Kluwer Academic.

— Scalable Shared Memory Multiprocessors. 352p. 1991. text 144.00 (*0-7923-9219-1*) Kluwer Academic.

Dubois, Michelle, jt. auth. see Nesbett, Peter T.

Dubois, Muriel L. Abenaki Captive. LC 92-23994. (J). (gr. 4-7). 1994. lib. bdg. 21.27 (*0-87614-753-8*, Carolrhoda) Lerner Pub.

***Dubois, Muriel L.** Alaska Facts & Symbols. LC 99-48481. (States & Their Symbols Ser.). (Illus.). 24p. (J). (ps-3). 2000. lib. bdg. 15.93 (*0-7368-0522-2*, Hilltop Bks) Capstone Pr.

— Argentina. LC 00-9788. (Countries of the World Ser.). (Illus.). 2000. write for info. (*0-7368-0811-6*, Bridgestone Bks) Capstone Pr.

— Ethiopia. LC 00-9668. (Countries of the World Ser.). (YA). 2001. write for info. (*0-7368-0813-2*, Bridgestone Bks) Capstone Pr.

— I Like Animals: What Can I Be? LC 00-21617. (What Can I Be? Ser.). (Illus.). 24p. (J). (ps-3). 2000. lib. bdg. 15.93 (*0-7368-0630-X*, Bridgestone Bks) Capstone Pr.

— I Like Computers: What Can I Be? LC 00-21354. (What Can I Be? Ser.). (Illus.). 24p. (J). (ps-3). 2000. lib. bdg. 15.93 (*0-7368-0631-8*, Bridgestone Bks) Capstone Pr.

— I Like Music: What Can I Be? LC 00-21250. (What Can I Be? Ser.). (Illus.). 24p. (J). (ps-3). 2000. lib. bdg. 15.93 (*0-7368-0632-6*, Bridgestone Bks) Capstone Pr.

— I Like Sports: What Can I Be? LC 00-21375. (What Can I Be? Ser.). (Illus.). 24p. (J). (ps-3). 2000. lib. bdg. 15.93 (*0-7368-0633-4*, Bridgestone Bks) Capstone Pr.

— Maryland: Facts & Symbols. LC 99-53463. (States & Their Symbols Ser.). (Illus.). 24p. (J). (ps-3). 2000. lib. bdg. 15.93 (*0-7368-0523-0*, Hilltop Bks) Capstone Pr.

— New Hampshire Facts & Symbols. LC 99-53461. (States & Their Symbols Ser.). (Illus.). 24p. (J). (ps-3). 2000. lib. bdg. 15.93 (*0-7368-0524-9*, Hilltop Bks) Capstone Pr.

— Wyoming Facts & Symbols. LC 99-53462. (States & Their Symbols Ser.). (Illus.). 24p. (J). (ps-3). 2000. lib. bdg. 15.93 (*0-7368-0529-X*, Hilltop Bks) Capstone Pr.

DuBois, Nelson F., jt. auth. see Kiewra, Kenneth H.

DuBois, Page. Centaurs & Amazons: Women & the Pre-History of the Great Chain of Being. (Women & Culture Ser.). (Illus.). 176p. 1991. pap. text 16.95 (*0-472-08153-5*, 08153) U of Mich Pr.

— Sappho Is Burning. LC 95-8407. 218p. 1995. 24.95 (*0-226-16755-0*) U Ch Pr.

— Sowing the Body: Psychoanalysis & Ancient Representations of Women. (Women in Culture & Society Ser.). (Illus.). xvi, 248p. 1996. 35.95 (*0-226-16757-7*) U Ch Pr.

— Sowing the Body: Psychoanalysis & Ancient Representations of Women. (Women in Culture & Society Ser.). (Illus.). 244p. 1999. pap. text 16.95 (*0-226-16758-5*) U Ch Pr.

DuBois, Paul. The Hospice Way of Death. LC 79-12326. 223p. 1980. 35.95 (*0-87705-415-0*, Kluwer Acad Hman Sci) Kluwer Academic.

***DuBois, Paul.** My SQL. 756p. 1999. pap. text 49.99 (*0-7357-0921-1*) New Riders Pub.

DuBois, Paul. Software Portability with Imake. Loukides, Mike, ed. (Computer Science). (Illus.). 390p. (Orig.). 1993. pap. 29.95 (*1-56592-055-4*) Thomson Learn.

Dubois, Paul. Software Portability with Imake. 2nd ed. Estabrook, Gigi, ed. LC 96-223955. (Illus.). 410p. 1996. pap. 32.95 (*1-56592-226-3*) Thomson Learn.

DuBois, Paul. Using CSH & TCSH. 242p. (Orig.). 1995. reprint ed. pap. 29.95 (*1-56592-132-1*) Thomson Learn.

DuBois, Paul M. & Hutson, Jonathan J. Bridging the Racial Divide: A Report on Interracial Dialogue in America. unabridged ed. LC 98-113990. 74p. 1997. pap. 10.00 (*0-9661626-0-9*) Ctr Liv Demo.

Dubois, Philip, ed. Judicial Reform. (Orig.). (C). 1982. pap. 15.00 (*0-918592-56-9*) Pol Studies.

Dubois, Philip L. & Feeney, Floyd. Lawmaking by Initiative: Issues, Options & Comparisons. LC 97-27078. (Representation Ser.: Vol. 4). 280p. 1998. text 30.00 (*0-87586-120-2*, 861202) Agathon.

Dubois, Philippe. Der Fotografische Akt: Geschichte und Theorie, Bd. 1. (GER., Illus.). 200p. 1997. pap. text 25.00 (*90-5705-057-9*, Verlag Kunst) Gordon & Breach.

***Dubois, Pierre.** Great Encyclopedia of Faeries. LC 99-31125. (Illus.). 184p. 2000. 24.50 (*0-684-86957-8*) S&S Trade.

DuBois, Random. Non-Sustainable Land Use Practices in Upland Areas & Their Relation to Coastal Livelihood Patterns: A Case Study from the Philippines. LC 90-11221. (Geography Ser.). (Illus.). 145p. 1991. pap. 14.50 (*0-685-39264-3*) U Ch Pr.

— Soil Erosion in a Coastal River Basin: A Case Study from the Philippines. LC 90-11221. (Research Papers: Vol. 232). (Illus.). 145p. 1991. pap. text 14.50 (*0-89065-139-6*) U Ch Pr.

DuBois, Robert A. Insurance Fraud & Motor Vehicle Collisions. 128p. (C). 1993. pap. text 34.95 (*1-884566-11-1*) Inst Police Tech.

Dubois, Shirley G. Gamal Abdel Nasser: Son of the Nile. (Illus.). 250p. 1972. 30.00 (*0-89388-048-5*) Okpaku Communications.

DuBois, Shirley G. Zulu Heart: A Novel. LC 73-92801. 1973. 20.00 (*0-89388-132-5*) Okpaku Communications.

Dubois, Sylvie. Vers une Approche Variationiste du Discours: Une Perspective Modulaire Pouor l'Usage et la Formation des Procedes Discoursifs. (American University Studies: Vol. 33, No. 13). (FRE., Illus.). X, 268p. 1997. text 45.95 (*0-8204-3122-2*) P Lang Pubng.

Dubois, T. The Seven Last Words of Christ: For Soli, Chorus, & Orchestra with Harp & Timpani. (ENG & LAT.). 80p. 1986. pap. 4.95 (*0-7935-5490-X*, 50323850) H Leonard.

Dubois, Theodora & Smith, Dorothy V. Staten Island Patroons. (Illus.). 1961. pap. 1.50 (*0-686-23393-X*) Staten Island.

Dubois, Thierry, et al. Dynamic Multilevel Methods & the Numerical Simulation of Turbulence. 2nd ed. LC 98-36472. (Mathematical Sciences Research Institute Publications). (Illus.). 328p. (C). 1999. 59.95 (*0-521-62165-8*) Cambridge U Pr.

***DuBois, Thomas.** Encyclopedia of World Mythology, 3 Vols. 2001. lib. bdg. 275.00 (*1-57607-211-8*) ABC-CLIO.

DuBois, Thomas A. Finnish Folk Poetry & the Kalevala. LC 95-15479. (New Perspectives in Folklore Ser.: Vol. 1). (Illus.). 342p. 1995. text 70.00 (*0-8153-1975-4*, H1895) Garland.

— Nordic Religions in the Viking Age. LC 99-22405. 1999. 19.95 (*0-8122-1714-4*) U of Pa Pr.

DuBois, William W. & Hodik, Barbara J. A Guide to Photographic Design. (Illus.). 128p. 1983. pap. text 22.00 (*0-13-370346-0*) P-H.

Dubon, Nissan D. Kitzur Dinei Neiros Shabbos Kodesh. 2nd ed. (ENG & HEB.). 110p. 1996. reprint ed. 13.00 (*0-8266-5211-5*) Kehot Pubn Soc.

Dubor, Francoise, tr. see Micale, Mark S., ed.

***DuBos, Denise.** Feng Shui... The Invisible Art of Communication. Olson, Syble, ed. 184p. 1999. ring bd. 24.00 (*0-9675436-0-6*) Concepts Plus.

Dubos, Jean, jt. ed. see Dubos, Rene Jules.

Dubos, Jean B. Critical Reflections on Poetry, Painting & Music, 3 vols., Set. LC 78-3659. (Music & Theatre in France in the 17th & 18th Centuries Ser.). reprint ed. 195.00 (*0-404-60170-7*) AMS Pr.

Dubos, Rene Jules. The Dreams of Reason: Science & Utopias. LC 61-11753. (George B. Pegram Lectures). (Illus.). 183p. reprint ed. pap. 56.80 (*0-8357-4276-8*, 203707400007) Bks Demand.

— A God Within. LC 76-37224. 320p. 1972. 32.50 (*0-684-12768-7*) Irvington.

— God Within. 1984. 25.00 (*0-684-17979-2*, Scribners Ref) Mac Lib Ref.

— Louis Pasteur: Free Lance of Science. (Series in Science). (Illus.). 462p. 1986. reprint ed. pap. 14.95 (*0-306-80262-7*) Da Capo.

— The Mirage of Health: Utopias, Progress, & Biological Change. 236p. 1987. pap. 16.00 (*0-8135-1260-3*); text 35.00 (*0-8135-1259-X*) Rutgers U Pr.

— Of Human Diversity. LC 73-78352. (Heinz Werner Lectures: No. 7). 1974. 9.00 (*0-914206-24-9*) Clark U Pr.

— Pasteur & Modern Science. LC 98-12395. (Illus.). 168p. 1998. reprint ed. pap. 29.95 (*1-55581-144-2*) ASM Pr.

— The Professor, the Institute, & DNA. LC 76-26812. (Illus.). 262p. 1976. 15.00 (*0-87470-022-1*) Rockefeller.

— Reason Awake: Science for Man. LC 70-111327. 280p. 1970. text 57.50 (*0-231-03181-5*) Col U Pr.

— So Human an Animal: How We Are Shaped by Surroundings & Events. LC 98-11413. 284p. 1998. pap. text 22.95 (*0-7658-0429-8*) Transaction Pubs.

Dubos, Rene Jules & Dubos, Jean, eds. The White Plague: Tuberculosis, Man, & Society. 277p. (C). 1987. reprint ed. pap. text 17.00 (*0-8135-1224-7*) Rutgers U Pr.

Duboscq, Genevieve. My Longest Night: A Twelve-Year-Old Heroine's Stirring Account of D-Day & After. Woodward, Richard S., tr. from FRE. LC 94-13980. (Illus.). 304p. 1994. reprint ed. pap. 11.45 (*1-55970-277-X*, Pub. by Arcade Pub Inc) Time Warner.

Dubose, Anita, jt. auth. see Pearlman, Daniel D.

DuBose, C. K., ed. see International Metallographic Exhibit (1979).

DuBose, Carolyn P. The Untold Story of Charles Diggs: The Public Figure, the Private Man. LC 97-77109. 276p. 1999. 25.00 (*0-9661356-0-1*) Barton Pub Hse.

DuBose, Edwin R. The Illusion of Trust: Toward a Medical Theological Ethics in the Postmodern Age. LC 94-34129. (Theology & Medicine Ser.: Vol. 5). 144p. 1995. lib. bdg. 92.50 (*0-7923-3144-3*, Pub. by Kluwer Academic) Kluwer Academic.

DuBose, Edwin R., et al, eds. A Matter of Principles? Ferment in U. S. Bioethics. LC 94-33. 400p. (C). 1994. 30.00 (*1-56338-081-1*) TPI PA.

DuBose, Edwin R., jt. ed. see Hamel, Ronald P.

DuBose, Estelle & DuBose, La Rocque. Cyrano de Bergerac Notes. (Cliffs Notes Ser.). 64p. 1971. pap. 4.95 (*0-8220-0346-5*, Cliff) IDG Bks.

DuBose, Frances L., jt. auth. see Cotter, Louise.

Dubose, Gaylan & Sebesta, Judith L. Farrago Latina: A Teacher Resource. LC 97-34993. 1997. pap. 20.00 (*0-86516-398-7*) Bolchazy-Carducci.

DuBose, J. & Vanegas, J., eds. Sustainable Development: Creating Agents of Change. 176p. 1996. write for info. (*0-939204-55-X*) Eng Found.

DuBose, La Rocque. For Whom the Bells Tolls Notes. (Cliffs Notes Ser.). 56p. 1965. pap. 4.95 (*0-8220-0497-6*, Cliff) IDG Bks.

DuBose, La Rocque, jt. auth. see DuBose, Estelle.

DuBose, Lou, jt. auth. see Ivins, Molly.

***Dubose, Martha.** Women of Mystery. (Illus.). 464p. 2000. 24.95 (*0-312-20942-8*, Minotaur) St Martin.

Dubose, Martha, ed. see Finley, Martha.

DuBose, Sybil. The Pastors' Wives Cookbook. Buford, Janine, ed. (Illus.). 352p. 1978. spiral bd. 13.95 (*0-918544-13-0*) Wimmer Bks.

DuBose, Terry J. Fetal Sonography. LC 95-5452. (Illus.). 416p. 1995. text 75.00 (*0-7216-5432-0*, W B Saunders Co) Harcrt Hlth Sci Grp.

DuBose, William P. A DuBose Reader. Armentrout, Donald S., ed. LC 84-51878. 256p. 1984. pap. 10.95 (*0-918769-06-X*) Univ South Pr.

Dubosque, D.C. Draw! Ocean Animals. 1994. 14.15 (*0-606-07450-3*, Pub. by Turtleback) Demco.

— Draw! Rainforest Animals. 1994. 14.15 (*0-606-07451-1*, Pub. by Turtleback) Demco.

DuBosque, Doug. Draw Cars. (J). 1998. 14.15 (*0-606-07448-1*, Pub. by Turtleback) Demco.

— Draw Cars. rev. ed. LC 97-25458. (Draw Bks.). (Illus.). 64p. (J). (gr. 2-8). 1997. pap. 8.95 (*0-939217-29-5*) Peel Prod.

— Draw Desert Animals. LC 95-51693. (Draw Bks.). (Illus.). 64p. (Orig.). (J). (gr. 4-7). 1996. pap. 8.95 (*0-939217-26-0*) Peel Prod.

— Draw Dinosaurs. LC 97-24684. (Draw! Bks.). (Illus.). 64p. (J). (gr. 2-8). 1997. pap. 8.95 (*0-939217-22-8*) Peel Prod.

— Draw Dinosaurs. 1998. 14.15 (*0-606-07449-X*, Pub. by Turtleback) Demco.

— Draw Grassland Animals. LC 95-51692. (Draw Bks.). (Illus.). 64p. (Orig.). (J). (gr. 4-7). 1995. pap. 8.95 (*0-939217-25-2*) Peel Prod.

— Draw Insects. (Draw Bks.). 63p. (J). (gr. 4-8). 1997. pap. 8.95 (*0-939217-28-7*) Peel Prod.

— Draw Ocean Animals. LC 94-26897. (Draw Bks.). (Illus.). 64p. (Orig.). (J). (gr. 3-9). 1994. pap. 8.95 (*0-939217-24-4*) Peel Prod.

— Draw Rainforest Animals. LC 94-69427. (Draw! Bks.). (Illus.). 63p. (Orig.). (J). (gr. 4-7). 1994. pap. 8.95 (*0-939217-23-6*) Peel Prod.

— Draw 3-D. LC 98-42174. (Draw! Bks.). Orig. Title: Learn to Draw 3-D. (Illus.). 64p. (J). (gr. 2-8). 1998. pap. 8.95 (*0-939217-14-7*) Peel Prod.

Dubosque, Doug. Learn to Draw Now! LC 90-27879. (Learn to Draw Ser.). 1991. 13.15 (*0-606-09531-4*, Pub. by Turtleback) Demco.

An Asterisk (*) at the beginning of an entry indicates that the title is appearing for the first time.

DuBosque, Doug C. Learn to Draw Now! LC 90-27879. (Illus.). 64p. (Orig.). (J). (gr. 4-7). 1991. pap. 8.95 (*0-939217-16-3*) Peel Prod.

Dubost, Thierry. Struggle, Defeat or Rebirth: Eugene O'Neill's Vision of Humanity. Dilys, Rosalind & McGarry, Christin, trs. LC 96-32268. 293p. 1997. lib. bdg. 39.95 (*0-7864-0265-2*) McFarland & Co.

DuBoulay, Benedict, jt. auth. see Thornton, Chris.

Duboule, Denis, ed. Guidebook to the Homeobox Genes. (Guidebook Ser. A Sambrook & Tooze Publication at Oxford University Press)). (Illus.). 292p. 1994. pap. text 45.00 (*0-19-859940-4*) OUP.

Dubouloz, M., jt. ed. see De Boer, J.

Duboux, J. P. Dictionary of Gastronomy - Hotel Industry - Tourism Vol. 1: German - English - French. (ENG, FRE & GER.). 608p. 1990. 105.00 (*3-907950-01-1*) IBD Ltd.

— Dictionary of Gastronomy - Hotel Industry - Tourism Vol. 2: English - French - German. (ENG, FRE & GER.). 608p. 1990. 119.00 (*3-907950-02-X*) IBD Ltd.

— Hotel-Tourism & Gastronomy Dictionary, 2 vols., Vol. 1. (ENG, FRE & GER.). write for info. (*0-8288-7718-1*) Fr & Eur.

— Hotel-Tourism & Gastronomy Dictionary, 2 vols., Vol. 2. (ENG, FRE & GER.). write for info. (*0-8288-7717-3*) Fr & Eur.

Dubov, David, ed. Yalkut Moshiach v'Geulah al Hatorah Vayeitzei (Messiah & Redemption from the Torah Portion Vayeitzei) An Anthology, Vol. 7. (HEB.). 712p. 1998. 15.00 (*0-8266-5907-1*) Kehot Pubn Soc.

Dubov, Dovid, ed. Yalkut Moshiach V'Geulah Al Hatorah Noach, Vol. 2.Tr. of Anthology on the Messiah & Redemption - Torah Portion Noach. (HEB.). 328p. 1996. 15.00 (*0-8266-5902-0*) Kehot Pubn Soc.

— Yalkut Moshiach V'Geulah Al Hatorah Va'yera, Vol. 4.Tr. of Anthology on the Messiah & Redemption - Torah Portion Va'yera. (HEB.). 474p. 1996. 15.00 (*0-8266-5904-7*) Kehot Pubn Soc.

— Yalkut Moshiach V'Geulal Al Hatorah Chayei Sarah, Vol. 5.Tr. of Anthology on the Messiah & Redemption - Torah Portion Chayei Sarah. (HEB.). 320p. 1997. 15.00 (*0-8266-5905-5*) Kehot Pubn Soc.

— Yalkut Moshrach V'Geulah Al Hatorah - Vayishlach, Vol. 8.Tr. of Compilation on Messiah & the Redemption from the Torah. 688p. 1998. 25.00 (*0-8266-5908-X*) Kehot Pubn Soc.

Dubov, Dovid, ed. Yalkut Moshiach V'Geulah Al Hatorah Toldos, Vol. 6.Tr. of Anthology on the Messiah & Redemption - Torah Portion Toldos. (HEB.). 816p. 1997. 25.00 (*0-8266-5906-3*) Kehot Pubn Soc.

Dubov, Dovid, ed. Yalkut Moshiach V'Geulah Al Hatorah Bereshis, Vol. 1.Tr. of Anthology on the Messiah & Redemption - Torah Bereshis. (HEB.). 440p. 1996. 15.00 (*0-8266-5901-2*) Kehot Pubn Soc.

— Yalkut Moshiach V'Geulah Al Hatorah Lech-Lecha, Vol. 3.Tr. of Anthology on the Messiah & Redemption - Torah Portion Lech-Lecha. (HEB.). 412p. 1996. 15.00 (*0-8266-5903-9*) Kehot Pubn Soc.

Dubov, Irving, ed. Contemporary Agricultural Marketing. LC 67-29414. 278p. reprint ed. pap. 86.20 (*0-608-14397-9*, 202177500023) Bks Demand.

Dubov, Nissan D. To Live & Live Again: An Overview of Techihas HaMeisim Based on the Classical Sources & on the Teachings of Chabad Chassidism. Kaploun, Uri, ed. LC 97-24333. 176p. 1995. 17.00 (*1-881400-18-2*) S I E.

Dubovec, Patricia, ed. see Reynolds, Terry.

Dubovitskij, V. A. The Ulam Problem of Optimal Motion of Line Segments. Balakrishnan, A. V., ed. LC 84-19035. (Translations Series in Mathematics & Engineering). 128p. 1985. text 58.00 (*0-911575-04-9*) Optimization Soft.

— The Ulam Problem of Optimal Motion of Line Segments. Ellis, J. T., tr. from RUS. LC 84-19035. xiii, 113p. 1985. 59.95 (*0-387-90946-X*) Spr-Verlag.

Dubovitsky, Victor. V Oktjobre - In October. Eydel, Igor, ed. (RUS., Illus.). 200p. 1997. 7.00 (*0-9661341-0-9*) Vic Publ.

Dubovoy, Sina. Civil Rights Leaders. LC 96-2920. (American Profiles Ser.). 144p. (J). 1997. 19.95 (*0-8160-3363-3*) Facts on File.

Dubovsky, Steven L. Concise Guide to Clinical Psychiatry. LC 88-3385. (Concise Guides Ser.). 216p. reprint ed. pap. 67.00 (*0-608-20025-5*, 207129700010) Bks Demand.

Dubovy, Andrew. Pilgrims of the Prairie. Bloch, Marie H., tr. from UKR. write for info. (*0-318-57394-6*) Ukrainian Cult Inst.

— Pilgrims of the Prairie: Pioneer Ukrainian Baptists in North Dakota. Bloch, Marie H., ed. (Illus.). 72p. (Orig.). 1983. pap. 4.50 (*0-317-00667-3*); lib. bdg. 8.50 (*0-317-00666-5*) Ukrainian Cult Inst.

Dubow, M., jt. auth. see Ackermann, H.

Dubow, Michael S., jt. ed. see Ackermann, Hans-W.

***Dubow, Saul.** The African National Congress. (Pocket Histories Ser.). 128p. 2000. pap. 9.95 (*0-7509-2193-5*) Sutton Publng.

Dubow, Saul. Scientific Racism in Modern South Africa. (Illus.). 332p. (C). 1995. text 64.95 (*0-521-47343-8*); pap. text 23.95 (*0-521-47907-X*) Cambridge U Pr.

Dubow, Saul, jt. auth. see Beinart, William.

Dubow, Saul, jt. ed. see Beinart, William.

Dubow, Saul, ed. see Sachs, Wulf.

DuBow, Wendy, ed. Conversations with Anais Nin. LC 94-20381. (Literary Conversations Ser.). 238p. 1994. pap. 15.95 (*0-87805-720-X*); text 39.50 (*0-87805-719-6*) U Pr of Miss.

Dubowitz. Muscle Disorders in Childhood. 2nd ed. 1995. text 102.00 (*0-7020-1437-0*, W B Saunders Co) Harcrt Hlth Sci Grp.

***Dubowitz, Howard & DePanfilis, Diane.** Handbook for Child Protection Practice. LC 99-5958. 2000. write for info. (*0-7619-1371-8*) Sage.

Dubowitz, Howard. Neglected Children: Research, Practice & Policy. LC 98-40296. 288p. 1999. 26.95 (*0-7619-0854-4*) Sage.

***Dubowitz, Howard.** Neglected Children: Research, Practice, & Policy. LC 98-40296. 320p. 1999. write for info. (*0-7619-1842-6*) Sage.

***Dubowitz, Howard, ed.** Neglected Children: Research, Practice & Policy. LC 98-40296. 320p. 1999. 55.00 (*0-7619-0853-6*) Sage.

Dubowitz, Libby & Dubowitz, Victor. The Neurological Assessment of the Pre-Term & Full-Term Newborn Infant. LC 65-80377. (Clinics in Developmental Medicine Ser.: No. 79). (Illus.). 104p. (C). 1991. text 33.95 (*0-521-41204-8*, Pub. by Mc Keith Pr) Cambridge U Pr.

Dubowitz, Lilly M., et al. The Neurological Assessment of the Preterm & Full-Term Newborn Infant. 2nd ed. (Clinics in Developmental Medicine Ser.: No. 148). (Illus.). 150p. (C). 2000. text 59.95 (*1-898683-15-8*, Pub. by Mc Keith Pr) Cambridge U Pr.

Dubowitz, Victor, ed. The Floppy Infant. 2nd ed. (Clinics in Developmental Medicine Ser.: Vol. 76). 158p. (C). 1993. text 34.95 (*0-521-41203-X*, Pub. by Mc Keith Pr) Cambridge U Pr.

Dubowitz, Victor, jt. auth. see Dubowitz, Libby.

Dubowski, Cathy. Aristocats. LC 94-74639. 64p. (J). 1996. pap. 3.95 (*0-7868-4053-6*, Pub. by Disney Pr) Little.

— Cat Showdown! (Sabrina, the Teenage Witch Ser.: No. 3). (Illus.). 32p. (J). (gr. 2-4). 1998. pap. 3.99 (*0-689-81878-5*, Simon Spot) Little Simon.

— Stone Soup. LC 97-23590. (Domino Readers Ser.). (Illus.). 24p. (J). (ps-1). 1998. pap. 5.95 (*1-887734-22-8*) Star Brght Bks.

***Dubowski, Cathy.** Strangeling. (So Weird Ser.: No. 4). 128p. (J). 2000. pap. 4.99 (*0-7868-1431-4*, Pub. by Disney Pr) Time Warner.

***Dubowski, Cathy & Dubowski, Mark.** Comic Book Criminal. (Mystery Files of Shelby Woo Ser.: No. 7). (J). (gr. 4-6). 1998. pap. 3.99 (*0-671-02007-2*, Minstrel Bks) PB.

— Rocky Bullwinkle the Movie. (Illus.). 144p. (J). (gr. 4-7). 2000. mass mkt. 3.99 (*0-689-82493-9*, Simon Spot) Litle Simon.

Dubowski, Cathy & Dubowski, Mark. The Rugrats Movie. (Rugrats Ser.). (Illus.). 128p. (J). (gr. 4-7). 1998. pap. 4.50 (*0-671-02106-0*, Minstrel Bks) PB.

Dubowski, Cathy, jt. auth. see Cardona, Jose.

Dubowski, Cathy E. Andrew Johnson: Rebuilding the Union. Gallin, Richard, ed. (History of the Civil War Ser.). (Illus.). 160p. (YA). (gr. 5 up). 1990. pap. 7.95 (*0-382-24054-5*) Silver Burdett Pr.

— Blast Off If You Dare! Stories from Space Mountain. LC 96-38222. (Illus.). 96p. (J). (gr. 2-6). 1997. pap. 3.50 (*0-7868-4107-9*, Pub. by Disney Pr) Time Warner.

— Camp Nowhere. (Junior Novel Ser.). 128p. (J). (gr. 3-7). 1994. pap. 3.95 (*0-7868-1013-0*, Pub. by Hyprn Ppbks) Little.

— Cave Boy. LC 87-23427. (Step into Reading Ser.: A Step 1 Book). (Illus.). 32p. (J). (ps-1). 1988. pap. 3.99 (*0-394-89571-1*, Pub. by Random Bks Yng Read) Random.

Dubowski, Cathy E. Cave Boy. (Step into Reading Ser.: A Step 1 Book). (J). (ps-1). 1988. 9.19 (*0-606-12216-8*, Pub. by Turtleback) Demco.

Dubowski, Cathy E. Disney's Flubber. 96p. (J). (gr. 3-7). 1997. pap. 4.95 (*0-7868-4136-2*, Pub. by Disney Pr) Time Warner.

— A Dog's Life. (Sabrina, the Teenage Witch Ser.: No. 9). (YA). (gr. 7-12). 1998. per. 4.50 (*0-671-01979-1*, Archway) PB.

— Goofy Visits Pluto: A Book about the Planets. LC 94-71788. (Illus.). 32p. (J). (ps-2). 1995. 12.95 (*0-7868-3024-7*, Pub. by Disney Pr) Little.

— Hercules Junior Novel. LC 96-71630. 96p. (J). (gr. 3-7). 1997. pap. 3.95 (*0-7868-4114-1*, Pub. by Disney Pr) Time Warner.

— Mulan. LC 97-80190. (Junior Novelization Ser.). (Illus.). 96p. (J). (gr. 3-7). 1998. pap. 3.95 (*0-7868-4222-9*, Pub. by Disney Pr) Time Warner.

— Muppet Treasure Island: The Movie Storybook. (Illus.). 32p. (J). (ps-3). 1996. 10.95 (*0-448-41280-2*, G & D) Peng Put Young Read.

— Robert E. Lee & the Rise of the South. (History of the Civil War Ser.). (Illus.). 160p. (YA). (gr. 5 up). 1990. pap. 7.95 (*0-382-24051-0*) Silver Burdett Pr.

— Super Bowl Switch: I Was Dan Marino Book Club Edition. (NFL/ABC Monday Night Football Club Ser.: No. 3). (J). 1997. pap. 3.95 (*0-7868-4243-1*) Hyprn Ppbks.

Dubowski, Cathy E., adapted by. Willow: The Storybook Based on the Movie. (Illus.). 64p. (J). (gr. k-5). 1988. lib. bdg. 8.99 (*0-394-99574-0*, Pub. by Random Bks Yng Read) Random.

Dubowski, Cathy E. & Dubowski, Mark. Picky Nicky. (All Aboard Reading Picture Readers Ser.). (Illus.). 32p. (J). (ps-1). 1996. pap. text 3.95 (*0-448-41295-0*, G & D) Peng Put Young Read.

— Pirate School. LC 95-23241. (All Aboard Reading Ser.: Level 2). (Illus.). 48p. (J). (gr. 1-3). 1996. pap. 3.95 (*0-448-41132-6*, G & D) Peng Put Young Read.

— Snug Bug. LC 94-22489. (All Aboard Reading Ser.: Level 1). (Illus.). 32p. (J). (ps-1). 1995. pap. 3.95 (*0-448-40849-X*, G & D) Peng Put Young Read.

— Snug Bug's Play Day, Level 1. LC 97-8290. (All Aboard Reading Ser.). (Illus.). 32p. (J). (ps-1). 1997. lib. bdg. 13.89 (*0-448-41652-5*, G & D) Peng Put Young Read.

Dubowski, Cathy E., et al. Chuckie's Big Wish. (Rugrats Chapter Bks.: No. 5). (Illus.). 64p. (J). (gr. 1-4). 1999. pap. 3.99 (*0-689-82895-0*, Simon Spot) Litle Simon.

***Dubowski, Cathy East.** Baby-Sitters & Company. (Full House Sisters Ser.). 160p. (J). (gr. 4-6). 2000. per. 3.99 (*0-671-04087-1*, Minstrel Bks) PB.

Dubowski, Cathy East. The Baby-Sitting Boss. (Full House Michelle Ser.: Vol. 26). 87p. (J). (gr. 1-5). 1999. per. 3.99 (*0-671-02156-7*) PB.

— Black Beauty. LC 89-62772. (Bullseye Step into Classics Ser.). 1993. 9.09 (*0-606-09081-9*, Pub. by Turtleback) Demco.

— Bonjour Alex! (Secret World of Alex Mack Ser.: No. 17). (J). (gr. 3-6). 1997. pap. 3.99 (*0-671-01373-4*, Minstrel Bks) PB.

— Bunk 3, Teddy & Me. (Full House Michelle Ser.). 96p. (J). (gr. 4-7). 1996. per. 3.99 (*0-671-56834-5*) PB.

— The Case of the Sea World Adventure, (Adventures of Mary-Kate & Ashley Ser.). (Illus.). 80p. (J). (gr. 2-4). 1996. pap. 3.99 (*0-590-86369-X*) Scholastic Inc.

***Dubowski, Cathy East.** The Case of the Slam Dunk Mystery: The Case Of The Slam Dunk Mystery. (New Adventures of Mary-Kate & Ashley Ser.). (Illus.). 96p. (J). (gr. 1-3). 2000. mass mkt. 4.25 (*0-06-106588-9*) HarpC Child Bks.

— The Case of the Surfing Secret With Other. (New Adventures of Mary-Kate & Ashley Ser.: Vol. 12). (Illus.). 78p. (J). (gr. 1-5). 1999. mass mkt. 4.25 (*0-06-106585-4*) HarpC.

Dubowski, Cathy East. Clean-up Catastrophe! (Secret World of Alex Mack Ser.: No. 6). (J). (gr. 3-6). 1996. pap. 3.99 (*0-671-56308-4*, Minstrel Bks) PB.

***Dubowski, Cathy East.** Cowboy Roy. LC 99-89375. (All Aboard Reading Ser.). (Illus.). (J). 2000. pap. text 3.99 (*0-448-41568-2*, G & D) Peng Put Young Read.

Dubowski, Cathy East. A Doll's Story. (Sabrina, the Teenage Witch Ser.: No. 6). (Illus.). 32p. (J). (gr. 1-6). 1998. pap. 3.99 (*0-689-81879-3*, Simon Spot) Litle Simon.

— Fastest Turtle in the West. 25th ed. (Full House Michelle Ser.: Vol. 25). 144p. (J). (gr. 4-7). 1999. pap. 3.99 (*0-671-02155-9*) S&S Trade.

***Dubowski, Cathy East.** Field Day Foul Up. (Full House Michelle & Friends Ser.). 96p. (J). (gr. 2-4). 2000. per. 3.99 (*0-671-04198-3*, Minstrel Bks) PB.

Dubowski, Cathy East. Fortune Cookie Fox. (Sabrina, the Teenage Witch Ser.: No. 26). 113p. (YA). (gr. 7-12). 1999. per. 4.50 (*0-671-02817-0*, Archway) PB.

— The Ghost in My Closet. (Full House Michelle Ser.: Vol. 5). 96p. (J). (gr. 4-7). 1995. per. 3.99 (*0-671-53573-0*) PB.

— Hercules. (J). 1997. pap. 3.95 (*0-7868-4196-6*, Pub. by Disney Pr) Little.

***Dubowski, Cathy East.** It's a Miserable Life! (Sabrina, the Teenage Witch Ser.: Vol. 34). 160p. 2000. 4.99 (*0-671-04071-5*) PB.

Dubowski, Cathy East. I've Got a Secret. (Full House Michelle Ser.). (J). (gr. 2-4). 1997. per. 3.99 (*0-671-00366-6*, Minstrel Bks) PB.

— The Little Princess. LC 93-14000. (Bullseye Step into Classics Ser.). 1994. 9.09 (*0-606-09564-0*, Pub. by Turtleback) Demco.

— My Best Friend Is a Movie Star. (Full House Michelle Ser.: Vol. 10). 144p. (J). (gr. 4-7). 1996. per. 3.99 (*0-671-56835-3*) PB.

— My Fourth-Grade Mess. (Full House Michelle Ser.). 96p. (J). (gr. 2-4). 1996. per. 3.99 (*0-671-53576-5*, PB Trade Paper) PB.

— My Ho- Ho- Horrible Christmas. (Full House Michelle Ser.: Vol. 17). 96p. (J). (gr. 4-7). 1997. per. 3.99 (*0-671-00836-6*) PB.

— My Life Is a Three Ring Circus. (Full House Michelle Ser.). (J). (gr. 2-4). 1998. per. 3.99 (*0-671-01730-6*, Minstrel Bks) PB.

— My Two Best Friends. (Full House Michelle Ser.). (Orig.). (J). (gr. 4-7). 1995. pap. 3.99 (*0-671-52271-X*, Minstrel Bks) PB.

— Peter Pan. LC 90-23077. (Bullseye Step into Classics Ser.). 1994. 9.09 (*0-606-06663-2*, Pub. by Turtleback) Demco.

— Pigs, Pies, & Plenty of Problems. (Full House Michelle & Friends Ser.: Vol. 28). 96p. (J). (gr. 4-7). 1999. per. 3.99 (*0-671-02152-4*) PB.

Dubowski, Cathy East. Pirate School. (All Aboard Reading Ser.). (J). 1996. 9.15 (*0-606-11751-2*, Pub. by Turtleback) Demco.

Dubowski, Cathy East. Pretty Good Magic. LC 87-4784. (Step into Reading Ser.: A Step 2 Book). (Illus.). 48p. (J). (ps-3). 1987. pap. 3.99 (*0-394-89068-X*, Pub. by Random Bks Yng Read) Random.

— Pretty Good Magic. (Step into Reading Ser.: A Step 2 Book). (J). (gr. 1-3). 1987. 9.19 (*0-606-12487-X*, Pub. by Turtleback) Demco.

— Psychic Kitty. (Sabrina, the Teenage Witch Ser.: No. 6). 96p. (J). (gr. 2-4). 1999. pap. 3.99 (*0-671-02582-9*) PB.

— Rocky Bullwinkle Metal Munching Mice. (Illus.). 64p. (J). (gr. 4-7). 1998. 3.99 (*0-689-82145-X*) S&S Childrens.

***Dubowski, Cathy East.** 7th Heaven: Four Years with the Camden Family. 240p. 2000. pap. 15.95 (*0-06-106624-9*, HarpEntertain) Morrow Avon.

Dubowski, Cathy East. Shark Attack! LC 98-14073. (Eyewitness Readers). (Illus.). 48p. (J). (gr. 2-3). 1998. pap. 3.95 (*0-7894-3440-7*); pap. 12.95 (*0-7894-3763-5*) DK Pub Inc.

***Dubowski, Cathy East.** Sink or Swim! (Secret World of Alex Mack Ser.: No. 29). (J). (gr. 3-6). 1998. pap. 3.99 (*0-671-02108-7*, Minstrel Bks) PB.

— Substitute Sister. (Full House Sisters Ser.). (Illus.). 160p. (J). (gr. 4-6). 2000. 3.99 (*0-671-04089-8*, Minstrel Bks) PB.

Dubowski, Cathy East. Take a Hike! (Secret World of Alex Mack Ser.: No. 7). (J). (gr. 3-6). 1996. pap. 3.99 (*0-671-56309-2*) PB.

— Tap Dance Trouble. (Full House Michelle Ser.). (J). (gr. 2-4). 1999. per. 3.99 (*0-671-02154-0*) PB.

— Truth Trap! (Secret World of Alex Mack Ser.: No. 21). (J). (gr. 3-6). 1997. pap. 3.99 (*0-671-01157-X*) PB.

***Dubowski, Cathy East.** Unlucky in Lunch. (Full House Michelle & Friends Ser.: Vol. 31). 96p. (J). (gr. 2-4). 2000. per. 3.99 (*0-671-04196-7*, Minstrel Bks) PB.

Dubowski, Cathy East. The Wish I Never Wished. (Full House Michelle Ser.: Vol. 27). 85p. (J). (gr. 1-5). 1999. per. 3.99 (*0-671-02151-6*) PB.

Dubowski, Cathy East & Dubowski, Mark. High Wire. (Mystery Files of Shelby Woo Ser.: Vol. 10). 144p. (J). (gr. 3-7). 1999. pap. 3.99 (*0-671-02694-1*, Archway) PB.

— Ice Mummy: The Discovery of a 5,000 Year-Old Man. LC 97-30998. (Step into Reading Ser.: A Step 3 Book). (Illus.). 48p. (J). (gr. 2-3). 1998. pap. 3.99 (*0-679-85647-1*) Random.

— Ice Mummy: The Discovery of a 5,000 Year-Old Man. LC 97-30998. (Step into Reading Ser.: A Step 3 Book). (Illus.). 48p. (J). (gr. 3-5). 1998. lib. bdg. 11.99 (*0-679-95647-6*) Random.

***Dubowski, Cathy East & Dubowski, Mark.** Rugrats in Paris. (Rugrats Ser.). (Illus.). (J). (ps-3). 2000. pap. 4.99 (*0-689-83394-6*, Simon Spot) Litle Simon.

— The Rugrats Movie Music Book. (Rugrats Ser.). (Illus.). 72p. (J). (ps-3). 1999. otabind 14.95 (*0-634-00514-6*) H Leonard.

Dubowski, Cathy East & Dubowski, Mark. Salem Goes to Rome. (Sabrina, the Teenage Witch Ser.). (J). (gr. 2-5). 1998. pap. 3.99 (*0-671-02773-5*) PB.

— Snug Bug's Play Day, Level 1. LC 97-8290. (All Aboard Reading Ser.). (Illus.). 32p. (J). (ps-1). 1997. pap. 3.95 (*0-448-41623-9*, G & D) Peng Put Young Read.

— Split Image. (Journey of Allen Strange Ser.: No. 3). (J). (gr. 3-6). 1999. pap. 3.99 (*0-671-02510-4*) PB.

Dubowski, Cathy East, see East Dubowski, Cathy.

Dubowski, Cathy East, jt. auth. see Dubowski, Mark.

Dubowski, Cathy East, jt. auth. see Waricha, Jean.

Dubowski, Jan J., ed. Laser Applications in Microelectronic & Optoelectronic Manufacturing II. Vol. 2991. LC 97-194518. 240p. 1997. 69.00 (*0-8194-2402-1*) SPIE.

***Dubowski, Jan J., et al, eds.** Laser Applications in Microelectronic & Optoelectronic Manufacturing IV. 546p. 1999. pap. text 120.00 (*0-8194-3088-9*) SPIE.

Dubowski, Jan J. & Dyer, Peter E., eds. Laser Applications in Microelectronic & Optoelectronic Manufacturing III. LC 98-233181. (Proceedings of SPIE Ser.: Vol. 3274). 354p. 1998. 99.00 (*0-8194-2713-6*) SPIE.

Dubowski, Mark. The King of Cats. (Sabrina, the Teenage Witch Ser.: No. 4). (J). (gr. 2-5). 1999. pap. 3.99 (*0-671-02105-2*, Minstrel Bks) PB.

— S. O. S. Titanic: The Disaster that Shocked the World. LC 98-25066. (Eyewitness Readers). 48p. (J). (gr. 2-3). 1998. 3.95 (*0-7894-3441-5*); 12.95 (*0-7894-3767-8*) DK Pub Inc.

Dubowski, Mark & Dubowski, Cathy East. Cat-TV. (Sabrina, the Teenage Witch Ser.: No. 1). (Illus.). (J). (gr. 2-4). 1998. pap. 3.99 (*0-671-02102-8*, Minstrel Bks) PB.

Dubowski, Mark, jt. auth. see Dubowski, Cathy.

Dubowski, Mark, jt. auth. see Dubowski, Cathy E.

Dubowski, Mark, jt. auth. see Dubowski, Cathy East.

DuBowy, Paul J. & Reeves, Richard P., eds. Constructed Wastelands for Animal Waste Management: Proceedings of Workshop, 4-6 April 1994, Lafayette, Indiana. LC 94-26888. 1994. 10.00 (*0-931682-46-0*) Purdue U Pubns.

Dubrava, Patricia. Holding the Light. Andrews, Nancy, ed. 112p. 1994. pap. 10.25 (*0-9614643-4-8*) James Andrews Co.

Dubravcic, Elizabeth V., et al. Assessing Vocational Teachers. 87p. 8.00 (*0-318-22040-7*, RD262) Ctr Educ Trng Employ.

— Evaluating Short-Term Skill Training. 58p. 1986. 6.25 (*0-318-22098-9*, RD261) Ctr Educ Trng Employ.

Dubray. Human Services for American Indians. 1992. mass mkt. 16.75 (*0-314-01356-3*) West Pub.

— Mental Health. 1993. mass mkt. 16.75 (*0-314-02889-7*) West Pub.

Dubreuil, Chisato O., jt. ed. see Fitzhugh, William W.

Dubreuil, G. Jouveau. Dravidian Architecture. ii, 47p. (C). 1987. reprint ed. 11.50 (*0-8364-2189-2*, Pub. by Usha) S Asia.

Dubreuil, Hyacinth. Robots or Men: French Workman's Experience in American Industry. Stein, Leon, ed. LC 77-70491. 1977. reprint ed. lib. bdg. 26.95 (*0-405-10163-5*) Ayer.

Dubreuil, John J. Florida Workers' Compensation Handbook. text 89.00 (*0-8205-4180-X*) Bender.

— Florida Workers' Compensation Handbook. 1988th ed. LC 98-23175. (Larson Ser.). 1998. write for info. (*0-8205-3736-5*) Bender.

Dubreuil, Linda. Crooked Letter: Linford Mystery Library. large type ed. 1993. pap. 14.95 (*0-685-67905-5*, Linford) Ulverscroft.

Dubreuil, Linda A. Crooked Letter. large type ed. (Linford Mystery Library). 368p. 1992. pap. 16.99 (*0-7089-7235-7*) Ulverscroft.

Dubreuil, Lorraine, ed. World Directory of Map Collections. 3rd ed. (IFLA Publications: Vol. 63). 310p. 1993. 80.00 (*3-598-21791-9*) K G Saur Verlag.

Dubreuil, P. Recueil Quadrilingue de Mots Usuels en Hydrologie. 113p. 1969. pap. 9.95 (*0-8288-6613-9*, M-6176) Fr & Eur.

***Dubrin.** The Active Manager. (SWC-General Business Ser.). 400p. 1999. pap. 22.95 (*0-324-02740-0*) Thomson Learn.

Dubrin. A Casebook of the Organizational Behavior of Man. 1996. pap. text. write for info. (*0-08-022976-X*, Pergamon Pr) Elsevier.

D

— Essentials of Management. 3rd ed. (GC - Principles of Management Ser.). 1994. student ed. 17.50 (*0-538-82941-9*) S-W Pub.

— Essentials of Management. 4th ed. LC 96-18537. (GC - Principles of Management Ser.). 560p. 1996. mass mkt. 36.95 (*0-538-85546-0*) S-W Pub.

— Leadership. LC 94-76500. (C). 1994. pap. text 54.76 (*0-395-65634-6*) HM.

— Leadership, 2 vols. 2nd ed. LC 97-72462. (C). 1997. pap. text 54.76 (*0-395-85664-7*) HM.

Dubrin & Ireland. Management & Organization. 2nd ed. 1999. 59.25 (*0-538-83621-0*) Sth-Wstrn College.

DuBrin, Andrew J. Applying Psychology: Individual & Organizational Effectiveness. 5th ed. LC 99-13193. Orig. Title: Effective Business Psychology. (Illus.). 477p. 1999. 74.00 (*0-13-083837-3*) P-H.

Dubrin, Andrew J. Bouncing Back: How to Stay in the Game When Your Career Is on the Line. 237p. 1998. text 25.00 (*0-7881-5903-8*) DIANE Pub.

— The Complete Idiot's Guide to Leadership. LC 97-73156. 336p. 1997. 16.95 (*0-02-861946-3*) Macmillan Gen Ref.

DuBrin, Andrew J. Essentials of Management. 2nd ed. 736p. (C). 1989. mass mkt. 27.50 (*0-538-80495-5*, GC63BA) S-W Pub.

— Essentials of Management. 3rd ed. LC 93-19469. (C). 1993. mass mkt. 36.50 (*0-538-82939-7*, GC63CA) S-W Pub.

***DuBrin, Andrew J.** Essentials of Management. 5th ed. LC 99-25803. 384p. 1999. pap. 47.95 (*0-324-00703-5*) Thomson Learn.

— Fundamentals of Organizational Behavior. 2nd ed. 2001. pap. 35.00 (*0-324-02281-6*) Thomson Learn.

DuBrin, Andrew J. Getting It Done: The Transforming Power of Self-Discipline. LC 94-42263. 235p. 1995. 22.95 (*1-56079-470-4*, Petersons Pacesetter) Petersons.

— Getting It Done: The Transforming Power of Self-Discipline. 235p. 1996. pap. text 14.95 (*1-56079-705-3*) Petersons.

— Human Relations. 6th ed. LC 96-7942. 320p. 1996. 55.00 (*0-13-400011-0*) P-H.

***DuBrin, Andrew J.** Human Relations: Interpersonal Job-Oriented Skills. 7th ed. 384p. 2000. pap. 42.67 (*0-13-010578-3*, Prentice Hall) P-H.

Dubrin, Andrew J. Human Relations for Career & Personal Success. 5th ed. LC 98-18986. 466p. (C). 1998. 68.00 (*0-13-924663-0*) P-H.

DuBrin, Andrew J. Looking Around Corners: The Art of Problem Prevention. 303p. 1999. pap. 16.95 (*1-886284-33-4*, Pub. by Chandler Hse) Natl Bk Netwk.

— Personal Magnetism: Discover Your Own Charisma & Learn to Charm, Inspire, & Influence Others. LC 97-11795. 208p. 1997. pap. 17.95 (*0-8144-7936-7*) AMACOM.

***DuBrin, Andrew J.** 10 Minute Guide to Leadership. 2nd ed. (10 Minute Guides). 168p. 2000. pap. text 10.95 (*0-02-863611-2*) Macmillan.

Dubrin, Andrew J. Winning Office Politics: Dubrin's New Guide for the '90s. 360p. 1990. pap. 14.95 (*0-13-964958-1*) P-H.

DuBrin, Andrew J. Your Own Worst Enemy: How to Overcome Career Self-Sabotage. 256p. 1993. pap. 14.95 (*0-8144-7861-1*) AMACOM.

Dubris, Maggie. Willieworld. (Illus.). 65p. 1998. pap. 6.95 (*0-9666328-2-6*) CUZ Ed.

Dubro, Alan. All about Kids & Eating Disorders. (Family Forum Library). 16p. 1992. 1.95 (*1-56688-016-5*) Bur For At-Risk.

— Coping with Angry, Acting-Out Children. (Family Forum Library). 16p. 1992. 1.95 (*1-56688-015-7*) Bur For At-Risk.

— Helping Children Handle Peer Pressure. (Family Forum Library). 16p. 1992. 1.95 (*1-56688-017-3*) Bur For At-Risk.

Dubro, Alec, jt. auth. see Kaplan, David E.

Dubrocard, Michel, ed. see Juvenal.

Dubroff, Rich. How Was the Game? LC 94-94135. 220p. 1994. 19.95 (*0-9640426-0-6*) Diamond Publshng.

Dubroff, Susanne. You & I. LC 94-76455. 54p. 1994. pap. 8.95 (*0-9637040-0-1*) Kinsman Pr.

Dubrov, A. P. Human Biorhythms & the Moon. (Illus.). 147p. (C). 1994. lib. bdg. 95.00 (*1-56072-145-6*) Nova Sci Pubs.

— The Symmetry of Biorhythms & Reactivity. Szamuely, H., tr. from RUS. x, 268p. 1989. text 455.00 (*2-88124-692-3*) Gordon & Breach.

Dubrovin, B. Mathematical Physics Reviews Vol. 9, Pt. 4: Hydrodynamics of Soliton Lattices, Vol. 9. (Soviet Scientific Reviews Ser.: Section C). 136p. 1993. pap. text 240.00 (*3-7186-5454-7*, Harwood Acad Pubs) Gordon & Breach.

Dubrovin, B. A., et al. Modern Geometry - Methods & Applications Pt. I: The Geometry of Surface, Transformation Groups & Fields. Burns, R. G., tr. (Graduate Texts in Mathematics Ser.: Vol. 93). (RUS., Illus.). 495p. 1984. 59.80 (*0-387-90872-2*) Spr-Verlag.

— Modern Geometry - Methods & Applications Pt. 1: The Geometry of Surfaces, Transformation Groups & Fields. 2nd ed. (Graduate Texts in Mathematics Ser.). (Illus.). xv, 468p. 1993. 65.95 (*0-387-97663-9*) Spr-Verlag.

— Modern Geometry - Methods & Applications Pt. 2: The Geometry & Topology of Manifolds. Burns, R. G., tr. LC 83-16851. (Graduate Texts in Mathematics Ser.: Vol. 104). (Illus.). xv, 448p. 1995. 65.95 (*0-387-96162-3*) Spr-Verlag.

— Modern Geometry - Methods & Applications Pt. 3: Introduction to Homology Theory. Ewing, J. H. et al, eds. Burns, R. G., tr. from RUS. (Graduate Texts in Mathematics Ser.: Vol. 124). (Illus.). 464p. 1990. 64.95 (*0-387-97271-4*) Spr-Verlag.

Dubrovin, M. Book of Russian Idioms Illustrated. (Illus.). 328p. (C). 1987. 75.00 (*0-7855-5353-3*, Pub. by Collets) St Mut.

Dubrovin, M. I. A Book of Russian Idioms Illustrated. LC 79-40433. (Illus.). 328p. 1981. 151.00 (*0-08-023594-8*, Pub. by Pergamon Repr) Franklin.

Dubrovin, Vivian. Create Your Own Storytelling Stories. LC 95-92399. (Illus.). 96p. (Orig.). (J). (gr. 4-6). 1995. pap. 12.95 (*0-9638339-1-X*) Storycraft Pub.

— Storytelling Adventures: Stories Kids Can Tell. LC 96-92370. (Illus.). 80p. (Orig.). (J). (gr. 3-8). 1997. pap. 14.95 (*0-9638339-2-8*) Storycraft Pub.

— Storytelling for the Fun of It: A Handbook for Children. LC 93-93694. 160p. (J). (gr. 4-7). 1994. pap. 16.95 (*0-9638339-0-1*) Storycraft Pub.

— Storytelling for the Fun of It: A Handbook for Children. 2nd rev. ed. LC 98-61152. (Illus.). 204p. (J). (gr. 4-6). 1999. pap. 19.90 (*0-9638339-3-6*) Storycraft Pub.

— Tradin' Tales with Grandpa: A Kid's Guide for Intergenerational Storytelling. (Illus.). 80p. (J). (gr. 3-7). 2000. 16.95 (*0-9638339-4-4*) Storycraft Pub.

Dubrovsky, Gertrude W. The Land Was Theirs: Jewish Farmers in the Garden State. LC 90-10740. (Judaic Studies). (Illus.). 272p. (C). 1992. pap. text 32.95 (*0-8173-0544-0*) U of Ala Pr.

Dubrovsky, Gertrude W., tr. see Schwartz, I. J.

***Dubrow, Eileen & Dubrow, Richard.** American Furniture of the Nineteenth Century. 2nd ed. (Illus.). 248p. 2000. 39.95 (*0-7643-1080-1*) Schiffer.

Dubrow, Eileen, jt. auth. see Dubrow, Richard.

Dubrow, Heather. Captive Victors: Shakespeare's Narrative Poems & Sonnets. LC 86-19627. 288p. (C). 1987. 42.50 (*0-8014-1975-1*) Cornell U Pr.

— Captive Victors: Shakespeare's Narrative Poems & Sonnets. LC 86-19627. 279p. reprint ed. pap. 86.50 (*0-608-20883-3*, 207198200003) Bks Demand.

— Echoes of Desire: English Petrachism & Its Counterdiscourses. LC 95-8916. 328p. 1995. text 47.50 (*0-8014-2966-8*) Cornell U Pr.

— Happier Eden: The Politics of Marriage in the Stuart Epithalamium. LC 89-71200. 320p. reprint ed. pap. 99.20 (*0-608-20882-5*, 207198100003) Bks Demand.

***Dubrow, Heather.** Shakespeare & Domestic Loss: Forms of Deprivation, Mourning & Recuperation. LC 98-46267. (Cambridge Studies in Renaissance Literature & Culture: Vol. 32). 260p. (C). 1999. 54.95 (*0-521-62633-1*) Cambridge U Pr.

Dubrow, Heather & Strier, Richard. The Historical Renaissance: New Essays on Tudor & Stuart Literature & Culture. 388p. 1989. pap. text 15.95 (*0-226-16766-6*) U Ch Pr.

— The Historical Renaissance: New Essays on Tudor & Stuart Literature & Culture. 416p. 1994. lib. bdg. 42.00 (*0-226-16765-8*) U Ch Pr.

Dubrow, Joanne, jt. auth. see Collay, Ryan.

Dubrow, Richard & Dubrow, Eileen. American Furniture of the 19th Century, 1840-1880. LC 82-50615. (Illus.). 248p. 1983. 30.00 (*0-916838-68-4*) Schiffer.

— Furniture Made in America, 1875-1905. 2nd rev. ed. 320p. 1998. pap. 24.95 (*0-7643-0595-6*) Schiffer.

— Styles of American Furniture, 1860-1960. LC 97-16558. (Illus.). 224p. 1997. 49.95 (*0-7643-0157-8*) Schiffer.

Dubrow, Richard, jt. auth. see Dubrow, Eileen.

Dubrowski, Emma L. HIV Tracing & Transmission in People in Working, Sports & Professional Populations: Index of New Information. rev. ed. 147p. 1997. 47.50 (*0-7883-1524-2*); pap. 44.50 (*0-7883-1525-0*) ABBE Pubs Assn.

Dubrowski, Janusz M., jt. auth. see Blazyca, George.

Dubrowski, Mark, ed. & illus. see Hermans, J. J.

DuBruck, Edelgard E. Aspects of Fifteenth-Century Society in the German Carnival Comedies: Speculum Hominis. LC 93-24706. (Studies in German Language & Literature: Vol. 13). 186p. 1993. text 79.95 (*0-7734-9328-X*) E Mellen.

— New Images of Medieval Women: Essays Toward a Cultural Anthropology. LC 87-26040. (Studies in Women & Religion). 1988. write for info. (*0-88946-523-1*) E Mellen.

DuBruck, Edelgard E., ed. New Images of Medieval Women: Studies Toward a Cultural Anthropology. LC 88-9351. (Medieval Studies: Vol. 1). 330p. 1988. lib. bdg. 99.95 (*0-88946-265-8*) E Mellen.

— La Passion Isabeau: Une Edition du Manuscript Fr. 996 de la Bibiotheque Nationale de Paris Avec une Introduction et des Notes. LC 90-5919. (American University Studies: Romance Languages & Literature: Ser. II, Vol. 141). VIII, 236p. (C). 1991. text 44.95 (*0-8204-1272-4*) P Lang Pubng.

DuBruck, Edelgard E. & Goller, Karl H., eds. Crossroads of Medieval Civilization: The City of Regensburg & Its Intellectual Milieu: A Collection of Essays. LC 83-63325. (Medieval & Renaissance Monograph Ser.: No. 5). (Illus.). 192p. reprint ed. pap. 59.60 (*0-8357-7536-4*, 203625100001) Bks Demand.

***DuBruck, Edelgard E. & Gusick, Barbara I., eds.** Death & Dying in the Middle Ages. LC 98-20807. (Studies in the Humanities: Vol. 45). (Illus.). xi, 515p. (C). 1999. text 71.00 (*0-8204-4127-9*) P Lang Pubng.

DuBruck, Edelgard E. & McDonald, William C., eds. The Current State of Research in Fifteenth-Century Literature: Germania - Romania. LC 96-17582. (Studies in Medieval Literature: Vol. 16). 220p. 1996. text 89.95 (*0-7734-8754-9*) E Mellen.

— Fifteenth-Century Studies, Vol. 16, 1990. LC 79-640105. 344p. reprint ed. pap. 106.70 (*0-7837-3335-6*, 202702300016) Bks Demand.

DuBruck, Edelgard E. & Mermier, Guy R., eds. Fifteenth Century Studies, Vol. 4. LC 79-640105. 240p. 1981. reprint ed. pap. 74.40 (*0-608-08231-7*, 202702300004) Bks Demand.

— Fifteenth Century Studies, Vol. 5. LC 79-640105. 248p. 1982. reprint ed. pap. 76.90 (*0-608-08232-5*, 202702300005) Bks Demand.

— Fifteenth Century Studies, Vol. 6. LC 79-640105. 340p. 1983. reprint ed. pap. 105.40 (*0-608-08233-3*, 202702300006) Bks Demand.

— Fifteenth Century Studies, Vol. 7. LC 79-640105. 364p. 1983. reprint ed. pap. 112.90 (*0-608-08234-1*, 202702300007) Bks Demand.

— Fifteenth Century Studies, Vol. 8. LC 79-640105. 308p. 1983. reprint ed. pap. 95.50 (*0-608-08235-X*, 202702300008) Bks Demand.

— Fifteenth Century Studies, Vol. 9. LC 79-640105. 270p. 1984. reprint ed. pap. 83.70 (*0-608-08236-8*, 202702300009) Bks Demand.

— Fifteenth Century Studies, Vol. 10. LC 79-640105. 306p. 1984. reprint ed. pap. 94.90 (*0-608-08237-6*, 202702300010) Bks Demand.

DuBruck, Edelgard E., jt. ed. see McDonald, William C.

DuBruck, Edelgard E., jt. ed. see Mermier, Guy R.

***Dubruiel, Michael.** Mention Your Request Here: The Church's Most Powerful Novenas. LC 99-75031. 144p. 2000. pap. 12.95 (*0-87973-341-1*) Our Sunday Visitor.

Dubruiel, Michael & Welborn, Amy. The Biblical Way of the Cross. LC 93-90827. (Illus.). 32p. (Orig.). 1994. pap. 1.75 (*0-87793-519-X*) Ave Maria.

DuBrul, E. F. Outlook for New Developments in the Machine Tool Industry. (Technical Papers: Vol. P74). (Illus.). 7p. 1930. pap. text 30.00 (*1-55589-151-9*) AGMA.

***Dubrul, Ronald C.** Apostolic & Humanic Gifts. (Ministering the Gifts Ser.: No. III). 74p. 1998. pap. 4.95 (*1-929138-14-8*, MINGI3) Christ Fellow Min.

— The Holy Ghost & Spiritual Gifts, (Ministering the Gifts Ser.: No. I). ii, 118p. 1998. pap. 9.95 (*1-929138-12-1*, MINGI1) Christ Fellow Min.

— How to Start Your Ministry. 60p. 1998. pap. 9.95 (*1-929138-07-5*, HOWSTA) Christ Fellow Min.

— The Mysteries of God Revealed. (Illus.). 262p. 1999. pap. 19.95 (*1-929138-24-5*, MYSTER) Christ Fellow Min.

— The Nine Spiritual Gifts. (Ministering the Gifts Ser.: No. II). ii, 118p. 1998. pap. 9.95 (*1-929138-13-X*, MINGI2) Christ Fellow Min.

— Releasing the Nature of God. 42p. 1998. pap. 5.00 (*1-929138-11-3*, RELEAS) Christ Fellow Min.

— The Six Secrets of Elijah: How You Can Succeed in God Even Though You're Only Human. (Illus.). 16p. 1998. pap. 2.95 (*1-929138-16-4*, SIXSEC) Christ Fellow Min.

— The Value of the Anointing. 14p. 1998. pap. 5.00 (*1-929138-09-1*, VALUE0) Christ Fellow Min.

— You Have Power Over the Devil! 136p. 2000. pap. 9.95 (*1-929138-33-4*, YOUHAV) Christ Fellow Min.

DuBrul, Sascha A. Carnival of Chaos: On the Road with the Nomadic Festival. 1997. pap. 8.00 (*1-57027-047-3*) Autonomedia.

Dubrule, Olivier. Geostatistics in Petroleum Geology. (AAPG Continuing Education Course Note Series: No. 38). (Illus.). 250p. 1998. pap. 30.00 (*0-89181-187-7*, 908) AAPG.

Dubrulle, B., et al, eds. Scale Invariance: From Axioms to Physical Mechanisms Course Held in Les Houches, 10-14 March, 1997. xx, 286p. 1998. pap. 79.95 (*3-540-64000-2*) Spr-Verlag.

Dubs, Homer H., tr. see Hsun-Tzu.

Dubsky, Ann, tr. see Hamann, Brigitte.

Dubsky, Ann, tr. see Kronberger, Hans & Lattacher, Siegbert.

Dubsky, Linda, jt. auth. see Hughes, Jonathan.

Dubsky-Rejsek. Czech-Spanish Dictionary: Cesko-Spanelsky Slovnik. (CZE & SPA.). 1240p. 1980. 35.00 (*0-8288-1083-4*, S39711) Fr & Eur.

***Dubsky, V.** Business Dictionary, Vol. 2. (FRE & CZE.). 1998. 75.00 (*0-320-01895-4*) Fr & Eur.

***Dubson, Michael, ed.** Ghosts in the Classroom: The Stories of College Adjunct Faculty - And the Price We All Pay. 172p. 2001. pap. 14.95 (*0-9658977-1-0*) Camels Back Bks.

Dubuc, R. English-French Bilingual Vocabulary of the Theatre: Vocaabulaire Bilingue du Theatre Anglais-Francais. (ENG & FRE.). 174p. 1981. pap. 19.95 (*0-8288-2167-4*, M14214) Fr & Eur.

Dubuc, Serge & Deslauriers, Gilles. Spline Functions & the Theory of Wavelets. LC 98-54441. (CRM Proceedings & Lecture Notes Ser.). 397p. 1999. 110.00 (*0-8218-0875-3*) Am Math.

Dubuc, Serge, jt. ed. see Belair, Jacques.

Dubucs, Jacques-Paul, ed. Philosophy of Probability. LC 93-24048. (Philosophical Studies in Philosophy: Vol. 56). 304p. 1993. lib. bdg. 169.50 (*0-7923-2385-8*, Pub. by Kluwer Academic) Kluwer Academic.

Dubuffet, Jean, et al. Jean Dubuffet: Forty Years of His Art. LC 84-51915. (Illus.). 96p. (Orig.). 1984. pap. 15.00 (*0-935573-02-X*) D & A Smart Museum.

DuBuisson-Hamel, Melany A. Dubuisson Dictionary. Hamel, Patrick E., ed. LC 98-85999. (Illus.). 970p. 1998. ring bd. 70.00 incl. cd-rom (*0-9665376-0-2*) Hamel Family.

DuBuisson-Hamel, Melany A. & Bonin. Dictionary Francais Regional du Berry-Bourbonnais. (FRE.). 160p. 1993. 49.95 (*0-320-00857-6*) Fr & Eur.

Dubuque, Tina. Parts of Speech. 1998. 4.95 (*1-55708-601-X*, MCR314) McDonald Pub Co.

Dubuque, Jean H. & Gleckner, Robert F. The Development of the Heavy Bomber, 1918-1944. (USAF Historical Studies: No. 6). 188p. 1951. pap. text 32.95 (*0-89126-030-7*) MA-AH Pub.

Dubuque Microcomputer Consultants Staff, et al. Safety Officer II, Macintosh Version. 188p. 1997. 2495.00 (*0-471-28820-9*, VNR) Wiley.

Dubuque, Nicholas & Dubuque, Susan. Kid Power Tactics for Dealing with Depression. 47p. (Orig.). (J). (gr. 4-8). 1996. pap. 10.95 (*1-882732-48-0*) Childswork.

Dubuque, Susan, jt. auth. see Dubuque, Nicholas.

Dubuque, Susan E. A Parent's Survival Guide to Childhood Depression. 85p. (Orig.). 1996. pap. 14.95 (*1-882732-49-9*) Childswork.

Dubus, Andre. Broken Vessels. 224p. 1991. 19.95 (*0-87923-885-2*) Godine.

— Broken Vessels: Essays by Andre Dubus. 224p. 1992. pap. 11.95 (*0-87923-948-4*) Godine.

— Dancing after Hours: Stories. 240p. 1996. 23.00 (*0-679-43107-1*) Knopf.

— Dancing after Hours: Stories. 1997. pap. 12.00 (*0-679-75114-9*) Vin Bks.

— Finding a Girl in America. LC 79-90371. 192p. 1980. pap. 11.95 (*0-87923-393-1*) Godine.

Dubus, Andre, III. House of Sand & Fog: A Novel. LC 98-35255. (Illus.). 368p. 1999. 24.95 (*0-393-04697-4*) Norton.

***Dubus, Andre, III.** House of Sand & Fog: A Novel. LC 99-44258. 365p. 2000. pap. 14.00 (*0-375-70841-3*) Vin Bks.

Dubus, Andre. The Last Worthless Evening: Four Novellas & Two Stories. LC 85-45530. 288p. 1986. 13.95 (*0-87923-642-6*) Godine.

— The Last Worthless Evening: Four Novellas & Two Stories. LC 86-45530. 288p. 1986. reprint ed. pap. 12.95 (*1-56792-067-5*) Godine.

— Meditations from a Movable Chair. large type ed. 234p. Date not set. 30.00 (*0-7862-1723-5*) Thorndike Pr.

***Dubus, Andre.** Meditations from a Movable Chair: Essays. (Vintage Contemporaries Ser.). 210p. 1999. pap. 12.00 (*0-679-75115-7*) Knopf.

— Meditations from a Movable Chair: Essays. LC 97-50551. 209p. 1998. 3.99 (*0-679-43108-X*) Random.

Dubus, Andre. Selected Stories. 496p. 1995. pap. 14.00 (*0-679-76730-4*) Random.

— Separate Flights. LC 74-25955. 224p. 1975. reprint ed. pap. 10.95 (*0-87923-123-8*) Godine.

— The Times Are Never So Bad. LC 82-48703. 192p. 1986. pap. 13.95 (*0-87923-641-8*) Godine.

— Voices from the Moon: A Novel. LC 84-47652. 160p. 1984. 12.95 (*0-87923-532-2*) Godine.

Dubus, Andre, et al. Four Sad Tales: Leslie in California; Final Grace; Window; Happily Ever After, 4 vols. (Illus.). 36p. (Orig.). 1988. pap. 32.00 (*0-913559-04-0*) Birch Brook Pr.

Dubus, Elizabeth N. Cajun: A Novel. (Arcadia Ser.). 394p. 1994. reprint ed. pap. 11.95 (*0-9636307-2-5*) Levee Pr LA.

Duby. Investigation Women 12th Century. Birrell, Jean, tr. LC 97-14198. 112p. 1997. lib. bdg. 45.00 (*0-226-16776-3*) U Ch Pr.

***Duby.** Women of 12th Century, Vol. 2. Birrell, Jean, tr. LC 98-139809. 144p. 1999. lib. bdg. 45.00 (*0-226-16783-6*) U Ch Pr.

— Women of 12th Century, Vol. 3. Vol. 3. 128p. 1998. pap. text 14.00 (*0-226-16786-0*) U Ch Pr.

— Women of 12th Century, Vol.2. Birrell, Jean, tr. LC 98-139809. 144p. 1999. pap. text 17.00 (*0-226-16784-4*) U Ch Pr.

Duby, George. Fondement d'un Nouvel Humanisme. (FRE., Illus.). lib. bdg. 150.00 (*0-8288-3948-4*) Fr & Eur.

Duby, Georges. The Age of the Cathedrals: Art & Society, 980-1420. Levieux, Eleanor & Thompson, Barbara, trs. LC 80-22769. (Illus.). vi, 320p. (C). 1983. pap. 17.95 (*0-226-16770-4*) U Ch Pr.

***Duby, Georges.** Art & Society in the Middle Ages. LC 99-58799.Tr. of Art et Societe Au Moyen Age. 128p. 2000. text 54.95 (*0-7456-2173-2*, Pub. by Polity Pr); pap. text 19.95 (*0-7456-2174-0*, Pub. by Polity Pr) Blackwell Pubs.

Duby, Georges. The Chivalrous Society. Postan, Cynthia, tr. from FRE. LC 74-81431. 254p. 1978. pap. 16.95 (*0-520-04271-9*, Pub. by U CA Pr) Cal Prin Full Svc.

— The Early Growth of the European Economy: Warriors & Peasants from the Seventh to the Twelfth Century. Clarke, Howard B., tr. from FRE. LC 73-16955. (World Economic History Ser.). 292p. 1978. pap. text 14.95 (*0-8014-9169-X*) Cornell U Pr.

— France in the Middle Ages, 987-1460: From Hugh Capet to Joan of Arc. Vale, Juliet, tr. from FRE. (History of France Ser.). 600p. (C). 1993. pap. text 29.95 (*0-631-18945-9*) Blackwell Pubs.

— Guerriers et Paysans. VIIe-XIIe Siecles: Premier Essor de l'Economie Europeenne. (Tel Ser.: No. 24). (FRE.). 308p. 1973. pap. 17.95 (*2-07-029542-7*) Schoenhof.

— Histoire de la France des Origines a Nos Jours. (FRE.). 1214p. 1995. 49.95 (*0-7859-9302-9*) Fr & Eur.

— History Continues. Goldhammer, Arthur, tr. LC 94-3893. 168p. 1994. 24.95 (*0-226-16775-5*) U Ch Pr.

— History Continues. Goldhammer, Arthur, tr. xvi, 150p. 1997. pap. text 14.95 (*0-226-16782-8*) U Ch Pr.

— History of Women in the West Vol. 4: Emerging Feminism from Revolution to World War, Vol. 4. Perrot, Michelle & Fraisse, Genevieve, eds. 1993. 29.95 (*0-674-40373-8*) Belknap Pr.

— The Knight, the Lady & the Priest: The Making of Modern Marriage in Medieval France. Bray, Barbara, tr. xx, 332p. 1993. pap. text 14.95 (*0-226-16768-2*) U Ch Pr.

— Love & Marriage in the Middle Ages. 232p. (C). 1996. reprint ed. pap. 14.95 (*0-226-16774-7*) U Ch Pr.

— Male Middle Age. 224p. 1993. 37.50 (*0-226-16773-9*) U Ch Pr.

— Medieval Marriage: Two Models from Twelfth-Century France. Forster, Elborg, tr. from FRE. LC 77-17255. (Johns Hopkins Symposia in Comparative History Ser.). 160p. 1991. reprint ed. pap. text 12.95 (*0-8018-4319-7*) Johns Hopkins.

— Rural Economy & Country Life in the Medieval West. LC 68-119833. xv, 600p. 1968. write for info. (0-7131-5120-X) OUP.

— Rural Economy & Country Life in the Medieval West. LC 98-20958. (Middle Ages Ser.). 632p. 1998. pap. 24.95 (0-8122-1674-1) U of Pa Pr.

— The Three Orders: Feudal Society Imagined. Goldhammer, Arthur, tr. LC 80-13158. 392p. 1980. 38.50 (0-226-16771-2, PHOEN) U Ch Pr.

— The Three Orders: Feudal Society Imagined. Goldhammer, Arthur, tr. LC 80-13158. 392p. 1982. pap. text 23.95 (0-226-16772-0) U Ch Pr.

— William Marshal: The Flower of Chivalry. 1987. pap. text. write for info. (0-07-541642-5) McGraw.

— William Marshal: The Flower of Chivalry. Howard, Richard, tr. from FRE. LC 85-42837. 136p. 1987. pap. 12.00 (0-394-75154-X) Pantheon.

— Women of the 12th Century: Eve & the Church. Birrell, Jean, tr. LC 97-14198. 104p. 1997. pap. 15.95 (0-226-16780-1) U Ch Pr.

— Women of the 12th Century: Eve & the Church, Vol. 3. 1998. lib. bdg. 30.00 (0-226-16785-2) U Ch Pr.

Duby, Georges, et al, eds. A History of Women in the West Vol. 3: Renaissance & Enlightenment Paradoxes, Vol. III. (Illus.). 608p. 1995. pap. 16.95 (0-674-40367-3, DAVHIX) Belknap Pr.

— A History of Women in the West Vol. III: Renaissance & Enlightenment Paradoxes, Vol. 3. (Illus.). 576p. (C). 1993. 29.95 (0-674-40372-X) Belknap Pr.

— History of Women in the West Vol. 5: Toward a Cultural Identity in the Twentieth Century, Vol. 5. 725p. (C). 1994. 29.95 (0-674-40374-6) Belknap Pr.

— History of Women in the West, Vol. 1: From Ancient Goddesses to Christian Saints. Goldhammer, Arthur, tr. from FRE. 572p. (C). 1994. pap. text 15.95 (0-674-40369-X) Belknap Pr.

Duby, Georges & Aries, Philippe, eds. A History of Private Life Vol. II: Revelations of the Medieval World, Vol. 2. Goldhammer, Arthur, tr. LC 86-18286. (Illus.). 672p. 1988. text 39.95 (0-674-39976-5) Belknap Pr.

— A History of Private Life Vol. II: Revelations of the Medieval World, Vol. 2. Goldhammer, Arthur, tr. (Illus.). 672p. (C). 1988. pap. text 19.95 (0-674-40001-1) Belknap Pr.

Duby, Georges & Pantel, Pauline S., eds. A History of Women in the West, Vol. I: From Ancient Goddesses to Christian Saints. Goldhammer, Arthur, tr. from FRE. (Illus.). 572p. (C). 1992. text 29.95 (0-674-40370-3) Belknap Pr.

Duby, Georges & Perrot, Michelle. Power & Beauty: Images of Women in Art. (Illus.). 192p. 1995. 50.00 (1-85043-612-6, Pub. by I B T) St Martin.

Duby, Georges, ed. see Aris, Philippe A.

Duby, P., jt. auth. see Gulley, D. A.

Duby, P. F., ed. see H.H. Kellogg International Symposium, Quantitative.

Dubyagin. Concise English-Russian & Russian-English Dictionary of the Underworld. (ENG & RUS.). 282p. 1993. 49.95 (0-7859-9227-8) Fr & Eur.

Duc Do, Hien. The Vietnamese Americans. LC 99-22706. (New Americans Ser.). 168p. 1999. 39.95 (0-313-29780-0, GR9780, Greenwood Pr) Greenwood.

Duc, Don R. Le, see Teeter, Dwight L., Jr. & Le Duc, Don R.

Duc, G., ed. Energy Metabolism, Nutrition & Growth in Premature Infants. (Journal: Biology of the Neonate: Vol. 52, Supplement 1). vi, 148p. 1988. pap. 46.25 (3-8055-4731-5) S Karger.

Duc, Nguyen Q., jt. ed. see Balaban, John.

Duca, Alfred M. & Loscutoff, Lynn L. The Best of Acrylic Painting. (Illus.). 144p. 1996. 24.99 (1-56496-268-7, Quarry Bks) Rockport Pubs.

Duca, Diane J. Nonprofit Boards: Roles, Responsibilities & Performances. LC 96-23264. 192p. 1996. 29.95 (0-471-13020-6) Wiley.

Duca, Louis F. Del, see Del Duca, Louis F.

Duca, Victoria, ed. see Rossie, John P.

Ducamp, Emmanuel, ed. Pavlovsk, 2 vols. (Illus.). 236p. boxed set 225.00 (2-909838-03-X, Pub. by A Gourcuff) Antique Collect.

Ducamp, Marc, jt. auth. see Reverchon, Alain.

Ducantman, Barbara S., jt. auth. see Cibas, Edmund S.

Ducas. Decline & Fall of Byzantium to the Ottoman Turks. annot. ed. Magoulias, Harry J., tr. & anno. by. LC 75-9949.Tr. of Historia Turco-Byzantina. (Illus.). 347p. reprint ed. pap. 107.60 (0-7837-3611-8, 204347700009) Bks Demand.

Ducas, Theodorus II. Opuscula Rhetorica. Tartaglia, L., ed. (Illus.). 320p. (C). text 100.00 (3-519-01863-2) B G Teubner.

***Ducasse, Alain.** America: Lands of Excellence. (Illus.). 2000. text 24.95 (2-84323-191-4, Pub. by Assouline) St Martin.

Ducasse, Alain & Dannenberg, Linda. Ducasse Flavors of France. LC 98-6963. (Illus.). 264p. 1998. 50.00 (1-57965-107-0, 85107) Artisan.

***Ducasse, Alain, et al.** L' Atelier of Alain Ducasse: The Artistry of a Master Chef & His Proteges. LC 99-86285. 250p. 2000. text 60.00 (0-471-37673-6) Wiley.

Ducasse, C. J. Paranormal Phenomena, Science, & Life after Death. LC 79-76282. (Parapsychological Monographs: No. 8). 1969. reprint ed. pap. 6.00 (0-912328-12-6) Parapsych Foun.

Ducasse, Isidore L., see Lautreamont, Comte D., pseud.

Ducastel, F. & Sofaer, E. Tropospheric Radiowave Propagation Beyond the Horizon. LC 65-16853. (International Series of Monographs in Electromagnetic Wave: Vol. 8). 1966. 125.00 (0-08-010974-8, Pub. by Pergamon Repr) Franklin.

Ducastelle, F., ed. Order & Phase Stability in Alloys. (Cohesion & Structure Ser.: Vol. 3). xiv, 512p. 1991. 216.50 (0-444-86973-5, North Holland) Elsevier.

Ducat. Constitutional Interpretation. 7th ed. LC 99-30165. (Political Science Ser.). 1999. 90.95 (0-534-52718-3) Wadsworth Pub.

***Ducat.** Constitutional Interpretation 2000. annuals 7th ed. (Political Science Ser.). 2000. suppl. ed. 18.00 (0-534-52720-5) Wadsworth Pub.

Ducat, Craig R. Constitutional Interpretation. 6th ed. LC 95-30453. 1600p. (C). 1995. 57.25 (0-314-05767-6) West Pub.

— Constitutional Interpretation. 6th ed. 100p. 1995. pap., suppl. ed. 19.00 (0-314-07015-X) West Pub.

— Constitutional Interpretation: Powers of the Government, Vol. 1. 7th ed. (Political Science Ser.). 1999. 54.95 (0-534-52713-2) Wadsworth Pub.

— Constitutional Interpretation: 1994 Supplement. 5th ed. Hannan, ed. 200p. 1995. pap. text 23.25 (0-314-04343-8) West Pub.

— Constitutional Interpretation: 1996 Supplement. 6th ed. (Political Science Ser.). 1996. pap. 16.50 (0-314-20626-4) Wadsworth Pub.

— Constitutional Interpretation Vol. 1: Powers of Government. 6th ed. 600p. 1995. 35.00 (0-314-06300-5) West Pub.

— Constitutional Interpretation Vol. 2: Rights of the Individual. 6th ed. 1000p. 1995. 35.00 (0-314-06301-3) West Pub.

— Constitutional Interpretation Vol. 2: Rights of the Individual. 7th ed. (Political Science Ser.). 1999. 54.95 (0-534-52714-0) Wadsworth Pub.

— Constitutional Interpretation, 1992 Supplement to. 5th ed. 100p. (C). 1992. pap. text 18.25 (0-314-01136-6) West Pub.

Ducat, Craig R. & Chase, Harold W. Constitutional Interpretation. 5th ed. Hannan, ed. 1503p. (C). 1992. text 65.25 (0-314-93366-2) West Pub.

— Constitutional Interpretation: Powers of Government. 5th ed. Hannan, ed. 900p. (C). 1992. pap. text 33.25 (0-314-93455-3) West Pub.

— Constitutional Interpretation: Rights of Individuals. 5th ed. Hannan, ed. 900p. (C). 1992. pap. text 42.50 (0-314-93456-1) West Pub.

Ducat, Craig R., ed. see Corwin, Edward S.

Ducat, Diane. Turning Points: The Career Guide for the New Century. LC 98-23017. (Illus.). 328p. 1998. pap. text 31.60 (0-13-727702-4) P-H.

Ducatel, Ken, ed. Employment & Technical Change in Europe: Work Organization, Skills & Training. 272p. 1994. 95.00 (1-85278-775-9) E Elgar.

***Ducatel, Ken, et al, eds.** The Information Society in Europe: Work & Like in an Age of Globalization. LC 99-48272. (Critical Media Studies). 320p. 2000. pap. 27.95 (0-8476-9590-5); text 71.00 (0-8476-9589-1) Rowman.

Ducatel, Ken, jt. ed. see Hepworth, Mark E.

Ducatenzeiler, Graciela, jt. auth. see Oxhorn, Philip.

Duce, D., ed. Distributed Computing Systems Programme. (Computing Ser.: No. 4). 320p. 1984. boxed set 75.00 (0-86341-023-5, CM004) INSPEC Inc.

Duce, D. A., et al, eds. User Interface Management & Design: Proceedings of the Workshop on User Interface Management Systems & Environments Lisbon, Portugal, June 4-6, 1990. (Eurographic Seminars Ser.). (Illus.). 344p. 1991. 82.95 (0-387-53454-7) Spr-Verlag.

Duce, Ivy O. How a Master Works. LC 75-17037. 791p. 1975. 17.95 (0-915828-01-4) Sufism Reoriented.

— What Am I Doing Here. LC 66-25818. 59p. 1978. reprint ed. pap. 1.20 (0-915828-05-7) Sufism Reoriented.

Duce, Joan, compiled by. Remember If You Will. large type ed. (Mainstream Ser.). 163p. 1988. reprint ed. 18.95 (1-85089-260-1, Pub. by ISIS Lrg Prnt) Transaction Pubs.

Duce, Robert A., jt. ed. see Liss, Peter S.

Duce, William. The Fine Art of Small Scale Woodturning. LC 98-40914. (Illus.). 1999. pap. 19.95 (0-8069-6301-8) Sterling.

Duceau, Eric. Microcomputer Dictionary: Dictionnaire Micro-Informatique. (FRE.). 191p. 1986. pap. 39.95 (0-7859-4743-4) Fr & Eur.

D'Ucel, Jeanne. Berber Art: An Introduction. LC NK1082.U3. (Illus.). 227p. reprint ed. pap. 70.40 (0-8357-7136-9, 200477200047) Bks Demand.

Ducellier, Alain. L' Albanie entre Byzance et Venise: Xe-XVe Siecles. (Collected Studies: No. CS248). (Illus.). 346p. (C). 1987. reprint ed. 124.95 (0-86078-196-8, Pub. by Variorum) Ashgate Pub Co.

DuCellier, Judith L., jt. auth. see Duke, James A.

Ducey, James E. Birds of the Untamed West: The History of Birdlife in Nebraska, 1750-1875. (Illus.). 303p. 1999. pap. 20.00 (0-9631699-5-5) Making Hist.

Duch, Barbara J., ed. see Allen, Deborah E.

Duch, K. Handbook of Cookery. (FRE, GER & ITA.). 1985. 75.00 (0-8288-7719-X) Fr & Eur.

Duch, Karl. Concise Encyclopedia of Culinary Terms, English, French, German, Italian: English, French, German, Italian. (ENG, FRE, GER & ITA.). 1110p. 1993. 150.00 (0-7859-9977-9) Fr & Eur.

***Duch, Mabel.** Easy-to-Make Puppets. Orig. Title: Primarily Puppets. (Illus.). 1999. pap. 22.20 (0-7857-2001-4) Econo-Clad Bks.

Duch, Mabel. Easy-to-Make Puppets. LC 93-15320. Orig. Title: Primarily Puppets. (Illus.). 64p. (J). (gr. 3-8). 1993. reprint ed. pap. 10.95 (0-8238-0300-7) Kalmbach.

Duch, Robert G. Successful Parish Leadership: Nurturing the Animated Parish. LC 89-64499. 224p. (Orig.). (C). 1990. pap. 12.95 (1-55612-353-1) Sheed & Ward WI.

Duch, W. GRMS or Graphical Representation of Model Spaces - Basics, Vol. 1. (Lecture Notes in Chemistry Ser.: Vol. 42). v, 189p. 1986. 32.95 (0-387-17169-X) Spr-Verlag.

Duchac, Joseph. Poems of Emily Dickinson: An Annotated Guide to the Commentary in English, 1978-1989. (G. K. Hall Reference Ser.). 525p. 1993. 70.00 (0-8161-7352-4, G K Hall & Co) Mac Lib Ref.

Duchac, Rene. La Sociologie des Migrations aux Etats-Unis Societe, Mouvements Sociaux & Ideologies. (Premier Serie, Etudes: No. 15). 1974. pap. 49.25 (90-279-7191-9) Mouton.

Duchacek, Ivo D. Nations & Men: An Introduction to International Politics. 3rd ed. LC 81-40916. 608p. 1982. reprint ed. pap. text 39.00 (0-8191-2260-2) U Pr of Amer.

Duchacek, Ivo D., et al, eds. Perforated Sovereignties & International Relations: Trans-Sovereign Contracts of Subnational Governments, 211. LC 87-36092. (Contributions in Political Science Ser.: No. 211). 256p. 1988. 65.00 (0-313-26180-6, DPD/) Greenwood.

Duchaine, Nina. The Literature of Police Corruption: A Selected, Annotated Bibliography, Vol. II. LC 76-30895. 1979. 12.50 (0-89444-008-X) John Jay Pr.

Duchak, Alicia. A-Z of Modern America. LC 98-34384. 1999. 75.00 (0-415-18755-9); pap. 24.99 (0-415-18756-7) Routledge.

Duchak, Kathleen D. The Three Bears. (Illus.). 28p. (J). (ps). 1994. 15.00 (0-9640865-0-6) Family Pubng.

Duchamp, jt. auth. see Pauli.

Duchamp, Marcel. Affectueusement, Marcel: Marcel Duchamp: The Selected Correspondence. Naumann, Francis M., ed. (Illus.). 448p. 1999. 39.50 (90-5544-249-6, Pub. by Ludion) Dist Art Pubs.

— Manual of Instructions for Etant Donnes: Il la Chuted'eau, Z'Legaz D'Eclairage. (Illus.). 56p. 1987. 40.00 (0-87633-072-3) Phila Mus Art.

***Duchamp, Marcel.** Marcel Duchamp: Respirateur. 2000. 39.95 (3-7757-0895-2) Gerd Hatje.

— Notes. Matisse, Paul, ed. & tr. by. from FRE. (Illus.). 128p. 2000. reprint ed. pap. 13.95 (1-878972-34-0, Pub. by Exact Change) Consort Bk Sales.

Duchamp, Marcel, jt. auth. see Naumann, Francis M.

Duchan. Filing Business Names, Bk. 2. 2nd ed. (KG - Filing/Records Management Ser.). 1982. mass mkt. 11.25 (0-538-25140-9) S-W Pub.

— Filing Names of People, Bk. 1. 2nd ed. (KG - Filing/Records Management Ser.). 1982. mass mkt. 11.25 (0-538-25130-1) S-W Pub.

Duchan & Schultheis. Filing Names of People Bk. ... 2nd ed. 1982. teacher ed. 13.50 (0-538-29872-3) S-W Pub.

Duchan, Judith F. Supporting Language Learning in Everyday Life. LC 94-29227. (School-Age Children Ser.). 224p. (Orig.). (C). 1994. pap. text 44.95 (1-56593-221-8, 0581) Thomson Learn.

Duchan, Judith F., et al, eds. Deixis in Narrative: A Cognitive Science Perspective. 536p. 1995. pap 55.00 (0-8058-1463-9); text 99.95 (0-8058-1462-0) L Erlbaum Assocs.

— Pragmatics: From Theory to Practice. LC 93-10009. 214p. 1993. pap. 55.00 (0-13-678988-9) P-H.

Duchane, Emma, ed. User's Manual, Advanced Fortran IV Utilities for Data General Computers. (Illus.). viii, 223p. 1980. pap. 20.00 (0-938876-03-1) Entropy Ltd.

DuCharme, Bob. The Operating Systems Handbook: UNIX, Open VMS, OS-400, VM & MVS. 1994. 49.50 (0-07-017891-7) McGraw.

Ducharme, Dede F. The Treasure in the Tiny Blue Tin. LC 97-15419. (Chaparral Books for Young Readers). (J). (gr. 5-8). 1998. pap. 11.95 (0-87565-180-1) Tex Christian.

Ducharme, Edward R. The Lives of Teacher Educators. 144p. (C). 1993. text 22.00 (0-8077-3257-5) Tchrs Coll.

Ducharme, Edward R., et al. Capturing the Vision: Reflections on NCATE's Redesign Five Years After. 1993. 14.00 (0-89333-105-8) AACTE.

Ducharme, Edward R., jt. ed. see Carlson, Robert V.

Ducharme, Edward R., jt. ed. see Wisniewski, Richard.

Ducharme, Elaine. Must I Turn the Other Cheek: Premature Forgiveness Obstructs Recovery from Sexual Abuse. 128p. pap. write for info. (0-9701695-0-7) den an prodns.

Ducharme, Jerry, tr. see Desbonnets, Theophile.

Ducharme, Louis, jt. ed. see De La Mothe, John.

***DuCharme, Mark.** Desire Series. 24p. 1999. pap. 5.00 (1-880743-12-4) Dead Metaphor.

— Near To. (Poetry New York Pamphlet Ser.: No. 25). 16p. 1999. pap. 5.00 (0-923389-41-5) Meet Eyes Bind.

Ducharme, Raymond, Jr., et al. A Bibliography for Teachers of Social Studies. LC 68-18106. (Social Studies Sources). 43p. reprint ed. pap. 30.00 (0-8357-7173-3, 202600700048) Bks Demand.

Ducharme, Raymond A., jt. ed. see Fink, Lawrence A.

Ducharme, Rejean. L' Avalee Des Avales. (FRE.). 1984. pap. 12.95 (0-7859-2005-6, 2070376222) Fr & Eur.

***Ducharme, Rejean.** The Daughter of Christopher Columbus. Browning, Will, tr. from FRE. (Prose Ser.: No. 44).Tr. of Jille de Christophe Columbe. 200p. 2000. pap. 18.00 (1-55071-106-7, , Pub. by Guernica Editions) Paul & Co Pubs.

Ducharme, Rejean. L' Hiver de Force. (FRE.). 283p. 1973. pap. 19.95 (0-7859-1670-9, 2070285006) Fr & Eur.

Ducharme, Robert. Art & Idea in the Novels of Bernard Malamud: Toward "The Fixer" (Studies in American Literature: No. 13). 1974. pap. text 37.70 (90-279-3212-3) Mouton.

***Ducharme, Robert.** XML: The Annotated Specification. 368p. 1999. pap. 44.99 (0-13-096275-9) Prntice Hall Bks.

— XML: The Annotated Specifications. 368p. 1998. pap. text 44.99 (0-13-082676-6, Prentice Hall) P-H.

Ducharme, Stephen & Stasiak, James W., eds. Organic Photorefractive Materials & Xerographic Photoreceptors, Vol. 2850. 218p. 1996. 56.00 (0-8194-2238-X) SPIE.

***Ducharme, Stephen & Stasiak, James W., eds.** Xerographic Photoreceptors & Organic Photoreactive Materials IV, Vol. #347. 1998. 69.00 (0-8194-2926-0) SPIE.

Ducharme, Stephen & Stasiak, James W., eds. Xerographic Photoreceptors & Organic Photoreactive Materials II. LC 98-122017. 246p. 1997. 59.00 (0-8194-2566-4) SPIE.

Ducharme, Allan, tr. see Requena, Yves.

Ducharte, Pierre L. Italian Comedy: The Improvisation, Scenarios, Lives, Attributes, Portraits & Masks of the Illustrious Characters of the Commedia Dell'arte. (Illus.). 1966. pap. 16.95 (0-486-21679-9) Dover.

Duchateau, Armand. Benin: Royal Art of Africa from the Museum Fur Volkerkunde, Vienna. LC 93-33986. 1994. 30.00 (0-89090-058-2) Mus Fine TX.

DuChateau, Paul. The Cauchy-Goursat Problem. LC 52-42839. (Memoirs Ser.: No. 1/118). 60p. 1972. pap. 16.00 (0-8218-1818-X, MEMO/1/118) Am Math.

Duchateau, Paul. Parameter Identification & Inverse Problems in Hydrology, Geology & Ecology. Gottlieb, Johannes, ed. LC 96-18938. (Water Science & Technology Library). 309p. (C). 1996. text 158.50 (0-7923-4089-2) Kluwer Academic.

DuChateau, Paul C. & Zachmann, D. W. Schaum's Outline of Partial Differential Equations. 256p. (C). 1986. pap. 14.95 (0-07-017897-6) McGraw.

Duchatelet, Bernard, ed. & pref. see Suares, Andre.

***Duchatschek, Mason.** Sales Utopia: How to Get the Right People, Doing the Right Things, Enough Times. LC 99-90793. (Illus.). 112p. 1999. pap. 14.95 (0-9674377-0-9) Perform Pr World.

***Duchaufour.** Handbook of Pedology. 274p. 1998. 66.00 (90-5410-782-0) Ashgate Pub Co.

Duchein, Michel, ed. Archives & Genealogical Sciences. (Archivum - International Review on Archives Ser.: Vol. 37). 254p. 1992. 58.00 (3-598-21237-2) K G Saur Verlag.

— International Review on Archives: Archive Legislation: Countries A-K, 40. 350p. 1995. 75.00 (3-598-21240-2) K G Saur Verlag.

Duchemin. Chateaubriand: Essais de Critique et d'Histoire. 23.75 (0-7859-0620-7, F58980) Fr & Eur.

Duchen, Claire. Feminism in France: From May '68 to Mitterand. 192p. (Orig.). (C). 1986. pap. 20.99 (0-7102-0455-8, Routledge Thoemms) Routledge.

— Women's Rights & Women's Lives in France, 1944-1968. LC 93-30843. 224p. (C). 1994. pap. 25.99 (0-415-00934-0) Routledge.

Duchen, Claire, ed. French Connections: Voices from the Women's Movement in France. LC 86-11347. 160p. 1987. text 22.50 (0-87023-547-8); pap. text 14.95 (0-87023-548-6) U of Mass Pr.

***Duchen, Claire & Bandhauer-Schhoffmann, Irene.** When the War Was Over: Women, War & Peace in Europe, 1940-1956. LC 00-21836. 2000. pap. write for info. (0-7185-0180-2, Pub. by Leicester U Pr) Cassell & Continuum.

Duchen, Jessica. Erich Wolfgang Korngold. LC 96-196289. (Twentieth Century Composers Ser.). (Illus.). 240p. 1996. pap. text 19.95 (0-7148-3155-7, Pub. by Phaidon Press) Phaidon Pr.

***Duchen, Jessica.** Gabriel Faure. (20th-Century Composers Ser.). (Illus.). 2000. pap. 24.95 (0-7148-3932-9) Phaidon Pr.

Duchene, A. S., et al, eds. The IRPA Guidelines on Protection Against Non-Ionizing Radiation. 129p. 1991. text 39.50 (0-07-105264-X) McGraw-Hill HPD.

Duchene, Francois. The Case of the Helmeted Airman: A Study of W. H. Auden's Poetry. LC 72-170234. 288p. 1972. write for info. (0-7011-1785-0) Chatto & Windus.

— Economic & Monetary Union in Europe. (New Ser.: No. 19). 1998. pap. 15.00 (0-86682-125-2) Ctr Intl Relations.

Duchene, Herve. Golden Treasures of Troy: The Dream of Heinrich Schliemann. Leggatt, Jeremy, tr. LC 95-79942. (Discoveries Ser.). (Illus.). 144p. 1996. pap. text 12.95 (0-8109-2825-6, Pub. by Abrams) Time Warner.

Duchene, Roger, ed. see Sevigne, Mme De.

Duchenen, Raphael, ed. see Sevigne, Mme De.

Duchesne, Alain. La Surprise, Larousse Dictionnaire des Sens Perdus. (FRE.). 288p. 1991. pap. 45.00 (0-7859-7642-6, 2033300315) Fr & Eur.

***Duchesne, Christiane.** Edmund & Amanda. LC 99-900525. 1999. 7.95 (1-894363-17-5) Doml & Friends.

Duchesne, Christiane. L' Ete Des Tordus. (Novels in the Premier Roman Ser.). (FRE.). 64p. (J). (gr. 2-5). 1996. pap. 7.95 (2-89021-176-2, Pub. by Les Editions) Firefly Bks Ltd.

Duchesne, Christiane. Lazarus Laughs. 13p. (J). 1977. pap. 5.95 (0-88862-157-4, Pub. by J Lorimer) Formac Dist Ltd.

— Lazarus Laughs. Allison, Rosemary, tr. from FRE. (Illus.). 13p. (J). 1977. 10.95 (0-88862-156-6, Pub. by J Lorimer) Formac Dist Ltd.

Duchesne, Christiane. Loonie Summer. (First Novels Ser.). (Illus.). 60p. (J). (gr. 1-4). 1995. mass mkt. 3.99 (0-88780-272-9, Pub. by Formac Publ Co); bds. 14.95 (0-88780-273-7, Pub. by Formac Publ Co) Formac Dist Ltd.

— The Loonies Arrive. (First Novels Ser.). (Illus.). 61p. (J). (gr. 1-4). 1995. mass mkt. 3.99 (0-88780-206-0, Pub. by Formac Publ Co); bds. 14.95 (0-88780-207-9, Pub. by Formac Publ Co) Formac Dist Ltd.

***Duchesne, Christiane & Marois, Carmen.** Cyrus, L'encyclopedie Racontee, Vol. 2. (Children's French Ser.).Tr. of Cyrus, the Storytelling Encyclopedia. (FRE., Illus.). 48p. (J). (gr. k-12). 2000. pap. 12.95 incl. audio (2-89517-034-7, Pub. by Coffragants) Penton Overseas.

— Cyrus, L'encyclopedie Racontee, Vol. 2. (Children's

D

French Ser.).Tr. of Cyrus, the Storytelling Encyclopedia. (FRE., Illus.). 48p. (YA). (gr. k-12). 2000. pap. 12.95 incl. audio (2-89517-030-4, Pub. by Coffragants) Penton Overseas.

— Cyrus, L'encyclopedie Racontee, Vol. 3. (Children's French Ser.).Tr. of Cyrus, the Storytelling Encyclopedia. (FRE.). 48p. (J). (gr. k-12). 2000. pap. 16.95 incl. audio compact disk (2-89517-035-5, Pub. by Coffragants) Penton Overseas.

Duchesne-Guillemin, J. The Western Response to Zoroaster. LC 72-9593. 112p. 1973. reprint ed. lib. bdg. 49.75 (0-8371-6590-3, DUWR, Greenwood Pr) Greenwood.

Duchesne-Guillemin, M. A Hurrian Musical Score from Ugarit: Sources & Monographs from the Ancient Near East, Vol. 2. (Sources & Monographs from the Ancient Near East). 32p. pap. 9.00 (0-89003-158-4) Undena Pubns.

Duchesne, Helen L. In Their Time. LC 97-95008. (Illus.). iv, 95p. 1997. pap. 11.95 (0-9661940-0-4) Bear Mtn.

Duchesne, Louis. Early History of the Christian Church from Its Foundations to the End of the Fifth Century, Vol. 1: To the End of the Third Century. 4th ed. Jenkins, Claude, tr. from FRE. 428p. 1965. 100.00 (0-614-00153-6); 100.00 (0-614-00258-3) Elliots Bks.

— Early History of the Christian Church from Its Foundations to the End of the Fifth Century, Vol. 3: The Fifth Century. Jenkins, Claude, tr. from FRE. 555p. 1960. 100.00 (0-614-00154-4); 100.00 (0-614-00259-1) Elliots Bks.

Duchesne, Lucie, tr. L'Autobus Magique Se Fait RtTir: Un Livre Sur les Deserts. (Magic School Bus Ser.).Tr. of Magic School Bus All Dried up: A Book about Deserts. (FRE., Illus.). 32p. (J). (gr. k-2). 1996. mass mkt. 5.99 (0-590-16043-5) Scholastic Inc.

Duchesne, Lucie, tr. see Beech, Linda.

Duchesne, Lucie, tr. see Herman, Gail.

Duchesne, Lucie, tr. see Nadler, Beth.

Duchesne, Lucie, tr. see Relf, Patricia.

Duchesne-Winter, Juan R. Narraciones de Testimonio en America Latina. 226p. 1992. pap. 11.50 (0-8477-3622-9) U of PR Pr.

Duchesneau, Claude & Veuthey, Michel. Music & Liturgy: The Universa Laus Document & Commentary. Inwood, Paul, tr. (Orig.). 1992. pap. text 9.95 (0-912405-98-8, Pastoral Press) OR Catholic.

Duchesneau, Claude, jt. auth. see Beguerie, Philippe.

Duchesneau, F. L' Empirisme de Locke. (International Archives of the History of Ideas Ser.: No. 57). 276p. 1973. lib. bdg. 112.50 (90-247-1349-8, Pub. by M Nijhoff) Kluwer Academic.

Duchesneau, Francois. La Physiologie des Lumieres: Empirisme, Modeles et Theories. 640p. 1982. lib. bdg. 287.50 (90-247-2500-3) Kluwer Academic.

***Duchess of Devonshire.** Garden at Chatsworth. 2000. 40.00 (0-670-89109-6) Viking Penguin.

Duchess of York. Dining with the Duchess: Making Everyday Meals a Special Occasion. 224p. 1997. 25.00 (0-02-862574-9, Pub. by Macmillan) S&S Trade.

Duchet-Suchaux, Gaston & Pastoureau, Michel. The Bible & the Saints. (Flammarion Iconographic Guides Ser.). (Illus.). 392p. 1994. pap. 24.95 (2-08-013564-3, Pub. by Flammarion) Abbeville Pr.

— The Bible & the Saints. (Flammarion Iconographic Guides Ser.). (Illus.). 392p. 1996. 45.00 (2-08-013575-9, Pub. by Flammarion) Abbeville Pr.

Ducheyne, P. & Christiansen, D. Bioceramics, Vol.6. 528p. 1994. text 135.00 (0-7506-1884-1) Buttrwrth-Heinemann.

Ducheyne, Paul & Hastings, Garth W., eds. Functional Behavior of Orthopedic Biomaterials, Vol. I. 176p. 1984. 105.00 (0-8493-6265-2, RD755, CRC Reprint) Franklin.

— Functional Behavior of Orthopedic Biomaterials, Vol. II. LC 83-3737. (Series in Structure Property Relationships of Biomaterials). 224p. 1984. 129.00 (0-8493-6266-0, RD755, CRC Reprint) Franklin.

— Metal & Ceramic Biomaterials: Strength & Surface, Vol. II. 184p. 1984. 108.00 (0-8493-6262-8, R857, CRC Reprint) Franklin.

— Metal & Ceramic Biomaterials: Structure, Vol. I. 136p. 1984. 83.00 (0-8493-6261-X, R857, CRC Reprint) Franklin.

Ducheyne, Paul, jt. ed. see Hastings, Garth W.

Duchin, Faye. Structural Economics: Measuring Change in Technology, Lifestyle & the Environment. LC 98-13576. 208p. 1998. text 35.00 (1-55963-606-8) Island Pr.

Duchin, Faye & Lange, Glenn-Marie. The Future of the Environment: Ecological Economic & Technical Change. LC 93-43254. (Illus.). 240p. (C). 1995. text 39.95 (0-19-508574-4) OUP.

— Trading Away Jobs: The Effects of the U. S. Merchandise Trade Deficit on Employment. (Working Papers: No. 102). 1990. 10.00 (0-944826-26-1) Economic Policy Inst.

Duchnowski, Albert J. Outcomes for Children & Youth with Emotional & Behavioral Disorders & Their Families: Programs & Evaluation Best Practices. Epstein, Michael H. & Kutash, Krista, eds. LC 97-21294. 1998. 44.00 (0-89079-750-1) PRO-ED.

Duchoissoir, A. R. The Fender Stratocaster. rev. ed. 72p. 1995. per. 14.95 (0-7935-4735-0, 00330027) H Leonard.

— The Fender Telecaster: The Detailed Story of America's Senior Solid Body Electric Guitar. 80p. 1991. otabind 14.95 (0-7935-0860-6, 00183003) H Leonard.

Duchon, Claude E., jt. auth. see Johnson, Howard L.

Duchon, P. Dictionary Patois Bourbonnais Canton de Varennes. (FRE.). 1978. reprint ed. 79.95 (0-320-00895-9) Fr & Eur.

Duchossoir, A. R. Gibson Electrics: the Classic Years: An Illustrated History from the Mid-30s to the Early 60s. (Illus.). 256p. 1998. otabind 24.95 (0-7935-9210-0) H Leonard.

***Duchossoir, A. R.** Guitar Identification: Fender - Gibson - Gretsch - Martin. 3rd ed. 56p. 1999. per. 9.95 (0-634-00672-X) H Leonard.

Duchossoir, Andre. Fender Stratocaster. (FRE., Illus.). 48p. 1985. reprint ed. pap. 6.95 (0-88188-388-3) H Leonard.

Duchovnay, Gerald. Humphrey Bogart: A Bio-Bibliography. LC 98-26538. (Popular Culture Bio-Bibliographies Ser.). 360p. 1999. lib. bdg. 69.50 (0-313-22338-6, Greenwood Pr) Greenwood.

Duchow, Paul G. & Meyers, Spike. Workbook & Exercises for Introduction to Computer Information Systems. 80p. (C). 1995. per. 15.95 (0-8403-9492-6) Kendall-Hunt.

Duchrow, Ulrich. Alternatives to Global Capitalism: Drawn from Biblical History, Designed for Political Action. 316p. (Orig.). 1998. reprint ed. pap. 19.95 (90-6224-976-0, Pub. by Uitgeverij Arkel) LPC InBook.

— Conflict over the Ecumenical Movement: Confessing Christ Today in the Universal Church. LC 81-196807. 463p. reprint ed. pap. 143.60 (0-7837-6009-4, 204581900008) Bks Demand.

Duchscherer, Paul. The Bungalow: America's Arts & Crafts Home. (Illus.). 128p. 1999. pap. 21.95 (0-14-025156-1, Viking Studio) Studio Bks.

— Inside Bungalow. LC 97-66505. 160p. 1997. 32.50 (0-670-87373-X) Viking Penguin.

— Outside the Bungalow: America's Arts & Crafts Garden. LC 99-70250. (Illus.). 192p. 1999. 32.95 (0-670-88355-7) Viking Penguin.

***Duchting, Hajo.** Cezanne. 1999. 19.99 (3-8228-7029-3) Benedikt Taschen.

Duchting, Hajo. Cezanne. (SPA.). 1996. pap. 19.99 (3-8228-0236-0) Taschen Amer.

— Delaunay. 1994. pap. 9.99 (3-8228-9327-7) Taschen Amer.

— Edouard Manet: Images of Parisian Life. (Pegasus Library). (Illus.). 128p. 1995. 25.00 (3-7913-1452-1, Pub. by Prestel) te Neues.

— Kandinsky. 1994. pap. 9.99 (3-8228-0542-4) Taschen Amer.

— Kandinsky. (SPA.). 1996. pap. 9.99 (3-8228-0225-5) Taschen Amer.

— Paul Klee: Painting Music. LC 97-36137. 128p. 1997. 25.00 (3-7913-1872-1, Pub. by Prestel) te Neues.

***Duchting, Hajo.** Seurat. 1999. pap. text 9.99 (3-8228-6510-9) Benedikt Taschen.

Duchy, George, jt. auth. see Westfall, Douglas.

***Ducibella, Jim.** Par Excellence: A Celebration of Virginia Golf. (Illus.). 256p. 2000. 29.95 (1-58261-103-3) Sports Pub.

Ducibella, Joseph W. Phonology of the Sicilian Dialects. LC 77-94206. (Catholic University of America. Studies in Romance Languages & Literatures: No. 10). reprint ed. 62.50 (0-404-50310-1) AMS Pr.

Ducie, Sonia. The Complete Illustrated Guide to Numerology: Using the Language of Numbers as a Personal Life Guide. (Illus.). 192p. 1999. pap. 19.95 (1-86204-568-2, Pub. by Element MA) Penguin Putnam.

***Ducie, Sonia.** Do It Yourself Numerology: How to Unlock the Secrets of Your Personality with Numbers. LC 98-29526. (Illus.). 224p. 1999. pap. 19.95 (1-86204-298-5, Pub. by Element MA) Penguin Putnam.

— Lucky Numbers Oracle: Discover the Power of Numerology. 2000. pap. 8.00 (0-7225-3880-4) Thorsons PA.

Ducie, Sonia. Numerology: Your Love & Relationship Guide. LC 98-55287. 208p. 1999. pap. 10.95 (1-86204-331-0, Pub. by Element MA) Penguin Putnam.

— Numerology: Your Personal Guide for Life. 178p. 1999. pap. 10.95 (1-86204-502-X, Pub. by Element MA) Penguin Putnam.

— Principles of Numerology: The Only Introduction You'll Ever Need. (Illus.). 160p. 1998. pap. 11.00 (0-7225-3580-5, Pub. by Thorsons MD) Natl Bk Netwk.

DuCille, Ann. Skin Trade. LC 96-16061. 240p. 1996. 32.50 (0-674-81081-3); pap. 16.95 (0-674-81084-8) HUP.

Duck, Daymond R. Daniel. LC 97-80894. (God's Word for the Biblically-Inept Ser.: Vol. 2). (Illus.). 352p. 1998. pap. 16.95 (0-914984-48-9) Starburst.

— On the Brink: Easy-to-Understand End-Time Bible Prophecy. LC 93-85140. 256p. 1995. pap. 11.95 (0-914984-58-6) Starburst.

***Duck, Daymond R.** Prophecies of the Bible. Richards, Larry, ed. (God's Word for the Biblically-Inept Ser.: No. 8). 352p. 2000. pap. 16.95 (1-892016-22-2, Pub. by Starburst) Natl Bk Netwk.

Duck, Daymond R. Revelation. Richards, Larry, ed. LC 97-68722. (God's Word for the Biblically-Inept Ser.: Vol. 1). (Illus.). 352p. 1997. pap. 16.95 (0-914984-98-5) Starburst.

Duck, Francis A. Physical Properties of Tissue: A Comprehensive Reference Work. (Illus.). 336p. 1990. text 94.00 (0-12-222800-6) Acad Pr.

Duck, Francis A., et al, eds. Ultrasound in Medicine. LC 98-48814. (Medical Science Ser.). 314p. 1998. 130.00 (0-7503-0593-2) IOP Pub.

Duck, Lloyd. Teaching with Charisma: A Teaching Styles Overview. (Illus.). 315p. (C). 1994. pap. text 19.95 (0-9639874-5-3) Chatelaine.

— Understanding American Education: Its Past, Practices & Promise. (Illus.). 480p. (Orig.). (C). 1996. pap. text 19.95 (0-9639874-8-8) Chatelaine.

Duck, Michael & Bishop, Peter. Data Communciations for Engineers. LC 97-112437. 270p. (C). 1996. pap. text 58.00 (0-201-42788-5) Addison-Wesley.

Duck, Peter W., ed. see Hall, Philip.

Duck, R. W., jt. ed. see McManus, J.

Duck, Ruth C. Circles of Care: Hymns & Songs. Clyde, Arthur G., ed. 144p. (Orig.). 1998. pap. 14.95 (0-8298-1204-0) Pilgrim OH.

— Finding Words for Worship: A Guide for Leaders. 160p. (Orig.). 1995. pap. 22.95 (0-664-25573-6) Westminster John Knox.

Duck, Ruth C., ed. Bread for the Journey: Resources for Worship. LC 81-5046. 96p. 1981. pap. 9.95 (0-8298-0423-4) Pilgrim OH.

— Flames of the Spirit. LC 85-6596. 128p. (Orig.). 1985. pap. 10.95 (0-8298-0537-0) Pilgrim OH.

Duck, Ruth C. & Tirabassi, Maren C., eds. Touch Holiness: Resources for Worship. LC 89-39435. 272p. (Orig.). 1990. pap. 14.95 (0-8298-0809-4) Pilgrim OH.

Duck, Ruth C., et al. Praising God: The Trinity in Christian Worship. LC 99-22981. 224p. 1999. pap. 22.00 (0-664-25777-1) Westminster John Knox.

Duck, Stephen W. Personal Relationships & Personal Constructs: A Study of Friendship Formation. LC 73-8193. 182p. reprint ed. pap. 56.50 (0-8357-9952-2, 201489800093) Bks Demand.

Duck, Steve. Human Relationships. 2nd ed. 288p. 1991. 49.95 (0-8039-8380-8); pap. 22.95 (0-8039-8381-6) Sage.

— Meaningful Relationships: Talking, Sense & Relating. (Series on Close Relationships: Vol. 8). 240p. (C). 1994. text 42.00 (0-8039-5702-5) Sage.

— Meaningful Relationships: Talking, Sense & Relating, No. 8. (Series on Close Relationships: Vol. 8). 240p. (C). 1994. pap. text 17.95 (0-8039-5703-3) Sage.

— Personal Relationships, Vol. 5. 1984. text 120.00 (0-12-222805-7) Acad Pr.

— Relating to Others. Manstead, Anthony S., ed. (Mapping Social Psychology Ser.). 192p. 1988. 42.50 (0-335-15339-9) OpUniv Pr.

— Relating to Others. 2nd ed. LC 98-36950. (Mapping Social Psychology Ser.). 1999. 75.00 (0-335-20164-4); pap. 24.95 (0-335-20163-6) OpUniv Pr.

— Social Context & Relationships. (Understanding Relationship Processes Ser.: Vol. 3). (Illus.). 184p. (C). 1993. text 39.95 (0-8039-5377-1); pap. text 18.95 (0-8039-5378-X) Sage.

— Understanding Relationships. LC 91-6658. 224p. 1991. pap. text 22.00 (0-89862-470-3) Guilford Pubns.

Duck, Steve, ed. Dynamics of Relationships. LC 93-48820. (Understanding Relationship Processes Ser.: Vol. 4). 1994. 39.95 (0-8039-5413-1); pap. 18.95 (0-8039-5414-X) Sage.

— Individuals in Relationships. (Understanding Relationship Processes Ser.: Vol. 1). (Illus.). 224p. (C). 1993. text 26.95 (0-8039-5156-6) Sage.

— Learning about Relationships. (Understanding Relationship Processes Ser.: Vol. 2). (Illus.). 224p. (C). 1993. text 39.95 (0-8039-5157-4); pap. text 18.95 (0-8039-5158-2) Sage.

— Personal Relationships Vol. 4: Dissolving Personal Relationships. 1982. text 120.00 (0-12-222804-9) Acad Pr.

Duck, Steve, et al, eds. Handbook of Personal Relationships: Theory, Research & Interventions. LC 96-10234. 896p. 1996. 234.95 (0-471-95913-8) Wiley.

Duck, Steve & Gilmour, Robin, eds. Personal Relationships Vol. 1: Studying Personal Relationships. LC 80-41360. 1981. text 120.00 (0-12-222801-4) Acad Pr.

— Personal Relationships Vol. 3: Personal Relationships in Disorder. LC 80-41360. 1981. text 120.00 (0-12-222803-0) Acad Pr.

Duck, Steve & Wood, Julia T. Confronting Relationship Challenges. (Understanding Relationship Processes Ser.: 5). 296p. 1995. text 39.95 (0-8039-5648-7); pap. text 21.95 (0-8039-5649-5) Sage.

Duck, Steve, jt. auth. see Mills, Rosemary S.

Duck, Steve, jt. auth. see Wood, Julia T.

Duck, Steve, jt. ed. see Montgomery, Barbara M.

Duck, Steve, jt. ed. see Perlman, Daniel.

Duck, Steven, jt. auth. see Perlman, Daniel.

Duckeck, Ghunter, jt. auth. see Hollik, W.

Ducker, Bruce. Bloodlines. LC 99-30774. 264p. 2000. 25.00 (1-57962-060-4) Permanent Pr.

— Failure at the Mission Trust. LC 86-25806. 275p. 1987. 16.95 (0-88191-046-5) Freundlich.

— Lead Us Not into Penn Station. LC 93-32742. 224p. 1994. 22.00 (1-877946-36-2) Permanent Pr.

— Marital Assets. LC 92-31161. 252p. 1993. 22.00 (1-877946-26-5) Permanent Pr.

Ducker, Carolyn A., jt. auth. see Hamilton, Kimberly A.

Ducker, James H. Men of the Steel Rails: Workers on the Atchison, Topeka & Santa Fe Railroad, 1869-1900. LC 82-17541. 244p. reprint ed. pap. 75.70 (0-7837-1839-X, 204204000001) Bks Demand.

Ducker, Kenneth J. & Kjerne, Daniel. Multipurpose Cadastre: Terms & Definitions. 12p. 1989. pap. 5.00 (0-614-06098-2, G428) Am Congrs Survey.

Ducker, Richard D. Subdivision Regulations in North Carolina: An Introduction. 16p. 1980. pap. 4.50 (1-56011-147-X) Institute Government.

Ducker, S. C. The Genus Chlorodesmis (Chlorophyta) in the Indo-Pacific Region. 1966. pap. 15.00 (3-7682-0511-8) Lubrecht & Cramer.

Ducker, Sophie C., ed. The Contented Botanist: Letters of W. H. Harvey about Australia & the Pacific. (The Miegunyah Press Ser.: No. 1:3). 430p. 1988. 69.95 (0-522-84341-7, Pub. by Melbourne Univ Pr) Paul & Co Pubs.

Ducker, T. B. & Brown, R. H., eds. Neurophysiology & Standards of Spinal Cord Monitoring. (Illus.). 400p. 1988. 127.00 (0-387-96634-X) Spr-Verlag.

Ducker, Thomas B., jt. ed. see Clark, Charles R.

Duckers, Alexander. George Grosz - The Graphic Work: Catalogue Raisonne. (ENG & GER., Illus.). 416p. 1996. reprint ed. 150.00 (1-55660-213-8) A Wofsy Fine Arts.

Duckers, Alexander, jt. auth. see Grosz, George.

Duckers, L. J. & Morton, J. Low Head Hydro-Electricity (C52) 57p. (C). 1988. 120.00 (0-7855-3810-0, Pub. by Interntl Solar Energy Soc) St Mut.

Duckers, L. J. & Morton, J., eds. Low Head Hydro-Electricity. (C). 1988. 125.00 (0-7855-4210-8, Pub. by Interntl Solar Energy Soc) St Mut.

Duckert, Audrey R., jt. auth. see Cassidy, Frederic G.

Duckert, Mary. Help! I'm a Sunday School Teacher. rev. ed. 128p. (Orig.). 1996. pap. 13.95 (1-57153-201-3) Curriculm Presbytrn KY.

— Who Touched the Remote Control? Television & Christian Choices for Children & Adults Who Care about Children. 1990. pap. 9.95 (0-377-00210-0) Friendship Pr.

— A World of Children's Games. LC 92-19619. (Illus.). 1993. pap. 19.95 (0-377-00261-5) Friendship Pr.

Duckert, Mary J., ed. see Fogle, Jeanne S.

Ducket, Mary Jean, ed. see Fogle, Jeanne S.

***Duckett.** 100 Secrets of the Carolina Coast. LC 99-86588. 288p. 2000. pap. write for info. (1-55853-813-5) Rutledge Hill Pr.

Duckett, Barbara, jt. auth. see Webb, Jane C.

***Duckett, Drew D.** Glimpses of Glory: The Regimental History of the 61st Illinois Volunteers. (Illus.). 170p. 1999. 18.50 (0-7884-1405-4, 1405) Heritage Bk.

Duckett, Eleanor S. Alfred the Great: The King & His England. LC 56-13050. 240p. 1958. pap. text 13.95 (0-226-16779-8, P29) U Ch Pr.

— Carolingian Portraits: A Study in the Ninth Century. (Ann Arbor Paperbacks Ser.). 320p. 1988. pap. text 17.95 (0-472-06157-7, 06157, Ann Arbor Bks) U of Mich Pr.

— Death & Life in the Tenth Century. (Ann Arbor Paperbacks Ser.). 376p. 1988. reprint ed. pap. 18.95 (0-472-06172-0, 06172, Ann Arbor Bks) U of Mich Pr.

— The Gateway to the Middle Ages: France & Great Britain. (Ann Arbor Paperbacks Ser.). 168p. 1988. reprint ed. pap. 17.95 (0-472-06050-3, 06050, Ann Arbor Bks) U of Mich Pr.

— The Gateway to the Middle Ages: Italy. (Ann Arbor Paperbacks Ser.). 240p. 1988. pap. 17.95 (0-472-06049-X, 06049, Ann Arbor Bks) U of Mich Pr.

— The Gateway to the Middle Ages: Monasticism. LC 61-2247. (Ann Arbor Paperbacks Ser.). 280p. 1988. pap. 17.95 (0-472-06051-1, 06051, Ann Arbor Bks) U of Mich Pr.

***Duckett, Eleanor S.** The Gateway to the Middle Ages: Monasticism. 262p. 1999. reprint ed. pap. text 15.00 (0-7881-6390-6) DIANE Pub.

Duckett, Jane. The Entrepreneurial State in China: Real Estate & Commerce Departments in Reform Era Tianjin. LC 98-2514. (Studies of China in Transition). 264p. (C). 1998. 90.00 (0-415-18741-9) Routledge.

Duckett, Judy B., et al, eds. Quality in Action. (Illus.). 90p. 1996. pap. text 55.00 (1-56395-063-4, PC97-960016) Am Assn Blood.

Duckett, Kermit E. A Laboratory Textbook for Introductory Astronomy. 5th ed. (Illus.). 320p. (Orig.). (C). 1998. pap. text, lab manual ed. 35.00 (0-89892-131-7) Contemp Pub Co of Raleigh.

Duckett, Margaret. Mark Twain & Bret Harte. LC 64-21709. (Illus.). 390p. reprint ed. 120.90 (0-8357-9734-1, 201009100068) Bks Demand.

Duckett, Maryellen, jt. auth. see Duckett, Randall.

Duckett, Michael J. Breaking the Money Barriers. 227p. 1999. pap. 19.95 (0-9668107-0-8, Pub. by Whitmire Pubg) ACCESS Pubs Network.

Duckett, Randall & Duckett, Maryellen. 100 Secrets of the Smokies. LC 98-5214. (Illus.). 224p. 1998. pap. 12.95 (1-55853-586-1) Rutledge Hill Pr.

Duckett, Serge. The Pathology of the Aging Human Nervous System. LC 90-6638. (Illus.). 505p. 1991. text 99.00 (0-8121-1355-1) Lppncott W & W.

Duckett, Serge, ed. Pediatric Neuropathology. LC 93-40970. (Illus.). 1500p. 1994. 169.00 (0-683-02680-1) Lppncott W & W.

***Duckett, Simon & Gilbert, Bruce.** Foundations of Spectroscopy. LC 99-43593. 1999. write for info. (0-19-850335-0) OUP.

Duckett, Steven W. Photoelectronic Processes & a Search for Exciton Mobility in Pure & Doped Alkali Halides. LC 79-135074. 145p. 1969. 25.00 (0-403-04496-0) Scholarly.

Duckham, Baron F. & Hume, J. R., eds. Transport History, Vol. 2, Nos. 1-3. LC 69-10856. (Illus.). 1970. 24.95 (0-678-05668-4) Kelley.

Duckitt, Hildegonda. Traditional South African Cookery. 184p. 1996. pap. 10.95 (0-7818-0490-6) Hippocrene Bks.

Duckitt, J. H., jt. auth. see Renshon, Stanley A.

Duckitt, John. The Social Psychology of Prejudice. LC 91-33889. 328p. 1992. 69.50 (0-275-94241-4, C4241, Praeger Pubs) Greenwood.

— The Social Psychology of Prejudice. LC 91-33889. 328p. 1994. pap. 26.95 (0-275-95099-9, Praeger Pubs) Greenwood.

Duckitt, John, jt. ed. see Renshon, Stanley A.

Duckles, Vincent H. & Keller, Michael A. Music Reference & Research Materials: An Annotated Bibliography. 4th rev. ed. 740p. 1998. text 40.00 (0-7881-5554-7) DIANE Pub.

— Music Reference & Research Materials: An Annotated Bibliography. 4th rev. ed. LC 92-12386. 740p. 1994. 45.00 (0-02-870822-9, Schirmer Books) Mac Lib Ref.

Ducklow, Mary E. 1930's Something: A Nice Neighborhood with Tall Trees. (Illus.). 145p. 1993. 29.95 (0-929682-03-3) Perin Pr.

***Duckro, Paul N.** Taking Control of Your Headaches: How to Get the Treatment You Need. 9p. 1999. pap. text 14.95 (1-57230-471-5) Guilford Pubns.

Ducks Staff. 161 Secrets of Waterfowling: Time Honored, Field Tested Waterfowling Tips & Advice from DU Members. Young, Matt, ed. (Illus.). 76p. 1995. pap. 10.95 (0-9617279-2-6, Pub. by Ducks Unltd) Willow Creek Pr.

D

An Asterisk (*) at the beginning of an entry indicates that the title is appearing for the first time.

***Ducks Unlimited Staff.** Waterfowler's Journal. (Illus.). 192p. 2000. 45.00 (*1-57223-386-9*) Willow Creek Pr.

Ducks Unlimited Staff, ed. Autumn Passages: A Ducks Unlimited Waterfowling Classics. LC 95-23523. 319p. 1995. 27.50 (*1-57223-026-6*, 0266) Willow Creek Pr.

— Dabblers & Divers: A Duck Hunter's Book. LC 96-24436. (Illus.). 160p. 1996. 39.95 (*1-57223-068-1*, 0681) Willow Creek Pr.

Ducksbury, Paul G. Parallel Array Processing. LC 86-2908. (Electrical & Electronic Engineering Ser.). 122p. 1986. text 44.95 (*0-470-20330-7*) P-H.

Duckson. Exercises in Physical Geography. 2nd ed. 1995. teacher ed. 14.06 (*0-697-25506-9*, WCB McGr Hill) McGrw-H Hghr Educ.

Duckson, Don W., Jr. Exercises in Physical Geography. 192p. (C). 1992. text. write for info. (*0-697-13147-5*, WCB McGr Hill) McGrw-H Hghr Educ.

— Exercises in Physical Geography. 2nd ed. 200p. (C). 1994. text. write for info. (*0-697-15783-0*, WCB McGr Hill) McGrw-H Hghr Educ.

Duckson, Don W. Exercises in Physical Geography. 3rd ed. LC 98-6986. 176p. 1998. spiral bd. 40.00 (*0-697-38493-4*) McGraw.

Duckstein, L., ed. Engineering Risk in Natural Resources Management. (NATO ASI Series E: Applied Sciences). 480p. (C). 1994. text 293.00 (*0-7923-3010-2*) Kluwer Academic.

Duckstein, Lucien & Plate, Erich J., eds. Engineering Reliability & Risk in Water Resources. (C). 1987. text 278.50 (*90-247-3492-4*) Kluwer Academic.

Duckstein, Lucien, jt. auth. see Bardossy, Andras.

Duckstein, Lucien, jt. auth. see Kroh, Aleksandra.

Duckwall, Byron, ed. see Theriault, Chris.

***Duckworth.** A Creative Approach to Music Fundamentals. 7th ed. (Music Ser.). 2000. 37.25 (*0-534-51768-4*) Wadsworth Pub.

Duckworth. Forty-Fifth Purdue Industrial Waste Conference. 880p. 1991. boxed set 139.00 (*0-87371-412-1*, L412) Lewis Pubs.

— Jane Austen: Emma Case Study. 2000. pap. text. write for info. (*0-312-20756-5*); pap. text. write for info. (*0-312-20757-3*) St Martin.

Duckworth, Alastair. The Improvement of the Estate: A Study of Jane Austen's Novels. 250p. 1994. reprint ed. pap. text 15.95 (*0-8018-4972-1*) Johns Hopkins.

Duckworth, Alistair. Howard's End: E. M.Forster's House of Fiction. (Twayne's Masterworks Ser.). 150p. 1992. 29.00 (*0-8057-8366-0*); pap. 18.00 (*0-8057-8566-3*) Macmillan.

Duckworth, Alistair, ed. see Forster, E. M.

***Duckworth, Antony.** Star Trusts. 102p. 1998. 75.00 (*0-9533599-0-5*, Pub. by Gostick Hall) Gaunt.

Duckworth, Bridget, jt. auth. see Ford, Jack R.

Duckworth, C., ed. Engineering in Textile Coloration. 1983. pap. 45.00 (*0-901956-31-7*, Pub. by Textile Inst) St Mut.

Duckworth, C. L. & Lanmuir, G. E. Clyde River & Other Steamers: Supplement. (C). 1987. 24.00 (*0-85174-421-4*) St Mut.

Duckworth, Colin. Steps to the High Garden. 350p. 1992. 26.95 (*0-7145-4155-9*); pap. 11.95 (*0-7145-4229-6*) Riverrun NY.

***Duckworth, Douglas C., et al.** Inorganic Mass Spectrometry: Fundamentals & Applications. Barshick, Christopher M., ed. LC 99-87830. (Practical Spectroscopy Ser.). 512p. 2000. 175.00 (*0-8247-0243-3*) Dekker.

Duckworth, Eleanor. The Having of Wonderful Ideas: And Other Essays on Teaching & Learning. 2nd rev. ed. LC 95-44974. 192p. (C). 1995. text 17.95 (*0-8077-3513-2*) Tchrs Coll.

— Learning with Breadth & Depth. 1979. pap. 2.50 (*0-918374-09-X*) City Coll Wk.

Duckworth, Eleanor & Experienced Teachers Group Staff, The. Teacher to Teacher: The Learning from Each Other. LC 97-20976. 1920p. (Orig.). 1997. text 42.00 (*0-8077-3653-8*); pap. text 18.95 (*0-8077-3652-X*) Tchrs Coll.

Duckworth, Eleanor, et al. Science Education: A Minds-on Approach for the Elementary Years. 216p. (C). 1990. text 49.95 (*0-8058-0543-5*) L Erlbaum Assocs.

Duckworth, Eleanor, tr. see Piaget, Jean.

Duckworth, George E. Foreshadowing & Suspense. (Studies in Comparative Literature: No. 35). 1970. reprint ed. pap. 75.00 (*0-8383-0021-9*) M S G Haskell Hse.

— The Nature of Roman Comedy: A Study in Popular Entertainment. 2nd ed. LC 93-27544. (Illus.). 496p. 1994. pap. 26.95 (*0-8061-2620-5*) U of Okla Pr.

Duckworth, H. E., ed. see International Conference on Nuclidic Masses Staff.

Duckworth, Harry W., ed. The English River Book: A North West Company Journal & Account Book of 1786. (Rupert's Land Record Society Ser.). 256p. (C). 1989. text 60.00 (*0-7735-0714-0*, Pub. by McG-Queens Univ Pr) CUP Services.

Duckworth, Henry T. The Church of the Holy Sepulchre. LC 78-63361. (BCL Ser.). (Illus.). reprint ed. 39.50 (*0-404-17014-5*) AMS Pr.

Duckworth, Ian. Cycling Australia: Bicycle Touring on the Sunny Continent. 224p. 1996. pap. text 5.98 (*0-933201-76-1*) MBI Pubg.

***Duckworth, Ian & Sudarshan, E. C .G.** 100 Years of Planck's Quantum. 550p. 2000. 86.00 (*981-02-4309-X*) World Scientific Pub.

***Duckworth, Jack.** The Judgment Ring Bk. 1: The Chinook River Princess. 224p. 2000. pap. 11.00 (*0-9679119-1-5*, Judgment Ring Bks) Expert Sys.

***Duckworth, John.** Goof-Proof Skits for Youth Ministry 2. (Illus.). 140p. 2000. pap. 14.99 (*0-7644-2142-5*) Group Pub.

Duckworth, John. High-Impact Worship Dramas: Quick-Prep Message Boosters for Pastors & Church Leaders. LC 98-56032. 144p. 1999. 16.99 (*0-7644-2096-8*) Group Pub.

***Duckworth, John.** Instant Skits for Children's Ministry. LC 99-28529. 1999. 16.99 (*0-7644-2095-X*) Group Pub.

Duckworth, John. The School Zone. 96p. (YA). (gr. 7-9). 1986. teacher ed. 2.80 (*0-89693-198-6*, Victor Bks) Chariot Victor.

Duckworth, Liz. God's Great Creation. (Illus.). 6p. (J). 1994. 5.99 (*1-56476-169-X*, 6-3169, Victor Bks) Chariot Victor.

Duckworth, M. La Mujer Decidida.Tr. of Decisive Woman. 6.99 (*1-56063-636-X*, 495103) Editorial Unilit.

Duckworth, M. Transforming Trouble. LC 97-114154. (Tapestry Collection). 96p. 1996. pap. 6.50 (*1-56476-416-8*, 6-3416, Victor Bks) Chariot Victor.

Duckworth, Marilyn. A Gap in the Spectrum. (New Zealand Classics Ser.). 184p. 1986. 9.95 (*0-19-558143-1*) OUP.

Duckworth, Marion. The Decisive Woman. 168p. (Orig.). 1993. pap. 1.80 (*1-56476-058-8*, Victor Bks) Chariot Victor.

— Healing for the Empty Heart. 176p. (Orig.). 1993. pap. 8.99 (*1-55661-314-8*) Bethany Hse.

— Pure Passion. LC 93-45044. (Tapestry Collection). 96p. (Orig.). 1994. pap. 6.50 (*1-56476-222-X*, 6-3222, Victor Bks) Chariot Victor.

— Remembering the Roses. LC 98-11953. 294p. 1998. pap. 9.99 (*1-57673-236-3*, Palisades OR) Multnomah Pubs.

— Remembering the Roses. large type ed. LC 99-33153. 1999. pap. 23.95 (*0-7862-2057-0*) Mac Lib Ref.

— Renewed on the Run. (Tapestry Collection). 108p. 1991. pap. 6.50 (*0-89693-878-6*, 6-1878, Victor Bks) Chariot Victor.

Duckworth, Mark & Mills, Gordon. Organising a Plain-Language Project. 67p. 1996. pap. 29.00 (*1-86287-243-0*, Pub. by Federation Pr) Gaunt.

Duckworth, Martin, jt. ed. see Ball, Martin J.

Duckworth, Mary, jt. auth. see Thuesen, Barbara W.

Duckworth, Michael. Oxford Business English: Grammar & Practice. (Illus.). 224p. 1996. pap. text 12.95 (*0-19-457068-1*) OUP.

Duckworth, Michael, jt. ed. see Ernst, Carl R.

Duckworth, Mick. Triumph & BSA Triples: The Complete Story of the Trident & Rocket 3. (Illus.). 192p. 1997. 34.95 (*1-86126-018-0*, Pub. by Crolwood) Motorbooks Intl.

Duckworth, Penelope. I Am: Teaching Sermons on the Incarnation. LC 98-20649. (Teaching Sermon Ser.). 96p. 1998. pap. 10.00 (*0-687-01359-3*) Abingdon.

Duckworth, Roger A. Mechanics of Fluids. LC 76-10368. (Introductory Engineering Ser.). (Illus.). 285p. reprint ed. pap. 88.40 (*0-608-30727-0*, 201960200013) Bks Demand.

Duckworth, T. The Lecture Notes on Orthopaedics. 3rd ed. (Lecture Notes Ser.). (Illus.). 400p. 1992. pap. 24.95 (*0-632-02781-9*) Blackwell Sci.

Duckworth, W. Donald, jt. auth. see Eichlin, Thomas D.

Duckworth, W. E., ed. Contract Research. 144p. 1991. lib. bdg. 96.00 (*0-7923-1449-2*) Kluwer Academic.

Duckworth, William. A Creative Approach to Music Fundamentals. 2nd ed. 339p. (C). 1984. pap. write for info. (*0-534-03753-4*) Wadsworth Pub.

— A Creative Approach to Music Fundamentals. 3rd ed. 358p. (C). 1988. pap. write for info. (*0-534-09420-1*) Wadsworth Pub.

— A Creative Approach to Music Fundamentals. 5th ed. 366p. 1994. mass mkt. 35.75 (*0-534-24696-6*) Wadsworth Pub.

— A Creative Approach to Music Fundamentals. 6th ed. LC 97-31421. (Music Ser.). (C). 1997. 60.95 (*0-534-52632-2*) Wadsworth Pub.

— Talking Music: Conversations with John Cage, Philip Glass, Laurie Anderson & Five Generations of American Experimental Composers. LC 98-43425. (Illus.). 504p. 1999. reprint ed. mass mkt. 16.95 (*0-306-80893-5*, Pub. by Da Capo) HarpC.

— 20 20: 20 New Sounds of the 20th Century. LC 98-45504. 15p. 1999. 30.00 (*0-02-864864-1*) Mac Lib Ref.

Duckworth, William & Fleming, Richard, eds. Sound & Light: La Monte Young Marian Zazeela. LC 55-58217. (Bucknell Review Ser.: Vol. 40, No. 1). (Illus.). 232p. 1997. 24.00 (*0-8387-5346-9*) Bucknell U Pr.

Duckworth, William, jt. ed. see Fleming, Richard.

Duclaux, Agnes M. French Ideal. LC 67-23209. (Essay Index Reprint Ser.). 1977. 20.95 (*0-8369-0393-5*) Ayer.

— French Procession. LC 68-8456. (Essay Index Reprint Ser.). 1977. 23.95 (*0-8369-0394-3*) Ayer.

— Twentieth Century French Writers. LC 67-22089. (Essay Index Reprint Ser.). 1977. 26.95 (*0-8369-1330-2*) Ayer.

Duclos, Denis. The Werewolf Complex: America's Fascination with Violence. Kapferer, Bruce & Gledhill, John, eds. Pingree, Amanda, tr. from FRE. LC 98-168150. (Global Issues Ser.). 256p. 1998. 49.50 (*1-85973-146-5*, Pub. by Berg Pubs); pap. 19.50 (*1-85973-151-1*, Pub. by Berg Pubs) NYU Pr.

Duclos, Donald P. Son of Sorrow: The Life, Works & Influence of Colonel William C. Falkner. LC 97-41970. 256p. 1997. pap. 54.95 (*1-57309-179-0*, Cath Scholar Pr) Intl Scholars.

— Son of Sorrow: The Life, Works & Influence of Colonel William C. Falkner, 1825-1889. LC 97-41970. 364p. 1997. 74.95 (*1-57309-180-4*) Intl Scholars.

Duclos, Jeanne. Dictionnaire du Francais d'Algerie. (FRE.). 159p. 1992. 49.95 (*0-7859-1012-3*, 2862531227) Fr & Eur.

Duclos, Paul, ed. see Mayeur, Jean-Marie & Hilaire, Yves-Marie.

Duclos, T. Dictionnaire de la Banque. (FRE.). 1998. 49.95 (*0-320-00393-0*) Fr & Eur.

Duclow, Geraldine, jt. auth. see Matheson, Katy.

Ducloy, M., et al, eds. Laser Spectroscopy X: Proceedings of the 10th International Conference, Font-Romeu, France, 16-21 June, 1991. 500p. 1992. text 130.00 (*981-02-0837-5*) World Scientific Pub.

Ducloy, Martial & Bloch, Daniel, eds. Quantum Optics of Confined Systems: Proceedings of the NATO Advanced Study Institute, Les Houches, France, May 23-June 2, 1995. LC 96-244. (NATO Advanced Science Institutes Ser.: Vol. 314, Pt. E). 416p. (C). 1996. text 217.50 (*0-7923-3974-6*) Kluwer Academic.

Duco, Joyce. Can You Cope with Happiness? LC 83-91233. 99p. (Orig.). 1983. pap. 6.95 (*0-9612896-0-0*) J Duco.

— Self-Image Is the Key. LC 86-90983. 71p. 1986. pap. 5.95 (*0-9612896-1-9*) J Duco.

— Workbook for Self Image Is the Key, Set. LC 89-92547. 26p. (Orig.). (J). (gr. 5-12). 1990. pap. 5.00 (*0-9612896-2-7*) J Duco.

Ducoff, Helen. The Hebrew Alphabet: Twenty-Two Letters & Numbers to Color. (Ruth Heller's Designs for Coloring Ser.). (Illus.). 48p. (J). (ps-8). 1991. pap. 4.95 (*0-448-40045-6*, G & D) Peng Put Young Read.

Ducommun, Debbiee. Rats! A Fun & Care Book. LC 97-32160. (Fun & Care Bks.). 112p. 1998. pap. 16.95 (*1-889540-05-6*) Bowtie Press.

***Ducor, Jerome.** Le Sutra d'Amida Preche Par le Buddha. (Etudes Asiatiques Suisses: Vol. 29). 216p. 1998. 35.95 (*3-906759-50-4*, Pub. by P Lang) P Lang Pubng.

Ducor, Phillipe G. Patenting the Recombinant Products of Biotechnology & Other Molecules. LC 98-194387. 208p. 1997. 87.00 (*90-411-0698-7*) Kluwer Academic.

Ducornet, Guy. Le Punching-Ball & la Vache a Lait: La Critique Universitaire Nord-Americaine Face au Surrealisme. LC 97-48645. (FRE.). 174p. 1994. pap. 30.00 (*0-941194-30-2*) Black Swan Pr.

Ducornet, Rikki. The Complete Butcher's Tales. LC 93-36127. 163p. 1994. 19.95 (*1-56478-043-0*) Dalkey Arch.

***Ducornet, Rikki.** The Complete Butcher's Tales. LC 93-36127. 176p. 1999. pap. 11.95 (*1-56478-229-8*, Pub. by Dalkey Arch) Chicago Distribution Ctr.

Ducornet, Rikki. The Cult of Seizure. 64p. 1989. pap. write for info. (*0-88984-132-2*) Porcup Quill.

***Ducornet, Rikki.** Entering Fire. 168p. (Orig.). 1999. pap. text 10.95 (*0-87286-355-7*) City Lights.

— The Fan-Maker's Inquisition. 2000. pap. 14.00 (*0-345-44104-4*) Ballantine Pub Grp.

— The Fan-Maker's Inquisition. Date not set. 13.00 (*0-8050-5927-X*, Owlet BYR) H Holt & Co.

Ducornet, Rikki. The Fan-Maker's Inquisition. LC 99-10246. 192p. 1999. 23.00 (*0-8050-5926-1*) H Holt & Co.

— Fountains of Neptune. 2nd ed. LC 91-33554. 224p. 1997. reprint ed. pap. 12.95 (*1-56478-155-0*) Dalkey Arch.

— The Jade Cabinet. LC 92-29129. 160p. 1993. 19.95 (*1-56478-021-X*) Dalkey Arch.

— The Jade Cabinet: A Novel. LC 92-29129. (American Literature Ser.). 160p. 1997. pap. 11.50 (*1-56478-173-9*) Dalkey Arch.

***Ducornet, Rikki.** The Monstrous & the Marvelous. LC 99-19319. 180p. 1999. pap. 12.95 (*0-87286-354-9*) City Lights.

Ducornet, Rikki. Phosphor in Dreamland. LC 95-17888. (Illus.). 174p. 1995. pap. 12.95 (*1-56478-084-8*) Dalkey Arch.

— The Stain. LC 95-16365. 230p. 1995. reprint ed. pap. 11.95 (*1-56478-085-6*) Dalkey Arch.

— The Word 'Desire' LC 97-6884. 208p. 1997. 22.00 (*0-8050-5173-2*) H Holt & Co.

— The Word 'Desire' 176p. 1998. pap. 12.00 (*0-8050-5174-0*) H Holt & Co.

Ducote, David, jt. auth. see Ducote, Roy.

Ducote, David, ed. see Ducote, Roy.

Ducote, Roy. The Hole Story. Ducote, David, ed. (Outdoor Classics Ser.). (Illus.). 116p. 1995. write for info. (*0-9637934-2-X*) D & R Outdr Classics.

Ducote, Roy & Ducote, David. Fish Tales. (Outdoor Classics Ser.). (Illus.). 112p. write for info. (*0-9637934-1-1*) D & R Outdr Classics.

***Ducovny, Amram.** Coney. 320p. 2000. 26.95 (*1-58567-067-7*, Pub. by Overlook Pr) Penguin Putnam.

Ducrocq, Marie-Pascale. Therese of Lisieux: A Vocation of Love. LC 81-20512. 77p. 1982. pap. 4.50 (*0-8189-0431-3*) Alba.

Ducrot, Jean-Marie. Textiltechnisches Woerterbuch: English-American-French-German-Spanish. (ENG, FRE & GER.). 535p. 1979. 350.00 (*0-7859-6868-7*) Fr & Eur.

Ducrot, O. & Todorov, Tzvetan. Les Comediens Francais du 17e Siecle Vol. 2: Dictionnaire Biographique. (FRE.). 475p. 1979. pap. 19.95 (*0-7859-4623-3*) Fr & Eur.

Ducrot, Oswald & Todorov, Tzvetan. Encyclopedic Dictionary of the Sciences of Language. Porter, Catherine, tr. LC 78-23901. 400p. 1979. pap. 19.95 (*0-8018-2857-0*) Johns Hopkins.

***Ducruix, Arnaud & Giege, Richard, eds.** Crystallization of Nucleic Acids & Proteins. 2nd ed. LC 99-15222. (The Practical Approach Ser.: No. 210). (Illus.). 464p. 2000. text 120.00 (*0-19-963679-6*); pap. text 60.00 (*0-19-963678-8*) OUP.

Duczko, W. Birka V--Filigree & Granulation Work of the Viking Period: An Analysis of Materials from Bjorko. (Illus.). 118p. 1985. lib. bdg. 33.50 (*91-7402-152-1*) Coronet Bks.

Duczynska, Ilona. Workers in Arms: The Austrian Schutzbund & the Civil War of 1934. LC 77-70970. 1978. 25.00 (*0-85345-410-8*, Pub. by Monthly Rev) NYU Pr.

Duda, jt. auth. see Wagner.

Duda, Deborah. Coming Home: A Guide to Dying at Home with Dignity. 426p. 1987. pap. 14.95 (*0-943353-31-0*) Aurora Press.

Duda, Frederick, jt. auth. see Creth, Shiela.

Duda, Halya. The Executive PowerPak: Maximum Leverage for Your First 90 Days. 53p. 495.00 (*1-882474-00-7*) H Duda.

Duda, Jan. My Devotional Diary: The Teen Years. 96p. 1992. pap. 5.99 (*0-570-03997-5*, 12-3025) Concordia.

Duda, Joan L., ed. Advances in Sport & Exercise Psychology Measurement. LC 97-77311. 510p. (C). 1998. text 49.00 (*1-885693-11-7*) Fit Info Tech.

Duda, Mark D. Virginia Wildlife Viewing Guide. LC 94-19271. (Falcon Guides Ser.). (Illus.). 96p. (Orig.). 1994. pap. 8.95 (*1-56044-292-1*) Falcon Pub Inc.

— Watching Wildlife: A Companion to the Watchable Wildlife Series. LC 95-26073. (Watchable Wildlife Ser.). (Illus.). 117p. 1995. pap. 9.95 (*1-56044-315-4*) Falcon Pub Inc.

Duda, Mark Damian. West Virginia Wildlife Viewing Guide. LC 98-26968. (Watchable Wildlife Ser.). (Illus.). 96p. 1999. pap. 8.95 (*1-56044-635-8*) Falcon Pub Inc.

Duda, Richard O. & Hart, Peter E. Pattern Classification & Scene Analyses. 512p. 1973. 98.00 (*0-471-22361-1*) Wiley.

Duda, Richard O., et al. Pattern Classification & Scene Analysis Part 1: Pattern Classification. 2nd ed. LC 99-29981. 624p. 2000. text 110.00 (*0-471-05669-3*, Wiley-Interscience) Wiley.

Duda, Walter H. Cement Data Book Vol. 1: International Process Engineering in the Cement Industry. 3rd ed. (ENG & GER.). 1985. 375.00 (*0-8288-0204-1*, M7317) Fr & Eur.

— Cement Data Book Vol. 2: Automation, Storage, Transportation, Dispatch. (ENG & GER.). 1984. 325.00 (*0-8288-0205-X*, M3900) Fr & Eur.

— Cement Data Book Vol. 3. (ENG & GER.). 1988. 250.00 (*0-8288-0206-8*, M3910) Fr & Eur.

Dudai, Moshe, jt. auth. see Wind, Gary G.

Dudai, Yadin. The Neurobiology of Memory: Concepts, Findings, Trends. (Illus.). 352p. 1989. pap. text 41.95 (*0-19-854229-1*) OUP.

Dudal, R. & Roy, R. N. Integrated Plant Nutrition Organization. LC 96-144321. (Fertilizer & Plant Nutrition Bulletins: 12). 432p. 1995. pap. 55.00 (*92-5-103665-9*) Food & Agri Org UN.

***Dudash, C. Michael.** Good News of Great Joy: The Christmas Story as Told in the Bible. 2000. 9.97 (*0-310-97957-9*) Zondervan.

Dudawaki, B., et al. Russian-Polish Political Dictionary. deluxe ed. (POL & RUS.). 726p. 1955. 29.95 (*0-8288-6866-2*, M-9114) Fr & Eur.

Dudbridge, Glen. Religious Experience & Lay Society in T'ang China: A Reading of Tai Fu's Kuang-I Chi. (Cambridge Studies in Chinese History, Literature & Institutions). (Illus.). 268p. (C). 1995. text 64.95 (*0-521-48223-2*) Cambridge U Pr.

Dudda, Frank. Die Binnenstruktur der Krankenversicherungstrager Nach dem Gesundheitsstrukturgesetz. (GER.). LX, 188p. 1996. 44.95 (*3-631-30790-X*) P Lang Pubng.

Duddeck, H. & Dietrich, W. Modern NMR-Spectroscopy. 230p. 1989. 39.95 (*0-387-91348-3*) Spr-Verlag.

— Structure Elucidation by Modern NMR: A Workbook. 2nd enl. rev. ed. (Illus.). 284p. 1992. pap. text 43.95 (*3-7985-0930-1*) Spr-Verlag.

Duddeck, H., jt. auth. see Dietrich, W.

Duddeck, Helmut, et al. Structure Elucidation by Modern NMR: A Workbook. 3rd rev. ed. (Illus.). 280p. 1998. pap., wbk. ed. 49.00 (*3-7985-1111-X*, Pub. by D Steinkopff) Spr-Verlag.

Dudden, Arthur P. The American Pacific: From the Old China Trade to the Present. (Illus.). 332p. (C). 1994. reprint ed. pap. text 21.95 (*0-19-508562-0*, 9016) OUP.

Dudden, Arthur P., ed. American Humor. 184p. 1989. pap. text 19.95 (*0-19-505054-1*) OUP.

Dudden, Arthur P. & Dynes, Russell R., eds. The Fulbright Experience Nineteen Forty-Six to Nineteen Eighty-Six. 345p. 1987. 39.95 (*0-88738-141-3*) Transaction Pubs.

Dudden, Faye E. Serving Women: Household Service in Nineteenth Century America. LC 83-1263. (Illus.). 352p. reprint ed. pap. 109.20 (*0-608-09077-8*, 206971100005) Bks Demand.

— Women in the American Theatre: Actresses & Audiences, 1790-1870. LC 93-40780. 270p. 1994. 37.50 (*0-300-05636-2*) Yale U Pr.

— Women in the American Theatre: Actresses & Audiences, 1790-1870. (Illus.). 270p. 1997. pap. 18.00 (*0-300-07058-6*) Yale U Pr.

Dudderar, Glenn R. Nature from Your Back Door. Johnson, Leslie, ed. (Illus.). 136p. (Orig.). 1991. 14.95 (*1-56525-001-X*, E-2323HC); pap. 9.95 (*1-56525-000-1*, E-2323) MSU Ext.

Duddington, C. L., jt. ed. see Carthy, J. D.

Duddington, Natalie, tr. see Goncharov, Ivan A.

Duddington, Natalie, tr. see Kliuchevsky, V. O.

Duddy, Patrick J. & Bahorik, J. Wesley. C & C Elementary School Science. (Illus.). 76p. (C). 1998. ring bd. 19.51 (*1-884768-04-0*) Charming Forge.

Duddy, Thomas. Mind, Self & Interiority. 208p. 1995. text 72.95 (*1-85972-153-2*, Pub. by Avebry) Ashgate Pub Co.

Dudeck, J., et al, eds. New Technologies in Hospital Information Systems. LC 97-75049. (Studies in Health Technology & Informatics: Vol. 45). 250p. Date not set. 86.00 (*90-5199-363-3*, 363-3) IOS Press.

Dudeck, J., jt. ed. see Prokosch, H. U.

Dudek. The Architecture of Schools & the New Learning Environments. 192p. 2000. pap. text 69.95 (*0-7506-3585-1*) Buttrwrth-Heinemann.

Dudek, Anthony, jt. auth. see Short, Thomas.

Dudek, Antoinette. Faith, Family & Friends, Vol. 3. 127p. (Orig.). (J). (gr. 1-2). 1993. pap. 13.30 (*1-55833-085-2*) Natl Cath Educ.

D

Dudek, Antoninette. Is There Room for Me? 66p. 1998. pap. 13.00 (*1-55833-196-4*) Natl Cath Educ.

***Dudek, Emily P.** Determining the Formulas of Copper(II)-Ethylenediamine Complex Ions by Spectrophotometry. (Modular Laboratory in Chemistry Ser.). 16p. (C). 1999. pap. text 1.50 (*0-87540-509-6*, STOI 5096) Chem Educ Res.

Dudek, Gerald, jt. auth. see Ault, Addison.

Dudek, Gregory & Jenkin, Michael. Computational Principles of Mobile Robotics. (Illus.). 300p. (C). 2000. pap. 22.95 (*0-521-56876-5*) Cambridge U Pr.

***Dudek, Gregory & Jenkin, Michael.** Computational Principles of Mobile Robotics. LC 99-18285. (Illus.). 300p. (C). 2000. 59.95 (*0-521-56021-7*) Cambridge U Pr.

Dudek, Louis. The Caged Tiger. LC 98-174888. 106p. 1997. write for info. (*0-921852-21-5*) Empyreal Press.

— Europe. 160p. 1991. pap. write for info. (*0-88984-115-2*) Porcup Quill.

— In Defence of Art: Critical Essays & Reviews. 302p. 1988. 29.95 (*0-919627-70-6*, Pub. by Quarry Pr); pap. 19.95 (*0-919627-72-2*, Pub. by Quarry Pr) LPC InBook.

Dudek, M. Architecture of the Kindergarten. (Illus.). 224p. (C). 1995. 80.00 (*0-419-19670-6*, E & FN Spon) Routledge.

***Dudek, Ronald W.** High-Yield Cell & Molecular Biology. LC 99-23316. (High Yield Ser.). 1999. pap. text 15.95 (*0-683-30359-7*) Lppncott W & W.

Dudek, Ronald W. High-Yield Embryology. LC 96-5667. (Illus.). 50p. 1996. 14.95 (*0-683-02714-X*) Lppncott W & W.

Dudek, Ronald W. High-Yield Embryology. 2nd ed. 50p. pap. text. write for info. (*0-7817-2132-6*) Lppncott W & W.

Dudek, Ronald W. High-Yield Gross Anatomy. LC 97-6715. (Illus.). 144p. 1997. pap. 14.95 (*0-683-18215-3*) Lppncott W & W.

— High-Yield Histology. LC 96-44885. (Illus.). 110p. 1997. write for info. (*0-683-02720-4*) Lppncott W & W.

Dudek, Ronald W. High-Yield Histology. 2nd ed. 232p. pap. text 15.95 (*0-7817-2134-2*) Lppncott W & W.

Dudek, Ronald W. & Fix, James D. Embryology. 2nd ed. LC 98-22361. (Board Review Ser.). 293p. 1998. 24.95 (*0-683-30272-8*) Lppncott W & W.

Dudek, Susan G. The Nutrition Handbook for Nursing Practice. 3rd ed. LC 96-26302. 864p. 1997. pap. text 31.95 (*0-397-55364-1*, Lippnctt) Lppncott W & W.

Dudek, Susan G. The Nutrition Handbook for Nursing Practice. 4th ed. 800p. pap. text 33.00 (*0-7817-2344-2*) Lppncott W & W.

DuDell, Gary. Teenagers, Drugs, & Growing Up. (Illus.). 170p. (Orig.). 1990. pap. 9.95 (*0-9627553-0-3*) C E Mendez Found.

Duden. Duden Dictionary of Borrowed Words: Duden Fremdwoerterbuch. (GER.). 813p. 1982. 49.95 (*0-8288-1958-0*, M14171) Fr & Eur.

— Duden Grammar of Modern Spoken German: Duden Grammatik der Deutschen Gegenwartssprache. (GER.). 804p. 1984. 49.95 (*0-8288-1959-9*, M14170) Fr & Eur.

— Duden Rechtschreibung der Deutschen Sprache und der Fremdwoerter. (GER.). 792p. 1980. 49.95 (*0-8288-1960-2*, M14167) Fr & Eur.

— Duden Scholar's Dictionary of Chemistry: Schulerduden-Die Chemie. (GER.). 424p. 1984. 35.00 (*0-8288-1310-8*, M15295) Fr & Eur.

— Duden Woertbuch Vol. 9: Richtiges. 3rd ed. (GER.). 803p. 1985. 49.95 (*0-614-00348-2*, M14175) Fr & Eur.

— Duden-Woerterbuch Geographischer Namen: Europa. 65.00 (*0-8288-7720-3*, M7345) Fr & Eur.

— Idiomatisches Woerterbuch, IBM PC Version. (GER.). 150p. 1994. write for info. (*0-614-00349-0*) Fr & Eur.

— Kleine Duden, 4 vols. (GER.). 75p. 1993. write for info. (*0-614-00350-4*, 3411058315) Fr & Eur.

— Schuelerduden - Geeschichte: Scholar's Duden Dictionary of History. (GER.). 603p. 1983. 39.95 (*0-8288-1491-0*, M15148) Fr & Eur.

— Schuelerduden - Politik und Gesellschaft. (GER.). 468p. 1985. 35.00 (*0-8288-2253-0*, M15260) Fr & Eur.

— Schuelerduden die Literatur. (GER.). 480p. 1980. 39.95 (*0-8288-1566-6*, M15163) Fr & Eur.

Duden, Barbara. Disembodying Women: Perspectives on Pregnancy & the Unborn. Hoinacki, Lee, tr. LC 93-17478. 128p. 1993. text 17.95 (*0-674-21267-3*) HUP.

— The Woman Beneath the Skin: A Doctor's Patients in Eighteenth-Century Germany. Dunlap, Thomas J., tr. from GER. 248p. (C). 1991. 33.95 (*0-674-95403-3*) HUP.

— Woman Beneath the Skin: A Doctor's Patients in Eighteenth-Century Germany. 256p. 1998. pap. text 15.95 (*0-674-95404-1*) HUP.

Duden Editorial Staff, jt. auth. see Broger, Achim.

Duden, Jane. Earthquake! On Shaky Ground LC 98-128791. (Cover-to-Cover Bks.). 56p. 1997. write for info. (*0-7807-6109-X*) Perfection Learn.

— The Giant Pandas of China. (Animals of the World Ser.). (Illus.). 24p. (J). (gr. k-3). 1997. lib. bdg. 14.00 (*0-531-11461-9*, Hlltop Bks) Capstone Pr.

— The Giant Pandas of China. LC 97-11369. (Animals of the World Ser.). (J). 1998. lib. bdg. write for info. (*1-56065-577-1*) Capstone Pr.

— 1950s. LC 89-34400. (Timelines Ser.). (Illus.). 48p. (J). (gr. 6). 1989. lib. bdg. 11.95 (*0-89686-476-6*, Crstwood Hse) Silver Burdett Pr.

— 1940s. LC 89-34401. (Timelines Ser.). (Illus.). 48p. (J). (gr. 6). 1989. lib. bdg. 11.95 (*0-89686-475-8*, Crstwood Hse) Silver Burdett Pr.

— 1970s. LC 89-34630. (Timelines Ser.). (Illus.). 48p. (J). (gr. 6). 1989. lib. bdg. 11.95 (*0-89686-478-2*, Crstwood Hse) Silver Burdett Pr.

— 1960s. LC 89-34399. (Timelines Ser.). (Illus.). 48p. (J). (gr. 6). 1989. lib. bdg. 11.95 (*0-89686-477-4*, Crstwood Hse) Silver Burdett Pr.

— The Sea Otters of California. (Animals of the World Ser.). (Illus.). 24p. (J). (gr. k-3). 1997. lib. bdg. 14.00 (*0-531-11464-3*, Hlltop Bks) Capstone Pr.

***Duden, Jane.** Vegetarianism for Teens. LC 00-39092. (Nutrition & Fitness for Teens Ser.). (Illus.). (YA). 2001. write for info. (*0-7368-0712-8*, LifeMatters Bks) Capstone Pr.

Duden, Jane & Stewart, Gail B. 1980s. LC 90-46827. (Timelines Ser.). (Illus.). 48p. (J). (gr. 6). 1991. lib. bdg. 11.95 (*0-89686-599-1*, Crstwood Hse) Silver Burdett Pr.

Duden, Jane, et al. Animals of the World. (Illus.). 24p. 47.80 (*0-7368-0455-2*, Bridgestone Bks) Capstone Pr.

Duden, Joan. The Sea Otters of California. LC 97-11368. (Animals of the World Ser.). (J). 1998. lib. bdg. write for info. (*1-56065-578-X*) Capstone Pr.

Duden Staff. Duden Vol. 5: Fremdworterbuch. 6th ed. (GER.). 864p. 1997. 59.95 (*0-320-00118-0*) Fr & Eur.

— Duden Vol. 9: Richtiges, Gutes Deutsch. 4th ed. (GER.). 864p. 1998. 59.95 (*0-320-00413-9*) Fr & Eur.

Dudeney, Henry E. Amusements in Mathematics. 1958. pap. 7.95 (*0-486-20473-1*) Dover.

Dudenhausen, J. W., jt. auth. see Pschyrembel, Willibald.

***Dudenhoefer, David.** The Panama Traveler: From Rainforest Adventures to Canal Cruises. (Illus.). 224p. (Orig.). 1999. pap. 13.95 (*0-942297-09-1*) Windham Bay.

***Dudenredaktion (Bibliographisches Institut) & Oxford University Press. Dictionary Dept. German Section.** The Oxford-Duden College German Dictionary: English-German, German-English. Clark, Michael & Thyen, Olaf, eds. LC 98-49986. 960p. 2000. pap. 11.95 (*0-19-860280-4*) OUP.

Duder, Tessa. In Lane Three, Alex Archer. 1991. 9.60 (*0-606-04943-6*, Pub. by Turtleback) Demco.

Duder, Tessa. Mercury Beach. LC 97-161409. 191p. 1997. write for info. (*0-14-038575-4*, PuffinBks) Peng Put Young Read.

Duder, Tessa & Nieuwenhuizen, Agnes. Crossing: Australian & New Zealand Short Stories. LC 96-216644. 313p. 1995. pap. write for info. (*1-86330-480-0*) Mdrin Au.

Duderstadt, Hank. The World's Weirdest Web Pages: And the People Who Create Them. LC 96-32857. 150p. 1996. pap. text 12.95 (*1-886411-12-3*) No Starch Pr.

***Duderstadt, James J.** Intercollegiate Athletics & the American University: A University President's Perspective. (Illus.). 250p. (C). 2000. 29.95 (*0-472-11156-6*, 11156) U of Mich Pr.

Duderstadt, James J. Nuclear Power. LC 79-12776. (Energy, Power & Environment Ser.: No. 3). (Illus.). 400p. reprint ed. pap. 124.00 (*0-7837-4321-1*, 204400700012) Bks Demand.

***Duderstadt, James J.** A University for the Twenty-First Century. LC 99-86823. 376p. 2000. text 47.50 (*0-472-11091-8*, 11091) U of Mich Pr.

Duderstadt, James J. & Hamilton, Louis J. Nuclear Reactor Analysis. 672p. (C). 1976. text 117.95 (*0-471-22363-8*) Wiley.

Duderstadt, James J. & Kikuchi, Chihiro. Nuclear Power: Technology on Trial. 240p. 1979. pap. text 19.95 (*0-472-06312-X*, 06312) U of Mich Pr.

Duderstadt, James J. & Martin, William R. Transport Theory. LC 78-13672. (Wiley-Interscience Publications). 623p. reprint ed. pap. 193.20 (*0-608-14600-5*, 202518600042) Bks Demand.

Duderstadt, Karen & Lagana, Kathleen. Ethical Decision Making for Perinatal Nurses. Wellman, Lynn G., ed. 1995. write for info. (*0-86525-065-0*) March of Dimes.

Dudev, T., jt. ed. see Galabov, B. S.

Dudevant, Jean F., see Sand, Maurice, pseud.

Dudevszky, Szabinka. Close-Up. Boeke, Wanda, tr. from DUT. LC 98-45085. (Illus.). 128p. (YA). (gr. 7-12). 1999. 15.95 (*1-886910-40-5*, Pub. by Front Str) Publishers Group.

Dudewicz, Edward J. Introduction to Statistics & Probability. LC 75-26827. (Series in Mathematical & Management Sciences: Vol. 1). 1976. text 195.00 (*0-03-086688-X*) Am Sciences Pr.

— Solutions in Statistics & Probability. 2nd ed. LC 93-72687. (American Sciences Press Series in Mathematical & Management Sciences: Vol. 3). (Illus.). 318p. (C). 1993. 195.00 (*0-935950-35-4*) Am Sciences Pr.

Dudewicz, Edward J., ed. The Frontiers of Modern Statistical Inference Procedures: Proceedings & Discussions of the IPASRAS Conference (First International Conference on Inference Procedures Associated with Statistical Ranking & Selection, East-West Center, Honolulu, July 1982) LC 83-72590. (American Sciences Press Series in Mathematical & Management Sciences: Vol. 10). 1985. 195.00 (*0-935950-07-9*) Am Sciences Pr.

***Dudewicz, Edward J., ed.** Modern Digital Simulation Vol. IV: Advances in Theory & Application of Distribution Fitting, Econometric Cointegrated Regression in Panel Data, System Reliability & Behrens-Fisher Problems. LC 99-73665. (Series in Mathematical & Management Sciences: Vol. 40). (Illus.). 190p. 1999. 195.00 (*0-935950-44-3*) Am Sciences Pr.

Dudewicz, Edward J., ed. Modern Digital Simulation Methodology Vol. III: Advances in Theory, Application, & Design--Electric Power Systems, Spare Parts Inventory, Purchase Interval & Incidence Modeling, Automobile Insurance Bonus-Malus Systems, Genetic Algorithms - DNA Sequence Assembly, Education, & Water Resource Case Studies. LC 97-71847. (American Sciences Press Series in Mathematical & Management Sciences: Vol. 39). (Illus.). 224p. 1997. 195.00 (*0-935950-43-5*) Am Sciences Pr.

— Modern Digital Simulation Methodology, II: Univariate & Bivariate Distribution Fitting, Bootstrap Methods, & Applications to CensusPES & CensusPlus of the U. S. Bureau of the Census, Bootstrap Sample Size, & Biology & Environment Case Studies. (Series in Mathematical & Management Sciences: Vol. 38). (Illus.). 240p. 1997. 195.00 (*0-935950-42-7*) Am Sciences Pr.

Dudewicz, Edward J., et al, eds. The Frontiers of Expert Systems & Artificial Intelligence Vol. 3: Proceedings of the ICOSCO-I Conference (First International Conference on Statistical Computing, Cesme, Izmir, Turkey, March-April 1987) LC 90-85326. (Series in Mathematical & Management Sciences: Vol. 27). 214p. 1990. 195.00 (*0-935950-29-X*) Am Sciences Pr.

***Dudewicz, Edward J., et al, eds.** Modern Mathematical, Management & Statistical Sciences I: Advances in Theory & Application. LC 99-72155. (American Series in Mathematical & Management Sciences: Vol. 41). (Illus.). 192p. 1999. pap. 195.00 (*0-935950-45-1*) Am Sciences Pr.

Dudewicz, Edward J. & Joo Ok Koo. The Complete Categorized Guide to Statistical Selection & Ranking Procedures. LC 80-68288. (American Sciences Press Series in Mathematical & Management Sciences: Vol. 6). 1982. text 195.00 (*0-935950-03-6*) Am Sciences Pr.

Dudewicz, Edward J. & Mishra, Satya N. Modern Mathematical Statistics. LC 87-14279. (Probability & Mathematical Statistics Ser.). 864p. 1988. text 95.95 (*0-471-81472-5*) Wiley.

Dudewicz, Edward J. & Ralley, Thomas G. The Handbook of Random Number Generation & Testing with TESTRAND Computer Code. LC 80-68286. (American Sciences Press Series in Mathematical & Management Sciences: Vol. 4). 1981. text 195.00 (*0-935950-01-X*) Am Sciences Pr.

Dudewicz, Edward J., et al. Modern Elementary Probability & Statistics with Statistical Programming in SAS, Minitab, & BMDP. LC 89-80812. 375p. 1989. pap. text 195.00 (*0-935950-19-2*) Am Sciences Pr.

Dudewicz, Edward J., jt. auth. see Karian, Zaven A.

Dudgeon. Multidimensional Signal Processing. (C). 2001. pap. 78.00 (*0-13-209206-9*, Macmillan Coll) P-H.

***Dudgeon, A. G.** Hidden Victory: The Battle of Habbaniya, May 1941. (Illus.). 2000. 27.99 (*0-7524-2001-1*, Pub. by Tempus Pubng) Arcadia Publng.

Dudgeon, Dan E. & Merser, Russell M. Multidimensional Digital Signal. 1995. pap. text 93.33 (*0-13-227638-0*) P-H.

Dudgeon, David. Patterns & Processes in Stream Ecology: A Synoptic Review of Hong Kong Running Waters. (Binnengewaesser Ser.: Band XXIX). (Illus.). viii, 150p. 1992. 56.00 (*3-510-40040-2*, Pub. by E Schweizerbartsche) Balogh.

— Patterns & Processes in Stream Ecology: A Synoptic Review of Hong Kong Running Waters. (Binnengewaesser Ser.: Vol. 29). (Illus.). 147p. 1992. lib. bdg. 62.50 (*0-685-67203-4*) Lubrecht & Cramer.

— Tropical Asian Streams: Zoobenthos, Ecology & Conservation. (Illus.). 844p. 1999. pap. 62.50 (*962-209-469-4*, 119751, Pub. by HK Univ Pr) Coronet Bks.

Dudgeon, David & Corlett, Richard. Hills & Streams: An Ecology of Hong Kong. (Illus.). 244p. 1994. 36.50 (*962-209-357-4*, Pub. by HK Univ Pr) Coronet Bks.

Dudgeon, David & Lam, Paul K. The Inland Waters of Tropical Asia & Australia: Conservation & Management. (International Association of Theoretical & Applied Limnology, Communications Ser.: No. 24). (Illus.). iv, 386p. 1994. pap. 76.00 (*3-510-52024-6*, Pub. by E Schweizerbartsche) Balogh.

Dudgeon, John, tr. see Berk, William.

Dudgeon, Piers. The Girl from Leam Lane: The Life & Writing of Catherine Cookson. LC 99-203781. (Illus.). 248p. 1998. pap. 11.95 (*0-7472-5660-8*, Pub. by Headline Bk Pub) Trafalgar.

— The Girl from Leam Lane: The Life & Writing of Catherine Cookson. large type ed. 336p. 1998. 29.99 (*0-7089-9039-8*) Ulverscroft.

Dudgeon, Piers, ed. The Country Child: An Illustrated Reminiscence. (Illus.). 192p. 1993. 29.95 (*0-7472-0677-5*, Pub. by Headline Bk Pub) Trafalgar.

Dudgeon, Ralph T. The Keyed Bugle. (Illus.). 282p. 1993. 34.50 (*0-8108-2645-3*) Scarecrow.

Dudiak, Andy, jt. auth. see Goeldner, Charles R.

Dudich, E. Contributions to the History of Geological Mapping: Proceedings of the Xth Inhigeo Symposium August 16-22, 1982, Budapest, Hungary. 441p. (C). 1984. 102.00 (*963-05-3616-1*, Pub. by Akade Kiado) St Mut.

Dudick, Thomas S. Profile for Profitability: Using Cost Control & Profitability Analysis. LC 72-4353. (Wiley Systems & Controls for Financial Management Ser.). 271p. reprint ed. 84.10 (*0-8357-9963-8*, 201561900095) Bks Demand.

Dudick, Thomas S., ed. How to Improve Profitability Through More Effective Planning. LC 75-20445. (Wiley Series on Systems & Controls for Financial Management). (Illus.). 375p. reprint ed. pap. 116.30 (*0-608-10148-6*, 201585000097) Bks Demand.

Dudick, Thomas S. & Cornell, Ross. Inventory Control for the Financial Executive. LC 79-10699. (Systems & Controls for Financial Management Ser.). (Illus.). 265p. reprint ed. pap. 82.20 (*0-7837-3510-3*, 205784300008) Bks Demand.

***Dudik, Evan Matthew.** Strategic Renaissance: New Thinking & Innovative Tools to Create Great Corporate Strategies... Using Insights from History & Science. LC 99-57944. 272p. 2000. 27.95 (*0-8144-0551-7*) AMACOM.

Dudish-Dozier, Donna. Modeling As a Career. 74p. 1993. pap. 10.00 (*0-9634826-1-0*) New Hope AL.

Dudkin, Lev. Iterative Aggregation Techniques in Soviet National Economic Planning. Tamberg, Andreas, ed. (Illus.). 127p. (Orig.). 1987. pap. text 75.00 (*1-55831-006-1*) Delphic Associates.

Dudko, Mary A. Barney's Alphabet Soup. Larsen, Margie, ed. LC 96-86256. (Barney Ser.). (Illus.). 18p. (J). (ps-k). 1997. bds. 4.95 (*1-57064-118-8*) Lyrick Pub.

— Barney's Clothes. LC 96-86252. (Barney Ser.). (Illus.). 20p. (J). (ps-k). 1997. bds. 3.95 (*1-57064-119-6*) Lyrick Pub.

Dudko, Mary A. & Larsen, Margie. Baby Bop Imagina. (Barney Ser.).Tr. of Baby Bop Pretends. (SPA., Illus.). 24p. (J). (ps-k). mass mkt. 3.25 (*1-57064-163-3*, Barney Publ) Lyrick Pub.

— Baby Bop Pretends. Dowdy, Linda C., ed. LC 93-74289. (Barney Ser.). (Illus.). 24p. (J). (ps-k). 1994. pap. 3.25 (*1-57064-022-X*) Lyrick Pub.

— Baby Bop's Counting Book. Hartley, Linda, ed. LC 93-77866. (Barney Ser.). (Illus.). 22p. (J). (ps-k). 1993. reprint ed. bds. 3.95 (*1-57064-006-8*) Lyrick Pub.

— Baby Bop's Foods. Dowdy, Linda C., ed. LC 93-74291. (Barney Ser.). (Illus.). 24p. (J). (ps-k). 1994. bds. 3.95 (*1-57064-014-9*) Lyrick Pub.

— Barney & Baby Bop at the Beach. LC 94-79380. (Barney Ser.). (Illus.). 14p. (J). (ps-k). 1995. bds. 7.95 (*1-57064-036-X*) Lyrick Pub.

— Barney's Book of Opposites. LC 94-72000. (Barney Ser.). (Illus.). 18p. (J). (ps-k). 1994. bds. 4.95 (*1-57064-016-5*) Lyrick Pub.

— Barney's Color Surprise. Hartley, Linda, ed. LC 93-77865. (Barney Ser.). (Illus.). 18p. (J). (ps-k). 1993. bds. 4.95 (*1-57064-007-6*) Lyrick Pub.

— Barney's Hats. Hartley, Linda, ed. LC 93-77016. (Barney Ser.). (Illus.). 24p. (J). (ps-k). 1993. pap. 2.25 (*1-57064-005-X*) Lyrick Pub.

— Barney's Weather Book. LC 94-79379. (Barney Ser.). (Illus.). 22p. (J). (ps-k). 1995. bds. 3.95 (*1-57064-037-8*) Lyrick Pub.

— BJ & Scooter. LC 95-75344. (Illus.). 24p. (J). 1995. pap. 3.25 (*1-57064-043-2*) Lyrick Pub.

— BJ's Fun Week. LC 94-72001. (Barney Ser.). (Illus.). 20p. (J). (ps-k). 1994. bds. 3.95 (*1-57064-015-7*) Lyrick Pub.

— A Day with Barney. Dowdy, Linda C., ed. LC 93-74292. (Barney Ser.). (Illus.). 26p. (J). (ps-k). 1994. bds. 3.95 (*1-57064-013-0*) Lyrick Pub.

Dudko, Mary A., jt. auth. see Larsen, Margie.

Dudko, Mary A., ed. see Larsen, Margie.

Dudko, Mary Ann. Los Sombreros de Barney. (SPA., Illus.). 24p. (J). 1997. pap. text 2.95 (*1-57064-162-5*) Lyrick Pub.

***Dudko, Mary Ann & Larsen, Margie.** Barney's Book of Foods. LC 99-66254. (Barney Ser.). (Illus.). 24p. (J). (ps-k). 2000. 5.95 (*1-57064-711-9*, 97962) Lyrick Pub.

Dudko, Mary Ann, jt. auth. see Larsen, Margie.

Dudley. Exploring the Past. 1995. pap. text. write for info. (*0-582-86142-X*, Pub. by Addison-Wesley) Longman.

— Supplement to 1894 "History of Dudley Family" 96p. 1993. reprint ed. pap. 18.00 (*0-8328-3798-9*); reprint ed. lib. bdg. 28.00 (*0-8328-3797-0*) Higginson Bk Co.

***DUDLEY & Gitelson.** American Elections: The Rules of the Game. 2000. pap. text. write for info. (*1-57259-821-2*) St Martin.

Dudley, Alan. Practical Guide Medical & Surgical Procedures. 179p. 1989. pap. text 49.50 (*0-433-00058-9*) Buttrwrth-Heinemann.

Dudley, Albert W., ed. History of the Township of Bybeary & Moreland in Philadelphia, PA. (Illus.). 415p. 1993. reprint ed. lib. bdg. 42.50 (*0-8328-2839-4*) Higginson Bk Co.

Dudley, Bev, ed. see Dudley, William H.

Dudley, Bill, ed. Opposing Viewpoints in American History, Vol. I. LC 95-33446. (Illus.). 352p. (J). (gr. 5-12). 1996. pap. text 21.20 (*1-56510-347-5*) Greenhaven.

Dudley, Bill, ed. Opposing Viewpoints in American History, Vol. I. LC 95-33446. (Illus.). 352p. (J). (gr. 5-12). 1996. lib. bdg. 37.44 (*1-56510-348-3*) Greenhaven.

Dudley, Brian A. Mathematical & Biological Interrelations. LC 77-7284. (Illus.). 329p. reprint ed. pap. 102.00 (*0-608-17693-1*, 203041300069) Bks Demand.

Dudley, Brian R. Fair or Foul: The Complete Soccer Guide for Fans & Players. LC 95-90304. (Illus.). 60p. (Orig.). 1995. pap. 11.95 (*1-887227-03-2*) Titan Pubng.

— Fair or Foul: The Complete Soccer Guide for Fans & Players. rev. ed. (Illus.). 60p. (Orig.). 1998. pap. 11.95 (*1-887227-28-8*) Titan Pubng.

— A Fan's Guide to American & Canadian Football. LC 95-90307. (Illus.). 68p. (Orig.). 1995. pap. 14.95 (*1-887227-02-4*) Titan Pubng.

— A Fan's Guide to NHL Hockey, Major League Baseball & NBA Basketball. LC 95-90306. (Illus.). 68p. (Orig.). 1995. pap. 14.95 (*1-887227-01-6*) Titan Pubng.

***Dudley, Brian R., ed.** The Greatest Speeches of President John F. Kennedy. 2nd rev. ed. 64p. 2000. pap. 14.95 (*1-887227-46-6*) Titan Pubng.

Dudley, Brian R., ed. see Kennedy, John F.

Dudley, Carl S. Basic Steps Toward Community Ministry: Guidelines & Models in Action. LC 91-72970. 147p. (Orig.). 1991. pap. 15.75 (*1-56699-048-3*, AL127) Alban Inst.

— Making the Small Church Effective. LC 78-2221. 1978. pap. 11.95 (*0-687-23044-6*) Abingdon.

— Next Step in Community Ministry: Hands-On Leadership. LC 95-83892. xviii, 138 p. 1996. pap. 15.75 (*1-56699-168-4*, AL172) Alban Inst.

Dudley, Carl S. & Johnson, Sally A. Energizing the Congregation: Images That Shape Your Church's Ministry. LC 92-29814. 144p. (Orig.). 1993. pap. 13.95 (*0-664-25359-8*) Westminster John Knox.

Dudley, Carl S. & Walrath, Douglas A., eds. Developing Your Small Church's Potential. 96p. (Orig.). 1988. pap. 12.00 (*0-8170-1120-X*) Judson.

Dudley, Charles E., Sr. Thou Who Hath Brought Us. LC 97-60576. 208p. 1997. boxed set 24.95 (*1-57258-086-0*) Teach Servs.

Dudley, Charles F., jt. auth. see Dunbar, Peter M.

Dudley, Charma D. Treating Depressed Children: A Therapeutic Manual of Cognitive Behavioral Interventions. LC 96-70515. 160p. 1997. text 49.95 (*1-57224-061-X*) New Harbinger.

Dudley, Christina, jt. auth. see Cox, Joyce.

Dudley, Christina, jt. auth. see Cox, Joyce K.

Dudley, Christina, ed. see Cox, Joyce.

Dudley, Christina/, jt. auth. see Cox, Joyce.

Dudley, Cliff. The Hidden Christian. LC 80-80657. 160p. 1980. 7.95 (*0-89221-074-5*) New Leaf.

Dudley, Cliff, jt. auth. see Kilpatrick, Paula.

Dudley, Cliff, jt. auth. see Tari, Mel.

Dudley, D. Dudley: History of the Dudley Family, 2 vols., Set. 1993. reprint ed. pap. 158.00 (*0-8328-3299-5*); reprint ed. lib. bdg. 168.00 (*0-8328-3298-7*) Higginson Bk Co.

Dudley, D. R. A History of Cynicism. 224p. 1980. reprint ed. pap. 20.00 (*0-89005-365-0*) Ares.

— A History of Cynicism from Diogenes to the Sixth Century A. D. 1974. 250.00 (*0-87968-137-3*) Gordon Pr.

Dudley, Darle. Handbook of Practical Gear Design. 688p. 1994. text 59.95 (*1-56676-218-9*) Technomic.

Dudley, Darle W. The Development of Long Life Epicyclic Gearing for Industrial Gas Turbines. (Technical Papers: Vol. P219.07). (Illus.). 28p. 1970. pap. text 30.00 (*1-55589-251-5*) AGMA.

— The Evolution of the Gear Art, Circa, 1966. (AGMA Technical Paper: Vol. P990.14). (Illus.). 20p. 1966. pap. text 30.00 (*1-55589-463-1*) AGMA.

— Proposed Application Factors for Industrial & High Speed Gearing. (Technical Papers: Vol. P159.02). (Illus.). 16p. 1969. pap. text 30.00 (*1-55589-204-3*) AGMA.

— Vehicle Gearing. (Technical Papers: Vol. P109.31). (Illus.). 17p. (Orig.). 1972. pap. text 30.00 incl. audio compact disk (*1-55589-200-0*) AGMA.

Dudley, Darle W. & Poritsky, H. Cutting & Hobbing Worms & Gears. (Technical Papers: Vol. P241). (Illus.). 30p. 1987. pap. text 30.00 (*1-55589-217-5*) AGMA.

Dudley, Darle W. & Zrodowski, J. J. Modern Marine Gears. (Technical Papers: Vol. P429.03). (Illus.). 52p. 1950. pap. text 30.00 (*1-55589-411-9*) AGMA.

Dudley, David L. My Father's Shadow: Intergenerational Conflict in African American Men's Autobiography. LC 91-8377. 192p. (C). 1991. text 27.95 (*0-8122-3081-7*) U of Pa Pr.

Dudley, Dean. History of the Council of Nice. Obaba, Al I., ed. (Illus.). 132p. 1925. pap. text 17.00 (*0-916157-19-9*) African Islam Miss Pubns.

— History of the First Council of Nice. (African Heritage Classical Research Studies). 124p. reprint ed. 15.00 (*0-938818-63-5*) ECA Assoc.

— History of the First Council of Nice. 7th ed. 125p. 1996. reprint ed. spiral bd. 11.00 (*0-7873-0299-6*) Hlth Research.

— History of the First Council of Nice: A World's Christian Convention A.D. 325, with a Life at Constantine. 125p. 1992. reprint ed. pap. 9.95 (*1-56459-165-4*) Kessinger Pub.

— History of the First Council of Nice: A World's Christian Convention A.D. 325, with a Life of Constantine. LC 98-11666. 128p. 1999. reprint ed. pap. 9.95 (*1-881316-03-3*) A&B Bks.

Dudley, Denise. Every Woman's Guide to Career Success. rev. ed. xii, 62p. (Orig.). 1991. 12.95 (*1-878542-25-7*, 12-0003) SkillPath Pubns.

Dudley, Denise, jt. auth. see Brown, Jerry.

Dudley, Dick. What Do You Give a Sick Tyrannosaurus Rex? (Dino Pop-up Joke Bks.). 12p. (J). (ps-3). 1992. 5.95 (*1-56288-179-5*) Checkerboard.

— Why Does a Brachiosaurus Have Such a Long Neck? (Dino Pop-up Joke Bks.). (J). (ps-3). 1992. 5.95 (*1-56288-178-7*) Checkerboard.

Dudley, Dick & Kong, Emilie. When Are Pteranodons Sad? (Dino Pop-up Joke Bks.). (Illus.). 12p. (J). (ps-2). 1992. 5.95 (*1-56288-180-9*) Checkerboard.

— Why Does an Apatosaurus Get Its Way? (Dino Pop-up Joke Bks.). (Illus.). 12p. (J). 1992. 5.95 (*1-56288-181-7*) Checkerboard.

Dudley, Donald G. Mathematical Foundations for Electromagnetic Theory. LC 94-3159. (Electromagnetic Waves Ser.). 264p. 1994. 59.95 (*0-7803-1022-5*, PC03715) Inst Electrical.

— Mathematical Foundations for Electromagnetic Theory. (IEEE/OUP Series on Electromagnetic Wave Theory). (Illus.). 264p. (C). 1997. text 65.00 (*0-19-859216-7*) OUP.

Dudley, Donald R. A History of Cynicism, from Diogenes to the 6th Century A. D. 224p. 1967. reprint ed. lib. bdg. 43.95 (*3-487-05916-9*) Lubrecht & Cramer.

Dudley, Dorothy. Forgotten Frontiers. LC 77-119663. (BCL Ser. I). reprint ed. 34.50 (*0-404-02188-3*) AMS Pr.

— Forgotten Frontiers: Dreiser & the Land of the Free. LC 75-144988. 485p. 1972. reprint ed. 18.00 (*0-403-00917-0*) Scholarly.

— Theatrum Majorum, the Cambridge of 1776: Diary of Dorothy Dudley. LC 73-140861. (Eyewitness Accounts of the American Revolution Ser.). (Illus.). 1971. reprint ed. 16.95 (*0-405-01228-4*) Ayer.

Dudley, Earl C., jt. auth. see Arkin, Stanley S.

Dudley, Edward. The Endless Text: "Don Quixote" & the Hermeneutics of Romance. LC 96-52143. (SUNY Series, The Margins of Literature). 316p. (C). 1997. text 65.50 (*0-7914-3525-3*); pap. text 21.95 (*0-7914-3526-1*) State U NY Pr.

Dudley, Edward, ed. The Development of National Library & Information Services: Papers Given at the First Library Association International Workshop, London, 1981. LC 82-240549. 214p. 1983. reprint ed. pap. 66.40 (*0-608-02485-6*, 206312900004) Bks Demand.

Dudley, Edward, jt. auth. see Crow, John A.

Dudley, Edward J. & Novak, Maximillian E., eds. The Wild Man Within: An Image in Western Thought from the Renaissance to Romanticism. LC 72-77191. 345p. reprint ed. pap. 107.00 (*0-608-15896-8*, 203079400074) Bks Demand.

Dudley, Edwards, ed. A Claim of Right for Scotland. 1989. 13.95 (*0-7486-6023-2*, Pub. by Polygon) Subterranean Co.

Dudley, Elizabeth. Start Exploring Forests: A Fact-Filled Coloring Book. (Start Exploring Ser.). (Illus.). 128p. (Orig.). (J). (gr. 2 up). 1989. pap. 8.95 (*0-89471-782-0*) Running Pr.

Dudley, Elizabeth, ed. The Unity of Evolutionary Biology: Proceedings of the Fourth International Congress of Systematic & Evolutionary Biology, 2 vols. LC 90-27811. (Illus.). 1160p. 1992. 125.00 (*0-931146-19-4*, Dioscorides) Timber.

Dudley, Ellen. The Savvy Adventure Traveler: What to Know Before You Go. LC 98-29343. (Illus.). 128p. 1998. pap. 15.95 (*0-07-018013-X*) Intl Marine.

— Slow Burn. LC 96-72364. (Illus.). 64p. 1997. pap. 10.00 (*0-944854-24-9*) Provincetown Arts.

— Slow Burn. LC 96-72364. (Poets Ser.: No. 6). (Illus.). 64p. 1998. 35.00 (*0-944854-25-7*) Provincetown Arts.

Dudley, Ellen & Seaborg, Eric. American Discoveries: Scouting the First Coast-to-Coast Recreational Trail. LC 96-23940. (Illus.). 304p. 1996. 24.95 (*0-89886-437-2*) Mountaineers.

Dudley, Ellen, jt. auth. see Seaborg, Eric.

Dudley, Eric & Haaland, Ane. Communicating Building for Safety: Guidelines for Methods of Communicating Technical Information to Local Builders & Householders. 80p. 1994. pap. 17.50 (*1-85339-183-2*, Pub. by Intermed Tech) Stylus Pub VA.

Dudley, Ernest. Dr. Morelle & the Drummer Girl. 256p. 1996. 19.50 (*0-7451-8679-3*, Black Dagger) Chivers N Amer.

— Nightmare for Dr. Morelle. 1998. 19.50 (*0-7540-8506-6*, Black Dagger) Chivers N Amer.

— The Return of Sherlock Holmes: Based upon the Play by J. E. Harold Terry & Arthur Rose. LC 93-1973. (Orig.). 1993. pap. 10.00 (*0-88734-272-8*) Players Pr.

***Dudley, Esther & Mealing, Stuart, eds.** Becoming Designers: Education & Influences. 160p. 2000. pap. 24.95 (*1-84150-032-1*, Pub. by Intellect) Intl Spec Bk.

***Dudley-Evans, Tony & St. John, Maggie-Jo.** Developments in ESP: A Multi-Disciplinary Approach. LC 98-30873. 1998. write for info. (*0-521-59329-8*); write for info. (*0-521-59675-0*) Cambridge U Pr.

Dudley, Frances & Talmage McLaurin. Weddings, 1. (Illus.). 167p. 1998. 39.95 (*0-9654149-4-9*) Florists Rev.

Dudley, Fred A., ed. The Relations of Literature & Science: A Selected Bibliography, 1930-1949. LC 50-4895. 146p. reprint ed. pap. 45.30 (*0-608-11226-7*, 200029400025) Bks Demand.

Dudley, G. F. & Richardson, J. J. Politics & Steel in Britain, 1967-1988: The Life & Times of the British Steel Corporation. 314p. 1990. text 82.95 (*1-85521-072-X*, Pub. by Dartmth Pub) Ashgate Pub Co.

***Dudley, Gary P.** The New Dudley Genealogies: The Descendants of William of Guilford. 111p. 1999. pap. 23.50 (*0-7884-1293-0*, D814) Heritage Bk.

Dudley, Geoffrey. Increase Your Learning Power. 1976. pap. 5.00 (*0-87980-085-2*) Wilshire.

***Dudley, Geoffrey A.** Double Your Learning Power: Master the Techniques of Successful Memory & Recall. 192p. 1998. pap. 10.00 (*0-7225-1211-2*) Thorsons PA.

Dudley, Geoffrey A. How to Understand Your Dreams. 1970. pap. 7.00 (*0-87980-066-6*) Wilshire.

Dudley, George A. A Workshop for Peace: Designing the United Nations Headquarters. LC 92-35859. (Architectural History Foundation Ser.). (Illus.). 429p. 1994. 70.00 (*0-262-04137-5*) MIT Pr.

Dudley, George W. & Goodson, Shannon L. Earning What You're Worth: The Psychology of Sales Call Reluctance. rev. ed. 448p. 1991. pap. 18.95 (*0-935907-03-3*) Behavioral Sci.

— The Psychology of Call-Reluctance: How to Overcome the Fear of Self-Promotion. LC 85-73334. 208p. (Orig.). 1986. reprint ed. 26.95 (*0-935907-00-9*); reprint ed. pap. 18.95 (*0-935907-01-7*) Behavioral Sci.

— The Psychology of Sales Call Reluctance: Earning What You're Worth in Sales. 4th rev. ed. LC 99-60831. Orig. Title: Psychology of Call Reluctance. 424p. 1999. pap. 22.95 (*0-935907-07-6*) Behavioral Sci.

Dudley, George W., et al. Earning What You're Worth: The Psychology of Sales Call Reluctance. rev. ed. 448p. 1995. pap. 22.95 (*0-935907-06-8*) Behavioral Sci.

— Earning What You're Worth? The Psychology of Sales Call Reluctance. rev. ed. 448p. 1995. 28.95 (*0-935907-05-X*) Behavioral Sci.

***Dudley Gold, Susan.** Asthma. LC 98-48584. (Health Watch Ser.). (J). 1999. write for info. (*0-382-42100-0*) Silver Burdett Pr.

Dudley Gold, Susan. Cystic Fibrosis. LC 98-48581. (Health Watch Ser.). (J). 1999. write for info. (*0-382-42094-2*) Silver Burdett Pr.

***Dudley Gold, Susan.** The Panama Canal Transfer: Controversy at the Crossroads. LC 98-47196. 1999. 25.69 (*0-8172-5762-4*) Raintree Steck-V.

Dudley Gold, Susan & Cournoyer, Jill. The History of Union Wharf, 1793-1998. LC 98-28345. (Illus.). 128p. 1998. boxed set 24.95 (*1-892168-01-4*) Custom Communs.

Dudley, Gordon H., jt. auth. see Sumich, James L.

Dudley, Grenae D. & Stewart, Carlyle F., III. Sankofa: Celebrations for the African American Church. LC 97-5600. 120p. (Orig.). 1997. pap. 12.95 (*0-8298-1179-6*) Pilgrim OH.

Dudley, H. A. & Waxman, B. P., eds. Scott: An Aid to Clinical Surgery. 4th ed. (Illus.). 320p. 1988. pap. text 25.00 (*0-443-03839-2*) Church.

Dudley-Higham, Mary. The Bellamys & Cornish Cousins of North Cornwall, England: A Case Study in Cornish Family History Research Spanning 400 Years. LC 97-77058. (Illus.). xvi, 185p. 1997. pap. 34.95 (*0-9662010-0-0*) Genesis Calif.

Dudley, J. Strategies for the Single Market, 1992. 400p. (C). 1989. 225.00 (*0-7855-5693-1*, Pub. by Inst Pur & Supply) St Mut.

Dudley, J. W., jt. ed. see Sprague, George F.

Dudley, Jack. Carteret Waterfowl Heritage. (Illus.). 152p. 1993. 40.00 (*0-9631815-2-1*) Decoy Mag.

Dudley, Jack C., ed. Custodial Staffing Guidelines for Educational Facilities. (Illus.). 92p. 1992. pap. 45.00 (*0-913359-66-1*) APPA VA.

Dudley, James R. Confronting the Stigma in Their Lives: Helping People with a Mental Retardation Label. LC 96-37186. 214p. (Orig.). 1997. text 49.95 (*0-398-06737-6*); pap. text 35.95 (*0-398-06738-4*) C C Thomas.

Dudley, Janice & Vidovich, Lesley, eds. The Politics of Education: Commonwealth Schools Policy, 1973-1993. 1995. pap. 65.00 (*0-86431-177-X*, Pub. by Aust Council Educ Res) St Mut.

Dudley, Joe L., Sr. Walking by Faith: I am, I Can & I Will. (Illus.). 180p. 1997. 25.95 (*0-939975-11-4*) Exec Pr NC.

Dudley, John. When Grief Visits School: Organizing a Successful Response. LC 95-60209. 176p. (Orig.). (C). 1995. pap. text 14.95 (*0-932796-71-0*) Ed Media Corp.

Dudley, John C., ed. History of the Town of Sutton, Massachusetts, Vol. 2. (Illus.). 634p. 1993. reprint ed. lib. bdg. 65.00 (*0-8328-3144-1*) Higginson Bk Co.

Dudley, Joseph I. Choteau Creek: A Sioux Reminiscence. LC 91-39285. x, 179p. 1998. pap. 10.00 (*0-8032-6611-1*, Bison Books) U of Nebr Pr.

— Choteau Creek: A Sioux Reminiscence. 176p. 1994. pap. 12.99 (*0-446-39519-6*) Warner Bks.

Dudley, Karen. Alligators & Crocodiles. LC 97-12104. (Untamed World Ser.). (Illus.). 64p. (J). (gr. 5-9). 1998. lib. bdg. 27.12 (*0-8172-4573-1*) Raintree Steck-V.

— Alligators & Crocodiles. (Untamed World Ser.). (Illus.). 64p. (J). (gr. 5-9). 1998. pap. 8.95 (*0-8172-8477-X*) Raintree Steck-V.

— Bald Eagles. LC 97-1271. (Untamed World Ser.). (Illus.). 64p. (J). (gr. 5-9). 1998. lib. bdg. 27.12 (*0-8172-4571-5*) Raintree Steck-V.

***Dudley, Karen.** Bald Eagles. (Untamed World Ser.). (J). 2000. pap. 8.95 (*0-7398-1681-0*) Raintree Steck-V.

Dudley, Karen. Elephants. LC 96-8367. (Untamed World Ser.). (Illus.). 64p. (J). (gr. 5-9). 1997. lib. bdg. 27.12 (*0-8172-4565-0*) Raintree Steck-V.

— Elephants. (Untamed World Ser.). 1998. pap. 8.95 (*0-8172-8009-X*) Raintree Steck-V.

— Giant Pandas. LC 96-23348. (Untamed World Ser.). (Illus.). 64p. (J). (gr. 5-9). 1997. lib. bdg. 27.12 (*0-8172-4566-9*) Raintree Steck-V.

— Giant Pandas. (Untamed World Ser.). 1998. pap. 8.95 (*0-8172-8010-3*) Raintree Steck-V.

— Wolves. LC 96-8365. (Untamed World Ser.). (Illus.). 64p. (J). (gr. 5-9). 1997. lib. bdg. 27.12 (*0-8172-4561-8*) Raintree Steck-V.

— Wolves. (Untamed World Ser.). (Illus.). 64p. (J). (gr. 5-9). 1998. pap. 8.95 (*0-8172-8475-3*) Raintree Steck-V.

***Dudley, Kathryn M.** Debt & Dispossession. LC 99-41110. 2000. 22.50 (*0-226-16911-1*) U Ch Pr.

Dudley, Kathryn M. The End of the Line: Lost Jobs, New Lives in Postindustrial America. LC 93-6041. 256p. 1994. 26.95 (*0-226-16908-1*) U Ch Pr.

— End of the Line: Lost Jobs, New Lives in Postindustrial America. 1997. pap. text 17.00 (*0-226-16910-3*) U Ch Pr.

Dudley, Lillian L. & Kinghorn, Harriet R. Songs to Sing & Picture: Grades PreK-2. 115p. (J). (ps-2). 1996. pap. text 17.50 (*1-56308-367-1*) Teacher Ideas Pr.

Dudley, Lynn M. & Guitjens, J. C. Agroecosystems & the Environment: Sources, Control, & Remediation of Potentially Toxic, Trace Element Oxyanions. LC 97-29875. 1998. 20.00 (*0-934394-12-1*) AAASPD.

Dudley, Mark. An Eye to the Sky. LC 91-33880. (Adventures in Space Ser.). (Illus.). 48p. (J). (gr. 5-6). 1992. lib. bdg. 12.95 (*0-89686-691-2*, Crstwood Hse) Silver Burdett Pr.

Dudley, Mark E. Brown vs. Board of Education (1954) School Desegregation. LC 93-32712. (J). 1994. text. write for info. (*0-02-736271-X*, New Dscvry Bks) Silver Burdett Pr.

— Brown vs. Board of Education (1954) School Desegregation. (Supreme Court Decisions Ser.). (Illus.). 96p. (YA). (gr. 6 up). 1995. lib. bdg. 18.90 (*0-8050-3657-1*) TFC Bks NY.

— Engle vs. Vitale (1962) Religion & the Schools. (Supreme Court Decisions Ser.). 96p. (YA). (gr. 6 up). 1995. lib. bdg. 18.90 (*0-8050-3916-3*) TFC Bks NY.

— Epilepsy. LC 95-25136. (Health Watch Ser.). (J). 1996. 15.95 (*0-89686-861-3*, Crstwood Hse) Silver Burdett Pr.

— Gideon v. Wainwright 1963: Right to Counsel. (Supreme Court Decisions Ser.). (Illus.). 96p. (YA). (gr. 6 up). 1995. lib. bdg. 18.90 (*0-8050-3914-7*) TFC Bks NY.

— United States vs. Nixon, 1974: Presidential Powers. LC 94-21863. (Supreme Court Decisions Ser.). 95p. (YA). (gr. 6 up). 1995. lib. bdg. 18.90 (*0-8050-3658-X*) TFC Bks NY.

Dudley, Mark E. & Spencer, Susan S. Epilepsy. LC 95-25136. (Health Watch Ser.). (J). (gr. 5). 1997. 5.95 (*0-382-39971-4*, Crstwood Hse) Silver Burdett Pr.

***Dudley-Marling, Curt.** If It Wasn't for School, Our Lives Would Be Perfect. 192p. 2000. pap. text 22.50 (*0-325-00101-4*) Heinemann.

Dudley-Marling, Curt. Uncertainty & the Whole Language Teacher: The Messy Reality of Classroom Practice. LC 96-53389. 1997. pap. text 22.50 (*0-435-07234-X*, 07234) Heinemann.

Dudley-Marling, Curt & Searle, Dennis. Who Owns Learning? Questions of Autonomy, Choice & Control. LC 94-27338. 213p. 1994. pap. text 23.00 (*0-435-08827-0*, 08827) Heinemann.

Dudley-Marling, Curt, jt. auth. see Rhodes, Lynn K.

Dudley-Marling, Curtis & Searle, Dennis. When Students Have Time to Talk . . . Creating Contexts for Learning Language. LC 91-12786. 147p. (C). 1991. pap. text 20.00 (*0-435-08588-3*, 08588) Heinemann.

Dudley, Martin, ed. Like a Two-Edged Sword: The Word of God in Liturgy & History. 220p. (Orig.). 1995. pap. 16.95 (*1-85311-115-5*, 845, Pub. by Canterbury Press Norwich) Morehouse Pub.

Dudley, Martin & Rowell, Geoffrey, eds. The Oil of Gladness. 160p. (Orig.). 1993. pap. text 10.95 (*0-8146-2245-3*) Liturgical Pr.

Dudley, Martin R., ed. The Collect in Anglican Liturgy: Texts & Sources, 1549-1989. 384p. (Orig.). 1994. pap. 24.95 (*0-8146-2308-5*, Liturg Pr Bks) Liturgical Pr.

Dudley, Maxine. The Prodigal Daughter: A Maundy Thursday Reconciliation Service. 1992. pap. 3.75 (*1-55673-563-4*, 9310) CSS OH.

Dudley, Michael. A Man in a Motel Room. (Chapbks.: No. 18). 40p. (Orig.). 1986. pap. 3.50 (*0-913719-84-6*, High Coo Pr) Brooks Books.

— Roasted Chestnuts. 24p. 1979. pap. 3.50 (*0-913719-10-2*, High Coo Pr) Brooks Books.

— Through the Green Fuse. 32p. 1983. pap. 3.50 (*0-913719-23-4*, High Coo Pr) Brooks Books.

Dudley, Michael K. Man, Gods, & Nature. pap. 12.95 (*1-878751-15-8*) Na Kane O Ka Malo.

Dudley, Michael K. & Agard, Keoni K. A Call for Hawaiian Sovereignty. rev. ed. LC 90-184941. 187p. 1993. reprint ed. 19.95 (*1-878751-08-5*); reprint ed. pap. 12.95 (*1-878751-09-3*) Na Kane O Ka Malo.

Dudley, Michael Kioni. A Hawaiian Nation I: Man, Gods & Nature. LC 90-184941. (Illus.). 169p. 1990. 19.95 (*1-878751-01-8*); pap. 12.95 (*1-878751-02-6*) Na Kane O Ka Malo.

Dudley, Michael Kioni & Agard, Keoni Kealoha. A Hawaiian Nation II: A Call for Hawaiian Sovereignty. LC 90-184941. 180p. (C). 1990. 19.95 (*1-878751-03-4*); pap. 12.95 (*1-878751-04-2*) Na Kane O Ka Malo.

Dudley Morrison, Susan. The Passenger Pigeon: Gone Forever. (Illus.). 48p. (J). (gr. 5-8). 1998. text 12.00 (*0-7881-5834-1*) DIANE Pub.

Dudley, N., et al. Bad Harvest. 1995. pap. 30.00 (*1-85383-188-3*, Pub. by Escan Pubns) Island Pr.

Dudley, N. A., jt. ed. see Muramatsu, R.

Dudley, Nan T., ed. see Maxwell, Lizzie.

Dudley, Nathan, jt. auth. see Cox, Joyce.

Dudley, Nathan, jt. auth. see Cox, Joyce K.

Dudley, Nigel, et al, eds. Land Is Life: Land Reform & Sustainable Agriculture. 144p. 1992. pap. 15.95 (*1-85339-146-8*, Pub. by Intermed Tech) Stylus Pub VA.

Dudley, Nigel & Stickland, Sue. G Is for EcoGarden: An A to Z Guide to a More Organically Healthy Garden. 192p. (Orig.). 1992. pap. 10.00 (*0-380-76522-5*, Avon Bks) Morrow Avon.

Dudley, Otis & Schnore, Leo F. Cultural, Behavioral, & Ecological Perspectives in the Study of Sociology. (Reprint Series in Social Sciences). (C). 1993. reprint ed. pap. text 5.00 (*0-8290-4108-7*, S-75) Irvington.

Dudley, Owen F. Will Men Be Like Gods: Humanitarianism or Human Happiness? 83p. 1979. 2.49 (*0-8199-0766-9*, Frncscn Herld) Franciscan Pr.

***Dudley, P.** HMS Submission. 240p. 1999. mass mkt. 15.99 (*0-352-33301-4*) Virgin Bks.

Dudley, Patti. Food with a View. 180p. 1993. 11.95 (*0-9638272-0-0*) Dudley Pr.

***Dudley, R. M.** Uniform Central Limit Theorems. LC 98-35562. (Cambridge Studies in Advanced Mathematics: No. 63). 450p. (C). 1998. 85.00 (*0-521-46102-2*) Cambridge U Pr.

***Dudley, R. M. & Norvaisa, R.** Differentiability of Six Operators on Nonsmooth Functions & P-Variation. Dold, A. et al, eds. LC 99-23639. (Lecture Notes in Mathematics Ser.: Vol. 1703). vii, 277p. 1999. pap. 49.00 (*3-540-65975-7*) Spr-Verlag.

Dudley, Richard M., et al, eds. Probability in Banach Spaces, VIII Vol. 30: Proceedings of the Eighth International Conference. LC 92-17649. xi, 510p. 1992. 109.00 (*0-8176-3657-9*) Birkhauser.

Dudley, Richard M., et al. Ecole d'Ete de Probabilites de Saint-Flour XII - 1982. (Lecture Notes in Mathematics Ser.: Vol. 1097). x, 396p. 1984. 54.95 (*0-387-13897-8*) Spr-Verlag.

***Dudley, Robert.** The Biomechanics of Insect Flight. LC 99-29653. 1999. text 49.50 (*0-691-04430-9*, Pub. by Princeton U Pr) Cal Prin Full Svc.

Dudley, Robert. A Briefe Report of the Militaire Services Done in the Low Countries by the Erle of Leicester. LC 72-192. (English Experience Ser.: No. 201). 36p. 1969. reprint ed. 20.00 (*90-221-0201-7*) Walter J Johnson.

Dudley, Robert, tr. see Thomas, a Kempis.

Dudley, Robert J. Think Like a Lawyer: How to Get What You Want by Using Advocacy Skills. LC 79-26488. 234p. 1980. text 29.95 (*0-88229-571-3*) Burnham Inc.

Dudley, Roger L. & Hernandez, Edwin I. Citizens of Two Worlds: Religion & Politics among American Seventh-Day Adventists. LC 92-71514. (Illus.). 322p. 1992. 15.99 (*0-943872-66-9*) Andrews Univ Pr.

Dudley, Sherwood, ed. see Devienne, Francois.

D

Dudley-Smith, Timothy. Great Is the Glory. LC 96-79605. 95p. 1997. pap. text 7.95 (*0-916642-64-X*, 1752) Hope Pub.
— John Stott: A Comprehensive Bibliography. LC 95-48954. 156p. (Orig.). 1996. pap. 12.99 (*0-8308-1865-0*, 1865) InterVarsity.
— John Stott: The Making of a Leader. LC 99-21813. 526p. 1999. 24.99 (*0-8308-2207-0*, 2207) InterVarsity.
— Lift Every Heart. LC 83-83215. 306p. 1984. pap. 19.95 (*0-916642-21-6*, 1037) Hope Pub.
— Praying with the English Hymn Writers. (Praying With...Ser.). 1990. pap. 5.95 (*0-687-86039-3*) Abingdon.
— A Voice of Singing. LC 92-74551. 65p. (C). 1993. pap. 9.95 (*0-916642-50-X*, 780) Hope Pub.
Dudley-Smith, Timothy, ed. Authentic Christianity: From the Writings of John Stott. LC 95-48952. 424p. 1996. 22.99 (*0-8308-1620-8*, 1620) InterVarsity.
Dudley, Steve, et al. Rare Birds Day by Day. (Illus.). 392p. 1996. text (*0-85661-102-6*) Poyser.
Dudley, Thelma J. Hurts Can Be Healed. LC 93-79272. (Reader Resource Ser.). 100p. (Orig.). 1993. pap. text 6.00 (*1-883667-02-X*) Christian Meth.
Dudley, Theodore R., ed. see Van Gelderen, D. M., et al.
Dudley, Thomas J. Pepperdine Management Simulation. unabridged ed. 112p. (C). 1998. pap. text 3.00 (*1-893260-03-8*) Harrison Pubg.
Dudley, Tim, jt. auth. see Sumrall, Lester.
Dudley, Tom. Entering the World of Plants. 2nd ed. 200p. (C). 1994. text 21.40 (*0-536-58727-2*) Pearson Custom.
Dudley, Trent, jt. auth. see Glover, Neal.
Dudley, Underwood. Elementary Number Theory. 2nd ed. LC 78-5661. (Mathematical Sciences Ser.). (Illus.). 272p. (C). 1978. pap. text 59.95 (*0-7167-0076-X*) W H Freeman.
— Mathematical Cranks. LC 92-69179. (MAA Spectrum Ser.). 384p. 1992. pap. 33.95 (*0-88385-507-0*, CRANKS) Math Assn.
— Numerology: or What Pythagoras Wrought. LC 97-74345. 329p. 1997. pap. 29.95 (*0-88385-524-0*) Math Assn.
— The Trisectors. LC 94-75575. 176p. 1994. pap. 9.99 (*0-88385-514-3*, TRI) Math Assn.
Dudley, Underwood, ed. Readings for Calculus. LC 92-62283. (Notes Ser.: Vol. 31). 1993. pap. text 38.50 (*0-88385-087-7*, NTE-31) Math Assn.
***Dudley, Walter.** I've Fallen & I Still Can't Get Up. 2000. pap. 14.95 (*1-891400-26-6*) Champion Pr.
Dudley, Walter & Lee, Min. Tsunami! 2nd ed. LC 98-24953. (Illus.). 376p. 1998. pap. 19.95 (*0-8248-1969-1*) UH Pr.
***Dudley, William.** Africa. LC 99-24848. (Opposing Viewpoints Ser.). 312p. (YA). (gr. 9-12). 2000. pap. 17.45 (*0-7377-0118-8*); lib. bdg. 27.45 (*0-7377-0119-6*) Greenhaven.
— American Slavery. LC 99-55866. (Turning Points in World History Ser.). 288p. 2000. 17.45 (*0-7377-0213-3*) Greenhaven.
— American Slavery. LC 99-55866. (Turning Points in World History Ser.). (Illus.). 288p. 2000. pap. 13.96 (*0-7377-0212-5*) Greenhaven.
— Endangered Oceans. LC 98-45933. (Opposing Viewpoints Ser.). 312p. 1999. pap. 17.45 (*0-7377-0062-9*) Greenhaven.
— Endangered Oceans. LC 98-45933. (Opposing Viewpoints Ser.). 312p. (J). 1999. lib. bdg. 27.45 (*0-7377-0063-7*) Greenhaven.
Dudley, William. The Environment: Distinguishing Between Fact & Opinion. LC 90-3819. (Opposing Viewpoints Juniors Ser.). (Illus.). 36p. (J). (gr. 3-6). 1990. lib. bdg. 16.20 (*0-89908-603-9*) Greenhaven.
— Media Violence. LC 98-22828. (Opposing Viewpoints Ser.). 186p. 1999. lib. bdg. 167.68 (*1-56510-945-7*) Greenhaven.
***Dudley, William.** Media Violence: Opposing Viewpoints. LC 98-22828. (Opposing Viewpoints Ser.). 186p. 1999. pap. 103.68 (*1-56510-944-9*) Greenhaven.
— The 1960s. LC 99-87776. (America's Decades Ser.). 360p. (YA). 2000. pap. 17.96 (*0-7377-0305-9*); lib. bdg. 22.45 (*0-7377-0306-7*) Greenhaven.
— Opposing Viewpoints in Social Issues. LC 99-30912. (Opposing Viewpoints Ser.). 192p. (YA). (gr. 9-12). 2000. 21.96 (*0-7377-0123-4*); pap. 13.96 (*0-7377-0122-6*) Greenhaven.
— Political Scandals. LC 00-29408. 2000. pap. write for info. (*0-7377-0518-3*) Greenhaven.
— Russia Today. LC 99-86133. (Opposing Viewpoints Ser.). 2000. pap. write for info. (*0-7377-0521-3*) Greenhaven.
Dudley, William. The U. S. Constitution: Locating the Author's Main Idea. LC 90-42328. (Opposing Viewpoints Juniors Ser.). (Illus.). 36p. (J). (gr. 3-6). 1990. lib. bdg. 16.20 (*0-89908-601-2*) Greenhaven.
— UFOs. LC 98-55488. (At Issue Ser.). 128p. 1999. pap. 13.70 (*0-7377-0070-X*) Greenhaven.
***Dudley, William.** UFOs. LC 98-55488. (At Issue Ser.). 128p. (gr. 7-12). 1999. lib. bdg. 21.20 (*0-7377-0071-8*) Greenhaven.
Dudley, William. The Vietnam War: Opposing Viewpoints. LC 97-9448. (Opposing Viewpoints Ser.). (Illus.). 284p. (J). (gr. 8). 1997. pap. 16.20 (*1-56510-700-4*); lib. bdg. 26.20 (*1-56510-701-2*) Greenhaven.
Dudley, William, ed. African Americans: Opposing Viewpoints. LC 96-18328. (Opposing Viewpoints Ser.). (Illus.). 1996. pap. 16.20 (*1-56510-521-4*); lib. bdg. 26.20 (*1-56510-522-2*) Greenhaven.
— The American Revolution: Opposing Viewpoints. LC 92-21795. (American History Ser.). 288p. (YA). 1992. pap. 16.20 (*1-56510-010-7*); lib. bdg. 26.20 (*1-56510-011-5*) Greenhaven.
— Asian Americans. LC 96-30439. (Opposing Viewpoints Ser.). (Illus.). (J). (gr. 5-12). 1997. pap. 16.20 (*1-56510-523-0*) Greenhaven.
— The Bill of Rights: Opposing Viewpoints. LC 93-4575. (American History Ser.). 312p. 1994. pap. 16.20 (*1-56510-087-5*); lib. bdg. 26.20 (*1-56510-088-3*) Greenhaven.
— The Creation of the Constitution: Opposing Viewpoints. (American History Ser.). (Illus.). 312p. 1995. pap. 16.20 (*1-56510-220-7*) Greenhaven.
— Epidemics: Opposing Viewpoints. LC 98-28458. (Opposing Viewpoints Ser.). (Illus.). 188p. (YA). (gr. 9-12). 1998. pap. 16.20 (*1-56510-940-6*) Greenhaven.
***Dudley, William, ed.** Epidemics: Opposing Viewpoints. LC 98-28458. (Opposing Viewpoints Ser.). (Illus.). (YA). (gr. 9-12). 1998. lib. bdg. 26.20 (*1-56510-941-4*) Greenhaven.
Dudley, William, ed. Homosexuality: Opposing Viewpoints. LC 92-40705. (Opposing Viewpoints Ser.). (Illus.). 216p. (YA). (gr. 10 up). 1993. pap. text 16.20 (*0-89908-456-7*) Greenhaven.
— The Industrial Revolution. (Opposing Viewpoints Ser.). (Illus.). (YA). (gr. 5-12). 1997. pap. 16.20 (*1-56510-706-3*); lib. bdg. 26.20 (*1-56510-707-1*) Greenhaven.
— Marijuana. LC 98-35006. (At Issue Ser.). 96p. (YA). (gr. 9-12). 1998. lib. bdg. 19.95 (*0-7377-0007-6*) Greenhaven.
***Dudley, William, ed.** Marijuana. LC 98-35006. (At Issue Ser.). 95p. (YA). (gr. 9-12). 1998. pap. 12.45 (*0-7377-0006-8*) Greenhaven.
Dudley, William, ed. The Middle East: Opposing Viewpoints. LC 91-43280. (Illus.). 264p. (YA). (gr. 10 up). 1992. pap. text 16.20 (*0-89908-160-6*) Greenhaven.
— Native Americans. LC 97-38334. (Opposing Viewpoints Ser.). (Illus.). (YA). (gr. 5-12). 1997. pap. 16.20 (*1-56510-704-7*); lib. bdg. 26.20 (*1-56510-705-5*) Greenhaven.
— The 1960s. LC 96-49282. (Opposing Viewpoints Ser.). (Illus.). (J). (gr. 5-12). 1996. pap. 16.20 (*1-56510-525-7*); lib. bdg. 26.20 (*1-56510-526-5*) Greenhaven.
— Opposing Viewpoints in American History, Vol. 2. LC 95-33446. (Illus.). 352p. (YA). (gr. 5-12). 1996. lib. bdg. 37.44 (*1-56510-350-5*) Greenhaven.
— Opposing Viewpoints in American History, Vol. II. LC 95-33446. (Illus.). 352p. (J). (gr. 5-12). 1996. pap. text 21.20 (*1-56510-349-1*) Greenhaven.
— Reconstruction: Opposing Viewpoints. (American History Ser.). (Illus.). 310p. 1995. pap. text 16.20 (*1-56510-226-6*, 2266); lib. bdg. 26.20 (*1-56510-227-4*, 2274) Greenhaven.
— Sexually Transmitted Diseases. LC 98-38040. (At Issue Ser.). 95p. (YA). (gr. 9-12). 1998. pap. 13.70 (*0-7377-0010-6*) Greenhaven.
***Dudley, William, ed.** Sexually Transmitted Diseases. LC 98-38040. (At Issue Ser.). 95p. (YA). (gr. 9-12). 1998. lib. bdg. 21.20 (*0-7377-0011-4*) Greenhaven.
Dudley, William, ed. World War I. (Opposing Viewpoints Ser.). (Illus.). (YA). (gr. 5-12). 1997. pap. 16.20 (*1-56510-702-0*); lib. bdg. 26.20 (*1-56510-703-9*) Greenhaven.
— World War II. LC 96-44978. (Opposing Viewpoints Ser.). (Illus.). (J). (gr. 5-12). 1997. pap. 16.20 (*1-56510-527-3*); lib. bdg. 26.20 (*1-56510-528-1*) Greenhaven.
Dudley, William & Szumski, Bonnie, eds. America's Future: Opposing Viewpoints. LC 89-25885. (Opposing Viewpoints Ser.). (Illus.). 312p. (YA). (gr. 10 up). 1990. pap. text 16.20 (*0-89908-423-0*) Greenhaven.
Dudley, William & Tipp, Stacey, eds. Iraq. LC 91-30036. (Current Controversies Ser.). 256p. (YA). (gr. 10 up). 1991. pap. text 16.20 (*0-89908-581-4*); lib. bdg. 26.20 (*0-89908-575-X*) Greenhaven.
Dudley, William, ed. see Woog, Adam.
Dudley, William H. Quandary 2000: The How to Guide for Developing & Implementing a Plan to Address the Y2K Computer Issues. 2nd rev. ed. Fuentes, Miguel & Dudley, Bev, eds. vi, 43p. 1998. 29.95 (*0-9669857-0-2*) JC Cnsltng.
Dudley, William S., ed. The Naval War of 1812 Vol. 1: 1812: A Documentary History. (Illus.). 714p. (C). 1985. 34.00 (*0-945274-06-8*) Naval Hist Ctr.
— The Naval War of 1812 Vol. 2: 1813: A Documentary History. (Illus.). 779p. (C). 1992. 43.00 (*0-685-71187-0*) Naval Hist Ctr.
Dudley, William S. & Crawford, Michael J., eds. The Naval War of 1812: A Documentary History, Vol. 1. LC 85-600565. 772p. 1985. 44.00 (*0-16-002042-5*, S/N 008-046-00112-0) USGPO.
Dudman, J. Division of Berlin, Set II. (Flashpoints Ser.). (Illus.). 80p. (YA). (gr. 7 up). 1988. lib. bdg. 23.93 (*0-86592-037-0*) Rourke Enter.
Dudman, John. Earthquake. LC 92-41510. (Violent Earth Ser.). (Illus.). 32p. (J). 1993. lib. bdg. 5.00 (*1-56847-000-2*) Raintree Steck-V.
— Volcano. LC 92-41511. (Violent Earth Ser.). (Illus.). 32p. (J). (gr. 2-7). 1993. lib. bdg. 21.40 (*1-56847-001-0*) Raintree Steck-V.
Dudman, K. JSP for Practical Program Design. LC 97-108055. 256p. 1996. pap. 39.95 (*0-387-91504-4*) Spr-Verlag.
Dudman, Martha T. Dawn: Short Stories & a Novella. 136p. (Orig.). 1990. pap. 8.95 (*0-913006-42-4*) Puckerbrush.
Dudman, Richard. Forty Days with the Enemy. LC 70-157097. (Illus.). 1972. pap. 2.45 (*0-87140-259-9*, Pub. by Liveright) Norton.
Dudney, Matt, et al. The Mandrell Family Cookbook. LC 99-28592. (Illus.). 175p. 1999. 19.95 (*1-55853-752-X*) Rutledge Hill Pr.
Dudoit, Mahealani, ed. He Oia Mau No Kakou: We Go On. 224p. 1998. pap. 12.95 (*0-9668220-0-5*) Kuleana Oiwi.
Dudok, G. A. Development of English Prose in the Nineteenth Century. (English Literature Ser.: No. 33). (C). 1970. reprint ed. pap. 12.95 (*0-8383-0022-7*) M S G Haskell Hse.
Dudon, Paul. St. Ignatius of Loyola. Young, William J., tr. LC 83-45591. reprint ed. 49.50 (*0-404-19884-8*) AMS Pr.
Dudovitz, Neal, jt. auth. see Fretz, Burton.
Dudovitz, Resa, ed. see Kuspit, Donald.
Dudovitz, Resa L., ed. Women in Academe. 118p. 1984. 19.25 (*0-08-030819-8*, 26/13, Pergamon Pr) Elsevier.
Dudrick, Stanley J., jt. ed. see Kirby, Donald F.
Dudson, Audrey M. Cheese Dishes: A Guide to Cheese Dishes from, 1750-1940. 128p. 1993. 35.00 (*0-9510126-1-4*, Pub. by R Dennis) Antique Collect.
Duduit, Michael. Abingdon Preaching Annual: 1998 Edition. 1997. 30.00 (*0-687-08209-9*); 30.00 (*0-687-08279-X*) Abingdon.
***Duduit, Michael.** The Abingdon Preaching Annual, 1999 Edition. 464p. 1998. 19.95 (*0-687-06722-7*) Abingdon.
Duduit, Michael, ed. Abingdon Preaching Annual 1998. 448p. 1997. 19.95 (*0-687-08329-X*) Abingdon.
— Communicate with Power: Insights from America's Top Communicators. 256p. 1998. pap. 14.99 (*0-8010-9060-1*) Baker Bks.
— Handbook of Contemporary Preaching. 656p. 1993. 34.99 (*0-8054-1550-5*, 4215-50) Broadman.
Duduit, Michael, ed. The Abingdon Preaching Annual 1996. 448p. 1995. 19.95 (*0-687-00121-8*) Abingdon.
— The Abingdon Preaching Annual, 1997 Edition. 448p. 1996. 29.95 incl. disk (*0-687-01986-9*); disk 29.95 (*0-687-01987-7*); mac hd 29.95 (*0-614-18851-2*) Abingdon.
Dudukovic, Milorad P. & Mills, Patrick L., eds. Chemical & Catalytic Reactor Modeling. LC 83-22378. (ACS Symposium Ser.: No. 237). 426p. 1984. lib. bdg. 65.95 (*0-8412-0815-8*) Am Chemical.
— Chemical & Catalytic Reactor Modeling. LC 83-22378. (ACS Symposium Ser.: Vol. 237). 436p. 1984. reprint ed. pap. 135.20 (*0-608-03068-6*, 206352100007) Bks Demand.
Duduman, Dumitru. Through the Fire: The True Story of a Romanian Pastor Facing Communist Persecution. 120p. 1991. pap. 8.95 (*1-879913-00-3*) Christ Creator.
— Through the Fire Without Burning. (Illus.). 198p. (Orig.). 1992. pap. 9.95 (*0-9635055-0-5*); disk. write for info. (*0-9635055-1-3*) Hand of Help.
Dudwick, Nora, jt. auth. see De Soto, Hermine G.
Dudycha, George J. Psychology for Law Enforcement Officers. (Illus.). 416p. 1982. 63.95 (*0-398-00482-X*); pap. 49.95 (*0-398-06098-3*) C C Thomas.
Dudyche, George J. Applied Psychology. LC 63-13748. (Illus.). 478p. reprint ed. pap. 148.20 (*0-8357-5688-2*, 201255300081) Bks Demand.
Dudziak, J. J., jt. auth. see Zong, C.
***Dudziak, Mary L.** Cold War Civil Rights: Race & the Image of American Democracy. LC 00-38515. (Politics & Society in Twentieth-Century America Ser.). (Illus.). 352p. 2000. 29.95 (*0-691-01661-5*) Princeton U Pr.
Dudzinski, Andrzej. Andrzej Dudzinski. 208p. 1998. 49.95 (*83-221-0672-6*) Gingko Press.
Dudzinski, George. Opportunities in Tool & Die. (Opportunities In . . . Ser.). (Illus.). 160p. pap. 11.95 (*0-8442-4048-6*, 40486, VGM Career) NTC Contemp Pub Co.
***Dudzinski, Kathleen.** Meeting Dolphins. LC 99-39069. 64p. (J). (gr. 4-6). 2000. per. 17.95 (*0-7922-7129-7*, Pub. by Natl Geog) S&S Trade.
Due, Andrea. The Atlas of the Bible Lands: History, Daily Life & Traditions. LC 98-35908. (Atlas Ser.). (Illus.). 62p. (J). (gr. 5-9). 1999. 19.95 (*0-87226-559-5*, 65595B, P Bedrick Books) NTC Contemp Pub Co.
— People & the Earth: An Environmental Atlas. LC 98-7395. (J). 1998. lib. bdg. 235.00 (*0-7172-9204-5*) Grolier Educ.
Due, Bodil. The Cyropaedia: Xenophon's Aims & Methods. LC 99-214691. 256p. (C). 1990. text 27.00 (*87-7288-246-8*, Pub. by Aarhus Univ Pr) David Brown.
Due, John F. Indirect Taxation in Developing Economies. rev. ed. LC 87-46310. (Johns Hopkins Studies in Development). 256p. 1988. reprint ed. pap. 79.40 (*0-608-03681-1*, 206450700009) Bks Demand.
— Sales Taxation: State & Local Structure & Administration. LC 82-13968. (Illus.). 368p. 1983. reprint ed. pap. 114.10 (*0-608-05952-8*, 206628900008) Bks Demand.
Due, John F. & Mikesell, John L. Sales Taxation. 2nd ed. 375p. (C). 1994. lib. bdg. 58.00 (*0-87766-627-X*) Urban Inst.
Due, John F., et al. Transportation Service to Small Rural Communities: Effects of Deregulation. LC 89-11151. (Illus.). 231p. 1990. reprint ed. pap. 71.70 (*0-608-00094-9*, 206085900006) Bks Demand.
Due, Linnea, ed. Hot Ticket. LC 97-4995. 232p. (Orig.). 1997. pap. 11.95 (*1-55583-379-9*) Alyson Pubns.
***Due, Linnea, ed.** Uniform Sex: Erotic Stories of Women in Service. 288p. 2000. pap. 12.95 (*1-55583-545-7*, Pub. by Alyson Pubns) Consort Bk Sales.
Due, Richard. Object Engineering: Managing Object Technology. (C). 1997. pap. text. write for info. (*0-8053-3118-2*) Addison-Wesley.
Due, Tananarive. The Between: A Novel. LC 95-2415. 288p. 1996. pap. 13.00 (*0-06-092726-7*) HarpC.
***Due, Tananarive.** The Black Rose: The Magnificent Story of Madam C. J. Walker, America's First Black Female Millionaire. 352p. 2000. 25.95 (*0-345-43960-0*) Ballantine Pub Grp.
Due, Tananarive. My Soul to Keep. LC 97-4992. 352p. 1998. pap. 15.00 (*0-06-105366-X*, HarperPrism) HarpC.
Due, William J. La, see La Due, William J.
Duebendorfer, Ernest M., jt. auth. see Rowland, Stephen M.
Dueber, Julianne. Juntos. (C). 1989. pap. text, wbk. ed. 15.00 (*0-13-512526-X*) P-H.
— Juntos: An Intermediate Course. 352p. (C). 1989. pap. text 33.75 (*0-13-512500-6*) P-H.
— Spanish Vocabulary. (SPA & ENG.). 256p. 1990. pap. 6.95 (*0-8120-4498-3*) Barron.
***Dueber, Julianne.** Ultimate High School Survival Guide: Make the Most of Your High School Experience. 275p. 1999. pap. 14.95 (*0-7689-0241-X*) Petersons.
Dueber, Ross E. & McKnight, Darren S. Chemical Principles Applied to Spacecraft Operations. LC 90-28269. 216p. (C). 1993. lib. bdg. 64.50 (*0-89464-036-4*) Krieger.
Dueck. Digital Applications: Lab Manual. (Electronics Technology Ser.). 1999. pap. 43.95 (*0-7668-1696-6*) Delmar.
— Digital Electronics. Date not set. pap. text, student ed. write for info. (*0-314-03267-3*) West Pub.
— Digital Electronics Principles. (Electronics Technology Ser.). 2000. pap. 89.95 (*0-7668-1160-3*); pap., lab manual ed. 25.00 (*0-7668-1161-1*) Delmar.
Dueck, Abe J. Moving Beyond Secession: The Mennonite Brethren Conference in Russia, 1872-1922. (Perspectives on Mennonite Life & Thought Ser.: No. 13). (Illus.). 179p. 1998. pap. 16.95 (*0-921788-47-9*) Kindred Prods.
Dueck, Adele. Anywhere but Here. (Northern Lights Young Novels Ser.). 112p. (YA). (gr. 4-9). 1996. pap. 8.95 (*0-88995-147-0*, Pub. by Red Deer) Genl Dist Srvs.
***Dueck, Daniela.** Strabo of Amasia: A Greek Man of Letters in Augustan Rome. LC 99-87661. 2000. write for info. (*0-415-21672-9*) Routledge.
Dueck, Dora. Under the Still Standing Sun. 279p. (Orig.). 1989. pap. 4.95 (*0-919797-93-8*) Kindred Prods.
Dueck, Elena R. de, see Cabrera, Sandra Z. & De Dueck, Elena R.
Dueck, Gerry, ed. Kids for the World: A Guidebook for Children's Mission Resources. 2nd rev. ed. (Illus.). 168p. 1996. pap. text 10.95 (*0-87808-768-0*, WCL768-0) William Carey Lib.
Dueck, Lynette. Sing Me No More. 128p. 1992. pap. 12.95 (*0-88974-046-1*, Pub. by Press Gang Pubs) LPC InBook.
Dueck, Robert K. Fundamentals of Digital Electronics. Contry, ed. LC 93-33038. 850p. (C). 1994. pap. 51.25 (*0-314-02424-7*) West Pub.
***Dueck, Stephan & Ivey, Monteria.** The Field Guide to White People. LC 99-88387. 96p. 2000. pap. 8.95 (*0-609-80542-8*, Three Riv Pr) Crown Pub Group.
Dueck, Walter. Family Documents: What They Are, Where They Are. LC 97-900873. 64p. 1997. pap. text 7.25 (*0-9682628-0-5*, Pub. by Wat5erside Hse) Assoc Pubs Grp.
Duecker, Werner W. & West, James R., eds. The Manufacture of Sulfuric Acid. LC 59-15498. (ACS Monograph Ser.: Vol. 144). (Illus.). 525p. 1959. reprint ed. pap. 162.80 (*0-608-06932-9*, 206714000009) Bks Demand.
Duedall, I. W. Papers from the 8th International Ocean Disposal Symposium 9-13 October 1989, Dubrovnik, Yugoslavia, Pt. I. 127p. 1991. pap. text 355.00 (*2-88124-797-0*) Gordon & Breach.
Duedall, I. W., ed. Second International Ocean Pollution Symposium, Beijing, China, 4-8 October, 1993, Vol. 2. 190p. 1995. pap. text 50.00 (*2-88449-050-7*) Gordon & Breach.
— Second International Ocean Pollution Symposium, Beijing, China, 4-8 October, 1993, Vol. 4. 115p. 1995. pap. text 50.00 (*2-88449-053-1*); pap. text 99.00 (*90-5699-017-9*) Gordon & Breach.
Duedall, Iver W., jt. ed. see Baumgartner, D. J.
Duedall, Iver. W., ed. see Capuzzo, Judith M. & Kester, Dana R.
Duedney, Daniel. Space: The High Frontier in Perspective. LC 82-50920. (Worldwatch Papers). 1982. pap. 5.00 (*0-916468-49-6*) Worldwatch Inst.
Duehr, Gary. Where Everyone Is Going To. 64p. 1999. pap. 11.00 (*1-879934-60-4*) St Andrews NC.
— Winter Light. LC 98-72331. (Stahlecker Ser.). 1999. pap. 12.95 (*1-884800-20-3*) Four Way Bks.
***Duehring, Erin.** Twenty-Three. 28p. 1999. pap. write for info. (*1-930254-02-4*) Premiere Gen.
Duekek, Christopher. Scuba Diving for Safety. 1978. pap. 6.95 (*0-02-499750-1*, Macmillan Coll) P-H.
Dueker, Alice K. Elder Law in New Jersey: Finding Solutions for Legal Problems. LC 99-32375. 150p. 2000. pap. 18.00 (*0-8135-2736-8*); text 40.00 (*0-8135-2735-X*) Rutgers U Pr.
Dueker, Christopher W. Scuba Diving Safety. LC 78-55789. 200p. 1979. pap. 6.95 (*0-89037-135-0*) Anderson World.
Dueker, Joyce S. The Power of Surrender. (Illus.). 51p. 1998. pap. 8.25 (*0-9614638-1-3*) Diving Safety.
***Dueker, Kenneth J., et al.** Strategies to Attract Auto Users to Public Transportation. LC 98-61201. (TCRP Report Ser.). 105 p. 1998. write for info. (*0-309-06307-8*) Natl Acad Pr.
Duel, Debra. William's Story. (Illus.). 48p. (Orig.). (J). (gr. k-8). 1992. pap. 9.95 (*1-880812-02-9*) S Ink WA.
Dueland, Joy. Barn Kitten, House Kitten. (Illus.). (J). (gr. 2-8). 1978. pap. 3.50 (*0-931942-00-4*) Phunn Pubs.
— The Blessings of Jesus. (Illus.). 1979. 8.95 (*0-931942-01-2*) Phunn Pubs.
— Dear Tabby. (Illus.). (J). (gr. 4-8). 1978. pap. 2.50 (*0-931942-02-0*) Phunn Pubs.
— God's Great Adventure. (Illus.). 111p. (J). (ps up). 1980. 8.95 (*0-685-08285-7*) Phunn Pubs.
— Kitten in the Manger. (Illus.). 32p. (J). (gr. 2-8). 1981. pap. 6.95 (*0-685-08286-5*) Phunn Pubs.
Duelist, Magazine. Magic: The Gathering Vol. 2: The Official Encyclopedia. 5th ed. LC 96-61056. (Illus.). 144p. 1997. pap. text 21.95 (*1-56025-150-6*, Thunders Mouth) Avalon NY.

D

Duell, jt. auth. see Smith.

Duelli-Klein, Renate, ed. So Far, So Good, So What? Women's Studies in the U. K. 100p. 1984. pap. 19.25 (*0-08-030816-3*, Pergamon Pr) Elsevier.

Duelli-Klein, Renate, jt. ed. see Bowles, Gloria.

Duellman, Elmer. Elmer's Price Guide to Toys, Vol. 1. (Illus.). 367p. 1994. pap. 29.95 (*0-89538-073-0*) L-W Inc.

— Elmer's Price Guide to Toys, Vol. II. (Illus.). 352p. 1996. pap. 29.95 (*0-89538-046-3*) L-W Inc.

Duellman, William E. Amphibian Species of the World: Additions & Corrections. Trueb, Linda, ed. (Special Publications: No. 21). 372p. pap. text 35.00 (*0-89338-045-8*) U KS Nat Hist Mus.

— Centrolenid Frogs from Peru. (Occasional Papers: No. 52). 11p. 1976. pap. 1.00 (*0-686-80349-3*) U KS Nat Hist Mus.

— Patterns of Distribution of Amphibians: A Global Perspective. LC 98-49449. 648p. 1999. 69.95 (*0-8018-6115-2*) Johns Hopkins.

— A Systematic Review of the Marsupial Frogs: Hylidae: Gastrotheca, of the Andes of Ecuador. (Occasional Papers: No. 22). 27p. 1974. pap. 1.00 (*0-686-80347-7*) U KS Nat Hist Mus.

— Three New Species of Centrolenid Frogs from the Pacific Versant of Ecuador & Colombia. (Occasional Papers: No. 88). 9p. 1981. 1.00 (*0-317-04856-2*) U KS Nat Hist Mus.

Duellman, William E. & Fritts, Thomas H. A Taxonomic Review of the Southern Andean Marsupial Frogs (Hylidae Gastrotheca) (Occasional Papers: No. 9). 37p. 1972. pap. 1.00 (*0-686-80344-2*) U KS Nat Hist Mus.

Duellman, William E. & Pyles, Rebecca A. A New Marsupial Frog: Hylidae: Gastrotheca, from the Andes of Ecuador. (Occasional Papers: No. 84). 13p. 1980. 1.00 (*0-317-04854-6*) U KS Nat Hist Mus.

Duellman, William E. & Trueb, Linda. Biology of Amphibians. LC 93-24401. 694p. (C). 1994. pap. text 39.95 (*0-8018-4780-X*) Johns Hopkins.

— The Systematic Status & Relationships of the Hylid Frog Nyctimantis Rugiceps Boulenger. (Occasional Papers: No. 58). 14p. 1976. pap. 1.00 (*0-686-80350-7*) U KS Nat Hist Mus.

Duellman, William E. & Veloso, Alberto. Phylogeny of Pleurodema: Anura: Leptodactylidae, a Biogeographic Model. (Occasional Papers: No. 64). 46p. 1977. pap. 1.00 (*0-686-80351-5*) U KS Nat Hist Mus.

Duellman, William E., jt. auth. see Lynch, John D.

Duellman, William E., jt. auth. see Rodriguez, Lily O.

Duellman, William Edward, jt. auth. see Lynch, John D.

Duemer, Joe & Simmerman, Jim, eds. Dog Music: Poetry about Dogs. (Illus.). 288p. 1995. text 16.95 (*0-312-13964-0*) St Martin.

Duemer, Joseph. Customs. LC 87-13791. (Contemporary Poetry Ser.). 104p. 1987. pap. 14.95 (*0-8203-0967-2*) U of Ga Pr.

— Dog Music. Simmerman, Jim, ed. (Illus.). 288p. 1997. pap. 9.95 (*0-312-15113-6*) St Martin.

— Static. 69p. 1996. pap. 12.00 (*0-937669-57-1*) Owl Creek Pr.

***Duemer, Joseph & Rakowski, David.** Making Musics: Contemporary Collaborations Between Poets & Composers. (Border Crossings Ser.: 8). 340p. 2000. 75.00 (*0-8153-2504-5*) Garland.

Duemler, David G. Bringing Life to the Stars. 206p. (C). 1993. pap. text 22.50 (*0-8191-8955-3*) U Pr of Amer.

— Bringing Life to the Stars. 206p. (C). 1993. lib. bdg. 47.50 (*0-8191-8954-5*) U Pr of Amer.

Duenas. Curso Basico de Correspondencia Comercial. 120p. 1982. text 10.12 (*0-07-017995-6*) McGraw.

— Curso Basico de Matematicas Comerciales. 172p. 1982. text 8.56 (*0-07-017994-8*) McGraw.

— Curso Basico de Mecanografia. 84p. 1982. text 9.88 (*0-07-017991-3*) McGraw.

— Curso Basico de Practicas Secretariales. 120p. 1982. text 10.56 (*0-07-017992-1*) McGraw.

Duenez, Ricardo. Optimizing Brown: An Indigenous Examination of Latino Roots, Values, & Rights. LC 97-106895. (Illus.). 60p. (Orig.). 1996. pap. 4.95 (*0-9655220-0-8*) Tlacatlihua Communs.

Duenk, Lester G., ed. Improving Vocational Curriculum. 3rd ed. LC 92-31261. 269p. 1993. 33.28 (*0-87006-031-7*) Goodheart.

Duenk, Lester G., et al. Auto Body Repair. 2nd ed. (gr. 9-12). 1984. text 45.75 (*0-02-662340-4*) Glencoe.

— Autobody Repair. 1984. student ed. 5.00 (*0-02-662320-X*) Glencoe.

Duenkel, Frieder, jt. auth. see Van Zyl Smit, Dirk.

Duensing, Edward. Talking to Fireflies, Shrinking the Moon: Activities for All Ages. (Illus.). 144p. (Orig.). 1997. pap. 15.95 (*1-55591-310-5*) Fulcrum Pub.

Duensing, Edward & Millmoss, A. B. Backyard & Beyond: A Guide for Discovering the Outdoors. (Illus.). 264p. 1992. pap. 14.95 (*1-55591-071-8*) Fulcrum Pub.

Duensing, Edward E. Information Sources in Urban & Regional Planning: A Directory & Guide to Reference Materials. LC 93-26775. 184p. (C). 1994. 24.95 (*0-88285-146-2*) Ctr Urban Pol Res.

— Information Sources in Urban & Regional Planning: A Directory & Guide to Reference Materials. 178p. 1994. 24.95 (*0-614-04060-4*) Transaction Pubs.

Duensing, Edward E., ed. America's Elderly: A Sourcebook. LC 88-6132. 197p. 1988. 1.00 (*0-88285-125-X*) Ctr Urban Pol Res.

Duensing, Paul H., tr. see Hamady, Walter S.

Duentzer, Heinrich. De Zenodoti Studiis Homericis. vii, 218p. 1981. reprint ed. write for info. (*3-487-07051-0*) G Olms Pubs.

Duenwald, Kimberley, tr. see Keller, Rudi.

Duenwald, Kimberley, tr. see Keller, Rudki.

Duer, Don. Penny Banks Around the World. LC 96-33470. 200p. (gr. 10). 1997. 49.95 (*0-7643-0019-9*) Schiffer.

— A Penny Saved: Still & Mechanical Banks. LC 93-85081. (Illus.). 176p. 1993. 59.95 (*0-88740-528-2*) Schiffer.

Duer, John. The Law & Practice of Marine Insurance, Deduced from a Critical Examination of the Adjudged Cases, the Nature & Analogies of the Subject, & the General Usage of Commercial Nations, 2 vols., Set. LC 72-37972. (American Law: The Formative Years). 1650p. 1972. reprint ed. 108.95 (*0-405-04010-5*) Ayer.

— The Law & Practice of Marine Insurance, Deduced from a Critical Examination of the Adjudged Cases, the Nature & Analogies of the Subject, & the General Usage of Commercial Nations, 2 vols., Vol. 1. LC 72-37972. (American Law: The Formative Years). 1650p. 1972. reprint ed. 54.95 (*0-405-04011-3*) Ayer.

— The Law & Practice of Marine Insurance, Deduced from a Critical Examination of the Adjudged Cases, the Nature & Analogies of the Subject, & the General Usage of Commercial Nations, 2 vols., Vol. 2. LC 72-37972. (American Law: The Formative Years). 1650p. 1972. reprint ed. 54.95 (*0-405-04012-1*) Ayer.

Duer, William A. A Course of Lectures on the Constitutional Jurisprudence of the United States, 1856. LC 99-16385. 2000. reprint ed. 85.00 (*1-58477-020-1*) Lawbk Exchange.

— Life of Lord Stirling: Collections of the N. J. Historical Society, Vol. II. (American Revolution Ser.: Vol. 4). (Illus.). 162p. 1997. 11.95 (*1-58057-018-6*, LOLS001B) Digital Antiq.

Duerbeck, H. W., jt. ed. see Flin, P.

Duerbeck, Hilmar, jt. auth. see Fischer, Daniel.

Duerbeck, Hilmar W. A Reference Catalog & Atlas of Galactic Novae. (C). 1987. text 145.50 (*90-277-2535-7*) Kluwer Academic.

Duerden, Brian I., et al, eds. Medical & Environmental Aspects of Anaerobes. 280p. 1992. 89.00 (*1-871816-13-0*, Pub. by Wrightson Biomed) Taylor & Francis.

Duerden, Brian I., et al. Microbiol & Parasitic Infection. 7th ed. 256p. 1993. pap. text 36.50 (*0-340-56018-5*, Pub. by E A) OUP.

Duerden, Bruce. Don't Break a Leg! A Manual for Theatre Safety. (Illus.). 30p. (Orig.). (YA). (gr. 9 up). 1996. pap. text 8.95 (*1-57514-020-9*, 5019) Encore Perform Pub.

Duerden, Richard. The Air's Nearly Perfect Elasticity. 1979. pap. 3.50 (*0-939180-08-1*) Tombouctou.

Duerdon, I. J., jt. auth. see Hearle, John W.

Duerfeldt, Pryse H., ed. see O'Dell, Richard F.

Duerichen, Norbert. Woodburning Stoves. (Illus.). 112p. pap. 7.95 (*0-88839-133-1*) Hancock House.

Duerig, Alfred W., jt. auth. see Kraus, Constantine R.

Duerig, M. & Laffer, U., eds. Tumorchirurgie und Lebensqualitaet. (Basler Beitraege zur Chirurgie Ser.: Vol. 2). (Illus.). x, 168p. 1989. 65.25 (*3-8055-5070-7*) S Karger.

Duerig, M., jt. ed. see Laffer, U.

Duerig, T. W., et al, eds. Engineering Aspects of Shape Memory Alloys. LC 90-2104. (Illus.). 511p. 1990. pap. 158.50 (*0-608-04998-0*, 206561600004) Bks Demand.

***Duerinckx, Andre J.** Coronary Magnetic Resonance Angiography. LC 99-53567. 2000. write for info. (*0-387-94959-3*) Spr-Verlag.

Duerinckx, Andre J., ed. MRI of the Cardiovascular System. (MRI Teaching File Ser.). 304p. 1993. text 76.00 (*0-88167-707-8*) Lppncott W & W.

Duerk, Donna & Campbell, David, eds. The Challenge of Diversity: EDRA Proceedings: 1984. 344p. 1984. 35.00 (*0-939922-05-3*) EDRA.

Duerk, Donna P. Architectural Programming: Information Management for Design. LC 93-10180. 258p. 1993. pap. text 49.95 (*0-442-01026-5*, VNR) Wiley.

Duerk, Donna P. Architectural Programming: Information Management for Design. 272p. 1993. pap. 54.95 (*0-471-28468-8*, VNR) Wiley.

Duerk, Judith. Circle of Stones: Woman's Journey to Herself. 2nd anniversary ed. LC 98-52771. (Circle of Stones Ser.: No. 1). 128p. (Orig.). 1999. pap. 13.95 (*1-880913-36-4*) Innisfree Pr.

***Duerk, Judith.** I Sit Listening to the Wind: Woman's Encounter Within Herself. 2nd rev. ed. LC 98-52771. (Circle of Stones Ser.: No. 2). 128p. (Orig.). 1999. pap. 13.95 (*1-880913-37-2*) Innisfree Pr.

Duerkop, Margaret, ed. see Wittgenstein, Herta.

Duerksen, Carl. Monterey Peninsula Sketches. (Illus.). 96p. (Orig.). 1997. mass mkt. 14.95 (*0-9657579-0-0*) C Duerksen.

***Duerksen, Carol.** God's Gift of Sex. (Fast Lane Bible Studies). 52p. (YA). 2000. pap. 9.95 (*0-87303-400-7*) Faith & Life.

Duerksen, Carol. Living Beyond Our Means: The Extravagance of Biblical Stewardship. (Generation Why: Vol. 2:3). 36p. (YA). (gr. 9-12). 1996. pap. 12.95 (*0-87303-267-5*) Faith & Life.

— Slickfester Dude Tells Bedtime Stories: Life Lessons from Our Animal Friends. LC 97-61515. (Illus.). 96p. (J). (gr. k-8). 1997. pap. 9.95 (*0-9648525-7-8*) Willowsprng.

— Understanding Gangs. (Fast Lane Bible Studies Ser.). 48p. (J). (gr. 7-9). 1995. pap. 9.95 (*0-87303-245-4*) Faith & Life.

***Duerksen, Carol & Knepp, Maynard.** Affair of the Heart. LC 98-61365. (Skye Ser.: Vol. 2). 178p. 1998. pap. 9.95 (*0-9648525-8-6*) Willowsprng.

Duerksen, Carol & Knepp, Maynard. Becca. LC 97-60524. (Jonas Ser.: Vol. 4). (Illus.). 160p. (Orig.). 1997. pap. 9.95 (*0-9648525-4-3*) Willowsprng.

— Hitched. LC 96-60896. (Jonas Ser.: Bk. 2). (Illus.). 144p. (Orig.). 1996. pap. 9.95 (*0-9648525-1-9*) Willowsprng.

— Preacher. LC 96-61387. (Jonas Ser.: Vol. 3). (Illus.). 136p. (Orig.). 1996. pap. 9.95 (*0-9648525-2-7*) Willowsprng.

— Runaway Buggy. LC 95-61742. (Jonas Ser.: Bk. 1). (Illus.). 144p. (Orig.). 1995. pap. 9.95 (*0-9648525-0-0*) Willowsprng.

— Twins. LC 97-61694. (Skye Ser.: Vol. 1). 196p. 1997. pap. 9.95 (*0-9648525-6-X*) Willowsprng.

Duerksen, Carol, et al. Through Fire & Water: An Overview of Mennonite History. LC 96-12242. (Illus.). 320p. (Orig.). 1996. pap. 15.99 (*0-8361-9015-7*) Herald Pr.

Duerksen, Lu & Nelson, Kathryn. Lawn Art, Kansas. LC 96-69167. (Illus.). 96p. (Orig.). 1996. pap. 12.95 (*0-9645085-8-3*) Prtnrshp Bk Servs.

Duerksen, Menno. Dear God, I'm Only a Boy. rev. ed. LC 95-60240. x, 406p. 1995. 21.95 (*0-945530-14-5*) Wordsworth KS.

Duerksen, Roland A., ed. see Shelley, Percy Bysshe.

Duerling, Nan. The New International Lesson Annual, 1995-96. 400p. (Orig.). 1995. pap. 11.95 (*0-687-19159-9*) Abingdon.

Duerling, Nan, ed. The New International Lesson Annual, 1999-2000. 140.00 (*0-687-02293-2*) Abingdon.

Duerling, Nan, ed. The New International Lesson Annual, 1999-2000. 488p. 1999. pap. 14.00 (*0-687-02303-3*) Abingdon.

— The New International Lesson Annual, 1996-97. 480p. (Orig.). 1996. pap. 12.50 (*0-687-00279-6*) Abingdon.

— The New International Lesson Annual, 1997-98. 488p. 1997. 12.95 (*0-687-01523-5*) Abingdon.

— The Word & You Vol. 1: A Lectionary-Based Exploration of the Bible. LC 97-16314. 248p. (Orig.). 1997. pap. 14.95 (*0-8298-1165-6*) Pilgrim OH.

— The Word & You Vol. 2: A Lectionary-Based Exploration of the Bible. 256p. (Orig.). 1998. pap. 14.95 (*0-8298-1241-5*) Pilgrim OH.

— The Word & You Vol. 3: A Lectionary-Based Exploration of the Bible. 264p. 1999. pap. 14.95 (*0-8298-1309-8*) Pilgrim OH.

Duerlinger, James P., ed. Ultimate Reality & Spiritual Discipline. (Contemporary Discussion Ser.). 237p. (C). 1984. text 22.95 (*0-913757-09-8*); pap. text 12.95 (*0-913757-08-X*) Paragon Hse.

Duermeier, Dennis, jt. ed. see Lombardo, Stan.

Duermueller, Urs. Towards a Varieties Grammar of English. 238p. 1982. pap. 16.00 (*3-261-05027-6*) P Lang Pubng.

Duerr, Art, jt. auth. see Hartman, Kane.

Duerr, Catherine. Hold Me Tightly: Devotions for Mothers of Young Children. 160p. 1996. pap. 8.99 (*0-570-04847-8*, 12-3284) Concordia.

***Duerr, Catherine.** Holding Hands. 1999. pap. 10.99 (*0-570-05398-6*); pap. text 10.99 (*0-570-05243-2*) Concordia.

— Holding Hands. LC 99-50850. 208p. 2000. pap. 10.99 (*0-570-05267-X*, 12-4052) Concordia.

Duerr, Charles. S&S Fun with Crostics, No. 9. 1994. pap. 8.00 (*0-671-88714-9*, Fireside) S&S Trade Pap.

***Duerr, Charles A.** Crostics. (Simon & Schuster Fun with Crostics Ser.). 64p. 1998. per. 8.00 (*0-684-84362-5*) S&S Trade Pap.

Duerr, Charles A. Fun with Crostics. 64p. 1999. per. 8.00 (*0-684-85943-2*) S&S Trade.

— Fun with Crostics, 20. 64p. 1998. per. 8.00 (*0-684-84277-7*) S&S Trade.

— Fun with Crostics, No. 14. 64p. 1996. per. 8.00 (*0-684-81881-7*) S&S Trade Pap.

— Fun with Crostics, Vol. 17. 64p. 1997. per. 8.00 (*0-684-83098-1*) S&S Trade.

— Fun with Crostics, Vol. 18. (Simon & Schuster Fun with Crostics Ser.). 1997. pap. 8.00 (*0-684-83501-0*, Fireside) S&S Trade Pap.

— Fun with Crostics Treasury, No. 2. 96p. 1996. pap. 8.00 (*0-684-82962-2*) S&S Trade.

***Duerr, Charles A.** Fun with Crostics Treasury: 75 Challenging Crostics from the Duerr Archive, Vol.3. (Simon & Schuster Crostics Ser.). 96p. 1998. pap. 8.00 (*0-684-84368-4*) S&S Trade.

— Fun with Crostics 21, Vol. 21. 64p. 1998. pap. 8.00 (*0-684-84361-7*, Fireside) S&S Trade Pap.

Duerr, Charles A. S&S Fun with Crostics, No. 12. 1995. pap. 8.00 (*0-684-80125-6*, Fireside) S&S Trade Pap.

— Simon & Schuster: Fun With Crostics #15, No. 15. 64p. 1996. per. 8.00 (*0-684-82430-2*, Fireside) S&S Trade Pap.

— Simon & Schuster Fun With Crostics, No. 7. 1993. pap. 8.00 (*0-671-86735-0*, Fireside) S&S Trade Pap.

— Simon & Schuster Fun with Crostics, No. 13. 64p. 1995. pap. 8.00 (*0-684-81391-2*, Fireside) S&S Trade Pap.

— Simon & Schuster Fun with Crostics, Vol. 24. 64p. 1999. per. 8.00 (*0-684-85942-4*, Fireside) S&S Trade Pap.

— Simon & Schuster Fun With Crostics #19, Vol. 19. (Simon & Schuster Fun with Crostics Ser.). 1997. per. 8.00 (*0-684-84273-4*, Fireside) S&S Trade Pap.

— Simon & Schuster's Fun with Crostics, No. 11. 64p. 1995. pap. 8.00 (*0-671-51130-0*, Fireside) S&S Trade Pap.

— Simon & Schuster's Fun with Crostics, No. 16. 1996. pap. 8.00 (*0-684-82959-2*, Fireside) S&S Trade Pap.

— Simon & Schuster's Fun with Crostics Series, No. 8. 1994. pap. 8.00 (*0-671-87220-6*, Fireside) S&S Trade Pap.

— Simon Schuster Fun with Crostics #23, Vol. 23. (Simon & Schuster Fun with Crostics Ser.). 64p. 1999. pap. 8.00 (*0-684-85941-6*) S&S Trade.

Duerr, Charles A., ed. Simon & Schuster Fun with Crostics, No. 10. 1994. pap. 8.00 (*0-671-89712-8*, Fireside) S&S Trade Pap.

Duerr, Edwin. Radio & Television Acting: Criticism, Theory & Practice. LC 78-138223. 417p. 1972. reprint ed. lib. bdg. 79.50 (*0-8371-5580-0*, DURT, Greenwood Pr) Greenwood.

***Duerr, Kathy.** Doctor Mom's Quick Reference Guide to Natural Health Care at Home. LC 99-67785. (Illus.). 80p. 2000. pap. 12.95 (*1-899171-18-5*, Pub. by Findhorn Pr) Words Distrib.

Duerr, William A. Forestry Economics As Problem Solving. 2nd ed. LC 87-73569. 400p. 1988. pap. 21.70 (*0-9613546-2-3*) W A Duerr.

— Introduction to Forest Resource Economics. 512p. (C). 1992. 70.63 (*0-07-017982-4*) McGraw.

Duerr, William A., ed. see Timber Supply Policy Conference Staff.

Duerrenmatt, Friedrich. The Deadly Game. 1966. pap. 5.25 (*0-8222-0284-0*) Dramatists Play.

Duerst-Lahti, Georgia & Kelly, Rita M. Gender Power, Leadership & Governance. LC 95-30132. 352p. 1995. pap. text 19.95 (*0-472-06610-2*, 06610) U of Mich Pr.

***Duerst, Marilyn D. & Hill, John W.** The Crimecracker Kids & the Bakeshop Break-In. (Illus.). 53p. (YA). (gr. 4 up). 1999. pap. 10.95 (*0-9678212-0-7*) Gravel Pit.

Duerst, Ulrich J., jt. auth. see Rau, Gustav.

Duerwald, W., ed. Mord - Selbstmord - Unfall. (Limited Volume Series: Gerichtliche Medizin im 19. Jahrhundert: Vol. 2). xvi, 338p. 1991. 71.50 (*3-8055-4779-X*) S Karger.

— Mord & Mordmotiv: Ein Gerichtsmedizinischer Pitaval Zusammengestellt aus Fachzeitschriften des 19. Jahrhunderts. (Gerichtliche Medizin im 19. Jahrhundert Ser.: Vol. 1). xx, 290p. 1987. 71.50 (*3-8055-4777-3*) S Karger.

Dues, Greg. Catholic Customs & Traditions: A Popular Guide. rev. ed. LC 92-80801. (Illus.). 224p. 1993. pap. 9.95 (*0-89622-515-1*) Twenty-Third.

— Enjoying God & Teaching Creatively: Insights & Ideas for More Effective Religion Classes. 183p. 1999. pap. 12.95 (*0-89622-976-9*) Twenty-Third.

— Seasonal Prayer Services for Teenagers. LC 90-71818. 80p. (Orig.). (gr. 7-12). 1991. pap. 9.95 (*0-89622-473-2*, C53) Twenty-Third.

Dues, Greg & Walkley, Barbara. Called to Parish Ministry: Identity, Challenges & Spirituality of Lay Ministers. LC 94-62158. 176p. (Orig.). 1995. pap. 12.95 (*0-89622-649-2*) Twenty-Third.

Duesberg, Peter. Inventing the AIDS Virus. 721p. 1996. 29.95 (*0-89526-470-6*) Regnery Pub.

— Inventing the AIDs Virus: The Truth Behind the World's Greatest Miscalculation. 1994. write for info. (*0-201-62466-4*) Addison-Wesley.

Duesberg, Peter & Yiamouyiannis, John. AIDS: The Good News is HIV Doesn't Cause It. (Illus.). 200p. (Orig.). 1995. pap. 15.00 (*0-913571-05-9*) Health Act Pr.

Duesberg, Peter H. Infectious AIDS: Have We Been Misled? LC 95-329397. 582p. 1995. 27.50 (*1-55643-204-6*); pap. 18.95 (*1-55643-195-3*) North Atlantic.

— Inventing the AIDS Virus. 722p. 1997. pap. 17.95 (*0-89526-399-8*) Regnery Pub.

Duesberg, Peter H., ed. AIDS: Virus or Drug Induced? (Contemporary Issues in Genetics & Evolution Ser.). 365p. (C). 1996. pap. text 55.50 (*0-7923-3961-4*) Kluwer Academic.

— AIDS: Virus or Drug Induced? LC 95-17475. (Contemporary Issues in Genetics & Evolution Ser.: Vol. 5). 365p. (C). 1996. lib. bdg. 227.50 (*0-7923-3552-X*) Kluwer Academic.

Duesberry, Joellyn, intro. Joellyn Duesberry: Recent Western Paintings. LC 90-62108. (Illus.). 1990. pap. 8.00 (*0-935037-36-5*) G Peters Gallery.

Duesbery, M. S., jt. ed. see Nabarro, F. R.

Duesenberg, H. Milton. Alaska Highway Expeditionary Force: A Roadbuilder's Story. LC 94-76660. (Illus.). 196p. 1995. reprint ed. 29.95 (*0-9640951-3-0*); reprint ed. pap. 19.95 (*0-9640951-2-2*) H & M Indus.

Duesenberg, Richard W. & King, Lawrence P. Sales & Bulk Transfers under the Uniform Commercial Code, 2 vols., Vol. 3 & 3a. 1966. ring bd. 465.00 (*0-8205-1612-0*) Bender.

Duesenberry, James, jt. auth. see Mayer, Thomas.

Dueser, Thorsten, jt. photos by see Lipton, Mimi.

Duesing, Bill. Living on the Earth: Eclectic Essays for a Sustainable & Joyful Future. 2nd ed. 222p. 1997. reprint ed. pap. 11.95 (*0-9659277-0-9*) Solar Farm.

Duesman, Jerome. Large Print Prayer Book. enl. large type ed. 1980. pap. 1.00 (*0-8189-0344-9*) Alba.

— Libro de Oraciones: Letra Grande. large type ed. (SPA.). 48p. 1994. pap. 1.00 (*0-8189-0705-3*) Alba.

Duespohl, T. Audean. Nursing Diagnosis Manual for the Well & Ill Client. 312p. 1986. pap. text 26.00 (*0-7216-1825-1*, W B Saunders Co) Harcrt Hlth Sci Grp.

Duester, Patricia A., ed. The Navy Seal Physical Fitness Guide. (Illus.). 282p. 1998. pap. text 40.00 (*0-7881-7362-6*) DIANE Pub.

Duesterberg, Thomas J. & Gordon, Kenneth. Competition & Deregulation in Telecommunications: The Case for a New Paradigm. LC 98-103994. 119p. 1997. pap. 12.95 (*1-55813-063-2*) Hudson Instit IN.

Duet, George & Duet, Karen F. The Business Security K-9: Selection & Training. (Illus.). 256p. 1995. per. 22.00 (*0-87605-439-4*) Howell Bks.

Duet, George, jt. auth. see Duet, Karen F.

Duet, Karen F. & Balabanov, Ivan. Advanced Schutzhund. LC 98-55573. (Illus.). 211p. 1999. 24.95 (*0-87605-730-X*) Howell Bks.

Duet, Karen F. & Duet, George. The Home & Family Protection Dog: Selection & Training. (Illus.). 256p. 1993. 25.95 (*0-87605-619-2*) Howell Bks.

Duet, Karen F., jt. auth. see Duet, George.

***Duetcsh, Jeffrey.** Teach Yourself to Read Music: A Guide for Pop, Rock, Blues & Jazz Singers. 80p. 1998. per. 19.95 incl. audio compact disk (*0-7935-9421-9*) H Leonard.

Duetsch, Larry L., ed. Industry Studies. 2nd ed. LC 98-3071. 384p. (C). (gr. 13). 1998. text 68.95 (*0-7656-0068-4*); pap. text 34.95 (*0-7656-0069-2*) M E Sharpe.

D

Duever, Michael J., et al. The Big Cypress National Preserve. 2nd ed. LC 86-60782. (National Audubon Society Research Report: No. 8). (Illus.). 455p. 1986. reprint ed. pap. 30.00 (*0-930698-22-3*) Natl Audubon.

Dueweke, Stephen. Playing Soldiers in the Dark. 294p. (Orig.). 1992. pap. 12.95 (*0-9624627-1-3*) Bagman Pr.

Duewel, Klaus, ed. Runische Schriftkultur in Kontinental-Skandin-Avischer und-Angelsaesischer Wechselbeziehung. (Ergaenzungsbaende zum Reallexikon der Germanischen Altertumskunde: Bd. 10). (GER.). 417p. (C). 1994. lib. bdg. 167.70 (*3-11-014328-3*) De Gruyter.

Duewel, Wesley. Ardiendo para Dios.Tr. of Ablaze for God. (SPA.). 295p. 1995. 9.99 (*1-56063-775-7*, 498564) Editorial Unilit.

***Duewel, Wesley.** More God, More Power: Filled & Transformed by the Holy Spirit. LC 99-58136. 2000. pap. 10.99 (*0-310-23085-3*) Zondervan.

Duewel, Wesley. Revival Fire. 368p. 1995. pap. 14.99 (*0-310-49661-6*) Zondervan.

Duewel, Wesley L. Ablaze for God. 352p. 1989. pap. 15.99 (*0-310-36181-8*) Zondervan.

— Cambie el Mundo a Traves de la Oracion. Araujo, Juan S., tr. from ENG.Tr. of Touch the World Through Prayer. (SPA.). 192p. (C). 1988. pap. 8.99 (*0-88113-045-1*) Caribe Betania.

— God's Great Salvation. 330p. (Orig.). 1991. pap. 9.00 (*1-880338-14-9*) Duewel Lit.

— Let God Guide You Daily. 224p. (Orig.). 1988. pap. 10.99 (*0-310-36171-0*, 17094P) Duewel Lit.

— Mighty Prevailing Power. 352p. 1990. pap. 14.99 (*0-310-36191-5*) Zondervan.

— La Oracion Poderosa Que Prevalece.Tr. of Mighty Prevailing Prayer. (SPA.). 400p. 1995. 10.99 (*1-56063-635-1*, 497729) Editorial Unilit.

— Touch the World Through Prayer. 304p. 1986. mass mkt. 5.99 (*0-310-36271-7*, 17093P) Zondervan.

Duewel, Wesley L. & Oxley, Beverly. Touch the World Through Prayer: Leader's Guide. 1990. pap. 11.95 (*0-911866-23-X*) LifeSprings Res.

Duey Bale. Survival, 6 Death Valley. LC 98-8422. (Survival Ser.). 168p. (J). (gr. 4-6). 1998. write for info. (*0-689-82117-4*) S&S Childrens.

Duey, K., jt. auth. see Bale, K. A.

Duey, Kathleen. Agnes May Gleason: Walsenburg, Colorado, 1932. LC 98-30243. (American Diaries Ser.). 144p. (J). (gr. 4-6). 1998. per. 3.99 (*0-689-82329-0*) Aladdin.

— Alexia Ellery Finsdale: San Francisco, 1906. LC 97-24652. 156p. (J). (gr. 4-6). 1997. per. 3.99 (*0-689-81620-0*) S&S Childrens.

— Alexia Ellery Finsdale: San Francisco, 1906. (American Diaries Ser.: No. 7). (J). (gr. 4-6). 1997. 9.09 (*0-606-12614-7*, Pub. by Turtleback) Demco.

***Duey, Kathleen.** Amelina Carrett: Thibodeau, Louisiana 1870. LC 99-13484. (American Diaries Ser.: No. 12). 144p. (J). (gr. 4-6). 1999. 3.99 (*0-689-82402-5*) S&S Childrens.

— Animal Book, No. 1. (J). Date not set. write for info. (*0-06-028293-2*); lib. bdg. write for info. (*0-06-029249-0*) HarpC Child Bks.

Duey, Kathleen. Anisett Lundberg: California, 1851. (American Diaries Ser.: No. 3). 144p. (J). (gr. 4-6). 1996. per. 3.99 (*0-689-80386-9*) Aladdin.

— Anisett Lundberg: California, 1851. (American Diaries Ser.: No. 3). (J). (gr. 4-6). 1996. 9.09 (*0-606-08987-X*, Pub. by Turtleback) Demco.

— Beware the Alien Invasion! (Alone in the Dark Ser.). (Illus.). 32p. (J). 2000. pap. text 3.95 (*1-891100-15-7*) Smart Kids Publ.

***Duey, Kathleen.** Blizzard: Estes Park, Colorado, 1886. 1998. 9.09 (*0-606-13827-7*, Pub. by Turtleback) Demco.

Duey, Kathleen. Boogeyman in the Basement! (Alone in the Dark Ser.). (Illus.). 32p. (J). 2000. pap. text 3.95 (*1-891100-12-2*) Smart Kids Publ.

— Cave-In: St. Claire, Pennsylvania, 1859. (Survival Ser.). 160p. (J). (gr. 3-8). 1998. pap. 3.99 (*0-689-82350-9*) Aladdin.

— Celou Sudden Shout: Idaho, 1826. LC 97-52936. (American Diaries Ser.: No. 9). 150p. (J). (gr. 4-6). 1998. per. 3.99 (*0-689-81622-7*) S&S Childrens.

— Celou Sudden Shout: Idaho, 1826. (American Diaries Ser.: No. 9). (J). (gr. 4-6). 1998. 9.09 (*0-606-13121-3*, Pub. by Turtleback) Demco.

— Double-Yuck Magic. 144p. (Orig.). (YA). 1991. pap. 2.99 (*0-380-76116-5*, Avon Bks) Morrow Avon.

— Earthquake: San Francisco, 1906. 1997. 9.09 (*0-606-13048-9*, Pub. by Turtleback) Demco.

— Ellen Elizabeth Hawkins: Mobeetie, Texas, 1886. LC 96-39818. (American Diaries Ser.). (Illus.). 144p. (J). (gr. 4-6). 1997. mass mkt. 3.99 (*0-689-81409-7*) Aladdin.

Duey, Kathleen. Ellen Elizabeth Hawkins: Mobeetie, Texas, 1886. (American Diaries Ser.: No. 6). (J). (gr. 4-6). 1997. 9.09 (*0-606-11037-2*, Pub. by Turtleback) Demco.

Duey, Kathleen. Emma Eileen Grove: Mississippi, 1865. (American Diaries Ser.: No. 2). (Illus.). 144p. (J). (gr. 4-6). 1996. per. 3.99 (*0-689-80385-0*) Aladdin.

— Emma Eileen Grove: Mississippi, 1865. (American Diaries Ser.: No. 2). (J). (gr. 4-6). 1996. 9.09 (*0-606-08986-1*, Pub. by Turtleback) Demco.

— Evie Peach: St. Louis, 1857. LC 97-35641. (American Diaries Ser.: No. 8). 144p. (J). (gr. 4-6). 1997. per. 3.99 (*0-689-81621-9*) S&S Childrens.

— Evie Peach: St. Louis, 1857, 8. (American Diaries Ser.: No. 8). (J). (gr. 4-6). 1997. 9.09 (*0-606-12615-5*, Pub. by Turtleback) Demco.

***Duey, Kathleen.** Fire: Chicago, 1871. 1998. 9.09 (*0-606-13828-5*, Pub. by Turtleback) Demco.

Duey, Kathleen. Flood, Mississippi, 1927. (J). 1998. 9.09 (*0-606-13829-3*, Pub. by Turtleback) Demco.

— Forest Fire: Hinckley, Minnesota, 1894, Vol. 10. LC 99-29036. (Survival Ser.: No. 10). 160p. (gr. 3-7). 1999. pap. 4.50 (*0-689-82928-0*, 076714004504) S&S Childrens.

— Josie Poe Palouse: Washington, 1943. (American Diaries Ser.: No. 13). (Illus.). 144p. (J). (gr. 3-7). 1999. per. 4.50 (*0-689-82930-2*, 076714004504) S&S Childrens.

***Duey, Kathleen.** Louisiana Hurricane, 1860. 256p. (YA). 2000. per. 4.99 (*0-671-03926-1*, Archway) PB.

— Louisiana Hurricane, 1860. (Illus.). (J). 2000. 10.34 (*0-606-18802-9*) Turtleback.

— Maddie Retta Lauren: Sandersville, Georgia, 1864. (American Diaries Ser.: No. 15). (Illus.). (J). (gr. 4-6). 2000. pap. 4.50 (*0-689-83377-6*) Aladdin.

— Maddie Retta Lauren, Sandersville, Georgia, C.S.A., 1864. (American Diaries Ser.: Vol. 15). 2000. 9.85 (*0-606-17902-X*) Turtleback.

Duey, Kathleen. Mary Alice Peale: Philadelphia, 1777. LC 96-16052. (American Diaries Ser.: No. 4). 176p. (J). (gr. 4-6). 1996. per. 3.99 (*0-689-80387-7*) S&S Childrens.

Duey, Kathleen. Mary Alice Peale: Philadelphia, 1777. (American Diaries Ser.: No. 4). (J). (gr. 4-6). 1996. 9.09 (*0-606-10739-8*, Pub. by Turtleback) Demco.

Duey, Kathleen. Mr. Stumpguss Is a Third Grader. (Illus.). 80p. (Orig.). (J). 1992. pap. 3.50 (*0-380-76939-5*, Avon Bks) Morrow Avon.

***Duey, Kathleen.** Nell Dunne: New York City, 1899. Vol. 15. 2000. 9.85 (*0-606-17903-8*) Turtleback.

Duey, Kathleen. Nowhere to Run, Nowhere to Hide! (Alone in the Dark Ser.). (Illus.). 32p. (J). 2000. pap. text 3.95 (*1-891100-14-9*) Smart Kids Publ.

***Duey, Kathleen.** Rosa Moreno: Hollywood, California, 1934. (American Diaries Ser.: No. 14). 144p. (J). (gr. 4-6). 1999. per. 4.50 (*0-689-83126-9*) Aladdin.

Duey, Kathleen. San Francisco Earthquake, 1906. 195p. (Orig.). (YA). 1999. mass mkt. 4.99 (*0-671-03602-5*, Archway) PB.

— Sarah Anne Hartford: Massachusetts, 1651. LC 95-39249. (American Diaries Ser.: No. 1). (Illus.). 144p. (J). (gr. 4-6). 1996. per. 3.99 (*0-689-80384-2*) Aladdin.

— Sarah Anne Hartford: Massachusetts, 1651. (American Diaries Ser.: No. 1). (J). (gr. 4-6). 1996. 9.09 (*0-606-08985-3*, Pub. by Turtleback) Demco.

— Stay Out of the Graveyard! (Alone in the Dark Ser.). (Illus.). 32p. (J). 2000. pap. text 3.95 (*1-891100-13-0*) Smart Kids Publ.

— Summer MacCleary: Virginia, 1749. (American Diaries Ser.: Vol. 10). (J). (gr. 3-7). 1998. 9.09 (*0-606-13120-5*, Pub. by Turtleback) Demco.

— Summer McCleary: Virginia, 1749. LC 98-7218. (American Diaries Ser.: No. 10). 144p. (J). (gr. 4-6). 1998. per. 3.99 (*0-689-81623-5*) S&S Childrens.

— The Third Grade's Skinny Pig. 80p. (Orig.). (J). (gr. 1). 1993. pap. 3.50 (*0-380-76730-9*, Avon Bks) Morrow Avon.

— Titanic, April 14, 1912. 1998. 9.09 (*0-606-13047-0*, Pub. by Turtleback) Demco.

— Willow Chase: Kansas Territory, 1847. LC 96-35021. (American Diaries Ser.). 144p. (J). (gr. 4-6). 1997. per. 3.99 (*0-689-81355-4*) Aladdin.

Duey, Kathleen. Willow Chase: Kansas Territory, 1847. (American Diaries Ser.: No. 5). (J). (gr. 4-6). 1997. 9.09 (*0-606-11036-4*, Pub. by Turtleback) Demco.

Duey, Kathleen & Bale, K. A. Flood, Mississippi, 1927, Vol. 5. LC 98-19349. (Survival Ser.: No. 5). 160p. (J). (gr. 3-7). 1998. pap. 3.99 (*0-689-82116-6*) Aladdin.

— Trainwreck: Kansas 1892, Vol. 8. LC 98-41011. (Survival Ser.: No. 8). 160p. 1999. per. 3.99 (*0-689-82543-9*) S&S Childrens.

Duey, Kathleen & Bale, Karen. Three of Hearts. 128p. (J). (gr. 3-7). 1998. pap. 3.99 (*0-380-78720-2*, Avon Bks) Morrow Avon.

Duey, Kathleen & Bale, Karen A. Blizzard, Estes Park, Colorado, 1886. LC 97-3172. (Survival Ser.). 160p. (J). (gr. 3-7). 1998. per. 3.99 (*0-689-81309-0*) S&S Childrens.

— Earthquake, San Francisco 1906, Bk. 2. LC 97-3578. (Survival Ser.). 160p. (J). (gr. 4-6). 1998. per. 3.99 (*0-689-81308-2*) Aladdin.

— Survival Series, Bk. 3. LC 97-52937. 160p. (J). (gr. 4-7). 1998. per. 3.99 (*0-689-81310-4*) S&S Childrens.

***Duey, Kathleen & Berry, Ron.** Crassy the Crude Beastie. (Beastie Buddies Ser.). (Illus.). 32p. (J). (ps-3). 2000. mass mkt. 3.95 (*1-891100-28-9*, Pub. by Smart Kids Publ) Penton Overseas.

— Glumby the Glumbling Beastie. (Beastie Buddies Ser.). (Illus.). 32p. (J). (ps-3). 2000. mass mkt. 3.95 (*1-891100-27-0*, Pub. by Smart Kids Publ) Penton Overseas.

— The Smart Kids Allowance System: Tool Kit. (Illus.). (J). (gr. 1-6). 2000. pap., boxed set 14.95 incl. audio (*1-891100-68-8*, Pub. by Smart Kids Publ) Penton Overseas.

Duey, Kathleen & Dodge, Bill. Swamp, Bayou Teche, Louisiana, 1851, Vol. 11. LC 99-35217. (Survival Ser.: No. 11). 160p. (J). (gr. 3-7). 1999. per. 3.99 (*0-689-82929-9*, 076714004504) Aladdin.

***Duey, Kathleen, et al.** Titanic, April 14, 1912. LC 97-38594. 160p. (J). (gr. 3-7). 1998. per. 3.99 (*0-689-81311-2*) Aladdin.

Duey, Kathleen, jt. auth. see Barnes, Mary.

Duey, Kathleen, jt. auth. see Berry, Rob.

Dufau, Micheline & D'Alelio, Ellen. Decouverte Du Poeme. (FRE.). 172p. (C). 1967. pap. text 37.00 (*0-15-517290-5*) Harcourt Coll Pubs.

Dufau, Micheline, tr. see Quinn, Esther C.

Dufaud, J. Dictionary French to Nord-Occitan. (FRE & PRO.). 1998. 95.00 (*0-320-00260-8*) Fr & Eur.

Dufault, Chuch, jt. auth. see Cox, Geof.

***Dufault, Richard.** Rules of Warfare 2: Silent Death Annex Book. Dennis, Donald G., ed. (Silent Death - The Next Millennium Ser.). (Illus.). 28p. (YA). (gr. 7 up). 1998. pap. 15.00 (*1-55806-382-X*, 7225) Iron Crown Ent Inc.

Dufault, Roseanna L. Metaphors of Identity: The Treatment of Childhood in Selected Quebecois Novels. LC 90-55832. 88p. 1991. 24.50 (*0-8386-3424-9*) Fairleigh Dickinson.

Dufault, Roseanna L., ed. Women by Women: The Treatment of Female Characters by Women Writers of Fiction in Quebec since 1980. LC 96-53873. 272p. 1997. 39.50 (*0-8386-3719-1*) Fairleigh Dickinson.

***Dufaux.** Dixie Road. 2000. pap. 10.95 (*1-56163-265-1*) NBM.

***Dufaux, Jean.** Raptors, Vol. 2. Johnson, Joe, tr. (Illus.). 64p. 2000. pap. 10.95 (*1-56163-260-0*) NBM.

***Dufaux, Jean & Marini, Enrico.** Raptors, Vol. 2. Johnson, Joe, tr. from FRE. (Illus.). 56p. 1999. pap. 10.95 (*1-56163-243-0*) NBM.

Dufay, Guillaume, et al. The Combinative Chanson: An Anthology. Maniates, Maria R., ed. (Recent Researches in Music of the Renaissance Ser.: Vol. RRR77). (Illus.). lxiii, 92p. 1989. pap. 50.00 (*0-89579-236-2*, RRR77) A-R Eds.

Dufeu, Bernard. Teaching Myself. Maley, Alan, ed. (Illus.). 224p. 1994. pap. text 14.95 (*0-19-437188-3*) OUP.

DUFEY. Instructors Manual. 3rd ed. (C). 2001. pap. text 24.00 (*0-201-60714-X*) Addison-Wesley.

Dufey, Gunter. Cases in International Finance. 3rd ed. (C). 2001. pap. text. write for info. (*0-201-60713-1*) Addison-Wesley.

Dufey, Gunter & Giddy, Ian H. The International Money Market. 2nd ed. LC 93-40621. 304p. 1994. pap. text 52.00 (*0-13-095407-1*) P-H.

— Readings in International Finance: 50 Cases & Problems. LC 86-3424. 416p. (C). 1987. pap. text 37.75 (*0-201-05127-3*) Addison-Wesley.

Dufey, Gunter & Giddy, Ian H., eds. Cases in International Finance. 2nd ed. LC 92-23755. (Illus.). 337p. (C). 1992. pap. text 45.00 (*0-201-51307-2*) Addison-Wesley.

Dufey, Gunter, ed. see Abbey, Augustus.

Dufey, Gunter, ed. see Brock, James L.

Dufey, Gunter, ed. see DeAngelo, Linda E.

Dufey, Gunter, ed. see Euh, Yoon-Dae.

Dufey, Gunter, ed. see Leonard, Paul A.

Dufey, Gunter, ed. see Rader, James.

Dufey, Gunter, ed. see Schillereff, Ronald L.

Dufey, Gunter, ed. see Smith, Charles H.

Dufey, Gunter, ed. see Smith, Francis G.

Dufey, Gunter, ed. see Tong, Hsin-Min.

Dufey, Gunter, ed. see Vonderembse, Mark A.

Dufey, Gunter, ed. see Wakabayashi, Mitsuru.

Dufey, Gunter, ed. see Wilson, Brent D.

Duff & Herman. Alternating Current Fundamentals. 6th ed. LC 99-23621. 1999. mass mkt. 61.95 (*0-7668-0961-7*) Delmar.

Duff, P. W. Personality in Roman Private Law. xiii, 241p. 1971. reprint ed. 27.50 (*0-8377-2026-5*, Rothman) W S Hein.

Duff, A., et al. Juries: A Hong Kong Perspective. 184p. (Orig.). 1992. pap. 34.50 (*962-209-306-X*, Pub. by HK Univ Pr) Coronet Bks.

Duff, A., jt. auth. see Reupke, P.

Duff, A. M., ed. see Duff, John W.

Duff, A. M., jt. tr. see Duff, John W.

Duff, Alan. Once Were Warriors. 208p. 1995. 19.95 (*0-8248-1762-1*) UH Pr.

— Once Were Warriors. LC 93-43507. 1995. pap. 11.00 (*0-679-76181-0*) Vin Bks.

— One Night Out Stealing. LC 95-13244. (Talanoa Ser.). 192p. (Orig.). 1995. pap. 12.95 (*0-8248-1684-6*) UH Pr.

— Translation. Maley, Alan, ed. (Illus.). 168p. 1989. pap. text 13.95 (*0-19-437104-2*) OUP.

Duff, Alan & Maley, Alan. Literature. (Illus.). 176p. 1990. pap. text 13.95 (*0-19-437094-1*) OUP.

Duff, Alan, jt. auth. see Maley, Alan.

Duff, Alexander. Treatise on the Deeds & Forms Used in the Constitution Transmission & Extinction of Feudal Rights. xi, 552p. 1999. reprint ed. 140.00 (*1-56169-446-0*) Gaunt.

***Duff, Alistair.** Information Society Studies. LC 99-49309. 260p. 2000. 90.00 (*0-415-21551-X*) Routledge.

***Duff, Andrew.** Treaty of Amsterdam: Text & Commentary. 2000. pap. 21.00 (*0-901573-65-5*) Fed Trust Ed Res.

Duff, Andrew. Understanding the Euro. 1999. pap. 19.95 (*0-901573-72-8*) Kogan Page Ltd.

***Duff, Andrew.** Unforseeable Circumstances of Mr. Gordon. 2000. pap. 8.00 (*0-901573-89-2*) Fed Trust Ed Res.

Duff, Andrew, et al. Maastricht & Beyond: Building the European Union. Pryce, Roy & Pinder, John, eds. LC 94-8621. 328p. (C). 1994. pap. 24.99 (*0-415-10818-7*, B3523) Routledge.

Duff, Anthony & Garland, David, eds. A Reader on Punishment. (Oxford Readings in Socio-Legal Studies). 358p. 1995. pap. text 21.00 (*0-19-876353-0*) OUP.

Duff, Antony. Criminal Attempts. LC 96-26275. (Oxford Monographs on Criminal Law & Justice). 448p. 1997. text 98.00 (*0-19-826268-X*) OUP.

***Duff, Antony.** Punishment, Communication, & Community. LC 99-49374. 288p. 2000. 45.00 (*0-19-510429-3*) OUP.

Duff, Antony, ed. Punishment. (International Research Library of Philosophy). 526p. 1993. 173.95 (*1-85521-312-5*, Pub. by Dartmth Pub) Ashgate Pub Co.

Duff, Carolyn & Cohen, Barbara. When Women Work Together: Using Our Strengths to Overcome Our Challenges. 300p. (Orig.). 1993. pap. 14.95 (*0-943233-53-4*) Conari Press.

Duff, Carolyn S. Learning from Other Women: How to Benefit from the Knowledge, Wisdom & Experience of Female Mentors. LC 99-28081. 208p. 1999. 22.95 (*0-8144-0455-3*) AMACOM.

— The Other Women: Challenge in the Workplace. (Illus.). (Orig.). 1990. pap. write for info. (*0-9624823-0-7*) WomenWorks.

Duff, Carolyn S., et al. The Other Women: A Workbook for Women Who Work with Women. (Illus.). (Orig.). 1989. pap. write for info. (*0-318-65968-9*) WomenWorks.

Duff, Charles. James Joyce & the Plain Reader. LC 78-164027. (Studies in Irish Literature: No. 16). 1971. reprint ed. lib. bdg. 75.00 (*0-8383-1329-9*) M S G Haskell Hse.

— The Lost Summer: The Heyday of the West End Theatre. 272p. 1996. pap. 17.95 (*0-435-07023-1*) Heinemann.

— Spanish for Beginners. (SPA.). 352p. (Orig.). 1971. pap. 14.00 (*0-06-463271-7*, EH 271) HarpC.

Duff, Charles & Makaroff, Dmitri. Russian for Beginners. (RUS.). 384p. 1971. pap. 15.00 (*0-06-463287-3*, EH 287) HarpC.

***Duff, Chris.** On Celtic Tides: One Man's Journey Around Ireland by Sea Kayak. (Illus.). 288p. 2000. pap. 13.95 (*0-312-26368-6*) St Martin.

Duff, Chris. On Celtic Tides: One Man's Journey Around Ireland by Sea Kayak. 2nd ed. LC 99-21989. 288p. 1999. text 23.95 (*0-312-20508-2*) St Martin.

Duff-Cooper, Andrew, ed. Contests: Cosmos 6. (Illus.). 200p. 1991. pap. 37.00 (*0-7486-0199-6*, Pub. by Edinburgh U Pr) Col U Pr.

Duff, D. G. & Sinclair, R. S. Giles's Laboratory Course in Dyeing. 4th ed. 1989. spiral bd. 65.00 (*0-901956-49-X*, Pub. by Textile Inst) St Mut.

***Duff, David.** Modern Genre Theory. LC 99-23077. (Critical Readers Ser.). 304p. (C). 1999. 79.95 (*0-582-36806-5*) Longman.

— Modern Genre Theory. LC 99-23077. (Critical Readers Ser.). 304p. 1999. pap. 30.73 (*0-582-36805-7*) Longman.

Duff, David. Romance & Revolution: Shelley & the Politics of a Genre. LC 93-34648. (Studies in Romanticism: No. 7). (Illus.). 288p. (C). 1994. text 64.95 (*0-521-45018-7*) Cambridge U Pr.

Duff, David, et al. Exploring the Domain of Accident Law: Taking the Facts Seriously. (Illus.). 464p. 1996. text 80.00 (*0-19-508797-6*) OUP.

Duff, Deborah, ed. see Brown, Hamilton & Stark, Nancy.

Duff, Deborah, ed. see Stark, Nancy.

Duff, Deborah L. A Metric Guide for Health Professionals on Dosages & Solutions, 3rd Edition. 3rd ed. (Illus.). 196p. 1994. pap. 22.00 (*0-920513-14-X*, W B Saunders Co) Harcrt Hlth Sci Grp.

Duff, Donald A., ed. Conservation Assessment for Inland Cutthroat Trout: Distribution, Status & Habitat Management Implications. (Illus.). 132p. (C). 1998. pap. text 30.00 (*0-7881-4567-3*) DIANE Pub.

Duff, E. Gordon. Early Printed Books. LC 68-25309. (Bibliophile Ser.: No. 83). (Illus.). 1968. reprint ed. lib. bdg. 75.00 (*0-8383-0936-4*) M S G Haskell Hse.

— The Printers, Stationers, & Book-Binders of Westminster & London from 1476 to 1535. LC 78-172540. (Illus.). reprint ed. 22.00 (*0-405-08467-6*, Pub. by Blom Pubns) Ayer.

— The Printers, Stationers & Bookbinders of West Minster & London from 1476 to 1535. 256p. 1972. 20.95 (*0-405-09135-4*) Ayer.

Duff, E. Gordon, ed. Information for Pilgrims Unto the Holy Land. LC 78-63464. reprint ed. 39.50 (*0-404-16536-2*) AMS Pr.

Duff, Edward G. A Century of English Book Trade. xxxv, 200p. 1985. reprint ed. lib. bdg. 59.00 (*0-7812-0647-2*) Rprt Serv.

Duff, Edward G., intro. Early English Printing: A Series of Facsimiles of All Types Used in England During the XVth Century, with Some of Those Used in the Printing of English Books Abroad. (Anglistica & Americana Ser.: No. 118). vii, 40p. 1974. reprint ed. 83.20 (*3-487-05153-2*) G Olms Pubs.

Duff, Frank. Miracles on Tap. 1961. pap. 5.00 (*0-910984-15-8*) Montfort Pubns.

Duff, G. F., ed. Tidal Energy: or Time & Tide Wait for No Man. (Illus.). 40p. 1984. 9.90 (*0-917853-02-4*, IO-15) Am Assn Physics.

Duff, Gail. The Barbecue Book. 2nd ed. (Illus.). 176p. 1993. pap. 9.95 (*1-85327-080-6*, Pub. by Prism Pr) Assoc Pubs Grp.

— Bread. 192p. 1995. 18.00 (*0-02-860396-6*) Macmillan.

— Eating Vegetarian. LC 99-18295. (In a Nutshell Ser.). (Illus.). 64p. 1999. 7.95 (*1-86204-482-1*, Pub. by Element MA) Penguin Putnam.

Duff, Gail. Fast Food, Real Food. (Illus.). 160p. (Orig.). 1993. pap. 15.95 (*1-85327-081-4*, Pub. by Prism Pr) Assoc Pubs Grp.

Duff, Gail. Loaf of Bread. 1998. 14.99 (*0-7858-1012-9*) Bk Sales Inc.

— Natural Beauty: Making & Using Pure & Simple Beauty Products. LC 97-31659. (Illus.). 128p. 1998. 19.95 (*0-7621-0032-X*, Pub. by RD Assn) Penguin Putnam.

— Natural Beauty: Making & Using Simple Beauty Products. LC 97-31659. 1998. pap. write for info. (*0-7621-0033-8*) RD Assn.

— Natural Fragrances: Outdoor Scents for Indoor Uses. LC 89-45219. (Illus.). 160p. 1989. 16.95 (*0-88266-554-5*, Garden Way Pub) Storey Bks.

— Natural Fragrances: Outdoor Scents for Indoor Uses. LC 89-45219. (Illus.). 160p. 1991. pap. 16.95 (*0-88266-683-5*, Garden Way Pub) Storey Bks.

— Oriental Vegetarian Cooking. (Illus.). 160p. (Orig.). 1989. pap. 12.95 (*0-89281-344-X*) Inner Tradit.

— Personalized Perfumes: More than 40 Recipes for Making Fragrances with Essential Oils. (Illus.). 80p. 1994. 16.00 (*0-671-88029-2*) S&S Trade.

— Seasonal Eating. LC 99-19656. (In a Nutshell). 64p. 1999. 7.95 (*1-86204-542-9*, Pub. by Element MA) Penguin Putnam.

D

Duff, George F. Partial Differential Equations. LC 56-4187. (Mathematical Expositions Ser.: No. 9). 258p. reprint ed. pap. 80.00 (*0-608-10040-4*, 201419300095) Bks Demand.

Duff, George F. & Naylor, D. Differential Equations of Applied Mathematics. LC 65-26844. 433p. reprint ed. pap. 134.30 (*0-608-30972-9*, 201259800081) Bks Demand.

Duff, Gerald. Calling Collect: Poems. LC 82-2819. 70p. reprint ed. pap. 30.00 (*0-608-04471-7*, 206521600001) Bks Demand.

— Graveyard Working. 185p. 1994. 18.00 (*1-880909-15-4*) Baskerville.

— Memphis Ribs. LC 98-87928. 209p. 1999. pap. 12.95 (*0-9664520-1-1*) Salvo Pr.

***Duff, Gerald.** Snake Song. LC 00-100611. 212p. 2000. pap. 14.95 (*0-9664520-8-9*) Salvo Pr.

Duff, Gerald. That's All Right, Mama. 278p. 1995. 21.00 (*1-880909-33-2*) Baskerville.

Duff-Gordon, Lucie. Letters from Egypt, 1863-1865. 2nd ed. LC 75-164794. (BCL Ser. I). reprint ed. 49.50 (*0-404-02189-1*) AMS Pr.

Duff, Howard. Astrological Types. 52p. 1948. 6.00 (*0-86690-084-5*, D1083-024) Am Fed Astrologers.

Duff, I. S. & Watson, G. A., eds. The State of the Art in Numerical Analysis. (The Institute of Mathematics & Its Applications Conference Ser.: No. 63). (Illus.). 576p. 1998. text 175.00 (*0-19-850014-9*) OUP.

Duff, I. S., et al. Direct Methods for Sparse Matrices. (Monographs on Numerical Analysis). (Illus.). 354p. 1989. pap. text 55.00 (*0-19-853421-3*) OUP.

Duff, J. D., tr. Civil War. (Loeb Classical Library: No. 220). 658p. 1928. 18.95 (*0-674-99242-3*) HUP.

Duff, J. D., tr. see Herzen, Aleksandr.

Duff, J. D., tr. see Rostovtzeff, Mikhail I.

Duff, James. Home Front. 1985. pap. 5.25 (*0-8222-0528-9*) Dramatists Play.

Duff, James G. History of the Mahrattas, Vols. I, II, & III. 1990. reprint ed. 35.00 (*81-85395-77-2*, Pub. by BR Pub) S Asia.

Duff, James H., et al. An American Vision: Three Generations of Wyeth Art. 1989. 24.95 (*0-318-41643-3*) Little.

Duff, James H., jt. auth. see Wyeth, Andrew.

***Duff, Joey & Conklin, Jean.** It Works, It Works, It Really Works! Life-Changing Truths Found Only in Christ. LC 99-90748. (Illus.). 168p. 1999. pap. 11.95 (*0-9673440-1-8*, Pub. by Carico Pr) Good Shepherd Pubns.

Duff, John, jt. auth. see Mohler, James.

Duff, John, ed. see Evanoff, Vlad.

Duff, John, ed. see Wood, Clement.

Duff, John R. & Herman, Stephen L. Alternating Current Fundamentals. 3rd ed. 576p. 1986. text 39.00 (*0-8273-2239-9*) Delmar.

— Alternating Current Fundamentals. 3rd ed. 576p. 1986. teacher ed. 15.00 (*0-8273-2240-2*) Delmar.

— Alternating Current Fundamentals. 4th ed. 1991. pap. 33.95 (*0-8273-4157-1*) Delmar.

— Alternating Current Fundamentals IG. 4th ed. 1991. pap., teacher ed. 15.00 (*0-8273-4159-8*) Delmar.

Duff, John W. A Literary History of Rome in the Silver Age: From Tiberius to Hadrian. 3rd ed. Duff, A. M., ed. LC 79-9906. 607p. 1979. reprint ed. lib. bdg. 47.50 (*0-313-20939-1*, DULH, Greenwood Pr) Greenwood.

Duff, John W. & Duff, A. M., trs. from LAT. Minor Latin Poets II. rev. ed. (Loeb Classical Library: No. 434). 434p. 1935. text 15.50 (*0-318-42567-X*) HUP.

Duff, Jon & Mohler, James. Laura Lemay's Web Workshop: Graphics & Web Page Design. LC 96-68245. 408p. 1996. 55.00 (*1-57521-125-4*) Sams.

Duff, Jon M. CADKEY Light: Computer Aided Design & Drafting for Engineers & Technology. (C). 1991. pap. text 44.20 (*0-13-117383-9*, 340401) P-H.

— Mastering 3D Studio. (General Engineering Ser.). 1996. pap., teacher ed. 10.50 (*0-534-95137-6*) PWS Pubs.

— PageMaker: Start to Finish. 528p. 1991. pap. 38.95 (*0-8273-4480-5*) Delmar.

Duff, Jon M. & Ross, William A. Freehand Sketching for Engineering Design. (General Engineering Ser.). 240p. (C). 1994. mass mkt. 34.95 (*0-534-93966-X*) PWS Pubs.

Duff, Jon M., jt. auth. see Luzadder, Warren J.

Duff, Karen, ed. see Holdt, Jacob.

***Duff, Karl.** Restoration of Marriage. LC 99-61133. 272p. 1999. pap. 13.95 (*1-57921-214-X*, Pub. by WinePress Pub) BookWorld.

Duff, Karl. Restoration of Men. 140p. (Orig.). 1990. pap. 9.99 (*1-56043-022-2*) Destiny Image.

— Teens, Sex & Happiness. 140p. (Orig.). 1994. pap. 9.99 (*1-56043-131-8*) Destiny Image.

Duff, Katherine E., et al. Atlas of Chrysophycean Cysts. LC 94-30346. (Developments in Hydrobiology Ser.: 99). (Illus.). 200p. (C). 1994. text 213.00 (*0-7923-3039-0*) Kluwer Academic.

Duff, M., et al. From Superstrings to Supergravity: Proceedings of the 26th Workshop of the Eloisatron Project. (Science & Culture Series - Physics). 324p. 1994. text 95.00 (*981-02-1461-8*) World Scientific Pub.

***Duff, M. J., ed.** The World in Eleven Dimensions: Supergravity, Supermembranes & Theory. (Studies in High Energy Physics, Cosmology & Gravitation). 500p. 1999. 49.00 (*0-7503-0672-6*, Pub. by IOP Pub) Am Intl Dist.

Duff, M. J., jt. auth. see Preston, K., Jr.

Duff, Margaret, tr. see Simenon, Georges.

Duff, Michael J. Intermediate-Level Image Processing. 1987. text 119.00 (*0-12-223325-5*) Acad Pr.

Duff, Michael J., ed. Computing Structures for Image Processing. 1983. text 119.00 (*0-12-223340-9*) Acad Pr.

Duff, Michael J., et al, eds. Supermembranes & Physics in 2 Plus 1 Dimensions. 468p. (C). 1990. text 118.00 (*981-02-0131-1*) World Scientific Pub.

Duff, Michael J. & Arnowitt, R. Strings '89: Proceedings. 1990. pap. 32.00 (*981-02-0006-4*); text 98.00 (*981-02-0005-6*) World Scientific Pub.

Duff, Mildred. The Story of Catherine Booth for Young People. 1979. pap. 6.99 (*0-88019-112-0*) Schmul Pub Co.

Duff, Mountstuart E. Grant, see Grant Duff, Mountstuart E., ed.

Duff, P., jt. auth. see Findlay, M. J.

Duff, P. M., ed. Holmes' Principles of Physical Geology. 4th ed. (Illus.). 807p. (Orig.). 1993. pap. 44.95 (*0-7487-4381-2*, Pub. by S Thornes Pubs) Trans-Atl Phila.

Duff, P. M. & Smith, A. J., eds. Geology of England & Wales. (Illus.). xx, 651p. (C). 1992. 126.00 (*0-903317-70-2*, 273, Pub. by Geol Soc Pub Hse); pap. 57.00 (*0-903317-71-0*, 274, Pub. by Geol Soc Pub Hse) AAPG.

Duff, Patrick, jt. auth. see Ling, Frank.

Duff, Patrick W. Personality in Roman Private Law. LC 70-138536. xiii, 241p. 1971. reprint ed. lib. bdg. 12.50 (*0-678-04544-5*) Kelley.

Duff, Peter. British Ships & Shipping. 1977. lib. bdg. 59.95 (*0-8490-1556-1*) Gordon Pr.

— Criminal Injuries Compensation. 1991. pap. 35.00 (*0-406-12131-1*, UK, MICHIE) LEXIS Pub.

Duff, Peter & Hutton, Neil, eds. Criminal Justice in Scotland. LC 98-44662. 432p. 1999. pap. 29.95 (*1-85521-899-2*) Ashgate Pub Co.

***Duff, Peter & Hutton, Neil, eds.** Criminal Justice in Scotland. LC 98-44662. 412p. 1999. text 87.95 (*1-85521-890-9*) Ashgate Pub Co.

Duff, R. A., ed. Philosophy & the Criminal Law: Principle & Critique. LC 97-25899. (Studies in Philosophy & Law). 272p. (C). 1998. text 54.95 (*0-521-55044-0*) Cambridge U Pr.

Duff, R. A., jt. ed. see Taft, T.

Duff, R. Eleanor, et al. Building Successful Parent-Teacher Partnerships. LC 79-91107. (Illus.). 84p. (Orig.). 1980. pap. 9.95 (*0-89334-053-7*) Humanics Ltd.

***Duff, Richard W.** Money Magic with Annuities: Great Ideas for Creative Investors. 1999. 19.95 (*1-882703-03-0*) RWD Ent.

— Money Magic with Annuities: Great Ideas for Creative Investors. 1999. pap. 19.95 (*1-882703-01-4*) RWD Ent.

Duff, Richard W. Preserving Family Wealth Using Tax Magic. 400p. (Orig.). 1995. pap. 16.95 (*0-425-14432-1*) Berkley Pub.

— Preserving Family Wealth Using Tax Magic: Strategies Worth Millions! LC 93-92696. (Illus.). 288p. 1992. 36.95 (*1-882703-07-3*) RWD Ent.

Duff, Scott A. The M1 Garand: Owner's Guide. 126p. 1995. pap. 16.95 (*1-888722-03-7*) S A Duff.

— The M1 Garand: Post World War II. 139p. 1989. pap. 19.95 (*1-888722-00-2*) S A Duff.

— The M1 Garand: Serial Numbers & Data Sheets. 101p. 1995. pap. 9.95 (*1-888722-05-3*) S A Duff.

— The M1 Garand: World War II. 320p. 1993. 69.95 (*1-888722-02-9*); pap. 34.95 (*1-888722-01-0*) S A Duff.

Duff, Scott A., et al. Arms for the Nation: Springfield Longarms. 73p. 1994. pap. 9.95 (*1-888722-04-5*) S A Duff.

Duff, Susan, jt. auth. see Woman's Day Editors.

Duff, Thomas A. Monarch Notes on Defoe's Robinson Crusoe. (Orig.). (C). 3.95 (*0-671-00821-8*, Arco) Macmillan Gen Ref.

Duff, W. Patrick, jt. auth. see Catanzarite, Valerian A.

Duff, William. Critical Observations on the Writings of the Most Celebrated Original Geniuses in Poetry (1770) LC 73-9526. 400p. 1973. reprint ed. lib. bdg. 60.00 (*0-8201-1119-8*) Schol Facsimiles.

— An Essay on Original Genius & Its Various Modes of Exertion in Philosophy & the Fine Arts. LC 64-10669. 328p. 1978. reprint ed. 60.00 (*0-8201-1261-5*) Schol Facsimiles.

***Duff, William.** Heads or Tails...You Die. LC 98-87027. (Illus.). 162p. 1999. pap. 11.95 (*1-56315-177-4*) SterlingHse.

***Duff, William E.** A Time for Spies: Theodore Stephanovich Mally & the Era of the Great Illegals. LC 99-6697. (Illus.). 256p. 1999. 29.95 (*0-8265-1352-2*) Vanderbilt U Pr.

Duff, William G. Electromagnetic Compatibility in Telecommunications. LC 88-80525. (Electromagnetic Interference & Compatibility Ser.: Vol. 7). (Illus.). 517p. 1988. 75.00 (*0-944916-07-4*) emf-emi Control.

— Fundamentals of Electromagnetic Compatibility. LC 88-80527. (Electromagnetic Interference & Compatibility Ser.: Vol. 1). (Illus.). 389p. 1988. 50.00 (*0-944916-01-5*) emf-emi Control.

Duff, Wilson. The Indian History of British Columbia: The Impact of the White Man. (Illus.). 160p. 1997. pap. 14.95 (*0-7718-9483-X*) U of Wash Pr.

Duff, Wilson. The Upper Stalo Indians of the Fraser River of B. C. fac. ed. (British Columbia Provincial Museum, Anthropology in British Columbia Ser.: No. 1). (Illus.). 138p. (C). 1952. reprint ed. pap. text 15.00 (*1-55567-784-3*) Coyote Press.

Duffaud, Briege. A Long Stem Rose. 384p. 1995. pap. 13.95 (*1-85371-502-6*, Pub. by Poolbeg Pr) Dufour.

Duffee, Carla & Turnbow, Julie. Fraction Fun: With the BarCulator & PieCulator. (FraConcept Ser.). (Illus.). 36p. (Orig.). 1995. pap., teacher ed. 5.00 (*1-890387-00-2*, KDY 340) Kaidy Educ.

Duffee, David. Correctional Management: Change & Control in Correctional Organizations. 407p. (C). 1986. reprint ed. pap. text 24.95 (*0-88133-246-1*) Waveland Pr.

— Corrections: Practice & Policy. 448p. (C). 1989. 69.06 (*0-07-557121-8*) McGraw.

Duffee, David E. Correctional Management: Change & Control in Correctional Organizations. (Criminal Justice Ser.). (Illus.). 1980. text 25.95 (*0-685-03805-X*) P-H.

Duffek, Karen. Bill Reid: Beyond the Essential Form. (Illus.). 64p. 1986. pap. 15.95 (*0-7748-0263-4*) U of Wash Pr.

Duffell, Roger. Engineering. 80p. (C). 1995. pap. 8.95 (*0-7453-0928-3*, Pub. by Pluto GBR) Stylus Pub VA.

Duffels, J. P. & Van der Laan, P. A. Catalogue of the Cicadoidea (Homoptera, Auchenorhyncha) 1956-1980. 1985. text 220.00 (*90-6193-522-9*) Kluwer Academic.

Duffens, Kurt, jt. auth. see Rickey, Brad.

Duffer, Allen P. Plan & Operation of the 1995 National Survey of Family Growth. LC 97-36607. (Vital & Health Statistics Ser.: Series 1, No. 37). 1997. write for info. (*0-8406-0531-5*) Natl Ctr Health Stats.

Duffer, Hiram, tr. see Greenfield, Guy.

Duffer, Hiram, tr. see LaHaye, Tim F.

Duffer, Hiram, tr. see West, Ross.

Duffer, Hiram F., Jr., tr. see Bunyan, John & Leavell, L. P.

Duffer, Hiran, tr. see McGee, Robert S.

Dufferin & Ava. Dufferin - Carnarvon Correspondence, 1874-1878, Vol. 33. Hamilton-Temple-Blackwood, Frederick T. et al, eds. LC 69-14508. 442p. 1969. reprint ed. lib. bdg. 75.00 (*0-8371-5073-6*, DUDC, Greenwood Pr) Greenwood.

Dufferwiel, Martin. Durham: A Thousand Years of History & Legend. (Illus.). 192p. 1997. 29.95 (*1-85158-885-X*, Pub. by Mainstream Pubng) Trafalgar.

***Duffet, Ann, et al.** Kids These Days '99 Vol. 2: What Americans Really Think about the Next Generation. (Illus.). 12p. 1999. pap. write for info. (*1-889483-61-3*) Public Agenda.

Duffet, Thomas, jt. auth. see Settle, Elkanah.

Duffett, Ann, jt. auth. see Farkas, Steve.

Duffett, Robert G. A Relevant Word: Communicating the Gospel to Seekers. 160p. 1995. pap. 16.00 (*0-8170-1233-8*) Judson.

Duffett-Smith, Peter. Easy PC Astronomy. (Illus.). 164p. (C). 1996. pap., pap. text 30.95 incl. 3.5 hd (*0-521-56052-7*) Cambridge U Pr.

Duffett-Smith, Peter J. Astronomy with Your Personal Computer. 2nd ed. (Illus.). 270p. (C). 1990. pap. 30.95 (*0-521-38995-X*); text 74.95 (*0-521-38093-6*) Cambridge U Pr.

— Practical Astronomy with Your Calculator. 3rd ed. (Illus.). 200p. 1989. text 54.95 (*0-521-35629-6*) Cambridge U Pr.

— Practical Astronomy with Your Calculator. 3rd ed. (Illus.). 200p. 1989. pap. 16.95 (*0-521-35699-7*) Cambridge U Pr.

Duffey, Barbara. Angels & Apparitions: True Ghost Stories from the South. unabridged ed. (Illus.). 216p. 1997. pap. 15.00 (*0-9659477-0-X*) Elysian Ent.

— Banshees, Bugles & Belles: True Ghost Stories of Georgia. LC 95-36423. (Illus.). 126p. (Orig.). 1995. pap. 15.00 (*1-883522-08-0*, Rockbridge) Howell Pr VA.

— Miracles from Heaven. unabridged ed. Orig. Title: In Search of Miracles. 180p. 1998. lib. bdg. 13.95 (*0-9659477-1-8*, 2) Elysian Ent.

Duffey, Bernard. A Poetry of Presence: The Writing of William Carlos Williams. LC 85-40760. (Wisconsin Project on American Writers Ser.). 352p. 1986. text 24.95 (*0-299-10470-2*) U of Wis Pr.

Duffey, Bernard I. The Chicago Renaissance in American Letters: A Critical History. LC 72-6193. 285p. 1973. reprint ed. lib. bdg. 55.00 (*0-8371-6461-3*, DUCR, Greenwood Pr) Greenwood.

— Poetry in America: Expression & Its Values in the Times of Bryant, Whitman, & Pound. LC 77-81281. 372p. reprint ed. pap. 115.40 (*0-608-18755-0*, 205223600068) Bks Demand.

***Duffey, Betsy.** Alien for Rent. (Illus.). 80p. (J). (gr. 2-5). 2000. pap. 4.50 (*0-440-41468-7*, Yearling) BDD Bks Young Read.

Duffey, Betsy. Alien for Rent. LC 98-19313. (Illus.). 80p. (J). (gr. 2-5). 1999. 14.95 (*0-385-32572-X*) Delacorte.

— A Boy in the Doghouse. LC 90-47751. (Illus.). 96p. (J). (gr. 2-6). 1993. pap. 3.95 (*0-671-86698-2*, Half Moon Paper) S&S Childrens.

— Boy in the Doghouse. 1993. 9.15 (*0-606-05169-4*, Pub. by Turtleback) Demco.

Duffey, Betsy. Camp Knock Knock. LC 95-619. 1996. 9.19 (*0-606-09124-6*, Pub. by Turtleback) Demco.

Duffey, Betsy. The Camp Knock Knock Mystery. (J). (gr. 3 up). 1997. pap. 3.99 (*0-440-91193-1*) Dell.

— The Camp Knock Knock Mystery. LC 96-16071. 1997. 9.19 (*0-606-11185-9*, Pub. by Turtleback) Demco.

— Coaster. LC 94-6487. 112p. (J). (gr. 5 up). 1994. 13.99 (*0-670-85480-8*, Viking Child) Peng Put Young Read.

Duffey, Betsy. Coaster. (J). 1996. 9.09 (*0-606-11277-0*, Pub. by Turtleback) Demco.

Duffey, Betsy. Coaster. (Illus.). 128p. (J). (gr. 5-9) 1996. pap. 4.99 (*0-14-036956-2*) Viking Penguin.

***Duffey, Betsy.** Cody's Secret Admirer. (Illus.). 96p. (J). (gr. 2-5). 2000. pap. 3.99 (*0-14-130565-7*, PuffinBks) Peng Put Young Read.

— Cody's Secret Admirer. (Illus.). (J). 2000. 9.44 (*0-606-18396-5*) Turtleback.

Duffey, Betsy. Cody's Secret Admirer. LC 97-26812. (gr. 3-4). 1998. 13.99 (*0-670-87400-0*) Viking Penguin.

— The Gadget War. (Illus.). (J). (gr. 2-5). 1991. 13.99 (*0-670-84152-8*, Viking Child) Peng Put Young Read.

— The Gadget War. (Young Puffin Read Alone Ser). (J). 1994. 9.19 (*0-606-06401-X*, Pub. by Turtleback) Demco.

***Duffey, Betsy.** Gadget War. (Illus.). (J). 2000. pap. 3.99 (*0-14-130708-0*, PuffinBks) Peng Put Young Read.

— Gadget War. (Illus.). (J). 2000. 9.34 (*0-606-18405-8*) Turtleback.

Duffey, Betsy. Hey, New Kid! LC 95-46309. (Illus.). 78p. (J). (gr. 4-7). 1996. 13.99 (*0-670-86760-8*, Viking Child) Peng Put Young Read.

— Hey, New Kid! (Puffin Chapters Ser.). (Illus.). 96p. (J). (gr. 2-5). 1998. pap. 3.99 (*0-14-038439-1*, PuffinBks) Peng Put Young Read.

— How to Be Cool in the Third Grade. LC 93-18618. (Illus.). 80p. (J). (gr. 2-5). 1993. 13.99 (*0-670-84798-4*, Viking Child) Peng Put Young Read.

— How to Be Cool in the Third Grade. 1999. pap. 3.99 (*0-14-130466-9*, PuffinBks) Peng Put Young Read.

— How to Be Cool in the Third Grade. (J). 1995. 9.19 (*0-606-07677-8*, Pub. by Turtleback) Demco.

— The Math Wiz. (Illus.). (J). (gr. 2-5). 1990. 13.99 (*0-670-83422-X*, Viking Child) Peng Put Young Read.

— The Math Wiz. (Illus.). 80p. (J). (gr. 2-5). 1997. pap. 3.99 (*0-14-038647-5*, PuffinBks) Peng Put Young Read.

— Math Wiz. (J). 1993. 9.19 (*0-606-05455-3*, Pub. by Turtleback) Demco.

— Puppy Love. (Pet Patrol Ser.: No. 1). (Illus.). 80p. (J). (gr. 2-6). 1994. pap. 4.99 (*0-14-034997-9*) Peng Put Young Read.

— Puppy Love. (J). 1995. 9.19 (*0-606-08007-4*, Pub. by Turtleback) Demco.

— Se Utterly Yours, Booker Jones. 128p. 1997. pap. write for info. (*0-14-038099-X*, PuffinBks) Peng Put Young Read.

***Duffey, Betsy.** Spot on Cody. (Illus.). 80p. (J). (gr. 2-5). 2000. pap. 3.99 (*0-14-130987-3*, PuffinBks) Peng Put Young Read.

Duffey, Betsy. Spotlight on Cody. LC 98-17461. (Illus.). 74p. (J). (gr. 2-5). 1998. pap. 14.99 (*0-670-88077-9*) Viking Penguin.

— Throw-Away Pets. (Pet Patrol Ser.). 1993. 9.19 (*0-606-08585-8*, Pub. by Turtleback) Demco.

— Utterly Yours, Booker Jones. LC 95-11143. (Illus.). 128p. (YA). (gr. 5 up). 1995. 14.99 (*0-670-86007-7*, Viking Child) Peng Put Young Read.

— Utterly Yours, Booker Jones. (J). 1997. 9.09 (*0-606-13061-6*, Pub. by Turtleback) Demco.

— Utterly Yours, Booker Jones. (Illus.). 128p. (J). (gr. 5-9). 1997. pap. 4.99 (*0-14-037496-5*) Viking Penguin.

— Virtual Cody. (Puffin Chapters for Readers on the Move Ser.). (Illus.). 96p. (J). (gr. 2-5). 1999. pap. 3.99 (*0-14-130350-6*, PuffinBks) Peng Put Young Read.

— Virtual Cody. LC 96-47356. (Illus.). 80p. (J). (gr. 2-5). 1997. 13.99 (*0-670-87470-1*) Viking Penguin.

— The Wild Things. (Pet Patrol Ser.). (J). 1993. 9.19 (*0-606-08008-2*, Pub. by Turtleback) Demco.

Duffey, Betsy & Dunbar, Fiona. Camp Knock Knock. 48p. (J). 1996. pap. 3.99 (*0-440-91305-5*) BDD Bks Young Read.

Duffey, David M. Expert Advice on Gun Dog Training. rev. ed. LC 85-21759. 288p. 1985. 19.95 (*0-8329-0411-2*, Winchester Pr) New Win Pub.

Duffey, Eliza B. The Relations of the Sexes. LC 73-20619. (Sex, Marriage & Society Ser.). 320p. 1974. reprint ed. 26.95 (*0-405-05824-1*) Ayer.

— What Women Should Know: Information for Wives & Mothers. LC 73-20620. (Sex, Marriage & Society Ser.). 324p. 1974. reprint ed. 24.95 (*0-405-05825-X*) Ayer.

Duffey, George H. A Development of Quantum Mechanics. 1983. text 211.50 (*90-277-1587-4*) Kluwer Academic.

***Duffey, George H.** Modern Physical Chemistry: A Molecular Approach. LC 00-35702. 2000. write for info. (*0-306-46395-4*) Plenum.

Duffey, Jenny N. Quittin' Time: An Ex-Smoker's Step-by-Step Plan for Beating Your Cigarette Addiction, Vol. 1. Welch, Bonnie, ed. (Orig.). 1993. 14.95 (*0-9642103-0-4*, TX3-677-725) Duffey Pubng.

Duffey, Michael E., jt. ed. see Lebenthal, Emanuel.

Duffey, Michael K. Peacemaking Christians: The Future of Just Wars, Pacifism & Nonviolent Resistance. LC 95-14284. (Illus.). 176p. 1995. pap. 14.95 (*1-55612-764-2*) Sheed & Ward WI.

Duffey, Peter. A Charmed Life: From Cornell to Concorde. (Illus.). 350p. 1998. 30.00 (*1-888962-10-0*) Paladwr Pr.

Duffey, Rick & Stephenson, Harry. Fifth House. 1979. 1.50 (*0-942582-01-2*) Erie St Pr.

Duffibe, Mary K., jt. auth. see Wharemaru, Heeni.

Duffie, Charles. The Mole & the Owl: A Romantic Fable about Braving the Wide World for Love. LC 98-140555. (Illus.). 104p. 1998. 18.95 (*1-57174-082-1*) Hampton Roads Pub Co.

Duffie, Darrell. Dynamic Asset Pricing Theory. 2nd ed. LC 95-32122. 328p. (C). 1996. text 49.50 (*0-691-02125-2*, Pub. by Princeton U Pr) Cal Prin Full Svc.

Duffie, J. Darrell. Security Markets: Stochastic Models. (Economic Theory, Econometrics & Mathematical Economics Ser.). (Illus.). 358p. 1988. 55.00 (*0-12-223345-X*) Acad Pr.

Duffie, John A. & Beckman, William A. Solar Engineering of Thermal Processes. 2nd ed. LC 90-25202. 944p. 1991. 140.00 (*0-471-51056-4*) Wiley.

Duffie, John A., jt. ed. see Boer, Karl W.

Duffie, John A., jt. ed. see Daniels, Farrington.

Duffie, Neil A., jt. auth. see Bollinger, John G.

Duffie, Patricia K. English Fundamentals. 889p. (C). 1996. pap. text, teacher ed., spiral bd. write for info. (*1-890601-01-2*); pap. text, student ed., spiral bd. write for info. (*1-890601-00-4*) P L Duffy.

— English Fundamentals - Plus Punctuation & More. (C). Date not set. pap. text, teacher ed., spiral bd. write for info. (*1-890601-07-1*); pap. text, student ed., spiral bd. write for info. (*1-890601-06-3*) P L Duffy.

— Vocabulary I. 251p. (C). 1996. pap. text, teacher ed., spiral bd. write for info. (*1-890601-03-9*); pap. text, student ed., spiral bd. write for info. (*1-890601-02-0*) P L Duffy.

D

An Asterisk (*) at the beginning of an entry indicates that the title is appearing for the first time.

— Vocabulary II. 837p. (C). 1996. pap. text, teacher ed., spiral bd. write for info. (1-890601-05-5); pap. text, student ed., spiral bd. write for info. (1-890601-04-7) P L Duffy.

Duffie, Sonia, ed. Reglamentos des Estado Libre Asociado de Puerto Rico No. 22: Autoridad de Acueducto y Alcantarillado.Tr. of Aqueduct & Sewer Authority. (SPA., Illus.). 1100p. 1998. ring bd. write for info. (0-327-05784-X, 47363-10) LEXIS Pub.

Duffield, Anne. Fiametta. large type ed. 400p. 1985. 27.99 (0-7089-1371-7) Ulverscroft.

Duffield, Barbara & Gleason, Mary A. Homelessness in America: Unabated & Increasing: A 10 Year Perspective. 82p. (C). 1999. pap. text 15.00 (0-7881-4139-2) DIANE Pub.

Duffield, C. G., jt. auth. see Welch, W.

Duffield, Camilla L., jt. auth. see Duffield, Lathel F.

***Duffield, Holley G.** Historical Dictionary of the Shakers. Woronoff, Jon, ed. LC 99-38149. (Historical Dictionaries of Religions, Philosophies & Movements Ser.: Vol. 28). 288p. 2000. 55.00 (0-8108-3683-1) Scarecrow.

***Duffield, Ian.** Representing Convicts: New Perspectives on Convict Forced Labour Migration. (New Historical Perspectives on Forced Migration Ser.). 2000. pap. text 28.95 (0-7185-0239-6) Leicester U Pr.

Duffield, Ian & Bradley, James. Representing Convicts: New Perspectives on Convict Forced Labour Migration. LC 96-24610. (New Historical Perspectives on Migration Ser.). 224p. 1997. 99.50 (0-7185-0075-X) Bks Intl VA.

Duffield, Ian, jt. auth. see Gundara, Jagdish S.

Duffield, J. W. Mason County Trees. (Illus.). 92p. 1998. pap. 8.00 (0-9635361-2-5) Burton Bks.

Duffield, James, jt. auth. see Slifer, Dennis.

Duffield, Jill, et al. Policy, Practice, & Provision for Children with Specific Learning Difficulties. LC 95-77822. 256p. 1995. 72.95 (1-85628-928-1, LC4706, Pub. by Avebry) Ashgate Pub Co.

Duffield, John S. Power Rules: The Evolution of NATO's Conventional Force Posture. LC 94-25006. xi , 386p. 1995. 49.50 (0-8047-2396-6) Stanford U Pr.

— World Power Forsaken: Political Culture, International Institutions, & German Security Policy after Unification. LC 97-39359. 408p. 1998. 49.50 (0-8047-3365-1) Stanford U Pr.

Duffield, John T. Duffield Family: Sketch of William Duffield of Venango Co., Pa., & His Descendants. (Illus.). 74p. 1997. reprint ed. pap. 15.00 (0-8328-8364-6); reprint ed. lib. bdg. 25.00 (0-8328-8363-8) Higginson Bk Co.

Duffield, John W., et al. Economic Value of Instream Flow in Montana's Big Hole & Bitterroot Rivers. 72p. 1997. reprint ed. 14.00 (0-89904-587-1, Bear Meadows Resrch Grp) Crumb Elbow Pub.

Duffield, Lathel F. & Duffield, Camilla L. Other Worlds, Other Beings. LC 97-90860. 1998. pap. 10.95 (0-533-12496-4) Vantage.

Duffield, Mark. Black Radicalism & Politics of De-Industrialisation: The Hidden History of Indian Foundry Workers in the West Midlands. (Research in Ethnic Relations Ser.). 230p. 1988. text 79.95 (0-566-05589-9, Pub. by Avebry) Ashgate Pub Co.

— War & Famine in Africa: Oxfam Research Discussion Papers. (Oxfam Research Discussion Papers). 36p. (C). Date not set. 15.95 (0-85598-161-X, Pub. by Oxfam Pub) Stylus Pub VA.

Duffield, Mark & Prendergast, John. Without Troops & Tanks: Humanitarism Intervention in Ethiopia & Eritrea. LC 94-28293. 350p. (C). 1994. 49.95 (1-56902-002-7); pap. 16.95 (1-56902-003-5) Red Sea Pr.

Duffield, Mary R. Plants for Dry Climates: How to Select, Grow & Enjoy. LC 98-36073. 1998. pap. 17.95 (1-55561-176-1) Fisher Bks.

***Duffield, Mary Rose & Jones, Warren.** Plants for Dry Climates. (Illus.). 192p. 2000. pap. 19.95 (1-55561-270-9) Fisher Bks.

Duffield, Nigel. Particles & Projections in Irish Syntax. LC 95-11030. (Studies in Natural Language & Linguistic Theory: Vol. 32). 374p. (C). 1995. text 161.50 (0-7923-3550-3) Kluwer Academic.

Duffield-Stoll, Anne Q. ZZYZX - History of an Oasis: San Bernardino County, California. (Illus.). 71p. (Orig.). 1995. pap. 9.00 (0-937048-49-6) Santa Susana.

Duffield, Wendell A. Volcanoes of Northern Arizona: Sleeping Giants of the Grand Canyon Region. Price, L. Greer, ed. LC 97-73191. (Illus.). 72p. 1998. pap. 14.95 (0-938216-58-9) GCA.

Duffield, Wendell A., et al. Tapping the Earth's Natural Heat. (Illus.). 63p. (C). 1995. pap. text 20.00 (0-7881-1922-2) DIANE Pub.

Duffieux, P. M. The Fourier Transform & Its Applications to Optics. LC 82-20302. (Wiley Series in Pure & Applied Optics). 217p. reprint ed. pap. 67.30 (0-7837-2830-1, 205764200006) Bks Demand.

***Duffill, Mark.** Mungo Park: Writer, Surgeon & West African Explorer. (Illus.). 112p. 1999. pap. write for info. (1-901663-15-9, Pub. by Natl Mus Scotland) A Schwartz & Co.

Duffin, Anne. Faction & Faith: Politics & Religion of the Cornish Gentry Before the Civil War. (Illus.). 280p. 1996. 55.00 (0-85989-435-5, Pub. by Univ Exeter Pr) Northwestern U Pr.

Duffin, Dacalyn. Langstaff: A Nineteenth-Century Medical Life. (Illus.). 400p. 1993. text 60.00 (0-8020-2908-6); pap. text 17.95 (0-8020-7414-6) U of Toronto Pr.

Duffin, Henry C. Thomas Hardy: A Study of the Wessex Novels, the Poems, & the Dynasts. LC 77-17945. 356p. 1978. reprint ed. lib. bdg. 37.50 (0-313-20109-9, DUTH, Greenwood Pr) Greenwood.

— Walter De La Mare, a Study of His Poetry. (Select Bibliographies Reprint Ser.). 1977. 23.95 (0-8369-5043-7) Ayer.

— Walter De La Mare, a Study of His Poetry. LC 71-95424. (Studies in Poetry: No. 38). 1970. reprint ed. lib. bdg. 75.00 (0-8383-0972-0) M S G Haskell Hse.

***Duffin, Jacalyn.** History of Medicine: A Scandalously Short Introduction. 1999. pap. text 24.95 (0-8020-7912-1) U of Toronto Pr.

Duffin, Jacalyn. To See with a Better Eye: A Life of R. T. H. Laennec. LC 97-19779. 456p. 1998. text 49.50 (0-691-03708-6, Pub. by Princeton U Pr) Cal Prin Full Svc.

Duffin, James M., compiled by. Guide to Records of the Sale of Commonwealth Property in the County of Philadelphia from 1780 to 1798. (Monograph Ser.: No. 2). 96p. (Orig.). 1996. pap. write for info. (1-887099-06-9) Geneal Soc Pa.

— Guide to the Mortgages of the General Loan Office of the Province of Pennsylvania, 1724-1756. (Monograph Ser.: No. 1). 160p. (Orig.). 1995. pap. 17.95 (1-887099-05-0) Geneal Soc Pa.

Duffin, Lorna, jt. ed. see Charles, Lindsey.

Duffin, Paul H. Knowledge Based Systems: Applications in Administrative Government. 148p. 1988. text 54.95 (0-470-21260-8) P-H.

***Duffin, Ross & Hillier, Paul, eds.** A Josquin Anthology. (Church Music Collections). 128p. 2000. pap. text 13.95 (0-19-353218-2) OUP.

***Duffin, Ross W.** A Performer's Guide to Medieval Music. 640p. 2000. 39.95 (0-253-33752-6) Ind U Pr.

Duffin, W. D., tr. see Duane, Michael.

Duffin, W. J. Electricity & Magnetism. 4th ed. 442p. (C). 1990. text 40.94 (0-07-707209-X) McGraw.

Duffin, W. J., tr. see DauNe, Michele.

Duffin, W. J., tr. see Ramade, Francois.

Duffley, Patrick J. English Infinitive English Lanquage Series. (English Language Ser.). 160p. (C). 1995. pap. text 32.00 (0-582-07135-6, 79350) Longman.

***Dufflied, Jeremy.** Oak Apples & Heavenly Kisses. 63p. 2000. pap. 11.95 (1-902096-61-4, Pub. by Headland Pubns) Intl Spec Bk.

Duffner. The Sorrowful & Immaculate Heart of Mary. 47p. 1.00 (0-911988-24-6, 37702) AMI Pr.

Duffner, Patricia K., jt. auth. see Cohen, Michael E.

Duffner, Robert W. Airborne Laser: Bullets of Light. LC 97-21335. (Illus.). 416p. (C). 1997. 34.95 (0-306-45622-2, Plenum Trade) Perseus Pubng.

***Dufford, Bob.** The Reign of God: Instrument Book. 24p. 1998. pap. 2.20 (0-915531-71-2) OR Catholic.

Dufford, Bob. The Reign of God Songbook. 1997. 8.95 (0-915531-69-0) OR Catholic.

Duffour, Jacqueline, jt. auth. see Levy, Andre.

Duffuaa, S., et al. Planning & Control of Maintenance Systems: Modeling & Analysis. LC 98-13431. 400p. 1998. 90.00 (0-471-17981-7) Wiley.

Duffus, C. M. & Slaughter, J. C. Seeds & Their Uses. LC 80-40283. 164p. reprint ed. pap. 50.90 (0-608-16312-0, 202667400051) Bks Demand.

Duffus, J., ed. Carcinogenicity of Inorganic Substances: Risks from Occupational Exposure. 1997. write for info. (0-85404-429-9) Am Chemical.

Duffus, J. E., jt. ed. see Whitney, E. D.

Duffus, J. H. Cancer & Workplace Chemicals. 1995. pap. 150.00 (0-948237-26-0) St Mut.

Duffus, J. H., ed. Substances of Abuse: An Assessment of Carcinogenicity. x, 124p. 1997. 113.00 (0-85404-447-7, 1607) Am Chemical.

Duffus, Nicole. Fragments. (Illus.). 48p. 1999. pap. 7.95 (0-9666100-3-2) Black Ink.

Duffus, Robert L. American Renaissance. LC 70-105679. reprint ed. 34.50 (0-404-02214-6) AMS Pr.

— The Santa Fe Trail. (Illus.). 1971. reprint ed. 39.00 (0-403-00918-9) Scholarly.

Duffus, Robert L. & Duffus, William M. The Innocents at Cedro: A Memoir of Thorstein Veblen & Some Others. LC 74-182193. vi, 163p. 1972. reprint ed. lib. bdg. 35.00 (0-678-00885-X) Kelley.

Duffus, Robert L. & Holt, L. Emmett, Jr. L. Emmett Holt: Pioneer of a Children's Century. LC 74-1683. (Children & Youth Ser.: Vol. 25). 310p. 1974. reprint ed. 28.95 (0-405-05960-4) Ayer.

Duffus, William M., jt. auth. see Duffus, Robert L.

Duffy. Annual Edit Online Psychology. 1999. pap. 6.32 (0-07-234602-7) McGraw.

— Auto Collision Repair Video Series IG. 96p. (C). 1998. teacher ed. 14.00 (0-8273-7792-4) Delmar.

— Basic Car Care: Survival Guide. (Automotive Technology Ser.). 1998. teacher ed. 12.00 (0-8273-7439-9); wbk. ed. 17.95 (0-8273-7438-0); pap. 30.95 (0-8273-7437-2) Delmar.

***Duffy.** Common Features of Microsoft Office 97. 2nd ed. 128p. (C). 1998. pap. text 19.00 (0-201-45923-X, Prentice Hall) P-H.

— Counseling. LC 98-48310. 744p. 1999. 85.00 (0-471-25461-4) Wiley.

Duffy. dBASE 5 for DOS: Tool Kit. (Management Information Systems Ser.). 1996. pap. 17.95 (0-7895-0185-6) Course Tech.

— Essential Dbase IV. 2nd ed. (Management Information Systems Ser.). 1996. pap. 18.95 (0-534-21882-2) S-W Pub.

— Essential DOS 5.0. 2nd ed. (Management Information Systems Ser.). 1996. pap. 18.95 (0-534-21883-0) S-W Pub.

— Essential Quattro Pro 4.0. 2nd ed. (Management Information Systems Ser.). 1996. pap. 18.95 (0-534-21884-9) S-W Pub.

***Duffy.** Fifty Blue Cats for Dad. 2002. pap. text. write for info. (0-7167-4088-5, Pub. by W H Freeman) VHPS.

Duffy. I-CAR Professional Auto Collision Repair. (Automotive Technology Ser.). 96p. 1996. teacher ed. 14.95 (0-8273-6501-2) Delmar.

***Duffy.** I-Car Professional Auto Collision Repair. 2nd ed. (C). 2000. pap. 53.25 (0-7668-1398-3) Thomson Learn.

Duffy. I-CAR Professional Automotive Collision Tech Man. (Automotive Technology Ser.). 224p. (C). 1996. mass mkt. 19.75 (0-8273-6502-0) Delmar.

— Ireland in the Middle Ages. LC 96-25753. 232p. 1997. text 69.95 (0-312-16389-4) St Martin.

— Lotus 5.0 for Windows: Tool Kit. (Management Information Systems Ser.). 1996. pap. 17.95 (0-7895-0402-2) Course Tech.

— Microsoft Access 97: Blue Ribbon Edition. 2nd ed. 176p. (C). 1998. pap. text 25.00 (0-201-44851-3, Prentice Hall) P-H.

— Microsoft Excel 97: Blue Ribbon Edition. 2nd ed. 224p. (C). 1998. pap. text 25.00 (0-201-44850-5, Prentice Hall) P-H.

— Microsoft Office 97: Professional, Blue Ribbon Edition. 2nd ed. 935p. (C). 1998. spiral bd. 64.00 (0-201-43860-7, Prentice Hall) P-H.

— Microsoft Windows 95 with Active Desktop & Windows 98. 2nd rev. ed. 144p. (C). 1998. pap. text 19.00 (0-201-45553-6, Prentice Hall) P-H.

— Microsoft Works, DOS Version. (Management Information Systems Ser.). 1996. pap. 32.95 (0-534-23623-5) S-W Pub.

— Motor Auto Body Repair - IG. 3rd ed. (Automotive Technology Ser.). 96p. 1998. teacher ed. 16.00 (0-8273-6859-3) Delmar.

— New Environments For Working. (Illus.). 192p. 1997. pap. write for info. (0-419-20990-5, E & FN Spon) Routledge.

— Personal Growth & Behavior 96. 16th annot. ed. 1996. teacher ed. (0-697-31672-6, WCB McGr Hill) McGrw-H Hghr Educ.

— Personal Growth & Behaviour. 14th ed. 1994. 12.74 (1-56134-284-X) McGraw.

— Personal Growth & Behaviour. 15th ed. 1995. 12.74 (1-56134-366-8) McGraw.

— PowerPoint 97: Blue Ribbon Edition. 2nd ed. 112p. (C). 1998. pap. text 25.00 (0-201-44852-1, Prentice Hall) P-H.

— Prog Ibm Persn Comp:ibm C Lang. (C). 1987. pap. text 25.00 (0-03-071481-8) Harcourt Coll Pubs.

— Psychology. 24th ed. 1994. 12.74 (1-56134-286-6) McGraw.

— Psychology. 25th ed. 1995. (1-56134-368-4, Dshkn McG-Hill) McGrw-H Hghr Educ.

— Psychology 1996/97. 26th annot. ed. 1996. teacher ed. (0-697-31677-7, WCB McGr Hill) McGrw-H Hghr Educ.

— Quality Software Applications for C++ (C). 2000. pap. 40.00 (0-13-261157-0) P-H.

— Questions in Irish History: Ireland 500-1170. 1992. pap. text. write for info. (0-582-09510-7, Pub. by Addison-Wesley) Longman.

— Read Me. (Management Information Systems Ser.). 1996. pap. 30.95 (0-7895-0556-8) S-W Pub.

— WordPerfect 6.1 for Windows: Tool Kit. (Management Information Systems Ser.). 1996. pap. 17.95 (0-7895-0689-0) Course Tech.

Duffy, ed. Pselli, Michaelis Vol. I: Philosophica Minora. (GRE.). 1992. 95.00 (3-8154-1955-7, T1955, Pub. by B G Teubner) U of Mich Pr.

Duffy & Hannay, P., eds. Architectural Knowledge: The New Professionalism. LC 98-38009. (Illus.). xvii, 217 p. 1997. pap. 39.99 (0-419-21000-8, E & FN Spon) Routledge.

***Duffy & Thurrott, Paul B.** Microsoft Office 97 Professional Applications & Visual Basic. 1999. pap. text 71.00 (0-201-67688-5) Addison-Wesley.

Duffy, jt. auth. see Scharff.

Duffy, jt. auth. see Swanson, Marie L.

***Duffy & Wong.** Community Psychology. 2nd ed. LC 99-40237. 330p. 1999. 69.00 (0-205-30598-9) Allyn.

Duffy, A. R., jt. auth. see Batelle Columbus Labs. Staff.

Duffy, A. R., jt. auth. see Kiefner, John F.

Duffy, Alex H., ed. The Design Productivity Debate. LC 97-26407. (Illus.). viii, 296p. 1997. 74.95 (3-540-76195-0) Spr-Verlag.

Duffy, B. Creativity & Imagination. LC 97-39366. (Supporting Early Learning Ser.). 1998. 78.95 (0-335-19872-4); pap. 21.95 (0-335-19871-6) OpUniv Pr.

Duffy, Bernard K. & Carpenter, Ronald H. Douglas MacArthur: Warrior As Wordsmith. 24. LC 96-2551. (Great American Orators Ser.: No. 24). 240p. 1997. lib. bdg. 69.50 (0-313-29148-9, Greenwood Pr) Greenwood.

Duffy, Bernard K. & Jacobi, Martin J. The Politics of Rhetoric: Richard M. Weaver & the Conservative Tradition, 51. LC 92-36514. (Contributions in Philosophy Ser.: No. 51). 244p. 1993. 62.95 (0-313-25713-2, DRC, Greenwood Pr) Greenwood.

Duffy, Bernard K. & Ryan, Halford R., eds. American Orators Before Nineteen Hundred: Critical Studies & Sources. LC 86-33610. 499p. 1987. lib. bdg. 115.00 (0-313-25129-0, DYO/, Greenwood Pr) Greenwood.

— American Orators of the Twentieth Century: Critical Studies & Sources. LC 86-10003. 490p. 1987. lib. bdg. 115.00 (0-313-24843-5, DFA/, Greenwood Pr) Greenwood.

Duffy, Bernard K., jt. ed. see Jackson, Lorraine D.

Duffy, Brian. Decade of Duffy's: Editorial Cartoons by Brian Duffy. LC 94-750. (Illus.). 152p. (C). 1994. pap. 14.95 (0-8138-2667-5) Iowa St U Pr.

— More of Duffy. (Illus.). 152p. 1995. pap. 14.95 (0-8138-2666-7) Iowa St U Pr.

Duffy, Brian, jt. auth. see McGee, James.

***Duffy, Bruce.** Last Comes the Egg. (Nonpareil Ser.: Vol. 91). 368p. 2000. pap. 16.95 (1-56792-124-8) Godine.

Duffy, Bruce. Last Comes the Egg. LC 96-43418. 359p. 1997. 22.50 (0-684-80883-8) S&S Trade.

— The World As I Found It. 570p. 1998. reprint ed. 29.95 (0-7351-0046-2) Replica Bks.

— The World As I Found It. rev. ed. 576p. 1997. pap. 15.00 (0-395-90057-3) HM.

Duffy, Carol A. Anvil New Poets 2. 166p. 1995. pap. 19.95 (0-85646-262-4, Pub. by Anvil Press) Dufour.

— I Wouldn't Thank You for a Valentine: Poems for Young Feminists. (Illus.). 112p. (YA). (gr. 7 up). 1995. 14.95 (0-8050-2756-4, Bks Young Read) H Holt & Co.

— Mean Time. 52p. 1993. pap. 14.95 (0-85646-247-0, Pub. by Anvil Press); pap. 17.95 (0-85646-303-5, Pub. by Anvil Press) Dufour.

— The Other Country. 56p. 1993. pap. 14.95 (0-85646-226-8, Pub. by Anvil Press) Dufour.

— Selling Manhattan. 64p. 1997. pap. 14.95 (0-85646-295-0, Pub. by Anvil Press) Dufour.

— Standing Female Nude. 62p. 1993. pap. 14.95 (0-85646-150-4, Pub. by Anvil Press) Dufour.

— Stopping for Death: Poems of Death & Loss. (Illus.). 144p. (YA). (gr. 7 up). 1996. 14.95 (0-8050-4717-4) H Holt & Co.

— William & the Ex-Prime Minister. 16p. 1992. pap. 14.95 (0-85646-253-5, Pub. by Anvil Press); pap. 7.95 (0-85646-254-3, Pub. by Anvil Press) Dufour.

Duffy, Carol A., ed. I Wouldn't Thank You for a Valentine: Poems for Young Feminists. (Illus.). (J). (gr. 6). 1997. reprint ed. pap. text 6.95 (0-8050-5545-2) H Holt & Co.

Duffy, Carol Ann. I Wouldn't Thank You for a Valentine: Poems for Young Feminists. 1997. 12.05 (0-606-13512-X, Pub. by Turtleback) Demco.

— Pamphlet, 1. 1999. pap. text 11.95 (0-85646-307-8) Anvil Pub.

***Duffy, Carol Ann.** The World's Wife. LC 99-87010. 128p. 2000. 22.00 (0-571-19985-2) Faber & Faber.

***Duffy, Carol Ann, ed.** Time's Tidings: Greeting the Twenty-First Century, an Anthology. 160p. 2000. pap. 18.95 (0-85646-313-2, Pub. by Anvil Press) Dufour.

Duffy, Catherine, jt. auth. see Scott, Emily.

Duffy, Cathy. Christian Home Educators' Curriculum Manual: Elementary Grades. rev. ed. LC 98-160057. (Illus.). 394p. 1997. pap. 19.95 (0-929320-09-3) Grove Pub.

***Duffy, Cathy.** Christian Home Educators' Curriculum Manual: Elementary Grades. 5th rev. ed. (Illus.). 504p. 2000. pap. 22.95 (0-929320-13-1, EG00) Grove Pub.

Duffy, Cathy. Christian Home Educators' Curriculum Manual: Junior - Senior High. 4th rev. ed. 400p. 1997. pap. 19.95 (0-929320-10-7) Grove Pub.

***Duffy, Cathy.** Christian Home Educators Curriculum Manual: Junior/Senior High. 5th rev. ed. (Illus.). 504p. 2000. pap. 22.95 (0-929320-14-X, JS00) Grove Pub.

Duffy, Cathy. Government Nannies: The Cradle-to-Grave Agenda of Goals 2000 & Outcome Based Education. 270p. (Orig.). (C). 1995. pap. 12.95 (1-56857-009-0) Noble Pub Assocs.

Duffy, Charles G. Young Ireland: A Fragment of Irish History, 1840-1850. LC 71-127257. (Europe 1815-1945 Ser.). 796p. 1973. reprint ed. lib. bdg. 79.50 (0-306-71119-2) Da Capo.

Duffy, Charles G., ed. The Ballad Poetry of Ireland. LC 72-13882. 256p. 1973. reprint ed. lib. bdg. 50.00 (0-8201-1116-3) Schol Facsimiles.

Duffy, Charles G., et al, eds. The Spirit of the Nation, 1845. (Hibernia Ser.). 368p. 1998. 105.00 (1-85477-223-6) Continuum.

Duffy, Chris. The Flag. Abreau, Kevin, ed. 157p. 1999. pap. 9.99 (1-892617-09-9) Conroca Pubg.

— The Last Promise. Abreau, Kevin, ed. LC 98-89316. 171p. 1999. pap. 9.99 (1-892617-08-0) Conroca Pubg.

Duffy, Christopher. Army of Frederick the Great. 1996. 37.50 (1-883476-02-X, Pub. by Emperors Pr) Combined Pub.

— The Fortress in the Age of Vauban & Frederick the Great, 1660-1789. (Siege Warfare Ser.: Vol. II). (Illus.). 400p. 1985. 50.00 (0-7100-9648-8, Routledge Thoemms) Routledge.

***Duffy, Christopher.** Instrument of War: The Austrian Army in the Seven Years War. (Illus.). 2000. 38.00 (1-883476-19-4, Pub. by Emperors Pr) Combined Pub.

Duffy, Christopher. Military Expert in the Age of Reason. 1998. pap. 12.99 (1-85326-690-6, Pub. by Wrdsworth Edits) Combined Pub.

***Duffy, Christopher.** Red Storm on the Reich. LC 99-47981. 2000. pap. write for info. (0-415-22829-8) Routledge.

Duffy, Christopher. Red Storm on the Reich: The Soviet March on Germany, 1945. (Illus.). 415p. 1993. reprint ed. pap. 14.95 (0-306-80505-7) Da Capo.

— Siege Warfare: Fortress in the Early Modern World 1494-1660. (Illus.). 304p. (C). 1997. pap. 27.99 (0-415-14649-6) Routledge.

Duffy, Christopher. Supplement: Microsoft Internet Explorer. 1997. teacher ed., suppl. ed. 24.00 (0-201-31523-8) Addisn-Wesley Iberoamer.

Duffy, Christopher. Suvarov: Campaigns in Italy & Switzerland. 1998. 35.00 (1-883476-18-6, Pub. by Emperors Pr) Combined Pub.

Duffy, Clinton T. Eighty-Eight Men & Two Women. LC 82-45663. reprint ed. 32.50 (0-404-62412-X) AMS Pr.

Duffy, D. E. & Santner, Thomas J. The Statistical Analysis of Discrete Data. (Texts in Statistics Ser.). (Illus.). 305p. 1989. 68.95 (0-387-97018-5) Spr-Verlag.

Duffy, Dan, ed. Not a War: American Vietnamese Fiction, Poetry & Essays. (Viet Nam Forum Ser.: No. 16). 316p. 1997. pap. 20.00 (0-614-31206-X) Yale U SE Asia.

— Vietnam Forum No. 14: Focus on Contemporary Fiction, the 1920's & Visits Home. 358p. 1993. pap. 15.00 (0-614-14929-0) Yale U SE Asia.

Duffy, Dan, jt. ed. see Tal, Kali.

Duffy, Daniel J. Quality Software Applications for C++ (Advances in Object Technology Ser.: Vol. 13). (Orig.). 1996. pap. 40.00 (*1-884842-35-6*, 2356) SIGS Bks & Multimedia.

Duffy, Daniel M. Benny Goes into Business. LC 98-33805. (Adventures of Benny & Watch: No. 5). 32p. (J). (gr. 1-3). 1999. pap. 3.95 (*0-8075-0637-0*) A Whitman.

— Benny's New Friend. LC 98-14070. (Adventures of Benny & Watch: No. 3). 32p. (J). (gr. 1-3). 1998. pap. 3.95 (*0-8075-0649-4*) A Whitman.

— The Magic Show Mystery. LC 98-30605. (Adventures of Benny & Watch: No. 4). 32p. (J). (gr. 1-3). 1998. pap. 3.95 (*0-8075-4939-8*) A Whitman.

— Meet the Boxcar Children. LC 98-6196. (Adventures of Benny & Watch: No. 1). 46p. (J). (gr. 1-3). 1998. pap. 3.95 (*0-8075-5034-5*) A Whitman.

— A Present for Grandfather. LC 98-6219. (Adventures of Benny & Watch: No. 2). 32p. (J). (gr. 1-3). 1998. pap. 3.95 (*0-8075-6625-X*) A Whitman.

— Watch Runs Away. LC 98-54892. (Adventures of Benny & Watch: No. 6). 32p. (J). (gr. 1-3). 1999. pap. 3.95 (*0-8075-8681-1*) A Whitman.

Duffy, Dave, ed. Backwoods Home Magazine: The Third Year. (Illus.). 384p. 1997. pap. 13.95 (*0-9655203-2-3*) Backwoods Home Mag Inc.

Duffy, David A. Principles of Automated Theorem Proving. LC 91-9103. (Wiley Professional Computing Ser.). 261p. 1991. reprint ed. pap. 81.00 (*0-608-05262-0*, 206580000001) Bks Demand.

Duffy, David C., jt. auth. see Nettleship, David N.

Duffy, Dean G. Advanced Engineering Mathematics. LC 97-33991. 656p. 1997. lib. bdg. 84.95 (*0-8493-7854-0*) CRC Pr.

Duffy, Dean G. Green's Functions with Applications. ring bd. write for info. (*1-58488-110-0*, Chap & Hall CRC) CRC Pr.

Duffy, Dean G. Solutions of Partial Differential Equations. (Illus.). 448p. 1986. 25.95 (*0-8306-0412-X*, 2612) McGraw-Hill Prof.

— Transform Methods for Solving Partial Differential Equations. LC 93-40215. 512p. 1994. boxed set 109.95 (*0-8493-7374-3*) CRC Pr.

Duffy, Dennis. Gardens, Covenants, Exiles: Loyalism in the Literature of Upper Canada, Ontario. LC 82-146241. 171p. reprint ed. pap. 53.10 (*0-7837-1233-2*, 204136900020) Bks Demand.

— John Richardson & His Works. (Canadian Author Studies). 42p. (C). 1983. pap. text 9.95 (*0-920763-41-3*, Pub. by ECW) Genl Dist Srvs.

— Sounding the Iceberg: An Essay on Canadian Historical Novels. 100p. (C). 1986. pap. text 14.00 (*0-920763-14-6*, Pub. by ECW) Genl Dist Srvs.

— A Tale of Sad Reality: John Richardson's Wacousta. (Canadian Fiction Studies: No. 20). 120p. (C). 1993. pap. text 14.95 (*1-55022-115-9*, Pub. by ECW) Genl Dist Srvs.

— A World under Sentence: John Richardson & the Interior. 180p. 1996. pap. 20.00 (*1-55022-250-3*, Pub. by ECW) Genl Dist Srvs.

Duffy, Donna, ed. see Thomas, John & Service, Robert W.

Duffy, Donna K. & Jones, Janet W. Teaching Within the Rhythms of the Semester. LC 94-41810. 281p. 1995. text 30.95 (*0-7879-0073-7*) Jossey-Bass.

Duffy, Eamon. Saints & Sinners: A History of the Popes. LC 97-60897. (Illus.). 320p. 1997. 35.00 (*0-300-07332-1*) Yale U Pr.

— Saints & Sinners: A/History of the Popes. (Illus.). 336p. 1999. pap. text 18.95 (*0-300-07799-8*) Yale U Pr.

— The Stripping of the Altars: Traditional Religion in England, 1400-1580. (Illus.). 608p. 1994. pap. 20.00 (*0-300-06076-9*) Yale U Pr.

Duffy, Edmund, jt. auth. see Harrison, S. L.

***Duffy, Elayn.** Proud Heart, Fair Lady. large type ed. 352p. 1999. 31.99 (*0-7089-4087-0*) Ulverscroft.

Duffy, Elizabeth A. & Goldberg, Idana. Crafting a Class: College Admissions & Financial Aid, 1955-1994. LC 97-5645. 336p. 1998. text 29.95 (*0-691-01683-6*, Pub. by Princeton U Pr) Cal Prin Full Svc.

Duffy, Enda. The Subaltern Ulysses. LC 93-47083. (C). 1994. pap. 18.95 (*0-8166-2329-5*); text 47.95 (*0-8166-2328-7*) U of Minn Pr.

Duffy, Erin, et al, eds. The Bahamas Index & Yearbook: 1994. 250p. 1995. text 100.00 (*0-932265-35-9*); pap. text 49.95 (*0-932265-36-7*) White Sound.

Duffy, F. H., et al. Clinical Electroencephalography & Topographic Brain Mapping. (Illus.). 355p. 1989. 137.00 (*0-387-96856-3*) Spr-Verlag.

Duffy, Francis. The Changing Workplace. Hannay, Patrick, ed. (Illus.). 192p. 1997. text 49.95 (*1-85454-120-X*) Chronicle Bks.

— The New Office: With 20 International Case Studies. LC 98-189791. (Illus.). 256p. 1997. 90.00 (*1-85029-891-2*, Pub. by Conran Octopus) Antique Collect.

***Duffy, Francis, et al.** Redesigning America's Schools: A Systems Approach to Improvement. (Illus.). 320p. 2000. text 44.95 (*1-929024-12-6*, 2012) CG Pubs Inc.

Duffy, Francis, et al. The Responsible Workplace. LC 92-37496. (Illus.). 240p. 1993. pap. 79.95 (*0-7506-0802-1*, Butterwrth Archit) Buttrwrth-Heinemann.

Duffy, Francis J. & Miller, William H. The New York Harbor Book. (Illus.). xvi, 208p. 1986. 22.50 (*0-931474-33-7*); pap. 17.95 (*0-931474-34-5*) TBW Bks.

Duffy, Francis M. Designing High-Performance Schools: A Practical Guide to Organizational Reengineering. (Illus.). 288p. 1996. boxed set 54.95 (*1-57444-010-1*) St Lucie Pr.

Duffy, Frank H. & Geschwind, Norman. Dyslexia: A Neuroscientific Approach. 223p. 1985. 57.00 (*0-316-19454-9*, Little Brwn Med Div) Lppncott W & W.

Duffy, Gerald G., ed. Reading in the Middle School. LC 74-23428. (Perspectives in Reading Ser.: No. 18). 220p. reprint ed. 68.20 (*0-608-15277-3*, 202959400061) Bks Demand.

Duffy, Gerald G. & Roehler, Laura R. Improving Classroom Reading Instruction: A Decision-Making Approach. 3rd ed. LC 92-26490. 512p. (C). 1993. 74.06 (*0-07-018034-2*) McGraw.

Duffy, Gillian. Hors D'oeuvres. Schwartz, Justin, ed. LC 98-5669. (Illus.). 144p. 1998. 23.00 (*0-688-14721-6*, Wm Morrow) Morrow Avon.

Duffy, Gloria, ed. see Stanford Arms Control Group Staff.

Duffy, H. Competitive Cities. (Illus.). 208p. (C). 1995. 55.00 (*0-419-19840-7*) Routledge.

Duffy, Helen, ed. see McBride, Mary & McBride, Veronica.

Duffy, Herbert S. William Howard Taft. rev. ed. (Illus.). 345p. 1998. reprint ed. pap. 14.95 (*1-888213-26-4*) Eastern National.

Duffy, J. C. Meet the Fusco Brothers! (Illus.). 128p. (Orig.). 1990. pap. 8.95 (*0-8362-1849-3*) Andrews & McMeel.

— Virtual Banality. LC 96-84114. (Fusco Brothers Collection). (Illus.). 128p. (Orig.). 1996. pap. 9.95 (*0-8362-2121-4*) Andrews & McMeel.

Duffy, J. C., ed. Health & Medical Aspects of Disaster Preparedness. (NATO - Challenges of Modern Society Ser.: Vol. 14). (Illus.). 200p. (C). 1990. text 107.00 (*0-306-43495-4*, Kluwer Plenum) Kluwer Academic.

Duffy, J. O., jt. auth. see Cowden, J. E.

Duffy, James. The Christmas Gang. 80p. (YA). 1991. pap. 2.99 (*0-380-71149-4*, Avon Bks) Morrow Avon.

— I-CAR Professional Automotive Collision Repair. LC 94-48561. (Trade, Technology & Industry Ser.). 544p. 1995. pap. 76.95 (*0-8273-6500-4*) Delmar.

— Radical Red. LC 93-12568. 144p. (J). (gr. 5-8). 1993. 15.00 (*0-684-19533-X*) Scribner.

— Uncle Shamus. LC 91-19217. 144p. (J). (gr. 4-6). 1992. lib. bdg. 13.95 (*0-684-19434-1*) Scribner.

Duffy, James, jt. ed. see Friedman, Joseph.

Duffy, James E. Auto Electricity & Electronics Technology. LC 97-35397. 1998. 42.64 (*1-56637-441-3*) Goodheart.

— Auto Engines Technology. LC 96-37209. (Illus.). 575p. 1997. text 42.64 (*1-56637-363-8*) Goodheart.

— Modern Automotive Technology. LC 99-10562. 2000. text 57.00 (*1-56637-610-6*) Goodheart.

Duffy, James E. Motor Auto Body Repair. 3rd ed. LC 96-47077. (Automotive Technology Ser.). 1997. mass mkt. 101.95 (*0-8273-6858-5*) Delmar.

Duffy, James E. Motor Autobody Repair. 3rd ed. (Automotive Repair Ser.). 1997. mass mkt., student ed. 20.50 (*0-8273-6786-4*) Delmar.

— Stay Tuned: My Life & the Business of Running the ABC Television Network. LC 97-3326. 424p. 1996. 24.95 (*0-935016-07-4*, Dunhill Pub Co) Zinn Pub Grp.

Duffy, James E. & Johanson, Chris. Auto Drive Trains Technology. LC 94-1440. (Illus.). 688p. (C). 1995. pap. text 43.96 (*1-56637-028-0*) Goodheart.

Duffy, James P. College Online: How to Take College Courses Without Leaving Home. LC 96-34881. 240p. 1997. pap. 14.95 (*0-471-12351-X*) Wiley.

— Hitler Slept Late: And Other Blunders That Cost the Nazis the War. LC 90-25350. 192p. 1991. 39.95 (*0-275-93667-8*, C3667, Praeger Pubs) Greenwood.

— How to Earn a College Degree Without Going to College. LC 81-40337. 192p. 1981. pap. 8.95 (*0-8128-6139-6*, Scrbrough Hse) Madison Bks UPA.

— How to Earn a College Degree Without Going to College. 2nd ed. 256p. 1994. pap. 15.95 (*0-471-30788-2*) Wiley.

— How to Earn an Advanced Degree Without Going to Graduate School. 2nd ed. 240p. 1994. pap. 14.95 (*0-471-30728-9*) Wiley.

— Learn While You Sleep. 224p. (Orig.). 1991. mass mkt. 4.50 (*0-380-76268-4*, Avon Bks) Morrow Avon.

— Lincoln's Admiral: The Civil War Campaigns of David Farragut. LC 96-34986. 288p. 1997. 27.95 (*0-471-04208-0*) Wiley.

Duffy, James P. & Ricci, Vincent L. Czars: Russia's Rulers for over One Thousand Years. LC 94-44654. (Illus.). 384p. (YA). 1995. 35.00 (*0-8160-2873-7*) Facts on File.

— Target Hitler: The Plots to Kill Adolf Hitler. LC 92-15695. 248p. 1992. 35.00 (*0-275-94037-3*, C4037, Praeger Pubs) Greenwood.

***Duffy, Jan.** Harvesting Experience: Reaping the Benefits of Knowledge. 296p. 1999. pap. 437.00 (*0-933887-80-9*) ARMA Intl.

Duffy, Jean. Le Ble en Herbe, Colette: Critical Monographs in English. 64p. 1993. pap. 32.00 (*0-85261-260-5*, Pub. by Univ of Glasgow) St Mut.

— Structuralism: Theory & Practice: Laclos, Critical Monographs in English. 104p. 1993. pap. 40.00 (*0-85261-319-9*, Pub. by Univ of Glasgow) St Mut.

Duffy, Jean H. Reading Between the Lines: Claude Simon & the Visual Arts. LC 98-127803. 288p. 1998. 44.95 (*0-85323-841-3*, Pub. by Liverpool Univ Pr); pap. 24.95 (*0-85323-851-0*, Pub. by Liverpool Univ Pr) Intl Spec Bk.

— Using French Vocabulary. LC 98-24723. (Illus.). 300p. (C). 1999. pap. 27.95 (*0-521-57851-5*); text 74.95 (*0-521-57040-9*) Cambridge U Pr.

Duffy, Jo & Zaffino, Jorge. Punisher: Assassin's Guild. 64p. 1988. 9.95 (*0-87135-460-8*) Marvel Entrprs.

Duffy, Jo, ed. see Miller, Frank.

Duffy, John. Economics Quick Review. (Cliffs Quick Reviews Ser.). (Illus.). 158p. (Orig.). (C). 1993. pap. text 7.95 (*0-8220-5324-1*, Cliff) IDG Bks.

— The Healers: A History of American Medicine. LC 78-27222. 385p. 1979. reprint ed. pap. 12.95 (*0-252-00743-3*) U of Ill Pr.

— A History of Public Health in New York City, 1625 - 1866,. Vol. 1. LC 68-25852. 620p. 1968. lib. bdg. 55.00 (*0-87154-212-9*) Russell Sage.

— The Sanitarians: A History of American Public Health. 344p. (C). 1992. pap. text 15.95 (*0-252-06276-0*) U of Ill Pr.

— The Sanitarians: A History of American Public Health. fac. ed. LC 89-5107. 341p. 1990. pap. 105.80 (*0-7837-7622-5*, 204737400007) Bks Demand.

— Vermont: An Illustrated History. LC 85-22621. 264p. 1985. 24.95 (*0-89781-159-3*) Am Historical Pr.

Duffy, John, ed. Alcohol & Illness: Health & Society. 224p. 1992. text 68.00 (*0-7486-0353-0*, Pub. by Edinburgh U Pr) Col U Pr.

— Coleridge's American Disciples: Selected Correspondence of James Marsh. LC 72-90497. 280p. 1973. 32.50 (*0-87023-121-9*) U of Mass Pr.

Duffy, John, ed. see Bassano, Sharron.

Duffy, John A. General Inorganic Chemistry. 2nd ed. LC 74-174665. (Illus.). 331p. reprint ed. pap. 102.70 (*0-8357-6591-1*, 203599800097) Bks Demand.

Duffy, John C. & McLaulin, J. Bryce. Psychiatry Specialty Board Review for the DSM-IV. (Continuing Education in Psychiatry & Psychology Ser.: No. 5). 128p. 1996. pap. 22.95 (*0-87630-788-8*) Brunner-Mazel.

Duffy, John-Charles. My Heart Cries Out to Thee. pap. write for info. (*0-88290-690-9*) Horizon Utah.

Duffy, John J. & Muller, H. Nicholas, III. An Anxious Democracy: Aspects of the 1830s, 58. LC 81-6387. (Contributions in American Studies: No. 58). 172p. 1982. 49.95 (*0-313-22727-6*, DUA/, Greenwood Pr) Greenwood.

Duffy, John J., ed. see Allen, Ethan.

***Duffy, John W.** Bruce Springsteen: In His Own Words. (In Their Own Words Ser.). (Illus.). 96p. 2000. pap. 15.95 (*0-7119-8039-X*) Omnibus NY.

Duffy, Joseph. Patrick: In His Own Words. 108p. 1988. reprint ed. pap. 6.95 (*0-86217-174-1*, Pub. by Veritas Pubns) St Mut.

***Duffy, Joseph.** Patrick in His Own Words. 147p. 2000. pap. 14.95 (*1-85390-525-9*, Pub. by Veritas Pubns) Irish Bks Media.

Duffy, Joseph. Statics & Kinematics with Applications to Robotics. (Illus.). 187p. (C). 1996. text 54.95 (*0-521-48213-5*) Cambridge U Pr.

Duffy, Joseph, jt. auth. see Crane, Carl D., III.

Duffy, Joseph R. Identification of Motor Speech Disorders: Reading Videofluoroscopic Studies & Planning Treatment. 1997. 110.00 incl. VHS (*1-58041-010-3*, 0112084) Am Speech Lang Hearing.

— Motor Speech Disorders: Substrates & Differential. (Illus.). 480p. (gr. 13). 1995. text 54.00 (*0-8015-6944-8*, 06944) Mosby Inc.

Duffy, Joseph T. Trading Advantage: Specific Techniques for Pinpointing High, Low, & Trend Change Points. 1992. pap. 95.00 (*0-930233-51-4*) Windsor.

Duffy, Joseph W. Power: Prime Mover of Technology. 2nd ed. (Illus.). 571p. (C). 1996. reprint ed. 108.00 (*1-878907-33-6*, RAN) TechBooks.

Duffy, Karen. Annual Editions: Personal Growth & Behavior, 97-98. 17th ed. 256p. (C). 1997. text 12.25 (*0-697-37336-3*) Brown & Benchmark.

— Annual Editions: Psychology, 97-98. 27th ed. 256p. (C). 1997. text 12.25 (*0-697-37346-0*, WCB McGr Hill) McGrw-H Hghr Educ.

***Duffy, Karen.** Model Patient: My Life as an Incurable Wise-ass. 288p. 2000. 24.00 (*0-06-019725-0*, Pub. by HarperTrade) HarpC.

Duffy, Karen. Personal Growth & Behavior, 1996-1997. annuals 16th ed. 256p. (C). 1996. text. write for info. (*0-697-31671-8*) Brown & Benchmark.

— Psychology, 1996-1997. annuals 26th ed. 288p. (C). 1995. text. write for info. (*0-697-31676-9*) Brown & Benchmark.

***Duffy, Karen.** Psychology 2000-2001. 30th ed. (Annual Editions Ser.). 240p. (J). 1999. pap. 16.56 (*0-07-236396-7*) McGrw-H Hghr Educ.

Duffy, Karen G. Personal Growth & Behavior, 98-99. 18th ed. (Annual Ser.). (Illus.). 240p. 1998. pap. text 12.25 (*0-697-39175-2*, Dshkn McG-Hill) McGrw-H Hghr Educ.

— Psychology, 98-99. 28th ed. (Annual Ser.). (Illus.). 240p. 1998. pap. text 12.25 (*0-697-39195-7*, Dshkn McG-Hill) McGrw-H Hghr Educ.

Duffy, Karen G., jt. auth. see Atwater, Eastwood.

Duffy, Karen G., ed. see Grosch, James W. & Olczak, Paul V.

***Duffy, Kate & Larsen, Bryan.** The Insiders' Guide to Salt Lake City. 2nd ed. (Insiders' Guide Travel Ser.). (Illus.). 376p. 1999. pap. 15.95 (*1-57380-121-6*, The Insiders Guide) Falcon Pub Inc.

Duffy, Katherine. The Erratic Behaviour of Tides. LC 98-131957. 54p. 1998. 19.95 (*1-901233-13-8*, Pub. by Dedalus); pap. 10.95 (*1-901233-12-X*, Pub. by Dedalus) Dufour.

Duffy, Katherine, jt. auth. see Campbell, Mike.

Duffy, Katy, jt. auth. see Wile, Darwin.

Duffy, Kevin. Children of the Forest: Africa's Mbuti Pygmies. (Illus.). 180p. (C). 1995. reprint ed. pap. text 11.50 (*0-88133-885-0*) Waveland Pr.

— Who Were Those Celts? xviii, 250p. (Orig.). 1996. pap. 24.00 (*0-7884-0505-5*, D822) Heritage Bk.

Duffy, Kevin R. Training on the Web: A Guide for Instructors & Designers. (Illus.). 256p. 1998. pap. 39.95 (*1-891832-00-X*) Lake Helen Publ.

Duffy, Kevin T. The Elsinore Appeal: People vs. Hamlet: The Funniest Court Case in 400 Years. 183p. 1998. text 20.00 (*0-7881-5742-6*) DIANE Pub.

Duffy, Larry & Tudor, Adrian. Les Lieux Interdits: Transgression & French Literature. 180p. 1998. pap. 25.00 (*0-85958-672-3*, Pub. by Univ of Hull Pr) Paul & Co Pubs.

Duffy, Laurie B. Who's Looking for Whom in Native American Ancestry. viii, 155p. 1997. pap. 16.00 (*0-7884-0751-1*, D824) Heritage Bk.

Duffy, Margaret. Brass Eagle. large type ed. 1991. 27.99 (*0-7089-2347-X*) Ulverscroft.

— Death of a Raven. large type ed. 1990. 27.99 (*0-7089-2202-3*) Ulverscroft.

— Man of Blood. large type ed. (Dales Mystery Ser.). 492p. 1994. pap. 18.99 (*1-85389-421-4*, Dales) Ulverscroft.

— Music in the Blood. large type ed. (Dales Large Print Ser.). 356p. 1998. pap. 19.99 (*1-85389-813-9*, Dales) Ulverscroft.

— Rook-Shoot. large type ed. (Dales Mystery Ser.). 392p. 1993. pap. 18.99 (*1-85389-399-4*) Ulverscroft.

Duffy, Mark, jt. auth. see Costa, Michael.

Duffy, Martin, jt. auth. see Nolan, Finbarr.

Duffy, Martin P., et al. Kentucky Estate Planning. xvii, 682p. 1996. 97.50 (*1-58757-016-5*, EH028) Univ of KY.

Duffy, Mary, jt. auth. see Arrington, Christian.

Duffy, Matt. Hothouse Transplants. LC 97-216531. 150p. (Orig.). 1997. pap. 11.95 (*0-929320-12-3*) Grove Pub.

***Duffy, Maureen.** A Fine Target. large type ed. 336p. 1999. pap. 20.99 (*1-85389-935-6*, Dales) Ulverscroft.

Duffy, Maureen. Purcell. (Illus.). 306p. 1996. pap. 15.95 (*1-85702-368-4*, Pub. by Fourth Estate) Trafalgar.

***Duffy, Maureen.** Restitution. large type unabridged ed. 315p. 1999. 26.95 (*0-7531-5956-2*, 159562, Pub. by ISIS Lrg Prnt) ISIS Pub.

Duffy, Michael. The Englishman & the Foreigner. LC 85-5943. (English Satirical Print Ser.). 368p. 1986. lib. bdg. write for info. (*0-85964-173-2*) Chadwyck-Healey.

Duffy, Michael, ed. Parameters of British Naval Power, 1650-1850. 170p. 1992. pap. text 23.95 (*0-85989-385-5*, Pub. by Univ Exeter Pr) Northwestern U Pr.

Duffy, Michael, jt. auth. see Knuttson, Anders.

Duffy, Neil, jt. auth. see Louw, Eric.

***Duffy, Page J. & Hubbell, Arlyn.** Understanding Web Development: Interactive Workbook. 273p. (C). 2000. pap. 26.67 (*0-13-025844-X*) P-H.

Duffy, Pat, et al, eds. HPER - Moving Toward the 21st Century. LC 93-39243. (Illus.). 352p. 1994. text 30.00 (*0-87322-405-1*, BDUF0405) Human Kinetics.

***Duffy, Patricia.** Index to Warrantee-Patentee Records of Westmoreland County, Pennsylvania. LC 99-72357. 53 p. 1999. per. 10.00 (*1-55856-292-3*, 253) Closson Pr.

Duffy, Patricia. Instructor's Guide: Setting Your Career & Life Direction, Landing a Job & Succeeding in Your Work. (Hire Learning, Schooling That Works Ser.). 1997. pap. text 14.95 (*1-56370-191-X*) JIST Works.

— Landing a Job. (Hire Learning, Schooling That Works Ser.). 1997. pap. text, wbk. ed. 6.95 (*1-56370-189-8*) JIST Works.

— Setting Your Career & Life Direction. (Hire Learning, Schooling That Works Ser.). 1997. pap. text, wbk. ed. 6.95 (*1-56370-188-X*) JIST Works.

— Succeeding in Your Work & Community. (Hire Learning, Schooling That Works Ser.). 1997. pap. text, wbk. ed. 6.95 (*1-56370-190-1*) JIST Works.

— Variations: Reading Skills-Oral Communication for Beginning Students of ESL. (Illus.). 224p. (C). 1986. pap. text 26.20 (*0-13-940503-8*) P-H.

Duffy, Patricia, jt. auth. see ABC Staff.

Duffy, Paul, jt. auth. see Kandalov, Andrei I.

Duffy, Paul, jt. auth. see Raymond, Boris.

Duffy, Paula B., ed. The Relevance of a Decade: Essays to Mark the First Ten Years of the Harvard Business School Press. LC 94-13037. 1994. 25.00 (*0-87584-576-2*) Harvard Busn.

— The Relevance of a Decade: Essays to Mark the First Ten Years of the Harvard Business School Press. 384p. (C). 1996. pap. 14.95 (*0-87584-687-4*) Harvard Busn.

Duffy, Philip E. Astrocytes: Normal, Reactive, & Neoplastic. LC 83-17754. 236p. 1983. reprint ed. pap. 73.20 (*0-608-00429-4*, 206114400007) Bks Demand.

***Duffy, Philip E.** The Head of the Bull: And Other Short Stories. LC 99-74619. x, 139p. 1999. pap. 12.95 (*0-9629651-3-8*) Chase Pub.

Duffy, Philip E. Moments. LC 91-71199. x, 146p. 1991. pap. 9.95 (*0-9629651-0-3*) Chase Pub.

— Undertones. LC 95-69549. xii, 148p. (Orig.). 1996. pap. 10.95 (*0-9629651-1-1*) Chase Pub.

Duffy, Philip G. B to B Marketing: Creating & Implementing a Successful Business-to-Business Marketing Program. 240p. 1992. text 29.95 (*1-55738-299-9*, Irwn Prfssnl) McGraw-Hill Prof.

Duffy, R. Quinn. The Road to Nunavut: The Progress of the Eastern Arctic Inuit since the Second World War. 368p. 1988. 27.95 (*0-7735-0619-5*, Pub. by McG-Queens Univ Pr) CUP Services.

Duffy, Ralph. Excel for Windows 95 Smartstart. LC 95-74884. 318p. 1995. 29.99 (*1-57576-032-0*) Que Educ & Trng.

Duffy, Regis & Gambatese, Angelus, eds. Made in God's Image: The Catholic Vision of Human Dignity. LC 98-40531. 192p. 1999. 14.95 (*0-8091-3850-6*) Paulist Pr.

Duffy, Regis A. An American Emmaus: Faith & Sacrament in the American Culture. 204p. 1995. pap. 15.95 (*0-8245-1540-4*) Crossroad NY.

Duffy, Regis A., ed. Alternative Futures for Worship Vol. I: General Introduction. 192p. 1987. pap. 9.95 (*0-8146-1493-0*) Liturgical Pr.

Duffy, Reid, jt. auth. see Ahern, Mike.

***Duffy, Richard.** Arlington - Twentieth-Century Reflection: Massachusetts. LC 99-69232. (Images of America Ser.). (Illus.). 128p. 2000. pap. 18.99 (*0-7385-0408-4*) Arcadia Publng.

Duffy, Richard. Brother Earth, Sister Sky. 1981. 1.50 (*0-942582-03-9*) Erie St Pr.

Duffy, Richard A. Arlington. (Images of America Ser.). 1997. pap. 16.99 (*0-7524-0851-8*) Arcadia Publng.

D

An Asterisk (*) at the beginning of an entry indicates that the title is appearing for the first time.

Duffy, Robert. The American Quiz Book. 134p. (YA). (gr. 7 up). 1992. pap. 6.95 (*1-85371-187-X*, Pub. by Poolbeg Pr) Dufour.
— The Children's Quiz Bk. 1. 2nd ed. 144p. 1992. pap. 6.95 (*1-85371-229-9*, Pub. by Poolbeg Pr) Dufour.
— Children's Quiz Book. 132p. (J). 1993. pap. 6.95 (*1-85371-020-2*, Pub. by Poolbeg Pr) Dufour.
— Poolbeg Quiz Book. 129p. 1988. pap. 6.95 (*1-85371-004-0*, Pub. by Poolbeg Pr) Dufour.
— Who Said That? A Book of Irish Lists. 104p. 1987. pap. 8.95 (*0-905169-99-9*, Pub. by Poolbeg Pr) Dufour.
Duffy, Robert J. Nuclear Politics in America: A History & Theory of Government Regulation. LC 97-19146. (Studies in Government & Public Policy). 336p. 1997. 45.00 (*0-7006-0852-4*); pap. 22.50 (*0-7006-0853-2*) U Pr of KS.
Duffy, Ron. Effective Listening Facilitator Guide. 2nd rev. ed. 116p. 1982. pap. text 15.00 (*0-943000-03-3*) Telstar Inc.
— Play Your Best. 83p. 1992. pap. write for info. (*0-9632496-0-6*) R Duffy.
Duffy, S. F., jt. ed. see Brinkman, C. R.
Duffy, Sarah Q., et al. Diagnosis & Procedure Combinations in Hospital Inpatient Data. 128p. (Orig.). (C). 1996. pap. text 35.00 (*0-7881-3716-6*) DIANE Pub.
***Duffy, Sean.** The Illustrated History of Ireland. (Illus.). 256p. 2000. 29.95 (*0-8092-2437-2*, 243720, Contemporary Bks) NTC Contemp Pub Co.
Duffy, Sean. Ireland in the Middle Ages. LC 96-25753. 232p. 1997. pap. 19.95 (*0-312-16390-8*) St Martin.
***Duffy, Sean, ed.** Medieval Dublin Vol. I: Proceedings of the Friends of Medieval Dublin Symposium 1999. 224p. 2000. 55.00 (*1-85182-537-1*, Pub. by Four Cts Pr); pap. 19.95 (*1-85182-580-0*, Pub. by Four Cts Pr) Intl Spec Bk.
Duffy, Sharon L., jt. auth. see Willoughby, Doris M.
***Duffy, Stella.** Beneath the Blonde. 256p. 2000. pap. 12.00 (*1-85242-711-6*) Serpents Tail.
Duffy, Stella. Beneath the Blonde: A Saz Martin Mystery. (Mask Noir Title Ser.). 240p. 1997. pap. text 13.99 (*1-85242-542-3*) Serpents Tail.
***Duffy, Stella.** Calendar Girl. 2000. pap. 12.00 (*1-85242-712-4*) Serpents Tail.
— Fresh, Flesh. 2000. 15.00 (*1-85242-616-0*) Serpents Tail.
Duffy, Stella. Wavewalker. (Mask Noir Ser.). 272p. (Orig.). 1996. pap. 13.99 (*1-85242-508-3*) Serpents Tail.
Duffy, Stephen. Paul Delaroche, 1797-1856. 1997. pap. text 40.00 (*0-900785-62-4*) Wallace Collect.
Duffy, Stephen, jt. auth. see Hedley, Joanne.
Duffy, Stephen J. The Dynamics of Grace: Perspectives in Theological Anthropology. (New Theology Studies). 400p. (Orig.). 1994. pap. 24.95 (*0-8146-5790-7*, M Glazier) Liturgical Pr.
— The Graced Horizon: Nature & Grace in Modern Catholic Thought. (Theology & Life Ser.: No. 37). 248p. (Orig.). 1992. pap. text 16.95 (*0-8146-5705-2*, M Glazier) Liturgical Pr.
Duffy, Stephen J., jt. auth. see Van Loon, Gary W.
***Duffy, Stephen W H.** Captain Blakeley & the Wasp: The Cruise of 1814. LC 99-26571. 1999. 34.95 (*1-55750-176-9*) Naval Inst Pr.
***Duffy, Steve.** The Night Comes On. xvi, 284p. 1998. 40.00 (*1-899562-44-3*) Ash-Tree.
Duffy, Susan. American Labor on Stage: Dramatic Interpretations of the Steel & Textile Industries in the 1930's, 72. LC 95-46420. (Contributions in Drama & Theatre Studies: Vol. 72). 176p. 1996. 55.00 (*0-313-29861-0*, Greenwood Pr) Greenwood.
Duffy, Susan, compiled by. The Political Left in the American Theatre of the 1930's: A Bibliographic Sourcebook. LC 92-10822. 218p. 1992. 32.00 (*0-8108-2577-5*) Scarecrow.
— Shirley Chisholm: A Bibliography of Writings by & about Her. LC 88-2073. 143p. 1988. 24.00 (*0-8108-2105-2*) Scarecrow.
***Duffy, Susan & Adalian, Paul T.** A Comprehensive Index to Artist & Influence: The Journal of Black American Cultural History, 1981-1999. LC 99-48166. (Black Studies: Vol. 8). 302p. 1999. 99.95 (*0-7734-7903-1*) E Mellen.
Duffy, Susan, ed. see Hughes, Langston.
Duffy, Thomas J. & Vergeer, Paul P. California Toxic Fungi. LC 77-76180. (Toxicology Monograph: No. 1). (Illus.). 1977. 2.00 (*0-918942-00-4*) Mycological.
Duffy, Thomas M., et al, eds. Designing Environments for Constructive Learning. LC 93-22188. (NATO ASI Series F: Computer & Systems Sciences, Special Programme AET: Vol. 105). 1993. 100.95 (*0-387-56452-7*) Spr-Verlag.
Duffy, Thomas M. & Jonassen, David, eds. Constructivism & the Technology of Instruction: A Conversation. 232p. 1992. pap. 29.95 (*0-8058-1272-5*) L Erlbaum Assocs.
Duffy, Thomas M., et al. Communication Pedagogy: Approaches to Teaching Undergraduate Courses in Communication. Shneiderman, Ben, ed. LC 92-15790. (Human-Computer Interaction Ser.). 272p. (C). 1992. pap. 39.50 (*0-89391-911-X*) Ablx Pub.
Duffy, Thomas P. The Best System: Basic Recordkeeping for a Small Business. LC 84-70087. 116p. 1984. 35.00 (*0-916115-00-3*) Challenge Pub Co.
Duffy, Thomas P., jt. auth. see Burrow, Gerard N.
Duffy, Tim. Access 97. 224p. (C). 1997. pap. text 25.00 (*0-201-31511-4*) Addison-Wesley.
— Basics of Microsoft Internet Explorer 5, Outlook 2000 & FrontPage 2000. (Illus.). 154p. 1999. pap. text 19.00 (*0-201-45920-5*) Addison-Wesley.
— Four Software Tools- Spanish. 1990. pap. write for info. (*968-7270-57-8*) Thomson Learn.
— Microsoft Access 2000. 230p. (C). 1999. pap. text 25.00 (*0-201-45916-7*, Prentice Hall) P-H.
— Microsoft Excel 2000. 238p. (C). 1999. pap. text 25.00 (*0-201-45914-0*, Prentice Hall) P-H.
Duffy, Tim. Microsoft Internet Explorer 4.0. 2nd ed. 80p. (C). 1998. pap. text 19.00 (*0-201-43868-2*, Prentice Hall) P-H.
— Microsoft Office 97: Professional, Blue Ribbon Edition. 2nd ed. 992p. (C). 1998. pap. text 62.67 (*0-201-43859-3*, Prentice Hall) P-H.
***Duffy, Tim.** Microsoft Office 2000 Certified Edition. 1000p. (C). 1999. spiral bd. 62.67 (*0-201-61188-0*, Prentice Hall) P-H.
— Microsoft PowerPoint 2000. 124p. (C). 1999. pap. text 25.00 (*0-201-45918-3*, Prentice Hall) P-H.
Duffy, Tim. Microsoft Windows 98. 104p. (C). 1999. pap. text 25.00 (*0-201-45910-8*, Prentice Hall) P-H.
***Duffy, Tim.** Microsoft Word 2000. 272p. (C). 1999. pap. text 25.00 (*0-201-45912-4*, Prentice Hall) P-H.
— Office 2000 Professional. 448p. (C). 1999. pap. text, teacher ed. write for info. (*0-201-45907-8*) Addison-Wesley.
Duffy, Tim. Plutarch's Lives: Exploring Virtue & Vice. LC 98-40794. 448p. 2000. text 95.00 (*0-19-815058-X*) OUP.
— Projects for Microsoft Office 2000: Professional Brief Edition. (Duffy Lab Series). 542p. (C). 1999. spiral bd. 49.00 (*0-201-61202-X*) Addison-Wesley.
— Tool Kit: Quattro Pro 4.0. 338p. (C). 1993. pap. 17.95 (*0-534-30252-1*) Course Tech.
Duffy, Tim. Windows 95. 112p. (C). 1997. pap. text 19.00 (*0-201-31517-3*) Addison-Wesley.
Duffy, Tim. Microsoft Word 97: Blue Ribbon Edition. 2nd ed. 272p. (C). 1998. pap. text 25.00 (*0-201-44849-1*, Prentice Hall) P-H.
Duffy, Timothy. Jesus Christ Is Lord: Poetic Praise. 1996. pap. 8.95 (*1-880451-21-2*) Rainbows End.
***Duffy, Trent & Welles, Toby.** Turning Point Inventions: The Clock. 80p. (J). (gr. 4). 2000. 17.95 (*0-689-82814-4*) Atheneum Yung Read.
Duffy, William, jt. ed. see Bly, Robert.
Duffy, Yvonne. All Things Are Possible. LC 81-83657. (Illus.). 1981. pap. 8.95 (*0-9607252-0-2*) A J Garvin.
Duflo, M. Random Iteractive Models. Wilson, Stephen S., tr. from FRE. LC 96-45470. (Applications of Mathematics Ser.: Vol. 34). (Illus.). 386p. 1997. 89.00 (*3-540-57100-0*) Spr-Verlag.
Duflo, M., et al, eds. The Orbit Method in Representation Theory. (Progress in Mathematics Ser.: No. 82). 225p. 1990. 60.50 (*0-8176-3474-6*) Birkhauser.
Duflo, M., jt. auth. see Dacunha-Castelle, D.
Dufner, Max, tr. & anno. see Wieland, Christoph M.
Dufner, Meinrad, jt. auth. see Gruen, Anselm.
Dufour. Colonial America: Testbank. Date not set. pap. text, teacher ed., suppl. ed. write for info. (*0-314-03270-3*) West Pub.
Dufour, Arnaud, jt. auth. see Ghernaouti-Helie, Solange.
Dufour, Carlos A. Lehre der "Proprietates Terminorum" Sinn & Referenz in Mittelalterlicher Logik. (Analytica Ser.). (GER.). 320p. (C). 1989. 99.00 (*3-88405-063-X*) Philosophia Pr.
Dufour, Charles L. Gentle Tiger: The Gallant Life of Roberdeau Wheat. LC 99-210677. (Illus.). 256p. 1999. pap. 14.95 (*0-8071-2391-9*) La State U Pr.
— The Night the War Was Lost. LC 93-47281. (Illus.). iv, 443p. (C). 1994. pap. 14.95 (*0-8032-6599-9*, Bison Books) U of Nebr Pr.
— Nine Men in Gray. LC 93-9529. (Illus.). xix, 372p. (C). 1993. reprint ed. pap. 16.00 (*0-8032-6596-4*, Bison Books) U of Nebr Pr.
DuFour, Christian. A Canadian Challenge. 1990. 17.94 (*0-88645-113-2*, Pub. by Inst Res Pub) Ashgate Pub Co.
Dufour, Christian. A Canadian Challenge: Le Defi Quebecois. 192p. 1995. per. 12.95 (*0-88982-105-4*, Pub. by Oolichan Bks) Genl Dist Srvs.
Dufour, D. Robert. Clinical Use of Laboratory Data: A Practical Guide. LC 97-12909. 656p. 1997. pap. 49.00 (*0-683-18017-7*) Lppncott W & W.
Dufour, E., jt. ed. see Najim, K.
Dufour, Francine, tr. see Ellison, George Vernon & Young, Loy.
Dufour, Francine, tr. & photos by see Ellison, George Vernon & Young, Loy.
Dufour-Gompers, Roger. Dictionnaire de la Violence et du Crime. (FRE.). 458p. 1992. pap. 115.00 (*0-7859-8148-9*, 2865862178) Fr & Eur.
Dufour, J., ed. see Bautier, Robert-Henri.
Dufour, J. M. & Raj, Baldev. New Developments in Time Series Econometrics. (Studies in Empirical Economics). (Illus.). vi, 250p. 1994. 107.95 (*0-387-91482-X*) Spr-Verlag.
Dufour, James T. California Environmental Compliance Handbook. 410p. (Orig.). (C). 1995. pap. text 99.00 (*1-57997-017-6*) CA Chamber Commerce.
— Cal/OSHA Compliance in 10 Practical Steps. 210p. (C). 1997. pap. 49.00 (*1-878630-87-3*) CA Chamber Commerce.
— Hazard Communication Handbook. 180p. (Orig.). (C). 1997. pap. text 35.00 (*1-878630-86-5*) CA Chamber Commerce.
— Hazardous Waste Management Supplement. 105p. (C). 1994. pap. text 49.00 (*1-57997-019-2*) CA Chamber Commerce.
Dufour, James T., ed. Cal-OSHA Organizer. (Orig.). (C). 1997. pap. text 25.00 (*1-57997-005-2*) CA Chamber Commerce.
Dufour, Jean. Felix Leclerc: D'une Etoile a L'Autre. (FRE., Illus.). 200p. 1998. pap. 59.95 (*2-86808-122-3*) Intl Scholars.
Dufour, Leon. Vocabulario de Teologia Biblica. 9th ed. (SPA.). 976p. 1977. 49.95 (*0-8288-5536-6*, S50205); pap. 49.95 (*0-8288-5539-0*, S50204) Fr & Eur.
***Dufour, Leon X.** Vocabulario de Teologia Biblica. (SPA.). 1998. pap. 24.95 (*0-8245-2153-6*) Crossroad NY.
Dufour, Liz, ed. see Radel, Cliff.
Dufour, Louis C., et al, eds. Surfaces & Interfaces of Ceramic Materials. (C). 1989. text 420.50 (*0-7923-0447-0*) Kluwer Academic.
Dufour, M. Dictionary Pali (Original Buddhist Terms) to French. (FRE & PLI.). 1998. 95.00 (*0-320-00302-7*) Fr & Eur.
Dufour, R., ed. see Colloque du Club Jules Gonin Staff & Assemblee de la Societe Suisse d'Ophthalmologie St.
DuFour, Richard. The Principal as Staff Developer. Sparks, Dennis, ed. 105p. (Orig.). 1991. pap. 21.95 (*1-879639-01-7*) Natl Educ Serv.
Dufour, Richard & Eaker, Robert. Fulfilling the Promise of Excellence: A Practitioners Guide to School Improvement. LC 86-40358. 270p. 1987. 24.95 (*0-915253-06-2*) Wilkerson Pub Co.
— Professional Learning Communities at Work: Best Practices for Enhancing Student Achievement. LC 98-160769. xx, 338p. 1998. pap. text 24.95 (*1-879639-60-2*) Natl Educ Serv.
DuFour, Richard, jt. auth. see Eaker, Robert.
Dufour, S. M. Over the Dead Line: Or Tracked by Bloodhounds, Giving the Author's Personal Experience During Eleven Months that He was Confined...As a (Confederate) Prisoner of War...; with Numerous & Varied Incidents & Anecdotes of His Prison Life. (Illus.). 283p. 1997. reprint ed. lib. bdg. 39.00 (*0-8328-6495-1*) Higginson Bk Co.
Dufourcq. Le Livre de l'Orgue Francais (1589-1789), 2 tomes, Set. 218.75 (*0-685-35984-0*) Fr & Eur.
Dufourcq, C. E. L' Iberie Chretienne et le Maghreb (XIIe-XVe Siecles) (Collected Studies: No. CS328). 376p. 1990. text 124.95 (*0-86078-275-1*, Pub. by Variorum) Ashgate Pub Co.
Dufoure, J., jt. ed. see Bothorel, J.
Dufournet, Jean, ed. Anthologie de la Poesie Lyrique Francaise des XIIe et XIIIe Siecles. (Poesie Ser.). (FRE.). 1987. pap. 16.95 (*2-07-032462-1*) Schoenhof.
Dufournet, Roger. Une Heure Avec Peguy. pap. 3.40 (*0-685-37048-8*) Fr & Eur.
Dufournet, Roger, ed. see Villon, Francois.
Dufraisse, Roger. Napoleon. 180p. (C). 1991. pap. 16.88 (*0-07-018045-8*) McGraw.
Dufrechou, L. F. Queenie's Diary. (Illus.). 206p. 1995. pap. 9.95 (*0-9644776-0-2*) L F Dufrechou.
Dufrene, Maurice. Three Hundred Five Authentic Art Nouveau Jewelry Designs. 48p. 1985. reprint ed. pap. 6.95 (*0-486-24904-2*) Dover.
Dufrene, Maurice & Duncan, Alastair, eds. Authentic Art Deco Interiors. (Illus.). 212p. 1990. 89.50 (*1-85149-119-8*) Antique Collect.
***Dufrene, Rebecca S.** His Gift to Me. 104p. 1999. pap. 12.95 (*1-58244-029-8*) Rutledge Bks.
Dufrenne, M. Jalons. (Phaenomenologica Ser.: No. 20). 230p. 1965. lib. bdg. 81.00 (*90-247-0252-6*, Pub. by M Nijhoff) Kluwer Academic.
Dufrenne, Mikel. Language & Philosophy. Veatch, Henry B., tr. LC 68-55630. (Illus.). 106p. 1968. reprint ed. lib. bdg. 49.50 (*0-8371-0396-7*, DULP, Greenwood Pr) Greenwood.
— The Phenomenology of Aesthetic Experience. Casey, Edward S. et al, trs. from FRE. LC 73-76806. (Studies in Phenomenology & Existential Philosophy).Tr. of Phenomenologie De L'experience Esthetique. 578p. (C). 1973. pap. 19.95 (*0-8101-0591-8*) Northwestern U Pr.
Dufrenne, Mikel, ed. Main Trends in Aesthetics & the Sciences of Art. LC 79-12758. (Main Trends in the Social & Human Sciences Ser.). 418p. (C). 1979. pap. 26.50 (*0-8419-0507-X*) Holmes & Meier.
Dufresne, Charles. Dictionnaire de l'Amerique Francaise. (ENG & FRE.). 396p. 1988. pap. 49.95 (*0-7859-8021-0*, 2760302164); lib. bdg. 69.95 (*0-8288-2594-7*) Fr & Eur.
***Dufresne, Chris.** My Life with Sylvia Browne: A Son Reflects on Life with His Psychic Mother. LC 99-44831. (Illus.). 176p. 2000. pap. 12.95 (*1-56170-667-1*, 5014) Hay House.
— The Reading Room: Memorable Experiences from the Psychic Work of Sylvia Browne. 240p. 2001. pap. 13.95 (*1-56170-760-0*, 5033) Hay House.
Dufresne, Craig R., et al, eds. Complex Craniofacial Problems. (Illus.). 556p. 1992. text 210.00 (*0-443-08624-9*) Church.
Dufresne, E. Faith That Makes Demand on Anointing. 1995. mass mkt. 6.00 (*0-940763-10-9*) E Dufresne Minist.
— Faithfulness: Road to Divine Promise. mass mkt. 5.99 (*0-940763-08-7*) E Dufresne Minist.
Dufresne, Ed. Devil, Don't Touch My Stuff. 90p. (Orig.). 1992. pap. 6.00 (*0-940763-04-4*) E Dufresne Minist.
— Fresh Oil from Heaven. rev. ed. 102p. 1992. pap. 6.00 (*0-940763-06-0*) E Dufresne Minist.
— Praying God's Word. 96p. 1992. mass mkt. 5.99 (*0-88368-240-0*) Whitaker Hse.
— The Prophet: Friend of God. rev. ed. 86p. 1993. pap. 6.00 (*0-940763-05-2*) E Dufresne Minist.
— There's a Healer in the House. (Orig.). 1993. pap. 6.00 (*0-940763-07-9*) E Dufresne Minist.
Dufresne, Isabelle & Block, Jean L. Famous for Fifteen Minutes: My Years with Andy Warhol. 304p. 1988. 18.95 (*0-15-130201-4*) Harcourt.
***DuFresne, Jim.** Alaska: Lonely Planet. 6th ed. (Travel Guides Ser.). (Illus.). 456p. 2000. pap. 18.95 (*0-86442-754-9*) Lonely Planet.
DuFresne, Jim. 50 Hikes in Michigan: The Best Walks, Hikes, & Backpacks in the Lower Peninsula. 2nd rev. ed. LC 98-54183. (Fifty Hikes Ser.). (Illus.). 300p. 1999. pap. 16.95 (*0-88150-455-6*, Pub. by Countryman) Norton.
— Glacier Bay National Park: A Backcountry Guide to the Glaciers & Beyond. LC 87-14294. (Illus.). 160p. (Orig.). 1987. pap. 10.95 (*0-89886-132-2*) Mountaineers.
— Isle Royale National Park: Foot Trails & Water Routes. 2nd ed. LC 83-24938. (Illus.). 136p. (Orig.). 1991. pap. 12.95 (*0-89886-283-3*) Mountaineers.
— Lonely Planet Alaska. 5th ed. (Illus.). 450p. 1997. pap. 16.95 (*0-86442-414-0*) Lonely Planet.
— Lonely Planet Backpacking in Alaska: A Walking Guide. (Illus.). 256p. 1995. pap. 13.95 (*0-86442-266-0*) Lonely Planet.
***Dufresne, Jim.** Michigan: Off the Beaten Path: A Guide to Unique Places. 5th ed. LC 99-21342. (Illus.). 225p. 1999. pap. 12.95 (*0-7627-0269-9*) Globe Pequot.
DuFresne, Jim. Michigan State Parks: A Complete Recreation Guide. LC 97-43534. (State Parks Ser.). (Illus.). 250p. 1998. pap. 16.95 (*0-89886-544-1*) Mountaineers.
***DuFresne, Jim.** Michigan's Best Campgrounds. 3rd rev. ed. Orig. Title: Camping Michigan: Lower Michigan's 75 Best Campgrounds. (Illus.). 2000. pap. 15.95 (*1-882376-73-0*, Pub. by Thunder Bay Pr) Partners Pubs Grp.
Dufresne, Jim. Michigan's Best Outdoor Adventures with Children. LC 90-37450. 240p. 1990. pap. 12.95 (*0-89886-249-3*) Mountaineers.
DuFresne, Jim. Porcupine Mountains Wilderness State Park: A Backcountry Guide for Hikers, Backpackers, & Winter Visitors. 2nd rev. ed. Orig. Title: Michigan's Porcupine Mountains Wilderness State Park. (Illus.). 160p. 1999. pap. 11.95 (*1-882376-64-1*) Thunder Bay Pr.
Dufresne, John. Louisiana Power & Light. LC 95-31672. 320p. 1995. pap. 12.95 (*0-452-27502-4*, Plume) Dutton Plume.
— Love Warps the Mind a Little. LC 97-39784. 336p. 1998. pap. 13.95 (*0-452-27898-8*) NAL.
— Love Warps the Mind a Little. LC 96-3112. 352p. 1997. 23.00 (*0-393-04013-5*) Norton.
— Love Warps the Mind a Little. 1998. pap. text. write for info. (*0-393-10166-5*) Norton.
— Love Warps the Mind a Little. large type ed. LC 97-9217. (Core Ser.). 553p. 1997. 26.95 (*0-7838-8127-4*, G K Hall Lrg Type) Mac Lib Ref.
— The Way That Water Enters Stone: Stories. 1997. pap. 10.95 (*0-452-27731-0*, Truman Talley) St Martin.
Dufresne, Marcel P., jt. auth. see Schulte, Henry.
Dufresne, Marie R. Evaluating Managed Care Networks: An Approach to Providing Cost-Effective Health Care to Employees. (Building Blocks Ser.: Vol. 20). (Illus.). 20p. (Orig.). 1995. pap. 24.95 (*1-57963-023-5*, A0040) Am Compensation.
Dufresne, Michel. Dictionnaire Nostradamus. (FRE.). 1989. 89.95 (*0-7859-8254-X*, 2-920176-54-4) Fr & Eur.
***Dufresne, Michele.** Cooking Thanksgiving Dinner. (Illus.). 1999. pap. 3.75 (*1-58453-034-0*) Pioneer MA.
— Early Emergent Set 2: Teacher Notes. 1999. pap. write for info. (*1-58453-042-1*) Pioneer MA.
— Emergent Set 2: Teacher Notes. Date not set. pap. 7.00 (*1-58453-073-1*) Pioneer MA.
— Emily Can't Sleep. (Illus.). 1999. pap. 3.75 (*1-58453-035-9*) Pioneer MA.
— Fruit Salad. (Illus.). 1999. pap. 3.75 (*1-58453-027-8*) Pioneer MA.
— Gabby Runs Away. (Illus.). Date not set. pap. 3.75 (*1-58453-072-3*) Pioneer MA.
— George's Show & Tell. (Illus.). 1999. pap. 3.75 (*1-58453-023-5*) Pioneer MA.
— A Snack for Roberto. (Illus.). 1999. pap. 3.75 (*1-58453-024-3*) Pioneer MA.
— Teachers Notes: Emergent 1. 1998. pap. 7.00 (*1-58453-022-7*) Pioneer MA.
Dufresne, Michele. Teachers Notes Set 1: Early Emergent. 1998. pap. 7.00 (*1-58453-020-0*) Pioneer MA.
Dufresne, Michele & Dickey, Laurel. Developing Books, Set 1. (Illus.). Date not set. pap. 16.50 (*1-58453-037-5*) Pioneer MA.
— Early Emergent Set 1: Classroom Collection. (Illus.). 1998. pap. 135.00 (*1-58453-049-9*) Pioneer MA.
— Emergent Books, Set 1. (Illus.). 1998. pap. write for info. (*1-58453-043-X*) Pioneer MA.
Dufresne, Michele, jt. auth. see Dickey, Laurel.
Dufresne, N. Daily Healing Bread from Gods Table. 1997. pap. 7.00 (*0-940763-11-7*) E Dufresne Minist.
***Dufresne, Nancy.** There Came a Sound from Heaven. (Illus.). 304p. 2000. 17.99 (*1-58568-205-5*) Sumrall Pubng.
***Dufresne, Todd.** Tales from the Freudian Crypt: The Death Drive in Text & Context. LC 99-39776. 1999. pap. text 19.95 (*0-8047-3885-8*) Stanford U Pr.
Dufresne, Todd, ed. Return of the French Freud. 252p. (C). 1997. pap. 19.99 (*0-415-91526-0*) Routledge.
— Return of the French Freud. 252p. (C). 1997. 65.00 (*0-415-91525-2*) Routledge.
Dufresne, Todd & Roazen, Paul. Freud under Analysis: History, Theory, Practice--Essays in Honor of Paul Roazeu. LC 96-49860. 344p. 1997. 60.00 (*0-7657-0057-3*) Aronson.
DuFresne, Tom. Loves Me . . . Loves Me Not: The Art of Choosing Who's Right for You (Includes Interactive Cards), Incl. cards. 90p. 1997. 24.95 (*0-9641461-3-4*) AP Pr.
Dufton, Jo S., jt. auth. see Johnson, Liliane.
Dufton, Jo S., jt. ed. see Everett, Joann M.
Dufty. Sugar Blues. 1993. 5.99 (*0-446-77701-3*) Warner Bks.
Dufty, William. Sugar Blues. 255p. 1986. reprint ed. mass mkt. 6.99 (*0-446-34312-9*, Pub. by Warner Bks) Little.
Dufty, William, jt. auth. see Holiday, Billie.
Dufur, Brett. Best of Missouri Hands: Profiles of the State's Fine Artists & Craftsmen. (Show Me Missouri Ser.). (Illus.). 136p. (Orig.). 1996. pap. 14.95 (*0-9646625-5-8*, MG3380) Pebble Pub.
— The Complete Katy Trail Guidebook: America's Longest

An Asterisk (*) at the beginning of an entry indicates that the title is appearing for the first time.

Rails-to-Trails Project. 4th rev. ed. (Show Me Missouri Ser.). (Illus.). 184p. (Orig.). 1998. pap. 14.95 (*0-9646625-0-7*, MG3390) Pebble Pub.

— Daytrip St. Louis. (Show Me Missouri Ser.). (Illus.). 224p. 1998. pap. 14.95 (*1-891708-00-7*) Pebble Pub.

— Exploring Missouri Wine Country. 2nd rev. ed. (Show Me Missouri Ser.). (Illus.). 208p. (Orig.). 1997. pap. 14.95 (*0-9646625-6-6*, MG3420) Pebble Pub.

Dufwa, Thamar E. Transcontinental Railroad Legislation, 1835-1862. Bruchey, Stuart, ed. LC 80-1279. (Railroads Ser.). 1981. lib. bdg. 20.95 (*0-405-13754-0*) Ayer.

Dugall, Berndt, ed. Handbuch der Historischen Buchbestande in Deutschland: Hessen M-Z & Rheinland-Pfalz A-Z, Bd. 6. (GER.). 368p. 1993. write for info. (*3-487-09580-7*) G Olms Pubs.

— Handbuch der Historischen Buchbestande in Deutschland, Vol. 5: Hessen A-L. 363p. 1992. 2535.00 (*3-487-09579-3*) G Olms Pubs.

Dugan. Bible Stories from the Book of Acts. 1994. pap. 7.95 (*1-55674-136-7*) Dugan Pubs Inc.

— Dugan Bible Dictionary. 1994. pap. text 7.95 (*1-55674-126-X*) Dugan Pubs Inc.

Dugan, Alan. Collected Poems. LC 76-89903. 212p. reprint ed. pap. 65.80 (*0-8357-8694-3*, 203371200087) Bks Demand.

— Poems of Alan Dugan. LC 79-144761. (Yale Series of Younger Poets: No. 57). reprint ed. 18.00 (*0-404-53857-6*) AMS Pr.

— Poems 6. 1989. 17.95 (*0-88001-199-8*) HarpC.

Dugan, Ann. Flatten Your Stomach for Men Over Forty. (Illus.). 1985. pap. 3.99 (*0-88176-249-0*) Pubns Intl Ltd.

Dugan, Ann, jt. auth. see Consumer Guide Editors.

Dugan, Ann, ed. see Association of Small Business Staff.

Dugan, Barbara. Good-Bye, Hello. LC 93-10989. 160p. (J). (gr. 5 up). 1994. 13.00 (*0-688-12447-X*, Grenwillow Bks) HarpC Child Bks.

— Loop the Loop. LC 90-21727. (Illus.). 32p. (J). (gr. k up). 1992. lib. bdg. 15.93 (*0-688-09648-4*, Grenwillow Bks) HarpC Child Bks.

— Loop the Loop. LC 90-21727. (Illus.). 32p. (J). (ps-3). 1992. 16.00 (*0-688-09647-6*, Grenwillow Bks) HarpC Child Bks.

— Loop the Loop. LC 92-40168. (Picture Puffin Ser.). (Illus.). (J). 1993. 10.19 (*0-606-05444-8*, Pub. by Turtleback) Demco.

Dugan, Barbara, jt. auth. see Swank, Roy L.

Dugan, Bill. Chief Joseph: War Chiefs. (War Chiefs Ser.: No. 2). 320p. (Orig.). 2000. mass mkt. 5.50 (*0-06-100388-3*, Harp PBks) HarpC.

— Crazy Horse. (War Chiefs Ser.: No. 3). 320p. 1999. mass mkt. 5.50 (*0-06-100448-0*, Harp PBks) HarpC.

— Geronimo. 320p. 1999. mass mkt. 5.50 (*0-06-100298-4*, Harp PBks) HarpC.

— Quanah Parker. (War Chiefs Ser.: No. 4). 320p. 2000. mass mkt. 5.50 (*0-06-100449-9*, Harp PBks) HarpC.

— Sitting Bull: An Epic Historical novel- the Glory & Tragedy of a Proud People & their Legendary Leader. (War Chiefs Ser.). 320p. 2000. mass mkt. 5.50 (*0-06-100660-2*, Harp PBks) HarpC.

Dugan, David, III, et al. Professional Responsibility in New Jersey (1992) 900p. ring bd. 85.00 (*0-685-65974-7*) NJ Inst CLE.

Dugan, Devin A. Expressions from the Heart. 1998. pap. write for info. (*1-57553-963-2*) Watermrk Pr.

Dugan, Eleanor. Sales Letters Ready to Go. Bethel, William, ed. (. . . Ready to Go! Ser.). (Illus.). 160p. 1995. pap. 14.95 (*0-8442-3566-0*, NTC Business Bks) NTC Contemp Pub Co.

Dugan, Eleanor, jt. auth. see Minninger, Joan.

Dugan, Eleanor, ed. see Minninger, Joan.

Dugan, Ellen. Picturing the South: 1860 to the Present; Photographers & Writers. 216p. 1996. 55.00 (*0-8118-1323-1*); pap. 29.95 (*0-8118-1343-6*) Chronicle Bks.

Dugan, Jack. Finally Something to Cheer About: A Fan's View of the 1991 Braves' Season. 181p. 1992. 10.95 (*0-942407-24-5*) Father & Son.

Dugan, Joanna, photos by. Taxi Driver Wisdom. LC 95-22085. (Illus.). 176p. 1996. 14.95 (*0-8118-1165-4*) Chronicle Bks.

Dugan, John R. Illusion & Reality: A Study of Descriptive Techniques in the Works of Guy de Maupassant. (De Proprietatibus Litterarum, Ser. Practica: No. 59). 1973. pap. text 36.95 (*90-279-2445-7*) Mouton.

Dugan, Karen, jt. auth. see Hurwitz, Johanna.

Dugan, Karen M. Yunmi & Halmoni's Trip. LC 96-22013. 32p. (J). (ps-3). 1997. 15.00 (*0-395-81180-5*) HM.

Dugan, Kathleen M. The Vision Quest of the Plains Indians: Its Spiritual Significance. LC 85-18768. (Studies in American Religion: Vol. 13). 272p. 1985. lib. bdg. 89.95 (*0-88946-659-9*) E Mellen.

Dugan, Kathleen M., jt. ed. see Sharma, Arvind.

Dugan, Lisa Scherver, jt. auth. see Bixler, Susan.

Dugan, Marcia P. Keys to Living with Hearing Loss. LC 96-54037. (Retirement Keys Ser.). 160p. (Orig.). 1997. pap. text 6.95 (*0-7641-0017-3*) Barron.

Dugan, Mark. Bandit Years: A Gathering of Wolves. LC 86-30045. (Western Legacy Ser.). (Illus.). 128p. (Orig.). 1987. pap. 10.95 (*0-86534-101-X*) Sunstone Pr.

— Knight of the Road: The Life of Highwayman Ham White. LC 90-39441. (Illus.). 197p. 1990. pap. 13.95 (*0-8040-0940-6*) Swallow.

— The Making of Legends: More True Stories of Frontier America. LC 97-4096. (Illus.). 300p. 1997. pap. 19.95 (*0-8040-0996-1*); text 36.95 (*0-8040-0995-3*) Swallow.

— Tales Never Told Around the Campfire: True Stories of Frontier America. LC 91-26183. 275p. 1992. pap. 17.95 (*0-8040-0955-4*) Swallow.

Dugan, Mark & Boessenecker, John. The Grey Fox: The True Story of Bill Miner - Last of the Old-Time Bandits. LC 91-50860. (Illus.). 284p. 1992. 24.95 (*0-8061-2435-0*) U of Okla Pr.

***Dugan, Meg Kennedy & Hock, Roger R.** It's My Life Now: Starting over after an Abusive Relationship or Domestic Violence. LC 99-44898. 208p. 2000. pap. 15.00 (*0-415-92358-1*) Routledge.

Dugan, Michael. The Emu Who Wanted to Be a Horse. LC 93-11736. (Voyages Ser.). (Illus.). (J). 1994. 4.25 (*0-383-03743-3*) SRA McGraw.

Dugan, Michael C., jt. ed. see Sarkar, Fazlul H.

Dugan, Michael E. Investment Return Handbook. 1993. pap. 7.95 (*1-882912-02-0*) Sunrise TN.

— Mortgage & Loan Payment Guide: A Valuable Reference Book for Anyone Who Borrows Money. (Illus.). 250p. 1998. 17.00 (*0-7881-5389-7*) DIANE Pub.

— Payment Tables Handbook. 1993. pap. 7.95 (*1-882912-03-9*) Sunrise TN.

Dugan, Patrick, ed. Wetland Conservation: A Review of Current Issues & Required Action. 96p. (C). 1990. pap. 15.00 (*2-8317-0015-9*, Pub. by IUCN) Island Pr.

— Wetlands In Danger: A World Conservation Atlas. LC 93-21729. (Illus.). 192p. (C). 1993. 45.00 (*0-19-520942-7*) OUP.

***Dugan, Peter V.** Medusa's Overbite. 95p. 1999. pap. 9.95 (*0-9651162-4-7*) Wysteria Ltd.

Dugan, R. E., jt. auth. see Jones, J. B.

Dugan, Robert, ed. see Highlights Editors.

Dugan, Robert E., jt. auth. see Coleman, James R.

Dugan, Roger C. Electrical Power Systems Quality. 448p. 1995. 59.95 (*0-07-018031-8*) McGraw.

Dugan, Roger C., et al. Electrical Power Systems Quality. 265p. 1997. 55.00 (*0-7803-3464-7*, PC5717-QOE) Inst Electrical.

Dugan, Sally. Measure for Measure: Fascinating Facts about Length, Weight, Time & Temperature. (Illus.). 128p. 1995. pap. 14.95 (*0-563-36900-0*, Pub. by BBC) Parkwest Pubns.

Dugan, Stewart, et al. Ploesti: The Great Ground-Air Battle of 1 August 1943. LC 97-31258. (Illus.). 318p. 1998. pap. 19.95 (*1-57488-144-2*) Brasseys.

Dugan, Thomas. A Modern Bestiary. LC 82-14515. (Illus.). 58p. (Orig.). 1982. pap. 9.95 (*0-940170-06-X*) Station Hill Pr.

— Photography Between Covers. 1979. 15.00 (*0-87992-012-2*) Visual Studies.

Dugan, Thomas K. Trip Across the Pond: A Personal Vietnam Experience. LC 92-72057. (Illus.). 286p. 1992. 19.95 (*1-878342-10-X*) Bentworth Pr.

DuGan, Thomas K. & Green, Susan L. Through the Eyes: A Venture Through America. LC 89-81541. (Illus.). 436p. (Orig.). (YA). (gr. 12). 1990. pap. 5.50 (*1-878342-07-X*) Bentworth Pr.

DuGan, Thomas K. & Housely, Jack. Abstract Thought & Profound Quotations: With Some of Thomas's Wonderous Thoughts. LC 96-84209. (Illus.). 104p. (Orig.). (YA). (gr. 10). 1995. pap. 10.00 (*1-878342-11-8*) Bentworth Pr.

Dugan, Tracy A., ed. Lifetime Memories, 1993-94: Summer Missions Handbook. rev. ed. 1993. pap. text 5.00 (*0-9621469-2-7*) Biola Student Missionary.

Dugan, William F. & Holmes, Richard. Derry. (Images of America Ser.). 1995. pap. 16.99 (*0-7524-0203-X*) Arcadia Publng.

Duganne, A. J. The Fighting Quakers. (Illus.). 120p. 1996. reprint ed. pap. 8.95 (*1-889246-03-4*) P A Schroeder.

Dugard, John. Human Rights & the South African Legal Order. LC 77-85536. 491p. reprint ed. pap. 152.30 (*0-608-17850-0*, 203263500080) Bks Demand.

***Dugard, John.** International Law: A South African Perspective, Vol. 1. 2nd ed. 517p. 2000. pap. 46.50 (*0-7021-5072-X*, Pub. by Blackstone Pr) Gaunt.

Dugard, John. International Law - A South African Perspective. LC 94-203413. 372p. 1994. pap. 36.50 (*0-7021-3071-0*, 15673, Pub. by Juta & Co) Gaunt.

— International Law on Abortion: A South African Perspective. xxxviii, 372p. 1994. 54.00 (*0-7021-3164-4*, Pub. by Juta & Co) Gaunt.

— Recognition & the United Nations. 208p. (C). 1987. 110.00 (*0-949009-00-8*, Pub. by Grotius Pubns Ltd) St Mut.

Dugard, John & Van den Wyngaert, Christine, eds. International Criminal Law & Procedure. (International Library of Criminology, Criminal Justice & Penology). 500p. 1996. text 189.95 (*1-85521-835-6*, Pub. by Dartmth Pub) Ashgate Pub Co.

Dugard, John, et al. Rights & Constitutionalism: The New South African Legal Order. LC 95-150973. 720p. 1994. 89.00 (*0-7021-3285-3*, Pub. by Juta & Co) Gaunt.

Dugard, L., et al, eds. Adaptive Systems in Control & Signal Processing, 1992: Selected Papers from the Fourth IFAC Symposium, Grenoble, France, 1-3 July 1992. 556p. 1995. pap. 100.00 (*0-08-042596-8*, Pergamon Pr) Elsevier.

Dugard, L. & Verriest, Erik I., eds. Stability & Control of Time-Delay Systems. LC 97-29314. (Lecture Notes in Control & Information Sciences: Vol. 228). xx, 317p. 1997. pap. 59.00 (*3-540-76193-4*) Spr-Verlag.

Dugard, Marie. Ralph Waldo Emerson, Sa Vie et Son Oeuvre. (BCL1-PS American Literature Ser.). 418p. 1992. reprint ed. lib. bdg. 99.00 (*0-7812-6707-2*) Rprt Serv.

Dugard, Martin. In-Line Skating Made Easy: A Manual for Beginners with Tips for the Experienced. LC 96-19861. (Made Easy Ser.). (Illus.). 176p. 1996. pap. 16.95 (*1-56440-903-1*) Globe Pequot.

***Dugard, Martin.** Knockdown: The Harrowing True Account of a Yacht Race Turned Deadly. 1999. 24.95 (*0-671-03878-8*) PB.

— Knockdown: The Harrowing True Story of a Yacht Race Turned Deadly. (Illus.). 264p. 2000. per. 13.95 (*0-671-03879-6*, PB Trade Paper) PB.

Dugard, Martin. On the Edge: Four True Stories of Extreme Outdoor Sports Adventures. (Sports Illustrated for Kids Ser.). 1995. 9.09 (*0-606-07967-X*) Turtleback.

Dugard, Martin. Surviving the Toughest Race on Earth. LC 97-32961. (Illus.). 175p. 1998. pap. 19.95 (*0-07-018129-2*) Intl Marine.

***Dugard, Martin.** Surviving the Toughest Race on Earth. 202p. 1999. pap. 12.95 (*0-07-135821-8*) McGraw.

DuGarm, Henry K. When Lilacs Bloom Again: A Novel Based on the Life & Times of Lincoln. LC 87-63213. 358p. (Orig.). 1988. pap. 5.50 (*0-942323-01-7*) N Amer Heritage Pr.

Dugas. Boltzmann's Conception. (Boston Studies in the Philosophy of Science). 1900. lib. bdg. write for info. (*90-277-0728-6*) Kluwer Academic.

Dugas, Andre, jt. auth. see Paillet, Jean-Pierre.

Dugas, Beverly W. Nursing Foundations: Canadian Perspectives. 1993. text. write for info. (*0-8385-7064-X*) Appleton & Lange.

Dugas, Beverly W. Tratado de Enfermeria Practica. 4th ed. 1986. pap. text 39.95 (*0-07-104008-0*) McGraw.

Dugas-Bonds, Pat. Due Season. rev. ed. Mitchell, Sarah, ed. 139p. (Orig.). (YA). 1992. 20.00 (*0-925022-00-4*) BDB Unlimited.

Dugas, Edmond, et al. Badminton Made Simple. 118p. 1989. pap. 16.95 (*0-912855-92-4*) E Bowers Pub.

Dugas, Florence. Sad Sister. 1999. pap. text 12.95 (*1-58419-000-0*) Masq Bks.

Dugas, H. Bioorganic Chemistry. 2nd ed. (Advanced Texts in Chemistry Ser.). (Illus.). xv, 651p. 1988. 65.00 (*0-387-96795-8*) Spr-Verlag.

***Dugas, H.** Bioorganic Chemistry: A Chemical Approach to Enzyme Action. 3rd ed. (Advanced Texts in Chemistry Ser.). (Illus.). 720p. 1999. pap. 49.95 (*0-387-98910-2*) Spr-Verlag.

Dugas, H., ed. Bioorganic Chemistry Frontiers, Vol. 1. (Illus.). 224p. 1990. 103.95 (*0-387-51931-9*) Spr-Verlag.

— Bioorganic Chemistry Frontiers, Vol. 2. (Illus.). 240p. 1991. 118.95 (*0-387-53365-6*) Spr-Verlag.

Dugas, H. & Penney, C. Bioorganic Chemistry: A Chemical Approach to Enzyme Action. (Advanced Texts in Chemistry Ser.). (Illus.). 508p. 1981. 42.00 (*0-387-90491-3*) Spr-Verlag.

Dugas, H. & Schmidtchen, F. P., eds. Bioorganic Chemistry Frontiers, Vol. 3. (Illus.). 280p. 1993. 142.95 (*0-387-56518-3*) Spr-Verlag.

Dugas, John. Structure & Agency in Explaining Democratization: Insights from the Colombian Case. LC 93-655022. (MacArthur Scholar Series, Occasional Paper: No. 23). 111p. (Orig.). 1994. pap. 4.00 (*1-881157-25-3*) In Ctr Global.

Dugas, Kristine, ed. see Wordsworth, William.

Dugas, Ludovic. Le Amitie Antique D'apres les Moeurs Populaires & les Theories Des Philosophes. LC 75-13263. (History of Ideas in Ancient Greece Ser.). (FRE.). 1976. reprint ed. 35.95 (*0-405-07305-4*) Ayer.

Dugas, Rene. A History of Mechanics. (Illus.). 671p. 1988. reprint ed. pap. text 14.95 (*0-486-65632-2*) Dover.

Dugas, Rene L., Sr. The French-Canadians in New England: Taftville, the Early Years. Gagnon, Richard, ed. LC 96-96259. (Illus.). 237p. 1995. reprint ed. 31.95 (*0-9652283-0-4*); reprint ed. pap. 24.95 (*0-9652283-1-2*) R L Dugas.

Dugatkin, Lee A. Cheating Monkeys & Citizen Bees: The Nature of Cooperation in Animals & Humans. LC 98-27768. 256p. 1999. 25.00 (*0-684-84341-2*) Free Pr.

***Dugatkin, Lee A.** Cheating Monkeys & Citizen Bees: The Nature of Cooperation in Animals & Humans. 2000. pap. 14.95 (*0-674-00167-2*) HUP.

Dugatkin, Lee A. Cooperation among Animals: An Evolutionary Perspective. (Oxford Series in Ecology & Evolution). (Illus.). 240p. 1997. pap. 35.00 (*0-19-508622-8*); text 70.00 (*0-19-508621-X*) OUP.

Dugatkin, Lee A. & Reeve, Hudson K., eds. Game Theory & the Study of Animal Behavior. LC 96-29891. (Illus.). 336p. 1998. text 80.00 (*0-19-509692-4*) OUP.

***Dugatkin, Lee Alan & Reeve, Hudson Kern, eds.** Game Theory & Animal Behavior. (Illus.). 336p. 2000. pap. text 34.95 (*0-19-513790-6*) OUP.

***Dugaw, Dianne.** Deep Play: John Gay & the Invention of Modernity. LC 00-31518. 2000. write for info. (*0-87413-731-4*) U Delaware Pr.

Dugaw, Dianne. Warrior Women & Popular Balladry, 1650-1850. (Cambridge Studies in Eighteenth-Century English Literature & Thought: No. 4). (Illus.). 256p. (C). 1989. text 64.95 (*0-521-37254-2*) Cambridge U Pr.

— Warrior Women & Popular Balladry, 1650-1850. LC 95-34137. xvi, 250p. 1995. pap. text 14.95 (*0-226-16916-2*) U Ch Pr.

Dugaw, Dianne, ed. The Anglo-American Ballad: A Folklore Casebook. LC 94-24348. (Folklore Casebks.: Vol. 8). 360p. 1995. text 20.00 (*0-8153-1747-6*, H1858) Garland.

Dugaw, Dianne, intro. The Female Soldier: or The Surprising Life & Adventures of Hannah Snell. LC 92-23097. (Augustan Reprints Ser.: No. 257). 1989. reprint ed. 14.50 (*0-404-70257-0*) AMS Pr.

Dugdale. Medical Diagnostics: Pocket Companion. 1992. pap. text 41.00 (*0-7216-3499-0*, W B Saunders Co) Harcrt Hlth Sci Grp.

Dugdale, A. M. & Stanton, K. M. Dugdale & Stanton: Professional Negligence. 3rd ed. Parkinson, J. E., ed. 610p. 1997. write for info. (*0-406-03258-0*, DSPN3, MICHIE) LEXIS Pub.

— Professional Negligence. (C). 1988. 500.00 (*0-7855-4056-3*, Pub. by Witherby & Co) St Mut.

Dugdale, A. M., et al. Dugdale, Furmston, Jones & Sherrin: 'A' Level Law. 3rd ed. 1996. pap. write for info. (*0-406-04835-5*, DALL3, MICHIE) LEXIS Pub.

— Professional Negligence. 2nd ed. 1989. 140.00 (*0-406-17911-5*, U.K., MICHIE) LEXIS Pub.

Dugdale, David E. Essentials of Electromagnetism. LC 93-5749. (C). 1993. text 64.95 (*1-56396-253-5*, AIP Pr) Spr-Verlag.

Dugdale, J. S. Dylan Thomas's Under Milk Wood. rev. ed. (Brodie's Notes Ser.). 91p. 1992. pap. 5.95 (*0-333-58208-X*, Pub. by Macmillan) Trans-Atl Phila.

— The Electrical Properties of Disordered Metals. (Cambridge Solid State Science Ser.). (Illus.). 254p. (C). 1995. text 80.00 (*0-521-26882-6*) Cambridge U Pr.

— Entropy & Its Physical Interpretation. LC 96-218083. 300p. 1996. 59.95 (*0-7484-0568-2*, Pub. by Tay Francis Ltd); pap. 29.95 (*0-7484-0569-0*, Pub. by Tay Francis Ltd) Taylor & Francis.

Dugdale, Joan. The Gripping Beast. 200p. 1994. pap. 16.95 (*0-7022-2577-0*, Pub. by Univ Queensland Pr) Intl Spec Bk.

— Struggle of Memory. (Orig.). 1991. pap. 16.95 (*0-7022-2315-8*, Pub. by Univ Queensland Pr) Intl Spec Bk.

Dugdale, John. Jaguar in America. LC 90-84488. (Illus.). 271p. 1993. 49.95 (*0-9635618-0-4*) BritBook Pub.

— Lengthening Shadows Before Nightfall. 104p. 1995. 50.00 (*0-944092-30-6*) Twin Palms Pub.

***Dugdale, John.** Life's Evening Hour. 2000. 45.00 (*0-9672484-2-6*) AGW Lithographers.

— Untitled Verse & Photograph. 112p. (J). 2000. lib. bdg. 17.49 (*0-7868-2470-0*, Pub. by Disney Pr) Little.

Dugdale, L. M., jt. auth. see Dixon, D. L.

Dugdale, Norman. Limbo. 60p. 1991. pap. 10.95 (*0-85640-468-3*, Pub. by Blackstaff Pr) Dufour.

Dugdale, Richard L. The Jukes. LC 79-38664. (Foundations of Criminal Justice Ser.). reprint ed. 21.50 (*0-404-09173-3*) AMS Pr.

— The Jukes: A Study in Crime, Pauperism, Disease, & Heredity. LC 74-112542. (Rise of Urban America Ser.). (Illus.). 1973. reprint ed. 18.95 (*0-405-02451-7*) Ayer.

Dugdale, William. The Baronage of England, Or an Historical Account of Our English Nobility, 2 vols., Set. 1295p. 1977. reprint ed. 323.70 (*3-487-06374-3*) G Olms Pubs.

Duge, Jean A. Tribo Babo: Chan Sanba. Vedrine, Emmanuel W. et al, eds. (Illus.). 71p. 1995. pap. 7.00 (*1-885566-05-0*) Oresjozef.

Duggal, K. S. Akal Takht & Other Seats of Sikh Polity. (C). 1995. 9.00 (*81-86112-37-5*, Pub. by UBS Pubs Dist) S Asia.

— Ranjit Singh: A Secular Sikh Sovereign. (C). 1989. 44.00 (*81-7017-244-6*, Pub. by Abhinav) S Asia.

— Ranjit Singh: A Secular Sikh Sovereign. (Illus.). 143p. 1993. lib. bdg. 35.00 (*0-948725-07-9*, Pub. by Tricolour Bks) Asia Pub Hse.

— Sain Bulleh Shah: The Mystic Muse. (C). 1996. 30.00 (*81-7017-341-8*, Pub. by Abhinav) S Asia.

— Select Sikh Scriptures 1 No. 1: Guru Nanak. (C). 1997. 22.00 (*81-7476-157-8*, Pub. by UBS Pubs Dist) S Asia.

— The Sikh Gurus: Their Lives & Teachings. 240p. 1996. 19.95 (*0-318-36784-X*) Asia Bk Corp.

— Sikh Gurus: Their Lives & Teachings. 1998. reprint ed. 12.00 (*81-85674-99-X*, Pub. by UBS Pubs) S Asia.

— Sikh People: Yesterday & Today. (C). 1994. text 7.50 (*81-85944-36-9*, Pub. by UBS Pubs Dist) S Asia.

***Duggal, K. S., tr.** Select Scriptures Vol. III: Guru Angad Dev, Guru Amar Das, Guru Ram Das, Guru Teg Bahadur, Bhaktas & Bhats. 1998. pap. 19.50 (*81-7476-092-X*, Pub. by UBS Pubs) S Asia.

— Select Sikh Scriptures Vol. IV: Guru Gobind Singh. 1999. pap. 19.50 (*81-7476-226-4*, Pub. by UBS Pubs) S Asia.

— Word Divine Guruvak: Gleanings Form Sri Guru Granth Saheb. 1999. pap. 20.00 (*81-7476-230-2*, Pub. by UBS Pubs) S Asia.

Duggal, K. S., jt. ed. see Cowasjee, Saros.

Duggal, Kartar S. Night of the Full Moon & Other Stories. (C). 1992. text 8.00 (*81-7201-228-4*, Pub. by National Sahitya Akademi) S Asia.

— Philosophy & Faith of Sikhism. LC 88-213598. 99p. (Orig.). 1988. pap. 10.95 (*0-89389-109-6*) Himalayan Inst.

Duggal, Krishan L. & Bejancu, Aurel. Lightlike Submanifolds of Semi-Riemannian Manifolds & Applications. LC 96-1346. (Mathematics & Its Applications Ser.: Vol. 364). 308p. (C). 1996. text 166.00 (*0-7923-3957-6*) Kluwer Academic.

***Duggal, Krishan L. & Sharma, Ramesh C.** Symmetries of Spacetimes & Riemannian Manifolds. LC 99-30731. (Mathematics & Its Applications Series). 1999. write for info. (*0-7923-5793-0*) Kluwer Academic.

Duggal, Krishan L., jt. ed. see Beem, John.

***Duggal, M. S., et al.** Restorative Techniques in Paediatric Dentistry: An Illustrated Guide to the Restoration of Extensively Carious Primary Teeth. rev. ed. (Illus.). 136p. 2000. 89.95 (*1-85317-592-7*, Pub. by Martin Dunitz) Thieme Med Pubs.

Duggal, Monty S., et al. Restorative Techniques in Paediatric Dentistry: An Illustrated Guide to the Restoration of Extensively Carious Primary Teeth. (Illus.). 134p. 1995. text 49.00 (*0-7216-6007-X*, W B Saunders Co) Harcrt Hlth Sci Grp.

Duggal, S. K. Building Materials. (Illus.). 390p. (C). 1998. text 51.00 (*90-5410-764-2*, Pub. by A A Balkema) Ashgate Pub Co.

***Duggal, Vijay.** CADD Primer: A General Guide to Computer Aided Design & Drafting - CADD, CAD. Zolli, Al & Rush, Sella, eds. LC 99-74579. (Illus.). 210p. 2000. 41.95 (*0-9629165-2-8*); pap. 32.95 (*0-9629165-9-5*) MailMax Pubg.

Duggan, et al. Contractual Non Disclosure. Date not set. text. write for info. (*0-582-87584-6*, Pub. by Addison-Wesley) Longman.

D

Duggan, A. J. Regulated Credit: The Sale Aspect. xxxix, 407p. 1986. 82.00 (*0-455-20691-0*, Pub. by LawBk Co) Gaunt.

Duggan, A. J., et al. Regulated Credit: The Credit & Security Aspects. lx, 848p. 1989. 127.50 (*0-455-20832-8*, Pub. by LawBk Co) Gaunt.

Duggan, Andrew & Murcott, David J. Lessons of the Future: Thriving Today By Understanding Tomorrow. LC 98-86065. 112p. 1999. pap. 9.95 (*0-9665329-0-2*, STS0210) Strtgc Tech Sltns.

Duggan, Ann S., et al. The Folk Dance Library, 5 Vols., Set. LC 79-7758. (Dance Ser.). (Illus.). 1980. reprint ed. lib. bdg. 115.95 (*0-8369-9305-5*) Ayer.

Duggan, Anne. Thomas Becket: A Textual History of His Letters. 1980. 59.00 (*0-19-822486-9*) OUP.

Duggan, Anne, ed. Queens & Queenship in Medieval Europe: Proceedings of a Conference Held at King's College, London, April 1995. LC 97-917. (Illus.). 384p. 1997. 90.00 (*0-85115-657-6*) Boydell & Brewer.

Duggan, Anne, ed. see Becket, Thomas.

***Duggan, Anne J., ed.** Nobles & Nobility in Medieval Europe: Concepts, Origins, Transformations. LC 99-87553. (Illus.). 352p. 2000. 75.00 (*0-85115-769-6*) Boydell & Brewer.

Duggan, Anne S., et al. 1905-Folk Dances of European Countries. (Anne Schley Duggan, 1905 Folk Dance Library). (Illus.). 160p. 1980. 23.95 (*0-8369-9285-7*) Bks for Libraries.

— 1905-Folk Dances of Scandinavia. (Anne Schley Duggan, 1905 Folk Dance Library). (Illus.). 118p. 1980. 23.95 (*0-8369-9284-9*) Bks for Libraries.

— 1905-Folk Dances of the United States & Mexico. (Anne Schley Duggan, 1905 Folk Dance Library). (Illus.). 159p. 1980. 23.95 (*0-8369-9287-3*) Bks for Libraries.

— 1905 Folk Dances of the British Isles. (Anne Schley Duggan, 1905 Folk Dance Library). 120p. 1980. 23.95 (*0-8369-9286-5*) Bks for Libraries.

— 1905-The Teaching of Folk Dance. (Anne Schley Duggan, 1905 Folk Dance Library). (Illus.). 116p. 1980. 23.95 (*0-8369-9283-0*) Bks for Libraries.

Duggan, Betty J. & Riggs, Brett H., eds. Studies in Cherokee Basketry: Including a Reprint of Decorative Art & Basketry of the Cherokee by Frank G. Speck. (Museum Occasional Paper Ser.: No. 9). 60p. 1991. pap. 10.00 (*1-880174-01-4*) U TN F H McClung.

Duggan, C., jt. auth. see Dugmore, C. W.

Duggan, Charles. Decretals & the Creation of the "New Law" in the Twelfth Century: Judges, Judgements, Equity & Law. LC 98-70353. (Variorum Collected Studies Ser.: Vol. 607). 350p. 1998. text 99.95 (*0-86078-680-3*, Pub. by Ashgate Pub) Ashgate Pub Co.

Duggan, Christopher. A Concise History of Italy. (Concise Histories Ser.). (Illus.). 334p. (C). 1994. pap. 17.95 (*0-521-40848-2*); text 54.95 (*0-521-40285-9*) Cambridge U Pr.

Duggan, Christopher & Wagstaff, Christopher, eds. Italy in the Cold War: Politics, Culture & Society, 1948-1958. 272p. 1995. 47.50 (*1-85973-038-8*) Berg Pubs.

Duggan-Cronin, Alfred M. The Bantu Tribes of South Africa, 4 vols. in 12 pts., Set. LC 74-15033. reprint ed. 450.00 (*0-404-12050-4*) AMS Pr.

D

***Duggan, Cynthia.** People of His Presence. 300p. 1998. pap. 10.99 (*1-884369-09-X*) McDougal Pubng.

Duggan, Cynthia. Seekers of His Face: Two Companies. Nigh, Kepler, ed. LC 99-165188. 210p. 1997. pap. 10.99 (*1-884369-58-8*, EBED Pubns) McDougal Pubng.

***Duggan, Diane.** Out Here by Ourselves: The Stories of Young People Whose Mothers Have AIDS. LC 00-35376. (Children of Poverty Ser.). 2000. write for info. (*0-8153-3621-7*) Garland.

Duggan, Francis X. Paul Elmer Moore. LC 66-24144. (Twayne's United States Authors Ser.). 1966. pap. text 4.95 (*0-8290-1868-9*); lib. bdg. 20.95 (*0-8057-0524-4*) Irvington.

Duggan, George C. The Stage Irishman. LC 70-91899. (Illus.). 1972. 23.95 (*0-405-08468-4*, Pub. by Blom Pubns) Ayer.

Duggan, Heather. Windows 3.1: A Tutorial to Accompany Peter Norton's Introduction to Computers. LC 93-45355. 1994. write for info. (*0-02-801329-8*) Glencoe.

Duggan, Hoyt N. & Turville-Petre, Thorlac, eds. Wars of Alexander. (SS 10 Ser.: No. 10). 468p. 1989. 75.00 (*0-19-722410-5*) OUP.

Duggan, J. L. & Morgan, I. L., eds. Application of Accelerators in Research & Industry: Proceedings of the Fourteenth International Conference, Vol. CP392. LC 97-71846. (AIP Conference Proceedings Ser.). (Illus.). xii, 1457p. 1997. 290.00 (*1-56396-652-2*) Am Inst Physics.

— Applications of Accelerators in Research & Industry: Proceedings of the 15th International Conference, 2 vols. (Conference Proceedings Ser.: Vol. 475). 1999. 280.00 (*1-56396-825-8*) Am Inst Physics.

Duggan, Janie P. Child of the Sea: A Chronicle of Puerto Rico. 1976. lib. bdg. 69.95 (*0-8490-1600-2*) Gordon Pr.

Duggan, Joseph B. & Duggan, Sandra. Edgar Cayce's Massage, Hydrotherapy & Healing Oils. (Illus.). 160p. (Orig.). 1995. reprint ed. pap. 16.95 (*0-917483-34-0*) InnerVision.

Duggan, Kevin. Access Method Systems Guide. LC 86-64009. (Illus.). 176p. 1987. spiral bd. 25.00 (*0-9613848-1-6*) MARIS.

— Macro Writing Guide. 60p. (C). 1987. pap., spiral bd. 12.95 (*0-9613848-2-4*) MARIS.

Duggan, Laara K. The Best Flowers for Midwest Gardens: The Plants You Need to Create Spectacular Low-Maintenance Gardens That Bloom with the Seasons-Year after Year. LC 95-47445. (Illus.). 208p. (Orig.). 1996. pap. 14.95 (*1-55652-263-0*) Chicago Review.

— The Best Plants for Midwest Gardens. LC 97-52710. 208p. 1998. pap. 14.95 (*1-55652-284-3*) Chicago Review.

***Duggan, Lisa.** Sapphic Slashers: Sex, Violence & American Modernity. LC 00-35426. (Illus.). 280p. 2000. pap. 17.95 (*0-8223-2617-5*) Duke.

— Sapphic Slashers: Sex, Violence, & American Modernity. LC 00-35426. (Illus.). 280p. 2000. lib. bdg. 49.95 (*0-8223-2609-4*) Duke.

Duggan, Lisa & Hunter, Nan D. Sex Wars: Sexual Dissent & Political Culture. 288p. (C). (gr. 13). 1995. pap. 17.99 (*0-415-91037-4*, B4372) Routledge.

Duggan, Lisa, jt. ed. see Berlant, Lauren.

***Duggan, M.** Guns of the Gambler. large type ed. 272p. 1999. pap. 18.99 (*0-7089-5491-X*, Linford) Ulverscroft.

Duggan, M. The Hangman's Noose. large type ed. (Linford Western Library). 272p. 1996. pap. 16.99 (*0-7089-7812-6*, Linford) Ulverscroft.

— Maverick Preacher. large type ed. (Linford Western Library). 272p. 1997. pap. 16.99 (*0-7089-5005-1*, Linford) Ulverscroft.

— The Tin Star. large type ed. (Western Ser.). 1994. pap. 16.99 (*0-7089-7598-4*, Linford) Ulverscroft.

— The Treacherous Trail. large type ed. (Linford Western Library). 288p. 1992. pap. 16.99 (*0-7089-7251-9*) Ulverscroft.

— Trouble in Big Spur. large type ed. (Linford Western Library). 272p. 1993. pap. 16.99 (*0-7089-7315-9*, Linford) Ulverscroft.

Duggan, Margaret M. English Literature & Backgrounds, 1660-1700. LC 89-34092. 552p. 1990. text 50.00 (*0-8240-8502-7*, 711) Garland.

Duggan, Mary & Grainger, Roger. Imagination, Identification & Catharsis in Theatre & Therapy. LC 97-197779. 176p. 1997. pap. write for info. (*1-85302-431-7*, Pub. by Jessica Kingsley) Taylor & Francis.

Duggan, Mary A. Powerful Parent Letters for K-3. LC 97-4818. 152p. 1997. 61.95 (*0-8039-6585-0*); pap. 27.95 (*0-8039-6586-9*) Corwin Pr.

Duggan, Mary K. Italian Music Incunabula: Printers & Type. LC 89-20270. (Illus.). 500p. 1991. 195.00 (*0-520-05785-6*, Pub. by U CA Pr) Cal Prin Full Svc.

Duggan, Mary K., ed. CD-ROM in the Library: Today & Tomorrow. (Professional Librarian Ser.). 130p. (C). 1990. 25.00 (*0-8161-1934-1*, Hall Reference) Macmillan.

Duggan, Maureen H. Mommy Doesn't Live Here Anymore. (Illus.). 48p. (Orig.). (J). (ps-7). 1987. pap. 8.95 (*0-944453-01-5*) B Brae.

***Duggan, Michael.** Unfair Dismissal. 1999. pap. 60.00 (*1-85811-231-1*, Pub. by CLT Prof) Gaunt.

— Wrongful Dismissal. 1999. pap. 60.00 (*1-85811-232-X*, Pub. by CLT Prof) Gaunt.

Duggan, Michael, ed. see Deal, Susan S.

Duggan, Michael A., et al, eds. The Computer Utility: Implications for Higher Education. LC 75-12104. 1969. 39.00 (*0-89197-708-2*) Irvington.

***Duggan, Paul.** Two Skeletons on the Telephone: And Other Poems from Tough City. 2000. pap. 7.95 (*0-7613-1399-0*) Millbrook Pr.

Duggan, Paul & Sylvestre, Daniel. Two Skeletons on the Telephone & Other Poems from Tough City. LC 99-20022. (J). (gr. 3-6). 1999. 20.40 (*0-7613-1451-2*) Millbrook Pr.

Duggan, Paul, tr. see Bello, Antonio.

Duggan, Paul, tr. see Cremona, Carlo.

Duggan, Paul, tr. see Desbonnets, Theophile.

Duggan, Paul, tr. see Manselli, Raoul.

Duggan, Paul, tr. see Salvail, Ghislaine.

Duggan, Paula. Making Sense of Federal Dollars: A Guide to Understanding Allocation Formulas. 2nd ed. 75p. 1996. pap. text 21.00 (*1-882061-63-2*) Northeast-Midwest.

Duggan, Robert. Parish Liturgy: A Handbook for Renewal. LC 96-1794. 192p. (Orig.). 1996. pap. 12.95 (*1-55612-909-2*, LL1909) Sheed & Ward WI.

***Duggan, Robert D.** Teaching Kids the Basics of Liturgy: Making the Rituals Meaningful. 96p. 2000. pap. 6.95 (*0-88347-409-3*, Pub. by T More) BookWorld.

Duggan, Robert D. & Kelly, Maureen A. The Christian Initiation of Children: Hope for the Future. LC 90-25973. 1991. pap. 9.95 (*0-8091-3258-3*) Paulist Pr.

Duggan, Sandra. Edgar Cayce's Guide to Colon Care: The First Step to Vibrant Health. (Illus.). 225p. (Orig.). 1995. pap. 19.95 (*0-917483-32-4*) InnerVision.

Duggan, Sandra, jt. auth. see Duggan, Joseph B.

Duggan, Sandra, jt. auth. see Gott, Richard.

Duggan, Stephen, jt. auth. see Fahey, Stephanie.

Duggan, Stephen P. The Eastern Question. LC 76-120209. (Columbia University. Studies in the Social Sciences: No. 39). reprint ed. 27.50 (*0-404-51039-6*) AMS Pr.

— A Professor at Large. LC 72-4507. (Essay Index Reprint Ser.). 1977. reprint ed. 30.95 (*0-8369-2942-X*) Ayer.

Duggan, T., ed. Third World Conference on Engineering Education, 3 vols. LC 92-81591. 1992. 492.00 (*1-56252-117-9*, 1894) Computational Mech MA.

— Third World Conference on Engineering Education: Industrial Links, Computers & Design, Vol. 3. LC 92-81951. 610p. 1992. 187.00 (*1-56252-120-9*, 1924) Computational Mech MA.

— Third World Conference on Engineering Education: Innovation, Teaching & Management, Vol. 2. LC 92-81951. 586p. 1992. 181.00 (*1-56252-119-5*, 1916) Computational Mech MA.

— Third World Conference on Engineering Education: International Quality & Environmental Issues, Vol. 1. LC 92-81951. 590p. 1992. 181.00 (*1-56252-118-7*, 1908) Computational Mech MA.

Duggan, T. V., ed. Third World Conference on Engineering Education: Industrial Links, Computers & Design. 610p. 1992. 187.00 (*1-85312-192-4*) Computational Mech MA.

— Third World Conference on Engineering Education: Innovation, Teaching & Management. 586p. 1992. write for info. (*1-85312-191-6*) Computational Mech MA.

— Third World Conference on Engineering Education: International Quality & Environmental Issues. 590p. 1992. 181.00 (*1-85312-190-8*) Computational Mech MA.

Duggan, T. V., et al, eds. Environmental Engineering Education & Training: Proceedings of the First International Conference. LC 93-83660. 528p. 1997. 134.00 (*1-85312-393-5*, 3935, Pub. by WIT Pr) Computational Mech MA.

Duggan, T. V. & Flavell, C. J., eds. Computational Methods & Testing for Engineering Integrity. LC 96-83304. 368p. 1996. 165.00 (*1-85312-412-5*) Computational Mech MA.

Duggan, T. V. & Mitchell, C. A., eds. Environmental Engineering Education. LC 97-65920. (Environmental Engineering Ser.: Vol. 1). 272p. 1997. text 142.00 (*1-85312-479-6*, 4796, Pub. by WIT Pr) Computational Mech MA.

Duggan, Terri, ed. see Welch, Tom, et al.

***Duggan, Thomas F.** Array-Driven Parallel Software Architecture. LC 96-84710. 450p. 1999. text 100.00 (*0-9642131-2-5*, Pub. by Frndship Sftware) COBOL Software.

Duggan, Thomas F. Financial Product Technology System: Alpha Test Reference Manual. LC 91-90591. 542p. 1991. lib. bdg. write for info. (*0-9642131-0-9*) Frndship Sftware.

— Parallel Software Architecture. LC 93-90692. 589p. 1993. lib. bdg. write for info. (*0-9642131-1-7*) Frndship Sftware.

Duggan, Timothy, ed. see Reid, Thomas.

Duggan, William R. Microeconomic Analysis of Southern African Agriculture. LC 85-12191. 271p. 1985. 59.95 (*0-275-90203-X*, C0203, Praeger Pubs) Greenwood.

— A Socioeconomic Profile of South Africa. LC 72-91715. (Special Studies in International Economics & Development). 1973. 39.50 (*0-275-28653-3*) Irvington.

Duggan, William R. & Civille, John R. Tanzania & Nyerere: A Study of Ujamaa & Nationhood. LC 76-18121. 298p. reprint ed. pap. 92.40 (*0-8357-7044-3*, 203354200086) Bks Demand.

Duggar, J. W. Staying in Touch. 96p. 1990. pap. 4.00 (*0-89114-174-X*) Baptist Pub Hse.

Duggar, John W. BMA of America (1950-1986) 332p. 1988. 10.00 (*0-89114-166-9*) Baptist Pub Hse.

— The Girl with the Missionary Heart. rev. ed. (Illus.). 110p. (YA). (gr. 7-12). 1995. pap. 7.99 (*0-89114-074-3*) Baptist Pub Hse.

Duggar, Lillie. A. J. Tomlinson. 1964. 15.95 (*0-934942-00-5*) White Wing Pub.

Dugger, ed. The History of Lesbian Hair: And Other Tales of Bent Life in a Straight World. LC 96-16293. (Illus.). 128p. 1996. pap. 10.95 (*0-385-48037-7*, Main St Bks) Doubleday.

Dugger, Albia, ed. see Sharpe, Jim, Jr.

Dugger, Elizabeth. Massachusetts & Western Connecticut. (Adventure Guide Ser.). (Illus.). 400p. 1999. pap. 17.95 (*1-55650-861-1*) Hunter NJ.

Dugger, Elizabeth L. Adventure Guide to Vermont. 2nd rev. ed. (Adventure Guides Ser.). (Illus.). 360p. 1999. pap. 15.95 (*1-55650-887-5*) Hunter NJ.

***Dugger, Jack T.** Find Your Cosmic Powers in Search of the Self: Who & What Are We? Where Have We Been? What's Next? How Do We Set There? etc. LC 99-93734. 116p. 2000. 16.95 (*0-533-13143-X*) Vantage.

Dugger, Jim. Business Letters for Busy People. 3rd ed. LC 95-36900. 256p. 1995. pap. 15.99 (*1-56414-196-9*) Career Pr Inc.

— Listen Up! Hear What's Really Being Said. LC 95-79755. (AMI How-to Ser.). 79p. 1995. per. 12.95 (*1-884926-40-1*, TAKE) Amer Media.

Dugger, Julia. Living Advent: A Daily Companion to the Lectionary, Cycle A. LC 94-76026. 64p. 1995. pap. 3.95 (*0-89243-696-4*) Liguori Pubns.

— Living Advent: A Daily Companion to the Lectionary, Cycle B. LC 94-76025. 64p. 1995. pap. 2.95 (*0-89243-697-2*) Liguori Pubns.

— Living Advent (Cycle C) A Daily Companion to the Lectionary. LC 94-76238. 64p. (Orig.). 1994. pap. 2.95 (*0-89243-698-0*) Liguori Pubns.

Dugger, Leonard P. The Man Who Owned the Hogs. LC 92-43933. 208p. 1993. boxed set 21.95 (*1-879384-18-3*) Cypress Hse.

Dugger, Mack, ed. Air Pollution Effects on Plant Growth. LC 74-26543. (ACS Symposium Ser.: No. 3). 1974. 21.95 (*0-8412-0223-0*) Am Chemical.

— Air Pollution Effects on Plant Growth. LC 74-26543. (ACS Symposium Ser.: Vol. 3). 160p. 1974. reprint ed. pap. 49.60 (*0-608-03551-3*, 206427000008) Bks Demand.

Dugger, Shepherd M. The Balsam Groves of Grandfather Mountain. (Illus.). 1974. 6.00 (*0-686-15218-2*) Puddingstone.

— The War Trails of the Blue Ridge. (Illus.). 1974. 6.00 (*0-686-15219-0*) Puddingstone.

Dugger, William E., Jr. & Gerrish, Howard H. Electronics Technology: Devices & Circuits. LC 93-25857. (Illus.). 656p. 1994. 41.28 (*0-87006-085-6*) Goodheart.

Dugger, William E., Jr., jt. auth. see Gerrish, Howard H.

Dugger, William M. Corporate Hegemony: Contributions in Economics & Economic History, 97. LC 89-2188. 223p. 1989. 57.95 (*0-313-26711-1*, DCT/, Greenwood Pr) Greenwood.

— Underground Economics: A Decade of Institutionalist Dissent. LC 90-19792. (Studies in Institutional Economics). 404p. (C). (gr. 13). 1991. text 88.95 (*0-87332-799-3*) M E Sharpe.

Dugger, William M., ed. Inequality: Radical Institutional Views on Race, Gender, Class, & Nation, 178. LC 96-3643. (Contributions in Economics & Economic History: No. 178). 304p. 1996. 65.00 (*0-313-30014-3*, Greenwood Pr) Greenwood.

— Radical Institutionalism: Contemporary Voices, 90. LC 88-32791. (Contributions in Economics & Economic History Ser.: No. 90). 162p. 1989. 49.95 (*0-313-26595-X*, DRL, Greenwood Pr) Greenwood.

***Dugger, William M. & Sherman, Howard J.** Reclaiming Evolution: A Marxist Institutionalist Dialogue on Social Change. LC 00-36892. (Advances in Social Economics Ser.). 2000. write for info. (*0-415-23264-3*) Routledge.

Dugger, William M. & Waller, William T., eds. The Stratified State: Radical Institutionalist Theories of Participation & Duality. LC 92-27890. (Studies in Institutional Economics Ser.). 280p. (C). (gr. 13). 1993. text 79.95 (*1-56324-020-3*) M E Sharpe.

Duggin, Richard. The Music Box Treaty. (Illus.). 1982. 20.00 (*0-317-40787-2*) Abattoir.

Duggirala, Gopala K., jt. auth. see Coomaraswamy, Ananda.

Duggleby, John. Artist in Overalls: The Life of Grant Wood. (Illus.). 48p. (YA). (gr. 4 up). 1996. 15.95 (*0-8118-1242-1*) Chronicle Bks.

— Story Painter: The Life of Jacob Lawrence. LC 98-4513. (J). (gr. 1-7). 1998. 16.95 (*0-8118-2082-3*) Chronicle Bks.

***Duggleby, Julia.** How to Be an Online Tutor. LC 99-44902. 176p. 2000. 65.95 (*0-566-08247-0*, Pub. by Gower) Ashgate Pub Co.

Dugin, Andrej, jt. auth. see Dugina, Olga.

***Dugina, Olga & Dugin, Andrej.** The Brave Little Tailor. LC 99-88543. (Illus.). 32p. (J). 2000. 15.95 (*0-8109-4113-9*, Pub. by Abrams) Time Warner.

Duginske. Band Saw Handbook. 1989. pap. 16.95 (*0-8273-5390-1*) Delmar.

— Bank Saw Pattern Book. (Sterling Publishing Co. Ser.). 1991. pap. 12.95 (*0-8273-5392-8*) Delmar.

Duginske, Mark. Band Saw Handbook. LC 89-35457. (Illus.). 319p. (Orig.). 1989. pap. 17.95 (*0-8069-6398-0*) Sterling.

— Band Saws: A Workshop Bench Reference. LC 98-50983. 1999. spiral bd. 17.95 (*0-8069-0680-4*) Sterling.

— Mastering Woodworking Machines. (Illus.). 245p. 1992. pap. 24.95 (*0-942391-98-5*, 70136) Taunton.

Dugis, Vinsensio, jt. auth. see Catley, Bob.

Dugmore, C. W. & Duggan, C. Studies in Church History Vol. 1: Papers Read at the First Winter & Summer Meetings of the Ecclesiastical History Society. 1964. 69.50 (*0-614-01797-1*) Elliots Bks.

Dugo, Carmen C. The Importance of the Don Quixote Myth in the Works of Antonio Buero Vallejo. LC 94-48926. 284p. 1995. text 89.95 (*0-7734-9015-9*) E Mellen.

Dugopoloski, Mark. College Algebra: Student Solutions Manual. 2nd ed. (C). 1999. text, student ed. write for info. (*0-201-34715-6*) Addison-Wesley.

***Dugopoloski, Mark.** Graphing Calculator Manual for College Algebra/College Algebra & Trigonometry/ Precalculus. 2nd ed. 224p. (C). 1998. pap. text 16.00 (*0-201-38397-7*) Addison-Wesley.

Dugopoloski, Mark. Precalculus. 2nd ed. 976p. (C). 1998. 91.00 (*0-201-34713-X*) Addison-Wesley.

— Precalculus: Teacher's Solution Manual. 2nd ed. (C). 1999. text, teacher ed. write for info. (*0-201-34714-8*) Addison-Wesley.

Dugopolski. Algebra for College Students. 2nd ed. 312p. 1999. pap., student ed. 19.38 (*0-07-232400-7*) McGraw.

— Algebra For College Students. 2nd ed. LC 99-40279. 1999. 52.25 (*0-07-232399-X*) McGraw.

DUGOPOLSKI. College Algebra. (C). 1995. text 24.00 (*0-201-62865-1*) Addison-Wesley.

Dugopolski. Elementary Algebra. 3rd ed. 1999. student ed. 19.38 (*0-07-229449-3*); text 51.00 (*0-07-229448-5*) McGraw.

— Interact Math to Accompany College Algebra & Trigonometry. 1996. 22.50 incl. 3.5 hd (*0-201-89995-7*) Addison-Wesley.

— Interact Math Windows to Accompany College Algebra & Trigonometry. (C). 1996. 25.00 incl. disk (*0-201-43019-3*) Addison-Wesley.

— Intermediate Algebra. 3rd ed. 1999. 51.00 (*0-07-229466-3*) McGraw.

— Intermediate Algebra. 3rd ed. 276p. 1999. student ed. 19.38 (*0-07-229468-X*) McGraw.

— Precalculus. 944p. (C). 1995. text 55.00 (*0-201-85964-5*) Addison-Wesley.

Dugopolski. Supplement. 2nd ed. 1996. 26.00 (*0-201-49910-X*) Addison-Wesley.

— Supplement: Elementary Algebra. 2nd ed. 1996. suppl. ed. 26.00 (*0-201-88947-1*) Addison-Wesley.

— Supplement College Algebra Trigonometry: W/graph Calculus option. 1995. suppl. ed. 67.00 (*0-201-89910-8*) Addison-Wesley.

***Dugopolski, Mark.** Algebra for College Students. 2nd ed. 864p. (C). 1999. 65.31 (*0-07-233233-6*) McGrw-H Hghr Educ.

Dugopolski, Mark. College Algebra. LC 93-47516. 720p. (C). 1994. text 80.00 (*0-201-52618-2*) Addison-Wesley.

— College Algebra (C). 1995. pap. text. write for info. (*0-201-83184-8*) Addison-Wesley.

— College Algebra. 2nd ed. LC 98-22932. 976p. (C). 1998. 86.00 (*0-201-34711-3*) Addison-Wesley.

— College Algebra & Trigonometry. (C). 1995. text. write for info. (*0-201-83185-6*) Addison-Wesley.

— College Algebra & Trigonometry. 2nd ed. LC 98-22889. 976p. (C). 1998. 91.00 (*0-201-34712-1*) Addison-Wesley.

An Asterisk (*) at the beginning of an entry indicates that the title is appearing for the first time.

***Dugopolski, Mark.** College Algebra & Trigonometry: Professional Copy. 2nd ed. 976p. 1998. text. write for info. (*0-201-38405-1*) Addison-Wesley.
Dugopolski, Mark. College Algebra Update: With Graphing Calculator Option/Emphasis. Poole, Bill, ed. LC 95-20659. 603p. (C). 1996. text 71.25 (*0-201-88953-6*) Addison-Wesley.
— Elementary Algebra. 2nd ed. LC 95-13813. 512p. (C). 1995. 84.00 (*0-201-59563-X*) Addison-Wesley.
— Elementary Algebra: Student Solutions Manual. 2nd ed. 208p. (C). 1996. pap. text 25.00 (*0-201-89514-5*) Addison-Wesley.
— Intermediate Algebra. 272p. (C). 1991. pap. text, student ed. 17.66 (*0-201-16896-0*); pap. text, student ed. 23.66 (*0-201-53348-0*) Addison-Wesley.
— Intermediate Algebra. 2nd ed. 688p. (C). 1995. text 75.00 (*0-201-59564-8*) Addison-Wesley.
— Intermediate Algebra. 2nd ed. 272p. (C). 1995. pap. text, student ed. 25.00 (*0-201-89515-3*) Addison-Wesley.
***Dugopolski, Mark.** Intermediate Algebra. 3rd ed. 704p. (C). 1999. 65.31 incl. cd-rom (*0-07-233232-8*) McGrw-H Hghr Educ.
Dugopolski, Mark. Intermediate Algebra: Answer Book. 2nd ed. (C). 1996. pap. text 20.00 (*0-201-84599-7*) Addison-Wesley.
Dugre, Donald. Essential Math for Beginning Chemistry & Physics. 80p. (C). 1993. spiral bd. 9.95 (*0-8403-8483-1*) Kendall-Hunt.
— General Chemistry in the Laboratory. 2nd ed. 134p. (C). 1997. pap. text, spiral bd. 20.95 (*0-7872-3433-8*, 41343301) Kendall-Hunt.
Dugre, Donald & Lin, Doris. Chemistry 101A. 128p. (C). 1995. pap. text, student ed., spiral bd. 11.95 (*0-7872-0529-X*) Kendall-Hunt.
Dugre, Tanya, tr. see Schmidt, Fran & Friedman, Alice.
Dugre, Tanya, tr. see Schmidt, Fran, et al.
Dugrenier, Ronald J. Computer Service Technician: The Definitive Guide to Software & Hardware Troubleshooting. (Illus.). 400p. (Orig.). 1996. pap. text 59.95 (*0-9631329-5-4*, CST1) Comp Etcetera.
DuGuay, G. E. & Treyz, George I. Endogenous Wage Determination: Its Significance for State Policy Analysis Models. (Discussion Papers: No. 120). 1980. pap. 10.00 (*1-55869-039-5*) Regional Sci Res Inst.
Duguay, R. Precis Pratique de Psychiatrie. 2nd ed. (FRE.). 756p. 1984. 125.00 (*0-8288-1802-9*, M15382) Fr & Eur.
Dugue, D., ed. Analytical Methods in Probability Theory: Proceedings. (Lecture Notes in Mathematics Ser.: Vol. 861). 183p. 1981. 31.95 (*0-387-10823-8*) Spr-Verlag.
Duguid, Ian M. Living in the Gap Between Promise & Reality: The Gospel According to Abraham. LC 99-28877. (Gospel According to the Old Testament Ser.). 192p. 1999. pap. 12.99 (*0-87552-652-7*) P & R Pubng.
Duguid, Julian. Green Hell. 1992. reprint ed. lib. bdg. 18.95 (*0-89966-959-X*) Buccaneer Bks.
Duguid, Naomi, jt. auth. see Alford, Jeffrey.
Duguid, Paul, jt. auth. see Brown, John Seely.
Duguid, William P. & Rosenberg, Lawrence M. Cellular Inter-Relationships in the Pancreas: Implications for Islet Transplantation. LC 96-34373. (Medical Intelligence Unit Ser.). (Illus.). 219p. 1996. 99.00 (*1-57059-403-1*) Landes Bioscience.
Duguran, Debbie & Hopkins, Margot. Thematic Learning Adventures for Young Children: Weekly Integrated Curriculum Units for the Whole Year. Keeling, Jan & Britt, Leslie, eds. (Illus.). 192p. (Orig.). (J). (ps). 1994. pap. text 14.95 (*0-86530-283-9*, 50-X) Incentive Pubns.
Duguy, R., ed. see International Conference on the Mediterranean Monk.
Duh, Quan-Yang, jt. auth. see Clark, Orlo H.
Duh, Samuel V. Blacks & AIDS: Causes & Origins. LC 91-15553. (Sage Series on Race & Ethnic Relations: Vol. 3). 163p. reprint ed. pap. 50.60 (*0-608-03373-1*, 205963700008) Bks Demand.
— Blacks & AIDS: Generic or Environmental Causes. (Series on Race & Ethnic Relations: Vol. 3). 224p. (C). 1991. 49.95 (*0-8039-4346-6*); pap. 24.00 (*0-8039-4347-4*) Sage.
Duhaime, Lloyd. Hear! Hear! One Hundred Twenty-Five Years of Debate in Canada's House of Commons. (Illus.). 224p. 1992. 19.95 (*0-7737-2644-6*) Genl Dist Srvs.
Duhaj, P., et al, eds. Amorphous Metallic Materials. 2nd ed. 480p. 1990. text 191.00 (*0-87849-601-7*, Pub. by Trans T Pub) Enfield Pubs NH.
— Amorphous Metallic Materials 3. 686p. (C). 1993. text 258.00 (*0-87849-655-6*, Pub. by Trans T Pub) Enfield Pubs NH.
Duhallow, Lord. Gaelic Titles & Forms of Address. 2nd rev. ed. 120p. 1997. reprint ed. lib. bdg. 14.95 (*0-940134-27-6*) Irish Genealog.
Duhamel. Le Notaire du Havre. (FRE.). (C). pap. 9.95 (*0-8442-1711-5*, VF1711-5) NTC Contemp Pub Co.
Duhamel, Denise. Girl Soldier. 70p. 1996. pap. 13.00 (*1-882329-05-8*) Garden St Pr.
— How the Sky Fell. 36p. (Orig.). 1996. pap. 6.00 (*1-888219-02-5*) Pearl Edit.
— Kinky. LC 96-19977. 96p. (Orig.). 1997. pap. 12.95 (*0-914061-61-5*) Orchises Pr.
— Smile! LC 92-91159. 100p. (Orig.). 1993. pap. 10.00 (*1-879294-04-4*) Warm Spring Pr.
— The Star-Spangled Banner: Poems. LC 98-50622. 84p. 1999. pap. 11.95 (*0-8093-2259-5*) S Ill U Pr.
— The Woman with Two Vaginas. 96p. (Orig.). (C). 1995. pap. 10.00 (*0-9634000-6-1*) Salmon Run.
Duhamel, Denise & Seaton, Maureen. Exquisite Politics. LC 97-61748. 80p. (Orig.). 1997. pap. 10.95 (*1-882688-15-5*) Tia Chucha Pr.
***Duhamel, Denise & Seaton, Maureen.** Oyl. 40p. 2000. pap. 8.00 (*1-888219-16-5*) Pearl Edit.
Duhamel du Monceau, Henri L. Decorative Floral Woodcuts of the Sixteenth Century. LC 98-9804. (Illus.). 1998. pap. 10.95 (*0-486-40206-1*) Dover.
Duhamel, Georges. America, the Menace: Scenes from the Life of the Future. Thompson, Charles M., tr. LC 73-13126. (Foreign Travelers in America, 1810-1935 Ser.). 236p. 1974. reprint ed. 23.95 (*0-405-05450-5*) Ayer.
— Cecile Parmi Nous. (Chronique Des Pasquier Ser.: Vol. VII). (FRE.). 1976. pap. 10.95 (*0-7859-1778-0*, 2070365530) Fr & Eur.
— Chronique des Pasquier. Incl. Cecile Parmi Nous. pap. 8.95 (*2-07-036553-0*); Combat Contre les Ombres. pap. 8.95 (*2-07-036841-6*); Desert de Bievres. pap. (*2-07-036473-9*); Jardin des Betes Sauvages. pap. (*2-07-036194-2*); Maitres. pap. 6.95 (*2-07-036525-5*); Notaire du Havre. pap. 8.95 (*2-07-036903-X*); Nuit de la Saint-Jean. pap. (*2-07-036440-2*); Passion de Joseph Pasquier. pap. 8.95 (*2-07-036985-4*); Suzanne et les Jeunes Hommes. pap. 9.95 (*2-07-036923-4*); Vue de la Terre Promise. pap. 6.95 Vue de la Terre Promise. pap. 5.95 (*2-07-036404-6*); Vol. 1. Notaire du Havre. 1963. Vol. 2. Jardin des Betes Sauvages. Vol. 3. Vue de la Terre Promise. Vol. 4. Nuit de la Saint-Jean. Vol. 5. Desert de Bievres. 1963. Vol. 6. Maitres. 1963. Vol. 7. Cecile Parminous. Vol. 8. Combat Contre les Ombres. 1963. Vol. 9. Suzanne et les Juenes Hommes. Vol. 10. Passion de Joseph Pasquier. 1963. 1963. write for info. (*0-318-63450-3*) Fr & Eur.
— Chronique des Pasquier, 10 tomes. Incl. Cecile Parmi Nous. pap. 8.95 (*2-07-036553-0*); Combat Contre les Ombres. pap. 8.95 (*2-07-036841-6*); Desert de Bievres. pap. (*2-07-036473-9*); Jardin des Betes Sauvages. pap. (*2-07-036194-2*); Maitres. pap. 6.95 (*2-07-036525-5*); Notaire du Havre. pap. 8.95 (*2-07-036903-X*); Nuit de la Saint-Jean. pap. (*2-07-036440-2*); Passion de Joseph Pasquier. pap. 8.95 (*2-07-036985-4*); Suzanne et les Jeunes Hommes. pap. 9.95 (*2-07-036923-4*); Vue de la Terre Promise. pap. 6.95 Vue de la Terre Promise. pap. 5.95 (*2-07-036404-6*); Vol. 1. Notaire du Havre. 1963. Vol. 2. Jardin des Betes Sauvages. Vol. 3. Vue de la Terre Promise. Vol. 4. Nuit de la Saint-Jean. Vol. 5. Desert de Bievres. 1963. Vol. 6. Maitres. 1963. Vol. 7. Cecile Parminous. Vol. 8. Combat Contre les Ombres. 1963. Vol. 9. Suzanne et les Juenes Hommes. Vol. 10. Passion de Joseph Pasquier. 1963. (FRE.). pap. write for info. (*0-318-51952-6*) Schoenhof.
— Chronique des Saisons Ameres. (FRE.). 232p. 1949. pap. 16.95 (*0-7859-5410-4*) Fr & Eur.
— Le Club des Lyonnais. (FRE.). 272p. 1929. pap. 16.95 (*0-7859-5544-5*) Fr & Eur.
— Le Combat Contre Les Ombres. (Chronique Des Pasquier Ser.: Vol. VIII). (FRE.). 304p. 1976. pap. 10.95 (*0-7859-1833-7*, 2070368416) Fr & Eur.
— Les Compagnons de l'Apocalypse. (FRE.). 1956. pap. 16.95 (*0-7859-5411-2*) Fr & Eur.
— Le Complexe de Theophile. (FRE.). 228p. 1958. pap. 16.95 (*0-7859-5412-0*) Fr & Eur.
— Confession de Minuit: Vie et Aventures de Salavin. 160p. 1973. write for info. (*0-318-63463-5*) Fr & Eur.
— Confession de Minuit: Vie et Aventures de Salavin. (Folio Ser.: No. 495). 160p. 1973. 8.95 (*2-07-036495-X*) Schoenhof.
— Consultation aux Pays d'Islam. (FRE.). 128p. 1947. pap. 16.95 (*0-7859-5421-X*) Fr & Eur.
— Cri des Profodeurs. (FRE.). 240p. 1951. pap. 16.95 (*0-7859-5414-7*) Fr & Eur.
— Le Desert De Bievres. (Chronique Des Pasquier Ser.: Vol. V). (FRE.). 1973. pap. 10.95 (*0-7859-1761-6*, 2070364739) Fr & Eur.
— Deux Hommes. (FRE.). 240p. 1924. pap. 16.95 (*0-7859-4877-5*) Fr & Eur.
— Discours aux Nuages. (FRE.). 276p. 1947. pap. 18.95 (*0-7859-5415-5*) Fr & Eur.
— Fables de Mon Jardin. (FRE.). 248p. 1936. pap. 16.95 (*0-7859-5416-3*) Fr & Eur.
— Israel, Clef de l'Orient. (FRE.). 112p. 1957. pap. 12.95 (*0-7859-5417-1*) Fr & Eur.
— Le Japon. (FRE.). 176p. 1953. pap. 16.95 (*0-7859-5561-5*) Fr & Eur.
— Le Jardin des Betes Sauvages. (Chronique des Pasquier Ser.: Vol. II). (FRE.). 192p. 1972. pap. 10.95 (*0-7859-1710-1*, 2070361942) Fr & Eur.
— Journal de Salavin. 11.95 (*0-685-37290-1*) Fr & Eur.
— Les Jumeaux de Vallangoujard. 9.95 (*0-686-55178-8*) Fr & Eur.
— La Legende de Saint Julien l'Hospitalier. (FRE., Illus.). 256p. 1974. 125.00 (*0-7859-1176-6*, 2225384126) Fr & Eur.
— Lieu d'Asile. (FRE.). 144p. 1940. pap. 10.95 (*0-7859-5418-X*) Fr & Eur.
— The Life of Martyrs. 1990. lib. bdg. 79.95 (*0-8490-4056-6*) Gordon Pr.
— Les Livres du Bonheur. (FRE.). 256p. 1957. pap. 15.95 (*0-7859-5562-3*) Fr & Eur.
— Lumieres sur Ma Vie Vol. 1: Inventaire de l'Aimbe (1884-1901) (FRE.). 244p. 1949. pap. 16.95 (*0-7859-5419-8*) Fr & Eur.
— Lumieres sur Ma Vie Vol. 2: Biographies de Mes Fantomer (1901-1906) (FRE.). 256p. 1949. pap. 9.95 (*0-7859-5420-1*) Fr & Eur.
— Lumieres sur Ma Vie Vol. 3: Le Temps de la Recherche (1906-1914) 9.95 (*0-686-55183-4*) Fr & Eur.
— Lumieres sur Ma Vie Vol. 4: La Pesee des Ames (1914-1919) (FRE.). 336p. 1949. pap. 16.95 (*0-685-73299-1*) Fr & Eur.
— Lumieres sur Ma Vie Vol. 5: Les Espoirs et les Epreuves (1919-1928) (FRE.). 1928. pap. 16.95 (*0-7859-5422-8*) Fr & Eur.
— Les Maitres. (Chronique Des Pasquier Ser.: Vol. VI). (FRE.). 256p. 1974. pap. 10.95 (*0-7859-1770-5*, 2070365255) Fr & Eur.
— Le Notaire du Havre. (Chronique Des Pasquier Ser.: Vol. I). (FRE.). 1972. pap. 10.95 (*0-7859-2210-5*, 207036903X) Fr & Eur.
— Nouvelles du Sombre Empire. (FRE.). 208p. 1960. pap. 16.95 (*0-7859-5424-4*) Fr & Eur.
— La Nuit de Saint-Jean. (Chronique Des Pasquier Ser.: Vol. IV). (FRE.). 192p. 1973. pap. 10.95 (*0-7859-1754-3*, 2070364402) Fr & Eur.
— La Nuit d'Orage. (FRE.). 262p. 1928. 14.95 (*0-7859-0040-3*, F99350) Fr & Eur.
— La Passion de Joseph Pasquier. (Chronique Des Pasquier Ser.: Vol. X). (FRE.). 276p. 1977. pap. 10.95 (*0-7859-1863-9*, 2070369854) Fr & Eur.
— La Pierre d'Horeb. (FRE.). 248p. 1974. pap. 10.95 (*0-7859-1787-X*, 2070365948) Fr & Eur.
— La Pierre d'Horeb. (Folio Ser.: No. 594). (FRE.). 286p. 1947. pap. 8.95 (*2-07-036594-8*) Schoenhof.
— La Possession du Monde. (FRE.). 240p. 1963. pap 18.95 (*0-7859-5425-2*) Fr & Eur.
— Problemes de Civilisation: Avec: Traite de Depart, Fables de ma Vie, La Medicine au 20e Siecle. (FRE.). 232p. 1962. pap. 16.95 (*0-7859-5426-0*) Fr & Eur.
— Querelles de Famille. (FRE.). 224p. 1959. pap. 16.95 (*0-7859-5427-9*) Fr & Eur.
— Recits des Temps de Guerre, 2 vols., Set. (FRE.). 720p. 1949. pap. 28.95 (*0-7859-5428-7*) Fr & Eur.
— Remarques sur les Memoires Imaginaires. (FRE.). 96p. 1934. pap. 16.95 (*0-7859-5563-1*) Fr & Eur.
— Salavin. (FRE.). 144p. 1972. 7.95 (*0-7859-0092-6*, M3393) Fr & Eur.
— Souvenirs de la Vie du Paradis. 204p. 9.95 (*0-686-55196-6*) Fr & Eur.
— Suzanne et les Jeunes Hommes. (Chronique Des Pasquier Ser.: Vol. IX). (FRE.). 374p. 1977. pap. 11.95 (*0-7859-1849-3*, 2070369234) Fr & Eur.
— Tel Qu'en Lui-Meme. 1973. 8.95 (*0-686-55197-4*) Fr & Eur.
— Tel Qu'en Lui-Meme. (Vie et Aventures De Salavin Ser.: Vol. II). (FRE.). 1973. pap. 10.95 (*0-7859-1730-6*, 2070363198) Fr & Eur.
— Trois Nouvelles. (Illus.). 25.00 (*0-686-55198-2*) Fr & Eur.
— Vie et Aventures de Salavin. (Illus.). 522p. 1959. write for info. (*0-318-63615-8*) Fr & Eur.
— Vie et Aventures de Salavin: Le Journal Salavin. (FRE.). 320p. 1970. pap. 10.95 (*0-7859-0090-X*, M3391) Fr & Eur.
— Voyage de Candide. 15.00 (*0-686-55201-6*) Fr & Eur.
— Le Voyage de Patrice Periot. (FRE.). 256p. 1983. pap. 12.95 (*0-7859-4724-8*) Fr & Eur.
— Vue de la Terre Promise. (Chronique Des Pasquier Ser.: Vol. III). (FRE.). 1973. pap. 10.95 (*0-7859-1749-7*, 2070364046) Fr & Eur.
— Vues sur Rimbaud. (FRE.). 256p. 1952. pap. 45.00 (*0-7859-5429-5*) Fr & Eur.
Duhamel, Georges & Vildrac, Charles. Notes sur la Technique Poetique. (FRE.). 50p. 1925. pap. 36.95 (*0-7859-5423-6*) Fr & Eur.
Duhamel, J. Dictionnaire Inattendu de Dieu: Citations. (FRE.). 1998. 65.00 (*0-320-00193-8*) Fr & Eur.
Duhamel, Olivier & Meny, Yves. Dictionnaire Constitutionnel. (FRE.). 1120p. 1992. 275.00 (*0-7859-0976-1*, 2130442560) Fr & Eur.
Duhamel, P. Albert. After Strange Fruit: Changing Literary Tastes in Post-World-War II Boston. 1980. 4.00 (*0-89073-063-6*, 224) Boston Public Lib.
Duhart, Karen J. Montgomery County, Ohio, Cemetery Inscriptions Vol. V: Book A - Dayton National Cemetery. Montgomery County Chapter OGS Staff, ed. LC 82-222963. (Illus.). 706p. 1998. pap. 35.00 (*1-887665-10-2*) MCC OGS.
***Duhart, Sharon.** From the Heart. 104p. 1999. pap. 11.00 (*0-8059-4572-5*) Dorrance.
Duhatschek, Eric, jt. auth. see Strachan, Al.
Duhaut-Cilly, Auguste B., et al. A Voyage to California, the Sandwich Islands & Around the World in the Years, 1826-1829. LC 98-36122. 317p. 1999. 29.95 (*0-520-21752-7*, Pub. by U CA Pr) Cal Prin Full Svc.
Duhem, B., jt. auth. see Courtecuisse, R.
Duhem, Bernard. Collins Watch Guide: Mushrooms & Toadstools. 1997. pap. 11.95 (*0-00-220102-X*, Pub. by HarpC) Trafalgar.
Duhem, P. Etudes Sur Leonard De Vinci: Ceux Qu'il a Lus et Ceux Qui L'ont Lu, 2 vols., 1. 850p. 1984. write for info. (*2-903928-13-4*) Gordon & Breach.
— Etudes Sur Leonard De Vinci: Ceux Qu'il a Lus et Ceux Qui L'ont Lu, 2 vols., 2. 850p. 1984. write for info. (*2-903928-14-2*) Gordon & Breach.
— Etudes Sur Leonard De Vinci: Ceux Qu'il a Lus et Ceux Qui L'ont Lu, 2 vols., Set. 850p. 1984. write for info. (*0-318-65451-2*) Gordon & Breach.
— Etudes Sur Leonard De Vinci: Les Precurseurs Parisiens de Galilee, 3 vols., Vol. 3. (FRE.). 1434p. 1983. pap. text 123.00 (*2-903928-12-6*) Gordon & Breach.
— Etudes Sur Leonard De Vinci: Les Precurseurs Parisiens de Galilee, 3 vols., Vol. 3. (FRE.). xiv, 605p. 1984. pap. text 37.00 (*2-903928-15-0*) Gordon & Breach.
— Etudes Sur Leonard de Vinci Vols. 1 - 2: Ceux Qu'il a Lus & Ceux Qui l'Ont Lu, 2 vols., Vol. 2. (FRE.). 355/474p. 1984. pap. text 73.00 (*2-903928-16-9*) Gordon & Breach.
Duhem, Pierre. Essays in the History & Philosophy of Science. Ariew, Roger & Barker, Peter, trs. from FRE. LC 95-52525. 312p. (C). 1996. pap. text 19.95 (*0-87220-308-5*); lib. bdg. 39.95 (*0-87220-309-3*) Hackett Pub.
— German Science. Lyon, John, tr. LC 91-21454. 162p. (C). 1991. 38.95 (*0-8126-9123-7*) Open Court.
— Premices Philosophiques. Jaki, Stanley L., ed. (Brill's Studies in Intellectual History: Vol. 3). 260p. 1987. 71.00 (*90-04-08117-8*) Brill Academic Pubs.
— To Save the Phenomena: An Essay on the Idea of Physical Theory from Plato to Galileo. Doland, Edmund & Maschler, Chaninah, trs. LC 71-77978. (Midway Reprint Ser.). xxvi, 120p. 1985. pap. text 9.95 (*0-226-16921-9*) U Ch Pr.
Duhem, Pierre M. The Evolution of Mechanics. Oravas, G. A., ed. (Genesis & Method Ser.: No. 1). Orig. Title: L' Evolution de la Mecanique. 234p. 1980. reprint ed. text 155.50 (*90-286-0688-2*) Kluwer Academic.
— Medieval Cosmology: Theories of Infinity, Place, Time, Void, & the Plurality of Worlds. Ariew, Roger, ed. LC 85-8115. xxxii, 634p. (C). 1987. pap. text 27.00 (*0-226-16923-5*) U Ch Pr.
— The Origins of Statics: The Sources of Physical Theory. Leneaux, Grant F. et al, trs. (Boston Studies in the Philosophy of Science). 632p. 1991. lib. bdg. 287.50 (*0-7923-0898-0*, Pub. by Kluwer Academic) Kluwer Academic.
Duheme, Jacqueline. Mrs. Kennedy Goes Abroad. LC 98-18686. (Illus.). 64p. 1998. 18.95 (*1-57965-123-2*, 85123) Artisan.
Duhig, Ian. The Bradford Count. 64p. (Orig.). 1991. pap. 13.95 (*1-85224-138-1*, Pub. by Bloodaxe Bks) Dufour.
— The Mersey Goldfish. 64p. 1996. pap. 16.95 (*1-85224-325-2*, Pub. by Bloodaxe Bks) Dufour.
— Nominies. LC 99-171046. 64p. 1998. pap. 16.95 (*1-85224-457-7*, Pub. by Bloodaxe Bks) Dufour.
Duhig, Stewart M. Huichica: Recollections of Stewart M. Duhig, Vol. I. (Illus.). 112p. (Orig.). 1990. pap. 18.95 (*0-9628217-0-5*) Duhig Pubns.
Duhl, D. N., ed. see International Symposium on Superalloys Staff.
Duhl, David, jt. auth. see Netherton, John.
Duhl, Leonard J. Health Planning & Social Change. 320p. 1986. 44.95 (*0-89885-301-X*, Kluwer Acad Hman Sci) Kluwer Academic.
— The Social Entrepreneurship of Change. 332p. (C). 1990. lib. bdg. 46.50 (*0-944473-02-4*) Pace Univ Pr.
Duhl, Leonard J. & Leopold, Robert L., eds. Mental Health & Urban Social Policy: A Casebook of Community Action. LC 68-54942. (Jossey-Bass Behavioral Science Ser.). 346p. reprint ed. 98.70 (*0-8357-9334-6*, 2013787) Bks Demand.
Duhling, Sallie R., et al. Catfish Grammar. 2nd ed. 240p. 1997. pap. text 25.95 (*0-89892-156-2*) Contemp Pub Co of Raleigh.
Duhn, John. The History of Political Theory & Other Essays. 249p. (C). 1996. text 59.95 (*0-521-49707-8*); pap. text 19.95 (*0-521-49784-1*) Cambridge U Pr.
Duhon Boudreaux, Gwendolyn M. This Woman's Life. LC 98-30721. 60p. 1998. pap. 14.95 (*0-7734-3090-3*, Mellen Poetry Pr) E Mellen.
Duhon Boudreaux, Gwendolyn M., ed. An Interdisciplinary Approach to Issues & Practices in Teacher Education. LC 98-38871. (Studies in Education: Vol. 38). 368p. 1998. text 89.95 (*0-7734-8246-6*) E Mellen.
Duhon, David. One Circle: How to Grow a Complete Diet in Less Than 1000 Square Feet. (Illus.). 199p. 1985. pap. 12.50 (*0-614-11404-7*) Ecology Action.
***Duhon, Gwendolyn M. & Manson, Tony.** Preparation, Collaboration & Emphasis on the Family in School Counseling for the New Millennium. LC 99-58572. (Studies in Education: Vol. 48). 300p. 2000. text 89.95 (*0-7734-7847-7*) E Mellen.
***Duhon, Gwendolyn M. & Manson, Tony, eds.** Implications for Teacher Education: Cross-Ethnic & Cross-Racial Dynamics of Instructions. LC 00-41144. (Studies in Education: Vol. 51). 200p. 2000. 79.95 (*0-7734-7695-4*) E Mellen.
Duhon, Remi. Fifty-Two Soul-Stirring Sermon Outlines. 124p. (Orig.). 1993. pap. 4.95 (*1-56794-036-6*, C2298) Star Bible.
Duhon-Ross, Alice, ed. Reaching & Teaching Children Who Are Victims of Poverty. LC 99-26084. (Symposium Ser.: Vol. 55). 216p. 1999. text 89.95 (*0-7734-7964-3*) E Mellen.
Duhon-Sells, Rose M., ed. Dealing with Youth Violence: What Schools & Communities Need to Know. 112p. (Orig.). 1995. pap. 18.95 (*1-879639-31-9*) Natl Educ Serv.
— Exploring Self Science Through Peace Education & Conflict Resolution. LC 97-48622. (Studies in World Peace: Vol. 6). 320p. 1998. text 99.95 (*0-7734-8451-5*) E Mellen.
— Parental Skills for Parenting Children of Color. LC 91-42619. (Illus.). 128p. 1992. lib. bdg. 59.95 (*0-7734-1655-2*) E Mellen.
Duhon-Sells, Rose M. & Pitts, Emma T., eds. An Interdisciplinary Approach to Multicultural Teaching & Learning. LC 95-41002. (Mellen Studies in Education: Vol. 24). 76p. 1996. 59.95 (*0-7734-8839-1*) E Mellen.
— A Vision of Multicultural Education for the Year 2000. LC 93-44824. 1994. text 79.95 (*0-7734-9427-8*) E Mellen.
***Duhon-Sells, Rose M., et al.** The Developmental Process of Positive Attitudes & Mutual Respect: A Multicultural Approach to Advocating School Safety. LC 99-45506. (Studies in World Peace: Vol. 11). 250p. 1999. text 69.95 (*0-7734-7886-8*) E Mellen.
Duhon, Susan T., jt. auth. see Wilkinson, Tony J.
Duhoux, Yves. L' Eteocretois: Les Textes - la Langue. (FRE., Illus.). viii, 335p. (C). 1982. 84.00 (*90-70265-05-2*, Pub. by Gieben) J Benjamins Pubng Co.
Duhring, Nathan. Immortality: Physically, Scientifically, Now: A Reasonable Guarantee of Bodily Preservation, a General Discussion, & Research Targets. 101p. 1991. pap. 11.95 (*1-880209-01-2*) Alcor Life Ext.
Duibhir, Ciaran O. Sinn Fein: The First Election, 1908. O'Duignean, Prionnsias, ed. (North Leitrim History Ser.). (Illus.). 52p. (Orig.). 1994. pap. 9.95 (*1-873437-02-1*, Pub. by Drumlin Pubns Ltd) Irish Bks Media.
Duich, Katarina, ed. see Salay, Cathy.

D

*Duie, Antione. Motives: Stories That Tell Why. 180p. 2000. pap. 18.00 (0-7388-2197-7) Xlibris Corp.

Duifhuis, H., et al, eds. Basic Issues in Hearing: Proceedings of the Eighth International Symposium on Hearing, Groningen. 470p. 1988. text 84.00 (0-12-223346-8) Acad Pr.

Duifhuis, H & Van Netten, S. Biophysics of Hair Cell S. 432p. 1993. text 121.00 (981-02-1522-3) World Scientific Pub.

*Duignan, Nancy. The Rhyme of My Life. LC 99-70718. (Illus.). 112p. 1999. pap. 10.00 (1-878149-45-8) Counterpoint Pub.

Duignan, P. A. & Macpherson, R. J., eds. Educative Leadership: A Practical Theory for Educational Administrators & Managers. 198p. 1992. 89.95 (0-7507-0058-0, Falmer Pr); pap. 34.95 (0-7507-0059-9, Falmer Pr) Taylor & Francis.

Duignan, Patricia R., jt. auth. see Vaz, Mark C.

Duignan, Peter. Bilingual Education: A Critique. LC 98-34869. (Hoover Essays Ser.: No. 22). 1998. pap. 5.00 (0-8179-3852-4) Hoover Inst Pr.

*Duignan, Peter. NATO: A History. LC 00-29567. 2000. write for info. (0-8179-9782-2) Hoover Inst Pr.

Duignan, Peter. The United States: A Hopeful Future. LC 93-12868. (Hoover Essays Ser.: No. 4). 50p. 1993. pap. 5.00 (0-8179-3672-6) Hoover Inst Pr.

Duignan, Peter, ed. The Library of the Hoover Institution on War, Revolution & Peace. LC 85-838. (Publication Ser.: No. 316). viii, 163p. 1985. lib. bdg. 22.95 (0-8179-8161-6) Hoover Inst Pr.

Duignan, Peter & Clendenen, Clarence. The United States & the African Slave Trade, 1619-1862. LC 77-20159. (Hoover Institution Studies). 72p. 1978. reprint ed. lib. bdg. 35.00 (0-313-20009-2, DUUS, Greenwood Pr) Greenwood.

Duignan, Peter & Gann, L. H. An Ambivalent Heritage: Euro-American Relations. LC 94-5916. (Hoover Essays Ser.: No. 7). 45p. 1994. pap. 5.00 (0-8179-3702-1) Hoover Inst Pr.
— Communism in Sub-Saharan Africa: A Reappraisal. LC 94-33511. (Hoover Essays Ser.: Vol. 8). 49p. 1994. pap. 5.00 (0-8179-3712-9) Hoover Inst Pr.
— Contemporary Europe & the Atlantic Alliance: A Political History. LC 97-3886. 448p. (C). 1997. text 83.95 (0-631-20589-6) Blackwell Pubs.
— Political Correctness: A Critique. LC 95-36921. (Hoover Essays Ser.: No. 11). 43p. 1995. pap. 5.00 (0-8179-3742-0) Hoover Inst Pr.
— The Rebirth of the West: The Americanization of the Democratic World, 1945-1958. 745p. (C). 1996. pap. text 29.95 (0-8476-8198-X) Rowman.

Duignan, Peter & Gann, L. H., eds. Colonialism in Africa, 1870-1960 Vol. 4: The Economics of Colonialism. (Publication Ser.: No. 127). 719p. 1975. reprint ed. pap. text 18.95 (0-8179-6272-7) Hoover Inst Pr.

Duignan, Peter & Gann, Lewis H., eds. Colonialism in Africa, 1870-1960, 5 vols. Incl. Vol. 5. Bibliography. 564p. 1974. text 139.95 (0-521-07859-8); write for info. (0-318-51277-7) Cambridge U Pr.
— The Debate in the United States over Immigration. LC 97-39555. (Publication Ser.: No. 444). 300p. 1997. pap. 19.95 (0-8179-9522-6) Hoover Inst Pr.

Duignan, Peter & Rabushka, Alvin, eds. The United States in the 1980s. LC 79-5475. (Publication Ser.: No. 228). 1980. 8.00 (0-8179-7281-1) Hoover Inst Pr.

Duignan, Peter, jt. auth. see Gann, L. H.

Duignan, Peter, jt. auth. see Gann, Lewis H.

Duignan, Peter, jt. auth. see Gunn, L. H.

Duignan, Peter J. & Gann, Lewis H. The Spanish Speakers in the United States: A History. LC 98-39212. 496p. 1998. pap. 39.50 (0-7618-1258-X) U Pr of Amer.

Duignan, Peter J., jt. ed. see Dorfman, Gerald A.

Duignan, P.R., jt. auth. see Vaz, M.C.

Duijker, Hubert C. Dictionnaire de Psychologie en Trois Langues, Vol. 2.Tr. of Dictionary of Psychology in 3 Languages. (ENG & GER.). 356p. 1977. ring bd. 165.00 (0-7859-4782-5, M4660) Fr & Eur.

Duijker, Hubert C. & Van Sijswijk, Maria. Dictionnaire de Psychologie en Trois Langues, 3 vols.Tr. of Dictionary of Psychology in 3 Languages. (ENG, FRE & GER.). 416p. 1977. ring bd. 165.00 (0-7859-0938-9, M-4661) Fr & Eur.

Duijker, Hubrecht. Alsace. (Wine Lover's Touring Guides Ser.). (Illus.). 144p. (Orig.). 1995. pap. 15.95 (1-85365-301-2, Pub. by Spectrum) Seven Hills Bk.
— Bordeaux: A Wine Lover's Touring Guide. (Illus.). 143p. 1998. pap. text 17.00 (0-7881-5967-4) DIANE Pub.
— Loire. (Wine Lover's Touring Guides Ser.). (Illus.). 144p. (Orig.). 1995. pap. 15.95 (1-85365-331-4, Pub. by Spectrum) Seven Hills Bk.
— Loire: A Wine Lover's Touring Guide. (Illus.). 143p. 1998. pap. text 17.00 (0-7881-5968-2) DIANE Pub.
— Touring in Wine Country: Burgundy. Johnson, Hugh, ed. 144p. 1996. pap. 21.95 (1-85732-580-X, Pub. by Reed Illust Books) Antique Collect.
— Touring in Wine Country: The Loire. Johnson, Hugh, ed. (Touring in Wine Country Ser.). (Illus.). 144p. 1997. pap. 21.95 (1-85732-876-0, Pub. by Mitchell Beazley) Antique Collect.

*Duijker, Hubrecht. Tuscany: Touring in Wine Country. rev. ed. (Touring in Wine Country Ser.). (Illus.). 144p. 2000. pap. text 21.95 (1-84000-247-6) Mitchell Beazley.
— The Wines of Chile. (Illus.). 240p. 2000. pap. 29.95 (90-274-6913-X, Pub. by Het Spec BV) Antique Collect.

*Duijker, Hubrecht & Ashley, Maureen. Bordeaux. rev. ed. (Touring in Wine Country Ser.). (Illus.). 144p. 2000. pap. text 21.95 (1-84000-246-8) Mitchell Beazley.
— Burgundy: Touring in Wine Country. rev. ed. (Touring in Wine Country Ser.). (Illus.). 144p. 2000. pap. text 21.95 (1-84000-245-X) Mitchell Beazley.

Duijker, Hubrecht & Broadbent, Michael. Bordeaux Wine Guide. 400p. 1998. text 50.00 (0-312-18276-7) St Martin.

Duijker, Hubrecht, jt. auth. see Johnson, Hugh.

Duijker, Hunbrecht. The Wine Atlas of Spain: And Traveller's Guide to the Vineyards. (Illus.). 240p. 1997. 45.00 (0-85533-910-1) Antique Collect.

Duijn, Bert V. & Wiltink, Anneke. Signal Transduction - Single Cell Techniques. LC 97-21326. (Springer Lab Manual Ser.). 300p. 1997. spiral bd. write for info. (3-540-62563-1) Spr-Verlag.

Duijn, Jacob J. The Long Wave in Economic Life. 240p. (C). 1983. text 37.95 (0-04-330330-7); pap. text 18.95 (0-04-330331-5) Routledge.

*Duijzings, Gerlachlus. Religion & the Politics of Identity in Kosovo. LC 00-23834. 2000. pap. write for info. (0-231-12099-0) Col U Pr.

*Duijzings, Gerlachus. Religion & the Politics of Identity in Kosovo. 2000. 27.50 (0-231-12098-2) Col U Pr.

Duiker. Duiker World History, Vol. 2. 1994. pap., student ed. 17.25 (0-314-04184-2) West Pub.

*Duiker. A History of East Asia. 2001. pap. 30.00 (0-534-56745-2) Thomson Learn.

Duiker. Reader for World History Vol. I: To 1800. 2nd ed. (History Ser.). 1998. pap. 23.95 (0-534-53122-9) Wadsworth Pub.
— Reader for World History Vol. II: Since 1500. 2nd ed. (History Ser.). 1998. pap. 23.95 (0-534-53123-7) Wadsworth Pub.
— 20th Century World. (History Ser.). 1998. pap. 11.00 (0-534-54874-1) Wadsworth Pub.

*Duiker. Twentieth Century World History. 2nd ed. 2001. pap. 26.00 (0-534-57879-9) Thomson Learn.

Duiker. World History. 2nd ed. 1999. mass mkt. 30.95 (0-314-22045-3) Wadsworth Pub.
— World History. 3rd ed. (History Ser.). 2000. 54.50 (0-534-57168-9) Wadsworth Pub.
— World History, Vol. I. 3rd ed. (History Ser.). 2000. 39.25 (0-534-57169-7) Wadsworth Pub.
— World History, Vol. II. 3rd ed. (History Ser.). 2000. 39.25 (0-534-57170-0) Wadsworth Pub.
— World History: Since 1500, Vol. 2. 2nd ed. (History). 1997. pap., wbk. ed. 8.75 (0-534-53125-3) Wadsworth Pub.
— World History: Testbank, Vol. 1. Date not set. pap. text, suppl. ed. write for info. (0-314-03271-1) West Pub.
— World History: Testbank, Vol. 2. Date not set. pap. text, teacher ed., suppl. ed. write for info. (0-314-03272-X) West Pub.
— World History Vol. I: To 1800. 2nd ed. (History Ser.). 1998. student ed. 15.25 (0-534-53128-8) Wadsworth Pub.
— World History Vol. II: Since 1500. 2nd ed. (History Ser.). 1998. student ed. 15.25 (0-534-53129-6) Wadsworth Pub.

*Duiker. World History in Brief. 2001. pap. 37.00 (0-534-57888-8) Thomson Learn.

Duiker. World History Since 1500, Vol. 2. 2nd ed. (History Ser.). 1998. pap., wbk. ed. 8.75 (0-534-53127-X) Wadsworth Pub.
— World History to 1500. 3rd ed. (History Ser.). 2000. 33.25 (0-534-57171-9) Wadsworth Pub.

*Duiker & Spielvogel. World History, Vol. 1. 3rd ed. (History Ser.). 2000. 17.25 (0-534-57173-5) Wadsworth Pub.
— World History, Vol. 2. 3rd ed. (History Ser.). 2000. 17.25 (0-534-57174-3) Wadsworth Pub.

Duiker & Spielvogel, Jackson J. Study Tips for World History, Vol. 1. 2nd ed. (History Ser.). 1998. pap. 5.25 (0-534-53138-5) Wadsworth Pub.
— Study Tips For World History,volume Ii: Since 1500, Vol. II. 2nd ed. (History). 1998. mass mkt. 5.25 (0-534-53144-X) Wadsworth Pub.

Duiker, William. Vietnam since the Fall of Saigon. 3rd rev. ed. LC 89-39990. (Monographs in International Studies, Southeast Asia Ser.: No. 56A). 401p. 1989. pap. 20.00 (0-89680-162-4) Ohio U Pr.

Duiker, William J. China & Vietnam: The Roots of Conflict. LC 86-81534. (Indochina Research Monographs: No. 1). 136p. 1986. pap. 10.00 (0-912966-89-0) IEAS.
— The Communist Road to Power in Vietnam. LC 80-22098. (Special Studies on South & Southeast Asia). 394p. 1981. text 46.00 (0-89158-794-2) Westview.
— The Communist Road to Power in Vietnam. 2nd ed. (C). 1996. pap. 35.00 (0-8133-8587-3, Pub. by Westview) HarpC.
— Historical Dictionary of Vietnam. LC 88-29721. (Asian Historical Dictionaries Ser.: No. 1). (Illus.). 285p. 1989. 34.50 (0-8108-2164-8) Scarecrow.
— Historical Dictionary of Vietnam. 2nd ed. LC 97-21952. (Asian/Oceanian Historical Dictionaries Ser.). 1997. 68.00 (0-8108-3351-4) Scarecrow.
— Ho Chi Minh. (Illus.). 704p. 2000. 35.00 (0-7868-6387-0, Pub. by Hyperion) Time Warner.
— Introduction to Vietnam: Land, History & Culture. rev. ed. Starr, Jerold M., ed. (Lessons of the Vietnam War Ser.). (Illus.). 32p. (C). 1991. pap. text 5.00 (0-945919-01-8) Ctr Social Studies.
— Sacred War: Nationalism & Revolution in a Divided Vietnam. LC 94-14473. 256p. (C). 1994. 22.81 (0-07-018030-X) McGraw.
— Twentieth Century World History. LC 98-39244. 400p. 1998. pap. 37.95 (0-534-54873-3) Wadsworth Pub.
— U. S. Containment Policy & the Conflict in Indochina. LC 93-41544. xii, 453p. 1994. 52.50 (0-8047-2283-8) Stanford U Pr.
— Vietnam: Revolution in Transit. 2nd ed. (Nations of the Modern World Ser.). (C). 1995. pap. 25.00 (0-8133-8589-X, Pub. by Westview) HarpC.
— Vietnam since the Fall of Saigon. rev. ed. LC 85-18912. (Monographs in International Studies, Southeast Asia Ser.: No. 56). 280p. reprint ed. pap. 86.80 (0-7837-6475-8, 204647900001) Bks Demand.

Duiker, William J. & Spielvogel, Jackson J. World History, 2 vols., Set. Baxter, ed. LC 93-36207. 1050p. (C). 1994. text 63.00 (0-314-02844-7) West Pub.
— World History, 2 vols., Vol. I. Baxter, ed. LC 93-36207. 756p. (C). 1994. pap. text 46.50 (0-314-02845-5) West Pub.
— World History, 2 vols., Vol. II. Baxter, ed. LC 93-36207. 701p. (C). 1994. pap. text 46.50 (0-314-02846-3) West Pub.
— World History: Comprehensive Edition. 2nd ed. LC 97-40042. (History Ser.). (C). 1997. 88.95 (0-534-53121-0) Wadsworth Pub.
— World History: To 1500. Baxter, ed. 522p. (C). pap. text 39.00 (0-314-03763-2) West Pub.
— World History: To 1500. 2nd ed. (History Ser.). 500p. (C). 1997. 53.95 (0-534-53120-2) Wadsworth Pub.
— World History Vol. I: To 1800. 2nd ed. (History Ser.). 724p. (C). 1997. 63.95 (0-534-53118-0) Wadsworth Pub.
— World History Vol. II: Since 1500. 2nd ed. (History Ser.). 1174p. (C). 1997. pap. 63.95 (0-534-53119-9) Wadsworth Pub.

Duin, Ann H. & Hansen, Craig J., eds. Nonacademic Writing: Social Theory & Technology. 344p. 1995. pap. 36.50 (0-8058-1628-3); text 89.95 (0-8058-1627-5) L Erlbaum Assocs.

Duin, Julia. Three Golden Looms. (Illus.). 128p. (J). 1997. 12.99 (0-7814-0013-9, Chariot Bks) Chariot Victor.
— Waiting for True Love: And Other Tales of Purity, Patience & Faithfulness. LC 97-36593. (Illus.). 96p. (J). (gr. k-2). 1997. 12.99 (0-7459-3816-7, Lion) Chariot Victor.

Duin, Spencer, et al. Case Studies of Just-in-Time Implementation at Westinghouse & IBM. American Production & Inventory Control Society St, ed. LC 86-71914. 50p. 1986. pap. 15.00 (0-935406-82-4) Am Prod & Inventory.

Duin, Steve & Richardson, Mike. Comics Between the Panels. LC 99-168704. 504p. 1998. 49.95 (1-56971-344-8) Dark Horse Comics.

Duina, Francesco G. Harmonizing Europe: Nation-States Within the Common Market. LC 98-30737. (SUNY Series in Global Politics). (Illus.). 176p. (C). 1999. pap. text 18.95 (0-7914-4178-4) State U NY Pr.
— Harmonizing Europe: The Global Market & the Endurance of History. LC 98-30737. (SUNY Series in Global Politics). 5p. (C). 1999. text 57.50 (0-7914-4177-6) State U NY Pr.

Duindam, Jeroen. Myths of Power: Norbert Elias & the Early-Modern European Court. 200p. (C). 1994. pap. 39.50 (90-5356-136-6, Pub. by Amsterdam U Pr); text 62.50 (90-5356-111-0, Pub. by Amsterdam U Pr) U of Mich Pr.

Duindam, S. Military Conscription: An Economic Analysis of the Labour Component in the Armed Forces. (Contributions to Economics Ser.). (Illus.). viii, 202p. 1999. pap. 53.00 (3-7908-1203-X) Spr-Verlag.

Duine, J. A., jt. ed. see Jongejan, J. A.

Duine, J. A., jt. ed. see Verseveld, H. W.

*Duinen, Martin T. Van. The Transorbital Intracranial Penetrating Injury. LC 99-40694. 1999. write for info. (0-7923-5915-1) Kluwer Academic.

Duininck, Guy. Grace for Powerful Christian Living. (Orig.). 1987. pap. 6.00 (0-929400-02-X) Masters Touch Pub Co.
— How to Harness a Vision. 50p. (Orig.). 1988. pap. 5.00 (0-929400-00-3) Masters Touch Pub Co.
— Praying for the Harvest. rev. ed. (Illus.). 163p. 1997. pap. 8.00 (0-929400-04-6) Masters Touch Pub Co.
— True or False? Judging Doctrine & Leadership. 509p. 1992. 15.95 (0-929400-03-8) Masters Touch Pub Co.

Duinker, J. C., jt. ed. see Kramer, C. J.

Duis, Perry R. Saloon: Public Drinking in Chicago & Boston, 1880-1920. 416p. 1999. pap. text 21.95 (0-252-06781-9) U of Ill Pr.

Duis, E. Good Old Times in McLean County Illinois, 2 vols. (Illus.). xviii, 940p. 1993. reprint ed. pap. text 53.00 (1-55613-694-3) Heritage Bk.

Duis, Perry. Challenging Chicago: Coping with Everyday Life, 1837-1920. LC 97-45252. (Illus.). 1998. 29.95 (0-252-02394-3) U of Ill Pr.

Duis, Perry & LaFrance, Scott. We've Got a Job to Do: Chicagoans & World War II. LC 92-14491. (Illus.). 152p. 1992. pap. 22.95 (0-913820-17-2) Chicago Hist.

Duis, Robin L. Cockatiel Color Genetics: Advanced Topics. (Illus.). 38p. (C). 1989. pap. text. write for info. (0-318-66536-0, 1020) Starbird Pubns.

Duisit, Lionel. Satire, Parodie, Calembour: Esquisse d'une Theorie des Devalues. (Stanford French & Italian Studies: No. 11). (FRE.). vi, 164p. 1978. pap. 56.50 (0-915838-26-5) Anma Libri.

Duisit, Vivian, ed. see Bailey, Richard, et al.

Duisit, Vivian, ed. see Polk, Dean L.

Duistermaat, H. Gorteria Supplement 3: Monograph of Arctium L. (Asteraceae) (Gorteria Ser.: No. 3). (Illus.). 143p. 1996. pap. 28.00 (90-71236-28-5, Pub. by Rijksherbarium) Balogh.

Duistermaat, J. J. The Heat Kernel Lefschetz Fixed Point Formula for the Spin-C Dirac Operator. LC 95-25828. (Progress in Nonlinear Differential Equations & Their Applications Ser.: Vol. 18). 247p. 1995. 42.50 (0-8176-3865-2) Birkhauser.

*Duistermaat, J. J. & Kolk, Johan A. C. Lie Groups. LC 99-50197. (Universitext Ser.). viii, 334p. 2000. pap. 48.00 (3-540-15293-8) Spr-Verlag.

Duistermaat, Johannes J. Fourier Integral Operators. (Progress in Mathematics Ser.: Vol. 130). 1995. write for info. (3-7643-3821-0) Birkhauser.
— Fourier Integral Operators. (Progress in Mathematics Ser.: Vol. 130). 142p. 1995. 42.50 (0-8176-3821-0) Birkhauser.

Duit, Reinders, jt. ed. see Glynn, Shawn M.

Duits, Carrie & Dorman, Adelle. Reaching Through Reading: Service Learning Adventures in Literature. LC 98-11045. (Illus.). 200p. 1998. pap. 23.00 (1-56308-514-3) Libs Unl.

Duits, Henk, ed. see Spies, Marijke.

Duivenvoorden, J. F. & Lips, J. M. A Land-Ecological Study of Soils, Vegetation, & Plant Diversity in Colombian Amazonia. (Tropenbos Technical Ser.: No. 12). (Illus.). 438p. 1995. pap. 80.00 (90-5113-024-4, Pub. by Backhuys Pubs) Balogh.

Duivenvoorden, J. F., jt. auth. see Lammerts Van Bueren, E. M.

Duivesteijn, Adri. The Hidden Assignment. 120p. Date not set. pap. 24.95 (90-72469-76-3) Dist Art Pubs.

*Dujardin. Business Organization & Leadership. 2nd ed. 1999. 52.00 (0-07-432697-X) McGraw.

Dujardin, Edouard. Ancient History of the God Jesus. 172p. 1993. spiral bd. 21.00 (0-7873-0300-3) Hlth Research.
— The Bays Are Sere Followed by Interior Monologue. (FRE.). 160p. 1991. text 37.50 (1-870352-70-X, Pub. by Libris) Paul & Co Pubs.
— Mallarme par un des Siens. LC 77-10259. reprint ed. 39.50 (0-404-16314-9) AMS Pr.
— We'll to the Woods No More. Gilbert, Stuart, tr. from FRE. LC 89-13019. Vol. 682. (Illus.). 176p. 1990. pap. 9.95 (0-8112-1113-4, NDP682, Pub. by New Directions) Norton.

*Dujarric, Robert. Korean Unification & After: The Challenge for U. S. Strategy. 106p. (C). 2000. pap. 16.95 (1-55813-070-5) Hudson Instit IN.

Dujarric, Robert, jt. auth. see Odom, William E.

Dujarrie, Robert, ed. Korea: Pivot of Security in Northeast Asia. 165p. 1997. pap. 12.95 (1-55813-064-0) Hudson Instit IN.

Dujcev, Ivan, intro. Bdinski Zbornik: Old Slavic Menologium A. D. 1360. 484p. (C). 1972. reprint ed. 123.95 (0-902089-40-4, Pub. by Variorum) Ashgate Pub Co.

Dujon, Diane & Withorn, Ann, eds. For Crying Out Loud: Women's Poverty in the United States. LC 96-30126. 414p. 1996. 40.00 (0-89608-530-9) South End Pr.
— For Crying Out Loud: Women's Poverty in the United States. 2nd ed. LC 96-30126. 414p. 1996. pap. 22.00 (0-89608-529-5) South End Pr.

Duk-Soo Park, jt. ed. see Lee, Sang-Oak.

Dukarich. Virtuoso WordPerfect 6.1. LC 96-215366. (C). 1995. pap. text 39.16 (0-395-74880-1) HM.

Dukarich, Cheryl L. Virtuoso Microsoft Word 6.0 for Windows: Assistant Tutorial. (C). 1996. text 10.47 (0-395-75939-0) HM.
— Virtuoso Microsoft Word 6.0 for Windows. 528p. (C). 1995. spiral bd. 42.76 incl. 3.5 hd (0-395-73788-5) HM.
— Virtuoso Microsoft Word 6.0 for Windows. (C). 1996. text, teacher ed. 11.96 (0-395-75938-2) HM.
— Virtuoso WordPerfect 6.1 for Windows: Assistant Tutorial. (C). 1996. text 10.47 (0-395-75940-4) HM.
— Virtuoso WordPerfect 6.1 for Windows. 560p. (C). 1995. spiral bd. 42.76 incl. 3.5 hd (0-395-73789-3) HM.
— Virtuoso WordPerfect 6.1 for Windows. (C). 1996. text, teacher ed. 11.96 (0-395-77447-0) HM.

Dukas. Cognitive Ecology. LC 97-36597. 420p. 1998. pap. text 30.00 (0-226-16933-2) U Ch Pr.

Dukas & Chabrier. Dukas' "The Sorcerer's Apprentice" & Charbrier's "Espana" in Full Score. 1998. pap. 11.95 (0-486-29826-4) Dover.

Dukas, Helen & Hoffmann, Banesh, eds. Albert Einstein, the Human Side: New Glimpses from His Archives. 176p. 1979. pap. 14.95 (0-691-02368-9, Pub. by Princeton U Pr) Cal Prin Full Svc.

Dukas, Helen, jt. auth. see Hoffmann, Banesh.

Dukas, P. Sorcerer's Apprentice: For the Piano. 28p. 1992. pap. 5.95 (0-7935-1745-1) H Leonard.

*Dukas, Reuven, ed. Cognitive Ecology. LC 97-36597. (Illus.). 448p. 1998. lib. bdg. 95.00 (0-226-16932-4) U Ch Pr.

Dukas, Vytas, ed. from RUS. Twelve Contemporary Russian Stories. LC 74-4969. 130p. 1977. 25.00 (0-8386-1491-4) Fairleigh Dickinson.

Duke. Biologically Active Phytochemicals & Their Activities Database. 28p. 1992. lib. bdg. 273.95 (0-8493-3671-6, TK) CRC Pr.
— Database of Phytochemical Constituents - Grass Herbs. 28p. 1992. lib. bdg. 273.95 (0-8493-3673-2, TK) CRC Pr.
— The Elusive Quest for European Security. LC 99-15389. 2000. text 69.95 (0-312-22402-8) St Martin.
— Too Rich: The Family Secrets of Doris Duke. 1996. 25.00 (0-06-172185-9) Harper SF.

Duke & Besst. Handbook of Bookbinding & Conservation. 42.95 (1-85928-047-1) Ashgate Pub Co.

Duke, Betty D. Jesse James Lived & Died in Texas. LC 98-48126. (Illus.). 248p. 1998. 21.95 (1-57168-287-2) Sunbelt Media.

Duke, A., jt. auth. see Stark, B.

Duke, A. H. & Gray, W. M. The Boatbuilders of Muskoka. (Illus.). 154p. reprint ed. pap. 29.95 (1-55046-074-9, Pub. by Boston Mills) Genl Dist Srvs.

Duke, Alastair. Reformation & Revolt in the Low Countries. 330p. 1991. 60.00 (1-85285-021-3) Hambledon Press.

Duke, Alastair, tr. see Lewis, Gillian & Pettegree, Andrew, eds.

Duke, Alex. Importing Oxbridge: English Residential Colleges & American Universities. LC 96-16980. 224p. 1997. 32.00 (0-300-06761-5) Yale U Pr.

Duke, Annette R., et al, eds. Legal Tactics: Self-Defense for Tenants in Massachusetts. LC 92-82124. 576p. 1993. pap. text 29.00 (0-944490-51-4) Mass CLE.

Duke, Barbara. Panache at Rose Hill. 1998. pap. text 14.95 (*0-9658397-0-2*) Panache Rose Hill.

Duke-Barbara, Brenda. Granny Grimes Visits. 70p. (YA). (gr. 5 up). 1998. pap. 5.99 (*1-57502-927-8*, PO2557) Morris Pubng.

Duke-Barber, Brenda. Come Spring. (Seasons of Love Ser.: No. 2). 176p. (Orig.). 1997. pap. 7.99 (*1-57502-499-3*, P01487) Morris Pubng.

— Hope of Autumn. 176p. 1998. pap. 7.99 (*1-57502-767-4*, PO2226) Morris Pubng.

***Duke-Barber, Brenda.** Love Mends a Broken Heart. 200p. 1999. pap. 8.99 (*0-7392-0292-8*, PO3630) Morris Pubng.

Duke-Barber, Brenda. Love's Memories. 206p. 1998. pap. 8.99 (*1-57502-929-4*, PO2556) Morris Pubng.

— A Summer of Love. (Season of Love Ser.: Bk. 3). 176p. 1997. pap. 7.99 (*1-57502-603-1*, PO1738) Morris Pubng.

Duke, Basil W. History of the Bank of Kentucky, 1792-1895. Bruchey, Stuart, ed. LC 80-1183. (Rise of Commercial Banking Ser.). (Illus.). 1981. reprint ed. lib. bdg. 17.95 (*0-405-13647-1*) Ayer.

— Reminiscences of General Basil W. Duke. 1997. write for info. (*1-57074-363-0*) Greyden Pr.

— Reminiscences of General Basil W. Duke, C. S. A. (Select Bibliographies Reprint Ser.). 1977. 36.95 (*0-8369-5150-6*) Ayer.

Duke, Benjamin C. Education & Leadership for the Twenty-First Century: Japan, America, & Britain. LC 90-28074. 184p. 1991. 52.95 (*0-275-93986-3*, C3986, Praeger Pubs) Greenwood.

Duke, Benjamin C., ed. Ten Educators from Japan: A Japanese Perspective. (Illus.). 200p. 1990. 42.50 (*0-86008-442-6*, Pub. by U of Tokyo) Col U Pr.

Duke, Benjamin C. O. The Japanese School: Lessons for Industrial America. LC 86-5002. 265p. 1986. 55.00 (*0-275-92053-4*, C2053, Praeger Pubs); pap. 22.95 (*0-275-92003-8*, B2003, Praeger Pubs) Greenwood.

Duke, Betty La, see La Duke, Betty.

Duke, Bill J. Smart Parenting: A Guide to Child Assessment & Therapeutic Interventions. 352p. (Orig.). 1996. pap. 19.95 (*0-9648838-3-X*) DCC Pubng.

Duke, C. B. Surface Science: The First Thirty Years. 1064p. 1994. pap. 59.75 (*0-444-81827-8*, North Holland) Elsevier.

Duke, C. B., ed. Surface Science: The First Thirty Years. 1064p. 1994. 123.50 (*0-444-81813-8*, North Holland) Elsevier.

Duke, Charles R. Writing Through Experience: A Process Approach. (C). 1997. 43.00 (*0-673-39208-2*) Addson-Wesley Educ.

Duke, Charles R. & Jacobsen, Sally A., eds. Poets' Perspectives: Reading, Writing & Teaching Poetry. LC 92-8499. 256p. (J). 1992. pap. text 18.50 (*0-86709-304-8*, 0304, Pub. by Boynton Cook Pubs) Heinemann.

Duke, Charles R., jt. ed. see Simpson, Robert J.

Duke, Chris. The Learning University: Towards a New Paradigm? (Cutting Edge Ser.). 160p. 1992. pap. 34.95 (*0-335-15653-3*) OpUniv Pr.

Duke, Chris, ed. Adult Education: International Perspectives from China. 272p. 1986. 37.50 (*0-7099-4509-4*, Pub. by C Helm) Routldge.

Duke, Cordia S. & Frantz, Joe B. Six Thousand Miles of Fence: Life on the XIT Ranch of Texas. (M. K. Brown Range Life Ser.: No. 1). (Illus.). 285p. (C). 1992. reprint ed. pap. 15.95 (*0-292-77564-4*) U of Tex Pr.

Duke, Cynthia. Element 115. 610p. mass mkt. 6.99 (*1-55197-310-3*) Picasso Publ.

Duke, D. J., et al, eds. BCS-FACS Northern Formal Methods Workshop: Proceedings of the BCS-FACS Northern Formal Methods Workshop, Ilkley, U. K., 23-24 September 1996. (Electronic Workshops in Computing Ser.). vi, 10p. 1997. pap. 59.95 (*3-540-76117-9*) Spr-Verlag.

Duke, D. J. & Evans, A. S., eds. 2nd BCS-FACS Northern Formal Methods Workshop: Proceedings of the 2nd BCS-FACS Northern Formal Methods Workshop, Ilkley, U. K., 14-15 July, 1997. (Electronic Workshops in Computing Ser.). vi, 11p. 1997. pap. 59.95 (*3-540-76215-9*) Spr-Verlag.

***Duke, D. J. & Puerta, A., eds.** Design, Specification & Verification of Interactive Systems '99: Proceedings of the Eurographics Workshop in Braga, Portugal, June 2-4, 1999. (Eurographics Ser.). (Illus.). ix, 280p. 1999. pap. 69.95 (*3-211-83405-2*) Spr-Verlag.

Duke, D. W., ed. Advances in Lattice Gauge Theories: Proceedings of the Conference on Advances in Lattice Gauge Theories, Tallahassee, Florida, April 10-13, 1985. 460p. 1985. 100.00 (*9971-5-0030-2*) World Scientific Pub.

Duke, D. W., et al, eds. Proceedings of the Conference on Measuring Chaos in the Human Brain, April 3-5, 1991, at the Supercomputer Computations Research Institute, Florida State University, Tallahassee, FL. LC 92-23707. 250p. (C). 1991. text 89.00 (*981-02-0701-8*) World Scientific Pub.

Duke, D. W. & Owens, J. F., eds. Perturbative Quantum Chromodynamics: Tallahassee, 1981. (AIP Conference Proceedings Ser.: No. 74). 477p. 1981. lib. bdg. 34.75 (*0-88318-173-8*) Am Inst Physics.

Duke, Daniel L. School Leadership & Instructional Improvement. 304p. (C). 1986. pap. 53.44 (*0-07-554970-0*) McGraw.

— The School That Refused to Die: Continuity & Change at Thomas Jefferson High School. LC 94-10030. (SUNY Series, Educational Leadership). 291p. (C). 1994. pap. text 20.95 (*0-7914-2332-8*) State U NY Pr.

— The School That Refused to Die: Continuity & Change at Thomas Jefferson High School. LC 94-10030. (SUNY Series, Educational Leadership). 291p. (C). 1995. text 57.50 (*0-7914-2331-X*) State U NY Pr.

— Teaching: An Introduction. 352p. (C). 1990. 57.19 (*0-07-557193-5*) McGraw.

— Teaching-The Imperiled Profession. LC 83-18181. 174p. (C). 1984. text 19.50 (*0-87395-788-1*) State U NY Pr.

Duke, Daniel L., ed. Helping Teachers Manage Classrooms. fac. ed. LC 82-70273. (Illus.). 173p. 1982. reprint ed. pap. 53.70 (*0-608-01026-X*, 2082502) Bks Demand.

— Teacher Evaluation Policy: From Accountability to Professional Development. LC 95-11832. (SUNY Series, Educational Leadership). 203p. (C). 1995. text 57.50 (*0-7914-2791-9*); pap. text 18.95 (*0-7914-2792-7*) State U NY Pr.

Duke, Daniel L. & Canady, Robert Lynn. School Policy. 224p. (C). 1991. 41.88 (*0-07-018028-8*) McGraw.

Duke, Daniel L. & Meckel, Adrienne M. Managing Student Behavior Problems. LC 80-10443. 206p. reprint ed. pap. 63.90 (*0-7837-1197-2*, 204172700023) Bks Demand.

Duke, Daniel L., jt. ed. see Stiggins, Richard J.

Duke, David. My Awakening: A Path to Racial Understanding. LC 98-86509. (Illus.). 736p. 1998. 29.95 (*1-892796-00-7*) Free Speech Pr.

Duke, David C. John Reed. (United States Authors Ser.: No. 516). 184p. 1987. 24.95 (*0-8057-7502-1*) Macmillan.

***Duke, David J., et al.** Premo: A Framework for Multimedia Middleware: Specification, Rationale & Java Binding. LC 99-52205. (Lecture Notes in Computer Science Ser.: Vol. 1591). xii, 254p. 1999. pap. 42.00 (*3-540-66720-2*) Spr-Verlag.

***Duke, Donald.** Electric Railways Around San Francisco Bay. LC 99-46646. 72p. 1999. 24.95 (*0-87095-115-7*) Gldn West Bks.

Duke, Donald. Incline Railways of Los Angeles & Southern California. LC 98-41927. (Illus.). 256p. 1998. 39.95 (*0-87095-114-9*) Gldn West Bks.

— Santa Fe Vol. 2: The Railroad Gateway to the American West: Passenger & Freight Service, the Harvey System, Steam & Diesel Locomotive, Etc. LC 95-21413. (Illus.). 268p. 1997. 59.95 (*0-87095-110-6*) Gldn West Bks.

Duke, Donald, jt. auth. see Krause, John.

Duke, Donald, ed. see Simburger, Edward J.

Duke, Drue. Alabama Tales: Anecdotes, Legends, & Stories from the Past. LC 93-32590. (Illus.). 168p. (Orig.). 1994. pap. 9.95 (*0-9630700-5-3*) Vision AL.

Duke, Dulcie. The Growth of a Medieval Town. 2nd ed. (Cambridge Introduction to World History Topic Bks.). (Illus.). 48p. (YA). (gr. 7 up). 1988. pap. 12.95 (*0-521-33725-9*) Cambridge U Pr.

Duke, E. A., ed. see Plato.

Duke, Elizabeth. Fair Trial. large type ed. 278p. 1994. 27.99 (*0-7505-0605-9*, Pub. by Mgna Lrg Print) Ulverscroft.

— The Husband Dilemma. (Romance Ser.: No. 417). 1999. mass mkt. 3.50 (*0-373-17417-9*, 1-17417-6) Harlequin Bks.

— Island Deception. large type ed. (Magna Large Print Ser.). 277p. 1997. 27.99 (*0-7505-1132-X*) Ulverscroft.

— Look-Alike Fiancee. (Romance Ser.: Vol. 395). 1998. mass mkt. 3.50 (*0-373-17395-4*, 1-17395-4) Harlequin Bks.

— Make-Believe Family. large type ed. 288p. 1996. 23.99 (*0-263-14383-X*, Pub. by Mills & Boon) Ulverscroft.

— Mariage a l'Improviste. (Azur Ser.: Vol. 753). (FRE.). 1999. mass mkt. 3.50 (*0-373-34753-7*, 1-34753-3) Harlequin Bks.

— Taming a Husband. (Australians Ser.: Bk. 11). 1999. per. 4.50 (*0-373-82583-8*, 1-82583-5, Harlequin) Harlequin Bks.

— To Catch a Playboy. large type ed. (Silhouette Ser.). 1996. 20.95 (*0-263-14417-8*) Mac Lib Ref.

— Wild Temptation. (Romance Ser.: No. 200). 1992. per. 2.89 (*0-373-03200-5*, 1-03200-2) Harlequin Bks.

Duke, Evelyn, ed. see Smith, Andy & Ward, Kirby.

Duke, Gerald R. Uncle Sam's Assassination Conspiracy. LC 92-93913. 100p. (Orig.). 1993. pap. write for info. (*0-9635221-0-8*) G R Duke.

Duke, Gordon L., et al. Behavior of Test Statistics in the Auditing Environment: An Empirical Study, Vol. 23. LC 85-72129. (Studies in Accounting Research). 178p. 1985. 12.00 (*0-86539-057-6*) Am Accounting.

Duke, Harvey. The Official Price Guide to Pottery & Porcelain. 8th ed. (Illus.). 512p. 1995. pap. 18.00 (*0-87637-893-9*) Hse Collectbls.

— Pottery & Porcelain. 9th ed. 1999. write for info. (*0-676-60091-3*) Hse Collectbls.

— Stangl Pottery. LC 92-50192. (Illus.). 168p. 1992. pap. 19.95 (*0-87069-674-2*) Krause Pubns.

Duke, J. Liaison Ways of a Woman. 1996. mass mkt. 6.95 (*0-7472-5443-5*, Pub. by Headline Bk Pub) Trafalgar.

— Seven Days. mass mkt. 6.95 (*0-7472-5094-4*, Pub. by Headline Bk Pub) Trafalgar.

Duke, J. A. Isthmian Ethnobotanical Dictionary. (C). 1988. 120.00 (*0-7855-2265-4*, Pub. by Scientific) St Mut.

Duke, Jacqueline, ed. see Ball, Michael.

Duke, Jacqueline, ed. see Blood-Horse Staff.

Duke, Jacqueline, ed. see Cable, Christina S.

Duke, Jacqueline, ed. see Holland, Robert.

Duke, Jacqueline, ed. see Livingston, Barbara D.

Duke, Jacqueline, ed. see Redden, Ric.

Duke, Jacqueline, ed. see Schweizer, Christina S.

Duke, Jacqueline, ed. see Squires, E. L.

Duke, James. In the Words of Our Mother. 60p. (Orig.). 1996. pap. text 9.95 (*1-887472-04-5*) Sunstar Pubng.

Duke, James, tr. see Schleiermacher, Friedrich Daniel Ernst.

***Duke, James A.** Dr. Duke's Essential Herbs: 13 Vital Herbs You Need to Disease Proof Your Body. (Illus.). 272p. 2000. pap. 14.95 (*1-57954-340-5*, Rodale Reach) Rodale Pr Inc.

— Dr Duke's Essential Herbs: The Only Herbs You Need to Disease-Proof Your Body, Boost You Energy, & Lengthen Your Life. (Illus.). 240p. 1999. 24.95 (*1-57954-183-6*) Rodale Pr Inc.

— La Farmacia Natural. 2000. pap. text 17.95 (*1-57954-262-X*) Rodale Pr Inc.

Duke, James A. Food Plants of North American Indians. Date not set. 40.00 (*0-8493-3663-5*) CRC Pr.

— Ginseng: A Concise Handbook. LC 88-35673. 1990. text 45.00 (*0-917256-32-8*) Ref Pubns.

— The Green Pharmacy. LC 97-6175. 528p. 1997. text 29.95 (*0-87596-316-1*) St Martin.

— The Green Pharmacy: New Discoveries in Herbal Remedies for Common Diseases & Conditions from the World's Foremost Authority on Healing Herbs. 507p. 1999. pap. 17.95 (*1-57954-124-0*) Rodale Pr Inc.

— The Green Pharmacy: The Ultimate Compendium of Natural Remedies from the World's Foremost Authority on Healing Herbs, Vol. 1. (Green Pharmacy Ser.). (Illus.). 617p. 1998. mass mkt. 7.99 (*0-312-96648-2*, Pub. by Tor Bks) St Martin.

***Duke, James A.** The Green Pharmacy Herbal Handbook: Your Comprehensive Reference to the Best Herbs for Healing. 2000. pap. 19.95 (*1-57954-184-4*, Rodale Reach) Rodale Pr Inc.

Duke, James A. Guide to Edible Weeds. 1999. pap. 17.95 (*0-375-70627-5*) Random.

— Handbook Biologically Active Phytochemicals & Their Activities. 208p. 1992. boxed set 156.95 (*0-8493-3670-8*, RM666) CRC Pr.

— Handbook of Agricultural Energy Potential in Developing Countries. 288p. 1987. lib. bdg. 32.95 (*0-8493-3644-9*) CRC Pr.

— Handbook of Agricultural Energy Potential of Developing Countries. 256p. 1987. lib. bdg. 32.95 (*0-8493-3642-2*); lib. bdg. 35.95 (*0-8493-3643-0*) CRC Pr.

— Handbook of Agricultural Energy Potential of Developing Countries, 4 vols., Set. 1045p. 1987. 99.00 (*0-8493-3640-6*, TP360) CRC Pr.

— Handbook of Edible Weeds. 256p. 1992. boxed set 62.95 (*0-8493-4225-2*, QK98) CRC Pr.

— Handbook of Legumes of World Economic Importance. LC 80-16421. (Illus.). 356p. 1981. 80.00 (*0-306-40406-0*, Plenum Trade) Perseus Pubng.

— Handbook of Medicinal Herbs. 696p. 1987. boxed set 393.95 (*0-8493-3630-9*, QP93) CRC Pr.

— Handbook of Medicinal Herbs. 2nd ed. Date not set. 125.00 (*0-8493-3631-7*) CRC Pr.

— Handbook of Northeastern Indian Medicinal Plants. LC 85-62814. (Bioactive Plants Ser.: Vol. 3). (Illus.). 212p. 1986. lib. bdg. 30.00 (*0-88000-142-9*) Quarterman.

— Herbs of the Bible: 2000 Years of Plant Medicine. LC 99-46121. 1999. 34.95 (*1-883010-66-7*, Pub. by Interweave) IPG Chicago.

— Isthmiam Ethnobotanical Dictionary. 3rd ed. 205p. (C). 1986. 410.00 (*81-85046-35-2*, Pub. by Scientific) St Mut.

— Isthmian Ethnobotanical Dictionary. (Illus.). 205p. 1986. text 72.00 (*0-318-32759-7*) Lubrecht & Cramer.

— Living Liqueurs. LC 85-62813. (Bioactive Plants Ser.: Vol. IV). (Orig.). 1987. pap. 15.00 (*0-88000-143-7*) Quarterman.

Duke, James A., compiled by. Handbook of Phytochemical Constituents of Grass Herbs & Other Economic Plants. 688p. 1992. boxed set 273.95 (*0-8493-3672-4*, SB351) CRC Pr.

Duke, James A., ed. Handbook of Nuts. 384p. 1988. lib. bdg. 239.00 (*0-8493-3636-8*, SF401) CRC Pr.

Duke, James A. & Achley, Alan A. Handbook of Proximate Analysis Tables of Higher Plants. 400p. 1986. 223.00 (*0-8493-3634-1*, TX557, CRC Reprint) Franklin.

Duke, James A. & Ayensu, Edward S. Medicinal Plants of China, 2 vols., Set. LC 84-4867. (Medicinal Plants of the World Ser.: No. 4). (Illus.). 1985. 99.00 (*0-917256-20-4*) Ref Pubns.

Duke, James A. & Beckstrom-Sternberg, Steve M. Handbook of Aromathematics (Mints) LC 96-8974. 480p. 1996. boxed set 169.95 (*0-8493-2665-6*) CRC Pr.

Duke, James A. & DuCellier, Judith L. CRC Handbook of Alternative Cash Crops. LC 93-25270. 544p. 1993. boxed set 187.95 (*0-8493-3620-1*, SB1111) CRC Pr.

Duke, James A. & Martinez, Rodolfo V. Amazonian Ethnobotanical Dictionary. LC 94-390. 224p. 1994. per. 57.95 (*0-8493-3664-3*) CRC Pr.

Duke, James A., et al. Ethnobotany in India. 1993. pap. 425.00 (*81-7233-066-9*, Pub. by Scientific Pubs) St Mut.

Duke, James A., jt. auth. see Foster, Steven.

Duke, James C., ed. Anesthesia Secrets. 2nd ed. (Secrets Ser.). 450p. 2000. text 39.00 (*1-56053-354-4*) Hanley & Belfus.

Duke, James C. & Rosenberg, Stuart G., eds. Anesthesia Secrets. LC 95-35457. (Secrets Ser.). (Illus.). 400p. 1995. pap. text 39.00 (*1-56053-153-3*) Hanley & Belfus.

Duke, James O. & Dunnavant, Tony L., eds. Christian Faith Seeking Understanding: Essays in Honor of H. Jack Forstmann. LC 97-31310. (C). 1997. text 40.00 (*0-86554-560-X*, MUP/H441) Mercer Univ Pr.

Duke, James O., jt. auth. see Stone, Howard W.

Duke, James O., jt. ed. see Toulouse, Mark G.

Duke, James T., ed. Latter-Day Saint Social Life, Vol. 12. LC 97-75396. 1998. 24.95 (*1-57008-396-7*) Bookcraft Inc.

Duke, Jas, et al. Industrial Woman. 205p. (C). 1990. 84.00 (*0-9590949-0-3*, Pub. by Pascoe Pub) St Mut.

Duke, Jerry. Recreational Dance Ballroom, Cajun & Country-Western. 110p. (C). 1996. pap. text 9.95 (*0-89641-277-6*) American Pr.

Duke, Kate. Archaeologists Dig for Clues. LC 95-10684. (Let's-Read-&-Find-Out Science Bks.: Level 2). (Illus.). 32p. (J). (gr. k-4). 1997. 15.95 (*0-06-027056-X*) HarpC Child Bks.

— Archaeologists Dig for Clues. LC 95-10684. (Let's-Read-&-Find-Out Science Bks.: Stage 2). (Illus.). 32p. (J). (gr. k-4). 1997. pap. 4.95 (*0-06-445175-5*, HarpTrophy) HarpC Child Bks.

— Archaeologists Dig for Clues. 2nd ed. LC 95-10684. (Let's-Read-&-Find-Out Science Bks.: Stage 2). (Illus.). 32p. (J). (gr. k-4). 1997. lib. bdg. 15.89 (*0-06-027057-8*) HarpC Child Bks.

Duke, Kate. Archaeologists Dig for Clues: Stage 2. (Let's Read-&-Find-Out Science Ser.). 1997. 10.15 (*0-606-11054-2*, Pub. by Turtleback) Demco.

Duke, Kate. Aunt Isabel Makes Trouble. 1999. pap. 5.99 (*0-14-056255-9*, PuffinBks) Peng Put Young Read.

— Aunt Isabel Tells a Good One. LC 91-14598. (Illus.). 32p. (J). (ps-2). 1992. 15.99 (*0-525-44835-7*, Dutton Child) Peng Put Young Read.

— Aunt Isabel Tells a Good One. 32p. (J). (ps-3). 1994. pap. 5.99 (*0-14-050534-2*, PuffinBks) Peng Put Young Read.

Duke, Kate. Aunt Isabel Tells a Good One. 1995. 10.19 (*0-606-07215-2*, Pub. by Turtleback) Demco.

Duke, Kate. Bedtime. LC 84-73140. (Guinea Pig Board Bks.). (Illus.). 10p. (J). (ps). 1986. pap. 5.99 (*0-525-44207-3*, Dutton Child) Peng Put Young Read.

— One Guinea Pig Is Not Enough. LC 97-21367. (Illus.). 48p. (J). 1998. 15.99 (*0-525-45918-9*, Dutton Child) Peng Put Young Read.

***Duke, Kate.** Twenty Is Too Many. LC 99-89376. (Illus.). (J). 2000. 15.99 (*0-525-42026-6*, Dutton Child) Peng Put Young Read.

Duke, Kate. What Bounces? LC 84-73138. (Guinea Pig Board Bks.). (Illus.). 10p. (J). (ps-2). 1986. pap. 5.99 (*0-525-44209-X*, Dutton Child) Peng Put Young Read.

Duke, Katherine. On the Brink of Ministry. unabridged ed. 1998. pap. 9.99 (*0-9666158-0-8*, 100) Marimae Publ.

Duke, Kenneth L., jt. auth. see Burnett-Balga, Beth.

Duke, Kerry. God at a Distance. LC 95-978. 1995. write for info. (*0-929540-19-0*) Pub Designs.

***Duke, Kerry.** My Sister's Keeper. LC 99-52032. 1999. pap. write for info. (*0-929540-23-9*) Pub Designs.

Duke, Kerry. Ox in the Ditch: Bible Interpretation As the Fundation of Christian Ethics. LC 93-24149. 1993. 6.95 (*0-929540-16-6*) Pub Designs.

Duke, L. Irene, jt. auth. see Hashway, Robert M.

Duke, Madelaine. Death at the Wedding. large type ed. (Linford Mystery Library). 249p. 1988. pap. 16.99 (*0-7089-6557-1*, Linford) Ulverscroft.

— Death of a Dandie Dinmont. large type ed. (Linford Mystery Library). 240p. 1988. pap. 16.99 (*0-7089-6614-4*, Linford) Ulverscroft.

— Death of a Holy Murderer. large type ed. (Linford Mystery Library). 224p. 1988. pap. 16.99 (*0-7089-6626-8*, Linford) Ulverscroft.

Duke, Marcus, ed. see Gilbert, John D.

***Duke, Marshall & Duke, Sara, eds.** What Works with Children: Wisdom & Reflections From People Who Have Devoted Their Careers to Kids. (Illus.). 2000. pap. 14.95 (*1-56145-200-9*) Peachtree Pubs.

Duke, Marshall, et al. Teaching Your Child the Language of Social Success. LC 96-4762. (Illus.). 192p. (Orig.). 1996. pap. 14.95 (*1-56145-126-6*) Peachtree Pubs.

Duke, Marshall, jt. auth. see Nowicki, Stephen, Jr.

Duke, Martin. The Development of Medical Techniques & Treatments: From Leeches to Heart Surgery. LC 90-4666. 270p. 1991. 37.50 (*0-8236-1232-5*) Intl Univs Pr.

— Tales My Stethoscope Told Me. LC 97-44275. (Illus.). 144p. 1998. pap. 10.00 (*1-56474-258-X*) Fithian Pr.

Duke, Mary A. Writing for "Real World" Reasons: A Ten Week Step-by-Step Outline for Writing, Producing & Performing Student's Original Works. LC 93-70816. (Illus.). 100p. (Orig.). 1993. pap. 18.95 (*1-883241-06-5*) Cognitive Pr.

Duke, Maurice. Chesapeake Bay Voices: Narratives from Four Centuries. (Illus.). 244p. 1993. pap. 19.95 (*0-87517-069-2*) Dietz.

— Chesapeake Bay Voices: Narratives of Four Centuries. (Illus.). 244p. 1993. 27.95 (*0-87517-077-3*) Dietz.

— Don't Carry Me Back: Narratives by Former Virginia Slaves. (Illus.). 180p. 1995. 19.95 (*0-87517-086-2*) Dietz.

Duke, Maurice, et al, eds. American Women Writers: Bibliographical Essays. LC 82-6156. 434p. 1983. lib. bdg. 49.95 (*0-313-22116-2*, DAW/, Greenwood Pr) Greenwood.

Duke, Maurice & Jordan, Daniel P., eds. A Richmond Reader, 1733-1983. LC 82-21921. 468p. reprint ed. pap. 145.10 (*0-608-20057-3*, 207132900011) Bks Demand.

— Tobacco Merchant: The Story of Universal Leaf Tobacco Company. LC 94-26776. 248p. 1994. lib. bdg. 27.50 (*0-8131-1892-1*) U Pr of Ky.

Duke Medical Center Child Development Staff. The Duke Guide to Baby's 1st Year. write for info. (*0-449-90317-6*) Fawcett.

Duke, Michael S. Blooming & Contending: Chinese Literature in the Post-Mao Era. LC 84-48641. (Studies in Chinese Literature & Society). 303p. pap. 94.00 (*0-608-05015-6*, 205967600004) Bks Demand.

Duke, Michael S., ed. Contemporary Chinese Literature: An Anthology of Post-Mao Fiction & Poetry. LC 85-10866. 138p. (gr. 13). 1985. pap. 34.95 (*0-87332-340-8*, East Gate Bk) M E Sharpe.

— Contemporary Chinese Literature: An Anthology of Post-Mao Fiction & Poetry. LC 85-10866. (Illus.). 143p. 1985. reprint ed. pap. 44.40 (*0-7837-9950-0*, 206067700006) Bks Demand.

— Modern Chinese Women Writers: Critical Appraisals. LC 89-36633. 290p. (gr. 13). 1989. 74.95 (*0-87332-536-2*, East Gate Bk); pap. 38.95 (*0-87332-623-7*, East Gate Bk) M E Sharpe.

— Worlds of Modern Chinese Fiction: Short Stories & Novellas from the People's Republic, Taiwan, & Hong Kong. LC 91-2564. 360p. (C). (gr. 13). 1991. 81.95 (*0-87332-757-8*, East Gate Bk); pap. 29.95 (*0-87332-758-6*, East Gate Bk) M E Sharpe.

D

An Asterisk (*) at the beginning of an entry indicates that the title is appearing for the first time.

Duke, Michael S., tr. Raise the Red Lantern. 272p. 1996. pap. 12.95 (*0-14-026030-7*) Viking Penguin.

Duke, Neville. Test Pilot. (Grub Street Aviation Classics Ser.). (Illus.). 224p. 1993. reprint ed. 29.95 (*0-948817-63-1*, Pub. by Grub St) Seven Hills Bk.

Duke, Neville & Lanchbery, Edward. Sound Barrier: The Story of High-Speed Flight. Gilbert, James B., ed. LC 79-7248. (Flight: Its First Seventy-Five Years Ser.). (Illus.). 1980. reprint ed. lib. bdg. 17.95 (*0-405-12160-1*) Ayer.

Duke of Bedford. The Neglected Issue: Some Essays on the Need for Monetary Reform. 1982. lib. bdg. 59.95 (*0-87700-355-6*) Revisionist Pr.

Duke of Windsor. A King's Story: The Memoirs of the Duke of Windsor. (Lost Treasures Ser.). (Illus.). 1999. pap. 24.95 (*1-85375-303-3*, Pub. by Prion) Trafalgar.

Duke, P. G. Points in Time: Structure & Event in a Late Northern Plains Hunting Society. LC 91-12002. (Illus.). 239p. 1991. reprint ed. pap. 74.10 (*0-608-08861-7*, 206950000004) Bks Demand.

Duke, P. J. & Michette, A. G. Modern Microscopies: Techniques & Applications. (Illus.). 266p. (C). 1989. text 102.00 (*0-306-43288-9*, Kluwer Plenum) Kluwer Academic.

Duke, Patricia, jt. auth. see Shepherd, Robert D.

Duke, Patty & Hochman, Gloria. A Brilliant Madness: Living with Manic-Depressive Illness. 368p. 1997. mass mkt. 7.50 (*0-553-56072-7*) Bantam.

Duke, Patty & Turan, Kenneth. Call Me Anna: The Autobiography of Patty Duke. 320p. 1988. mass mkt. 7.50 (*0-553-27205-5*) Bantam.

Duke, Paul, ed. see Johnson, Haynes.

***Duke, Philip.** Synchrotron Radiation: Production & Properties. (Oxford Series on Synchrotron Radiation: 3). (Illus.). 304p. 2000. text 120.00 (*0-19-851758-0*) OUP.

***Duke, Philip & Matlock, Gary.** Points, Pit Houses & Pioneers: Tracing Durango's Archaeological Past. 136p. 1999. 45.00 (*0-87081-519-9*) Univ Pr Colo.

— Points, Pithouses & Pioneers: Tracing Durango's Archaeological Past. 136p. 1999. pap. 24.95 (*0-87081-556-3*) Univ Pr Colo.

Duke, Philip & Matlock, Gary, eds. The State of Colorado Archaeology. (Memoir Ser.: No. 5). 1992. pap. text 12.95 (*1-888400-02-1*) Colo Archaeol.

Duke, Philip & Wilson, Michael C., eds. Beyond Subsistence: Plains Archaeology & the Postprocessual Critique. LC 94-11820. 320p. 1995. pap. text 29.95 (*0-8173-0799-0*) U of Ala Pr.

Duke Private Sector Conference Staff. The Academic Health Center & Health Care Reform: Proceedings of the Duke Private Sector Conference, 1994. Snyderman, Ralph et al, eds. LC 95-7174. (Illus.). 126p. reprint ed. pap. 39.10 (*0-608-09725-X*, 206989200007) Bks Demand.

Duke, Rebecca. A Journey Through Gloucestershire & the Cotswolds. (Journey Through...Ser.). (Illus.). 64p. (Orig.). 1994. pap. 8.95 (*0-7117-0607-7*) Seven Hills Bk.

— A Journey Through the Peak District. (Journey Through...Ser.). (Illus.). 64p. (Orig.). 1994. pap. 8.95 (*0-7117-0606-9*) Seven Hills Bk.

— A Journey Through Yorkshire. (Journey Through...Ser.). (Illus.). 64p. (Orig.). 1994. pap. 8.95 (*0-7117-0608-5*) Seven Hills Bk.

Duke, Robert A. Boat Renovation Guide. 2000. 34.95 (*0-07-135597-9*) McGraw.

Duke, Robert E. Holistic Health. 272p. 1985. 14.95 (*0-88282-011-7*) New Horizon NJ.

— How to Help Your Learning-Challenged Child Be a Winner. LC 92-63125. 160p. 1993. pap. 13.95 (*0-88282-076-1*) New Horizon NJ.

— Hypnotherapy for Troubled Children. 220p. 1984. text 29.95 incl. audio (*0-8290-1030-0*) Irvington.

— Hypnotherapy for Troubled Children. 1994. 14.95 (*0-88282-007-9*) New Horizon NJ.

Duke, Rodney K. The Persuasive Appeal of the Chronicler. (JSOT Supplement Ser.: No. 88). 192p. 1990. 57.50 (*1-85075-228-1*, Pub. by Sheffield Acad) CUP Services.

Duke, Romare. Hot Snake Nights: A Low Down Delta Blues Story. 320p. 1985. mass mkt. 5.99 (*0-87067-891-4*, Holloway House) Holloway.

Duke, Sandra Y. Gusty Winds May Exist. 36p. Date not set. pap. write for info. (*0-9659895-1-8*) Whiskey Light.

— Shots in the Morning. (Illus.). 53p. 1997. pap. 6.50 (*0-9659895-2-6*) Whiskey Light.

— Too Much Hallucinogenic Coffee. 34p. 1997. pap. 5.00 (*0-9659895-0-X*) Whiskey Light.

Duke, Sara, jt. ed. see Duke, Marshall.

Duke, Simon. The New European Security Disorder. LC 94-21686. 1994. text 59.95 (*0-312-12371-X*) St Martin.

Duke, Simon W. United States Military Forces & Installations in Europe. (SIPRI Publication). (Illus.). 462p. 1989. text 85.00 (*0-19-829132-9*) OUP.

Duke, Stephen O., ed. Herbicide-Resistant Crops: Agricultural, Economic, Environmental, Regulatory, & Technological Aspects. LC 95-43474. 432p. 1995. lib. bdg. 99.95 (*1-56670-045-0*, L1045) Lewis Pubs.

— Weed Physiology, Vol. I: Reproduction & Ecophysiology. 176p. 1985. lib. bdg. 159.00 (*0-8493-6313-6*, SB611) CRC Pr.

Duke, Stephen O., et al, eds. Pest Control with Enhanced Environmental Safety. LC 93-12098. (ACS Symposium Ser.: No. 524). (Illus.). 358p. 1993. text 95.00 (*0-8412-2638-5*, Pub. by Am Chemical) OUP.

Duke, Stephen O. & Rebeiz, Constantin A., eds. Porphyric Pesticides: Chemistry, Toxicology & Pharmaceutical Applications. LC 94-16418. (ACS Symposium Ser.: No. 559). 318p. 1994. text 85.00 (*0-8412-2923-6*, Pub. by Am Chemical) OUP.

Duke, Susan, jt. auth. see Weiss, LeAnn.

Duke, Thomas S. Celebrated Criminal Cases of America: Reprinted with Corrections & with Index Added. LC 79-172594. (Criminology, Law Enforcement, & Social Problems Ser.: No. 184). (Illus.). 682p. 1991. 45.00 (*0-87585-184-3*) Patterson Smith.

Duke University Commonwealth Studies Center Staff. The American Economic Impact of Canada. Publication Number 12. LC 81-4163. 176p. 1981. reprint ed. lib. bdg. 59.50 (*0-313-23056-0*, AIAI, Greenwood Pr) Greenwood.

Duke University Library Staff. Dante Gabriel Rossetti. Baum, Paull F., ed. LC 31-11769. reprint ed. 21.50 (*0-404-05414-5*) AMS Pr.

Duke University, School of Forestry Staff. Mineral Nutrition of Trees: A Symposium. LC SD0390.D85. (Duke University, School of Forestry Bulletin Ser.: No. 15). (Illus.). 200p. reprint ed. pap. 62.00 (*0-7837-6042-6*, 204585500008) Bks Demand.

Duke University Staff. In Memoriam, William Kenneth Boyd. LC 74-115997. (Trinity College Historical Papers: No. 22). reprint ed. 30.00 (*0-404-51772-2*) AMS Pr.

— Trinity College Historical Society Historical Papers, Series 1-32. LC 74-115989. reprint ed. 900.00 (*0-404-51750-1*) AMS Pr.

— Trinity College Historical Society Papers, Series 1: Reconstruction & State Biography. reprint ed. 30.00 (*0-404-51751-X*) AMS Pr.

— Trinity College Historical Society Papers, Series 10, 1914: 1914. reprint ed. 30.00 (*0-404-51760-9*) AMS Pr.

— Trinity College Historical Society Papers, Series 11, 1915: 1915. reprint ed. 30.00 (*0-404-51761-7*) AMS Pr.

— Trinity College Historical Society Papers, Series 12, 1916: 1916. reprint ed. 30.00 (*0-404-51762-5*) AMS Pr.

— Trinity College Historical Society Papers, Series 13, 1919: 1919. reprint ed. 30.00 (*0-404-51763-3*) AMS Pr.

— Trinity College Historical Society Papers, Series 14, 1922: 1922. reprint ed. 30.00 (*0-404-51764-1*) AMS Pr.

— Trinity College Historical Society Papers, Series 15, 1925: 1925. reprint ed. 30.00 (*0-404-51765-X*) AMS Pr.

— Trinity College Historical Society Papers, Series 2: Legal & Biographical Studies. reprint ed. 30.00 (*0-404-51752-8*) AMS Pr.

— Trinity College Historical Society Papers, Series 3: Gov. W. W. Holden & Revolutionary Documents. reprint ed. 30.00 (*0-404-51753-6*) AMS Pr.

— Trinity College Historical Society Papers, Series 4, 1900: 1900. reprint ed. 30.00 (*0-404-51754-4*) AMS Pr.

— Trinity College Historical Society Papers, Series 5, 1905: 1905. reprint ed. 30.00 (*0-404-51755-2*) AMS Pr.

— Trinity College Historical Society Papers, Series 6, 1906: 1906. reprint ed. 30.00 (*0-404-51756-0*) AMS Pr.

— Trinity College Historical Society Papers, Series 7, 1907: 1907. reprint ed. 30.00 (*0-404-51757-9*) AMS Pr.

— Trinity College Historical Society Papers, Series 8, 1908-1909: 1908-1909. reprint ed. 30.00 (*0-404-51758-7*) AMS Pr.

— Trinity College Historical Society Papers, Series 9, 1912: 1912. reprint ed. 30.00 (*0-404-51759-5*) AMS Pr.

Duke University Tropical Forestry Symposium Staff. Proceedings of the Duke University Tropical Forestry Symposium, April 21-26, 1965. LC SD0131.D85. (Duke University, School of Forestry Bulletin Ser.: No. 18). 213p. reprint ed. pap. 66.10 (*0-7837-6045-0*, 204585800008) Bks Demand.

Duke, Vernon. Listen Here. 1963. 14.95 (*0-685-06621-5*); pap. 10.95 (*0-8392-5010-X*) Astor-Honor.

Duke, Vic & Crolley, Liz. Football, Nationality & the State. LC 96-23692. 1996. pap. write for info. (*0-582-29306-5*) Longman.

Duke, Vic, jt. auth. see Edgell, Stephen.

Duke, Walter G. Duke: Henry Duke, Councilor, & His Descendants & Connections, Comprising Partial Records of Many Allied Families. (Illus.). 452p. 1994. reprint ed. pap. 69.50 (*0-8328-4034-3*); reprint ed. lib. bdg. 79.50 (*0-8328-4033-5*) Higginson Bk Co.

Duke, William. Sustainable Competition in Global Telecommunications: From Principle to Practice. 45p. 1998. pap. text 12.00 (*0-89843-225-1*) The Aspen Inst.

Duke, William, jt. ed. see Campbell, Meg.

Duke, Winifred, ed. Trial of Field & Gray, No. 1. (Notable British Trials Ser.). vi, 302p. 1995. reprint ed. 93.00 (*1-56169-168-2*) Gaunt.

— Trial of Harold Greenwood, No. 1. (Notable British Trials Ser.). xi, 347p. 1995. reprint ed. 145.00 (*1-56169-167-4*) Gaunt.

— The Trials of Frederick Nodder (The Mona Tinsley Case) (Notable British Trials Ser.). xiii, 242p. 1995. reprint ed. 77.00 (*1-56169-182-8*) Gaunt.

Dukehart, Morton M. Dukehart: My Heritage: Collection of Authenticated Biographical Sketches of the Author's Ancestors Dating from the Thirty Years' War (1618-48) & Continuing to (1947) (Illus.). 160p. 1997. reprint ed. pap. 25.00 (*0-8328-8366-2*); reprint ed. lib. bdg. 35.00 (*0-8328-8365-4*) Higginson Bk Co.

Dukek, W. G. & Strauss, K. H., eds. Factors in Using Kerosine Jet Fuel of Reduced Flash Point - STP 688. 113p. 1979. pap. 15.00 (*0-8031-0340-9*, STP688) ASTM.

Dukek, William G., jt. ed. see Strauss, Kurt H.

Dukelow, David. Transpluto. 31p. 1992. pap. 4.95 (*0-935127-26-7*) ACS Pubns.

Dukelow, S. G. The Control of Boilers. 2nd ed. 412p. 1991. 76.00 (*1-55617-330-X*, A330-X) ISA.

Dukelow, Sam G. The Control of Boilers. LC 86-20190. (Illus.). 314p. 1986. reprint ed. pap. 97.40 (*0-7837-1637-0*, 204193000024) Bks Demand.

Dukelow, Samuel G. Improving Boiler Efficiency. 2nd ed. LC TH7470.D85. 182p. 1985. reprint ed. pap. 56.50 (*0-608-01351-X*, 206209100002) Bks Demand.

Dukelow, W. Richard. The Alpha Males: An Early History of the Regional Primate Research Center. (Illus.). 228p. (Orig.). (C). 1995. lib. bdg. 46.50 (*0-7618-0099-9*) U Pr of Amer.

— Graduate Student Survival. (Illus.). 88p. 1980. pap., spiral bd. 20.95 (*0-398-04068-0*) C C Thomas.

Dukelow, W. Richard, ed. Nonhuman Primate Models for Human Diseases. LC 82-4519. 208p. 1983. 123.00 (*0-8493-6466-3*, RB125, CRC Reprint) Franklin.

Dukel'skaia, L. A. English Art of Sixteen-Nineteenth Centuries. (RUS.). 120p. 1983. pap. 30.00 (*0-7855-1542-9*) St Mut.

Dukelskaya, L. English Art in the Hermitage. 1981. 100.00 (*0-7855-7265-1*) St Mut.

Dukeminier. Gilbert Future Interests & Perpetuities. 4th ed. 1996. pap. text 17.95 (*0-15-900218-4*) Harcourt Legal.

— Gilbert Property. 13th ed. 1991. 21.95 (*0-15-900032-7*) Harcourt Legal.

Dukeminier, Jesse. Property. 3rd ed. 1344p. 1993. 56.00 (*0-316-19523-5*, Aspen Law & Bus) Aspen Pub.

— Wills & Trusts. 5th ed. 1168p. 1995. 55.00 (*0-316-19522-7*, Aspen Law & Bus) Aspen Pub.

Dukeminier, Jesse & Johanson, Stanley M. Wills, Trusts, & Estates. 1168p. 1995. teacher ed. write for info. (*0-316-19495-6*, 94956) Aspen Law.

— Wills, Trusts & Estates. 3rd ed. LC 83-82694. 1140p. (C). 1984. 38.95 (*0-316-19514-6*, Aspen Law & Bus) Aspen Pub.

Dukeminier, Jesse & Krier, James E. Property. 1344p. 1993. teacher ed. write for info. (*0-316-19524-3*, 95243) Aspen Law.

— Property. 4th ed. LC 97-33583. 1998. boxed set 64.00 (*1-56706-648-8*) Aspen Law.

Dukepoo, Frank. The Elder American Indian. LC 77-83494. (Elder Minority Ser.). 62p. 1980. 9.50 (*0-916304-33-7*) SDSU Press.

Duker, Pieter C. Teaching the Developmentally Handicapped Communicative Gesturing: A How-to-Do Book. (Modern Approaches to the Diagnosis & Instruction of Multi-Handicapped Children Ser.: Vol. 22). viii, 160p. 1989. 40.75 (*90-265-0940-5*) Swets.

Duker, Sam. Individualized Instruction in Mathematics. LC 72-5739. 1972. 26.50 (*0-8108-0533-2*) Scarecrow.

Duker, William F. A Constitutional History of Habeas Corpus. 13. LC 79-6834. (Contributions in Legal Studies: No. 13). 349p. 1980. 49.95 (*0-313-22264-9*, DHC/, Greenwood Pr) Greenwood.

Dukert, Joseph M., jt. auth. see Landsberg, Hans H.

Dukes. Resolving Public Conflict. 220p. 1997. text 69.95 (*0-7190-4512-6*) St Martin.

Dukes, jt. auth. see Gibson.

Dukes, Ashley. Modern Dramatists. LC 67-23210. (Essay Index Reprint Ser.). 1977. 20.95 (*0-8369-0396-X*) Ayer.

Dukes, Ashley, et al. Plays of Today, Vol. 3. LC 76-132137. (Play Anthology Reprint Ser.). 1977. 21.95 (*0-8369-8216-9*) Ayer.

Dukes, Charlie. Good Morning . . . But the Nightmares Never End. LC 97-44486. 1997. 21.95 (*0-9641423-2-5*) Tales Pr.

Dukes, Donald E. In This City, We Dance: Thelma. Usher, Brenda & Ellison, Ruth, eds. (Illus.). 328p. (Orig.). 1996. write for info. (*0-9653638-0-5*) Nexphrase Pub.

Dukes, Duane, jt. ed. see Kratcoski, Peter C.

Dukes, E. Load & Speed Conditions of Wormgear Drives. (Technical Papers: Vol. P60). (Illus.). 16p. 1929. pap. text 30.00 (*1-55589-419-4*) AGMA.

— Load & Speed Conditions of Wormgear Drives, Pt. 2. (Technical Papers: Vol. P61). (Illus.). 16p. 1930. pap. text 30.00 (*1-55589-420-8*) AGMA.

***Dukes, E. Franklin, et al.** Reaching for Higher Ground in Conflict Resolution: How to Build Shared Expectations & Commitments. LC 00-9232. 2000. 37.95 (*0-7879-5058-0*) Jossey-Bass.

Dukes, Eugene D. Magic & Witchcraft in the Dark Ages. LC 95-39869. 322p. (C). 1996. pap. text 29.00 (*0-7618-0148-0*); lib. bdg. 44.00 (*0-7618-0147-2*) U Pr of Amer.

Dukes, Eva, tr. & afterword by see Wiesenthal, Simon.

Dukes, George H., Jr. Science & Religion - Steppingstones & Stumblingblocks. LC 98-92177. 121p. 1999. 16.50 (*0-9655380-2-8*); pap. 13.50 (*0-9655380-1-X*) Poplar Petal.

— Trees of Mississippi & Other Woody Plants. LC 96-92727. (Illus.). 276p. 1997. 36.00 (*0-9655380-0-1*) Poplar Petal.

Dukes, Gramham & Mildred, M., eds. Responsibility for Drug Induced Injury: A Reference Book for Lawyers, the Health Profession & Manufacturers. LC 97-78442. 1998. 125.00 (*90-5199-387-0*) IOS Pr.

***Dukes, Jack.** Mississippi High. 296p. 2000. pap. 19.95 (*0-9700270-0-1*) Wild Dove Pub.

Dukes, Johnathan. Blindsighted. 1998. pap. write for info. (*1-889505-25-0*) White Wing Pub.

Dukes, Jonnie. The Lost Chronicles of Love. 64p. (Orig.). 1997. pap. 6.95 (*0-9641606-2-5*) Easy Break.

Dukes, M. N., ed. Drug Utilization Studies: Methods & Uses. (WHO Regional Publications: No. 45). viii, 218p. 1993. pap. text 36.00 (*92-890-1308-7*, 1310045) World Health.

— Meyler's Side Effects of Drugs: An Encyclopedia of Adverse Reactions & Interactions. 12th ed. (Side Effects of Drugs Ser.: Vol. 12). xxii,1308p. 1992. 316.00 (*0-444-89524-8*) Elsevier.

Dukes, M. N. & Aronson, J. K. Side Effects of Drugs Annual 15, 1991, Vol. 15. 586p. 1991. 216.50 (*0-444-89171-4*) Elsevier.

Dukes, M. N. & Aronson, J. K., eds. Side Effects of Drugs Annual 16: A Yearly Critical Survey of the World's Literature on Adverse Reactions to Drugs. 646p. 1993. 221.00 (*0-444-89657-0*) Elsevier.

Dukes, M. N. G., ed. Meyler's Side Effects of Drugs: An Encyclopedia of Adverse Reactions & Interactions. 13th ed. 1610p. 1996. 316.00 (*0-444-82405-7*) Elsevier.

Dukes, Mark, et al. Greatest Moments in Iowa Hawkeyes Football History. Fitzgerald, Francis J., ed. (Illus.). 223p. 1997. 34.95 (*1-57243-261-6*) Triumph Bks.

Dukes, Norman. The Reckless Sleeper. Kaplan, Peter, ed. LC 75-23871. 1975. 2.00 (*0-915176-11-4*) Pourboire.

Dukes, Paul. Catherine the Great & the Russian Nobility: A Study Based on the Materials of the Legislative Commission of 1767. LC 67-13802. 281p. reprint ed. pap. 80.10 (*0-608-12205-X*, 2024441) Bks Demand.

— Culture & the Revolution. 256p. 1990. text 49.00 (*0-86187-788-8*, Pub. by P P Pubs) Cassell & Continuum.

— A History of Russia: Medieval, Modern, Contemporary. 2nd ed. LC 90-3366. 437p. (C). 1990. reprint ed. text 64.95 (*0-8223-1078-3*) Duke.

— A History of Russia: Medieval, Modern, Contemporary. 2nd ed. LC 90-3366. 437p. (C). 1990. reprint ed. pap. text 26.95 (*0-8223-1096-1*) Duke.

— A History of Russia: Medieval, Modern, Contemporary, c. 882-1996. 3rd ed. LC 97-15047. 430p. 1997. write for info. (*0-8223-2082-7*); pap. 23.95 (*0-8223-2096-7*) Duke.

— The Making of Russian Absolutism, 1613-1801. 2nd ed. (History of Russia Ser.). 256p. (C). 1990. pap. 44.00 (*0-582-00324-5*, 78647) Longman.

— Russia under Catherine the Great, 2 vols., 1. 1978. 12.00 (*0-89250-106-5*) Orient Res Partners.

— Russia under Catherine the Great, 2 vols., 2. 1978. 12.00 (*0-89250-105-7*) Orient Res Partners.

— Russia under Catherine the Great, 2 vols., Set. 1978. 24.00 (*0-89250-104-9*) Orient Res Partners.

Dukes, Paul, ed. Frontiers of European Culture. LC 96-31328. 264p. 1997. text 89.95 (*0-7734-8925-8*) E Mellen.

***Dukes, Paul, et al.** Russia & the Wider World in Historical Perspective: Essays for Paul Dukes LC 99-40355. 2000. text 68.00 (*0-312-22926-7*) St Martin.

Dukes, Paul, jt. ed. see Brotherstone, Terry.

Dukes, Paul, ed. see Porshnev, B. F.

Dukes, Richard L. Worlds Apart: Collective Action in Simulated Agrarian & Industrial Societies. (Theory & Decision Library). 206p. (C). 1990. lib. bdg. 114.50 (*0-7923-0620-1*) Kluwer Academic.

Dukes, Roland, jt. auth. see Dyckman, Thomas.

Dukes, Roland, jt. auth. see Dyckman, Thomas R.

Dukes, Roland E. An Empirical Investigation of the Effects of Statement of Financial Accounting Standards No. 8 on Security Return Behavior. LC 78-74875. (Financial Accounting Standards Board Research Report Ser.). (Illus.). 102p. (Orig.). 1978. pap. 3.00 (*0-910065-07-1*) Finan Acct Found.

Dukharin, Nikolai. Science at the Crossroads. 228p. 1971. 35.00 (*0-7146-2868-9*, Pub. by F Cass Pubs) Intl Spec Bk.

Dukhin, Stanislaw S., et al. Dynamics of Adsorption at Liquid Interfaces: Theory, Experiment, Application. LC 95-7868. (Studies in Interface Science: Vol. 1). 604p. 1995. text 275.50 (*0-444-88117-4*) Elsevier.

Dukkipati, Rao V. & Amyot, Joseph R. Computer-Aided Simulation in Railway Dynamics. (Mechanical Engineering Ser.: Vol. 61). (Illus.). 448p. 1987. text 175.00 (*0-8247-7787-5*) Dekker.

Dukler, A. E. Gas Liquid Flow in Pipelines: I-Research Results. 200p. 1969. pap. 5.00 (*0-318-12631-1*, L20169) Am Gas Assn.

Dukler, Sofiya, ed. see Trubetskaya, Ellayda.

Duknovych, Aleksandr. Virtue Is More Important Than Riches. Rusinko, Elaine, ed. & tr. by. 85p. 1995. 34.00 (*0-88033-290-5*, 393, Pub. by East Eur Monographs) Col U Pr.

Dukor, P., et al, eds. Cell Mediated Reactions, Miscellaneous Topics Vol. 3: PAR, Pseudo-Allergic Reactions, Involvement of Drugs & Chemicals. (Illus.). viii, 160p. 1982. 68.75 (*3-8055-0960-X*) S Karger.

— Cytotoxic & Complement Mediated Reactions. (Par Pseudo-Allergic Reactions, Involvement of Drugs & Chemicals Ser.: Vol. 2). (Illus.). viii, 144p. 1980. 56.75 (*3-8055-0666-X*) S Karger.

— Genetic Aspects Anaphylactoid Reactions. (Par Pseudo-Allergic Reactions, Involvement of Drugs & Chemicals Ser.: Vol. 1). (Illus.). xiv, 310p. 1980. 113.25 (*3-8055-0537-X*) S Karger.

— Idiopathic & Food or Drug-Induced PAR. (Par Pseudo-Allergic Reactions, Involvement of Drugs & Chemicals Ser.: Vol. 4). (Illus.). viii, 196p. 1985. 104.50 (*3-8055-3798-0*) S Karger.

Dukore, B. F. Dramatic Theory & Criticism. LC 73-9778. (C). 1974. text 55.50 (*0-03-091152-4*, Pub. by Harcourt Coll Pubs) Harcourt.

Dukore, Bernard F. Barnestorm: The Plays of Peter Barnes. LC 95-4207. (Studies in Modern Drama: Vol. 5). 328p. 1995. text 50.00 (*0-8153-1134-6*, H1654) Garland.

***Dukore, Bernard F.** Sam Peckinpah's Feature Films. LC 99-6064. 256p. 1999. pap. 18.95 (*0-252-06802-5*) U of Ill Pr.

— Sam Peckinpah's Feature Films. LC 99-6064. (Illus.). 256p. 1999. 49.95 (*0-252-02486-9*) U of Ill Pr.

Dukore, Bernard F. Where Laughter Stops: Pinter's Tragicomedy. LC 76-15590. (Literary Frontiers Ser.). 80p. 1976. pap. 9.95 (*0-8262-0208-X*) U of Mo Pr.

Dukore, Bernard F., ed. Bernard Shaw & Gabriel Pascal. (Selected Correspondence of Bernard Shaw Ser.: Vol. 3). (Illus.). 224p. 1996. text 40.00 (*0-8020-3002-5*) U of Toronto Pr.

Dukore, Bernard F. & Gerould, Daniel C. Avant Garde Drama: A Casebook. (J). 1976. pap. 8.50 (*0-690-00848-1*) HarpC Child Bks.

Dukore, Bernard F., ed. see Shaw, George Bernard.

An Asterisk (*) at the beginning of an entry indicates that the title is appearing for the first time.

Dukore, Bernard F., ed. & intro. see Shaw, George Bernard.

Dukstra. Flora Tristan: Feminism in the Age of George Sand. 217p. (C). 49.95 (*0-7453-0316-1*, Pub. by Pluto GBR); pap. 18.95 (*0-7453-0450-8*, Pub. by Pluto GBR) Stylus Pub VA.

Dukthas, Ann. In the Time of the Poisoned Queen. LC 97-31614. 273p. 1998. text 22.95 (*0-312-18030-6*) St Martin.

— The Prince Lost to Time. 1996. mass mkt. 5.99 (*0-312-95843-9*) St Martin.

— A Time for the Death of a King. 1995. mass mkt. 4.99 (*0-312-95613-4*); mass mkt. 4.99 (*0-614-15605-X*) St Martin.

— Time of Murder at Mayerling, Vol. 1. 1997. mass mkt. write for info. (*0-312-96338-6*) St Martin.

Dul, J. & Weerdmeester, B. A. Ergonomics for Beginners: A Quick Reference Guide. 146p. 1993. pap. 19.95 (*0-7484-0079-6*, Pub. by Tay Francis Ltd) Taylor & Francis.

Dula. Before the Fall: Innsmouth Adventures Prior to the Great Raid of 1928. (Pendragon Roleplaying Ser.). 1998. pap. text 11.95 (*1-56882-135-2*) Chaosium.

Dula, Annette & Goering, Sara. It Just Ain't Fair: The Ethics of Health Care for African Americans. LC 93-43780. 1994. pap. 19.95 (*0-275-95057-3*, Greenwood Pr) Greenwood.

Dula, Annette & Goering, Sara, eds. It Just Ain't Fair: The Ethics of Health Care for African Americans. LC 93-43780. 336p. 1994. 69.50 (*0-275-94494-8*, Praeger Pubs) Greenwood.

Dula, Giora & Schultz, Reinhard. Diagram Cohomology & Isovariant Homotopy Theory. LC 94-14405. (Memoirs of the American Mathematical Society Ser.: No. 527). 82p. 1994. pap. 31.00 (*0-8218-2589-5*) Am Math.

Dulac, jt. auth. see Madrigal, Margarita.

Dulac, Colette. Shortcut to French. (J). (gr. 9 up). 1977. pap. text 5.45 (*0-88345-300-2*, 18441); audio 25.00 (*0-685-79306-0*, 58442) Prentice ESL.

— Shortcut to French. 1987. pap. text 25.00 (*0-13-809195-1*) Prentice ESL.

Dulac, Colette, jt. auth. see Madrigal, Margarita.

Dulac, Edmund. F Was a Fanciful Frog: Edmund Dulac's Limericks. (Illus.). 28p. 1993. 8.95 (*1-55859-640-2*, Abbeville Kids) Abbeville Pr.

Dulac, Gerry & Parascenzo, Marino. On Course: A Guide to the Region's Public Golf Courses. Alward, Debra, ed. 1998. pap. 9.75 (*0-9657325-1-7*) Pittsbrgh Post-Gazette.

Dulac, Glen J. The Color Coded Alphabet: The Best Coloring Book Ever. (Reading & Writing & Coloring Ser.). (Illus.). (J). (gr. k-3). 1991. pap. 5.00 (*0-9628227-4-4*) Desert Bks.

— The Color Coded Alphabet, an Alphabet for Easy Reading: The Alphabet as It Has Never Been Seen Before. (Illus.). (J). (ps-2). 1990. 49.50 (*0-9628227-2-8*) Desert Bks.

Dulac, Olivier, et al, eds. Infantile Spasms & West Syndrome. 310p. 1994. text 86.00 (*0-7020-1777-9*, W B Saunders Co) Harcrt Hlth Sci Grp.

Dulack, Tom. Breaking Legs. 1992. pap. 5.25 (*0-8222-0147-X*) Dramatists Play.

— Diminished Capacity. 1998. pap. 5.25 (*0-8222-1686-8*) Dramatists Play.

— Incommunicado. 1990. pap. 5.25 (*0-8222-0565-3*) Dramatists Play.

— Solomon's Child. 1985. pap. 5.25 (*0-8222-1051-7*) Dramatists Play.

Dulacska, E. Soil Settlement Effects on Buildings. (Developments in Geotechnical Engineering Ser.: Vol. 69). xx,448p. 1992. 208.00 (*0-444-98689-8*) Elsevier.

***Dulai, Phinder.** Basmati Brown. 2000. pap. 11.95 (*0-88971-172-0*) Nightwood Edns.

Dulaney, et al. Microtech U. S. A MCSE Training Guide: Microsoft TCP IP. 1998. 53.49 (*1-56205-906-8*, New Riders Sftwre) MCP SW Interactive.

Dulaney, Benjamin L. Dulaney: Something about the Dulaney (Dulany) Family & Sketch of the Southern Cobb Family. (Illus.). 94p. 1997. reprint ed. pap. 18.00 (*0-8328-8368-9*); reprint ed. lib. bdg. 28.00 (*0-8328-8367-0*) Higginson Bk Co.

DuLaney, Cora A. Anderson. The Andersons from the Great Fork of the Patuxent. (Illus.). 223p. 1997. reprint ed. pap. 34.00 (*0-8328-7271-7*); reprint ed. lib. bdg. 44.00 (*0-8328-7270-9*) Higginson Bk Co.

***Dulaney, Emmett.** A+ Certification Interactive. (Illus.). 552p. 1999. pap. text, wbk. ed. 49.99 (*0-13-084847-6*) P-H.

— MCSE Exam 70-240: Microsoft Windows 2000 Accelerated Exam for MCPS Certified on Microsoft Window. 600p. 2000. pap. text 39.99 (*0-7897-2387-5*) Que.

Dulaney, Emmett. MCSE Fast Track: Internet Information Server 4. LC 98-86319. 1998. pap. 19.99 (*1-56205-936-X*) New Riders Pub.

— MCSE Fast Track: Networking Essentials. LC 98-86325. 1998. pap. 19.99 (*1-56205-939-4*) New Riders Pub.

— MCSE Fast Track: TCP/IP. LC 98-86320. 1998. pap. 19.99 (*1-56205-937-8*) New Riders Pub.

— MCSE Fast Track: WIndows NT Server 4. LC 98-86318. 1998. pap. 19.99 (*1-56205-935-1*) New Riders Pub.

— MCSE Fast Track: Windows NT Server 4 Enterprise. LC 98-86322. 1998. pap. 19.99 (*1-56205-940-8*) New Riders Pub.

— MCSE Fast Track: Windows NT Workstation 4. LC 98-86321. 1998. pap. 19.99 (*1-56205-938-6*) New Riders Pub.

— Netware Solutions & Shortcuts Batch File Programming for Administrators. 1995. pap. 39.95 incl. disk (*1-55851-310-8*, M&T Bks) IDG Bks.

— The Network Starter Kit. LC 94-34770. (Illus.). 518p. (Orig.). 1994. pap. 29.99 (*1-56205-403-1*) New Riders Pub.

***Dulaney, Emmett.** Sams Teach Yourself MCSE Windows 2000 Accelerated Exam in 14 Days. (Teach Yourself... in 14 Days Ser.). (Illus.). 2000. pap. 35.00 (*0-672-31903-9*) Sams.

Dulaney, Emmett. 6 in 1. (MCSE Fast Track Ser.). 1998. pap. 89.99 (*1-56205-909-2*) New Riders Pub.

Dulaney, Emmett, et al. MCSE TestPrep: Windows NT Workstation 4. 400p. 1997. 24.99 (*1-56205-848-7*) New Riders Pub.

***Dulaney, Emmett A.** I-Net+ Exam Cram. LC 00-22668. (Exam Cram Ser.). (Illus.). 400p. 2000. pap. write for info. (*1-57610-673-X*) Coriolis Grp.

— Visual Basic 6.0 Brief Course. LC 98-52360. (Illus.). 2000. write for info. (*0-02-805813-5*) Glencoe.

Dulaney, Emmett A. Visual Basic 6.0 Brief Course. LC 98-52360. 2000. 5.25 hd. write for info. (*0-02-805814-3*) Glencoe.

***Dulaney, Emmett A.** Visual Basic 6.0 Complete Course. LC 98-52104. (Illus.). 2000. write for info. (*0-02-805812-7*) Glencoe.

— Visual Basic 6.0 Complete Course. LC 98-52104. (Illus.). 2000. write for info. (*0-02-805811-9*) Glencoe.

Dulaney, Kim. I Believe I Can Fly! The R. Kelly Story. 1998. 9.95 (*1-891636-03-0*) Unique Exp.

— I Love Me! 1998. 9.95 (*1-891636-02-2*) Unique Exp.

***Dulaney, Kim.** Maya's Magic. (Fuzzy-Feeling Bks.). (Illus.). (J). (ps-3). 1999. pap. 8.25 (*1-891636-04-9*, 1003) Unique Exp.

Dulaney, Kim. Who Am I? The Royal Family. (Fuzzy-Feeling Bks.). (Illus.). (J). (ps-3). 1999. pap. 8.25 (*1-891636-06-5*, 1001) Unique Exp.

***Dulaney, Kim L.** My Lost Dream. (Fuzzy-Feeling Bks.). (J). 1999. pap. 8.25 (*1-891636-07-3*) Unique Exp.

— My Pest. (Fuzzy-Feeling Bks.). (Illus.). (J). (gr. 1-4). 1999. pap. 8.25 (*1-891636-05-7*, 1006) Unique Exp.

Dulaney, Kim L. Woman to Woman: A Collection of Essays & Poems LC 99-177470. 52 p. 1998. 12.95 (*1-891636-01-4*) Unique Exp.

Dulaney, Miriam F. Humor, Rumor & Romance in Old Jonesborough (Tennessee) (Illus.). 56p. (Orig.). 1991. pap. 4.95 (*0-932807-61-5*) Overmountain Pr.

Dulaney, Paul S. The Architecture of Historic Richmond. LC 68-14089. 222p. reprint ed. pap. 68.90 (*0-7837-2430-6*, 204257800005) Bks Demand.

Dulaney, Sara. The Complete Idiot's Guide to Single Parenting. LC 98-85423. (Illus.). 352p. 1999. pap. text 16.95 (*0-02-862409-2*) Macmillan Gen Ref.

Dulaney, W. Marvin. Black Police in America. LC 95-19359. (Blacks in the Diaspora Ser.). (Illus.). 216p. 1996. pap. 14.95 (*0-253-21040-2*) Ind U Pr.

Dulaney, W. Marvin & Underwood, Kathleen, eds. Essays on the American Civil Rights Movement. LC 92-45792. (Walter Prescott Webb Memorial Lectures: No. 26). (Illus.). 112p. 1993. 23.95 (*0-89096-540-4*) Tex A&M Univ Pr.

Dulany, Daniel. Maryland & the Empire, 1773: The Antilon-First Citizen Letters. Onuf, Peter S., ed. LC 73-8128. (Maryland Bicentennial Studies). 250p. reprint ed. pap. 77.50 (*0-7837-0047-4*, 204029400016) Bks Demand.

Dulany, Donelson E. & Logan, Gordon D., eds. Views & Varieties of Automaticity. (Special Issue of the American Journal of Psychology Ser.: Vol. 105, No. 2). 160p. 1992. pap. text 12.50 (*0-252-06266-3*) U of Ill Pr.

***Dulany, Emmett.** MCSE Windows 2000 Core 4 Exam Guide Kit: Covers Exams 70-210, 70-215, 70-216, 70-217. (Illus.). 2000. pap. 120.00 (*0-7897-2415-4*) Que.

Dulany, Peggy, et al, contrib. by. Promoting U. S. Economic Relations with Africa: Report of an Independent Task Force. 1998. pap. 5.00 (*0-87609-215-6*) Coun Foreign.

Dulat, Karin B., jt. auth. see Wells, L. Fargo.

Dulaure, Jacques-Antoine. The Gods of Generation. LC 72-9635.Tr. of De Divinites Generatrices. reprint ed. 49.50 (*0-404-57433-5*) AMS Pr.

Dulay, Heidi, et al. The Language II. (Illus.). 316p. 1982. pap. text 16.95 (*0-19-502553-9*) OUP.

Dulay, Heidi C., ed. see Teachers of English to Speakers of Other Languages.

Dulbecco, Renato. The Design of Life. 466p. (C). 1990. reprint ed. pap. 30.00 (*0-300-04477-1*) Yale U Pr.

— Encyclopedia of Human Biology. 2nd ed. 1997. text 234.00 (*0-12-226971-3*); text 234.00 (*0-12-226972-1*); text 234.00 (*0-12-226973-X*); text 233.00 (*0-12-226974-8*); text 233.00 (*0-12-226975-6*); text 233.00 (*0-12-226976-4*); text 233.00 (*0-12-226977-2*); text 233.00 (*0-12-226979-9*) Acad Pr.

— Encyclopedia Of Human Biology. 2nd ed. 1997. text 233.00 (*0-12-226978-0*) Acad Pr.

Dulbecco, Renato, ed. Encyclopedia of Human Biology, 9 vols. 2nd ed. (Illus.). 5200p. 1997. text 2100.00 (*0-12-226970-5*) Morgan Kaufmann.

— Encyclopedia of Human Biology, 8 vols., Vols. 1-3. (Illus.). 6600p. 1991. 731.25 (*0-12-226748-6*) Acad Pr.

— Encyclopedia of Human Biology, 8 vols., Vols. 4-6. (Illus.). 6600p. 1991. 731.25 (*0-12-226749-4*) Acad Pr.

— Encyclopedia of Human Biology, 8 vols., Vols. 7-8. (Illus.). 6600p. 1991. 487.50 (*0-12-226750-8*) Acad Pr.

***Dulbecco, Renato, et al, eds.** Frontiers of Life, 4 vol., Set. 2400p. 2000. 1000.00 (*0-12-077340-6*) Acad Pr.

Dulbecco, Renato & Ginsberg, Harold S. Virology. 2nd ed. LC 65-10705. (Illus.). 425p. 1988. text 41.95 (*0-397-50905-7*, Lippnctt) Lppncott W & W.

Dulberger, Judith A. Mother Donit Fore the Best: Correspondence of a Nineteenth-Century Orphan Asylum. (Illus.). 272p. (C). 1996. pap. 17.95 (*0-8156-0341-X*, DUMDP) Syracuse U Pr.

Dulcan, Mina K., ed. Helping Parents, Youth, & Teachers Understanding Medications for Behavioral & Emotional Problems: A Resource Book of Medication Information Handouts. LC 98-16698. 196p. 1998. spiral bd. 39.95 (*0-88048-794-1*, 8794) Am Psychiatric.

Dulcan, Mina K. & Martini, D. Richard. Concise Guide to Child & Adolescent Psychiatry. 2nd ed. LC 98-22463. (Concise Guide Ser.). 400p. 1998. pap. text 22.95 (*0-88048-905-7*, 8905) Am Psychiatric.

Dulchavsky, Scott A. Alexander J. Walt: Reflections. LC 99-10277. 1999. 29.95 (*0-8143-2831-8*) Wayne St U Pr.

Dulcinos, Donald P. Pioneer of Inner Space: The Life of Fitz Hugh Ludlow, Hasheesh Eater. (Illus.). 320p. 1998. pap. 14.00 (*1-57027-071-6*) Autonomedia.

Dulcken, H. W., tr. Emperor's New Clothes.Tr. of Kejserens nye klaeder. (J). 1982. 9.95 (*0-690-04150-0*) HarpC Child Bks.

Dulcken, H. W., ed. see Rose, D.

Dulcy, Faye H., ed. Aquatics: A Revived Approach to Pediatric Management. LC 83-85. (Physical & Occupational Therapy in Pediatrics Ser.: Vol. 3, No. 1). 92p. 1983. text 39.95 (*0-86656-215-X*) Haworth Pr.

Duleep, Harriet O. & Wunnava, Phanindra V., eds. Immigrants & Immigration Policy: Individual Skills, Family Ties, & Group Identities. LC 95-54003. (Contemporary Studies in Economic & Financial Analysis: Vol. 79). 392p. 1996. 78.50 (*0-7623-0076-0*) Jai Pr.

Dulek, Ronald E., jt. auth. see Fielden, John S.

Duley, Irene, et al. PKD Patient's Manual: Understanding & Living with Autosomal Dominant Polycystic Kidney Disease. 2nd rev. ed. Rueb, Wendy et al, eds. (Illus.). 68p. 1995. teacher ed. 15.00 (*0-9614567-4-4*) PKR Foundation.

Duley, W. W. UV Lasers: Effects & Applications in Materials Science. LC 97-673. (Illus.). 418p. (C). 1996. text 100.00 (*0-521-46498-6*) Cambridge U Pr.

Duley, Walter & Shibata, Kimihiro, eds. 1996 International Congress on Applied Lasers & Electro-Optics Proceedings. (Illus.). 968p. 1997. pap. text 160.00 (*0-912035-54-4*, 581) Laser Inst.

— 1996 International Congress on Applied Lasers & Electro-Optics Proceedings: Lasers & Electro-Optics for Automotive Manufacturing. (TCALEO 96 Ser.: Vol. 82). (Illus.). 173p. 1997. pap. text 60.00 (*0-912035-55-2*, 582) Laser Inst.

Duley, Walter W. Laser Processing & Analysis of Materials. LC 82-18611. 476p. 1983. 110.00 (*0-306-41067-2*, Plenum Trade) Perseus Pubng.

— Laser Welding. LC 98-15242. 251p. 1998. 94.95 (*0-471-24679-4*, Wiley-Interscience) Wiley.

***Dulfano, Cecilia.** The Quilt of My Life. LC 99-96753. 2000. pap. 9.95 (*0-533-13337-8*) Vantage.

Dulffer, Jost. Nazi Germany 1933-1945: Faith in the Fuhrer & Pursuit of a War of Annihilation. LC 95-31743. 256p. 1996. pap. text 19.95 (*0-340-61393-9*, Pub. by E A) OUP.

Dulffer, Jost. Nazi Germany 1933-1945: Faith in the Fuhrer & Pursuit of a War of Annihilation. McMurry, Dean S., tr. LC 95-31743. 288p. 1996. text 49.95 (*0-340-65265-9*, Pub. by E A) St Martin.

Dulfon, Alan, ed. see Bennett, Matthew.

Dulfon, Alan, ed. see Sanan.

Dulfon, Alan, ed. see Thakur, Bhaktivinoda.

Dulfur, Brett, jt. auth. see Borwick, Jim.

Duliani, Mario. The City Without Women. Mazza, Antonio, tr. & intro. by. 220p. 1995. 24.95 (*0-88962-566-2*) Mosaic.

— The City Without Women. Mazza, Antonio, tr. & intro. by. 220p. 1996. 24.95 (*0-88962-531-X*); pap. 14.95 (*0-88962-530-1*) Mosaic.

***Duliba, Lee E. & Shand, Tom W.** Young Fire Equipment Corporation, 1932-1991. (Photo Archives Ser.). (Illus.). 128p. 2000. pap. 32.95 (*1-58388-015-1*, 130666AE, Pub. by Iconografix) Motorbooks Intl.

Dulikravich, G. S., et al, eds. Developments in Electrorheological Flows - 1995: Proceedings of the ASME International Mechanical Engineering Congress & Exposition, 1995, San Francisco, CA. LC 95-81277. (1995 ASME International Mechanical Engineering Congress & Exposition Ser.: FED-Vol. 235/MD-Vol. 71). 84p. 1995. 50.00 (*0-7918-1761-X*, H01043) ASME.

Dulikravich, G. S. & Woodbury, K. A., eds. Proceedings of the 32nd National Heat Transfer Conference, Baltimore, Maryland, August 8-12, 1997, Vol. 2. (HTD Ser.: Vol. 340). 172p. 1997. 80.00 (*0-7918-1807-1*, H01088) ASME Pr.

Dulikravich, George S., jt. auth. see Tanaka, M.

Dulin, C. I., ed. Ireland Transition: The Postal History of the Transitional Period 1922 - 1925. 394p. (C). 1992. 200.00 (*0-9517095-1-8*, Pub. by MacDonnell Whyte) St Mut.

***Dulin, Daniel L.** The Littlest Volcano. (Illus.). 16p. (J). (ps-2). 2000. pap. write for info. (*0-9677274-1-3*) BlacKat Pubng.

Dulin, John J., et al. Electronic Communications. (Illus.). 656p. 1990. pap. 24.95 (*0-8306-3365-0*) McGraw-Hill Prof.

Dulin, John J., jt. auth. see Veley, Victor F.

Dulin, Laura, tr. see Gonzalbo, Pablo Escalante.

Dulin, Laura, tr. see Linares, Frederico Navarrete.

Dulin, Robert O., Jr., jt. auth. see Garzke, William, Jr.

Dulin, Robert O., Jr., jt. auth. see Garzke, William H., Jr.

Duling. The New Testament. 4th ed. (C). 1999. text. write for info. (*0-15-507856-9*) Harcourt Coll Pubs.

Duling, Dennis C. Jesus Christ Through History. 324p. (C). 1979. pap. text 41.50 (*0-15-547370-0*, Pub. by Harcourt Coll Pubs) Harcourt.

Duling, Dennis C. & Perrin, Norman. The New Testament: Proclamation & Parenesis, Myth & History. 3rd ed. Ferm, Robert L., ed. LC 93-79968. 512p. (C). 1994. pap. text 47.50 (*0-15-500378-X*, Pub. by Harcourt Coll Pubs) Harcourt.

Duling, Gretchen A. Oral Life Histories of One-Room Schoolhouse Teachers: Voices from the Recitation Bench. LC 97-29258. 316p. 1997. text 99.95 (*0-7734-4250-2*) E Mellen.

Duling, Irl N., 3rd, ed. Compact Sources of Ultrashort Pulses. (Cambridge Studies in Modern Optics: Ser. 18). (Illus.). 448p. (C). 1995. text 89.95 (*0-521-46192-8*) Cambridge U Pr.

Duling, Jean. Winds of Time. LC 94-68579. 160p. 1995. 12.95 incl. audio (*0-8158-0508-X*) Chris Mass.

Duling, Sandy. Short Bike Rides Vermont: Rides for the Casual Cyclist. 2nd ed. LC 99-37031. (Short Bike Rides Ser.). (Illus.). 224p. 2000. pap. text 11.95 (*0-7627-0404-7*) Globe Pequot.

Dulka, Doreen, jt. auth. see Dulka, Ed.

Dulka, Ed & Dulka, Doreen. Colombian Jungle Escape. 175p. (Orig.). 1992. pap. 5.99 (*0-87508-092-8*) Chr Lit.

***Dulka, J. G., ed.** Steroid Action on Brain & Behavior: 10th Annual Workshop, Los Angeles, California, November 1998. (Brain, Behavior & Evolution Ser.: Vol. 54, No. 1). (Illus.). 70p. 1999. pap. 25.25 (*3-8055-6969-6*) S Karger.

Dulken, Stephen Van, see Van Dulken, Stephen, ed.

Dull, Christine, jt. auth. see Dull, Ralph.

Dull, Harold. Bodywork Tantra: On Land & in Water. (Illus.). 51p. (Orig.). 1987. pap. 10.95 (*0-944202-00-4*) Harbin Springs.

— Watsu: Freeing the Body in Water. 2nd rev. ed. LC 93-77503. v, 160p. 1997. pap. 20.00 (*0-944202-11-X*) Harbin Springs.

Dull, Henrietta. Southern Cooking. LC 88-19299. (Illus.). 352p. 1989. reprint ed. 24.95 (*0-87797-151-X*) Cherokee.

Dull, Jack L., ed. see Ch'u, T'ung-tsu.

Dull, Jack L., ed. see Hsu, Cho-yun.

Dull, Jonathan R. A Diplomatic History of the American Revolution. LC 85-5306. (Illus.). 224p. 1985. pap. 18.00 (*0-300-03886-0*) Yale U Pr.

Dull, Kay E., ed. see Midwestern Food & Social Policy Conference Staff.

Dull, Paul S. A Battle History of the Imperial Japanese Navy: 1941-1945. LC 77-77933. (Illus.). 402p. 1978. 37.95 (*0-87021-097-1*) Naval Inst Pr.

Dull, Ralph & Dull, Christine. Soviet Laughter, Soviet Tears: An American Couple's Six-Month Adventure in a Ukrainian Village. Atkinson, Rebecca, ed. (Illus.). 384p. 1991. 23.50 (*0-9628038-6-3*) Stillmore Pr.

Dull, Terry R. The Owner's Manual for New Business Ventures: How to Uncover a Legitimate Business Opportunity & Start Smart...a Reference Guide. Donaldson, Kim, ed. LC 93-83994. (Illus.). 160p. (Orig.). 1993. pap. text 19.95 (*1-883416-00-0*) Nat Home Ofc.

Dullea. Alternative Technologies to Regulated Cleaning Solvents: A Growing Industry. LC 96-128180. 224p. 1995. 2650.00 (*1-56965-036-5*, C-192) BCC.

Dullea, Henrik N. Charter Revision in the Empire State: The Politics of New York's 1967 Constitutional Convention. LC 97-7475. 449p. (Orig.). 1997. pap. 24.95 (*0-914341-49-9*) Nelson Rockefeller Inst Govt.

Dullea, Henrik N., jt. ed. see Benjamin, Gerald.

Dullemeyer, P., jt. ed. see Zweers, G. A.

***Dullerud, G. E. & Paganini, F.** A Course in Robust Control Theory: A Convex Approach. LC 99-46358. (Texts in Applied Mathematics Ser.: Vol. 36). (Illus.). 384p. 2000. 59.95 (*0-387-98945-5*) Spr-Verlag.

Dullerud, Geir E. Control of Uncertain Sampled-Data Systems. (Systems & Control Ser.). 177p. 1995. 47.00 (*0-8176-3851-2*) Birkhauser.

Dulles, Allen. The Boer War: A History. 1974. 250.00 (*0-87968-184-5*) Gordon Pr.

— Great Spy Stories. 1992. 7.98 (*0-89009-717-8*) Bk Sales Inc.

— Great True Spy Stories. 1992. 7.98 (*0-89009-716-X*) Bk Sales Inc.

Dulles, Allen W. From Hitler's Doorstep: The Wartime Intelligence Reports of Allen Dulles, 1942-1945. Petersen, Neal H., ed. 768p. 1996. 85.00 (*0-271-01485-7*) Pa St U Pr.

— Germany's Underground. LC 78-746. 207p. 1978. reprint ed. lib. bdg. 35.00 (*0-313-20287-7*, DUGU, Greenwood Pr) Greenwood.

***Dulles, Allen W.** Germany's Underground: The Anti-Nazi Resistance. LC 99-58434. 240p. 1999. pap. text 15.00 (*0-306-80928-1*, Pub. by Da Capo) HarpC.

Dulles, Allen W. The Marshall Plan. LC 92-15793. 160p. 1993. 30.00 (*0-85496-350-2*) Berg Pubs.

Dulles, Allen W. & Armstrong, Hamilton F. Can We Be Neutral? (Select Bibliographies Reprint Ser.). 1977. reprint ed. 19.95 (*0-8369-6686-4*) Ayer.

Dulles, Avery. The Assurance of Things Hoped For: A Theology of Christian Faith. 320p. 1997. reprint ed. pap. 16.95 (*0-19-510973-2*) OUP.

— The Catholicity of the Church. 208p. 1987. pap. text 19.95 (*0-19-826695-2*) OUP.

— Church Authority in American Culture; Church Authority in American Culture/The Second Cardinal B. LC 99-11107. 1999. pap. text 14.95 (*0-8245-1788-1*) Crossroad NY.

— Church Membership As a Catholic & Ecumenical Problem. (Pere Marquette Lectures). 1974. 15.00 (*0-87462-506-8*) Marquette.

— The Craft of Theology: From Symbol to System. 240p. 1995. pap. 29.95 (*0-8245-1456-4*) Crossroad NY.

***Dulles, Avery.** A History of Apologetics. 326p. 1999. pap. 28.00 (*1-57910-224-7*) Wipf & Stock.

D

Dulles, Avery. Models of Revelation. LC 82-45243. 1983. 16.95 (*0-385-17975-8*) Doubleday.
— Models of Revelation. 2nd ed. LC 92-25800. 365p. 1992. reprint ed. pap. 17.50 (*0-88344-842-4*) Orbis Bks.
— Models of the Church. LC 77-11246. 256p. 1991. reprint ed. pap. 11.95 (*0-385-13368-5*, Image Bks) Doubleday.
***Dulles, Avery.** The New World of Faith. LC 00-130460. 176p. 2000. pap. 14.95 (*0-87973-692-5*) Our Sunday Visitor.
Dulles, Avery. The Priestly Office: A Theological Reflection. LC 97-5289. 96p. (Orig.). 1997. pap. 7.95 (*0-8091-3716-X*) Paulist Pr.
— Splendor of Faith: The Theological Vision of Pope John Paul II. LC 99-11634. 208p. 1999. pap. text 19.95 (*0-8245-1792-X*) Crossroad NY.
— A Testimonial to Grace & Reflections on a Theological Journey. 50th anniversary rev. ed. Orig. Title: A Testimonial to Grace. 160p. 1996. 24.95 (*1-55612-904-1*, LL1904) Sheed & Ward WI.
Dulles, Avery & Granfield, Patrick. The Theology of the Church: A Bibliography. LC 98-45037. 176p. 1999. 14.95 (*0-8091-3847-6*) Paulist Pr.
Dulles, Avery, tr. see Rousselot, Pierre.
Dulles, Eleanor L. The French Franc: 1914-1928. Wilkins, Mira, ed. LC 78-3910. (International Finance Ser.). (Illus.). 1979. reprint ed. lib. bdg. 53.95 (*0-405-11214-9*) Ayer.
Dulles, Foster R. America in the Pacific. LC 73-86595. (American Scene Ser.). 1969. reprint ed. 37.50 (*0-306-71431-0*); reprint ed. pap. text 11.95 (*0-685-01351-0*) Da Capo.
— American Policy Toward Communist China, 1949-1969. LC 70-184974. (C). 1972. pap. text. write for info. (*0-88295-728-7*) Harlan Davidson.
— Eastward Ho! LC 73-90632. (Essay Index Reprint Ser.). 1977. 21.95 (*0-8369-1256-X*) Ayer.
— A History of Recreation: America Learns to Play. 2nd ed. LC 65-25489. (Illus.). (C). 1965. 39.50 (*0-89197-498-9*); pap. text 19.95 (*0-8290-1781-X*) Irvington.
— Old China Trade. LC 70-111470. reprint ed. 32.50 (*0-404-02216-2*) AMS Pr.
— Twentieth Century America. 582p. 1972. 28.95 (*0-8369-2898-9*) Bks for Libraries.
Dulles, Foster R., jt. auth. see Dubofsky, Melvyn.
Dulles, John F. Federal Immigration Law Enforcement in the Southwest: Civil Rights Impacts on Border Communities. (Illus.). 125p. 1998. pap. text 25.00 (*0-7881-7197-6*) DIANE Pub.
Dulles, John F., et al. Minutes of Telephone Conversations of John Foster Dulles & of Christian Herter, 1953-1961. LC 86-892621. (Presidential Documents Ser.). 11 p. 1980. write for info. (*0-89093-356-1*) U Pubns Amer.
— The Papers of John Foster Dulles & of Christian A. Herter, 1953-1961. LC 87-15979. (The Presidential Documents Ser.). 24p. 1986. write for info. (*0-89093-890-3*); write for info. (*0-89093-891-1*) U Pubns Amer.
Dulles, John W. Carlos Lacerda, Brazilian Crusader Vol. 1: The Years, 1914-1960. (Illus.). 513p. 1991. text 42.50 (*0-292-71125-5*) U of Tex Pr.
— Carlos Lacerda, Brazilian Crusader Vol. II: 1960-1977. (Illus.). 864p. 1996. text 50.00 (*0-292-71581-1*) U of Tex Pr.
— Castello Branco: The Making of a Brazilian President. LC 77-99279. (Illus.). 544p. 1978. 49.95 (*0-89096-043-7*) Tex A&M Univ Pr.
— President Castello Branco: Brazilian Reformer. LC 79-5281. (Illus.). 568p. 1981. 39.95 (*0-89096-092-5*) Tex A&M Univ Pr.
— The Sao Paulo Law School & the Anti-Vargas Resistance (1938-1945) LC 85-15069. (Illus.). 286p. 1986. pap. 88.70 (*0-7837-8956-4*, 204966900002) Bks Demand.
Dulles, Wink. Fielding's Bahamas. 304p. 1996. pap. text 16.95 (*1-56952-105-0*) Fielding Wrldwide.
— Fielding's Guide to Thailand: Including Cambodia Laos & Myanmar. 1996. pap. 18.95 (*1-56952-069-0*) Fielding Wrldwide.
— Fieldings Southern Vietnam on Two Wheels. 1995. pap. 15.95 (*1-56952-064-X*) Fielding Wrldwide.
— Fielding's Vietnam Including Cambodia & Laos. Knoles, Kathy, ed. (Illus.). 512p. 1997. pap. 19.95 (*1-56952-154-9*) Fielding Wrldwide.
Dullien, F. A. Introduction to Industrial Gas Cleaning. 458p. 1988. text 99.00 (*0-12-223652-1*) Acad Pr.
— Porous Media: Fluid Transport & Pore Structure. 2nd ed. (Illus.). 574p. 1991. text 82.00 (*0-12-223651-3*) Acad Pr.
Dullum, Kare B., jt. auth. see Stonehill, Arthur I.
Dulmage, K. Basic Typing Skills. 96p. (Orig.). (C). 1986. pap. text 19.95 (*0-273-02465-5*) Trans-Atl Phila.
Dulman, Marc. House Wine. 86p. (Orig.). 1988. pap. 5.95 (*0-9620955-9-1*) GldnGate.
Dulong, Gaston. Dictionnaire Correctif du Francais au Canada. (FRE.). 1968. write for info. (*0-7859-8030-X*, 2-7637-6363-4) Fr & Eur.
Dulong, John. French-Canadian Genealogical Research. (Illus.). 74p. 1995. pap. 8.00 (*0-614-10198-0*) L I S I Pr.
Dulpers, Juliane. Voulez - Vous Voler Avec Moi: Eine Studie Zur Franzosischsprachigen Dichtung Hans Arps. (GER.). 270p. 1997. 51.95 (*3-631-31776-X*) P Lang Pubng.
Duls, L. D. Richard II in the Early Chronicles. LC 73-80355. (Studies in English Literature: No. 79). 274p. 1975. pap. text 46.15 (*90-279-3326-X*) Mouton.
Dulsey, Bernard M., tr. see Icaza, Jorge.
Dulski, Thomas R., ed. A Manual for the Chemical Analysis of Metals, No. 25. LC 96-1836. (Manual Ser.: Vol. 25). (Illus.). 260p. 1996. text 89.00 (*0-8031-2066-4*, MNL25) ASTM.
Dultz, Marc. Perfect General 2: The Official Strategy Guide. 1995. pap. 19.95 (*1-55958-766-0*) Prima Pub.
Dultz, Mark, told to. This Means War: The Official Strategy Guide. 265p. 1996. pap. text 19.95 (*0-7615-0176-2*) Prima Pub.
Dultz, Mary Alice Bozzo. Animals. 1995. 6.95 (*1-55708-451-3*, MCC897) McDonald Pub Co.
Dultz, Ron. The Amazing Poetry of Ron Dultz. (Illus.). 56p. 1986. pap. 5.95 (*0-9601636-6-2*) R Dultz.
— The Collected Poetry of Ron Dultz. Towbin, Ruth, ed. LC 84-91082. (Illus.). 165p. 1984. 12.00 (*0-9601636-2-X*); pap. 7.00 (*0-9601636-3-8*) R Dultz.
— Educating the Entire Person. Towbin, Ruth, ed. LC 78-52911. 108p. (C). 1984. reprint ed. 10.00 (*0-9601636-1-1*) R Dultz.
— Educating the Entire Person: An Original Theory of Learning & Teaching. Towbin, Ruth, ed. LC 78-52911. 128p. (C). 1984. reprint ed. pap. 10.00 (*0-9601636-0-3*) R Dultz.
— Hainesville. Towbin, Ruth, ed. LC 84-91137. 195p. 1984. pap. 6.00 (*0-9601636-4-6*) R Dultz.
— A New Approach to Human Psychology. unabridged ed. 124p. (Orig.). 1996. mass mkt. 10.00 (*0-9601636-8-9*) R Dultz.
Dultzin, Deborah. Cuasares en los Confines del Universo. (Ciencia para Todos Ser.). (SPA.). pap. 6.99 (*968-16-2795-4*, Pub. by Fondo) Continental Bk.
Duly, Leslie C. British Land Policy at the Cape, Seventeen Ninety-Five to Eighteen Forty-Four: A Study of Administrative Procedures in the Empire. LC 67-29574. 246p. reprint ed. 76.30 (*0-8357-9097-5*, 201790000010) Bks Demand.
Dum, Adam, ed. see Kim, Sung Ho & Yuan, Tina.
Dum, Mary. The Computerized Appraisal Office. LC 96-25410. 1996. write for info. (*0-922154-29-5*) Appraisal Inst.
Duma, Gerald, ed. Earthquake Engineering: Proceedings of the 10th European Conference, Vienna, Austria, August 28, Sept. 2, 1994, 4 vols. (Illus.). 2900p. 1995. 492.00 (*90-5410-528-3*, Pub. by A A Balkema) Ashgate Pub Co.
Dumagaindin, Iris, ed. see Benefiel, Robert.
Dumagan, Jesus C. & Hackett, John W. U. S. Trends in Eating Away from Home, 1982-89: A Survey by Eating Occasion, Type of Foodservice Establishment, & Kind of Food. (Illus.). 70p. (C). 1997. reprint ed. pap. text 25.00 (*0-7881-3701-8*) DIANE Pub.
Dumaine. Vest Pocket Guide to Technical Writing. 1997. pap. text 17.95 (*0-13-614264-8*) P-H.
Dumaine, Bob, jt. auth. see Dolin, Eric Jay.
Dumaine, Deborah. Write to the Top: Writing for Corporate Success. rev. ed. 1989. pap. 14.00 (*0-679-72346-3*) Vin Bks.
Dumaine, Deborah & Better Communications Staff. Vest-Pocket Guide to Business Writing. 452p. (C). 1997. text 27.95 (*0-13-440355-X*); pap. text 18.95 (*0-13-440348-7*) P-H.
DuMais, Richard. Fifty Ski Tours in Jackson Hole & Yellowstone. (Illus.). 125p. (Orig.). 1990. pap. 14.95 (*1-884709-03-6*) High Peak Bks.
— Great American Rock Climbs. (Illus.). 120p. 1995. pap. 21.95 (*1-884709-04-4*) High Peak Bks.
Dumanski, Julian, et al. Indicators of Land Quality & Sustainable Land Management: An Annotated Bibliography. LC 98-14346. (Environmentally & Socially Sustainable Development Studies & Monographs). 132p. 1998. pap. 22.00 (*0-8213-4208-8*, 14208) World Bank.
Dumarcay, Jacques & Smithies, Michael. Cultural Sites of Burma, Thailand, & Cambodia. (Illus.). 138p. 1996. text 55.00 (*967-65-3070-0*) OUP.
— Cultural Sites of Malaysia, Singapore, & Indonesia. LC 97-19878. (Illus.). 144p. (C). 1998. 38.00 (*983-56-0028-7*) OUP.
Dumarche & Pouessel. The Hundred Years War. (Illus.). (J). 1993. write for info. (*0-237-51279-3*) EVN1 UK.
Dumarest, Noel. Notes on Cochiti, New Mexico. LC 20-23196. (American Anthropological Association Memoirs Ser.: No. 27). 1919. 25.00 (*0-527-00526-6*) Periodicals Srv.
DuMars, Charles T., et al, eds. Pueblo Indian Water Rights: Struggle for a Precious Resource. LC 84-2490. 183p. 1984. 29.50 (*0-8165-0832-1*) U of Ariz Pr.
Dumas. Financial Securities: Market Equilibrium & Pricing Methods. 1995. pap. 39.00 (*0-412-53880-6*) Thomson Learn.
Dumas, jt. auth. see Shurpin.
Dumas, Alexandre. Acte. (FRE.). 1984. pap. 10.95 (*0-7859-3237-2*, 2266041479) Fr & Eur.
— Adventures in Caucasia. Murch, Alma E., ed. LC 75-16415. (Illus.). 205p. 1975. reprint ed. lib. bdg. 59.50 (*0-8371-8187-9*, DUAC, Greenwood Pr) Greenwood.
— Alexandre Dumas' Adventures in Czarist Russia. Murch, Alma E., ed. LC 75-11422. (Illus.). 208p. 1975. reprint ed. lib. bdg. 35.00 (*0-8371-8188-7*, DUCZR, Greenwood Pr) Greenwood.
— Ange Pitou. (FRE.). 13.95 (*0-8288-9972-X*, F60222) Fr & Eur.
— Ange Pitou, 2 vols., 1. 1989. pap. 23.95 (*0-7859-3320-4*, 2870273142) Fr & Eur.
— Ange Pitou, 2 vols., 2. 1989. pap. 23.95 (*0-7859-3321-2*, 2870273150) Fr & Eur.
***Dumas, Alexandre.** Ange Pitou, Vol. I. 252p. 2000. pap. 9.95 (*0-594-02966-X*) Eightn Hundrd.
Dumas, Alexandre. Ascanio. (FRE., Illus.). 600p. 1956. 7.95 (*0-8288-9973-8*, F60232) Fr & Eur.
— The Black Tulip. 1976. 23.95 (*0-8488-1290-5*) Amereon Ltd.
— The Black Tulip. (Oxford World Classics Ser.). 288p. 2000. pap. 11.95 (*0-19-283750-8*) OUP.
— The Black Tulip. 1990. reprint ed. lib. bdg. 21.95 (*0-89966-684-1*) Buccaneer Bks.
— The Black Tulip. (Pocket Classic Ser.). (Illus.). 256p. 1992. reprint ed. pap. 6.00 (*0-7509-0028-8*, Pub. by Sutton Pub Ltd) Intl Pubs Mktg.
— Camille. 1972. mass mkt. 5.95 (*0-451-52398-9*, Sig Classics) NAL.
— Camille. Heron, Matilde, tr. from FRE. LC 76-170697. 1977. reprint ed. 14.95 (*0-8369-8887-6*) Ayer.
— Le Capitaine Pamphile. (FRE.). 230p. 1977. pap. 24.95 (*0-7859-5519-4*) Fr & Eur.
— Charles the Seventh at the Homes of His Great Vassals: A Tragedy in Five Acts. Trench-Bonett, Dorothy, tr. from FRE. LC 90-63426. 126p. (Orig.). 1991. pap. 10.95 (*1-879360-00-4*) Noble Pr.
— Le Chevalier de Maison Rouge. (FRE.). 1989. pap. 23.95 (*0-7859-3312-3*, 2870272839) Fr & Eur.
— Le Collier de la Reine. (FRE.). 1973. 23.95 (*0-8288-9739-5*, 2070501337) Fr & Eur.
— Le Collier de la Reine, Vol. 1. (FRE.). 1989. pap. 23.95 (*0-7859-3313-1*, 2870272928) Fr & Eur.
— Le Collier de la Reine, Vol. 2. (FRE.). 1989. pap. 23.95 (*0-7859-3314-X*, 2870272936) Fr & Eur.
***Dumas, Alexandre.** The Companions of Jehu. 252p. 2000. pap. 9.95 (*0-594-02841-8*) Eightn Hundrd.
Dumas, Alexandre. Le Comte de Monte-Cristo. (FRE.). 1981. 99.50 (*0-8288-3442-3*, F120780) Fr & Eur.
— Le Comte de Monte-Cristo. (FRE.). (C). pap. 11.25 (*0-8442-1232-6*, VF1232-6) NTC Contemp Pub Co.
— Le Comte de Monte-Cristo. (Pleiade Ser.). (FRE.). 1476p. 1981. pap. 75.95 (*2-07-010979-8*) Schoenhof.
— Le Comte de Monte-Cristo, 3 vols., 1. 1988. pap. 12.95 (*0-7859-3089-2*) Fr & Eur.
— Le Comte de Monte-Cristo, 3 vols., 2. 1988. pap. 12.95 (*0-7859-3090-6*) Fr & Eur.
— Le Comte de Monte-Cristo, 3 vols., 3. 1988. pap. 12.95 (*0-7859-3092-2*) Fr & Eur.
— Le Comte de Monte-Cristo, 2 tomes, Set. Bornecque, Henri, ed. (Class. Garnier Ser.). pap. 19.90 (*0-685-34891-1*) Fr & Eur.
***Dumas, Alexandre.** La Comtesse de Charny. 252p. 2000. pap. 9.95 (*0-594-01414-X*) Eightn Hundrd.
Dumas, Alexandre. La Comtesse de Charny, 4 vols. (FRE.). 1989. pap. 95.00 (*0-7859-3332-8*, 2870273193); pap. 23.95 (*0-685-68143-2*) Fr & Eur.
— La Comtesse de Charny, 4 vols., 1. (FRE.). 1989. pap. 95.00 (*0-7859-3322-0*, 2870273169) Fr & Eur.
— La Comtesse de Charny, 4 vols., 2. (FRE.). 1989. pap. write for info. (*0-7859-3323-9*, 2870273177) Fr & Eur.
— La Comtesse de Charny, 4 vols., 3. (FRE.). 1989. pap. write for info. (*0-7859-3324-7*, 2870273185) Fr & Eur.
Dumas, Alexandre. Le Contesse de Charny, 2 vols. (FRE.). 15.95 (*0-8288-9974-6*, F60320); 23.95 (*0-685-57706-6*, 2070501337) Fr & Eur.
Dumas, Alexandre. Corsican Brothers. 1976. 20.95 (*0-8488-1291-3*) Amereon Ltd.
— Corsican Brothers. 68p. 1983. reprint ed. lib. bdg. 15.95 (*0-89966-317-6*) Buccaneer Bks.
— The Count of Monte Cristo. Date not set. lib. bdg. 27.95 (*0-614-30405-9*) Amereon Ltd.
— The Count of Monte Cristo. 1976. 29.95 (*0-8488-0478-3*) Amereon Ltd.
— The Count of Monte Cristo. Bair, Lowell, tr. 448p. 1984. mass mkt. 5.95 (*0-553-21350-4*, Bantam Classics) Bantam.
— The Count of Monte Cristo. 1976. lib. bdg. 39.95 (*0-89968-147-6*, Lghtyr Pr) Buccaneer Bks.
— The Count of Monte Cristo. (Classics Illustrated Ser.). (Illus.). 52p. (YA). 1990. pap. 4.95 (*1-57209-005-7*) First Classics.
— The Count of Monte Cristo. Vogel, Malvina, ed. (Great Illustrated Classics Ser.: Vol. 28). (Illus.). 240p. (J). (gr. 3-6). 1993. 9.95 (*0-86611-979-5*) Playmore Inc.
— The Count of Monte Cristo. 1996. 25.95 (*0-679-60199-6*) Random.
— The Count of Monte Cristo. 1998. pap. 4.99 (*0-8125-6568-1*, Pub. by Tor Bks) St Martin.
— The Count of Monte Cristo. 1956. 11.05 (*0-606-00491-2*, Pub. by Turtleback) Demco.
— The Count of Monte Cristo. Buss, Robin, tr. & intro. by. LC 97-152697. 1997. pap. 12.95 (*0-14-044615-X*) Viking Penguin.
— The Count of Monte Cristo. (Classics Library). 1998. pap. 3.95 (*1-85326-733-3*, 7333WW, Pub. by Wrdsworth Edits) NTC Contemp Pub Co.
— The Count of Monte Cristo. abr. ed. 509p. 1988. mass mkt. 6.95 (*0-451-52195-1*, Sig Classics) NAL.
— The Count of Monte Cristo. abr. ed. (Classics for Young Readers Ser.). (Illus.). 400p. (YA). (gr. 4-7). 1996. pap. 4.99 (*0-14-037353-5*, PuffinBks) Peng Put Young Read.
— The Count of Monte Cristo, Vol. I. 448p. 1998. pap. 14.95 (*0-89526-347-5*, Pub. by Regnery Pub) Natl Bk Netwk.
— The Count of Monte Cristo, Vol. II. 448p. 1998. pap. 14.95 (*0-89526-346-7*, Pub. by Regnery Pub) Natl Bk Netwk.
— Les Crimes Celebres. 320p. 1961. 8.95 (*0-7859-0697-5*) Fr & Eur.
— A Critical Edition of La Route de Thebes by Alexandre Dumas Fils. Lewis, H. D., ed. LC 98-37625. (Studies in French Literature: Vol. 29). 284p. 1998. text 89.95 (*0-7734-8241-5*) E Mellen.
***Dumas, Alexandre.** La Dame Aux Camelias. Coward, David, tr. (Oxford World's Classics Ser.). 244p. 2000. pap. text 9.95 (*0-19-283638-2*) OUP.
Dumas, Alexandre. La Dame aux Camelias. unabridged ed. (FRE.). pap. 7.95 (*2-87714-205-1*, Pub. by Bookking Intl) Distribks Inc.
— La Dame de Monsoreau. (FRE., Illus.). 256p. 1972. 17.95 (*0-8288-9975-4*, F60346) Fr & Eur.
— D'Artagnan the King Maker. 1976. 24.95 (*0-8488-0358-2*) Amereon Ltd.
— The Demi-Monde. Squier, E. G., tr. from FRE. LC 87-7395. 164p. 1987. reprint ed. lib. bdg. 29.50 (*0-86527-364-2*) Fertig.
— Dumas on Food: Selections from Le Grand Dictionnaire de Cuisine. Davidson, Alan & Davidson, Jane, trs. LC 79-321517. 327p. 1978. reprint ed. pap. 101.40 (*0-7837-2020-3*, 204229500002) Bks Demand.
— Excursions sur les Bords du Rhin. (FRE.). 1991. pap. 20.95 (*0-7859-3401-4*) Fr & Eur.
— Le Faiseur. (FRE.). 312p. 1981. 39.95 (*0-7859-1208-8*, 205000169X) Fr & Eur.
— La Femme aux Camelias. (FRE.). 1975. pap. 11.95 (*0-7859-1812-4*, 2070367045) Fr & Eur.
— Fille du Regent. (FRE.). 8.95 (*0-8288-9976-2*, F60402) Fr & Eur.
— Georges. Rivers, W. Napoleon et al, eds. (FRE.). (YA). 1990. 7.95 (*0-87498-082-8*); pap. 5.95 (*0-87498-083-6*) Assoc Pubs DC.
— Georges. (FRE.). 512p. 1974. pap. 10.95 (*0-7859-1782-9*, 2070365670) Fr & Eur.
— Georges. (Folio Ser.: No. 567). (FRE.). 512p. 8.95 (*2-07-036567-0*) Schoenhof.
— La Guerre des Femmes. 8.95 (*0-686-55818-9*) Fr & Eur.
— The Lady of the Camellias. 1994. 5.50 (*0-87129-449-4*, L81) Dramatic Pub.
— Lethal Arrogance. LC 99-31677. 416p. 1999. text 29.95 (*0-312-22251-3*) St Martin.
— Lettrines, Vol. 1. (FRE.). 288p. 1977. 16.95 (*0-7859-1200-2*, 2859560262) Fr & Eur.
— Louise de la Valliere. Coward, David, ed. & intro. by. (Oxford World's Classics Ser.). 764p. 1998. pap. 14.95 (*0-19-283465-7*) OUP.
— Louise de la Valliere. 1994. reprint ed. lib. bdg. 37.95 (*1-56849-274-X*) Buccaneer Bks.
— The Man in the Iron Mask. (Classics Illustrated Study Guides Ser.). (Illus.). 1997. mass mkt. 4.99 (*1-57840-037-6*, Pub. by Acclaim Bks) Penguin Putnam.
— The Man in the Iron Mask. (Illustrated Classics Collection 4). 64'p. 1994. pap. 4.95 (*0-7854-0750-2*, 40503) Am Guidance.
— The Man in the Iron Mask. 1976. 27.95 (*0-8488-1293-X*) Amereon Ltd.
— The Man in the Iron Mask. 1976. lib. bdg. 35.95 (*0-89968-146-8*, Lghtyr Pr) Buccaneer Bks.
— The Man in the Iron Mask. Coward, David, ed. & intro. by. (Oxford World's Classics Ser.). 654p. 1998. pap. 11.95 (*0-19-283842-3*) OUP.
— The Man in the Iron Mask. Farr, Naunerle C., ed. (Now Age Illustrated IV Ser.). (Illus.). (J). (gr. 4-12). 1978. student ed. 1.25 (*0-88301-340-1*); pap. text 2.95 (*0-88301-316-9*) Pendulum Pr.
— The Man in the Iron Mask. LC 98-65626. (Illus.). (J). (gr. 4-7). 1998. pap. 3.99 (*0-679-89433-0*, Pub. by Random Bks Yng Read) Random.
— The Man in the Iron Mask. LC 98-47663. 448p. 1998. pap. 14.95 (*0-89526-348-3*, Pub. by Regnery Pub) Natl Bk Netwk.
— The Man in the Iron Mask. 592p. 1998. pap. 4.99 (*0-8125-6499-5*, Pub. by Tor Bks) St Martin.
***Dumas, Alexandre.** The Man in the Iron Mask. 1998. 10.09 (*0-606-13594-4*, Pub. by Turtleback) Demco.
Dumas, Alexandre. The Man in the Iron Mask. rev. ed. Rogers, Jacqueline, tr. 464p. 1992. mass mkt. 6.95 (*0-451-52564-7*, Sig Classics) NAL.
— The Man in the Iron Mask. rev. ed. 496p. 1998. mass mkt. 6.99 (*0-451-19700-3*, Sig) NAL.
— The Man in the Iron Mask Readalong. (Illustrated Classics Collection 4). 64p. 1994. pap. 14.95 incl. audio (*0-7854-0766-9*, 40505) Am Guidance.
***Dumas, Alexandre.** Marguerite De Valois. 252p. 2000. pap. 9.95 (*0-594-02836-1*) Eightn Hundrd.
Dumas, Alexandre. Masked Ball & Other Stories. Bell, A. Craig, tr. & intro. by. LC 98-115360. (Pocket Classics Ser.). 128p. 1997. pap. 12.95 (*0-7509-1467-X*, Pub. by Sutton Pub Ltd) Intl Pubs Mktg.
***Dumas, Alexandre.** Memoirs of a Physician. 252p. 2000. pap. 9.95 (*0-594-02976-7*) Eightn Hundrd.
— Memoirs of a Physician, Vol. II. 252p. 2000. pap. 9.95 (*0-594-02981-3*) Eightn Hundrd.
— Memoirs of a Physician, Vol. III. 252p. 2000. pap. 9.95 (*0-594-03016-1*) Eightn Hundrd.
Dumas, Alexandre. Mes Memoires, 5 vols., 4. 16.50 (*0-686-55825-1*) Fr & Eur.
— Mes Memoires, 5 vols., 5. 1968. 16.50 (*0-685-57721-X*) Fr & Eur.
— Mes Memoires, 5 vols., Set. 95.00 (*0-8288-9977-0*, F60460) Fr & Eur.
— Un Metier de Seigneur. (FRE.). 260p. 1991. 24.95 (*0-7859-1185-5*, 2268012883) Fr & Eur.
— Mille et un Fantomes. (FRE.). 238p. 1980. pap. 7.95 (*0-7859-5573-9*) Fr & Eur.
— Mon Dictionnaire de Cuisine. (FRE.). 1998. 29.95 (*0-320-00207-1*) Fr & Eur.
***Dumas, Alexandre.** Monsieur de Chauvelin's Will. 252p. 2000. pap. 9.95 (*0-594-01561-8*) Eightn Hundrd.
Dumas, Alexandre. Les Oeuvres Completes d'Alexandre Dumas, 48 vols., Set. 1000.00 (*0-686-55828-6*) Fr & Eur.
***Dumas, Alexandre.** The Page of the Duke of Savoy. 252p. 2000. pap. 9.95 (*0-594-03021-8*) Eightn Hundrd.
— Les Quarante-Cinq. 12.50 (*0-686-55830-8*) Fr & Eur.
Dumas, Alexandre. Queen Margot. LC 94-7600. 542p. (J). 1994. pap. 14.45 (*0-7868-8082-1*, Pub. by Hyperion) Time Warner.
***Dumas, Alexandre.** The Queen's Necklace. 252p. 2000. pap. 9.95 (*0-594-03006-4*) Eightn Hundrd.
— The Queen's Necklace, Vol. II. 252p. 2000. pap. 9.95 (*0-594-03011-0*) Eightn Hundrd.
Dumas, Alexandre. La Reine Margot. (FRE.). 1992. pap. 16.95 (*0-7859-3287-9*, 2277232793) Fr & Eur.

D

An Asterisk (*) at the beginning of an entry indicates that the title is appearing for the first time.

— La Reine Margot. unabridged ed. (FRE.). pap. 8.95 (*2-87714-188-8*, Pub. by Bookking Intl) Distribks Inc.
— La Reine Margot: Dame De Monsoreau: Les Quarante-Cinq. (FRE.). 1680p. 1988. pap. 65.00 (*0-7859-2192-3*, 2715213638) Fr & Eur.
***Dumas, Alexandre.** La Reine Margot: Literature in Translation. (Oxford World's Classics Ser.). 560p. 1999. pap. 13.95 (*0-19-283844-X*) OUP.
Dumas, Alexandre. Road to Monte Cristo. 405p. Date not set. 27.95 (*0-8488-2634-5*) Amereon Ltd.
— Salvator, 4 vols. 1976. pap. 9.95 (*0-685-73335-1*) Fr & Eur.
— Short Stories, 10 Vols. LC 72-5898. (Short Story Index Reprint Ser.). 1977. reprint ed. 55.95 (*0-8369-4212-4*) Ayer.
— The Son of Monte Cristo. 1976. 20.95 (*0-8488-1294-8*) Amereon Ltd.
— Theatre Complet, Vol. 1. (FRE., Illus.). 588p. 1974. 33.95 (*0-7859-0067-5*, M2279) Fr & Eur.
— Theatre Complet: Christine ou Stockholm, Fontainebleau et Rome, Vol. 1, Pt. 6. (FRE.). 186p. 1976. pap. 27.95 (*0-7859-5434-1*) Fr & Eur.
— Theatre Complet: Flesque de Lavagna, Vol. 1, Pt. 4. (FRE.). 166p. 1976. pap. 22.95 (*0-686-55208-3*) Fr & Eur.
— Theatre Complet: Henry III et sa Cour, Vol. 1, Pt. 5. (FRE.). 152p. 1976. pap. 22.95 (*0-7859-5433-3*) Fr & Eur.
— Theatre Complet: La Chasse et l'Amour, la Noce et l'Enterrement, Vol. 1, Pt. 2. (FRE.). 126p. 1976. pap. 22.95 (*0-7859-5431-7*) Fr & Eur.
— The Three Musketeers. (Classics Illustrated Study Guides Ser.). (Illus.). 1997. mass mkt. 4.99 (*1-57840-029-5*, Pub. by Acclaim Bks) Penguin Putnam.
— The Three Musketeers. 1976. 29.95 (*0-8488-1295-6*) Amereon Ltd.
***Dumas, Alexandre.** The Three Musketeers. (Illus.). 712p. (gr. 8-12). 1999. 17.95 (*0-375-40657-3*) Everymns Lib.
— The Three Musketeers. Le Clercq, Jacques, tr. from ENG. LC 99-34768. 684p. (gr. 4-11). 1999. 24.95 (*0-679-60332-8*) Modern Library Prakashan.
Dumas, Alexandre. The Three Musketeers. Bair, Lowell, tr. LC 98-10575. (Illus.). 656p. (J). (gr. 4-7). 1998. 25.00 (*0-688-14583-3*, Wm Morrow) Morrow Avon.
— The Three Musketeers. Coward, David, ed. & intro. by. (Oxford World's Classics Ser.). 704p. 1999. pap. 8.95 (*0-19-283575-0*) OUP.
— The Three Musketeers. (Illustrated Junior Library). (Illus.). 320p. (J). (gr. 4-6). 1953. 15.99 (*0-448-06024-8*, G & D) Peng Put Young Read.
— The Three Musketeers. Vogel, Malvina, ed. (Great Illustrated Classics Ser.: Vol. 15). (Illus.). 240p. (J). (gr. 3-6). 1990. 9.95 (*0-86611-966-3*) Playmore Inc.
— The Three Musketeers. LC 98-47661. 416p. 1998. pap. 14.95 (*0-89526-349-1*, Pub. by Regnery Pub) Natl Bk Netwk.
***Dumas, Alexandre.** The Three Musketeers. (Signature Classics Ser.). (Illus.). 776p. 1999. 24.95 (*1-58279-035-3*) Trident Pr Intl.
Dumas, Alexandre. The Three Musketeers. (Bantam Classics Ser.). 1984. 11.05 (*0-606-02468-9*, Pub. by Turtleback) Demco.
— The Three Musketeers. (Classics Library). 576p. 1997. pap. 3.95 (*1-85326-040-1*, j0401WW, Pub. by Wrdsworth Edits) NTC Contemp Pub Co.
— The Three Musketeers. abr. ed. (Puffin Classics Ser.). (Illus.). 224p. (YA). (gr. 4-7). 1995. pap. 4.99 (*0-14-036747-0*, PuffinBks) Peng Put Young Read.
— The Three Musketeers. adapted ed. 1976. pap. 5.25 (*0-8222-1140-8*) Dramatists Play.
***Dumas, Alexandre.** The Three Musketeers. deluxe ed. (Signature Classics Ser.). (Illus.). 776p. 1999. 29.95 (*1-58279-047-7*) Trident Pr Intl.
Dumas, Alexandre. The Three Musketeers. unabridged ed. Bair, Lowell, tr. from FRE. LC 00-3693. (Bantam Classics Ser.). 545p. (J). 1984. mass mkt. 5.95 (*0-553-21337-7*, Bantam Classics) Bantam.
— The Three Musketeers. 2nd ed. (Illustrated Classic Book Ser.). (Illus.). 61p. (J). (gr. 3 up). 1998. reprint ed. pap. text 4.95 (*1-56767-251-5*) Educ Insights.
— The Three Musketeers: Acting Edition. (Illustrated Classics Collection 2). 64p. 1994. pap. 4.95 (*0-7854-0675-1*, 40421) Am Guidance.
— The Three Musketeers: Acting Edition. (Illus.). 96p. 1995. pap. text 1.00 (*0-486-28326-7*) Dover.
— The Three Musketeers: Acting Edition. (Regents Illustrated Classics Ser.). 62p. (YA). (gr. 7-12). 1987. pap. text 3.75 (*0-13-920463-6*, 20533) Prentice ESL.
— The Three Musketeers: Acting Edition. LC 93-42782. (Bullseye Step into Classics Ser.). 108p. (J). (gr. 2-6). 1994. pap. 3.99 (*0-679-86017-7*, Pub. by Random Bks Yng Read) Random.
— The Three Musketeers: Acting Edition. (J). 1994. mass mkt. 4.99 (*0-8125-3602-9*, Pub. by Tor Bks) St Martin.
— The Three Musketeers: Acting Edition. Sudley, Lord, tr. 720p. 1982. pap. 9.95 (*0-14-044025-9*, Penguin Classics) Viking Penguin.
— The Three Musketeers: Acting Edition. abr. ed. Hochman, Eleanor, tr. & rev. by. 608p. (J). (gr. 7). 1991. reprint ed. mass mkt. 6.95 (*0-451-52547-7*, W8107, Sig Classics) NAL.
— The Three Musketeers: Acting Edition. 1984. reprint ed. lib. bdg. 28.95 (*0-89968-148-4*, Lghtyr Pr) Buccaneer Bks.
— The Three Musketeers Readalong. (Illustrated Classics Collection 2). 64p. 1994. pap. 14.95 incl. audio (*0-7854-0691-3*, 40423) Am Guidance.
— The Tower. Wood, Charles, tr. (Oberon Bks.). 160p. 1997. pap. 12.95 (*1-870259-60-2*) Theatre Comm.
— Les Trois Mousquetaires. (FRE.). 1800p. 1962. 95.00 (*0-7859-1098-0*, 2070101800); 115.00 (*0-8288-3443-1*, F60650) Fr & Eur.
— Les Trois Mousquetaires. (FRE.). (C). pap. 11.25 (*0-8442-1229-6*, VF1229-6) NTC Contemp Pub Co.
— Les Trois Mousquetaires. deluxe ed. (Pleiade Ser.). (FRE.). 82.95 (*2-07-010180-0*) Schoenhof.
— Les Trois Mousquetaires. unabridged ed. (FRE.). 1999. pap. 7.95 (*2-87714-198-5*, Pub. by Bookking Intl) Distribks Inc.
— Les Trois Mousquetaires, Tome I. (FRE.). 448p. 1973. pap. 11.95 (*0-7859-1771-3*, 2070365263) Fr & Eur.
— Les Trois Mousquetaires, Tome II. (FRE.). 448p. 1973. pap. 11.95 (*0-7859-1772-1*, 2070365271) Fr & Eur.
— Les Trois Mousquetaires & Vingt Ans Apres. 1800p. 45.00 (*0-686-56508-8*) Fr & Eur.
— Le Trou de L'Enfer. (FRE.). 364p. 1980. pap. 34.95 (*0-7859-5435-X*) Fr & Eur.
— La Tulipe Noire. Simon, Rene, ed. (FRE., Illus.). 188p. 1983. pap. 11.95 (*0-7859-4670-5*) Fr & Eur.
— Twenty Years After. 1976. 28.95 (*0-8488-1296-4*) Amereon Ltd.
— Twenty Years After. LC 99-188043. (Illus.). 880p. 1998. pap. 14.95 (*0-19-283843-1*) OUP.
— Twenty Years After. 467p. 1981. reprint ed. lib. bdg. 31.95 (*0-89968-229-4*, Lghtyr Pr) Buccaneer Bks.
— The Vicomte de Bragelonne, or Ten Years Later. Coward, David, ed. & intro. by. (Oxford World's Classics Ser.). 766p. 1998. pap. 14.95 (*0-19-283463-0*) OUP.
— Vingt Ans Apres. Samaran, Charles, ed. (Coll. Prestige). 12.95 (*0-685-34894-6*) Fr & Eur.
— Vingt Ans Apres, 2 tomes. (Coll. GF). 1961. pap. 9.00 (*0-685-11621-2*) Fr & Eur.
— Vingt Ans Apres, 2 vols. 1975. write for info. (*0-318-63616-6*) Fr & Eur.
— Vingt Ans Apres. Samaran, Charles, ed. (Class. Garnier Ser.). 1989. pap. 20.95 (*0-7859-3150-3*, 2253050520) Fr & Eur.
— Vingt Ans Apres, Tome I. (FRE.). 544p. 1975. pap. 11.95 (*0-7859-1803-5*, 2070366820) Fr & Eur.
— Vingt Ans Apres, Tome II. (FRE.). 544p. 1975. pap. 12.95 (*0-7859-1804-3*, 2070366839) Fr & Eur.
— Voyage en Calabre. (FRE.). 1989. pap. 24.95 (*0-7859-3316-6*, 2870272979) Fr & Eur.
***Dumas, Alexandre.** The War of Women. 252p. 2000. pap. 9.95 (*0-594-02996-1*) Eighth Hundrd.
— The War of Women, Vol. II. 252p. 2000. pap. 9.95 (*0-594-03001-3*) Eighth Hundrd.
Dumas, Alexandre & Bassan, Fernande. Theatre Complet: Comment Je Devins Auteur Dramatique. Ivanhoe, Vol. 1, Pt. 1. (FRE.). 144p. 1976. pap. 22.95 (*0-7859-5430-9*) Fr & Eur.
Dumas, Alexandre & Raffalli, Bernard. La Dame aux Camelias. 1975. write for info. (*0-318-63468-6*) Fr & Eur.
— La Dame aux Camelias. (Folio Ser.: No. 704). (FRE.). 1975. 9.95 (*2-07-036704-5*) Schoenhof.
Dumas, Alexandre & Rizvi, S. N. The Three Musketeers. 156p. 1997. pap. 20.00 (*81-209-0218-1*, Pub. by Pitambar Pub) St Mut.
Dumas, Alexandre, et al. Quinze Aventures de Mousquetaires. 256p. 1976. 9.95 (*0-686-55831-6*) Fr & Eur.
— Quinze Chasses au Tresor. (Illus.). 224p. 1974. 9.95 (*0-686-55832-4*) Fr & Eur.
Dumas, Alexandre, ed. see Eluard, Paul.
Dumas, Alexandre, ed. see Hugo, Victor.
Dumas, Ann. Degas's Mlle. Fiocre in Context. (Illus.). 46p. 1988. pap. 5.95 (*0-87273-116-2*) Bklyn Mus.
Dumas, Ann & Tinterow, Gary. The Private Collection of Edgar Degas. Polizzotti, Mark, tr. from FRE. LC 97-17882. 1997. pap. 35.00 (*0-87099-799-8*) Metro Mus Art.
Dumas, Ann, et al. Impressionism: Paintings Collected by European Museums. LC 98-45847. (Illus.). 272p. 1999. 39.95 (*0-8109-6383-3*, Pub. by Abrams) Time Warner.
— The Private Collection of Edgar Degas. Polizzotti, Mark, tr. from FRE. LC 97-17882. (Illus.). 320p. 1997. 75.00 (*0-8109-6512-7*, Pub. by Abrams) Time Warner.
— The Private Collection of Edgar Degas. Polizzotti, Mark, tr. from FRE. LC 97-17882. 1997. pap. 45.00 (*0-87099-797-1*) Metro Mus Art.
Dumas, Barbara, ed. see Bullock, Harold B.
***Dumas, Bianca Cowan.** Tia Luisa, the Magical Cook: A Tale in English & Spanish. LC 99-64692. (SPA & ENG., Illus.). 32p. (J). (gr. k-4). 2000. pap. 7.95 (*0-9669645-4-3*, AlterLingo) OHollow.
Dumas, Charles E. The Effects of Government Deficits: A Comparative Analysis of Crowding out. LC 85-19423. (Essays in International Finance Ser.: No. 158). 52p. 1985. pap. text 10.00 (*0-88165-065-X*) Princeton U Int Finan Econ.
Dumas, Didier, et al. Sons, Lovers & Fathers: Understanding Male Sexuality. Trager, Anne, tr. from FRE. LC 96-31300. 200p. 1997. 35.00 (*0-7657-0033-6*) Aronson.
Dumas, Eric, jt. auth. see Card, Remy.
Dumas, Ernest, compiled by. The Clintons of Arkansas: An Introduction by Those Who Know Them Best. LC 93-12648. 208p. (C). 1993. pap. 16.00 (*1-55728-288-9*) U of Ark Pr.
Dumas, Evelyn. The Bitter Thirties in Quebec. Bennett, Arnold, tr. from FRE. Orig. Title: Dans le Sommeil de nos os. 157p. 1975. 36.99 (*0-919618-53-7*, Pub. by Black Rose); pap. 7.99 (*0-919618-54-5*, Pub. by Black Rose) Consort Bk Sales.
Dumas, Frank R. Claim Paid: A Consumer's Guide Through the Insurance Claims Maze. LC 89-51782. 191p. (Orig.). 1990. pap. 15.95 (*0-9624813-5-1*) Stratton Pr.
Dumas, Gerald. An Afternoon in Waterloo Park. LC 87-31731. (Great Lakes Bks.). (Illus.). 154p. 1988. reprint ed. pap. 14.95 (*0-8143-2039-2*) Wayne St U Pr.
Dumas, Glenda. The Rootworker. 256p. (Orig.). 1992. mass mkt. 3.95 (*0-87067-387-4*) Holloway.
— The Rootworker. (Orig.). 1983. pap. 1.95 (*0-87067-711-X*, BH711) Viking Penguin.
***Dumas, Glenda F.** Respect You Draw & Color Book Bk. 1: Respect. 34p. (J). (ps-2). 1999. mass mkt. 9.99 (*1-930457-00-6*) Glendas Pl.
— Respect You Draw & Color Book Bk. 2: Do Unto Others As You Would Have Them Do Unto You. 36p. (J). (ps-2). 1999. mass mkt. 9.99 (*1-930457-02-2*) Glendas Pl.
— Respect You Draw & Color Book Bk. 3: Cleanliness. 36p. (J). (ps-2). 1999. mass mkt. 9.99 (*1-930457-04-9*) Glendas Pl.
— Respeto Tu Libro Para Dibujar y Colorear Libro 1: Respeto.Tr. of Respect You Draw & Color Book. (SPA.). 34p. (J). (ps-2). 1999. mass mkt. 9.99 (*1-930457-01-4*) Glendas Pl.
— Respeto Tu Libro Para Dibujar y Colorear Libro 3: Limpieza.Tr. of Respect You Draw & Color Book. (SPA.). 36p. (J). (ps-2). 1999. mass mkt. 9.99 (*1-930457-05-7*) Glendas Pl.
Dumas, H. S., et al, eds. Hamiltonian Dynamical Systems: History, Theory, & Applications. LC 94-44179. (IMA Volumes in Mathematics & its Applications Ser.: Vol. 63). 1995. 83.95 (*0-387-94437-0*) Spr-Verlag.
Dumas, Henry. Goodbye, Sweetwater: New & Selected Stories. (Contemporary Fiction Ser.). 370p. 1988. pap. 14.95 (*0-938410-58-X*, Thunders Mouth) Avalon NY.
Dumas, J., ed. see Desnos, Robert.
Dumas, Jacques. Registering Title to Land: A Series of Lectures Delivered at Yale. 106p. 1985. reprint ed. 30.00 (*0-8377-0522-3*, Rothman) W S Hein.
***Dumas, Jennifer.** Car Crashes & Other Sad Stories. 2000. pap. 29.99 (*3-8228-6411-0*) Taschen Amer.
Dumas, John, ed. see Dumas, Lynda.
***Dumas, Joseph S. & Redish, Janice C.** A Practical Guide to Usability Testing. 2nd ed. 416p. 1999. pap. 24.95 (*1-84150-020-8*, Pub. by Intellect) Intl Spec Bk.
Dumas Lachtman, Ofelia. Call Me Consuelo. LC 96-50201. (Illus.). 152p. (YA). (gr. 3-7). 1997. pap. 9.95 (*1-55885-187-9*, Pinata Bks) Arte Publico.
— Girl from Playa Blanca: An Entertaining Adventure Story for Young People That Will Stimulate... 1995. 13.05 (*0-606-13428-X*, Pub. by Turtleback) Demco.
Dumas, Lloyd J. The Overburdened Economy: Uncovering the Causes of Chronic Unemployment, Inflation, & National Decline. 256p. 1986. pap. 14.95 (*0-520-06169-1*, Pub. by U CA Pr) Cal Prin Full Svc.
Dumas, Lloyd J. & Etzioni, Amitai, eds. The Socio-Economics of Conversion from War to Peace. LC 94-48186. (Studies in Socio-Economics). (Illus.). 354p. (YA). (gr. 13). 1995. text 77.95 (*1-56324-528-0*) M E Sharpe.
Dumas, Lloyd J. & Thee, Marek. Making Peace Possible: The Promise of Economic Conversion. (Illus.). 208p. 1999. 150.00 (*0-08-037252-X*, Pub. by Pergamon Repr) Franklin.
Dumas, Lloyd J., ed. see Etzioni, Amitai.
Dumas, Lynda. Rachel & the Royal Garden. Dumas, John, ed. LC 96-86146. (Illus.). 99p. (J). (gr. k-4). 1997. 14.95 (*1-888934-82-4*) Central OR Coast.
Dumas, M. C., ed. see Eluard, Paul.
Dumas, Marc. Die Theologische Deutung der Erfahrung des Nichts Im Deutschen Werk Paul Tillichs (1919-1930) (Europaische Hochschulschriften Ser.: Reihe 23, Bd. 479). (GER.). XI, 216p. 1993. 39.80 (*3-631-45815-0*) P Lang Pubng.
Dumas, Marc, jt. auth. see Jastremski, Michael S.
Dumas, Marcelle, ed. see Eluard, Paul.
Dumas, Marie-Claire, jt. auth. see Desnos, Robert.
Dumas, Marlene. Francis Bacon. (Illus.). 200p. 1996. pap. text 45.00 (*88-8158-027-6*, Pub. by Charta) Dist Art Pubs.
— Marlene Dumas. LC 99-475008. (Contemporary Artists Ser.). 1999. pap. 29.95 (*0-7148-3823-3*) Phaidon Press.
***Dumas, Michael.** Progress in Human African Trypanosomiasis, Sleeping Sickness. LC 98-31567. 1998. 159.00 (*2-287-59655-0*) Spr-Verlag.
Dumas, Mildred. God's Diet for His People. large type ed. LC 98-93744. viii, 235p. (Orig.). 1998. pap. 11.95 (*0-9667905-0-2*) Dumas Ent.
Dumas, Paul, jt. ed. see Carr, G. Lawrence.
Dumas, Paul, jt. ed. see Williams, Gwyn.
***Dumas, Philippe.** A Farm. (Creative Editions Ser.). (Illus.). 40p. (YA). (gr. 6 up). 1999. 39.95 (*1-56846-169-0*, Creat Educ) Creative Co.
Dumas, R. & Fulachier, L., eds. Structure of Complex Turbulent Shear Flow: Marseille, France, 1982, Proceedings. (International Union of Theoretical & Applied Mechanics Symposia Ser.). (Illus.). 444p. 1983. 76.95 (*0-387-12156-0*) Spr-Verlag.
Dumas, Sharron G. As You Are. 40p. 1996. pap. 7.00 (*0-8059-3882-6*) Dorrance.
***Dumas, Timmy.** 24 Reasons Why African Americans Suffer. 144p. 1999. pap. 12.95 (*0-913543-63-2*, Pub. by African Am Imag) IPG Chicago.
Dumas, Timothy. Greentown: Murder & Mystery in Greenwich, America's Wealthiest Community. LC 97-52342. 304p. 1998. 24.45 (*1-55970-441-1*, Pub. by Arcade Pub Inc) Time Warner.
— A Wealth of Evil: The True Story of a Murder in America's Richest Community. (Illus.). 322p. 1999. mass mkt. 7.50 (*0-446-60732-0*, Pub. by Warner Bks) Little.
Dumat, Andrea L. Medicare Claims Management for Home Health Agencies. LC 98-32279. 1999. 149.00 (*0-8342-1220-X*, 1220X) Aspen Pub.
DuMaurier, George. Martian. 1988. reprint ed. lib. bdg. 59.00 (*0-7812-0458-5*) Rprt Serv.
— Peter Ibbetson. 1988. reprint ed. lib. bdg. 49.00 (*0-7812-0022-9*) Rprt Serv.
— Trilby. 1994. reprint ed. lib. bdg. 32.95 (*1-56849-527-7*) Buccaneer Bks.
Dumay, Regine. Como Hacerle Amor A Un Hombre. (SPA.). 142p. 1997. pap. text 11.98 (*968-13-1703-3*) Libros Fronteras.
Dumazy, Francoise Chaniac. Top 10 Guide to Paris. (Top Ten Travel Guides Ser.). (Illus.). 200p. 1999. pap. 14.95 (*1-891382-04-7*) Intrntnlst.
Dumbarton Oaks Collection Staff. Pre-Columbian Art. Benson, Elizabeth P., ed. LC 76-8176. 21p. 1976. lib. bdg. 30.00 (*0-226-68981-6*) U Ch Pr.
Dumbarton Oaks Staff & Maguire, Henry P. Materials Analysis of Byzantine Pottery. LC 96-49564. 1998. 78.00 (*0-88402-251-X*) Dumbarton Oaks.
Dumbauld, Edward. The Bill of Rights & What It Means Today. LC 78-12307. (Illus.). 242p. 1979. reprint ed. lib. bdg. 65.00 (*0-313-21215-5*, DUBR, Greenwood Pr) Greenwood.
— Constitution of the United States. LC 64-11324. (Illus.). 521p. reprint ed. 161.60 (*0-8357-9722-8*, 201621100002) Bks Demand.
— The Declaration of Independence & What It Means Today. LC JK0128.D887. 208p. reprint ed. pap. 64.50 (*0-608-13295-0*, 205215300044) Bks Demand.
— Sayings of Jesus. (Illus.). 196p. (C). 1988. reprint ed. pap. text 20.00 (*0-8191-6753-3*) U Pr of Amer.
— Thomas Jefferson & the Law. LC 78-5742. (Illus.). 1978. 42.50 (*0-8061-1441-X*) U of Okla Pr.
Dumbezil, Georges. The Riddle of Nostradamus: A Critical Dialogue. LC 98-32013. (Parallax Ser.). 1999. write for info. (*0-8018-6129-2*) Johns Hopkins.
Dumbleton, John H., jt. ed. see Black, Jonathan.
Dumbleton, Mike. Dial-a-Croc. 1995. 11.15 (*0-606-08725-7*, Pub. by Turtleback) Demco.
Dumbleton, Susanne, ed. see Roseberry, C. R.
Dumbrajs, T. Y., tr. see Barbashov, B. M. & Nesterenko, V. V.
***Dumbrell, John.** A Special Relationship: Anglo-American Relations in the Cold War & After. LC 00-40458. (Illus.). 2000. write for info. (*0-333-62249-9*) St Martin.
Dumbrell, John, ed. Vietnam & the Antiwar Movement. 190p. 1989. text 77.95 (*0-566-05684-4*, Pub. by Avebry) Ashgate Pub Co.
Dumbrell, R. Understanding Antique Wine Bottles. (Understanding Ser.). (Illus.). 340p. 1983. 29.50 (*0-907462-14-6*) Antique Collect.
Dumbrell, W. J. Covenant & Creation: A Theology of the Old Testament Covenants. (Biblical & Theological Classics Library: Vol. 12). 217p. 1997. reprint ed. pap. text 9.99 (*0-85364-771-2*, Pub. by Paternoster Pub) OM Literature.
Dumbuya, Peter A. Tanganyika under International Mandate, 1919-1946. (C). 1995. lib. bdg. 42.50 (*0-7618-0063-8*) U Pr of Amer.
Dumcombe, Frank R., et al. Katonah: History of a New York Village & Its People. (Illus.). 515p. 1997. reprint ed. lib. bdg. 55.00 (*0-8328-6160-X*) Higginson Bk Co.
Dumelle, Grace, jt. auth. see Cohen, Gail.
Dumelle, Grace, ed. see Johnson, Therese.
Dumenil, Annie, jt. auth. see Edmiston, William F.
Dumenil, Gerard & Levy, Dominique. The Economics of the Profit Rate: Competition, Crises, & Historical Tendencies in Capitalism. LC 93-9720. (New Directions in Modern Economics Ser.). 416p. 1993. 100.00 (*1-85278-760-0*) E Elgar.
Dumenil, Lynn. Freemasonry & American Culture, 1880-1930. LC 84-42594. 324p. reprint ed. pap. 100.50 (*0-7837-4329-7*, 204403300012) Bks Demand.
— The Modern Temper: American Culture & Society in the 1920s. Foner, Eric, ed. 352p. 1995. pap. text 13.00 (*0-8090-1566-8*) Hill & Wang.
Dumeril, Auguste H., et al. Mission Scientifique au Mexique et dans l'Amerique Centrale . . . Recherches Zoologiques: Etude Sur les Reptiles, Avec Atlas, 2 vols. Sterling, Keir B., ed. LC 77-81098. (Biologists & Their World Ser.). (FRE., Illus.). 1978. reprint ed. lib. bdg. 121.95 (*0-405-10680-7*) Ayer.
Dumery, Henry. The Problem of God in Philosophy of Religion: A Critical Examination of the Category of the Absolute & the Scheme of Transcendence. Courtney, Charles, tr. (Studies in Phenomenology & Existential Philosophy). 135p. 1964. pap. 19.95 (*0-8101-0606-X*) Northwestern U Pr.
Dumesic, James A., et al. The Microkinetics of Heterogeneous Catalysis. LC 92-36488. (Professional Reference Book Ser.). 316p. 1993. text 69.00 (*0-8412-2214-2*, Pub. by Am Chemical) OUP.
Dumesnil. Gustave Flaubert, l'Homme et l'Oeuvre. 18.50 (*0-685-34907-1*, F62440) Fr & Eur.
Dumesnil, ed. see Flaubert, Gustave.
Dumesnil, Maurice. Claude Debussy: Master of Dreams. LC 78-23438. 326p. 1979. reprint ed. lib. bdg. 65.00 (*0-313-20775-5*, DUCB, Greenwood Pr) Greenwood.
— Claude Debussy, Master of Dreams. (Music Book Index Ser.). 326p. 1992. reprint ed. lib. bdg. 89.00 (*0-7812-9500-9*) Rprt Serv.
Dumestre, Marcel. A Church at Risk: The Challenge of Spiritually Hungry Adults. LC 97-4143. 192p. (Orig.). 1997. pap. 19.95 (*0-8245-1461-0*, Herdr & Herdr) Crossroad NY.
Dumestre, Marcel, ed. How to Read Church History: From the Beginnings to the 15th Century. (Adult Christian Formation Program Ser.: Vol. 1). 79p. 1992. pap. 4.95 (*0-8245-7004-9*, Herdr & Herdr) Crossroad NY.
— How to Read Church History Vol. 1: Facilitator's Guide. pap. 5.95 (*0-8245-7005-7*) Crossroad NY.
— How to Read Church History Vol. 2: Facilitator's Guide. (Adult Christian Formation Program Ser.). pap. 5.95 (*0-8245-7007-3*) Crossroad NY.

D

An Asterisk (*) at the beginning of an entry indicates that the title is appearing for the first time.

— How to Read Church History Vol. 2: Participants Guide. (Adult Christian Formation Program Ser.). pap. 4.95 (*0-8245-7006-5*) Crossroad NY.

— How to Understand the Sacraments - Participant Guide. (Adult Christian Formation Program Ser.). 1997. pap. 5.95 (*0-8245-7013-8*) Crossroad NY.

Dumett. Gentlemanly Capitalism & British Imperialism: The New Debate on Empire. LC 98-52959. 248p. (C). 1999. pap. 32.06 (*0-582-32782-2*) Longman.

Dumett, Raymond E. El Dorado in West Africa: The Gold Mining Frontier, African Labor, & Colonial Capitalism in the Gold Coast, 1875-1900. LC 97-46494. 235p. 1998. text 44.95 (*0-8214-1197-7*) Ohio U Pr.

— El Dorado in West Africa: The Gold Mining Frontier, African Labor, & Colonial Capitalism in the Gold Coast, 1875-1900. LC 97-46494. 235p. 1998. pap. text 19.95 (*0-8214-1198-5*) Ohio U Pr.

Dumey, Raymond. French-German, German-French Legal Dictionary: Dictionnaire Juridique Francais-Allemand-Francais. (FRE & GER.). 850p. 1982. 175.00 (*0-8288-0383-8*, M6425) Fr & Eur.

DuMez, Judy. Understanding & Regulating Markets. LC 99-15385. 2000. text 69.95 (*0-312-22622-5*) St Martin.

Dumezil. Loki. 1990. lib. bdg. 34.95 (*0-226-16977-4*) U Ch Pr.

Dumezil, Georges. Archaic Roman Religion, Vol. 1. Krapp, Philip, tr. LC 96-14884. Vol. 1. 394p. 1996. text 45.00 (*0-8018-5482-2*) Johns Hopkins.

— Archaic Roman Religion, Vol. 1. Krapp, Philip, tr. LC 96-14884. 394p. 1996. reprint ed. pap. text 18.95 (*0-8018-5480-6*) Johns Hopkins.

— Archaic Roman Religion, Vol. 2. Krapp, Philip, tr. LC 96-14884. 321p. 1996. text 45.00 (*0-8018-5483-0*) Johns Hopkins.

— Deesses Latines et Mythes Vediques. Bolle, Kees W., ed. LC 77-79121. (Mythology Ser.). (FRE.). 1978. reprint ed. lib. bdg. 19.95 (*0-405-10533-9*) Ayer.

— Destiny of a King. Hiltebeitel, Alf, tr. (Midway Reprint Ser.). 164p. 1973. lib. bdg. 18.00 (*0-226-16975-8*) U Ch Pr.

— Destiny of a King. Hiltebeitel, Alf, tr. (Midway Reprint Ser.). 168p. 1988. pap. text 14.95 (*0-226-16976-6*) U Ch Pr.

Dumezil, Georges. From Myth to Fiction. Coltman, Derek, tr. from FRE. 266p. 1973. lib. bdg. 26.50 (*0-226-16972-3*) U Ch Pr.

Dumezil, Georges. Horace et les Curiaces. Bolle, Kees W., ed. (Mythology Ser.). (FRE.). 1978. reprint ed. lib. bdg. 19.95 (*0-405-10534-7*) Ayer.

— Mitra-Varuna: An Essay on Two Indo-European Representations of Sovereignty. Coltman, Derek, tr. from FRE. LC 87-34052. 189p. 1988. 26.95 (*0-942299-12-4*); pap. 13.50 (*0-942299-13-2*) Zone Bks.

— Riddle of Nostradamus: A Critical Dialogue. LC 98-32013. 1999. 39.95 (*0-8018-6128-4*) Johns Hopkins.

Dumezil, Georges & Eliade, Mircea. Archaic Roman Religion, Vol. 2. Krapp, Philip, tr. LC 96-14884. 321p. 1996. reprint ed. pap. text 18.95 (*0-8018-5481-4*) Johns Hopkins.

Dumicich, John, ed. Picture It. (Illus.). 208p. (YA). (gr. 10-12). 1987. pap. text 19.40 (*0-13-676149-6*, 18677) Prentice ESL.

Dumicich, John & Root, Christine. Drawing on Experience: The Fundamentals of Good Writing. LC 95-17741. 170p. (C). 1995. pap. 21.25 (*0-07-018022-9*) McGraw.

***Duminuco, Vincent.** Jesuit Ratio Studiorum of 1599: 400th Anniversary Perspectives. 2000. pap. text. write for info. (*0-8232-2047-8*) Fordham.

— Jesuit Ratio Studiorum of 1599: 400th Anniversary Perspectives. 2000. 29.95 (*0-8232-2046-X*) Fordham.

Duminy, Andrew & Ballard, Charles, eds. The Anglo-Zulu War: New Perspectives. (Illus.). 200p. 1981. pap. 17.95 (*0-86980-244-5*, Pub. by Univ Natal Pr) Intl Spec Bk.

Duminy, Andrew, ed. see Guest, Bill.

Dumit, J., jt. ed. see Davis-Floyd, R.

Dumit, Joseph, jt. ed. see Downey, Gary L.

Dumitiu, Severian. Polysaccharides in Medicinal Applications. LC 96-15856. (Illus.). 816p. 1996. text 225.00 (*0-8247-9540-7*) Dekker.

Dumitrache, I., et al. Supplemental Ways for Improving International Stability, 1998 (Swiis'98) A Proceedings Volume from the Ifac Conference, Sinaia, Romania, 14-16 May, 1998. LC 98-41671. 1998. write for info. (*0-08-043231-X*) Elsevier.

Dumitras, Dan C., jt. ed. see Vlad, Valentin I.

***Dumitrescu, C. & Seleacu, V., eds.** Proceedings of the 1st International Conference on Smarandache Type Notions in Number Theory. LC 98-185610. (Smarandache Bks.). (ENG & FRE., Illus.). 250p. (C). 1998. pap. 39.95 incl. VHS (*1-879585-58-8*) Erhus Univ Pr.

Dumitrescu, C. & Seleacu, V., eds. Some Notions & Questions in Number Theory. LC QA0241.. (Illus.). 65p. reprint ed. pap. 30.00 (*0-608-10449-3*, 207108400008) Bks Demand.

Dumitrescu, C., ed. see Intl. Conference on Smarandache Type Nothing in Nu.

Dumitrescu, Constantin & Popescu, Marcela. The Smarandache Function in Number Theory. Tilton, Homer, ed. LC 97-146933. (Illus.). 100p. (C). 1996. pap. 9.99 (*1-879585-47-2*) Erhus Univ Pr.

Dumitrescu, Constantin & Seleacu, V. The Smarandache Function. LC 97-146933. 137p. reprint ed. pap. 42.50 (*0-608-10468-X*, 207108600008) Bks Demand.

***Dumitrescu, D.** Evolutionary Computation. LC 00-30348. (International Series on Computational Intelligence). (Illus.). 424p. 2000. boxed set 119.95 (*0-8493-0588-8*) CRC Pr.

Dumitrescu, D. Illustrated English-Rumanian Dictionary of Construction & Building Materials. (ENG & RUM., Illus.). 636p. 1981. write for info. (*0-8288-0216-5*, M15592) Fr & Eur.

***Dumitrescu, D., et al.** Fuzzy Sets & Their Application to Clustering & Training. LC 99-88763. 664p. 2000. boxed set 89.95 (*0-8493-0589-6*) CRC Pr.

Dumitrescu, Ion. Electrographic Imaging in Medicine & Biology. 1992. 25.95 (*0-85435-045-4*) C W Daniel.

Dumitrescu, Ion & Kenyon, Julian N. Electrographic Imaging in Medicine & Biology. (Illus.). 316p. pap. 38.95 (*0-8464-4189-6*) Beekman Pubs.

Dumitrescu, L., jt. ed. see Brun, R.

Dumitrescu, L. Z., jt. ed. see Brun, R.

Dumitrescu, L. Z., ed. see International Symposium on Shock Waves Staff.

Dumitriu, ed. Polysaccharides. LC 98-16717. (Illus.). 1176p. 1998. text 250.00 (*0-8247-0127-5*) Dekker.

Dumitriu, Helene. Good Drug Regulatory Practices: A Regulatory Affairs Quality Manual. LC 97-26489. (Good Drug Development Ser.: Vol. 1). (Illus.). 300p. 1997. ring bd. 169.00 (*1-57491-051-5*) Interpharm.

Dumitriu, Petru. To the Unknown God. Kirkup, James, tr. from FRE. LC 82-5722. 256p. 1984. 11.95 (*0-8164-2424-1*) Harper SF.

Dumitriu, Severian. Polymeric Biomaterials. (Illus.). 864p. 1993. text 250.00 (*0-8247-8969-5*) Dekker.

***Dumitru, Cyra S.** What the Body Knows. 96p. 1999. pap. 10.00 (*1-877603-76-7*, Pub. by Pecan Grove) Herveys Bklink.

Dumitru, Cyra S., et al. Keeping Company: Poems by Poetry & Company. (Illus.). 93p. (Orig.). 1996. pap. 10.95 (*1-877603-35-X*) Pecan Grove.

Dumitru, Daniel. Electrodiagnostic Medicine. (Illus.). 1300p. 1995. text 153.00 (*1-56053-071-5*) Hanley & Belfus.

Dumke, Glenn S. The Boom of the Eighties in Southern California. 5th ed. (Illus.). 326p. 1991. reprint ed. 24.95 (*0-87328-003-2*) Huntington Lib.

Dumke, Klaus. AIDS the Deadly Seed: An Anthropological & Epidemiological Investigation of a Modern Epidemic & Its Significance. Orig. Title: AIDS - Die Vodliche Befruchtung. 148p. 1991. pap. 22.95 (*1-85584-130-4*, Pub. by R Steiner Pr) Anthroposophic.

Dumke, Nicolette M. Allergy Cooking with Ease: The No Wheat, Milk, Eggs, Corn, Soy, Yeast, Sugar, Grain & Gluten Cookbook. LC 91-67061. 320p. 1992. pap. 14.95 (*0-914984-42-X*) Starburst.

— Easy Breadmaking for Special Diets: Use Your Bread Machine, Food Processor, or Mixer to Make the Bread You Need Quickly & Easily. LC 95-77917. 256p. (Orig.). 1996. pap. 14.95 (*1-887624-02-3*) Adapt Bks.

— Five Years Without Food: The Food Allergy Survival Guide How to Overcome Your Food Allergies & Recover Good Health. LC 97-93899. 320p. (Orig.). 1998. pap. 19.95 (*1-887624-04-X*) Adapt Bks.

— A Preview of the Allergy Diet Guide & Cookbook. 52p. (Orig.). 1995. pap. 6.95 (*1-887624-03-1*) Adapt Bks.

Dumkee, Nicolette M. The EPD Patient's Cooking & Lifestyle Guide. expanded rev. ed. 52p. 1995. pap. 6.95 (*1-887624-01-5*) Adapt Bks.

Dumler, Helmut & Burkhardt, Willi P. The High Mountains of the Alps. LC 93-28903. (Illus.). 224p. 1994. 45.00 (*0-89886-378-3*) Mountaineers.

Dumler, Susan, illus. see Barr, Barbara.

Dumm, Demetrius. Cherish Christ above All: The Bible in the Rule of Benedict. LC 96-4740. 176p. 1996. pap. 12.95 (*0-8091-3646-5*, 3646-5) Paulist Pr.

— Flowers in the Desert: A Spirituality of the Bible. LC 98-18570. 1998. pap. 14.95 (*1-879007-29-0*) St Bedes Pubns.

Dumm, Judy R. The Flying Ferry Boat: An Amazing San Francisco Adventure. LC 97-9153. (Illus.). 192p. (J). (gr. 3-6). 1997. pap. 8.99 (*0-9637217-0-4*) Peak Exp Art.

Dumm, Robert. Instead of Scales. pap. 8.95 (*0-943748-35-6*) Ekay Music.

— Pumping Ivory. 220p. (YA). pap. 16.95 (*0-943748-36-4*, PF0606) Ekay Music.

Dumm, Thomas L. Democracy & Punishment: Disciplinary Origins of the United States. LC 87-40147. (Rhetoric of the Human Sciences Ser.). 224p. (C). 1987. pap. text 16.95 (*0-299-11404-X*) U of Wis Pr.

— Michel Foucault & the Politics of Freedom. (Modernity & Political Thought Ser.: Vol. 9). 167p. 1996. 44.00 (*0-8039-3864-0*); pap. 19.95 (*0-8039-3865-9*) Sage.

— Politics of the Ordinary. LC 98-40234. 240p. 1999. text 55.00 (*0-8147-1896-5*) NYU Pr.

***Dumm, Thomas L.** Politics of the Ordinary. LC 98-40234. 215p. 1999. pap. 18.50 (*0-8147-1897-3*) NYU Pr.

Dumm, Thomas L. United States. (Contestations Ser.). (Illus.). 256p. 1994. text 39.95 (*0-8014-3002-X*); pap. text 16.95 (*0-8014-8190-2*) Cornell U Pr.

Dumm, Thomas L., jt. ed. see Dolan, Frederick M.

Dummelow, J. The One Volume Bible Commentary. 1993. 39.95 (*0-933062-28-1*) R H Sommer.

Dummer, Alexander. Practice Book for the Regents Competency Test in Global Studies. 167p. 1990. student ed. 8.95 (*0-910307-22-9*) Comp Pr.

Dummer, Beeke. Von der Narration zur Deskription: Generative Textkonstitution bei Jean Ricardou, Claude Simon und Philippe Sollers. (B. A. S. L. Ser.: Vol. 14). (GER.). 219p. 1988. 38.00 (*90-6032-220-7*, Pub. by B R Gruner) Humanities.

Dummer, G. W. Electronic Inventions & Discoveries: Electronics from Its Earliest Beginnings to the Present Day. 4th ed. LC 97-31264. 1997. pap. 42.00 (*0-7503-0493-6*) Institute of Personal Magnetism.

Dummer, G. W. & Davies, E. Electronic Inventions & Discoveries: Electronics from Its Earliest Beginnings to the Present Day. 4th rev. ed. LC 97-31264. (Illus.). 284p. 1997. 137.00 (*0-7503-0376-X*) IOP Pub.

Dummer, G. W., et al. An Elementary Guide to Reliability. 5th ed. LC 97-180297. 112p. 2000. pap. text 24.95 (*0-7506-3553-3*) Buttrwrth-Heinemann.

— Newnes Dictionary of Electronics. 4th ed. LC 99-461824. 400p. 1999. 36.95 (*0-7506-4331-5*) Buttrwrth-Heinemann.

Dummer, Geoffrey W. Semiconductor Technology, 1975. 1976. pap. 35.00 (*0-08-019976-3*, Pergamon Pr) Elsevier.

— Semiconductor Technology, 1977. 1977. pap. 43.00 (*0-08-022148-3*, Pergamon Pr) Elsevier.

— Semiconductor Technology, 1978. 1979. pap. 57.00 (*0-08-024205-7*, Pergamon Pr) Elsevier.

Dummer, Geoffrey W., ed. Semiconductor & Microprocessor Technology, 1981: Selected Papers Presented at the 1981 Annual Seminex Technical Seminar & Exhibition, London, U. K. 144p. 1982. pap. 47.00 (*0-08-028722-0*, Pergamon Pr) Elsevier.

— Semiconductor Technology, 1976. 1977. pap. 35.00 (*0-08-020983-1*, Pergamon Pr) Elsevier.

Dummer, Geoffrey W. & Griffin, N. B. Environmental Testing Technology for Electronics & Materials. LC 62-19284. (International Series of Monographs on Electronics & Instrumentation: Vol. 15). 1962. 198.00 (*0-08-013514-5*, Pub. by Pergamon Repr) Franklin.

Dummer, Geoffrey W. & Robertson, J. M. Manufacturers A-Z: Anglo American Microelectronics Data 1968-69, 2 vols., Set. LC 68-20388. 1968. 1330.00 (*0-08-012880-7*, Pub. by Pergamon Repr) Franklin.

Dummer, Geoffrey W. & Wells, Malvern, eds. Semiconductor & Microprocessor Technology, 1980: Selected Papers Presented at the Annual SEMINEX Technical Seminar & Exhibition, London, U. K. 190p. 1981. pap. 48.00 (*0-08-028674-7*, Pergamon Pr) Elsevier.

Dummer, Geoffrey W., et al. An Elementary Guide to Reliability. 3rd ed. 60p. 1986. text 27.00 (*0-08-033460-1*, Pub. by PPL); pap. text 16.00 (*0-08-033459-8*, Pub. by PPL) Elsevier.

Dummer, Geoffrey W., ed. see SEMINEX Staff.

Dummer, Jeremiah. Defence of the New-England Charters. LC 71-141122. (Research Library of Colonial Americana). 1972. reprint ed. 20.95 (*0-405-03333-8*) Ayer.

Dummer, Lucinda A. Christmas Makes Me Crazy: A Spiritual & Practical Guide to Enjoying the Holidays. LC 92-74211. (Illus.). 128p. (Orig.). 1992. pap. 9.95 (*0-9634533-0-0*) DTS Pr.

Dummer, Richard G., jt. ed. see Burg, Gunter.

Dummer, Shirley. Lost Love. 188p. 1994. pap. 8.00 (*0-9633479-2-6*) Dummer Pub.

— Therese, My Love. 216p. (Orig.). 1987. pap. 8.00 (*0-9633479-1-8*) Dummer Pub.

— We've Climbed the Mountains. 164p. 1992. pap. 8.00 (*0-9633479-0-X*) Dummer Pub.

Dummet, Michael. The Seas of Language. (Illus.). 502p. 1996. pap. text 24.95 (*0-19-823621-2*) OUP.

Dummett, Ann, ed. Towards a Just Immigration Policy. (C). 1988. 21.00 (*0-900137-26-6*, Pub. by NCCL) St Mut.

Dummett, Ann & Martin, Ian. British Nationality: The Agin Guide to the New Law. (C). 1988. 21.00 (*0-946088-10-1*, Pub. by NCCL) St Mut.

Dummett, Ann & Nichol, Andrew. Subjects, Citizens, Aliens, & Others: Nationality & Immigration Law. (Law in Context Ser.). 336p. (C). 1994. pap. text 25.95 (*0-297-82026-5*) Northwestern U Pr.

— Subjects, Citizens, Aliens, & Others: Nationality & Immigration Law. (Law in Context Ser.). 336p. (C). 1990. 57.50 (*0-297-82025-7*) W S Hein.

Dummett, Leonie, jt. auth. see Valletutti, Peter J.

***Dummett, Michael.** Elements of Intuitionism. 2nd ed. (Oxford Logic Guides Ser.: Vol. 39). 336p. 2000. text 100.00 (*0-19-850524-8*) OUP.

Dummett, Michael. Frege: Philosophy of Language. 2nd ed. 708p. (C). 1993. pap. 28.00 (*0-674-31931-1*) HUP.

— Frege: Philosophy of Mathematics. 224p. (C). 1991. 46.50 (*0-674-31935-4*) HUP.

— Frege: Philosophy of Mathematics. 352p. 1995. pap. text 22.50 (*0-674-31936-2*, DUMFRY) HUP.

— Frege & Other Philosophers. 344p. 1991. text 85.00 (*0-19-824870-9*) OUP.

— Frege & Other Philosophers. (Illus.). 344p. 1996. pap. text 19.95 (*0-19-823628-X*) OUP.

— The Interpretation of Frege's Philosophy. 480p. 1987. pap. 28.50 (*0-674-45976-8*) HUP.

— The Logical Basis of Metaphysics. LC 90-39999. (William James Lectures). 376p. 1991. 49.50 (*0-674-53785-8*, DUMLOG) HUP.

— The Logical Basis of Metaphysics. (William James Lectures). 376p. (C). 1993. pap. 23.95 (*0-674-53786-6*) HUP.

— Origins of Analytical Philosophy. LC 93-3772. 208p. 1994. 40.50 (*0-674-64472-7*) HUP.

— Origins of Analytical Philosophy. 208p. 1996. pap. 17.95 (*0-674-64473-5*) HUP.

— Principles of Electoral Reform. LC 96-40027. 208p. 1997. text 65.00 (*0-19-829247-3*); pap. text 24.95 (*0-19-829246-5*) OUP.

— Truth & Other Enigmas. LC 77-12777. 528p. 1978. 58.50 (*0-674-91075-3*) HUP.

— Truth & Other Enigmas. LC 77-12777. 528p. 1981. pap. 24.95 (*0-674-91076-1*) HUP.

— Voting Procedures. (Illus.). 318p. 1985. 75.00 (*0-19-876188-0*) OUP.

Dummett, Michael A. Frege. LC 73-177708. xxv, 698 p. 1973. write for info. (*0-7156-0659-X*) G Duckworth.

Dummett, Nanci L. Self-paced Business Mathematics. (Math). 410p. (C). 1979. mass mkt. 14.00 (*0-534-00616-7*) PWS Pubs.

— Self-paced Business Math. 2nd. 2nd ed. LC 81-23626. (Math). 425p. 1982. mass mkt. 21.50 (*0-534-01155-1*) PWS Pubs.

***Dummies Press Staff.** MCSE Internet Explorer 5 for Dummies. 496p. 2000. pap. 29.99 incl. cd-rom (*0-7645-0522-X*) IDG Bks.

Dummies Press Staff & Rachui, Scott. MCSE Exchange Server 5.5 for Dummies. LC 99-62292. (Illus.). 496p. 1999. pap. 29.99 incl. cd-rom (*0-7645-0481-9*) IDG Bks.

Dummies Press Staff & Rathbone, Andy. Windows 95. LC 96-75107. (Dummies 101 Ser.). (Illus.). 256p. 1996. pap. 24.99 incl. disk (*1-56884-631-2*) IDG Bks.

***Dummies Technical Press Staff.** A+ Certification for Dummies Flash Cards. (For Dummies Ser.). 250p. 1999. pap. 24.99 incl. cd-rom (*0-7645-0556-4*) IDG Bks.

— ACT! X for Windows for Dummies: Quick Reference. LC 99-66085. (For Dummies). (Illus.). 224p. 1999. spiral bd. 12.99 (*0-7645-0562-9*) IDG Bks.

Dummies Technical Press Staff. Banking Online for Dummies. LC 99-60535. (For Dummies Ser.). 384p. 1999. pap. 24.99 incl. cd-rom (*0-7645-0458-4*) IDG Bks.

— Digital Video for Dummies. (For Dummies Ser.). 384p. 1999. pap. 24.99 incl. cd-rom (*0-7645-0023-6*) IDG Bks.

— MCSE Core Four for Dummies, 4 vols. (For Dummies Ser.). 1900p. 1998. pap. 99.99 incl. cd-rom (*0-7645-0526-2*) IDG Bks.

— MCSE Core Four for Dummies. 2nd ed. 1900p. 1999. pap. 99.99 incl. cd-rom (*0-7645-0627-7*) IDG Bks.

— MCSE CP/IP for Dummies Flash Cards. (For Dummies Ser.). 250p. 1999. pap. 24.99 incl. cd-rom (*0-7645-0552-1*) IDG Bks.

***Dummies Technical Press Staff.** MCSE Exchange Server 5.5 For Dummies Flash Cards. (For Dummies Ser.). 250p. 2000. pap. 24.99 incl. cd-rom (*0-7645-0631-5*) IDG Bks.

— MCSE Exchange Server 5.5 for Dummies Training Kit. (For Dummies Ser.). 568p. 1999. pap. 49.99 incl. cd-rom (*0-7645-0619-6*) IDG Bks.

— MCSE Internet Information Server 4 for Dummies Flash Cards. (For Dummies Ser.). 250p. 1999. pap. 24.99 incl. cd-rom (*0-7645-0555-6*) IDG Bks.

— MCSE Networking Essentials for Dummies Flash Cards. (For Dummies Ser.). 250p. 1999. pap. 24.99 incl. cd-rom (*0-7645-0554-8*) IDG Bks.

— MCSE Networking Essentials for Dummies Training Kit. (For Dummies Ser.). 448p. 1999. pap. 49.99 incl. cd-rom (*0-7645-0621-8*) IDG Bks.

— MCSE Tcp/IP for Dummies Training Kit. (For Dummies Ser.). 512p. 1999. pap. 49.99 incl. cd-rom (*0-7645-0620-X*) IDG Bks.

— MCSE Windows Networking Server 4 for Dummies Training Kit. (For Dummies Ser.). 568p. 1999. pap. 49.99 incl. cd-rom (*0-7645-0616-1*) IDG Bks.

— MCSE Windows Networking Server 4 in the Enterprise for Dummies Training Kit. (For Dummies Ser.). 604p. 1999. pap. 49.99 incl. cd-rom (*0-7645-0617-X*) IDG Bks.

— MCSE Windows Networking Workstation 4 for Dummies Training Kit. (For Dummies Ser.). 528p. 1999. pap. 49.99 incl. cd-rom (*0-7645-0618-8*) IDG Bks.

— Mcse Windows Nt Server 4 in the Enterprise For Dummies Flash Cards. 250p. 1999. pap. 24.99 incl. cd-rom (*0-7645-0551-3*) IDG Bks.

— MCSE Windows NT Workstation 4 for Dummies Flash Cards. (For Dummies Ser.). 250p. 1999. pap. 24.99 incl. cd-rom (*0-7645-0553-X*) IDG Bks.

— MCSE Windows NT 4 Server for Dummies Flash Cards. (For Dummies Ser.). 250p. 1999. pap. 24.99 incl. cd-rom (*0-7645-0550-5*) IDG Bks.

— MCSE Windows 95 for Dummies Flash Cards. (For Dummies Ser.). 250p. 1999. pap. 24.99 incl. cd-rom (*0-7645-0549-1*) IDG Bks.

— MCSE Windows 98 for Dummies Flash Cards. (For Dummies Ser.). 250p. 2000. pap. 24.99 incl. cd-rom (*0-7645-0630-7*) IDG Bks.

Dummies Technical Press Staff. Microsoft Visual Studio 6 for Dummies. LC QA76.76.A65M334 1998. (For Dummies Ser.). 500p. 1998. pap. 29.99 incl. cd-rom (*0-7645-0374-X*) IDG Bks.

***Dummies Technical Press Staff.** Network+ Certification for Dummies Flash Cards. (For Dummies Ser.). 250p. 2000. pap. 24.99 incl. cd-rom (*0-7645-0628-5*) IDG Bks.

Dummies Technical Press Staff. Starting an Online Business for Dummies. LC 98-89940. (For Dummies Ser.). 384p. 1999. pap. 24.99 incl. cd-rom (*0-7645-0464-9*) IDG Bks.

— Travel Planning Online for Dummies. LC G155.A1V333 1998. (For Dummies Ser.). 384p. 1998. pap. 24.99 incl. cd-rom (*0-7645-0438-X*) IDG Bks.

***Dummies Technical Press Staff.** Virtual Private Networks for Dummies. (For Dummies Ser.). 360p. 1999. pap. 24.99 (*0-7645-0590-4*) IDG Bks.

Dummies Technical Press Staff, jt. auth. see Angell, David.

Dummies Technical Press Staff, jt. auth. see Cummings, Steve.

Dummies Technical Press Staff, jt. auth. see Dyszel, Bill.

Dummies Technical Press Staff, jt. auth. see Harvey, Greg.

Dummies Technical Press Staff, jt. auth. see Holder, Wayne.

Dummies Technical Press Staff, jt. auth. see Komando, Kim.

Dummies Technical Press Staff, jt. auth. see Robinette, Michelle.

Dummies Technical Press Staff, jt. auth. see San Filippo, John.

Dummies Technical Press Staff, jt. auth. see Vander Veer, Emily.

Dummies Technical Press Staff, jt. auth. see Weverka, Peter.

Dummies Technical Press Staff, jt. auth. see Wolf, Douglas J.

***Dummies Technology Press Staff, ed.** PCs for Dummies Quick Reference. (For Dummies Ser.). 224p. 2000. spiral bd. 12.99 (*0-7645-0722-2*) IDG Bks.

***Dummit, David.** Abstract Algebra. 2nd ed. 912p. 1999. text 96.95 (*0-471-36857-1*) Wiley.

Dummit, David & Foote, Richard. Abstract Algebra. 2nd ed. 898p. (C). 1998. text 88.00 (*0-13-569302-0*, Prentice Hall) P-H.

Dummy. Patch of Blue: Frst. 1989. mass mkt. 3.50 (*0-446-73863-8*, Pub. by Warner Bks) Little.

Dumoga, John. Africa Between East & West. LC 76-77360. (Background Ser.). 1969. 18.95 (*0-8023-1214-4*) Dufour.

Dumol, Paul A. The Metaphysics of Reading Underlying Dante's "Commedia" The "Ingegno" LC 97-8501. (Studies in the Humanities: Literature-Politics-Society: No. 35). XVI, 239p. (C). 1999. 49.95 (*0-8204-3781-6*) P Lang Pubng.

Dumon, Jean-Francois, et al. YAG Laser Bronchoscopy. LC 84-26310. 128p. 1985. 47.95 (*0-275-91311-2*, C1311, Praeger Pubs) Greenwood.

Dumond, Annie H. Annie Nelles. Baxter, Annette K., ed. LC 79-8788. (Signal Lives Ser.). 1980. reprint ed. lib. bdg. 42.95 (*0-405-12836-3*) Ayer.

Dumond, Don E. The Eskimos & Aleuts. rev. ed. (Ancient Peoples & Places Ser.). (Illus.). 180p. 1987. pap. 16.95 (*0-500-27479-7*, Pub. by Thames Hudson) Norton.

— The Machete & the Cross: Campesino Rebellion in Yucatan. LC 96-32949. (Illus.). xvii, 573p. 1997. text 60.00 (*0-8032-1706-4*) U of Nebr Pr.

Dumond, Dwight L. Antislavery Origins of the Civil War in the United States. LC 80-12505. 133p. 1980. reprint ed. lib. bdg. 45.00 (*0-313-22378-5*, DUAO, Greenwood Pr) Greenwood.

— A Bibliography of Antislavery in America. LC 61-9306. 130p. reprint ed. pap. 40.30 (*0-8357-7176-8*, 205108100074) Bks Demand.

Dumond, Dwight L., jt. ed. see Barnes, Gilbert H.

Dumond, Dwight L., ed. see Birney, James G.

DuMond, Jesse W., ed. see Millikan, Robert Andrews.

Dumond, John, et al. Maturing Weapon Systems for Improved Availability at Lower Costs. LC 94-6662. 1994. pap. 13.00 (*0-8330-1513-3*, MR-338-A) Rand Corp.

Dumond, K. J. & Merlin, Ann. New York City: A Pictorial Guide. Du Bois, Anne, ed. 64p. 1992. pap. 8.95 (*1-56540-033-X*) Impact Photograph.

Dumond, M. Trilingual Lexicon of Cookie & Pastry Making. (ENG, FRE & GER.). 128p. 1988. pap. 49.95 (*0-8288-7725-4*) Fr & Eur.

Dumond, Michael. Coping with Life after High School. rev. ed. Rosen, Roger, ed. (Coping Ser.). (YA). (gr. 7-12). 1988. lib. bdg. 17.95 (*0-8239-0781-3*) Rosen Group.

— Respect Between the Sexes. (Illus.). 115p. (Orig.). (YA). (gr. 9-12). 1995. pap. 6.95 (*1-57515-084-0*) PPI Pubng.

Dumond, Val. Doin' the Puyallup: An Illustrated History of the Western Washington Fair Since 1900. (Illus.). 270p. (Orig.). 1991. 32.95 (*0-9613673-2-6*) V Dumond.

— The Elements of Nonsexist Usage: A Guide to Inclusive Spoken & Written English. 90p. 1991. pap. 4.95 (*0-13-368911-5*) Macmillan Gen Ref.

— Grammar for Grownups: A Guide to Grammar & Usage for Everyone Who Has to Put Words on Paper Effectively. LC 92-33204. 256p. 1994. pap. 12.00 (*0-06-272043-0*, Harper Ref) HarpC.

— Visiting Olympia. (Color-A-Story Ser.). (Illus.). 24p. (Orig.). (J). (gr. 1-4). 1983. pap. 2.75 (*0-933992-39-4*) Coffee Break.

Dumond, Val, ed. see Fritchman, Samara C. Kezele.

Dumond, Val, ed. see Steele, Patrick M.

Dumond, Val, ed. see Thompson, JeVon.

Dumond, Val, ed. see Writers Roundtable Authors Staff.

Dumond, Valerie, ed. see Wynett, Stanley & Wynett, Jonathan.

Dumont. Sociology 340 Reader. 1994. 30.25 (*0-07-018115-2*) McGraw.

***Dumont, Charles.** Pathway of Peace: Cistercian Wisdom According to Saint Bernard. LC 99-30965. (Cistercian Studies: Vol. CS187). 259p. 1999. write for info. (*0-87907-687-9*) Cistercian Pubns.

Dumont, Charles. Pathway of Peace: Cistercian Wisdom According to Saint Bernard. LC 99-30965. (Cistercian Studies). 259p. 1999. pap. write for info. (*0-87907-787-5*) Cistercian Pubns.

Dumont d'Urville, Jules-Sebastien-Cesar. Two Voyages to the South Seas. Rosenman, Helen, tr. from FRE. & retold by by. LC 92-22735. (Illus.). 340p. 1992. reprint ed. pap. 96.90 (*0-608-04395-8*, 2065176) Bks Demand.

Dumont, Ella E. Ella Elgar Bird Dumont: An Autobiography of a West Texas Pioneer. (Barker Texas History Center Ser.: No. 6). (Illus.). 272p. 1988. 22.95 (*0-292-78089-3*) U of Tex Pr.

Dumont, Eric. Timidez Mucha...Poca...Nada. (SPA.). 164p. 1997. pap. text 13.98 (*968-13-3133-8*) Edit Diana.

Dumont, Gabriel. Gabriel Dumont Speaks. Barnholden, Michael, tr. 80p. (Orig.). 1993. pap. 10.95 (*0-88922-323-8*) Genl Dist Srvs.

Dumont, Gabriel P. Parallele de Plans des Plus Belles Salles de Spectacles d'Italie et de France. LC 68-17155. (FRE., Illus.). 1972. reprint ed. 43.95 (*0-405-08469-2*, Pub. by Blom Pubns) Ayer.

Dumont, H. J., et al, eds. Intrazooplankton Predation. (C). 1990. text 257.50 (*0-7923-0808-5*) Kluwer Academic.

— Limnology & Marine Biology in the Sudan. (Developments in Hydrobiology Ser.). 1984. text 289.00 (*90-6193-772-8*) Kluwer Academic.

— Studies on the Ecology of Tropical Zooplankton. LC 93-43395. (Developments in Hydrobiology Ser.: Vol. 92). 304p. (C). 1994. text 255.50 (*0-7923-2639-3*) Kluwer Academic.

Dumont, H. J. & Green, J., eds. Rotatoria. (Developments in Hydrobiology Ser.: No. 1). 268p. 1980. text 234.00 (*90-6193-754-X*) Kluwer Academic.

Dumont, H. J. & Tundisi, J. G. Tropical Zooplankton. (Developments in Hydrobiology Ser.: No. 23). 344p. 1984. text 270.00 (*90-6193-774-4*) Kluwer Academic.

Dumont, H. J., ed. see Bayly, I. A.

Dumont, H. J., ed. see Dussart, B. H. & Defaye, D.

Dumont, H. J., ed. see Korovchinsky, N. M.

Dumont, H. J., ed. see Nogrady, T., et al.

Dumont, H. J., ed. see Reddy, Y. Ranga.

Dumont, H. J., ed. see Segers, H.

Dumont, H. J., ed. see Smirnov, N. N.

Dumont, J. E., et al. Hormones & Cell Regulation. (ENG & FRE.). 136p. 1990. 150.00 (*0-8288-7375-5*, 2855984432) Fr & Eur.

Dumont, J. J., ed. Learning Disabilities Vol. 2: Cognitive, Social, & Remedial Aspects. xii, 208p. 1989. 55.50 (*90-265-0984-7*) Swets.

Dumont, Jacques E., et al, eds. Advances in Cyclic Nucleotide Research: Fourth International Conference on Cyclic Nucleotides, Brussels, Belgium, July 22-26, 1980, Vol. 14. fac. ed. LC 71-181305. (Illus.). 756p. 1993. pap. 200.00 (*0-7837-7234-3*, 204706200014) Bks Demand.

Dumont, Jean, et al, eds. Corps Universel Diplomatique: Supplement. 5 vols. LC 72-953. reprint ed. lib. bdg. write for info. (*0-404-01820-3*) AMS Pr.

— Corps Universel Diplomatique du Droit des Gens, 8 vols. LC 72-164796. reprint ed. lib. bdg. write for info. (*0-404-01810-6*) AMS Pr.

Dumont, Jean-Michael & Marion, Remy. On the Trail of Whales. LC 98-4550. (Nature Travel Guides Ser.). (Illus.). 128p. 1998. pap. 11.95 (*0-7641-0598-1*) Barron.

Dumont, Jean-Paul. Les Ecoles Presocratiques. (FRE.). 1991. pap. 24.95 (*0-7859-1672-5*, 2070326101) Fr & Eur.

— The Headman & I: Ambiguity & Ambivalence in the Fieldworking Experience. rev. ed. (Illus.). 211p. (C). 1992. reprint ed. pap. text 12.50 (*0-88133-627-0*) Waveland Pr.

— Visayan Vignettes: Ethnographic Traces of a Philippine Island. LC 91-37573. (Illus.). 246p. 1992. pap. text 19.95 (*0-226-16955-3*); lib. bdg. 46.00 (*0-226-16954-5*) U Ch Pr.

Dumont, Jeanne M. Pleadings & Pretrial Practice: A Deskbook for Connecticut Litigators. LC 95-104164. iii, 157 p. 1994. write for info. (*0-910051-33-X*) CT Law Trib.

Dumont, K. P. Sclerotinaceae 2: Lambertella. (Memoirs Ser.: Vol. 22 (1)). (Illus.). 178p. 1971. pap. 10.50 (*0-89327-074-1*) NY Botanical.

***DuMont, Katie.** The New Macrame. (Illus.). 2000. 24.95 (*1-57990-163-8*) Lark Books.

— The New Macrame: Contemporary Knotted Jewelry & Accessories. LC 99-37032. (Illus.). 128p. 2000. 18.95 (*1-57990-127-1*) Lark Books.

— Picture Perfect Framing: Making, Matting, Mounting, Embellishing, Displaying, & More. LC 00-28227. (Illus.). 128p. 2000. write for info. (*1-57990-165-4*, Pub. by Lark Books) Sterling.

***Dumont, Kitty.** Die Sozialpsychologie Der Ddr: Eine Wissenschaftshistorische Untersuchung. (Beitrage Zur Geschichte der Psychologie Ser.). 282p. 1999. 48.95 (*3-631-35213-1*) P Lang Pubng.

Dumont, Louis. Affinity As a Value: Marriage Alliance in South India with Comparative Essays on Australia. LC 82-13468. (Illus.). 240p. (C). 1983. 26.50 (*0-226-16964-2*) U Ch Pr.

— Essays on Individualism: Modern Ideology in Anthropological Perspective. LC 86-1477. x, 284p. (C). 1986. 33.00 (*0-226-16956-1*) U Ch Pr.

— Essays on Individualism: Modern Ideology in Anthropological Perspective. LC 86-1477. x, 294p. 1997. pap. text 17.95 (*0-226-16958-8*) U Ch Pr.

— From Mandeville to Marx: The Genesis & Triumph of Economic Ideology. LC 76-8087. (Midway Reprint Ser.). 246p. 1983. pap. text 15.95 (*0-226-16966-9*) U Ch Pr.

— German Ideology: From France to Germany & Back. 250p. 1996. reprint ed. pap. text 14.95 (*0-226-16953-7*) U Ch Pr.

— Germany Ideology: From France to Germany & Back. 260p. 1995. 32.50 (*0-226-16952-9*) U Ch Pr.

— Homo Hierarchicus: The Caste System & Its Implications. rev. ed. Gulati, Basia M., tr. LC 80-16480. 544p. 1981. pap. text 22.00 (*0-226-16963-4*, P601) U Ch Pr.

Dumont, Louis. A South Indian Subcaste: Social Organization & Religion of the Pramalai Kallar. Moffatt, Michael, ed. & tr. by. Morton, L. et al, trs. (French Studies on South Asia). (Illus.). 524p. 1986. text 38.00 (*0-19-561785-1*) OUP.

Dumont, M. Treatise on Judicial Evidence: Extracted from the Manuscripts of Jeremy Bentham. xvi, 366p. 1981. reprint ed. 45.00 (*0-8377-0318-2*, Rothman) W S Hein.

Dumont, Marie-Jeanne, ed. Anatole de Baudot, Rassegna 68. (Illus.). 110p. 1997. pap. 35.00 (*88-85322-26-3*, Pub. by Birkhauser) Princeton Arch.

Dumont, Marilyn. A Really Good Brown Girl. LC 97-193123. 80p. 1996. pap. 12.95 (*0-919626-76-9*, Pub. by Brick Bks) Genl Dist Srvs.

Dumont, Matthew. Therapists in the Community: Changing the Conditions That Produce Psychopathology. LC 94-37986. 200p. 1994. reprint ed. pap. text 40.00 (*1-56821-405-7*) Aronson.

Dumont, Matthew P. Treating the Poor: A Personal Sojourn Through the Rise & Fall of Community Mental Health. 2nd ed. Kaplan, Judy, ed. LC 92-97289. 149p. (Orig.). 1994. 26.95 (*0-9634975-1-0*) Dymphna Pr.

-Treating the Poor: A Personal Sojourn Through the Rise & Fall of Community Mental Health. 2nd ed. Kaplan, Judy, ed. LC 92-97289. 149p. (Orig.). 1994. pap. 15.95 (*0-9634975-0-2*) Dymphna Pr.

The author, a well known activist, writer & psychiatrist, played a significant role in the community mental health movement of the 60s & 70s. The book describes its antecedents & subsequent destruction against the social, economic & political events of recent American history. As a practitioner of 16 years in a low-income, immigrant community, he tells vivid stories which demonstrate how poverty drives people crazy & how the prevention & control of mental illness requires community organization, pollution control, jobs & housing as much as case finding & treatment. Documented with research & personal experience, the book is also a critique of biological psychiatry with its emphasis on genetic etiologies & reliance on drugs. It warns against privatization, managed care, & the continued medical hegemony of mental health as part of current models of health care "reform." Call or write for information to order: Dymphna Press, Box 44, Belmont, MA 02178. 617-489-2126. *Publisher Paid Annotation.*

Dumont, Michele, et al. Quebec Women: A History. Gannon, Roger & Gill, Rosalind, trs. 396p. pap. 17.95 (*0-88961-101-7*, Pub. by Womens Pr) LPC InBook.

Dumont, Ninda, ed. Heart 2 Heart Scraps & Scribbles: A Scrapbook Sort of Journal & a Sketchbook Sort of Album. (Illus.). 64p. (J). (gr. 3-8). 1996. spiral bd. 12.95 (*0-9640713-2-0*) Fine Print.

***Dumont, Ninda, ed.** My Heart 2 Heart Autograph Album. (Illus.). 80p. (J). 1999. 5.95 (*1-892951-01-0*) Fine Print.

— My Heart 2 Heart Girlfriends' Book. (Illus.). 64p. (J). 1999. 11.95 (*1-892951-02-9*) Fine Print.

Dumont, Ninda, ed. My Heart Two Heart Diary: Blue Dog Edition. (Illus.). 128p. (J). 1996. 11.95 (*0-9640713-4-7*) Fine Print.

— My Heart 2 Heart Diary: Broccoli Edition. (Illus.). 128p. (J). 1998. 11.95 (*0-9640713-9-8*) Fine Print.

— My Heart 2 Heart Diary: Indigo Puppy Edition. (Illus.). 64p. (J). 1998. 11.95 (*0-9640713-8-X*) Fine Print.

— My Heart 2 Heart Diary: Keyhole Edition. 128p. (J). (gr. 4-8). 1994. 10.95 (*0-9640713-0-4*) Fine Print.

— My Heart 2 Heart Diary: Wordy Birdy Edition. 1997. 12.95 (*0-9640713-6-3*) Fine Print.

— My Heart 2 Heart Scraps & Pockets. (J). 1997. 14.95 (*0-9640713-3-9*) Fine Print.

— My Heart 2 Heart Travel Diary. (Illus.). 64p. (J). 1998. pap. 11.95 (*0-9640713-7-1*) Fine Print.

Dumont, Raeann. The Sky Is Falling: Understanding & Coping with Phobias, Panic & Obsessive-Compulsive Disorders. 352p. 1996. 25.00 (*0-393-03848-3*) Norton.

— The Sky Is Falling: Understanding & Coping with Phobias, Panic & Obsessive-Compulsive Disorders. LC 95-30992. 320p. (C). 1997. pap. 13.95 (*0-393-31603-3*) Norton.

Dumont, Renbe. Is Cuba Socialist? LC 74-164690. 159 p. 1974. write for info. (*0-233-96255-7*) Andre Deutsch.

Dumont, Rene & Mottin, Marie-France. Strangehold on Africa. 272p. 1984. 56.00 (*0-389-20466-8*, 08027) B&N Imports.

DuMont, Rosemary R. Reform & Reaction: The Big City Public Library in American Life. 21. LC 77-71864. (Contributions in Librarianship & Information Science Ser.: No. 21). 153p. 1977. 55.00 (*0-8371-9549-3*, DRR/, Greenwood Pr) Greenwood.

Dumont, Theron. Art & Science of Personal Magnetism. reprint ed. 15.00 (*0-911662-38-3*) Yoga.

— Power of Concentration. reprint ed. 15.00 (*0-911662-39-1*) Yoga.

— The Solar Plexus. reprint ed. pap. 3.00 (*0-911662-40-5*) Yoga.

Dumont, Theron Q. Advanced Course in Personal Magnetism. 281p. 1972. reprint ed. 15.00 (*0-911662-46-4*) Yoga.

— The Art & Science of Personal Magnetism: The Secrets of Mental Fascination. 191p. 1993. spiral bd. 15.50 (*0-7873-0301-1*) Hlth Research.

— The Art & Science of Personal Magnetism: The Secrets of Mental Fascination. 196p. 1996. reprint ed. pap. 12.00 (*1-56459-877-2*) Kessinger Pub.

— The Master Mind: The Key to Mental Power, Development & Efficiency. 276p. 1980. reprint ed. 15.00 (*0-911662-66-9*) Yoga.

— Mental Therapeutics. 235p. 1972. reprint ed. 15.00 (*0-911662-47-2*) Yoga.

— The Solar Plexus: Abdominal Brain. 64p. 1996. reprint ed. pap. 10.00 (*0-7873-0302-X*) Hlth Research.

— The Solar Plexus: or Abdominal Brain. 64p. 1998. reprint ed. pap. 5.00 (*1-885395-09-4*) Book Tree.

Dumont, William & Bryan, Mary G. Passports Issued by Governors of Georgia, 1810 to 1820. 112p. 1964. 8.00 (*0-915156-28-8*, 28) Natl Genealogical.

Dumont, William H. Colonial Georgia Genealogical Data 1748-1783. 77p. 1978. 7.50 (*0-915156-36-9*) Natl Genealogical.

Dumontier, Paul E., et al. Vancouver: Ulysses Travel Guide. (Ulysses Travel Guide Ser.). 1996. pap. 10.95 (*0-614-12866-8*) Ulysses Travel.

Dumortier, Freddy & Roussarie, Robert. Canard Cycles & Center Manifolds. LC 96-2234. (Memoirs of the American Mathematical Society Ser.: No. 577). 96p. 1996. pap. 35.00 (*0-8218-0443-X*, MEMO/ 21/577) Am Math.

Dumouchel, Christophe, jt. ed. see Yule, Andrew J.

***Dumouchel, J. Robert, ed.** Government Assistance Almanac 2000-2001: The Guide to Federal Domestic Financial & Other Programs. 14th ed. 1000p. 2000. lib. bdg. 195.00 (*0-7808-0342-6*) Omnigraphics Inc.

Dumouchel, Paul, ed. Violence & Truth: On the Work of Rene Girard. LC 87-61959. vi, 289p. 1988. 39.50 (*0-8047-1338-3*) Stanford U Pr.

Dumoulin, Heinrich. The Development of Chinese Zen. 146p. 1990. reprint ed. pap. 15.00 (*957-9482-16-0*) Oriental Bk Store.

***Dumoulin, Heinrich.** History of Zen Buddhism. 2nd ed. 2000. reprint ed. pap. 26.95 (*81-215-0958-0*, Pub. by M Manoharial) S Asia.

Dumoulin, Heinrich. Understanding Buddhism: Key Themes. O'Leary, Joseph S., tr. from GER. 192p. (Orig.). 1993. pap. 14.95 (*0-8348-0297-X*) Weatherhill.

— Zen Buddhism: A History: India & China. rev. ed. 386p. 1994. 20.00 (*0-02-897109-4*) P-H.

— Zen Enlightenment: Origins & Meaning. LC 78-27310. 188p. 1979. pap. 13.95 (*0-8348-0141-8*) Weatherhill.

Dumoulin, Michel & Dutrieue, Anne-Myriam. La Lingue Europeenne de Cooperation Economique, 1946-1981. 280p. 1993. 40.80 (*3-906750-74-4*) P Lang Pubng.

Dumpe, Bert. X-Rayed Without Consent: Computer Health Hazards. Kepple, Stephen, ed. (Illus.). 388p. (Orig.). 1989. 19.75 (*0-9622907-0-X*) Ergotec Assn.

Dumper, Michael. Islam & Israel: Muslim Religious Endowments & the Jewish State. 192p. 1994. pap. 12.00 (*0-88728-270-9*) Inst Palestine.

— The Politics of Jerusalem since 1967. (Institute for Palestine Studies). (Illus.). 320p. 1996. 31.00 (*0-231-10640-8*) Col U Pr.

Dumpit, Darlene. The New Mellenium: Do You Have the Time? LC 98-88882. 112p. 1999. pap. 12.95 (*1-56167-464-8*) Am Literary Pr.

Dumpleton, John. Law & Order: The Story of the Police. (Junior Reference Ser.). (Illus.). (J). (gr. 3-7). 1983. reprint ed. 14.95 (*0-7136-1079-4*) Dufour.

— Make Your Own Booklet. LC 79-3815. (Illus.). 1980. pap. 2.95 (*0-8008-5058-0*) Taplinger.

Dumroese, Kas, jt. auth. see Svingen, Daniel N.

Dumroese, R. Kasten, jt. auth. see Landis, Thomas D.

Dumur, Guy. Histoire des Spectacles. (Historique Ser.). 2040p. 48.95 (*0-686-56460-X*) Fr & Eur.

— Histoire Generale des Techniques, Vol. 1: Origines de la Civilisation Technique. (FRE.). 2038p. 1965. 135.00 (*0-7859-4543-1*) Fr & Eur.

Dumville, David, ed. see Hughes, Kathleen.

Dumville, David N. Britons & Anglo-Saxons in the Early Middle Ages. (Collected Studies: No. CS379). 352p. 1993. 115.95 (*0-86078-332-4*, Pub. by Variorum) Ashgate Pub Co.

— English Caroline Script & Monastic History: Studies in Benedictinism, A.D. 950-1030. (Studies in Anglo-Saxon History: No. VI). (Illus.). 222p. (C). 1993. 75.00 (*0-85115-323-2*) Boydell & Brewer.

— Histories & Pseudo-Histories of the Insular Middle Ages. (Collected Studies: No. CS316). (Illus.). 352p. 1990. text 117.95 (*0-86078-264-6*, Pub. by Variorum) Ashgate Pub Co.

— Liturgy & the Ecclesiastical History of Late Anglo-Saxon England: Four Studies. LC 92-34651. (Studies in Anglo-Saxon History: Vol. 5). 204p. (C). 1992. 75.00 (*0-85115-331-3*, Boydell Pr) Boydell & Brewer.

***Dumville, David N.** Saint Patrick: AD 493-1993, Vol. 13. (Studies in Celtic History). 344p. 1999. pap. 35.00 (*0-85115-733-5*) Boydell & Brewer.

Dumville, David N., ed. The Anglo-Saxon Chronicle 1 MS F: Facsimile Edition. fac. ed. (Illus.). 110p. (C). 1995. 150.00 (*0-85991-125-X*, DS Brewer) Boydell & Brewer.

Dumville, David N., jt. ed. see Blackburn, Mark A.

Dumville, John P., ed. see Williams, John A.

Dumych, Daniel Martin. Niagara Falls. (Images of America Ser.). 128p. 1996. pap. 16.99 (*0-7524-0432-6*) Arcadia Pubing.

— Niagara Falls, Vol. II. (Images of America Ser.). (Illus.). 128p. 1998. pap. 16.99 (*0-7524-1201-9*) Arcadia Pubing.

Dun & Bradstreet Information Services Staff. Chemical Industry Report on ISO 9000: A Report Featuring Statistical Profile of the Industry, Registered Company List, Fully Tabulated Survey Results, Executive Summary. LC 97-3413. 1997. text 295.00 (*0-7863-1165-7*) McGraw.

Dun & Bradstreet Staff. America's Corporate Families & International Affiliates, 1996, 3 vols. Incl. Vol. III. International Affiliates, 1996. 1996. 495.00 (*1-56203-476-6*); Vols. I & II. America's Corporate Families, 1996. 1996. 495.00 900.00 (*0-614-25655-0*) Dun & Bradstreet.

— The Career Guide: Dun's Employment Opportunities Directory. 1995. 495.00 (*1-56203-459-6*) Dun & Bradstreet.

— The Directory of Key Manufacturing Companies in People's Republic of China. 1626p. 1995. 495.00 (*962-7240-13-3*) Dun & Bradstreet.

— Dun & Bradstreet Business Rankings, 1996: Public & Private Businesses Ranked Within Industry & State. 1996. 485.00 (*1-56203-473-1*) Dun & Bradstreet.

— Dun & Bradstreet Census of American Business. 1996. 395.00 (*1-56203-472-3*) Dun & Bradstreet.

— Dun & Bradstreet Consultants Directory, 1996. 1995. 425.00 (*1-56203-460-X*) Dun & Bradstreet.

— Dun & Bradstreet Directory of Service Companies, 1996. 1995. 500.00 (*1-56203-462-6*) Dun & Bradstreet.

— Dun & Bradstreet Industrial Guide: The Metalworking Directory, 1996/97, 3 vols. 1996. 795.00 (*1-56203-489-8*) Dun & Bradstreet.

— Dun & Bradstreet Million Dollar Directory, 1996. 1996. 1350.00 (*1-56203-471-5*) Dun & Bradstreet.

D

— Dun & Bradstreet Regional Business Directories: 54 Separate Economic Areas. 1995. pap. write for info. (*1-56203-244-5*) Dun & Bradstreet.

— Dun & Bradstreet Regional Business Directories: 54 Separate Economic Areas, 54. 1996. cd-rom. write for info. (*0-614-24669-5*) Dun & Bradstreet.

— Dun & Bradstreet's Million Dollar Directory, 1996. 1996. 5295.00 incl. cd-rom (*1-56203-477-4*) Dun & Bradstreet.

— Dun's Guide to Key Decision Makers in Hong Kong. 305p. 1996. 380.00 (*962-7240-06-0*) Dun & Bradstreet.

— Exporters' Encyclopedia, 1995-1996. 1995. 495.00 (*1-56203-402-2*) Dun & Bradstreet.

— The ISO 9000 Survey: Comprehensive Data & Analysis of U. S. Registered Companies, 1996. LC 96-1228. (Illus.). 208p. 1996. text 150.00 (*0-7863-0901-6*, Irwn Prfssnl) McGraw-Hill Prof.

— Latin America 25,000, 1996. 1995. pap. 250.00 (*0-614-25654-2*); disk 295.00 (*1-56203-551-7*) Dun & Bradstreet.

— Principal International Businesses: The World Marketing Directory. 3336p. 1995. 595.00 (*1-56203-461-8*) Dun & Bradstreet.

— Reference Book of Corporate Managements: America's Corporate Leaders, 1996, 3 vols. 1996. 795.00 (*1-56203-469-3*) Dun & Bradstreet.

— Taiwan's Leading Corporations. 755p. 1995. 380.00 (*957-99683-0-6*) Dun & Bradstreet.

— Who Owns Whom Directories, 6 vols. Incl. Vol. 1: Australia & Far East. 939p. 1995. 395.00 (*0-901491-24-1*); Vol. 2: North America. 1032p. 1995. 445.00 (*0-901491-19-5*); Vols. 3 & 4: United Kingdom., 2 vols. 1376p. 1995. 395.00 (*0-901491-09-8*); Vols. 5 & 6: Continental Europe., 2 vols. 1885p. 1995. 395.00 (*0-901491-14-4*); 1300.00 (*0-614-25163-X*) Dun & Bradstreet.

— Dun & Bradstreet Guide to Your Investment, 1998: The Year-Round Investment Sourcebook for Managing Your Personal Finance. 464p. 1998. pap. 19.95 (*0-06-273510-1*) HarpC.

Dun, John & Higonnet, Rene. The Banking Institutions, Bullion Reserves, & Non Legal Tender Note Circulation of the United Kingdom Statistically Investigated. LC 82-48219. (Gold, Money, Inflation & Deflation Ser.). 227p. 1983. lib. bdg. 22.00 (*0-8240-5229-3*) Garland.

Dun, Nae J. & Perlman, Robert L., eds. Neurobiology of Acetylcholine. 590p. 1987. 120.00 (*0-306-42493-2*, Plenum Trade) Perseus Pubng.

Dunaetz, Robert, ed. see International SAMPE Symposium & Exhibition Staff.

Dunaevsky, V. V., tr. see Kragel'skii, I. V. & Mikhin, N. M.

Dunagan, Ann. Teaching with God's Heart for the World, Vol. 2. (Illus.). 256p. (Orig.). 1995. ring bd. 49.95 (*0-9645420-1-3*) Fam Mission.

Dunagan, Dianne E., jt. auth. see Odom-Winn, Danni.

Dunagan, Hermelinda G. Spanish/English Reference Guide for the Professional: A Dictionary of Financial & Legal Terminology. (ENG & SPA.). 432p. 1995. 79.00 (*1-880047-36-5*) Creative Des.

Dunagin, Richard L. Beyond These Walls: Building the Church in a Built-Out Neighborhood. LC 98-46440. 144p. 1999. pap. 15.00 (*0-687-08596-9*) Abingdon.

Dunahoo, Kermit L., jt. auth. see Berger, Peter W.

Dunai, jt. auth. see Chekhov, Anton.

***Dunaif, Andrea E.** Brigham & Women's Hospital Guide to Womens Health & Wellness. 320p. 2001. 27.95 (*0-7370-1623-X*) Time-Life Educ.

Dunand, Francoise. Mummies: A Voyage Through Eternity. (Discoveries Ser.). (Illus.). 128p. 1994. pap. 12.95 (*0-8109-2886-8*, Pub. by Abrams) Time Warner.

Dunand, Ghislaine. L' Impudeur. (FRE.). 189p. 1991. pap. 10.95 (*0-7859-2162-1*, 2070383679) Fr & Eur.

Dunant, Ghislaine. Brazen. Lamont, Rosette C., tr. 202p. 1996. pap. 12.95 (*1-56201-090-5*) FoxRock.

Dunant, Sarah. Fatlands: A Hannah Wolfe Mystery. 256p. 1994. reprint ed. pap. 21.00 (*1-883402-82-4*) S&S Trade.

***Dunant, Sarah.** Mapping the Edge. 2001. 25.00 (*0-375-50323-4*) Random.

Dunant, Sarah. Under My Skin. large type ed. 382p. 1996. pap. 20.95 (*0-7862-0621-7*) Thorndike Pr.

— Under My Skin: A Hannah Wolfe Novel. LC 95-13115. 288p. 1995. 20.00 (*0-684-81521-4*) S&S Trade.

Dunar, Andrew & McBride, Dennis. Building Hoover Dam: An Oral History of the Great Depression. LC 92-44170. (Twayne's Oral History Ser.: No. 11). 350p. 1993. 27.95 (*0-8057-9110-8*, Twyne); pap. 15.95 (*0-8057-9133-7*, Twayne) Mac Lib Ref.

***Dunar, Andrew J.** Power to Explore: A History of Marshall Space Flight Center, 1960-1990. 723p. 2000. boxed set 49.00 (*0-16-058992-4*) USGPO.

Dunar, Andrew J. The Truman Scandals & the Politics of Morality. LC 84-2205. 224p. 1997. 24.00 (*0-8262-0443-0*); pap. 16.95 (*0-8262-1118-6*) U of Mo Pr.

Dunar, Andrew J. & McBride, Dennis. Building Hoover Dam: An Oral History of the Great Depression. (Illus.). 350p. 1999. reprint ed. pap. text 16.00 (*0-7881-6235-7*) DIANE Pub.

Dunas, Diane. Preservers Journal: Putting down What You Put Up. 96p. 1996. per. 9.95 (*0-914667-17-3*) Culinary Arts Ltd.

Dunas, Felice. Passion Play: Ancient Secrets for a Lifetime of Health & Happiness Through Sensational Sex. 272p. 1998. pap. 14.00 (*1-57322-698-X*, Riverhd Trade) Berkley Pub.

Dunas, Felice & Goldberg, Philip. Passion Play: Ancient Secrets for a Lifetime of Health & Happiness Through Sensational Sex. LC 97-8420. (Illus.). 304p. 1997. 24.95 (*1-57322-076-0*, Riverhead Books) Putnam Pub Group.

***Dunas, Jeff.** House of Blues. 1998. text 50.00 (*0-89381-844-5*) N Point Pr.

— State of the Blues. 1998. pap. write for info. (*0-89381-843-7*) N Point Pr.

Dunas, Jeff. State of the Blues: The Living Legacy of the Delta. LC 98-84500. (Illus.). 144p. 1998. 76.00 (*0-89381-799-6*) Aperture.

***Dunas, Jeff.** State of the Blues - Delta Blues. 1998. pap. write for info. (*0-89381-842-9*) N Point Pr.

Dunathan, A. T. The American BB Gun: A Collectors Guide. (Illus.). 158p. 1997. 30.00 (*1-884849-22-9*) R&R Bks.

Dunaway. From Hook to Table. LC 73-14110. 1974. 4.95 (*0-02-533900-1*) Macmillan.

Dunaway, et al. Private Market Financing for Developing Countries. (World Economic & Financial Surveys Ser.). 1995. pap. 20.00 (*1-55775-469-1*) Intl Monetary.

Dunaway, Baxter. The Law of Distressed Real Estate, 4 vols., Set. LC 85-4161. (Real Property - Zoning Ser.). 1985. ring bd. 495.00 (*0-87632-461-8*) West Group.

Dunaway, Baxter, ed. FIRREA: Law & Practice, 3 vols. LC 92-25688. (Real Property - Zoning Ser.). 1992. ring bd. 395.00 (*0-87632-820-6*) West Group.

***Dunaway, David K.** Aldous Huxley, Recollected: An Oral History, Updated Edition. 254p. 1998. 65.00 (*0-7619-9064-X*); pap. 19.95 (*0-7619-9065-8*) AltaMira Pr.

Dunaway, David K. How Can I Keep from Singing: Pete Seeger. (Quality Paperbacks Ser.). (Illus.). 416p. 1990. pap. 13.95 (*0-306-80399-2*) Da Capo.

Dunaway, David K. & Baum, Willa K., eds. Oral History: An Interdisciplinary Anthology. 2nd ed. LC 96-25385. (American Association for State & Local History Book Ser.). (Illus.). 432p. 1996. 65.00 (*0-7619-9188-3*); pap. 24.95 (*0-7619-9189-1*) AltaMira Pr.

Dunaway, Faye & Sharkey, Betsy. Looking for Gatsby: My Life. (Illus.). 416p. 1998. per. 14.00 (*0-671-67526-5*, PB Trade Paper) PB.

— Looking for Gatsby: My Life. LC 95-34651. 480p. 1995. 24.50 (*0-684-80841-2*) Simon & Schuster.

Dunaway, George M., et al. Family Legacies: An Anthology. LC 89-63138. (Illus.). 144p. (Orig.). 1989. pap. 7.95 (*0-9624376-0-3*) JoLee Enterprises.

Dunaway, James, jt. auth. see Brereton, Thomas.

Dunaway, John. Simone Weil. (World Authors Ser.: No. 723). 152p. 1984. 24.95 (*0-8057-6570-0*, Twyne) Mac Lib Ref.

Dunaway, John M. Double Vocation: Christian Presence in Twentieth-Century French Fiction. LC 96-68094. 204p. 1996. lib. bdg. 37.95 (*1-883479-14-2*) Summa Pubns.

— The Metamorphoses of the Self: The Mystic, the Sensualist, & the Artist in the Works of Julien Green. LC 78-88007. (Studies in Romance Languages: No. 19). 125p. reprint ed. pap. 38.80 (*0-7837-5814-6*, 204548100006) Bks Demand.

Dunaway, John M., ed. Exiles & Fugitives: The Letters of Jacques & Raissa Maritain, Allen Tate, & Caroline Gordon. LC 92-18979. (Southern Literary Studies). (Illus.). 144p. (C). 1992. text 25.00 (*0-8071-1779-X*) La State U Pr.

Dunaway, John M. & Springsted, Eric O. The Beauty That Saves: Essays on Aesthetics & Language in Simone Weil. 224p. 1996. text 35.00 (*0-86554-500-6*, MUP/H392) Mercer Univ Pr.

Dunaway, Laramie. Hungry Women. 464p. (Orig.). 1990. mass mkt. 4.95 (*0-446-35294-2*, Pub. by Warner Bks) Little.

— Lessons in Survival. 1995. pap. write for info. (*0-446-67067-7*) Warner Bks.

***Dunaway, Michele.** A Little Office Romance. (American Romance Ser.: Bk. 848). 2000. mass mkt. 4.25 (*0-373-16848-9*, 1-16848-3) Harlequin Bks.

Dunaway, Robert, jt. auth. see Remer, Daniel.

***Dunaway, Suzanne.** No Need to Knead: Handmade Italian Breads in 90 Minutes. LC 99-24912. (Illus.). 272p. 1999. text 24.95 (*0-7868-6427-3*, Pub. by Hyperion) Time Warner.

Dunaway, Vic. Baits, Rigs & Tackle. 1998. pap. 11.95 (*0-936240-14-8*) Wickstrom.

— The Best of Waterfront View. LC 88-51540. (Orig.). 1989. 16.95 (*0-936240-05-9*); pap. 9.95 (*0-936240-03-2*) Wickstrom.

— From Hook to Table. rev. ed. (Illus.). 224p. 1991. 14.95 (*0-936240-07-5*); pap. 9.95 (*0-936240-04-0*) Wickstrom.

— Sport Fish of Florida, 1. 1999. pap. text 16.95 (*0-936240-16-4*) Wickstrom.

***Dunaway, Vic.** Sport Fish of the Gulf of Mexico. (Illus.). 2000. pap. text 16.95 (*0-936240-18-0*) Wickstrom.

Dunaway, Vic. Vic Dunaway's Complete Book of Baits, Rigs & Tackle. 1989. pap. 8.95 (*0-936240-12-1*) Wickstrom.

— Vic Dunaway's Complete Book of Baits, Rigs & Tackle. 6th rev. ed. (Illus.). 224p. 1984. reprint ed. pap. 6.95 (*0-936240-02-4*) Wickstrom.

Dunaway, Vic, et al, eds. Florida Sportsman Tide Atlas, 1992. (Illus.). 112p. (Orig.). 1991. pap. 4.95 (*0-936240-08-3*) Wickstrom.

Dunaway, Wayland F. History of the James River & Kanawha Company. (Columbia University. Studies in the Social Sciences: No. 236). reprint ed. 32.50 (*0-404-51236-4*) AMS Pr.

— Reminiscences of a Rebel. (Army of Northern Virginia Ser.). (Illus.). 170p. (C). 1996. reprint ed. 25.00 (*0-935523-56-1*) Butternut & Blue.

— The Scotch-Irish of Colonial Pennsylvania. LC 79-52943. 273p. 1997. reprint ed. 20.00 (*0-8063-0850-8*) Genealog Pub.

Dunaway, Wilma A. The First American Frontier: Transition to Capitalism in Southern Appalachia, 1700-1860. LC 95-2790. (Fred W. Morrison Series in Southern Studies). (Illus.). 468p. (C). 1996. pap. text 24.95 (*0-8078-4540-X*); lib. bdg. 59.95 (*0-8078-2236-1*) U of NC Pr.

Dunay, David. Truck Company Fireground Operations Study Guide. rev. ed. 81p. 1991. pap. 11.95 (*0-945250-11-8*) Davis Pub Co.

Dunay, R. E. & Hailwood, E., eds. Non-Biostratigraphical Methods of Dating & Correlation. (Geological Society Special Publication Ser.: No. 89). (Illus.). 272p. 1995. 100.00 (*1-897799-30-6*, 330, Pub. by Geol Soc Pub Hse) AAPG.

***Dunayer, Joan.** Animal Equality: Language & Liberation. 240p. 2000. 50.00 (*1-873797-28-1*, Pub. by New Clarion); pap. 24.95 (*1-873797-27-3*, Pub. by New Clarion) Paul & Co Pubs.

***Dunayeskaya, Raya.** Marxism & Freedom: From 1776 until Today. LC 99-87116. 400p. 2000. pap. 24.95 (*1-57392-819-4*, Humanity Bks) Prometheus Bks.

Dunayevskaya, Raya. Kapitalizm Panstwowy I Wschodnioeuropejskie Bunty. Wislanka, Urszula, tr. from ENG.Tr. of State-Capitalism & the East European Revolts. (POL.). 48p. 1990. pap. 3.00 (*0-914441-29-9*) News & Letters.

— The Marxist-Humanist Theory of State-Capitalism. 200p. (Orig.). 1992. pap. 8.50 (*0-914441-30-2*) News & Letters.

— Marx's Capital & Today's Global Crisis. 108p. (Orig.). 1978. pap. 2.00 (*0-914441-11-6*) News & Letters.

— The Myriad Global Crises of the 1980's & the Nuclear World since World War II. 64p. 1986. pap. 2.00 (*0-914441-27-2*) News & Letters.

— Nationalism, Communism, Marxist-Humanism & the Afro-Asian Revolutions. 3rd ed. 48p. 1984. pap. 1.25 (*0-914441-06-X*) News & Letters.

— New Essays: Post-Mao China, Dialectics of Liberation, Trotsky as Theoretician. (Illus.). 50p. (Orig.). 1977. pap. 2.00 (*0-914441-37-X*) News & Letters.

— The Philosophic Moment of Marxist-Humanism. xii, 52p. 1989. pap. 3.00 (*0-914441-38-8*) News & Letters.

— Rosa Luxemburg, Women's Liberation, & Marx's Philosophy of Revolution. 2nd ed. 276p. 1991. text 32.50 (*0-252-01838-9*); pap. text 15.95 (*0-252-06189-6*) U of Ill Pr.

— Russia As State-Capitalist Society: The Original Historical Analysis. 27p. (Orig.). 1973. pap. 1.00 (*0-914441-23-X*) News & Letters.

— State Capitalism & Marx's Humanism, or Philosophy & Revolution: China, Russia, U. S. A. 62p. (Orig.). 1967. pap. 0.50 (*0-914441-10-8*) News & Letters.

— Twenty-Five Years of Marxist-Humanism in the U. S. A History of Worldwide Revolutionary Developments. (Illus.). 30p. (Orig.). 1980. pap. 1.50 (*0-914441-20-5*) News & Letters.

— Women's Liberation & the Dialectics of Revolution: Reaching for the Future. LC 96-14153. 308p. 1996. pap. 16.95 (*0-8143-2655-2*) Wayne St U Pr.

Dunayevskaya, Raya, jt. auth. see Phillips, Andy.

Dunbabin, J. P. Rural Discontent in 19th Century Britain. LC 73-94070. 320p. (C). 1975. 39.95 (*0-8419-0146-5*) Holmes & Meier.

***Dunbabin, Jean.** France in the Making 843-1180. 2nd ed. (Illus.). 476p. 2000. pap. text 24.95 (*0-19-820846-4*) OUP.

Dunbabin, Jean. A Hound of God: Pierre de la Palud & the Fourteenth Century Church. 224p. 1991. 75.00 (*0-19-822291-2*) OUP.

Dunbabin, John. International Relations since 1945 V1 Cold War. LC 93-28429. (Post War World Ser.: Vol. 1). 496p. (C). 1995. pap. 52.00 (*0-582-49365-X*) Addison-Wesley.

— INTL RELS SINCE 1945 V1. LC 93-28429. (Post War World Ser.). (C). 1995. text 104.50 (*0-582-22866-2*) Longman.

— INTL RELS SINCE 1945 V2. LC 93-28429. (Post War World Ser.). (C). 1995. text 90.50 (*0-582-22719-4*) Longman.

***Dunbabin, Katherine.** Mosaics of the Greek & Roman World. LC 98-38082. (Illus.). 384p. (C). 1999. write for info. (*0-521-46143-X*) Cambridge U Pr.

Dunbabin, T. J. The Greeks & Their Eastern Neighbours. (Illus.). 96p. 1979. pap. 15.00 (*0-89005-317-0*) Ares.

— The Western Greeks. 504p. 1991. 30.00 (*0-89005-300-6*) Ares.

***Dunbar.** Happy Days for Mouse & Mole. (J). 2000. pap. 6.95 (*0-552-52978-8*, Pub. by Transworld Publishers Ltd) Trafalgar.

— Heisey Glass: The Early Years, 1896-1924. LC 99-68145. (Illus.). 176p. 2000. pap. 26.95 (*0-87341-885-9*) Krause Pubns.

— Mouse & Mole. (J). 2000. 15.95 (*0-385-40198-1*, Pub. by Transworld Publishers Ltd) Trafalgar.

Dunbar. Ten Little Mice. LC 99-187658. (C). 1999. pap. 5.95 (*0-15-201991-X*) Harcourt.

***Dunbar.** Very Special Mouse & Mole. (J). 2000. pap. 6.95 (*0-552-52977-X*, Pub. by Transworld Publishers Ltd) Trafalgar.

Dunbar, ed. Touring Club: Italy. (Illus.). 448p. 1997. pap. 25.00 (*1-885254-26-1*, Pub. by Monacelli Pr) Penguin Putnam.

***Dunbar, A.** Masterpieces of African-American Eloquence, 1818-1913: Descriptions, Analyses, Characters, Plots, Themes, Critical Evaluations & Significance of Major Works of Fiction, Non-Fiction, Drama & Poetry. 2000. pap. 12.95 (*0-486-41142-7*) Dover.

Dunbar, Alice. The Goodness of St. Rocque. LC 77-161258. (Black Heritage Library Collection). 1977. reprint ed. 22.95 (*0-8369-8817-5*) Ayer.

***Dunbar, Amanda.** Guided by Angels: Divinely Inspired Paintings by Amanda Dunbar. (Illus.). 128p. 2000. 35.00 (*1-56352-635-2*) Longstreet.

Dunbar, Andrea. Rita, Sue & Bob Too with the Arbor & Shirley. (Methuen New Theatrescripts Ser.). 103p. (C). 1988. pap. 8.95 (*0-413-18340-8*, A0244) Heinemann.

Dunbar, Andrew & Lahn, Dean. Body Piercing. 80p. 1999. pap. 19.95 (*0-312-20268-7*, St Martin Griffin) St Martin.

Dunbar, Ann. Alice in Arts Administration. LC 86-50755. (Illus.). 65p. 1986. 7.50 (*0-939855-00-3*) Woodchuck Pr.

Dunbar, Anthony P. Against the Grain: Southern Radicals & Prophets, 1929-1959. LC 81-1782. (Illus.). ix, 306p. 1981. text 32.50 (*0-8139-0892-2*) U Pr of Va.

Dunbar, Arlo, ed. see Montana, Montie, Jr.

Dunbar, B. S. Two-Dimensional Electrophoresis & Immunological Techniques. LC 86-30393. (Illus.). 388p. (C). 1988. spiral bd. 44.50 (*0-306-42839-3*, Kluwer Plenum) Kluwer Academic.

Dunbar, B. S. & O'Rand, M. G. A Comparative Overview of Mammalian Fertilization. (Illus.). 480p. (C). 1991. text 115.00 (*0-306-43841-0*, Kluwer Plenum) Kluwer Academic.

Dunbar, Baxter. Insurance Commander: How to Sell Property & Casualty Business Insurance. LC 93-74125. 333p. (Orig.). 1994. pap. text 59.95 (*0-9626747-9-6*) Busn Insu Pub.

Dunbar, Bob W. The Holy Sabbath Morning: A Novel of the Alamo. 338p. 1998. pap. 17.95 (*1-892896-79-6*) Buy Books.

Dunbar, Bonnie S. Two-Dimensional Electrophoresis & Immunological Techniques. LC 86-30393. (Illus.). 388p. (C). 1988. 85.00 (*0-306-42439-8*, Plenum Trade) Perseus Pubng.

Dunbar, Bonnie S., ed. Protein Blotting: A Practical Approach. LC 93-42043. (Practical Approach Ser.: No. 140). (Illus.). 266p. 1994. pap. text 55.00 (*0-19-963437-8*) OUP.

Dunbar, Burton L. & Feagin, Susan L. Drawings: Reaffirming the Media. (Illus.). 32p. (Orig.). 1994. pap. 10.00 (*0-914489-14-3*) Univ Miss-KC Art.

Dunbar, Burton L. & Olszewski, Edward J., eds. Drawings in Midwestern Collections Vol. 1: Early Works. (Illus.). 200p. (C). 1996. text 42.50 (*0-8262-1062-7*) U of Mo Pr.

Dunbar, C., jt. auth. see Harte, J. P.

Dunbar, Carl O. New Species of Devonian Fossils from Western Tennessee. (Connecticut Academy of Arts & Sciences Ser., Trans.: Vol. 23). 1920. pap. 49.50 (*0-685-22834-7*) Elliots Bks.

Dunbar, Catherine. Dance of the Golden Peacock. 291p. 1996. 27.00 (*0-340-59443-8*, Pub. by Hodder & Stought Ltd) Trafalgar.

***Dunbar, Catherine.** False Images. LC 00-101816. 282p. 2000. pap. 14.95 (*1-890208-38-8*) Poisoned Pen.

Dunbar, Catherine. Sunlight Across the Plains. 264p. 1995. mass mkt. 10.95 (*0-340-59442-X*, Pub. by Hodder & Stought Ltd) Trafalgar.

Dunbar, Charles E. Painted Scenery. 200p. (Orig.). 1994. pap. 7.95 (*0-9640309-0-X*) C E D Prods.

Dunbar, Charles F. Chapters on the Theory & History of Banking. Bruchey, Stuart, ed. LC 80-1145. (Rise of Commercial Banking Ser.). 1981. reprint ed. lib. bdg. 20.95 (*0-405-13648-X*) Ayer.

— Economic Essays. 1977. 19.95 (*0-8369-6971-5*, 7852) Ayer.

Dunbar, Charles F., compiled by. Laws of the United States Relating to Currency, Finance & Banking from 1789 to 1896. rev. ed. LC 69-16856. (Library of Money & Banking History). iv, 310p. 1969. reprint ed. 20.00 (*0-678-00476-5*) Kelley.

Dunbar, Charles F., ed. Laws of the United States Relating to Currency, Finance & Banking from 1789 to 1891. LC 68-28627. 309p. reprint ed. lib. bdg. 22.50 (*0-8371-4585-6*, DULU, Greenwood Pr) Greenwood.

Dunbar, Clement, et al. Assignments Expostiton. 12th ed. LC 96-16752. 490p. (C). 1997. pap. text 39.06 (*0-673-98085-5*) Addson-Wesley Educ.

— Assignments in Exposition. 12th ed. LC 96-16752. (C). 1996. teacher ed. write for info. (*0-673-98240-8*) Addson-Wesley Educ.

Dunbar, David. The Outdoor Traveler's Guide to Canada. LC 90-48520. (Outdoor Traveler's Guides Ser.). (Illus.). 400p. (Orig.). 1991. pap. 12.50 (*1-55670-169-1*) Stewart Tabori & Chang.

Dunbar, David, et al. Exploring Canada's Spectacular National Parks. deluxe ed. LC 95-24289. (Illus.). 1995. write for info. (*0-7922-2963-0*) Natl Geog.

Dunbar, David, jt. auth. see National Parks & Conservation Association Staff.

Dunbar, Dirk. The Balance of Nature's Polarities in New-Paradigm Theory. LC 93-31503. (Reshaping of Psychoanalysis Ser.: Vol. 6). XIV, 165p. (C). 1994. text 31.95 (*0-8204-2310-6*) P Lang Pubng.

Dunbar, Dorothy. A Song for Robbie. LC 96-22158. 55p. (Orig.). 1996. pap. 5.00 (*0-88734-362-7*) Players Pr.

Dunbar, Edward M., jt. auth. see Brooks, David.

Dunbar, Elton. Primer for Clients (Humor) 1972. pap. 2.00 (*0-911214-47-X*) Rational Isl.

Dunbar, Fiona. My Secret Brother. (Illus.). 32p. (J). (ps-1). 1994. 17.95 (*0-09-176402-5*, Pub. by Hutchnson) Trafalgar.

Dunbar, Fiona, jt. auth. see Duffey, Betsy.

Dunbar, Florence W., jt. auth. see Kerr, Willard A.

Dunbar, Frederick C., et al. Estimating Future Claims: Case Studies from Mass Tort & Product Liability Litigation. LC 96-45684. 250p. 1996. pap. text 115.00 (*0-9636246-8-7*) Andrews Pubns.

Dunbar, Gary S., compiled by. Biographical Dictionary of American Geography in the Twentieth Century. 2nd rev. ed. LC 96-812. 130p. 1996. pap. 15.00 (*0-938909-00-2*) Geosci Pubns LSU.

Dunbar, Gary S., ed. Modern Geography: An Encyclopedic Survey. LC 90-3742. 239p. 1990. text 20.00 (*0-8240-5343-5*, H1197) Garland.

Dunbar, George. Data Analysis for Psychology. LC 97-14582. (Illus.). 192p. 1997. pap. text 22.95 (*0-340-69136-0*) OUP.

— Data Analysis for Psychology. LC 97-14582. (Illus.). 192p. (C). 1997. text 60.00 (*0-340-69133-6*) OUP.

An Asterisk (*) at the beginning of an entry indicates that the title is appearing for the first time.

Dunbar, Harry B. A Brother Like Me: A Memoir. LC 94-61310. 240p. 1995. 21.95 (*0-9643654-0-5*) Queenhyte Pubs.

Dunbar, Helen F. Emotions & Bodily Changes: A Survey of Literature on Psychosomatic Interrelationships, 1910-1953. 4th ed. LC 75-16699. (Classics in Psychiatry Ser.). 1976. reprint ed. 99.95 (*0-405-07426-3*) Ayer.

Dunbar, Henry. A Complete Concordance to the Comedies & Fragments of Aristophanes. 2nd enl. rev. ed. x, 398p. 1985. reprint ed. 128.70 incl. 3.5 hd (*3-487-05017-X*) G Olms Pubs.

Dunbar, Ian. Dachshund. LC 98-46331. (Essential Ser.). 96p. 1999. pap. 7.95 (*1-58245-023-4*) Howell Bks.

— Dog Behavior. LC 98-39314. (Owner's Guide to a Happy, Healthy Pet Ser.). (Illus.). 144p. 1998. 12.95 (*0-87605-236-7*) Howell Bks.

— Dog Behavior. (Illus.). 224p. 1989. 17.95 (*0-86622-800-4*, H-1016) TFH Pubns.

***Dunbar, Ian.** The Essential African Grey. Higdon, Pamela Leis, ed. LC 98-33423. (Essential Ser.). (Illus.). 92p. 1999. pap. 7.95 (*1-58245-028-5*) Howell Bks.

Dunbar, Ian. The Essential Australian Shepherd. LC 98-45863. (Essential Ser.). (Illus.). 92p. 1999. pap. 7.95 (*1-58245-026-9*) Howell Bks.

— The Essential Cockatiel. LC 98-45862. (Essential Ser.). (Illus.). 92p. 1999. pap. 7.95 (*1-58245-027-7*) Howell Bks.

***Dunbar, Ian.** The Essential Dalmatian. LC 98-48816. (Essential Ser.). (Illus.). 92p. 1999. pap. 7.95 (*1-58245-024-2*) Howell Bks.

Dunbar, Ian. The Essential Pit Bull. LC 98-46323. (Essential Ser.). (Illus.). 92p. 1999. pap. 7.95 (*1-58245-022-6*) Howell Bks.

— The Essential Poodle. LC 98-42618. 1999. 7.95 (*1-58245-020-X*) Howell Bks.

— How to Teach a New Dog Old Tricks: Sirus Puppy Training. (Illus.). 200p. 1996. pap. 17.95 (*1-888047-06-2*) J & K Pubs.

— Pug. LC 98-46322. 96p. 1999. pap. 7.95 (*1-58245-025-0*) Howell Bks.

***Dunbar, Ian, ed.** Cocker Spaniel. LC 99-17756. (Howell Book House's Essential Ser.). (Illus.). 92p. 1999. pap. 7.95 (*1-58245-068-4*) Howell Bks.

Dunbar, Ian, ed. The Essential Boxer. LC 99-12403. (Essential Ser.). (Illus.). 92p. 1999. pap. 7.95 (*1-58245-067-6*) Howell Bks.

— The Essential Maltese. LC 98-55111. (Essential Ser.). (Illus.). 92p. 1999. pap. 7.95 (*1-58245-084-6*) Howell Bks.

— The Essential Miniature Schnauzer. LC 99-10094. (Essential Ser.). (Illus.). 92p. 1999. pap. 7.95 (*1-58245-069-2*) Howell Bks.

— The Essential Shetland Sheepdog. LC 99-10089. (Essential Ser.). (Illus.). 92p. 1999. pap. 7.95 (*1-58245-070-6*) Howell Bks.

— The Essential Siberian Husky. LC 99-24335. (Essential Ser.). (Illus.). 96p. 1999. pap. 7.95 (*1-58245-071-4*) Howell Bks.

— The Essential West Highland White Terrier. LC 99-20754. (Essential Ser.). (Illus.). 96p. 1999. pap. 7.95 (*1-58245-085-4*) Howell Bks.

— The Essential Yorkshire Terrier. LC 99-19604. (Essential Ser.). (Illus.). 96p. 1999. pap. 7.95 (*1-58245-073-0*) Howell Bks.

— Pomeranian. LC 99-12404. (Howell Book House's Essential Ser.). (Illus.). 92p. 1999. pap. 7.95 (*1-58245-074-9*) Howell Bks.

Dunbar, Ian & Langdon, Anthony. Tough Justice: Sentencing & Penal Policies in the 1990s. LC 98-181991. vi, 173p. 1998. pap. 40.00 (*1-85431-725-3*, Pub. by Blackstone Pr) Gaunt.

Dunbar, Ian & McDonald, Malcolm B. Market Segmentation: A Step-by-Step Approach to Creating Profitable Market Segments. 271p. 1995. pap. 42.50 (*0-333-63723-2*, Pub. by Macmillan) Trans-Atl Phila.

Dunbar, Ian, jt. auth. see McDonald, Malcolm.

***Dunbar, Inga.** Barbara Pitcairn. large type ed. LC 00-28645. 2000. write for info. (*0-7862-2565-3*) Thorndike Pr.

— Dragon's Isle. large type ed. 384p. 1999. 31.99 (*0-7505-1332-2*, Pub. by Mgna Lrg Print) Ulverscroft.

— The Rose of Redayre. large type ed. 352p. 1999. 31.99 (*0-7505-1299-7*, Pub. by Mgna Lrg Print) Ulverscroft.

Dunbar, Jake. Crashers. 160p. (J). (gr. 3-7). Date not set. pap. write for info. (*0-7373-0303-4*, 03034W, Pub. by Lowell Hse) NTC Contemp Pub Co.

Dunbar, James. Tick-Tock. LC 97-14874. (Illus.). 32p. (J). (gr. 1-3). 1998. 19.93 (*1-57505-251-2*, Carolrhoda) Lerner Pub.

— When I Was Young. LC 98-33799. (Picture Books Ser.). 32p. (J). (gr. k-3). 1999. 15.95 (*1-57505-359-4*, Carolrhoda) Lerner Pub.

***Dunbar, James & Swift, Jonathan.** Gulliver's Travels. LC 99-43288. (Eyewitness Classics Ser.). (Illus.). 64p. (J). (gr. 2-5). 2000. 14.95 (*0-7894-5307-X*, D K Ink) DK Pub Inc.

Dunbar, James, jt. auth. see Dunbar, Joyce.

Dunbar, Jan. The Overlay of Random & Order: Selected Poems by Jan Dunbar. LC 97-67160. 128p. 1997. pap. 11.95 (*1-889087-02-5*) P S A Pr.

Dunbar, John B., jt. ed. see Tarazi, Robert C.

Dunbar, John R. The Combat at the Barrier. (Illus.). 1967. 12.50 (*0-910330-13-1*) Grant Dahlstrom.

Dunbar, John T. Highland Costume. 62p. (C). 1989. pap. 21.00 (*0-901824-74-7*, Pub. by Mercat Pr Bks) St Mut.

Dunbar, Joyce. The Baby Bird. LC 96-45001. (Illus.). 32p. (J). (ps-k). 1998. 15.99 (*0-7636-0322-8*) Candlewick Pr.

— Eggday. LC 98-42791. (Illus.). 32p. (J). (ps-3). 1999. 15.95 (*0-8234-1510-4*) Holiday.

— Four Fierce Kittens. (Illus.). 32p. (J). 1992. 13.95 (*0-590-45535-4*, Scholastic Hardcover) Scholastic Inc.

***Dunbar, Joyce.** Gander's Pond. LC 98-14049. (Read Me Ser.). (Illus.). 24p. (J). (ps-2). 1999. 9.99 (*0-7636-0722-3*, Pub. by Candlewick Pr) Penguin Putnam.

— Gander's Pond. LC 98-14049. (Panda & Gander Stories Ser.). (Illus.). (J). 1998. pap. write for info. (*0-7636-0721-5*) Candlewick Press.

— The Glass Garden. (Illus.). 32p. (J). (gr. k-4). 1999. 18.99 (*0-7112-1350-X*) F Lincoln.

Dunbar, Joyce. I Want a Blue Banana! LC 90-5361. (Illus.). 1991. 12.95 (*0-685-52465-5*) HM.

— Indigo & the Whale. LC 95-3629. (Illus.). 32p. (J). (gr. k-3). 1997. 13.95 (*0-8167-3802-5*) BrdgeWater.

***Dunbar, Joyce.** Kingfisher Read-Aloud Storybook. LC 99-88380. (Illus.). 80p. (J). (ps-2). 2000. pap. 10.95 (*0-7534-5297-9*, Kingfisher) LKC.

— Mouse & Mole Have a Party. (J). 2000. pap. 6.95 (*0-552-54557-0*, Pub. by Transworld Publishers Ltd) Trafalgar.

Dunbar, Joyce. Oops-a-Daisy! And Other Talks for Toddlers. LC 94-74045. (Illus.). 32p. (J). (ps). 1997. reprint ed. pap. 4.99 (*0-7636-0143-8*) Candlewick Pr.

— Panda's New Toy. LC 98-14045. (Read Me Ser.). (Illus.). 24p. (J). (gr. k-2). 1999. 9.99 (*0-7636-0724-X*, Pub. by Candlewick Pr) Penguin Putnam.

— The Pig Who Wished. LC 98-28832. (Toddlers Storybook Ser.). (Illus.). 32p. (J). 1999. 9.95 (*0-7894-3487-3*) DK Pub Inc.

***Dunbar, Joyce.** Pig Who Wished. LC 98-28832. (Toddlers Storybook Ser.). (Illus.). 32p. (J). (ps). 2000. pap. text 5.95 (*0-7894-5748-2*, D K Ink) DK Pub Inc.

Dunbar, Joyce. Pomegranate Seeds. LC 98-14046. (Panda & Gander Stories Ser.). (Illus.). (J). 1998. pap. write for info. (*0-7636-0707-X*) Candlewick Press.

— The Sand Children. LC 98-46852. (Illus.). 32p. (J). (ps-3). 1999. 15.95 (*1-56656-309-7*, Pub. by Interlink Pub) Kane-Miller Bk.

— The Secret Friend. LC 98-14048. (Panda & Gander Stories Ser.). (Illus.). (J). 1998. pap. write for info. (*0-7636-0719-3*) Candlewick Pr.

— The Secret Friend. LC 98-14048. (Read Me Ser.). (Illus.). 24p. (J). (ps-2). 1999. 9.99 (*0-7636-0720-7*, Pub. by Candlewick Pr) Penguin Putnam.

— The Spring Rabbit. (Illus.). 32p. (J). (ps-2). 1998. reprint ed. pap. 6.99 (*0-440-41458-X*, Yearling) BDD Bks Young Read.

— Tell Me Something Happy Before I Go to Sleep. LC 97-38562. (Illus.). 32p. (J). (ps-3). 1998. 16.00 (*0-15-201795-X*) Harcourt.

— Ten Little Mice. LC 89-36463. (Illus.). 32p. (J). (ps-1). 1990. 13.95 (*0-15-200601-X*, Gulliver Bks) Harcourt.

— Ten Little Mice. LC 89-36463. (Illus.). 32p. (C). (ps-1). 1992. pap. 23.95 (*0-15-284614-X*, Gulliver Bks) Harcourt.

— Ten Little Mice. 1995. 10.20 (*0-606-09957-3*, Pub. by Turtleback) Demco.

— Ten Little Mice. large type ed. LC 89-36463. (Illus.). 32p. (J). (ps-1). 1995. pap. 6.00 (*0-15-200770-9*, Gulliver Bks) Harcourt.

— This Is the Star. LC 95-50730. (Illus.). 36p. (J). 1996. 16.00 (*0-15-200851-9*) Harcourt.

— This Is the Star. LC 95-50730. (Illus.). 32p. (C). 1998. pap. 6.00 (*0-15-201910-3*) Harcourt.

***Dunbar, Joyce.** The Very Small. (Illus.). 32p. (J). (ps-3). 2000. 16.00 (*0-15-202346-1*, Harcourt Child Bks) Harcourt.

Dunbar, Joyce & Craig, Helen. The Bowl of Fruit. LC 98-14046. (Read Me Ser.). (Illus.). 24p. (J). (ps-2). 1999. 9.99 (*0-7636-0706-1*, Pub. by Candlewick Pr) Penguin Putnam.

Dunbar, Joyce & Dunbar, James. Jugg. (J). 1980. 15.00 (*0-85967-596-3*, Pub. by Scolar Pr) Ashgate Pub Co.

***Dunbar, June, ed.** Jose Limn: An Artist Re-Viewed. (Choreography & Dance Studies: Vol. 21). (Illus.). 168p. 1999. text 42.00 (*90-5755-121-7*, Harwood Acad Pubs) Gordon & Breach.

***Dunbar, Kathleen.** Journey of the Blue Woman. unabridged ed. 106p. (Orig.). 1999. pap. 8.00 (*1-879665-27-1*) Cyborg Prods.

Dunbar, Lee. Automobilia. LC 98-85220. 160p. 1998. pap. 29.95 (*0-7643-0624-3*) Schiffer.

Dunbar, Leila. More Motorcycle Collectibles. (Schiffer Book for Collectors Ser.). (Illus.). 192p. 1997. pap. 29.95 (*0-7643-0333-3*) Schiffer.

— Motorcycle Collectibles. LC 96-644. (Illus.). 216p. (YA). (gr. 10-13). 1996. pap. write for info. (*0-88740-947-4*) Schiffer.

***Dunbar, Lin.** Ferns of the Coastal Plain: Their Lore, Legends & Uses. (Illus.). 165p. 1999. reprint ed. pap. text 17.00 (*0-7881-6730-8*) DIANE Pub.

Dunbar, Louise B. A Study of "Monarchical" Tendencies in the United States: From 1776 to 1801. (BCL1 - U. S. History Ser.). 164p. 1991. reprint ed. lib. bdg. 69.00 (*0-7812-6112-0*) Rprt Serv.

Dunbar, Marc W., jt. auth. see Dunbar, Peter M.

***Dunbar, Margaret.** Remembering a Love (A Widow's Inside Journey) 96p. 2000. pap. write for info. (*1-57197-233-1*, Pub. by Pentland Pr) Assoc Pubs Grp.

Dunbar, Maurice, et al. Hooked on Books: Everybody's Guide to Book Collecting. rev. ed. Whitaker, R. L., ed. 1997. 24.95 (*0-9654129-4-6*) Smarts Pub.

Dunbar, Maury. Books & Collectors. 208p. 1980. text 11.95 (*0-686-27441-5*) Book Nest.

Dunbar, Max. Essays from a Life: Scotland, Canada, Greenland, Denmark. (Illus.). 210p. 1995. text 49.95 (*0-7735-1384-1*) McG-Queens Univ Pr.

Dunbar, Maxwell J. Environment & Good Sense: An Introduction to Environmental Damage & Control in Canada. LC 72-171563. (Environmental Damage & Control in Canada Ser.: No. 1). (Illus.). 100p. reprint ed. pap. 31.00 (*0-7837-1161-1*, 204169000022) Bks Demand.

Dunbar, Michael. Make a Windsor Chair with Michael Dunbar. LC 83-50681. (Illus.). 176p. 1985. pap. 19.95 (*0-918804-21-3*) Taunton.

— Restoring, Tuning, & Using Classic Woodworking Tools. LC 89-35456. (Illus.). 256p. 1989. pap. 19.95 (*0-8069-6670-X*) Sterling.

Dunbar, Nan, ed. Birds. 800p. 1997. pap. text 49.95 (*0-19-815083-0*) OUP.

Dunbar, Nan, ed. & comment see Aristophanes.

***Dunbar, Natalie.** Best of Friends. 2000. pap. 8.95 (*1-58571-007-5*, Pub. by Genesis Press) BookWorld.

Dunbar-Nelson, Alice. The Works of Alice Dunbar-Nelson, Vol. 3. Hull, Gloria T., ed. (Schomburg Library of Nineteenth-Century Black Women Writers). (Illus.). 352p. 1988. text 35.00 (*0-19-505252-8*) OUP.

Dunbar-Nelson, Alice M., ed. Masterpieces of Negro Eloquence: African-American Women Writers, 1910-1940 by Dunbar-Nelson. LC 96-44327. 1996. 30.00 (*0-7838-1424-0*, Hall Reference) Macmillan.

***Dunbar, Nicholas.** Inventing Money: Long-Term Capital Management & the Search for Risk-Free Profits. 262p. 1999. 29.95 (*0-471-89999-2*) Wiley.

Dunbar-Ortiz, Roxanne. Red Dirt: Growing up Okie. (Haymarket Ser.). 1998. pap. 15.00 (*1-85984-152-7*, Pub. by Verso) Norton.

Dunbar-Ortiz, Roxanne. Red Dirt: Growing up Okie. LC 97-13070. 1997. 25.00 (*1-85984-856-7*, Pub. by Verso) Norton.

Dunbar, Patsy, jt. auth. see Dunbar, R.

Dunbar, Paul Laurence. As Old As Darkness. 77p. 1998. pap. 8.00 (*1-56411-203-9*) Untd Bros & Sis.

— Best Stories of Paul Laurence Dunbar. Brawley, B., ed. (Notable American Authors Ser.). 1992. reprint ed. lib. bdg. 75.00 (*0-7812-2715-1*) Rprt Serv.

— Candle-Lightin' Time. LC 76-164797. (Illus.). reprint ed. 19.50 (*0-404-00030-4*) AMS Pr.

— The Collected Poetry of Paul Laurence Dunbar. LC 92-37190. 354p. (C). 1993. pap. 18.95 (*0-8139-1438-8*) U Pr of Va.

— Collected Works. 1990. reprint ed. lib. bdg. 75.00 (*0-7812-2706-2*, 1514); reprint ed. write for info. (*0-318-67714-8*); reprint ed. write for info. (*0-318-67715-6*); reprint ed. write for info. (*0-318-67716-4*); reprint ed. write for info. (*0-318-67717-2*); reprint ed. write for info. (*0-318-67718-0*); reprint ed. write for info. (*0-318-67719-9*); reprint ed. write for info. (*0-318-67720-2*); reprint ed. write for info. (*0-318-67721-0*) Rprt Serv.

— Complete Poems. (Notable American Authors Ser.). 1992. reprint ed. lib. bdg. 75.00 (*0-7812-2710-0*) Rprt Serv.

Dunbar, Paul Laurence. Complete Poems of Paul Laurence Dunbar. Date not set. lib. bdg. 23.95 (*0-8488-1704-4*) Amereon Ltd.

Dunbar, Paul Laurence. The Complete Poems of Paul Laurence Dunbar. 289p. 1993. reprint ed. pap. 10.95 (*0-317-05269-1*) Hakims Pubs.

— The Complete Poems of Paul Laurence Dunbar. 289p. reprint ed. pap. 10.95 (*0-396-07895-8*) Hakims Pubs.

— The Fanatics. LC 70-81110. (Black Heritage Library Collection). 320p. 1977. 41.95 (*0-8369-8555-9*) Ayer.

— The Fanatics. LC 70-81110. (Black Heritage Library Collection). 320p. 1991. pap. 29.95 (*0-88143-128-1*) Ayer.

— The Fanatics. LC 70-84687. 312p. 1969. reprint ed. lib. bdg. 59.50 (*0-8371-1264-8*, DUT&) Greenwood.

— The Fanatics. (Notable American Authors Ser.). 1992. reprint ed. lib. bdg. 75.00 (*0-7812-2713-5*) Rprt Serv.

— Folks from Dixie. LC 72-101281. (Short Story Index Reprint Ser.). 1977. 17.95 (*0-8369-3218-8*) Ayer.

— Folks from Dixie. LC 73-81111. (Black Heritage Library Collection). (Illus.). 1977. 17.95 (*0-8369-8659-7*) Ayer.

— Four Collections of Poetry: Includes Howdy Honey Howdy, Li'l Gal, Poems of Cabin & Field, & When Malindy Sings. (C). 1991. 54.95 (*0-88143-121-4*) Ayer.

— Heart of Happy Hollow. LC 77-81112. (Short Story Index Reprint Ser.). (C). 1977. reprint ed. 41.95 (*0-8369-3318-4*) Ayer.

— Heart of Happy Hollow. LC 77-81112. (Short Story Index Reprint Ser.). (C). 1991. reprint ed. pap. 29.95 (*0-88143-127-3*) Ayer.

— Howdy Honey Howdy. LC 79-78993. (Black Heritage Library Collection). (Illus.). 1977. 35.95 (*0-8369-8556-7*) Ayer.

— Howdy Honey Howdy. LC 73-164799. (Illus.). reprint ed. 19.50 (*0-404-00035-5*) AMS Pr.

— Howdy Honey Howdy. (C). 1991. reprint ed. pap. 22.95 (*0-88143-133-8*) Ayer.

— Joggin' erlong. LC 78-83921. (Black Heritage Library Collection). (Illus.). 1977. 35.95 (*0-8369-8557-5*) Ayer.

— Joggin' erlong. (C). 1991. reprint ed. pap. 22.95 (*0-88143-124-9*) Ayer.

***Dunbar, Paul Laurence.** Jump Back, Honey. 40p. (J). 1999. pap. 16.99 (*0-7868-0573-0*, Pub. by Disney Pr) Time Warner.

Dunbar, Paul Laurence. Jump Back, Honey. LC 98-54252. (Illus.). 40p. (J). (gr. k-3). 1999. lib. bdg. 17.49 (*0-7868-2406-9*, Pub. by Hyprn Child) Little.

***Dunbar, Paul Laurence.** Jump Back, Honey. Bryan, Ashley, ed. LC 98-54252. (Illus.). 40p. (J). (gr. k-3). 1999. 16.99 (*0-7868-0464-5*, Pub. by Hyprn Child) Time Warner.

Dunbar, Paul Laurence. Li'l' Gal. LC 75-78992. (Black Heritage Library Collection). (Illus.). 1977. 35.95 (*0-8369-8558-3*) Ayer.

— Li'l Gal. LC 73-164800. (Illus.). reprint ed. 19.50 (*0-404-00034-7*) AMS Pr.

— Li'l' Gal. (Illus.). 1991. reprint ed. pap. 22.95 (*0-88143-131-1*) Ayer.

— The Love of Landry. LC 70-81113. (Black Heritage Library Collection). 1977. reprint ed. 35.95 (*0-8369-8559-1*) Ayer.

— The Love of Landry. LC 70-81113. (Black Heritage Library Collection). 1991. reprint ed. pap. text 24.95 (*0-88143-126-5*) Ayer.

— The Love of Landry. LC 72-88408. 200p. 1969. reprint ed. lib. bdg. 59.50 (*0-8371-1810-7*, DUL&) Greenwood.

— The Love of Landry. (Notable American Authors Ser.). 1992. reprint ed. lib. bdg. 75.00 (*0-7812-2712-7*) Rprt Serv.

— Lyrics of a Lowly Life. LC 70-78996. (American Negro: His History & Literature. Series 2). (C). 1975. reprint ed. 36.95 (*0-405-01858-4*) Ayer.

— Lyrics of a Lowly Life. LC 70-78996. (American Negro: His History & Literature. Series 2). (C). 1991. reprint ed. pap. 27.95 (*0-88143-129-X*) Ayer.

— Lyrics of Love & Laughter. 1993. reprint ed. lib. bdg. 89.00 (*0-7812-5359-4*) Rprt Serv.

— Lyrics of Lowly Life. 224p. 1984. pap. 9.95 (*0-8065-0922-8*, Citadel Pr) Carol Pub Group.

— Lyrics of Lowly Life. (Notable American Authors Ser.). 1992. reprint ed. lib. bdg. 75.00 (*0-7812-2709-7*) Rprt Serv.

— Lyrics of Sunshine & Shadow. LC 70-83919. (Black Heritage Library Collection). 1977. 35.95 (*0-8369-8561-3*) Ayer.

— Lyrics of Sunshine & Shadow. LC 77-164801. reprint ed. 19.50 (*0-404-00038-X*) AMS Pr.

— Lyrics of Sunshine & Shadow. (Illus.). 1991. reprint ed. pap. 22.95 (*0-88143-125-7*) Ayer.

— Lyrics of the Hearthside. LC 70-164802. reprint ed. 19.50 (*0-404-00037-1*) AMS Pr.

— Lyrics of the Hearthside. LC 74-83920. (Black Heritage Library Collection). (C). 1977. reprint ed. 38.95 (*0-8369-8562-1*) Ayer.

— Lyrics of the Hearthside. LC 74-83920. (Black Heritage Library Collection). (C). 1991. reprint ed. pap. 27.95 (*0-88143-135-4*) Ayer.

— Majors & Minors. LC 76-83918. (Black Heritage Library Collection). 1977. 35.95 (*0-8369-8563-X*) Ayer.

— Majors & Minors. 1991. reprint ed. pap. 22.95 (*0-88143-123-0*) Ayer.

— Majors & Minors. (Notable American Authors Ser.). 1992. reprint ed. lib. bdg. 75.00 (*0-7812-2708-9*) Rprt Serv.

— Oak & Ivy. (Notable American Authors Ser.). 1992. reprint ed. lib. bdg. 75.00 (*0-7812-2707-0*) Rprt Serv.

— Poems of Cabin & Field. LC 72-83917. (Black Heritage Library Collection). (Illus.). 1977. 35.95 (*0-8369-8564-8*) Ayer.

— Poems of Cabin & Field. LC 74-164803. (Illus.). reprint ed. 19.50 (*0-404-00041-X*) AMS Pr.

Dunbar, Paul Laurence. Poems of Cabin & Field. (Illus.). 1991. reprint ed. pap. 22.95 (*0-88143-132-X*) Ayer.

Dunbar, Paul Laurence. Selected Poems. LC 97-22682. (Dover Thrift Editions Ser.). (Illus.). 80p. 1998. pap. 1.00 (*0-486-29980-5*) Dover.

— Speakin' O' Christmas & Other Christmas & Special Poems. LC 73-18574. (Illus.). reprint ed. 19.50 (*0-404-11385-0*) AMS Pr.

***Dunbar, Paul Laurence.** Sport of the Gods, 1. 1999. mass mkt. 5.95 (*0-451-52755-0*) NAL.

Dunbar, Paul Laurence. Sport of the Gods. LC 69-18588. (American Negro: His History & Literature. Series 2). 262p. (C). 1978. reprint ed. 38.95 (*0-405-01859-2*) Ayer.

— Sport of the Gods. LC 69-18588. (American Negro: His History & Literature. Series 2). 262p. (C). 1991. reprint ed. pap. 27.95 (*0-88143-136-2*) Ayer.

— Sport of the Gods. (Notable American Authors Ser.). 1992. reprint ed. lib. bdg. 75.00 (*0-7812-2714-3*) Rprt Serv.

— Strength of Gideon. LC 69-18589. 1991. reprint ed. pap. write for info. (*0-88143-137-0*) Ayer.

— Strength of Gideon & Other Stories. LC 69-18589. (American Negro: His History & Literature. Series 2). (Illus.). (C). 1974. reprint ed. 38.95 (*0-405-01860-6*) Ayer.

— Three Collections of Poetry: Joggin' erlong; Lyrics of Sunshine & Shadow; Majors & Minors. (Illus.). (C). 1991. 43.95 (*0-88143-122-2*) Ayer.

— The Uncalled: A Novel. LC 78-164804. reprint ed. 19.50 (*0-404-00042-8*) AMS Pr.

— The Uncalled: A Novel. LC 71-81116. (Black Heritage Library Collection). (C). 1977. reprint ed. 38.95 (*0-8369-8567-2*) Ayer.

— The Uncalled: A Novel. LC 71-81116. (Black Heritage Library Collection). (C). 1991. reprint ed. pap. 26.95 (*0-88143-130-3*) Ayer.

— The Uncalled: A Novel. LC 70-104443. reprint ed. lib. bdg. 9.50 (*0-8398-0374-5*) Irvington.

— The Uncalled: A Novel. (Notable American Authors Ser.). 1992. reprint ed. lib. bdg. 75.00 (*0-7812-2711-9*) Rprt Serv.

— When Malindy Sings. LC 79-83916. (Black Heritage Library Collection). (Illus.). 1977. 19.95 (*0-8369-8568-0*) Ayer.

— When Malindy Sings. LC 71-164805. (Illus.). reprint ed. 19.50 (*0-404-00039-8*) AMS Pr.

Dunbar, Peter M. The Condominium Concept: A Practical Guide for Officers, Owners & Directors of Florida Condominiums. 6th rev. ed. 352p. 1996. pap. 18.95 (*0-937569-16-X*) Suncoast Prof Pub.

— The Homeowners Association Manual. 3rd rev. ed. LC 98-100558. 1997. pap. 14.95 (*0-937569-17-8*) Suncoast Prof Pub.

Dunbar, Peter M. & Dudley, Charles F. The Law of Florida Homeowners' Associations. 3rd rev. ed. LC 98-115009. 1997. pap. 15.95 (*0-937569-18-6*) Suncoast Prof Pub.

D

*__Dunbar, Peter M. & Dunbar, Marc W.__ The Homeowners Association Manual. 4th rev. ed. 176p. 1999. pap. 14.95 (*0-9667496-2-6*) Aras Pubg.

Dunbar, Peter M. & Dunbar, Marc W. Resident Owned Community Guide for Florida Cooperatives. 368p. 1998. pap. 19.95 (*0-9667496-1-8*) Aras Pubg.

Dunbar, Prescott N. New Orleans Museum of Art: The First 75 Years. LC 90-6002. (Illus.). 456p. 1990. 24.95 (*0-8071-1604-1*) La State U Pr.

Dunbar, R. & Dunbar, Patsy. Social Dynamics of Gelada Baboons. (Contributions to Primatology Ser.: Vol. 6). (Illus.). 176p. 1975. 77.50 (*3-8055-2137-5*) S Karger.

Dunbar, Robert. 1980-1989. (Yearbooks in Science Ser.). (Illus.). 80p. (J). (gr. 5-8). 1995. lib. bdg. 20.40 (*0-8050-3438-2*) TFC Bks NY.

— Secret Lands: The World of Patricia Lynch. 1999. 14.95 (*0-86278-575-8*) OBrien Pr.

Dunbar, Robert, ed. Enchanted Journeys: Fifty Years of Irish Writing for Children. (Illus.). 192p. 1998. 14.95 (*0-86278-518-9*, Pub. by OBrien Pr) Irish Amer Bk.

Dunbar, Robert E. A Doctor Discusses Learning to Cope with Arthritis Rheumatism & Gout. (Illus.). (Orig.). 1990. pap. 6.00 (*0-318-37504-4*) Budlong.

— Homosexuality. LC 95-18088. (Issues in Focus Ser.). (Illus.). 104p. (YA). (gr. 6 up). 1995. lib. bdg. 20.95 (*0-89490-665-8*) Enslow Pubs.

— How to Debate. 2nd ed. LC 93-11959. (Speak Out! Write On! Ser.). 96p. (YA). (gr. 7-12). 1994. lib. bdg. 24.00 (*0-531-11122-9*) Watts.

Dunbar, Robert G. Forging New Rights in Western Waters. LC 82-13421. 291p. reprint ed. pap. 90.30 (*0-7837-1841-1*, 204204100001) Bks Demand.

Dunbar, Robin. Grooming, Gossip & the Evolution of Language. LC 96-15934. (Illus.). 240p. 1997. 22.95 (*0-674-36334-5*) HUP.

— Grooming, Gossip & the Evolution of Language. (Illus.). 240p. 1998. pap. 14.00 (*0-674-36336-1*) HUP.

— The Trouble with Science. LC 96-17482. 224p. 1996. pap. 14.00 (*0-674-91019-2*) HUP.

Dunbar, Robin, ed. Human Reproductive Decisions: Biological & Social Perspectives: Proceedings of the Thirteenth Annual Symposium of the Galton Institute, London, 1993. LC 94-32721. 1995. text 79.95 (*0-312-12436-8*) St Martin.

Dunbar, Robin, et al, eds. The Evolution of Culture: An Interdisciplinary View. LC 99-26791. 272p. 1999. text 55.00 (*0-8135-2730-9*); pap. text 24.00 (*0-8135-2731-7*) Rutgers U Pr.

Dunbar, Robin I. Reproductive Decisions: An Economic Analysis of Gelada Baboon Social Strategies. LC 84-42584. (Monographs on Behavior & Ecology). 276p. 1984. reprint ed. pap. 78.70 (*0-608-02925-4*, 2063990) Bks Demand.

Dunbar, Ronald W. & Hieke, Adolf E. Building Fluency in English: Conversation Management. (Illus.). 250p. (C). 1985. pap. text 12.50 (*0-13-086117-0*) P-H.

Dunbar, Ronald W., jt. auth. see Hieke, Adolf E.

Dunbar, Ruth. The White Tide. 256p. (Orig.). 1993. pap. 8.95 (*1-878903-07-1*) Nosado Pr.

Dunbar, Sandra B., et al, eds. Sudden Cardiac Death: Past, Present, & Future. LC 96-47804. (American Heart Association Monograph Ser.). (Illus.). 440p. 1997. 78.00 (*0-87993-666-5*) Futura Pub.

D

Dunbar, Seymour. History of Travel in America, 4 vols., Set. LC 68-23283. (Illus.). 1968. reprint ed. lib. bdg. 195.00 (*0-8371-0063-1*, DUHT) Greenwood.

— History of Travel in America, 4 vols., Vol. 1. LC 68-23283. (Illus.). 1968. reprint ed. lib. bdg. 55.00 (*0-8371-1791-7*, DUHA) Greenwood.

— History of Travel in America, 4 vols., Vol. 2. LC 68-23283. (Illus.). 1968. reprint ed. lib. bdg. 55.00 (*0-8371-0873-X*, DUHB) Greenwood.

— History of Travel in America, 4 vols., Vol. 3. LC 68-23283. (Illus.). 1968. reprint ed. lib. bdg. 55.00 (*0-8371-0874-8*, DUHC) Greenwood.

— History of Travel in America, 4 vols., Vol. 4. LC 68-23283. (Illus.). 1968. reprint ed. lib. bdg. 55.00 (*0-8371-0875-6*, DUHD) Greenwood.

Dunbar, Sophie. A Bad Hair Day: An Eclaire Mystery. (Eclaire Mystery Ser.: No. 3). 296p. 1998. reprint ed. mass mkt. 5.95 (*1-890768-08-1*) Intrigue Press.

— Behind Eclaire's Doors: An Eclaire Mystery. (Eclaire Mystery Ser.: No. 1). 296p. 1998. reprint ed. mass mkt. 5.95 (*1-890768-10-3*) Intrigue Press.

*__Dunbar, Sophie.__ Fashion Victims. 336p. 2001. 23.95 (*1-890768-29-4*, Pub. by Intrigue Press) Midpt Trade.

Dunbar, Sophie. Redneck Riviera: An Eclaire Mystery. 290p. 1998. mass mkt. 5.50 (*1-890768-06-5*) Intrigue Press.

*__Dunbar, Sophie.__ Shiveree. LC 98-51073. (Eclaire Mystery Ser.: 4). 320p. 1999. 22.95 (*1-890768-11-1*) Intrigue Press.

— Shiveree. (Eclaire Mysteries Ser.: 4). 416p. 2000. mass mkt. 5.95 (*1-890768-24-3*) Intrigue Press.

Dunbar, Tony. City of Beads. 256p. 1996. mass mkt. 5.99 (*0-425-15578-1*, Prime Crime) Berkley Pub.

— The Crime Czar: A Tubby Dubonnet Mystery. (Tubby Dubonnet Mysteries Ser.). 240p. 1998. mass mkt. 5.99 (*0-440-22658-9*) Dell.

— Crooked Man. 208p. 1996. mass mkt. 4.99 (*0-425-15138-7*) Berkley Pub.

*__Dunbar, Tony.__ Lucky Man. 240p. 1999. mass mkt. 5.99 (*0-440-22662-7*) Dell.

Dunbar, Tony. Shelter from the Storm. 224p. 1998. mass mkt. 5.99 (*0-425-16644-9*) Berkley Pub.

— Shelter from the Storm. large type ed. LC 98-22095. (Large Print Book Ser.). 1998. 22.95 (*1-56895-607-X*) Wheeler Pub.

— Trick Question. 1997. mass mkt. 5.99 (*0-425-16092-0*, Prime Crime) Berkley Pub.

— Trick Question. large type ed. LC 97-5824. (Cloak & Dagger Ser.). 332p. 1997. 23.95 (*0-7862-1086-9*) Thorndike Pr.

Dunbar, Virgil. Why Christ Can't Be Pictured: God Is Not Like Art. 244p. 1994. pap. 14.95 (*1-886096-00-7*, Pub. by Priceless Prnting) Rapids Christian.

Dunbar, William. The Poems, 3 vols., Set. Small, John, ed. (Anglistica & Americana Ser.: No. 136). (Illus.). 1973. reprint ed. 161.20 (*3-487-04650-4*) G Olms Pubs.

— The Poems of William Dunbar. LC 70-161970. reprint ed. 29.00 (*0-403-01321-6*) Scholarly.

*__Dunbar, William.__ Selected Poems. 144p. 2000. pap. 16.95 (*1-85754-446-3*, Pub. by Carcanet Pr) Paul & Co Pubs.

Dunbar, William. William Dunbar Poems. LC 74-161966. 159p. 1958. reprint ed. 29.00 (*0-403-01339-9*) Scholarly.

Dunbar, Willis F. & May, George S. Michigan: A History of the Wolverine State. 3rd rev. ed. (Illus.). 784p. 1995. pap. 30.00 (*0-8028-7055-4*) Eerdmans.

Dunbar, Wylene. Margaret Cape: A Novel. LC 96-48108. 352p. (C). 1997. 23.00 (*0-15-100248-7*) Harcourt.

Dunbaradom Higher Learning Staff. Dunbarodom Higher Learning. Date not set. pap. text 22.17 (*0-395-88154-4*) HM.

Dunbaugh, Edwin L. The Era of the Joy Line: A Saga of Steamboating on Long Island Sound, 43. LC 81-6293. (Contributions in Economics & Economic History Ser.: No. 43). (Illus.). 363p. 1982. 55.00 (*0-313-22888-4*, DEJ/, Greenwood Pr) Greenwood.

— Night Boat to New England, 1815-1900, 128. LC 91-22368. (Contributions in Economics & Economic History Ser.: No. 116). (Illus.). 384p. 1992. 65.00 (*0-313-27733-8*, DNB, Greenwood Pr) Greenwood.

— Whistles Echo on the Bay. Eppich, Linda & Martinez, Marta V., eds. (Illus.). 20p. (Orig.). 1996. 5.00 (*0-932840-12-4*) RI Hist Soc.

Dunbaugh, Edwin L. & Thomas, William D. William H. Webb: Shipbuilder. LC 89-50473. (Illus.). xiv, 240p. 1989. 35.00 (*0-9622631-0-9*) Webb Inst Naval Arch.

Dunbaugh, Edwin L., ed. see Jones, Harry & Jones, Timothy.

Dunbaugh, Edwin L., ed. see Mueller, Edward A.

*__Dunbier, Lonnie Pierson & Kmack, Marcia.__ Augustus W. Dunbier: Paint for Love of Color. (Illus.). 2000. pap. 24.95 (*1-889921-09-2*, Pub. by Western Edge Pr) Mountain Pr.

Dunbier, Roger. The Dunbier Art Companion: American Picture Prices. (Illus.). 310p. 1989. 35.00 (*0-685-30118-4*) Genus.

Dunboyne, Lord, ed. The Trial of John George Haigh: The Acid Bath Murder. (Notable British Trials Ser.). 271p. 1995. reprint ed. 81.00 (*1-56169-190-9*) Gaunt.

Duncan. Agricultural Futures & Options. LC 98-51052. 240p. 1999. 60.00 (*0-07-134922-7*) McGraw.

— Baroque Sonatas: For Flute & Guitar. 1990. 7.95 (*0-685-32138-X*, T669) Hansen Ed Mus.

— Clinical Epilepsy. 1996. text 76.00 (*0-443-04936-X*, W B Saunders Co) Harcrt Hlth Sci Grp.

Duncan. Eyelid Myoclinia with Absences. 130p. 31.00 (*0-86196-550-7*, Pub. by J Libbey Med) Bks Intl VA.

Duncan. Four Catalonian Songs: Flute & Guitar. 1990. 6.95 (*0-685-32123-1*, T668) Hansen Ed Mus.

— Just Like a Mama. (J). 1997. 14.95 (*0-689-80584-5*) S&S Childrens.

— Landscape Interpretation. text 112.00 (*0-471-98529-5*); pap. text 37.00 (*0-471-98530-9*) Wiley.

— Lone Mothers, Paid Work & Gender. LC 99-21783. 1999. text 65.00 (*0-312-22432-X*) St Martin.

*__Duncan.__ Marketing Communication. 2001. 63.74 (*0-256-21476-X*) McGraw.

— Past Imperative. 2000. 22.00 (*0-380-97260-3*) Morrow Avon.

Duncan & Vanhuss. Keyboarding/Typewriting. 5th ed. 1990. student ed. 17.50 (*0-538-28155-3*) S-W Pub.

Duncan & Vanhuss, Susie H. Advanced Key & Typewriting. 5th ed. (TE - Keyboarding Ser.). (C). 1990. wbk. ed. 42.95 (*0-538-14862-4*) S-W Pub.

— Advanced Keyboarding/Typewriting. 5th ed. (Keyboarding Ser.). 1991. pap., lab manual ed. 9.95 (*0-538-14861-6*) S-W Pub.

— College Keyboarding Advanced Course. 6th ed. (TE - Keyboarding Ser.). (C). 1994. mass mkt. 32.25 (*0-538-70857-3*) S-W Pub.

— College Keyboarding & Typewriting: WordPerfect Formatting. 12th ed. (TE - Keyboarding Ser.). 1991. 34.95 (*0-538-20942-9*) S-W Pub.

— College Keyboarding & Typewriting Intensive. 12th ed. (TE - Keyboarding Ser.). 1991. 72.95 (*0-538-20905-4*) S-W Pub.

— College Keyboarding & Typwriting: WordPerfect Formatting. 12th ed. (TE - Keyboarding Ser.). 1991. 34.95 (*0-538-20941-0*) S-W Pub.

— College Keyboarding Introductory Course. 6th ed. (TE - Keyboarding Ser.). (C). 1994. mass mkt. 32.25 (*0-538-70850-6*) S-W Pub.

— College Keyboarding Lab Materials. 6th ed. (TE - Keyboarding Ser.). (C). 1994. mass mkt., lab manual ed. 11.25 (*0-538-70851-4*) S-W Pub.

— College Keyboarding Lab Materials Lesson. 6th ed. (TE - Keyboarding Ser.). (C). 1994. mass mkt. 12.50 (*0-538-70855-7*); mass mkt. 14.00 (*0-538-70858-1*) S-W Pub.

— College Keyboarding Typewriting Intensive. 12th ed. (Keyboarding Ser.). (C). 1991. 58.95 (*0-538-20935-6*) S-W Pub.

— Document Production Course, L121-180, College Keyboarding. 13th ed. LC 93-1746. (TE - Keyboarding Ser.). (C). 1994. mass mkt. 32.25 (*0-538-70809-3*) S-W Pub.

— Introduction to Keyboarding/Typewriting. 5th ed. (Keyboarding Ser.). (C). 1990. wbk. ed. 33.25 (*0-538-14842-X*) S-W Pub.

— Keyboarding/Typewriting: Advanced (T30) 5th ed. (TE - Keyboarding Ser.). 1991. 33.95 (*0-538-14860-8*) S-W Pub.

— MLS College Keyboarding: Basic Course. 12th ed. (TE - Keyboarding Ser.). 1991. pap., student ed. 6.95 (*0-538-70139-0*) S-W Pub.

— MLS College Keyboarding: Document Production. Advanced. 12th ed. (TE - Keyboarding Ser.). (C). 1990. mass mkt. 36.00 (*0-538-70138-2*) S-W Pub.

— MLS College Keyboarding: Formatting, Intermediate. 12th ed. (TE - Keyboarding Ser.). (C). 1990. mass mkt. 36.00 (*0-538-70129-3*) S-W Pub.

— Typewriting: Intermediate. 5th ed. (TE - Keyboarding Ser.). 1991. pap. 33.95 (*0-538-14850-0*) S-W Pub.

Duncan & Warner. College Keyboarding, Vol. 2. 13th ed. (TE - Keyboarding Ser.). (C). 1994. pap., suppl. ed. 7.00 (*0-538-70822-0*) S-W Pub.

— College Keyboarding & Typewriting. 12th ed. (TE - Keyboarding Ser.). 1990. 169.95 (*0-538-20852-X*) S-W Pub.

— College Keyboarding & Typewriting: Formatting Template for WordPerfect. 12th ed. (TE - Keyboarding Ser.). 1990. pap. 34.95 (*0-538-20953-4*) S-W Pub.

— College Keyboarding & Typewriting: Micropace. 12th ed. (TE - Keyboarding Ser.). 1990. 105.95 (*0-538-20867-8*) S-W Pub.

— College Keyboarding & Typewriting, Document Production, Micro Assistant. 12th ed. (TE - Keyboarding Ser.). 1990. 34.95 (*0-538-20849-X*) S-W Pub.

— College Keyboarding & Typewriting Int Microguide WordPerfect. 12th ed. (TE - Keyboarding Ser.). 1990. 20.95 (*0-538-20878-3*) S-W Pub.

— College Keyboarding & Typewriting, Micro Assistant. 12th ed. (TE - Keyboarding Ser.). 1990. 34.95 (*0-538-20847-3*) S-W Pub.

— College Keyboarding Document Production. 12th ed. (TE - Keyboarding Ser.). 1990. 34.95 (*0-538-20846-5*) S-W Pub.

— College Keyboarding Document Production. 13th ed. (TE - Keyboarding Ser.). (C). 1994. 38.00 (*0-538-70882-4*) S-W Pub.

— College Keyboarding Formatting Micro Assistant. 12th ed. (TE - Keyboarding Ser.). 1990. 34.95 (*0-538-20845-7*) S-W Pub.

— College Keyboarding Microcomputer Material. 12th ed. (TE - Keyboarding Ser.). 1990. 75.95 (*0-538-20957-7*) S-W Pub.

— College Keyboarding Microcomputer Material. 12th ed. (TE - Keyboarding Ser.). 1990. 75.95 (*0-538-20958-5*) S-W Pub.

— College Keyboarding Typewriting: Lab Material. 11th ed. (TE - Keyboarding Ser.). 1985. pap. 18.95 (*0-538-20781-7*) S-W Pub.

— College Keyboarding/Typewriting. 12th ed. (TE - Keyboarding Ser.). 1994. text 25.95 (*0-538-71066-7*) S-W Pub.

— College Keyboarding/Typewriting. 13th ed. (TE - Keyboarding Ser.). (C). 1994. pap., student ed., suppl. ed. 7.00 (*0-538-70823-9*); mass mkt., wbk. ed. 11.25 (*0-538-70810-7*); mass mkt., lab manual ed. 14.00 (*0-538-70812-3*); mass mkt., lab manual ed. 12.50 (*0-538-70811-5*) S-W Pub.

— College Keyboarding/Typing 1-60. 13th ed. (TE - Keyboarding Ser.). (C). 1994. mass mkt., suppl. ed. 7.00 (*0-538-70821-2*) S-W Pub.

Duncan, et al. College Keyboarding Test. 11th ed. (TE - Keyboarding Ser.). 1986. 6.95 (*0-538-27582-0*) S-W Pub.

— College Keyboarding/Typing Intensive Basic. 11th ed. (TE - Keyboarding Ser.). 1986. text 41.95 (*0-538-20280-7*) S-W Pub.

— College Keyboarding/Typing Intermediate. 11th ed. (TE - Keyboarding Ser.). 1986. text 39.95 (*0-538-20290-4*) S-W Pub.

— Microsoft Word 6.0-7.0 College Keyboard - Complete. 14th ed. LC 98-131509. (TA - Typing/Keyboarding Ser.). (C). 1998. pap. 81.95 (*0-538-71538-3*) S-W Pub.

Duncan, jt. auth. see Barlow.

Duncan, jt. auth. see Vanhuss.

Duncan, jt. auth. see Vanhuss, Susie H.

Duncan, jt. auth. see Wood.

Duncan, A. & Berney, Charlotte. San Jose: A Museum of Reflections, Joseph Schuett American Photographer. (Illus.). 104p. 1997. 100.00 (*0-9660374-1-3*, 01); pap. 29.95 (*0-9660374-0-5*, 01) Bingham Gallery.

Duncan, A. A. The Edinburgh History of Scotland Vol. 1: The Making of the Kingdom. 705p. (C). 1986. pap. 75.00 (*0-901824-83-6*, Pub. by Mercat Pr Bks) St Mut.

Duncan, A. A., ed. The Acts of Robert I, 1306-29. (Regesta Regum Scottorum Ser.: No. 5). 500p. 1989. 130.00 (*0-85224-543-2*, Pub. by Edinburgh U Pr) Col U Pr.

Duncan, A. A., ed. see Barbour, John.

Duncan, A. M., tr. see Kepler, Johannes.

Duncan, A. R. On the Nature of Persons. LC 89-28145. (John MacMurray Studies: Vol. 1). X, 148p. (C). 1990. text 47.95 (*0-8204-1241-4*) P Lang Pubng.

Duncan, Acheson J. Quality Control & Industrial Statistics. 5th ed. 1125p. (C). 1986. text 61.00 (*0-256-03535-0*, Irwn McGrw-H) McGrw-H Hghr Educ.

Duncan, Adrian. Doing Time on Planet Earth. 1993. pap. 16.95 (*1-85230-190-2*, Pub. by Element MA) Penguin Putnam.

Duncan, Al. Master Plan. 1999. pap. text 12.95 (*0-9663533-3-1*) Ambassador Hse.

Duncan, Alan, et al, eds. Pediatric Intensive Care. (Illus.). 288p. 1998. pap. 52.00 (*0-7279-1073-6*, Pub. by BMJ Pub) Login Brothers Bk Co.

Duncan, Alastair. American Art Deco. LC 98-61182. (Illus.). 288p. 1999. reprint ed. pap. 34.95 (*0-500-28093-2*, Pub. by Thames Hudson) Norton.

— Art Deco. LC 88-50231. (World of Art Ser.). (Illus.). 210p. 1988. pap. 14.95 (*0-500-20230-3*, Pub. by Thames Hudson) Norton.

— Art Deco Furniture: The French Designers. LC 91-67310. (Illus.). 192p. 1997. reprint ed. pap. 27.50 (*0-500-27660-9*, Pub. by Thames Hudson) Norton.

— Art Nouveau. LC 93-61372. (World of Art Ser.). (Illus.). 216p. 1994. pap. 14.95 (*0-500-20273-7*, Pub. by Thames Hudson) Norton.

— Louis Comfort Tiffany. (Library of American Art). (Illus.). 160p. 1992. 45.00 (*0-8109-3862-6*, Pub. by Abrams) Time Warner.

— Modernism: Modernist Design, 1880-1940. (Illus.). 256p. 1998. 59.50 (*1-85149-274-7*) Antique Collect.

— Orrefors Glass. LC 96-145363. (Illus.). 320p. 1996. 89.50 (*1-85149-224-0*) Antique Collect.

— Paris Salons: 1895-1914, Objets D'Art & Metalware. (Illus.). 576p. 1999. 99.50 (*1-85149-304-2*) Antique Collect.

— Paris Salons Ceramics & Glass. (Paris Salons Ser.). (Illus.). 350p. 1998. 99.50 (*1-85149-229-1*) Antique Collect.

— The Paris Salons, 1895-1914: Furniture, Vol. 3. (Illus.). 392p. 1995. 99.50 (*1-85149-190-2*) Antique Collect.

— The Paris Salons, 1895-1914: Jewellery. (Illus.). 306p. 1994. 89.50 (*1-85149-168-6*) Antique Collect.

— The Paris Salons, 1895-1914: Jewellery. (Jewellery: Vol. 1). (Illus.). 350p. 1994. 89.50 (*1-85149-159-7*) Antique Collect.

Duncan, Alastair & De Bartha, Georges. Art Nouveau & Art Deco Bookbinding: French Masterpieces, 1880-1940. (Illus.). 200p. 1989. 67.50 (*0-685-25301-5*) Abrams.

Duncan, Alastair, et al. Tiffany Meisterwerke. Auffhammer, W., tr. (ENG & GER., Illus.). 160p. (C). 1989. 84.00 (*3-8170-2017-1*, Pub. by Knstvrlag Weingrtn) Intl Bk Import.

Duncan, Alastair, jt. ed. see Dufrene, Maurice.

Duncan, Albert. The Old Prater Mill. LC 90-92905. (Illus.). 70p. (Orig.). 1990. pap. text 6.95 (*0-9626306-0-8*) Duncan-Everden.

Duncan, Alex & Howell, John, eds. Structural Adjustment & the African Farmer. LC 92-11274. 214p. (C). 1992. pap. 25.00 (*0-435-08073-3*, 08073) Heinemann.

Duncan, Alice F. Miss Viola & Uncle Ed Lee. LC 95-30292. (Illus.). 40p. (J). (ps-3). 1999. 16.00 (*0-689-80476-8*) Atheneum Yung Read.

— The National Civil Rights Museum Celebrates Everyday People. LC 94-15831. (Illus.). 64p. (J). (gr. 2-6). 1996. pap. 6.95 (*0-8167-3503-4*, Troll Medallion) Troll Communs.

— Willie Jerome. LC 94-10444. (Illus.). 32p. (J). (gr. k-3). 1995. mass mkt. 15.00 (*0-02-733208-X*, Mac Bks Young Read) S&S Childrens.

Duncan, Alistair. Laws & Order in Eighteenth-Century Chemistry. LC 96-165706. (Illus.). 262p. 1996. text 90.00 (*0-19-855806-6*) OUP.

— The Noble Heritage: Jerusalem & Christianity - A Portrait. 1974. 17.95 (*0-86685-011-2*) Intl Bk Ctr.

*__Duncan, Andres.__ Trouble Spots: The World Atlas of Strategic Information. 2000. 34.95 (*0-7509-2171-4*, Pub. by Sutton Publng) Intl Pubs Mktg.

*__Duncan, Andrew.__ Britain on Backroads. 2nd ed. (On Backroads Ser.). (Illus.). 256p. 2000. pap. 16.95 (*1-55650-895-6*) Hunter NJ.

— Charming Small Hotels Austria. 3rd ed. (Charming Small Hotels Ser.). (Illus.). 224p. 2000. pap. 14.95 (*1-55650-898-0*) Hunter NJ.

— Charming Small Hotels Ireland. (Charming Small Hotels Ser.). (Illus.). 224p. 2000. pap. 14.95 (*1-55650-892-1*) Hunter NJ.

— Charming Small Hotels Southern France. 2nd ed. (Charming Small Hotels Ser.). (Illus.). 224p. 2000. pap. 14.95 (*1-55650-893-X*) Hunter NJ.

Duncan, Andrew. Edinburgh. (C). 1988. 30.00 (*1-85368-030-3*, Pub. by New5 Holland) St Mut.

— Egypt. (C). 1989. 35.00 (*1-85368-046-X*, Pub. by New5 Holland) St Mut.

*__Duncan, Andrew.__ France on Backroads. 3rd ed. (On Backroads Ser.). (Illus.). 256p. 2000. pap. 16.95 (*1-55650-894-8*) Hunter NJ.

Duncan, Andrew. India. (C). 1989. 50.00 (*1-85368-047-8*, Pub. by New5 Holland) St Mut.

— London Neighborhoods. LC 97-188747. (Illus.). 208p. 1997. pap. 15.95 (*0-8442-9478-0*, 94780) NTC Contemp Pub Co.

— Oxford. (Illus.). (C). 1989. 25.00 (*1-85368-055-9*, Pub. by New5 Holland) St Mut.

— The River Thames. (C). 1989. 50.00 (*1-85368-054-0*, Pub. by New5 Holland) St Mut.

— Secret London: Exploring the Hidden City, with Original Walks & Unusual Places to Visit. (Walking Ser.). 192p. 1998. pap. 14.95 (*0-8442-9705-4*, 97054, Natl Textbk Co) NTC Contemp Pub Co.

— Walking London. (Illus.). 184p. 1992. 14.95 (*1-56757-009-7*) Appleton Comms.

— Walking London: Thirty Original Walks in & Around London. 2nd ed. (Illus.). 192p. 1999. pap. 14.95 (*0-8442-0144-8*, 01448) NTC Contemp Pub Co.

— Walking London: Thirty Original Walks in & Around the Capital. 128p. (C). 1989. 110.00 (*1-85368-073-7*, Pub. by New5 Holland) St Mut.

Duncan, Andrew & Opatowski, Michel. War in the Holy Land: From Meggido to the West Bank. LC 99-194106. (Illus.). 256p. 1998. 39.95 (*0-7509-1500-5*, Pub. by Sutton Pub Ltd) Intl Pubs Mktg.

An Asterisk (*) at the beginning of an entry indicates that the title is appearing for the first time.

Duncan, Andrew J., et al, eds. Combinatorial & Geometric Group Theory, Edinburgh, 1993: Proceedings of ICMS Workshop Held at Heriot-Watt University, 23 March to 8 April 1993. (London Mathematical Society Lecture Note Ser.: No. 204). (Illus.). 335p. (C). 1995. pap. text 47.95 (*0-521-46595-8*) Cambridge U Pr.

Duncan, Andrew J. & McKay, Raymond E., Jr. Business Valuations for Lawyers. 1991. 30.00 (*0-943856-34-5*, 455) SC Bar CLE.

***Duncan, Andy.** Beluthahatchie & Other Stories. 310p. 2000. 23.95 (*0-9655901-1-9*, Pub. by Golden Gryphon) IPG Chicago.

Duncan, Andy, jt. auth. see Nicholas, Geoff.

Duncan, Angus. History, Science, the Law, & Watershed Recovery in the Grande Ronde: A Case Study. 82p. 1998. pap. 7.00 (*1-881826-11-2*) OR Sea Grant.

Duncan, Ann. Speaking Beyond the Podium. 4th ed. 232p. (C). 1999. spiral bd. 29.95 (*0-7872-5712-5*, 41571201) Kendall-Hunt.

Duncan, Anthony. Elements of Celtic Christianity. (Elements of...Ser.). (Illus.). 144p. (Orig.). 1997. pap. 9.95 (*1-86204-138-5*, Pub. by Element MA) Penguin Putnam.

— The Lord of the Dance: An Essay in Mysticism. 2nd ed. 117p. (Orig.). 1996. reprint ed. pap. 10.95 (*0-9650839-5-0*) Sun Chalice.

— Mind of Christ. 1993. pap. 14.95 (*1-85230-185-6*, Pub. by Element MA) Penguin Putnam.

— The Sword in the Sun: Dialogue with an Angel. (Illus.). 212p. (Orig.). 1997. pap. 14.95 (*0-9650839-4-2*) Sun Chalice.

— The Temple of the Spirit: A Christian View of Life. 136p. 1998. pap. 12.95 (*0-9650839-2-6*) Sun Chalice.

***Duncan, Anthony.** The Way of Transcendence: The Mystery We Call God. 152p. 2001. pap. 12.95 (*1-928754-02-3*) Sun Chalice.

Duncan, Archibald A., ed. see Dickinson, W. Croft.

Duncan, B. Allen. Flute Etudes. 36p. 1990. pap. text 7.95 (*0-931759-42-0*) Centerstream Pub.

— Flutists Daily Dozen. 80p. (Orig.). 1988. pap. text 7.95 (*0-931759-27-7*) Centerstream Pub.

Duncan, Baird. Big Color. 1924. write for info. (*0-688-16939-2*, Wm Morrow) Morrow Avon.

Duncan, Baird. Printed Matter: Bound for Glory. 1999. 45.00 (*0-688-16938-4*, Wm Morrow) Morrow Avon.

Duncan Baird Publishers Staff. Hot Sites. 1997. 39.95 (*0-688-15774-2*, Wm Morrow) Morrow Avon.

Duncan, Barbara R. & Arch, Davey. Living Stories of the Cherokee. LC 97-35037. (Illus.). 272p. 1998. 29.95 (*0-8078-2411-9*); pap. 15.95 (*0-8078-4719-4*) U of NC Pr.

Duncan, Barry L., et al. Changing the Rules: A Client-Directed Approach to Therapy. LC 92-1550. (Family Therapy Ser.). 284p. 1992. lib. bdg. 38.00 (*0-89862-108-9*) Guilford Pubns.

— Psychotherapy with Impossible Cases: The Efficient Treatment of Therapy Veterans. LC 96-35581. 256p. (C). 1997. 35.00 (*0-393-70246-4*) Norton.

Duncan, Barry L., jt. auth. see Murphy, John J.

Duncan, Barry L., jt. auth. see Rock, Joseph W.

Duncan, Ben. High Performance Audio Power Amplifiers. LC 97-100523. 463p. 1996. text 69.95 (*0-7506-2629-1*) Buttrwrth-Heinemann.

***Duncan, Ben.** High Performance Audio Power Amplifiers. 2nd ed. 544p. 2000. 85.95 (*0-7506-4822-8*) Buttrwrth-Heinemann.

Duncan, Betty D. & Isaac, Golda. Ferns & Allied Plants of Victoria, Tasmania & South Australia: With Distribution Maps for the Victorian Species. (Illus.). 270p. 1994. pap. 29.95 (*0-522-84595-9*, Pub. by Melbourne Univ Pr) Paul & Co Pubs.

Duncan, Beverly. Christmas in the Stable. LC 88-37953. (Illus.). 32p. (J). 1996. pap. 5.00 (*0-15-201385-7*) Harcourt.

Duncan, Beverly. Christmas in the Stable. (J). 1996. 10.20 (*0-606-13274-0*, Pub. by Turtleback) Demco.

Duncan, Beverly, jt. auth. see Duncan, Otis D.

Duncan, Bill & Jones, Stephen. Sale of Land in Queensland. 4th ed. 370p. 1996. 110.00 (*0-455-21372-0*, Pub. by LawBk Co); pap. 75.00 (*0-455-21373-9*, Pub. by LawBk Co) Gaunt.

Duncan, Billie. Beneath the Desk. Whitebird, J., ed. (Illus.). 84p. 1997. pap. 16.00 (*0-930324-36-6*) Wings Pr.

Duncan, Blackwell S. Custom Cabinets. 1993. 27.95 (*0-8306-4171-8*); pap. 15.95 (*0-8306-4172-6*) McGraw-Hill Prof.

Duncan, Brett. Fingerpicking Guitar Licks. (Progressive Ser.). 1997. pap. text 14.95 incl. cd-rom (*0-947183-70-1*) Koala Pubns.

— Fingerpicking Guitar Solos. (Progressive Ser.). (Illus.). 1997. pap. 14.95 incl. audio compact disk (*1-875726-36-5*) Koala Pubns.

— Introducing Blues Guitar. (Illus.). 1997. pap. text 14.95 incl. cd-rom (*1-875726-29-2*) Koala Pubns.

— Introducing Lead Guitar. (Illus.). 1997. pap. text 14.95 incl. audio compact disk (*1-875726-02-0*) Koala Pubns.

— Introducing Rhythm Guitar. (Illus.). 1997. pap. text 14.95 incl. audio compact disk (*1-875726-01-2*) Koala Pubns.

— Lead Guitar Licks. (Progressive Ser.). (Illus.). 1997. pap. 14.95 incl. audio compact disk (*1-875726-00-4*) Koala Pubns.

— Lead Guitar Solos. (Progressive Ser.). (Illus.). 1997. pap. text 14.95 incl. cd-rom (*1-875726-37-3*) Koala Pubns.

— Rock Guitar Licks. 1997. pap. 14.95 (*0-947183-74-4*) Koala Pubns.

— Rock Guitar Method. (Progressive Ser.). (Illus.). 1997. pap. text 14.95 incl. cd-rom (*0-947183-92-2*) Koala Pubns.

— Rock Guitar Technique. 1997. pap. 14.95 (*0-947183-91-4*) Koala Pubns.

— Slide Guitar Licks. 1997. pap. 14.95 (*0-947183-58-2*) Koala Pubns.

— Slide Guitar Technique. 1997. pap. 14.95 (*0-947183-59-0*) Koala Pubns.

Duncan, Bruce. The German Storm & Stress. 1999. 58.00 (*1-57113-101-9*) Camden Hse.

— Lovers, Parricides & Highwaymen: Aspects of Sturm und Drang Drama. LC 99-18276. 260p. 1999. 60.00 (*1-57113-086-1*) Camden Hse.

— Pray Your Way. pap. write for info. (*0-232-52019-4*) S Asia.

Duncan, Bruce, tr. see Achim von Arnim, Ludwig.

Duncan, C. Easy Classic Guitar Duets. 48p. 1993. pap. 17.95 (*0-7935-1795-8*, 00697244) H Leonard.

— Easy Classical Guitar Duets. 48p. 1993. pap. 14.95 (*0-7935-1794-X*, 00697243) H Leonard.

Duncan, C. Modern Approach to Classical Guitar, Pt. 1. 56p. 1984. pap. 7.95 (*0-7935-2627-2*, 00699204) H Leonard.

— Modern Approach to Classical Guitar Bk. 1: With Soundsheet. 1981. pap. 6.95 (*0-88188-946-6*, 00699200) H Leonard.

— Modern Approach to Classical Guitar Bk. 2: With Soundsheet. 1982. pap. 6.95 (*0-7935-2712-0*, 00699201) H Leonard.

— Modern Approach to Classical Guitar Pt. 2: Repertoire. 72p. 1985. pap. 7.95 (*0-7935-3322-8*, 00699208) H Leonard.

Duncan, C. & Stocks, E. G. The Installation of Electrical Circuits, Bk. 2. 92p. (C). 1985. pap. 24.00 (*0-85973-011-5*, Pub. by S Thornes Pubs) St Mut.

***Duncan, C. H.** College Keyboarding. 14th ed. (C). 1999. pap. 33.95 (*0-538-72248-7*) Sth-Wstrn College.

Duncan, C. J., ed. Calcium, Oxygen Radicals & Cellular Damage. (Society for Experimental Biology Seminar Ser.: No. 46). (Illus.). 234p. (C). 1991. text 90.00 (*0-521-38068-5*) Cambridge U Pr.

Duncan, C. J., jt. auth. see Scott, Susan.

***Duncan, C. S.** A Fait Accompli: A True, Extraordinary Account of Undying Love. 226p. 2000. pap. 8.75 (*0-9679283-0-3*) Transcode.

Duncan, C. Thom. And Some Cried Fraud. 1997. pap. 4.00 (*1-57514-303-8*, 1009) Encore Perform Pub.

— Matters of the Heart. 1997. pap. 4.00 (*1-57514-304-6*, 1010) Encore Perform Pub.

Duncan, Carol. The Aesthetics of Power: Essays in Critical Art History. LC 92-20448. (New Art History & Criticism Ser.). (Illus.). 256p. (C). 1993. pap. text 22.95 (*0-521-42187-X*) Cambridge U Pr.

— Civilizing Rituals: Inside Public Art Museums. LC 94-31251. (Re Visions Ser.). (Illus.). 224p. (C). (gr. 13). 1995. pap. 20.99 (*0-415-07012-0*, C0141) Routledge.

Duncan, Catherine. Paul Strand: The World on My Doorstep. (Aperture Ser.). (Illus.). 142p. 1997. pap. 37.95 (*0-89381-579-9*) Aperture.

— Paul Strand: The World on My Doorstep, the Years 1950 to 1976. 1994. 68.00 (*0-89381-545-4*) Aperture.

Duncan, Catherine, jt. auth. see Eskildsen, Ute.

Duncan, Charles. The Absent Man: The Narrative Craft of Charles W. Chesnutt. LC 98-22063. 214p. 1998. 32.95 (*0-8214-1239-6*) Ohio U Pr.

— The Art of Classical Guitar Playing. (Art of Ser.). (Illus.). 132p. (Orig.). 1980. pap. text 19.95 (*0-87487-079-8*) Summy-Birchard.

— Classical Guitar 2000. 94p. 1993. pap. text 18.95 (*0-87487-681-8*) Summy-Birchard.

— Guitar at Sight. 98p. (Orig.). 1997. pap. text 16.95 (*0-9627832-6-9*) Guitar Solo.

Duncan, Charles, des. Christmas with the Classical Guitar. 48p. 1991. pap. text 7.95 (*0-87487-408-4*) Summy-Birchard.

Duncan, Charles H. & VanHuss, Susie H. South-Western College Keyboarding: Complete Course with WordPerfect 5.1. 13th ed. LC 93-33854. (C). 1994. mass mkt. 46.00 (*0-538-71258-9*) S-W Pub.

Duncan, Charles H., et al. College Keyboarding: Formatting with WordPerfect 5.1. 13th ed. LC 93-5224. (C). 1994. mass mkt. 32.25 (*0-538-70867-0*) S-W Pub.

Duncan, Charles H., et al. College Keyboarding: Windows Complete Course. 13th ed. 1995. pap. 62.25 (*0-538-71392-5*) Thomson Learn.

Duncan, Charles H., et al. College Keyboarding - Typewriting: Formatting Course. 13th ed. LC 93-13638. (C). 1994. mass mkt. 32.25 (*0-538-70808-5*) S-W Pub.

— College Keyboarding - Typewriting: Introductory Course with WordPerfect 5.1. 13th ed. LC 92-45164. (C). 1993. mass mkt. 32.25 (*0-538-70865-4*) S-W Pub.

— College Keyboarding for Windows Formatting with Microsoft Word 6.0 & WordPerfect 6.0. 13th ed. (C). 1995. mass mkt. 50.95 (*0-538-70868-9*) S-W Pub.

— South-Western College Keyboarding. 13th ed. LC 93-27530. (C). 1994. mass mkt. 32.25 (*0-538-71041-1*) S-W Pub.

— Southwestern College Keyboarding for Windows Document Processing with Microsoft Word 6.0 & WordPerfect 6.0. 13th ed. (C). 1995. mass mkt. 50.95 (*0-538-71042-X*) S-W Pub.

Duncan, Charles T. Terhune Family History. LC 97-78020. 1998. 44.95 (*1-57860-055-3*) Guild Pr IN.

Duncan, Charles T., ed. see McCoy, Keith.

Duncan, Christopher, tr. see Guglielmi, Joseph.

Duncan, Christopher M. The Anti-Federalists & Early American Political Thought. LC 94-7159. 256p. 1995. lib. bdg. 32.00 (*0-87580-189-7*) N Ill U Pr.

***Duncan, Christopher M.** Fugitive Theory: Political Theory, the Southern Agrarians & America. LC 99-48924. 272p. 2000. 65.00 (*0-7391-0088-2*) Lxngtn Bks.

Duncan-Clark, S. J. Progressive Movement, Its Principles & Its Programme. LC 72-164808. reprint ed. 36.50 (*0-404-02217-0*) AMS Pr.

Duncan, Colin. Low Pay: Its Causes & the Post-War Trade Union Response. LC 81-30555. (Social Policy Research Monographs: No. 3). (Illus.). 175p. reprint ed. pap. 54.30 (*0-8357-8940-3*, 203333300085) Bks Demand.

Duncan, Colin A. The Centrality of Agriculture: Between Humankind & the Rest of Nature. (Illus.). 344p. 1996. 49.95 (*0-7735-1363-9*, Pub. by McG-Queens Univ Pr) CUP Services.

Duncan, Colin A. & Tandy, David W., eds. From Political Economy to Anthropology: Situating Economic Life in Past Societies, Vol. 3. LC 93-73927. 186p. 1994. 48.99 (*1-895431-89-1*, Pub. by Black Rose); pap. 19.99 (*1-895431-88-3*, Pub. by Black Rose) Consort Bk Sales.

Duncan, Craig. Advanced Fiddling. 120p. 1997. pap. 22.95 incl. audio compact disk (*0-7866-2953-3*, 93971BCD) Mel Bay.

Duncan, Craig. Blues Fiddling Classics. 1994. 17.95 incl. audio compact disk (*0-7866-1855-8*, 95159BCD) Mel Bay.

Duncan, Craig. The Cajun Fiddle. 104p. 1997. spiral bd. 22.95 incl. audio compact disk (*0-7866-3139-2*, 95383BCD) Mel Bay.

— Christmas Melodies for Violin Solos. 96p. 1995. pap. 10.95 (*0-7866-1670-9*, 95702) Mel Bay.

— The Craig Duncan Master Fiddle Solo Collection. 152p. 1999. pap. 19.95 (*0-7866-3387-5*, 96995) Mel Bay.

Duncan, Craig. Deluxe Fiddling Method. 1981. 18.95 incl. audio (*0-87166-627-8*, 93742P) Mel Bay.

— Deluxe Fiddling Method. 104p. 1981. spiral bd. 10.95 (*0-87166-612-X*, 93742); audio 9.98 (*0-87166-626-X*, 93742C) Mel Bay.

Duncan, Craig. Deluxe Fiddling Method. 104p. 1981. spiral bd. 24.95 incl. audio compact disk (*0-7866-1660-1*, 93742CDP) Mel Bay.

Duncan, Craig. Deluxe Fiddling Method. 1995. vdisk 29.95 (*0-7866-0623-1*, 93742VX) Mel Bay.

— Deluxe Fiddling Method. 1995. audio compact disk 15.98 (*0-7866-1646-6*, 93742CD) Mel Bay.

Duncan, Craig. Easiest Fiddling. 32p. 1996. pap. 14.95 incl. audio compact disk (*0-7866-0727-0*, 95602BCD) Mel Bay.

Duncan, Craig. Easy Solos for Beginning Cello. (Building Excellence Ser.). 40p. 1991. pap. 5.95 (*1-56222-243-0*, 94659) Mel Bay.

— Easy Solos for Beginning Viola. (Building Excellence Ser.). 40p. 1991. pap. 5.95 (*1-56222-244-9*, 94660) Mel Bay.

— Easy Solos for Beginning Violin. (Building Excellence Ser.). 40p. 1991. pap. 5.95 (*1-56222-192-2*, 94582) Mel Bay.

— Essential Scales & Stds. Vln. 401p. 1993. pap. 6.95 (*1-56222-891-9*, 95052) Mel Bay.

***Duncan, Craig.** Famous Fiddlin' Tunes. 32p. 2000. pap. 5.95 (*0-7866-4927-5*, 98431BCD) Mel Bay.

Duncan, Craig. Fiddling Chord Book. 72p. 1992. pap. 8.95 (*1-56222-428-X*, 94683) Mel Bay.

Duncan, Craig. A Fiddling Christmas. 108p. 1996. pap. 12.95 (*0-7866-2580-5*, 96466) Mel Bay.

— Fiddling Handbook. 80p. 1997. pap. 17.95 incl. audio compact disk (*0-7866-3210-0*, 94111BCD) Mel Bay.

Duncan, Craig. Rhythmic Studies for Beginning Viola. (Building Excellence Ser.). 32p. 1991. pap. 5.95 (*1-56222-245-7*, 94661) Mel Bay.

— Solo Pieces for the Intermediate Violinist. 60p. 1993. pap. 7.95 (*1-56222-801-3*, 94877) Mel Bay.

***Duncan, Craig.** Student Cellist: Bach. 48p. 1998. pap. 8.95 (*0-7866-1340-8*, 97033) Mel Bay.

— Student Cellist: Handel. 48p. 1998. pap. 8.95 (*0-7866-1459-5*, 97034) Mel Bay.

— The Student Violinist: Beethoven: Beginning-Intermediate Level. 48p. 1997. pap. 8.95 (*0-7866-3075-2*, 96799) Mel Bay.

— The Student Violinist: Beginning-Intermediate Level. 48p. 1997. pap. 8.95 (*0-7866-2359-4*, 96211) Mel Bay.

— The Student Violinist: Beginning-Intermediate Level. 48p. 1997. pap. 8.95 (*0-7866-3012-4*, 96797) Mel Bay.

— Student Violinists: Bach: Beginning-Intermediate Level. 48p. 1997. pap. 8.95 (*0-7866-2117-6*, 96173) Mel Bay.

— The Student Violist: Bach. 48p. 1998. pap. 8.95 (*0-7866-3266-6*, 97039) Mel Bay.

— The Student Violist: Handel. 48p. 1997. pap. 8.95 (*0-7866-3267-4*, 97048) Mel Bay.

Duncan, Craig. Technical Studies for Beginning Cello. (Building Excellence Ser.). 32p. 1991. pap. 5.95 (*1-56222-213-9*, 94599) Mel Bay.

— Technical Studies for Beginning Violin. (Building Excellence Ser.). 32p. 1991. pap. 5.95 (*1-56222-164-7*, 94559) Mel Bay.

— Top Fiddle Solos: Intermediate to Advanced. 120p. 1997. spiral bd. 22.95 incl. audio compact disk (*0-7866-3513-4*, 94095BCD) Mel Bay.

***Duncan, Craig.** Violin Solos on Early American Hymn Tunes. 112p. 1999. 14.95 (*0-7866-3503-7*, 97119) Mel Bay.

Duncan, Craig. You Can Teach Yourself Fiddling. 80p. 1990. pap. 9.95 (*1-56222-003-9*, 94430); pap. 18.95 incl. audio (*1-56222-521-9*, 94430P); audio 9.98 (*1-56222-004-7*, 94430C); audio compact disk 15.98 (*0-7866-0382-8*, 94430CD) Mel Bay.

— You Can Teach Yourself Fiddling. 1992. VHS 29.95 (*1-56222-316-X*, 94717VX) Mel Bay.

***Duncan, Craig.** You Can Teach Yourself Fiddling. 80p. 1998. pap. 17.95 incl. audio compact disk (*0-7866-4407-9*, 94430BCD) Mel Bay.

Duncan, Craig, et al. Complete Fiddling Book. (Complete Book). 208p. 1990. pap. 19.95 (*0-87166-837-8*, 94367) Mel Bay.

— Complete Fiddling Book. (Complete Book). 1995. vdisk 29.95 (*0-7866-0621-5*, 94367VX) Mel Bay.

Duncan, Cyndi & Patrick, Georgie. Colorado Cookie Collection. (Colorado Collection: No. 1). (Illus.). 216p. (Orig.). 1989. pap., spiral bd. 14.95 (*0-9626335-0-X*) C&G Pub CO.

— Cookie Exchange. LC 95-107875. (Colorado Collection: Vol. 3). (Illus.). 140p. 1994. pap. 12.95 (*0-9626335-4-2*) C&G Pub CO.

***Duncan, Cyndi & Patrick, Georgie.** Cookie Exchange. rev. ed. (Colorado Collection: No. 3). 168p. 1999. per. 12.95 (*0-9626335-8-5*) C&G Pub CO.

Duncan, Cyndi & Patrick, Georgie. Nothin' but Muffins. (Colorado Collection: No. 2). (Illus.). 96p. (Orig.). 1991. pap., spiral bd. 12.95 (*0-9626335-1-8*) C&G Pub CO.

— Quick Crockery Cooking: A One Foot in the Kitchen Cookbook. (Illus.). 168p. 1997. per. 14.95 (*0-9626335-5-0*) C&G Pub CO.

— Quick Mexican Cooking: A One Foot in the Kitchen Cookbook. LC 98-92651. (Illus.). 168p. 1998. 14.95 (*0-9626335-6-9*) C&G Pub CO.

— Quick Soups 'n Salads. (One Foot in the Kitchen Cookbook Ser.: No. 3). (Illus.). 168p. 1999. pap. 14.95 (*0-9626335-7-7*) C&G Pub CO.

Duncan, Cynthia M. Rural Poverty in America. LC 91-18655. 328p. 1992. 65.00 (*0-86569-013-8*, T013, Auburn Hse); pap. 24.95 (*0-86569-014-6*, R014, Auburn Hse) Greenwood.

Duncan, Cynthia M. Worlds Apart: Why Poverty Persists in Rural America. LC 98-44964. 256p. 1999. 30.00 (*0-300-07628-2*) Yale U Pr.

***Duncan, Cynthia M.** Worlds Apart: Why Poverty Persists in Rural America. 256p. 2000. pap. 15.95 (*0-300-08456-0*) Yale U Pr.

Duncan, Dan & Anno, J. N. Basic Thermal Science & Engineering for Nuclear Technology Vol. 1: Fundmental Aspects. 380p. (C). 1994. pap. text 28.00 (*1-57074-190-5*) Greyden Pr.

Duncan, Daniel W., jt. auth. see Beard, Jeffrey L.

***Duncan, Dave.** The Crooked House: Book Two of the King's Daggers. LC 99-69745. Vol. 2. 256p. (J). (gr. 7 up). 2000. mass mkt. 4.99 (*0-380-80099-3*) Morrow Avon.

Duncan, Dave. Destiny of the Sword. (Seventh Sword Ser.: Bk. 3). 338p. 1988. mass mkt. 5.99 (*0-345-35293-9*, Del Rey) Ballantine Pub Grp.

— Emperor & Clown. 469p. (Orig.). 1992. mass mkt. 5.99 (*0-345-36631-X*, Del Rey) Ballantine Pub Grp.

— Faery Lands Forlorn. (Man of His Word Ser.: Pt. 2). 352p. (Orig.). 1991. mass mkt. 5.99 (*0-345-36629-8*, Del Rey) Ballantine Pub Grp.

— Future Indefinite: Round Three of the Great Game. 496p. 1998. mass mkt. 6.50 (*0-380-78131-X*, Eos) Morrow Avon.

***Duncan, Dave.** The Gilded Chain: A Tale of the King's Blades. (King's Blades Ser.). 432p. (Orig.). 1999. mass mkt. 6.99 (*0-380-79126-9*) Morrow Avon.

— The Gilded Chain: A Tale of the King's Blades. LC 98-18691. 352p. 1998. pap. 23.00 (*0-380-97460-6*, Eos) Morrow Avon.

Duncan, Dave. The Hunters' Haunt. (Orig.). 1995. mass mkt. 5.99 (*0-345-38459-8*, Del Rey) Ballantine Pub Grp.

— Lord of the Fire Lands: A Tale of the King's Blades. LC 99-33277. 368p. 1999. 23.00 (*0-380-97461-4*, Avon Bks) Morrow Avon.

***Duncan, Dave.** Lord of the Fire Lands: A Tale of the King's Blades. 480p. 2000. mass mkt. 6.99 (*0-380-79127-7*) Morrow Avon.

Duncan, Dave. Magic Casement. (The Wizards of Fantasy Promotion: Pt. 1). 320p. (Orig.). 1990. mass mkt. 4.95 (*0-345-36628-X*, Del Rey) Ballantine Pub Grp.

— Past Imperative: Round 1 of the Great Game. 464p. 1996. mass mkt. 6.50 (*0-380-78129-8*, Avon Bks) Morrow Avon.

— Perilous Seas. 352p. (Orig.). 1991. mass mkt. 5.99 (*0-345-36630-1*, Del Rey) Ballantine Pub Grp.

— Present Tense: Round Two of the Great Game, Vol. 2. 432p. (Orig.). 1997. mass mkt. 5.99 (*0-380-78130-1*) Morrow Avon.

— The Reaver Road. (Orig.). 1992. mass mkt. 4.99 (*0-345-37481-9*, Del Rey) Ballantine Pub Grp.

***Duncan, Dave.** Sir Stalwart: Book One of the King's Daggers. LC 99-94643. Vol. 1. 256p. (J). 1999. mass mkt. 4.99 (*0-380-80098-5*, Avon Bks) Morrow Avon.

— Sky of Swords: A Tale of the King's Blades. LC 00-37539. 368p. 2000. 23.00 (*0-380-97462-2*, Avon Bks) Morrow Avon.

Duncan, Dave. The Stricken Field. 368p. 1994. mass mkt. 5.99 (*0-345-38874-7*) Ballantine Pub Grp.

— The Stricken Field, Pt. 3. LC 93-3174. 1993. 19.00 (*0-345-37898-9*, Del Rey) Ballantine Pub Grp.

— Upland Outlaws. (Handful of Men Ser.: Pt. 2). 288p. 1993. mass mkt. 5.99 (*0-345-38477-6*, Del Rey) Ballantine Pub Grp.

Duncan, David. Best American Card Games: A Deal of Fresh Excitement for Every Player. 169p. 1995. pap. 8.95 (*0-572-01542-9*, Pub. by Foulsham UK) Assoc Pubs Grp.

Duncan, David Douglas. A Secret Garden: Photographers of the Imagination. (Illus.). 80p. 19.95 (*0-9633849-1-0*) D D Duncan.

— Thor. LC 93-2163. (Illus.). 96p. 1993. 27.95 (*1-55821-237-X*) Lyons Pr.

— Yo-Yo: Kidnapped in Provence. (Illus.). 72p. 1999. 24.95 (*1-55821-962-5*) Lyons Pr.

Duncan, David E. Calendar: Humanity's Epic Struggle to Determine a True & Accurate Year. LC 98-10434. 240p. 1998. 23.00 (*0-380-97528-9*, Avon Bks) Morrow Avon.

— Hernando de Soto: A Savage Quest in the Americas. LC E125.S7D86 1997. (Illus.). 608p. 1997. pap. 21.95 (*0-8061-2977-8*) U of Okla Pr.

***Duncan, David Ewing.** Calendar: Humanity's Epic Struggle to Determine a True & Accurate Year. 352p. 1999. reprint ed. pap. 13.50 (*0-380-79324-5*, Avon Bks) Morrow Avon.

Duncan, David J. The Brothers K. 656p. 1996. reprint ed. pap. 13.95 (*0-553-37849-X*) Bantam.

D

An Asterisk (*) at the beginning of an entry indicates that the title is appearing for the first time.

— Duncan. 2001. write for info. (0-385-46863-6) Doubleday.

— River Teeth: Stories & Writings. LC 94-47570. 272p. 1996. reprint ed. pap. 13.95 (0-553-37827-9) Bantam.

— The River Why. 304p. (Orig.). 1984. pap. 13.95 (0-553-34486-2) Bantam.

— The River Why. LC 82-5508. 320p. (Orig.). 1983. 22.00 (0-87156-321-5, Pub. by Sierra) Random.

Duncan, David R. & Litwiller, Bonnie H. Problem Solving with Number Patterns. (Classroom Activities Ser.: No. 1). (Illus.). 158p. 1987. pap. text 9.50 (0-912047-06-2) Sch Sci Math.

***Duncan, Dayton.** Lewis & Clark: The Journey of The Corps of Discovery. 1999. pap. 25.00 (0-375-70652-6) Knopf.

— Miles from Nowhere: Tales from America's Contemporary Frontier. (Illus.). 352p. 2000. pap. 16.95 (0-8032-6627-8, Bison Books) U of Nebr Pr.

— Out West: A Journey Through Lewis & Clark's America. (Illus.). 464p. 2000. reprint ed. pap. 18.95 (0-8032-6626-X, Bison Books) U of Nebr Pr.

Duncan, Dayton. Out West: An American Journey. (Illus.). 448p. 1988. pap. 13.95 (0-14-008362-6, Penguin Bks) Viking Penguin.

— People of the West. (West (Television Program) Ser.). (Illus.). 128p. (J). (gr. 3-7). 1996. 19.95 (0-316-19627-4) Little.

Duncan, Dayton, et al. Lewis & Clark: The Journey of the Corps of Discovery. LC 97-73823. (Illus.). 288p. 1997. 40.00 (0-679-45450-0) Knopf.

Duncan, Debbie. Joy of Reading: One Family's Fun-Filled Guide to Reading Success. LC 97-35073. 240p. (Orig.). (J). 1998. pap. 14.95 (1-877810-45-2, JOY) Rayve Prodns.

— When Molly Was in the Hospital: A Book for Brothers & Sisters of Hospitalized Children. LC 94-67525. (Minimed Ser.: Vol. 1). (Illus.). 40p. (J). (ps-7). 1994. 12.95 (1-877810-44-4, MOLL) Rayve Prodns.

Duncan, Deborah. Vikings: With Stand-Up Scenes to Cut Out & Glue Together. pap. 7.95 (0-906212-81-2, Pub. by Tarquin Pubns) Parkwest Pubns.

Duncan, Debra, ed. see Galus, Lisa & Galus, Elizabeth B.

Duncan, Denis. Be Still & Know... (C). 1994. pap. 40.00 (0-85305-332-4, Pub. by Arthur James) St Mut.

— Health & Healing. 144p. (C). 1988. pap. text 45.00 (0-7152-0615-X) St Mut.

Duncan, Denis, ed. Creative Silence. (C). 1990. pap. 29.00 (0-85305-222-0, Pub. by Arthur James) St Mut.

— A Day at a Time. (C). 1990. pap. 35.00 (0-85305-283-2, Pub. by Arthur James) St Mut.

Duncan Designers Staff. Christmas Collectibles. Thompson, Bill, ed. 52p. 1993. pap. text 9.95 (0-916809-71-4) Scott Pubns MI.

***Duncan, Diane.** Becoming a Primary School Teacher. 120p. 1999. pap. 16.95 (1-85856-104-3, Trentham Bks) Stylus Pub VA.

Duncan, Dierdre M., ed. Working with Bilingual Language Disability. (Therapy in Practice Ser.). 230p. 1989. pap. 19.95 (0-412-33940-4) Chapman & Hall.

Duncan, Don. Physics 120. (C). 1997. pap. text 19.88 (1-56870-275-2) RonJon Pub.

— Physics 121. (C). 1997. text 22.17 (1-56870-274-4) RonJon Pub.

***Duncan, Donna & Lockhart, Laura.** I-Search, You Search, We All Learn to Research: A How-to-Do-It Manual for Teaching Elementary School Students to Solve Information Problems. LC 99-89993. (How-to-Do-It Ser.). 159p. 2000. pap. 45.00 (1-55570-381-X) Neal-Schuman.

Duncan, Doree, et al, eds. Life into Art: Isadora Duncan & Her World. LC 93-1737. 1993. 40.00 (0-393-03507-7) Norton.

Duncan, Douglas. Ben Jonson & the Lucianic Tradition. LC 78-18093. 260p. reprint ed. pap. 74.10 (0-8357-7125-3, 2030590) Bks Demand.

Duncan, E. R., ed. Dimensions of World Food Problems. LC 77-1663. (Illus.). 327p. 1977. reprint ed. pap. 101.40 (0-608-00018-3, 206078400006) Bks Demand.

Duncan, Earlene, et al. Usher's Syndrome: What It Is, How to Cope, & How to Help. (Illus.). 106p. 1988. pap. 21.95 (0-398-06099-1) C C Thomas.

— Usher's Syndrome: What It Is, How to Cope, & How to Help. (Illus.). 106p. (C). 1988. text 34.95 (0-398-05481-9) C C Thomas.

Duncan, Earlene, jt. ed. see Prickett, Hugh T.

Duncan-Eaves, T. C., ed. see Richardson, Samuel.

Duncan, Ed E. The Complete Guide to Planning Your Family Reunion. LC 93-70485. 83p. (Orig.). 1993. pap. 9.95 (0-9636044-0-6) Cleve-Coast.

Duncan, Edmondstoune. Opera Stories of To-Day & Yesterday. 227p. 1991. reprint ed. lib. bdg. 79.00 (0-7812-9334-0) Rprt Serv.

— The Story of the Carol. LC 89-49707. (Illus.). xii, 253p. 1992. reprint ed. lib. bdg. 40.00 (1-55888-921-3) Omnigraphics Inc.

Duncan, Edmonstoune, ed. Lyrics from Old Song Books. LC 77-168780. (Granger Index Reprint Ser.). 1977. reprint ed. 30.95 (0-8369-6300-8) Ayer.

Duncan Edwards, Pamela. Barefoot: Escape on the Undergroud Railroad. LC 95-44863. (Illus.). 32p. (J). (gr. k-4). 1999. pap. 5.95 (0-06-443519-9, HarpTrophy) HarpC Child Bks.

Duncan, Elizabeth E., jt. auth. see Klingensmith, Patricia J.

Duncan, Eric. Growing up Memories, Bk. I. (Illus.). 350p. 1999. pap. text 6.99 (1-888347-02-3, Veritas Press); cd-rom 11.99 (1-888347-01-5, Veritas Press) Donnchad.

— Growing-Up Memories Bk. II: The Turmoil of Adolescence. (Illus.). 350p. Date not set. 25.00 (1-888347-05-8, Veritas Press); pap. text 6.99 (1-888347-06-6, Veritas Press) Donnchad.

— Growing-Up Memories Bk. III: Father to Father. (Illus.). 400p. 1999. 25.00 (1-888347-07-4, Veritas Press); pap. text 6.99 (1-888347-08-2, Veritas Press) Donnchad.

— To Hell & Back: Over the Brink. LC 95-83404. (Illus.). 103p. (Orig.). 1995. pap. text 9.95 (1-888347-00-7) Donnchad.

— Unaccountable. (Illus.). 500p. 2000. pap. text 5.99 (1-888347-14-7, Enigma); cd-rom 24.00 (1-888347-13-9, Enigma) Donnchad.

Duncan, Erin, et al, eds. Proceedings of the Twelfth West Coast Conference on Formal Linguistics (WCCFL 12) Proceedings of the West Coast Conference on Formal Linguistics, Vol. 12. 611p. 1995. pap. 24.95 (1-881526-33-X) CSLI.

Duncan, Fiona. Amsterdam up Close. (Illus.). 160p. 1994. pap. 12.95 (0-8442-9453-5, 94535) NTC Contemp Pub Co.

— Central Italy: Florence, Tuscany, Umbria, the Marches, Northern Lazio. 2nd ed. (Passport's Trip Planners & Guides Ser.). 240p. 1999. pap. 17.95 (0-8442-2549-5, Passprt Bks) NTC Contemp Pub Co.

Duncan, Fiona & Glass, Leonie. Manhattan up Close: District to District, Street by Street. (Illus.). 160p. 1994. pap. 12.95 (0-8442-9450-0, 94500, Passprt Bks) NTC Contemp Pub Co.

Duncan, Fiona, et al. London up Close: District to District, Street to Street. (Illus.). 176p. 1994. pap. 12.95 (0-8442-9451-9, 94519, Passprt Bks) NTC Contemp Pub Co.

Duncan, Forbes. Hindustani & English: Accompanied by a Reverse Dictionary. 1986. 39.95 (0-8288-1742-1, M6271) Fr & Eur.

Duncan, Forbes, jt. auth. see Kilgour, R.

Duncan, Frances. Dragonhunt. 128p. pap. 4.95 (0-88961-068-1, Pub. by Womens Pr) LPC InBook.

Duncan, Francis. Rickover & the Nuclear Navy: The Discipline of Technology. LC 89-39097. (Illus.). 480p. 1990. 29.95 (0-87021-236-2) Naval Inst Pr.

Duncan, Francis, jt. auth. see Hewlett, Richard G.

Duncan, Fraser, tr. see Arsac, Jacques.

Duncan, Fred J. Super Jesus: A Collection of Doctrinal Essays. 128p. (Orig.). 1997. pap. write for info. (0-614-26624-6) Pennington TX.

— Super Jesus: A Collection of Doctrinal Essays. 128p. (Orig.). 1998. pap. 12.00 (0-614-30084-3) Pennington TX.

Duncan, G. The Lachenalia Handbook. (Annals of Kirstenbosch Botanic Gardens Ser.: Vol. 17). (Illus.). 71p. 1988. pap. 15.00 (0-620-11953-5, Pub. by Natl Botanical Inst) Balogh.

— Physics in the Life Sciences. 2nd ed. 1990. pap. 39.95 (0-632-01778-3) Blackwell Sci.

Duncan, G. I. The High Court of Delegates. LC 85-81805. (Cambridge Studies in English Legal History). 345p. 1986. reprint ed. 85.00 (0-912004-44-4) Gaunt.

Duncan, Gena, jt. auth. see White, Lois.

Duncan, George. Marks of Christian Maturity: Becoming the Kind of Christian God Wants You to Be. 159p. 1987. pap. 4.95 (0-310-55282-6, 19028P) Zondervan.

— Quiet Time. 1997. pap. 10.99 (0-907927-63-7) Emerald House Group Inc.

***Duncan, George.** Streetwise Direct Marketing: How to Use the Internet, Direct Mail & Other Media to Generate Direct Sales. (Streetwise Ser.). (Illus.). 352p. 2000. pap. 19.95 (1-58062-439-1) Adams Media.

Duncan, George B. Preacher among the Prophets. 176p. 1985. reprint ed. pap. 5.95 (0-930577-00-0) N Burleson.

Duncan, George H. Code Name Identical. 96p. 1997. pap. 19.95 (1-56311-370-8) Turner Pub KY.

Duncan, Glen. Hope. LC 97-37359. 352p. 1998. 23.95 (1-57322-094-9, Riverhead Books) Putnam Pub Group.

— Hope. 336p. 1999. pap. text 13.00 (1-57322-732-3, Riverhead Books) Putnam Pub Group.

***Duncan, Glen A.** Goodbye Green: How Extremists Stole the Environmental Movement from Middle America & Killed It. 182p. 2000. pap. 14.95 (0-936783-26-5, Pub. by Merril Pr) Midpt Trade.

Duncan, Gra Delle. Dinosaurs & Cousin Armadillo. (J). (gr. 3-4). 1990. pap. 3.95 (0-89015-744-8) Sunbelt Media.

Duncan, Graham. The Map Reader. 28p. 1987. pap. 3.00 (0-9613465-6-6) Great Elm.

Duncan, Greg & Brooks-Gunn, Jeanne. Consequences of Growing up Poor. 640p. 1999. pap. 24.95 (0-87154-144-0) Russell Sage.

Duncan, Greg & Brooks-Gunn, Jeanne, eds. Consequences of Growing up Poor. LC 96-53161. 640p. (C). 1997. text 49.95 (0-87154-143-2) Russell Sage.

Duncan, Greg J. Years of Poverty, Years of Plenty. 200p. 1984. text 28.95 (0-472-00702-5, 00702) U of Mich Pr.

Duncan, Greg J., et al. A Validation Study of Economic Survey Data. LC 85-14434. (Institute for Social Research, Research Report). 136p. (Orig.). reprint ed. pap. 42.20 (0-7837-5249-0, 204498500005) Bks Demand.

Duncan, Greg J., jt. auth. see Morgan, James N.

Duncan, Gregory, ed. see Malm, Kiyoko.

Duncan, Guri. My Mother Was a Grapevine. LC 93-73403. 1994. 10.00 (0-9638803-1-4) Driftwood Pr.

Duncan, Guri, ed. see Dupuis, Carolyn C.

Duncan, H. C. & Pradhan, G. P. Cosmo Dictionary of English Nepali. 399p. (C). 1991. 60.00 (0-89771-071-1, Pub. by Ratna Pustak Bhandar) St Mut.

Duncan, Hall. Off Our Rockers LC 98-70391. 145 p. 1998. write for info. (0-9661367-1-3) ICHH.

***Duncan, Harley T.** West of Appomattox. 212p. 2000. pap. 12.95 (1-58345-404-7) Domhan Bks.

Duncan, Harry. Doors of Perception. 99p. 1987. reprint ed. pap. 16.50 (0-935072-12-8); reprint ed. pap. text. write for info. (0-318-62980-1) W T Taylor.

— Doors of Perception: Essays in Book Typography. 104p. 1987. pap. 16.50 (0-614-16148-7) Oak Knoll.

***Duncan-Hawthorne, Mary.** Spiritual Poems by a Young Black Female. (Illus.). 32p. 1999. pap. 7.99 (0-9675155-0-5) Duncan Hawthorne.

Duncan, Helen. Duncan's Dictionary for Nurses. 2nd ed. 816p. 1989. pap. 36.95 (0-8261-6200-2) Springer Pub.

— Duncan's Dictionary for Nurses. 2nd ed. 816p. 1989. 73.95 (0-8261-6201-0) Springer Pub.

— Lisa. 144p. 1998. pap. 6.95 (0-9652813-4-5) Dello & Assoc.

— Love Contracts. 144p. 1998. pap. 6.95 (0-9652813-3-7) Dello & Assoc.

— Saying Goodbye: When It's over. 160p. 1999. mass mkt. 14.95 (1-892873-00-1) Ginger Pubns.

Duncan, Hugh D. Communication & Social Order. 528p. 1985. pap. 29.95 (0-87855-971-X) Transaction Pubns.

— Culture & Democracy: The Struggle for Form in Society & Architecture in Chicago & the Middle West During the Life & Times of Louis H. Sullivan. 525p. (Orig.). 1988. pap. 29.95 (0-88738-746-2) Transaction Pubns.

Duncan, Ian, ed. see Buchan, John.

Duncan, Ian, ed. see Doyle, Arthur Conan.

Duncan, Ian, ed. see Hudson, William.

Duncan, Ian, ed. see Scott, Sir Walter.

Duncan, Ian, ed. & intro. see Scott, Sir Walter.

Duncan, Ida R. The Complete Book of Needlecraft. LC 61-15020. (Illus.). 1972. pap. 3.95 (0-87140-265-3, Pub. by Liveright) Norton.

Duncan, Irma. Duncan Dancer. LC 79-7759. (Dance Ser.). 1980. reprint ed. lib. bdg. 41.95 (0-8369-9288-1) Ayer.

Duncan, Isadora. Art of the Dance. Cheney, Sheldon W., ed. LC 71-85671. (Illus.). 1969. 19.95 (0-87830-005-8, Thtre Arts Bks) Routledge.

— Isadora Speaks: Writings & Speeches. Rosemont, Franklin, ed. & intro. by. (Illus.). 160p. (Orig.). 1994. pap. 12.00 (0-88286-227-8) C H Kerr.

— My Life. 384p. 1996. pap. 14.00 (0-87140-158-4, Norton Paperbks) Norton.

— My Life. (American Biography Ser.). 376p. 1991. reprint ed. lib. bdg. 79.00 (0-7812-8115-6) Rprt Serv.

***Duncan, J., ed.** Pipeline Protection: Proceedings International Conference Edinburgh, Scotland, 1999. (BHR Group Conference Ser.: No. 37). 332p. 1999. 340.00 (1-86058-214-1) Prof Eng Pubng.

Duncan, J. Alastair, frwd. The Art Work of Louis C. Tiffany. (Illus.). 134p. 1987. reprint ed. 70.00 (0-938290-06-1) Apollo.

***Duncan, J. D. H.** Feather in the Wind. (Real Life Ser.). vi, 250p. 1999. pap. 8.95 (1-930277-00-8) Sparow Hse Inc.

Duncan, J. Ligon. Moses' Law for Modern Government: The Intellectual & Sociological Origins of the Christian Reconstructionist Movement. 40p. 1996. pap. text 7.95 (1-884416-18-7) A Press.

Duncan, J. Ligon, III, jt. auth. see Hall, David W.

Duncan, J. Ligon, III, ed. see Carruthers, S. W.

Duncan, J. Ligon, III, ed. see Girardeau, John L.

Duncan, J. Ligon, III, ed. see Henry, Matthew.

Duncan, J. Ligon, III, ed. see Macleod, Donald.

Duncan, J. Ligon, III, ed. see Palmer, B. M.

Duncan, J. Ligon, III, ed. see Witsius, Herman.

Duncan, J. M. & Torrance, Lesley, eds. Techniques for the Rapid Detection of Plant Pathogens. (Illus.). 256p. 1991. 125.00 (0-632-03066-6) Blackwell Sci.

Duncan, J. P. & Law, K. K. Computer-Aided Sculpture: Of Arbitrary & Analytical Surfaces. (Illus.). 172p. 1989. text 47.95 (0-521-36303-9) Cambridge U Pr.

Duncan, J. Robert & Prasse, Keith W. Veterinary Laboratory Medicine: Clinical Pathology. 2nd ed. LC 85-19786. (Illus.). 293p. 1986. reprint ed. pap. 90.90 (0-608-00014-0, 206078000006) Bks Demand.

Duncan, J. Robert, et al. Veterinary Laboratory Medicine. 3rd ed. LC 94-1554. (Illus.). 308p. 1994. text 42.95 (0-8138-1917-2) Iowa St U Pr.

Duncan, J. Robert, jt. ed. see Nielsen, Klaus.

Duncan, Jacci. Washington for Women. LC 97-7164. 160p. 1996. pap. text 16.95 (1-56833-088-X) Madison Bks UPA.

Duncan, Jacci & Whittaker, Lynn P. The Women's History Guide to Washington. LC 97-49147. (Illus.). 192p. 1998. pap. 14.00 (0-9647124-3-1) C River Pr.

Duncan, James & Gregory, Derek, eds. Writes of Passage: Travel Writing Place & Ambiguity. LC 98-8225. (Illus.). 4p. (C). 1999. 85.00 (0-415-16013-8) Routledge.

Duncan, James S. The City As Text: The Politics of Landscape Interpretation in the Kandyan Kingdom. (Cambridge Human Geography Ser.). (Illus.). 243p. (C). 1990. text 80.00 (0-521-35305-X) Cambridge U Pr.

Duncan, James S., et al, eds. Information Processing in Medical Imaging: 15th International Conference, IPMI'97, Poultney, Vermont, U. S. A., June 9-13, 1997, Proceedings. LC 97-20852. (Lecture Notes in Computer Science Ser.: No. 1230). xvi, 557p. 1997. pap. 85.00 (3-540-63046-5) Spr-Verlag.

Duncan, James S. & Gregory, Derek. Writes of Passage: Reading Travel Writing. LC 98-8225. vi, 225 p. 1999. pap. 25.99 (0-415-16014-6) Routledge.

Duncan, James S. & Ley, David. Place - Culture - Representation. LC 92-37659. (Illus.). 368p. (C). 1993. pap. 25.99 (0-415-09451-8, B2362) Routledge.

Duncan, James S., jt. auth. see Barnes, Trevor J.

Duncan, James S., jt. ed. see Agnew, John.

Duncan, Jane. Brave Janet Reachfar. LC 74-8693. (Illus.). 32p. (J). (ps-3). 1975. 7.95 (0-8164-3130-2, Clarion Bks) HM.

— Janet Reachfar & the Kelpie. LC 75-44166. (Illus.). 32p. (J). (ps-3). 1976. 7.50 (0-685-02316-8, Clarion Bks) HM.

— My Friend Cousin Emmie. large type ed. 1978. 27.99 (0-7089-0136-0) Ulverscroft.

— My Friend Martha's Aunt. large type ed. 416p. 1983. 27.99 (0-7089-1041-6) Ulverscroft.

— My Friend Muriel. large type ed. 434p. 1982. 27.99 (0-7089-0846-2) Ulverscroft.

— My Friend Muriel. 1993. reprint ed. lib. bdg. 18.95 (1-56849-235-9) Buccaneer Bks.

— My Friend Sandy. large type ed. 432p. 1983. 27.99 (0-7089-0955-8) Ulverscroft.

— My Friend Sashie. 1993. reprint ed. lib. bdg. 18.95 (1-56849-232-4) Buccaneer Bks.

— My Friend the Swallow. large type ed. 1985. 15.95 (0-7089-1253-2) Ulverscroft.

— My Friends George & Tom. 1993. reprint ed. lib. bdg. 18.95 (1-56849-234-0) Buccaneer Bks.

— My Friends the Miss Boyds. large type ed. 414p. 1982. 27.99 (0-7089-0818-7) Ulverscroft.

— My Friends the Miss Boyds. 1993. reprint ed. lib. bdg. 18.95 (1-56849-233-2) Buccaneer Bks.

— My Friends the Mrs. Millers. large type ed. 1984. 15.95 (0-7089-1157-9) Ulverscroft.

Duncan, Jane, ed. see Jackson, Lyman C.

Duncan, Jane C. Careers in Veterinary Medicine. rev. ed. (Careers in Depth Ser.). (Illus.). (YA). (gr. 7-12). 1994. pap. 9.95 (0-8239-1719-3); lib. bdg. 16.95 (0-8239-1678-2) Rosen Group.

Duncan, Janie. Technology Assisted Teaching Techniques. (Language Resource Handbook Ser.: No. 5). (Illus.). 112p. 1987. pap. text 2.00 (0-86647-022-0) Pro Lingua.

Duncan, Janie L., jt. auth. see Clark, Raymond C.

Duncan, Jeffrey L. The Power & Form of Emerson's Thought. LC 73-85043. 121p. reprint ed. pap. 37.60 (0-7837-0200-0, 204049600017) Bks Demand.

***Duncan, Jeffrey L.** The Town Mouse & the Country Mouse. 47p. 2000. pap. 5.95 (0-87129-961-5, TC3) Dramatic Pub.

Duncan, Jeffrey L., jt. auth. see Cawelti, G. Scott.

Duncan, Jenni. Helping Children Cope with Divorce. LC 98-88817. 120p. 1999. pap. 19.95 (0-88177-270-4, DR270) Discipleship Res.

Duncan, Jennifer. Indian Programs: Tribal Priority Allocations Do Not Target the Neediest Tribes. (Illus.). 47p. (C). 1999. text 20.00 (0-7881-7929-2) DIANE Pub.

***Duncan, Jennifer.** Sanctuary & Other Stories. (New Writers Ser.). (Illus.). 188p. 2000. (0-919688-56-X) DC Books.

Duncan, Jerry R., et al. Agricultural Safety & Health for Engineers. Baker, L. D., ed. LC 94-72086. 100p. 1994. pap. text 22.25 (0-929355-51-2, M0894) Am Soc Ag Eng.

Duncan, Jim. Practical Math Skills - Intermediate Level. (Illus.). 64p. (J). (gr. 4-6). 1989. student ed. 8.99 (0-86653-465-2, GA1070) Good Apple.

— Practical Math Skills - Junior High Level. (Illus.). 64p. (J). (gr. 7-9). 1989. student ed. 8.99 (0-86653-466-0, GA1071) Good Apple.

— Practical Math Skills - Primary Level. (Illus.). 64p. (J). (gr. 1-3). 1989. student ed. 8.99 (0-86653-464-4, GA1069) Good Apple.

Duncan, Jim, jt. auth. see Rubin, Louis D., Sr.

Duncan, Jody. Making of Dragonheart. 160p. 1996. pap. 16.00 (1-57297-109-6) Blvd Books.

Duncan, Jody, jt. auth. see Bouzereau, Laurent.

Duncan, John. The Elements of Complex Analysis. LC QA0331.D85. 323p. reprint ed. pap. 100.20 (0-608-30988-5, 201602500097) Bks Demand.

— Travels in Western Africa in 1845 & 1846, 2 vols. 1968. reprint ed. 95.00 (0-7146-1804-7, Pub. by F Cass Pubs) Intl Spec Bk.

***Duncan, John.** UFOs. (Unexplained Ser.). 32p. (YA). (gr. 5 up). 1999. pap. 5.95 (0-7641-1062-4) Barron.

Duncan, John & Walton, John. Heroes for Victoria 1837-1901. 200p. (C). 1991. 125.00 (0-946771-38-3, Pub. by Spellmnt Pubs) St Mut.

Duncan, John & Webb, Edwin. Blitz over Britain. 192p. (C). 1991. 100.00 (0-946771-89-8, Pub. by Spellmnt Pubs) St Mut.

Duncan, John, jt. auth. see Forty, George.

***Duncan, John B.** The Origins of the Chosŏn Dynasty. LC 00-29876. (Korean Studies of the Henry M. Jackson School of International Studies). (Illus.). 400p. 2000. 60.00 (0-295-97985-2) U of Wash Pr.

Duncan, John D., Jr. A Crimson Fountain for Harlingscourt. Ashton, Sylvia, ed. LC 75-774. 1976. 22.95 (0-87949-038-1) Ashley Bks.

Duncan, John E. The Sea Chain. LC 85-73918. (Illus.). 439p. 1986. pap. 12.95 (0-914166-23-9) Americana Rev.

Duncan, John E., see Tuttle, Sam, pseud.

Duncan, John J., Jr., ed. Aviation Security & Anti-Terrorism Efforts: Hearing Before the Committee on Transportation & Infrastructure, U. S. House of Representatives. 205p. (C). 1998. pap. text 35.00 (0-7881-4963-6) DIANE Pub.

Duncan, John R., tr. see Barton, Karel.

Duncan, Johnny. You Might Be a Nigger. 150p. 1998. pap. 10.95 (1-57502-702-X, PO1982) Morris Pubng.

Duncan-Jones, Katherine. Sir Philip Sidney, Courtier Poet. LC 91-65391. (Illus.). 384p. 1991. reprint ed. pap. 119.10 (0-608-07886-7, 205999300010) Bks Demand.

Duncan-Jones, Katherine, ed. see Shakespeare, William.

Duncan-Jones, Katherine, ed. see Sidney, Philip.

Duncan-Jones, Richard. Money & Government in the Roman Empire. LC 93-31989. (Illus.). 320p. (C). 1994. text 85.00 (0-521-44192-7) Cambridge U Pr.

— Money & Government in the Roman Empire. (Illus.). 320p. (C). 1998. pap. text 27.95 (0-521-64829-7) Cambridge U Pr.

Duncan, Joseph E. Milton's Earthly Paradise: A Historical Study of Eden. LC 71-187167. (Minnesota Monographs in the Humanities: No. 5). (Illus.). 347p. reprint ed. pap. 107.60 (0-8357-8953-5, 203321800085) Bks Demand.

Duncan, Joseph W. & Grass, Andrew. Statistics for the 21st Century: Proposals for Improving Statistics for Better Decision Making. 336p. (Orig.). 1995. text 45.00 (0-7863-0328-X, Irwn Prfssnl) McGraw-Hill Prof.

An Asterisk (*) at the beginning of an entry indicates that the title is appearing for the first time.

Duncan, Joseph W. & Gross, Andrew C. Statistics for the 21st Century: Proposals for Improving Statistics for Better Decision Making. 230p. (Orig.). 1993. pap. 14.95 (*1-56203-310-7*, Irwn Prfssnl) McGraw-Hill Prof.

Duncan, Joy R., ed. see Duncan, Ray H.

Duncan, Joyce, jt. auth. see Bradshaw, Steve.

Duncan, Judith. Better Than Before. (Intimate Moments Ser.: No. 421). 1992. mass mkt. 3.39 (*0-373-07421-2*, 5-07421-6) Harlequin Bks.

— Beyond All Reason: Wide Open Spaces. (Intimate Moments Ser.). 1993. per. 3.50 (*0-373-07536-7*, 5-07536-1) Silhouette.

— Driven to Distraction (Romantic Traditions) (Intimate Moments Ser.). 1996. per. 3.99 (*0-373-07704-1*, 1-07704-9) Silhouette.

— Marriage of Agreement: Conveniently Wed. (Intimate Moments Ser.). 2000. mass mkt. 4.25 (*0-373-07975-3*, 1-07975-5) Silhouette.

— Murphy's Child: Families Are Forever. (Intimate Moments Ser.: No. 946). 1999. per. 4.25 (*0-373-07946-X*, 1-07946-6) Silhouette.

— The Return of Eden McCall. LC 95-15837. (Intimate Moments Ser.). 248p. 1995. per. 3.75 (*0-373-07651-7*, 1-07651-2) Silhouette.

— A Special Request. (To Mother with Love Ser.). 1993. pap. 4.99 (*0-685-61546-4*) Silhouette.

— That Same Old Feeling. (Intimate Moments Ser.). 1994. per. 3.50 (*0-373-07577-4*, 1-07577-9) Harlequin Bks.

Duncan, Julian S. Public & Private Operation of Railways in Brazil. (Columbia University. Studies in the Social Sciences: No. 367). reprint ed. 29.50 (*0-404-51367-0*) AMS Pr.

Duncan, Justin. Fire Protection Systems. LC 93-45429. 1994. 29.95 (*0-912524-78-2*) Busn News.

— Hydronics Technology. LC 94-23005. 1995. 37.95 (*0-912524-87-1*) Busn News.

— Plumbing Technology. Turpin, Joanna, ed. LC 93-11615. (Illus.). 384p. 1994. text 29.95 (*0-912524-76-6*) Busn News.

Duncan, K. A. Community Health Information Systems: Lessons for the Future. LC 97-39549. 1998. 44.00 (*1-56793-071-9*) Health Admin Pr.

Duncan, Karen, jt. auth. see Blum, Bruce I.

Duncan, Kate & Carney, Eunice. A Special Gift: The Kutchin Beadwork Tradition. LC 97-41710. (Illus.). xx, 104p. 1998. pap. 19.95 (*0-912006-88-9*, 6889) U of Alaska Pr.

***Duncan, Kate & Cultural Environment Movement.** Liberating Alternatives: The Founding Convention of the Cultural Environment Movement. LC 99-17257. (Hampton Press Communication Ser.). 1999. pap. 21.95 (*1-57273-199-0*) Hampton Pr NJ.

***Duncan, Kate C.** 1001 Curious Things: Ye Olde Curiosity Shop & Native American Art. (Illus.). 248p. 2001. 35.00 (*0-295-98010-9*) U of Wash Pr.

Duncan, Kate C. Some Warmer Tone: Alaska Athabaskan Bead Embroidery. Smetzer, Mary B., ed. (Illus.). 64p. (Orig.). 1984. pap. 12.00 (*0-931163-00-5*) U Alaska Museum.

Duncan, Kate C., jt. auth. see Hail, Barbara A.

***Duncan, Katherine.** Creative Collage for Crafters: Techniques, Projects, Inspirations. (Illus.). 128p. 2000. write for info. (*1-57990-173-5*, Pub. by Lark Books) Sterling.

Duncan, Katherine. Dualities & Dichotomies: The Works of John Briggs. (Illus.). 27p. (Orig.). (C). 1990. pap. 10.00 (*0-9619219-3-5*) Polk Mus Art.

***Duncan, Katherine.** Fabulous Felt Crafts: 50 Creative & Colorful Projects to Make. LC 99-54242. (Illus.). 128p. 2000. pap. 17.95 (*1-57990-156-5*, Pub. by Lark Books) Sterling.

Duncan, Katherine. Fired Up! Hot Designs & Cool Techniques for Painting Pottery. LC 98-48215. (Illus.). 128p. 1999. pap. 18.95 (*1-57990-088-7*, Pub. by Lark Books) Random.

— Jeffrey Kronsnoble: A Retrospective, 1964-1988. (Illus.). 30p. (C). 1990. pap. 12.00 (*0-9619219-2-7*) Polk Mus Art.

Duncan, Katherine, ed. see Auth, Betty.

Duncan, Katherine, ed. see King, Peter W.

Duncan, Ken, jt. auth. see Schultz-Ela, Dan.

***Duncan, Kenn.** Models & Friends: Photobooks. (Illus.). 1998. 44.95 (*3-925443-73-8*) Janssen.

Duncan, Kenneth, et al, eds. Land & Labour in Latin America: Essays on the Development of Agrarian Capitalism in the Nineteenth & Twentieth Centuries. LC 76-11076. (Cambridge Latin American Studies: No. 26). 549p. reprint ed. pap. 156.50 (*0-608-12076-6*, 2024573) Bks Demand.

Duncan, King, ed. King's Treasury of Dynamic Humor. 256p. 1991. 14.95 (*0-936497-06-8*) Seven Worlds.

— Mule Eggs & Topknots. rev. ed. LC 86-63997. 220p. (Orig.). 1991. 14.95 (*0-936497-05-X*) Seven Worlds.

— Who's Afraid of a Hinged-Tail Bingbuffer? Object Lessons for Children. LC 87-90466. 144p. (Orig.). 1987. pap. 7.50 (*0-936497-02-5*) Seven Worlds.

Duncan, King & Akers, Angela. Amusing Grace: Humor to Heal Mind, Soul, & Body. 2nd ed. 466p. (Orig.). 1996. pap. 14.95 (*0-936497-11-4*) Seven Worlds.

Duncan, King, jt. auth. see Clark, Rebecca.

Duncan, Kirin, jt. auth. see Saratoga.

Duncan, Kunigunde. Blue Star: The Story of Corabelle Fellows, Teacher at Dakota Missions, 1884-1888. LC 89-39848. (Illus.). xxxiv, 216p. 1989. pap. 8.95 (*0-87351-245-6*, Borealis Book) Minn Hist.

Duncan, L. C. The Medical Department of the U. S. Army in the Civil War. Date not set. lib. bdg. 27.95 (*0-8488-0996-3*) Amereon Ltd.

Duncan, L. Wallace. History of Montgomery County: By Its Own People, Containing Sketches of Our Pioneers...& Biographies of Their Worthy Successors. (Illus.). 852p. 1997. reprint ed. lib. bdg. 85.00 (*0-8328-6721-7*) Higginson Bk Co.

Duncan-Lacoste, Lisbeth, jt. auth. see Esposito, Chris.

Duncan, Larry W., jt. ed. see Timmer, L. W.

Duncan, Leland L. & Kelly, Liam. The Face of Time: Photographs of County Leitrim. LC 96-117321. 80p. 1995. 39.95 (*1-874675-59-7*) Dufour.

Duncan, Leland L., jt. ed. see Phillimore, W. P.

***Duncan, Leonard C.** Beyond Phonics. 42p. 1999. spiral bd. 20.00 (*0-941414-32-9*) LCD.

— Greek Roots Bk. 1: -ology (Study) 66p. 1999. spiral bd. 13.00 (*0-941414-33-7*) LCD.

— Greek Roots Bk. 2: Arith (Numbers) 40p. 1999. spiral bd. 13.00 (*0-941414-34-5*) LCD.

— Greek Roots Bk. 3: Psych/Soma (Mind/Body) 42p. 1999. spiral bd. 13.00 (*0-941414-35-3*) LCD.

— Greek Roots Bk. 4: Phobia/Mania (Fear/Desire) 34p. 1999. spiral bd. 13.00 (*0-941414-36-1*) LCD.

— Greek Roots Bk. 5: Path (Diseases) 38p. 1999. spiral bd. 13.00 (*0-941414-37-X*) LCD.

— Greek Roots Bk. 6: Therap (Cure) 38p. 1999. spiral bd. 13.00 (*0-941414-38-8*) LCD.

Duncan, Leonard C. Greek Roots J-Ology. (Illus.). 140p. (J). (gr. 6-12). Date not set. spiral bd. 25.00 (*0-941414-01-9*) LCD.

***Duncan, Leonard C.** Homonyms & Homographs. 46p. 1999. spiral bd. 20.00 (*0-941414-39-6*) LCD.

Duncan, Leonard C. How to Teach Phonics. 74p. 1996. spiral bd. 20.00 (*0-941414-25-6*) LCD.

— 99 Nursery Rhymes. (Illus.). 110p. (J). 1995. spiral bd. 20.00 (*0-941414-15-9*) LCD.

— Number Words. 148p. 1984. spiral bd. 25.00 (*0-941414-07-8*) LCD.

— Phonics First, Bk. 1. (Illus.). 88p. (J). (gr. 1-6). 1996. student ed., spiral bd. 20.00 (*0-941414-20-5*) LCD.

— Phonics First, Bk. 2. (Illus.). 76p. (J). (gr. 1-6). 1996. student ed., spiral bd. 20.00 (*0-941414-21-3*) LCD.

— Phonics First Bk. 3: The Words That Phonics Can't Teach. (Illus.). 82p. (J). (gr. 1-6). 1996. student ed., spiral bd. 20.00 (*0-941414-22-1*) LCD.

— Phonics First Bk. 4: Introduction to Words of More Than One Syllable. (Illus.). 110p. (J). (gr. 1-6). 1996. student ed., spiral bd. 20.00 (*0-941414-23-X*) LCD.

— Phonics in 90 Days: Lesson Plans for Teachers. 80p. Date not set. teacher ed., spiral bd. 20.00 (*0-941414-19-1*) LCD.

— Sounds of the Letters. (Illus.). 80p. 1999. spiral bd. 20.00 (*0-941414-24-8*) LCD.

— Words of Liberty. (Illus.). 58p. 1995. spiral bd. 15.00 (*0-941414-08-6*) LCD.

Duncan, Linda B. The Cowboy Gourmet Guide: A Bona Fide Bible of Good Lives & Good Living. LC 93-95060. (Illus.). 100p. 1994. lib. bdg. write for info. (*0-9633751-1-3*) TX Marquee Pub.

Duncan, Lois. Daughters of Eve. 272p. (YA). 1990. mass mkt. 4.99 (*0-440-91864-2*) Dell.

Duncan, Lois. Daughters of Eve. 1979. 9.60 (*0-606-02081-0*, Pub. by Turtleback) Demco.

Duncan, Lois. Don't Look Back. 192p. (YA). 1990. mass mkt. 4.99 (*0-440-20729-0*, LLL BDD) BDD Bks Young Read.

Duncan, Lois. Don't Look Back. 1989. 10.09 (*0-606-03232-0*, Pub. by Turtleback) Demco.

Duncan, Lois. Down a Dark Hall. 192p. (YA). (gr. 5-9). 1990. mass mkt. 4.99 (*0-440-91805-7*, LLL BDD) BDD Bks Young Read.

— Down a Dark Hall. (J). 1990. mass mkt. 6.95 (*0-440-80223-7*) Dell.

Duncan, Lois. Down a Dark Hall. 181p. (YA). (gr. 7 up). pap. 4.99 (*0-8072-1370-5*) Listening Lib.

— Down a Dark Hall. 1974. 9.60 (*0-606-02048-9*, Pub. by Turtleback) Demco.

Duncan, Lois. Gallows Hill. LC 96-43641. 240p. (YA). (gr. 7 up). 1997. 15.95 (*0-385-32331-X*, Delacorte Pr Bks) BDD Bks Young Read.

— Gallows Hill. 240p. (YA). 1998. mass mkt. 4.99 (*0-440-22725-9*) BDD Bks Young Read.

— A Gift of Magic. 240p. (YA). 1999. mass mkt. 4.99 (*0-440-22847-6*) BDD Bks Young Read.

Duncan, Lois. A Gift of Magic. LC 70-150053. 1971. 9.09 (*0-606-03419-6*, Pub. by Turtleback) Demco.

Duncan, Lois. Gift of Magic. (YA). (gr. 6 up). 1990. per. 3.99 (*0-671-72649-8*, Archway) PB.

***Duncan, Lois.** Gift of Magic. (Illus.). (J). 1999. 10.34 (*0-606-17033-2*, Pub. by Turtleback) Demco.

Duncan, Lois. I Know What You Did Last Summer. 208p. (YA). 1999. mass mkt. 4.99 (*0-440-22844-1*) BDD Bks Young Read.

— I Know What You Did Last Summer. (YA). (gr. 7 up). 1990. pap. 3.99 (*0-671-73589-6*, PB Trade Paper) PB.

— I Know What You Did Last Summer. (J). 1997. mass mkt. 4.99 (*0-671-01722-5*, Archway) PB.

Duncan, Lois. I Know What You Did Last Summer. (J). 1975. 9.60 (*0-606-02652-5*, Pub. by Turtleback) Demco.

— I Know What You Did Last Summer. 1990. 10.34 (*0-606-17034-0*, Pub. by Turtleback) Demco.

Duncan, Lois. Killing Mr. Griffin. 224p. (YA). (gr. 7 up). 1990. mass mkt. 4.99 (*0-440-94515-1*, LLL BDD) BDD Bks Young Read.

Duncan, Lois. Killing Mr. Griffin. 223p. (YA). (gr. 7 up). pap. 4.50 (*0-8072-1373-X*) Listening Lib.

— Killing Mr. Griffin. 1978. 10.09 (*0-606-01739-9*, Pub. by Turtleback) Demco.

— Killing Mr. Griffin, Class Set. unabridged ed. (J). 1997. 109.80 incl. audio (*0-7887-2712-5*, 46300) Recorded Bks.

— Killing Mr. Griffin, Homework Set. unabridged ed. (J). 1997. 56.75 incl. audio (*0-7887-1898-3*, 40634) Recorded Bks.

Duncan, Lois. Locked in Time. 224p. (YA). (gr. 7-12). 1986. mass mkt. 4.99 (*0-440-94942-4*, LLL BDD) BDD Bks Young Read.

— Locked in Time. (J). 1985. 9.60 (*0-606-03022-0*, Pub. by Turtleback) Demco.

***Duncan, Lois.** Longest Hair in the World. LC 98-53372. 32p. (J). (gr. k-2). 1999. 15.95 (*0-385-32113-9*) BDD Bks Young Read.

— The Longest Hair In The World. (J). 2001. pap. 5.99 (*0-440-41239-0*) BDD Bks Young Read.

— Magic of Spider Woman. (Illus.). (J). 2000. pap. 5.99 (*0-590-46156-7*) Scholastic Inc.

Duncan, Lois. The Magic of Spider Women. LC 95-17366. (Illus.). (J). 1996. write for info. (*0-590-46095-1*) Scholastic Inc.

— Night Terrors. (J). 1997. per. 3.99 (*0-689-80724-4*, S&S Childrens.

— Night Terrors: Stories of Shadow & Substance. 1997. 9.09 (*0-606-13662-2*, Pub. by Turtleback) Demco.

— Psychic Connections: A Journey into the Mysterious World of Psychic. 272p. (YA). 1995. pap. 12.95 (*0-385-32072-8*) Delacorte.

— Ransom. 1966. 10.09 (*0-606-03390-4*, Pub. by Turtleback) Demco.

— Ransom. 176p. (YA). (gr. 7-12). 1986. reprint ed. mass mkt. 4.99 (*0-440-97292-2*) BDD Bks Young Read.

— Stranger with My Face. 240p. (YA). (gr. 7-12). 1990. mass mkt. 4.99 (*0-440-98356-8*, LLL BDD) BDD Bks Young Read.

Duncan, Lois. Stranger with My Face. 235p. (YA). (gr. 7 up). pap. 4.99 (*0-8072-1371-3*) Listening Lib.

— Stranger with My Face. (Laurel-Leaf Suspense Ser.). (J). 1981. 9.60 (*0-606-01798-4*, Pub. by Turtleback) Demco.

— Stranger with My Face. unabridged ed. (Young Adult Cliffhangers Ser.). (YA). (gr. 7 up). 1993. audio 15.98 (*0-8072-1834-0*, JRH117SP) Listening Lib.

Duncan, Lois. Summer of Fear. 224p. (YA). (gr. 7 up). 1977. mass mkt. 4.99 (*0-440-98324-X*, LLL BDD) BDD Bks Young Read.

Duncan, Lois. Summer of Fear. 224p. (YA). (gr. 7 up). pap. 4.99 (*0-8072-1372-1*) Listening Lib.

Duncan, Lois. Summer of Fear. (Laurel-Leaf Suspense Ser.). (J). 1976. 9.09 (*0-606-02179-5*, Pub. by Turtleback) Demco.

— They Never Came Home. 1969. 9.60 (*0-606-04828-6*, Pub. by Turtleback) Demco.

— They Never Came Home. 192p. (YA). 1990. reprint ed. mass mkt. 4.99 (*0-440-20780-0*, LLL BDD) BDD Bks Young Read.

— The Third Eye. 224p. (YA). (gr. 6-12). 1991. mass mkt. 4.99 (*0-440-98720-2*, LLL BDD) BDD Bks Young Read.

— The Third Eye. 220p. (YA). (gr. 7). 1984. 15.95 (*0-316-19553-7*) Little.

— The Third Eye. (YA). 1985. 9.60 (*0-606-00474-2*, Pub. by Turtleback) Demco.

— Trapped! Cages of Mind & Body. Gutierrez, Rudy, ed. 240p. (J). (gr. 7). 1999. per. 4.99 (*0-689-83082-3*) Aladdin.

— Trapped! Cages of the Mind & Body. LC 97-18049. 228p. (J). (gr. 7 up). 1998. 16.00 (*0-689-81335-X*) S&S Bks Yung.

— The Twisted Window. 192p. (YA). (gr. k-12). 1988. mass mkt. 4.99 (*0-440-20184-5*, LLL BDD) BDD Bks Young Read.

Duncan, Lois. Twisted Window. (Laurel-Leaf Suspense Ser.). (J). 1987. 9.60 (*0-606-04076-5*, Pub. by Turtleback) Demco.

Duncan, Lois. Who Killed My Daughter: The True Story of a Mother's Search for Her Daughter's Murderer. 368p. 1994. mass mkt. 6.99 (*0-440-21342-8*) Dell.

— Wonder Kid Meets the Evil Lunch Snatcher. LC 87-26490. 76p. (J). (gr. 4-7). 1990. pap. 4.95 (*0-316-19561-8*) Little.

— Wonder Kid Meets the Evil Lunch Snatcher. (Springboard Bks.). (J). 1988. 9.70 (*0-606-04591-0*, Pub. by Turtleback) Demco.

Duncan, Lois, ed. Night Terrors: Stories of Shadow & Substance. LC 95-44901. 176p. (YA). (gr. 7 up). 1996. per. 16.00 (*0-689-80346-X*) S&S Bks Yung.

***Duncan, Lois, ed.** On the Edge: Stories at the Brink. LC 99-54262. (Illus.). 224p. (J). (gr. 7-12). 2000. per. 17.00 (*0-689-82251-0*) S&S Bks Yung.

Duncan, Lois M. I Heard from God, I Think? 200p. 2000. ring bd. 12.75 (*0-9635410-2-1*) Beginnings.

— Novice Duncan's Useful Guide for Starting Herbs from Seed. (Illus.). 34p. (Orig.). 1997. pap. 2.00 (*0-9635410-1-3*) Beginnings.

Duncan, Louis C. The Medical Department of the United States in the Civil War. 400p. 1987. reprint ed. 28.50 (*0-942211-30-8*) Olde Soldier Bks.

Duncan, M. C. Masonic Ritual. rev. ed. 21.95 (*0-685-22033-8*) Wehman.

Duncan, Malcolm. Masonic Ritual & Monitor, 2 pts. 1946. pap. 13.00 (*0-911164-22-7*) Powner.

Duncan, Malcolm C. Duncan Masonic Ritual & Monitor. 1976. pap. 13.00 (*0-679-50626-8*) Random.

— Duncan's Masonic Ritual & Monitor. 288p. 1976. pap. 5.95 (*0-685-03267-1*) McKay.

— Duncan's Masonic Ritual & Monitor. 288p. 1986. 20.00 (*0-679-50979-8*) McKay.

— Duncan's Masonic Ritual & Monitor: Or a Guide to the Three Symbolic Degrees of the Ancient York Rite & to the Degrees of Mark Master, Past Master, Most Excellent Master & the Royal Arch. Explained & Interpreted by Copious Notes & Numerous Engravings. 281p. 1995. reprint ed. pap. 16.95 (*1-56459-488-2*) Kessinger Pub.

Duncan, Margaret C., et al, eds. Explorations in the Field of Play. (Play & Culture Studies Ser.). 350p. 1998. pap. 39.50 (*1-56750-371-3*) Ablx Pub.

— Explorations in the Field of Play, Vol. 1. (Play & Culture Studies Ser.). 350p. 1998. 73.25 (*1-56750-370-5*) Ablx Pub.

Duncan, Margo A., jt. auth. see Young, David G.

Duncan, Marie & Farrell, Betty. Celebrate the Seasons with Ribbon Embroidery by Machine: More Than 30 New Projects from the Authors of Ribbon Embroidery by Machine & More Ribbon Embroidery by Machine. LC 98-84105. (Illus.). 112p. 1998. pap. 19.95 (*0-87341-623-6*, SFCR) Krause Pubns.

— Hand Sewn by Machine. LC 99-61454. 128p. 1999. pap. 21.95 (*0-87341-799-2*) Krause Pubns.

— More Ribbon Embroidery by Machine. LC 97-73026. (Illus.). 96p. (Orig.). 1997. pap. 21.95 (*0-8019-9047-5*, BCUR) Krause Pubns.

— Ribbon Embroidery by Machine. LC 96-20437. (Illus.). 96p. 1996. pap. 18.95 (*0-8019-8783-0*) Krause Pubns.

Duncan, Marijane D. My Mother's Arm Swings the Broom with Mine. Duncan, Nancy G., ed. LC 93-73402. (Illus.). 900p. 1994. 30.00 (*0-9638803-0-6*) Driftwood Pr.

Duncan, Marilyn P., ed. The Guide to Texas State Agencies. 10th rev. ed. (Illus.). 330p. 1998. pap. 60.00 (*0-89940-328-X*) LBJ Sch Pub Aff.

Duncan, Marion B., jt. auth. see Duncan, Wilbur H.

***Duncan, Marion H.** Customs & Superstitions of Tibetans. 1998. pap. 22.00 (*81-7303-127-4*) Book Faith.

Duncan, Mark. On Target with Mark Duncan: An Illustrated Pocket Guide to Handgun Accuracy. (Illus.). 52p. (Orig.). 1984. pap. 4.95 (*0-9613502-0-2*) Duncan Gun.

Duncan, Mark, ed. Section Lines: A Manitoba Anthology. 1997. pap. 9.95 (*0-88801-127-X*, Pub. by Turnstone Pr) Genl Dist Srvs.

Duncan, Martha G. Romantic Outlaws, Beloved Prisons: The Unconscious Meanings of Crime & Punishment. 288p. (C). 1996. text 30.00 (*0-8147-1880-9*) NYU Pr.

Duncan, Martha Grace. Romantic Outlaws, Beloved Prisons: The Unconscious Meanings of Crime & Punishment. 1999. pap. text 19.00 (*0-8147-1881-7*) NYU Pr.

Duncan, Marti. Being & Breakfast. 1975. 4.00 (*0-686-71049-5*) Windless Orchard.

Duncan, Marvin & Stam, Jerome M., eds. Financing Agriculture into the Twenty-First Century. LC 98-22831. 232p. 1998. text 69.00 (*0-8133-3254-0*, Pub. by Westview) HarpC.

— Financing Agriculture into the Twenty-First Century. (C). 1999. pap. 19.95 (*0-8133-3255-9*) Westview.

Duncan, Mary & Marsh, Christine. Fatal Accident Claims. 150p. 1993. 60.00 (*1-85190-191-4*, Pub. by Tolley Pubng) St Mut.

Duncan, Mary E., jt. auth. see Grossman, Gary M.

Duncan, Melba J. The New Executive Assistant: Advice for Succeeding in Your Career. LC 96-51841. (Illus.). 256p. 1997. pap. 12.95 (*0-07-018241-8*) McGraw.

Duncan, Michael. Advances in Metal & Semiconductor Clusters, Vol. 4. 1998. 109.50 (*0-7623-0058-2*) Jai Pr.

— Costly Mission. 144p. 1996. pap. 9.95 (*0-912552-96-4*) MARC.

Duncan, Michael & Gerstler, Amy. Georganne Deen. (Illus.). 20p. 1997. pap. 10.00 (*1-889195-11-1*, Pub. by Smart Art Pr) RAM Publications.

Duncan, Michael & Wolff, Theodore F. Joyce Treiman. LC 97-20203. (Illus.). 180p. 1997. 50.00 (*1-55595-141-4*, Pub. by Hudson Hills) Natl Bk Netwk.

***Duncan, Michael A., ed.** Advances in Metal & Semiconductor Clusters, Vol. 5. 1999. 109.50 (*0-7623-0492-8*) Jai Pr.

Duncan, Michael A., ed. Advances in Metal & Semiconductor Clusters: Cluster Reactions, Vol. 2. 213p. 1994. 109.50 (*1-55938-704-1*) Jai Pr.

— Advances in Metal & Semiconductor Clusters: Spectroscopy & Dynamics, Vol. 1. 314p. 1993. 109.50 (*1-55938-171-X*) Jai Pr.

— Advances in Metal & Semiconductor Clusters: Spectroscopy & Structure, Vol. 3. 221p. 1995. 109.50 (*1-55938-788-2*) Jai Pr.

Duncan, Mike. Reach Your Goals in Spite of the Old Boy Network: A Guide for African American Employees. Reid, Nancy G. & Goode, Delores, eds. LC 90-93039. 190p. 1990. 16.95 (*1-878647-00-8*) APU Pub Grp.

Duncan, Mitchell G. Diccionario de Sociologia. 2nd ed. (SPA.). 240p. 1986. 24.95 (*0-7859-5799-5*) Fr & Eur.

Duncan, Nancy, ed. Body Space: Destabilising Geographies of Gender & Sexuality. LC 96-589. (Illus.). 288p. (C). 1996. 85.00 (*0-415-14441-8*); pap. 22.99 (*0-415-14442-6*) Routledge.

Duncan, Nancy G., ed. see Duncan, Marijane D.

Duncan, Nigel, et al. Employment Law in Practice. 2nd ed. (Inns of Court School of Law Ser.). 207p. 1998. pap. 48.00 (*1-85431-716-4*, 15592, Pub. by Blackstone Pr) Gaunt.

— Employment Law in Practice. 3rd ed. 207p. 1999. pap. 50.00 (*1-85431-900-0*, Pub. by Blackstone Pr) Gaunt.

***Duncan, Nigel, et al.** Employment Law in Practice. 4th ed. (Inns of Court School of Law Ser.). 209p. 2000. pap. 46.00 (*1-84174-003-9*, Pub. by Blackstone Pr) Gaunt.

Duncan, Norman. Battles Royal Down North. LC 70-125209. (Short Story Index Reprint Ser.). (Illus.). 1977. 19.95 (*0-8369-3576-4*) Ayer.

— Harbor Tales Down North. LC 72-121536. (Short Story Index Reprint Ser.). (Illus.). 1977. 21.95 (*0-8369-3492-X*) Ayer.

— The Way of the Sea. LC 76-121537. (Short Story Index Reprint Ser.). 1977. 23.95 (*0-8369-3493-8*) Ayer.

D

An Asterisk (*) at the beginning of an entry indicates that the title is appearing for the first time.

Duncan, Otis D. An Examination of the Problem of Optimum City Size. Zuckerman, Harriet & Merton, Robert K., eds. LC 79-8994. (Dissertations on Sociology Ser.). (Illus.). 1980. lib. bdg. 28.95 (*0-405-12965-3*) Ayer.

— The Measurement of Population Distribution. (Reprint Series in Social Sciences). (C). 1993. reprint ed. pap. text 2.30 (*0-8290-2663-0*, S-378) Irvington.

— Notes on Social Measurement: Historical & Critical. LC 83-62503. (Russell Sage Foundation 75th Anniversary Ser.). 272p. 1984. 34.95 (*0-87154-219-6*) Russell Sage.

Duncan, Otis D. & Duncan, Beverly. Negro Population of Chicago. LC 57-5271. 399p. reprint ed. 123.70 (*0-8357-9651-5*, 201575400003) Bks Demand.

Duncan, Otis D., et al. Introduction to Structural Equation Models. (Studies in Population). 1975. text 59.95 (*0-12-224150-9*) Acad Pr.

— Metropolis & Region. LC 77-86393. (Resources for the Future Ser.). (Illus.). 608p. reprint ed. 64.50 (*0-404-60331-9*) AMS Pr.

— Metropolis & Region. LC 60-10656. 607p. reprint ed. pap. 188.20 (*0-7837-3133-7*, 204285400006) Bks Demand.

— Social Change in a Metropolitan Community. LC 73-76764. 136p. 1973. pap. 14.95 (*0-87154-216-1*) Russell Sage.

— Statistical Geography: Problems in Analyzing Areal Data. LC 77-7890. (Illus.). 190p. 1977. reprint ed. lib. bdg. 35.00 (*0-8371-9676-0*, DUSG, Greenwood Pr) Greenwood.

Duncan, Otis D., jt. ed. see Hauser, Philip M.

Duncan, P. Horses & Grasses: A Study of Horses & Their Impact on the Camargue. (Ecological Studies: Vol. 87). (Illus.). xiv, 287p. 1991. 128.00 (*0-387-97543-8*) Spr-Verlag.

Duncan, Pamela, ed. Balance (Proceedings) 112p. 1990. pap. 21.00 (*0-912452-73-0*, P-66) Am Phys Therapy Assn.

Duncan, Patricia A. Pat's Sourdough & Favorite Recipes. 2nd ed. 200p. 1991. reprint ed. spiral bd. 14.95 (*0-9625098-1-7*) TAP Pub.

***Duncan, Patricia B.** Hunterdon County New Jersey 1895 Census Pt. 1: Alexandria - Junction. 212p. 1999. pap. 34.00 (*0-7884-1310-4*) Heritage Bk.

— Hunterdon County, New Jersey, 1895 State Census Pt. II: Kingwood-West Amwell. 225p. 1999. pap. 34.50 (*0-7884-1332-5*, D852) Heritage Bk.

Duncan, Patricia E. Moonbeams & Starlight. 1990. write for info. (*0-9626313-0-2*) Leprechauns Unltd.

Duncan, Patricia J. Ingles Hecho Facil: English Made Simple. 384p. 1996. pap. 12.95 (*0-385-48186-1*) Doubleday.

***Duncan, Patricia J.** Jennifer Lopez. 1999. mass mkt. 4.99 (*0-312-97085-4*, St Martins Paperbacks) St Martin.

Duncan, Patricia J. Ricky Martin: La Vida Loca. 128p. 1999. mass mkt. 10.99 (*0-446-67628-4*, Pub. by Warner Bks) Little.

— Salma Hayek. LC 99-205938. 1999. mass mkt. 5.99 (*0-312-96982-1*, St Martins Paperbacks) St Martin.

Duncan, Patricia J., tr. see Giardinelli, Mempo.

Duncan, Patricia J., tr. see Toscana, David.

Duncan, Patrick S. Courage under Fire. 1996. mass mkt. 5.99 (*1-57297-183-5*) Blvd Books.

***Duncan, Paul.** Alfred Hitchcock. 96p. 2000. pap. 5.95 (*1-903047-00-5*, Pub. by Pocket Essentials) Trafalgar.

— David Lynch. 2000. pap. 5.95 (*1-903047-06-4*, Pub. by Pocket Essentials) Trafalgar.

— Film Noir. 2000. pap. 5.95 (*1-903047-08-0*, Pub. by Pocket Essentials) Trafalgar.

— Hong Kong's Heroic Bloodshed. 2000. pap. 5.95 (*1-903047-07-2*, Pub. by Pocket Essentials) Trafalgar.

— Insight Pocket Guide Cape Town with Map. rev. ed. (Illus.). 2000. pap. 12.95 (*1-58573-018-1*) Langenscheidt.

— Noir Fiction. 2000. pap. 5.95 (*1-903047-11-0*, Pub. by Pocket Essentials) Trafalgar.

— Orson Welles. 2000. pap. 5.95 (*1-903047-04-8*, Pub. by Pocket Essentials) Trafalgar.

Duncan, Paul. Rome. LC 94-68184. (Illustrated Travel Guides from Thomas Cook Ser.). (Illus.). 192p. (Orig.). 1994. pap. 12.95 (*0-8442-9077-7*, Passprt Bks) NTC Contemp Pub Co.

***Duncan, Paul.** Stanley Kubrick. 96p. 2000. pap. 5.95 (*1-903047-01-3*, Pub. by Pocket Essentials) Trafalgar.

Duncan, Paul. Traditional Houses of Rural Italy. (Illus.). 160p. 1993. 27.50 (*1-55859-637-2*) Abbeville Pr.

— Traditional Houses of Rural Italy. (Illus.). 160p. 1997. pap. 17.95 (*0-7892-0432-0*) Abbeville Pr.

***Duncan, Paul.** Woody Allen. 2000. pap. 5.95 (*1-903047-05-6*, Pub. by Pocket Essentials) Trafalgar.

Duncan, Paul, jt. auth. see Cook, Matthew.

***Duncan, Peggy.** Just Show Me Which Button to Click! Computer Training for Busy People. LC 99-91133. (Illus.). xii, 196p. 2000. pap. 24.99 (*0-9674728-0-6*) PSC Pr.

Duncan, Peter. Children of the Revolution: The Screenplay. 1997. pap. 17.95 (*0-86819-503-0*, Pub. by Currency Pr) Accents Pubns.

— Russian Nationalism & the New Foreign Policy. (Former Soviet South Ser.). 60p. 1997. pap. 12.95 (*1-86203-050-2*, Pub. by Royal Inst Intl Affairs) Brookings.

— Winemaking with Concentrates. (Illus.). 96p. (Orig.). 1995. pap. 14.95 (*1-85486-118-2*, Pub. by Nexus Special Interests) Trans-Atl Phila.

Duncan, Peter, jt. auth. see Acton, Bryan.

Duncan, Peter J. Sosa. 224p. 1998. pap. 5.99 (*0-684-86342-1*) S&S Trade.

Duncan, Peter J. The Soviet Union & India. (Chatham House Papers on Foreign Policy). (Orig.). 1989. pap. write for info. (*0-415-00212-5*) Routledge.

Duncan, Peter J., jt. ed. see Pravda, Alex.

Duncan Peterson Publishing Ltd. Staff. The Book of Rules: A Visual Guide to the Laws of Every Commonly Played Sport & Game. Paluch, Mark, ed. LC 98-24910. (Illus.). 223p. 1998. 24.95 (*0-8160-3919-4*, Checkmark) Facts on File.

Duncan Ph.D, William A. 1994 Essentials with CPE. 94th ed. (C). 1994. pap. text 59.00 (*0-15-602249-4*) Harcourt Coll Pubs.

***Duncan, Phil.** Basic Blues Harp. 32p. 2000. pap. 5.95 (*0-7866-5078-8*, 98584BCD) Mel Bay.

— Basic Chromatic Harmonica. 32p. 2000. pap. 5.95 incl. audio compact disk (*0-7866-5080-X*, 98586BCD) Mel Bay.

Duncan, Phil. Bluegrass & Country Music for Harmonica. 56p. 1997. 17.95 incl. audio compact disk (*0-7866-2873-1*, 93990BCD) Mel Bay.

— Blues Harp. 84p. 1982. pap. 9.95 (*0-87166-890-4*, 93814) Mel Bay.

Duncan, Phil. Blues Harp. 84p. 1982. pap. 17.95 incl. audio (*0-7866-0939-7*, 93814P) Mel Bay.

Duncan, Phil. Blues Harp. 1985. audio 9.98 (*1-56222-355-0*, 93814C) Mel Bay.

— Blues Harp. 1995. vdisk 24.95 (*0-7866-0464-6*, 93814VX) Mel Bay.

— Blues Harp. 84p. 1996. pap., spiral bd. 17.95 incl. audio compact disk (*0-7866-2855-3*, 93814BCD) Mel Bay.

Duncan, Phil. Christmas Songs for Harmonica. 48p. 1996. pap. 15.95 incl. audio compact disk (*0-7866-2638-0*, 95156BCD) Mel Bay.

— Chromatic Harmonica: Beginning Level. 32p. 1997. pap. 0.95 (*0-7866-2456-6*, 96291) Mel Bay.

— Chromatic Harmonica Solos. 76p. 1996. pap. 18.95 incl. audio compact disk (*0-7866-0327-5*, 95404BCD) Mel Bay.

Duncan, Phil. Complete Chromatic Harmonica Method. 120p. 1983. pap. 11.95 (*0-87166-831-9*, 93890) Mel Bay.

Duncan, Phil. Complete Chromatic Harmonica Method. 120p. 1983. spiral bd. 26.95 incl. audio compact disk (*0-7866-1839-6*, 93890) Mel Bay.

Duncan, Phil. Complete Chromatic Harmonica Method. 1995. vdisk 24.95 (*0-7866-0815-3*, 93890VX) Mel Bay.

— Complete Chromatic Harmonica Method. 1996. audio compact disk 15.98 (*0-7866-1838-8*, 93890CD) Mel Bay.

— Deluxe Harmonica Method. 1981. pap. 9.95 (*0-87166-382-1*, 93737); audio 9.98 (*0-87166-383-X*, 93737C) Mel Bay.

Duncan, Phil. Deluxe Harmonica Method. 112p. 1981. pap. 24.95 incl. audio compact disk (*0-7866-0602-9*, 93737CDP) Mel Bay.

Duncan, Phil. Deluxe Harmonica Method. 1993. 17.95 incl. audio (*0-87166-384-8*, 93737P); audio compact disk 15.98 (*0-7866-0601-0*, 93737CD) Mel Bay.

— Deluxe Harmonica Method. 1994. vdisk 19.95 (*0-7866-0182-5*, 93737VX) Mel Bay.

— Easiest Blues Harp Book. 24p. 1991. pap. 3.95 (*1-56222-303-8*, 94673) Mel Bay.

***Duncan, Phil.** Favorite Harmonica Songs. 32p. 2000. pap. 5.95 (*0-7866-5079-6*, 98585BCD) Mel Bay.

— Great Hits for Harmonica. 76p. 1996. pap. 9.95 (*0-7866-0328-3*, 95405); pap. 18.95 incl. audio (*0-7866-1318-1*, 95405P) Mel Bay.

— Harmonicare Chart. 4p. 1992. pap. 3.95 (*1-56222-351-8*, 94752) Mel Bay.

Duncan, Phil. Hymns for Harmonica. 112p. 1982. spiral bd. 8.95 (*0-87166-691-X*, 93861) Mel Bay.

***Duncan, Phil.** Irish Melodies for Harmonica. 152p. 1998. pap. 22.95 incl. audio compact disk (*0-7866-2920-7*, 96656BCD) Mel Bay.

Duncan, Phil. Jazz Harp. 84p. 1997. spiral bd. 17.95 incl. audio compact disk (*0-7866-3091-4*, 94058BCD) Mel Bay.

— You Can Teach Yourself Blues Harp. 84p. 1992. pap. 9.95 (*1-56222-309-7*, 94698); audio 9.98 (*1-56222-330-5*, 94698C) Mel Bay.

Duncan, Phil. You Can Teach Yourself Blues Harp. 84p. 1992. pap. 17.95 (*0-7866-4405-2*, 94698BCD) Mel Bay.

Duncan, Phil. You Can Teach Yourself Blues Harp. 1993. 24.95 incl. audio compact disk (*0-7866-1095-6*, 94698CDP); pap. 18.95 incl. audio (*1-56222-517-0*, 94698P); audio compact disk 15.98 (*0-7866-0384-4*, 94698CD) Mel Bay.

— You Can Teach Yourself Blues Harp. 1995. VHS 24.95 (*0-7866-0172-8*, 94698VX) Mel Bay.

Duncan, Phil, et al, eds. Politics in America 1996. LC 93-11559. 1541p. 1995. pap. 54.95 (*0-87187-844-5*) Congr Quarterly.

Duncan, Phil & Musselwhite, Charlie. Power Harp. 96p. 1997. spiral bd. 19.95 incl. cd-rom (*0-7866-2875-8*, 94359BCD) Mel Bay.

Duncan, Phil, ed. see CQ Inc. Staff.

Duncan, Phil, jt. ed. see Lawrence, Christine C.

Duncan, Philip D., et al, eds. Politics in America 1996. LC 93-11559. 1541p. 1995. 89.95 (*0-87187-843-7*) Congr Quarterly.

Duncan, Philip D. & Nutting, Brian, eds. Politics in America 2000: The 106th Congress. 1650p. 1999. 98.95 (*1-56802-470-3*); pap. 55.95 (*1-56802-471-1*) CQ Pr.

Duncan, Phillip K., ed. Current Topics in Organizational Behavior Management. LC 82-11685. (Journal of Organizational Behavior Management: Vol. 3, No. 3). 111p. 1982. text 39.95 (*0-86656-198-6*) Haworth Pr.

Duncan, R., ed. Militant Workers: Labour & Class Conflict on the Clyde, 1900-1950. 200p. (C). 1989. pap. 30.00 (*0-7855-6974-X*, Pub. by J Donald) St Mut.

— SPECT Imaging of the Brain. LC 96-28961. (Developments in Nuclear Medicine Ser.). 260p. (C). 1997. text 169.00 (*0-7923-4186-4*) Kluwer Academic.

Duncan, R. & McIvor, A. Militant Workers: Labour & Class Conflict on the Clyde, 1900-1950. 200p. (C). 1996. pap. 30.00 (*0-85976-373-0*, Pub. by J Donald) St Mut.

Duncan, R. & Weston-Smith, Miranda. Encyclopedia of Ignorance: Everything You Ever Wanted to Know about the Unknown. LC 77-30376. 1977. reprint ed. 204.00 (*0-08-021238-7*, Pub. by Pergamon Repr) Franklin.

Duncan, R. & Weston-Smith, Miranda, eds. The Encyclopaedia of Medical Ignorance: The Mind & Body in Health & Disease. LC 83-4785. (Illus.). 240p. 1984. 114.00 (*0-08-024515-3*, 37, Pub. by Pergamon Repr) Franklin.

— The Encyclopedia of Ignorance, Vol. 1 & 2. 1978. 21.00 (*0-685-04001-1*, Pergamon Pr) Elsevier.

Duncan, R., jt. auth. see Parry, Martin.

Duncan, R., ed. see Krapiec, Mieczyslaw A.

***Duncan, R. Bruce.** CFIDs, Fibromyalgia & the Virus-Allergy Link: Hidden Viruses, Allergies, & Uncommon Fatigue/Pain Disorders. LC 00-22098. (Illus.). 340p. 2000. pap. 39.95 (*0-7890-1073-9*, Hawrth Medical); lib. bdg. 79.95 (*0-7890-1072-0*, Hawrth Medical) Haworth Pr.

Duncan, R. M. & Roberts, D. Legal Studies for New South Wales. 2nd ed. 504p. 1992. pap. 47.00 (*0-409-30432-8*, Austral, MICHIE) LEXIS Pub.

Duncan, R. M., ed. see Sender, Ramon J.

***Duncan, R. R. & Carrow, R. N.** Seashore Paspalum: The Environmental Turfgrass. LC 99-87984. (Illus.). 175p. 2000. 65.00 (*1-57504-141-3*, Ann Arbor Press) Sleeping Bear.

Duncan, R. S. Duncan Family Register of Lewis Duncan & Harriet Kinnaird, His Wife, with Numerous Biographical Sketches. (Illus.). 88p. 1997. reprint ed. pap. 17.00 (*0-8328-8372-7*); reprint ed. lib. bdg. 27.00 (*0-8328-8371-9*) Higginson Bk Co.

Duncan, Ralph & Wren, James E. Electrical Wiring. 7th ed. LC 99-461913. (Illus.). 262p. 1999. pap. text 32.95 (*0-89606-351-8*) Am Assn Voc Materials.

***Duncan, Ray H.** The MLM Binary Plan: A Comprehensive Look at Network Marketing's Most Controversial. Duncan, Joy R., ed. (Illus.). 64p. 1999. 9.95 (*1-929746-01-6*) Double Dia.

— The MLM Road Map: A Step-by-Step System of Building a Network Marketing Dowline. Duncan, Joy R., ed. (Illus.). 128p. 1999. 19.95 (*1-929746-00-8*) Double Dia.

Duncan, Rea L. Down to Earth: Wisdom, Wit & Great Advice from a Connecticut Garden. 160p. 1995. pap. 14.95 (*0-9648033-0-5*) CT Mag.

Duncan, Richard, ed. Agricultural Futures & Options: A Guide to Using North American & European Markets. (Illus.). 240p. 1992. 185.00 (*1-85573-075-8*, Pub. by Woodhead Pubng) Am Educ Systs.

Duncan, Richard F. & Lyons, William H. The Law & Practice of Secured Transactions: Working with Article 9. LC 87-3695. 450p. 1987. ring bd. 55.00 (*0-318-22530-1*, 00603) Law Journal.

Duncan, Richard F. & Lyons, William H. The Law & Practice of Secured Transactions: Working with Article 9. 450p. 1987. ring bd. 95.00 (*0-318-23684-2*) NY Law Pub.

Duncan, Richard R. Lee's Endangered Left. LC 98-33689. (Illus.). 400p. 1998. 29.95 (*0-8071-2291-2*) La State U Pr.

Duncan, Richard R., compiled by. Theses & Dissertations on Virginia History: A Bibliography. ix, 217p. 1986. pap. 10.00 (*0-88490-136-X*) Library of VA.

Duncan, Richard R., ed. Alexander Neil & the Last Shenandoah Valley Campaign: Letters of an Army Surgeon to His Family, 1864. LC 96-26375. (Illus.). 140p. 1996. 19.95 (*0-942597-95-8*) White Mane Pub.

Duncan, Robert. Architectural Graphics & Communication. 3rd ed. 268p. 1996. pap., per. 38.95 (*0-7872-2037-X*, 41203701) Kendall-Hunt.

— Architectural Graphics & Communication Problems. 3rd ed. 324p. (C). 1996. spiral bd. 40.95 (*0-7872-2163-5*, 41216301) Kendall-Hunt.

— Bending the Bow. LC 68-15879. 1968. pap. 9.95 (*0-8112-0033-7*, NDP255, Pub. by New Directions) Norton.

Duncan, Robert. The Cruising Guide to the New England Coast. 12th ed. 49.95 (*0-393-04858-6*) Norton.

Duncan, Robert. Faust Foutu: A Comic Masque By Robert Dunkan. LC 85-14833. (Illus.). 96p. 1985. reprint ed. pap. write for info. (*0-88268-019-6*) Station Hill Pr.

— Fictive Certainties. LC 85-11417. 320p. 1985. 9.95 (*0-8112-0944-X*, Pub. by New Directions) Norton.

— Ground Work: Before the War. LC 84-4889. 192p. 1984. pap. 10.95 (*0-8112-0896-6*, NDP571, Pub. by New Directions) Norton.

— Ground Work II: In The Dark. LC 87-1103. 1988. 19.95 (*0-8112-1041-3*, Pub. by New Directions) Norton.

— Ground Work II: In The Dark. LC 87-1103. Vol. 647. 90p. 1988. pap. 9.95 (*0-8112-1042-1*, NDP647, Pub. by New Directions) Norton.

— A Little Endarkenment, & in My Poetry You Will Find Me. 48p. 1997. 7.00 (*1-887289-23-2*) Rodent Pr.

— The Opening of the Field. rev. ed. LC 72-93976. 96p. 1973. pap. 6.95 (*0-8112-0480-4*, NDP356, Pub. by New Directions) Norton.

— Roots & Branches. LC 64-24233. 1969. reprint ed. pap. 9.95 (*0-8112-0034-5*, NDP275, Pub. by New Directions) Norton.

— Selected Poems. Bertholf, Robert J., ed. LC 92-35812. 160p. 1993. 22.95 (*0-8112-1227-0*, Pub. by New Directions) Norton.

— Selected Poems: Revised & Enlarged. 2nd enl. rev. ed. Bertholf, Robert J., ed. LC 96-43881. (New Directions Paperbook Ser.). 192p. 1997. pap. 12.95 (*0-8112-1345-5*, NDP838, Pub. by New Directions) Norton.

— A Selected Prose. Bertholf, Robert J., ed. LC 94-12983. 208p. 1995. 24.95 (*0-8112-1278-5*, Pub. by New Directions) Norton.

— Writing, Writing. (Orig.). 1971. pap. 5.00 (*0-932264-15-8*) Trask Hse Bks.

— The Years As Catches. 1977. 3.00 (*0-685-80007-5*) Oyez.

Duncan, Robert & Rea, David, eds. Synthesis of Results from Scientific Drilling in the Indian Ocean. LC 92-34422. (Geophysical Monograph Ser.: Vol. 70). 1993. 48.00 (*0-87590-822-5*) Am Geophysical.

Duncan, Robert B., text. Cutwater: Speedboats & Launches from the Golden Days of Boating. (Illus.). 160p. 1993. 29.95 (*1-879301-04-0*) Top Ten Pub.

Duncan, Robert C., et al. Introductory Biostatistics for the Health Sciences. 2nd ed. LC 82-23822. 249p. (C). 1989. mass mkt. 35.50 (*0-8273-4230-6*) Delmar.

Duncan, Robert E., ed. see Farmer, Charles K.

Duncan, Robert E., ed. see Goetz, G. D.

Duncan, Robert E., ed. see Maya.

Duncan, Robert G., ed. see Marder, William & Marder, Estelle.

Duncan, Robert L., jt. auth. see Hobbs, Jack A.

Duncan, Roderic. How to Sue for up to $25,000...& Win! Suing & Defending a Case in Municipal Court Without a Lawyer. 2nd ed. Elias, Steve & Leonard, Robin, eds. LC 96-15517. (Illus.). 368p. 1997. reprint ed. pap. 29.95 (*0-87337-344-8*) Nolo com.

Duncan, Roderic & Siegel, Warren. How to Change Child Support in California. 4th ed. LC 97-30723. (Illus.). 368p. 1998. 19.95 (*0-87337-421-5*) Nolo com.

***Duncan, Roderic & Siegel, Warren.** How to Raise or Lower Child Support in California. 5th ed. LC 99-40252. 2000. pap. 24.95 (*0-87337-555-6*) Nolo com.

Duncan, Roger. Eastward: A Maine Cruise in a Friendship Sloop. 210p. 1995. 10.95 (*0-942396-73-1*) Blackberry ME.

Duncan, Roger F. Coastal Maine: A Maritime History. 540p. 1992. 39.95 (*0-393-03048-2*) Norton.

***Duncan, Roger F.** Dorothy Elizabeth: Building a Traditional Wooden Schooner. (Illus.). 2000. 27.95 (*0-393-04904-3*) Norton.

Duncan, Roger F., et al. The Cruising Guide to the New England Coast: Including the Hudson River, Long Island Sound, & the Coast of New Brunswick. (Illus.). 750p. 1995. 45.00 (*0-393-03639-1*) Norton.

Duncan, Ronald C., jt. ed. see Claessens, Stijn.

Duncan, Ronald Frederick Henry. Collected Plays. 368p. 1971. 19.95 (*0-246-64004-9*) Boulevard.

— The Perfect Mistress: And Other Stories. LC 76-465470. 143 p. (J). 1969. write for info. (*0-246-98564-X*) Grfton HrprCllns.

Duncan, Ronald Frederick Henry, ed. Writings of Gandhi. (C). 1993. text 9.00 (*0-8364-2890-0*, Pub. by Rupa) S Asia.

Duncan, Ronald J. The Ceramics of Raquira, Colombia: Gender, Work, & Economic Change. LC 98-11727. (Illus.). 304p. 1998. 49.95 (*0-8130-1615-0*) U Press Fla.

***Duncan, Ronald J.** Crafts, Capitalism & Women: The Potters of la Chamba, Colombia. (Illus.). 280p. 2000. 59.95 (*0-8130-1774-2*) U Press Fla.

Duncan, Ronald J., ed. Investigacion Social en Puerto Rico. LC 80-23445. 289p. 1980. pap. 8.00 (*0-913480-44-4*); text 13.00 (*0-913480-45-2*) Inter Am U Pr.

— Social Research in Puerto Rico: Science, Humanism & Society. LC 83-12635. 255p. 1984. pap. 8.00 (*0-913480-57-6*) Inter Am U Pr.

Duncan, Ronald J., et al. Manual de Tecnicas de Investigacion Social. LC 80-23411. (Illus.). 73p. 1980. 5.00 (*0-913480-46-0*) Inter Am U Pr.

Duncan, Ronny R., jt. auth. see Carrow, Robert N.

Duncan-Rose, Caroline, et al, eds. On Language Rhetorica, Phonologica, Syntactica: A Festschrift for Robert P. Stockwell from His Friends & Colleagues. 520p. 1988. lib. bdg. 89.95 (*0-415-00312-1*) Routledge.

Duncan, Russell. Freedom's Shore: Tunis Campbell & the Georgia Freedmen. LC 86-6914. (Brown Thrasher Bks.). (Illus.). 175p. 1986. pap. 14.95 (*0-8203-0905-2*) U of Ga Pr.

***Duncan, Russell.** Where Death & Glory Meet: Colonel Robert Gould Shaw & the 54th Massachusetts Infantry. LC 99-28857. (Illus.). 163p. 1999. 35.00 (*0-8203-2135-4*); pap. 15.95 (*0-8203-2136-2*) U of Ga Pr.

Duncan, Russell, ed. Blue-Eyed Child of Fortune: The Civil War Letters of Colonel Robert Gould Shaw. xxxii, 448p. 1994. pap. 12.50 (*0-380-72168-6*, Avon Bks) Morrow Avon.

— Blue-Eyed Child of Fortune: The Civil War Letters of Colonel Robert Gould Shaw. LC 91-46644. (Illus.). 448p. 1992. 29.95 (*0-8203-1459-5*) U of Ga Pr.

Duncan, Russell, jt. ed. see Morton, Marian J.

Duncan, Russell, ed. see Shaw, Robert G.

Duncan, S. Blackwell. Basic Woodturning: A Layman's Introduction & Guide. (Illus.). 320p. 1986. 24.95 (*0-671-61367-7*) P-H.

— Build Your Own Log Home from Scratch. 2nd ed. (Illus.). 352p. 1988. 25.95 (*0-8306-9481-1*, 3081); pap. 16.95 (*0-8306-9081-6*, 3081) McGraw-Hill Prof.

— The Essence of the United States. (Orig.). 1997. pap. 9.95 (*0-9642409-1-2*) Wstrn Research.

— Small-Scale Model Railroads. (Illus.). 160p. 1990. pap. 12.95 (*0-8306-3518-1*, 3518) McGraw-Hill Prof.

— Whole House Remodeling Guide. (Illus.). 340p. 1989. 28.95 (*0-8306-9281-9*); pap. 19.95 (*0-8306-3281-6*) McGraw-Hill Prof.

Duncan, Sally J., jt. auth. see Cleary, Barbara A.

Duncan, Sara Jeannette, pseud. The Imperialist. 320p. 1996. pap. 8.95 (*0-7710-9978-9*) McCland & Stewart.

— Set in Authority. Warkentin, Germaine, ed. 250p. 1995. pap. 12.95 (*1-55111-080-6*) Broadview Pr.

Duncan, Seymour W. Seymour Duncan's Guide to Guitar Electronics. (Illus.). 300p. (Orig.). 1997. pap. 29.95 (*1-884883-07-9*) Vintage Guitar.

An Asterisk (*) at the beginning of an entry indicates that the title is appearing for the first time.

Duncan, Simon & Edwards, Rosalind, eds. Single Mothers in International Context: Mothers or Workers? LC 97-3476. (Gender & Society Ser.). 176p. 1997. 69.95 (*0-7484-0363-9*, Pub. by Tay Francis Ltd); pap. 22.95 (*0-7484-0364-7*, Pub. by Tay Francis Ltd) Taylor & Francis.

— Single Mothers in International Contexts: Mothers or Workers? LC 97-3476. (Feminist Perspectives on the Past & Present Ser.). 285p. 1997. pap. 24.95 (*1-85728-791-6*, Pub. by UCL Pr Ltd) Taylor & Francis.

Duncan, Simon, jt. auth. see Barlow, James.

Duncan, Sondra, jt. ed. see Geiger, Peter.

Duncan, Starkey & Fiske, Donald W. Face-to-Face Interaction: Research, Methods & Theory. LC 77-1841. 377p. reprint ed. pap. 116.90 (*0-7837-1211-1*, 204174300023) Bks Demand.

Duncan, Stephen. Citizen Warriors: America's National Guard & Reserve Forces & the Politics of National Security. LC 96-42301. 432p. 1997. 24.95 (*0-89141-609-9*) Presidio Pr.

Duncan, Stephen F. A Genre in Hindusthani Music (Bhajans) As Used in the Roman Catholic Church, No.12. LC 98-47116. (Roman Catholic Studies). 152p. 1998. 69.95 (*0-7734-8273-3*) E Mellen.

Duncan, Steven M. A Primer of Modern Virtue Ethics. 124p. (Orig.). (C). 1995. pap. text 17.50 (*0-8191-9875-7*) U Pr of Amer.

Duncan, Susan. Joey Moses. (Illus.). 96p. (J). (gr. 5-8). 1998. pap. 10.95 (*1-880812-28-2*) S Ink WA.

Duncan, Susan Kirsch. Levittown: The Way We Were. (Illus.). 112p. 1999. pap. 10.95 (*0-930545-18-4*) Maple Hill Pr.

Duncan, T. Exploring Physics, Vol. 1. (gr. 11-12). pap. text 7.50 (*0-7195-2043-6*) Transatl Arts.

Duncan, T. Gcse Physics. 3rd ed. text 29.95 (*0-7195-5301-6*, Pub. by John Murray) Trafalgar.

Duncan, T. Bentley. Atlantic Islands: Madeira, the Azores, & the Cape Verdes in Seventeenth-Century Commerce & Navigation. LC 72-80157. (Studies in the History of Discoveries). (Illus.). 320p. (C). 1972. lib. bdg. 25.00 (*0-226-17001-2*) U Ch Pr.

Duncan, T. E. & Pasik-Duncan, B., eds. Stochastic Theory & Adaptive Control. LC 92-27045. (Lecture Notes in Control & Information Sciences: Vol. 184). 1992. 133.95 (*0-387-55962-0*) Spr-Verlag.

Duncan, T. Michael. A Compilation of Chemical Shift Tensors. 2nd rev. ed. (Illus.). 200p. (C). 1996. text 39.95 (*0-917903-11-0*); pap. text 24.95 (*0-917903-14-5*) Farragut Pr.

Duncan, T. Michael & Reimer, Jeffrey A. Chemical Engineering Design & Analysis: An Introduction. LC 98-16452. (Cambridge Series in Chemical Engineering). (Illus.). 338p. (C). 1998. text 80.00 (*0-521-63041-X*); pap. text 34.95 (*0-521-63956-5*) Cambridge U Pr.

Duncan, Terence. Powell's Army No. 1: Unchained Lightning. 224p. 1987. mass mkt. 2.50 (*0-8217-1994-7*, Zebra Kensgtn) Kensgtn Pub Corp.

— Powell's Army No. 2: Apache Raiders. 224p. 1987. mass mkt. 2.50 (*0-8217-2073-2*, Zebra Kensgtn) Kensgtn Pub Corp.

Duncan, Terry E., et al. An Introduction to Latent Variable Growth Modeling: Concepts, Issues & Applications. LC 98-41005. (Quantitative Methodology Ser.). 208p. 1999. 45.00 (*0-8058-3060-X*) L Erlbaum Assocs.

Duncan, Theodore G. Over 55: A Handbook on Health. 668p. 1982. 99.95 (*0-89859-726-9*) L Erlbaum Assocs.

Duncan, Thom. Moroni Smith: In the Land of Zarahemla. 167p. 1991. pap. 10.98 (*0-88290-415-9*) Horizon Utah.

— Novell Netware Lite: Simplified Network Solutions: A Practical Guide to Installing & Running a Peer-to-Peer Local Area Network. (Illus.). 272p. 1992. pap. 24.95 (*1-55958-186-7*) Prima Pub.

— Thom Duncan's Guide to Netware Shareware. LC 93-86994. 224p. 1994. pap. 29.95 (*1-55958-514-5*) Prima Pub.

Duncan, Thomas. A Taxonomic Study of the Ranunculus Hispidus Michaux Complex in the Western Hemisphere. LC 80-10493. (University of California Publications in Social Welfare: No. 77). (Illus.). 131p. reprint ed. pap. 40.70 (*0-608-18179-X*, 203289800081) Bks Demand.

Duncan, Thomas & Muvandi, Ityai. How Fast is Fertility Declining in Botswana & Zimbabwe. LC 94-29584. (Discussion Papers, 258, Africa Technical Department Ser.). 44p. 1994. pap. 22.00 (*0-8213-2993-6*, 12993) World Bank.

Duncan, Thomas R. Driving Brand Value: Using Integrated Marketing to Manage Profitable Shareholder Relationships. LC 97-1667. 1997. 24.95 (*0-7863-0822-2*, Irwn Prfssnl) McGraw-Hill Prof.

— How to Buy & Restore Wicker Furniture. LC 82-73902. (Illus.). 166p. 1983. pap. 15.95 (*0-9609480-1-5*); lib. bdg. 22.95 (*0-9609480-0-7*) Sylvan Bks.

***Duncan, Todd.** Closing the Gap: Getting from Where You Are to Where You Want to Be. 2000. pap. 12.99 (*0-8499-5597-1*) J Countryman.

Duncan, Todd. The Power! To Be Your Best! Creating & Maintaining the Life You Deserve. (Illus.). xxi, 337p. 1998. 24.95 (*0-9665134-0-1*) T Duncan Grp.

***Duncan, Todd.** The Power! To Be Your Best! Creating & Maintaining the Life You Deserve. LC 99-36581. 1999. 21.99 (*0-8499-1621-6*) Word Pub.

— Wealth: 9 1/2 Steps to Financial, Physical & Spiritual Abundance. 2000. write for info. (*0-8499-1653-4*) Word Pub.

Duncan, Tom, et al. Alaska Place Names Pronunciation Guide. LC 76-620956. (Elmer E. Rasmuson Library Occasional Papers: No. 4). 29p. 1975. pap. text 2.00 (*0-937592-00-5*) U Alaska Rasmuson Lib.

Duncan, Tom, jt. auth. see Moriarty, Sandra.

Duncan, Veronica. Towards Achieving Maat: Communication Patterns in African Americans. 274p. (C). 1998. per. 44.95 (*0-7872-5396-0*, 41539601) Kendall-Hunt.

Duncan, W., ed. Paediatric Oncology. (Recent Results in Cancer Research Ser.: Vol. 88). (Illus.). 170p. 1983. 76.00 (*0-387-12349-0*) Spr-Verlag.

Duncan, W. & Traves, S. Due Diligence. 1995. 110.00 (*0-455-21333-X*, Pub. by LawBk Co); pap. 85.00 (*0-455-21332-1*, Pub. by LawBk Co) Gaunt.

Duncan, W. D. Commercial Leases. xxxviii, 239p. 1989. 43.50 (*0-455-20918-9*, Pub. by LawBk Co) Gaunt.

— Commercial Leases. 2nd ed. 1993. 60.00 (*0-455-21184-1*, Pub. by LawBk Co) Gaunt.

— Commercial Leases in Australia. 3rd ed. LC 98-213252. 349 p. 1998. write for info. (*0-455-21579-0*) LawBk Co.

— Real Estate Agency Law in Queensland. 2nd ed. xxx, 348p. 1990. pap. 49.00 (*0-455-21009-8*, Pub. by LawBk Co) Gaunt.

Duncan, W. D., ed. Commercial & Property Law: Australian Studies in Law. 216p. 1991. 58.00 (*1-86287-068-3*, Pub. by Federation Pr) Gaunt.

— Joint Ventures Law in Australia. 467p. 1994. 79.00 (*1-86287-126-4*, Pub. by Federation Pr) Gaunt.

Duncan, W. D. & Weld, H. A. The Standard Land Contract in Queensland. 3rd ed. c, 370p. 1990. pap. 65.00 (*0-455-20952-9*, Pub. by LawBk Co) Gaunt.

Duncan, W. D. & Willmott, Lindy. Mortgages Law in Australia. 2nd ed. 432p. 1996. pap. 50.00 (*1-86287-193-0*, Pub. by Federation Pr) Gaunt.

— Real & Personal Securities. 294p. 1990. pap. 53.00 (*1-86287-035-7*, Pub. by Federation Pr) Gaunt.

Duncan, W. D., jt. auth. see Christensen, S. A.

Duncan, W. Jack. Management: Ideas & Actions. LC 98-15512. 288p. (C). 1999. text 65.00 (*0-19-511846-4*); pap. text 39.95 (*0-19-511847-2*) OUP.

Duncan, W. Jack, et al, eds. Handbook of Healthcare Management. LC 97-13926. 610p. 1997. text 89.95 (*1-55786-833-6*) Blackwell Pubs.

Duncan, W. Jack, et al. Strategic Management of Health Care Organizations. 3rd ed. LC 97-12153. (Illus.). 960p. 1997. text 79.95 (*1-55786-968-5*) Blackwell Pubs.

Duncan, W. Raymond. The Soviet Union & Cuba: Interests & Influences. Rubinstein, Alvin Z., ed. LC 84-26296. 240p. 1985. 55.00 (*0-275-90088-6*, C0088, Praeger Pubs); pap. 15.95 (*0-275-91662-6*, B1662, Praeger Pubs) Greenwood.

Duncan, Walter J. Color Doppler in Clinical Cardiology. (Illus.). 176p. (C). 1988. text 155.00 (*0-03-014267-9*, Pub. by SCP) Harcourt.

Duncan, Wendy A. Engendering School Learning: Science, Attitudes & Achievement among Girls & Boys in Botswana. (Studies in Comparative Education: No. 16). xvi, 222p. (Orig.). 1989. pap. 65.50 (*91-7146-754-8*) Coronet Bks.

***Duncan, Wilbur H.** Trees of the Southeastern United States. (Illus.). 336p. 2000. pap. 22.95 (*0-8203-2271-7*) U of Ga Pr.

Duncan, Wilbur H. & Duncan, Marion B. The Smithsonian Guide to Seaside Plants of the Gulf & Atlantic Coast: From Louisiana to Massachusetts, Exclusive of Lower Peninsular Florida. LC 85-22095. (Illus.). 410p. 1987. pap. 29.95 (*0-87474-387-7*) Smithsonian.

— Wildflowers of the Eastern United States. LC 98-43314. (Wormsloe Foundation Publications). (Illus.). 380p. 1999. 29.95 (*0-8203-2107-9*) U of Ga Pr.

Duncan, Wilbur H. & Kartesz, John T. Vascular Flora of Georgia: An Annotated Checklist. LC 80-22014. 158p. (C). 1981. pap. 17.00 (*0-8203-0538-3*) U of Ga Pr.

Duncan, William. Substantial Rehab - New Construction No. 3: Housing Production Manual. Cashman, Jude & Werwath, Peter, eds. (Housing Production Manuals Ser.). 1990. student ed. 35.00 (*0-942901-04-5*) Enterprise Fnd.

Duncan, William J., ed. Miscellaneous Papers, Principally Illustrative of Events in the Reigns of Queen Mary & King James Sixth. LC 79-164807. (Maitland Club, Glasgow. Publications: No. 26). reprint ed. 32.50 (*0-404-52981-X*) AMS Pr.

— Notices & Documents Illustrative of the Literary History of Glasgow During the Greater Part of Last Century. (Maitland Club, Glasgow. Publications: No. 14). reprint ed. 41.50 (*0-404-52947-X*) AMS Pr.

***Duncan-Williams, Nicholas.** Birthing the Promises of God in Trevail. 3rd ed. (It Is Time to Pray Ser.). Orig. Title: Taking the Promises of God in Battle. 112p. 1999. reprint ed. pap. 10.00 (*1-929533-00-4*, 01BH-00799) Bishop Hse.

— Born with a Destiny. 2nd ed. Orig. Title: You Are Destined to Succeed!. 174p. 1999. reprint ed. pap. 10.00 (*1-929533-01-2*, 01BH-00800) Bishop Hse.

***Duncanson, Joann Snow.** Who Gets the Yellow Bananas? And Other Wry Thoughts on the Human Condition. LC 99-87047. 160p. 2000. pap. 14.95 (*0-914339-83-4*, Pub. by P E Randall Pub) U Pr of New Eng.

Duncanson, Michael E. Best Canoe Trails of Southern Wisconsin. rev. ed. LC 74-77134. (Illus.). 68p. 1995. pap. 12.95 (*0-915024-44-6*) Trails Media.

***Duncanson, Neil.** Sexual Bullying. 224p. (C). 1999. text 75.00 (*0-415-21372-X*) Routledge.

— Sexual Bullying: Gender Conflict & Pupil Culture in Secondary Schools. LC 98-33129. 1999. pap. 24.99 (*0-415-19113-0*) Routledge.

Dunccan, Phil. Complete Harmonica Book. (Complete Book). 240p. 1992. pap. 19.95 (*1-56222-280-5*, 94713); audio 9.98 (*1-56222-339-9*, 94713C) Mel Bay.

— Complete Harmonica Book. (Complete Book). 1993. pap. 26.95 incl. audio (*0-7866-1101-4*, 94713P) Mel Bay.

Dunckel, Jacqueline. Keeping Customers Happy: Strategies for Success. 3rd ed. 200p. 1994. pap. 9.95 (*0-88908-790-3*) Self-Counsel Pr.

Dunckel, Mona. Escape. LC 98-35287. (Illus.). 101p. (J). 1999. pap. 6.49 (*1-57924-068-2*) Bob Jones Univ.

Duncker, Alfred P., jt. ed. see Ory, Marcia G.

***Duncker, Arne.** Hans Kohlhase: Die Geschichte einer Fehde in Sachsen und Brandenburg zur Zeit der Reformation. (Rechtshistorische Reihe Ser.). 564p. 1999. 79.95 (*3-631-34694-8*) P Lang Pubng.

Duncker, H. R. & Fleischer, G., eds. Functional Morphology of Vertebrates. LC 85-17538. 752p. 1985. 175.00 (*0-89574-207-1*, Pub. by Gustav Fischer) Balogh.

Duncker, Henrick. Hay on the Highway. 1996. 34.95 (*952-90-4830-0*) Finnish State.

Duncker, Karl. On Problem-Solving. Lees, Lynne S., tr. LC 73-138621. (Illus.). 113p. 1972. reprint ed. lib. bdg. 35.00 (*0-8371-5733-1*, DUPS, Greenwood Pr) Greenwood.

***Duncker, Patricia.** The Doctor: A Novel. LC 99-57062. 384p. 2000. 24.00 (*0-06-019601-7*, Ecco Press) HarperTrade.

Duncker, Patricia. Hallucinating Foucault. LC 98-20941. 192p. 1998. pap. 12.00 (*0-375-70185-0*) Vin Bks.

— Hallucinating Foucault. 2nd ed. LC 96-35092. 192p. 1996. 21.00 (*0-88001-499-7*) HarpC.

— Monsieur Shoushana's lemon Trees. LC 97-31152. 1998. 22.95 (*0-88001-604-3*) HarpC.

Duncker, Patricia & Wilson, Vicky, eds. Cancer: Through the Eyes of Ten Women. LC 98-211628. 256p. 1996. 16.00 (*0-04-440980-X*, Pub. by Pandora) NYU Pr.

Dunckey, David D. Iowa Legal Forms: Residential Real Estate, 1982-1993. (Iowa Legal Forms Ser.). 400p. ring bd. 85.00 incl. disk (*0-685-49486-1*, MICHIE) LEXIS Pub.

— Iowa Legal Forms: Residential Real Estate, 1982-1993. (Iowa Legal Forms Ser.). 400p. 1989. suppl. ed. 15.00 (*0-88063-012-4*, MICHIE) LEXIS Pub.

— Iowa Legal Forms: Residential Real Estate, 1982-1993. (Iowa Legal Forms Ser.). 1993. suppl. ed. 28.50 (*0-685-74346-2*, MICHIE) LEXIS Pub.

Duncklee, A. M. Duncklee: Sketch of the Duncklee Family & a History of the Descendants of David Duncklee of Amherst, NH, & His Sister Hannah Duncklee Howe of Milford. 260p. 1993. reprint ed. pap. 39.50 (*0-8328-3666-4*); reprint ed. lib. bdg. 49.50 (*0-8328-3665-6*) Higginson Bk Co.

Duncklee, John. Coyotes I Have Known. LC 95-41766. 150p. 1996. 29.95 (*0-8165-1611-1*); pap. 15.95 (*0-8165-1614-6*) U of Ariz Pr.

***Duncklee, John.** Genevieve of Tombstone. 320p. 1999. pap. 4.99 (*0-8439-4628-8*, Leisure Bks); mass mkt. 4.99 Dorchester Pub Co.

Duncklee, John. Good Years for the Buzzards. LC 94-2451. 165p. 1994. 15.95 (*0-8165-1454-2*) U of Ariz Pr.

— Quest for the Eagle Feather. Max, Jill, ed. LC 97-8794. (Illus.). 112p. (J). (gr. 3-6). 1997. pap. 6.95 (*0-87358-657-3*, Rising Moon Bks) Northland AZ.

— Quest for the Eagle Feather. Max, Jill, ed. LC 97-8794. (Illus.). 104p. (J). (gr. 3-7). 1997. lib. bdg. 12.95 (*0-87358-668-9*, Rising Moon Bks) Northland AZ.

Duncombe, Alice E. Handbook for Telephone Ministry. 1975. spiral bd. 9.95 (*0-89985-110-X*) Christ for the Nations.

Duncombe, Charles. Duncombe's Free Banking: An Essay on Banking, Currency, Finance, Exchanges & Political Economy. LC 68-27852. (Library of Money & Banking History). 356p. 1969. reprint ed. 45.00 (*0-678-00530-3*) Kelley.

Duncombe, Giles. Trial per Pais: or The Law of England Concerning Juries by NisiPruis & C. Helmholz, R. H. & Reams, Bernard D., eds. LC 79-91755. 1997. reprint ed. 95.00 (*0-89941-041-3*, 311350) W S Hein.

Duncombe, John. The Feminiad: A Poem. LC 92-25464. (Augustan Reprints Ser.: No. 207). 1981. reprint ed. 14.50 (*0-404-70207-4*, PR3429) AMS Pr.

Duncombe, Raynor L., ed. Dynamics of the Solar System. (I.A.U. Symposia Ser.: No. 81). 1979. lib. bdg. 117.50 (*90-277-0976-9*) Kluwer Academic.

Duncombe, Raynor L., et al. The Stability of Planetary Systems: Reprinted from Celestial Mechanics Vol. 34, Nos. 1-4. 1985. text 293.00 (*90-277-1961-6*) Kluwer Academic.

Duncombe, Raynor L., ed. see Seidelmann, P. Kenneth.

Duncombe, Stephen. Notes from Underground: Zines & the Politics of Alternative Culture. LC 97-29603. 1997. pap. 19.00 (*1-85984-158-9*, Pub. by Verso) Norton.

Duncombe, William, jt. auth. see Bahl, Roy.

Duncraft Staff. Audubon Tips for Backyard Birdfeeding. Dunn, Sharon, ed. (Illus.). 24p. (Orig.). 1995. pap. 4.95 (*0-9647129-0-3*) Duncraft.

Dundas, Carl. Compendium of Election Laws, Practices & Cases of Selected Commonwealth Countries. 812p. 1996. pap. 99.95 (*0-85092-463-4*, Pub. by Comm Sec) Stylus Pub VA.

— Compendium of Election Laws, Practices & Cases of Selected Commonwealth Countries. 540p. 1998. pap. 99.95 (*0-85092-533-9*, Pub. by Comm Sec); pap. 99.95 (*0-85092-542-8*, Pub. by Comm Sec) Stylus Pub VA.

— Compendium of Election Laws, Practices & Cases of Selected Commonwealth Countries. 500p. 1998. pap. 99.95 (*0-85092-575-4*, Pub. by Comm Sec) Stylus Pub VA.

Dundas, Charles. African Crossroads. LC 76-45443. 242p. 1977. reprint ed. lib. bdg. 65.00 (*0-8371-9089-4*, DUAF, Greenwood Pr) Greenwood.

Dundas, Evalyn T. Symbols Come Alive in the Sand. (Illus.). 151p. 1989. pap. 16.95 (*0-904575-41-1*) Sigo Pr.

Dundas, Francis. Dundas - Hesselius. (Illus.). 122p. 1996. reprint ed. pap. 19.00 (*0-8328-5593-6*); reprint ed. lib. bdg. 29.00 (*0-8328-5592-8*) Higginson Bk Co.

Dundas, George, ed. see Virgil.

***Dundas, Glen.** Tangled up in Tapes: A Recording History of Bob Dylan. 1999. pap. 40.00 (*0-9698569-2-X*) SMA2 servs.

Dundas, James L. Cap Guns: With Values. LC 95-45515. (Collectors Bks.). (Illus.). 160p. 1996. pap. 29.95 (*0-88740-960-1*) Schiffer.

— Collecting Whistles. LC 95-21502. (Illus.). 128p. (Orig.). 1995. pap. 19.95 (*0-88740-859-1*) Schiffer.

***Dundas, James L.** Collecting Yo-Yos. (Illus.). 129p. 1999. pap. 16.95 (*0-7643-1010-0*) Schiffer.

Dundas, James L. Licensing Exams for Refrigeration, Air Conditioning, & Heating: 4000 Questions & Answers. rev. ed. LC 94-4632. 1994. 29.95 (*0-912524-89-8*) Busn News.

— Toys That Shoot & Other Neat Stuff. 112p. 1998. pap. 29.95 (*0-7643-0554-9*) Schiffer.

Dundas, Judith. Pencils Rhetorique: Renaissance Poets & the Art of Painting. LC 91-51090. 1993. 44.50 (*0-87413-459-5*) U Delaware Pr.

— The Spider & the Bee: The Artistry of Spenser's Faerie Queene. LC 83-18253. (Illus.). 248p. 1986. text 24.95 (*0-252-01118-X*) U of Ill Pr.

Dundas, Mamie. The Proof. 40p. 1986. 40.00 (*0-7223-1993-2*, Pub. by A H S Ltd) St Mut.

Dundas, Mary J., jt. auth. see Bohlman, Herbert M.

Dundas, Richard J. Twentieth Century Brass Musical Instruments in the United States LC 86-90264. x, 58 p. 1986. 9.95 (*0-9617093-0-8*) R J Dundas Pubns.

— Twentieth Century Brass Musical Instruments in the United States. 3rd rev. ed. LC 99-175864. (Illus.). 86p. (Orig.). 1998. reprint ed. pap. 12.50 (*0-9617093-1-6*) R J Dundas Pubns.

Dundas, Vince & Strong, George. Readers, Writers & Parents Learning Together. (Illus.). 140p. (C). 1991. ring bd. 295.00 (*1-878450-10-7*, 514) R Owen Pubs.

— Readers, Writers & Parents Learning Together: Parent Handbook, 5 vols., Set Only. 113p. (C). 1991. pap. text 59.00 (*1-878450-11-5*, 515) R Owen Pubs.

Dundass, Samuel R. & Keller, George. Crossing the Plains to California in 1849 & Crossing the Plains to California in 1850. 170p. 1983. 19.95 (*0-87770-291-8*) Ye Galleon.

Dundatscheck, Eric P. Sustineo Alas: Keep Them Flying. LC 93-90390. (Illus.). 275p. (Orig.). 1993. pap. 14.95 (*0-9636497-0-1*) Erisys.

Dunday, John, ed. see Rudolph, Thomas & Richmond, Floyd.

Dunde, Siegfried R. Woerterbuch der Religionspsychologie. (GER.). 368p. 1993. 125.00 (*0-7859-8445-3*, 3579002864) Fr & Eur.

Dundee Conference on Numerical Analysis Staff. Numerical Analysis, 1989: Proceedings of the 13th Dundee Conference, June 1989. Griffiths, D. F. & Watson, G. A., eds. LC 89-13163. (Pitman Research Notes in Mathematics Ser.: Vol. 228). 295p. 1990. reprint ed. pap. 91.50 (*0-608-03597-1*, 206442000009) Bks Demand.

Dundee, Harold A. & Rossman, Douglas E. Amphibians & Reptiles of Louisiana. LC 88-12873. (Illus.). 316p. (C). 1996. pap. 22.95 (*0-8071-2077-4*) La State U Pr.

Dundee, John G. Letters. Smythe, George, ed. LC 76-164808. (Bannatyne Club, Edinburgh. Publications: No. 15). reprint ed. 34.50 (*0-404-52715-9*) AMS Pr.

Dundee, Mark, jt. auth. see Meyen, Victor B.

Dundee, Mark W. Qualified Domestic Relations Order: Forms & Worksheets 2nd ed. LC 98-193442. (Panel Answer Bks). 1998. write for info. (*0-7355-0120-3*) Panel Pubs.

— Qualified Domestic Relations Order Answer Book: Forms & Worksheets. annuals LC 97-200589. 1560p. 1997. pap. 96.00 (*1-56706-381-0*, 63810) Panel Pubs.

Dundee, Wayne & Sublet, Jesse. Gryphon Double: Black Lake; The Teflon Babe, No. 2. 2nd ed. 416p. 1995. per. 12.00 (*0-614-06207-1*) Gryphon Pubns.

Dunderdale, J., ed. Energy & the Environment, No. 81. 1990. 127.00 (*0-85186-647-6*) CRC Pr.

Dundervill, Robert F., ed. Defense Conversion Strategies: Proceedings of the NATO Advanced Study Institute, Pitlochry, Perthshire, Scotland, U. K., July 2-14, 1995. LC 96-48875. (NATO Advanced Science Institutes Ser.). 644p. (C). 1997. lib. bdg. 360.50 (*0-7923-4364-6*) Kluwer Academic.

Dundes, Alan. Analytic Essays in Folklore. (Studies in Folklore: No. 2). 1975. pap. text 41.55 (*90-279-3231-X*) Mouton.

— Cinderella: A Casebook. LC 81-43334. (Folklore Casebks.). 331p. 1982. text 15.00 (*0-8240-9295-3*) Garland.

— Cinderella: A Casebook. LC 88-40186. 328p. (C). 1988. pap. text 19.95 (*0-299-11864-9*) U of Wis Pr.

— Folklore Matters. LC 88-32616. (C). 1993. pap. 15.00 (*0-87049-776-6*) U of Tenn Pr.

— Folklore Theses & Dissertations in the United States. LC 75-29244. (Publications of the American Folklore Society, Bibliographical & Special Ser.). 630p. reprint ed. pap. 195.30 (*0-8357-7737-5*, 203609400002) Bks Demand.

— From Game to War & Other Psychoanalytic Essays on Folklore. LC 97-19215. 160p. 1997. text 32.50 (*0-8131-2031-4*); pap. text 17.00 (*0-8131-0933-7*) U Pr of Ky.

— Holy Writ as Oral Lit: The Bible as Folklore. LC 98-42449. 176p. 1999. 55.00 (*0-8476-9197-7*) Rowman.

— Holy Writ As Oral Writ: The Bible As Folklore. LC 98-42449. 176p. 1999. pap. 15.95 (*0-8476-9198-5*, Pub. by Rowman) Natl Bk Netwk.

— Interpreting Folklore. LC 79-2969. 320p. 1980. pap. 14.95 (*0-253-20240-X*, MB-240) Ind U Pr.

— Life Is Like a Chicken Coop Ladder: A Study of German National Character Through Folklore. LC 88-27955. (Illus.). 192p. (C). 1989. reprint ed. pap. 15.95 (*0-8143-2038-4*) Wayne St U Pr.

— Parsing Through Customs: Essays by a Freudian Folklorist. LC 87-1675. 208p. (C). 1987. text 22.95 (*0-299-11260-8*) U of Wis Pr.

D

— Sometimes the Dragon Wins: Yet More Urban Folklore from the Paperwork Empire. LC 95-2880. (Illus.). 15p. 1996. 45.00 (*0-8156-2690-8*); pap. 19.95 (*0-8156-0371-1*) Syracuse U Pr.

— Two Tales of Crow & Sparrow: A Freudian Folkloristic Essay on Caste & Untouchability. LC 97-25277. 164p. 1997. 52.50 (*0-8476-8456-3*); pap. 18.95 (*0-8476-8457-1*) Rowman.

— The Vampire: A Casebook. LC 98-10399. 184p. 1998. 45.00 (*0-299-15920-5*); pap. 16.95 (*0-299-15924-8*) U of Wis Pr.

Dundes, Alan, ed. The Cockfight: A Casebook. LC 93-30545. 1994. 58.00 (*0-299-14050-4*); pap. 19.95 (*0-299-14054-7*) U of Wis Pr.

— The Evil Eye: A Casebook. LC 91-31862. 328p. (C). 1992. reprint ed. pap. 15.95 (*0-299-13334-6*); reprint ed. lib. bdg. 19.95 (*0-299-13330-3*) U of Wis Pr.

— International Folkloristics: Classic Contributions by the Founders of Folklore. LC 99-29463. 272p. 1999. pap. 22.95 (*0-8476-9515-8*); text 65.00 (*0-8476-9514-X*) Rowman.

— Mother Wit from the Laughing Barrel: Readings in the Interpretation of Afro-American Folklore. rev. ed. LC 90-40867. 640p. (C). 1991. reprint ed. pap. text 23.00 (*0-87805-478-2*) U Pr of Miss.

— Sacred Narrative: Reading in the Theory of Myth. LC 83-17921. (Illus.). 352p. 1984. pap. 19.95 (*0-520-05192-0*, Pub. by U CA Pr) Cal Prin Full Svc.

— Sacred Narrative: Readings in the Theory of Myth. LC 83-17921. (Illus.). 362p. reprint ed. pap. 112.30 (*0-7837-4817-5*, 204446400003) Bks Demand.

— Varia Folkloria. (World Anthropology Ser.). (Illus.). xii, 280p. 1978. 50.80 (*90-279-7720-8*) Mouton.

— The Walled-Up Wife: A Casebook. LC 96-1225. (Illus.). 222p. 1996. 50.00 (*0-299-15070-4*); pap. 16.95 (*0-299-15074-7*) U of Wis Pr.

Dundes, Alan & Pagter, Carl R. Never Try to Teach a Pig to Sing: Still More Urban Folklore from the Paperwork Empire. LC 90-28451. (Humor in Life & Letters Ser.). (Illus.). 436p. 1991. pap. 19.95 (*0-8143-2358-8*); text 39.95 (*0-8143-2357-X*) Wayne St U Pr.

— When You're up to Your Ass in Alligators: More Urban Folklore from the Paperwork Empire. LC 87-3056. (Humor in Life & Letters Ser.). (Illus.). 272p. 1987. pap. 17.95 (*0-8143-1867-3*) Wayne St U Pr.

***Dundes, Alan & Pagter, Carl R.** Why Don't Sheep Shrink When It Rains? A Further Collection of Photocopier Folklore. LC 99-32839. (Illus.). 256p. 1999. pap. 24.95 (*0-8156-0600-1*) Syracuse U Pr.

Dundes, Alan & Pagter, Carl R. Work Hard & You Shall Be Rewarded: Urban Folklore from the Paperwork Empire. LC 92-11158. (Humor in Life & Letters Ser.). (Illus.). 248p. (C). 1992. reprint ed. pap. 16.95 (*0-8143-2432-0*) Wayne St U Pr.

Dundes, Alan, jt. ed. see Edmunds, Lowell.

Dundes, Alan, jt. ed. see Mieder, Wolfgang.

Dundes, Alan, ed. see Ramanujan, A. K.

Dundes, Alan, jt. ed. see Renteln, Alison D.

Dundes, Alan, pref. see Ramanujan, A. K.

Dundon, H. Dwyer. Occupational Therapy Examination Review: 800 Multiple-Choice Questions with Referenced, Explanatory Answers. 5th ed. 245p. (C). 1988. pap. text 26.95 (*0-8385-7204-9*, A7204-9) Appleton & Lange.

***Dundon, R. W. & Jainer, J. L.** A Philosophy of Social Sciences: An Interdisciplinary Approach. LC 99-43354. 1999. 34.00 (*1-56072-730-6*) Nova Sci Pubs.

Dundore, Nathan. Dundore: Genealogical Record of the Dundore Family in America. (Illus.). 58p. 1997. reprint ed. pap. 11.00 (*0-8328-8374-3*); reprint ed. lib. bdg. 21.00 (*0-8328-8373-5*) Higginson Bk Co.

Dundore, P., jt. auth. see Bostwick, David G.

Dundy, Melanie Richardson. Westward Ho with Ollie Ox! (Illus.). 56p. (J). (gr. k-5). Date not set. per. 12.95 (*0-9674491-4-6*) MDCT Pubng.

Dune, Eduard M. Notes of a Red Guard. Koenker, Diane P. & Smith, S. A., eds. & trs. by. from RUS. LC 92-18937. (Illus.). 328p. (C). 1993. text 37.50 (*0-252-01972-5*); pap. text 16.95 (*0-252-06277-9*) U of Ill Pr.

Dunedin Youth Guild Staff. Suncoast Seasons. (Illus.). 430p. 1984. 13.95 (*0-9613858-0-4*) Dunedin Youth.

***Dunegan, Lizann.** Hike America: Oregon. (Illus.). 2000. pap. 17.95 (*0-7627-0762-3*) Globe Pequot.

Dunegan, Lizann. Mountain Bike America: Oregon: An Atlas of Oregon's Greatest Off-Road Bicycle Rides. Adams, Scott E., ed. (Illus.). 224p. 2000. pap. 15.95 (*1-882997-10-7*, Pub. by Beachway Pr) Globe Pequot.

Duneier, Mitchell. Poor Black Women Untitled. Date not set. text. write for info. (*0-374-23582-1*) FS&G.

Duneier, Mitchell. Sidewalk. (Illus.). 388p. 1999. 25.00 (*0-374-26355-8*) FS&G.

***Duneier, Mitchell.** Sidewalk. 2000. pap. write for info. (*0-374-52614-1*) FS&G.

— Sidewalk. (Illus.). 416p. 2001. pap. 15.00 (*0-374-52725-3*) FS&G.

Duneier, Mitchell. Slim's Table: Race, Respectability, & Masculinity. (Illus.). 200p. 1992. 19.95 (*0-226-17030-6*) U Ch Pr.

— Slim's Table: Race, Respectability, & Masculinity. abr. ed. (Illus.). viii, 192p. (C). 1994. pap. 11.00 (*0-226-17031-4*) U Ch Pr.

Duneier, Mitchell, jt. auth. see Giddens, Anthony.

Duner, Bertil. The Bear, the Cubs, & the Eagle: Soviet Bloc Interventionism in the Third World & the U. S. Response. 204p. 1987. text 75.95 (*0-566-05631-3*, Pub. by Dartmth Pub) Ashgate Pub Co.

Duner, Bertil, ed. An End to Torture: Torture & Other Barbarous Practices. LC 98-8239. 256p. 1998. pap. 25.00 (*1-85649-622-8*) Zed Books.

— An End to Torture: Torture & Other Barbarous Practices. LC 98-8239. 256p. 1998. text 69.95 (*1-85649-621-X*) Zed Books.

Dunes of Dare Garden Club Staff. Wildflowers of the Outer Banks: Kitty Hawk to Hatteras. LC 79-18927. (Illus.). 183p. reprint ed. pap. 56.80 (*0-7837-6856-7*, 204668500003) Bks Demand.

Dunetz, Bryant & Summers, Charles K. ISDN: How to Get a High-Speed Connection to the Internet. LC 95-45824. 346p. 1996. pap. 22.95 (*0-471-13326-4*) Wiley.

Dunetz, Martin R. You & Your Assets: A Practical Guide to Financial Management & Estate Planning. LC 96-52480. (Illus.). 176p. 1997. text 14.95 (*1-56833-091-X*) Madison Bks UPA.

Dunetz, Nancy S. Language Development Through Content: Our People & Their Stories. 128p. 1987. pap. text 15.00 (*0-201-11205-1*) Addison-Wesley.

Dunev, Michael, et al. Alek Rapoport: An Artist's Journey. (Illus.). 120p. 1997. pap. 30.00 (*0-9661190-0-2*) M Dunev.

Dunfee, Susan N. Beyond Servanthood: Christianity & the Liberation of Women. LC 88-27856. 192p. (Orig.). (C). 1989. lib. bdg. 38.00 (*0-8191-7223-5*) U Pr of Amer.

Dunfee, Thomas W. & Gibson, Frank F. Modern Business Law: The Regulatory Environment. 3rd ed. (C). 1995. pap., student ed. 31.25 (*0-07-018217-5*) McGraw.

Dunfee, Thomas W., et al. Modern Business Law. 3rd ed. LC 94-40587. 1376p. (C). 1995. 90.94 (*0-07-018212-4*) McGraw.

Dunfee, Thomas W., jt. auth. see Donaldson, Thomas.

Dunfee, Thomas W., jt. ed. see Donaldson, Thomas.

Dunfie, Chris. Normandy: Gold Beach. (Battleground Europe Ser.). 1999. pap. text 16.95 (*1-58097-008-7*) Combined Pub.

Dunfield, David. Exploring Osaka. (Exploring Japan Ser.). (Illus.). 160p. 1993. pap. 14.95 (*0-8348-0271-6*) Weatherhill.

Dunford. Bibliography of Women Artists & Designers of Europe since 1800, Vol. 1. LC 97-39199. 1998. 100.00 (*0-8161-0596-0*) Mac Lib Ref.

Dunford, Andrew, jt. auth. see Eldin, Sue.

Dunford, Betty & Ridgell, Reilly. Pacific Neighbors: The Islands of Micronesia, Melanesia, & Polynesia. (Illus.). 192p. (J). (gr. 4-9). 1996. text 44.95 (*1-57306-022-4*) Bess Pr.

Dunford, C. Kent. A Testament of Our Times. 1993. 8.95 (*0-88494-878-1*) Bookcraft Inc.

Dunford, Charles L. Nuclear Data Evaluation Methodology: Proceedings of the Symposium. 700p. 1993. text 178.00 (*981-02-1285-2*) World Scientific Pub.

Dunford, Christopher, jt. auth. see Pulliam, H. Ronald.

Dunford, Elizabeth P. The Hawaiians of Old. (Illus.). 220p. (J). (gr. 4 up). 1990. pap., teacher ed. 9.95 (*0-935848-09-6*) Bess Pr.

— The Hawaiians of Old. rev. ed. (Illus.). 220p. (J). (gr. 4 up). 1990. pap., student ed. 8.95 (*0-935848-08-8*); text 34.95 (*0-935848-43-6*) Bess Pr.

Dunford, Fred & O'Brien, Greg. Secrets in the Sand: The Archaeology of Cape Cod & the Islands. (Illus.). 1997. 30.00 (*0-940160-63-3*) Parnassus Imprints.

Dunford, H. B., et al. The Biological Chemistry of Iron. 1982. text 206.50 (*90-277-1444-4*) Kluwer Academic.

Dunford, H. Brian. Heme Peroxidases. LC 98-28908. 528p. 1999. 195.00 (*0-471-24244-6*) Wiley.

***Dunford, Jill W.** Teach Me Mommy: A Preschool Learning Guide. 3rd rev. enl. ed. (Illus.). 285p. (J). (ps-1). 2000. pap. 23.95 (*0-931151-01-5*) Gloucester Cres.

Dunford, John. Her Majesty's Inspectorate of Schools since 1944: Standard Bearers or Turbulent Priests? LC 97-37986. 272p. 1998. 49.50 (*0-7130-0210-7*, Pub. by Woburn Pr); pap. 25.00 (*0-7130-4028-9*, Pub. by Woburn Pr) Intl Spec Bk.

Dunford, John, jt. auth. see Chitty, Clyde.

Dunford, Martin. Belgium & Luxembourg. 2nd ed. 432p. 1999. pap. 17.95 (*1-85828-427-9*, Pub. by Rough Guides) Penguin Putnam.

— Nueva York en Vivo. (SPA.). 375p. 1992. pap. 39.95 (*0-7859-7561-6*, 84207459600) Fr & Eur.

Dunford, Martin & Hollard, Jack. The Real Guide: New York. 3rd ed. LC 93-19249. (Real Guides Ser.). 1993. pap. 13.00 (*0-671-79822-7*, P-H Travel) Prntice Hall Bks.

Dunford, Martin & Lee, Phil. Belgium & Luxembourg. (Rough Guides Ser.). (Illus.). 416p. 1997. pap. 17.95 (*1-85828-222-5*, Penguin Bks) Viking Penguin.

Dunford, Martin, et al. Holland. (Rough Guides Ser.). (Illus.). 400p. 1997. pap. 17.95 (*1-85828-229-2*, Penguin Bks) Viking Penguin.

Dunford, Mick. France. (Modern Industrial World Ser.). (Illus.). 48p. (J). (gr. 6-8). 1994. lib. bdg. 24.26 (*1-56847-263-3*) Raintree Steck-V.

Dunford, Mick & Kafkalas, Grigorio, eds. Cities, Regions & the New Europe. 256p. 1992. text 65.00 (*1-85293-221-X*) St Martin.

Dunford, Mick & Kafkalas, Grigoris, eds. Cities & Regions in the New Europe: The Global-Local Interplay & Spatial Development Strategies. 256p. (Orig.). 1991. 190.00 (*0-471-94525-0*) Wiley.

Dunford, Neilson & Schwartz, Jacob T. Linear Operators Pt. 1: General Theory. (Classics Library). 872p. 1988. pap. 89.95 (*0-471-60848-3*) Wiley.

— Linear Operators Pt. 2: Spectral Theory, Vol. 2. (Classics Library). 1088p. 1988. pap. 195.00 (*0-471-60847-5*) Wiley.

— Linear Operators Pt. 3: Spectral Operators, Vol. 3. (Classics Library). 688p. 1988. pap. 165.00 (*0-471-60846-7*) Wiley.

***Dunford, R. W., et al, eds.** X-ray & Inner-Shell Processes: 18th International Conference. LC 99-69958. (AIP Conference Proceedings Ser.: Vol. 506). (Illus.). xv, 694p. 2000. 135.00 (*1-56396-713-8*) Am Inst Physics.

Dunford, R. W. & Calaprice, F. P., eds. Workshop on Polarized 3He Beams & Targets (Princeton, NJ, 1984) LC 85-48026. (AIP Conference Proceedings Ser.: No. 131). 224p. 1985. lib. bdg. 39.25 (*0-88318-330-7*) Am Inst Physics.

Dunford, Randall E. Healthy House-Cleaning Tips: Useful Solutions to a More Dust-Free Home. (Illus.). 32p. (Orig.). 1992. pap. text 3.95 (*0-9628093-2-2*) NuDawn Pub.

— Your Health & the Indoor Environment: A Complete Guide to Better Health Through Control of the Indoor Atmosphere. 2nd rev. ed. LC 90-92083. (Illus.). 272p. (Orig.). 1994. pap. 12.95 (*0-9628093-4-9*) NuDawn Pub.

Dunford, Randy. Clean Your House Safely & Effectively Without Harmful Chemicals. 157p. 1993. pap. 12.95 (*1-882330-24-2*) Magni Co.

Dunford, Richard. Dunford Organisational Behavior. (C). 1999. pap. text. write for info. (*0-201-17769-2*) Addison-Wesley.

***Dunford, Warren.** Soon to Be a Major Motion Picture: A Novel. 256p. 2000. pap. 12.95 (*1-55583-582-1*, Pub. by Alyson Pubns) Consort Bk Sales.

Dung-Dkar Blo-Bzang 'Phrim-Las. The Merging of Religious & Secular Rule in Tibet. 135p. 1991. pap. 7.15 (*7-119-00672-X*, 17E-2324P) Cypress Co.

Dung, Van Tien. Our Great Spring Victory: An Account of the Liberation of South Vietnam. Speagens, John, tr. LC 76-58106. 275p. 1977. 25.00 (*0-85345-409-4*, Pub. by Monthly Rev) NYU Pr.

Dung, Viet N. Extending Modules. LC 94-31198. 1994. pap. 55.00 (*0-582-25382-9*, Pub. by Addison-Wesley) Longman.

Dungan. Electronic Communication Systems. 3rd ed. 192p. (C). 1998. mass mkt. 26.25 (*0-8273-8629-X*) Delmar.

— Electronic Communication Systems 3E IG. 128p. 1998. 31.95 (*0-8273-8625-7*) Delmar.

— Electronic Communications Systems. 3rd ed. LC 97-31917. 816p. (C). 1998. mass mkt. 100.95 (*0-8273-8624-9*) Delmar.

— Linear Integrated Circuits: Experiments. (Electronics Technology Ser.). 1984. pap. 27.00 (*0-8273-3840-6*) Delmar.

Dungan, Anita B., ed. see Dungan, Thomas P.

Dungan, Christopher & Ridings, Donald. Business Law. deluxe ed. (Barron's Business Library). 320p. 1990. pap. 17.95 (*0-8120-4189-5*) Barron.

Dungan, David L., ed. Interrelations of the Gospels: Bibliotheca Ephemeridum Theologicarum Lovaniensium 95. xxx, 672p. 1991. text 75.00 (*90-6186-396-1*, MUP-P088) Mercer Univ Pr.

Dungan, David L., jt. ed. see Cartlidge, David R.

Dungan, David Laird. A History of the Synoptic Problem: The Canon, the Text, the Composition & the Interpretation. LC 97-49895. 544p. 1999. 39.95 (*0-385-47192-0*) Doubleday.

Dungan, F. Alvin. The Next Step: A Daily Walk in Recovery. McBride, Christy, ed. LC 93-9834. 220p. (Orig.). 1993. pap. 11.95 (*1-880292-10-6*) LangMarc.

Dungan, Frank R. Electronic Communications Systems. 2nd ed. LC 92-21491. 673p. 1993. mass mkt. 93.95 (*0-8273-5843-1*) Delmar.

— Electronic Communications Systems: Instructor's Guide. 2nd ed. 86p. 1993. 16.00 (*0-8273-5845-8*) Delmar.

— Electronic Communications Systems Lab Manual. 2nd ed. 169p. 1993. lab manual ed. 25.00 (*0-8273-5846-6*) Delmar.

— Experiments in OP Amps & Linear Integrated Circuits. 2nd ed. 1992. pap. 38.95 (*0-8273-5072-4*) Delmar.

— Op Amps & Lic for Technology. 2nd ed. 1992. mass mkt. 56.25 (*0-8273-5086-4*) Delmar.

— OP Amps & Linear Integrated Circuits for Technicians. 2nd ed. 1992. teacher ed. 16.00 (*0-8273-5087-2*) Delmar.

Dungan, Marilyn. Snakebird. unabridged ed. LC 98-73589. (Laney McVey Ser.: Vol. 1). 256p. 1999. pap. 11.95 (*0-9666478-5-8*) Arcane Books.

***Dungan, Marilyn.** The Tape. LC 99-94562. (Laney McVey Ser.: Vol. 2). 246p. 2000. pap. 12.95 (*0-9666478-6-6*) Arcane Books.

Dungan, Miles. Distant Drums. (Illus.). 184p. (Orig.). 1994. pap. 15.95 (*0-86281-384-0*, Pub. by Appletree Pr) Irish Bks Media.

Dungan, Myles. Irish Voices from the Great War. 224p. 1995. 35.50 (*0-7165-2573-9*, Pub. by Irish Acad Pr) Intl Spec Bk.

— They Shall Not Grow Old: Irish Soldiers Remember the Great War. 208p. 1997. boxed set 30.00 (*1-85182-347-6*, Pub. by Four Cts Pr) Intl Spec Bk.

Dungan, Thomas P. John Dongan of Dublin, an Elizabethan Gentleman & His Family. Dungan, Anita B., ed. (Illus.). 246p. 1996. 24.50 (*0-9663239-0-4*) Dungan Bks.

— A Quest for Origins: The Search for the Parentage of William Dungan, Perfumer of St. Martin-in-the-Fields. (Illus.). 65p. 1997. pap. 12.00 (*0-9663239-1-2*) Dungan Bks.

Dungar, R., et al, eds. Numerical Models in Geomechanics: International Symposium, Zurich, 13-17 September 1982. 831p. (C). 1982. text 252.00 (*90-6191-225-3*, Pub. by A A Balkema) Ashgate Pub Co.

Dungar, R. & Studer, J. A., eds. Geomechanical Modelling in Engineering Practice. 409p. (C). 1986. text 220.00 (*90-6191-518-X*, Pub. by A A Balkema) Ashgate Pub Co.

Dungeons & Dragons Staff. Dragon Dice Randomizers. 1981. 3.00 (*0-394-51840-3*) Random.

Dungey, Joan M. Interactive Bulletin Boards as Teaching Tools. 80p. 1989. pap. 9.95 (*0-8106-3340-X*) NEA.

Dungey, Melba, ed. WVPS, 1995 Contest Winners: West. 88p. write for info. (*0-9643888-1-2*) West VA Poetry.

— WVPS, 1994 Contest Winners: Anthology. 1994. 76p. 1994. write for info. (*0-9643888-0-4*) West VA Poetry.

Dunglison, Robley. Human Health. Rosenkrantz, Barbara G., ed. LC 76-25660. (Public Health in America Ser.). 1977. reprint ed. lib. bdg. 39.95 (*0-405-09815-4*) Ayer.

Dungundji, James. Topology. 447p. (C). 1988. text 71.88 (*0-697-06889-7*, WCB McGr Hill) McGrw-H Hghr Educ.

Dungworth, Richard. Attacking. (Soccer School Ser.). (Illus.). 32p. (J). (gr. 3 up). 1998. pap. 5.95 (*0-7460-2911-X*); lib. bdg. 13.95 (*0-88110-966-5*, Usborne) EDC.

— Dead Ball Skills. (Soccer School Ser.). (Illus.). 32p. (J). (gr. 3-7). 1997. pap. 5.95 (*0-7460-2448-7*, Usborne) EDC.

— Dead Ball Skills. (Soccer School Ser.). (Illus.). 32p. (J). (gr. 3 up). 1997. lib. bdg. 13.95 (*0-88110-909-6*, Usborne) EDC.

— Famous Women. (Famous Lives Ser.). (Illus.). 48p. (J). (gr. 5 up). 1997. pap. 7.95 (*0-7460-2404-5*, Usborne) EDC.

— Famous Women. (Famous Lives Ser.). (Illus.). 48p. (J). (gr. 5 up). 1999. 15.95 (*0-88110-889-8*, Usborne) EDC.

Dungworth, Richard. Windows for Beginners. (Computer Guides Ser.). (Illus.). 48p. (YA). (gr. 4 up). 1996. pap. 9.95 (*0-7460-2335-9*, Usborne) EDC.

Dungworth, Richard. Windows for Beginners. (Computer Guides Ser.). (Illus.). 48p. (YA). (gr. 5 up). 1996. lib. bdg. 17.95 (*0-88110-852-9*, Usborne) EDC.

Dungworth, Richard & Wingate, Philippa. The Usborne Book of Famous Women: From Nefertiti to Diana. (Usborne Kid Kits Ser.). (Illus.). (YA). (gr. 5-9). 1998. 16.95 (*1-58086-018-4*, Usborne) EDC.

Dungworth, Richard, et al. Famous Lives. (Famous Lives Ser.). (Illus.). 240p. (J). (gr. 5 up). 1998. pap. 19.95 (*0-7460-3033-9*, Usborne); lib. bdg. 27.95 (*0-88110-998-3*, Usborne) EDC.

Dungworth, Richard, jt. auth. see Harvey, Gill.

Dungworth, Richard, jt. auth. see Wingate, Philippa.

Dunham. Childhood of Famous Americans Thurgood Marshall. LC 98-4080. (Illus.). 192p. 1998. per. 4.99 (*0-689-82042-9*) S&S Childrens.

— Organizationl Behavior. 4th ed. (C). 1997. pap. text, teacher ed., suppl. ed. 22.50 (*0-673-55994-7*) Addson-Wesley Educ.

Dunham & Pierce. Management. (C). 1989. pap., student ed. 23.33 (*0-673-39802-1*) Addson-Wesley Educ.

— Managing. (C). 1990. pap. text, student ed. 25.00 (*0-673-46168-8*) Addson-Wesley Educ.

Dunham, Aileen. Political Unrest in Upper Canada, 1815-1836. LC 74-3751. 210p. 1975. reprint ed. lib. bdg. 59.50 (*0-8371-7474-0*, DUPU, Greenwood Pr) Greenwood.

— Political Unrest in Upper Canada, 1815-1836. (BCL1 - History - Canada Ser.). 210p. 1991. reprint ed. lib. bdg. 79.00 (*0-7812-6370-0*) Rprt Serv.

Dunham, Alison B. & Freeman, Jessica B. Recruiting Love: Using the Business Skills You Have to Find the Love You Want. (Illus.). 240p. 1998. pap. 11.95 (*1-890723-19-3*) Cyclone Bks.

Dunham, Anne, photos by. Mindfulness & Home: Poetry & Prose from a Prairie Landscape. (Illus.). 115p. (Orig.). 1997. pap. write for info. (*0-9636224-4-7*) Rose Hill Bks.

Dunham, Bandhu S. Contemporary Lampworking: A Practical Guide to Shaping Glass in the Flame. LC 95-14682. 1995. 37.95 (*0-934252-56-4*, Pub. by Hohm Pr) SCB Distributors.

— Contemporary Lampworking: A Practical Guide to Shaping Glass in the Flame. 2nd rev. ed. (Illus.). 384p. 1997. text 36.95 (*0-9658972-0-6*) Salusa Glass.

Dunham, Barrows, tr. see Ker, John & Malloch, David.

Dunham, Betty. Oliver Township Cemetery, Kalkaska County, Michigan. (Illus.). 34p. 1990. pap. 6.00 (*0-940133-26-1*) Kinseeker Pubns.

Dunham, C. Michael & Cowley, R. Adams, eds. Shock Trauma: Critical Care Manual. LC 91-22232. 520p. reprint ed. pap. 161.20 (*0-608-07377-6*, 206760400009) Bks Demand.

Dunham, Carroll. Tibet: Reflections from the Wheel of Life. (Illus.). 204p. 1993. 55.00 (*1-55859-218-0*) Abbeville Pr.

Dunham, Chester F. Dunahm Genealogy, & Related Families Billings, Powell, Hice, Gray, Root, Andrus. (Illus.). 160p. 1997. reprint ed. pap. 24.50 (*0-8328-8370-0*); reprint ed. lib. bdg. 34.50 (*0-8328-8369-7*) Higginson Bk Co.

Dunham, Chip. Abandon Ship! An Overboard Collection. (Illus.). 128p. (Orig.). 1992. pap. 8.95 (*0-8362-1895-7*) Andrews & McMeel.

— Overboard. (Illus.). 128p. (Orig.). 1991. pap. 8.95 (*0-8362-1880-9*) Andrews & McMeel.

Dunham, Corydon B. Fighting for the First Amendment: Stanton of CBS vs. Congress & the Nixon White House. LC 97-17517. 248p. 1997. 24.95 (*0-275-96027-7*, Praeger Pubs) Greenwood.

***Dunham, Donald Carl.** Assignment Bucharest: An American Diplomat's View of the Communist Takeover of Romania. 200p. 2000. 39.95 (*973-9432-06-9*, Pub. by Ctr Romanian Studies) Intl Spec Bk.

Dunham, Dows. The Barkal Temples. (Illus.). 124p. text 60.00 (*0-87846-108-6*, Pub. by Mus Fine Arts Boston) D Brown Bk Co.

***Dunham, Gary.** How to Buy a Computer: Plain & Simple. (Illus.). 48p. 1999. 5.95 (*0-9641339-7-0*) E T C Pub.

Dunham, George R. & Quinlan, David A. U. S. Marines in Vietnam: The Bitter End, 1973-1975. (Illus.). 315p. (Orig.). (C). 1995. pap. text 45.00 (*0-7881-1877-3*) DIANE Pub.

An Asterisk (*) at the beginning of an entry indicates that the title is appearing for the first time.

Dunham, Glory. The Wings of Christmas. 1998. pap. 4.50 (*1-57514-327-5*, 1178) Encore Perform Pub.

Dunham, H. Warren. Social Realities & Community Psychiatry. LC 74-10967. 252p. 1976. 42.95 (*0-87705-215-8*, Kluwer Acad Hman Sci) Kluwer Academic.

— Social Systems & Schizophrenia: Selected Papers. LC 80-14193. 316p. 1980. 69.50 (*0-275-90472-5*, C0472, Praeger Pubs) Greenwood.

Dunham, H. Warren, jt. auth. see Faris, Robert E.

Dunham, Harold H. Government Handout: A Study in the Administration of the Public Lands 1875-1891. LC 80-27052. (American Scene Ser.). 1970. reprint ed. lib. bdg. 42.50 (*0-306-71433-7*) Da Capo.

Dunham, Harvey. Adirondack French Louie: Early Life in the Northwoods. 6th ed. (Illus.). 290p. 1987. reprint ed. pap. 16.00 (*0-932052-57-6*) North Country.

Dunham, Henry W. Community & Schizophrenia: An Epidemiological Analysis. LC 65-13720. (Lafayette Clinic Monographs in Psychiatry: No. 1). (Illus.). 339p. reprint ed. pap. 105.10 (*0-7837-3829-3*, 204365000010) Bks Demand.

— Sociological Theory & Mental Disorder. LC 59-9323. (Illus.). 311p. reprint ed. pap. 96.50 (*0-7837-3597-9*, 204346200009) Bks Demand.

Dunham, Henry W. & Weinberg, S. Kirson. The Culture of the State Mental Hospital. LC 59-11472. 309p. reprint ed. pap. 95.80 (*0-608-16569-7*, 202766700055) Bks Demand.

Dunham, I. W. Genealogy of Deacon John Dunham of Plymouth, Massachusettes, 1589-1669 & His Descendants. 384p. 1989. reprint ed. pap. 47.00 (*0-8328-0499-1*); reprint ed. lib. bdg. 55.00 (*0-8328-0498-3*) Higginson Bk Co.

Dunham, Jack. Stress in Teachers: Past, Present & Future. 1998. pap. 37.95 (*1-86156-082-6*) Whurr Pub.

— Stress in Teaching. 2nd ed. LC 91-44817. 224p. (C). (gr. 13). 1992. text 85.00 (*0-415-06634-4*, A7511) Routledge.

Dunham, James H. Religion of Philosophers. LC 78-80386. (Essay Index Reprint Ser.). 1977. 23.95 (*0-8369-1059-1*) Ayer.

Dunham, Jeff. Database Performance Tuning Handbook. LC 97-35362. (Series on Data Warehousing & Data Management). (Illus.). 778p. 1997. 59.95 incl. cd-rom (*0-07-018244-2*) McGraw.

Dunham, John B., ed. Guide to Coastal Outcrops of the Monterey Formation of Western Santa Barbara County, California. (Illus.). 36p. (Orig.). 1987. pap. 7.00 (*1-878861-16-6*) Pac Section SEPM.

Dunham, John H. Twice Told Tales: The Families of Irvine Hockaday Dunham & Martin Baskett Dunham in Callaway 1870-1930. (Illus.). 132p. 1991. lib. bdg. 10.00 (*0-9627098-8-3*) B Wyman.

Dunham, Judith. American Safari LC 99-24594. (Travel Adventures Ser.). 1999. 19.95 (*1-56331-834-2*) Discovery Channel.

— The Art of the Trout Fly. LC 88-2063. (Illus.). 132p. 1988. 19.95 (*0-87701-528-7*) Chronicle Bks.

***Dunham, Judith.** Backcountry Treks. LC 00-20084. (Travel Adventures Ser.). (Illus.). 2000. write for info. (*1-56331-926-8*) Discovery.

Dunham, Judith, jt. auth. see Horn, Jane.

Dunham, Judith, ed. see Bassham, Ben & Cordova, Ruben C.

Dunham, Judith, ed. see Murphy, Pat.

Dunham, Katharine. Kasamance: A Fantasy. LC 73-92612. (J). (gr. 7 up). 1974. 25.00 (*0-89388-128-7*) Okpaku Communications.

Dunham, Katherine. Island Possessed. LC 93-46117. 292p. (C). 1994. pap. 11.95 (*0-226-17113-2*) U Ch Pr.

— Katherine Dunham's Journey to Accompong. LC 78-135595. (Illus.). 162p. (C). 1972. reprint ed. lib. bdg. 35.00 (*0-8371-5187-2*, DJA&, Greenwood Pr) Greenwood.

— Katherine Dunham's Journey to Accompong: American Autobiography. 162p. 1995. lib. bdg. 69.00 (*0-7812-8507-0*) Rprt Serv.

— A Touch of Innocence. LC 79-7760. (Dance Ser.). 1980. reprint ed. lib. bdg. 35.95 (*0-8369-9289-X*) Ayer.

— A Touch of Innocence: Memoirs of Childhood. LC 93-46125. 320p. (C). 1994. pap. 12.95 (*0-226-17112-4*) U Ch Pr.

***Dunham, Kenneth R.** Bigelow's Virus Troubleshooting Pocket Reference. (Pocket References Ser.). 2000. pap. 19.99 (*0-07-212627-2*) Osborne-McGraw.

Dunham, Kenneth R. Dunham-Singletary Genealogy. (Illus.). 207p. 1987. text 23.50 (*0-9616641-1-8*) Royal Pr.

Dunham, Maxie. Living the Psalms. 1990. pap. 12.95 (*0-687-60683-7*) Abingdon.

Dunham, Molly, ed. The Wild Side of Maryland: An Outdoor Guide. LC 97-70224. (Illus.). 276p. (Orig.). 1997. pap. 14.95 (*0-9649819-4-7*) Baltimore Sun.

Dunham, Montrew. Abner Doubleday, Young Baseball Pioneer. LC 93-45400. (Illus.). 192p. (J). (gr. 3-7). 1995. mass mkt. 4.95 (*0-689-71788-1*) Aladdin.

— Abner Doubleday, Young Baseball Pioneer. (Childhood of Famous Americans Ser.). 1995. 10.05 (*0-606-07172-5*, Pub. by Turtleback) Demco.

— Childhood of Famous Americans Langston Hughes: Young Black Poet. LC 93-21128. (Illus.). 192p. (J). (gr. 3-7). 1995. mass mkt. 4.95 (*0-689-71787-3*) Aladdin.

— Childhood of Famous Americans Mahalia Jackson: Young Gospel Singer. LC 93-34072. (Illus.). 192p. (J). (gr. 3-7). 1995. mass mkt. 4.95 (*0-689-71786-5*) Aladdin.

— John Muir, Young Naturalist. LC 97-29092. (Childhood of Famous Americans Ser.). (Illus.). 192p. (J). 1998. per. 4.99 (*0-689-81996-X*) Aladdin.

***Dunham, Montrew.** John Muir, Young Naturalist. (Childhood of Famous Americans Ser.). 1998. 10.09 (*0-606-13539-1*, Pub. by Turtleback) Demco.

Dunham, Montrew. Langston Hughes, Young Black Poet. (Childhood of Famous Americans Ser.). (J). 1995. 10.30 (*0-606-07770-7*) Turtleback.

— Mahalia Jackson, Young Gospel Singer. (Childhood of Famous Americans Ser.). (J). 1995. 10.05 (*0-606-07829-0*) Turtleback.

— Neil Armstrong: Young Flyer. (Illus.). 192p. (J). (gr. 3-7). 1996. per. 4.99 (*0-689-80995-6*) S&S Trade.

— Neil Armstrong, Young Pilot. (Childhood of Famous Americans Ser.). 1996. 10.09 (*0-606-11674-5*, Pub. by Turtleback) Demco.

— Roberto Clemente: Young Ball Player. LC 96-37326. (Childhood of Famous Americans Ser.). (Illus.). 192p. (J). (gr. 4-6). 1997. per. 4.99 (*0-689-81364-3*) Aladdin.

— Roberto Clemente, Young Ball Player. (Childhood of Famous Americans Ser.). 1997. 10.09 (*0-606-11803-9*, Pub. by Turtleback) Demco.

***Dunham, Montrew.** Ronald Reagan: Young Leader. (Childhood of Famous Americans Ser.). (Illus.). 192p. (J). 1999. per. 4.99 (*0-689-83006-8*) Aladdin.

Dunham, N. J. A History of Jerauld County, South Dakota. (Illus.). 441p. 1993. reprint ed. lib. bdg. 47.50 (*0-8328-3475-0*) Higginson Bk Co.

Dunham, Nancy, ed. see Stryk, Lucien, et al.

Dunham, Paul, Jr. Evaluation for Physical Education. (Illus.). 400p. (C). 1994. pap. text 34.95 (*0-89582-277-6*) Wadsworth Pub.

Dunham, Philip, jt. ed. see Moore, Chris.

Dunham, Roger, jt. auth. see Alpert, Geoffrey.

Dunham, Roger, jt. auth. see Alpert, Geoffrey P.

Dunham, Roger C. Spy Sub: A Top Secret Mission to the Bottom of the Pacific. 1997. mass mkt. 6.99 (*0-451-40797-0*, Onyx) NAL.

— Spy Sub: A Top Secret Mission to the Bottom of the Pacific. (Illus.). 256p. 1996. 29.95 (*1-55750-178-5*) Naval Inst Pr.

Dunham, Roger G. & Alpert, Geoffrey P., eds. Critical Issues in Policing: Contemporary Readings. 3rd rev. ed. LC 97-205582. (Illus.). 651p. (C). 1997. pap. text 29.95 (*0-88133-947-4*) Waveland Pr.

Dunham, Roger G., jt. auth. see Alpert, Geoffrey P.

Dunham, Roger G., jt. auth. see Cromwell, Paul E.

Dunham, S. T., jt. ed. see Nelson, J. S.

Dunham, Scott, jt. auth. see Ball, Steve.

Dunham, Scott H., jt. auth. see Pepe, Stephen P.

Dunham, Steve, ed. see Bonire, Josiah.

Dunham, Steve, ed. see Sadiku, Matthew N.

Dunham, Susan. Sculpting & Making a Toddler Doll - Head to Toe. LC 96-193203. (Illus.). 128p. 1996. pap. 19.95 (*0-87588-457-1*, 5038) Hobby Hse.

Dunham, Tacy. Discover Marin State Parks: Angel Island, Mt. Tamalpais, China Camp, Tomales Bay, Olompali. rev. ed. (Marin Trail Guide Ser.). (Illus.). 56p. 1989. reprint ed. pap. 6.95 (*0-685-27206-0*) Cttnwd Pr.

— Hiking West Marin: Trail Guide for Pt. Reyes & Mt. Tamalpais Watershed. rev. ed. (Marin Trail Guide Ser.). (Illus.). 56p. 1989. reprint ed. pap. 6.95 (*0-685-27207-9*) Cttnwd Pr.

— Marin Bike Paths: A Guide to Easy Rides & Interesting Sights. rev. ed. (Marin Trail Guide Ser.). (Illus.). 56p. (Orig.). 1989. reprint ed. pap. 6.95 (*0-685-27208-7*) Cttnwd Pr.

— Marin Headlands Trail Guide: Golden Gate National Recreation Area. rev. ed. (Marin Trail Guide Ser.). (Illus.). 56p. 1989. reprint ed. pap. 6.95 (*0-685-27204-4*) Cttnwd Pr.

— Nature Walks & Easy Hikes: A Family Guide to Marin Trails. rev. ed. (Marin Trail Guide Ser.). (Illus.). 56p. 1989. reprint ed. pap. 6.95 (*0-685-27205-2*) Cttnwd Pr.

— Sunday Outings: A Guide to Scenic Drives & Historical Sights in Marin County. (Marin Trail Guide Ser.). (Illus.). 56p. (Orig.). 1989. reprint ed. pap. 6.95 (*0-685-27209-5*) Cttnwd Pr.

— Wandering Marin Trails: A Hiking Guide to Trails of Central Marin. rev. ed. (Marin Trail Guide Ser.). (Illus.). 56p. 1989. reprint ed. pap. 6.95 (*0-685-44725-1*) Cttnwd Pr.

Dunham, Tracy. The Changing Trail. LC 98-96232. 192p. 1998. 18.95 (*0-8034-9310-X*, Avalon Bks) Bouregy.

***Dunham, Tracy.** The Eureka Trail. LC 99-94437. 192p. 1999. 18.95 (*0-8034-9370-3*, Avalon Bks) Bouregy.

Dunham, Tracy. The Ghost Trail. LC 97-93732. (Mythmaker Ser.: No. 4). 192p. 1997. lib. bdg. 18.95 (*0-8034-9250-2*, Avalon Bks) Bouregy.

— The Long Trail Home. LC 96-96762. (Mythmaker Ser.: No. 3). 192p. 1996. 18.95 (*0-8034-9176-X*, Avalon Bks) Bouregy.

— The Trail of Mythmaker. LC 95-94893. (Mythmaker Ser.: No. 2). 192p. 1995. 18.95 (*0-8034-9151-4*, Avalon Bks) Bouregy.

Dunham, Troy. Pine Needle National Park Visitor Guide: America's Favorite Fictitious National Park. LC 90-82942. (Illus.). 112p. (Orig.). 1990. pap. 12.95 (*1-877967-07-6*) Cttnwd Pr.

Dunham, V. L., jt. auth. see Bryant, J. A.

Dunham, Vera Sandomirsky. In Stalin's Time: Middleclass Values in Soviet Fiction. 2nd ed. LC 90-42414. (Studies of the Harriman Institute). 320p. (C). 1990. reprint ed. pap. text 19.95 (*0-8223-1085-6*) Duke.

Dunham, Vera Sandomirsky, tr. see Akhmatova, Anna Andreevena.

Dunham, W. B. New York Insurance Law, 4 vols. 1991. 530.00 (*0-8205-1484-5*) Bender.

Dunham, W. V., Jr. Texas Criminal Defense Forms Annotated. 410p. 1984. ring bd. 135.00 (*1-878337-19-X*) Knowles Pub Inc.

Dunham, William. Euler: The Master of Us All. LC 98-88271. (Dolciani Mathematical Expositions Ser.: Vol. 22). 212p. 1999. pap. text 29.95 (*0-88385-328-0*) Math Assn.

— The Mathematical Universe: An Alphabetical Journey Through the Great Proofs, Problems, & Personalities. LC 93-48720. (Illus.). 314p. 1994. 24.95 (*0-471-53656-3*) Wiley.

Dunham, William C. The Euro Directory: Executive Search & Selection Firms in Europe. 471p. 1994. 125.00 (*0-614-04615-7*) Recruiting & Search.

Dunham, William H., Jr. Lord Hasting's Indentured Retainers, 1461-1483: The Lawfulness of Livery & Retaining under the Yorkists & the Tudors. (Connecticut Academy of Arts & Sciences Ser., Trans.: Vol. 39). 1955. pap. 69.50 (*0-685-22896-7*) Elliots Bks.

Dunham, William H. Radulphi de Hengham Summae. (Cambridge Studies in English Legal History). xxxix, 94p. 1986. reprint ed. 45.00 (*0-912004-45-2*) Gaunt.

Dunham, William J., jt. auth. see Connors, Richard J.

Dunham, William W. Journey Through Genius: The Great Theorems of Mathematics. 320p. 1991. pap. 14.95 (*0-14-014739-X*, Penguin Bks) Viking Penguin.

— Journey Through Genius: The Great Theorems of Mathematics. LC 89-27366. 320p. 1990. 29.95 (*0-471-50030-5*) Wiley.

— The Mathematical Universe. LC 93-48720. (Illus.). 320p. 1997. pap. 19.95 (*0-471-17661-3*) Wiley.

Dunham, Wolcott B. Insurance M & A: A Practical Approach to Structuring Complex Transactions. LC 98-230540. (Corporate Law & Practice Course Handbook Ser.). 504 p. 1998. 129.00 (*0-87224-516-0*) PLI.

Dunham, Wolcott B. & Practising Law Institute Staff. Insurance M&A: A Practical Approach to Structuring Complex Transactions. LC 97-229141. (Corporate Law & Practice Course Handbook Ser.). 456p. 1997. 129.00 (*0-87224-392-3*) PLI.

***Dunhill, Alfred.** The Pipe Book. 304p. 2000. 9.99 (*0-517-16187-7*) Random Hse Value.

Dunhill, Alfred. The Pipe Book. LC 98-46883. (Illus.). 262p. 1999. reprint ed. 25.00 (*1-55821-776-2*) Lyons Pr.

Dunhill, Priscilla, jt. auth. see Grossman, John.

Dunhill, Thomas F. Chamber Music. (Select Bibliographies Reprint Ser.). 1977. reprint ed. 17.95 (*0-8369-9935-5*) Ayer.

— Mozart's String Quartets. LC 77-104260. 1970. reprint ed. lib. bdg. 38.50 (*0-8371-3919-8*, DUMQ, Greenwood Pr) Greenwood.

— Mozart's String Quartets, 2 vols. 1990. reprint ed. lib. bdg. 140.00 (*0-7812-9017-1*) Rprt Serv.

— Sullivan's Comic Operas: A Critical Appreciation. (Music Ser.). 256p. 1981. reprint ed. lib. bdg. 32.50 (*0-306-76080-0*) Da Capo.

Dunhill, Tina, et al. Sleeping Rough: Stories of the Night. 162p. (C). 1991. pap. 14.95 (*0-413-45401-0*, A0637, Methuen Drama) Methn.

Dunhouse, Mary B. International Directory of Children's Literature. LC 85-29372. 138p. reprint ed. pap 42.80 (*0-7837-5332-2*, 204507200005) Bks Demand.

Dunhouse, Mary B., ed. International Directory of Children's Literature: A Directory of Children's Literature. LC 85-81551. 136p. (J). 1985. 24.95 (*0-914746-44-8*) G Kurian.

Dunicliff, Joy. Mary Howitt: Another Lost Victorian Writer. LC 93-168845. 264 p. 1992. write for info. (*1-85634-102-X*) Excalibur.

Dunigan, Erin. Microtech U. S. A. MCSE Training Guide: Windows NT Workstation 4. 1998. 53.49 (*1-56205-902-5*, New Riders Sftwre) MCP SW Interactive.

***Dunigan, John.** Essential Golf: Everything You Need to Know & How to Learn It! LC 98-96930. (Illus.). 192p. 1999. pap. 20.00 (*0-9669375-0-3*) Golf Bet.

— The Secret of the Golf Swing. (Illus.). 84p. 2000. pap. 18.95 (*0-9669375-1-1*) Golf Bet.

Dunigan, Mike & Parker, J. B. Resplandores: Cap & Rays 8 Reales of the Republic of Mexico. LC 97-61923. 460p. 1997. text 125.00 (*0-9662935-0-9*) Sup Stamp.

Duniho, Terence. Actual Type - Determining Who You Really Are. 32p. Date not set. pap. write for info. (*1-878287-32-X*) Type & Temperament.

— Creativity & Risk in the Workplace. Date not set. pap. write for info. (*1-878287-36-2*) Type & Temperament.

— Freud & Jung: Patterns in Conflict. Date not set. pap. write for info. (*1-878287-29-X*) Type & Temperament.

— Making Good Decisions. 1989. pap. 2.50 (*1-878287-28-1*) Type & Temperament.

— Patterns of Preference. Date not set. pap. write for info. (*1-878287-33-8*) Type & Temperament.

— Wellness vs. Neurotic Styles: Holistic or Monomanic Use of the Four Functions. 1991. pap. 5.95 (*1-878287-31-1*) Type & Temperament.

— Your Shadow Side - The Fourth Function: Achilles' Heel & Pearl of Great Price. 36p. 1991. pap. 5.95 (*1-878287-30-3*) Type & Temperament.

Dunikoski, Robert H. Computers & Information Processing Today with BASIC. 3rd ed. Perlee, Clyde, ed. 401p. (C). 1988. mass mkt. 51.00 (*0-314-64976-X*) West Pub.

— Computers & Information Processing Today Without BASIC. 3rd ed. Perlee, Clyde, ed. 401p. (C) 1988. mass mkt. 52.50 (*0-314-64975-1*) West Pub.

Dunin, Elsie I. South Slavic Dances in California: A Compendium for the Years, 1924-1977. LC 79-63063. 1979. 10.00 (*0-918660-11-4*) Ragusan Pr.

Dunin, Elsie I. & Ruyter, Nancy L. Yugoslav Dance: An Introduction & List of Sources Available in United States Libraries. LC 80-51688. 100p. 1981. per. 10.00 (*0-918660-12-2*) Ragusan Pr.

Dunin, Ivan. The Well of Days. 316p. Date not set. 24.95 (*0-8488-2254-4*) Amereon Ltd.

Duning, Becky S. & Pittman, Von V., eds. Distance Education Symposium 3: Policy & Administration. LC 98-146707. (ACSDE Research Monograph Ser.: No. 11). 88p. (Orig.). 1996. pap. text 30.00 (*1-877780-14-6*) ACSDE.

Dunis, Christian. Exchange Rate Forecasting. 1990. text 60.00 (*1-55738-100-3*, Irwn Prfssnl) McGraw-Hill Prof.

— Forecasting Financial Markets. LC 96-22532. 324p. 1996. 110.00 (*0-471-96653-3*) Wiley.

— Non-Linear Modelling of High Frequency Financial Time-Series. LC 97-44713. (Series in Financial Economics & Quantitative Analysis). 320p. 1998. 133.95 (*0-471-97464-1*) Wiley.

***Dunis, Christian L.** Advances in Quantitative Asset Management. LC 99-86380. (Studies in Computational Finance). 2000. write for info. (*0-7923-7778-8*) Kluwer Academic.

Dunitz, J., jt. auth. see Heilbronner, E.

Dunitz, J. D., et al, eds. Luminescence & Energy Transfer. (Structure & Bonding Ser.: Vol. 42). (Illus.). 133p. 1980. 58.95 (*0-387-10395-3*) Spr-Verlag.

Dunitz, Jack D. X-Ray Analysis & the Structure of Organic Molecules. LC 78-15588. (Illus.). 514p. (C). 1995. reprint ed. 105.00 (*3-906390-14-4*, Wiley-VCH) Wiley.

Dunitz, Jay. Pacific Light. Levitt, Peter, ed. (Illus.). 112p. 1989. 95.00 (*0-941831-23-X*) Beyond Words Pub.

Dunitz, Robin J. California Murals Postcard: Postcard Book, Featuring Images from Painting the Town. (Illus.). 61p. 1998. pap. 9.95 (*0-9632862-7-7*) RJD Ent.

— Los Angeles Murals: A Book of Postcards. (Illus.). 61p. (Orig.). 1995. pap. 9.95 (*0-9632862-3-4*) RJD Ent.

— Los Angeles Murals by African-American Artists: A Book of Postcards. (Illus.). 61p. (Orig.). 1995. pap. 9.95 (*0-9632862-2-6*) RJD Ent.

— Street Gallery: A Guide to One Thousand Murals of Los Angeles County. LC 92-97162. (Illus.). 469p. 1993. pap. 24.95 (*0-9632862-1-8*) RJD Ent.

— Street Gallery: Guide to over 1000 Los Angeles Murals. 1998. pap. text 45.00 (*0-9632862-8-5*) RJD Ent.

Dunitz, Robin J. & Prigoff, James. Painting the Towns: Murals of California. (Illus.). 304p. 1997. pap. 29.95 (*0-9632862-4-2*) RJD Ent.

— Painting the Towns: Murals of California. unabridged ed. (Illus.). 304p. 1997. 49.95 (*0-9632862-5-0*) RJD Ent.

***Dunitz, Robin J. & Prigoff, James.** Walls of Heritage, Walls of Pride: African American Murals. LC 00-29133. (Illus.). 280p. 2000. boxed set 60.00 (*0-7649-1339-5*, A567) Pomegranate Calif.

***Duniway, Abigail Scott.** Edna & John: A Romance of Idaho Flat. Shein, Debra, ed. LC 99-53703. (Illus.). 244p. 2000. pap. 19.95 (*0-87422-188-9*) Wash St U Pr.

Duniway, David. Dr. Luke A. Port, Builder of Deepwood: An Urban Report - From England to Salem, Oregon & San Diego, California. LC 89-12608. (Illus.). 94p. (Orig.). 1989. pap. 11.00 (*0-943297-01-X*) Marion Coun Hist Soc.

Duniway, David C., jt. ed. see Holmes, Kenneth L.

Dunk, Klaus Von der, see Buff, Wolfram & Von der Dunk, Klaus.

Dunk, Thomas W. It's a Working Man's Town: Male Working-Class Culture. LC 92-246444. 208p. 1991. 65.00 (*0-7735-0861-9*, Pub. by McG-Queens Univ Pr) CUP Services.

— It's a Working Man's Town: Male Working-Class Culture. 208p. 1995. pap. 22.95 (*0-7735-1304-3*, Pub. by McG-Queens Univ Pr) CUP Services.

Dunkel. Theory & Practice in Listening. (College ESL Ser.). (J). 1996. mass mkt. 19.95 (*0-8384-5930-7*) Heinle & Heinle.

Dunkel, F., jt. ed. see Van Zyl Smit, Dirk.

Dunkel, Frieder, jt. ed. see Van Zyl Smit, Dirk.

Dunkel, Harold B. & Pillet, Roger A. French in the Elementary School: Five Years Experience. LC 62-12631. 156p. reprint ed. pap. 48.40 (*0-608-10701-8*, 201996200015) Bks Demand.

Dunkel, Johann G. Historisch-Kritische Nachrichten von Verstorbenen Gelehrten und Deren Schriften, 3 vols., Set. 2596p. 1968. reprint ed. write for info. (*0-318-70765-9*) G Olms Pubs.

Dunkel, Manuela. Fortbildung und Unschulung Unter Transformationsbedingungen. (Illus.). XIX, 255p. 1997. 54.95 (*3-631-31934-7*) P Lang Pubng.

Dunkel, Norbert W. & Schuh, John. Advising Student Groups & Organizations. LC 97-21125. (Higher & Adult Education Ser.). 1997. pap. 29.95 (*0-7879-1033-3*) Jossey-Bass.

Dunkel, Norbert W. & Spencer, Cindy L., eds. Advice for Advisers: The Development of a Residence Hall Association. 230p. 1998. pap. text 37.00 (*0-945109-00-8*) Assn Coll U Hse.

Dunkel, Pat & Gorder, Christine. Start with Listening. 256p. (J). 1987. mass mkt. 7.95 (*0-8384-2821-5*, Newbury) Heinle & Heinle.

— Start with Listening. 256p. (J). (gr. 9 up). 1987. mass mkt. 12.50 (*0-8384-2820-7*, Newbury) Heinle & Heinle.

Dunkel, Patricia. Advanced Listening Comprehension. 2nd ed. (College ESL Ser.). 187p. (J). 1996. mass mkt. 31.95 (*0-8384-4842-9*) Heinle & Heinle.

Dunkel, Patricia & Lim, Phyllis L. Intermediate Listening Comprehension. 184p. (J). 1982. pap. 19.95 (*0-8384-2966-1*, Newbury) Heinle & Heinle.

— Intermediate Listening Comprehension. 184p. (J). 1991. audio 95.95 (*0-8384-2965-3*, Newbury) Heinle & Heinle.

— Intermediate Listening Comprehension: Understanding & Recalling Spoken English. 2nd ed. LC 93-27953. 208p. (J). 1993. mass mkt. 26.95 (*0-8384-4838-0*) Heinle & Heinle.

Dunkel, Patricia & Pialorsi, Frank. Advanced Listening Comprehension. 187p. (J). 1982. pap. 24.50 (*0-8384-2963-7*, Newbury) Heinle & Heinle.

D

An Asterisk (*) at the beginning of an entry indicates that the title is appearing for the first time.

Dunkel-Schetter, C., jt. auth. see Stanton, A. L.

Dunkel, Stuart E. The Audition Process: Anxiety Management & Coping Strategies. LC 89-37075. (Juilliard Performance Guides Ser.: No. 3). 200p. 1990. pap. 16.95 (*0-945193-35-1*) Pendragon NY.

Dunkelberg, Anne. Expanding the Medicaid Program in Texas: Funding Issues & Alternatives. 237p. 1988. reprint ed. pap. 10.00 (*0-89940-861-3*) LBJ Sch Pub Aff.

— Texas Medicaid in Perspective. (Illus.). 159p. (Orig.). (C). 1995. pap. text 35.00 (*0-7881-1535-9*) DIANE Pub.

Dunkelberg, John S. & Sulock, Joseph M. Cases In Financial Management. 2nd ed. LC 96-29420. 384p. 1996. pap. 52.95 (*0-471-11043-4*) Wiley.

Dunkelberger, David L., jt. auth. see Lutz, John T.

Dunkelberger, Dottie. Household Hints Your Mother Never Told You. 2nd ed. (Illus.). 120p. 1989. per. 8.95 (*1-877633-00-3*) Luthers.

Dunkeld, Colin, jt. auth. see Hall, Betty L.

Dunkell, Samuel. Goodbye Insomnia, Hello Sleep. LC 94-18114. (Illus.). 256p. 1994. 18.95 (*1-55972-247-9*, Birch Ln Pr) Carol Pub Group.

Dunkelman, Ben. Dual Allegiance: Freud as A Modern Jew. 336p. 1976. mass mkt. 5.95 (*0-88780-127-7*, Pub. by Formac Publ Co) Formac Dist Ltd.

Dunkelman, Mark H. Gettysburg's Unknown Soldier. LC 98-40342. 304p. 1999. 45.00 (*0-275-96294-6*, Praeger Pubs) Greenwood.

Dunkels, Marjorie. Donkey Wrinkles & Tales. 80p. 1990. pap. 21.00 (*0-85131-274-8*, Pub. by J A Allen) St Mut.

Dunker. European Community Aeronautics Research. 5 vols., Set. 1996. text 200.00 (*0-471-95177-3*) Wiley.

Dunker, Marilee. Walker's Point. LC 97-33838. (Portraits Ser.). 272p. 1997. pap. 8.99 (*1-55661-997-9*) Bethany Hse.

Dunker, Marilee P. Days of Glory, Seasons of Night. rev. ed. 176p. (C). 1984. reprint ed. pap. 7.95 (*0-310-45501-4*, 12040P) Zondervan.

Dunker, R., ed. Advances in Bearing Design & Instrumentation: Techniques for Aero-Engines. (European Community-Aeronautics Research Ser.). 154p. 1996. 110.00 (*0-471-95363-6*) Wiley.

— Advances in Engine Technology. (European Community-Aeronautics Research Ser.). 372p. 1995. 160.00 (*0-471-95102-1*) Wiley.

Dunkerley, Charlotte. Working with Soft Furnishings: A Practical Guide to Professional Techniques. LC 96-229402. (Illus.). 160p. 1996. 29.95 (*0-7063-7408-8*, Pub. by WrLock) Sterling.

— Working with Soft Furnishings: A Practical Guide to Professional Techniques. (Illus.). 160p. 1998. pap. 19.95 (*0-7063-7735-4*, Pub. by WrLock) Sterling.

Dunkerley, David, jt. auth. see Clegg, Stewart.

Dunkerley, James. The Pacification of Central America: Political Change in the Isthmus, 1987-1993. LC 93-46843. 180p. (C). 1994. pap. 19.00 (*0-86091-648-0*, Pub. by Verso) Norton.

— Political Suicide in Latin America: And Other Essays. LC 91-38676. 278p. (C). 1992. pap. 19.00 (*0-86091-560-3*, A6411, Pub. by Verso) Norton.

***Dunkerley, James.** Warriors & Scribes: Essays in the History & Politics of Latin America. 240p. 2000. 60.00 (*1-85984-754-4*, Pub. by Verso); pap. 20.00 (*1-85984-272-0*) Verso.

Dunkerley, James, jt. ed. see Bulmer-Thomas, Victor.

Dunkerley, Joy. International Comparisons of Energy Consumption. LC 78-4334. 256p. 1978. pap. 15.00 (*0-8018-2129-0*) Johns Hopkins.

— Trends in Energy Use in Industrial Societies: An Overview. LC 80-8022. (Resources for the Future Ser.: No. R-19). 167p. reprint ed. pap. 51.80 (*0-608-18088-2*, 203215000078) Bks Demand.

Dunkerley, Joy, ed. International Comparisons of Energy Consumption: Proceedings of a Workshop. LC 78-4334. (Resources for the Future Ser.: No. R-10). (Illus.). 252p. reprint ed. pap. 78.20 (*0-608-18087-4*, 203214900078) Bks Demand.

Dunkerley, Joy, et al. Energy Strategies for Developing Nations. LC 80-8774. 265p. 1981. pap. 16.95 (*0-8018-2597-0*) Resources Future.

Dunkerley, Michael. The Jobless Economy? Computer Technology in the World of Work. LC 96-26100. 120p. (C). 1996. 60.95 (*0-7456-1577-5*); pap. 27.95 (*0-7456-1578-3*) Blackwell Pubs.

Dunkerley, William J. The Faithful Centurion: A Saga of Faith. LC 90-20112. 240p. (Orig.). 1991. pap. 9.95 (*0-931832-78-0*) Fithian Pr.

***Dunkerly, James.** Americana: The Americas in the World Around 1850. (Illus.). 600p. 2000. 40.00 (*1-85984-753-6*, Pub. by Verso) Norton.

***Dunkerton, Jill, et al.** Durer to Veronese: Sixteenth-Century Paintings in the National Gallery. LC 99-25852. (Illus.). 317p. 1999. 65.00 (*0-300-07220-1*) Yale U Pr.

Dunkerton, Jill, et al. Giotto to Durer: Early Renaissance Painting in the National Gallery. (Illus.). 408p. (C). 1991. pap. 35.00 (*0-300-05082-8*) Yale U Pr.

Dunkerton, Jill, jt. auth. see Hirst, Michael.

Dunkin. Encyclopedia of Teaching. (Advances in Education Ser.). 1987. 70.00 (*0-08-034251-5*, Pergamon Pr) Elsevier.

Dunkin, A. C., jt. ed. see Taverner, M. R.

Dunkin, Alan. Galapagos: Mendel's Escape: The Official Strategy Guide. LC 97-69764. (Secrets of the Game Ser.). 144p. 1997. per. 19.99 (*0-7615-1312-4*) Prima Pub.

Dunkin, Ian R. Matrix-Isolation Techniques: A Practical Approach. (The Practical Approach Ser.). (Illus.). 252p. 1998. text 105.00 (*0-19-855863-5*) OUP.

Dunkin, Paul. How to Catalog a Rare Book. 2nd rev. ed. LC 72-6515. 117p. reprint ed. pap. 36.30 (*0-608-14575-0*, 202492200039) Bks Demand.

Dunkins, Betty M. & Gray, Joy. The Perfect Choice: The Ultimate Party & Wedding Location Guide. 2nd rev. ed. Parker, Nancy, ed. LC 97-94688. viii, 359p. 1998. pap. 19.95 (*0-9641379-1-7*) Gray McPherson.

Dunkins, Betty M. & Gray-Miott, Joy. The Perfect Choice: Wedding Location Guide. LC 93-81089. 294p. 1994. pap. 19.95 (*0-9641379-0-9*) Gray McPherson.

Dunkl, Charles F. & Ramirez, Donald E. Topics in Harmonic Analysis. LC 73-153387. (Century Mathematics Ser.). (C). 1971. 37.50 (*0-89197-454-7*) Irvington.

Dunkle, Alice. Successful People: What Makes Them That Way? 1987. pap. text 14.00 (*0-910609-14-4*) Gifted Educ Pr.

Dunkle, David S. Guide to Pension & Profit Sharing Plans: Taxation, Selection, & Design. (Commercial Law Publications). 1552p. 1984. text 115.00 (*0-07-018227-2*) Shepards.

Dunkle, Harvey I., tr. see Drach, Albert.

Dunkle, Harvey I., tr. see Gregor, Henry.

Dunkle, Harvey I., tr. see Klinger, Kurt.

Dunkle, Harvey I., tr. see Skwara, Erich W.

Dunkle, Harvey I., tr. see Von Starhemberg, Heinrich.

Dunkle, Jac L. & Edwards, Martha S. The No Leftovers! Child Care Cookbook: Kid-Tested Recipes & Menus for Centers & Home-Based Programs. LC 92-15973. (Illus.). 210p. (Orig.). 1992. pap. 14.95 (*0-934140-64-2*, 5211) Redleaf Pr.

Dunkle, Margaret, jt. auth. see Ingpen, Robert.

Dunkle, Robert J. & Lainhart, Ann S. The Town Records of Roxbury, Massachusetts, 1647 to 1730: Being Volume One of the Original. LC 97-12907. 1997. 35.00 (*0-88082-065-9*) New Eng Hist.

Dunkle, Ruth, jt. ed. see Harel, Zev.

Dunkle, Ruth E. & Wykle, May L., eds. Decision Making in Long-Term Care: Factors in Planning. 224p. 1988. 24.95 (*0-8261-5970-2*) Springer Pub.

Dunkle, Sidney W. Dragonflies of the Florida Peninsula, Bermuda & the Bahamas. (Illus.). 154p. 1989. pap. 16.95 (*0-945417-23-3*) Sci Pubs.

***Dunkle, Sidney W.** Dragonflies Through Binoculars: A Field & Finding Guide to Dragonflies of North America. (Butterflies (or Other) Through Binoculars Ser.). (Illus.). 352p. 2000. pap. 29.95 (*0-19-511268-7*) OUP.

Dunkle, W. E. A Birds Eye View. LC 88-11370. 1988. 17.95 (*0-943929-00-8*) J Sellers Pr.

Dunkle, W. E. A Trial in San Serra. 451p. mass mkt. 5.99 (*1-55197-553-X*) Picasso Publ.

Dunkleberger, Jeff. Ace the MCSE. 1998. pap. 24.99 (*0-07-134270-2*) Osborne-McGraw.

***Dunklee, Dennis R.** If You Want to Lead, Not Just Manage: A Primer for Principals. LC 00-8180. (One-Off Ser.). (Illus.). 176p. 2000. pap. 22.95 (*0-7619-7647-7*); lib. bdg. 51.95 (*0-7619-7646-9*) Corwin Pr.

Dunklee, Dennis R. You Sound Taller on the Telephone: A Practitioner's View of the Principalship. LC 98-51238. 280p. 1999. 67.95 (*0-8039-6849-3*); pap. 30.95 (*0-8039-6850-7*) Corwin Pr.

Dunklee, Dennis R., jt. auth. see Shoop, Robert J.

Dunkleman, Martha L. Central Italian Painting, Fourteen Hundred - Fourteen Sixty-Five: An Annotated Bibliography. (Reference Books - Art History). 388p. (C). 1986. 75.00 (*0-8161-8546-8*, Hall Reference) Macmillan.

Dunkley, ed. see Defresny.

Dunkley, ed. see Pere, Vernice W.

***Dunkley, Diana.** Two-Hour No-Sew Decorating. LC 99-56903. (Illus.). 128p. 2000. 27.95 (*0-8069-9978-0*) Sterling.

Dunkley, Graham. The Free Trade Adventure: Australia, the Uruguay Round & Globalism. LC 98-128336. 208p. 1996. pap. 34.95 (*0-522-84680-7*, Pub. by Melbourne Univ Pr) Paul & Co Pubs.

***Dunkley, Graham.** Free Trade Adventure: The WTO the Uruguay Round & Globalism. LC 99-51631. 2000. pap. 27.50 (*1-85649-769-0*); text 69.95 (*1-85649-768-2*) Zed Books.

Dunkley, J. & Kirton, W. Voices in the Air: French Dramatists & the Resources of Language. 200p. 1993. 90.00 (*0-85261-340-7*, Pub. by Univ of Glasgow) St Mut.

Dunkley, John J., jt. auth. see Yule, Andrew J.

Dunklin, Philip I. Best Practices in Utility Quality Initiatives. Smith, L. Dennis & Hope, Dee, eds. (Illus.). 100p. 1998. spiral bd. 98.00 (*1-891790-01-3*) Chartwell Inc.

— The Chartwell AMR Report, 1999. 4th rev. ed. Couret, Jacques & Smith, L. Dennis, eds. (Illus.). 436p. 1998. spiral bd. 975.00 (*1-891790-15-3*) Chartwell Inc.

— Chartwell's Case Studies in Energy Sales & Marketing: Advertising & New Products & Services. Smith, L. Dennis, III & Shumake, Rodney, eds. (Energy Sales & Marketing Ser.: Vol. 1). 99p. 1999. spiral bd. 150.00 (*1-891790-18-8*) Chartwell Inc.

— Chartwell's Case Studies in Energy Sales & Marketing: Strategic Alliances & Customer Choice. Smith, L. Dennis, III & Shumake, Rodney, eds. (Energy Sales & Marketing Ser.: Vol. 2). 93p. 1999. spiral bd. 150.00 (*1-891790-19-6*) Chartwell Inc.

***Dunklin, Philip I.** Chartwell's Guide to E-Commerce in the Energy Industry, 2 vols. Smith, L. Dennis et al, eds. 536p. 1999. spiral bd. 1495.00 (*1-891790-29-3*) Chartwell Inc.

— Competition in the Energy Industry: The First Wave. Smith, L. Dennis et al, eds. 1999. spiral bd. 495.00 (*1-891790-28-5*) Chartwell Inc.

Dunkling. London. 1984. pap. text. write for info. (*0-582-74905-0*, Pub. by Addison-Wesley) Longman.

— Mike's Lucky Day. 1984. pap. text. write for info. (*0-582-52973-5*, Pub. by Addison-Wesley) Longman.

Dunkling & Wright Staff. Dictionary of Pub Names. (Reference Library). 320p. 1998. pap. 6.95 (*1-85326-334-6*, 3346WW, Pub. by Wrdsworth Edits) NTC Contemp Pub Co.

Dunkling, Leslie. The Guinness Drinking Companion. 224p. 1995. 22.95 (*1-55821-380-5*) Lyons Pr.

— Mike's Best Summer. (American Structural Readers Stage Ser.: No. 1). (Illus.). 16p. 1989. pap. text 6.31 (*0-582-79885-X*, 75124) Longman.

— Mikes Lucky Day, 1. (Longman Originals Ser.). 1996. pap. text 5.51 (*0-582-07499-1*) Addison-Wesley.

Dunkling, Leslie & Gosling, William. New American Dictionary of Baby Names. 496p. 1991. mass mkt. 6.99 (*0-451-17107-1*, Sig) NAL.

Dunkman, William E. Qualitative Credit Control. (Columbia University. Studies in the Social Sciences: No. 395). reprint ed. 32.50 (*0-404-51395-6*) AMS Pr.

Dunlap, A. R. Dutch & Swedish Place-Names in Delaware. LC 57-62613. 66p. pap. 2.50 (*0-87413-110-3*) U Delaware Pr.

Dunlap, Albert J. Mean Business: How I Save Bad Companies & Make Good Ones Great. 304p. 1997. per. 14.00 (*0-684-84406-0*, Fireside) S&S Trade Pap.

Dunlap, Albert J. & Andleman, Bob. Mean Business: How I Save Bad Companies & Make Good Companies Great. 1996. 25.00 (*0-614-19862-3*, Times Bks) Crown Pub Group.

Dunlap, Anne, ed. see Dunlap, Cas.

Dunlap, B. J., ed. see Academy of Marketing Science Staff.

Dunlap-Berg, Larry. The Environment. (Lifesearch Ser.). 64p. (Orig.). 1994. pap. 4.95 (*0-687-77878-6*) Abingdon.

Dunlap, Carol. The Culture Vulture: A Guide to Style, Period & Ism. LC 93-1394. (Illus.). 320p. 1995. pap. 19.95 (*0-471-14423-1*) Wiley.

***Dunlap, Cas.** Beach Breezes. Dunlap, Anne, ed. (Illus.). 213p. 1999. pap. 9.95 (*0-9670420-2-X*, 103) Cas Dunlap.

— It's New to Us. Dunlap, Anne, ed. (Illus.). 196p. 1998. reprint ed. mass mkt. 9.95 (*0-9670420-1-1*, 102) Cas Dunlap.

— Southern Lights. Dunlap, Anne, ed. (Illus.). 185p. 1998. reprint ed. mass mkt. 9.95 (*0-9670420-0-3*, 101) Cas Dunlap.

Dunlap, Dan, jt. auth. see Cassady, Jim.

***Dunlap, David & Vecchione, Joe.** Sacred Sights in New York. (Illus.). 128p. 2000. pap. 14.00 (*1-929439-01-6*) City & Co.

***Dunlap, Deborah.** Historic Pensacola Photographs. Appleyard, John & Soule, Laura, eds. (Illus.). 160p. 1999. 49.95 (*1-929727-00-3*, HPP-001) Historic Pensa.

Dunlap, Diane M. & Schmuck, Patricia A., eds. Women Leading in Education. LC 94-7301. 444p. (C). 1994. text 74.50 (*0-7914-2215-1*); pap. text 24.95 (*0-7914-2216-X*) State U NY Pr.

Dunlap, Donald & Zea, Philip M. The Dunlap Cabinetmakers: A Tradition in Craftmanship. (Illus.). 224p. 1994. 49.95 (*0-8117-0990-6*) Stackpole.

***Dunlap, E. Scott.** Motor Carrier Safety: A Guide to Regulatory Compliance. LC 99-51410. (Occupational Safety & Health Guide Ser.). 313p. 2000. 89.95 (*1-56670-356-5*) Lewis Pubs.

Dunlap, Edward A., jt. auth. see Chapman, Loring F.

Dunlap, Ellen S., et al. A Quarter Century of Visiting Fellowships at the American Antiquarian Society, 1972-97. (Illus.). 56p. 1998. pap. 9.50 (*0-944026-89-3*) Am Antiquarian.

Dunlap, Elvira, ed. see Cota-Robles, Patricia D.

Dunlap, Franklin & Perrill, John H. The Adventures of Talldorf & Small: The Myth, Bk. 1. 546p. (Orig.). 1990. pap. 15.00 (*0-9626555-0-3*) Wilderness Road.

Dunlap, G. D. Dutton's Navigation & Piloting. 44.95 (*0-87021-163-3*) Naval Inst Pr.

Dunlap, G. D., jt. auth. see Shufeldt, H. H.

Dunlap, Gertrude F. Fox Point Remembered: Early Development in New Castle, Delaware. (Illus.). 89p. (Orig.). 1992. pap. text 34.95 (*0-941375-49-8*) DIANE Pub.

Dunlap, Harry. Dear Mother-in-Law. LC 96-97004. 274p. (Orig.). (YA). 1996. pap. 16.95 (*1-57502-303-2*, P01037) Morris Pubng.

Dunlap, Helen D., jt. auth. see Moss, Robert A.

Dunlap, Howard G. Social Aspects of a Verb Form: Native Atlanta Fifth-Grade Speech - The Present Tense of Be. (Publications of the American Dialect Society: Nos. 61 & 62). 96p. 1974. pap. text 10.50 (*0-8173-0661-7*) U of Ala Pr.

Dunlap, J. E. & Wayner, John. Knowing the Numbers: Gain & Retain Control of Your Practice. 128p. 1990. 44.95 (*0-87814-355-6*) PennWell Bks.

Dunlap, Jay C., jt. ed. see Hall, Jeffrey C.

Dunlap, Jessie, jt. auth. see Schuler, Charles A.

Dunlap, Jim. Critter Chronicles. (Illus.). 168p. (Orig.). 1993. pap. 12.95 (*1-55622-312-9*, Seaside Pr) Wordware Pub.

— Only, the Last Dinosaur. LC 94-39155. (Illus.). 152p. 1994. pap. 8.95 (*1-55622-382-X*, Rep of TX Pr) Wordware Pub.

— Pete the Python: The Further Adventures of Mark & Deke. 160p. 1996. pap. 8.95 (*1-55622-508-3*, Seaside Pr) Wordware Pub.

— Slithering Around Texas. LC 93-34488. (Illus.). 208p. 1993. pap. 12.95 (*1-55622-313-7*, Rep of TX Pr) Wordware Pub.

— They Don't Have to Die: Home & Classroom Care for Small Animals. LC 90-12685. (Illus.). 280p. (Orig.). 1990. pap. 12.95 (*1-55622-193-2*, Seaside Pr) Wordware Pub.

— They Don't Have to Die: Home & Classroom Care for Small Animals. 2nd ed. LC 96-44549. 288p. (Orig.). 1996. pap. 12.95 (*1-55622-533-4*, Seaside Pr) Wordware Pub.

Dunlap, Jon & Waren, William. Low-Income Housing: Overview of State-Federal Issues. (State-Federal Issue Brief Ser.: Vol. 5, No. 3). 22p. 1992. pap. text 6.50 (*1-55516-897-3*, 8500-0503) Natl Conf State Legis.

Dunlap, Jonathan C. America's Newcomers: A State & Local Policymakers' Guide to Immigration Immigrant Policy. 32p. 1993. 10.00 (*1-55516-930-9*, 9353) Natl Conf State Legis.

— America's Newcomers: Health Care Issues for New Americans. 18p. 1993. 10.00 (*1-55516-928-7*, 9359) Natl Conf State Legis.

Dunlap, Jonathan C., jt. auth. see Morse, Ann.

Dunlap, Judith. Faith Formation: A Parish Planning Workbook. (Follow Me! Ser.). 1998. pap. 9.95 (*1-881307-12-3*, B7123) Natl Pastoral LC.

— Jesus Lives: Faith Stories for Young Children. (God Is Calling Ser.). 80p. (J). (gr. 2-5). 1997. pap. 8.95 (*0-86716-285-6*) St Anthony Mess Pr.

— Spirit with Us: Faith Stories for Young Children. (God Is Calling Ser.). 88p. (J). (gr. 2-5). 1997. pap. 8.95 (*0-86716-289-9*) St Anthony Mess Pr.

— Together Time: Spirit with Us: Activities for Your Children. (Together Time Ser.). 64p. (J). (gr. 2-5). 1997. pap. 9.95 (*0-86716-290-2*) St Anthony Mess Pr.

— Together Time: Yahweh Calls: Activities with Young Children. (Together Time Ser.). (Illus.). 72p. (J). (gr. 2-5). 1997. pap. 9.95 (*0-86716-281-3*) St Anthony Mess Pr.

— Yahweh Calls: Faith Stories for Young Children. (Faith Stories Ser.). (Illus.). 80p. (J). (gr. 2-5). 1997. pap. 8.95 (*0-86716-280-5*) St Anthony Mess Pr.

Dunlap, Judith & Suttman, Carleen. Praying All Ways. Kielbasa, Marilyn, ed. (Horizons Ser.: Level 1, Minicourse 6). (Illus.). 56p. (Orig.). (YA). (gr. 9). 1996. pap. text, student ed. 9.95 (*0-88489-364-2*) St Marys.

Dunlap, Judith & Wiodarski, Mary C. Together Time: Jesus Lives: Activities with Ages 11 to 14. (Together Time Ser.). 64p. (J). (gr. 6-9). 1997. pap. text 9.95 (*0-86716-288-0*) St Anthony Mess Pr.

— Together Time: Jesus Lives: Activities with Young Children. (Together Time Ser.). 64p. (J). 1997. pap. 9.95 (*0-86716-286-4*) St Anthony Mess Pr.

Dunlap, Judith & Wiodavski, Mary C. God Is Calling: Leader's Guide. 160p. 1997. pap., teacher ed. 15.95 (*0-86716-293-7*) St Anthony Mess Pr.

— Together Time: Yahweh Calls: Activities with Ages 11 to 14. (Together Time Ser.). 64p. (J). (gr. 6-9). 1997. pap. 9.95 (*0-86716-284-8*) St Anthony Mess Pr.

Dunlap, Julie. Birds in the Bushes: A Story about Margaret Morse Nice. (Carolrhoda Creative Minds Bks.). (Illus.). (J). 1996. lib. bdg. 19.93 (*1-57505-006-4*, Carolrhoda) Lerner Pub.

— Extraordinary Horseshoe Crabs. LC 98-6990. 48p. (J). (gr. 2-5). 1999. 22.60 (*1-57505-293-8*, Carolrhoda) Lerner Pub.

— Eye on the Wild: A Story about Ansel Adams. (Creative Minds Biographies Ser.). (Illus.). 56p. (J). (gr. 3-6). 1995. pap. 5.95 (*0-87614-966-2*, First Ave Edns) Lerner Pub.

— Parks for the People: A Story about Frederick Law Olmsted. LC 93-40988. (Carolrhoda Creative Minds Bks.). (Illus.). (J). (gr. 3-6). 1994. lib. bdg. 19.95 (*0-87614-824-0*, Carolrhoda) Lerner Pub.

Dunlap, Julie & Maguire, Kerry. Eye on the Wild: A Story about Ansel Adams. LC 94-42172. (Creative Minds Biographies Ser.). (Illus.). 64p. (J). (gr. 3-6). 1995. lib. bdg. 19.93 (*0-87614-944-1*, Carolrhoda) Lerner Pub.

***Dunlap, Karen Brown.** Effective Editor: How to Lead Your Staff to Better Writing & Teamwork. 2000. pap. 18.95 (*1-56625-142-7*) Bonus Books.

Dunlap, Katherine M., jt. auth. see Bigger, Margaret G.

Dunlap, Kathi. Mathematics for Health Occupations. 200p. (C). 1991. mass mkt. 28.50 (*0-8273-4173-3*) Delmar.

Dunlap, Knight. Habits: Their Making & Unmaking. LC 77-184102. 336p. 1949. pap. 3.95 (*0-87140-267-X*, Pub. by Liveright) Norton.

— Mysticism, Freudianism & Scientific Psychology. (Select Bibliographies Reprint Ser.). 1977. reprint ed. 19.95 (*0-8369-5838-1*) Ayer.

Dunlap, Lauren G. & Fruge-Brown, Kathleen. And I, Francis: The Life of Francis of Assisi in Word & Image. large type ed. (Illus.). 128p. 1996. 19.95 (*0-8264-0867-2*) Continuum.

***Dunlap, Lauren G. & Fruge-Brown, Kathleen.** And I, Francis: The Life of Francis of Assisi in Word & Image. 120p. 2000. reprint ed. pap. 16.95 (*0-8264-1272-6*) Continuum.

Dunlap, Leslie, jt. auth. see Ortiz, Darwin.

Dunlap, Leslie W. American Historical Societies: 1790-1860. LC 73-16331. (Perspectives in American History Ser.: No. 7). ix, 238p. 1974. reprint ed. lib. bdg. 35.00 (*0-87991-343-6*) Porcupine Pr.

Dunlap, Linda L. An Introduction to Early Childhood Special Education. LC 96-41886. 368p. 1997. 67.00 (*0-205-18440-5*) Allyn.

— An Introduction to Early Childhood Special Education. (C). 1998. pap., teacher ed. write for info. (*0-205-26546-4*, T6546-0) Allyn.

Dunlap, Lloyd A., ed. see Scripps, John L.

***Dunlap, Michelle Robin.** Voices of Community Volunteering & Service-Learning: Student Perspective on Working with Children & Families. 2000. pap. 17.95 (*0-8476-9116-0*) Rowman.

Dunlap, Olga, tr. see Clement, M. Olivier.

Dunlap, Orrin E., Jr. Marconi: The Man & His Wireless. rev. ed. LC 72-161142. (History of Broadcasting: Radio to Television Ser.). 1976. reprint ed. 35.95 (*0-405-03563-2*) Ayer.

— The Outlook for Television. 1977. 23.95 (*0-405-03564-0*, 11231) Ayer.

D

— Radio's One Hundred Men of Science. LC 70-128235. (Essay Index Reprint Ser.). 1977. 27.95 (0-8369-1916-5) Ayer.

Dunlap, Patricia R. Riding Astride: The Frontier in Women's History. LC 95-21682. (Illus.). 220p. (C). 1996. 26.50 (0-912869-17-8); pap. 18.95 (0-912869-18-6) Arden Pr.

Dunlap, R. A. Experimental Physics: Modern Methods. (Illus.). 390p. (C). 1988. text 68.00 (0-19-504949-7) OUP.

— The Golden Ratio & Fibonacci Numbers. LC 97-28758. 650p. 1997. 34.00 (981-02-3264-0) World Scientific Pub.

Dunlap, Rikk. The Angel of Dreams: A Fable of Hope. unabridged ed. LC 98-90287. 144p. 1998. pap. 12.95 (0-9664409-0-0) Self Hope.

Dunlap, Riley E., et al, eds. Public Reactions to Nuclear Waste: Citizens' Views of Repository Siting. LC 93-6980. (Illus.). 384p. (C). 1993. text 54.95 (0-8223-1355-3); pap. text 24.95 (0-8223-1373-1) Duke.

Dunlap, Riley E. & Mertig, Angela G., eds. American Environmentalism: The U. S. Environmental Movement, 1970-1990. 115p. 1992. pap. 21.95 (0-8448-1730-9, Crane Russak) Taylor & Francis.

***Dunlap, Ruth L.** Dunlap Lads & Lasses: Descendants of Samuel Dunlap of Lancaster County, Pennsylvania, to Virginia, Ohio, & Beyond. unabridged ed. (Illus.). 182p. 1998. 27.50 (0-9666788-0-X) Ruth L Dunlap.

Dunlap, Samuel F. Sod, the Mysteries of Adonai. LC 92-81766. (Secret Doctrine Reference Ser.). 240p. 2000. reprint ed. pap. 16.00 (0-913510-62-9) Wizards.

— Sod, the Son of Man. 2nd ed. LC 92-81768. (Secret Doctrine Reference Ser.). (Illus.). 192p. 1998. reprint ed. pap. 14.00 (0-913510-61-0) Wizards.

Dunlap, Sarah V. The Jewish Community of Cape Ann: An Oral History. LC 98-88680. (Illus.). ix, 302p. 1998. 25.00 (0-9667776-0-3) Cape Ann Jewish Comm.

Dunlap, Shirlee. Circle of Light. (Illus.). 183p. (Orig.). 1982. pap. 7.95 (0-942494-19-9) Coleman Pub.

Dunlap, Susan. High Fall. large type ed. LC 95-3697. (Large Print Bks.). 1995. pap. 19.95 (1-56895-093-4) Wheeler Pub.

Dunlap, Susan. No Immunity: A Kiernan O'Shaughnessy Mystery. 1999. mass mkt. 5.99 (0-440-22480-2) Dell.

***Dunlap, Susan.** No Immunity: A Kiernan O'Shaughnessy Mystery. LC 99-46184. 1999. pap. 22.95 (1-56895-782-3, Wheeler) Wheeler Pub.

Dunlap, Susan J. Counseling Depressed Women. LC 97-14697. (Counseling & Pastoral Theology Ser.). 1997. pap. 16.00 (0-664-25667-8) Westminster John Knox.

***Dunlap, Thomas.** Nature & the English Diaspora: Environment & History in the United States, Canada, Australia, & New Zealand. (Studies in Environment & History: No. 17). (Illus.). 368p. (C). 1999. 59.95 (0-521-65173-5); pap. 19.95 (0-521-65700-8) Cambridge U Pr.

Dunlap, Thomas, tr. see Bracher, Karl D.

Dunlap, Thomas, tr. see Deichmann, Ute.

Dunlap, Thomas, tr. see Ladner, Gerhart B.

Dunlap, Thomas, tr. see Schwan, Gesine.

Dunlap, Thomas, tr. see Stolleis, Michael.

Dunlap, Thomas, tr. see Van Rossum, Gerhard D.

Dunlap, Thomas, tr. see Wolfram, Herwig.

Dunlap, Thomas J., tr. see Blickle, Peter.

Dunlap, Thomas J., tr. see Duden, Barbara.

Dunlap, Thomas J., tr. & illus. see Wolfram, Herwig.

Dunlap, W. Crawford, ed. see International Conference on Hot Electrons in Semic.

Dunlap, William. Adaptations of European Plays. LC 87-35629. 248p. 1988. 50.00 (0-8201-1428-6) Schol Facsimiles.

— Collected Works. 1990. reprint ed. lib. bdg. 75.00 (0-7812-2716-X, 1515); reprint ed. write for info. (0-318-67722-9); reprint ed. write for info. (0-318-67723-7); reprint ed. write for info. (0-318-67724-5); reprint ed. write for info. (0-318-67725-3); reprint ed. write for info. (0-318-67726-1); reprint ed. write for info. (0-318-67727-X) Rprt Serv.

— Diary of William Dunlap, 3 vols., 1 bk. LC 78-84204. 1000p. 1972. 63.95 (0-405-08474-9, Pub. by Blom Pubns) Ayer.

— Diary of William Dunlap, 1766-1839: The Memoirs of a Dramatist, Theatrical Manager, Painter, Critic, Novelist, & Historian. (American Biography Ser.). 502p. 1991. reprint ed. lib. bdg. 129.00 (0-7812-8116-4) Rprt Serv.

— Five Plays of William Dunlap. LC 91-12032. 368p. 1991. reprint ed. 50.00 (0-8201-1454-5) Schol Facsimiles.

— Four Plays, 1789-1812. LC 76-46978. 300p. 1976. lib. bdg. 50.00 (0-8201-1283-6) Schol Facsimiles.

— A History of New York, for Schools. (Notable American Authors Ser.). 1992. reprint ed. lib. bdg. 75.00 (0-7812-2722-4) Rprt Serv.

— History of the American Theater. (Notable American Authors Ser.). 1992. reprint ed. lib. bdg. 75.00 (0-7812-2719-4) Rprt Serv.

— History of the New Netherlands. (Notable American Authors Ser.). 1992. reprint ed. lib. bdg. 75.00 (0-7812-2723-2) Rprt Serv.

— History of the Rise & Progress of the Arts of Design in the United States. (Notable American Authors Ser.). 1992. reprint ed. lib. bdg. 270.00 (0-7812-2720-8) Rprt Serv.

— History of the Rise & Progress of the Arts of Design in the United States, 3 vols., 1. rev. ed. Bayley, Frank W. et al, eds. LC 65-16236. (Illus.). 1972. 30.95 (0-405-08471-4, Pub. by Blom Pubns) Ayer.

— History of the Rise & Progress of the Arts of Design in the United States, 3 vols., 2. rev. ed. Bayley, Frank W. et al, eds. LC 65-16236. (Illus.). 1972. 30.95 (0-405-08472-2, Pub. by Blom Pubns) Ayer.

— History of the Rise & Progress of the Arts of Design in the United States, 3 vols., 3. rev. ed. Bayley, Frank W. et al, eds. LC 65-16236. (Illus.). 1972. 30.95 (0-405-08473-0, Pub. by Blom Pubns) Ayer.

— History of the Rise & Progress of the Arts of Design in the United States, 3 vols., Set. rev. ed. Bayley, Frank W. et al, eds. LC 65-16236. (Illus.). 1972. 90.95 (0-405-08470-6, Pub. by Blom Pubns) Ayer.

— The Life of Charles Brockden Brown. (Notable American Authors Ser.). 1992. reprint ed. lib. bdg. 75.00 (0-7812-2718-6) Rprt Serv.

— The Life of Charles Brockden Brown, Vol. 1. 1988. reprint ed. lib. bdg. 75.00 (0-7812-0361-9) Rprt Serv.

— Memoir of George Fred Cooke. (Notable American Authors Ser.). 1992. reprint ed. lib. bdg. 75.00 (0-7812-2717-8) Rprt Serv.

— Musical Works. LC 79-24504. 1979. 50.00 (0-8201-1348-4) Schol Facsimiles.

— Thirty Years Ago; or The Memoirs of a Water-Drinker. (Notable American Authors Ser.). 1992. reprint ed. lib. bdg. 75.00 (0-7812-2721-6) Rprt Serv.

Dunlap, William, et al. Manual of Ground Water Sampling Procedures. 96p. 1981. 15.00 (1-56034-026-6, T029) Natl Grnd Water.

— Manual of Ground Water Sampling Procedures. 96p. (C). 1987. 160.00 (0-7855-6704-6, Pub. by Scientific) St Mut.

Dunlavy, Colleen A. Politics & Industrialization: Early Railroads in the United States & Prussia. LC 93-17455. (Studies in American Politics: Historical, International, & Comparative Perspectives). 283p. (C). 1993. text 49.50 (0-691-04769-3, Pub. by Princeton U Pr) Cal Prin Full Svc.

Dunlavy, John. Manifesto: or A Declaration of the Doctrines & Practice of the Church of Christ. LC 74-134416. reprint ed. 49.50 (0-404-08460-5) AMS Pr.

Dunlavy, Kathy. I Can Write All Through the Year. 160p. teacher ed. 12.99 (0-86653-743-0, GA1458) Good Apple.

— Learn & Grow from A to Z: Learning Centers & Activities for Young Children. (Illus.). 160p. (J). (ps-2). 1992. student ed. 14.99 (0-86653-682-5, GA1416) Good Apple.

Dunlavy, Kathy & Carroll, Jeri A. More Little Books to Make & Read. 176p. 1995. teacher ed. 13.99 (1-56417-720-3, GA1539) Good Apple.

Dunlavy, Kathy, jt. auth. see Carroll, Jeri.

***Dunlay, Thomas W.** Kit Carson & the Indians. LC 99-85995. (Illus.). 632p. 2000. 45.00 (0-8032-1715-3) U of Nebr Pr.

Dunlea, Anne. Vision & the Emergence of Meaning: Blind & Sighted Children's Early Language. (Illus.). 216p. (C). 1990. text 64.95 (0-521-30496-2) Cambridge U Pr.

Dunlea, Nancy. The Courtesy Book. LC 93-80030. (Illus.). 128p. (J). (gr. 4-8). 1993. reprint ed. pap. 7.95 (1-882420-07-1) Hearth KS.

Dunlea, William. Anne Hutchinson & the Puritans: An Early American Tragedy. 296p. (Orig.). 1993. pap. 10.95 (0-8059-3434-0) Dorrance.

— Artie Shaw: Rebel with a Clarinet. 272p. 1999. pap. 16.00 (0-8059-4332-3) Dorrance.

Dunleavy, jt. ed. see Ashe, pseud.

Dunleavy, Aidan O., et al, eds. Studies in the Sociology of Sport. LC 82-16807. 402p. (C). 1982. pap. 15.00 (0-912646-78-0) Tex Christian.

Dunleavy, Deborah. The Language Beat. 96p. (C). 1992. pap. text 16.50 (0-435-08615-4, 08615) Heinemann.

Dunleavy, Gareth W. Douglas Hyde. (Irish Writers Ser.). 92p. 1975. 8.50 (0-8387-7883-6); pap. 1.95 (0-8387-7975-1) Bucknell U Pr.

Dunleavy, Gareth W., jt. auth. see Dunleavy, Janet E.

Dunleavy, Gareth W., ed. see Hyde, Douglas.

Dunleavy, James F., jt. auth. see Ballantyne, Duncan S.

Dunleavy, Janet E. George Moore: The Artist's Vision, the Storyteller's Art. LC 75-125793. 156p. 1975. 26.50 (0-8387-7757-0) Bucknell U Pr.

Dunleavy, Janet E., ed. Re-Viewing Classics of Joyce Criticism. 240p. 1991. text 39.95 (0-252-01774-9); pap. text 14.95 (0-252-06166-7) U of Ill Pr.

Dunleavy, Janet E., et al, eds. Joycean Occasions: Essays from the Milwaukee James Joyce Conference. LC 89-40758. 248p. 1991. 42.50 (0-87413-402-1) U Delaware Pr.

Dunleavy, Janet E. & Dunleavy, Gareth W. Douglas Hyde: A Maker of Modern Ireland. LC 90-40120. (Illus.). 475p. 1991. 45.00 (0-520-06684-7, Pub. by U CA Pr) Cal Prin Full Svc.

Dunleavy, Janet E., ed. see Hyde, Douglas.

***Dunleavy, Mairead.** Dress in Ireland: A History. (Illus.). 192p. 1999. pap. 29.95 (1-898256-84-5, Pub. by Collins Press) Irish Bks Media.

Dunleavy, Patricia G., ed. Georgia Lawyers & Their Profession: A Self-Examination, 1987. 124p. 1989. pap. text 11.00 (1-55816-001-9) ICLE Georgia.

***Dunleavy, Patrick.** Developments in British Politics, No. 6. LC 00-35264. 2000. write for info. (0-312-23515-1) St Martin.

Dunleavy, Patrick. Developments in British Politics, Vol. 4. 1993. pap. text 45.00 (0-333-58014-1, Pub. by Macmillan) Humanities.

— Developments in British Politics 5. LC 97-27504. 1997. pap. 19.95 (0-312-21010-8) St Martin.

— The Politics of Mass Housing in Britain, 1945-1975: A Study of Corporate Power & Professional Influence in the Welfare State. (Illus.). 1981. 55.00 (0-19-827426-2) OUP.

Dunleavy, Patrick, jt. ed. see Rhodes, R. A.

Dunlevy, Crystal. Appleton & Lange's Review of Respiratory Care. 2nd rev. ed. LC 94-23439. (C). 1994. pap. text 39.95 (0-8385-8414-4, A8414-3) Appleton & Lange.

— Respiratory Care Pharmacology. 5th ed. (Illus.). 145p. 1998. wbk. ed. write for info. (0-8151-2004-4) Mosby Inc.

Dunlevy, Crystal L. & Douce, F. Herbert. Basic Respiratory Therapy. (C). 1999. 34.95 (0-8385-0566-X) Appleton & Lange.

***Dunlevy, John N., ed.** Portfolio Management. 2000. 75.00 (1-883249-64-3) F J Fabozzi.

Dunlevy, Marion B., jt. auth. see Maxwell, Alice S.

Dunlevy, Maurice. Feature Writing. 145p. (C). 1988. 41.00 (0-7300-0541-0, Pub. by Deakin Univ) St Mut.

— Interviewing Techniques for Newspapers. 143p. (C). 1995. pap. 20.00 (0-86828-186-7, Pub. by Deakin Univ) St Mut.

Dunley, Dorothea, et al. For Mother, with Love: Makeshift Mama - The Notorious Mrs. Carlton - The Virtues of Patience. (Zebra Romance Ser.). 256p. 1998. pap. 4.99 (0-8217-5892-6, Zebra Kensgtn) Kensgtn Pub Corp.

***Dunlop.** Digital Mobile Communications. LC 99-32468. 464p. 1999. 135.00 (0-471-98792-1) Wiley.

Dunlop, A., et al. Materials under Irradiation. (Solid State Phenomena Ser.: Vols. 30-31). 512p. 1992. text 192.00 (0-87849-651-3, Pub. by Trans T Pub) Enfield Pubs NH.

Dunlop, Alan, ed. The Scottish Ministers Widows Fund, 1743-1993. 160p. (C). 1992. 85.00 (0-86153-153-1, Pub. by St Andrew) St Mut.

Dunlop, Alexander, jt. ed. see Miller, David L.

Dunlop, Anne. The Pineapple Tart. 263p. 1992. pap. 10.95 (1-85371-169-1) Dufour.

Dunlop, Beth. Arquitectonica. (Illus.). 224p. 1991. pap. 40.00 (1-55835-043-8) AIA Press.

— Arts & Crafts Houses, Vol. 2. (Architecture 3s Ser.). 1999. 19.95 (0-7148-3874-8) Phaidon Pr.

— Building a Dream: The Art of Disney Architecture. (Illus.). 224p. 1996. 39.95 (0-8109-3142-7, Pub by Abrams) Time Warner.

— City Icons. (Architecture 3s Ser.). 1999. 19.95 (0-7148-3873-X) Phaidon Pr.

— Classics. (Twentieth-Century Ser.). 1999. 19.95 (0-7148-3868-3) Phaidon Pr.

— Frank Lloyd Wright: Decorative Objects, Prints, Drawings, Florida Projects. LC 84-73354. (Illus.). 61p. (Orig.). 1984. pap. 9.99 (1-880511-06-1) Bass Museum.

— Havana: The Photography of Hans Engels. 1999. 39.95 (3-7913-2157-9) Prestel.

***Dunlop, Beth.** A House for My Mother: Architects Build for Their Families. LC 98-49795. (Illus.). 200p 1999. pap. 34.95 (1-56898-173-2) Princeton Arch.

Dunlop, Beth. Houses: Europe. (Twentieth-Century Ser.). 1999. 19.95 (0-7148-3870-5) Phaidon Pr.

— Masterpieces. (Arts & Crafts Ser.). 1999. 19.95 (0-7148-3876-4) Phaidon Pr.

— National Trust Guide: Miami & South Florida. (Illus.). 316p. 1999. pap. text 19.95 (0-471-18018-1) Wiley.

Dunlop, Beth, jt. auth. see Lombard, Joanna.

Dunlop, Beth, jt. auth. see Schezen, Roberto.

***Dunlop, Bill & Fountain-Blacklidge, Marcia.** The Indians of Hungry Hollow. 236p. 2000. pap. 19.95 (0-472-08653-7, 08653); text 39.50 (0-472-11115-9, 11115) U of Mich Pr.

***Dunlop, Carolyn C.** The Russian Court Chapel Choir: 1796-1917. (Music Archive Publications Ser.: Series F, Vol. 1). 204p. 1999. text 39.00 (90-5755-026-1, Harwood Acad Pubs) Gordon & Breach.

***Dunlop, Carolyn C., ed.** Bakhmetev to Lyapunov: Music of the Russian Court Chapel II. (Music Archive Publications Ser.: Series F, Vol. 1, Part 2). 184p. 1999. text 42.00 (90-5755-075-X, Harwood Acad Pubs) Gordon & Breach.

— Galuppi to Vorotnikov: Music of the Russian Court Chapel Choir I. (Music Archive Publications Ser.: Series F, Vol. 1, Part 1). 176p. 1999. text 41.00 (90-5755-042-3, Harwood Acad Pubs) Gordon & Breach.

Dunlop, Charles E. & Fetzer, James H. Glossary of Cognitive Science. LC 92-27750. (Glossary for Research, Reading, & Writing Ser.). 160p. 1993. 12.95 (1-55778-566-X); pap. 8.95 (1-55778-567-8) Paragon Hse.

***Dunlop, Cheryl J.** Follow Me as I Follow Christ: A Manual for Teaching Children in a Church Setting. LC 00-41845. 2000. write for info. (0-8024-1094-4) Moody.

Dunlop, D. M., ed. Muntakhab Siwan Al-Hikmah of Abu Sulaiman As-Sijistani. (Near & Middle East Monographs: No. 4). (ARA.). 1979. text 73.10 (90-279-3377-4) Mouton.

Dunlop, Dale. Exploring Nova Scotia. 192p. 1995. pap. 19.95 (0-88780-324-5) Formac Dist Ltd.

— Exploring Nova Scotia: A Guide to 500+ Unique Adventures & Activities. 1998. pap. text 16.95 (0-88780-422-5) Formac Dist Ltd.

Dunlop, David J. & Ozdemir, Ozden. Rock Magnetism: Fundamentals & Frontiers. (Cambridge Studies in Magnetism: No. 3). (Illus.). 594p. (C). 1997. text 125.00 (0-521-32514-5) Cambridge U Pr.

Dunlop, David W. & Martins, J. M., eds. An International Assessment of Health Care Financing: Lessons for Developing Countries. LC 95-8983. (EDI Seminar Ser.). 206p. 1996. pap. 22.00 (0-8213-3253-8, 13253) World Bank.

Dunlop, Douglas. Arab Civilization to AD 1500. (Arab Background Ser.). 368p. 1971. 45.00 (0-86685-012-0, LDL0120, Pub. by Librairie du Liban) Intl Bk Ctr.

Dunlop, Ed. Let's Play a Bible Game! 48 Reproducible Scripture Games & Puzzles for the Overhead Projector. Wray, Rhonda, ed. LC 95-36395. (Illus.). 208p. 1995. pap. 14.95 (1-56608-013-4, B183) Meriwether Pub.

— More! Overhead Projector Games. Brewer, Karen, ed. (Illus.). 48p. (J). (gr. 1-6). 1996. teacher ed. 10.99 (0-7847-0507-0, 03510) Standard Pub.

***Dunlop, Ed.** Mouse on a Mission: 54 Bible Review Games to Reinforce Your Lessons. (Illus.). 220p. (gr. 4-7). 1999. pap. 0.00 (0-87398-570-2) Sword of Lord.

Dunlop, Ed. Overhead Projector Games. Brewer, Karen, ed. (Illus.). 48p. (J). (gr. 1-6). 1996. teacher ed. 10.99 (0-7847-0506-2, 03509) Standard Pub.

— Teaching with Bible Games: "Kid-Tested" Contests to Make Christian Education Fun. Wray, Rhonda, ed. LC 93-16857. (Illus.). 224p. 1993. pap. 12.95 (0-916260-94-1, B108) Meriwether Pub.

Dunlop, Eileen. Finn's Island. LC 91-55027. 128p. (YA). (gr. 4-6). 1992. 13.95 (0-8234-0910-4) Holiday.

— Finn's Search. LC 93-44880. 160p. (J). (gr. 4-6). 1994. 14.95 (0-8234-1099-4) Holiday.

— The Ghost by the Sea. 192p. (J). (gr. 4-6). 1996. 15.95 (0-8234-1264-4) Holiday.

— The House on the Hill. 1992. 8.60 (0-606-12344-X, Pub. by Turtleback) Demco.

— The House on the Hill. 160p. (J). (gr. 2-9). 1989. reprint ed. pap. 3.50 (0-8167-1323-5) Troll Communs.

***Dunlop, Eileen.** A Royal Ring of Gold. (Illus.). 128p. 1999. pap. 9.95 (0-86315-292-9) Anthroposophic.

Dunlop, Eileen. Stones of Destiny. 142p. (J). (gr. 4-7). 1994. pap. 7.95 (1-85371-307-4, Pub. by Poolbeg Pr) Dufour.

— Tales of St. Columba. 136p. (J). (gr. 4 up). 1992. pap. 7.95 (1-85371-134-9, Pub. by Poolbeg Pr) Dufour.

— Tales of St. Patrick. 144p. (J). (gr. 4-6). 1996. 15.95 (0-8234-1218-0) Holiday.

— Waters of Life. 172p. 1996. pap. 8.95 (1-85371-691-X, Pub. by Poolbeg Pr) Dufour.

— Websters' Leap. LC 95-2075. (Illus.). 176p. (J). (gr. 4-6). 1995. 15.95 (0-8234-1193-1) Holiday.

Dunlop, Ethel. The Soft Curve. LC 92-74836. (Illus.). 128p. (Orig.). 1993. pap. 11.95 (0-9627680-5-7) Inkwell CA.

Dunlop, F., jt. ed. see De Coninck, J.

Dunlop, Francis, ed. see Kolnai, Aurel.

Dunlop, Frank & Dale, Jim. Scapino! - Full. 94p. 1975. pap. 5.95 (0-87129-639-X, S12) Dramatic Pub.

— Scapino! - Special Book. 1975. pap. 9.95 (0-87129-374-9, S13) Dramatic Pub.

— Scapino! One Act Version. 1975. pap. 3.95 (0-87129-183-5, S11) Dramatic Pub.

Dunlop, Geoffrey, tr. see Roth, Joseph.

Dunlop, Geoffrey, tr. see Werfel, Franz.

Dunlop-Hebert, Carol, tr. see Blais, Marie-Claire.

Dunlop-Hebert, Carol, tr. see Robertson, Heather.

***Dunlop, Ian.** Louis XIV. (Illus.). 512p. 2000. text 27.95 (0-312-26196-9) St Martin.

Dunlop, Ian, jt. auth. see Warren, Lynne.

Dunlop, J. Telecommunications Engineering. 3rd ed. 616p. 1994. pap. 57.95 (0-412-56270-7, Chap & Hall NY) Chapman & Hall.

Dunlop, Jack, jt. auth. see Belford, James N.

Dunlop, James A., ed. Juicio Critico de los Poetas Espanoles Contemporaneos: Juan Martinez Villergas. 260p. 1995. lib. bdg. 35.00 (0-8191-9928-1) U Pr of Amer.

Dunlop, James J. Leading the Association: Striking the Right Balance Between Staff & Volunteers. Bowers, Heidi H., ed. 148p. 1989. pap. 49.50 (0-88034-038-X) Am Soc Assn Execs.

Dunlop, Jean. The Clan MacKenzie. (Johnston & Bacon Clan Histories Ser.). (Illus.). 32p. 1993. reprint ed. pap. 8.95 (0-8063-5003-2, 9603) Clearfield Co.

— The Clan MacKintosh. (Johnston & Bacon Clan Histories Ser.). (Illus.). 32p. 1993. reprint ed. pap. 8.95 (0-8063-5002-4, 9602) Clearfield Co.

Dunlop, Jocelyn & Denman, R. P. English Apprenticeship & Child Labor: A History. 1976. lib. bdg. 59.95 (0-8490-1770-X) Gordon Pr.

Dunlop, John. A Precarious Belonging: Presbyterians & the Conflict in Ireland. 144p. 1996. pap. 16.95 (0-85640-559-0, Pub. by Blackstaff Pr) Dufour.

Dunlop, John B. The Faces of Contemporary Russian Nationalism. LC 83-42554. 376p. 1983. reprint ed. pap. 116.60 (0-608-03293-X, 206381100007) Bks Demand.

— The New Russian Nationalism, 16. (Washington Papers: Vol. 16). 1985. 47.95 (0-275-90191-2, Praeger Pubs) Greenwood.

— The Rise of Russia & the Fall of the Soviet Empire. 394p. 1993. pap. text 18.95 (0-691-00173-1, Pub. by Princeton U Pr) Cal Prin Full Svc.

— Russia Confronts Chechnya: Roots of a Separatist Conflict. LC 97-51840. (Illus.). 248p. (C). 1998. text 59.95 (0-521-63184-X); pap. text 18.95 (0-521-63619-1) Cambridge U Pr.

Dunlop, John B., et al, eds. Solzhenitsyn in Exile: Critical Essays & Documentary Materials. LC 85-10821. (Publication Ser.: No. 305). xv, 416p. 1985. lib. bdg. 19.95 (0-8179-8051-2) Hoover Inst Pr.

Dunlop, John C. History of Prose Fiction, 2 vols. Wilson, Henry, ed. LC 71-95396. 1969. reprint ed. 90.00 (0-404-02218-9) AMS Pr.

— History of Roman Literature. 1977. 79.95 (0-8369-7266-X, 8065) Ayer.

Dunlop, John D. The New Russian Nationalism, 16. (Washington Papers: No. 116). 192p. 1985. pap. 11.95 (0-275-91665-0, B1665, Praeger Pubs) Greenwood.

Dunlop, John T. Business & Public Policy. LC 80-81866. (Harvard Business School Publications). 135p. (C). 1980. 11.00 (0-87584-119-8) HUP.

— Dispute Resolution: Negotiation & Consensus Building. LC 83-27531. 316p. 1984. 57.95 (0-86569-123-1, Auburn Hse) Greenwood.

— Fact Finding Report: Commission on the Future of Worker-Management Relations. (Illus.). 163p. (Orig.). (C). 1994. pap. text 40.00 (0-7881-1491-3) DIANE Pub.

— Industrial Relations Systems. rev. ed. LC 92-42569. (Harvard Business School Press Classics Ser.). 1993. pap. 24.95 (0-87584-334-4) Harvard Busn.

D

— Industrial Relations Systems: Harvard Business School Press Classics. rev. ed. 1993. text 39.95 (*0-07-103415-3*) McGraw.

— Wage Determination under Trade Unions. LC 50-58147. (Reprints of Economic Classics Ser.). xi, 230p. 1966. reprint ed. 35.00 (*0-678-00137-5*) Kelley.

Dunlop, John T., ed. Automation & Technological Change. LC 62-17597. 1962. 3.95 (*0-317-02946-0*, 05449-C) Am Assembly.

Dunlop, John T. & Zack, Arnold M. Mediation & Arbitration of Employment Disputes. LC 97-16797. 223p. 1997. 36.95 (*0-7879-0847-9*) Jossey-Bass.

Dunlop, John T., ed. see Slichter, Sumner H.

Dunlop, Lane, ed. from JPN. A Late Chrysanthemum: 21 Stories from the Japanese. 180p. 1991. reprint ed. pap. 12.95 (*0-8048-1578-X*) Tuttle Pubng.

Dunlop, Lane, tr. Autumn Wind & Other Stories. 210p. (Orig.). 1994. pap. 11.95 (*0-8048-1921-1*) Tuttle Pubng.

Dunlop, Lane, jt. auth. see Ponge, Francis.

Dunlop, Lane, tr. see Kawabata, Yasunari.

Dunlop, Lane, tr. see Nagai Kafu, pseud.

Dunlop, Lane, tr. see Ponge, Francis.

Dunlop, Lane, tr. see Shiga Naoya.

Dunlop, Laurence. Patterns of Prayer in the Psalms. 160p. (Orig.). 1984. 9.95 (*0-8164-2377-6*) Harper SF.

***Dunlop, M. H.** Gilded City: Style & Spectacle in the American City, 1880-1910. 288p. 2000. 25.00 (*0-688-17144-3*, Wm Morrow) Morrow Avon.

Dunlop, M. H. Sixty Miles from Contentment: Traveling the Nineteenth-Century American Interior. 288p. 1996. pap. 15.00 (*0-465-03366-0*) Basic.

— Sixty Miles from Contentment: Traveling the Nineteenth-Century American Interior. (C). 1998. pap. 19.00 (*0-8133-3432-2*, Pub. by Westview) HarpC.

Dunlop, Paul H. The Jokelson Collection of Antique Cameo Incrustation. (Illus.). 128p. 1991. 60.00 (*0-9619547-3-6*) Papier Presse.

Dunlop, Philip. Short Latin Stories. 80p. 1987. pap. text 10.95 (*0-521-31592-1*) Cambridge U Pr.

Dunlop, R. Cancer: Palliative Care. Rubens, R., ed. LC 97-36628. (Focus on Cancer Ser.). 200p. 1997. pap. 45.00 (*3-540-19974-8*) Spr-Verlag.

Dunlop, Reginald. Come Fly with Me: Your Nineties Guide to Becoming a Professional Flight Attendant. 92p. 1992. pap. text 15.95 (*0-9632749-9-6*) Maxamillian.

Dunlop, Reginald M. Is It a Scam? Seeing & Avoiding Those Ripoffs! 212p. 1994. pap. 12.95 (*0-9632749-8-8*) Maxamillian.

***Dunlop, Robert.** Teach Yourself Directx 7 Programming in 24 Hours. 450p. 1999. pap. 24.99 (*0-672-31634-X*) Sams.

Dunlop, Robert & Hockley, Jo. Hospital-Based Palliative Care Teams: The Hosptial-Hospice Interface. 2nd ed. LC 98-22223. (Illus.). 174p. 1998. pap. text 34.50 (*0-19-262980-8*) OUP.

Dunlop, Robert, jt. auth. see Carson, Alan.

Dunlop, Robert H. & Williams, David J. The Illustrated History of Veterinary Medicine. (Illus.). 704p. (gr. 13). 1995. text 92.00 (*0-8016-3209-9*, 03209) Mosby Inc.

Dunlop, S. & Gerbaldi, M., eds. Stargazers. (Illus.). xvii, 232p. 1989. 42.95 (*0-387-50230-0*) Spr-Verlag.

Dunlop, S., tr. see Encrenaz, T. & Bibring, J. P.

Dunlop, S., tr. see Montenbruck, Oliver & Pfleger, T.

Dunlop, S., tr. see Montenbruck, O. & Pfleger, T.

Dunlop, Storm. Weather & Forecasting. (Field Guide Ser.). 160p. 1987. pap. 10.95 (*0-02-013700-1*) Macmillan.

— Weather Photoguide. 1996. pap. 8.00 (*0-00-470829-6*) Collins.

***Dunlop, Storm.** Wild Guide Night Sky. (Illus.). 1999. 14.95 (*0-00-220127-5*, Pub. by HarpC) Trafalgar.

Dunlop, Storm, tr. see Brunier, Serge.

Dunlop, Storm, tr. see Heidmann, Jean.

Dunlop, Storm, tr. see Martinez, Patrick, ed.

Dunlop, Storm, tr. see Montenbruck, Oliver & Pfleger, T.

Dunlop, W. S. Lee's Sharpshooters: Or The Forefront of Battle: A Story of Southern Valor That Never Has Been Told. (Illus.). 499p. 2000. reprint ed. 50.00 (*0-89029-064-4*) Morningside Bkshop.

Dunlop, William. Caruso for the Children, & Other Poems. LC 97-65389. 96p. (Orig.). 1997. pap. 9.95 (*0-9651210-2-X*) Rose Alley Pr.

Dunmire, Marj. National Parks of Alaska. (Illus.). 48p. (YA). (gr. 2 up). 1991. pap. 4.95 (*0-942559-07-X*) Pegasus Graphics.

— Not Even Footprints. (Illus.). 72p. (Orig.). (J). (gr. 2). 1987. pap. 4.95 (*0-942559-04-5*) Pegasus Graphics.

— Rocky Mountain Sketches. (Illus.). 24p. (J). 1978. pap. 4.95 (*0-942559-00-2*) Pegasus Graphics.

— Water Birds. (Illus.). 48p. (YA). (gr. 2 up). 1990. pap. 4.95 (*0-942559-06-1*) Pegasus Graphics.

— Wildlife of Cactus & Canyon Country. large type ed. (Illus.). 48p. (YA). (gr. 2 up). 1988. pap. 4.95 (*0-942559-05-3*) Pegasus Graphics.

Dunmire, Marjorie. Mountain Wildlife. (Illus.). 48p. (Orig.). (J). (gr. 2 up). 1986. pap. 4.95 (*0-942559-03-7*) Pegasus Graphics.

Dunmire, Marjorie S. Faces of the Forests. (Illus.). 64p. (Orig.). (J). (gr. 3 up). 1998. pap. 5.95 (*0-942559-08-8*) Pegasus Graphics.

Dunmire, Robert B., et al. Basic Chemistry One. 160p. (C). 1994. pap. text 11.95 (*0-8403-7873-4*) Kendall-Hunt.

Dunmire, Susan M. & Paris, Paul M. Atlas Emergency Procedures. LC 93-25118. (Illus.). 240p. 1994. text 79.00 (*0-7216-3682-9*, W B Saunders Co) Harcrt Hlth Sci Grp.

Dunmire, William W. & Tierney, Gail D. Wild Plants & Native Peoples of the Four Corners. LC 97-2372. (Illus.). 320p. 1997. pap. 22.50 (*0-89013-319-0*) Museum NM Pr.

— Wild Plants of the Pueblo Province: Exploring Ancient & Enduring Uses. (Illus.). 1995. 29.95 (*0-89013-282-8*); pap. 22.50 (*0-89013-272-0*) Museum NM Pr.

***Dunmore.** Expedition of The St. Jean-baptiste to the Pacific. 1998. 52.95 (*0-904180-11-5*) Ashgate Pub Co.

— Go Fox. (J). 2000. pap. 5.95 (*0-552-52963-X*, Pub. by Transworld Publishers Ltd) Trafalgar.

Dunmore, Charles W. Studies in Etymology. (Texts Ser.). 402p. 1993. pap. 19.95 (*0-941051-29-3*) Focus Pub-R Pullins.

Dunmore, Charles W. & Fleischer, Rita M. Medical Terminology: Exercises in Etymology. 2nd ed. LC 85-4350. 305p. (C). 1985. pap. 29.95 (*0-8036-2946-X*) Davis Co.

Dunmore, D. B. System Development Auditing: Traditional & New Development Methodologies & Packaged Software. (Illus.). 354p. 1988. text 60.00 (*0-940706-22-9*) Management Advisory Pubns.

Dunmore, Helen. Apple Fall. 1983. pap. 12.95 (*0-906427-43-6*, Pub. by Bloodaxe Bks) Dufour.

— Bestiary. LC 97-171761. 64p. 1997. pap. 15.95 (*1-85224-401-1*, Pub. by Bloodaxe Bks) Dufour.

***Dunmore, Helen.** Brother Brother, Sister Sister. (Illus.). 128p. (J). 2000. mass mkt. 4.50 (*0-439-11322-9*) Scholastic Inc.

— Love of Fat Men. large type unabridged ed. 189p. 1999. 26.95 (*0-7531-5898-1*, 158981, Pub. by ISIS Lrg Prnt) ISIS Pub.

— Poetry Quartets 5: Women Poets. 2000. 26.95 incl. audio (*1-85224-499-2*, Pub. by Bloodaxe Bks) Dufour.

Dunmore, Helen. Raw Garden. LC 88-51310. 64p. 1988. pap. 10.95 (*1-85224-074-1*, Pub. by Bloodaxe Bks) Dufour.

— Sea Skater. 72p. 1986. pap. 11.95 (*1-85224-006-7*, Pub. by Bloodaxe Bks) Dufour.

— Short Days Long Nights: New & Selected Poems. 192p. (Orig.). 1991. pap. 18.95 (*1-85224-150-0*, Pub. by Bloodaxe Bks) Dufour.

— A Spell of Winter. 1999. pap. write for info. (*0-316-19794-7*) Little.

— Talking to the Dead. 304p. 1998. pap. 12.95 (*0-316-19645-2*) Little.

— Talking to the Dead. large type ed. LC 97-31634. (Core Ser.). 281p. 1997. lib. bdg. 25.95 (*0-7838-8329-3*, G K Hall Lrg Type) Mac Lib Ref.

***Dunmore, Helen.** With Your Crooked Heart. LC 99-53739. 256p. 2000. 24.00 (*0-87113-773-9*, Atlntc Mnthly) Grove-Atltic.

— With Your Crooked Heart. large type ed. LC 99-48320. (General Ser.). 2000. pap. 23.95 (*0-7862-2301-4*) Thorndike Pr.

Dunmore, Helen. Your Blue-Eyed Boy. LC 97-40078. 288p. (gr. 8). 1998. 23.95 (*0-316-19738-6*) Little.

— Your Blue-Eyed Boy. 288p. 1999. pap. 13.00 (*0-316-19747-5*, Back Bay) Little.

Dunmore, Helen et al. Recovering a Body. 64p. 1995. pap. 14.95 (*1-85224-289-2*, Pub. by Bloodaxe Bks) Dufour.

Dunmore, John. Who's Who in Pacific Navigation. LC 91-19280. (Illus.). 320p. (C). 1992. text 34.00 (*0-8248-1350-2*) UH Pr.

Dunmore, Mary V. On the Cutting Edge - A Great American Surgeon: Richard B. Cattell, M.D. LC 91-60402. (Illus.). 256p. 1991. 29.95 (*0-9628738-0-2*) Jones Riv Pr.

Dunmore, Simon, ed. & selected by see Shakespeare, William.

Dunmore, Spencer. Above & Beyond: The Canadians' War in the Air, 1939-1945. LC 97-140958. (Illus.). 400p. 1997. 29.95 (*0-7710-2928-4*) McCland & Stewart.

***Dunmore, Spencer.** In Great Waters: The Epic Story of the Battle of the Atlantic, 1939-1945. (Illus.). 360p. 2000. text 24.95 (*0-7710-2929-2*) McCland & Stewart.

Dunmore, Spencer. Reap the Whirlwind: The Untold Story of 6 Group Canadas Bomber Force of World War II. 438p. 1997. pap. text 19.99 (*0-7710-2926-8*) McCland & Stewart.

— Squadron. 330p. 1996. mass mkt. 6.99 (*0-7710-2919-5*) McCland & Stewart.

— Wings for Victory: The Remarkable Story of the British Commonwealth Air Training Plan in Canada. (Illus.). 400p. 1994. 23.95 (*0-7710-2927-6*) McCland & Stewart.

— Wings for Victory: The Remarkable Story of the British Commonwealth Air Training Plan in Canada. (Illus.). 400p. 1996. pap. text 19.99 (*0-7710-2918-7*) McCland & Stewart.

***Dunn.** American Government. 2nd ed. 192p. (C). 1999. pap. text, student ed. 21.00 (*0-321-03835-5*) Addson-Wesley Educ.

Dunn. Art & Design Resource Book. Date not set. pap. text. write for info. (*0-582-02448-X*, Pub. by Addison-Wesley) Longman.

***Dunn.** Cunning of Unreason. 2000. pap. 18.00 (*0-465-01748-7*, Pub. by Basic) HarpC.

Dunn. I'll Never Forgive My Heart. (Piano-Vocal-Guitar Ser.). 6p. 1994. pap. 3.95 (*0-7935-4287-1*, 00351048) H Leonard.

— Psychology: A Concise Introduction. 2nd ed. (C). 1995. pap. text, student ed. 276.50 (*0-03-012852-8*, Pub. by Harcourt Coll Pubs) Harcourt.

— Riffs & Reciprocities: Prose Poems. 112p. 1999. pap. 12.00 (*0-393-31957-1*) Norton.

— Stat Data Anal Behav Sciences. 2000. 55.50 (*0-07-234764-3*) McGraw.

— Teaching World History. 1999. pap. text 46.95 (*0-312-18327-5*) St Martin.

Dunn, ed. American Government: A Comparative Approach. 2nd ed. LC 99-21256. 318p. (C). 1999. pap. text 48.00 (*0-321-01201-1*) Addson-Wesley Educ.

— Bldg Confdnc Commnct Cus. (C). 1996. text 38.44 (*0-321-01245-3*) Addson-Wesley Educ.

Dunn & Morris. The Composite Novel: The Short Story Cycle on Transition. 1995. pap. 16.95 (*0-8057-9235-X*, Hall Reference) Macmillan.

Dunn, et al. Test Questions Social Animal. 7th ed. 1994. 16.00 (*0-7167-2704-8*) W H Freeman.

Dunn, jt. auth. see Boyatis.

Dunn, jt. ed. see Crosby.

Dunn, A., jt. auth. see Vervest, P.

Dunn, A. D. & Rudorf, W. D. Carbon Disulphide in Organic Chemistry. 1989. text 89.95 (*0-470-21441-4*) P-H.

Dunn, A. J., jt. ed. see Nemeroff, Charles B.

***Dunn, Alan.** Exotic Sugar Flowers for Cakes. 2000. 24.95 (*1-85391-802-4*, Pub. by Merehurst Ltd) Tuttle Pubng.

Dunn, Alan. Floral Wedding Cakes & Sprays. (Illus.). 1999. pap. 24.95 (*1-85391-604-8*) Tuttle Pubng.

***Dunn, Alan R.** The CadCARD Slidechart 5.0: For AutoCAD 2000. 2000. 17.99 (*0-9678891-1-1*) Autograph Tech Serv.

— The CadCARD Slidechart 4.0: For AutoCAD r13/14. 1997. 17.99 (*0-9678891-0-3*) Autograph Tech Serv.

***Dunn, Alison, ed.** The Voluntary Sector, the State & the Law. 2000. 50.00 (*1-84113-067-2*, Pub. by Hart Pub) Intl Spec Bk.

Dunn, Allan & Underwood, John. How to Succeed in the Music Business. (Illus.). 88p. 1985. pap. 9.95 (*0-86001-454-1*, AM19977) Music Sales.

Dunn, Allan J. The Flower of Fate. Reginald, R. & Melville, Douglas, eds. LC 77-84219. (Lost Race & Adult Fantasy Ser.). 1978. reprint ed. lib. bdg. 26.95 (*0-405-10974-1*) Ayer.

Dunn, Amy J., jt. ed. see Zeise, Lauren.

Dunn, Andrew. The Children's Atlas of Scientific Discoveries & Inventions. LC 96-38358. (Children's Atlases Ser.). 96p. (J). (gr. 2-6). 1997. lib. bdg. 27.40 (*0-7613-0220-4*) Millbrook Pr.

— The Children's Atlas of Scientific Discoveries & Inventions. LC 96-38358. (Illus.). 96p. (J). (gr. 2-6). 1997. pap. 14.95 (*0-7613-0241-7*) Millbrook Pr.

— Fog, Mist & Smog. LC 97-22354. (Living with the Weather Ser.). 1998. 25.69 (*0-8172-5053-0*) Raintree Steck-V.

Dunn, Angela. Mathematical Bafflers. rev. ed. (Illus.). 217p. 1980. reprint ed. pap. 6.95 (*0-486-23961-6*) Dover.

— Second Book of Mathematical Bafflers. 84th ed. (Puzzles, Amusements, Recreations Ser.). (Illus.). 192p. (Orig.). 1983. pap. 5.95 (*0-486-24352-4*) Dover.

Dunn, Ann. Olde Women. 60p. 1995. 12.00 (*0-9648305-1-5*) Urthona Pr.

Dunn, Anne, jt. auth. see Guest, Barbara.

Dunn, Anne M. Grandmother's Gift: Stories from the Anishinabeg. 160p. (J). 1997. pap. text 12.95 (*0-930100-72-7*) Holy Cow.

***Dunn, Anne M.** Summer Thunder: Retold Tales. 2000. pap. 13.95 (*0-930100-70-0*) Holy Cow.

Dunn, Anne M. When Beaver Was Very Great: Stories to Live by. LC 95-75453. (Illus.). 224p. 1995. 18.95 (*1-883953-08-1*); pap. 13.95 (*1-883953-07-3*) Midwest Trad.

Dunn, April L. DecoSerging: Decorative Serging Techniques. Teufel, Linda C., ed. (Illus.). 144p. (Orig.). 1997. pap. 25.00 (*0-9641201-2-7*) Dragon Threads.

Dunn, Arlene, ed. Brookman Price Guide for Disney Stamps. 2nd ed. (Illus.). 248p. 1998. per. 19.95 (*0-936937-45-9*) Krause Pubns.

Dunn, Arliene, ed. see Dunn, Troy & Klunder, Virgil.

Dunn, Arthur W. From Harrison to Harding: A Personal Narrative, Covering a Third of a Century, 1888-1921, 2 vols., Set. (American Biography Ser.). 1991. reprint ed. lib. bdg. write for info. (*0-7812-8117-2*) Rprt Serv.

— Gridiron Nights: Humorous & Satirical Views of Politics & Statesmen, Presented by the Dining Club. LC 73-19141. (Politics & People Ser.). (Illus.). 402p. 1974. reprint ed. 30.95 (*0-405-05866-7*) Ayer.

Dunn, B. M. Structure & Function of the Aspartic Proteinases: Genetics, Structure & Mechanisms. (Advances in Experimental Medicine & Biology Ser.: Vol. 306). (Illus.). 608p. (C). 1991. text 165.00 (*0-306-44052-0*, Kluwer Plenum) Kluwer Academic.

Dunn, Barbara & Edwards, Janet R. Lonely Planet Diving & Snorkeling Guide to Texas: Includes Inland, Coastal, & Offshore Sites. 2nd ed. LC 96-8596. (Pisces Diving & Snorkeling Guides Ser.). 96p. (Orig.). 1996. pap. 14.95 (*1-55992-091-2*, 2091, Pisces Books) Lonely Planet.

Dunn, Barbara & Myers, Stephan. Lonely Planet Diving & Snorkeling Guide to Texas. (Diving & Snorkeling Guides Ser.). 96p. 1990. 14.95 (*1-55992-032-7*, Pisces Books) Lonely Planet.

Dunn, Ben. Proteases of Infectious Agents. LC 98-89642. 282p. 1999. 69.95 (*0-12-420510-0*) Acad Pr.

Dunn, Ben M., jt. ed. see Pennington, Michael W.

Dunn, Betty. Ju-Ju Swallowed a Penny. (Illus.). 90p. (Orig.). 1994. pap. 7.50 (*0-9640603-0-2*) Badger Pubns.

— Legends Lost. (Illus.). 98p. (Orig.). 1995. pap. 6.50 (*0-9640603-8-8*) Badger Pubns.

Dunn, Bill. Boomer Trek. LC 96-61787. 144p. (Orig.). 1997. pap. write for info. (*1-883893-86-0*) WinePress Pub.

— Boot: An L. A. P. D. Officer's Rookie Year. LC 96-12726. 320p. 1996. 23.00 (*0-688-14713-5*, Wm Morrow) Morrow Avon.

Dunn, Bill N. Greater in Europe. 85p. 1985. 40.00 (*0-7212-0731-6*, Pub. by Regency Pr GBR) St Mut.

Dunn, Bob, ed. see Detchon, Jack.

Dunn, Bob, ed. see Howe, Bobby & Waiters, Tony.

Dunn, Bob, ed. see Waiters, Tony.

Dunn, Bob, ed. see Waiters, Tony & Cowan, Jane.

Dunn, Bob, ed. see Waiters, Tony & Howe, Bobby.

Dunn, Brian, jt. auth. see Yaeger, Michael.

Dunn, Brian, ed. see Dovell, Michael.

Dunn, Bruce S., et al, eds. Sol-Gel Optics IV. LC 98-122028. 67p. 1997. pap. 107.00 (*0-8194-2558-3*) SPIE.

Dunn, C. Desire. 1989. mass mkt. 2.95 (*0-446-93174-8*, Pub. by Warner Bks) Little.

Dunn, C., jt. ed. see Pallister, C.

Dunn, C. D., ed. Current Concepts in Erythropoiesis. LC 82-13389. (Illus.). 429p. reprint ed. pap. 133.00 (*0-608-17285-5*, 202963400062) Bks Demand.

Dunn, Carla, jt. auth. see Stoel-Gammon, Carol.

Dunn, Carola. The Babe & the Baron. 224p. 1997. mass mkt. 4.99 (*0-8217-5543-9*, Zebra Kensgtn) Kensgtn Pub Corp.

— Crossed Quills. (Zebra Regency Romance Ser.). 224p. 1998. mass mkt. 4.99 (*0-8217-6007-6*, Zebra Kensgtn) Kensgtn Pub Corp.

***Dunn, Carola.** Crossed Quills. large type ed. LC 99-41967. (Romance Ser.). 1999. 27.95 (*0-7838-8770-1*, G K Hall & Co) Mac Lib Ref.

Dunn, Carola. Dead in the Water. 256p. 1998. text 22.95 (*0-312-19181-2*) St Martin.

***Dunn, Carola.** Death at Wentwater Court. (Daisy Dalrymple Mysteries Ser.). (Illus.). (J). 2000. mass mkt. 5.99 (*1-57566-750-9*) Kensgtn Pub Corp.

Dunn, Carola. Ginnie Come Lately. (Regency Romance Ser.). 1993. per. 2.99 (*0-373-31208-3*, 1-31208-1) Harlequin Bks.

— Ginnie Come Lately. 1999. per. 3.75 (*0-373-31229-6*) Harlequin Bks.

— Ginnie Come Lately. large type ed. 350p. 1995. 23.99 (*0-263-14429-1*, Pub. by Mills & Boon) Ulverscroft.

— The Improper Governess. (Zebra Romance Ser.). 256p. 1998. pap. 4.99 (*0-8217-5889-6*, Zebra Kensgtn) Kensgtn Pub Corp.

***Dunn, Carola.** The Improper Governess. large type ed. (G. K. Hall Romance Ser.). 2000. 27.95 (*0-7838-8974-7*, G K Hall Lrg Type) Mac Lib Ref.

Dunn, Carola. The Man in the Green Coat. 192p. 1987. 16.95 (*0-8027-0937-0*) Walker & Co.

— Mayhem & Miranda. 224p. 1997. mass mkt. 4.99 (*0-8217-5766-0*, Zebra Kensgtn) Kensgtn Pub Corp.

— Miss Hartwell's Dilemma. 224p. 1988. 17.95 (*0-8027-1041-7*) Walker & Co.

— Miss Hartwell's Dilemma. large type ed. LC 90-10939. 341p. 1990. reprint ed. 18.95 (*1-56054-014-1*) Thorndike Pr.

— Murder on the Flying Scotsman. LC 96-31780. 240p. 1996. text 21.95 (*0-312-15175-6*) St Martin.

***Dunn, Carola.** Rattle His Bones: A Daisy Dairymple Mystery. LC 00-27854. 256p. 2000. 22.95 (*0-312-20572-4*, Minotaur) St Martin.

Dunn, Carola. Requiem for a Mezzo. large type ed. 291p. 1996. pap. 21.95 (*0-7838-1857-2*, G K Hall Lrg Type) Mac Lib Ref.

— The Road to Gretna. (Regency Romance Ser.: No. 173). 1992. mass mkt. 2.99 (*0-373-31173-7*, 1-31173-7) Harlequin Bks.

— Scandal's Daughter. 320p. 1996. mass mkt. 4.50 (*0-8217-5273-1*, Zebra Kensgtn) Kensgtn Pub Corp.

***Dunn, Carola.** Snowflake Kittens. 1999. mass mkt. 4.99 (*0-8217-6450-0*) Kensgtn Pub Corp.

Dunn, Carola. Styx & Stones: A Daisy Dalrymple Mystery. 2nd ed. LC 99-22067. 240p. 1999. text 22.95 (*0-312-20592-9*) St Martin.

— Thea's Marquis. 1999. per. 3.75 (*0-373-31223-7*) Harlequin Bks.

— Tudor Secret. 1995. pap. 4.50 (*0-8217-5172-7*) NAL.

— Two Corinthians. large type ed. LC 90-44227. 340p. 1990. reprint ed. lib. bdg. 18.95 (*1-56054-049-4*) Thorndike Pr.

— The Winter Garden Mystery. large type ed. 326p. 1995. 23.95 (*0-7838-1487-9*, G K Hall Lrg Type) Mac Lib Ref.

Dunn, Carola, et al. A Christmas Courtship. 352p. 1996. mass mkt. 4.99 (*0-8217-5464-5*, Zebra Kensgtn) Kensgtn Pub Corp.

— Once Upon a Kiss. (Zebra Regency Romance Ser.). 255p. 1999. mass mkt. 4.99 (*0-8217-6210-9*) Kensgtn Pub Corp.

— Once upon a Time. 288p. 1998. pap. 4.99 (*0-8217-5995-7*) Kensgtn Pub Corp.

— A Winter Wedding. 256p. 1998. mass mkt. 4.99 (*0-8217-5828-4*, Zebra Kensgtn) Kensgtn Pub Corp.

***Dunn, Carola, et al.** Wonderful & Wicked. (Zebra Regency Romance Ser.). 256p. 2000. mass mkt. 4.99 (*0-8217-6630-9*, Zebra Kensgtn) Kensgtn Pub Corp.

Dunn, Caroline, jt. auth. see Patton, James R.

***Dunn, Carolyn.** Fourth of July. (American Indian Chapbook Ser.: Vol. I, No. 1). 20p. (C). 2000. pap. 5.00 (*1-928708-10-2*) That Painted Horse.

— Hidden Creek Journal: Haiku & Other Verse from the Center of the World. 50p. 2000. pap. 9.95 (*1-928708-12-9*) That Painted Horse.

— Outfoxing Coyote: Poems. Allen, Paula Gunn, ed. (Paula Gunn Allen American Indian Poets Ser.: No. 1). 90p. 2000. pap. 13.95 (*1-928708-08-0*) That Painted Horse.

— A Pie Went By. LC 98-16790. 32p. (J). (ps-1). Date not set. pap. 4.95 (*0-06-443649-7*) HarpC Child Bks.

— A Pie Went By. LC 98-16790. 32p. (J). (ps-1). 2000. 14.95 (*0-06-028807-8*); lib. bdg. 14.89 (*0-06-028808-6*) HarpC Child Bks.

— Plant Biology. 128p. (C). 1999. spiral bd. 31.95 (*0-7872-6310-9*, 41631001) Kendall-Hunt.

Dunn, Carolyn. Real Kings Don't Do Ballet. (J). 2001. 15.95 (*0-688-16176-6*, Grenwillow Bks); lib. bdg. 15.89 (*0-688-16177-4*, Grenwillow Bks) HarpC Child Bks.

Dunn, Carolyn & Comfort, Carol, eds. Through the Eye of the Deer: An Anthology of Native American Women Writers. LC 99-52696. 288p. 1999. pap. 16.95 (*1-879960-58-3*, Pub. by Aunt Lute Bks) SPD-Small Pr Dist.

Dunn, Carrie. Exploring the Spirituality of Menstruation: A Cross-Cultural Search into the Religious Symbolic & Mythological Power of Menstruation. (Illus.). 125p. (Orig.). (C). 1990. pap. 8.95 (*0-945086-37-7*) Sunlight Prodns.

Dunn, Catherine. The Black Swan. large type ed. 1990. 27.99 (*0-7089-2169-8*) Ulverscroft.

— The Bluebell Wood. large type ed. (Linford Romance Library). 1991. pap. 16.99 (*0-7089-7055-9*) Ulverscroft.

Dunn, Catherine & Mohler, Dorothy A., eds. Pioneering Women at the Catholic University of America. 112p. 1991. pap. 9.95 (*0-8132-0749-5*, DUPWP) Cath U Pr.

Dunn, Catherine E., ed. see Symposium in Comparative Literature (3rd: 1968, Ca.

Dunn, Charles. Conversations in Paint: A Notebook of Fundamentals. LC 95-21366. (Illus.). 208p. 1995. pap. 19.95 (*1-56305-664-X*, 3664) Workman Pub.

— Learning with Leonard & Friends: From A to Z. large type ed. Ovange, Sheila & Groller, Scott, eds. LC 98-90168. (Illus.). 64p. (J). (ps-1). 1998. text 17.95 (*0-9663240-3-X*) C C Dunn.

Dunn, Charles J. Everyday Life in Traditional Japan. (Illus.). 208p. 1977. pap. 12.95 (*0-8048-1384-1*) Tuttle Pubng.

Dunn, Charles W. American Political Theology: Historical Perspective & Theoretical Analysis. LC 84-13308. 195p. 1984. 57.95 (*0-275-91146-2*, C1146, Praeger Pubs); pap. 17.95 (*0-275-91603-0*, B1603, Praeger Pubs) Greenwood.

— Constitutional Democracy in America: A Reappraisal. LC 86-17802. (Illus.). 487p. reprint ed. pap. 151.00 (*0-7837-4749-7*, 204455800004) Bks Demand.

— Highland Settler: A Portrait of the Scottish Gael in Nova Scotia. LC 53-7025. 191p. reprint ed. pap. 59.30 (*0-8357-6379-X*, 203573300096) Bks Demand.

Dunn, Charles W., Sr. How to Be Happy in an Unhappy World. 141p. (Orig.). 1986. pap. 8.95 (*0-89084-318-X*, 028282) Bob Jones Univ.

***Dunn, Charles W.** The Scarlet Thread of Scandal: Morality & the American Presidency. LC 99-41042. 200p. 2000. 24.95 (*0-8476-9606-5*, Pub. by Rowman) Natl Bk Netwk.

Dunn, Charles W., ed. American Government: A Comparative Approach. (C). 1997. pap., student ed. 28.00 (*0-06-502237-8*) Addison-Wesley.

Dunn, Charles W. & Byrnes, Edward T., eds. Middle English Literature. LC 89-78116. 564p. 1990. text 30.00 (*0-8240-5298-6*, 1330); pap. text 20.95 (*0-8240-5297-8*, 1330) Garland.

Dunn, Charles W. & Woodard, J. David. The Conservative Tradition in America. 208p. (C). 1996. pap. text 14.95 (*0-8476-8167-X*); lib. bdg. 60.50 (*0-8476-8166-1*) Rowman.

Dunn, Charles W., jt. auth. see Bloomfield, Morton W.

***Dunn, Charleta J.** Sisk--Book of Ages. LC 99-175564. xiii, 1081p. 1998. write for info. (*0-8328-9581-4*) Higginson Bk Co.

Dunn, Charlotte. Poetic Creativity. 52p. (Orig.). 1993. pap. 4.95 (*0-9622849-6-3*) Papito.

Dunn, Charlotte V. Otto. LC 99-189022. (Illus.). 240p. 1998. pap. 20.00 (*1-57502-867-0*, PO2362, SchlMate) Morris Pubng.

Dunn, Chris. Provinces: Canadian Provincial Politics. 400p. 1996. pap. 27.95 (*1-55111-090-3*) Broadview Pr.

Dunn, Chris, jt. auth. see Bretherton, Michael.

Dunn, Christopher. The Giza Power Plant: Technologies of Ancient Egypt. LC 98-3949. (Illus.). 288p. 1998. pap. 18.00 (*1-879181-50-9*) Bear & Co.

— The Institutionalized Cabinet: Governing the Western Provinces. LC 96-129064. (Canadian Public Administration Ser.). 352p. 1995. 60.00 (*0-7735-1283-7*, Pub. by McG-Queens Univ Pr) CUP Services.

Dunn, Christopher A., jt. auth. see Kaye, Harvey.

Dunn Communications, Ltd., ed. see Waiters, Tony & Cowan, Jane.

Dunn Communications Ltd. Staff, ed. see Waiters, Tony.

Dunn, Connie. Internet Publishing with Microsoft Word 7.0. 1997. pap. text 29.95 (*1-55622-580-6*) Wordware Pub.

Dunn, Craig. Iron Men, Iron Will: The Nineteenth Indiana Regiment of the Iron Brigade. LC 95-77509. (Illus.). 300p. 1995. 29.95 (*1-878208-65-9*); pap. 24.95 (*1-878208-64-0*) Guild Pr IN.

***Dunn, Craig L.** Harvestfields of Death: The Twentieth Indiana Volunteers of Gettysburg. LC 99-65148. 334p. 1999. 29.95 (*1-57860-039-1*) Guild Pr IN.

— Harvestfields of Death: The Twentiety Indiana Volunteers of Gettysburg. LC 99-65148. 334p. 1999. pap. 24.95 (*1-57860-038-3*) Guild Pr IN.

***Dunn, Cynthia & Chadwick, Gary.** Protecting Study Volunteers in Clinical Research. Allen, Whitney, ed. 200p. 1999. pap. 59.00 (*0-9673029-1-9*) CenterWatch.

Dunn, D. C., jt. auth. see Goldie, B. S.

Dunn, D. Ellwood. Liberia. LC 96-129637. (World Bibliographical Ser.). 252p. 1995. lib. bdg. 77.50 (*1-85109-178-5*) ABC-CLIO.

Dunn, D. Elwood & Holsoe, Svend E. Historical Dictionary of Liberia. LC 84-23524. (African Historical Dictionaries Ser.: No. 38). (Illus.). 304p. 1985. 31.00 (*0-8108-1767-5*) Scarecrow.

***Dunn, D. Elwood, et al.** Historical Dictionary of Liberia. LC 00-44654. (African Historical Dictionaries Ser.). 2000. write for info. (*0-8108-3876-1*) Scarecrow.

Dunn, D. Gregory, jt. auth. see Fishell, Randy.

Dunn, D. Judith. Friends Matter: The Beginnings. 1995. 10.00 (*0-449-90931-X*) Fawcett.

Dunn, Dale M., jt. auth. see Pence, Barbara C.

Dunn, Dalmer D. Financing Presidential Campaigns. LC 72-64. (Brookings Institution Studies in Presidential Selection). 184p. reprint ed. pap. 57.10 (*0-608-12180-0*, 202537300043) Bks Demand.

Dunn, Dana. The Practical Researcher: A Student Guide to Conducting Psychological Research. LC 98-26089. 408p. 1998. pap. 48.13 (*0-07-018323-6*) McGraw.

Dunn, Dana, ed. Workplace/Women's Place: An Anthology. LC 96-48794. 380p. (C). 1998. pap. text. write for info. (*0-935732-81-0*) Roxbury Pub Co.

***Dunn, Dana & Waller, David V.** Analyzing Social Problems: Essays & Exercises. 2nd ed. LC 99-30357. 227p. 1999. pap. 29.67 (*0-13-083228-6*) P-H.

Dunn, Dana, et al. Exploring Social Relationships. 140p. 1995. pap. text 27.80 (*0-13-304460-2*) P-H.

Dunn, Dana, jt. ed. see Dubeck, Paula.

Dunn, Daniel M. Building Confidence in Communication. (C). 1997. pap. text 38.66 (*0-673-39929-X*) Addson-Wesley Educ.

Dunn, Danielle & Dunn, Jessica. A Teen's Guide to Getting Published: The Only Writer's Guide Written by Teens for Teens. 83p. 1997. pap. 14.95 (*1-882664-22-1*) Prufrock Pr.

Dunn, David. Delivering Health Care to Refugees: Cross-Cultural Training to Enhance the Delivery of Quality Health Care to Culturally Diverse Persons. 32p. 1992. 5.00 (*0-940723-08-5*) SIIS.

— Sky Drift. LC 80-80806. (Illus.). 90p. 1979. 13.50 (*0-939044-27-7*) Lingua Pr.

— Try Giving Yourself Away. 3rd ed. LC 74-102032. 146p. 1998. reprint ed. pap. 10.00 (*0-9613203-3-8*) Updegraff.

***Dunn, David.** Why Do Whales & Children Sing? A Guide to Listening in Nature. LC 99-61987. 96p. 1999. pap. 17.95 (*0-945401-03-5*, Pub. by EarthEar) New Leaf Dist.

***Dunn, David, ed.** Harry Partch: An Anthology of Critical Perspectives. (Illus.). 208p. 1999. text 64.00 (*90-5755-065-2*, Harwood Acad Pubs) Gordon & Breach.

Dunn, David, ed. A History of the Evangelical & Reformed Church. LC 90-33153. 406p. 1990. reprint ed. pap. 16.95 (*0-8298-0855-8*) Pilgrim OH.

Dunn, David, jt. auth. see Gaburo, Kenneth.

Dunn, David C. & Menzies, Donald. Laparoscopic Hernia Repair: Problems & Solutions. 160p. 1995. 99.95 (*0-86542-908-1*) Blackwell Sci.

Dunn, David C. & Rawlinson, Nigel. Surgical Diagnosis & Management: A Guide to General Surgical Care. 3rd ed. LC 98-14103. (Illus.). 736p. 1999. pap. 44.95 (*0-86542-718-6*) Blackwell Sci.

Dunn, David C. & Watson, Christopher J. Laparoscopic Cholecystectomy: Problems & Solutions. (Illus.). 160p. 1992. 70.00 (*0-632-03444-0*) Blackwell Sci.

Dunn, David H. The Politics of Threat: Minuteman Vulnerability in American National Security Policy. LC 97-13669. 289p. 1997. text 65.00 (*0-312-17611-2*) St Martin.

Dunn, David H., jt. ed. see Bowen, Wyn Q.

***Dunn, Declan.** The Complete Insiders Guide to Associate & Affiliate Programs: Discover How to Dramatically Increase Your Revenues Through Quick, Strategic Positioning on the Internet. 126p. 1998. ring bd. 112.00 (*1-930336-02-0*) Adnet Intl.

— Director of Sales. 125p. 1996. ring bd. 97.00 (*1-930336-00-4*) Adnet Intl.

— Director of Sales, Set. unabridged ed. 1997. 97.00 incl. audio (*1-930336-06-3*) Adnet Intl.

— E-Business Maximum Cash Flow. 205p. 1997. ring bd. 197.00 (*1-930336-01-2*) Adnet Intl.

— Net Profits: How to Win the Internet Game. 2000. cd-rom 17.97 (*1-930336-09-8*) Adnet Intl.

— Net Profits: Winning the Internet Game. 200p. 2000. pap. write for info. (*1-930336-07-1*) Adnet Intl.

— Net Profits: How to Win the Internet Game Pt. 2: Proven Success of the $65,000 Affiliate, the $750,000 Super Affiliate, & the $600,000/6-Week Performance Network, 2 CDs. 200p. 2000. pap. 47.00 incl. cd-rom (*1-930336-10-1*) Adnet Intl.

— Winning the Affiliate Game. 97p. 1999. ring bd. 97.00 (*1-930336-03-9*) Adnet Intl.

— Winning the Affiliate Game: The Mastermind Sessions, Set. unabridged ed. 1999. 39.97 incl. audio (*1-930336-05-5*) Adnet Intl.

Dunn, Delmer D. Politics & Administration at the Top: Lessons from down Under. LC 97-4770. (Series in Policy & Institutional Studies). 194p. 1997. pap. 19.95 (*0-8229-5650-0*); text 45.00 (*0-8229-4045-0*) U of Pittsburgh Pr.

Dunn, Dennis D. Every Child Is Our Child: A Plan for Education That Leaves No Child Behind. 1992. write for info. (*0-9633280-0-X*) Dunn & Hargitt.

Dunn, Dennis J. Caught Between Roosevelt & Stalin: America's Ambassadors to Moscow. LC 97-23033. (Illus.). 384p. (C). 1998. 32.50 (*0-8131-2023-3*) U Pr of Ky.

Dunn, Dennis J., ed. Religion & Communist Society: Selected Papers from the Second World Congress for Soviet & East European Studies. 165p. (Orig.). 1983. pap. 12.00 (*0-933884-29-X*) Berkeley Slavic.

Dunn, Diane, jt. auth. see Dunn, Phil.

Dunn, Dianna K., jt. auth. see Dunn, Gary A.

Dunn, Dick. New Faces in the Frame: A Guide to Marriage & Parenting in the Blended Family. LC 97-220270. 224p. 1997. pap. text 12.95 (*0-8054-9817-6*, LifeWy Press) LifeWay Christian.

Dunn, Dick. Preparing to Marry Again. LC 98-88823. 96p. 1999. pap. 14.95 (*0-88177-276-3*, DR276, Pub. by Discipleship Res) P B D Inc.

— Willing to Try Again: Steps Toward Blending a Family. LC 92-33555. 128p. 1993. pap. 12.00 (*0-8170-1185-4*) Judson.

Dunn, Donald J. Noter Up. 1986. ring bd. 80.00 (*0-89941-439-7*, 303800) W S Hein.

Dunn, Donald J., jt. auth. see Jacobstein, J. Myron.

Dunn, Donald J., ed. see Jacobstein, J. Myron & Mersky, Ray M.

Dunn, Donald J., ed. see Jacobstein, J. Myron & Mersky, Roy M.

Dunn, Donald J., jt. ed. see Mersky, Roy M.

Dunn, Douglas. Dazhan. 2nd rev. ed. LC 88-1296. 244p. 1988. pap. 6.95 (*0-944363-00-8*) Word Wizards.

— Extro-Dynamics. LC 94-11592. (Illus.). 200p. (Orig.). 1994. pap. 8.95 (*0-944363-23-7*) Word Wizards.

— Footnotes: Six Choreographers. (Illus.). 192p. 1998. text 22.00 (*90-5701-042-9*, 810581); pap. text 18.00 (*90-5701-082-8*, 810584) Gordon & Breach.

— New & Selected Poems, 1966-1988. (Modern European Poets Ser.). 240p. 1989. 17.95 (*0-88001-177-7*) HarpC.

Dunn, Douglas, ed. The Essential Browning. (Essential Poets Ser.: Vol. 13). 192p. 1990. pap. 8.00 (*0-88001-195-5*) HarpC.

— The Oxford Book of Scottish Short Stories. 504p. 1996. reprint ed. pap. 15.95 (*0-19-282521-6*) OUP.

Dunn, Douglas, jt. auth. see Shafer, Ross.

Dunn, Durwood. An Abolitionist in the Appalachian South: Ezekiel Birdseye on Slavery, Capitalism, & Seperate Statehood in East Tennessee, 1841-1846. LC 96-25271. (Illus.). 304p. 1997. 36.00 (*0-87049-964-5*) U of Tenn Pr.

— Cades Cove: The Life & Death of a Southern Appalachian Community, 1818-1937. LC 87-18212. (Illus.). 288p. 1988. pap. 16.95 (*0-87049-559-3*); lib. bdg. 32.00 (*0-87049-554-2*) U of Tenn Pr.

Dunn, E., ed. see Metallurgical Society of AIME Staff.

Dunn, Earl V., et al, eds. Disseminating Research - Impacting Practice. LC 94-10317. (Research Methods for Primary Care Ser.: Vol. 6). 1994. pap. 26.00 (*0-8039-5706-8*) Sage.

— Disseminating Research - Impacting Practice, No. 6. LC 94-10317. (Research Methods for Primary Care Ser.: Vol. 6). 1994. 58.00 (*0-8039-5705-X*) Sage.

Dunn, Edgar S., Jr. The Development of the U. S. Urban System: Industrial Shifts, Implications, Vol. II. LC 81-47619. 266p. 1983. 75.00 (*0-8018-2638-1*) Resources Future.

Dunn, Edgar S. The Development of the U. S. Urban System Vol. I: Concepts, Structures, Regional Shifts. LC 79-2180. (Illus.). 227p. reprint ed. pap. 70.40 (*0-7837-6144-9*, 204372600001) Bks Demand.

Dunn, Edgar S., Jr. Economic & Social Development: A Process of Social Learning. LC 70-134691. (Resources for the Future Ser.). 342p. 1971. 24.50 (*0-8018-1198-8*) Johns Hopkins.

Dunn, Edgar S. Social Information Processing & Statistical Systems-Change & Reform. LC 74-5289. 256p. reprint ed. pap. 79.40 (*0-608-11176-7*, 205157000089) Bks Demand.

Dunn, Edith B. Cooking Made Easy with a Touch of the Welsh. Pritchard, John & Pritchard, Gerylin, eds. (Illus.). 336p. 1988. pap. 19.95 (*0-914207-05-9*) Cornucopia Pubns.

Dunn, Edmond J. What Is Theology? Foundational & Moral. LC 97-60965. 272p. 1998. pap. 12.95 (*0-89622-742-1*) Twenty-Third.

Dunn, Edward T. What Is This Thing Called Love? LC 95-90975. (Orig.). 1996. pap. 8.95 (*0-533-11804-2*) Vantage.

***Dunn, Eileen.** Conscious Divorce: With Forgiveness Comes Freedom. (Illus.). 104p. 2000. pap. 9.95 (*1-885003-62-5*, Pub. by R D Reed Pubs) Midpt Trade.

— Our Haunting Good-Byes: The Journey from Grief to Life. 104p. 2000. pap. 9.95 (*1-885003-61-7*, Pub. by R D Reed Pubs) Midpt Trade.

Dunn, Elizabeth, jt. auth. see Stickland, Laurie

Dunn, Elizabeth, jt. ed. see Hann, Chris.

Dunn, Elizabeth G. The FUNDACEN Experience: Factors for Success & Failure in a Guatemalan Land Purchase-Sale Program. (Research Paper Ser.: Vol. 107). viii, 133p. (C). 1992. pap. 7.00 (*0-934519-17-X*, RP107) U of Wis Land.

Dunn, Ellen C. The Gallican Saint's Life & the Late Roman Dramatic Tradition. LC 88-25784. 176p. 1989. reprint ed. pap. 54.60 (*0-7837-9196-8*, 204989800004) Bks Demand.

Dunn, Elsie M. Innocence Lost Vol. 1: Life As a Teenage Mother. Carr, Dorothy, ed. (Illus.). 64p. (YA). 1997. pap. 4.95 (*0-9661227-4-7*) Media Graphix.

Dunn, Elwood D. & Tarr, Byron S. Liberia. (Profiles of Africa Ser.). 1996. text 26.50 (*0-86531-736-4*) Westview.

Dunn, Erica. The Complete Bird Feeder Book. write for info. (*0-393-03932-3*) Norton.

***Dunn, Erica H.** Birds at Your Feeder. LC 98-35661. 1999. 29.95 (*0-393-04737-7*) Norton.

Dunn, Ernest. Black Experience. 428p. 1996. pap. text, per. 41.95 (*0-7872-1400-0*) Kendall-Hunt.

Dunn, Esther C. Shakespeare in America. LC 68-21212. (Illus.). 1972. reprint ed. 20.95 (*0-405-08475-7*, Pub. by Blom Pubns) Ayer.

Dunn, Ethel, jt. auth. see Dunn, Stephen P.

Dunn, F., et al, eds. Ultrasonic Tissue Characterization. (Illus.). 250p. 1996. 139.00 (*4-431-70162-1*) Spr-Verlag.

Dunn, Finlay. American Farming & Food. 1980. lib. bdg. 75.00 (*0-8490-3185-0*) Gordon Pr.

Dunn, Finley P., Jr., ed. Song of the Outer Banks: A Poem in Twelve Cantos. (Illus.). 105p. (Orig.). 1989. pap. write for info. (*0-318-64790-7*) Gresham Pubns.

Dunn, Francis M. Tragedy's End: Closure & Innovation in Euripidean Drama. 264p. (C). 1996. text 49.95 (*0-19-508344-X*) OUP.

Dunn, Frank. Paul's Later Life & Letters. 1983. pap. 1.00 (*0-88027-101-9*) Firm Foun Pub.

Dunn, Frederick S. Peace-Making & the Settlement with Japan. LC 81-6223. 210p. 1981. reprint ed. lib. bdg. 59.50 (*0-313-23076-5*, DUPM, Greenwood Pr) Greenwood.

— Practice & Procedure of International Conferences. LC 70-158959. reprint ed. 31.50 (*0-404-02221-9*) AMS Pr.

Dunn, G., et al. Modelling Covariances & Latent Variables Using EQS. (Illus.). 208p. (Orig.). 1993. ring bd. 41.95 (*0-412-48990-2*, Chap & Hall CRC) CRC Pr.

Dunn, G. H., jt. ed. see Maerk, T. D.

Dunn, G. P., et al. Some Properties of the Bank Model. LC HG1588.D86. (Bank of England. Discussion Papers. Technical Ser.: No. 9). 115p. reprint ed. pap. 35.70 (*0-608-12570-9*, 202397800035) Bks Demand.

Dunn, G. T. Bad Blood. large type ed. (Linford Western Library). 272p. 1996. pap. 16.99 (*0-7089-7955-6*, Linford) Ulverscroft.

— Cold Welcome in Paradise. large type ed. (Dales Large Print Ser.). 212p. 1996. pap. 18.99 (*1-85389-694-2*, Dales) Ulverscroft.

— Ride on Angry Land. large type ed. 272p. 1998. pap. 17.99 (*0-7089-5377-8*, Linford) Ulverscroft.

Dunn, Gary. Descubre Mariposas. University of Mexico City Staff, tr. (Descubre - Spanish Ser.).Tr. of Discover Butterflies. (SPA., Illus.). 48p. (J). (gr. 3-6). 1993. lib. bdg. 16.95 (*1-56674-048-7*, HTS Bks) Forest Hse.

Dunn, Gary A. Beginner's Guide to Observing & Collecting Insects. LC 95-119743. (Illus.). 92p. 1994. pap. 8.95 (*1-884256-12-0*) Yng Entomol.

— Caring for Insect Livestock: An Insect Rearing Manual. (YES Special Publications: No. 8). 96p. 1993. pap. text 8.95 (*1-884256-10-4*) Yng Entomol.

— Insect Life Cycle Studies Unit III: Entomology. (Illus.). 36p. (J). (gr. 5-7). 1998. reprint ed. pap. text 15.00 (*0-7881-4323-9*) DIANE Pub.

— Insects of the Great Lakes Region. LC 95-50882. 336p. (C). 1996. pap. 18.95 (*0-472-06515-7*, 06515); text 42.50 (*0-472-09515-3*, 09515) U of Mich Pr.

— Project B. U. G. S. (Illus.). 128p. 1994. pap. 9.95 (*1-884256-13-9*) Yng Entomol.

Dunn, Gary A. YES International Entomology Resource Guide: The Insect Study Sourcebook. 4th ed. (YES Special Publications: No. 1). 90p. 1992. pap. text 5.95 (*1-884256-07-4*) Yng Entomol.

Dunn, Gary A. & Dunn, Dianna K. Insect Identification Guide. 4th ed. LC 98-140937. (Illus.). 72p. 1998. pap. 8.95 (*1-884256-16-3*) Yng Entomol.

Dunn, Geoffrey. Santa Cruz Is in the Heart. 185p. 1990. 12.95 (*0-932319-02-5*) Capitola Bk.

Dunn, George, Jr. & McGill, Kevin. The Throws Manual. 2nd ed. (Illus.). 160p. 1994. pap. 18.50 (*0-911521-39-9*) Tafnews.

Dunn, George E., ed. A Gilbert & Sullivan Dictionary. LC 72-125070. (Music Ser.). 1971. reprint ed. lib. bdg. 25.00 (*0-306-70007-7*) Da Capo.

Dunn, Gloria. From Making a Living to Having a Life: A Book for the Working Challenged. Rosenbush, Amanita, ed. LC 97-80933. (Illus.). 272p. 1999. pap. 17.95 (*0-9660867-5-9*) Violin Pub.

***Dunn, Graham.** Statistics in Psychiatry. 224p. 1999. pap. text 37.50 (*0-340-67668-X*, Pub. by E A) OUP.

Dunn, Graham & Everitt, Brian S. Clinical Biostatistics: An Introduction to Evidence-Based Medicine. LC 95-171090. (An Arnold Publication). 160p. 1999. pap. 35.00 (*0-340-59531-0*, Pub. by E A) OUP.

Dunn, Graham, jt. auth. see Everitt, Brian S.

Dunn, Graham, jt. ed. see Everitt, Brian S.

Dunn, H. P. The Doctor & Christian Marriage. LC 92-15244. 1992. pap. 9.95 (*0-8189-0642-1*) Alba.

— Ethics for Doctors, Nurses, & Patients. LC 93-44150. 158p. 1994. pap. 8.95 (*0-8189-0688-X*) Alba.

Dunn, Halbert L. High Level Wellness. 7th ed. (Positive Health Bookshelf Ser.013, Vol. 1). 1972. 9.95 (*0-87948-002-5*) Beatty.

Dunn, Hampton. Florida's Historic Courthouses. LC 98-41618. 1998. 34.95 (*0-9653759-5-1*) Hallmark Pubng.

— Tampa: A Pictorial History. Morgan, Nancy, ed. LC 85-4450. (Portrait of American Cities Ser.). (Illus.). 224p. 1995. reprint ed. pap. 14.95 (*0-89865-409-2*) Donning Co.

Dunn, Hank. Hard Choices for Loving People: CPR, Artificial Feeding, Comfort Measures Only & the Elderly Patient. 3rd rev. ed. 44p. 1994. pap. 3.50 (*1-928560-00-8*) A & A Pubs.

***Dunn, Hank.** Light in the Shadows: Meditations While Living with a Life-Threatening Illness. 52p. 1999. pap. 3.50 (*1-928560-01-6*) A & A Pubs.

Dunn, Harold. The World According to Kids: Wit & Wisdom from the Elementary School Classroom. 96p. 1992. pap. 6.95 (*0-930753-11-9*) Spect Ln Pr.

Dunn, Henry. Guatemala, or, the Republic of Central America. xviii, 328p. 1981. reprint ed. 20.00 (*0-87917-075-1*) La Tienda.

Dunn, Henry G., ed. Sequelae of Low Birthweight. LC 65-80534. (Clinics in Developmental Medicine Ser.: No. 95-96). (Illus.). 306p. (C). 1991. text 69.95 (*0-521-41215-3*, Pub. by Mc Keith Pr) Cambridge U Pr.

Dunn, Henry T. Recollections of Dante Gabriel Rossetti & His Circle. Pedrick, Gale, ed. LC 73-129379. reprint ed. 29.50 (*0-404-02222-7*) AMS Pr.

Dunn, Herb. Jackie Robinson: Young Sports Trailblazer. LC 98-45623. (Childhood of Famous Americans Ser.). (Illus.). 192p. 1999. per. 4.99 (*0-689-82453-X*) Aladdin.

***Dunn, Herb.** Joe Dimaggio: Young Sports Hero. (Childhood of Famous Americans Ser.). (Illus.). 192p. (J). (gr. 3-7). 1999. per. 4.99 (*0-689-83186-2*) Aladdin.

Dunn, Hilda, jt. auth. see Glanbman, Michael.

Dunn, Hopeton, ed. Globalization, Communications & Caribbean Identity. LC 95-17952. 224p. 1995. text 55.00 (*0-312-12764-2*) St Martin.

D

Dunn, I. J. Biological Reaction Engineering: Principles, Applications & Modelling with PC Simulation. (Illus.). 438p. 1992. 295.00 (*3-527-28511-3*, Wiley-VCH) Wiley.

Dunn, Ilene. Dreams. 6p. 1995. write for info. (*1-887975-03-9*) Romance & Miracles.

— Soul Food. 10p. 1995. write for info. (*1-887975-02-0*) Romance & Miracles.

Dunn, Ilene L. I Am. (Illus.). 10p. 1995. write for info. (*1-887975-00-4*) Romance & Miracles.

— We Are. 10p. 1995. write for info. (*1-887975-01-2*) Romance & Miracles.

Dunn, Irene B. Out of the Night: A Story of Tragedy & Hope from a Survivor of the 1959 Montana - Yellowstone Earthquake. 128p. 1998. 10.95 (*1-879628-16-3*, Plaudit Pr) Keokee ID.

Dunn, Irving S., et al. Fundamentals of Geotechnical Analysis. LC 79-13583. 414p. 1980. text 103.95 (*0-471-03698-6*) Wiley.

— Fundamentals of Geotechnical Analysis. 27p. 1980. pap. text, student ed. 6.00 (*0-471-04997-2*) Wiley.

Dunn, J. Allan. Language & Society in Post-Communist Europe Selected Papers from the Fifth World Congress of Central & East European Studies, Warsaw, 1995. LC 98-54304. 1999. text 59.95 (*0-312-22232-7*) St Martin.

Dunn, J. E., et al, eds. Shock Induced Transitions & Phase Structures in General Media. LC 93-4682. (IMA Volumes in Mathematics & Its Applications Ser.: Vol. 52). 1993. 69.95 (*0-387-94084-7*) Spr-Verlag.

— Shock Induced Transitions & Phase Structures in General Media. LC 93-4682. (IMA Volumes in Mathematics & Its Applications: Vol. 52). (Illus.). 250p. 1993. write for info. (*3-540-94084-7*) Spr-Verlag.

Dunn, J. J., jt. auth. see Alter, Harvey.

Dunn, J. M. Stratford & Midland Junction Railway. 72p. (C). 1985. 50.00 (*0-85361-214-5*) St Mut.

Dunn, J. Michael & Epstein, George, eds. Modern Uses of Multiple-Valued Logic. (Episteme Ser.: No. 2). 343p. 1977. text 171.00 (*90-277-0747-2*, D Reidel) Kluwer Academic.

Dunn, J. Michael & Gupta, Anil, eds. Truth or Consequences: Essays in Honor of Nuel Belnap. 392p. (C). 1990. lib. bdg. 201.00 (*0-7923-0920-0*, Pub. by Kluwer Academic) Kluwer Academic.

***Dunn, J. P., Jr.** Massacres of the Mountains: A History of the Indian Wars of the Far West. (Illus.). ix, 784p. 2000. write for info. (*1-58218-203-5*); pap. write for info. (*1-58218-204-3*) Digital Scanning.

Dunn, J. R. Days of Cain. 384p. 1998. mass mkt. 3.99 (*0-380-79049-1*, Eos) Morrow Avon.

***Dunn, J. R.** Days of Cain. 1998. 9.09 (*0-606-13319-4*, Pub. by Turtleback) Demco.

— Full Tide of Night. 312p. 1999. mass mkt. 5.99 (*0-380-79050-5*, Eos) Morrow Avon.

Dunn, J. R. This Side of Judgment. LC 93-23696. 1994. 21.95 (*0-15-100076-X*) Harcourt.

Dunn, Jack. The Vatican Boys: A Novel about Church Corruption. unabridged ed. 220p. 1997. pap. 10.95 (*0-9662602-0-1*) Modern Memoirs.

Dunn, Jacob P. Indiana: A Redemption from Slavery. enl. ed. LC 72-3754. (American Commonwealths Ser.: No. 12). reprint ed. 49.50 (*0-404-57212-X*) AMS Pr.

— True Indian Stories: With Glossary of Indiana Indian Names. (Illus.). 320p. 1997. reprint ed. lib. bdg. 37.50 (*0-8328-6643-1*) Higginson Bk Co.

Dunn, Jacob P., jt. ed. see Woolen, William W.

Dunn, James. Unity & Diversity in the New Testament: An Inquiry into the Character of Earliest Christianity. 2nd ed. LC 89-20659. 528p. (C). 1990. pap. 25.00 (*0-334-02436-6*) TPI PA.

Dunn, James A., Jr. Driving Forces: The Automobile, Its Enemies & the Politics of Mobility. LC 98-25420. 250p. 1998. 44.95 (*0-8157-1964-7*); pap. 18.95 (*0-8157-1963-9*) Brookings.

Dunn, James D. The Acts of the Apostles. LC 97-129183. (Narrative Commentaries Ser.). 384p. (Orig.). 1996. pap. 22.00 (*1-56338-192-3*) TPI PA.

— Christian Liberty: A New Testament Prospective. (Didsbury Lectures). xi, 115p. 1993. reprint ed. pap. 13.99 (*0-85364-528-0*, Pub. by Paternoster Pub) OM Literature.

— Commentary on Colossians & Philemon: A Commentary on the Greek Text. LC 95-26758. (New International Greek Testament Commentary Ser.). 336p. 1996. 32.00 (*0-8028-2441-2*) Eerdmans.

— The Epistle to the Galatians. (Black's New Testament Commentary Ser.: No. 9). 400p. 1993. 24.95 (*1-56563-036-X*) Hendrickson MA.

— The Evidence for Jesus. LC 85-22540. 128p. (Orig.). 1986. pap. 16.95 (*0-664-24698-2*) Westminster John Knox.

— Jesus & the Spirit: A Study of the Religious & Charismatic Experience of Jesus & the First Christians As Reflected in the New Testament. LC 96-49933. 527p. 1997. pap. 30.00 (*0-8028-4291-7*) Eerdmans.

— Jesus' Call to Discipleship: Understanding Jesus Today. 151p. (C). 1992. pap. text 10.95 (*0-521-42481-X*) Cambridge U Pr.

— Jesus, Paul, & the Law: Studies in Mark & Galatians. rev. ed. 320p. 1990. pap. 24.95 (*0-664-25095-5*) Westminster John Knox.

— Romans 9-16. (Biblical Commentary Ser.: Vol. 38B). 29.99 (*0-8499-0252-5*) Word Pub.

— Romans 1-8. (Biblical Commentary Ser.: Vol. 38A). 29.99 (*0-8499-0237-1*) Word Pub.

— The Theology of Paul the Apostle. LC 97-23189. 844p. 1997. 45.00 (*0-8028-3844-8*) Eerdmans.

Dunn, James D., ed. The Theology of Paul's Letter to the Galatians. LC 93-9. (New Testament Theology Ser.). 179p. (C). 1993. text 54.95 (*0-521-35127-8*); pap. text 16.95 (*0-521-35953-8*) Cambridge U Pr.

Dunn, James D. G. 1 Corinthians. (New Testament Guides Ser.: No. 7). 118p. 1995. pap. 12.50 (*1-85075-742-9*, Pub. by Sheffield Acad) CUP Services.

Dunn, James D. G., ed. Jews & Christians: The Parting of the Ways, A. D. 70 to 135. LC 98-32398. 404p. 1999. pap. 39.00 (*0-8028-4498-7*) Eerdmans.

Dunn, James D. G. & Suggate, Alan M. Justice of God. 87p. 1997. reprint ed. pap. 7.99 (*0-85364-562-0*, Pub. by Paternoster Pub) OM Literature.

Dunn, James P., jt. auth. see Mendeloff, Albert.

Dunn, James R. & Kinney, John E. Conservative Environmentalism: Reassessing the Means, Redefining the Ends. LC 96-3620. 296p. 1996. 62.95 (*0-89930-993-3*, Quorum Bks) Greenwood.

Dunn, James T. The Saint Croix: Midwest Border River. LC 79-52970. (Illus.). xv, 310p. 1979. reprint ed. pap. 12.95 (*0-87351-141-7*) Minn Hist.

— St. Paul's Schubert Club: A Century of Music, 1882-1982. 103p. 1983. 5.00 (*0-912373-02-4*) Schubert.

— Saving the River: The St. Croix River Association. (Illus.). 56p. (Orig.). 1986. pap. 7.50 (*0-9617292-0-1*) St Croix River Assn.

Dunn, James T., ed. see Taylor, Elizabeth.

Dunn, Jane, ed. see Woolf, Virginia.

Dunn, Jean, ed. see Maharaj, Nisargadatta.

Dunn, Jeanette M. Nutrifacts: A Quick Reference for Nutrition in HIV Care. Mutzabaugh, Camle A. et al, eds. (Illus.). 1997. pap. write for info. (*1-891814-02-8*) Found Care Mgmt.

Dunn, Jeanette M. & Mutzebaugh, Carole A. Nutrition in Cancer Care: A Quick Reference for Nutritional Oncology. Garritson, Brenda & Adams, Lizbeth, eds. (Illus.). viii, 132p. 1997. pap. write for info. (*1-891814-03-6*) Found Care Mgmt.

Dunn, Jeffrey D. Reappraising Social Security: Toward an Alternative System. 244p. 1982. pap. 5.95 (*0-89940-850-8*) LBJ Sch Pub Aff.

Dunn, Jerry. Idiom Savant. 320p. 1998. pap. 12.95 (*0-8050-5093-0*) H Holt & Co.

— Idiom Savant. 1996. pap. 10.00 (*0-684-80019-5*) S&S Trade.

— Idiom Savant: Slang As It Is Slung. LC 96-52529. 1997. 25.00 (*0-8050-5094-9*) H Holt & Co.

— Leader Makers: 12 Steps Developing People & Getting Lean. (Illus.). 238p. 1998. pap. 39.95 (*1-57502-870-0*, PO2368) Morris Pubng.

Dunn, Jerry C. & Young, Donald. The Rocky Mountain States. LC 96-40545. (Smithsonian Guides to Historic America Ser.). 464p. 1998. pap. 19.95 (*1-55670-639-1*) Stewart Tabori & Chang.

Dunn, Jerry C., et al. National Geographic's Driving Guides to America. LC 96-37340. 1996. write for info. (*0-7922-3427-8*) Natl Geog.

Dunn, Jerry G. & Palmer, Bernard. God Is for the Alcoholic. expanded rev. ed.Tr. of Deus e a Favor do Alcoolatra. 236p. pap. 10.99 (*0-8024-3284-0*, 152) Moody.

Dunn, Jerry L. Words for Abundant Living. 200p. 1998. pap. 9.95 (*1-57502-862-X*, PO2353) Morris Pubng.

Dunn, Jessica, jt. auth. see Dunn, Danielle.

Dunn, Jim. David Coulthard - The Flying Scotsman. (Illus.). 176p. 1995. pap. 21.95 (*1-85260-530-8*, Pub. by J H Haynes & Co) Motorbooks Intl.

Dunn, Jim, jt. auth. see Veronico, Nicolas.

Dunn, Jimmy, jt. auth. see Manocchio, Anthony J.

Dunn, Jo. Painful People & How to Deal with Them. 1998. pap. 13.95 (*0-7322-5737-9*) HarpC.

Dunn, Joanna Valente, see Valente Dunn, Joanna.

Dunn, Joe, ed. see Church, W. H.

Dunn, Joe P. & Preston, Howard L., eds. The Future South: A Historical Perspective for the Twenty-First Century. LC 90-45170. 264p. 1991. text 34.95 (*0-252-01776-5*); pap. text 14.95 (*0-252-06167-5*) U of Ill Pr.

Dunn, Joe P. & Starr, Jerold M. How the U. S. Fought the War. rev. ed. (Lessons of the Vietnam War Ser.). (Illus.). 32p. (C). 1991. pap. text 5.00 (*0-945919-05-0*) Ctr Social Studies.

Dunn, John. Advertising. LC 96-35920. (Overview Ser.). (Illus.). (YA). (gr. 4-12). 1996. lib. bdg. 22.45 (*1-56006-182-0*) Lucent Bks.

— La Agonia Del Pensamiento Politico Occidental (Western Political Theory in the Face of the Future) (SPA.). 240p. (C). 1996. pap. 16.95 (*0-521-55566-3*) Cambridge U Pr.

— Auditing: Theory & Practice. LC 90-19558. 1991. 34.10 (*0-13-051277-X*) P-H.

— Auditing: Theory & Practice. 2nd ed. LC 95-46383. 1998. write for info. (*0-13-240896-1*) P-H.

***Dunn, John.** Cunning of Unreason: Making Sense of Politics. 400p. 2000. 30.00 (*0-465-01747-9*, Pub. by Basic) HarpC.

Dunn, John. Learning about Rights. 80p. (C). 1993. pap. text 21.00 (*0-900137-37-1*, Pub. by NCCL) St Mut.

— Modern Revolutions: An Introduction to the Analysis of a Political Phenomenon. 382p. (C). 1989. pap. text 19.95 (*0-521-37814-1*) Cambridge U Pr.

— The Political Thought of John Locke: An Historical Account of the Argument of the 'Two Treatises of Government' 306p. 1983. pap. text 24.95 (*0-521-27139-8*) Cambridge U Pr.

— Real Estate Law Revision Manual. LC 97-125867. 350p. (C). 1996. mass mkt. 38.95 (*0-314-09848-8*) West Pub.

— Western Political Theory in the Face of the Future. 2nd ed. (Canto Book Ser.). 153p. (C). 1993. pap. 11.95 (*0-521-43755-5*) Cambridge U Pr.

Dunn, John, ed. Democracy. 302p. 1994. pap. text 16.95 (*0-19-827934-5*) OUP.

— Textbook of Small Animal Medicine. (Illus.). 1100p. (C). 1998. text 125.00 (*0-7020-1582-2*, Pub. by W B Saunders) Saunders.

Dunn, John & Harris, Ian, eds. Aquinas, 10 vols., Set. Incl. Plato No. 1., 2 vols. Fine, G. LC 97-8555. 1088p. 1997. 350.00 (*1-85898-097-6*); No. 2. Aristotle., 2 vols. Bradley, A. C. LC 97-8554. 1232p. 1997. 400.00 (*1-85898-098-4*); No. 3. Augustine., 2 vols. Baynes, N. LC 97-8553. 1056p. 1997. 345.00 (*1-85898-099-2*); No. 5. Machiavelli., 2 vols. Chabod, F. LC 97-8552. 1264p. 1997. 400.00 (*1-85898-101-8*); No. 7. Grotius., 2 vols. LC 97-17562. 1232p. 1997. 400.00 (*1-85898-103-4*); No. 8. Hobbes., 3 vols. Dowey, J. LC 97-12054. 1864p. 1997. 610.00 (*1-85898-104-2*); No. 9. Locke., 2 vols. Burns, J. LC 97-24828. 1232p. 1997. 400.00 (*1-85898-105-0*); No. 10. Hume., 2 vols. Forbes, D. LC 97-17549. 1168p. 1997. 380.00 (*1-85898-106-9*); Set. Aquinas., 2 vols. Maritain, Jacques. LC 97-12053. 1136p. 1997. 370.00 (*1-85898-100-X*); (Great Political Thinkers Ser.: Vol. 4). 1997. 3975.00 (*1-85898-096-8*) E Elgar.

Dunn, John, et al. The British Empiricists: Locke, Berkeley, Hume. (Past Masters Ser.). 304p. 1992. pap. text 13.95 (*0-19-283068-6*) OUP.

Dunn, John, jt. auth. see Ableman, Paul.

Dunn, John A., ed. Sm'algyax: A Reference Dictionary & Grammar of the Coast Tsimshian Language. LC 94-31488. 255p. 1995. pap. text 22.50 (*0-295-97419-2*) U of Wash Pr.

***Dunn, John B.** Dr. John's Traveling Magic Show. 15p. 2000. pap. 4.00 (*1-58193-188-3*) Brown Bag Prods.

Dunn, John F., ed. see Krieger, Richard.

Dunn, John L., et al. Field Guide to the Birds of North America. 3rd rev. ed. LC 00-265098. (Illus.). 464p. 1999. per. 21.95 (*0-7922-7451-2*, Pub. by Natl Geog) S&S Trade.

Dunn, John M. The Civil Rights Movement. LC 97-27443. (World History Ser.). (Illus.). (YA). (gr. 4-12). 1997. lib. bdg. 22.45 (*1-56006-310-6*) Lucent Bks.

— Contemporary Crisis of the Nation State. 224p. 1995. pap. text 26.95 (*0-631-19263-8*) Blackwell Pubs.

— The Enlightenment. LC 98-8373. (World History Ser.). (Illus.). (YA). (gr. 4-12). 1998. lib. bdg. 23.70 (*1-56006-242-8*) Lucent Bks.

***Dunn, John M.** Life During the Black Death. LC 99-23791. (Way People Live Ser.). (Illus.). 112p. (YA). (gr. 6-9). 2000. lib. bdg. 23.70 (*1-56006-542-7*) Lucent Bks.

Dunn, John M. Special Physical Education. 7th adapted ed. 656p. (C). 1996. text. write for info. (*0-697-38187-0*) Brown & Benchmark.

— Winterwise: A Backpacker's Guide. 2nd rev. ed. LC 95-15220. (Illus.). 194p. 1997. pap. 12.95 (*0-935272-80-1*) ADK Mtn Club.

Dunn, John M. & Fait, Hollis F. Special Physical Education. 7th ed. LC 95-81071. 608p. (C). 1996. text. write for info. (*0-697-12623-4*) Brown & Benchmark.

— Special Physical Education: Adapted, Individualized, Developmental. 6th ed. 608p. (C). 1989. text. write for info. (*0-697-08624-0*) Brown & Benchmark.

Dunn, John T., ed. see Ziskin, Jay.

Dunn, John W., ed. Colorado Legal & Business Forms: Contracts, Gifts, Trusts, & Wills, & Real Property Forms. LC 95-80998. 750p. 1995. text. write for info. (*0-7620-0020-1*) West Group.

Dunn, Jon. Field Guide to Warblers of North America, 001. LC 97-12213. (Illus.). 400p. 1997. 30.00 (*0-395-38971-2*); pap. 20.00 (*0-395-78321-6*) HM.

Dunn, Joseph. Grammar of the Portuguese Language. (C). 1977. reprint ed. 10.00 (*0-87535-023-2*) Hispanic Soc.

— No Vipers in the Vatican. LC 96-156022. 236p. (Orig.). 1996. pap. 15.95 (*1-85607-167-7*, Pub. by Columba Press) Whitecap Bks.

— Transformed Lives. LC 98-37139. (Membership Ser.). 1998. 7.95 (*0-87604-413-5*) ARE Pr.

Dunn, Joseph, ed. see Kyle, Louisa V.

Dunn, Joy B., ed. Land in Common: Illustrated History of Jackson County, Oregon. (Illus.). 192p. 1996. 24.95 (*0-943388-11-2*) South Oregon.

Dunn, Judith, jt. ed. see Booth, Alan.

Dunn, Judith F., ed. Connections Between Emotion & Understanding in Development Vol. 9, Nos. 2 & 3: A Special Issue of "Cognition & Emotion" 180p. 1995. 65.00 (*0-86377-921-2*) L Erlbaum Assocs.

Dunn, Judith F., jt. ed. see Boer, Fritz.

Dunn, Judith F., jt. ed. see Booth, Alan.

Dunn, Judy. The Beginnings of Social Understanding. LC 88-766. (Developing Child Ser.). (Illus.). 240p. 1988. 35.95 (*0-674-06453-4*) HUP.

— Distress & Comfort. LC 76-30319. (Developing Child Ser.). 137p. reprint ed. pap. 42.50 (*0-7837-5933-9*, 204573200007) Bks Demand.

— From One Child to Two. LC 94-25563. 1995. pap. 10.00 (*0-449-90645-0*, Columbine) Fawcett.

— The Little Duck. LC 75-36467. (Pictureback Ser.). (Illus.). 32p. (J). (ps-1). 1976. pap. 3.25 (*0-394-83247-7*, Pub. by Random Bks Yng Read) Random.

— The Little Kitten. LC 82-16711. (Pictureback Ser.). (Illus.). 32p. (J). (ps-4). 1983. pap. 3.25 (*0-394-85818-2*, Pub. by Random Bks Yng Read) Random.

— The Little Lamb. LC 76-24167. (Pictureback Library Editions). (Illus.). (J). (ps-2). 1977. pap. 3.25 (*0-394-83455-0*, Pub. by Random Bks Yng Read) Random.

— The Little Pig. LC 86-42956. (Pictureback Ser.). (Illus.). 32p. (J). (ps-3). 1987. pap. 2.25 (*0-394-88774-3*) Random Bks Yng Read.

— The Little Puppy. LC 84-2031. (Pictureback Ser.). (Illus.). 32p. (J). (ps-3). 1984. pap. 3.25 (*0-394-86595-2*, Pub. by Random Bks Yng Read) Random.

— The Little Rabbit. LC 79-5241. (Pictureback Ser.). (Illus.). 32p. (J). (ps). 1980. pap. 3.25 (*0-394-84377-0*, Pub. by Random Bks Yng Read) Random.

— The Little Rabbit. 1980. 8.45 (*0-606-12399-7*, Pub. by Turtleback) Demco.

— Sisters & Brothers. LC 84-19343. (Developing Child Ser.). (Illus.). 192p. 1985. pap. text 8.50 (*0-674-80981-5*) HUP.

— Sisters & Brothers. LC 84-19343. (Developing Child Ser.). (Illus.). 192p. 1985. 26.95 (*0-674-80980-7*) HUP.

— Young Children's Close Relationships: Beyond Attachment. (Individual Differences & Development Ser.: Vol. 4). (Illus.). 160p. (C). 1993. text 48.00 (*0-8039-4490-X*); pap. text 13.99 (*0-8039-4491-8*) Sage.

Dunn, Judy & Kendrick, Carol. Siblings: Love, Envy, & Understanding. LC 81-7251. (Developing Child Ser.). (Illus.). 304p. 1982. 36.50 (*0-674-80735-9*) HUP.

Dunn, Judy, et al. Sibling Relationships Vol. 10: Their Causes & Consequences. Brody, Gene H., ed. (Advances in Applied Developmental Psychology Ser.). (Illus.). 263p. 1996. pap. 39.50 (*1-56750-181-8*) Ablx Pub.

— Sibling Relationships Vol. 10: Their Causes & Consequences. Brody, Gene H., ed. LC 96-136098. (Advances in Applied Developmental Psychology Ser.: Vol. 10). (Illus.). 263p. 1996. text 73.25 (*1-56750-180-X*) Ablx Pub.

Dunn, Judy, jt. ed. see Plomin, Robert.

Dunn, Judy, jt. ed. see Shaffer, David.

Dunn, Judy, ed. & pref. see Cairns, Ed.

Dunn, Julie, ed. Jud Fine. LC 88-81581. (Illus.). 48p. 1988. pap. 16.00 (*0-911291-15-6*, Pub. by Fellows Cont Art) RAM Publications.

Dunn, Julie, jt. auth. see Bozzi, Julie.

Dunn, Julie, ed. see Tazzi, Pier L.

Dunn, Julie, ed. see Yard, Sally.

Dunn, Kara L., ed. see Cox, Donald D.

***Dunn, Kate.** Exit Through the Fireplace: The Great Days of Rep. (Illus.). 304p. 1999. text 35.00 (*0-7195-5475-6*, Pub. by John Murray) Trafalgar.

Dunn, Katherine. Attic. 1990. mass mkt. 9.99 (*0-446-39152-2*, Pub. by Warner Bks) Little.

Dunn, Katherine. The Book of Slice. (Illus.). (Orig.). 1989. pap. 4.95 (*0-9624513-0-4*) City Roses News.

— Death Scenes: A Homicide Detective's Scrapbook. Tejaratchi, Sean, ed. (Illus.). 182p. 1995. pap. 19.95 (*0-922915-29-6*) Feral Hse.

— Geek Love. 355p. 1990. mass mkt. 13.99 (*0-446-39130-1*, Pub. by Warner Bks) Little.

— Guyana. (Illus.). 96p. 1996. 60.00 (*0-944092-41-1*) Twin Palms Pub.

Dunn, Katherine. Truck. 1990. mass mkt. 10.99 (*0-446-39153-0*, Pub. by Warner Bks) Little.

Dunn, Katherine. Why Do Men Have Nipples? And Other Low-Life Answers to Real-Life Questions. 1992. reprint ed. mass mkt. 6.99 (*0-446-39412-2*, Pub. by Warner Bks) Little.

Dunn, Keith & Flanagan, Stephen J., eds. NATO in the Fifth Decade. 242p. (C). 1992. pap. text 40.00 (*0-941375-53-6*) DIANE Pub.

Dunn, Kenneth & Dunn, Rita. The Complete Guide to the Learning Styles Inservice System. LC 98-30269. 226p. (C). 1998. pap. 33.00 (*0-205-27441-2*, Longwood Div) Allyn.

Dunn, Kenneth, jt. ed. see Dunn, Rita.

Dunn, Kenneth J. & Dunn, Rita S. Situational Leadership for Principals: The School Administrator in Action. LC 82-11211. 228p. 1983. 18.95 (*0-686-84595-1*, Parker Publishing Co) P-H.

— Teaching Students Through Their Individual Learning Styles: A Practical Approach. (Illus.). 336p. 1978. text 81.00 (*0-87909-808-2*, R80821) P-H.

Dunn, Kenneth J., jt. auth. see Dunn, Rita S.

Dunn, Kevin. Pretexts of Authority: The Rhetoric of Authorship in the Renaissance Preface. LC 93-6279. xvi, 198p. 1994. 35.00 (*0-8047-2284-6*) Stanford U Pr.

Dunn, Kimberley, jt. auth. see Viegas, Steven F.

Dunn, Kylie. The Sound Sleuth. (Illus.). 104p. (J). (gr. k-2). 1997. pap. 10.95 (*0-673-36390-2*, GoodYrBooks) Addson-Wesley Educ.

Dunn, L. & Capobianco, R. J. Studies of Reading & Arithmetic in Mentally Retarded Boys. (SRCD M Ser.: Vol. 19, No. 1). 1954. pap. 25.00 (*0-527-01560-1*) Periodicals Srv.

Dunn, L. C. Anthropometric Study of Hawaiians of Pure & Mixed Blood. Tozzer, Alfred M., ed. (HU PMP Ser.). 1928. pap. 15.00 (*0-527-01220-3*) Periodicals Srv.

Dunn, Larry, jt. auth. see Murray, Michael.

Dunn, Leo J., ed. see American College of Obstetricians & Gynecologists.

Dunn, Leslie C. A Short History of Genetics: The Development of Some of the Main Lines of Thought, 1864-1939. LC 91-18890. (History of Science & Technology Reprint Ser.). (Illus.). 286p. (C). 1991. reprint ed. pap. text 24.95 (*0-8138-0447-7*) Iowa St U Pr.

Dunn, Leslie C. & Jones, Nancy A., eds. Embodied Voices: Representing Female Vocality in Western Culture. (Illus.). 272p. 1997. pap. text 22.95 (*0-521-58583-X*) Cambridge U Pr.

Dunn, Lewis A. Controlling the Bomb: Nuclear Proliferation in the 1980s. LC 81-16086. 223p. reprint ed. pap. 69.20 (*0-7837-5307-1*, 208032800005) Bks Demand.

— The Emerging Nuclear Suppliers: Some Guidelines for Policy. (CISA Working Papers: No. 61). 24p. (Orig.). 1988. pap. 15.00 (*0-86682-078-7*) Ctr Intl Relations.

Dunn, Lloyd. Inbetweening. 56p. (Orig.). 1989. pap. 3.00 (*0-926935-22-4*) Runaway Spoon.

Dunn, Lloyd, et al. Peabody Language Development Kit, Lesson Manual 1 - Level P. 1981. pap. text 47.95 (*0-88671-026-X*, 8551) Am Guidance.

— Peabody Language Development Kit, Level P Lesson Manual 2. rev. ed. 1981. pap. text 47.95 (*0-88671-027-8*, 8552) Am Guidance.

— Peabody Language Development Kit, Level P Teachers Guide. 1981. teacher ed. 12.95 (*0-88671-028-6*, 8554) Am Guidance.

— Peabody Language Development Kit, Level 1 Lesson Manual 1. 1981. pap. text 47.95 (*0-88671-030-8*, 8701) Am Guidance.
— Peabody Language Development Kit, Level 1, Lesson Manual 2. 1981. pap. text 47.95 (*0-88671-031-6*, 8702) Am Guidance.
— Peabody Language Development Kit, Level 1 Teachers Guide. 1981. teacher ed. 12.95 (*0-88671-032-4*, 8704) Am Guidance.
Dunn, Lois, tr. see Freeman, Lory.
Dunn, Lois B. You Need Family Devotions. (Christian Living Ser.). 32p. 1990. pap. 3.50 (*0-8341-1380-5*) Beacon Hill.
Dunn-Long, Barbara, jt. auth. see Milchovich, Sue K.
Dunn, Louise. Hiring In-Home Help. (Orig.). 1990. pap. 95.00 (*1-877592-16-1*) GSH&MC.
Dunn, Louise, ed. see Beedle, Joyce.
Dunn, Louise M., jt. auth. see Laird, Gerald F.
Dunn, Lynne K., jt. auth. see Kuehl, Warren F.
Dunn, M. Illustrator's Figure Reference Manual. 1989. 22.98 (*1-55521-033-3*) Bk Sales Inc.
Dunn, M. Douglas & Practising Law Institute Staff. Utility Restructuring: Negotiating, Structuring, & Documenting the Deal. LC 99-159959. (Corporate Law & Practice Course Handbook Ser.). 720p. 1998. 129.00 (*0-87224-529-2*) PLI.
Dunn, M. H., jt. auth. see Maitland, Arthur.
Dunn, M. J., jt. auth. see Pennington, S.
Dunn, M. J., jt. ed. see Horton, R.
Dunn, M. L., ed. Mechanics & Materials for Electronic Packaging Vol. 3: Coupled Field Behavior in Materials: 1994 International Mechanical Engineering Congress & Exposition, Chicago, Illinois - November 6-11, 1994. LC 94-79149. (AMD Ser.: Vol. 193). 88p. 1994. 40.00 (*0-7918-1442-4*, G00937) ASME.
Dunn, Manuela, ed. Haiku: The Poetry of Zen. LC 96-33723. (Box of Zen Ser.). 64p. (J). 1998. 9.70 (*0-7868-6251-3*, Pub. by Hyperion) Time Warner.
— Koans: The Lessons of Zen. LC 96-33724. 64p. (J). 1998. 9.70 (*0-7868-6252-1*, Pub. by Hyperion) Time Warner.
***Dunn, Manuela, ed.** Sayings: The Wisdom of Zen. LC 96-33725. (Box of Zen Ser.). (Illus.). 64p. (J). 1998. 9.70 (*0-7868-6253-X*, Pub. by Hyperion) Time Warner.
Dunn, Margaret. Paradigms & Paradoxes in the Life & Letters of Sigrid Undset. LC 93-11754. 122p. (C). 1993. lib. bdg. 35.00 (*0-8191-9280-5*) U Pr of Amer.
Dunn, Margaret M. & Morris, Ann R. The Composite Novel: The Short Story Cycle in Transition. LC 94-34996. (Twayne's Studies in Literary Themes & Genres: No. 6). 232p. 1995. 33.00 (*0-8057-0966-5*, Twyne) Mac Lib Ref.
Dunn, Margery G., ed. Exploring Your World: The Adventure of Geography. rev. ed. LC 93-1849. (Illus.). 608p. (J). (ps-6). 1993. 31.95 (*0-87044-762-9*); write for info. (*0-87044-959-1*) Natl Geog.
***Dunn, Marilyn Faherty.** Medieval Monasticism. (Illus.). 320p. 2000. 64.95 (*0-631-13463-8*) Blackwell Pubs.
Dunn, Maritza O., jt. ed. see Butterworth, Taia.
Dunn, Mark. Frank's Life. 98p. (YA). (gr. 10 up). 1998. pap. 5.60 (*0-87129-858-9*, F66) Dramatic Pub.
Dunn, Marvin. Black Miami in the Twentieth Century. LC 97-20262. (Florida History & Culture Ser.). (Illus.). 416p. 1997. 29.95 (*0-8130-1530-8*) U Press Fla.
Dunn, Mary, compiled by. Index to Pennsylvania's Colonial Records Series. 228p. 1996. reprint ed. 20.00 (*0-8063-1332-3*, 1545) Genealog Pub.
Dunn, Maryjane. Emergency Spanish for Firefighters. Slick, Sam L., ed. 52p. 1997. ring bd. 49.50 (*1-888467-07-X*) Command Spanish.
Dunn, Maryjane & Davidson, Linda K. The Pilgrimage to Santiago de Compostela: A Comprehensive Annotated Bibliography. LC 94-8769. (Medieval Bibliographies Ser.: Vol. 18). (Illus.). 568p. 1994. text 20.00 (*0-8240-7220-0*, H1380) Garland.
Dunn, Maryjane, jt. auth. see Davidson, Linda K.
Dunn, Maryjane, jt. ed. see Slick, Sam L.
Dunn, Maryjane, tr. see Davidson, Linda, et al, eds.
Dunn, Marylois. The Man in the Box: A Story from Vietnam. Richards, Jerri S., ed. (Illus.). 104p. (Orig.). (YA). (gr. 6-12). 1997. pap. 12.50 (*1-887303-16-2*) Blu Lantern Pub.
Dunn, Marylois, jt. auth. see Mayhar, Ardath.
Dunn, Maureen, tr. see Shinpoch, Jan, et al.
***Dunn-Merritt, Sheila.** Natural Treatments for Osteoporosis. (Natural Pharmacist Ser.). 2000. pap. 9.99 (*0-7615-3010-X*) Prima Pub.
Dunn-Merritt, Sheila & Patrick, Judy L. The Natural Pharmacist Guide to Osteoporosis. LC 98-33112. 208p. 1999. per. 6.99 (*0-7615-1618-2*) Prima Pub.
Dunn, Michael. A Concise History of New Zealand Painting. 2nd rev. ed. (Illus.). 188p. 1991. text 30.00 (*976-8097-07-8*) Gordon & Breach.
— Contemporary Painting in New Zealand. LC 96-218602. (Illus.). 240p. 1997. text 39.00 (*976-641-008-9*, ECU50, Harwood Acad Pubs) Gordon & Breach.
***Dunn, Michael.** The Good Death Guide: Everything You Wanted to Know but Were Afraid to Ask. (Pathways Ser.). (Illus.). 208p. 2000. pap. 24.95 (*1-85703-559-3*, Pub. by How To Bks) Trans-Atl Phila.
— The Good Death Guide: Everything You Wanted to Know but Were Afraid to Ask. 208p. 2000. pap. 15.95 (*1-85703-560-7*, Pub. by How To Bks) Midpt Trade.
Dunn, Michael A. The Black Racism Index: A Great American Guilt Trip. 136p. 1999. pap. 13.00 (*0-8059-4547-4*) Dorrance.
Dunn, Michael J. Mistaken Identity. 290p. mass mkt. 4.99 (*1-55197-259-X*) Picasso Publ.
Dunn, Michael J., ed. Renal Eicosanoids. (Illus.). 438p. 1989. 105.00 (*0-306-43320-6*, Plenum Trade) Perseus Pubng.
Dunn, Michael J., et al, eds. Prostaglandins & the Kidney: Biochemistry, Physiology, Pharmacology & Clinical Applications. LC 82-18117. 438p. 1982. 95.00 (*0-306-41054-0*, Kluwer Plenum) Kluwer Academic.
Dunn, Mike. Bridge of No Return. 368p. (Orig.). 1996. mass mkt. 5.99 (*0-380-78060-7*, Avon Bks) Morrow Avon.
— Quicksilver. 448p. (Orig.). 1993. mass mkt. 5.50 (*0-380-77160-8*, Avon Bks) Morrow Avon.
— Sidewinder. 1991. mass mkt. 4.95 (*0-380-76371-0*, Avon Bks) Morrow Avon.
— Task Force. 480p. (Orig.). 1992. mass mkt. 4.99 (*0-380-76373-7*, Avon Bks) Morrow Avon.
Dunn, Miriam. Kim & Ting. 1981. pap. 3.95 (*0-85363-137-9*) OMF Bks.
— Let's Look at Malaysia. 1986. pap. 1.95 (*9971-972-48-4*) OMF Bks.
***Dunn, Nancy.** Golf's Greenland, Vol. 1. Mustard, Kirk, ed. (Illus.). 28p. (J). (gr. 4). 1999. pap. write for info. (*0-9673330-0-8*) Swing Play.
Dunn, Nancy E. The 1995 Office Computing Bible: Using Personal Computers at Work. (Illus.). 575p. 1999. reprint ed. pap. text 15.00 (*0-7881-6502-X*) DIANE Pub.
Dunn, Nell. Grandmothers Talking. large type ed. 22.95 (*1-85695-077-8*, Pub. by ISIS Lrg Prnt) Transaction Pubs.
***Dunn, Nell.** Up the Junction. 128p. 2000. pap. text 13.00 (*1-58243-066-7*, Pub. by Counterpt DC) HarpC.
Dunn, Olive J. Basic Statistics: A Primer for the Biomedical Sciences. 2nd ed. (Probability & Mathematical Statistics: Applied Probability & Statistics Section Ser.). 218p. 1977. 159.95 (*0-471-22744-7*) Wiley.
Dunn, Olive J., et al. Applied Statistics: Analysis of Variance & Regression. 2nd ed. LC 86-24649. (Probability & Mathematical Statistics: Applied Probability & Statistics Section Ser.). 464p. 1987. 159.95 (*0-471-81269-2*) Wiley.
Dunn, Olive Jean & Clark, Virginia. Basic Statistics: A Primer for the Biomedical Sciences. 3rd ed. 288p. 2000. text 84.95 (*0-471-35422-8*) Wiley.
Dunn, Oliver, tr. see Columbus, Christopher.
***Dunn, Opal.** Acka Backa Boo: Playground Games from Around the World. LC 99-58509. (Illus.). 48p. (J). (gr. k-3). 2000. 16.95 (*0-8050-6424-9*) H Holt & Co.
Dunn, Opal. Help Your Child with a Foreign Language. (Berlitz Kids Ser.). 1998. pap. 10.95 (*2-8315-6806-4*) Berlitz.
— Hippety-Hop, Hippety-Hay: Growing with Rhymes from Birth to Age Three. LC 98-8105. (Illus.). 46 p. (J). (ps). 1999. 16.95 (*0-8050-6081-2*) H Holt & Co.
***Dunn, Opal.** Little Boat. (Track-Me-Back Board Bks.). 12p. (J). 2000. bds. 5.95 (*0-8050-6416-8*) H Holt & Co.
— Little Car. (Track-Me-Back Board Bks.). 12p. (J). 2000. bds. 5.95 (*0-8050-6417-6*) H Holt & Co.
— Little Plane. (Track-Me-Back Board Bks.). 12p. (J). 2000. bds. 5.95 (*0-8050-6418-4*) H Holt & Co.
— Little Train. (Track-Me-Back Board Bks.). 12p. (J). 2000. bds. 5.95 (*0-8050-6419-2*) H Holt & Co.
Dunn, Opal. Un, Deux, Trois: My First French Rhymes. (Illus.). 24p. (J). (ps up). 1995. 18.95 incl. audio (*0-8120-8402-0*) Barron.
— Un, Deux, Trois: Premieres Comptines Francaises. (FRE., Illus.). 24p. (J). (ps up). 1995. 12.95 incl. audio (*0-8120-8153-6*) Barron.
Dunn, P. D. Energy for Development...What Are the Solutions? 75p. (C). 1985. 150.00 (*0-7855-4200-0*, Pub. by Interntl Solar Energy Soc) St Mut.
Dunn, P. D., jt. auth. see Reay, David A.
Dunn, P. M. & McIlwaine, G., eds. Perinatal Audit: A Report Produced for the European Association of Perinatal Medicine. 44p. 1996. pap. 18.00 (*1-85070-933-5*) Prthnon Pub.
Dunn, Patricia. Children's Book of Irish Fairy Tales. (J). 1988. pap. 10.95 (*0-85342-843-3*) Dufour.
— 1870 Biblical Story Performances. (Illus.). 64p. (J). (gr. 1-3). 1950. student ed. 12.99 (*0-86653-492-X*, GA1072) Good Apple.
***Dunn, Patricia.** Greater Expectations: Challenging Ways of Knowing in the English & Writing Classroom. 2001. pap. text. write for info. (*0-86709-570-9*, Pub. by Boynton Cook Pubs) Heinemann.
Dunn, Patricia. Learning Re-Abled: The Learning Disability Controversy & Composition Studies. LC 95-9316. 232p. 1995. pap. text 24.50 (*0-86709-360-9*, 0360, Pub. by Boynton Cook Pubs) Heinemann.
— Math Trivial Pursuit - Intermediate Level. (Illus.). 64p. (J). (gr. 4-6). 1989. student ed. 12.99 (*0-86653-468-7*, GA1073) Good Apple.
— Math Trivial Pursuit - Junior High Level. (Illus.). 64p. (J). (gr. 7-9). 1989. student ed. 12.99 (*0-86653-469-5*, GA1074) Good Apple.
Dunn, Patricia A. Manual of Maternal-Newborn Nursing. LC 96-3206. 450p. 1996. spiral bd. 29.95 (*0-316-19659-2*) Lppncott W & W.
Dunn, Patrick J. Priesthood: A Re-Examination of the R. C. Theology. LC 90-37005. 244p. (Orig.). 1990. pap. 12.95 (*0-8189-0581-6*) Alba.
Dunn, Patrick R. Mr. Austin's Commercial Bartending Basics. Orig. Title: Professional Bartending Basics. (Illus.). 62p. (Orig.). 1985. reprint ed. pap. 4.95 (*0-9613869-1-6*) Texas Cedar Pr.
Dunn, Paul H. Christmas: Do You Hear What I Hear. 112p. 1997. reprint ed. 13.95 (*1-882723-31-7*, Pub. by Gold Leaf Pr) Origin Bk Sales.
— In Humility Our Savior. LC 97-30635. 128p. 1997. 14.95 (*1-882723-30-9*, Pub. by Gold Leaf Pr) Origin Bk Sales.
— The Light of Liberty. LC 98-25166. 2000. 19.95 (*1-882723-32-5*) Gold Leaf Pr.
— Meaningful Living. LC 98-33634. 2000. 19.95 (*1-882723-33-3*) Gold Leaf Pr.
— Success Formulas. LC 98-34288. 2000. 19.95 (*1-882723-34-1*) Gold Leaf Pr.
***Dunn, Paul H. & Eyre, Richard M.** The Birth We Call Death. LC 99-28287. 96p. 1999. pap. 10.95 (*1-56236-239-9*, Pub. by Aspen Bks) Origin Bk Sales.
Dunn, Pete J., jt. auth. see Cooper, Susan B.
Dunn, Peter. Goatkeeper's Veterinary Book. 3rd ed. (Illus.). 198p. 1994. 34.95 (*0-85236-279-X*, Pub. by Farming Pr) Diamond Farm Bk.
***Dunn, Peter C.** Gateways into Electronics, 1. LC 98-45207. 696p. 2000. 89.95 (*0-471-25448-7*) Wiley.
Dunn, Peter J., jt. auth. see Kluka, Darlene A.
Dunn, Peter M., jt. auth. see Grinter, Lawrence E.
Dunn, Peter N. Spanish Picaresque Fiction: A New Literary History. LC 92-36854. 352p. 1993. text 39.95 (*0-8014-2800-9*) Cornell U Pr.
Dunn, Phil & Dunn, Diane. Echoes of the Melody: A Spiritual Warrior's Handbook. 283p. (Orig.). 1990. pap. 11.95 (*0-9625763-0-1*) Blue Eagle Pub.
***Dunn, Philip, et al, trs.** The Illustrated Rumi: A Treasury of Wisdom from the Poet of the Soul. (Illus.). 256p. 2000. 29.95 (*0-06-062017-X*) Harper SF.
Dunn, Phillip. Creating Curriculum in Art. 96p. 1995. 18.00 (*0-937652-88-1*, 256) Natl Art Ed.
Dunn, Phillip B. A Guide to Ancestral Research - London. (Illus.). 120p. 1987. 9.95 (*0-9619260-7-4*) Manuscript UT.
Dunn, Phillip C. Promoting School Art: A Practical Approach. 61p. (C). 1987. pap. 12.00 (*0-937652-42-3*, 224) Natl Art Ed.
Dunn, Phillip C., jt. ed. see Johnson, Thomas L.
Dunn, Phoebe, photos by. Baby's Animal Friends. LC 87-61462. (Chunky Bks. Ser.). (Illus.). 28p. (J). (ps). 1988. 3.99 (*0-394-89583-5*, Pub. by Random Bks Yng Read) Random.
— Farm Animals. LC 83-61244. (Chunky Bks. Ser.). (Illus.). 24p. (J). (gr. k-1). 1988. 3.99 (*0-394-86254-6*, Pub. by Random Bks Yng Read) Random.
Dunn, R. A., et al. The Florida Lawn Handbook: Best Management Practices for the Selection, Establishment & Maintenance of Florida Lawngrasses. 2nd ed. Black, Robert J. & Ruppert, Kathleen C., eds. (Illus.). 224p. 1995. pap. 8.00 (*0-916287-13-0*, SP45) Univ Fla Food.
Dunn, R. D., ed. see Camden, William.
Dunn, R. Jeffrey & Singh, Udai P., eds. Landfill Closures - Environmental Protection & Land Recovery: Proceedings of Sessions Sponsored by the Environmental Geotechnics Committee of the Geotechnical Engineering Division & the Solid Waste Engineering Committee of the Environmental Engineering Division of the American Society of Civil Engineers in Conjunction with the ASCE Convention in San Diego, California, October 23-27, 1995. (Geotechnical Special Publications: Vol. 53). 248p. 1995. 31.00 (*0-7844-0119-5*) Am Soc Civil Eng.
Dunn, R. L., jt. ed. see Gebelein, Charles G.
Dunn, Ralph, jt. auth. see Rogers, Bob.
Dunn-Rankin, Patricia. Vocabulary. 3rd ed. (C). 1989. pap. text, teacher ed. 11.56 (*0-07-018320-1*) McGraw.
— Vocabulary. 3rd ed. 224p. (C). 1990. pap. 35.00 (*0-07-018319-8*) McGraw.
Dunn-Rankin, Peter. Fishing the Reefs: A Guide to Topwater Spinning in Hawai'i & the South Pacific. (Illus.). 80p. 1994. pap. 12.95 (*1-56647-090-0*) Mutual Pub HI.
Dunn, Ray. 20,000 Gallons of Chowder: And Other Recipes for the Semi-Adventurous. Borgias, Alaine, ed. (Illus.). 112p. Date not set. pap. 12.95 (*0-9667283-3-5*) Mama Colophon.
Dunn, Ray & Gorman, Taimi D. The Colophon Cafe Best Soups Vol. 1: A Collection of Fine Soups from the Legendary Colophon Cafe. Date not set. spiral bd. 9.95 (*0-9667283-0-0*) Mama Colophon.
Dunn, Ray & Gorman, Taimi F. The Colophon Cafe Best Recipes Vol. 2: The Most Requested Recipes of the Legendary Colophon Cafe. Date not set. spiral bd. 8.95 (*0-9667283-1-9*) Mama Colophon.
Dunn, Richard. Jane Eyre. 3rd ed. (Norton Critical Editions Ser.). pap. write for info. (*0-393-97542-8*) Norton.
Dunn, Richard. Leading from the Back of the Line (Leaders Book) 80p. (Orig.). 1992. pap. 1.00 (*1-56476-002-2*, 6-3002, Victor Bks) Chariot Victor.
— Leading from the Back of the Line (Student Book) 48p. (Orig.). (YA). 1992. pap. 0.60 (*1-56476-003-0*, 6-3003, Victor Bks) Chariot Victor.
— Narrow Gauge to No Man's Land. (Illus.). 203p. 1990. 38.95 (*0-9615467-2-7*) Benchmark Ltd.
— Relapse & the Addict. 24p. (Orig.). 1986. pap. 2.00 (*0-89486-393-2*, 5410B) Hazelden.
— Where Do You Think Sex Came From? 48p. (YA). 1991. pap., student ed. 0.60 (*0-89693-195-1*, Victor Bks) Chariot Victor.
— Where Do You Think Sex Came From? 96p. 1991. teacher ed. 1.00 (*0-89693-194-3*, Victor Bks) Chariot Victor.
— Why Not Love All of Me? 72p. 1991. teacher ed. 1.00 (*0-89693-182-X*, 6-1182, Victor Bks) Chariot Victor.
— Why Not Love All of Me? 48p. (YA). 1991. pap., student ed. 0.60 (*0-89693-183-8*, 6-1183, Victor Bks) Chariot Victor.
Dunn, Richard, jt. auth. see Dornan, Peter.
Dunn, Richard, tr. see Zampaglione, Gerardo.
***Dunn, Richard J.** David Copperfield: An Annotated Bibliography. LC 99-25556. 1999. write for info. (*0-404-62470-7*) AMS Pr.
Dunn, Richard J. Oliver Twist: Whole Heart & Soul. (Masterwork Studies). 180p. 1993. 23.95 (*0-8057-9426-3*, Twyne); pap. 13.95 (*0-8057-8579-5*, Twyne) Mac Lib Ref.
Dunn, Richard J., ed. Approaches to Teaching Dickens' David Copperfield. LC 84-1046. (Approaches to Teaching World Literature Ser.: No. 5). x, 152p. 1985. pap. 18.00 (*0-87352-484-5*, AP05P); lib. bdg. 37.50 (*0-87352-483-7*, AP05C) Modern Lang.
***Dunn, Richard J. & Tandy, Ann M.** David Copperfield: An Annotated Bibliography, 1981-1998. LC 99-59956. (Studies in the Nineteenth Century). 2000. write for info. (*0-404-64453-8*) AMS Press.
Dunn, Richard J., ed. see Bronte, Charlotte.
Dunn, Richard J., ed. see Bronte, Emily Jane.
Dunn, Richard L. & Ottenbrite, Raphael M., eds. Polymeric Drugs & Drug Delivery Systems. LC 91-23423. (ACS Symposium Ser.: No. 469). (Illus.). 313p. 1991. text 85.00 (*0-8412-2105-7*, Pub. by Am Chemical) OUP.
Dunn, Richard M. Geoffrey Scott & the Berenson Circle: Literary & Aesthetic Life in the Early 20th Century. LC 97-47573. (Studies in British Literature: Vol. 34). (Illus.). 352p. 1998. text 99.95 (*0-7734-8488-4*) E Mellen.
Dunn, Richard R. & Senter, Mark H. Reaching a Generation for Christ: A Comprehensive Guide to Youth Ministry. LC 97-201507. 704p. 1997. 35.99 (*0-8024-9348-3*, 263) Moody.
Dunn, Richard S. The Age of Religious Wars, 1559-1715. 3rd ed. (History of Modern Europe Ser.). (Illus.). (C). 1998. pap. write for info. (*0-393-96150-8*) Norton.
***Dunn, Richard S.** Sugar & Slaves: The Rise of the Planter Class in the English West Indies, 1624-1713. LC 99-89856. (Published for the Omohundro Institute of Early American History & Culture, Williamsburg, Virginia Ser.). (Illus.). 379p. 2000. pap. 16.95 (*0-8078-4877-8*) U of NC Pr.
Dunn, Richard S. Sugar & Slaves: The Rise of the Planter Class in the English West Indies, 1624-1713. (Illus.). 384p. 1973. reprint ed. pap. 15.95 (*0-393-00692-1*) Norton.
Dunn, Richard S., contrib. by. The Laws & Liberties of Massachusetts: Reprinted from the Unique Copy of the 1648 Edition in the Henry E. Huntington Library. LC 98-8646. 1998. 29.95 (*0-87328-173-X*) Huntington Lib.
Dunn, Richard S., et al, eds. The Journal of John Winthrop, 1630-1649. LC 95-52489. (John Harvard Library). (Illus.). 704p. 1996. 100.00 (*0-674-48425-8*) Belknap Pr.
Dunn, Richard S. & Yeandle, Laetitia, eds. The Journal of John Winthrop, 1630-1649. abr. ed. LC 96-20644. (John Harvard Library). (Illus.). 384p. 1996. 39.95 (*0-674-48426-6*); pap. 19.95 (*0-674-48427-4*) Belknap Pr.
Dunn, Rita. How to Implement & Supervise a Learning Style Program. LC 96-9955. 1996. pap. 10.95 (*0-87120-259-X*) ASCD.
Dunn, Rita & Dunn, Kenneth, eds. Practical Approaches to Individualizing Staff Development for Adults. LC 97-33710. 160p. 1998. 49.95 (*0-275-96066-8*, Praeger Pubs) Greenwood.
Dunn, Rita & Griggs, Shirley A. Learning Styles: Quiet Revolution in American Secondary Schools. 88p. 1988. 9.00 (*0-88210-209-5*) Natl Assn Principals.
— Multiculturalism & Learning Style: Teaching & Counseling Adolescents. LC 94-36775. 296p. 1995. 59.95 (*0-275-94762-9*, Praeger Pubs) Greenwood.
Dunn, Rita, jt. auth. see Dunn, Kenneth.
Dunn, Rita A. & Griggs, Shirley. Multiculturalism & Learning Style: Teaching & Counseling Adolescents. LC 94-36775. 200p. 1998. pap. 24.95 (*0-275-96480-9*, Praeger Pubs) Greenwood.
Dunn, Rita C. & DeBello, Thomas. Improved Test Scores, Attitudes & Behaviors in America's Schools: Supervisors' Success Stories. LC 99-14842. 248p. 1999. 59.95 (*0-89789-687-4*, Bergin & Garvey) Greenwood.
Dunn, Rita S. & Dunn, Kenneth J. Administrator's Guide to New Programs for Faculty Management & Evaluation. 1976. text 24.95 (*0-13-008623-1*, Parker Publishing Co) P-H.
— Teaching Elementary Students Through Their Individual Learning Styles: A Practical Approach. 464p. (J). (gr. 3-6). 1992. 69.00 (*0-205-13221-9*, Longwood Div) Allyn.
— Teaching Secondary School Students Through Their Individual Learning Styles: Practical Approaches for Grades 7-12. 496p. (C). 1993. 69.00 (*0-205-13308-8*) Allyn.
Dunn, Rita S. & Griggs, Shirley A. Learning Styles & the Nursing Profession. LC 97-49117. 1998. write for info. (*0-88737-771-8*) Natl League Nurse.
Dunn, Rita S., et al. The Giftedness in Every Child: Unlocking Your Child's Unique Talents, Strengths & Potential. (Science Editions Ser.). 224p. 1992. 22.95 (*0-471-52803-X*) Wiley.
— Teaching Young Children Through Their Individual Learning Styles: Practical Approaches for Grades K-2. LC 93-13944. 480p. (C). 1993. 69.00 (*0-205-15271-6*, H52715, Longwood Div) Allyn.
Dunn, Rita S., jt. auth. see Dunn, Kenneth J.
***Dunn, Rita Stafford & Griggs, Shirley A.** Practical Approaches to Using Learning Styles in Higher Education. LC 99-40321. 280p. 2000. write for info. (*0-89789-703-X*, Bergin & Garvey) Greenwood.
Dunn, Robert. The Possibility of Weakness of Will. LC 85-24784. 192p. (C). 1987. pap. 14.95 (*0-915145-98-7*); lib. bdg. 32.95 (*0-915145-99-5*) Hackett Pub.
— Transactional Filing: An Integreated Approach. 37p. 1998. pap. 16.50 (*1-878204-58-0*) APIS Inc.
Dunn, Robert & Hemingway, Ernest. Ernest Hemingway's The Sun Also Rises. (Barron's Book Notes Ser.). (C). 1984. pap. 2.50 (*0-8120-3443-0*) Barron.
Dunn, Robert G. Identity Crises: A Social Critique of Postmodernity. LC 97-39564. 1998. 49.95 (*0-8166-3072-0*); pap. 19.95 (*0-8166-3073-9*) U of Minn Pr.
Dunn, Robert H. Dunn-Crostics, Vol. 1. 48p. (Orig.). 1993. pap., student ed. 7.95 (*1-884202-00-4*) Systs Qual Sftware.
Dunn, Robert L. Recovery of Damages for Fraud. 2nd ed. 440p. 1995. 110.00 (*0-915544-26-1*) Lawpress CA.

D

— Recovery of Damages for Lost Profits, 2 vols. 5th ed. LC 98-65672. (Little Guy's Investment Ser.). 1170p. 1998. 160.00 (*0-915544-28-8*) Cromwell-Smith.

Dunn, Robert M., Jr. The Canada-U. S. Capital Market. LC 78-71657. (Canadian-U. S. Prospect Ser.). 148p. 1978. pap. 6.00 (*0-88806-046-7*) Natl Planning.

***Dunn, Robert M.** International Economics. 5th ed. 608p. 2000. pap. 40.99 (*0-415-20880-7*); text 125.00 (*0-415-20879-3*) Routledge.

Dunn, Robert M., Jr. The Many Disappointments of Flexible Exchange Rates. LC 83-26543. (Essays in International Finance Ser.: No. 154). 36p. 1983. pap. text 10.00 (*0-88165-061-7*) Princeton U Int Finan Econ.

Dunn, Robert M. & Ingram, James C. International Economics. 4th ed. LC 95-36677. 576p. 1995. text 86.95 (*0-471-11669-6*) Wiley.

Dunn, Robert M., Jr. & Neftci, Salih N. Economic Growth among Industrialized Countries: Why the United States Lags. LC 80-81478. (Committee on Changing International Realities Ser.). 77p. 1980. 5.50 (*0-89068-053-1*) Natl Planning.

Dunn, Robert W. American Foreign Investments. Richt, Adrian, ed. LC 76-5003. (American Business Abroad Ser.). 1976. reprint ed. 39.95 (*0-405-09272-5*) Ayer.

— The Americanization of Labor. LC 74-22740. (Labor Movement in Fiction & Non-Fiction Ser.). reprint ed. 41.50 (*0-404-58492-6*) AMS Pr.

Dunn, Ron. Will God Heal Me? Faith in the Midst of Suffering. LC 97-6732. 240p. 1997. 18.99 (*1-57673-100-6*, Multnomah Bks) Multnomah Pubs.

Dunn, Ronald. Don't Just Stand There, Pray Something: Secrets of Effective Prayer. LC 92-40879. 276p. 1992. pap. 12.99 (*0-8407-4393-9*) Nelson.

— The Faith Crisis. Chao, Lorna Y., tr. (CHI.). 1985. pap. write for info. (*0-941598-30-6*) Living Spring Pubns.

Dunn, Rose. Finance Principles for the Health Information Manager. (Illus.). 254p. 1999. pap. text 62.00 (*1-58426-006-8*, AB120899) Am Hlth Info.

— Haimann's Supervisory Management for Health Care. 6th ed. LC 97-10575. 464p. (C). 1997. text. write for info. (*0-697-25155-1*, WCB McGr Hill) McGrw-H Hghr Educ.

Dunn, Ross E. Adventures of Ibn Battuta, a Muslim Traveler of the Fourteenth Century. 1994. pap. 18.95 (*0-520-06743-6*, Pub. by U CA Pr) Cal Prin Full Svc.

— Resistance in the Desert: Moroccan Responses to French Imperialism, 1881-1912. LC 76-52597. (Illus.). 291p. reprint ed. pap. 90.30 (*0-608-20425-0*, 207167800002) Bks Demand.

Dunn, Ross E. & Vigilante, David, eds. Bring History Alive! A Sourcebook for Teaching World History. (Illus.). 321p. (Orig.). 1996. pap. text 17.95 (*0-9633218-6-2*) Natl Ctr Hist.

Dunn, Ross E., tr. see Battuta, Ibn.

Dunn, Ruben J. & Morris, John. The Crash Put Simply: October, 1987. LC 88-17992. 186p. 1988. 49.95 (*0-275-93133-1*, Praeger Pubs) Greenwood.

***Dunn, Samantha.** Failing Paris. 1999. 27.95 (*1-902881-01-X*, Pub. by Toby Pr Ltd) Toby Pr.

— Failing Paris. 146p. 2000. pap. 12.95 (*1-902881-17-6*, Pub. by Toby Pr Ltd) Toby Pr.

Dunn, Sara & Scholefield, Alan, eds. Poetry for the Earth. 288p. 1992. pap. 10.00 (*0-449-90599-3*, Columbine) Fawcett.

***Dunn, Sarah S.** Innovative Piecing. LC 00-44568. (Successful Quilting Library). 2000. write for info. (*1-57954-130-8*) Rodale Pr Inc.

— Rotary Cutting & Speed Piecing. LC 99-87180. (Successful Quilting Library). 2000. 19.95 (*1-57954-192-5*) Rodale Pr Inc.

Dunn, Seamus. Facets of the Conflict in Northern Ireland, Vol. 1. LC 94-27907. 1995. text 75.00 (*0-312-12280-2*) St Martin.

***Dunn, Seamus & Dawson, Helen.** An Alphabetical Listing of Word, Name & Place in Northern Ireland & the Living Language of Conflict. (Symposium Ser.: Vol. 57). 336p. 2000. pap. 99.95 (*0-7734-7711-X*) E Mellen.

Dunn, Seamus & Fraser, T. G., eds. Europe & Ethnicity: World War I & Contemporary Ethnic Conflict. LC 96-7153. 232p. (C). 1996. 80.00 (*0-415-11995-2*); pap. 24.99 (*0-415-11996-0*) Routledge.

Dunn, Seamus & Morgan, Valerie. The IBM Personal Computer for Beginners. (Illus.). 320p. 1984. pap. 12.95 (*0-13-448259-X*) P-H.

Dunn, Seymour. Golf Fundamentals: Orthodoxy of Style. LC 85-31688. (Illus.). 288p. 1983. reprint ed. 14.95 (*0-914178-89-X*) Golf Digest.

Dunn, Shannon. Microsoft Visual J++ 6.0 Developer's Workshop. LC 98-30227. 560p. 1998. 44.99 incl. cd-rom (*1-57231-925-9*) Microsoft.

Dunn, Sharon, ed. see Allen, Harold.

Dunn, Sharon, ed. see Duncraft Staff.

Dunn, Sharon A. We Bring Her Flowers. LC 90-3626. 96p. (Orig.). 1990. pap. 8.95 (*0-931832-62-4*) Fithian Pr.

Dunn, Sheldon M. How to Expand & Upgrade PCs. 300p. 1998. pap. 24.99 (*0-7897-1672-0*) Que.

Dunn, Shelia A. Primary Care Consultant. LC 97-42363. (Illus.). 704p. (C). (gr. 13). 1998. text 49.95 (*0-8151-2950-5*, 29682) Mosby Inc.

Dunn, Sheri. Bearly Any Fat: Low Fat, Low Sugar, Low Salt Cookbook. (Illus.). 162p. (Orig.). 1988. pap. 12.95 (*0-9620860-0-2*) S Dunn.

— Bearly Any Fat Too. (Illus.). 192p. 1993. pap. text 12.95 (*0-9620860-1-0*) S Dunn.

Dunn, Shirley. Celluloid Collectibles: Identification & Value Guide. (Illus.). 144p. 1996. pap. 14.95 (*0-89145-672-4*, 4636) Collector Bks.

Dunn, Shirley, ed. see Wiltse, Leah.

Dunn, Shirley W. The Mohicans & Their Land, 1609-1730. 3rd ed. LC 94-18080. (Illus.). 350p. 1994. pap. 24.00 (*0-935796-49-5*) Purple Mnt Pr.

Dunn, Shirley W. & Bennett, Allison P. Dutch Architecture Near Albany: The Polgreen Photographs. LC 96-16987. (Illus.). 144p. (Orig.). 1996. pap. 25.00 (*0-935796-74-6*) Purple Mnt Pr.

Dunn, Sonja. Butterscotch Dreams: Chants for Fun & Learning. LC 89-30384. 111p. (Orig.). (C). 1987. pap. text 16.50 (*0-435-08497-6*, 08497) Heinemann.

— Crackers & Crumbs: Chants for Whole Language. LC 89-78077. 96p. (C). 1990. pap. text 17.00 (*0-435-08528-X*, 08528) Heinemann.

— Gimme a Break, Rattlesnake! unabridged ed. (Illus.). 56p. (J). (ps up). 1996. pap. 6.95 (*0-7737-5696-5*) STDK.

— Keeping Fit. 2nd ed. (Let Me Read Ser.). (Illus.). 8p. (J). (ps-k). 1995. bds. 2.95 (*0-673-36265-5*, GoodYrBooks) Addson-Wesley Educ.

Dunn, Stephen. Between Angels. 1990. pap. 11.95 (*0-393-30658-5*) Norton.

— A Circus of Needs. LC 78-59800. (Poetry Ser.). 1978. pap. 11.95 (*0-915604-15-9*) Carnegie-Mellon.

***Dunn, Stephen.** Different Hours: Poems. 2000. 22.00 (*0-393-04986-8*) Norton.

Dunn, Stephen. The Fall & Rise of the Asiatic Mode of Production. 240p. (Orig.). 1982. pap. 14.95 (*0-7100-9053-6*, Routledge Thoemms) Routledge.

— Full of Lust & Good Usage. LC 76-12129. (Classic Contemporaries Ser.). 1985. reprint ed. pap. 12.95 (*0-88748-148-5*) Carnegie-Mellon.

— Landscape at the End of the Century. 96p. 1992. pap. 9.95 (*0-393-30853-7*) Norton.

— Landscape at the End of the Century: Poems. 1991. 17.95 (*0-393-02972-7*) Norton.

— Loosestrife: Poems. LC 96-1238. 80p. 1996. 19.00 (*0-393-03982-X*) Norton.

— Loosestrife: Poems. LC 96-1238. 96p. 1998. pap. 11.00 (*0-393-31683-1*) Norton.

— New & Selected Poems, 1974-1994. LC 93-33212. 1994. 22.00 (*0-393-03618-9*) Norton.

— New & Selected Poems, 1974-1994. 320p. 1995. pap. 15.00 (*0-393-31300-X*) Norton.

— Not Dancing. LC 84-70175. (Poetry Ser.). 77p. 1984. 12.95 (*0-88748-000-4*) Carnegie-Mellon.

— Riffs & Reciprocities: Prose Pairs. LC 97-31238. 112p. 1998. 19.95 (*0-393-04630-3*) Norton.

— Walking Light: Essays & Memoirs. LC 92-31578. 224p. 1993. 20.95 (*0-393-03488-7*) Norton.

Dunn, Stephen. The Wonderful Way Home: An Adventure in Haiti, One. (Illus.). 16p. (J). (ps-5). 1990. pap. 6.95 (*0-9679937-2-5*, 20520, Pub. by Bapt Haiti) Mountain Maid.

Dunn, Stephen P. & Dunn, Ethel. Encyclopedia of Modern Separatist Movements. 300p. 1996. lib. bdg. 65.00 (*0-87436-752-2*) ABC-CLIO.

Dunn, Stephen P., tr. see Zdravomyslov, A. G., et al, eds.

Dunn, Steve, jt. auth. see Williams, Bruce R.

Dunn-Strohecker, Martha & Tippett, Deborah T. You: Living, Learning & Caring. LC 98-20608. 1998. text 42.64 (*1-56637-472-3*) Goodheart.

Dunn, Susan. The Deaths of Louis XVI: Regicide & the French Political Imagination. LC 93-39519. 192p. 1994. text 32.50 (*0-691-03429-X*, Pub. by Princeton U Pr) Cal Prin Full Svc.

Dunn, Susan. Sister Revolutions: French Lightning, American Light. (Illus.). 256p. 1996. 26.00 (*0-571-19050-2*) Faber & Faber.

— Sister Revolutions: French Lightning, American Light. LC 99-18178. 258p. 1999. text 26.00 (*0-571-19900-3*) Faber & Faber.

***Dunn, Susan.** Sister Revolutions: French Lightning, American Light. (Illus.). 272p. 2000. pap. 14.00 (*0-571-19989-5*) Faber & Faber.

Dunn, Susan & Larson. Design Technology: Children's Engineering. 230p. 1989. pap. 29.95 (*1-85000-590-7*, Falmer Pr) Taylor & Francis.

Dunn, Susan, jt. auth. see Heaps, Kelly S.

Dunn, Susan, jt. ed. see Jacobsohn, Gary J.

Dunn, Suzannah. Darker Days Than Usual. 128p. (Orig.). 1993. pap. 10.99 (*1-85242-172-X*) Serpents Tail.

Dunn, Tamara, ed. The Second Rainbow Book of Simulations. (Illus.). 200p. (Orig.). 1986. pap. 9.95 (*0-932471-06-4*) Falsoft.

Dunn, Teresa W. Jackson County, Georgia Superior Court Records, 1796-1803. 360p. (C). 1994. text. write for info. (*1-883793-06-8*) Wolfe Pubng.

***Dunn, Teri.** Cottage Gardens. LC 99-12469. (For Your Garden Ser.). 1999. pap. text 12.95 (*1-56799-784-8*, Friedman-Fairfax) M Friedman Pub Grp Inc.

Dunn, Teri. Fountains & Cascades. LC 99-17311. 1999. pap. text 12.95 (*1-56799-745-7*, Friedman-Fairfax) M Friedman Pub Grp Inc.

***Dunn, Teri.** Garden Accessories. (Illus.). 2000. 24.98 (*1-58663-030-X*) M Friedman Pub Grp Inc.

Dunn, Teri. Garden Antiques & Collectibles. LC 99-31052. (For Your Garden Ser.). 1999. pap. text 12.95 (*1-56799-785-6*, Friedman-Fairfax) M Friedman Pub Grp Inc.

***Dunn, Teri.** Garden Gates & Arches. (For Your Garden Ser.). (Illus.). 72p. 2000. pap. 12.95 (*1-56799-924-7*, Friedman-Fairfax) M Friedman Pub Grp Inc.

Dunn, Teri. Gardeners Favorites: 600 Essential Plants for Your Garden. 704p. 1999. 34.98 (*1-56799-813-5*, MetroBooks) M Friedman Pub Grp Inc.

***Dunn, Teri.** Hanging Baskets & Planters. (For Your Garden Ser.). (Illus.). 72p. 2000. pap. 12.95 (*1-56799-955-7*, Friedman-Fairfax) M Friedman Pub Grp Inc.

Dunn, Teri. 100 Favorite Garden Wildflowers. LC 99-18983. (One Hundred Favorite Ser.). (Illus.). 120p. 1999. 15.98 (*1-56799-641-8*, MetroBooks) M Friedman Pub Grp Inc.

— 100 Favorite Herbs. LC 98-152307. (Illus.). 120p. 1998. 15.98 (*1-56799-526-8*, MetroBooks) M Friedman Pub Grp Inc.

— 100 Favorite Perennials. LC 96-34520. (Illus.). 120p. 1998. 15.98 (*1-56799-527-6*, MetroBooks) M Friedman Pub Grp Inc.

— 100 Favorite Plants for Shade. LC 99-18982. (One Hundred Favorite Ser.). (Illus.). 120p. 1999. 15.98 (*1-56799-653-1*, MetroBooks) M Friedman Pub Grp Inc.

— 100 Favorite Roses. LC 96-34521. (Illus.). 120p. 1997. 15.98 (*1-56799-435-0*, Friedman-Fairfax) M Friedman Pub Grp Inc.

— Potting Places. LC 99-17299. 1999. text 24.95 (*1-56799-768-6*) M Friedman Pub Grp Inc.

Dunn, Terry. The T'ai Chi Ruler: Chinese Yoga for Health & Longevity. 128p. (Orig.). 1996. pap. text 15.95 (*0-938045-14-8*) Dragon Door.

Dunn, Terry L. Guide to Global Environmental Issues. LC 97-38572. 192p. (Orig.). 1997. pap. text 19.95 (*1-55591-956-1*) Fulcrum Pub.

Dunn, Thomas, ed. Renaissance Singer. LC 75-20077. 1976. 13.75 (*0-911318-10-0*) E C Schirmer.

Dunn, Thomas, ed. see Fontana, Giovanni Battista.

Dunn, Thomas G., jt. auth. see Pike, Frank.

Dunn, Thomas P., ed. Clockworks: A Multimedia Bibliography of Works Useful for the Study of the Human - Machine Interface in SF, 37. LC 93-1069. (Bibliographies & Indexes in World Literature Ser.: No. 37). 344p. 1993. lib. bdg. 85.00 (*0-313-27305-7*, DWG/, Greenwood Pr) Greenwood.

Dunn, Thomas P. & Erlich, Richard D., eds. The Mechanical God: Machines in Science Fiction, 1. LC 81-13429. (Contributions to the Study of Science Fiction & Fantasy Ser.: No. 1). 284p. 1982. 65.00 (*0-313-22274-6*, DME/, Greenwood Pr) Greenwood.

Dunn, Thomas P., jt. ed. see Erlich, Richard D.

Dunn, Timothy J. The Militarization of the U. S. - Mexico Border, 1978-1992: Low Intensity Conflict Doctrine Comes Home. LC 94-42964. (Border & Migration Studies). (Illus.). xii, 307 p. (C). 1995. pap. 14.95 (*0-292-71580-3*) U of Tex Pr.

— The Militarization of the U. S. Mexico Border, 1978-1992: Low Intensity Conflict Doctrine Comes Home. LC 94-42964. (Border & Migration Studies). (Illus.). 256p. (C). 1995. text 35.00 (*0-292-71579-X*) U of Tex Pr.

Dunn, Tom. Pulitzer Prizewinning Playwrights. 280p. 1995. 24.95 (*0-435-08688-X*, 08688) Heinemann.

Dunn, Tricia & King, Katie. Gold Medal Ice Hockey for Women & Girls: Tricia Dunn & Katie King, Gold Medal Winning Members of the U. S. Women's Olympic Ice Hockey Team. LC 98-74421. (Illus.). 256p. 1999. pap. 15.95 (*1-886284-37-7*, Pub. by Chandler Hse) Natl Bk Netwk.

Dunn, Troy. Industry Secrets: Inside Techniques That Will Save You Thousands. Klunder, Virgil L., ed. LC 91-70193. (Illus.). 60p. (Orig.). 1990. pap. 19.95 (*1-879499-23-1*) Caradium Pub.

— Life Is a Football Game. 1998. pap. 3.95 (*1-57734-138-4*, 01113151) Covenant Comms.

— The Locator: A Step-by-Step Guide to Finding Lost Families, Friends & Loved One Any Where Any Time. LC 99-37144. 336p. 2000. pap. 17.95 (*0-385-49452-1*) Doubleday.

Dunn, Troy & Klunder, Virgil. The Locator: The Complete Guide to Finding Family, Friends & Loved Ones. large type ed. Dunn, Arliene, ed. (Illus.). 720p. 1992. ring bd., lthr. 199.00 (*1-879499-06-1*) Caradium Pub.

Dunn, Vincent. Collapse of Burning Buildings: A Guide to Fireground Survival. (Illus.). 287p. (C). 1988. student ed. 15.00 (*0-87814-903-1*); text 39.95 (*0-87814-902-3*) Fire Eng.

***Dunn, Vincent.** Command & Control of Fires & Emergencies LC 99-29952. 1999. write for info. (*0-912212-84-5*) Fire Eng.

Dunn, Vincent. Safety & Survival on the Fireground. 377p. 1992. 39.95 (*0-912212-23-3*) Fire Eng.

Dunn, Vincent A. Cattle-Raids & Courtships: Medieval Narrative Genres in a Traditional Context. LC 88-37675. (Garland Monographs in Medieval Literature: Vol. 2). 288p. 1989. text 20.00 (*0-8240-4428-2*, 866) Garland.

Dunn, Virginia, et al. Civil Litigation, 1998-99. 3rd ed. (Inns of Court School of Law Ser.). 347p. 1998. pap. 42.00 (*1-85431-774-1*) Gaunt.

— Civil Litigation, 1997/98. 2nd ed. (Inns of Court School of Law Ser.). 347p. 1997. pap. 40.00 (*1-85431-678-8*, Pub. by Blackstone Pr) Gaunt.

Dunn, W. L., jt. auth. see Douthwaite, G. K.

Dunn, Waldo H. English Biography. (Channels of English Literature Ser.: No. 3). reprint ed. 43.50 (*0-404-07813-3*) AMS Pr.

Dunn, Walter S., Jr. Frontier Profit & Loss: The British Army & the Fur Traders, 1760-1764, 180. LC 97-48580. (Contributions in American History Ser.: Vol. 180). 216p. 1998. 59.95 (*0-313-30605-2*, Greenwood Pr) Greenwood.

Dunn, Walter S. Hitler's Nemesis: The Red Army, 1930-1945. LC 94-8345. 256p. 1994. 59.95 (*0-275-94894-3*, Praeger Pubs) Greenwood.

— Kursk: Hitler's Gamble, 1943. LC 97-7179. 216p. 1997. 57.95 (*0-275-95733-0*, Praeger Pubs) Greenwood.

***Dunn, Walter S., Jr.** Soviet Blitzkrieg: The Battle for White Russia, 1944. LC 99-36041. 252p. 2000. lib. bdg. 55.00 (*1-55587-880-6*) L Rienner.

Dunn, Walter S. The Soviet Economy & the Red Army, 1930-1945. LC 95-7016. 272p. 1995. 65.00 (*0-275-94893-5*, Praeger Pubs) Greenwood.

Dunn, Walter S., Jr. Walworth County. LC 98-87780. (Images of America Ser.). 128p. (Orig.). 1998. pap. write for info. (*0-7524-1356-2*) Arcadia Publng.

Dunn, Wendy. Childhood. (C). 1994. pap., student ed. 21.88 (*0-07-061235-8*) McGraw.

— Infancy, Childhood & Adolescence: Development in Context. (C). 1991. text, student ed. 21.87 (*0-07-061215-3*) McGraw.

Dunn, Wendy, jt. auth. see Morey, Janet N.

Dunn, Wilbur R. Full Measure of Devotion: The Eighth New York Volunteer Heavy Artillery, Pt. I. LC 97-94750. (Illus.). 368p. 1997. pap. write for info. (*1-57502-653-8*, PO1849) Morris Pubng.

— Full Measure of Devotion: The Eighth New York Volunteer Heavy Artillery, 2 vols., Pt. II. (Illus.). 341p. 1997. pap. 29.95 (*1-57502-654-6*, PO1850) Morris Pubng.

— Full Measure of Devotion Vols. I & II: The Eighth New York Volunteer Heavy Artillery. (Orig.). 1997. pap. 29.95 (*1-57502-656-2*, PO1849 & 1850) Morris Pubng.

Dunn, William. The Baby Bust: A Generation Comes of Age. LC 93-71267. 213p. 1993. pap. 29.95 (*0-936889-21-7*) American Demo.

— St. Edward's University: A Centennial History. LC 80-53738. (Illus.). 444p. 1986. 34.95 (*0-938472-01-1*) St Edwards Univ.

— Selling the Story: The Layman's Guide to Collecting & Communicating Demographic Information. LC 91-58811. 245p. (C). 1992. 24.95 (*0-936889-14-4*); pap. 29.95 (*0-936889-15-2*) American Demo.

Dunn, William, ed. Social Values & Public Policy. (Orig.). (C). 1981. pap. 15.00 (*0-918592-44-5*) Pol Studies.

Dunn, William & Nagel, Stuart S., eds. Policy Analysis Vol. 6: Perspectives, Concepts, & Methods. LC 85-23152. (Public Policy Ser.). 396p. 1986. 73.25 (*0-89232-371-X*) Jai Pr.

Dunn, William, jt. auth. see Bryant, Barbara E.

Dunn, William E. Spanish & French Rivalry in the Gulf Region of the U. S., 1678-1702: The Beginnings of Texas & Pensacola. (Select Bibliographies Reprint Ser.). 1977. reprint ed. 20.95 (*0-8369-5792-X*) Ayer.

Dunn, William H. The Sale of a Small Business. (Orig.). 1984. suppl. ed. 65.00 (*0-933808-02-X*) Busn Sale Inst.

Dunn, William J. Pacific Microphone. LC 88-12193. (Military History Ser.: No. 8). (Illus.). 416p. 1988. 24.95 (*0-89096-339-8*) Tex A&M Univ Pr.

Dunn, William N. The Experimenting Society Vol. 11: Essays in Honor of Donald T. Campbell. (Policy Studies Review Annual Ser.). 256p. 1997. text 32.95 (*1-56000-193-3*) Transaction Pubs.

— Public Policy Analysis: An Introduction. 2nd ed. 480p. (C). 1993. 56.00 (*0-13-738550-1*) P-H.

Dunn, William N. & Kelly, Rita M., eds. Advances in Policy Studies since 1950: Policy Studies Review Annual, Vol. 10. 420p. (C). 1991. text 89.95 (*0-88738-421-8*) Transaction Pubs.

Dunn, William N., jt. ed. see Nagel, Stuart S.

Dunn, William N., jt. ed. see Obradovic, Josip.

Dunn, William P. Sir Thomas Browne, a Study in Religious Philosophy. 2nd ed. LC 50-10370. 192p. reprint ed. pap. 59.60 (*0-8357-7022-2*, 203321900085) Bks Demand.

Dunn, William R. Fighter Pilot: The First American Ace of World War II. (Illus.). 272p. 1996. pap. 18.00 (*0-8131-0867-5*) U Pr of Ky.

— Fighter Pilot: The First American Ace of World War II. LC 82-40172. 268p. reprint ed. pap. 83.10 (*0-7837-5801-4*, 204546700006) Bks Demand.

— I Stand by Sand Creek. (Illus.). 1985. 7.95 (*0-88342-249-2*) Old Army.

Dunn, William R., jt. auth. see Mackay, Gilbert F.

***Dunn, Winnie W.** Best Practice Occupational Therapy: In Community Service with Children & Families. (Illus.). 400p. 2000. pap. text 42.00 (*1-55642-456-6*) SLACK Inc.

— Best Practice Occupational Therapy: In Community Service with Children & Families Instruction Manual. 32p. (C). 2000. pap. text. write for info. (*1-55642-457-4*) SLACK Inc.

Dunn, Winnie W. Pediatric Occupational Therapy: Facilitating Effective Service Provision. LC 89-43515. 420p. 1990. pap. 42.00 (*1-55642-014-5*) SLACK Inc.

Dunn, Zellie, ed. see Amsler, Kevin.

Dunn, Zellie, ed. see Rother, Herbert & Rother, Charlotte.

Dunna, J. Mick. Horse-Scents. 1995. 5.50 (*0-87129-561-X*, H20) Dramatic Pub.

Dunnagan, Harry D. A War to Win: Company B 813th Tank Destroyers. Warner, Vicki H., ed. (Illus.). 214p. 1992. 17.95 (*0-9631959-1-3*) Royall Dutton Bks.

Dunnagan, William R. A Survey of Lubbock's Growth As a Medical Center, 1909-1954. 65p. 1980. 5.00 (*0-911618-05-8*) Mus Texas.

Dunnage, Jonathan. The Italian Police & the Rise of Fascism: A Case Study of the Province of Bologna, 1897-1925. LC 97-5457. 216p. 1997. 57.95 (*0-275-95268-1*, Praeger Pubs) Greenwood.

Dunnahoo, Terry. Boston's Freedom Trail. LC 94-470. (Places in American History Ser.). (Illus.). 72p. (J). 1994. pap. 7.95 (*0-382-24762-0*, Dillon Silver Burdett) Silver Burdett Pr.

— Boston's Freedom Trail. LC 94-470. (Places in American History Ser.). (J). 1999. lib. bdg. 22.00 (*0-87518-623-8*) Silver Burdett Pr.

— How to Survive High School. (Issues Ser.). (Illus.). 112p. (YA). (gr. 9-12). 1994. pap. 6.95 (*0-531-15705-9*) Watts.

— How to Survive High School: A Student's Guide. LC 92-41700. (Issues Ser.). (Illus.). 112p. (YA). (gr. 9-12). 1993. lib. bdg. 24.00 (*0-531-11135-0*) Watts.

— The United States Mint. LC 98-33152. 2000. write for info. (*0-382-42135-3*, Dillon Silver Burdett) Silver Burdett Pr.

Dunnahoo, Terry J. The Plymouth Plantation. LC 93-39625. (Places in American History Ser.). (Illus.). 72p. (J). (gr. 4 up). 1995. lib. bdg. 14.95 (*0-382-24968-2*) Silver Burdett Pr.

— Sacramento, California. LC 96-111172. (Places in American History Ser.). (Illus.). 72p. (J). 1996. pap. 7.95 (*0-382-39334-1*); lib. bdg. 14.95 (*0-382-39333-3*) Silver Burdett Pr.

Dunnahoo, Terry J., jt. auth. see Silverstein, Herma.

D

Dunnam. Galatians, Ephesians, Philippians, Colossians & Philemon. (Mastering the Old & New Testament Ser.: Vol. 8). pap. 14.99 (*0-8499-3324-2*) Word Pub.
— Workbook on Loving Jesus. 1995. pap. 8.95 (*0-687-61441-4*) Abingdon.

Dunnam, Donald E. Cooking Triumphs of a Tightwad. LC 98-90374. 1998. pap. 11.95 (*0-533-12772-6*) Vantage.

Dunnam, Maxie. Alive in Christ. 1987. 16.30 (*0-687-00994-4*) Abingdon.
— Exodus. (Communicator's Commentary Ser.: Vol. 2). 295p. 22.99 (*0-8499-0407-2*) Word Pub.
— Galatians, Ephesians, Philippians, Colossians, Philemon. (Communicator's Commentary Ser.: Vol. 8). 420p. 22.99 (*0-8499-0161-8*) Word Pub.
— Jesus' Claims - Our Promics. 1982. 8.95 (*0-687-60569-5*) Abingdon.
— Jesus' Claims - Our Promises: A Study of the "I Am" Sayings of Jesus. LC 84-51831. 128p. 1984. pap. 10.00 (*0-8358-0502-6*) Upper Room Bks.
— Let Me Say That Again: Maxims for Spiritual Living. 128p. 1996. 12.00 (*0-8358-0769-X*) Upper Room Bks.
— Living the Psalms: A Confidence for All Seasons. LC 90-83523. 160p. 1990. pap. 10.00 (*0-8358-0622-7*) Upper Room Bks.
— Pack up Your Troubles. LC 92-42037. (Protestant Pulpit Exchange Ser.). 1993. pap. 8.95 (*0-687-09755-X*) Abingdon.
— Perceptions: Observations on Everyday Life. 2nd deluxe ed. 80p. (Orig.). 1990. reprint ed. pap. 9.95 (*0-917851-59-5*) Bristol Hse.
— That's What the Man Said. 1989. pap. 8.95 (*0-687-61161-X*) Abingdon.

Dunnam, Maxie. That's What the Man Said: The Sayings of Jesus. 128p. 1989. pap. 10.00 (*0-8358-0599-9*) Upper Room Bks.

Dunnam, Maxie. This Is Christianity: With Leader's Guide. 1998. pap. 10.00 (*0-687-08410-5*) Abingdon.
— Unless We Pray: Brief Lessons on the Practice of Prayer. Williams, Karen, ed. LC 97-27913. 160p. 1998. 12.00 (*0-8358-0841-6*, UR841) Upper Room Bks.
— Workbook of Intercessory Prayer. 1989. pap. 8.95 (*0-687-61374-4*) Abingdon.
— The Workbook of Living Prayer: 20th Anniversary Edition. 20th anniversary ed. 144p. 1994. pap., wbk. ed. 10.00 (*0-8358-0718-5*) Upper Room Bks.
— The Workbook on Becoming Alive in Christ. 1986. pap. text 8.95 (*0-687-61379-5*) Abingdon.
— The Workbook on Becoming Alive in Christ. 160p. 1986. pap. 10.00 (*0-8358-0542-5*) Upper Room Bks.
— The Workbook on Christians under Construction & in Recovery. 160p. 1993. pap. 10.00 (*0-8358-0683-9*) Upper Room Bks.
— The Workbook on Coping As Christians. 160p. 1988. pap. 10.00 (*0-8358-0581-6*) Upper Room Bks.
— The Workbook on Loving the Jesus Way. 168p. 1995. pap. 10.00 (*0-8358-0729-0*) Upper Room Bks.
— Workbook on Spiritual Disciplines. LC 83-51402. 160p. 1984. pap. text 10.00 (*0-8358-0479-8*) Upper Room Bks.
— Workbook on the Christ. 1992. pap. 8.95 (*0-687-61370-1*) Abingdon.
— The Workbook on the Christian Walk. 144p. 1992. pap. 10.00 (*0-8358-0640-5*) Upper Room Bks.

Dunnam, Maxie & Reisman, Kimberly D. The Workbook on Virtues & the Fruit of the Spirit. Williams, Karen F., ed. LC 98-17290. 160p. 1998. pap., wbk. ed. 10.00 (*0-8358-0854-8*, UR854) Upper Room Bks.

Dunnam, Maxie & Reisman, Kimberly Dunnam. The Workbook on the Seven Deadly Sins. LC 97-9331. 160p. 1997. pap., wbk. ed. 10.00 (*0-8358-0714-2*, UR 714) Upper Room Bks.

Dunnam, Maxie D. The Christian Way: A Wesleyan View of our Spiritual Journey. 112p. 1987. pap. 6.95 (*0-310-20741-X*, 06330P) Zondervan.
— The Devil at Noonday: Battling Temptation in Daily Life. 185p. 1996. 14.99 (*0-7852-7876-1*) Nelson.
— Exodus. (Mastering the Old & New Testament Ser.: Vol. 2). pap. 14.99 (*0-8499-3541-5*) Word Pub.
— Going on to Salvation: A Study in the Wesleyan Tradition. LC 90-62269. 128p. 1990. pap. 9.95 (*0-88177-100-7*, DR100) Discipleship Res.
— Workbook of Intercessory Prayer. LC 78-65617. 1979. pap. 10.00 (*0-8358-0382-1*) Upper Room Bks.

Dunnan, Nancy. Dun & Bradstreet Guide to Your Investments, 1990. 1990. pap. 12.95 (*0-685-30576-7*) HarperTrade.
— Dun & Bradstreet Guide to Your Investments, 1996. 1996. 35.00 (*0-06-271583-6*) Harper SF.

***Dunnan, Nancy.** Dunnan's Guide to Your Investment$ The Year-Round Investment Sourcebook for Managing Your Personal Finances 2000 Edition. 464p. 2000. pap. 22.00 (*0-06-273691-4*, HarpRes) HarpInfo.
— How to Invest $50-$5,000: The Small Investor's Step-by-Step, Dollar-by-Dollar Plan for Low-Risk, High-Value Investing. 7th ed. LC 98-51548. 160p. 1999. pap. 12.95 (*0-06-273656-6*) HarpC.

Dunnan, Nancy. How to Invest Fifty Dollars to Five Thousand Dollars: The Small Investor's Step-by-Step Dollar-by-Dollar Plan for Low Risk, High-Yield Investing. 3rd ed. LC 90-55497. 128p. (Orig.). 1991. pap. 7.95 (*0-00-003265-4*, Harper Ref) HarpC.
— How to Survive & Thrive in the Recession of Nineteen Ninety-One. 1991. pap. 3.95 (*0-380-76609-4*, Avon Bks) Morrow Avon.
— Never Balance Your Checkbook on Tuesday: And 300 More Financial Lessons You Can't Afford Not to Know. LC 98-44042. 256p. (Orig.). 1999. pap. 9.00 (*0-06-273659-0*) HarpC.
— Never Call Your Broker on Monday: And 300 Other Financial Lessons You Can't Afford Not To Know. LC 96-3018. 256p. (Orig.). 1997. pap. 8.50 (*0-06-270164-9*, Harper Ref) HarpC.

***Dunnan, Nancy.** Never Short a Stock on Wednesday: And 300 More Financial Lessons You Can't Afford Not to Know, LC 99-56970. 256p. 2000. pap. 9.50 (*0-06-273727-9*) HarpC.

Dunnan, Nancy. One Europe. (YA). 1992. pap. 4.80 (*0-395-62470-3*) HM.
— One Europe. LC 91-30083. (Headliners Ser.). 64p. (J). (gr. 5-8). 1992. pap. 6.95 (*1-878841-96-3*) Millbrook Pr.

Dunnan, Nancy & Pack, Jay J. Market Movers. 352p. (Orig.). 1993. mass mkt. 14.99 (*0-446-39340-1*, Pub. by Warner Bks) Little.

Dunnan, Nancy, jt. auth. see Teison, Herbert.

Dunnan, Nancy, jt. auth. see Tuckerman, Nancy.

Dunnavant, Anthony L, et al. Founding Vocation & Future Vision: The Self-Understanding of the Disciples of Christ. LC 98-32159. 136p. 1999. pap. 14.99 (*0-8272-1024-8*) Chalice Pr.

Dunnavant, Anthony L. Restructure: Four Historical Ideals in the Campbell-Stone Movement of the Polity of the Christian Church (Disciples of Christ) LC 90-36892. (American University Studies: Theology & Religion: Ser. VII, Vol. 85). 265p. (C). 1993. text 27.95 (*0-8204-1420-4*) P Lang Pubng.

Dunnavant, Keith, jt. auth. see Welden, W. Edgar.

Dunnavant, Michelle. Josh & Jennie & George's Velocipede. (Rail Rales Ser.: Vol. 4). (Illus.). 20p. (J). (ps up). 1998. mass mkt. 5.00 (*1-892136-03-1*) Lionel MI.
— Josh & Jennie Discover Chessie. (Rail Tales Ser.: Vol. 1). (Illus.). 20p. (J). (ps up). 1997. mass mkt. 5.00 (*1-892136-00-7*) Lionel MI.
— Josh & Jennie Ride the Super Chief. unabridged ed. (Rail Tales Ser.: Vol. 2). (Illus.). 20p. (J). (ps up). 1997. mass mkt. 5.00 (*1-892136-01-5*) Lionel MI.
— Josh & Jennie Save the Day. (Rail Tales Ser.: Vol. 3). (Illus.). 20p. (J). (ps up). 1997. mass mkt. 5.00 (*1-892136-02-3*) Lionel MI.

Dunnavant, Robert, Jr. Decatur: Yankee Foothold in Dixie. Gentry, Phillip, ed. (Illus.). 220p. (Orig.). 1995. pap. write for info. (*0-9642084-1-5*) Pea Ridge Pr.
— The Railroad War: N. B. Forrest's 1864 Raid Through Northern Alabama & Middle Tennessee. Langley, Roland, ed. LC 94-61417. (Illus.). 180p. (Orig.). 1994. pap. 16.95 (*0-9642084-0-7*) Pea Ridge Pr.

Dunnavant, Sandra, et al. The Maple Leaf: A Civil War Shipwreck. 2nd ed. Cole, Vicki, ed. (Series of Lesson Plans: Ser. 2, No. 18). (Illus.). 12p. (J). (gr. k-12). 1997. write for info. (*1-889030-11-2*) FL Div Hist Res.
— One Room Schoolhouses of Florida. 2nd ed. (Series of Lesson Plans: Ser. 2, No. 20). (Illus.). 16p. (J). (gr. k-12). 1997. write for info. (*1-889030-10-4*) FL Div Hist Res.
— Steamboats in 19th Century Florida. 2nd ed. (Series of Lesson Plans: Series 2, No. 19). (Illus.). 16p. (J). (gr. k-12). 1997. write for info. (*1-889030-13-9*) FL Div Hist Res.

Dunnavant, Sylvia. Celebrating Life: African American Women Speak Out about Breast Cancer. Egiebor, Sharon, ed. LC 95-60852. (Illus.). 256p. 1995. pap. 19.95 (*0-9643211-4-9*) USFI.

Dunnavant, Tony L., jt. ed. see Duke, James O.

Dunne. Retailing. (C). 1998. pap. text, teacher ed. 40.00 (*0-03-024819-1*) Harcourt Coll Pubs.
— Retailing. 3rd ed. LC 97-77645. (C). 1998. text 84.00 (*0-03-024758-6*, Pub. by Harcourt Coll Pubs) Harcourt.

Dunne & Lusch, Robert F. Retailing. 2nd ed. (SB - Marketing Education Ser.). (C). 1994. mass mkt. 99.95 (*0-538-84136-2*) S-W Pub.

Dunne, et al. Stanford Environmental Law Journal, 1990, Vol. 9. 197p. (Orig.). 1990. pap. 15.00 (*0-942007-34-4*) Stanford Enviro.

Dunne, Agnes C., jt. auth. see Le Gros, Clark F.

Dunne, Alex. Answer Guide to How to Become a Candidate Master. 1995. pap. text 4.95 (*0-938650-38-6*) Thinkers Pr.

***Dunne, Alex.** Chess is Still Alive! (Illus.). 2000. pap. 17.95 (*0-938650-56-4*) Thinkers Pr.

Dunne, Alex. LDL Sicilian. 1995. pap. 5.00 (*0-938650-42-4*) Thinkers Pr.
— Modern Postal Masterpieces. Long, Robert B., ed. (Illus.). 141p. 1994. pap. 16.95 (*0-938650-70-X*) Thinkers Pr.

Dunne, Andrew P. International Theory: To the Brink & Beyond, 378. LC 96-18227. (Contributions in Political Science Ser.). 224p. 1996. 57.95 (*0-313-30078-X*) Greenwood.

Dunne, Anne. The Unconstitutional Family. pap. text. write for info. (*1-85475-136-0*, IE, MICHIE) LEXIS Pub.

Dunne, Brenda J., jt. auth. see Jahn, Robert F.

Dunne, Carrin. Buddha & Jesus: Conversations. 112p. 1975. pap. 10.95 (*0-87243-057-X*) Templegate.
— Calming the Storm. 110p. 1994. pap. 10.95 (*0-87243-205-X*) Templegate.

Dunne, Catherine. In the Beginning. LC 97-201001. 288p. 1998. pap. 17.95 (*0-224-04426-5*, Pub. by Jonathan Cape) Trafalgar.

Dunne, Catherine B. Interior Designing for All Five Senses. unabridged ed. LC 98-17153. (Illus.). 192p. 1998. text 30.00 (*0-307-44069-9*) St Martin.

Dunne, Christine. Cuidado! El Espanol es Divertido! The Complete Sourcebook to Create Engaging Cultural Experiences for Beginning Spanish Students. (Illus.). 117p. (Orig.). 1994. pap., teacher ed. 19.95 (*1-885126-01-8*) Laurelwood NY.
— Vorsicht! Deutsch macht Spass! The Complete Sourcebook to Create Engaging Cultural Experiences for Beginning German Students. (Illus.). 109p. (Orig.). 1994. pap., teacher ed. 19.95 (*1-885126-00-X*) Laurelwood NY.

Dunne, Christine & Adasiak, Kathy T. Attention! Le Francais, C'est Marrant! The Complete Sourcebook to Create Engaging Cultural Experiences for Beginning French Students. (Illus.). 112p. (Orig.). 1996. pap., teacher ed. 19.95 (*1-885126-02-6*) Laurelwood NY.

***Dunne, Claire.** Carl Jung: Wounded Healer of the Soul: An Illustrated Portrait. (Illus.). 258p. 2000. 39.95 (*0-930407-49-0*, Pub. by Parabola Bks); pap. 24.95 (*0-930407-50-4*, Pub. by Parabola Bks) IPG Chicago.

Dunne, Clare. People under the Skin. 216p. (C). 1990. 70.00 (*0-7855-6626-0*, Pub. by Pascoe Pub) St Mut.

Dunne, Colin. Rye in the '20s. 1978. 15.95 (*0-405-09141-9*, 19506) Ayer.

Dunne, David, jt. auth. see Baritz, Tony.

Dunne, Dominick. Another City, Not My Own: A Novel in the Form of a Memoir. 406p. 1999. mass mkt. 7.99 (*0-345-43051-4*) Ballantine Pub Grp.
— Another City, Not My Own: A Novel in the Form of a Memoir. 1999. mass mkt. 7.99 (*0-449-00419-8*, Crest) Fawcett.
— Fatal Charms & Other Tales of Today & the Mansions of Limbo. LC PS3554.U492A6 1999. 509p. 1999. pap. 14.95 (*0-345-43059-X*) Ballantine Pub Grp.
— An Inconvenient Woman. 1999. mass mkt. 6.99 (*0-345-43053-0*) Ballantine Pub Grp.
— The Mansions of Limbo. 1999. 14.95 (*0-449-00437-6*) Fawcett.
— The Mansions of Limbo. large type ed. (General Ser.). 440p. 1992. pap. 16.95 (*0-8161-5371-X*, G K Hall Lrg Type) Mac Lib Ref.
— People Like Us. 1999. mass mkt. 6.99 (*0-345-43054-9*) Ballantine Pub Grp.
— People Like Us. 464p. 1990. mass mkt. 6.99 (*0-553-27891-6*) Bantam.
— A Season in Purgatory. 464p. 1994. mass mkt. 6.99 (*0-553-29076-2*) Bantam.
— Season in Purgatory. 1999. mass mkt. 6.99 (*0-345-43055-7*) Ballantine Pub Grp.
— Sins of the Sons. 1997. 25.00 (*0-517-58387-9*) Random Hse Value.
— The Two Mrs. Grenvilles. 1999. mass mkt. 6.99 (*0-345-43056-5*) Ballantine Pub Grp.
— The Two Mrs. Grenvilles. 384p. 1986. mass mkt. 6.99 (*0-553-25891-5*) Bantam.
— The Way We Lived Then: Recollections of a Well-Known Name Dropper. LC 99-17616. (Illus.). 224p. 1999. 27.50 (*0-609-60388-4*, Crown) Crown Pub Group.

Dunne, E. Excerpts from a Bush Pilot's Diary. 274p. (Orig.). 1992. pap. 12.95 (*0-9644370-0-7*) Dryden Publ.

Dunne, Edward F. Cardiac Radiology. LC RC0683.R3D8. (Illus.). 268p. reprint ed. pap. 83.10 (*0-608-11200-3*, 205542100022) Bks Demand.

***Dunne, Elisabeth.** The Learning Society: International Perspectives on Core Skills in Higher Education. LC 99-491044. 228p. 1999. 65.00 (*0-7494-2895-3*, Kogan Pg Educ) Stylus Pub VA.

Dunne, Elizabeth & Bennett, Neville S. Talking & Learning in Groups. (Classroom Skills Ser.). (Illus.). 256p. (C). 1993. pap. text 13.95 (*0-333-55180-X*, A9897) Routledge.

Dunne, Faith. Places in the System: New Directions for the Vocational Education of Rural Women. 16p. 1985. 2.75 (*0-318-22167-5*, OC108) Ctr Educ Trng Employ.

Dunne, Finley P. Mr. Dooley & the Chicago Irish: The Autobiography of a Nineteenth-Century Ethnic Group. Fanning, Charles, ed. LC 87-13228. 357p. 1976. reprint ed. pap. 110.70 (*0-7837-9106-2*, 204990800004) Bks Demand.
— Mr. Dooley in Peace & in War. LC 88-20662. (Prairie State Bks.). 176p. 1988. 11.95 (*0-252-06040-7*) U of Ill Pr.
— Mr. Dooley in Peace & War. 1972. 250.00 (*0-87968-249-3*) Gordon Pr.
— Mr. Dooley in the Hearts of His Countrymen. 1972. 250.00 (*0-87968-248-5*) Gordon Pr.
— Mr. Dooley in the Hearts of His Countrymen. 1968. reprint ed. 13.00 (*0-403-00096-3*) Scholarly.
— Mr. Dooley's Opinions. 1973. 250.00 (*0-87968-161-6*) Gordon Pr.
— Mr. Dooley's Opinions. 1977. reprint ed. 59.00 (*0-403-08562-4*) Scholarly.
— Mr. Dooley's Philosophy. LC 73-10444. (American Humorists Ser.). 267p. reprint ed. lib. bdg. 22.00 (*0-8398-0376-1*) Irvington.
— Observations by Mr. Dooley. 1973. 250.00 (*0-8490-0746-1*) Gordon Pr.

Dunne, Finley P. & Schaaf, Barbara C. Mr. Dooley - Wise & Funny - We Need Him Now. 310p. (Orig.) 1987. pap. 8.95 (*0-942936-11-6*) Lincoln-Herndon Pr.

Dunne, Gary, ed. Fruit. LC 95-223779. 1995. pap. 10.95 (*1-875243-15-1*) LPC InBook.

Dunne, George C. & McDougall, Kristin A. Mesozoic Paleogeography of the Western United States-II. 500p. (Orig.). 1993. pap. 33.00 (*1-878861-64-6*) Pac Section SEPM.

Dunne, Gerald. Self-Dual Chern-Simons Theories, Vol. X. Beiglbock, W. et al, eds. (Lecture Notes in Physics Ser.: No. M 36). 217p. 1995. 49.95 (*3-540-60257-7*) Spr-Verlag.

Dunne, Gerald T. Hugo Black & the Judicial Revolution. 1977. text 36.50 (*0-8290-0344-4*) Irvington.
— The Missouri Supreme Court: From Dred Scott to Nancy Cruzan. (Illus.). 240p. 1993. text 34.95 (*0-8262-0826-6*) U of Mo Pr.

***Dunne, Gerry.** Preventing Violence in Our Schools. (Illus.). 144p. (YA). (gr. 4-12). 1999. pap. text 21.95 (*1-880396-65-3*) Jalmar Pr.

Dunne, Gerry & Hadley, George. Magic Circle: Preschool & Kindergarten Activity Guide. (Illus.). 117p. (J). 1996. spiral bd. 21.95 (*1-56499-031-1*, IP9031) Innerchoice Pub.

Dunne, Gerry, et al. Impact: A Self-Esteem Based Skill Development Program for Secondary Students. 1990. pap., teacher ed. 39.95 (*0-9625486-1-8*, IP486Z) Innerchoice Pub.
— Impact: A Self-Esteem Based Skill Development Program Kit for Secondary Students. (YA). (gr. 9-12). 1993. teacher ed., boxed set 99.95 (*1-56499-039-7*, IP4861) Innerchoice Pub.

Dunne, Gillian A. Lesbian Lifestyles: Women's Work & the Politics of Sexuality. 240p. 1996. text 50.00 (*0-8020-4104-3*); pap. text 18.95 (*0-8020-7951-2*) U of Toronto Pr.

Dunne, Gillian A., ed. Living "Difference" Lesbian Perspectives on Work & Family Life. LC 98-38652. 1998. pap. 14.95 (*1-56023-115-7*, Harrington Park) Haworth Pr.
— Living "Difference" Lesbian Perspectives on Work & Family Life. LC 98-38652. 167p. 1998. 39.95 (*0-7890-0537-9*, Harrington Park) Haworth Pr.

Dunne, H. P. The Mooncusser. 368p. 1994. 23.00 (*1-885173-03-2*) Write Way.

Dunne, J. F., jt. ed. see Bankowski, Z.

Dunne, Jane, ed. Dinner by Design. (Illus.). 158p. 1994. spiral bd. 25.00 (*0-941447-03-0*) Amer Ctr Design.

Dunne, John. The City of the Gods: A Study in Myth & Mortality. 156p. 1978. pap. 11.50 (*0-268-00726-8*) U of Notre Dame Pr.
— Shrines of Ireland. 126p. 1989. pap. 22.00 (*1-85390-028-1*, Pub. by Veritas Pubns) St Mut.

Dunne, John G. Crooning. 1991. pap. 9.95 (*0-671-74031-8*, Touchstone) S&S Trade Pap.
— Harp. 1990. pap. 8.95 (*0-671-72514-9*, Touchstone) S&S Trade Pap.
— Monster: Living off the Big Screen. 1998. pap. 12.00 (*0-375-75024-X*) Vin Bks.
— The Studio. LC 97-36329. 1998. pap. 13.00 (*0-375-70008-0*) Vin Bks.

***Dunne, John J.** Irish Ghosts. rev. ed. Orig. Title: Haunted Ireland. (Illus.). 114p. 2000. pap. 16.95 (*0-86281-766-8*, Pub. by Appletree Pr) Irish Bks Media.

Dunne, John S. The Church of the Poor Devil: Reflections on a Riverboat Voyage & a Spiritual Journey. LC 83-14548. (C). 1983. pap. text 10.50 (*0-268-00746-2*) U of Notre Dame Pr.
— The Homing Spirit: A Pilgrimage of the Mind, of the Heart, of the Soul. LC 97-17553. 1997. pap. 16.00 (*0-268-01112-5*) U of Notre Dame Pr.
— The House of Wisdom: A Pilgrimage. LC 93-22813. (C). 1993. reprint ed. pap. text 13.00 (*0-268-01103-6*) U of Notre Dame Pr.
— Love's Mind: An Essay on Contemplative Life. LC 93-13910. (C). 1993. text 23.00 (*0-268-01303-9*) U of Notre Dame Pr.

***Dunne, John S.** Love's Mind: An Essay on Contemplative Life. LC 93-13910. 170p. 2000. reprint ed. pap. 14.00 (*0-268-01331-4*, Pub. by U of Notre Dame Pr) Chicago Distribution Ctr.

Dunne, John S. The Music of Time: Words & Music & Spiritual Friendship. LC 95-47364. 232p. (C). 1996. text 25.00 (*0-268-01423-X*) U of Notre Dame Pr.
— The Mystic Road of Love. LC 99-22330. 200p. 1999. 25.00 (*0-268-01445-0*); pap. 16.00 (*0-268-01446-9*) U of Notre Dame Pr.
— Reading the Gospel. 168p. 2000. 18.00 (*0-268-01667-4*, Pub. by U of Notre Dame Pr); pap. 11.00 (*0-268-01668-2*, Pub. by U of Notre Dame Pr) Chicago Distribution Ctr.
— The Reasons of the Heart: A Journey into Solitude & Back Again into the Human Circle. LC 79-18513. 1979. reprint ed. pap. 11.50 (*0-268-01606-2*) U of Notre Dame Pr.
— A Search for God in Time & Memory. LC 76-20165. 1977. reprint ed. pap. 15.00 (*0-268-01673-9*) U of Notre Dame Pr.
— Time & Myth. LC 74-32289. 128p. 1975. reprint ed. pap. 9.50 (*0-268-01828-6*) U of Notre Dame Pr.
— The Way of All the Earth: Practical Judgement & the Lure of Technique: Experiments in Truth & Religion. LC 78-1575. 1978. reprint ed. pap. 18.00 (*0-268-01928-2*); reprint ed. text 29.00 (*0-268-01927-4*) U of Notre Dame Pr.

Dunne, Joseph. Back to the Rough Ground: Practical Judgement & the Lure of Technique: Experiments in Truth & Religion. LC 91-50564. (Revisions: A Series of Books on Ethics: Vol. 11). (C). 1992. text 53.00 (*0-268-00689-X*) U of Notre Dame Pr.
— Back to the Rough Ground: Practical Judgement & the Lure of Technique: Experiments in Truth & Religion. LC 97-35478. (Revisions: A Series of Books on Ethics). 512p. (C). 1997. pap. 22.00 (*0-268-00705-5*) U of Notre Dame Pr.

Dunne, Kerry & Campbell, Ian R., eds. Unravelling the Labyrinth: Decoding Text & Language - Festschrift for Eric Lowson Marson. LC 97-30899. 174p. 1997. pap. 42.95 (*0-8204-3195-8*) P Lang Pubng.
— Unravelling the Labyrinth: Decoding Text & Language - Festschrift for Eric Lowson Marson. LC 97-30899. 174p. 1997. 42.95 (*3-631-30385-8*) P Lang Pubng.

Dunne, Mairead, et al. Kenya. LC 96-52703. (Country Insights Ser.). (J). 1998. 25.69 (*0-8172-4790-4*) Raintree Steck-V.

***Dunne, Mark.** Horses: A Guide to Carrots, Cantering & Sugar Cubes. LC 00-25682. (Illus.). 112p. 2000. 9.95 (*1-57145-659-7*, Laurel Glen Pub) Advantage Pubs.

Dunne, Mary G. Blood-Sport Memorial: A Spiritual Service for the Yearly Human Rights Commemoration in Memory of Circumcised Children & All Victims of Genital Mutilation. 53p. (Orig.). (C). 1995. pap. text 27.95 (*1-884090-10-9*) Ecumenics Intl.

D

Dunne, Michael. Metapop: Self-Referentiality in Contemporary American Popular Culture. LC 91-35995. (Studies in Popular Culture). 208p. 1992. text 30.00 (*0-87805-548-7*) U Pr of Miss.

Dunne, Michael, ed. Hawthorne's Narrative Strategies. LC 94-43866. 224p. 1995. text 37.50 (*0-87805-761-7*) U Pr of Miss.

Dunne, Pam B. Creative Drama: A Complete Sourcebook for Church & School. 191p. 1987. reprint ed. pap. 24.00 (*1-888657-01-4*) Drama Thrpy Inst.

— Creative Journal. (Illus.). 63p. 1995. pap. 18.00 (*1-888657-04-9*) Drama Thrpy Inst.

— The Creative Therapeutic Thinker. 2nd ed. (Illus.). 75p. 1993. pap. 18.00 (*1-888657-02-2*) Drama Thrpy Inst.

— Drama Therapy Activities for Parents & Children: An Exercise Handbook. 2nd ed. 53p. 1992. pap. 18.00 (*1-888657-05-7*) Drama Thrpy Inst.

— Media in Drama Therapy: An Exercise Handbook. 64p. 1988. pap. 18.00 (*1-888657-03-0*) Drama Thrpy Inst.

— The Narrative Therapist & the Arts. (Illus.). 256p. (Orig.). 1992. pap. 40.00 (*1-888657-06-5*) Drama Thrpy Inst.

— Theatre for Young People: A Creative Workbook. (Illus.). 52p. (Orig.). 1993. pap. 18.00 (*1-888657-00-6*) Drama Thrpy Inst.

Dunne, Patrick, jt. auth. see Lusch, Robert F.

Dunne, Patrick J. & McInturff, Susan L. Respiratory Home Care. LC 97-18412. (Illus.). 207p. (C). 1997. pap. text 24.95 (*0-8036-0154-9*) Davis Co.

Dunne, Patrick M. Retailing. 3rd ed. (C). 1998. pap. text 29.50 (*0-03-022132-3*) Harcourt Coll Pubs.

Dunne, Patrick M. & Obenhouse, Susan. Product Management: A Reader. LC 80-22355. 182p. reprint ed. pap. 56.50 (*0-608-12626-8*, 202542700043) Bks Demand.

Dunne, Patrick M., et al. Retailing. (C). 1991. text. write for info. (*0-538-81443-8*, SF65AA) S-W Pub.

Dunne, Paul, ed. Quantitative Marxism. 220p. (C). 1990. 61.95 (*0-7456-0647-4*) Blackwell Pubs.

***Dunne, Paul E.** Red Hat Linux 6.0 Application Development Tools With CDROM. 1999. pap. 44.95 (*0-07-134147-1*) McGraw.

Dunne, Pete. Before the Echo: Essays on Nature. LC 94-22910. (Corrie Herring Hooks Ser.). (Illus.). 152p. 1995. 19.95 (*0-292-71578-1*) U of Tex Pr.

— Feather Quest. 1999. pap. 14.00 (*0-452-26876-1*, Plume) Dutton Plume.

— More Tales of a Low-Rent Birder. LC 93-47657. (Illus.). 125p. (C). 1994. 18.95 (*0-292-71572-2*) U of Tex Pr.

— Small-Headed Flycatcher: Seen Yesterday; He Didn't Leave His Name & Other Stories. LC 97-43354. (Illus.). 152p. 1998. pap. 14.95 (*0-292-71600-1*) U of Tex Pr.

— Small-Headed Flycatcher & Seen Yesterday & He Didn't Leave His Name: And Other Stories. LC 97-43354. (Illus.). 152p. 1998. 25.00 (*0-292-71599-4*) U of Tex Pr.

— Tales of a Low-Rent Birder. LC 93-37749. (Illus.). 176p. (C). 1994. reprint ed. pap. 11.95 (*0-292-71574-9*) U of Tex Pr.

— The Wind Masters: The Lives of North American Birds of Prey. LC 95-18314. (Illus.). 268p. 1995. 22.95 (*0-395-65235-9*) HM.

Dunne, Pete & Sutton, Clay. Hawks in Flight: Flight Identification of North American Migrant Raptors. (Illus.). 254p. 1989. pap. 13.00 (*0-395-51022-8*) HM.

Dunne, Peter. Feather Quest. LC 99-22725. 1999. pap. 16.00 (*0-395-92790-0*) HM.

Dunne, Peter, et al. New Jersey at the Crossroads of Migration. LC 89-14554. (Illus.). 74p. 1989. pap. 8.00 (*0-9624065-0-3*) NJ Audubon Soc.

Dunne, Philip. How Green Was My Valley: The Screenplay for the Darryl F. Zanuck Film Production. (Illus.). 105p. 1990. 35.00 (*0-944166-04-0*) Santa Teresa Pr.

Dunne, Richard, jt. auth. see Wragg, Edward C.

Dunne, Sean. Against the Storm. 48p. 1985. pap. 10.95 (*0-85105-440-4*, Pub. by Smyth) Dufour.

***Dunne, Sean.** In My Father's House. 2000. pap. 17.95 (*1-85235-264-7*, Pub. by Gallery Pr) Dufour.

Dunne, Sean. An Introduction to Irish Poetry. 68p. 14.95 incl. audio (*0-946005-35-4*, OS 10682, Pub. by Ossian) Music Sales.

— The Road to Silence: An Irish Spiritual Oddyssey. 79p. (Orig.). 1994. pap. 9.95 (*1-874597-12-X*, Pub. by New Island Books) Irish Bks Media.

— The Sheltered Nest. 58p. 1992. pap. 12.95 (*1-85235-084-9*) Dufour.

— Time & the Island. LC 96-139994. 62p. 1996. pap. 12.95 (*1-85235-180-2*) Dufour.

Dunne, Sean, ed. The College: A Photographic History of University College, Cork. (Illus.). 105p. 1995. 29.95 (*1-85918-057-4*, Pub. by Cork Univ) Intl Spec Bk.

— Ireland Anthology, Vol. 1. LC 98-16112. 1998. text 30.00 (*0-312-18429-8*) St Martin.

— Poets of Munster. Date not set. pap. 18.95 (*0-85646-122-9*, Pub. by Anvil Press) Dufour.

— Poets of Munster. 224p. 1985. 29.95 (*0-85646-121-0*, Pub. by Anvil Press) Dufour.

Dunne, Seban & O'Brien, George. The Ireland Anthology. LC 98-120209. xxxi, 455 p. 1997. write for info. (*0-7171-2519-X*, Pub. by Gill & MacMill) St Mut.

Dunne, Stephen M., jt. auth. see Birnbaum, William S.

Dunne, Susan, jt. auth. see Pybus, Victoria.

Dunne, Tad. We Cannot Find Words. 1985. pap. 6.95 (*0-87193-262-8*) Dimension Bks.

***Dunne, Tad.** We Love You Matty: Meeting Death with Faith. Morgan, John D., ed. LC 99-46089. (Death, Value & Meaning Ser.). (Illus.). 196p. 2000. pap. 29.95 (*0-89503-203-1*) Baywood Pub.

Dunne, Thomas & Leopold, Luna B. Water in Environmental Planning. LC 78-8013. (Illus.). 818p. (C). 1978. pap. text 74.95 (*0-7167-0079-4*) W H Freeman.

***Dunne, Tim, et al, eds.** The Eighty Years Crisis 1919-1999. 246p. (C). 2000. pap. 24.95 (*0-521-66783-6*) Cambridge U Pr.

Dunne, Tim & Wheeler, Nicholas J., eds. Human Rights in Global Politics. LC 98-35137. (Illus.). 360p. (C). 1999. 64.95 (*0-521-64138-1*); pap. 24.95 (*0-521-64643-X*) Cambridge U Pr.

Dunne, Tim, jt. auth. see Warren, Bernie.

Dunne, Timothy. Inventing International Society: A History of the English School. LC 98-17291. (St. Antony's Ser.). 240p. 1998. text 65.00 (*0-312-21545-2*) St Martin.

Dunne, W. M. Thomas F. McManus & the American Fishing Schooners: An Irish-American Success Story. (American Maritime Library Ser.: Vol. XIV). (Illus.). xi, 406p. 1994. 39.95 (*0-913372-69-2*) Mystic Seaport.

Dunne, Wilbert V. Honeymoon in Merida. (Illus.). 64p. (Orig.). 1995. pap. 10.00 (*1-56474-123-0*) Fithian Pr.

— The Ides of September: The Story of Patrick Bryan, an Early Californian. (Illus.). 64p. (Orig.). 1993. pap. 8.95 (*1-56474-060-9*) Fithian Pr.

Dunne, William P. Is It a Saint's Name? 1977. pap. 2.50 (*0-89555-024-5*) TAN Bks Pubs.

Dunnebier-Frauenberg, Martha. I Am. 1998. pap. write for info. (*1-57553-778-8*) Watermrk Pr.

Dunnell, R. C. The Prehistory of Fishtrap, Kentucky. LC 72-90078. (Publications in Anthropology: No. 75). 1972. pap. 7.00 (*0-913516-08-2*) Yale U Anthro.

Dunnell, Robert C. & Hall, Edwin C. Archaeological Essays in Honor of Irvin B. Rouse. 1979. 67.70 (*90-279-7834-4*) Mouton.

Dunnell, Robert C., jt. ed. see Meltzer, David J.

Dunnell, Ruth W. The Great State of White & High: Buddhism & State Formation in Eleventh-Century Xia. LC 95-31978. 1996. text 49.00 (*0-8248-1719-2*) UH Pr.

Dunnen, Emile Den, see Den Dunnen, Emile.

Dunner, David L. Current Psychiatric Therapy II, Vol. 2. 2nd ed. Fletcher, Judy & Lefebvre, Yolaine, eds. LC 96-16730. (Illus.). 624p. 1997. text 78.00 (*0-7216-5989-6*, W B Saunders Co) Harcrt Hlth Sci Grp.

Dunner, David L., et al. Relatives at Risk for Mental Disorder. LC 87-42919. (American Psychopathological Association Ser.). 336p. 1988. reprint ed. pap. 104.20 (*0-608-00330-1*, 206104700007) Bks Demand.

Dunner, Donald R. & Gholz, Charles L. Court of Appeals for the Federal Circuit: Review of Patent Practice & Procedure, 2 vols., Set. (Patent Law & Practice Ser.). 1973. ring bd. 280.00 (*0-8205-1261-3*) Bender.

Dunner, Peter M. Pioneer Jesuits in Northern Mexico. LC 78-10566. (Illus.). 227p. 1979. reprint ed. lib. bdg. 59.75 (*0-313-20653-8*, DUPJ, Greenwood Pr) Greenwood.

Dunnett. Understanding Economy. 1982. pap. text. write for info. (*0-582-44646-5*, Pub. by Addison-Wesley) Longman.

Dunnett, Andrew. Understanding the Economy. 2nd ed. LC 86-7197. xiii, 290p. 1987. write for info. (*0-582-44652-X*) Longman.

— Understanding the Economy. 3rd ed. LC 91-43361. xiv, 310p. 1992. write for info. (*0-582-09749-5*) Addison-Wesley.

Dunnett, Charles W., jt. auth. see Bechhofer, Robert E.

Dunnett, Dorothy. Caprice & Rondo: House of Niccolo. LC 97-49458. 592p. 1998. 27.50 (*0-679-45477-2*) Knopf.

— Caprice & Rondo: The Seventh Book of the House of Niccolo. LC 97-49458. (Illus.). 576p. 1999. pap. 15.00 (*0-375-70612-7*) Knopf.

— Checkmate. 1976. 34.95 (*0-8488-1292-1*) Amereon Ltd.

— Checkmate. 425p. 1983. lib. bdg. 39.95 (*0-89966-319-2*) Buccaneer Bks.

— Checkmate. 608p. 1997. pap. 14.00 (*0-679-77748-2*) Vin Bks.

— The Disorderly Knights. 1976. 31.95 (*0-8488-1297-2*) Amereon Ltd.

— The Disorderly Knights. LC 96-45599. 1997. pap. 14.00 (*0-679-77745-8*) Vin Bks.

— The Disorderly Knights. 334p. 1981. reprint ed. lib. bdg. 39.95 (*0-89966-295-1*) Buccaneer Bks.

— The Game of Kings. 1976. 22.95 (*0-8488-1298-0*) Amereon Ltd.

— The Game of Kings. 425p. 1983. lib. bdg. 39.95 (*0-89966-318-4*) Buccaneer Bks.

— The Game of Kings. LC 96-46867. 1997. pap. 14.00 (*0-679-77743-1*) Vin Bks.

***Dunnett, Dorothy.** Gemini. LC 00-25027. 688p. 2000. 27.50 (*0-679-45478-0*); 27.50 (*0-375-41083-X*) Knopf.

Dunnett, Dorothy. King Hereafter. LC 99-158596. 736p. 1998. pap. 16.00 (*0-375-70403-5*) Vin Bks.

— King Hereafter: A Novel. 1976. 45.95 (*0-8488-1299-9*) Amereon Ltd.

— King Hereafter: A Novel. 721p. 1991. reprint ed. lib. bdg. 44.95 (*0-89966-808-9*) Buccaneer Bks.

— Niccolo Rising: The First Book of the House of Niccolo. LC 86-45306. (House of Niccolo Series: Vol. I). 470p. 1999. pap. 15.00 (*0-375-70477-9*) Vin Bks.

— Niccolo Rising: The First Book of the House of Niccolo. 1992. reprint ed. lib. bdg. 33.95 (*0-89966-963-8*) Buccaneer Bks.

— Pawn in Frankincense. 1976. 33.95 (*0-8488-1300-6*) Amereon Ltd.

— Pawn in Frankincense. LC 96-45598. 1997. pap. 14.00 (*0-679-77746-6*) Vin Bks.

— Pawn in Frankincense. 425p. 1983. reprint ed. lib. bdg. 39.95 (*0-89966-321-4*) Buccaneer Bks.

— Queen's Play. 1976. 21.95 (*0-8488-1301-4*) Amereon Ltd.

— Queen's Play. LC 96-46882. 1997. pap. 14.00 (*0-679-77744-X*) Vin Bks.

— Queen's Play. 425p. 1983. reprint ed. lib. bdg. 39.95 (*0-89966-320-6*) Buccaneer Bks.

— Race of Scorpions: Third Book of the House of Niccolo. LC 89-45292. (House of Niccolo Series: Vol. III). 534p. 1999. pap. 15.00 (*0-375-70479-5*) Vin Bks.

— The Ringed Castle. 1976. 32.95 (*0-8488-1302-2*) Amereon Ltd.

— The Ringed Castle. LC 97-6673. 544p. 1997. pap. 14.00 (*0-679-77747-4*) Vin Bks.

— The Ringed Castle. 425p. 1983. reprint ed. lib. bdg. 39.95 (*0-89966-322-2*) Buccaneer Bks.

— Scales of Gold: Fourth Book of the House of Niccolo. (Illus.). 528p. 1999. pap. 15.00 (*0-375-70480-9*) Knopf.

— Send a Fax to the Kashbah. 1992. 21.95 (*0-15-180812-0*) Harcourt.

— The Spring of the Ram: Second Book of the House of Niccolo. LC 87-37847. Vol. II. 469p. 1999. pap. 15.00 (*0-375-70478-7*) Vin Bks.

— The Spring of the Ram: Second Book of the House of Niccolo. 1992. reprint ed. lib. bdg. 33.95 (*0-89966-964-6*) Buccaneer Bks.

***Dunnett, Dorothy.** To Lie with Lions: The Sixth Book of the House of Niccolo. (House of Niccolo Series). (Illus.). 672p. 1999. pap. 15.00 (*0-375-70482-5*) Vin Bks.

— Unicorn Hunt: The Fifth Book of the House of Niccolo. (House of Niccolo Series). 688p. 1999. pap. 15.00 (*0-375-70481-7*) Vin Bks.

Dunnett, N. G., jt. ed. see Leitner, L. M.

Dunnett, Ninian. Out on the Edge. 1999. pap. 15.00 (*0-86241-777-5*) Interlink Pub.

Dunnett, Peter J. The World Newspaper Industry. 288p. 1988. text 52.50 (*0-7099-0834-2*, Pub. by C Helm) Routldge.

***Dunnett, S. B. & Bjorklund, A., eds.** Functional Neural Transplantation 2. (Progress in Brain Research Ser.). 2000. write for info. (*0-444-50109-6*, Excerpta Medica) Elsevier.

***Dunnett, Stephen B., et al, eds.** Neural Transplantation Methods. (Neuromethods Ser.: No. 36). (Illus.). 576p. 1999. 125.00 (*0-89603-793-2*) Humana.

Dunnett, Stephen B. & Bjorklund, Anders T., eds. Functional Neural Transplantation, No. 2. LC 94-7297. (Advances in Neuroscience Ser.: Vol. 2). (Illus.). 608p. 1994. text 145.00 (*0-7817-0068-X*) Lppncott W & W.

— Neural Transplantation: A Practical Approach. (Practical Approach Ser.: Vol. 98). (Illus.). 232p. 1992. 85.00 (*0-19-963286-3*); pap. text 46.50 (*0-19-963285-5*) OUP.

***Dunnett, Walter M.** Apercu du Nouveau Testament. (Discovery Ser.).Tr. of New Testament Survey. (FRE., Illus.). 108p. 1999. pap. text. write for info. (*2-912377-03-X*, Editions SAFT) Africa Theolog Trng.

— New Testament Survey. (Discovery Ser.). Orig. Title: Broadening Your Biblical Horizons - New Testament Survey. (Illus.). 110p. 1999. pap. text. write for info. (*1-891110-02-0*, ATTS Pubns) Africa Theolog Trng.

Dunnett, Walter M. New Testament Survey: Broadening Your Biblical Horizons. LC 63-7410. 96p. 1963. pap. text 9.95 (*0-910566-03-8*) Evang Trg Assn.

— Revelation. (Survey of the Scriptures Study Guides Ser.). 1995. pap. 8.99 (*1-56570-006-6*) Meridian MI.

Dunnette. Personnel Selection & Placement. (Psychology). 1967. mass mkt. 14.75 (*0-8185-0311-4*) Brooks-Cole.

Dunnette, David A. & O'Brien, Robert J., eds. The Science of Global Change: The Impact of Human Activities on the Environment. LC 91-40724. (Symposium Ser.: No. 483). (Illus.). 506p. 1992. 99.95 (*0-8412-2197-9*) Am Chemical.

Dunnette, David A., jt. auth. see Laenen, Antonius.

Dunnette, Marvin D., et al, eds. Handbook of Industrial & Organizational Psychology, Vol. 4. 2nd ed. 896p. 1993. 89.95 (*0-89106-044-8*, 7458, Davies-Black Pub) Consulting Psychol.

Dunnette, Marvin D. & Fleishman, Edwin A., eds. Human Performance & Productivity Vols. 1-3, Set. 304p. 1982. 49.95 (*0-89859-085-X*) L Erlbaum Assocs.

Dunnette, Marvin D. & Hough, Leaetta M., eds. Handbook of Industrial & Organizational Psychology, Vol. 1. 2nd ed. 784p. 1991. 79.95 (*0-89106-041-3*, 7455, Davies-Black Pub) Consulting Psychol.

— Handbook of Industrial & Organizational Psychology, Vol. 2. 2nd ed. 984p. 1991. 89.95 (*0-89106-042-1*, 7456, Davies-Black Pub) Consulting Psychol.

— Handbook of Industrial & Organizational Psychology, Vol. 3. 2nd ed. 1120p. 1991. 89.95 (*0-89106-043-X*, 7457, Davies-Black Pub) Consulting Psychol.

Dunnewald, Ann & Sanford, Diane G. PostPartum Survival Guide. LC 94-67045. (Illus.). 288p. (Orig.). 1994. pap. 14.95 (*1-879237-80-6*) New Harbinger.

Dunnewald, Hans-Bernhard, jt. auth. see Freund, Walter.

Dunnewold, Ann L. Evaluation & Treatment of Postpartum Emotional Disorders. LC 96-47166. (Practitioner's Resource Ser.). 112p. (Orig.). 1997. pap. 17.45 (*1-56887-024-8*, ETPEBP, Prof Resc Pr) Pro Resource.

Dunnewold, Jane. Complex Cloth: A Comprehensive Guide to Surface Design. Lowe, Melissa, ed. LC 96-26494. (Illus.). 164p. (Orig.). 1996. pap. 34.95 (*1-56477-149-0*, B264, Fiber Studio Pr) Martingale & Co.

— 15 Beads: A Guide to Creating One-of-a-Kind Beads. Lowe, Melissa, ed. LC 98-18137. (Illus.). 80p. 1998. pap. 18.95 (*1-56477-214-4*, B343) Martingale & Co.

Dunney, Joseph A. Church History in the Light of the Saints. LC 74-2196. (Essay Index Reprint Ser.). 1977. reprint ed. 27.95 (*0-518-10162-2*) Ayer.

Dunnick, N. Reed. Textbook of Uroradiology. 3rd ed. 608p. text 129.95 (*0-7817-2389-2*) Lppncott W & W.

Dunnick, N. Reed & American College of Radiology Staff. Genitourinary Disease (Fifth Series) Test & Syllabus. LC 98-37827. (Professional Self-Evaluation Program Ser.). 1998. 230.00 (*1-55903-043-7*) Am Coll Radiology.

Dunnick, N. Reed, et al. Textbook of Uroradiology. (Illus.). 505p. 1990. 125.00 (*0-683-02696-8*) Lppncott W & W.

— Textbook of Uroradiology. 2nd ed. LC 96-14722. (Illus.). 650p. 1996. 125.00 (*0-683-02697-6*) Lppncott W & W.

Dunnicliff, John. Geotechnical Instrumentation for Monitoring Field Performance. 608p. 1993. pap. 99.00 (*0-471-00546-0*) Wiley.

Dunnigan, Alice A. The Fascinating Story of Black Kentuckians: Their Heritage & Tradition. (YA). 1990. 29.45 (*0-87498-088-7*); 8.00 (*0-87498-089-5*) Assoc Pubs DC.

Dunnigan, Ann, tr. see Chekhov, Anton.

Dunnigan, Ann, tr. see Ferrucci, Franco.

Dunnigan, Ann, tr. see Tolstoy, Leo.

Dunnigan, Brian L. The British Army at Mackinac, 1812-1815. Armour, David A., ed. LC 83-109767. (Reports in Mackinac History & Archaeology: No. 7). (Illus.). 56p. (Orig.). 1981. pap. 6.00 (*0-911872-40-X*) Mackinac St Hist Pks.

— Forts Within a Fort: Niagara's Redoubts. (Illus.). 104p. (Orig.). 1989. pap. 7.95 (*0-941967-08-5*) Old Fort Niagara Assn.

— A History & Guide to Old Fort Niagara. (Illus.). 72p. (Orig.). 1985. pap. 3.50 (*0-941967-01-8*) Old Fort Niagara Assn.

— King's Men at Mackinac: The British Garrisons, 1780-1796. Armour, David A., ed. LC 74-172729. (Reports in Mackinac History & Archaeology: No. 3). (Illus.). 38p. (Orig.). 1973. pap. 6.00 (*0-911872-19-1*) Mackinac St Hist Pks.

— Siege - 1759: The Campaign Against Niagara. 2nd rev. ed. (Illus.). 168p. (Orig.). 1996. pap. 14.95 (*0-941967-15-8*) Old Fort Niagara Assn.

Dunnigan, Brian L. & Scott, Patricia K. Old Fort Niagara in Four Centuries: A History of Its Development. (Illus.). 64p. (Orig.). 1991. pap. 4.50 (*0-941967-12-3*) Old Fort Niagara Assn.

Dunnigan, Brian L., ed. see Pouchot, Pierre.

***Dunnigan, Brian Leigh.** The Necessity of Regularity in Quartering Soldiers: The Organization, Material Culture & Quartering of the British Soldier at Michilimackinac. (Illus.). 80p. 1999. pap. 12.95 (*0-911872-72-8*) Mackinac St Hist Pks.

Dunnigan, J. A., ed. see California State University at Northridge, Office.

***Dunnigan, James.** Dirty Little Secrets of the Vietnam War: Military Information Your're Not Supposed to Know. 400p. 2000. pap. 15.95 (*0-312-25282-X*) St Martin.

Dunnigan, James & Masterson, Daniel. The Way of the Warrior: Business Tactics & Techniques from History's Twelve Greatest Generals. LC 97-20324. 224p. 1997. text 21.95 (*0-312-17061-0*) St Martin.

Dunnigan, James, jt. auth. see Masterson, Daniel.

Dunnigan, James F. Digital Soldiers. 336p. 1998. pap. 15.95 (*0-312-18239-2*) St Martin.

— Digital Soldiers: The Evolution of High-Tech Weaponry & Tomorrow's Brave New Battlefield. LC 96-18924. 400p. 1996. text 25.95 (*0-312-14588-8*) St Martin.

***Dunnigan, James F.** Dirty Little Secrets of the Twentieth Century. LC 99-15807. 336p. 1999. pap. 14.00 (*0-688-17068-4*, Quil) HarperTrade.

— Pap War-h to Mak. 3rd rev. ed. LC 93-6568. 1993. pap. 16.00 (*0-688-12157-8*, Wm Morrow) Morrow Avon.

Dunnigan, James F. Victory at Sea: World War II in the Pacific. 624p. 1996. pap. 16.00 (*0-688-14947-2*, Wm Morrow) Morrow Avon.

Dunnigan, James F. & Bay, Austin. A Quick & Dirty Guide to War: Briefings on Present & Potential Wars. 3rd rev. ed. (Illus.). 416p. 1991. pap. 15.00 (*0-688-10033-3*, Quil) HarperTrade.

Dunnigan, James F. & Nofi, Albert A. Dirty Little Secrets: Military Information You're Not Supposed to Know. 468p. 1992. pap. 15.00 (*0-688-11270-6*, Quil) HarperTrade.

— Dirty Little Secrets of the Vietnam War. LC 98-40892. (Thomas Dunne Bk.). 400p. 1998. text 27.50 (*0-312-19857-4*) St Martin.

— The Pacific War Encyclopedia, 2 vols. LC 97-15634. (Illus.). 800p. 1998. 125.00 (*0-8160-3439-7*, Checkmark) Facts on File.

***Dunnigan, James F. & Nofi, Albert A.** The Pacific War Encyclopedia. (Illus.). 800p. 2000. pap. 24.95 (*0-8160-4393-0*, Checkmark) Facts on File.

Dunnigan, James F. & Nofi, Albert A. Shooting Blanks: War-Making That Doesn't Work. 516p. 1995. pap. 15.00 (*0-688-14066-1*, Quil) HarperTrade.

Dunnigan, John, jt. auth. see Cooke, Ned.

Dunnigan, John P. Deep-Rooted Conflict & the IRA Cease-Fire. LC 95-17933. 126p. (Orig.). (C). 1995. 42.00 (*0-8191-9967-2*); pap. 19.50 (*0-8191-9968-0*) U Pr of Amer.

Dunnigan, Timothy & Catlin, Amy. Hmong Art: Tradition & Change. (Illus.). 168p. 1986. pap. 30.00 (*0-932718-19-1*) Kohler Arts.

Dunnigan, Timothy P. Modern Military Cadence. 228p. 1997. pap. 10.00 (*0-9679910-0-5*) Tyler Enter.

— Running with Modern Military Cadence, Vol. 2. 128p. 1999. pap. 9.00 (*0-9679910-1-3*) Tyler Enter.

— U. S. Army Awards & Decorations: A Complete Guide to Setting up Dress Uniforms & Wearing Awards. (Illus.). 55p. 1996. pap. 18.00 (*0-9679910-2-1*) Tyler Enter.

Dunnigan, William. New Blueprints for Gains in Stocks & Grains & One Way Formula for Trading in Stocks & Commodities. Mack, Donald, ed. (Traders Masterclass Ser.). 304p. 1997. 55.00 (*0-273-63096-2*) F T P-H.

Dunnihoo, Dale R. Fundamentals of Gynecology & Obstetrics. 2nd ed. LC 92-6271. (Illus.). 720p. 1992. pap. text 42.00 (*0-397-51284-8*) Lppncott W & W.

Dunnill, R. P. & Colvin, M. P. Clinical & Resuscitative Data: A Compendium of Intensive, Medical, & Anaesthetic Resuscitative Data. 5th ed. LC 97-18409. 1998. 39.95 (*0-86542-788-7*) Blackwell Sci.

Dunning. Earth Metals & Their Processes. 1993. pap. text 16.76 (*0-314-02921-4*) West Pub.

— Intro to Programmable Controllers LM. 160p. 1998. lab manual ed. 16.95 (*0-8273-7867-X*) Delmar.

— Intro to Programmable Logic Controllers. 2nd abr. rev. ed. 96p. 1998. text, teacher ed. 12.95 (*0-8273-7868-8*) Delmar.

— Let's Talk about Rocks. 1966. 5.95 (*0-87505-125-1*) Borden.

Dunning, jt. auth. see Brown.

Dunning, A. J. Extremes: Reflections on Human Behavior. LC 92-378. 1992. 19.95 (*0-15-129476-3*) Harcourt.

Dunning, Al. Reining, Completely Revised: The Guide for Training & Showing Winning Reining Horses. rev. ed. Close, Pat, ed. LC 97-100900. (Illus.). 215p. 1996. pap. 15.95 (*0-911647-39-2*) Western Horseman.

Dunning, Anthony, jt. auth. see Anderla, Georges.

Dunning, Chester S., ed. & tr. see Margeret, Jacques.

***Dunning, Chester S. L.** Russia's First Civil War: The Time of Troubles & the Founding of the Romanov Dynasty. LC 00-28817. (Illus.). 2000. write for info. (*0-271-02074-1*) Pa St U Pr.

Dunning, Chris. Courage Alone: The Italian Air Force, 1940-1943. Ketley, Barry, ed. (Illus.). 272p. 1999. 49.95 (*1-902109-02-3*, Pub. by Hikoki Pubns) Howell Pr VA.

Dunning, David, jt. auth. see Dunning, Mary.

Dunning-Davies, Jeremy. Concise Thermodynamics: Principles & Applications in Physical Science & Engineering. 150p. 1997. pap. text 29.95 (*1-898563-15-2*, Pub. by Horwood Pub) Paul & Co Pubs.

Dunning, Dianne. Cathedral Cuisine: St. Mary's Basilica Cathedral of the Assumption, Covington KY. (Illus.). 235p. 1997. 15.00 (*0-9660124-1-0*) St Marys Basilica.

Dunning, Eric. Sport Matters: Sociological Studies of Sport, Violence, & Civilisation. LC 98-47958. 1999. 85.00 (*0-415-06413-9*) Routledge.

Dunning, Eric & Rojek, Chris, eds. Sport & Leisure in the Civilizing Process: Critique & Counter-Critique. 320p. (Orig.). 1992. text 50.00 (*0-8020-2804-7*); pap. text 19.95 (*0-8020-7679-3*) U of Toronto Pr.

Dunning, Eric, tr. see Elias, Norbert.

Dunning, F. B., et al, eds. Experimental Methods in the Physical Sciences Vol. 29C: Atomic, Molecular & Optical Physics: Electromagnetic Radiation. LC 97-175575. (Illus.). 406p. (C). 1997. text 125.00 (*0-12-475977-7*) Morgan Kaufmann.

Dunning, F. B. & Hulet, Randall G., eds. Experimental Methods in the Physical Science Vol. 29B: Atomic, Molecular & Optical Physics: Atoms & Molecules, Vol. 29B. LC 96-204083. (Illus.). 435p. (C). 1996. text 99.00 (*0-12-475976-9*) Acad Pr.

— Experimental Methods in the Physical Sciences: Atomic, Molecular & Optical Physics: Charged Particles, Vol. 29A. Orig. Title: Methods of Experimental Physics. (Illus.). 463p. (C). 1995. text 104.00 (*0-12-475974-2*) Acad Pr.

Dunning, F. W., et al, eds. Mineral Deposits of Europe Vol. 2: Southeast Europe. 304p. 1982. text 98.00 (*0-900488-63-8*) IMM-North Am.

Dunning, Gary. Introduction to Programmable Logic Controllers. LC 97-39868. 448p. 1998. 61.95 (*0-8273-7866-1*) Delmar.

— Introduction to Programmable Logic Controllers. 2nd ed. (Electrical Trades Ser.). (C). 2001. pap. text 41.25 (*0-7668-1768-7*); pap. text 15.75 (*0-7668-1769-5*) Delmar.

Dunning, Glenna, jt. ed. see Johnson, Julia.

Dunning, H. Ray. Biblical Resources for Holiness Preaching Vol. 2: From Text to Sermon. 359p. 1993. boxed set 37.99 (*0-8341-1465-8*) Beacon Hill.

— Grace, Faith & Holiness: A Wesleyan Systematic Theology. 672p. 1988. 49.99 (*0-8341-1219-1*) Beacon Hill.

— A Layman's Guide to Sanctification. 96p. 1991. pap. 6.99 (*0-8341-1387-2*) Beacon Hill.

— A Layman's Guide to the Apostles' Creed. 88p. 1995. pap. 7.99 (*0-8341-1552-2*) Beacon Hill.

— Reflecting the Divine Image: Christian Ethics in Wesleyan Perspective. LC 97-45119. 156p. 1998. pap. 14.99 (*0-8308-1545-7*, 1545) InterVarsity.

— Search the Scriptures Vol. 13: Pastoral Epistles. 1958. pap. 1.99 (*0-8341-0023-1*) Beacon Hill.

— Search the Scriptures, New Testament Vol. 15: James, Peter, John, Jude. 1960. pap. 1.99 (*0-8341-0025-8*) Beacon Hill.

— Search the Scriptures, Old Testament Vol. 19: Nahum, Haggai. 1967. pap. 1.99 (*0-8341-0046-0*) Beacon Hill.

Dunning, H. Ray, ed. A Community of Faith: Celebrating the Church of Jesus Christ & Its Mission to the World. LC 97-3837. 80p. (Orig.). 1997. pap. 9.99 (*0-8341-1665-0*) Beacon Hill.

— The Second Coming: A Wesleyan Approach to the Doctrine of Last Things. 276p. (Orig.). 1995. kivar 23.99 (*0-8341-1525-5*) Beacon Hill.

Dunning, H. Ray & Wiseman, eds. Biblical Resources for Holiness Preaching, 2 vols. 2nd ed. 828p. 1993. 64.99 (*0-8341-1508-5*) Beacon Hill.

Dunning, H. Ray & Wiseman, Neil B., eds. Biblical Resources for Holiness Preaching Vol. 1: From Text to Sermon. 466p. 1990. 39.99 (*0-8341-1339-2*) Beacon Hill.

Dunning, H. Ray, jt. auth. see Greathouse, William.

Dunning, H. Ray, jt. auth. see Strickland, William J.

Dunning, Harold. Trade Unions & Migrant Workers: A Workers' Education Guide. vi, 40p. (Orig.). 1985. pap. 9.00 (*92-2-105241-9*) Intl Labour Office.

— Trade Unions & Vocational Training: A Workers' Education Guide. ii, 83p. (Orig.). 1984. pap. 9.00 (*92-2-103522-0*) Intl Labour Office.

Dunning, James B. Echoing God's Word: Formation for Catechists & Homilists in a Catechumenal Church. LC 92-32824. 313p. 1993. pap. 16.00 (*0-929650-63-8*, ECHO) Liturgy Tr Pubns.

Dunning, James M. Dental Care for Everyone: Problems & Proposals. (Illus.). 240p. 1976. 25.95 (*0-674-19790-9*) HUP.

Dunning, Jeanne. Affirmative Actions: Recognizing a Cross-Cultural Practice in Contemporary Art. 48p. (Orig.). 1993. pap. write for info. (*0-9637817-6-6*) Schl Art Inst.

***Dunning, Jennifer.** Alvin Ailey: A Life in Dance. (Illus.). 468p. 2000. reprint ed. text 30.00 (*0-7881-9089-X*) DIANE Pub.

Dunning, Jennifer. Alvin Ailey: A Life in Dance. LC 97-42644. (Illus.). 496p. 1998. reprint ed. pap. 16.95 (*0-306-80825-0*) Da Capo.

Dunning, Jennifer, et al. Great Performances: A Celebration. LC 97-36264. (Illus.). 256p. 1997. pap. 24.95 (*0-912333-55-3*) BB&T Inc.

Dunning, Joan. From the Redwood Forest: Ancient Trees & the Bottom Line: A Headwaters Journey. LC 98-26963. (Illus.). xi, 272 p. 1998. pap. 24.95 (*1-890132-11-X*) Chelsea Green Pub.

— The Loon: Voice of the Wilderness. LC 85-50055. (Illus.). 144p. 1985. 17.95 (*0-89909-080-X*, 80-950-7) Yankee Bks.

— Secrets of the Nest: The Family Life of North American Birds. (Illus.). 210p. 1999. pap. 15.95 (*0-395-71820-1*, Pub. by HM) Chelsea Green Pub.

Dunning, John. Booked to Die. large type ed. (Niagara Large Print Ser.). 420p. 1996. 27.99 (*0-7089-5836-2*) Ulverscroft.

— Booked to Die. LC 91-26889. 384p. 1993. reprint ed. mass mkt. 5.99 (*0-380-71883-9*, Avon Bks) Morrow Avon.

— The Bookman's Wake. 448p. 1996. per. 5.99 (*0-671-56782-9*) PB.

— The Bookman's Wake. 1995. 21.00 (*0-684-80003-9*) S&S Trade.

— Deadline. 1997. mass mkt. 5.99 (*0-671-00352-6*) PB.

— The Holland Suggestions. 1997. per. 6.99 (*0-671-00353-4*) PB.

— On the Air: The Encyclopedia of Old-Time Radio. LC 96-41959. 840p. 1998. 55.00 (*0-19-507678-8*) OUP.

***Dunning, John.** Two O'Clock Eastern Wartime. 2001. 26.00 (*0-7432-0195-7*) Scribner.

Dunning, John H. Alliance Captialism & Global Business. LC 96-25974. 400p. (C). 1997. 85.00 (*0-415-14828-6*) Routledge.

— American Investment in British Manufacturing Industry. Bruchey, Stuart & Bruchey, Eleanor, eds. LC 76-5004. (American Business Abroad Ser.). (Illus.). 1976. 33.95 (*0-405-09273-3*) Ayer.

— American Investment in British Manufacturing Industry. 2nd rev. ed. LC 97-47604. 360p. (C). 1998. 100.00 (*0-415-18411-8*); pap. 32.99 (*0-415-18412-6*) Routledge.

— Booked to Die: A Mystery Introducing Cliff Janeway. 288p. 1992. 19.95 (*0-684-19383-3*, Scribners Ref) Mac Lib Ref.

— The Globalization of Business. LC 92-42817. 320p. (C). 1993. pap. 31.95 (*0-415-09611-1*) Thomson Learn.

— Multinational Enterprises, Technology & Competitiveness. 350p. 1988. text 60.00 (*0-04-445175-X*) Routledge.

Dunning, John H., ed. Governments, Globalization & International Business. LC 96-52308. (Illus.). 536p. (C). 1997. text 95.00 (*0-19-829068-3*) OUP.

— Governments, Globalization & International Business. LC 99-31581. (Illus.). 536p. 1999. pap. text 29.95 (*0-19-829605-3*) OUP.

— The Multinational Enterprise. 1971. text 65.00 (*0-04-330189-4*) Routledge.

***Dunning, John H., ed.** Regions, Globalization & Knowledge-Based Economy. (Illus.). 400p. 2000. text 75.00 (*0-19-829536-7*) OUP.

Dunning, John H., ed. Theory of Transnational Corporations. (Readings in Transnational Corporations Ser.). 272p. 1996. pap. 29.95 (*0-415-14106-0*) Routledge.

— The United Nations Library on Transnational Corporations, 4 vols., Vols. 1-4, Set A. 1792p. (C). (gr. 13). 1993. text, boxed set 745.00 (*0-415-08554-3*, A9635) Routledge.

— The United Nations Library on Transnational Corporations, 4 vols., Vols. 5-8, Set B. 1590p. (C). (gr. 13). 1993. text, boxed set 745.00 (*0-415-08555-1*, A9639) Routledge.

— The United Nations Library on Transnational Corporations, 4 vols., Vols. 9-12, Set C. 1590p. (C). (gr. 13). 1993. text, boxed set 745.00 (*0-415-08556-X*, A9643) Routledge.

— The United Nations Library on Transnational Corporations, 4 vols., Vols. 13-16, Set D. LC 93-19014. 1590p. (C). (gr. 13). 1993. text, boxed set 745.00 (*0-415-08557-8*, A9647) Routledge.

— The United Nations Library on Transnational Corporations, 4 vols., Vols. 17-20, Set E. 1831p. (C). (gr. 13). 1994. text, boxed set 745.00 (*0-415-08558-6*, A9651) Routledge.

— The United Nations Library on Transnational Corporations: International Business & the Development of the World Economy, 20 vols. 8275p. (C). 1994. 3325.00 (*0-415-08559-4*, B4705) Routledge.

Dunning, John H. & Hamdani, Khalil A., eds. The New Globalism & Developing Countries. LC 99-490580. 346p. 1997. pap. 29.95 (*92-808-0944-X*, Pub. by UN Univ Pr) Brookings.

Dunning, John H. & International Trade & Finance Association Staff. Globalization, Trade, & Foreign Direct Investment. LC 98-19613. (International Business & Economics Ser.). 1998. 60.00 (*0-08-043369-3* Pergamon Pr) Elsevier.

Dunning, John H. & Narula, Rajneesh. Foreign Direct Investment & Governments: Catalysts for Economic Restructuring. LC 97-21653. (Routledge Studies in International Business & the World Economy). 455p. (C). 1998. pap. 32.99 (*0-415-17355-8*) Routledge.

Dunning, John H. & Narula, Rajneesh, eds. Foreign Direct Investment & Economic Restructuring: Catalyst for Change. LC 95-4620. (International Business Ser.). (Illus.). 480p. (C). (gr. 13). 1995. 85.00 (*0-415-11820-4*) Routledge.

Dunning, John H., jt. ed. see Boyd, Gavin.

Dunning, John S. Portraits of Tropical Birds. LC 85-24552. (Illus.). 174p. 1985. reprint ed. 30.00 (*0-915180-27-8*) Harrowood Bks.

— Retratos de Aves Tropicales. Guarnaccia, John & Villamil, Mercedes, trs. from ENG. LC 85-24553. Orig. Title: Portraits of Tropical Birds. (SPA., Illus.). 174p. 1985. 30.00 (*0-915180-28-6*) Harrowood Bks.

— South American Birds: A Photographic Aid to Identification. LC 88-6299. (Illus.). 352p. 1989. 47.50 (*0-915180-25-1*); pap. 35.00 (*0-915180-26-X*) Harrowood Bks.

Dunning, Lorry. John Deere Tractor Data Book: Two-Cylinder Models Through 1960. LC 96-29855. (Tractor Data Bks.). (Illus.). 176p. 1996. pap. 11.95 (*0-7603-0228-6*) MBI Pubg.

— Ultimate American Farm Tractor Data Book: Nebraska Test Tractors 1920-1960. LC 99-25558. (Farm Tractor Data Bk.). (Illus.). 272p. 1999. pap. 19.95 (*0-7603-0477-7*) MBI Pubg.

Dunning, Mary & Dunning, David. Good Apple & Wonderful Word Games. 144p. (J). (gr. 3-7). 1981. 13.99 (*0-86653-053-3*, GA 254) Good Apple.

Dunning, N. A., et al, eds. The Farmers' Alliance History & Agricultural Digest. LC 74-30629. (American Farmers & the Rise of Agribusiness Ser.). (Illus.). 1975. reprint ed. 78.95 (*0-405-06798-4*) Ayer.

Dunning, Pam. Riding School. 1993. pap. 18.95 (*0-8120-1883-4*) Barron.

Dunning, Phillip. Sequel to a Verdict. 1962. pap. 5.25 (*0-8222-1010-X*) Dramatists Play.

Dunning, R. W. Social & Economic Change among the Northern Ojibwa. LC 60-50269. 1959. pap. text 9.95 (*0-8020-6131-1*) U of Toronto Pr.

Dunning, R. W., ed. A History of the Counties of Somerset, Vol. 5. (Victoria History of the Counties of England Ser.). (Illus.). 256p. 1985. 135.00 (*0-19-722764-3*) OUP.

— A History of the County of Somerset: Andersfield, Cannington, & North Petherton Hundreds (Bridgwater & Neighboring Parishes), Vol. 6. (Victoria History of the Counties of England Ser.). (Illus.). 380p. 1993. 115.00 (*0-19-722780-5*) OUP.

— Somerset, Vol. IV. (Victoria History of the Counties of England Ser.). (Illus.). 286p. 1979. 110.00 (*0-19-722747-3*) OUP.

***Dunning, Robert.** The History of the County of Somerset, Vol. VII. (Illus.). 304p. 2000. text 125.00 (*0-19-722792-9*) OUP.

Dunning, Roy. Cric Crac! Teaching & Learning French Through Story-Telling. LC 97-5031. (ENG & FRE.). 180p. 1997. 79.00 (*1-85359-389-3*, Pub. by Multilingual Matters); pap. 28.95 (*1-85359-388-5*, Pub. by Multilingual Matters) Taylor & Francis.

— French for Communication, 1979-1990, Vol. 990. LC 93-29930. 190p. 1994. 69.00 (*1-85359-224-2*, Pub. by Multilingual Matters); pap. 24.95 (*1-85359-223-4*, Pub. by Multilingual Matters) Taylor & Francis.

Dunning, Stephen. Do You Fear No One. (Illus.). 32p. 1982. pap. 4.95 (*0-942908-05-8*) Pancake Pr.

Dunning, Stephen. Do You Fear No One. (Illus.). 36p. 1982. pap. 11.00 (*0-942908-13-9*) Pancake Pr.

Dunning, Stephen. Good Words. Bixby, Robert, ed. 24p. (Orig.). 1991. pap. 6.00 (*0-9624453-3-9*) March Street Pr.

— Menominee. (Illus.). (Orig.). 1987. pap. 10.00 (*0-9608802-3-2*) Years Pr.

— Running with Bill. (Illus.). 22p. (Orig.). 1985. pap. 10.00 (*0-9608802-2-4*) Years Pr.

Dunning, Stephen, et al, compiled by. Refelctions on a Gift of Watermelon Pickle & Other Modern Verse. large type ed. 1995. 50.50 (*0-614-09606-5*, L-78696-00) Am Printing Hse.

Dunning, Stephen, et al, eds. Reflections on a Gift of Watermelon Pickle & Other Modern Verse. LC 66-8763. (Illus.). 144p. (J). (gr. 7 up). 1967. 20.00 (*0-688-41231-9*) Lothrop.

Dunning, Stephen & Stafford, William. Getting the Knack: 20 Poetry Writing Exercises. LC 92-36710. 203p. (YA). 1992. 15.95 (*0-8141-1848-8*) NCTE.

Dunning, Stephen N. Dialectical Readings: Three Types of Interpretation. LC 96-34938. 1997. 45.00 (*0-271-01647-7*); pap. 19.95 (*0-271-01648-5*) Pa St U Pr.

— The Tongues of Men. LC 79-10729. (American Academy of Religion. Dissertation Ser.: No. 27). 272p. reprint ed. pap. 84.40 (*0-7837-5410-8*, 204517400005) Bks Demand.

Dunning, T. P., jt. ed. see Bliss, Alan J.

Dunning, Thom H., Jr., ed. Advances in Molecular Electronic Structure Theory, Vol. 3. Date not set. 109.50 (*1-55938-859-5*) Jai Pr.

— Advances in Molecular Electronic Structure Theory: Calculation & Characterization of Molecular Potential Energy Surfaces, Vol. 1. 275p. 1990. 109.50 (*0-89232-956-4*) Jai Pr.

— Advances in Molecular Electronic Structure Theory: Molecular Approaches to Materials Chemistry, Vol. 2. 209p. 1995. 109.50 (*0-89232-957-2*) Jai Pr.

Dunning, Trisha. Care of People with Diabetes: A Manual of Nursing Practice. LC 93-46697. 188p. 1994. pap. 26.95 (*0-632-03876-4*) Blackwell Sci.

Dunning, William A. Essays on the Civil War & Reconstruction. LC 79-37151. (Essay Index Reprint Ser.). 1977. reprint ed. 32.95 (*0-8369-2494-0*) Ayer.

— Reconstruction, Political & Economic, 1865-1877. (History - United States Ser.). 378p. 1993. reprint ed. lib. bdg. 89.00 (*0-7812-4818-3*) Rprt Serv.

Dunning, William V. Changing Images of Pictorial Space: A History of Spatial Illusion in Painting. (Illus.). 272p. (C). 1992. pap. 17.95 (*0-8156-2508-1*) Syracuse U Pr.

— The Roots of Postmodernism. LC 94-5936. 336p. (C). 1994. pap. text 35.80 (*0-13-097387-4*) P-H.

Dunning, William V. & Mahmoud, Ben. Advice to Young Artists in a Postmodern Era. LC 97-46913. 1998. 28.95 (*0-8156-0526-9*) Syracuse U Pr.

***Dunning, William V. & Mahmoud, Ben.** Advice to Young Artists in a Postmodern Era. 208p. 2000. pap. 16.95 (*0-8156-0630-3*) Syracuse U Pr.

Dunningan, James F. Dirty Little Secrets of World War II: Military Information No One Told You... (Illus.). 468p. 1996. pap. 14.00 (*0-688-12288-4*, Quil) HarperTrade.

Dunninger, J. Monument to Magic. 1974. 14.95 (*0-8184-0160-5*) Carol Pub Group.

Dunning,Jr, John B., ed. Handbook of Avian Body Masses. 384p. 1992. boxed set 104.95 (*0-8493-4258-9*, QL967) CRC Pr.

***Dunnington, A.** Easy Guide to the Reti Open. (Cadogen Chess Ser.). 1998. pap. text 18.95 (*1-85744-518-X*) Cadgn Bks.

— Ultimate Kings: Indian Attack. 1999. pap. text 22.95 (*0-7134-8222-2*) B T B.

Dunnington, Angus. The Chigorin Queen's Gambit. LC 96-78268. (New American Batsford Chess Library). 160p. 1997. pap. 20.95 (*1-879479-46-X*) ICE WA.

— How to Play the King's Indian Attack. 144p. 1995. pap. 16.95 (*0-8050-2933-8*, Pub. by Batsford Chess) H Holt & Co.

***Dunnington, Angus.** 101 Winning Chess Strategies. (Illus.). 128p. 2000. pap. 17.95 (*1-901983-22-6*, Pub. by Gambit) BHB Intl.

Dunnington, Angus. Pawn Power. 88p. 1995. pap. 11.95 (*0-8050-3578-8*, Pub. by Batsford Chess) H Holt & Co.

***Dunnington, Angus.** Winning Unorthodox Openings. 2000. pap. text 19.95 (*1-85744-285-7*) Cadgn Bks.

Dunnington, Angus. Winning with the Catalan. LC 97-71888. (Illus.). 144p. (Orig.). 1997. pap. 19.50 (*1-879479-69-9*) ICE WA.

Dunnington, Ann L. Hellcoal Annual, No. 4. 1978. pap. 3.00 (*0-916912-11-6*) Hellcoal Pr.

Dunnington, Ann L., ed. Hellcoal Annual, No. 5. 1979. pap. text 3.00 (*0-685-91298-1*) Hellcoal Pr.

— Hellcoal Review, Vol. 5, No. 1. 1978. pap. text 2.50 (*0-685-91299-X*) Hellcoal Pr.

— Prose & Poetry, Vol. 4, No. 1. 1978. pap. 2.50 (*0-916912-33-7*) Hellcoal Pr.

Dunnington, George A. History & Progress of the County of Marion: From Its Earliest Settlement by the Whites, Together with Biographical Sketches of Its Most Prominent Citizens. (Illus.). 162p. 1997. reprint ed. lib. bdg. 25.00 (*0-8328-6949-X*) Higginson Bk Co.

Dunnington, Jacqueline. Viva Guadalupe! The Virgin in New Mexican Popular Art. (Illus.). 88p. (Orig.). 1997. pap. 19.95 (*0-89013-321-2*) Museum NM Pr.

Dunnington, Jacqueline Orsini. Guadalupe: Our Lady of New Mexico. LC 99-13729. (Illus.). 128p. 1999. pap. 24.95 (*0-89013-336-0*, Pub. by Museum NM Pr) U of NM Pr.

***Dunnington, Jacqueline Orsini.** Guadalupe: Our Lady of New Mexico. (Illus.). 128p. 1999. 45.00 (*0-89013-335-2*, Pub. by Museum NM Pr) U of NM Pr.

Dunnom, D., ed. Health Effects of Synthetic Silica Particulates-STP 732. 223p. 1981. 24.00 (*0-8031-0734-X*, STP732) ASTM.

Dunnston, Mark. Paseos: Poems from Hollywood. 13p. 1998. pap. 5.00 (*0-89642-439-1*) Linden Pubs.

Dunny, Gary M., et al, eds. Genetics & Molecular Biology of Streptococci, Lactococci, & Enterococci. LC 91-2846. 318p. reprint ed. pap. 98.60 (*0-608-08636-3*, 206915900003) Bks Demand.

Dunny, Gary M. & Winans, Stephen C., eds. Cell-Cell Signaling in Bacterial. LC 98-44808. (Illus.). 328p. 1998. 89.95 (*1-55581-149-3*) ASM Pr.

Duno. Power Pups & Fat Cats. 1999. text. write for info. (*0-312-24531-9*) St Martin.

Duno, Steve. Anti-Aging for Dogs. Simon, John M., ed. LC 98-22879. 224p. 1998. pap. 16.95 (*0-312-19060-3*) St Martin.

***Duno, Steve.** Bad Dog! A Quick-Fix A-Z Problem Solver for Your Dog's Bad Behavior. 224p. 2000. pap. 5.99 (*0-312-97582-1*, St Martins Paperbacks) St Martin.

Duno, Steve. Everything Cat Book. LC 97-6929. 1997. pap. text 12.95 (*1-55850-710-8*) Adams Media.

***Duno, Steve.** The Kiss Guide to Golf. LC 99-50662. (Keep It Simple Ser.). (Illus.). 2000. 18.95 (*0-7894-5978-7*) DK Pub Inc.

— No, Kitty! A Quick-Fix A-Z Problem Solver for Your Cat's Bad Behavior. 224p. 2000. pap. 5.99 (*0-312-97581-3*, St Martins Paperbacks) St Martin.

— Plump Pups & Fat Cats. LC 99-34014. (Illus.). 208p. (ps-3). 1999. pap. 14.95 (*0-312-24436-3*) St Martin.

Duno, Steve, jt. auth. see Baer, Nancy.

Duno, Steve, jt. auth. see Simon, John.

Dunod Staff. Dictionnaire des Composants Electroniques. (FRE.). 256p. 1994. pap. 75.00 (*0-7859-7730-9*, 2100012932) Fr & Eur.

D

An Asterisk (*) at the beginning of an entry indicates that the title is appearing for the first time.

Dunon, D., et al, eds. Adhesion in Leukocyte Homing & Differentiation. (Current Topics in Microbiology & Immunology Ser.: Vol. 184). (Illus.). 260p. 1993. write for info. (*3-540-56756-9*) Spr-Verlag.

Dunon, D., et al. Adhesion in Leukocyte Homing & Differentiation. (Current Topics in Microbiology & Immunology Ser.: Vol. 184). 230p. 1993. 150.95 (*0-387-56756-9*) Spr-Verlag.

***DuNour, Shlomo.** Adiel. 2000. write for info. (*1-902881-32-X*, Pub. by Toby Pr Ltd); pap. 15.95 (*1-902881-33-8*, Pub. by Toby Pr Ltd) Toby Pr.

Dunoyer, Alphonse. The Public Prosecutor of the Terror: Antoine Quentin Fouquier-Tinville. 1977. lib. bdg. 59.95 (*0-8490-2489-7*) Gordon Pr.

Dunoyer, Cecilia. Marguerite Long: A Life in French Music, 1874-1966. LC 93-9354. (Illus.). 1993. 29.95 (*0-253-31839-4*) Ind U Pr.

Dunphy. Volleyball Today. Date not set. pap. text, teacher ed. write for info. (*0-314-91108-1*) West Pub.

Dunphy, A. Working Drawings for Residential Interior. 1991. pap. write for info. (*0-442-00388-9*, VNR) Wiley.

Dunphy, Alicia, ed. see Roberts, Paul.

Dunphy, Catherine. Blt. (Degrassi Book Ser.). 164p. (J). (gr. 6-9). 1995. pap. 4.95 (*1-55028-372-3*); bds. 16.95 (*1-55028-374-X*) Formac Dist Ltd.

— Caitlin. (Degrassi Book Ser.). 159p. (J). (gr. 6-9). 1995. mass mkt. 4.95 (*1-55028-255-7*); bds. 16.95 (*1-55028-253-0*) Formac Dist Ltd.

***Dunphy, Dexter & Griffiths, Andrew.** The Sustainable Corporation: Organisational Renewal in Australia. LC 98-201819. 256p. 1999. pap. 24.95 (*1-86448-752-6*, Pub. by Allen & Unwin Pty) Paul & Co Pubs.

Dunphy, Eamon. Only a Game: The Diary of a Professional Footballer. 224p. pap. 13.95 (*0-14-010290-6*, Pub. by Pnguin Bks Ltd) Trafalgar.

Dunphy, Edward P. The UNIX Industry & Open Systems in Transition: A Guidebook to Managing Change. 2nd ed. 616p. 1994. 39.95 (*0-471-60608-1*) Wiley.

Dunphy, Jack. John Fury: A Novel in Four Parts. LC 76-6338. (Irish Americans Ser.). 1976. reprint ed. 25.95 (*0-405-09333-0*) Ayer.

Dunphy, Joan S., jt. auth. see Ferguson, Trudi.

Dunphy, Joan S., ed. see Balsamo, William & Carpozi, George, Jr.

Dunphy, Joan S., ed. see Dicks, Shirley.

Dunphy, Joan S., ed. see Gediman, Judith S. & Brown, Linda P.

Dunphy, Joan S., ed. see O'Leary, K. Daniel.

Dunphy, Joan S., ed. see Weiner, Marcella B. & Starr, Bernard D.

***Dunphy, Lynn M. & Winland-Brown, Jill E.** Primary Care: The Art & Science of Advanced Practice Nursing. 2000. text 99.00 (*0-8036-0589-7*) Davis Co.

Dunphy, Lynne M., jt. auth. see Winland-Brown, Jill E.

Dunphy, Lynne M. Hektor, see Hektor Dunphy, Lynne M.

Dunphy, Madeleine. Here Is the African Savanna. LC 98-30007. (Illus.). 32p. (J). 1999. lib. bdg. 14.99 (*0-7868-2134-5*, Pub. by Hyperion) Little.

— Here is the African Savanna. LC 98-30007. 32p. (J). 1999. 14.99 (*0-7868-0162-X*, Pub. by Hyperion) Time Warner.

— Here Is the Arctic Winter. LC 92-72022. (Illus.). 32p. (J). (ps-3). 1993. lib. bdg. 14.89 (*1-56282-337-X*, Pub. by Hyprn Child) Little.

Dunphy, Madeleine. Here Is the Arctic Winter. LC 92-72022. (Illus.). 32p. (J). (ps-3). 1993. 14.95 (*1-56282-336-1*, Pub. by Hyprn Child) Time Warner.

Dunphy, Madeleine. Here Is the Coral Reef. LC 97-20886. (Illus.). 32p. (J). (ps-3). 1998. 14.95 (*0-7868-0163-8*, Pub. by Hyprn Child) Time Warner.

— Here Is the Tropical Rain Forest. (Here is Ser.). (J). 1997. 11.15 (*0-606-13476-X*, Pub. by Turtleback) Demco.

— Here Is the Tropical Rain Forest. LC 93-24850. (Illus.). 32p. (J). (ps-3). 1997. reprint ed. pap. 5.95 (*0-7868-1212-5*, Pub. by Hyprn Ppbks) Little.

— Here Is the Tropical Rainforest. LC 93-24850. (Illus.). 32p. (J). (ps-3). 1994. 14.95 (*1-56282-636-0*, Pub. by Hyprn Child) Little.

— Here Is the Wetland. LC 95-37206. (Illus.). 32p. (J). (ps-3). 1996. 14.95 (*0-7868-0164-6*, Pub. by Hyprn Child); lib. bdg. 14.89 (*0-7868-2136-1*, Pub. by Hyprn Child) Little.

Dunphy, Madeleine, ed. Here Is the Coral Reef. LC 97-20886. (Illus.). 32p. (J). (ps-3). 1998. lib. bdg. 15.49 (*0-7868-2135-3*, Pub. by Hyprn Child) Little.

Dunphy, Marv & Wilde, Rod. Volleyball Today. Perlee, Clyde, ed. 223p. (C). 1991. pap. 19.25 (*0-314-83711-6*) West Pub.

***Dunphy, Michael J.** The Kids' Karate Book & Karate Belt. LC 99-13138. (Illus.). 128p. (J). (gr. 3-6). 1999. pap. 12.95 (*0-7611-1609-5*) Workman Pub.

Dunphy, Paul, ed. see Green, Douglas.

Dunphy, Philip W., ed. Career Development for the College Student. 5th ed. LC 80-26933. 128p. 1981. pap. 7.50 (*0-910328-02-1*) Sulzburger & Graham Pub.

Dunphy, R. Graeme, tr. see Seybold, Klaus.

Dunphy, Richard. The Making of Fianna Fail Power in Ireland, 1923-1948. 356p. 1995. text 75.00 (*0-19-820474-4*) OUP.

Dunphy, Robert T. Moving Beyond Gridlock: Traffic & Development. LC 96-61394: (Illus.). 180p. (Orig.). 1996. pap. 45.95 (*0-87420-803-3*, T03) Urban Land.

— Twelve Tools for Improving Mobility & Managing Congestion. 1991. pap. text 24.95 (*0-87420-718-5*, T11) Urban Land.

Dunphy, Robert T. & Lin, Ben C. Transportation Management Through Partnerships. LC 89-52210. 224p. 1991. 45.95 (*0-87420-698-7*, T10) Urban Land.

Dunphy, Robert T., et al. Transportation & Growth: Myth & Fact. 16p. 1996. pap. text 12.95 (*0-87420-788-6*, T15) Urban Land.

Dunphy, Thomas & Cummins, Thomas J., compiled by. Remarkable Trials of All Countries: Particularly of the United States, Great Britain, Ireland & France: With Notes & Speeches of Counsel. Containing Thrilling Narratives of Fact from the Court-Room, Also Historical Reminiscences of Wonderful Events. vi, 464p. 1981. reprint ed. lib. bdg. 68.00 (*0-8377-0512-6*, Rothman) W S Hein.

***Dunphy, Wilde.** Volleyball Today. 2nd ed. LC 99-33874. (Health Sciences Ser.). 1999. 29.95 (*0-534-35836-5*) Wadsworth Pub.

Dunpont, Marc. Walking Out of Spiritual Abuse. 192p. 12.99 (*1-85240-219-9*, Pub. by SOV5) R G Mitchell Bks.

Dunraven, Windham T. The Great Divide: Travels in the Upper Yellowstone in the Summer of 1874. LC 67-26059. (Illus.). 423p. reprint ed. pap. 131.20 (*0-608-16036-9*, 203313600084) Bks Demand.

Dunrea, Oliver. Essie & Miles. text. write for info. (*0-374-39992-1*) FS&G.

Dunrea, Oliver. The Painter Who Loved Chickens. LC 94-27562. (Illus.). 32p. (J). (ps-3). 1995. 15.00 (*0-374-35729-3*) FS&G.

Dunrea, Olivier. Appearing Tonight! Mary Heather Elizabeth Livingstone. LC 98-13094. (Illus.). 32p. (J). (ps-3). 2000. text 15.00 (*0-374-30455-6*) FS&G.

***Dunrea, Olivier.** Bear Noel. LC 99-27600. (Illus.). 32p. (J). (ps-3). 2001. 16.00 (*0-374-39990-5*) FS&G.

Dunrea, Olivier. Eppie M. Says... LC 89-8134. (Illus.). 32p. (J). (ps-2). 1990. lib. bdg. 14.95 (*0-02-733205-5*, Mac Bks Young Read) S&S Childrens.

— Noggin & Boggin in the Garden. 2nd ed. (Let Me Read Ser.). (Illus.). 16p. (J). (ps-1). 1995. pap. 2.95 (*0-673-36237-X*, GoodYrBooks) Addson-Wesley Educ.

— The Painter Who Loved Chickens. LC 94-4243. (J). (gr. 2 up). 1995. text 14.95 (*0-02-733209-8*, Mac Bks Young Read) S&S Childrens.

— Painter Who Loved Chickens. (Illus.). 32p. (gr. k-3). 1998. pap. text 5.95 (*0-374-45708-5*) FS&G.

— Painter Who Loved Chickens. 1998. 11.15 (*0-606-13693-2*, Pub. by Turtleback) Demco.

— The Tale of Hilda Louise. LC 95-33511. 32p. (J). (ps-3). 1996. 16.00 (*0-374-37380-9*) FS&G.

— The Trow-Wife's Treasure. LC 96-24030. 32p. (J). (ps-3). 1998. 16.00 (*0-374-37792-8*) FS&G.

— The Writing Process: One Writer's Approach to Writing with Children. Heltshe, Mary A., ed. (Illus.). 72p. (C). 1990. pap. 11.50 (*0-9627288-0-2*) Stonetrow Studio.

***Dunrud, C. Richard.** Engineering Geology Applied to the Design & Operation of Underground Coal Mines. (Illus.). 134p. 2000. pap. text 30.00 (*0-7881-8739-2*) DIANE Pub.

Dunrud, Carl M., et al. Let's Go! 85 Years of Adventure. (Illus.). 112p. 1998. pap. 19.95 (*0-9652942-1-8*) WordsWorth.

Duns, J. & Davison, M. Trade Practices & Consumer Protection: Cases & Materials. LC 95-166227. 700p. 1994. pap. write for info. (*0-409-30421-2*, MICHIE) LEXIS Pub.

Dun's Marketing Services Staff. Top Fifty Thousand Companies. 1988. 350.00 (*0-918257-19-0*) Dun & Bradstreet.

Duns, Scotus John. Duns Scotus on the Will & Morality. Frank, William A., ed. Wolter, Allan B., tr. from LAT. LC 97-2325. 340p. 1997. pap. text 24.95 (*0-8132-0895-5*) Cath U Pr.

— Duns Scotus on the Will & Morality. Wolter, Allan B., tr. & selected by by. LC 85-14907. 553p. 1986. reprint ed. pap. 171.50 (*0-7837-9193-3*, 204989400004) Bks Demand.

Dunsany, Edward J. Book of Wonder. LC 72-6079. (Short Story Index Reprint Ser.). 1977. reprint ed. 21.95 (*0-8369-4213-2*) Ayer.

— The Curse of the Wise Woman. 315p. reprint ed. lib. bdg. 24.95 (*0-88411-650-6*) Amereon Ltd.

— A Dreamer's Tales. LC 70-101803. (Short Story Index Reprint Ser.). 1977. 29.95 (*0-8369-3191-2*) Ayer.

— The Glittering Gate. LC 94-20190. 1994. pap. 5.00 (*0-88734-323-6*) Players Pr.

— Last Book of Wonder. LC 76-101282. (Short Story Index Reprint Ser.). (Illus.). 1977. 18.95 (*0-8369-3219-6*) Ayer.

— The Lost Silk Hat. LC 94-20189. 1994. pap. 5.00 (*0-88734-335-X*) Players Pr.

— Time & the Gods. LC 76-113659. (Short Story Index Reprint Ser.). 1977. 18.95 (*0-8369-3388-5*) Ayer.

Dunsany, Lord. The Charwoman's Shadow. 1999. pap. 12.00 (*0-345-43192-8*, Del Rey) Ballantine Pub Grp.

— The Fourth Book of Jorkens. 1994. reprint ed. lib. bdg. 29.95 (*1-56849-275-8*) Buccaneer Bks.

— Ghosts of the Heaviside Layer & other fantasms. (Illus.). x, 354 p. 1980. 20.00 (*0-913896-14-4*) Owlswick Pr.

— The Gods of the Mountain. LC 94-19076. 1994. pap. 5.00 (*0-88734-332-5*) Players Pr.

— The Hashish Man & Other Stories. LC 96-45809. 160p. (Orig.). 1996. pap. 11.95 (*0-916397-45-9*) Manic D Pr.

— A Night at an Inn. unabridged ed. Landes, William-Alan, ed. LC 97-10228. 55p. (Orig.). 1997. pap. 5.00 (*0-88734-398-8*) Players Pr.

— Tales of Three Hemispheres. LC 76-8950. (Illus.). 130p. 1976. 15.50 (*0-913896-04-7*) Owlswick Pr.

Dunsby, Jonathan. Performing Music: Shared Concerns. (Illus.). 112p. 1996. reprint ed. pap. text 13.95 (*0-19-816642-7*) OUP.

Dunsby, Jonathan M. Structural Ambiguity in Brahms: Analytical Approaches to Four Works. Fortune, Nigel, ed. LC 81-24. (Studies in British Musicology). 128p. 1981. reprint ed. pap. 39.70 (*0-8357-1159-5*, 207003300063) Bks Demand.

Dunscomb, J. Richard, ed. see Norberg, John.

Dunscomb, S. Whitney, Jr. Bankruptcy: A Study in Comparative Legislation. LC 78-82250. (Columbia University. Studies in the Social Sciences: No. 6). reprint ed. 29.50 (*0-404-51006-X*) AMS Pr.

Dunsdorfs, Edgars. The Baltic Dilemma. 15.00 (*0-8315-0148-0*) Speller.

***Dunseath, Kirsty.** A Second Skin: Women Write about Clothes. 1999. pap. 13.95 (*0-7043-4588-9*, Pub. by Womens Press) Trafalgar.

Dunselman, Ron. In Place of the Self: How Drugs Work. Langham, Tony & Peters, Plym, trs. (Illus.). 304p. 1995. 43.95 (*1-869890-72-8*, Pub. by Hawthorn Press) Anthroposophic.

Dunseny, Edward J. The Golden Doom. LC 94-17622. 1994. pap. 5.00 (*0-88734-322-8*) Players Pr.

— King Argimenes & the Unknown Warrior. Landes, William-Alan, ed. & intro. by. LC 94-16747. 1994. pap. 5.00 (*0-88734-333-3*) Players Pr.

Dunseth, Joyce S. Teddy Bear Dreams: A Children's Story. (Illus.). 32p. (J). 1992. pap. 14.00 (*1-882792-00-9*) Proctor Pubns.

Dunseth, Ric. Selecting Wines for Food. 160p. (Orig.). 1997. pap. 12.95 (*1-56550-064-4*) Vis Bks Intl.

Dunsford, Cathie. Cowrie. 123p. 1994. pap. 12.95 (*1-875559-28-0*, Pub. by SpiniFex Pr) LPC InBook.

Dunsing, Richard J. You & I Have Simply Got to Stop Meeting This Way. enl. ed. LC 78-2516. 172p. reprint ed. pap. 53.40 (*0-608-15491-1*, 202967700062) Bks Demand.

Dunskaya, Irina. Security Practices at Soviet Scientific Research Facilities. Dash, Barbara, ed. 143p. (Orig.). 1983. pap. text 75.00 (*1-55831-007-X*) Delphic Associates.

Dunsker, Eric. Surfing the Stock Market. Date not set. pap. 18.00 (*0-9667766-0-7*) Haimish Pr.

Dunsker, Stewart B. Anterior Cervical Spine Surgery. Whitecloud, Thomas S., III, ed. LC 93-18054. (Principles & Techniques in Spine Surgery Ser.). 160p. 1993. text 105.00 (*0-7817-0050-7*) Lppncott W & W.

Dunsker, Stewart B., ed. Cervical Spondylosis - Sponsored by the Subcommittee on Continuing Education II (Expanded Program), American Association of Neurological Surgeons, & Congress of Neurological Surgeons. fac. ed. LC 79-5395. (Seminars in Neurological Surgery Ser.). (Illus.). 229p. pap. 71.00 (*0-7837-7229-7*, 204706900005) Bks Demand.

Dunsmore, Donald J. Safety Measures for Use in Outbreaks of Communicable Disease. 99p. 1986. pap. text 17.00 (*92-4-154206-3*, 1150250) World Health.

Dunsmore, H. E., jt. auth. see Theobald, William.

***Dunsmore, H.E. & Theobald, William.** Internet Resources for Leisure & Tourism. 2nd ed. 300p. 1999. pap. text 59.95 (*981-00-9329-2*) Buttrwrth-Heinemann.

Dunsmore, Lillian D. & Dunsmore, Richard A. The Shredding of Families. 100p. (Orig.). 1994. pap. 14.00 (*0-9640590-0-2*) Fallowfield.

Dunsmore, Richard A., jt. auth. see Dunsmore, Lillian D.

Dunsmore, Rikki, jt. auth. see Maragos, James E.

Dunsmore, Roger, et al. Earth's Mind: Essays in Native Literature. LC 97-4872. 227p. 1997. pap. 17.95 (*0-8263-1798-7*) U of NM Pr.

Dunsmore, S. Nepalese Textiles. (Illus.). 204p. 1994. pap. 35.00 (*0-7141-2510-5*) U of Wash Pr.

Dunsmuir, Tom. The Cure for the Meanies, No. 2. LC 97-40953. (J). 1998. pap. 3.25 (*0-679-89121-8*, Pub. by Random Bks Yng Read) Random.

— The Queen's New Clothes, No. 1. LC 97-40955. (J). 1998. pap. 3.25 (*0-679-89120-X*, Pub. by Random Bks Yng Read) Random.

Dunson, Josh. Freedom in the Air: Song Movements of the Sixties. LC 80-11678. 127p. 1980. reprint ed. lib. bdg. 38.50 (*0-313-22393-9*, DUFA, Greenwood Pr) Greenwood.

Dunson, Miriam. A Very Present Help: Psalm Studies for Older Adults. LC 99-23298. 100p. 1999. pap. 10.95 (*0-664-50034-X*) Geneva Press.

Dunson, Mirlam S. Facing Forward in Older Adult Ministry: Resources for the Congregation. (Older Adult Issues Ser.). 50p. 1999. pap. 4.50 (*0-664-50089-7*) Geneva Press.

Dunst, Carl. Key Characteristics & Features of Family Support Programs. (Guidelines for Effective Practice Ser.). (Orig.). 1995. pap. 7.00 (*1-885429-10-X*) Family Resource.

Dunst, Carl J., et al, eds. Supporting & Strengthening Families: Methods, Strategies & Practices. LC 93-50893. 252p. 1994. pap. 30.00 (*0-914797-94-8*) Brookline Bks.

Dunst, Carl J., et al. Enabling & Empowering Families: Principles & Guidelines for Practice. (Illus.). 220p. 1989. pap. 24.95 (*0-914797-59-X*) Brookline Bks.

Dunst, J. Late Sequelae in Oncology. 250p. 1995. 145.00 (*0-387-56936-7*) Spr-Verlag.

Dunst, J. & Sauer, R., eds. Late Sequelae in Oncology. LC 94-45370. (Medical Radiology Ser.). 1995. write for info. (*3-540-56936-7*) Spr-Verlag.

Dunstan. A Primer of Veterinary Anatomic. 1993. write for info. (*0-397-51102-7*) Lppncott W & W.

***Dunstan.** Warrior Company: Europa Militaria #25. 64p. 2000. pap. 19.95 (*1-86126-191-8*, Pub. by Cro1wood) Motorbooks Intl.

Dunstan, A. C., ed. see Carey, Elizabeth.

Dunstan, Bob. The Book of Falmouth & Penryn. 1977. 40.00 (*0-86023-002-3*) St Mut.

Dunstan, F. & Pickles, J., eds. Statistics in Medicine. (Institute of Mathematics & Its Applications Conference Series, New Ser.: New Series 29). (Illus.). 288p. 1991. text 79.00 (*0-19-853662-3*) OUP.

Dunstan, G. R., ed. The Human Embryo: Aristotle & the Arabic & European Traditions. (Illus.). 248p. 1990. text 59.00 (*0-85989-340-5*, Pub. by Univ Exeter Pr) Northwestern U Pr.

Dunstan, G. R. & Maruice, F. D. Science & Sensibility. 1982. 30.00 (*0-7855-1116-4*) St Mut.

Dunstan, G. R. & Shinebourne, Elliot A., eds. Doctors' Decisions: Ethical Conflicts in Medical Practice. (Illus.). 264p. 1989. 52.00 (*0-19-261631-5*) OUP.

Dunstan, Helen. Conflicting Counsels to Confuse the Age: A Documentary Study of Political Economy in Qing China, 1644-1840. LC 95-46073. (Michigan Monographs in Chinese Studies: No. 73). 1996. text 50.00 (*0-89264-115-0*) Ctr Chinese Studies.

Dunstan, Jeffrey, jt. auth. see Chapman, Judith D.

Dunstan, John. Soviet Schooling in the Second World War. LC 96-43240. 256p. 1997. text 65.00 (*0-312-16601-X*) St Martin.

— V. N. Soroka-Rosinsky (1882-1960), Soviet Teacher, In Fact & Fiction: The Double Exposure of Vikniksor. LC 91-14083. (Slavic Studies: Vol. 2). 140p. 1991. lib. bdg. 69.95 (*0-7734-9779-X*) E Mellen.

Dunstan, Peta & Tristam, eds. Anglican Religious Communities Year Book. 160p. 1998. pap. 7.95 (*0-88028-199-5*, 1479) Forward Movement.

Dunstan, Phyllis, et al. Friendship Fun! LC 97-222301. (Illus.). 48p. (J). 1997. write for info. (*0-7853-2324-4*) Pubns Intl Ltd.

Dunstan, Ralph. A Cyclopaedic Dictionary of Music. LC 72-14060. 642p. 1973. reprint ed. lib. bdg. 85.00 (*0-306-70559-1*) Da Capo.

— Cyclopaedic Dictionary of Music. 4th ed. 632p. 1993. reprint ed. lib. bdg. 149.00 (*0-7812-9710-9*) Rprt Serv.

***Dunstan, Roger.** Construction Defect Litigation & the Condominium Market, Vol. 7. 9p. 1999. pap. write for info. (*1-58703-117-5*, CRB Note 6) CA St Libry.

— Gambling in California. 137p. 1997. pap. write for info. (*1-58703-060-8*) CA St Libry.

— Indian Casinos in California. 28p. 1998. pap. write for info. (*1-58703-094-2*, CRB-98-015) CA St Libry.

— Local Government Revenue & Expenditures since Proposition 13: A Historical Primer. 31p. 1993. pap. write for info. (*1-58703-012-8*, CRB-93-006) CA St Libry.

— Overview of New York City's Fiscal Crisis. 10p. 1995. pap. write for info. (*1-58703-033-0*) CA St Libry.

Dunstan, Simon. British Armoured Cars. (Orig.). 1990. pap. 29.00 (*1-85368-994-7*, Pub. by New5 Holland) St Mut.

— Challenger Main Battle Tank. (Illus.). 48p. 1996. pap. 12.95 (*1-85532-485-7*, Pub. by Ospry) Stackpole.

***Dunstan, Simon.** Challenger Squadron. (Europa Militaria Ser.: Vol. 29). (Illus.). 64p. 2000. 19.95 (*1-86126-301-5*, 129767AE, Pub. by Cro1wood) Motorbooks Intl.

Dunstan, Simon. Flak Jackets: Twentieth Century Military Body Armour. (Men-at-Arms Ser.: No. 157). (Illus.). 48p. pap. 11.95 (*0-85045-569-3*, 9089, Pub. by Ospry) Stackpole.

— Guards: The British Army's Household Division. 1996. pap. text 16.95 (*1-85915-062-4*, Pub. by Windrow & Green) Motorbooks Intl.

— Warrior Company. (Europa Militaria Ser.). (Illus.). 64p. 1998. pap. 16.95 (*1-85915-079-9*, Pub. by Windrow & Green) Motorbooks Intl.

Dunstan, Stephen. Tarot Poems. 56p. 1980. pap. 9.95 (*0-906427-10-X*, Pub. by Bloodaxe Bks) Dufour.

Dunstan, William E. The Ancient Near East, Vol. 1. LC 97-71994. 352p. (C). 1997. text 44.00 (*0-03-035299-1*, Pub. by Harcourt Coll Pubs) Harcourt.

Dunstedter, Deborah W. Flying Dreams. (Illus.). 69p. 1998. 19.95 (*1-882935-26-8*) Westphalia.

Dunsten, Mark. Brouhahas: Poems from Hollywood. 11p. 1998. pap. 5.00 (*0-89642-583-5*) Linden Pubs.

— California Dreams: Poems From Hollywood. 11p. 1998. pap. 5.00 (*0-89642-600-9*) Linden Pubs.

— Communion: Poems from Hollywood. 11p. 1998. pap. 5.00 (*0-89642-603-3*) Linden Pubs.

— Episodes of Winds: Poems from Hollywood. 11p. 1998. pap. write for info. (*0-89642-604-1*) Linden Pubs.

***Dunsten, Mark.** Fizz: Poems from Holywood. 11p. (Orig.). 1999. pap. 5.00 (*0-89642-717-X*) Linden Pubs.

Dunsten, Mark. Fugues: Poems from Hollywood. 11p. 1999. pap. 5.00 (*0-89642-649-1*) Linden Pub.

***Dunsten, Mark.** In Our Time: Poems from Hollywood. 11p. 1999. pap. 5.00 (*0-89642-843-5*) Linden Pubs.

— Interludes: Poems from Hollywood. 11p. (Orig.). 1999. pap. 5.00 (*0-89642-716-1*) Linden Pubs.

Dunsten, Mark. Pavanes: Poems from Hollywood. 11p. 1998. pap. 5.00 (*0-89642-582-7*) Linden Pubs.

— Radiance: Poems from Hollywood. 11p. 1999. pap. 5.00 (*0-89642-647-5*) Linden Pub.

— Ragbook: Poems from Hollywood. 11p. 1998. pap. 5.00 (*0-89642-601-7*) Linden Pubs.

— Rollick: Poems from Hollywood. 19p. 1998. pap. 5.00 (*0-89642-394-8*) Linden Pubs.

— Songtime: Poems from Hollywood. 11p. 1998. pap. 5.00 (*0-89642-602-5*) Linden Pubs.

— Sprints: Poems from Hollywood. 11p. 1998. pap. 5.00 (*0-89642-581-9*) Linden Pubs.

— Strudel: Poems from Hollywood. 21p. 1998. pap. 5.00 (*0-89642-396-4*) Linden Pubs.

***Dunsten, Mark.** Syllabub: Poems from Hollywood. 11p. 1999. pap. 5.00 (*0-89642-845-1*) Linden Pubs.

— Themes: Poems from Hollywood. 11p. (Orig.). 1999. pap. 5.00 (*0-89642-718-8*) Linden Pubs.

Dunsten, Mark. Tweaks: Poems from Hollywood. 11p. 1999. pap. 5.00 (*0-89642-648-3*) Linden Pub.

***Dunsten, Mark.** Yearns: Poems from Hollywood. 11p. 1999. pap. 5.00 (*0-89642-844-3*) Linden Pubs.

Dunsten, Mark. Yolks: Poems From Hollywood. 11p. 1998. pap. 5.00 (*0-89642-599-1*) Linden Pubs.

Dunsten, Mark, jt. auth. see Whitecap Books Staff.

Dunster, Charles, jt. auth. see Meadowcourt, Richard.

Dunster, D. Arups on Engineering. 289p. 1996. 175.00 (*3-433-02637-8*) Wiley.

An Asterisk (*) at the beginning of an entry indicates that the title is appearing for the first time.

Dunster, David. Key Buildings of the Twentieth Century Vol. 1: Houses, 1900-1944. LC 85-42945. (Illus.). 107p. 1985. reprint ed. pap. 33.20 (*0-608-04404-0*, 206518600001) Bks Demand.
— Key Buildings of the Twentieth Century Vol. 2: Houses, 1945-1989. (Illus.). 104p. 1990. pap. text 54.95 (*0-408-50029-8*) Buttrwrth-Heinemann.
— Key Buildings of the Twentieth Century Vol. 2: Houses, 1945-1989. LC 85-42945. (Illus.). 121p. 1990. reprint ed. pap. 34.50 (*0-608-04405-9*, 2065186) Bks Demand.
Dunster, David, et al. Robert Stern: An Architectural Monograph. (Illus.). 124p. pap. 24.95 (*0-312-68755-9*) St Martin.
Dunster, David, jt. auth. see Scully, Vincent.
Dunster, Julian. Arboriculture & the Law in Canada. McCullem, Emily, ed. 227p. (C). 1997. pap. text 45.00 (*1-881956-19-9*) Int Soc Arboricult.
Dunster, Julian & Dunster, Katherine. Dictionary of Natural Resource Management. LC 96-158111. (Illus.). 379p. 1996. 90.00 (*0-7748-0503-X*, S922) U of Wash Pr.
Dunster, Katherine, jt. auth. see Dunster, Julian.
Dunster, Mark. Aberdare. 23p. (Orig.). 1995. pap. 5.00 (*0-89642-278-X*) Linden Pubs.
— Ace. 26p. (Orig.). 1985. pap. 4.00 (*0-89642-126-0*) Linden Pubs.
— Advances: Poems from Hollywood. 11p. 1999. pap. 5.00 (*0-89642-785-4*) Linden Pubs.
— Advantages: Poems from Hollywood. 14p. 1998. pap. 5.00 (*0-89642-456-1*) Linden Pubs.
— Advertising. 12p. (Orig.). 1991. pap. 4.00 (*0-89642-201-1*) Linden Pubs.
— Agathon's Supper. 14p. (Orig.). 1993. pap. 4.00 (*0-89642-216-X*) Linden Pubs.
— Ahmed. 25p. (Orig.). 1986. pap. 4.00 (*0-89642-140-6*) Linden Pubs.
***Dunster, Mark.** Alarms: Poems from Hollywood. 11p. 1999. pap. 5.00 (*0-89642-729-3*) Linden Pubs.
— Alembic: Poems from Hollywood. 11p. 2000. pap. 5.00 (*0-89642-991-1*) Linden Pubs.
Dunster, Mark. Alerts: Poems from Hollywood. 11p. 1999. pap. 5.00 (*0-89642-657-2*) Linden Pubs.
— Aliment: Poems from Hollywood. 11p. 1998. pap. 5.00 (*0-89642-486-3*) Linden Pubs.
— Aliquots: Poems from Hollywood. 11p. 1998. pap. 5.00 (*0-89642-535-5*) Linden Pubs.
— Allegations: Poems from Hollywood. 11p. 1999. pap. 5.00 (*0-89642-781-1*) Linden Pubs.
***Dunster, Mark.** Allegrettos: Poems from Hollywood. 11p. 1999. pap. 5.00 (*0-89642-896-6*) Linden Pubs.
Dunster, Mark. Aloes: Poems from Hollywood. 63p. (Orig.). 1985. pap. 6.00 (*0-89642-119-8*) Linden Pubs.
— Amleth. 1979. pap. 4.00 (*0-89642-056-6*) Linden Pubs.
— Amphitryon. 11p. (Orig.). 1993. pap. 4.00 (*0-89642-223-2*) Linden Pubs.
— Ana: Poems from Hollywood. 11p. 1999. pap. 5.00 (*0-89642-633-5*) Linden Pubs.
— Analects: Poems From Hollywood. 11p. 1998. pap. 5.00 (*0-89642-562-2*) Linden Pubs.
— Analgesics: Poems from Hollywood. 23p. 1998. pap. 5.00 (*0-89642-434-0*) Linden Pubs.
— Anchors: Poems from Hollywood. 11p. 1999. pap. 5.00 (*0-89642-782-X*) Linden Pubs.
***Dunster, Mark.** And So On: Poems from Hollywood. 11p. 1999. pap. write for info. (*0-89642-664-5*) Linden Pubs.
Dunster, Mark. And Then Some: Poems from Hollywood. 11p. 1999. pap. 5.00 (*0-89642-668-8*) Linden Pubs.
— Andronicus. 19p. (Orig.). (YA). (gr. 9-12). 1996. pap. 5.00 (*0-89642-297-6*) Linden Pubs.
— Angel. 1972. 4.00 (*0-89642-011-6*) Linden Pubs.
— Animal Tales. 9p. (Orig.). 1989. pap. 4.00 (*0-89642-172-4*) Linden Pubs.
***Dunster, Mark.** Anthems: Poems from Hollywood. 11p. 1999. pap. 5.00 (*0-89642-777-3*) Linden Pubs.
Dunster, Mark. Antony & Cleopatra. 36p. (Orig.). (YA). (gr. 9-12). 1996. pap. 5.00 (*0-89642-307-7*) Linden Pubs.
— Antony Begins. (Antony Ser.: Pt. 4). 26p. (Orig.). 1994. pap. 5.00 (*0-89642-229-1*) Linden Pubs.
***Dunster, Mark.** Apercus: Poems from Hollywood. 11p. 1999. pap. 5.00 (*0-89642-899-0*) Linden Pubs.
Dunster, Mark. Aperitives: Poems from Hollywood. 21p. 1997. pap. 5.00 (*0-89642-358-1*) Linden Pubs.
***Dunster, Mark.** Apertures: Poems from Hollywood. 11p. 1999, pap. 5.00 (*0-89642-888-5*) Linden Pubs.
Dunster, Mark. Archpriest. 11p. (Orig.). (YA). 1994. pap. 4.00 (*0-89642-241-0*) Linden Pubs.
— Ardon. 23p. (Orig.). 1995. pap. 5.00 (*0-89642-280-1*) Linden Pubs.
***Dunster, Mark.** Areana: Poems from Hollywood. 11p. 1999. pap. 5.00 (*0-89642-839-7*) Linden Pubs.
Dunster, Mark. Armin. 22p. (Orig.). 1982. pap. 4.00 (*0-89642-094-9*) Linden Pubs.
***Dunster, Mark.** As It Were: Poems from Hollywood. 11p. 1999. pap. 5.00 (*0-89642-720-X*) Linden Pubs.
Dunster, Mark. Attars: Poems from Hollywood. 39p. (Orig.). 1988. pap. 6.00 (*0-89642-155-4*) Linden Pubs.
***Dunster, Mark.** Auras: Poems from Hollywood. 11p. 1999. pap. 5.00 (*0-89642-864-8*) Linden Pubs.
Dunster, Mark. Avatars: Poems from Hollywood. 11p. 1999. pap. 5.00 (*0-89642-756-0*) Linden Pubs.
— Bacon's Fall: James, Pt. 5. 31p. (Orig.). 1993. pap. 5.00 (*0-89642-226-7*) Linden Pubs.
— Bacon's Rise: James, Pt. 2. 38p. (Orig.). 1994. pap. 5.00 (*0-89642-227-5*) Linden Pubs.
***Dunster, Mark.** Badges: Poems from Hollywood. 11p. 1999. pap. 5.00 (*0-89642-836-2*) Linden Pubs.
Dunster, Mark. Badr. 13p. (Orig.). 1988. pap. 4.00 (*0-89642-158-9*) Linden Pubs.
***Dunster, Mark.** Balladry: Poems from Hollywood. 11p. 1999. pap. 5.00 (*0-89642-970-9*) Linden Pubs.
Dunster, Mark. Ballads: Poems from Hollywood. 15p. 1998. pap. 5.00 (*0-89642-468-5*) Linden Pubs.
— Bards & Ballads: Poems from Hollywood. 11p. 1999. pap. 5.00 (*0-89642-689-0*) Linden Pubs.
— Basilio. 10p. (Orig.). 1991. pap. 4.00 (*0-89642-198-8*) Linden Pubs.
— Basks: Poems from Hollywood. 25p. 1998. pap. 5.00 (*0-89642-395-6*) Linden Pubs.
— Bat: A Play. 24p. 1998. pap. 5.00 (*0-89642-398-0*) Linden Pubs.
— Batteries: Poems from Hollywood. 11p. 1998. pap. 5.00 (*0-89642-536-3*) Linden Pubs.
— Beach: Cliff. (Rin Ser.: Pt. 24). 23p. 1998. pap. write for info. (*0-89642-399-9*) Linden Pubs.
— Beauty. 10p. (Orig.). 1990. pap. 4.00 (*0-89642-185-6*) Linden Pubs.
— Believe the Green. 18p. (Orig.). 1996. pap. 5.00 (*0-89642-300-X*) Linden Pubs.
***Dunster, Mark.** Bell & Candle: Poems from Hollywood. 11p. 1999. pap. 5.00 (*0-89642-969-5*) Linden Pubs.
Dunster, Mark. Bell Songs: Poems from Hollywood. 11p. 1999. pap. 5.00 (*0-89642-638-6*) Linden Pubs.
***Dunster, Mark.** Benisons: Poems from Hollywood. 11p. 1999. pap. 5.00 (*0-89642-714-5*) Linden Pubs.
Dunster, Mark. Bestirments: Poems from Hollywood. 11p. 1999. pap. 5.00 (*0-89642-783-8*) Linden Pubs.
***Dunster, Mark.** Bevies: Poems from Hollywood. 11p. 2000. pap. 5.00 (*0-89642-994-6*) Linden Pubs.
Dunster, Mark. Bhagavad. 9p. (Orig.). 1993. pap. 4.00 (*0-89642-215-1*) Linden Pubs.
— Bibelots: Poems from Hollywood. 14p. (Orig.). (YA). (gr. 9-12). 1997. pap. 5.00 (*0-89642-351-4*) Linden Pubs.
— Bicentennials. 1977. pap. 4.00 (*0-89642-003-5*) Linden Pubs.
— Birds. 30p. (Orig.). 1987. pap. 4.00 (*0-89642-144-9*) Linden Pubs.
***Dunster, Mark.** Bits & Pieces: Poems from Hollywood. 11p. 1999. pap. 5.00 (*0-89642-841-9*) Linden Pubs.
Dunster, Mark. Bleats: Poems from Hollywood. 11p. 1999. pap. 5.00 (*0-89642-725-0*) Linden Pubs.
— Blex. 16p. (Orig.). 1994. pap. 4.00 (*0-89642-243-7*) Linden Pubs.
— Body & Soul. 1979. pap. 4.00 (*0-89642-057-4*) Linden Pubs.
— Boons: Poems from Hollywood. 17p. (Orig.). (YA). (gr. 9-12). 1997. pap. 5.00 (*0-89642-378-6*) Linden Pubs.
***Dunster, Mark.** Boughs: Poems from Hollywood. 11p. 1999. pap. 5.00 (*0-89642-874-5*) Linden Pubs.
— Bounces: Poems from Hollywood. 11p. 1999. pap. 5.00 (*0-89642-893-1*) Linden Pubs.
— Bounds: Poems from Hollywood. 11p. 1999. pap. 5.00 (*0-89642-882-6*) Linden Pubs.
Dunster, Mark. Bounty: Poems from Hollywood. 16p. 1998. pap. 5.00 (*0-89642-467-7*) Linden Pubs.
— A Boys Beginning. 17p. 1984. pap. 4.00 (*0-89642-108-2*) Linden Pubs.
— Brandy. (Rin Ser.: Part 13). 1977. pap. 4.00 (*0-89642-000-0*) Linden Pubs.
— Bread. 27p. (Orig.). (YA). (gr. 9-12). 1995. pap. 5.00 (*0-89642-292-5*) Linden Pubs.
— Bread & Circuses. 28p. (Orig.). 1997. pap. 5.00 (*0-89642-344-1*) Linden Pubs.
— Bret (Rin, Pt. 23) A Play. LC 77-356479. 1976. 4.00 (*0-89642-012-4*) Linden Pubs.
— A Broken Window: Poems from Hollywood. 11p. 1999. pap. 5.00 (*0-89642-677-7*) Linden Pubs.
— Brother Lawrence. (Rin Ser.: Pt. 25). 47p. (Orig.). 1987. pap. 4.00 (*0-89642-153-8*) Linden Pubs.
***Dunster, Mark.** Brouhaha: Poems from Hollywood. 11p. 1999. pap. 5.00 (*0-89642-981-4*) Linden Pubs.
Dunster, Mark. Brutus. (Antony Ser.: Pt. 6). (Orig.). 1980. pap. 4.00 (*0-89642-063-9*) Linden Pubs.
***Dunster, Mark.** Bubbles: Poems from Hollywood. 11p. 1999. pap. 5.00 (*0-89642-920-2*) Linden Pubs.
Dunster, Mark. Buel. 19p. 1991. pap. 4.00 (*0-89642-197-X*) Linden Pubs.
— Bulwark: Poems from Hollywood. 11p. 1999. pap. 5.00 (*0-89642-672-6*) Linden Pubs.
— Butterflies: Poems from Hollywood. 11p. 1999. pap. 5.00 (*0-89642-678-5*) Linden Pubs.
— Buzzes: Poems from Hollywood. 11p. 1998. pap. 5.00 (*0-89642-548-7*) Linden Pubs.
***Dunster, Mark.** By the Way: Poems from Hollywood. 11p. 1999. pap. 5.00 (*0-89642-870-2*) Linden Pubs.
Dunster, Mark. Cachous: Poems from Hollywood. 11p. 1999. pap. 5.00 (*0-89642-750-1*) Linden Pubs.
— Cadences. 18p. (Orig.). (YA). (gr. 9-12). 1996. pap. 5.00 (*0-89642-326-3*) Linden Pubs.
— Caesar. (Borgia Ser.: Pt. 3). 1979. pap. 4.00 (*0-89642-049-3*) Linden Pubs.
— Caesars Fall: Antony, Pt. 3. 1978. pap. text 4.00 (*0-89642-045-0*) Linden Pubs.
— Caesar's Rise. (Antony Ser.: Pt. 1). 40p. (Orig.). 1986. pap. 5.00 (*0-89642-134-1*) Linden Pubs.
***Dunster, Mark.** Cajoles: Poems from Hollywood. 11p. 1999. pap. 5.00 (*0-89642-982-2*) Linden Pubs.
Dunster, Mark. Cakewalks: Poems from Hollywood. 11p. 1999. pap. 5.00 (*0-89642-704-8*) Linden Pubs.
— Calends: Poems from Hollywood. 28p. (Orig.). 1992. pap. 5.00 (*0-89642-203-8*) Linden Pubs.
— California Songs. 19p. (Orig.). 1996. pap. 5.00 (*0-89642-301-8*) Linden Pubs.
— Calixes: Poems from Hollywood. 12p. 1998. pap. 5.00 (*0-89642-454-5*) Linden Pubs.
— Callis. 39p. (Orig.). 1994. pap. 5.00 (*0-89642-247-X*) Linden Pubs.
— Cam. LC 74-437961. (Rin Ser.: Pt. 47). 1974. 4.00 (*0-89642-013-2*) Linden Pubs.
— Candid. 14p. (Orig.). 1991. pap. 4.00 (*0-89642-193-7*) Linden Pubs.
— Candles: Poems from Hollywood. 11p. 1998. pap. 5.00 (*0-89642-495-2*) Linden Pubs.
— Canterville. 19p. (Orig.). 1985. pap. 4.00 (*0-89642-122-8*) Linden Pubs.
— Canticles: Poems from Hollywood. 11p. 1999. pap. 5.00 (*0-89642-691-2*) Linden Pubs.
— Cantilenas: Poems from Hollywood. 11p. 1998. pap. 5.00 (*0-89642-463-4*) Linden Pubs.
— Cantillations: Poems from Hollywood. 19p. 1998. pap. 5.00 (*0-89642-457-X*) Linden Pubs.
***Dunster, Mark.** Cantos: Poems from Hollywood. 11p. 1999. pap. 5.00 (*0-89642-779-X*) Linden Pubs.
Dunster, Mark. Cantus: Poems from Hollywood. 13p. 1998. pap. 5.00 (*0-89642-464-2*) Linden Pubs.
— Capers. (Poems from Hollywood Ser.). 64p. (Orig.). 1986. pap. 6.00 (*0-89642-131-7*) Linden Pubs.
— Caprices. 24p. (Orig.). (YA). (gr. 9-12). 1996. pap. 5.00 (*0-89642-327-1*) Linden Pubs.
— Caprioles. 24p. (Orig.). 1996. pap. 5.00 (*0-89642-315-8*) Linden Pubs.
***Dunster, Mark.** Caracoles: Poems from Hollywood. 11p. 1999. pap. 5.00 (*0-89642-807-9*) Linden Pubs.
Dunster, Mark. Caravans: Three Books of Poems. 57p. (Orig.). 1981. pap. 4.00 (*0-89642-071-X*) Linden Pubs.
— Carillons: Poems from Hollywood. 11p. 1998. pap. 5.00 (*0-89642-553-3*) Linden Pubs.
— Carnivals: Poems from Hollywood. 17p. (YA). (gr 9-12). 1997. pap. 5.00 (*0-89642-380-8*) Linden Pubs.
— Carols: Songs from Hollywood. 11p. 1999. pap. 5.00 (*0-89642-637-8*) Linden Pubs.
— Cascades: Poems from Hollywood. 11p. 1998. pap. 5.00 (*0-89642-490-1*) Linden Pubs.
— Catches Poems from Hollywood. 11p. 1998. pap. 5.00 (*0-89642-571-1*) Linden Pubs.
— Catherine. (Borgia Ser.: Pt. 2). 49p. (Orig.). 1980. pap. 4.00 (*0-89642-067-1*) Linden Pubs.
— Catherine. (Henry the Eighth Ser.: Pt. 2). 22p. (Orig.). 1984. pap. 4.00 (*0-89642-111-2*) Linden Pubs.
***Dunster, Mark.** Caught in the Act: Poems from Hollywood. 11p. 1999. pap. 5.00 (*0-89642-811-7*) Linden Pubs.
Dunster, Mark. Cavalcades. 17p. (YA). (gr. 9-12). 1996. pap. 5.00 (*0-89642-324-7*) Linden Pubs.
— Cavatinas: Poems from Hollywood. 11p. 1999. pap. 5.00 (*0-89642-793-5*) Linden Pubs.
— Celebrations: Poems from Hollywood. 11p. 1998. pap. 5.00 (*0-89642-446-4*) Linden Pubs.
— Cento: Poems from Hollywood. 28p. (YA). (gr. 9-12). 1997. pap. 5.00 (*0-89642-371-9*) Linden Pubs.
— Ceramics Poems from Hollywood. 11p. 1998. pap. 5.00 (*0-89642-569-X*) Linden Pubs.
— Ceremonies: Poems from Hollywood. 11p. 1999. pap. 5.00 (*0-89642-753-6*) Linden Pubs.
— Challenges: Poems from Hollywood. 11p. 1998. pap. 5.00 (*0-89642-525-8*) Linden Pubs.
— Changes: Poems from Hollywood. 11p. 1998. pap. 5.00 (*0-89642-555-X*) Linden Pubs.
— Chanties: Poems from Hollywood. 12p. 1998. pap. 5.00 (*0-89642-469-3*) Linden Pubs.
— Chants: Poems from Hollywood. 13p. 1998. pap. 5.00 (*0-89642-466-9*) Linden Pubs.
— Chapter & Verse: Poems from Hollywood. 19p. 1998. pap. 5.00 (*0-89642-427-8*) Linden Pubs.
***Dunster, Mark.** Charades: Poems from Hollywood. 11p. 1999. pap. 5.00 (*0-89642-766-8*) Linden Pubs.
Dunster, Mark. Charades: Poems from Hollywood. 11p. 1999. pap. 5.00 (*0-89642-792-7*) Linden Pubs.
— Cheers: Poems from Hollywood. 11p. 1999. pap. 5.00 (*0-89642-702-1*) Linden Pubs.
— Chimney. 14p. (Orig.). (J). 1990. pap. 4.00 (*0-89642-180-5*) Linden Pubs.
— Chinoiseries. 17p. 1998. pap. 5.00 (*0-89642-417-0*) Linden Pubs.
***Dunster, Mark.** Chitchat: Poems from Hollywood. 11p. 2000. pap. 5.00 (*0-89642-987-3*) Linden Pubs.
Dunster, Mark. Chorales: Poems from Hollywood. 43p. (Orig.). 1996. pap. 5.00 (*0-89642-319-0*) Linden Pubs.
— Chris. (Rin Ser.: Pt. 14). (Orig.). 1978. pap. 4.00 (*0-89642-044-2*) Linden Pubs.
***Dunster, Mark.** Chrysalis: Poems from Hollywood. 11p. 1999. pap. 5.00 (*0-89642-913-X*) Linden Pubs.
Dunster, Mark. Churn: Poems from Hollywood. 11p. 1998. pap. 5.00 (*0-89642-493-6*) Linden Pubs.
Dunster, Mark. Cirrus. 20p. (Orig.). (YA). (gr. 9-12). 1996. pap. 5.00 (*0-89642-331-X*) Linden Pubs.
Dunster, Mark. Clay. LC 74-165104. 1973. 4.00 (*0-89642-014-0*) Linden Pubs.
— Cleopatra: Antony, Part 11. 37p. 1984. pap. 4.00 (*0-89642-115-5*) Linden Pubs.
***Dunster, Mark.** Clues: Poems from Hollywood. 11p. 1999. pap. 5.00 (*0-89642-887-7*) Linden Pubs.
Dunster, Mark. Coffers: Poems from Hollywood. 11p. 1998. pap. 5.00 (*0-89642-475-8*) Linden Pubs.
***Dunster, Mark.** Collations: Poems from Hollywood. 11p. (Orig.). 1999. pap. 5.00 (*0-89642-842-7*) Linden Pubs.
Dunster, Mark. Collections: Poems from Hollywood. 11p. 1999. pap. 5.00 (*0-89642-671-8*) Linden Pubs.
— Collects: Poems from Hollywood. 19p. (Orig.). (YA). (gr. 9-12). 1997. pap. 5.00 (*0-89642-354-9*) Linden Pubs.
***Dunster, Mark.** Compasses: Poems from Hollywood. 11p. 1999. pap. 5.00 (*0-89642-764-1*) Linden Pubs.
Dunster, Mark. Compendia: Poems from Hollywood. 11p. 1998. pap. 5.00 (*0-89642-511-8*) Linden Pubs.
— Compendium: Poems from Hollywood. 11p. 1998. pap. write for info. (*0-89642-497-9*) Linden Pubs.
— Concoctions: Poems from Hollywood. 11p. 1999. pap. 5.00 (*0-89642-786-2*) Linden Pubs.
***Dunster, Mark.** Connections: Poems from Hollywood. 11p. 1999. 5.00 (*0-89642-966-0*) Linden Pubs.
— Continuities: Poems from Hollywood. 11p. 1999. pap. 5.00 (*0-89642-838-9*) Linden Pubs.
Dunster, Mark. Contours: Poems from Hollywood. 11p. 1998. pap. 5.00 (*0-89642-519-3*) Linden Pubs.
***Dunster, Mark.** Contrasts: Poems from Hollywood. 11p. 2000. pap. 5.00 (*0-89642-992-X*) Linden Pubs.
Dunster, Mark. Controls: Poems from Hollywood. 11p. 1999. pap. 5.00 (*0-89642-695-5*) Linden Pubs.
— Coriolanus. 34p. (Orig.). (YA). (gr. 9-12). 1996. pap. 5.00 (*0-89642-298-4*) Linden Pubs.
— Corky: Kel, Pt. 2. (Rin Ser.: Pt. 29). 82p. (Orig.). 1981. pap. 5.00 (*0-89642-072-8*) Linden Pubs.
— Correspondences: Poems from Hollywood. 11p. 1998. pap. 5.00 (*0-89642-528-2*) Linden Pubs.
— Cory. (Rin Ser.: Pt. 51). 55p. (Orig.). 1984. pap. 4.00 (*0-89642-117-1*) Linden Pubs.
***Dunster, Mark.** Coryphaeus: Poems from Hollywood. 11p. 1999. pap. 5.00 (*0-89642-937-7*) Linden Pubs.
Dunster, Mark. Cotillions. 23p. (Orig.). 1996. pap. 5.00 (*0-89642-317-4*) Linden Pubs.
***Dunster, Mark.** Countercues: Poems from Hollywood. 11p. 1999. pap. 5.00 (*0-89642-868-0*) Linden Pubs.
Dunster, Mark. Coverture: Poems from Hollywood. 11p. 1999. pap. 5.00 (*0-89642-666-1*) Linden Pubs.
— Crazy Book No. 1: Poems from Hollywood. 11p. 1998. pap. 5.00 (*0-89642-550-9*) Linden Pubs.
***Dunster, Mark.** Criterions: Poems from Hollywood. 11p. 1999. pap. 5.00 (*0-89642-765-X*) Linden Pubs.
— Croons: Poems from Hollywood. 11p. 1999. pap. 5.00 (*0-89642-715-3*) Linden Pubs.
Dunster, Mark. Cross Currents: Poems from Hollywood. 11p. 1998. pap. 5.00 (*0-89642-501-0*) Linden Pubs.
— Crossroads: Poems from Hollywood. 11p. 1998. pap. 5.00 (*0-89642-576-2*) Linden Pubs.
— Crosswinds: Poems from Hollywood. 11p. 1998. pap. 5.00 (*0-89642-502-9*) Linden Pubs.
***Dunster, Mark.** Croutons: Poems from Hollywood. 11p. 1999. pap. 5.00 (*0-89642-825-7*) Linden Pubs.
Dunster, Mark. Crumbs: Poems from Hollywood. 11p. 1999. pap. 5.00 (*0-89642-708-0*) Linden Pubs.
— Crumwell. (Henry the Eighth Ser.: Pt. 4). 41p. (Orig.). 1982. pap. 4.00 (*0-89642-085-X*) Linden Pubs.
— Crunches: Poems from Hollywood. 11p. 1999. pap. 5.00 (*0-89642-707-2*) Linden Pubs.
— Currents: Poems from Hollywood. 11p. 1998. pap. 5.00 (*0-89642-575-4*) Linden Pubs.
— Cuttings: Poems from Hollywood. 11p. 1998. pap. 5.00 (*0-89642-586-X*) Linden Pubs.
— Cymbeline. 40p. (Orig.). 1995. pap. 5.00 (*0-89642-272-0*) Linden Pubs.
— Dancers. (Rin Ser.: Pt. 18). 36p. (Orig.). 1986. pap. 4.00 (*0-89642-133-3*) Linden Pubs.
— A Day in Phoenix. 13p. 1994. pap. 4.00 (*0-89642-248-8*) Linden Pubs.
***Dunster, Mark.** Decals: Poems from Hollywood. 11p. 1999. pap. 5.00 (*0-89642-834-6*) Linden Pubs.
— A Decoction of Herbs: Poems from Hollywood. 11p. 1999. pap. 5.00 (*0-89642-908-3*) Linden Pubs.
Dunster, Mark. Descants: Poems from Hollywood. 27p. (Orig.). 1990. pap. 5.00 (*0-89642-179-1*) Linden Pubs.
— Destinies: Poems from Hollywood. 17p. 1998. pap. 5.00 (*0-89642-422-7*) Linden Pubs.
— Dialogue. 15p. (Orig.). 1985. pap. 4.00 (*0-89642-120-1*) Linden Pubs.
— Diamond. 17p. (Orig.). 1994. pap. 4.00 (*0-89642-238-0*) Linden Pubs.
***Dunster, Mark.** Diaries: Poems from Hollywood. 11p. 1999. pap. 5.00 (*0-89642-897-4*) Linden Pubs.
Dunster, Mark. Dicta: Poems from Hollywood. 18p. (Orig.). (YA). (gr. 9-12). 1997. pap. 5.00 (*0-89642-355-7*) Linden Pubs.
— Dido. 14p. (Orig.). 1994. pap. 4.00 (*0-89642-237-2*) Linden Pubs.
— Dionysius. 13p. (Orig.). 1994. pap. 4.00 (*0-89642-242-9*) Linden Pubs.
— Directions: Poems from Hollywood. 11p. 1999. pap. 5.00 (*0-89642-659-9*) Linden Pubs.
— Disquisitions: Poems from Hollywood. 20p. 1998. pap. 5.00 (*0-89642-419-7*) Linden Pubs.
***Dunster, Mark.** Distillate: Poems from Hollywood. 11p. 1999. pap. 5.00 (*0-89642-881-8*) Linden Pubs.
Dunster, Mark. Distinctions: Poems from Hollywood. 11p. 1998. pap. 5.00 (*0-89642-544-4*) Linden Pubs.
— Dit. LC 78-100964. 1978. pap. 4.00 (*0-89642-004-3*) Linden Pubs.
— Ditties: Poems from Hollywood. 12p. 1998. pap. 5.00 (*0-89642-465-0*) Linden Pubs.
— Divagations: Poems from Hollywood. 11p. 1999. pap. 5.00 (*0-89642-622-X*) Linden Pubs.
— Dogs, 2 vols. (Animals Ser.: Pt. 1). (Orig.). 1979. pap. 8.00 (*0-89642-058-2*) Linden Pubs.
— Domack. 15p. 1988. pap. 4.00 (*0-89642-157-0*) Linden Pubs.
— Doors: Poems from Hollywood. 11p. 1998. pap. 5.00 (*0-89642-549-5*) Linden Pubs.
— Doricio. 11p. (Orig.). (J). 1989. pap. 4.00 (*0-89642-170-8*) Linden Pubs.
***Dunster, Mark.** Dovetails: Poems from Hollywood. 11p. 1999. pap. 5.00 (*0-89642-732-3*) Linden Pubs.
— Down & Dirty: Poems from Hollywood. 11p. 1999. pap. 5.00 (*0-89642-910-5*) Linden Pubs.
Dunster, Mark. Drams: Poems from Hollywood. 11p. 1999. pap. 5.00 (*0-89642-705-6*) Linden Pubs.
— Dray. 11p. (Orig.). 1989. pap. 4.00 (*0-89642-176-7*) Linden Pubs.
***Dunster, Mark.** Dream Assembly: Poems from Hollywood. 11p. 1999. pap. 5.00 (*0-89642-923-7*) Linden Pubs.
Dunster, Mark. Dreams. 20p. (Orig.). (YA). (gr. 9-12). 1996. pap. 5.00 (*0-89642-302-6*) Linden Pubs.
— Driftwood: Poems from Hollywood. 15p. 1998. pap. 5.00 (*0-89642-410-3*) Linden Pubs.

D

An Asterisk (*) at the beginning of an entry indicates that the title is appearing for the first time.

— Driss. 62p. (Orig.). 1982. pap. 4.00 (0-89642-088-4) Linden Pubs.
— Druce. (Rin Ser.: Part 2). 1976. pap. 4.00 (0-89642-015-9) Linden Pubs.
***Dunster, Mark.** Drumsticks: Poems from Hollywood. 11p. 1999. pap. 5.00 (0-89642-915-6) Linden Pubs.
— Drupes: Poems from Hollywood. 11p. 1999. pap. 5.00 (0-89642-763-3) Linden Pubs.
— Dubs: Poems from Holywood. 11p. 1999. pap. 5.00 (0-89642-925-3) Linden Pubs.
Dunster, Mark. Duct: Poems from Hollywood. 11p. 1999. pap. 5.00 (0-89642-760-9) Linden Pubs.
— Duel. 10p. (Orig.). 1989. pap. 4.00 (0-89642-173-2) Linden Pubs.
***Dunster, Mark.** Echelons: Poems from Hollywood. 11p. 1999. pap. 5.00 (0-89642-871-0) Linden Pubs.
— Echoes: Poems from Hollywood. 11p. 1999. pap. 5.00 (0-89642-796-X) Linden Pubs.
Dunster, Mark. Eckel. 28p. (Orig.). 1989. pap. 5.00 (0-89642-177-5) Linden Pubs.
— Eclogs: Poems from Hollywood. 11p. 1999. pap. 5.00 (0-89642-698-X) Linden Pubs.
— Edulcorants: Poems from Hollywood. 17p. 1998. pap. 5.00 (0-89642-432-4) Linden Pubs.
— Efton. 22p. (Orig.). 1995. pap. 5.00 (0-89642-275-5) Linden Pubs.
— Elaborations: Poems from Hollywood. 11p. 1998. pap. write for info. (0-89642-616-5) Linden Pubs.
***Dunster, Mark.** Elixirs: Poems from Hollywood. 11p. 1999. pap. 5.00 (0-89642-800-1) Linden Pubs.
Dunster, Mark. Ella. LC 75-212842. 87p. (Orig.). 1975. pap. 4.00 (0-89642-016-7) Linden Pubs.
— Emerson Impressions. 21p. (Orig.). (YA). 1994. pap. 5.00 (0-89642-245-3) Linden Pubs.
— Emily Pt. 1: Charles. 46p. (Orig.). 1975. pap. 4.00 (0-89642-017-5) Linden Pubs.
— Emily Pt. 2: Squire. 29p. (Orig.). 1987. pap. 5.00 (0-89642-152-X) Linden Pubs.
— Emily Pt. 3: Gib. 29p. (Orig.). (YA). 1994. pap. 5.00 (0-89642-239-9) Linden Pubs.
***Dunster, Mark.** Emporiums: Poems from Hollywood. 11p. 1999. pap. 5.00 (0-89642-662-9) Linden Pubs.
Dunster, Mark. Endo. 20p. (Orig.). 1989. pap. 4.00 (0-89642-171-6) Linden Pubs.
— Enid. 55p. (Orig.). 1975. pap. 4.00 (0-89642-018-3) Linden Pubs.
***Dunster, Mark.** Entropies: Poems from Hollywood. 11p. 1999. pap. 5.00 (0-89642-876-1) Linden Pubs.
Dunster, Mark. Ephemera: Poems from Hollywood. 20p. (Orig.). (YA). (gr. 9-12). 1997. pap. 5.00 (0-89642-377-8) Linden Pubs.
***Dunster, Mark.** Epiphanies: Poems from Hollywood. 11p. 1999. pap. 5.00 (0-89642-817-6) Linden Pubs.
Dunster, Mark. Erastus. 80p. (Orig.). 1975. pap. 4.00 (0-89642-019-1) Linden Pubs.
— Escapes: Poems from Hollywood. 18p. (Orig.). (YA). (gr. 9-12). 1997. pap. 5.00 (0-89642-343-3) Linden Pubs.
— Essays: Poems from Hollywood. 11p. 1998. pap. 5.00 (0-89642-532-0) Linden Pubs.
— Et Cetera: Poems from Hollywood. 11p. 1999. pap. 5.00 (0-89642-658-0) Linden Pubs.
***Dunster, Mark.** Evensong: Poems from Hollywood. 11p. 1999. pap. 5.00 (0-89642-974-1) Linden Pubs.
Dunster, Mark. Events & Transformations: Poems from Hollywood. 11p. 1998. pap. 5.00 (0-89642-537-1) Linden Pubs.
— Everyman. 10p. 1994. pap. 4.00 (0-89642-249-6) Linden Pubs.
— Exaltations: Poems from Hollywood. 15p. 1998. pap. 5.00 (0-89642-458-8) Linden Pubs.
— Excapades: Poems from Hollywood. 11p. 1999. pap. 5.00 (0-89642-627-0) Linden Pubs.
— Excursions: Poems from Hollywood. 19p. (Orig.). (YA). (gr. 9-12). 1996. pap. 5.00 (0-89642-322-0) Linden Pubs.
— Excursions: Poems from Hollywood. 14p. (Orig.). 1997. pap. 5.00 (0-89642-368-9) Linden Pubs.
***Dunster, Mark.** Excursus: Poems from Hollywood. 11p. 1999. pap. 5.00 (0-89642-728-5) Linden Pubs.
— Exempla: Poems from Hollywood. 11p. 1999. pap. 5.00 (0-89642-747-1) Linden Pubs.
Dunster, Mark. Exhilarations: Poems from Hollywood. 20p. (Orig.). 1997. pap. 5.00 (0-89642-367-0) Linden Pubs.
— Exorbitance: Poems from Hollywood. 11p. 1998. pap. 5.00 (0-89642-611-4) Linden Pubs.
— Exordiums: Poems from Hollywood. 22p. (Orig.). (YA). (gr. 9-12). 1997. pap. 5.00 (0-89642-348-4) Linden Pubs.
— Experiment. 13p. (Orig.). 1988. pap. 4.00 (0-89642-164-3) Linden Pubs.
— Explicatives: Poems From Hollywood. 11p. 1998. pap. 5.00 (0-89642-572-X) Linden Pubs.
***Dunster, Mark.** Extracts: Poems from Hollywood. 11p. 1999. pap. 5.00 (0-89642-961-X) Linden Pubs.
Dunster, Mark. Extravaganzas: Poems from Hollywood. 11p. 1999. pap. 5.00 (0-89642-623-8) Linden Pubs.
— Exuberations: Poems from Hollywood. 11p. 1998. pap. 5.00 (0-89642-455-3) Linden Pubs.
— Exultations: Poems from Hollywood. 13p. 1998. pap. 5.00 (0-89642-449-9) Linden Pubs.
— Fables: Poems from Hollywood. 19p. (Orig.). (YA). (gr. 9-12). 1997. pap. 5.00 (0-89642-374-3) Linden Pubs.
— Facetiae: Poems from Hollywood. 11p. 1999. pap. 5.00 (0-89642-755-2) Linden Pubs.
— Fan. 27p. (Orig.). 1995. pap. 6.00 (0-89642-252-6) Linden Pubs.
— Fandangos: Poems from Hollywood. 11p. 1999. pap. 5.00 (0-89642-636-X) Linden Pubs.
— Fangs: Poems from Hollywood. 11p. 1998. pap. 5.00 (0-89642-527-4) Linden Pubs.
— Fantasmas. 17p. (Orig.). 1996. pap. 5.00 (0-89642-336-0) Linden Pubs.
— Farms. 57p. (Orig.). 1984. pap. 4.00 (0-89642-116-3) Linden Pubs.
— Fasces, Bazaars, Ariosos: Three Books of Poems. 1979. pap. 4.00 (0-89642-051-5) Linden Pubs.
***Dunster, Mark.** Fasciations: Poems from Hollywood. 11p. 1999. pap. 5.00 (0-89642-724-2) Linden Pubs.
Dunster, Mark. Fascicles: Poems from Hollywood. 20p. (Orig.). (YA). (gr. 9-12). 1996. pap. 5.00 (0-89642-334-4) Linden Pubs.
— Fascicules: Poems from Hollywood. 11p. 1999. pap. 5.00 (0-89642-742-0) Linden Pubs.
— Fasciculi: Poems from Hollywood. 11p. 1999. pap. 5.00 (0-89642-726-9) Linden Pubs.
— Fascines: Poems from Hollywood. 11p. (Orig.). (YA). (gr. 9-12). 1997. pap. 5.00 (0-89642-353-0) Linden Pubs.
— Fat Man. 53p. (Orig.). 1981. pap. 4.00 (0-89642-081-7) Linden Pubs.
— Fathoms: Poems from Hollywood. 11p. 1999. pap. 5.00 (0-89642-682-3) Linden Pubs.
***Dunster, Mark.** Fauns: Poems from Hollywood. 11p. 1999. pap. 5.00 (0-89642-719-6) Linden Pubs.
Dunster, Mark. Faust. 22p. (Orig.). 1994. pap. 5.00 (0-89642-230-5) Linden Pubs.
— Faustus. 33p. (Orig.). 1995. pap. 5.00 (0-89642-265-8) Linden Pubs.
— Faux Pases: Poems from Hollywood. 11p. 1999. pap. 5.00 (0-89642-674-2) Linden Pubs.
***Dunster, Mark.** Favonius: Poems from Hollywood. 11p. 1999. pap. 5.00 (0-89642-824-9) Linden Pubs.
— Favors: Poems from Hollywood. 11p. 1999. pap. 5.00 (0-89642-692-0) Linden Pubs.
Dunster, Mark. Feigns: Poems from Hollywood. 11p. 1998. pap. 5.00 (0-89642-615-7) Linden Pubs.
***Dunster, Mark.** Felonies: Poems from Hollywood. 11p. 1999. pap. 5.00 (0-89642-953-9) Linden Pubs.
Dunster, Mark. Festivals: Poems from Hollywood. 15p. 1997. pap. 5.00 (0-89642-356-5) Linden Pubs.
— Fiddlesticks: Poems from Hollywood. 11p. 1999. pap. 5.00 (0-89642-661-0) Linden Pubs.
***Dunster, Mark.** Findings: Poems from Hollywood. 11p. 1999. pap. 5.00 (0-89642-721-8) Linden Pubs.
Dunster, Mark. Fire Island: Blue. (Rin Ser.: Part 40). 56p. 1988. pap. 6.00 (0-89642-160-0) Linden Pubs.
***Dunster, Mark.** Firecrackers: Poems from Hollywood. 11p. 1999. pap. 5.00 (0-89642-745-5) Linden Pubs.
Dunster, Mark. Fires: Poems from Hollywood. 11p. 1998. pap. write for info. (0-89642-552-5) Linden Pubs.
— Firestones: Poems from Hollywood. 21p. 1998. pap. 5.00 (0-89642-409-X) Linden Pubs.
— Firks: Poems from Hollywood. 11p. 1999. pap. 5.00 (0-89642-770-6) Linden Pubs.
***Dunster, Mark.** Fissures: Poems from Hollywood. 11p. 1999. pap. 5.00 (0-89642-840-0) Linden Pubs.
Dunster, Mark. Flairs: Poems from Hollywood. 11p. 1999. pap. 5.00 (0-89642-758-7) Linden Pubs.
— Flambeaus: Poems from Hollywood. 12p. 1998. pap. 5.00 (0-89642-442-1) Linden Pubs.
— Flamingos: Poems from Hollywood. 11p. 1999. pap. 5.00 (0-89642-641-6) Linden Pubs.
— Flight: Poems from Hollywood. 11p. 1999. pap. 5.00 (0-89642-628-9) Linden Pubs.
— Flights: Poems from Hollywood. 11p. 1999. pap. 5.00 (0-89642-773-0) Linden Pubs.
— Florizal. 20p. (Orig.). 1995. pap. 5.00 (0-89642-277-1) Linden Pubs.
***Dunster, Mark.** Flourishes: Poems from Hollywood. 11p. 1999. pap. 5.00 (0-89642-860-5) Linden Pubs.
— Fluidities & Agitations: Poems from Hollywood. 11p. 1999. pap. 5.00 (0-89642-748-X) Linden Pubs.
Dunster, Mark. Flyings: Poems from Hollywood. 11p. 1999. pap. 5.00 (0-89642-687-4) Linden Pubs.
***Dunster, Mark.** Foils: Poems from Hollywood. 11p. 1999. pap. 5.00 (0-89642-900-8) Linden Pubs.
Dunster, Mark. Folderols: Poems from Hollywood. 11p. 1999. pap. 5.00 (0-89642-774-9) Linden Pubs.
— Folkways: Poems from Hollywood. 22p. (Orig.). (J). (gr. 9-12). 1997. pap. 5.00 (0-89642-370-0) Linden Pubs.
— Follicles: Poems from Hollywood. 21p. 1997. pap. 5.00 (0-89642-369-7) Linden Pubs.
— Foofaraw: Poems from Hollywood. 11p. 1999. pap. 5.00 (0-89642-688-2) Linden Pubs.
***Dunster, Mark.** Foofaraws: Poems from Hollywood. 11p. 1999. pap. 5.00 (0-89642-795-1) Linden Pubs.
Dunster, Mark. Forayings: Poems from Hollywood. 29p. (Orig.). (YA). (gr. 9-12). 1997. pap. 5.00 (0-89642-373-5) Linden Pubs.
***Dunster, Mark.** Forms: Poems from Hollywood. 11p. 1999. pap. 5.00 (0-89642-693-9) Linden Pubs.
— Fountains: Poems from Hollywood. 11p. 1999. pap. 5.00 (0-89642-731-5) Linden Pubs.
Dunster, Mark. Fourdroyants: Poems from Hollywood. 16p. 1998. pap. 5.00 (0-89642-461-8) Linden Pubs.
— Fox. 68p. (Orig.). 1980. pap. 4.00 (0-89642-064-7) Linden Pubs.
***Dunster, Mark.** Foyer: Poems from Hollywood. 11p. 1999. pap. 5.00 (0-89642-947-4) Linden Pubs.
Dunster, Mark. Friends. 12p. (Orig.). 1990. pap. 4.00 (0-89642-186-4) Linden Pubs.
— Fringes: Poems from Hollywood. 11p. 1998. pap. 5.00 (0-89642-514-2) Linden Pubs.
***Dunster, Mark.** Frisks: Poems from Hollywood. 11p. 1999. pap. 5.00 (0-89642-924-5) Linden Pubs.
Dunster, Mark. Frivolities: Poems from Hollywood. 11p. (Orig.). (YA). (gr. 9-12). 1997. pap. 5.00 (0-89642-352-2) Linden Pubs.
— Frolics: Poems from Hollywood. 11p. 1998. pap. 5.00 (0-89642-587-8) Linden Pubs.
— Frontiers: Poems from Hollywood. 11p. 1998. pap. 5.00 (0-89642-522-3) Linden Pubs.
— Fudge: Poems from Hollywood. 12p. 1998. pap. 5.00 (0-89642-480-4) Linden Pubs.
***Dunster, Mark.** Full Tilt: Poems from Hollywood. 11p. 1999. pap. 5.00 (0-89642-959-8) Linden Pubs.
Dunster, Mark. Further Music. 24p. (Orig.). (YA). (gr. 9-12). 1996. pap. 5.00 (0-89642-312-3) Linden Pubs.
***Dunster, Mark.** Fusions: Poems from Hollywood. 11p. (Orig.). 1999. pap. 5.00 (0-89642-914-8) Linden Pubs.
Dunster, Mark. Gage. 13p. (Orig.). 1985. pap. 4.00 (0-89642-130-9) Linden Pubs.
— Galore: Poems from Hollywood. 11p. 1999. pap. 5.00 (0-89642-787-0) Linden Pubs.
***Dunster, Mark.** Gamuts: Poems from Hollywood. 11p. 1999. pap. 5.00 (0-89642-858-3) Linden Pubs.
Dunster, Mark. Gareth. 43p. 1977. pap. 4.00 (0-89642-005-1) Linden Pubs.
***Dunster, Mark.** A Gate to Gardens: Poems from Hollywood. 11p. 1999. pap. 5.00 (0-89642-964-4) Linden Pubs.
Dunster, Mark. Gatherings: Poems from Hollywood. 18p. (Orig.). (YA). (gr. 9-12). 1997. pap. 5.00 (0-89642-349-2) Linden Pubs.
— Gaul: Antony, Pt. 5. 31p. (Orig.). 1994. pap. 5.00 (0-89642-228-3) Linden Pubs.
— Geneva. (Rin Ser.: Part 41). 1977. pap. 4.00 (0-89642-020-5) Linden Pubs.
— Genie: Poems from Hollywood. 11p. 1998. pap. 5.00 (0-89642-546-0) Linden Pubs.
— Getting a Part. 9p. (Orig.). 1992. pap. 4.00 (0-89642-211-9) Linden Pubs.
— Gilgamesh. 12p. (Orig.). 1992. pap. 4.00 (0-89642-204-6) Linden Pubs.
— Giveaways: Poems from Hollywood. 11p. 1998. pap. 5.00 (0-89642-545-2) Linden Pubs.
***Dunster, Mark.** Glass-House Rocks: Poems from Hollywood. 11p. 1999. pap. 5.00 (0-89642-950-4) Linden Pubs.
Dunster, Mark. Glorias: Poems from Hollywood. 22p. 1998. pap. 5.00 (0-89642-408-1) Linden Pubs.
— Glosses Poems from Hollywood. 11p. 1998. pap. 5.00 (0-89642-573-8) Linden Pubs.
— Glyphs: Poems from Hollywood. 24p. 1997. pap. 5.00 (0-89642-359-X) Linden Pubs.
***Dunster, Mark.** Glypts: Poems from Hollywood. 11p. 1999. pap. 5.00 (0-89642-939-3) Linden Pubs.
— Going with the Flow: Poems from Hollywood. 11p. 1999. pap. 5.00 (0-89642-806-0) Linden Pubs.
Dunster, Mark. The Golden Sword. 17p. (Orig.). 1995. pap. 4.00 (0-89642-268-2) Linden Pubs.
***Dunster, Mark.** Gone Wild: Poems from Hollywood. 11p. 1999. pap. 5.00 (0-89642-943-1) Linden Pubs.
Dunster, Mark. Goodeve. 17p. (Orig.). (YA). 1995. pap. 5.00 (0-89642-290-9) Linden Pubs.
— Gotham. 14p. (Orig.). 1985. 4.00 (0-89642-123-6) Linden Pubs.
***Dunster, Mark.** Grabbag: Poems from Hollywood. 11p. 1999. pap. 5.00 (0-89642-971-7) Linden Pubs.
— Graphics: Poems from Hollywood. 11p. 1999. pap. 5.00 (0-89642-863-X) Linden Pubs.
— Graphs: Poems from Hollywood. 11p. 1999. pap. write for info. (0-89642-849-4) Linden Pubs.
Dunster, Mark. Griggs. 47p. 1979. pap. 4.00 (0-89642-048-5) Linden Pubs.
— Grist: Poems from Hollywood. 18p. 1996. pap. 5.00 (0-89642-340-9) Linden Pubs.
— Guiles: Poems from Hollywood. 11p. 1998. pap. 5.00 (0-89642-481-2) Linden Pubs.
***Dunster, Mark.** Gumbo: Poems from Hollywood. 11p. 1999. pap. 5.00 (0-89642-818-4) Linden Pubs.
Dunster, Mark. Hafts: Poems from Hollywood. 13p. 1998. pap. 5.00 (0-89642-479-0) Linden Pubs.
— Hamlet. 39p. (Orig.). 1995. pap. 5.00 (0-89642-259-3) Linden Pubs.
***Dunster, Mark.** Hangups: Poems from Hollywood. 11p. 1999. pap. 5.00 (0-89642-954-7) Linden Pubs.
Dunster, Mark. Happenings: Poems from Hollywood. 11p. 1998. pap. 5.00 (0-89642-568-1) Linden Pubs.
— Happens: Poems from Hollywood. 11p. 1998. pap. 5.00 (0-89642-503-7) Linden Pubs.
— Hart. 13p. (Orig.). 1986. pap. 4.00 (0-89642-135-X) Linden Pubs.
— Harvests: Poems from Hollywood. 11p. 1998. pap. 5.00 (0-89642-500-2) Linden Pubs.
— Hash. (Rin, Fathers. The Village Plays, Pt. 3, Sheridan Square Ser.: Pt. 12). 59p. (Orig.). 1984. pap. text 5.00 (0-89642-109-0) Linden Pubs.
— Haslemere. LC 78-100953. (Rin Ser.: Pt. 9). 1978. pap. 4.00 (0-89642-001-9) Linden Pubs.
— Heaps: Poems from Hollywood. 11p. 1998. pap. 5.00 (0-89642-592-4) Linden Pubs.
— Henry 4. 18p. (Orig.). 1995. pap. 4.00 (0-89642-273-9) Linden Pubs.
— Henry VIII. 17p. (Orig.). (YA). (gr. 9-12). 1996. pap. 5.00 (0-89642-305-0) Linden Pubs.
— Henry 5. 16p. (Orig.). (YA). (gr. 9-12). 1996. pap. 5.00 (0-89642-304-2) Linden Pubs.
— Henry 6, Pt. 1. 26p. (Orig.). 1995. pap. 5.00 (0-89642-281-X) Linden Pubs.
— Henry 6, Pt. 2. 26p. (Orig.). 1995. pap. 5.00 (0-89642-282-8) Linden Pubs.
— Henry 6, Part 3, Pt. 3. 28p. 1995. pap. 5.00 (0-89642-283-6) Linden Pubs.
— Heritage. 11p. (Orig.). 1991. pap. 4.00 (0-89642-200-3) Linden Pubs.
— Herod. (Antony Ser.: Pt. 9). 23p. (Orig.). 1983. pap. 4.00 (0-89642-105-8) Linden Pubs.
— Heroes. (Rin Ser.: Pt. 21). 25p. (Orig.). 1985. pap. 4.00 (0-89642-129-5) Linden Pubs.
***Dunster, Mark.** Heydays: Poems from Hollywood. 11p. 1999. pap. 5.00 (0-89642-916-4) Linden Pubs.
Dunster, Mark. Highroads: Poems from Hollywood. 17p. 1998. pap. 5.00 (0-89642-392-1) Linden Pubs.
— Highs: Poems from Hollywood. 11p. 1998. pap. 5.00 (0-89642-478-2) Linden Pubs.
— Highways: Poems from Hollywood. 28p. 1998. pap. 5.00 (0-89642-403-0) Linden Pubs.
— Hilts: Poems from Hollywood. 12p. 1998. pap. 5.00 (0-89642-476-6) Linden Pubs.
— Hit & Miss: Poems from Hollywood. 11p. 1999. pap. 5.00 (0-89642-669-6); pap. 5.00 (0-89642-670-X) Linden Pubs.
— Hoards: Poems from Hollywood. 11p. 1999. pap. 5.00 (0-89642-690-4) Linden Pubs.
— Hodgepodge: Poems from Hollywood. 13p. 1998. pap. 5.00 (0-89642-441-3) Linden Pubs.
***Dunster, Mark.** Hoists: Poems from Hollywood. 11p. 1999. pap. 5.00 (0-89642-889-3) Linden Pubs.
Dunster, Mark. Holds: Poems from Hollywood. 11p. 1998. pap. 5.00 (0-89642-605-X) Linden Pubs.
— Hollywood Headlight. 11p. (Orig.). 1992. pap. 4.00 (0-89642-213-5) Linden Pubs.
— Hollywood Poems. 80p. (Orig.). 1983. pap. 5.00 (0-89642-095-7) Linden Pubs.
***Dunster, Mark.** Honeycomb: Poems from Hollywood. 11p. 1999. pap. 5.00 (0-89642-949-0) Linden Pubs.
Dunster, Mark. Honeyswuggles: Poems from Hollywood. 11p. 1999. pap. 5.00 (0-89642-675-0) Linden Pubs.
— Hoop, 2 vols., Set. 140p. (Orig.). 1980. pap. 8.00 (0-89642-070-1) Linden Pubs.
***Dunster, Mark.** Hoopla: Poems from Hollywood. 11p. 1999. pap. 5.00 (0-89642-830-3) Linden Pubs.
Dunster, Mark. Hootenanny: Poems from Hollywood. 11p. 1999. pap. 5.00 (0-89642-642-4) Linden Pubs.
***Dunster, Mark.** Horizons: Poems from Hollywood. 11p. 2000. pap. 5.00 (0-89642-997-0) Linden Pubs.
— Hornets' Nests: Poems from Hollywood. 11p. 1999. pap. 5.00 (0-89642-975-X) Linden Pubs.
— Hornswoggler: Poems from Hollywood. 11p. 2000. pap. 5.00 (0-89642-993-8) Linden Pubs.
Dunster, Mark. Horsetails. 15p. (Orig.). (YA). (gr. 9-12). 1996. pap. 5.00 (0-89642-310-7) Linden Pubs.
— Hullabaloos: Poems from Hollywood. 11p. 1998. pap. 5.00 (0-89642-574-6) Linden Pubs.
— Hurlyburly: Poems from Hollywood. 11p. 1998. pap. 5.00 (0-89642-518-5) Linden Pubs.
— Hymnal: Poems from Hollywood. 11p. (Orig.). (YA). (gr. 9-12). 1997. pap. 5.00 (0-89642-357-3) Linden Pubs.
— Ichabod. 15p. (Orig.). 1986. pap. 4.00 (0-89642-138-4) Linden Pubs.
— Idiosyncrasies: Poems from Hollywood. 11p. 1998. pap. 5.00 (0-89642-609-2) Linden Pubs.
***Dunster, Mark.** Idle Addle: Poems from Hollywood. 11p. 1999. pap. 5.00 (0-89642-956-3) Linden Pubs.
Dunster, Mark. If & How: Poems from Hollywood. 11p. 1999. pap. 5.00 (0-89642-651-3) Linden Pub.
— Illuminations: Poems from Hollywood. 11p. 1998. pap. 5.00 (0-89642-577-0) Linden Pubs.
***Dunster, Mark.** Immortelles: Poems from Hollywood. 11p. 1999. pap. 5.00 (0-89642-909-1) Linden Pubs.
Dunster, Mark. Impecunities: Poems from Hollywood. 11p. 1998. pap. 5.00 (0-89642-542-8) Linden Pubs.
— Impossibilities: Poems from Hollywood. 22p. 1998. pap. 5.00 (0-89642-425-1) Linden Pubs.
***Dunster, Mark.** In the Mix: Poems from Hollywood. 11p. 1999. pap. 5.00 (0-89642-797-8) Linden Pubs.
Dunster, Mark. Incentives: Poems from Hollywood. 11p. 1998. pap. 5.00 (0-89642-578-9) Linden Pubs.
— Incursions. 20p. (Orig.). (YA). (gr. 9-12). 1996. pap. 5.00 (0-89642-338-7) Linden Pubs.
***Dunster, Mark.** Indexes: Poems from Hollywood. 11p. 1999. 5.00 (0-89642-968-7) Linden Pubs.
Dunster, Mark. Indiscretions: Poems from Hollywood. 11p. 1999. pap. 5.00 (0-89642-727-7) Linden Pubs.
— Infare. 23p. (Orig.). 1983. pap. 4.00 (0-89642-098-1) Linden Pubs.
***Dunster, Mark.** Influences: Poems from Hollywood. 11p. 1999. pap. 5.00 (0-89642-872-9) Linden Pubs.
Dunster, Mark. Inklings: Poems from Hollywood. 11p. 1998. pap. 5.00 (0-89642-499-5) Linden Pubs.
— Inlets: Poems from Hollywood. 11p. 1998. pap. 5.00 (0-89642-494-4) Linden Pubs.
— Inroads. (Poems from Hollywood Ser.). 51p. 1987. pap. 6.00 (0-89642-143-0) Linden Pubs.
— Ins & Outs: Poems from Hollywood. 20p. (Orig.). (YA). (gr. 9-12). 1997. pap. 5.00 (0-89642-375-1) Linden Pubs.
***Dunster, Mark.** Insights: Poems from Hollywood. 11p. 1999. pap. 5.00 (0-89642-917-2) Linden Pubs.
Dunster, Mark. Intaglios: Poems from Hollywood. 11p. 1999. pap. 5.00 (0-89642-769-2) Linden Pubs.
— Intermezzos. 15p. (Orig.). 1996. pap. 5.00 (0-89642-316-6) Linden Pubs.
— Interventions: Poems from Hollywood. 11p. 1998. pap. 5.00 (0-89642-543-6) Linden Pubs.
— Introits: Poems from Hollywood. 18p. (Orig.). 1996. pap. 5.00 (0-89642-337-9) Linden Pubs.
— Intrusions: Poems from Hollywood. 11p. 1998. pap. 5.00 (0-89642-491-X) Linden Pubs.
— Invitations: Poems from Hollywood. 11p. 1998. pap. text 5.00 (0-89642-565-7) Linden Pubs.
— Irritants: Poems from Hollywood. 11p. 1998. pap. 5.00 (0-89642-589-4) Linden Pubs.
— Ish. (Rin Ser.: Pt. 32). 51p. (Orig.). 1984. pap. 4.00 (0-89642-113-9) Linden Pubs.
***Dunster, Mark.** Jagged Edge: Poems from Hollywood. 11p. 1999. pap. 5.00 (0-89642-847-8) Linden Pubs.
Dunster, Mark. Jeff. (Rin Ser.: Pt. 30). 23p. (Orig.). 1983. pap. 4.00 (0-89642-096-5) Linden Pubs.

An Asterisk (*) at the beginning of an entry indicates that the title is appearing for the first time.

— Jekyll. 14p. (Orig.). 1986. pap. 4.00 (*0-89642-137-6*) Linden Pubs.

***Dunster, Mark.** Jellies & Buns: Poems from Hollywood. 11p. 1999. pap. 5.00 (*0-89642-878-8*) Linden Pubs.

— Jetsam: Poems from Hollywood. 11p. 1999. 5.00 (*0-89642-967-9*) Linden Pubs.

Dunster, Mark. Jewel. 29p. (Orig.). (YA). 1995. pap. 5.00 (*0-89642-271-2*) Linden Pubs.

— Jiggs. (Rin Ser.: Pt. 49). 82p. (Orig.). 1981. pap. 5.00 (*0-89642-076-0*) Linden Pubs.

— Jigs: Poems from Hollywood. 11p. 1998. pap. 5.00 (*0-89642-538-X*) Linden Pubs.

— Jinxes: Poems from Hollywood. 11p. 1999. pap. 5.00 (*0-89642-660-2*) Linden Pubs.

— Jipsies, Otherwise, Raphael. 38p. 1984. pap. 4.00 (*0-89642-110-4*) Linden Pubs.

***Dunster, Mark.** Jives: Poems from Hollywood. 11p. 1999. pap. 5.00 (*0-89642-861-3*) Linden Pubs.

Dunster, Mark. Joy, Otherwise, Seasong. 19p. 1985. pap. 4.00 (*0-89642-121-X*) Linden Pubs.

— Julius Caesar: A Play. 24p. (Orig.). (YA). (gr. 9-12). 1996. pap. 5.00 (*0-89642-306-9*) Linden Pubs.

— Junkets: Poems from Hollywood. 12p. 1998. pap. 5.00 (*0-89642-462-6*) Linden Pubs.

— Kansas. (John Brown Ser.: Pt. 1). 31p. (Orig.). 1984. pap. 4.00 (*0-89642-107-4*) Linden Pubs.

— Karma: Poems from Hollywood. 16p. (Orig.). 1996. pap. 5.00 (*0-89642-308-5*) Linden Pubs.

— Katherine Howard. (Henry the Eighth Ser.: Pt. 5). 1979. pap. 4.00 (*0-89642-047-7*) Linden Pubs.

***Dunster, Mark.** Keynotes: Poems from Hollywood. 11p. 1999. pap. 5.00 (*0-89642-852-4*) Linden Pubs.

— Keys: Poems from Hollywood. 11p. 1999. pap. 5.00 (*0-89642-932-6*) Linden Pubs.

Dunster, Mark. Kids, Alias, Haloween. LC 78-314767. (Holiday Ser.: Pt. 1). 1978. pap. 4.00 (*0-89642-040-X*) Linden Pubs.

***Dunster, Mark.** Kilters: Poems from Hollywood. 11p. 1999. pap. 5.00 (*0-89642-712-9*) Linden Pubs.

Dunster, Mark. King John. 23p. (Orig.). (YA). 1995. pap. 5.00 (*0-89642-286-0*) Linden Pubs.

— Kip. (Rin Ser.: Part 33). 79p. (Orig.). 1975. pap. 4.00 (*0-89642-022-1*) Linden Pubs.

— Kit. (Rin Ser.: Pt. 45). (Orig.). 1980. pap. 5.00 (*0-89642-060-4*) Linden Pubs.

— Knightwood. 1973. 4.00 (*0-89642-023-X*) Linden Pubs.

— Knolls. 11p. (Orig.). 1998. pap. 5.00 (*0-89642-561-4*) Linden Pubs.

— Konichiwa: Poems from Hollwood. 11p. 1999. pap. 5.00 (*0-89642-652-1*) Linden Pub.

— Lambence: Poems from Hollywood. 17p. 1998. pap. 5.00 (*0-89642-406-5*) Linden Pubs.

— Laramie. 83p. (Orig.). 1975. pap. 4.00 (*0-89642-024-8*) Linden Pubs.

— Lauds: Poems from Hollywood. 11p. 1998. pap. 5.00 (*0-89642-559-2*) Linden Pubs.

— Laura. 19p. 1988. pap. 4.00 (*0-89642-163-5*) Linden Pubs.

— Laves: Poems from Hollywood. 12p. 1998. pap. 5.00 (*0-89642-489-8*) Linden Pubs.

— Lays: Poems from Hollywood. 13p. 1998. pap. 5.00 (*0-89642-474-X*) Linden Pubs.

— Lear. 27p. (Orig.). 1995. pap. 4.00 (*0-89642-253-4*) Linden Pubs.

— Leavings: Poems from Hollywood. 11p. 1998. pap. 5.00 (*0-89642-520-7*) Linden Pubs.

— Legacy: Poems from Hollywood. 11p. 1998. pap. 5.00 (*0-89642-554-1*) Linden Pubs.

***Dunster, Mark.** Legibilities: Poems from Hollywood. 11p. 1999. pap. 5.00 (*0-89642-663-7*) Linden Pubs.

— Leis: Poems from Hollywood. 11p. 1999. pap. 5.00 (*0-89642-744-7*) Linden Pubs.

Dunster, Mark. Lelia. 24p. (Orig.). 1993. pap. 5.00 (*0-89642-217-8*) Linden Pubs.

***Dunster, Mark.** Lemonade: Poems from Hollywood. 11p. 1999. pap. 5.00 (*0-89642-879-6*) Linden Pubs.

Dunster, Mark. Lenitives: Poems from Hollywood. 13p. 1998. pap. 5.00 (*0-89642-430-8*) Linden Pubs.

— Lens: Poems from Hollywood. 27p. 1998. pap. 5.00 (*0-89642-390-5*) Linden Pubs.

— Leonardo Thoughts. 10p. (Orig.). 1995. pap. 4.00 (*0-89642-257-7*) Linden Pubs.

— Les: Kel, Pt. 1. (Rin Ser.: Pt. 28). 60p. 1981. pap. 4.00 (*0-89642-075-2*) Linden Pubs.

***Dunster, Mark.** Letters from the Dead: Poems from Hollywood. 11p. 1999. pap. 5.00 (*0-89642-936-9*) Linden Pubs.

Dunster, Mark. Light: Poems from Hollywood. 24p. 1998. mass mkt. 5.00 (*0-89642-391-3*) Linden Pubs.

***Dunster, Mark.** Light Spirit: Poems from Hollywood. 11p. 1999. pap. 5.00 (*0-89642-730-7*) Linden Pubs.

— Lilts: Poems from Hollywood. 11p. 1999. pap. 5.00 (*0-89642-855-9*) Linden Pubs.

Dunster, Mark. Lint. 24p. (Orig.). 1983. pap. 4.00 (*0-89642-100-7*) Linden Pubs.

***Dunster, Mark.** Lo & Behold: Poems from Hollywood. 11p. 1999. pap. 5.00 (*0-89642-942-3*) Linden Pubs.

Dunster, Mark. Lodes: Poems from Hollywood. 11p. 1998. pap. 5.00 (*0-89642-438-3*) Linden Pubs.

— Lolls: Poems from Hollywood. 11p. 1999. pap. 5.00 (*0-89642-645-9*) Linden Pubs.

— Loose Ends: Poems from Hollywood. 11p. 1999. pap. 5.00 (*0-89642-788-9*) Linden Pubs.

— Loris. (Rin Ser.: Pt. 1). (Orig.). 1980. pap. 4.00 (*0-89642-062-0*) Linden Pubs.

— Los Angeles Poems: Poems from Hollywood. 11p. 1998. pap. 5.00 (*0-89642-558-4*) Linden Pubs.

— Lost. 12p. (Orig.). 1990. pap. 4.00 (*0-89642-187-2*) Linden Pubs.

— Luck. 15p. (Orig.). 1987. pap. 4.00 (*0-89642-147-3*) Linden Pubs.

— Madrigals. 27p. (Orig.). 1996. pap. 5.00 (*0-89642-318-2*) Linden Pubs.

— Magnitudes: Poems from Hollywood. 11p. 1998. pap. 5.00 (*0-89642-507-X*) Linden Pubs.

— The Malcontent. 21p. (Orig.). 1994. pap. 4.00 (*0-89642-246-1*) Linden Pubs.

***Dunster, Mark.** Manege: Poems from Hollywood. 11p. 1999. pap. 5.00 (*0-89642-808-7*) Linden Pubs.

Dunster, Mark. Maneuvers: Poems from Hollywood. 11p. 1998. pap. 5.00 (*0-89642-516-9*) Linden Pubs.

— Manna: Poems from Hollywood. 12p. 1998. pap. 5.00 (*0-89642-429-4*) Linden Pubs.

— Marga. (Rin Ser.: Pt. 4). 61p. (Orig.). 1982. pap. 4.00 (*0-89642-086-8*) Linden Pubs.

— Marsh King. 10p. (Orig.). (J). 1990. pap. 4.00 (*0-89642-184-8*) Linden Pubs.

— Mary. LC 78-112416. (Henry the Eighth Ser.: Pt. 3). 1978. pap. 4.00 (*0-89642-043-4*) Linden Pubs.

— Masks: Poems from Hollywood. 20p. 1998. pap. 5.00 (*0-89642-404-9*) Linden Pubs.

— Massachusetts. (John Brown Ser.: Pt. 2). 1978. pap. 4.00 (*0-89642-041-8*) Linden Pubs.

Dunster, Mark. Maul. 32p. (Orig.). (YA). 1995. pap. 5.00 (*0-89642-233-X*) Linden Pubs.

Dunster, Mark. Mazurkas: Poems from Hollywood. 11p. 1998. pap. 5.00 (*0-89642-567-3*) Linden Pubs.

— Medley: Poems from Hollywood. 11p. 1998. pap. 5.00 (*0-89642-585-1*) Linden Pubs.

— Medleys: Poems from Hollywood. 12p. (Orig.). (gr. 9-12). 1997. pap. 5.00 (*0-89642-379-4*) Linden Pubs.

— Melisar. 25p. (Orig.). 1994. pap. 5.00 (*0-89642-240-2*) Linden Pubs.

— Melmoth. 13p. (Orig.). 1995. pap. 4.00 (*0-89642-285-2*) Linden Pubs.

— Mementoes: Poems from Hollywood. 11p. 1999. pap. 5.00 (*0-89642-790-0*) Linden Pubs.

— Merchant of Venice. 21p. 1995. pap. 4.00 (*0-89642-255-0*) Linden Pubs.

— Meridians. 37p. (Orig.). (YA). (gr. 9-12). 1996. pap. 5.00 (*0-89642-294-1*) Linden Pubs.

— Mermaid. 41p. 1982. pap. 4.00 (*0-89642-087-6*) Linden Pubs.

— Merry Wives. 25p. (Orig.). (YA). 1995. pap. 5.00 (*0-89642-289-5*) Linden Pubs.

— Messages: Poems from Hollywood. 20p. 1998. pap. 5.00 (*0-89642-448-0*) Linden Pubs.

— Messes. 24p. (Orig.). (YA). (gr. 9-12). 1996. pap. 5.00 (*0-89642-313-1*) Linden Pubs.

***Dunster, Mark.** Meteors: Poems from Hollywood. 11p. 1999. pap. 5.00 (*0-89642-853-2*) Linden Pubs.

Dunster, Mark. Midsummer Night. 22p. (Orig.). 1995. pap. 4.00 (*0-89642-258-5*) Linden Pubs.

— Mildew: Poems from Hollywood. 19p. 1998. pap. 5.00 (*0-89642-416-2*) Linden Pubs.

— Miles. LC 75-177113. (Rin Ser.: Pt. 39). 1974. 4.00 (*0-89642-025-6*) Linden Pubs.

***Dunster, Mark.** Minarets: Poems from Hollywood. 11p. 1999. pap. 5.00 (*0-89642-928-8*) Linden Pubs.

Dunster, Mark. Minstrelsy: Poems from Hollywood. 15p. 1998. pap. 5.00 (*0-89642-473-1*) Linden Pubs.

— Minutiae: Poems from Hollywood. 11p. 1998. pap. 5.00 (*0-89642-531-2*) Linden Pubs.

— Mirth: Poems from Hollywood. 11p. 1998. pap. 5.00 (*0-89642-539-8*) Linden Pubs.

— Miser. 2nd rev. ed. 39p. (Orig.). 1982. pap. 4.00 (*0-89642-093-0*) Linden Pubs.

— Mishmash: Poems from Hollywood. 11p. 1998. pap. 5.00 (*0-89642-513-4*) Linden Pubs.

— Mr. Jings. 80p. (Orig.). 1975. pap. 4.00 (*0-89642-027-2*) Linden Pubs.

— Mittrin. 15p. (Orig.). 1987. pap. 4.00 (*0-89642-151-1*) Linden Pubs.

***Dunster, Mark.** Moments Before They Come: Poems from Hollywood. 11p. 1999. pap. 5.00 (*0-89642-799-4*) Linden Pubs.

— Moments More in Us: Poems from Hollywood. 11p. 1999. pap. 5.00 (*0-89642-804-4*) Linden Pubs.

Dunster, Mark. Moneymakers. (Rin Ser.: Pt. 17). 37p. (Orig.). 1982. pap. 4.00 (*0-89642-090-6*) Linden Pubs.

— The Moon. 10p. (Orig.). (J). 1993. pap. 4.00 (*0-89642-220-8*) Linden Pubs.

— More & More: Poems from Hollywood. 11p. 1998. pap. 5.00 (*0-89642-613-0*) Linden Pubs.

***Dunster, Mark.** Motets: Poems from Hollywood. 11p. 1999. pap. 5.00 (*0-89642-778-1*) Linden Pubs.

Dunster, Mark. Motley: Poems from Hollywood. 11p. 1999. pap. 5.00 (*0-89642-699-8*) Linden Pubs.

— Motorcycles. LC 77-155954. (Rin Ser.: Pt. 7). 1978. pap. 4.00 (*0-89642-006-X*) Linden Pubs.

— Moviemakers. (Rin Ser.: Pt. 16). 49p. (Orig.). 1982. pap. 4.00 (*0-89642-089-2*) Linden Pubs.

— Movings: Poems from Hollywood. 11p. 1998. pap. 5.00 (*0-89642-533-9*) Linden Pubs.

— Mrs. Wiggs. 16p. (Orig.). 1992. pap. 4.00 (*0-89642-210-0*) Linden Pubs.

***Dunster, Mark.** Muffins: Poems from Hollywood. 11p. 2000. pap. 5.00 (*0-89642-989-X*) Linden Pubs.

Dunster, Mark. Munchausen Exploits. 11p. (Orig.). 1992. pap. 4.00 (*0-89642-205-4*) Linden Pubs.

— Murder. (James Ser.: Pt. 3). 38p. (Orig.). 1990. pap. 5.00 (*0-89642-189-9*) Linden Pubs.

— Muse: Poems from Hollywood. 11p. 1998. pap. write for info. (*0-89642-498-7*) Linden Pubs.

— Mused: Poems from Hollywood. 11p. 1998. pap. 5.00 (*0-89642-510-X*) Linden Pubs.

— Muses: Poems from Hollywood. 11p. 1998. pap. 5.00 (*0-89642-505-3*) Linden Pubs.

— Musing: Poems from Hollywood. 11p. 1998. pap. 5.00 (*0-89642-509-6*) Linden Pubs.

***Dunster, Mark.** Musings: Poems from Hollywood. 11p. 1999. pap. 5.00 (*0-89642-809-5*) Linden Pubs.

Dunster, Mark. My Sin: Poems from Hollywood. 11p. 1998. pap. 5.00 (*0-89642-523-1*) Linden Pubs.

— Myrna: Rin, Pt. 10. 30p. 1982. pap. 4.00 (*0-89642-084-1*) Linden Pubs.

— Myrrhs: A Book of Poems for the Los Angeles Bicentennial. 20p. (Orig.). 1981. pap. 4.00 (*0-89642-078-7*) Linden Pubs.

— Mystics. 13p. (Orig.). 1993. pap. 4.00 (*0-89642-218-6*) Linden Pubs.

— The Nan Shan. 1977. pap. 4.00 (*0-89642-007-8*) Linden Pubs.

— Nard. (Poems from Hollywood Ser.). 70p. (Orig.). 1984. pap. 5.00 (*0-89642-114-7*) Linden Pubs.

— Ned. LC 74-172084. (Rin Ser.: Pt. 3). 1973. 4.00 (*0-89642-028-0*) Linden Pubs.

— Nefton. 24p. (Orig.). (YA). 1995. pap. 5.00 (*0-89642-288-7*) Linden Pubs.

— Negligentia: Poems from Hollywood. 11p. 1998. pap. 5.00 (*0-89642-614-9*) Linden Pubs.

— Nephew. 9p. (Orig.). 1988. pap. 4.00 (*0-89642-161-9*) Linden Pubs.

— Nerit. 48p. (Orig.). 1988. pap. 4.00 (*0-89642-159-7*) Linden Pubs.

***Dunster, Mark.** New Wine in Old Bottles: Poems from Hollywood. 11p. 1999. pap. 5.00 (*0-89642-980-6*) Linden Pubs.

Dunster, Mark. New York. LC 74-229035. 1973. 4.00 (*0-89642-029-9*) Linden Pubs.

***Dunster, Mark.** Nibbles: Poems from Hollywood. 11p. 1999. pap. 5.00 (*0-89642-918-0*) Linden Pubs.

Dunster, Mark. No Question: Poems from Hollywood. 11p. 1999. pap. 5.00 (*0-89642-650-5*) Linden Pub.

— Nogs: Poems from Hollywood. 18p. 1998. pap. 5.00 (*0-89642-412-X*) Linden Pubs.

***Dunster, Mark.** Nothings: Poems from Hollywood. 11p. 1999. pap. 5.00 (*0-89642-985-7*) Linden Pubs.

— Now & Then: Poems from Hollywood. 11p. 1999. pap. 5.00 (*0-89642-740-4*) Linden Pubs.

Dunster, Mark. Nutcrack. 11p. (Orig.). (J). (gr. 1-7). 1990. pap. 4.00 (*0-89642-190-2*) Linden Pubs.

***Dunster, Mark.** Nuts: Poems from Hollywood. 11p 1999. pap. 5.00 (*0-89642-722-6*) Linden Pubs.

— Oasis: Poems from Hollywood. 11p. 1999. pap. 5.00 (*0-89642-902-4*) Linden Pubs.

— Octaves: Poems from Hollywood. 11p. 1999. pap. 5.00 (*0-89642-960-1*) Linden Pubs.

Dunster, Mark. Octavian: Prolog to Actium, Antony, Pt. 10. 50p. (Orig.). 1981. pap. 4.00 (*0-89642-074-4*) Linden Pubs.

— Oddies: Poems from Hollywood. 11p. 1999. pap. 5.00 (*0-89642-759-5*) Linden Pubs.

— Oddities: Poems from Hollywood. 11p. 1998. pap. 5.00 (*0-89642-450-2*) Linden Pubs.

— Odds & Ends: Poems from Hollywood. 11p. 1999. pap. 5.00 (*0-89642-772-2*) Linden Pubs.

***Dunster, Mark.** Of Things: Poems from Hollywood. 11p. 1999. pap. 5.00 (*0-89642-884-2*) Linden Pubs.

Dunster, Mark. Offerings. 28p. (Orig.). (YA). (gr. 9-12). 1996. pap. 5.00 (*0-89642-325-5*) Linden Pubs.

— Ofice. LC 78-105243. 1978. pap. 4.00 (*0-89642-010-8*) Linden Pubs.

***Dunster, Mark.** Olibanum & Myrrh: Poems from Hollywood. 11p. 1999. pap. 5.00 (*0-89642-948-2*) Linden Pubs.

Dunster, Mark. Olio: Poems from Hollywood. 12p. 1998. pap. 5.00 (*0-89642-440-5*) Linden Pubs.

— Olivier. 12p. (Orig.). 1993. pap. 4.00 (*0-89642-222-4*) Linden Pubs.

***Dunster, Mark.** On & On: Poems from Hollywood. 11p. 1999. pap. 5.00 (*0-89642-903-2*) Linden Pubs.

— On the Way: Poems from Hollywood. 11p. 1999. pap. 5.00 (*0-89642-810-9*) Linden Pubs.

Dunster, Mark. Onsets. 17p. (Orig.). (YA). (gr. 9-12). 1996. pap. 5.00 (*0-89642-333-6*) Linden Pubs.

***Dunster, Mark.** Onslaughts: Poems from Hollywood. 11p. 1999. pap. 5.00 (*0-89642-963-6*) Linden Pubs.

Dunster, Mark. Opposites: Poems from Hollywood. 11p. 1999. pap. 5.00 (*0-89642-680-7*) Linden Pubs.

***Dunster, Mark.** Opus: Poems from Hollywood. 11p. 1999. pap. 5.00 (*0-89642-821-4*) Linden Pubs.

— Orbits: Poems from Hollywood. 11p. 1999. pap. 5.00 (*0-89642-813-3*) Linden Pubs.

Dunster, Mark. Oris. 13p. (Orig.). 1991. pap. 4.00 (*0-89642-199-6*) Linden Pubs.

— Othello. 24p. (Orig.). 1995. pap. 5.00 (*0-89642-261-5*) Linden Pubs.

***Dunster, Mark.** Out & About: Poems from Hollywood. 11p. 1999. pap. 5.00 (*0-89642-739-0*) Linden Pubs.

Dunster, Mark. Outcomes: Poems from Hollywood. 11p. 1998. pap. write for info. (*0-89642-606-8*) Linden Pubs.

— Outlets: Poems from Hollywood. 11p. 1998. pap. 5.00 (*0-89642-504-5*) Linden Pubs.

— Over & Out: Poems from Hollywood. 11p. 1999. pap. 5.00 (*0-89642-665-3*) Linden Pubs.

— Overtures. 20p. (Orig.). (YA). (gr. 9-12). 1996. pap. 5.00 (*0-89642-328-X*) Linden Pubs.

— Overviews: Poems from Hollywood. 11p. 1999. pap. 5.00 (*0-89642-634-3*) Linden Pubs.

— Packet. 18p. (Orig.). (YA). (gr. 9-12). 1996. pap. 5.00 (*0-89642-335-2*) Linden Pubs.

— Page. 30p. (Orig.). 1990. pap. 5.00 (*0-89642-181-3*) Linden Pubs.

***Dunster, Mark.** Palliatives: Poems from Hollywood. 11p. 1999. pap. 5.00 (*0-89642-951-2*) Linden Pubs.

Dunster, Mark. Parade: Poems from Hollywood. 11p. 1999. pap. 5.00 (*0-89642-626-2*) Linden Pubs.

— Parrol. 29p. (Orig.). 1989. pap. 4.00 (*0-89642-174-0*) Linden Pubs.

— Parsnips: Poems from Hollywood. 11p. 1998. pap. 5.00 (*0-89642-524-X*) Linden Pubs.

— Parthia. (Antony Ser.: Pt. 7). (Orig.). 1979. pap. 4.00 (*0-89642-055-8*) Linden Pubs.

— Partitas: Poems from Hollywood. 11p. 1999. pap. 5.00 (*0-89642-621-1*) Linden Pubs.

— Passacaglias: Poems From Hollywood. 12p. 1998. pap. 5.00 (*0-89642-560-6*) Linden Pubs.

***Dunster, Mark.** Passion Songs: Poems from Hollywood. 11p. 1999. pap. 5.00 (*0-89642-837-0*) Linden Pubs.

— Passionate: Poems from Hollywood. 11p. 1999. pap. 5.00 (*0-89642-835-4*) Linden Pubs.

Dunster, Mark. Pastiches: Poems from Hollywood. 11p. 1999. pap. 5.00 (*0-89642-734-X*) Linden Pubs.

***Dunster, Mark.** Paths: Poems from Hollywood. 11p. 1999. pap. 5.00 (*0-89642-957-1*) Linden Pubs.

— Paths to the Wind: Poems from Hollywood. 11p. 1999. pap. 5.00 (*0-89642-962-8*) Linden Pubs.

Dunster, Mark. Pats. 24p. (Orig.). (YA). (gr. 9-12). 1996. pap. 5.00 (*0-89642-303-4*) Linden Pubs.

— Pavilions: Poems from Hollywood. 19p. (Orig.). (YA). (gr. 9-12). 1996. pap. 5.00 (*0-89642-330-1*) Linden Pubs.

— Peccadillos: Poems from Hollywood. 13p. 1998. pap. 5.00 (*0-89642-435-9*) Linden Pubs.

— Peekaboo: Poems from Hollywood. 11p. 1999. pap. 5.00 (*0-89642-735-8*) Linden Pubs.

— Pegasus. 27p. (Orig.). (YA). (gr. 9-12). 1996. pap. 5.00 (*0-89642-314-X*) Linden Pubs.

— Pendules: Poems from Hollywood. 11p. 1999. pap. 5.00 (*0-89642-757-9*) Linden Pubs.

— Pergola: Poems from Hollywood. 11p. 1998. pap. 5.00 (*0-89642-484-7*) Linden Pubs.

— Periapts, Amulets, Inflections: Three Books of Poems. 1978. pap. 4.00 (*0-89642-002-7*) Linden Pubs.

— Periclus. 22p. 1995. pap. 5.00 (*0-89642-276-3*) Linden Pubs.

— Petruchio. 20p. (Orig.). 1995. pap. 5.00 (*0-89642-267-4*) Linden Pubs.

— Physostegia: Poems from Hollywood. 24p. (Orig.). (YA). (gr. 9-12). 1997. pap. 5.00 (*0-89642-362-X*) Linden Pubs.

— Pinkie: Alias Witches. (Holiday Ser.: Pt. 11: Halloween). 36p. (Orig.). 1990. pap. 5.00 (*0-89642-188-0*) Linden Pubs.

— Pip. (Rin Ser.: Pt. 53). 1979. pap. 4.00 (*0-89642-052-3*) Linden Pubs.

— Pistachios: Poems from Hollywood. 11p. 1998. pap. 5.00 (*0-89642-540-1*) Linden Pubs.

***Dunster, Mark.** Pizazz: Poems from Hollywood. 11p. 1999. pap. 5.00 (*0-89642-857-5*) Linden Pubs.

Dunster, Mark. Plank: Poems from Hollywood. 11p. 1998. pap. 5.00 (*0-89642-556-8*) Linden Pubs.

— Playboy. (Rin Ser.: Pt. 43). 1974. 4.00 (*0-89642-030-2*) Linden Pubs.

— Plumes: Poems from Hollywood. 11p. 1999. pap. 5.00 (*0-89642-654-8*) Linden Pubs.

— Plunder: Poems from Hollywood. 20p. 1998. 5.00 (*0-89642-424-3*) Linden Pubs.

— Poo: Poems from Hollywood. 11p. 1998. pap. 5.00 (*0-89642-564-9*) Linden Pubs.

— Poof Tales: Poems from Hollywood. 11p. 1998. pap. 5.00 (*0-89642-547-9*) Linden Pubs.

— Poopoo: Poems from Hollywood. 11p. 1998. pap. 5.00 (*0-89642-563-0*) Linden Pubs.

— The Pope. (Borgia Ser.: Pt. 1). 36p. (Orig.). 1984. pap. 4.00 (*0-89642-112-0*) Linden Pubs.

— Portraits. 2nd ed. LC 76-358986. 140p. 1976. pap. 5.00 (*0-89642-031-0*) Linden Pubs.

— Ports of Call: Poems from Hollywood. 16p. 1998. pap. 5.00 (*0-89642-413-8*) Linden Pubs.

— Poses: Poems from Hollywood. 1998. pap. 5.00 (*0-89642-515-0*) Linden Pubs.

— Possibilities: Poems from Hollywood. 15p. 1998. pap. 5.00 (*0-89642-431-6*) Linden Pubs.

— Postmortem. 19p. (Orig.). 1983. pap. 4.00 (*0-89642-099-X*) Linden Pubs.

— Postures: Poems from Hollywood. 11p. 1998. pap. 5.00 (*0-89642-521-5*) Linden Pubs.

***Dunster, Mark.** Potluck: Poems from Hollywood. 11p. 1999. pap. 5.00 (*0-89642-738-2*) Linden Pubs.

Dunster, Mark. Potpourris: Poems from Hollywood. 17p. 1998. pap. 5.00 (*0-89642-400-6*) Linden Pubs.

— Prances: Poems from Hollywood. 24p. (Orig.). 1997. pap. 5.00 (*0-89642-363-8*) Linden Pubs.

— Prayers: Poems from Hollywood. 11p. 1998. pap. 5.00 (*0-89642-557-6*) Linden Pubs.

— Preachments: Poems from Hollywood. 11p. 1999. pap. 5.00 (*0-89642-736-6*) Linden Pubs.

— Prefaces: Poems from Hollywood. 17p. (Orig.). (YA). (gr. 9-12). 1997. pap. 5.00 (*0-89642-350-6*) Linden Pubs.

— Prial. 32p. (Orig.). 1995. pap. 6.00 (*0-89642-270-4*) Linden Pubs.

***Dunster, Mark.** Prime: Poems from Hollywood. 11p. 1999. pap. 5.00 (*0-89642-827-3*) Linden Pubs.

Dunster, Mark. Primer. 10p. (Orig.). (YA). (gr. 9-12). 1996. pap. 5.00 (*0-89642-320-4*) Linden Pubs.

— Prince Hal. 18p. (Orig.). 1995. pap. 4.00 (*0-89642-274-7*) Linden Pubs.

— Prisms. 21p. (Orig.). (YA). (gr. 9-12). 1997. pap. 5.00 (*0-89642-341-7*) Linden Pubs.

— Progressions. 38p. (Orig.). (YA). (gr. 9-12). 1996. pap. 5.00 (*0-89642-323-9*) Linden Pubs.

***Dunster, Mark.** Projections: Poems from Hollywood. 11p. 1999. pap. 5.00 (*0-89642-710-2*) Linden Pubs.

Dunster, Mark. Prometheus: A Play. 10p. (Orig.). (J). 1995. pap. 5.00 (*0-89642-284-4*) Linden Pubs.

— Propriums. 30p. (Orig.). (YA). (gr. 9-12). 1995. pap. 5.00 (*0-89642-293-3*) Linden Pubs.

— Prosper. 24p. (Orig.). 1995. pap. 5.00 (*0-89642-266-6*) Linden Pubs.

D

An Asterisk (*) at the beginning of an entry indicates that the title is appearing for the first time.

— Psalms: Poems from Hollywood. 11p. 1999. pap. 5.00 (*0-89642-771-4*) Linden Pubs.

***Dunster, Mark.** Pungenee: Poems from Hollywood. 11p. 1999. pap. 5.00 (*0-89642-733-1*) Linden Pubs.

— Purlieus: Poems from Hollywood. 11p. 1999. pap. 5.00 (*0-89642-921-0*) Linden Pubs.

— Purs of My Thumb: Poems from Hollywood. 11p. 2000. pap. 5.00 (*0-89642-990-3*) Linden Pubs.

— Purviews: Poems from Hollywood. 11p. 1999. pap. 5.00 (*0-89642-927-X*) Linden Pubs.

Dunster, Mark. Putties: Poems from Hollywood - A Play by Mark Dunster. 32p. 1996. pap. 5.00 (*0-89642-433-2*) Linden Pubs.

— Putty: Poems from Hollywood. 11p. 1998. pap. 5.00 (*0-89642-608-4*) Linden Pubs.

***Dunster, Mark.** Quaintnesses: Poems from Hollywood. 11p. 1999. pap. 5.00 (*0-89642-885-0*) Linden Pubs.

— Quatrains: Poems from Hollywood. 11p. 1999. pap. 5.00 (*0-89642-984-9*) Linden Pubs.

— Quest: Poems from Hollywood. 11p. 1999. pap. 5.00 (*0-89642-713-7*) Linden Pubs.

— ? Poems from Hollywood. 11p. 1999. pap. 5.00 (*0-89642-848-6*) Linden Pubs.

— Quintessences: Poems from Hollywood. 11p. 1999. pap. 5.00 (*0-89642-883-4*) Linden Pubs.

Dunster, Mark. Rab. 14p. (Orig.). 1987. pap. 4.00 (*0-89642-150-3*) Linden Pubs.

— Ragdoll. 12p. (Orig.). 1986. pap. 4.00 (*0-89642-142-2*) Linden Pubs.

— Ralegh. (James Ser.: Pt. 1). 21p. (Orig.). 1989. pap. 4.00 (*0-89642-169-4*) Linden Pubs.

***Dunster, Mark.** Rambles: Poems from Hollywood. 11p. 1999. pap. 5.00 (*0-89642-934-2*) Linden Pubs.

Dunster, Mark. Ransom. 15p. (Orig.). 1986. pap. 4.00 (*0-89642-132-5*) Linden Pubs.

— Rap. 17p. (Orig.). 1987. pap. 4.00 (*0-89642-146-5*) Linden Pubs.

***Dunster, Mark.** Raptures: Poems from Hollywood. 11p. 1999. pap. 5.00 (*0-89642-931-8*) Linden Pubs.

Dunster, Mark. Rebirth. 9p. (Orig.). 1993. pap. 4.00 (*0-89642-224-0*) Linden Pubs.

— Red. (Rin Ser.: Pt. 46). 1979. pap. 5.00 (*0-89642-054-X*) Linden Pubs.

— Reels: Poems from Hollywood. 11p. 1998. pap. 5.00 (*0-89642-471-5*) Linden Pubs.

***Dunster, Mark.** Refuge: Poems from Hollywood. 11p. 1999. pap. 5.00 (*0-89642-905-9*) Linden Pubs.

— Relating. 16p. (Orig.). 1988. pap. 4.00 (*0-89642-162-7*) Linden Pubs.

Dunster, Mark. Remoulades: Poems from Hollywood. 11p. 1999. pap. 5.00 (*0-89642-655-6*) Linden Pubs.

***Dunster, Mark.** Rendezvouses: Poems from Hollywood. 11p. 1999. pap. 5.00 (*0-89642-850-8*) Linden Pubs.

Dunster, Mark. Ret. 12p. (Orig.). 1990. pap. 4.00 (*0-89642-183-X*) Linden Pubs.

***Dunster, Mark.** Revelations: Poems from Hollywood. 11p. 1999. pap. 5.00 (*0-89642-826-5*) Linden Pubs.

Dunster, Mark. Revels: Poems from Hollywood. 17p. 1998. pap. 5.00 (*0-89642-405-7*) Linden Pubs.

— Rhapsodies: Poems from Hollywood. 12p. (Orig.). (YA). (gr. 9-12). 1997. pap. 5.00 (*0-89642-347-6*) Linden Pubs.

— Richard II. 21p. (Orig.). (YA). 1995. pap. 5.00 (*0-89642-287-9*) Linden Pubs.

— Richard III. 26p. (Orig.). 1995. pap. 6.00 (*0-89642-263-1*) Linden Pubs.

— Ricks: Poems from Hollywood. 13p. 1998. pap. 5.00 (*0-89642-483-9*) Linden Pubs.

***Dunster, Mark.** Rigadoons: Poems from Hollywood. 11p. 1999. pap. 5.00 (*0-89642-930-X*) Linden Pubs.

Dunster, Mark. Rinwood. 21p. (Orig.). 1984. pap. 4.00 (*0-89642-118-X*) Linden Pubs.

— Rites & Choruses: Three Books of Poems. 1980. pap. 4.00 (*0-89642-059-0*) Linden Pubs.

— Riven. 11p. 1995. pap. 5.00 (*0-89642-264-X*) Linden Pubs.

— River Wind: Poems from Hollywood. 11p. 1999. pap. 5.00 (*0-89642-683-1*) Linden Pubs.

— River Wine: Poems from Hollywood. 11p. 1999. pap. 5.00 (*0-89642-685-8*) Linden Pubs.

— Robin Hood. 34p. (Orig.). 1988. pap. 5.00 (*0-89642-166-X*) Linden Pubs.

— Rock. (Rin Ser.: Part 48). 1977. pap. 4.00 (*0-89642-008-6*) Linden Pubs.

— Roils: Poems from Hollywood. 17p. 1998. mass mkt. 5.00 (*0-89642-393-X*) Linden Pubs.

— Romeo. 30p. (Orig.). 1995. pap. 5.00 (*0-89642-254-2*) Linden Pubs.

— Romps: Poems from Hollywood. 17p. (Orig.). (YA). (gr. 9-12). 1997. pap. 5.00 (*0-89642-346-8*) Linden Pubs.

— Rondos: Poems from Hollywood. 19p. (Orig.). 1997. pap. 5.00 (*0-89642-366-2*) Linden Pubs.

— Ror. (Rin Ser.: Pt. 50). 50p. (Orig.). 1981. pap. 4.00 (*0-89642-080-9*) Linden Pubs.

— Rothage. 23p. (Orig.). 1987. pap. 4.00 (*0-89642-154-6*) Linden Pubs.

— Roulades: Poems from Hollywood. 27p. (Orig.). 1989. pap. 4.00 (*0-89642-167-8*) Linden Pubs.

***Dunster, Mark.** Roundelays: Poems from Hollywood. 11p. 1999. pap. 5.00 (*0-89642-952-0*) Linden Pubs.

Dunster, Mark. Rubaiyat. 14p. (Orig.). 1992. pap. 4.00 (*0-89642-214-3*) Linden Pubs.

— Runes: Poems from Hollywood. 11p. 1999. pap. 5.00 (*0-89642-751-X*) Linden Pubs.

— Ruscisilva Poems: Poems from Hollywood. 11p. 1999. pap. 5.00 (*0-89642-686-6*) Linden Pubs.

— Ry: A Play. 1977. 4.00 (*0-89642-032-9*) Linden Pubs.

— Salome. 16p. (Orig.). 1995. pap. 4.00 (*0-89642-251-8*) Linden Pubs.

— Salves: Poems from Hollywood. 11p. 1998. pap. 5.00 (*0-89642-579-7*) Linden Pubs.

— Samson. 8p. 1994. pap. 4.00 (*0-89642-250-X*) Linden Pubs.

— Sands: Poems from Hollywood. 11p. 1998. pap. 5.00 (*0-89642-607-6*) Linden Pubs.

— Sarabands: Poems from Hollywood. 26p. 1997. pap. 5.00 (*0-89642-382-4*) Linden Pubs.

***Dunster, Mark.** Sardanas: Poems from Hollywood. 11p. 1999. pap. 5.00 (*0-89642-976-8*) Linden Pubs.

Dunster, Mark. Savors: Poems from Hollywood. 11p. 1998. pap. 5.00 (*0-89642-482-0*) Linden Pubs.

***Dunster, Mark.** Sawdust: Poems from Hollywood. 11p. 1999. pap. 5.00 (*0-89642-911-3*) Linden Pubs.

Dunster, Mark. Scattershot: Poems from Hollywood. 11p. 1999. pap. 5.00 (*0-89642-676-9*) Linden Pubs.

***Dunster, Mark.** Scissures: Poems from Hollywood. 11p. 1999. pap. 5.00 (*0-89642-946-6*) Linden Pubs.

— Scooping the Wind: Poems from Hollywood. 11p. 1999. pap. 5.00 (*0-89642-741-2*) Linden Pubs.

Dunster, Mark. Scraps: Poems from Hollywood. 18p. 1998. pap. 5.00 (*0-89642-418-9*) Linden Pubs.

— Scrooge. 16p. (Orig.). 1983. pap. 4.00 (*0-89642-101-5*) Linden Pubs.

— Scrutinies: Poems from Hollywood. 11p. 1999. pap. 5.00 (*0-89642-701-3*) Linden Pubs.

***Dunster, Mark.** Scurrilities: Poems from Hollywood. 11p. 1999. pap. 5.00 (*0-89642-798-6*) Linden Pubs.

Dunster, Mark. Seamaid. 10p. 1992. pap. 4.00 (*0-89642-208-9*) Linden Pubs.

— Search. 10p. (Orig.). 1992. pap. 4.00 (*0-89642-212-7*) Linden Pubs.

— Seeking the Wind: Poems from Hollywood. 11p. 1998. pap. 5.00 (*0-89642-485-5*) Linden Pubs.

***Dunster, Mark.** Segues: Poems from Hollywood. 11p. 1999. pap. 5.00 (*0-89642-803-6*) Linden Pubs.

Dunster, Mark. Sequences: Poems from Hollywood. 11p. 1999. pap. 5.00 (*0-89642-632-7*) Linden Pubs.

***Dunster, Mark.** Sessions: Poems from Hollywood. 11p. 1999. pap. 5.00 (*0-89642-955-5*) Linden Pubs.

Dunster, Mark. Sev. 14p. (Orig.). 1993. pap. 4.00 (*0-89642-221-6*) Linden Pubs.

***Dunster, Mark.** Shadow & Substance: Poems from Hollywood. 11p. 1999. pap. 5.00 (*0-89642-833-8*) Linden Pubs.

— Shadow Catcher: Poems from Hollywood. 11p. 1999. pap. 5.00 (*0-89642-922-9*) Linden Pubs.

Dunster, Mark. Shapes: Poems from Hollywood. 11p. 1999. pap. 5.00 (*0-89642-656-4*) Linden Pubs.

— Shards: Poems from Hollywood. 19p. 1998. pap. 5.00 (*0-89642-407-3*) Linden Pubs.

— Shining. 14p. (Orig.). 1993. pap. 4.00 (*0-89642-219-4*) Linden Pubs.

— Shortcuts: Poems from Hollywood. 11p. 1999. pap. 5.00 (*0-89642-789-7*) Linden Pubs.

***Dunster, Mark.** Shred Ends: Poems from Hollywood. 11p. 1999. pap. 5.00 (*0-89642-867-2*) Linden Pubs.

— Side Streams: Poems from Hollywood. 11p. 1999. pap. 5.00 (*0-89642-776-5*) Linden Pubs.

Dunster, Mark. Sidebars: Poems from Hollywood. 11p. 1999. pap. 5.00 (*0-89642-684-X*) Linden Pubs.

— Sideshows: Poems from Hollywood. 11p. 1999. pap. 5.00 (*0-89642-697-1*) Linden Pubs.

***Dunster, Mark.** Sigils: Poems from Hollywood. 11p. 1999. pap. 5.00 (*0-89642-894-X*) Linden Pubs.

Dunster, Mark. Signal: Poems from Hollywood. 11p. 1998. pap. 5.00 (*0-89642-517-7*) Linden Pubs.

***Dunster, Mark.** Silt: Poems from Hollywood. 11p. (Orig.). 1999. pap. 5.00 (*0-89642-933-4*) Linden Pubs.

Dunster, Mark. Situations: Poems from Hollywood. 16p. 1998. pap. 5.00 (*0-89642-436-7*) Linden Pubs.

— Six Loves. (Rin Ser.: Pt. 5). 1978. pap. 4.00 (*0-89642-046-9*) Linden Pubs.

— Skelton. rev. ed. (Henry the Eighth Ser.). 13p. (Orig.). 1988. pap. 4.00 (*0-89642-156-2*) Linden Pubs.

***Dunster, Mark.** Sketches: Poems from Hollywood. 11p. 1999. pap. 5.00 (*0-89642-898-2*) Linden Pubs.

Dunster, Mark. Skip. LC 74-281770. (Rin Ser.: Pt. 27). 1973. 4.00 (*0-89642-033-7*) Linden Pubs.

— Skitch. 50p. (Orig.). 1982. pap. 4.00 (*0-89642-092-2*) Linden Pubs.

— Slapdashes: Poems from Hollywood. 20p. (Orig.). (YA). (gr. 9-12). 1997. pap. 5.00 (*0-89642-376-X*) Linden Pubs.

***Dunster, Mark.** Slaw: Poems from Hollywood. 11p. (Orig.). 1999. pap. 5.00 (*0-89642-935-0*) Linden Pubs.

— Slaws: Poems from Hollywood. 11p. 1999. pap. 5.00 (*0-89642-929-6*) Linden Pubs.

— Slinks: Poems from Hollywood. 11p. 1999. pap. 5.00 (*0-89642-958-X*) Linden Pubs.

Dunster, Mark. Slurps: Poems from Hollywood. 11p. 1999. pap. 5.00 (*0-89642-794-3*) Linden Pubs.

— Slutch: Poems from Hollywood. 11p. 1998. pap. 5.00 (*0-89642-477-4*) Linden Pubs.

***Dunster, Mark.** Smirks: Poems from Hollywood. 11p. 1999. pap. 5.00 (*0-89642-973-3*) Linden Pubs.

— Snips: Poems from Hollywood. 11p. (Orig.). 1999. pap. 5.00 (*0-89642-912-1*) Linden Pubs.

Dunster, Mark. Soars: Poems from Hollywood. 29p. 1998. pap. 5.00 (*0-89642-389-1*) Linden Pubs.

— Sojourner Truth. 12p. (Orig.). 1983. pap. 4.00 (*0-89642-106-6*) Linden Pubs.

***Dunster, Mark.** Some More: Poems from Hollywood. 11p. 1999. pap. 5.00 (*0-89642-829-X*) Linden Pubs.

— Some Yule Logs for the Xmas Fire: Poems from Hollywood. 11p. 1999. pap. 5.00 (*0-89642-820-6*) Linden Pubs.

— Someplace: Poems from Hollywood. 11p. 1999. pap. 5.00 (*0-89642-978-4*) Linden Pubs.

— Something: Poems from Hollywood. 11p. 1999. pap. 5.00 (*0-89642-823-0*) Linden Pubs.

— Something Else: Poems from Hollywood. 11p. 1999. pap. 5.00 (*0-89642-828-1*) Linden Pubs.

— Something More: Poems from Hollywood. 11p. 1999. pap. 5.00 (*0-89642-814-1*) Linden Pubs.

Dunster, Mark. Somethings: Poems from Hollywood. 23p. 1998. pap. 5.00 (*0-89642-421-9*) Linden Pubs.

***Dunster, Mark.** Somewhat: Poems from Hollywood. 11p. 1999. pap. 5.00 (*0-89642-877-X*) Linden Pubs.

Dunster, Mark. Songs: Poems from Hollywood. 16p. 1998. pap. 5.00 (*0-89642-460-X*) Linden Pubs.

— Songs & Gardens: Poems from Hollywood. 11p. 1998. pap. write for info. (*0-89642-496-0*) Linden Pubs.

— Songs & Profiles. 31p. (Orig.). (YA). (gr. 9-12). 1996. pap. 5.00 (*0-89642-299-2*) Linden Pubs.

***Dunster, Mark.** Songs for Anytime: Poems from Hollywood. 11p. 1999. pap. 5.00 (*0-89642-869-9*) Linden Pubs.

— Songs of the Woods: Poems from Hollywood. 11p. 1999. pap. 5.00 (*0-89642-743-9*) Linden Pubs.

Dunster, Mark. Soul Feast: Poems from Hollywood. 11p. 1998. pap. 5.00 (*0-89642-590-8*) Linden Pubs.

— Soul Fest: Poems from Hollywood. 11p. 1998. pap. 5.00 (*0-89642-591-6*) Linden Pubs.

— Soul Train: Poems from Hollywood. 11p. 1998. pap. 5.00 (*0-89642-612-2*) Linden Pubs.

— Souled. 18p. (Orig.). (YA). (gr. 9-12). 1996. pap. 5.00 (*0-89642-309-3*) Linden Pubs.

***Dunster, Mark.** Source & Entrance: Poems from Holywood. 11p. 1999. pap. 5.00 (*0-89642-831-1*) Linden Pubs.

Dunster, Mark. Sourdines: Poems from Hollywood. 11p. 1998. pap. 5.00 (*0-89642-506-1*) Linden Pubs.

— Space: Poems from Hollywood. 11p. 1998. pap. 5.00 (*0-89642-526-6*) Linden Pubs.

— Sparkles: Poems from Hollywood. 11p. 1998. pap. 5.00 (*0-89642-619-X*) Linden Pubs.

— Spasm: Poems from Hollywood. 13p. 1998. pap. 5.00 (*0-89642-447-2*) Linden Pubs.

— Spasms: Poems from Hollywood. 11p. 1999. pap. 5.00 (*0-89642-709-9*) Linden Pubs.

— Spawns: Poems from Hollywood. 11p. 1999. pap. 5.00 (*0-89642-767-6*) Linden Pubs.

***Dunster, Mark.** Spectrum: Poems from Hollywood. 11p. 1999. pap. 5.00 (*0-89642-856-7*) Linden Pubs.

— Spelunks & Feretories: Poems from Hollywood. 11p. 1999. pap. 5.00 (*0-89642-919-9*) Linden Pubs.

Dunster, Mark. Spiceways: Poems from Hollywood. 1p. 1998. pap. 5.00 (*0-89642-588-6*) Linden Pubs.

— Spike. (Rin Ser.: Pt. 42 - Nightpeople Pt. 2). 37p. (Orig.). 1986. pap. 5.00 (*0-89642-141-4*) Linden Pubs.

— Spins: Poems from Hollywood. 17p. 1998. pap. 5.00 (*0-89642-428-6*) Linden Pubs.

— Splendor: Poems from Hollywood. 11p. 1998. pap. 5.00 (*0-89642-617-3*) Linden Pubs.

***Dunster, Mark.** Splurge: Poems from Hollywood. 11p. 1999. pap. 5.00 (*0-89642-802-8*) Linden Pubs.

Dunster, Mark. Sponge: Poems from Hollywood. 11p. 1998. pap. 5.00 (*0-89642-472-3*) Linden Pubs.

— Spoon. 20p. (Orig.). 1994. pap. 5.00 (*0-89642-234-8*) Linden Pubs.

***Dunster, Mark.** Sprees: Poems from Hollywood. 11p. 1999. pap. 5.00 (*0-89642-873-7*) Linden Pubs.

Dunster, Mark. Spring. 10p. (Orig.). 1993. pap. 4.00 (*0-89642-225-9*) Linden Pubs.

***Dunster, Mark.** Squibs: Poems from Hollywood. 11p. 1999. pap. 5.00 (*0-89642-711-0*) Linden Pubs.

— Stance & Comment: Poems from Hollywood. 11p. 1999. pap. 5.00 (*0-89642-832-X*) Linden Pubs.

Dunster, Mark. Star. 11p. (Orig.). 1991. pap. 4.00 (*0-89642-202-X*) Linden Pubs.

— Stashes: Poems from Hollywood. 11p. 1999. pap. 5.00 (*0-89642-752-8*) Linden Pubs.

— Steaks: Poems from Hollywood. 11p. 1999. pap. 5.00 (*0-89642-754-4*) Linden Pubs.

***Dunster, Mark.** Stew: Poems from Hollywood. 11p. 1999. pap. 5.00 (*0-89642-890-7*) Linden Pubs.

Dunster, Mark. A Stick for the Fire: Poems from Hollywood. 11p. 1999. pap. write for info. (*0-89642-653-X*) Linden Pubs.

— Stig. 1978. pap. 4.00 (*0-89642-042-6*) Linden Pubs.

— Still: Poems from Hollywood. 16p. 1998. pap. 5.00 (*0-89642-401-4*) Linden Pubs.

***Dunster, Mark.** Stirs: Poems from Hollywood. 11p. 1999. pap. 5.00 (*0-89642-723-4*) Linden Pubs.

Dunster, Mark. Storkwood. rev. ed. (Rin Ser.: Pt. 8). 62p. (Orig.). 1980. pap. 4.00 (*0-89642-066-3*) Linden Pubs.

— A Story with No Point: Poems from Hollywood. 19p. 1998. 5.00 (*0-89642-423-5*) Linden Pubs.

— Storytell: Poems from Hollywood. 11p. 1998. pap. 5.00 (*0-89642-530-4*) Linden Pubs.

— Strange Sermons: Poems from Hollywood. 11p. 1998. pap. 5.00 (*0-89642-618-1*) Linden Pubs.

— Strategies: Poems from Hollywood. 11p. 1999. pap. 5.00 (*0-89642-700-5*) Linden Pubs.

— Strathspeys: Poems from Hollywood. 11p. 1998. pap. 5.00 (*0-89642-470-7*) Linden Pubs.

***Dunster, Mark.** Streusel: Poems from Hollywood. 11p. 1999. pap. 5.00 (*0-89642-801-X*) Linden Pubs.

Dunster, Mark. Stuff: Poems from Hollywood. 29p. 1997. pap. 5.00 (*0-89642-386-7*) Linden Pubs.

— Stuyvesant. 23p. (Orig.). 1991. pap. 5.00 (*0-89642-194-5*) Linden Pubs.

— Succubus. 11p. 1991. pap. 4.00 (*0-89642-196-1*) Linden Pubs.

***Dunster, Mark.** Suckets: Poems from Hollywood. 11p. 1999. pap. 5.00 (*0-89642-761-7*) Linden Pubs.

Dunster, Mark. Summerton. 21p. (Orig.). (YA). (gr. 9-12). 1996. pap. 5.00 (*0-89642-295-X*) Linden Pubs.

***Dunster, Mark.** Sun & Shade. 11p. 1999. pap. 5.00 (*0-89642-906-7*) Linden Pubs.

— Sun & Shadow: Poems from Hollywood. 11p. 1999. pap. 5.00 (*0-89642-866-4*) Linden Pubs.

— Superfluities: Poems from Hollywood. 11p. 1999. pap. 5.00 (*0-89642-805-2*) Linden Pubs.

Dunster, Mark. Surrey: Henry the Eighth, Pt. 6. 1980. pap. 4.00 (*0-89642-061-2*) Linden Pubs.

— Swallows: Poems from Hollywood. 11p. 1999. pap. 5.00 (*0-89642-791-9*) Linden Pubs.

— Swirls: Poems from Hollywood. 11p. 1998. pap. 5.00 (*0-89642-534-7*) Linden Pubs.

— Sylvan. 23p. (Orig.). 1995. pap. 4.00 (*0-89642-256-9*) Linden Pubs.

— Talismans: Poems from Hollywood. 11p. 1999. pap. 5.00 (*0-89642-749-8*) Linden Pubs.

***Dunster, Mark.** Talking to the Wind: Poems from Hollywood. 11p. 2000. pap. 5.00 (*0-89642-988-1*) Linden Pubs.

— Tarantula: Poems from Hollywood. 11p. 1999. pap. 5.00 (*0-89642-979-2*) Linden Pubs.

Dunster, Mark. Teacher. 15p. (Orig.). 1985. pap. 4.00 (*0-89642-127-9*) Linden Pubs.

— Tecumseh. 1979. pap. 4.00 (*0-89642-053-1*) Linden Pubs.

***Dunster, Mark.** Tendrils: Poems from Hollywood. 11p. 1999. pap. 5.00 (*0-89642-875-3*) Linden Pubs.

— Tesserao. 11p. 1999. pap. 5.00 (*0-89642-851-6*) Linden Pubs.

Dunster, Mark. Text & Compasses: Poems from Hollywood. 11p. 1999. pap. 5.00 (*0-89642-679-3*) Linden Pubs.

***Dunster, Mark.** Thaws: Poems from Hollywood. 11p. 1999. pap. 5.00 (*0-89642-940-7*) Linden Pubs.

Dunster, Mark. Theo. 14p. (Orig.). 1988. pap. 4.00 (*0-89642-165-1*) Linden Pubs.

— Therapies. 14p. (Orig.). (YA). (gr. 9-12). 1996. pap. 5.00 (*0-89642-329-8*) Linden Pubs.

— Thief. 24p. (Orig.). 1983. pap. 4.00 (*0-89642-097-3*) Linden Pubs.

— Thing That's Yours: Poems from Hollywood. 16p. 1998. pap. 5.00 (*0-89642-459-6*) Linden Pubs.

— Things. 12p. (Orig.). 1990. pap. text 4.00 (*0-89642-182-1*) Linden Pubs.

— Thinks: Poems from Hollywood. 11p. 1998. pap. 5.00 (*0-89642-566-5*) Linden Pubs.

***Dunster, Mark.** This & That: Poems from Hollywood. 11p. 1999. pap. 5.00 (*0-89642-822-2*) Linden Pubs.

Dunster, Mark. This Just In: Poems from Hollywood. 11p. 1999. pap. 5.00 (*0-89642-768-4*) Linden Pubs.

— Thit. 14p. (Orig.). 1992. pap. 4.00 (*0-89642-207-0*) Linden Pubs.

— Thor Bridge: A Play. 1989. 4.00 (*0-89642-178-3*) Linden Pubs.

— Thread Ends: Poems from Hollywood. 16p. 1998. pap. 5.00 (*0-89642-445-6*) Linden Pubs.

— Three Ladies of Bagdad. 24p. (Orig.). 1989. pap. 5.00 (*0-89642-175-9*) Linden Pubs.

***Dunster, Mark.** Thresholds: Poems from Hollywood. 11p. 1999. pap. 5.00 (*0-89642-812-5*) Linden Pubs.

— Through the Keyhole: Poems from Hollywood. 11p. 1999. pap. 5.00 (*0-89642-986-5*) Linden Pubs.

Dunster, Mark. Tib. (Holiday Ser.: Pt. 6: Easter). 77p. (Orig.). 1981. pap. 5.00 (*0-89642-077-9*) Linden Pubs.

— Tiger. (Holiday Ser.: Pt. 4: New Years Eve). 79p. (Orig.). 1980. pap. 4.00 (*0-89642-068-X*) Linden Pubs.

***Dunster, Mark.** Tilts: Poems from Hollywood. 11p. 1999. pap. 5.00 (*0-89642-901-6*) Linden Pubs.

Dunster, Mark. Tim. (Rin Ser.: Pt. 20). 25p. (Orig.). 1987. pap. 4.00 (*0-89642-145-7*) Linden Pubs.

— Timmon. 22p. (Orig.). 1996. pap. 5.00 (*0-89642-296-8*) Linden Pubs.

***Dunster, Mark.** Tisane: Poems from Hollywood. 11p. 1999. pap. 5.00 (*0-89642-907-5*) Linden Pubs.

Dunster, Mark. Titch. 24p. 1983. pap. 4.00 (*0-89642-103-1*) Linden Pubs.

— Toccatas: Poems from Hollywood. 12p. 1997. pap. 5.00 (*0-89642-381-6*) Linden Pubs.

— Torches: Poems from Hollywood. 23p. (Orig.). (YA). (gr. 9-12). 1997. pap. 5.00 (*0-89642-361-1*) Linden Pubs.

— Toss-Ups: Poems from Hollywood. 11p. 1999. pap. 5.00 (*0-89642-780-3*) Linden Pubs.

***Dunster, Mark.** Touch & Go: Poems from Hollywood. 11p. 1999. pap. 5.00 (*0-89642-895-8*) Linden Pubs.

Dunster, Mark. Touchstones: Poems from Hollywood. 11p. 1999. pap. 5.00 (*0-89642-624-6*) Linden Pubs.

***Dunster, Mark.** Touchstones: Poems from Hollywood. 11p. 1999. pap. 5.00 (*0-89642-977-6*) Linden Pubs.

Dunster, Mark. Touts Poems from Hollywood. 11p. 1998. pap. 5.00 (*0-89642-570-3*) Linden Pubs.

— Tracy. (Rin Ser.: Pt. 54). (Orig.). 1981. pap. 4.00 (*0-89642-079-5*) Linden Pubs.

— Trade Winds: Poems from Hollywood. 17p. 1998. pap. 5.00 (*0-89642-415-4*) Linden Pubs.

— Trails. 32p. (Orig.). 1991. pap. 5.00 (*0-89642-191-0*) Linden Pubs.

— Travels: Poems from Hollywood. 11p. 1998. pap. 5.00 (*0-89642-580-0*) Linden Pubs.

***Dunster, Mark.** Treasures: Poems from Hollywood. 11p. 1999. pap. 5.00 (*0-89642-938-5*) Linden Pubs.

Dunster, Mark. Treatises: Poems from Hollywood. 11p. 1998. pap. 5.00 (*0-89642-610-6*) Linden Pubs.

— Trellis: Poems from Hollywood. 15p. 1998. pap. 5.00 (*0-89642-487-1*) Linden Pubs.

— Trent. 33p. (Orig.). 1982. pap. 4.00 (*0-89642-091-4*) Linden Pubs.

— Trex. 24p. (Orig.). 1994. pap. 5.00 (*0-89642-235-6*) Linden Pubs.

***Dunster, Mark.** Triptychs: Poems from Hollywood. 11p. 1999. pap. 5.00 (*0-89642-983-0*) Linden Pubs.

Dunster, Mark. Triumphs: Poems from Hollywood. 11p. 1999. pap. 5.00 (*0-89642-694-7*) Linden Pubs.

An Asterisk (*) at the beginning of an entry indicates that the title is appearing for the first time.

— Trock. 31p. (Orig.). 1995. pap. 5.00 (*0-89642-269-0*) Linden Pubs.
— Troilus. 37p. (Orig.). 1995. pap. 5.00 (*0-89642-291-7*) Linden Pubs.
— The Trojan War. 20p. (YA). (gr. 9-12). 1996. pap. 5.00 (*0-89642-339-5*) Linden Pubs.
— Trolls: Poems from Hollywood. 16p. (Orig.). (YA). (gr. 9-12). 1997. pap. 5.00 (*0-89642-342-5*) Linden Pubs.
— Trouble: Poems from Hollywood. 11p. 1998. pap. 5.00 (*0-89642-551-7*) Linden Pubs.
— Troy. LC 74-437973. (Rin Ser.: Pt. 31). 1974. 4.00 (*0-89642-035-3*) Linden Pubs.
— Truce. (Drex Ser.: Pt. 2). 1979. pap. 4.00 (*0-89642-050-7*) Linden Pubs.
— Tuck. (Holiday Ser.: Pt. 2: Thanksgiving). 55p. (Orig.). 1981. pap. 4.00 (*0-89642-073-6*) Linden Pubs.
— Twins. LC 75-192367. (Rin Ser.: Pt. 35). 1975. 4.00 (*0-89642-036-1*) Linden Pubs.
— Twirls: Poems from Hollywood. 11p. 1999. pap. 5.00 (*0-89642-635-1*) Linden Pubs.
— Two Men. 18p. 1983. pap. 4.00 (*0-89642-102-3*) Linden Pubs.
— Ty Pt. 1: Night People. (Rin Ser.: Pt. 19). 34p. (Orig.). 1987. pap. 5.00 (*0-89642-149-X*) Linden Pubs.
— Tylo. 25p. (Orig.). 1995. pap. 5.00 (*0-89642-279-8*) Linden Pubs.
— Unguents: Poems from Hollywood. 17p. 1998. pap. 5.00 (*0-89642-426-X*) Linden Pubs.
— Unimportances: Poems from Hollywood. 11p. 1998. pap. 5.00 (*0-89642-508-8*) Linden Pubs.
— Up & Down: Poems from Hollywood. 11p. 1999. pap. 5.00 (*0-89642-696-3*) Linden Pubs.
***Dunster, Mark.** Upheavals: Poems from Hollywood. 11p. 2000. pap. 5.00 (*0-89642-996-2*) Linden Pubs.
Dunster, Mark. Variorums: Poems from Hollywood. 29p. (Orig.). (YA). (gr. 9-12). 1997. pap. 5.00 (*0-89642-372-7*) Linden Pubs.
— Velleities: Poems from Hollywood. 11p. 1998. pap. 5.00 (*0-89642-529-0*) Linden Pubs.
— Venues. 25p. (Orig.). (YA). (gr. 9-12). 1996. pap. 5.00 (*0-89642-311-5*) Linden Pubs.
***Dunster, Mark.** Verbatim: Poems from Hollywood. 11p. 1999. pap. 5.00 (*0-89642-854-0*) Linden Pubs.
— Verve: Poems from Hollywood. 11p. 1999. pap. 5.00 (*0-89642-880-X*) Linden Pubs.
— Verves: Poems from Hollywood. 11p. 1999. pap. 5.00 (*0-89642-865-6*) Linden Pubs.
— Vestiges: Poems from Hollywood. 11p. 1999. pap. 5.00 (*0-89642-965-2*) Linden Pubs.
— Vestures: Poems from Hollywood. 11p. 2000. pap. 5.00 (*0-89642-998-9*) Linden Pubs.
Dunster, Mark. Views: Poems from Hollywood. 11p. 1999. pap. 5.00 (*0-89642-784-6*) Linden Pubs.
— Virginia. (James Ser.: Pt. 4). 79p. (Orig.). 1975. pap. 4.00 (*0-89642-037-X*) Linden Pubs.
— Virginia. (John Brown Ser.: Pt. 3). 34p. (Orig.). 1983. reprint ed. pap. 4.00 (*0-89642-104-X*) Linden Pubs.
— Visions: Poems from Hollywood. 11p. 1999. pap. 5.00 (*0-89642-703-X*) Linden Pubs.
— Vistas: Poems from Hollywood. 17p. (Orig.). (YA). (gr. 9-12). 1997. pap. 5.00 (*0-89642-345-X*) Linden Pubs.
— Vivas: Poems from Hollywood. 11p. 1999. pap. 5.00 (*0-89642-625-4*) Linden Pubs.
— Voyage: Poems from Hollywood. 11p. 1998. pap. 5.00 (*0-89642-492-8*) Linden Pubs.
Dunster, Mark. Vulp. 27p. (Orig.). 1994. pap. 5.00 (*0-89642-236-4*) Linden Pubs.
Dunster, Mark. Wanderer. 11p. (Orig.). 1992. pap. 4.00 (*0-89642-209-7*) Linden Pubs.
***Dunster, Mark.** Wassail: Poems from Hollywood. 11p. 1999. pap. 5.00 (*0-89642-815-X*) Linden Pubs.
Dunster, Mark. Water from the Well: Poems from Hollywood. 19p. 1998. pap. 5.00 (*0-89642-402-2*) Linden Pubs.
***Dunster, Mark.** Water in the Skillet: Poems from Hollywood. 11p. 1999. pap. 5.00 (*0-89642-737-4*) Linden Pubs.
Dunster, Mark. Watersheds: Poems from Hollywood. 11p. 1999. pap. 5.00 (*0-89642-673-4*) Linden Pubs.
— Ways In: Poems from Hollywood. 32p. 1997. pap. 5.00 (*0-89642-364-6*) Linden Pubs.
— Webster. (John Brown, First Prolog Ser.). 1977. pap. 4.00 (*0-89642-009-4*) Linden Pubs.
— Wedding Day. 53p. (Orig.). 1986. pap. 5.00 (*0-89642-139-2*) Linden Pubs.
— Weekend. LC 74-438797. (Rin Ser.: Pt. 6). 1974. 4.00 (*0-89642-038-8*) Linden Pubs.
— Weens: Poems from Hollywood. 11p. 1998. pap. 5.00 (*0-89642-541-X*) Linden Pubs.
— Wellings: Poems from Hollywood. 17p. 1998. pap. 5.00 (*0-89642-411-1*) Linden Pubs.
— Wells: Poems from Hollywood. 21p. 1997. pap. 5.00 (*0-89642-360-3*) Linden Pubs.
***Dunster, Mark.** What You Will: Poems from Hollywood. 11p. 1999. pap. 5.00 (*0-89642-746-3*) Linden Pubs.
— Which End Is Up? Poems from Hollywood. 11p. 1999. pap. 5.00 (*0-89642-945-8*) Linden Pubs.
— Whimsies: Poems from Hollywood. 11p. 1999. pap. 5.00 (*0-89642-972-5*) Linden Pubs.
— Whimsies: Poems from Hollywood. 11p. 2000. pap. 5.00 (*0-89642-999-7*) Linden Pubs.
Dunster, Mark. Whirlwinds: Poems from Hollywood. 11p. 1999. pap. 5.00 (*0-89642-620-3*) Linden Pubs.
— Whitbread: Poems from Hollywood. 11p. 1998. pap. 5.00 (*0-89642-512-6*) Linden Pubs.
***Dunster, Mark.** Whitman Log: Poems from Hollywood. 18p. 1999. pap. 6.00 (*0-89642-891-5*) Linden Pubs.
— Whizzes: Poems from Hollywood. 11p. 1999. pap. 5.00 (*0-89642-941-5*) Linden Pubs.
— Whoopee: Poems from Hollywood. 11p. 1999. pap. 5.00 (*0-89642-892-3*) Linden Pubs.
— Whoosh: Poems from Hollywood. 11p. 2000. pap. 5.00 (*0-89642-995-4*) Linden Pubs.
Dunster, Mark. Wildfire: Poems from Hollywood. 12p. 1998. pap. 5.00 (*0-89642-437-5*) Linden Pubs.
***Dunster, Mark.** Wind Tales: Poems from Hollywood. 11p. 1999. pap. 5.00 (*0-89642-904-0*) Linden Pub.
Dunster, Mark. Wind Trips: Poems from Hollywood. 11p. 1999. pap. 5.00 (*0-89642-706-4*) Linden Pubs.
— Windfalls: Poems from Hollywood. 11p. 1998. pap. 5.00 (*0-89642-488-X*) Linden Pubs.
***Dunster, Mark.** Windows: Poems from Hollywood. 11p. 1999. pap. 5.00 (*0-89642-762-5*) Linden Pubs.
Dunster, Mark. Winds. 26p. (Orig.). 1996. 5.00 (*0-89642-321-2*) Linden Pubs.
— Wings: Poems from Hollywood. 11p. 1998. pap. 5.00 (*0-89642-584-3*) Linden Pubs.
— Wink. 40p. (Orig.). 1994. pap. 5.00 (*0-89642-231-3*) Linden Pubs.
— Winter. (Rin Ser.: Pt. 36). 47p. (Orig.). 1985. pap. 5.00 (*0-89642-125-2*) Linden Pubs.
— The Winter War Pt. 2: Antony. 42p. 1985. pap. 5.00 (*0-89642-124-4*) Linden Pubs.
— Wishbones: Poems from Hollywood. 15p. 1998. pap. 5.00 (*0-89642-414-6*) Linden Pubs.
— Wolsey. (Henry the Eighth: Pt. 1). 54p. (Orig.). 1980. pap. 4.00 (*0-89642-069-8*) Linden Pubs.
— Words to the Wind: Poems from Hollywood. 11p. 1999. pap. 5.00 (*0-89642-667-X*) Linden Pubs.
— Worlds: Poems from Hollywood. 11p. 1999. pap. 5.00 (*0-89642-681-5*) Linden Pubs.
— Worth. 11p. (Orig.). 1992. pap. 4.00 (*0-89642-206-2*) Linden Pubs.
— Wreaks: Poems from Hollywood. 11p. 1999. pap. 5.00 (*0-89642-775-7*) Linden Pubs.
***Dunster, Mark.** Written by a Waker from a Dream: Poems from Hollywood. 11p. 1999. pap. 5.00 (*0-89642-846-X*) Linden Pubs.
Dunster, Mark. Yeast: Poems from Hollywood. 11p. 1999. pap. 5.00 (*0-89642-646-7*) Linden Pubs.
— York: Being the Story of Mrs. Osgoods Will. 50p. (Orig.). 1981. pap. 4.00 (*0-89642-082-5*) Linden Pubs.
***Dunster, Mark.** You Never Can Tell: Poems from Hollywood. 11p. 1999. pap. 5.00 (*0-89642-886-9*) Linden Pubs.
— Yule Log for the Xmas-Tale Fire Spinners. 11p. 1999. pap. 5.00 (*0-89642-816-8*) Linden Pubs.
Dunster, Mark. Zand. 52p. (Orig.). 1994. pap. 6.00 (*0-89642-244-5*) Linden Pubs.
***Dunster, Mark.** Zeniths: Poems from Hollywood. 11p. 1999. pap. 5.00 (*0-89642-859-1*) Linden Pubs.
— Zephyrs: Poems from Hollywood. 11p. 1999. pap. 5.00 (*0-89642-819-2*) Linden Pubs.
Dunster, Mark. Zests: Poems from Hollywood. 19p. 1998. pap. 5.00 (*0-89642-420-0*) Linden Pubs.
— Zings: Poems from Hollywood. 11p. 1999. pap. 5.00 (*0-89642-640-8*) Linden Pubs.
— Zond. 45p. (Orig.). (J). 1989. pap. 5.00 (*0-89642-168-6*) Linden Pubs.
***Dunster, Mark.** Zones: Poems from Hollywood. 11p. 1999. pap. 5.00 (*0-89642-862-1*) Linden Pubs.
Dunster, Mark. Zora. 19p. (Orig.). 1985. pap. 4.00 (*0-89642-128-7*) Linden Pubs.
— Zorro. 17p. (Orig.). 1995. pap. 4.00 (*0-89642-262-3*) Linden Pubs.
Dunster, Mark & Brown, John. Sumner: John Brown, Second Prolog. 1980. pap. 4.00 (*0-89642-065-5*) Linden Pubs.
Dunster, Mark, ed. see Shakespeare, William.
Dunster, S. Henry Dunster & His Descendants. (Illus.). 343p. 1989. reprint ed. pap. 51.00 (*0-8328-0501-7*); reprint ed. lib. bdg. 59.00 (*0-8328-0500-9*) Higginson Bk Co.
***Dunsterville-Branch, Hilary.** Venezuela: The Bradt Travel Guide. 3rd ed. (Illus.). 192p. 1999. pap. text 18.95 (*1-898323-89-5*) Bradt Pubns.
Dunsterville, E., jt. auth. see Dunsterville, G. C.
Dunsterville, G. C. & Dunsterville, E. Orchid Hunting in the Lost World (And Elsewhere in Venezuela) (Illus.). 280p. (C). 1988. write for info. (*0-923096-00-0*) Amer Orchid Soc Inc.
Dunsterville, Jane. The Glass Painting Book. (Illus.). 128p. 1997. 24.95 (*0-7153-0428-3*, Pub. by D & C Pub) Sterling.
Dunsterville, Jane & Dunsterville, John. Glass Painting Projects: Decorative Glass for Beautiful Interiors. (Illus.). 144p. 1999. 27.99 (*0-89134-971-5*, North Lght Bks) F & W Pubns Inc.
Dunsterville, John, jt. auth. see Dunsterville, Jane.
Dunston, Alfred G., Jr. The Black Man in the Old Testament & Its World. LC 91-78315. 175p. 1992. 35.00 (*0-86543-304-6*); pap. 11.95 (*0-86543-305-4*) Africa World.
Dunston, Mark. Arroyos: Poems from Hollywood. 11p. 1998. pap. 5.00 (*0-89642-443-X*) Linden Pubs.
— Cubeb: Poems from Hollywood. 15p. 1998. pap. 5.00 (*0-89642-451-0*) Linden Pubs.
— Miscellany: Poems from Hollywood. 11p. 1998. pap. 5.00 (*0-89642-444-8*) Linden Pubs.
— Odd Drink: Poems from Hollywood. 14p. 1998. pap. 5.00 (*0-89642-452-9*) Linden Pubs.
Dunston, Mark S. Street Signs: An Identification Guide of Symbols of Crime & Violence. LC 91-66378. (Illus.). 256p. (Orig.). 1992. pap. 14.95 (*1-879411-13-X*); VHS 29.95 (*1-879411-14-8*) Perf Dimensions Pub.
Dunstone, N. & Gorman, M. L., eds. Mammals As Predators: The Proceedings of a Symposium Held by the Zoological Society of London & the Mammal Society, London, 22-23 November 1991. LC 92-39591. (Illus.). 508p. (C). 1993. text 125.00 (*0-19-854067-1*, Clarendon Pr) OUP.
Dunstone, Nigel & Gorman, Martyn L., eds. Behavior & Ecology of Riparian Mammals. (Symposia of the Zoological Society of London Ser.: No. 71). (Illus.). 379p. (C). 1998. text 95.00 (*0-521-63101-7*) Cambridge U Pr.
Dunstone, Nigel, jt. ed. see Entwistle, Abigail.
Dunstone, Virginia. Why Do I Do What I Do? How to Understand Yourself & Others. (Illus.). 348p. (Orig.). 1995. pap. 15.95 (*0-9638282-0-7*) Gate Pubng.
Dunteman, George H. Introduction to Linear Models. LC 83-19623. (Illus.). 357p. 1984. reprint ed. pap. 110.70 (*0-608-01158-4*, 205945800001) Bks Demand.
— Introduction to Multivariate Analysis. LC 83-19139. (Illus.). 237p. 1984. reprint ed. pap. 73.50 (*0-608-01159-2*, 205945900001) Bks Demand.
— Principal Components Analysis, No. 69. (Quantitative Applications in the Social Sciences Ser.: Vol. 69) 96p. (C). 1989. pap. text 10.95 (*0-8039-3104-2*) Sage.
Duntemann, Jeff. Assembly Language: Step-by-Step. LC 92-16665. 448p. 1992. pap. 39.99 (*0-471-57814-2*) Wiley.
***Duntemann, Jeff.** Assembly Language Step-by-Step Programming with DOS & Linux. 2nd ed. LC 00-20611. 612p. 2000. pap. text 49.99 (*0-471-37523-3*) Wiley.
Duntemann, Jeff. Latte Frontrunner. 400p. 1996. pap. text 29.99 (*1-57610-004-9*) Coriolis Grp.
— Latte' Programming Explorer. 500p. 1996. pap. text 39.99 incl. cd-rom (*1-57610-005-7*) Coriolis Grp.
— Turbo Pascal Solutions. (C). 1988. pap. 24.33 (*0-673-18584-2*, Scott Frsmn) Addson-Wesley Educ.
Duntemann, Jeff, ed. see Cilwa, Paul.
Duntemann, Jeff, ed. see Mischel, Jim.
Dunten, Joseph F. Dunten-Dunton, 1644-1997. LC 98-165426. 279p. 1998. pap. 22.50 (*0-7884-0859-3*, D857) Heritage Bk.
Dunthorn, David J., jt. ed. see Leitz, Christian.
Dunthorne, Gordon. Flower & Fruit Prints of the 18th & Early 19th Centuries: Their History, Makers & Uses, with a Catalogue Raisonne of the Works in Which They Are Found. (Illus.). 289p. 1996. reprint ed. 75.00 (*1-888262-05-2*) Martino Pubng.
Dunton, Chris. Make Man Talk True: Nigerian Drama in English since 1970. (New Perspectives on African Literature Ser.: No. 5). 226p. 1992. lib. bdg. 85.00 (*0-905450-87-6*, Pub. by H Zell Pubs) Seven Hills Bk.
— Nigerian Theatre in English. 1998. 100.00 (*1-873836-71-6*) Bowker-Saur.
Dunton, Chris & Palmberg, Mai. Human Rights & Homosexuality in Southern Africa. 2nd ed. 48p. (Orig.). 1996. pap. 22.50 (*91-7106-402-8*, Pub. by Almqvist Wiksell) Coronet Bks.
Dunton, Darlene. Complete Bonsai Handbook. 169p. 1978. pap. 12.95 (*0-8128-6008-X*, Scrbrough Hse) Madison Bks UPA.
Dunton, David J. & Trumbore, Harry. What You Can Do for Her When She's Expecting. LC 98-50125. (Illus.). 96p. 1999. pap. 9.95 (*1-58063-055-3*, Pub. by Renaissance) St Martin.
Dunton, David J., ed. see Horowitz, Shel.
Dunton, Dorothy M. All This Day Fine: Mellie's Life at Sea with Captain Frank. LC 98-84388. (Illus.). 96p. 1998. pap. 12.50 (*0-89725-341-8*, 1865, Penobscot Pr, Picton Pr.
Dunton, Gardner. The Letters of World War I Pilot in the Army Air Corps. 252p. 1977. pap. text 36.95 (*0-89126-028-5*) MA-AH Pub.
Dunton, John. The Dublin Scuffle. 352p. 1999. pap. 75.00 (*1-85182-446-4*, Pub. by Four Cts Pr) Intl Spec Bk.
— A True Journal of the Sally Fleet, with the Proceedings of the Voyage. LC 71-25745. (English Experience Ser.: No. 242). 26p. 1970. reprint ed. 20.00 (*90-221-0242-4*) Walter J Johnson.
Dunton, Loren & Banta, Kim C. Preserving Family Wealth & Peace of Mind: Estate Planning: Caring for & Communicating to Your Family Though the Legacies You Leave. 225p. 1994. text 27.50 (*1-55738-832-6*, Irwn Prfssnl) McGraw-Hill Prof.
Dunton, Sabina & Miller, Kathy A. Counselfile. McNeely, Richard A., ed. LC 82-50626. (Illus.). 150p. (Orig.). (C). 1982. 27.50 (*0-943562-50-3*) Well Aware.
Dunton, Sabina M. & Fanning, Melody S. Smoking: Facilitator's Manual. McNeely, Richard A., ed. (Well Aware About Health Risk Reduction Ser.). (Illus.). 186p. (Orig.). 1982. 29.95 (*0-943562-51-1*) Well Aware.
— Smoking: Workbook. McNeely, Richard A., ed. (Well Aware About Health Risk Reduction Ser.). (Illus.). 109p. (Orig.). 1982. pap. 8.50 (*0-943562-52-X*) Well Aware.
Dunton, Trevor, jt. auth. see Preston, Charlotte.
Duntze, Dorothee. The Twelve Days of Christmas. LC 91-32359. (Illus.). 64p. (J). (gr. 1-4). 1996. pap. 6.95 (*1-55858-608-3*, Pub. by North-South Bks NYC) Chronicle Bks.
Duntze, Dorothee. The Life of Jesus: Adapted from NRSV. LC 93-28776. 105p. (J). 1993. 14.95 (*0-8146-2303-4*) Liturgical Pr.
Duntze, Klaus. Die Verantwortung der Kirche Fur das Grobstadtische Gemeinwesen: Eine Untersuchung zum Verhaltnis von Kirchlicher Arbeit und Stadtentwicklung in Berlin (West) von 1968 Bis 1985 Unter Besonderer Berucksichtigung des Bezirks Kreuzberg. (Europaische Hochschulschriften Ser.: Reihe 22, Bd. 243). (GER., Illus.). 460p. 1993. 60.80 (*3-631-45482-1*) P Lang Pubng.
Duntzer, Heinrich, ed. see Herder, Johann G.
Dunung, Sanjyot P. Doing Business in Asia: The Complete Guide. 2nd ed. LC 98-40364. (Business & Management Ser.). 608p. 1998. pap. 34.95 (*0-7879-4283-9*) Jossey-Bass.
Dunwell, Anna. Guide to 400 Best Children's & Adults Books about Family. 100p. 1998. spiral bd. 42.00 (*1-891657-18-6*, S2991) Lift Every Voice.
— Guide to the 400 Best Children's & Adults Multicultural Books about New York. 100p. 1998. spiral bd. 24.95 (*1-891657-30-5*, S2992) Lift Every Voice.
— Guide to the 400 Best Children's & Adult's Multicultural Books about Immigration & Moving. Date not set. spiral bd. 42.00 (*1-891657-29-1*, S2990) Lift Every Voice.
— Guide to the 400 Best Children's & Adults Books about Religion. 50p. (J). (gr. k-12). 1999. spiral bd. 24.95 (*1-891657-19-4*, S2598) Lift Every Voice.
— Guide to the 400 Best Children's & Adults Multicultural Books about History. 50p. (J). (gr. k-12). 1999. spiral bd. 24.95 (*1-891657-20-8*, S2599) Lift Every Voice.
— Guide to the 400 Best Children's & Adults Books about Math Numbers & Alphabets. 50p. (J). 1999. spiral bd. 24.95 (*1-891657-21-6*, S2600) Lift Every Voice.
— Guide to the 400 Best Children's & Adults Multicultural Books about People of Middle Eastern Descent. 50p. (J). (gr. k-12). 1999. spiral bd. 24.95 (*1-891657-31-3*, S2993) Lift Every Voice.
— Guide to the 400 Best Children's & Adults Books about School. 50p. (J). 1999. spiral bd. 24.95 (*1-891657-32-1*, S3080) Lift Every Voice.
— Guide to the 400 Best Children's & Adults Books about Grandparents. 50p. (J). (gr. k-12). 1999. spiral bd. 24.95 (*1-891657-33-X*, S3079) Lift Every Voice.
Dunwell, Frances. The Hudson River Highlands. (Illus.). 320p. 1991. pap. 23.50 (*0-231-07043-8*) Col U Pr.
Dunwell, Steve. Extraordinary Boston. rev. ed. LC 94-79004. (Illus.). 128p. 1994. reprint ed. 35.00 (*0-9643015-0-4*) Back Bay Boston.
— Harvard: A Living Portrait. rev. ed. (Illus.). 144p. 1995. 37.50 (*0-9643015-1-2*) Back Bay Boston.
— Massachusetts. Patrick, James B., ed. (Scenic Discovery Ser.). (Illus.). 120p. reprint ed. 30.00 (*0-940078-04-X*) Foremost Pubs.
— Rhode Island: A Scenic Discovery. Patrick, James B., ed. (Scenic Discovery Ser.). 120p. 1983. 25.00 (*0-940078-03-1*) Foremost Pubs.
Dunwell, Steve, photos by. Massachusetts: A Scenic Discovery. rev. ed. LC 97-71381. (Illus.). 120p. 1997. 35.00 (*0-9643015-3-9*) Back Bay Boston.
Dunwich, Gerina. Candlelight Spells. 193p. (Orig.). 1988. pap. 12.00 (*0-8065-1106-0*, Citadel Pr) Carol Pub Group.
— Circle of Shadows: A Collection of Goddess - Inspired Poetry & Magickal Verse. LC 91-73793. (Illus.). 52p. (Orig.). 1990. pap. 8.00 (*0-9628638-0-7*) Golden Isis Pr.
— The Concise Lexicon of the Occult. 215p. 1990. pap. 7.95 (*0-8065-1191-5*, Citadel Pr) Carol Pub Group.
— Everyday Wicca: Magickal Spells Throughout the Year. LC 97-7924. (Illus.). 200p. 1997. pap. 10.95 (*0-8065-1869-3*, Citadel Pr) Carol Pub Group.
***Dunwich, Gerina.** Exploring Spellcraft: How to Create & Cast Effective Spells. 224p. 2001. pap. 12.99 (*1-56414-494-1*, New Page Bks) Career Pr Inc.
Dunwich, Gerina. The Magic of Candle Burning. (Citadel Library of the Mystic Arts). 195p. 1989. pap. 6.95 (*0-8065-1141-9*, Citadel Pr) Carol Pub Group.
— Magick Portions: HOQ to Prepare & Use Homemade Aphrodisiacs, Oils, Brews & Much More. LC 97-51860. 176p. 1998. pap. text 10.95 (*0-8065-1982-7*, Citadel Pr) Carol Pub Group.
***Dunwich, Gerina.** The Pagan Book of Halloween: A Complete Guide to the Magick, Incantations, Recipes, Spells & Lore. (Illus.). 224p. 2000. pap. 11.00 (*0-14-019616-1*) Penguin Putnam.
Dunwich, Gerina. Wicca A to Z: A Modern Witch's Encyclopedia. LC 97-25999. 224p. 1997. pap. text 10.95 (*0-8065-1930-4*, Citadel Pr) Carol Pub Group.
— Wicca Book of Days: Legend & Lore for Every Day of the Year. (Illus.). 176p. 1995. pap. 9.95 (*0-8065-1685-2*, Citadel Pr) Carol Pub Group.
— Wicca Candle Magick. 192p. Date not set. pap. 9.95 (*0-8065-1831-6*, Citadel Pr) Carol Pub Group.
— Wicca Craft: The Book of Herbs, Magick & Dreams. 192p. Date not set. pap. 9.95 (*0-8065-1238-5*, Citadel Pr) Carol Pub Group.
— The Wicca Garden: A Modern Witch's Book of Magickal & Enchanted Herbs & Plants. (Citadel Library of the Mystic Arts). 192p. 1996. pap. 10.95 (*0-8065-1777-8*, Citadel Pr) Carol Pub Group.
— Wicca Love Spells: How to Attract a Lover, Make a Former Lover Return to You...& Much, Much More. LC 95-50273. (Illus.). 206p. 1996. pap. 10.95 (*0-8065-1782-4*) Carol Pub Group.
— Wicca Source Book: A Complete Guide for the Modern Witch. rev. ed. 266p. 1998. pap. 12.00 (*0-8065-2027-2*, Citadel Pr) Carol Pub Group.
— The Wicca Source Book: Complete Guide for the Modern Witch. 208p. Date not set. pap. 10.95 (*0-8065-1830-8*, Citadel Pr) Carol Pub Group.
— The Wicca Spellbook. LC 93-43436. 204p. Date not set. pap. 10.95 (*0-8065-1476-0*, Citadel Pr) Carol Pub Group.
— Wiccan Prophecy: A Practical Guide to the Mystical Guide of Divination. LC 97-8641. (Illus.). 200p. 1997. pap. 10.95 (*0-8065-1864-2*, Citadel Pr) Carol Pub Group.
— The Wiccan's Dictionary of Prophecy & Omens. (Illus.). 160p. 1999. pap. 12.00 (*0-8065-2067-1*, Citadel Pr) Carol Pub Group.
— Your Magickal Cat: Feline Magick, Lore, & Worship. LC 99-31181. (Illus.). 176p. 1999. pap. 12.00 (*0-8065-2094-9*, Citadel Pr) Carol Pub Group.
Dunwiddie, Peter, jt. auth. see Vickery, Peter D.
Dunwiddie, Peter W. Changing Landscapes: A Pictorial Field Guide to a Century of Change on Nantucket. (Illus.). 48p. (Orig.). 1992. pap. write for info. (*0-9607340-5-8*) Nantucket Hist Assn.

D

An Asterisk (*) at the beginning of an entry indicates that the title is appearing for the first time.

Dunwiddie, Thomas V. & Lovinger, David M., eds. Presynaptic Receptors in the Mammalian Brain. (Illus.). 272p. 1993. 109.00 (*0-8176-3651-X*) Birkhauser.
***Dunwoodie, Duane.** A Solo Act. 2000. pap. 6.95 (*0-552-54524-4*, Pub. by Transworld Publishers Ltd) Trafalgar.
Dunwoodie, Peter. Writing from Algeria. LC 98-37816. 342p. 1999. text 80.00 (*0-19-815972-2*) OUP.
Dunwoody, H. H., et al. Weather Proverbs. 1977. lib. bdg. 69.95 (*0-8490-2813-2*) Gordon Pr.
Dunwoody, Ken, ed. Great Whitetail Hunts: And the Lessons They Taught. LC 95-60953. 240p. 1995. 19.95 (*0-9633315-2-3*) Venture Pr MT.
Dunwoody, M. J., jt. auth. see Dicks, Warren.
***Dunwoody, Richard.** Hands & Heels. 2000. 35.95 (*1-85225-262-6*, Pub. by Transworld Publishers Ltd) Trafalgar.
Dunwoody, Sharon. Reconstructing Science for Public Consumption: Journalism As Science Education. 104p. 1993. 60.00 (*0-7300-1604-8*, ESC810, Pub. by Deakin Univ) St Mut.
Dunworth, J., jt. auth. see Amphlett, C.
Dunworth, Jeanne M., jt. auth. see Kell, Michael J.
***Dunworth, John.** The Dollar-a-Year Principal: Miracle at Munson. LC 00-130150. (Illus.). 261p. 2000. 29.95 (*0-9628917-4-6*) Watersun MA.
Dunworth, Terence & Saiger, Aaron J. State Strategic Planning under the Drug Formula Grant Program: An Evaluation. 137p. (Orig.). (YA). (gr. 12 up). 1994. pap. text 30.00 (*0-7881-0781-X*) DIANE Pub.
DuoDuo Staff. DuoDuo: Crossing the Sea: Poems in Exile - Poems in China. Robinson, Lee & Li Ming Yu, trs. from CHI. LC 98-191537. 136p. 1998. pap. 11.95 (*0-88784-562-2*, Pub. by Hse of Anansi Pr) Genl Dist Srvs.
***Duome, Joseph J.** "Return to Yesterday" (... ritorno a jeri ...) 2000. 25.00 (*0-7388-0744-3*); pap. 18.00 (*0-7388-0745-1*) Xlibris Corp.
Duong, Dai. Cong San Dang Lung Lung Tro Lai.Tr. of Communists Are Coming Back. (VIE.). 650p. 1999. pap. 20.00 (*1-889880-05-1*) Nguoi Dan.
Duong, Pham C. Vietnamese Peasants under French Domination 1861-1945. LC 85-7499. (Monographs: No. 24). (Illus.). 240p. (Orig.). 1985. pap. 26.00 (*0-8191-4715-X*) U Pr of Amer.
Duong, Phan Huy, tr. see Huong, Duong Tho.
Duong, Phan Huy, tr. see Vu, Tran.
***Duong, T. C.** The Naked Humanity & the Art of Living: What Can Be Learned from Life & Humankind. LC 99-90351. 200p. 1999. 24.95 (*0-9670180-0-5*) Think Pond.
Duornek, Richard. Your First Job Interview. 10p. 1991. pap. 3.50 (*0-937652-55-5*) Natl Art Ed.
Dupa, Johnny. Geek Redemption: What's Wrong with Being a Geek? How to Stop Being One. LC 99-60081. (Illus.). 250p. (Orig.). 1999. pap. 15.95 (*0-9670088-0-8*, AAMPGRE1) AAM Pr MD.
Dupagne, Michel & Seel, Peter B. High-Definition Television: A Global Perspective. LC 97-28423. (Illus.). 344p. 1997. 49.95 (*0-8138-2925-9*) Iowa St U Pr.
Dupaigne, Bernard. The History of Bread. LC 99-22309. 256p. 1999. 60.00 (*0-8109-3438-8*, Pub. by Abrams) Time Warner.
Dupaquier, Carolyn. Focus on Reading & Writing: Intermediate Level. LC 97-41536. 240p. 1997. pap. text 23.10 (*0-201-69422-0*) Addison-Wesley.
Duparc, Henri. Complete Songs. 112p. 1995. pap. 9.95 (*0-486-28466-2*) Dover.
Dupas, Brenda, jt. ed. see Casey, Barbara.
Dupas, H. Lexique Civilisation Germanique. (FRE.). 1998. 65.00 (*0-320-00148-2*) Fr & Eur.
Dupasquier, A. Positron Spectroscopy of Solids. LC 94-73354. 780p. (gr. 12). 1995. 170.00 (*90-5199-203-3*) IOS Press.
***Dupasquier, P.** Sunday with Grandpa. (J). 1998. text 19.95 (*0-86264-791-6*, Pub. by Random) Trafalgar.
Dupasquier, Philippe. Andy's Pirate Ship. 32p. (J). 1995. 11.95 (*0-8050-3154-5*) H Holt & Co.
— A Busy Day at the Airport. (Illus.). (J). (ps up). 1996. pap. 5.99 (*1-56402-591-8*) Candlewick Pr.
— A Busy Day at the Building Site. (Illus.). (J). (ps up). 1996. pap. 5.99 (*1-56402-592-6*) Candlewick Pr.
— A Busy Day at the Garage. (Illus.). (J). (ps-3). 1996. pap. 5.99 (*1-56402-590-X*) Candlewick Pr.
— A Busy Day at the Harbor. LC 95-71628. (Illus.). 32p. (J). (gr. k-3). 1996. pap. 5.99 (*1-56402-837-2*) Candlewick Pr.
— A Busy Day at the Train Station. LC 95-71630. (Illus.). 32p. (J). (gr. k-3). 1996. pap. 5.99 (*1-56402-838-0*) Candlewick Pr.
— The Great Escape. LC 95-67535. (Illus.). 40p. (J). (gr. 1-4). 1996. pap. 7.99 (*1-56402-850-X*) Candlewick Pr.
DuPaul, George J. & Stoner, Gary. ADHD in the Schools: Assessment & Intervention Strategies. LC 93-46055. (School Practitioner Ser.). 269p. 1994. lib. bdg. 33.00 (*0-89862-245-X*, 2245) Guilford Pubns.
Dupayrat, J. Chemical & Technological Dictionary of Biological Sciences English-French. 2nd ed. (ENG & FRE.). 229p. 1996. pap. 72.50 (*2-7430-0101-1*, Pub. by Technique et Documentation) IBD Ltd.
Dupayrat, Jacques. Chemical & Technical Dictionary of Biological Sciences: English - French. 2nd ed. (ENG & FRE.). 232p. 1996. 125.00 (*0-7859-9293-6*) Fr & Eur.
— Chemical & Technological Dictionary of Biological Sciences: Dictionnaire Chimique & Technologique des Sciences Biologiques. 2nd ed. (ENG & FRE.). 138p. 1993. reprint ed. pap. 85.00 (*0-8288-0781-7*, F63490) Fr & Eur.
Dupayrat, Jacques, ed. Dictionary of Biomedical Acronyms & Abbreviations. 2nd ed. 172p. 1990. pap. 176.50 (*0-471-92649-3*) Wiley.
Dupee, Frederick W. Henry James. LC 72-9047. (American Men of Letters Ser.). (Illus.). 301p. 1973. reprint ed. lib. bdg. 35.00 (*0-8371-6566-0*, DUHE, Greenwood Pr) Greenwood.
— The King of Cats: And Other Remarks on Writers & Writing. exp. ed. 275p. (C). 1984. pap. 12.50 (*0-226-17287-2*); lib. bdg. 28.00 (*0-226-17286-4*) U Ch Pr.
Dupee, Michael. How to Get on Jeopardy & Win: Valuable Information from a Champion. LC 98-26500. 1998. pap. 12.95 (*0-8065-9833-6*); pap. text 12.95 (*0-8065-1991-6*, Citadel Pr) Carol Pub Group.
Dupenois, Charles. High Is the Mountain: A Short Trilogy of Mystery, Adventure & Spiritual Comments. 96p. 1996. pap. 39.95 (*0-85439-469-9*, Pub. by St Paul Pubns) St Mut.
Duper, Linda L. 160 Ways to Help the World: Community Service Projects for Young People. 192p. (J). (gr. 5-12). 1996. pap. 9.95 (*0-8160-3503-2*) Facts on File.
— 160 Ways to Help the World: Community Service Projects for Young People. LC 95-34223. 192p. (YA). 1996. 19.95 (*0-8160-3324-2*) Facts on File.
Dupere, Phyllis. Seekonk in the Twentieth Century. (Images of America Ser.). pap. 16.99 (*0-7524-0923-9*) Arcadia Publng.
Dupertius, C. Wesley, jt. auth. see Hooton, E. A.
Dupertuis, Atilio R. Liberation Theology: A Study in Its Soteriology. (Andrews University Seminary Doctoral Dissertation Ser.: Vol. 9). 376p. 1987. pap. 19.99 (*0-943872-42-1*) Andrews Univ Pr.
Dupeux, Georges. French Election Study, 1958. 1974. write for info. (*0-89138-100-7*) ICPSR.
Duphar, P., et al. Behavioral Pharmacology of 5-HT. 528p. (C). 1989. text 89.95 (*0-8058-0135-9*) L Erlbaum Assocs.
Duphorn, Klaus, et al. Die Deutsche Ostseekueste. (Sammlung Geologischer Fuehrer Ser.: Band 88). (GER., Illus.). viii, 288p. 1995. 30.00 (*3-443-15065-9*, Pub. by Gebruder Borntraeger) Balogh.
Dupiechain, Loida S., tr. see Burns Knight, Margy.
Dupin, Henri. La Courtoisie au Moyen Age: (d'apres les textes du XII et du XIII siecle) LC 78-63496. 176p. reprint ed. 42.50 (*0-404-17144-3*) AMS Pr.
Dupin, Jacques. Miro. (Great Monographs). (Illus.). 480p. 1993. 500.00 (*84-343-0727-8*) Elliots Bks.
— Miro's Engravings, 1961-1973: With Two Original Woodcuts. (Illus.). 248p. 1989. 375.00 (*1-55660-248-0*) A Wofsy Fine Arts.
— Miro's Engravings, 1928-1960: A Catalogue Raisonne with Two Original Woodcuts. (Illus.). 192p. 1984. 375.00 (*1-55660-058-5*) A Wofsy Fine Arts.
— Selected Poems. Bree, Germaine, ed. Auster, Paul et al, trs. from FRE. LC 92-53715. (French Poetry in Translation Ser.). 191p. (Orig.). 1992. pap. 11.95 (*0-916390-52-7*) Wake Forest.
Dupin, Jacques, text. Joan Miro. (Illus.). 35p. 1996. pap. 20.00 (*1-879173-31-X*) Locks Gallery.
***Dupin, Jacques & Lelong-Mainaud, Ariane.** Joan Miro Vol. I: Catalogue Raisonne Paintings, 1908-1930. (Illus.). 247p. 1999. 180.00 (*2-86882-031-X*, Pub. by G Lelong) Hacker.
— Joan Miro Vol. II: Catalogue Raisonne Paintings, 1931-1941. (Illus.). 258p. 2000. 150.00 (*2-86882-038-7*, Pub. by G Lelong) Hacker.
Dupin, Jacques, jt. auth. see Carandente, Giovanni.
***Dupin-Spriet, T. & Spriet, A.** Memento de l'Investigateur Promoteur. 70p. 1999. 52.25 (*3-8055-6844-4*) S Karger.
Dupin-Spriet, T., jt. auth. see Spriet, A.
Dupin-Spriet, Therese, jt. auth. see Spriet, A.
Dupin-Spriet, Therese, jt. auth. see Spriet, Alain.
Dupire, Beatrice, ed. see St. Laurent, Yves.
Dupis, Diane L., jt. auth. see Englebert, Phyllis.
Duplaa, Cristina & Barnes, Gwendolyn, eds. Las Nacionalidades del Estado Espanol: Una Problematica Cultural. LC 86-60528. (ENG & SPA.). 254p. (Orig.). 1986. pap. text 8.95 (*0-910235-11-2*) Prisma Bks.
Duplacey, James. Amazing Forwards. LC 96-12619. (J). (gr. 7 up). 1996. mass mkt. 5.95 (*0-688-15025-X*, Wm Morrow) Morrow Avon.
— Amazing Forwards, Hockey Superstars. (Hockey Superstars Ser.). (J). 1996. 11.15 (*0-606-11465-3*, Pub. by Turtleback) Demco.
— Annotated Rules of Hockey: An Official Publication of the National Hockey League. Diamond, Dan, ed. (Illus.). 192p. 1996. pap. text 17.95 (*1-55821-466-6*) Lyons Pr.
— Centers. unabridged ed. (Hockey's Hottest Ser.). (Illus.). 32p. (J). (gr. 1-4). 1999. pap. 4.95 (*1-55074-592-1*, Pub. by Kids Can Pr) Genl Dist Srvs.
Duplacey, James. Champion Defencemen. (Hockey Superstars Ser.). (Illus.). 40p. (J). 1997. pap. 6.95 (*1-55074-390-2*) Kids Can Pr.
Duplacey, James. Champion Defensemen. LC 00-551334. (Hockey Superstars Ser.). 40p. (gr. 3-7). 1997. mass mkt. 5.95 (*0-688-15688-6*, Wm Morrow) Morrow Avon.
— Champion Defensemen. (Hockey Superstars Ser.). (J). 1997. 11.15 (*0-606-11466-1*, Pub. by Turtleback) Demco.
— Defensemen. unabridged ed. (Hockey's Hottest Ser.). (Illus.). 32p. (J). (gr. 1-4). 1999. pap. 4.95 (*1-55074-594-8*, Pub. by Kids Can Pr) Genl Dist Srvs.
— Goalies. (Hockey's Hottest Ser.). 32p. (J). (gr. 2-5). 1999. 6.95 (*1-55074-561-1*) Kids Can Pr.
Duplacey, James. Great Goalies. (Hockey Superstars Ser.). (Illus.). 40p. (J). 1996. pap. 6.95 (*1-55074-185-3*) Kids Can Pr.
Duplacey, James. Great Goalies. (J). 1996. mass mkt. 5.95 (*0-688-15021-7*, Wm Morrow) Morrow Avon.
— Great Goalies. (Hockey Superstars Ser.). (J). 1996. 11.15 (*0-606-11467-X*, Pub. by Turtleback) Demco.
— Hockey Superstars: Top Rookies. LC 96-11705. (J). 1996. reprint ed. pap. 5.95 (*0-688-15023-3*, Wm Morrow) Morrow Avon.
— Hockey's Hottest Centers. (Illus.). 32p. 1999. pap. 6.95 (*1-55074-681-2*, Pub. by Kids Can Pr) Genl Dist Srvs.
— Hockey's Hottest Defensemen, 1. (Illus.). 32p. 1999. pap. 6.95 (*1-55074-683-9*, Pub. by Kids Can Pr) Genl Dist Srvs.
Duplacey, James. The Leafs vs. the Canadiens: The NHL's Top Teams. (Hockey Superstars Ser.). (Illus.). 32p. (J). 1996. pap. 6.95 (*1-55074-358-9*) Kids Can Pr.
Duplacey, James. Muhammed Ali: Athlete, Activist, Ambassador. (Champion Sports Biography Ser.). (Illus.). 96p. (YA). (gr. 7-12). 1999. pap. 8.95 (*1-894020-50-2*) Warwick Publ.
— The NHL Today's Stars - Tomorrow's Legends. 112p. 14.99 (*1-57215-237-0*, JG2370) World Pubns.
***Duplacey, James.** Rules of Hockey: An Anecdotal Look at the Rules of Hockey & How They Came to Be. rev. ed. (Illus.). 2000. pap. 19.95 (*1-58574-052-7*) Lyons Pr.
— Top Rookies. (Hockey Superstars Ser.). (Illus.). 40p. (J). 1995. pap. 6.95 (*1-55074-252-3*) Kids Can Pr.
Duplacey, James. Top Rookies. (Hockey Superstars Ser.). (J). 1996. 11.15 (*0-606-11468-8*, Pub. by Turtleback) Demco.
— Wingers. (Hockey's Hottest Ser.). 32p. (J). 1999. 6.95 (*1-55074-596-4*) Kids Can Pr.
***Duplacey, James & Zweig, Eric.** A Century of Hockey Heroes: 100 of the Greatest All-Time Stars. (NHL Coolest Books on Earth Ser.). (Illus.). 208p. (YA). (gr. 3 up). 1999. pap. 16.99 (*1-58184-062-4*) Somerville Hse.
Duplain, Jacques, jt. auth. see Belanger, Francine.
Duplan, J. F. & Chapiro, A., eds. Advances in Radiation Research: Physics & Chemistry, 2 vols. LC 72-92724. 668p. 1973. 238.00 (*0-677-15780-0*) Gordon & Breach.
***Duplantier, F. R.** Politickles: Limericks Lampooning the Liberal Left. LC 99-88628. (Illus.). 120p. 2000. pap. 14.95 (*0-936783-25-7*, Pub. by Merril Pr) Midpt Trade.
Duplantier, F. R., ed. see Raitport, Eli.
Duplantis, Cathy. Keeping a Clean Heart. (Mini-Bks.). 16p. 1993. pap. 1.00 (*0-89274-645-9*, HH-645) Harrison Hse.
Duplantis, Jesse. The Battle of Life. (Mini-Bks.). 16p. 1993. pap. 1.00 (*0-89274-675-0*, HH-675) Harrison Hse.
***Duplantis, Jesse.** Breaking The Power of Natural Law: How to Be Free of Sickness, Disease, Addiction & Depression B. 1999. 17.99 (*1-57794-224-8*) Harrison Hse.
Duplantis, Jesse. Don't Be Affected by the World's Message. (Mini-Bks.). 16p. 1993. pap. 7.00 (*0-89274-676-9*, HH-676) Harrison Hse.
— God Is Not Enough, He's Too Much! LC 98-114029. 224p. 1997. 14.99 (*1-57794-020-2*, HH2-020) Harrison Hse.
— Heaven: Close Encounters of the God Kind. write for info. (*0-614-24938-4*); write for info. (*0-614-24965-1*) Harrison Hse.
— Heaven: Close Encounters of the God Kind. 192p. (C). 1996. 14.99 (*0-89274-943-1*, HH-943) Harrison Hse.
***Duplantis, Jesse.** Jambalaya for the Soul: 51 Humorous Stories & Cajun Recipes from the Bayou. (Illus.). 2000. pap. 11.99 (*1-57794-304-X*) Harrison Hse.
Duplantis, Jesse. Keep Your Foot on the Devil's Neck. (Mini-Bks.). 16p. 1993. pap. 1.00 (*0-89274-648-3*, HH-648) Harrison Hse.
— Leave It in the Hands of a Specialist. (Mini-Bks.). 16p. 1993. pap. 1.00 (*0-89274-646-7*, HH-646) Harrison Hse.
— The Ministry of Cheerfulness. large type ed. 80p. 1994. pap. 5.99 (*0-89274-799-4*, HH-799) Harrison Hse.
— One More Night with the Frogs. (Mini-Bks.). 16p. 1993. pap. 1.00 (*0-89274-649-1*, HH-649) Harrison Hse.
— The Return of Jesus. (Mini-Bks.). 16p. 1993. pap. 1.00 (*0-89274-647-5*, HH-647) Harrison Hse.
— Running Toward Your Giant. (Mini-Bks.). 16p. 1993. pap. 1.00 (*0-89274-644-0*, HH-644) Harrison Hse.
Duplatre, Olivier. Eben: Signifie et Fonctions. (Germanistische Linguistik - Monographien: Bd. 1). (GER.). 376p. 1996. write for info. (*3-487-10079-7*) G Olms Pubs.
Duplechain Duhon, Maxine. Duplechin Descendants: Genealogical Research of Over 600 Duplechin's. Fuqua, Linda, ed. (Illus.). 166p. 1986. pap., per. 22.00 (*0-9617489-0-7*, TXU 237-556) Duplechain Pub.
Duplechan, Larry. Tangled up in Blue. 272p. 1990. pap. 8.95 (*0-312-05167-0*) St Martin.
Dupleix, Andre. 15 Days of Prayer with Pierre Teilhard de Chardin. Hebert, Victoria & Sabourin, Denis, trs. from FRE. LC 99-34433. 128p. 1999. reprint ed. pap. 7.95 (*0-7648-0490-1*) Liguori Pubns.
Dupleix, Jill. Bread Tomato Garlic: Quick Cooking with 3 Main Ingredients. LC 98-55115. (Illus.). 160p. 1999. pap. 25.00 (*1-57959-022-5*, SOMA) BB&T Inc.
DuPlessis, David & Slosser, Bob. A Man Called Mr. Pentecost. LC 76-53322. 247p. 1977. pap. 7.99 (*0-88270-184-3*) Bridge-Logos.
Duplessis, G. Wonders of Engraving. 340p. 1989. reprint ed. pap. 35.00 (*0-87556-178-0*) Saifer.
DuPlessis, J. P., ed. Fluid Transport in Porous Media. LC 97-65677. (Advances in Fluid Mechanics Ser.: Vol. 13). 320p. 1997. 147.00 (*1-85312-429-X*, 429X) Computational Mech MA.
DuPlessis, Rachel B. Draft 32: Renga. 56p. 1998. write for info. (*0-9667655-0-8*) Beautifulswimmer.
— Draft X: Letters. 32p. (Orig.). 1991. pap. 6.00 (*0-935162-10-0*) Singing Horse.
— Drafts. 99p. (Orig.). 1991. pap. 9.50 (*0-937013-37-4*) Potes Poets.
— Drafts 15 - XXX, the Fold. 91p. (C). 1996. pap. 12.00 (*0-937013-65-X*) Potes Poets.
— H. D. The Career of That Struggle. LC 86-45393. (Key Women Writers Ser.). 170p. 1986. 32.00 (*0-253-32702-4*); pap. 9.95 (*0-253-20400-3*, MB-400) Ind U Pr.
***DuPlessis, Rachel B.** The Objectivist Nexus: Essays in Cultural Poetics. (Modern & Contemporary Poetics Ser.). 376p. 1999. text 49.95 (*0-8173-0974-8*) U of Ala Pr.
DuPlessis, Rachel B. Tabula Rosa. 110p. 1987. pap. 8.50 (*0-937013-19-6*) Potes Poets.
DuPlessis, Rachel B., ed. The Selected Letters of George Oppen. LC 89-23772. (Illus.). 471p. (Orig.). (C). 1990. text 49.95 (*0-8223-1017-1*); pap. text 23.95 (*0-8223-1024-4*) Duke.
***DuPlessis, Rachel B. & Quartermain, Peter.** The Objectivist Nexus: Essays in Cultural Poetics. LC 98-58047. (Modern & Contemporary Poetics Ser.). 380p. 1999. pap. text 24.95 (*0-8173-0973-X*) U of Ala Pr.
DuPlessis, Rachel B., jt. ed. see Friedman, Susan S.
DuPlessis, Rachel Blau, see Snitow, Ann & Blau DuPlessis, Rachel, eds.
DuPlessis, Robert S. Lille & the Dutch Revolt: Urban Stability in an Era of Revolution, 1500-1582. (Studies in Early Modern History). (Illus.). 390p. (C). 1991. text 89.95 (*0-521-39415-5*) Cambridge U Pr.
— Transitions to Capitalism in Early Modern Europe. LC 96-50037. (New Approaches to European History Ser.: Vol. 10). (Illus.). 344p. (C). 1997. text 59.95 (*0-521-39465-1*); pap. text 18.95 (*0-521-39773-1*) Cambridge U Pr.
Duplessis, Shirley. Hidden in the Woods: The Story of Kokadjo. (Illus.). 212p. 1997. pap. 12.95 (*1-890454-00-1*) Moosehead Communs.
Duplessis, Yves. Surrealism. Capon, Paul, tr. LC 77-17880. 158p. 1978. reprint ed. lib. bdg. 55.00 (*0-313-20110-2*, DUSU, Greenwood Pr) Greenwood.
Duplessis, Yvonne. The Paranormal Perception of Color. LC 75-19563. (Parapsychological Monographs: No. 16). 1975. pap. 8.00 (*0-912328-27-4*) Parapsych Foun.
Duplessy, Jean-Claude & Spyridakis, Marie-Therese, eds. Long-Term Climatic Variations: Data & Modelling. LC 94-12952. 1994. 229.00 (*0-387-58112-X*) Spr-Verlag.
Duplex, Mary H. Mystery at Maple Street Park. LC 93-28466. (J). 1994. pap. 1.97 (*0-8163-1187-0*) Pacific Pr Pub Assn.
— The Mystery on Oak Street & Other Stories. (Illus.). 96p. (Orig.). (J). (gr. 6-8). 1995. pap. 5.95 (*0-8198-4778-X*) Pauline Bks.
Duplex, Mary H., et al. Quiet Times with Jesus. LC 92-20278. (J). (ps). 1992. pap. 10.99 (*0-8280-0678-4*) Review & Herald.
Duplij, Steven. Alien. Carbone, Joyce, ed. (Illus.). 54p. (Orig.). 1995. pap. 5.95 (*1-878116-51-7*) JVC Bks.
— Angel. limited ed. Carbone, Joyce, ed. 126p. (Orig.). 1997. pap. 8.95 (*1-878116-64-9*) JVC Bks.
DuPoet, P. D., ed. Report on Protein Engineering R & D Programmes in Europe (1994) 169p. (C). 1998. reprint ed. pap. text 30.00 (*0-7881-7127-5*) DIANE Pub.
Duponceau, Peter S., tr. see Holm, Thomas C.
DuPont - UCLA Symposium on Molecular Strategies fo. Molecular Strategies for Crop Protection: Proceedings of a DuPont - UCLA Symposium on Molecular Strategies for Crop Protection, Held in Steamboat Springs, Colorado, March 30-April 6, 1986. Arntzen, Charles J. & Ryan, Clarence, eds. LC 86-34284. (UCLA Symposia on Molecular & Cellular Biology Ser.: Vol. 48). 465p. reprint ed. pap. 144.20 (*0-7837-2841-7*, 205763100006) Bks Demand.
Dupont, Alan. The Environment & Security in Pacific Asia. (Adelphi Papers 311). (Illus.). 94p. 1998. pap. text 24.95 (*0-19-922370-X*) OUP.
Dupont-Auberville, M. Full Color Historic Textile Designs. LC 95-10905. 112p. 1995. pap. 19.95 (*0-486-28718-1*) Dover.
Dupont, B., ed. Immunobiology of HLA, 2 vols., Vols. 1 & 2. (Illus.). 1408p. 1989. 548.00 (*0-387-96826-1*) Spr-Verlag.
DuPont, Betty, jt. auth. see Schlaich, Joan.
DuPont, Betty, jt. ed. see Schlaich, Joan.
***DuPont, Chantal.** Reiki. (Pocket Healing Bks.). (Illus.). 22p. 2000. pap. 4.95 (*965-494-102-3*) Astrolog Pub.
Dupont, Connie Hull. Mike Myers. LC 99-34328. (Illus.). 64p. 1999. 17.95 (*0-7910-5236-2*) Chelsea Hse.
Dupont, Desiree. Love Me Forever. LC 97-178736. 142p. 1996. pap. 12.95 (*81-7328-065-7*) Intl Spec Bk.
DuPont, Elizabeth N. Landscaping with Native Plants in the Middle-Atlantic Region. Williams, Wick, ed. LC 78-21194. (Illus.). 1978. 7.95 (*0-940540-02-9*) Brandywine Conserv.
Dupont, Etienne C. & Walker, Cathy. Molecular - Cellular Mechanisms of Immunomodulatory Drugs. 1993. write for info. (*0-8493-4809-9*, 4809, CRC Reprint) Franklin.
Dupont, Florence. Daily Life in Ancient Rome. 1994. pap. 29.95 (*0-631-19395-2*) Blackwell Pubs.
DuPont, H. A. DuPont: Early Generations of the DuPont & Allied Families, 2 vols. (Illus.). 802p. 1998. reprint ed. pap. 119.50 (*0-8328-8380-8*); reprint ed. lib. bdg. 129.50 (*0-8328-8379-4*) Higginson Bk Co.
DuPont, H. L., ed. Use of Quinolones in Travel Medicine: Second Conference on International Travel Medicine. (Illus.). 56p. 1992. 21.95 (*0-387-54778-9*) Spr-Verlag.
Dupont, Henry. Emotional Development, Theory & Applications: A Neo-Piagetian Perspective. LC 93-43067. 152p. 1994. 55.00 (*0-275-94839-0*, Praeger Pubs) Greenwood.
DuPont, Herbert L. & Steffen, Robert. Textbook of Travel Medicine & Health. LC 98-147351. 370p. 1997. boxed set 135.00 incl. cd-rom (*1-55009-037-2*) DEKR.
DuPont, Herbert L., jt. auth. see Steffen, Robert.
Dupont, Inge & Mayo, Hope, eds. Morgan Library Ghost Stories. LC 90-82150. (Illus.). 107p. 1990. 24.95 (*0-8232-1283-1*) Fordham.

An Asterisk (*) at the beginning of an entry indicates that the title is appearing for the first time.

Dupont, J. E., jt. ed. see Numez, J.

Dupont, Jacqueline. Cholesterol Systems in Insects & Animals. 160p. 1982. 79.95 (*0-8493-5315-7*, QL495) CRC Pr.

Dupont, Jacqueline & Osman, Elizabeth M., eds. Cereals & Legumes in the Food Supply. LC 87-16796. (Illus.). 382p. (Orig.). 1987. reprint ed. pap. 118.50 (*0-608-00081-7*, 206084400006) Bks Demand.

***Dupont, Jerry.** The Common Law Abroad: Reception of British Laws & Institutions in the Former Empire. LC 00-34156. 2000. write for info. (*0-8377-3125-9*, Rothman) W S Hein.

DuPont, John E. Philippine Birds. 490p. 1971. 60.00 (*0-913176-03-6*, Delaware Estuary) Weidner & Sons.

— South Pacific Birds. 230p. 1976. 50.00 (*0-913176-04-4*, Delaware Estuary) Weidner & Sons.

Dupont, John E., jt. auth. see Weaver, Clifton S.

Dupont, Judith, ed. see Ferenczi, Sandor.

DuPont, Kay. Business Etiquette & Professionalism: Your Guide to Career Success. Brett, Elaine, ed. LC 89-81952. (Fifty-Minute Ser.). (Illus.). 117p. (Orig.). 1990. pap. 10.95 (*1-56052-032-9*) Crisp Pubns.

— Handling Diversity in the Workplace: Communication Is the Key. Miller, Karen M., ed. LC 96-80413. (How-to Book Ser.). 104p. (Orig.). 1997. pap. 12.95 (*1-884926-72-X*, DIVER) Amer Media.

Dupont, Lieven & Fijnaut, Cyrille, eds. Criminal Law. 1991. ring bd. write for info. (*0-318-68489-6*) Kluwer Law Intl.

Dupont, Lieven & Fijnaut, Cyrille J. C. F., eds. Criminal Law, 3 vols. (International Encyclopedia of Laws Ser.). 1991. ring bd. 477.00 (*90-6544-937-X*) Kluwer Law Intl.

DuPont, Lonnie H. Oksana Baiul. LC 98-21901. (Female Figure Skating Legends Ser.). (Illus.). 64p. (J). (gr. 2 up). 1998. lib. bdg. 16.95 (*0-7910-4201-4*) Chelsea Hse.

Dupont, Lonnie Hull. Mike Myers. LC 99-34328. (Galaxy of Superstars Ser.). (Illus.). 64p. (YA). (gr. 3-7). 1999. pap. 9.95 (*0-7910-5336-9*) Chelsea Hse.

Dupont, Louis. Development Planning: The Test of Facts. 274p. (C). 1996. lib. bdg. 47.00 (*0-7618-0264-9*) U Pr of Amer.

***Dupont, Luc.** Images That Sell: 500 Ways to Create Great Ads. 267p. 1999. pap. 24.95 (*0-9699834-4-1*) White Rock Pubng.

Dupont, Luc. 1001 Advertising Tips. (Illus.). 290p. 1996. pap. 19.95 (*0-9699834-0-9*) White Rock Pubng.

DuPont, M. Kay. Business Etiquette & Professionalism: Your Guide to Career Success. 2nd rev. ed. (Crisp 50-Minute Ser.). (Illus.). 112p. 1998. pap. 10.95 (*1-56052-475-8*) Crisp Pubns.

— Don't Let Your Participles Dangle in Public! (Illus.). 152p. (Orig.). 1984. pap. 12.95 (*0-9614927-0-8*) Comm Connect.

Dupont, Marc A. The Church of the 3rd Millennium. LC 97-195641. 182p. 1997. pap. 10.99 (*1-56043-194-6*, Revival Pr) Destiny Image.

Dupont, Marie. Your First Kitten. (YF Ser.). (Illus.). 32p. (Orig.). (YA). 1991. pap. 2.29 (*0-86622-061-5*, YF-118) TFH Pubns.

Dupont, Nicole. Sex Diary of Nicole Dupont. 1997. mass mkt. 6.95 (*0-7472-5680-2*, Pub. by Headline Bk Pub) Trafalgar.

Dupont, P. Porcelaines Francaises. (FRE.). 192p. 1991. pap. 195.00 (*0-8288-7303-8*, 270590330) Fr & Eur.

DuPont, Pete. What in the World Is Going On? (Excellence in Education Ser.). 15p. (Orig.). 1992. pap. text 3.00 (*1-878802-03-8*) J M Ashbrook Ctr Pub Affairs.

Dupont, Philippe. Cheetah. (Animal Close-Ups Ser.). (Illus.). (J). 1992. 12.40 (*0-606-18023-0*) Turtleback.

Dupont, Philippe. The Cheetah: Fast As Lightning. LC 92-70579. (Animal Close-Ups Ser.). (Illus.). 28p. (J). (ps-3). 1992. pap. 6.95 (*0-88106-425-4*) Charlesbridge Pub.

Dupont, Pierre. How Levesque Won. Fischman, Sheila, tr. 136p. 1977. pap. 14.95 (*0-88862-130-2*, Pub. by J Lorimer) Formac Dist Ltd.

Dupont, Pierre, jt. auth. see Cook, Robert M.

Dupont, R. & Reynolds, J. Accident & Emergency Management: Problems & Solutions. 187p. 1991. pap. 84.95 (*0-471-18804-2*, Wiley-VCH) Wiley.

Dupont, R. Ryan, et al. Bioremediation: Design & Application. LC 97-14812. (Innovative Site Remediation Technology: Vol. 1). (Illus.). 450p. 1998. 104.95 (*1-883767-17-2*) Am Acad Environ.

***Dupont, R. Ryan, et al.** Pollution Prevention. LC 99-47203. 498p. 1999. write for info. (*1-56670-495-2*) Lewis Pubs.

Dupont, R. Ryan, jt. auth. see Theodore, Louis.

Dupont, Ralph P. Dupont on Connecticut Civil Practice, 2 vols. LC 96-76381. 1996. 160.00 (*1-55834-328-8*, 83074-10, MICHIE) LEXIS Pub.

Dupont, Ralph P. Dupont on Connecticut Civil Practice: 2000 Edition, 2 Vols. pap. 199.00 (*0-327-10205-5*) LEXIS Pub.

— Dupont on Connecticut Civil Practice: 2000 Edition, 2 vols. Incl. Vol. 1. Dupont on Connecticut Civil Practice: 2000 Edition. 1999. (*0-327-04902-2*); Vol. 2. Dupont on Connecticut Civil Practice: 2000 Edition. 1999. (*0-327-04903-0*); 1900p. 1999. write for info. (*0-327-04901-4*) LEXIS Pub.

Dupont, Ralph P. Dupont on Connecticut Civil Practice, 1998 Edition, Vol. 1. 1600p. 1998. 175.00 (*0-327-00487-8*, 83075-12) LEXIS Pub.

— Dupont on Connecticut Civil Practice, 1998 Edition, Vol. 2. 1600p. 1998. 175.00 (*0-327-00488-6*, 83076-12) LEXIS Pub.

DuPont, Robert L., Jr. Getting Tough on Gateway Drugs: A Guide for the Family. LC 84-14595. 332p. 1984. pap. 12.95 (*0-88048-046-7*, 8046) Am Psychiatric.

DuPont, Robert L. The Selfish Brain: Learning from Addiction. 589p. 1997. 32.95 (*0-88048-686-4*, 8686) Am Psychiatric.

***DuPont, Robert L.** Selfish Brain: Learning from Addiction. LC 99-87111. 580p. 2000. pap. 18.00 (*1-56838-363-0*) Hazelden.

DuPont, Robert L., ed. Crack Cocaine: A Challenge for Prevention. (Illus.). 71p. (Orig.). (C). 1994. pap. text 25.00 (*0-7881-0579-5*) DIANE Pub.

— Stopping Alcohol & Other Drug Use Before It Starts: The Future of Prevention. (Illus.). 99p. (C). 1996. reprint ed. pap. text 25.00 (*0-7881-2965-1*) DIANE Pub.

DuPont, Robert L. & McGovern, John P. A Bridge to Recovery: An Introduction to 12-Step Programs. LC 93-26758. 159p. 1994. 24.50 (*0-88048-669-4*, 8669) Am Psychiatric.

DuPont, Robert L., et al. The Anxiety Cure: An Eight-Step Program for Getting Well. LC 97-44043. 256p. 1998. pap. 14.95 (*0-471-24701-4*) Wiley.

Dupont, Robert L., jt. ed. see Bischof, Gunter.

Dupont-Sommer, A. The Essene Writings from Qumran. Vermes, Geza, tr. 1990. 25.25 (*0-8446-2012-2*) Peter Smith.

Dupont, Stephen. Steam: India's Last Steam Trains. (Illus.). 120p. 1999. 45.00 (*1-899235-27-2*, Pub. by Dewi Lewis) Dist Art Pubs.

Dupont, Veronique. Decentralized Industrialization & Urban Dynamics: The Case of Jetpur in West India. LC 95-926. 532p. 1995. 36.00 (*0-8039-9236-X*) Sage.

DuPont, Yves. Catholic Prophecy. 1994. pap. 5.50 (*0-89555-015-6*) TAN Bks Pubs.

Dupont, Yves, tr. see Pius, X, pseud.

Duportal, Marguerite. Bearing Your Troubles Well: Your Path to Peace in Difficult Times. abr. ed. LC 98-34299. 128p. 1998. pap. 9.95 (*0-918477-81-6*) Sophia Inst Pr.

Dupotet de Sennevoy, Jean. An Introduction to the Study of Animal Magnetism. LC 75-36837. (Occult Ser.). 1976. reprint ed. 33.95 (*0-405-07950-8*) Ayer.

Dupoux, Emmanuel, jt. auth. see Mehler, Jacques A.

Dupper, Thom. Human Side of Intranets: Content, Style & Politics. LC 98-125656. 272p. 1997. per. 54.95 (*1-57444-175-2*) St Lucie Pr.

Duppler, Dana, jt. auth. see Connors, Dean.

Dupra, Lyle E. We Delivered: The U.S. Navy Armed Guard. (Illus.). 170p. 1997. pap. 23.95 (*0-89745-212-7*) Sunflower U Pr.

Duprae dal Poggetto, Maria Grazia Ciardi. Small Renaissance Bronzes. LC 74-861518. (Cameo Ser.). 157 p. 1970. write for info. (*0-600-01246-8*) P HM.

Duprat, Gerard, et al, eds. European Democratic Culture. (What Is Europe? Ser.). (Illus.). 216p. (C). 1995. pap. 25.99 (*0-415-12419-0*, C0490) Routledge.

— European Democratic Culture. (What Is Europe? Ser.). (Illus.). 216p. (C). (gr. 13). 1995. 80.00 (*0-415-12418-2*, C0489) Routledge.

Duprat, M., ed. Electrochemical Methods in Corrosion Research: Proceedings of International Symposium, 2nd, Toulouse, France, July 1985. (Materials Science Forum Ser.: Vol. 8). 644p. 1986. pap. text 187.00 (*0-87849-550-9*, Pub. by Trans T Pub) Enfield Pubs NH.

DuPratz, M. L. & Fortier, Alcee. History of Louisiana, Vol. 2. rev. ed. Carrigan, J. A. et al, eds. 1972. 50.00 (*0-87511-138-6*) Claitors.

DuPrau, Jeanne. Adoption: The Facts, Feelings & Issues of a Double Heritage. rev. ed. Steltenpohl, Jane, ed. 128p. (YA). (gr. 7 up). 1990. pap. 5.95 (*0-671-69329-8*, Julian Messner); lib. bdg. 12.95 (*0-671-69328-X*, Julian Messner) Silver Burdett Pr.

***DuPrau, Jeanne.** Cloning. LC 99-28320. (Overview Ser.). (Illus.). 128p. (YA). (gr. 6-9). 2000. lib. bdg. 23.70 (*1-56006-583-4*) Lucent Bks.

DuPrau, Jeanne. The Earth House. 128p. 1992. 16.95 (*0-942257-32-4*) New Chapter Pr.

Dupraz, C., jt. ed. see Signore, Monique.

Dupraz, Christian, jt. auth. see Auclair, D.

Dupre, jt. auth. see Motter.

Dupre, Alexandra. Men's Wear: A Guide to Designing Wearable Art for Men. 160p. 1996. pap. 14.95 (*0-89145-865-4*, 4598, Am Quilters Soc) Collector Bks.

Dupre, Ben, ed. The Living World. (Illus.). 160p. (J). (gr. 3-9). 1993. 40.00 (*0-19-910142-6*) OUP.

— Science & Technology. (Illus.). 160p. (J). (gr. 3-9). 1993. 40.00 (*0-19-910143-4*) OUP.

Dupre, Celine. French - English Vocabulary of Clothing. (ENG & FRE.). 173p. 1989. pap. 49.95 (*0-8288-9386-1*) Fr & Eur.

— Vocabulary of the Shoe: Vocabulaire de la Chaussure. (ENG & FRE.). 48p. 1982. pap. 19.95 (*0-8288-0741-8*, F37380) Fr & Eur.

Dupre, Celine, ed. see Lanecki, Francois.

Dupre, Cindy & Bulkin, Rena. Frommer's Florida on $40 a Day. 640p. 1996. 18.95 (*0-02-861136-5*) Macmillan.

Dupre, Dalmation D. The Crawfish Cookbook. Barbre, Sylvia J., ed. (Illus.). 32p. 1982. pap. 2.95 (*0-9604580-0-X*) T Chacheres.

Dupre, Daniel S. Transforming the Cotton Frontier: Madison County, Alabama, 1800-1840. LC 97-16094. (Illus.). 344p. 1997. text 40.00 (*0-8071-2193-2*) La State U Pr.

Dupre, Denise, jt. auth. see Lane, Harold E.

DuPre, Gabrielle. Ariane. 1988. pap. 4.50 (*0-317-67195-2*) St Martin.

Dupre, Henri. Purcell. LC 74-24071. reprint ed. 21.50 (*0-404-12899-8*) AMS Pr.

Dupre, Huntley. Lazare Carnot, Republican Patriot. LC 75-29217. (Perspectives in European History Ser.: No. 5). viii, 343p. 1975. reprint ed. lib. bdg. 45.00 (*0-87991-612-5*) Porcupine Pr.

Dupre, Jean-Paul. Barron's Illustrated Fact Finder: An Encyclopedia for Young Children. 2nd ed. (Illus.). 320p. (J). (gr. 2 up). 1995. pap. 14.95 (*0-8120-9404-2*) Barron.

Dupre, John. The Disorder of Things: Metaphysical Foundations of the Disunity of Science. LC 92-12930. (Illus.). 320p. 1993. 43.50 (*0-674-21260-6*) HUP.

— The Disorder of Things: Metaphysical Foundations of the Disunity of Science. (Illus.). 320p. 1995. pap. text 20.50 (*0-674-21261-4*, DUPDIX) HUP.

Dupre, John, ed. The Latest on the Best: Essays on Evolution & Optimality. LC 86-27226. 359p. 1987. 47.50 (*0-262-04090-5*) MIT Pr.

Dupre, Judith. La Boda de la Ratoncita - The Mouse Bride. (J). 1995. pap. text 12.95 (*1-56014-583-8*) Santillana.

— Bridges: A History of the World's Most Famous & Important Spans. LC 97-28291. (Illus.). 128p. (YA). (gr. 7). 1999. 24.98 (*1-884822-75-4*) Blck Dog & Leventhal.

***Dupre, Judith.** Churches. 160p. 2000. 35.00 (*0-06-019438-3*) HarpC.

Dupre, Judith. Native American Rock Art: A Petroglyph Stamp Kit for All Ages. (Illus.). 64p. (J). 1997. 24.95 (*0-8118-1611-7*) Chronicle Bks.

— Skyscrapers: A History of the World's Most Famous & Important Skyscrapers. (Illus.). 128p. 1996. 24.98 (*1-884822-45-2*) Blck Dog & Leventhal.

***Dupre, Lonnie.** Green Expedition: Where Ice Is Born. (Illus.). 160p. 2000. 24.95 (*1-55971-707-6*, NorthWord Pr) Creat Pub Intl.

Dupre, Louis. Christian Spirituality, Vol. 3. Vol. 18. 592p. 1989. 49.50 (*0-8245-0766-5*) Crossroad NY.

— Metaphysics & Culture. (Aquinas Lectures). 1994. pap. 15.00 (*0-87462-161-5*) Marquette.

— Passage to Modernity: An Essay in the Hermeneutics of Nature & Culture. 1995. pap. 18.00 (*0-300-06501-9*) Yale U Pr.

***Dupre, Louis.** Symbols of the Sacred. 168p. 2000. pap. 20.00 (*0-8028-4748-X*) Eerdmans.

Dupre, Louis. Transcendent Selfhood: The Loss & Rediscovery of the Inner Life. 1984. 9.20 (*0-8164-0306-6*) Harper SF.

Dupre, Louis, et al, eds. Christian Spirituality: Post-Reformation & Modern, Vol. 3. (World Spirituality Ser.). (Illus.). 592p. 1991. reprint ed. pap. 24.95 (*0-8245-1144-1*) Crossroad NY.

Dupre, Louis & Wiseman, James A., eds. Light from Light: An Anthology of Christian Mysticism. 256p. 1988. pap. 22.95 (*0-8091-2943-4*) Paulist Pr.

Dupre, Louis K. Religious Mystery & Rational Reflection. LC 97-24216. 159p. 1997. pap. 20.00 (*0-8028-4325-5*) Eerdmans.

Dupre, Lyn. Bugs in Writing. 2nd rev. ed. LC 97-46656. (Illus.). 704p. (C). 1998. pap. text 19.95 (*0-201-37921-X*) Addison-Wesley.

— BUGS in Writing: A Guide to Debugging Your Prose. LC 94-29807. 688p. (C). 1994. pap. text 19.95 (*0-201-60019-6*) Addison-Wesley.

Dupre, M. J. The Classification & Structure of C-Algebra Bundles. LC 79-17975. (Memoirs Ser.: No. 21/222). 77p. 1979. pap. 17.00 (*0-8218-2222-5*, MEMO/21/222) Am Math.

Dupre, Marcel. 8 Short Preludes on Gregorian Themes. 20p. 1998. pap. text 5.95 (*0-87487-604-4*) Summy-Birchard.

Dupre, Paul. Encyclopedie des Citations. 14th ed. (FRE.). 1959. 66.50 (*0-7859-0772-6*, F-C1020) Fr & Eur.

— Encyclopedie du Bon Francais Dans L'usage Contemporain, 3 vols., Set. (FRE.). 2900p. 1959. 160.00 (*0-8288-6844-1*, M-6179) Fr & Eur.

Dupre, Rick. Agassu: Legend of the Leopard King. (Picture Bks.). (Illus.). 40p. (J). (gr. 1-4). 1993. lib. bdg. 19.93 (*0-87614-764-3*, Carolrhoda) Lerner Pub.

— The Wishing Chair. LC 92-38880. (Illus.). 32p. (J). (ps-3). 1993. lib. bdg. 14.95 (*0-87614-774-0*, Carolrhoda) Lerner Pub.

Dupre, Wilhelm. Religion in Primitive Cultures: A Study in Ethnophilosophy. (Religion & Reason Ser.: No. 9). 366p. 1975. text 56.95 (*90-279-7531-0*) Mouton.

Dupree. Effective Small Business Planning. 1996. pap. text 11.80 (*0-13-578279-1*) P-H.

Dupree, A. Hunter. Science in the Federal Government: A History of Policies & Activities. LC 86-45456. 488p. 1986. reprint ed. pap. text 18.95 (*0-8018-3381-7*) Johns Hopkins.

— Science in the Federal Government: A History of Policies & Activities to 1940. Cohen, I. Bernard, ed. LC 79-7959. (Three Centuries of Science in America Ser.). (Illus.). 1980. reprint ed. lib. bdg. 42.95 (*0-405-12540-2*) Ayer.

Dupree, A. K. & Lago, M. T., eds. Formation & Evolution of Low Mass Stars. (C). 1988. text 237.50 (*90-277-2782-1*) Kluwer Academic.

Dupree, A. K., jt. ed. see Bonnet, Robert L.

Dupree, Andrea K., jt. ed. see Pallavicini, Roberto.

Dupree, C. Bruce. Coming Home Auburn! Whatley, Carole, ed. (Illus.). 48p. (Orig.). (J). (gr. 1-4). 1995. pap. 12.95 (*0-9647431-1-6*) Red Rover.

— Homecoming Alabama! Whatley, Carol, ed. (Illus.). 48p. (Orig.). (J). (gr. 1-4). 1995. pap. 12.95 (*0-9647431-0-8*) Red Rover.

Dupree, Christine. Erotic Escapades for Longtime Lovers: Fun & Daring Ways to Keep the Thrill Alive. LC 99-21001. (Illus.). 192p. 1999. 19.95 (*1-55972-502-8*, Birch Ln Pr) Carol Pub Group.

DuPree, David. Grant Hill Fantasy Basketball Journal '97. 300p. 1997. pap. 11.95 (*0-9636895-8-4*) Fantasy Spts.

DuPree, Don K., ed. see Harrison, Charles.

Dupree, Edison. Prosthesis: Poems. LC 94-24525. 1994. 18.00 (*1-878325-10-8*); pap. 9.95 (*1-878325-11-6*) Bluestem Press.

— A Rapid Transit. (Poetry Chapbook Ser.). (Illus.). 27p. (Orig.). 1988. pap. write for info. (*0-9624274-3-8*) NC Writers Network.

Dupree, Garland C. & Namanny, Dorothy C. Legal Office Typing with Practical Applications. 2nd ed. (C). 1984. mass mkt. 19.25 (*0-538-11970-5*, K97) S-W Pub.

Dupree, Herbert & Dupree, Sherry. Busy Bookworm: Good Conduct Book. (Illus.). (J). (gr. k-5). 1980. pap. 2.25 (*0-9600962-8-0*) Displays Sch.

DuPree, Herbert C., jt. auth. see DuPree, Sherry S.

Dupree, Lisa, ed. see Bryan, Luis A. & Bryan, Eric A.

Dupree, Louis. Afghanistan. LC 76-154993. 802p. reprint ed. pap. 200.00 (*0-7837-1431-9*, 204178600023) Bks Demand.

***Dupree, M. Tina.** Hot T. I. P. S. on Public Speaking. 64p. 1999. 11.97 (*0-9665531-1-X*) Motivatnl Train Ctr.

Dupree, Madris. My Lord Beaumont. (Intrigue Ser.). 1994. per. 3.99 (*0-373-28813-1*, 1-28813-3) Harlequin Bks.

Dupree, Marguerite W. Family Structure in the Staffordshire Potteries, 1840-1880. (Oxford Historical Monographs). (Illus.). 426p. 1995. text 85.00 (*0-19-820400-0*) OUP.

DuPree, Mary. Musical Americans: A Biographical Dictionary, 1918-1926. LC 97-18294. (Reference Books in Music: Vol. 23). 317p. 1997. 37.95 (*0-914913-13-1*, Fallen Lef Pr) Scarecrow.

Dupree, Nancy H., jt. auth. see Anderson, Ewan W.

Dupree, Nathalie. Nathalie Dupree Cooks Everyday Meals from a Well-Stocked Pantry: Strategies for Shopping Less & Eating Better. LC 94-31426. 1995. 22.50 (*0-517-59735-7*) C Potter.

— Nathalie Dupree Cooks Quick Meals for Busy Days: 180 Delicious Timesaving Recipes. 1996. 22.50 (*0-614-96288-9*) C Potter.

— Nathalie Dupree's Comfortable Entertaining: At Home with Ease & Grace. LC 98-19871. (Illus.). 336p. 1998. 29.95 (*0-670-87885-5*) Viking Penguin.

Dupree, Robert S., et al. The Muses. LC 94-34955. (Entities Trilogy Ser.). 131p. (Orig.). 1994. pap. 20.00 (*0-911005-26-9*) Dallas Inst Pubns.

Dupree, Robert S., tr. & contrib. by see Bachelard, Gaston.

Dupree, Sherry, jt. auth. see Dupree, Herbert.

DuPree, Sherry S. The African-American Holiness Pentecostal Movement: An Annotated Bibliography. LC 94-20225. (Religious Information Systems Ser.: Vol. 4). (Illus.). 650p. 1995. text 50.00 (*0-8240-1449-9*, SS526) Garland.

— Biographical Dictionary of African-American, Holiness-Pentecostals: 1880-1990. LC 89-12590. 386p. (Orig.). 1989. pap. 23.95 (*0-9616056-9-3*) Mid Atl Reg Pr.

— What You Always Wanted to Know about the Card Catalog but Were Afraid to Ask. 1988th rev. ed. LC 77-87133. (Illus.). (J). (gr. k-6). 1988. pap. 6.95 (*0-9600962-3-X*) Displays Sch.

DuPree, Sherry S. & DuPree, Herbert C. African American Good News (Gospel) Music. LC 92-37092. (Illus.). 156p. (Orig.). 1993. pap. 19.95 (*1-877971-08-1*) Mid Atl Reg Pr.

— Exposed! F.B.I. Unclassified Reports on Churches & Church Leaders. LC 92-33480. (Illus.). 66p. (Orig.). 1992. pap. 13.95 (*1-877971-09-X*) Mid Atl Reg Pr.

DuPree, Sherry S., jt. auth. see Stewart, Alexander C.

Dupree, Toy Kim, jt. auth. see Scherber, Amy.

***Dupret, Baudouin, et al.** Legal Pluralism in the Arab World. (Arab & Islamic Laws Ser.: Vol. 18). 304p. 1999. 105.00 (*90-411-1105-0*) Kluwer Law Intl.

Dupret, S., jt. auth. see Pauchet, Victor.

Duprey, Daniel. L' Universalite de "Bien" Linguistique et Philosophie du Langage. (Sciences pour la Communication Ser.: Vol. 44). (FRE.). xxxix, 200p. 1995. 41.95 (*3-906754-06-5*, Pub. by P Lang) P Lang Pubng.

***Duprey, John W.** Turbolinux Bible. (Bible Ser.). (Illus.). 648p. 2000. pap. text 39.99 (*0-7645-4702-X*) IDG Bks.

Duprey, Kenneth. Old Houses on Nantucket. (Illus.). 1986. pap. 14.95 (*0-8038-5399-8*) Archit CT.

Dupriez, Bernard. Gradus: Dictionary of Literary Devices. Halsall, Albert W., tr. 564p. 1991. pap. 24.95 (*0-8020-6803-0*); text 65.00 (*0-8020-2756-3*) U of Toronto Pr.

Dupuch, Etienne. Tribune Story. (Illus.). 1968. 12.00 (*0-685-20643-2*) Transatl Arts.

Dupuis. Handy Science Answer Book. 2nd ed. LC 98-231245. (Illus.). xv, 580p. 1997. 16.95 (*0-7876-1013-5*) Visible Ink Pr.

Dupuis, Adrian M., ed. Nature, Aims, & Policy. LC 70-100373. (Readings in the Philosophy of Education Ser.). 358p. reprint ed. pap. 111.00 (*0-608-30917-6*, 202225500026) Bks Demand.

Dupuis, Adrian M. & Gordon, Robin L. Philosophy of Education in Historical Perspective. 2nd ed. LC 96-43224. 318p. 1996. pap. text 24.50 (*0-7618-0548-6*) U Pr of Amer.

Dupuis, Ann. Santa's Secret: A Gatecrasher Adventure with "All the Rules You Need to Know" 2nd ed. (Illus.). 24p. 1998. pap. 4.95 (*1-887154-05-1*, GGG3003) Grey Ghost Press.

***Dupuis, Ann, et al.** GURPS Old West: Adventure on the American Frontier. 2nd ed. (GURPS Ser.). (Illus.). 128p. 2000. pap. 19.95 (*1-55634-439-2*) S Jackson Games.

Dupuis, Ann, ed. see Masters, Phil & Brooks, Alison.

Dupuis, Carolyn C. The Lilac House. Duncan, Guri, ed. 280p. 1997. 25.00 (*0-9638803-2-2*) Driftwood Pr.

Dupuis, David. Sawchuk: The Troubles & Triumphs of the World's Greatest Goalie. LC 99-161058. (Illus.). 320p. 1999. 19.95 (*0-7737-3117-2*) Genl Dist Srvs.

***Dupuis, David.** Sawchuk: The Troubles & Triumphs of the World's Greatest Goalie. large type ed. LC 99-161058. (Illus.). 328p. 1999. pap. 13.95 (*0-7737-6064-4*, Pub. by Stoddart Publ) Genl Dist Srvs.

Dupuis, Diane, ed. see Morgan, Bradley J.

Dupuis, Diane L. Cities of the U. S. West, Vol. 2. 3rd ed. 1997. 115.00 (*0-8103-8393-4*) Gale.

D

DuPuis, E. Melanie & Vandergeest, Peter, eds. Creating the Countryside: The Politics of Rural & Environmental Discourse. LC 95-5167. (Conflicts in Urban & Regional Development Ser.). (Illus.). (C). 1996. pap. text 24.95 (*1-56639-360-4*); lib. bdg. 69.95 (*1-56639-359-0*) Temple U Pr.

Dupuis, Elizabeth A., jt. ed. see Anghelescu, Hermina G.

Dupuis, Francois. Cavalier History of Surrealism. 128p. 1999. pap. text 9.95 (*1-873176-94-5*) AK Pr Dist.

Dupuis, Hector & Legare, Romain. Dictionnaire des Synonymes et des Antonymes. (FRE.). 608p. 1975. 39.95 (*0-8288-5860-8*, M6180) Fr & Eur.

Dupuis, Hector, et al. Lexique de la Fabrication du Refrigerateur: Francais-Anglais. (ENG & FRE.). 66p. 1975. pap. 5.95 (*0-8288-5929-9*, M9240) Fr & Eur.

Dupuis, Hector, jt. auth. see Connington.

Dupuis, Hector, jt. auth. see Mousset.

Dupuis, Henriette & Comeau, Cecile. English French Lexicon of Industrial Safety Vol. 2: Control of Noise & Vibrations. (ENG & FRE.). 67p. 1987. pap. 29.95 (*0-8288-9382-9*) Fr & Eur.

Dupuis, J., jt. ed. see Neuner, Josef.

Dupuis, Jacques. Toward a Christian Theology of Religious Pluralism. LC 97-2515. 700p. 1997. 50.00 (*1-57075-125-0*) Orbis Bks.

— Toward a Christian Theology of Religious Pluralism. LC 99-22418. 448p. 1999. pap. 25.00 (*1-57075-264-8*) Orbis Bks.

— Who Do You Say I Am? Introduction to Christology. LC 93-45599. 200p. 1994. pap. 23.00 (*0-88344-940-4*) Orbis Bks.

Dupuis, Joseph. Journal of a Residence in Ashanti. 502p. 1966. 75.00 (*0-7146-1805-5*, Pub. by F Cass Pubs) Intl Spec Bk.

Dupuis, Marc & Dawson, John, eds. European Cases in Retailing. LC 98-27031. 272p. 1998. pap. 36.95 (*0-631-20730-9*) Blackwell Pubs.

Dupuis, Mary M., ed. Reading in the Content Areas: Research for Teachers. LC 83-8577. 87p. reprint ed. pap. 30.00 (*0-8357-4311-X*, 203710900007) Bks Demand.

Dupuis, Mary M. & Merchant, Linda K., eds. Reading Across the Curriculum: A Research Report for Teachers. LC 92-10123. 1992. 21.95 (*0-927516-33-0*) ERIC-REC.

Dupuis, Michael, et al. Are Today's Seminaries Catholic? (Illus.). 271p. (Orig.). 1990. pap. text 8.45 (*0-935952-75-6*) Angelus Pr.

Dupuis, Michel. Pronoms et Visages: Lecture de'Emmanuel Levinas. (Phaenomenologica Ser.: No. 134). 240p. (C). 1996. lib. bdg. 118.00 (*0-7923-3655-0*, Pub. by Kluwer Academic) Kluwer Academic.

Dupuis, Paul & Ellis, Richard S. A Weak Convergence Approach to the Theory of Large Deviations. LC 96-27513. (Wiley Series in Probability & Mathematical Statistics). 504p. 1997. 99.95 (*0-471-07672-4*) Wiley.

Dupuis, Paul, jt. auth. see Kushner, Harold J.

Dupuis, Richard. From the Mouth of God: Changing Life Struggles to Powerful Energy. LC 98-71008. 160p. 1998. pap. 14.95 (*1-58151-009-8*) BookPartners.

— Money Matters: What Stockbrokers Don't Always Tell You. 1991. pap. 12.95 (*0-9623830-0-7*) Companion Bks.

Dupuis, Richard A., jt. ed. see Rosell, Garth M.

Dupuis, Robert. Bunny Berigan: Elusive Legend of Jazz. LC 99-21408. (Illus.). xxii, 392p. 1993. 24.95 (*0-8071-1648-3*) La State U Pr.

Dupuis, S. Jacques. Jesus Christ at the Encounter of World Religions. Barr, Robert R., tr. from FRE. LC 91-7840. (Faith Meets Faith Ser.).Tr. of Jesus Christ a la Recontre Des Religions. 1991. pap. 20.00 (*0-88344-723-1*) Orbis Bks.

Dupuis-Yakouba, A. Les Gow, ou, Chasseurs du Niger: Legendes Songai de la Region de Tombouctou. (B. E. Ser.: No. 124). (FRE.). 30.00 (*0-8115-3053-1*) Periodicals Srv.

Dupuy. Focus on Nutrition. 1995. 13.75 (*0-697-40359-9*, WCB McGr Hill) McGraw-H Hghr Educ.

Dupuy, Alex. Haiti in the New World Order: The Limits of the Democratic Revolution. LC 96-36190. 6p. (C). 1996. pap. 26.00 (*0-8133-2114-X*, Pub. by Westview) HarpC.

Dupuy, Edward J. Autobiography in Walker Percy: Repetition, Recovery, & Redemption. LC 95-23388. (Southern Literary Studies). 184p. (C). 1996. text 27.50 (*0-8071-2012-X*) La State U Pr.

Dupuy, Eliza A. The Cancelled Will. LC 78-164559. (American Fiction Reprint Ser.). 1977. reprint ed. 35.95 (*0-8369-7035-7*) Ayer.

— Dethroned Heiress. LC 76-76923. (American Fiction Reprint Ser.). 1977. 20.95 (*0-8369-7002-0*) Ayer.

Dupuy, Francois. The Customer's Victory: From Corporation to Cooperation. LC 98-31070. 157p. 1999. pap. 18.95 (*0-253-21289-8*); text 49.95 (*0-253-33528-0*) Ind U Pr.

Dupuy, Harold J. The Construction & Utility of Three Indexes of Intellectual Achievement. Stevenson, Taloria, ed. Incl. Differential-Intellectual-Development (DID) Index (U. S. Children & Youth 6-17 Years) 1977. Index of Intellectual Development (ID) 1977. Socio-Intellectual-Status (SIS) Index. 1977. (Series 2: No. 74). 1977. Set pap. text 1.85 (*0-8406-0106-9*) Natl Ctr Health Stats.

Dupuy, J., ed. see NATO Advanced Study Institute Staff.

Dupuy, J., jt. ed. see Wright, A. F.

***Dupuy, Jean-Pierre.** The Mechanization of the Mind: On the Origins of Cognitive Science. DeBevoise, M. B., tr. (New French Thought Ser.). (Illus.). 240p. 2000. 29.95 (*0-691-02574-6*) Princeton U Pr.

Dupuy, Jean-Pierre, ed. Self-Deception & Paradoxes of Rationality. LC 98-3095. (Lecture Notes Ser.: Vol. 69). 224p. (C). 1998. text 64.95 (*1-57586-069-4*); pap. text 22.95 (*1-57586-068-6*) CSLI.

Dupuy, Marigny J., jt. auth. see Berman, Matt.

***Dupuy, R. Ernest.** The Compact History of the Civil War. 512p. 2000. 9.98 (*1-56731-393-0*, MJF Bks) Fine Comms.

Dupuy, R. Ernest. St. Vith: Lion in the Way: The 106th Infantry Division in World War II. (Divisional Ser.: 30th). (Illus.). 284p. 1986. reprint ed. 39.95 (*0-89839-092-3*) Battery Pr.

Dupuy, R. Ernest & Dupuy, Trevor N. Brave Men & Great Captains. 300p. 1993. reprint ed. pap. 23.95 (*1-883833-01-9*) Depuy Inst.

— Brave Men & Great Captains. 1995. reprint ed. pap. 23.95 (*0-9638692-2-1*) NOVA Pubns.

— The Compact History of the Civil War. 512p. 1993. mass mkt. 15.99 (*0-446-39432-7*, Pub. by Warner Bks) Little.

Dupuy, Rene-Jean. The Right to Development at the International Level. 458p. 1980. lib. bdg. 129.00 (*90-286-0990-3*) Kluwer Academic.

— The Settlement of Disputes on the New Natural Resources: Workshop, 1982. 1983. lib. bdg. 129.00 (*90-247-2901-7*) Kluwer Academic.

Dupuy, Rene-Jean, ed. The Development of the Role of the Security Council: Peace-Keeping & Peace-Building Workshop 1992 - Colloque 1992. (Recueil des Cours, Colloque Ser.). 516p. (C). 1993. lib. bdg. 158.00 (*0-7923-2318-1*) Kluwer Academic.

— The Future of International Law in a Multicultural World (Workshop 1983) 1984. lib. bdg. 129.00 (*90-247-3070-8*) Kluwer Academic.

— The Future of the International Law of the Environment. (Hague Academy of International Law Recueil des Cours, Colloque Ser.). 1985. lib. bdg. 129.00 (*90-247-3239-5*) Kluwer Academic.

***Dupuy, Rene-Jean, ed.** A Handbook on International Organizations. 2nd ed. (Recueil des Cours Ser.: Vol. 87). 1000p. 1998. 257.00 (*90-411-1119-0*) Kluwer Law Intl.

Dupuy, Rene-Jean, ed. The Right to Health As a Human Right: Colloquim 1978 of the Hague Academy of International Law. 513p. 1979. lib. bdg. 129.00 (*90-286-1028-6*) Kluwer Academic.

Dupuy, Rene-Jean & Vighes, Daniel, eds. A Handbook on the New Law of the Sea, Vol. 1. (Recueil des Cours, Colloque Ser.). 900p. 1991. lib. bdg. 235.00 (*0-7923-0924-3*) Kluwer Academic.

Dupuy, Rene-Jean & Vignes, Daniel, eds. A Handbook on the New Law of the Sea. (Recueil des Cours, Colloque Ser.: Vol. 2). 882p. (C). 1991. lib. bdg. 235.00 (*0-7923-1063-2*) Kluwer Academic.

DuPuy, Richard E. Automotive Brake Systems. 2nd rev. ed. (Illus.). 656p. 1997. pap. 49.00 (*1-57932-079-1*) Chek-Chart.

— Fuel Systems & Emission Controls. 3rd rev. ed. (Illus.). 737p. 1997. pap. 49.00 (*1-57932-117-8*) Chek-Chart.

DuPuy, Richard K. Automotive Electrical & Electronic Systems. 3rd rev. ed. (Illus.). 848p. 1997. pap. 49.00 (*1-57932-123-2*) Chek-Chart.

— Automotive Engine Repair & Rebuilding. 2nd rev. ed. (Illus.). 761p. 1998. pap. 49.00 (*1-57932-120-8*) Chek-Chart.

DuPuy, Richard K., ed. see Check-Chart Publication Staff.

Dupuy-Sullivan, Francoise. Paysages Francais sur Fond D'Amerique. LC 94-41995. (FRE., Illus.). 309p. 1995. pap. 34.95 (*0-7734-1945-4*) E Mellen.

Dupuy, T. N. Understanding War: History & Theory of Combat. 312p. 1992. 31.95 (*0-85052-293-5*, Pub. by Leo Cooper) Trans-Atl Phila.

Dupuy, Trevor N. Attrition: Forecasting Battle Casualties & Equipment Losses in Modern War. 1990. pap. 19.95 (*0-9638692-3-X*) NOVA Pubns.

— The Evolution of Weapons & Warfare. LC 80-781. 358p. reprint ed. 111.00 (*0-7837-6668-8*, 204628000011) Bks Demand.

— The Evolution of Weapons & Warfare. (Quality Paperbacks Ser.). 358p. 1990. reprint ed. pap. 13.95 (*0-306-80384-4*) Da Capo.

— Future Wars: The World's Most Dangerous Flashpoints. 432p. 1993. mass mkt. 6.50 (*0-446-36421-5*, Pub. by Warner Bks) Little.

— Harper Encyclopedia of Military Biography. 834p. 1995. 17.98 (*0-7858-0437-4*) Bk Sales Inc.

— How to Defeat Saddam Hussein. 1991. mass mkt. 4.95 (*0-446-36263-8*, Pub. by Warner Bks) Little.

— If War Comes. 1991. pap. 19.95 (*0-915979-27-6*) NOVA Pubns.

— Understanding Defeat: How to Recover from Loss in Battle to Gain Victory in War. 1995. reprint ed. pap. 24.95 (*0-9638692-4-8*) NOVA Pubns.

Dupuy, Trevor N., ed. International Military & Defense Encyclopedia, 6 vols., 1. (Illus.). 3344p. 1993. 225.00 (*0-02-881061-9*) Brasseys.

— International Military & Defense Encyclopedia, 6 vols., 2. (Illus.). 3344p. 1993. 225.00 (*0-02-881062-7*) Brasseys.

— International Military & Defense Encyclopedia, 6 vols., 3. (Illus.). 3344p. 1993. 225.00 (*0-02-881063-5*) Brasseys.

— International Military & Defense Encyclopedia, 6 vols., 4. (Illus.). 3344p. 1993. 225.00 (*0-02-881064-3*) Brasseys.

— International Military & Defense Encyclopedia, 6 vols., 5. (Illus.). 3344p. 1993. 225.00 (*0-02-881065-1*) Brasseys.

— International Military & Defense Encyclopedia, 6 vols., 6. (Illus.). 3344p. 1993. 225.00 (*0-02-881066-X*) Brasseys.

— International Military & Defense Encyclopedia, 6 vols., Set. (Illus.). 3344p. 1993. 1300.00 (*0-02-881011-2*) Brasseys.

Dupuy, Trevor N., et al. Dictionary of Military Terms. LC 85-26592. 233p. 1986. 42.00 (*0-8242-0717-3*) Wilson.

— Har Enc Military His. 4th ed. LC 92-17853. (Illus.). 1760p. 1993. 75.00 (*0-06-270056-1*, Harper Ref) HarpC.

— Hitler's Last Gamble: The Battle of the Bulge, December 1944-January 1945. LC 94-19460. 624p. 1995. pap. 18.00 (*0-06-092196-X*, Perennial) HarperTrade.

Dupuy, Trevor N., jt. auth. see Dupuy, R. Ernest.

Dupuy, Trevor Nevitt. Evolution of Weapons & Warfare. LC 80-781. 1980. 14.95 (*0-672-52050-8*) Sams.

DuPuy, William, jt. auth. see Wilbur, Ray L.

Dupuy, William A. Our Bird Friends & Foes. (Illus.). 1990. 15.00 (*0-8446-0601-4*) Peter Smith.

Dupuy, Yves & Rolland, Gerard. Manual de Control de Gestion. (SPA.). 329p. 1992. pap. 31.00 (*84-7978-044-4*, Pub. by Ediciones Diaz) IBD Ltd.

Duqennoy, Jacques. The Ghosts in the Cellar. LC 97-37583. (Illus.). 48p. (J). (ps-3). 1998. lib. bdg. 12.00 (*0-15-201775-5*) Harcourt.

Duque, Angel M., ed. see Menendez Pidal, Ramon.

Duque, Angel Montenegro, see Montenegro Duque, Angel.

Duque, Luis & Cubillos, Julio C. Arqueologia de San Agustin: Alto de Lavapatas. (SPA., Illus.). 192p. (C). 1988. pap. 8.50 (*1-877812-15-3*, BR005, Pub. by Banco de la Repub) UPLAAP.

Duquennoy, Antoine & Mayor, Michael, eds. Binaries As Tracers of Stellar Formation. (Illus.). 302p. (C). 1993. text 74.95 (*0-521-43358-4*) Cambridge U Pr.

Duquennoy, Jacques. Ghost's Dinner. 1994. 9.89 (*0-606-11375-4*, Pub. by Turtleback) Demco.

— Ghosts Trip to Loch Ness. LC 96-11675. (Illus.). 52p. (J). 1996. 11.00 (*0-15-201440-3*) Harcourt.

— Operation Ghost. LC 98-43351. 48p. (J). 1999. 13.00 (*0-15-202182-5*, Harcourt Child Bks); pap. 6.00 (*0-15-202203-1*, Harcourt Child Bks) Harcourt.

Duquesne, Jacques. Jesus: An Unconventional Biography. Spencer, Catherine, tr. LC 98-3000. 304p. 1997. 24.00 (*0-7648-0061-2*, Liguori Triumph) Liguori Pubns.

— Jesus: An Unconventional Biography. Spencer, Catherine, tr. LC 98-3000. 304p. 1998. reprint ed. pap. 16.00 (*0-7648-0198-8*, Liguori Triumph) Liguori Pubns.

Duquest, William, et al, eds. Youth Sport: A Social Approach. (Illus.). 248p. 1994. pap. 29.95 (*90-70289-99-7*) Paul & Co Pubs.

Duquet, Denis & Lachapell, Mark. Auto Guide, 1987. 1988. pap. 17.95 (*0-8050-0881-0*) H Holt & Co.

Duquet, Denis, et al. New Car Report, 1996. (Illus.). 428p. 1995. pap. 19.95 (*0-88266-746-7*) Storey Bks.

Duquet, Marc. Collins Watch Guide: Birds in Winter. 1997. pap. 11.95 (*0-00-220100-3*, Pub. by HarpC) Trafalgar.

— Collins Watch Guide: Birds of the Countryside. (Illus.). 1997. pap. 11.95 (*0-00-220087-2*, Pub. by HarpC) Trafalgar.

Duquet-Picard, Diane, jt. auth. see Boivin, Gilles.

Duquet, Richard. Actively Seeking Nutrition. 27p. 1978. pap. 2.00 (*0-934332-20-7*) LEpervier Pr.

Duquet, William & Day, James A., eds. Kinanthropometry, No. IV. LC 93-34093. 320p. (C). 1993. 115.00 (*0-419-16770-6*, E & FN Spon) Routledge.

Duquette & Cain. Fitness Assessment. 200p. (C). 1997. spiral bd., wbk. ed. 26.95 (*0-7872-4229-2*) Kendall-Hunt.

Duquette, Anne M. Anniversary Waltz. (Great Escapes Ser.). 1994. per. 3.99 (*0-373-83272-9*, 1-83272-4) Harlequin Bks.

— The Dinosaur Lady. (Romance Ser.). 1994. per. 2.99 (*0-373-03328-1*, 1-03328-1) Harlequin Bks.

— Finding Father: (Family Man) LC 95-13576. (Superromance Ser.). 298p. 1995. per. 3.75 (*0-373-70644-8*, 1-70644-9) Harlequin Bks.

— Her Own Ranger. (Superromance Ser.: Bk. 849). 1999. per. 4.25 (*0-373-70849-1*, 1-70849-4) Harlequin Bks.

— In the Arms of the Law. 1997. per. 3.99 (*0-373-70759-2*, 1-70759-5) Harlequin Bks.

— On the Line: Back to the Ranch. (Romance Ser.). 1993. per. 2.99 (*0-373-03289-7*, 1-03289-5) Harlequin Bks.

— Rescued by Love. 1993. per. 2.89 (*0-373-03253-6*, 1-03253-1) Harlequin Bks.

— Rescued by Love. large type ed. LC 93-13223. 277p. 1993. lib. bdg. 14.95 (*1-56054-760-X*) Thorndike Pr.

— She Caught the Sheriff. (Harlequin Super Romance Ser.: No. 700). 1996. per. 3.99 (*0-373-70700-2*, 1-70700-9) Harlequin Bks.

— She's the Sheriff: Home on the Ranch. (Harlequin Super Romance Ser.: No. 787). 298p. 1998. mass mkt. 4.25 (*0-373-70787-8*, 1-70787-6) Harlequin Bks.

— Toute une Eternite D'Amour. (Horizon Ser.). (FRE.). 1997. pap. 3.50 (*0-373-39433-0*, 1-39433-7) Harlequin Bks.

***Duquette, Anne Marie.** A Lethal Combination. 2000. mass mkt. 9.95 (*1-55279-018-5*, Pub. by Picasso Publ) Baker & Taylor.

Duquette, David. Timber Solutions Manual. LC 96-93136. (Illus.). 360p. (Orig.). (C). 1997. pap. text 49.95 (*0-9656181-0-2*) Argulus Pub.

Duquette, David A. Hooftrimming for Horseowners: Step by Step Guide to Daily Hoof Care, Hoof Handling & Trimming. rev. ed. 52p. 1994. pap. 12.95 (*0-945782-02-0*) HFH Pubns.

— Horseshoeing for Horseowners: A Step by Step Guide to Daily Hoof Care, Hoof Handling, Trimming & Shoeing. rev. ed. (Illus.). 80p. 1994. pap. 19.95 (*0-945782-03-9*) HFH Pubns.

Duquette, Donald N. Advocating for the Child in Protection Proceedings: A Guide for Child Advocates. 160p. 1990. 25.95 (*0-669-21465-5*) Lxngtn Bks.

Duquette, George, ed. Classroom Methods & Strategies for Teaching at the Secondary Level. LC 97-29961. (Studies in Education: Vol. 14). 228p. 1997. text 89.95 (*0-7734-8647-X*) E Mellen.

Duquette, George S., jt. ed. see Malave, Lilliam.

Duquette, Georges. The Undiscovered Country. rev. ed. LC 93-24146. 64p. 1995. pap. 14.95 (*0-7734-2767-8*, Mellen Poetry Pr) E Mellen.

Duquette, Georges, ed. Second Language Practice: Classroom Strategies for Deveoping Communicative Competence. LC 95-30458. 200p. 1995. 69.00 (*1-85359-306-0*, Pub. by Multilingual Matters); pap. 24.95 (*1-85359-305-2*, Pub. by Multilingual Matters) Taylor & Francis.

***Duquette, Jerold J.** Regulating the National Pastime: Baseball & Antitrust. LC 99-16060. 184p. 1999. 59.95 (*0-275-96535-X*) Greenwood.

DuQuette, John. Adicora Venezuela: The Gringo's Windsurfing Map & Guide. LC 97-69467. (Illus.). 54p. 1997. 19.95 (*1-889748-02-1*) Cleveland Map Co.

Duquette, Keith. The House Book. LC 98-15820. (Illus.). 32p. (J). (ps-3). 1999. 15.99 (*0-399-23183-8*) Putnam Pub Group.

DuQuette, Lon M. Angels Demons & Gods of the New Millennium: Musings on Modern Magick. LC 97-9199. (Illus.). 192p. (Orig.). 1997. pap. 16.95 (*1-57863-010-X*) Weiser.

— The Magic of Thelema: A Handbook of the Rituals of Aleister Crowley. LC 93-10004. (Illus.). 288p. (Orig.). 1993. pap. 15.95 (*0-87728-778-3*) Weiser.

— My Life with the Spirits: The Adventures of a Modern Magician. LC 99-20559. (Illus.). 208p. 1999. pap. 14.95 (*1-57863-120-3*) Weiser.

Duquette, Lon M. Tarot of Ceremonial Magick. 1997. pap. text 14.95 (*1-57281-041-6*, BK718) US Games Syst.

— Tarot of Ceremonial Magick: A Pictorial Synthesis of Three Great Pillars of Magick (Astrology, Enochian Magick, Goetia) LC 95-14649. 304p. 1995. pap. 14.95 (*0-87728-764-3*) Weiser.

DuQuette, Lon M., jt. auth. see Hyatt, Christopher S.

Duquette-May, Christy, ed. see Butker, Mabel & Butker, Burton.

Duquette, Michel. Building New Democracies: Economic & Social Reform in Brazil, Chile, & Mexico. (Studies in Comparative Political Economy & Public Policy). (Illus.). 287p. 1999. pap. 19.95 (*0-8020-8209-2*); text 50.00 (*0-8020-4402-6*) U of Toronto Pr.

Duquetteke. Ripping Day Picnic. 1999. pap. 3.95 (*0-14-054251-5*) NAL.

***Duquid, Iain.** Ezekiel. LC 99-30790. (NIV Application Commentary Ser.). 1999. 24.99 (*0-310-21047-X*) Zondervan.

Duquin, Christopher J., jt. auth. see Duquin, Lorene H.

Duquin, Lorene H. Could You Ever Come Back to the Catholic Church? LC 96-40145. (Orig.). 1997. pap. 9.95 (*0-8189-0789-4*) Alba.

— They Called Her the Baroness: The Life of Catherine de Hueck Doherty. LC 95-34825. (Illus.). 356p. 1995. 19.95 (*0-8189-0753-3*) Alba.

Duquin, Lorene H. & Duquin, Christopher J. Could You Ever Become a Catholic Priest? LC 98-13335. 184p. 1998. pap. 9.95 (*0-8189-0816-5*) Alba.

Duquoc, Christian, et al, eds. Mysticism & the Institutional Crisis. (Concilium Ser.). 130p. (Orig.). 1994. pap. 15.00 (*0-88344-879-3*) Orbis Bks.

— Pilgrimage. (Concilium Ser.). 115p. 1996. pap. 15.00 (*1-57075-073-4*) Orbis Bks.

Duquoc, Christian & Floristan, Casiano. Job & the Silence of God. (Concilium Ser.: Vol. 169). 128p. (Orig.). 1983. 6.95 (*0-8164-2449-7*) Harper SF.

Duquoc, Christian, jt. auth. see Floristan, Casiano.

Dur, A. Mobius Functions, Incidence Algebras & Power Series Representations. (Lecture Notes in Mathematics Ser.: Vol. 1202). xi, 134p. 1986. 35.95 (*0-387-16771-4*) Spr-Verlag.

Dur O, D. F., ed. see Adrian, Richard H., et al.

***Durack, Gary & Robinson, J. Paul.** Emerging Tools for Single Cell Analysis: Advances in Optical Measurement Technologies. LC 99-51911. 352p. 2000. 129.95 (*0-471-31575-3*) Wiley.

Durack, Mary. The Rock & the Sand. LC 75-424996. 336 p. 1969. write for info. (*0-09-455710-1*) Trafalgar.

Durack, Richard, jt. auth. see Cole, Beverly.

***Durack, Terry.** Noodle. LC 99-24105. (Illus.). 208p. 1999. 27.00 (*1-57959-053-5*, SOMA) BB&T Inc.

Duraiappah, Anantha K. Global Warming & Economic Development: A Holistic Approach to International Policy Co-Operation & Co-Ordination. LC 92-47021. (AICE - Advances in Computational Economics Ser.: No. 2). 244p. (C). 1993. lib. bdg. 147.00 (*0-7923-2149-9*) Kluwer Academic.

***Durakovic, Ferida & Simic, Amela.** Heart of Darkness. Simon, Greg, ed. LC 98-39977. (Terra Incognito Ser.: Vol. 3). 109p. 1999. pap. 14.00 (*1-877727-91-1*, Pub. by White Pine) SPD-Small Pr Dist.

Durall, Wilbur I., jt. auth. see Obert, Leonard.

Duran. Communication Connections: Introduction to Human Communication. (Speech & Theater Ser.). 2001. pap. 30.00 (*0-534-55809-7*) Wadsworth Pub.

Duran, Anne. Just a Minute Games: Got a Minute? Play a Game. 3rd rev. ed. ii, 52p. (Orig.). (J). 1996. reprint ed. pap. 8.00 (*1-889645-02-8*) Cabin Fev Pubg.

Duran, Antonio E., ed. National Advisory Council on Migrant Health: 1993 Recommendations. (Illus.). 93p. (C). 1999. reprint ed. pap. text 20.00 (*0-7881-7617-X*) DIANE Pub.

Duran, Bonnie, jt. auth. see Duran, Eduardo.

Duran, Carlos, jt. ed. see Al-Zaibag, Muayed.

Duran, Carlos, tr. see Freeman, Don.

Duran, Carmen & Cuchi, Paloma. Promoviendo un Futuro Saludable: Manual de Entrenamiento para Jovenes Promotores de Salud.Tr. of Promoting a Healty Future. (SPA., Illus.). 200p. 1997. pap. text. write for info. (*0-9658448-1-1*) LatAm Youth.

— Promoviendo un Futuro Saludable: Manual de Entrenamiento para Jovenes Promotores de Salud. unabridged ed.Tr. of Promoting a Healty Future. (SPA., Illus.). 200p. 1997. text. write for info. (*0-9658448-0-3*) LatAm Youth.

An Asterisk (*) at the beginning of an entry indicates that the title is appearing for the first time.

Duran, Cathi. The Lemonade Handbook: Seeing Everyday Lemons in a Positive Light. Caton, Patrick, ed. LC 97-71653. 168p. 1997. pap. 5.95 (*1-56245-307-6*) Great Quotations.

Duran, Cheli. Hildilid's Night. 1996. 10.19 (*0-606-09413-X*, Pub. by Turtleback) Demco.

Duran, Cheryl M. Gatekeepers in Ethnolinguistic Communities. LC 92-33265. (Information Management, Policies & Services Ser.). 232p. 1993. pap. 39.50 (*0-89391-996-9*); text 73.25 (*0-89391-891-1*) Ablx Pub.

Duran, Daniel F. Latino Communication Patterns. Cortes, Carlos E., ed. LC 79-6203. (Hispanics in the United States Ser.). (Illus.). 1981. lib. bdg. 55.95 (*0-405-13154-2*) Ayer.

Duran, Diego. The History of the Indies of New Spain. Heyden, Doris, tr. & anno. by. LC 93-48624. (Civilization of the American Indian Ser.: Vol. 210). (Illus.). 744p. 1994. 57.50 (*0-8061-2649-3*) U of Okla Pr.

Duran, Eduardo & Duran, Bonnie. Native American Postcolonial Psychology. LC 94-13400. (SUNY Series in Transpersonal & Humanistic Psychology). 227p. (C). 1995. pap. text 20.95 (*0-7914-2354-9*) State U NY Pr.

Duran, Elva. Teaching Students with Moderate-Severe Disabilities, Including Autism: Strategies for Second Language Learners in Inclusive Settings. 2nd ed. LC 96-23691. Orig. Title: Teaching the Moderately & Severely Handicapped Student & Autistic Adolescent. 416p. 1996. text 79.95 (*0-398-06700-7*); pap. text 58.95 (*0-398-06701-5*) C C Thomas.

— Vocational Training & Employment of the Moderately & Severely Handicapped & Autistic Adolescent with Particular Emphasis to Bilingual Special Education. (Illus.). 182p. 1992. pap. 27.95 (*0-398-06101-7*) C C Thomas.

— Vocational Training & Employment of the Moderately & Severely Handicapped & Autistic Adolescent with Particular Emphasis to Bilingual Special Education. (Illus.). 182p. (C). 1992. text 41.95 (*0-398-05801-6*) C C Thomas.

Duran, Esperanza, jt. ed. see Valenta, Jiri.

***Duran, Gloria.** Maria de Estrada: Gypsy Conquistadora. LC 99-16679. 227p. (YA). 1999. pap. 14.95 (*1-891270-01-X*, Pub. by Lat Am Lit Rev Pr) Consort Bk Sales.

Duran, Gloria & Duran, Manuel. Autoretratos y Espejos: Self Portraits & Reflections. 1977. pap. write for info. (*0-318-54912-3*) P-H.

Duran, Grace Z., jt. ed. see Artiles, Alfredo J.

Duran, Helen C. Mexican Recipe Shortcuts or Casserolization of the Classics. (Wild & Woolly West Ser.). (Illus.). 52p. (Orig.). 1983. pap. 3.50 (*0-86541-013-5*) Filter.

Duran, Ignacio, jt. auth. see Decker, David R.

Duran, Jacques. Physics of Granular Materials. Reisinger, A., tr. LC 98-31321. (Partially Ordered Systems Ser.). (Illus.). 314p. 1999. 59.95 (*0-387-98656-1*) Spr-Verlag.

Duran, Jacques & Katamba, Francis, eds. Fronteirs Phonology. LC 94-27527. (Linguistics Library). 1995. text 69.95 (*0-582-08268-4*) Longman.

Duran, James C. Norman Thomas. Bowman, Sylvia E., ed. LC 73-15831. (Twayne's United States Authors Ser.). 173p. 1974. text 20.95 (*0-8057-0727-1*) Irvington.

Duran, Jane. Breathe Now, Breathe. 64p. 1996. pap. 13.95 (*1-870612-52-3*, Pub. by Enitha Pr) Dufour.

— Epistemics: Epistemic Justification Theory Naturalized & the Computational Model of Mind. LC 88-33792. 102p. (C). 1989. lib. bdg. 32.00 (*0-8191-7328-2*) U Pr of Amer.

— Knowledge in Context: Naturalized Epistemology & Sociolinguistics. LC 93-6474. 220p. (Orig.). (C). 1994. pap. text 23.95 (*0-8476-7832-6*); lib. bdg. 59.50 (*0-8476-7831-8*) Rowman.

— Philosophies of Science & Feminist Theories. LC 98-102367. 224p. (C). 1997. pap. text 25.00 (*0-8133-3325-3*, Pub. by Westview) HarpC.

— Toward a Feminist Epistemology. 256p. (C). 1990. lib. bdg. 58.00 (*0-8476-7635-8*) Rowman.

— Toward a Feminist Epistemology. 288p. 1990. pap. 21.95 (*0-8476-7989-6*) Rowman.

Duran, Jennie, ed. see Akens, David S. & Klein, Eugene L.

Duran, Joe, jt. auth. see Sauer, Charles.

Duran, Laurel. The Blue Cord: A Semi-Autobiographical Novel. Baldinger, Jo Ann, ed. LC 95-92113. 294p. (Orig.). 1995. pap. 13.95 (*0-9646909-0-X*) DuirSoul Bks.

Duran, Leo, ed. Plays of Old Japan. LC 77-94339. (One-Act Plays in Reprint Ser.). 1978. reprint ed. 20.00 (*0-8486-2037-2*) Roth Pub Inc.

Duran, Luis H. Songs of Love & Wind. Russell-Pineda, Diana, tr. from ENG. LC 92-72431. (Illus.). 224p. (Orig.). 1992. pap. 10.00 (*0-9623552-9-1*) Ed Arcas.

Duran, Manuel. Cervantes. LC 74-7006. (World Authors Ser.: No. 329). 192p. 1974. 28.95 (*0-8057-2206-8*, Twyne) Mac Lib Ref.

— Luis de Leon. LC 79-19352. (Twayne's World Authors Ser.). 1971. lib. bdg. 20.95 (*0-8057-2524-5*) Irvington.

— Reason in Exile Vol. 13: Essays on Catalan Philosophers. LC 93-46253. (Catalan Studies: Vol. 13). 104p. (C). 1994. text 27.95 (*0-8204-2361-0*) P Lang Pubng.

Duran, Manuel & Kluback, William, trs. Luis de Leon: Names of Christ. (Classics of Western Spirituality Ser.). (C). 1984. 14.95 (*0-8091-0346-X*); pap. 11.95 (*0-8091-2561-7*) Paulist Pr.

Duran, Manuel, jt. auth. see Duran, Gloria.

Duran, Martin J. The Original Computer Idiot PC User's Guide. (Idiot Ser.). (Illus.). 192p. (Orig.). pap. 15.95 (*1-879986-40-X*) SoftMark CA.

— The Original Computer Idiot PC User's Guide: For IBM PC's & Compatibles. (Idiot Ser.). (Illus.). 192p. (Orig.). 1992. pap. 15.95 (*1-879986-00-0*) SoftMark CA.

Duran, Maureen Gallagher, jt. auth. see Cole, Deborah D.

Duran, Meliha S. & Laumbach, Karl W., eds. Fourth Jornada Mogollon Conference, Oct. 1985, Collected Papers. 259p. 1988. pap. 18.00 (*1-887523-01-4*) Human Systs Res.

Duran, Melina S., et al. Jewels of the Desert: Collects from the First Dump at White Sands Missile Range. unabridged ed. LC 97-74738. (Illus.). 140p. 1997. pap. 12.00 (*1-887523-13-8*) Human Systs Res.

Duran, Nadira & Gatti, Donna W. When Angels Speak: Messages from the Keepers of the Lion's Gate. 2nd ed. 136p. 1999. reprint ed. pap. 9.95 (*1-58446-007-5*, Legacy OH) Temple Pubg.

Duran, Nadira, jt. auth. see Wolfe, Donna.

Duran, Nelson, tr. see Lasaga, Jose I.

Duran, Paul, ed. see Akens, David S. & Klein, Eugene L.

Duran, Paul A. A Practical Guide to Analog Behavioral Modeling for IC System Design. LC 98-33840. 1998. 115.00 (*0-7923-8276-5*) Kluwer Academic.

Duran, Phil L. Developing the Survival Attitude: A Guide for the New Officer. LC 98-188130. 112p. (C). 1997. pap. text 9.95 (*1-889031-14-3*) Looseleaf Law.

Duran, Richard, jt. ed. see Freedle, Roy O.

Duran, Richard P., ed. Latino Language & Communicative Behavior. (Advances in Discourse Processes Ser.: Vol. 6). 384p. 1981. pap. 42.50 (*0-89391-093-7*); text 78.50 (*0-89391-038-4*) Ablx Pub.

Duran, Roberto T. Reality Ribs. LC 93-20055. 112p. 1993. pap. 11.00 (*0-927534-35-5*) Biling Rev-Pr.

Duran, Roberto T., et al. Triple Crown: Chicano, Puerto Rican & Cuban American Poetry. LC 87-70081. 168p. 1987. pap. 14.00 (*0-916950-71-9*) Biling Rev-Pr.

Duran, Ruben & Fischer, George W. The Genus Tilletia. LC 61-40321. (Illus.). 144p. reprint ed. pap. 44.70 (*0-8357-8144-5*, 203410500088) Bks Demand.

Duran, Victor M. A Marxist Reading of Fuentes, Vargas Llosa & Puig. 136p. (C). 1993. lib. bdg. 38.00 (*0-8191-9305-4*) U Pr of Amer.

— Que Es y Como Se Hace el Analisis y Diagnostico de la Realidad en la CLAT. (SPA.). 130p. (Orig.). 1987. pap. 8.00 (*0-917049-10-1*) Saeta.

— Teoria de Organizacion de la Clase Trabajadora. (SPA.). 126p. (Orig.). 1987. pap. 8.00 (*0-917049-12-8*) Saeta.

— Teoria y Tecnica del Analisis y Diagnostico de la Empresa en el Sistema Capitalista. (SPA.). 128p. (Orig.). 1987. pap. 8.00 (*0-917049-11-X*) Saeta.

Duranceau, Andre, jt. auth. see Jamieson, Glyn G.

Duranceau, Steven J., et al. Effects of Electrical Grounding on Pipe Integrity & Shock Hazard. LC 96-206489. (Illus.). 250p. 1996. pap. 195.00 (*0-89867-861-7*, 90702) Am Water Wks Assn.

— Impact of Wet-Pipe Fire Sprinkler Systems on Drinking Water Quality. LC 97-44422. 1998. write for info. (*0-89867-943-5*) Am Water Wks Assn.

***Durand & Barlow.** Abnormal Psychology: An Introduction. 2nd ed. (Psychology Ser.). 1999. pap. 41.50 incl. cd-rom (*0-534-50687-9*) Wadsworth Pub.

— Abnormal Psychology: An Introduction. 2nd ed. (Psychology Ser.). (C). 2000. text, student ed. 17.25 (*0-534-36861-1*) Wadsworth Pub.

Durand, jt. auth. see Barlow.

Durand, Arthur A. Stalag Luft III: The Secret Story. (Illus.). 432p. 1999. pap. 19.95 (*0-8071-2443-5*) La State U Pr.

Durand, B. Kerogen: Insoluble Organic Matter from Sedimentary Rocks. (Illus.). 550p. (C). 1980. 935.00 (*2-7108-0371-2*, Pub. by Edits Technip) Enfield Pubs NH.

— Thermal Phenomena in Sedimentary Basins: 1st IPF Exploration & Production Research Conference, Bordeaux, 1983. (Illus.). 352p. 1984. 430.00 (*2-7108-0481-6*, Pub. by Edits Technip) Enfield Pubs NH.

Durand, B., et al, eds. The Mediterranean Basins: Tertiary Extension Within the Alpine Orogen. (Geological Society Special Publication Ser.: No. 156). 584p. 1999. 148.00 (*1-86239-033-9*, Pub. by Geol Soc Pub Hse) AAPG.

Durand-Barthez, Manuel. Etre Autrichien: La Problematique de la Faute Chez les Ecrivains Autrichiens du Debut du Siecle. (Publications Universitaires Europeennes Ser.: Series 1, Vol. 1594). (FRE.). 452p. 1997. 59.95 (*3-906754-86-3*, Pub. by P Lang) P Lang Pubng.

***Durand, Bud & Jacobs, Connie, frwds.** Moving DARPA Technologies into the Marketplace. (Illus.). 51p. (C). 2000. reprint ed. pap. text 20.00 (*0-7567-0064-7*) DIANE Pub.

Durand, Celia C. Durand: Genealogy of the Durand Family: Record of the Descendants of Francis Jos. Durand Together with Biographical Notes & Some Family Letters. 136p. 1997. reprint ed. pap. 21.00 (*0-8328-8382-4*); reprint ed. lib. bdg. 31.00 (*0-8328-8381-6*) Higginson Bk Co.

Durand-Charre, Madeleine. The Microstructure of Superalloys. 140p. 1998. text 45.00 (*90-5699-097-7*) Gordon & Breach.

***Durand, D.** Nuclear Dynamics in the Nucleonic Regime. (Fundamental & Applied Nuclear Physics Ser.). 1999. 200.00 (*0-7503-0537-1*) IOP Pub.

***Durand, Dave.** Perpetual Motivation: How to Light Your Fire & Keep It Burning. Jamison, Warren, ed. 2000. pap. 12.00 (*0-9675631-0-0*) ProBalance.

Durand, David. Bank Stock Prices & the Bank Capital Problem. (Occasional Papers: No. 54). 86p. 1957. reprint ed. 22.40 (*0-87014-368-9*) Natl Bur Econ Res.

— Basic Yields of Corporate Bonds, 1900-1942. (Technical Papers: No. 3). 40p. 1942. reprint ed. 20.00 (*0-87014-448-0*); reprint ed. mic. film 20.00 (*0-685-61235-X*) Natl Bur Econ Res.

— Risk Elements in Consumer Installment Financing. (Financial Research Program II: Studies in Consumer Installment Financing: No. 8). 128p. 1941. reprint ed. 33.30 (*0-87014-124-4*) Natl Bur Econ Res.

Durand, David & Winn, Willis J. Basic Yields of Bonds, 1926-1947: Their Measurement & Pattern. (Technical Papers: No. 6). 48p. 1947. reprint ed. 20.00 (*0-87014-451-0*); reprint ed. mic. film 20.00 (*0-685-61272-4*) Natl Bur Econ Res.

Durand, David, jt. auth. see Jones, Lawrence A.

Durand, David G., jt. auth. see DeRose, Steven J.

Durand de Bousingen, Denis, jt. auth. see Rogers, Arthur.

Durand, Dianne. Smocking: Techniques, Projects & Designs. (Illus.). 56p. 1979. pap. 3.95 (*0-486-23788-5*) Dover.

Durand-Drouhin, Jean-Louis & Szwengrub, Lili-Marie. Trends Selected & Annotated Bibliographies Analyses, 3 vols., Set. LC 80-41523. (Rural Community Studies in Europe). reprint ed. 372.00 (*0-08-032651-X*, Pub. by Pergamon Repr) Franklin.

Durand-Drouhin, Jean-Louis & Szwengrub, Lili-Marie, eds. Rural Community Studies in Europe: Trends, Selected & Annotated Bibliographies, Analyses, Vol. I. LC 80-41523. (Publications of the Vienna Centre). (Illus.). 342p. 1981. 149.00 (*0-08-021384-7*, Pub. by Pergamon Repr) Franklin.

Durand, Edward D., jt. auth. see Durand, Mary E.

Durand, Eugene. The Story of the Seventh-Day Adventist Church. Wheeler, Gerald, ed. (Harvesttime Ser.). 32p. (Orig.). 1986. pap. 0.89 (*0-8280-0320-3*) Review & Herald.

Durand-Forest, J. De, see Nowotny, K. A., comment.

Durand, Francisco & Silva, Eduardo, eds. Organized Business, Economic Change & Democracy in Latin America. ii, 297p. 1998. pap. 24.95 (*1-57454-048-3*) U Miami N-S Ctr.

Durand-Gordon, Lara, ed. see Ritchey, Brenda.

Durand, Herve. Dictionnaire Des Examens Biologiques et Investigations Paracliniques. 3rd ed. (FRE.). 488p. 1991. pap. 110.00 (*0-7859-7917-4*, 2704006687) Fr & Eur.

— Dictionnaire des Malades: Choix des Examens Complementaires. (FRE.). 316p. 1989. pap. 79.95 (*0-7859-7916-6*, 2704005982) Fr & Eur.

Durand, Ian & Bliss, Robert. ISO 9000 Video Seminar. (C). 1992. student ed. 24.95 (*1-883495-01-6*) Int Qual Systs.

Durand, Ian & Cormaci, April. The ISO 9000 Registration Workbook. rev. ed. LC 94-218078. 1994. 49.95 (*1-883495-04-0*) Int Qual Systs.

Durand, J. B. Labor Force in the United States (1890-1960), Vol. 2. (Demographic Monographs). xx, 290p. 1968. text 191.00 (*0-677-01550-X*) Gordon & Breach.

Durand, J. R. & Leveque, Ch. Flore et Faune Aquatiques de l'Afrique Sahelo-Soudanienne (The Aquatic Flora & Fauna of Sahel-Sudanian Africa), Vol. 1. (Initiations Documentations Techniques Ser.: No. 45).Tr. of Aquatic Flora & Fauna of Sahel-Sudanian Africa. (FRE., Illus.). 390p. 1980. pap. 28.00 (*2-7099-0522-1*, Pub. by LInstitut Francais) Balogh.

— Flore et Faune Aquatiques de l'Afrique Sahelo-Soudanienne (The Aquatic Flora & Fauna of Sahel-Sudanian Africa) Initiations Documentations Techniques, Vol. 2. (Initiations Documentations Techniques Ser.: No. 45).Tr. of Aquatic Flora & Fauna of Sahel-Sudanian Africa. (FRE., Illus.). 484p. 1981. pap. 34.00 (*2-7099-0585-X*, Pub. by LInstitut Francais) Balogh.

Durand, Jacques. Generative & Non-Linear Phonology: Longman Linguistics Library. (Linguistics Library). (Illus.). 400p. (C). 1990. text 49.50 (*0-582-05303-X*, 78491) Longman.

Durand, Jacques, ed. Dependency & Non-Linear Phonology. LC 85-24265. 352p. 1986. 59.95 (*0-7099-0894-6*, Pub. by C Helm) Routldge.

Durand, Jacques, ed. see Katamba, Francis.

Durand, James R. The Life & Adventures of James R. Durand. Brooks, George S., ed. (Illus.). 160p. 1995. pap. 9.95 (*0-939218-08-9*) Chapman Billies.

Durand, Jannic, jt. auth. see Alcouffe, Daniel.

***Durand, Jean-Nicolas-Louis.** Precis of the Lectures on Architecture: With, Graphic Portion of the Lectures on Architecture. LC 99-57591. (Illus.). 352p. 2000. 55.00 (*0-89236-580-3*, Getty Res Inst) J P Getty Trust.

Durand, John. Life & Times of A. B. Durand. 232p. 1993. reprint ed. lib. bdg. 79.00 (*0-7812-5269-5*) Rprt Serv.

Durand, John & Chinard, Gilbert. Un Francais en Virginie: Avec une Introd et des Notes par Gilbert Chinard. 1979. 19.95 (*0-405-10589-4*) Ayer.

Durand, John & Miller, A. T. The Business of Trading in Stocks. LC 67-28631. 1967. reprint ed. pap. 13.00 (*0-87034-019-0*) Fraser Pub Co.

Durand, John, jt. ed. see Stillman, William J.

Durand, John, tr. see Taine, Hippolyte A.

Durand, John D. The Labor Force in Economic Development: A Comparison of International Census Data, 1946-1966. LC 75-2988. 277p. 1975. reprint ed. pap. 85.90 (*0-7837-9332-4*, 206007300004) Bks Demand.

Durand, Jorge & Massey, Douglas S. Miracles on the Border: Retablos of Mexican Migrants to the United States. LC 94-32080. (Illus.). 216p. 1995. pap. 25.95 (*0-8165-1497-6*); lib. bdg. 52.00 (*0-8165-1471-2*) U of Ariz Pr.

Durand, Jose. Garcilaso Inca de la Vega: An American Humanist, a Tribute to Jose Durand. Anadon, Jose, ed. LC 97-21481. 248p. (C). 1998. 45.00 (*0-268-01182-6*) U of Notre Dame Pr.

Durand, Jose & Anadon, Jose. Garcilaso Inca de la Vega: An American Humanist: A Tribute to Jose Durand. LC 97-21481. 245p. 1998. pap. 20.00 (*0-268-01037-4*) U of Notre Dame Pr.

Durand, Kathryn S. Critical Thinking: Developing Skills for Radiography. LC 98-32464. 268p. 1999. pap. 29.99 (*0-8036-0343-6*) Davis Co.

Durand, Larry, ed. see Hubbard, Larry E.

Durand-Lasserve, Alain. Requirements for Establishing Land-Information Systems in Cities in Sub-Saharan Africa. LC 92-27326. (Urban Management Program, Urban Management & Land Ser.: Vol. 8). (FRE.). 114p. 1994. pap. 22.00 (*0-8213-2267-2*, 12267) World Bank.

Durand, Loup. Daddy. 1990. mass mkt. 5.95 (*0-446-35917-3*, Pub. by Warner Bks) Little.

— Daddy. large type ed. (Large Print Books, General Ser.). 571p. 1990. lib. bdg. 21.95 (*0-8161-4862-7*, G K Hall Lrg Type) Mac Lib Ref.

— Jaguar. 448p. 1992. mass mkt. 5.99 (*0-8217-3842-9*, Zebra Kensgtn) Kensgtn Pub Corp.

Durand, Loyal & Pondrom, Lee G., eds. High Energy Physics, 1980: International Conference, Madison Wisconsin, 2 pts. (AIP Conference Proceedings Ser.: No. 68). 1622p. 1981. lib. bdg. 85.00 (*0-88318-167-3*) Am Inst Physics.

***Durand, Marielle.** The Deaf & Silly Bird of Russia. 2000. write for info. (*1-58235-514-2*) Watermrk Pr.

Durand, Mark, jt. auth. see Barlow, David H.

Durand, Mary E. & Durand, Edward D. Bennett Family History: William Bennett & Grace Davis (m. 1789); Their Ancestry & Their Descendants. (Illus.). 220p. 1997. reprint ed. pap. 34.00 (*0-8328-7489-2*); reprint ed. lib. bdg. 44.00 (*0-8328-7488-4*) Higginson Bk Co.

Durand, Maurice & Huan, Nguyen T. An Introduction to Vietnamese Literature. 232p. 1985. text 46.00 (*0-231-05852-7*) Col U Pr.

Durand, Maurice, jt. auth. see Huard, Pierre A.

Durand, Michel. Les Romans Berlinois de Clara Viebig (1860-1952) Vol. 19: Contribution a l'Etude du Naturalisme Tardif en Allemagne. (Etudes & Documents Ser.: Serie 3). (FRE.). 428p. 1993. 55.80 (*3-906750-84-1*) P Lang Pubng.

Durand, Oswald. Rires et Pleurs; Poesies, 2 pts. (B. E. Ser.: No. 3). (FRE.). 1896. 60.00 (*0-8115-2954-1*) Periodicals Srv.

Durand, P. & O'Brien, J. S., eds. Genetic Errors of Glycoprotein Metabolism. (Illus.). 220p. 1983. 68.95 (*0-387-12066-1*) Spr-Verlag.

Durand, Paul C. Where the Waters Gather & the Rivers Meet. (Illus.). 165p. 1994. 14.95 (*0-9641469-0-8*) P C Durand.

Durand, Phillipe. Designer Desserts. (Illus.). 192p. 1996. 55.00 (*0-471-16064-4*) Wiley.

Durand, Robert. The Ages of J. LC 73-76636. (Hip-Pocket Ser.: No. 1). 1973. pap. 2.50 (*0-87922-020-1*) Christophers Bks.

Durand, T. Index Generum Phanerogamorum. 722p. (C). 1979. text 450.00 (*0-89771-601-9*, Pub. by Intl Bk Distr) St Mut.

— Index Generum Phanerogamorum. 722p. 1979. reprint ed. 450.00 (*0-7855-6653-8*, Pub. by Intl Bk Distr) St Mut.

Durand, V. Mark. Abnormal Psychology: An Introduction. 2nd ed. LC 99-42478. (Psychology). 470p. (C). 1999. mass mkt. 84.95 (*0-534-35427-0*) Brooks-Cole.

— Childhood Behavior Disorders. 3rd ed. 144p. (C). 1995. pap. text, per. 37.95 (*0-7872-1313-6*, 41131301) Kendall-Hunt.

— Severe Behavior Problems: A Functional Communication Training Approach. LC 90-44746. (Treatment Manuals for Practitioners Ser.). 183p. 1990. pap. text 21.00 (*0-89862-217-4*) Guilford Pubns.

Durand, V. Mark & Barlow, David H. Abnormal Psychology: An Introduction. (Psychology Ser.). 550p. (C). 1996. mass mkt. 53.25 (*0-534-20364-7*); mass mkt. write for info. (*0-534-34294-9*); mass mkt., student ed. 14.75 (*0-534-34295-7*) Brooks-Cole.

— Abnormal Psychology: An Introduction, Test Bank. 1996. mass mkt. write for info. (*0-534-34296-5*) Brooks-Cole.

Durand, V. Mark & Crimmins, Daniel B. Motivation Assessment Scale: Administration Guide & Set of 25 Forms. unabridged ed. 90p. 1992. spiral bd. 55.00 (*1-882322-29-0*, 2003) Monaco & Assocs.

— The Motivation Assessment Scale (MAS) Administration Guide. 64p. (Orig.). (C). 1992. pap. text 49.00 (*1-882322-00-2*) Monaco & Assocs.

Durand, V. Mark, jt. auth. see Barlow, David H.

Durand, Vincent M. Sleep Better! A Guide to Improving Sleep for Children with Special Needs. LC 97-28102. 1997. 21.95 (*1-55766-315-7*) P H Brookes.

Durand, William F. Adventures in the Navy, in Education, Science, Engineering & the War: A Life Story. LC 53-2031. 228p. reprint ed. pap. 70.70 (*0-8357-5203-8*, 201330600087) Bks Demand.

Durando, Furio. Ancient Greece: The Dawn of the Western World. LC 97-14192. (Illus.). 292p. 1997. 60.00 (*1-55670-601-4*) Stewart Tabori & Chang.

— Splendours of Ancient Greece. LC 98-159811. 292p. 1997. write for info. (*0-500-01824-3*) Thames Hudson.

Durang, Charles. The Fashionable Dancer's Casket. LC 96-28995. (Illus.). 192p. 1996. reprint ed. pap. 9.95 (*1-55709-444-6*) Applewood.

— The Theatrical Rambles of Mr. & Mrs. John Greene. Slout, William L., ed. LC 84-11165. (Clipper Studies in the Theater: No. 1). 142p. 1987. pap. 19.00 (*0-89370-460-1*) Millefleurs.

Durang, Christopher. Baby with the Bathwater. 1984. pap. 5.25 (*0-8222-0084-8*) Dramatists Play.

Durang, Christopher. Betty's Summer Vacation. Date not set. pap. 5.95 (*0-8222-1766-X*) Dramatists Play.

— Betty's Summer Vacation. LC 99-51709. 112p. 2000. pap. 13.00 (*0-8021-3661-3*, Pub. by Grove-Atltic) Publishers Group.

— Beyond Therapy. LC 83-131370. 1983. pap. text 5.50 (*0-573-60574-2*) French.

Durang, Christopher. Christopher Durang Vol. 1: 27 Short Plays. LC 96-222339. (Contemporary Playwrights Ser.). 432p. 1995. pap. 19.95 (*1-880399-89-X*) Smith & Kraus.

— Christopher Durang Vol. I: 27 Short Plays. LC 96-222339. (Contemporary American Playwrights Ser.: Vol. 1). 432p. 1995. 35.00 (*1-57525-023-3*) Smith & Kraus.

— Christopher Durang Vol. II: Complete Full-Length Plays, Vol. II. LC 96-51133. (Contemporary American Playwrights Ser.). 432p. (Orig.). 1997. 35.00 (*1-57525-017-9*) Smith & Kraus.

— Christopher Durang Explains It All for You. LC 90-36867. 304p. 1990. pap. 12.95 (*0-8021-3232-4*, Grove) Grove-Atltic.

— Durang, Durang: And Other Short Plays. 1996. pap. 5.25 (*0-8222-1460-1*) Dramatists Play.

— Laughing Wild. rev. ed. LC 96-158360. 1996. pap. 5.25 (*0-8222-1528-4*) Dramatists Play.

Durang, Christopher. Laughing Wild & Baby with the Bathwater. LC 88-13938. 176p. 1989. pap. 10.00 (*0-8021-3130-1*, Grove) Grove-Atltic.

— The Marriage of Bette & Boo. 1986. pap. 5.25 (*0-8222-0736-2*) Dramatists Play.

Durang, Christopher. The Marriage of Bette & Boo. LC 86-33468. 112p. 1987. pap. 13.00 (*0-8021-3365-7*, Grove) Grove-Atltic.

— Naomi in the Living Room & Other Short Plays . . . 1998. pap. 9.75 (*0-8222-1448-2*) Dramatists Play.

— Sister Mary Ignatius Explains It All for You & The Actor's Nightmare. rev. ed. 1996. pap. 5.25 (*0-8222-1576-4*) Dramatists Play.

— Three Short Plays by Christopher Durang. 1979. pap. 5.25 (*0-8222-0341-3*) Dramatists Play.

— Titanic. 1983. pap. 5.25 (*0-8222-1155-6*) Dramatists Play.

— The Vietnamization of New Jersey (An American Tragedy) 1978. pap. 5.25 (*0-8222-1208-0*) Dramatists Play.

Durang, Christopher & Innaurato, Albert. The Idiots Karamazov. 1980. pap. 5.25 (*0-8222-0553-X*) Dramatists Play.

Duranske, Benjamin, ed. see Petty, Carolyn A.

Durant, Alan. Conditions of Music. LC 84-16408. 256p. (C). 1985. pap. text 21.95 (*0-88706-017-X*) State U NY Pr.

***Durant, Alan.** Leggs United: The Phantom Footballer. large type ed. (Illus.). (J). 1999. pap. write for info. (*0-7540-6084-5*, Galaxy Child Lrg Print) Chivers N Amer.

Durant, Alan. Mouse Party. LC 94-38904. (J). 1996. 11.19 (*0-606-09637-X*, Pub. by Turtleback) Demco.

— Vampire & Werewolf Stories. LC 98-33660. (Story Library). (Illus.). (J). (gr. 4-9). Date not set. 7.95 (*0-7534-5162-X*, Kingfisher) LKC.

— Vampire & Werewolf Stories. LC 98-33660. (Story Library Ser.). 224p. (J). (gr. 4-10). 1998. pap. 7.95 (*0-7534-5152-2*) LKC.

Durant, Alan & Fabb, Nigel. Literary Studies in Action. LC 89-10465. 256p. (C). 1990. pap. 24.99 (*0-415-02945-7*, A3649) Routledge.

Durant, Alan, jt. auth. see Fabb, Nigel.

Durant, Ariel, jt. auth. see Durant, Will.

Durant, Charles. Exposition: A New Theory of Animal Magnetism. LC 79-75313. (Hypnosis & Altered States of Consciousness Ser.). 225p. 1982. reprint ed. lib. bdg. 27.50 (*0-306-76075-4*) Da Capo.

Durant, Charlotte T. Miss Mary McLeod Bethune: The Life of a Beautiful African American Woman. Pye, Ethel, ed. (Illus.). 40p. (Orig.). (J). (ps-1). 1992. pap. 4.00 (*0-913678-21-X*) New Day Pr.

Durant, Charlotte T., ed. see Adrine-Robinson, Kenyette.

Durant, Charlotte T., ed. see Ceasor, Ebraska D.

Durant, Clarence W. Roman Afternoon, 2019 A. D., 3 vols., Vol. 1. 116p. 1984. pap. 7.95 (*0-915153-03-3*) Gold Star Pr.

***Durant, David N.** Bess of Hardwick: Portrait of an Elizabethan Dynast. 274p. (C). 1999. pap. 28.95 (*0-7206-1078-8*, Pub. by P Owen Ltd) Dufour.

Durant, David N. The Handbook of British Architectural Styles. (Illus.). 208p. 1992. pap. 19.95 (*0-7126-4862-3*, Pub. by Barrie & Jenkins) Trafalgar.

— Where Queen Elizabeth Slept & What the Butler Saw: A Treasury of Historical Terms from the Sixteenth Century to the Present. 352p. 1998. pap. 14.95 (*0-312-19569-9*) St Martin.

Durant, David S. Ann Radcliffe's Novels: Experiments in Setting. Varma, Devendra P., ed. LC 79-8450. (Gothic Studies & Dissertations). 1980. lib. bdg. 26.95 (*0-405-12665-4*) Ayer.

Durant, Freddie O. The Donaldson Mansion. LC 80-53470. 415p. 1984. 13.95 (*0-86632-000-8*); pap. 3.95 (*0-317-05215-2*) Shane Pub.

Durant, Frederick C., III, ed. Between Sputnik & the Shuttle: New Perspectives on American Astronautics, 1957-1980. (American Astronautical Society History Ser.: Vol. 3). (Illus.). 350p. 1981. pap. text 30.00 (*0-87703-149-5*) Univelt Inc.

Durant, Frederick C., ed. Between Sputnik & the Shuttle: New Perspectives on American Astronautics, 1957-1980. (AAS History Ser.: Vol. 3). (Illus.). 350p. 1981. 40.00 (*0-87703-145-2*, Am Astronaut Soc) Univelt Inc.

Durant, Frederick C. & James, George S., eds. First Steps Towards Space. (AAS History Ser.: Vol. 6). 318p. 1986. 45.00 (*0-87703-243-2*, Am Astronaut Soc); pap. 35.00 (*0-87703-244-0*, Am Astronaut Soc) Univelt Inc.

Durant, Helen, jt. auth. see Durant, Kenneth.

Durant, Isadore. Death among the Fossils: Who Killed the Notorious Anthropologist in Africa? LC 98-40790. 266p. 1999. 21.95 (*0-8263-1950-5*) U of NM Pr.

Durant, Jane. Colors of Supervision. 80p. (Orig.). 1995. pap. text, per. 11.95 (*0-7872-0581-8*) Kendall-Hunt.

Durant, John, frwd. The Way Science Works: An Illustrated Exploration of Technology in Action. (Illus.). 288p. 1995. 35.00 (*0-02-860822-4*) Macmillan Info.

Durant, John & Miller, Jonathan, eds. Laughing Matters, a Serious Look at Humour. LC 89-135282. (Illus.). 144p. reprint ed. pap. 44.70 (*0-7837-1594-3*, 204188600024) Bks Demand.

Durant, Judith & Campbell, Jean. The Beader's Companion. LC 98-3277. (Illus.). 1998. spiral bd. 19.95 (*1-883010-56-X*) Interweave.

Durant, Judith, ed. see Chou, Hsaio Chin.

Durant, Judith, ed. see Lees, Laura & Mason, Kris.

Durant, Kenneth & Durant, Helen. The Adirondack Guide-Boat. LC 80-80778. (Illus.). xvii, 250p. 1980. pap. 19.95 (*0-87742-125-0*) Adirondack Mus.

Durant, Lucius, jt. auth. see Watkins, Kathleen P.

Durant, Lucius, jt. auth. see Watkins, Kathy.

Durant, Mark Alice, jt. text see Stainback, Charles Ashley.

Durant, Mary. In Pursuit of the Mouse. 256p. 1999. pap. 9.95 (*0-452-27262-9*, Plume) Dutton Plume.

Durant, Mary & Harwood, Michael. This Curious Country Badlands National Park. limited ed. (Illus.). 64p. 1988. pap. 7.95 (*0-912410-08-6*) Badlands Natl Hist.

Durant, Mary, jt. auth. see Crowder, Carol.

Durant, Penny R. Bubblemania. LC 93-38274. 96p. (J). (gr. 3 up). 1994. pap. 3.99 (*0-380-77373-2*, Avon Bks) Morrow Avon.

— Exploring the World of Animals. (Try This! Ser.). 48p. (J). (gr. 3-5). 1995. lib. bdg. 20.80 (*0-531-20128-7*) Watts.

— Exploring the World of Plants. (Try This! Ser.). (Illus.). 48p. (J). (gr. 3-5). 1995. lib. bdg. 20.80 (*0-531-20126-0*) Watts.

— Prize-Winning Science Fair Projects. 144p. (J). (gr. 3-7). 1992. pap. 2.95 (*0-590-44019-5*) Scholastic Inc.

Durant, Penny Raife. When Heroes Die. LC 91-48267. (J). 1995. mass mkt. 3.95 (*0-689-71835-7*) Aladdin.

— When Heroes Die. LC 91-48267. 144p. (YA). (gr. 5 up). 1992. 15.00 (*0-689-31764-6*) Atheneum Yung Read.

Durant, Penny Raife. When Heroes Die. 1995. 9.05 (*0-606-08373-1*, Pub. by Turtleback) Demco.

Durant, Robert F. The Administrative Presidency Revisited: Public Lands, the BLM, & the Reagan Revolution. LC 91-14098. (SUNY Series on the Presidency). 401p. (C). 1992. text 21.50 (*0-7914-0959-7*) State U NY Pr.

— When Government Regulates Itself: EPA, TVA, & Pollution Control in the 1970s. LC 84-22058. 210p. 1985. pap. 65.10 (*0-608-05194-2*, 206573100001) Bks Demand.

Durant, Samuel W. History of Ingham & Eaton Counties: With Illustrations & Biographical Sketches of Their Prominent Men & Pioneers. (Illus.). 586p. 1997. reprint ed. lib. bdg. 59.50 (*0-8328-6761-6*) Higginson Bk Co.

Durant, Samuel W., intro. History of Kalamazoo County, Michigan. (Illus.). 552p. 1993. reprint ed. lib. bdg. 57.00 (*0-8328-3221-9*) Higginson Bk Co.

Durant, Samuel W. & Pierce, Henry B. History of Saint Lawrence County, N. Y., 1749-1878, with Illustrations & Biographical Sketches of Prominent Men & Pioneers. (Illus.). 521p. 1995. reprint ed. lib. bdg. 53.00 (*0-8328-4476-4*) Higginson Bk Co.

Durant, Stephen C., jt. auth. see Lundberg, Steven W.

Durant, Stuart. C. F. A. Voysey. (Architectural Monographs). (Illus.). 128p. 1992. pap. 38.00 (*0-312-05205-7*) St Martin.

Durant, Stuart & Low, Angus. Palais des Machines: Paris 1889 Charles-Louis-Ferdinand Dutert. LC 95-150965. (Architecture in Detail Ser.). (Illus.). 60p. (C). 1994. pap. 29.95 (*0-7148-2930-7*, Pub. by Phaidon Press) Phaidon Pr.

Durant, Sybrina, jt. auth. see Johnson, Sandi.

Durant, Sylvia. A Better Man, Vol. 2. 35p. (Orig.). 1996. pap. 6.00 (*0-9641133-7-6*) Pocket Perks.

— A Better Woman. 35p. (Orig.). 1993. pap. 6.00 (*0-9641133-1-7*) Pocket Perks.

Durant, Thomas J., Jr. & Knottnerus, J. David, eds. Plantation Society & Race Relations: The Origins of Inequality. LC 98-35372. 280p. 1999. 59.95 (*0-275-95808-6*, Praeger Pubs) Greenwood.

Durant, Will. The Age of Faith. (Story of Civilization Ser.: Vol. 4). (Illus.). 1198p. 1993. 17.98 (*1-56731-015-X*, MJF Bks) Fine Comms.

— Anatole France: The Man & His Work. 1992. lib. bdg. 259.95 (*0-8490-5569-5*) Gordon Pr.

— Caesar & Christ. (Story of Civilization Ser.: Vol. 3). (Illus.). 752p. 1993. 17.98 (*1-56731-014-1*, MJF Bks) Fine Comms.

— The Life of Greece. (Story of Civilization Ser.: Vol. 2). (Illus.). 758p. 1993. 17.98 (*1-56731-013-3*, MJF Bks) Fine Comms.

— Our Oriental Heritage. (Story of Civilization Ser.). (Illus.). 1052p. 1993. 17.98 (*1-56731-012-5*, MJF Bks) Fine Comms.

— The Reformation. (Story of Civilization Ser.: Vol. 6). (Illus.). 1030p. 1993. 17.98 (*1-56731-017-6*, MJF Bks) Fine Comms.

— The Renaissance. (Story of Civilization Ser.: Vol. 5). (Illus.). 778p. 1993. 17.98 (*1-56731-016-8*, MJF Bks) Fine Comms.

— Story of Philosophy. 543p. 1991. per. 6.99 (*0-671-73916-6*) PB.

— The Story of Philosophy: The Lives & Opinions of the Great Philosophers. 432p. 1967. pap. 15.00 (*0-671-20159-X*) S&S Trade.

Durant, Will & Durant, Ariel. Age of Faith. (Story of Civilization Ser.: Vol. 4). (Illus.). 1200p. 1980. 35.00 (*0-671-01200-2*) S&S Trade.

— The Age of Louis the Fourteenth. (Story of Civilization Ser.: Vol. 8). (Illus.). 816p. 1980. 35.00 (*0-671-01215-0*) S&S Trade.

— The Age of Louis XIV. (Story of Civilization Ser.: Vol. 8). (Illus.). 806p. 1993. 17.98 (*1-56731-019-2*, MJF Bks) Fine Comms.

— The Age of Napoleon. (Story of Civilization Ser.: Vol. 11). (Illus.). 874p. 1993. 17.98 (*1-56731-022-2*, MJF Bks) Fine Comms.

— The Age of Napoleon. LC 75-6888. (Story of Civilization Ser.: Vol. 11). (Illus.). 880p. 1980. 35.00 (*0-671-21988-X*) S&S Trade.

— The Age of Reason Begins. (Story of Civilization Ser.: Vol. 7). (Illus.). 736p. 1993. 17.98 (*1-56731-018-4*, MJF Bks) Fine Comms.

— The Age of Reason Begins. (Story of Civilization Ser.: Vol. 7). (Illus.). 736p. 1980. 35.00 (*0-671-01320-3*) S&S Trade.

— The Age of Voltaire. (Story of Civilization Ser.: Vol. 9). (Illus.). 896p. 1993. 17.98 (*1-56731-020-6*, MJF Bks) Fine Comms.

— The Age of Voltaire. (Story of Civilization Ser.: Vol. 9). (Illus.). 1980. 35.00 (*0-671-01325-4*) S&S Trade.

— Caesar & Christ: A History of Roman Civilization from Its Beginnings to A.D. 337. (Story of Civilization Ser.: Vol. 3). (Illus.). 752p. 1980. 40.00 (*0-671-11500-6*) S&S Trade.

— The Lessons of History. 118p. 1993. 7.98 (*1-56731-024-9*, MJF Bks) Fine Comms.

— The Lessons of History. LC 68-19949. 128p. 1968. 22.00 (*0-671-41333-3*) S&S Trade.

— The Life of Greece. (Story of Civilization Ser.: Vol. 2). (Illus.). 768p. 1980. 40.00 (*0-671-41800-9*) S&S Trade.

— The Reformation. (Story of Civilization Ser.: Vol. 6). (Illus.). 1040p. 1980. 40.00 (*0-671-61050-3*) S&S Trade.

— The Renaissance. (Story of Civilization Ser.: Vol. 5). (Illus.). 784p. 1980. 35.00 (*0-671-61600-5*) S&S Trade.

— Rousseau & Revolution. (Story of Civilization Ser.: Vol. 10). (Illus.). 1098p. 1993. 17.98 (*1-56731-021-4*, MJF Bks) Fine Comms.

— Rousseau & Revolution. (Story of Civilization Ser.: Vol. 10). (Illus.). 1140p. 1967. 35.00 (*0-671-63058-X*) S&S Trade.

— The Story of Civilization: Complete Set, 11 vols., Set, Vols. 1-11. 1993. 175.00 (*1-56731-023-0*, MJF Bks) Fine Comms.

Durante, Daniel C. Sade Ou l'Ombre des Lumieres. (Eighteenth-Century French Intellectual History Ser.: Vol. 7). (FRE., Illus.). 129p. (C). 1998. text 41.95 (*0-8204-3785-9*) P Lang Pubng.

Durante, F., et al. Recueil des Cours de l'Academie de Droit International de la Haye: Collected Courses of the Hague Academy of International Law, Vol. 152 (1976-iv) 478p. 1980. lib. bdg. 129.00 (*90-286-0590-8*) Kluwer Academic.

Durante, Georgia. The Company She Keeps. LC 98-36737. (Illus.). 456p. 1998. 24.95 (*1-58029-105-8*, Celebrity Bks) Hambleton-Hill.

***Durante, Robert.** The Dialectic of Self & Story: Reading & Story Telling in Contemporary American Fiction. (Literary Criticism & Cultural Theory Ser.). 250p. 2000. 60.00 (*0-8153-3759-0*) Garland.

Durante, Sheila R., jt. auth. see Rord, Elinor R.

Duranteau, Andre. Diccionario de Medicina. (SPA.). 396p. 1987. 39.95 (*0-7859-5809-6*) Fr & Eur.

— Elementary Dictionary of Medicine: Dictionnaire Elementaire de Medicine. (FRE.). 576p. 1981. 59.95 (*0-8288-1803-7*, M15411) Fr & Eur.

Durantel, J. St. Thomas et le Pseudo-Denis. (Medieval Studies). (FRE.). reprint ed. lib. bdg. 48.00 (*0-697-00036-2*) Irvington.

Duranti, Alessandro. From Grammar to Politics: Linguistic Anthropology in a Western Samoan Village. LC 93-18095. 1994. 55.00 (*0-520-08245-1*, Pub. by U CA Pr); pap. 17.95 (*0-520-08385-7*, Pub. by U CA Pr) Cal Prin Full Svc.

— Linguistic Anthropology. LC 96-44608. (Textbooks in Linguistics). (Illus.). 420p. (C). 1997. text 64.95 (*0-521-44536-1*); pap. text 24.95 (*0-521-44993-6*) Cambridge U Pr.

Duranti, Alessandro & Goodwin, Charles, eds. Rethinking Context: Language As an Interactive Phenomenon. (Studies in the Social & Cultural Foundations of Language: No. 11). 371p. (C). 1992. pap. text 30.95 (*0-521-42288-4*) Cambridge U Pr.

***Duranti, Francesca.** Left-Handed Dreams. LC 00-22737. 2000. 20.00 (*1-883285-19-4*) Delphinium.

***Duranti, Francesca & Sartarelli, Stephen.** The House on Moon Lake: A Novel. LC 00-35888. 2000. 13.95 (*1-883285-20-8*) Delphinium.

***Duranti, Luciana.** Diplomatics: New Uses for an Old Science. 198p. 1998. 45.00 (*0-8108-3528-2*) Scarecrow.

Durantini, Mary F. The Child in Seventeenth-Century Dutch Painting. LC 81-21852. (Studies in the Fine Arts: Iconography: No. 7). (Illus.). 406p. reprint ed. pap. 125.90 (*0-8357-1292-3*, 207048100096) Bks Demand.

Durantis, Gulielmus. The Symbolism of Churches & Church Ornaments. 1980. lib. bdg. 64.95 (*0-8490-3166-4*) Gordon Pr.

— Symbolism of Churches & Church Ornaments: A Translation of the First Book of the Rationale Divinorum Officiorum. Neale, John M. & Webb, Benjamin, eds. reprint ed. 28.00 (*0-404-04653-3*) AMS Pr.

Duranty, Walter. Curious Lottery & Other Tales of Russian Justice. LC 78-101805. (Short Story Index Reprint Ser.). 1977. 19.95 (*0-8369-3193-9*) Ayer.

Durao, D. F., et al, eds. Combusting Flow Diagnostics: Proceedings of the NATO Advanced Study Institute Montechoro, Algarve, Portugal, April 16-27, 1990. 576p. 1991. text 272.50 (*0-7923-1521-9*) Kluwer Academic.

— Instrumentation for Combustion & Flow in Engines. (C). 1988. text 218.00 (*0-7923-0034-3*) Kluwer Academic.

Durao, D. F., ed. see Adrian, Richard H., et al.

Duras, Claire De, see De Duras, Claire.

Duras, Madame De, see De Duras, Madame.

Duras, Marguerite. Agatha & Savannah Bay: 2 Plays. Limoli, Howard, tr. from FRE. 160p. (Orig.). 1992. pap. 14.00 (*0-942996-16-X*) Post Apollo Pr.

— Amant de la Chine du Nord. (Folio Ser.: No. 2509). (FRE.). 237p. 1991. pap. 23.95 (*2-07-038809-3*) Schoenhof.

— L' Amante Anglaise. (Imaginaire Ser.). (FRE.). 1967. 13.95 (*2-07-070750-4*) Schoenhof.

— L' Amour. (Folio Ser.: No. 2918). (FRE.). 8.95 (*2-07-038553-1*) Schoenhof.

Duras, Marguerite. L' Apres-Midi de Monsieur Andesmas. (Imaginaire Ser.). (FRE.). pap. 10.95 (*2-07-028664-9*) Schoenhof.

Duras, Marguerite. Barrage Contre le Pacifique. (Folio Ser.: No. 882). (FRE.). 1950. pap. 9.95 (*2-07-036882-3*) Schoenhof.

— Un Barrage Contre le Pacifique. (FRE.). 1977. pap. 11.95 (*0-8288-3635-3*, M5666) Fr & Eur.

— Des Journees Entieres Dans les Arbres. (Gallimard Ser.). (FRE.). 238p. 1954. 25.95 (*2-07-022096-6*) Schoenhof.

— Destroy, She Said. Bray, Barbara, tr. from FRE. LC 86-45522. 144p. 1970. pap. 7.95 (*0-8021-5154-X*, Grove) Grove-Atltic.

— Detruire, Dit-Elle. (FRE.). 1969. pap. 14.95 (*0-7859-0042-X*, F99780) Fr & Eur.

— Dix Heures et Demie de Soir en Ete. (FRE.). 1985. pap. 10.95 (*0-8288-3636-1*, F99790) Fr & Eur.

— Dix Heures et Demie du Soir en Ete. (Folio Ser.: No. 1699). (FRE.). pap. 6.95 (*2-07-037699-0*) Schoenhof.

— Duras: Plays One. (Oberon Bks.). 240p. 1998. pap. 18.95 (*1-870259-78-5*, Pub. by Theatre Comm) Consort Bk Sales.

— L' Eden Cinema. (FRE.). 153p. 1989. pap. 10.95 (*0-7859-2118-4*, 2070381390) Fr & Eur.

— L' Eden Cinema. (Folio Ser.: No. 2051). (FRE.). pap. 8.95 (*2-07-038139-0*) Schoenhof.

— Four Novels: The Square; Moderato Cantabile; 10:30 on a Summer Night; The Afternoon of Mr. Andesmas. Seaver, Richard et al, trs. from FRE. LC 90-46533. 272p. 1965. reprint ed. pap. 12.00 (*0-8021-5111-6*, Grove) Grove-Atltic.

— Four Plays. (Oberon Bks.). 184p. 1997. pap. 16.95 (*1-870259-28-9*) Theatre Comm.

— Hiroshima Mon Amour. (FRE.). 1972. pap. 10.95 (*0-8288-3637-X*, F99801) Fr & Eur.

— Hiroshima Mon Amour. Seaver, Richard, tr. from FRE. LC 61-8011. (Illus.). 112p. 1987. pap. 10.00 (*0-8021-3104-2*, Grove) Grove-Atltic.

— Hiroshima Mon Amour. (Folio Ser.: No. 9). (FRE.). 1960. pap. 6.95 (*2-07-036009-1*) Schoenhof.

— Impudents. (Folio Ser.: No. 2325). (FRE.). 1992. pap. 9.95 (*2-07-038490-X*) Schoenhof.

— India Song. Bray, Barbara, tr. from FRE. LC 75-16763. 146p. 1989. pap. 8.95 (*0-8021-3135-2*, Grove) Grove-Atltic.

— India Song. (Imaginaire Ser.). (FRE.). 152p. 1973. 12.95 (*2-07-072386-0*) Schoenhof.

— The Lover. LC 99-166709. 1998. pap. 10.00 (*0-375-70052-8*) Random.

— The Malady of Death. Bray, Barbara, tr. from FRE. LC 83-49427.Tr. of La/Maladie de la Mort. 64p. 1988. pap. 7.95 (*0-8021-3036-4*, Grove) Grove-Atltic.

— The Man Sitting in the Corridor. Bray, Barbara, tr. 48p. 1991. pap. 5.95 (*1-56201-006-9*) FoxRock.

— Le Marin de Gibraltar. (FRE.). 1977. pap. 13.95 (*0-8288-3638-8*, F99870) Fr & Eur.

Duras, Marguerite. Le Marin de Gibraltar. (Folio Ser.: No. 943). (FRE.). 429p. 1977. 10.95 (*2-07-036943-9*) Schoenhof.

Duras, Marguerite. Moderato Cantabile. 1958. pap. 8.95 (*0-685-11399-X*) Fr & Eur.

— Moderato Cantabile. (FRE.). 112p. 1980. pap. write for info. (*0-7859-4725-6*) Fr & Eur.

— Moderato Cantabile. (FRE.). (C). pap. 13.95 (*0-8442-1975-4*, VF1975-4) NTC Contemp Pub Co.

— Nathalie Granger. (FRE.). 200p. 1973. 27.95 (*0-8288-9600-3*, 207028915X) Fr & Eur.

— Le Navire Night. (FRE.). 1989. pap. 10.95 (*0-8288-3639-6*) Fr & Eur.

— Le Navire Night. (Folio Ser.: No. 2009). (FRE.). 1989. pap. 6.95 (*2-07-038097-1*) Schoenhof.

— No More. Howard, Richard, tr. from FRE. & afterword by. by. LC 97-46209. Orig. Title: C'Est Tout. 128p. 1998. pap. 17.00 (*1-888363-65-7*) Seven Stories.

— The North China Lover. Hafrey, Leigh, tr. LC 92-53729. 240p. 1992. 19.95 (*1-56584-018-6*, Pub. by New Press NY) Norton.

— The North China Lover. LC 92-53729. 240p. 1993. pap. 10.00 (*1-56584-043-7*, Pub. by New Press NY) Norton.

— Les Petits Chevaux de Tarquinia. (FRE.). 1973. pap. 10.95 (*0-7859-2195-8*, 207036187X) Fr & Eur.

— Les Petits Chevaux de Tarquinia. (Folio Ser.: No. 187). (FRE.). pap. 8.95 (*2-07-036187-X*) Schoenhof.

— Practicalities. LC 89-77419. (Illus.). 143p. 1992. pap. 9.95 (*0-8021-3311-8*, Grove) Grove-Atltic.

— The Ravishing of Lol Stein. Seaver, Richard, tr. 1986. pap. 11.00 (*0-394-74304-0*) Pantheon.

— Ravissement de Lol V. Stein. (Folio Ser.: No. 810). (FRE.). 190p. 1976. pap. 6.95 (*2-07-036810-6*) Schoenhof.

— Le Ravissement de Lol V. Stein. (FRE.). 1976. pap. 10.95 (*0-8288-3641-8*, F99841) Fr & Eur.

— The Sailor from Gibraltar. 1986. pap. text 11.95 (*0-7145-0511-0*) Riverrun NY.

— Le Square. (FRE.). 1990. pap. 10.95 (*0-8288-3642-6*, F42630) Fr & Eur.

— Square. Begue, Claude M., ed. 1965. pap. text. write for info. (*0-685-16005-X*) Macmillan.

— Square. (Folio Ser.: No. 2158). (FRE.). 1990. pap. 6.95 (*2-07-038224-9*) Schoenhof.

An Asterisk (*) at the beginning of an entry indicates that the title is appearing for the first time.

— Summer Rain: A Novel. Bray, Barbara, tr. from FRE.Tr. of La/Pluie d'Ete. 160p. 1993. reprint ed. pap. 9.00 (*0-02-073040-3*) Macmillan.
— Theatre Vol. 1: Avec: Les Eaux et Forets, le Square, la Musica. (Gallimard Ser.). (FRE.). 176p. 1956. 26.95 (*2-07-022103-2*) Schoenhof.
— Theatre, Vol. 2: Suzanne Andler, des Journees Entieres Dans les Arbres, Yes Peut-Etre?, le Shape, Etc. (Gallimard Ser.). (FRE.). 298p. 1968. pap. 29.95 (*2-07-026964-7*) Schoenhof.
— Theatre, Vol. 2: Suzanne Andler, des Journees Entieres Dans les Arbres, Yes Peut-Etre?, le Shape, Etc., 3. (Gallimard Ser.). (FRE.). 298p. 1968. 25.95 (*2-07-070175-1*) Schoenhof.
— Les Viaducs de la Seine et Oise. (Coll. Le Manteau d'Arlequin). pap. 8.95 (*0-685-34112-7*) Fr & Eur.
— Le Vice-Consul. (Imaginaire Ser.). (FRE.). 216p. 1965. 11.95 (*2-07-029844-2*) Schoenhof.
— La Vie Tranquille. (FRE.). 1982. pap. 10.95 (*0-8288-3643-4*, M11315) Fr & Eur.
— La Vie Tranquille. (Folio Ser.: No. 1341). (FRE.). 222p. 1944. 8.95 (*2-07-037341-X*) Schoenhof.
— The War: A Memoir. 1987. pap. 6.95 (*0-07-545159-X*) McGraw.
— The War: A Memoir. Bray, Barbara, tr. from FRE. 192p. 1994. pap. 10.00 (*1-56584-221-9*, Pub. by New Press NY) Norton.
— Writing. Polizzotti, Mark, tr. from FRE. LC 98-21440.Tr. of Ecrire. 78p. (Orig.). 1998. pap. 15.95 (*1-57129-053-2*, Lumen Eds) Brookline Bks.

Duras, Marguerite & Gauthier, Xaviere. Les Parleuses, Vol. 44. (FRE.). 25p. 1974. 31.95 (*0-8288-9922-3*, F33220) Fr & Eur.
Duras, Marguerite & Porte, Michelle. Les Lieux de Marguerite Duras. (FRE., Illus.). 117p. 1977. 19.95 (*0-8288-9921-5*, F33080) Fr & Eur.
Duras, Marguerite, et al. Marguerite Duras: Etude sur l'Oeuvre Litteraire, Theatrale et Cinematographique de Marguerite Duras. (Illus.). 200p. 1976. 14.95 (*0-8288-9601-1*) Fr & Eur.
Duras, Marquerite. Hiroshima Mon Amour Level B. text 8.95 (*0-88436-998-6*) EMC-Paradigm.
Durasov, Gennady. Beloved Sufferer: The Life & Mystical Revelations of a Russian Eldress, Schemanun Macaria. (Modern Matericon Ser.). (Illus.). 278p. 1995. pap. 10.00 (*0-938635-87-5*) St Herman Pr.
Durastanti, Sylvie. Venice & the Veneto. LC 97-31397. (Illus.). 180p. 1998. 45.00 (*0-7892-0166-6*) Abbeville Pr.
Durate, Alex. Miracle Food of the East: The Story of the Wakame Spore. 95p. 1995. pap. text 8.00 (*1-891036-02-5*) Nutri Tapes.
Duray, Chery, jt. auth. see Schoyer, Linda.
***Durbach, Andrea.** Upington. (Illus.). 288p. 2000. pap. 16.95 (*1-86508-063-2*, Pub. by Allen & Unwin Pty) IPG Chicago.
Durbach, Errol. A Doll's House: Ibsen's Myth of Transformation. (Twayne's Masterwork Studies: No. 75). 168p. (C). 1991. 23.95 (*0-8057-9403-4*, Twyne) Mac Lib Ref.
***Durback, Christina Bigatel.** FAQs about Confirmation: What You Want to Know. (Illus.). 16p. (YA). (gr. 7-12). 2000. write for info. (*0-937997-80-3*) Hi-Time Pflaum.
Durback, Robert, ed. Seeds of Hope: A Henri Nouwen Reader. rev. ed. 320p. 1997. pap. 11.95 (*0-385-49049-6*, Image Bks) Doubleday.
Durbal, Bryan & Bubenheimer, Glen. Collectors Guide to Vintage Televisions Identification. LC 99-214300. 198p. 1999. pap. text 15.95 (*1-57432-126-9*) Collector Bks.
D'Urban, Benjamin. The Peninsular Journal, 1808-17. 376p. 1989. 37.50 (*0-947898-87-5*, 5574) Stackpole.
Durban, Manuel & Safir, Margery. Earth Tones: The Poetry of Pablo Neruda. LC 80-8095. 250p. 1981. reprint ed. pap. 77.50 (*0-7837-3697-5*, 205787500009) Bks Demand.
Durban, Pam. All Set about with Fever Trees, & Other Stories. LC 95-13562. 1995. pap. 12.95 (*0-8203-1775-6*) U of Ga Pr.
— The Laughing Place: A Novel. Grossman, Barbara, ed. 352p. 1993. 21.00 (*0-684-19258-6*, Scribners Ref) Mac Lib Ref.
— The Laughing Place: A Novel. 352p. 1995. pap. 13.00 (*0-312-13110-0*) St Martin.
***Durban, Pam.** So Far Back. 256p. 2000. 23.00 (*0-312-26869-6*, Picador USA) St Martin.
Durband, Alan. Playbill 1. 152p. (C). 1989. pap. 11.95 (*0-7487-0180-X*) Dufour.
Durband, Alan, ed. see Shakespeare, William.
***Durband, D. & Pearson, J. R. A., eds.** Non-Linear Singularities in Deformation & Flow: Proceedings: IUTAM Symposium on Non-Linear Singularities in Deformation & Flow (1997: Haifa, Israel) LC 98-54487. 360p. 1999. 170.00 (*0-7923-5349-8*) Kluwer Academic.
Durbano, Linda. Two-Hour Painted Wood Projects. LC 95-23016. (Illus.). 144p. 1996. 24.95 (*0-8069-1399-1*) Sterling.
Durber, Susan. Silence in Heaven: A Book of Women's Preaching. 1994. pap. 16.00 (*0-334-01543-X*) TPI PA.
Durbin. Getting Money to Do Good: An Overview of Federal Funding Opportunities for Local YMCAs. 2nd ed. 76p. 1997. spiral bd. write for info. (*0-88011-814-8*, Y5341, YMCA USA) Human Kinetics.
Durbin, jt. auth. see Bixler.
Durbin, Margaret. And Featuring Bailey Wellcom as the Biscuit. (Illus.). 150p. (YA). 1999. pap. 11.00 (*1-886383-88-X*, Little Blue) Pride & Imprints.
Durbin, Alan C., jt. auth. see Bixler, C. Temple.
Durbin, Andrew J. Organizational Behavior: An Applied Perspective. LC 96-42472. (GI - Organizational Behavior Ser.). 1996. pap. 49.95 (*0-538-85776-5*) S-W Pub.

Durbin Carson, Betty J. & Durbin Wooley, Doris M. Our Ewing Heritage, 2 vols., Set. (Illus.). 944p. (Orig.). 1995. pap. text 60.50 (*0-7884-0236-6*) Heritage Bk.
Durbin, Charles, ed. Cardinal Is Her Color: One Hundred Fifty Years of Achievement at William Jewell College. LC 98-75075. (Illus.). 188p. 1999. 29.95 (*0-9671241-0-7*) W Jewell Coll.
Durbin, David & Borba, Philip S., eds. Workers' Compensation Insurance: Claim Costs, Prices, & Regulation. LC 92-22576. (C). 1992. lib. bdg. 110.00 (*0-7923-9170-5*) Huebner Foun Insur.
Durbin, Evan F. The Politics of Democratic Socialism: An Essay on Social Policy. LC 71-83799. 384p. 1969. reprint ed. 45.00 (*0-678-06513-6*) Kelley.
— Problems of Economic Planning: Papers on Planning & Economics. LC 68-29483. (Reprints of Economic Classics Ser.). x, 214p. 1968. reprint ed. 35.00 (*0-678-06514-4*) Kelley.
***Durbin, Frederic S.** Dragonfly. LC 99-27612. 1999. 22.95 (*0-87054-175-7*) Arkham.
Durbin, Gail. Developing Museum Exhibitions for Lifelong Learning: Problems & Prospects. 200p. 1996. pap. 50.00 (*0-11-290552-8*, Pub. by Statnry Office) Balogh.
Durbin, J. Distribution Theory for Tests Based on the Sample Distribution Function. (CBMS-NSF Regional Conference Series in Applied Mathematics: No. 9). vi, 64p. 1973. reprint ed. pap. text 19.00 (*0-89871-007-3*) Soc Indus-Appl Math.
Durbin, John R. College Algebra. 3rd ed. (C). 1993. pap. text 29.50 (*0-07-018351-1*) McGraw.
— College Algebra & Trigonometry. 2nd ed. LC 87-28039. 608p. 1988. text 84.95 (*0-471-62545-0*) Wiley.
— Modern Algebra: An Introduction. 3rd ed. LC 91-21511. 368p. (C). 1991. text 89.95 (*0-471-51001-7*) Wiley.
— Modern Algebra: An Introduction. 4th ed. LC 99-13830. 328p. 1999. text 92.95 (*0-471-32147-8*) Wiley.
— Trigonometry. LC 86-28193. 416p. 1987. text 84.95 (*0-471-03366-9*) Wiley.
Durbin, Kathie. Tongass: Pulp Politics & the Fight for the Alaska Rainforest. LC 99-40408. (Illus.). 336p. 1999. pap. 19.95 (*0-87071-466-X*) Oreg St U Pr.
— Tree Huggers: Victory, Defeat & Renewal in the Northwest Ancient Forest Campaign. 304p. 1998. pap. 14.95 (*0-89886-569-7*) Mountaineers.
Durbin, L. D., ed. see Symposium on Instrumentation for the Process Indus.
Durbin, Mary E., et al. The Empowerment Process: Centering Social Ministry in the Life of the Local Christian Community. LC 93-47222. 144p. (Orig.). 1994. pap. 12.95 (*0-8091-3478-0*) Paulist Pr.
Durbin, Mike & Herbst, Dan. From Gutterballs to Strikes. LC 97-24595. (Illus.). 176p. 1997. pap. 14.95 (*0-8092-3058-5*, 305850, Contemporary Bks) NTC Contemp Pub Co.
Durbin, Paul. Kissing Frogs: The Practical Use of Hypnotherapy. 270p. 1996. pap. text, per. 19.95 (*0-7872-1934-7*) Kendall-Hunt.
— Kissing Frogs: The Practical Use of Hypnotherapy. 2nd ed. LC 99-180746. 288p. 1998. per. 19.95 (*0-7872-4986-6*) Kendall-Hunt.
Durbin, Paul T. Dictionary of Concepts in the Philosophy of Science. LC 87-32293. (Reference Sources for the Social Sciences & Humanities Ser.: No. 6). 376p. 1988. lib. bdg. 59.95 (*0-318-32545-4*, DDI/, Greenwood Pr) Greenwood.
— Philosophy of Technology. 2nd ed. 216p. (C). 1989. lib. bdg. 160.00 (*0-7923-0139-0*, Pub. by Kluwer Academic) Kluwer Academic.
— Research in Philosophy & Technology, Vol. 7. Mitcham, Carl et al, eds. 304p. 1984. 78.50 (*0-89232-505-4*) Jai Pr.
— Social Responsibility in Science, Technology, & Medicine. LC 92-72013. 232p. (C). 1993. 31.50 (*0-934223-27-0*) Lehigh Univ Pr.
Durbin, Paul T., ed. Broad & Narrow Interpretations of Philosophy of Technology. 212p. (C). 1990. lib. bdg. 129.50 (*0-7923-0684-8*, Pub. by Kluwer Academic) Kluwer Academic.
— Critical Perspectives on Nonacademic Science & Engineering. LC 89-64066. (Research in Technology Studies: Vol. 4). 304p. 1991. 45.00 (*0-934223-15-7*) Lehigh Univ Pr.
— Europe, America, & Technology: Philosophical Perspectives. (Philosophy & Technology Ser.: No. 8). 272p. 1991. lib. bdg. 160.50 (*0-7923-1254-6*, Pub. by Kluwer Academic) Kluwer Academic.
— Technology & Contemporary Life. 328p. (C). 1987. pap. text 67.50 (*90-277-2571-3*, D Reidel); lib. bdg. 139.00 (*90-277-2570-5*, D Reidel) Kluwer Academic.
— Technology & Responsibility. (Philosophy & Technology Ser.: No. 3). 404p. (C). 1987. lib. bdg. 139.00 (*90-277-2415-6*, D Reidel) Kluwer Academic.
— Technology & Responsibility. (Philosophy & Technology Ser.: No. 3). 404p. 1989. pap. text 66.50 (*90-277-2416-4*) Kluwer Academic.
Durbin, Paul T. & Rapp, Friedrich, eds. Philosophy & Technology. 357p. 1983. text 214.50 (*90-277-1576-9*, D Reidel) Kluwer Academic.
Durbin, R., et al. Biological Sequence Analysis: Probabilistic Models of Proteins & Nucleic Acids. (Illus.). 368p. (C). 1998. pap. text 34.95 (*0-521-62971-3*) Cambridge U Pr.
Durbin, Richard D. The Wisconsin River: An Odyssey Through Time & Space. (Illus.). 270p. (C). 1997. 27.50 (*0-9658559-0-2*) Spring Freshet.
Durbin, Trish. Collected Classics of Soaring. (Illus.). 275p. 1988. text 20.00 (*0-9620668-0-X*) AZ Soaring Assn.
***Durbin, William.** American Haiku of the Soke. 1998. pap. write for info. (*1-57553-760-5*) Watermrk Pr.
Durbin, William. Arnold Palmer. LC 97-43915. (Golf Legends Ser.). (Illus.). 64p. (YA). (gr. 3 up). 1999. 7.95 (*0-7910-4562-5*) Chelsea Hse.

— The Broken Blade. LC 96-22114. 176p. (YA). (gr. 5 up). 1997. 14.95 (*0-385-32224-0*, Delacorte Pr Bks) BDD Bks Young Read.
— The Broken Blade. (J). 1998. 9.60 (*0-606-13228-7*, Pub. by Turtleback) Demco.
— The Broken Blade. (Illus.). 176p. (YA). (gr. 5-9). 1998. reprint ed. pap. 4.50 (*0-440-41184-X*, YB BDD) BDD Bks Young Read.
***Durbin, William.** The Journal of Otto Peltonen: A Finnish Immigrant. LC 00-21919. (My Name Is America Ser.). (Illus.). 208p. (YA). (gr. 4-7). 2000. 10.95 (*0-439-09254-X*) Scholastic Inc.
Durbin, William. The Journal of Sean Sullivan: A Transcontinental Railroad Worker, Nebraska & Points West, 1867. LC 98-47705. (My Name Is America Ser.). (Illus.). 188p. (J). (gr. 4-8). 1999. 10.95 (*0-439-04994-6*, Pub. by Scholastic Inc) Penguin Putnam.
***Durbin, William.** Mastering Kempo. (Illus.). 192p. 2000. pap. 19.95 (*0-7360-0350-9*) Human Kinetics.
Durbin, William. Tiger Woods: Golf Star. LC 97-43783. (Golf Legends Ser.). (Illus.). 64p. (YA). (gr. 3 up). 1999. 7.95 (*0-7910-4563-3*) Chelsea Hse.
— Tiger Woods: Golf Star. LC 97-40746. (Black Americans of Achievement Ser.). (Illus.). 144p. (YA). (gr. 5 up). 1999. 19.95 (*0-7910-4651-6*); pap. 8.95 (*0-7910-4687-7*) Chelsea Hse.
Durbin, William. Wintering. LC 98-25546. 208p. (YA). (gr. 5 up). 1999. 14.95 (*0-385-32598-3*) BDD Bks Young Read.
***Durbin, William.** Wintering. (Illus.). 208p. (J). 2000. pap. 4.50 (*0-440-22759-3*, Yearling) BDD Bks Young Read.
Durbin Wooley, Doris M., jt. auth. see Durbin Carson, Betty J.
Durborow, Louis L. Annual Report Card State of California & Counties: 1997 Edition. (Illus.). v, 140p. (Orig.). 1996. pap. 39.95 (*1-889718-07-6*) Strat Planners.
— Annual Report Card State of Illinois & 102 Counties. 144p. 1996. pap. 39.95 (*1-889718-01-7*) Strat Planners.
— Annual Report Card State of Indiana & Counties: 1997 Edition. (Illus.). v, 140p. (Orig.). 1996. pap. 39.95 (*1-889718-04-1*) Strat Planners.
— Annual Report Card State of Michigan & Counties: 1997 Edition. (Illus.). v, 140p. (Orig.). 1996. pap. 39.95 (*1-889718-02-5*) Strat Planners.
— Annual Report Card State of New York & Counties: 1997 Edition. (Illus.). v, 131p. (Orig.). 1996. pap. 39.95 (*1-889718-05-X*) Strat Planners.
— Annual Report Card State of Ohio & 88 Counties. 124p. (Orig.). 1996. pap. 39.95 (*1-889718-00-9*) Strat Planners.
— Annual Report Card State of Pennsylvania & Counties: 1997 Edition. (Illus.). v, 131p. (Orig.). 1996. pap. 39.95 (*1-889718-06-8*) Strat Planners.
— Annual Report Card State of Wisconsin & Counties: 1997 Edition. (Illus.). v, 130p. (Orig.). 1996. pap. 39.95 (*1-889718-03-3*) Strat Planners.
Durbridge, Francis. Dead to the World. large type ed. 1978. 27.99 (*0-7089-0120-4*) Ulverscroft.
Durbridge, Francis. The Other Man. 21.95 (*0-7540-8542-2*, Black Dagger) Chivers N Amer.
Durbridge, Francis. The Other Man. large type ed. 1977. 12.00 (*0-85456-547-7*) Ulverscroft.
— A Time of Day. 190p. 1998. 19.50 (*0-7540-8522-8*, Black Dagger) Chivers N Amer.
Durby, Katrina A. Enjoy a Simpler Life: The Secret to Happiness. 200p. 1998. pap. 13.95 (*0-9670223-9-8*) Westwood.
Durcan, Jim, jt. auth. see Kirkbride, Paul S.
Durcan, Paul. The Berlin Wall Cafe. 70p. 1985. pap. 10.95 (*0-85640-348-2*, Pub. by Blackstaff Pr) Dufour.
— Going Home to Russia: Poems. LC 87-18576. 102p. 1987. pap. 11.95 (*0-85640-386-5*, Pub. by Blackstaff Pr) Dufour.
— Greetings to Our Friends in Brazil: 100 Poems. 1999. 23.00 (*1-86046-607-9*) HarpCollins.
— Jesus & Angela: Poems. LC 88-7430. 98p. 1989. pap. 12.95 (*0-85640-407-1*, Pub. by Blackstaff Pr) Dufour.
***Durcan, Paul.** Poetry Quartets 4: Irish Poets. 2000. 26.95 incl. audio (*1-85224-498-4*, Pub. by Bloodaxe Bks) Dufour.
Durcan, Philomena. A Celtic Garden. LC 94-96813. (Illus.). 80p. 1998. 19.95 (*0-9631982-2-X*) Celtic Design.
— Celtic Spirals. Feinler, Elizabeth, ed. LC 91-78387. (Illus.). 1998. 17.95 (*0-9631982-1-1*) Celtic Design.
Durch, Jane S., ed. see Institute of Medicine, Committee on Pediatric Emer.
Durch, Jane S., ed. see Institute of Medicine, Committee on Using Performa.
Durch, William J. ABM Treaty & Western Security. LC 87-26978. 128p. 1987. text 22.50 (*0-88730-264-5*, HarpBusn) HarpInfo.
***Durch, William J.** Constructing Regional Security: The Role of Arms Transfers, Arms Control & Reassurance. LC 00-41726. 2000. write for info. (*0-312-23645-X*) St Martin.
Durch, William J. The United Nations Peacekeeper of American Policies & Uncivilizations. LC 96-34880. 416p. 1996. text 49.95 (*0-312-12930-0*) St Martin.
Durch, William J., ed. The Evolution of U. N. Peacekeeping: Case Studies & Comparative Analysis. 544p. 1993. pap. 19.95 (*0-312-10401-4*) St Martin.
— National Interests & the Military Use of Space. 286p. 1984. text 34.95 (*0-88410-974-7*, HarpBusn) HarpInfo.
— U. N. Peacekeeping, American Policy, & the Uncivil Wars of the 1990s. 416p. (Orig.). 1996. pap. 19.95 (*0-312-16075-5*) St Martin.
Durcharme, Stanley H. & Gill, Kathleen M. Sexuality after Spinal Cord Injury: Answers to Your Questions. 192p. 1996. pap. 24.95 (*1-55766-265-7*, 2657) P H Brookes.
Durchholtz, Eric. The Promise of Eden: A Novel. 208p. 1999. pap. 14.95 (*0-9670297-0-8*, 10018) Concrete Bks.

Durchholz, Daniel, jt. auth. see Graff, Gary.
Durchholz, Patricia. Defining Mission: Comboni Missionaries in North America. LC 99-30961. (Illus.). 384p. 1999. 33.00 (*0-7618-1427-2*) U Pr of Amer.
Durchholz, Reiner & Richter, Gernot. Compositional Data Objects: The IMC/IMCL Reference Manual. fac. ed. LC 92-25262. (Wiley Professional Computing Ser.). (Illus.). 199p. reprint ed. pap. 61.70 (*0-608-00987-3*, 206184300012) Bks Demand.
Durchschlag, H., jt. ed. see Jaenicke, R.
Durckheim, Karlfried G. The Japanese Cult of Tranquility. rev. ed. LC 91-29005. 128p. 1974. pap. 9.95 (*0-87728-738-4*) Weiser.
— Way of Transformation. 1990. pap. 10.95 (*0-04-292020-5*) Routledge.
— The Way of Transformation: Daily Life As Spiritual Exercise. 1988. pap. 10.95 (*0-685-44222-5*) Routledge.
Durczak, Jerzy. Selves Between Cultures: Contemporary American Bicultural Autobiography. LC 98-20403. 225p. 1998. 74.95 (*1-57309-319-X*); pap. 54.95 (*1-57309-318-1*) Intl Scholars.
Durdem, Kent. Gifts of an Eagle. 6th ed. LC 72-83075. (Illus.). 160p. (YA). 1980. reprint ed. pap. 12.50 (*0-9653321-0-1*) K D Prods.
Durden, Angela K. Nine Stupid Things People Do to Mess up Their Resume: And 16 Ways to Avoid the Traps. 80p. Date not set. pap. 11.95 (*0-9701356-0-2*) Writer Hire.
Durden, Charles. The Fifth Law of Hawkins. 1991. mass mkt. 4.99 (*0-8125-0952-8*) Tor Bks.
Durden, Chris. Learn about Texas Insects. Zappler, Georg, ed. (Illus.). 60p. (J). (gr. 1-6). 1999. pap. 7.95 (*1-885696-27-2*, Pub. by TX Prks & Wldlife) U of Tex Pr.
Durden, Lance A., jt. auth. see Barnard, Susan M.
Durden, Leslie, ed. see Belknap, Bryan.
Durden, Leslie, ed. see Bundschuh, Rick.
Durden, Leslie, ed. see Burgen, Jim.
Durden, Leslie, ed. see St. Clair, Barry.
Durden, Leslie, ed. see Warden, Michael.
Durden, Robert F. Carter G. Woodson: Father of African-American History. LC 97-30243. (African-American Biographies Ser.). (Illus.). 128p. (YA). (gr. 6 up). 1998. lib. bdg. 20.95 (*0-89490-946-0*) Enslow Pubs.
— The Dukes of Durham, 1865-1929. LC 74-83785. (Illus.). xiv, 295p. 1987. reprint ed. pap. text 19.95 (*0-8223-0743-X*) Duke.
— The Gray & the Black: The Confederate Debate on Emancipation. LC 72-79330. 317p. 1972. pap. 90.40 (*0-7837-8453-8*, 2049258) Bks Demand.
***Durden, Robert F.** The Gray & the Black: The Confederate Debate on Emancipation. 328p. 2000. pap. 19.95 (*0-8071-2557-1*) La State U Pr.
Durden, Robert F. James Shepherd Pike: Republicanism & the American Negro, 1850-1882. LC 57-6284. 263p. reprint ed. pap. 81.60 (*0-608-13864-9*, 202376000033) Bks Demand.
— Lasting Legacy to the Carolinas: The Duke Endowment, 1924-1994. LC 97-31427. 1998. 55.95 (*0-8223-2151-3*) Duke.
— The Launching of Duke University, 1924-1949. LC 92-27499. (Illus.). 588p. 1993. text 32.95 (*0-8223-1302-2*) Duke.
— Reconstruction Bonds & Twentieth-Century Politics: South Dakota Versus North Carolina, 1904. LC 62-10051. 290p. reprint ed. 89.90 (*0-8357-9116-5*, 201790100010) Bks Demand.
— The Self-Inflicted Wound: Southern Politics in the Nineteenth Century. LC 84-29173. (New Perspectives on the South Ser.). 160p. 1985. 20.00 (*0-8131-0307-X*) U Pr of Ky.
Durden, Theresa, ed. see Barclay, Alistair & Halpin, Claire.
Durden, William G. & Tangherlini, Arne E. Smart Kids: How Academic Talents Are Developed & Nurtured in America. LC 92-40190. 346p. 1994. text 27.50 (*0-88937-112-1*) Hogrefe & Huber Pubs.
Durdin, Tillman, et al. New York Times Report from Red China. 1976. pap. 1.95 (*0-380-01363-0*, Avon Bks) Morrow Avon.
Durdy, James D. Car Smart: Used Vehicle Evaluation Guide. (Illus.). 36p. (Orig.). 1992. pap. 4.95 (*1-887430-04-0*) Global Inc.
Durdy, James D., jt. auth. see Global Inc. Staff.
Durdy, Katrina A. Enjoy a Simpler Life: An A-Z Guide for Downscaling to the Essentials. unabridged ed. 112p. 1998. pap. 9.95 (*1-887430-28-8*) Global Inc.
— Let's Get Organized: Protect Your Loved Ones with an Organized Account of Affairs. unabridged ed. 1998. pap. 9.95 (*1-887430-48-2*) Global Inc.
Dure, Leon, jt. ed. see Schilperoort, Robert A.
Dureau, Christian. Dictionnaire Mondial des Chanteurs. (FRE.). 1989. 59.95 (*0-7859-8149-7*, 2-86594-048-9) Fr & Eur.
Durell, Ann. The Diane Goode Book of American Folk Tales & Songs. (Illus.). 64p. (J). (ps up). 1996. pap. 6.99 (*0-14-055953-1*, PuffinBks) Peng Put Young Read.
Durell, J. C. V. The Historic Church: An Essay on the Conception of the Christian Church & Its Ministry in the Sub-Apostolic Age. 328p. 1997. pap. 25.00 (*1-57910-075-9*) Wipf & Stock.
Durell, J. L., ed. see International Nuclear Physics Conference Staff.
Durelle, Yvon & Fraser, Raymond. The Fighting Fisherman. 282p. 1981. mass mkt. 5.95 (*0-88780-114-5*, Pub. by Formac Publ Co) Formac Dist Ltd.
Duren, Donald. Our Enemy Destroyed. LC 90-93244. 196p. 1990. per. write for info. (*0-8187-0124-2*) Harlo Press.
Duren, Lista & McDonald, Wil. Build Your Own Home Darkroom. rev. ed. (Illus.). 160p. (C). 1990. reprint ed. pap. 17.95 (*0-936262-04-4*) Amherst Media.

D

An Asterisk (*) at the beginning of an entry indicates that the title is appearing for the first time.

Duren, P., et al. A Century of Mathematics in America, Pt. II. LC 88-22155. (HMATH Ser.: Vol. 2). 585p. 1989. text 87.00 (*0-8218-0130-9*, HMATH/2C) Am Math.

Duren, Peter, et al. The Bieberbach Conjecture: Proceedings of the Symposium on the Occasion of the Proof. LC 86-10843. (SURV Ser.: Vol. 21). 218p. 1986. reprint ed. pap. 58.00 (*0-8218-1521-0*, SURV/21) Am Math.

***Duren, Peter L.** Theory of HP Spaces. 2000. pap. 8.95 (*0-486-41184-2*) Dover.

Duren, Peter L. Univalent Functions. (Grundlehren der Mathematischen Wissenschaften Ser.: Vol. 259). (Illus.). 382p. 1983. 99.95 (*0-387-90795-5*) Spr-Verlag.

Duren, Peter L., ed. A Century of Mathematics in America, Pt. I. LC 88-22155. (History of Mathematics Ser.: Vol. 1). 477p. 1988. reprint ed. text 75.00 (*0-8218-0124-4*, HMATH/1C) Am Math.

Duren, Peter L., et al, eds. A Century of Mathematics in America, Pt. III. LC 88-22155. (History of Mathematics Ser.: Vol. 3). 675p. 1989. text 93.00 (*0-8218-0136-8*, HMATH/3C) Am Math.

Duren, Peter L., jt. auth. see Gehring, Frederick W.

Duren, Peter L., jt. ed. see Zdravkovska, Smilka.

Duren, Stephen E., jt. auth. see Ramey, David W.

Duren, William L. Dusen - Gayden Family Record. (Illus.). 74p. 1997. reprint ed. pap. 14.50 (*0-8328-8392-1*); reprint ed. lib. bdg. 24.50 (*0-8328-8391-3*) Higginson Bk Co.

Durenne, A. Ornamental Ironwork. LC 98-167579. (Illus.). 128p. 1998. pap. 10.95 (*0-486-29811-6*) Dover.

Durepos, Joseph, ed. see Teresa, Madre.

Durer, Albrecht. Complete Engravings, Etchings, & Dry Points of Albrecht Durer. Strauss, Walter L., ed. (Illus.). 235p. (Orig.). 1972. pap. 13.95 (*0-486-22851-7*) Dover.

— Complete Woodcuts of Albrecht Durer. Kurth, Willi, ed. (Illus.). 285p. 1963. pap. 12.95 (*0-486-21097-9*) Dover.

— A Course in the Art of Measurement with Compass & Ruler: Underweysung der Messung, 1525. (Printed Sources of Western Art Ser.). (GER., Illus.). 180p. 1981. reprint ed. boxed set 65.00 (*0-915346-52-4*) A Wofsy Fine Arts.

— Drawings. Appelbaum, Stanley & Woelfflin, H., eds. (Illus.). 176p. 1970. reprint ed. pap. 10.95 (*0-486-22352-3*) Dover.

— Drawings of Durer. Longstreet, Stephen, ed. (Master Draughtsman Ser.). (Illus.). 1964. pap. 4.95 (*0-87505-160-X*) Borden.

— Durer's Record of Journeys to Venice & the Low Countries. enl. unabridged ed. (Illus.). 160p. 1995. pap. 7.95 (*0-486-28348-8*) Dover.

— Human Figure: Dresden Sketchbook. Strauss, Walter L., ed. & tr. by. 335p. 1972. reprint ed. pap. 18.95 (*0-486-21042-1*) Dover.

— Of the Just Shaping of Letters: From the Applied Geometry of Albrecht Durer, Book 3. Nichol, R. T., tr. (Illus.). 43p. 1965. pap. 5.95 (*0-486-21306-4*) Dover.

Durer, C. S., ed. see Witkiewicz, Stanislaw I.

Durer, Ulbrecht. Etchings of Albrecht Durer. 81p. 1984. reprint ed. pap. text 25.00 (*0-87556-376-7*) Saifer.

Dures, Alan. How & Why: The English Civil War. (C). 1990. 95.00 (*0-7855-7553-7*) St Mut.

D

Duret, Elsa, jt. auth. see Ngo, Brian.

Duret, Pierre, ed. New Generation of Two-Stroke Engines for the Future (A)? Proceedings of the International Seminar Held in Rueil-Malmaison, France, November 29-30, 1993. 224p. (C). 1993. pap. 395.00 (*2-7108-0654-1*, Pub. by Edits Technip) Enfield Pubs NH.

Duret, Theodore. Manet & the French Impressionists. Crawford Flitch, J. E., tr. (Select Bibliographies Reprint Ser.). 1977. reprint ed. 26.95 (*0-8369-6687-2*) Ayer.

Durette, Jackie, jt. auth. see Soderberg, K. A.

Durey, David D. & Cotton, Ray. Steps Toward Ministry Vol. 2: One-to-One Mentoring for Effective Ministry. LC 98-208866. 109p. 1997. pap. 9.00 (*0-9656237-2-6*) Fnd of Hope.

Durey, David D. & Goldberg, Chuck. Steps Toward Balancing Life's Demands Vol. 3: One-to-One Mentoring for Effective Living. 2nd rev. ed. LC 98-209908. Orig. Title: Mentoring for Leadership Development. (Illus.). 100p. 1997. pap. 9.00 (*0-9656237-1-8*) Fnd of Hope.

Durey, Michael. Transatlantic Radicals & the Early American Republic. LC 96-49216. 540p. 1997. 45.00 (*0-7006-0823-0*) U Pr of KS.

— With the Hammer of Truth: James Thomson Callender & America's Early National Heroes. 225p. 1990. text 35.00 (*0-8139-1278-4*) U Pr of Va.

Durey, Michael, ed. Andrew Bryson's Ordeal: An Epilogue to the 1798 Rebellion. LC 98-189073. (Irish Narrative Ser.). 128p. 1998. pap. 12.95 (*1-85918-144-9*, Pub. by Cork Univ) Stylus Pub VA.

D'Urfe, Jim P. Sailing Beyond the Sea. LC 96-70985. 228p. (Orig.). 1996. pap. 8.95 (*1-882972-86-4*) Queenship Pub.

Durfee, Edmund & Tokoro, Mario, eds. Proceedings of the Second International Conference on Multiagent Systems. (Illus.). 476p. (Orig.). 1996. pap. text 59.95 (*1-57735-013-8*) AAAI Pr.

Durfee, Edmund H. Coordination of Distributed Problem Solvers. (C). 1988. text 113.00 (*0-89838-284-X*) Kluwer Academic.

Durfee, Elizabeth D., intro. Faces in the Parlor: Eighteenth & Nineteenth Century Portraits from Vermont Collections, Exhibition catalog. (Illus.). 40p. 1989. pap. 7.00 (*0-934658-05-6*) R H Flem Mus.

Durfee, Harold A. Foundational Reflections: Studies in Contemporary Philosophy. 304p. 1987. lib. bdg., student ed. 155.50 (*90-247-3504-1*, Pub. by M Nijhoff) Kluwer Academic.

Durfee, Harold A. & Rodier, David F., eds. Phenomenology & Beyond: The Self & Its Language. 182p. (C). 1989. lib. bdg. 138.50 (*0-7923-0511-6*, Pub. by Kluwer Academic) Kluwer Academic.

Durfee, Mary. A Vision for Lake Superior. (Pew Case Studies in International Affairs). 50p. (C). 1995. pap. text 3.50 (*1-56927-164-X*, GU Schl Foreign) Geo U Inst Dplmcy.

Durfee, Mary, jt. auth. see Rosenau, James N.

D'Urfey, Thomas. Butler's Ghost. LC 84-13916. 224p. 1985. reprint ed. 50.00 (*0-8201-1399-9*) Schol Facsimiles.

Durfey, Thomas C. & Ferrier, James A. Religious Broadcast Management Handbook. 1987. pap. 15.99 (*0-310-39741-3*, 12258P) Zondervan.

Durfield. Como Hablares de Sexo.Tr. of How to Speak to Your Children about Sex. 1995. pap. 9.99 (*0-88113-122-9*) Caribe Betania.

Durfield, Renee, jt. auth. see Durfield, Richard.

Durfield, Richard & Durfield, Renee. Raising Them Chaste. 192p. (Orig.). 1991. pap. 9.99 (*1-55661-171-4*) Bethany Hse.

***Durgan, Dorrana.** Tooth & Claw. (Star Trek : No. 60). 2001. mass mkt. 6.99 (*0-671-04211-4*, Star Trek) PB.

Durgananda, Swami, intro. Everything Happens for the Best: A Book of Contemplations. 48p. (Orig.). 1993. pap. 4.75 (*0-911307-28-1*) SYDA Found.

— The Light of the Guru: The Celebration of Guru Purnima. 56p. (Orig.). 1994. pap. 4.75 (*0-911307-32-X*) SYDA Found.

Durgananda, Swami, ed. see Muktananda, Swami.

Durgin & Hanan. Pharmacy Assisting for the Technician. 2nd ed. LC 98-54627. (Allied Health Ser.). 464p. (C). 1999. pap. 49.95 (*0-7668-0458-5*) Delmar.

***Durgin & Hanan.** Pharmacy Assisting for the Technician, IML. 2nd ed. 80p. 1999. teacher ed. 17.95 (*0-7668-0464-X*) Delmar.

Durgin, Doranna. Barrenlands. 352p. 2000. per. 5.99 (*0-671-87872-7*) Baen Bks.

— Changespell. 352p. 2000. mass mkt. 5.99 (*0-671-87765-8*) PB.

— Dun Lady's Jess. (Orig.). 1994. per. 4.99 (*0-671-87617-1*) Baen Bks.

***Durgin, Doranna.** Seer's Blood. 352p. 2000. per. 6.99 (*0-671-57877-4*) PB.

Durgin, Doranna. Touched by Magic. 352p. 1996. per. 5.99 (*0-671-87737-2*) Baen Bks.

— Wolf Justice. 400p. 2000. mass mkt. 5.99 (*0-671-87891-3*) Baen Bks.

***Durgin, Doranna.** Wolverine's Daughter. 320p. 2000. per. 6.99 (*0-671-57847-2*) Baen Bks.

Durgin, Jane & Hanan, Zachary. Pharmacy Practice for Technicians: Instructor's Guide. 96p. 1994. 16.00 (*0-8273-5905-5*) Delmar.

Durgin, Jane & Hanan, Zachary, eds. Pharmacy Practice for Technicians. LC 92-48679. 478p. (C). 1993. mass mkt. 33.50 (*0-8273-4660-3*) Delmar.

Durgin, Jean B., jt. auth. see Ross, Beverly B.

Durgin, Max W. FORTRAN 77. (Illus.). 316p. (Orig.). (C). 1982. pap. text 22.50 (*0-935920-04-8*, Ntl Pubs Blck) P-H.

— Subset FORTRAN-77. (Illus.). 320p. (Orig.). 1983. pap. text 24.95 (*0-935920-11-0*, Ntl Pubs Blck) P-H.

Durgin, Patrick F. Pundits Scribes Pupils. 44p. 1998. 7.00 (*0-937013-88-9*, Pub. by Potes Poets) SPD-Small Pr Dist.

Durgin, Philip B. & Young, Thomas M., eds. Leak Detection for Underground Storage Tanks. LC 93-14690. (Special Technical Publication Ser.: No. 1161). (Illus.). 240p. 1993. 39.00 (*0-8031-1858-9*, USTANKS) ASTM.

Durgin, Winslow. Separation Poems. 5.00 (*0-318-11911-0*) Great Raven Pr.

— Traces - Fire. 5.00 (*0-686-15294-8*) Great Raven Pr.

***Durgnat, Raymodn.** WR-Mysteries of the Organism. (BFI Modern Classics Ser.). (Illus.). 96p. 1999. pap. 10.95 (*0-85170-720-3*, Pub. by British Film Inst) Ind U Pr.

Durgo, A. S., ed. Russia Changes: The Events of August 1991 & the Russian Constitution. (Illus.). 162p. 1992. lib. bdg. 125.00 (*1-56072-079-4*) Nova Sci Pubs.

Durgunoglu, Aydin & Verhoeven, Ludo, eds. Literacy Development in a Multilingual Context: Cross-Cultural Perspectives. LC 97-43202. 250p. 1998. write for info. (*0-8058-2442-1*); pap. write for info. (*0-8058-2443-X*) L Erlbaum Assocs.

Durham & Curry. Ohio Real Property, Vol. 2. 5th ed. LC 96-79576. 834p. 1997. text 85.00 (*1-55834-436-5*, 62955-11, MICHIE) LEXIS Pub.

***Durham, Joel.** Fear Effect: Prima's Official Strategy Guide. LC 99-69779. (Illus.). 93p. (YA). 2000. pap. 14.99 (*0-7615-2603-X*, Prima Games) Prima Pub.

Durham, Joel. Outcast. LC 99-62822. (Illus.). 229p. 1999. pap. 19.99 (*0-7615-2209-3*) Prima Pub.

— Wargasm: Official Strategy Guide. LC 98-68703. 1999. pap. 19.99 (*0-7615-2036-8*) Prima Pub.

Durham, Alan L. Patent Law Essentials: A Concise Guide. LC 98-20133. 240p. 1999. 69.50 (*1-56720-242-X*, Quorum Bks) Greenwood.

Durham, Alexis M. Crisis & Reform. LC 93-79051. 377p. 1994. pap. 29.00 (*0-316-19710-6*) Little.

Durham, Anne. The Romantic Doctor Rydon. large type ed. (Linford Romance Library). 272p. 1987. pap. 8.95 (*0-7089-6446-X*, Linford) Ulverscroft.

— The Stubborn Tide. large type ed. 1990. 27.99 (*0-7089-2299-6*) Ulverscroft.

— Tender Bondage. large type ed. 1990. 27.99 (*0-7089-2216-3*) Ulverscroft.

— The Unreachable Star. large type ed. 1990. 27.99 (*0-7089-2170-1*) Ulverscroft.

Durham, Bill. Steamboats & Modern Steam Launches. enl. rev. ed. Spurlock, Pat, ed. (Elliott Bay Classics: Vol. 3). (Illus.). 698p. 1997. 59.95 (*0-9641204-3-7*) Boat Hse.

Durham, Bill, ed. see Mitchell, Richard M.

***Durham, Bobby.** Up in Fairmont & Other Out of Body Experiences. (Illus.). 77p. 1999. 10.95 (*0-7414-0005-7*) Buy Books.

Durham, Carolyn A. The Contexture of Feminism: Marie Cardinal & Multicultural Literacy. 312p. 1991. text 34.95 (*0-252-01811-7*); pap. text 15.95 (*0-252-06184-5*) U of Ill Pr.

— Double Takes: Culture & Gender in French Films & Their American Remakes. LC 98-3920. (Contemporary French Culture & Society Ser.). (Illus.). 260p. 1998. pap. 21.95 (*0-87451-874-1*); text 45.00 (*0-87451-873-3*) U Pr of New Eng.

Durham, Carolyn R., tr. see Alves, Miriam.

Durham, Charles, jt. auth. see Pruitt, Kristin A.

Durham, Charles W. & McColgan, Kristin P., eds. Spokesperson Milton: Voices in Contemporary Criticism. LC 93-47329. 1995. 42.50 (*0-945636-65-2*) Susquehanna U Pr.

***Durham, Charles W. & Pruitt, Kristin A., eds.** All in All. LC 98-28760. (Illus.). 272p. 1999. 45.00 (*1-57591-016-0*) Susquehanna U Pr.

Durham, Charles W., jt. ed. see McColgan, Kristin P.

Durham, D. R., et al. MI92--Technologies, Economics, Information for Global Partnership Realignments: Presented at Manufacturing International '92 March 29-april 1, 1992, Dallas, Texas / LC 92-160696. ix, 499p. 1992. write for info. (*0-7918-0763-0*) ASME.

Durham, D. R., ed. see Metallurgical Society of AIME Staff.

Durham, Daniel. Song to Tame the Storm. 1990. 7.95 (*0-941720-83-7*) Slough Pr TX.

Durham, David & Yavatkar, Raj. Inside the Internet's Resource ReSerVation Protocol: Foundations for Quality Service. LC 99-21790. (Illus.). 384p. 1999. 44.99 (*0-471-32214-8*) Wiley.

***Durham, David A.** Gabriel's Story. LC 00-25291. (Illus.). 2001. 22.95 (*0-385-49814-4*) Doubleday.

Durham, David L. California's Geographic Names: A Gazetteer of Historic & Modern Names of the State. LC 98-2858. 1694p. 1998. 195.00 (*1-884995-14-4*) Word Dancer.

Durham, Deborah L. Atlas of CT Pathology. Biello, Lisa, ed. 192p. 1996. text 42.00 (*0-7216-6415-6*, W B Saunders Co) Harcrt Hlth Sci Grp.

— Atlas of MR Pathology. Durham, Lisa, ed. LC 96-8867. 208p. 1996. text 42.00 (*0-7216-6416-4*, W B Saunders Co) Harcrt Hlth Sci Grp.

Durham, Dick. The Last Sailorman. 168p. 1990. 42.00 (*0-86138-067-3*, Pub. by T Dalton) St Mut.

Durham, Eleanor, jt. ed. see Durham, James.

***Durham, Emma.** Floods. LC 99-56298. (Restless Planet Ser.). (Illus.). 48p. (J). (ps-3). 2000. lib. bdg. 25.69 (*0-7398-1329-3*) Raintree Steck-V.

Durham, Flora. The Lesions. 36p. (Orig.). 1996. pap. 4.00 (*1-882550-17-X*) Quiet Lion Pr.

Durham, Frank. Elmer Rice. (Twayne's United States Authors Ser.). 1970. reprint ed. lib. bdg. 20.95 (*0-8057-0616-X*) Irvington.

Durham, Frank & Purrington, Robert D. The Frame of the Universe. LC 82-12990. (Illus.). 1985. pap. text 21.00 (*0-231-05393-2*) Col U Pr.

— Some Truer Method: Reflections on the Heritage of Newton. 256p. 1990. text 46.50 (*0-231-06896-4*) Col U Pr.

Durham, G. Homer. The Discourses of Wilford Woodruff. deluxe ed. 1990. 11.95 (*0-88494-000-4*) Bookcraft Inc.

***Durham, Gary N. & Marr, W. Allen.** Field Instrumentation for Soil & Rock. LC 99-46576. (STP Ser.: No. 1358). (Illus.). 415p. 1999. text 74.00 (*0-8031-2604-2*) ASTM.

Durham, George. Taming the Nueces Strip: The Story of McNelly's Rangers. (Illus.). 198p. 1962. pap. 10.95 (*0-292-78048-6*) U of Tex Pr.

Durham, Glenda P. International Export Management Group, Inc. Corporate Capabilities. (Illus.). 32p. (Orig.). 1984. pap. text 5.00 (*0-89904-084-5*) Crumb Elbow Pub.

***Durham, Helen & McCormack, Timothy L.** The Changing Face of Conflict & the Efficacy of International Humanitarian Law. LC 99-35401. (International Humanitarian Law Ser.). 1999. 111.00 (*90-411-1180-8*) Kluwer Law Intl.

Durham Historic Association, Committee of Volunteers. Durham, New Hampshire: A History, 1900-1985. LC 85-16313. (Illus.). 400p. 1985. 25.00 (*0-914659-15-4*) Phoenix Pub.

Durham Historical Society Staff. Durham. LC 98-87325. (Images of America Ser.). 1998. write for info. (*0-7524-1337-6*) Arcadia Publng.

Durham, J. C., jt. auth. see Young, C. S.

Durham, J. Frank. Epistles from Pap: Letters from the Man Known As the Will Rogers of Indiana. LC 97-74001. 200p. 1997. 22.95 (*1-57860-010-3*) Guild Pr IN.

Durham, Jack L. Acid Rain: A Student's First Sourcebook. (Illus.). 59p. (Orig.). (C). 1994. pap. text 15.00 (*0-7881-1492-1*) DIANE Pub.

Durham, James. Song of Solomon. (Geneva Commentaries Ser.). 460p. 1982. reprint ed. 23.99 (*0-85151-352-2*) Banner of Truth.

Durham, James & Durham, Eleanor, eds. Soldier of the Cross: The Civil War Diary & Correspondence of Rev. Andrew Jackson Hartsock. (Illus.). 275p. (Orig.). 1979. pap. 41.95 (*0-89126-076-5*) MA-AH Pub.

Durham, James & Thomas, Virginia. The Sacred Buffalo: The Lakota Way for a New Beginning. LC 96-142691. (Illus.). 200p. (Orig.). 1996. pap. 19.95 (*0-87364-868-4*) Paladin Pr.

Durham, James C. To Write, Write: Writing. 240p. (gr. 9-12). 1981. pap. 8.95 (*0-88334-144-1*) Longman.

Durham, James G., jt. auth. see Curry, Robert M.

Durham, James R. Secular Darkness: Religious Right Involvement in Texas Public Education, 1963-1989. LC 94-11507. (American University Studies: Vol. 167). XI, 124p. (C). 1995. text 33.95 (*0-8204-2543-5*) P Lang Pubng.

Durham, Jean, et al, eds. Tar Heels Cooking for Ronald's Kids. (Illus.). 184p. 1988. 13.95 (*0-9620949-0-0*) R McDonald Hse.

Durham, Jennifer L. Benjamin Franklin: A Biographical Companion. LC 97-41976. (Illus.). 322p. 1997. lib. bdg. 55.00 (*0-87436-931-2*, FN-1717) ABC-CLIO.

— Crime in America. LC 96-9077. 318p. 1996. lib. bdg. 45.00 (*0-87436-841-3*) ABC-CLIO.

***Durham, Jennifer L.** World Cultural Leaders of the Twentieth Century, 2 vols. Stansky, Peter, ed. (Illus.). 800p. 2000. 150.00 (*1-57607-038-7*) ABC-CLIO.

Durham, Jerfene N. School Days. 40p. 1999. pap. 8.00 (*0-8059-4516-4*) Dorrance.

Durham, Jerry, jt. ed. see Cohen, Felissa.

Durham, Jerry D. & Lashley, Felissa R., eds. The Person with HIV/AIDS: Nursing Perspectives. 3rd ed. LC 99-16258. (Illus.). 518p. 1999. text 54.95 (*0-8261-1293-5*) Springer Pub.

Durham, Jerry D., jt. ed. see Cohen, Felissa L.

Durham, Jimmie. A Certain Lack of Coherence: Writings on Art & Cultural Politics. 256p. 1993. 19.95 (*0-947753-04-4*, Pub. by Kala Pr) SPD-Small Pr Dist.

— Columbus Day. 104p. (C). 1983. pap. 8.95 (*0-931122-30-9*) West End.

Durham, John. Exodus. (Biblical Commentary Ser.: Vol. 3). 29.99 (*0-8499-0202-9*) Word Pub.

— Football's Match up Zone Coverages. LC 98-43212. (Illus.). 128p. 1999. pap. 15.00 (*1-890450-04-9*) Harding Pr.

Durham, John, ed. Worship Beyond the Usual: An Echo of the Voice of John W. Carlton. 134p. 1993. text 11.95 (*0-86554-413-1*, MUP-H335) Mercer Univ Pr.

Durham, John G. Report on the Affairs of British North America, 3 vols., Set. LC 73-117388. 1970. reprint ed. lib. bdg. 150.00 (*0-678-00647-4*) Kelley.

Durham, John I., ed. see Southeastern Baptist Theological Seminary Staff.

Durham, John W. Football's Modern Zone Blocking. LC 97-32429. (Illus.). 112p. 1997. pap. 14.00 (*1-890450-01-4*) Harding Pr.

— Football's Modular Defense: A Simplified Multiple System. LC 85-21667. 154p. (C). 1986. text 27.95 (*0-13-324179-3*, Parker Publishing Co) P-H.

Durham, Karl. The Dead Revived: A Novel of Suspense. LC 98-89013. 325p. 1998. 25.00 (*0-7388-0175-5*); pap. 15.00 (*0-7388-0176-3*) Xlibris Corp.

Durham, Katherine C., jt. auth. see Rush, Susan D.

Durham, Keith. The Border Reivers. (Men-at-Arms Ser.: No. 275). (Illus.). 279p. 1994. pap. 11.95 (*1-85532-417-2*, 9247, Pub. by Ospry) Stackpole.

Durham, Ken. Santa Anna: Prisoner of War in Texas. Steely, Skipper, ed. (Illus.). 125p. 1986. 17.95 (*0-915263-09-2*); pap. 9.95 (*0-915263-10-6*) Wright Pr.

— Santa Anna: Prisoner of War in Texas. Steely, Skipper, ed. (Illus.). 184p. 1998. reprint ed. pap. 15.95 (*0-915263-02-5*) Wright Pr.

Durham, Kenneth & Kennedy, Bruce. The New High-Tech Manager: Six Rules for Success in Changing Times. LC 97-3746. 201p. 1997. 63.00 (*0-89006-926-3*) Artech Hse.

Durham, Kenneth M., jt. auth. see House, H. Wayne.

Durham, Kenneth R. Faith & Ingenuity: LeTourneau University's First Fifty Years. 1995. write for info. (*0-89865-955-8*) Donning Co.

Durham, Lewis E., ed. see Hilarion.

Durham, Lisa, ed. see Durham, Deborah L.

Durham, Louise. Louise Durman's Recipes upon Request. (Illus.). pap. text 12.00 (*1-881092-00-3*) Knoxville News-Sentinel.

Durham, Lowell M. Abravanel! LC 89-37172. (Illus.). 227p. reprint ed. pap. 70.40 (*0-7837-6868-0*, 204669800003) Bks Demand.

Durham, Lyn. Marie No. 2: Mystery at the Paris Ballet. LC 96-39353. (Girlhood Journeys Ser.: Bk. 2). (J). 1997. 12.95 (*0-689-81205-1*) S&S Childrens.

Durham, Martin. Women & Fascism. LC 98-4916. 208p. (C). 1998. 75.00 (*0-415-12279-1*, D5926); pap. 24.99 (*0-415-12280-5*, D5930) Routledge.

Durham, Mary E. High Albania. LC 70-135803. (Eastern Europe Collection). xii, 352 p. 1971. reprint ed. 43.95 (*0-405-02745-1*) Ayer.

— Some Tribal Origins, Laws & Customs of the Balkans. LC 76-44710. (Illus.). reprint ed. 44.50 (*0-404-15856-0*) AMS Pr.

Durham, Mary L. & La Fond, John Q. Back to the Asylum: The Future of Mental Health Law in the United States. 280p. 1992. text 47.50 (*0-19-505520-9*) OUP.

***Durham, Meenakshi Gigi & Kellner, Douglas, eds.** Media & Cultural Studies. 2000. 79.95 (*0-631-22095-X*); pap. 34.95 (*0-631-22096-8*) Blackwell Pubs.

Durham, Merle. The Lone Star State Divided: Texans & the Civil War. LC 94-1984. (Illus.). 136p. (J). (gr. 4 up). 1994. lib. bdg. 14.95 (*0-937460-97-4*) Hendrick-Long.

Durham, Michael S. Desert Between the Mountains. LC 97-13619. (Illus.). 320p. 1997. 30.00 (*0-8050-4161-3*) H Holt & Co.

***Durham, Michael S.** Desert Between the Mountains: Mormons, Miners, Padres, Mountain Men, & the Opening of the Grea. LC 99-23572. 352p. 1999. pap. text 18.95 (*0-8061-3186-1*) UN.

Durham, Michael S. & Young, Donald. The Desert States. LC 96-40547. (Smithsonian Guide to Historic America Ser.). 446p. 1998. 19.95 (*1-55670-641-3*) Stewart Tabori & Chang.

An Asterisk (*) at the beginning of an entry indicates that the title is appearing for the first time.

Durham, Michael S., et al. The Mid-Atlantic States. LC 96-40540. (Smithsonian Guide to Historic America Ser.). 495p. 1998. pap. 19.95 (*1-55670-634-0*) Stewart Tabori & Chang.

***Durham, Norris M., et al, eds.** The State of Dermatoglyphics: The Science of Finger & Palm Prints. LC 00-33950. (Mellen Studies in Anthropology : Vol. 2). 384p. 2000. 99.95 (*0-7734-7636-9*) E Mellen.

Durham, Norris M. & Plato, Chris C., eds. Trends in Dermatoglyphic Research. (Studies in Human Biology). 328p. 1990. lib. bdg. 135.00 (*0-7923-0963-4*) Kluwer Academic.

Durham, Philip. Down These Mean Streets a Man Must Go: Raymond Chandler's Knight. LC 63-21075. 183p. reprint ed. pap. 56.80 (*0-7837-2077-7*, 204235100004) Bks Demand.

Durham, Philip & Jones, Everett L. The Negro Cowboys. LC 83-6446. (Illus.). x, 278p. 1983. reprint ed. pap. 11.00 (*0-8032-6560-3*, Bison Books) U of Nebr Pr.

***Durham, Robert.** First 1000 Words & Pictures Book. (Illus.). (J). 2000. 9.99 (*1-57866-092-0*) Galahad Bks.

Durham, Robert K. The Atcheson, Topeka, & Santa Fe Railroad: Steam Locomotives & Trains 1935-1956. LC 97-77026. (Steam Ser.). (Illus.). 72p. 1997. pap. text 21.00 (*1-891427-00-8*) Durham Publng.

— Baltimore & Ohio: Steam Locomotives & Trains 1935 to 1938. LC 96-92641. (Steam of the Thirties Ser.). (Illus.). 48p. 1995. pap. 21.00 (*0-9644480-3-3*) Durham Publng.

***Durham, Robert K.** Burlington Railroad Vol. 15: Steam Locomotives & Trains 1941-1952. LC 98-74605. (Illus.). 72p. 1999. pap. 21.00 (*1-891427-04-0*) Durham Publng.

Durham, Robert K. Erie: Steam Locomotives & Trains 1933-37. LC 95-92280. (Steam of the Thirties Ser.). (Illus.). 56p. 1995. pap. 21.00 (*0-9644480-1-7*) Durham Publng.

***Durham, Robert K.** Great Northern & Northern Pacific Railroads Vol. 16: Steam Trains & Locomotives, 1932-1959. LC 99-72747. (Illus.). 74p. 1999. pap. 21.00 (*1-891427-06-7*) Durham Publng.

— Illinois Central Railroad Vol. 17: Steam Trains & Locomotives, 1891-1956. (Illus.). 64p. 2000. pap. 21.00 (*1-891427-05-9*) Durham Publng.

Durham, Robert K. Lackawanna: Steam Locomotives & Trains, 1934-1937. LC 97-91798. (Steam of the Thirties Ser.). (Illus.). 72p. 1997. pap. 21.00 (*0-9644480-8-4*) Durham Publng.

— The Milwaukee Road: Steam Locomotives & Trains 1930-1954. LC 98-73837. (Steam Ser.: Vol. 14). (Illus.). 66p. 1998. pap. 21.00 (*1-891427-02-4*) Durham Publng.

— New Jersey Central: Steam Locomotives & Trains 1934 to 1937. LC 95-96119. (Steam of the Thirties Ser.). (Illus.). 52p. 1996. pap. 21.00 (*0-9644480-4-1*) Durham Publng.

— New York Central: Steam-Locomotives & Trains from 1933 to 1943. 2nd rev. ed. LC 94-69691. (Steam of the Thirties Ser.). (Illus.). 64p. 2000. pap. 21.00 (*0-9644480-0-9*) Durham Publng.

***Durham, Robert K.** Norfolk & Western Railroads; Inc. Virginian, Clinchfield RR's Vol. 18: Steam Trains & Locomotives 1938-1956. (Illus.). 72p. 2000. pap. 21.00 (*1-891427-07-5*) Durham Publng.

Durham, Robert K. Pennsylvania: Steam - Locomotives & Trains from 1931-1938. 2nd rev. ed. LC 95-92377. (Steam of the Thirties Ser.). (Illus.). 80p. 1999. pap. 21.00 (*0-9644480-2-5*) Durham Publng.

— Reading Railroad: Steam Locomotives & Trains 1936-1956. LC 97-68394. (Steam Ser.). (Illus.). 71p. 1997. pap. 21.00 (*0-9644480-9-2*) Durham Publng.

— Seaboard Air Line: Steam Trains & Locomotives 1935 to 1937. LC 96-96170. (Steam of the Thirties Ser.). (Illus.). 52p. 1996. pap. 21.00 (*0-9644480-5-X*) Durham Publng.

— The Southern Pacific Railroad: Steam Locomotives & Trains 1936-1956. LC 98-71415. (Steam Ser.: Vol. 13). (Illus.). 76p. 1998. pap. 21.00 (*1-891427-03-2*) Durham Publng.

— Southern Railway Vol. 7: Steam-Locomotives & Trains 1935 to 1937 Includes N & PBLRR; Norfolk Southern; Atlantic CSTLINE. LC 96-96625. (Illus.). 52p. 1996. pap. 21.00 (*0-9644480-6-8*) Durham Publng.

— Union Pacific Railroad: Steam Locomotives & Trains, 1936-1956. LC 98-72199. (Steam Ser.). (Illus.). 72p. 1998. pap. 21.00 (*1-891427-01-6*) Durham Publng.

***Durham, Roger S., ed.** The Blues in Gray: The Civil War Journal of William Daniel Dixon & the Republican Blues Daybook. LC 00-9343. (Illus.). 496p. (C). 2000. text 46.00 (*1-57233-101-1*, Pub. by U of Tenn Pr) U Ch Pr.

Durham, Ron. Happily Ever After: And Other Myths About Divorce. LC 92-21506. 132p. (Orig.). 1993. pap. 8.99 (*1-56476-069-3*, 6-3069, Victor Bks) Chariot Victor.

— Jacob I Loved: A Novel. Curtiss, Carol, ed. 214p. 1995. 12.99 (*1-886763-03-8*) Higley.

Durham, Ron & DeGraffenried, Doug. The Higley Lesson Commentary 2000-2001, Vol. 68. Reagan, Wesley C., ed. (Illus.). 52p. 13.99 (*1-886763-16-X*, Pub. by Higley) Spring Arbor Dist.

— The Higley Lesson Commentary 2000-2001, Vol. 68. large type ed. Reagan, Wesley C., ed. 52p. 12.99 (*1-886763-18-6*, Pub. by Higley) Spring Arbor Dist.

Durham, Ron, et al. Higley Lesson Commentary, Vol. 66. Reagan, Wesley C., ed. (Illus.). 1998. 15.99 (*1-886763-11-9*); pap. 12.99 (*1-886763-10-0*) Higley.

— Higley Lesson Commentary, Vol. 66. large type ed. Reagan, Wesley C., ed. (Illus.). 1998. pap. 11.99 (*1-886763-12-7*) Higley.

— Higley Lesson Commentary 1997-1998, Vol. 65. Reagan, Wesley C., ed. (Illus.). 528p. 1997. text 15.99 (*1-886763-08-9*); pap. text 12.99 (*1-886763-07-0*) Higley.

— Higley Lesson Commentary 1997-1998, Vol. 65. large type ed. Reagan, Wesley C., ed. (Illus.). 528p. 1997. pap. text 11.99 (*1-886763-09-7*) Higley.

— Higley Sunday School Commentary 1996-97. Reagan, Wesley C., ed. (Illus.). 1997. 14.99 (*1-886763-05-4*); pap. 11.99 (*1-886763-04-6*) Higley.

Durham, Ron, ed. see Barna, George.

Durham, Ron, ed. see Cannistraci, David.

Durham, Scott. Phantom Communities: The Simulacrum & the Limits of Postmodernism. LC 97-43145. 1998. 49.50 (*0-8047-3071-7*); pap. 18.95 (*0-8047-3336-8*) Stanford U Pr.

Durham, Scott. Yale French Studies, 91: Genet In the Language of the Enemy. 1996. pap. 19.00 (*0-300-07175-2*) Yale U Pr.

Durham, Stephen R., ed. ABC of Allergies. 66p. 1998. pap. text 25.50 (*0-7279-1236-4*, Pub. by BMJ Pub) Login Brothers Bk Co.

Durham, Steven R., jt. ed. see Naclerio, Robert M.

Durham, Taylor R., jt. auth. see LaPlante, Josephine M.

Durham, Thomas. Serbia: The Rise & Fall of a Medieval Empire. 152p. (C). 1989. pap. 25.00 (*1-85072-060-6*, Pub. by W Sessions) St Mut.

Durham, Thomas L. Beginning Tonal Dictation. 323p. (C). 1994. pap. text 26.95 (*0-88133-797-8*) Waveland Pr.

— Tonal Harmonic Dictation: A Workbook. (Illus.). 134p. (C). 1987. 28.00 (*0-8191-6283-3*) U Pr of Amer.

Durham, Tony. Computing Horizons. (Illus.). 252p. (C). 1988. pap. text 23.75 (*0-201-18046-4*) Addison-Wesley.

Durham, W. Cole, tr. see Viehweg, Theodor.

Durham, Walter T. Before Tennessee: The Southwest Territory, 1790-1796: A Narrative History of the Territory of the United States South of the River Ohio. (Illus.). 327p. 1990. 24.95 (*0-9627696-0-6*) Rocky Mt Hist Assn.

— Reluctant Partners: Nashville & the Union, July 1, 1863, to June 30, 1865. (Illus.). 320p. 1987. 19.95 (*0-9615966-1-9*) TN His Soc.

— Volunteer Forty-Niners: Tennesseans & the California Gold Rush. LC 97-21090. (Illus.). 352p. 1997. 29.95 (*0-8265-1298-4*) Vanderbilt U Pr.

— Wynnewood: Bledsoe's Lick, Castalian Springs, Tennessee. LC 94-79974. (Illus.). 104p. 1994. 8.95 (*0-9644297-1-3*) Sumner Cnty Hist.

***Durham, Walter T., ed.** Rebellion Revisited: A History of Sumner County, Tennessee from 1861-1870. (Tennessee Heritage Library Bicentennial Collection). 395p. 1999. 19.95 (*1-57736-151-2*, Hillsboro Pr) Providence Hse.

Durham, Walter T. & Thomas, James W. A Pictorial History of Sumner County, Tennessee, 1786-1986. LC 86-62487. (Illus.). 152p. 1986. 24.95 (*0-9644297-0-5*) Sumner Cnty Hist.

Durham, Walter T., et al. A Celebration of Houses Built Before 1900 in Sumner County, Tennessee. (Illus.). 152p. 1995. 45.00 (*0-9644297-2-1*) Sumner Cnty Hist.

Durham, Weldon B., ed. American Theatre Companies, 1888-1930. LC 85-30213. 551p. 1987. lib. bdg. 125.00 (*0-313-25359-5*, DHT/, Greenwood Pr) Greenwood.

— American Theatre Companies, 1931-1986. LC 88-32039. 605p. 1989. lib. bdg. 125.00 (*0-313-25360-9*, DTP/, Quorum Bks) Greenwood.

— American Theatre Companies, 1749-1887. LC 84-27947. 606p. 1986. lib. bdg. 125.00 (*0-313-20886-7*, DAT/, Greenwood Pr) Greenwood.

Durham, William C. Durham: The Name & Family of Durham. (Illus.). 99p. 1997. reprint ed. pap. 18.00 (*0-8328-8386-7*); reprint ed. lib. bdg. 28.00 (*0-8328-8385-9*) Higginson Bk Co.

Durham, William H. Coevolution: Genes, Culture, & Human Diversity. xxiv, 651p. 1991. 75.00 (*0-8047-1537-8*) Stanford U Pr.

— Scarcity & Survival in Central America: Ecological Origins of the Soccer War. LC 78-55318. (Illus.). xx, 209p. 1979. pap. 13.95 (*0-8047-1154-2*) Stanford U Pr.

Durham, William H., ed. Annual Review of Anthropology, Vol. 24. LC 72-82136. 1995. lib. bdg. 47.00 (*0-8243-1924-9*) Annual Reviews.

— Annual Review of Anthropology, Vol. 25. LC 72-82136. 1996. text 49.00 (*0-8243-1925-7*) Annual Reviews.

***Durham, William H., ed.** Annual Review of Anthropology, Vol. 28. LC 72-82160. 652p. 1999. 110.00 (*0-8243-1928-1*) Annual Reviews.

Durham, William H., et al, eds. Annual Review of Anthropology, Vol. 22. LC 72-82136. 1993. text 44.00 (*0-8243-1922-2*) Annual Reviews.

— Annual Review of Anthropology, Vol. 23. LC 72-82136. 1994. text 47.00 (*0-8243-1923-0*) Annual Reviews.

— Annual Review of Anthropology, Vol. 26. LC 72-82136. 1997. text 55.00 (*0-8243-1926-5*) Annual Reviews.

Durham, William H., jt. ed. see Painter, Michael.

Durham, Williar H. Critical Essays of the Eighteenth Century, 1700-1725. (BCL1-PR English Literature Ser.). 445p. 1992. reprint ed. lib. bdg. 99.00 (*0-7812-7000-6*) Rprt Serv.

Durhan, Ron & De Graffenried, Doug. The Higley Lesson Commentary 2000-2001, Vol. 68. Reagan, Wesley C., ed. (Illus.). 52p. 17.99 (*1-886763-17-8*, Pub. by Higley) Spring Arbor Dist.

Durheim, Erma. The Depression of the Dirty Thirties: Howard & Erma's Life. LC 92-30365. 1992. 19.95 (*0-87770-516-X*) Ye Galleon.

Duri, A. A. The Historical Formation of the Arab Nation: A Study in Identity & Consciousness. Conrad, Lawrence I., tr. 400p. 1988. lib. bdg. 95.00 (*0-7099-3471-8*, Pub. by C Helm) Routldge.

Duric, L., jt. auth. see Bratska, M.

Duric, Ladislav. Essentials of Educational Psychology. (Educational Sciences Ser.). 160p. 1990. pap. 23.00 (*1-85302-054-0*) Taylor & Francis.

Duric, N. & Crane, P., eds. The Interpretation of Modern Synthesis Observation of Galaxies. (ASP Conference Series Proceedings: Vol. 18). 275p. 1991. 34.00 (*0-937707-37-6*) Astron Soc Pacific.

Durica. Dejiny Slovenska a Slovakov. (SLO.). 288p. 1996. write for info. (*80-08-01427-X*, Pub. by Slov Pegagog Naklad) IBD Ltd.

Durica, Karen M. Literature Links to Phonics: A Balanced Approach. 150p. 1996. pap. text 22.00 (*1-56308-353-1*) Teacher Ideas Pr.

Durie, B. G., ed. Current & Potential Applications for Erythropoietin. (Journal: Acta Haematologica: Vol. 87, Suppl. 1, 1992). (Illus.). vi, 34p. 1992. pap. 17.50 (*3-8055-5617-9*) S Karger.

Durie, Brian G., jt. auth. see Gahrton, Gosta.

Durie, Brian G., jt. auth. see Russell, Diane H.

***Durie, Bruce.** E-Business: How to Make Money Running a Business on the Internet. 144p. 2000. pap. 14.95 (*1-85703-643-3*, Pub. by How To Bks) Midpt Trade.

Durie, John. Film Marketing Handbook. 1996. pap. text 29.95 (*84-88773-00-5*, Pub. by British Film Inst) Ind U Pr.

Durie, John, et al. Marketing & Selling Your Film Around the World: A Guide for Independent Filmmakers. (Illus.). 260p. 1998. pap. 22.95 (*1-879505-43-6*) Silman James Pr.

Durie, M. H. Te Mana Te Kawanatanga: The Politics of Maori Self-Determination. LC DU423.P63D87 1998. (Illus.). 288p. 1998. pap. text 45.00 (*0-19-558367-1*) OUP.

Durie, Mark & Ross, Malcolm, eds. The Comparative Method Reviewed: Regularity & Irregularity in Language Change. (Illus.). 336p. 1996. text 85.00 (*0-19-506607-3*) OUP.

Durie, Mason. Whaiora: Maori Health Development. LC 94-233384. (Illus.). 192p. 1995. pap. text 37.50 (*0-19-558316-7*) OUP.

— Whaiora: Maori Health Development. 2nd ed. 256p. 1999. pap. text 26.00 (*0-19-558403-1*) OUP.

Durie, R. A., ed. The Science of Victorian Brown Coal: Structure, Properties & Consequences for Utilisation. (Illus.). 720p. 1992. text 165.00 (*0-7506-0420-4*) Buttrwrth-Heinemann.

Durier, Roland & Michelot, Christian. Recent Developments in Optimization: Seventh French-German conference on Optimization. LC 95-30519. (Lecture Notes in Economics & Mathematical Systems Ser.: No. 429). 1995. write for info. (*0-387-60041-8*) Spr-Verlag.

Duries, Vanessa. The Ties That Bind. (Orig.). 1996. mass mkt. 6.50 (*1-56333-510-7*) Masquerade.

— The Ties That Bind. 2nd ed. (Orig.). 1998. reprint ed. mass mkt. 6.95 (*1-56333-688-X*) Masquerade.

***Durieux, Delphine.** Lakes. (Illus.). 80p. 1999. 29.95 (*3-929078-88-0*, Kehayoff) te Neues.

Durieux, Gilbert, et al. French Financial Markets. (International Financial Markets Ser.). 288p. 1995. 155.00 (*1-85573-116-9*, Pub. by Woodhead Publng) Am Educ Systs.

Durieux, Marcel E. Lysophosphatidate Signaling: Cellular Effects & Molecular Mechanisms. LC 95-4044 (Molecular Biology Intelligence Unit Ser.). 244p. 1995. 89.00 (*1-57059-248-9*) Landes Bioscience.

Durieux, Philippe. Enciclopedia de la Construccion: Encyclopedia of Construction, 10 vols., Set. (SPA.). 4118p. 1984. 1095.00 (*0-8288-5407-6*, S50540) Fr & Eur.

***Duriez, Colin.** The C. S. Lewis Encyclopedia: A Complete Guide to His Life, Thought & Writings. LC 99-48055. Orig. Title: The C. S. Lewis Handbook. 256p. 2000. reprint ed. pap. 17.99 (*1-58134-136-9*) Crossway Bks.

Durif, A. Crystal Chemistry of Condensed Phosphates. LC 95-2312. (Illus.). 424p. (C). 1995. text 120.00 (*0-306-44878-5*, Kluwer Plenum) Kluwer Academic.

Durif, A., jt. auth. see Averbuch-Pouchot, M.

Durig, Alexander. Autism & the Crisis of Meaning. LC 95-15368. 312p. (C). 1996. text 59.50 (*0-7914-2813-3*); pap. text 19.95 (*0-7914-2814-1*) State U NY Pr.

Durig, J. R. & Sullivan, J. F., eds. Twelfth International Conference on Raman Spectroscopy: Proceedings of the Twelfth International Conference on Raman Spectroscopy, 13-17 August 1990, Columbia, South Carolina. LC 90-12450. (Illus.). 961p. 1990. pap. 200.00 (*0-608-05258-2*, 206579600001) Bks Demand.

Durig, James R., ed. Analytical Applications of FT-IR to Molecular & Biological Systems. (NATO Advanced Study Institutes Series C, Mathematical & Physical Sciences: No. 57). 607p. 1980. text 206.50 (*90-277-1145-3*) Kluwer Academic.

— Chemical, Biological, & Industrial Applications of Infrared Spectroscopy. LC 85-16719. (Illus.). 417p. 1985. pap. 129.30 (*0-608-05259-0*, 206579700001) Bks Demand.

— Vibrational Spectra & Structure, Vol. 1. LC QC0454.V5V53. 208p. 1972. reprint ed. pap. 64.50 (*0-608-08520-0*, 205508300001) Bks Demand.

— Vibrational Spectra & Structure, 2 vols., Vol. 2. LC 72-87850. (Illus.). 431p. 1975. reprint ed. pap. 133.70 (*0-7837-0855-6*, 204116400002) Bks Demand.

— Vibrational Spectra & Structure, 2 vols., Vol. 3. LC 72-87850. (Illus.). 342p. 1975. reprint ed. pap. 106.10 (*0-7837-0856-4*, 204116400003) Bks Demand.

— Vibrational Spectra & Structure: Vibrartional Intensities, 22. 342p. 1995. 288.00 (*0-444-82295-X*) Elsevier.

Durig, James R. & Klabunde, Kenneth J. Second International Conference on Low Temperature Chemistry: Proceedings of the Second International Conference on Low Temperature Chemistry: 4-9 August 1996, University of Missouri-Kansas City, Kansas City, Missouri. LC 96-31007. 1996. pap. 10.00 (*1-886157-11-1*) BkMk.

Durig, James R., ed. see Mukhtarov, E. I. & Zhizhin, G. N.

Duriga, James. The Kern County Trivia Book. 105p. 1998. mass mkt. 6.95 (*1-889991-06-6*) Seneca-Secor.

Duriga, Jim. The Proverbial Leroy. (Illus.). (Orig.). 1996. pap. text 4.95 (*1-889991-00-7*) Seneca-Secor.

— Traveling at Warp 7: A Search for Star Trek. 110p. (Orig.). 1998. pap. text 7.95 (*1-889991-02-3*) Seneca-Secor.

— The Unofficial Kern County Activity Guide. (Illus.). 193p. 1996. lab manual ed. 4.95 (*1-889991-01-5*) Seneca-Secor.

During, E. D. Corrosion Atlas. 256p. 1991. ring bd. 250.75 (*0-444-89093-9*) Elsevier.

During, E. D. D., compiled by. Corrosion Atlas: A Collection of Illustrated Case Histories. 3rd expanded rev. ed. LC 97-191387. 810p. 1997. 862.00 (*0-444-82616-5*) Elsevier.

During, H. J. Taxonomical Revision of the Garovaglioideae (Pterobryaceae, Musci) (Bryophytorum Bibliotheca Ser.: No. 12). (Illus.). 1977. lib. bdg. 48.00 (*3-7682-1161-4*) Lubrecht & Cramer.

During, Ingemar. Die Harmonienlehre des Klaudios Ptolemaios. LC 78-66554. (Ancient Philosophy Ser.). 513p. 1982. lib. bdg. 62.00 (*0-8240-9600-2*) Garland.

— Ptolemaios und Porphyrios Uber die Musik. 293p. 1987. reprint ed. write for info. (*3-487-07932-1*) G Olms Pubs.

During, Ingemar, ed. Porphyrius (Philosophus), Kommentar Zur Harmonielehre Des Ptolemaios. xlii, 217p. 1978. reprint ed. write for info. (*0-318-71001-3*) G Olms Pubs.

During, Ingemar, ed. see Ptolemy, Claudius.

During, Jean, et al. The Art of Persian Music. LC 90-43217. (Illus.). 280p. 1991. 50.00 (*0-934211-22-1*) Mage Pubs Inc.

During, Simon. The Cultural Studies Reader. 2nd ed. LC 98-51656. 1999. pap. 25.00 (*0-415-13754-3*) Routledge.

— Cultural Studies Reader. 2nd ed. LC 98-51656. 1999. 85.00 (*0-415-13753-5*) Routledge.

— Patrick White. (Australian Writers Ser.). 120p. 1996. pap. text 26.00 (*0-19-553497-2*) OUP.

***During, W. E., et al.** New Technology-Based Firms at the Turn of the Century. LC 00-25523. 2000. write for info. (*0-08-043791-5*, Pergamon Pr) Elsevier.

Durini, Lucrezia D. Joseph Beuys: The Felt Hat. (Illus.). 267p. 1997. pap. 24.95 (*88-85203-48-5*) Dist Art Pubs.

Duris, Charles S., jt. auth. see Moursand, David G.

Durish, Jack. WordPerfect 5.1 Creative Applications. 1992. pap. 29.95 incl. disk (*0-915391-74-0*) Slawson Comm.

Durivage, Oliver E. The Stage-Struck Yankee. Meserve, Walter J., ed. & intro. by. (On Stage, America! Ser.). 17p. 1996. spiral bd. 3.95 (*0-937657-25-5*) Feedbk Theabks & Prospero.

DuRivage, Virginia L., ed. New Policies for the Part-Time & Contingent Workforce. LC 92-28670. (Economic Policy Institute Ser.). 155p. (C). (gr. 13). 1992. text 70.95 (*1-56324-164-1*); pap. text 36.95 (*1-56324-165-X*) M E Sharpe.

Durix, Jean-Pierre. Mimesis, Genres & Post-Colonial Discourse: Deconstructing Magic Realism LC 98-3656. viii, 206 p. 1998. write for info. (*0-333-73224-3*, Pub. by Macmillan) St Martin.

— The Writer Written: The Artist & Creation in the New Literatures in English, 21. LC 87-7518. (Contributions to the Study of World Literature Ser.: No. 21). 177p. 1987. 45.00 (*0-313-25894-5*, DXA/, Greenwood Pr) Greenwood.

Durizch, M. L., jt. auth. see Littleton, J. T.

Durk, Dan. Prey. LC 98-66732. 400p. 1998. pap. 7.99 (*0-8100-101-5*) Natl Writ Pr.

Durka. Structural Mechanics. 4th ed. 1989. pap. text. write for info. (*0-582-01851-X*, Pub. by Addison-Wesley) Longman.

— Sturctural Mechanics. 5th ed. (C). 1996. pap. 54.95 (*0-582-25199-0*, Pub. by Addison-Wesley) Longman.

Durka, Gloria. The Joy of Being a Catechist. LC 96-142745. (Spirit Life Ser.). 1995. pap. 4.95 (*1-878718-27-4*, Resurrection Pr) Catholic Bk Pub.

— Praying with Hildegard of Bingen. Koch, Carl, ed. (Companions for the Journey Ser.). (Illus.). 120p. (Orig.). 1991. pap. 8.95 (*0-88489-254-9*) St Marys.

— Praying with Julian of Norwich. Koch, Carl, ed. (Companions for the Journey Ser.). (Illus.). 107p. 1989. pap. 8.95 (*0-88489-221-2*) St Marys.

Durka, Gloria & Smith, Joanmarie. Family Ministry. 216p. (Orig.). 1983. 7.95 (*0-86683-762-0*) Harper SF.

Durkacz, Victor E. The Decline of the Celtic Languages. LC 96-169888. 272p. 1996. pap. 48.00 (*0-85976-428-1*, Pub. by J Donald) St Mut.

Durkacz, Victor E., et al. Financial Planning for New Businesses. fac. ed. LC 85-17927. 265p. 1985. reprint ed. pap. 82.20 (*0-608-00993-8*, 206185000012) Bks Demand.

Durkan, Andrew. Spirits & Liqueurs. (Illus.). 192p. 1998. pap. 9.95 (*0-8442-0038-7*, 00387, Teach Yrslf) NTC Contemp Pub Co.

Durkan, Michael J. & Brandes, R. Seamus Heaney: A Reference Guide. 1996. 45.00 (*0-8161-7389-3*, G K Hall Lrg Type) Mac Lib Ref.

Durkee, Cornelius E., compiled by. Reminiscences of Saratoga. (Illus.). 316p. 1997. reprint ed. lib. bdg. 37.00 (*0-8328-6219-3*) Higginson Bk Co.

Durkee, Deborah J. Easy Day Hikes in Yosemite. (Illus.). 40p. (Orig.). 1985. pap. 4.50 (*0-939666-43-X*) Yosemite Assn.

Durkee, John B. Parts Cleaning Handbook Without CFCs: How to Manage the Change. 110p. 1994. pap. 39.95 (*1-56990-143-0*) Hanser-Gardner.

Durkee, Lee. Rides of the Midway. 25.95 (*0-393-04971-X*) Norton.

***Durkee, Michael P.** Ballot Box Navigator: A Legal Guide to Land Use Initiatives & Referenda. 2000. 50.00 (*0-923956-66-2*) Solano Pr.

Durkee, Noura. The King, the Prince & the Naughty Sheep. (Illus.). 24p. (J). (gr. 1-5). 1999. 10.00 (*1-879402-58-0*) Tahrike Tarsile Quran.

D

An Asterisk (*) at the beginning of an entry indicates that the title is appearing for the first time.

***Durkee, Noura.** The Loyal Ansar. Quraishi-Ahmed, Huda et al, eds. (Stories of the Sahabah Ser.: Vol. 3). (Illus.). 170p. (YA). (gr. 7-10). 1999. pap. text 10.00 (1-56316-452-3) Iqra Intl Ed Fdtn.

Durkee, Noura. Maryann & Her Baby. (Illus.). 22p. (J). (gr. 1-5). 1999. 10.00 (1-879402-60-2) Tahrike Tarsile Quran.

— Short Surahs Workbook. Ghazi, Abidullah & Ghazi, Tasneema, eds. (Illus.). 42p. 1994. student ed. 4.00 (1-56316-103-6) Iqra Intl Ed Fdtn.

— Yunus in the Whale, Vol. 1. (Illus.). 25p. (J). (gr. 1-5). 1999. 10.00 (1-879402-59-9) Tahrike Tarsile Quran.

Durkee, Noura, ed. see Al-Ahsan, Abdullah.

Durkee, Noura, ed. see Ghazi, Abidullah & Ghazi, Tasneema.

Durkee, Noura, ed. see Ghazi, Abidullah & Ghazi, Tasneema K.

Durkee, Noura, ed. see Ghazi, Tasneema.

***Durkee, Sarah.** Lucky Duck. LC 99-87425. (Between the Lions Ser.). (Illus.). (J). 2000. 7.99 (0-307-16502-7, Goldn Books) Gldn Bks Pub Co.

***Durkee, Sarah & Prebenna, David.** The Lucky Duck. LC 99-87425. (J). 2000. 10.99 (0-307-36502-6) Gldn Bks Pub Co.

Durken, Mary Cabrini, tr. see Dilasser, Maurice.

Durkheim, Emile. The Division of Labor in Society. Hall, W. D., tr. 350p. (C). 1984. pap. 16.95 (0-02-907960-8) Free Pr.

— The Division of Labor in Society. 416p. 1997. pap. 17.95 (0-684-83638-6) S&S Trade.

— Division of Labor in Society: Some Notes on Occupational Groups. (Reprint Series in Social Sciences). (C). 1993. reprint ed. pap. text 2.30 (0-8290-3848-5, S-76) Irvington.

— Durkheim on Religion. Pickering, W. S. F., ed. LC 94-15084. (AAR Texts & Translations Ser.: No. 6). 388p. 1994. pap. 19.95 (1-55540-981-4, 010206) OUP.

— Education & Sociology. LC 55-11002. 1956. pap. 19.95 (0-02-907920-9) Free Pr.

— The Elementary Forms of the Religious Life. Swain, Joseph W., tr. 1965. pap. 16.95 (0-02-908010-X) Free Pr.

— The Elementary Forms of the Religious Life. Fields, Karen E., tr. 500p. 1995. 35.00 (0-02-907936-5) Free Pr.

— The Elementary Forms of the Religious Life. Fields, Karen E., tr. 1995. pap. 19.95 (0-02-907937-3) Free Pr.

— The Elementary Forms of the Religious Life. 2nd ed. Swain, Joseph W., tr. LC 76-369730. 471p. reprint ed. pap. 146.10 (0-608-11932-6, 202327600032) Bks Demand.

— Emile Durkheim on Institutional Analysis. Traugott, Mark, ed. LC 77-25105. (Heritage of Sociology Ser.). 1978. 23.00 (0-226-17330-5) U Ch Pr.

— Emile Durkheim on Morality & Society. Bellah, Robert N., ed. LC 73-76594. (Heritage of Sociology Ser.). lvi, 288p. (C). 1975. pap. text 13.00 (0-226-17336-4, P565) U Ch Pr.

— Ethics & the Sociology of Morals. Hall, Robert T., tr. & intro. by. LC 93-5459. (Great Minds Ser.). 135p. 1993. reprint ed. pap. 8.95 (0-87975-845-7) Prometheus Bks.

— Moral Education: A Study in the Theory & Application of the Sociology of Education. Wilson, Everett K., tr. LC 59-6815. 288p. 1973. pap. 17.95 (0-02-908320-6) Free Pr.

— Professional Ethics & Civic Morals. Brookfield, Cornelia, tr. LC 83-12653. 228p. (C). 1983. reprint ed. lib. bdg. 75.00 (0-313-24114-7, DUPR, Greenwood Pr) Greenwood.

— Professional Ethics & Civic Morals. 2nd ed. (Illus.). 304p. (C). 1992. pap. 24.99 (0-415-06225-X) Routledge.

— The Rules of Sociological Method. 1982. pap. 16.95 (0-02-907940-3) Free Pr.

— Selected Writings. Giddens, Anthony, ed. 282p. 1972. pap. text 19.95 (0-521-09712-6) Cambridge U Pr.

Durkheim, Emile. Socialism & Saint-Simon (Le Socialisme) Gouldner, Alvin W., ed. LC 58-8736. 282p. reprint ed. pap. 87.50 (0-608-11959-8, 202319900032) Bks Demand.

Durkheim, Emile. Sociology & Philosophy. Pocock, D. F., tr. LC 54-2835. 1974. pap. 13.95 (0-02-908580-2) Free Pr.

— Suicide. 1966. pap. 16.95 (0-02-908660-4) Free Pr.

— Suicide. 416p. 1997. pap. 17.95 (0-684-83632-7) Free Pr.

Durkheim, Emile & Mauss, Marcel. Primitive Classification. Needham, Rodney, tr. LC 63-9737. 113p. 1967. pap. text 13.00 (0-226-17334-8, P273) U Ch Pr.

Durkheim, Emile, et al. Society & Solitude. LC 95-40641. (Lynchburg College Symposium Readings Ser.: Vol. 5). 1995. pap. text. write for info. (0-7618-0129-4) U Pr of Amer.

Durkin, jt. auth. see Ferguson.

Durkin, Andrew & Cousins, John. Teach Yourself Wine Appreciation. 192p. 1995. pap. text 9.95 (0-8442-3644-6, Teach Yrslf) NTC Contemp Pub Co.

Durkin, Dolores. Children Who Read Early: Two Longitudinal Studies. LC 66-25980. 190p. 1966. reprint ed. pap. 58.90 (0-608-02761-8, 206382700007) Bks Demand.

— Getting Reading Started: A Textbook for Early Childhood Educators Responsible for Readiness & Beginning Reading Instruction. 200p. (C). 1981. pap. text 24.00 (0-205-07559-2, H75591) Allyn.

— Phonics, Linguistics & Reading. LC 72-87115. 100p. 1972. pap. 10.95 (0-8077-1258-2) Tchrs Coll.

— Teaching Them to Read. 5th ed. 1989. text 45.00 (0-205-11706-6, H17064) Allyn.

— Teaching Them to Read. 6th ed. LC 92-17718. 475p. 1992. 78.00 (0-205-13915-9) Allyn.

— Teaching Them to Read: Examination Copy. 6th ed. 448p. (C). 1992. pap. write for info. (0-205-14772-0, H4772-3) Allyn.

Durkin, Helen. The Group in Depth. LC 64-7550. 378p. (Orig.). 1966. 57.50 (0-8236-2240-1) Intl Univs Pr.

Durkin, James. This War Is an Awful Thing: Civil War Letters of the National Guards, the 19th & 90th Pennsylvania Volunteers. (Illus.). 300p. 1994. 27.50 (0-9631314-1-9) J M S Civil War.

Durkin, James, ed. & pref. see Smedley, Charles.

Durkin, Jim. Life with a Purpose - Chinese Edition. Kuan, Jensen, tr. (CHI.). 71p. 1987. pap. 5.00 (1-56582-099-1) Christ Renew Min.

Durkin, Joe, et al. Blackstone's Guide to the Transport & Works Act, 1992. 190p. 1992. 16.95 (1-85431-241-3, Pub. by Blackstone Pr) Gaunt.

Durkin, John. Expert Systems: Design & Development. (Illus.). 768p. (C). 1993. text 60.00 (0-02-330970-9, Macmillan Coll) P-H.

Durkin, John F. & Newton, Joe. Running to the Top of the Mountain. (Illus.). 350p. (Orig.). (YA). (gr. 9-12). 1988. pap. text 24.95 (0-9621313-0-X) J & J Win Edge.

Durkin, Joseph, ed. Swift Potomac's Lovely Daughter: Two Centuries at Georgetown Through Students' Eyes. LC 89-48744. (Illus.). 446p. (Orig.). 1990. pap. 14.95 (0-87840-501-1) Georgetown U Pr.

Durkin, Kevin. Developmental Social Psychology: An Introduction. (Illus.). 640p. (C). 1995. pap. 36.95 (0-631-14829-9) Blackwell Pubs.

Durkin, Kevin & Shire, Beatrice, eds. Language in Mathematical Education: Research & Practice. 256p. 1991. pap. 41.95 (0-335-09366-3) OpUniv Pr.

Durkin, Lisa L., ed. see Faggella, Kathy.

Durkin, Lisa L., ed. see Faggella, Kathy & Horowitz, Janet.

Durkin, Lisa L., ed. see Hayes, Martha A. & Faggella, Kathy.

Durkin, Lisa L., ed. see Hayes, Martha A., et al.

Durkin, Lisa L., ed. see Perez, Jeannine.

Durkin, Lisa L., ed. see Spann, Mary B.

Durkin, M., ed. see Eltringham, R. J., et al.

Durkin, Mary. Thinking Through Class Discussion: The Hilda Taba Approach. LC 93-60802. 115p. 1993. pap. text 19.95 (1-56676-055-0) Scarecrow.

Durkin, Mary Brian. Be Not Afraid, I Am with You: Prayers for Healing. 168p. 1999. pap. 6.95 (0-88489-583-1) St Marys.

Durkin, Mary C. & Dierks, Sheila D. Jubilee Journal: A Workbook on Forgiving for the Millennium. 128p. 1998. spiral bd., wbk. ed. 9.00 (0-9658137-0-3) Woven Word.

Durkin, Mary D. Heal Me, Lord: Ecumenical Prayerbook for Hospitals. 63p. 1987. pap. 1.95 (0-8199-0911-4, Frncscn Herld) Franciscan Pr.

Durkin, Mary G. Making Your Family Work. 176p. (Orig.). 1990. mass mkt. 4.50 (0-446-35835-5, Pub. by Warner Bks) Little.

Durkin, Mary G., jt. auth. see Greeley, Andrew M.

Durkin, Patrick. The Deer Hunters: Tactics, Lore, Legacy & Allure of American Deer Hunting. LC 97-73778. (Illus.). 208p. 1997. 29.95 (0-87341-537-X, BOD) Krause Pubns.

Durkin, Patrick, ed. see Alsheimer, Charles J.

Durkin, Patrick, ed. see Clancy, Gary.

Durkin, Patrick, ed. see Miller, Greg.

Durkin, Patrick, ed. see Ozogas, John.

Durkin, Peter, jt. auth. see Ferguson, Virginia.

Durkin, Rosemary D. Ohio Probate, 1998 Cumulative Supplement. 2nd ed. 100p. 1998. suppl. ed. write for info. (0-327-00517-3, 6896011) LEXIS Pub.

Durko, Sandy V., ed. see Michelson, Maureen R.

Durkon. The Tarot of the Orishas: The Deck. (ENG & SPA.). 1997. 19.95 (1-56718-843-5) Llewellyn Pubns.

Durkon, Rosemary. Ohio Probate. 2nd ed. 135.00 (0-327-11243-3) LEXIS Pub.

Durkon, Rosemary. Ohio Probate, 1999 Supplement. 2nd ed. 250p. 1999. ring bd. write for info. (0-327-01498-9, 6896012) LEXIS Pub.

Durkota, Alan, et al. The Imperial Russian Air Service: Famous Pilots & Aircraft & World War I. LC 95-83553. (Illus.). 550p. 1995. 79.95 (0-9637110-2-4) Flying Machines.

Durkota, Alan E. Medal of Honor Vol. 1: Aviators of World War One. (Illus.). 112p. 1998. pap. 24.95 (1-891268-03-1) Flying Machines.

Durksen, Menno. Dear God, I'm Only a Boy. rev. ed. LC 95-60240. x, 406p. 1995. pap. 17.95 (0-945530-13-7) Wordsworth KS.

Durlabhji, Subhash & Marks, Norton E., eds. Japanese Business: Cultural Perspectives. LC 91-42663. 402p. (C). 1993. pap. text 24.95 (0-7914-1252-0) State U NY Pr.

Durlach, jt. auth. see Halpern.

Durlach, J. & Altura, B. M., eds. Magnesium & the Cardiovascular System Journal Vol. 4, Nos. 5-6: Magnesium. (Illus.). vi, 134p. 1986. pap. 62.75 (3-8055-4282-8) S Karger.

— Magnesium, Diabetes & Carbohydrate Metabolism Journal: Magnesium, Vol. 2, Nos. 4-6. (Illus.). iv, 172p. 1984. pap. 85.25 (3-8055-3865-0) S Karger.

Durlach, J., jt. ed. see Halpern, M. J.

Durlach, Nathaniel I., ed. see National Research Council Staff.

Durlach, Theresa M. The Relationship Systems of the Tlingit, Haida, & Tsimshian. LC 73-3547. (American Ethnological Society Publications: No. 11). reprint ed. 31.50 (0-404-58161-7) AMS Pr.

Durlacher, Ed, ed. The Play Party Book: Singing Games for Children. (Illus.). 38p. (J). (ps-5). 1945. 9.50 (0-8159-6505-2) Devin.

Durlacher, Gerhard. Drowning: Growing up in the Third Reich. 106p. 1994. pap. 12.99 (1-85242-282-3) Serpents Tail.

— The Search. Masotty, Susan, tr. 182p. 1998. pap. 14.99 (1-85242-540-7) Serpents Tail.

— Stripes in the Sky: A Wartime Memoir. Massotty, Susan, tr. from DUT. 112p. (Orig.). 1992. pap. 13.95 (1-85242-202-5) Serpents Tail.

Durlacher, James V. Freedom from Fear Forever. McGill, Guy, ed. LC 94-62181. (Illus.). 245p. 1995. pap. 18.95 (0-9645713-1-5) Van Ness Pub.

Durlacher, Jennifer, jt. ed. see Blauvelt, Euan.

***Durlacher, Julian.** Cocaine: Its History & Lore. (Drugs the Hard Facts Ser.). (Illus.). 80p. 2000. pap. 9.95 (1-85868-863-9, Pub. by Carlton Bks Ltd) Natl Bk Netwk.

— Ecstasy: Its History & Lore. (Drugs the Hard Facts Ser.). (Illus.). 80p. 2000. pap. 9.95 (1-85868-862-0, Pub. by Carlton Bks Ltd) Natl Bk Netwk.

— Heroin: Its History & Lore. (Drugs the Hard Facts Ser.). (Illus.). 80p. 2000. pap. 9.95 (1-85868-860-4, Pub. by Carlton Bks Ltd) Natl Bk Netwk.

— Speed: Its History & Lore. (Drugs the Hard Facts Ser.). (Illus.). 80p. 2000. pap. 9.95 (1-85868-861-2, Pub. by Carlton Bks Ltd) Natl Bk Netwk.

Durlak, Joseph A. Program Implementation in Preventive Trials. Ferrari, Joseph R., ed. LC 98-3323. 94p. 1998. 29.95 (0-7890-0523-9) Haworth Pr.

— School-Based Prevention Programs for Children & Adolescents. (Development Clinical Psychology & Psychiatry Ser.: Vol. 34). 136p. (C). 1995. 42.00 (0-8039-5631-2); pap. 18.95 (0-8039-5632-0) Sage.

— Successful Prevention Programs for Children & Adolescents. LC 97-18250. (Issues in Clinical Child Psychology Ser.). 256p. (C). 1997. 45.00 (0-306-45645-1, Plenum Trade) Perseus Pubng.

Durland, Frances C. Creative Dramatics for Children: A Practical Manual for Teachers & Leaders. LC 75-1493. 188p. reprint ed. pap. 58.30 (0-7837-0208-6, 204051500018) Bks Demand.

Durland, M. A. Gears & Pinions of Equal Strength. (Technical Papers: Vol. P39A). (Illus.). 6p. 1924. pap. text 30.00 (1-55589-174-8) AGMA.

Durland, Mary M. Mr. Thank You So Muchly. (Illus.). 32p. (J). (gr. k-2). 1994. 8.95 (0-9643013-0-X) Hidden Brook Pr.

Durland, Stanley. Where Angels Tread. 456p. 1998. 25.00 (0-9661118-0-X) Indian Stream.

Durland, Steven, ed. see Apple, Jacki.

Durland, Steven, jt. ed. see Burnham, Linda F.

Durland, William. Apocalypse Witness. LC 88-61520. (Orig.). 1988. pap. 4.00 (0-87574-279-3) Pendle Hill.

— God or Nations: Radical Theology for the Religious Peace Movement. 309p. (Orig.). 1989. pap. 16.95 (1-879175-03-7) Fortkamp.

***Durland, William R.** William Penn, James Madison & the Historical Crisis in American Federalism. LC 00-39452. (Studies in American History: Vol. 28). 308p. 2000. 99.95 (0-7734-7698-9) E Mellen.

Durling, Nancy V., ed. Jean Renart & the Art of Romance: Essays on Guillaume de Dole. LC 96-53088. (Illus.). 256p. 1997. 49.95 (0-8130-1495-6) U Press Fla.

Durling, Nancy V., ed. & tr. see Renart, Jean.

Durling, Nancy Vine, jt. auth. see Terry, Patricia Ann.

Durling, R. J., ed. Galenus Latinus I. (Ars Medica Ser.: Vol. 6). (C). 1976. text 184.65 (3-11-005759-X) De Gruyter.

Durling, Richard J. A Catalogue of Sixteenth Century Printed Books in the National Library of Medicine. 698p. 1999. reprint ed. 75.00 (1-57898-137-9) Martino Pubng.

— A Dictionary of Medical Terms in Galen. LC 92-39986. (Studies in Ancient Medicine: No. 5). (ENG & GRE.). xiii, 344p. 1993. 148.00 (90-04-09754-6) Brill Academic Pubs.

Durling, Richard J., jt. ed. see Kudlien, Fridolf.

Durling, Robert & Martinez, Ronald L. Time & the Crystal: Studies in Dante's "Rime Petrose" 1990. 60.00 (0-520-06488-7, Pub. by U CA Pr) Cal Prin Full Svc.

Durling, Robert M. The Figures of the Poet in Renaissance Epic. LC 65-22060. 292p. reprint ed. pap. 90.60 (0-608-10998-3, 200296600016) Bks Demand.

Durling, Robert M., ed. Petrarch's Lyric Poems. 624p. 1976. pap. 22.00 (0-674-66348-9) HUP.

Durling, Robert M., ed. see Petrarca, Francesco.

Durling, Robert M., ed. & tr. see Dante Alighieri.

Durman, Hilda. Her Father's Partner. large type ed. (Dales Large Print Ser.). 255p. 1995. pap. 18.99 (1-85389-538-5, Dales) Ulverscroft.

— Kit's Benefactor. large type ed. (Dales Large Print Ser.). 209p. 1995. pap. 18.99 (1-85389-537-7, Dales) Ulverscroft.

Durman, Hilda A. Artist in Love. large type ed. (Linford Romance Library). 272p. 1989. pap. 16.99 (0-7089-6645-4, Linford) Ulverscroft.

— Call from Greenacres. large type ed. (Linford Romance Library). 240p. 1989. pap. 16.99 (0-7089-6697-7, Linford) Ulverscroft.

— Cure for Love. large type ed. 1991. pap. 16.99 (0-7089-6975-5) Ulverscroft.

— A Heart of Stone. large type ed. (Linford Romance Library). 288p. 1993. pap. 16.99 (0-7089-7412-0) Ulverscroft.

— Meadow's End. large type ed. 1990. pap. 16.99 (0-7089-6876-7, Linford) Ulverscroft.

— Seeds of Jealousy. large type ed. (Linford Romance Library). 1991. pap. 16.99 (0-7089-7049-4) Ulverscroft.

— The Twain Shall Meet. large type ed. (Linford Romance Library). 304p. 1993. pap. 16.99 (0-7089-7331-0, Linford) Ulverscroft.

— Valley of the Sun. large type ed. 230p. 1993. pap. 18.99 (1-85389-367-6, Dales) Ulverscroft.

Durman, Karel. Lost Illusions: Russian Policies Towards Bulgaria in 1877-1887. (Uppsala Studies on the Soviet Union & Eastern Europe: No. 1). (Orig.). 1988. pap. 40.00 (91-554-2153-9, Pub. by Uppsala Univ Acta Univ Uppsaliensis) Coronet Bks.

— The Time of the Thunderer: Mikhail Katkov, Russian Nationalist Extremism & the Failure of the Bimarkian System, 1871-1887. 609p. 1988. text 104.00 (0-88033-134-8, Pub. by East Eur Monographs) Col U Pr.

Durmin, M. Learn to Play Beethoven. (Piano Classics Ser.). (Illus.). 64p. (J). (gr. 1 up). 1994. lib. bdg. 17.95 (0-88110-676-3, Usborne) EDC.

— Learn to Play Beethoven. (Piano Classics Ser.). (Illus.). 64p. (J). (gr. 4-7). 1994. pap. 9.95 (0-7460-1026-5, Usborne) EDC.

Durnan, J. Richard. Mountain Biking the White Mountains (West) LC 98-6249. (Illus.). 160p. 1998. pap. 10.95 (1-56044-663-3) Falcon Pub Inc.

Durnan, Mary H. & Smith, Carla, eds. History of Marshall County Indiana, 1836-1986. (Illus.). 576p. 1986. lib. bdg. 60.00 (0-9617303-0-7) Marshall Hist.

Durnbaugh, Donald F. The Believers' Church: The History & Character of Radical Protestantism. LC 85-7599. 328p. 1985. reprint ed. pap. 15.99 (0-8361-1271-7) Herald Pr.

— The Brethren in Colonial America. (Illus.). 659p. 1996. 15.95 (0-87178-110-7, 8107) Brethren.

— European Origins of the Brethren. 463p. 1958. 15.95 (0-87178-256-1, 8561) Brethren.

— Fruit of the Vine: A History of the Brethren, 1708-1995. LC 96-22415. 689p. 1996. 49.95 (0-87178-003-8, 8038) Brethren.

— Pragmatic Prophet: The Life of M. R. Zigler. LC 89-34973. 416p. 1989. pap. 12.95 (0-87178-717-2, 8172) Brethren.

— Pragmatic Prophet: The Life of M. R. Zigler. LC 89-34973. (Illus.). 440p. 1989. 24.95 (0-87178-715-6, 8156) Brethren.

Durnbaugh, Donald F., ed. Meet the Brethren. (Illus.). 120p. 1995. reprint ed. pap. 8.00 (0-936693-11-8) Brethren Encyclopedia.

— On Earth Peace. 412p. 1978. pap. 9.95 (0-87178-660-5, 8605) Brethren.

Durnbaugh, Donald F., jt. auth. see Eberly, William R.

Durnbaugh, Donald F., ed. see Zigler, M. R.

Durnbaugh, Hedwig T. The German Hymnody of the Brethren, 1720-1903. Eberly, William R., ed. (Monographs: No. 1). (Illus.). 336p. 1986. 25.00 (0-936693-21-5) Brethren Encyclopedia.

Durnbaugh, Hedwig T., tr. see Skeie, Eyvind.

Durnberg, Steffi, jt. auth. see Rubio, Maggie.

Durnell, Hazel B. The America of Carl Sandburg. LC 90-46584. (Illus.). 276p. 1990. reprint ed. 34.95 (0-87797-206-0) Cherokee.

Durney, Bernard R. & Sofia, Sabatino, eds. The Solar Angular Velocity. (C). 1987. text 193.50 (90-277-2523-3) Kluwer Academic.

***Durney, Carl H. & Christensen, Douglas A.** Basic Introduction to Bioelectromagnetics LC 99-29332. 184p. 1999. boxed set 59.95 (0-8493-1198-5) CRC Pr.

Durney, Lawrence J. Graham's Electroplating Handbook. 4th ed. 1984. text 105.00 (0-442-22002-2) Chapman & Hall.

— Trouble in Your Tank? 185p. 1988. 20.00 (0-685-44516-X) Am Electro Surface.

— Trouble in Your Tank? Handbook for Solving Plating Problems. 3rd ed. 1996. 39.95 (1-56990-200-3) Hanser-Gardner.

***Durney, Ryan.** Prairie Town. (Illus.). 8p. (J). (gr. k-2). 2000. pap. 3.75 (1-58323-014-9) Seedling Pubns.

Durnford, D. Ground Water & the Vadose Zone. 1994. pap. write for info. (0-442-01636-0, VNR) Wiley.

Durnford-Slater, John. Commando: Memoirs of a Fighting Commando in World War II. (Illus.). 222p. 1991. 26.95 (1-55750-125-4) Naval Inst Pr.

Durnil, Gordon K. Is America Beyond Reform? LC 97-23770. 1997. 25.95 (0-9651213-9-9) Sligo Pr.

— The Making of a Conservative Environmentalist: With Reflections on Government, Industry, Scientists, the Media, Education, Economic Growth, the Public, the Great Lakes, Activists, & the Sunsetting of Toxic Chemicals. LC 94-24989. 216p. 1995. text 19.95 (0-253-32873-X) Ind U Pr.

Durnin, John. Toward Educational Engineering. LC 81-40101. (Illus.). 134p. (Orig.). (C). 1982. pap. text 17.00 (0-8191-2436-2) U Pr of Amer.

Durnin, Michael. Learn to Play Mozart. (Learn to Play Ser.). (Illus.). 64p. (J). (gr. 4-7). 1993. pap. 9.95 (0-7460-0964-X, Usborne) EDC.

Durning. Gender & Architecture. LC 99-45847. 304p. (C). 2000. text 95.00 (0-471-98532-5); pap. text 32.95 (0-471-98533-3) Wiley.

Durning, Alan B. Action at the Grassroots: Fighting Poverty & Environmental Decline. (Orig.). (C). 1989. pap. 5.00 (0-916468-89-5) Worldwatch Inst.

— Apartheid's Environmental Toll. (Orig.). (C). 1990. pap. 5.00 (0-916468-96-8) Worldwatch Inst.

— How Much Is Enough? The Consumer Society & the Future of the Earth. LC 92-15410. (Worldwatch Environmental Alert Ser.). 200p. 1992. pap. 9.95 (0-393-30891-X) Norton.

— Poverty & the Environment: Reversing the Downward Spiral. (Orig.). (C). 1989. pap. 5.00 (0-916468-93-3) Worldwatch Inst.

Durning, Alan B. & Brough, Holly. Taking Stock: Animal Farming & the Environment. 70p. (Orig.). 1991. pap. 5.00 (1-878071-04-1) Worldwatch Inst.

Durning, Alan B., jt. auth. see Flavin, Christopher.

Durning, Alan T. The Car & the City, Vol. 3. (New Reports: No. 3). 74p. (Orig.). 1996. pap. text 9.95 (1-886093-03-2) NW Environ Watch.

— Guardians of the Land: Indigenous Peoples & the Health of the Earth. 70p. (Orig.). 1992. pap. 5.00 (1-878071-13-0) Worldwatch Inst.

D

An Asterisk (*) at the beginning of an entry indicates that the title is appearing for the first time.

— Saving the Forests: What Will It Take? 70p. (Orig.). 1993. pap. 5.00 (*1-878071-18-1*) Worldwatch Inst.

— This Place on Earth: Home & the Practice of Permanence. LC 96-20592. 302p. 1996. 22.95 (*1-57061-040-1*) Sasquatch Bks.

— This Place on Earth: Home & the Practice of Permanence. 336p. 1997. reprint ed. pap. 14.95 (*1-57061-127-0*) Sasquatch Bks.

Durning, Alan T. & Crowther, Christopher D. Misplaced Blame: The Real Roots of Population Growth. Chu, Ellen W., ed. LC 95-68006. (New Report Ser.: No. 5). 41p. (Orig.). (YA). (gr. 11-12). 1997. pap. 9.95 (*1-886093-05-9*) NW Environ Watch.

Durning, Alan T., jt. auth. see Ryan, John C.

Durning, Dan W. Distributing Georgia's General Purpose Local- Option Sales Tax Revenue. 38p. (Orig.). 1992. pap. 5.00 (*0-89854-156-5*) U of GA Inst Govt.

Durning, Danny W., ed. Mortgage Revenue Bonds: Housing Markets, Home Buyers & Public Policy. 288p. (C). 1991. lib. bdg. 102.00 (*0-7923-9180-2*) Kluwer Academic.

Durning-Lawrence, Edwin. Bacon Is Shake-Speare: Together with a Reprint of Bacon's Promus of Formularies & Elegancies. 316p. 1996. reprint ed. pap. 24.95 (*1-56459-541-2*) Kessinger Pub.

— Bacon Is Shake-speare, Together with a Reprint of Bacon's "Promus of Formularies & Elegancies" (BCL1-PR English Literature Ser.). 286p. 1992. reprint ed. lib. bdg. 79.00 (*0-7812-7287-4*) Rprt Serv.

***Durning-Lawrence, Lady.** Notes & Illustrations Covering the Family History of James Smith of Coventry (b. 1731-d. 1794) & His Descendants. fac. ed. 156p. 1999. reprint ed. 34.00 (*0-8328-9968-2*) Higginson Bk Co.

Durning, Mary J., jt. auth. see Durning, William P.

Durning, Nancy, ed. see Durning, William P. & Durning, Mary J.

Durning, Nancy, ed. see Martin, Gary.

Durning, William P. & Durning, Mary J. The Scotch-Irish Who Came to America: A Genealogical History. Durning, Nancy & Harris, Margaret, eds. LC 97-149073. (Illus.). 232p. (Orig.). 1998. pap. 17.95 (*0-9601868-4-0*) Irish Family Names.

Duro, A., jt. ed. see Felice, E. De.

Duro, Carol J., jt. auth. see Duro, Peter A.

Duro, I. & Hysa, R. Albanian-English Dictionary: Fjalor Shqip Anglisht. (ALB & ENG.). 510p. 1981. 24.95 (*0-8288-0537-7*, M6767) Fr & Eur.

Duro, Paul. The Academy & the Limits of Painting in Seventeenth-Century France. LC 96-36824. (Cambridge Studies in New Art History & Criticism). (Illus.). 312p. (C). 1997. text 85.00 (*0-521-49501-6*) Cambridge U Pr.

Duro, Paul, ed. The Rhetoric of the Frame: Essays on the Boundaries of the Artwork. LC 96-19427. (Cambridge Studies in New Art History & Criticism). (Illus.). 336p. (C). 1996. text 85.00 (*0-521-46148-0*); pap. text 30.95 (*0-521-56629-0*) Cambridge U Pr.

Duro, Peter A. & Duro, Carol J. You Don't Know My God. LC 85-81388. 238p. (Orig.). 1985. pap. 5.95 (*0-9615955-0-7*) Emmanuel Christian.

Duro, Robert & Sandstro, Bjorn. The Basic Principles of Marketing Warfare. LC 87-8317. 176p. 1987. text 186.50 (*0-471-91545-9*) Wiley.

***Duro, Stephen.** The Best of Bach. 71p. 2000. pap. text 10.95 (*0-7119-7951-0*, AM956637) Music Sales.

— The Best of Beethoven. 71p. 2000. pap. 10.95 (*0-7119-7950-2*, AM956626) Music Sales.

— The Best of Mozart. 71p. 2000. pap. text 10.95 (*0-7119-7949-9*, AM956648) Music Sales.

— Easy Classic Tunes for Clarinet. 1999. pap. text 12.95 (*0-8256-1777-4*, M961895) Music Sales.

— Easy Classic Tunes for Flute. 39p. 1999. pap. text 12.95 (*0-8256-1775-8*, AM961873) Music Sales.

Duro, Stephen. Joy of English Music for Piano. 1996. pap. text 12.95 (*0-7119-4671-X*, AM92594) Omnibus NY.

Duro, Stephen, contrib. by. I Can Play That: Folk Songs. 1994. 12.95 (*0-7119-3629-3*, AM91366) Omnibus NY.

Duro, Stephen, selected by. I Can Play That! Classics. (Illus.). 48p. 1992. pap. 12.95 (*0-7119-3088-0*, AM89927) Music Sales.

Duro, Stephen. The Joy of First Piano Collection. 64p. 1999. pap. 12.95 (*0-7119-7292-3*, AM952765) Omnibus NY.

Durocher, Claude & Ives, Vera, eds. BBQ Breads: The City Dweller's Guide to Baking Bread Products in a Gas Grill. 160p. 1998. pap. 20.00 (*0-9668958-0-0*) C Tremblay.

Durocher, Joseph F. & Goodman, Raymond J., Jr. The Essentials of Tableside Cookery. (Illus.). (Orig.). 1978. pap. text 5.00 (*0-937056-00-6*, F&B22) Cornell U Sch Hotel.

Durocher, Joseph F., jt. auth. see Baraban, Regina S.

Durocher, Leo. Dodgers & Me: Inside Story: American Autobiography. 284p. 1995. lib. bdg. 79.00 (*0-7812-8508-9*) Rprt Serv.

Duronio, Margaret A. & Loessin, Bruce A. Effective Fund Raising in Higher Education: Ten Success Stories. LC 91-8426. (Higher & Adult Education - Policy, Leadership & Administration Ser.). 271p. 1991. text 40.45 (*1-55542-360-4*) Jossey-Bass.

Duronio, Margaret A. & Temple, Eugene R. Fund Raisers: Their Careers, Stories, Concerns, & Accomplishments. LC 96-3462. (Nonprofit Sector Ser.). 221p. 1997. 30.95 (*0-7879-0307-8*) Jossey-Bass.

DuRose, Paulette, ed. see Lindell, Colleen & Hersh, William R.

Duroselle, Jean B. France & the United States: From the Beginnings to the Present Day. Coltman, Derek, tr. from FRE. LC 78-1467. (United States in the World: Foreign World Perspectives Ser.). 1978. lib. bdg. 18.00 (*0-226-17408-5*) U Ch Pr.

***Duroselle, Jean-Baptiste.** Todo Imperio Precera. 465p. 1999. pap. 21.99 (*968-16-5471-4*) Fondo CA.

Durosimi, Eldred. Childhood in African Literature. (African Literature Today Ser.). 1998. pap. 18.95 (*0-86543-673-8*) Africa World.

Durosimi, Eldred, et al, eds. The Questions of Language in African Literature Today. LC 91-64141. (African Literature Today Ser.: Vol. 17). 190p. (C). 1991. 45.00 (*0-86543-214-7*); pap. 14.95 (*0-86543-215-5*) Africa World.

Durosimi-Jones, Eldred. Childhood in African Literature. (African Literature Today Ser.). 192p. 1998. 59.95 (*0-86543-672-X*) Africa World.

Duroska, Lud & Schiffer, Don. Football Rules in Pictures. rev. ed. (Illus.). 80p. (YA). 1991. reprint ed. pap. 9.95 (*0-399-51689-1*, Perigee Bks) Berkley Pub.

Durost, Walter N. Children's Collecting Activity Related to Social Factors. LC 75-176734. (Columbia University. Teachers College. Contributions to Education Ser.: No. 535). reprint ed. 37.50 (*0-404-55535-7*) AMS Pr.

Durouchoux, Philippe & Prantzos, Nikos, eds. Gamma-Ray Line Astrophysics. LC 91-55492. (AIP Conference Proceedings Ser.: No. 232). (Illus.). 544p. 1991. lib. bdg. 95.00 (*0-88318-875-9*) Am Inst Physics.

Duroussoff, Nicolai. Frank O. Gehry The Architect's Studio. 1999. pap. text 21.00 (*87-90029-35-6*) Louisana.

Duroux, Paul-Emile. Dictionnaire des Anthropologistes. (FRE.). 336p. 1974. pap. 59.95 (*0-8288-6018-1*, M6182) Fr & Eur.

Durova, Nadezhda. The Cavalry Maiden: Journals of a Russian Officer in the Napoleonic Wars. Zirin, Mary F., tr. & notes by. LC 87-45395. (Indiana-Michigan Series in Russian & East European Studies). (RUS., Illus.). 282p. 1988. 35.00 (*0-253-31372-4*) Ind U Pr.

— The Cavalry Maiden: Journals of a Russian Officer in the Napoleonic Wars. Zirin, Mary F., tr. & notes by. LC 87-45395. (Indiana-Michigan Series in Russian & East European Studies). (RUS., Illus.). 282p. 1989. pap. 16.95 (*0-253-20549-2*) Ind U Pr.

Durozoi, G. Dictionnaire de Philosophie. (FRE.). 407p. 1997. 37.95 (*0-320-00434-1*) Fr & Eur.

Durozoi, Gerard. Dictionnaire de l'Art Moderne Contemporain. (ENG & FRE.). 700p. 1992. 225.00 (*0-7859-8056-3*, 2850252662) Fr & Eur.

— Dictionnaire de Philosophie. 2nd ed. (FRE.). 367p. 1990. 45.00 (*0-7859-7724-4*, 2091801135) Fr & Eur.

***Durozoi, Gerard.** History Surrealist Movement. 1999. 95.00 (*0-226-17411-5*) U Ch Pr.

Durphy, Michael, jt. auth. see Sonkin, Daniel J.

Durphy, Rosemarie & Sullivan, Mary. That First Bite - Chance or Choice? A Working Guide Empowering Choice for Those with Eating Disorders. 128p. (Orig.). 1992. pap. 7.95 (*0-9631517-6-2*) Jeremiah Pr.

Durr. Johann Sebastian Bach's St John Passion: Genesis, Transmission & Meaning. Clayton, Alfred, tr. LC 99-32937. (Illus.). 208p. 2000. text 45.00 (*0-19-816240-5*) OUP.

Durr, Hilda, jt. auth. see Kincaid, Eloise.

***Durr, Jerry. The Truth is Beyond Belief: Some Thoughts to Make You Think about the Power of Your Thoughts. Thomas, Jean, ed. LC 99-96089. 224p. 2000. 12.95 (*0-9674954-1-5*) Peppertree Pub.**
With this deeply insightful book, "The Truth is Beyond Belief", the author "re-minds" you of the powerful role your ordinary thoughts & beliefs continually play in the way you experience this truly extraordinary life. He focuses you on how your thoughts about another person, the world or God mean nothing & everything. They mean nothing because they so often have nothing to do with how the other actually is. And they mean everything because they have everything to do with how you will see & experience them. With a single contemplative thought on each page, you are reminded how your thoughts often do more to separate you from the perfection of yourself, other people, the world & God, than they do to connect you. Each idea has been carefully formed to help you reflect on & then move beyond the illusory thoughts of the mind in order to see the perfection of The Truth that really is Beyond Belief! Peppertree Publications, c/o BookMasters, Inc. 1-800-247-6553. *Publisher Paid Annotation.*

Durr, Kay. Ancient Egyptian Names for Dogs. LC 96-11498. (Illus.). 144p. (Orig.). 1996. pap. 11.95 (*0-931866-91-X*) Alpine Pubns.

Durr, Michael & Walker, Dwayne. Micro-to-Mainframe: Creating an Integrated Environment. write for info. (*0-318-59577-X*) Addison-Wesley.

***Durr, Robert.** Down in Bristol Bay: High Tides, Hangovers & Harrowing Experiences on Alaska's Last Frontier. LC 99-21748. (Illus.). 240p. 1999. text 23.95 (*0-312-20529-5*) St Martin.

Durr, Ruth E. A Shelter from Compassion. LC 56-6375. (Orig.). 1956. pap. 4.00 (*0-87574-087-1*) Pendle Hill.

Durr, Volker, et al, eds. Imperial Germany. LC 84-40571. (Monatshefte Occasional Volumes Ser.: Vol. 3). (Illus.). 205p. reprint ed. pap. 63.60 (*0-608-20426-9*, 207167900002) Bks Demand.

— Nietzsche: Literature & Values. LC 87-40145. (Monatshefte Occasional Volumes Ser.: Vol. 6). 229p. 1988. reprint ed. pap. 71.00 (*0-608-07440-3*, 206766700009) Bks Demand.

Durra, Joseph, jt. auth. see Liu, Victoria.

Durra, Joseph B., jt. auth. see Liu, Victoria.

Durran, C. P. Dublin Decorative Plasterwork. 1967. 35.00 (*0-693-01112-2*) Transatl Arts.

Durran, D. R. Numerical Methods for Geophysical Fluid Dynamics. Marsden, J. E. & Sirov, L., eds. LC 98-24739. (Applied Mathematical Sciences Ser.). 460p. 1998. 49.95 (*0-387-98376-7*) Spr-Verlag.

Durran, Osman, et al, eds. The New Germany: Literature & Society after Unification. 1995. 35.00 (*1-85075-560-4*, Pub. by Sheffield Acad) CUP Services.

Durrance, Dick. Dick Durrance "The Man on the Medal" The Life & Times of America's First Great Ski Racer. Jerome, John, ed. LC 95-92551. (Illus.). 192p. 1995. 39.50 (*0-9648473-0-2*) D Durrance.

***Durrance, Dick.** Golfers. (Illus.). 160p. 2000. 27.95 (*0-7407-1096-6*) Andrews & McMeel.

Durrance, Eric M. Radioactivity in Geology: Principles & Applications. (Geology Ser.). 1987. text 69.95 (*0-470-20389-7*) P-H.

Durrance, Joan. Armed for Action: Library Response to Citizen Information Needs. LC 83-15400. 190p. 1984. 45.00 (*0-918212-71-5*) Neal-Schuman.

— Meeting Community Needs with Job & Career Services: A How-to-Do-It Manual. LC 94-16462. (How-to-Do-It Manuals for Libraries Ser.: No. 42). 252p. 1994. 49.95 (*1-55570-177-9*) Neal-Schuman.

Durrani, A. M. Prostate Cancer Detection & Cure. Billac, Pete, ed. LC 97-66581. (Illus.). 120p. (Orig.). 1997. pap. 9.95 (*0-943629-30-6*) Swan Pub.

— The Truth about Vasectomy & Reversal. Billac, Pete, ed. LC 97-65578. (Illus.). 96p. (Orig.). 1997. pap. 9.95 (*0-943629-29-2*) Swan Pub.

Durrani, Osman. Fictions of Germany: Images of the German Nation in the Modern Novel. 240p. 1994. 50.00 (*0-7486-0491-X*, Pub. by Edinburgh U Pr) Col U Pr.

Durrani, Tariq S., et al, eds. Applications of Transputers Three. (Transputer & Occam Engineering Ser.). 900p. (gr. 12). 1991. 145.00 (*90-5199-064-2*, Pub. by IOS Pr) IOS Press.

Durrant, Amanda. My Book of Gymnastics. LC 93-24978. (Illus.). 32p. (J). (gr. k-4). 1993. lib. bdg. 21.40 (*1-56847-125-4*) Raintree Steck-V.

Durrant, C. J. The Atmosphere of the Sun. (Illus.). 184p. 1988. 74.00 (*0-85274-375-0*) IOP Pub.

Durrant, Christopher J., jt. ed. see Bruzek, Anton.

Durrant, Colin & Welch, Graham. Making Sense of Music: Foundations for Music Education. (Cassell Education Ser.). (Illus.). 192p. 1995. 80.00 (*0-304-33084-1*); pap. 29.95 (*0-304-33082-5*) Continuum.

Durrant, George D. Don't Forget the Star. 1982. pap. 5.95 (*0-88494-467-0*) Bookcraft Inc.

— Look at the Sky. 1994. 10.95 (*0-88494-925-7*) Bookcraft Inc.

— Love at Home - Starring Grandpa. LC 95-81232. 1995. pap. 7.95 (*1-57008-197-2*) Bookcraft Inc.

— True to the Faith. 1998. 14.95 (*1-57008-469-6*) Bookcraft Inc.

Durrant, Jennifer & Hoole, John, texts. Durrant, Jennifer: Recent Paintings. (Illus.). 1980. pap. 21.00 (*0-905836-19-7*, Pub. by Museum Modern Art) St Mut.

Durrant, John D. & Lovrinic, Jean H. Bases of Hearing Sciences. 3rd ed. 304p. 1995. text 42.00 (*0-683-02737-9*) Lppncott W & W.

Durrant, Jolene. Never Never Never Will She Stop Loving You. LC 98-91376. (Illus.). 32p. (J). (gr. 3 up). 1998. pap. 9.95 (*0-9663567-5-6*) JoBiz.

***Durrant, Jolene.** Never Never Never Will She Stop Loving You: The Adoption Love Story of Angel Annie. rev. ed. LC 99-72088. (Illus.). 40p. (YA). (gr. k up). 1999. pap. 6.95 (*0-9663567-9-9*) JoBiz.

Durrant, Lindsey. Paint Effects. 1999. pap. 11.95 (*0-85532-875-4*) Srch Pr.

Durrant, Lynda. The Beaded Moccasins. LC 97-16288. 185p. (gr. 5-8). 1998. 15.00 (*0-395-85398-2*, Clarion Bks) HM.

***Durrant, Lynda.** Beaded Moccasins: The Story of Mary Campbell. (Illus.). (J). 2000. pap. 4.50 (*0-440-41591-8*, Yearling) BDD Bks Young Read.

— Betsy Zane, the Rose of Fort Henry. (Illus.). 176p. (J). (gr. 4-7). 2000. 15.00 (*0-395-97899-8*, Clarion Bks) HM.

Durrant, Lynda. Echohawk. 192p. (gr. 5-9). 1998. pap. 4.50 (*0-440-41438-5*) BDD Bks Young Read.

— Echohawk. LC 96-2113. 192p. (J). (gr. 5-9). 1996. 14.95 (*0-395-74430-X*, Clarion Bks) HM.

— Turtle Clan Journey. LC 98-22710. 176p. (YA). (gr. 5-9). 1999. 15.00 (*0-395-90369-6*, Clarion Bks) HM.

Durrant, Michael. Creative Strategies for School Problems: Solutions for Psychologists & Teachers. 192p. (C). 1995. 23.00 (*0-393-70190-5*) Norton.

— Residential Treatment: A Cooperative, Competency-Based Approach to Therapy & Program Design. 240p. (C). 1993. 27.95 (*0-393-70154-9*) Norton.

Durrant, Samuel W. & Peirce, Henry B. History of Saint Lawrence County, New York 1749-1878. LC 84-103114. (Illus.). 914p. 1983. reprint ed. 50.00 (*0-932334-52-0*, NY45006) Hrt of the Lakes.

Durrant, Stephen, jt. auth. see Earl, James W.

Durrant, Stephen, jt. auth. see Shankman, Steven.

Durrant, Stephen D. Mammals of Utah: Taxonomy & Distribution. (Museum Ser.: Vol. 6). 549p. 1952. 15.00 (*0-686-80278-0*) U KS Nat Hist Mus.

— The Pocket Gophers (Genus Thomomys) of Utah. (Museum Ser.: Vol. 1, No. 1). 82p. 1946. pap. 4.25 (*0-686-80277-2*) U KS Nat Hist Mus.

Durrant, Stephen W. The Cloudy Mirror: Tension & Conflict in the Writings of Sima Qian. LC 94-43357. (Series in Chinese Philosophy & Culture). 226p. (C). 1995. pap. text 16.95 (*0-7914-2656-4*) State U NY Pr.

— The Cloudy Mirror: Tension & Conflict in the Writings of Sima Qian. LC 94-43357. (SUNY Series in Chinese Philosophy & Culture). 226p. (C). 1995. text 49.50 (*0-7914-2655-6*) State U NY Pr.

Durrant-Whyte, Hugh F. Integration, Coordination & Control of Multi-Sensor Robot Systems. (C). 1987. text 95.50 (*0-89838-247-5*) Kluwer Academic.

Durrbach, Felix. Choix d'Inscriptions de Delos. (Subsidia Epigraphica Ser.: Vol. VI). (GER.). iii, 294p. 1976. reprint ed. write for info. incl. 3.5 hd (*3-487-05998-3*) G Olms Pubs.

Durrbach, Felix, ed. Choix d'inscriptions de Delos. xii, 288p. 1977. 30.00 (*0-89005-190-9*) Ares.

Durrel, Bryant. Trinity Field Report: Psi Laws. (Trinity Ser.). (Illus.). 24p. 1999. pap. 4.95 (*1-56504-769-9*, 9203) White Wolf.

Durrell, Ann, ed. The Diane Goode Book of American Folk Tales & Songs. (Illus.). 64p. (J). (ps-3). 1999. pap. 5.99 (*0-14-038252-6*, PuffinBks) Peng Put Young Read.

Durrell, Bryant. Noblesse Oblige: The Book of Houses. (Changeling: The Dreaming Ser.). 1998. pap. text 18.00 (*1-56504-719-2*) White Wolf.

Durrell, Bryant, et al. Trinity Player's Guide. (Trinity Ser.). (Illus.). 224p. 1999. pap. 22.95 (*1-56504-768-0*, 9010) White Wolf.

Durrell, Cordell. Geologic History of Feather River Country, California. 1988. pap. 25.00 (*0-520-05691-4*, Pub. by U CA Pr) Cal Prin Full Svc.

Durrell, Dennis, jt. illus. see Gonzalez, Ric.

Durrell, Gerald. The Ark's Anniversary. large type ed. (Windsor Ser.). 216p. 1992. 23.95 (*0-86220-495-X*, G K Hall Lrg Type) Mac Lib Ref.

— The Aye-Aye & I. (Illus.). 256p. 1993. 22.45 (*1-55970-204-4*, Pub. by Arcade Pub Inc) Time Warner.

— The Battle for Castle Cockatrice. LC 98-31428. 208p. (YA). (gr. 5-9). 1999. pap. 4.95 (*0-06-440780-2*) HarpC Child Bks.

— Catch Me a Colobus. large type ed. 1978. 27.99 (*0-7089-0094-1*) Ulverscroft.

— The Fantastic Dinosaur Adventure. LC 89-49099. (Illus.). 96p. (J). (gr. 2-5). 1990. pap. 16.95 (*0-671-70871-6*) S&S Trade.

— Golden Bats & Pink Pigeons. large type ed. 1980. 12.00 (*0-7089-0415-7*) Ulverscroft.

— The Keeper. (Illus.). 32p. (J). 1991. pap. write for info. (*1-85479-087-0*, Pub. by M OMara) Trafalgar.

— Marrying off Mother: And Other Stories. 208p. 1993. reprint ed. pap. 10.45 (*1-55970-213-3*, Pub. by Arcade Pub Inc) Time Warner.

— The Mockery Bird. large type ed. 1983. 15.95 (*0-7089-0901-9*) Ulverscroft.

— My Family & Other Animals. 1983. 22.50 (*0-8446-6073-6*) Peter Smith.

— My Family & Other Animals. 1959. pap. 12.99 (*0-14-001399-7*, Penguin Bks) Viking Penguin.

***Durrell, Gerald.** My Family & Other Animals. LC 99-46458. (Penguin Nature Classics Ser.). 288p. (J). 2000. pap. 12.95 (*0-14-028902-X*, Penguin Bks) Viking Penguin.

— The Overloaded Ark. (Illus.). 238p. 1987. pap. 14.95 (*0-571-05371-8*) Faber & Faber.

Durrell, Gerald. The Talking Parcel. LC 74-23367. (Illus.). (J). (gr. 4-7). 1975. 12.95 (*0-397-31608-9*) HarpC Child Bks.

— Toby the Tortoise. (Illus.). 32p. (J). 1992. pap. write for info. (*1-85479-069-2*, Pub. by M OMara) Trafalgar.

— Two in the Bush. large type ed. 1980. 12.00 (*0-7089-0516-1*) Ulverscroft.

— The Whispering Land. (Illus.). 224p. 1975. pap. 7.95 (*0-14-002083-7*, Penguin Bks) Viking Penguin.

— The Whispering Land. large type ed. 334p. 1980. 27.99 (*0-7089-0474-2*) Ulverscroft.

— A Zoo in My Luggage. 192p. 1976. pap. 8.95 (*0-14-002084-5*, Penguin Bks) Viking Penguin.

Durrell, Harold C. Durell Family: Descendants of Peter of Newton, Mass. & Moses of Gloucester, Mass. (Illus.). 48p. 1997. reprint ed. pap. 9.50 (*0-8328-8384-0*); reprint ed. lib. bdg. 19.50 (*0-8328-8383-2*) Higginson Bk Co.

— Durell Genealogy: Descendants of Philip. (Illus.). 204p. 1997. reprint ed. pap. 31.00 (*0-8328-8388-3*); reprint ed. lib. bdg. 41.00 (*0-8328-8387-5*) Higginson Bk Co.

Durrell, Julie. Here Comes Peter Cottontail. LC 98-164856. (J). 1998. 6.95 (*0-694-01156-8*) HarpC Child Bks.

Durrell, Julie. The Pudgy Book of Farm Animals. (Pudgy Board Bks.). 18p. (J). (ps). 1984. bds. 3.99 (*0-448-10211-0*, G & D) Peng Put Young Read.

Durrell, Julie, jt. illus. see McNulty, Faith.

Durrell, Lawrence. Acte: A Play. (Illus.). 76p. 1966. 16.95 (*0-910278-27-X*) Boulevard.

— The Alexandria Quartet, 4 vols. 1991. reprint ed. pap. 51.80 (*0-14-015317-9*, Penguin Bks) Viking Penguin.

— Antrobus Complete. LC 85-6995. (Illus.). 202p. 1990. pap. 14.95 (*0-571-13603-6*) Faber & Faber.

— Balthazar. large type ed. LC 99-16630. 1999. pap. 26.95 (*0-7838-8718-3*) Mac Lib Ref.

— Balthazar. 1991. reprint ed. pap. 12.95 (*0-14-015321-7*, Penguin Bks) Viking Penguin.

— Bitter Lemons. 1976. 22.95 (*0-8488-0480-5*) Amereon Ltd.

— Bitter Lemons. 256p. 1996. pap. 10.95 (*1-56924-839-7*) Marlowe & Co.

***Durrell, Lawrence.** Clea. large type ed. (G. K. Hall Perennial Bestsellers Ser.). 2000. 25.95 (*0-7838-8975-5*, G K Hall Lrg Type) Mac Lib Ref.

Durrell, Lawrence. Clea. 1991. reprint ed. pap. 12.95 (*0-14-015322-5*, Penguin Bks) Viking Penguin.

— Esprit de Corps: Sketches from Diplomatic Life. (Illus.). 90p. 1981. pap. 9.95 (*0-571-05667-9*) Faber & Faber.

— Justine. 272p. Date not set. 22.95 (*0-8488-2255-2*) Amereon Ltd.

— Justine. LC 99-23231. 1999. 25.95 (*0-7838-8644-6*) Macmillan Gen Ref.

— Justine. 1991. reprint ed. pap. 12.95 (*0-14-015319-5*, Penguin Bks) Viking Penguin.

D

— Lawrence Durrell: Conversations. Ingersoll, Earl G., ed. LC 97-25070. 264p. 1998. 41.50 (*0-8386-3723-X*) Fairleigh Dickinson.

— Monsieur Ou le Prince des Tenebres. (FRE.). 338p. 1976. pap. 29.95 (*0-7859-2193-1*, 207029515X) Fr & Eur.

***Durrell, Lawrence.** Mountolive. large type ed. LC 99-47952. 2000. 25.95 (*0-7838-8820-1*, G K Hall & Co) Mac Lib Ref.

Durrell, Lawrence. Mountolive. 1991. reprint ed. pap. 12.95 (*0-14-015320-9*, Penguin Bks) Viking Penguin.

— Nunquam. (FRE.). 448p. 1980. pap. 11.95 (*0-7859-1910-4*, 2070371719) Fr & Eur.

***Durrell, Lawrence.** Nunquam. 1999. per. 119.85 (*0-671-78072-7*, Pocket Books) PB.

Durrell, Lawrence. Pope Joan. Royidis, Emmanuel, tr. from GRE. & adapted by by. LC 82-81088. 176p. 1984. 22.50 (*0-87951-963-0*, Pub. by Overlook Pr) Penguin Putnam.

— Pope Joan. LC 84-7116. 160p. 1997. reprint ed. pap. 13.95 (*0-87951-786-7*, Pub. by Overlook Pr) Penguin Putnam.

— Prospero's Cell: A Guide to the Landscape & Manners of the Island of Corfu. LC 96-24352. 150p. 1996. pap. 10.95 (*1-56924-766-8*) Marlowe & Co.

— Provence. 192p. 1994. pap. 11.45 (*1-55970-247-8*, Pub. by Arcade Pub Inc) Time Warner.

— Reflections on a Marine Venus: A Companion to the Landscape of Rhodes. LC 96-76839. 200p. 1996. pap. 10.95 (*1-56924-791-9*) Marlowe & Co.

— Sicilian Carousel. 1997. pap. text 12.95 (*1-56924-783-8*) Marlowe & Co.

— Spirit of Place. Thomas, Alan G., ed. (Illus.). 432p. 1997. pap. text 13.95 (*1-56924-722-6*) Marlowe & Co.

— The Spirit of Place: Letters & Essays on Travel. Thomas, Alan G., ed. 432p. 1984. pap. 8.95 (*0-918172-17-9*) Leetes Isl.

— Tunc. (FRE.). 1979. pap. 11.95 (*0-7859-1896-5*, 2070371220) Fr & Eur.

— White Eagles over Serbia. LC 95-17743. 200p. 1995. 19.45 (*1-55970-312-1*, Pub. by Arcade Pub Inc) Time Warner.

Durrell, Lawrence. White Eagles over Serbia. LC 58-7779. 1957. 26.95 (*0-87599-030-4*) S G Phillips.

Durrell, Lawrence & Miller, Henry. The Durrell Miller Letters 1935-80. MacNiven, Ian S., ed. LC 88-9847. (Illus.). 528p. 1988. 26.95 (*0-8112-1043-X*, Pub. by New Directions) Norton.

Durrell, Lawrence, ed. see Lawrence, D. H.

Durrell, Lawrence, ed. see Miller, Henry.

Durrell, Margaret. Whatever Happened to Margo? (Illus.). 226p. 1996. 29.95 (*0-233-98917-X*, Pub. by Andre Deutsch) Trafalgar.

Durrell, Martin. Hammer's German Grammar & Usage. 3rd ed. (Illus.). 544p. 1997. pap. 29.95 (*0-8442-2208-9*) NTC Contemp Pub Co.

— Practicing German Grammar: A Workbook. 2nd ed. (GER & ENG., Illus.). 256p. 1997. pap., wbk. ed. 15.95 (*0-8442-2209-7*, 22097) NTC Contemp Pub Co.

— Using German: A Guide to Contemporary Usage. 288p. (C). 1992. pap. 24.95 (*0-521-31556-5*); text 69.95 (*0-521-42077-6*) Cambridge U Pr.

***Durrell, Martin.** Using German Synonyms. LC 99-56319. 346p. (C). 2000. 64.95 (*0-521-46552-4*); pap. 22.95 (*0-521-46954-6*) Cambridge U Pr.

Durrell, Martin, et al. Hammer's German Grammar & Usage: Exercises. 192p. 1993. pap. 14.95 (*0-340-58336-3*, B0094, Pub. by E A) Routldge.

Durrenberger, Dorothy, jt. auth. see Durrenberger, E. Paul.

Durrenberger, Dorothy, jt. tr. see Durrenberger, Paul.

Durrenberger, E. Paul. Gulf Coast Soundings: People & Policy in the Mississippi Shrimp Industry. LC 95-49243. (Rural America Ser.). 184p. (C). 1996. 29.95 (*0-7006-0759-5*); pap. 17.95 (*0-7006-0760-9*) U Pr of KS.

— Icelandic Essays: Explorations in the Anthropology of Modern Life. 1994. pap. 12.95 (*0-945213-17-4*) Rudi Pub.

— It's All Politics: South Alabama's Seafood Industry. 240p. (C). 1992. text 34.95 (*0-252-01910-5*) U of Ill Pr.

— Lisu Religion. (Occasional Papers: Vol. 13). 44p. 1989. pap. 9.95 (*1-877979-13-9*) SE Asia.

Durrenberger, E. Paul, ed. State Power & Culture in Thailand. LC 95-61260. (Southeast Asia Studies: Vol. 44). 216p. 1996. pap. 20.00 (*0-938692-60-7*); lib. bdg. 32.00 (*0-938692-59-3*) Yale U SE Asia.

Durrenberger, E. Paul & Durrenberger, Dorothy. The Saga of Gunnlaugur Snake's Tongue: With an Essay on the Structure & Translation of the Saga. LC 91-50425. 128p. 1992. 26.50 (*0-8386-3465-6*) Fairleigh Dickinson.

Durrenberger, E. Paul & Palsson, Gisli, eds. The Anthropology of Iceland. LC 89-4657. (Illus.). 286p. 1989. pap. text 15.95 (*0-87745-499-X*) U of Iowa Pr.

Durrenberger, E. Paul, jt. ed. see Palsson, Gisli.

Durrenberger, E. Paul, jt. ed. see Thu, Kendall M.

Durrenberger, Paul & Durrenberger, Dorothy, trs. The Saga of Havardur of Isafjord. (Icelandic Saga Studies). 104p. 1996. 22.95 (*1-874312-19-2*, Pub. by Hisarlik Pr) Intl Spec Bk.

Durrenberger, Paul & Tannenbaum, Nicola. Analytical Perspectives on Shan Agriculture & Village Economics. (Monographs: No. 37). 112p. 1990. 25.00 (*0-938692-45-3*); pap. 15.00 (*0-685-57339-7*) Yale U SE Asia.

Durrenmatt. Die Physiker. (GER.). (C). Date not set. 11.95 (*0-8442-2946-6*, X2946-6) NTC Contemp Pub Co.

— Der Richter und Sein Henker. (GER.). (C). 1978. 9.95 (*0-8442-2750-1*, X2750-1) NTC Contemp Pub Co.

— Der Verdacht. (GER.). (C). 1987. 9.95 (*0-8442-2861-3*, X2861-3) NTC Contemp Pub Co.

Durrenmatt, Friedrich. Der Besuch der Alten Dame, 001. Ackermann, Paul K., ed. LC 60-3863. (GER.). (YA). (gr. 11-12). 1960. pap. 28.76 (*0-395-04089-2*) HM.

— Conversation at Night with a Despised Character: A Curriculum for Our Times. MacDonald, Robert D., tr. 23p. (C). 1947. pap. 3.50 (*0-87129-790-6*, C32) Dramatic Pub.

Durrenmatt, Friedrich. Drei Horspiele. Regensteiner, Henry, ed. LC 79-22768. (GER.). 1980. pap. text 9.95 (*0-8290-0116-6*) Irvington.

— Episode on an Autumn Evening. Karminski, Gabriel, tr. 1959. 3.50 (*0-87129-445-1*, E16) Dramatic Pub.

***Durrenmatt, Friedrich.** Judge & His Hangman. 2000. pap. 10.00 (*0-226-17438-7*) U Ch Pr.

Durrenmatt, Friedrich. The Physicists. Kirkup, James, tr. from GER. LC 91-20775. 96p. 1964. pap. 10.00 (*0-8021-5088-8*, Grove) Grove-Atltic.

— Die Physiker. Helbling, Robert E., ed. (GER., Illus.). 188p. (Orig.). 1965. text 18.95 (*0-19-500908-8*) OUP.

— Plays & Essays. Sander, Volkmar, ed. LC 56-12398. (German Library: Vol. 89). 316p. 1982. 39.50 (*0-8264-0257-7*); pap. 19.95 (*0-8264-0267-4*) Continuum.

***Durrenmatt, Friedrich.** The Promise. 2000. pap. 10.00 (*0-226-17440-9*) U Ch Pr.

— Der Richter und Sein Henker. 001. Gillis, William & Neumaier, J. J., eds. (C). 1972. pap. 28.76 (*0-395-04499-5*) HM.

Durrenmatt, Friedrich. Romulus. adapted ed. 1963. pap. 5.25 (*0-8222-0961-6*) Dramatists Play.

***Durrenmatt, Friedrich.** Selected Writings, Vol. 1. 1999. 30.00 (*0-226-17426-3*) U Ch Pr.

— Selected Writings, Vol. 2. 1999. 30.00 (*0-226-17429-8*) U Ch Pr.

— Selected Writings, Vol. 3. 1999. 30.00 (*0-226-17432-8*) U Ch Pr.

— Suspicion. 2000. pap. 10.00 (*0-226-17436-0*) U Ch Pr.

Durrenmatt, Friedrich. The Visit. Bowles, Patrick, tr. from GER. LC 62-16341. 112p. 1987. pap. 10.00 (*0-8021-3066-6*, Grove) Grove-Atltic.

Durrenmatt, Friedrich & Selz, Peter H. Varlin, 1900 - 1977: Paintings. Ross, Felice & Levitt, Mimi, trs. LC 85-63886. (Illus.). 56p. (Orig.). 1986. pap. 12.00 (*0-936827-01-7*) C Bernard Gallery Ltd.

Durrett. Essentials of Probability. 1994. 14.50 (*0-534-19231-9*) Brooks-Cole.

— Probability: Theory & Examples. 2nd ed. 1995. 36.50 (*0-534-24319-3*) Brooks-Cole.

Durrett, Charles R., jt. auth. see McCamant, Kathryn M.

***Durrett, Deanne.** The Abortion Conflict: A Pro/Con Issue. LC 98-33213. (Hot Pro/Con Issues Ser.). (Illus.). 64p. (YA). (gr. 6 up). 2000. lib. bdg. 19.95 (*0-7660-1193-3*) Enslow Pubs.

— Dominique Moceanu. LC 98-17195. (People in the News Ser.). (Illus.). 144p. (J). (gr. 4-12). 1999. lib. bdg. 23.70 (*1-56006-099-9*) Lucent Bks.

Durrett, Deanne. Healers. annot. ed. LC 96-23072. (American Indian Lives Ser.). (Illus.). 144p. (J). (gr. 5-12). 1996. 19.95 (*0-8160-3406-0*) Facts on File.

***Durrett, Deanne.** Teen Privacy Rights: Hot Issues. LC 00-8413. 2000. write for info. (*0-7660-1374-X*) Enslow Pubs.

Durrett, Deanne. Unsung Heroes of World War II: The Story of the Navajo Code Talkers. LC 97-50083. (Library of American Indian History). (Illus.). 122p. (YA). (gr. 6 up). 1998. 19.95 (*0-8160-3603-9*) Facts on File.

Durrett, Deanne & Kallen, Stuart A. Native American Chiefs & Warriors. LC 99-13227. (History Makers Ser.). (Illus.). 112p. (YA). (gr. 4 up). 1999. lib. bdg. 17.96 (*1-56006-364-5*) Lucent Bks.

Durrett, H. John, ed. Color & the Computer. LC 86-17344. (Illus.). 299p. 1987. text 108.00 (*0-12-225210-1*) Acad Pr.

Durrett, John C., jt. ed. see Culp, Robert D.

Durrett, R. Essentials of Stochastic Processes. Casella, G. et al, eds. LC 99-14733. (Texts in Statistics Ser.). 304p. 1999. 69.95 (*0-387-98836-X*) Spr-Verlag.

Durrett, R. & Bramson, M., eds. Perplexing Problems in Probability: Festschrift in Honor of Harry Kesten. LC 99-14285. (Progress in Probability Ser.: Vol. 44). (Illus.). 432p. 1999. 79.95 (*0-8176-4093-2*) Birkhauser.

Durrett, R. & Kesten, Harry, eds. Random Walks, Brownian Motion & Interacting Particle Systems. (Progress in Probability Ser.: Vol. 28). xii, 472p. 1991. 80.50 (*0-8176-3509-2*) Birkhauser.

Durrett, R. & Pinsky, M. Geometry of Random Motion. LC 88-13964. (Contemporary Mathematics Ser.: No. 73). 337p. 1988. pap. 41.00 (*0-8218-5081-4*, CONM/73) Am Math.

Durrett, Reuben T. John Filson: The First Historian of Kentucky. (Notable American Authors Ser.). 1992. reprint ed. lib. bdg. 90.00 (*0-7812-2725-9*) Rprt Serv.

— Traditions of the Earliest Visits of Foreigners to North America. (Notable American Authors Ser.). 1992. reprint ed. lib. bdg. 75.00 (*0-7812-2726-7*) Rprt Serv.

Durrett, Richard. The Essentials of Probability. 269p. 1993. pap. 64.95 (*0-534-19230-0*) Wadsworth Pub.

— Stochastic Calculus: A Practical Introduction. LC 96-24642. (Probability & Stochastics Ser.). 352p. 1996. boxed set 84.95 (*0-8493-8071-5*, QA274) CRC Pr.

Durrett, Richard, ed. Particle Systems, Random Media & Large Deviations. LC 85-6181. (Contemporary Mathematics Ser.: Vol. 41). 380p. 1985. reprint ed. pap. 44.00 (*0-8218-5042-3*, CONM/41C) Am Math.

Durrett, Richard A. Probability: Theory & Example. LC 90-37802. 453p. (C). 1991. text 55.75 (*0-534-13206-5*) Wadsworth Pub.

— Probability: Theory & Example. 2nd ed. LC 90-37802. (C). 1995. pap. 110.95 (*0-534-24318-5*) Wadsworth Pub.

Durrie, D. S. Bibliographic Genealogica Americana. 1972. 59.95 (*0-87968-733-9*) Gordon Pr.

— A Genealogical History of the Holt Family in the United States: More Particularly the Descendants of Nicholas Holt of Newbury & Andover, Mass., 1634-1644 & of William Holt of Newhaven, Conn. 367p. reprint ed. pap. 47.50 (*0-8328-0674-9*); reprint ed. lib. bdg. 57.50 (*0-8328-0673-0*) Higginson Bk Co.

Durrill, Wayne K. War of Another Kind: A Southern Community in the Great Rebellion. (Illus.). 304p. 1994. pap. text 19.95 (*0-19-508923-5*) OUP.

Durron, Daskin R. Civil Rights: Index of Modern Information. rev. ed. LC 88-47546. 153p. 1994. 47.50 (*0-7883-0680-4*); pap. 44.50 (*0-7883-0681-2*) ABBE Pubs Assn.

***Durrschmidt, Jorg.** Everyday Lives in the Global City: The Delinking of Locale & Mileiu. LC 00-30821. 2000. write for info. (*1-84142-011-5*, Pub. by UCL Pr Ltd) Taylor & Francis.

Durrschmidt, Monika. Beitrage zur Kenntnis der Desmidiaceen des Banado Cruces, Provinz Valdivia, Chile. (Bibliotheca Phycologica Ser.: No. 73). (GER., Illus.). 138p. 1985. pap. text 48.00 (*3-7682-1430-3*) Lubrecht & Cramer.

Durrwell, Francois-Xavier. Mary: Icon of the Spirit & of the Church. 123p. (C). 1996. pap. 39.95 (*0-85439-364-1*, Pub. by St Paul Pubns) St Mut.

Durrwell, Francois Xavier. The Spirit of the Father & of the Son. 64p. (C). 1990. 39.00 (*0-85439-321-8*, Pub. by St Paul Pubns) St Mut.

***Durschmied, Erik.** The Hinge Factor. LC 99-89506. 416p. 2000. 25.95 (*1-55970-515-9*, Pub. by Arcade Pub Inc) Time Warner.

Durschmied, Erik. Shooting Wars. 3.99 (*5-553-40843-1*) World Pr Ltd.

Dursht, K., ed. see Girlirz, A.

Durslag, Mel, jt. auth. see Linn, Ed.

Durso, Asunta, jt. auth. see Langston, Melissa.

Durso, D., jt. ed. see Silk, E.

Durso, Francis T. & Nickerson, Raymond S. Handbook of Applied Cognition. LC 98-47298. 904p. 1999. 108.95 (*0-471-97765-9*) Wiley.

Durso, Joe, jt. auth. see Block, Mervin.

Durso, Joe, jt. auth. see Hall, Monty.

Durso, Joseph M. & Burgess-Durso, Lori. Better Golf Through Better Practice. 130p. 1993. lib. bdg. 14.95 (*0-9633760-0-4*) Intl Acad Golf.

Durst. Organic Chemistry. 2nd ed. 1987. teacher ed. 23.12 (*0-07-018399-6*) McGraw.

Durst, ed. Introduction to Corporate Finance. (C). 1989. pap. text, student ed. 21.00 (*0-673-38347-4*) Addson-Wesley Educ.

Durst, et al. Modern New York Discovery, Vol. 1. LC 82-84231. 1989. 115.00 (*0-317-00659-2*) West Group.

— Modern New York Discovery, Vol. 1. 1993. suppl. ed. 65.00 (*0-317-03233-X*) West Group.

Durst-Andersen, Per. Mental Grammar Russian Aspect & Related Issues. (Illus.). 268p. (Orig.). 1992. pap. 18.95 (*0-89357-229-2*) Slavica.

Durst, Carol. I Knew You Were Coming So I Baked a Cake: More Than 130 Delicious Delectable Desserts. LC 97-23889. (Illus.). 256p. 1997. 24.50 (*0-684-81490-0*) Simon & Schuster.

Durst, Charles E. Noise Reduction. 2nd ed. (ABC Pocket Guide for the Field Ser.). (Illus.). 40p. (C). 1985. pap. text 7.95 (*1-56016-025-X*) ABC TeleTraining.

Durst, F., et al, eds. Developments in Laser Techniques & Applications to Fluid Mechanics: Proceedings of the 7th International Symposium, Lisbon, Portugal, 11-14 July, 1994. LC 95-45828. 486p. 1995. 199.00 (*3-540-60236-4*) Spr-Verlag.

— Turbulent Shear Flows 8: Selected Papers from the Eighth International Symposium on Turbulent Shear Flows, Munich, FRG, September 9-11, 1991. LC 92-32190. 1992. 48.95 (*0-387-55740-7*) Spr-Verlag.

— Turbulent Shear Flows 5. (Illus.). 380p. 1987. 168.95 (*0-387-16885-0*) Spr-Verlag.

— Turbulent Shear Flows 9. 490p. 1995. 157.95 (*0-387-57704-1*) Spr-Verlag.

— Turbulent Shear Flows 1: Proceedings of the First International Symposium, Pennsylvania State University, University Park, Pennsylvania, April 18-20, 1977. (Illus.). 1979. 72.95 (*0-387-09041-X*) Spr-Verlag.

— Turbulent Shear Flows 7: Selected Papers from the Seventh International Symposium on Turbulent Shear Flows, Stanford University, U. S. A., August 21-23, 1989. (Illus.). 352p. 1991. 163.95 (*0-387-53177-7*) Spr-Verlag.

Durst, F., et al. Principles & Practice of Laser-Doppler Anemometry. 2nd ed. 1981. text 177.00 (*0-12-225260-8*) Acad Pr.

— Two-Phase Momentum, Heat & Mass Transfer in Chemical, Process & Energy Engineering Systems. 1979. text 92.00 (*0-07-079166-X*) McGraw.

Durst, G. Michael. Management by Responsibility. (Illus.). 206p. 1987. pap. 24.00 (*0-9602552-1-4*) Train Sys.

— Napkin Notes: On the Art of Living. LC 79-50554. (Illus.). 230p. 1988. pap. 15.00 (*0-9602552-0-6*) Train Sys.

— Responsibility: The South African Imperative. (Illus.). 208p. (C). 1997. 24.00 (*0-620-21472-4*) Train Sys.

Durst, H. Dupont & Gokel, George W. Experimental Organic Chemistry. 2nd ed. 672p. (C). 1986. text 66.00 (*0-07-018398-8*) McGraw.

— Microscae Experiments in Organic Chemistry. text. write for info. (*0-07-018405-4*) McGraw.

Durst, John E., Jr. & Fuchsberg, Abraham. New York Courtroom Evidence. 2nd ed. 400p. 1993. spiral bd. 120.00 (*0-250-40706-X*, MICHIE) LEXIS Pub.

Durst, John E., Jr., jt. auth. see Fuchsberg, Abraham.

Durst, Lorraine S. United States Numismatic Auction Catalogs: A Bibliography. lib. bdg. 25.00 (*0-915262-44-4*) S J Durst.

Durst, Lorraine S. & Durst, Sanford J. World Gold Coin Value Guide. LC 80-51832. 1981. pap. 9.00 (*0-915262-54-1*) S J Durst.

— World Silver Coin Value Guide. LC 80-51831. 1981. pap. 9.00 (*0-686-64441-7*); lib. bdg. 12.00 (*0-915262-46-0*) S J Durst.

Durst, Maribeth & Schaeffer, E. Marilyn. A Cultural Analysis of Student Life at a Liberal Arts College. 140p. 1992. lib. bdg. 69.95 (*0-7734-9634-3*) E Mellen.

Durst, Matthias. Die UVP in Parallelen und Konzentrierten Verfahren: Eine Untersuchung unter Besonderer Berucksichtigung Europarechtlicher Vorgaben Am Beispiel Immissionsschutzrechtlicher und gentechnischer Anlagen. (Europaische Hochschulschriften Ser.: Reihe 2, Vol. 2338). 285p. 1998. pap. 51.95 (*3-631-31817-0*) P Lang Pubng.

Durst, Mose. The Strategies of Love. LC 87-12389. 184p. 1987. lib. bdg. 79.95 (*0-88946-209-7*) E Mellen.

***Durst, Russel K. & National Council of Teachers of English Staff.** Collision Course: Conflict, Negotiation & Learning in College Composition. LC 99-12766. 208p. 1999. write for info. (*0-8141-0742-7*) NCTE.

Durst, Russel K., jt. ed. see Newell, George E.

Durst, S. Copyright Practice & Procedure. LC 83-71260. 1984. pap. 10.00 (*0-685-10798-1*); lib. bdg. 15.00 (*0-942666-22-4*) S J Durst.

Durst, S., ed. Private Bankers of U. S. - Canada. LC 88-73214. 1989. pap. 10.00 (*0-942666-59-3*) S J Durst.

Durst, S., ed. see Curtis, James.

Durst, Sanford J. Comprehensive Guide to American Colonial Coinage. LC 75-32796. (Illus.). 1998. pap. 25.00 (*0-915262-02-9*) S J Durst.

— Contemporary World Gold Coins: Comprehensive Catalog. (Illus.). 128p. 1975. 10.00 (*0-915262-01-0*) S J Durst.

— Investor-Collector Guidebook. LC 76-40813. (Illus.). 1977. lib. bdg. 20.00 (*0-915262-07-X*) S J Durst.

Durst, Sanford J., ed. Early American Coppers Anthology. LC 76-62837. (Eleven Various Reference Bks.). (Illus.). 1977. reprint ed. lib. bdg. 85.00 (*0-915262-08-8*) S J Durst.

Durst, Sanford J., jt. auth. see Durst, Lorraine S.

Durst, Sanford J., jt. auth. see Reisman, Daniel.

Durst, Seymour, jt. auth. see Alpern, Andrew.

Durst, Shirley, ed. see Brown, Arlene.

Durst, Shirley J., ed. see Brown, Arlene.

Durst, Shirley J., ed. see Mammen, Lori.

Durst, Shirley J., ed. see Watson, Pat.

Durst, Sonda. Every Astrologer Has Been There, 2 vols., Vol. 2. LC 77-92772. 56p. 1977. 8.50 (*0-86690-182-5*, D1085-014) Am Fed Astrologers.

Durst, Steve. Aquarius Age, 2000: Starlife. (Illus.). 32p. 1999. pap. 20.00 (*0-9670903-0-X*) Aquarius Age.

Durst, Walter & Vogt, Werner. Bucket Wheel Excavator. 450p. 1988. text 130.00 (*0-87849-075-2*, Pub. by Trans T Pub) Enfield Pubs NH.

***Durstewitz, Jeff & Williams, Ruth.** Younger Than That Now: A Shared Passage from the Sixties. LC 99-53697. 352p. 2000. 23.95 (*0-553-10649-X*, Spectra) Bantam.

Durstin, Larry. Still Looking: A Novel Concerning Single Men. LC 90-70653. (Illus.). 249p. (Orig.). 1996. pap. 11.95 (*1-877978-14-0*, FLF Pr) FL Lit Foundation.

Durstine, J. Larry, ed. see American College of Sports Medicine Staff.

Durston, Christopher. Charles I. LC 97-43684. (Lancaster Pamphlets Ser.). 96p. (C). 1998. pap. 11.99 (*0-415-14340-3*) Routledge.

— James First. LC 92-44013. (Lancaster Pamphlets Ser.). 96p. (C). 1993. pap. 13.99 (*0-415-07779-6*, B2378) Routledge.

Durston, Christopher & Eales, Jacqueline, eds. Culture of English Puritanism, 1560-1700. LC 96-139776. 304p. 1996. text 49.95 (*0-312-15801-7*) St Martin.

Durston, Christopher, jt. auth. see Doran, Susan.

Durston, Diane. Kyoto: 7 Paths to the Heart of the City. (Illus.). 64p. (Orig.). (C). 1992. pap. 19.95 (*4-8381-0094-9*, Pub. by Mitsumura Suiko Shoin) Weatherhill.

— The Living Traditions of Old Kyoto. LC 94-15413. (Illus.). 112p. 1995. 28.00 (*4-7700-1870-3*) Kodansha.

— Old Kyoto: A Guide to Traditional Shops, Restaurants, & Inns. LC 85-45709. (Illus.). 240p. (Orig.). 1987. pap. 17.00 (*0-87011-757-2*) Kodansha.

***Durston, Linda M.** Keiko's Journey Home. LC 99-31963. 72p. (YA). (gr. 5-8). 2000. lib. bdg. 23.90 (*0-7613-1500-4*) Millbrook Pr.

Dursy, David D. Steps Toward Spiritual Growth: One-to-One Mentoring for Effective Spiritual Development, Vol. 1. 3rd rev. ed. Orig. Title: The Twelve Steps Toward Ministry. (Illus.). 84p. 1996. pap. 9.00 (*0-9656237-0-X*) Fnd of Hope.

Durth, Werner & Honold, Klaus, contrib. by. Rudiger Kramm: Buildings & Projects. (Illus.). 216p. 1999. 89.00 (*3-932565-03-7*, Pub. by Edition A Menges) Natl Bk Netwk.

Duru, G. Econometrics of Health Care. (C). 1991. lib. bdg. 191.50 (*0-7923-0766-6*) Kluwer Academic.

Duru, Mary S., jt. ed. see Perry, Gail.

Durucan, C. Continuing Education in British Universities. (C). 1986. 60.00 (*1-85041-005-4*, Pub. by Univ Nottingham) St Mut.

Durum, Scott K. & Muegge, Kathrin, eds. Cytokine Knockouts. LC 97-39690. (Contemporary Immunology Ser.: Vol. 1). (Illus.). 512p. 1997. 125.00 (*0-89603-368-6*) Humana.

Durusau, Patrick. High Places in Cyberspace: A Guide to Biblical & Religious Studies, Classics & Archaeological Resources on the Internet. 2nd ed. LC 98-45570. (Scholars Press Handbook Ser.). 400p. 1998. pap. 29.95 (*0-7885-0492-4*, 001511) Duke.

An Asterisk (*) at the beginning of an entry indicates that the title is appearing for the first time.

*DuRussel, Raymond H. The End of This System of Things. Hintz, Pat, ed. 264p. 2000. 20.00 (0-615-11317-6) R H DuRussel.

DuRussel, Raymond H. Relax, Your Life Is Predestined. LC 97-67281. 200p. (Orig.). 1997. pap. 12.95 (1-882792-43-2) Proctor Pubns.

Durvan Staff. Diccionario Durvan de la Lengua Espanola. (SPA.). 1312p. 1977. 69.95 (0-8288-5333-9, S11956) Fr & Eur.

— Diccionario Enciclopedico Durvan: Durvan Encyclopedic Dictionary, 12 vols., Set. (SPA.). 5632p. 1978. 995.00 (0-8288-5131-X, S12265) Fr & Eur.

— Diccionario Enciclopedico Ilustrado Deca90, 12 vols., Set. (SPA.). 1991. 1295.00 (0-7859-6258-1, 8476772211) Fr & Eur.

— Diccionario Enciclopedico Ilustrado Deca90, Vol. 1. (SPA., Illus.). 524p. 1991. 125.00 (0-7859-6490-8) Fr & Eur.

— Diccionario Enciclopedico Ilustrado Deca90, Vol. 3. (SPA.). 520p. 1991. 125.00 (0-7859-6260-3, 8476772246) Fr & Eur.

— Diccionario Enciclopedico Ilustrado Deca90, Vol. 4. (SPA.). 524p. 1991. 125.00 (0-7859-6261-1, 8476772254) Fr & Eur.

— Diccionario Enciclopedico Ilustrado Deca90, Vol. 6. (SPA.). 520p. 1991. 125.00 (0-7859-6263-8, 8476772270) Fr & Eur.

— Diccionario Enciclopedico Ilustrado Deca90, Vol. 7. (SPA.). 520p. 1991. 125.00 (0-7859-6264-6, 8476772289) Fr & Eur.

— Diccionario Enciclopedico Ilustrado Deca90, Vol. 8. (SPA.). 516p. 1991. 125.00 (0-7859-6265-4, 8476772297) Fr & Eur.

— Diccionario Enciclopedico Ilustrado Deca90, Vol. 9. (SPA.). 520p. 1991. 125.00 (0-7859-6266-2, 8476772300) Fr & Eur.

— Diccionario Enciclopedico Ilustrado Deca90, Vol. 10. (SPA.). 520p. 1991. 125.00 (0-7859-6267-0, 8476772319) Fr & Eur.

— Diccionario Enciclopedico Ilustrado Deca90, Vol. 11. (SPA.). 550p. 1991. 125.00 (0-7859-6268-9, 8476772327) Fr & Eur.

— Diccionario Enciclopedico Ilustrado Deca90, Vol. 12. 512p. 1991. 125.00 (0-7859-6269-7, 8476772335) Fr & Eur.

— Gran Enciclopedia del Mundo, 23 vols., Set. (SPA.). 12550p. 1977. 2250.00 (0-8288-5443-2, S12307) Fr & Eur.

Durward, Brian R., et al. Functional Human Movement: Measurement & Analysis. LC 99-17156. 256p. 1999. text 51.00 (0-7506-2607-0) Buttrwrth-Heinemann.

Durwell, Francoise-Xavier. Holy Spirit of God. 1992. pap. 19.95 (0-225-66453-4, 6348, Pub. by G Chapman) Morehouse Pub.

Durwood, Thomas A., et al. The History of the Civil War Series, 10 vols. (Illus.). 1600p. (YA). (gr. 5 up). 1990. pap. 79.50 (0-382-24044-8) Silver Burdett Pr.

Dury, Alan. Speak English Well: The Sounds of English. (C). 1988. text 80.00 (1-85122-062-3, Pub. by Domino Bks Ltd) St Mut.

Dury, G. H. Environmental Systems. LC 80-29151. (Orig.). 1981. 19.95 (0-435-08001-6); teacher ed. 6.00 (0-435-08002-4) Ashgate Pub Co.

— The Face of the Earth. 5th ed. (Illus.). 250p. (C). 1986. pap. text 16.95 (0-04-551130-6) Routledge.

Dury, John. The Reformed Librarie-Keeper with a Supplement to the Reformed-School, As Subordinate to Colleges in Universities. LC 92-24284. (Augustan Reprints Ser.: No. 220). 1983. reprint ed. 14.50 (0-404-70220-1, Z665) AMS Pr.

Duryea, E. D. University & College Governing Boards: From the Middle Ages to the Twentieth Century. Altbach, Philip, ed. (Garland Studies in Higher Education). 200p. 1997. text 30.00 (0-8153-2119-8) Garland.

*Duryea, E. D. & Williams, Donald T. Corporate Autonomy in Academe. LC 99-38674. (Reference Library of Social Science). 2000. write for info. (0-8153-3376-5) Garland.

Duryea, Edwin D. & Fisk, Robert S. Faculty Unions & Collective Bargaining. LC 72-11968. (Jossey-Bass Higher Education Ser.). 254p. reprint ed. pap. 78.80 (0-608-14792-3, 202565300045) Bks Demand.

Duryea, Mary L. & Brown, Gregory N., eds. Seedling Physiology & Reforestation Success. (Forestry Sciences Ser.). 1984. text 154.50 (90-247-2949-1) Kluwer Academic.

Duryea, Mary L. & Dougherty, Phillip M. Forest Regeneration Manual. (Forestry Sciences Ser.). (C). 1991. pap. text 107.00 (0-7923-0960-X); lib. bdg. 202.00 (0-7923-0959-6) Kluwer Academic.

Duryea, Mary L. & Landis, Thomas D., eds. Forestry Nursery Manual: Production of Barefoot Seedlings. (Forestry Sciences Ser.). 1984. text 232.00 (90-247-2913-0) Kluwer Academic.

Duryea, Merle J., et al. The Duryea Automotive Era in Reading, PA. 32p. 1996. pap. text 4.95 (1-887762-04-3) His Soc Brks Cnty.

Duryee, John S. The Study of Neurosis. LC 84-18699. 300p. (C). 1984. text 29.95 (0-940524-02-3); pap. text 19.95 (0-940524-03-1) G Handwerk.

*Duryee, Lynn. My Treehouse. Wise, Noreen, ed. (Lemonade Collection). 160p. (YA). (gr. 5 up). 2000. pap. 8.95 (1-58584-283-4) Huckleberry CT.

Durzan, Don J., jt. auth. see Bonga, J. M.

Durzan, Don J., jt. ed. see Bonga, J. M.

Durzok, J. Worterbuch Kunstoffprufung. (ENG & GER.). 200p. 1991. lib. bdg. 125.00 (0-8288-3600-0, 3527280359) Fr & Eur.

Dusa, Joan. The Medieval Dalmatian Cities: Development & Transformation. LC 90-6145. (American University Studies: History: Ser. IX, Vol. 94). 157p. (C). 1992. text 35.95 (0-8204-1286-4) P Lang Pubng.

Dusabek, F. & Bukva, V., eds. Modern Acarology: Proceedings of the 8th International Congress of Acarology, Held in Ceske Budejovice, Czechoslovakia, 6-11 August 1990, 2 vols., Set. (Illus.). 1572p. 1991. 190.00 (90-5103-054-1, Pub. by SPB Acad Pub) Balogh.

Dusablon, M. Cooking with Tofu. 1983. pap. 2.95 (0-88266-288-0, Storey Pub) Storey Bks.

— Winter Squash & Pumpkins. 1983. pap. 2.95 (0-88266-230-9, Storey Pub) Storey Bks.

DuSablon, Mary A. America's Collectible Cookbooks: The History, the Politics, the Recipes. LC 93-49602. (Illus.). 229p. 1994. 24.95 (0-8214-1057-1); pap. 15.95 (0-8214-1077-6) Ohio U Pr.

— Cincinnati Recipe Treasury: The Queen City's Culinary Heritage. LC 82-14773. (Illus.). 229p. 1989. reprint ed. pap. 14.95 (0-8214-0933-6) Ohio U Pr.

— Walking the Steps of Cincinnati. LC 97-49210. (Illus.). 176p. 1998. pap. 17.95 (0-8214-1227-2) Ohio U Pr.

Dusbin, Dominique, et al. Economic Evaluation of Community Options to Limit CO2 Emissions at the Horizon 2005 & 2010: Final Report / LC 98-196589. 1998. 35.00 (92-828-2873-5, Pub. by Comm Europ Commun) Bernan Associates.

Duschl, Richard A. Restructuring Science Education: The Importance of Theories & Their Development. 176p. (C). 1990. text 30.00 (0-8077-3006-8); pap. text 16.95 (0-8077-3005-X) Tchrs Coll.

Duschl, Richard A. & Hamilton, Richard J., eds. Philosophy of Science, Cognitive Psychology, & Educational Theory & Practice. LC 91-22633. (SUNY Series in Science Education). 287p. (C). 1992. text 24.50 (0-7914-1053-6) State U NY Pr.

Duschl, Richard A., ed. see Aue, A., et al.

Duschl, W. J., et al, eds. Variability of Active Galaxies: Proceedings of a Workshop of the Sonderforschungsbereich Held at Heidelberg, Germany, 3-5 September. (Lecture Notes in Physics Ser.: Vol. 377). xii, 312p. 1991. 50.95 (0-387-53860-7) Spr-Verlag.

Duschl, W. J., jt. ed. see Wagner, S. J.

Duschl, Wolfgang J., ed. Theory of Accretion Disks - 2: Proceedings of the NATO Advanced Research Workshop, Garching, Germany, March 16-22, 1993. LC 93-23735. (NATO Advanced Study Institutes Series C, Mathematical & Physical Sciences). 440p. 1993. text 267.50 (0-7923-2609-1) Kluwer Academic.

Duse, Phillip M. Phil Duse Versus the Tyranny of DOD: (Intelligence & Investigative Agencies) LC 99-172589. 140p. 1998. 35.00 (0-9666309-0-4); 30.00 (0-9666309-1-2) Debtors Arbitration.

Duseau, Janice A. Deborah: Woman Warrior of God. 16p. (Orig.). 1989. pap. text. write for info. (0-318-65837-2) Word Power Pub.

— Eve: Woman in God's Image. 16p. (Orig.). 1989. pap. write for info. (0-318-65840-2) Word Power Pub.

— God Wants You to Have Children. 16p. (Orig.). 1989. pap. write for info. (0-318-65842-9) Word Power Pub.

— Mary Magdelene: God's New Covenant Woman. 16p. (Orig.). 1989. pap. write for info. (0-318-65835-6) Word Power Pub.

— Mary, the Mother of Jesus: God's Woman of Obedience. 16p. (Orig.). 1989. pap. write for info. (0-318-65836-4) Word Power Pub.

— Pain Free Childbirth: Your Right. 16p. (Orig.). 1989. pap. write for info. (0-318-65841-0) Word Power Pub.

— Ruth: God's Loving Woman. 16p. (Orig.). 1989. pap. write for info. (0-318-65838-0) Word Power Pub.

— Sarah: God's Covenant Woman. 16p. (Orig.). 1989. pap. write for info. (0-318-65839-9) Word Power Pub.

Duseau, Michael J., Sr. Temptation Beat It! Let Go & Let God. 96p. (Orig.). 1989. pap. write for info. (0-318-65834-8) Word Power Pub.

Dusek, Dorothy E. Weight Management the Fitness Way. 336p. (Orig.). 1989. pap. 37.50 (0-86720-416-8) Jones & Bartlett.

Dusek, Dorothy E., jt. auth. see Girdano, Daniel A.

Dusek, Dorthy E. & Girdano, Daniel A. Emotional Risk Factors: The New Science of Health & Illness. rev. ed. LC 92-80753. 174p. 1995. pap. 12.95 (0-9633305-2-7) Paradox CO.

Dusek, Jerome B., et al, eds. Teacher Expectancies. (Psychology of Teaching & Instruction Ser.). 408p. (C). 1985. 79.95 (0-89859-443-X) L Erlbaum Assocs.

Dusek, K. Pharmacy-Thermomechanics-Elastomers-Telechelics. (Advances in Polymer Science Ser.: Vol. 76). (Illus.). 200p. 1986. 77.00 (0-387-15830-8) Spr-Verlag.

Dusek, K., ed. Epoxy Resins & Composites III. (Advances in Polymer Science Ser.: Vol. 78). (Illus.). 170p. 1986. 78.00 (0-387-15936-3) Spr-Verlag.

— Polymer Networks. (Advances in Polymer Science Ser.: Vol. 44). (Illus.). 164p. 1982. 73.95 (0-387-11471-8) Spr-Verlag.

— Responsive Gels: Volume Transitions I. (Advances in Polymer Science Ser.: Vol. 109). (Illus.). 290p. 1993. 171.95 (0-387-56791-7) Spr-Verlag.

— Responsive Gels: Volume Transitions II. (Advances in Polymer Science Ser.: Vol. 110). (Illus.). 260p. 1993. 145.00 (0-387-56970-7) Spr-Verlag.

Dusek, Mikulas. Die Thraker im Karpatenbecken. (Publications of the Henri Frankfort Foundation: No. 4). xiv, 210p. 1978. pap. write for info. (90-6032-108-1) B R Gruner.

Dusek, Val. The Holistic Inspiration of Physics: The Underground History of Electromagnetic Theory. LC 99-14095. 352p. (C). 1999. text 60.00 (0-8135-2634-5); pap. text 28.00 (0-8135-2635-3) Rutgers U Pr.

Dusen, Barry Van, see Perkins, Simon.

Dusen, Barry W. Van, see Bird Observer Staff & Van Dusen, Barry W.

Dusen, Bill Van, see Van Dusen, Bill.

Dusen, Chris Van, see Sayers, Jack.

Dusenberry, David B. Life at Small Scale: The Behavior of Microbes. LC 96-28629. (Illus.). 250p. 1996. text 32.95 (0-7167-5060-0) W H Freeman.

Dusenberry, Donald O., et al. Effects of Construction on Structures: Proceedings of the Geo-Institute of the American Society of Civil Engineers Geo-Congress '98: Boston, Massachusetts, October 18-21, 1998. LC 98-38899. (Geotechnical Special Publication Ser.). 128p. 1998. 29.00 (0-7844-0391-0) Am Soc Civil Eng.

Dusenberry, Phil. Star Wars And Other Skirmishes in the Advertising Business. 1999. text 24.95 (0-670-86309-2) Viking Penguin.

Dusenberry, Verne. The Montana Cree: A Study in Religious Persistence. LC 97-43208. (Illus.). 296p. (Orig.). 1998. pap. 15.95 (0-8061-3025-3) U of Okla Pr.

Dusenbery, David B. Sensory Ecology: How Organisms Acquire & Respond to Information. LC 92-2278. 558p. (C). 1992. pap. text 56.95 (0-7167-2333-6) W H Freeman.

Dusenbery, E. B. The Nekropoleis. (Samothrace Ser.: Vol. 11). 1252 pages in 2p. 1998. text 500.00 (0-691-03679-9, Pub. by Princeton U Pr) Cal Prin Full Svc.

Dusenbery, Harris. North Apennines & Beyond with the 10th Mountain Division. LC 98-72371. (Illus.). 272p. 1998. pap. 14.95 (0-8323-0522-7) Binford Mort.

— Ski the High Trail: World War Two Ski Troopers in the High Colorado Rockies. LC 91-70989. (Illus.). 176p. 1991. pap. 12.95 (0-8323-0485-9) Binford Mort.

Dusenbery, Wylma D. Wylma's La Trouvaille Cookbook: The Simple Joy of Cajun Cooking. (Illus.). 80p. 1993. reprint ed. spiral bd. 14.95 (0-944064-05-1) Paupieres Pub.

Dusenbury, Teri. Tatting Butterflies. LC 97-22707. (Illus.). 32p. (Orig.). 1997. pap. text 3.95 (0-486-29665-2) Dover.

— Tatting Hearts. LC 94-17257. (Needlework Ser.). (Illus.). 32p. (Orig.). 1994. pap. 3.50 (0-486-28071-3) Dover.

Duser, Guy Van, see Van Duser, Guy.

Dusewicz, Russell A. & Beyer, Francine S. Dimensions of Excellence Scales (DOE) Survey Instruments for School Improvement. 70p. 1990. reprint ed. pap. 21.95 (1-56602-024-7) Research Better.

Dusgate, Richard H. Conquest of Northern Nigeria. 316p. 1985. 45.00 (0-7146-3227-9, Pub. by F Cass Pubs) Intl Spec Bk.

Dush, David M., et al. Psychosocial Assessment in Terminal Care. LC 86-22801. (Hospice Journal: Vol. 2, No. 3). 150p. 1987. text 39.95 (0-86656-461-6) Haworth Pr.

DuShane, Graham P. Supplemental Drawings for Embryology. LC 55-5121. 49p. 1955. reprint ed. pap. 30.00 (0-608-10343-8, 202409100035) Bks Demand.

Dusharme, Susan, jt. auth. see Dillane, Christina.

Dusheck, jt. auth. see Tobin.

Dusheck, Jennie, jt. auth. see Tobin, Allan.

Dushkin, Alexander M. Living Bridges: Memories of an Educator. 320p. 1975. boxed set 39.95 (0-87855-179-4) Transaction Pubs.

Dushkin Publishing Group Staff. Annual Editions: International Business, 1996-1997. 3rd ed. (C). 1995. text 13.50 (0-256-21653-3, Irwn McGrw-H) McGrw-H Hghr Educ.

— Annual Editions: Marketing, 1996-1997. 3rd ed. (C). 1996. text 13.25 (0-256-22751-9, Irwn McGrw-H) McGrw-H Hghr Educ.

— Dushkin Annual Editions Management, 1994-1995. annuals 3rd ed. (C). 1995. text 13.57 (0-256-21543-X, Irwn McGrw-H) McGrw-H Hghr Educ.

Dushkin Publishing Group Staff & Siegel, Carolyn F. Dushkin 96-97 Marketing Annual. (C). 1996. text 34.00 (0-256-23115-X, Irwn McGrw-H) McGrw-H Hghr Educ.

Dushkina, Natalia, jt. auth. see Prevost, Dyranda.

Dusik, Barbel, comment. Hitler: Vom Weimarer Parteitag bis zur Reichstagswahl, Juli 1926-Mai 1928, Vol. 2. 881p. 1992. lib. bdg. 75.00 (3-598-21932-6) K G Saur Verlag.

Dusinberre. Alice to the Lighthouse. LC 98-44053. 352p. 1999. pap. 19.95 (0-312-22057-X) St Martin.

Dusinberre, Deke, et al, trs. The Geopolitics of Drugs 1996 Edition: Observatoire Geopolitique des Drogues. (Illus.). 224p. 1996. text 65.00 (1-55553-262-4) NE U Pr.

Dusinberre, Deke, tr. see Arnaud, Claude.

Dusinberre, Deke, tr. see Baldassari, Anne.

Dusinberre, Deke, tr. see Chastel, Andre.

Dusinberre, Juliet. Shakespeare & the Nature of Women. 2nd ed. 356p. 1996. pap. 19.95 (0-312-15975-0); text 59.95 (0-312-15972-2) St Martin.

— Virginia Woolf's Renaissance: Woman Reader or Common Reader? LC 96-61309. 288p. 1997. text 29.95 (0-87745-576-7); pap. text 14.95 (0-87745-577-5) U of Iowa Pr.

Dusinberre, William. Henry Adams, the Myth of Failure. LC 79-16096. 262p. reprint ed. pap. 81.30 (0-8357-6806-6, 203548900095) Bks Demand.

— Them Dark Days: Slavery in the American Rice Swamps. (Illus.). 576p. 1996. text 65.00 (0-19-509021-7) OUP.

*Dusinberre, William. Them Dark Days: Slavery in the American Rice Swamps. LC 99-55812. (C). 2000. pap. 30.00 (0-8203-2210-5) U of Ga Pr.

Dusink, L. M. & Hall, P. A., eds. Software Re-use, Utrecht, 1989: Proceedings of the Software Re-use Workshop 23-24 November 1989, Utrecht, The Netherlands. 176p. 1991. 43.95 (0-387-19652-8) Spr-Verlag.

Duska, Ronald, jt. auth. see Bowie, Norman E.

Duska, Ronald F., ed. Rerum Novarum - A Symposium Celebrating 100 Years of Catholic Social Thought. LC 91-47947. (Symposium Ser.: Vol. 29). (Illus.). 260p. 1992. lib. bdg. 89.95 (0-7734-9447-2) E Mellen.

Duska, Ronald F., jt. auth. see Walton, Clarence C.

Duskin, J. Simplicial Methods & the Interpretation of "Triple" Cohomolgy. LC 75-20008. (Memoirs Ser.: No. 3/163). 135p. 1975. pap. 21.00 (0-8218-1863-5, MEMO/3/163) Am Math.

*Duskin, J. Eric. Stalinist Reconstruction & the Confirmation of a New Elite, 1945-1953. LC 00-41512. 2000. write for info. (0-333-91894-0, Pub. by Macmillan) St Martin.

Duskis, Michael, ed. see Spurgeon, Charles H.

Duskis, Neil, jt. auth. see Barlowe, Wayne D.

Duskis, Ronald A. Groceries: How to Use Them for Any Good Reason. 3rd ed. Cura, Saraya, ed. & illus. by. Griffin, James, illus. 100p. 1995. spiral bd. 20.00 (0-9647252-0-7) Advan Hlth Tech.

Duskova, Libuse, jt. ed. see Vachek, Josef.

Duskova, Libuse, tr. see Mathesius, Vilem.

Dusoir, Lind L., ed. see James, Henry.

Duspiva, W., jt. auth. see Biemer, E.

Duss, John S. The Harmonists: A Personal History. LC 79-187439. (American Utopian Adventure Ser.). (Illus.). xviii, 425p. 1972. reprint ed. lib. bdg. 49.50 (0-87991-013-5) Porcupine Pr.

Dussan, Christopher. Historia de Italia. (SPA., Illus.). 460p. 1996. pap. 18.95 (0-521-55568-X) Cambridge U Pr.

Dussart, B. & Defaye, D. Repertoire Mondial des Crustaces Copepodes des Eaux Interieures, No. 3: Harpacticoides. LC 89-70852. (Crustaceana Supplements Ser.: No. 16). (FRE.). vii, 384p. 1990. pap. 97.00 (90-04-09191-2) Brill Academic Pubs.

Dussart, B. H. & Defaye, D. Guides to the Identification of Microinvertebrates of the Continental Waters of the World Vol. 7: Introduction to Copepoda. Dumont, H. J., ed. (Illus.). vi, 277p. 1995. pap. 75.00 (90-5103-098-3, Pub. by SPB Acad Pub) Balogh.

Dussart, Bernard. Crustaces Copepodes Calanoides des Eaux Interieures Africaines. LC 89-10017. (Crustaceana Supplements Ser.: No. 15). (FRE., Illus.). ix, 205p. (Orig.). 1989. pap. 94.50 (90-04-09053-3) Brill Academic Pubs.

— Limnologie: L'Etude des Eaux Continentales. 2nd ed. (FRE., Illus.). 680p. 1992. lib. bdg. 180.00 (2-85004-067-3, Pub. by Editions Boubees) Lubrecht & Cramer.

*Dussart, Francoise. The Politics of Ritual in an Aboriginal Settlement: Kinship, Gender & the Currency of Knowledge. LC 00-36548. (Series in Ethnographic Inquiry). (Illus.). 2000. write for info. (1-56098-393-0) Smithsonian.

Dussauge, Jan-Paul, jt. auth. see Smits, Alexander J.

Dussauge, Pierre, et al. Strategic Technology Management. LC 91-39732. 228p. 1992. 110.00 (0-471-93418-6) Wiley.

Dussault, Jean H. & Walker, Peter, eds. Congenital Hypothyroidism. LC 83-15331. (Basic & Clinical Endocrinology Ser.: No. 2). (Illus.). 496p. reprint ed. pap. 153.80 (0-7837-4319-X, 204400500012) Bks Demand.

Dussault, Jean H., jt. ed. see Burrow, Gerard N.

Dusseau. Informal History of Saunders. 1988. pap. text 85.00 (0-7216-2801-X, W B Saunders Co) Harcrt Hlth Sci Grp.

D'Usseau, Arnaud & Gow, James. Deep Are the Roots. 1947. pap. 5.25 (0-8222-0296-4) Dramatists Play.

D'Usseau, Emmanuel. Nous, les Jeunes: Level Two. 1990. text 58.50 (0-15-381750-X) Harcourt.

— Nouveaux Copains: Level One. 1989. text 56.50 (0-15-381700-3) Harcourt.

Dusseau, John L., jt. auth. see Sloane, Sheila B.

Dusseau, Lizbeth. The Applicant. (Orig.). 1997. mass mkt. 6.50 (1-56333-501-8) Masquerade.

— The Applicant. 2nd ed. (Orig.). 1998. reprint ed. mass mkt. 6.95 (1-56333-670-7) Masquerade.

— The Best of Lizbeth Dusseau. 1998. mass mkt. 6.95 (1-56333-630-8) Masquerade.

— Caroline's Contract. 2nd ed. (Orig.). 1998. reprint ed. mass mkt. 6.95 (1-56333-672-3) Masquerade.

— Trinkets. 2nd ed. (Orig.). 1998. reprint ed. mass mkt. 6.95 (1-56333-668-5) Masquerade.

Dussek, Ian. Motoring Specials. (Album Ser.: no. 266). (Illus.). 32p. 1989. pap. 6.25 (0-7478-0118-5, Pub. by Shire Pubns) Parkwest Pubns.

— Sports Cars. 1989. pap. 25.00 (0-85263-850-7, Pub. by Shire Pubns) St Mut.

Dussek, Jan L. Jan Ladislav Dussek - Selected Piano Works Pt. 1: Sonatas for Piano 4-Hands. Craw, H. Allen, ed. (Recent Researches in Music of the 19th & Early 20th Centuries Ser.: Vol. RRN1). (Illus.). xxiii, 104p. 1979. pap. 45.00 (0-89579-122-6) A-R Eds.

— Jan Ladislav Dussek - Selected Piano Works Pt. 2: Solo Piano Works. Craw, H. Allen, ed. (Recent Researches in Music of the 19th & Early 20th Centuries Ser.: Vol. RRN2). (Illus.). 125p. 1979. pap. 45.00 (0-89579-123-4) A-R Eds.

Dussek, Johann L. Collected Works, 6 vols. LC 79-75313. (Music Ser.). 1978. 59.50 (0-685-74233-4) Da Capo.

— Collected Works, 6 vols., 1. LC 79-75313. (Music Ser.). 1978. 59.50 (0-306-77271-X) Da Capo.

— Collected Works, 6 vols., 2. LC 79-75313. (Music Ser.). 1978. 59.50 (0-306-77272-8) Da Capo.

— Collected Works, 6 vols., 3. LC 79-75313. (Music Ser.). 1978. 59.50 (0-306-77273-6) Da Capo.

— Collected Works, 6 vols., 4. LC 79-75313. (Music Ser.). 1978. 59.50 (0-306-77274-4) Da Capo.

— Collected Works, 6 vols., 5. LC 79-75313. (Music Ser.). 1978. 59.50 (0-306-77275-2) Da Capo.

— Collected Works, 6 vols., 6. LC 79-75313. (Music Ser.). 1978. 59.50 (0-306-77276-0) Da Capo.

— Collected Works, 6 vols., Set. LC 79-75313. (Music Ser.). 1978. 325.00 (0-685-45906-3) Da Capo.

D

Dussel, Enrique. The Church in Latin America, 1492-1992. 512p. 1994. 150.00 (*0-86012-180-1*, Pub. by Srch Pr) St Mut.

— Ethics & Community.Tr. of Etica Comunitaria. 272p. 1994. pap. 27.00 (*0-86012-162-3*, Pub. by Srch Pr) St Mut.

— The Underside of Modernity: Apel, Ricoeur, Rorty, Taylor, & the Philosophy of Liberation. Mendieta, Eduardo, ed. & tr. by. LC 95-32838. 256p. (C). 1996. text 60.00 (*0-391-03932-6*) Humanities.

— The Underside of Modernity: Apel, Ricoeur, Rorty, Taylor, & the Philosophy of Liberation. Mendieta, Eduardo, ed. & tr. by. 248p. 1998. reprint ed. pap. 19.95 (*0-391-04081-2*) Humanities.

Dussel, Enrique D. Ethics & the Theology of Liberation. McWilliams, Bernard F., tr. LC 77-22179. 191p. reprint ed. pap. 59.30 (*0-8357-8872-5*, 203348700086) Bks Demand.

— History & the Theology of Liberation: A Latin American Perspective. Drury, John, tr. LC 75-21773. 205p. reprint ed. pap. 63.60 (*0-8357-8910-1*, 203350100086) Bks Demand.

— A History of the Church in Latin America: Colonialism to Liberation (1492-1979) Neely, Alan, tr. & rev. by. LC 81-17483. 384p. reprint ed. pap. 119.10 (*0-608-17877-2*, 203272400080) Bks Demand.

— Philosophy of Liberation. Martinez, Aquilina & Morkovsky, Christine, trs. from SPA. LC 85-5103. 223p. reprint ed. pap. 69.20 (*0-608-20205-3*, 207146400012) Bks Demand.

Dussel, Enrique D. & Mendieta, Eduardo. The Underside of Modernity: Apel, Ricoeur, Rorty, Taylor, & the Philosophy of Liberation LC 99-10398. 1999. write for info. (*1-57392-396-6*, Humanity Bks) Prometheus Bks.

***Dusseldorf, Kunsthalle, ed.** Heaven: A Book That Will Break Your Heart. (Illus.). 256p. 1999. pap. 45.00 (*3-89322-935-3*, Pub. by Dr Cantz sche Druckerei GmbH) Dist Art Pubs.

Dussen, W., ed. see Collingwood, R. G.

Dussen, W. J. Van der, see Van der Dussen, W. J.

Dusser, Daniel, jt. ed. see Chretien, Jacques.

Dussere, Carolyn, tr. see Ernst, Herzog.

Dusserre, Michelle, ed. see U. S. A. Gymnastics Staff.

Dusserre Telmon, Pierre. Dictionnaire Vivant du Batiment et des Travaux Publics. (FRE.). 181p. 1988. pap. 59.95 (*0-7859-8258-2*, 2950329802) Fr & Eur.

DuSsette, Kamille M. Walking on Hot Coals. 82p. (Orig.). 1989. pap. write for info. (*0-9621430-0-6*) K M duSsette.

Dussinger, John. The Discourse of the Mind in the 18th Century Fiction. LC 73-94032. (Studies in English Literature: No. 80). 215p. 1974. pap. text 64.65 (*90-279-3222-0*) Mouton.

Dussinger, John A. In the Pride of the Moment: Encounters in Jane Austen's World. LC 89-31597. (Illus.). 227p. reprint ed. pap. 70.40 (*0-608-09668-7*, 206978300006) Bks Demand.

Dussinger, Marshall A. Amish Country: Land of Buggies, Bears, Barns, Bridges, Bonnets & Barefeet. (Illus.). 1980. pap. 3.95 (*0-935456-00-7*) Stel-Mar.

— Amish Country Address Book. (Illus.). 28p. 1987. pap. 4.95 (*0-935456-02-3*) Stel-Mar.

Dussling, Jennifer. Balto Beware! (Illus.). 24p. (J). (ps-3). Date not set. pap. text. write for info. (*0-448-41114-8*, G & D) Peng Put Young Read.

— Bossy Kiki. (Puzzle Place Ser.). (Illus.). 32p. (J). (ps-1). 1996. lib. bdg. 13.99 (*0-448-41330-2*, G & D) Peng Put Young Read.

— Bug Off! LC 97-8785. (Eek! Stories to Make You Shriek Ser.). (Illus.). 48p. (J). (gr. 1-3). 1997. 13.89 (*0-448-41726-X*, G & D); pap. 3.95 (*0-448-41646-8*, G & D) Peng Put Young Read.

Dussling, Jennifer. Bug Off! (Eek! Stories to Make You Shriek Ser.). 1997. 9.15 (*0-606-11172-7*, Pub. by Turtleback) Demco.

Dussling, Jennifer. Bugs! Bugs! Bugs! LC 98-14975. (Eyewitness Readers). (Illus.). 32p. (J). (gr. 1-3). 1998. 12.95 (*0-7894-3762-7*); pap. 3.95 (*0-7894-3438-5*) DK Pub Inc.

— The Bunny Slipper Mystery. (Muppet All Aboard Reading Ser.: Level 2). (Illus.). 32p. (J). (gr. 1-3). 1997. lib. bdg. 13.99 (*0-448-41615-8*, G & D) Peng Put Young Read.

— The Bunny Slipper Mystery, Level 2. (Muppet All Aboard Reading Ser.). (Illus.). 32p. (J). (gr. 1-3). 1997. pap. 4.95 (*0-448-41562-3*, G & D) Peng Put Young Read.

— Construction Trucks: An All Aboard Book. LC 98-8668. (All Aboard Bks.). (Illus.). 32p. (J). (ps-3). 1998. mass mkt. 2.99 (*0-448-41885-1*, G & D) Peng Put Young Read.

— Creep Show. (Eek! Stories to Make You Shriek Ser.). (Illus.). 48p. (J). (gr. 1-3). 1996. pap. 3.99 (*0-448-41272-1*, G & D) Peng Put Young Read.

Dussling, Jennifer. Creep Show. LC 95-18331. (Eek! Stories to Make You Shriek Ser.). 1996. 9.15 (*0-606-09171-8*, Pub. by Turtleback) Demco.

— Dinosaur Eggs. (All Aboard Reading Ser.). (Illus.). 48p. (J). (ps-3). 2000. 13.89 (*0-448-42094-5*, G & D); pap. 3.99 (*0-448-42093-7*, G & D) Peng Put Young Read.

— Dinosaur Eggs: Level 2. (All Aboard Reading Ser.). (Illus.). (J). 2000. 9.44 (*0-606-18850-9*) Turtleback.

Dussling, Jennifer. The Dinosaurs of the Lost World: Jurassic Park. LC 97-70584. (All Aboard Reading Ser.: Level 3). (Illus.). 32p. (Orig.). (J). (gr. 2-4). 1997. pap. 4.95 (*0-448-41575-5*, G & D) Peng Put Young Read.

— Don't Call Me Names! (Puzzle Place Ser.). (Illus.). 32p. (Orig.). (J). (ps-1). 1996. pap. 4.95 (*0-448-41312-4*, G & D) Peng Put Young Read.

— Gargoyles: Monsters in Stones. LC 98-42133. (All Aboard Reading Ser.). (Illus.). 1999. 13.89 (*0-448-41962-9*, G & D) Peng Put Young Read.

— Gargoyles: Monsters in Stones. LC 98-42133. (All Aboard Reading Ser.). (Illus.). 48p. (gr. 1-3). 1999. pap. 3.99 (*0-448-41961-0*, G & D) Peng Put Young Read.

***Dussling, Jennifer.** Giant Squid: Mystery of the Deep. LC 99-20822. (All Aboard Reading Ser.). (Illus.). 48p. (J). 1999. pap. 13.89 (*0-448-42085-6*, Tuffy) Putnam Pub Group.

Dussling, Jennifer. A Heart for the Queen of Hearts. LC 99-214678. (Jewel Sticker Stories Ser.). (Illus.). 24p. (J). (ps-2). 1998. mass mkt. 3.99 (*0-448-41864-9*, G & D) Peng Put Young Read.

***Dussling, Jennifer.** In a Dark Dark House. (Illus.). (J). 1999. pap. 11.05 (*0-613-12772-2*) Econo-Clad Bks.

Dussling, Jennifer. In a Dark, Dark House. (All Aboard Reading Picture Readers Ser.). (Illus.). 32p. (J). 1995. pap. 3.95 (*0-448-40970-4*, G & D) Peng Put Young Read.

***Dussling, Jennifer.** The 100-Pound Problem. LC 99-42679. (Math Matters Ser.). (Illus.). (J). (gr. k-2). 2000. pap. 4.95 (*1-57565-095-9*) Kane Pr.

Dussling, Jennifer. Pink Snow: And Other Weird Weather, Level 2. LC 98-14336. (All Aboard Reading Ser.). (Illus.). 48p. (J). (gr. 1-3). 1998. lib. bdg. 13.89 (*0-448-41887-8*, G & D); mass mkt. 3.99 (*0-448-41858-4*, G & D) Peng Put Young Read.

***Dussling, Jennifer.** Planets. (All Aboard Reading Ser.). (Illus.). 48p. (J). (gr. 1-3). 2000. 13.89 (*0-448-42416-9*, Planet Dexter); pap. 3.99 (*0-448-42406-1*, Planet Dexter) Peng Put Young Read.

Dussling, Jennifer. A Simple Wish 8 x 8. LC 97-72382. (Simple Wish Ser.). (Illus.). 24p. (Orig.). (J). (gr. k-3). 1997. pap. 3.95 (*0-448-41637-9*, G & D) Peng Put Young Read.

— Slinky, Scaly Snakes. LC 98-25068. (Eyewitness Readers). 48p. (J). (gr. 1-3). 1998. 3.95 (*0-7894-3439-3*); pap. 12.95 (*0-7894-3766-X*) DK Pub Inc.

— The Stars. LC 95-24763. (All Aboard Reading Ser.: Level 1). (Illus.). 32p. (J). (ps-1). 1996. pap. 3.99 (*0-448-41148-2*, G & D) Peng Put Young Read.

— Stars. (All Aboard Reading Ser.). (Illus.). 32p. (J). (ps-1). 1996. lib. bdg. 13.99 (*0-448-41149-0*, G & D) Peng Put Young Read.

— Tall Tale Trouble. LC 97-74999. 1998. pap. text 3.99 (*0-448-41719-7*, G & D) Peng Put Young Read.

— Under the Sea. (Books & Stuff Ser.). (Illus.). 24p. (J). (gr. 1-5). 1995. pap. 7.95 (*0-448-40078-2*, G & D) Peng Put Young Read.

— A Very Strange Dollhouse. LC 95-46793. (Eek! Stories to Make You Shriek Ser.). (Illus.). 48p. (J). (gr. 1-3). 1996. pap. 3.95 (*0-448-41311-6*, G & D); lib. bdg. 13.99 (*0-448-41346-9*, G & D) Peng Put Young Read.

— Very Strange Dollhouse. (Eek! Stories to Make You Shriek Ser.). 1996. 9.15 (*0-606-10963-3*, Pub. by Turtleback) Demco.

Dussourd, J. L., ed. see American Society of Mechanical Engineers Staff.

Dussuage, Pierre & Garrette, Bernard. Managing Strategic Alliances. LC 98-53082. 254p. 1999. 43.95 (*0-471-97492-7*) Wiley.

Dust, A. I. Charles Cotton's Works, 1663-1665: Critical Editions of "The Valiant Knight" & "Scarronides" LC 91-41637. (Renaissance Imagination Ser.). 488p. 1992. text 20.00 (*0-8153-0452-8*) Garland.

Dust, Babaloo R. Living Out of the Moment: 100 Ways to Obtain Happiness Through Total Denial. 80p. 1995. pap. 6.95 (*0-8048-3073-8*) Tuttle Pubng.

Dust, Patrick H., intro. Ortega y Gasset & the Question of Modernity. (Hispanic Issues Ser.: No. 5). 387p. (Orig.). 1989. pap. 12.95 (*0-910235-34-1*) Prisma Bks.

***Dust, W. O.** Key to the Universe - God's Story. 256p. (C). 2001. pap. 16.95 (*0-9674734-0-3*) Whisp Of Dust.

Dustan, Guillame. In My Room. 128p. 1998. pap. 12.99 (*1-85242-590-3*) Serpents Tail.

Dustan, Jane, jt. auth. see Zurcher, Arnold J.

Dustdar, Schahram, jt. auth. see Angelides, Marios C.

Duster, Alfreda M., ed. see Wells, Ida B.

Duster, Troy & Garrett, Karen, eds. Cultural Perspectives on Biological Knowledge. LC 83-27174. (Modern Sociology Ser.). 208p. 1984. text 73.25 (*0-89391-059-7*) Ablx Pub.

Dustin & Wassell. History of Dwight, Illinois, from 1853 to 1894. (Illus.). 153p. 1997. reprint ed. lib. bdg. 21.50 (*0-8328-5737-8*) Higginson Bk Co.

Dustin, Daniel L. The Wilderness Within: Journeys in Self-Discovery. 152p. 1993. pap. 6.95 (*1-882708-52-0*) Inst Leisure.

— The Wilderness Within: Reflections on Leisure & Life. (Illus.). 153p. 1999. pap. 19.95 (*1-57167-253-2*) Sagamore Pub.

Dustin, Daniel L., et al. Stewards of Access/Custodians of Choice: A Philosophical Foundation for the Park & Recreation Profession. 2nd ed. 112p. 1995. pap. text 13.95 (*1-57167-009-2*) Sagamore Pub.

Dustin, Dick, jt. auth. see George, Rickey L.

***Dustin, Elfriede, et al.** Automated Software Testing: Introduction, Management & Performance. LC 99-25423. 608p. (C). 1999. pap. text 44.95 (*0-201-43287-0*) Addison-Wesley.

Dustin, Fred. The Custer Tragedy: Events Leading up to & Following the Little Big Horn Campaign of 1876. LC 87-5696. (Echoes of the Little Big Horn Ser.: Vol. 2). (Illus.). 310p. (C). 1988. reprint ed. 45.00 (*0-912783-10-9*) Upton & Sons.

Dustin, Ginny. At Grandma's Knee. (Illus.). 48p. (Orig.). 1992. pap. text. write for info. (*1-880551-03-9*) Silver Hill.

— Songs of the Miller's Maid. (Illus.). 50p. 1991. 30.00 (*1-880551-00-4*) Silver Hill.

Dustin, J., jt. auth. see Hardwick, J.

Dustman, Karen D. Ferrets! A Fun & Care Book. LC 97-32168. (Fun & Care Bks.). (Illus.). 112p. 1998. pap. 16.95 (*1-889540-00-5*) Bowtie Press.

***Dustman, Karen D.** The Woman's Fix-It Guide to Kitchen Makeovers: Incredibly Simple Ways to Spice Up Your Space. (Woman's Fix-It Ser.: Vol. 3). 2000. pap. 15.95 (*1-886284-49-0*, Pub. by Chandler Hse) Natl Bk Netwk.

Dustman, Karen Dale. The Woman's Fix-It Book: Incredibly Simple Weekend Projects & Everyday Home Repair. LC 97-77694. 120p. 1998. pap. 14.95 (*1-886284-14-8*, Pub. by Chandler Hse) Natl Bk Netwk.

***Duston, Dwight, frwd.** Ballistic Missile Defense Organization (BMDO) Technology Applications Report (1998) (Illus.). 80p. 2000. pap. text 20.00 (*0-7881-8581-0*) DIANE Pub.

Duston, Robert. A Guide to Writing Job Descriptions under the ADA. 60p. 1992. 10.00 (*1-878240-16-1*) Coll & U Personnel.

— Hiring: Do's & Don'ts for Interviewers under the ADA. 32p. 1992. 7.50 (*1-878240-17-X*) Coll & U Personnel.

Duston, Robert L. & Robbins, Scott. A Practical Guide to Implementing the Family & Medical Leave Act. 153p. 1993. 85.00 (*1-878240-29-3*) Coll & U Personnel.

Duston, Robert L. & Robins, Scott. A Practical Guide to Implementing the Family & Medical Leave Act, 1996 Supplement. 1997. 65.00 (*1-878240-56-0*) Coll & U Personnel.

Duston, Robert L., et al. ADA Compliance Manual for Higher Education: A Guide to Title I. 242p. 1992. 90.00 (*1-878240-20-X*) Coll & U Personnel.

Duston, Thomas E. Recycling Solid Waste: The 1st Choice for Private & Public Sector Management. LC 92-31709. 224p. 1993. 55.00 (*0-89930-754-X*, DRG, Quorum Bks) Greenwood.

Duszak, Anna, ed. Culture & Styles of Academic Discourse. LC 97-16450. (Trends in Linguistics, Studies & Monographs: Vol. 104). viii, 362p. 1997. lib. bdg. 177.95 (*3-11-015249-5*) Mouton.

***Duszynski, Susan.** Pediatric ECG Interpreation - A Self Study Text. 3rd rev. ed. Hirshy-Wolkenheim, Becki Jo, ed. (Illus.). 189p. 2000. pap. 65.00 (*1-930605-01-3*, 106003) Maxishare.

— Pocket Reference for Pediatric ECG's. 3rd rev. ed. (Illus.). 76p. 2000. pap. 13.00 (*1-930605-00-5*, 104001) Maxishare.

Dutch & Monroe. Earth Science. (Earth Science Ser.). 1998. mass mkt., student ed. 15.50 (*0-314-20888-7*) West Pub.

— Earth Science with Infotrac. (Earth Science Ser.). 1997. 51.00 incl. cd-rom (*0-534-54101-1*) Wadsworth Pub.

Dutch, Bill & Vanderburgh, George A. August Derleth: A Bibliographical Checklist. (Illus.). 76p. (Orig.). 1996. pap. 10.00 (*1-896648-14-2*) Battered Silicon.

Dutch, Boling. Magia de la Sonrisa. (SPA.). 1997. pap. text 9.98 (*968-403-340-0*) Selector.

Dutch Chemical Industry Association Staff, jt. ed. see Dutch Institute for the Working Environment Staff.

Dutch Committee for Long Term Environmental Policy, ed. The Environment: Towards a Sustainable Future. (Environment & Policy Ser.). 620p. (C). 1993. pap. text 75.00 (*0-7923-2656-3*) Kluwer Academic.

Dutch Institute for the Working Environment Staff & Dutch Chemical Industry Association Staff, eds. Chemical Safety Sheets: Working Safely with Hazardous Chemicals. (C). 1991. lib. bdg. 124.00 (*0-7923-1258-9*) Kluwer Academic.

Dutch, Oswald. The Errant Diplomat: The Life of Franz von Papen. LC 78-63665. (Studies in Fascism: Ideology & Practice). 320p. reprint ed. 41.50 (*0-404-16928-7*) AMS Pr.

— Hitler's Twelve Apostles. LC 75-93333. (Essay Index Reprint Ser.). 1977. 21.95 (*0-8369-1286-1*) Ayer.

Dutch, Steve I. & Monroe, James S. Earth Science. LC 97-14327. 1997. pap. 57.95 (*0-314-20111-4*) Wadsworth Pub.

Dutcher. Dutcher's Hematologic Morphology. 1994. text 500.00 (*1-56815-023-7*) Mosby Inc.

Dutcher, Bill. Managing IP Addresses: How to Number your Network for Growth & Change. LC 99-49094. 310p. 1999. pap. 49.99 (*0-471-25484-3*) Wiley.

Dutcher, Douglas. Bible Prophecies 1998 Thru 2005. 2nd rev. ed. LC 97-91893. 130p. 1997. pap. 5.95 (*0-9658500-1-3*, 0153) Smith Pubns FL.

Dutcher, George N. Voyage Round the World. (Illus.). 44p. 1998. pap. 5.50 (*1-877703-44-3*) Pavilion Pr.

Dutcher, J. P. & Wiernik, P. H. Handbook of Hematologic & Oncologic Emergencies. LC 87-7374. (Illus.). 372p. (C). 1988. text 85.00 (*0-306-42646-3*, Kluwer Plenum) Kluwer Academic.

Dutcher, Janice P., ed. Modern Transfusion Therapy, 2 vols., Vol. 1. 336p. 1989. lib. bdg. 225.00 (*0-8493-6247-4*, RM171) CRC Pr.

— Modern Transfusion Therapy, 2 vols., Vol. II. 384p. 1989. lib. bdg. 216.00 (*0-8493-6248-2*, RM171) CRC Pr.

***Dutcher, Jim, ed.** Wolves at Our Door: 2001 Engagement Calendar. (Illus.). 114p. 2000. 13.95 (*0-9702294-1-0*) Glyph Pubng Arts.

— Wolves at Our Door: 2001 Wall Calendar. (Illus.). 24p. 2000. 12.95 (*0-9702294-0-2*) Glyph Pubng Arts.

Dutcher, Jim, jt. auth. see McCall, Karen.

Dutcher, June & Framke, Janet J. The New Airedale Terrier. (Complete Breed Bk.). (Illus.). 256p. 1991. 25.95 (*0-87605-007-0*) Howell Bks.

Dutcher, Laura H. Herbie the Owl Who Couldn't Hoot. (Illus.). 32p. (J). (ps-2). 1994. pap. 6.95 (*0-9643149-0-8*) Dutcher & Apperson.

Dutcher, Mary. Nicaragua: Violations of the Laws of War by Both Sides, February-December 1985. 44p. (Orig.). (C). 1986. pap. text 6.50 (*0-9613249-3-7*) WOLA.

***Dutcher-McLeod, Andrea.** Surfacing Soliloquy. LC 99-71730. (Illus.). 46p. 1999. pap. 12.95 (*1-890622-69-9*) Leathers Pub.

Dutcher, R. M., ed. see International Symposium on Comparative Leukemia Re.

Dutcher, R. R., ed. Field Description of Coal - STP 661. 76p. 1978. pap. 7.50 (*0-8031-0349-2*, STP661) ASTM.

Dutcher, Russell K., III. Middlesex County, New Jersey Militia, 1791-1795: Compiled Records with Biographical Sketches of the Officers of Selected Companies, Including a Roster of the Middlesex County Militia, 1775-1783. (Illus.). 275p. 1996. pap. 26.50 (*0-8063-4516-0*) Clearfield Co.

Dutcher, Salem, jt. auth. see Jones, Charles C., Jr.

Dutcher-Walls, Patricia. Narrative Art, Political Rhetoric: The Case of Athalia & Joash. (Journal for the Study of the Old Testament Supplement Ser.: No. 209). 198p. 1996. 57.50 (*1-85075-577-9*, Pub. by Sheffield Acad) CUP Services.

Dutchess County Genealogical Society Staff. Census with Index, 1810: Dutchess County, New York. 181p. 1990. reprint ed. lib. bdg. 20.00 (*1-56012-107-6*, 100) Kinship Rhinebeck.

Dutchess of St. Albans. Where Time Stood Still: A Portrait of Oman. (Illus.). 160p. 1982. 11.95 (*0-7043-2247-1*, Pub. by Quartet) Charles River Bks.

Dutchess of York. Budgie at Bendick's Point. (Illus.). 40p. (J). (ps-1). 1989. per. 14.00 (*0-671-67684-9*) Aladdin.

— Budgie the Little Helicopter. (Illus.). 40p. (J). (ps-1). 1989. mass mkt. 14.00 (*0-671-67683-0*) S&S Bks Yung.

Dute, Roland & Peterson, Curt. Plant Biology Laboratory Manual. 3rd ed. 212p. (C). 1996. spiral bd. 21.99 (*0-8403-9336-9*) Kendall-Hunt.

***Duteil, Francoise P.** Studien Zur Pradikation: Eine Analyse der Verbalperiphrasen der Phase Im Franzosischen. (GER., Illus.). 192p. 1999. 35.00 (*3-631-33816-3*) P Lang Pubng.

Duteil, Francoise P. Le Verbe Francais en Conjugaison Orale. (FRE., Illus.). 204p. 1997. 38.95 (*3-631-30504-4*) P Lang Pubng.

***DuTemple, Lesley A.** Coral Reefs. LC 99-38212. (Overview Ser.). (Illus.). 128p. (YA). (gr. 6-9). 2000. lib. bdg. 23.70 (*1-56006-597-4*) Lucent Bks.

— Jacques-Yves Cousteau. LC 99-38342. (A&E Biography Ser.). (Illus.). 128p. (YA). (gr. 6-9). 2000. 25.26 (*0-8225-4979-4*, Lerner Publctns) Lerner Pub.

Dutemple, Lesley A. Moose. LC 97-24685. (Early Bird Nature Books Ser.). (Illus.). (J). 1997. lib. bdg. 19.93 (*0-8225-3031-7*) Lerner Pub.

***Dutemple, Lesley A.** North American Cranes. LC 98-4519. 48p. (J). (gr. 2-5). 1999. 22.60 (*1-57505-302-0*, Carolrhoda) Lerner Pub.

***DuTemple, Lesley A.** North American Moose. LC 99-37091. (Nature Watch Bks.). (Illus.). 48p. (J). (gr. 4-7). 2000. 23.93 (*1-57505-426-4*, Carolrhoda) Lerner Pub.

Dutemple, Lesley A. Polar Bears. LC 97-4131. (Early Bird Nature Bks.). (Illus.). (J). (ps-4). 1997. lib. bdg. 19.95 (*0-8225-3025-2*, Lerner Publctns) Lerner Pub.

DuTemple, Lesley A. Seals & Sea Lions. LC 98-30303. (Overview Ser.). (Illus.). 128p. (YA). (gr. 4-12). 1998. lib. bdg. 22.45 (*1-56006-473-0*) Lucent Bks.

***DuTemple, Lesley A.** Sweden. LC 99-30142. (Overview Ser.). (Illus.). 144p. (YA). (gr. 6-9). 2000. lib. bdg. 23.70 (*1-56006-588-5*) Lucent Bks.

DuTemple, Lesley A. Tigers. (Early Bird Nature Bks.). (Illus.). (J). 1996. lib. bdg. 19.95 (*0-8225-3010-4*, Lerner Publctns) Lerner Pub.

— Whales. LC 95-30803. (Early Bird Nature Bks.). 48p. (J). (gr. 1-3). 1996. lib. bdg. 19.95 (*0-8225-3008-2*, Lerner Publctns) Lerner Pub.

DuTemple, Leslie A. Oil Spills. LC 99-21614. (Overview Ser.). (Illus.). 128p. (YA). (gr. 4-12). 1999. lib. bdg. 23.70 (*1-56006-524-9*) Lucent Bks.

Dutery, Polly. Barbeque. 36p. (Orig.). 1983. pap. 2.75 (*0-940844-21-4*) Wellspring.

— Casseroles. 36p. (Orig.). 1981. pap. 2.75 (*0-940844-04-4*) Wellspring.

— Hors d'Oeuvres. 36p. (Orig.). 1981. pap. 3.25 (*0-940844-03-6*) Wellspring.

— Hors d'Oeuvres II. 36p. (Orig.). 1983. pap. 3.25 (*0-940844-13-3*) Wellspring.

— Slim & Trim. 36p. (Orig.). 1982. pap. 3.25 (*0-940844-11-7*) Wellspring.

Dutery, Polly & Van Roden, Joanne. Salads for All Occasions. 36p. (Orig.). 1992. pap. 3.25 (*0-940844-48-6*) Wellspring.

Dutescu, D., tr. see Banus, Maria, et al.

Dutfield, Graham, jt. auth. see Posey, Darrell A.

Dutfield, Michael. A Marriage of Inconvenience: The Persecution of Ruth & Seretse Khama. 256p. 1990. text 24.95 (*0-04-440495-6*) Routledge.

Duthac, Janine. Your Inner Journey to the Real: Finding Your True Self & the Art of Joyful Relating. (Illus.). 128p. 1998. pap. 19.95 (*0-85207-319-4*, Pub. by C W Daniel) Natl Bk Netwk.

Duthie, Alan S. How to Choose Your Bible Wisely. 2nd ed. 244p. 1995. reprint ed. pap. 16.99 (*0-85364-615-5*, Pub. by Paternoster Pub) OM Literature.

Duthie, Alexander. The Greek Mythology: A Reader's Handbook. 2nd ed. LC 78-12988. (Illus.). 168p. 1979. reprint ed. lib. bdg. 49.75 (*0-313-21077-2*, DUGM, Greenwood Pr) Greenwood.

Duthie, Beth, ed. see Ainslie, Patricia.

Duthie, Christine. True Stories: Nonfiction Literacy in the Primary Classroom. LC 96-3417. (Illus.). 176p. 1996. pap. text 17.00 (*1-57110-026-1*) Stenhse Pubs.

Duthie, Dorothy B., ed. see Ford, Beatrice.

Duthie, Edmund H., Jr. & Katz, Paul R. Practice of Geriatrics. 3rd ed. Kersey, Ray, ed. LC 97-22941. (Illus.). 544p. (C). 1998. text 85.00 (*0-7216-6599-3*, W B Saunders Co) Harcrt Hlth Sci Grp.

An Asterisk (*) at the beginning of an entry indicates that the title is appearing for the first time.

Duthie, Elizabeth A., ed. Modell's Drugs in Current Use & New Drugs, 1998. 44th ed. 288p. 1998. 27.95 (*0-8261-7657-7*) Springer Pub.
— Modell's Drugs in Current Use & New Drugs 1999. 45th ed. 304p. 1999. pap. 29.95 (*0-8261-7658-5*) Springer Pub.

Duthie, G. Andrew. Microsoft Visual InterDev 6.0 Enterprise Developer's Workshop. LC 98-42528. 500p. 1998. pap. 49.99 (*0-7356-0568-8*) Microsoft.

Duthie, H. C., jt. auth. see Contant, H.

Duthie, J. F. Flora of the Upper Gangetic Plainand of the Adjacent Siwalik & Sub-Himalayan Tracts. 1049p. 1973. 125.00 (*0-7855-3048-7*, Pub. by Intl Bk Distr) St Mut.
— The Fodder Grasses of Northern India. (C). 1978. text 50.00 (*0-7855-6012-2*, Pub. by Scientific) St Mut.
— The Fodder Grasses of Northern India, 2 vols., 1. (C). 1987. reprint ed. 80.00 (*81-85046-01-8*, Pub. by Scientific) St Mut.
— The Fodder Grasses of Northern India, 2 vols., 2. (C). 1987. reprint ed. 350.00 (*0-7855-3020-7*, Pub. by Scientific) St Mut.

Duthie, J. F., ed. Flora of the Upper Gangetic Plain & of the Adjacent Siwalik & Sub-Himalayan Tracts, 3 vols. in 2. 1049p. (C). 1973. text 300.00 (*0-89771-602-7*, Pub. by Intl Bk Distr) St Mut.

Duthie, J. F., tr. The Orchids of North Western Himalaya. (C). 1988. 200.00 (*0-7855-3278-1*, Pub. by Scientific) St Mut.

Duthie, Niall. The Duchess's Dragonfly. 176p. 1993. (*1-897580-30-4*) Phoenix Hse.

Duthie, P. E., ed. see Osborne, D. R.

***Duthie, Pam.** Continuous Bloom. LC 99-88588. (Illus.). 328p. 2000. 39.95 (*1-883052-23-8*) Ball Pub.

Duthie, Robert & Bentley, George, eds. Mercer's Orthopaedic Surgery. 9th ed. (Arnold Publication). (Illus.). 1376p. 1996. text 145.00 (*0-340-55163-1*) OUP.

Duthie, Robert B., et al. The Management of Musculoskeletal Problems in the Haemophilias. 2nd ed. (Illus.). 298p. 1994. text 110.00 (*0-19-262317-6*) OUP.

Duthie, Ruth. Florists' Flowers & Societies. (Illus.). 98p. 1988. 10.00 (*0-85263-953-8*, Pub. by Shire Pubns) Lubrecht & Cramer.

Duthuit, Claude. Henri Matisse: Catalogue Raisonne des Ouvrages Illustres. (FRE., Illus.). 509p. 1988. 570.00 (*2-904852-01-8*) Ursus Bks.

Duthuit, Claude & Bois, Yve-Alain. Henri Matisse: Catalogue Raisonne de l'Oeuvre Sculpte Etabli avec la Collaboration de Wanda de Guebriant. (FRE., Illus.). 416p. 1997. 270.00 (*2-904852-04-2*, 38584, Pub. by C Duthuit) Ursus Bks.

Duthuit, Claude, jt. auth. see Duthuit-Matisse, Marguerite.

Duthuit-Matisse, Marguerite & Duthuit, Claude. Henri Matisse: Catalogue Raisonne de l'Oeuvre Grave Etabli avec la Collaboration de Francoise Garnaud, 2 vols. (FRE., Illus.). 1983. 660.00 (*2-904852-00-X*) Ursus Bks.

Dutilh, Nauta, jt. auth. see Verloop, Peter.

Dutille, H. Kenneth. Lewiston & Auburn. (Images of America Ser.). 1995. pap. 16.99 (*0-7524-0220-X*) Arcadia Publng.

Dutka, jt. auth. see Liu, Dickson.

Dutka, Alan. Competitive Intelligence for the Competitive Edge. LC 98-8554. (Illus.). 336p. 1999. 39.95 (*0-8442-0293-2*, 02932, NTC Business Bks) NTC Contemp Pub Co.

***Dutka, Alan.** Competitive Intelligence for the Competitive Edge. LC 98-8554. (Illus.). 240p. 2000. pap. 19.95 (*0-658-00059-4*, 000594) NTC Contemp Pub Co.

Dutka, Alan F. AMA Handbook for Customer Satisfaction: A Complete Guide to Research, Planning, & Implementation. (Illus.). 240p. 1995. 49.95 (*0-8442-3454-0*, NTC Business Bks) NTC Contemp Pub Co.
— AMA Handbook for Customer Satisfaction: A Complete Guide to Research, Planning, & Implementation. (Illus.). 240p. 1995. pap. 24.95 (*0-8442-3586-5*, NTC Business Bks) NTC Contemp Pub Co.

Dutka, Anna B., jt. auth. see Ginzberg, Eli.

Dutka, B. J., jt. ed. see Hadley, A. W.

Dutka, Bernard J., ed. Membrane Filtration: Applications, Techniques, & Problems. LC 81-4103. (Pollution Engineering & Technology Ser.: Vol. 17). (Illus.). 628p. reprint ed. pap. 194.70 (*0-608-08931-1*, 206956600005) Bks Demand.

Dutka, Bernard J. & Bitton, Gabriel. Toxicity Testing Using Microorganisms, Vol. I. 168p. 1986. 103.00 (*0-8493-5256-8*, RA1199, CRC Reprint) Franklin.
— Toxicity Testing Using Microorganisms, Vol. II. 240p. 1986. 123.00 (*0-8493-5257-6*, RA1199, CRC Reprint) Franklin.

Dutkiewicz, Piotr J. & Jackson, Robert, eds. NATO Looks East. LC 98-6823. 208p. 1998. 55.00 (*0-275-96059-5*, Praeger Pubs) Greenwood.

Dutkina, Galina. Moscow Days: Life & Hard Times in the New Russia. Fitzpatrick, Catherine A., tr. 208p. 1996. 23.00 (*1-56836-066-5*) Kodansha.

Dutky, Paul. The Bombproof Roll & Beyond. LC 93-7348. 180p. 1993. pap. 14.95 (*0-89732-085-9*) Menasha Ridge.

***Dutlinger, Anne D., ed.** Art, Music & Education As Strategies for Survival: Theresienstadt, 1941-1945. (Illus.). 204p. 2000. 75.00 (*1-928746-10-1*); pap. 45.00 (*1-928746-11-X*) Herodias.

Dutoit, Thierry. An Introduction to Text-to-Speech Synthesis. LC 97-11352. (Text, Speech, & Language Technology Ser.). 1997. text 113.50 (*0-7923-4498-7*) Kluwer Academic.

Dutoit, Thomas, ed. see Derrida, Jacques.

Dutoit, Thomas, tr. see Derrida, Jacques.

Dutoit, Ulysse, jt. auth. see Bersani, Leo.

Dutot, Charles. Political Reflections on the Finances & Commerce of France. LC 76-146461. (Reprints of Economic Classics Ser.). xiii, 304p. 1974. reprint ed. lib. bdg. 57.50 (*0-678-00842-6*) Kelley.

Dutour, L. C. & Nowotny, J., eds. External & Internal Surfaces in Metal Oxides. (Materials Science Forum Ser.: Vol. 29). 320p. 1988. text 116.00 (*0-87849-542-8*, Pub. by Trans T Pub) Enfield Pubs NH.

Dutourd, Jean. L' Ame Sensible. (FRE.). 248p. 1985. pap. 11.95 (*0-7859-2018-8*, 2070376834) Fr & Eur.
— Au Bon Beurre. (Folio Ser.: No. 260). (FRE.). 375p. 1952. pap. 9.95 (*2-07-036260-4*) Schoenhof.
— Au Bon Buerre ou Dix Ans de la Vie d'un Cremier. (FRE.). 1982. pap. 11.95 (*0-7859-1717-9*, 2070362604) Fr & Eur.
— Le Dejeuner Du Lundi. (FRE.). 342p. 1986. pap. 12.95 (*0-7859-2042-0*, 2070377563) Fr & Eur.
— Le Demi-Solde. (FRE.). 192p. 1983. pap. 10.95 (*0-7859-1978-3*, 2070374882) Fr & Eur.
— Dogs Head. Chancellor, Robin, tr. LC 97-51257. 149p. 1998. pap. 12.00 (*0-226-17492-1*) U Ch Pr.
— Les Horreurs De l'Amour, Tome I. (FRE.). 1980. pap. 12.95 (*0-7859-1911-2*, 2070371816) Fr & Eur.
— Les Horreurs De l'Amour, Tome II. (FRE.). 1980. pap. 11.95 (*0-7859-1912-0*, 2070371824) Fr & Eur.
— Les Taxis de la Marne. (FRE.). 224p. 1973. pap. 11.95 (*0-7859-1767-5*, 2070365069) Fr & Eur.
— Une Tete de Chien. (FRE.). 154p. 1988. pap. 10.95 (*0-7859-2103-6*, 2070380866) Fr & Eur.

Dutra, Francis A. & Dos Santos, Joao C., eds. The Portuguese & the Pacific Vol. 1: Proceedings of the International Colloquium, 1993. LC 95-83243. (Publication Ser.: No. 10). 451p. (Orig.). (C). 1995. pap. 25.00 (*0-942208-29-3*) Bandanna Bks.

Dutra, Ines de Castro, et al. Parallelism & Implementation of Logic & Constraint Logic Programming. LC 99-23165. 379p. 1999. lib. bdg. 98.00 (*1-56072-673-3*) Nova Sci Pubs.

Dutre, Willy L. A European Transient Simulation Model for Thermal Solar Systems. 1985. text 293.00 (*90-277-2051-7*) Kluwer Academic.
— Simulation of Thermal Systems: A Modular Program with an Interactive Preprocessor (EMGP3) (C). 1991. text 313.00 (*0-7923-1235-X*) Kluwer Academic.
— Simulation of Water Based Thermal Solar Systems: Eursol - An Interactive Program. (C). 1991. text 146.50 (*0-7923-1236-8*) Kluwer Academic.

DuTremolet deLacheisseri, E. Magnetostriction: Theory & Applications - Magnetoelasticity. 432p. 1993. lib. bdg. 149.00 (*0-8493-6934-7*, QC754) CRC Pr.

***Dutrenit, Gabriela.** Learning & Knowledge Management in the Firm: From Knowledge Accumulation to Strategic Capabilities. LC 99-41929. (New Horizons in the Economics of Innovation Ser.). 352p. 2000. 100.00 (*1-84064-204-1*) E Elgar.

Dutrieue, Anne-Myriam, jt. auth. see Dumoulin, Michel.

Dutrizac, J. E. & Ji, J. Electrorefining & Electrowinning, 111. Ramachandran, V., ed. (Illus.). 736p. write for info. (*0-87339-437-2*) Minerals Metals.

Dutro, J. T., Jr., et al, eds. AGI Data Sheets. 3rd rev. ed. LC 89-32854. (Illus.). 294p. 1990. pap. 43.75 (*0-922152-01-2*) Am Geol.

Dutro, J. T., Jr., jt. auth. see Cooper, G. A.

Dutro, J. Thomas, Jr. & Pfefferkorn, Herman W., eds. Neuvieme Congres International de Stratigraphie et de Geologie du Carbonifere: Compte Rendu: Paleontology, Paleoecology, Paleogeography, Vol. 5. LC 83-19147. 556p. 1986. pap. 77.00 incl. 5.25 hd (*0-8093-1172-0*) S Ill U Pr.

Dutro, Jack. Night Light: A Story for Children Afraid of the Dark. LC 91-19612. (Illus.). 32p. (J). (ps-2). 1991. 11.95 (*0-945354-37-1*) Am Psychol.

Dutro, Orville. Saga of Kettle Falls. (Illus.). 44p. (Orig.). 1988. pap. 4.95 (*0-940151-06-5*) Statesman-Exam.

Dutschke, C. W., et al, eds. Medieval & Renaissance Manuscripts in the Claremont Libraries. (UC Publications in Catalogs & Bibliographies: Vol. III). 1987. 55.00 (*0-520-09644-4*, Pub. by U CA Pr) Cal Prin Full Svc.

Dutschke, Consuelo W. Guide to Medieval & Renaissance Manuscripts in the Huntington Library, 2 vols. 880p. 1989. 95.00 (*0-87328-082-2*) Huntington Lib.

Dutschke, Michael, jt. ed. see Michaelowa, Axel.

Dutson, Judith. Getting Your First Horse. LC 98-25941. (Horse-Wise Guide Ser.). (Illus.). 176p. 1998. pap. 19.95 (*1-58017-078-1*) Storey Bks.

Dutson, T. R. & Pearson, A. M. Quality Attributes & Their Measurement in Meat, Poultry & Fish Products: Advances in Meat Research, Vol. 9. 505p. 1995. 239.00 (*0-8342-1305-2*) Aspen Pub.

***Dutt.** Inside Pakistan 52 Years Outlook. 2000. 72.50 (*81-7648-157-2*, Pub. by Ashish Pub Hse) S Asia.
— War & Peace in Kargil Sector. 2000. 78.00 (*81-7648-151-3*, Pub. by BR Pub) S Asia.

Dutt, Amitava K., ed. New Directions in Analytical Political Economy. LC 93-50633. 368p. 1994. 95.00 (*1-85898-032-1*) E Elgar.

Dutt, Amitava K., et al, eds. The State, Markets & Development: Beyond the Neoclassical Dichotomy. 240p. 1994. 90.00 (*1-85278-929-8*) E Elgar.

Dutt, Amitava K. & Amadeo, Edward J. Keynes's Third Alternative: The Neo-Ricardian Keynesians & the Post-Keynesians. (New Directions in Modern Economics Ser.). (Illus.). 208p. 1990. text 80.00 (*1-85278-354-0*) E Elgar.

Dutt, Amitava K. & Jameson, Kenneth P., eds. New Directions in Development Economics. 208p. 1992. text 90.00 (*1-85278-535-7*) E Elgar.

Dutt, Ashok K., ed. The Asian City: Processes of Development, Characteristics & Planning. LC 94-31375. (GeoJournal Library). 408p. (C). 1994. lib. bdg. 234.00 (*0-7923-3135-4*) Kluwer Academic.
— Medical Geography South & Southeast Asia. (Illus.). 78p. 1981. pap. 24.00 (*0-08-026762-9*, Pergamon Pr) Elsevier.
— Southeast Asia. 4th ed. (C). 1996. text 49.95 (*0-8133-1562-X*); pap. text 21.95 (*0-8133-1563-8*) Westview.
— Southeast Asia: A Ten Nation Region. LC 96-26424. (GeoJournal Library). 352p. (C). 1996. lib. bdg. 169.00 (*0-7923-4171-6*) Kluwer Academic.

Dutt, Ashok K. & Costa, Frank J., eds. Perspectives on Planning & Urban Development in Belgium. LC 92-22979. (GeoJournal Library: Vol. 22). 244p. (C). 1992. text 127.50 (*0-7923-1885-4*) Kluwer Academic.

Dutt, Clemens, tr. see Engels, Friedrich & Marx, Karl.

Dutt, Gurusaday. Folk Arts & Crafts of Bengal: The Collected Papers. (C). 1990. text 47.50 (*81-7046-045-X*, Pub. by Seagull Bks) S Asia.

Dutt, Indu, tr. see Tagore, Rabindranath.

Dutt, K. C., ed. Who's Who of Sanskrit Scholars in India, 1991. (C). 1995. 32.00 (*81-7201-689-1*, Pub. by Indian Pubs) S Asia.

Dutt, N. K. Origin & Growth of Caste in India. 340p. 1986. reprint ed. 18.00 (*0-8364-1677-5*) S Asia.

Dutt, Nalinaksha. Buddhist Sects in India. 1978. pap. 8.50 (*0-89684-044-1*, Pub. by Motilal Bnarsidass) S Asia.
— Buddhist Sects in India. 2nd ed. 1977. 9.00 (*0-88386-971-3*) S Asia.
— Early History of the Spread of Buddhism & the Buddhist Schools. LC 78-72429. reprint ed. 42.00 (*0-404-17293-8*) AMS Pr.
— Early Monastic Buddhism. 1981. reprint ed. 12.50 (*0-8364-0815-2*, Pub. by Mukhopadhyaya) S Asia.
— Mahayana Buddhism. 1976. reprint ed. 11.00 (*0-8364-0430-0*) S Asia.
— Mahayana Buddhism. rev. ed. 1978. 22.00 (*0-89684-032-8*, Pub. by Motilal Bnarsidass) S Asia.

Dutt, R. & Ray, A. K. Dirac & Feynman: Pioneers in Quantum Mechanics. 1993. write for info. (*81-224-0493-6*, Pub. by Wiley Estrn) Franklin.

Dutt, R. C. Nation Building in India. 1987. 29.00 (*81-7062-019-8*, Pub. by Lancer India) S Asia.
— Retreat of Socialism in India: Two Decades Without Nehru, 1964-1984. 219p. (C). 1987. 20.00 (*81-7017-217-9*, Pub. by Abhinav) S Asia.
— Socialism of Jaharwalal Nehru. 1981. 18.50 (*0-8364-0708-3*, Pub. by Abhinav) S Asia.
— Socialism of Jawaharlal Nehru. 284p. 1981. 24.95 (*0-318-36638-X*) Asia Bk Corp.
— State Enterprises in Developing Countries: The Indian Experience. 1990. 33.00 (*81-7017-272-1*, Pub. by Abhinav) S Asia.

Dutt, R. C., ed. Challenges to the Polity. (C). 1988. 17.50 (*0-8364-2390-9*, Pub. by Lancer International) S Asia.

Dutt, R. Palme. Whither China? 1967. pap. 0.40 (*0-87898-021-0*) New Outlook.

Dutt, Romesh C. Civilization in the Buddhist Age (B.C. Three Hundred Twenty to Five Hundred A.D. 1990. reprint ed. 7.50 (*81-85395-75-6*, Pub. by Low Price) S Asia.
— The Economic History of India, 2 vols. in 1. 1990. reprint ed. 21.50 (*81-85418-01-2*, Pub. by Low Price) S Asia.
— History of India from the Earliest Times to the Sixth Century, B.C. LC 72-14391. (History of India Ser.: No. 1). reprint ed. 90.00 (*0-404-09001-X*) AMS Pr.

Dutt, Sagarika. The Politicization of the United Nations Specialized Agencies: A Case Study of UNESCO. LC 94-13281. 340p. 1994. 99.95 (*0-7734-9106-6*) E Mellen.

Dutt, Sagarika, jt. auth. see Bakut tswah Bakut.

Dutt, Shoshee C. Historical Studies & Recreations, 2 vols, Set. LC 72-13307. (Essay Index Reprint Ser.). 1977. reprint ed. 56.95 (*0-8369-8155-3*) Ayer.

Dutt, Sukumar. Buddhist Monks & Monasteries of India: Their History & Their Contribution to Indian Culture. (C). 1989. 26.00 (*81-208-0498-8*, Pub. by Motilal Bnarsidass) S Asia.

Dutt, Trevor P. Gynecology. Scott, Sir Walter, ed. (Medico-Legal Practitioner Ser.). 300p. 1996. write for info. (*1-85941-215-7*, Pub. by Cavendish Pubng) Gaunt.

Dutt, U. C. The Materia Medica of the Hindus. 1989. reprint ed. 46.50 (*0-8364-2540-5*, Pub. by Mittal Pubs Dist) S Asia.
— The Materia Medica of the Hindus. (C). 1995. reprint ed. 30.00 (*0-8364-2915-X*, Pub. by Mittal Pubs Dist) S Asia.

Dutt, Vishnu. Gandhi, Nehru & the Challenge. 1979. 14.00 (*0-8364-0322-3*) S Asia.

Dutta. Biological Nitrogen Fixation in Rice Production. 1990. 60.00 (*0-88258-052-3*) Howard U Pr.

Dutta, A. K. Indian Artifacts: A Study of Indian Arts & Crafts. (Illus.). 208p. 1984. text 39.00 (*0-685-14050-4*) Coronet Bks.

Dutta, A. S. Small Peptides: Chemistry, Biology, & Clinical Studies. LC 93-11629. (Pharmacochemistry Library: Vol. 19). 632p. 1993. 300.00 (*0-444-88655-9*) Elsevier.

Dutta, Abhijit. Christian Missionaries on the Indigo Question in Bengal (1855-1861) (C). 1989. 20.00 (*81-85195-23-4*, Pub. by Minerva) S Asia.
— Nineteenth Century Bengal Society & the Christian Missionaries. (C). 1992. 23.00 (*81-85195-40-4*, Pub. by Minerva) S Asia.

Dutta, Addie, jt. auth. see Proctor, Robert W.

***Dutta, Ajit Singh.** A Father's Poems. (Illus.). 88p. 2000. pap. 10.95 (*0-615-11750-3*) DROVNAS Grp.

Dutta, Aloke. Tabla: Lessons & Practice. 2nd ed. (Illus.). 190p. (Orig.). 1995. pap. 30.00 incl. audio (*0-9646771-0-5*) A Dutta.

Dutta, Anima. Assam Vaishnavism. (C). 1989. 24.00 (*81-7099-173-0*, Pub. by Mittal Pubs Dist) S Asia.

Dutta, Arup K. Nature Quiz. (Illus.). x, 122p. 1991. 15.95 (*81-220-0237-4*) Advent Bks Div.

Dutta, B., et al. Game Theory & Economic Applications: Proceedings of the International Conference Held at the Indian Statistical Institute, New Delhi, India, December 18-22, 1990. LC 92-28524. (Lecture Notes in Economics & Mathematical Systems Ser.: Vol. 389). 1992. 94.95 (*0-387-55886-1*) Spr-Verlag.

Dutta, Bahskar & Dutta Majumdar, D., eds. Recent Advances in Statistical Physics: Proceedings of the International Base Symposium on Statistical Physics. 176p. (C). 1987. text 81.00 (*9971-5-0369-7*) World Scientific Pub.

Dutta, Bahskar, ed. see Mookherjee, Dilip & Ray, Debraj.

Dutta, Bhaskar, ed. Welfare Economics. (Oxford in India Readings Ser.). (Illus.). 266p. 1998. reprint ed. pap. text 11.95 (*0-19-564599-5*) OUP.
— Welfare Economics & India. (India Readings: Themes in Economics Ser.). (Illus.). 264p. 1994. text 29.95 (*0-19-563103-X*) OUP.

Dutta, Bhaskar, et al, eds. Theoretical Issues in Development Economics. (Illus.). 312p. 1993. text 32.00 (*0-19-563171-4*) OUP.

Dutta, D. C. The Income Tax Law. (C). 1990. 200.00 (*0-89771-274-9*) St Mut.
— On Contract, the Indian Contract Act, 1872. (C). 1990. 210.00 (*0-89771-231-5*) St Mut.
— Text Book of Gynecology. (C). 1989. 135.00 (*0-89771-375-3*, Pub. by Current Dist) St Mut.
— Text Book of Obstetrics. (C). 1989. 265.00 (*0-89771-374-5*, Pub. by Current Dist) St Mut.

Dutta, D. C., et al, eds. Concurrent Engineering - 1992. (PED Ser.: Vol. 59). 472p. 1992. 72.50 (*0-7918-1090-9*, G00734) ASME.

Dutta, H. M., jt. ed. see Munshi, J. S.

Dutta, Hiran M., jt. auth. see Datta-Munshi, J. S.

***Dutta, Indrani.** Japanese Invasion of India (1944) Myth or Reality? 1999. 19.00 (*81-87502-05-3*, Pub. by Spectrum) S Asia.

Dutta, Jan. Asia-Pacific Economies: Promises & Challenges. (Research in International Business & Finance Ser.: Vol. 6A). 1987. 78.50 (*0-89232-851-7*) Jai Pr.
— Asia-Pacific Economies: Promises & Challenges. (Research in International Business & Finance Ser.: Vol. 6B). 1987. 78.50 (*0-89232-852-5*) Jai Pr.
— Research in International Business & Finance Vol. 6: Promises & Challenges. Lang, Larry et al, eds. (Research in International Business & Finance Ser.: Vol. 6). 1987. 157.00 (*0-89232-647-6*) Jai Pr.

Dutta, K. K. Some Aspects of Criminal Law. LC 97-913913. xiii, 184p. 1998. 26.00 (*81-7024-917-1*, Pub. by APH Pubng) Nataraj Bks.
— Treatise on Criminal Law. 625p. (C). 1984. 240.00 (*0-7855-1390-6*) St Mut.

Dutta, Kavita. MCQs for the PLAB Examination. 288p. 1998. pap. text 32.50 (*0-7506-4004-9*) Buttrwrth-Heinemann.

Dutta, Kedar N. Sachitra Guljar Hagar: A Pen Picture of Calcutta in the Late 19th Century. Dutta, Satyabrata, tr. (C). 1990. text 22.00 (*0-8364-2592-8*, Pub. by Firma KLM) S Asia.

Dutta, Kedarnatha & Das, Shukavak. Svalikhita Jivani: The Autobiography of Srila Bhaktivinda Thakur. 180p. 1994. pap. 25.00 (*1-889756-29-6*) Sanskrit Relgns Inst.

Dutta, Krishna & Robinson, Andrew, eds. Selected Letters of Rabindranath Tagore. LC 96-38903. (University of Cambridge Oriental Publications: No. 53). (Illus.). 594p. (C). 1997. text 100.00 (*0-521-59018-3*) Cambridge U Pr.

Dutta, M., ed. Research in Asian Economic Studies, Vol. 8. 1998. 78.50 (*0-7623-0199-6*) Jai Pr.
— Research in Asian Economic Studies Vol. 7: Asia Pacific Economic Cooperation: Theory & Practice, 2 vols. 556p. 1996. 157.00 (*0-7623-0119-8*) Jai Pr.

Dutta, M., et al, eds. Essays in Regional Economic Studies. LC 82-71901. (Acorn Economic Communication Ser.: No. 1). xii, 289p. 1983. 33.50 (*0-89386-005-0*) Acorn NC.

Dutta, M. J. Economics, Econometrics & the LINK: Essays in Honor of Lawrence R. Klein. LC 94-34470. (Contributions to Economic Analysis Ser.: Vol. 226). 608p. 1995. 117.00 (*0-444-81787-5*) Elsevier.

Dutta Majumdar, D., et al, eds. Research in Asian Economic Studies Vol. 2: China's Modernization & Open Economic Policy. 449p. 1991. 78.50 (*1-55938-033-0*) Jai Pr.

Dutta Majumdar, D. & Zhongli, Zhang, eds. Research in Asian Economic Studies, 2 vols., Vol. 1. 1989. 157.00 (*0-89232-986-6*) Jai Pr.
— Research in Asian Economic Studies: Asian Industrialization: Changing Economic Structures, Vol. 1, Pt. A. 359p. 1989. 78.50 (*0-89232-987-4*) Jai Pr.
— Research in Asian Economic Studies: Asian Industrialization: Changing Economic Structures, Vol. 1, Pt. B. 377p. 1989. 78.50 (*0-89232-988-2*) Jai Pr.
— Research in Asian Economic Studies: Chinas Economic Reform, 1978-1988, Vol. 3. 300p. 1991. 78.50 (*1-55938-314-3*) Jai Pr.
— Research in Asian Economic Studies Vol. 4: Asian Economic Regimes: An Adaptive Innovation Paradigm. 1992. 157.00 (*1-55938-429-8*) Jai Pr.
— Research in Asian Economic Studies Vol. 5: Asia-Pacific Economics: 1990's & Beyond. 474p. 1994. 78.50 (*1-55938-616-9*) Jai Pr.

Dutta Majumdar, D., jt. ed. see Dutta, Bahskar.

Dutta, Manoranjan. Economic Regionalization in the Asia-Pacific: Challenges to Economic Cooperation. LC 98-9827. 336p. 1999. 95.00 (*1-85898-825-X*) E Elgar.

Dutta, Manoranjan, ed. Studies in U. S. - Asia Economic Relations. LC 83-70889. (Acorn Economic Communication Ser.: No. 2). xvi, 578p. 1985. 48.50 (*0-89386-010-7*) Acorn NC.

D

Dutta, Monoranjan. Sculptures of Assam. 1990. 96.00 (*81-7186-001-X*, Pub. by Agam) S Asia.
Dutta, N. Kanta. Nutritional Relation of Soils. 176p. 1990. 85.00 (*81-7041-457-1*, Pub. by Scientific Pubs) St Mut.
Dutta, N. M. Contribution to the Flora of Calcutta & Its Neighbourhood. Ganguy, A. K., ed. 1985. 85.00 (*0-7855-0725-6*, Pub. by Current Dist) St Mut.
Dutta, Narendra N. Obscure Religious Practices among Some Vaisnavas of Assam. (C). 1990. text 28.50 (*0-8364-2590-1*, Pub. by Punthi Pus) S Asia.
Dutta, P. K. Neutralism: Theory & Practice. 327p. 1978. 16.95 (*0-318-37249-5*) Asia Bk Corp.
Dutta, P. K., ed. Drug Control. (C). 1990. 125.00 (*0-89771-182-3*) St Mut.
Dutta, P. K., jt. auth. see Sahay, B. N.
Dutta, Prajit K. Games That We Play: Introduction to Game Theory & Its Application. (Illus.). 830p. 1999. 60.00 (*0-262-04169-3*) MIT Pr.
Dutta, R. L. Elementary Inorganic Chemistry. 1985. 90.00 (*0-7855-0727-2*, Pub. by Current Dist) St Mut.
— Inorganic Chemistry. 1985. 79.00 (*0-317-38778-2*, Pub. by Current Dist) Mosby Inc.
***Dutta, Reginald.** The Right Way to Keep Pet Fish. 10th rev. ed. (Illus.). 160p. 2001. pap. 7.95 (*0-7160-2114-5*, Pub. by Elliot RW Bks) Midpt Trade.
Dutta-Roy, Amit. LAN Technology & Concepts: Ethernet & Token-Ring Systems. 1993. text 39.95 (*0-07-018395-3*) McGraw.
Dutta, S. Ambivalence in Hardy. LC 99-13316. 1999. text 59.95 (*0-312-22183-5*) St Martin.
Dutta, S. K. Biological Nitrogen Fixation Associated with Rice Production. 1991. 62.50 (*81-204-0560-9*, Pub. by Oxford IBH) S Asia.
— DNA Systematics Vol. 2: Plants. LC 85-21285. 1986. reprint ed. 124.00 (*0-8493-5821-3*, CRC Reprint) Franklin.
Dutta, S. K., ed. DNA Systematics. 288p. 1986. 138.00 (*0-8493-5820-5*, QP624); 135.00 (*0-317-05983-1*) Franklin.
Dutta, S. K. & Winter, W. P. DNA Systematics Vol. III: Human & Higher Primates, Vol. 3. rev. ed. LC 85-21285. 224p. 1990. 125.00 (*0-8493-5822-1*, QP624) Franklin.
Dutta, Saroj. Land System in Northern India: c. AD 400-700. LC 95-910426. 232p. (C). 1995. 31.00 (*81-215-0657-3*, Pub. by M Manoharial) Coronet Bks.
Dutta, Satyabrata, tr. see Dutta, Kedar N.
Dutta, Sibani. Public Expenditure & Economic Development. 395p. 1986. 42.00 (*81-7024-020-4*, Pub. by Ashish Pub Hse) S Asia.
Dutta, Sisir K. & Millis, Richard M., eds. Biological Effects of Electropollution: Brain Tumors & Experimental Models. LC 86-82834. (Illus.). x, 245p. (C). 1986. text 48.00 (*0-9617314-1-9*) Info Ventures Inc.
Dutta, Soumitra & Manzoni, J. F. Process Reengineering, Organizational Change & Performance Improvement. LC 98-19210. (INSEAD Global Management Ser.). 1998. write for info. (*0-07-709436-0*) McGraw.
Dutta, Sudipt. Family Business in India. LC 96-35428. 1996. 38.95 (*0-8039-9326-9*) Sage.
Dutta, Sukanta K., jt. auth. see Mohanty, Sashi B.
Dutta, Sunil, tr. see Ghalib, Mirza A.
Dutta, Swapna, tr. see Parashuram.
Dutta, V. R., ed. Rural Poverty & Economic Change in India. 167p. 1992. text 25.00 (*0-685-37817-9*, Pub. by Radiant Pubs) S Asia.
Dutter, Barry. Everything I Really Need to Know I Learned from Television. (Illus.). 80p. 1992. pap. 7.95 (*1-55783-122-X*) Applause Theatre Bk Pubs.
— The Shy Guy's Guide to Dating. LC 98-5090. 272p. 1998. pap. 13.95 (*0-312-18757-2*) St Martin.
Dutter, Barry & Kurth, Steve. In a Perfect World. Carle, Cliff, ed. 2000. pap. 6.95 (*1-57644-093-1*) CCC Pubns.
Dutter, R. & Grossmann, W. COMPSTAT 1994: Proceedings in Computational Statistics. 576p. 1994. 156.95 (*3-7908-0793-1*) Spr-Verlag.
Duttmann, Alexander G. At Odds with AIDS: Thinking & Talking about a Virus. Gilgen, Peter & Scott-Curtis, Conrad, trs. from GER. LC 96-14817. (Meridian: Crossing Aesthetics Ser.). 1996. 37.50 (*0-8047-2437-7*); pap. 12.95 (*0-8047-2438-5*) Stanford U Pr.
Duttmann, Martina & Zwoch, Felix, eds. Bauwelt Berlin Annual 1998: Chronology of Building Events 1996-2001: 1998. (Bauwelt Berlin Annuals Ser.). (Illus.). 192p. 1999. pap. 45.00 (*3-7643-6015-1*, Pub. by Birkhauser) Princeton Arch.
— Bauwelt Berlin Annual, 1997: Chronology of Building Events 1996 to 2001: 1997. (Bauwelt Berlin Ser.). (Illus.). 192p. 1998. pap. 45.00 (*3-7643-5843-2*, Pub. by Birkhauser) Princeton Arch.
— Bauwelt Berlin Annual 1996: A Chronicle of Architecture 1996-2001. (Illus.). 192p. 1997. pap. 44.50 (*3-7643-5664-2*, Pub. by Birkhauser) Princeton Arch.
— Bauwelt Berlin Annual 1996: Chronik der Baulichen Ereignisse, 1996-2001. (GER., Illus.). 192p. 1997. pap. 44.50 (*3-7643-5663-4*, Pub. by Birkhauser) Princeton Arch.
Dutto, G. & Craddock, M. K. Cyclotrons & Their Applications: Proceedings of the 13th International Conference. 972p. 1993. text 178.00 (*981-02-1130-9*) World Scientific Pub.
Dutton. Politics & Diplomacy. 248p. 1998. text 59.50 (*1-86064-112-1*, Pub. by I B T) St Martin.
— Understanding Optical Communication. LC 99-183122. 800p. (C). 1998. pap. text 64.99 (*0-13-020141-3*) P-H.
Dutton, ed. A New Berceo Manuscript. (Exeter Hispanic Text Ser.: No. 32). 122p. Date not set. pap. text 17.95 (*0-85989-104-6*, Pub. by Univ Exeter Pr) Northwestern U Pr.
Dutton, jt. auth. see Rice, H.
Dutton, Allen A. A Mythology for the 21st Century: Mythologie pour le Vingt-et-Unieme Siecle. Eason, Pat & Hawkins, Mary, eds. Grobe, Edwin P., tr. (ENG & FRE., Illus.). 70p. (Orig.). 1990. pap. 25.00 (*0-9625682-0-1*) Jeckwoe Pub.
Dutton, Anne. Triangles on a Roll: It's Play Time. (Illus.). 40p. 1995. pap. 12.95 (*0-9646198-1-4*) Quilter Ranch.
Dutton, B., et al. Diccionario Esencial Diafora Espanol-Ingles-Espanol.Tr. of Essential Diafore Spanish-English-Spanish Dictionary. (ENG & SPA.). 425p. 1981. 19.95 (*0-8288-2326-X*, S40509) Fr & Eur.
Dutton, Bertha P. American Indians of the Southwest. enl. rev. ed. LC 80-52274. (Illus.). 317p. 1983. pap. 16.95 (*0-8263-0704-3*) U of NM Pr.
— Southwest Indians Bk. 2: Hopi, Acoma, Tewa, Zuni. (J). (gr. 1-9). 1992. pap. 4.95 (*0-88388-062-8*) Bellerophon Bks.
Dutton, Bertha P., jt. auth. see Hewett, Edgar L.
Dutton, Bertha P., jt. auth. see Olin, Caroline.
Dutton, Bob & Anderson, Beth. Personal & Comprehensive Testimony: The P. A. C. T. Plan. Thompson, Rachel, ed. 148p. 1993. student ed. 42.00 (*0-9636798-0-5*) Creat Artforms.
Dutton, Brian, ed. see Berceo, Bonzalo.
Dutton, Brian, ed. see Berceo, Gonzalo.
Dutton, Brian, ed. see De Berceo, Gonzalo.
Dutton, Brian, ed. see Gordonio, Bernardo.
***Dutton, Brunella N.** 750 Italian Verbs & Their Uses. Zamir, Jan R. & Zamir, Sonia N., eds. LC 98-22784. (750 Verbs & Their Uses Ser.). 391p. 1999. pap. 17.95 (*0-471-01627-6*) Wiley.
Dutton, Charles J. The Samaritans of Molokai. (Select Bibliographies Reprint Ser.). 1977. reprint ed. 25.95 (*0-8369-5733-4*) Ayer.
Dutton Childrens Bks. Staff. Who's at the Door?, 1 vol. (ps-2). 1999. 8.99 (*0-525-46158-2*, Dutton Child) Peng Put Young Read.
Dutton Childrens Books Staff. Humpty Dumpty: And Other Nursery Rhymes. LC 96-217755. (Illus.). 14p. (J). (ps). 1996. pap. 6.99 (*0-525-45675-9*, Dutton Child) Peng Put Young Read.
Dutton Childrens Books Staff, ed. Mr. Potato Goes to Washington. (J). 1999. 6.99 (*0-525-45626-0*, Dutton Child) Peng Put Young Read.
Dutton, Daryl A. & Krausz, M., eds. The Concept of Creativity in Science & Art. (Martinus Nijhoff Philosophy Library: No. 6). 1984. pap. text 61.50 (*90-247-3127-5*, Pub. by M Nijhoff) Kluwer Academic.
Dutton, Daryl A., jt. ed. see Ashour-Abdalla, Maha.
Dutton, David. Anthony Eden: A Life & Reputation. LC 97-8824. (Illus.). 606p. 1997. reprint ed. pap. text 24.95 (*0-340-69139-5*) OUP.
— Austen Chamberlain: Gentleman in Politics. 373p. 1986. 49.95 (*0-86360-018-2*) Transaction Pubs.
— British Politics since 1945: The Rise, Fall & Rebirth of Consensus. 2nd ed. (Historical Association Studies). 208p. (C). 1997. pap. text 16.95 (*0-631-20320-6*) Blackwell Pubs.
Dutton, Diana B. Worse Than the Disease: Pitfalls of Medical Progress. 544p. (C). 1992. pap. text 24.95 (*0-521-39557-7*) Cambridge U Pr.
Dutton, Donald G. The Abusive Personality: Violence & Control in Intimate Relationships. LC 98-23645. 214p. 1998. lib. bdg. 29.00 (*1-57230-370-0*) Guilford Pubns.
— The Domestic Assault of Women: Psychological & Criminal Justice Perspectives. 320p. (C). 1988. pap. text 29.00 (*0-205-11323-0*, H13238) Allyn.
— The Domestic Assault of Women: Psychological & Criminal Justice Perspectives. 2nd expanded rev. ed. (Illus.). 256p. 1994. pap. 24.95 (*0-7748-0462-9*) U of Wash Pr.
Dutton, Donald G. & Golant, Susan K. The Batterer: A Psychological Profile. 224p. 1997. pap. 14.00 (*0-465-03388-1*, Pub. by Basic) HarpC.
Dutton, Dorothy & Humphries, Carly. A Rendezvous with Colorado History. LC 99-165308. (Illus.). 200p. (J). (gr. 4). 1999. text 24.95 (*0-9642420-2-8*) Sterling Ties.
Dutton, Dorothy & Humphries, Caryl. How to Do a Rendezvous. (Illus.). teacher ed. 7.95 (*0-9642420-1-X*) Sterling Ties.
— A Rendezvous with Idaho History. (Illus.). (J). 1994. text 26.95 (*0-9642420-0-1*) Sterling Ties.
Dutton-Douglas, Mary A., et al, eds. Feminist Psychotherapies: Integration of Therapeutic & Feminist Systems. LC 88-16705. (Developments in Clinical Psychology Ser.: Vol. 9). 320p. (C). 1989. text 73.25 (*0-89391-387-1*) Ablx Pub.
Dutton, Ellen. LAN Security Handbook. LC 94-19132. 1994. 39.95 incl. disk (*1-55851-387-6*, M&T Bks) IDG Bks.
Dutton, Fred. Life on the Great Lakes: A Wheelsman's Story. Ellis, William D., ed. LC 90-49241. (Great Lakes Bks.). (Illus.). 176p. 1991. pap. 16.95 (*0-8143-2261-1*, Great Lks Bks); text 29.95 (*0-8143-2260-3*, Great Lks Bks) Wayne St U Pr.
Dutton, G. F. Some Branch Against the Sky: The Practice & Principles of Marginal Gardening. (Illus.). 207p. 1997. 29.95 (*0-88192-409-1*) Timber.
Dutton, G. J. Glucuronidation of Drugs & Other Compounds. 288p. 1980. 129.95 (*0-8493-5295-9*, RM301) CRC Pr.
Dutton, Gail. A Matter of Trust: The Guide to Gestational Surrogacy. LC 96-93105. 230p. (Orig.). 1997. pap. 21.95 (*0-9655966-0-5*) Clouds Pub.
Dutton, Geoffrey. A Hierarchical Coordinate System for Geoprocessing & Cartography. LC 98-41285. (Lecture Notes in Earth Sciences Ser.). 231p. 1999. pap. 119.00 (*3-540-64980-8*) Spr-Verlag.
— Out in the Open. 1995. 39.95 (*0-7022-2681-5*, Pub. by Univ Queensland Pr) Intl Spec Bk.
Dutton, Geoffrey, ed. Country Childhoods. (Orig.). 1992. pap. 14.95 (*0-7022-2434-0*, Pub. by Univ Queensland Pr) Intl Spec Bk.
Dutton, Geoffrey F. The Concrete Garden. 64p. (Orig.). 1991. pap. 14.95 (*1-85224-141-1*, Pub. by Bloodaxe Bks) Dufour.
— Squaring the Waves. 60p. 1986. pap. 11.95 (*1-85224-007-5*, Pub. by Bloodaxe Bks) Dufour.
Dutton, H. J., jt. ed. see Emken, Edward A.
Dutton, Harry J. & Lenhard, Peter. A Synchronous Transfer: Asychronous Transfer Mode - A Technical Overview. LC 96-128096. 336p. (C). 1995. pap. 69.00 (*0-13-520446-1*) P-H.
Dutton, Ian S. Writing Operating Procedures for Process Plants. LC 94-29180. 1995. write for info. (*0-412-99341-4*) Chapman & Hall.
Dutton, J. C. & Purtell, L. P., eds. Separated Flows, 1993. LC 93-71636. (FED Ser.: Vol. 149). 217p. 1993. pap. 45.00 (*0-7918-0957-9*, H00789) ASME.
Dutton, Jane E., jt. auth. see Cooperrider, David L.
Dutton, Joan P. Plants of Colonial Williamsburg: How to Identify 200 of Colonial America's Flowers, Herbs, & Trees. LC 76-50633. (Illus.). 193p. 1979. pap. 12.95 (*0-87935-042-3*) Colonial Williamsburg.
Dutton, Joan P., jt. auth. see Booth, Letha.
Dutton, John A. Dynamics of Atmospheric Motion. LC 94-25265. (Illus.). 640p. 1999. pap. text 17.95 (*0-486-68486-5*) Dover.
— The Scientific Objectives, Philosophy & Management of the MOCAT Project. LC 77-136104. 141p. 1969. 19.00 (*0-403-04497-9*) Scholarly.
***Dutton, John, pseud.** St. Giles's Fair. unabridged ed. (Dreamguard Trilogy Ser.: Vol. 1). (Illus.). 303p. (J). 2000. pap. 12.95 (*0-9577556-0-0*) Samara.
— Tiger's Island. unabridged ed. (Dreamguard Trilogy Ser.: Vol. 2). (Illus.). viii, 245p. (J). Date not set. pap. 12.95 (*0-9577556-1-9*) Samara.
Dutton, Jonathan J. Atlas of Clinical & Surgical Orbital Anatomy. LC 93-11266. (Illus.). 256p. 1994. text 177.00 (*0-7216-5427-4*, W B Saunders Co) Harcrt Hlth Sci Grp.
***Dutton, Jonathon J., et al.** Diagnostic Atlas of Orbital Diseases. LC 99-49762. (Illus.). 220p. 2000. text. write for info. (*0-7216-8273-1*, W B Saunders Co) Harcrt Hlth Sci Grp.
Dutton, June. The Adventures of the S. S. Happiness Crew: Cap'n Joshua's Super Secret: 3rd Adventure. (Illus.). 1982. 5.95 (*0-915696-50-9*) Determined Prods.
— A Christmas Cook Book. (Illus.). 1978. pap. 2.50 (*0-915696-06-1*) Determined Prods.
— Fourth Adventure of the S. S. Happiness Crew: Visit to a Magic Mountain. (Illus.). (J). 1983. 5.95 (*0-915696-64-9*) Determined Prods.
— Hope Is a Handful of Dreams. LC 77-90655. (Illus.). 1978. 5.95 (*0-915696-10-X*) Determined Prods.
Dutton, June, text. Snoopy & the Gang Out West. LC 82-71284. (Illus.). (J). 1983. 6.95 (*0-915696-55-X*); 5.00 (*0-915696-82-7*) Determined Prods.
Dutton, June & Hill, Eric. The Adventures of the S. S. Happiness Crew: Cap'n Joshua's Dangerous Dilemma : 1st Adventure. (Illus.). 1982. reprint ed. 5.95 (*0-915696-36-3*) Determined Prods.
— The Adventures of the S. S. Happiness Crew: Mystery in the Middle of the Ocean: 2nd Adventure. LC 81-65682. (Illus.). 1981. 5.95 (*0-915696-48-7*) Determined Prods.
Dutton, June & Perl, Susan. Faith, Hope & Charity. LC 77-78293. (Illus.). 5.95 (*0-915696-46-0*) Determined Prods.
Dutton, June, jt. auth. see Schulz, Charles M.
Dutton, Ken. Art of Control Engineering. 800p. (C). 1996. pap. text 37.61 (*0-582-23633-9*) Addison-Wesley.
Dutton, Ken, et al. Art of Control Engineering. LC 97-172297. 820p. (C). 1997. pap. text 78.95 (*0-201-17545-2*) Addison-Wesley.
Dutton, Kenneth R. The Perfectible Body: The Western Ideal of Male Physical Development. LC 94-38092. (Illus.). 400p. 1995. pap. 24.95 (*0-8264-0787-0*) Continuum.
Dutton, Kenneth R., jt. auth. see Laura, Ronald S.
Dutton, Lyn, et al. Military Space. (Air Power: Aircraft, Weapons Systems & Technology Ser.). (Illus.). 200p. 1990. 40.00 (*0-08-037346-1*, 3004, Pub. by Brasseys) Brasseys.
Dutton, Marsha, ed. see Aelred of Rievaulx.
Dutton, Mary A. Empowering & Healing the Battered Woman: A Model for Assessment & Intervention. LC 92-7826. 224p. 1992. 34.95 (*0-8261-7130-3*) Springer Pub.
Dutton, Michael, ed. Streetlife China. LC 98-8136. (Modern China Ser.). (Illus.). 272p. (C). 1999. 54.95 (*0-521-63141-6*); pap. 19.95 (*0-521-63719-8*) Cambridge U Pr.
Dutton, Michael R. Policing & Punishment in China: From Patriarchy to "the People" (Illus.). 401p. (C). 1992. text 80.00 (*0-521-40097-X*) Cambridge U Pr.
***Dutton, Monte.** At Speed: The People, Places & Fans of NASCAR. LC 99-86478. (Illus.). 192p. 2000. pap. 15.95 (*1-57488-261-9*) Brasseys.
— Jeff Gordon. GHB Publishers Staff, ed. (Sport Snaps Ser.). (Illus.). (YA). 2000. pap. text 12.95 (*1-892920-31-X*) G H B Pubs.
Dutton, Paul, ed. Carolingian Civilization: A Reader. 360p. 1993. pap. 24.95 (*1-55111-003-2*) Broadview Pr.
— Charlemagne's Courtier: The Complete Einhard. (Readings in Medieval Civilizations & Cultures Ser.: Vol. 3). 280p. (C). 1998. pap. 12.95 (*1-55111-134-9*) Broadview Pr.
Dutton, Paul, jt. ed. see Stouck, Mary-Ann.
Dutton, Paul E. The Politics of Dreaming in the Carolingian Empire. LC 93-38615. (Regents Studies in Medieval Culture). (Illus.). xviii, 346p. 1994. text 50.00 (*0-8032-1653-X*) U of Nebr Pr.
Dutton, Paul E. & Kessler, Herbert L. The Poetry & Paintings of the 1st Bible of Charles the Bald. LC 97-4833. (Recentiores Ser.). 198p. (C). 1998. text 69.50 (*0-472-10815-8*, 10815) U of Mich Pr.
Dutton, Paul E., jt. ed. see Murray, Alexander C.
Dutton, R. E. Duttonism, Two Hundred Lessons. 62p. 1993. reprint ed. spiral bd. 15.50 (*0-7873-0303-8*) Hlth Research.
Dutton, Rebecca. Clinical Reasoning in Physical Disabilities. LC 94-24714. (Illus.). 304p. 1995. 29.00 (*0-683-02740-9*) Lppncott W & W.
***Dutton, Richard.** Ben Johnson. LC 99-20661. 232p. 1999. pap. 28.60 (*0-582-21506-4*) Addison-Wesley.
— Licensing, Censorship & Authorship in Early Modern England. LC 00-40452. 2000. write for info. (*0-312-23624-7*) St Martin.
Dutton, Richard. Mastering the Revels: The Regulation & Censorship of English Renaissance Drama. LC 90-72125. (Illus.). 327p. 1991. text 37.95 (*0-87745-335-7*) U of Iowa Pr.
— Modern Tragicomedy & the British Tradition. LC 86-40072. 256p. 1986. pap. 14.95 (*0-8061-2025-8*) U of Okla Pr.
Dutton, Richard, jt. auth. see Wilson, Wilson.
Dutton, Richard, ed. see Hammond, Paul.
Dutton, Richard, ed. see Jonson, Ben.
Dutton, Richard, ed. see Middleton, Thomas.
Dutton, Richard, ed. see Sidney, Philip.
Dutton, Richard P. Anesthesia Guide. LC 94-27187. 416p. 1994. pap. text 34.95 (*0-316-19958-3*, Little Brwn Med Div) Lppncott W & W.
Dutton, Richard P., et al. Anesthesiologist's Guide to the OR: Prepped. 1994. write for info. (*0-614-32032-1*) Little.
Dutton, Rick & Freitao, Walter O. Nexus: Live Action Roleplaying. Brooks, Les, ed. (Play This Bk.: Vol. 1). (Illus.). 136p. (Orig.). 1994. pap. 19.95 (*1-56882-030-5*, 6500) Chaosium.
Dutton, Robert R. Saul Bellow. rev. ed. (United States Authors Ser.: No. 181). 232p. (C). 1982. 24.95 (*0-8057-7353-3*) Macmillan.
Dutton, Robert W., ed. VLSI Logic Synthesis & Design. 326p. (gr. 12). 1991. 120.00 (*90-5199-046-4*, Pub. by IOS Pr) IOS Press.
Dutton, Robert W. & Yu, Zhiping. Technology CAD: Computer Simulation of IC Processes & Devices. LC 93-20663. (International Engineering & Computer Science Ser.: No. 243). 400p. (C). 1993. text 127.50 (*0-7923-9379-1*) Kluwer Academic.
Dutton, Roderic. An Arab Family. LC 85-10272. (Families the World Over Ser.). (Illus.). 32p. (J). (gr. 2-5). 1985. lib. bdg. 18.60 (*0-8225-1660-8*, Lerner Publctns) Lerner Pub.
— Changing Rural Systems in Oman: The Khabura Project. LC 97-44000. 1998. write for info. (*0-7103-0607-5*, Pub. by Kegan Paul Intl) Col U Pr.
Dutton, Roderic, et al. Arid Land Resources & Their Management: Jordan's Desert Martin. LC 97-48326. 300p. 1998. 212.50 (*0-7103-0612-1*, Pub. by Kegan Paul Intl) Col U Pr.
Dutton, S. P. Depositional Systems & Hydrocarbon Resource Potential of the Pennsylvanian System, Palo Duro & Dalhart Basins, Texas Panhandle. (Geological Circular Ser.: GC 80-8). (Illus.). 49p. 1980. pap. 1.50 (*0-318-13665-1*) Bur Econ Geology.
Dutton, S. P., et al. Geologic Controls on Reservoir Properties of Low-Permeability Sandstone, Frontier Formation, Moxa Arch, Southwestern Wyoming. (Reports of Investigations: No. 234). (Illus.). xxp. (Orig.). 1995. pap. 9.50 (*0-614-11612-0*) Bur Econ Geology.
— Geology & Geohydrology of the Palo Duro Basin, Texas Panhandle, A Report on the Progress of Nuclear Waste Isolation Feasibility Studies (1978) (Geological Circular Ser.: GC 79-1). (Illus.). 99p. 1979. pap. 2.50 (*0-686-29328-2*) Bur Econ Geology.
— Petroleum Potential of the Palo Duro Basin, Texas Panhandle. (Reports of Investigations: RI 123). (Illus.). 87p. 1982. pap. 5.00 (*0-318-03264-3*) Bur Econ Geology.
Dutton, S. P., jt. auth. see Kreitler, C. W.
***Dutton Staff.** Tiger. (Animal Planet Ser.). 1999. pap. 6.99 (*0-525-46282-1*) NAL.
Dutton, Thom. Celtic Charms. (Illus.). ii, 25p. 1998. pap. 10.00 (*1-892811-01-4*, CCMB) Cape Side.
Dutton, Thomas A., ed. Voices in Architectural Education: Cultural Politics & Pedagogy. LC 91-9593. (Critical Studies in Education & Culture). 328p. 1991. 62.95 (*0-89789-253-4*, H253, Bergin & Garvey) Greenwood.
Dutton, Thomas A. & Mann, Lisa H., eds. Reconstructing Architecture: Critical Discourses & Social Practices. (Pedagogy & Cultural Practices Ser.: Vol. 5). 336p. (C). 1996. pap. 21.95 (*0-8166-2809-2*); text 54.95 (*0-8166-2808-4*) U of Minn Pr.
Dutton, Thomas E., jt. auth. see Demetriou, Andrew J.
Dutton, Tom & Tyron, Darrell, eds. Language Contact & Change in the Austronesian World. (Trends in Linguistics, Studies & Monographs: No. 77). 693p. (C). 1994. lib. bdg. 213.85 (*3-11-012786-5*, 170-94) Mouton.
***Dutton, Victoria.** Bead Book: A Step-by-Step-Guide to the Creative Art of Beading. 1998. 16.98 (*1-880908-96-4*) Todtri Prods.
Dutton, Victoria. Traditional Coutry Crafts, 1. 1998. pap. text 12.98 (*1-880908-39-5*) Todtri Prods.
Dutton, William. Society On The Line: Information Politics in the Digital Age. (Illus.). 416p. 1999. text 89.00 (*0-19-877461-3*) OUP.
— Society on the Line: Information Politics in the Digital Age. (Illus.). 416p. 1999. pap. text 29.95 (*0-19-877460-5*) OUP.

D

— William Shakespeare Vol. 1: A Literary Life. 1994. pap. 18.95 (*0-312-12357-4*) St Martin.

Dutton, William & Kraemer, Kenneth L. Modeling As Negotiating: The Political Dynamics of Computer Models in the Public Process. Voigt, Melvin J., ed. LC 84-28429. (Communication & Information Science Ser.). 280p. 1985. text 73.25 (*0-89391-261-1*) Ablx Pub.

Dutton, William H., ed. Information & Communication Technologies: Visions & Realities. (Illus.). 484p. 1996. text 88.00 (*0-19-877459-1*); pap. text 28.00 (*0-19-877496-6*) OUP.

Dutton, Yasin, ed. see Al-Furqan Islamic Heritage Foundation (London, England).

***Duttons Children's Books Staff.** World Greatest Dog. (Animal Planet Ser.). (Illus.). 24p. (J). (ps-3). 2000. pap. 6.99 (*0-525-46500-6*, Dutton Child) Peng Put Young Read.

Duttweiler, Michael W., jt. auth. see Greene, H. David.

***Dutwin, Phyllis.** Writing the Easy Way. 3rd ed. LC 99-46423. 220p. 2000. pap. write for info. (*0-7641-1206-6*) Barron.

Dutwin, Phyllis, jt. auth. see Diamond, Harriet.

Duty, Earl. How to Build a Dune Buggy. (Illus.). 264p. 1998. pap. 19.95 (*1-880524-26-0*) Cars & Parts.

Duty, Guy. Divorce & Remarriage. LC 96-2485. 16p. 1967. text 14.99 (*0-87123-097-6*) Bethany Hse.

Duuren, B. L. Van, see Van Duuren, B. L., ed.

Duuren, Bob Van, see Van Duuren, Bob.

Duursma, E. K. & Carroll, J. Environmental Compartments: Equilibria & Assessment of Processes Between Air, Water, Sediments & Biota. LC 96-23139. 1996. write for info. (*0-387-61039-1*) Spr-Verlag.

— Environmental Compartments: Equilibria & Assessment of Processes Between Air, Water, Sediments & Biota. LC 96-23139. 277p. 1996. 74.95 (*3-540-61039-1*) Spr-Verlag.

Duursma, E. K., ed. see Baretta-Bekker, H. G.

Duursma, Jorri. Fragmentation & the International Relations of Micro-State. (Cambridge Studies in International & Comparative Law). 486p. (C). 1996. text 95.00 (*0-521-56360-7*) Cambridge U Pr.

Duus. Japan Unbolted. LC 96-86768. 226p. 1996. pap. text 15.95 (*0-312-11681-0*) St Martin.

— The Rise of Modern Japan, 2 vols. 2nd ed. (C). 1997. pap. text 27.96 (*0-395-74604-3*) HM.

Duus, Erling. Danish American Journey. 134p. 1971. pap. 10.00 (*1-881946-01-0*) Gauntlet Bks.

Duus, Masayo. The Japanese Conspiracy: The Oahu Sugar Strike of 1920. LC 99-17701. 375p. 1999. pap. 18.95 (*0-520-20485-9*, Pub. by U CA Pr) Cal Prin Full Svc.

Duus, Masayo U. The Japanese Conspiracy: The Oahu Sugar Strike of 1920. Cary, Beth, tr. LC 99-17701. 375p. 1999. 55.00 (*0-520-20484-0*, Pub. by U CA Pr) Cal Prin Full Svc.

— Unlikely Liberators: The Men of the 100th & the 442nd. Duus, Peter, tr. from JPN. LC 87-6013. (Illus.). 288p. 1987. 24.95 (*0-8248-1081-3*) UH Pr.

Duus, Olaus F. Frontier Parsonage. Scott, Franklyn D., ed. LC 78-15205. (Scandinavians in America Ser.). 1979. reprint ed. lib. bdg. 17.95 (*0-405-11632-2*) Ayer.

Duus, Peter. The Abacus & the Sword: The Japanese Penetration of Korea, 1859-1910. (Twentieth-Century Japan Ser.: Vol. 4). 498p. 1997. 55.00 (*0-520-08614-7*, Pub. by U CA Pr) Cal Prin Full Svc.

— The Abacus & the Sword: The Japanese Penetration of Korea, 1895-1910. (Twentieth-Century Japan: The Emergence of a World Power Ser.). 498p. 1998. pap. text 19.95 (*0-520-21361-0*, Pub. by U CA Pr) Cal Prin Full Svc.

— Feudalism in Japan. 3rd ed. LC 92-35470. (Studies in World Civilization). 160p. (C). 1993. pap. 17.50 (*0-07-018412-7*) McGraw.

— Party Rivalry & Political Change in Taisho Japan. LC 68-21972. (Harvard East Asian Ser.: No. 35). 328p. reprint ed. pap. 101.70 (*0-608-30372-0*, 200549000054) Bks Demand.

— Topical Diagnosis in Neurology. 3rd ed. Lindenberg, Richard, tr. LC 97-31483. (Flexibook Ser.). (Illus.). 516p. 1997. text 33.00 (*0-86577-305-X*) Thieme Med Pubs.

— Topical Diagnosis in Neurology: Anatomy, Physiology, Signs & Symptoms. 3rd ed. Lindenberg, Richard, tr. from ENG. LC 97-31483. 1997. write for info. (*3-13-612802-8*) Thieme Med Pubs.

Duus, Peter, ed. The Cambridge History of Japan Vol. 6: The Twentieth Century. (Illus.). 896p. 1989. text 120.00 (*0-521-22357-1*) Cambridge U Pr.

Duus, Peter, et al, eds. The Japanese Informal Empire in China, 1895-1937. LC 88-28311. (Illus.). 484p. 1989. reprint ed. pap. 150.10 (*0-608-04531-4*, 206527400001) Bks Demand.

— The Japanese Wartime Empire, 1931-1945. LC 95-37203. 440p. 1996. text 52.50 (*0-691-04382-5*, Pub. by Princeton U Pr) Cal Prin Full Svc.

Duus, Peter, tr. see Duus, Masayo U.

Duv, Gloria. How to Run a Successful Mail Order Business by Defrauding the Public: A Semi-Serious Guide to Illusory Riches. 82p. 1995. pap. 14.95 (*0-9627647-5-2*) Space Eagle.

D'Uva. Film Financing: Independent Producers. 144p. 1993. pap. 12.95 (*0-685-69318-X*) Prof Pr NC.

Duva, Joseph W. & Mamorsky, Jeffrey D., eds. Journal of Health Care Benefits. 126.00 (*0-685-69671-5*, HBEN) Warren Gorham & Lamont.

Duva, Joy, jt. auth. see Cole, Elizabeth.

Duva, Nicholas, compiled by. Somebody Real. (Illus.). 192p. (Orig.). (J). (gr. 5-12). 1973. 6.95 (*0-912834-01-3*); pap. 3.95 (*0-912834-04-8*) Am Faculty Pr.

Duval, Anjela. A Modern Breton Political Poet - Anjela Duval: A Biography & an Anthology. Timm, Lenora A., ed. & tr. by. LC 89-29829. (Studies in French Literature: Vol. 5). 296p. 1990. lib. bdg. 89.95 (*0-88946-570-3*) E Mellen.

Duval, C. Dictionnaire de la Chimie et de Ses Applications. 3rd ed.Tr. of Dictionary of Chemistry & Its Applications. (FRE.). 1100p. 1977. 450.00 (*0-8288-5383-5*, M6183) Fr & Eur.

Duval, Cynthia. Figures from Life: Porcelain Sculpture from the Metropolitan Museum of Art: 1740-1780. Outland, Wendy, ed. (Illus.). 101p. (Orig.). (C). 1992. pap. 20.00 (*1-878390-01-5*) Mus St Pete.

Duval, Cynthia, ed. Gladys Shafran Kashdin: In Retrospect. (Illus.). 48p. 1996. pap. 12.00 (*1-878293-12-5*) Tampa Mus Art.

Duval, Cynthia & Karcheski, Walter J. Medieval & Renaissance Splendor: The Romance of Arts, Armor & Works of Art from the John Woodman Higgins Armary. LC 83-83306. (Illus.). 160p. (Orig.). 1984. pap. 9.95 (*0-916758-15-X*) Ringling Mus Art.

Duval, Elizabeth W. T. E. Lawrence: A Bibliography. LC 74-185877. (Reference Ser.: No. 44). 1972. reprint ed. lib. bdg. 75.00 (*0-8383-1385-X*) M S G Haskell Hse.

Duval, Frank. A Survivor's Manual for Sexual Addiction & Other Sexual Disorders: Resources for the Sexually Broken & the Christian Community. Phelan, James, ed. LC 98-91230. 70p. 1998. pap. write for info. (*1-57502-733-X*, PO2047) Morris Pubng.

Duval, J. H. Svengali's Secrets & Memoirs of the Golden Age. 1958. 12.00 (*0-8315-0014-X*) Speller.

Duval, James K. The Heart of Selling. 96p. 1994. per. 9.95 (*0-8403-7867-X*) Kendall-Hunt.

Duval, Joe. God, Man, & Institutions: The Ultimate Ethic Is Here. 36p. 1997. pap. 10.00 (*0-9618680-1-5*) Rights Pr.

— Punch-Drunk in America: Reviving the American Revolutionary Movement. 120p. (Orig.). 1987. pap. 10.00 (*0-9618680-0-7*) Rights Pr.

DuVal, John, tr. see Reyes, Sandra, ed.

Duval, John C. The Adventures of Big-Foot Wallace, Texas Ranger & Hunter. 1993. reprint ed. lib. bdg. 75.00 (*0-7812-5877-4*) Rprt Serv.

— Early Times in Texas. 1993. reprint ed. lib. bdg. 75.00 (*0-7812-5876-6*) Rprt Serv.

— Early Times in Texas; or, the Adventures of Jack Dobell. Major, Mabel & Smith, Rebecca W., eds. LC 86-6971. (Illus.). xxv, 286p. 1986. reprint ed. pap. 14.95 (*0-8032-6567-0*, Bison Books) U of Nebr Pr.

Duval, John T., tr. Fabliaux, Fair & Foul. LC 91-44327. 208p. 1992. pap. 12.95 (*0-86698-114-4*, P12) Pegasus Pr.

Duval, Karen C., tr. see Schipper, Kristofer.

Duval, Leon. The Bromeliads. Rothenberg, Michael, ed. Love, Doris, tr. from FRE. (Illus.). 154p. 1990. 22.00 (*1-878471-01-5*) Big Bridge Pr.

Duval, Marguerite. The King's Garden. LC 81-15934. Orig. Title: La Planete Des Fleurs. (Illus.). 527p. reprint ed. pap. 163.40 (*0-7837-4346-7*, 204405600012) Bks Demand.

***Duval, Monique.** Persistence of Yellow: A Book of Recipes for Life. (Illus.). 2000. 19.95 (*1-888387-38-6*) Compendium Inc.

Duval, Paul. Ken Danby: The New Decade. (Illus.). 196p. 1984. 50.00 (*0-7737-2030-8*) Genl Dist Srvs.

— Ken Danby: The New Decade. (Illus.). 196p. 1987. pap. 24.95 (*0-7737-5137-8*) Genl Dist Srvs.

Duval, Paul, frwd. Michael Thompson: Passion over Reason. LC 95-189558. (Illus.). 72p. (C). 1994. pap. 15.00 (*0-919423-94-9*) W Laurier U Pr.

Duval, Quinton. Dinner Music. LC 84-824. (Lost Roads Ser.: No. 25). 56p. (Orig.). 1984. pap. 5.95 (*0-918786-28-2*) Lost Roads.

Duval, R. Shannon, jt. auth. see Mitcham, Carl.

Duval, R. Shannon, jt. auth. see Terkel, Susan N.

Duval, Raymond. Semiosis et Pensee Humaine: Registres Semiotiques et Apprentissages Intellectuels. (Exploration Ser.). (FRE.). xi, 396p. 1995. 55.95 (*3-906754-32-4*, Pub. by P Lang) P Lang Pubng.

Duval, Robert D., jt. auth. see Mooney, Christopher Z.

Duval, Shelley, et al. Consistency & Cognition: A Theory of Causal Attribution. 176p. (C). 1983. text 29.95 (*0-89859-220-8*) L Erlbaum Assocs.

Duval, Stu. Volcano Adventures. (Science Comic Bks.). (YA). (gr. 4-7). 1998. pap. text 8.95 (*957-8741-76-6*) Large Nature.

— Wildlife Adventure. (Science Comic Bks.). (J). (gr. 4-7). 1998. pap. text 8.95 (*957-8741-74-X*) Large Nature.

Duval, Yves-Marie. L' Extirpation de l'Arianisme en Italie du Nord et en Occident: Remini (359/60) et Aquilee (381), Hilaire de Poitiers (+367/8) et Ambroise de Milan (+397) LC 98-3739. (Variorum Collected Studies Ser.: Vol. 611). 384p. 1998. text 112.95 (*0-86078-764-8*, Pub. by Ashgate Pub) Ashgate Pub Co.

— Histoire et Historiographie en Occident aux IVe et Ve Siecles. LC 97-9728. (Variorum Collected Studies Ser.: Vol. 577). (FRE.). 384p. 1997. text 115.95 (*0-86078-628-5*, Pub. by Variorum) Ashgate Pub Co.

Duvall. Anthropology. 8th ed. 1996. pap. text, teacher ed. write for info. (*0-13-575283-3*) Allyn.

Duvall. Anthropology. 8th ed. 208p. (C). 1996. pap. text, student ed. 23.00 (*0-13-371881-6*) P-H.

Duvall. Cultural Anthropology. 8th ed. 1996. pap. text, teacher ed. write for info. (*0-13-575366-X*) Allyn.

Duvall. Grasping God's Word. Date not set. 24.99 (*0-310-22832-8*) HarpC.

DuVall, Audre, jt. auth. see Henriques, Gary.

Duvall, Brian & Kershner, Robert M. Ophthalmic Medications & Pharmacology. LC 97-41938. (Basic Bookshelf for Eyecare Professionals Ser.). (Illus.). 144p. 1997. pap. 26.00 (*1-55642-328-4*, 63284) SLACK Inc.

***Duvall, Brian, et al.** Cataract & Glaucoma for Eyecare Paraprofessionals (BBS) LC 99-27975. (Basic Bookshelf for Eyecare Professionals Ser.). 144p. 1999. pap. 24.00 (*1-55642-335-7*, D1627) SLACK Inc.

Duvall Curran, Pamela & Curran, George. Collectible California Raisins: An Unauthorized Guide, with Values. LC 97-80354. (Illus.). 128p. 1998. pap. 19.95 (*0-7643-0433-X*) Schiffer.

DuVall, D. Audre, jt. auth. see Henriques, Gary A.

Duvall, D. C., jt. auth. see Wissler, Clark.

Duvall, D. C., jt. tr. see Wissler, Clark.

Duvall, David, et al, eds. Chemical Signals in Vertebrates Vol. 4: Ecology, Evolution, & Comparative Biology. LC 86-17013. 754p. 1986. 125.00 (*0-306-42382-0*, Plenum Trade) Perseus Pubng.

***Duvall, Deborah L.** Tahlequah: The Cherokee Nation. (Images of America Ser.). (Illus.). 128p. 1999. pap. 18.99 (*0-7385-0289-8*) Arcadia Publng.

DuVall, George K., ed. see Timiadis, Emilianos.

DuVall, J. Barry. Contemporary Manufacturing Processes. (Illus.). 608p. (C). 1995. pap. text 42.64 (*1-56637-158-9*) Goodheart.

DuVall, J. Barry, et al. Getting the Message: The Technology of Communication. LC 79-57016. (Technology Ser.). 384p. (J). 1981. mass mkt. 25.95 (*0-87192-123-5*) Delmar.

Duvall, J. Scott, jt. auth. see Guthrie, George H.

***Duvall, Jack.** Victory without Violence. (Illus.). 415p. 2000. pap. 29.95 (*0-312-22864-3*) St Martin.

Duvall, Janet L. Intermediate Sign Language & Deaf Culture. (Illus.). 93p. (Orig.). (C). 1990. pap. text 19.95 (*1-882457-01-3*) Sharp Image.

— Law Enforcement & the Deaf. rev. ed. (Illus.). 210p. (C). 1992. pap. text 32.50 (*1-882457-00-5*) Sharp Image.

— Sign Language & Deaf Culture. rev. ed. (Illus.). 166p. (C). 1994. pap. text 29.50 (*1-882457-02-1*) Sharp Image.

Duvall, Jill D. The Cayuga. LC 91-3038. (New True Books Ser.). (Illus.). 48p. (J). (ps-3). 1991. lib. bdg. 21.00 (*0-516-01123-5*) Childrens.

— Chef Ki Is Serving Dinner! (Our Neighborhood Ser.). (J). 6.95 (*0-516-26148-7*) Childrens.

— Chef Ki Is Serving Dinner! LC 96-34902. (Our Neighborhood Ser.). (Illus.). 32p. (J). (gr. 1-2). 1997. lib. bdg. 19.50 (*0-516-20313-4*) Childrens.

— Congressional Committees. LC 96-48495. (Democracy in Action Ser.). (YA). (gr. 7-12). 1997. lib. bdg. 24.00 (*0-531-11343-4*) Watts.

— Meet Rory Hohenstein, a Professional Dancer. LC 96-34906. (Our Neighborhood Ser.). (Illus.). (J). (gr. k-2). 1997. lib. bdg. 19.50 (*0-516-20312-6*) Childrens.

— Meet Rory Hohenstein, a Professional Dancer. (Our Neighborhood Ser.). (J). (gr. k-2). 1997. pap. 6.95 (*0-516-26149-5*) Childrens.

— Mr. Duvall Reports the News. (Our Neighborhood Ser.). (J). pap. 6.95 (*0-516-26150-9*) Childrens.

— Mr. Duvall Reports the News. LC 96-34915. (Our Neighborhood Ser.). (Illus.). (J). 1997. lib. bdg. 19.50 (*0-516-20316-9*) Childrens.

— The Mohawk. LC 90-21166. (New True Books Ser.). (Illus.). 48p. (J). (gr. k-4). 1991. pap. 5.50 (*0-516-41115-2*) Childrens.

— The Mohawk. LC 90-21166. (New True Books Ser.). (Illus.). 48p. (J). (ps-3). 1991. lib. bdg. 21.00 (*0-516-01115-4*) Childrens.

— Ms. Moja Makes Beautiful Clothes. LC 96-34907. (Our Neighborhood Ser.). (Illus.). 1997. lib. bdg. 19.50 (*0-516-20314-2*) Childrens.

— Ms. Moja Makes Beautiful Clothes. (Our Neighborhood Ser.). (J). (gr. k-2). 1997. pap. 6.95 (*0-516-26151-7*) Childrens.

— The Tuscarora. LC 91-3037. (New True Books Ser.). 48p. (J). (gr. 2-4). 1991. pap. 5.50 (*0-516-41128-4*) Childrens.

— The Tuscarora. LC 91-3037. (New True Books Ser.). (Illus.). 48p. (J). (ps-3). 1991. lib. bdg. 21.00 (*0-516-01128-6*) Childrens.

— Who Keeps the Water Clean? Ms. Schindler! LC 96-34908. (Our Neighborhood Ser.). (Illus.). (J). (gr. 1-2). 1997. lib. bdg. 19.50 (*0-516-20315-0*) Childrens.

— Who Keeps the Water Clean? Ms. Schindler! (Our Neighborhood Ser.). (J). (gr. 1-2). 1997. pap. 6.95 (*0-516-26152-5*) Childrens.

Duvall, John N. Faulkner's Marginal Couple: Invisible, Outlaw & Unspeakable Communities. 184p. 1990. 22.50 (*0-292-75114-1*) U of Tex Pr.

Duvall, John N. Toni Morrison's Fictions: Modernist Authenicity & Postmodern. text. write for info. (*0-312-23402-3*) St Martin.

Duvall, Lindsay O. James City County, Virginia, 1634-1659, Vol. 4. (Virginia Colonial Abstracts, Series II). 1979. reprint ed. 17.50 (*0-89308-065-9*) Southern Hist Pr.

— Lancaster County, Virginia Records, Vol. 2. (Virginia Colonial Abstracts, Series II). 1979. reprint ed. 17.50 (*0-89308-063-2*) Southern Hist Pr.

— Northumberland County, Virginia, 1678-1713, Vol. 1. (Virginia Colonial Abstracts, Series II). 160p. 1979. reprint ed. pap. 20.00 (*0-89308-062-4*) Southern Hist Pr.

— Prince George County, Virginia, Vol. 6. (Virginia Colonial Abstracts, Series II). 80p. 1978. reprint ed. pap. 17.50 (*0-89308-067-5*) Southern Hist Pr.

— The Virginia Company of London, 1607-1624, Vol. 3. (Virginia Company of London 1607-1624, Series 2). 118p. 1978. reprint ed. 17.50 (*0-89308-064-0*) Southern Hist Pr.

— York County, Virginia Wills, Deeds, Orders, 1657-1659, Vol. 5. (Virginia Colonial Abstracts, Series II). 94p. 1978. reprint ed. 17.50 (*0-89308-066-7*) Southern Hist Pr.

***Duvall, Lisa.** Assessment Book for Successful Science. (C). 1999. pap. text 29.95 (*1-56870-372-4*) RonJon Pub.

— Lab Practicals for the Life Sciences. 1999. pap. text 16.95 (*1-56870-373-2*) RonJon Pub.

— Phasing into Successful Science - Chemistry & Physics. (C). 1999. pap. text 26.95 (*1-56870-371-6*) RonJon Pub.

— Phasing into Successful Science - Earth & Science. 1999. pap. text 26.95 (*1-56870-370-8*) RonJon Pub.

— Phasing into Successful Science-Life. 1999. pap. text 26.95 (*1-56870-369-4*) RonJon Pub.

Duvall, Lynn. Respecting Our Differences: A Guide to Getting Along in a Changing World. LC 94-7164. 1994. 18.05 (*0-606-06694-2*, Pub. by Turtleback) Demco.

DuVall, Nell. Domestic Technology: A Chronology. 552p. 1988. 45.00 (*0-8161-8913-7*, Hall Reference) Macmillan.

Duvall, P. F. & Husch, L. S. Embedding Coverings into Bundles with Applications. LC 82-8742. (Memoirs of the American Mathematical Society Ser.: No. 38/263). 53p. 1982. pap. 16.00 (*0-8218-2263-2*, MEMO/38/263) Am Math.

Duvall, Paula. The New World of Eating. (Illus.). 470p. 1994. 19.95 (*0-9645980-0-0*) P Duvall Nutrit.

Duvall, Ralph G. History of Shelter Island, from Its Settlement in 1652 to the Present Time, 1932. (Illus.). 229p. 1997. reprint ed. lib. bdg. 32.00 (*0-8328-6238-X*) Higginson Bk Co.

DuVall, Richard. Just for the Birds: The Woodpecker & Others with Light Profiles. LC 90-62572. 48p. 1988. 4.95 (*0-914546-89-9*) Rose Pub.

— Sleepy Hollow Moon. (Illus.). 55p. 1993. per. 5.00 (*0-914546-93-7*) Rose Pub.

DuVall, Rick. Building Character & Community in the Classroom, Vol. 2330. Cicciarelli, Joellyn T., ed. (Illus.). 96p. (J). (ps-1). 1997. pap. text 9.98 (*1-57471-224-1*, 2330) Creat Teach Pr.

Duvall, Robert. The Apostle. 1998. pap. 12.00 (*0-425-16607-4*) Berkley Pub.

Duvall, Steven F., et al. Parents As Reading Tutors. 28p. 1996. pap. 7.50 (*1-57035-054-X*, 81PARENT) Sopris.

Duvant, G. & Lions, J. L. Inequalities in Mechanics & Physics. John, C., tr. from FRE. (Grundlehren der Mathematischen Wissenschaften Ser.: Vol. 219). (Illus.). 400p. 1976. 112.95 (*0-387-07327-2*) Spr-Verlag.

Duve, Christian De, see De Duve, Christian.

Duve, Sandra S., ed. see Slovak World Congress Staff.

Duveau, Georges. Eighteen Forty-Eight: The Making of a Revolution. 288p. 1984. pap. 13.50 (*0-674-54348-3*) HUP.

Duveen, Denis I. Bibliotheca Alchemica et Chemica: Annotated Catalogue of Printed Books on Alchemy, Chemistry, Etc., 2 vols. annot. ed. 695p. 1995. reprint ed. 85.00 (*1-888262-26-5*) Martino Pubng.

Duveen, Gerard & Lloyd, Barbara, eds. Social Representations & the Development of Knowledge. 205p. (C). 1990. text 59.95 (*0-521-36368-3*) Cambridge U Pr.

Duveen, Gerard, ed. see Jodelet, Denise.

Duveen, Gerard, ed. see Moscovici, Serge.

Duvell, Andrea. Struktur und Funktion Linearer Plasmide bei dem Phytopatogenen Ascomyceten Claviceps Purpurea. (Bibliotheca Mycologica Ser.: Vol. 126). (GER., Illus.). 108p. 1989. pap. 40.00 (*0-318-41530-5*, Pub. by Gebruder Borntraeger) Balogh.

Duvenage, Pieter, ed. & intro. see Rusen, Jorn.

Duverger, Maurice. The French Political System. North, Barbara & North, Robert, trs. LC 58-5538. (Chicago Library of Comparative Politics Ser.). (Illus.). 239p. reprint ed. pap. 74.10 (*0-608-10210-5*, 201122600074) Bks Demand.

DuVerlie, Claud, ed. & pref. see De Verneil, Marie.

Duvernay, Joe. I Begin: Poems, Essays, Thoughts & Observations. LC 97-90811. 176p. 1998. 17.95 (*0-533-12488-3*) Vantage.

— Offering. 64p. 1998. pap. 7.00 (*0-8059-4352-8*) Dorrance.

Duverney, Guichard J. A Treatise of the Organ of Hearing. LC 77-147969. reprint ed. 41.50 (*0-404-08221-1*) AMS Pr.

***DuVernois, Michael.** Topics in Cosmic Ray Astrophysics. (Horizons in World Physics Ser.: Vol. 230). 251p. 1999. lib. bdg. 79.00 (*1-56072-658-X*) Nova Sci Pubs.

Duvernoy, Claude. Controversy of Zion. LC 86-63886. 224p. 1987. reprint ed. pap. 7.95 (*0-89221-144-X*) New Leaf.

Duvernoy, Henri M. The Human Brain: Surface, Three-Dimensional Sectional Anatomy & MRI. Alhinc, J., tr. (Illus.). vii, 354p. 1992. 185.00 (*0-387-82260-7*) Spr-Verlag.

— The Human Brain Stem & Cerebellum: Surface, Structure, Vascularization & Three-Dimensional Sectional Anatomy with MRI. LC 94-46338. (Radiology, Neurosurgery Anatomy Ser.). (Illus.). 480p. 1995. 235.00 (*0-387-82503-7*) Spr-Verlag.

— The Human Brain Stem & Cerebellum: Surface, Structure, Vascularization, Three Dimensional Sectional Anatomy, & MRI. (Illus.). 480p. 1995. 235.00 (*3-211-82503-7*) Spr-Verlag.

— The Human Hippocampus. (Illus.). 160p. 1988. 125.00 (*0-387-00375-4*) Spr-Verlag.

Duvernoy, Henri M. & Bourgouin, P. The Human Hippocampus: Functional Anatomy, Vascularization & Serial Sections with MRI. 2nd expanded rev. ed. LC 97-35996. (Illus.). 125p. 1997. write for info. (*3-540-63205-0*) Spr-Verlag.

Duvernoy, Henri M. & Cabanis, Emmanuel A. The Human Brain: Surface, Three-Dimensional Sectional Anatomy with MRI & Vascularization. LC 99-22443. 1999. write for info. (*3-211-82260-7*) Spr-Verlag.

Duvernoy, J. B. The School of Mechanism: Fifteen Etudes for the Piano, Op. 120. Seifert, Hans T., ed. (Carl Fischer Music Library: No. 361). 1904. pap. 6.50 (*0-8258-0112-5*, L361) Fischer Inc NY.

Duvert. When Jonathan Died. 1995. per. 12.95 (*0-85449-154-6*, Pub. by Gay Mens Pr) LPC InBook.

Duvert, Michel, jt. ed. see De Barandiaran, Jose M.

D

An Asterisk (*) at the beginning of an entry indicates that the title is appearing for the first time.

Duvignaud, Jean. L' Or de la Republique. (FRE.). 1984. pap. 17.95 (*0-7859-1995-3*, 2070375641) Fr & Eur.

Duvillier, Fabienne. Publicity & Communications Bilingual Dictionary. 464p. 1990. lib. bdg. 150.00 (*0-8288-2609-9*, F83360) Fr & Eur.

Duvivier-Dodds, Eleanora. Apollo's Lover. 96p. (YA). (gr. 10-12). 1997. pap. 8.00 (*0-8059-4121-5*) Dorrance.

Duvivier, Roger, jt. auth. see Richter, Patricia.

DuVivier, Roxanne S. Diagnosis & Treatment in Education: A Handbook for Applying the Impressionistic Models System in Teaching & Student Development. 128p. (Orig.). (C). 1992. pap. text 21.50 (*0-8191-8672-4*) U Pr of Amer.

Duvoisin, Roger. Petunia. anniversary ed. (Illus.). (J). 1962. 15.95 (*0-394-80865-7*) Knopf Bks Yng Read.

Duvoisin, Roger C. & Plaitakis, Andreas, eds. The Olivopontocerebellar Atrophies. fac. ed. LC 84-9861. (Advances in Neurology Ser.: No. 41). (Illus.). 304p. pap. 94.30 (*0-7837-7268-8*, 204703700005) Bks Demand.

Duvoisin, Roger C. & Sage, Jacob I. Parkinson's Disease: A Guide for Patient & Family. 4th ed. 200p. 1995. pap. text 26.00 (*0-7817-0312-3*) Lppncott W & W.

Duvoism, R. C., jt. ed. see Birkmayer, W.

Duvvury, Vasumathi K. Play, Symbolism & Ritual: A Study of Tamil Brahmin Women's Rites of Passage. LC 89-14564. (American University Studies: Anthropology & Science: Ser. XI, Vol. 41). (Illus.). X, 251p. (C). 1991. text 46.95 (*0-8204-1108-6*) P Lang Pubng.

DuWatt, Betsy & Dillon, Molly B., eds. Industries in Transition Review. 1995. 1500.00 (*1-56965-337-2*, DIT94) BCC.

Duwayer, P. Beatles: The Ultimate Encyclopedia. 1996. 19.98 (*0-7858-0715-2*) Bk Sales Inc.

Duwe, Gert & Roth, Leo, eds. Kunst und Humanismus in den Niederlanden des 15. bis 17. Jahrhunderts. (GER., Illus.). 240p. 1995. 44.95 (*3-631-48122-5*) P Lang Pubng.

Duwell, Martin, et al, eds. The ALS Guide to Australian Writers: A Bibliography 1963-1990. LC 93-226785. (Studies in Australian Literature). 366p. 1993. pap. 19.95 (*0-7022-2439-1*, Pub. by Univ Queensland Pr) Intl Spec Bk.

Duwell, Martin, jt. ed. see Dixon, R. M.

Duxbury. Fundamental Oceanography. 3rd ed. LC 97-53175. 1998. 43.50 (*0-697-37453-X*, Dshkn McG-Hill) McGrw-H Hghr Educ.

— Fundamentals of Oceanography. 2nd ed. 1995. teacher ed. 21.87 (*0-697-26672-9*, WCB McGr Hill) McGrw-H Hghr Educ.

***Duxbury.** Fundamentals of Oceanography. 4th ed. 2000. 35.20 (*0-07-290434-8*) McGraw.

Duxbury. Introduction to the World's Oceans. 4th ed. 1994. teacher ed. 12.81 (*0-697-13598-5*) McGraw.

— Introduction to the World's Oceans. 5th ed. 1996. teacher ed. 23.75 (*0-697-28275-9*, WCB McGr Hill) McGrw-H Hghr Educ.

— Repeated Financial Decisions. LC 99-30109. 90p. 1999. pap. 85.00 (*0-471-72028-3*) Wiley.

Duxbury, Alison B. An Introduction to the World's Oceans. 6th ed. 224p. 1999. pap., student ed. 26.88 (*0-07-303604-8*) McGraw.

Duxbury, Alison B. & Duxbury, Alyn C. Fundamentals of Oceanography. 2nd ed. 308p. (C). 1995. text 52.20 (*0-697-26671-0*, WCB McGr Hill) McGrw-H Hghr Educ.

— Fundamentals of Oceanography. 2nd ed. 320p. (C). 1997. per. write for info. (*0-07-114169-3*, WCB McGr Hill) McGrw-H Hghr Educ.

— An Introduction to the World's Oceans. 3rd ed. 464p. (C). 1990. text. write for info. (*0-697-09765-X*, WCB McGr Hill) McGrw-H Hghr Educ.

— An Introduction to the World's Oceans. 4th ed. 496p. (C). 1993. text 56.55 (*0-697-13597-7*, WCB McGr Hill) McGrw-H Hghr Educ.

— An Introduction to the World's Oceans. 4th ed. 496p. (C). 1993. text, student ed. 23.75 (*0-697-13599-3*, WCB McGr Hill) McGrw-H Hghr Educ.

— An Introduction to the World's Oceans. 5th ed. LC 95-83694. 496p. (C). 1996. text. write for info. (*0-697-28273-2*, WCB McGr Hill) McGrw-H Hghr Educ.

Duxbury, Alison B. & Sverdrup, Keith A. Fundamentals of Oceanography. 2nd ed. 140p. (C). 1995. text, student ed. 21.87 (*0-697-29298-3*, WCB McGr Hill) McGrw-H Hghr Educ.

Duxbury, Alison B., jt. auth. see Duxbury, Alun C.

Duxbury, Allison B. & Duxbury, Alyn C. Fundamentals of Oceanography. 304p. (C). 1992. text. write for info. (*0-697-14646-4*) Brown & Benchmark.

Duxbury, Alun C. & Duxbury, Alison B. Intro to Worlds Oceans. (Illus.). 475p. 1984. text 31.16 (*0-201-11348-1*) Addison-Wesley.

***Duxbury, Alyn C.** Introduction to the World's Oceans. 6th ed. LC 98-55196. 1999. 62.25 (*0-07-303603-X*) McGraw.

Duxbury, Alyn C., jt. auth. see Duxbury, Alison B.

Duxbury, Alyn C., jt. auth. see Duxbury, Allison B.

Duxbury-Duxbury. Introduction to the World's Oceans. 3rd ed. 1990. teacher ed. 14.06 (*0-697-09766-8*) McGraw.

Duxbury, Geoffrey. Infrared Vibration-rotation Spectroscopy: From Free Radicals to the Infrared Sky. LC 99-15116. 468p. 2000. 225.00 (*0-471-97419-6*) Wiley.

Duxbury, Janell R. Rockin' the Classics & Classicizin' the Rock: A Selectively Annotated Discography, 14. LC 84-22419. (Discographies Ser.: No. 14). 188p. 1985. lib. bdg. 52.95 (*0-313-24605-X*, DUR/, Greenwood Pr) Greenwood.

Duxbury, Janell R., compiled by. Rockin' the Classics & Classicizin' the Rock: A Selectively Annotated Discography; First Supplement, 43. LC 91-7899. (Discographies Ser.: No. 43). 192p. 1991. lib. bdg. 55.00 (*0-313-27542-4*, DRA, Greenwood Pr) Greenwood.

***Duxbury, Joe.** The Difficult Patient. 192p. 2000. pap. 35.00 (*0-7506-3838-9*) Buttrwrth-Heinemann.

Duxbury, Neil. Patterns of American Jurisprudence. 530p. 1995. text 59.00 (*0-19-825850-X*) OUP.

— Patterns of American Jurisprudence. 530p. 1997. reprint ed. pap. text 27.00 (*0-19-826491-7*) OUP.

— Random Justice: On Lotteries & Legal Decision-Making. LC 99-24515. (Illus.). 192p. 1999. text 60.00 (*0-19-826825-4*) OUP.

Duxbury, P. M. & Pence, T. J. Dynamics of Crystal Surfaces & Interfaces: Proceedings of a Workshop Held in Traverse City, Michigan, August 4-8, 1996. LC 97-15447. (Fundamental Materials Research Ser.). 260p. (C). 1997. 95.00 (*0-306-45619-2*, Plenum Trade) Perseus Pubng.

Duxbury, P. M., jt. auth. see Thorpe, M. F.

Duxbury, R. & Morton, S. Blackstone's Statutes on Environmental Law. 2nd ed. 463p. 1995. pap. 28.00 (*1-85431-484-X*, Pub. by Blackstone Pr) Gaunt.

Duxbury, R. M. Telling & Duxbury: Planning Law & Procedure. 10th ed. 1996. pap. write for info. (*0-406-99374-2*, TDPL10, MICHIE) LEXIS Pub.

Duy, Hoang Chu, tr. see Prucha, Isabel D.

***Duy, Nguyen.** Distant Road: Selected Poems of Nguyen Duy. Bowen, Kevin & Chung, Nguyen Ba, trs. from VIE. LC 99-27584. 257p. 1999. pap. 15.95 (*1-880684-61-6*, Pub. by Curbstone) SPD-Small Pr Dist.

Duy Tu Tran. German-Vietnamese Dictionary of Engineering: Woerterbuch der Technik Deutsch - Vietnamesisch. (GER & VIE.). 504p. 1982. 75.00 (*0-8288-2159-3*, M15528) Fr & Eur.

Duyckinck, W. C. & Cornell, J. Duyckinck & Allied Families, Being a Record of the Descendants of Evert Duyckinck Who Settled in New Amsterdam, now N.Y., in 1638. 256p. 1991. reprint ed. pap. 41.00 (*0-8328-1998-0*); reprint ed. lib. bdg. 51.00 (*0-8328-1997-2*) Higginson Bk Co.

Duyff. World Foods. Date not set. text. write for info. (*0-314-07143-1*) West Pub.

— World Foods. annot. ed. Date not set. text, teacher ed. write for info. (*0-314-07144-X*) West Pub.

Duyff, Roberta, jt. auth. see McKissack, Patricia.

Duyff, Roberta L. The American Dietetic Association's Complete Food & Nutrition Guide: The Most Comprehensive & Up-to-Date Resource on Healthy Food Choices from the World's Foremost Experts. (Illus.). 644p. 1996. 39.95 (*1-56561-098-9*) Wiley.

— Big Bug Book of Exercise. McKissack, Patricia & McKissack, Fredrick, eds. LC 87-61656. (Big Bug Bks.). (Illus.). 24p. (Orig.). (J). (gr. k-1). 1987. pap. text 4.95 (*0-88335-771-2*) Milliken Pub Co.

Duyff, Roberta L., et al. Nutrition, Health, & Safety for Preschool Children. LC 94-4626. 1994. 22.00 (*0-02-802089-8*) Glencoe.

Duyff, Roberta L., jt. auth. see McKissack, Patricia C.

Duyfhuizen, Bernard. Narratives of Transmission. LC 91-58803. 280p. 1992. 36.50 (*0-8386-3472-9*) Fairleigh Dickinson.

Duyker, Edward. Nature's Argonaut: Daniel Solander, 1733-1782. 400p. 1998. 49.95 (*0-522-84753-6*, Pub. by Melbourne Univ Pr) Paul & Co Pubs.

— An Officer of the Blue: Marc-Joseph Marion Dufresne, South Sea Explorer 1724-1772. LC 94-166017. (Miegunyah Press Ser.: No. 1:15). 256p. 1994. 39.95 (*0-522-84565-7*, Pub. by Melbourne Univ Pr) Paul & Co Pubs.

— Tribal Guerillas: The Santals of West Bengal & the Naxalite Movement. (Illus.). 228p. 1987. 19.95 (*0-19-561938-2*) OUP.

Duyker, Edward, ed. A Woman on the Goldfields: Emily Skinner's Diary. LC 95-213903. 144p. 1996. 39.95 (*0-522-84652-1*, Pub. by Melbourne Univ Pr) Paul & Co Pubs.

Duyker, Edward & Tingbrand, Per. Daniel Solander: Collected Correspondence, 1733-1782. LC 96-110868. 320p. 1995. 61.00 (*82-00-22454-6*) Scandnvan Univ Pr.

Duyker, Edward & Tingbrand, Per, eds. Daniel Solander: Collected Correspondence, 1753-1782. LC 95-176756. (Miegunyah Press Ser.: No. 2:4). 524p. 1995. 69.95 (*0-522-84636-X*, Pub. by Melbourne Univ Pr) Paul & Co Pubs.

Duyn Hill, Mary Van, see Van Duyn Hill, Mary.

Duyn, Mona Van, see Van Duyn, Mona.

Duyne, Marie A. Van, see Van Duyne, Marie A.

Duyne, Petrus C. Van, see Van Duyne, Petrus C.

Duyshart, Bruce. The Digital Document. LC 97-44809. (Illus.). 256p. 1998. text 59.95 (*0-7506-3602-5*, Butterwrth Archit) Buttrwrth-Heinemann.

Duysters, Geert. The Dynamics of Technical Innovation: The Evolution & Development of Information Technology. LC 95-39636. 272p. 1996. 95.00 (*1-85898-400-9*) E Elgar.

Duyvendak, Jan J., tr. see Ching-Shan.

Duyvis, Paul D., et al. Furniture/Sculpture. (Illus.). 72p. 1998. pap. 17.00 (*90-6918-190-8*, Pub. by Boymans Mus) Dist Art Pubs.

Duz, M. D. Astral Medicine: A Practical Treatise & Therapeutics Combining Astrology, Diet & Homeopathic Medicine. 1991. lib. bdg. 67.95 (*0-8490-4305-0*) Gordon Pr.

— A Practical Treatise of Astral Medicine & Therapeutics. 252p. 1996. reprint ed. pap. 16.00 (*0-7873-0304-6*) Hlth Research.

— A Practical Treatise of Astral Medicine & Therapeutics. 257p. 1996. reprint ed. pap. 14.95 (*1-56459-684-2*) Kessinger Pub.

Duzee, E. P. Van, see Van Duzee, E. P.

Duzer, Leslie Van, see Kleinman, Kent & Van Duzer, Leslie, eds.

Duzer, Leslie Van, see Van Duzer, Leslie.

Duzgunes, N., ed. Mechanisms & Specificity of HIV Entry into Host Cells. (Advances in Experimental Medicine & Biology Ser.: Vol. 300). (Illus.). 222p. (C). 1991. text 102.00 (*0-306-44008-3*, Kluwer Plenum) Kluwer Academic.

Duzgunes, Nejat, et al, eds. Membrane Fusion Techniques, Pt. A. (Methods in Enzymology Ser.: Vol. 220). (Illus.). 433p. 1993. text 94.00 (*0-12-182121-8*) Acad Pr.

— Membrane Fusion Techniques, Vol. 221, Pt. B. (Methods in Enzymology Ser.). (Illus.). 462p. 1993. text 89.00 (*0-12-182122-6*) Acad Pr.

Duzinkiewicz, Janusz. Fateful Transformations: The Four Years' Parliament & the Constitution of May 3, 1791. 488p. 1993. 75.50 (*0-88033-265-4*, 368, Pub. by East Eur Monographs) Col U Pr.

Duz'minskii, A. S. & Leyland, B. N., eds. Ageing & Stabilisation of Polymers. (Illus.). xiv, 280p. 1971. 55.00 (*0-444-20076-2*) Elsevier.

Dvane, Marl. The Key to Peace & Progress: Self-Esteem & Enlightment. 360p. 1995. 19.95 (*0-9646422-0-4*) Esse Bear Enter.

***D'Vari, Marisa.** Script Magic: Subconscious Techniques to Conquer Writer's Block. LC 99-38020. 2000. 18.95 (*0-941188-74-4*) M Wiese.

Dveksler, Gabriela, jt. ed. see Dieffenbach, Carl.

Dvell, Persis & Rubin, David, eds. Lepton & Photon Interactions: XVI International Symposium. LC 94-70079. (AIP Conference Proceedings Ser.: No. 302). 837p. 1994. text 830.00 (*1-56396-106-7*) Am Inst Physics.

DVGS-Technologiezentrum Wasser Staff, jt. auth. see American Water Works Association Research Foundati.

DVGW Staff. Lexikon der Gastechnik. (GER.). 472p. 1990. 150.00 (*0-7859-8484-4*, 3802722868) Fr & Eur.

D'ville, Linda G., ed. see Rubenstein, Edward.

Dvillers, C. & Chaline, Jean. Evolution: An Evolving Theory. Reimer, Thomas, tr. from FRE. (Illus.). 265p. 1993. write for info. (*3-540-54674-X*) Spr-Verlag.

D'Vincent, Cynthia. The Whale Family Book. LC 97-48377. 64p. (J). (gr. 1-5). 1998. pap. 8.95 (*1-55858-947-3*, Pub. by North-South Bks NYC) Chronicle Bks.

— The Whale Family Book. LC 90-7403. (Illus.). 60p. (J). (gr. 5 up). 1992. pap. 15.95 (*0-88708-148-7*, Picture Book Studio) S&S Childrens.

Dvir. Clinical Biomechanics. LC 99-37691. (C). 2000. text. write for info. (*0-443-07945-5*) Harcrt Hlth Sci Grp.

Dvir, Azriel & Mashat, Mazal. My Little Siddur. 68p. (J). 8.95 (*0-915361-87-6*) Lambda Pubs.

Dvir, Zeevi. Isokinetics: Testing, Interpretation & Clinical Applications. (Illus.). 199p. 1994. text 54.00 (*0-443-04794-4*) Church.

Dvirnak, M. Ingrid. The Work of the Clerk. 2nd rev. ed. 64p. (Orig.). 1996. pap. 8.00 (*0-8170-1253-2*) Judson.

***Dvoeglazov, Valeri V.** Photon & Poincare Group. (Contemporary Fundamental Physics Ser.). 356p. 1999. lib. bdg. 135.00 (*1-56072-718-7*) Nova Sci Pubs.

Dvorackova, Ivana, ed. Aflatoxins & Human Health. 274p. 1989. lib. bdg. 166.00 (*0-8493-4628-2*, RA1242) CRC Pr.

***Dvorak.** Research Trends in Solid Mechanics. LC 99-48376. 1999. 119.00 (*0-08-043572-6*, Pergamon Pr) Elsevier.

Dvorak, A. J., ed. see DOE Technical Information Center Staff.

Dvorak, A. M. Blood Cell Biochemistry Vol. 4: Basophil & Mast Cell Degranulation & Recovery. (Illus.). 415p. (C). 1991. text 105.00 (*0-306-43752-X*, Kluwer Plenum) Kluwer Academic.

— Human Mast Cells. (Advances in Anatomy & Cell Biology Ser.: Vol. 114). (Illus.). 110p. 1989. pap. 94.00 (*0-387-50374-9*) Spr-Verlag.

Dvorak, Ann M. Diagnostic Ultrastructural Pathology I: Text Atlas Case Studies, Vol. 1. 512p. 1992. boxed set 156.95 (*0-8493-4404-2*, RB643) CRC Pr.

Dvorak, Ann M. & Monahan-Earley, Rita A. Diagnostic Ultrastructural Pathology III: A Text-Atlas of Case Studies Emphasizing Endocrine & Hematopoietic Systems, Vol. 3. LC 94-47673. 464p. 1995. boxed set 314.95 (*0-8493-9474-0*, 9474) CRC Pr.

Dvorak, Ann M. & Monahan-Earley, Rita A., eds. Diagnostic Ultrastructural Pathology II: A Text-Atlas of Case Studies Emphasizing Respiratory & Nervous Systems, Vol. 2. LC 94-47018. Vol. 2. 416p. 1995. boxed set 344.95 (*0-8493-4490-5*, 4490) CRC Pr.

Dvorak, Antonin. Chamber Works for Piano & Strings. 352p. 1988. pap. 15.95 (*0-486-25663-4*) Dover.

— Complete Slavonic Dances for Piano Four Hands. 144p. 1992. pap. 9.95 (*0-486-27019-X*) Dover.

***Dvorak, Antonin.** Dvorak: Complete Piano Works I. 1999. pap. 7.95 (*963-9155-19-5*) Kone Music.

— Dvorak: Complete Piano Works II. 1999. pap. 7.95 (*963-9155-20-9*) Kone Music.

— Dvorak: Complete Piano Works III. 1999. pap. 7.95 (*963-9155-21-7*) Kone Music.

Dvorak, Antonin. Humoresques & Other Works for Solo Piano. 160p. 1999. pap. 9.95 (*0-486-28355-0*) Dover.

***Dvorak, Antonin.** Palm Pilot. 2000. pap. 34.99 (*0-13-026113-0*) P-H.

Dvorak, Antonin. Slavonic Dances, Op. 46, in Full Score. 303p. 1987. pap. 13.95 (*0-486-25394-5*) Dover.

Dvorak, Antonin. So Many Songs: Es Zog Manch Lied a Cappalla from in the World of Nature. 8p. 1986. pap. 1.25 (*0-7935-5505-1*, 50319370) H Leonard.

Dvorak, Antonin. Symphonies Nos. 6 & 7 in Full Score. 288p. 1994. pap. 16.95 (*0-486-28026-8*) Dover.

— Symphony No. 8 in G Major, Op. 88, Symphony No. 9 in E Minor, Op. 95 ("New World") in Full Score. 272p. 1984. pap. 13.95 (*0-486-24749-X*) Dover.

— Symphony Number 9 in E Minor OP 95. 1998. pap. text 2.95 (*0-486-29892-2*, 741733Q) Dover.

Dvorak, August, et al. Typewriting Behavior: Psychology Applied to Teaching & Learning Typewriting. (Illus.). 521p. 1936. 30.00 (*0-935309-12-8*) Freelance Comm.

Dvorak, G. J., ed. Inelastic Deformation of Composite Materials: Proceedings of the IUTAM Symposium on Inelastic Deformation of Composite Materials. (International Union of Theoretical & Applied Mechanics Symposia Ser.). (Illus.). 752p. 1991. 121.95 (*0-387-97458-X*) Spr-Verlag.

— Mechanics of Composite Materials. 184p. 1983. pap. text 40.00 (*0-317-02631-3*, H00273) ASME.

Dvorak, J. & Dvorak, V. Checklist of Manual Medicine. Sturm, A. et al, eds. Gilliar, Wolfgang G., tr. from GER. (Flexibook Ser.). (Illus.). 180p. 1991. pap. text 18.00 (*0-86577-386-6*) Thieme Med Pubs.

Dvorak, J. & Novak, L., eds. Soil Conservation & Silviculture. LC 93-47987. (Developments in Soil Science Ser.: Vol. 23). 420p. 1994. 251.50 (*0-444-98792-4*) Elsevier.

Dvorak, J. J. & Mastrolorenzo, G. The Mechanisms of Recent Vertical Crustal Movements in Campi Flegrei Caldera, Southern Italy. (Special Papers: No. 263). (Illus.). 66p. 1991. pap. 12.00 (*0-8137-2263-2*) Geol Soc.

Dvorak, Jack, et al. Journalism Kids Do Better: What Research Tells Us about High School Journalism. LC 94-4006. 1994. 24.95 (*0-927516-40-3*) ERIC-REC.

Dvorak, Jim, jt. auth. see Rostoker, William.

Dvorak, Jiri, et al. Manual Medicine - Diagnostics. 2nd ed. (Illus.). 1990. text 85.00 (*0-86577-306-8*) Thieme Med Pubs.

Dvorak, Johanna J., ed. Fire Trucks in Action. (J). (ps-2). 1995. 14.95 incl. VHS (*0-9660245-0-8*) High Profiles.

Dvorak, John C. PC Magazine Buyer's Guide to PCs, Printers, & Monitors, 1992. (Guide to...Ser.). 410p. (Orig.). 1991. pap. 19.95 (*1-56276-004-1*, Ziff-Davis Pr) Que.

— PC Magazine 1996 Computer Buyer's Guide. 1995. pap. text 19.95 (*1-56276-343-1*, Ziff-Davis Pr) Que.

Dvorak, John C., ed. PC Magazine 1995 Computer Buyer's Guide. rev. ed. (Buyer's Guide Ser.). 528p. (Orig.). 1994. pap. 19.95 (*1-56276-251-6*, Ziff-Davis Pr) Que.

Dvorak, John C., jt. auth. see Osborne, Adam.

Dvorak, Karen A., ed. Social Science Research for Agricultural Technology Development: Spatial & Temporal Dimensions. (Illus.). 260p. 1993. text 80.00 (*0-85198-806-7*) OUP.

Dvorak, Katharine L. An African-American Exodus: The Segregation of the Southern Churches. LC 90-23383. (Chicago Studies in the History of American Religion Ser.: Vol. 4). 256p. 1991. 50.00 (*0-926019-25-2*) Carlson Pub.

Dvorak, Otakar. Antonin Dvorak, My Father. Polansky, Paul J., ed. 192p. 1993. 25.00 (*0-9636734-0-8*) Czech Hist.

Dvorak, Paul F., tr. see Hermlin, Stephan.

Dvorak, Paul F., tr. see Schneider, Robert.

Dvorak, Paul F., tr. see Unseld, Joachim.

Dvorak, Paul F., tr. & afterword by see Kolleritsch, Alfred.

Dvorak, R. & Henrard, J., eds. Long-Term Evolution of Planetary Systems. (C). 1989. text 278.00 (*0-7923-0120-X*) Kluwer Academic.

Dvorak, R. R. The Magic of Drawing & the Artist's Drawing Pad. 2nd ed. (Illus.). 150p. 1993. pap. 16.95 (*0-945625-04-9*) Inkwell Pr.

— The Pocket Drawing Book: On to the Basics. (Illus.). 162p. (Orig.). 1987. reprint ed. pap. 9.95 (*0-945625-00-6*) Inkwell Pr.

— The Pocket Drawing Book & the Pocket Drawing Pad. 2nd ed. (Illus.). 160p. 1993. reprint ed. pap. 12.95 (*0-945625-02-2*) Inkwell Pr.

Dvorak, Robert R. The Artists Drawing Pad. (Illus.). 160p. (YA). (gr. 5 up). 1993. pap. 16.95 (*0-945625-01-4*) Inkwell Pr.

— Drawing Without Fear. (Illus.). 144p. (Orig.). (J). 1997. pap. 18.95 (*0-945625-05-7*) Inkwell Pr.

— Experiential Drawing. Hicks, Tony, ed. LC 91-55519. (Illus.). 120p. (Orig.). 1991. pap. 15.95 (*1-56052-065-5*) Crisp Pubns.

— The Magic of Drawing. (Illus.). 160p. (Orig.). (YA). (gr. 5 up). 1993. pap. 16.95 (*0-945625-03-0*) Inkwell Pr.

— Productivity at the Workstation: Wellness & Fitness at Your Desk. Crisp, Michael G., ed. LC 89-82344. (Fifty-Minute Ser.). (Illus.). 100p. (Orig.). 1990. pap. 10.95 (*1-56052-041-8*) Crisp Pubns.

Dvorak, Rudolf & Henrard, Jacques. The Dynamical Behaviour of Our Planetary System: Proceedings of the 4th Alexander von Humboldt Colloquium on Celestial Mechanics, Ramsau, Austria, 1996. LC 97-11142. 428p. 1997. text 200.50 (*0-7923-4548-7*) Kluwer Academic.

Dvorak, Rudolf & Henrard, Jacques, eds. Qualitative & Quantitative Behavior of Planetary Systems: Proceedings of the Third Alexander von Humboldt Colloquium on Celestial Mechanics. LC 93-17750. 406p. (C). 1993. text 196.50 (*0-7923-2339-4*) Kluwer Academic.

Dvorak, Thomas L. & Floyd, Richard L. Best Music for Beginning Band: A Selective Repertoire Guide to Music & Methods for Beginning Band. Margolis, Bob, ed. (Orig.). (C). Date not set. pap. write for info. (*0-931329-04-3*, BMBB) Manhattan Beach.

Dvorak, Thomas L., et al. Best Music for High School Band: A Selective Repertoire Guide for High School Bands & Wind Ensembles. Margolis, Bob, ed. 124p. (Orig.). (C). 1993. pap. 39.95 (*0-931329-03-5*, BMHSB) Manhattan Beach.

D

An Asterisk (*) at the beginning of an entry indicates that the title is appearing for the first time.

D

An Asterisk (*) at the beginning of an entry indicates that the title is appearing for the first time.

Dwivedi, M. N., tr. from SAN. Yogasutras of Patanjali. 2nd ed. 159p. 1983. reprint ed. 9.50 (*81-7030-091-6*, Pub. by Motilal Bnarsidass) S Asia.
Dwivedi, O. P. India's Environmental Policies, Programmes & Stewardship. LC 97-14129. 1997. text 65.00 (*0-312-17649-X*) St Martin.
***Dwivedi, O. P. & Gow, Lain.** From Bureaucracy to Public Management: The Administrative Culture of the Government of Canada. 224p. 1999. pap. 19.95 (*1-55111-271-X*) Broadview Pr.
Dwivedi, O. P. & Henderson, Keith, eds. Public Administration in World Perspective. LC 90-10712. (Illus.). 428p. 1990. text 49.95 (*0-8138-0154-0*) Iowa St U Pr.
Dwivedi, O. P. & Vajpeyi, Dhirendra K., eds. Environmental Policies in the Third World: A Comparative Analysis, 350. LC 94-27948. (Contributions in Political Science Ser.: Vol. 350). 248p. 1995. 65.00 (*0-313-29397-X*, Greenwood Pr) Greenwood.
Dwivedi, O. P., et al. Governing India: Issues Concerning Public Policy, Institutions, & Administration. LC 98-902043. xxi, 411 p. 1998. write for info. (*81-7018-970-5*) BR Pub.
Dwivedi, O. P., jt. ed. see Jabbra, Joseph G.
Dwivedi, O. P., jt. ed. see Tremblay, R. C.
Dwivedi, P. S., ed. Essays on Indian Painting: Bilingual. (Karl Khandalavala Felicitation Volume Ser.). 142p. 1991. 25.00 (*0-685-62632-6*, Pub. by Kala Prakashan) Nataraj Bks.
Dwivedi, P. S., et al, eds. Essays on Indian Art & Culture. (Professor R. Das Gupta Felicitation Volume Ser.). (Illus.). 172p. 1992. 39.95 (*0-685-62629-6*, Pub. by Kala Prakashan) Nataraj Bks.
Dwivedi, Prem S. Durga (Theme in Varanasi Wall Painting) (C). 1993. 28.00 (*81-85133-82-4*, Pub. by Eastern Bk Linkers) S Asia.
Dwivedi, R. C., ed. Studies in Mimamsa. (C). 1994. text 34.00 (*81-208-1109-7*, Pub. by Motilal Bnarsidass) S Asia.
Dwivedi, R. C., ed. see Pandey, K. C.
Dwivedi, R. C., ed. see Pandey, Kanti C.
***Dwivedi, S.** The Broken Flute. 1998. pap. 30.00 (*81-86982-22-1*, Pub. by Business Pubns) St Mut.
Dwivedi, S. N., ed. Robotics & Factories of the Future. 650p. 1985. 135.95 (*0-387-15015-3*) Spr-Verlag.
Dwivedi, S. N., et al, eds. CAD-CAM, Robotics, & Factories of the Future Vols. 1-2: Proceedings of the International Conference, 5th, 2 vols. (Illus.). 1991. 110.00 (*0-685-74373-X*) Spr-Verlag.
— CAD-CAM, Robotics, & Factories of the Future Vols. 1-2: Proceedings of the International Conference, 5th, 2 vols., Set. (Illus.). 1991. 198.00 (*0-685-50989-3*) Spr-Verlag.
— CAD-CAM, Robotics, & Factories of the Future Vols. 1-2: Proceedings of the International Conference, 5th, 2 vols., Vol. 1: Concurrent Engineering. (Illus.). xxxi, 584p. 1991. 126.95 (*0-387-53399-0*) Spr-Verlag.
— CAD-CAM, Robotics, & Factories of the Future Vols. 1-2: Proceedings of the International Conference, 5th, 2 vols., Vol. 2: Flexible Automation. (Illus.). xxxii, 637p. 1991. 126.95 (*0-387-53400-8*) Spr-Verlag.
D'Wolf, John. A Voyage to the North Pacific. LC 98-17251. 150p. 1998. pap. 14.95 (*0-87770-620-4*) Ye Galleon.
— A Voyage to the North Pacific. 2nd ed. LC 98-17251. 1998. 19.95 (*0-87770-560-7*) Ye Galleon.
***Dwor-Frecaut, Dominique, et al.** Asian Corporate Recovery: Findings from Firm-Level Surveys in Five Countries. LC 00-24442. 2000. write for info. (*0-8213-4634-2*) World Bank.
Dworak, Kara, jt. auth. see Benz, Cheryl.
Dworak, Paul, jt. auth. see Ottman, Robert W.
Dworak, Robert J. Taxpayers, Payers Guide to Revolt: Perspectives on the Taxpayers Revolt. LC 80-135. 259p. 1980. 59.95 (*0-275-90473-3*, C0473, Praeger Pubs) Greenwood.
Dworetsky, M. M., et al, eds. Peculiar vs. Normal Phenomena in A-Type & Related Stars. (ASP Conference Series Proceedings: Vol. 44). 696p. 1993. 34.00 (*0-937707-63-5*) Astron Soc Pacific.
Dworetz, Steven M. The Unvarnished Doctrine: Locke, Liberalism, & the American Revolution. LC 89-35756. 264p. 1994. pap. text 18.95 (*0-8223-1470-3*) Duke.
Dworetzky. Abnormal Psychology. (Psychology Ser.). 1919. pap. text 48.00 (*0-534-35692-3*) Brooks-Cole.
— Child Development. 5th ed. Date not set. pap. text, teacher ed. write for info. (*0-314-02169-8*) West Pub.
— Child Development. 5th ed. 1993. mass mkt., student ed. 14.75 (*0-314-02170-1*) West Pub.
— Human Development. Date not set. pap. text, student ed. 18.50 (*0-314-79791-2*) West Pub.
— Human Development. 2nd ed. 1995. mass mkt., student ed. 16.50 (*0-314-06815-5*) West Pub.
— Introduction to Child Development. 6th ed. (Psychology Ser.). 1995. student ed. 15.75 (*0-314-20115-7*) Brooks-Cole.
— Introduction to Child Development. 7th ed. 2000. pap. text, student ed. 18.00 (*0-534-35985-X*) Thomson Learn.
— Psychology. 5th ed. Date not set. pap. text, teacher ed. write for info. (*0-314-03273-8*); pap. text, teacher ed. write for info. (*0-314-03274-6*); pap. text, student ed. 20.00 (*0-314-03725-X*) West Pub.
— Psychology: Testbank. 5th ed. Date not set. pap. text, suppl. ed. write for info. (*0-314-03275-4*) West Pub.
Dworetzky, John. Human Development. 1988. mass mkt. 43.75 (*0-314-62481-3*) West Pub.
Dworetzky, John P. Human Development, A Lifespan Approach. 2nd ed. LC 94-41823. 648p. (C). 1995. mass mkt. 82.95 (*0-314-04533-3*) West Pub.
— Introduction to Child Development. 5th ed. Perlee, Clyde, ed. LC 92-39465. 550p. (C). 1993. text 45.50 (*0-314-01135-8*) West Pub.
— Introduction to Child Development. 6th ed. LC 96-12902. 550p. 1996. text 80.95 (*0-314-06748-5*) West Pub.
— Introduction to Child Development. 7th ed. (Psychology Ser.). (C). 2000. text 55.95 (*0-534-35443-2*) Brooks-Cole.
— Psychology. 5th ed. Perlee, Clyde, ed. LC 93-41549. 650p. (C). 1994. text 60.00 (*0-314-02478-6*) West Pub.
Dworin, Christopher, ed. see Starr, Philip, et al.
Dworin, Christopher D., ed. see Armstrong, William H.
Dworin, Christopher D., ed. see Branton, Lawrence S.
Dworin, Christopher D., ed. see Crawford, James E. & Martin, Neil B.
Dworin, Christopher D., ed. see Matos, Paula C.
Dworin, Christopher D., ed. see Merritt, Valerie J.
Dworin, Christopher D., ed. see Moskovitz, Myron.
Dworin, Christopher D., ed. see Moskovitz, Myron, et al.
Dworin, Christopher D., ed. see Pearl, Richard M.
Dworin, Christopher D., ed. see Sproul, Curtis C. & Rosenberry, Katharine N.
Dworin, Christopher D., ed. see Walker, Robert L.
Dworin, Christopher D., ed. see Wennergren, Kenneth H. & Mondon, Kathryn T.
Dworin, Lawrence. Profits in Buying & Renovating Homes. 304p. (Orig.). 1990. pap. 19.75 (*0-934041-57-1*) Craftsman.
— Renovating & Restyling Older Homes: The Professional's Guide to Maximum Value Remodeling. (Illus.). 416p. (Orig.). 1996. pap. 33.50 (*1-57218-029-3*) Craftsman.
Dwork, Bernard. Generalized Hypergeometric Functions. (Oxford Mathematical Monographs). 200p. 1990. 65.00 (*0-19-853567-8*) OUP.
— An Introduction to G-Functions. LC 94-2414. (Annals of Mathematics Studies: No. 133). 352p. 1994. text 69.50 (*0-691-03675-6*, Pub. by Princeton U Pr); pap. text 39.50 (*0-691-03681-0*, Pub. by Princeton U Pr) Cal Prin Full Svc.
— Lectures on P-Adic Differential Equations. (Grundlehren der Mathematischen Wissenschaften Ser.: Vol. 253). (Illus.). 304p. 1982. 149.95 (*0-387-90714-9*) Spr-Verlag.
Dwork, Deborah. Children with a Star: Jewish Youth in Nazi Europe. LC 90-23908. (Illus.). 384p. (C). 1993. reprint ed. pap. 20.00 (*0-300-05447-5*) Yale U Pr.
— War Is Good for Babies & Other Young Children. 300p. 1987. 45.00 (*0-422-60660-X*, 1200, Pub. by Tavistock) Routldge.
Dwork, Deborah & Jan van Pelt, Robert. Auschwitz: 1270 to the Present. LC 95-40275. (Illus.). 416p. 1996. 35.00 (*0-393-03933-1*) Norton.
Dwork, Deborah & Van Pelt, Robert J. Auschwitz: 1270 to the Present. (Illus.). 472p. 1997. pap. 22.50 (*0-393-31684-X*) Norton.
Dwork, John, jt. auth. see Getz, Michael.
Dwork, John D., jt. auth. see Getz, Michael M.
***Dworkin.** Treatment of the Dysarthrias. 2001. pap. 55.00 (*0-7693-0030-8*) Singular Publishing.
***Dworkin, Aaron P.** They Said I Wasn't Really Black. 80p. 1999. pap. write for info. (*0-9675385-0-5*) Ethnovibe Pubng.
Dworkin, Andrea. Intercourse. 288p. 1988. per. 13.95 (*0-02-907971-3*) Free Pr.
— Intercourse. LC 97-188998. 1997. per. 13.00 (*0-684-83239-9*) Free Pr.
— Letters from a War Zone. LC 93-13114. 344p. 1992. reprint ed. pap. 14.95 (*1-55652-185-5*, Lawrence Hill) Chicago Review.
— Life & Death. LC 96-38335. 1997. 22.50 (*0-684-83512-6*) Free Pr.
— Mercy. LC 91-18157. 344p. 1991. 22.00 (*0-941423-69-7*); pap. 13.95 (*0-941423-88-3*) FWEW.
— The New Woman's Broken Heart: Short Stories. LC 79-55919. 56p. (Orig.). 1980. pap. 4.00 (*0-9603628-0-0*) Frog in Well.
***Dworkin, Andrea.** Scapegoat: The Jews, Israel & Womens Liberation. LC 99-53819. 448p. 2000. 27.50 (*0-684-83612-2*) Free Pr.
Dworkin, Andrea, jt. ed. see MacKinnon, Catharine A.
Dworkin, Andrea S., jt. auth. see Kallas, William R.
Dworkin, Andrea S., jt. auth. see Kellas, William R.
Dworkin, Anthony G., ed. Teacher Burnout in the Public Schools: Structural Causes & Consequences for Children. LC 86-5713. (SUNY Series, Educational Leadership). 241p. (C). 1986. pap. text 24.95 (*0-88706-349-7*) State U NY Pr.
— Teacher Burnout in the Public Schools: Structural Causes & Consequences for Children. LC 86-5713. (SUNY Series, Educational Leadership). 241p. (C). 1986. text 74.50 (*0-88706-348-9*) State U NY Pr.
Dworkin, Anthony G. & Dworkin, Rosalind J. The Minority Report. 3rd ed. LC 98-87890. (C). 1998. pap. text 56.00 (*0-03-047534-1*, Pub. by Harcourt Coll Pubs) Harcourt.
Dworkin, Avish & Dworkin, Nancy. Problem Solving Assessment. Kratoville, Betty Lou, ed. 219p. (Orig.). 1988. pap. text 16.50 (*0-87879-593-6*) Acad Therapy.
Dworkin, Barry R. Learning & Physiological Regulation. LC 92-564. (John D. & Catherine T. MacArthur Foundation Series on Mental Health & Development). (Illus.). 232p. (C). 1993. 26.50 (*0-226-17600-2*) U Ch Pr.
Dworkin, Casey. Aquatic Effects of Acid Deposition. 144p. 1989. per. 12.95 (*0-8019-7990-0*) NP-Chilton.
— How to Buy a FAX Machine: In Five Easy Lessons. (Illus.). 40p. (Orig.). 1988. pap. 2.95 (*0-317-92524-5*) Personal Tech Rsch.
Dworkin, Craig. Signature-Effects. 32p. 1997. 5.00 (*1-891190-51-2*) Atelos.
Dworkin, Daniel S., jt. auth. see Cook, Alicia S.
Dworkin, Dennis. Cultural Marxism in Postwar Britain: History, the New Left, & the Origins of Cultural Studies. LC 96-43000. (Post-Contemporary Interventions Ser.). 328p. 1997. pap. text 16.95 (*0-8223-1914-4*); lib. bdg. 49.95 (*0-8223-1909-8*) Duke.
Dworkin, Dennis, jt. auth. see Burton, Stacy.
Dworkin, Dennis L. & Roman, Leslie G., eds. Views Beyond the Border Country: Raymond Williams & Cultural Politics. LC 92-11709. (Critical Social Thought Ser.). 352p. (C). (gr. 13). 1992. pap. 21.99 (*0-415-90276-2*, A4262) Routledge.
Dworkin, Gerald. The Theory & Practice of Autonomy. (Cambridge Studies in Philosophy). 192p. 1988. pap. text 20.95 (*0-521-35767-5*) Cambridge U Pr.
Dworkin, Gerald, ed. Mill's "On Liberty" Critical Essays. LC 97-1792. (Critical Essays on the Classics Ser.). 206p. 1997. 36.00 (*0-8476-8488-1*); pap. 13.95 (*0-8476-8489-X*) Rowman.
— Morality, Harm & the Law. 208p. (C). 1994. pap. 24.00 (*0-8133-8711-6*, Pub. by Westview) HarpC.
Dworkin, Gerald & Taylor, Richard. Blackstone's Guide to the Copyright, Designs & Patents Act, 1988. 464p. 1989. pap. 46.00 (*1-85431-023-2*, Pub. by Blackstone Pr) Gaunt.
Dworkin, Ira B. Sherlock Takes a Wife & Other Modern Tales. LC 93-90974. (Illus.). 100p. (Orig.). 1994. pap. 10.00 (*0-9639979-0-4*) Creative Writers.
Dworkin, James B. Owners vs. Players: Baseball & Collective Bargaining. LC 81-3472. 320p. 1981. 29.95 (*0-86569-072-3*, Auburn Hse) Greenwood.
Dworkin, James P. & Culatta, Richard. Dworkin-Culatta Oral Mechanism Examination. (Illus.). 76p. (Orig.). (C). 1980. 13.00 (*0-938820-00-1*) Edgewood KY.
Dworkin, James P. & Hartman, David E. Cases in Neurogenic Communicative Disorders: A Workbook. 2nd ed. LC 93-30762. (Illus.). 416p. (Orig.). (C). 1993. pap. text, wbk. ed. 55.00 (*1-56593-264-1*, 0586) Thomson Learn.
— Cases in Neurogenic Communicative Disorders: A Workbook & Audio Tape Set: & Aphasia, Apraxia of Speech, & Dysarthria Samples: Audiotape, Manual & Test Stimuli. 2nd ed. (Illus.). 428p. (Orig.). (C). 1993. pap., wbk. ed. 65.00 (*1-56593-310-9*, 0602) Thomson Learn.
Dworkin, James P. & Meleca, Robert J. Vocal Pathologies: Diagnosis, Treatment & Case Studies. LC 96-24941. 346p. 1996. pap., student ed. 55.00 (*1-56593-623-X*, 1292) Thomson Learn.
Dworkin, James P., jt. auth. see Hartman, David E.
Dworkin, James Paul. Motor Speech Disorders. 351p. (C). (gr. 13). 1991. text 49.95 (*1-55664-223-7*) Mosby Inc.
Dworkin, James R., jt. ed. see Chelius, James.
Dworkin, M., ed. The Prokaryotes: An Evolving Electronic Resource for the Microbiological Community. 3rd ed. 1999. 295.00 (*0-387-14254-1*) Spr-Verlag.
***Dworkin, Mark J.** Mayas, Aztecs & Incas: Mysteries of Ancient Civilizations of Central & South America. (Illus.). 144p. (gr. 10-12). 1999. reprint ed. pap. text 17.00 (*0-7881-6589-5*) DIANE Pub.
Dworkin, Martin, ed. Dewey on Education: Selections, with an Introduction & Notes. LC 59-15893. (Classics in Education Ser.). (Illus.). 134p. 1959. pap. text 9.00 (*0-8077-1263-9*) Tchrs Coll.
— Microbial Cell-Cell Interactions. (Illus.). 369p. 1991. text 69.00 (*1-55581-037-3*) ASM Pr.
Dworkin, Martin & Kaiser, Dale, eds. Myxobacteria 2. LC 92-48477. (Illus.). 385p. 1993. 69.00 (*1-55581-060-8*) ASM Pr.
Dworkin, Martin, jt. ed. see Shapiro, James A.
Dworkin, Martin S., ed. The Literature of Cinema, 48 bks., Set. (Series One). 1970. 2045.00 (*0-405-01600-X*) Ayer.
— The Literature of Cinema, 15 bks., Set. (Series Two). 1972. reprint ed. 353.00 (*0-405-03887-9*) Ayer.
Dworkin, Nancy, jt. auth. see Dworkin, Avish.
Dworkin, Paul H. NMS Pediatrics. 2nd ed. (National Medical Ser.). 460p. 1991. 27.00 (*0-683-06246-8*) Lppncott W & W.
— NMS Pediatrics. 4th ed. 675p. 30.00 (*0-683-30637-5*) Lppncott W & W.
Dworkin, Paul H., ed. Pediatrics. 3rd ed. LC 95-37175. (National Medical Series for Independent Study). 679p. 1996. 30.00 (*0-683-06245-X*) Lppncott W & W.
Dworkin, Rita, jt. auth. see Adelman, Irving.
Dworkin, Robert H., jt. ed. see Lenzenweger, Mark F.
Dworkin, Roger B. Limits: The Role of the Law in Bioethical Decision Making. LC 95-50697. (Medical Ethics Ser.). 224p. 1996. text 35.00 (*0-253-33075-0*) Ind U Pr.
***Dworkin, Ronald.** Sovereign Virtue: The Theory & Practice of Equality. LC 00-20071. 512p. 2000. pap. text 35.00 (*0-674-00219-9*) HUP.
Dworkin, Ronald M. Freedom's Law: The Moral Reading of the American Constitution. 408p. 1996. 35.00 (*0-674-31927-3*) HUP.
— Freedom's Law: The Moral Reading of the American Constitution. 416p. 1997. pap. text 16.95 (*0-674-31928-1*) HUP.
— Freedom's Law: The Moral Reading of the American Constitution. LC 97-43239. 420p. 1997. reprint ed. lib. bdg. 36.95 (*0-7351-0006-3*) Replica Bks.
— Law's Empire. LC 85-28566. 486p. 1986. 37.50 (*0-674-51835-7*) Belknap Pr.
— Law's Empire. LC 85-28566. 486p. 1990. pap. text 19.95 (*0-674-51836-5*) Belknap Pr.
— Life's Dominion: An Argument about Abortion, Euthanasia & Individual Freedom. LC 93-42582. 1994. pap. 13.00 (*0-679-73319-1*) Vin Bks.
— A Matter of Principle. LC 84-25122. 480p. 1985. 39.00 (*0-674-55460-4*) HUP.
— A Matter of Principle. 480p. 1985. pap. 19.50 (*0-674-55461-2*) HUP.
— Taking Rights Seriously. 308p. 1977. 40.50 (*0-674-86710-6*) HUP.
— Taking Rights Seriously. 386p. 1977. pap. 18.00 (*0-674-86711-4*) HUP.
Dworkin, Ronald M., ed. The Philosophy of Law. (Oxford Readings in Philosophy Ser.). 190p. 1977. pap. text 21.95 (*0-19-875022-6*) OUP.
Dworkin, Ronald W. The Rise of the Imperial Self: America's Culture Wars in Augustinian Perspective. LC 96-2178. 270p. (C). 1996. pap. text 25.95 (*0-8476-8219-6*); lib. bdg. 62.50 (*0-8476-8218-8*) Rowman.
Dworkin, Rosalind J. Researching Persons with Mental Illness. (Applied Social Research Methods Ser.: Vol. 30). 160p. (C). 1992. text 42.00 (*0-8039-3603-6*) Sage.
Dworkin, Rosalind J., jt. auth. see Dworkin, Anthony G.
Dworkin, Steven N. & Billick, David J. Lexical Studies of Medieval Spanish Texts: A Bibliography of Concordances, Glossaries, Vocabularies & Selected Word Studies. 2nd expanded rev. ed. (Bibliographical Ser.: No. 11). xiii, 209p. 1993. 25.00 (*0-940639-89-0*) Hispanic Seminary.
Dworkin, Susan. The Book of Candy. LC 96-23706. 360p. 1996. 20.00 (*1-56858-078-9*) FWEW.
***Dworkin, Susan.** Miss America, 1945: Bess Myerson & the Year That Changed Our Lives. LC 98-18445. 240p. 1999. pap. 18.95 (*1-55704-381-7*, Pub. by Newmarket) Norton.
Dworkin, Susan, jt. auth. see Beer, Edith Hahn.
Dworkin, Susan, jt. auth. see Lopez, Charlotte.
Dworkin, Susan, jt. auth. see White, Jeanne.
Dworkin, Terry M., jt. auth. see Barnes, A. James.
Dworkin, Walter. Price Guide to Holt-Howard Collectibles & Other Related Ceramicwares of the 50s & 60s. LC 97-80622. (Illus.). 160p. 1998. pap. 24.95 (*0-87341-517-5*, HHCK) Krause Pubns.
Dworkin Wright, Elena, ed. Ask a Riddle Big Book, Unit 4. (Networks Ser.). (J). (gr. 1). 1991. pap. 19.50 (*0-88106-727-X*, N140) Charlesbridge Pub.
Dworkin Wright, Elena, ed. see Muzik, Katy.
Dworkis, Janis Leibs, jt. auth. see Waldman, Jackie.
Dworkis, Sam. Recovery Yoga: Practical Guide for the Chronically Ill. LC 97-6239. 224p. 1997. pap. 15.00 (*0-517-88399-6*) Crown Pub Group.
Dworschak, F. Operation & Application of Electrostatic Accelerators: Proceedings of the 31st Symposium of No. 350p. 1999. 78.00 (*981-02-3852-5*) World Scientific Pub.
Dworski, Susan, jt. auth. see Thum, Robert.
Dworsky, Alan & Sansby, Betsy. Conga Drumming: A Beginner's Guide to Playing with Time. (Illus.). 160p. (Orig.). 1994. pap. text 24.95 incl. audio compact disk (*0-9638801-0-1*) Dancing Hands.
***Dworsky, Alan & Sansby, Betsy.** How to Play Djembe: West African Rhythms for Beginners. 96p. (C). 2000. pap. 24.95 (*0-9638801-4-4*, Pub. by Dancing Hands) SCB Distributors.
Dworsky, Alan & Sansby, Betsy. A Rhythmic Vocabulary: A Musician's Guide to Understanding & Improvising with Rhythm. LC 97-91788. (Illus.). 208p. (Orig.). 1997. pap. text 29.95 incl. audio compact disk (*0-9638801-2-8*) Dancing Hands.
— World-Beat & Funk Grooves: Playnig a Drumset the Easy Way. (Illus.). 128p. 1999. pap. text 24.95 incl. cd-rom, audio compact disk (*0-9638801-3-6*) Dancing Hands.
Dworsky, Alan L. Little Book of Oral Argument. LC 91-22872. xii, 77p. 1991. pap. 9.95 (*0-8377-0557-6*, Rothman) W S Hein.
Dworsky, Alan L. Little Book on Legal Writing. 2nd ed. LC 92-8448. xvii, 142p. 1992. pap. 11.95 (*0-8377-0560-6*, Rothman) W S Hein.
Dworsky, Alan L. User's Guide to the "Bluebook" 15th rev. ed. LC 91-31634. vi, 54p. 1991. pap. 5.50 (*0-8377-0558-4*, Rothman) W S Hein.
— User's Guide to the Bluebook: Revised for the 16th Edition of the "Bluebook" 16th rev. ed. LC 96-48351. vi, 58p. 1996. pap. 7.95 (*0-8377-0563-0*, Rothman) W S Hein.
Dworsky, Lawrence N. Modern Transmission Line Theory & Application. LC 88-2753. 250p. (C). 1988. reprint ed. lib. bdg. 34.95 (*0-89464-276-6*) Krieger.
Dworsky, Leonard B., ed. see Social & Economic Aspects of Water Resources Devel.
Dworsky, Richard F., ed. see Symposium on Water Resources Related to Mining & E.
Dwoskin, Stephen. Film Is: The International Free Cinema. LC 75-7685. (Illus.). 272p. 1978. reprint ed. 22.95 (*0-87951-036-6*, Pub. by Overlook Pr); reprint ed. pap. 10.95 (*0-87951-072-2*, Pub. by Overlook Pr) Penguin Putnam.
— Ha, Ha! La Solution Imaginaire. LC 93-83657. (Illus.). 128p. 1993. pap. 16.50 (*0-912292-99-7*) Smith.
Dwoyer, D. L., et al, eds. Finite Elements: Theory & Application. (Illus.). 235p. 1988. 105.95 (*0-387-96610-2*) Spr-Verlag.
— Theoretical Approaches to Turbulence. LC 85-14765. (Applied Mathematical Sciences Ser.: Vol. 58). (Illus.). xii, 373p. 1985. 89.95 (*0-387-96191-7*) Spr-Verlag.
Dwoyer, D. L., jt. ed. see Noor, A. K.
Dwyer. College Algebra. 2nd ed. (Math). Date not set. 52.00 (*0-314-12629-5*) Brooks-Cole.
— Easy Microwave Cooking. 1993. mass mkt. write for info. (*0-312-92618-9*) St Martin.
— Fundamentals of Economics. (HB - Economics Ser.). 1995. mass mkt. 39.95 (*0-538-85119-8*) S-W Pub.
— Over Coming Speech Fright. (C). 1997. pap. text 26.75 (*0-15-505328-0*) Harcourt Coll Pubs.
— Precalculus. 2000. mass mkt. 74.95 (*0-534-35287-1*) Brooks-Cole.
***Dwyer.** Precalculus. (Mathematics Ser.). (C). 2000. text 12.00 (*0-534-37903-6*) Brooks-Cole.

D

An Asterisk (*) at the beginning of an entry indicates that the title is appearing for the first time.

Dwyer. Precalculus. 2000. mass mkt., student ed. 30.95 (*0-534-35289-8*) Brooks-Cole.

Dwyer. The Problem of Pornography. 2nd ed. (Philosophy Ser.). (C). 1919. text 21.00 (*0-534-50978-9*) Wadsworth Pub.

***Dwyer & Gruenwald.** College Algebra & Trigonometry: A Contemporary Approach. 2nd ed. (Mathematics Ser.). 2000. text 18.75 (*0-534-36995-2*) Brooks-Cole.

Dwyer & Gruenwald. Graphing Calculator Manual College Algebra W/graphing 2nd ed. (Math Ser.). 1999. pap. text 10.00 (*0-534-37432-8*) Brooks-Cole.

— Graphing Calculator Manual: College Algegbra & Trigonometry W/graphing. 2nd ed. (Math Ser.). 1999. pap. text 10.00 (*0-534-37433-6*) Brooks-Cole.

***Dwyer & Gruenwald.** Trigonometry. 2001. pap. 54.00 (*0-534-38118-9*) Brooks-Cole.

***Dwyer, Adrian.** Reflections on the Mysteries of the Rosary. 2000. pap. 8.00 (*0-8059-4991-7*) Dorrance.

Dwyer, Amy S., jt. auth. see Stewart, Terence P.

Dwyer, Augusta. On the Line: Life on the U. S. - Mexican Border. 200p. (Orig.). (C). 1994. pap. text 16.00 (*0-85345-897-9*, Pub. by Monthly Rev) NYU Pr.

Dwyer, B. M. & Tooher, J. G. Butterworths Statutes - Property & Conveyancing Law Victoria. 400p. 1996. pap. write for info. (*0-409-31219-3*, MICHIE) LEXIS Pub.

Dwyer, Brian, jt. auth. see Letovsky, Robert.

***Dwyer, Britta C.** Anna Klumpke: A Turn-of-the-Century Painter & Her World. LC 99-13060. 1999. text 35.00 (*1-55553-386-8*) NE U Pr.

Dwyer, Carol A. Cursive Writing: Grades 3-4. (I Know It! Book Ser.). (Illus.). 32p. (J). (gr. 3-4). 1984. pap., student ed. 2.49 (*0-938256-02-5*, 02002) Sch Zone Pub Co.

Dwyer, Charles. Managing People. 2nd ed. 200p. (C). 1996. pap. text, per. 36.95 (*0-7872-2828-1*, 41282801) Kendall-Hunt.

Dwyer, Charles E. The Shifting Sources of Power & Influence. LC 92-74648. 80p. (Orig.). (C). 1993. pap. text 25.95 (*0-924674-12-1*) Am Coll Phys Execs.

Dwyer, Charles P. The Homestead Builder: Practical Hints for Handy-Men. 10th ed. LC 98-4206. (Illus.). 160p. 1998. pap. 12.95 (*1-55821-728-2*) Lyons Pr.

Dwyer, Christopher. Chile: Major World Nations. (Major World Nations Ser.). (Illus.). 144p. (YA). (gr. 5 up). 1999. lib. bdg. 19.95 (*0-7910-4734-2*) Chelsea Hse.

— The Dominican Americans. (Peoples of North America Ser.). (Illus.). 120p. (J). (gr. 5 up). 1991. lib. bdg. 19.95 (*0-87754-872-2*) Chelsea Hse.

— Robert Peary & the Quest for the North Pole. Goetzmann, William H., ed. (World Explorers Ser.). (Illus.). 120p. (YA). (gr. 5 up). 1992. lib. bdg. 19.95 (*0-7910-1316-2*) Chelsea Hse.

Dwyer, Clifford S. Index to Series I of American Loyalists Claim. 153p. 1989. pap. 14.00 (*0-935931-64-3*) Iberian Pub.

Dwyer, Corinne A. Loon Legends. LC 88-60995. (Illus.). 96p. 1988. pap. 9.95 (*0-87839-046-4*) North Star.

Dwyer, D. J. C. I. I. Life Assurance Salesmanship & Marketing, No. 910. (C). 1981. suppl. ed. 230.00 (*0-7855-4283-3*, Pub. by Witherby & Co) St Mut.

Dwyer, D. J., ed. China Now: An Introductory Survey with Readings. LC 73-87225. (Illus.). 520p. reprint ed. pap. 161.20 (*0-608-11639-4*, 202252600027) Bks Demand.

Dwyer, Daisy H., ed. Law & Islam in the Middle East. LC 89-18545. Orig. Title: Law & Islam in the Contemporary Middle East. 168p. 1990. 52.95 (*0-89789-151-1*, H151, Bergin & Garvey) Greenwood.

Dwyer, Daisy H. & Bruce, Judith, eds. A Home Divided: Women & Income in the Third World. LC 88-4938. 304p. 1988. 45.00 (*0-8047-1485-1*) Stanford U Pr.

— A Home Divided: Women & Income in the Third World. 303p. (C). 1993. pap. 15.95 (*0-8047-2213-7*) Stanford U Pr.

Dwyer, Dale E., ed. see Marlowe, Lynn G., et al.

Dwyer, Daniel J. & Hoffmann, Friedrich M., eds. Surface Science of Catalysis: In Situ Probes & Reaction Kinetics. LC 91-41322. (Symposium Ser.: No. 482). (Illus.). 364p. 1992. text 65.00 (*0-8412-2189-8*, Pub. by Am Chemical) OUP.

Dwyer, David. Ariana Olisvos: Her Last Works & Days. LC 76-8752. 80p. 1976. lib. bdg. 15.00 (*0-87023-218-5*) U of Mass Pr.

— College Algebra. 2nd ed. Date not set. pap. 18.95 (*0-534-35149-2*) Brooks-Cole.

Dwyer, David & Gruenwald, Mark. College Algebra: A Contemporary Approach. 2nd ed. LC 99-41146. 685p. 1999. text 79.95 (*0-534-35147-6*) Brooks-Cole.

— College Algebra & Trigonometry. LC 96-45932. 1997. mass mkt. 50.75 (*0-314-09970-0*) West Pub.

Dwyer, David J., jt. auth. see Osborn, Donald W.

Dwyer, Denis & Smith, David D., eds. Ethnicity & Development: Geographical Perspectives. LC 95-47705. 304p. 1996. 100.00 (*0-471-96354-2*) Wiley.

Dwyer, Denis J. China: The Next Decades. 1996. pap. (*0-582-10164-6*) Addison-Wesley.

— People & Housing in Third World Cities: Perspectives on the Problem of Spontaneous Settlements. 2nd ed. LC 74-84346. (Illus.). 310p. reprint ed. pap. 96.10 (*0-8357-6252-1*, 203451000090) Bks Demand.

Dwyer, Dennis. Beyond Jargon: What You Need to Know about Mediation - A Canadian Perspective. 128p. pap. 12.95 (*0-9698752-6-6*) Shloreline.

Dwyer, Derek & Corby, Jill. More Fun with Science: Practice at Home. (Illus.). 24p. (Orig.). (J). (gr. 3-5). 1992. pap., student ed. 2.95 (*0-7214-3240-9*, S9115-3, Ladybrd) Penguin Putnam.

***Dwyer, Diana.** Interpersonal Relationships. LC 99-38469. (Modular Psychology Ser.). 2000. pap. write for info. (*0-415-19624-8*) Routledge.

Dwyer, Diane. The Golden Bridge to Freedom: Techniques for Self-Mastery. 56p. 1997. pap. 10.00 (*0-9658355-0-2*) I AM Pubns.

Dwyer, Edward J., jt. auth. see Wright, John W.

Dwyer, Ellen. Homes for the Mad: Life Inside Two Nineteenth-Century Asylums. 281p. 1987. text 40.00 (*0-8135-1182-8*) Rutgers U Pr.

Dwyer, F. James, et al, eds. Environmental Toxicology & Risk Assessment Vol. 6: Modeling & Risk Assessment. (Illus.). 565p. 1997. text 107.00 (*0-8031-2474-0*) ASTM.

Dwyer, Francis G., jt. ed. see Stucky, Galen D.

Dwyer, Francis M., jt. ed. see Moore, David M.

Dwyer, Frank. The Annotated AA Handbook: A Companion to the Big Book. LC 95-26653. 432p. 1996. pap. 20.00 (*1-56980-075-8*) Barricade Bks.

— Georges-Jacques Danton. (World Leaders Past & Present Ser.). (Illus.). 120p. (YA). (gr. 5 up). 1987. lib. bdg. 19.95 (*0-87754-519-7*) Chelsea Hse.

— Henry VIII. (World Leaders Past & Present Ser.). (Illus.). 120p. (YA). (gr. 5 up). 1988. lib. bdg. 19.95 (*0-87754-530-8*) Chelsea Hse.

— James I. (World Leaders Past & Present Ser.). (Illus.). 120p. (YA). (gr. 5 up). 1988. lib. bdg. 19.95 (*1-55546-811-X*) Chelsea Hse.

Dwyer, Frank, tr. see Bulgakov, Mikhail Afanasevich.

Dwyer, Frank, tr. see Chekhov, Anton.

Dwyer, Frank, tr. see Gorky, Maxim.

Dwyer, Gerald P., Jr. & Hafer, R. W., eds. The Stock Market: Bubbles, Volatility, & Chaos. (C). 1989. lib. bdg. 86.50 (*0-7923-9029-6*) Kluwer Academic.

Dwyer, Gruenwald. College Algebra & Trigonometry with Graphing: Study Guide. 2nd ed. 1999. pap. text 15.00 (*0-534-37186-8*) Brooks-Cole.

***Dwyer, Gruenwald.** Interactive Algebra Plus Student College Algebra & Trigonometry with graph. 2nd ed. (Mathematics Ser.). 2000. pap. 10.00 (*0-534-37744-0*) Brooks-Cole.

— Interactive Algebra Plus Student Version College Algebra with Graphing. 2nd ed. (Mathematics Ser.). 2000. pap. 10.00 (*0-534-37746-7*) Brooks-Cole.

Dwyer, Helen, ed. Index Biographique Francais, 4 vols., Set. 2400p. 1993. 1055.00 (*0-86291-801-4*) U Pubns Amer.

***Dwyer, J.** The Launch Manual: An Introduction to the Principles of World Takeover. 2nd rev. ed. LC 00-90386. 221p. 2000. pap. 10.95 (*0-9658366-6-5*) Chairman Pubns.

Dwyer, Jack. The Launch Manual: A Young Person's Introduction to the Principles of World Takeover. LC 97-91731. (Illus.). 275p. (YA). (gr. 10 up). 1998. pap. 10.95 (*0-9658366-5-7*) Chairman Pubns.

***Dwyer, Jackie.** Flowers. LC 99-49973. (Readers Nature Bks.). (Illus.). (J). 2000. lib. bdg. 14.60 (*0-8239-5677-6*, PowerKids) Rosen Group.

— Fruits. LC 99-49795. (Readers Nature Bks.). (Illus.). (J). 2000. lib. bdg. 14.60 (*0-8239-5678-4*, PowerKids) Rosen Group.

Dwyer, James. Private Pilot's Blue Book. LC 76-41837. 1977. write for info. (*0-685-81548-X*) Macmillan.

Dwyer, James A., tr. see Klaiber, Walter.

Dwyer, James G. Religious Schools vs. Children's Rights. LC 98-14863. 224p. 1998. 29.95 (*0-8014-3426-2*) Cornell U Pr.

Dwyer, Janet & Hodge, Ian. Countryside in Trust: Land Management by Conversation, Recreation & Amenity Organization. 314p. 1996. 80.00 (*0-471-94871-3*) Wiley.

Dwyer, Jeffrey R., jt. auth. see Madison, Michael T.

Dwyer, Jeffrey W. & Coward, Raymond T. Gender, Families & Elder Care. (Focus Editions Ser.: Vol. 138). (Illus.). 312p. 1992. 59.95 (*0-8039-3932-9*); pap. 26.00 (*0-8039-3933-7*) Sage.

Dwyer, Jeffrey W. & Coward, Raymond T., eds. Gender, Families & Elder Care. LC 91-40695. (Sage Focus Editions Ser.: No. 138). 278p. 1992. pap. 86.20 (*0-608-05065-2*, 206562000005) Bks Demand.

Dwyer, Jim. Earth Works: Recommended Fiction & Nonfiction about Nature & the Environment for Adults & Young Adults. 507p. (Orig.). 1995. pap. 49.95 (*1-55570-194-9*) Neal-Schuman.

— Lake Superior Gold: An Amateur's Guide to Prospecting in the Lake Superior Region. LC 92-14659. 1992. pap. 9.95 (*0-87839-067-7*) North Star.

Dwyer, Jim, et al. Two Seconds under the World: Terror Comes to America - The Conspiracy Behind the World Trade Center Bombing. (Illus.). 322p. 1997. reprint ed. text 24.00 (*0-7881-5136-3*) DIANE Pub.

Dwyer, Joan. Personal Health Notes. 124p. 1999. pap. write for info. (*0-7392-0111-5*, PO3008) Morris Pubng.

***Dwyer, Johanna & Rippe, James.** Lifestyle Nutrition. (Illus.). 208p. 2000. pap. 32.95 (*0-632-04548-5*) Blackwell Sci.

Dwyer, John. Body at War: The Story of Our Immune System. (Illus.). 416p. 1994. pap. 14.95 (*1-86373-484-8*, Pub. by Allen & Unwin Pty) IPG Chicago.

— Church History: Twenty Centuries of Catholic Christianity. rev. ed. 448p. 1998. pap. text 18.95 (*0-8091-3830-1*) Paulist Pr.

***Dwyer, John.** The Unknown Sky: A Novel of the Moon. unabridged ed. LC 99-90874. 364p. 1999. pap. 12.99 (*0-9673984-0-1*) J W Dwyer.

Dwyer, John, ed. A Sea of Talk. LC 90-27279. 106p. (Orig.). (C). 1991. pap. text 16.50 (*0-435-08582-4*, 08582) Heinemann.

Dwyer, John B. Commandos from the Sea: The History of Amphibious Special Warfare in World War II & the Korean War. LC 98-209631. (Illus.). 288p. 1998. 44.95 (*0-87364-960-5*) Paladin Pr.

— Scouts & Raiders: The Navy's First Special Warfare Commandos. LC 92-30384. 224p. 1993. 55.00 (*0-275-94409-3*, C4409, Praeger Pubs) Greenwood.

— Seaborne Deception: The History of U. S. Navy Beach Jumpers. LC 91-27817. 192p. 1992. 52.95 (*0-275-93800-X*, C3800, Praeger Pubs) Greenwood.

***Dwyer, John B.** To Wire the World: Perry M. Collins & the North Pacific Telegraph Expedition. LC 00-23941. 192p. 2000. 64.00 (*0-275-96755-7*, C6755, Praeger Pubs) Greenwood.

Dwyer, John C. Human Sexuality: A Christian View. LC 87-61923. 172p. (Orig.). 1988. pap. 8.95 (*1-55612-076-1*) Sheed & Ward WI.

— The Word Was Made Flesh: An Introduction to the Theology of the New Testament. LC 88-63858. 160p. (Orig.). (C). 1989. pap. 10.95 (*1-55612-251-9*) Sheed & Ward WI.

Dwyer, John F. Customer Diversity & the Future Demand for Outdoor Recreation. (Illus.). 58p. (C). 1998. pap. text 15.00 (*0-7881-7514-9*) DIANE Pub.

— Customer Diversity & the Future Demand for Outdoor Recreation. (Illus.). 64p. 1997. reprint ed. 14.00 (*0-89904-585-5*, Cascade Expedit); reprint ed. pap. 7.40 (*0-89904-586-3*, Cascade Expedit) Crumb Elbow Pub.

Dwyer, John J. Stonewall. LC 98-8712. 1998. pap. 14.99 (*0-8054-1663-3*) Broadman.

Dwyer, John P. & Bergsund, Marika F. Dwyer & Bergsund, Federal Environmental Laws. annot. ed. Lawyers Cooperative Publishing Staff, ed. LC 96-76297. 2000p. 1996. pap. text. write for info. (*0-7620-0063-5*) West Group.

Dwyer, John P. & Menell, Peter S. Property Law & Policy: A Comparative Institutional Perspective. LC 97-30646. (University Casebook Ser.). 1060p. 1998. text 41.25 (*1-56662-533-5*) Foundation Pr.

Dwyer, Joseph D., ed. Slovenes in the United States & Canada: A Bibliography. LC 81-83551. (IHRC Ethnic Bibliography Ser.: No. 3). (Illus.). xiv, 196p. 1981. pap. text 8.95 (*0-932833-02-0*) Immig His Res.

Dwyer-Joyce, Alice. The Chieftain. large type ed. (Ulverscroft Large Print Ser.). 304p. 1997. 27.99 (*0-7089-3717-9*) Ulverscroft.

— Cry the Soft Rain. large type ed. 288p. 1996. 27.99 (*0-7089-3514-1*) Ulverscroft.

— Danny Boy. large type ed. 1981. 27.99 (*0-7089-0579-X*) Ulverscroft.

— Doctor Ross of Harton. large type ed. 304p. 1983. 27.99 (*0-7089-0927-2*) Ulverscroft.

***Dwyer-Joyce, Alice.** Gibbet Fen. large type ed. 248p. 1999. 31.99 (*0-7089-4133-8*) Ulverscroft.

Dwyer-Joyce, Alice. The Gingerbread House. large type ed. 1978. 12.00 (*0-7089-0101-8*) Ulverscroft.

— The Glitter-Dust. large type ed. 361p. 1982. 27.99 (*0-7089-0747-4*) Ulverscroft.

— The Pennybox. large type ed. 304p. 1995. 27.99 (*0-7089-3237-1*) Ulverscroft.

— Prescription for Melissa. large type ed. 263p. 1980. 27.99 (*0-7089-0437-8*) Ulverscroft.

— The Rainbow Glass. large type ed. 304p. 1995. 27.99 (*0-7089-3327-0*) Ulverscroft.

— The Storm of Wrath. large type ed. (Large Print Ser.). 416p. 1994. 27.99 (*0-7089-3015-8*) Ulverscroft.

— The Swiftest Eagle. large type ed. (Large Print Ser.). 352p. 1997. 27.99 (*0-7089-3700-4*) Ulverscroft.

Dwyer, Judith A. Vision & Values: Ethical Viewpoints in the Catholic Tradition. LC 99-19947. 208p. 1999. 19.95 (*0-87840-742-1*) Georgetown U Pr.

Dwyer, Judith A., ed. The New Dictionary of Catholic Social Thought. LC 94-4264. 1056p. (Orig.). 1994. 79.50 (*0-8146-5526-2*, M Glazier) Liturgical Pr.

— Questions of Special Urgency: The Church in the Modern World Two Decades after Vatican II. LC 86-218. 251p. (Orig.). reprint ed. pap. 77.90 (*0-7837-6319-0*, 204603400010) Bks Demand.

Dwyer, Karen. Conquer Your Speechfright. LC 97-74863. (C). 1997. pap. text 19.50 (*0-15-508177-2*, Pub. by Harcourt Coll Pubs) Harcourt.

Dwyer, Karen K. Easy Livin' Low-Calorie Microwave Cooking. 4th ed. (Illus.). 160p. 1990. pap. 14.95 (*0-312-03821-6*) St Martin.

— Easy Livin' Microwave Cooking. 4th ed. 1989. pap. 14.95 (*0-312-02910-1*) St Martin.

Dwyer, Kathleen M. What Do You Mean I Have a Learning Disability? (Illus.). 32p. (YA). (gr. 5-9). 1991. 14.95 (*0-8027-8102-0*); lib. bdg. 15.85 (*0-8027-8103-9*) Walker & Co.

— What Do You Mean I Have Attention Deficit Disorder? LC 95-44556. (Illus.). 48p. (J). (gr. k-9). 1996. 14.95 (*0-8027-8392-9*); lib. bdg. 15.85 (*0-8027-8393-7*) Walker & Co.

***Dwyer, Kelly.** Self-Portrait with Ghosts. 2000. mass mkt. 6.99 (*0-425-17696-7*) Berkley Pub.

— Self-Portrait with Ghosts. LC 98-8715. 320p. 1999. 23.95 (*0-399-14440-4*, G P Putnam) Peng Put Young Read.

Dwyer, Kelly. The Tracks of Angels. large type ed. LC 94-921. 342p. 1994. lib. bdg. 23.95 (*0-7862-0193-2*) Thorndike Pr.

Dwyer, Kevin. Arab Voices: Human Rights & Culture. 350p. 1991. 50.00 (*0-520-07490-4*, Pub. by U CA Pr); pap. 17.95 (*0-520-07491-2*, Pub. by U CA Pr) Cal Prin Full Svc.

— Arab Voices: The Human Rights Debate in the Middle East. 245p. 1996. pap. 15.50 (*0-614-21618-4*, 47) Kazi Pubns.

***Dwyer, Kevin.** Ireland - The Inner Island. (Illus.). 2000. 39.95 (*1-898256-91-8*, Pub. by Collins Press) Dufour.

Dwyer, Kevin. Moroccan Dialogues: Anthropology in Question. LC 82-15167. 327p. 1982. reprint ed. pap. 101.40 (*0-608-03727-3*, 206455200009) Bks Demand.

— Moroccan Dialogues: Anthropology in Question. (Illus.). 297p. (C). 1987. reprint ed. pap. text 13.95 (*0-88133-293-3*) Waveland Pr.

Dwyer, Kevin, photos by. Ireland-Our Island Home: An Aerial Tour Around Ireland's Coastline. (Illus.). 158p. 1997. 39.95 (*1-898256-20-9*, Pub. by Collins Press) Dufour.

***Dwyer, Laurie S.** Geographies of New Femininities. (Illus.). 225p. 2000. pap. 27.53 (*0-582-32024-0*) Longman.

Dwyer, Liz. Playtime Crafts & Activities: Fun Things to Make & Do. LC 93-73232. (Illus.). 32p. (J). (gr. 2-7). 1994. pap. 4.95 (*1-56397-348-0*) Boyds Mills Pr.

Dwyer, M. J., ed. The Performance of Off-Road Vehicles & Machines: Proceedings of the 8th International ISTVS Conference, Cambridge, August 1984. 120p. 1984. pap. 33.00 (*0-08-031655-7*, Pergamon Pr) Elsevier.

Dwyer, Maureen, intro. New Woman, New Church, New Priestly Ministry: Proceedings of the Second Conference on the Ordination of Roman Catholic Women. LC 89-183386. (Illus.). 178p. (Orig.). (C). 1980. pap. 5.00 (*0-9623386-0-5*) Women's Ord Conf.

Dwyer, Meaghan, ed. see Greeley, Hugh P., et al.

***Dwyer, Michael J.** Over the Side Mickey: A First Hand Account of the 1997 Newfoundland Seal Hunt. (Illus.). 148p. 1999. pap. 14.95 (*1-55109-253-0*) Nimbus Publ.

Dwyer, Mindy. Aurora: A Tale of the Northern Lights. LC 97-11295. (Illus.). 32p. (J). 1997. 15.95 (*0-88240-494-6*, Alaska NW Bks) Gr Arts Ctr Pub.

— Coyote in Love. LC 96-52627. (Illus.). 32p. (J). (ps up). 1997. 15.95 (*0-88240-485-7*, Alaska NW Bks) Gr Arts Ctr Pub.

***Dwyer, Mindy.** Quilt of Dreams. LC 00-36270. (Illus.). (J). 2000. pap. write for info. (*0-88240-521-7*, Alaska NW Bks) Gr Arts Ctr Pub.

Dwyer, Mindy, jt. auth. see Laverde, Arlene.

Dwyer, Nancy. FluxAttitudes. Lauf, Cornelia, ed. (Illus.). 56p. 1992. pap. 24.50 (*1-56466-038-9*, Pub. by Imschoot) Dist Art Pubs.

Dwyer, O. E. Boiling Liquid-Metal Heat Transfer. LC 75-11012. (Nuclear Science Technology Ser.). (Illus.). 1976. text 44.00 (*0-89448-000-6*, 300008) Am Nuclear Soc.

***Dwyer, P. A.** Standard Review Plan for Physical Protection Plans for the Independent Storage of Spent Fuel & High-level Radioactive Waste. 30p. 1998. pap. 2.75 (*0-16-062754-0*) USGPO.

Dwyer, Paulinus, jt. auth. see MacKenthun, Carole.

Dwyer, Peter J., et al, eds. Social Division, Economy & Schooling. 126p. (C). 1985. 65.00 (*0-7300-0336-1*, Pub. by Deakin Univ) St Mut.

Dwyer, Philip. Sense & Subjectivity: A Study of Wittgenstein & Merleau-Ponty. LC 89-37713. (Studies in Epistemology, Psychology & Psychiatry: Vol. 2). xii, 223p. 1990. 79.00 (*90-04-09205-6*) Brill Academic Pubs.

Dwyer, Philip G., compiled by. Charles-Maurice de Talleyrand, 1754-1838: A Bibliography, Vol. 4. LC 95-22753. (Bibliographies of World Leaders Ser.: Vol. 4). 232p. 1996. lib. bdg. 75.00 (*0-313-29354-6*, Greenwood Pr) Greenwood.

***Dwyer, Rachel.** All You Want is Money, All You Need Is Love: Sex & Romance in Modern India. LC 99-47860. 224p. 1999. 69.95 (*0-304-70320-6*); pap. 22.95 (*0-304-70321-4*) Continuum.

Dwyer, Rachel. Teach Yourself Gujarati: A Complete Course for Beginners. LC 94-65934. (GUJ., Illus.). 256p. 1995. pap. 16.95 (*0-8442-3775-2*, Teach Yrslf) NTC Contemp Pub Co.

— Teach Yourself Gujarati Complete Course for Beginners, Set. (Teach Yourself Ser.). (GUJ.). 256p. 1996. pap. 25.95 incl. audio (*0-8442-3877-5*, Teach Yrslf) NTC Contemp Pub Co.

Dwyer, Rex, jt. auth. see Rozycki, William.

Dwyer, Richard A. Boethian Fictions: Narratives in the Medieval French Versions of the Consolatio Philosophiae. LC 75-36477. (Medieval Academy Bks.: No. 83). 1976. 20.00 (*0-910956-57-X*) Medieval Acad.

Dwyer, Richard A. & Lingenfelter, Richard E. Lying on the Eastern Slope: James Townsend's Comic Journalism on the Mining Frontier. LC 84-2251. (Illus.). 175p. 1984. reprint ed. pap. 54.30 (*0-608-04495-4*, 206524000001) Bks Demand.

Dwyer, Richard E. Labor Education in the U. S. An Annotated Bibliography. LC 77-21572. 292p. 1977. 26.50 (*0-8108-1058-1*) Scarecrow.

Dwyer, Robert F. & Tanner, John F. Business Marketing. LC 98-21676. (Irwin-McGraw-Hill Series in Marketing). 1998. write for info. (*0-256-22133-2*, Irwn Prfssnl) McGraw-Hill Prof.

Dwyer, Ruth, jt. ed. see Petrie, Graham.

Dwyer, Ruth A. Malcolm St. Clair: His Films, 1919-1945. LC 94-15371. (Filmmakers Ser.: No. 38). (Illus.). xxvii, 250p. 1997. 42.00 (*0-8108-2709-3*) Scarecrow.

***Dwyer, Simon, ed.** Rapid Eye Movement Vol. 4: The Best of the Classic Counter-Culture Journal. (Rapid Eye Ser.: No. 4). 256p. 2000. pap. 24.95 (*1-871592-69-0*, Pub. by Creation Books) Subterranean Co.

Dwyer, Simon, ed. Rapid Eye 1. rev. ed. (Illus.). 256p. 1996. pap. 19.95 (*1-871592-22-4*) Creation Books.

— Rapid Eye 3. rev. ed. (Illus.). 256p. 1995. pap. 19.95 (*1-871592-24-0*) Creation Books.

— Rapid Eye 2. rev. ed. (Illus.). 256p. 1996. pap. 19.95 (*1-871592-23-2*) Creation Books.

Dwyer, Susan. The Problem of Pornography. LC 94-18082. 264p. 1994. 28.95 (*0-534-22044-4*) Wadsworth Pub.

Dwyer, Susan & Feinberg, Joel. The Problem of Abortion. 3rd ed. LC 96-19686. (Philosophy Ser.). (C). 1996. 33.95 (*0-534-50514-7*) Wadsworth Pub.

Dwyer, T. Life & Death at Work: Industrial Accidents As a Case of Socially Produced Error. (Studies in Work & Industry). (Illus.). 335p. (C). 1991. text 59.50 (*0-306-43949-2*, Kluwer Plenum) Kluwer Academic.

Dwyer, T. Ryle. Big Fellow, Long Fellow: A Joint Biography of Collins & de Valera. LC 98-34378. 256p. 1999. text 35.00 (*0-312-21919-9*) St Martin.

— De Valera: The Man & the Myths. 370p. (Orig.). 1992. pap. 14.95 (*1-85371-180-2*, Pub. by Poolbeg Pr) Dufour.

— Eamon de Valera. 2nd ed. (Gill's Irish Lives Ser.). (Illus.). 151p. 1998. reprint ed. pap. 13.95 (*0-7171-2685-4*, Pub. by Gill & MacMill) Irish Bks Media.

— Fallen Idol: Haughey's Controversial Career. LC 97-212330. 250p. 1998. pap. 12.95 (*1-85635-202-1*, Pub. by Mercier Pr) Irish Amer Bk.

— Michael Collins: The Man Who Won The War. 160p. 1997. pap. 12.95 (*0-85342-931-6*, Pub. by Mercier Pr) Irish Amer Bk.

— Strained Relations: Ireland at Peace & the U. S. A. at War 1941-1945. 1988. 52.50 (*0-389-20774-8*, N8333) B&N Imports.

Dwyer, T. Ryle, ed. De Valera: The Man & the Myths. rev. ed. 340p. (Orig.). 1991. 45.00 (*1-85371-121-7*, Pub. by Poolbeg Pr) Dufour.

***Dwyer, Terry.** The Change Agent. 108p. 2000. pap. 14.95 (*1-928704-77-8*, Fusion Pr) Authorlink.

Dwyer, Terry. How to Write an Astrological Synthesis: A Guide for Students. 95p. 1999. pap. 14.95 (*0-8464-4947-1*) Beekman Pubs.

Dwyer, Thomas A. & Critchfield, Margot A. A Bit of Applesoft BASIC. (Illus.). 240p. 1985. pap. 12.95 (*0-201-11161-6*) Addison-Wesley.

Dwyer, Thomas W. Simply Public Relations: Public Relations Made Challenging, Complete & Concise! 210p. (C). 1992. pap. text 19.95 (*0-913507-25-3*) New Forums.

Dwyer, Timothy. The Motif of Wonder in the Gospel of Mark. LC 96-147332. (JSNT Supplement Ser.: No. 128). 243p. 1996. 70.00 (*1-85075-603-1*, Pub. by Sheffield Acad) CUP Services.

Dwyer, Timothy, ed. Newell Lectureships 1, Vol. 1. 1992. 16.95 (*0-87162-638-1*, D3075) Warner Pr.

Dwyer, Timothy, ed. see Jewett, Robert.

Dwyer, Timothy, ed. see Oswalt, John N. & Lane, William L.

***Dwyer, Tom.** Broad Street. 2000. pap. write for info. (*1-928781-20-9*) Hollis Bks.

Dwyer, Tom. A Guide to the Allegheny National Forest. (Illus.). 122p. 1999. pap. 12.00 (*0-9666045-0-4*) Trailside Pub.

Dwyer, Tom, jt. auth. see Zamchyn, Sylva.

Dwyer, Vincent. Lift Your Sails: The Challenge of Being a Christian. LC 98-24352. 176p. 1998. reprint ed. pap. 15.95 (*0-8264-1139-8*) Continuum.

Dwyer, William, jt. auth. see Ledbetter, Richard.

Dwyer, William, jt. auth. see Murrell, Dan.

Dwyer, William G., et al, eds. Stable & Unstable Homotopy. LC 98-11194. (Fields Institute Communications Ser.: Vol. 19). 316p. 1998. 79.00 (*0-8218-0824-9*, FIC/19) Am Math.

Dwyer, William L. The Goldmark Case: An American Libel Trial. LC 84-40326. 304p. 1984. 18.95 (*0-295-96163-5*) U of Wash Pr.

Dwyer, William M. The Day Is Ours! A Inside View of the Battles of Trenton & Princeton, November 1776-January 1777. LC 98-24044. (Illus.). 448p. (C). 1998. pap. 20.00 (*0-8135-2608-6*) Rutgers U Pr.

Dwyer, William O. Earth's Eleventh Hour: Environmental Readings from the Washington Post Writers Group. LC 94-237320. 419p. 1994. pap. 30.00 (*0-205-16002-6*) Allyn.

Dwyer, William O., jt. auth. see Leeming, Frank C.

Dwyer, William O., jt. auth. see Murrell, Dan S.

Dwyre, Bill, ed. see Murray, Jim.

Dy, Manuel B. Values in Philippine Culture & Education. LC 94-4724. (Series III, Asia: Vol. 7). 205p. 1994. 45.00 (*1-56518-040-2*); pap. 17.50 (*1-56518-041-0*) Coun Res Values.

Dy, Manuel B., et al. Civil Society in Chinese Context. LC 96-20810. (Cultural Heritage & Contemporary Change Series III: Vol. 15). 1997. pap. 17.50 (*1-56518-084-4*) Coun Res Values.

Dyachkov, P. N., jt. auth. see Levinson, A. A.

Dyadkin, Iosif G. Unnatural Deaths in the U. S. S. R., 1928-1954. Deruguine, Tania, tr. from RUS. LC 82-8455. (Illus.). 80p. (Orig.). 1983. pap. text 21.95 (*0-87855-919-1*) Transaction Pubs.

Dyahoff, Margaret O., et al. Nucleic Acid Sequence Database, Vol 1. LC 81-84122. (Illus.). xiv, 214p. (Orig.). 1981. text 35.00 (*0-912466-09-X*) Natl Biomedical.

Dyak, Miriam. Dying. LC 78-70873. 1978. pap. 3.00 (*0-934678-00-6*) New Victoria Pubs.

— Fire under Water. LC 77-78508. 1977. pap. 3.00 (*0-934678-01-4*) New Victoria Pubs.

— In Celebration of Planet Earth. 36p. (Orig.). 1988. pap. 7.00 (*0-942396-53-7*) Blackberry ME.

— The Voice Dialogue Facilitator's Handbook Pt. 1: A Step by Step Guide to Working with the Aware Ego. LC 98-94077. (Illus.). 1999. pap. 32.50 (*0-9668390-0-5*) LIFE Energy.

D'yakonov, Eugene G. Optimization in Solving Elliptic Problems. McCormick, Steve, ed. 592p. 1995. lib. bdg. 89.95 (*0-8493-2872-1*, 2872) CRC Pr.

Dyakonova, Yelena M., jt. ed. see Braginsky, Vladimir I.

D'yakov, Y. T., et al. Psychology & General Sociology Reviews: Population Biology of Phytopathogenic Fungi & Plants, Vol. 4. Turpaev, E. T. & Yaslokov, A. V., eds. (Soviet Scientific Reviews Ser.: Vol. 4, Pt. 2). iv, 96p. 1989. text 108.00 (*3-7186-5001-0*) Gordon & Breach.

Dyal, Donald H., et al. Historical Dictionary of the Spanish American War. LC 95-33076. 392p. 1996. lib. bdg. 89.50 (*0-313-28852-6*, Greenwood Pr) Greenwood.

Dyal, Donald H., jt. auth. see Dethloff, Henry C.

Dyal, Donald H., jt. auth. see Kelsey, Mavis P., Sr.

Dyall-Smith, D. & Marks, R., eds. Dermatology at the Millennium: The Proceedings of the 19th World Congress of Dermatology. LC 99-10220. (Illus.). 812p. 1999. 120.00 (*1-85070-005-2*) Prthnon Pub.

Dyall-Smith, Delwyn & O'Brien, T. Dermatological Discoveries of the 20th Century. LC 99-10463. (Illus.). 38p. 1999. pap. 34.95 (*1-85070-085-0*) Prthnon Pub.

Dyar, M. D., et al, eds. Mineral Spectroscopy: A Tribute to Roger G. Burns. LC 96-77227. (Special Publication: No. 5). (Illus.). xiv, 400p. (C). 1996. write for info. (*0-941809-04-8*) Geochemical Soc.

Dyas, Dee. Images of Faith in English Literature, 700-1550: An Introduction. LC 96-52219. (Medieval & Renaissance Library). 344p. (C). 1997. pap. text 64.69 (*0-582-30192-0*) Longman.

Dyas, Denise. Images of Faith in English Literature, 700-1550: An Introduction. LC 96-52219. (Medieval & Renaissance Library). 344p. (C). 1997. pap. 30.13 (*0-582-30191-2*) Longman.

Dyas, Ronald D. Screenwriting for Television & Film. 368p. (C). 1993. text. write for info. (*0-697-13761-9*) Brown & Benchmark.

Dyason, Duncan. Miracle Children. 1998. pap. 6.99 (*0-340-72184-7*, Pub. by Hodder & Stought Ltd) Trafalgar.

Dyba, Olga I., et al, eds. Obscured Catastrophe of SWIFT II & Its Lessons: The Emperor's New Clothes or the Eclipse in Technology. LC 93-90808. (Illus.). 108p. (Orig.). 1997. per. 138.00 (*0-9638406-0-6*) Comp Res & Innovat.

Dyba, Thomas J. The Story of the Only Home Abraham Lincoln Ever Owned. (Illus.). 16p. (Orig.). 1977. reprint ed. pap. 1.70 (*0-931090-00-8*) I B C Pubns.

Dyball, G. E. Mathematics for Technician Engineers: Levels 4 & 5. 384p. 1983. write for info. (*0-07-084664-2*) McGraw.

Dyballa, Cynthia D., et al. The Tug Hill Program: A Regional Planning Option for Rural Areas. LC 81-8999. (New York State Study Ser.). (Illus.). 189p. reprint ed. pap. 58.60 (*0-8357-3979-1*, 203667700005) Bks Demand.

Dyban, A. P. & Baranov, V. S. Cytogenetics of Mammalian Embryonic Development. (Illus.). 376p. 1988. 79.00 (*0-19-854584-3*) OUP.

Dybbig, Kent. The Scheme Programming Language. 2nd ed. (The: ANSI Scheme). 272p. (C). 1996. pap. 55.00 (*0-13-454646-6*) P-H.

Dybbroe, Susanne, et al, eds. The Faroe Islands. (North Atlantic Studies: No. 1, Pt. 1). (Illus.). 63p. (C). 1989. pap. 19.95 (*87-983424-0-1*, Pub. by Aarhus Univ Pr) David Brown.

Dybbroe, Susanne & Moller, Poul B., eds. Greenland: Nationalism & Cultural Identity Comparative Perspective. (North Atlantic Studies: No. 1, Pt. 2). (Illus.). 71p. (C). 1991. pap. 19.95 (*87-983424-4-4*, Pub. by Aarhus Univ Pr) David Brown.

— Local Organisation, Cultural Identity & National Integration in the North Atlantic. (North Atlantic Studies: No. 3, Pt. 1). (Illus.). 68p. (Orig.). (C). 1991. pap. 19.95 (*87-983424-8-7*, Pub. by Aarhus Univ Pr) David Brown.

Dybdahl, Claudia S., jt. auth. see Shaw, Donna G.

Dybek, Stuart. Childhood & Other Neighborhoods. 2nd ed. 201p. 1995. reprint ed. pap. 12.00 (*0-88001-415-6*) HarpC.

Dybek, Stuart & Hirshfield, Jane, eds. Ploughshares Spring, 1998: Stories & Poems Edited by Stuart Dabek & Jane Hirshfield, Vol. 24, No. 1. 225p. 1998. pap. 9.95 (*0-933277-22-9*) Ploughshares.

Dybiec, David A., ed. Slipp' Away: The Loss of Black-Owned Farms. LC 88-81218. (Illus.). 80p. (Orig.). 1988. pap. 6.00 (*0-914422-16-2*) Glenmary Res Ctr.

Dybjer, P., jt. ed. see Pitts, A.

Dybjer, Peter, et al, eds. Types for Proofs & Programs: International Workshop TYPES '94, Bastad, Sweden, June 6-10, 1994 Proceedings. LC 95-44954. (Lecture Notes in Computer Science Ser.: Vol. 996). 202p. 1995. 43.00 (*3-540-60579-7*) Spr-Verlag.

Dybkov, V. P. Growth Kinetics of Chemical Compound Layers. 180p. 1995. pap. 70.00 (*1-898326-34-7*, Pub. by CISP) Balogh.

Dyboski, Roman. Outlines of Polish History. LC 78-24236. 285p. 1979. reprint ed. lib. bdg. 65.00 (*0-313-20831-X*, DYOP, Greenwood Pr) Greenwood.

Dyboski, Roman, ed. see Hill, Richard.

Dybovskaia, V. & Kirillova, I. Dictionnaire Geologique: Francais-Russe: French - Russian Dictionary of Geology. deluxe ed. (FRE & RUS.). 406p. 1958. 19.95 (*0-8288-6847-6*, M-9099) Fr & Eur.

Dybowski, C. R., jt. auth. see Gerstein, B. C.

Dybwad, G. L. & Bliss, Joy V. Annotated Bibliography: World's Columbian Exposition, Chicago 1893. LC 91-77456. (Illus.). 459p. (Orig.). 1992. pap. 39.95 (*0-9631612-0-2*) Bk Stops Here.

— Chicago Day at the World's Columbian Exposition Illustrated with Candid Photographs. LC 97-92955. (Illus.). 140p. 1997. 34.95 (*0-9631612-3-7*) Bk Stops Here.

— James A. Michener: The Beginning Teacher & His Textbooks. limited ed. LC 95-79641. (Illus.). 104p. 1995. 29.95 (*0-9631612-1-0*) Bk Stops Here.

Dybwad, Gunnar. Challenges in Mental Retardation. LC 64-14238. 299p. reprint ed. 92.70 (*0-8357-9059-2*, 201100100071) Bks Demand.

Dybwad, Gunnar & Bersani, Hank, eds. New Voices: Self-Advocacy by Persons with Disabilities. 274p. (C). 1996. pap. text 29.95 (*1-57129-004-4*) Brookline Bks.

***Dybwad, Gunnar & Bersani, Hank A.** Responding to the Challenge: Current Issues & International Developments in Developmental Disabilities. LC 99-35778. (Essays in Honor of Gunner Dybwad Ser.). 238p. 1999. 29.95 (*1-57129-075-3*) Brookline Bks.

Dybwad, Rosemary F. Perspectives on a Parent Movement: The Revolt of Parents of Children with Intellectual Limitations. LC 90-35065. 186p. (Orig.). 1990. pap. text 17.95 (*0-914797-74-3*) Brookline Bks.

Dyce, Alexander. A Few Notes on Shakespeare. LC 71-164813. reprint ed. 34.50 (*0-404-02228-6*) AMS Pr.

— Remarks on Mister J. P. Collier's & Mister C. Knight's Edition of Shakespeare. LC 79-164815. reprint ed. 44.50 (*0-404-02230-8*) AMS Pr.

— Strictures on Mr. Colliers New Edition of Shakespeare, 1858. LC 72-164816. reprint ed. 42.50 (*0-404-02231-6*) AMS Pr.

Dyce, Alexander, ed. Timon, a Play. LC 75-16481. reprint ed. 29.50 (*0-404-02229-4*) AMS Pr.

Dyce, Alexander, ed. see Akenside, Mark.

Dyce, Alexander, ed. see Bentley, Richard.

Dyce, Alexander, ed. see Skelton, John.

Dyce, K. M., et al. Textbook of Veterinary Anatomy. 2nd ed. (Illus.). 992p. 1995. text 89.00 (*0-7216-4961-0*, W B Saunders Co) Harcrt Hlth Sci Grp.

Dych, William, ed. Anthony DeMello: Writings Selected & with an Introduction by William Dych, S. J. LC 99-17007. (Modern Spiritual Masters Ser.). 140p. 1999. pap. 14.00 (*1-57075-283-4*) Orbis Bks.

***Dych, William V.** Karl Rahner. (Illus.). 2000. pap. 21.95 (*0-225-66889-0*) G Chapman.

Dych, William V. The Mystery of Faith: A Christian Creed for Today. 104p. 1995. pap. text 7.95 (*0-8146-5514-9*, M Glazier) Liturgical Pr.

***Dych, William V.** Thy Kingdom Come: Jesus & the Reign of God. LC 99-12422. 1999. pap. text 19.95 (*0-8245-1793-8*) Crossroad NY.

Dyche, Jill, jt. auth. see Ginsburg, David.

Dyche, June. Educational Program Development for Employees in Health Care Agencies. 384p. (Orig.). 1982. pap. text 23.50 (*0-9609732-0-6*) Tri-Oak.

— Keeping Your Baby Safe: A Guidebook for You to Protect Your Child. (Illus.). 70p. 1994. per. 5.95 (*0-9609732-4-9*) Tri-Oak.

Dyche, Thomas W. A New General English Dictionary. (Anglistica & Americana Ser.: No. 81). 912p. 1972. reprint ed. 154.70 (*3-487-04398-X*) G Olms Pubs.

Dyches, Richard W. & Mustachio, Thomas. A Child's First Catholic Dictionary. LC 94-71885. (Illus.). 112p. (J). (gr. k-3). 1994. 15.95 (*0-87793-525-4*) Ave Maria.

***Dyches, Tina Taylor.** Guide to Writing Quality Individualized Education Programs: What's Best for Students with Disabilities. 79p. 1999. pap. text 17.00 (*0-205-31692-1*) P-H.

Dychtwald, Ken. Age Power: How the 21st Century Will Be Ruled by the New Old. LC 99-32738. 320p. 1999. 24.95 (*0-87477-954-5*, Tarcher Putnam) Putnam Pub Group.

***Dychtwald, Ken.** Age Power: How the 21st Century Will Be Ruled by the New Old. 2000. pap. 24.95 (*1-58542-041-7*, Tarcher Putnam) Putnam Pub Group.

Dychtwald, Ken. Age Wave: Choices & Challenges for Our New Future. 400p. 1990. pap. 14.95 (*0-553-34806-X*) Bantam.

— Bodymind. rev. ed. 320p. 1986. pap. 12.95 (*0-87477-375-X*, Tarcher Putnam) Putnam Pub Group.

— Healthy Aging: Challenges & Solutions. LC 98-39726. 448p. Date not set. pap. 49.00 (*0-8342-1042-8*, 10428) Aspen Pub.

***Dychtwald, Ken.** Healthy Aging: Challenges & Solutions. LC 98-39726. 448p. 1999. 49.00 (*0-8342-1363-X*) Aspen Pub.

Dychtwald, Ken, et al. New Directions in Eldercare Services: Cooperation along a Continuum. 1990. pap. 44.95 (*0-685-71203-6*) McGraw.

***Dychwaldt, Ken.** Age Power: How the 21st Century Will Be Ruled by the New Old. 288p. 2000. reprint ed. pap. 13.95 (*1-58542-043-3*, Tarcher Putnam) Putnam Pub Group.

Dyck, jt. auth. see Mulej.

Dyck, Andrew, ed. Epimerismi Homerici: Pars Altera: Epimerismos Continens Qui Ordine Alphabetico Traditi Sunt. (Sammlung Griechischer und Lateinischer Grammatiker Ser.: Vol. 5/2). (GER.). viii, 1034p. (C). 1995. lib. bdg. 684.60 (*3-11-012742-3*) De Gruyter.

Dyck, Andrew R. A Commentary on Cicero, De Officiis. LC 96-45128. 760p. (C). 1997. text 72.50 (*0-472-10719-4*, 10719) U of Mich Pr.

Dyck, Andrew R., ed. Epimerismi Homerici: Pars Prior: Epimerismos Continens Qui Ad Iliadis Librum A Pertinent. (LAT.). 340p. 1983. 215.40 (*3-11-006556-8*) De Gruyter.

Dyck, Anthony van, see Van Dyck, Anthony.

Dyck, C. J., ed. Something Meaningful for God. LC 80-10975. (MCC Story Ser.: Vol. 4). 408p. (Orig.). 1981. pap. 7.99 (*0-8361-1244-X*) Herald Pr.

Dyck, C. J., et al, eds. The Writings of Dirk Philips. Keeney, William E. et al, trs. from DUT. LC 91-31658. (Classics of the Radical Reformation Ser.: Vol. 6). 672p. 1992. text 44.99 (*0-8361-3111-8*) Herald Pr.

Dyck, Cornelius J. An Introduction to Mennonite History: A Popular History of the Anabaptists & the Mennonites. 3rd rev. ed. LC 93-9203. 456p. (Orig.). 1993. pap. 16.99 (*0-8361-3620-9*) Herald Pr.

— Something Meaningful for God. Kreider, Robert S. & Lapp, John A., eds. LC 82-10975. (Mennonite Central Committee Story Ser.: No. 4). 399p. reprint ed. pap. 113.80 (*0-608-06026-7*, 2066357) Bks Demand.

— Spiritual Life in Anabaptism. LC 95-31471. 312p. (Orig.). 1996. pap. 19.99 (*0-8361-9024-6*) Herald Pr.

Dyck, Cornelius J. & Martin, Dennis, eds. The Mennonite Encyclopedia, Vol. 5. LC 55-4563. 962p. 1990. text 90.00 (*0-8361-3105-3*) Herald Pr.

Dyck, E. F. Apostrophes to Myself. 1987. pap. text 6.95 (*0-88982-077-5*, Pub. by Oolichan Bks) Genl Dist Srvs.

— Pisscat Songs. 40p. 1984. pap. 7.50 (*0-919626-23-8*, Pub. by Brick Bks) Genl Dist Srvs.

***Dyck, Edna M. & Dyck, Jennifer.** Where the Wheat Waves. LC 00-133089. iv, 144p. 2000. pap. 10.95 (*0-9702096-0-6*) Flagleaf Pr.

Dyck, Elfrieda, jt. auth. see Dyck, Peter.

Dyck, Elmer, ed. The Act of Bible Reading: A Multidisciplinary Approach to Biblical Interpretation. LC 95-48966. 180p. (Orig.). 1996. pap. 12.99 (*0-8308-1623-2*, 1623) InterVarsity.

Dyck, George, jt. auth. see Raber, Merill F.

Dyck, Harry R. Van, see Van Dyck, Harry R.

Dyck, Harvey L., ed. The Pacifist Impulse in Historical Perspective. 448p. 1996. text 70.00 (*0-8020-0777-5*) U of Toronto Pr.

Dyck, Harvey L., ed. A Mennonite in Russia: The Diaries of Jacob D. Epp, 1851-1880. (Illus.). 448p. 1991. text 60.00 (*0-8020-2788-1*) U of Toronto Pr.

Dyck, Ian & Morlan, Richard E. The Sjovold Site: A River Crossing Campsite in the Northern Plains. LC 96-185660. (Mercury Ser.: ASC No. 642). (Illus.). 642p. 1995. pap. 39.95 (*0-660-14033-0*, Pub. by CN Mus Civilization) U of Wash Pr.

Dyck, Ian, jt. ed. see Chase, Malcolm.

Dyck, Jennifer, jt. auth. see Dyck, Edna M.

Dyck, Jonathan E. The Theocratic Ideology of the Chronicler. LC 98-16756. (Biblical Interpretation Ser.). xii, 258p. 1998. 79.50 (*90-04-11146-8*) Brill Academic Pubs.

Dyck, Karen Van, see Van Dyck, Karen.

Dyck, Madelyn B., tr. see Berta of Vilich.

Dyck, Maria J. Van, see Van Dyck, Maria J.

Dyck, Martin. Novalis & Mathematics. LC 76-164817. (North Carolina. University. Studies in the Germanic Languages & Literatures: No. 27). reprint ed. 37.50 (*0-404-50927-4*) AMS Pr.

Dyck-Mulej. Self-Transformation of the Forgotten Four-Fifths. LC 98-196855. 408p. (C). 1998. per. 51.95 (*0-7872-5113-5*, 41511301) Kendall-Hunt.

Dyck, Nicholas B. Van, see Van Dyck, Nicholas B.

***Dyck, Noel, ed.** Games, Sports & Cultures. (Illus.). 224p. 2000. 65.00 (*1-85973-312-3*, Pub. by Berg Pubs); pap. 19.50 (*1-85973-317-4*, Pub. by Berg Pubs) NYU Pr.

Dyck, Noel & Waldram, James B., eds. Anthropology, Public Policy & Native Peoples in Canada. 368p. 1993. 65.00 (*0-7735-0961-5*, Pub. by McG-Queens Univ Pr); pap. 22.95 (*0-7735-0978-X*, Pub. by McG-Queens Univ Pr) CUP Services.

***Dyck, Norma.** Reading Comprehension Lessons: Using Text Structures to Improve Expository Text Comprehension. 126p. 2000. pap., teacher ed. 29.95 (*1-893206-05-X*) Curriculum Solns.

Dyck, Norma & Pemberton, Jane. A Dozen Tools for Paras, Vol. 1. 45p. 1997. pap. text 12.50 (*0-9659517-3-1*) Curriculum Solns.

Dyck, Norma & Thurston, Linda P. Getting the Message Across: A Para's Guide to Communication. 33p. 1998. pap. text 12.50 (*0-9659517-7-4*, 3002) Curriculum Solns.

Dyck, Norma, et al. Behavior Management Guide for Paras. 60p. 1998. pap. 15.00 (*0-9659517-8-2*, 3003) Curriculum Solns.

Dyck, Norma J. How to Adapt Text for Struggling Readers. 48p. 1999. spiral bd. 15.00 (*1-893206-02-5*) Curriculum Solns.

Dyck, Norma J. & Kaff, Marilyn. Essential Skills for Paras. 32p. 1999. spiral bd. 12.50 (*1-893206-03-3*) Curriculum Solns.

Dyck, Norma J., et al. Creating Inclusive Schools: A New Design for All Students. 2nd ed. 200p. 1998. 29.95 (*1-893206-00-9*) Curriculum Solns.

Dyck, Peter & Dyck, Elfrieda. Up from the Rubble. LC 91-12848. (Illus.). 384p. (Orig.). 1991. pap. 15.99 (*0-8361-3559-8*) Herald Pr.

***Dyck, Peter J.** Getting Home Before Dark: Stories of Wisdom for All Ages. LC 00-38842. 272p. 2000. pap. 14.99 (*0-8361-9135-8*) Herald Pr.

Dyck, Peter J. The Great Shalom. LC 90-33739. (Illus.). 96p. (Orig.). 1990. pap. 6.99 (*0-8361-3528-8*) Herald Pr.

— A Leap of Faith: True Stories for Young & Old. LC 90-32837. 120p. (Orig.). 1990. pap. 7.99 (*0-8361-3523-7*) Herald Pr.

— Shalom at Last. LC 92-11199. (Illus.). 128p. (Orig.). (J). (ps-8). 1992. pap. 6.99 (*0-8361-3615-2*) Herald Pr.

— Storytime Jamboree. LC 93-50209. (Illus.). 184p. (J). (gr. 1-5). 1994. pap. 6.99 (*0-8361-3667-5*) Herald Pr.

Dyck, Peter J. & Thomas, P. K. Diabetic Neuropathy. 2nd ed. Ross, Allan, ed. LC 97-39762. (Illus.). 464p. (C). 1998. text 125.00 (*0-7216-6182-3*, W B Saunders Co) Harcrt Hlth Sci Grp.

Dyck, Peter J., et al. Diabetic Neuropathy. (Illus.). 336p. (C). 1987. text 110.00 (*0-7216-2125-2*, W B Saunders Co) Harcrt Hlth Sci Grp.

— Peripheral Neuropathy, 2 vols., Set. 3rd ed. LC 92-11721. (Illus.). 1845p. 1992. text 415.00 (*0-7216-3242-4*, W B Saunders Co) Harcrt Hlth Sci Grp.

Dyck, Sarah, ed. The Silence Echoes: Memoirs of Trauma & Tears. (Mennonite Reflections Ser.). (Illus.). xii, 236p. 1997. pap. 17.50 (*0-9698762-7-0*) Pandora Pr.

Dyck, Walter. Katalog Mathematischer und Mathematisch-Physikalischer Modelle, Apparate und Instrumente. (GER.). 1997. 168.00 (*3-487-09865-2*) G Olms Pubs.

Dyckhoff, H. & Finke, U. Cutting & Packing in Production & Distribution: A Typology & Bibliography. (Contributions to Management Science Ser.). (Illus.). x, 248p. 1992. 65.95 (*0-387-91426-9*) Spr-Verlag.

Dyckhoff, H., et al. Operations Research Proceedings, 1993. 576p. 1994. 143.95 (*0-387-57862-5*) Spr-Verlag.

Dyckhoff, Roy, ed. Extensions of Logic Programming: Proceedings of the 4th International Workshop, ELP '93, St. Andrews, U. K., March 29 - April 1, 1993. LC

D

An Asterisk (*) at the beginning of an entry indicates that the title is appearing for the first time.

94-15491. (Lecture Notes in Computer Science; Lecture Notes in Artificial Intelligence Ser.: Vol. 798). 1994. write for info. (*0-387-58025-5*) Spr-Verlag.

Dyckhoff, Roy, et al, eds. Extensions of Logic Programming: Proceedings of the 5th International Workshop, ELP '96, Leipzig, Germany, March 28-30, 1996. (Lecture Notes in Computer Science: Vol. 1050). 318p. 1996. 56.00 (*3-540-60983-0*) Spr-Verlag.

Dyckman. Intermediate Accounting, Vol. 1. 4th ed. 1997. pap., student ed. 31.25 (*0-256-16838-5*) McGraw.

— Intermediate Accounting, Vol. 2. 4th ed. 1997. pap., student ed. 31.25 (*0-256-16835-0*) McGraw.

— Intermediate Accounting WP, Vol. 1. 4th ed. 1997. pap. 33.13 (*0-256-16830-X*) McGraw.

— Intermediate Accounting WP, Vol. 2. 4th ed. 1997. pap. 31.25 (*0-256-16831-8*) McGraw.

Dyckman, et al. International Accounting with Canadian Financial Cases. 6th ed. 1992. 60.74 (*0-256-12795-6*) McGraw.

Dyckman, Dan. Hidden Dimensions. Date not set. 3.99 (*0-517-17634-3*) Random Hse Value.

Dyckman, Katharine M., jt. auth. see Carroll, L. Patrick.

***Dyckman, Lawrence J.** Food Assistance: Efforts to Control Fraud & Abuse in the WIC Program Can Be Strengthened. (Illus.). 57p. (C). 2000. pap. text 20.00 (*0-7881-8724-4*) DIANE Pub.

***Dyckman, Lawrence J. & Cheston, Richard.** Food Stamp Program: Various Factors Have Led to Declining Participation. (Illus.). 46p. (C). 2000. pap. text 20.00 (*0-7881-8718-X*) DIANE Pub.

***Dyckman, Lawrence J. & Summers, Robert C., eds.** Food Safety: U. S. Lacks a Consistent Farm-to-Table Approach to Egg Safety. 65p. (C). 1999. pap. text 20.00 (*0-7881-8461-X*) DIANE Pub.

Dyckman, Lawrence J., et al. Public Housing: HUD Should Improve the Usefulness & Accuracy of Its Management Assessment Program. (Illus.). 61p. 1998. reprint ed. pap. text 20.00 (*0-7881-4331-X*) DIANE Pub.

Dyckman, Lise & Thompson, George A., eds. Bobst & Beyond: A Guide to Graduate Research in New York City with a Directory of Research Library Collections & Archives. (Illus.). 104p. (C). 1994. pap. write for info. (*0-9641374-0-2*) NYU Ofc Advert.

Dyckman, T. R. Investment Analysis & General Price-Level Adjustments, Vol. 1. (Studies in Accounting Research). 76p. 1969. 12.00 (*0-86539-013-4*) Am Accounting.

Dyckman, Thomas. Ready Notes to Accompany Intermediate Accounting, Vol. 1. 4th ed. 1997. pap., student ed. 23.44 (*0-07-000582-6*) McGrw-H Hghr Educ.

— Ready Notes to Accompany Intermediate Accounting, Vol.2. 4th ed. (C). 1997. pap. 23.44 (*0-07-000583-4*) McGrw-H Hghr Educ.

Dyckman, Thomas & Dukes, Roland. Intermediate Accounting: Chapters 1-6. 2nd rev. ed. 336p. (C). 1991. pap. text. write for info. (*0-256-11305-X*, Irwn McGrw-H) McGrw-H Hghr Educ.

— Intermediate Accounting: Working Papers. 488p. (C). 1992. text, suppl. ed. 26.25 (*0-256-10900-1*, Irwn McGrw-H) McGrw-H Hghr Educ.

Dyckman, Thomas R. The Effects of the Issuance of the Exposure Draft & FASB Statement No. 19 on the Security Returns of Oil & Gas Producing Companies. LC 79-50567. (Financial Accounting Standards Board Research Report Ser.). (Illus.). 84p. (Orig.). 1979. pap. 3.00 (*0-910065-08-X*) Finan Acct Found.

— Intermediate Accounting. 2nd ed. (C). 1992. text 69.95 (*0-256-13274-7*, Irwn McGrw-H) McGrw-H Hghr Educ.

— Intermediate Accounting, Chapters 1-26. 4th ed. LC 97-25532. 1997. text 63.60 (*0-256-16825-3*, Irwn McGrw-H) McGrw-H Hghr Educ.

Dyckman, Thomas R. & Dukes, Roland. Intermediate Accounting: Chapter 1-14, Vol. 1. 3rd ed. 760p. (C). 1994. text, student ed. 21.87 (*0-256-13128-7*, Irwn McGrw-H) McGrw-H Hghr Educ.

Dyckman, Thomas R. & Morse. Efficient Capital Markets & Accounting: A Critical Analysis. 2nd ed. (Illus.). 112p. (C). 1986. pap. text 20.95 (*0-317-29659-0*) P-H.

Dyckman, Thomas R., et al. Intermediate Accounting, 2 vols. 3rd ed. Incl. Vol. 1. Intermediate Accounting., 2 vols. 3rd ed. LC 94-37819. 792p. (C). 1994. text 44.25 (*0-256-13174-0*, Irwn McGrw-H); Vol. 2. Intermediate Accounting., 2 vols. 3rd ed. LC 94-37819. 672p. (C). 1994. text 37.95 (*0-256-13175-9*, Irwn McGrw-H); LC 94-37819. (Series in Undergraduate Accounting). 1400p. (C). 1994. Set text 79.50 (*0-256-13123-6*, Irwn McGrw-H) McGrw-H Hghr Educ.

***Dyckman, Thomas R., et al.** Intermediate Accounting. 4th ed. LC 98-155820. (Illus.). 1999. write for info. (*0-07-115237-7*, Irwn Prfssnl) McGraw-Hill Prof.

— Intermediate Accounting. 5th ed. LC 00-27786. 2001. write for info. (*0-07-241223-2*) Gregg-McGraw.

Dyckman, Thomas R., et al. Intermediate Accounting: Chapters 1-14, Vol. I. 4th ed. 1997. 46.25 (*0-256-16864-4*, Irwn Prfssnl) McGraw-Hill Prof.

— Intermediate Accounting: Chapters 15-25, Vol. II. 4th ed. 1997. 39.69 (*0-256-16867-9*, Irwn Prfssnl) McGraw-Hill Prof.

— Intermediate Accounting: Student Spreadsheet Applications, Vol. 2. 3rd ed. 40p. (C). 1995. text, pap. text, student ed. 15.50 incl. 3.5 hd (*0-256-19631-1*, Irwn McGrw-H) McGrw-H Hghr Educ.

— Intermediate Accounting Chapters 1-14, Vol. 1. 3rd ed. 368p. (C). 1994. text 28.75 (*0-256-13124-4*, Irwn McGrw-H) McGrw-H Hghr Educ.

— Intermediate Accounting Ready Notes 2: Chapters 15-25. 3rd ed. 256p. (C). 1995. text 24.37 (*0-256-20906-5*, Irwn McGrw-H) McGrw-H Hghr Educ.

— Intermediate Accounting, Standard Version. 544p. (C). 1992. text, student ed. 26.25 (*0-256-10899-4*, Irwn McGrw-H) McGrw-H Hghr Educ.

— Intermediate Accounting Working Papers Chapters 1-14, 2. 3rd ed. 368p. (C). 1995. text 28.75 (*0-256-13126-0*, Irwn McGrw-H) McGrw-H Hghr Educ.

— Intermediate Accounting Working Papers Chapters 15-24, Vol. 2. 3rd ed. 344p. (C). 1995. text 28.75 (*0-256-13127-9*, Irwn McGrw-H) McGrw-H Hghr Educ.

Dycus, Barbara. God's Design for Broken Lives: Rebuilding after Divorce. 208p. 1994. pap. 6.95 (*0-88243-344-X*, 02-0344) Gospel Pub.

Dycus, Stephen. National Defense & the Environment. LC 95-20878. 306p. 1996. pap. 22.00 (*0-87451-735-4*); text 50.00 (*0-87451-675-7*) U Pr of New Eng.

Dycus, Stephen, et al. National Security Law. 2nd ed. 916p. 1997. teacher ed., boxed set 58.00 (*0-316-09335-1*, 93351) Aspen Law.

***Dyczewski, Leon.** Values in the Tradition of the Polish Culture. LC 99-50272. (Cultural Heritage & Contemporary Change Ser.). 1999. pap. write for info. (*1-56518-142-5*) Coun Res Values.

Dyczewski, Leon & Kromkowski, John, eds. Private & Public Social Inventions in Modern Society: Polish Philosophical Studies II. LC 93-11928. (Cultural Heritage & Contemporary Change Series IVA: Vol. 2). 330p. 1994. 45.00 (*1-56518-050-X*); pap. 17.50 (*1-56518-051-8*) Coun Res Values.

Dyczkowski, Mark S. The Doctrine of Vibration: An Analysis of the Doctrines & Practices Associated with Kashmir Shaivism. LC 86-14552. (SUNY Series in the Shaiva Traditions of Kashmir). 297p. (C). 1987. pap. text 21.95 (*0-88706-432-9*) State U NY Pr.

— The Doctrine of Vibration: An Analysis of the Doctrines & Practices Associated with Kashmir Shaivism. LC 86-14552. (SUNY Series in the Shaiva Traditions of Kashmir). 297p. (C). 1987. text 65.50 (*0-88706-431-0*) State U NY Pr.

***Dyczok, Marta.** The Grand Alliance & Ukranian Refugees. 290p. 2000. text 69.95 (*0-312-23192-X*) St Martin.

— Ukraine Vol. 5: Movement Without Change, Change Without Movement. 150p. 2000. 33.00 (*90-5823-025-2*, Harwood Acad Pubs); pap. 19.95 (*90-5823-026-0*, Harwood Acad Pubs) Gordon & Breach.

Dydak, J. & Segal, J. Shape Theory: An Introduction. (Lecture Notes in Mathematics Ser.: Vol. 688). 1978. 33.95 (*0-387-08955-1*) Spr-Verlag.

Dyde, J. A. & Smih, R. E., eds. Present State of Thoracic Surgery. 300p. 1981. pap. 59.00 (*0-8464-1218-7*) Beekman Pubs.

Dyde, S. W., tr. see Hegel, Georg Wilhelm Friedrich.

Dyde, Walter F. Public Secondary Education in Canada. LC 72-176736. (Columbia University. Teachers College. Contributions to Education Ser.: No. 345). reprint ed. 37.50 (*0-404-55345-1*) AMS Pr.

Dydek. Health Risks Analysis for Toxic Air Pollutants. Date not set. 69.95 (*0-87371-567-5*, L567) Lewis Pubs.

D'Ydewalle, G. & Lens, W., eds. Cognition in Human Motivation & Learning. 304p. (Orig.). 1981. pap. 42.50 (*90-6186-099-7*, Pub. by Leuven Univ) Coronet Bks.

D'Ydewalle, Gery, et al, eds. Deductive Reasoning & Strategies. LC 99-43475. 321p. 1999. write for info. (*0-8058-3238-6*) L Erlbaum Assocs.

D'Ydewalle, Gery & Lens, Willy, eds. Cognition in Human Motivation & Learning. LC 80-23715. 304p. 1981. text 59.95 (*0-89859-067-1*) L Erlbaum Assocs.

D'Ydewalle, Gery & van Rensbergen, Johan, eds. Perception & Cognition: Advances in Eye Movement Research. LC 93-12440. (Studies in Visual Information Processing: Vol. 4). (Illus.). 436p. 1993. 146.50 (*0-444-89938-3*, North Holland) Elsevier.

— Visual & Oculomotor Functions: Advances in Eye Movement Research. LC 94-3974. (Studies in Visual Information Processing: Vol. 5). 474p. 1994. 155.75 (*0-444-81808-1*, North Holland) Elsevier.

Dydinski, Krzysztof. Lonely Planet Poland. 3rd ed. 552p. 1999. pap. 19.95 (*0-86442-655-0*) Lonely Planet.

***Dydnski, Krzysztof.** Krakow. (Illus.). 176p. 2000. pap. 14.95 (*0-86442-698-4*) Lonely Planet.

Dydo, Ulla, ed. & intro. see Stein, Gertrude.

Dydynski, Krzysztof. Lonely Planet Colombia: Travel Survival Kit. 2nd ed. (Illus.). 544p. 1995. pap. 15.95 (*0-86442-234-2*) Lonely Planet.

— Lonely Planet Venezuela. 2nd ed. (Illus.). 400p. 1998. pap. 19.95 (*0-86442-514-7*) Lonely Planet.

— Lonely Planet Venezuela: Travel Survival Kit. (Illus.). 336p. 1994. pap. 14.95 (*0-86442-229-6*) Lonely Planet.

Dye. American Politics in Media Age. 4th ed. (C). 1992. pap. text, teacher ed. 28.00 (*0-534-16777-2*) Harcourt Coll Pubs.

— Beginning Bobbin Lace. 1998. pap. 6.95 (*0-486-25416-X*) Dover.

— The Irony of Democracy. 11th ed. (C). 1998. pap. text, teacher ed. 44.50 (*0-15-505802-9*, Pub. by Harcourt Coll Pubs) Harcourt.

— The Irony of Democracy. 11th ed. (C). 1999. text 56.00 (*0-15-505800-2*, Pub. by Harcourt Coll Pubs) Harcourt.

— Politics in America. 2nd ed. 1996. pap. text, teacher ed. write for info. (*0-13-258310-0*) Allyn.

— Politics in America. 3rd ed. LC 98-27686. 708p. 1998. 65.33 (*0-13-095689-9*) P-H.

— Politics in America. 3rd ed. (C). 1998. pap. text, student ed. 18.67 (*0-13-095903-0*) P-H.

— Politics of America in Texas. 2nd ed. 1997. pap. text, student ed. 20.80 (*0-13-259276-2*) P-H.

— Power & Society. 7th ed. (Political Science Ser.). (C). 1995. pap. text, student ed. 17.95 (*0-534-26071-3*) Wadsworth Pub.

— Power & Society. 8th ed. (C). 1998. pap. text, student ed. 24.00 (*0-15-507233-1*) Harcourt.

— Principles of Corporate Finance. 1998. pap. text 19.35 (*0-13-679911-6*) P-H.

Dye, Alan. Cuban Sugar in the Age of Mass Production: Technology & the Economics of the Sugar Central, 1899-1929. LC 97-6657. 400p. 1998. 55.00 (*0-8047-2819-4*) Stanford U Pr.

Dye, Barbara L. A Driving Tour of the Palos Verdes Peninsula. (Illus.). 136p. (Orig.). 1989. pap. 7.95 (*0-9620050-0-2*) Point Vicente.

***Dye, Bob.** Hawai'i Chronicles III: World War II in Hawai'i, from the Pages of Paradise of the Pacific. LC 00-23410. (Illus.). 2000. pap. write for info. (*0-8248-2289-7*) UH Pr.

Dye, Bob. Merchant Prince of the Sandalwood Mountains: Afong & the Chinese in Hawai'i. LC 96-25678. (Illus.). 336p. 1997. text 35.00 (*0-8248-1772-9*, Latitude Twenty) UH Pr.

Dye, Bob, ed. Hawai'i Chronicles: Island History from the Pages of Honolulu Magazine. LC 96-7380. (Illus.). 232p. 1996. pap. 15.95 (*0-8248-1829-6*, Kolowalu Bk) UH Pr.

— Hawai'i Chronicles II: Contemporary Island History from the Pages of Honolulu Magazine. LC 97-37409. (Illus.). 296p. 1997. pap. 19.95 (*0-8248-1984-5*) UH Pr.

Dye, C. & Phillips, M. Guidelines for Cost-Effectiveness Analysis of Vector Control. (PEEM Guidelines Ser.: No. 3). 192p. 1993. pap. text 29.70 (*0-614-08055-X*, 1933026) World Health.

***Dye, Carson F.** Leadership in Healthcare: Values at the Top. LC 99-47342. (Ache Management Ser.). 145p. 2000. pap. 42.00 (*1-56793-114-6*, LHC-1090) Health Admin Pr.

Dye, Carson F. Protocols for Health Care Executive Behavior: A Factor for Success. LC 93-14057. 231p. 1993. text 42.00 (*1-56793-000-X*, 0934) Health Admin Pr.

***Dye, Charles.** Oracle Distributed Systems. Russell, Deborah, ed. (Illus.). 548p. 1999. pap. 39.95 incl. disk (*1-56592-432-0*) OReilly & Assocs.

Dye, Christina. Alcohol: How Drinking Affects Health & Nutrition. rev. ed. 2000. pap. 0.50 (*0-89230-191-0*) Do It Now.

— Amyl/Butyl Nitrite & Nitrous Oxide. rev. ed. 2000. pap. 0.50 (*0-89230-081-7*) Do It Now.

— Angel Dust: New Facts about PCP. rev. ed. 2000. pap. 0.50 (*0-89230-165-1*) Do It Now.

— Children of Alcoholics: Growing up Unheard. rev. ed. 1999. pap. 0.50 (*0-89230-197-X*) Do It Now.

— Cocaine: Waking up to a Nightmare. rev. ed. 2000. pap. 0.50 (*0-89230-102-3*) Do It Now.

— Crack: Cocaine Squared. rev. ed. 2000. pap. 0.50 (*0-89230-214-3*) Do It Now.

— Designer Drugs: Deadly by Design. 1999. pap. 0.50 (*0-89230-182-1*) Do It Now.

— Drugs, Alcohol & Pregnancy. rev. ed. 2000. pap. 3.50 (*0-89230-190-2*) Do It Now.

— Drugs & the Body: A New Way to Understand Psychoactive Chemicals. rev. ed. 1999. pap. 3.50 (*0-89230-233-X*) Do It Now.

— Everyday Drugs & Pregnancy: Alcohol, Tobacco & Caffeine. rev. ed. 2000. pap. 0.50 (*0-89230-192-9*) Do It Now.

— Hangovers: The Agony after the Ecstasy. rev. ed. 2000. pap. 0.50 (*0-89230-146-5*) Do It Now.

— Health Wise: A Handbook on Healthy Aging. rev. ed. 1992. pap. 3.50 (*0-89230-232-1*) Do It Now.

— Ice: Speed, Smoke & Fire. rev. ed. 2000. pap. 0.50 (*0-89230-236-4*) Do It Now.

— Living with AIDS: A Survival Guide. rev. ed. 1999. pap. 0.50 (*0-89230-235-6*) Do It Now.

— Safer Sex: How Safe Is Safe? rev. ed. 2000. pap. 0.50 (*0-89230-221-6*) Do It Now.

— Smoke Signals: Smoking & You. rev. ed. 2000. pap. 0.50 (*0-89230-208-9*) Do It Now.

Dye, Colin. Listening to God, Vol. 9. (Sword of the Spirit Ser.). 1999. pap. write for info. (*1-85240-208-3*, Pub. by SOV5) R G Mitchell Bks.

— Reaching the Lost, Vol. 8. 1999. pap. write for info. (*1-85240-207-5*) SOV5.

Dye, Dale. Outrage: A Novel of Beirut. 1988. 17.95 (*0-316-20010-7*) Little.

***Dye, Dan & Beckloff, Mark.** Amazing Gracie: A Dog's Tale. (Illus.). 160p. 2000. 18.95 (*0-7611-1957-X*) Workman Pub.

Dye, Dan & Beckloff, Mark. Short Tails & Treats from Three Dog Bakery. (Illus.). 128p. (Orig.). 1996. pap. 14.95 (*0-8362-2155-9*) Andrews & McMeel.

— Three Dog Bakery Cookbook: Over 50 Recipes for All-Natural Treats for Your Dog. (Illus.). 80p. 1998. 12.95 (*0-8362-6919-5*) Andrews & McMeel.

Dye, Daniel S. Chinese Lattice Designs. LC 74-82205. (Illus.). 469p. 1974. reprint ed. pap. 11.95 (*0-486-23096-1*) Dover.

— A Grammar of Chinese Lattice. (Illus.). 469p. reprint ed. 35.00 (*957-9482-40-3*, ATE008, Pub. by SMC Pub) Antique Collect.

— The New Book of Chinese Lattice Designs. (Pictorial Archive Ser.). (Illus.). 128p. (Orig.). 1981. pap. 7.95 (*0-486-24128-9*) Dover.

Dye, David & Moore, Paul. Drafting & Design with AutoCAD LT. (Illus.). 608p. (Orig.). 1995. pap. 30.00 (*1-56205-501-1*) New Riders Pub.

Dye, David H. & Brister, Ronald C., eds. The Protohistoric Period in the Mid-South, 1500-1700: Proceedings of the 1983 Mid-South Archaeological Conference. LC 86-620009. (Archaeological Report Ser.: No. 18). (Illus.). xiv, 102p. 1986. pap. text 5.00 (*0-938896-49-0*) Mississippi Archives.

— The Tchula Period in the Mid-South & Lower Mississippi Valley. LC 86-620005. (Mississippi Department of Archives & History Archaeological Reports: No.17). (Illus.). 138p. (Orig.). 1986. pap. text 5.00 (*0-938896-48-2*) Mississippi Archives.

Dye, David H. & Cox, Cheryl A., eds. Towns & Temples along the Mississippi. LC 89-32994. (Illus.). 312p. 1990. pap. text 29.95 (*0-8173-0455-X*) U of Ala Pr.

Dye, Dylotta. The Mandatory Parties. 32p. (Orig.). (J). 1994. pap. 3.90 (*1-885148-01-1*) Lavots Press.

— "Sweat" Triumph of Selfworth. 48p. (Orig.). (J). 1994. pap. 3.90 (*1-885148-00-3*) Lavots Press.

Dye, Edward. Let's Make a Law. (Illus.). 12p. (gr. 4-12). 1983. 9.95 (*0-910141-03-7*, KP117) Kino Pubns.

— Take Me to Your Leader: A Game about Presidential Elections. (Illus.). 12p. (gr. 4-12). 1982. 9.95 (*0-910141-02-9*, KP116) Kino Pubns.

Dye, Ellis, ed. see Saine, Thomas P.

Dye, Frederick N. Champion of Women & the Unborn: Horatio Robinson Storer, M. D. LC 99-19740. 1999. write for info. (*0-88135-266-7*) Watson Pub Intl.

Dye, Gillian. Bobbin Lace Braid. (Illus.). 144p. 1979. 6.00 (*0-8231-5055-0*) Robin & Russ.

Dye, Harold E. Shadow of a Man. LC 95-72408. 64p. 1995. pap. 8.95 (*1-881576-75-2*) Providence Hse.

***Dye, Helen S.** The Johns Connections. 549p. 1999. pap. 42.50 (*0-7884-1218-3*, D192) Heritage Bk.

Dye, Holly S. 100 Best Ideas for Primary Math. (One Hundred Best Ideas Ser.). (Illus.). 112p. (J). (gr. k-3). 1994. pap., teacher ed. 9.95 (*1-57310-003-X*) Teachng & Lrning Co.

Dye, Ira. The Fatal Cruise of the Argus: Two Captains in the War of 1812. LC 94-17810. (Illus.). 388p. 1994. 37.95 (*1-55750-175-0*) Naval Inst Pr.

Dye, Jane. Aromatherapy for Women & Children: Pregnancy & Childbirth. 103p. 1992. pap. 15.95 (*0-85207-226-0*, Pub. by C W Daniel) Natl Bk Netwk.

— Aromatherapy in Pregnancy & Childbirth. 192p. (Orig.). 1991. pap. 23.95 (*0-8464-1536-4*) Beekman Pubs.

— First Steps in Aromatherapy. 1996. pap. 7.95 (*0-85207-292-9*, Pub. by C W Daniel) Natl Bk Netwk.

Dye, Jessee. From Country Boy to Combat Medic. 169p. 1995. lib. bdg. write for info. (*0-9622415-2-0*) Pubs Syndication.

Dye, Joan & Frankfort, Nancy. Spectrum II. (Spectrum Ser.). 1987. pap. text, teacher ed. 14.00 (*0-13-826769-3*, 20266) Prentice ESL.

Dye, John S. History of the Plots & Crimes of the Great Conspiracy to Overthrow Liberty in America. LC 76-75508. (Select Bibliographies Reprint Ser.). 1977. 30.95 (*0-8369-5006-2*) Ayer.

Dye, Kitty. Maconaquah's Story: The Saga of Frances Slocum. LC 96-765780. (Illus.). 110p. (YA). (gr. 7-12). 1996. pap. 8.95 (*0-9642058-2-3*) InChem Pubng.

Dye, Marguerite L. A Smile, a Chuckle or a Loud Guffaw: or What Happened When I Wasn't Looking. 84p. (Orig.). 1996. pap. 12.95 (*1-890175-00-5*) Armadillo Poetry.

***Dye, Mimi.** Spiritual Songs of Hildegard. 1998. audio 9.95 (*0-87793-922-5*) Ave Maria.

Dye, Nancy S. & Woloch, Nancy. Main Problems in American History Vol. 4: The Emergence of the "New Woman," 1870-1920 & New Women: From the 1920s to the Present. abr. ed. (PaperBook Series in History). (Illus.). 128p. (C). 1996. pap. text 2.25 (*1-877891-35-5*) Paperbook Pr Inc.

Dye, Nancy S., jt. ed. see Frankel, Noralee.

Dye, Norman E. & Granberg, Helge O. Radio Frequency Transistors: Principles & Practical Applications. (EDN Ser.). (Illus.). 288p. 1993. 49.95 (*0-7506-9059-3*) Buttrwrth-Heinemann.

Dye, Pete & Shaw, Mark. Bury Me in a Pot Bunker. LC 98-45115. (Illus.). 256p. 1999. pap. 14.95 (*0-8092-2681-2*, 268120, Contemporary Bks) NTC Contemp Pub Co.

***Dye, Rebecca.** World Problems. (Illus.). 96p. (YA). (gr. 5). 1999. pap. text 10.95 (*1-58037-099-3*, Pub. by M Twain Media) Carson-Dellos.

***Dye, Sean.** Painting with Water-Soluble Oils. (Illus.). 144p. 2001. pap. 28.99 (*1-58180-033-9*, North Lght Bks) F & W Pubns Inc.

Dye, Steve & Baylin, Frank. The GPS Manual: Principles & Applications. (Illus.). 248p. (Orig.). 1997. pap. 40.00 (*0-917893-29-8*) Baylin Pubns.

Dye, Suzanne. Tropical Heat. 1997. mass mkt. 1.78 (*0-8217-5772-5*) Kensgtn Pub Corp.

Dye, Thomas, jt. auth. see Gray, Virginia.

Dye, Thomas R. American Politics in the Media Age. 5th ed. (C). 1999. pap. text 43.00 (*0-15-507886-0*) Harcourt.

***Dye, Thomas R.** Policymaking: From the Top Down. (Illus.). 208p. (C). 2000. pap. text 21.95 (*1-889119-33-4*, Chatham House Pub) Seven Bridges.

Dye, Thomas R. Politics in America. 2nd ed. 1996. text 65.00 (*0-13-257007-6*) P-H.

***Dye, Thomas R.** Politics in America. 4th ed. LC 00-29805. 2000. write for info. (*0-13-027109-8*) P-H.

Dye, Thomas R. Politics in Florida. LC 98-10060. 234p. (C). 1998. pap. text 25.80 (*0-13-690330-4*) P-H.

***Dye, Thomas R.** Politics in States & Communities. 10th ed. LC 99-29096. 536p. 1999. 56.00 (*0-13-020680-6*) P-H.

Dye, Thomas R. Politics Sunshine Politics. 48p. (C). 1995. pap. text 4.00 (*0-13-229600-4*) P-H.

— Power & Society. 8th ed. LC 97-77100. 384p. (C). 1998. pap. text 57.00 (*0-15-508080-6*) Harcourt.

— Understanding Public Policy. 9th ed. LC 97-25918. 360p. (C). 1997. 50.67 (*0-13-639105-2*) P-H.

— Who's Running America? The Clinton Years: The Clinton Years. 6th ed. LC 94-9675. 320p. 1994. pap. text 38.60 (*0-13-123241-X*) P-H.

Dye, Thomas R., et al, eds. The Political Legitimacy of Markets & Governments. LC 89-71749. (Political Economy & Public Policy Ser.: Vol. 7). 215p. 1990. 78.50 (*1-55938-103-5*) Jai Pr.

Dye, Thomas R., et al. American Politics in the Media Age. 4th ed. LC 91-15973. 352p. (C). 1991. pap. text 51.50 (*0-534-16776-4*) Harcourt.

D

— Politics America: The Texas Edition. 2nd ed. LC 96-38827. 963p. 1996. 74.67 (*0-13-257015-7*) P-H.

Dye, Thomas R., jt. ed. see Domhoff, G. William.

Dye, William M. Moslem Egypt & Christian Abyssinia. LC 78-97365. 500p. 1969. reprint ed. lib. bdg. 49.75 (*0-8371-2432-8*, DYM&) Greenwood.

Dyen, I. Sanskrit Indeclinables of the Hindu Grammarians & Lexicographers. (Language Dissertations Ser.: No. 31). 1939. pap. 25.00 (*0-527-00777-3*) Periodicals Srv.

Dyen, Isidore. Linguistic Subgrouping & Lexicostatistics. LC 73-82418. (Janua Linguarum, Series Minor: No. 175). (Illus.). 251p. 1975. pap. text 56.95 (*90-279-3054-6*) Mouton.

— A Sketch of Trukese Grammar. (American Oriental Society Essays Ser.: 4). 1964. pap. 3.00 (*0-685-00308-6*) Am Orient Soc.

— Spoken Malay. Incl. Units 1-12. LC 74-176207. v, 192p. 1974. pap. 15.00 (*0-87950-160-X*); LC 74-176207. (Spoken Language Ser.). (C). 1974. Set pap. (*0-685-04718-0*) Spoken Lang Serv.

Dyen, Isidore, ed. Lexicostatistics in Genetic Linguistics: Proceedings of the Yale Conference, Yale University, April 3-4, 1971. (Janua Linguarum, Series Major: No. 69). 1973. 52.35 (*90-279-2497-X*) Mouton.

Dyen, Isidore, et al. An Indoeuropean Classification: A Lexicostatistical Experiment. LC 90-70403. (Transactions Ser.: Vol. 82, Pt. 5). (Illus.). 112p. (C). 1992. pap. 16.00 (*0-87169-825-0*, T825-KRJ) Am Philos.

Dyer. Architectural Desktop. (C). 2000. pap. 45.00 (*0-7668-1774-1*) Delmar.

***Dyer.** Cold Night in Paradise. 2000. pap. 25.00 (*0-8133-3774-7*, Pub. by Westview) HarpC.

Dyer. Labors of a Modern Hercules. 512p. 1990. 50.00 (*0-07-103231-2*) McGraw.

Dyer, jt. auth. see Heagy.

Dyer, jt. auth. see Hutchinson.

Dyer, jt. auth. see Mitchell.

Dyer, A., ed. see Conference on Progress in Ion Exchange (1995: Wrex.

Dyer, A., jt. ed. see Williams, P. A.

Dyer, Alan. A Biography of James Parker, Colonial Printer: 1715-1770. LC 80-52545. xviii, 421p. 1982. 49.50 (*0-87875-202-1*) Whitston Pub.

Dyer, Alan. Decline & Growth in English Towns, 1400-1640. (New Studies in Economic & Social History: Vol. 13). 90p. (C). 1995. text 34.95 (*0-521-55272-9*); pap. text 10.95 (*0-521-55781-X*) Cambridge U Pr.

— An Introduction to Zeolite Molecular Sieves. fac. ed. LC 88-5524. 165p. 1994. pap. 51.20 (*0-7837-6374-3*, 204608600010) Bks Demand.

— Liquid Scintillation Counting Practice. LC 82-100882. (Illus.). 114p. 1980. reprint ed. pap. 35.40 (*0-608-18843-3*, 203049900069) Bks Demand.

— Space. 1. LC 98-53123. (Pathfinders Ser.: Vol. 4). (Illus.). 64p. (J). (gr. 3-9). 1999. lib. bdg. 18.99 (*1-57584-299-8*, Pub. by Rdrs Digest) S&S Trade.

— Space. LC 98-53123. (Pathfinders Ser.: Vol. 4). (Illus.). 64p. (J). (gr. 4-7). 1999. 16.99 (*1-57584-291-2*, Pub. by Rdrs Digest) Random.

Dyer, Alan, compiled by. James Fenimore Cooper: An Annotated Bibliography of Criticism, 16. LC 91-27084. (Bibliographies & Indexes in American Literature Ser.: No. 16). 320p. 1991. lib. bdg. 65.00 (*0-313-27919-5*, DJF/, Greenwood Pr) Greenwood.

Dyer, Alan, ed. Gas Chemistry in Nuclear Reactors & Large Industrial Plant: Proceedings of the Conference, University of Salford, U. K., April 21-24, 1980. LC 82-104413. 295p. reprint ed. pap. 91.50 (*0-608-14542-4*, 202481000038) Bks Demand.

Dyer, Alan, jt. auth. see Dickinson, Terence.

Dyer, Allen R. Ethics & Psychiatry: Toward Professional Definition. LC 87-1337. 176p. 1988. text 12.95 (*0-88048-225-7*, 8225) Am Psychiatric.

Dyer, Amye, ed. see Tam, Vivienne.

Dyer, Andrea L., et al. PPC's 5500 Deskbook, 2 vols. Incl. Vol. 1. 1997. ring bd. (*0-7646-0135-0*); Vol. 2. 1997. ring bd. (*0-7646-0136-9*); 150.00 (*1-56433-895-9*); 150.00 (*0-7646-0134-2*) Prctnrs Pub Co.

Dyer, Angela & Lobello, Peter. Lobello LC 99-196429. 92p. 1997. write for info. (*0-06-237790-6*, E Burlingame Bks) HarpC.

Dyer, Annie I. Administration of Home Economics in City Schools: A Study of Present & Desired Practices in the Organization of the Home Economics Program. LC 76-176737. (Columbia University. Teachers College. Contributions to Education Ser.: No. 318). reprint ed. 37.50 (*0-404-55318-4*) AMS Pr.

Dyer, Anthony. The Big Five. 2nd limited ed. LC 95-61875. (Illus.). 224p. 1996. 100.00 (*1-882458-10-9*) Trophy Rm Bks.

***Dyer, Arlene T.** Ya Tienes el Empleo! Y Ahora Que? 2nd ed. (SPA.). 64p. 1999. pap. text 9.95 (*1-57464-007-0*) Reyd Pubns.

— You Got the Job!... Now What? A Survival Guide for New Employees. (Illus.). 2000. pap. 9.95 (*1-57464-006-2*) Reyd Pubns.

Dyer, Barbara, jt. auth. see Vaughan, Roger J.

Dyer, Barbara, ed. see Nothdurft, William E.

Dyer, Barbara, ed. see Smith, Rodney T.

Dyer, Barbara F. Camden & Rockport. (Images of America Ser.). 1995. pap. 16.99 (*0-7524-0232-3*) Arcadia Publng.

— Vessels of Camden. (Images of America Ser.). 1998. write for info. (*0-7385-0014-3*) Arcadia Publng.

Dyer, Betsey D. & Obar, Robert A. Tracing the History of Eukaryotic Cells: The Enigmatic Smile. LC 93-26798. (Critical Moments in Paleobiology & Earth History Ser.). 335p. 1984. 58.50 (*0-231-07592-8*) Col U Pr.

— Tracing the History of Eukaryotic Cells: The Enigmatic Smile. LC 93-26798. (Critical Moments in Paleobiology & Earth History Ser.). 335p. 1994. pap. 29.00 (*0-231-07593-6*) Col U Pr.

Dyer, Bob, ed. see Dewald, Louise.

Dyer, Brainerd. The Public Career of William M. Evarts. (Publications of the University of California Humanities Research Institute: Vol. 2). 1933. pap. 30.00 (*0-686-17390-2*) R S Barnes.

— The Public Career of William M. Evarts. LC 72-87565. (American Scene Ser.). 279p. 1969. reprint ed. lib. bdg. 35.00 (*0-686-42966-4*) Da Capo.

Dyer, Brenda. Power Play-Individuals in Conflict: Liiterary Selections for Students of English. 2nd ed. LC 97-157018. 256p. (C). 1996. pap. text 32.33 (*0-13-122046-2*) P-H.

Dyer, C., ed. Doctors, Patients & the Law. (Illus.). 240p. 1992. pap. 39.95 (*0-632-03442-4*) Blackwell Sci.

Dyer, C., jt. auth. see Berlins, Marcel.

Dyer, Carolyn S. & Romalov, Nancy T., eds. Rediscovering Nancy Drew. LC 95-8514. (Illus.). 297p. 1995. 24.95 (*0-87745-500-7*); pap. 14.95 (*0-87745-501-5*) U of Iowa Pr.

Dyer, Ceil. Best Recipes from the Backs of Boxes, Bottles, Cans & Jars. 608p. 1989. 9.98 (*0-88365-737-6*); 11.98 (*0-88365-827-5*) Galahad Bks.

— Best Recipes from the Backs of Boxes, Bottles, Cans, & Jars. 608p. 1992. pap. 14.95 (*0-88486-063-9*) Arrowood Pr.

Dyer, Ceil. Ceil Dyer's Wok Cookery. 1977. 7.95 (*0-912656-76-X*) Berkley Pub.

Dyer, Ceil. Great Desserts. 320p. 1996. 9.98 (*0-88365-964-6*) Galahad Bks.

— The Newport Cookbook. rev. ed. (Illus.). 256p. reprint ed. pap. 5.95 (*0-940078-08-2*) Foremost Pubs.

***Dyer, Charles.** Old Testament Explorer: Discovering the Essence, Background & Meaning of Every Book in the Old Testament. 700p. 2000. 29.99 (*0-8499-1447-7*) Word Pub.

Dyer, Charles & Hattelberg, Greg. The Christian Traveler's Guide to the Holy Land. (Illus.). 224p. 1998. pap. 19.99 (*0-8054-0156-3*) Broadman.

Dyer, Charles E. Official Record of the Old Settlers Society of Racine County: With Historical Address. (Illus.). 84p. 1997. reprint ed. pap. 16.00 (*0-8328-6983-X*) Higginson Bk Co.

Dyer, Charles H. Babilonia Renace.Tr. of Rise of Babylon. (SPA.). 236p. 1991. pap. 6.99 (*1-56063-082-5*, 498415) Editorial Unilit.

— The Power of Personal Integrity. LC 96-43750. 230p. 1997. pap. 9.99 (*0-8423-4884-0*) Tyndale Hse.

— World News & Bible Prophecy. 303p. 1993. pap. 9.99 (*0-8423-5017-9*) Tyndale Hse.

Dyer, Charles H. & Hunt, Angela E. The Rise of Babylon: Sign of the End Times. (Illus.). 236p. 1991. pap. 8.99 (*0-8423-5618-5*) Tyndale Hse.

Dyer, Christopher. Everyday Life in Medieval England. 304p. 1994. 60.00 (*1-85285-112-0*) Hambledon Press.

***Dyer, Christopher.** The New Penguin Economic History of Britain. 1999. write for info. (*0-7139-9162-3*, A Lane) Viking Penguin.

Dyer, Christopher. Standards of Living in the Later Middle Ages. (Cambridge Medieval Textbooks Ser.). (Illus.). 320p. (C). 1989. text 59.95 (*0-521-25127-3*); pap. text 22.95 (*0-521-27215-7*) Cambridge U Pr.

Dyer, Christopher L. & McGoodwin, James R., eds. Folk Management in the World's Fisheries: Lessons for Modern Fisheries Management. (Illus.). 330p. 1994. 34.95 (*0-87081-325-0*) Univ Pr Colo.

Dyer, Colin. Beginning Research in Psychology: A Practical Guide to Research Methods & Statistics. (Illus.). 448p. (C). 1995. pap. 30.95 (*0-631-18929-7*) Blackwell Pubs.

— Population & Society in Twentieth Century France. LC 77-2908. (Illus.). 256p. (C). 1978. 42.00 (*0-8419-0308-5*) Holmes & Meier.

Dyer, Constance E., ed. The Canon Production System: Creative Involvement of the Total Workforce. Campbell, Alan, tr. from JPN. LC 85-63498. (Illus.). 251p. 1987. 40.00 (*0-915299-06-2*) Productivity Inc.

— El Sistema de Produccion de Canon: Participacion Creativa Del Personal. (Illus.). 276p. (Orig.). 1991. pap. 35.00 (*84-87022-69-3*) Productivity Inc.

Dyer, Constance E., jt. auth. see Jackson, Thomas L.

Dyer, D., et al. Measuring & Improving the Efficiency of Boilers. Gyftopoulos, Elias P. & Cohen, Karen C., eds. (Industrial Energy-Conservation Manuals Ser.: No. 3). 120p. 1982. 20.00 (*0-262-04067-0*) MIT Pr.

Dyer, Daniel. Jack London: Sons of the Wolf. LC 96-29910. 240p. (YA). (gr. 7-9). 1997. 17.95 (*0-590-22216-3*) Scholastic Inc.

— Jack London's The Call of the Wild for Teachers. LC 96-29525. 96p. (Orig.). 1997. pap., teacher ed. 14.95 (*0-8061-2933-6*) U of Okla Pr.

Dyer, Daniel, ed. see London, Jack.

Dyer, Daniel, ed. & notes see London, Jack.

Dyer, David L. Darts in Los Angeles. LC 83-51647. (Illus.). 177p. (Orig.). 1984. pap. 4.95 (*0-930103-01-7*); lib. bdg. 11.95 (*0-930103-00-9*) Travl Guides.

Dyer, David O., Sr. Is Stamp Collecting the Hobby for You? LC 98-85952. iii, 159 p. (Orig.). 1998. pap. 14.95 (*0-9663393-1-2*) Truman Publ.

Dyer, Davis. TRW: Pioneering Technology & Innovation 1900-1994. 1995. text 35.00 (*0-07-103624-5*) McGraw.

— TRW: Pioneering Technology & Innovation, 1900-1996. LC 97-30659. 1998. 60.00 (*0-87584-606-8*) Harvard Busn.

Dyer, Davis & Dennis, Michael Aaron. Architects of Information Advantage: The Mitre Corporation Since 1958. LC 98-50027. 1998. write for info. (*1-58192-012-1*) Community Comm.

Dyer, Davis, jt. ed. see Brinkley, Alan.

***Dyer, Diana.** A Dietitian's Cancer Story: Information & Inspiration for Recovery & Healing from a 3-Time Cancer Survivor. LC 99-90175. (Illus.). 64p. 1999. pap. 10.00 (*0-9667238-1-3*) Swan Press MI.

***Dyer, Dolores A.** Plank House. LC 00-25459. (Native American Homes Ser.). 2000. write for info. (*1-55916-248-1*) Rourke Pubns.

***Dyer, Donald.** Jung's Thoughts on God: The Religious Depths of the Psyches. LC 99-59295. 224p. 2000. pap. 18.95 (*0-89254-049-4*, Pub. by Nicolas-Hays) Weiser.

***Dyer, Donald L.** The Romanian Dialect of Moldova: A Study in Language & Politics. LC 99-51521. (Studies in Linguistics & Semiotics). 228p. 1999. 89.95 (*0-7734-8037-4*) E Mellen.

Dyer, Donald L., ed. Studies in Moldovan: The History, Culture, Language, & Contemporary Politics of the People of Moldova. 250p. 1996. 35.00 (*0-88033-351-0*, 454, Pub. by East Eur Monographs) Col U Pr.

Dyer, E. Otis. Swamp Yankee. LC 94-92172. (Illus.). 240p. (Orig.). 1994. pap. 18.00 (*0-88492-052-6*) W S Sullwold.

Dyer, E. R., ed. Dyer Solar Terrestrial Physics, 4 vols., Vol. 2. 1971. pap. text 99.50 (*90-277-0211-X*) Kluwer Academic.

Dyer, E. R., ed. see International Symposium on Solar-Terrestial Physic.

Dyer, Edwin M., III. Muzzle Velocity: The Weaponry Guide for Thundering Steel. (Illus.). 24p. (Orig.). (C). 1993. pap. text 5.00 (*0-9631504-1-3*) Minds In One Prods.

— OPFur: The Anthropomorphic Supplement for Thundering Steel. (Illus.). 36p. (Orig.). (C). 1993. pap. text 7.00 (*0-9631504-2-1*) Minds In One Prods.

— Thundering Steel: The Role-Playing - Combat Game of Warfare in the Near Future. (Illus.). 200p. (Orig.). 1991. pap. 28.95 (*0-9631504-0-5*) Minds In One Prods.

Dyer, Esther R. Cooperation in Library Service to Children. LC 77-28190. 160p. reprint ed. pap. 49.60 (*0-608-15226-9*, 202749100055) Bks Demand.

— Cultural Pluralism & Children's Media. LC 78-25845. (School Media Centers: Focus on Trends & Issues Ser.: No. 1). 87p. reprint ed. pap. 30.00 (*0-7837-5970-3*, 204577200007) Bks Demand.

***Dyer, Frank J.** Psychological Consultation in Parental Rights Cases. LC 99-29101. 300p. 1999. lib. bdg. 35.00 (*1-57230-474-X*) Guilford Pubns.

Dyer, Frank J., jt. auth. see McCann, Joseph T.

Dyer, G. W. Democracy in the South Before the Civil War. LC 72-11343. (American South Ser.). 1980. reprint ed. 18.95 (*0-405-05059-3*) Ayer.

Dyer, Gary. British Satire & the Politics of Style, 1789-1832. (Studies in Romanticism: Vol. 23). 278p. (C). 1997. text 59.95 (*0-521-56357-7*) Cambridge U Pr.

Dyer, Geoff. But Beautiful: A Book about Jazz. LC 95-24549. (Illus.). 205p. 1996. 21.00 (*0-86547-490-7*) N Point Pr.

— But Beautiful: A Book about Jazz. 240p. 1997. pap. text 12.00 (*0-86547-508-3*) N Point Pr.

— Out of Sheer Rage: Wrestling with D. H. Lawrence. LC 97-33053. 256p. 1998. 23.00 (*0-86547-533-4*) N Point Pr.

***Dyer, Geoff.** Out of Sheer Rage: Wrestling with D. H. Lawrence. 256p. 1999. pap. 13.00 (*0-86547-540-7*) N Point Pr.

— Paris Trance: A Romance. LC 98-47522. 272p. 1999. 22.00 (*0-374-22981-3*) FS&G.

— Paris Trance: A Romance. 272p. 2000. pap. 13.00 (*0-86547-600-4*) N Point Pr.

Dyer, Geoff, ed. see Gedney, William J.

Dyer, George. Privileges of the University of Cambridge, 2 vols. reprint ed. 135.00 (*0-404-07306-9*) AMS Pr.

Dyer, George L., Jr. Forty Poems for "T" The Fun of Writing Poetry. (Illus.). 99p. (YA). (gr. 6-9). 16.95 (*1-57532-261-7*, Pub. by Press-Tige Pub) Baker & Taylor.

Dyer, Gerri M., ed. see Foundation for Crime Prevention & Education Staff.

Dyer, Gillian. Advertising As Communication. (Studies in Communication). 250p. 1982. pap. 14.95 (*0-416-74530-X*, NO. 3662) Routledge.

— Advertising As Communication. (Studies in Communication). 224p. (C). 1982. pap. 17.99 (*0-415-02781-0*, NO. 3661) Routledge.

Dyer, Goeff, et al. Open City, Vol. 9. 1999. pap. text 8.00 (*1-890447-20-X*) Open City Bks.

Dyer, Graham. Class, State & Agricultural Productivity in Egypt: Study of the Inverse Relationship Between Farm Size & Land Productivity. LC 96-39385. (Library of Peasant Studies: No. 15). 240p. (Orig.). (C). 1997. 49.50 (*0-7146-4707-1*, Pub. by F Cass Pubs); pap. 24.50 (*0-7146-4245-2*, Pub. by F Cass Pubs) Intl Spec Bk.

Dyer, H. R. Recommendations for Preparing the Criticality Safety Evaluation of Transportation Packages. 57p. 1997. pap. 6.00 (*0-16-062835-0*) USGPO.

Dyer, Heather. Stories Jesus Told. Incl. Good Shepherd. (Illus.). 1980. 2.50 (*0-89191-283-5*); House Built on Sand. (Illus.). 1980. 2.50 (*0-89191-288-6*); Prodigal Son. (Illus.). 1980. 2.50 (*0-89191-285-1*); Rich Man. (Illus.). 1980. 2.50 (*0-89191-287-8*); (Illus.). (J). (gr. 1-4). 1980. reprint ed. write for info. (*0-318-51435-4*) Cook.

Dyer, Henry. The Evolution of Industry. LC 72-5044. (Technology & Society Ser.). 322p. 1972. reprint ed. 23.95 (*0-405-04696-0*) Ayer.

Dyer Heritage '86 Committee Staff. A History of Dyer, Tennessee Community. 256p. 1986. 49.95 (*0-938021-00-1*) Turner Pub KY.

Dyer, Hilary, jt. auth. see Morris, Anne.

Dyer, James. Ancient Britain. LC 98-125392. 176p. (C). 1997. pap. 29.99 (*0-415-15151-1*) Routledge.

— Bedfordshire. (Country Guide Ser.: No. 12). (Illus.). 112p. pap. 12.50 (*0-7478-0269-6*, Pub. by Shire Pubns) Parkwest Pubns.

— Discovering Archaeology in England & Wales. 1989. pap. 30.00 (*0-85263-705-5*, Pub. by Shire Pubns) St Mut.

***Dyer, James.** Discovering Archaeology in England & Wales. (Handbook Ser.). (Illus.). 128p. 1999. pap. 10.50 (*0-7478-0333-1*, Pub. by Shire Pubns) Parkwest Pubns.

Dyer, James. Discovering Prehistoric England. 1989. pap. 14.75 (*0-7478-0197-5*, Pub. by Shire Pubns) St Mut.

Dyer, James. Hillforts of England & Wales. (Archaeology Ser.: No. 16). (Illus.). 54p. pap. 10.50 (*0-7478-0180-0*, Pub. by Shire Pubns) Parkwest Pubns.

Dyer, James. Teaching Archaeology in Schools. 1989. pap. 25.00 (*0-85263-622-9*, Pub. by Shire Pubns) St Mut.

Dyer, James, jt. auth. see Grinsell, Leslie V.

Dyer, James A. Applications of Absorption Spectroscopy of Organic Compounds. 1965. pap. text 37.00 (*0-13-038802-5*) P-H.

Dyer, James A., jt. auth. see Bernstein, Robert A.

Dyer, James S. & Shapiro, Roy D. Management Science-Operations Research: Cases & Readings. LC 81-19703. 274p. (C). 1982. pap. text 20.00 (*0-471-86554-0*) Wiley.

Dyer, James S. & Shapiro, Roy D., eds. Management Science-Operations Research: Cases & Readings. LC 81-19703. 400p. reprint ed. pap. 124.00 (*0-7837-3509-X*, 205784200008) Bks Demand.

Dyer, Jane. Animal Crackers: Bedtime. (Illus.). 12p. (J). (ps). 1998. 4.95 (*0-316-19660-6*) Little.

— Animal Crackers: Nursery Rhymes. (Illus.). 12p. (J). (ps). 1998. 5.95 (*0-316-19643-6*) Little.

— The Little Brown Bear in I Won't Take a Nap. (Illus.). 32p. (J). 2000. write for info. (*0-316-19764-5*) Little.

— Moo, Moo Peekaboo. LC 85-61530. (Illus.). (J). (ps). 1986. 4.99 (*0-394-87883-3*, Pub. by Random Bks Yng Read) Random.

Dyer, Jane. Little Red Riding Hood. LC 85-70289. (Pudgy Pal Board Bks.). 18p. (J). (ps). 1985. bds. 3.95 (*0-448-10227-7*, G & D) Peng Put Young Read.

— The Random House Book of Bedtime Stories. LC 94-2631. 160p. (J). (gr. 1 up). 1994. 19.00 (*0-679-80832-9*) Random.

Dyer, Jane. Animal Crackers: A Delectable Collection of Pictures, Poems, & Lullabies for the Very Young. LC 93-4244. 64p. (J). (gr. k-3). 1996. 17.95 (*0-316-19766-1*) Little.

Dyer, Jeffrey M., jt. auth. see Doshi, Mahendra R.

Dyer, Jerry & Pepper, Clayton, eds. Keeping Converts & Restoring the Erring. 1982. pap. 4.35 (*0-89137-205-9*) Quality Pubns.

***Dyer, Jerry L.** Tar Heel Born: Dyer Family from Lincoln Co., N. C. 484p. 1999. pap. 72.00 (*0-8328-9912-7*); lib. bdg. 82.00 (*0-8328-9911-9*) Higginson Bk Co.

Dyer, Joel. Harvest of Rage: Why Oklahoma City Is Only the Beginning. LC 98-26117. 336p. (C). 1998. pap. text 17.00 (*0-8133-3293-1*, Pub. by Westview) HarpC.

— The Perpetual Prisoner Machine: How America Profits from Crime. LC 99-45576. 318p. 2000. 26.00 (*0-8133-3507-8*, Pub. by Westview) HarpC.

Dyer, John, ed. see Gunnufson, Kent.

Dyer, John A. & Lee, David A. Atlas of Extraocular Muscle Surgery. 2nd ed. LC 84-18090. 256p. 1984. 59.95 (*0-275-91427-5*, C1427, Praeger Pubs) Greenwood.

Dyer, John P. From Shiloh to San Juan: The Life of "Fightin' Joe" Wheeler. LC 61-10832. (Southern Biography Ser.). (Illus.). 275p. (C). 1992. pap. 14.95 (*0-8071-1809-5*) La State U Pr.

Dyer, Joyce. In a Tangled Wood: An Alzheimer's Journey. LC 96-11354. 184p. 1996. 22.50 (*0-87074-396-1*); pap. 12.95 (*0-87074-397-X*) SMU Press.

Dyer, Joyce, ed. Bloodroot: Reflections on Place by Appalachian Women Writers. LC 97-45570. (Illus.). 304p. 1998. 28.00 (*0-8131-2059-4*) U Pr of Ky.

***Dyer, Joyce, ed.** Bloodroot: Reflections on Place by Appalachian Women Writers. LC 99-89873. (Illus.). 312p. 2000. reprint ed. pap. 17.00 (*0-8131-0983-3*) U Pr of Ky.

Dyer, Judith & Schram, Frederick R. A Manual of Invertebrate Paleontology. (Illus.). 165p. (Orig.). (C). 1983. pap. text 8.25 (*0-87563-237-8*) Stipes.

***Dyer, K. R.** Estuaries: A Physical Introduction. LC 97-14903. 210p. 1998. pap. 44.95 (*0-471-97471-4*) Wiley.

— Estuaries: A Physical Introduction. 2nd ed. LC 97-14903. 210p. 1998. 100.00 (*0-471-97470-6*) Wiley.

Dyer, Kathleen & Luce, Stephen C. Teaching Practical Communication Skills. Browder, Diane M., ed. LC 96-8706. (Innovations Ser.). (Illus.). 30p. (Orig.). 1996. pap. 21.95 (*0-940898-42-X*) Am Assn Mental.

Dyer, Keith D. The Prophecy on the Mount: Mark 13 & the Gathering of the New Community. (International Theological Studies: Vol. 2). 338p. (C). 1998. pap. text 50.95 (*3-906759-71-7*) P Lang Pubng.

Dyer, Keith R. Estuaries: A Physical Introduction. LC 72-8598. (Illus.). 156p. reprint ed. pap. 48.40 (*0-608-17937-X*, 202789200057) Bks Demand.

Dyer, Ken, ed. Sportswomen Towards 2000: A Celebration. 286p. (C). 1989. pap. 135.00 (*0-909120-93-5*, Pub. by U of Adelaide) St Mut.

Dyer, L. R., jt. auth. see Coppen, J. J.

Dyer, L. S. A Practical Approach to Bank Lending. 243p. (C). 1990. pap. 125.00 (*0-85297-181-8*, Pub. by Chartered Bank) St Mut.

— A Practical Approach to Bank Lending. 2nd ed. 232p. 1980. 130.00 (*0-85297-084-6*, Pub. by Chartered Bank) St Mut.

Dyer, L. S., jt. auth. see Hutchinson, H. H.

***Dyer, Larry.** Baptism: The Believer's First Obedience. 2000. pap. 4.99 (*0-8254-2497-6*) Kregel.

An Asterisk (*) at the beginning of an entry indicates that the title is appearing for the first time.

Dyer, Lee & Holder, Gerald W., eds. Human Resource Management: Evolving Roles & Responsibilities. LC 88-21252. (ASPA/BNA Ser.: Vol. 1). 288p. 1988. reprint ed. pap. 89.30 (*0-608-00749-8*, 206154000010) Bks Demand.

Dyer, Lois F. The Cowboy Takes a Wife. (Special Edition Ser.). 1998. per. 4.25 (*0-373-24198-4*, 1-24198-3) Silhouette.

— He's Got His Daddy's Eyes. 1997. per. 3.99 (*0-373-24129-1*, 1-24129-8) Silhouette.

— Lonesome Cowboy. 1996. per. 3.99 (*0-373-24038-4*, 1-24038-1) Silhouette.

— The Only Cowboy for Caitlin: Family Arch. (Special Edition Ser.: No. 1253). 1999. per. 4.25 (*0-373-24253-0*, 1-24253-6) Silhouette.

***Dyer, Lois F.** Le Poison du Doute. (Amours d'Aujourd'Hui Ser.: No. 338). (FRE.). 1999. mass mkt. 5.50 (*0-373-38338-X*, 1-38338-9) Harlequin Bks.

***Dyer, Lois Faye.** Cattleman's Courtship. (Special Edition Ser.: Vol. 133). 2000. mass mkt. 4.50 (*0-373-24306-5*) Silhouette.

Dyer, Louis, ed. see Plato.

Dyer, M. H. Dyer's Index to Land Grants in West Virginia. (Illus.). 948p. 1992. reprint ed. lib. bdg. write for info. (*0-8328-2579-4*) Higginson Bk Co.

Dyer, M. Phillip. Beneath a Broken Moon. Benson, Carol, ed. LC 96-94997. (Illus.). 96p. (Orig.). 1996. pap., per. 12.00 (*0-9654931-0-5*) Bl Moon Pr ME.

Dyer, Marcelene, jt. auth. see Dyer, Wayne W.

***Dyer, Margaret Adams.** Inspirational Poems of Yesterday & Today. LC 97-91223. (Illus.). 49p. (YA). 2000. pap. 9.95 (*0-533-12598-7*) Vantage.

Dyer, Mary H. A Ship in the Harbor. LC 93-84468. 160p. (Orig.). 1993. pap. 8.95 (*1-882587-00-6*) Paradigm San Diego.

***Dyer, Mary H.** Year of Jubliee: A Guidebook for Women Reinventing Their Lives. 249p. 1999. pap. 18.95 (*0-9666448-7-5*) Dandelion Seed.

Dyer, Michael. Capable Citizens & Improvident Democrats: The Scottish Electoral System, 1884-1929. 208p. 1990. pap. 33.00 (*1-898218-23-4*) St Mut.

Dyer, Michael, ed. Men of Property & Intelligence: The Scottish Electoral System Prior to 1884. 176p. 1990. pap. 33.00 (*1-898218-22-6*) St Mut.

Dyer, Michael G. Cleanroom Approach to Quality Software Development. LC 91-37245. (Series in Software Engineering Practice). 224p. 1992. 52.00 (*0-471-54823-5*) Wiley.

Dyer, Murray. The Weapon on the Wall. 1979. 28.95 (*0-405-10599-1*) Ayer.

Dyer, Nancy & Homeyer, Pat. A Practical Education Program for the Diabetic Client Within the Rehabilitation Setting. LC RC0660.D84. (American Foundation for the Blind Practice Ser.). 153p. reprint ed. pap. 47.50 (*0-7837-0144-6*, 204043400016) Bks Demand.

Dyer, Nancy Joe, ed. El Mio Cid del Taller Alfonsi: Version en Prosa en la Primera Cronica General y en la Cronica. (Ediciones Criticas Ser.: Vol. 6). (SPA.). 237p. 1995. 23.00 (*0-936388-72-2*) Juan de la Cuesta.

Dyer, Nigel & Watkins, Trevor, eds. Marketing Insurance: A Practical Guide. (C). 1988. 400.00 (*0-7855-4081-4*, Pub. by Witherby & Co) St Mut.

Dyer, Oliver. Great Senators of the United States Forty Years Ago. LC 72-8557. (Essay Index Reprint Ser.). 1977. reprint ed. 21.95 (*0-8369-7344-5*) Ayer.

— History of the Battle of Lake Erie. 264p. 1985. reprint ed. lib. bdg. 44.00 (*0-7812-0891-2*) Rprt Serv.

Dyer, P. & Middleton, D., eds. Histocompatibility Testing: A Practical Approach. LC 92-38629. (Practical Approach Ser.). 326p. 1993. 85.00 (*0-19-963364-9*) OUP.

— Histocompatibility Testing: A Practical Approach. LC 92-38629. (Practical Approach Ser.). (Illus.). 326p. 1993. pap. text 49.95 (*0-19-963363-0*) OUP.

Dyer, Paul L. The Ultimate Job Search Survival Guide: Find the Job You Really Want & Get Hired. LC 98-11994. (Ultimate Guides Ser.). 304p. pap. 14.95 (*0-7689-0009-3*) Petersons.

Dyer, Peter E., jt. ed. see Dubowski, Jan J.

Dyer, Peter E., jt. ed. see Shields, Harry.

Dyer, R. A. Flora of Southern Africa Series, Vol. 27, Pt. 4. 91p. 1980. 25.00 (*0-621-04737-6*, Pub. by Natl Botanical Inst) Balogh.

Dyer, R. Allen. Ceropegia, Brachystelma & Riocreuxia in Southern Africa. (Illus.). 274p. 1983. 99.00 (*90-6191-227-X*, Pub. by A A Balkema) Ashgate Pub Co.

Dyer, R. Allen, jt. auth. see Reid, C.

Dyer, Raymond. Her Father's Daughter: The Work of Anna Freud. LC 82-11334. 352p. 1983. 45.00 (*0-87668-627-7*) Aronson.

Dyer, Raymond B., ed. Handbook of Basic Vascular & Interventional Radiology. (Illus.). 275p. 1992. text 83.00 (*0-443-08840-3*) Church.

Dyer, Richard. Brief Encounter. (Illus.). 72p. 1994. pap. 10.95 (*0-85170-362-3*, Pub. by British Film Inst) Ind U Pr.

— The Matter of Images: Essays on Representations. LC 92-37765. (Illus.). 240p. (C). 1993. pap. 20.99 (*0-415-05719-1*, A9988) Routledge.

— Now You See It: Studies on Lesbian & Gay Film. (Illus.). 352p. (C). 1990. pap. 22.99 (*0-415-03556-2*, A4864) Routledge.

— Only Entertainment. (Illus.). 176p. (C). (gr. 13). 1992. pap. 19.99 (*0-415-05717-5*, A9586) Routledge.

***Dyer, Richard.** Seven. (BFI Modern Classics Ser.). (Illus.). 88p. 1999. pap. 10.95 (*0-85170-723-8*, Pub. by British Film Inst) Ind U Pr.

Dyer, Richard. Stars. (Illus.). 204p. 1982. pap. 12.95 (*0-85170-085-3*, Pub. by British Film Inst) Ind U Pr.

— Stars. 2nd rev. ed. LC 98-150751. (Illus.). 224p. 1998. 49.95 (*0-85170-648-7*, Pub. by British Film Inst); pap. 16.95 (*0-85170-643-6*, Pub. by British Film Inst) Ind U Pr.

— White. LC 96-11485. (Illus.). 284p. (C). 1997. pap. 19.99 (*0-415-09537-9*) Routledge.

— White. LC 96-11485. (Illus.). 284p. (C). 1997. 75.00 (*0-415-09536-0*) Routledge.

Dyer, Richard & Vincendeau, Ginette, eds. Popular European Cinema. LC 91-40138. (Illus.). 280p. (C). 1992. pap. 22.99 (*0-415-06803-7*, A9576) Routledge.

Dyer, Robert. Showdown at Total Wreck. large type ed. (Linford Western Large Print Ser.). 272p. 1998. pap. 17.99 (*0-7089-5269-0*) Ulverscroft.

Dyer, Robert A., jt. ed. see Chang, Louis W.

Dyer, Robert L. Jesse James & the Civil War in Missouri. LC 93-50793. (Missouri Heritage Readers Ser.). (Illus.). 104p. (C). 1994. pap. 8.95 (*0-8262-0959-9*) U of Mo Pr.

Dyer, Robert L. & Von Sachsen-Altenburg, Hans. Duke Paul of Wuerttemberg on the Missouri Frontier, 1823, 1830, 1851. (Illus.). 264p. 1997. 19.95 (*0-9661902-0-3*); pap. 14.95 (*0-9661902-1-1*) Pekitanoui.

Dyer, Rod & Spark, Ron. Fit to Be Tied: Vintage Ties of the 1940s & Early '50s. (Illus.). 96p. 1987. 27.50 (*0-89659-756-3*) Abbeville Pr.

Dyer, Scott & Beach, Nancy. The Source: A Resource Guide for Using Creative Arts in Church Services. 352p. 1996. pap. 49.99 (*0-310-50021-4*) Zondervan.

Dyer, Sue. Partner Your Project. LC 96-70849. (Illus.). xvi, 234p. 1997. 34.95 (*0-9652243-0-9*) Pendulum Pubng.

Dyer, Susan K. Manual of Procedures for Private Law Libraries: 1984 Supplement. LC 84-11589. (AALL Publications Ser.: No. 21). ix, 130p. 1984. suppl. ed. 22.50 (*0-8377-0119-8*, Rothman) W S Hein.

Dyer, Susan K., jt. auth. see American Association of Law Librarians Staff.

Dyer, Svetlana R. Grammatical Analysis of the Lao Ch'i-Ta: With an English Translation of the Chinese Text. (Faculty of Asian Studies Monographs: Vol. 3). (Illus.). 556p. 1997. pap. text 50.00 (*0-909879-18-4*, Pub. by Aust Nat Univ) UH Pr.

Dyer, T. A. A Way of His Own. LC 81-350. 160p. (YA). (gr. 7 up). 1990. pap. 6.95 (*0-395-54969-8*) HM.

Dyer, T.A. Way of His Own. 1981. 11.05 (*0-606-04844-8*, Pub. by Turtleback) Demco.

Dyer, Thomas G. Secret Yankees: The Union Circle in Confederate Atlanta. LC 98-28165. (War, Society & Culture Ser.). (Illus.). 392p. 1999. 29.95 (*0-8018-6116-0*) Johns Hopkins.

— Theodore Roosevelt & the Idea of Race. LC 79-20151. 182p. (C). 1992. pap. text 14.95 (*0-8071-1808-7*) La State U Pr.

— The University of Georgia: A Bicentennial History, 1785-1985. LC 84-232. 448p. 1984. 34.95 (*0-8203-0725-4*) U of Ga Pr.

Dyer, Traci, ed. Mother Voices: Real Women Write about Growing into Motherhood. 256p. 1999. pap. 12.95 (*1-887166-45-9*) Sourcebks.

Dyer, W. Gibb, Jr. The Entrepreneurial Experience: Confronting Career Dilemmas of the Start-up Experience. LC 91-39474. (Management Ser.). 288p. 1992. 36.95 (*1-55542-417-1*) Jossey-Bass.

Dyer, Walter A. Gulliver the Great: And Other Dog Stories. LC 72-5906. (Short Story Index Reprint Ser.). 1977. reprint ed. 26.95 (*0-8369-4210-0*) Ayer.

— Many Dogs There Be. LC 71-122695. (Short Story Index Reprint Ser.). 1977. 18.95 (*0-8369-3528-4*) Ayer.

Dyer, Wayne W. El Cielo Es El Limite. 1997. pap. text 17.98 (*968-419-382-3*) Grijalbo Edit.

Dyer, Wayne W. Construye Tu Destino. 1997. pap. text 14.98 (*84-253-9654-9*) Grijalbo Edit.

— Everyday Wisdom. LC 93-36208. 176p. 1993. pap. 5.95 (*1-56170-076-2*, 154) Hay House.

— Gifts from Eykis. 1989. mass mkt. 6.99 (*0-671-68461-2*) S&S Trade.

— Manifest Your Destiny: The Nine Spiritual Principles for Getting Everything You Want. LC 96-48248. 192p. 1997. 23.00 (*0-06-017528-1*) HarpC.

— Manifest Your Destiny: The Nine Spiritual Principles for Getting Everything You Want. LC 96-48248. 192p. 1998. pap. 13.00 (*0-06-092892-1*) HarpC.

— Manifest Your Destiny: The Nine Spiritual Principles for Getting Everything You Want. 240p. 1999. mass mkt. 6.99 (*0-06-109494-3*, Harp PBks) HarpC.

Dyer, Wayne W. Manifest Your Destiny: The Nine Spiritual Principles for Getting Everything You Want. abr. ed. 1997. audio 18.00 (*0-694-51778-X*, CPN 2620) HarperAudio.

Dyer, Wayne W. One Hundred & One Ways to Transform Your Life. 1995. pap. text 5.95 (*1-56170-169-6*) Hay House.

— 101 Ways to Transform Your Life. 112p. 1998. pap. 9.95 (*1-56170-493-8*) Hay House.

— Pulling Your Own Strings. 320p. 1994. mass mkt. 6.50 (*0-06-109224-X*, Harp PBks) HarpC.

— Pulling Your Own Strings. 1979. mass mkt. 4.95 (*0-380-44388-0*, Avon Bks) Morrow Avon.

Dyer, Wayne W. Pulling Your Own Strings: Dyer,&Wayne W. abr. ed. 1991. audio 18.00 (*1-55994-433-1*, CPN 1888) HarperAudio.

Dyer, Wayne W. Pulling Your Own Strings: Dynamic Techniques for Dealing with Other People & Living Life as You Choose. LC 77-23368. 288p. 1993. reprint ed. pap. 13.00 (*0-06-091975-2*, Perennial) HarperTrade.

— Real Magic. 368p. 1993. mass mkt. 6.99 (*0-06-109150-2*, Harp PBks) HarpC.

— Sky's the Limit. 1990. per. 6.99 (*0-671-72565-3*) PB.

— Staying on the Path. LC 94-38239. 208p. 1995. pap. 6.95 (*1-56170-126-2*, 152) Hay House.

— Tus Zonas Erroneas. (SPA.). 1997. pap. text 14.98 (*968-419-174-X*) Grijalbo Edit.

— Tus Zonas Magicas. 1997. pap. text 18.00 (*970-05-0436-0*) Grijalbo Edit.

— Tus Zonas Sagradas Decidete A Ser Libre. 1997. pap. text 15.98 (*970-05-0808-0*) Grijalbo Edit.

— What Do You Really Want for Your Children? 400p. 1986. mass mkt. 6.99 (*0-380-69957-5*, Avon Bks) Morrow Avon.

— What Do You Really Want for Your Children? write for info. (*0-318-60256-3*) S&S Trade.

— Wisdom of the Ages: A Modern Master Brings Eternal Truth into Everyday Life. LC 98-23756. 288p. 1998. 22.00 (*0-06-019231-3*) HarpC.

***Dyer, Wayne W.** Wisdom of The Ages: A Modern Master Brings Eternal Truths into Everyday LifeDyer,&Wayne W. 1998. audio 18.00 (*0-694-52055-1*) HarperAudio.

— Wisdom of the Ages: Australian Edition. 2000. pap. 12.00 (*0-06-095351-9*) HarpC.

Dyer, Wayne W. You'll See It When You Believe It. 288p. 1990. reprint ed. mass mkt. 6.99 (*0-380-70658-X*, Avon Bks) Morrow Avon.

— Your Erroneous Zones. 320p. 1993. mass mkt. 6.50 (*0-06-109148-0*, Harp PBks) HarpC.

— Your Erroneous Zones. 1977. mass mkt. 4.95 (*0-380-01669-9*, Avon Bks) Morrow Avon.

— Your Erroneous Zones: Step-by-Step Advice for Escaping the Trap of Negative Thinking & Taking Control of Your Life. LC 91-2718. 288p. 1993. reprint ed. pap. 13.00 (*0-06-091976-0*, Perennial) HarperTrade.

Dyer, Wayne W. Your Erroneous Zones: Step-by-Step Advice for Escaping the Trap of Negative Thinking & Taking Control of Your Life. unabridged ed. 1991. audio 12.00 (*1-55994-432-3*, CPN 1887) HarperAudio.

Dyer, Wayne W. Your Sacred Self: Making the Decision to Be Free. 400p. 1996. mass mkt. 6.99 (*0-06-109475-7*) HarpC.

Dyer, Wayne W. Your Sacred Self: Making the Decision to Be Free, Set. abr. ed. 1995. audio 18.00 (*0-694-51526-4*, CPN 2480) HarperAudio.

Dyer, Wayne W., reader. Real Magic: Creating Miracles in Everyday Life. abr. ed. 1992. audio 18.00 (*1-55994-667-9*, CPN 2315) HarperAudio.

Dyer, Wayne W. & Dyer, Marcelene. A Promise Is a Promise: An Almost Unbelievable Story of a Mother's Unconditional Love & What It Can Teach Us. LC 96-9125. 112p. 1996. 14.00 (*1-56170-348-6*, 851) Hay House.

Dyer, Wayne W., jt. auth. see Vriend, John.

Dyer, William, jt. auth. see Parks, Don.

Dyer, William G. Contemporary Issues in Management & Organization Development. LC 82-8732. 224p. 1983. 15.96 (*0-201-10348-6*) Addison-Wesley.

— Modern Theory & Method in Group Training. LC 80-24641. 268p. (C). 1981. reprint ed. text 23.00 (*0-89874-280-3*) Krieger.

— Team Building: Current Issues & New Alternatives. 3rd ed. (Illus.). 154p. (C). 1994. pap. text 40.00 (*0-201-62882-1*) Addison-Wesley.

— Team Building: Issues & Alternatives. (Organization Development Ser.). 1977. pap. 11.95 (*0-201-01191-3*) Addison-Wesley.

— Team Building: Issues & Alternatives. 2nd ed. LC 86-20635. (Organization Development Ser.). 160p. (C). 1987. pap. text 26.95 (*0-201-18037-5*) Addison-Wesley.

Dyer, William G. & Kunz, Phillip R. 10 Critical Keys for Highly Effective Mormon Families. LC 94-68468. 205p. 1994. pap. 12.95 (*1-55517-155-9*) CFI Dist.

Dyer, William G., et al. The Challenge of Management. 640p. (C). 1989. VHS, disk. write for info. (*0-318-67017-8*) Dryden Pr.

Dyer, William P. Activities of the Elementary School Principal for the Improvement of Instruction: The Kind of Supervisory Program Which a City Superintendent of Schools Should Set up for His Elementary School Principals. LC 70-176738. (Columbia University. Teachers College. Contributions to Education Ser.: No. 274). reprint ed. 37.50 (*0-404-55274-9*) AMS Pr.

Dyer-Witheford, Nick. Cyber-Marx: Cycles & Circuits of Struggle in High-Technology Capitalism. LC 98-58056. 1999. 21.95 (*0-252-06795-9*) U of Ill Pr.

— Cyber-Marx: Cycles & Circuits of Struggle in High-Technology Capitalism. LC 98-58056. 416p. 1999. 49.95 (*0-252-02479-6*) U of Ill Pr.

Dyers, C. Las Noticias Mundiales y la Profecia Biblica.Tr. of World News & Bible Prophecy. (SPA.). 274p. pap. 9.99 (*1-56063-950-4*, 498210) Editorial Unilit.

Dyers, J. A., jt. auth. see Mulholland, Kenneth.

Dyers, Jeffrey M., jt. auth. see Doshi, Mahendra R.

Dyes, John C. Nesting Birds of the Coastal Islands: A Naturalist's Year on Galveston Bay. LC 92-29457. (Corrie Herring Hooks Ser.: No. 22). (Illus.). 163p. 1993. text 24.95 (*0-292-71567-6*) U of Tex Pr.

Dyess, A. Eugene. Faithing: A Reconstructive Method. LC 94-21259. 410p. (Orig.). (C). 1994. pap. text 37.50 (*0-8191-9602-9*) U Pr of Amer.

Dyess, Ernest L. Divine Appointments: In the Master's Vineyard. LC 98-91691. (God, If You're Real, Let the Cow Be in the Pen When I Get Home Ser.). (Illus.). 259p. 1998. pap. 9.95 (*0-9641704-1-8*) Pebble Hill.

— God, If You're Real, Let the Cow Be in the Pen When I Get Home: Experiencing the Reality of God. LC 94-71770. (Illus.). 289p. (Orig.). 1994. pap. 9.99 (*0-9641704-0-X*) Selah Hse Pub.

Dyet, James. Out of the Rough: Meditations for Golfers. LC 96-6444. 160p. 1996. 12.99 (*0-7852-7659-9*) Nelson.

Dyet, John F., et al. Textbook of Endovascular Procedures. LC 99-40814. (Illus.). 795p. 2000. text. write for info. (*0-443-06541-1*, W B Saunders Co) Harcrt Hlth Sci Grp.

Dyett, Linda, jt. auth. see Green, Annette.

Dygard, Thomas J. Backfield Package. LC 92-6315. 208p. (YA). (gr. 7 up). 1992. 14.00 (*0-688-11471-7*, Wm Morrow) Morrow Avon.

— Forward Pass. (J). 1990. 10.09 (*0-606-04674-7*, Pub. by Turtleback) Demco.

— Game Plan. LC 92-47252. 224p. (YA). (gr. 7 up). 1993. 14.00 (*0-688-12007-5*, Wm Morrow) Morrow Avon.

— Game Plan. LC 94-45663. (J). 1995. pap. 4.99 (*0-14-036970-8*, PuffinBks) Peng Put Young Read.

— Game Plan. (J). 1995. 10.09 (*0-606-07555-0*, Pub. by Turtleback) Demco.

— Halfback Tough. 1989. 9.09 (*0-606-01303-2*, Pub. by Turtleback) Demco.

— Infield Hit. LC 94-32914. (Illus.). 208p. (YA). (gr. 7 up). 1995. 16.00 (*0-688-14037-8*, Wm Morrow) Morrow Avon.

Dygard, Thomas J. Infield Hit. 1997. 10.09 (*0-606-10999-4*, Pub. by Turtleback) Demco.

Dygard, Thomas J. Infield Hit. LC 96-38204. 1997. pap. 4.99 (*0-14-037935-5*) Viking Penguin.

— Outside Shooter. (J). 1987. 10.09 (*0-606-04767-0*, Pub. by Turtleback) Demco.

— Quarterback Walk-On. 1989. 10.09 (*0-606-02293-7*, Pub. by Turtleback) Demco.

— Rebounder. LC 94-51257. 192p. (YA). (gr. 7 up). 1994. 16.00 (*0-688-12821-1*, Wm Morrow) Morrow Avon.

— Rebounder. 192p. (YA). (gr. 5 up). 1996. pap. 4.99 (*0-14-037702-6*, PuffinBks) Peng Put Young Read.

Dygard, Thomas J. Rebounder. 1996. 9.09 (*0-606-08853-9*, Pub. by Turtleback) Demco.

Dygard, Thomas J. River Danger. LC 97-36362. 151p. (J). (gr. 7-12). 1998. 15.95 (*0-688-14852-2*, Wm Morrow) Morrow Avon.

— The Rookie Arrives. 176p. (J). (gr. 5-9). 1989. pap. 4.99 (*0-14-034112-9*, PuffinBks) Peng Put Young Read.

Dygard, Thomas J. Rookie Arrives. (J). 1988. 10.09 (*0-606-04309-8*, Pub. by Turtleback) Demco.

Dygard, Thomas J. Running Wild. LC 96-10182. 208p. (YA). (gr. 7 up). 1996. 15.00 (*0-688-14853-0*, Wm Morrow) Morrow Avon.

— Running Wild. LC 97-50530. (Illus.). 176p. (J). (gr. 5-9). 1998. pap. 4.99 (*0-14-038687-4*, PuffinBks) Peng Put Young Read.

— Running Wild. 1998. 10.09 (*0-606-13753-X*, Pub. by Turtleback) Demco.

***Dygard, Thomas J.** Second Stringer. 192p. (YA). (gr. 7-12). 1998. 15.00 (*0-688-15981-8*, Wm Morrow) Morrow Avon.

Dygard, Thomas J. Soccer Duel. 1990. 10.09 (*0-606-02459-X*, Pub. by Turtleback) Demco.

— Tournament Upstart. (J). 1989. 10.09 (*0-606-04350-0*, Pub. by Turtleback) Demco.

Dygard, Thomas J. Wilderness Peril. 1991. 10.09 (*0-606-05048-5*, Pub. by Turtleback) Demco.

Dygdon, John & Spencer, Henry. Basic Technical Drawing. 1980. 62.56 (*0-02-232150-0*) Glencoe.

Dygdon, Judith A. The Culture & Lifestyle-Appropriate Social Skills Intervention Curriculum (CLASSIC) A Program for Socially Valid Social Skills Training. LC 92-72154. 1993. pap. 15.95 (*0-88422-119-9*) Clinical Psych.

Dygert, Charles B. Success Is a Team Effort. 95p. 1993. pap. 6.95 (*1-884182-00-3*) Motivat Ent.

Dygert, Charles B. & Jacobs, Rich. The Culture of Success. (Orig.). 1996. pap. text 6.95 (*1-884182-01-1*) Motivat Ent.

Dygert, Clare, ed. see Lindquist, Robert A.

Dygert, Janice. Red Horse & the Buffalo Robe Man. Gilliland, Hap, ed. (Indian Culture Ser.). (Illus.). 36p. (J). (gr. 4-8). 1978. pap. 4.95 (*0-89992-074-8*) Coun India Ed.

Dyhouse. No Distinction of Sex? Women in British Universities, 1870-1939. LC 95-875. (Women's History Ser.). 1995. 75.00 (*1-85728-458-5*, Pub. by UCL Pr Ltd); pap. write for info. (*1-85728-459-3*, Pub. by UCL Pr Ltd) Taylor & Francis.

Dyhr, Timothy M., jt. auth. see Gillette, Laurence N.

Dyienkowski, John S. Professional Responsibility, Standards, Rules & Statutes, 1997-1998 Edition. 10th ed. 1031p. (C). 1997. pap. text. write for info. (*0-314-21220-5*) West Pub.

Dyja, Eddie. BFI Film & Television Handbook, 1999. (Distributed for the British Film Institute Ser.). 446p. Date not set. pap. 35.00 (*0-85170-682-7*, Pub. by British Film Inst) Ind U Pr.

***Dyja, Eddie.** BFI Film & Television Handbook, 2000. 424p. 2000. pap. 35.00 (*0-85170-764-5*, Pub. by British Film Inst) Ind U Pr.

Dyja, Eddie. BFI Film & Television Handbook, 1996. 1996. pap. text 28.95 (*0-85170-552-9*, Pub. by British Film Inst) Ind U Pr.

— BFI Film & Television Handbook 1997. 1998. pap. 35.00 (*0-85170-637-1*, Pub. by British Film Inst) Ind U Pr.

— BFI Film & Television Handbook, 1998. 1998. pap. 35.00 (*0-85170-652-5*, Pub. by British Film Inst) Ind U Pr.

Dyja, Thomas. Play for a Kingdom: A Novel. LC 96-53875. 384p. (C). 1997. 25.00 (*0-15-100267-3*) Harcourt.

— Play for a Kingdom: A Novel. (Illus.). 428p. (C). 1998. pap. 14.00 (*0-15-600629-4*, Harvest Bks) Harcourt.

Dyja, Thomas, jt. ed. see Balliett, Will.

Dyjak, Elisabeth. I Should Have Listened to the Moon. Ashby, Ruth, ed. 144p. (J). 1993. reprint ed. per. 2.99 (*0-671-73830-5*, Minstrel Bks) PB.

Dyk, Gregory Van, see Van Dyk, Gregory.

Dyk, J. W. On Tracing the Line of Syntactic Dependence: A Computer-Assisted Study of the Old Testament Hebrew Participal Constructions. LC 95-101514. 1994. pap. 33.00 (*90-5383-278-5*, Pub. by VU Univ Pr) Paul & Co Pubs.

Dyk, John Van, see Van Dyk, John.

Dyk, Stephen H. Van, see Van Dyk, Stephen H.

Dykas, Christine. The Hunter's Woods. 1989. write for info. (*0-318-65386-9*) Pr MacDonald & Reinecke.

D

Dyke, A. L. Dyke's Automobile & Gasoline Engine Encyclopedia, 1921 Edition. unabridged ed. (Illus.). 945p. 1992. reprint ed. pap. 29.95 (*1-57002-072-8*) Univ Publng Hse.

Dyke, Annette Van, see Van Dyke, Annette.

Dyke, Beth Van, see Van Dyke, Beth.

Dyke, Bill & Jones, Bill. The Horse Business: An Investor's Guide. (Illus.). 1974. 10.00 (*0-912830-22-0*) Printed Horse.

Dyke, C., jt. auth. see Lee, F.

Dyke, Carl Van, see Van Dyke, Carl.

Dyke, Carol H. Summer Folly. large type ed. 1991. pap. 16.99 (*0-7089-6976-3*) Ulverscroft.

Dyke, Carrie Van, see Van Dyke, Carrie.

Dyke, Charles. The Evolutionary Dynamics of Complex Systems: A Study in Biosocial Complexity. (Monographs in History & Philosophy of Biology). 174p. 1987. text 55.00 (*0-19-505176-9*) OUP.

Dyke, Cornelius M., jt. auth. see Lee, K. Francis.

Dyke, D. C. Van, see Van Dyke, D. C.

Dyke, Daniel. Michael & the Dragon: or Christ Tempted & Satan Foiled. unabridged ed. 275p. 1997. reprint ed. 29.95 (*1-889058-06-8*) Old Paths Pubns.

Dyke, Della Van, see Van Dyke, Della.

Dyke, Della Van, see Nakken, Jane & Van Dyke, Della.

Dyke, Frances van, see Van Dyke, Frances.

Dyke, George V. Comparative Experiments with Field Crops. 2nd ed. (Charles Griffin Bks.). (Illus.). 280p. 1988. text 85.00 (*0-19-520633-9*) OUP.

Dyke, Henry Van, see Van Dyke, Henry.

Dyke, Jan Van, see Van Dyke, Jan.

Dyke, John Van, see Van Dyke, John.

Dyke, Jon M. Van, see Van Dyke, Jon M.

Dyke, Kate Van, see Van Dyke, Kate.

Dyke, Knox Van, ed. Bioluminescence & Chemiluminesence Instruments & Applications, Set, Vols. I & II. 256p. 1985. 174.00 (*0-8493-5863-9*, QP517) CRC Pr.

***Dyke, Larry & McLeroy, Leigh.** Revealing the Beauty. LC 99-31947. (Illus.). 160p. 1999. 65.00 (*0-8054-2140-8*) Broadman.

Dyke, Louis van, see Van Dyke, Louis.

Dyke, Milton Van, see Van Dyke, Milton, ed.

Dyke, Milton Van, see Lumley, John L. & Van Dyke, Milton, eds.

Dyke, Milton Van, see Van Dyke, Milton.

Dyke, Nancy B. Conflict Prevention: Strategies to Sustain Peace in the Post-Cold War World. (Aspen Institute Conferences on International Peace & Security Ser.: No. 3). 164p. 1997. pap. 10.00 (*0-89843-205-7*) The Aspen Inst.

***Dyke, Nancy B.** International Poverty Gap: Investing in People & Technology to Build Sustainable Pathwaysout. 2000. pap. 10.00 (*0-89843-272-3*) The Aspen Inst.

Dyke, Nancy B. Managing Conflict in the Post-Cold War World: The Role of Intervention: Report of the Aspen Institute Conference. (Aspen Institute Conferences on International Peace & Security Ser.). 123p. 1996. pap. 10.00 (*0-89843-192-1*) The Aspen Inst.

Dyke, Nancy B., ed. Persistent Poverty in Developing Countries: Determining the Causes & Closing the Gaps. 150p. 1998. pap. 12.95 (*0-89843-237-5*) The Aspen Inst.

Dyke, P. P. An Introduction to Laplace Transforms & Fourier Series. LC 98-47927. (Springer Undergraduate Mathematics Ser.). (Illus.). xii, 248p. 1999. pap. 39.95 (*1-85233-015-5*, Pub. by Spr-Verlag) Spr-Verlag.

Dyke, P. P. & Heaps, Norman S., eds. Jonsmod Eighty-Two: A Workshop of the Joint North Sea Modelling Group on Mathematical Models of the North Sea & Surrounding Continental Shelf Seas, Heriot-Watt University, Edinburgh, U. K., Sept. 1-3, 1982. 136p. 1984. pap. 26.00 (*0-08-031425-2*, Pergamon Pr) Elsevier.

Dyke, Patricia M., jt. auth. see Schiller, Pamela.

Dyke, Patt Van, see Van Dyke, Patt, ed.

Dyke, Paul C. Van, see Van Dyke, Paul C.

Dyke, Paul Van, see Van Dyke, Paul.

***Dyke, Peter C.** Cyberdiary: A Year in the Life of an Average Man. unabridged ed. Cummins, P. D., ed. LC 00-103205. (Illus.). 160p. 2000. pap. 30.00 (*0-9618819-3-3*) Foghrn Pr.

Dyke, Peter C. High Times at Happy Ranch: Living with the Big "C" LC 98-92669. (Illus.). 274p. 1998. pap. 25.00 (*0-9618819-1-7*) Foghrn Pr.

Dyke, Philip. Modelling Marine Processes. LC 96-3937. 1996. write for info. (*0-614-12742-4*) P-H.

Dyke, Richard W. Mr. Atomic Energy: Congressman Chet Holifield & Atomic Energy Affairs, 1945-1974, 241. LC 89-12005. (Contributions in Political Science Ser.: No. 241). 467p. 1989. 65.00 (*0-313-26244-6*, DYM/, Greenwood Pr) Greenwood.

Dyke, Richard W. & Gannon, Francis X. Chet Holifield: Master Legislator & Nuclear Statesman. LC 95-44386. (Illus.). 392p. (C). 1999. lib. bdg. 45.00 (*0-7618-0171-5*) U Pr of Amer.

Dyke, S. E. Thoughts on the American Flintlock Pistol. LC 74-24435. (Illus.). 52p. 1974. pap. 15.00 (*0-87387-070-0*) Shumway.

Dyke, Stanley F. The Chemistry of Enamines. LC 72-78893. (Cambridge Chemistry Texts Ser.). 101p. 1973. reprint ed. pap. 31.40 (*0-608-08118-3*, 2024440) Bks Demand.

— Organic Spectroscopy: An Introduction. 2nd ed. LC 78-40163. (Illus.). 290p. reprint ed. pap. 89.90 (*0-8357-6585-7*, 203598000097) Bks Demand.

Dyke Parks, Van, see Parks, Van Dyke.

Dyke, Vanessa Van, see Van Dyke, Vanessa.

***Dykema, Earl.** Focus Your Ministry: Developing a Congregational Plan. 96p. 1999. ring bd. 49.95 (*1-56212-422-6*, 1930-0860) CRC Pubns.

Dykema, Frank E. Belgian Sheepdogs. (KW Ser.). (Illus.). 192p. 1990. 9.95 (*0-86622-787-3*, KW-195) TFH Pubns.

***Dykema, Owen W.** An Excellent Adventure in Aviation: Navy Flight Training Circa 1950. 96p. 1999. pap. 14.95 (*0-9660705-4-2*) Dykema Pub Co.

Dykema, Owen W. Legacy of the War Orphans: How We Lost World War II. 37p. 1998. pap. 9.95 (*0-9660705-1-8*) Dykema Pub Co.

— Letters from the Bird Barge. (Illus.). 214p. 1997. pap. 19.95 (*0-9660705-0-X*) Dykema Pub Co.

***Dykema, Owen W.** Unstable Combustion: Trials & Tribulations of a Rocket Scientist. 42p. 1999. pap. 9.95 (*0-9660705-3-4*) Dykema Pub Co.

Dykema, Peter A. & Oberman, Heiko A., eds. Anticlericalism in Late Medieval & Early Modern Europe. LC 92-21783. (Studies in Medieval & Reformation Thought: Vol. 51). xi, 704p. 1994. 272.00 (*90-04-09518-7*) Brill Academic Pubs.

Dykeman, Amy, ed. Automated Acquisitions: Issues for the Present & Future. (Acquisitions Librarian Ser.: Vol. 1). 285p. 1989. 59.95 (*0-86656-913-8*) Haworth Pr.

Dykeman, Cass, ed. Maximizing School Guidance Program Effectiveness: A Guide for School Administrators & Program Directors. 156p. (C). 1998. pap. text 15.00 (*1-56109-083-2*, EC233) CAPS Inc.

Dykeman, Douglas D., et al. Human Adaptations & Cultural Change in the Greater Southwest. 322p. 1989. pap. 29.00 (*1-56349-060-9*, RS32) AR Archaeol.

Dykeman, Peter A. Field Guide to North American Wild Edible Plants. 1991. 24.95 (*1-55654-017-5*) Times Mir Mag Bk Div.

Dykeman, Peter A., jt. auth. see Elias, Thomas S.

Dykeman, Therese B. The Neglected Canon: 9 Women Philosophers from the 12th to the 20th Century. (New Feminist Perspectives Ser.: No. 67). 384p. 1997. 58.50 (*0-8476-8420-2*); pap. 19.95 (*0-8476-8421-0*) Rowman.

Dykeman, Therese B., ed. American Women Philosophers, 1650-1930: Six Exemplary Thinkers. LC 93-9573. (Illus.). 404p. 1993. text 109.95 (*0-7734-9266-6*) E Mellen.

Dykeman, Wilma. Battle of Kings Mountain 1780, with Fire & Sword. 80p. 1991. per. 6.50 (*0-16-061643-3*) USGPO.

Dykeman, Wilma. Explorations. LC 84-52024. 265p. 1984. pap. 10.95 (*0-9613859-7-9*) Wakestone Bks.

— The Far Family. (Illus.). 372p. 1988. reprint ed. 14.95 (*0-9613859-4-4*); reprint ed. pap. 9.95 (*0-9613859-5-2*) Wakestone Bks.

— The French Broad. (Illus.). 382p. 1992. pap. 12.95 (*0-9613859-8-7*) Wakestone Bks.

— Haunting Memories: Echoes & Images of Tennessee's Past. LC 95-41759. (Illus.). 88p. (C). 1996. 32.50 (*0-87049-930-0*) U of Tenn Pr.

— Return the Innocent Earth. 2nd ed. 444p. 1994. pap. 14.95 (*1-884450-01-6*) Wakestone Bks.

— The Tall Woman. LC 62-11580. 315p. 1999. reprint ed. pap. 9.95 (*0-9613859-1-X*) Wakestone Bks.

— Tennessee: A History. rev. ed. 240p. 1993. reprint ed. pap. 10.95 (*0-9613859-9-5*) Wakestone Bks.

— Tennessee Woman: An Infinite Variety. (Illus.). 128p. 1993. 14.95 (*1-884450-00-8*) Wakestone Bks.

Dykeman, Wilma & Stokely, James. Seeds of Southern Change: The Life of Will Alexander. 368p. (C). 1976. reprint ed. pap. 7.00 (*0-393-00813-4*) Norton.

Dykeman, Wilma & Stokely, Jim. Great Smoky Mountains: At Home in the Smokies. LC 84-600108. (Official National Park Handbook Ser.: No. 125). 1984. pap. 8.50 (*0-912627-22-0*) Natl Park Serv.

Dyken, Barbara M. Van, see Van Dyken, Seymour & Van Dyken, Barbara M.

Dyken, Donald Van, see Van Dyken, Donald.

Dyken, M., jt. ed. see Orgogozo, J. M.

Dyken, Seymour Van, see Van Dyken, Seymour.

Dykens, Elisabeth, et al. Behavior & Development in Fragile X Syndrome. (Developmental Clinical Psychology & Psychiatry Ser.: Vol. 28). (Illus.). 112p. (C). 1993. text 42.00 (*0-8039-4887-5*); pap. text 18.95 (*0-8039-4888-3*) Sage.

Dyker, David. National Economies Europe. 337p. (C). 1992. 108.00 (*0-582-05918-6*) Addison-Wesley.

— National Economies of Europe. 337p. (C). 1995. pap. 56.00 (*0-582-05881-3*) Addison-Wesley.

Dyker, David, ed. see Wolverton, Dave.

Dyker, David A. The European Economy. 2nd ed. LC 98-35474. 1999. write for info. (*0-582-29803-2*) Longman.

— The Future of the Soviet Economic Planning System. LC 84-27594. 172p. (gr. 13). 1988. pap. text 42.95 (*0-87332-479-X*) M E Sharpe.

— The Future of the Soviet Economic Planning System. LC 84-27594. (Illus.). 182p. 1985. reprint ed. pap. 56.50 (*0-7837-9979-9*, 206070600006) Bks Demand.

— The National Economies of Europe. LC 92-12829. 1992. pap. text 32.25 (*0-685-72518-9*, 79413) Longman.

Dyker, David A., ed. The European Economy. LC 92-10139. (C). 1992. pap. text 37.50 (*0-582-05883-X*, 79414) Longman.

— The European Economy. LC 92-10139. 364p. (C). 1995. 113.00 (*0-582-05919-4*, 79434) Longman.

— Foreign Direct Investment & Technology Transfer in the Former Soviet Union. LC 98-50844. 336p. 1999. 80.00 (*1-85898-917-5*) E Elgar.

— The Soviet Union under Gorbachev: Prospects for Reform. LC 87-15432. 240p. 1987. lib. bdg. 37.50 (*0-7099-4519-1*, Pub. by C Helm) Routldge.

— The Technology of Transition: Science & Technology Policies for Transition Countries. LC 97-168521. (Illus.). 304p. 1997. 49.95 (*1-85866-050-5*); pap. text 26.95 (*1-85866-051-3*) Ctrl Europ Univ.

***Dyker, David A. & Radoisevic, Slavo.** Innovation & Structural Change in Post-Socialist Countries: A Quantitative Approach. LC 99-46156. (NATO ASI Ser.). 1999. write for info. (*0-7923-5976-3*) Kluwer Academic.

Dyker, David A. & Vejvoda, Ivan, eds. Yugoslavia& After. LC 96-36265. 268p. (C). 1997. pap. text 25.31 (*0-582-24637-7*, Pub. by Addison-Wesley) Longman.

Dykes, jt. auth. see Mckeague.

Dykes, Andrea, tr. see Jung, Emma & Von Franz, Marie-Louise.

Dykes, Andrea, tr. see Von Franz, Marie-Louise.

Dykes, David L. An Easy Course in Using WordPerfect. 358p. 1991. pap. 9.95 (*0-931011-37-X*) Grapevine Pubns.

Dykes, David O. Do Angels Really Exist? Separating Fact from Fantasy. LC 95-78013. 192p. 1996. pap. 10.99 (*1-56384-105-3*) Huntington Hse.

***Dykes, Donald & Verbanic, Carl.** Rauch Guide to U. S. Rubber Industry. (Illus.). 300p. (C). 1999. pap. 445.00 (*0-932157-06-8*) Impact Mrkting.

Dykes, Donald, jt. auth. see Verbanic, Carl.

Dykes, Donald, ed. see Rauch, James A.

Dykes, Donald, jt. ed. see Verbanic, Carl.

Dykes, Fran, ed. see Hall, Frances S.

Dykes, Harvey, jt. auth. see Williams, A. C.

Dykes, James B. Crossword Busters. 1996. mass mkt. 5.99 (*0-425-15419-X*) Berkley Pub.

Dykes, Jeff C., jt. auth. see Dobie, J. Frank.

Dykes, Joan. HarperCollins College Outline Introduction to Calculus. LC 91-58268. (Outline Ser.). 256p. (C). 1992. pap. 15.00 (*0-06-467125-9*, Harper Ref) HarpC.

— HCO Elementary Algebra. LC 90-56204. (College Outline Ser.). (Illus.). 304p. 1991. pap. 15.00 (*0-06-467118-6*, Harper Ref) HarpC.

— HCO Intermediate Algebra. LC 91-55387. (College Outline Ser.). 368p. 1992. pap. 14.00 (*0-06-467137-2*, Harper Ref) HarpC.

Dykes, M. T. A Time to Kill. LC 82-6811. 1989. pap. 12.95 (*0-87949-223-6*) Ashley Bks.

Dykes, Mary Ann. The Herb Book. McDaniel, Jodi, ed. LC 97-186679. (Illus.). 112p. (Orig.). 1996. pap. 14.95 (*0-9651890-0-7*) HealingLink Srvs.

***Dykes, Mary Ann.** The Herb Book II. rev. ed. Tracey, Deborah, ed. xii, 144p. 2000. pap. 22.00 (*0-9651890-1-5*) HealingLink Srvs.

Dykes, Patricia C. Psychiatric Clinical Pathways: An Interdisciplinary Approach. LC 98-5909. 400p. 1998. 60.00 (*0-8342-1156-4*, 11564) Aspen Pub.

Dykes, Patricia C. & Wheeler, Kathleen, eds. Planning, Implementing & Evaluating Critical Pathways: A Guide for Health Care Survival into the 21st Century. LC 97-16500. 184p. 1997. 34.95 (*0-8261-9790-6*) Springer Pub.

Dykes, Spike, jt. auth. see Bobo, Mike.

Dykes, Tomoko T., tr. see Tsuchiya, Yukio.

Dykes, William R. The Genus Iris. 1974. reprint ed. 35.00 (*0-486-23037-6*) Dover.

— A Handbook of Garden Irises. LC 75-42381. (Illus.). 1976. reprint ed. write for info. (*0-685-78307-3*) Theophrastus.

Dykewoman, Elana. Beyond the Pale. LC PS3564.A27B4 1997. 1997. pap. 15.95 (*0-88974-074-7*, Pub. by Press Gang Pubs) LPC InBook.

Dykewomon, Elana. Nothing Will Be As Sweet As the Taste. 1995. pap. 9.99 (*0-906500-57-5*) LPC InBook.

Dykgraaf & Bolt. Little Ones Need Jesus. 57p. 1996. pap. 2.95 (*1-56212-162-6*) CRC Pubns.

Dykgraff, Diane & Fennema, Deb. Story Hour: Year One. LC 99-164579. 658p. (J). 1998. ring bd. 96.95 (*1-56212-339-4*, 1950-1000) CRC Pubns.

***Dykinga, Jack W., photos by.** Desert: The Mojave & Death Valley. LC 99-25454. (Illus.). 143p. 1999. 49.50 (*0-8109-3238-5*, Pub. by Abrams) Time Warner.

Dykinga, Jack W., photos by. The Secret Forest. LC 92-34880. (Illus.). 154p. 1993. reprint ed. pap. 47.80 (*0-608-04140-8*, 206487300011) Bks Demand.

— The Sonoran Desert. (Illus.). 167p. 1997. pap. 24.95 (*0-8109-2669-5*, Pub. by Abrams) Time Warner.

— Stone Canyons of the Colorado Plateau. LC 95-40455. (Illus.). 128p. 1996. 45.00 (*0-8109-4468-5*, Pub. by Abrams) Time Warner.

Dykman, Charlene A., jt. auth. see Ruthstrom, Carl R.

Dykman-Gastwirth, Esther, compiled by. Determination, Courage, Destiny. LC 92-30855. 1992. write for info. (*0-9622584-2-3*) Oceanco Ltd.

Dykman, Judy & Whitley, Colleen. The Silver Queen: Her Royal Highness Suzanne Bransford Emery Holmes Delitch Engalitcheff, 1859-1942. (Illus.). 200p. 1998. pap. 19.95 (*0-87421-237-5*) Utah St U Pr.

— The Silver Queen: Her Royal Highness Suzanne Bransford Emery Holmes Delitch Engalitcheff, 1859-1942. (Illus.). 200p. 1998. 34.95 (*0-87421-240-5*) Utah St U Pr.

Dykova, Iva & Lom, Jiri. Protozoan Parasites of Fishes. (Developments in Aquaculture & Fisheries Science Ser.: Vol. 26). 316p. 1992. 207.50 (*0-444-89434-9*) Elsevier.

Dykova, Iva, jt. auth. see Lom, Jiri.

Dykson, Wayne. TEC X Windows. 1991. pap. write for info. (*0-201-41897-5*) Addison-Wesley.

Dykstal, Timothy, jt. ed. see Backscheider, Paula R.

Dykstra. Physical Chemistry: Modern Introduction. (C). 1997. teacher ed. write for info. (*0-13-633017-7*, Macmillan Coll) P-H.

***Dykstra.** Rhythms 1999. pap. text 29.07 (*0-395-91807-3*) HM.

Dykstra, Andrew. The Kanji ABC. LC 76-58964. (Illus.). 186p. 1990. pap. text 16.00 (*0-917880-00-5*) Kanji Pr.

— Kanji One-Two-Three. LC 82-14007. (Illus.). 220p. (Orig.). 1990. pap. text 16.00 (*0-917880-01-3*) Kanji Pr.

— Laughing Stories of Old Japan. 120p. 1987. pap. 8.95 (*0-917880-03-X*) Kanji Pr.

Dykstra, Ann M. Region, Economy, & Party: The Roots of Party Formation in Pennsylvania, 1820-1860. (Nineteenth Century American Political & Social History Ser.). 400p. 1990. reprint ed. 25.00 (*0-8240-4065-1*) Garland.

Dykstra, Art. Outcome Management: Achieving Outcomes for People with Disabilities. Lubertozzi, Alex, ed. (Illus.). 162p. 1995. 27.50 (*1-57654-000-6*) High Tide Pr.

— Outcome Management: Achieving Outcomes for People with Disabilities. (Illus.). 162p. 1996. reprint ed. 27.50 (*0-9653744-0-8*) High Tide Pr.

— When Bad Things Happen in Good Organizations. 175p. 2001. 24.50 (*0-9653744-2-4*) High Tide Pr.

Dykstra, Art, jt. ed. see Dykstra, Thane.

Dykstra, B. Amusement Park, USA: Piano Amusement Song. 43p. 1985. pap. 6.95 (*0-89898-270-7*) Centerstream Pub.

— Great Ragtime Tunes: Simplified & Arranged for Piano. 48p. 1983. pap. 5.95 (*1-57424-089-7*, Centerbrook Publishing) Centerstream Pub.

— It's a Ragtime Christmas: Christmas Songs for Piano in the Ragtime Style. (Illus.). 44p. 1985. pap. 5.95 (*1-57424-088-9*, Centerbrook Publishing) Centerstream Pub.

Dykstra, Brian. Peter Rabbit Plays Piano. 46p. (Orig.). 1988. pap. text 7.95 (*0-931759-29-3*) Centerstream Pub.

Dykstra, Clifford E. Introduction to Quantum Chemistry. 301p. (C). 1993. pap. text 26.40 (*0-13-701293-4*) P-H.

Dykstra, Craig R. Growing in the Life of Faith: Education & Christian Practices. LC 99-11554. 192p. 1999. pap. 18.95 (*0-664-50033-1*) Geneva Press.

Dykstra, D. P. & Heinrich, R. FAO Model Code of Forest Harvesting Practice. 96p. 1996. pap. 27.00 (*92-5-103690-X*, F3690X, Pub. by FAO) Bernan Associates.

Dykstra, Darrell I. Egypt in the Nineteenth Century: The Impact of Europe Upon a Non-Western Society. (Orig.). (YA). (gr. 10-12). 1979. pap. text 6.00 (*0-932098-15-0*) UM Ctr MENAS.

Dykstra, David L. The Shifting Balance of Power: American-British Diplomacy in North America, 1842-1848. LC 99-18694. 288p. 1999. 39.00 (*0-7618-1363-2*) U Pr of Amer.

Dykstra, Dewey I., jt. auth. see Fuller, Robert G.

Dykstra, Gerald, et al, eds. Composition: Guided-Free. LC 73-76064. 1974. pap. text 3.95 (*0-8077-2385-1*); pap. text 3.95 (*0-8077-2386-X*) Tchrs Coll.

— Composition: Guided-Free. LC 73-76064. 1974. teacher ed. 3.95 (*0-8077-2383-5*); pap. text 3.95 (*0-8077-2387-8*) Tchrs Coll.

Dykstra, Gerald, et al. Composition: Guided Free Program 5, Grades 5-7. 1978. pap. text 3.95 (*0-8077-2389-4*) Tchrs Coll.

— Composition: Guided Free Program 7, Grades 7-9. 1978. pap. text 3.95 (*0-8077-2391-6*) Tchrs Coll.

— Composition: Guided Free Program 8, Grades 8-10. 1978. pap. text 3.95 (*0-8077-2392-4*) Tchrs Coll.

— Teachers Manual for Composition: Guided-Free for Programs 5 Through 8. LC 73-76064. (Illus.). 42p. reprint ed. pap. 30.00 (*0-608-08846-3*, 206948500004) Bks Demand.

Dykstra, Gino, jt. auth. see Bailey, Keith.

Dykstra, Gino, ed. see Bailey, Keith.

Dykstra, Gino, illus. see Bailey, Keith.

Dykstra, Linda H. Marriage Owner's Manual. 2nd rev. ed. (Illus.). xvii, 214p. 1998. pap. 14.95 (*0-9665503-0-7*) Medit Ctr Grnd.

Dykstra, M. J. Biological Electron Microscopy: Theory, Techniques & Troubleshooting. (Illus.). 380p. (C). 1992. text 54.50 (*0-306-44277-9*, Kluwer Plenum) Kluwer Academic.

Dykstra, Mary. Precis: A Primer. rev. ed. LC 87-17617. 280p. 1988. reprint ed. pap. 23.50 (*0-8108-2060-9*) Scarecrow.

Dykstra, Michael J. A Manual of Applied Techniques for Biological Electron Microscopy. LC 93-23118. (Illus.). 272p. (C). 1993. text 39.50 (*0-306-44449-6*, Kluwer Plenum) Kluwer Academic.

Dykstra, Monique. My Heart on the Yukon River. LC 97-26116. (Illus.). 136p. (Orig.). 1997. pap. 24.95 (*0-87422-157-9*) Wash St U Pr.

Dykstra, Pearl A. Next of (Non) Kin: The Importance of Primary Relationships for Adults' Well Being. viii, 248p. 1990. 40.75 (*90-265-1104-3*) Swets.

Dykstra, Pearl A., jt. ed. see Van Wissen, Leo J. G.

Dykstra, R. L., et al, eds. Advances in Order Restricted Statistical Inference. (Lecture Notes in Statistics Ser.: Vol. 37). (Illus.). viii, 295p. 1986. 79.95 (*0-387-96419-3*) Spr-Verlag.

Dykstra, Robert C. Counseling Troubled Youth. LC 97-20101. (Counseling & Pastoral Theology Ser.). 1997. pap. 16.00 (*0-664-25654-6*) Westminster John Knox.

***Dykstra, Robert C.** Discovering a Sermon: Personal Pastoral Preaching. 2000. pap. 18.99 (*0-8272-0627-5*) Chalice Pr.

Dykstra, Robert R. Bright Radical Star: Black Freedom & White Supremacy on the Hawkeye Frontier. LC 92-15672. 360p. 1993. text 58.50 (*0-674-08180-3*) HUP.

— Bright Radical Star: Black Freedom & White Supremacy on the Hawkeye Frontier. LC 97-5570. (Illus.). 366p. 1997. pap. 29.95 (*0-8138-2308-0*) Iowa St U Pr.

— The Cattle Towns. LC 83-6485. (Illus.). xii, 412p. 1983. reprint ed. pap. 15.00 (*0-8032-6561-1*, Bison Books) U of Nebr Pr.

Dykstra, Thane & Dykstra, Art, eds. Handbook for Qualified Mental Retardation Professionals. 300p. 2001. lib. bdg. 49.95 (*0-9653744-3-2*) High Tide Pr.

Dykstra, Yoshiko, tr. see Kajiyama, Toshiyuki.

Dykstra, Yoshiko K., tr. & anno. see Chingen.

Dylan, Bob. The Best of Bob Dylan. 71p. 1997. pap. text 17.95 (*0-7119-7003-3*, AM950060) Music Sales.

— Bob Dylan: Harmonica. 1996. pap. text 16.95 (*0-7119-5196-9*, AM931240) Omnibus NY.

D

— Bob Dylan Anthology: 50 More Songs from the Pen of One of This Generation's Most Distinct..., Vol. 2. 1996. pap. 21.95 (*0-8256-1530-5*, AM 934384) Music Sales.
— Bob Dylan (Leatherette Folio) (Illus.). 178p. 1993. pap. 21.95 (*0-8256-1367-1*, AM91466) Music Sales.
***Dylan, Bob.** Bob Dylan Rock Score. 2000. pap. 19.95 (*0-7119-2194-6*) Music Sales.
Dylan, Bob. Classic Dylan. (Illus.). 176p. 1992. pap. 21.95 (*0-8256-1289-6*, AM80185) Music Sales.
— The Consise Bob Dylan. 50p. 1997. pap. text 24.95 (*0-7119-5780-0*, AM937200) Music Sales.
— Dylan: World Gone Wrong. 1994. pap. 14.95 (*0-8256-1402-3*, AM91775) Music Sales.
— Good As I Been to You. (Illus.). 32p. 1993. pap. 12.95 (*0-8256-1511-9*, AM91048) Music Sales.
— Lyrics, 1962-1985. 2nd ed. 500p. 1985. 35.00 (*0-394-54278-9*) Knopf.
— Lyrics, 1962-1998. rev. ed. LC 97-17101. 1999. 35.00 (*0-679-43913-7*) Villard Books.
***Dylan, Bob.** Man Gave Names to All the Animals. LC 98-28826. (Illus.). 32p. (J). (ps-2). 1999. 16.00 (*0-15-202005-5*, Harcourt Child Bks) Harcourt.
Dylan, Bob. Tarantula: Poems. LC 93-37274. 160p. 1993. pap. 13.95 (*0-312-10554-1*) St Martin.
Dylan, Jamie. Guide to Owning a Bichon Frise: AKC Rank #30. (Guide to Owning Ser.). (Illus.). 64p. 1995. pap. 6.95 (*0-7938-1868-0*, RE-318) TFH Pubns.
***Dylewski, Mary.** Science: A Reference for Students & Parents. 64p. (J). (gr. 3-7). 1999. pap. 6.95 (*0-8167-5526-4*) Troll Communs.
D'yley, Enid F. Animal Fables & Other Tales Retold: Africa in the New World. LC 87-73226. 40p. (Orig.). (J). (gr. 1-7). 1989. 12.95 (*0-86543-075-6*); pap. 5.95 (*0-86543-076-4*) Africa World.
Dylis, N., jt. auth. see Sukachev, V.
Dyllansow Truran Staff. Canow Kernow. (C). 1989. 40.00 (*0-907566-25-1*, Pub. by Dyllansow Truran) St Mut.
— The Carols of Thomas Merritt. (C). 1989. 40.00 (*0-9506431-7-3*, Pub. by Dyllansow Truran) St Mut.
— Names for the Cornish. (C). 1989. 25.00 (*0-907566-94-4*, Pub. by Dyllansow Truran) St Mut.
Dyllansow Truran Staff, ed. Cornish Voices. (C). 1989. 50.00 (*0-907566-21-9*, Pub. by Dyllansow Truran) St Mut.
Dylong, John. The Spirituality of Work: Visual Artists. 48p. 1995. pap. 2.95 (*0-87946-126-8*) ACTA Pubns.
Dym. Atlas of Minor Oral Surgery. Date not set. text. write for info. (*0-7216-7977-3*, W B Saunders Co) Harcrt Hlth Sci Grp.
Dym, Clive L. Engineering Design: A Synthesis of Views. (Illus.). 223p. (C). 1994. pap. text 23.95 (*0-521-47760-3*) Cambridge U Pr.
— Introduction to the Theory of Shells. rev. ed. 160p. 1990. 52.95 (*1-56032-052-4*) Hemisp Pub.
— Stability Theory & Its Applications to Structural Mechanics. (Mechanics of Elastic Stability Ser.: No. 3). 200p. 1974. text 87.50 (*90-286-0094-9*) Kluwer Academic.
Dym, Clive L. & Ivey, Elizabeth. Principles of Mathematical Modeling. LC 79-65441. (Computer Science & Applied Mathematics Ser.). 261p. 1980. text 71.00 (*0-12-226550-5*) Acad Pr.
Dym, Clive L. & Levitt, Ray E. Knowledge-Based Systems in Engineering. 432p. 1991. teacher ed. write for info. (*0-07-018564-6*) McGraw.
— Knowledge-Based Systems in Engineering. 432p. (C). 1991. text 74.75 (*0-07-018563-8*) McGraw.
***Dym, Clive L. & Little, Patrick.** Engineering Design: A Project-Based Introduction. LC 99-26896. 304p. 1999. pap. 40.95 (*0-471-28296-0*) Wiley.
Dym, Clive L. & Shames, Irving H. Energy & Finite Element Methods in Structural Mechanics: SI Units Edition. 1991. write for info. (*81-224-0749-8*, Pub. by Wiley Estrn) Franklin.
Dym, E. D. Subject Analysis Methodologies. (Books in Library & Information Sciences: 47). (Illus.). 512p. 1985. text 99.75 (*0-8247-7354-3*) Dekker.
Dym, H. Topics in Interpolation Theory. LC 97-8157. (Operator Theory, Advances & Applications Ser.). 1997. write for info. (*0-8176-5723-1*) Birkhauser.
Dym, H., et al, eds. Topics in Interpolation Theory. LC 97-8157. (Operator Theory Ser.: No. 95). 450p. 1997. 130.00 (*3-7643-5723-1*) Birkhauser.
Dym, Harry. J Contractive Matrix Functions, Reproducing Kernel Hilbert Spaces & Interpolation. LC 89-6802. (CBMS Regional Conference Series in Mathematics: No. 71). 160p. 1989. pap. 25.00 (*0-8218-0722-6*, CBMS/71) Am Math.
Dym, Harry, et al, eds. Topics in Operator Theory Systems & Networks, Vol. 12. (Operator Theory Ser.). 300p. 1984. 75.00 (*3-7643-1550-4*) Birkhauser.
Dym, Harry & McKean, Henry P. Fourier Series & Integrals. (Probability & Mathematical Statistics Ser.). 1985. pap. text 59.00 (*0-12-226451-7*) Acad Pr.
Dym, Harry, et al. The Gohberg Anniversary Collection, 2 vols., Set. 900p. 1989. 267.00 (*0-8176-2283-7*) Birkhauser.
— The Gohberg Anniversary Collection: The Calgary Conference & Matrix Theory Papers, Vol. 1. (Operator Theory Ser.: No. 40). 504p. 1989. 139.00 (*0-8176-2307-8*) Birkhauser.
— The Gohberg Anniversary Collection: Topics in Analysis & Operator Theory, Vol. 2, No. 41. 500p. 1989. 156.00 (*0-8176-2308-6*) Birkhauser.
Dym, Joseph B. Product Design with Plastics: A Practical Manual. LC 82-3091. (Illus.). 288p. (C). 1982. 32.95 (*0-8311-1141-0*) Indus Pr.
Dymacek, Wayne M. & Sharp, Henry. Introduction to Discrete Mathematics. LC 97-5717. 720p. (C). 1997. 63.75 (*0-07-018566-2*) McGraw.
Dymally, Mervyn M., jt. auth. see Elliot, Jeffrey M.
Dymalski, Stacy. Interleaf Exercise Book, 5. LC 94-66166. 224p. (C). 1993. pap. 46.95 (*1-56690-041-7*) Thomson Learn.
— Interleaf Tips & Tricks, 5. LC 94-65057. 528p. 1994. pap. 54.95 (*1-56690-050-6*) Thomson Learn.
Dyman, Jenni. Lurking Feminism: The Ghost Stories of Edith Wharton. LC 94-36238. (American University Studies Series XXIV: American Literature: Vol. 62). XX, 199p. (C). 1996. text 44.95 (*0-8204-2697-0*) P Lang Pubng.
Dymkowski, Christine. Harley Granville Barker: A Preface to Modern Shakespeare. LC 84-46123. (Illus.). 240p. 1986. 42.50 (*0-918016-82-7*) Folger Bks.
Dymkowski, Christine, ed. see Shakespeare, William.
Dymling, Claes, ed. Architect Sigurd Lewerentz, 2 vols. Incl. Vol. I. Photographs of the Work. LC 98-191349. (Illus.). 180p. 1997. 99.50 (*91-7988-025-8*, Pub. by Byggforlaget); Vol. II. Drawings. LC 98-191349. (Illus.). 128p. 1997. 99.50 (*91-7988-027-4*, Pub. by Byggforlaget); LC 98-191349. (Illus.). 308p. 1997. 197.50 (*91-7988-066-5*, Pub. by Byggforlaget) Coronet Bks.
Dymmoch, Michael A. Incendiary Designs. LC 98-19413. 304p. 1998. 22.95 (*0-312-19245-2*, Thomas Dunne) St Martin.
— The Man Who Understood Cats. 224p. 1995. mass mkt. 4.99 (*0-380-72265-8*, Avon Bks) Morrow Avon.
Dymnikov, V. & Filatov, A. H. Mathematics of Climate Modeling. LC 96-47912. 346p. 1997. write for info. (*3-7643-3915-2*) Birkhauser.
Dymnikov, V. P. & Filatov, A. N. Mathematics of Climate Modelling. LC 96-47912. 300p. 1996. 64.50 (*0-8176-3915-2*) Birkhauser.
Dymock, A. Materia Medica of W. India. (C). 1986. 140.00 (*0-7855-2264-6*, Pub. by Scientific) St Mut.
Dymock, Eric. The Jaguar File. (Illus.). 416p. 1998. 46.95 (*0-85429-983-1*, Pub. by GT Foulis) Haynes Manuals.
— Jim Clark: Tribute to a Champion. LC 96-79738. 256p. 1997. write for info. (*0-85429-982-3*, Pub. by GT Foulis) Haynes Manuals.
— Saab. (Illus.). 192p. 1997. 56.95 (*0-85429-981-5*) Haynes Manuals.
Dymock, W. Pharmacographia Indica, Vols. 1-3. (C). 1988. 410.00 (*0-7855-2266-2*, Pub. by Scientific) St Mut.
Dymoke, Juliet. Cassie's Captain. large type ed. (Ulverscroft Large Print Ser.). 544p. 1998. 29.99 (*0-7089-3892-2*) Ulverscroft.
— A Fragile Marriage. large type ed. 528p. 1996. 27.99 (*0-7089-3536-2*) Ulverscroft.
— The Making of Molly March. large type ed. (Ulverscroft Large Print Ser.). 528p. 1997. 27.99 (*0-7089-3734-9*) Ulverscroft.
— Winter's Daughter. large type ed. 752p. 1995. 27.99 (*0-7089-3293-2*) Ulverscroft.
Dymond, Andrew, jt. auth. see Kayani, Rogati A.
Dymond, Bill, jt. auth. see Hart, Michael.
***Dymond, Christine.** Designer Doodles: 12 International Designs for You to Hand-Colour & Frame. (Illus.). 2000. pap. 9.95 (*0-85532-858-4*) Srch Pr.
***Dymond, D. S.** An Atlas of Myocardial Infarction. 2nd ed. (Illus.). 2001. write for info. (*1-84214-024-8*) Prthnon Pub.
Dymond, David, ed. The Register of Thetford Priory, 1518-1540, Pt. 2. LC 96-144310. (Records of Social & Economic History, New Series British Academy: No. 25). (Illus.). 548p. 1997. text 95.00 (*0-19-726161-2*) OUP.
— The Register of Thetford Priory, 1482-1517, Vol. 1. LC 96-144310. (Records of Social & Economic History, British Academy New Ser.). (Illus.). 406p. (C). 1996. text 95.00 (*0-19-726160-4*) OUP.
Dymond, David, jt. auth. see Betterton, Alec.
Dymond, Detta, ed. see Dymond, Kenneth M.
Dymond, Detta, ed. see Dymond, Kenneth N.
Dymond, Dorothy W. "God, How Do I Talk to You?" A Children's Color & Workbook on Prayer. 2nd ed. (Illus.). 36p. (J). (gr. 4-6). 1995. reprint ed. pap., spiral bd. 9.95 (*0-9665322-0-1*) Jewel Pr FL.
Dymond, Duncan S. An Atlas of Myocardial Infraction: And Related Cardiovascular Complications. LC 94-21976. (Encyclopedia of Visual Medicine Ser.). 136p. 1994. 85.00 (*1-85070-505-4*) Prthnon Pub.
Dymond, J. N., et al. Rare Birds in Britain & Ireland. (Illus.). 480p. 1990. text (*0-85661-053-4*) Poyser.
Dymond, Jonathan. War, an Essay. 1973. 59.95 (*0-8490-1275-9*) Gordon Pr.
Dymond, Kenneth F., jt. ed. see Carruthers, George R.
Dymond, Kenneth M. Assessment Coordinator's Handbook: Planning for a Well-Orchestrated Software Appraisal. Dymond, Detta, ed. 41p. (Orig.). 1997. pap. text 35.00 (*0-9646008-1-1*) Process Transition.
— A Guide to the CMM: Understanding the Capability Maturity Model for Software. Dymond, Detta, ed. LC 95-92116. (Illus.). 221p. (Orig.). 1998. pap. text 28.00 (*0-9646008-0-3*) Process Transition.
Dymond, Kenneth N. Una Guia del CMM: Comprender el Modelo de Madurez de Capacidad del Software. Dymond, Detta, ed. Grupo SOMEPRO Staff, tr. (SPA., Illus.). 1997. pap. text 35.00 (*0-9646008-2-X*) Process Transition.
Dymond, Lura. Concord's Dynamic Half Century: 1940s to the Present. Parks, Lori, ed. LC 99-73075. (Illus.). 250p. 2000. 39.95 (*1-886483-37-X*, Pub. by Heritge Media) Sunbelt Pubns.
Dymond, Ruby. Threads of Circumstance. 206p. 1987. 30.00 (*0-7212-0733-2*, Pub. by Regency Pr GBR) St Mut.
***Dymond, Steve.** Researching British Military Medals. (Illus.). 128p. 2000. 34.95 (*1-86126-282-5*, 129776AE, Pub. by Crolwood) Motorbooks Intl.
Dymshits, Valery. Facing West: Oriental Jews of Central Asia & the Caucasus. LC 98-184836. (Illus.). 128p. 1998. pap. 30.00 (*90-400-9216-8*, Pub. by Waandrs) Consort Bk Sales.
Dymski, J. Daniel. A Caregiver's Companion: Ministering to Older Adults. LC 98-44186. 176p. 1999. pap. 8.95 (*0-87793-673-0*) Ave Maria.
Dymski, Gary & Pollin, Robert, eds. New Perspectives in Monetary Macroeconomics: Explorations in the Tradition of Hyman P. Minsky. LC 93-45596. 424p. 1994. text 70.00 (*0-472-10472-1*, 10472) U of Mich Pr.
Dymski, Gary A. Bank Merger Wave: The Economic Causes & Social Consequences of Financial Consolidation. LC 98-37065. (Issues in Money, Banking, & Finance Ser.). 344p. 1999. text 69.95 (*0-7656-0382-9*) M E Sharpe.
— The Bank Merger Wave: The Economic Causes & Social Consequences of Financial Consolidation. LC 98-37065. (Issues in Money, Banking, & Finance Ser.). 344p. 1999. pap. text 27.95 (*0-7656-0383-7*) M E Sharpe.
Dymski, Gary A., et al, eds. Transforming the U. S. Financial System: Equity & Efficiency for the 21st Century. LC 93-23796. (Economic Policy Institute Ser.). 384p. (C). (gr. 13). 1993. text 87.95 (*1-56324-268-0*); pap. text 42.95 (*1-56324-269-9*) M E Sharpe.
Dymsza, William A. & Vambery, Robert G., eds. International Business Knowledge: Managing International Functions in the 1990's. LC 86-20460. 593p. 1986. 42.95 (*0-275-92308-8*, C2308, Praeger Pubs) Greenwood.
Dynamic Learning Staff. Getting Audiences on Feet. 104p. 1998. per. 24.95 (*0-7872-5444-4*, 41544401) Kendall-Hunt.
— Not Just Games: Strategic Uses of Experiential Learning to Drive Business Results. 86p. 1996. pap. text, per. 19.95 (*0-7872-1985-1*) Kendall-Hunt.
Dynamic Publishing Editors. Essiac - Concept Herbal Essence: The Ultimate Optimizer & Detoxifier. (You Need to Know about This Ser.: Vol. 1). 48p. 1996. 4.95 (*0-9651551-0-2*) Dynamic Pubng.
Dynamic Solutions Staff. Color Separation Demo. (Illus.). 49.95 (*0-8273-8025-9*, Pub. by Delmar) Thomson Learn.
— Color Trapping Demo. (Illus.). 49.95 (*0-8273-8024-0*, Pub. by Delmar) Thomson Learn.
Dynatech Corporation Staff. Electrically Insulating Thermally Conducting Copper Materials. 88p. 1962. 13.20 (*0-317-34519-2*, 14) Intl Copper.
Dynatech R-D Company, jt. auth. see Haines, D. M.
Dynatech R-D Company Staff & Walker, D. H. Use & Conservation of Natural Gas in the Steel Industry. 115p. 1977. pap. 5.50 (*0-318-12727-X*, M60377) Am Gas Assn.
Dyncan, Ronny R. International Germplasm Transfer: Past & Present. LC 96-1969. (Special Publication Ser.: Vol. 23). 206p. 1995. 30.00 (*0-89118-540-2*) Crop Sci Soc Am.
Dyne, Barbara Van, see Van Dyne, Barbara.
Dyne, Glen Van, see Van Dyne, Glen.
Dyne, Glen Van, see Bowers, Curt & Van Dyne, Glen.
Dyne, Glen Van, see Van Dyne, Glen.
Dyne, Michael. The Right Honourable Gentleman. 1967. pap. 5.25 (*0-8222-0951-9*) Dramatists Play.
Dynerman, Susan B. Are Our Kids All Right? Answers to the Tough Questions about Child Care Today. 384p. 1995. pap. text 12.95 (*1-56079-576-X*) Petersons.
Dynes, Russell R. & Tierney, Kathleen J., eds. Disasters, Collective Behavior, & Social Organization. LC 93-46766. (C). 1994. 49.50 (*0-87413-498-6*) U Delaware Pr.
Dynes, Russell R., jt. ed. see Dudden, Arthur P.
Dynes, Wayne R. Homosexuality: A Research Guide. LC 85-45109. 880p. 1987. text 20.00 (*0-8240-8692-9*) Garland.
— Turning the Corner: Abstraction at the End of the Twentieth Century. LC 97-177348. (Illus.). 32p. 1997. pap. 5.00 (*1-885998-09-0*) Hunter College.
Dynes, Wayne R., ed. Encyclopedia of Homosexuality, 2 vols. LC 89-28128. 1522p. 1990. 150.00 (*0-8240-6544-1*) Garland.
— Ethnographic Studies of Homosexuality. LC 92-14694. (Studies in Homosexuality: Vol. 2). 424p. 1992. text 94.00 (*0-8153-0547-8*) Garland.
Dynes, Wayne R. & Donaldson, Stephen, eds. Asian Homosexuality. LC 92-15208. (Studies in Homosexuality: Vol. 3). (Illus.). 392p. 1992. text 77.00 (*0-8153-0548-6*) Garland.
— History of Homosexuality in Europe & America. LC 92-12980. (Studies in Homosexuality: Vol. 5). 448p. 1992. text 77.00 (*0-8153-0550-8*) Garland.
— Homosexual Themes in Literary Studies, 8. LC 92-13897. (Studies in Homosexuality: Vol. 8). 416p. 1992. text 94.00 (*0-8153-0553-2*) Garland.
— Homosexuality & Government, Politics & Prisons. LC 92-13896. (Studies in Homosexuality: Vol. 10). (Illus.). 456p. 1992. text 94.00 (*0-8153-0555-9*) Garland.
— Homosexuality & Homosexuals in the Arts. LC 92-14722. (Studies in Homosexuality: Vol. 4). (Illus.). 464p. 1992. text 94.00 (*0-8153-0549-4*) Garland.
— Homosexuality & Medicine, Health & Science. LC 92-13993. (Studies in Homosexuality: Vol. 9). 360p. 1992. text 88.00 (*0-8153-0554-0*) Garland.
— Homosexuality in the Ancient World. LC 92-13991. (Studies in Homosexuality: Vol. 1). (Illus.). 520p. 1992. text 110.00 (*0-8153-0546-X*) Garland.
— Lesbianism. LC 92-15643. (Studies in Homosexuality: Vol. 7). 416p. 1992. text 77.00 (*0-8153-0552-4*) Garland.
— Sociology of Homosexuality. LC 92-13735. (Studies in Homosexuality: Vol. 13). (Illus.). 432p. 1992. text 99.00 (*0-8153-0768-3*) Garland.
Dynkin, E. B. Markov Processes & Related Problems of Analysis. LC 81-38438. (London Mathematical Society Lecture Note Ser.: No. 54). 320p. reprint ed. pap. 91.20 (*0-608-17519-6*, 2030605) Bks Demand.
Dynkin, E. B., et al. Eleven Papers on Analysis, Probability & Topology. LC 51-5559. (Translations Ser.: Series 2, Vol. 12). 342p. 1959. reprint ed. 38.00 (*0-8218-1712-4*, TRANS2/12) Am Math.
— Five Papers on Algebra & Group Theory. LC QA0385.. (American Mathematical Society, Translations Series 2: Vol. 6). 487p. 1957. pap. text 151.00 (*0-608-05160-8*, 202965900062) Bks Demand.
***Dynkin, E. B., et al.** Selected Papers of E. B. Dynkin. LC 99-35175. 798p. 1999. 128.00 (*0-8218-1065-0*) Am Math.
Dynkin, E. B., et al. Six Lectures Delivered at the International Congress of Mathematicians in Stockholm, 1962. LC 51-5559. (Translations Ser.: Series 2, Vol. 31). 84p. 1963. 23.00 (*0-8218-1731-0*, TRANS2/31) Am Math.
Dynkin, E. G., et al. Mathematical Problems: An Anthology. (Pocket Mathematical Library). viii, 70p. 1967. text 128.00 (*0-677-20710-7*) Gordon & Breach.
Dynkin, Eugene B. An Introduction to Branching Measure-Valued Processes. LC 94-16257. (CRM Monographs: Vol. 6). 134p. 1994. text 48.00 (*0-8218-0269-0*, CRMM/6) Am Math.
Dynneson, Thomas L. & Gross, Richard E. Designing Effective Instruction for Secondary Social Studies. 2nd ed. LC 98-22982. 489p. (C). 1998. 72.00 (*0-13-791732-5*, Merrill Coll) P-H.
Dynneson, Thomas L., jt. ed. see Gross, Richard E.
Dyogot, Ekaterina. Contemporary Painting in Russia. (Illus.). 240p. 1995. text 35.00 (*976-8097-29-9*) Gordon & Breach.
Dyomin, Mikhail. Blatnoi. LC 80-54025. (RUS.). 364p. (Orig.). 1981. pap. 18.50 (*0-89830-027-4*) Russica Pubs.
— Perekrestki Sudeb: Dve povesti. LC 80-54024. (RUS.). 307p. 1983. 29.00 (*0-89830-071-1*); pap. 21.00 (*0-89830-033-9*) Russica Pubs.
— Ryzhii D'Iavol. LC 87-60055. 300p. (Orig.). 1987. pap. 18.00 (*0-89830-110-6*) Russica Pubs.
— Taezhnyi Brodiaga. LC 84-62843. 336p. (Orig.). 1986. pap. 19.00 (*0-89830-094-0*) Russica Pubs.
Dyorak, Max. Idealism & Naturalism in Gothic Art. LC 67-22143. (Illus.). 282p. reprint ed. pap. 87.50 (*0-608-11241-0*, 202207200024) Bks Demand.
Dyos, G. T. & Farrell, T., eds. Electrical Resistivity Handbook. (IEE Materials & Devices Ser.: No. 10). 744p. 1992. 195.00 (*0-86341-266-1*, Pub. by Peregrinus) Dist Unknown.
Dyos, H. J. & Wolff, Michael, eds. Victorian City: Images & Realities, 2 vols. (Illus.). 1352p. (C). 1999. 325.00 (*0-415-19325-7*, D5975) Routledge.
Dyott, R. B. Elliptical Fiber Waveguides. LC 94-44501. 250p. 1995. 37.00 (*0-89006-477-6*) Artech Hse.
Dyrberg, T., ed. The Role Viruses & the Immune System in Diabetes Mellitus. (Current Topics in Microbiology & Immunology Ser.: Vol. 156). (Illus.). 160p. 1990. 95.00 (*0-387-51918-1*) Spr-Verlag.
Dyrberg, Torben. The Circular Structure of Power: Politics, Identity, Community. 1997. 60.00 (*1-85984-846-X*, Pub. by Verso); pap. 20.00 (*1-85984-152-X*, Pub. by Verso) Norton.
Dyrbye, C. D. Wind Load on Structures. LC 96-30346. 244p. 1997. 125.00 (*0-471-95651-1*) Wiley.
***Dyrbye, Helen, et al.** The Xenophobe's Guide to the Danes. (Xenophobe's Guides Ser.). 64p. 1999. pap. 5.95 (*1-902825-24-1*) Oval Bks.
Dyrcz-Freeman, Dosia, tr. see Birenbaum, Halina.
Dyregrov, Atle. Grief in Children: A Handbook for Adults. 144p. 1991. pap. 19.95 (*1-85302-113-X*) Taylor & Francis.
Dyrek, Jerald P. "Nonton" - "The Search For" Anthropic Signature Particles. 320p. 1997. 37.50 (*0-9645447-6-8*); 37.50 (*0-9645447-5-X*) Dyrek-Seaways.
— United States Merchant Marine: Guide to Seaman Opportunities. 2nd ed. LC 94-92148. (Illus.). 432p. 1997. pap. 69.95 (*0-9645447-4-1*) Dyrek-Seaways.
— United States Merchant Marine: Guide to Seaman Opportunities. 2nd rev. ed. LC 94-92148. 432p. 1996. pap. text 69.95 (*0-9645447-0-9*) Dyrek-Seaways.
Dyrenfurth, M., jt. ed. see Blandow, D.
Dyrenfurth, Michael J. Literacy for a Technological World. 37p. 1984. 3.75 (*0-318-22145-4*, IN266) Ctr Educ Trng Employ.
Dyreson, Mark. Making the American Team: Sport, Culture, & the Olympic Experience. LC 97-4663. (Sport & Society Ser.). 296p. 1997. 18.95 (*0-252-06654-5*); text 44.95 (*0-252-02349-8*) U of Ill Pr.
***Dyreson, Patricia A.** A Very Special Egg. (Illus.). 22p. (J). (ps-2). 1999. pap. 8.95 (*0-9676135-0-7*) P A Dyreson.
Dyring, Anna. The Structure of the Nucleon: Precision Measurements of Parton Distributions at Small X. (Uppsala Dissertations from the Faculty of Science Ser.: No. 9). (Illus.). 135p. (Orig.). 1995. pap. 39.50 (*91-554-3608-0*) Coronet Bks.
Dyrness, C. T., jt. auth. see Franklin, Jerry F.
Dyrness, Wayne. Apple Programming Secrets "They Didn't Want You to Know" (Illus.). 256p. 1986. 27.95 (*0-13-039215-4*) P-H.
***Dyrness, William.** Themes in Old Testament Theology. (Biblical & Theological Classics Library: Vol. 24). 218p. 1998. reprint ed. pap. 9.99 (*0-85364-883-2*, Pub. by Paternoster Pub) OM Literature.
Dyrness, William A. The Earth Is God's: A Theology of North American Culture. LC 97-22919. (Faith & Cultures Ser.). 144p. (Orig.). 1997. pap. 16.00 (*1-57075-151-X*) Orbis Bks.
— How Does America Hear the Gospel? fac. ed. LC 89-39253. (Illus.). 176p. 1989. reprint ed. pap. 54.60 (*0-7837-7951-8*, 204770700008) Bks Demand.

D

***Dyrness, William A.** Let the Earth Rejoice: A Biblical Theology of Holistic Mission. 224p. 1998. pap. 20.00 (*1-57910-125-9*) Wipf & Stock.

Dyrness, William A. Let the Earth Rejoice: A Biblical Theology of Holistic Mission. LC 84-82346. 216p. (C). 1991. reprint ed. pap. 18.00 (*0-9602638-3-7*) Fuller Seminary.

— Themes in Old Testament Theology. LC 79-2380. 252p. 1980. pap. 14.99 (*0-87784-726-6*, 726) InterVarsity.

Dyrness, William A., jt. auth. see Engel, James F.

Dyroff, Adolf. Die Ethik der Alten Stoa. Vlastos, Gregory, ed. LC 78-19350. (Morals & Law in Ancient Greece Ser.). (GER & GRE.). 1979. reprint ed. lib. bdg. 33.95 (*0-405-11540-7*) Ayer.

Dyrud, Keith P. The Quest for the Rusyn Soul: The Politics of Religion & Culture in Eastern Europe & in America, World War I, 1890. LC 91-77488. 160p. 1992. 29.50 (*0-944190-10-3*) Balch IES Pr.

Dyrud, Keith P., et al. The Other Catholics. 1978. 36.95 (*0-405-10820-6*) Ayer.

***Dyrud, Loiell.** The Quest for Freedom. 2000. pap. write for info. (*1-58572-042-9*) Ambasdor Pubns.

Dysart, Benjamin C., III & Clawson, Marion, eds. Managing Public Lands in the Public Interest. LC 87-38117. 157p. 1988. 55.00 (*0-275-92990-6*, C2990, Praeger Pubs) Greenwood.

— Public Interest in the Use of Private Lands: Environmental Regeneration. LC 89-3913. 200p. 1989. 57.95 (*0-275-92991-4*, C2991, Praeger Pubs) Greenwood.

Dysart, David L. The Role of the Painting in the Works of Theodor Storm. LC 91-29512. (North American Studies in Nineteenth-Century German Literature: Vol. 11). 161p. (C). 1992. text 35.95 (*0-8204-1690-8*) P Lang Pubng.

Dysart, Dinah & Fink, Hannah. Asian Women Artists. 132p. 1996. text 29.95 (*976-641-077-1*, Pub. by Craftsman House) Gordon & Breach.

Dysart, Jane, ed. Computers in Libraries '98 Conference Proceedings, March 2-4, 1998. 216p. 1998. pap. 15.00 (*1-57387-051-X*) Info Today Inc.

— Internet Librarian '97 Proceedings. 147p. 1997. pap. 10.00 (*1-57387-049-8*) Info Today Inc.

Dysart, Jane I., et al, contrib. by. Internet Librarian '98 Proceedings: The Internet Conference & Exhibition for Librarians & Information Managers. 260p. 1998. pap. 15.00 (*1-57387-067-6*) Info Today Inc.

Dysart, Norman. Bodandy: The Bull. large type ed. (Illus.). 28p. 1999. mass mkt. 7.00 (*0-9654503-1-7*) Dysart Divrsfied.

— Inventing: Can Be Hazardous to Your Health. large type ed. 1999. mass mkt. 7.00 (*0-9654503-2-5*) Dysart Divrsfied.

Dyscolus, Apollonius, jt. auth. see Householder, Fred W.

Dysinger, William. Heaven's Lifestyle Today: Your Health in the Context of Revelation 14. Scoggins, Rebecca, ed. 160p. 1997. pap. 12.95 (*1-57847-003-X*) Genl Conf Svnth-day.

Dysken, jt. ed. see Gibbons, Robert D.

Dyskstra, Andrew. Kanji Ichi Ni. (Kanji Ser.). (Illus.). 208p. (Orig.). (C). 1992. pap. text 16.00 (*0-917880-02-1*) Kanji Pr.

Dyslexia Institute Staff, ed. An ABC Picture Gallery: An ABC of Contemporary Illustrators. (Illus.). 64p. 1999. pap. 14.99 (*0-434-80472-X*) Buttrwrth-Heinemann.

Dyson. Orion. 1999. write for info. (*0-8050-5985-7*) H Holt & Co.

Dyson. Weapons & Hope: International Edition. 1984. 17.95 (*0-06-337037-9*) HarpC.

Dyson, A. Etching & Engraving. Date not set. pap. text. write for info. (*0-582-41347-8*, Pub. by Addison-Wesley) Longman.

Dyson, A. E. The Inimitable Dickens: A Reading of the Novels. LC 70-106204. 303 p. 1970. write for info. (*0-333-06328-7*) Macmillan.

Dyson, A. E., jt. auth. see Cox, C. B.

Dyson, Alan & Gains, Charles, eds. Rethinking Special Needs in Mainstream Schools: Toward the Year 2000. 160p. 1993. pap. 32.50 (*1-85346-221-7*, Pub. by David Fulton) Taylor & Francis.

***Dyson, Alan & Millward, Alan.** Schools & Special Needs: Issues of Innovation & Inclusion. 256p. 2000. pap. 24.95 (*0-7619-6442-8*, Pub. by P Chapman); lib. bdg. 74.00 (*0-7619-6441-X*, Pub. by P Chapman) Sage.

Dyson, Alan, et al. New Directions in Special Needs: Innovation in Mainstream Schools. LC 97-175377. 208p. 1997. pap. 24.95 (*0-304-70024-X*) Continuum.

Dyson, Anne H. Multiple Worlds of Child Writers: Friends Learning to Write. (Early Childhood Education Ser.). 336p. 1989. text 42.00 (*0-8077-2972-8*); pap. text 22.95 (*0-8077-2971-X*) Tchrs Coll.

— Social Worlds of Children Learning to Write in an Urban Primary School. LC 93-25086. (Language & Literacy Ser.). 288p. (C). 1993. text 43.00 (*0-8077-3296-6*); pap. text 19.95 (*0-8077-3295-8*) Tchrs Coll.

— What Difference Does Difference Make? Teacher Reflections on Diversity, Literacy, & the Urban Primary School. LC 96-23993. 158p. (Orig.). 1997. pap. text 16.95 (*0-8141-5657-6*) NCTE.

— Writing Superheroes: Contemporary Childhood, Popular Culture, & Classroom Literacy. LC 97-1488. (Language & Literacy Ser.). (Illus.). 264p. 1997. 46.00 (*0-8077-3640-6*); pap. 21.95 (*0-8077-3639-2*) Tchrs Coll.

Dyson, Anne H. & Genishi, Celia. Language Assessment in the Early Years. Green, Judith & Wallat, Cynthia, eds. LC 84-3074. (Language & Learning for Human Service Professions Ser.: Vol. 4). 276p. (C). 1984. pap. 39.50 (*0-89391-246-8*) Ablx Pub.

— The Need for Story: Cultural Diversity in Classroom & Community. 350p. (Orig.). 1996. pap. text 22.95 (*0-8077-3596-5*) Tchrs Coll.

Dyson, Anne H. & Genishi, Celia, eds. The Need for Story: Cultural Diversity in Classroom & Community. (Illus.). 259p. (Orig.). 1994. pap. text 22.95 (*0-8141-3300-2*) NCTE.

Dyson, Anne H., jt. auth. see Genishi, Celia.

Dyson, Anne J. & Palmer, Helen H. English Novel Explication: Criticisms to 1972. (Novel Explication Ser.). vi, 329p. (C). 1973. lib. bdg. 45.00 (*0-208-01322-9*) Shoe String.

Dyson, Anthony. Looking, Making & Learning: Thinking about Art & Design in the Primary School. 112p. (Orig.). 1989. 20.95 (*0-8464-1417-1*) Beekman Pubs.

— Pictures to Print: The Nineteenth-Century Engraving Trade. (Illus.). 234p. 1985. 35.00 (*0-916271-02-1*) BkPr Ltd.

— Pictures to Print: The Nineteenth-Century Engraving Trade. deluxe ed. (Illus.). 234p. 1985. 115.00 (*0-916271-03-X*) BkPr Ltd.

Dyson, Anthony & Harris, John, eds. Experiments on Embryos. 224p. 1989. 49.95 (*0-415-00749-6*, A3624) Routledge.

Dyson, Anthony E. The Crazy Fabric: Essays in Irony. LC 72-10871. (Essay Index Reprint Ser.). 1977. reprint ed. 18.95 (*0-8369-7214-7*) Ayer.

Dyson, B., jt. auth. see Dyson, Henry V.

Dyson, B. F., et al, eds. Aspects of Materials Metrology & Standards for Structural Performance. LC 93-12669. 1993. write for info. (*1-85861-027-3*, Pergamon Pr) Elsevier.

Dyson, B. F. & Hayhurst, D. R., eds. Materials & Engineering Design: The Next Decade. 500p. 1989. text 110.00 (*0-901462-65-9*, Pub. by Inst Materials) Ashgate Pub Co.

Dyson, Betty, jt. auth. see Dyson, Clegg.

Dyson, Betty, jt. ed. see Jones, Sheila.

Dyson, Brian. A Guide to Local Studies in East Yorkshire. 250p. 1985. 60.00 (*0-907033-33-4*) St Mut.

— Pepper in the Blood. 1996. pap. text 12.95 (*0-9652958-3-4*) Chatham Intl.

Dyson, Byron H., jt. auth. see Forkner, John L.

***Dyson, Cindy.** Brandon Lee. LC 00-26021. (They Died Too Young Ser.). 2000. pap. 16.95 (*0-7910-5858-1*) Chelsea Hse.

— Janet Jackson: Singer. (Black Americans of Achievement Ser.). (Illus.). 144p. 2000. 19.95 (*0-7910-5283-4*); pap. text 9.95 (*0-7910-5284-2*) Chelsea Hse.

Dyson, Clegg & Dyson, Betty. Follow Me. (Kingdom Kids Ser.). 40p. (J). (gr. 3-7). 1995. pap., wbk. ed. 5.99 (*1-884553-15-X*) Discipleshp.

— The Servant King. (Kingdom Kids Ser.). 40p. (J). (gr. 3-7). 1994. pap., wbk. ed. 5.99 (*1-884553-20-6*) Discipleshp.

Dyson, David H. Suggestions for Successful Living: Positive Ideas for the 7 Areas of Life. 72p. 1994. reprint ed. pap. 10.00 (*0-9640187-0-5*) Leave A Legacy.

Dyson, E., et al. Yarn Production & Properties. 96p. 1974. 80.00 (*0-7855-7237-6*) St Mut.

Dyson, Esther. Release 2.1: A Design for Living in the Digital Age. LC 98-34486. 384p. 1998. reprint ed. pap. 14.00 (*0-7679-0012-X*) Broadway BDD.

Dyson, Frances & Kahn, Douglas. Telesthesia. (Illus.). 24p. (Orig.). 1991. pap. 5.00 (*0-930495-12-8*) San Fran Art Inst.

Dyson, Freeman. Origins of Life. 2nd ed. LC 99-21079. (Illus.). 125p. 1999. pap. 12.95 (*0-521-62668-4*) Cambridge U Pr.

Dyson, Freeman J. Imagined Worlds. LC 96-31042. (Jerusalem-Harvard Lectures). (Illus.). 224p. 1997. 22.00 (*0-674-53908-7*) HUP.

— Imagined Worlds. 224p. 1998. pap. 14.00 (*0-674-53909-5*) HUP.

— Innenansichten: Erinnerungen in die Zukunft. Zehnder, Jeanette, tr. from ENG. (Science & Society Ser.: No. 38). Orig. Title: Disturbing the Universe. (GER.). 288p. (C). 1981. 19.95 (*0-8176-1200-9*) Birkhauser.

— Selected Papers of Freeman Dyson: With Commentary. LC 96-6211. (Collected Works Ser.: Vol. 5). (Illus.). 601p. 1996. text 59.00 (*0-8218-0561-4*, CWORKS/5) Am Math.

***Dyson, Freeman J.** The Sun, The Genome, & the Internet: Tools of Scientific Revolution. 2000. pap. 10.95 (*0-19-513922-4*) OUP.

Dyson, Freeman J. The Sun, the Genome & the Internet: Tools of Scientific Revolutions. LC 98-53830. 144p. 1999. 22.00 (*0-19-512942-3*) OUP.

Dyson, Freeman J., et al. Values at War: Selected Tanner Lectures on the Nuclear Crisis. McMurrin, Sterling M., ed. LC 83-21705. 142p. (Orig.). reprint ed. pap. 44.10 (*0-8357-3273-8*, 203949400013) Bks Demand.

Dyson, Geoffrey H. The Mechanics of Athletics. 7th rev. ed. LC 77-3430. (Illus.). 264p. 1978. 37.95 (*0-8419-0309-3*) Holmes & Meier.

Dyson, George. New Music. (Select Bibliographies Reprint Ser.). 1977. 19.95 (*0-8369-5231-6*) Ayer.

— The New Music. 151p. 1990. reprint ed. lib. bdg. 59.00 (*0-7812-9010-4*) Rprt Serv.

— Progress of Music. LC 79-93334. (Essay Index Reprint Ser.). 1977. 20.95 (*0-8369-1287-X*) Ayer.

Dyson, George B. Darwin among the Machines: The Evolution of Global Intelligence. LC 98-87226. 304p. 1998. pap. text 15.00 (*0-7382-0030-1*) Perseus Pubng.

Dyson, Guy. The Kendrick Kindred. 1973. pap. 10.00 (*0-87511-685-X*) Claitors.

Dyson, Henry V. & Butt, John E. Augustans & Romantics, Sixteen Eighty-Nine to Eighteen Thirty. 2nd rev. ed. reprint ed. 39.00 (*0-403-03061-7*) Somerset Pub.

Dyson, Henry V. & Dyson, B. Augustans & Romantics, Sixteen Eighty-Nine to Eighteen Thirty. 1988. reprint ed. lib. bdg. 65.00 (*0-7812-0133-0*) Rprt Serv.

Dyson, Hope & Tennyson, Charles, eds. Dear & Honoured Lady. LC 72-151284. 152p. 1975. 20.00 (*0-8386-7922-6*) Fairleigh Dickinson.

Dyson-Huds. Turkana Pastoralists. (C). 2000. pap. text 20.50 (*0-15-502801-4*) Harcourt.

Dyson, J. E. & Carling, E. B., eds. Kinematics & Dynamics of Diffuse Astrophysical Media: Proceedings of the 8th Manchester Conference, Held at the University of Manchester, 22-26 March 1993. LC 94-22249. 420p. (C). 1994. text 336.00 (*0-7923-2992-9*) Kluwer Academic.

Dyson, J. E. & Williams, D. A. The Physics of the Interstellar Medium. 2nd ed. LC 97-16359. (Graduate Series in Astronomy). 1997. 137.00 (*0-7503-0306-9*); pap. 40.00 (*0-7503-0460-X*) IOP Pub.

Dyson, J. R. Accounting for Non-Accounting Students. 4th ed. xiv, 543p. (Orig.). 1997. pap. 57.50 (*0-273-62575-6*, Pub. by Pitman Pub) Trans-Atl Phila.

— Intermediate Accounting. 500p. (C). 1987. 65.00 (*1-870941-29-2*) St Mut.

Dyson, Jeremy. Bright Darkness: The Lost Art of the Supernatural Horror Film. LC 96-42358. 282p. 1997. pap. 21.95 (*0-304-34038-3*) Continuum.

— Bright Darkness: The Lost Art of the Supernatural Horror Film. LC 96-42358. (Illus.). 1997. 70.00 (*0-304-70037-1*) Continuum.

Dyson, Jeremy & Gattis, Mark. The Essex Files: To Basildon & Beyond. 128p. 1997. pap. 15.95 (*1-85702-747-7*) Fourth Estate.

Dyson, John. The Black Marshal. large type ed. (Linford Western Library Ser.). 240p. 1997. pap. 16.99 (*0-7089-5126-0*, Linford) Ulverscroft.

— Black Pete - Outlaw. large type ed. (Linford Western Library). 272p. 1993. pap. 16.99 (*0-7089-7434-1*, Linford) Ulverscroft.

— Blood Brothers. large type ed. 256p. 1998. pap. 17.99 (*0-7089-5191-0*) Ulverscroft.

— Bullwhip. large type ed. (Dales Large Print Ser.). 199p. 1996. pap. 18.99 (*1-85389-619-5*, Dales) Ulverscroft.

***Dyson, John.** Bushwhacked! large type ed. 256p. 1998. pap. 19.99 (*1-85389-890-2*, Dales) Ulverscroft.

Dyson, John. China Race. large type ed. 512p. 1986. 11.50 (*0-7089-8337-5*, Charnwood) Ulverscroft.

— The Crooked Sheriff. large type ed. (Linford Western Library). 272p. 1997. pap. 16.99 (*0-7089-7986-6*, Linford) Ulverscroft.

— Death at Sombrero Rock. large type ed. (Linford Western Library). 272p. 1996. pap. 16.99 (*0-7089-7884-3*) Ulverscroft.

— The Gambling Man. large type ed. (Dales Large Print Ser.). 1995. pap. 18.99 (*1-85389-547-4*, Dales) Ulverscroft.

***Dyson, John.** Horse Dreamer. large type ed. 240p. 2000. pap. 18.99 (*0-7089-5630-0*, Linford) Ulverscroft.

— The Horsehead Trail. 248p. 2000. 18.99 (*0-7089-5683-1*) Ulverscroft.

Dyson, John. The Lawless Land. large type ed. 1994. pap. 16.99 (*0-7089-7593-3*, Linford) Ulverscroft.

— Lousy Reb. large type ed. (Dales Large Print Ser.). 242p. 1997. pap. 18.99 (*1-85389-764-7*, Dales) Ulverscroft.

***Dyson, John.** Sidewinder. large type ed. 240p. 1999. pap. 18.90 (*0-7089-5492-8*, Linford) Ulverscroft.

Dyson, John. Spirit of Sail. 1990. 17.98 (*0-88365-766-X*) Galahad Bks.

***Dyson, John.** A Town Called Troublesome. large type ed. 256p. 1998. pap. 18.99 (*0-7089-5430-8*) Ulverscroft.

Dyson, John. The Train Robbers. large type ed. (Dales Large Print Ser.). 229p. 1995. pap. 18.99 (*1-85389-522-9*, Dales) Ulverscroft.

— Westward with Columbus. LC 90-15566. (Illus.). 64p. (J). (gr. 4-7). 1993. pap. 6.95 (*0-590-43847-6*) Scholastic Inc.

— Westward with Columbus: A Time Quest Book. LC 90-15566. 64p. (J). (gr. 4-7). 1991. 15.95 (*0-590-43846-8*, Scholastic Hardcover) Scholastic Inc.

Dyson, K. K., tr. see Tagore, Rabindranath.

***Dyson, Katharine D.** The 100 Best Romantic Resorts of the World: Perfect Places in All Price Ranges for Honeymooners & Others. 3rd ed. (One Hundred Best Resorts Ser.). (Illus.). 352p. 2000. pap. 19.95 (*0-7627-0624-4*) Globe Pequot.

Dyson, Kenneth. Elusive Union: The Process of Economic & Monetary Union in Europe. LC 94-19952. 320p. (C). 1995. text 75.75 (*0-582-25132-X*, 77020, Pub. by Addison-Wesley) Longman.

— The Politics of German Regulation. 250p. 1992. 72.95 (*1-85521-273-0*, Pub. by Dartmth Pub) Ashgate Pub Co.

Dyson, Kenneth & Featherstone, Kevin. The Road to Maastricht: Negotiating Economic & Monetary Union. LC 99-25739. 888p. 2000. 135.00 (*0-19-828077-7*); pap. text 45.00 (*0-19-829638-X*) OUP.

Dyson, Kenneth & Humphreys, Peter, eds. Politics of the Communications Revolution in Western Europe. 224p. 1986. 35.00 (*0-7146-3284-8*, Pub. by F Cass Pubs) Intl Spec Bk.

Dyson, Kenneth H. Combatting Long-Term Unemployment in Europe: Local-EEC Relations. 256p. 1989. 59.95 (*0-415-03127-3*, A3483) Routledge.

Dyson, Kenneth H., ed. Local Authority & New Technologies: The European Dimension. 192p. 1988. lib. bdg. 52.50 (*0-7099-4570-1*, Pub. by C Helm) Routldge.

Dyson, Kenneth H. & Humphreys, Peter, eds. The Political Economy of International Communications: International & European Dimensions. 320p. (C). (gr. 13). 1990. text 85.00 (*0-415-03794-8*, A5552) Routledge.

Dyson, Kenneth H. & Wilks, Stephen, eds. Industrial Crisis: A Comparative Study of the State & Corporate Decline. LC 83-9518. 290p. 1983. 32.50 (*0-312-51239-2*) St Martin.

Dyson, Ketaki K., tr. see Tagore, Rabindranath.

Dyson, Linda. Partnership: An Innovative Curriculum for Disaffected & Disadvantaged Young People. 128p. 1992. pap. 24.95 (*1-85346-210-1*, Pub. by David Fulton) Taylor & Francis.

Dyson, Lowell K. Farmers' Organizations, 10. LC 85-17529. (Encyclopedia of American Institutions Ser.: No. 10). 398p. 1986. lib. bdg. 65.00 (*0-313-22149-9*, DYA/, Greenwood Pr) Greenwood.

— Red Harvest: The Communist Party & American Farmers. LC 81-8200. 271p. reprint ed. pap. 84.10 (*0-8357-5550-9*, 203516900093) Bks Demand.

***Dyson, Marianne J.** Homework Help on the Internet. LC 00-27415. (Illus.). 64p. (J). (gr. 4-7). 2000. pap. 3.96 (*0-439-20892-0*) Scholastic Inc.

Dyson, Marianne J. Space Station Science: Life in Free Fall. LC 98-45994. (Illus.). 128p. (J). (gr. 4-9). 1999. 16.95 (*0-590-05889-4*, Pub. by Scholastic Inc) Penguin Putnam.

Dyson, Mary, jt. ed. see Harding, Rachel.

Dyson, Michael. Boys to Men. 1997. 23.00 (*0-679-43645-6*) Random.

Dyson, Michael E. Between God & Gangsta' Rap: Bearing Witness to Black Culture. 240p. (C). 1996. 27.50 (*0-19-509898-6*) OUP.

— Between God & Gansta Rap: Bearing Witness to Black Culture. 240p. 1997. reprint ed. pap. 14.95 (*0-19-511569-4*) OUP.

— From God to Gangsta' Rap: Bearing Witness to Black Culture. (C). 1996. 25.00 (*0-614-15452-9*) OUP.

— Making Malcolm: The Myth & Meaning of Malcolm X. 256p. 1996. reprint ed. pap. 10.95 (*0-19-510285-1*) OUP.

— Race Rules: Navigating the Color Line. LC 97-5433. 240p. 1997. pap. 12.00 (*0-679-78156-0*) Vin Bks.

— Reflecting Black: African-American Cultural Criticism. (American Culture Ser.: Vol. 9). 352p. (C). 1993. pap. 19.95 (*0-8166-2143-8*) U of Minn Pr.

***Dyson, Michael Eric.** I May Not Get There with You: The True Martin Luther King, Jr. LC 99-40478. 416p. 2000. 24.50 (*0-684-86776-1*) Free Pr.

— I May Not Get There With You: The True Martin Luther King Jr. 432p. 2000. pap. 15.00 (*0-684-83037-X*, Fireside) S&S Trade Pap.

Dyson, N. & Smith, R. M. Chromatographic Integration Methods. 2nd ed. (RSC Chromatography Monographs). 220p. 1998. 94.95 (*0-85404-510-4*) Spr-Verlag.

Dyson, N. A. An Introduction to Nuclear Physics with Applications in Medicine & Biology. LC 81-6720. (Physics & Medicine in Biology Ser.). 260p. 1982. text 79.95 (*0-470-27277-5*) P-H.

— X-Rays in Atomic & Nuclear Physics. 2nd ed. (Illus.). 414p. (C). 1990. text 125.00 (*0-521-26280-1*) Cambridge U Pr.

Dyson, Norman. Chromatographic Integration Methods. 1990. 105.00 (*0-85186-587-9*) CRC Pr.

Dyson, Peter. Dictionary of Networking. 3rd ed. LC 99-62864. 464p. 1999. pap. 29.99 (*0-7821-2461-5*) Sybex.

— Mastering Microsoft Internet Information Server 4. LC 97-66376. (Illus.). 944p. 1997. pap. text 49.99 incl. cd-rom (*0-7821-2080-6*) Sybex.

— Mastering SCO Unix. 1998. pap. text 44.99 (*0-7821-2262-0*) Sybex.

— The Network Press Dictionary of Networking. 2nd ed. LC 95-70853. 416p. 1995. pap. text 22.99 (*0-7821-1818-6*, Network Pr) Sybex.

— The PC User's Essential Accesible Pocket Dictionary. 2nd ed. LC 95-69363. 656p. 1995. 14.99 (*0-7821-1684-1*) Sybex.

— UNIX Complete. (Complete Ser.). 1024p. 1999. pap. 19.99 (*0-7821-2528-X*) Sybex.

***Dyson, Peter.** Windows 98 Instant Reference. 2nd ed. LC 99-65202. 320p. 1999. pap. text 14.99 (*0-7821-2616-2*) Sybex.

***Dyson, Peter & Coleman, Pat.** Windows 2000 Professional: In Record Time. 4th ed. 512p. 2000. 44.95 (*0-7821-2450-X*) Sybex.

Dyson, R. H., et al. From Athens to Gordion: The Papers of a Memorial Symposium for Rodney S. Young. DeVries, Keith, ed. (University Museum Papers: Vol. I). (Illus.). xix, 168p. (Orig.). (C). 1980. pap. 20.00 (*0-934718-35-0*) U Museum Pubns.

***Dyson, R. W.** Quaestio de Potestate Papae - Rex Pacificus: An Enquiry into the Power of the Pope: A Critical Edition & Translation. LC 99-43563. (Texts & Studies in Religion : Vol. 83). 104p. 1999. text 59.95 (*0-7734-7955-4*) E Mellen.

Dyson, R. W. Three Royalist Tracts, 1296-1302, 1 Vol. 162p. 1999. 72.00 (*1-85506-608-4*) Thoemmes Pr.

Dyson, R. W., ed. & tr. see Augustine, Saint.

Dyson, R. W., tr. see James of Viterbo.

***Dyson, Robert G. & O'Brien, Frances A.** Strategic Development: Methods & Models. LC 97-45636. 346p. 1998. pap. 79.50 (*0-471-97495-1*) Wiley.

Dyson, Robert H., Jr., ed. see Muscarella, Oscar W.

Dyson, Robert H., Jr., ed. see Winter, Irene J.

Dyson, Rose A. Mind Abuse: Media Violence in an Information Age. 1999. 48.99 (*1-55164-153-4*, Pub. by Black Rose) Consort Bk Sales.

Dyson, Rose Anne. Mind Abuse: Media Violence in an Information Age. 250p. 1999. pap. 19.99 (*1-55164-152-6*, Pub. by Black Rose) Consort Bk Sales.

Dyson, Rudolph L. Heart People: The Voice of the Medu-Neters. Smith, Abbygail et al, eds. (Illus.). 177p. 1990. pap. 12.00 (*0-9626733-0-7*) Heart Pubns.

Dyson, Stephen. The Commonware & Brittle Ware: Final Report IV, Part 1, Fascicle 3. LC 43-2669. pap. 28.00 (*0-685-71742-9*) J J Augustin.

— Tank Twins: East End Brothers in Arms, 1943-45. (Illus.). 224p. 1994. 27.95 (*0-85052-274-9*, Pub. by Leo Cooper) Trans-Atl Phila.

D

An Asterisk (*) at the beginning of an entry indicates that the title is appearing for the first time.

Dyson, Stephen G. HELP! WordPerfect 6.0. (Help! Ser.). 880p. 1993. pap. 27.95 (*1-56276-014-9*, Ziff-Davis Pr) Que.

Dyson, Stephen L. Ancient Marbles to American Shores: Classical Archaeology in the United States. LC 98-21208. (Illus.). 320p. 1998. 35.00 (*0-8122-3446-4*) U of Pa Pr.

— Community & Society in Roman Italy. LC 91-20070. (Ancient Society & History Ser.). 416p. 1991. text 48.00 (*0-8018-4175-5*) Johns Hopkins.

— The Creation of the Roman Frontier. LC 84-42881. 337p. 1985. reprint ed. pap. 104.50 (*0-7837-8584-4*, 204939900011) Bks Demand.

Dyson, Steve. French-English Glossary on Spot, Remote Sensing & Their Applications. (ENG & FRE.). 339p. 1992. pap. 195.00 (*0-7859-0508-1*, 2950157106) Fr & Eur.

— French-English Glossary on the Spot, Remote Sensing & Their Applications. (Illus.). 339p. (C). 1992. 400.00 (*2-9501571-0-6*, Pub. by Edits Technip) Enfield Pubs NH.

***Dyson, Sue.** The Bluffer's Guide to Secretaries: Bluff Your Way in Secretaries. (Bluffer's Guides Ser.). 64p. 2000. pap. 5.95 (*1-902825-59-4*) Oval Bks.

Dyson, Sue. A Far Tomorrow. 512p. 1997. pap. 11.95 (*0-7472-4953-9*, Pub. by Headline Bk Pub) Trafalgar.

— Migraines: A Natural Approach. LC 98-84064. (Natural Approach Ser.). (Illus.). 240p. 1998. pap. 10.95 (*1-56975-140-4*) Ulysses Pr.

Dyson, T., ed. India's Historical Demography: Studies in Famine, Disease & Society. (SOAS Collected Papers on South Asia: No. 8). (Illus.). 304p. (C). 1996. text 48.00 (*0-913215-43-0*, Pub. by Curzon Pr Ltd) UH Pr.

Dyson, Tim. Population & Food: Global Trends & Future Prospects. LC 95-38227. (Global Environmental Change Ser.). 256p. (C). 1996. pap. 22.99 (*0-415-11975-8*) Routledge.

Dyson-Vines, Pamela L. Somsey. 96p. 1998. pap. 9.00 (*0-8059-4381-1*) Dorrance.

Dyson, W. H. Studies in Christian Mysticism. 1977. lib. bdg. 69.95 (*0-8490-2702-0*) Gordon Pr.

***Dysonwilliams, Barbara.** Enter Justice. LC 99-93811. 2000. 22.95 (*0-533-13168-5*) Vantage.

Dyssegaard, Elisabeth Kallick, tr. see Anderson, Lena.

Dyssegaard, Elisabeth Kallick, tr. see Lindgren, Astrid.

Dyssegaard, Elisabeth Kallick, tr. see Lindgren, Barbro.

Dyssli, Bernard, jt. ed. see Deimann, Sven.

Dysson, Brian, ed. The Modern Academic Library: Essays in Memory of Philip Larkin. LC 89-117023. 177p. reprint ed. pap. 54.90 (*0-608-08883-8*, 206952000004) Bks Demand.

Dystaeyen, F. Van & Verschoren, A. Reflectors & Localization: Application to Sheaf Theory. LC 78-31333. (Lecture Notes in Pure & Applied Mathematics Ser.: Vol. 41). 176p. reprint ed. pap. 54.60 (*0-608-08998-2*, 206963300005) Bks Demand.

Dystar Television Staff. Georgia Stories: A Teacher's Guide. (Illus.). 76p. 1996. pap. text, teacher ed. 10.00 (*1-892720-24-8*) GA Public Brdcstng.

Dyster, Barrie. Servant & Master: Building & Running the Grand Houses of Sydney, 1788-1850. (Illus.). 260p. 1990. pap. 19.95 (*0-86840-395-4*, Pub. by New South Wales Univ Pr) Intl Spec Bk.

Dyster, Barrie, jt. auth. see Meredith, David.

Dyster, Floy, jt. auth. see Shannon, Patricia J.

***Dyszel.** Microsoft Outlook 2000. LC 98-99798. (Windows for Dummies Ser.). 384p. 1999. pap. 19.99 (*0-7645-0471-1*); spiral bd. 12.99 (*0-7645-0472-X*) IDG Bks.

Dyszel, Bill. Microsoft Outlook 98 for Windows for Dummies. LC 98-85133. 384p. 1998. pap. 19.99 (*0-7645-0393-6*) IDG Bks.

— Microsoft Outlook 98 for Dummies Quick Reference. LC 98-85430. (For Dummies). 224p. 1998. spiral bd. 12.99 (*0-7645-0394-4*) IDG Bks.

***Dyszel, Bill.** Palm Computing for Dummies. 408p. 1999. pap. 24.99 incl. cd-rom (*0-7645-0581-5*) IDG Bks.

Dyszel, Bill & Dummies Technical Press Staff. Microsoft Outlook for Dummies. LC 96-80190. (Illus.). 384p. 1997. pap. 19.99 (*0-7645-0080-5*) IDG Bks.

— Microsoft Outlook 97 for Windows for Dummies Quick Reference. LC 97-70738. 202p. 1997. spiral bd. 12.99 (*0-7645-0184-4*) IDG Bks.

Dytham, Calvin. Choosing & Using Statistics: A Biologists Guide. LC 98-28514. (Illus.). 1999. pap. 39.95 (*0-86542-653-8*) Blackwell Sci.

Dytrych, Denise D. Christmas Party Celebrations: 71 New & Exciting Party Plans for Holiday Fun. LC 97-22238. 160p. 1997. pap. 11.95 (*0-918420-33-4*) Brighton Pubns.

Dyugaev, A. M. Physics Reviews Vol. 14, Pt. 3: The Theory of Quantum Nondegenerate Liquids, Vol. 14. (Soviet Scientific Reviews Ser.: Section A). 177p. 1991. text 192.00 (*3-7186-5040-1*, Harwood Acad Pubs) Gordon & Breach.

Dyville, Jack. Barabbas... Out of Darkness: A One-Act Drama. 21p. 1998. pap. 3.50 (*0-88680-449-3*, C449-3) I E Clark.

— Those Magical Red Sneaks: A 2-Act Musical Comedy. (Illus.). 51p. 1996. pap. 4.50 (*0-88680-429-9*) I E Clark.

Dyville, Jack, jt. auth. see Nelson, Ken.

Dyzenhais, David. Judging the Judges & Ourselves: Truth, Reconciliation & the Apartheid Legal Order. 200p. 1998. 40.00 (*1-901362-94-9*) Hart Pub.

Dyzenhaus, David. Hard Cases in Wicked Legal Systems: South African Law in the Perspective of Legal Philosophy. (Illus.). 312p. 1991. text 75.00 (*0-19-825292-7*, 12228) OUP.

— Law As Politics: Carl Schmitt's Critique of Liberalism. LC 98-13618. 1998. write for info. (*0-8223-2227-7*); pap. 18.95 (*0-8223-2244-7*) Duke.

— Legality & Legitimacy: Carl Schmitt, Hans Kelsen & Hermann Heller in Weimar Republic. LC 97-11502. 304p. 1997. text 75.00 (*0-19-826062-8*) OUP.

— Legality & Legitimacy: Carl Schmitt, Hans Kelsen & Hermann Heller in Weimar Republic. 304p. 1999. pap. text 29.95 (*0-19-829846-3*) OUP.

Dyzenhaus, David & Ripstein, Arthur, eds. Ethics & the Law: Readings in Legal Philosophy. (Toronto Studies in Philosophy). 352p. 1996. text 55.00 (*0-8020-0896-8*); pap. text 21.95 (*0-8020-7878-8*) U of Toronto Pr.

***D'Zailo, Joe.** Things I Know Journal. (Oh No! Collection Ser.). 1999. 9.95 (*0-8118-2426-8*) Chronicle Bks.

***Dzaki, Tohru & Yildiz, Fatma.** Die Umma Texte Ans den Archaologischen Museem Zu Istanbul. (GER.). 285p. 2000. 60.00 (*1-883053-57-9*) CDL Pr.

***Dzamba, Andrew.** Managing Accounting Systems & Technology 2000 Yearbook. annuals (Illus.). 200p. 2000. pap. 199.00 (*1-58673-025-8*) IOMA.

— Retirement Plans for Not-For-Profit Organizations with CD-ROM. 400p. 2000. pap. 91.00 incl. cd-rom (*0-15-607214-9*) Harcourt Prof.

Dzamba, Andrew. Retirement Plans For Not-for-profit Organizations, 1999 Ed. 1998. pap. text 79.00 (*0-15-606283-6*) Assessment Sys.

***Dzamba, Andrew.** 2000 Retirement Plans for Not-for-Profit Organzation. 400p. 1999. pap. text 85.00 (*0-15-606991-1*) Harcourt.

***Dzamba, Andy & Prescott, Janice, eds.** The 1999 Managing HR Information Systems Yearbook. (Illus.). 200p. 1999. pap. 199.00 (*1-58673-008-8*) IOMA.

D'Zamko, Mary E. & Hedges, William D. Helping Exceptional Children Succeed in the Regular Classroom. 1984. 22.95 (*0-317-39625-0*, Busn) P-H.

Dzarnouski, Judy R. What to Do: Life. 114p. (Orig.). 1997. pap. 10.00 (*0-9659109-0-3*) J R Phillips.

***Dzatko, Dave, et al.** AGP System Architecture. 2nd ed. LC 99-44737. (PC Systems Architecture Ser.). 400p. 1999. pap. text 39.95 (*0-201-70069-7*) Addison-Wesley.

Dzau, Victor J., ed. Tissue Renin-Angiotensin System: Physiologic & Pharmacologic Implications. LC 73-3001. (Circulation Monographs: No. 12). 78p. 1988. 9.60 (*0-87493-261-0*) Am Heart.

Dzau, Victor J., jt. ed. see Rubanyi, Gabor M.

Dzelainis, Martin, ed. see Milton, John.

Dzelepy, E. N. The Spanish Plot. 1972. 59.95 (*0-8490-1105-1*) Gordon Pr.

Dzelzainis, Martin, jt. auth. see Chernaik, Warren L.

Dzelzkalns, Lee Ann F. View from the Mountaintop: A Journey into Wholeness: A Contemplative, Inspirational Book of Poems. Foster, Rhonda, ed. LC 95-80180. (Illus.). 110p. (Orig.). 1995. pap. 11.95 (*1-881300-01-3*) Ageless.

***Dzeroski, S., et al, eds.** Inductive Logic Programming: Proceedings of the 9th International Conference, ILP-99, Bled, Slovenia, June 24-27, 1999. LC 99-32073. (Lecture Notes in Computer Science Ser.: Vol. 1634). viii, 303p. 1999. pap. 56.00 (*3-540-66109-3*) Spr-Verlag.

Dzever. Perspectives on Economic Integration & Business Strategy in the Asia-Pacific Region. LC 96-44474. 247p. 1997. text 69.95 (*0-312-17275-3*) St Martin.

Dzhafarov, T. D., jt. ed. see Abdullayev, G. B.

Dzhafarov, Taiar D., jt. auth. see Abdullaev, Gasan M.

Dzhagarov, Georgi. The Public Prosecutor. Alexieva, Marguerite, tr. from BUL. 112p. 1969. 16.95 (*0-910278-16-4*) Boulevard.

Dzhamalov, R. & Safronov, Y. Elsevier's Dictionary of Geoenvironmental & Natural Disasters. 468p. 1998. 169.50 (*0-444-82906-7*, Excerpta Medica) Elsevier.

Dzhamalov, Roald G., et al. Elsevier's Dictionary of Hydrological & Hydrogeological Environment: Russian - English, English - Russian. (ENG & RUS.). 510p. 1992. 250.00 (*0-8288-9301-2*) Fr & Eur.

Dzhamay, A., tr. see Arnol'd, V. I., et al, eds.

Dzhaparidze, K. Parameter Estimation & Hypothesis Testing in Spectral Analysis of Stationary Time Series. Kotz, Samuel I., tr. from DUT. (Series in Statistics). vi, 324p. 1985. 74.95 (*0-387-96141-0*) Spr-Verlag.

Dzhincharadze, A. Marketing: Defining Dictionary. 224p. (C). 1991. text 80.00 (*0-569-09911-0*, Pub. by Collets) St Mut.

Dzhumadanova, Ana, jt. auth. see Hubenova, Milka.

***Dzhuraev, A.** Singular Partial Differential Equations. LC 99-46247. (Monographs & Surveys in Pure & Applied Mathematics). 195p. 1999. write for info. (*1-58488-144-5*, Chap & Hall CRC) CRC Pr.

Dzhuraev, Abduhamid. Degenerate & Other Problems. 328p. 1992. ring bd. 136.95 (*0-582-09636-7*, LM9636, Chap & Hall CRC) CRC Pr.

— Methods of Singular Integral Equations, Vol. 60. (Monographs & Surveys in Pure & Applied Mathematics). 328p. 1992. boxed set 132.00 (*0-582-08373-7*, LM8373, Chap & Hall CRC) CRC Pr.

Dzhuraev, Abduhamid, jt. auth. see Begehr, Henrich G.

Dziadulewicz, Stanislaw. Herbarz Rodzin Tatarskich W Polsce. (POL.). 240p. 1994. 190.00 (*0-614-02649-0*) Szwede Slavic.

Dziak, Jack, ed. see Grant, Natalie.

***Dziak, Michael.** Telecommuting Success: A Practical Guide for Staying in the Loop While Working Away from the Office. 2001. pap. 16.95 (*1-57112-109-9*) Park Ave.

Dziczek, Ed, ed. see Stasey, Bobbie.

Dziech, Aaron & Houser, Donald R. Refinements in Root Stress Predictions Or Edges of Helical Gear Teeth. (Technical Papers: Vol. 97FTM14). (Illus.). 9p. 1997. pap. text 30.00 (*1-55589-708-8*) AGMA.

Dziech, Billie W. & Hawkins, Michael W. Sexual Harassment in Higher Education: Reflections & New Perspectives. Altbach, Philip, ed. LC 98-14229. (Garland Studies in Higher Education: Vol. 12). 191p. 1998. 50.00 (*0-8153-2036-1*, SS1034) Garland.

Dziech, Billie W. & Schudson, Charles B. On Trial: America's Courts & Their Treatment of Sexually Abused Children. rev. ed. LC 90-23545. 240p. 1991. reprint ed. pap. 17.00 (*0-8070-0415-4*) Beacon Pr.

Dziech, Billie W. & Vilter, William R., eds. Prisoners of Elitism: The Community College's Struggle for Stature. LC 85-644753. (New Directions for Community Colleges Ser.: No. CC 78). 130p. 1992. pap. 22.00 (*1-55542-750-2*) Jossey-Bass.

Dziech, Billie W. & Weiner, Linda. The Lecherous Professor: Sexual Harassment on Campus. 2nd ed. 288p. 1990. pap. text 15.95 (*0-252-06118-7*) U of Ill Pr.

Dziedzic. Twentieth-Century Literary Criticism, Vol. 74. 500p. 1998. 140.00 (*0-7876-2018-1*, GML00198-111455) Visible Ink Pr.

— Twentieth-Century Literary Criticism, Vol. 75. 500p. 1998. 140.00 (*0-7876-2019-X*, GML00198-111456) Visible Ink Pr.

— Twentieth-Century Literary Criticism, Vol. 76. 500p. 1998. 140.00 (*0-7876-2022-X*, GML00198-111459) Visible Ink Pr.

Dziedzic. Twentieth Century Literature, Vol. 62. 500p. 1996. text 150.00 (*0-8103-9307-7*) Gale.

— Twentieth Century Literature, Vol. 63. 500p. 1996. text 150.00 (*0-8103-9309-3*) Gale.

— Twentieth Century Literature, Vol. 64. 500p. 1996. text 150.00 (*0-7876-0778-9*) Gale.

Dziedzic, Eugene E., jt. auth. see Pula, James S.

Dziegielewska, K. M. & Brown, William H. Fetuin. LC 94-44100. (Molecular Biology Intelligence Unit Ser.). 180p. 1995. 89.00 (*1-57059-213-6*) Landes Bioscience.

Dziegielewska, K. M., jt. ed. see Saunders, N. R.

Dziegielewski, Benedykt, et al. Lessons Learned from the California Drought (1987-1992) National Study of Water Management During Drought. (Illus.). 277p. (C). 1997. reprint ed. pap. text 40.00 (*0-7881-4163-5*) DIANE Pub.

***Dziegielewski, Sophia.** The Changing Face of Health Care Social Work: A Guide for Professional Empirical Practice. LC 97-52604. (Illus.). 320p. 1998. 59.95 (*0-8261-1196-3*) Springer Pub.

Dzieglelewski, Sophia F., jt. auth. see Colby, Ira C.

Dzielak, Ted & Greiner, Lynn. Injured at Work: A Guide for Washington Workers. write for info. (*0-318-61780-5*) Natl Lawyers Guild.

— Injured at Work: A Guide for Washington Workmen's Compensation. LC 84-40664. (Illus.). 152p. 1985. pap. 9.95 (*0-295-96220-8*) U of Wash Pr.

Dzielska, Maria. Hypatia of Alexandria. Lyra, F., tr. (Revealing Antiquity Ser.: No. 8). 176p. 1995. text 35.00 (*0-674-43775-6*, DZIHYP) HUP.

— Hypatia of Alexandria. Lyra, F., tr. (Revealing Antiquity Ser.: No. 8). 176p. 1996. pap. 14.00 (*0-674-43776-4*) HUP.

Dziemianowicz, Stefan R. The Annotated Guide to Unknown & Unknown Worlds. LC 93-202547. (Starmont Studies in Literary Criticism: No. 13). 212p. 1991. pap. 23.00 (*1-55742-140-4*) Millefleurs.

Dziemianowicz, Stefan R., et al, eds. Horrors! 365 Scary Stories. LC 98-213793. xviii, 734p. 1998. write for info. (*0-7607-0141-5*) B&N Imports.

Dziemianowicz, Stefan R., ed. see Stoker, Bram, et al.

Dziemidko, Helen. The Complete Book of Energy Medicines: Choosing Your Path to Health. LC 99-28518. (Illus.). 192p. 1999. pap. 18.00 (*0-89281-845-X*) Inner Tradit.

Dziemidok, Bohdan. The Comical: A Philosophical Analysis. Janiak, Marek, tr. LC 92-40290. (Nijhoff International Philosophy Ser.: Vol. 47). (ENG & POL., Illus.). 1992. text 155.50 (*0-7923-2103-0*) Kluwer Academic.

Dziemidok, Bohdan & McCormick, Peter, eds. On the Aesthetics of Roman Ingarden: Interpretations & Assessments. 312p. (C). 1988. lib. bdg. 147.00 (*0-7923-0071-8*, Pub. by Kluwer Academic) Kluwer Academic.

Dzienkowski, John S. Professional Responsibility: Standards, Rules & Statutes, 1998-1999. abr. ed. (Miscellaneous Ser.). 650p. 1998. 16.00 (*0-314-23247-8*) West Pub.

— Professional Responsibility Standards, Rules & Statutes. 11th abr. ed. 500p. (C). 1997. pap. text, supp. ed. write for info. (*0-314-21225-6*) West Pub.

— Professional Responsibility, Standards, Rules, & Statutes, 1998-1999 Edition. (Pamphlet Ser.). 1000p. 1998. 21.00 (*0-314-23246-X*) West Pub.

— Selected Statutes, Rules & Standards on the Legal Profession: 1994 Edition. 1050p. 1994. pap. text. write for info. (*0-314-04331-4*) West Pub.

Dzienkowski, John S., ed. Professional Responsibility Standards, Rules & Statutes, 1996-97 Edition. 975p. 1996. pap. text. write for info. (*0-314-09976-X*) West Pub.

Dzienkowski, John S., ed. Professional Responsibility: Standards, Rules & Statutes (1995-1996 Ed) 996p. (C). pap. 19.00 (*0-314-06788-4*) West Pub.

— Professional Responsibility: Standards, Rules & Statutes (1995-1996 Ab.Ed) abr. ed. 492p. (C). Date not set. pap. 14.00 (*0-314-06839-2*) West Pub.

Dzienkowski, John S., jt. auth. see Sutton, John F., Jr.

Dzierzynski, Nellie, tr. see Biernacki, Wladyslaw.

Dziewanowska, Ada. Polish Folkdances & Songs: A Step by Step Guide. LC 97-26137. (ENG & POL., Illus.). 800p. 1997. 39.50 (*0-7818-0420-5*) Hippocrene Bks.

Dziewanowski, M. K. The Communist Party of Poland: An Outline of History. LC 75-18050. (Russian Research Center Studies: No. 32). 431p. reprint ed. pap. 133.70 (*0-7837-1690-7*, 205722000024) Bks Demand.

Dziewanowski, M. Kamil. A History of Soviet Russia & Its Aftermath. 5th ed. LC 96-30522. 448p. (C). 1996. pap. text 57.00 (*0-13-260746-8*) P-H.

— War at Any Price: World War II in Europe, 1939-1945. 2nd ed. 400p. (C). 1990. pap. text 36.00 (*0-13-946658-4*) P-H.

Dziggel, Oliver C., jt. auth. see Enderlyn, Allyn.

Dzik, Stanley J. Aircraft Detail Design Manual. 3rd ed. Rice, Michael S., ed. (Illus.). 99p. 1977. pap. 18.50 (*0-87994-011-5*) Aviat Pub.

Dzimba, John. South Africa's Destabilization of Zimbabwe, 1980-89. LC 97-19534. 224p. 1998. text 69.95 (*0-312-17669-4*) St Martin.

Dzindzeleta, Jerry. Secret Rooms Secret Compartments: How You Can Design Them to Protect Your Valuables. (Illus.). 80p. 1990. spiral bd. 29.95 (*0-9671139-0-3*) Secret Rooms.

Dzinkowski, John. Professional Responsibility Standards, Rules & Statutes, 1996-97. abr. ed. 500p. 1996. pap. text. write for info. (*0-314-09975-1*) West Pub.

Dziob, John. A Young Surgeon Goes to War: An Autobiography. 96p. 1999. pap. 10.00 (*0-8059-4727-2*) Dorrance.

Dziobek, Claudia, ed. see Group of Green Economists Staff.

Dziong, Zbigniew. ATM Network Resource Management. LC 97-15265. (Computer Communications Ser.). (Illus.). 300p. 1997. pap. 60.00 (*0-07-018546-8*) McGraw.

Dziuba, Mark. Blues Guitar. (National Guitar Workshop Arts). 1997. pap. 7.50 (*0-88284-849-6*, 17840); pap. 17.45 incl. audio compact disk (*0-88284-848-8*, 17839) Alfred Pub.

— Guitar Rock. (National Guitar Workshop Arts Ser.). 1997. pap. 17.45 incl. audio compact disk (*0-88284-847-X*, 17822) Alfred Pub.

— Introducing Alternate Tunings. (Alfred Handy Guide Ser.). 1995. pap. 4.50 (*0-88284-651-5*, 7018); pap. 6.95 (*0-88284-650-7*, 14108) Alfred Pub.

— Rock Guitar. (National Guitar Workshop Arts). 1997. pap. 7.50 (*0-88284-850-X*, 17820) Alfred Pub.

— Stand Alone Blues & Beyond. (Alfred's Handy Guide Ser.). 1995. pap. 12.95 incl. audio compact disk (*0-88284-733-3*) Alfred Pub.

— Stand Alone Fusion. (Alfred's Handy Guide Ser.). 1995. pap. 12.95 incl. audio compact disk (*0-88284-732-5*) Alfred Pub.

— Stand Alone Fusion. (Alfred Handy Guide Ser.). 32p. 1992. reprint ed. pap. 9.95 incl. audio (*0-88284-542-X*, 4429) Alfred Pub.

Dziubenko, B.V. Modeling & Design of Twisted Tube Heat Exchangers. LC 99-44188. 1998. write for info. (*1-56700-123-8*) Begell Hse.

Dziunikowski, B. Comprehensive Analytical Chemistry Vol. XXIV: Energy Disperse X-Ray Fluorescence Analysis. Svehla, Gyula I., ed. (Illus.). xx,432p. 1990. 330.00 (*0-444-98897-1*) Elsevier.

Dziura, Ceceila & Ellis, Jack. Oh, What Joy Is This Journey. 50p. 1994. pap. 6.95 (*0-9643594-1-3*) Aljen Pubng.

Dzivba, Mark. Stand Alone Blues & Beyond. (National Guitar Workshop Arts Ser.). 1994. pap. 12.95 incl. audio compact disk (*0-88284-642-6*, 11288) Alfred Pub.

Dziweciolowski, Ryszard, jt. auth. see Busher, Peter E.

Dziwirek, Katarzyna, ed. see Farrell, Patrick & Mejias-Bikandi, Errapel.

Dzobo, N. K. Melagbe "A Life Affirming African Theology" LC 94-69482. 131p. (Orig.). (C). 1995. pap. text 15.00 (*0-943324-38-6*) Omenana.

Dzombak, David A. Surface Complexation Modeling: Hydrous Ferric Oxide. LC 89-35596. 416p. 1990. 175.00 (*0-471-63731-9*) Wiley.

***Dzorgbo, Dan-Bright S.** Ghana in Search of Development: The Challenge of Governance, Economic Management & Institution Building. (Making of Modern Africa Ser.). 392p. 2000. text 83.95 (*0-7546-1211-2*, Pub. by Ashgate Pub) Ashgate Pub Co.

Dzorgbo, Dan-Bright S. Ghana in Search of Development: The Challenge of Governance, Economic Management & Institution Building. LC 98-235699. ix, 302 p. 1998. pap. 47.50 (*91-506-1315-4*, Pub. by Uppsala Universitet) Coronet Bks.

Dzrbasjan, M. M., et al. Seventeen Papers on Functions of Complex Variables. LC 51-5559. (Translations Ser.: Series 2, Vol. 32). 393p. 1963. 44.00 (*0-8218-1732-9*, TRANS2/32) Am Math.

Dzuback, Mary A. Robert M. Hutchins: Portrait of an Educator. (Centennial Publication Ser.). (Illus.). 404p. 1991. 24.95 (*0-226-17710-6*) U Ch Pr.

Dzubow, Leonard M., ed. Cosmetic Dermatologic Surgery. LC 97-51986. (Illus.). 350p. 1998. text 135.00 (*0-397-51740-8*) Lppncott W & W.

Dzugan, Jerry, pref. Training & Technology for Safety at Sea: Summary Proceedings. (Alaska Sea Grant Report: No. 92-01). 60p. (Orig.). 1992. pap. 7.00 (*1-56612-011-X*) AK Sea Grant CP.

Dzugan, Jerry & Falvey, Dan. Spawn, Spat & Sprains: A Manual for Aquaculture Safety in Alaska. (Aquaculture Note Ser.: AN-17). (Illus.). 84p. 1998. pap. 6.00 (*1-56612-055-1*) AK Sea Grant CP.

Dzugan, Jerry & Jensen, S. Clark. Water Wise: Safety for the Recreational Boater. (Marine Advisory Bulletin Ser.: MAB-51). (Illus.). 200p. 1999. pap. 19.98 (*1-56612-058-6*) AK Sea Grant CP.

Dzuikas, Linas. Emergency Medicine. 304p. 1999. text 50.00 (*0-07-452910-2*) McGraw-Hill HPD.

Dzulynski, Stanislaw & Sanders, John E. Current Marks on Firm Mud Bottoms. (Connecticut Academy of Arts & Sciences Ser., Trans.: Vol. 42). 1962. pap. 49.50 (*0-685-22890-8*) Elliots Bks.

Dzur, Carlos Lopez, tr. see Professional Truck Driver Institute, Inc. Staff.

Dzurik, Andrew A. Water Resources Planning. 256p. (C). 1990. lib. bdg. 44.95 (*0-8476-7391-X*, R7391) Rowman.

D

— Water Resources Planning. 2nd rev. ed. LC 96-23295. 368p. (C). 1996. lib. bdg. 47.50 (*0-8476-8081-9*) Rowman.

Dzurik, R., et al, eds. Kidney Metabolism & Function. (Developments in Nephrology Ser.). 1986. text 209.50 (*0-89838-749-3*) Kluwer Academic.

D'Zurilla, Thomas J. & Nezu, Arthur M. Problem-Solving Therapy: A Social Competence Approach to Clinical Intervention. 2nd ed. LC 98-48399. (Behavior Therapy & Behavioral Medicine Ser.). (Illus.). 256p. 1999. 42.95 (*0-8261-1266-8*) Springer Pub.

Dzurinko, Mary K., jt. auth. see Newman, Diane.

Dzurnak, Janet. So, You Really Want a Horse. (Illus.). 56p. 1998. pap. 8.00 (*0-8059-4398-6*) Dorrance.

Dzuro, Don, ed. Ohio Bottles. 5th rev. ed. LC 99-220125. 557p. 1999. pap. write for info. (*0-9672032-0-1*) OH Bottle Club.

Dzwonchyk, Wayne M. Brief History of the United States Army in World War 2: The United States Army Campaigns of World War 2. 52p. 1992. pap. 3.00 (*0-16-035956-2*) USGPO.

Dzwonkoski, Peter. American Literary Publishing Houses, 1900-1980. (Dictionary of Literary Biography Ser.: Vol. 46). 400p. 1986. text 155.00 (*0-8103-1724-9*) Gale.

Dzwonkoski, Peter, ed. American Literary Publishing Houses 1638-1899, 2 vols., Set. (Dictionary of Literary Biography Ser.: Vol. 49). 715p. 1986. text 296.00 (*0-8103-1727-3*) Gale.

Dzwonkowski, Ed. How You Can Become a Millionaire: Your Lifetime Guide for Building Wealth & Achieving Financial Independence. LC 98-96176. 288p. 1998. pap. 19.95 (*0-9663822-1-8*) Grt Spirit.

Dzwonkowski, Ron, ed. The Suicide Machine: Understanding Jack Kevorkian, the People Who Came to Him, & the Issue of Assisted Suicide. 200p. 1997. pap. 11.95 (*0-937247-73-1*) Detroit Pr.

Dzyadyk, V. K. Approximation Methods for Solutions of Differential & Integral Equations. 325p. 1995. 197.50 (*90-6764-194-4*, Pub. by VSP) Coronet Bks.

Dzyubenko, B. V., et al. Unsteady Heat Mass Transfer. 1990. 175.00 (*0-89116-884-2*) Hemisp Pub.

***Dmann, Martina.** Bauwelt Berlin Annual 1999/2000. (Illus.). 192p. 2000. pap. 49.95 (*3-7643-6279-0*) Birkhauser.

D

An Asterisk (*) at the beginning of an entry indicates that the title is appearing for the first time.